THE OXFORD ENGLISH DICTIONARY

SECOND EDITION

THE OXFORD ENGLISH DICTIONARY

First Edited by

JAMES A. H. MURRAY, HENRY BRADLEY, W. A. CRAIGIE
and C. T. ONIONS

COMBINED WITH

A SUPPLEMENT TO THE OXFORD ENGLISH DICTIONARY

Edited by

R. W. BURCHFIELD

AND RESET WITH CORRECTIONS, REVISIONS
AND ADDITIONAL VOCABULARY

THE OXFORD ENGLISH DICTIONARY

SECOND EDITION

Prepared by

J. A. SIMPSON *and* E. S. C. WEINER

VOLUME V

Dvandva–Follis

CLARENDON PRESS · OXFORD

Oxford University Press, Walton Street, Oxford OX2 6DP
Oxford New York Toronto
Delhi Bombay Calcutta Madras Karachi
Petaling Jaya Singapore Hong Kong Tokyo
Nairobi Dar es Salaam Cape Town
Melbourne Auckland
and associated companies in
Berlin Ibadan

Oxford is a trade mark of Oxford University Press

© Oxford University Press 1989
First published 1989
Reprinted (with corrections) 1991

British Library Cataloguing in Publication Data
Oxford English dictionary.—2nd ed.
1. English language-Dictionaries
I. Simpson, J. A. (John Andrew), 1953-
II. Weiner, Edmund S. C., 1950-
423
ISBN 0-19-861217-6 (vol. V)
ISBN 0-19-861186-2 (set)

Library of Congress Cataloging-in-Publication Data
The Oxford English dictionary.—2nd ed.
prepared by J. A. Simpson and E. S. C. Weiner
Bibliography: p.
ISBN 0-19-861217-6 (vol. V)
ISBN 0-19-861186-2 (set)
1. English language—Dictionaries. I. Simpson, J. A.
II. Weiner, E. S. C. III. Oxford University Press.
PE1625.087 1989
423—dc19   88-5330

Data capture by ICC, Fort Washington, Pa.
Text-processing by Oxford University Press
Typesetting by Pindar Graphics Origination, Scarborough, N. Yorks.
Manufactured in the United States of America by
Rand McNally & Company, Taunton, Mass.

KEY TO THE PRONUNCIATION

THE pronunciations given are those in use in the educated speech of southern England (the so-called 'Received Standard'), and the keywords given are to be understood as pronounced in such speech.

I. *Consonants*

b, d, f, k, l, m, n, p, t, v, z *have their usual English values*

g as in *go* (gəʊ)

h ... *ho!* (həʊ)

r ... *run* (rʌn), *terrier* ('tɛrɪə(r))

(r) ... *her* (hɜː(r))

s ... *see* (siː), *success* (sək'sɛs)

w ... *wear* (wɛə(r))

hw... *when* (hwɛn)

j ... *yes* (jɛs)

θ as in *thin* (θɪn), *bath* (bɑːθ)

ð ... *then* (ðɛn), *bathe* (beɪð)

ʃ ... *shop* (ʃɒp), *dish* (dɪʃ)

tʃ ... *chop* (tʃɒp), *ditch* (dɪtʃ)

ʒ ... *vision* ('vɪʒən), *déjeuner* (deʒøne)

dʒ ... *judge* (dʒʌdʒ)

ŋ ... *singing* ('sɪŋɪŋ), *think* (θiŋk)

ŋg ... *finger* ('fɪŋgə(r))

(FOREIGN AND NON-SOUTHERN)

ʎ as in It. *serraglio* (ser'raʎo)

ɲ ... Fr. *cognac* (kɔɲak)

x ... Ger. *ach* (ax), Sc. *loch* (lɒx), Sp. *frijoles* (fri'xoles)

ç ... Ger. *ich* (ɪç), Sc. *nicht* (nɪçt)

ɣ ... North Ger. *sagen* ('zaːɣən)

c ... Afrikaans *baardmannetjie* ('baːrtmanəci)

ɥ ... Fr. *cuisine* (kɥizin)

Symbols in parentheses are used to denote elements that may be omitted either by individual speakers or in particular phonetic contexts: e.g. *bottle* ('bɒt(ə)l), *Mercian* ('mɜːʃ(ɪ)ən), *suit* (s(j)uːt), *impromptu* (ɪm'prɒm(p)tjuː), *father* ('fɑːðə(r)).

II. *Vowels and Diphthongs*

SHORT

ɪ as in *pit* (pɪt), *-ness*, (-nɪs)

ɛ ... *pet* (pɛt), Fr. *sept* (sɛt)

æ ... *pat* (pæt)

ʌ ... *putt* (pʌt)

ɒ ... *pot* (pɒt)

ʊ ... *put* (pʊt)

ə ... *another* (ə'nʌðə(r))

(ə) ... *beaten* ('biːt(ə)n)

i ... Fr. *si* (si)

e ... Fr. *bébé* (bebe)

a ... Fr. *mari* (mari)

ɑ ... Fr. *bâtiment* (bɑtimã)

ɔ ... Fr. *homme* (ɔm)

o ... Fr. *eau* (o)

ø ... Fr. *peu* (pø)

œ ... Fr. *boeuf* (bœf) *coeur* (kœr)

u ... Fr. *douce* (dus)

ʏ ... Ger. *Müller* ('mʏlər)

y ... Fr. *du* (dy)

LONG

iː as in *bean* (biːn)

ɑː ... *barn* (bɑːn)

ɔː ... *born* (bɔːn)

uː ... *boon* (buːn)

ɜː ... *burn* (bɜːn)

eː ... Ger. *Schnee* (ʃneː)

ɛː ... Ger. *Fähre* ('fɛːrə)

aː ... Ger. *Tag* (taːk)

oː ... Ger. *Sohn* (zoːn)

øː ... Ger. *Goethe* ('gøːtə)

yː ... Ger. *grün* (gryːn)

NASAL

ɛ̃, æ̃ as in Fr. *fin* (fɛ̃, fæ̃)

ã ... Fr. *franc* (frã)

ɔ̃ ... Fr. *bon* (bɔ̃)

œ̃ ... Fr. *un* (œ̃)

DIPHTHONGS, etc.

eɪ as in *bay* (beɪ)

aɪ ... *buy* (baɪ)

ɔɪ ... *boy* (bɔɪ)

əʊ ... *no* (nəʊ)

aʊ ... *now* (naʊ)

ɪə ... *peer* (pɪə(r))

ɛə ... *pair* (pɛə(r))

ʊə ... *tour* (tʊə(r))

ɔə ... *boar* (bɔə(r))

aɪə as in *fiery* ('faɪərɪ)

aʊə ... *sour* (saʊə(r))

The incidence of main stress is shown by a superior stress mark (') preceding the stressed syllable, and a secondary stress by an inferior stress mark (ˌ), e.g. *pronunciation* (prəˌnʌnsɪ'eɪʃ(ə)n).

For further explanation of the transcription used, see *General Explanations*, Volume I.

LIST OF ABBREVIATIONS, SIGNS, ETC.

Some abbreviations listed here in italics are also in certain cases printed in roman type, and vice versa.

a. (in Etym.)	adoption of, adopted from
a (as *a* 1850)	*ante*, 'before', 'not later than'
a.	adjective
abbrev.	abbreviation (of)
abl.	ablative
absol.	absolute, -ly
Abstr.	(in titles) *Abstract, -s*
acc.	accusative
Acct.	(in titles) *Account*
A.D.	*Anno Domini*
ad. (in Etym.)	adaptation of
Add.	Addenda
adj.	adjective
Adv.	(in titles) *Advance, -d, -s*
adv.	adverb
advb.	adverbial, -ly
Advt.	advertisement
Aeronaut.	(as label) in Aeronautics; (in titles) *Aeronautic, -al, -s*
AF., AFr.	Anglo-French
Afr.	Africa, -n
Agric.	(as label) in Agriculture; (in titles) *Agriculture, -al*
Alb.	Albanian
Amer.	American
Amer. Ind.	American Indian
Anat.	(as label) in Anatomy; (in titles) *Anatomy, -ical*
Anc.	(in titles) *Ancient*
Anglo-Ind.	Anglo-Indian
Anglo-Ir.	Anglo-Irish
Ann.	Annals
Anthrop., *Anthropol.*	(as label) in Anthropology; (in titles) *Anthropology, -ical*
Antiq.	(as label) in Antiquities; (in titles) *Antiquity*
aphet.	aphetic, aphetized
app.	apparently
Appl.	(in titles) *Applied*
Applic.	(in titles) *Application, -s*
appos.	appositive, -ly
Arab.	Arabic
Aram.	Aramaic
Arch.	in Architecture
arch.	archaic
Archæol.	in Archæology
Archit.	(as label) in Architecture; (in titles) *Architecture, -al*
Arm.	Armenian
assoc.	association
Astr.	in Astronomy
Astrol.	in Astrology
Astron.	(in titles) *Astronomy, -ical*
Astronaut.	(in titles) *Astronautic, -s*
attrib.	attributive, -ly
Austral.	Australian
Autobiogr.	(in titles) *Autobiography, -ical*
A.V.	Authorized Version
B.C.	Before Christ
B.C.	(in titles) British Columbia
bef.	before
Bibliogr.	(as label) in Bibliography; (in titles) *Bibliography, -ical*
Biochem.	(as label) in Biochemistry; (in titles) *Biochemistry, -ical*
Biol.	(as label) in Biology; (in titles) *Biology, -ical*
Bk.	*Book*
Bot.	(as label) in Botany; (in titles) *Botany, -ical*
Bp.	Bishop
Brit.	(in titles) *Britain, British*
Bulg.	Bulgarian
Bull.	(in titles) *Bulletin*
c (as *c* 1700)	*circa*, 'about'
c. (as 19th c.)	century
Cal.	(in titles) *Calendar*
Cambr.	(in titles) *Cambridge*
Canad.	Canadian
Cat.	Catalan
catachr.	catachrestically
Catal.	(in titles) *Catalogue*
Celt.	Celtic
Cent.	(in titles) *Century, Central*
Cent. Dict.	Century Dictionary
Cf., cf.	*confer*, 'compare'
Ch.	Church
Chem.	(as label) in Chemistry; (in titles) *Chemistry, -ical*
Chr.	(in titles) *Christian*
Chron.	(in titles) *Chronicle*
Chronol.	(in titles) *Chronology, -ical*
Cinemat., *Cinematogr.*	in Cinematography
Clin.	(in titles) *Clinical*
cl. L.	classical Latin
cogn. w.	cognate with
Col.	(in titles) *Colonel, Colony*
Coll.	(in titles) *Collection*
collect.	collective, -ly
colloq.	colloquial, -ly
comb.	combined, -ing
Comb.	Combinations
Comm.	in Commercial usage
Communic.	in Communications
comp.	compound, composition
Compan.	(in titles) *Companion*
compar.	comparative
compl.	complement
Compl.	(in titles) *Complete*
Conc.	(in titles) *Concise*
Conch.	in Conchology
concr.	concrete, -ly
Conf.	(in titles) *Conference*
Congr.	(in titles) *Congress*
conj.	conjunction
cons.	consonant
const.	construction, construed with
contr.	contrast (with)
Contrib.	(in titles) *Contribution*
Corr.	(in titles) *Correspondence*
corresp.	corresponding (to)
Cotgr.	R. Cotgrave, *Dictionarie of the French and English Tongues*
cpd.	compound
Crit.	(in titles) *Criticism, Critical*
Cryst.	in Crystallography
Cycl.	(in titles) *Cyclopædia, -ic*
Cytol.	(in titles) *Cytology, -ical*
Da.	Danish
D.A.	*Dictionary of Americanisms*
D.A.E.	*Dictionary of American English*
dat.	dative
D.C.	District of Columbia
Deb.	(in titles) *Debate, -s*
def.	definite, -ition
dem.	demonstrative
deriv.	derivative, -ation
derog.	derogatory
Descr.	(in titles) *Description, -tive*
Devel.	(in titles) *Development, -al*
Diagn.	(in titles) *Diagnosis, Diagnostic*
dial.	dialect, -al
Dict.	Dictionary; *spec.*, the *Oxford English Dictionary*
dim.	diminutive
Dis.	(in titles) *Disease*
Diss.	(in titles) *Dissertation*
D.O.S.T.	*Dictionary of the Older Scottish Tongue*
Du.	Dutch
E.	East
Eccl.	(as label) in Ecclesiastical usage; (in titles) *Ecclesiastical*
Ecol.	in Ecology
Econ.	(as label) in Economics; (in titles) *Economy, -ics*
ed.	edition
E.D.D.	*English Dialect Dictionary*
Edin.	(in titles) *Edinburgh*
Educ.	(as label) in Education; (in titles) *Education, -al*
EE.	Early English
e.g.	*exempli gratia*, 'for example'
Electr.	(as label) in Electricity; (in titles) *Electricity, -ical*
Electron.	(in titles) *Electronic, -s*
Elem.	(in titles) *Element, -ary*
ellipt.	elliptical, -ly
Embryol.	in Embryology
e.midl.	east midland (dialect)
Encycl.	(in titles) *Encyclopædia, -ic*
Eng.	England, English
Engin.	in Engineering
Ent.	in Entomology
Entomol.	(in titles) *Entomology, -logical*
erron.	erroneous, -ly
esp.	especially
Ess.	(in titles) *Essay, -s*
et al.	*et alii*, 'and others'
etc.	et cetera
Ethnol.	in Ethnology
etym.	etymology
euphem.	euphemistically
Exam.	(in titles) *Examination*
exc.	except
Exerc.	(in titles) *Exercise, -s*
Exper.	(in titles) *Experiment, -al*
Explor.	(in titles) *Exploration, -s*
f.	feminine
f. (in Etym.)	formed on
f. (in subordinate entries)	form of
F.	French
fem. (rarely f.)	feminine
fig.	figurative, -ly
Finn.	Finnish
fl.	*floruit*, 'flourished'
Found.	(in titles) *Foundation, -s*
Fr.	French
freq.	frequent, -ly
Fris.	Frisian
Fund.	(in titles) *Fundamental, -s*
Funk or *Funk's Stand. Dict.*	*Funk and Wagnalls Standard Dictionary*
G.	German
Gael.	Gaelic
Gaz.	(in titles) *Gazette*
gen.	genitive
gen.	general, -ly
Geogr.	(as label) in Geography; (in titles) *Geography, -ical*

Geol.	(as label) in Geology; (in titles) *Geology, -ical*	
Geom.	in Geometry	
Geomorphol.	in Geomorphology	
Ger.	German	
Gloss.	Glossary	
Gmc.	Germanic	
Godef.	F. Godefroy, *Dictionnaire de l'ancienne langue française*	
Goth.	Gothic	
Govt.	(in titles) *Government*	
Gr.	Greek	
Gram.	(as label) in Grammar; (in titles) *Grammar, -tical*	
Gt.	Great	
Heb.	Hebrew	
Her.	in Heraldry	
Herb.	among herbalists	
Hind.	Hindustani	
Hist.	(as label) in History; (in titles) *History, -ical*	
hist.	historical	
Histol.	(in titles) *Histology, -ical*	
Hort.	in Horticulture	
Househ.	(in titles) *Household*	
Housek.	(in titles) *Housekeeping*	
Ibid.	*Ibidem*, 'in the same book or passage'	
Icel.	Icelandic	
Ichthyol.	in Ichthyology	
id.	*idem*, 'the same'	
i.e.	*id est*, 'that is'	
IE.	Indo-European	
Illustr.	(in titles) *Illustration, -ted*	
imit.	imitative	
Immunol.	in Immunology	
imp.	imperative	
impers.	impersonal	
impf.	imperfect	
ind.	indicative	
indef.	indefinite	
Industr.	(in titles) *Industry, -ial*	
inf.	infinitive	
infl.	influenced	
Inorg.	(in titles) *Inorganic*	
Ins.	(in titles) *Insurance*	
Inst.	(in titles) *Institute, -tion*	
int.	interjection	
intr.	intransitive	
Introd.	(in titles) *Introduction*	
Ir.	Irish	
irreg.	irregular, -ly	
It.	Italian	
J., (J.)	(quoted from) Johnson's *Dictionary*	
(Jam.)	Jamieson, *Scottish Dict.*	
Jap.	Japanese	
joc.	jocular, -ly	
Jrnl.	(in titles) *Journal*	
Jun.	(in titles) *Junior*	
Knowl.	(in titles) *Knowledge*	
l.	line	
L.	Latin	
lang.	language	
Lect.	(in titles) *Lecture, -s*	
Less.	(in titles) *Lesson, -s*	
Let., Lett.	letter, letters	
LG.	Low German	
lit.	literal, -ly	
Lit.	Literary	
Lith.	Lithuanian	
LXX	Septuagint	
m.	masculine	
Mag.	(in titles) *Magazine*	
Magn.	(in titles) *Magnetic, -ism*	
Mal.	Malay, Malayan	
Man.	(in titles) *Manual*	
Managem.	(in titles) *Management*	
Manch.	(in titles) *Manchester*	
Manuf.	in Manufacture, -ing	
Mar.	(in titles) *Marine*	

masc. (*rarely* m.)	masculine	
Math.	(as label) in Mathematics; (in titles) *Mathematics, -al*	
MDu.	Middle Dutch	
ME.	Middle English	
Mech.	(as label) in Mechanics; (in titles) *Mechanics, -al*	
Med.	(as label) in Medicine; (in titles) *Medicine, -ical*	
med.L.	medieval Latin	
Mem.	(in titles) *Memoir, -s*	
Metaph.	in Metaphysics	
Meteorol.	(as label) in Meteorology; (in titles) *Meteorology, -ical*	
MHG.	Middle High German	
midl.	midland (dialect)	
Mil.	in military usage	
Min.	(as label) in Mineralogy; (in titles) *Ministry*	
Mineral.	(in titles) *Mineralogy, -ical*	
MLG.	Middle Low German	
Misc.	(in titles) *Miscellany, -eous*	
mod.	modern	
mod.L	modern Latin	
(Morris),	(quoted from) E. E. Morris's *Austral English*	
Mus.	(as label) in Music; (in titles) *Music, -al; Museum*	
Myst.	(in titles) *Mystery*	
Mythol.	in Mythology	
N.	North	
n.	neuter	
N. Amer.	North America, -n	
N. & Q.	*Notes and Queries*	
Narr.	(in titles) *Narrative*	
Nat.	(in titles) *Natural*	
Nat. Hist.	in Natural History	
Naut.	in nautical language	
N.E.	North East	
N.E.D.	*New English Dictionary,* original title of the *Oxford English Dictionary* (first edition)	
Neurol.	in Neurology	
neut. (*rarely* n.)	neuter	
NF., NFr.	Northern French	
No.	Number	
nom.	nominative	
north.	northern (dialect)	
Norw.	Norwegian	
n.q.	no quotations	
N.T.	New Testament	
Nucl.	Nuclear	
Numism.	in Numismatics	
N.W.	North West	
N.Z.	New Zealand	
obj.	object	
obl.	oblique	
Obs., obs.	obsolete	
Obstetr.	(in titles) *Obstetrics*	
occas.	occasionally	
OE.	Old English (= Anglo-Saxon)	
OF., OFr.	Old French	
OFris.	Old Frisian	
OHG.	Old High German	
OIr.	Old Irish	
ON.	Old Norse	
ONF.	Old Northern French	
Ophthalm.	in Ophthalmology	
opp.	opposed (to), the opposite (of)	
Opt.	in Optics	
Org.	(in titles) *Organic*	
orig.	origin, -al, -ally	
Ornith.	(as label) in Ornithology; (in titles) *Ornithology, -ical*	
OS.	Old Saxon	
OSl.	Old (Church) Slavonic	
O.T.	Old Testament	
Outl.	(in titles) *Outline*	
Oxf.	(in titles) *Oxford*	
p.	page	
Palæogr.	in Palæography	

Palæont.	(as label) in Palæontology; (in titles) *Palæontology, -ical*	
pa. pple.	passive participle, past participle	
(Partridge),	(quoted from) E. Partridge's *Dictionary of Slang and Unconventional English*	
pass.	passive, -ly	
pa.t.	past tense	
Path.	(as label) in Pathology; (in titles) *Pathology, -ical*	
perh.	perhaps	
Pers.	Persian	
pers.	person, -al	
Petrogr.	in Petrography	
Petrol.	(as label) in Petrology; (in titles) *Petrology, -ical*	
(Pettman),	(quoted from) C. Pettman's *Africanderisms*	
pf.	perfect	
Pg.	Portuguese	
Pharm.	in Pharmacology	
Philol.	(as label) in Philology; (in titles) *Philology, -ical*	
Philos.	(as label) in Philosophy; (in titles) *Philosophy, -ic*	
phonet.	phonetic, -ally	
Photogr.	(as label) in Photography; (in titles) *Photography, -ical*	
phr.	phrase	
Phys.	physical; (*rarely*) in Physiology	
Physiol.	(as label) in Physiology; (in titles) *Physiology, -ical*	
Pict.	(in titles) *Picture, Pictorial*	
pl., plur.	plural	
poet.	poetic, -al	
Pol.	Polish	
Pol.	(as label) in Politics; (in titles) *Politics, -al*	
Pol. Econ.	in Political Economy	
Polit.	(in titles) *Politics, -al*	
pop.	popular, -ly	
Porc.	(in titles) *Porcelain*	
poss.	possessive	
Pott.	(in titles) *Pottery*	
ppl. a., pple. adj.	participial adjective	
pple.	participle	
Pr.	Provençal	
pr.	present	
Pract.	(in titles) *Practice, -al*	
prec.	preceding (word or article)	
pred.	predicative	
pref.	prefix	
pref., Pref.	preface	
prep.	preposition	
pres.	present	
Princ.	(in titles) *Principle, -s*	
priv.	privative	
prob.	probably	
Probl.	(in titles) *Problem*	
Proc.	(in titles) *Proceedings*	
pron.	pronoun	
pronunc.	pronunciation	
prop.	properly	
Pros.	in Prosody	
Prov.	Provençal	
pr. pple.	present participle	
Psych.	in Psychology	
Psychol.	(as label) in Psychology; (in titles) *Psychology, -ical*	
Publ.	(in titles) *Publications*	
Q.	(in titles) *Quarterly*	
quot(s).	quotation(s)	
q.v.	*quod vide*, 'which see'	
R.	(in titles) *Royal*	
Radiol.	in Radiology	
R.C.Ch.	Roman Catholic Church	
Rec.	(in titles) *Record*	
redupl.	reduplicating	
Ref.	(in titles) *Reference*	
refash.	refashioned, -ing	
refl.	reflexive	
Reg.	(in titles) *Register*	

reg.	regular	str.	strong	*Trop.*	(in titles) *Tropical*
rel.	related to	*Struct.*	(in titles) *Structure, -al*	Turk.	Turkish
Reminisc.	(in titles) *Reminiscence, -s*	*Stud.*	(in titles) *Studies*	*Typog., Typogr.*	in Typography
Rep.	(in titles) *Report, -s*	subj.	subject		
repr.	representative, representing	*subord. cl.*	subordinate clause	ult.	ultimately
Res.	(in titles) *Research*	subseq.	subsequent, -ly	*Univ.*	(in titles) *University*
Rev.	(in titles) *Review*	subst.	substantively	unkn.	unknown
rev.	revised	*suff.*	suffix	*U.S.*	United States
Rhet.	in Rhetoric	superl.	superlative	U.S.S.R.	Union of Soviet Socialist
Rom.	Roman, -ce, -ic	Suppl.	Supplement		Republics
Rum.	Rumanian	*Surg.*	(as label) in Surgery;	usu.	usually
Russ.	Russian		(in titles) *Surgery, Surgical*		
		s.v.	*sub voce,* 'under the word'	*v., vb.*	verb
S.	South	Sw.	Swedish	var(r)., vars.	variant(s) of
S.Afr.	South Africa, -n	s.w.	south-western (dialect)	*vbl. sb.*	verbal substantive
sb.	substantive	*Syd. Soc. Lex.*	Sydenham Society, *Lexicon*	*Vertebr.*	(in titles) *Vertebrate, -s*
sc.	*scilicet,* 'understand' or		*of Medicine & Allied*	*Vet.*	(as label) in Veterinary
	'supply'		*Sciences*		Science;
Sc., Scot.	Scottish	syll.	syllable		(in titles) *Veterinary*
Scand.	(in titles) *Scandinavia, -n*	Syr.	Syrian	*Vet. Sci.*	in Veterinary Science
Sch.	(in titles) *School*	Syst.	(in titles) *System, -atic*	viz.	*videlicet,* 'namely'
Sc. Nat. Dict.	*Scottish National Dictionary*			*Voy.*	(in titles) *Voyage, -s*
Scotl.	(in titles) *Scotland*	*Taxon.*	(in titles) *Taxonomy, -ical*	*v.str.*	strong verb
Sel.	(in titles) *Selection, -s*	techn.	technical, -ly	*vulg.*	vulgar
Ser.	Series	*Technol.*	(in titles) *Technology, -ical*	*v.w.*	weak verb
sing.	singular	*Telegr.*	in Telegraphy		
Sk.	(in titles) *Sketch*	*Teleph.*	in Telephony	W.	Welsh; West
Skr.	Sanskrit	(Th.),	(quoted from) Thornton's	wd.	word
Slav.	Slavonic		*American Glossary*	Webster	*Webster's* (*New*
S.N.D.	*Scottish National Dictionary*	*Theatr.*	in the Theatre, theatrical		*International*) *Dictionary*
Soc.	(in titles) *Society*	*Theol.*	(as label) in Theology;	*Westm.*	(in titles) *Westminster*
Sociol.	(as label) in Sociology;		(in titles) *Theology, -ical*	WGmc.	West Germanic
	(in titles) *Sociology, -ical*	*Theoret.*	(in titles) *Theoretical*	*Wks.*	(in titles) *Works*
Sp.	Spanish	Tokh.	Tokharian	w.midl.	west midland (dialect)
Sp.	(in titles) *Speech, -es*	tr., transl.	translated, translation	WS.	West Saxon
sp.	spelling	*Trans.*	(in titles) *Transactions*		
spec.	specifically	*trans.*	transitive	(Y.),	(quoted from) Yule &
Spec.	(in titles) *Specimen*	*transf.*	transferred sense		Burnell's *Hobson-Jobson*
St.	Saint	*Trav.*	(in titles) *Travel(s)*	*Yrs.*	(in titles) *Years*
Stand.	(in titles) *Standard*	*Treas.*	(in titles) *Treasury*		
Stanf.	(quoted from) *Stanford*	*Treat.*	(in titles) *Treatise*	*Zoogeogr.*	in Zoogeography
	Dictionary of Anglicised	*Treatm.*	(in titles) *Treatment*	*Zool.*	(as label) in Zoology;
	Words & Phrases	*Trig.*	in Trigonometry		(in titles) *Zoology, -ical*

Signs and Other Conventions

Before a word or sense

† = obsolete
‖ = not naturalized, alien
¶ = catachrestic and erroneous uses

In the listing of Forms

1 = before 1100
2 = 12th c. (1100 to 1200)
3 = 13th c. (1200 to 1300), etc.
5-7 = 15th to 17th century
20 = 20th century

In the etymologies

* indicates a word or form not actually found,
  but of which the existence is inferred
:— = normal development of

The printing of a word in SMALL CAPITALS indicates that further information will be found under the word so referred to.

.. indicates an omitted part of a quotation.

~ (in a quotation) indicates a hyphen doubtfully present in the original; (in other text) indicates a hyphen inserted only for the sake of a line-break.

PROPRIETARY NAMES

THIS Dictionary includes some words which are or are asserted to be proprietary names or trade marks. Their inclusion does not imply that they have acquired for legal purposes a non-proprietary or general significance nor any other judgement concerning their legal status. In cases where the editorial staff have established in the records of the Patent Offices of the United Kingdom and of the United States that a word is registered as a proprietary name or trade mark this is indicated, but no judgement concerning the legal status of such words is made or implied thereby.

dvandva ('dvandvə). *Philol.* Also dwandwa. [Skr. *dvandvá*, the repeated nom. of *dva* pair, couple.] In full ***dvandva compound***. A compound word in which the elements are related to each other as if joined by a copula.

1846 MONIER WILLIAMS *Elem. Gram. Sanscr.* ix. 158 Native grammarians class compound nouns under ..*dwandwa*, or those formed by the aggregation into one compound of two or more nouns..which, if uncompounded, they would all be in the same case, connected by a copulative conjunction [etc.]. **1932** W. L. GRAFF *Lang. & Languages* iii. 119 A dvandva compound is one in which the relationship between the two constituents may be rendered by the conjunction *and*; for example, *prince-consort*. **1946** *Trans. Philol. Soc. 1945* 86 The compound *śiloñcha-* then came to be misunderstood as a dvandva. **1962** A. CAMPBELL in Davis & Wrenn *Eng. & Medieval Stud.* 18 The lays seem to have preserved the dvandva compound, a type otherwise unknown in Germanic.

dvornik ('dvɔːnɪk). [Russ. *dvórnik*, f. *dvor* courtyard.] A house-porter.

1903 *Westm. Gaz.* 17 Jan. 10/1 The duties of the dvorniks, a sort of assistant police. **1919** H. S. WALPOLE *Secret City* I. xxii. 160, I said good-night to every one. I could hear their laughter as I waited at the bottom of the stairs for the Dvornik to let me out. **1923** *Blackw. Mag.* Feb. 203/2 The 'dvornik' had been with the family for years.

dwa-grass: see TWA-GRASS.

†**dwale**, *sb.*[1] and *a.* *Obs.* Forms: α. 1 dweola, dwola, dwala, 3 dwole, dwale, 3–4 duale. [In sense 1, a variant of DWELE *sb.*, = OE. **dwela*, *dweola*, *dwola*, error, heresy, madness; in sense 2 app. aphetic for OE. *ȝedweola*, *-dwola*, etc. error, heresy, madness, also heretic, deceiver; f. ablaut-series *dwel-*, *dwal-*, *dwol-*: see DWELL *v.* Cf. OE. *dwol-* in comb. 'erring, heretical', and Goth. *dwals* 'foolish'.]

1. Error, delusion; deceit, fraud.

[*c* **900** tr. *Bæda's Hist.* II. xii. [xv.] (1890) 142 Seo mæȝd þreo ȝear in ȝedwolan wæs lifiende.] *c* **950** *Lindisf. Gosp.* Matt. xxvii. 64 And bið ðin hlætmesto duola wyrse from ærra. *c* **975** *Rushw. Gosp.* Matt. vi. 24 Ne maȝun ȝe gode ðeowiȝe & dwale. *a* **1250** *Owl & Night.* 823 Ȝif the vox mist of al this dwole, At than ende he cropth to hole. *c* **1250** *Gen. & Ex.* 4055 Wið win, and wlite, & bodi, & dwale. *a* **1300** *Cursor M.* 12841 Þe godds lamb, þan clenge sale þis wreched werld fra sinful duale. *Ibid.* 14197 Qua walkes on nightertale O dreching oft he findes duale.

2. Heretic, deceiver, transgressor.

[*c* **1000** ÆLFRIC *Hom.* (Th.) I. 290 Þa forwearð eac þes ȝedwola mid his ȝedwylde. *c* **1000** *Blickl. Hom.* 7 þone ealdan ȝedwolan (= Satan).] *c* **1200** ORMIN 7454 Off all þiss laþe læredd follc.. Wass maȝȝstredwale, an defless þeww, þat Arriuss wass nemmnedd. *a* **1250** *Prov. Ælfred* 414 in *O.E. Misc.* 126 Ne myd manyes cunnes tales; ne chid þu wiþ nenne dwales. *c* **1250** *Gen. & Ex.* 1220 Til god him bad is wiues tale Listen, and don a-wei ðat dwale. *Ibid.* 3404 Ietro listnede moyses tale, Of him and pharaon ðe dwale.

3. *attrib.* or *adj.* Heretical, perverse.

c **1250** *Gen. & Ex.* 20 Lucifer, ðat deuel dwale.

4. *Comb.*, as **dwal-kenned** *a.*, heretical.

c **1200** ORMIN 7441 þatt þurrh dwallkennde lare Tahhtenn & turrndenn lawedd follc To lefenn wrang o Criste.

dwale (dweɪl), *sb.*[2] Also 6–7 **dwall**, 7 **dwaile**. [prob. from Scandinavian: cf. ON. *dvöl*, *dvalar*, delay, *dvali* (Haldors.) delay, sleep, Sw. *dvala* trance, Da. *dvale* dead sleep, trance, torpor, *dvaledrik* soporiferous draught, *dvalebær* narcotic berry; from same root as DWALE *sb.*[1]]

†1. A stupefying or soporific drink. *Obs.* (Prob. in many instances, the juice or infusion of Belladonna: see 2.)

a **1300** *Cursor M.* 26323 (Cott.) Lech þat suld.. giue him for to drinc duale. *c* **1340** *Ibid.* 17708 (Trin.) þei fel as þei had dronken dwale. *c* **1386** CHAUCER *Reeve's T.* 241 Hem neded no dwale. This Millere hath so wisely bibbed Ale. **1393** LANGL. *P. Pl.* C. XXIII. 379 The frere with his fisik þis folke haþ enchaunted, And doþ men drynke dwale. *c* **1480** *Crt. of Love* 998 Aryse anon, quod she, whate? have ye dronken dwale? **1585** LUPTON *Thous. Notable Th.* (1675) 73 Dwale.. makes one to sleep while he is cut, or burned by cauterizing. **1606** BRETON *Ourania* Mij, As one receiving Opium or Dwall, Deprived of vital sence doth deadly fall.

2. The Deadly Nightshade, *Atropa Belladonna*.

In early use sometimes applied to a species of Winter Cherry (*Physalis somnifera*), and perhaps to other plants of similar properties.

14.. *Receipts* in *Rel. Ant.* I. 324 For to take alle maner of byrdys.. take juse of dwale and menche the corne theryn; and ley yt ther the byrdes hawnten, and wher they have eten therof, they shalle slepe. *c* **1440** *Promp. Parv.* 134/1 Dwale, herbe, *morella sompnifera*, *vel mortifera*. **1538** TURNER *Libellus*, Dwale, *Solanum soporiferum*. **1552** HULOET, Dwale, herbe hauynge a redde berrye within a bladder lyke a cherye, *alkakengi*. **1597** GERARDE *Herbal* II. li. §1. 269 Dwale or sleeping nightshade hath round blackish stalks sixe foote high. **1608** R. JOHNSON *Seven Champ.* II. M iv, As heavy a sleepe as if they had drunke the juyce of dwaile or the seede of poppie. **1861** MISS PRATT *Flower. Pl.* IV. 71 Dwale, or Deadly Nightshade.

†3. In *Her.* sometimes used for *sable*. *Obs.*

1562 LEIGH *Armorie* (1597) 100b, For Azure, perwinke: for Sable, dwale. **1727–51** CHAMBERS *Cycl.*, *Dwale*, or *dwal* in heraldry.. used by such as blazon with flowers and herbs, instead of colours and metals, for sable, or black.

dwalm, dwam (dwɑːm), *sb.* *Sc.* and *north. dial.* Forms: 6–9 dwawm, 8 dwaam, 9 dwam, dwalm, dwaum. [orig. *dwalm*, a deriv. of the verbal ablaut series mentioned under DWELL: cf. OE. *dwolma* confusion, chaos, abyss, OHG. *twalm*, MDu. *dwelm* stunning, stupefaction, giddiness, OS. *dwalm* delusion.] A swoon, a fainting fit.

1500–20 DUNBAR *Poems* lxxiv. 17 Sic deidlie dwawmes so mischeifaislie.. hes my hairt ouirpast. **1566** *Let.* 23 Oct. in Keith *Hist. Ch. & St. Scotl.* II. App. (1734) 133 Hir Majestie.. hes had sum Dwaumes of Swouning, quhilk puttis Men in sum Feir. *a* **1774** FERGUSSON *Cauler Water* Poems (1845) 25 Though.. ony inward dwaam should seize us. **1816** SCOTT *Old Mort.* xxxix, 'Sae he fell out o' ae dwam into another.' **1837** R. NICOLL *Poems* (1842) 151 Last Sabbath, as I sang the Psalm, I fell into an unco dwaum. **1892** *Northumbld. Gloss.*, *Dwalm*, a slight illness, a faint fit. (Also in Glossaries of E. Yorkshire.)

dwalm, dwam, *v.* *Sc.* and *north. dial.* [f. DWALM *sb.*] *intr.* To faint, swoon; to become unconscious; also, to sicken or fail in health.

1500–20 DUNBAR *Poems* xxvii. 50 His hairt a littill dwamyng tuke. **1513** DOUGLAS *Æneis* III. v. 55 Ȝit thus, at last said eftir hir dwalmyng. **1576** *Trial Eliz. Dunlop* in P.H. Brown *Scot. bef. 1700* (1893) 212 That causit hir to dwam. **1892** *Northumbld. Gloss.* s.v., Ah dwalmed off to sleep. **1895** IAN MACLAREN *Bonnie Brier Bush* 31 He begood to dwam in the end of the year.

dwang (dwæŋ). *Sc.* [cf. Du. *dwang* force, compulsion, constraint, f. *dwingen* to force.]

1842–76 GWILT *Encycl. Archit.* Gloss, *Dwang*, a term used in Scotland to denote the short pieces of timber employed in strutting a floor.

dwarf (dwɔːf), *sb.* and *a.* Pl. -fs; Forms: α. 1 duerȝ, dweorȝ, dweorh, 2 dwæruh, 4 dweruȝ, 4–5 dwerȝ(e, 5 dwergh, dwargh(e, duergh, dwerk, 5–6 *Sc.* duerch(e, dorche, DROICH. β. 4 dweruf, 4–5 dwerf(e, dwerff(e, (dwrfe), 5–7 dwarfe, 6–7 dwarff(e, 7 dwearf, 5– dwarf. γ. 4 duerwe, durwe, dwarw, 5 dwerwh(e, dwerwe, dwerowe, duorow. δ. 5 dwery, duery, dueri. [Comm. Teut.: OE. *dweorȝ*, *dweorh* (:—*dwerg*), = OFris. *dwirg*, OLG. **dwerg* (MDu. *dwerch*, Du. *dwerg*, MLG. *dwerch*, *dwarch*, LG. *dwark*, *dwarf* (Brem. Wbch.), *dorf*), OHG. *twerg* (MHG. *twerc*, Ger. *zwerg*), ON. *dvergr*, (Sw., Da. *dverg*):—OTeut. **dwergo-z*:—Aryan type **dhwérgʷhos*, represented phonetically in Gr. by *σέρφος* (:—**τϝέρφος*) 'midge'. In English the word shows interesting phonetic processes: (1) the original guttural and vowel came down in Sc. *duerch*, *duergh* (whence *dorch*, and by metathesis DROICH). (2) In Eng. *dweorȝ* became regularly *dwarf* (*eor*—: *ar* as in *bark*; *ȝ*—: *f* as in *enough*, *draft*). But (3) the pl. *dweorȝas* became *dwerwhes*, *dwerwes*, *dwerows*, *dwarrows*; and (4) the inflected form *dweorȝe-* gave *dwerȝhe*, *dweryhe*, *dwerye*, *dwery*. From these, by 'levelling', arose corresponding forms of the nom. sing. Parallel forms appear in *bargh*, *barf*, *barrow*, *burrow*, *berry*, from OE. *beorȝ* (:—*berg*) hill, and *burgh*, *borough*, *burrow*, *bury*, *Brough*, (bɒrf, brʊf), from OE. *burȝ* town.]

A. *sb.* 1. a. A human being much below the ordinary stature or size; a pygmy.

α. *a* **700** *Epinal Gloss.* 686 *Nanus vel pumilio*, duerȝ [so *Erfurt* and *Cott.*]. *a* **800** *Erfurt Gloss.* 1176 *Humiliamanus*, duerh. *c* **1050** *Supp. Ælfric's Voc.* in Wr.-Wülcker 190/17 *Pygmæus*.. dweorȝ. **11..** *Semi-Sax. Voc.* ibid. 539/20 *Nanus*, dwæruh. **13..** *Sir Beues* 2526 (MS. A.) Eueri man me clepede dweruȝ. *c* **1400** MAUNDEV. (Roxb.) xxxii. 147 Þai er lytill, lyke dwerghs. *a* **1400–50** *Alexander* 1752 Slike a dwinyng, a dwaȝe & a dwerȝe as þi-selfe, A grub, a grege out of grace. *c* **1450** HOLLAND *Howlat* 650 That wretchit dorche. **1460** *Lybeaus Disc.* 481 (Mätz.) The dwerk Teondeleyn Tok the stede be the rayne. **1483** *Cath. Angl.* 111/2 A Dwarghe, *tantillus*. **1508** KENNEDIE *Flyting w. Dunbar* 395 Duerch [*v.r.* derch], I sall ding the.

β. *c* **1325** *Gloss W. de Biblesw.* in Wright *Voc.* 167 *Neym*, a dwarw (dweruf). **1387** TREVISA *Higden* (Rolls) I. 231 A dwerf of þe kynrede of Mesenis. *Ibid.* IV. 301. *c* **1400** MAUNDEV. (1839) viii. 98 Ȝacheus the Dwerf, that clomb up in to the Sycomour Tre. **14..** *Nom.* in Wr.-Wülcker 689/14 *Hic tantillus*, a dwarf. *a* **1450** *Le Morte Arth.* 2058 A dwerffe shulde wende by hyr syde. **1590** SPENSER *F.Q.* I. i. 6 Behind her farre away a Dwarfe did lag. **1668** WOOD *Life* 24 July, Edward Price, dwarff, belonging to Mert. Coll., buried. **1711** ADDISON *Spect.* No. 99 ⁋5 The Damsel.. to avoid Scandal, must have a Dwarf for her Page. **1843–46** GROVE *Corr. Phys. Forces* 3 If a dwarf on the shoulders of a giant can see further than the giant, he is no less a dwarf in comparison with the giant.

fig. **1707** NORRIS *Humility* v. 197 A dwarf in goodness.

γ. **13..** *K. Alis.* 6266 Durwes al so he bysette Thikke and schort and gud sette. *c* **1320** *Sir Tristr.* 2062 Þe duerwe yseiȝe her ginne Þer he sat in þe tre. *c* **1440** *Promp. Parv.* 134/2 Dwerowe (*K.* dwerwh, *H.*, *P.* dwerwe, *W.* dwerfe), *nanus*. *c* **1475** *Pict. Voc.* in Wr.-Wülcker 806/9 *Hic omunculus*, a duorow.

δ. **1412–20** LYDG. *Chron. Troy* IV. xxxiii. (ed. 1555), No dwery is but lyke a gyaunt longe. **1430–40** —— *Bochas* III. i. (MS. *Rawl. C* 448 *lf.* 63 a/1) But it may falle a dwery [*ed.* **1554**, *lf.* 70 b/2 Drewry] in his riht Toutraie a geaunt for al his gret myht. *Ibid.* VI. i. viii. (MS. *Bodl.* 263 *lf.* 298) Now as a crepil lowe coorbed doun, Now a duery [*MS. Rawl. C* 448 *lf.* 123 a, dueri] and now a Champioun.

b. One of a supposed race of diminutive beings, who figure in Teutonic and esp. Scandinavian mythology and folk-lore; often identified with the elves, and supposed to be endowed with special skill in working metals, etc.

1770 BP. PERCY tr. *Mallet's North. Antiq.* v. (1847) 98 They made of his skull the vault of heaven, which is supported by four dwarfs, named North, South, East, and West. **1818** W. TAYLOR in *Monthly Mag.* XLVI. 26 The history of Laurin, king of the dwarves. **1834** LYTTON *Pilgrims of Rhine* xxvi, The aged King of the Dwarfs that preside over the dull realms of lead. **1846** J. E. TAYLOR *Fairy Ring* Notes 363 The notion that the wicked elves or dwarfs had the power to steal children before their baptism is found also.. in Iceland.

2. a. An animal or plant much below the ordinary height or size of its kind or species.

1664 EVELYN *Kal. Hort.* (1729) 222 The Crab-stock for Standards: For Dwarfs Stocks of the Paradise or Sweet-Apple-Kernel. **1719** LONDON & WISE *Compl. Gard.* 113 The Beauty of Dwarfs consists in a low Stem, an open Head. **1785** MARTYN *Rousseau's Bot.* xiv. 158 You will be glad to entertain this pretty dwarf [the Persian Iris]. **1880** MISS BIRD *Japan* I. 170 The wistaria.. As a dwarf, it covers the hills and roadsides, and as an aggressive liana it climbs the tallest trees.

b. *Astr.* One of the class of smaller stars of greater density as distinguished from the larger diffuse stars or 'giants'; without qualification or as ***dwarf star*** the term usu. denotes a star of the class comprising the majority of main-sequence stars (including the sun), as distinguished from a ***white dwarf*** (WHITE *a.*).

1912 [see GIANT B. 1 c]. **1913** *Observatory* Aug. 326 One can predict the real brightness of a dwarf star from a knowledge of its spectrum. **1921** *Discovery* Sept. 236/1 After this stage is reached and the star attains a certain density, it falls off rapidly in temperature, and becomes a cooling dwarf. **1956** H. S. JONES in A. Pryce-Jones *New Outl. Mod. Knowl.* II. 114 Other stars are so small that their diameters are less than one-hundredth of the Sun's. Such stars are called dwarfs. **1968** P. MOORE *Sky At Night* II. xxix. 214 It used to be thought that a typical star.. would end its career as a feeble Red Dwarf.

3. *attrib.* and *Comb.*, as ***dwarf-armour***, ***-king***; ***dwarf-worked*** (wrought by the dwarfs) adj.

a **1661** HOLYDAY *Juvenal* 240 The pygmie-warriour runs to fight In his dwarf-armour. **1853** DICKENS *Lett.* (1880) I. 317 Happy if I could do her any dwarf service. **1865** KINGSLEY *Herew.* iv, A gold ring.. right royally dwarf-worked. **1884** CHILD *Ballads* II. xli. 361/2 A dwarf-king, elf-king, hill-king.

B. *adj.*

1. a. Of or pertaining to a dwarf; dwarfish; of unusually small stature or size; diminutive; pygmy.

1634 RANDOLPH *Muses' Looking-gl.* v. i, Their stature neither dwarf nor giantish. **1686** PLOT *Staffordsh.*, Those little dwarf Spirits, we call Elves and Fairies. **1870** HOOKER *Stud. Flora* 342 Salix herbacea; very dwarf. **1880** MISS BRADDON *Just as I am* vii, There were dwarf bookcases between the windows. **1882** *Garden* 25 Feb. 126/3 The sweet perfumed double yellow Wallflower.. is much dwarfer than the old well-known yellow.

b. *transf.* Small, puny, stunted.

1634 FITZ-GEFFRAY *Bless. Birthd.* 23 (T.) Great is this mysterie of godlinesse Exceeding man's dwarf wit.

2. a. Used as the specific or trivial name of plants and animals of a height or size much below the average of their kind. See the sbs.

1597 GERARDE *Herbal* I. ii. (1633) 3 Dwarfe Grasse is one of the least of Grasses. **1598** FLORIO, *Garzetta*.. Also a dwarfe Hearon, or myre dramble. **1641** FRENCH *Distill.* i. (1651) 39 Ebulus or Dwarfe Elder. **1712** J. JAMES tr. *Le Blond's Gardening* 149 Dwarf-Box.. is made use of for planting the.. Edgings of Borders. **1832** *Veg. Subst. Food* 220 The dwarf kidney-bean.. a native of India.. erroneously called the French bean. **1861** MISS PRATT *Flower. Pl.* V. 66 Dwarf Birch.. a low shrub.

b. *dwarf wainscoting*: see quot. 1823. *dwarf-wall*, any low wall; *spec.* one which forms the basis of a palisade or railing, or which supports the joists under a floor.

1722 DE FOE *Plague* (1884) 37 A Dwarf-wall with a Palisadoe on it. **1823** P. NICHOLSON *Pract. Build.* 584 *Dwarf-wainscotting*, that wainscotting which does not reach to the usual height. *Ibid.*, *Dwarf-walls*, those of less height than the story of a building. **1842–76** GWILT *Encycl. Archit.* Gloss., *Dwarf Wainscoting*.. usually three, four, five or six feet high. Sometimes called a *Dado*. *Dwarf Walls*.. sometimes the joists of a ground floor rest upon dwarf walls. **1892** *Law Times Rep.* LXVII. 487/1 Protected by dwarf walls on each side of the cutting.

Hence **'dwarfdom**, state of a dwarf. **'dwarfess**, (*rare*), a female dwarf. **'dwarfism**, a dwarfed condition (in animals or plants). **'dwarflike** *a.* **'dwarfship**, the personality of a dwarf.

a **1618** SYLVESTER *Epist.* i. *Arctophilo to Arctoa* Wks. 1880 II. 331/1 To see his dwarfship court you to my face. **1670** J. SMITH *Eng. Improv. Reviv'd* 74 Dwarf-like trees. **1830** COLERIDGE *Ch. & St.* 111 With its dwarfdom exaggerated by the contrast. **1835** ANSTER tr. *2nd Pt. Faustus* II. (1887) 118 The dwarfess fair. **1847** TENNYSON *Princ.* VII. 111 Half-crushed among the rest A dwarf-like Cato cower'd. **1865** *Morn. Star* 18 July, Upon the origin of dwarfism in animals .. The cause of dwarfism the writer supposes to be an accelerated development.

dwarf (dwɔːf), *v.* [f. prec. sb.]

1. *trans.* To render dwarf or dwarfish; to hinder from growing to the natural size; to stunt in growth.

a **1626** BACON *New Atl.* (1886) 180 We make them greater or taller than their kind is; and contrariwise dwarf them and stay their growth. **1711** ADDISON *Spect.* No. 98 ⁋1 The

whole Sex is in a manner dwarfed and shrunk into a race of Beauties that seems almost another Species. **1851** CARPENTER *Man. Phys.* (ed. 2) 251 Such a limitation of the supply, as would dwarf a Plant to any considerable extent, would be fatal to the life of an Animal. **1859** DARWIN *Orig. Spec.* ix. 255 The seedlings were miserably dwarfed.

2. *transf.* and *fig.* To render small, puny, or insignificant in extent, nature, character, mind, etc.

1638 W. GILBERTE in *Ussher's Lett.* (1686) 494 He dwarfs his Understanding. **1690** CHILD *Disc. Trade* (1694) 219 Undoubtedly high Customs do as well dwarf Plantations as Trade. **1752** HUME *Ess. & Treat.* (1777) I. 125 Not being dwarfed by the restraint of authority. **1856** EMERSON *Eng. Traits, Wealth* Wks. (Bohn) II. 74 The incessant repetition of the same hand-work dwarfs the man, robs him of his strength, wit, and versatility.

3. To cause to look or seem small, as by the near presence of a much higher or larger object, or by removal to a distance. *lit.* and *fig.*

1850 *Chambers' Papers for People* IV. 3 It overshadowed and dwarfed the sinking throne of the Merovingian kings of France. **1870** DISRAELI *Lothair* xxxi, There was an immense chandelier suspended in each of these rooms.. dwarfing the apartments. **1894** FENN *In Alpine Valley* I. 40 A herd of these [goats] on the other side of the valley, seemed to be dwarfed to the size of rabbits.

4. *intr.* To become dwarf or dwarfed.

1833 TENNYSON *Poems* 132 By him [Mark Antony] great Pompey dwarfs and suffers pain. **1880** L. WALLACE *Ben-Hur* 7 The region where the herbage began to dwarf.

Hence **'dwarfing** *vbl. sb.* and *ppl. a.*

1626 BACON *Sylva* §536 Dwarfing requireth a slow Putting forth, and lesse Vigour of Mounting. **1823** BYRON *Juan* VIII. lxvi, Tall and strong.. Beyond the dwarfing city's pale abortions. **1846** J. BAXTER *Libr. Pract. Agric.* (ed. 4) I. 113 The process of dwarfing is another illustration of the fact that leaf-buds can be converted into flower-buds.

dwarfed (dwɔːft), *ppl. a.* [f. DWARF *v.* + -ED[1].] Rendered dwarf-like; stunted in growth.

1849 ROBERTSON *Serm.* Ser. I. ii. (1866) 29 A dwarfed, stunted.. religion. **1859** JEPHSON *Brittany* ix. 134 Dwarfed and gnarled oaks.

Hence **'dwarfedness.**

1886 W. F. WARREN in *Homilet. Rev.* Jan. 53 All our deformities, all our dwarfedness.

'dwarfify, *v. nonce-wd.* [f. DWARF + -FY.] *trans.* To dwarf.

1816 J. GILCHRIST *Phil. Etym.* 187 The.. dwarfifying tendency of [this] kind of learning.

dwarfish ('dwɔːfɪʃ), *a.* [f. DWARF *sb.* + -ISH.] Approaching the size of a dwarf, dwarf-like; of a stature or size below the average; pygmy, puny.

1565–73 COOPER *Thesaurus, Homuncio*.. a litle man: a dwarfishe fellow. **1590** SHAKS. *Mids. N.* III. ii. 295. **1607** TOPSELL *Four-f. Beasts* (1658) 23 In Ferraria among other strange beasts, they nourish dwarvish Asses. **1681** DRYDEN *Sp. Friar* Ded., A dwarfish thought, dressed up in gigantic words. **1774** GOLDSM. *Nat. Hist.* (1776) II. 219 A whole race of the dwarfish breed is often found to come down from the north. **1825** MACAULAY *Ess., Milton* (1854) I. 22 The days.. of dwarfish talents and gigantic vices. **1852** *Beck's Florist* Aug. 183 It has a dwarfish habit, is a profuse bloomer.

Hence **'dwarfishly** *adv.*; **'dwarfishness.**

1656 *Artif. Handsom.* 75 Shrunk to a dwarfishnesse and epitomized to a Decimo-sexto. **1755** JOHNSON, *Dwarfishly*, like a dwarf. **1841–4** EMERSON *Ess.* Ser. II. i. (1876) 38 To express themselves symmetrically and abundantly, not dwarfishly and fragmentarily. **1850** MISS MITFORD in L'Estrange *Life* (1870) III. xii. 217 Written by a Miss Brontë, a clergyman's daughter, diminutive almost to dwarfishness.

dwarfism ('dwɔːfɪz(ə)m). [f. DWARF *sb.* + -ISM.] The condition or character of being a dwarf or considerably undersized.

1891 *Brit. Med. Jrnl.* 5 Dec. 1187/2 When found as a racial feature dwarfism appears to be propagated indefinitely. **1919** *Nature* 3 Nov. 304/1 One of these forms of dwarfism is known to medical men as achondroplasia, because the growth of cartilage is particularly affected. **1934** [see ACHONDROPLASIA]. **1958** *Times* 1 July (Agric. Suppl.) p. vi/3 The genetics of dwarfism, over-simplified in the beginning, are now being studied thoroughly. The only present advice on how to avoid it is to breed for size. **1962** R. H. SMYTHE *Anat. Dog Breeding* 19 Toy Pomeranians are examples of true dwarfism.

dwarfling ('dwɔːflɪŋ). [f. DWARF *sb.* + -LING.] A small dwarf; a pygmy. Also *attrib.*

a **1618** SYLVESTER *Woodman's Bear* xxxiii, When the Dwarfling did perceive me, Me, Love's most rebellious scorner. **1887** *Pall Mall G.* 19 Sept. 6/1 Giant trees they are, and throw the dwarfling oaks into the shade.

dwarf-man. [f. DWARF *sb.* and *a.* + MAN *sb.*[1]] A very small man; a dwarf.

1877 *Encycl. Brit.* VII. 568/2 The dwarf man.. was less attractive than the dwarf boy. **1922** JOYCE *Ulysses* 380 It was upheld by four dwarfmen of that country. **1955** TOLKIEN *Return of King* 202 A sort of small dwarf-man.

'dwarfness. [f. DWARF *sb.* + -NESS.] The quality of being a dwarf; diminutiveness.

1658 J. ROBINSON *Eudoxa* Pref. 3 Neither the meannesse of the Superficies, nor dwarfnesse of the Bulk. *a* **1661** FULLER *Worthies* I. (1662) 116 His Expression, little Cleark.. referred not to his stature, but dwarfness in learning. **1880** P. GILLMORE *On Duty* 147 Peach, apple, and walnut-trees, the dwarfness of which did not take away from the general dreariness.

dwarfy ('dwɔːfɪ), *a.* [f. as prec. + -Y[1].] Of the nature of or resembling a dwarf; dwarfish.

1607 NORDEN *Surv. Dial.* (1608) 233 A kind of smal hungry dwarffy thistle. **1775** ROMANS *Hist. Florida* App. 66 Where you see the timber of a dwarfy and shrubby growth. **1851** *Beck's Florist* Dec. 281 If it has but few and short roots, the flower will be poor and dwarfy.

dwaum, dwawm, var. of DWALM.

dway-berry. *Obs.* or *dial.* [cf. DWALE *sb.*[2], and Da. *dvale-bær.*] The berry of the Deadly Nightshade.

1605 PLAT *Delightes for Ladies*, Recipe 70 Dwayberies that do somewhat resemble blacke cherries, called in Latine by the name of *Solanum lethale.* **1819** *Banquet* 91 On dway-berries and daffodils to gaze. **1878** BRITTEN & HOLLAND *Plant-n.*

dwble, obs. Sc. form of DOUBLE.

†**dwele,** *sb. Obs.* Also 3–4 dweole, 4 dwelle. [= OE. **dwela*, **dweola* (*dwola, dwala*), or aphetic for *ȝedwela, -dweola, -dwola*, in same sense, f. root *dwel-*, as in next. Cf. DWALE *sb.*[1]] A going astray; error, delusion, deceit.

[*c* **900** tr. *Bæda's Hist.* I. viii. (1890) 42 Se ȝedweola wæs on ðam Nyceaniscan sinoþe ȝe iðerad.] *a* **1225** *Ancr. R.* 62 Louerd.. wend awei mine eien vrom þe worldes dweole. *c* **1275** *Passion our Lord* 525 in *O.E. Misc.* 52 þenne wrþ þe laste dwele wurse to alegge. *c* **1275** *Orison of our Lady* 35 ibid. 160 Iluued ich habbe gomen and gleo.. Al þat is dweole wel i seo. *a* **1300** *Sarmun* xxvii. in *E.E.P.* (1862) 4 þeiȝ freris prech of heuen and helle.. al þat him þenchit bot dwelle. *a* **1350** *Life Jesu* 149 (Mätz.) It nis bote dwele.

†**dwele,** *v. Obs.* Forms: 1 dwelian, dweliȝan, 2–4 dwele. [OE. *dwelian* (*dweolian, dwolian*), app.:—**dwelôjan*, f. *e*-grade of ablaut series *dwel-, dwal-, dwol-*: see DWELL.]

1. *intr.* To wander, go astray; to err, be deluded.

c **900** tr. *Bæda's Hist.* IV. iii. (1890) 270 þurh monige stowe dwoliende. *Ibid.* xxvii. 362 To ðæm dwoliȝendum læcedomum deofolȝylda. *c* **1000** ÆLFRIC *Hom.* I. 384 þæt he swa lange on ðam holte.. dwelode. *c* **1000** *Ags. Gosp.* Matt. xxii. 29 Ȝe dweliaþ and ne cunnon haliȝe ȝe-writu. *c* **1175** *Lamb. Hom.* 109 Ȝif þe larðeu dwelað hwa bið siððan his larþeu. *a* **1300** *E.E. Psalter* lvii[i]. 4 þai dweled fra magh.

2. *intr.* To be torpid, to be stunned, to swoon.

13.. *Seuyn Sag.* (W.) 770 The cradel turnd up so doun on ground, Up so doun, in hire feghting, That the child lai dweling.

dwell (dwɛl), *v.* Pa. t. and pa. pple. **dwelt,** now rarely **dwelled** (dwɛld). Forms: 1 dwellan, 3 (*Orm.*) dwellenn, 3–6 duell(e, (4 dewelle, dowelle), 4–6 duel, dwelle, 4–7 dwel, 4– dwell. *Pa. t.* α. 1 dwealde, 3 dwalde, dualde, duelde, 4–5 dwelde, dwellede, 4– dwelled (4–6 -id, -yd). β. 4 duelit, dwelte, 4–5 dwellet, -it, 4– dwelt. [OE. *dwęllan*, pa. t. **dwalde, dwealde*, (later also *dwęlian, -ede, -ode*) to lead astray, hinder, delay; also *intr.* (for *refl.*) to go astray, err; to be delayed, tarry, stay; corresp. to OHG. *twellan*, ON. *dvęlja* to retard, delay, *intr.* to stop, MDu. *dwellen* to stun, make giddy, perplex:—OTeut. **dwaljan*, causal of strong vb. of ablaut series *dwel-, dwal-, dwol-, (dul-)*, repr. by OHG. *gitwelan* to be stunned, benumbed, torpid, also to cease, leave off, give up, OS. *fordwelan* to cease, leave off, OE. pa. pple. *ȝedwolen* gone astray, gone wrong, perverted; from an Aryan root *dhwel, dhul*, appearing in Skr. *dhwṛ, dhūr* to mislead, deceive.]

†**1.** *trans.* To lead into error, mislead, delude; to stun, stupefy. *Obs.*

c **888** K. ÆLFRED *Boeth.* xxxv. §5 Me þincþ þæt þu me dweliȝe [*MS. Cott.* dwelle]. *Ibid.*, Ðu rædest ær þæt ic þe dwealde. Ac me þincþ selfum þæt ic þe nauht ne dwelode [*MS. Cott.* dwelle]. *c* **1000** ÆLFRIC *Hom.* II. 492 þa.. drymen.. ferdon him ætforan mid heora scincræfte, þæt folc dweliende. *a* **1300** *Cursor M.* 17708 þei fell als þai in duale war dueld [*Gött.* delued]. *Ibid.* 28031 Quen yee sa bede your war to sell, þe fole marchandis eth to duell.

†**2.** To hinder, delay. (Only OE.)

a **1000** *Riddles* xii. (*Exeter Bk.* lf. 103 b) Ic dysȝe dwelle.

†**3.** *intr.* To tarry, delay; to desist from action.

c **1200** ORMIN 9938 He nollde nohht þatt aniȝ shollde dwellenn Ne draȝhenn nohht fra daȝȝ to daȝȝ. *Ibid.* 13218 [He] Ne dwalde nohht to kiþenn himm. þatt god tatt himm was awwnedd. *c* **1300** [see DWELLING 1]. *a* **1325** *Prose Psalter* xliii[i]. 25 Arise vp, Lord; whi dwellestou? *c* **1386** CHAUCER *Nun's Pr. T.* 330 Thilke tale is al to longe for to telle, And eek it is ny day, I may nat dwelle. **1470–85** MALORY *Arthur* XI. vii, I drede we dwelle ouer longe from the sege.

4. To abide or continue for a time, in a place, state, or condition. *Obs.* or *arch.*

c **1200** ORMIN 5576 Himm reoweþþ þatt he dwelleþþ her Swa swiþe lange onn eorþe. *a* **1300** *Cursor M.* 17288 + 393 Sir, dwelle withe vus, for it is nerhand night. *c* **1380** WYCLIF *Wks.* (1880) 318 Crist duelled in preyere al þe nyȝt. *a* **1483** *Liber Niger* in *Househ. Ord.* 66 If any sergeaunt.. dwelle in arerages, he to be sent into the ward of Marchalcye. **1550** CROWLEY *Epigr.* 26 They be determined styll in their synne to dwell. **1596** SHAKS. *Merch. V.* I. iii. 157 Ile rather dwell in my necessitie. **1670** BROOKS *Wks.* (1867) VI. 390 A man.. would dwell in this contemplation of heaven, and be loath to come out of it. **1797** GODWIN *Enquirer* I. vi. 40 Their lines dwell upon our memory. **1896** J. DAVIDSON *Fleet Street Eclogues* 25 Fainter Voices Echo about the air and dwell and die.

†**b.** *to let dwell*: to let (things) remain as they are, let alone, let be. *Obs.*

c **1435** *Torr. Portugal* 2105 Let we now this children dwelle, And speke we more of Desonelle.

c. Of a horse: (*a*) To be slow in raising the feet from the ground in stepping. (*b*) To pause before taking a fence.

1737 BRACKEN *Farriery Impr.* (1757) II. 48 They.. are apt.. to interfere or cut, and to dwell upon the Ground (as the Jockeys term it). *Ibid.* 76 The Horse that takes long Steps, and dwells upon the Ground. **1885** *Sat. Rev.* 14 Feb. 206/1 Horses that 'dwell' at their fences are in our opinion, most objectionable hunters.

d. *Mech.* To pause. See DWELL *sb.* 2.

1836 [see DWELLING 4]. **1888** C. P. BROOKS *Cotton Manuf.* 61 The slay dwells longer at the healds than at the cloth.

5. ***to dwell on, upon*** (†*in*): to spend time upon or linger over (a thing) in action or thought; to remain with the attention fixed on; now, *esp.* to treat at length or with insistence, in speech or writing; also, to sustain (a note) in music. (The most frequent current use in speech.)

[*c* **1400** *Lanfranc's Cirurg.* 69 He dwellide on þe cure, and I wente my wey. *c* **1470** HENRY *Wallace* II. 246 Thai chargyt the geyler nocht on him to duell, Bot bryng him wp out of that vgly sell To jugisment.] **1513** DOUGLAS *Æneis* I. Prol. 246 Quhat suld I langar on his errouris dwell? **1581** MULCASTER *Positions* xliv. (1887) 285 Not to dwel longer on this point. **1594** SHAKS. *Rich. III*, v. iii. 100 Enterchange of sweet Discourse, Which so long sundred Friends should dwell vpon. **1652** J. WRIGHT tr. *Camus' Nature's Paradox* 222 Not to dwell any longer in these lawless proceedings. **1709** STEELE *Tatler* No. 28 ¶13 That Letter dwells upon the Unreasonableness of the Allies. **1816** KEATINGE *Trav.* (1817) II. 33 The mind.. can make the eye dwell on the more pleasing parts. **1834** MEDWIN *Angler in Wales* I. 274 Now she dwells on a single note. **1848** MILL *Pol. Econ.* I. v. §3 (1876) 42 This proposition requires to be somewhat dwelt upon. **1875** JOWETT *Plato* (ed. 2) IV. 495 [Plato] is constantly dwelling on the importance of regular classification.

†**6.** To continue in existence, to last, persist; to remain after others are taken or removed. *Obs.*

13.. *Guy Warw.* (Caius) 294 Yf I my sorowe hir doo not telle, Allas, wrecche, how shall y duelle? **1393** *Test. Ebor.* (Surtees) I. 186, I will that this place dwell still to my wyfe and to my childer. *c* **1400** *Lanfranc's Cirurg.* 49 For so þe schap of þe lyme [= limb] mai dwelle faire and strengere. **1401** *Pol. Poems* (Rolls) II. 83, I have chosen ȝou alle, that ȝe gon and beren fruyte, and ȝour fruyte may dwellyn.

7. To remain (in a house, country, etc.) as in a permanent residence; to have one's abode; to reside, 'live'. (Now mostly superseded by *live* in spoken use; but still common in literature.)

c **1250** *Gen. & Ex.* 1106 Quile ðat loth dwelledde ðor. **1303** R. BRUNNE *Handl. Synne* Prol. 65 Y dwelled yn þe pryorye Fyftene ȝere yn cumpanye. **1470–85** MALORY *Arthur* I. xvii, His mayster Bleyse that dwelde in Northumberland. **1574** *Nottingham Rec.* IV. 156 The tenemente.. wherein George Taylor lately dwelled. **1651** HOBBES *Leviath.* III. xxxviii. 240 The King that dwelleth in Heaven. **1798** WORDSW. *We are Seven*, Two of us at Conway dwell, And two are gone to sea. **1874** GREEN *Short Hist.* i. §1. 3 As they fought side by side on the field, so they dwelled side by side on the soil.

transf. and *fig.* **1340** HAMPOLE *Pr. Consc.* 294 Bot na drede in þair hertes may dwelle. *c* **1450** tr. *De Imitatione* II. i. 40 Reste in þe passion of crist, & dwelle gladly in hys holy woundes. **1667** MILTON *P.L.* I. 250 Farewel happy Fields Where Joy for ever dwells. **1751** JORTIN *Serm.* (1771) IV. i. 114 A faith which dwells in the heart. **1847** A. M. GILLIAM *Trav. Mexico* 177, I admire the love of country that dwells in the bosoms of Englishmen.

†**8.** *trans.* To occupy as a place of residence; to inhabit. *Obs.*

1520 SIR R. ELYOT *Will* in *Elyot's Gov.* (1883) I. App. A. 315 The tenement that she dwellith in Sarum. **1671** MILTON *P.R.* I. 330 We.. Who dwell this wild, constrained by want. **1799** W. TAYLOR in *Monthly Mag.* VII. 139 And now I dwell the cloister, sweep the ailes.

†**9.** To cause to abide *in. Obs.*

1667 MILTON *P.L.* XII. 487 The promise of the Father, who shall dwell His Spirit within them.

Hence **dwelling** *ppl. a.*, remaining, lasting, abiding; † **dwelt** *ppl. a.*, inhabited.

c **1380** WYCLIF *Serm.* Sel. Wks. I. 293 Apostlis chosen preestis.. and maden hem dwellinge curatis. **1610** BROUGHTON *Job* xxxiv. 13 Who settled all the dwelt-land. **1650** TRAPP *Comm. Lev.* xix. 17 The neglect of this dutie breeds dwelling suspicions. **1872** A. SHADWELL in J. E. Morgan *University Oars* (1873) 316 The blade long enough in the water to secure a dwelling stroke.

dwell, *sb.* Also 4 duell, dwel. [f. DWELL *v.* (Cf. ON. *dvöl* stay, delay.)] The action or an act of dwelling.

†**1.** Delay, stay, stoppage. ***withoute(n dwell***: without delay, straightway. *Obs.*

a **1300** *Cursor M.* 2831 Ne mak ȝee in þe plain na duell. *Ibid.* 12992 Fle sathanas, wit-vten duell. *c* **1380** *Sir Ferumb.* 648 þe iantail knyȝt.. spak with-oute duelle. *Ibid.* 2646 þat myn host may come withoute dwel.

2. *Mech.* A slight pause in the motion of a part of a machine to give time for the completion of the operation effected by the particular part. **b.** The brief continuation of pressure in taking an impression with a hand-press.

1841 *Specif. Darker's Patent* No. 9065. 7 A dwell of sufficient length to insert the wire [in a carpet loom]. **1885** *Specif. J. Jardine's Patent* No. 4960. 4, I am enabled to give a similar rest or dwell to the carriages at each extremity of their motion. **1890** *Iron* XXXV. 269/1 This positive

standstill lasts.. during the whole portion of the stroke [of the press], which is technically called the dwell.

dweller ('dwɛlə(r)). [f. DWELL *v.* + -ER[1].]

1. One who dwells or resides (in a place); an inhabitant, resident.

1382 WYCLIF *Isa.* xviii. 3 Alle ȝee dwelleris of the world. *c* **1460** FORTESCUE *Abs. & Lim. Mon.* vi. (1885) 123 Dwellers vppon owre costes. **1512** *Act 4 Hen. VIII*, c. 2 §1 The owner or dweller of the howse.. then beyng theryn. **1674** N. FAIRFAX *Bulk & Selv.* 186 Enough to hold all the dwellers of it and their children. **1791** COWPER *Iliad* I. 332 The rude dwellers on the mountain-heights. **1834** LYTTON *Pompeii* I. v, The dwellers in a sunny clime.

2. With *on*: see DWELL *v.* 5.

c **1600** SHAKS. *Sonn.* cxxv, Dwellers on form and favour.

3. A horse that 'dwells' at a fence.

1885 *Sat. Rev.* 14 Feb. 206/1 Dwellers require very careful handling, for.. if hurried at their fences they will run into them instead of jumping.

Hence †'**dwelleress**, a female dweller. *Obs.*

1382 WYCLIF *Jer.* xxi. 13 To thee, dwelleresse [*c* **1440** *MS. Bodl.* 277 dwelstere] of the sadde valey, and wilde feld.

dwelling ('dwɛlɪŋ), *vbl. sb.* [f. DWELL *v.* + -ING[1].] The action of the verb DWELL.

†**1.** Delaying, delay; tarrying. *Obs.*

c **1330** *Havelok* 1352 Loke that thou dwellen nouth: Dwelling haueth ofte scathe wrouth. *c* **1330** R. BRUNNE *Chron. Wace* (Rolls) 4965 Bot com, & make no dwellynge. *c* **1374** CHAUCER *Boeth.* I. metr. i. 1 (Camb. MS.) Myn vnpietous lyf draweth a long vnagreable dwellynges [*ingratas moras*] in me. *c* **1475** *Rauf Coilȝear* 239 For my dwelling to nicht, I dreid me for blame.

b. With *on, upon*: see DWELL *v.* 5.

1832 B'NESS BUNSEN in Hare *Life* I. ix. 380 It will not bear dwelling upon.

2. Continued, esp. habitual, residence; abode. Also *fig.*

1382 WYCLIF *Dan.* v. 21 With feeld assis his dwellynge was. *c* **1400** *Rom. Rose* 6208 Ne no wight may, by my clothing, Wite with what folk is my dwellyng. **1586** A. DAY *Eng. Secretary* II. (1625) 51 My dwelling with Master L. continued.. even to this present day. **1648** GAGE *West Ind.* xviii. 124 The healthiest and pleasantest place of dwelling that ever I came into.

†**b.** 'Residence', accommodation. *Obs.*

c **1460** FORTESCUE *Abs. & Lim. Mon.* xvii. (1885) 151 He hath be þe yere iij. li. x[d], be sydes his dwellynge in þe logge. **1535** COVERDALE *2 Kings* ii. 19 There is good dwellynge in this cite.. but the water is euell.

3. *concr.* A place of residence; a dwelling-place, habitation, house.

1340 HAMPOLE *Pr. Consc.* 1368 Na syker duellyng fynde we here. **1382** WYCLIF *John* xiv. 2 In the hous of my fadir ben manye dwellingis. **14..** *Voc.* in Wr.-Wülcker 594/41 *Mansio*, a dwellynge. **1535** COVERDALE *1 Esdras* ix. 37 The children of Israel were in their dwellynges. **1613** PURCHAS *Pilgrimage* (1614) 749 They have no dwelling but their boats. **1667** MILTON *P.L.* VII. 183 Good will To future men, and in thir dwellings peace. **1726** *Adv. Capt. R. Boyle* 43, I went back to my Dwelling. **1863** GEO. ELIOT *Romola* I. xx, A street of high silent-looking dwellings.

fig. **1655** STANLEY *Hist. Philos.* I. (1701) 40/1 Enclosed in the narrow dwelling of the Mind. **1713** BERKELEY *Guardian* No. 3 ¶1 That bosom which ought to be the dwelling of sanctity and devotion.

4. *attrib.* and *Comb.*, as ***dwelling cave, chamber, cottage, space,*** †***stead, tent,*** etc.; ***dwelling action*** (see DWELL *v.* 4 d). Also DWELLING-HOUSE, -PLACE.

a **1300** *Cursor M.* 14709 (Gött.) His duelling stede sal last in hell. *a* **1340** HAMPOLE *Psalter* xxxviii. 17 Na duellynge stede haf i here. **1607** TOPSELL *Serpents* (1658) 793 The Sea-tortoises of India are so big, that with one of them they cover a dwelling Cottage. **1718** BERKELEY *Tour in Italy* Wks. 1871 IV. 593 The dwelling-seat of the Prince of Caserta. **1780** COXE *Russ. Disc.* 132 One of the dwelling-caves of the savages. **1836** *Specif. Stansfeld's Patent* No. 7130. 2 Producing a gradual pressure and dwelling action of the lay or slay. **1891** *Month* LXXIII. 25 Freight-cars.. turned into dwelling-caves for the ballast-men.

Hence '**dwellingless** *a.*, without a dwelling; possessing or containing no dwelling.

1882 *Blackw. Mag.* Feb. 244 A melancholy expanse—treeless, dwellingless, manless. **1894** *Month* May 68 Whether they be styled dwellers in waggons, or be dwellingless.

'**dwelling-house.** A house occupied as a place of residence, as distinguished from a house of business, warehouse, office, etc.

1450-1530 *Myrr. our Ladye* 111 She mote make god mercyfull to vs, that was made hys dwellynge howse. **1592** *Nottingham Rec.* IV. 238 Makinge his barnes into dwellyn houses. **1616** SURFL. & MARKH. *Country Farme* 6 You must chuse the higest peece of ground to build your dwelling house vpon. **1777** ROBERTSON *Hist. Amer.* (1783) II. 190 Even in a village of the rudest Indians there are.. dwelling-houses. **1893** SELOUS *Trav. S. E. Africa* 251 A comfortable dwelling-house and several outhouses.

'**dwelling-place.** A place of abode.

c **1380** WYCLIF *Sel. Wks.* III. 197 þei.. han not here a dwellynge-place for evere. *c* **1400** MAUNDEV. (Roxb.) viii. 32 Na kirk, ne na chapell, ne oþer dwellyng place. **1551** T. WILSON *Logike* (1580) 78 b, None can tell almoste now a daies, where the good menne dooe dwell. Or if thei have dwellyng places still, yet fewe can finde them at home. **1667** MILTON *P.L.* II. 57 For thir dwelling place Accept this dark opprobrious Den of shame. **1818** BYRON *Ch. Har.* IV. clxxvii, Oh! that the Desart were my dwelling place. **1889** JESSOPP *Coming of Friars* iii. 119 The monastery was the common dwelling-place; the convent was the society of persons inhabiting it.

†'**dwelster.** *Obs. rare.* [f. DWELL *v.* + -STER.] A female dweller.

c **1440** [see DWELLERESS].

†**dwelth.** *Obs.* Also 3 **dweoleð, dweoluhðe, dweolðe.** [OE. type **dweluða*, **dweoluða*, from root *dwel-*: see DWELE, DWELL.] Error, delusion.

a **1225** *Ancr. R.* 224 þet heo was igon a dweoleð [*v.r.* o dweole]. *a* **1240** *Ureisun* 93 in *Cott. Hom.* 195 Alle kunnes dweoluhðe. *Ibid.* 148 þet.. ne dweolðe me ne derie. *c* **1420** *Chron. Vilod.* 3149 So seke he was þat he speke o dwelthe.

†'**dweomercræft.** *Obs.* [f. OE. **dwimer*, **dweomer*, in *ȝedwimer*, *ȝedwomer* illusion, sorcery, necromancy, *ȝedwimere* juggler, sorcerer + *cræft*, CRAFT.] Jugglery, magic art.

c **1205** LAY. 30634 And Peluz hit wiste anan þurh his dweomer-cræften.

dweomerlayk = prec.: see DEMERLAYK.

dwer, var. DOWER *sb.*[1] *Obs.*

†**dwere.** *Obs.* Also **dwer.** [Etymology unknown. (Cf. DISWERE.)] Doubt, dread.

c **1440** CAPGRAVE *Life St. Kath.* IV. 1165 Thou seyde to hem thei shulde not be in dwere What thei shulde speke. *c* **1440** HYLTON *Scala Perf.* (W. de W. 1494) II. xi, Therfore fallen some in dowte and dwere.. wheder they synned in tyme of temptacyon or noo. *c* **1450** LONELICH *Grail* lxvi. 18 Thus bothe the ladyes Enterid were In that same Abbey with-Owten dwere. *c* **1450** *Cov. Myst.* Prol. (Shaks. Soc.) 17 Alle woundere sore and have gret dwere. *c* **1460** *Towneley Myst.* (Surtees) 302 That maide us alle to be in dwere.

dwerf, dwergh, dwerowe, obs. ff. DWARF.

dwerg (dwɜːg). Pseudo-archaic form of DWARF *sb.* after OE. *dwerg*.

1892 KIPLING *Lett. Trav.* (1920) 76 A puff of the warm night wind among the flares set the whole line off again in a crazy dance of dwergs. **1892** —— *Seven Seas* (1896) 124 And the troll and gnome and dwerg, and the Gods of Cliff and Berg Were about me and beneath me and above.

dwete, obs. form of DUTY.

†**dwild.** *Obs.* Also 3 (*Orm.*) **dwilde, dwillde.** [OE. *dwyld* (*dwila*):—**d(w)ulði* (:—*dhúlti*), from *u-* grade of **dwelan* to err: see DWELL, DWALE.] Error, heresy.

O.E. Chron. an. 1122 Feole dwild wearen ȝeseoȝen and ȝeheord. *Ibid.* an. 1129 Nu wærð swa mycel dwyld on Cristendom. *c* **1200** ORMIN 11147 þurrh hæþenndom and dwilde. [Also in 10 other places.]

dwile (dwaɪl). *dial.* Also **dwily, dwyle.** [cf. Du. *dweil* mop, f. *dweilen* to mop.] A house-flannel, floor-cloth, or mop (see also quot. *a* 1825).

1823 E. MOOR *Suffolk Words* 117 *Dwily*, a towel. *a* **1825** R. FORBY *Vocab. E. Anglia* (1830) I. 101 *Dwile.* 1. A refuse lock of wool. 2. A mop made of them. 3. Any coarse rubbing rug. **1887** E. R. SUFFLING *Land of Broads* (illustr. ed.) xvii. 251 *Dwyle*, a dishcloth. **1962** A. JOBSON *Window in Suffolk* vi. 100 She called a house-flannel a *dwile*.

dwindle ('dwɪnd(ə)l), *v.* [A dimin. derivative of DWINE *v.*: cf. KINDLE *v.*[2] Prob. of dialect origin: in Shaks., but little used before 1650.]

1. *intr.* To become smaller and smaller; to shrink, waste away, decline.

1596 SHAKS. *1 Hen. IV*, III. iii. 3 Bardolph, am I not falne away vilely.. doe I not bate? doe I not dwindle? **1605** —— *Macb.* I. iii. 23 Wearie Sev'nights, nine times nine, Shall he dwindle, peake, and pine. **1649** BLITHE *Eng. Improv. Impr.* (1652) 107 Corne will fall flat and dwindle or rot. *a* **1661** FULLER *Worthies, Middlesex* (R.), It grindeth the grain beforehand, making it to dwindle away almost to nothing. **1711** BUDGELL *Spect.* No 150 ¶1 Little Insults and Contempts, which.. seem to dwindle into nothing when a Man offers to describe them. **1764** GOLDSM. *Trav.* 126 Man seems the only growth that dwindles here. **1831** EARL OF ELGIN in *Croker Papers* 15 July, [The] Opposition.. dwindling down to thirty or forty. **1855** MACAULAY *Hist. Eng.* III. 285 The party which on the first day of the session had rallied round Athol had dwindled away to nothing. **1875** JOWETT *Plato* (ed. 2) III. 163 Polygamist peoples.. dwindle in numbers.

In *pa. pple.* (constructed with *be*), denoting the resulting condition. (See also 2.)

a **1674** CLARENDON *Hist. Reb.* VIII. §145 The rest were dwindled away. **1700** T. BROWN tr. *Fresny's Amusem. Ser. & Com.* 130 Honour and Arms.. is now almost dwindled into an Airy nothing. **1863** KINGSLEY *Water-Bab.* iii. (1878) 134 Whether the fall be dwindled to a single thread.

b. *fig.* To decline in quality, value, or estimation; to degenerate, 'sink'.

1678 BUTLER *Hud.* III. ii. 644 For Saints in Peace degenerate And dwindle down to reprobate. *a* **1704** T. BROWN *Sat. Fr. King* Wks. 1730 I. 59 Thou that hast look'd so fierce, and talk'd so big, In thy old age to dwindle to a Whig. **1757** BURKE *Abridgm. Eng. Hist.* Wks. 1842 II. 517 The ancient prætors dwindled into his legates. **1874** GREEN *Short Hist.* 142 The writers dwindle into mere annalists whose view is bounded by the abbey precincts.

†**c.** To shrink (with fear). *Obs. rare.* (Prob. a misuse owing to two senses of *shrink*.)

1610 B JONSON *Alch.* V. iv, *Fac.* Did you not heare the coyle, About the dore? *Sub.* Yes, and I dwindled with it.

2. *trans.* To reduce gradually in size, cause to shrink into small dimensions.

a **1661** FULLER *Worthies* III. (1662) 56 Divine Justice, insensibly dwindling their Estates. **1679** *Prot. Conformist* 4 These Monsters.. have dwindled the Wolf into a Fox. **1710** *Pict. of Malice* 12 Dwindling the Prince below the Pigmy Size. **1867** G. GILFILLAN *Night* I. 13 Like a star.. When dwindled by the moon to small sharp point.

Hence '**dwindling** *vbl. sb.* and *ppl. a.*; '**dwindler**, one who dwindles; '**dwindlement** (*nonce-wd.*), dwindling, shrinking.

1654 GAYTON *Pleas. Notes* II. ii. 38 The Monks were.. not dwindlers, but of ample size. **1664** H. MORE *Antid. Idol.* 73 *Illuminatrix cordium*.. would be but a dwindling Title. **1857** H. REED *Lect. Brit. Poets* II. xv. 200 A dwarfish and dwindling race. **1863** MRS. OLIPHANT *Salem Ch.* i. 22 With a sensation of dreadful dwindlement. **1884** *Spectator* 12 July 902/1 The dwindling of their majority.

'**dwindle,** *sb. rare.* [f. prec. vb.] The process of dwindling; gradual diminution or decline. **b.** *concr.* A dwindled or shrunken object.

1779-81 JOHNSON *L.P., Milton* Wks. II. 128 The hope of every day growing greater in the dwindle of posterity. **1782** ELPHINSTON *Martial* III. xciii. 173 Three hairs, and four teeth, are the dwindle Fell Chronus allows thy command. **1847-78** HALLIWELL, *Dwindle*, a poor sickly child. *Kent.*

dwindled ('dwɪnd(ə)ld), *ppl. a.* [f. as prec. + -ED[1].] That has wasted away, or become gradually less; shrunken; reduced to insignificance.

1602 MARSTON *Ant. & Mel.* I. Wks. 1856 I. 14 He hath a dwindled legge. **1796** BURKE *Regic. Peace* iv. Wks. IX. 86 The degenerate and pusillanimous impatience of our dwindled race. **1828** SCOTT *F.M. Perth* xxxii, A poor dwindled dwarf. **1850** ROBERTSON *Serm.* Ser. III. vii. 97 This dwindled Humanity of ours.

†**dwindling** ('dwɪndlɪŋ), *sb. Obs. rare.* [f. DWINDLE + -ING[3]: cf. DWINING *sb.*] A thing that dwindles or has dwindled away.

a **1653** PLAT *Garden of Eden* (1653) 39 Your pompions will prove but dwindlings.

dwine (dwaɪn), *v.* Now *Sc.*, *dial.*, and *arch.* Forms: 1 **dwínan,** 3-8 **dwyne,** (4 **duin(e,** 5 **dwynne,** 6 **dwinne,** *Sc.* **duyn(e),** 4- **dwine.** [OE. *dwínan, dwán, dwinen*, an original Teut. strong vb., represented by ON. *dvína* (Sw. *dvina*, MDu. *dwînen*, early mod.Du. *dwijnen* (Kilian 1599), Du. *verdwijnen* to vanish, disappear), MLG. and LG. *dwînen*. The strong inflexions are not found after OE. period. Cf. also FORDWINE.]

1. *intr.* To waste or pine away; to decline in vigour, languish, fade, wither.

c **1000** *Sax. Leechd.* I. 82 Ðonne dwineþ seo wamb sona. *c* **1050** *Gloss.* in Wr.-Wülcker 506/35 *Tabuerunt*, dwinan. *a* **1300** *Cursor M.* 23695 Wit sere colurs; þat neuermar sal dime ne duine. *c* **1350** *Will. Palerne* 578 Sche dwined awaie boþe daies and niȝtes. *c* **1380** WYCLIF *Serm.* Sel. Wks. II. 34 [It] comeþ above þe erþe soone, but it dwyneþ anoon. **1513** DOUGLAS *Æneis* IX. vii. 149 Lyke as the purpour flour.. Dwynis away, as it doith faid or de. *a* **1598** ROLLOCK *Sel. Wks.* (Wodrow Soc.) II. 591 John's faith and Peter's zeal were languishing and dwining. *a* **1605** MONTGOMERIE *Misc. Poems* xxii. 4 My hevy hairt, Quhilk daylie duyns, bot nevir dees. *a* **1818** MACNEILL *Poet. Wks.* (1844) 98 See how he's dwining wi' care. **1825** BROCKETT *N.C. Gloss.*, *Dwine*, to pine, to be in a decline or consumption. **1886** LADY VERNEY in *Gd. Words* 181 Put the plant into a splendid.. vase, in which it dwined and dwindled. **1889** *Spectator* 21 Dec., A race, which.. must, to use a fine though half-forgotten word, begin to dwine away.

2. *trans.* To cause to pine or waste away. *rare.*

1597 MONTGOMERIE *Cherrie & Slae* 752 His deidly drouth; Quhilk pynis him, and dwynis him To deid. **1894** CROCKETT *Raiders* (ed. 3) 360, I will dwine your flesh on your bones.

Hence **dwined** *ppl. a.*; **dwining** *vbl. sb.* and *ppl. a.*; also **dwine** *sb.*, decline, wane.

? *a* **1366** CHAUCER *Rom. Rose* 360 Drye and dwyned al for elde. **1536** BELLENDEN *Cron. Scot.* (1821) II. 60 Ambrose.. fell in ane dwinand seiknes. **1583** STANYHURST *Æneis* II. (Arb.) 61 His old dwynd carcas. **1718** *Wodrow Corr.* (1843) II. 403 Our dwining, sinking condition. **1820** *Blackw. Mag.* June 280, I' the dwine o' the moon. **1830** SCOTT *Demonol.* ix. 289 For long dwining and ill heal.

†'**dwining,** *sb. Obs. rare.* [f. DWINE *v.* + -ING[3].] One who pines away, a sickly creature.

a **1400-50** *Alexander* 1752 Slike a dwinyng, a dwaȝe, and a dwerȝe as þi-selfe.

dwle, dwly, obs. forms of DOLE *sb.*[2], DULY.

dwme, dwole, obs. forms of DOOM, DWALE.

dwr, dwresse, obs. forms of DOOR, DURESS.

dwrfe, obs. form of DWARF.

dwt., abbreviation for *pennyweight*: see D.

dwte, dwwe, obs. forms of DUTY, DUE.

dy (daɪ). [a. Sw. *dy* mire, ooze (H. von Post 1862, in *K. Sven. Vetenskaps-Akad. Handl.* 1), f. ON. *dý*, perh. f. Gmc. **dunhia*, rel. to **dungia*, the antecedent of OE. *dung* DUNG (see Falk and Torp); but the etym. of the ON. word is disputed.] A type of sediment rich in organic matter deposited in unproductive lakes.

1936 S. A. WAKSMAN *Humus* iv. 66 Formation of 'dy', or colloidal humus material, in environments supplying amounts of air that are limited as a result of water cover. **1939** W. H. TWENHOFEL *Princ. Sedimentation* ii. 88 Black muds.. have been differentiated into *gyttja*.. and *dy* if the

organic matter was brought to the lakes in colloidal form. **1957** G. E. Hutchinson *Treat. Limnol.* I. xvii. 882 The distinction between autochthonous (*gyttja*) and allochthonous (*dy*) organic sediments was early made by the Swedish students of sedimentation.

dy, obs. form of DIE.

dy, dyah: see DAYE.

dya, dya-, var. DIA *Obs.* drug; obs. f. DIA-.

dyad (ˈdaɪæd). Also 7 diad. [ad. L. *dyas, dyad-*, a. Gr. δυάς, δυάδ-, the number two.]

1. The number two; a group of two; a couple. Cf. DUAD 1.

1675 R. Burthogge *Causa Dei* 244 Now a Monad and a Diad, or One and Two, makes Three. **1678** Cudworth *Intell. Syst.* 372 The Writer..doth affirm Pythagoras to have asserted Two Substantial Principles Self-existent, a Monad and a Dyad. **1809** W. Irving *Knickerb.* (1849) 37 Pythagoras likewise inculcated the famous numerical system of the monad, dyad, and triad. **1885** F. Hall in *Ballantyne's Sánkhya Aphorisms* 224 The gross product of Nature, viz., the great elements and the dyad of bodies.

2. In specific uses: **a.** *Chem.* An atom, radical, or element that has the combining power of two units, i.e. of two atoms of hydrogen.

1865 *Reader* 1 Apr. 372/2 Each of these atoms combines usually with three monads, or with one dyad and one monad. **1873** *Fownes' Chem.* (ed. 11) 250 Sulphur, selenium, and tellurium, are usually regarded as dyads.

b. *Biol.* A secondary unit of organization consisting of an aggregate of monads. Hence ***dyaddeme***.

1883 [see DEME].

c. *Pros.* A group of two lines having different rhythms.

1885 B. L. Gildersleeve *Pindar* p. liii, Dyads and triads there are in Pindar, but they do not disturb the rhythmical working of the odes.

d. *Math.* An operator *ab* so defined that *F.* (*ab*) = (*F.a*)*b* for all *F*, where *a* and *b* are vectors and *F* is any linear vector function.

1884 J. W. Gibbs *Coll. Wks.* (1928) II. II. iii. 53 An expression of the form $a\lambda$ or $\beta\mu$ will be called a dyad. **1933** H. B. Phillips *Vector Anal.* x. 217 A linear equation satisfied by dyads will remain valid if each dyad is replaced by the dot or cross product of its two vectors. **1969** Ll. G. Chambers *Course Vector Anal.* vi. 181 Consider now the dyad, or indefinite product of two vectors a and b, ab... This has the properties that (ab). F = a(b. F) and F. (ab) = (F. a)b.

3. *attrib.* or as *adj.* = DYADIC.

1869 Roscoe *Elem. Chem.* 266 Copper is a dyad element. **1881** *Athenæum* 26 Mar. 433/1 He has also prepared the hydrate and oxalate of the dyad radical ($C_2H_2Hg_3O_2$).

dyad, dyaf, dyaþ, ME. (Kentish) forms of DEAD, DEAF, DEATH *sb.*

dyadeeme, obs. form of DIADEM.

dyadic (daɪˈædɪk), *a.* (*sb.*) [ad. Gr. δυαδικ-ός of the number two.] Of or pertaining to a dyad or group of two. ***dyadic arithmetic***: binary arithmetic, in which the radix is 2. ***dyadic disyntheme***: see DUADIC.

1727–51 Chambers *Cycl.* s.v. *Arithmetic*, Binary or Dyadic Arithmetic is that, wherein only two figures, unity, or 1, and 0, are used. **1800** *Monthly Mag.* X. 43 The dyadic arithmetic proposes to express all numbers by two characters, 1 and 0... Thus, 1 is represented by 1, 2 by 10, 4 by 100, and 8 by 1000. **1882** Schaff *Encycl. Relig. Knowl.* III. 2395 Up to 360, the whole development [of the doctrine of the Trinity] was markedly dyadic.

b. *Chem.* Of the atomic constitution of a dyad.

1873 *Fownes' Chem.* 395 Cadmium, like zinc, is dyadic.

B. *sb.* **1.** = *dyadic arithmetic*.

[**1845** J. M. Mackie *Leibnitz* 187 Leibnitz invented the Dyadik or reckoning with zero and unity.]

2. *Math.* Any quantity formed by the addition or subtraction (or both) of dyads.

1884 J. W. Gibbs *Coll. Wks.* (1928) II. II. iii. 53 An expression consisting of any number of dyads united by the signs + or − will be called a *dyadic binomial*, *trinomial* etc., ..or, more briefly, a *dyadic*. The latter term will be used so as to include the case of a single dyad. **1924** C. E. Weatherburn *Adv. Vector Anal.* v. 81 Then r′ = r·ai + r·bj + r·ck. We write this more briefly r′ = r·(ai + bj + ck), where the expression in brackets is an operator called a dyadic. **1969** Ll. G. Chambers *Course Vector Anal.* vi. 189 Dyadics may be formed in which the vector operator ∇ is a component part.

Dyak (ˈdaɪæk). Also **Daya(c)k, Dayakker.** [f. Mal. *dayak* up-country.] A member of one of the aboriginal peoples inhabiting parts of Borneo and Sarawak, often divided into ***Land Dyaks*** and ***Sea Dyaks***; the language of these peoples. Also *attrib.* or *adj.*

1836 *Penny Cycl.* V. 189/2 The mines are only wrought by the Dayacks. **1840** J. Brooke *Jrnl.* 2 Oct. in E. Hahn *J. Brooke of Sarawak* (1953) iv. 51 The arrival of various Dyak tribes. **1876** *Encycl. Brit.* IV. 58/1 The Dyaks, Dayaks, or Dayakkers are..broken into numerous tribes. **1880** *Ibid.* V. 818/1 Among the other languages which have been reduced to writing and grammatically analysed are the Balinese..the Dayak, and the Macassarese. **1882** *Jrnl. Straits Branch R. Asiatic Soc.* (1883) Dec. 213 (*title*) Sea Dyak religion. *Ibid.*, They may be regarded as the racial gods of the Sea-Dyaks. **1893** Russan & Boyle *Orchid Seekers* xii. 134 Squatting on their 'tail-mats' to the Collector's right hand..were the Dyaks; on the left lay the Malays. *Ibid.* xiii. 151 On every side rose cries of terror in Malay and Dyak. **1924** D. H. Lawrence in *Adelphi* I. 883 How apparently untamed the savage may be, Dyak or Hottentot, you may be sure he is grinding upon his own..ideas. **1937** *Discovery* Jan. 7/1 The Dyak tribes. *Ibid.*, The inhabitants inland are divided into two distinct races, known as the Sea and Land Dyaks. **1957** W. R. Geddes *Nine Dyak Nights* v. 44 *Orang Kaya*, meaning 'Rich Man'..is not a traditional Dyak title—the words are not even Dyak, but Malay. **1966** L. W. Jones *Pop. Borneo* iii. 35 A half of the Dyak population..had disappeared in ten years as a result of forced labour, slavery, sickness and the sword. **1968** *Listener* 4 Apr. 427/2 West Borneo['s]..population of one and a half million Dayaks and Chinese.

dyakis-dodecahedron (ˈdaɪəkɪsˌdəʊdɪkəˈhiːdrən). *Cryst.* [f. Gr. δυάκις twice, f. δύο two + DODECAHEDRON.] A crystalline form contained by twenty-four trapezoidal planes having two sides equal; = DIPLOHEDRON, DIPLOID.

1881 H. Bauerman *Textbk. Syst. Min.* 54 The same relation holds good with its hemihedral form, the dyakisdodecahedron which under similar conditions passes into a pentagonal dodecahedron. **1883** M. F. Heddle in *Encycl. Brit.* XVI. 355 The dyakisdodecahedron..has twelve short, twelve long, and twenty-four intermediate edges.

dyakne, obs. form of DEACON.

dyal-, dyam-, dyap-: see DIAL-, etc.

dyarchal, etc.: see DIARCHAL *a.*, etc.

dyarchy. Erroneous spelling of DIARCHY.

Dyas (ˈdaɪæs). *Geol.* [a. Gr. δυάς: see DYAD. After *Trias*.] A name for the Permian system.

1876 Page *Adv. Text-bk. Geol.* xv. 273 The lower red sandstones and magnesian limestones—the Dyas or double group of German geologists. **1887** *Athenæum* 29 Jan. 163/2 In the place of Murchison's term 'Permian'..he follows continental geologists in using Marcou's rather awkward word 'Dyas'.

Hence **Dyassic** (daɪˈæsɪk), *a.*, Permian.

1878 Lawrence tr. *Cotta's Rocks Class.* 105 Rocks belonging unmistakably to the Rothliegende or Dyassic age.

dyaster, dyastole: see DIA-.

dyat(t, obs. form of DIET.

dyaue, ME. (Kentish) form of DEAF.

dybbuk (ˈdɪbʊk). Also **dibbuk.** Pl. **dybbukim, dybbuks.** [Heb. *dibbūḳ*, f. *dāḇaḳ* to cling, cleave.] In Jewish folk-lore, the malevolent spirit of a dead person that enters and controls the body of a living person until exorcized.

1903 *Jewish Encycl.* IV, *Dibbukim*, transmigrated souls. 'Dibbuḳ'..is a colloquial equivalent, common among the superstitious Jews in eastern European countries, for a migrant soul. **1926** Alsberg & Katzin tr. 'S. Ansky' (*title*) The dybbuk. **1929** T. Wolfe *Look Homeward, Angel* (1930) xxx. 431 An old Jew who muttered jargon into a rabbi's beard as if saying a spell against Dybbuks. **1959** *Times* 30 Dec. 9/1 *The Tenth Man* is about a Jewish girl who thinks she is possessed by a dybbuk, or demon.

dycare, obs. form of DIKER.

dyce, dice (daɪs), *adv. Naut.* [History obscure.] Assumed to mean 'thus'.

*c*1860 H. Stuart *Seaman's Catech.* 40 What is the meaning of 'very well thus'; 'dice and no higher'? Her head is in a very good direction, but no closer to the wind. **1867** Smyth *Sailor's Word-bk.* s.v., 'Very Well Dyce.' (See *Thus.*) *Ibid.*, *Thus, Very Well Thus*, or *Dyce*, the order to the helmsman to keep the ship in her present direction, when sailing close-hauled.

dyce, dycer, obs. forms of DICE, DICER.

dych(e, dycht, dycke, obs. ff. DITCH, DIGHT, DIKE *sb.*[1]

dyctee, -ye, obs. forms of DITTY *sb.*

dydapper, -dopper, obs. ff. DIDAPPER.

dyde, obs. form of DEAD, DEED, DID, DIED.

dydle, var. DIDLE *sb.*

dye (daɪ), *sb.* Forms: 1 **déaȝ, déah**, 3–4 **dehe**, 6–9 **die**, 7– **dye.** [OE. had *déaȝ*, *déah* fem., gen. *déaȝe* (:—OTeut. **daugâ-*), for which a ME. *dehe* (= *deaȝe, deȝe*) is known in 13th c. This would give later *deye, dey*, also (as with DIE *v.* and EYE) *dye, die*. The word is not known thenceforth till the 16th c., when we find *die*: see the vb.

(The OTeut. **daugâ-* indicates an ablaut series *deug-, daug-, dug-*, Aryan **dheuk-*, etc., to which Kluge (*Engl. Stud.* XI. 511) refers also L. *fūcus*, and *fūcāre* to dye.)]

1. a. Colour or hue produced by, or as by, dyeing; tinge, hue.

*c*1000 Ælfric *Voc.* in Wr.-Wülcker 152/18 *Tinctura*, deah. *c*1000 Ælfric *Hom.* II. 254 Se wolcn-reada wæfels..mid ðære deaȝe hiwe. *a*1300 *Prayer to Our Lady* 20 in *O.E. Misc.* 193 And mi tohte rude iturnd al in-to oðre dehe [*rimes* bisehe, ehe, leihe]. **1589** Greene *Menaphon* (Arb.) 41 Girt with a crimson roobe of brightest die. **1663** Butler *Hud.* I. i. 243 His tawny Beard In..cut and dye so like a Tile. **1698** Fryer *Acc. E. India & P.* 24 Till..we ploughed deeper Water, North East, or a Cærulean dye. **1706** Addison *Rosamond* II. iii, Deck'd with flow'rs of various dies. **1740** Somerville *Hobbinol* III. 358 Fragrant Spice, or Silks of costly Die. **1812** J. Wilson *Isle of Palms* III. 88 Wings and crests of rainbow dyes.

b. *fig.* Chiefly in such phrases as ***a crime, fact,*** etc. ***of blackest*** or ***deepest dye***, and the like.

1601 Cornwallyes *Ess.* xvii, I never yet saw griefe of so deepe a Dye. **1605** *Tryall Chev.* III. iii. in Bullen *O. Pl.* III. 314 True vertues dye is such That malice cannot stayne nor envy tuch. **1665** Sir T. Herbert *Trav.* (1677) 244 A Treason of an ugly dye. **1752** A. Murphy *Gray's-Inn Jrnl.* No. 5. §1 A Fact..of as Glaring a Die as I have ever known. **1819** Mackintosh *Sp. Ho. Com.* 2 Mar. Wks. 1846 III. 370 Crimes..of the blackest die. **1885** *Manch. Exam.* 16 June 4/7 He is a criminal of the deepest dye.

2. a. A material or matter used for dyeing; *esp.* colouring matter in solution.

*c*1000 Ælfric *Voc.* in Wr.-Wülcker 152/19 *Coccus*, read deah. *c*1000 *Ags. Gloss.* ibid. 244/30 *Fucus*, deaȝ *uel* telȝ. **1660** F. Brooke tr. *Le Blanc's Trav.* 26 Wood called Sorba, much like Brasill, but makes a very deep dye. **1805** Southey *Madoc in W.* xiv, Cheese of curd-like whiteness, with no foreign die Adulterate. **1816** J. Smith *Panorama Sc. & Art* II. 527 Dyes..which require no mordant, are called permanent or great dyes. **1856** Stanley *Sinai & Pal.* vi. (1858) 269 The purple shellfish..supplied the Phœnician merchants with their celebrated dye.

b. As a constituent or property of the cloth.

1835 Ure *Philos. Manuf.* 200 When the dye is very fast, the cloth may be passed repeatedly through the machines..without being affected.

3. *attrib.* and *Comb.*, as ***dye-drug, -pot, -trial, -vat*** (***-fat***); **dye-bath, dye-beck**, the wide shallow vessel containing the dyeing liquid; also the colouring matter therein contained; **dye-coupled, -coupling** *Photogr.* (see quot. 1958); **dye laser**, a tunable laser based on the intense fluorescence of certain organic dyes; **dye-stone**, an iron limestone, used as a dye in U.S.; **dye-stuff, dye-ware**, a substance which yields a dye; **dye-works**, works in which dyeing is carried on. Also DYE-HOUSE, -WOOD.

1875 *Ure's Dict. Arts* III. 168 But in its state of freshness its volume becomes troublesome in the *dye-bath. *Ibid.* I. 611 The mordant..is apt to give up a portion from the cloth in the *dyebeck. **1879** *Cassell's Techn. Educ.* III. 198/2 A solution of it is made in the dyebeck—a long vessel containing the dye in solution. **1943** C. Duncan *Man. Miniat. Camera* (ed. 2) x. 100 (*heading*) Toning with a *dye-coupled developer. **1958** M. L. Hall et al. *Newnes' Compl. Amat. Photogr.* xxxv. 328 *Dye-coupled Developing.* Where a wide range of colours is required probably the best method is provided by dye-coupling developers. The general principle is that the by-products of the developer giving the silver image will couple up with another compound, to produce a coloured substance. **1842** Bischoff *Woollen Manuf.* II. 267 The duties upon oil, *dye-drugs, and every other impost. **1640** Parkinson *Theat. Bot.* (1644) 602 A blew and purple scumme that riseth on the *Dyfat which is taken off and dried. **1675** Brooks *Gold. Key* Wks. 1867 V. 55 Wool which never received the least tincture in the dye-fat. **1967** *Chem. & Engin. News* 19 June 38/1 Organic *dye lasers, barely a year old, may be much more versatile than people have supposed. **1977** *Jrnl. R. Soc. Arts* CXXV. 763/2 The dye-laser..has made the laser, essentially a fixed frequency device, tunable. **1891** 'Ganconagh' *J. Sherman & Dhoya* II. iii. 57 Some mischievous goblin always runs off with the *dye-pot. **1930** E. Pound *XXX Cantos* xvii. 78 Dye-pots in the torch-light. **1837** *Penny Cycl.* IX. 225/1 *Dye-stuffs can penetrate the minute pores of vegetable and animal fibres only when presented to them in a state of solution. **1842** Bischoff *Woollen Manuf.* II. 41 Low prices of oil and *dye-wares. **1837** *Penny Cycl.* IX. 226/2 Each of the great *dye-works in Alsace.

dye (daɪ), *v.* Pa. t. and pple. **dyed**; pr. pple. **dyeing.** Forms: 1 **déaȝian, déȝian**, 4–5 **deyen, deien, dyen**, (5 **dyȝen, dyne**, 6 **dei**), 4–9 **die**, 4– **dye.** [OE. *déaȝian* (:—OTeut. **daugôjan*), f. *déaȝ* DYE *sb.* (The convenient distinction in spelling between *die* and *dye* is quite recent. Johnson's Dict. spells both *die*; Addison has both as *dye*.)]

1. a. *trans.* To diffuse a colour or tint through; to tinge with a colour or hue; to colour, stain.

*a*1000 *Aldhelm Gl.* (Napier, *O.E. Gl.*) I. 1208 *Fucare*, deaȝian. *Ibid.* 5196 *Inficere*, deaghian. *Ibid.* 5330 *Coloratis*, deaȝedum. **1398** Trevisa *Barth. De P.R.* XIX. viii. (1495) 866 Red clothe dieth the vtter parti of water yf it is layed there vnder. *Ibid.*, Many thynges dyeth and colouryth thynges wythout and not wythin: as it fareth in peynture. *c*1500 *Melusine* xxxi. 229 The dyches watre was as tourned & dyed with theyre blood. **1667** Milton *P.L.* x. 1009 So much of Death her thoughts Had entertaind, as di'd her Cheeks with pale. **1720** Gay *Poems* (1745) II. 258 My hands with blood of innocence are dy'd. **1826** Cooper *Mohicans* (1829) I. iii. 45 It fell, dying the waters with its blood. **1892** Gardiner *Student's Hist. Eng.* 9 They dyed their faces in order to terrify their enemies.

b. *spec.* To impregnate (any tissue or the like) with a colour, to fix a colour in the substance of, or to change the hue of by a colouring matter.

*c*1386 Chaucer *Nun's Pr. Epil.* 12 Him nedeth nat his colour for to dyen With brasil. *c*1400 *Lanfranc's Cirurg.* 180 þow schalt die hise heeris if þei ben white, wiþ tincture þat ben forseid. **1465** *Mann. & Househ. Exp.* 178 Saffe he axithe alowanse ffor dyeynge xvj. ȝerdys cloth .xj.d. *a*1577 Gascoigne *Flowers*, etc. Wks. (1587) 309 Nor useth art, in deing of hir heare. **1654** tr. *Martini's Conq. China* 34 Black and purple horse-hair, which they die and dress most curiously. **1816** J. Smith *Panorama Sc. & Art* II. 527 The most usual stuffs or materials which are required to be dyed, are wool, silk, cotton, and linen.

fig. **1576** Fleming *Panopl. Epist.* 418 As it were dye your wit in their unchaungeable colours. *a*1700 Dryden (J.), All white, a virgin saint she sought the skies; For marriage, though it sullies not, it dies.

c. Phrase: ***to dye in*** (***the***) ***wool, in grain***, to subject to the action of a colouring matter while

the material is in the raw or primitive state; the effect of which is more thorough and lasting than when done after it is 'made up'. *lit.* and *fig.* (See also GRAIN *sb.*[1] 10 b; WOOL *sb.* 1 g.)

c **1386** [see sense 2 a] **1579–80** NORTH *Plutarch* (1676) 65 If he had not through institution and education (as it were) died in wool the manners of children. **1679** *Lond. Gaz.* No. 1449/4 A peice of half Ell green double Camblet dyed in the Wool. **1798** EDGEWORTH *Pract. Educ.* II. 351 Dyed in grain, means dyed into the substance of the material so that the dye can't be washed out.

2. Various constructions: **a.** with the colour as object.

c **1386** CHAUCER *Sqr.'s T.* 503 So depe in greyn he dyed [*Lansd.* deiede] his coloures. *c* **1386** —— *Frankl. Prol.* 53 Colours ne knowe I none..But..swiche as men dye [so all 6 texts; *Wright* deyen] or peynte. **1530** PALSGR. 515/2 This dyer dyeth none other coloures but onely scarlets. *c* **1600** SHAKS. *Sonn.* xcix, The purple pride..In my love's veins thou hast too grossly dyed. **1875** *Ure's Dict. Arts* II. 173 Green..is produced by dyeing a blue over a yellow or a yellow over a blue.

b. with *complement*: To dye (a thing) *red, blue,* etc., or *of* (*into, to*) some colour.

1412–20 LYDG. *Chron. Troy* I. v, Whose blewe is lightly dyed into grene. **1486** *Bk. St. Albans* A ij b, It hade need to be died other green or blwe. **1590** SPENSER *F.Q.* II. i. 39 A stream of gore..into a deepe sanguine dide the grassy grownd. **1717** LADY M. W. MONTAGU *Let. to C'tess Mar* 1 Apr., They die their nails a rose colour. **1753** CHAMBERS *Cycl. Supp.* s.v. *Dyeing*, He uses it daily to dye any thing woollen to a scarlet colour. **1875** *Ure's Dict. Arts* II. 164 Moses speaks of a raiment dyed blue. **1883** *Manch. Guardian* 30 Oct. 8/4 The rain..in this red sandstone country soon dyes the stream of a dark red. **1891** C. GRAVES *Field of Tares* 62, I saw a lovely flush rise in her cheeks and dye her sweet white throat into crimson.

c. *absol.* or with *compl.* only.

1436 *Pol. Poems* (Rolls) II. 180 The madre and woode that dyers take on hande To dyne wyth. **1467** in *Eng. Gilds* (1870) 383 Wher they be persones ynogh..to dye, carde, or spynne. **1596** SHAKS. *1 Hen. IV*, II. iv. 16 They call drinking deepe, dying Scarlet. **1862** LINDLEY *Sch. Bot.* 56 Genista tinctoria..Dyes yellow.

3. *intr.* for *pass.* To take a colour or hue (well or badly) in the process of dyeing.

Mod. This material dyes very well.

Hence **dyed** *ppl. a.*

c **1645** HOWELL *Lett.* VI. 9 Alderman Cockeins project of transporting no White Cloths but Died. **1863–72** WATTS *Dict. Chem.* II. 354 A piece of dyed cotton. **1876** A. ARNOLD in *Contemp. Rev.* June 30 A henna-dyed follower of Islam.

dye, obs. form of DIE *v.* and *sb.*

d'ye. Colloq. contraction of *do ye, do you.*

1697 [see HOW-DO-YOU-DO 1]. **1773** [see DO *v.* 26]. *a* **1832** [see DO *v.* A. 2 d]. **1866** J. W. GRAVES in *People's Eng. Songs* (1903) 9 D'ye ken John Peel..? **1922** JOYCE *Ulysses* 420 D'ye ken bare socks?

dyeable ('daɪəb(ə)l), *a.* [f. DYE *v.* + -ABLE.] That can be dyed. Hence **dyea'bility.**

1934 WEBSTER, Dyeable. **1939** *Nature* 19 Aug. 313/2 It [*sc.* the structure of the rayon fibre] is responsible for the amount of swelling, the dyeability, and the resistance to creasing. **1969** *Sci. Jrnl.* July 78/1 The sheath polymer not engaged in bond formation remains distributed along the fibre where it can still contribute to properties of abrasion resistance, covering power and dyeability. **1970** *Ibid.* Jan. 23/1 New techniques for producing coloured, patterned effects on dyeable fabrics have been developed.

dyead, dyeath, dyeaue, obs. ff. DEAD, DEATH, DEAF.

dyedral, obs. var. DIHEDRAL.

'dye-house[1]. The building in which a dyer carries on his work.

1465 *Mann. & Househ. Exp.* 179 Edward Bernard that dweld in hys dyhowse. **1545** *Act 37 Hen. VIII*, c. 12 §9 Wheare anny personne shall demyse any dyehouse or Brewhouse. **1697** *Lond. Gaz.* No. 3261/4 Some of them Broke open a Dye-House at Bow. **1876** BANCROFT *Hist. U.S.* VI. xxx. 87 Trees, useful in the workshop and the dye-house.

dye-house[2], dial. var. of DEY-HOUSE (Grose).

dyeing ('daɪɪŋ), *vbl. sb.* Also 6–9 **dying.** [f. DYE *v.* + -ING[1].] The process of impregnating with colour; esp. the fixing of colours in solution in textile and other absorbent substances.

c **1000** ÆLFRIC *Hom.* II. 464 Ne mihte se wuldorfulla Salomon, ne nan eorðlic cyning swa wlitige deagunge his hræglum begytan swa swa rose hæfð. **1530** PALSGR. 213/2 Dieng with colour, *taincture.* **1548** *Act 2 & 3 Edw. VI*, c. 26 Preamb., White Ashes..are very necessarie..for the..dyinge and scowringe of wollen clothe. **1731–59** MILLER *Gard. Dict.* (ed. 7) s.v. *Cæsalpinia*, The Brasiletto wood which is much used in Dying. **1877** C. O'NEILL in *Encycl. Brit.* VII. 570/2 The term dyeing..is usually confined to the colouring of textile fibrous materials by penetration.

b. *attrib.* and *Comb.*, as *dyeing-drug, -earth, -goods, -herb, -liquor, -material, -stuff, -wood,* etc.; also **dyeing-frame,** one on which articles are hung when dipped simultaneously into the dye.

1530 PALSGR. 213/2 Dieng fatte or leed, *couier.* **1670** R. COKE *Disc. Trade* 34 All sorts of Dying stuffs, Hides, [etc.]. **1725** DE FOE *Voy. round World* (1840) 161 Dying-woods and dying-earths. **1735** BERKELEY *Querist* §509 Saffron, dying drugs, and the like produce. **1813** SIR H. DAVY *Agric. Chem.* (1814) 73 Dyeing materials are furnished by leaves, or the petals of flowers. **1875** *Ure's Dict. Arts* II. 792 When the dyeing-frame is raised up out of the copper, it should be tilted on one side.

dye-line, dyeline ('daɪlaɪn). [f. DYE *sb.* + LINE *sb.*] = DIAZO, DIAZOTYPE; also, a print or copy prepared by this process. Freq. *attrib.*

1951 *O & M Bull.* Oct. 23 The simplicity of the dyeline process and the cheapness of diazo papers..have led to the development of equipment for ordinary office use. *Ibid.* 24 The Mervac Copier..is suitable both for the preparation of the transparent master and as a dyeline printer for the subsequent production of additional copies. **1953** *Jrnl. Photogr. Sci.* I. 78/1 Photographic copies of documents may be of many different types; they may differ in the process used (silver, dye line, or blueprint). **1959** *Economist* 21 Mar. 1087/2 Dyeline, or Diazo processes have been used for many years in drawing offices, but have been introduced in small fast-copying machines only since the war.

dyep, obs. (Kentish) form of DEEP.

dyeper, obs. form of DIAPER.

dyer ('daɪə(r)). Also 4 **dighere, dyhȝere,** 6–7 **dyar, dier, -ar.** [f. DYE *v.* : OE. type **déaȝere.*]

1. One whose occupation is to dye cloth and other materials.

1369 in Riley *Lond. Mem.* (1868) 337 Victor de Male, dighere. *c* **1386** CHAUCER *Prol.* 362 A Webbe, a Dyere, and a Tapicer. *a* **1400** in *Eng. Gilds* (1870) 359 þe mayster dyhȝeres of peyntours in þe citee. **1562** BULLEYN *Bk. Simples* 47 b, With this Diars colour their Wolle withall. *a* **1610** HEALEY *Theophrastus* (1636) To Rdr., A great water-pot like a Diers fat. **1724** SWIFT *Drapier's Lett.* Wks. 1755 V. II. 94 A piece of black and white stuff just sent from the dyer. **1838** T. THOMSON *Chem. Org. Bodies* 368 Indigo employed by the dyers or calico-printers.

b. A variety of grape.

1865 *Daily Tel.* 20 July, Grapes are already in the market, and the especial one known as the 'dyer', from being used to colour various wines, is beginning to blush.

2. Combinations of *dyer's*: **a. dyer's bath** = DYE-BATH; †**dyer's grain,** the coccus insect, kermes; **dyer's spirit,** tin tetrachloride, employed as a mordant. **b.** In the names of plants used for dyeing: **dyer's alkanet, bugloss,** *Anchusa tinctoria* (*Ure's Dict. Arts* 1875); **dyer's broom, whin,** *Genista tinctoria,* also called **dyer's green-weed,** DYER'S WEED, and *woadwaxen*; **dyer's grape,** *Phytolacca decandra* (Miller *Plant-n.* 1884); **dyer's-moss,** archil; **dyer's oak,** *Quercus infectoria,* the galls of which yield a dye; **dyer's rocket,** *Reseda Luteola,* also called **dyer's yellow-weed; dyer's woad,** *Isatis tinctoria* (see WOAD).

1591 PERCIVALL *Sp. Dict.*, The tree whereon diers grayne groweth, *Coccus infectorius.* **1597** GERARDE *Herbal* III. xviii. (1633) 1317 The Greenweeds..do grow to dye clothes with. It is called..in English Diers Greenweed. **1854** S. THOMSON *Wild Fl.* III. (ed. 4) 236 The..yellow-flowered *Genista tinctoria,* or dyer's-green weed, or woad-waxen. **1860** OLIVER *Less. Bot.* (1886) 124 Dyer's Woad (*Isatis tinctoria*). **1861** MISS PRATT *Flower Pl.* I. 157 *Reseda Luteola,* Dyer's Rocket. *Ibid.* II. 81 *Genista tinctoria,* Woad-waxen, Dyer's-whin, Dyer's weed, or Greenweed.

dyer, obs. form of DIER, one who dies.

'dyer's weed. A name given to plants that yield a dye: esp. Yellow-weed or Weld, *Reseda Luteola*; also Dyer's greenweed or Woadwaxen, *Genista tinctoria,* and Dyer's woad, *Isatis tinctoria.*

1578 LYTE *Dodoens* I. xlvii. 68 Of Dyers weede..The leaues of this herbe are..not much vnlike the leaues of Woad..It is vsed of Dyers to colour and dye their clothes into greene, and yellow. **1649** BLITHE *Eng. Improv. Impr.* (1653) 224 In our English Welde or Dyars-Weed. **1794** MARTYN *Rousseau's Bot.* xx. 280 Dyers-weed or Weld grows common in barren pastures, dry banks, and on walls. **1861** MISS PRATT *Fl. Pl.* II. 81 [see prec.]. **1866** *Treas. Bot.*, Dyer's-weed..also..*Isatis tinctoria. Ibid.* s.v. *Reseda, R. Luteola,* the Weld, Yellow-weed, or Dyer's Weed.

dyery ('daɪərɪ). [f. DYE + -(E)RY.] A place where dyeing is carried on; a dyeing establishment.

1762 tr. *Busching's Syst. Geog.* V. 609 In this town are manufactures of stuffs and linen, as also a dyery. **1884** J. PAYNE 1001 *Nts.* VIII. 298 The door of the dyery.

dyery, obs. form of DAIRY.

dyester ('daɪstə(r)). Now *Sc. arch.* Also 4 **diestere, -are,** 5 **deyster.** [f. DYE *v.* + -STER. Cf. DEXTER *sb.*] = DYER.

a **1350** *Childh. Jesus* 1158 (Mätz.) He cam to a diestare, And seide he coupe of his mestere, þis diestere with oute blame Of þis hadde game. **1497** *Will of J. Thomlynson* (Somerset Ho.), I John Thomlynson of Coventry, Deyster. **1818** SCOTT *Hrt. Midl.* vii, That dyester's pole is good enough for the homicide. **1857** A. JEFFREY *Roxburghshire* II. iii. 120 In 1736 Robert Dick, a dyester, was summoned.

dyety, dyeve, obs. forms of DEITY, DIVE *v.*

'dye-wood. Wood yielding a dye.

1699 DAMPIER *Voy.* (R.), Here are dye-woods, as fustick, &c. **1812–16** J. SMITH *Panorama Sc. & Art* I. 92 Several woods..of foreign production, such as dyewoods..we pass over. **1863–72** WATTS *Dict. Chem.* II. 354 This is a style of calico-printing in which one or more mordants are mixed with dye-wood decoctions or other coloured solutions.

dyf-: see DIF-.

dygne, dygnyte, obs. ff. DIGNE, DIGNITY.

dygogram ('daɪgəʊgræm). [See quot. 1862.] A diagram consisting of a curve showing the variation of the horizontal component of the force of magnetism exerted upon the ship's compass-needle by the iron in the ship's composition while making a circuit or curve.

1862 A. SMITH *Deviat. Ship's Compass* App. ii. 151 Graphic representations of the amount and direction of the forces which act on the magnetic needle. These representations are designated by the general name of 'Dygo-gram', a contraction for 'Dynamo-gonio-gram' or 'Force and angle diagram'. **1881** MAXWELL *Electr. & Magn.* II. 73 Such a curve, by means of which the direction and magnitude of the force on the compass is given in terms of the magnetic course of the ship, is called a Dygogram.

dygre, obs. f. DEGREE.

dying ('daɪɪŋ), *vbl. sb.* Forms: see DIE *v.*[1] [f. DIE *v.*[1] + -ING[1].] The action of the verb DIE.

1. a. Ceasing to live, expiring, decease, death.

1297 R. GLOUC. (1724) 485 Hunger & deiinge of men. *a* **1340** HAMPOLE *Psalter* cvi. 20 He toke þaim out of þaire diyngis. **1526–34** TINDALE *2 Cor.* iv. 10 And we all wayes beare in oure bodyes the dyinge of the Lorde Iesus. **1626** BACON *Sylva* §448 The Dying, in the Winter, of the Roots or Plants that are Annual. **1893** HUXLEY *Evolut. & Ethics* 9 Life seems not worth living except to escape the bore of dying.

b. *transf.* and *fig.* See DIE *v.* Also with *advs.* ***dying-back***: see DIE *v.*[1] 14, DIE-BACK.

1750 *Phil. Trans.* XLVI. 413 At the dying of the Stream, it is often two Feet higher than the Main Tide. **1855** BAIN *Senses & Int.* II. i. §16 The gradual dying away of a motion. **1884** J. A. H. MURRAY in *13th Addr. Philol. Soc.* 7 The history of the dying-out of Cornish. **1921** *Times Lit. Suppl.* 8 Sept. 574/3 Its silviculture is very difficult, more especially the question of the dying-back of its seedlings. **1959** *Jrnl. R. Hort. Soc.* LXXXIV. 483 Many plants..suffer some dying back of their top growth.

2. *attrib.* Of, belonging to, or relating to dying or death, as ***dying bed, command, day, declaration, fit, groan, prayer, shriek, time, tree, wish, word,*** etc. Cf. DEATH *sb.* 18 a. (In some of these, the *vbl. sb.* has come to be identified with the *ppl. a.*)

1580 J. STUBBS in *Lett. Lit. Men* (Camden) 41 The glad tydings..half revived my wife almost in a dyeng bedd. **1593** SHAKS. *Lucr.* 1266 Dying fear through all her body spread. **1599** SANDYS *Europæ Spec.* (1632) 90 To have a sight of her sometime before their dying-dayes. **1620** QUARLES *Jonah* (1638) 45 Like pinioned pris'ners at the dying tree. **1711** ADDISON *Spect.* No. 70. ¶8 The Scotch Earl falls; and with his Dying Words encourages his men to revenge his Death. **1784** COWPER *Task* III. 328 The sobs and dying shrieks Of harmless Nature. **1872** WHARTON *Law-Lexicon* (ed. 5) 273/2 Death-bed or Dying Declarations are constantly admitted in evidence. **1884** TENNYSON *Becket* Prol. 19 A dead man's dying wish should be of weight. *Mod.* I shall remember it to my dying day.

'dying, *ppl. a.* [f. as prec. + -ING[2].] That dies.

1. a. Departing from this life; at the point of death, moribund; mortal.

c **1450** tr. *De Imitatione* II. xii. 59 Know for certein þat þou must lede a dieng lif. **1563** WINȜET *Wks.* (1890) II. 63 He had leuir the dethe of the deand sinnar, than that he suld returne and leue. **1598** SYLVESTER *Du Bartas* II. i. IV. *Handicrafts* 422 He..buries there his dying-living seeds. **1704** RAY in *Lett. Lit. Men* (Camden) 206, I look upon my self as a dying man. **1821** SHELLEY *Ginevra* 81 The dying violet. **1860–1** FLO. NIGHTINGALE *Nursing* 71 Oh! how much might be spared to the dying!

b. *dying god* (also with capitals), a god whose death is commemorated annually, typifying the seasonal death of vegetation.

1890 J. G. FRAZER *Golden Bough* II. iii. 206 If we ask why a dying god should be selected to take upon himself and carry away the sins and sorrows of the people, it may be suggested that in the practice of using the divinity as a scapegoat we have a combination of two customs which were at one time distinct and independent. *Ibid.* 207 These features become at once intelligible if we suppose that the Death was not merely the dying god of vegetation, but also a public scapegoat. **1911** *Ibid.* (ed. 3) III. (*title*) The Dying God. **1912** *Ibid.* VII. i. 33 In that case..we should have to confess that Greece had what we may call its Good Friday and its Easter Sunday long before the events took place in Judaea which diffused these two annual commemorations of the Dying and Reviving God over a great part of the civilised world. **1947** C. S. LEWIS *Miracles* xiv. 138 The records..show us a Person who *enacts* the part of the Dying God, but whose thoughts and words remain quite outside the circle of religious ideas to which the Dying God belongs. **1952** O. R. GURNEY *Hittites* vii. 137 He may have been a typical 'dying god' like Adonis, Attis, and Osiris, representing the vital forces of nature which appear to die in winter and revive in the spring.

2. *transf.* and *fig.* See DIE *v.*

1590 SPENSER *F.Q.* II. vii. 36 Another did the dying bronds repayre With yron tongs. **1592** SHAKS. *Ven. & Ad.* 338 As a dying coal revives with wind. **1697** DRYDEN *Virg. Georg.* IV. 382 Dying Murmurs of departing Tides. **1713** POPE *Prol. Cato* 14 Such Tears as Patriots shed for dying Laws. **1820** SHELLEY *Liberty* xix, As a brief insect dies with dying day.

Hence **'dyingly** *adv.*, in a dying manner, in dying; **'dyingness,** dying or languishing quality.

1435 MISYN *Fire of Love* II. xii. 103 Deyngly I sal wax stronge. **1556** J. HEYWOOD *Spider & F.* lix. 46 As both sides shall liue: euermore dyingly. *a* **1625** FLETCHER *Love's Pilgr.* IV. iii, I can dyingly and boldly say I know not your dishonour. **1700** CONGREVE *Way of World* III. v, Tenderness

becomes me best, a sort of dyingness. **1823** *New Monthly Mag.* VIII. 276 To sing faintly, sweetly, and as it were dyingly. **1955** E. BOWEN *World of Love* v. 98 She could not suffer dyingness to usurp.

Dyirbal (djɜːrbəl), *sb.* (and *a.*) Also **Chirpal, Tjirbal**, etc. [Native name.] An Australian Aboriginal language spoken in the vicinity of Tully and Atherton in N.E. Queensland; the people speaking this language. Also *attrib.* or as *adj.*

1901 W. E. ROTH *N. Queensland Ethnogr.* III. 3 CHI = Chirpal blacks to be found at Atherton, etc. **1910** *Rec. Austral. Museum* VIII. I. 91 At Atherton, the natives.. belong to three groups or tribes speaking..chirpal, ngaikungo and ngachan. **1939** *Oceania* IX. 442 The Ngatjan, Mamu, Tjirbal, Mudju and perhaps Ngaikungo may have not simply two moieties, but three phratries. **1968** *Lingua* XXI. 104 The main aim of this paper is to discuss.. the semantic basis of noun class membership in Dyirbal. **1972** R. M. W. DIXON (*title*) The Dyirbal language of North Queensland. **1977** C. F. & F. M. VOEGELIN *Classification & Index World's Lang.* 278 *Yara.* Inland and along the coast of east central Queensland, opposite the Great Barrier Reef... Djirbal = Djirubal = Tjirbal, [etc.]. **1977** *Language* LIII. 288 Dyirbal.., a northeastern Australian language, has four noun classifiers. **1984** *Verbatim* Summer 6/2 Chloe.. worked out principles of gender in Dyirbal (involving a knowledge of Dyirbal science).

dyit, Sc. var. of DITE *sb.*[1], *Obs.*

dyke, etc., a frequent spelling of DIKE *sb.*[1], etc.

dyker, dylaye, obs. forms of DICKER, DELAY.

dylde (in phr. ***God dylde you***): see YIELD *v.*

dyle, dyll(e, obs. forms of DILL.

dylectable, obs. var. DELECTABLE.

dyluuye, var. DILUVY *Obs.*, deluge, flood.

dymaxion (daɪˈmæksɪən), *a.* Also **Dymaxion.** [Arbitrary; see note below.] In the philosophies of construction and design of R. Buckminster Fuller: yielding the greatest possible efficiency in terms of the available technology, 'doing the most with the least'. Hence ***dymaxion car, house, map***, etc.

In a private communication (July 1969) Mr. Buckminster Fuller said that the word was coined for him in 1929 by his business associates as a 'word-portrait' of him and his work. They were concerned to form a euphonious word of four syllables based on words that occurred in Fuller's own description of his prototype (*Dymaxion*) house, viz. *dy*(*namism*, *max*(*imum*, and *ion*.

1929 R. B. FULLER in *Archit. Forum* July 104 (*caption*) Elevation and Isometric Drawing of the Dymaxion House. **1934** *Sat. Rev.* 2 June 1/1 The author [*sc.* H. G. Wells], during his recent visit to America, with the new Dymaxion car. **1960** R. W. MARKS *Dymaxion World of B. Fuller* 9/1 Another dimension of this Weltenschauung is expressed by the term *Dymaxion*, a label Fuller has used to qualify the implication of his various inventions, developments, and projected ideas. *Ibid.* 34/1 The Dymaxion bathroom was designed by Fuller for ultimate production in plastics, when plastics had been developed to an adequate point. *Ibid.* 49/1 The Dymaxion map was not a shadow projection, as are other global maps, but a topological transfer of a high frequency form of Fuller's totally-triangulated systems from the surface of a sphere to the equivalent triangular spaces on the faces of a polyhedron. **1962** R. DAVENPORT in R. B. Fuller *Epic Poem on Industrialization* p. vi, At his own factory in Bridgeport he designed and built the first Dymaxion car.

dymbe, dyme, dymme, obs. forms of DIM.

dyme, obs. form of DEEM, *v.*, DIME.

dymisent, dymyceynt, -sen(t, -son: see DEMICEINT, *Obs.*

dymonde, obs. form of DIAMOND.

dyna-. In the derivatives of Gr. δύνα-σθαι to be able, δύναμις power, *y* (= Gr. υ) is etymologically short, and is so treated in pronouncing dictionaries down to the middle of the 19th c. But popular usage (esp. since *dynamite* came into vogue) tends to give the *y* the diphthongal pronunciation (aɪ) in all these words, though (dɪn-) is still preferred by some in *dynamic* and its family, and app. by most scholars in *dynasty* and its family.

dyna, obs. form of DINAR.

dynactiˈnometer. ? *Obs.* [f. Gr. δύν(αμις power + ἀκτίς (ἀκτῖν-) ray + μέτρον measure: see -METER, and cf. ACTINOMETER.] An instrument designed to measure the intensity of the photogenic rays, and to compute the power of object-glasses.

1851 M. CLAUDET in *Philos. Mag.*

dynagraph (ˈdaɪnəgrɑːf, -æ-, dɪn-). [f. Gr. δύνα(μις power + -γραφος writer, -GRAPH.] The name given in the United States to a machine of the same character as the *dynamometer car* on some English Railways, used for mechanically reporting the condition of a railway line, the speed of a train, and the power used in traversing a given distance.

These elements are recorded on a paper ribbon moved by means of gearing from one of the axles of the car or van which carries the machine.

1890 in *Century Dict.*

†ˈ**dynam.** *Obs.* [a. F. *dyname* (also *dynamie*), 'a unit of power, the force necessary to raise in a given time 1000 kilogrammes to a height of 1 metre'; f. Gr. δύναμις power, force.] 'A term proposed by Dr. Whewell, as expressive of a pound or other unit, in estimating the effect of mechanical labour.' Craig 1847. (See also DYNE.)

dynaˈmagnite, early name for DYNAMOGEN, q.v.

dyname (ˈdaɪnəm). *Physics.* [a. Ger. *dyname*, f. Gr. δύναμις: see DYNAM.] A force or a force and a couple, the resultant of all the forces acting together on a body.

1866 J. PLÜCKER *Fundam. Views Mech.* in *Phil. Trans.* CLVI. 362 If any number of given forces.. act upon or pass through given points, according to the fundamental laws of statics, the *resulting effect* is obtained by adding the six coordinates of the forces.. In the general case I propose to call the cause producing the resulting effect *dyname*. *Ibid.* 363 A dyname, determined by its six linear coordinates.. represents the effect produced by two forces not intersecting each other. *Ibid.* 369 A dyname may be resolved into pairs of forces, the forces of all pairs constitute a linear complex.

dynameter (daɪ-, dɪˈnæmɪtə(r): see DYNA-). [mod. f. Gr. δύνα(μις power + μέτρ-ον measure; or shortened from DYNAMOMETER.] An instrument for measuring the magnifying power of a telescope; = DYNAMOMETER 2.

a **1828** WEBSTER cites RAMSDEN. **1837** GORING & PRITCHARD *Microgr.* 67 View the image..formed in the visual pencil of an engiscope, with a dynameter of very delicate divisions. **1878** LOCKYER *Stargazing* 116 The image can be measured with tolerable accuracy by Mr. Berthon's dynameter.

Hence **dynaˈmetric, dynaˈmetrical** *adjs.*, of or pertaining to a dynameter.

1828 WEBSTER, *Dynametrical.*

dynamic (daɪ-, dɪˈnæmɪk: see DYNA-), *a.* and *sb.* [ad. F. *dynamique* (Leibnitz 1692. Dict. Acad. 1762), ad. Gr. δυναμικός powerful, f. δύναμις power, strength.]

A. *adj.* **1.** Of or pertaining to force producing motion: often opposed to *static.*

1827 D. GILBERT in *Phil. Trans.* CXVII. 26 Mr. Watt.. assumed one pound raised one foot high for what has been called in other countries the dynamic unit. **1843–46** GROVE *Corr. Phys. Forces* (ed. 1) 13 A comparative view of the corpuscular and dynamic theories of heat. **1850** *Ibid.* (ed. 2) 74, I have used..the terms dynamic and static to represent the different states of magnetism. **1847** J. DWYER *Princ. Hydraul. Engineer.* 94 The horse's power is principally used by Engineers in this country as a Dynamic unit. **1855** H. SPENCER *Princ. Psychol.* (1872) II. VI. xi. 138 We find light producing a dynamic effect..in those molecular re-arrangements which it works in certain crystals. **1860** TYNDALL *Glac.* II. xix. 331 According to the dynamic view ..heat is regarded as a motion. **1881** ARMSTRONG *Address Brit. Assoc.* in *Nature* No. 619. 449 Such is the richness of coal as a store of mechanical energy that a pound of coal, even as used in the steam-engine, produces a dynamic effect about five times greater than a pound of gunpowder burnt in a gun.

2. Of or pertaining to force in action or operation; active.

1862 TYNDALL *Mountaineer.* i. 6 What would man be without Nature? A mere capacity, if such a thing be conceivable alone; potential, but not dynamic. **1863** —— *Heat* v. 137 While in the act of falling, the energy of the weight is active. It may be called *actual* energy, in antithesis to *possible*, or..*dynamic* energy, in antithesis to *potential.* *Ibid.* 138 As potential energy disappears, dynamic energy comes into play.

3. *transf.* and *fig.* **a.** Active, potent, energetic, effective, forceful.

1856 EMERSON *Eng. Traits, Lit.* Wks. (Bohn.) II. 105 Their dynamic brains hurled off their words, as the revolving stone hurls off scraps of grit. **1876** GEO. ELIOT *Dan. Der.* I. i, What was the secret of form or expression which gave the dynamic quality to her glance? **1878** LECKY *Eng. in 18th C.* I. i. 14 It [Greek intellect] has been the great dynamic agency in European civilisation.

b. Opposed to *static.*

1876 C. P. MASON *Eng. Gram.* (ed. 21) 117 (To borrow a metaphor from mechanics) the adjective is a *static attribute*, the verb is a *dynamic attribute.*

4. Of, according to, or pertaining to the science of DYNAMICS: as the *dynamic* theory of the tides.

1838–51 NICHOL *Archit. Heav.* (ed. 9) 196 A sure dynamic theorem. **1891** E. PEACOCK *N. Brendon* II. 416 The dynamic laws which cause a pump to act.

5. *Med.* **a.** Functional, in contradistinction to *organic*; as in ***dynamic disease.*** **b.** With Hahnemann and his followers: Of the nature of some immaterial or 'spiritual' influence. †**c.** Attended with a morbid increase of vital action, sthenic (*obs.*).

dynamic school: a name given to the Stahlians, or followers of Stahl, as attributing the vital phenomena to the operation of an internal force or power acting for the most part independently of external causes. (*Syd. Soc. Lex.*)

[**1829** see ADYNAMIC.] **1834** *Good's Study Med.* (ed. 4) IV. 272 Dr. Stoker..has divided dropsies into two kinds, dynamic and adynamic. **1855** J. R. REYNOLDS *Dis. Brain* ix, The simple fact of convulsions is proof of dynamic (functional) disease. **1881** J. G. GLOVER in *Encycl. Brit.* XII. 128/1 (*Homœopathy*), Underlying all his [Hahnemann's] system..was the idea that the causes of disease were impalpable, immaterial, spiritual, dynamic. **1882** *Med. Temp. Jrnl.* I. 114 A dynamic narcosis of the ultimate fibres of sensation.

6. In the Kantian philosophy: Relating to the reason of existence of an object of experience.

dynamic relations, the relations between objects as forming parts of one connected experience: viz. the relations of substance and accident, of cause and effect, and of substances acting upon each other. ***dynamic category***, a category that expresses one of the dynamic relations. ***dynamic synthesis***, a synthesis which is guided by the dynamic categories.

7. Relating to the existence or action of some force or forces; applied esp. to a theory that accounts for matter, or for mind, as being merely the action of forces: see DYNAMISM 1.

dynamic theory of Kant, a theory according to which matter was conceived to be constituted by two antagonistic principles of attraction and repulsion.

1817 COLERIDGE *Biog. Lit.* I. ix. 150 We had both equal obligations to the polar logic and dynamic philosophy of Giordano Bruno.

8. *Mus.* Of, pertaining to, or indicating the volume of sound from a musical instrument or in a musical performance. Also *transf.*

1893 J. S. SHEDLOCK tr. *Riemann's Dict. Mus.* 226/1 The natural dynamic shading of a musical phrase is therefore *crescendo*..and *diminuendo*... Dynamic and agogic shadings must be used with economy. **1931** G. JACOB *Orchestral Technique* iii. 29 It is excellent as a bass-strengthener, however, in dynamic ranges of *mf* and upwards. **1941** *B.B.C. Gloss. Broadc. Terms* 10 *Dynamic range*, range of intensities within which the volume of a programme fluctuates. **1948** *Penguin Music Mag.* June 129 Fearless attack, great volume, and subtle dynamic changes.

9. ***dynamic braking*** = ***electric braking***; ***dynamic equator*** (see quot. 1883); ***dynamic metamorphism*** (also ***dynamical m.***) Geol., metamorphism produced by mechanical forces; ***dynamic pressure***, the pressure in a fluid that is due to its motion.

1930 *Engineering* 24 Jan. 105/1 Driven by two 100 h.p. mill-type motors..equipped with solenoid and dynamic braking. **1950** *Ibid.* 22 Dec. 528/2 Slip-ring induction motors with dynamic braking. **1883** *Encycl. Brit.* XVI. 165/1 The line connecting all the points where the magnetic intensity is least is called the dynamic equator. **1893** *Jrnl. Geol.* I. 854 The dynamic metamorphism of the eruptive rocks occurring in it. **1965** A. HOLMES *Princ. Phys. Geol.* (ed. 2) viii. 170 Since the main process is dynamic, slate is said to be a product of dynamic metamorphism. **1919** A. B. EASON *Flow & Measurem. Air & Gases* ix. 163 Threlfall.. mentions tests made upon a Pitot tube in which..there was a large suction effect, and..the difference between the static and dynamic pressures was of the form $H = k(u)^n$, where *n* was greater than 2. **1949** O. G. SUTTON *Sci. of Flight* ii. 36 The dynamic pressure of the flow..is the pressure felt on the nose of a body at the point where the impinging stream is actually brought to rest. **1970** A. C. KERMODE *Flight without Formulae* 43 A fluid can exert pressure for two reasons: first because of its movement... The pressure due to movement we will call dynamic pressure.

B. *sb.* **1.** = DYNAMICS, q.v.

1873 CLIFFORD *Syllabus of Lectures* in *Math. Papers* (1882) 516 The science which teaches under what circumstances particular motions take place..is called Dynamic.. It is divided into two parts, *Static*..and *Kinetic*. **1878** —— (*title*) Elements of Dynamic: an Introduction to the Study of Motion and Rest in Solid and Fluid Bodies.

2. = Dynamic theory: see A. 7.

1884 tr. *Lotze's Metaph.* 305 As Kant does in the course of his 'Proof' of this 'Precept No. 1' of his 'Dynamic'.

3. Energizing or motive force.

1894 H. DRUMMOND *Ascent of Man* 270 The Struggle for Life, as life's dynamic, can never wholly cease. **1896** *Advance* (Chicago) 16 July 80/1 There is lack of dynamic. There is lack of direct soul-changing power.

4. *Mus.* = DYNAMICS 3.

[**1884** H. RIEMANN (*title*) Musikalische Dynamik und Agogik.] **1959** D. COOKE *Lang. Music* iii. 159 The minor system, soft dynamic, and slow tempo.

dynamical (daɪ-, dɪˈnæmɪkəl), *a.* [f. as prec. + -AL[1].]

1. Of or pertaining to the science of DYNAMICS.

1812–16 PLAYFAIR *Nat. Phil.* (1819) II. 271 An elementary exposition of the dynamical principles employed in these investigations. **1833** HERSCHEL *Astron.* viii. 266 As an abstract dynamical proposition. **1869** HUXLEY in *Sci. Opinion* 28 Apr. 486/3 Strict deductions from admitted dynamical principles.

2. Of or pertaining to force or mechanical power: = DYNAMIC *a.* 1, 2.

dynamical electricity, current electricity, as exhibited in the galvanic battery, and in electromotive appliances. ***d. metamorphism***: see prec. 9.

1828 WEBSTER, *Dynamical*, pertaining to strength or power. **1843–46** GROVE *Corr. Phys. Forces* (ed. 1) 15 Nor do we by any of our ordinary methods test heat in any other way than by its purely dynamical action. **1855** H. SPENCER *Princ. Psychol.* (1872) II. VI. xi. 138 In this purely dynamical action consists the production of sound. **1860** MAURY *Phys. Geog. Sea* ii. §108 The dynamical forces which are expressed by the Gulf Stream. **1862** SIR H. HOLLAND *Ess.* i. 14 On the mutual convertibility of heat and dynamical force. **1880** HAUGHTON *Phys. Geog.* iii. 96 In a permanent condition of dynamical equilibrium. **1881** SIR W. THOMSON in *Nature*

No. 619. 435 High potential..is the essential for good dynamical economy in the electric transmission of power. **1889** Dynamical metamorphism [see DYNAMO-METAMORPHISM 2].

b. *transf.* Cf. DYNAMIC *a.* 3 b.

1870 S. H. HODGSON *The. Practice* II. iv. §93. 11 The distinction between the statical and dynamical mode of perception gives the distinction between noun and verb. [See also s.v. DYNAMICALLY.]

3. Applied to inspiration conceived as an endowing with divine power, in opposition to a 'mechanical' inspiration in which the medium is the mere tool or instrument of the Deity.

1841 MYERS *Cath. Th.* III. xvi. 60 The method in which it [Divine Influence] has been exerted on man has been dynamical rather than merely mechanical. **1846** HARE *Mission Comf.* (1850) 299 Andrewes..was disposed to look at the work of the Spirit rather as mechanical, than as dynamical or organical. **1856** J. MACNAUGHT *Doctrine Inspir.* vi. (1857) 6 If a living man..be 'moved by the Spirit', it can, assuredly, only be by a strengthening, or enlarging, or adding to the number of the faculties of that living man—that is, by 'dynamical' inspiration.

4. Of or pertaining to DYNAMISM (sense 1).

1845 MAURICE *Mor. & Met. Philos.* in *Encycl. Metrop.* 579/1 That high form of dynamical philosophy which was contained in the poems of Empedocles of Agrigentum. **1850** —— *Mor. & Met. Philos.* (ed. 2) 85 The natural philosophers of Greece are divided into the dynamical and mechanical—Thales being assigned to the former class.

5. *Med.* Functional: = DYNAMIC 5 a.

1861 T. J. GRAHAM *Pract. Med.* 19 Another element of disease in the dynamical condition of a part, appears to be an alteration in the relation between the tissues and the blood.

dy'namically, *adv.* [f. prec. + -LY².] **a.** In a dynamic or dynamical manner or way; in the way of a force in action or in motion; from the point of view of dynamics.

1833 HERSCHEL *Astron.* viii. 267 A straight line, dynamically speaking, is the only path which can be pursued by a body absolutely free. **1836** MACGILLIVRAY tr. *Humboldt's Trav.* xxvii. 411 Manifesting its power, at great distances, only dynamically, by shaking the crust of our planet in linear directions. **1870** S. H. HODGSON *The. Practice* II. iv. §93. 8 The distinction of noun and verb.. seems to me to be the distinction between an object considered statically, and one, perhaps the same object, considered dynamically..A verb is a noun in motion, a noun is a verb at rest. **1881** MIVART *Cat* 9 The animal may be considered statically or dynamically.

b. *Mus.* With regard to dynamics (sense 3).

1939 A. COPLAND *What to listen for in Music* vii. 95 They [*sc.* percussion instruments] are generally used in one of three ways: to sharpen rhythmic effects, dynamically to heighten the sense of climax, or to add color to the other instruments. **1947** A. EINSTEIN *Mus. Romantic Era* xi. 136 The overture to the *Francs Juges*..is most delicately modeled both orchestrally and dynamically.

dynamicism (daɪˈnæmɪsɪz(ə)m). = DYNAMISM 2.

1947 E. BOWEN *Coll. Impressions* (1950) I. 18 A life of inner dynamicism which covered, geographically, little space. **1948** L. SPITZER *Linguistics & Lit. Hist.* 183 Falstaff, perhaps, comes very close to the French figures, only that his belly does not make him fit for dynamicism.

dynamicist (daɪˈnæmɪsɪst). [f. DYNAMIC(S + -IST 2.] One who studies dynamics.

1956 *Nature* 18 Feb. 321/1 It is particularly important that meteorologists (especially dynamicists) should develop the difficult studies of individual clouds. **1957** G. E. HUTCHINSON *Treat. Limnol.* I. v. 251 Some empirical work was done in the eighteenth century, largely by engineers, but it seldom conformed to the expectations of the deductive dynamicists. **1971** *Nature* 23 Apr. 491/3 The assumptions that are made by planetary dynamicists regarding the state of the Earth's interior in the geological past are particularly difficult to investigate.

dyna'micity. *Chem.* A synonym of *valency* or *atomicity*.

In mod. Dicts.

dynamics (daɪ-, dɪˈnæmɪks). [Plural of DYNAMIC, after earlier names of sciences in -ICS, q.v.]

1. a. The branch of Physics which treats of the action of Force: in earlier use restricted to the action of force in producing or varying motion, and thus opposed to *Statics* (which treats of rest or equilibrium under the action of forces); more recently (see quots. 1863-67), the name *Kinetics* has been introduced for the former, Dynamics being taken in a more comprehensive (and more etymological) sense, to include Statics and Kinetics. But the earlier usage, in which Statics and Dynamics are treated as co-ordinate, is still retained by some physicists, and has largely influenced the popular and transferred applications of the word and its derivatives. Also called DYNAMIC.

1788-89 HOWARD *Royal Encycl.*, *Dynamics* is the science of moving powers; more particularly of the motion of bodies that mutually act on one another. **1804** ROBISON *Mechan. Philos.* Pref., The general doctrines of Dynamics are the basis of Mechanical Philosophy. **1812-16** PLAYFAIR *Nat. Phil.* (1819) I. 57 This part of Dynamics would lead to the consideration of Central Forces. **1829** *Nat. Philos., Mech.* I. i. 1 (U.K.S.) In the second part, which is called dynamics, bodies are considered as submitted to the action of forces which are not in equilibrium. **1863** THOMSON & TAIT *Sketch of Elem. Dynamics* 1 Dynamics is the science which investigates the action of Force..Dynamics is divided into two parts, Statics and Kinetics. **1867** —— *Nat. Philos.* Pref. 2 Keeping in view the proprieties of language, and following the example of the most logical writers, we employ the term Dynamics in its true sense as the science which treats of the action of *force*, whether it maintains relative rest, or produces acceleration of relative motion. The two corresponding divisions of Dynamics are thus conveniently entitled *Statics* and *Kinetics*. **1871** TYNDALL *Fragm. Sc.* (1879) I. i. 17 We deal with statics, not with dynamics.

b. That branch of any science in which force or forces are considered.

e.g. ***geological dynamics***, that branch of geology which treats of the nature and operation of the forces by which the earth's surface has been affected, as distinguished from that which treats of the existing condition of the surface, and the order and characteristics of the strata.

1843 MILL *Logic* VI. x. §5 (1856) II. 505 [With Comte] Social Dynamics is the theory of society considered in a state of progressive movement; while Social Statics is the theory of the *consensus* already spoken of as existing among the different parts of the social organism. **1845** GRAVES *Rom. Law* in *Encycl. Metrop.* 768/1 He treats rather of the *dynamics* than of the *statics* of law—rather of those events or *forces* by which classes of rights begin, are modified or terminate, than of those rights and duties which accompany a given *stationary* legal relation. **1863** LYELL *Antiq. Man* xv. 313 It is for those to decide who are conversant with dynamics of glacier motion.

2. *transf.* The moving physical or moral forces in any sphere, or the laws by which they act.

1833 CHALMERS *Const. Man* (1835) I. vi. 236 To unsettle the moral dynamics which nature hath established there. **1843** J. MARTINEAU *Chr. Life* (1867) 189 The great storehouse of our spiritual dynamics. **1849** BUCHANAN *10 Years' Confl.* (1852) II. 392 Conscience seemed to be a force as little known to the dynamics of politicians in the nineteenth as in the seventeenth century. **1867** *Cornh. Mag.* Jan. 25 No comprehensive theory of the dynamics of æsthetic evolution has yet been propounded.

3. *Mus.* The variation in, or amount of, volume of sound from a musical instrument or in a musical performance. Also *transf.*

1883 in *Encycl. Dict.* **1908** *Jrnl. Folk-Song Soc.* III. III. 155 He will..find no difficulty in keeping well together with the record, as regards rhythms, twiddles, added syllables dynamics, etc. **1939** A. COPLAND *What to listen for in Music* iii. 25 Merely by changing the dynamics, that is, by playing it loudly and bravely or softly and timidly, one can transform the emotional feeling of the very same succession of notes. **1942** E. BLOM *Mus. England* vii. 116 The new instrument, capable of producing not only harmony but a range of dynamics undreamt of by harpsichord players. **1962** A. NISBETT *Technique Sound Studio* 252 Graphical representation of the envelope (or dynamics) of a single note may show separate distinctive features.

†**dynamide.** A generic term proposed by Berzelius to include the 'imponderables', caloric, light, electricity, and magnetism, in substitution for *fluid*. (*Syd. Soc. Lex.* 1883.)

dyna'mimeter, dynami'ometer, forms more etymologically correct, proposed and by some used, instead of DYNAMOMETER.

dynamism (ˈdaɪn-, ˈdɪnəmɪz(ə)m). [f. Gr. δύναμις power, force + -ISM. In mod.F. *dynamisme*.]

1. A philosophical system, theory, or doctrine, which seeks to explain the phenomena of the universe by some immanent force or energy.

Applied to an ancient doctrine of the Ionic philosophers, who explained the motion of bodies by such principles as love and hatred; to the doctrine of Leibnitz that all substance involves force; and to modern theories that mechanical energy is substance, or that the doctrine of energy is sufficient to explain the constitution of the universe.

1857 W. FLEMING *Vocab. Philos.* (1858) 148 *Dynamism*, the philosophy of Leibnitz, that all substance involves *force*. **1866** *Contemp. Rev.* II. 552 To distinguish the dynamism of Goethe from that of Diderot, to show how this dynamism is related to the free pantheistic doctrine which emerged in Goethe's mind from the dogmatic system of..Spinoza. **1875** LEWES *Probl. Life & Mind* IV. iv. §77 II. 316 Two great systems embrace all minor systems: Atomism and Dynamism..The Dynamist theory regards Matter as constituted by unextended centres of force. **1876** MANNING in *Contemp. Rev.* Nov. 1030 Mr. Kirkman, as a champion of Dynamism, has challenged single-handed all Atomists and Materialists. **1891** tr. *Didon's Jesus Christ* 14 The dynamism of Thales and Pherecydes gave place to the atomism of Democritus.

2. The mode of being of force or energy; operation of force. Now usu., energizing or dynamic action, energy, 'drive'.

1831 CARLYLE in Froude *Life in Lond.* (1882) II. vii. 144 These all build on mechanism; one spark of dynamism, of inspiration, were it in the poorest soul, is stronger than they all. **1874** LEWES *Probl. Life & Mind* I. 111 That which by its definition is not substantial at all, but pure dynamism. **1880** *Times* 20 Nov. 5/4 The seismograph on Mount Vesuvius indicates great subterranean dynamism. **1885** L. OLIPHANT *Sympneumata* 211 Apparent miracle by the dynamism of touch. **1887** —— *Fash. Philos.* 19 The one contains a vital element in its dynamism which the other does not. **1940** *Economist* 20 July 70/1 Admiral Yonai's Ministry was brought down by the Army simply on the grounds of 'insufficient dynamism'. **1951** R. FIRTH *Elem. Social Org.* v. 165 The primitive artist had hardly anything like the theory of æsthetic dynamism lying behind the use of the Chinese brush. **1955** P. HERON *Changing Forms of Art* 148 The solid earth itself is far too convulsed to be really convincing in the long run *as* the solid earth. I enjoy these landscapes very much, but their unity is violated by so much 'dynamism'. **1966** G. N. LEECH *Eng. in Advertising* vi. 65 Board-room clichés which imply the dynamism, success, and health of the firm's activities.

3. *Med.* 'The theory of the origin of disease from change or alteration of vital force.' (*Syd. Soc. Lex.*)

Hence **'dynamist**, (*a*) One who studies or deals with dynamics; (*b*) One who holds the doctrine of dynamism. **dyna'mistic** *a.*, of, pertaining to, or of the nature of dynamism; according to the doctrine of dynamists.

1856 DOVE *Logic Chr. Faith* v. i. §2. 275 The dynamist.. treating of levers which..have neither breadth nor thickness, and contain no material, is an absolute Idealist. **1883** *Encycl. Brit.* XVI. 719/1 It is usual..to speak of two kinds of monarchianism,—the dynamistic and the modalistic. By monarchians of the former class Christ was held to be..constituted the Son of God simply by the infinitely high degree in which he had been filled with Divine wisdom and power.

‖**dynamitard.** [f. DYNAMITE, after Fr. *communard*. (Not in recognized Fr. use, though it may have occurred in French newspapers.)] = DYNAMITER.

1882 *Pall Mall G.* 28 Oct. 1/2 'Red Spectre in France.' The public confession that the 'dynamitards' had paralyzed the administration of justice. **1883** *Ibid.* 2 Feb. 1/2 The Dynamitards have not secured the return of a single deputy even for the 'reddest' constituency in France. **1883** *Athenæum* 29 Dec. 876/1 A melodrama..dealing with the proceedings of English dynamitards. **1892** G. B. SHAW *Fabian Soc.* 5 Not that we were dynamitards..how innocent we were of any practical acquaintance with explosives. **1917** T. E. LAWRENCE *Lett.* (1938) 232 The Ageyl dynamitards were inefficient, and our supply of dynamite small.

dynamite (ˈdaɪnəmaɪt, ˈdɪn-), *sb.* [mod. f. Gr. δύναμις force + -ITE, by Alfred Nobel the inventor.]

1. a. A high explosive prepared from nitro-glycerine mixed, for greater safety in carriage and use, with some inert absorptive substance.

1867 *Specif. Newton's Patent* No. 1345. 3 Causing it [nitro-glycerine] to be absorbed in porous unexplosive substances, such as charcoal, silica.. whereby it is converted into a powder, which I call dynamite or Nobel's safety powder. **1868** *Daily Tel.* 15 July, Other experiments demonstrated the great velocity imparted to fragments of shells charged with dynamite. **1875** *Ann. Reg.* 120 A clockwork which was timed to cause the explosion of the dynamite. **1883** *Fortn. Rev.* May 641 Dynamite..consists of nitro-glycerine absorbed in an infusorial siliceous earth called 'Kieselguhr'.

b. *fig.* Something or someone potentially unsettling, dangerous, or disastrous.

1922 HART CRANE *Let.* 23 Jan. (1965) 78 Another small magazine, full of compressed dynamite. **1926** J. BLACK *You can't Win* (1927) xiv. 199 I'm dynamite with them old brums in the cribs. **1945** P. CHEYNEY *I'll say she Does!* v. 128, I call it goddam urgent. It's dynamite. **1961** *Countryman* 441 The 'Church question' is still dynamite in the field of education. **1970** 'W. HAGGARD' *Hardliners* vi. 62 He had reason to be cautious for the proposal..had been naked political dynamite.

c. Heroin or a similar narcotic (see quots.). *slang* (orig. *U.S.*).

1924 G. C. HENDERSON *Keys to Crookdom* xxiv. 301 So powerful was the 'kick' of heroin that it was called 'dynamite'. **1938** *Amer. Speech* XIII. 183/2 *Dynamite.* 1. Bootleg dope with an unusually high narcotic content... 2. A knockout dose given to an addict under the guise of narcotics. **1967** M. CULPAN *In Deadly Vein* vii. 149 'A little bit of horse? Some dynamite?' Horse was heroin; so was dynamite.

2. *attrib.*, as ***dynamite bomb***, ***outrage***, etc.; **dynamite cruiser**, a cruiser armed with dynamite guns; **dynamite gun**, a pneumatic gun for throwing dynamite shells, or other high explosives.

1880 *Daily News* 13 Dec., What was to be said of the dynamite affair at Bantry. **1883** *Ibid.* 14 Sept. 2/7 The various dynamite outrages committed in Glasgow. **1883** *Pall Mall G.* 6 Apr. 7/1 The dynamite conspiracy. **1886** *World* 12 May 8 The dynamite bomb exploded among the Chicago police. **1888** *Times* 2 Oct. 3/2 To have shown that the dynamite shells could be successfully fired from an ordinary gun. *Ibid.*, The dynamite gun is a new instrument which has its own functions in time of war. *Ibid.*, After the gun has been properly tested on board the dynamite cruiser.

'dynamite, *v.* [f. prec. sb.] *trans.* To shatter or wreck by the explosion of dynamite; to mine or charge with dynamite. Also *fig.*

1881 H. CROSBY in *Independent* (N.Y.) No. 1684 Finally Utah should be dynamited. **1883** A. M. SULLIVAN in *Pall Mall G.* 20 Mar. 7/1 Our homes are in the midst of the cities that are, forsooth, to be kerosined and dynamited. **1892** *L'pool Daily Post* 4 Aug. 5/9 Threat to dynamite New York Bankers. **1903** *Westm. Gaz.* 30 July 3/1 Mr. Chamberlain.. tried to dynamite discussion by declaring that the rejection of the Bill would mean the infringement of treaty obligation. **1938** *Amer. Speech* XIII. 156/1 *Dynamite an order*, to rush an order through as quickly as possible.

dynamiter (ˈdaɪnəmaɪtə(r), ˈdɪn-). [f. DYNAMITE *v.* + -ER.] One who employs dynamite and similar explosives for unlawful purposes; esp. as a means of attacking existing governments or political systems.

1883 *U.S. Newspaper* 16 May, There is a rumor that dynamiters intend to damage the Welland canal. **1884** *American* VIII. 294 You do not find a good citizen..under

the hat of a dynamiter and an assassin. **1885** STEVENSON *Dynamiter* 116 Under this alias, you follow the profession of a dynamiter.

‖**dynamiteur** (dinamitœ:r). [mod.F.] = prec.
1883 *Spectator* 14 Apr. 472/2 The Dynamiteurs—we had better adopt the French word at once—may yet secure.. fanatics as agents. **1886** J. D. CHAMPLIN *Chron. Coach* i. 6 The tall column..which the dynamiteurs had threatened with their bombs only a few nights before.

dynamitic (daɪnə'mɪtɪk, 'dɪn-), *a.* [f. DYNAMITE *sb.* + -IC.] Of or pertaining to dynamite; having to do with dynamite, or dynamiters.
1882 GOLDW. SMITH in *19th Cent.* June 887 If he did, a more dynamitic rival would immediately pluck him down. **1885** *Sat. Rev.* 24 Jan. 102/2 To receive subscriptions for carrying on dynamitic warfare. **1895** *N. Amer. Rev.* Apr. 463 The father of Nihilism and of dynamitic anarchy.
Hence **dyna'mitical** *a.*, in same sense: **dyna'mitically** *adv.*, by way of dynamite.
1886 *Pall Mall G.* 2 Oct. 1/1, I have had neither part nor lot in any secret Fenian or dynamitical operations. **1887** *Congregationalist* (U.S.) 17 Feb., The Irish attempts, at New York, Paris, and elsewhere, dynamitically to blow up England on behalf of Ireland. **1892** *Illustr. Lond. News* 8 Oct. 450/3 His dynamitical and tyrannicidal schemes.

dynamitism ('daɪnəmaɪˌtɪz(ə)m, 'dɪn-). [-ISM.] The principles and practice of the dynamiter; the use of dynamite and similar explosives for the destruction of life and property, as a method of attacking a government, nation, or person.
1883 *American* VI. 36 Unqualified repudiation of assassination and dynamitism. **1891** *Pall Mall G.* 4 Aug. 3/3 He was indicted, not for dynamitism, but for Fenianism.

'dynamitist. [f. as prec. + -IST.] One who practises or favours dynamitism; a dynamiter.
1882 *Sat. Rev.* 8 July 45/1 Reports of the intentions of the American-Irish dynamitists. **1885** HOLYOAKE *Let.* in *Daily News* 7 Feb. 3/8 While Dynamitists and State Socialists appear as lurid figures on the horizon of society.

dynamize ('daɪn-, 'dɪnəmaɪz), *v. Med.* [see -IZE.] *trans.* To endow with power. In *Homœopathy*, To increase the power of (medicines) by trituration or succussion. Hence **dynami'zation**.
1855 *Household Wds.* XII. 69 Monstrous assertions of the curative power of the 'high dynamisation' of medicinal substances. **1881** J. G. GLOVER in *Encycl. Brit.* XII. 127/1 The most characteristic feature of Hahnemann's practice—the 'potentizing', 'dynamizing', of medicinal substances. **1883** *Syd. Soc. Lex.*, *Dynamisation*..used by the homœopathists to denote the accession or freeing of active powers produced in a medicine by pounding it or shaking violently the bottle in which it is contained.

dynamo-, an element, derived from Gr. δύναμις 'power, force', used to form combinations and derivative words, as **dynamo-e'lectric** *a.*, pertaining to current (formerly called dynamic) electricity; also, pertaining to the conversion of dynamical into electrical energy, as in ***dynamo-electric machine, machinery***: see next. Cf. also DYNAMO-METAMORPHISM.
1882 *Deschanel's Nat. Phil.* (ed. 6) 795 Machines constructed on this principle [that of Siemens and Wheatstone] are called dynamo-electric.

dynamo ('daɪnəməʊ), *sb.* Pl. -os. [Abbreviated from *dynamo-machine*, itself short for *dynamo-electric machine.*] **a.** *Electr.* A machine for converting energy in the form of mechanical power into energy in the form of electric currents, by the operation of setting conductors (usually in the form of coils of copper wire) to rotate in a magnetic field.
The full name ***dynamo-electric machine*** was given by Siemens in 1867, to distinguish his invention from the ***magneto-electric machines*** previously used, in which the electric current was generated by means of a permanent magnet. But in the shortened form *dynamo* (recommended by Prof. S. P. Thompson early in 1882), the use of the word has been extended so as to include all forms of these machines: see quot. 1884.
[**1882** *Times* 2 Dec. 5 Professor Thompson said that the name 'dynamo-electric machine' was first applied by Dr. Werner Siemens in a communication made in January, 1867, to the Berlin Academy. He there described a machine for generating electric currents by the application of mechanical power, the currents being induced in the coils of a rotating armature by the action of electro-magnets which were themselves excited by the currents so generated. The machine was, in fact, a self-exciting dynamo.]
1875 *Specif. Clark's Patent* No. 4311. 2 Dynamo-electric machine. **1878** S. P. THOMPSON in *Engineering* 20 Dec. 300 Such machines were more powerful than those in which only steel magnets were used; and they have received the name *dynamo-electric machines. Ibid.*, The cost of producing electric currents of any required power is now simply the cost of..a dynamo-machine and a steam-engine, and of the coal and labour necessary to supply and attend to them. **1880** *Print. Trades Jrnl.* No. 32. 26 Instructions..for depositing Copper by the battery, or by the Dynamo-machine. **1882** *Athenæum* 5 Aug. 179/2 The word 'dynamo' is now being used as a noun in the place of 'dynamo-electric machine', and from its convenience it will probably soon become the generic term. **1884** S. P. THOMPSON *Dynamo-electric Mach.* 3 A dynamo is a dynamo, in fact, whether its magnets be excited by the whole of its own current, or by a part of its own current, or by a current from an independent source. *Ibid.* 4 The arbitrary distinction between so-called magneto-electric machines and dynamo-electric machines fails when examined carefully. In all these machines a magnet, whether permanently excited, independently excited, or self-excited, is employed to provide a field of magnetic force. *Ibid.* xi. 199 (Heading) The magneto-dynamo or magneto-electric machine. **1885** *Athenæum* No. 2985. 54 Efficiency and economic coefficient of dynamos, the series dynamo and the shunt dynamo being separately considered. **1916** *Autocar Handbk.* (ed. 6) xvii. 240 Electric lighting failed to secure adoption until the complete system involving the fitting of a dynamo upon the car came forward. **1936** *Encycl. Sports* 212/2 Many firms make cheap, light, and reliable dynamos driven off the edge of the front or rear tire.
b. *fig.*
1892 G. MEREDITH *Let.* 4 Feb. (1970) II. 1064 Ask Jim whether his whirring dynamo of a brain has flung to nothing Will's questions. **1904** E. DOWDEN *Browning* 327 Any stream of moral electricity worked from a dynamo of the will. **1938** *Time* 24 Oct. 2/2 In short, I am to be..the 'alter ego' of a human dynamo. **1963** D. OGILVY *Confess. Advert. Man* (1964) i. 18, I have to rely on..empirical techniques for spotting creative dynamos.

dynamogen (daɪn-, dɪ'næməʊdʒɪn). [mod. f. DYNAMO- + -GEN taken in sense of 'producing', 'producer'.] Nitromagnite; a high explosive (for which the name 'dynamagnite' was first proposed), consisting of a mixture of nitro-glycerine and prepared hydrocarbonate of magnesia. Known in U.S. as 'Hercules powder'.
1882 *Daily News* 30 May 6/2 A new explosive has been invented by M. Petri, a Viennese engineer. The name given to it is dynamogen..The charge of dynamogen is in the form of a solid cylinder.

dynamogeny (daɪn-, dɪnə'mɒdʒɪnɪ). [mod. f. DYNAMO- + Gr. -γενεια production; see -GENY.] Production of increased nervous activity; dynamization of nerve-force.
1887 *Fortn. Rev.* May 742 The views recently propounded by Professor Brown-Séquard upon what he calls nervous 'dynamogeny'. *Ibid.*, Inhibition in one nervous sphere is often accompanied with dynamogeny in another. **1895** tr. *Max Nordau's Degeneration* 28 A feeling of pleasure is always connected with dynamogeny, or the production of force; every living thing, therefore, instinctively seeks for dynamogenous sense-impressions.
So **dynamo'genesis** = DYNAMOGENY; **dynamo'genic** *a.*, of or pertaining to dynamogeny; **dyna'mogenous** *a.*, having the property of generating or producing force; **dyna'mogenously** *adv.*
1883 L. BRUNTON in *Nature* 8 Mar. 436 M. Brown-Séquard supposes that in each layer of the cerebro-spinal system there are both dynamogenic elements and inhibitory elements for the subjacent segments. **1887** *Fortn. Rev.* May 742 Recent researches by Dr. Féré have thrown additional light upon these 'dynamogenic' or 'force-producing' processes. **1895** tr. *Max Nordau's Degeneration* 28 Many sense-impressions operate enervatingly and inhibitively on the movements; others, on the contrary, make these more powerful, rapid and active; they are 'dynamogenous', or 'force-producing'. *Ibid.* 29 Pictures operating dynamogenously, and producing feelings of pleasure.

dynamograph ('daɪn-, 'dɪnəməʊgrɑ:f, -æ-). [mod. f. DYNAMO- + Gr. -γραφος writer: see -GRAPH.] An instrument for recording the amount of force exerted.
1851 *Offic. Catal. Gt. Exhib.* III. 1014 A dynamograph, for ascertaining the average strength of draught. Invented by Adam Chevalier de Burg. **1871** HAMMOND *Dis. Nerv. Syst.* p. xix, The Dynamograph is of great value in the diagnosis of diseases of the nervous system. **1878** HAMILTON *Nerv. Dis.* 26 The dynamograph..a combination of the dynamometer and the writing part of the sphygmograph, is advocated as a valuable aid in diagnosis.
Hence **ˌdynamo'graphic** *a.*, pertaining to a dynamograph.
1895 PRITCHARD tr. *Marey's Movement* ix. 52 The areas of the curves which are described by the dynamographic needle express the exact equivalent of the force employed.

ˌdynamometa'morphism. [f. DYNAMO- + METAMORPHISM.]
1. The transformation of energy from one mode of action to another.
1896 *Yale Univ. Grad. Course Instruct.* 58 Effects of dynamo-metamorphism.
2. *Geol.* = *dynamic metamorphism* (DYNAMIC *a.* and *sb.* A. 9). So **ˌdynamometa'morphic** *a.*
1888 J. P. IDDINGS tr. *Rosenbusch's Microsc. Physiogr. Rock-Making Min.* 223 The product of a dynamo-metamorphic alteration of plagioclase. **1889** *Geol. Mag.* 243 Rosenbusch..seeking to bring clearly into view the consideration that the special kind of metamorphism referred to is only produced when the mechanical forces effect movement, and thus do work, suggested the term Dynamical metamorphism or dynamometamorphism. **1904** *Nature* 4 Aug. 317/2 The observations of..Barrois in Brittany thus receive confirmation from the stronghold of the dynamometamorphic school. **1909** F. P. MENNELL *Introd. Petrol.* xix. 152 It is usual to discriminate between dynamo- and pyrometamorphic types. *Ibid.*, These rocks which owe their immediate characters to dynamometamorphism..are usually grouped together under the name of schists. **1966** *McGraw-Hill Encycl. Sci. & Technol.* VIII. 296a/2 Cataclastic rocks are mechanically sheared and crushed. They represent products of dynamometamorphism, or kinetic metamorphism.

dynamometer (daɪn-, dɪnə'mɒmɪtə(r): see DYNA-). [ad. F. *dynamomètre* (in Lunier, *Dict. des Sciences*, 1805), f. DYNAMO- + Gr. μέτρ-ον measure.]
1. a. A name of instruments of various kinds for measuring the amount of energy exerted by an animal, or expended by a motor or other engine in its work, or by the action of any mechanical force.
1810 *Q. Rev.* Aug. 59 Some experiments made..with a new instrument, invented by Regnier, which he calls a dynamometer, for the purpose of ascertaining the comparative strength which individuals are capable of exerting. **1823** *Mech. Mag.* No. 14. 209 The Dynamometer of Regnier, which enables us to ascertain easily the comparative strength of men. **1862** *Lond. Rev.* 23 Aug. 176 The draught-power of the engine was noted by a spiral spring dynamometer, capable of registering up to 8 tons. **1879** THOMSON & TAIT *Nat. Phil.* I. I. 488 The name 'dynamometer', besides, appears to be badly formed from the Greek; and for designating an instrument for *measurement of force*, I would suggest that the name may with advantage be changed to *dynamimeter.* **1895** PRITCHARD tr. *Marey's Movement* ix. 146 Dynamometers are constructed on the principle that an elastic body is distorted in proportion to the degree of force applied.
fig. **1854** LOWELL *Cambridge 30 Y. Ago* Pr. Wks. 1890 I. 88 An accurate dynamometer of Willard's punch or Porter's flip. **1890** B. L. GILDERSLEEVE *Ess. & Stud.* 245 He saluted his wife as a moral dynamometer.
b. *attrib.*, as **dynamometer car**, a railway vehicle with equipment for continuously measuring and recording the force exerted by the locomotive pulling it and other information about the running of the train.
1879 *Railroad Gaz.* 30 May 298/2 Mr. F. M. Wilder..has during the past year been occupied..in perfecting a dynamometer car. *Ibid.* 298/3 The train consisted of 45 loaded cars, with a caboose and the dynamometer car. **1953** W. W. HAY *Railroad Engin.* I. xi. 153 Many of the test data used in deriving drawbar pull, tonnage ratings, and other locomotive performance data are obtained with a dynamometer car.
2. An instrument for measuring the magnifying power of a telescope: also called DYNAMETER.
1832 *Nat. Philos., Optic. Instr.* iv. §18. 11 (U.K.S.) The magnifying power of telescopes may be ascertained..by means of a dynamometer. **1890** G. F. CHAMBERS *Handbk. Astron.* VII. i, Shifting the Dynamometer until the two internal edges exactly touch the circumference of the image.
Hence **dynamo'metric, -'metrical** (also **dynami-**) *a.*, of or pertaining to the measurement of force; **dyna'mometry**, the measurement of force.
1837 *Ann. Electr., Magn. & Chem.* I. 444 The mechanical effect..was estimated at half the force of a man. I shall apply it hereafter to an exact dynamometric apparatus. **1864** WEBSTER, *Dynamometric, -al.* **1868** DUNCAN *Ins. World* Introd. 23 In order to measure the muscular strength of man, or of animals..many different dynamometric apparatuses have been invented, composed of springs, or systems of unequal levers. **1870** *Daily News* 14 Nov., Thorough Test of Double Ploughs..To carry out the dynamometrical experiments. **1879** THOMSON & TAIT *Nat. Phil.* I I. §437 If we..apply the proper amount of force at each end of the dynamimetric rope or chain. **1891** *Athenæum* 7 Mar. 316/1 Further Contributions to Dynamometry.

dyna'mopathy. A synonym of *Homœopathy*, in reference to the 'dynamization' of drugs. (*S.S.Lex.*)

dynamoscope (dɪ'næməʊskəʊp). [a. F. *dynamoscope* (Collongues 1862), f. DYNAMO- + Gr. -σκοπος, -SCOPE.] An instrument devised for the prosecution of *dynamoscopy*.
dyna'moscopy [Fr. *-opie*]; Collongues' name for a special form of auscultation for the observation of the sound called *bruit rotatoire*, a hollow rumbling heard in living muscular tissue, esp. in the tips of the fingers, and supposed to proceed from fibrillary contraction of the muscles.

dynamotor ('daɪnəməʊtə(r)). [f. DYNA- + MOTOR *sb.*] A combined electric motor and generator with one field magnet and two armatures, or with one armature upon which are two windings, one which receives current as a motor and the other which generates current as a dynamo.
1908 *Westm. Gaz.* 30 Mar. 5/2 For starting purposes supplementary power is obtained by means of an electric machine, best described as a dynamotor. **1910** *Hawkins's Electr. Dict.* 133/2 Another form of dynamotor is called the continuous alternating transformer. **1942** *Electronic Engin.* June 36/2 The basic power supply is 24v. from the aircraft battery, and this operates a compact dynamotor.

dynast ('dɪn-, 'daɪnæst: see DYNA-). Also 7 di-. [ad. late L. *dynastēs*, a. Gr. δυναστής lord, chief, ruler, f. δύνασθαι to be able, powerful. Cf. F. *dynaste* (16th c.). Milton used the Gr. and L. accus. pl. *dynastas* in English context.] One in power; a ruler, lord, chief, potentate, esp. a hereditary ruler; a member or founder of a dynasty.
1631 WEEVER *Anc. Fun. Mon.* 652 The ancient stemme of Des Ewes, Dynasts or Lords of the Dition of Kessell in the Dutchie of Gelderland. **1632** BURTON *Anat. Mel.* II. iii. III. (ed. 4) 332 How many great Cæsars, mighty monarches,

tetrarches, dynastes, Princes, liued in his daies. **1638** SIR T. HERBERT *Trav.* (ed. 2) 113 Shaw-Mahomet an Arabian Dinast. **1648** MILTON *Tenure Kings* Wks. (1847) 237/1 Therefore did his Mother the Virgin Mary give such praise to God..that he had..cut down dynastas or proud monarchs from the throne. **1725** tr. *Dupin's Eccl. Hist. 17th C.* I. v. 121 They might probably be Dynasts of that Country. **1874** MAHAFFY *Soc. Life Greece* iv. 116 Miltiades the elder was a sort of prince or dynast in Attica.

dynastic (dɪn-, daɪˈnæstɪk), *a.* (*sb.*) [ad. Gr. δυναστικ-ός, f. δυναστής: see prec., and cf. F. *dynastique* (admitted 1878 into Acad. Dict.).] Of, pertaining to, or connected with a dynasty or dynasties.

1828 WEBSTER, *Dynastic*, relating to a dynasty or line of kings. **1850** MRS. BROWNING *Poems* I. 74 An alien tyranny, With its dynastic reasons of larger bones And stronger sinews. **1863** BRYCE *Holy Rom. Emp.* vi. (1875) 77 The first of the dynastic quarrels of modern Europe.

†**B.** *sb.* = DYNAST. *Obs. rare*$^{-0}$.

1623 COCKERAM, *Dynasticke*, one of great rule and power. *Ibid.* II, A Great Ruler, *Potentate, Dinastick.*

dyˈnastical, *a.* [f. as prec. + -AL[1].] = prec.

1730 DALE (*title*) The History and Antiquities of Harwich and Dovercourt, topographical, dynastical, and political. **1880** DISRAELI *Endym.* III. xxiii. 232 Monarchical, not dynastical institutions.

Hence **dyˈnastically** *adv.*

1858 GLADSTONE *Homer* I. 243 Those [nations] which are designated dynastically from the head of a ruling family.

dyˈnasticism. [f. DYNASTIC *a.* + -ISM.] The dynastic principle; the system of ruling dynasties.

1872 GOLDW. SMITH in *Fortn. Rev.* Mar. 260 Look round Europe, and you will see that Legitimacy is dead, and that the sand of Dynasticism has nearly run. **1884** —— in *Contemp. Rev.* Sept. 315 Its attempt to make election extinguish itself in favour of dynasticism.

dynastidan (dɪn-, daɪˈnæstɪdən). *Entom.* [f. mod.L. *Dynastidæ*, f. *Dynastes* as a generic name.] A member of the *Dynastidæ*, a family of large beetles including the *Dynastes* or Hercules-beetle.

1835 KIRBY *Hab. & Inst. Anim.* II. xx. 365 The mighty Dynastidans appear to feed upon putrescent timber.

dynasty (ˈdɪnəstɪ, daɪ-). [a. F. *dynastie* (15–16th c.), ad. late L. *dynastīa*, ad. Gr. δυναστεία power, lordship, domination, f. δυναστής DYNAST.]

1. Lordship, sovereignty, power; régime. Now *rare* or *Obs.*

1613 PURCHAS *Pilgrimage* (1614) 69 They tell..of divers Dynasties or governments in this countrey of Babylon. *a* **1656** USSHER *Ann.* vi. (1658) 196 The King bestowed a far better Dynasty or Principality upon him in Asia. **1664** H. MORE *Myst. Iniq.* 439 The Dynasties or Polities of the Nations, the Secular Kingdomes and Powers. **1850** H. MILLER *Footpr. Creat.* xv. (1874) 295 During the present dynasty of probation and trial.

2. A succession of rulers of the same line or family; a line of kings or princes.

1460 CAPGRAVE *Chron.* 23 Than entered that lond [Egipte] they of Tebes, tyl xxxvi. dynasties had regned. **1614** RALEIGH *Hist. World* II. ii. §2 (R.) The account of the dynasties..agreeth for the most part, if not altogether, with the histories of the Assyrians, Trojans, Italians, and others, etc. **1677** HALE *Prim. Orig. Man.* II. iii. 146 He digested the successive Governments of the Egyptians into 32 Dynasties. **1790** BURKE *Fr. Rev.* 19 At some time or other..all the beginners of dynasties were chosen by those who called them to govern. **1844** H. H. WILSON *Brit. India* II. 53 Disaffected to the ruling dynasty of Nepal.

b. *transf.* and *fig.*

1800 J. REEVES *On Ps.* 18 (T.) The next dynasty of theologists, the schoolmen. **1857** H. REED *Lect. Brit. Poets* vii. 234 The annals of a dynasty of noble poets. **1866** FERRIER *Grk. Philos.* I. xii. 363 Aristotle..was fitted to found a new dynasty in philosophy.

dynatron (ˈdaɪnətrɒn). [f. DYNA- + -TRON.] (See quots.)

1918 A. W. HULL in *Proc. Inst. Radio Engin.* VI. 35 A new, hot cathode, three electrode vacuum tube, the dynatron, is described. **1918** *Wireless World* June 148 The dynatron utilises the secondary emission of electrons by a plate upon which the primary electrons fall. **1932** *B.B.C. Techn. Tables & Gloss.* 48/2 *Dynatron*, a thermionic valve, generally with four electrodes, which can be arranged to have negative resistance over a portion of its grid volt anode current characteristic, and used, by virtue of this property, to generate continuous oscillations. **1944** *Electronic Engin.* Mar. 432/3 The dynatron does not work on the feedback principle as in the case of most oscillators.

dyndille, obs. form of DINDLE *v.*

dyne (daɪn). *Physics.* [a. F. *dyne*, taken from Gr. δύναμις force, δύνασθαι to be powerful.]

The unit of force in the centimetre-gramme-second (C.G.S.) system, i.e. a unit equivalent to that force which, acting for one second on a mass of one gramme, gives it a velocity of one centimetre per second.

In France the term had been proposed at an earlier date in a different sense: see quot. 1842.

[**1842** *Mech. Mag.* XXXVI. 192 The Industrial Society of Mulhausen..observe, that the usual estimation of horse-power is not uniform, and propose that the unit for France should be the force required to raise one kilogramme to the height of a metre in a second. To this unit they propose that the name of *dyne*..should be applied.] **1873** *Brit. Assoc. Rep.* 223 As regards the name to be given the C.G.S. unit of force, we recommend that it be a derivative of the Greek δύναμις. The form *dynamy* appears to be most satisfactory to etymologists. *Dynam* is equally intelligible, but awkward in sound to English ears. The shorter form, *dyne*..will probably be generally preferred in this country. *Ibid.* 224 The weight of a gramme, at any part of the earth's surface, is about 980 dynes, or rather less than a kilodyne. **1874** MAXWELL *Poem* in *Life* (1882) 633 This string, you said, is strained too far, 'Tis forty dynes at least too tight. **1889** A. W. POYSER *Magnet. & Electr.* 97 By a charge of one unit is meant that charge on a very small body, which, if placed at a distance of one centimetre from an equal and similar charge, repels it with a force of one dyne.

-dyne (daɪn), *suffix*, forming sbs. repr. Gr. δύναμις power, used in the formation of scientific, esp. electrical, terms. Examples: *aerodyne, amplidyne, autodyne, heterodyne.*

dyneer, -er(e, dynner, -or, obs. ff. DINNER.

dynein (ˈdaɪniːn). *Biochem.* [f. DYNE + -IN[1], -EIN (see quot. 1965).] A protein with ATPase activity that is responsible for the movement of cilia, flagella, and sperm tails; **dynein arm**, a short transverse projection from a ciliary microtubule, composed of dynein.

1965 GIBBONS & ROWE in *Science* 23 July 424/2 We propose the term 'dynein' (*dyne*, force; *-in*, protein) to describe..adenosine triphosphatase proteins associated with motile structures. **1974** *Sci. Amer.* Oct. 50/2 If the ciliary microtubules could 'walk along' one another by means of their dynein arms, one could envisage that, given the right sequence of activity and appropriate shear resistance with the axoneme, bends would form. **1979** *Nature* 7 June 532/1 The force required for motion of cilia, eukaryotic flagella and sperm tails is generated by the dynein arms... The dynein arms have been shown to contain Mg^{2+}-ATPases. **1985** *Sci. Amer.* Oct. 99/1 In cilia and flagella tubulin links with a flexible protein known as dynein.

Dynel, dynel (ˈdaɪnəl). orig. *U.S.* [Proprietary term.] A synthetic fibre that is a copolymer of vinyl chloride and acrylonitrile and resembles wool; also, the fabric made from it.

1950 *Trade Marks Jrnl.* 20 Dec. 1094/1 Dynel. Yarns and threads, all of synthetic textile materials. Union Carbide & Carbon Corporation. **1952** *Economist* 2 Feb. 282/2 There is ..war..in the textile industry, that between wool and the new synthetic substitutes—dynel, dacron and others. **1962** J. T. MARSH *Self-Smoothing Fabrics* ii. 10 Dynel goods should not be heated above about 120° C for the fibre contains a high proportion of vinyl chloride. **1967** *Daily Tel.* 18 Jan. 13/7 A dress made completely of Dynel hair.

dyng(e, obs. forms of DING. *v.*[1]

dyng(e, Sc. var. of DIGNE *a. Obs.* worthy, etc.

dyngnete, obs. form of DIGNITY.

dynle, dynt, obs. ff. DINDLE, DINT.

dynode (ˈdaɪnəʊd). [f. Gr. δύν(αμις power + ELECTR)ODE.] An electrode which emits secondary electrons.

1939 L. M. MYERS *Electron Optics* v. 307 These secondary emitting surfaces are termed the dynodes, and this term is applicable to all other forms of secondary emitting surfaces in electron multipliers. **1952** *Electronic Engin.* May 214/1 Only recently..has it been found possible to manufacture dynode surfaces with an operating life of 1000 hours. **1953** *Ibid.* Feb. 48/2 An electron multiplier having beryllium-oxide coated dynodes. **1965** *New Scientist* 2 Sept. 558/3 The image is formed by directing the secondary electrons to the first dynode or phosphorescent screen of the electron multiplier.

Dyophysite (daɪˈɒfɪzaɪt). *Theol.* [ad. late Gr. δυοφυσῖται (found in 5th c. beside διφυσῖται, DIPHYSITE, which was a more etymological form), f. δύο two + φύσις nature.] A holder of the doctrine of the co-existence of two natures, the divine and the human, in Christ: opposed to the Monophysites. Hence **Dyophyˈsitic, Dyophyˈsitical** *a.*, of or pertaining to Dyophysites; **Dyˈophysitism**, the doctrine of the Dyophysites.

1860 EDERSHEIM tr. *Kurtz's Ch. Hist.* I. §82. 5 Felix II of Rome..leader of the Dyophysites. **1882** CAVE & BANKS tr. *Dorner's Chr. Doctrine* 216 This monothelistic formula of union maintained by Heraclius and Zenon, retained no place between Dyophysites and Monophysites. *Ibid.* 219 In opposition to all theories of confusion the Church held to Dyophysitism and Dyotheletism. **1882–3** SCHAFF *Encycl. Relig. Knowl.* I. 461 An attempt to reconstruct the Lutheran theory [of Christology] on a modern critical and ethical instead of a dyophysitic basis.

dyot, obs. f. DIET.

Dyothelete, -ite (daɪˈɒθɪliːt, -aɪt), *a.* and *sb. Theol.* [f. Gr. δύο two + θελητής, agent-n. from θέλ-ειν to will: lit. a 'two-willer'. Opposed to μονοθελήτης a 'one-willer'. The ending in *-ite* is conformed to words of that termination. A more etymological form would be *dithelete*.] **a.** *adj.* Holding the doctrine that Christ had two wills, a divine and a human. **b.** *sb.* A holder of this doctrine; an opponent of MONOTHELETISM.

Hence **Dyotheˈletian, Dyotheˈletic, -ˈitic, Dyotheˈletical** *adjs.*, of or pertaining to the Dyotheletes; **Dyˈotheletism, dyˈothelism**, the doctrine that Christ had two wills.

1848 S. DAVIDSON tr. *Gieseler's Eccl. Hist.* II. 174 The doctrines of the Duothelites and Monothelites. **1860** EDERSHEIM tr. *Kurtz's Ch. Hist.* I. §82. 8 After that [A.D. 680] Dyotheletism was universally received as orthodox doctrine. **1882** CAVE & BANKS tr. *Dorner's Chr. Doctrine* 220 The decision of the Dyothelitic Council of the year 680: 'The human will remains in unity with the Divine, because it is always determined by the omnipotent drawing of the Logos'. **1882–3** SCHAFF *Encycl. Relig. Knowl.* I. 458 [Impersonality of human nature of Christ] seems inconsistent with the dyotheletic theory. *Ibid.* II. 1560 The dyothelite views were defended by the Roman legates. *Ibid.* The doctrine of two wills in Christ, dyothelism, was formally defined and accepted by a synod of the Lateran (649). **1887** HEARD *Russian Ch.* i. 2 The monotheletian patriarchs and the dyotheletian popes mutually anathematized each other.

dyphone (ˈdaɪfəʊn). *Mus.* [f. Gr. δύο two + φωνή sound, tone. But the etymological form is *diphone*, Gr. δίφωνος.] The 'double lute', invented by Thomas Mace in 1672.

1676 T. MACE *Musick's Mon.* II. xli. 203 Concerning the Dyphone: or Double-Lute, The Lute of Fifty Strings. *Ibid.* 206 Since we are Thus Joyned Both in One, Henceforth Our Name shall be The Lute Dyphone. **1880** W. H. HUSK in Grove *Dict. Mus.* II. 185 He [Mace] in 1672 invented a lute of 50 strings, which he termed the Dyphone, or Double Lute.

dypnosophistick, erron. f. DEIPNO-.

dyptic(k, obs. ff. DIPTYCH.

dyr-: see DER-, DIR-.

dyre, obs. f. DIRE *a.*, DOOR, DURE *v.*

dyrege, obs. form of DIRGE.

dyrk(e, dyrse, obs. forms of DARK, DRESS *v.*

dyrupcionne, obs. f. DIRUPTION.

c **1450** *Mirour Saluacioun* 2963 Josephs cote in no parte felt payne of dyrupcionne.

dys, obs. f. DICE; see DIE *sb.*[1]

dys-: obs. spelling of DIS-, in many words.

dys- (dɪs), *prefix*, repr. Gr. δυσ- [= Skr. *dus-*, OTeut. **tuz-*, OHG. *zúr-* (Ger. *zer-*), ON. *tor-*, OE. *tó-* in *to-break*, etc.] 'inseparable prefix, opp. to εὖ [see EU-], with notion of *hard, bad, unlucky*, etc.; destroying the good sense of a word, or increasing its bad sense' (Liddell and Scott). In Eng. used in many words, chiefly scientific, derived or compounded from Greek; the more important of these are entered as Main words; others (mostly pathological) follow here.

dysanˈgelical *a.* (*nonce-wd.*), used in opposition to *evangelical*; **dyˈsarthria** [Gr. ἄρθρον joint, articulation], defective or deranged articulation in speaking; whence **dyˈsarthric** *a.*, belonging to dysarthria; **dysarthrosis** (dɪsɑːˈθrəʊsɪs) [Gr. ἄρθρωσις articulation], (*a*) faulty articulation or congenital dislocation of a joint; (*b*) = *dysarthria*; **dysbasia** (-ˈbeɪsɪə) [Gr. βάσις stepping, step], difficulty in walking; **dyschezia** (-ˈkiːzɪə) [Gr. χέζ-εῖν to defecate + -IA[1]], difficult or painful defecation; **dyscholic** (-ˈkɒlɪk), *a.* [Gr. χολή bile], arising from bilious disorder (*nonce-wd.*); **dyschromaˈtopsia, -ˈchromatopsy** [Gr. χρωματ- colour + -οψία seeing, sight], deranged vision of colours, colour-blindness; hence **dyschromaˈtoptic** *a.*, colour-blind; **ˈdyschronous** *a.*, not agreeing as to time, separate as to time; *spec.* in *Ecology*, not overlapping in period of blooming; **dysciˈnesia**: see *dyskinesia*; **dysepuˈlotic, -ical** *adjs.* [Gr. ἐπουλωτικός (Galen) promoting cicatrization], difficult to heal or cicatrize; **dysgenesis** (-ˈdʒɛnɪsɪs) [Gr. γένεσις production], difficulty in breeding; *spec.* used by Broca for that degree of sexual affinity in which the offspring are sterile among themselves, but capable of producing (sterile) offspring with either of the parental races (*Syd. Soc. Lex.* 1883); so **dysgenesic** (-dʒɪˈnɛsɪk), *a.* [F. *dysgénésique*]; **dysgeogenous** (-dʒiːˈɒdʒɪnəs), *a.* [ad. F. *dysgéogène* (Thurmann 1849), f. Gr. γῆ, γεω- earth + *-gène*, taken in sense 'producing'], not readily decomposing into good soil; the opposite of *eugeogenous*; **dysgraˈmmatical** *a.*, pertaining to faults of speech arising from disease; **dysˈidrosis** (also *dyshi-*) [Gr. ἱδρώς sweat], a disease of the sweat-glands, in which the sweat is retained and produces swellings; **dyskiˈnesia** (also *dysci-*) [Gr. δυσκινησία (Hippoc.)], a class of diseases in which voluntary motion is impeded; **dyslalia** (dɪˈsleɪlɪə), **dyslaly** (ˈdɪsləlɪ) [Gr. λαλία speaking], derangement or impediment in speech, *spec.* that due to defects in the organs of speech or motor nerves; **dysˈlexia** [Gr. λέξις 'speaking'

(here taken in sense 'reading'), first formed as G. *dyslexie* (R. Berlin 1883, in *Med. Correspondenz-Blatt des Württemberg. ärztl. Landesvereins* LIII. 209)], a difficulty in reading due to affection of the brain; *spec.* = *word-blindness* (WORD *sb.* 29); hence **dys'lectic**, **dys'lexic** *adjs.* and *sbs.*; **dyslogia** (-'ləʊdʒɪə) [Gr. -λογία speaking, speech]: see quot.; hence **dys'logical** *a.*; **dys'metria** [Gr. μέτρον measure], inability to control the range of movement in a muscular action; **dysnomy** ('dɪsnəmɪ) [Gr. δυσνομία lawlessness, f. νόμος law], a bad system of law (*rare*—^{0}); **dys'opia**, **dys'opsia**, **-'opsy** [Gr. ὤψ (ὠπ-) eye, face, -οψία sight, vision], defect or derangement of vision (Hooper *Med. Dict.* 1811); **dyso'rexia**, **-xy** [Gr. δυσορεξία (Galen)], defective or depraved appetite; **dyspareunia** (-pə'ru:nɪə) [Gr. πάρευνος (f. παρά beside + εὐνή bed) lying beside or with + -IA^1], difficult or painful sexual intercourse; **dysphasia** (-'feɪzɪə) [Gr. δύσφατος hard to utter, -φασία speaking], derangement in speech due to confusion or loss of ideas arising from affection of the brain (*Syd. Soc. Lex.* 1883); hence **dysphasic** (-'fæzɪk), *a.*; **dysphemia** (-'fi:mɪə) [Gr. δυσφημία ill language], stammering (see quots.); hence **dys'phemic**, one who stutters; **dysphonia** (-'fəʊnɪə), **dysphony** ('dɪsfənɪ), [Gr. δυσφωνία 'harshness of sound'], difficulty of speaking arising from affection of the vocal organs; hence **dysphonic** (-'fɒnɪk), *a.*, affected with dysphonia; **dys'photic** *a. Ecology* [Gr. φῶς, φωτ- light], poorly lighted, used *esp.* of those depths in oceans, lakes, etc., where some light penetrates but brings about little or no photosynthesis; also erron. **disphotic**; **dys'pneumony** *nonce-wd.* [Gr. πνεύμων lung], disease or affection of the lungs; **dys'rhythmia**, an abnormal or disordered rhythm; *spec.*, an abnormal rhythm in the electrical waves shown in an electroencephalogram; hence **dys-'rhythmic** *a.* and *sb.*; **dys'spermatism** [Gr. σπερματισμός emission of semen (LXX.)], impeded emission of semen (Hooper *Med. Dict.* 1811); **dysthesia** (-'θi:sɪə), **dysthesy** ('dɪsθɪsɪ) [Gr. δυσθεσία], a bad condition or habit of body; hence **dysthetic** (-'θɛtɪk), *a.*; **dysthymia** (-'θaɪmɪə) [Gr. δυσθυμία despondency], despondency or depression; **dys'thymic** (-'θɪmɪk), *a.* [f. Gr. δύσθῡμ-ος desponding + -IC], affected with despondency or depression of spirits; *sb.*, a person affected with dysthymia; **dystocia** (-'təʊsɪə), **dystokia**, incorrectly **-tochia** (-'tɒkɪə) [Gr. δυστοκία], difficult or painful childbirth; hence **dys'tocial** *a.*; **dystome** ('dɪstəʊm), **dystomic** (dɪ'stɒmɪk), **dystomous** ('dɪstɒməs), *adjs. Min.* [Gr. δύστομος hard to cut], having imperfect fracture; cleaving with difficulty; **dystrophia** (-'trɒfɪə), **dystrophy** ('dɪstrəfɪ) [Gr. -τροφία nourishment], defective nourishment (*Syd. Soc. Lex.* 1883); hence **dy'strophic** *a.*, (*a*) pertaining to or characterized by dystrophy; (*b*) *Ecology* [ad. G. *dystroph* (A. Thienemann *Binnengewässer Mitteleuropas* (1925) iv. 198, 201)], of a lake: having much dissolved organic matter.

1834 SOUTHEY *Corr. w. Caroline Bowles* (1881) 318 What I call the *Dysangelical party. **1878** *Ziemssen's Cycl. Med.* XIV. 613 The latter [lalopathia] thus includes *dysarthrias (including dyslalias and dysphasias). *Ibid.* 612 *Dysarthric disturbances of speech. **1890** GOULD *New Med. Dict.* 138/1 **Dysbasia*, difficulty of walking. Proposed instead of abasia, since in the affection there is rarely absolute inability to walk. **1962** R. N. DEJONG in A. B. Baker *Clin. Neurol.* (ed. 2) I. i. 52 In the hysterical dysbasia there is often marked swaying from side to side. **1848** DUNGLISON *Dict. Med. Sci.* (ed. 7) *Dyschezia. **1915** R. KNOX *Radiography* I. 233 Dyschezia, in which the passage through the colon is normal, but defaecation is inefficiently performed. **1969** M. PAULSON *Gastroenterologic Med.* xlv. 1196/1 Rectal constipation (dyschezia, simple constipation, simple retention) may be defined as a failure of the defecation reflex. **1889** *Ch. Q. Rev.* 441 Views..formed under the predominating influence of eucholic and *dyscholic expressions of thought prevalent at the time. **1890** H. ELLIS *Criminal* iii. 117 *Dyschromatopsia has been found common. **1886** *Sat. Rev.* 10 Apr. 515 A *dyschromatoptic patient. **1902** *Science* 4 July 5/1 Consciousness..can make synchronous impressions dyschronous in their effects, and *dyschronous impressions synchronous. **1924** *Ecology* V. 393 A species, genus or family which does not overlap [in blooming time] with any of its relatives, or a group which contains species which do not overlap with their relatives, may be called *dyschronous*. **1753** CHAMBERS *Cycl. Supp.*, **Dysepulotica*, in medicine, great ulcers beyond cure. **1851-60** MAYNE *Expos. Lex.*, *Dysepuloticus*.. difficult to be healed..*dysepulotic. **1657** TOMLINSON *Renou's Disp.* 205 The ulcer is sometimes left *dysepulotical. **1878** BARTLEY tr. *Topinard's Anthrop.* II. vii. 369 M. Broca has defined the various degrees of sexual affinity..thus:—Abortive, Agenesic, *Dysgenesic, without offspring; Paragenesic, Eugenesic, with offspring. **1863** J. G. BAKER *N. Yorksh.* 152 The *dysgeogenous hills..a range of calcareous hills which are somewhat lower in altitude. **1888** F. A. LEES *Flora West Yorksh.* 65 Dysgeogenous Rocks..are homogeneous in nature, hard or moderately so, very permeable to water, etc. **1878** *Ziemssen's Cycl. Med.* XIV. 793 [Faults of speech] which arise from disease and which we designate by the term **dysgrammatical derangements*. **1876** DUHRING *Dis. Skin* 236 **Dysidrosis*. Fox has described this disease. **1706** PHILLIPS (ed. Kersey), **Dyscinesia*. **1879** G. HEWITT in Reynolds *Syst. Med.* V. 702 Uterine dyskinesia is one of the earliest symptoms of uterine flexion. **1883** *Syd. Soc. Lex.*, *Uterine Dyscinesia*. Graily Hewett's term for inability to walk or move, or perform certain of the ordinary motions of the body, without producing pain referable to the uterus. **1851-60** MAYNE *Expos. Lex.*, **Dyslalia*. **1856** *Househ. Words* Nov. 465 Learnedly speaking, stammering is an idiopathic *dyslaly. **1876** *Ziemssen's Cycl. Med.* XIV. 612 It is usual to designate those [lesions of articulation] which depend clearly upon gross mechanical defects in the external apparatuses of speech and their motor nerves as *dyslalia* in contradistinction to the true or *central dysarthrosis*. **1886-8** W. R. GOWERS *Dis. Nerv. Syst.* (1892) I. 297 The cerebral symptom..'*dyslexia' a peculiar intermitting difficulty in reading. **1888** *Arch. Ophthalmol.* XVII. 307 The term 'dyslexia'..signifies an inability to read to one's self or aloud for a short time. **1957** L. E. TRAVIS *Handbk. Speech Path.* (1959) ii. 54 *Dyslexia*, partial inability to read characterized by associative learning difficulty; a form of dysphasia. **1960** *New Scientist* 15 Sept. 738/2 There might be a special category of reading backwardness which could be delimited and termed 'specific dyslexia'—though the deplorable name of 'word blindness' should be avoided. **1964** L. KAISER in D. Abercrombie et al. *Daniel Jones* 108 Several factors may lead to dyslexia. **1961** M. CRITCHLEY in *Trans. Ophthalmological Soc. U.K.* LXXXI. 473 Some *dyslexics cannot place in correct serial order days of the week or months of the year. *Ibid.*, Poor muscular co-ordination has often been witnessed in the younger dyslexic children. **1964** L. KAISER in D. Abercrombie et al. *Daniel Jones* 108 The right hand..may be undeveloped in the dyslectic child. **1965** *Sunday Times* 10 Oct. 58/4 The most inspiriting contender for the title of the World's Greatest Dyslexic: Hans Christian Andersen. **1966** *Sat. Rev.* 16 Apr. 82/1 (*heading*) Teaching the dyslexic child. **1883** *Syd. Soc. Lex.*, **Dyslogia*, a defect of speech in which the individual words are correctly formed, but are so put together as to express a disturbance of thought. **1878** *Ziemssen's Cycl. Med.* XIV. 790 An instance of *dyslogical paragraphia. **1911** T. L. STEDMAN *Pract. Med. Dict.* 257/2 **Dysmetria*, a form of dysergia in which the subject is unable to arrest a muscular movement at the desired point or, sometimes, to prevent an involuntary reverse movement. **1913** G. HOLMES in White & Jellife *Mod. Treatm. Nerv. & Mental Dis.* II. xiv. 630 Cerebellar disease produces a disproportion in the elements of a movement, and there results therefrom what Babinski has termed a dysmetria. **1952** *New Biol.* XIII. 55 The dysmetria characteristic of cerebellar disease consists in an incapacity to stop a movement at the intended place, with resulting overswing. **1970** *Nature* 19 Sept. 1228/2 Dysmetria will result from the malfunctioning of both cerebellar nuclei and cerebellar cortex. **1623** COCKERAM, **Dysnomie*, ill ordering of lawes. **1656** BLOUNT *Glossogr.*, **Dysopsie*, dimness, ill sight. **1706** PHILLIPS, **Dysorexia*, a decay or want of Appetite. **1828** WEBSTER, *Dysorexy*, a bad or depraved appetite; a want of appetite. *Coxe*. **1873** R. BARNES *Clin. Hist. Dis. Women* vi. 61 We want a word to express the condition of difficult or painful performance of the sexual function... I have determined to adopt the word '*dyspareunia'. **1962** *Lancet* 12 May 1011/2 An assortment of pains in various sites, sexual frigidity, dyspareunia, and general nervousness, fears, and depression. **1878** *Ziemssen's Cycl. Med.* XIV. 613 Dysarthric and *dysphasic disturbances taken together constituting what are properly considered as true disturbances of speech. **1894** C. F. COXWELL in *Intercolonial Q. Jrnl. Med. & Surg.* I. 3 *Dysphemia, or stammering, is regarded by most persons as an annoying trick. **1933** S. M. STINCHFIELD *Speech Disorders* vi. 116 Dysphemia is defined as intermittent and variable nervous disorders of speech accompanying certain psychoneuroses. **1940** *Q. Jrnl. Speech* Apr. 203 *Dysphemia*, speech difficulty, usually related to a psychoneurotic or nervous condition. **1957** L. E. TRAVIS *Handbk. Speech Path.* (1959) ii. 55 *Dysphemia*, a nervous disorder of speech arising from psychological disturbance; includes stuttering. **1894** C. F. COXWELL in *Intercolonial Q. Jrnl. Med. & Surg.* I. 3 The *dysphemic can speak, as a rule, tolerably well in private. **1706** PHILLIPS, **Dysphonia*, a Difficulty of Speech, occasion'd by an ill-Disposition of the Organs. **1866** A. FLINT *Princ. Med.* (1880) 309 There is dysphonia, but not complete loss of voice. **1872** COHEN *Dis. Throat* 164 At other times the patient wakes up in the morning aphonic or *dysphonic. **1903** W. R. FISHER tr. *Schimper's Plant Geogr.* III. v. iii. 811 The flora of the *dysphotic region is composed almost exclusively of microphytes. **1958** P. LAKE *Physical Geogr.* (ed. 4) xviii. 424 The water column can..be divided into..the disphotic zone with insufficient light for photosynthesis. **1970** B. H. MCCONNAUGHEY *Introd. Marine Biol.* i. 17 Below the euphotic zone are the dysphotic, or mesopelagic, depths extending down to about 1000 metres. **1839** STERLING *Let.* 30 June in Carlyle *Life* III. i, Rather I think from dyspepsia than *dyspneumony. **1909** *Cent. Dict.* Suppl., *Dysrhythmia. **1939** *Jrnl. Amer. Med. Assoc.* CXIII. 1002/2 [Electro-encephalographic] records were made..of twenty-six patients who had cerebral dysrhythmia. **1962** *Listener* 7 June 994/2 In all susceptible patients bursts of abnormal electric activity of the brain (so-called dysrhythmia) could be induced by flicker from the stroboscope. **1965** W. R. BRAIN *Speech Disorders* (ed. 2) xiii. 150 The dysrhythmias [of speech] include cluttering and stuttering. **1969** W. CLELAND et al. *Med. & Surg. Cardiol.* ii. 43 Absence of the P wave may be due to sinoatrial block or atrial dysrhythmia. **1941** W. G. LENNOX *Science & Seizures* (ed. 3) xi. 90 These 'asymptomatic *dysrhythmic' individuals form a reservoir from which persons with seizures are drawn. **1944** *Proc. R. Soc. Med.* XXXVII. 319 Comparison between dysrhythmics in whom fits occur and those in whom they do not occur may be artificial. **1965** W. R. BRAIN *Speech Disorders* (ed. 2) xiii. 150 Truncated dysrhythmic and incoherent utterance. **1822-34** GOOD *Study Med.* (ed. 4) II. 605 Followed by secondary symptoms or a syphilitic *dysthesy. *Ibid.* I. 282 Persons of weakly and inelastic fibres, and *dysthetic habits. **1844** DUNGLISON *Med. Dict.* 254/2 **Dysthymia*, depression, despondency. **1944** H. J. EYSENCK in *Jrnl. Mental Sci.* XC. 855 The term 'affective disorder' or 'dysthymia' is suggested for the anxiety-depression-obsessional group. **1847** CRAIG, **Dysthymic*, desponding; depressed in mind. **1864** WEBSTER, *Dysthymic*, affected with despondency; depressed in spirits; dejected. **1947** *Brit. Jrnl. Psychol.* May 135 Twenty-five female dysthymics. **1961** *New Scientist* 26 Oct. 225 An anxious neurotic patient, or dysthymic. **1706** PHILLIPS, **Dystocia*, a Difficulty of bringing forth. **1811** HOOPER *Med. Dict.*, *Dystochia*. **1828** M. RYAN *Man. Midwifery* 308 In consequence of difficult, tedious and *dystocial labors. **1847** CRAIG, **Dystomic*, in Mineralogy, having an imperfect fracture or cleavage. **1864** WEBSTER, *Dystome*, *Dystomic*, *Dystomous*. **1893** S. D'ODIARDI *Med. Electr.* 54 The agents of demolition or elimination, called *dystrophics or denutrients. **1893** *Brit. Med. Jrnl.* 4 Nov. 998 The dystrophic view of sclerosis. **1931** R. N. CHAPMAN *Animal Ecology* xvi. 305 The *dystrophic lake, or brown-water lake, is found among peat bogs. **1959** J. CLEGG *Freshwater Life Brit. Isles* (ed. 2) ii. 38 The so-called *Dystrophic* lake..which is generally understood to be a lake with a bottom composed of peaty humus and very soft, acid water. **1967** G. E. HUTCHINSON *Treat. Limnol.* II. xxii. 380 The water color involved in the separation of Thienemann's dystrophic type is ordinarily regarded as due to extractives from bog soils and peat. **1886** W. R. GOWERS *Dis. Nerv. Syst.* I. 386 Idiopathic Muscular Atrophy..Muscular *Dystrophy.

‖**dysæsthesia** (dɪsɪs'θi:sɪə). *Path.* [L., a. Gr. δυσαισθησία (Galen) insensibility, f. δυσαίσθητος insensible, f. δυσ- (DYS-) + αἰσθε- to feel: cf. ÆSTHESIS, ANÆSTHESIA.]

Difficulty or derangement of sensation, or of any bodily senses; also applied to a class of diseases of which this is a symptom.

1706 PHILLIPS, *Dysæsthesia*, a difficulty or fault in sensation. **1822-34** GOOD *Study Med.* (ed. 4) III. 210 The common technical name for the genus is dysæsthesia. **1889** *Lancet* 28 Dec. 1331/1 Hyperæsthesia or dysæsthesia of one or more nerves.

So **dysæsthetic** (-'θɛtɪk), *a.*, relating to or affected with dysæsthesia.

dysamay, obs. f. DISMAY.

dysanalyte (dɪ'sænəlaɪt). *Min.* [ad. Ger. *dysanalit*, Knop, 1877), ad. Gr. δυσανάλυτ-ος hard to analyse.] A columbo-titanate of lime, in black cubical crystals.

1877 *Amer. Jrnl. Sc.* Ser. III. XIV. 243.

dysar, **dysarde**, obs. ff. DICER, DIZZARD.

dysbink, var. of *dish-bink*: see DISH *sb.* 10.

dyscalculia (dɪskæl'kju:lɪə). *Med.* [f. DYS- + CALCUL(ATE *v.*^{1} + -IA^1.] Severe disturbance of the ability to calculate, resulting from cerebral injury.

1953 M. CRITCHLEY *Parietal Lobes* vii. 208 Dyscalculia is the fourth characteristic feature of the Gerstmann syndrome... The most striking defects are apparent when the patient attempts to make calculations upon paper. **1964** —— *Developmental Dyslexia* vi. 38 There may exist a higher-level dyscalculia, made up partly at any rate by an inability to visualise numbers. **1965** W. R. BRAIN *Speech Disorders* (ed. 2) iii. 27 Dyscalculias of the spatial type indicate a lesion of the right hemisphere. **1965** LUCHSINGER & ARNOLD *Voice-Speech-Language* II. B. i. 596/1 True dyscalculia is present when the processes of calculation are disturbed independently of the reading act and in all forms of mathematical manipulation.

dyscece, **-cencion**, **-cend**, **-cept**, **-ceyte**, **-ceyue**, obs. ff. DECEASE, DESCENSION, DISSENSION, DESCEND, DECEIT, DECEIVE.

dysclasite ('dɪskləsaɪt). *Min.* [Named 1834, f. Gr. δυσ- (DYS-) + κλάσ-ις breaking, fracture + -ITE; from its toughness.] A synonym of OKENITE.

1835 C. U. SHEPARD *Min.* 175.

†**dy'scrase**, *v. Obs.* Also 4-7 **discrase**, 6 **discrayse**, 7 **discraze**. [f. *dyscrasie*, DYSCRASY, or prob. a. OF. **discraser*, f. *discrasie*. In 15-16th c. evidently viewed as a deriv. of *crase*, CRAZE *v.*, and used accordingly.] *trans.* To affect with a dyscrasy; to distemper, disorder.

c **1380** WYCLIF *Serm.* Sel. Wks. II. 215 Bi occasioun of þes two errours many oþer men ben discrasid. *c* **1440** LYDG. *Secrees* 1213 Helthe of body, discrasyng of syknesse. **1504** ATKYNSON tr. *De Imitatione* I. xiii, A bell..whether it be hole and of perfite sounde or dyscrased. **1574** NEWTON *Health Mag.* Ep. 4 Sufficient to cure the discrased. **1576** —— *Lemnie's Complex.* (1633) 45 Wherby health..if it happen to be discrazed and impaired..may againe be restored. **1610** BARROUGH *Meth. Physic* (N.), So they..do first by this evil demeanour shake and discrase them [their bodies].

‖**dyscrasia** (dɪ'skreɪsɪə). Also 7 **dis-**. [med.L., a. Gr. δυσκρασία bad temperament (of body, air, etc.), f. δυσ- (DYS-) + κρᾶσις mixing, tempering.] = DYSCRASY.

c **1400** *Lanfranc's Cirurg.* 54 A Wounde þat haþ enpostym or an yuel discrasiam—þat is to seie out of kynde distemperid, eiþer to cold eiþer to hoot. **1677** GILPIN *Demonol.* (1867) 65 The souls of men have their general discrasias and disaffections, as our bodies have. **1859** TODD *Cycl. Anat.* V. 413/1 We find these alterations associated with a general dyscrasia.

Hence **dys'crasial** *a.*, of the nature of, belonging to, or arising from dyscrasia.

1874 VAN BUREN *Dis. Genit. Org.* 23 Acute dyscrasial disease—typhus, small-pox, etc.

dyscrasic (dɪˈskræzɪk), *a.* [mod. f. DYSCRASIA + -IC.] Of the nature of, arising from, or affected with dyscrasia; dyscratic.
1874 JONES & SIEV. *Pathol. Anat.* (ed. 2) 227 This form is ..of a dyscrasic character. **1876** BARTHOLOW *Mat. Med.* (1879) 161 A dyscrasic state induced by the enormous amount of alkali.

dyscrasite (ˈdɪskrəsaɪt). *Min.* Also dis-. [f. Gr. δυσκρασία bad mixture + -ITE.] Antimonial silver, a native alloy of silver and antimony in variable proportions (Ag_2Sb, Ag_3Sb, Ag_3Sb_2), found in the Harz Mountains, etc.
1852 C. U. SHEPARD *Min.* 300 Arsenical silver..is harder than discrasite. **1868** DANA *Min.* 35 Dyscrasite.

dyscrasy (ˈdɪskrəsɪ), *sb.* Also 5-8 discrasie, -cie, -cy. [a. OF. *dyscrasie* (13-14th c. in Hatz.-Darm.), ad. med.L. *dyscrāsia*: see above.] A bad or disordered condition of the body (originally supposed to arise from disproportionate mixture of the 'humours': cf. DISTEMPER, -ANCE, -ATURE); morbid diathesis; distemper. (Now more usually in Latin form DYSCRASIA, q.v.)
c **1400** *Lanfranc's Cirurg.* 57 Þe drie discrasie þou schalt knowe bi þe smalnes of þe lyme. **1533** ELYOT *Cast. Helthe* II. x. (1539) 27 b, Nutmigges, with their swete odour comforte ..also the brayn in colde discrasies. *Ibid.* IV. 75 b, I will somewhat wryte of two dyscrasyes of the body. **1650** VENNER *Via Recta* (1650) 9 A dyscrasie, a putting of the body and spirit out of frame. **1646** J. WHITAKER *Uzziah* 22 Physicians observe in crasie bodies, that a sudden *eucrasie* is the forerunner of some *discrasie*. **1756** C. LUCAS *Ess. Waters* III. 154 A discrasy of the juices. **1822-34** GOOD *Study Med.* (ed. 4) IV. 364 Dependent upon a dyscrasy or intemperament of the blood.
b. *transf.* and *fig.* Disorder.
1647 JER. TAYLOR *Lib. Proph.* Ep. Ded. 2 The perpetuall Meditation of my private Troubles, and the publike Dyscrasy. **1647** CUDWORTH *Serm.* 1 Cor. xv. 57 (1676) 81 Sin is but a disease and Dyscrasie in the soul. **1817** J. GILCHRIST *Intell. Patrimony* 40 Giving..nutriment to social dyscrasy.
Hence †**dyscrasy** *v. Obs. rare.* = DYSCRASE.
c **1400** *Lanfranc's Cirurg.* 85 If þei ben discrasid [*v.r.* discrasyede], remeue þilke discrasie wiþ þat, þat is contrarie. **1670** MAYNWARING *Vita Sana* iii. 40 A discrasyed body.

†**dys'cratic**, *a. Obs.* [f. Gr. δύσκρᾱτος of bad temperament, distempered + -IC.] Affected with dyscrasy; distempered.
1684 tr. *Bonet's Merc. Compit.* XIX. 739 The Blood being habitually weak and withal dyscratick or intemperate.

dyscrease, -crece, -cres, obs. var. ff. DECREASE.

dyse, obs. f. DICE (DIE *sb.*[1]); var. DISE (= ADZE).

dysease, dyseis, obs. ff. DISEASE.

†**dysen'terial**, *a. Obs.* [f. L. *dysenteria* DYSENTERY + -AL[1].] = DYSENTERIC 1.
1600 W. VAUGHAN *Direct. for Health* (1633) 76 Use it to stop the fluxe, whether it be sudden, or humorall, or dissenteriall. **1612** WOODALL *Surg. Mate* Wks. (1653) 185. **1725** BRADLEY *Fam. Dict.* s.v. *Strawberry*, To stop the Whites and Dysenterial Fluxes.

dysenteric (dɪsɛnˈtɛrɪk), *a.* Also 8 dissentrick. [ad. L. *dysenteric-us*, a. Gr. δυσεντερικ-ός liable to or afflicted with dysentery, f. δυσεντερία: see DYSENTERY.]
1. Belonging to or of the nature of dysentery.
1727 BRADLEY *Fam. Dict.* s.v. *Flux*, A Dysenterick Flux. **1764** GRANGER *Sugar Cane* 114. **1846** G. E. DAY tr. *Simon's Anim. Chem.* II. 382 In dysenteric diarrhœa. **1876** DAVIS *Polaris Exp.* xix. 410 [It] produced a dysenteric effect.
b. Used for curing dysentery. *rare.*
1703 DAMPIER *Voy.* (1729) III. 459 The Dissentrick Vomit, a leaning plant.
2. Affected with or suffering from dysentery.
1822-34 GOOD *Study Med.* (ed. 4) II. 248 Twelve dysenteric patients. **1831** TRELAWNEY *Adv. Younger Son* I. 288 Noisy and filthy as the draggletailed dysenteric cockatoo.

†**dysen'terical**, *a. Obs.* = prec.
1601 HOLLAND *Pliny* II. 331 If the flux be from the stomack, or dysentericall. **1677** GILPIN *Demonol.* (1867) 393 Calanus, an Indian philosopher, being dysenterical, obtained leave of Alexander to burn himself for more quick despatch. **1684** BOYLE *Porousn. Anim. & Solid Bod.* iii. 29 A Flux, for the most part dysenterical.

dysenteriform (dɪsɛnˈtɛrɪfɔːm), *a.* [f. L. *dysenteria* + -FORM.] Having the appearance or symptoms of dysentery.
1880 *Med. Temp. Jrnl.* Oct. 5 Dysenteriform evacuations.

†**dysen'terious**, *a. Obs.* [f. as prec. + -OUS.] = DYSENTERIC 2.
a **1654** GATAKER 186 (L.) A dysenterious person, that can relish nothing.

dysentery (ˈdɪsəntərɪ). Also 4-7 diss-, (dyss-), 6-7 dis-, (7 disc-); 4-8 -erie. *β.* (in L. form) 4-7 dissenteria, (4 -aria), 6-7 dis-, dysenteria. [a. OF. *dissenterie* (13th c. *dissintere*), ad. L. *dysenteria* (Pliny, etc.), a. Gr. δυσεντερία, f. δυσέντερος afflicted in the bowels, f. δυσ- (DYS-) + ἔντερα bowels.]
A disease characterized by inflammation of the mucous membrane and glands of the large intestine, accompanied with griping pains, and mucous and bloody evacuations.
1382 WYCLIF *Acts* xxviii. 8 The fadir of Puplius..trauelid with feueres and dissenterie or flix. **1447** BOKENHAM *Seyntys* (Roxb.) 259 That dyssentyrye of comon usage The reed flyx ys clepyd in oure langwage. **1547** BOORDE *Brev. Health* cvi. 40 The disentery or exulceracion of the guttes. **1601** HOLLAND *Pliny* XXVIII. ix. (R.), For the dysenterie or bloudie flix. **1649** *Thomasson Tracts* (Br. Mus.) CCCCXLII. vi. 51 Other necessities encreased the discentery in our leaguer. **1708** SWIFT *Predict. for* 1708 Wks. 1755 II. I. 153 On the 20th cardinal Portocarero will die of a dysentery. **1767** T. HUTCHINSON *Hist. Mass.* II. iv. 419 Many of our men had..fallen into dysenteries. **1781** GIBBON *Decl. & F.* II. xli. 544 The dysentery swept away one-third of their army. **1869** E. A. PARKES *Pract. Hygiene* (ed. 3) 69 Dysentery also is decidedly produced by impure water.
attrib. **1822-34** GOOD *Study Med.* (ed. 4) I. 265 Rolander, who, like Linnæus, ascribed dysentery to the dysentery-tick, or *acarus dysenteriæ*.
b. A disease of bees.
1816 KIRBY & SP. *Entomol.* (1828) I. iv. 90. **1846** J. BAXTER *Libr. Pract. Agric.* (ed. 4) I. 97 The chief diseases of bees.. are dysentery or looseness, torpor, falling in flight from vertigo or giddiness, and vermin.

dyser, obs. form of DICER, DISOUR.

dyses, -esse, dyshese, etc., obs. ff. DISEASE.

dysfunction (dɪsˈfʌŋkʃən). [f. DYS- + FUNCTION *sb.*] Any abnormality or impairment of function. Hence **dys'functional** *a.*, **dys'functionally** *adv.*, **dys'functioning** *vbl. sb.*
1916 in *Gould's Practitioner's Med. Dict.* (ed. 3) 307/2. **1927** HENDERSON & GILLESPIE *Text-Bk. Psychiatry* xi. 355 An aplasia or dysfunction of the tissues. **1933** *Mind* XLII. 114 The physiological [point of view] (which subordinates neural to glandular, circulatory, etc., dysfunctioning). **1936** *Brit. Med. Jrnl.* 28 Mar. 630/1 The school of endocrine dysfunction incriminates variously the thyroid, parathyroid, ovarian, and pituitary glands. **1949** R. K. MERTON *Social Theory & Social Struct.* (1951) I. i. 51 Unintended consequences of action are..those which are irrelevant to the system which they affect neither functionally nor dysfunctionally. **1952** T. PARSONS *Social System* ii. 35 They must be counteracted by 'mechanisms of control' unless dysfunctional consequences are to ensue. **1959** G. D. MITCHELL *Sociology* I. ii. 38 That it is functional..for mothers of young children to go out to work does not mean that it is not dysfunctional for the well-being of their children. **1959** B. WOOTTON *Social Sci.* vii. 225 A social judgment is still implied in the decision to rank the thieving tendency together with its bodily concomitants as symptoms of disease or dysfunction. **1969** R. BLACKBURN in Cockburn & Blackburn *Student Power* 186 Thus the 1929 crash was 'dysfunctional' for capitalism and so was the Chinese People's Liberation Army 'dysfunctional' for the social order of Nationalist China in the nineteen thirties and forties. **1971** *Optometry Today* (Amer. Optometric Assoc.) 12 Corrective lenses or visual training techniques to correct or improve the perceptual-motor dysfunction.

dysgenic (dɪsˈdʒɛnɪk), *a.* [f. DYS- + -GENIC.] Exerting a detrimental effect on the race, tending towards racial degeneration, *spec.* opposed to *eugenic*. Hence **dys'genically** *adv.*
1915 W. R. INGE *Outspoken Ess.* (1919) 41 Its [*sc.* frequent war's] dysgenic effect, by eliminating the strongest and healthiest of the population, while leaving the weaklings at home to be the fathers of the next generation. **1922** *Edin. Rev.* July 46 Encouraging the dysgenic art of fortune-hunting. **1926** *Spectator* 1 May 804/2 Conceptive control has been an almost entirely harmful or dysgenic factor. **1928** G. B. SHAW *Intell. Woman's Guide Socialism* xxxviii. 150 Division of society into classes, with the resultant dysgenic restrictions on marriage. **1934** C. P. BLACKER *Chances of Morbid Inheritance* iv. 122 If our propaganda succeeds another barrier against dysgenic marriages will have gone. **1937** A. HUXLEY *Ends & Means* viii. 79 A residual population, dysgenically selected for its lack of spirit and intellectual gifts. *Ibid.* ix. 90 So far as individuals are concerned, war selects dysgenically. **1971** *Daily Tel.* 5 Oct. 14/2 The 'two child family' or 'Zero Population Growth'.. have the merit that they are less dysgenic than is the present irresponsible propagation.
B. *sb. pl.* [Cf. EUGENIC *sb.*] Racial degeneration, or its study.
1920 A. HUXLEY in *London Mercury* June 182 A process which we may be permitted to call dysgenics—the carrying on of the species by the worst members. **1951** *New Biol.* XI. 24 Eugenics or dysgenics..are necessarily in progress all the time. **1958** *Times Lit. Suppl.* 11 July 386/3 Racial dilution, dysgenics, and national and social loss of status. **1970** *New Scientist* 28 May 438/3 'Dysgenics', as Shockley describes it, has to do with 'retrogression evolution'.

dysgraphia (dɪsˈgræfɪə). *Med.* [f. DYS- + Gr. γραφία writing.] Inability to write coherently (as a manifestation of brain damage). Hence **dys'graphic** *a.* and *sb.* Cf. AGRAPHIA.
1934 H. C. WARREN *Dict. Psychol.* 87/1 *Dysgraphia*, a cerebral disorder characterized by inability to write. **1953** M. CRITCHLEY *Parietal Lobes* vii. 208 Agraphia, or better, dysgraphia, forms the third cardinal feature of Gerstmann's syndrome. This may take the form of a disturbance in the execution of letters..or of words. **1962** A. L. BENTON in J. Money *Reading Disability* 84 So-called 'parietal' dyslexia,.. is associated with severe dysgraphia, all aspects of writing being disturbed. **1963** B. HAIGH tr. *Luria's Restoration of Function after Brain Injury* v. 183 In less extensive lesions the disintegration of writing takes the form of dysgraphia.. and examination of the writing of such patients reveals a disturbance of the clear distinction of the sounds of words, confusion between closely related phonemes, and other signs of a defect of acoustic analysis. **1964** M. CRITCHLEY *Developmental Dyslexia* vi. 36 The true 'dysgraphic' is an adult of at least normal education, who has developed a difficulty in expressing himself on paper as the result of a disease. **1970** —— *Aphasiology* i. 11 Not every instance of poor writing in cases of cerebral disease is dysgraphic.

dysiȝ, dysioyn, obs. ff. DIZZY, DISJOIN.

dyslexia, dyslexic: see DYS-

dyslogistic (dɪsləʊˈdʒɪstɪk), *a.* Also erron. dis-. [f. DYS- + stem of *eu-logistic* (without reference to Gr. δυσλόγιστος 'hard to calculate, ill-calculated, misguided').]
Expressing or connoting disapprobation or dispraise; having a bad connotation; opprobrious. (The opposite of *eulogistic.*)
1802-12 BENTHAM *Ration. Jud. Evid.* (1827) I. 146 Under the name of revenge, or malice, or some other such dyslogistic name. **1810** —— *Packing* (1821) 15 Packing:—a name which, from the application at that time but too frequently made of the practice..has acquired a dyslogistic tinge: serving at present to express, not merely the practice itself, but the sentiment of disapprobation excited by the idea of it. **1825** SYD. SMITH *Wks.* (1859) II. 70/2 Mischievous fallacies also circulate from the convertible use of what Mr. B. is pleased to call dyslogistic and eulogistic terms. **1838** *Tait's Mag.* V. 67 A political adventurer (we use the word in its dyslogistic sense). **1887** *Spectator* 2 July 888/2 The dyslogistic names, by which it pleases each side to denominate its opponents.

dyslo'gistically, *adv.* [f. prec. + -AL[1] + -LY[2].] In a dyslogistic manner; in dispraise.
1862 F. HALL *Hindu Philos. Syst.* 166 The latter is applied to them dyslogistically. **1874** SIDGWICK *Meth. Ethics* (1877) 204 'Caution' is used dyslogistically; at least a man is said to be too cautious, or over-cautious, when he deliberates too much or too often.

dyslogy (ˈdɪslədʒɪ). *nonce-wd.* [f. DYS- + stem of *eu-logy*. (There was no corresp. Gr.)] Dispraise, censure: the opposite of *eulogy*.
1837 CARLYLE *Mirabeau* Misc. Ess. 1872 V. 267 In the way of eulogy and dyslogy..there may doubtless be a great many things set forth concerning this Mirabeau.

dysluite (ˈdɪsluːaɪt). *Min.* [arbitrary f. DYS- + Gr. λύ-ειν to loose, dissolve + -ITE.] A variety of gahnite or zinc spinel, containing manganese: from the difficulty of decomposing it for analysis.
1821 *Jrnl. Acad. Nat. Sc.* (Philad.) II. 287 Dysluite, a new mineral.

dyslysin (ˈdɪslɪsɪn). *Chem.* [arbitrary f. DYS- + Gr. λύσ-ις solution + -IN.] (See quots.)
1851-60 MAYNE *Expos. Lex.*, *Dyslysin*, term for a substance got from bilin digested with dilute hydrochloric acid with alcohol. **1863-72** WATTS *Dict. Chem.* II. 360 *Dyslysin*, $C_{24}H_{36}O_3$. Dyslysin is an amorphous substance.. insoluble in water, acids, potash-ley, and alcohol (hence the name), but soluble in ether.

dysme, obs. form of DIME.

‖**dysmenorrhagia** (ˌdɪsmɛnəʊˈreɪdʒɪə). *Path.* [See DYS-.] = next.
1885 W. ROBERTS *Treat. Urin. & Renal Dis.* III. xiv. (ed. 4) 678 In women who are subject to dysmenorrhagia.

‖**dysmenorrhœa** (-ˈriːə). *Path.* Also -rhea. [See DYS-.] Difficult or painful menstruation.
1810 R. THOMAS *Mod. Pract. Physic* (ed. 3) 532. **1873** E. H. CLARKE *Sex in Educ.* (1880) 23 Those grievous maladies which torture a woman's earthly existence, called leucorrhoea, amenorrhoea, dysmenorrhoea..and the like.
Hence **dysmeno'rrhœal**, **dysmeno'rrhœic** *adjs.*
1859 TODD *Cycl. Anat.* V. 644/1 These dysmenorrheal membranes present all the characteristics of a true decidual structure. **1873** E. H. CLARKE *Sex in Educ.* 62 Pale, weak, neuralgic, dyspeptic, hysterical..dysmenorrhoeic girls and women.

dysmerism (ˈdɪsmərɪz(ə)m). *Biol.* [f. Gr. δυσ- (DYS-) + μερισμός division into parts (MERISM).] The aggregation of unlike or irregularly arranged parts in the formation of an organism. So **dysme'ristic** *a.*, having the character of such an aggregation. **dysmerogenesis** (ˌdɪsmərəʊˈdʒɛnɪsɪs) [Gr. μέρος part, γένεσις production], the formation of an organism by successive production of parts which are unlike or irregularly arranged; hence **ˌdysmeroge'netic** *a.*, marked by or resulting from dysmerogenesis. **'dysmeroˌmorph** (-mɔːf) [Gr. μορφή form], an organic form or organism resulting from dysmerogenesis; hence **ˌdysmero'morphic** *a.*, having the character of a dysmeromorph. (Opposed to *eumerism*, *eumeristic*, etc.)
1881 E. R. LANKESTER in *Encycl. Brit.* XII. 555/1 (*Hydrozoa*) According to this second hypothesis..the tendency to bud-formation has all along acted concurrently with a powerful synthetic tendency, so that new units have from the first made but a gradual and disguised appearance. This is 'dysmerogenesis', and such aggregates as exhibit it may be called dysmeristic. *Ibid.* 555/2 Ordinary cell-division is an example of eumerogenesis; free-formation of

nuclei, as in the fertilized ovum of Arthropoda, is dysmerogenesis. A synctium is usually a synthesized eumeromorph, but may be a dysmeromorph.

dysodont (ˈdɪsəʊdɒnt), *a. Zool.* [f. DYS- + Gr. ὀδούς, ὀδοντ- tooth.] Belonging to the order *Dysodonta* of bivalve molluscs, having obsolete or irregular hinge-teeth.

dysodyle, -ile (ˈdɪsəʊdaɪl). *Min.* [a. F. *dysodyle* (Cordier 1808) f. Gr. δυσώδης ill-smelling, stinking + ὕλη matter: cf. CACODYL.] A very inflammable hydrocarbon occurring in masses of a yellowish or greenish colour, and foliated structure, which emits a fetid odour when burned.

1809 *Nicholson's Jrnl.* XXIV. 223 On the Dusodile, a new Species of Mineral. **1814** T. ALLAN *Min. Nomen.* 12 Dysodile. **1887** *Dana's Man. Min.* 349 Dysodile.. containing several per cent of sulphur.

dysour, -owre, obs. forms of DICER, DISOUR.

dysparych, obs. form of DISPARAGE.

dyspathy (ˈdɪspəθɪ). *rare.* Also 9 (erron.) **dis-**. [In sense 1, ad. Gr. δυσπάθεια insensibility, f. δυσπαθής impassive, f. δυς- (DYS-) + πάθος, παθε- feeling. In sense 2, = obs. F. *dispathie* 'an Antipathie or naturall disagreement' (Cotgr.), obs. It. *dispathía* (Florio), taken as the opposite of Gr. συμπάθεια, L. *sympathīa*, It. *simpathía* (Florio), *simpatía*, F. *sympathie*, SYMPATHY, and sometimes spelt *dispathy*, as if the first element were L. *dis-* (DIS-), and the sense rather 'difference of feeling'.]

†**1.** *Med.* (See quot. 1883.) *Obs.*

1541 R. COPLAND *Galyen's Terap.* 2 Ej, They do vse these names, Dyspathies, Metasyncrises, Imbecyllitees, fyrmytudes, and sondry other such names. **1883** *Syd. Soc. Lex.*, *Dyspathia*, old term..for indisposition to, or non-susceptibility of, a disease. Also, a severe disease.

2. The opposite of *sympathy*; antipathy, aversion, dislike; disagreement of feeling or sentiment.

1603 FLORIO *Montaigne* II. xxxvii. (1632) 428 It may well be, I have received from them that natural dyspathie unto physicke. **1651** BIGGS *New Disp.* Summary 73 A discourse touching the causes of Sympathie and Dyspathy. **1803** SOUTHEY in Robberds *Mem. W. Taylor* (1843) I. 439 With enough dispathy always to keep conversation wakeful. **1829** —— *Sir T. More* I. 18 Notwithstanding many discrepancies and some dispathies between us. **1884** H. S. WILSON *Stud. Hist.* 326 Woman-like, she was a partisan; she felt sympathy or dyspathy; she loved favourites, and she loathed antagonists.

So **dyspaˈthetic** *a.*, marked by 'dyspathy' or aversion; the reverse of *sympathetic*.

1886 LOWELL *Lett.* (1894) II. 315 What you say of Carlyle is sympathetic (as it should be) and not dyspathetic.

dyspayr(e, -peir(e, -pere, obs. ff. DESPAIR.

‖**dyspepsia** (dɪˈspɛpsɪə). [a. L. *dyspepsia* (Cato), a. Gr. δυσπεψία indigestion, f. δύσπεπτ-ος: see DYSPEPTIC.] Difficulty or derangement of digestion; indigestion: applied to various forms of disorder of the digestive organs, esp. the stomach, usually involving weakness, loss of appetite, and depression of spirits.

[**1657** *Physical Dict.*, *Duspepnia*, ill concoction.] **1706** PHILLIPS (ed. Kersey), *Dyspepsia*, a Difficulty of Digestion, or Fermentation in the Stomach and Guts. **1805** *Med. Jrnl.* XIV. 569 Report of Diseases in the..Practice of one of the Physicians of the Finsbury Dispensary..Diarrhœa, 15; Dysenteria, 2; Dyspepsia, 10. **1842** A. COMBE *Physiol. Digestion* (ed. 4) 263 Rapid eating almost invariably leads to overloading the stomach; and when to this is added a total disregard of the quietude necessary for digestion, what can be expected to follow but inveterate dyspepsia? **1854** C. BRONTE *Let.* in Mrs. Gaskell *Life* 430 Headache and dyspepsia are my worst ailments. **1862** *Lancet* 13 Sept. 278 A French writer calls dyspepsia 'the remorse of a guilty stomach'.

fig. **1865** LOWELL *Thoreau* Pr. Wks. 1890 I. 362 Every possible form of intellectual and physical dyspepsia brought forth its gospel. **1885** *Pall Mall G.* 1 Jan. 3/2 The Christian life, in order to be healthy and strong, wanted exercise as well as feeding; too many were content to feed without serving, the consequence being spiritual dyspepsia.

Hence **dysˈpepsia** *v. nonce-wd.*, to affect with dyspepsia.

1848 *Q. Rev.* Dec. (Hoppe), It gravels and dyspepsias him. **1849** F. B. HEAD *Stokers & P.* iii. (1851) 38 To lose sight of his luggage..dyspepsias him beyond description.

dyspepsy (dɪˈspɛpsɪ). Also 7 **-ie**, 7-9 **dis-**. [a. F. *dyspepsie* (17th c.) or ad. L. *dyspepsia*: see prec.] = DYSPEPSIA (which is now more usual).

1656 BLOUNT *Glossogr.*, *Dyspepsie*. **1661** LOVELL *Hist. Anim. & Min.* 366 The imbecility of the stomach, which is a vice of the concocting faculty..and it's called apepsy, bradyspepsy, or dispepsy and diaphthora. **1817** *Gentl. Mag.* LXXXVII. II. 365 He was, at first, attacked with diarrhœa, afterwards with dispepsy. **1829** SOUTHEY *Epistle* in *Anniversary* 18 By bile, opinions, and dyspepsy sour. **1848** LOWELL *Fable for Critics* 106 Brought to death's door of a mental dyspepsy.

dyspeptic (dɪˈspɛptɪk), *a.* (*sb.*) [f. Gr. δύσπεπτος difficult of digestion, f. δυσ- (DYS-) + πεπτός cooked, digested: after Gr. πεπτικός able to digest.]

†**1.** Difficult of digestion; causing dyspepsia; indigestible. *Obs. rare.*

1694 WESTMACOTT *Script. Herb.*, It is..more solid, course, and dispeptic than that of wheat.

2. Of or belonging to dyspepsia.

1809 *Med. Jrnl.* XXI. 269 This dyspeptic state of the stomach. **1875** H. C. WOOD *Therap.* (1879) 188 Decided dyspeptic symptoms.

b. *fig.* Showing depression of spirits like that of a person suffering from dyspepsia; morbidly despondent or gloomy.

1894 *Forum* (U.S.) Aug. 732 There is no throwing up of the hands in despair—no dyspeptic politics, to put it briefly.

3. Subject to or suffering from dyspepsia.

1822-34 GOOD *Study Med.* (ed. 4) I. 443 Common to the hysteric, dyspeptic, and choleric. **1844** DICKENS *Mart. Chuz.* (C.D. ed.) 171 Dyspeptic individuals bolted their food in wedges. **1884** *Pall Mall G.* 16 Oct. 1 Carlyle..was a kind of dyspeptic Mount Sinai.

B. *sb.* A person subject to or suffering from dyspepsia.

1822-34 GOOD *Study Med.* (ed. 4) I. 157 The sedentary and studious dyspeptic. **1866** MRS. STOWE *Lit. Foxes* 34 It is almost impossible for a confirmed dyspeptic to act like a good Christian; but a good Christian ought not to become a confirmed dyspeptic. **1893** G. ALLEN *Scallywag* II. 98 She had the usual surprising appetite of the sallow American dyspeptic.

dysˈpeptical, *a. rare.* [f. prec. + -AL.] = prec.

1831 CARLYLE *Sart. Res.* II. iv. We are poor, unfriended, dyspeptical, bashful. **1831** —— in Froude *Life in Lond.* (1882) II. 169 She had been for three years violently dyspeptical.

dysˈpeptically, *adv.* [f. prec. + -LY².] In a dyspeptic manner (*lit.* and *fig.*).

a **1859** DE QUINCEY *Posth. Wks.* (1893) II. iv. 102 A man ..dyspeptically incapable of command at forty-two. **1866** DICKENS in J. Forster *Life* VIII. vii. 354 Half strangled with my cold, and dyspeptically gloomy and dull.

‖**dysphagia** (dɪsˈfeɪdʒɪə). *Path.* Rarely in anglicized form **dysphagy** (ˈdɪsfədʒɪ). [mod.L. f. DYS- + Gr. -φαγία eating. So mod.F. *disphagie* (1805 Lunier).] Difficulty of swallowing (as a symptom of some disease or affection).

1783 W. KEIR in *Med. Commun.* I. 160 This case exhibits an instance of a species of dysphagia. **1822-34** GOOD *Study Med.* (ed. 4) I. 78 Dysphagy, strictly speaking, is not a disease itself. **1892** GOWERS *Dis. Nerv. Syst.* I. 293 Dysphagia may be added to the other paralytic symptoms.

Hence **dysphagic** (dɪsˈfædʒɪk), *a.*, relating to or affected with dysphagia (*Syd. Soc. Lex.* 1883).

dysphemism (ˈdɪsfɪmɪz(ə)m). [f. DYS- + *-phemism* as in EUPHEMISM; cf. F. *dysphémisme*.] The substitution of an unpleasant or derogatory word or expression for a pleasant or inoffensive one; also, a word or expression so used; opp. EUPHEMISM. Hence **dyspheˈmistic** *a.*, of the nature of or containing such an expression.

1884 L. A. TOLLEMACHE *Safe Studies* 142 The great system which Comte, and other assailants, call by the euphemism, or dysphemism, of Catholicism. [**1927** A. CARNOY *La Science du Mot* xxii. 351 Le dysphémisme..est impitoyable, brutal, moqueur. Il est une réaction contre le pédantisme, la raideur et la prétention, mais aussi contre la noblesse et la dignité dans le langage.] **1933** *John o' London's* 7 Oct., Professor Carnoy, the distinguished French philologist, has coined the word 'dysphemism' as a set-off to 'euphemism', to which it is directly opposed... 'It consists, above all, in the substitution for dignified or simply normal terms, of expressions borrowed from spheres more vulgar, familiar, and joyous.' **1940** E. PARTRIDGE in *S.P.E. Tract* LV. 181 A minor species of dysphemism is the pejorative suffix, as in 'robustious'. **1955** *Archivum Linguisticum* VII. 159 Mothers addressing their babies as *Sübling* etc., are clearly unaware of the dysphemistic force of the suffix. **1962** *John o' London's* 14 June 583/1 'Robber' may also be one of those political dysphemisms used to discredit a nationalist rebel.

dysphoria (dɪsˈfɔərɪə). [ad. Gr. δυσφορία malaise, discomfort, f. δύσφορος hard to bear, f. δυσ- DYS- + φέρειν to bear.] A state or condition marked by feelings of unease or (mental) discomfort (see quots.). Hence **dysphoric** (dɪsˈfɒrɪk) *a.*, pertaining to, characteristic of, or characterized by dysphoria.

1842 DUNGLISON *Dict. Med. Sci.* (ed. 3) 248/1 *Dysphoria*, dissatisfaction, restlessness, suffering. **1933** *Jrnl. R. Anthrop. Inst.* LXIII. 511 *Kunta kunta* means more than merely immoral; it is used for an *incestuous* marriage..when a condition of dysphoria results; when the people feel "shamed'. **1934** WEBSTER, Dysphoric. **1951** PARSONS & SHILS *Toward Gen. Theory of Action* II. ii. 142 Such a dysphoric feeling..may be called *guilt*. **1959** G. D. MITCHELL *Sociology* II. v. 81 The social *euphoria*, or well-being, has been turned into a state of *dysphoria*.

dyspite, obs. form of DESPITE.

dysplasia (dɪˈspleɪzɪə). *Path.* [mod.L., f. DYS- + Gr. πλάσις moulding, conformation, f. πλάσσειν to form, mould + -IA¹.] Abnormal development or growth of tissues, cells, etc.

1935 *Edinb. Med. Jrnl.* XLII. 550 Study of this male skull led to the conclusion that the primary dysplasia was of the skull-base. **1962** *Lancet* 6 Jan. 46/1 Dysplasias of the external ears and of the eyes. **1962** R. H. SMYTHE *Anat. Dog Breeding* 159 Hip dysplasia does not seem to be a particularly painful condition.

dysplastic (dɪˈsplæstɪk), *a. Path.* [ad. G. *dysplastisch* (E. Kretschmer *Körperbau und Character* (1921) v. 53), f. DYS- + Gr. πλαστός formed, f. πλάσσειν to form, mould: see -IC.] Of, or characterized by, abnormal growth or development (of tissues, cells, etc.). Also as *sb.*, a dysplastic person.

1925 W. J. H. SPROTT tr. *Kretschmer's Physique & Character* v. 65 We understand under 'dysplastic' such forms of growth as vary very markedly from the average and commonest form of the type in question. *Ibid.* 67 The dysgenital groups to which so many of the schizophrene dysplastics bear..resemblances. **1939** *Nature* 9 Sept. 469/2 Properly designed exercises..can be used to correct faults of carriage..and fit the mildly dysplastic to take their place without shame among the euplastic. **1949** M. MEAD *Male & Female* xiv. 286 Girls and boys who are so physically immature and dysplastic. **1964** M. CRITCHLEY *Developmental Dyslexia* v. 17 Most neurologists, however, would be reluctant to visualise in developmental dyslexia any focal brain lesion, dysplastic, traumatic or otherwise.

‖**dyspnœa** (dɪspˈniːə). *Path.* [L. *dyspnœa*, a. Gr. δύσπνοια difficulty of breathing, f. δύσπνοος, f. δυσ- (DYS-) + πνοή breath, breathing.] Difficulty of breathing; laborious breathing.

1681 tr. *Willis' Rem. Med. Wks.* Vocab., *Dyspnœa*, a pursiness or shortness of breathing. **1707** FLOYER *Physic. Pulse-Watch* 144 This happens in Dyspnæas, Pains, Diseases of the Stomach, Liver, Head. **1754-64** SMELLIE *Midwif.* II. 27 She was seized with a dry cough, violent dyspnœa, etc. **1843** SIR T. WATSON *Lect. Princ. & Pract. Phys.* xxxviii. (L.), In dyspnœa the breathing is almost always difficult when the patient is lying flat on his back. **1890** *Lancet* 27 Sept. 663/2 Obesity develops the systemic circulation to the full capacity of the lungs, so that the least exertion will produce dyspnœa.

Hence **dyspˈnœal** *a.*, of or belonging to dyspnœa; **dyspˈnœic** [Gr. δυσπνοϊκός] (also erron. **dyspˈnœtic, -etic**) *a.*, of the nature of, characteristic of, accompanied by, or affected with dyspnœa.

1822-34 GOOD *Study Med.* (ed. 4) I. 467 Gold-refiners become dyspnœtic from inhaling the vapour of aquafortis. **1866** A. FLINT *Princ. Med.* (1800) 245 Diseases terminating rapidly with dyspnœic symptoms. **1874** JONES & SIEV. *Pathol. Anat* (ed. 4) 31 Without experiencing any notable dyspnœal distress.

dysporomorph (ˈdɪspərəʊˌmɔːf). *Zool.* [f. *Dysporus* name of a genus of gannets + Gr. -μορφος -FORM.] A bird of the division *Dysporomorphæ* in Huxley's classification, including the pelicans, gannets, cormorants, etc. So ˌ**dysporoˈmorphic** *a.*, belonging to the *Dysporomorphæ*.

dyspoyle, dyspyghte: see DE-.

dysprosium (dɪˈsprəʊzɪəm). *Chem.* [mod.L., f. Gr. δυσπρόσιτος difficult of access; named by L. de Boisbaudran 1886, in *Compt. Rend.* CII. 1004, who showed that the 'holmium oxide' of de Cleve was a mixture containing compounds of holmium and of dysprosium (see HOLMIA).] A paramagnetic metallic element of the lanthanide series, present in yttria-rich minerals such as gadolinite and forming yellowish green salts in which it is trivalent. Symbol Dy; atomic number 66; atomic weight 162·5.

1886 *Jrnl. Chem. Soc.* L. 667 The earths which do not show the bands of holmium but give the bands of dysprosium are relatively rich in terbia. **1906** *Nature* 5 Apr. 551/2 The isolation and some atomic characters of dysprosium. **1962** *New Scientist* 27 Dec. 724 The RCA laser of the solid-state type (using dysprosium in calcium fluoride). **1966** PHILLIPS & WILLIAMS *Inorg. Chem.* II. xix. 18 Dysprosium is strongly ferromagnetic below −168° C. and exhibits a remarkable magnetic anisotropy. **1967** *New Scientist* 20 July 158/3 Accurately machined pole-pieces, such as could be turned out of dysprosium or holmium, would ensure better symmetry than currently used iron-free magnet coils.

dysprosody (dɪˈsprɒsədɪ). *Med.* [f. DYS- + PROSODY.] A speech disorder affecting inflexion, stress, and rhythm, sometimes found in aphasic conditions.

1947 G. H. MONRAD-KROHN in *Brain* LXX. 405 (*heading*) Dysprosody, or altered 'Melody of Language'. **1965** W. R. BRAIN *Speech Disorders* (ed. 2) 114 Disturbances of inflexion, stress and rhythm, termed dysprosody by Monrad-Krohn..may make the speech [in Broca's aphasia] sound as though pronounced by a foreigner. **1970** ESPIR & ROSE *Basic Neurol. Speech* v. 27 Disturbances of inflexion, stress and rhythm (dysprosody) are other features which may occur.

dyss (dɪs). *Archæol.* Also **dysse**. Pl. **dysser**. [ad. Da. *dysse*.] (See quot. 1970.)

1938 A. SERNER *'Dyss' Burial* i. 8 The Younger Stone Age begins with the 'dyss' period. *Ibid.* 27 My research below intends to show that the oldest form of megalithic tombs in South Scandinavia, the rectangular simple dolmen called below 'dyss' by me, is spread in prehistoric times outside South Scandinavia. **1947** V. G. CHILDE *Dawn Europ. Civilization* (ed. 4) x. 179 One classical method of disposal of the dead..which gives its name to the whole period in Denmark, was ceremonial burial in a megalithic dolmen or dyss. In its oldest form a dyss is a small chamber formed by

four uprights supporting a single large capstone, and less than 6ft long by 2 ft. wide. **1968** G. JONES *Hist. Vikings* I. i. 18 Builders of dolmen and dysse. **1970** BRAY & TRUMP *Dict. Archaeol.* 78 *Dyss*, a megalithic cist of the final stage of the Danish Early Neolithic... The oldest dysser are slab cists roofed with capstones and containing from one to six skeletons. The burial chamber is covered with a mound which rises to the height of the capstone and has a retaining kerb of stones.

dyssaue, -ayue, dyssayt, -eyte, obs. forms of DECEIVE, DECEIT.

dyssche, dysse, obs. ff. DISH, DAIS, DICE.

dyssease, -ees, -ese, etc., obs. ff. DECEASE, DISEASE.

dyssende, -ente, obs. forms of DESCEND.

dyssour, var. DISOUR *Obs.*

dyssypers, corrupt f. DOUZEPERS *Obs.*

dysteleology (ˌdɪstɛliːˈɒlədʒɪ). [ad. Ger. *dysteleologie* (Häckel), f. DYS-, here taken in privative sense + *teleologie* TELEOLOGY.] The doctrine of purposelessness, or denial of 'final causes', in nature (opp. to TELEOLOGY); the study of apparently functionless rudimentary organs in animals and plants, as held to sustain this doctrine.

1874 MIVART in *Contemp. Rev.* XXIV. 371 Dysteleology is a term which Professor Haeckel, of Jena, has devised to denote the study of the 'purposelessness' of organs. **1875** *Ibid.* XXVI. 950. **1879** tr. *Haeckel's Evol. Man* I. 109 The science of Rudimentary Organs, which we may call, in reference to their philosophical consequences, the Doctrine of Purposelessness, or Dysteleology.

Hence **ˌdysteleoˈlogical** *a.*, relating to dysteleology; showing absence of purpose or design; **ˌdysteleˈologist**, a believer in dysteleology; one who denies final causes in nature.

1874 MIVART in *Contemp. Rev.* XXIV. 371 Arguments analogous to some of the Dysteleological arguments of today. **1879** tr. *Haeckel's Evol. Man* I. v. 111 The favorite phrase 'the moral ordering of the world' is also shown in its true light by the dysteleological facts. **1883** L. F. WARD *Dynam. Sociol.* I. 173 (Cent.) Dysteleologists, without admitting a purpose, had not felt called upon to deny the fact.

dyster, var. DYESTER.

dystopia (dɪˈstəʊpɪə). [mod.L., f. DYS- + U)TOPIA.] An imaginary place or condition in which everything is as bad as possible; opp. UTOPIA (cf. CACOTOPIA). So **dysˈtopian** *sb.*, one who advocates or describes a dystopia; **dysˈtopian** *a.*, of or pertaining to a dystopia; **dysˈtopianism**, dystopian quality or characteristics.

1868 J. S. MILL in *Hansard Commons* 12 Mar. 1517/1 It is, perhaps, too complimentary to call them Utopians, they ought rather to be called dys-topians, or caco-topians. What is commonly called Utopian is something too good to be practicable; but what they appear to favour is too bad to be practicable. **1952** NEGLEY & PATRICK *Quest for Utopia* xvii. 298 The *Mundus Alter et Idem* [of Joseph Hall] is..the opposite of *eutopia*, the ideal society: it is a *dystopia*, if it is permissible to coin a word. **1962** C. WALSH *From Utopia to Nightmare* 11 The 'dystopia' or 'inverted utopia'. *Ibid.* 12 Stories..that seemed in their dystopian way to be saying something important. *Ibid.* ii. 27 A strand of utopianism or dystopianism. **1967** *Listener* 5 Jan. 22 The modern classics—Aldous Huxley's *Brave New World* and George Orwell's *Nineteen Eighty Four*—are dystopias. They describe not a world we should like to live in, but one we must be sure to avoid. **1968** *New Scientist* 11 July 96/3 It is a pleasant change to read some hope for our future... I fear that our real future is more likely to be dystopian.

dysuric (dɪˈsjʊərɪk), *a.* [ad. Gr. δυσουρικός, f. δυσουρία DISURY: see -IC.] Pertaining to or affected with dysury (Webster, 1864).

dysury (ˈdɪsjʊərɪ). *Path.* Forms: 6 dyssurye, 6–7 dissurie, -ry, 6–8 disury, 7 dysurie, 7- dysury. Also in Lat. form dysuria (dɪˈsjʊərɪə). [a. OF. *dissurie* (14th c.), mod.F. *dysurie*, ad. L. *dysūria* (Coelius), a. Gr. δυσουρία retention of urine, f. *δύσουρος adj., f. δυσ- (DYS-) + οὖρον urine.] Difficulty in passing urine; a disorder characterized by difficult or painful urination.

1398 TREVISA *Barth. De P.R.* VII. lv. (1495) 268 Somtyme the wayes ben alle stoppyd and pyssynge is all forbode, and that euyl hyghte Dissuria. **1527** ANDREW *Brunswyke's Distyll. Waters* Kij, Good agaynst strangury and dyssurye. **1547** BOORDE *Brev. Health* cvii. 40 b, It is named the Disury. **1684** tr. *Bonet's Merc. Compit.* III. 60 Old Men, who labour of a most cruel Dysury from a great Stone. **1748** tr. *Renatus' Distemp. Horses* 266 If he stales with Difficulty, it is called a Dysury. **1800** *Med. Jrnl.* III. 26 She had dysuria during the night. **1837** BICKERSTETH *Life of Franke* vii. 208 The complaint so frequently attendant upon old age, the dysury.

dysyn, dysyng, obs. forms of DIZEN, DICING.

dyt-: see also DIT-.

dytiscid (dɪˈtɪsɪd). *a.* and *sb.* [f. *Dytiscus*, a genus of water-beetles, mod.L. corruption of *Dyticus*, a. Gr. δυτικός able to dive, f. δύειν to dive.] Pertaining to the *Dytiscidæ*, a family of water-beetles. Also as *sb.* Hence **dytiˈscidiform** *a.*

1866 E. C. RYE *Brit. Beetles* x. 64 When ponds, etc., are dried up in the summer, the *Dytiscides* take to the wing. **1882** *Sci. Trans. R. Dublin Soc.* 2nd Ser. II. 207 The most important characteristics of the Dytiscid head besides its short, broad form, are first, its great extension transversely behind the eyes..and second, the great extension of the eyes on the under surface. *Ibid.* 228 Its [*sc.* Omophron's] epimeron is Dytiscidiform in shape... With respect to the size of the anterior pieces [of the mesothorax of Pelobius] it is Dytiscid rather than Carabid. **1950** F. BALFOUR-BROWNE *Brit. Water Beetles* II. xii. 250 Sub-aquatic eggs of many insects, including those of Dytiscids, develop quite well on damp cotton-wool. *Ibid.* 252 The Symmetrid or Dytiscid type has rounded and very numerous suckers.

dytiscus (dɪˈtɪskəs). [mod.L. (Linnæus *Systema Naturæ* (ed. 10, 1758) I. 411): see DYTISCID *a.*] A member of the genus of water-beetles so named. Also *attrib.*

1866 E. C. RYE *Brit. Beetles* x. 63 The females of *Dytiscus* are, however, sometimes found without these dorsal furrows. **1895** L. C. MIALL *Nat. Hist. Aquatic Insects* i. 39 No one can hunt long for water-insects without coming across the rapacious Dytiscus. **1902** C. CORNISH *Naturalist on Thames* 26 The great carnivorous water-beetle, the dytiscus..will rise by night from the surface of the Thames. *Ibid.*, A dytiscus beetle. **1952** M. K. WILSON tr. *Lorenz's King Solomon's Ring* iii. 17 A larva of the water-beetle Dytiscus. *Ibid.*, The Dytiscus larva..is a slim, streamlined insect, rather more than two inches long. **1969** R. F. CHAPMAN *Insects* xvi. 308 The fore legs of *Dytiscus* and some other beetles bear suckers.

dytone, Sc. form of DITTON *Obs.*, a phrase.

dyvise, dyvys(e, obs. ff. DEVICE, DEVISE.

dyvour (ˈdaɪvə(r)). *Sc.* ? *Obs.* Also 6 dyver, 7–8 dyvor, -ar, 9 divor. [Origin uncertain.

According to Skene, 'called *dyvour*, because he does his *devore* to his creditours'. But this is not logical; and it leaves the vowel and stress of the first syllable unexplained. The phrase ' drowned in debt' in quots. 1597 and 1636, with the later 'over head and ears in debt', suggests that it may be the same word as *diver.*]

A bankrupt; hence *gen.* one in debt; a beggar.

1508 DUNBAR *Tua Mariit Wemen* 410 Deid is now that dyvour, & dollin in erd. **1583** *Satir. Poems Reform.* xlv. 278 Lyk ane dyver, thair he deis. **1597** SKENE *De Verb. Sign.*, *Dyovr*, *Dyvour*, vtherwaies Bair-man, quha being involved and drowned in debtes, and not able to pay or satisfie the same: For eschewing of prison and vther paines, makis cession and assignation of al his gudes and geare, in favoures of his creditoures: And dois his devour and dewtie to them. **1636** RUTHERFORD *Lett.* (1862) I. 194, I am as deeply drowned in His debt as any dyvour can be. **16..** *Court of Sess. Rec.* in Cramond *Ann. Banff* (1891) I. 318 *note*, The Court of Session enacted that the dyvours habit be a coat or upper garment..whereof one half to be of a yellow and the other of a brown colour..with uppermost hose on his legs half brown and half yellow. **1693** *Sc. Presbyt. Eloq.* (1738) 101 The Saints in Heaven are nothing but Christ's..beggarly Dyvars, a Pack of redeem'd Sinners. **1769** in Cramond *Ann. Banff* (1891) I. 318 The magistrates..ordained him to put on and wear the dyvour's habit: he was thereafter dismissed wearing the said dyvour's habit. **1824** SCOTT *Redgauntlet* let. xi, 'Well, you dyvour bankrupt,..have you brought me my rent?' **18..** GALT *Town Drummer*, He was..a divor bodie, with no manner of conduct. **1836** *Act 6 & 7 Will. IV*, c. 56 § 18 It shall not be lawful to ordain the Debtor to wear the Dyvour's Habit.

†**ˈdyvoury.** *Sc. Obs.* [f. prec. + -Y.] Bankruptcy; beggary.

1597 SKENE *De Verb. Sign.* s.v. *Dyovr, Dyvour*, Diverse shamefull formes of dyuourie, ar vsed and observed. **1661** R. BAILLIE in Z. Boyd *Zion's Flowers* (1855) App. 35/2 Help your..friends out of beggary and dyvoury if you can.

dywte, rare obs. form of DUTY.

dyyss, obs. form of DICE: see DIE *sb.*[1]

dyzar, var. of DISOUR, *Obs.*

dyzerde, -ert, var. DIZZARD, *Obs.*

‖**dzeren** (ˈdzɪərɛn). Also -on, -in. [Native name in Mongolia, *dséren* (Pallas *Zoogr. Rosso-Asiatica* 251), more properly *dzēren*, f. *dzēr* reddish-yellow, rufous. (Prof. Pozdneyev of St. Petersburg.)] The Mongolian antelope, *Procapra gutturosa.*

1834 *Penny Cycl.* II. 73/2 The dzerens inhabit the dry arid deserts of Central Asia...particularly the desert of Gobi.

dzhu: see DIZZUE.

‖**dziggetai, dzh-** (ˈdzɪgətaɪ, dʒ-). Also dschikketaei, dshikketei, dshiggetai, dzigguetai, dzigithai, dziggethai, gicquetei, djiggetai, jiggetai. [Mongolian *dschiggetéi* (Pallas *Zoogr. Rosso-Asiatica* 262), more properly *tchikhitei*, eared, long-eared, f. *tchikhi* ear (Pozdneyev).] A species of equine quadruped native to Central Asia, *Equus hemionus.* It approaches the mule in appearance.

1793 PENNANT *Hist. Quad.* (ed. 3) I. 4 *Dshikketaei* or Wild Mule. *Ibid.* 7 The Mongalians call them *Dshikketaei*, which signifies the *eared*. *Ibid.* 11 The manners of the *Koulan* or wild ass, are very much the same with those of the wild horse and the Dshikketaei. **1825** T. M. HARRIS *Nat. Hist. Bible* s.v. *Ass* §4 The *Gicquetei* of Professor Pallas, the wild mule of Mongalia. **1834** MCMURTRIE *Cuvier's Anim. Kingd.* 102 *Equus hemionus.* (The Dzigguetai.) A species which, as to its proportions, is intermediate between the horse and the ass, and lives in troops in the sandy deserts of Central Asia. **1834** *Phys. Geog.* 54/2 (U.K.S.) Thus the quagga [and] the zebra ..answer to the ass and the jiggetai of Asia. **1839** *Penny Cycl.* XV. 330/1 Wild animals are numerous, especially hares, antelopes, dshiggetais or wild asses. **1847–9** TODD *Cycl. Anat.* IV. 1. 714 The second species admitted by Zoologists to form a distinct race is the Dzigguetai. **1870** BLAINE *Encycl. Rur. Sports* §77 That direct link between the horse and ass, known to the moderns as the *dziggetai*, or *Equus hemionus.*

dzo, var. DSO.

dzong, var. JONG.

Dzongkha (ˈdzɒŋka). Also Den-jong-ke, Ḍrug-kä, etc. [Tibetan: see quot. 1979.] A Tibetan dialect used as the official language of Bhutan.

1909 CONRADY & KONOW in G. A. Grierson *Linguistic Survey India* III. I. 14 Bhōṭiā of Bhutan or Ḍrug-kä. **1964** G. L. HARRIS et al. *U.S. Army Area Handbk. Nepal Sikkim & Bhutan* 412 One of the most widely spoken dialects—probably Den-jong-ke—is Bhutan's language of administration and education. **1964** *Statesman's Year Bk. 1964–5*, 822 The language is Dzongkha, akin to Tibetan. **1967** P. P. KARAN *Bhutan* viii. 75/1 The most widely spoken dialect—Druk-ke—is Bhutan's official language. **1974** *Encycl. Brit. Macropædia* II. 879/1 A large number of school textbooks are being produced in Dzongkha (a Tibetan dialect), the official language of Bhutan. **1979** M. V. ARIS *Bhutan* p. xvii, Since the 17th century..there has..developed an official idiom known as 'Dzongkha'..'the language of the fortress'.., a polished form of the village patois of the Ngalong people. **1981** *Whitaker's Almanack 1982* 798/2 The official language is Dzongkha, a dialect of Tibetan.

E

E (iː), the fifth letter of the Roman alphabet, represents historically the Semitic ∃, which originally expressed a sound resembling that of *h*, but was adopted by the Greeks (and from them by the Romans) as a vowel, the pronunc. of which probably varied from the 'mid-front' (e) to the 'low front' (ɛ) vowels of Bell's system. In the Roman, as in the earliest Greek alphabet, the letter represented the long as well as the short quantity of the vowel. There are reasons for believing that in OE. the short *e* had two sounds, possibly (e) and (ɛ); the OE. long *é* seems to have been sounded approximately as (eː).

The sounds now expressed by E in standard English are the following:

(1) (iː) in b*e* (biː) (4) (iː/ɪ)in acm*e* ('ækmiː, 'ækmɪ)
(2) (ɪə) in h*e*re (hɪə(r)) (5) (ɛ) in b*e*d (bɛd)
(3) (ɛə) in th*e*re (ðɛə(r)) (6) (ɜː) in al*e*rt (ə'lɜːt)

Exceptional sounds are (7) (eɪ) in *e*h!, (8) (ɪ) in *E*ngland, *E*nglish, and (9) (ɑː) occurring before *r* in cl*e*rk, s*e*rgeant, and in various proper names, as B*e*rkeley, H*e*rtford.

In unaccented syllables it has the obscure sounds:
(10)(ɪ) in r*e*main (rɪ'mein), add*e*d ('ædɪd)
(11)(ə) in mom*e*nt ('məʊmənt), fath*e*r ('fɑːðə(r))
(12) the mere voice-glide (ə) as in sadd*e*n ('sæd(ə)n).

In foreign words not fully naturalized certain other sounds occur: the Fr. *en* occas. retains in Eng. use its two sounds of (ɑ̃) and (æ̃), as in *ennui* (ɑ̃nyi), *bon-chretien* (bɔ̃kretjæ̃); the Fr. unaccented *e* preserves the sound of (ə) in words like *eau-de-vie* (o də vi); and the Fr. *é* that of (e) in a few words, as *café* (kafe).

E is also the first element in many vowel-digraphs, most of which have more than one pronunciation.

(1) *Ea* is usually sounded (iː), as in *bead* (biːd); exceptionally as (eɪ) in *break*, *great*, *steak*. It frequently represents (ɛ) in cases where that sound descends from a long vowel or diphthong, either original, as in *thread* (θrɛd), *dead* (dɛd), or acquired in ME. through position, as in *stead* (stɛd). When followed by *r* it has the sounds of (ɪə) as in *ear* (ɪə(r)), of (ɛə) as in *pear* (pɛə(r)), and of (ɜː) as in *earth* (ɜːθ), (ɑː) as in *heart* (hɑːt). In final unaccented syllables it sometimes becomes (ɪ) as in *guinea* ('gɪnɪ).

(2) *Eau*, found only in words of Fr. origin, is sounded (juː) in *beauty* and its derivatives, and (iː) in a few proper names, as *Beauchamp* ('biːtʃəm); in all other cases it is (əʊ) or (o), as in *bureau* ('bjuːrəʊ), *rouleau* (rulo).

(3) *Ee* has the sound of (iː) as in *feel* (fiːl), and before *r* that of (ɪə), as in *peer* (pɪə(r)). In *been* many persons sound it as (ɪ); it has also this sound in *breeches* ('brɪtʃɪz), *coffee* ('kɒfɪ).

(4) *Ei* has the sound of (iː) chiefly in the combination *cei*, as in *receive*; also in *teil*, and in Sc. words, as *teind*. In other cases its usual sound is (eɪ), as in *vein*. In *either*, *neither*, it is variously sounded (iː) and (aɪ). In a few words, on account of German or Greek etymology, it is pronounced (aɪ), as in *eider-down*, *ophicleide*. In unaccented final syllables it becomes (ɪ), as in *foreign* ('fɒrɪn), *sovereign*.

(5) *Eo* (as a digraph) is sounded (iː) in *people*, (ɛ) in *leopard*, and (əʊ) in *yeoman*.

(6) *Eu* has the sound of (juː), and when followed by *r* that of (jʊə), as in *euphony*, *Europe*. (After *l* or *r* the first element in these diphthongs is wholly or partially obscured: see L, R.) In a few Fr. words not fully naturalized *eu* retains its original sounds (œ) and (ø).

(7) *Ew* has the sound of (juː), as in *new* (njuː), *Matthew*.

(8) *Ey* is sounded (iː) in *key*, and (eɪ) in *obey*, *they*, *prey*; it occurs most frequently in unaccented final syllables, with the sound (ɪ), as in *donkey* ('dɒŋkɪ), *money*. In *eye* and its derivatives and compounds it is pronounced (aɪ).

The cases in which E is silent are very numerous.

The rule may be laid down that (except in foreign words not fully naturalized as to form) a final *e* is never sounded when there is another vowel in the word. The silent *e* is due primarily to the ME. obscure *-e* (:—OE. *a*, *e*, *o*, *u*, or a. Fr. *e*), which continued to be written long after it ceased to be sounded. In imitation of the cases in which the silent *e* had this historical justification, it was in 16th c. very frequently added to almost all words ending phonetically with a cons.; when the preceding vowel was short and accented, the final cons. was doubled, as in *bludde*, *bedde* for *blood*, *bed*; a mute *e* after a single cons. implied that the preceding vowel was long. In our present spelling the use of silent *e* has been greatly narrowed, but it is retained in the following cases: (1) When it serves to indicate that the vowel in the syllable is long; e.g. in *wine* (waɪn) compared with *win* (wɪn), *paste* (peɪst) compared with *past* (pɑːst, pæst). When the quantity of the vowel is already shown by the use of a digraph, the *e* is no longer added, e.g. in *soon*, *mean* (in 16th c. often *soone*, *meane*), unless the final cons. is *s*, *z*, or the voiced *th* (ð), as in *house*, *breeze*, *sheathe*. (2) When a word ends phonetically with certain consonants which custom does not permit to be written in a final position, as *v*, and *l*, *r* after consonants. (3) Where the silent *e* affects the pronunc. of a preceding *c* or *g*. (4) After *s* or *z* preceded by a cons., as in *purse*, *pulse*, *corpse*, *bronze*, *furze*. (5) In words like *infinite*, *rapine*, etc., where the vowel of the final syllable has become short since the establishment of the existing rules of spelling; and in words adopted from Fr. (6) In some anomalous cases of diverse origin, as *are*, *were*, *come*, *done*, *gone*, *some*, *one*, *none*. The silent *e* is omitted before flexional suffixes beginning with a vowel, as in *moving*; before *-able* it has been usually retained, as in *moveable*, *loveable*, *unmistakeable*, though many writers now prefer to omit it, esp. when the vb. is a polysyllable. Before suffixes beginning with a cons. the mute *e* is nearly always written; in *abridgment*, *acknowledgment*, *fledgling*, *judgment*, *nursling*, it is commonly omitted, but usage is divided except in the last instance; in this Dictionary the *e* is retained after *dg*, in accordance with general English analogies.

The following are illustrations of the literary use of the letter:

a. simply.

c **1000** ÆLFRIC *Gram.* (1880) 6 þa syx ongynnað of ðam stæfe e. **1668** O. PRICE in Ellis *E.E. Pronunc.* I. iii. (1867) 81 E soundes like, ee, in be, euen, euening, England, English, etc. **1865** MISS YONGE *Clever Wom. of Fam.* I. x. 249, I can very easily alter the L into an E.

b. as representing the sound of which it is the usual symbol.

1340 HAMPOLE *Pr. Consc.* 485 If þe child a woman be, When it es born it says 'e, e'..þe first letter..of Eve.

II. Used as a symbol, with reference to its place (5th) in the alphabet, or (2nd) in the series of vowels; also on various other grounds.

1. E, e, *e* is used to denote anything occupying the fifth place in a series (cf. A, B, C).

2. in *Music.* E is the name of the 3rd note of the diatonic scale of C major, corresponding to *mi* in the Sol-fa notation. Also the scale or key which has that note for its tonic.

1848 RIMBAULT *First Bk. Pianof.* 54 Every black key except B-flat and E-flat. **18..** *As it was Written* 229 A leap of the bow and fingers back to A and E.

3. in *Logic*: A universal negative.

1827 WHATELY *Logic* (1850) 49.

4. *Naut.* E. The second class of rating on Lloyd's books for the comparative excellence of merchant ships. (Adm. Smyth.)

5. *Math.* The lower-case e or *e* denotes: **a.** The quantity 2·71828.., the base of Napier's system of logarithms. **b.** The ECCENTRICITY of a conic.

1860 SALMON *Conic Sect.* xi. (1879) 161 The quantity *e* is called the eccentricity of the curve. **1873** B. WILLIAMSON *Diff. Calc.* i. 21 The system [of logarithms] whose base is *e*.

6. in *Dynamics*: *e* is the symbol of the coefficient of restitution or of elasticity.

1856 TAIT & STEELE *Dynam. Particle* x. (1871) 344 Let *e* be the coefficient of restitution.

7. in *Electricity. e* stands for the electro-motive force of a single cell, E for the sum of such forces.

1885 S. P. THOMPSON *Electr. & Magn.* §345.

8. in *Chem.* E represents the element Erbium.

9. ***E-layer***, ***-region***: a stratum in the ionosphere, above the D-layer, that reflects medium frequency radiation; = *Heaviside layer*.

1930, **1935** [see D. II. 1 c]. **1955** *Sci. Amer.* Sept. 128/2 The E layer (extending from about 60 to 90 miles above the earth's surface). **1959** DAVIES & PALMER *Radio Stud. Universe* ix. 162 Far below the F-region is the E-region which is centred at a height of 110 km.

10. ***E-type***, a type of 'Jaguar' sports-car.

1961 *Autocar* 17 Mar. 403/2 Independent rear suspension is still a rarity on British cars, and Jaguar have not introduced it on the E-type without a great deal of investigation. **1964** J. WELCOME *Hard to Handle* v. 56 The note of the 'E' type's exhaust. **1967** L. DEIGHTON *Expensive Place* v. 41 On the corner an E-type was parked.

11. e, a symbol used chiefly on the packaging of certain foodstuffs and other products to indicate that they comply with relevant EEC directives; *spec.* printed with the indication of weight or volume, and stating the average contained; also (cap.) on washing-powder packs, etc.; also ***E-pack***.

1972 tr. *EEC Directive 71/316* in *European Communities Secondary Legislation* (Foreign & Commonwealth Office) XII. 301 The final ratification mark is composed of two stamps: (a) the first consists of the small letter '*e' containing:—in the top half, the capital letter indicating the State where the primary examination takes place..in the lower half, the number indicating the examining agent or office; [etc.]. **1975** *Monthly Rev. Inst. Trading Standards* Mar. 50/1 The E.3 cartons will start to replace Giant sizes in January, the E.2 replaces Large sizes from February and the conversion from Regular to E.1 and Family to E.5 will be completed in June. **1975** *Measuring Instruments (EEC Requirements) Regulations* No. 1173. Schedule 1 para. 5 The mark of EEC initial verification is composed of two stamps. .. The first stamp consists of a letter 'e'. **1975** *Grocer* 8 Mar. 7 The Soap and Detergent Industry Association have issued amended amounts for their packed weights of Euro-size (E-packs) products. **1984** A. SCRIVENER in *Halsbury's Laws Eng.* (ed. 4) L. para. 39 The EEC mark..is a lower case letter 'e'.

b. ***E number***, a code number preceded by the letter E, assigned to an additive that accords with EEC Food Additive directives, and listed as an ingredient on the packaging of food or drink; also, an E number itself, as *E200*, etc.

1977 *Grocer* 31 Dec. 31/3 Other labelling disagreement stems from EEC Commission recommendations that all additives be declared by their name or by their 'E' number (an 'E' number means the additive has been approved). **1981** *Statutory Instruments 1980* III. II. 6105 Lecithins E322..Alginic acid E400 [etc.]. **1984** M. HANSSEN *E for Additives* 9 All foods made after 1 January 1986 will (except for flavourings) have to have the 'E' number or the actual name in the list of ingredients. **1986** *Financial Times* 7 June (Suppl.) p. xiv/8 A merry dance of dietary fibre, polyunsaturates and E-numbers.

III. Abbreviations.

a. E. = various proper names, as Edward, Ellen; = Engineer(s) in *C.E.* and *R.E.*; **b.** = East, a point of the compass; **c. E.A.**, **E/A**, enemy aircraft; **E.A.M.**, Ethnikon Apeleutherotikon Metopon ([Greek] National Liberation Front); **E.B.S.**, emergency bed service; **E.C.**, European Community; **E.C.G.**, electrocardiogram; **E.C.T.**, electro-convulsive therapy; **ECU**, **ecu** [after F. *écu*: see ÉCU], European Currency Unit; **E.D.C.**, European Defence Community; **E.D.D.**, English Dialect Dictionary; **E.D.P.**, **e.d.p.**, electronic data processing; **E.D.S.**, English Dialect Society; **EDTA**, ethylenediamine tetra-acetic acid; also, ethylenediamine tetra-acetate; **E.E.**, Early English (see EARLY *a.* 4 b); **E.E.**, **E. & O.E.** (*Comm.*) = errors (and omissions) excepted; **E.E.C.**, European Economic Community; **E.E.G.**, electro-encephalogram (see ELECTRO-); **E.E.T.S.**, Early English Text Society; **EFL**, English as a foreign language; cf. *TEFL*, *TOEFL* s.v. T 6 a; **E.F.T.A.** (see EFTA as a main entry); **e.g.** = EXEMPLI GRATIA, for the sake of example; **E.H.P.**, effective (or electrical) horse-power; **E.H.T.**, extra high tension; **E.I.**, East India; **E.I.C.**, East India(n) Company; **E.L.A.S.**, Ethnikos (or Ellinikos) Laikos Apeleutherotikos Stratos (National (or Greek) Popular Liberation Army); **E.L.D.O.** (see quot. 1962); **ELT**, English language teaching; **E.M.** = Earl Marshal; **E.M.F.**, **e.m.f.**, electromotive force; **EMP**, electromagnetic pulse (as emitted by an atmospheric nuclear explosion); **E.N.I.A.C.**, also *eniac* (see quots.); **E.N.S.A.** (see ENSA as a main entry); **E.N.T.**, ear, nose, and throat; **E.P.**, electro-plate(d); **E.P.**, extended-play (record) (see quot. 1962); **E.P.A.** (*U.S.*), Environmental Protection Agency; **E.P.D.**, excess profits duty; **EPG**, Eminent Persons Group; **E.P.N.S.**, electro-plated nickel silver; **EPOS**, electronic point of sale; cf. *POS* s.v. P II; **E.P.T.**, excess profits tax; **E.P.U.**, European Payments Union; **ER** (*U.S.*), emergency room; **E.R.A.** (*Baseball*), earned run average; **ERA** (*U.S.*), Equal Rights Amendment; **ESL**, English as a second language; cf. *TESL* s.v. T 6 a; **E.S.N.**, **e.s.n.**, educationally subnormal; **ESP**, English for special (or specific) purposes; **E.S.P.**, extra-sensory perception (see EXTRA-SENSORY *a.*); **E.S.R.**, **e.s.r.**, electron spin resonance; **E.S.R.O.** (see quot. 1961); **E.S.T.**, Eastern Standard Time (in the eastern parts of the U.S and Canada); **E.S.T.**, electro-shock (or electric shock) treatment (see ELECTRO-); **E.S.U.**, **e.s.u.**, electrostatic unit (see ELECTROSTATIC *a.*); **ET**, extra-terrestrial (being); popularized by the film of this name (1982); **E.T.A.**, estimated time of arrival; **E.T.A.** ('ɛtə) [Basque, acronym f. the initial letters of *Euzkadi ta Azkatasuna* Basque Homeland and Liberty], the name of a Basque separatist organization formed in 1959; **E.T.D.**, estimated time of departure; **e.V.**, **eV**, electron volt; **E.V.A.**, extravehicular activity (activity outside a space-craft).

1916 T. E. LAWRENCE *Lett.* (1938) 214 The feed-block of one of the *E.A. German Maxims. **1942** 'B. J. ELLAN' *Spitfire* 42 A faint silhouette even if the E/A was not actually illuminated. **1944** *Time* 16 Oct. 45/3 The Greek resistance forces wore the insignia of *E.A.M. (left-wing National Liberation Front) or E.L.A.S. (E.A.M.'s fighting arm). **1945** *Spectator* 21 Sept. 265/1 There were those..who

regarded E.A.M. as little more than a group of unscrupulous adventurers who were employing the brigand bands of E.L.A.S. to seize power by violent means. **1966** P. P. ARGENTI *Occupation of Chios* vi. 61 The Communist E.A.M. ('Εθνικὸν Ἀπελευθερωτικὸν Μέτωπον, i.e. National Freedom Front). **1973** *Business Week* 1 Dec. 37/1 (*heading*) Europe: The *EC feud over nuclear fuel. **1980** *Daily Tel.* 6 Dec. 18 The abbreviation EEC is now taboo... 'The European Community' is the Council [of Ministers]'s approved designation, with the abbreviation EC. **1986** *Ibid.* 4 Jan. 12/6 It's the EC now, the European Community, a syntactical change intended to heighten our feeling of Europeanness. **1952** *E.C.G. [see *electrocardiogram* s.v. ELECTRO-]. **1962** *Lancet* 5 May 946/2 The first three cases show that ST and T-wave depression can occur in the left chest leads of E.C.G.s in acute pulmonary embolism... The reasons for these E.C.G. changes are debatable. **1970** *Guardian* 28 May 4/1 M. Rey, president of the EEC Commission in Brussels, yesterday forecast the *écu (crown) as the name of the future European currency... [It] would..stand for 'European Currency Unit'. **1972** *Times* 5 Jan. 15/2 The European currency unit, the Ecu, failed to make an impact. **1983** *Times* 2 July 6/6 The European Commission yesterday agreed a supplementary budget for this year which would use up every single European currency unit (ECU) available to the EEC budget. *Ibid.*, The proposed budget totals 2,380m ecus. **1952** *Times* 22 May 5/4 (*heading*) *E.D.C. talks end in Paris. **1954** *Encounter* Nov. 51/1 And so [certain elements of the Right] were led to oppose EDC, which was conceived precisely in order to safeguard France against the extreme risks of German rearmament pure and simple. **1960** *Electronic Engin.* Mar. 153/2 In the early days of business *e.d.p. it was not unusual for the manufacturer's programmers and analysts to guide, control, and even supplement the efforts of the user's personnel. **1960** *Times Rev. Industry* Dec. 3/1 Electronic data processing (E.D.P.). **1873** *N. & Q.* 4th Ser. XII. 342/1 Walter W. Skeat, Hon. Sec. *E.D.S. [**1950** *Proc. Soc. Exper. Biol. & Med.* LXXIV. 415/1 Ethylenediamine tetra-acetic acid (E.D.T.A.A.).] **1951** *Plant Physiol.* XXVI. 542 The use of *EDTA was tested in mass culture conditions under daylight illumination in the greenhouse. **1959, 1964** [see *ethylenediamine tetra-acetic acid* s.v. ETHYLENE 2]. **1966** PHILLIPS & WILLIAMS *Inorg. Chem.* II. xx. 82 For the complexes of ethylenediaminetetraacetate, $EDTA^{4-}$.., the stability orders are IIIA > IIA > IA, [etc.]. **1977** *Time* 31 Jan. 42/1 The grime was removed with cotton swabs wet with an aqueous solution called E.D.T.A. **1877** G. F. CHAMBERS *Handbk. Sussex* 26 The Ch... is chiefly Perpendicular, with an *E.E. tower. **1966** *Listener* 3 Feb. 166/2 Things like that little E.E. job in Palermo, now closed, could not possibly be mistaken for any Sicilian place of worship. **1958** *Times Rev. Industry* July 75/1 Exchanges with the other members of *E.E.C. accounted for 27 per cent. of imports. **1961** *Listener* 10 Aug. 196/2 The preferences British goods enjoyed on the Australian market would disappear if Britain joined E.E.C. **1969** *Times* 27 Jan. 10/6 Union thinking..is strongly against exchanging present guaranteed prices for any 'target' prices on the E.E.C. model. **1867** SKEAT *Piers Plowman* p. xii, My tract published for the *E.E.T.S. in 1866. **1891** SCHICK *Lydgate's Temple of Glas* p. xii, Dr. Erdmann's forthcoming edition of the *Story of Thebes*, for the E.E.T.S. **1958** *Times Lit. Suppl.* 17 Jan. 35/1 Few E.E.T.S. introductions can show such grace, style and wit. **1965** *Language Learning* XV. 131 Future plans are to hire regularly trained *EFL teachers for part of the staff. **1986** *Times Educ. Suppl.* 9 May 109/2 (Advt.), Qualified/Experienced E.F.L. Teachers required for Summer Courses. **1682** R. BAXTER *Answer to Mr. Dodwell* 226 What if they hold, *e.g. Arrianism, Socinianism, Manichisme, &c... Are they not Heretical? **1818** MOORE *Fudge Fam. Paris* (ed. 5) 106 Like him, Tiberius loved his joke, On matters, too, where few can bear one; *E.g.* a man, cut up, or broke Upon the wheel—a devilish fair one! **1871** B. JOWETT *Dial. Plato* I. 110 In this or that passage—e.g. in the explanation of good as pleasure. **1892** J. WRIGHT *Primer Gothic Lang.* viii. 42 In the former case they are said to be voiced (e.g. the mediæ), and in the latter voiceless (e.g. the tenues). **1922** JOYCE *Ulysses* 700 Requisite farming implements, e.g., an end-to-end churn. **1970** J. McN. DODGSON *Place-Names of Cheshire* p. xlv, Sources whose dates cannot be fixed to a particular year are dated by century (e.g. 12, 13 etc.), by regnal year (e.g. E1, H2 etc.) or a range of years (e.g. 1189–1217). **1920** *Conquest* June 360/1 An average of about £50 per *E.H.P. at power house must be allowed. **1948** *Electronic Engin.* XX. 160 The circuit.. derives its H.T. from the *E.H.T. supply which feeds the cathode ray tube. **1814** *Statutes 54 Geo. III* Index 2/2 *E.I. Co... Cap. xxxiv. The East India Company. **1898** J. J. M. INNES *Sir H. Lawrence* 103 The E.I. Board. **1944, 1945** *E.L.A.S. [see E.A.M. above]. **1945** W. S. CHURCHILL *Victory* (1946) 7, I have been told that I made a mistake in under-rating the power of the Communist-directed E.L.A.S. **1966** P. P. ARGENTI *Occupation of Chios* vi. 67 E.L.A.S. ('Εθνικὸς Λαϊκὸς Ἀπελευθερωτικὸς Στρατός, i.e. National Popular Liberation Army). **1962** *Daily Tel.* 22 Feb. 24/4 ESRO is independent of the European Launcher Development Organisation (*ELDO), ..which seeks European support for converting Britain's abandoned Blue Streak defence rocket into a satellite launcher. **1967** (*title*) *E.L.T. Selections..Articles from the journal *English Language Teaching*. **1969** *Eng. Lang. Teaching* Oct. 63 Experimental summer school on ELT methods in northern Nigeria. **1977** P. STREVENS *New Orientations Teaching Eng.* v. 56 The principal British cover term is *English language teaching* (ELT), which normally excludes English as the mother tongue. **1881** HEAVISIDE in *Jrnl. Soc. Telegr. Engin.* X. 271 The phase of the current is behind that of the *E.M.F. **1905** N. H. SCHNEIDER *Study Electr.* 76 The e.m.f. is raised. **1963** *N.Y. Times* 26 July 10/8 The so-called '*EMP' or electromagnetic pulse, induced by a major explosion has widespread effects. **1983** *Listener* 15 Sept. 7/2 EMP would also, en passant, knock out huge numbers of satellites. **1946** *N.Y. Times* 15 Feb. 1/7 The *Eniac, known more formally as 'the electronic numerical integrator and computer', has not a single moving mechanical part. **1946** *Lancet* 30 Nov. 795/1 Another war secret now disclosed is an electrical calculating machine which has been built in the United States and has been called an 'electronic brain', or more accurately an Electronic Numerical Integrator and Computer—ENIAC. **1947** *Ann. Reg. 1946* 392 The one [electronic calculating machine] which has gained most publicity is the Electronic Numerical Integrator and Automatic Calculator (E.N.I.A.C.). **1944** *Dorland's Med. Dict.* 503/2 *E.N.T. Abbreviation for *ear, nose* and *throat*. **1952** 'R. GORDON' *Doctor in House* xiv. 154 The E.N.T. clinic was busy..for the London atmosphere silted up patients' sinuses and roughened their lungs. *c* **1895** *Catal. R.S. Rowell, Oxford* 43 Best *E.P. Entrée Dish 50/-. **1954** *Gramophone* May 491/2 The second batch of *EPs to appear. *Ibid.* Sept. 165/2 The other side of the new EP. *Ibid.*, Two of them..now make an EP appearance. **1962** A. NISBETT *Technique Sound Studio* 252 *E.P.* (*extended play*) *record*, a 45 rpm 7-inch fine groove record which may carry more material than a coarse-groove 10 or 12-inch 78. **1970** *Time* 23 Nov. 42/3 When *EPA opens for business on Dec. 2, it will take over 15 component parts of five different (and often conflicting) agencies. **1976** *N.Y. Times* 11 Dec. 1/3 (*heading*) E.P.A. faults 208,000 cars. **1984** *N.Y. Rev. Bks.* 19 Aug. 14/3 She has done more for the environment today than during her entire tenure at E.P.A. **1921** *Times* 4 Feb. 11/4 The End of *E.P.D. **1986** *Guardian* 13 May 12/2 The return to South Africa this week of the Commonwealth 'Eminent Persons Group' (*EPG) ought to remind Pretoria that the outside world has not forgotten apartheid. **1986** EPG [see *Eminent Persons Group* s.v. EMINENT *a.* 2 e]. **1897** *Illustr. Price List* (Edward Morrison, Parsonstown) 22, *E.P.N.S. Preserve Dish with Glass, 9/-. E.P. Butter with Glass, 3/6. **1949** *Canning Handbk. Electro-Plating* (ed. 16) xxi. 338 For best quality hotel plate and E.P.N.S. spoons and forks it is customary to give a deposit of 0.002 inch in thickness. **1970** *Daily Tel.* (Colour Suppl.) 24 Apr. 3/2 If he's after antiques you know he's an amateur if he takes EPNS stuff and reproduction porcelain and ignores the real thing. **1980** *Which Computer?* June 37 We look briefly at *EPOS 80, a conference and exhibition this month in Kensington which is devoted to POS systems and applications. **1985** *Times* 6 Aug. 23/8 Electronic point of sale (EPOS) systems..link cash registers to larger computers for data processing. **1940** *Economist* 6 Jan. 3/1 There is the unknown yield of *E.P.T. **1950** *Times* (Suppl.) 18 Sept. p. iv/5 A number of European countries, ..might not have felt justified in exposing themselves to the inevitable risks of *E.P.U. **1965** *Acronyms & Initialisms Dict.* (Gale Research Co.) 266 *ER, Emergency Room (Medicine). **1976** *N.Y. Times Mag.* 23 May 80 Deborah Scher is waiting in the ER. A huddle of nurses moves to the side as Basil wheels the stretcher in. **1949** P. CUMMINGS *Dict. Sports* 121/2 *Earned run average*... Abbreviation: *ERA. **1975** *New Yorker* 23 June 46/2 At contract-renewal time, earned-run averages below 3.30 are invariably mentioned by pitchers; an E.R.A. close to or above the 4.00 level will always be brought up by management. **1973** *Americana Ann.* 747/2 Acting 32 minutes after the vote, Hawaii became the first state to ratify *ERA. **1981** *Gossip* (Holiday Special) 52/3 How would you explain your position on the ERA (Equal Rights Amendment) and feminism—your personal view? **1967** C. C. CATE in *Calif. Jrnl. Educ. Research* XVIII. 184 (*title*) Test behaviour of *ESL students. **1985** *Toronto Sun* 10 Oct. 55/1 Volunteers are needed to conduct tours of the hospital for schoolchildren and pupils of E.S.L. classes. **1955** *Special Schools Jrnl.* June 13/2, I have a strong conviction that Mary is not *E.S.N. at all. On the orthodox tests of intelligence she certainly gains a score which puts her in the upper level of the E.S.N. group. **1960** *Where?* III. 13/2 *Educationally Subnormal* (*ESN*), an expression used to describe children whose I.Q. is between about 55 and about 80. **1976** *Studies in Sci. Educ.* (Univ. Leeds) III. 63 *ESP requires that teachers of English should define the aims of each language course with great precision, and devise teaching syllabuses and materials that lead only to those ends. **1977** P. STREVENS *New Orientations Teaching Eng.* viii. 89 'English for Special Purposes' (ESP)..is generally used in circumstances in which the command of English being imparted relates to a specific job, or subject, or purpose. **1982** *English World-Wide* III. I. 92 Lines of interest and research..have converged in the attention currently being paid to ESP. **1955** *Jrnl. Chem. Physics* XXIII. 2441/2 The other two dichloro compounds each give a pair of additional *ESR lines. **1972** R. A. JACKSON *Mechanism* iv. 53 Spectroscopic techniques, particularly n.m.r., e.s.r., u.v., and mass spectroscopy may be used to provide evidence for intermediates. **1976** *Ann. Rev. Microbiol.* XXX. 458 The molecular environments within cell membranes have been studied with the use of..electron spin resonance (ESR). **1961** *Engineering* 21 July 71/1 In the scientific field there would be close cooperation with the proposed European Space Research Organization (*E.S.R.O.). **1968** *Times* 19 Nov. 6/8 Britain is not getting value for money from the European Space Research Organization (Esro). **1937** *Printers Ink Monthly* Apr. 53/1 *EST, a term used by NBC to denote Eastern Standard Time. **1966** *Punch* 4 May 658/2 The National Broadcasting Company found a sponsor willing to put the British General Election up on prime time (9.30 EST to be precise). **1957** S. H. KRAINES *Mental Depressions* xvi. 456 Many names are given to this technique and its modifications: electric shock therapy (*E.S.T.), shock therapy (S.T.), electrocoma (E.C.), electric treatments (E.T.), electroconvulsive therapy (E.C.T.), [etc.]. *Ibid.*, In the Manic-Depressive Illness, E.S.T. has proved to be of value in shortening the illness. **1969** L. L'ABATE in C. M. Franks *Behavior Therapy* III. xiv. 480 More concrete mediators in general psychiatric practice would be drugs, EST, and allied ancillary practices. **1957** T. STURGEON *Thunder & Roses* 189 The xenologists and *e-t mineralogists who were crazy enough to work out there. **1982** *Nature* 23 Sept. 377/1 A pop-eyed, stick-figured ET.. looks out from the cover of *The Biology of Human Conduct*. **1983** *Ibid.* 27 Jan. 291/1 (*heading*) Can honeycomb weathering be ET? **1939** *Flight* 26 Oct. 335/1 A quickly estimated *E.T.A., too, will narrow down the area of search if the next outstanding landmark fails to turn up. **1958** 'N. SHUTE' *Rainbow & Rose* vi. 231 E.T.A. is seven-fifteen. **1963** *Times* 12 Jan. 6/5 All are said to be members of a movement known as *E.T.A., which stands for Euzkadi ta Azkatasuna (Basque country and liberty). **1973** *Times* 18 Jan. 1/2 ETA..sources in Biarritz said they could not say what would happen to the industrialist. **1980** *Guardian Weekly* 16 Mar. 10 In an election which seems to have been fair, both the Basque extremist organisation ETA and the Spanish national police kept off the streets. **1939** *Jrnl. R. Aeronaut. Soc.* XLIII. 85 Three hours before the *E.T.D. of the aircraft. **1965** *Newsweek* 14 June 30/3 White climbed into a new 'extravehicular activity' (*EVA) suit. **1969** *Daily Tel.* 24 Feb. 21/3 In connection with the space-walk, Schweikart who 'will go Eva' (extra-vehicular activity) said 'I am looking forward to it'.

e, obs. form of HE; obs. Sc. form of EYE.

e-, *prefix*[1], ME. *ē-*:—OE. *ǣ-*, accented form of *a-*. See A- *pref.* 1 and Æ- *pref.*

e-, *prefix*[2], occas. variant of Y-. *Obs.*

e-, *prefix*[3], L. *ē-*, shortened form of *ex-*, out of, occurring in words ad. or f. L., as *emit, evacuate*; see EX-.

ea ('iːə). *dial.* [repr. OE. *éa*, ME. *Æ sb.*[1] river.] A river, running water. Still in use in Lanc.; in the fen-country applied to the canals for drainage, in which sense it is usually spelt *eau* [as if a. F. *eau* water]. Also *attrib.* See also AA[1].

[*c* **1000** ÆLFRIC *Gen.* ii. 14 Seo feorðe ea ys ȝehaten Eufrates.] **1781** J. HUTTON *Tour to Caves* Gloss. (E.D.S.) *Ea*, a river along the sands on the sea shore. **1861** SMILES *Lives Engineers* I. 63 They..surveyed the new eaus and sluices..after which they returned to Ely. **1865** KINGSLEY *Herew.* xx, They rowed away for Crowland, by many a mere and many an ea. **1875** *Whitby Gloss.* (E.D.S.), *Ea-coorse*, or Eau-course, the water-channel.

each (iːtʃ), *a.* (quasi-*pron.*) Forms: *α.* 1 ǽlc, œ́lc, 2–3 ælc, ælch, 3 alc, alch, 1–2 elc, 2–3 elch, (2 helch, 3 elhc), 2 ach(e, (ec), 3 æche, 3–6 ech(e, 5–6 eich, eyche, eache, 6– each. *β.* 1 ylc, 3–4 ilc, (3 il), 3–5 ilk(e, (3 *Orm.* illc, illk), 6– *Sc.* (see ILK). *γ.* 2 ulch, 3–4 ilch(e, 5 ylche, 2, 4–5 uch(e, 4–6 ich(e, 5–6 ych(e. *δ.* 1 ȝehwilc, -hwelc, -hwylc, 2 iwilch (iwil, iwi), iwulc(h, uwilch, (uwlch, uwil), (3 *Orm.* iwhillc), 4 uich. *ε.* 1 ǽȝ- (œ́ȝ-, éȝ-)hwilc, -hwelc, -hwylc, -wylc, 2 aiȝhwilc, ewilch, eilc, 3 ewc (*accus.* eulne), 2–4 euch. [The historical forms inseparable from this word represent three distinct but nearly synonymous words in OE.

1. OE. *ǽlc*, app. = OFris. *ellîk, elk, êk*, Du. *elk*, OHG. *eogilîh* (MHG. *iegelîh*, mod.G. *jeglich*):—WGer. phrase **aiwo(n galîko-z*, corresp. to OE. *á ȝelíc* (see A *adv.*, AY, and ALIKE). The phrase may perhaps best be explained as evolved from the adverbial **aiwo(n galîkô* 'ever alike', = the frequent OHG. *eogilîcho*. In OE. (as in OFris. and Du.) the second word seems to have lost the prefix *ȝe-*, and the *i* of **á-líc*, **álic*, produced the umlaut in the first syllable. (See, however, 3 below.) The OE. *ǽlc* with long vowel is perhaps the ancestor of our modern form; but already in the OE. period the vowel was dialectally shortened, and appears as *ælc, elc*, and *ylc*. The two former gave rise to such ME. forms as *alc(h, ache, elch*; the OE. *ylc* seems to be recorded only in the (Mercian) Vesp. Psalter, but must have been widely diffused, as it became in southern ME. *ulch* (*ü*), *ilch*, in west midland *uch* (*ü*), *ich*, and in east midland and north. ILK, which still survives in north. dial. and in Sc. (In *Havelok* the form *ilc, ilk* is occas. reduced to *il* before a cons.)

2. OE. *ȝehwilc* = OHG. *gihwelîh* (see Y- and WHICH). This is the source of early ME. *iwilch, iwulch*, probably also of *uwilch, uich*; it is possible also that the 14–15th c. *uch(e* may be from this source instead of being a continuation of the earlier *uch* (*ü*) from OE. *ylc*. (Layamon writes *iwildel, iwidel* for *iwilc del*; similarly the Lambeth Homilies have *uwil* before cons., and accus. *uwilne*.)

3. OE. *ǽȝ-* (*œ́ȝ-, éȝ-*)*hwilc* = OHG. *eogihwelîh*, f. WGer. **aiwo(n*, OE. *á, ó*, AY, always + **gahwalîko-z* = OE. *ȝehwilc* (see above). (The umlaut is supposed to be due to the *i* in *ȝi-*, earlier form of the prefix *ȝe-*.) This word seems to be represented in ME. by the forms *ewilc* (*eulne* for **eulcne* accus. occurs once in Layamon), *euych, eilc, ewc, euch*; the forms *eich, eyche*, in 15–16th c. may possibly in some cases belong to this series rather than to *a*, to which they are referred above.]

A. Illustration of Forms.

α. *c* **825** *Vesp. Psalter* civ. 35 And sloȝ oelc frumbearn. *c* **1000** *Ags. Gosp.* Matt. vii. 17 Ælc god treow byrð gode wæstmas. *c* **1175** *Lamb. Hom.* 13 Ic eou wulle werien wið elcne herm. *Ibid.* 75 Ec of heom wrat..his uers. *c* **1175** *Cott. Hom.* 217 þenche ȝie ælc word of him swete. *c* **1200** *Trin. Coll. Hom.* 29 Elch pine of helle is fremed on þre fold wise. *Ibid.* 31 Ðus deuel eggeð ælch man on his herte. *Ibid.* 91 Elhc cristene man makeð þis dai..processio. *Ibid.* 99 Eches mannes soule. *Ibid.* 145 Hie clensede heo seluen of ache synne. *c* **1205** LAY. 13113 Wende æche oðer þat hit weoren heore broðer. *Ibid.* 14850 Habbe alc god mon his rihte. *Ibid.* 29056 We þe wulleð ȝelden sixti hundred punden to alches ȝeres firsten. *c* **1430** *Syr Gener.* xxxiii, And eache a Prince bryng his semble. *a* **1500** *MS. Sloane* No. 1986 f. 30 in *Dom. Archit.* III. 69 In halle make fyre at eyche a mele. *a* **1500** *Miracle Plays* (1838) 17 Leeve you not this eich one? **1570** B. GOOGE *Pop. Kingd.* 52 Eche heart was then peruersely

bent. *a* **1580** *Ld. Vaux* in Farr's *S.P.* 303 Why doest thou put thy trust In things eiche made of clay. **1593** HOOKER *Eccl. Pol.* I. ii. (1611) 3 That which doth assigne vnto each thing the kinde.

β. *c* **825** *Vesp. Psalter* lxxvii[i]. 51 And sloȝ ylc frumbearn on eorðan. *c* **1250** *Gen. & Ex.* 119 Ilk gres, ilc wurt, ilc birðhel tre. *a* **1300** *Havelok* 1740 Il man to þer he cam fro. *Ibid.* 2112 Of his mouth it com il del. **1340** HAMPOLE *Pr. Consc.* 584 Þus foul with-in ilk man es. *c* **1430** *Syr Tryam.* 1511 At ylke stroke the fyre owt braste.

γ. *c* **1175** *Lamb. Hom.* 65 Ulche dei. *a* **1200** *Moral Ode* 90 in *Cott. Hom.* 165 Uches monnes þonc. *c* **1200** *Trin. Coll. Hom.* 181 Ilch man of his wise noteð his swinch. **1307** *Elegy Edw. I*, xi, In uch bataille thou hadest pris. *c* **1330** *Arth. & Merl.* 3666 Ich of hem wel noble was. *c* **1340** *Cursor M.* 35 (Trin.) Vche fruyt, þat men may fynde. *c* **1380** WYCLIF *Sel. Wks.* III. 431 Ilche man þat is ordeyned of God to be dampned. *c* **1400** *Destr. Troy* 4046 Now wete yche wegh. *c* **1450** MYRC 416 Vche dayes bred. **1538** STARKEY *England* I. ii. §3 (1871) 29 Ychone in hym selfe. *Ibid.* 38 Loue euery man iche other.

δ. *c* **825** *Vesp. Psalter* xiv. 9 Ðæghwelce dæg æcera þusend. *c* **1000** *Ags. Gosp.* ... *c* **825** *Vesp. Psalter* xi[i]. 2 Ða idlan spreocende is anra ȝehwelc to ðæm nestan. *c* **1175** *Lamb. Hom.* 11 Halden from uwilche swinke. *Ibid.* 13 Uwil mon. *Ibid.* 17 God..hauet ihaten uwilne..mon. *Ibid.* 121 Seh ut on iwulche half. *Ibid.* 133 Wið iwilche cristene monne þe he to sendeð his halie iwriten. *c* **1200** ORMIN 10784 Iwhillc man. *c* **1205** LAY. 25664 Þat lond iwelde iwidel. *Ibid.* 25880 He þe awalt iwildel. *c* **1275** *Luve Ron* 125 in *O.E. Misc.* 97 Þarinne is vich balewes bote. —— *Pains of Hell* 151 *ibid.* 151 And heore ineward uych del..Eft heo werpeþ al in al.

ε. *a* **1000** *Metr. Boeth.* xiv. 9 Æȝhwelce dæȝ æcera þusend. *c* **1000** *Ags. Gosp.* Matt. vi. 34 Æȝhwylc [*c* **1160** *Hatton G.* aiȝhwilc] dæȝ hæfð ȝenoh on hys aȝenum ymbhoȝan. *c* **1175** *Lamb. Hom.* 17 Þet þu beode eilcmon al swa þu waldest þet me dude þe. *Ibid.* 93 Ewilcum of þan wurhtan. *c* **1205** LAY. 596 Þe king..heihte eulne mon. *a* **1225** *Leg. Kath.* 1231 On euch [*Cotton MS.* ewc] wise in þe world. *a* **1240** *Lofsong* in *Cott. Hom.* 205 On euche half abuten.

B. Signification and uses.

I. As adj. used *attrib.*

1. Every (individual of a number) regarded or treated separately.

The early use of *each* corresponded closely to the mod. use of its compound EVERY (= *ever each*), the only difference being that it has always been possible to use *each* when only two things are referred to. Thus a sentence with a sing. subject preceded by *each* would (formerly) have been but slightly if at all altered in meaning by the substitution of a plural subject preceded by *all*. In modern usage *each* has assumed the sense of the Lat. *quisque*, and implies a distribution of the predicate or object parallel with the distribution of the subject (or conversely). An exception to this rule results from the fact that we cannot use *every* when only two persons or things are spoken of, so that in this case *each* retains its original extended use.

a. followed immediately by a sb. (In OE. sometimes pl.; afterwards always sing.)

c **1000** *Sax. Leechd.* I. 310 Ælce wunde hyt ȝehæleþ. *a* **1123** *O.E. Chron.* an. 1101 Rotb't ælce ȝeare sceolde..þreo þusend marc habban. *c* **1250** *Gen. & Ex.* 581 Ilc wateres springe here strengðe undede. *c* **1350** *Will. Palerne* 1488 Uch wiȝh þat it wist. *c* **1380** WYCLIF *Serm.* lxxxvii. Sel. Wks. I. 301 Ebreus clepen ech water a see. *c* **1420** *Sir Amadace* l, Iche mon in thayre degre. **1482** *Marg. Paston's Will* in *Lett.* 861 III. 283, I wulle that ich houshold being my tenaunt there have vjd. **1598** J. DICKENSON *Greene in Conc.* (1878) 153 The bodyes each-sickenesse may be expelled by choyce of symples. **1664** EVELYN *Kal. Hort.* (1729) 187 Gard'ners had need each Star as well to know..as Sea-men. **1742** YOUNG *Nt. Th.* II. 286 Each night we die, Each morn are born anew. **1820** KEATS *Lamia* 572 Before each lucid panel fuming stood A censer. **1874** MORLEY *Compromise* (1886) 123 Each citizen of the latter is an incorporated member of the former.

†**b.** with *a* or *an* (*one*) before the sb. (= mod. *each, every*). *Obs.* (For Sc. examples see ILKA.)

c **1175** *Lamb. Hom.* 87 Þet heo sculden offrien of elchan hiwscipe gode an lomb. *c* **1200** ORMIN 5726 Illc an unnclene lusst. *a* **1300** *E.E. Psalter* lxxxviii[ix]. 13 In ilka land. *c* **1350** *Will. Palerne* 511 Vch a burn of þis world worschipeþ him one. **1393** LANGL. *P. Pl.* C. XXIII. 19 He dronk of eche a diche. **1432** *Test. Ebor.* II. (1855) 22, I wite to ilka prest.. iiiijd. *c* **1456** *Tourn. Tottenham* 112 in *Percy Reliq.*, In ycha stede ther thay me se.

c. with *one* used absol. (often distributing a pl. subject or object; cf. 4). In mod. use generally superseded by *every one*, or by *each* absol. For Sc. examples see ILKANE.

971 *Blickl. Hom.* 127 Æt æȝhwylcum anum þara hongaþ leohtfæt. *c* **1200** ORMIN 503 Þatt illc an shollde witenn wel. *a* **1225** *Leg. Kath.* 57 Euchan bi his euene. *c* **1250** *Gen. & Ex.* 1379 Him and ilc-on his kamel Wið watres drinc ghe quemede wel. **1330** R. BRUNNE *Chron.* 165 With þo ladies ilkone. *c* **1340** *Gaw. & Gr. Knt.* 96 Leue vchon oþer. **1420** *E.E. Wills* (1882) 52, I will þat ilkon off þe other thre ordirs ..haue x marc. **1513** DOUGLAS *Æneis* VII. vi. 55 The fader of goddis ichone. **1513** BRADSHAW *St. Werburge* (1848) 113 She ..kyssed them ycheon. **1535** COVERDALE *Isa.* xiii. 14 Euery man shal turne to his owne people, & fle echone. **1631** T. POWELL *Tom All Trades* 153 Every each one respectively.

d. Phrases. *on* (†*in*) *each side*, †*on each a side*: (now usually = *on both sides*; formerly also = *on every side*). In same sense, †*on, in each half*. *each day*: †used *attrib.* and in genitive case in sense 'every day', as applied to clothing, etc. †*each other*..: = *every other* (i.e. every alternate)... †*each a deal*, †*each deal*: every whit. †*each kins*: of every kind, every kind of; the northern form appears in one word as ILKIN. *each way*: a betting term denoting that a horse, etc., has been backed for both a win and a place; also *attrib.* and *transf.*

1375 BARBOUR *Bruce* XVI. 367 The..lord of dowglass ay Had spyis out on ilka syde. *c* **1420** *Chron. Vilod.* 724 Wepyng and sorwyng in yche a syde. **1551** TURNER *Herbal* D vj a, It groweth..of iche syde of the hygh way.

c **1205** LAY. 14745 Bruttes..heom to-holden in æchere halue. *a* **1225** *Leg. Kath.* 19 On euch half [= on every side]. **1422** *Will of Clanbowe* (Som. Ho.) Myn echedaies gowne. **1748** RICHARDSON *Clarissa* (1811) VI. 363 It ended in a compromise for a fee each other time.

a **1300** *Cursor M.* 1364 Had vnderstanden wele..ilk [*F.* ilka] dele. *c* **1325** *Chron. Eng.* in Ritson *Metr. Rom.* II. 303 The traitour uchadel Sende hit to Denemarke. *c* **1400** *St. Alexius* (Vern.) 334 Rædde hit siþen vchadel. *c* **1440** *Generydes* 697 His thought was sett oon hir yche deell.

a **1250** *Prov. Alfred* 384 in *O.E. Misc.* 126 Uyches cunnes madmes. *c* **1250** *Gen. & Ex.* 220 Ilc kinnes beste.

1869 *Cassell's Mag.* IV. 170/2 One pound on Blue Gown each way. **1897** E. H. COOPER *Mr. Blake* vi, I'll just go and put a little bit on Highborn for this race..; only fifty pounds or so each way. **1926** [see BRADBURY]. **1929** *Star* 21 Aug. 16/2, I should think he may be a good each-way bet. **1930** *Daily Mail* 17 June 14/2 Sun Glory..has a useful each-way chance. **1951** E. RICKMAN *Come racing with Me* x. 84 A very small bet 'each way'. **1963** *Times* 15 Feb. 11/4 Why should Britain back the 625 line horse to win when we can place an each-way bet on the dual standard?

e. *ever each*: original form of EVERY, q.v.

†**2.** After *without* (*buton*): = ANY. Cf. ALL A. 4.

c **897** K. ÆLFRED *Gregory's Past.* xl. 288 Butan ælcum eȝe. *c* **1175** *Cott. Hom.* 227 Acenned of þe feder on hefene buton elcer moder. *c* **1300** *Beket* 480 Withoute ech delay.

II. Absol. (quasi-*pron.*)

3. With reference to a sb. going before, or followed by *of*. Sometimes incorrectly with pl. vb.

a **1000** *Cædmon's Gen.* 1521 (Gr.) Ælc hine selfa begrindeþ gastes dugeðum. *c* **1330** [see A. γ]. *c* **1386** CHAUCER *Monkes T.* 163 He..maked ech of hem to been his thral. **1588** J. UDALL *Demonstr. Discip.* (Arb.) 50 If God do vsually bestow doctrine and exhortation vpon seuerall persons, wherein eche is found to excell. **1678** R. BARCLAY *Apol. Quakers* xi. §7. 354 Each made it their work to retire inwardly to the Measure of Grace in themselves. **1739** CHESTERF. *Lett.* I. xxv. 93 Each of these verses have five feet. **1782** COWPER *Gilpin* 213 All and each that pass'd that way Did join in the pursuit. **1837** J. H. NEWMAN *Par. Serm.* (ed. 2) III. xxii. 354 Each has his own place marked out for him. **1871** MORLEY *Voltaire* (1886) 3 Each did much to..purify the spiritual self-respect of mankind.

4. a. Distributing a plural subj. or obj. So ***equal each to each***, said in Geometry of corresponding parts.

c **1000** *Ags. Gosp.* Matt. xx. 9 Þa onfengon hiȝ ælc his pening. *c* **1400** *Beryn* 83 Lo! howe the clowdis worchyn, eche to mete his mach. *c* **1510** MORE *Picus* Wks. (1557) 9/1 Eche of them after their deseruing. **1572** MASCALL *Govt. Cattle, Horses* (1627) 151 Turmerick, long Pepper, graines of Bay-berries, of ech a halfe peny worth. **1697** DRYDEN *Virg. Georg.* IV. 258 Studious of Honey, each in his Degree. **1790** BURKE *Fr. Rev.* 19 His majesty's heirs and successors, each in his time and order. **1840** LARDNER *Geom.* 164 The component plates..being equal..each to each in magnitude. **1848** MACAULAY *Hist. Eng.* I. 309 The lords of the bed-chamber [had] a thousand a year each.

†**b.** *Each* (uninflected) has been occas. used to distribute a pron. in genit. pl.

1615 CHAPMAN *Odyss.* XII. 149 Two rocks..whose each strength binds The boist'rous waves in from the high-flown winds. **1704** ROWE *Ulyss.* II. i. 944 The massie Goblets.. Whose each capacious Womb..Portended witless Mirth.

c. Often with reference to price; = *apiece*.

Mod. They cost sixpence each. I paid sixpence each for them.

5. *each other*: used as a reciprocal pronoun in acc., dat., or genit. case; = *one another*.

Originally this was a phrase construed as in 4, *each* being the subject, and *other* (inflected in OE. *óðerne, óðres, óðrum*, etc.) being governed in acc., genit., or dat. by a verb, prep., or sb. This use still occurs arch. or poet. (*each to other*, etc.). The words have however long become a compound (cf. Du. *elkander*), so that we can say *to each other, of each other*, etc. To use the word as a nom. ('We know what each other are doing') is a vulgarism occasionally heard.

a **1000** *Battle of Maldon* 234 Us is eallum þearf ðæt ure æȝhwylc oðerne bylde. *c* **1200** *Trin. Coll. Hom.* 149 Þat we sholden biwepen ure elch oðres sinne. **1258** *Proclam. Hen. III* in Stubbs *Sel. Chart.* 388 Þæt æhc oþer helpe þæt for to done. **1398** TREVISA *Barth. De P.R.* v. xxix. (1495) 140 Foules that lyue by blode ete not eche other. **1480** CAXTON *Chron. Eng.* ccxxiii. 222 Thousandes fell to the grounde eche vp other. **1485** MALORY *Arthur* II. vi, We wil helpe eche other. **1523** LD. BERNERS *Froiss.* I. cxi. 133 [He] saluted them eche after other. **1538** STARKEY *England* I. 2 Ych one to the profyt of other. **1594** T. B. *La Primaud. Fr. Acad.* II. 338 Helping eche other so farre as wee may. **1615** WADSWORTH in Bedell *Lett.* (1624) 7 How these two could be..members..participant each of other. **1647** CLARENDON *Hist. Reb.* I. (1702) I. 37 Justled each the other too much. **1667** MILTON *P.L.* IV. 682 Responsive each to others note. **1709** STEELE *Tatler* No. 47 ¶2 These Two Lovers seem'd.. made for each other. **1816** J. WILSON *City of Plague* II. iii. 11 That we may see each other's faces. **1821** KEATS *Isabel* xxi, Each unconfines His bitter thoughts to other. **1828** SCOTT *F.M. Perth* II. 24 To defy each other to mortal combat.

C. Combinations.

Certain phrases beginning with *each* were formerly written as single words (cf. *everybody*): as *each a dele* (*ilkadel, uchadel*), *each day's* (*echedaies*, cf. Sc. *ilkaday*), *each man* (*eilcmon, eacheman*), *each one* (*echone, ichone*, ILKANE); see examples under A, B. See also ILKIN.

each, var. f. ECHE *v. Obs.*

†**'each-'where.** *Obs.* [f. EACH + WHERE.] Everywhere, in every part, on every side.

c **1430** *Cursor M.* 13981 (Trin.) Iesus preched vche where. *a* **1541** WYATT *Poet. Wks.* (1861) 50 Each where where man doth live. **1553** *Short Catech.* in *Liturgies, etc. Edw. VI* (1844) 507 His Godhead is in such sort eachwhere, that it filleth both heaven and earth. *a* **1649** DRUMM. OF HAWTH. *Poems* Wks. (1711) 43 From dark sepulchres each where.

†**'eadi**, *a. Obs.* Forms: 1 éadiȝ, 2–4 eadi, 2–3 ædi, ædiȝ, edi, eddi. [Com. Teut.: OE. *éadiȝ* = OSax. *ôdag*, OHG. *ôtag*, ON. *auðigr*, wealthy, happy, Goth. *audags* happy, f. OTeut. **auðo-m, auðo-z* riches + *-go-*; see -Y.]

1. Rich, wealthy, luxurious.

a **1000** *Crist* 1497 (Bosw.) Earm ic wæs..ðæt ðu wurde eadiȝ. *c* **1175** *Lamb. Hom.* 115 Þet he mid wohȝe ne ofsitte ne ermne ne eadine. *a* **1200** *Moral Ode* 227 in *Lamb. Hom.* 173 Understondeð nu to me edi [*other MSS.* eadi, edye, ædi] men and arme. *c* **1205** LAY. 2361 An eorð-hus eadi & feier.

2. Happy, fortunate, well-omened. Also, Blessed, saintly; said of persons and their actions.

c **825** *Vesp. Psalter* cxviii. (cxix.) 1 Eadȝe unwemme in weȝe. *a* **1000** *Guthlac* (Gr.) 147 Siððan biorȝ ȝestæh Eadiȝ oretta. *c* **1175** *Lamb. Hom.* 47 Ædie and blessede beon alle þeo þe ihereð godes weordes and heom athaldeð. *a* **1225** *Ancr. R.* 142 Heo holden hire up mid hore lif holinesse, ant mid hore eadie bonen. *c* **1250** *Gen. & Ex.* 2086 'Me wore leuere,' quad Ioseph, 'Of eddi dremes rechen swep.' *c* **1315** SHOREHAM 129 The eadi levedy [*i.e.* the Blessed Virgin].

Hence †**ædiȝleȝȝc** (Orm.) [see -LOCK], happiness, prosperity. †**eadily** *adv.*, in a blessed or fortunate manner. †**eadiness**, happiness, prosperity; blessedness.

a **1000** *Beowulf* (Gr.) 100 Swa þa driht-guman dreamum lifdon eadiȝlice. *c* **1200** *Trin. Coll. Hom.* 33 Þe fulle edinesse of paradis. *c* **1200** ORMIN 5706 Þe sexte seollþess ædiȝleȝȝc. *a* **1225** *Ancr. R.* 328 Edmodnesse eadiliche bigileð ure Louerd. *a* **1240** *Ureisun* in *Cott. Hom.* 189 Þu hauest þin edinesse, and ti muchele heh-schipe.

eadish, obs. form of EDDISH.

eadmede, -mod, var. ff. EDMEDE, *Obs.*, humility, EDMOD *a.*, humble.

†**'eadness.** *Obs.* Forms: 1 eadnis, 2 ednesse. [OE. *éadnis*, f. *éad* wealth = OHG. *ôt, ôd*, ON. *auðr*:—OTeut. **auðo-m, auðo-z*; see -NESS. (The OE. *éad* adj. wealthy is of doubtful genuineness.) Cf. EADI, EADINESS.] Happiness, luxury.

a **1000** *Runic Poems* (Gr.) 4 Os byð..eorla ȝehwam eadnis and tohyht. *c* **1200** *Trin. Coll. Hom.* 75 Ednesse letteð þe mannes shrifte.

eager, var. form of EAGRE, tidal wave.

eager ('iːgə(r)), *a.* Forms: 3–7 egre, 4–5 egor, egyr, 4–6 egir, 5 eegre, 5–6 aygre, 6 eigre, eygre, eger, egar, aeygre, 7 ægre, 6– eager. [a. OF. *aigre* sharp, keen, sour:—L. *acre-m* acc. of *acer* sharp, pungent, swift, strenuous.

(Senses 1, 2, 4, 5 are taken from Fr.; 6 seems a specially Eng. development.)]

I. Of material things or physical conditions.

†**1. a.** Pungent, acrid, keen to the taste or other senses. Of medicines: Sharp or violent in operation. Of diseases: Acute, severe. *Obs.*

c **1374** CHAUCER *Boeth.* (1868) I. v. 25 A more myȝty and more egre medicine. **1544** PHAËR *Regim. Lyfe* (1546) I j, Those diseases are excedynge egre, sharp and almost importable of peyne. **1574** NEWTON *Health Mag.* 14 To mingle..sweete and toothsome with sower and eigre. *c* **1600** SHAKS. *Sonn.* cxviii, To make our appetites more keene With eager compounds we our pallat vrge. **1601** HOLLAND *Pliny* XIX. v, Of all this bulbous kind, the Sea-onyon is reputed chiefe..there is not any more ægre and biting than it.

b. Said of cold (after quot. 1602).

1602 SHAKS. *Ham.* I. iv. 2 It is a nipping and an eager ayre. **1854** J. KENNEDY *Swallow B.* (1860) 100 Imparted an eager chilliness to the atmosphere. **1884** STEVENSON *New Arab. Nts.* 180 The eager air of the seaside.

†**c.** *fig.* Of words: Biting, keen. *Obs.*

c **1386** CHAUCER *Melibeus'* ¶212 Thou shalt rather..flee fro the sweete wordes of flaterynge preiseres than fro the egre wordes of thy freend. **1593** SHAKS. *3 Hen. VI*, II. vi. 68 Vex him with eager Words. —— *Rich. II*, I. i. 49 The bitter clamour of two eager tongues.

†**2.** *spec.* Sour, acid, tart. *Obs.* [So Fr. *aigre.*]

c **1350** *Med. MS.* in *Archæol.* XXX. 352 Eysyl or egyr wyn. *c* **1460–70** *Bk. Quintessence* 4 Corrupt wiyn, þat is, rotyn, but not egre. **1575** *Art of Planting* 39 The wylde and eager Cherry tree. **1602** SHAKS. *Ham.* I. v. 69 It doth posset And curd like Aygre droppings into Milke. *a* **1717** PARNELL *Hermit* 39 Bread of the coursest sort, with eager wine. **1727** BRADLEY *Fam. Dict.* I. s.v. *Brewing*, It was hard to brew Drink which would be fine before it was eager.

3. †**a.** Of a cutting instrument: Sharp (*obs. rare.*) **b.** *techn.* Of certain tools: 'Biting' keenly.

c **1611** CHAPMAN *Iliad* x. 150 The eager razor's edge. **1831** J. HOLLAND *Manuf. Metals* II. 139 [The tool represented in the figure] is what the artisan calls an eager tool, and is used for roughing the work; it has a..semicircular edge, so formed as to bite keenly.

†**4.** Of metals: Imperfectly tempered, brittle. *Obs.* [So Fr. *aigre*, opposed to *doux.*]

1580 NORTH *Plutarch* 378 The Iron Coyn of Sparta..was so eager and brittle by means of this temper, that, etc. **1690** LOCKE *Hum. Und.* III. vi. §35 Gold will be sometimes so eager..that it will as little endure the Hammer as Glass itself. **1763–6** W. LEWIS in *Phil. Trans.* XCIII. 78 *note*, Iron or steel..render gold hard and eager.

II. Of living beings or their attributes.

†5. a. Strenuous, ardent, impetuous; fierce, angry. Said of persons, their actions and attributes. *Obs.*

1297 R. GLOUC. 80 þis Britones were so egre..þat þo Romaynes and here kyng gonne fle atte laste. c1380 *Sir Ferumb.* 144 Roland answerede wyþ egre mod. c1400 *Destr. Troy* 5445 Ymasus, yrfull, egor of wille. 1475 *Bk. Noblesse*, Cruell and egre werre. 1485 MALORY *Arthur* I. xiv (1817) With an egyr countenaunce. 1513 DOUGLAS *Æneis* IX. xi. 28 Egyr of thar wyllis. 1555 *Fardle Facions* Pref. 17 Echone contendeth with eigre mode and bitter dispute. 1610 HOLLAND *Camden's Brit.* II. 137 His most ægre enemy. 1667 *Decay Chr. Piety* x. §1. 298 Glut the eagerest malice. 1733 CHEYNE *Eng. Malady* II. viii. §7 (1734) 201 When the Conflict..is very hot, brisk, and eager, we all agree to call it a Fever.

†b. Of beasts and birds of prey: Fierce, savage. Also *transf. Obs.*

c1386 CHAUCER *Clerkes T.* 1143 Egre as is a Tygre. 1530 PALSGR. 311/1 Egar, fierce..as a wyld beest is. 1583 STANYHURST *Æneis* I. (Arb.) 21 The southwynd mercilés eager.

6. a. Of persons: Full of keen desire or appetite; impatiently longing to do or obtain something. Const. *inf.*; *after*, *for*, †*of* (the thing desired); *about*, *in*, † *upon* (a task, matter, or concern). Also of desires or appetites: Intense, impatient. **eager beaver** [BEAVER[1] (cf. 1 d)]: a glutton for work; an over-zealous or officious person; also *attrib.* and *transf.* (*colloq.*, orig. *U.S.*).

c1400 *Destr. Troy* 3753 Menelay the mighty was.. Auntrus in armys, eger of wer. 1561 NORTON & SACKV. *Gorboduc* 1008 After bloud so eigre were thy thirst. 1596 SPENSER *F.Q.* I. viii. 6 Eger greedinesse. 1647 CLARENDON *Hist. Reb.* I. I. 40 He..found others to be less eager in the pursuit of his Friendship. 1695 BLACKMORE *Pr. Arth.* IX. 432 Eager of fame, and of the promis'd Prize. 1719 DE FOE *Crusoe* (1840) I. 319 The Captain was so eager..that he could hardly have Patience to let him come so near as to be sure of him. 1732 LAW *Serious C.* xii. (ed 2) 189 He is eager upon it. 1751 JOHNSON *Rambl.* No. 153 ¶5 Eager of any intelligence that might increase it. 1759 ROBERTSON *Hist. Scot.* I. II. 133 She had become acquainted with the eager and impatient temper of the nation. 1769 —— *Chas. V*, III. VII. 2 He was eager for war. 1793 BURKE *Corr.* (1844) IV. 177, I am not now so eager about your coming to town as I was. 1796 MORSE *Amer. Geog.* I. 291 The enemy..being eager in plundering the baggage of the dead. 1836 THIRLWALL *Greece* III. xix. 106 They are..eager for foreign expeditions. 1849 RUSKIN *Sev. Lamps* v. §10. 146 How much of imperfection..the eyes of those eager builders could endure. 1883 *Manch. Exam.* 26 Nov. 4/2 Makers are not eager to book fresh orders. 1943 *Daily Nebraskan* 7 Nov., Eager Beaver, anyone who has the slightest conception of what physics is all about. 1947 *Sat. Even. Post* 16 Aug. 122/1 Before photostating my application, some eager beaver..helpfully typed the address. 1948 *Time* 5 July 1/1 It would be futile to play that game against Republican Earl Warren, one of the foremost spokesmen of the eager-beaver West. 1958 E. DUNDY *Dud Avocado* I. i. 11 The Eager-Beaver-Culture-Vulture with the list ten yards long, who *just* manages to get it all crossed off before she collapses of aesthetic indigestion each night. 1959 *Observer* 24 May 27/8 The British pack were like a set of eager beavers. 1959 *Spectator* 29 May 753/1 Well-meaning state social workers ..and eager-beaver politicos lavish with praise and perquisites, are not helping him.

b. Of actions, gestures, looks, etc.: Characterized by or manifesting alacrity or impatient desire.

Phrases like *eager conflict*, *pursuit*, originally belonged rather to 5, but modern feeling connects them with this sense.

1697 DRYDEN *Virg. Georg.* II. 645 Early Visitants, With eager Eyes devouring..The breathing Figures of Corinthian Brass. 1732 BERKELEY *Alciphr.* ii. §16 Wks. 1871 II. 84 Those gentlemen who are called men of pleasure, from their eager pursuit of it. 1853 ROBERTSON *Serm.* Ser. III. xi. (1876) 131 An epistle abounding with the most earnest and eager controversy. 1866 G. MACDONALD *Ann. Q. Neighb.* xiii. (1878) 253 The unconsciously eager way in which he looked at the eatables. 1873 BUCKLE *Civilis.* viii. 457 Eager in upholding rights of kings.

†7. *spec.* Hungry (? orig. techn. in *Falconry*). Of the eyes: Hungry-looking. *Obs.*

1486 *Bk. St. Albans* Cvj, The hawke will be very eegre and gleetous of the seekeness. 1575 TURBERV. *Bk. Falconrie* 160 When your falcons be skoured and cleane so as beyng sharp set they may be called hungrie hawkes, or as faulconers tearme them eagre hawkes. 1693 W. ROBERTSON *Phraseol. Gen.* 516 Eager or sharp set, i.e. hungry. 1712 STEELE *Spect.* No. 266 ¶2 Her eyes were wan and eager. 1766 ANSTEY *Bath Guide* v. 75 Your Frenchman so eager, With all his Soup Meagre.

III. *Comb.*, as ***eager-eyed***, ***-hearted***, ***-looking*** adjs.; also †**eager-dulce**, **-sweet** *a.*, acid and sweet. [Cf. AIGRE-DOUX, AGRODOLCE.]

1820 KEATS *Eve St. Agnes* iv, The carved angels, ever eager-eyed. 1805 WORDSW. *Incid. Favourite Dog* 11 Every dog is eager-hearted. 1825 *Bro. Jonathan* II. 77 His eager-looking red eyes. 1548 UDALL *Erasm. Par. Luke* 3 a, The eagredulce sauce of the paraphrase. *Ibid.* Pref. 5 b, If with vinegre it be made eagredulce. *Ibid.* 3 Eagredulce. 1616 SURFL. & MARKH. *Countr. Farm* 416 As concerning Ciders ..the eager sweet are much better..than the harsh sweet.

†'**eager**, *v. Obs.* Also 4-5 egren. [ad. OF. *aigrier*, *aigroier*; cf. prec.] *trans.* To excite, irritate, provoke; in quot. 1581 to irritate physically; also *refl.* to become exasperated.

c1374 CHAUCER *Boeth.* (1868) IV. vi. 141 þe nature of som man is so..vncouenable þat..pouerte..myȝte raþer egren hym to done felonies. c1400 *Destr. Troy* 7329 He angurt hym full euyll, & egerd hym with. 1581 MULCASTER *Positions* xvi. (1887) 77 They that be gawled or byled within, may neither runne nor wrastle, for eagering the inward.

eagerly ('iːgəlɪ), *adv.* [f. EAGER *a.* + -LY[2].]

†1. Sharply, pungently, keenly; violently, harshly, severely. *Obs.*

1377 LANGL. *P. Pl.* B. XIX. 376 þanne welled water for wikked werkes, Egerlich ernynge out of mennes eyen. c1450 *Knt. de la Tour* (1868) 82 The more the synne is abhominable the egerlyer thei be tempted bi the deuelle. 1480 CAXTON *Ovid's Met.* XI. xxi, I am more aigrely tempested, than he was wyth the floodes of the see. 1553 BALE *Vocacyon* in *Harl. Misc.* (Malh.) I. 341 Within ii dayes after was I sick agayn, so egerly, etc. 1603 KNOLLES *Hist. Turks* (1621) 650 Raine, which frose so eagerly..that it seemed the depth of Winter had..been come in.

†b. *to bear eagerly* [tr. *acide ferre*, Vulg.; cf. also Lat. *ægre ferre*, which may have been sometimes confused]: to take amiss, be grieved at. *Obs.*

1382 WYCLIF *Ecclus.* iv. 9 Egreli or heuyly bere thou not in thi soule. 1491 CAXTON *Vitas Patr.* (W. de W.) I. xxxv. (1495) 29 a/1, Whyche thynge..Cypryan bare aygrely. 1598 CHAPMAN *Iliad* I. 99 Agamemnon rose, eagerly bearing all.

†2. Angrily, fiercely, bitterly, malignantly. *Obs.*

1377 LANGL. *P. Pl.* B. XVI. 64 Egrelich he loked on me. c1450 LONELICH *Grail* xxxvii. 698 A lyown that loked ful egerlye. 1609 B. JONSON *Sil. Wom.* II. ii. 81 Him she loves most, she will seeme to hate eagerliest.

3. Impetuously, swiftly. (Now only in phrases like *eagerly pursuing*, which approach sense 4).

1330 R. BRUNNE *Chron.* 39 To þe cite þei went egrely, & did þo kynges fle. 1375 BARBOUR *Bruce* VI. 427 Douglas.. full egirly Assalit. c1450 *Merlin* x. 158 He..rode a-gein hym full egerly. 1613 SHAKS. *Hen. VIII*, III. ii. 240 How eagerly ye follow my disgraces. 1655 EARL ORRERY *Parthen.* (1676) 23 Who were eagerly pursuing the Parthians.

4. In an eager manner; with impatient desire, promptitude, or alacrity.

1601 SHAKS. *Jul. C.* v. iii. 7 Brutus..hauing some aduantage on Octauius, Tooke it too eagerly. 1719 DE FOE *Crusoe* (1840) II. viii. 184 Eagerly hungry. 1781 GIBBON *Decl. & F.* III. 114 The oath of fidelity was eagerly taken by every order of the state. 1855 MACAULAY *Hist. Eng.* III. 546 An unprincipled minister eagerly accepted the services of these mercenaries. 1867 SMILES *Huguenots Eng.* x. (1880) 156 Thanksgivings..in which the people eagerly took part.

eagerness ('iːgənɪs). [f. EAGER *a.* + -NESS.] The state or quality of being EAGER.

†1. a. Pungency of taste. b. Acidity, sourness.

1490 ARNOLDE *Chron.* (1811) 112 Alle maner auenturs.. of alle the sayd wynes, lecage forth and egirnesse of the same oonly excepte. 1558 WARDE tr. *Alexis' Secr.* (1568) 106 a, Sugre for to moderate the eygrenesse of the Alome. 1601 HOLLAND *Pliny* XIX. viii, Senvie..stewed in some convenient liquor, in such sort, as a man shal not.. complaine of any eagernesse that it hath. 1713 *Lond. & Country Brew.* II. (1743) 104 By..Boiling, the Wort is.. more able to resist Eagerness and Putrefaction.

†2. Acerbity, bitterness, irritability. *Obs.*

1475 *Bk. Noblesse* 4 Ire, egrenesse, and feersnesse is holden for a vertu in the lion. 1571 GOLDING *Calvin on Ps.* xviii. I. 56 Saul had persecuted him with greater furie and egrenesse than all the rest. 1624 BEDELL *Lett.* ii. 47 This eagrenesse is not mutuall.

†3. Of metals: Defective temper, brittleness.

1622 MALYNES *Anc. Law-Merch.* 289 It taketh away the eagrenesse of Brasse.

4. Keenness, swiftness.

1831 J. HOLLAND *Manuf. Metals* I. 290 These stones [grindstones for cutlery] are of a peculiar grit, and cut with great eagerness.

†5. Impetuosity, fierceness. *Obs.*

c1400 *Melayne* 915 Aftir armours he askede tytte, For egernesse he loughe. 1485 MALORY *Arthur* I. xv (1817) They were so couragyous that many Knyghtes shoke..for egrenes. 1665 MANLEY *Grotius' Low-C. Warrs* 417 Nor the Sea it self, can put a stop to their [bears'] eagerness. 1678 EARL MURRAY in *Lauderdale Pap.* (1885) III. lxxx. 131 The Kinge..becaem paell and he shouke withe eagernes.

6. Keenness of appetite or desire; impatient haste to do or obtain something. Const. *of*, *for*, or *inf.*

1486 *Bk. St. Albans* A vij b, Mony an hawke for egernesse when he shulde nomme a fowle he seesith bot the federis. 1589 PUTTENHAM *Eng. Poesie* (1869) 239 Industrie is a liuely and vnweried search and occupation in honest things, egernesse is an appetite in base and small matters. 1665 BOYLE *Occas. Refl.* (1675) 69 We..find not..that Satisfaction..that the Eagerness of our unruly Appetites promises us. 1697 DRYDEN *Virg. Georg.* Ded., An eagerness of Learning more. 1741 RICHARDSON *Pamela* I. 18 'What say'st thou my Girl?' said he, with some Eagerness. 1870 BRYANT *Homer* I. VI. 184 Let no man through eagerness for spoil Linger behind the rest.

eagle ('iːg(ə)l), *sb.* Forms: 4-7 egle, 5 egylle, 6 aegle, 6-7 ægle, 6- eagle; also 4-5 a negle, neggle. [ME. *egle*, a. OF. *egle*, *aigle* = Pr. *aigla*, It. *aquila*, Sp., Pg. *aguila*:—L. *aquila*.]

1. a. The name commonly given to any of the larger Diurnal Birds-of-prey which are not Vultures; though some birds are accounted Eagles by ornithologists which are smaller than certain Buzzards. Two species of Eagle are natives of Britain; the Golden Eagle (*Aquila chrysaëtus*), almost confined in these islands to the mountainous parts of Scotland and Ireland; and the Sea, or White-tailed Eagle (*Haliaëtus albicilla*) found on the coasts of the same countries. Much resembling the latter is the Bald or White-headed Eagle (*H. leucocephalus*), the emblematic bird of the United States of America. Freq. in U.S. allusive use, esp. as a symbol of liberty or freedom.

The strength, keen vision, graceful and powerful flight of the eagle are proverbial, and have given to him the title of the king of birds.

c1380 WYCLIF *Serm.* xxx. Sel. Wks. II. 110 Lyke to a fleynge egle. 1382 —— *Jer.* iv. 13 Swiftere than eglis his hors. c1475 *Voc.* in Wr-Wülcker 701 *Hec aquila*, a negylle. *Ibid.* 761 A egyle. 1535 COVERDALE *Obad.* 4 Though thou wentest vp as hye as the Aegle. 1606 HOLLAND *Sueton.* 81 An Ægle snatched a peece of bread out of his hand. 1607 SHAKS. *Timon* IV. iii. 224 These moyst Trees, That haue out-liu'd the Eagle. 1766 PENNANT *Zool.* (1768) I. 123 Eagles are remarkable for their longevity. 1798 T. G. FESSENDEN *Orig. Poems* (1806) 4 The Eagle of Freedom with rapture behold, Overshadow our land with his plumage of gold! 1862 LOWELL *Poet. Wks.* (1879) 391/2 Ninety miles off as the eagle flies. 1865 *Trans. Ill. Agric. Soc.* 1861-2 V. 203 The clang of mighty forges, fashioning out the sinews of war, to guard the eagle of liberty. 1872 'MARK TWAIN' *Speeches* (1910) 415 You won't mind a body bragging a little about his country on the Fourth of July. It is a fair and legitimate time to fly the eagle. 1878 BROWNING *La Saisiaz* 25 Can I make my eye an eagle's? 1904 *N.Y. Even. Post* 14 Sept. 1 Mr. Fassett was toying with those dear but haggard phrases.. and generally making the eagle scream. 1942 R. G. LILLARD *Desert Challenge* 194 He introduced the orator of the day.. and for a while the eagle screamed.

b. with prefixed word defining the species.

1688 I. CLAYTON in *Phil. Trans.* XVII. 989 The largest I take to be that they call the Grey Eagle. 1790 PENNANT *Tour in Scotl.* II. 24 Sea Eagles breed in ruined towers, but quit the country in winter; the black eagles continue there the whole year. 1803 *Pic Nic* No. 6 (1806) I. 224 The fierce bald-eagle, tyrant of thy native woods. 1865 GOULD *Birds of Australia* I. 9 The natural disposition of the Wedge-tailed Eagle leads it to frequent the interior portion of the country.

c. *fig.* (often with allusion to 2 a, b.)

1611 SHAKS. *Cymb.* v. v. 473 Our princely Eagle Th' Imperiall Caesar. 1664 MARVELL *Corr.* Wks. 1872-5 II. 126 Those two Sonnes of the Russian Eagle. 1821 SHELLEY *Hellas* 47 Russia's famish'd eagles Dare not to prey beneath the crescent's light. 1847 TENNYSON *Princ.* IV. 64 Hope, a poising eagle. 1893 *Congress Rec.* 16 Oct. 2561/2 The grand old man, known as the Bald Eagle of Rhode Island rose to reply.

d. *Golf.* A score of two under bogey or par.

1922 C. LEITCH *Golf* xii. 202 Barnes..holed his putt for a 3, so securing what is known in American golfing parlance as an 'eagle'. 1926 WODEHOUSE *Heart of Goof* iv. 135 When he had got that 'eagle' on the third, he had looked bored. 1927 *Observer* 3 Apr. 29/1 [He] let loose a whole flock of 'birdies' and 'eagles' with which he captured the remainder of the holes. 1928 *Daily Express* 9 July 17/7 He accomplished an 'eagle' two for the 351 yards. 1966 WODEHOUSE *Plum Pie* ii. 66 It was on the fourth green, after he had done an eagle, that he spoke again.

2. A figure of the bird used for any purpose: a. as an ensign in the Roman army, and as an ensign and badge in the French army under the empire.

?a1400 *Morte Arth.* 360 Hys egle to touche, þat borne es in his banere. 1601 HOLLAND *Pliny* I. 273 Caius Marius.. ordained, that the legions..should haue the Egle for their standard. 1720 OZELL *Vertot's Rom. Rep.* II. XI. 161 Cinna flatter'd Valerius..that Sylla's Soldiers..would soon desert to his Eagles. 1812 WELLINGTON *Disp.* 21, 24 July in *Examiner* 24 Aug. 535/2 The Eagles and Colours taken from the enemy. 1815 J. W. CROKER in *Papers* (1884) I. iii. 73 The broken eagles which the French soldiers wore on the fronts of their caps. 1862 MERIVALE *Rom. Emp.* (1865) IV. xxxviii. 348 Their eagles were retained as trophies.

b. as an armorial bearing; *esp.* of the Holy Roman Empire, and of the various modern empires, as the Austrian, French, German, and Russian. Also as the badge of an order of knighthood.

c1386 CHAUCER *Monkes T.* 393 The feeld of snow, with thegle of blak ther-Inne. 1705 *Lond. Gaz.* No. 4182/1 A new Order of Knighthood, called the Order of the White Eagle. 1707 *Ibid.* No. 4354/2 Knight of the Order of the Prussian Eagle. 1845 S. AUSTIN tr. *Ranke's Hist. Ref.* I. I. 149 The.. cities..which bear the imperial eagle in their arms.

c. as the sign (or appellation) of an inn.

1556 *Chron. Gr. Friars* (1852) 75 At the syne of the Eggylle.

d. *U.S.* = *eagle button* (10).

1789 W. MACLAY *Deb. Senate* (1880) 97 The Cincinnati had seats allotted for themselves—worn their eagles at their button-holes. 1812 *Niles' Weekly Reg.* II. 131/1 Cockades and eagles..have been bought and made.

e. *U.S. Mil.* A device worn on the shoulder, indicating the rank of a colonel.

1861 *Army Regulations* (U.S.) 485 Shoulder-Straps.. For a Colonel—..a silver-embroidered spread eagle on the centre of the strap. 1865 L. N. BOUDRYE *Fifth N.Y. Cavalry* 184 Col. Hull..was killed. He was a gallant young officer, who had but recently borne the eagle.

3. Applied to certain objects made in the form of an eagle; such as a brass (or wooden) lectern in a church; the ampulla containing the anointing oil used at coronations; a clasp for a belt, etc.

1766 ENTICK *London* IV. 213 The reader's desk is an inclosure..in which is a..brass pillar supporting an eagle. 1820 A. TAYLOR *Glory of Regal.* 61 A spoon into which the oil is poured from the beak of the eagle. 1836 PARKER *Gloss. Archit.* I. 287 A common form for brass lecterns..is that of an eagle..with wings expanded to receive the book. 1842 TENNYSON *Godiva* 43 She..Unclasp'd the wedded eagles of her belt. 1852 THACKERAY *Esmond* II. vi, Mr. Tusher..read from the eagle.

4. The asterism *Aquila*, one of the northern constellations. †*eagle-star*, Altair or α Aquilæ.

1551 RECORDE *Cast. Knowl.* 264 Towarde the southe, is the Egle, includynge 9 starres. **1601** HOLLAND *Pliny* II. 522 From the Egle-star. **1868** LOCKYER *Heavens* (ed. 3) 329 In the west appears Altair, in the Eagle.

5. A coin bearing the image of the bird; *spec.* a coin of base metal current in England at the accession of Edward I; a gold coin of the United States, value ten dollars. ***double-eagle***: a U.S. coin worth twenty dollars.

[*c* **1350** W. HEMINGBURGH *Chronicon* (1849) II. 187 Monetas..pessimi metalli, pollardorum, crocardorum.. aquilarum, etc.] **1753** CHAMBERS *Cycl. Supp.* s.v., He.. decry'd the use of these Eagles, and other the like kinds of base coin. **1786** in *Amer. Museum* (1789) II. 182 There shall be two gold coins; one..to be stamped with the impression of the American eagle, and to be called an eagle. **1789** *Gazette of U.S.* (N.Y.) 14 July (Th.), The Eagle containing 10 dollars of 50d. is worth 2 guineas, and rather more. **1809** T. G. FESSENDEN *Pills Poetical* 16 Were eagles, in embargo times, As plentiful as cents and dimes. **1816** *Niles' Weekly Reg.* IX. 370/2 The president tendered several eagles in gold to cover the costs. *a* **1850** ROSSETTI *Dante & Circ.* I. (1874) 209 Quite a glut of eagle-pieces. **1854** M. J. HOLMES *Tempest & Sunshine* xiii. 84 At the same time managing to slip an eagle into the hands of the honest clerk. **1860** BARTLETT *Dict. Amer.* s.v., There are also double-eagles of twenty dollars, as well as half and quarter-eagles. **1905** T. DIXON *Clansman* 139 A beggar asked him for a night's lodging, and he tossed him a gold eagle.

6. *sea eagle*: †**a.** properly the White-tailed Eagle (*Haliaëtus albicilla*), which older writers confounded with the Osprey or so-called Fishing Eagle. Pennant, *Brit. Zool.* (1766) 140, refers to Sibbald as having applied this name to the Skua.

1766 PENNANT *Brit. Zool.* 63.

b. a species of Skate, *Myliobates marginata*. [So Fr. *aigle de mer*; see quot.]

1847 CARPENTER *Zool.* §584 The Myliobates receives its common name of Sea-eagle from having the pectoral fins of extreme breadth, so that it much resembles a bird of prey with its wings expanded.

†**7.** *Arch.* The gable of a house; the pediment of a temple. [transl. L. *aquila*, Gr. ἀετός, ἀέτωμα.]

1682 WHELER *Journ. Greece* v. 360 The Figures of the Front, which the Antients called the Eagle. *Ibid.* 388 On the highest point of the Eagle is a broad Stone laid. **1751** CHAMBERS *Cycl.* s.v.

†**8.** *Cant.* 'The winning Gamester' (*New Cant. Dict.* 1725). *Obs.*

9. *Angling.* A kind of artificial fly.

1867 F. FRANCIS *Angling* x. (1880) 360 There are two Eagles, the grey and yellow.

10. *Comb.* **a.** attrib., as *eagle-bark, -claw, -eye, -flight, -height, -plume, -plumage, -radiance, -speed, -spirit, -standard*; **b.** objective, as *eagle-baffling* adj., *-bearer*; **c.** parasynthetic deriv., as *eagle-billed, -pinioned, -sighted, -winged* adjs.; *eagle-like* adj. and adv. Also **eagle button**, a button bearing the device of an eagle, **eagle-cock**, a weather-cock; **eagle-fisher**, the Osprey; †**eagle-flower**, the Balsam (*Impatiens Balsamina*); **eagle-ray, -skate** (= sense 6 b); †**eagle-wit**, a person of penetrating intellect. Also EAGLE-EYED, -HAWK, -OWL, -STONE.

1821 SHELLEY *Prometh. Unb.* I. i. 20 This wall of *eagle-baffling mountain. **1875** BROWNING *Aristoph. Apol.* Aiskhulos' bronze-throat *eagle-bark at blood. **1658** ROWLAND *Moufet's Theat. Ins.* 939 The mouth forked and *Eagle-bill'd. **1897** J. L. ALLEN *Choir Invis.* ii. 15 As he joined them, three other young men—Federalists—sauntered past, wearing black cockades, with an *eagle button on the left side. **1883** *Fisheries Exhib. Catal.* 195 *Eagle-claw trap. **1667** E. CHAMBERLAYNE *St. Gt. Brit.* I. III. x. (1743) 213 On it was a Cross..and on that an *Eagle-cock of Copper gilt. [**1603** CHETTLE, etc. *Patient Grissil* (1841) 12 Women have *eagle's eyes To pry even to the heart.] **1819** J. Q. ADAMS in C. Davies *Metr. Syst.* III. (1871) 120 The eagle eyes of informers. **1855** LONGF. *Hiaw.* x. 145 Hiawatha ..hardly touched his *eagle-feathers As he entered at the doorway. **1849** C. ST. JOHN *Tour Suthld.* I. 24 A shepherd told us of a nest of the *Eagle Fisher. **1851** GALLENGA tr. *Mariotti's Italy* 337 *Eagle-flight of genius was out of the question with him. **1741** *Compl. Fam.-Piece* II. iii. 386 Trees and Shrubs which are now in Flower, as..Genistella, *Eagle Flower. **1786** CHAMBERS *Cycl.* (ed. Rees) s.v. *Balsamine*, The other [species] is from China..most commonly called the immortal eagle-flower. **1884** TENNYSON *Becket* 29 At such an *eagle-height I stand. *a* **1600** J. BRYAN *Ps.* cxxvii. in Farr's *S.P.* 335 *Eagle-like his fame shall mount. *a* **1626** R. HARRIS *Hezekiah's Recov.* (1630) 29 Good men will bless God for an eagle-like body. **1800** BURNS *Wks.* III. 301 Dangers, *eagle-pinioned, bold, Soar around each cliffy hold. **1811** SCOTT *Roderick* 28 Morena's *eagle-plume adorned his crest. **1813** SCOTT *Trierm.* II. ix, *Eagle-plumage deck'd her hair. **1717** FENTON *Poems* 160 (Jod.) The nectar'd sweets supply *Eagle-radiance to the faded eye. **1856** GOSSE *Marine Zool.* II. 151 Myliobatis (Cuv.) *Eagle Ray. Head projecting; pectorals extended like wings. **1588** SHAKS. *L.L.L.* IV. iii. 226 What peremptory *Eagle-sighted eye Dares looke? **1637** HEYWOOD *Roy. Kings* I. i. Wks. 1874 VI. 7, I was borne Eagle-sighted, and to gaze In the Suns fore-head. **1641** J. JACKSON *True Evang. T.* II. 113 S. John having written his Eagle-sighted Gospel. **1882** *St. James's Gaz.* 15 Mar. 6/1 The formidable sting-ray, *eagle-skate, or *thère*. **1725** POPE *Odyss.* I. 413 Abrupt, with *eagle-speed she cut the sky. **1817** BYRON *Lament Tasso* 2 *Eagle-spirit of a child of song. **1811** SCOTT *Roderick* 42 On *eagle-standards and on arms he gazed. **1593** SHAKS. *Rich. II*, I. iii. 129 The *eagle-winged pride Of sky-aspiring and ambitious thoughts. **1675** J. SMITH *Chr. Relig. Appeal* II. 12 The Eagle-wing'd Evangelist. **1864** PUSEY *Lect. Daniel* iii. 112 The eagle-winged lion of Daniel. **1665** GLANVILL *Sceps. Sci.* xx, 129 Aristotle would have fainted before he had flown half so far, as that *Eagle-wit [Descartes].

eagle (ˈiːg(ə)l), *v. nonce-wd.* [f. the sb.] *intr.* To fly as an eagle. Also, *to eagle it.*

1652 BENLOWES *Theoph. To my fancy, &c.*, Eagling 'bove transitory Sphears. **1868** R. BUCHANAN *Wallace* I. ii, Thou'dst play the eagle in thy borrowed plumage; Whose are the feathers wherewith thou wouldst eagle it?

†ˈ**eagled**, *ppl. a. Obs. or nonce-wd.* [f. EAGLE *sb.* + -ED².] **a.** Furnished with the image of an eagle; having an eagle or eagles. **b.** Resembling an eagle in form or action; eagle-like.

1618 BOLTON *Florus* (1636) 296 Hee carried upon his own shoulders the Eagled Ensigne into the Camp. **1660** WATERHOUSE *Arms & Arm.* 115 Souldiers haue the start of Scholars in their Eagled strength.

ˈ**eagle-ˌeyed**, *a.* [see EAGLE 10 c.] Having an eye like an eagle; keen-sighted. *lit.* and *fig.*

1601 BP. BARLOW *Eagle & Body* (1609) E iv a, Faith, being Eagle eyed, can..see the maiestie of God. **1625** HART *Anat. Ur.* II. iii. 65 The most eagle-eyed Physitian. *a* **1703** BURKITT *On N.T.* John viii. 11 It is a false zeal that is eagle-eyed abroad, and blind at home. **1800** WEEMS *Washington* v. (1877) 35 The eagle-eyed friendship of Mr. Waller quickly discovered him.

eagle-ˈhawk. **1.** Transl. of Fr. *aigle-autour*, Cuvier's name for a South American bird of prey of the genus *Morphnus*, called *Spizaëtus* by Vieillot.

The name is found in Griffith's transl. (1829) of Cuvier's *Règne Animal*, but never came into English use.

2. An Australian bird of prey, *Uroaëtus audax*.

1827 in J. Bischoff *Van Diemen's Land* (1832) 177 The eagle-hawk pouncing upon them for his prey. **1848** J. GOULD *Birds of Australia* I. pl. 1 *Aquila Fucosa*..Wedge-tailed Eagle. Eagle Hawk, Colonists of New South Wales. *a* **1882** H. C. KENDALL *Poems* (1886) 159 The fierce-featured eagle-hawk flies—afraid as a dove is afraid. **1911** C. E. W. BEAN *'Dreadnought' of Darling* xii. 105 A big black eagle-hawk. **1965** H. FRAUCA *Bk. Austral. Wild Life* 93 Some cattlemen..suggested that the local wedgetails be classified as vermin because they were scratching the cattle. One cattleman said that two of his cows had been 'badly scratched by them eagle-hawks'.

ˈ**eagle-ˌowl.** A nocturnal bird of prey (*Bubo ignavus*), the largest of the Owl tribe inhabiting Europe.

1678 RAY *Willughby's Ornith.* 99 The great Horn-Owl or Eagle-Owl. **1766** PENNANT *Zool.* 71 The great eagle owl has once been shot in Yorkshire. **1849** KNOX *Ornith. Rambles* 186 There has been for many years a magnificent living collection of Eagle owls at Arundel Castle.

ˈ**eagleship.** *nonce-wd.* [f. EAGLE *sb.* + -SHIP.] The position or dignity of an eagle.

1748 RICHARDSON *Clarissa* (1811) IV. 24, I always illustrated my eagleship, by aiming at the noblest quarries.

†ˈ**eagless.** *Obs. rare*⁻⁰. [ad. OF. *aiglesse*.] A female eagle.

1611 COTGR., *Aiglesse*, an Eaglesse; a henne Eagle.

ˈ**eagle-ˈstone.** [See AETITES, and quot. 1601.] = AETITES.

c **1440** *Bone Flor.* 390 An egyll and a charbokull stone. **1601** HOLLAND *Pliny* II. 590 The Ægle-stones called Aëtites ..it is said that..without them the Ægles cannot hatch. **1686** *Lond. Gaz.* No. 2126/4 An Eagle Stone, tied up in a piece of black Ribon..lost the 29th Instant. **1753** CHAMBERS *Cycl. Supp.* s.v. *Ætites*, The finest and most valued of all the eagle-stones, are accidental states of one or other of our common pebbles. **1796** MORSE *Amer. Geog.* II. 16 Norway produces crystals..thunder stones, and eagle-stones. **1879** *Syd. Soc. Lex.* s.v. *Aetites*, The eagle-stone; a stone, hollow and containing another substance within it; the..shell of clay-iron stone; the..nucleus, of variable composition.

eaglet (ˈiːglɪt). Also 7 **eglet.** [a. Fr. *aiglette*, dim. of *aigle* EAGLE; see -ET¹.] **a.** A young eagle.

1572 BOSSEWELL *Armorie* II. 68 b, This birde Ossifraga.. bryngeth vp the Eaglet so cast out. **1628** WITHER *Brit. Rememb.* v. 1660 When Eglets are first taught to flye. **1795** SOUTHEY *Joan of Arc* x. 377 Went like eaglets to the prey. **1832** TENNYSON *Œnone* 208 The callow eaglet.

b. as a charge in heraldry.

1611 GUILLIM *Heraldry* III. xvii. 158 On a bend gules, three Eaglets displaied. **1864** BOUTELL *Heraldry Hist. & Pop.* xiv. §1 (ed. 3) 158 The well-known Shield of Piers de Gaveston..vert, six eaglets or.

ˈ**eagle-wood.** Also 8 **agal-wood.** [transl. F. *bois d'aigle*, Pg. *pao d'aguila*, a perversion of Malayālam *ayil*, or some other vernacular form of Skr. *aguru* (Yule). Cf. AGALLOCH.]

Another name for AGALLOCH or CALAMBAC, q.v.

[**1516** BARBOSA (Lisbon) 393 (Y.) Aguila, cada Farazola de 300 a 400 (fanams)]. **1712** tr. *Pomet's Hist. Drugs* I. 59 The Portuguese call it Eagle-wood. **1774** NIEBUHR *Des. de l'Arabie* xxxiv. (Y.) Un bois nommé par les Anglois Agal-wood, et par les Indiens de Bombay Agar. **1854** HOOKER *Himal. Jrnls.* (1855) II. 318 (Y.) The eagle-wood..is much sought for its fragrant wood. **1864** *Sat. Rev.* 9 July 67 Trees containing the eagle-wood, resins, and dye-woods. **1871** ALABASTER *Wheel of Law* 86 A second [palace] of nine stories, constructed entirely of eagle-wood.

†ˈ**eaglify**, *v. Obs.* [f. EAGLE + -FY.] *trans.* To make into an eagle or like an eagle.

1592 WARNER *Alb. Eng.* VII. xxxvii, Had the Sunne been up..(such pride bewitch'd my wit To Egel-fie my selfe) I had assayed to soar to it. **1628** WITHER *Brit. Rememb.* v. 1595 The Kites that flye Above the clouds, themselves to Eaglifie.

†ˈ**eagly**, *a. Obs. rare*⁻¹. [f. EAGLE + -Y¹.] Eagle-like, aquiline.

1624 SANDERSON *Serm.* I. 222 The sharpest and most eagly eye.

eagre (ˈeɪgə(r), ˈiːgə(r)). Forms: α. (2, 8 **higra**), 7 **higre**, 7- **hygre, hyger.** β. (? 6,) 7 **agar**, (9 *dial.* **ager**), 7-9 **eagre**, 8 **eger, egre**, (9 **ægir, ægre**, *pseudo-arch.* **eygre**), 7- **eager, eagre.** [Of unknown etymology. The conjecture which connects it with the OE. *éagor, égor*, occurring in comb., app. with sense 'flood, ocean', is untenable, because the OE. ȝ in such a position would have become *y* in mod.E. Nor can it be a. ON. *ægir* ocean, sea-god, as the inflexional *-r* would in that case have disappeared.

The identity of *eagre* with *higre* (latinized as *higra* by William of Malmesbury) seems clear from the sense, but is difficult to account for phonologically. The usual pronunc. in the neighbourhood of the Humber and Trent is (ˈeɪgə(r)); the 17th (? 16th) c. spelling *agar* seems to be a phonetic rendering of this or its antecedent. The Dicts. give (ˈiːgə(r)). Identity with ACKER is not clearly indicated by the sense, and is very doubtful.]

A tidal wave of unusual height, caused by the rushing of the tide up a narrowing estuary; = BORE *sb.*³ Chiefly with reference to the Humber (and Trent) and the Severn.

α. [*c* **1125** WILL. OF MALMESB. *Gest. Pontific* (Rolls) 292 [The Bore on the Severn] Nautæ certe gnari, cum vident illam Higram (sic enim Anglici vocant) venire, navem obvertunt, et per medium secantes violentiam ejus eludunt.] **1612** DRAYTON *Poly-olb.* vii. 101 With whose tumultuous waues Shut up in narrower bounds, the Higre wildly raues. **1623** J. TAYLOR (Water P.) *Wherry-Ferry Voy.* Wks. II. 11/1 The Flood..hath lesse mercy then Beare, Wolfe or Tyger, And..it is called the Hyger. **1704** STEELE *Lying Lover*, Such a Roll of the Tides as the Sailors corruptly call the Higre, instead of the Eager. **1817** STARK *Hist. Gainsburgh* (1843) 522 A curious phenomenon is observed in the Trent called the Eagre or Hygre.

β. [**1592** LYLY *Gallathea* I. i, [The scene is beside the Humber] Neptune..sendeth a Monster called the *Agar*, against whose comming the waters rose, the fowles flie away, etc.] **1647** SPRIGGE *Anglia Rediv.* (1854) 76 A sudden surprisal of the tide called Eager. **1646** SIR T. BROWNE *Pseud. Ep.* (1650) 312 Those Agars and impetuous flows. **1685** DRYDEN *Threnodia August.* iv, His manly heart..like an eagre rode in triumph oer the tide. **1759** JOHNSON *Idler* No. 49 ⁋ 12 He forded rivers where the current roared like the Egre of the Severn. **1851** SIR F. PALGRAVE *Norm. & Eng.* I. 323 The Eager or Eau-guerre, so remarkable in the mouth of the Severn. **1862** DANA *Man. Geol.* 653 In the eagre of the Amazon, the whole tide passes up the stream in five or six waves..each twelve to fifteen feet high. **1863** JEAN INGELOW *High Tide* Lindis..at the eygre's breast Flung uppe her weltering walls. **1870** E. PEACOCK *Ralf. Skirl.* II. 87 He would..get on a pink and go up wi' th'ager.

eahte, obs. form of AUGHT, property.

eaise, obs. form of EASE.

eal, obs. form of AWL.

eald, obs. form of ELD, OLD.

ealdor, ealdor-, WS. ff. of ALDOR, ALDOR-.

ealdren, obs. and dial. form of ELDER.

eam, variant of EME, *Obs.*, uncle.

eam, obs. form of *am*: see BE *v.*

Eames (iːmz). The name of Charles *Eames* (1907–78), U.S. architect and designer, used *attrib.* in ***Eames chair*** to designate a chair designed by Eames, or in the functional style popularized by him, esp. one made of moulded plastic or plywood and used in modern office furniture.

1946 *Mag. of Art* May 180 The Eames' chair shows an adjustment of the four legs so that a leg extends to the rear and front. **1949** *Interiors* July 99/2 What sets the Eames chair apart is that it is a total design package, integrating new techniques with modern art forms into a unified design. **1952** 'E. BOX' *Death in Fifth Position* iv. 107 He sat down in an Eames chair. **1964** *Time* 20 Mar. 97/2 A novel by Vienna's Heimito von Doderer is rather like an Eames chair draped with an antimacassar. **1978** *Jrnl. R. Soc. Arts* CXXVI. 767/2 The moulded plywood Eames chairs, which were innovatory and sold throughout the world.

ean, *v.* Forms: 1 **éanian**, 4 **enen, enye(n**, 5 **enyn**, 6 **eane, eyne**, 7- **ean.** (*Pa. pple.* 4 **eindyd.**) [OE. *éanian* = Du. dial. *oonen* of same meaning; Prof. Sievers considers the OTeut. type to be **aunôjan*, f. **aw-jâ* EWE.

The current identification with OE. *éacnian* to bring forth does not account for the specialized sense, and the supposed loss of the *c* lacks analogy.]

trans. Of ewes: To bring forth lambs, to yean. Also *intr.* See YEAN.

a **1000** *Lamb. Ps.* lxxvii[i]. 70 (Bosw.) He ȝenam hine of eowedum sceapa, fram eaniȝendum he ȝenam hine. **1387** TREVISA *Higden* (Rolls) IV. 451 An hoyffer..enyed a lomb.

1398 —— *Barth. De P.R.* XVIII. iv. (1495) 757 Lambes whyche ben eindyd in spryngyng tyme. **1440** *Promp. Parv.* 140 Enyn, *feto*. **1555** EDEN *Decades W. Ind.* (Arb.) 329 A lambe newly eyned. **1580** NORTH *Plutarch* 582 An Ewe that had eaned a Lamb. *c* **1640** J. SMYTH *Lives Berkeleys* (1883) I. 243 Eaned and nursed up such a couple of twins as the kingdome..could not parralell. **1750** W. ELLIS *Mod. Husbandm.* IV. i. 115 (E.D.S.) When the ewe has lately eaned. **1864** in WEBSTER. **1965** *Times* 18 Feb. 14/6 The.. ewes who were due to ean..were driven down..to the fold.

Hence **'eaned** *ppl. a.*, born (of lambs); **'eaning** *vbl. sb.*, the action of bearing lambs; also *attrib.*, as in ***eaning-mood***, ***-time***; **'eanling**, a young lamb.

1596 SHAKS. *Merch. V* I. iii. 80 All the eanelings which were streakt and pied. **1599** *Broughton's Lett.* vii. 24 Your selfe-conceiuing phantasie, being euer in the eaning mood. **1661** LOVELL *Hist. Anim. & Min.* 88 Salt is to be given to them after eaning. **1637** B. JONSON *Sad Sheph.* I. iv. (1640) 134 And both [ewes and rams] do feed, As either promised to increase your breed At eaning-time. **1639** G. DANIEL *Ecclus.* xlvi. 47 When he the Ean-ling offer'd. *a* **1648** —— *Eclog.* v. 57 Dire, as y Smiting Haile to new-ean'd Lambs.

-ean, *suffix*. Var. of -AN, after L. *-aeus*, *-eus*, orig. representing *-e-* (in names ending in *-(a)ea*, *-es*, *-eus*) + -AN, as *antipodean*, *crustacean*, *European*, *Herculean*, *Linn(a)ean*, *Promethean*; also added to names in *-as*, *-os*, *-us* after Gr. *-eios*, *-aios*, as *Pythagorean*, *Sisyphean*, *Theocritean*, etc.

eani, obs. f. ANY.

ear (ɪə(r)), *sb.*[1] Forms: 1-2 éare, 3-6 ere, (3 ire, 4 ȝhere, er, erre, 5 heer, here, 6 heare) 4-6 eere, yere, 5 eire, 6-7 eare, 6- ear. *Pl.* **ears**; also 1-2 earan, 1 earo, -u, 2-4 earen, 4 eeren, eren, (heren, ern). [Common Teut.: OE. *éare* wk. neut. = OFris. *âre*, OS. *ôre*, *ôra* (MDu. *ōre*, *oore*, Du. *oor*), OHG. *ôra* (MHG. *ôre*, mod.G. *ohr*), ON. *eyra* (Sw. *öra*, Da. *öre*), Goth. *ausô*:—OTeut. *('auson-), *au'zon-*, cogn. with L. *auris* (:—**ausis*), Gr. *οὖς*, Lith. *ausis*, OSlav. *ucho*, OIr. *ó*, of same meaning.]

I. The organ of hearing in men and animals. Anatomists distinguish (1) The ***external ear***, consisting of the pinna (the portion which projects outside the head) and the meatus or passage leading thence to (2) the ***middle ear***, or tympanum, a cavity in the substance of the temporal bone, separated from the external meatus by a membrane called the ***membrana tympani***; (3) the ***internal ear***, or labyrinth, which is a complex cavity hollowed out of the bone. In popular language *ear* is often used for the external ear or the pinna alone.

1. a. The external ear.

a **1000** *Riddles* lxxxviii. 3 (Gr.) Wiht..hæfde an eaȝe and earan twa. *a* **1300** *Cursor M.* 18836 His hare..Bi his eres skailand sumdele. *c* **1386** CHAUCER *Prol.* 556 Reed as the brustles of a sowes erys. **1556** *Chron. Gr. Friars* (1852) 79 Vij gentylmen of Kent sett on the pyllery..and one of eche of ther erys cut of. **1562** J. HEYWOOD *Prov. & Epigr.* (1867) 43 Hir eares might well glow, For all the towne talkt of hir. **1661** LOVELL *Hist. Anim. & Min.* Introd., The eares..are divided..in the hart, and pilous in the rat. **1746** W. THOMPSON *R.N. Advoc.* (1757) 34 They would not have let their Ears appear quite so long, had they suspected, etc. *c* **1750** J. NEWTON *Jrnl.* (1836) 64 Some of them said that their ears burned on their heads to hear me speak to such a man. **1832** TENNYSON *Miller's Dau.* xxii, I would be the jewel That trembles in her ear.

b. With certain defining words: a particular shape or appearance of the ear. ***button ear***: in dogs, an ear falling in front, and hiding the inside. ***rose ear***: one folding at the back and disclosing the inside. ***asylum ear***, ***insane ear***: a disease of the ear common among the insane in asylums.

c. Phrases. ***about one's ears***: said of a shower of blows or missiles, a conflagration, a falling house; also *fig.* ***on one's ear***, drunk. ***over*** (***head and***) ***ears***, ***up to the ears***: *fig.* deeply immersed *in*. ***dry behind*** (occas. in the U.S. ***back of***) ***the ears***, adult, experienced, mature; also, ***wet behind the ears***, immature, naïve. ***to prick*** (***up***) ***one's ears***: as a horse when full of animation; *fig.* of persons, to assume an attitude of expectant attention. †***to hang one's ears***: to be cowed, discouraged. ***to have***, ***hold***, ***take by the ears***: to keep or obtain a secure hold upon (a person); so also, ***to pull or drag by the ears***, i.e. violently, roughly; ***to lead by the ears***: to keep in abject dependence. †***to pull one by the ear*** [? after L. *vellere auriculam*]: *fig.* to compel one's attention. ***to have*** (or ***keep***) ***one's ear(s) to the ground***, (fig.) to be on the alert regarding rumours or the trend of public opinion; ***out on one's ear***, dismissed, ejected ignominiously. †***to shake one's ears***: (? as a dog when wet); also, ? to make the best of a bad bargain; also, to show contempt or displeasure. ***to be willing to give one's ears***: to be ready to make any sacrifice.

1652 WARREN *Unbelievers* (1654) 24 All Sodome was.. flaming about the ears of the Inhabitants. **1823** BYRON *Juan* XIV. x, I have brought this world about my ears, and eke The other: that's to say, the clergy.

1906 E. DYSON *Fact'ry 'Ands* xiv. 180 It's these cheap 'n' easy shickers rollin' round on their ear what brings discredit on beer. **1921** K. S. PRICHARD *Black Opal* ii. 17 The old chap has 'got on his ear' in Sydney. **1932** J. VAN DRUTEN *Behold, We Live* I. 17, I shall be on my little ear if I don't get some food soon.

a **1553** UDALL *Royster D.* I. i. (Arb.) 12 If any woman smyle, Vp is he to the harde eares in loue. **1663** PEPYS *Diary* 2 Oct., My wife, who is over head and ears in getting her house up. **1768** GRAY in *Corr. N. Nicholls* (1843) 80, I am over head and ears in writings. **1839** W. IRVING *Wolfert's R.* (1855) 213, I..was up to my ears in law. **1889** W. B. YEATS *Let.* Sept. (1954) 136, I am up to the ears in Irish novelists. **1966** *Listener* 6 Jan. 15/1 He..is up to his ears in work.

1914 *Dialect Notes* IV. 105 *Dry back of the ears*, mature; —of persons. **1931** BROPHY & PARTRIDGE *Songs Brit. Soldier* (ed. 3) 375 Wet behind the ears, a term of reproach imputing ignorance or youth. **1939** *Amer. Speech* XIV. 264 The classic chastening phrase applied to the adolescent who feels that he is grown is that he 'isn't dry behind the ears yet'. **1939** J. STEINBECK *Grapes of Wrath* ix. 109 When you bastards get dry behin' the ears, you'll maybe learn to let an ol' fella sleep. **1962** J. F. STRAKER *Coil of Rope* vii. 71 You're still wet behind the ears, darling. It's time you grew up. **1968** W. J. BURLEY *Three Toed Pussy* iv. 68, I am not an abortionist but neither am I wet behind the ears. I've been around.

1610 SHAKS. *Temp.* IV. i. 275 At which like Vnback't colts they prick't their eares. **1678** EARL MURRAY in *Lauderdale Papers* (1885) III. lxxxiv. 147 They begine now to hange ther ears..A gentilman tould me..he saw the E. Kincarden & dyvers others..all out of humor. *a* **1891** *Mod.* I pricked up my ears when I heard your name mentioned.

a **1555** RIDLEY *Wks.* 206 Bertram was the first that pulled me by the ear and brought me from the common error of the Romish Church. **1581** SIDNEY *Apol. Poetrie* (Arb.) 62 For Poesie must not be drawne by the eares, it must be gently led. **1590** *Pasquil's Apol.* I. C b, They have all vowed to hale thee out of thy trenches by the head and eares. **1600** HOLLAND *Livy* XXVI. 592 They would home to their very houses and pluck them out by the eares. *c* **1645** HOWELL *Lett.* (1655) II. xxviii. 39 Which Countries..the Spaniard holds as one would do a Woolf by the ear, fearing they should run away. **1884** MARY HICKSON *Ireland in 17th C.* I. Introd. 9 The chiefs..led the ignorant credulous masses by the ears after them.

1920 *Nat. Rev.* Apr. 142 On the eve of a Presidential Election campaign, when practical politicians have their ears to the ground. **1955** G. GREENE *Quiet American* III. i. 190 What's the gossip of the market, Tom? You fellows certainly do keep your ears to the ground. **1966** 'H. CALVIN' *Italian Gadget* ix. 146 Honestly, the way I've had my ear to the ground, I simply don't see it.

1951 M. KENNEDY *Lucy Carmichael* VI. ii. 294 If I pipe down and give no trouble I'm safe. If not, I'll be out on my ear. **1953** J. TRENCH *Docken Dead* ix. 129 I'm going to throw the sleuth out on his ear.

1583 GOLDING *Calvin on Deut.* viii. 45 When Gods threatnings are vttered vnto vs a great many of vs do but shake our eares at them. **1606** CHAPMAN *Mons. D'Olive* II. (D.) Shooke mine eares And lickt my lipps, as if I begg'd attention. *c* **1645** HOWELL *Lett.* (1655) I. §i. xxi. 32 They shut their Gates against him, and made him go shake his ears, and to shift for his lodging. **1747** H. WALPOLE *Lett.* I. 166 (D.) How merry my ghost will be, and shake its ears, to hear itself quoted as a person of consummate prudence.

1796–1801 T. G. FESSENDEN *Orig. Poems* (1806) 128 Jove tells his peers He'd give his ears For such an hour as this is. **1853** DICKENS *Bleak Ho.* xxxix. 395 There are people in London who would give their ears to be you. **1883** W. NORRIS *No New Th.* I. vii. 176 Many a man would give his ears to be allowed to call two such charming young ladies by their Christian names.

d. †***to go, come, fall, together by the ears, be by the ears***: said of animals fighting; hence of persons, to be at variance (*obs.*). So ***to set*** (***persons***) ***by the ears***: to put them at variance.

1539 TAUERNER *Erasm. Prov.* (1552) 22 The apes.. skambled and went together by yᵉ eares for the nuttes. **1579** TOMSON *Calvin's Serm. Tim.* 280/1 When we be together by the eares like dogs and cattes. **1603** KNOLLES *Hist. Turkes* 1184 They fell together by the eares about the matter, some taking part with the old General, and some with the new. **1663** BUTLER *Hud.* I. I. 4 When hard Words..Set Folks together by the ears, And made them fight. **1725** DE FOE *Voy. round W.* (1840) 67 They would fall together by the ears about who should go with you. **1755** SMOLLETT *Quix.* (1803) II. 225 In one place, we fight for a sword; in another for a horse; in short, we are all by the ears together. **1793** GOUVR. MORRIS in Sparks *Life & Writ.* (1832) II. 282, I saw clearly that France and England would at length get by the ears. **1868** G. DUFF *Pol. Surv.* (1868) 40 Does it [Turkey] fancy that it will obtain security for itself by setting Greek and Bulgarian by the ears?

†**e.** ***to sleep on the*** (***right or left***) ***ear***: to sleep lying on one side. ***to be able to sleep on both ears*** [after L.: 'you may sleep at ease on which ear you like', Ter. *Heaut.* I. ii. 100]: to be free from anxiety.

a **1663** BRAMHALL *Wks.* (1842-4) III. 518 (D.), I will remove this scruple out of his mind that he may sleep securely upon both ears. **1768** TUCKER *Lt. Nat.* (1805) VII. 485 Young people..will need no more than one nap..if they turn upon the other ear to take a second, they should be taught to look on it as an intemperance.

f. In allusion to the loss of ears as a punishment. † ***(not to dare) for one's ears***; cf. *for one's life*, and mod. *colloq.* 'It would be as much as his ears were worth'.

1607 TOPSELL *Serpents* 640 The Drones do willingly contain themselves in their own cells..the younger not daring for their ears to break into their fathers Lands.

†**g.** ***wine of one ear***: good wine. [A French idiom of obscure origin.]

1653 URQUHART *Rabelais* I. v, [The wine] is of one eare, well wrought, and of good wooll.

h. ***to get*** (a person) ***up on his ears***, to make him indignant; so ***to be on one's ear***; ***to get up*** or ***go off on one's ear*** (U.S.), to rouse or bestir oneself.

1871 L. H. BAGG *4 Years at Yale* 44 A man somewhat offended or indignant is said to be *on his ear*. **1871** *Galveston News* 4 May (De Vere), They..said that I was lightning, when I got up on my ear. **1882** W. D. HOWELLS *Mod. Instance* II. xxix. 144 'I can cut your acquaintance fast enough,..if you're really on your ear!' 'I'm on my ear,' said Ricker. **1889** FARMER *Americanisms* s.v., *To get up or go off on one's ear*, to bestir oneself; to rouse oneself to a great effort. **1907** M. C. HARRIS *Tents of Wickedness* III. iv. 255, I only hope Paul Fairfax won't read it and get on his ear!

i. ***Oh my ears and whiskers!***, a joc. exclamation.

1865 'L. CARROLL' *Alice in Wonderland* i. 7 Alice..was just in time to hear it [*sc.* the White Rabbit] say..'Oh my ears and whiskers, how late it's getting!' **1956** M. STEWART *Wildfire at Midn.* iii. 33 He gave a little bark of laughter. 'Oh my ears and whiskers!' **1963** 'M. ERSKINE' *House in Belmont Square* i. 20 Oh, my ears and whiskers! Why didn't you say so before?

2. The internal and middle ear, together or separately; also the three portions as a whole.

1398 TREVISA *Barth. De P.R.* III. xviii. (1495) 64 The couenable lymme to herynge is a gristyl-bone set in the eere. **1615** CROOKE *Body of Man* 611 The Sounds..are carried through the curled Meanders of the Eares to the Auditory Nerue. **1808** *Med. Jrnl.* XIX. 387 The Muscles of the Middle Ear. **1861** HULME tr. *Moquin-Tandon* II. I. 50 In the lowest animals the ear is reduced to a sack filled with a special fluid.

3. a. With reference to its function: The organ of hearing. ***to speak in the ear***: to whisper, speak privately. Proverb, ***Walls have ears***, i.e. there may be listeners anywhere.

c **825** *Vesp. Psalter* ix. 38 Lustas heortan heara ȝeherde eare ðin. *c* **1000** *Ags. Gosp.* Matt. xiii. 15 Hiȝ hefelice mid earum ȝehyrdon [*c* **1160** *Hatton* earen]. *c* **1200** *Trin. Coll. Hom.* 181 Eien lokeð and eare lusteð. *a* **1225** *Ancr. R.* 98 Sing ine min earen. *a* **1300** *Cursor M.* 5140 A messager, þat spak al still in his er. *c* **1380** WYCLIF *Serm.* cxl. Sel. Wks. II. 28 Here he þes wordis, wiþ ere and herte. *c* **1384** CHAUCER *H. Fame* 2068 Tho thinges that I herde there, What a loude and what in eere. **1432–50** tr. *Higden* (1865) I. 411 If thou putte thyne eiere to hit thou schalle here a maruellous sownde. *a* **1450** *Knt. de la Tour* (1868) 27 He rouned in one of his felawes heres. **1620** SHELTON *Quix.* IV. vii. 53 They say Walls have Ears. **1662** GERBIER *Princ.* 27 To inform either of them in the ear what may be the best for them to choose. **1697** DRYDEN *Virg. Georg.* IV. 801 A buzzing Sound of Bees his Ears alarms. **17..** COWPER *Ep.* ii. 4 Nor ear heard huntsman's halloo. **1859** TENNYSON *Elaine.* 893 Till the ear Wearies to hear it.

b. with adjs. expressing the character or disposition of the person listening, as *vulgar*, *polite*, *fastidious*, *willing*, *sympathetic*, *patient*.

1593 HOOKER *Eccl. Pol.* I. xvi, Plausible to vulgar eares. **1631** R. BYFIELD *Doctr. Sabb.* 32 This is abhorring to Christian..eares. *a* **1703** BURKITT *On N.T.* Mark ix. 8 The obedient ear honours Christ more than..the applauding tongue. **1875** JOWETT *Plato* (ed. 2) III. 511 Things unfit for ears polite.

c. *transf.* and *fig.* esp. as attributed to the mind, the heart, etc., or to quasi-personified objects.

c **1400** *Apol. Loll.* 36 Wiþ þe eeris & een of his hert. **1526** *Pilgr. Perf.* (W. de W. 1531) 146 No persone may receyue.. the counseyles of the holy goost, excepte he haue a spirituall eare. **1596** SHAKS. *Merch. V.* II. v. 35 Stop my houses eares, I meane my casements. **1651** HOBBES *Leviath.* II. xxiii. 126 Those that are appointed to receive the Petitions..of the People..are as it were the publique Eare. **1728** ADDISON *Ps.* xix, In reason's ear they all rejoice. **1853** MAURICE *Proph. & Kings* xx. 350 There was an ear in an Assyrian..people which could be opened to hear God's word. **1864** BURTON *Scot. Abr.* I. ii. 103 The illustrious Eastern conqueror, whose name fills the ear of fame.

d. *fig.* Phrases, ***to open one's ears***, ***incline one's ear(s***, ***lend an ear*** (***one's ears***), †***lay to one's ears***: to listen (see *give ear* in 6). ***to bow down one's ear***: to listen graciously. †***to cast aside one's ear***: to listen casually. ***to be all ears***: to be eagerly attentive. ***to close***, ***stop one's ears***, ***turn*** (†***give***) ***a deaf ear***: to refuse to listen. †***to hear of both ears***: to hear both sides, be impartial. †***not to hear of that ear***: to be wilfully obtuse on a certain subject, 'to be deaf on that side of the head'. ***to go in at one ear and out at the other***: said of discourse that produces no impression on the hearer's mind. ***to have itching ears*** (after 2 *Tim.* iv. 3): to be eager to hear novelties. ***to tickle the ear(s***: to gratify with agreeable sounds; hence to flatter, coax; so also, †***to stroke the ears***. ***to believe one's ears***, to credit that one can have heard aright (chiefly with negative expressed or implied). ***to bite one's ear***, see BITE *v.* 16.

c **1375** *Lay-Folks Mass-bk.* B. 585 Bow doun þin eren. *c* **1430** *Syr Tryam.* 59 *note*, If ye wyll..laye to your eere, Of adventres ye shall here. **1604** DEKKER *Honest Wh.* I. i. Wks. 1873 II. 9 *Viola.* Then lend me your eares. *Fust.* Mine eares are yours deare sister. **1611** BIBLE *Prov.* iv. 20 My sonne,.. incline thine eare vnto my sayings. **1611** —— *Ps.* xxxi. 2 Bowe downe thine eare to me. **1632** B. JONSON *Magn. Lady* I. i. (D.) Hang your ears this way, and hear his praises. **1670** G. H. *Hist. Cardinals* I. III. 74, I..began to open my ears, the better to understand so efficacious a proof. **1878** MORLEY *Carlyle, Crit. Misc.* 202 These are possibilities to which he will lend no ear.

c **1430** LYDG. *Bochas* III. xxv. 969 a, Of hap, as he kest his eare aside, He, of two porters, the counsaile did espie. **1786** tr. *Beckford's Vathek* (1868) 88 He was all ear to her charming voice. **1865** TROLLOPE *Belton Est.* xv. 174, I am all ears.

a **1300** *Cursor M.* 19452 (Gött.) þa wreches.. gun þair erin for to ditt. **1548** HALL *Chron. Rich. III*, 24 (Halliw.) She began.. to relent and to geve to them no deffe are. **1600** HOLLAND *Livy* XXXIII. xlvii. 850 Scipio Africanus for a long time gave the deafe eare.. unto them. **1611** SHAKS. *Wint. T.* v. i. 201 [The king of] Bohemia stops his eares. **1835** THIRLWALL *Greece* I. vii. 272 She had turned a deaf ear to the persuasions by which they sought to prevail on her.

1624 SANDERSON *Serm.* I. 239 Our unthankfulness, how foul it is.. But we cannot abide to hear on this ear. **1705** HICKERINGILL *Priest-Cr.* II. v. 50 A Man of Understanding .. is not apt to pass sentence till he hear of both Ears, and have well pondered, Pro and Con.

c **1400** *Rom. Rose* 5154 For alle yede oute at oon ere That in that other she dide lere. **1583** GOLDING *Calvin on Deut.* xxi. 125 [A sermon] goes in at the one eare and out at the other. **1726** AMHERST *Terræ Fil.* xxxiii. 173 Let it go in at one ear, and out at the other; never report it again. **1862** MRS. GASKELL *Let.* ? 16 May (1966) 923 You know things so often go in at one ear with him & out at another that it will be as well to be quite sure. **1930** 'BRENT OF BIN BIN' *Ten Creeks Run* v. 52 You might hear a lot that isn't true if you listen to gossip. It's best to let such things go in one ear and out the other.

a **1668** DENHAM *Sp. agst. Peace at Close Comm.* xi, Did I for this take pains.. To stroke the people's ears?

1807 LAMB *Tales fr. Shakes.* I. 200 Lear at first could not believe his eyes or ears, nor that it was his daughter who spoke so unkindly. *a* **1885** 'H. CONWAY' *Living or Dead* (1886) viii, He.. blamed my partner, who could scarcely believe his ears.

4. *transf.* Used in *sing.* and *pl.* for: The sense of hearing, auditory perception (cf. similar use of *eye*, *palate*). ***in the ears*** (rarely ***ear***) ***of***: within the hearing of, so as to be heard by. (Orig. a Biblical Hebraism, and now somewhat *arch.*) ***to come to the ear(s of***: to come to (a person's) knowledge by hearing; said of facts, reports, etc. † ***at first ear***: on the first hearing.

1297 R. GLOUC. 492 It com the kinge to ere. **1375** BARBOUR *Bruce* v. 449 The tithandis.. Com to the cliffurdis ere. **1382** WYCLIF *Luke* iv. 21 This scripture is fulfillid in ȝoure eeris. **1646** SIR T. BROWNE *Pseud. Ep.* I. v. 17 A third cause of common Errors is.. a believing at first eare what is delivered by others. **1749** CHESTERF. *Lett.* 9 Dec. (1870) 158 Most people have ears, but few have judgment.

5. (in *sing.* only) The faculty of discriminating sounds; *esp.* that of accurately recognizing musical intervals. More fully ***musical ear***, ***ear for music***. Similarly, ***an ear for verse***, etc. ***to sing or play by ear***: i.e. without the aid of written music. Fig. phr. ***to play (it***, etc.) ***by ear***, to proceed step by step according to results.

1526 *Pilgr. Perf.* (W. de W. 1531) 158 b, In the psalmody .. haue a good eare. **16..** PEPYS *Diary* (1879) IV. 139 Singing with my wife, who has lately begun to learn.. though her eare is not good. **1674** PLAYFORD *Skill Mus.* II. 110 To learn to play by rote or ear without Book. **1712** STEELE *Spect.* No. 313 ¶9, I have no Ear for Musick. **1779** COWPER *Lett.* Wks. (1876) 40, I am convinced.. that he has no ear for poetical numbers. **1789** BELSHAM *Ess.* I. xii. 220 The ear distinguishes verse from prose. **1837** DISRAELI *Venetia* II. i. (1871) 104 A fine ear for music. **1839** *Edin. Rev.* July 496 Miss Austen is like one who plays by ear, while Miss Martineau understands the science. **1873** L. TROUBRIDGE *Life amongst Troubridges* (1966) 7 She plays the piano *beautifully* and can play anything by ear. **1874** SAYCE *Philol.* vi. 246 The musical ear is.. the creation of a high civilisation. **1961** L. GRIBBLE *Wantons die Hard* xiii. 161 'I'm playing this by ear,' he grunted once when the American queried the devious route he was following. **1961** A. SMITH *East-Enders* xi. 183 'What happens then?' 'I don't know... We're playing it by ear at the moment.' **1962** A. NISBETT *Technique Sound Studio* xi. 195 The relative [sound] levels are judged by ear.

6. Voluntary hearing, listening, attention. Chiefly in phrases like ***to give ear***: to listen attentively. ***to have*** (***win, gain***) ***a person's ear***: to have (obtain) his favourable attention.

1503 HAWES *Examp. Virt.* vi. 83 Gyuynge god ere vnto the vteraunce. **1587** HARRISON *England* II. i. (1877) I. 23 Your request deserveth little consideration and lesse eare. **1611** COTGR., *Ouye*, eare, attention, hearing. **1655** MRQ. WORCESTER *Cent. Inv.* in Dircks *Life* (1865) 384 Never refused me his ear to any reasonable motion. **1701** W. WOTTON *Hist. Rome* Alex. i. 463 They.. would.. sell his Ear, pretending Interest where they had none. **1710** STEELE *Tatler* No. 1 ¶7 Mr. Kidney.. has the Ear of the greatest Politicians. **1727** DE FOE *Syst. Magic.* I. iv. (1840) 103 On condition that thou wilt now.. give ear to my instructions. **1826** E. IRVING *Babylon* II. vi. 97 Some messenger powerful enough to take their ear and be heard. **1884** *Times* (weekly ed.) 31 Oct. 14/3 To gain the ear of the House.

II. An object resembling the external ear in shape or relative position.

†**7.** One of the auricles of the heart. *Obs.*

1398 TREVISA *Barth. De P.R.* v. xxxvi. (1495) 149 Thyse two pyeces ben callyd the eeres of the herte. **1541** R. COPLAND *Guydon's Quest. Chirurg.*, The hert hath two eares .. yᵗ serue for to let the ayre in and out. **1604** E. GRIMSTONE *Hist. Siege Ostend* 196 The bullet had peirced through his heart, and had stayed in the left eare. **1671** GREW *Anat. Plants* I. vii. §4 The Fibers of the Ears of the Heart.

8. a. The handle of a pitcher or drinking vessel, and *dial.* of many other things.

[Cf. Ger. *öhr* (:—OHG. *ôri*, perh. = OE. *ýre*, ? spike at the back of an axe), *öse* (:—MHG. *œse*, f. base of OTeut. *'auson, au'zon* = EAR); Eng. employs the primary word in this sense instead of a derivative as in Ger.]

c **1440** *Promp. Parv.* 141 Ere of a vesselle, *ansa*. **1522** *MS. Acc. St. John's Hosp., Canterb.*, For a new bayle & an ere.. of the bukket. **1534** in Peacock *Eng. Ch. Furniture* (1866) 211 Item an other basen of latten withowt erys weynge vli. **1602** PLAT *Delightes for Ladies* liv, A deep bottomed bason.. with two eares of Iron to hange it. **1697** DRYDEN *Virg.* (1806) I. 135 His empty can, with ears half worn away, Was hung on high. **1782** COWPER *Gilpin* 61 Each bottle had a curling ear.

b. The part of a bell by which it is hung; a similar part on the ram of a pile-driver, by which it is lifted; 'the lugs or ear-shaped rings fastened on the larger bombs or mortar shells for their convenient handling with shell-hooks' (Adm. Smyth).

1484 *Churchw. Acc. Wigtoft, Lincolnsh.* (Nichols 1797) 80 Paide.. for makyng.. an ere to yᵉ for bell. **1872** ELLACOMBE *Bells of Ch.* i. 4 The various parts of a bell may be described as.. the ear or cannon on its top.. by which it is hung.

9. a. *Mech.* A projection on the side or edge of a piece of machinery or a tool; serving as a handle or attachment, as one of a pair of supports on opposite sides, or for other purposes.

1677 MOXON *Mech. Exerc.* (1703) 2 At the Ear of the upper Bellows board is fastened a Rope. **1874** KNIGHT *Dict. Mech.*, *Ear*, one of the two projecting parts on the portions of an eccentric strap by which they are bolted together. *Ibid. Ear*, in *Printing*, a projection on the edge of the frisket; or one on the edge of the composing-rule. **1876** HILES *Catech. Organ* iv. (1878) 27 Flue-pipes [of an organ].. are often furnished with ears, that is, pieces of metal or wood projecting from each side of the mouth.

†**b.** Used by Dryden in the description of a Roman plough [transl. L. *auris*].

1697 DRYDEN *Virg. Georg.* I. 252 A fastned Beam prepare, On either side the Head produce an Ear.

10. ***ears of a pump***: 'the support of the bolt for the handle or break' (Adm. Smyth).

11. *Naut.* See quot.

c **1850** *Rudim. Navig.* (Weale) 116 Ears of boats, the knee-pieces at the fore-part on the outside, at the height of the gunwale.

12. *Bot.* and *Conch.* = AURICLE 2.

1688 R. HOLME *Armoury* II. 85/1 The Ears, or fines, are such leaves as grow on the foot stalk, either naturally small, or through extravagancy above nature uses. **1755** *Gentl. Mag.* XXV. 32 Ear, is the flat part that in some bivalves spreads from the Cardo, or joint, as in a scalop. **1854** WOODWARD *Mollusca* II. 258 Shell hyaline, posterior ears obsolete, anterior prominent. **1861** MISS PRATT *Flower. Pl.* III. 183 Corolla with two ears at the base, which remain and crown the fruit.

13. The part of a cap coming over the ears.

c **1830** MRS. SHERWOOD *Houlston Tracts* III. lxxvii. 8 The ears of her mob cap untied for the benefit of the air.

14. ***artificial ear***: an ear-trumpet in the form of a natural ear.

15. *pl.* A citizens'-band radio, its antenna, or the vehicle carrying it; in phr. ***to have one's ears on***, to be listening to or operating a CB radio. *slang* (chiefly *U.S.*).

1976 *Daily Progress* (Charlottesville, Va.) 27 Apr. (Advt.), CB spoken here.. *Ears*, a vehicle with a CB antenna. **1976** *CB Mag.* June 9/1 Now you can let all the 'good buddies' know that you've got your ears on and you're ready to modulate! **1976** PERKOWSKI & STRAL *Joy of CB* xi. 127 With antennas as high as 60 feet above the ground, however, there is the possibility that your ears may obstruct air navigation if you are close to an airport. **1977** *New Scientist* 30 June 764 Because of overcrowding, many a CB enthusiast (called an 'apple') is strapping an illegal linear amplifier ('boots') on to his transceiver ('ears') which is limited by the Federal Communications Commission ('Big Daddy' in the US) to an output power of no more than five watts.

III. *Comb.* and *attrib.*

16. General relations: **a.** attributive (portions or natural appendages of the ear), as ***ear-drum***, ***-lobe***, ***ridge***, ***-root***, ***-sac***, ***-tip***, ***-tuft***; (ornaments worn in the ear), as ***ear-jewel***, ***-pendant***; (surgical instruments for operating on or examining the ear), as ***ear-douche***, ***-lamp***, ***-nozzle***, ***-scoop***, ***-speculum***, ***-spoon***, ***-syringe***; **b.** objective, as ***ear-protector***, ***-whisperer***; †***ear-bussing***, ***-catching***, ***-crucifying***, ***-deafening***, †***-deafing***, ***-erecting***, ***-kissing***, ***-piercing***, ***-pleasing***, ***-splitting***, ***-stunning*** adjs., ***ear-tickling*** adj. and vbl. sb.; **c.** locative and instrumental, as ***ear-labour***; ***ear-cropped***, ***-directed***, ***-hard*** adjs.

1605 SHAKS. *Lear* II. i. (Qo.), You have heard of the news .. I meane the whisper'd ones, for they are yet but *ear bussing [*folios* here kissing] arguments. **1839** DARBY *Introd. Beaum. & Fl.* (1839) I. 25 Fletcher's *ear-catching language. **1646** J. HALL *Poems, To Mr. Hall*, Thou need'st no nose-lesse monuments display Or *Ear-cropp'd Images. **1789** WOLCOTT (P. Pindar) *Subj. for Paint.* Wks. 1812 II. 110 Raising such *ear-crucifying noise. **1611** SHAKS. *Wint. T.* III. i. 9 The *eare-deaff'ning Voyce o' th' Oracle. **1644** BULWER *Chirol.* 8 The noise of some *eare-deafing crowd. **1812** G. COLMAN *Br. Grins, Lady of Wreck* II. xxvi, *Ear-directed by the sound. **1645** RUTHERFORD *Tryal & Tri. Faith* (1845) 63 There is carnosity on the *ear-drum. **1798** EDGEWORTH *Pract. Educ.* (1822) I. 166 The much-enduring ear-drum of the nursery-maid. **1784** COWPER *Task* III. 9 He chirrups brisk his *ear-erecting steed. **1731–1800** BAILEY, **Ear Hard*, spoken of a Horse. **1725** DE FOE *Voy. round W.* (1840) 126 Made the other pull off his two *ear-jewels also. *a* **1593** H. SMITH *Wks.* (1866) I. 325 But as we pray, so we hear; the one is a lip-labour and the other is an *ear-labour. **1859** R. BURTON *Centr. Afr.* in *Jrnl. R.G.S.* XXIX. 130 All distend the *ear-lobe: a hole is bored with a needle.. and is enlarged by inserting bits of cane. **1648** tr. *Senault's Par. upon Job* 416 An *Ear-pendant of gold. **1604** SHAKS. *Oth.* III. iii. 352 Th' *Eare-piercing Fife. **1853** KINGSLEY *Hypatia* xxix. 362 Wail on wail, long, wild, ear-piercing, rang along the vaulted roofs. **1641** W. HOOKE *New Eng. Teares* Pref. A ij b, As for this Sermon, expect not *eare-pleasing, but heart-affecting phrases in it. **1884** *Health Exhib. Catal.* 156/1 *Ear Protector for winter. **1853** KANE *Grinnell Exp.* xxx. (1856) 263, I wear an *ear-ridge, a tiara, to speak heroically, of wolf-skin. **1616** SURFL. & MARKH. *Countr. Farm* 128 Your Horse.. sweateth much, especially in his flanks, at his *eare-roots, and in such like vsuall places. **1709** *Lond. Gaz.* No. 4540/8 A.. Bay Gelding.. hath large slouch Ears.. very large Ear-roots. **1882** W. K. PARKER in *Trans. Linn. Soc.* II. III. 166 The huge *ear-sacs are quite perfect as to cartilage. **1895** *Arnold & Sons' Catal. Surg. Instrum.* 83 *Ear scoop and Eye spud. **1928** V. G. CHILDE *Most Anc. East* viii. 189 Tweezers.. were combined with prickers and earscoops in regular reticules. **1966** *Punch* 7 Sept. 344/2 Diggers in the newly excavated Roman villa in Hampshire have found a lot of ear-scoops. **1884** *Pall Mall G.* 10 Sept. 4/1 The trombones seemed.. to drown everything else by their *ear-splitting tones. *c* **1325** *Gloss W. de Bibbesworth* in Wright *Voc.* (1857) 146 Cakenole *gloss* *herespon. **1878** *Sunday at Home* 6 July 424/2, I made several purchases, such as.. ear spoons. **1921** *Chambers's Jrnl.* 763/2 Toilet implements as toothpick, tweezers, ear-spoon. **1937** *Jrnl. R. Anthrop. Inst.* 322 Inca metalwork includes many small objects such as pins, pincers, earspoons, etc. **1969** E. H. PINTO *Treen* 323 The prevalence of ear spoons in *étuis*. **1885** TENNYSON *Tires.* 11 That *ear-stunning hail of Ares. **1884** *Academy* 10 May 303/1 There is no *ear-tickling, or mere writing for effect. **1801** SOUTHEY *Lett.* (1856) I. 182 It puzzles me how he has learnt to round his sentences so ear-ticklingly. **1856** KANE *Arct. Expl.* I. xxix. 395 A crescent of black marking the *ear-tips. **1871** DARWIN *Desc. Man* II. xiii. 71 Elegant *ear-tufts are occasionally present. **1549** OLDE *Erasm. Paraphr. Ephesians* Prol., Seduced.. by sedicious *eare-whisperours.

17. Special comb.: **ear-biter** *slang*, † (*a*) *U.S.*, a special agent of the Post Office *obs.*; (*b*) an habitual borrower of money, a cadger; hence **ear-biting** *vbl. sb.*; **ear-bob** (now *vulgar* or *humorous*), = EAR-DROP; **ear-bone**, a bone of the ear; †**ear-bored** *ppl. a.* (see BORE *v.*¹ 1 c); **ear-bow**, an ornament for a horse's ear; **ear-brisk** *a.* (see quot.); **ear-brush** = AURILAVE (see quot.); **ear-bulb** (*Anat.*), the membranous labyrinth and the cochlea together; **ear-cap** (see quot.); **ear-chamber**, the cavity of the internal ear; **ear-clip**, an ear-ring, esp. one that clips on; **ear-conche** (*Anat.*), the concha or external ear; †**ear-confession**, auricular confession; **ear-cornet**, a kind of ear-trumpet; **ear-cough**, a 'cough excited through irritation of the external ear' (*Syd. Soc. Lex.*); **ear-covert**, a tuft of feathers covering the ear in birds, = AURICULAR B. a; **ear-deep** *a.*, reaching the ears only; **ear-defenders** *pl.*, (a pair of) plugs or ear-muffs designed to protect the ear-drums from damage by loud or persistent noise; †**ear-dove**, obs. name of some bird (see quot.); †**ear-dropper**, an eaves-dropper; **ear-exercise**, an exercise for training the musical ear; †**ear-finger**, the little finger, often put in the ear, = AURICULAR B. b; **ear-flap**, the lobe or the loose part of the ear; the external ear generally; also, a flap of material covering the ear; hence **ear-flapped** *a.*; **ear-fly**, a gad-fly belonging to the genus *Chrysops*, esp. *C. vittatus*, which attacks the ears of horses; †**ear-gristle**, the cartilage of the ear, the external ear; **ear-guard**, (*a*) one who prevents a person from hearing; (*b*) a protection for the ears; (*c*) *slang* (see quot. 1941); **ear-hole**, the aperture of the ear; *dial.* used for the ear itself; **ear-hoop** *U.S.*, an ear-ring; †**ear-knowledge**, knowledge obtained by hearsay; **ear-lap**, the lobe of the ear; also the external ear as a whole; **ear-lappet**, ? = *ear-covert*; = *ear-tab*; †**ear-leaf** (*Bot.*), the cotyledon of a plant; **ear-lechery** (see quot.); **ear-lid** (see quot.); **ear-lock**, a lock of hair over or above the ear; **ear-muff** orig. *U.S.*, a protection for the ears, in cold weather, from noise, etc.; **ear-nosed** *a.*, *Conch.* (see quot.); **ear-phone**, (*a*) a device applied to the ears for listening in to radio broadcasting; (*b*) a device to aid defective hearing; (*c*) a woman's hair-style (current in the 1920s) of a shape reminiscent of the listening device; **ear-piece**, an apparatus or a part of one designed to be fitted to the ear, as of a telephone or a radio receiver; **ear-pieces**, **ear-plate**, part of a helmet covering the ears; **ear-plug**, (*a*) an ornament worn in the lobe of the ear; (*b*) a wad of cotton wool, wax, or other substance placed in the ear to prevent an inrush of cold air or water, or to exclude excessive noise; **ear-port** (see quot.); **ear-reach**, = EAR-SHOT; †**ear-rentingly** *adv.*, ? for *ear-rendingly*, but cf. EAR-RENT; **ear-roll**, in a leather helmet, a roll of leather behind the ear; **ear-room** (cf. *house-room*); †**ear-rowner**, an ear-whisperer; **ear-say**, erroneously used for *hearsay*; **ear-scalp** (*Anat.*), the skin covering the ears; **ear-shell** (see quot.); †**ear-shrift**, auricular

confession; †**ear-sore**, something disagreeable to the ear (cf. EYESORE); **ear-sore** *a.* (*dial.*), irritable, ill-tempered; †**ear-spectacle**, an ear-trumpet; **ear-stone**, an otolith; **ear-string** (cf. *eye-strings, heart-strings*); **ear-stud**, a stud, freq. ornamented, worn in a hole pierced through the lobe of the ear; **ear-tab** *U.S.*, a tab, esp. one affixed to either side of a fur cap, to protect the ear in cold weather (= TAB 13); also, = *ear-phone* (a); **ear-training** *vbl. sb.*, the cultivating of the ability to distinguish and reproduce sounds and rhythms in speech or music; †**ear-wire** (see quot. 1685); **ear-worm**, ? = EAR-WIG; *fig.* a secret counsellor; **ear-wort**, a plant supposed to be good for curing deafness, *Dysophila auricularis* (*Syd. Soc. Lex.*). Also EAR-ACHE, -DROP, -MARK, -MARKED, -PICK, -RING, -SHOT, -TRUMPET, -WAX, -WISE, -WITNESS, q.v.

1855 J. HOLBROOK *Ten Yrs. among Mail Bags* 27 The restoration of the '*ear-biters' (as they were then sometimes facetiously called). **1934** *Bulletin* (Sydney) 17 Oct. 21/2 No ..earbiters anxious to give you a moral for the lars'. **1940** WODEHOUSE *Eggs, Beans & Crumpets* 19 Two things which rendered Oofy Prosser a difficult proposition for the ear-biter. **1954** —— *Jeeves & Feudal Spirit* i. 10 It is not often that one is confronted with ear-biting on so majestic a scale, a fiver till next Wednesday being about the normal tariff. **1648** GAGE *West Ind.* xii. (1655) 56 Her *eare-bobs of some considerable Jewels. **1869** *Pall Mall G.* 4 He purchased a pair of ear-bobs. **1938** M. K. RAWLINGS *Yearling* xii. 123 Now you jest give me them ear-bobs, you pirate. **1681** GREW *Musæum* I. v. i. 82 Part of the *Ear-Bone of a Whale. **1901** *Jrnl. R. Microsc. Soc.* 138 Ear-bones of Opossum. **1915** SHIPLEY & MACBRIDE *Zool.* (ed. 3) 644 The evolution of the ear-bones in Mammalia. **1658** *2nd Narr. Late Parl.* in *Select. fr. Harl. Misc.* (1793) 433 The *ear-bored slavish citizens. **1691** E. TAYLOR *Behmen's Theos. Phil.* 64 Are voluntary Ear-boared Slaves. **1796** W. FELTON *Carriages* II. 148 The *Earbows are of stiff leather, and covered with lace, or tape. **1731–1800** BAILEY, **Ear Brisk* , when he [a horse] carries his Ears forward. **1851** S. JUDD *Margaret* II. viii. (1871) 281 He was an ear-brisk and high-necked critter. **1874** KNIGHT *Dict. Mech.*, **Ear-brush*, a toilet instrument for cleaning the ear. **1836–9** TODD *Cycl. Anat.* II. 529/2 The *ear-bulb..consists of a hard external case. **1847** CRAIG, **Ear-cap*, a cover for the ears against the cold. **1963** *Times* 4 May 6/4 They will admire the earcaps knitted to protect the horses from flies. **1854** OWEN in *Circ. Sc.* (*c* 1865) II. 65/2 They contribute..to the formation of the *ear-chamber. **1945** A. SELWYN *Retail Jeweller's Handbk.* viii. 100 To the diamond mounters must be credited the idea of a new ornament, the *ear-clip (*not* same as clip-on earring); this lies over the lobe and follows the ear up for a short way. **1951** *Catal. of Exhibits, South Bank Exhib., Festival of Britain* 39/1 Gold, sapphire and diamond clip, with ear clips and ring. **1958** *Times* 15 Dec. 11/6 Citrine, diamond and 18 ct. gold Earclips. **1875** BLAKE *Zool.* 86 There are no *earconches, lips, teeth, epiglottis..nor scrotum. **1549** ALLEN tr. *Jude's Par. Rev.* 37 The articles of auricular and *eare confession, of purgatorye. **1877** BURNET *Ear* 326 *Ear-cough was known to medical men a long time ago. **1828** STARK *Elem. Nat. Hist.* I. 233 Head, nape of the neck, and *ear-coverts pale yellow. *a* **1843** SOUTHEY *Tri. Woman* 376 Content with *ear-deep melodies. **1915** *Illustr. London News* 16 Jan. 72 (*caption*) *Ear-defenders for British: a Device to prevent deafening by big guns. **1917** W. OWEN *Let.* 9 Jan. (1967) 424 There is a Howitzer just 70 or 80 yards away... I can't tell you how glad I am you got me the ear-defenders. **1934** *Discovery* Dec. 345/2 Ear-defenders, small plugs which limit the intensity applied to the ear drum. **1961** *Flight* LXXX. 933/3 Headsets incorporating ear defender fittings. **1725** SLOANE *Jamaica* II. 304 It had two spots of each side of the neck of a dark colour, whence the name of *Ear-Dove. *a* **1670** HACKET *Abp. Williams* II. 81 (D), An *ear-dropper might hear such things talk'd at cock-pits and dancing schools. **1887** *Birmingham Instit. Mag.* Sept. 23 The classes in Harmony—*Ear Exercises, and Sight Singing. *c* **1000** ÆLFRIC *Gram.* (Z.) 298 *Auricularis*, *ear-finger. **1644** BULWER *Chirol.* 179 To becken with the Eare-finger is their usuall concise expression. **1859** O. W. HOLMES *De Sauty* Pretermit thy whittling, wheel thine *ear-flap toward me, Thou shalt hear them answered. **1876** LANKESTER *Hist. Creation* I. i. 13 Our long-eared ancestors ..moved their large ear-flaps freely. **1907** *Yesterday's Shopping* (1969) 882/2 Motor caps... Seal fur caps, with earflaps. **1968** W. GARNER *Deep, Deep Freeze* xxi. 198 He let down the ear-flaps of his fur hat. **1894** A. CONAN DOYLE *S. Holmes* 2 Sherlock Holmes, with his sharp, eager face framed in his *ear-flapped travelling cap. **1925** E. F. NORTON *Fight for Everest, 1924* 51 Ear-flapped caps. **1806** M. LEWIS *Orig. Jrnls.* (1905) V. 87 Found here [are] the butterflies, common house and blowing flies, the horse flies, except the gold coloured *ear fly. **1917** SANDERSON & PEAIRS *School Entom.* 136 The Horse-flies. *Tabanidæ*... Some are called Ear-flies, some Gad-flies. **1656** DUGARD *Gate Lat. Unl.* §206. 57 To the ears are fitted the *ear-gristles, being broad to reflect the sounds, and hollowed with turnings to carry them inwards. **1647** WARD *Simp. Cobler* 62 Your *Ear-guard will keep farre enough from you what ever I have said. **1939** AUDEN & ISHERWOOD *Journey to War* ii. 50 Chinese in skin caps with ear-guards like airmen's helmets. **1941** BAKER *Dict. Austral. Slang* 27 *Earguards*, small side-whiskers. **1691** RAY *Creation* (1714) 152 Have very small ears and *ear-holes as the cetaceous fishes have. **1923** MANCHON *Le Slang* s.v., Give 'im a plug in the ear-hole! **1962** *John o' London's* 11 Jan. 27/3 Before you know it you'll be out on your earhole. **1966** *New Statesman* 25 Feb. 265/2 [In the Wallis Islands] a man can be fined two dollars for entering church with a piece of tobacco stuck in his earhole. **1808** *Massachusetts Spy* 18 May (Th.), A large assortment of *Earhoops, of different sizes. **1845** S. JUDD *Margaret* I. x. 64 Many wore ear-hoops of pinchbeck, large as a dollar. **1624** HEYWOOD *Gunaik.* IV. 186 In all this banding of their disreputation..nothing ever came within the compasse of his *eare knowledge. *c* **1000** ÆLFRIC *Voc.* in Wr.-Wülcker 157 *Pinnula*, *earlæppa, *uel* ufweard eare. **1561** HOLLYBUSH *Hom. Apoth.* 13 Pull ye patient sore by ye earlap vpwardly. **1880** E. OPPERT *Forbid. L.* iv. 126 The hat is..attached by strings round the earlaps. **1884** tr. *Lotze's Logic* 40 Aristotle gives risibility as a property of man, Hegel..the ear-lap; both distinguish man from the brutes. **1864** B. TAYLOR *H. Thurston* vi. 79 Woodbury recognised, projecting between *ear-lappets of fur, the curiously-planted nose..which belonged to the Rev. Mr. Waldo. **1868** DARWIN *Anim. & Pl.* I. vii. 244 The breeds which..have red ear-lappets. **1869** Ear-lappet [see LAPPET *sb.* 4]. **1718** BRADLEY *Gardening* (1731) 285 If any seed has had Moisture enough to put forth its Radicle never so little, and is after that check'd before the *Ear-Leaves appear. **1737** M. GREEN *Spleen* (1738) 20 Hir'd to praise with stallion pen, Serve the *ear-lechery of men. **1552** HULOET, *Eare lydde, or over-parte of the eare, *pinnula*. **1871** T. H. HUXLEY *Anat. Vert.* 250 The tympanic membranes [of the crocodile] are exposed, but a cutaneous valve, or earlid, lies above each, and can be shut down over it. **1930** *Times* 3 July 10/5 Nature..has not provided against assaults upon the hearing, and we have no 'ear-lid' by which we can shut out noise. *c* **1775** WELCH in *Harper's Mag.* (1883) Oct. 736/1 A musket ball [struck] the pin out of the hair of his *ear-lock. **1809** W. IRVING *Knickerb.* (1861) 183 His hair strutting out on each side in stiffly pomatumed ear-locks. **1867** J. R. LOWELL *Poems* (1912) 578 His ear-locks gray, striped with a foxy brown, Were braided up to hide a desert crown. **1859** *Rep. Comm. Pat. 1858* (U.S.) II. 572 William P. Ware..[patented an] *Ear, Cheek, and Chin Muff..July 6, 1858. **1889** *Kansas Times & Star* 30 Nov., A young chap got off a train from the South today... Said they wore no flannels, gloves or earmuffs down at Shreveport. **1906** E. DYSON *Fact'ry 'Ands* xvi. 215 Well, y' orter wear ear muffs this bitin' weather. **1940** *Chambers's Techn. Dict.* 276/2 *Ear muffs.* 1. Pads of rubber or similar material which are placed on head telephone receivers to minimise discomfort during long use. 2. Large pads for reducing the effect of noise on factory workers. **1954** A. W. FIELDING *Hide & Seek* ii. 29 Theatrical side-whiskers as thick and furry as ear-muffs. **1705** I. PETIVER in *Phil. Trans.* XXV. 1954 This is distinguisht from the last in being..*Ear-nosed, viz. inclining more towards one end of the hinge. **1924** *Glasgow Herald* 24 Dec. 6 With a slight effort of the imagination we can forget *earphones and valves. **1927** *Radio Times* 22 Apr. 145/1 One might even suppose that you had never in your life put on a pair of earphones or listened to a loud speaker. **1928** J. F. BARNHILL *Nose, Throat & Ear* 583 Ear phones..are the most serviceable present means of aiding impaired hearing. **1964** M. DRABBLE *Garrick Year* iv. 57, I spent hours trying to put my hair into earphones. **1965** *Punch* 17 Mar. 404/3 Only two of the sound films.. have subtitles, the others being shown with 'earphone commentary'. **1967** *Lebende Sprachen* XII. 136/2 *Earphones, headphones*, a device worn in or on the ear for listening to a sound source. *a* **1843** SOUTHEY *Comm.-Pl. Bk.* Ser. II. (1849) 644 The morion should be without *ear-pieces. **1853** W. O. MARKHAM tr. *Skoda's Auscult.* 29 The ear-piece may be convex, concave, or plane, provided the disk forming it be large enough to close the ear completely. **1882** *Leisure Hour* XXXI. 312/1 In front of the coil is placed a thin disc of iron (H), which is fitted into an ear-piece (I) [of the telephone]. **1904** F. LYNDE *Grafters* xxvii. 352 The train-master dropped the ear-piece of the telephone. **1909** *Practitioner* Dec. 862 The ear-pieces should fit closely and accurately into the external auditory meatus. **1916** 'BOYD CABLE' *Action Front* 185 The earpiece receiver strapped tightly over one ear. **1923** A. HUXLEY *Antic Hay* x. 156 For business, tortoiseshell rims and nickel ear-pieces lend incisive poise. **1928** GALSWORTHY *Swan Song* I. iv. 29 Soames..took up the earpieces of the wireless. **1962** *Which?* Feb. 42/2 Table I shows which radios had earpieces, sometimes included in the price. **1622** F. MARKHAM *Bk. War* I. ix. §3. 34 A Spanish Morian..bound downe with lined *eare-plates vnderneath his chinne. **1904** *Nature* 9 June 138/1 Numerous copper ornaments..such as pendants and *ear-plugs. **1904** *Daily Chron.* 5 Sept. 8/3 We should like..to see the use of ear-plugs spread, for many cases of ear trouble are brought into activity by the inrush of water during diving or swimming. **1940** *Nature* 17 Aug. 219/2 The methods of protection of the ears against explosive sounds are very simple. One of these, the earplug, has..always been used extensively by gunners and others in the presence of intensive noise. **1955** E. POUND *Classic Anthol.* II. 140 In the old Capital officers wore ear-plugs fittingly Of sea stones (common jade). **1959** *Daily Tel.* 19 Aug. 10/5 B.O.A.C. stewardesses, ground receptionists and other staff who have to work near jet airliners are to have miniature ear plugs. **1751** SMOLLETT *Per. Pic.* xcix. Wks. (1797) IV. 461 Your *ear-ports will let in the sound. **1642** FULLER *Holy & Prof. St.* v. xviii. II. §6 Some invisible eare might lie in ambush within the *Eare-reach of his words. **1593** NASHE *Christ's T.* (1613) 63 Roaring and *eare-rentingly exclaiming. **1909** *Westm. Gaz.* 23 Sept. 12/3 One of the regulations was that competitors had to wear *ear-rolls to facilitate their hearing when other riders wished to overtake them. **1922–3** *Halford Cycle Co. Ltd.* 110 Helmets. Leather, with Ear Rolls. *a* **1656** BP. HALL *Select Th.* §48 Som there are that will not give so much as *ear-room to the Word of Truth. ? **1388** WIMBELDON *Serm.* in Hatton MS. 57 p. 11 (Halliw.) It is good that every lorde of the comunte be not lad bi folis, nor bi noon othir *ere-rownerys. **1817** COLERIDGE *Biog. Lit.* I. iii. 53, I have only *ear-say evidence. **1872** MIVART *Elem. Anat.* 396 This part is distributed to the *ear-scalp and the muscles of the mouth. **1753** CHAMBERS *Cycl. Supp.*, *Ear Shell, *auris marina*, in natural history, the name of a genus of shell-fish. **1838** *Penny Cycl.* XII. 14/2 This section of Gastropods [Haliotidæ] commonly called 'Ear-shells' or 'Sea-ears'. **1554** T. SAMPSON in Strype *Eccl. Mem.* III. App. xviii. 50 But this is so far from their *ear-shrift. **1604** BABINGTON *Notes Levit.* Wks. (1637) 385 Our Popish Teachers would gather an argument for their Auricular Confession and Eare-shrift. **1594** CAREW *Huarte's Exam. Wits* viii. (1596) 106 It is rather an head-ach than an *eare-sore. *a* **1704** T. BROWN *Wks.* (1760) I. 306 (D.) The perpetual jangling of the chimes..is no small ear-sore to us. **1626** BACON *Sylva* §285 Mark whether any Sound abroad in the open Air, will not be heard distinctly, from further distance, than without that Instrument; being (as it were) an *Eare-spectacle. **1854** BADHAM *Halieut.* 171 The large *ear-stones, which..characterise all the members of the present group [the gurnard group]. **1810** SOUTHEY *Kehama*, The *ear-strings throb as if they were rent. [**1873** *Young Englishwoman* Sept. 443/1 The most recherché..is the small diamond earring, riveted into the ear like a stud.] **1939–40** *Army & Navy Stores Catal.* 463/1 Pair Cultured Pearl *Earstuds. **1961** *Times* 6 June 22/6 A pair of circular-cut diamond earstuds. **1966** R. PETRIE *Dead Loss* vi. 44, I could get stud earrings, vulgar-big, from Woolworths... Big white plastic ear-studs. **1855** *Knickerbocker* Feb. 199 In stable-yards, old-looking black boys, in cat-skin caps, with *ear-tabs to them. **1909** *N.Y. Even. Post* 28 Jan. (Th.), With the first really cold weather of the winter, there appeared on Broadway the vendors of ear-tabs. **1922** *Short Stories* Feb. 36/1 An experience much like the one I had had in the wireless station... Sprague gave me one set of ear tabs and took the other for himself. **1899** F. G. SHINN *Elem. Ear-Training* I. p. iii, The author believes that the placing of the subject of direct *ear-training in a prominent position in schemes of musical education, will..raise the standard demanded of public and private performances. **1921** H. E. PALMER *Princ. Language-Study* 17 If his ear-training is neglected during the elementary stage, he will replace foreign sounds by native ones. **1929** I. C. WARD *Phonetics Eng.* (1931) iii. 17 Ear-training exercises. **1947** *Penguin Music Mag.* May 49 The lessons should be as varied as possible: a little ear-training, a little sight-reading.., a few finger exercises. **1659** FELTHAM *Low Countries* (1677) 54 Their *Ear-wyres have so nipt in their Cheeks. **1685** COOKE *Marrow of Chirurg.* (ed. 4) V. i. 221 The Ear-wires worn by women to fix their Head-clothes too to keep them on. **1598** tr. *Linschoten's Voy.* I. xl. 84/2 They [in India] can hardly kepe any paper..from wormes, which are like *eare-wormes. *a* **1670** HACKET *Abp. Williams* II. 152 There is nothing in the oath to protect such an ear-worm, but he may be appeached.

ear (ɪə(r)), *sb.*[2] Forms: 1 éar, eher, æhher, æchir, 2 eher, 3 er, 3–5 ere, 5 eere, ȝer, 6–7 eare, 7– ear. For Sc. forms see ICKER. [OE. *éar* (WS.), *eher*, *æhher* (Northumb.), *æchir* (? Mercian) = OHG. *ehir*, *ahir*, (MHG. *eher* neut., mod.G. *ähre* fem., Du. *aar*), ON. *ax* (Sw., Da. *ax*), Goth. *ahs* (genit. *ahsis*) neut.:—OTeut. **ahoz-*, of same meaning = Lat. *acus* (genit. *-ĕris*) neut., husk of corn. Words radically of the same origin and signification are AWN, AIL *sb.*[2]]

a. A spike or head of corn; the part of a cereal plant which contains its flowers or seeds. ***in*** (†OE. ***on***) ***the ear, in ear***: said of corn when in the stage at which it bears ears; cf. *in flower*.

a **800** *Corp. Gloss.* 1892 *Spicas*, ear. *c* **1000** *Ags. Gosp.* Matt. xii. 1 Hys leorning-cnihtas..ongunnun pluccian þa ear [*c* **950** *Lindisf.* eheru; *c* **975** *Rushw.* æchir; *c* **1160** *Hatton* ear]. *Ibid.* Mark iv. 28 Syþþan fullne hwæte on þam eare [*c* **950** *Lindisf.* eher; *c* **975** *Rushw.* æhher; *c* **1160** *Hatton* eare]. *c* **1250** *Gen. & Ex.* 2104, Vii. eares wexen fette of coren. **1297** R. GLOUC. 490 Tho grene corn in Somer ssolde curne, To foule wormes muchedel the eres gonne turne. **1398** TREVISA *Barth. De P.R.* XVII. clvi. (1495) 707 The heedis of corn eres ben arerid vpwarde. *c* **1420** *Pallad. on Husb.* VII. 16 Now gynneth barly ripe and is to amende Er the eere to breke and shedde it. **1483** *Cath. Angl.* 116 An Ere of corne; *spica, arista*. *c* **1489** CAXTON *Sonnes of Aymon* 136 We oughte to ryde now..while the corne is in the eere. **1523** FITZHERB. *Husb.* §13 Sprot-barley hath a flat eare. **1611** BIBLE *Ex.* ix. 31 Barley was in the ear. **1740** SOMERVILLE *Hobbinol* II. (1749) 133 The ripen'd Grain, whose bending Ears Invite the Reaper's Hand. **1819** J. Q. ADAMS in C. Davies *Metr. Syst.* III. (1871) 93 Thirty-two kernels of wheat from the middle of the ear. **1821** CLARE *Vill. Minstr.* I, Marking each little object on his road, An insect, sprig of grass, and ear of grain.

b. ***ear of corn***, a head of maize. Also *ellipt. N. Amer.*

1622 *Mourt's Relation* 21 We..found a fine new Basket full of very faire corne of this yeare, with some 36. goodly eares of corne. *c* **1665** P. E. RADISSON *Voyages* (1885) 78 Each takes an ear of corne and putts in their mouths. **1831** J. M. PECK *Guide for Emigrants* II. 156 The ears [of Virginia corn] are usually five or six feet, and often more from the ground. **1880** WEBSTER Suppl. s.v. *Head*, In the U.S., *ear* is used of Indian corn alone. **1894** *Vermont Agric. Rep.* XIV. 42 The ears (grain and cobs) are of course digestible. **1958** *Edmonton* (Alberta) *Jrnl.* 26 July 39/4 The staff..reported harvesting about 300 ears of Altagold corn.

†**ear**, *sb.*[3] *Obs. rare*$^{-1}$. Forms: 5 yere, 7 eare. [f. EAR *v.*] The action of ploughing; a ploughing. Also in *comb.*, as ***ear-land, -time***.

c **1460** *Towneley Myst.* 12 At yere time I sew fare corn. **1616** SURFL. & MARKH. *Countr. Farm* 35 Hee shall giue the second eare vnto those his grounds that are most barren. **1693** W. ROBERTSON *Phraseol. Gen.* 516 Ear-land, *arvum*.

ear, *sb.*[4] *dial.* 'A west country term for a place where hatches prevent the influx of the tide' (Adm. Smyth).

1847 HALLIW. (Somerset.)

ear (ɪə(r)), *v.*[1] *Obs.* exc. *arch.* Forms: 1 eriȝan, 1–2 erien, (3 ærien), 3–5 ere(n, (eer), 6–8 eare, 7– ear. (3–5 here, 5 eryyn, eiere, 6 eire, eyr, 6–8 *Sc. dial.* are, 7 ayre.) [Common Teut.: OE. *ęrian* = OFris. *era*, ODu. *erien*, OHG. *erran*, *erren*, (MHG. *eren*, *ern*, early mod.G. *aren*), ON. *erja*, Goth. *arjan*:—OTeut. **arjan*, f. WAryan root **ar* to plough, whence Gr. *ἀρό-ειν*, L. *ar-āre*, Ir. *airim*.]

1. *trans.* To plough, till (the ground); also, to turn *up* (the ground), to throw *up* (an object) with a plough.

c **888** K. ÆLFRED *Boeth.* xiv. 4 (Gr.) þeah him mon eriȝan scyle æcera þusend. *c* **1000** ÆLFRIC *Gram.* xxiv. 135 Hæfst ðu æceras to eriȝenne. **1340–70** *Alex. & Dind.* 201 For ye non erþe ne eren. *c* **1440** *Promp. Parv.* 141 Eryyn londe, *aro*. *c* **1420** *Pallad. on Husb.* I. 184 To tille a felde man must.. eree it uppe bydene. **1513** DOUGLAS *Æneis* VII. ix. 140 And wyth ane hundreth plewis the land he aryt. **1526** *Pilgr. Perf.* (W. de W. 1531) 23 After that he tempereth it with dong, than eareth it, soweth it, and haroweth it. **1587** HARRISON

England I. xxiv. (1877) I. 361 A siluer saucer..was eared vp by a plough. **1601** HOLLAND *Pliny* I. 505 When you ere it [the ground] vp with the plough. **1607** NORDEN *Surv. Dial.* 181 A plow will ayre an Acre a day. **1721–1800** BAILEY, To *Ear*, or *Are*, to till, plough, or fallow the Ground. **1855** SINGLETON *Virgil* I. 83 But if you'll ear the soil For wheaten harvest.

b. *absol.*

a **1000** *Ags. Gosp.* Luke xvii. 7 Hwylc eower hæfþ eriȝendne þeow. *c* **1205** LAY. 10030 Heo gunnen to ærien. **1297** R. GLOUC. 21 Heo..erede and sewe, So þat in lutel while gôde cornes hem grew. *c* **1430** LYDG. *Bochas* I. xix. (1554) 35 b, If ye not had hered in my calf. **1483** CAXTON *Gold. Leg.* 74/4 The oxen erid in the ploughe. **1526** TINDALE 1 *Cor.* ix. 10 That he which eareth should ear in hope. *c* **1630** in RISDON *Surv. Devon* §77 (1810) 78 Plough with a golden coulter, And eare with a gilded shere.

2. *transf.* and *fig.*

c **1386** CHAUCER *Knts. T.* 28, I wolde have told you fully.. But all this thing I moste as now forbere. I have..a large feeld to ere. **1483** CAXTON *Gold. Leg.* 271/3 With the plough of his tonge erye the feldes unresonable. **1558** PHAËR *Æneid* II. F ij, Long pilgrimage you haue to pas, huge feelde of seas to eare. **1600** FAIRFAX *Tasso* I. xiv. 22 The field of loue, with plow of vertue eared. **1606** SHAKS. *Ant. & Cl.* I. iv. 49 Make the Sea serue them; which they eare and wound With keeles.

Hence **eared**, **earing** *ppl. adjs.*; **earer** *sb.*, a ploughman.

1382 WYCLIF *Isa.* xxviii. 24 Whether al day shal ere the erere, that he sowe. *c* **1384** CHAUCER *H. Fame* I. 485 Without toune, house, or tree..or eared land. *c* **1440** *Promp. Parv.* 141 Eryar of londe, *arator*. **1565** CALFHILL *Answ. Treat. Crosse* (1846) 178 He maketh many mysteries of the Cross: as the hoised sail, the earing plough, the blowing winds. **1594** ?GREENE *Selimus* Wks. 1881–3 XIV. 244 The vnmanured land, Which answeres not his earers greedie mind.

ear (ɪə(r)), *v.*² Also 7 eare. [f. EAR *sb.*²] **a.** *intr.* Of corn: To produce ears, come into ear.

1442 *Three K. Cologne* (Bedf. MS.) vii, [In Palestine] atte Cristemasse barly bygynneth to ere. **1610** G. FLETCHER *Christ's Vict.* in Farr's *S.P.* (1848) 56 Thou with corn canst make this stone to eare. **1776** BARKER in *Phil. Trans.* LXVI. 373 The barley..not earing well on account of the dry season. **1797** HOLCROFT *Stolberg's Trav.* (ed. 2) III. lxxvii. 157 The rye was..beginning to ear.

b. Of maize. *N. Amer.*

1624 CAPT. J. SMITH *Virginia* VI. 239 The stalke was first set, began to eare ere it came to halfe growth, and the last not like to yeeld any thing at all. **1896** *Vermont Agric. Rep.* XV. 71 Usually it [*sc.* the Red Cob] does not ear.

†**ear**, *v.*³ *Obs.* [f. EAR *sb.*¹; in some cases perh. a misspelling for *hear*.] *trans.* To give ear to.

1583 STANYHURST *Æneis* IV. (Arb.) 117 You Gods..Eare this I doe craue you. *a* **1626** FLETCHER *Two Noble Kinsm.* III. i, Thou knew'st..I ear'd her language.

ear, dial. var. of NERE, kidney.

†ˈ**earable**, *a. Obs.* exc. *dial.* Forms: 5–7 **erable**, 5 **errabull**, 6–7 **errable**, (**herabul**), **ereable**, 6–7 **earable**. [f. EAR *v.*¹ + -ABLE.] Capable of being ploughed; fit for tillage. Also *absol.* as quasi-*sb.* Cf. ARABLE.

1475 CAXTON *Jason* (1477) 118 Good londe erable and fayr medowes plente. **1486** *Bk. St. Albans* E vj, On felde or in errabull londe. **1552** HULOET, Ereable, or rather arable lande. **1598** GRENEWEY *Tacitus' Germanie* iii. (1622) 265 Their earable land they change by yeeres. **1693** W. ROBERTSON *Phraseol. Gen.* 516 Earable, *arabilis*.

ˈ**ear-ache.** [f. EAR *sb.*¹]

1. Pain in the drum of the ear; otalgia.

1789 W. BUCHAN *Dom. Med.* (1790) 361 When the ear-ach proceeds from insects, or any hard body sticking in the ear. **1863** FR. KEMBLE *Resid. Georgia* 63 A poor woman suffering dreadfully from the earache.

2. *dial.* The Field Poppy. (Britten and Holland.)

†ˈ**earal** *a.* ? *nonce-wd.* That addresses the ear.

1658 HEWYT *Serm.* 34 (Todd) They are not true penitents who are merely earal, verbal, and worded men, that speak more than they really intend.

earand, dial. f. ERRAND.

earar, var. of ERER, sooner.

ear-bash (ˈɪəbæʃ), *v. trans.* and *intr. slang* (chiefly *Austral.*). [f. EAR *sb.*¹ + BASH *v.*²] To talk inordinately (to someone). Hence **ear-bashing** *vbl. sb.* and *ppl. a.*; **ear-basher**, a chatterer; a bore.

1944 L. GLASSOP *We were Rats* xxxvi. 205 'Time for you bastards to do some spine bashing,' said one. 'Are you going to sit there ear bashing all night?' **1944** R. J. OAKES in *Austral. Short Stories* (1951) 374 The little ear-bashing engineer would take him along. **1953** K. TENNANT *Joyful Condemned* iii. 22 She was ear-bashing me all over tea. **1955** 'N. SHUTE' *Requiem for Wren* (1956) v. 121 The Commander escaped after a quarter of an hour of ear-bashing. **1956** S. HOPE *Diggers' Paradise* xvii. 157 Most golf clubs have a share of 'ear-bashers' as the Aussies call the type who verbally replay their strokes *ad nauseum* [*sic*] at the 'nineteenth'. **1957** I. CROSS *God Boy* (1958) x. 81 We went on ear-bashing each other like that for the next hour or so. **1962** *Daily Tel.* 24 Nov. 1/6 (*heading*) Ear-bashing exercise by Mr. Wigg. [*Ibid.*, Mr. Wigg bashes the ear as once he bashed the square.] **1966** 'L. LANE' *ABZ of Scouse* II. 32 *Ear-basher*, one who talks too much; a garrulous person.

ear-cockle (ˈɪəˌkɒk(ə)l). [? f. EAR *sb.*² + COCKLE in some sense, perhaps the name of the weed.] 'A disease of wheat and other graminaceous plants caused by the presence of vibriones in the seed' (*Syd. Soc. Lex.*).

1836–9 TODD *Cycl. Anat.* II. 113/2.

ear-drop (ˈɪədrɒp). [f. EAR *sb.*¹ + DROP *sb.*]

1. An ornamental pendant worn in the ear.

1720 DEFOE *Capt. Singleton* 211 A few Diamonds in the Ear-drops. **1861** [see ALBERT 1]. **1936** L. C. DOUGLAS *White Banners* ix. 201 While finding the jabot, she had come upon a pair of long imitation-jade eardrops.

2. *transf.* The popular name of the flower of the common fuchsia. (Britten and Holland.)

eared (ɪəd), *ppl. a.*¹ [f. EAR *sb.*¹ + -ED.]

1. Furnished with ears (in various senses); in *Bot.* = AURICULATE. ***eared owl***: a species of owl which has tufts on the head resembling ears.

1434 *E.E. Wills* (1882) 101 A litill panne of brasse y-ered. **1594** BLUNDEVIL *Exerc.* v. xii. (ed. 7) 556 He is eared and tailed like a Rat. **1677** PLOT *Nat. Hist. Oxfordsh.* 103 This stone is..eared on both sides. **1854** WOODWARD *Mollusca* (1856) 256 Shell sub-orbicular..beaks approximate, eared. **1867** *Athenæum* No. 2094. 812/2 A white cap and eared head-dress. **1883** *Fisheries Exhib. Catal.* (ed. 4) 176 C, A group of Eared Seals.

b. With defining word: Having (large, open, etc.) ears. Also LOP-EARED, PRICK-EARED, etc. †***four-eared***: ? = four-armed (said of a market cross).

1514 *MS. Acc. St. John's Hosp. Canterb.*, Rec...for land at þe fower yeryd cros. **1724** *Lond. Gaz.* No. 6324/3 A Cart-like Gelding..a little Wide Ear'd. **1813** SOUTHEY *Roderick* VI, The whole people heard..open-ear'd, the sound. **1825** MRS. SHERWOOD *Old Times* 11, Her hair..was combed neatly under a round-eared cap.

†**2.** (Cf. L. *auriti canes* in Apuleius.) *Obs.*

1607 TOPSELL *Four-f. Beasts* 111 Dogs..are called.. fierce, subtil, sounding, bold, eared for attention, affable, swift.

eared (ɪəd), *ppl. a.*² Also 4 **eeryd**. [f. EAR *sb.*² and *v.*² + -ED.] Of corn or similar plants: Having ears; in *Her.* having ears of a certain tincture. Also, That has come into ear.

1398 TREVISA *Barth. De P.R.* XI. vi. (1495) 393 Dewe gendrid in corrupt ayre..corrumpyth grene corn whan it is eeryd. **1563** HYLL *Garden.* (1593) 105 The flour also is eared, much like to an ear of corne. **1589** R. HARVEY *Pl. Perc.* (1590) 21 A crop of toward youth, so well eared, that they put vs in hope of a timely haruest. **1610** GUILLIM *Heraldrie* III. ix. 111 Three Wheate stalkes, bladed and Eared all proper. **1623** E. WYNNE in Whitbourne *Newfoundland* 108 We have Wheate, Barly, Oates & Beanes both eared and codded. **1870** RUSKIN in *Daily Tel.* 7 Oct., If one could only consider it as much a victory to get a barren field sown as to get an eared field stripped.

†**earestay.** ? Mistake for *caresaye*, obs. f. KERSEY.

1611 in J. Jeaffreson *Middlesex County Rec.* II. 71 Unam peciam linei vocatam Earestayes.

earewe, obs. form of ARROW.

earfth, var. of ARVETH, *Obs.*

earful (ˈɪəfʊl). *colloq.* [f. EAR *sb.*¹ + -FUL 2.] As much (talk) as one's ears can take in at one time; a large quantity (*of* talk, gossip, etc.); a strong reprimand, a 'piece of one's mind'.

1917 R. W. LARDNER *Gullible's Travels* (1926) 27, I and my Missus and Mrs. Hatch clubbed together on the straps and I got a earful o' the real dope. **1922** S. FORD *Trilby May crashes In* x. 159 A parlor Bolshevist..had started to give me an earful about the downtrodden. **1927** A. CLARKE *Son of Learning* III. 56, I have heard an earful of good stories. **1929** W. R. BURNETT *Little Caesar* IV. i. 106, I want the boys to get an earful. Go ahead and spill it. *Ibid.* ii. 119 I'll have to go over and give that bird an earful. **1944** W. STEVENS *Let.* 13 Mar. (1967) 462 He said that the Germans had not changed since Tacitus described them. Considering that I was only waiting for the shop to open, this was rather an earful. **1945** L. A. G. STRONG *Othello's Occupation* 49 She got one of the hottest earfuls I ever heard. **1946** F. SARGESON *That Summer* 56, I tried to get an earful when I heard somebody out on the landing-place. **1964** *Times* 11 Feb. 11/7, I used to put a bottle on the seat and if it rolled off when the pupil let his clutch out, he got an earful.

‖ˈ**earik.** [Ir. *eiric.*] Compensation, fine.

1586 J. HOOKER *Girald. Irel.* in Holinshed II. 23/2 When earike or composition is made among the late people for anie murther.

†ˈ**earing**, *vbl. sb.*¹ *Obs.* [f. EAR *v.*¹ + -ING.] The action of ploughing; a ploughing. Also *attrib.*, as in ***earing-time***.

c **1440** *Promp. Parv.* 141 Eryynge of londe, *aracio*. **1580** BARET *Alv.* E 15 The first earing, or tilth of land. **1611** BIBLE *Ex.* xxxiv. 21 In earing time and in haruest thou shalt rest. **1616** SURFL. & MARKH. *Countr. Farm* 537 Wheat or mesling especially doe desire to haue three earings before they bee sowne.

ˈ**earing**, *vbl. sb.*² [f. EAR *v.*²] The process of coming into ear. Also *concr.* (see quot. 1750).

a **1547** T. KEY *Erasm. Par. Mark* (1548) iv. 17 It widdered awaye before it came to earing. *a* **1682** SIR T. BROWNE *Tracts* 41 Many grains are lost which come not to sprouting or earing. **1750** W. ELLIS *Mod. Husbandm.* III. i. 27 (E.D.S.) The shoot or earing of young wheat.

earing (ˈɪərɪŋ), *sb. Naut.* Also 7–9 **earring**. [? f. EAR *sb.*¹ + -ING¹; possibly however = EARRING. (See quot. 1627.)] 'One of a number of small ropes employed to fasten the upper corner of a sail to the yard' (Adm. Smyth). Also *attrib.*

1626 CAPT. SMITH *Accid. Yng. Seamen* 15 The trusses, the lifts, the earring, the cat harpings. **1627** —— *Seaman's Gram.* v. 23 The Earing is that part of the bunt rope which at all the foure corners of the saile is left open as it were a ring. **1762–9** FALCONER *Shipw.* II. 153 The weather-earings and the lee they past. **1774** *Westm. Mag.* II. 429 We're all Macaronies from earing to clue. **1840** R. DANA *Bef. Mast* iv. 9 Our new second mate used to..have the weather earing passed before there was a man upon the yard. *c* **1860** H. STUART *Seaman's Catech.* 19 Head earring strops [are] used ..For hauling out and securing the head earrings. *Ibid.* 45 The head earrings [are] handed up to the earing men on the yard. *Ibid.* 46 The first and second reef earrings.

†ˈ**earish**, *a. Obs. rare.* [f. EAR *sb.*¹ + -ISH.] Auricular (confession).

1554 BECON *Comfort. Epist.* in *Prayers* (1844) 201 Their rising up consisteth in popish penance, in feigned contrition, in earish confession.

earl (ɜːl) *sb.* Forms: 1–4 **eorl**, 2 **ærl**, 3 **ȝierl**, 3–6 **erl**, (4 **erldl**, **erld**, **erel**, **errel**, 5 **erell**, **errille**), 4–6 **ȝerl**, 5–7 **erle**, 5 **urle**, **ȝorle**, 6–7 **yerle**, **earle**, 9 *Sc.* **yerl**, 7– **earl**. See also JARL, YARL. [OE. *eorl* = OSax. *erl* (= sense 1 b below), ON. *earl*, later *iarl*, nobleman, chieftain:—OTeut. **erlo-z*.

Some scholars refer the word to the Aryan root **ers*, comparing Gr. ἔρσην, ἄρσην male; cf. also EARNEST *a.* and *sb.*¹ The ON. runic spelling *erilaR* seems however unfavourable to this view. The notion that *eorl* is a corruption of *ealdor* is wholly untenable.]

†**1.** A man of noble rank, as distinguished from a *ceorl*, CHURL, or ordinary freeman. Only in OE.

?*a* **616** *Laws of Ethelbert* ⁋13 Gif on eorles tune man mannan ofslæhþ xii scillinga ȝebete. *a* **1000** *Byrhtnoth* 132 Eode swa anræd eorl to þam ceorle.

†**b.** In OE. poetry used for: A warrior, a brave man, a man generally.

Beowulf 357 þær Hroðgar sæt..mid his eorla ȝedriht. *a* **1000** *Riddles* xlvii. 6 (Gr.) Ealra wæron fife eorla and idesa. *a* **1000** *Crist* 546 (Gr.) Hwite cwoman eorla eadgiefan englas togeanes. *a* **1000** *Cædmon's Gen.* 1844 þa com ellenrof eorl siðian Abraham.

†**2.** In late OE.: A Danish under-king (see JARL); hence (under Cnut and his successors) the viceroy or governor of one of the great divisions of England, Wessex, Northumbria, Mercia, etc. (In this sense practically synonymous with the native title of ALDERMAN.) *Obs.* exc. *Hist.*

c **906** *Laws of Edw. & Guthrum* ⁋12 Gif man ȝehadodne.. forræde..þonne sceal him cyng beon oþþon eorl þær on lande..for mæȝ and for mund boran. *c* **1042** *Chart. Leofric* in *Cod. Dipl.* IV. 72 Leofric eorl and his ȝebedda habbað ȝeunnen twa land for Godes lufan. *a* **1123** *O.E. Chron.* (Laud) an. 1048 Man sette þa Odda to eorle ofer Defenascire, & ofer Sumersæton, etc. **1761** HUME *Hist. Eng.* I. iii. 72 Canute..created Thurkill earl or duke of East Anglia.

3. After the Norman Conquest regarded as equivalent to the Lat. *comes* COUNT.

†**a.** *generally.* Applied to all feudal nobles and princes bearing the Romanic title of Count; also *Hist.* to the officers called *comites* under the later Roman empire. In ME. often used as the typical designation of a great noble. *Obs.* (In *Hist.* use COUNT is now always employed in this sense.)

c **1175** *Cott. Hom.* 231 Se hlaford into þar halle come, mid his dierewurd ȝeferede, mid ærlen and aldren. *a* **1200** *Moral Ode* 324 in *Trin. Coll. Hom.* 230 We mihten habben more ..þan ȝierles and kinges. *a* **1300** *Cursor M.* 13270 Noght o riche kinges kin Ne of erel þan gret baron. *c* **1380** WYCLIF *Wks.* (1880) 386 Dukis & erlis, barons & knyȝtis. **1387** TREVISA *Higden* (Rolls) VI. 251 Rouland eorl of þe paleys. *c* **1400** *Destr. Troy* 4068 Ascalaphus, a skathil duke..And Helminus, a hede vrle, hadyn to-gedur Thretty shippes. *c* **1420** *Chron. Vilod.* 269, Duke, Errelle, and eke Baroun. *c* **1440** *Promp. Parv.* 141 Erle, lorde, *comes*. **1483** CAXTON *G. de la Tour* E vj, The sone of an erle of that land. **1577** HOLINSHED *Chron.* I. 72/2 Nectaridus one of the emperours house earle of the sea coast, hauing charge of the parties towards the sea, was slaine. **1655** M. CARTER *Hon. Rediv.* (1660) 51 We used the word Earl for gentle or noble. **1799** H. HUNTER tr. *St. Pierre* I. 354 Christianity..wrested in France enormous possessions out of the hands of the Earls and Barons.

b. *spec.* In England, Scotland, and Ireland, the title of a specific order of rank, corresponding to *Count* in the nobility of other European nations; in the modern peerage an earl ranks next below a marquis, and next above a viscount.

Under the Norman kings the title of earl (count) implied the governorship or the feudal lordship of a COUNTY; subsequently the territorial designation (Earl of Derby, of Leicester) became, as in other degrees of the peerage, purely formal, and in some cases a surname is used instead (as Earl Brownlow, Earl Cowper). When a duke or a marquis has an earldom as his second title, this is 'by courtesy' given to his eldest son: thus the heir of the Duke of Northumberland is Earl Percy, of the Marquis of Winchester, the Earl of Wiltshire.

a **1123** *O.E. Chron.* an. 1101 þurh þone eorl Rodbert of Normandie þe mid unfriðe hider to lande fundode. **1140** *Ibid.*, On þis gær wolde þe king Stephne tæcen Rodbert eorl of Gloucestre. **1297** R. GLOUC. 523 He..bileuede the erl marschal & the erl of Chestre there. **1375** BARBOUR *Bruce* II. 234 Twa Erlis alsua with him war. **1473** WARKW. *Chron.* 1 Lord Stafforde was made Erle of Devynshire. **1536** WRIOTHESLEY *Chron.* (1875) I. 41 Moste of the Kings Councell, as erles, lordes and nobles of this realme. **1556** *Chron. Gr. Friars* 54 Sir John Dudley that was amrelle of the

see was made yerle of Warwyk. **1593** SHAKS. *2 Hen. VI*, II. ii. 79 The Earle of Warwick Shall one day make the Duke of Yorke a King. **1768** BLACKSTONE *Comm.* I. I. xii. 310 An earl is a title of nobility. **1816** SCOTT *Old Mort.* 293 Levied an armed regiment under the Yerl of Angus.

†**4.** A director, superintendent.

1483 CAXTON *Gold. Leg.* 382/1 Thenne the erle of the sacrefyses gaue moche money.

5. *Comb.* †**earl-right.** (Only in OE. and *Hist.*)

c **1030** *Laws of Cnut* in Thorpe *Laws* 81 Gif þeȝen ȝeþeah þæt he wearð to eorle þonne wæs he syþþan eorl-rihtes weorðe. **1875** STUBBS *Const. Hist.* I. v. 80 The..man who has 'thriven to eorl-right', or who has his forty hides.

earl, *v.*[1] *Sc.* [var. of ARLE *v.*] To 'fasten' by earnest-money, pledge, betroth.

c **1375** ? BARBOUR *St. Agnes* 26 In takine of wedinge He erlis þaime with his rynge. *a* **1810** TANNAHILL *My Mary*, The heavenly vow I got, That earled her my own.

†**earl,** *v.*[2] ? *nonce-wd.* [? f. EARL *sb.*] *trans.* ? To be the lord of.

a **1400–50** *Alexander* 4646 Alexander, that aire · þat erles all þe werd.

†**ear-lage.** *rare*⁻¹. (See quot.)

1607 TOPSELL *Four-f. Beasts* 439 The ear-lages or ear-laps of a Mule.

earldom ('ɜːldəm). [f. EARL *sb.* + -DOM.] The domain or territory governed by an earl (*obs.* exc. *Hist.*); the rank or dignity of an earl.

a **1123** *O.E. Chron.* an. 1053 (Laud MS.) Feng Ælfgar eorl to ðam eorldome þe Harold ær ahte. **1297** R. GLOUC. 523 Sir Peris de Roches..The king ȝet..erldom of Gloucestre. **1387** TREVISA *Higden* (Rolls) II. 85 Two and þritti schires ..þat now beeþ i-cleped erldoms. **1495** *Act 2 Hen. VII*, xxxiii. §2 Londes and tenementes parcelles of the seid Erledome of Marche. **1530** PALSGR. 49 *Conte*, an erledom. **1594** SHAKS. *Rich. III*, IV. ii. 93, I clayme the gift..Th' Earledome of Hertford, Which you haue promised. **1682** DRYDEN *Satyr* 124 Others with Titles and new Earldoms Caught. *a* **1745** SWIFT *Lett.* (1768) IV. 317 [Henry II] bequeathed that earldom [Anjou] to the second [son] in his last sickness. **1841** W. SPALDING *Italy & It. Isl.* II. 118 Robert Guiscard, about 1059, united in his own person all these earldoms. **1848** MACAULAY *Hist. Eng.* I. 537 His marquisate became extinct; but his son was permitted to inherit the ancient earldom. **1874** *Daily News* 17 Feb. 3/4 The accession of Viscount St. Lawrence to the earldom of Howth.

fig. **1393** LANGL. *P. Pl.* C. III. 88 The erldom of enuye and yre he hym grauntep.

earled *ppl. a. nonce-wd.* Turned into an earl.

1606 EARL NORTHAMPTON in *True & Perf. Relat.* Pp 3 b, As the Prior of Duresme [wondered] of his Earled Bishop.

earless ('ɪəlɪs), *a.*[1] [f. EAR *sb.*[1] + -LESS.]

1. Having no ears: **a.** of human beings and animals; **b.** of drinking vessels, etc. (cf. EAR *sb.*[1] 7); **c.** *Conch.* of bivalve shells.

1611 COTGR., *Essoreillé*..earelesse, without eares. **1796** MORSE *Amer. Geog.* I. 105 Earless mammot [*misspelt for* marmot]. **1828** *Blackw. Mag.* XXIII. 598 He was..earless, eyeless, cheekless, noseless, and chinless. **1854** WOODWARD *Mollusca* (1856) 261 Aucella..left umbo prominent, earless. **1870** E. PEACOCK *Ralf Skirl.* II. 136 Dainty little earless china cups.

2. Destitute of the sense of hearing, or of musical ear. Also *poet.* of places: Where nothing can be heard.

1802 WORDSW. *Sonn. To Toussaint l'Ouv.*, In some deep dungeon's earless den. **1865** ALEX. SMITH *Summ. Skye* I. 180 Weary of singing his songs to the earless rocks and sea waves. **1876** MISS YONGE *Womank.* vi. 44 Just as the earless are given up as to music.

earless ('ɪəlɪs), *a.*[2] [f. EAR *sb.*[2]] Of stalks of corn: Destitute of ears.

? *a* **1400** *Chester Pl., Death Abel* I. (1843) 38 *Cain.* Thes earles cornes..offer I will to daye.

earlet ('ɪəlɪt). [f. EAR *sb.*[1] + -LET; in sense 1 after BRACELET.]

†**1.** An ear-ring. *Obs.*

1609 BIBLE (Douay) *Prov.* xxv. 12 A golden earlet.

2. Anything resembling a small ear. †**a.** An auricle of the heart. **b.** *Bot.* = AURICLE 2. **c.** ? An attachment to a church bell.

1668 CULPEPPER & COLE *Barthol. Anat.* II. vii. 107 The parts of the Heart..are either externally seen, as the Earlets. *c* **1720** W. GIBSON *Farrier's Guide* I. iii. (1738) 27 There belong also to the Heart, two Auricles or Earlets. **1865** tr. *Hugo's Hunchback* IV. iii. (Chapman and H.) 144 He seized the brazen monster by the earlets. **1883** *Syd. Soc. Lex.*, *Earlet*, an ear-like appearance produced by an indentation in the leaves of some of the foliose Hepaticæ.

d. = TRAGUS, esp. when largely developed as in some bats.

1837 *Penny Cycl.* VII. 25/2 The ears are large, insulated and lateral, with an internal earlet. **1845** *Encycl. Metrop.* XXV. 1072/1 Ears large, the tragus or earlet always existing. **1904** *Speaker* 24 Dec. 315/2 The earlet, a curious development of the tragus in insectivorous bats. **1957** *Encycl. Brit.* V. 596/2 The 'earlet', or tragus, is generally large in the insectivorous bats but is never present in the Megachiroptera nor in the insectivorous Rhinolophidae.

†'**earlierness.** *Obs.* [f. *earlier*, compar. deg. of EARLY *a.* + -NESS.] The quality of being more early, priority.

1674 N. FAIRFAX *Bulk & Selv.* Cont., A Moreness of worlds, and Earlyerness of this world, stand upon the same untrusty bottom.

†'**earlily,** *adv. Obs.* [f. EARLY *a.* + -LY[2].] At an early period or stage.

1669 PEPYS *Diary* 4 Mar., And so I parted, with great content that I had so earlily seen him there. **1678** BP. WETENHALL *Office of Preaching* 742 That it [preaching] was earlily required of the Presbyters, we have already seen out of the pretended Apostolical constitutions. **1713** STEELE *Englishman* No. 46. 302, I thus earlily let go my Fire against the Pretender's Friends.

earliness ('ɜːlɪnɪs). [f. EARLY *a.* + -NESS.] The state or condition of being early; formerly also, promptitude, zeal.

a **1626** DONNE *Serm.* 245 There is a youth in our age and an earlinesse acceptable to God in every action. **1640** BP. HALL *Episc.* I. xii. 52 Our owne Authours are..alledged for the earlinesse of this Apostasie. **1682** *Addr. fr. Worcester* in *Lond. Gaz.* No. 1707/5 Our former Earliness and Stability in Duty, had given us the Character of the Loyal City of Worcester. **1820** SCOTT *Monast.* xx, That we may strive to-morrow, with the sun's earliness, to wake a stag from his lair. **1866** MRS. GASKELL *Wives & Dau.* I. 328 No one objected to the earliness of his call.

†'**earlings,** *sb. pl. Obs.* [? f. EAR *sb.*[1] + -LING.] Possibly a transl. of Fr. *oreillettes* 'wires about a woman's head' (Miège *Fr. Dict.* 1701); cf. *ear-wires.*

1660 *Rates* in *Act Tonnage & Poundage 12 Chas. II*, 16 Earlings, the Groce cont. 12 dozen, *jl.* **1721** C. KING *Brit. Merch.* I. 290 Catlings, Earlings, Outnall, Thred, Ticking, Copperas [in list of Imports from France].

earlishness ('ɜːlɪʃnɪs). *nonce-wd.* [f. EARL *sb.* + -ISH + -NESS; OE. had *eorlisc* (= earlish) in the sense 'noble, like an earl'.] The distinctive quality of an earl.

1876 M. COLLINS *Blacksm. & Schol.* II. 120 The Earl had no particular earlishness about him.

'**Earl** '**Marshal.** A high officer of state, formerly the deputy of the CONSTABLE as judge of the *curia militaris* or court of chivalry. The title was originally 'marshal', but one of the holders of the dignity became in 1189 Earl of Pembroke, and it has never since been held by a person of lower rank than an earl. The office is now hereditary in the line of the Dukes of Norfolk, its functions being now confined to the presidency of the Heralds' College and the right of appointing its officers, and to certain purely ceremonial duties.

The equivalent Scottish office of *marischal* became in 14th c. hereditary in the family of Keith; in 1458 the holder of the office was created an earl under the title of Earl Marischal; the last Earl Marischal was attainted in 1716.

1297 R. GLOUC. (Rolls ser.) 10733 Willam þe erl marschal deide þulke ȝer alas. **1495** *Act 11 Hen. VII*, xxxv. Preamb., The..office of Erle Marchall of this Realme. **1603** DRAYTON *Bar. Wars* (R.) Being earl-marshall..welcomes her ashore. **1766** ENTICK *London* IV. 27 The four pursuivants..are also created by the earl-marshal. **1837** *Penny Cycl.* IX. 242/1 Earl Marshal of England..orders all great ceremonials.

earlship ('ɜːlʃɪp). In OE. eorlscipe. [f. EARL *sb.* + -SHIP. In sense 2 the word is of later and independent formation.]

†**1.** Manliness, bravery; nobility, lordship. Only in OE.

Beowulf 1727 (Gr.) Eard and eorlscipe. *a* **1000** *Widsith* 37 (Gr.) No hwæðre he ofer Offan eorlscype fremede.

2. The dignity or office of an earl (*Hist.*). Also, ***your earlship***: used as a humorous or quasi-*arch.* form of address.

1792 H. BROOKE *Fool of Quality* V. 268 Allow me to repair my omission by presenting to your earlship her little highness Abenaide [*ed.* 1 **1770** *has* your lordship]. **1828** SCOTT *F.M. Perth* III. 295, I thank your noble earlship. **1883** H. M. KENNEDY tr. *Ten Brink's E.E. Lit.* 115 The formation of the new great earlships.

early ('ɜːlɪ), *a.* and *sb.* Forms: 3 **earlich,** 4–5 **erli, erly,** 6 **yerly,** 7 **earely,** 6– **early.** [See the *adv.* Not found in OE., and only rarely in ME.; probably evolved from the adv. Cf. the equivalent ON. *árligr*, which is also of rare occurrence.]

A. *adj.* **I.** Absolutely or relatively near to the beginning of a portion of time: opposed to *late.*

When used with a sb. denoting a division of time, it sometimes gives to the latter a partitive sense: thus *the early spring* = the early part of the spring; *the early morning* = the early part of the morning; similarly *the early nineteenth century*, etc.

1. With reference to the time of day.

a. Belonging to the first part of the morning; that exists, takes place, appears, or does something in the first part of the morning. Proverb, ***The early bird gets the worm***; hence ***early bird***, humorously = early riser.

In *early riser, early rising*, the first word may either be taken as an adj., or the phrase may be treated as a combination in which the first element is the adv. (cf. *well-doer, -doing*). The former view seems most in accordance with the modern grammatical consciousness, and is supported by the analogy of the similar phrase in quot. 1225.

a **1225** *Ancr. R.* 258 His earlich ariste from deað to liue. **1398** TREVISA *Barth. De P.R.* IX. xxii. (1495) 360 Mane the erly dawnynge makyth ende of the nyght lytyll and lytyll. *c* **1450** *Sir Beues* (MS. *M.*) 1929 Beuys sayde: 'Yet is it but erly day!' **1594** SHAKS. *Rich. III*, V. iii. 209 The early Village Cock Hath twice done salutation to the Morne. **1611** BIBLE *Hosea* vi. 4 Your goodnesse is as a morning cloud, and as the early dew it goeth away. *c* **1645** HOWELL *Lett.* II. xiv, He that hath once got the fame of an early riser, may sleep till noon. **1667** MILTON *P.L.* IV. 642 Sweet is the breath of morn, her rising sweet, With charm of earliest Birds. **1785** COWPER *Tiroc.* 765 Where early rest makes early rising sure. **1808** J. BARLOW *Columb.* I. 356 Whose watchful priest would meet, with matin blaze, His earlier God. **1833** R. HOGG *Let.* in Lockhart *Scott* (1839) IX. 111 He asked me if I was an early riser. **1866** *Arab. Nts.* 487 It was time to get up for early prayers before sunrise.

b. Relatively near to the beginning of the day (or night). Of events or actions: Taking place at an hour relatively not far advanced, or before the usual hour. ***small-and-early***: applied in the 19th c. to evening parties; colloq. also as quasi-*sb.*

1848–60 BARTLETT *Dict. Amer.*, The meeting will begin at early candle-light. **1865** DICKENS *Mut. Fr.* I. xi. 83 Mrs. Podsnap added a small and early evening to the dinner.

c. ***to keep early hours***: to rise and retire early. ***early habits***: habits of keeping early hours. Hence colloq. the adj. is applied to persons.

1754 RICHARDSON *Grandison* V. xvii. 114 Early hours..and ease, without hurry, will do every thing. **1781** COWPER *Retirem.* 429 What early philosophic hours he keeps. *Mod.* They are early people, and seldom go out in the evening.

†**d.** *absol.* = Early morning, early hour. *Obs.*

1382 WYCLIF *Ecclus.* xviii. 26 Fro erli vnto euen the tyme shal ben chaunged. **1604** SHAKS. *Oth.* II. iii. 7 To morrow with your earliest, Let me haue speech with you.

2. Relatively near to the beginning of the year. Of things or events: Appearing or occurring relatively soon in the year; *esp.* of plants with regard to their time of bearing flowers or fruit.

1526 TINDALE *James* v. 7 Untill he receave the yerly and the latter rayne. **1597** SHAKS. *2 Hen. IV*, I. iii. 38 In an early Spring, We see th' appearing buds, which to proue fruite, Hope giues not so much warrant. **1632** MILTON *L'Allegro* 89 If the earlier season lead. **1664** EVELYN *Kal. Hort.* (1729) 192 Fruits and Flowers, are more early or tardy..according as the Soil and Situation are qualify'd by Nature or Accident. **1697** DRYDEN *Virg. Georg.* I. 67 Ev'n in this early Dawning of the Year. **1811** W. SPENCER *Poems* 98 Sere, sere was ev'ry earlier rose. **1861** MISS PRATT *Flower. Pl.* V. 204 Early Purple Orchis.

3. With reference to a lifetime.

a. Pertaining to or connected with childhood or youth. **b.** Relatively near to the beginning of a lifetime or career. (Sometimes contextually = premature, too early.)

1630 LORD *Banians* 62 They marry about the seventh year ..that the parents might before death see their children disposed, which commeth to pass by these earely conjunctions. **1705** ADDISON *Italy* (Ded.), I had a very early Ambition to recommend my self to Your Lordship's Patronage. **1742** YOUNG *Nt. Th.* v. 899 Early, not sudden, was Narcissa's fate. **1771** *Junius Lett.* xlix. 256 The duke.. was in life your earliest friend. **1780** COWPER *Progr. Err.* 354 Our most important are our earliest years. **1848** MACAULAY *Hist. Eng.* II. 109 Henry Wharton,..whose early death was soon after deplored by men of all parties. **1875** EMERSON *Lett. & Soc. Aims., Poet & Imag.* Wks. (Bohn) III. 158 Music and rhyme are among the earliest pleasures of the child. **1875** JOWETT *Plato* (ed. 2) V. 36 The man who is to be good at anything must have early training.

¶ Used by Byron for: Youthful, young.

1814 BYRON *Lara* I. xx, Blest are the early hearts and gentle hands That mingle therein well-according bands. **1818** —— *Juan* I. xliii, Lucretius' irreligion is too strong For early stomachs.

4. a. Belonging or relating to the initial stage of a historical epoch, of the history of a people, of the world, of a science, etc.; ancient. So ***early history, early records.***

1672–5 COMBER *Comp. Temple* (1702) 558 There are no More, or earlyer Laws than these. **1747** COLLINS *Passions* 2 While yet in early Greece she sung. **1787** BONNYCASTLE *Astron.* i. 3 Astronomy is a science of the earliest antiquity. **1794** SULLIVAN *View Nat.* I. 106 Anaxagoras seems to have been one of the earliest philosophers..who held this doctrine. **1821** CRAIG *Lect. Drawing* vii. 373 The early engravers..never attempted to express more than the drawing and the actual light and shadows. **1848** MACAULAY *Hist. Eng.* I. 593 After the fashion of an earlier generation. *Ibid.* II. 399 Early fathers of the Church. **1851** RUSKIN *Stones Ven.* (1874) I. viii. 90 Wherever we find the level.. square occurring..in early Northern work. **1875** JOWETT *Plato* (ed. 2) III. 1, In the early Church he exercised a real influence. **1875** FORTNUM *Maiolica* 92 Two large and finely painted early dishes.

b. *Archit.* **Early English**: the name commonly applied to the period of English architecture succeeding the so-called 'Norman', and usually described as extending from A.D. 1175 to 1275; also the style characteristic of that period; also called ***Early Pointed, First Pointed.***

1807 G. MILLERS *Descr. Cathedral Ch. Ely* 17 Sketch of the Characteristics of English Church Architecture. 1. Age. —Saxon..2. Age.—Norman..3. Age.—Early English; from 1200 to 1300, comprehending the reigns of John, Hen. III. and Edw. I. **1851** RUSKIN *Stones Ven.* I. 106 The Early English capital is, therefore, a barbarism of triple grossness. **1879** SIR G. SCOTT *Lect. Archit.* I. 123 The round moulded capital is characteristic of the English Early Pointed. *Ibid.* 138 The Early Pointed style was from 1175 to 1275.

5. a. *generally.* Connected with the initial part of any division of time, any continuous action, etc.; also, anterior in comparison with something else; timely, done or taking place

without delay, or before it is too late. In compar. and superl. = former, foremost (in time).

1767 GOOCH *Wounds* I. 191 This consideration shou'd engage our earliest and closest attention to the rules. 1791 BURKE *App. Whigs* Wks. VI. 9 Made men remiss in early precaution. 1795 SOUTHEY *Joan of Arc* IX. 303 Fear not for Burgundy!.. Our earliest scouts Shall tell his homeward march. 1814 SCOTT *Ld. of Isles* VI. iii, Bruce's earliest cares restore That speechless page to Arran's shore. 1882 PEBODY *Eng. Journalism* xxi. 153 The early part of this century.

b. Of future dates and events: Not remote, near at hand.

1857 LIVINGSTONE *Trav.* Introd. 8 There being no prospect of an early peace. *Mod.* An early date has been fixed for the ceremony. Please reply at your earliest convenience.

II. 6. With reference to serial order: Occupying a position near the beginning.

1707 *Lond. Gaz.* No. 4333/8 They will Advance Money upon early Tallies. *Mod.* The early chapters of the book. The early prime numbers.

III. 7. a. Special collocations: as, **early American** *a.*, belonging to or characteristic of the colonial and post-Revolutionary period in America; **early-closer**, one whose place of business is closed one afternoon in the week; **early closing**, orig. designating a movement for the reduction of the daily hours of labour in wholesale and retail trades; now, the system by which business premises are closed for the day at the end of the morning on a particular day of the week; also, the closing of public houses earlier at night; also *attrib.* or *adj.*; **early days**, early in time for something (to happen, etc.); **early leaver**, a pupil who leaves school without completing the full course of study; hence ***early leaving***; **early Victorian** *a.*, belonging to or characteristic of the early years of Queen Victoria's reign, its literature, fashions, etc.; also as *sb.*; so ***early Victorianness***; **early wood**, the less dense part of the annual ring of a tree.

1895 *Critic* 9 Nov. 310/2 (*title*) Early American paintings at the Metropolitan Museum. 1915 W. A. DYER (*title*) Early American craftsmen. 1922 *Country Life* Sept. 45/1 Furniture from the workshop of Duncan Phyfe holds distinctly a place of its own in the history of early American utilitarian art. 1926 *Ladies' Home Jrnl.* Sept. 98/4 There was first of all a charm created by the primitive simplicity of the antique Early American furniture as seen against nut-brown panelings of old pine. 1937 E. ST. V. MILLAY *Conversation at Midnight* II. 47 They fill the place so full of Early American furniture that there isn't a comfortable chair in the house. 1945 O. NASH *Many Long Years Ago* (1954) 96 He was too Early-American to write for advice from Emily Post. 1863 *Sat. Rev.* 17 Jan. 78/1 The public would look with a more favourable eye upon the early closers if [etc.]. 1906 *Daily Chron.* 28 July 7/6 Thus giving early-closers and Saturday-afternooners a chance. 1845 *Chambers's Edin. Jrnl.* 25 Aug. 123/1 Those who are striving for the early closing of shops. 1846 *Punch* 11 Apr. 165/1 (*heading*) The Early Closing Movement. 1849 *Hogg's Weekly Instructor* III. 24/2 The Metropolitan Early Closing Society. 1851 *Household Words* 1 Nov. 126/2 That early-closing movement which has fastened the portals of all those magnificent palaces of linen-drapery. 1881 *Ibid.* 12 Nov. 53/2 That Saturday 'early closing'.. must be a vast boon to shop-people. 1888 *Boy's Own Paper* Christmas Number 34/1 Wednesday was our early-closing day. 1902 *Encycl. Brit.* XXXII. 685/2 Scottish Early Closing of Public-houses Act. 1534 T. MORE *Wks.* (1557) 1156/1 She telleth hym then that it is but earely dayes, & he shal com time inough. 1739–40 RICHARDSON *Pamela* (1740) I. xiv. 26 'Tis early Days with Pamela; and she does not yet think of a Husband. 1828 J. CONSTABLE *Let.* 25 Apr. (1962) 244 No impediments have yet arisen, and it is early days. 1935 G. HEYER *Death in Stocks* xi. 145 It's early days yet. 1957 *Times* 23 Dec. 11/2 As regards the current year, it is early days to express any considered opinion, but trading conditions are bad. 1951 *Times Educ. Suppl.* 12 Jan. 21/1 That there is a substantial number of early leavers is not to be disputed. *Ibid.* 21/2 To tolerate early leaving is to destroy the structure and purpose of the grammar school. 1878 C. L. EASTLAKE *Hints Household Taste* (ed. 4) vi. 161 Fifty years hence most of our early 'Victorian' upholstery will have fallen into useless lumber. 1883 *Eng. Illustr. Mag.* Nov. 89/2 The late Georgian or early Victorian age. 1896 *Lady's Realm* Dec. 129/1, I was a youth—in the mahogany age—early Victorian, you know. 1895 F. HARRISON (*title*) Studies in early Victorian literature. 1906 *Fortn. Rev.* Nov. 880 We invite the humour of the gods if we look down on the early Victorians. 1908 *Westm. Gaz.* 31 Oct. 15/3 The bonnets.. were positively early-Victorian in size, and quite early-Victorian in the dainty pale silk frillings which framed most becomingly the face and the hair. 1959 *N. & Q.* CCIV. 123/1 Mr. G. M. Young's excellent two-volume survey of *Early Victorian England* began in 1830. 1914 WODEHOUSE *Man Upstairs* 181 It was the gruesome Early Victorianness of it all that took the heart out of him. 1914 S. J. RECORD *Mech. Prop. Wood* II. 44 The inner portion [of the annual ring] was formed early in the season, when growth was comparatively rapid and is known as early wood. 1931 G. A. GARRATT *Mech. Prop. Wood* II. 115 That [wood] originally nearest the pith, which was formed in the spring of the year and is consequently known as springwood or early wood, is generally more open textured and of lighter colour than the outer portion of the ring. 1967 F. D. SILVESTER *Timber* iv. 26 The discoloration tends to be uneven as if a stain.. has bled into the early wood portion of the growth rings.

b. In collocations used *attrib.*; *spec.* **early-warning**, used of equipment, bases, etc., designed for the early detection of aerial, etc., attacks; also *fig.*

1897 M. KINGSLEY *Trav. W. Africa* 65 The pottery has a very early-man look about it. 1900 *Westm. Gaz.* 9 Jan. 2/1 The shock of that early-dawn disaster. 1906 *Daily Chron.* 2 June 9/1 The abolition of early-season events for two-year-olds. 1909 *Westm. Gaz.* 23 Apr. 8/2 Much of the early-morning work is performed entirely alone. 1916 R. FROST *Let.* 8 Aug. (1964) 41 Regarded as an attack of early-marriage nerves, it seems even a little funny. 1946 A. LEE *German Air Force* iv. 44 With no early warning system to help them operate fighters economically.., the Polish Air Force could not be expected to survive. 1949 E. COXHEAD *Wind in West* iii. 61 The first recipient of her early-morning tea. 1956 *Ann. Reg. 1955* 135 President Eisenhower's 'early warning' plan.. for a mutual exchange of military blueprints and aerial reconnaissance by Russia and America. 1958 *Listener* 17 July 78/1 The early warning missile station is about to be constructed. 1961 *Flight* LXXX. 654/1 The same hardware and techniques used to launch an orbiting scientific capsule can also be used to orbit an early-warning satellite. 1970 *Daily Tel.* 28 Apr. 2/3 An early warning system to alert doctors of the latest drug, Mandrax, being misused has been called for.

B. *sb.* **a.** An early fruit or vegetable. Chiefly *pl.*

1846 *Times* 13 Feb., Regents.. kidneys, earlies, Scotch reds. 1883 R. FREMLIN *Potato* 4 Second Earlies and Late Sorts. 1900 *Daily News* 10 Sept. 2/3 Hops... A few samples of earlies were offered at market to-day. 1925 *Daily Mail* 25 Apr. (Advt.), Chrysanthemums. A nice collection of well rooted outdoor earlies. 1961 J. SEYMOUR *Fat of Land* iv. 53 In March we start potato planting. We plant a few earlies and later a lot of main crop.

b. *pl.* Early years or days.

1927 'A. HORN' (*title*) The Ivory Coast in the earlies. 1928 *Sunday Express* 24 June 8/5 So much for the old show days in the earlies. 1936 *Times Lit. Suppl.* 22 Feb. 167/2 A sheep-droving expedition on the scale of the one described here was more common in the 'earlies' of Australia than now.

early ('ɜːlɪ), *adv.* Forms: 1 *Northumb.* árlíce, ǽrlíce, 2–4 erliche, 3 earliche, 4 erlike, erli, erely, eerly, arliche, orly, *Sc.* airlie, 3–4 arli, 4–5 erly, 5 ȝerlyche, yerely, *north.* 4–5 areli, -ly, 4–6 *Sc.* ar-, ayr-, airly, 5 *Sc.* yarly, 6 yerle, 6–7 earely, 6– early. [OE. *árlíce* (= ON. *árliga*) f. **ár* (= ON. *ár*) positive deg. of *ǽr* ERE + *-líce* -LY². The ME. forms with *o* descend directly from this; the OE. var. *ǽrlíce* (with umlaut or assimilation to *ǽr*) gave rise to *arli, erli* (whence the mod form).]

I. Near the beginning of a period of time.

1. With reference to the time of day.

a. In the first part of the morning.

c950 *Lindisf. Gosp.* John viii. 2 And ærlice [c975 *Rushw.* arlice] æftersona cuom in temple. c1200 *Trin. Coll. Hom.* 13 Erliche rise, and gernliche seche chireche. a1225 *Ancr. R.* 20 Siggeð.. prime iþe winter erliche. a1300 *Cursor M.* 2817 Bot arli [1340 *Fairf.* erly], ar men well moght see, þe angls badd loth do him flee. c1320 *Seuyn Sag.* (W.) 203 The child.. ros arliche amorewen. 1330 R. BRUNNE *Chron.* (1810) 32 He suld fynd a palmere orly at morn. 1375 BARBOUR *Bruce* v. 554 For to riss airly euirilk day. c1380 WYCLIF *Wks.* (1880) 460 He wakide eerly to his puple. c1420 *Chron. Vilod.* 785 In Asterre day ȝerlyche in þe mornyng. c1425 WYNTOUN *Cron.* IX. i. 65 Rycht airly in til þe dawing. 1513 DOUGLAS *Æneis* VIII. viii. 23 At morrow full ayrly Eneas haistis vp, and mycht nocht ly. 1513 BRADSHAW *St. Werburge* (1848) 165 This Judith.. rose up yerle. 1535 COVERDALE *Ps.* cxviii[xix]. 147 Early in yᵉ mornynge do I crie vnto the. 1592 SHAKS. *Rom. & Jul.* v. iii. 188 What misadventure is so earely vp? a1665 J. GOODWIN *Filled w. Spirit* (1867) 113 Early up and never the nearer. 1711 STEELE *Spect.* No. 49 ¶2 Young Fellows.. who rise early for no other purpose but to publish their Laziness. 1832 TENNYSON *May Queen*, Call me early, mother dear. 1884 J. HAWTHORNE in *Harper's Mag.* Feb. 433/2 You must get up early to get the better of a man who has been a parson.

b. Relatively near to the beginning of the day (or night); at an hour not far advanced.

1495 *Act 11 Hen. VII*, xxii. §4 Laborers.. late commyng unto their werke, erly departing therefro. 1832 G. DOWNES *Lett. Cont. Countries* I. 458 We resumed our journey early. 1801 SOUTHEY *Thalaba* IV. xviii, Earlier the night came on. 1850 TENNYSON *In Mem.* cvii, A bitter day that early sank Behind a purple-frosty bank Of vapour.

c. *early and late*: at all hours, continuously, incessantly.

c1330 *Assump. Virg.* (BM. MS.) 302 Erliche & late to gladen þee. c1325 *E.E. Allit. P.* A. 392 What lyf ȝe lede, erly & late. c1440 *York Myst.* xxii. 124 Be subgette to þi souereyne Arely and late. 1590 *Pasquil's Apol.* I. C iij b, His conuersation among them.. was.. all manner of seasons, earely, and late. [1621 QUARLES *Esther* (1717) 28 Prayr.. finds admittance, whether earl' or late.] 1766 GOLDSM. *Vic. W.* xx, I was up early and late.

2. Relatively near to the beginning of the year.

1626 BACON *Sylva* §421 An Early-Comming Fruit. 1664 EVELYN *Kal. Hort.* (1729) 191 Early-set Anemonies. 1795 BURKE *Th. on Scarcity* Wks. VII. 406 All the early sown grain recovered itself. *Mod.* Some of the species flower very early.

3. With reference to a lifetime.

a. In childhood or youth. **b.** At a time relatively near to the beginning of a lifetime or career. (Sometimes contextually = too early, prematurely.)

a1225 *Leg. Kath.* 116 Hire fader hefde iset hire earliche to lare. c1340 *Cursor M.* (Edinb. MS.) 23046 Þat.. arlik to god þaim tok. 1612–15 BP. HALL *Contempl. O.T.* XII. iv, Samuel began his acquaintance with God early. 1697 DRYDEN *Virg. Georg.* III. 265 Early begin the stubborn Child to break. 1767 FORDYCE *Serm. Yng. Wom.* II. xii. 200 She lost her father early. 1815 *Scribbleomania* 252 Where the seeds of virtue are early planted. 1835 WILLIS *Pencillings* I. xiv. 105 The early-learnt history of the family. 1871 MORLEY *Voltaire* (1886) 107 Voltaire perceived very early in life that to be needy was to be dependent.

4. At or near the beginning of a historical epoch, of the history of the nation, the world, a science, etc.; far back in date, anciently.

c1340 *Cursor M.* 9001 (Fairfax MS.), Allas arly [*v.r.* arli, erly] þis gile be-gan. Þat adam þat was formast man.. was begiled þorou a wife. 1658 SIR T. BROWNE *Hydriot.* ii. 7 The Romans themselves were early in no small numbers. 1774 GOLDSM. *Nat. Hist.* (1776) IV. 312 The Americans early found out its useful qualities. 1848 MACAULAY *Hist. Eng.* I. 317 As early as the reign of Elizabeth.

5. a. *generally.* In the initial part of any division of time, any continuous action, etc. Also, at a time anterior with respect to something else; in good time, without delay, before it is too late.

1655 MILTON *Sonn. 'Avenge, O Lord'* 14 That from these may grow A hundredfold, who.. Early may fly the Babylonian woe. 1697 DRYDEN *Virg. Georg.* III. 545 Early they stall their Flocks and Herds. 1701 W. WOTTON *Hist. Rome* Alex. i. 457 This Abuse was early redrest. 1807 T. JEFFERSON *Writ.* (1830) IV. 71 He very early saw that the fidelity of the western country was not to be shaken. 1857 BUCKLE *Civiliz.* I. vii. 456 This great and salutary reaction began early in the present century. 1863 H. COX *Instit.* I. vi. 41 A Parliament.. may.. be convened earlier for dispatch of business. 1872 RAYMOND *Mines* 200 Early in December the weather becomes too cold and stormy.

b. *early on* [f. *earlier on* after LATER ON], at an early stage.

1928 D. L. SAYERS *Bellona Club* xv. 170 'It might have been *given* him earlier.'.. 'Well—not too early on, Peter. Suppose he had died a lot too soon.' 1942 A. L. ROWSE *Cornish Childhood* iv. 82, I was a very 'forward' child: very early on throwing my bottle out over the cradle. 1953 D. D. C. P. MOULD *Ireland of Saints* viii. 103 The difficulties surrounding the relation between philosophy and the Christian revelation and faith had been studied from early on in the Church's history. 1958 *Spectator* 1 Aug. 175/3 Two of the principal characters.. are involved early on in a session of the Law.

II. 6. Referring to serial order. Near the beginning of the series.

Mod. His name appears very early in the list.

earlyish ('ɜːlɪɪʃ), *a.* and *adv.* [f. EARLY *a.* + -ISH¹ 3.] Somewhat early; at an early hour; = *early on.*

1838 MRS. GASKELL *Let.* 17 July (1966) 18 We set off earlyish 4 o'clock say. 1927 W. DEEPING *Kitty* xxviii. 352 It was earlyish, and the big room—empty and noiseless—.. seemed to envelope old Jermyn with velvet arms. 1950 in K. Jackson *Lang. & Hist. Early Brit.* (1953) II. xi. 294 Its epigraphy.. is earlyish. 1963 *Times* 23 Jan. 12/7 The wheels of their cars, in which they hoped to make an earlyish get-away, were already jammed with ice. 1968 H. R. F. KEATING *Inspector Ghote hunts Peacock* ix. 116 'It was early,' he said. 'Quite earlyish. Say about seven.. give or take five minutes either side.'

†**'earman.** *Obs. rare.* In 3 hearman. [f. stem of EAR *v.*¹ + MAN.] A cultivator.

c1230 *Hali Meid.* 47 All swuch as weren ear ha gulten his earste hearmen.

'ear-mark, *sb.* [f. EAR *sb.*¹ + MARK *sb.*]

1. A mark in the ear of a sheep or other animal, serving as a sign of ownership.

1523 FITZHERB. *Husb.* §52 Se that they [the sheep] be well marked, both eare-marke, pitche-marke, and radel-marke. 1681 *Lond. Gaz.* No. 1625/4 Lost.. a White Mare.. no Ear-mark. 1683 *Col. Rec. Penn.* I. 65 Punishmᵗ for those yᵗ shall presume to alter their Neighbours Eare or Brand Mark. 1725 BRADLEY *Fam. Dict.* II. s.v. *Marking*, Some mark them with Raddle and make Ear Marks.

2. *transf.* and *fig.* A 'stamp', mark of ownership, identifying mark.

1577–87 HARRISON in Holinshed *Descr. Brit.* xx. 115 This proverbe hath.. been used as an eare marke of their dissimulation. 1622 R. HAWKINS *Voy. S. Sea* (1847) 67 We should see foure, five, and more, which had, as it were, our eare-marke; one hurt upon the backe, another neere the tayle, another about the fynnes. 1670 BROOKS *Wks.* (1867) VI. 99 God makes this the ear-mark of his people, that they are children that will not lie. 1672 MARVELL *Reh. Transp.* I. 151 Fanatick Money hath no Ear-mark. 1879 TROLLOPE *Thackeray* 201 His [Thackeray's] most besetting sin in style,—the little earmark by which he is most conspicuous.

3. The mark of teeth in the ear.

1837–40 HALIBURTON *Clockm.*, They said it was a biter bit, and they came.. to see which critter would get the ear-mark.

'ear-mark, *v.* Also earmark. [partly f. prec. sb.; partly f. EAR *sb.*¹ + MARK *v.*]

1. *trans.* To mark (animals) in the ear as a sign of ownership or identity; *fig.* to mark (anything) as one's own, make its identity recognizable, by a special sign. Hence **'ear-marked** *ppl. a.*

1591 SPENSER *M. Hubberd* 188 Least we.. for eare marked beasts abroad be bruted. 1612 R. CARPENTER *Soules Sent.* 76, I will heere let them passe as eare-markt slaues of Sathan. 1641 BEST *Farm. Bks.* (1856) 4 It is a goode way to earemarke lambes as they fall. 1882 *Standard* 2 Jan. 5 The troubles which an ear-marked cheque avoids. 1882 MONTAGUE WILLIAMS *Def. Dr. Lamson* in *Times* 14 Mar., Why did the prisoner go down to Wimbledon and earmark his visit by, etc.

†**2.** (*nonce-use.*) To mark a person by cutting his ears (in the pillory).

1660 S. FISHER *Rusticks Alarm* Wks. (1679) 125 The Practice of.. pilloring, gagging, Ear-marking, Noseslitting.

3. To set aside (money, etc.) for a particular purpose. So **'ear-marking** *vbl. sb.* (also *concr.*). Also *fig.*

[*a* **1868** W. STEBBING in M. Pattison *Acad. Org.* i. 13 Corporate property..unearmarked..by the donor.] **1890** *Spectator* 28 June, With large sums ear-marked and accumulating for the extinction of licences. **1893** *Times* 28 Apr. 9/4 A perfectly arbitrary earmarking of moneys paid into a common fund. **1928** *Manch. Guardian Weekly* 31 Aug. 179/2 Sundry amounts of sovereigns were 'ear-marked' for the Commonwealth Bank of Australia. **1929** S. MCKENNA *Happy Ending* III. ii, I need only earmark sufficient time in the summer for certain people whose hospitality I've accepted. **1931** *Economist* 10 Jan. 64/2 The usual year-end earmarkings have cut down the usual gain, so that the year may end with the total under earmark virtually unchanged at around $135,000,000. **1966** *New Statesman* 22 July 123/2 Already the unions give about £270,000 to Transport House without ear-markings.

'ear-ˌminded, *a. Psychol.* [f. EAR *sb.*¹ + MINDED *a.*] Having a marked tendency to carry on mental operations most readily by auditory images; thinking in sounds.

1888 *Pop. Sci. Monthly* XXXIII. 604 Tests for distinguishing between an eye-minded and an ear-minded person..reveal whether the words are better apprehended by the eye or by the ear. **1900** W. B. SECOR in *Amer. Jrnl. Psychol.* XI. 228 Notwithstanding the fact that he was decidedly visual, he had a strong tendency to be ear-minded. **1901** E. B. TITCHENER *Exper. Psychol.* I. I. 196 The purely ear-minded man would recognise persons, things and places by the sounds connected with them. **1925** C. FOX *Educational Psychol.* iv. 76 Classification into ear-minded, eye-minded, etc.

Hence **'ear-ˌmindedness.**

1888 [see *eye-mindedness* s.v. EYE *sb.*¹ 28.] **1893** *Jrnl. Proc. & Addresses Nat. Educ. Assoc. U.S.* XXXII. 780 Some..did show extreme eye-mindedness, and others..showed extreme ear-mindedness. **1902** BALDWIN *Dict. Philos.* II. 571 The varying prominence which visual and auditory and muscular processes occupy in different minds—eye-mindedness, ear-mindedness, motor-mindedness.

†**earn,** *sb. Obs. rare.* [OE. *ærn* = (by metathesis) ON. *rann*, Goth. *razn*:—OTeut. **razno(m*; cogn. with REST. The OE. word is chiefly found in compounds, as *bere-ern*, *hordern*; see quots. under BARN, SALTERN.] A place, dwelling, hut.

a **1000** *Laws of Ine* 57 (Bosw.) Bireþ into his ærne. **1664** *Floddan F.* iii. 25 Who had been shroud in shepherds earn.

earn (ɜːn), *v.*¹ Forms: α. 1 earnian, 2-4 ernie(n, erne(n, 5 arne, 6-7 earne, 7- earn. β. 1 ȝeearnian, 2 ȝearnien, iarnien, iernien, 6 ȝarn, yerne, yearne, yarn, (9 *dial.* yearn, yarn). [OE. *earnian*, *ȝe-earnian*, repr. an OTeut. type **aznôjan*, f. **aznâ* (ON. *ǫnn*) labour, properly field-labour, connected with Goth. *asans*, OHG. *aran* (whence MHG. *erne*, mod.G. *ernte*) harvest, Goth. *asneis*, OHG. *esni* hired labourer, OE. *esne* serf, labourer, man. The primary sense is therefore 'to obtain as the reward of labour'. The OE. *earnian* corresponds in meaning with OHG. *arnên*, but in form with OHG. *arnôn*, which derives its sense 'to reap' independently from the sb.

The ME. forms with initial ȝ or *y* may in some cases descend from OE. *ȝe-earnian*; the mod. dial. forms with *y* prob. represent the simple vb.; cf. *yerth*, *yale* for *earth*, *ale* (OE. *ealo*).]

1. *trans.* To render an equivalent in labour or service for (wages); hence, to obtain or deserve (money, praise, any advantage) as the reward of labour. In early use in wider sense: To deserve; to obtain as a recompense. (In OE. the simple vb. governs the genit. case, the compound *ȝe-earnian* the accusative.)

c **888** K. ÆLFRED *Boeth.* in Sweet *Ags. Reader* (ed. 5) ix. 47 Wuton agifan ðæm esne [Orpheus] his wif, for ðæm he hi hæfð ȝeearnad mid his hearpunga. *a* **1000** *Guthlac* 767 (Gr.) Soðfæstra saula..earniað on eorðan ecan lifes. *a* **1175** *Cott. Hom.* 223 þat hi sceoldan mid edmodnisse & mid hersamnisse ȝearnie þa wuniunge on hefe rice. *c* **1175** *Lamb. Hom.* 93 þet ðeo edmode isomnunge iernade et gode, þet muchel er þe engles..forluren. *a* **1529** SKELTON *Vox Populi* I. 339 Yoke man..trewly his goodes to yerne. **1529** LYNDESAY *Complaynt* 50 Lang seruyce ȝarnis ay reward. **1591** NASHE *Prognost.* 23 Many shall drinke more than they can yearne. *a* **1687** PETTY *Pol. Arith.* (1690) 107 There was earned in four years..the summe of four Millions. **1771** *Junius Lett.* liv. 286 These praises..have been dearly earned. **1833** HT. MARTINEAU *Loom & Lugg.* I. i. 8 Do they all earn wages? **1851** MAYHEW *Lond. Labour* I. 359, 'I must..yearn my own living.' **1851** RUSKIN *Mod. Paint.* II. III. I. xv. §11 The effort of men to earn, rather than to receive, their salvation. **1863** BARRY *Dockyard Econ.* 147 Go into any private workshop where old men are earning as much as young men, and you will find that they *are* earning it.

b. Of qualities or actions: To procure as a direct consequence (a name, reputation, etc.) *for* a person.

1596 SPENSER *F.Q.* VI. I. 40 The which shal nought to you but foule dishonor yearne. **1876** GREEN *Short Hist.* iii. §7 (1882) 148 The stern justice of his rule earned the hatred of the disorderly baronage. *Mod.* His eccentricities had earned for him the nickname of 'The Madman'.

c. Of money invested; also of an implement, etc.: To be the means of producing (an income or money return).

1887 *Times* (weekly ed.) 30 Sept. 1/4 The line..would earn at least four per cent.

†**d.** *intr.* To do work *for* (a reward or result).

1589 WARNER *Alb. Eng.* VI. xxx. (1612) 148 Now Mars..Anchises and Adonis..May earne for babes, for Vulcan shall be parent at their birth.

†**2.** *absol.* To deserve *well* or *ill*. *Obs.* [cf. L. *bene mereri.*]

961 EADGIFU *Charter* in Sweet *Ags. Reader* (ed. 5) 55 Heo ne dorste..hem swa leanian swa he hire to ȝeearnud hæfde. **1622** DEKKER, etc. *Virgin Mart.* IV. i. Wks. 1873 IV. 59 A piece of Roman gold With Cæsar's stamp, such as he sends his captains When in the wars they earn well.

3. [cf. OHG. *arnôn* to reap.] To glean. *dial.*

1876 *Mid. Yorksh. Gloss.* (E.D.S.).

Hence **earned** *ppl. a.*, purchased by an equivalent in labour; *esp.* in phrases ***well-earned, hardly-earned.***

1855 MACAULAY *Hist. Eng.* III. 75 The well earned promotion. **1885** *Pall Mall G.* 10 Feb. 11/2 Unearned incomes should be taxed before earned incomes.

†**earn,** *v.*² *Obs.* exc. *dial.* [app. identical with ME. *erne* (repr. both OE. *iernan*, metathetic var. of *rinnan*, RUN, and the causative *ærnan* = *ręnnan*): in OE. the prefix-vbs. *ȝe-rinnan*, *ȝe-ręnnan*, occur in the senses 'curdle, cause to curdle'; the pple. *ȝeurnen* 'curdled' is found in *Leechdoms* II. 230, 272, III. 278.] *intr.* To curdle. Also *trans.* To curdle (milk), esp. for making into cheese.

1674 RAY *N.C. Wds.* 16 To *Earn*, to run as cheese doth..Var. Dial. **1724** RAMSAY *Tea-T. Misc.* (1733) I. 86 The kirns to kirn and milk to earn. **1769** MRS. RAFFALD *Eng. Housekpr.* (1778) 250 When it [new milk] is ready to boil put in a quart of good cream, earn it. **1877** E. PEACOCK *N.-W. Linc. Gloss.* (E.D.S.) *Earn*, to curdle with rennet.

†**earn,** *v.*³ *Obs.* Forms: (? 1 eornian), 6 erne, earne, 7 earn. [app. a var. of YEARN:—OE. *ȝeornian*; cf. dial. *ear* for *year*. All the senses of the present word, exc. 3, also belong to the form YEARN. The OE. *eornian* to murmur (Bosw.-T. in pres. pple. *eorniȝende*), *eornfulnes* solicitude, *eornlice* diligently (*Leechdoms* I. 190), seem to show that the two forms go back to an early period; see Sievers *Ags. Gram.* (ed. 2) §212.

Prof. Skeat (s.v. YEARN) considers that *earn*, *yearn* to grieve (sense 2 below) are of distinct origin from *earn*, *yearn* in the sense to desire. He regards the former as a corruption of ME. ERME. But the development of sense from 'desire' to 'sorrow' presents no serious difficulty; and there is no clear evidence of confusion between the two words.]

1. *intr.* To desire strongly, to long. Also, *to earn it.* (? refl.)

1579 SPENSER *Sheph. Cal.* Mar. 76 My courage earnd it to awake. **1596** —— *F.Q.* I. i. 3 His hart did earne To proue his puissance.

2. To be affected with poignant grief or compassion; also impers. ***it earns me.***

1599 SHAKS. *Hen. V*, II. iii. 3 My manly heart doth erne..for Falstaffe hee is dead, and wee must erne therefore. **1601** —— *Jul. C.* II. ii. 129 That every like is not the same..the heart of Brutus earnes to think upon. **1614** B. JONSON *Barth. Fair* IV. vi, Alas poore wretch! how it earnes my heart for him! **1651** P. STERRY *England's Deliverance* (1652) 26, I do..with bowels tenderly Earning, warn and intreat, etc.

3. ? To tremble. *rare*⁻⁰.

1611 COTGR., *Frissonner*, to tremble, quake, shrug, shiuer, didder, shudder, earne, through cold or feare.

4. Of hounds, deer, etc.: To utter a prolonged cry. See EARNING *vbl. sb.*² 2.

†**earn,** *adv. Obs. rare.* [app. ME. *eorne*, OE. *ȝeorne* eagerly, anxiously; cf. EARN *v.*³] Earnestly, longingly.

1230 *Ancr. R.* 44 Crieð him eorne merci & forgiuenesse. **1656** TRAPP *Comm. Matt.* vii. 11 Who doubts but they prayed earn and earnestly, when they were in Bocardo.

earn, var. form of ERNE, eagle.

'earn-bleater, -bliter. *dial.* [Derivation unknown; this and OE. *hæferblæte*, *hæfenblæte*, name of some bird, 'bicoca, bugium', prov. Eng. *hammerbleat* snipe, may possibly be various corruptions of the same word.]

'A Scotch name for the snipe.' (Jamieson.)

1768 ROSS *Helenore* 58 (Jam.) The earn-bleater or the muirfowl's craw, Was like to melt her very heart awa.

'earner, *sb.*¹ [f. EARN *v.*¹ + -ER¹; cf. *wage-earner* (see WAGE *sb.* 4b.] **1.** One who or that which earns.

1612 ROWLANDS *Knaue of Harts* 23 Make my hands the earners of my meate. **1614** CORNWALLIS in Gutch *Coll. Cur.* I. 162 Nor make him so dear an earner of our monies. **1886** *Manch. Exam.* 3 Nov. 5/5 The wives of wage earners.

2. *spec.* An activity that brings in money for the person engaged in it; *esp.* in phr. ***a nice little earner***, a means of making easy or illicit profit. *colloq.*

1970 G. F. NEWMAN *Sir, you Bastard* 7 His earner had come on top. **1982** *Observer* 15 Aug. 22/7 A 'nice little earner' is anything that brings in easy money, often but not always criminally. **1985** *Trucking Internat.* May–June 45/1 Vernon sells it at a very low margin to keep the price down — he sees it as a service to his customers, rather than an 'earner' in its own right. **1987** *Sunday Tel.* 24 May 35/1 The family letting rooms on the quiet, or the person who has a 'nice little earner' on the side.

earnest ('ɜːnɪst), *sb.*¹ Forms: 1 eornust, -ost, -est, 3 eornest, ȝorneste, 3-5 erneste, 3-6 ernest, 5 erneyst, 4-6 ernes, 6 earnes, 6- earnest. [OE. *eornust* fem. = OHG. *ernust* fem., neut., MHG. *ernest*, mod.G. *ernst* masc., MDu. *ernst*, *aernst* (of similar meaning):—OTeut. **ernusti*, perh. f. root **ers*, found also in ERRE (*obs.*) anger. A different ablaut form of the same root, with similar suffix, appears to exist in OE. *ornest* wager of battle, ON. *orrosta*, late OE. *orrest* battle.

The form *ernes* may possibly represent a distinct word:—OE. *ȝeornes*, (*ȝeornnes*) eagerness, strength of desire; cf. EARN *v.*³; it was however in 15th c. completely identified with the present word.]

†**1.** Ardour in battle; in wider sense, intense passion or desire. *Obs.*

c **1205** LAY. 16480 þer wes fehte swiþe stor, eornest ful sturne. *c* **1250** *Ibid.* 16468 To fihte mid folle ȝorneste. **1297** R. GLOUC. (1810) 121 Vortimer with gret power and god ernest ynow. *c* **1385** CHAUCER *L.G.W.* 1285 The hote ernest [*v.r.* hervest] is al overblowe. *c* **1400** *Rom. Rose* 4840 And whanne they han her lust geten The hoote ernes they al foryeten.

2. Seriousness, serious intention, as opposed to jest or play; *esp.* in phrase ***in (*†*for) earnest, in good (sober, sad) earnest.*** In OE. *on eornest* means 'earnestly', also 'in reality'. In mod. use ***to be in earnest***, applied to persons, has sometimes an emphatic sense = to be earnest.

c **1000** WULFSTAN *Addr. to English* in Sweet *Ags. Reader* (ed. 5) 111 Gif we on eornost æniȝe scame cuðan. *c* **1250** *Gen. & Ex.* 411 Adam is to eue cumen, More for erneste ðan for gamen. *a* **1340** HAMPOLE *Psalter* v. 6 Til perfite man it falles not to leghe nouþer in ernest ne in gamen. **1430** LYDG. *Chron. Troy* I. v And this contek in ernes and in game Departed was betwixt love and shame. *Ibid.* I. vi, It is an ernest and no game. *c* **1440** *Promp. Parv.* 14/2 Arneste or erneste, seryowste. *c* **1489** CAXTON *Sonnes of Aymon* 328 Is it erneste that ye speke? *c* **1535** DEWES *Introd. Fr.* in *Palsgr.* 927 In earnes, *a certes*, For earnes, *pour certes*, Of earnes, *de certes*. **1570** *Marriage Wit & Sc.* IV. i. in Hazl. *Dodsley* II. 362 But in good earnest, madam, speak—off or on? **1636** RUTHERFORD *Lett.* lxxv. (1862) I. 193, It were good to be beginning in sad earnest to find out God. **1645** MILTON *Colast.* Wks. (1851) 373, I deal not now with this caitiff, never worth my earnest, and now not seasonable for my jest. **1729** BP. BUTLER *Serm.*, *Self-Deceit* 475 It never in earnest comes into their thoughts. **1745** WESLEY *Answ. Ch.* 15, I am in great Earnest when I declare once more, that I have a deep conviction. **1855** PRESCOTT *Philip II*, II. vi. (1857) 102 It was no feint, but a surprise meditated in good earnest. **1875** JOWETT *Plato* (ed. 2) I. 207 Are you in jest or in real earnest?

†**b.** ME. phrase: ***erte(n to ernest***: to conduct to a serious result; ***erte(n in ernest***: to bring seriously to pass. [Cf. OHG. *uuart giuuentit in guota ernust* 'factus est in agonia' Graff.]

c **1400** *Destr. Troy* 2942 Ertes ay to euyll ende & ernyst by the last. *Ibid.* 11634 For ertyng his exile in ernest.

earnest ('ɜːnɪst), *sb.*² Forms: 3 dat. or acc. ernesse, 4 ernes, eernes, 5 ernys, 5-6 ernest, (5 arneste), 6- earnest. [Of obscure etymology: presumably connected with the synonymous *erles* (see ARLES), ERRES (a. OFr. *erres* pl.); possibly it was altered from these after the analogy of derivatives in -NESS.

The alleged OF. *ernes*, frequently given as the etymon, is spurious (Prof. Paul Meyer); the Welsh *ernes* is borrowed from Eng. At an early period app. confused with EARNEST *sb.*¹, the notion being that an 'earnest' was so called as showing that a bargain was made 'in earnest'.]

1. Money, or a sum of money, paid as an instalment, esp. for the purpose of securing a bargain or contract. Also *fig.* A foretaste, instalment, pledge, of anything afterwards to be received in greater abundance. †Phrase, ***on (in, for) earnest***: by way of earnest, as an instalment or foretaste.

The lit. sense is now nearly confined to law-books, and the fig. use, which retains its currency chiefly on account of its occurrence in the Bible, has almost ceased to be consciously metaphorical.

a **1225** *Juliana* 17 Nu þu schalt on alre earst as on ernesse swa beon ibeaten wið bittere besmen. **1380** WYCLIF *Sel. Wks.* I. 142 Crist toke ernes here in þis world. *Ibid.* III. 61 He hadde answere of God, þat was eernes herto. **1424** R. FLORE in *E.E. Wills* (1882) 59, I haue paied him a noble on ernest. *c* **1440** *Promp. Parv.* 14/2 Arneste or hanselle [or ernest *H.P.*, ansal *K.*]. **1463** *Mann. & Househ. Exp.* 157 Item, my mastyr payd to hym in ernest that schuld make my ladys cloke, iijs. iiijd. **1499** *Nottingham Borough Rec.* MS. 1378. 5 Reseyved of ernys iijd. **1509** BARCLAY *Shyp of Folys* (1874) II. 115 Thy ernest is layde, the bargen must abyde. It may nat be broke. **1581** MARBECK *Bk. of Notes* 685 As ye see,..after all bargaines, there is a signe thereof made, eyther clapping of hands..or giving some earnest. **1611** SHAKS. *Cymb.* I. v. 65 It is an earnest of a farther good. **1633** T. ADAMS *Exp. 2 Peter* iv. 11 An earnest seals the bargain. **1712** STEELE *Spect.* No. 432 ⁋12 The Earnest given me of something further intended in my Favour. **1800** A. ADDISON *Reports* 133 Plaintiff paid a guinea earnest. **1814** WORDSW. *Excursion* I, The primrose flower Peeped forth, to give an earnest of the Spring. *a* **1830** MACKINTOSH *More* Wks. 1846 I. 397 The enthusiastic admiration with which the superior few feel an earnest of their own higher powers. **1845** STEPHEN *Laws Eng.* II. 69 If such portion be accepted by way of earnest. **1850** TENNYSON *In Mem.* xcvii, The days she never can forget Are earnest that he loves her yet.

b. *Comb.*, ***earnest-money, -giver***, EARNEST-PENNY.

1557 in Turner *Records of Oxford* 266 The ernyst money of the towne rents. **1616** SIR R. BOYLE in *Lismore Papers* (1886) I. 136, I delivered to..Capn. Wm. Hull xxli ster: as earnest money to buy casks for ffumadoes. **1698** VANBRUGH *Prov. Wife* III. i, I'm none of your earnest-givers. **1826** KENT *Comm. Amer. Law* (1873) II. xxxix. 494 If, therefore, earnest money be given..the contract is binding.

†**2.** *Cant.* (See quot.) *Obs.*

1673 R. HEAD *Canting Acad.* 37 *Tip me my Earnest*, Give me my Share or Divident. **1725** *New Cant. Dict.*

†'**earnest**, *sb.*^{3} *Obs.* ? Mistake for OE. *ornest* single combat; the ground for the concluding statement in the quot. is unknown.

1591 LAMBARDE *Arch.* (1635) 44 If a French man doe appeale an English man of..murder, the French man may defend himselfe by Battaile, which was then termed in English, Ernest; a word that we keep yet, saying, when wee see a man fight, hee is an Ernest.

earnest ('ɜːnɪst), *a.* Forms: 1 eorneste, 3, 6 ernest, (3 ernexst), 5 ernyst (? 7 earst), 6– earnest. [OE. *eorneste*, f. EARNEST *sb.*^{1}; in ME. no unequivocal examples have been found; perh. the word died out in OE., and was afterwards developed afresh from the attrib. use of the sb.]

1. Of persons: Serious, as opposed to trifling; usually in emphatic sense, intensely serious, gravely impassioned, in any purpose, feeling, conviction, or action; sincerely zealous. Of feelings, convictions, etc.: Intense, ardent. Of actions or words: Proceeding from or implying intensity of feeling or conviction.

In mod. use the word tends to exclude the notion of ungoverned or violent feeling, which in some earlier examples is prominent; cf. quot. 1670 under EARNESTNESS.

c **1000** ÆLFRIC *Hom.* (Thorpe) I. 386 Mid eornestum mode. *a* **1300** *Cursor M.* 26351 Clene and reuful..stedfast, ernexst, willi [? *read* ernest-willi]. *c* **1400** *Destr. Troy* 2713 The ernyst speche..of Elinus the Bysshop. **15..** R. WEAVER *Lusty Juv.* in Hazl. *Dodsley* II. 99 Of an earnest professor of Christs Gospel Thou madest me an hypocrite. **1563** MAN tr. *Musculus' Common Pl.* 372 a, Anye earnest or curiouse search thereof. **1581** SAVILE *Tacitus' Agricola* (1622) 186 Being yoong hee had addicted himselfe to the study of philosophie in earnester sort. **1591** SHAKS. *2 Hen. VI*, III. ii. 316 My tongue should stumble in mine earnest words. **1593** HOOKER *Eccl. Pol.* II. i. (1611) 54 An earnest longing desire to see things brought to a peaceable end. **1594** SHAKS. *Rich. III*, I. iii. 87, I..haue been An earnest aduocate to plead for him. **1611** BIBLE *Hebr.* ii. 1 We ought to giue the more earnest heede. **1628** EARLE *Microcosm.*, *Flatterer*, His chiding may seem but the earnester commendation. **1658** DEKKER, etc. *Witch Edmont.* III. i. Wks. 1873 IV. 391 I'll not turn from it, if you be earst Sir. **1716–8** LADY M. W. MONTAGUE *Lett.* I. xxxvii. 141 The good lady..was very earnest in serving me of everything. **1793** SOUTHEY *Triumph of Wom.* 240 What though her Priests in earnest terror call On all their host of Gods to aid? **1830** D'ISRAELI *Charles I*, III. vi. 114 There was a good deal of earnest impetuosity in his temper. **1841–4** EMERSON *Ess. Self-Reliance* Wks. (Bohn) I. 26 All history resolves itself..into the biography of a few stout and earnest persons. **1858** *Edin. Rev.* No. 217. 183 To [Arnold]..we owe the substitution of the word 'earnest' for its predecessor 'serious'. **1860** TYNDALL *Glac.* I. §22. 160 To say one earnest word in connexion with this ascent.

b. Const. *for*, or *inf.* Somewhat *rare*.

c **1665** MRS. HUTCHINSON *Mem. Col. Hutchinson* (1846) 302 The presbyterian faction were earnest to have the army disbanded. **1676** TEMPLE *Let.* in Wks. 1731 II. 420 The Swede is earnest for a Peace. **1853** *Arab. Nts.* 377 Saony,.. was earnest with the King to give the signal to the executioner. **1855** PRESCOTT *Philip II*, I. I. v. 61 Caraffa [was] earnest to introduce the inquisition.

c. *transf.*

1843 CARLYLE *Past & Pr.* (1858) 166 For the Earth, I say, is an earnest place. **18..** LONGF. *Psalm of Life*, Life is real, life is earnest. **1851** CARLYLE *Sterling*, The Bible, most earnest of books.

d. Comb. ***earnest-hearted, -mild*** adjs.

1850 MRS. BROWNING *Poems* II. 409 If a little maid,.. Should sigh within it, earnest-mild, This reed will answer evermore. **1860** *Sat. Rev.* IX. 53/2 A thoroughly good and earnest-hearted man.

†**2.** Of animals: Excited. *Obs. rare.*

1609 C. BUTLER *Fem. Mon.* i. (1623) C ij, If they [bees] be so earnest that you fear stinging your hands.

3. Of things: Demanding serious consideration; weighty, important.

1544 ASCHAM *Toxoph.* (Arb.) 26 We scholers have more ernest and weightie matters in hand. **1753** RICHARDSON *Grandison* (1781) I. xxv. 180 Sir Charles had earnest business in town.

†'**earnest**, *adv. Obs.* [OE. had *eornoste* adv., perh. instrum. case of *eornost*, EARNEST *sb.*^{1}, or f. the adj.; the later word is merely an advbl. use of the adj.] = EARNESTLY.

1629 J. COLE *Of Death* 44 The lesse the bodily members are occupied, the more earnester hee withdrawes himselfe to his cogitations. **1709** STRYPE *Ann. Ref.* I. xlvii. 516 Had not profited with that Queen, so earnest was she bent against the Duke of Chastelherault. **1791** COWPER *Iliad* IV. 453 Earnest they sued for an auxiliar band.

†'**earnest**, *v.*^{1} *Obs. rare.* [f. EARNEST *sb.*^{1} or *a.*] *trans.* **a.** To use in earnest. **b.** To render earnest.

1602 *Pastor Fido* E j (N.) Let's prove among ourselves our armes in jest, That when we come to earnest them with men, We may them better use. **1603** FLORIO *Montaigne* III. viii. (1632) 519 The study and plodding on bookes, is a languishing and weake kinde of motion, and which heateth or earnesteth nothing.

†'**earnest**, *v.*^{2} *Obs.* Also 5 ernest. [f. the adj.] To secure by giving or taking earnest.

1447 BOKENHAM *Seyntys* (1835) 120 A nothir lovere.. Wyth the ryng of hys feyth hath ernestyd me. **1630** LORD *Banians* Introd., I was willing to earnest my love to mee by this injunction. **1695** J. ST. N. *Widow's Mite* 28 Election made sure, confirmed, sealed, witnessed, earnested by the peculiar Spirit of Adoption.

†'**earnestful.** *obs.* [f. EARNEST *sb.*^{1} + -FUL.]

1. Important; = EARNEST *a.* 3.

c **1386** CHAUCER *Clerkes T.* 1175 Lat us stynte of ernestful matere. **1534** WHITTINTON *Tullyes Offices* I. (1540) 60 If so be of seryous and ernestfull maters, let hym vse grauytie.

2. = EARNEST *a.* 1. Also as quasi-*adv.*

1430 *A.B.C. Aristotle* in *Babees Bk.* (1868) 11 E to elenge, ne to excellent, ne to eernesful neiþer. **1533** BELLENDEN *Livy* I. (1822) 73 Quhen the king wes behaldin this man maist earnistfull. **1563** DAVIDSON *Answ. Kennedy* in *Misc. Wodr. Soc.* (1844) 186 Zour Lordship's earnestfull and godly desyre.

Hence †'**earnestfully** *adv.*

1375 BARBOUR *Bruce* VIII. 144 He ansuerd ernystfully.

earnestly ('ɜːnɪstlɪ), *adv.* [f. EARNEST *a.* + -LY^{2}.] In an earnest manner; in a manner indicating earnestness. (In OE.: In truth, in reality; also in the Gospels transl. *ergo*, *itaque*, Vulg.)

c **1000** *Ags. Gosp.* Matt. xx. 9 Eornostlice þa ðæ ȝecomon þa embe þa endlyften tide comon, þa onfengon hig ælc hys pening. *a* **1000** *Laws of Cnut* (Eccl.) xv. Sunnan-dæȝes cypingce we forbeodaþ eac eornostlice. *a* **1300** *Cursor M.* 26932 þi scrift agh to be mad hernestly, noght als intent o wayn-glori. *c* **1325** *E.E. Allit. P.* B. 1240 He enteres in ful ernestly, in yre of his hert. *c* **1400** *Destr. Troy* 6490 Carion ..full ernestly with Ector auntrid to fight. *c* **1440** *Promp. Parv.* 142 Ernestly, *seriose*. **1535** COVERDALE *Tobias* ix. 3 Now seist thou how earnestly Raguel hath requyred me. **1544** BALE *Chron. Sir J. Oldcastell* in *Harl. Misc.* (Malh.) I. 268 Than loked the Lord Cobham ærnestly vpon the archbishopp. **1552** ABP. HAMILTON *Catech.* (1884) 3 He so ernestly maid supplicatioun to thame. **1596** SHAKS. *Merch. V.* IV. i. 121. **1609** BIBLE (Douay) *Zech.* xii. *comm.*, The other Jewes most earnestly persecuted Christians. **1712** ADDISON *Spect.* No. 89 ¶3 Reflexions which I earnestly recommend to the Thoughts of my fair Readers. **1849** RUSKIN *Sev. Lamps* iv. §33. 123 The most earnestly imitative treatment. **1855** PRESCOTT *Philip. II*, i. (1857) 8 He had..endeavoured earnestly to do his duty to the best of his abilities. **1863** FR. KEMBLE *Resid. Georgia* 55 A..pair of chickens, which he offered most earnestly to S——. **1871** FREEMAN *Norm. Conq.* (1876) IV. xx. 155 We know enough of Hereward to make us earnestly long to know more.

earnestness ('ɜːnɪstnɪs). [f. EARNEST *a.* + -NESS.] The state or quality of being earnest.

1561 T. NORTON *Calvin's Inst.* IV. xx. 162 They must watch with all care, earnestnesse, and diligence. **1670** WALTON *Lives* III. 158 Never expressing an earnestness.. but an humble Gravity sutable to the Aged. **1779** JOHNSON *Lett.* (1788) II. ccvii. 55 Keep your mind quiet, do not think with earnestness even of your health. **1833** LAMB *Elia* (1860) 361 Sawing, every one with the might and earnestness of a Demiurgus. **1849** ROBERTSON *Serm.* Ser. I. ii. (1866) 32 Earnestness; that is, sincerity of purpose. **1848** W. H. KELLY tr. *L. Blanc's Hist. Ten Y.* II. 581 The discussion began with warmth on one side, and grave earnestness on the other.

†'**earnest-,penny.** *Obs.* [f. EARNEST *sb.*^{2} + PENNY.] A small sum of money (prob. orig. a literal penny) paid as earnest to secure a bargain; cf. *bargain-penny*, *fastening-penny*.

1508 *Nottingham Borough Rec.* MS. 1383. 10 Recepit.. unum denarium argenti ut pro an ernest peny. **1552** HULOET, Bynde wyth an earnest penye, *obæro*. **1562** EDEN *Let.* in *1st Eng. Bks. Amer.* (Arb.) Pref. 43/2, Xxli thereof to be lotted to me for an earnest penye to begynne the booke. **1629** W. COWPER *Heaven Open.* 119 It is customable to men to giue an earnest penny in buying and selling. **1760** MAIR *Tyro's Dict.* (1820) 10 *Arrha*, an earnest-penny.

b. *fig.* (In 16th and 17th c. freq. in religious use.)

1533 TINDALE *Supper of Lord* 19 That assured saving health and earnest-penny of everlasting life. **1571** R. EDWARDS *Damon & P.* in Hazl. *Dodsley* IV. 59 Then for an earnest-penny take this blow. **1579** TOMSON *Calvin's Serm. Tim.* 927/2 Ye spirite of God..is the earnest peny of our adoption. **1662** J. CHANDLER *Van Helmont's Oriat.* 281, I offered them an earnest-penny, to take me along with them as a companion and witnesse. **1676** WYCHERLEY *Pl. Dealer* IV. ii, Presents from me ..the earnest-pence for our love-bargain.

†'**earnesty.** *Obs. rare.* Also 6 yrnesty. [f. EARNEST *a.* + -TY.] Earnestness.

1572 ABP. PARKER *Corr.* (1853) 419 With some earnesty to prefer his honour and true religion. **1591** HORSEY *Trav.* (1857) 361 This was done with such yrnesty that for the tyme it was a great obstacle in our proceedings.

†'**earnful**, *a. Obs.* exc. *dial.* [app. a var. of YEARNFUL; for the relations between the two forms cf. EARN *v.*^{3}] Anxious, full of longing desire; sorrowful. Hence '**earnfully** *adv.*

[*a* **1000** *Ags. Gosp.* Matt. xiii. 22 Eornfullness [*v.r.* ȝeornfullnes] þisse woruldE.] *c* **1500** *Noble Lyfe* II. lxxxix, He cryeth eurnefulli ho, ho! **1575** T. ROGERS *Sec. Coming Christ* 47/1 Their woofull cries..their earnefull plaintes. **1581** STUDLEY *Seneca's Hercules Œt.* 191 b, Philomele.. earnefully did mone Her tender Itis death. **1587** T. HUGHES *Arthur* IV. ii. in Hazl. *Dodsley* IV. 323 A deep and earnful sigh. **1596** LODGE *Marg. Amer.* 136 Weeping piteously in so erneful manner. **1633** P. FLETCHER *Pisc. Ecl.* v. viii. The earnful smart Which eats my breast. **1875** PARISH *Sussex Gloss.*, *Ernful*, sad, lamentable.

earning ('ɜːnɪŋ), *vbl. sb.*^{1} [f. EARN *v.*^{1} + -ING^{1}; in OE. *earnung*, *ȝeearnung.*]

1. The action of giving labour as an equivalent for wages, of acquiring money by labour. Also *attrib.*

1872 *Daily News* 3 May 6/1 The men who have earned them [laurels] and know what the earning cost. **1884** *Pall Mall G.* 4 Oct. 1/1 The real earning power of the property.

b. *concr.* in pl.: The amount of money which a person acquires or becomes entitled to by his labour; also, the income produced by invested capital.

1732 *Acc. of Workhouses* 29 To know their earnings, and to give an account to the trustees. **1776** ADAM SMITH *W. N.* I. i. vi. 56 The whole is commonly considered as the earnings of his labour. **1848** MACAULAY *Hist. Eng.* I. 416 The earnings of the peasant were very different in different parts of the kingdom. **1888** *Daily News* 16 Feb. 2/1 The gross earnings of railways have increased.

†**2.** The fact of deserving, merit; *concr.* that which one deserves. *Obs.*

c **1020** WULFSTAN *Homily* in Sweet *Ags. Reader* xvi. 16 Mid miclan earnungan we ȝeearnodon þa yrmða þe on us sittað. *c* **1175** *Lamb. Hom.* 19 Crist us ȝef moni freo ȝeue.. nawiht for ure ernunge bute for his muchele mildheortnesse. *c* **1200** *Trin. Coll. Hom.* 171 Ðanne wule he ..demen elch man after his erninge.

†**3.** *pl.* Gain, profit. *Obs.*

a **1200** *Moral Ode* (Egerton MS.) 161 in *E.E.P.* (1862) 32 3if we serueden god so we doð erninges, more we haueden of heuene þanne eorles oþer kinges. [*But other texts read* erminges.] **1703** PENN in *Pa. Hist. Soc. Mem.* IX. 182 Now is the time to make earnings in the islands. **1675** BROOKS *Gold. Key* Wks. 1867 V. 15 If thou wouldst make any earnings of thy reading this treatise, then thou must—Read, and believe what thou readest.

†'**earning**, *vbl. sb.*^{2} *Obs.* [f. EARN *v.*^{3}; = YEARNING.]

1. Longing desire; poignant grief or compassion.

1631 R. H. *Arraignm. Whole Creature* xii. §4. 131 The strong movings of his hart, and the earnings of his affections. **1711** STEELE *Spect.* No. 95 ¶1 The generous Earnings of Distress in a manly Temper.

2. The act of uttering the prolonged cry of hounds or deer.

1575 LANEHAM *Let.* (1871) 13 The earning of the hoounds in continuauns of their crie. **1631** R. H. *Arraignm. Whole Creature* xiii. §4. 219 The young Fawne with earning.

earning ('ɜːnɪŋ), *vbl. sb.*^{3} *dial.* Also **yearning.** [f. EARN *v.*^{2} + -ING^{1}.]

1. The curdling of milk for cheese.

1782 A. MONRO *Compar. Anat.* (ed. 3) 40 It is this fourth stomach with the milk curdled in it, that is commonly taken for earning of milk. **1784** TWAMLEY *Dairying* 31 To allow the Milk to stand an Hour, in earning, or after the Runnet is put in. *Ibid.* 45 A very material circumstance to be attended to in Cheese-making, is the time..when the Milk is at rest, called earning time.

2. The means of curdling milk; rennet. Also *attrib.*, as in ***earning-bag, -skin.*** Also **earning-grass** = BUTTERWORT.

1615 MARKHAM *Eng. Housew.* II. vi. (1668) 149 When your Runnet or Earning is fit to be used. **1727** BRADLEY *Fam. Dict.* I. s.v. *Cheese*, Go to the Pot where the Earning Bag hangs, and take so much of the Earning..as will serve for the Proportion of Milk. **1775** LIGHTFOOT *Flora Scot.* (1792) 1131 (Jam.) *Pinguicula vulgaris*, Steep-grass, Earning-grass. **1778** *Fam. Acc. Bk.* in E. Peacock *N.-W. Linc. Gloss.* (E.D.S.) A calf-head and a piece of earning-skin. *c* **1820** *Cottagers of Glenburnie* 202 (Jam.) Mrs. MacClarty then took down a bottle of rennet, or yearning, as she called it. **1863** ATKINSON *Danby Provinc. N. Riding Yorksh.*

earock, var. form of EIRACK.

'**ear-,pick, -'picker.** [f. EAR *sb.*^{1}] An instrument for clearing the ear of wax, etc.; also *fig.*

1483 *Cath. Angl.* 116 An Erepyke, *aurifricium*. **1568** *Richmond. Wills* (1853) 227 To James Gybson my godson.. one silver ear pick. **1580** HOLLYBAND *Treas. Fr. Tong*, *Vne cure oreille*, an eare picker. **1592** LYLY *Midas* v. ii. 63, I protest by cissars, brush & combe; bason ball & apron; by razor, earepike & rubbing clothes. **1614** T. ADAMS in Spurgeon *Treas. Dav.* Ps. xxvi. 10 Alas! poor truth, that she must now be put to the charge of a golden earpick, or she cannot be heard. **1634** S. ROWLEY *Noble Sold.* II. i, Is the king at leisure..to heare a Souldier speake. I am no eare-picker To sound his hearing that way. **1700** *Transactioneer* 21 He Acts all the uncouth Faces, of a Transactioneer pausing over a China Earpicker. **1825** HONE *Every-day Bk.* I. 1255 Tweezers with an ear-pick.

†'**ear-,rent.** *Obs.* [perh. orig. f. EAR *sb.*^{3} + RENT; but used (? punningly) with allusion to EAR *sb.*^{1}] ? Some kind of agricultural rent. In quots. used punningly for: **a.** The loss of a person's ears in the pillory. **b.** The 'tax' imposed on a listener's patience by a profitless or noisy talker.

1610 B. JONSON *Alch.* I. i, Raskalls would runne themselves from breath to see..you t' haue but a Hole to thrust your heads in, For which you should pay Eare-rent. **1624** MASSINGER *Renegado* III. ii, You speak not tempests, nor take ear-rent from A poor shopkeeper.

'**ear-ring, earring.** Also 1 ear-hring, 5 aryng, 6 earing(e, eare ryng(e. [f. EAR *sb.*^{1}]

1. A ring worn in the lobe of the ear for ornament; often used for a pendant or 'drop.'

c **1000** ÆLFRIC *Exod.* xxxii. 2 Nymaþ ȝyldene ear-hringas of eower wifa earon. **1468** *Medulla Gram.* in *Cath. Angl.* 45 *Inauris*, þe Aryng in the ere. **1535** COVERDALE *Judg.* viii. 24 For in so moch as yᵉ men were Ismaelites, they had earinges. —— *Ezek.* xvi. 12, I put..eare rynges vpon thyne eares. **1600** HAKLUYT *Voy.* (1810) III. 454, I send your honour two earerings. *a* **1643** G. SANDYS (J.) They..gave the precious earrings that they wore. **1701** LADY M. W. MONTAGUE *Lett.* II. xliv. 18 Her earrings..were two diamonds shaped exactly like pears. **1814** SCOTT *Wav.* xviii, A pair of gold earrings. **1876** BANCROFT *Hist. U.S.* III. xi. 174 The lifeless frame, dressed as became a war-chief, glittered with belts, and ear-rings.

2. *dial.* The common fuchsia. (Britten and Holland.)

'ear-ringed, *a.* [f. EAR-RING + -ED².] Wearing ear-rings.

a **1846** B. R. HAYDON *Autobiogr.* (1927) III. xiii. 235 We were saluted as we entered by one of those ear-ringed, red-capped blackguards. **1883** J. PAYN *Thicker than Water* xvi, The ear-ringed, ringleted sailors. **1892** STEVENSON & OSBOURNE *Wrecker* viii. 123 Some ear-ringed fisher of the bay. **1920** *Chambers's Jrnl.* 561/1 His black-browed, ear-ringed kind knew him of an older race. **1924** J. BUCHAN *Three Hostages* xiii. 192 The earringed Jewess.

†**earsh.** *Obs.* exc. *dial.* [A slurred pronunc. of EDDISH; see also ARRISH.]

a. A stubble field. **b.** = Eddish or aftermath.

1622 MAY *Virgil's Georg.* (L.) Fires oft are good on barren earshes made. **1875** PARISH *Sussex Gloss.*, *Earsh*, a stubble field; as a wheat earsh, a barley earsh.

earshot ('ɪəʃɒt). [f. EAR *sb.*¹ + SHOT; after *bowshot*, etc.] The distance at which the voice may be heard; hearing.

1607 BEAUM. & FL. *Wom. Hater* I. iii, Hark you Sir, there may perhaps be some within ear-shots. **1713** *Guardian* No. 71 (1756) I. 315 Within ear-shot of one of those little ambitious men. **1844** DISRAELI *Coningsby* II. vi. 75 Tadpole and Taper..withdrew to a distant sofa, out of earshot, and indulged in confidential talk. **1856** MRS. BROWNING *Aur. Leigh* III. 1001 She was..not in earshot of the things Outspoken o'er the heads of common men.

earst, obs. var. ERST; ? also of EARNEST *a.*

eart, obs. form of *art*: see BE *v.*

earth (ɜːθ), *sb.*¹ Forms: *α.* 1–4 **eorðe,** 1– *Northumb.* **eorðu, eorðe,** 2 **horðe,** 3–6 **erð(e,** 4–5 **irthe, urth(e,** 4–6 **yerth(e, herthe,** 5 **ȝerþ, yorth,** 6 **earthe, yearth(e, (erith),** 8–9 *Sc.* **yirth,** 9 *Sc.* and *dial.* **yearth, orth,** 6– **earth.** *β.* 3–5 **erd(e,** 6 **eard, eird,** 8 **yird,** 9 *Sc.* and *north. dial.* **yird, yeird, eard.** [Common Teut.: OE. *eorþe*, wk. fem., corresponds to OS. *ertha* wk. fem. (MDu. *aerde*, *erde*, Du. *aarde*), OHG. *erda* str. and wk. fem. (MHG., mod.G. *erde*), ON. *iǫrð* (Sw., Da. *jord*), Goth. *airþa* str. fem.:—OTeut. **erþâ*, (? WGer.) *erþôn-*; without the dental suffix the word appears in OHG. *ero* earth, Gr. ἔρα-ζε on the ground; no other non-Teutonic cognates are known to exist, the plausible connexion with WAryan root **ar*, to plough, being open to serious objection.

With the northern and Sc. forms with *-d* cf. ME. *dede* for *death*; the change of *-þ* into *-d* is rare at the end of a word, though in medial positions it is frequent in Sc. The northern forms of the present word were in the early ME. period graphically coincident with those of ERD, and in some phrases the two words seem to have been confused.]

(Men's notions of the shape and position of the earth have so greatly changed since Old Teutonic times, while the language of the older notions has long outlived them, that it is very difficult to arrange the senses and applications of the word in any historical order. The following arrangement does not pretend to follow the development of ideas.)

A. Simple uses. **I.** The ground.

1. Considered as a mere surface. † ***to win earth on***: to gain ground upon; ***to lose earth***: to lose ground.

Beowulf 1533 Wearp ða wunden mæl..þæt hit on eorðan læȝ stið and stylecȝ. *c* **1000** ÆLFRIC *Hom.* in Sweet *Ags. Reader* (ed. 5) 85 Iohannes..astrehte his lichoman to eorðan on langsummum gebede. *c* **1200** ORMIN 8073 Forr he [Herod] warrþ seoc, and he bigann To rotenn bufenn eorþe. **1330** R. BRUNNE *Chron. Wace* (Rolls) 13860 þey wyþ-drowen hem, & erþe þey les. **1375** BARBOUR *Bruce* IV. 284 The Kyng..Wes laid at erd. *c* **1400** *Destr. Troy* 6817 Sum [he] hurlit to þe hard yerth. *c* **1435** *Torr. Portugal* 657 Twenty fote he garde hyme goo, Thus erthe on hym he wane. **1611** SHAKS. *Wint. T.* v. i. 199 They kneele, they kisse the Earth. **1664** EVELYN *Kal. Hort.* (1729) 192 Let your Gardiner endeavour to apply the Collateral Branches of his Wall-Fruits..to the Earth or Borders. **1847** TENNYSON *Princ.* v. 486 Part roll'd on the earth and rose again.

2. Considered as a solid stratum.

a **1300** *Cursor M.* 4699 þe erth it clang, for drught and hete. *c* **1340** *Ibid.* (Fairf.) 16784 The day was derker then the night þe erthe quoke with-alle. **1562** BULLEYN *Bk. Simples* 57 a, The people..are constrained to inhabite in Caves, under the yearth. **1567** MAPLET *Gr. Forest* 8 b, Of Gemmes, some are found in the earthes vaines, & are digged vp with Metalles. **1790** COWPER *Iliad* III. 339 Who under earth on human kind avenge Severe, the guilt of violated oaths. [**1865** *Frost & Fire* II. 182 Them is what we call marble stones; they grow in the yearth].

†**3.** Considered as a place of burial; *esp.* in phrase ***to bring (a person) to (the) earth.*** *Obs.*

c **1205** LAY. 4283 To gadere come his eorles & brohten hime to eorðe. *c* **1305** *Edm. the Conf.* 594 in *E.P.P.* (1862) 86 Ded he com iwis & þer he was ibroȝt an vrþe. **1387** *E.E. Wills* (1882) 2 Y be-quethe iii.*li* to bringe me on erthe. **1541** *Bury Wills* (1850) 261 [William Clovyer, of Chelsworth, charged his wife] to brynge me vnto the herthe honestly accordynge to my value. *Ibid.* 141, I commytt my body to be buryed in the churche erthe. **1590** MARLOWE *Edw. II*, v. i, Every earth is fit for burial.

4. The hole or hiding-place of a burrowing animal, as a badger, fox, etc.; also *fig.* ***to run to earth***: to chase (the quarry) to its earth; *fig.* to capture or find (something sought for) after a long search. Similarly ***to go to earth***, said of the quarry; also *fig.*

1575 TURBERV. *Bk. Venerie* 187 If you..put the Terryer into an earth where foxes be or Badgerdes, they will leave that earth. **1611** COTGR. *Accul*,..the bottome..of a foxes, or badgers earth. **1719** DE FOE *Crusoe* (1840) I. xi. 183 Frighted hare fled to cover, or fox to earth. **1781** P. BECKFORD *Hunting* (1802) 332, I recommend to you, to turn them into large covers and strong earths. **1828** SCOTT *F.M. Perth* I. 311, I am ready to take you to any place of safety you can name..But you cannot persuade me that you do not know what earth to make for. **1845** DARWIN *Voy. Nat.* vi. (1879) 113 They were generally near their earths, but the dogs killed one. **1857** KINGSLEY *Two Y. Ago* xxviii, Frightened—beat—run to earth myself, although I talked so bravely of running others to earth just now. **1859** TENNYSON *Enid* 253 And onward to the fortress rode the three..'So,' thought Geraint, 'I have track'd him to his earth'. **1876** [see RUN *v.* 42 *fig.*]. **1888** *Spectator* 7 Jan. 20/2 All the men who helped to run to earth the various members of the Ruthven family..were richly rewarded. **1913** *Punch* 26 Feb. 153/1 Men who used to go to earth behind evening papers on the entrance of a woman now spring to their feet in platoons without a moment's hesitation. **1917** M. WEBB (*title*) Gone to Earth. **1950** R. MACAULAY *World my Wilderness* xvi. 194 The policeman..turned back to assist his colleagues in flushing Barbary, so mysteriously gone to earth. **1953** 'F. O'CONNOR' *Stories* 63 Eventually he would run her to earth in some snug with a couple of cronies.

5. The soil as suited for cultivation; sometimes with a defining word denoting the nature or quality of the soil.

c **950** *Lindisf. Gosp.* Luke xiii. 7 Hrendas forðon ða ilca to huon uutedlice eorðo ȝi-onetað. *c* **1200** *Trin. Coll. Hom.* 155 Sum ful on þe gode eorðe and þat com wel forð. *c* **1340** *Cursor M.* 27268 (Fairf.) Tilmen..better þaire awen erþ tilis. *c* **1440** *Promp. Parv.* 141 Erye, or erthe [erde *K*], *terra*, *humus*, *tellus*. *c* **1420** *Pallad. on Husb.* I. 81 The bitterest erthe & werst that thou canst thinke. **1523** FITZHERB. *Husb.* §13 To plowe his barley-erthe. **1557** *Lanc. Wills* (1854) I. 143 On close lyeinge nerest unto James Bailies called the merled earthe. **1617** MARKHAM *Caval.* III. 29 When you finde the chase to runne ouer any faire earth, as either ouer More, Medow, Heath [etc.] all which my countrymen of the North call skelping earths. **1751** CHAMBERS *Cycl.* s.v. *Earth*, By means of sand it is, that the fatty earth is rendered fertile. **1821** MRS. WHEELER *Westmorld. Dial.* 71 They racken his earth is as gud as onny ith parrish.

6. *Electr.* The ground considered as the medium by which a circuit is completed. Hence used for: Connection of a wire conductor with the earth, either accidental (with the result of leakage of current or dangerous differences of potential) or intentional (as for the purpose of providing a return path for a telegraph current, etc.). (Cf. GROUND *sb.* 15 b.)

[**1773** H. CAVENDISH *Jrnl.* 9 Feb. in *Electr. Researches* (1879) 267 It was suspected that this increase of separation of the balls before they closed was owing to the wire designed to carry off the el[ectricity] to earth not conducting fast enough.] **1868** L. CLARK *Elem. Treat. Electr. Measurement* vi. 42 The earth connections should therefore be carefully looked to occasionally. If a station have a defective earth, and have two wires leading to it, the evil will generally disclose itself. **1870** R. FERGUSON *Electr.* 250 An 'earth', however, is generally put at each station. **1876** PREECE & SIVEWRIGHT *Telegraphy* 225 Upon no account whatever is a leaden gas-pipe to be employed for the purpose of affording earth. *Ibid.* 243 Earths are indicated by an increase in the strength of the current at the sending end, and by a decrease in the strength, or the entire cessation of it, at the other end. *Ibid.* 253 If the earth at B is bad while that at A and at C is good, then a part of A's current, on reaching B, instead of going to earth there, will take the course of the wire to C, working C's apparatus, and go to earth at C. **1901** L. M. WATERHOUSE *Conduit Wiring* 17 When the cables are pulled through, the braiding (and perhaps the rubber) is torn off and the result is a bad 'earth' at some future time. **1911** *Encycl. Brit.* XXVI. 523/2 The signals received on such sensitive instruments..are liable to be disturbed by the return currents of other systems..and to obviate this it is necessary to form the 'earth' for the cable a few miles out at sea. **1966** *Buying Secondhand* (Consumers' Assoc.) 71 Earth is always green or green/yellow except in German-made appliances where earth is red.

II. The world on which we dwell.

7. The dry land, as opposed to the sea.

c **1000** ÆLFRIC *Gen.* i. 10 And God geciȝde þa driȝnisse eorðan. *c* **1160** *Hatton Gosp.* Matt. xxiii. 15 ȝe befareð sæ and eorðan. *c* **1250** *Gen. & Ex.* 116 Ðe ðridde dai..was water and erðe o sunder sad. *a* **1300** *Cursor M.* 383 þe watris all he calid þe se, þe drey he calid erd. **1382** WYCLIF *Gen.* i. 10 God clepid the drie erthe. **1667** MILTON *P.L.* VII. 624 The seat of men, Earth, with her nether Ocean circumfus'd. **1712–4** POPE *Rape Lock* IV. 119 Sooner let earth, air, sea to Chaos fall. **1826** J. WILSON *Noct. Ambr.* Wks. I. 6 There's sae strong a spirit of life hotchin over yearth and sea.

8. The world as including land and sea; as distinguished from the (material) heaven.

Beowulf 92 (Gr.) Se ælmihtiȝa eorðan w[orhte]. *c* **1175** *Lamb. Hom.* 139 Sunnen dei was iseȝan þet formeste liht buuen eorðe. *c* **1205** LAY. 4154 He somenede ferd Swulc nes næuere eær on erde. *c* **1250** *Gen. & Ex.* 40 Of noȝt Was heuene and erðe samen wroȝt. *c* **1320** *Cast. Loue* 95 God atte begynnynges Hedde i-maad heuene wiþ ginne..And þe eorþe þer-after þer-wiþ. **1698** KEILL *Exam. Th. Earth* (1734) 127 What proportion all the Rivers in the Earth bear to the Po. **1747** J. SCOTT *Christ. Life* III. 489 Spreading..even to the utmost ends of the earth. *a* **1813** A. WILSON *Rab & Ringan* Poet. Wks. (1846) 147 He ca'd the kirk the church, the yirth the globe. **1854** TOMLINSON *Arago's Astron.* 99 Men for a long while regarded the earth as a boundless plain.

9. a. Considered as the present abode of man; frequently contrasted with heaven or hell. In poet. and rhet. use often without the article.

c **1000** *Ags. Gosp.* Matt. xxviii. 18 Me is ȝeseald ælc anweald on heofonan and on eorþan [**950** *Lindisf.* on eorðo]. *c* **1175** *Lamb. Hom.* 47 Heo on eorðe ȝeueð reste to alle eorðe þrelles wepmen and wifmen of heore þrel weorkes. *a* **1300** *Cursor M.* 29280 Crist has here in irthe leuyd þe hele of cristendom and heuyd. *Ibid.* 71 [Scho] saues me first in herth fra syn, And heuen blys me helps to wyn. *c* **1380** WYCLIF *Sel. Wks.* III. 515 To conquere alle seculer lordship in þis eorþe. *c* **1400** *Apol. Loll.* 8 Wat þu byndist vpon ȝerþe, it schal be boundoun al so in heuin. *c* **1420** *Chron. Vilod.* 462 Shalle not long wᵗ ȝou in urthe a byde. *c* **1430** *Life St. Kath.* (1884) 13 And he..loueth hir chastite a monge alle þe virgyns in erthe. *c* **1500** *Lancelot* 128 For in this erith no lady is so fare. **1546** *Primer Hen. VIII*, 74 To whom..In heaven & yerth be laud and praise. Amen. **1597** J. PAYNE *Royal Exch.* 37, I came not to send peace in to the yerthe but warr. **1601** SHAKS. *Jul. C.* I. iii. 45 Those that haue knowne the Earth so full of faults. **1667** MILTON *P.L.* IX. 99 O Earth! how like to Heav'n, if not preferr'd More justly. **1697** DRYDEN *Virg. Georg.* IV. 813 Mighty Cæsar..On the glad Earth the Golden Age renews. **1813** HOGG *Queen's Wake* 182 But Kilmeny on yirth was nevir mayre seine. **1858** TRENCH *Parables* ii. (1877) 15 Earth is not a shadow of heaven, but heaven..a dream of earth.

b. *transf.* The inhabitants of the world.

1549 *Bk. Com. Prayer, Benedicite*, O let the Earth, speak good of the Lord. **1611** BIBLE *Gen.* xi. 1 The whole earth was of one language.

c. In the intensive expression ***on earth***, chiefly in interrogative and negative contexts. Also, with a superlative, used as an intensive phr.

1774 GOLDSM. *Retal.* 103 With no reason on earth to go out of his way, He turned and he varied full ten times a day. **1847** J. CARLYLE *Let.* 15 July (1883) I. 389 If I could have done anything on earth but cry. **1859** PRINCESS ROYAL *Let.* 26 Aug. in R. Fulford *Dearest Child* (1964) 207, I cannot see what on earth he can have of very urgent business here in November. **1862** THACKERAY *Philip* (1872) 228 What scheme on (h)earth are you driving at? **1873** 'MARK TWAIN' & WARNER *Gilded Age* 29 I've got the biggest scheme on earth—and I'll take you in! **1876** R. BROUGHTON *Joan* xiii, You people really have the worst small-beer in Europe. Where on earth did you get it? **1882** MRS. J. H. RIDDELL *Daisies & Buttercups* I. iv. 121 What on earth did it all matter to me? **1885** 'F. ANSTEY' *Tinted Venus* 128 Why on earth was she making this dead set at him? **1910** WODEHOUSE *Psmith in City* xviii. 158 Master Edward Waller..in frocks, looking like a gargoyle;..in sailor suit, looking like nothing on earth.

d. Colloq. phr. ***the earth***, used in intensive expressions indicative of great or excessive ambition, cost, expense, etc.; ***to cost the earth***: see COST *v.* 1 d.

1928 WODEHOUSE *Money for Nothing* vii. 132 What's the matter with you that you always want the earth? **1952** —— *Barmy in Wonderland* xiv. 137, I pay a director the earth. Where is he? **1958** *Engineering* 4 Apr. 427/2 The customer has a perfect right to ask for the earth, but the supplier, if he is wise, will not necessarily let him have it. **1961** A. CHRISTIE *Pale Horse* xii. 129 Would it be terribly expensive?.. She'd heard they charged the earth.

10. a. Considered as a sphere, orb, or planet.

c **1400** *Rom. Rose* 5339 Erthe, that bitwixe is sett The sonne and hir [the moon]. **1555** EDEN *Decades W. Ind.* Cont. (Arb.) 45 A demonstration of the roundenesse of the earth. **1658** CULPEPPER *Astrol. Judgem. Dis.* 18 The Earth is a great lump of dirt rolled up together, and..hanged in the Air. **1726** tr. *Gregory's Astron.* I. 403 The Place of the Aphelion or Perihelion of the Earth. **1796** H. HUNTER tr. *St. Pierre's Stud. Nat.* (1799) I. Introd. 32 The Earth is lengthened out at the Poles. **1854** BREWSTER *More Worlds* Introd. 2 The earth is a planet.

†**b.** *transf.* A world resembling the earth; a (supposed) habitable planet.

1678 CUDWORTH *Intell. Syst.* 381 He affirmed..the Moon [to be] an earth, having Mountains and Valleys, Cities and Houses in it. **1684** T. BURNET *Th. Earth* I. 168 We will consider..the rest of the earths, or of the planets within our heavens. **1841** LANE *Arab. Nts.* I. 23, This is the 1st, or highest, of 7 earths.

III. †**11.** [? After L. *terra*.] A country, land; portion of the earth's surface. *Obs.*

c **950** *Lindisf. Gosp.* John iii. 22 Æfter ðas cum se hælend ..in iudea eorðu [**975** *Rushw.* eorðo]. *a* **1300** *Cursor M.* 5484 Ioseph..first was berid in þat contre, Siþen born til his erth was he. *c* **1382** WYCLIF *Ezek.* xxi. 2 Sone of man..prophecy thou aȝens the erthe of Israel. *c* **1435** *Torr. Portugal* 1325 They yave Ser Torent that he wan, Both the erth and the woman. **1556** LAUDER *Tract.* (1864) 270 And..ȝe be nocht feird But doute for to possesse the eird. **1595** SHAKS. *John* II. i. 344 This hand That swayes the earth this Climate ouerlookes. **1628** HOBBES *Thucyd.* (1822) 41 The Athenians have the spirit not to be slaves to their earth.

IV. As a substance or material.

12. a. The material of which the surface of the ground is composed, soil, mould, dust, clay.

a **1000** *Guthlac* 351 (Gr.) þeah min ban and blod butu ȝeweorðen eorðan to eacan. *a* **1175** *Cott. Hom.* 221 God.. cweð þat he wolde wercan man of eorðan. *a* **1300** *Cursor M.* 928 Vnto þat erth þou was of tan. *a* **1300** *Havelok* 740 A litel hus to maken of erthe. **1340** HAMPOLE *Pr. Consc.* 427 Askes and pouder, erthe and clay. **1534** LD. BERNERS *Gold. Bk. M. Aurel.* (1546) C v, To graue..in erthe, and other sculptures. **1664** EVELYN *Kal. Hort.* (1729) 193 Now is your Season for Circumposition by Tubs or Baskets of Earth. **1708** J. C. *Compl. Collier* (1845) 15 Mould, Sand, Gravil or Clay (all which I call Earth). **1806** *Gazetteer Scotl.* 54 Alternate strata of earth and limestone. **1836** THIRLWALL *Greece* II. xiv. 213 The envoys..undertook to give earth and water. **1865** G.

MACDONALD *A. Forbes* III. 168 'Sober floories that smell o' the yird like'.

†**b.** Clay as material for pottery. *Obs.*

1526 *Pilgr. Perf.* (W. de W. 1531) 69 He wolde euer be serued in vessels of erth. **1660** *Act 12 Chas. II*, iv. Sched. s.v. *Bottles*, Bottles..of Earth or Stone the dozen.

c. In *Sugar-making.* A layer of earth spread over the raw sugar in the process of refining.

1752 CHAMBERS *Cycl.* s.v. *Sugar*, When the second earth is taken off, they cleanse the surface of the sugar with a brush.

13. a. As the type of dull, dead matter.

1593 SHAKS. *Rich. II*, III. iii. 78 Dar'st thou, thou little better thing then earth, Divine his downfall?

b. As a disparaging term for precious metal.

1612 W. PARKES *Curtaine Dr.* (1876) 34 My bagges are full ..with the white and red earth of the world.

c. Used for: The body. Cf. *dust*, *clay*.

a **1600** SHAKS. *Sonn.* cxlvi, Poore soule the center of my sinfull earth. **1611** BEAUM. & FL. *Maid's Trag.* v. (1679) 19 This earth of mine doth tremble, and I feel A stark affrighted motion in my blood. **1822** SHELLEY *Hellas* 21 The indignant spirit cast its mortal garment Among the slain—dead earth upon the earth.

14. Earth as one of the four so-called 'elements'. Also, in pre-scientific chemistry, one of the supposed five (or six) elements; see quot. 1778.

a **1300** *Fragm. Pop. Sc.* (Wright) 267 Of this four elementz ech quik thing y-maked is, Of urthe, of water, and of eyr, and of fur, i-wis. **1393** GOWER *Conf.* III. 92 Four elements there ben diverse, The first of hem men erthe call. **1564** P. MOORE *Hope Health* I. iii. 5 The yearth is the loweste and heauiest element. **1601** SHAKS. *Twel. N.* I. v. 294 You should not rest Betweene the elements of ayre and earth. **1778** *Dict. of Art & Sciences*, s.v. *Element*, The elements..to which all bodies may be..reduced are..Water..Air..Oil..Salt.. Earth.

15. *Chem.* (See quots.) In mod. use restricted to certain metallic oxides, agreeing in having little taste or smell, and in being uninflammable, *e.g.* magnesia, alumina, zirconia, and the 'alkaline earths' baryta, lime, strontia.

a **1728** WOODWARD (J.) Earths are opake, insipid, and, when dried, friable, or consisting of parts easy to separate, and soluble in water. **1751** SIR J. HILL *Mat. Med.* (J.) The five genera of earths are, 1. Boles, 2. Clays, 3. Marls, 4. Ochres, 5. Tripelas. **1791** HAMILTON *Berthollet's Dyeing* I. i. I. i. 22 They unite with acids, alkalis..and some earths, principally alumine. **1814** SIR H. DAVY *Agric. Chem.* 12 Four Earths generally abound in soils, the aluminous, the siliceous, the calcareous, and the magnesian. **1863–79** WATTS *Dict. Chem.* II. 360 *Earths*, this name is applied to the oxides of the metals, barium, strontium, etc.

B. earth- in *comb.*

I. General relations.

1. attributive. **a.** Pertaining to the earth as a world, or as a globe or planet; as in ***earth-child***, ***-god***, ***-goddess***, ***-history***, ***-line***, ***-lord***, ***-magic***, ***-measure***, ***-noise***, ***-pole***, ***-power***, ***-surface***, ***-time***, ***-year***. **b.** Pertaining to the ground, dwelling or existing on, near, or below the surface of the ground, as in ***earth-beetle***, ***-bird***, ***-damp***, ***-fly***, ***-hole***. **c.** Pertaining to the crust of the earth, as in ***earth-throe***, ***-tremor***. **d.** Pertaining to the earth in relation to electricity, as in ***earth-resistance***. **e.** Characteristic of earth as a substance, as in ***earth-colour***, (hence ***earth-coloured*** adj.), ***-smell***, ***-tint***, ***-tone***; composed of earth, as in ***earth-bank***, ***-bottom***, ***-envelope***, ***-mound***, ***-wall***.

1866 KINGSLEY *Herew.* xix. 236 He went along the *earth-banks of his ancient home. **1601** HOLLAND *Pliny* II. 379 A kind of *earth-beetles called tauri, i. Buls. *a* **1225** *Ancr. R.* 132 þeos..beoþ *eorð briddes, & nesteð o þer eorðe. **1883** F. G. HEATH in *Century Mag.* Dec. 169/1 Over the original *earth-bottom of the cave is a bed or layer of considerable thickness. **1906** *Westm. Gaz.* 2 June 6/2 *Earth-child, struggle no more. **1931** BLUNDEN *To Themis* 56 Age cannot wither you, Tiny philosopher, Earth-child, musician. **1935** T. S. ELIOT *Murder in Cathedral* i. 12 The labourer bends to his piece of earth, *earth-colour, his own colour. **1918** D. H. LAWRENCE *New Poems* 50 The waste all dry..Stirring with *earth-coloured life. **1814** SCOTT *Wav.* xxxvii, The light usually carried by a miner..certain to be extinguished should he encounter the more formidable hazard of *earth-damps or pestiferous vapours. **1884** H. R. HAWEIS in *Longm. Mag.* Dec. 191 The *earth-envelope of mind is not the measure of mind. **1731** MEDLEY *Kolben's Cape G. Hope* II. 176 There is a sort of Flies at the Cape which the Europeans call *Earth-flies. **1871** SWINBURNE *Poems* (1904) II. 124 The *earth-god Freedom. **1904** *Folk-Lore* Sept. 312 As an embodiment of the earth-god the king was responsible for the fruits of the earth. **1878** GLADSTONE *Prim. Homer* 74 We have no acknowledged *earth-goddess in the poems. **1880** A. WALLACE *Isl. Life* 83 The opposite belief, which is now rapidly gaining ground among the students of *earth-history. *c* **1200** *Trin. Coll. Hom.* 139 He turnde..fro mennes wunienge to wilde deores, and ches þere crundel to halle and *eorðhole to bure. **1866** G. M. HOPKINS *Jrnl.* 6 May (1959) 135 A charming day, sky pied with clouds, near the *earth-line egg-blue. **1907** KIPLING *Twenty Poems* (1918) 2 They are concerned with matters hidden—under the earth-line their altars are. **1628** GAULE *Pract. The.* 42 The *Earth-Lords [Adam's] honour now layd in the dust. **1944** BLUNDEN *Shells by Stream* 13 Something between a castle and a cave..For that earth-lord to pace. **1901** 'L. MALET' *Hist. R. Calmady* VI. x. 603 All this, the unity and secrecy of the place..circling them about with something of *earth-magic. **1928** C. DAY LEWIS *Country Comets* 9 For his was the simpleness Born of earth-magic. **1570** BILLINGSLEY *Euclid* XII. xviii. 389 It was nedefull for Mechanicall *earthmeasures, not to be ignorant of the measure and contents of the circle. **1875** EMERSON *Lett. & Soc. Aims, Immortality* Wks. (Bohn) III. 280 The Pyramids..and cromlechs and *earth-mounds much older. **1850** BROWNING *Poems* II. 435, I can hear it 'Twixt my spirit And the *earth-noise, intervene. **1847** EMERSON *Poems* (1857) 32 From the *earth-poles to the line. **1887** *Spectator* 7 May 626/1 The *earth-powers which dwell in the billows, the rain, the frost, and the air. **1870** R. FERGUSON *Electr.* 243 The *earth resistance to the current..is next to nothing. **1895** K. GRAHAME *Golden Age* 14 The air was wine, the moist *earth-smell wine. **1942** T. S. ELIOT *Little Gidding* i. 7 There is no earth smell Or smell of living thing. **1883** PROCTOR in *Contemp. Rev.* Oct. 566 An extent of *earth-surface to be measured. *Ibid.* Tens of thousands of human beings have..been destroyed by *earth-throes. **1951** A. C. CLARKE *Sands of Mars* ii. 15 We keep normal *Earth-time —Greenwich Meridian—aboard the [space-]ship. **1951** S. SPENDER tr. *Rilke's Life of Virgin Mary* 47 Something endured Still, rest of earth-time, canker withered. **1865** *Daily Tel.* 27 Oct. 3/1 The colour of these tiles is a deep *earth-tint. **1973** T. PYNCHON *Gravity's Rainbow* I. 149 All in some nameless *earth tone—a hedge-green, a clay-brown, a touch of oxidation, a breath of the autumnal. **1984** *Homes & Land in Gatorland* (Fla.) 17 Apr. 3/1 (Advt.), Fieldstone complements this cheerful 3 bdr. Decorated in earthtones. **1887** G. H. DARWIN *Earthquakes* in *Fortn. Rev.* Feb. 274 These troublesome changes are called *earth tremors. **1884** *Athenæum* 16 Aug. 217/3 Dr. Bruce also pointed out traces ..of the vallum or *earthwall. **1953** E. F. RUSSELL *Somewhere a Voice* (1965) 18 It would take them most of an *Earth-year to reach the fortieth parallel.

2. objective. **a.** (sense 1), as ***earth-tilling***, ***-worker*** vbl. sbs.; ***earth-baking***, ***-convulsing***, ***-delving***, ***-incinerating***, ***-piercing***, ***-trading*** ppl. adjs. **b.** (senses 7, 8), as ***earth-measuring*** vbl. sb.; †***earths-amazing***, ***earth-crossing***, ***-destroying***, ***-devouring***, ***-embleming***, ***-over-gazing***, ***-refreshing***, ***-vexing*** ppl. adjs. **c.** (sense 9), as ***earth-poring***, ***-seeking*** ppl. adjs. **d.** (sense 12), as ***earth-grubber***, ***-maker***, ***-scraper***; ***earth-eating*** vbl. sb. and ppl. adj.; ***earth-wheeling*** vbl. sb.

1624 QUARLES *Job* (1717) 221 Jehovah did at length unshroud His *Earths-amazing language. **1847** EMERSON *Poems* (1857) 143 *Earth-baking heat. **1819** SHELLEY *Prometh. Unb.* IV. (1878) II. 132 *Earth-convulsing behemoth. **1886** PROCTOR in *19th Cent.* May 692 A special *earth-crossing family of Comets. **1592** SHAKS. *Ven. & Ad.* 687 Where *earth-deluing Conies keepe. *a* **1631** DRAYTON *Wks.* IV. 1540 (Jod.) This all drowning *earth-destroying shower. *c* **1605** MONTGOMERIE *Poems* 39 (Jod.) The *earth devouring anguish of despair. **1852** TH. ROSS tr. *Humboldt's Trav.* II. xxiv. 499 These examples of *earth-eating in the torrid zone appear very strange. **1869** tr. *Pouchet's Universe* (1871) 22 There are a tolerably large number of earth-eating tribes in North America. **1839** BAILEY *Festus* x. (1848) 108 The sacrificial ox, *earth-embleming. *c* **1630** DRUMM. OF HAWTH. *Poems* Wks. (1711) 33/2 The earth and *earth-embracing sea did shake. **1870** BRYANT *Homer* I. IX. 274 They offered prayer To earth-embracing Neptune. **1883** PROCTOR in *Contemp. Rev.* Oct. 566 The *earth-fashioning power of vulcanian forces. **1661** K. W. *Conf. Charac.*, *Usurer* (1860) 74 This miserable *earthgrubber doth.. acquire this trash with vexation. **1869** SPURGEON *Treas. Dav.* Ps. xv. 2 True believers do not..bend double as earth-grubbers. **1801** HUNTINGTON *Bank of Faith* 34 Finding nothing could be done with the *earth-holders, I.. determined to build my stories in the heaven. **1598** J. DICKENSON *Greene in Conc.* (1878) 134 *Earth-incinerating Aetnas wombe big swolne with flames. **1719** DE FOE *Crusoe* (1840) II. xiv. 285 Potters and *earth-makers; that is to say, people that tempered the earth for the China ware. **1570** BILLINGSLEY *Euclid* XII. xviii. 389 Geometria, that is, *Earthmeasuring. **1816** BYRON *Ch. Har.* III. xci, The peak Of *earth-o'ergazing mountains. **1839** BAILEY *Festus* xix. (1848) 206 The broad and upturned base Of that *earth-piercing altar pyramid. **1646** G. DANIEL *Poems* Wks. 1878 I. 24 High, and purged Soules Leave Time and Place, to dull *earthporing fooles. *a* **1631** DRAYTON *Wks.* II. 4–9 (Jod.) The *earth-refreshing Sun..his golden head doth run Far under us. **1615** T. ADAMS *Spiritual Navig.* 34 *Earth scrapers..that would dig to the Center to exhale riches. **1646** G. DANIEL *Poems* Wks. 1878 I. 13 A low bruit Affection..which binds In Sensuall Fetters, lowe *Earth-seeking minds. **1875** E. WHITE *Life in Christ* I. i. (1878) 3 Wearing so many crowns, as *Earth-subduer, Legislator. **1387** TREVISA *Higden* (Rolls) III. 31 þis kyng [Azarias] louede wel *erþe telynge. **1382** WYCLIF *1 Cor.* iii. 9 ȝe ben the erthe tilyinge of God. **1592** SHAKS. *Rom. & Jul* I. ii. 25 *Earthtreading starres, that make darke heauen light. **1611** —— *Cymb.* v. iv. 42 This *earth-vexing smart. **1477** in *York Myst.* Introd. 21 *note*, Garthyners, *erthe wallers, pavers, dykers. **1885** SIR R. RAWLINSON in *Pall Mall G.* 17 Jan. 1/2 Stockport, where men had been set to test work at *earth-wheeling. **1872** H. MACMILLAN *True Vine* ii. 57 '*Earth-worker,' as the original word for husbandman should be rendered.

3. instrumental with passive pple., as ***earth-blinded***, ***-dimmed***, ***-fed***, ***-rampired***, ***-stained***, ***-worn***.

1831 CARLYLE *Sart. Res.* III. viii, Thou the *Earth-blinded summonest both Past and Future. **1884** W. G. HORDER in *Chr. World Pulpit* 12 Nov. 310/3 Our *earth-dimmed souls. **1605** B. JONSON *Volpone* III. vii, *Earth-fed Minds That never tasted the true Heav'n of love. **1649** G. DANIEL *Trinarch.*, *Hen. V*, cli, *Earth-rampeir'd Ears, expect the Drum to Call. **1827** KEBLE *Chr. Y. 24th Sund. after Trin.*, The *earth-stained spright Whose wakeful musings are of guilt and fear. **1866** E. PEACOCK *Eng. Ch. Furniture* 177 The *earth-worn face of the living.

4. adverbial with adjs. or vbl. sbs. Chiefly locative and originative (in, on, near to the earth; from, of the earth), and similative (as the earth); as in ***earth-bedded***, ***-bound*** (also *transf.* and *fig.*, and indicating motion towards the earth), ***-bowed***, ***-bred***, ***-burrower***, ***-coloured***, ***-creeping***, ***-ejected***, ***-gaping***, ***-grovelling***, ***-lent***, ***-long***, ***-low***, ***-made***, ***-nurtured***, ***-proud***, ***-rooted***, ***-sprung***, ***-turned***, ***-undone***, ***-wide***.

1813 SCOTT *Rokeby* II. xv, Yon *earth-bedded jetting-stone. **1605** SHAKS. *Macb.* IV. i. 96 Who can..bid the Tree Vnfixe his *earth-bound Root? **1869** W. JAMES *Coll. Ess. & Rev.* (1920) 1, The 'Sadducees', as our author [*sc.* a spiritualist] loves to call the earth-bound portion of the community. **1931** C. DAY LEWIS *From Feathers to Iron* xv. 31 Earth's first faint tug at the earthbound soul. **1935** *Discovery* Feb. 43/1 To an earth-bound rocket pressure is more important than velocity. **1950** S. SPENDER *Sel. Poems Whitman* 11 With all his loftiness and idealism, he is peculiarly earth-bound. **1865** G. SMITH *Autumn* iv. in *Macm. Mag.* XIII. 54 *Earth-bow'd trees. **1594** ? GREENE *Selimus* Wks. 1881–3 XIV. 285 *Earth-bred brethren, which once Heapte hill on hill to scale the starrie skie. **1603** H. CROSSE *Vertues Commw.* (1878) 90 Earth-bred wormes, ..will stand vpon termes of gentilitie. **1622** MAY *Heir* in Hazl. *Dodsley* II. 517 The earth-bred thoughts of his gross soul. **1883** WOOD in *Longm. Mag.* Dec. 162 The mole is an *earth-burrower. **1877** *Daily News* 1 Nov. 5/7 We reached Biela at dark, *earth-coloured, wet and out of spirits. **1581** SIDNEY *Apol. Poesie* (1622) 530 So *earth-creeping a mind, that it cannot lift itself vp to looke to the skies of Poetry. **1819** SHELLEY *Prometh. Unb.* II. ii, The earth-creeping breeze. **1886** PROCTOR in *19th Cent.* May 694 The orbit.. had been that of the *earth-ejected comet. **1596** FITZ-GEFFREY *Sir F. Drake* (1881) 31 *Earth-gaping Chasma's, that mishap aboades. **1642** H. MORE *Song of Soul* I. III. xxxviii, This Province..is hight *earth-grovelling Aptery. **1839** BAILEY *Festus* vi. (1848) 61 With every *earthlent ray of every star Holy and special influences are. **1903** W. S. BLUNT *7 Golden Odes* 15 Herds knelt, their necks stretched *earth-long. **1935** C. DAY LEWIS *Time to Dance* 55 Earth-long and heaven-outfacing woes. **1600** TOURNEUR *Transf. Met.* cclxxxii, With fleecy Wooll, that hung on *earth-low brakes. **1849** HARE *Par. Serm.* II. 416 Everything *earth-made has a weight in it which drags it down to earth. **1881** H. PHILLIPS tr. *Chamisso's Faust* 15 Woe and wail! earth-born, *earth-nurtured! **1868** HAWTHORNE *Amer. Note-bks.* (1879) I. 218 Weary *earth-plodders. **1847** EMERSON *Poems* (1857) 70 *Earth-proud, proud of the earth which is not theirs. **1871** G. MACDONALD *Songs of Days & Nts.* 51 The long grass..an *earth-rooted sea. **1614** R. TAYLOR *Hog lost Pearl* in *Dodsley* (1780) VI. 412 Tortur'd by the weak assailments Of *earth-sprung griefs. *a* **1849** J. C. MANGAN *Poems* (1850) 74 Earthsprung mothers, of an earthly name, Doomed to die. **1618** BRAITHWAIT *Descr. Death*, *Earth-turned, mole-eied, flesh-hook, that puls us hence. **1850** MRS. BROWNING *Poems* I. 313 As one God-satisfied and *earth-undone. **1864** R. S. HAWKER *Quest. Sangraal* 4 The *Earthwide Judge, Pilate the Roman.

II. Special comb.: **earth-almond** = CHUFA; **earth-bags** = *sand-bags* (Adm. Smyth); see *earth-sack*; **earth-balls**, truffles, *Tuber cibarium* (Britten and Holland); †**earth-bath**, a kind of medical treatment in which the patient was buried up to the shoulders in the ground; **earth-battery** (*Electr.*), a battery formed by burying two voltaic elements in the earth some distance apart; **earth-bed**, a bed upon the ground; the grave; †**earth-bind**, some creeping plant; **earth-bob**, a maggot, the larva of a beetle; †**earth-coal**, coal as distinguished from charcoal; **earth-car** (see quot.); **earth-chestnut** = EARTH-NUT; †**earth-chine**, a cleft in the earth; **earth-closet**, a substitute for a water-closet, in which earth is used as a deodorising agent; **earth colour**, **pigment**, a pigment obtained from native earth, as the ochres and umbers; so **earth white**; **earth-current** (*Electr.*), an irregular current due to the earth, which affects telegraph wires so as to render them temporarily useless for communication; †**earth-dog**, a terrier; **earth-drake**, mod. rendering of OE. *eorð-draca* earth-dragon; †**earth-flax**, some mineral, possibly asbestos; **earth-flea**, **earth-fly**, = CHIGOE; **earth-foam**, a variety of Aphrite; **earth-fork**, a digging fork; **earth-gall**, the Lesser Centaury, *Erythræa Centaurium*; **earth-hog** = AARD-VARK; **earth-house**, an underground chamber or dwelling; *fig.* the grave; **earth-hunger**, a disease characterized by a morbid craving for eating earth; *fig.* desire to possess land, greed of territory; †**earth-ivy** = GROUND-IVY; †**earth-lice**, transl. L. *pedunculi terræ* (see quot.); **earth-life**, terrestrial existence; **earth-man**, (*a*) a human being (or occas. a mythical creature) whose life and instincts are closely allied with the natural or material (as opposed to the spiritual) world; (*b*) esp. in science fiction, an inhabitant or native of the planet Earth; also **earthsman**, **earth-woman**; **earth-marl**, marl containing a large proportion of clay; **earth-moss**, the genus *Phascum* (Britten and Holland); **Earth-Mother** [tr. G. *erdmutter*], in mythology and folklore, a spirit or being taken as a symbol of the earth; a sensual and maternal woman; also = MOTHER EARTH 1; **earth-mouse**, the plant *Lathyrus tuberosus* (Britten and Holland); **earth-mover** orig. *U.S.*, a vehicle or machine designed for the excavation or shifting of large quantities of earth; so **earth-moving** *ppl. a.*; **earth-moving** *vbl. sb.*, (*a*) =

EARTHQUAKE; (*b*) the process of moving large quantities of earth during excavation, etc.; **earth-oil**, petroleum; **earth-pig**, transl. Du. *aardvarken* = AARD-VARK; **earth-pillar** (*Geol.*), a pillar-like mass of earth (see quot.); †**earth-planet**, *nonce-wd.*, a fugitive, wanderer; **earth-plate** (*Electr.*), a metal plate buried in the earth, connected with a telegraph battery in order that the circuit may be completed by the earth; †**earth-puff**, a puff-ball fungus (Nares); **earth-return** (*a*) *Electr.*, an earthed return circuit, as distinguished from a metallic return; also *attrib.*; (*b*) *attrib.*, returning to the planet Earth; †**earth-ric** (Orm. *eorþeriche*), the earth-realm, earth as a region; **earth-rind**, rhetorically used for 'crust of the earth'; also *fig.*; **earth-sack**, a sack filled with earth, used as a fascine in fortifications; **earth satellite**, an artificial satellite projected into orbit around the earth; also *attrib.*; **earth-sculpture**, the physical processes by which the form of the earth's surface is altered; **earth-shaker**, also **earth-shaking** *ppl. a.*, chiefly used as epithets of Poseidon or Neptune; *ppl. a.*, also *fig.*; **earth-shaking** *vbl. sb.*, formerly = EARTHQUAKE; **earth-shine** (*Astron.*) = EARTH-LIGHT; **earth-shock**, a convulsion of the earth; †an earthquake; †**earth-shrew**, the Shrew-mouse; **earth-side**, *nonce-wd.*, earthward side or aspect; also *attrib.* or as *adj.*, and used adverbially; **earth-smoke**, the plant Fumitory (Britten and Holland); **earth-soul**, (*a*) *Philos.*, the supposed collective consciousness of the earth, including as its parts the consciousnesses of all earth's inhabitants (cf. ANIMA MUNDI); (*b*) the soul of a former earth-dweller; **earth-spider**, the Tarantula; **earth-spring**, in electrical machines a spring connected with the earth; **earth-star**, a fungus so called from its stellate shape when lying on the ground; also as *nonce-wd.*, applied to the earth considered as a 'star', and to luminous objects resembling stars; **earth-stopper**, one who is employed to stop up the 'earths' or holes of foxes; **earth-table** (*Arch.*), see quot.; **earth-tongue** (*Bot.*), Eng. rendering of the name of the genus *Geoglossum* (Treas. Bot.); **earth-wave**, a seismic wave in the solid crust of the earth; **earth-wax** = OZOCERITE; **earth-wire** *Electr.*, wire carried from a conductor into the earth, esp. to prevent contact from the leakage of current from one wire into another; hence **earth-wire** *v.*, **-wired** *ppl. a.*, **-wiring** *vbl. sb.*; **earth-wolf**, transl. Du. AARDWOLF, q.v.; **earth-woman** (see *earth-man* above). Also EARTH-APPLE, -BOARD, -BORN, -DIN, -FAST, -LESS, -LIGHT, -MAD, -WISE, -WORK, -WORM.

1856 *Rep. Comm. Pat.: Agric. 1855* (U.S.) p. xiii, The *Earth Almond, or *Chufa*, (*Cyperus esculentus*), a small tuberous esculent, from the south of Spain, has naturalised itself to our climate and soil. **1860** Earth-almond [see CHUFA]. **1765** *Nat. Hist.* in *Ann. Reg.* 108/2 The *Earth-bath ..may be used with safety only from the end..of May to.. October. *a* **1300** *Cursor M.* 6962 Ioseph bans þai wit ham ledd, þar þai þam grof in *erth bedd. **1637** NABBES *Microcosm.* in *Dodsley* IX. 163 My earth-bed wet with nightly tears. **1877** BROWNING *La Saisiaz* 118 Of all earth-beds, to your mind Most the choice for quiet, yonder. **1579** LANGHAM *Gard. Health* (1633) 205 Headache of rheume, put in the iuyce of white *Earthbinde into the nose. **1740** R. BROOKES *Art of Angling* I. iii. 13 The *Earth-Bob or White-Grub is a Worm with a red Head. **1787** BEST *Angling* (ed. 2) 57 The best bait for them in the winter is, the earth bob, it is the spawn of the beetle. **1874** KNIGHT *Dict. Mech.*, **Earth-car* = dumping-car, a car for transporting gravel and stone in railway operations. *c* **1220** *Bestiary* 402 [A fox] goð o felde to a furg, and falleð ðarinne, In eried lond er *erð-chine. **1870** *Eng. Mech.* 18 Mar. 661/3 He had converted a privy into an *earth-closet. **1871** NAPHEYS *Prev. & Cure Dis.* I. viii. 233 The dry earth-closet is especially valuable. **1807** SOUTHEY *Espriella's Lett.* (1814) I. 12 They burn *earth-coal everywhere. **1913** N. HEATON *Hurst's Man. Painters' Colours* (ed. 5) v. 155 Iron oxide is also the colouring principle of the group of pigments known as '*earth colours'. **1951** *Oxf. Jun. Encycl.* VII. 325/1 Examples of such earth colours are yellow ochre, siennas (dark yellows), and umbers (browns). **1872** *Phil. Mag.* XLIII. 186 It is almost impossible to have two earth-plates inserted any distance apart without a difference of tension, ..This is due in some cases to *earth-currents. **1879** THOMSON & TAIT *Nat. Phil.* I. I. §376 An unknown and every varying electromotive force..due to the earth (producing what is commonly called the 'earth-current'). **1616** SURFL. & MARKH. *Countr. Farm* 699 The hunting of the Foxe and Broke..is to be performed with *earth-dogs. *a* **1000** *Beowulf* (Gr.) 2711 Sio wund..þe him se *eorð-draca ær ȝeworhte. **18..** OGILVIE, s.v. *Earth-drake*, cites W. SPALDING. **1695** WOODWARD (J.) Of English talc, the coarser sort is called plaister, or parget; the finer, *earth flax, or salamander's hair. **1872** WATTS *Dict. Chem.* I. 349 A soft friable variety of it [aphrite] called *earth-foam. *c* **1000** *Sax. Leechd.* II. 186 Centaurian sume hatað hyrde wyrt sume *eorð ȝeallan. **1611** COTGR., *Repeyret*, Feuerwort, Earthgall, Centorie the lesse. **1884** MILLER *Plant Names* 40 Earth-gall, Erythræa Centaurium and other plants of the Gentian tribe. **1731** MEDLEY *Kolben's Cape G. Hope* II. 118 The *Earth-hogs..are not unlike the European hogs, excepting that their colour approaches to a red. *c* **1000** *Sax. Leechd.* II. 146 Romane him..worhton *eorþ hus for þære lyfte wilme. *c* **1205** LAY. 2381 Seouen ȝer wes Astrild i þissen eorð huse [**1250** erþ huse]. *a* **1856** LONGF. *Grave* 28 Loathsome is that earth-house and grim within to dwell. **1856** EMERSON *Eng. Traits* vii. *Truth* Wks. (Bohn) II. 53 The *earth-hunger, or preference for property in land, which is said to mark the Teutonic nations. **1884** *Graphic* 4 Oct. 342/2 The Boers.. whose earth hunger is notorious, will gradually 'eat-up' all the surrounding territories. *c* **1050** *Voc.* in Wr.-Wülcker 299 *Hedera nigra*, *eorðifiȝ. *c* **1265** *Voc. Plant-names* in Wr.-Wülcker 558 *Hedera nigra*, oerþiui. **1561** HOLLYBUSH *Hom. Apoth.* 37 a, Take the lesse Shaving girss..and Earth yvy, of eche two handfull. **1601** HOLLAND *Pliny* II. 379 Some tearme them, Pedunculos terræ, *earth-lice. **1906** W. DE MORGAN *Joseph Vance* xix. 191 The black Shadow that oppressed me was bidden to..scatter itself over the remainder of my *earth-life. **1906** *Daily Chron.* 28 May 3/4 One brief day—as long as seven years of this earth-life. **1922** O. LODGE *Raymond Revised* 47 Humour does not cease with earth-life. **1958** *New Statesman* 15 Mar. 353/2 The spy from Outer Space..will be happy to discover..an authentic smell, that is, of mid-century earth-life in general. **1860** H. B. TRISTRAM *Great Sahara* i. 18 A negro from Timbuctoo engaged to remove the plague, and taught sacrifices to the '*Earth-men', or demons who roam the earth. These are believed to be harmless when once they have obtained a human residence. **1904** G. K. CHESTERTON *G. F. Watts* 126 He would see giants and the sea..and brown earth-men and red earth-women lying in the heaps of greens and browns and reds. **1905** *Daily Chron.* 16 Mar. 8/2 The sensual earth-man must be killed, beyond all chances of reviving, before the man after the divine pattern and will can live. **1930** A. H. KRAPPE *Sci. Folk-Lore* i. 20 In at least one type [of fairy tale], the story of the Earthman, the helper, a dwarf, sometimes a witch, has to be overcome by the hero first. **1936** C. S. LEWIS *Alleg. Love* vii. 312 Mammon is the gold-hoarding earthman of immemorial tradition, the gnome. **1947** W. K. RICHMOND *Poetry & People* i. 14 At heart we are still Saxons, and deeper still we are countryfolk, peasants, earth-men. **1949** R. HEINLEIN *Red Planet* (1963) i. 3 The Mars creature saw an elderly pale Earthman. **1960** *Guardian* 26 Aug. 2/7 If their site did indeed become the set of the space film, the corps members would not be suitable for the parts of earth-men. **1770–4** A. HUNTER *Georg. Ess.* (1803) I. 226 *note*, A very considerable number of *earth-marls are of a stony hardness. **1831** *Brit. Husb.* I. 311 The origin of earth-marl is a subject of curious inquiry. **1904** *Edin. Rev.* Jan. 38 The Indian women disraimented still enact the ancient ritual of the Rain-Goddess or *Earth-Mother. **1906** *Inst. Mag.* Apr. 312 When the great, good Earth-Mother saw this, she called to April and sent her back to gain a victory over her malicious enemy. **1907** *Academy* 31 Aug. 837/1 Soft to his neck earth-mother clings. **1961** S. LLOYD *Art Anc. Near East* iii. 82 His symbolic marriage with Inanna, the 'earth-mother'. **1962** *John o'London's* 31 May 529/2 An earth-mother barmaid. **1859** *All Y. Round* No. 32. 126 The *earth-mouse (Lathyrus tuberosus), which the French peasant will not cultivate because, he says, it walks underground. **1382** WYCLIF *Matt.* xxiv. 7 *Erthemouyngis schulen be by placis. **1939** *Civil Engineering* XXXIV. 228 (*title*) The development of earth moving equipment for highway construction. **1941** *Agricultural Engineering* XXII. 19/1 Earth moving makes up the principal portion of construction work. *Ibid.* 24/1 Profit by experience of earth movers. **1959** *B.S.I. News* June 10/2 Giant earth-mover tyres. **1963** *Times* 24 Jan. 11/7 The earthmover, the caterpillar tractor. **1968** *Daily Tel.* 1 Nov. 19/4 Three or four heavy earth-moving vehicles started levelling the adjacent land. **1755** BAKER in Dalrymple *Or. Rep.* I. 172 (Y.) About 200 Families..employed in getting *Earth-oil out of Pitts. **1785** G. FORSTER tr. *Sparrman's Voy. Cape Gd. Hope* I. 270 The *aard-varken*, or *earth-pig, which, probably, is a species of *manis*. **1962** M. BURTON *Syst. Dict. Mammals* 195 (*heading*) Aardvark, earth-pig, ant-bear (*Orycteropus afer*). **1923** L. C. MARTIN *Colour & Methods of Colour Reprod.* vi. 73 Generally speaking, the '*earth pigments' are the most stable and satisfactory. **1870** LYELL *Student's Geol.* vi. (ed. 4) 82 *Earth-pillars with stones on their tops are relics of the country worn away all around them. **1591** FLORIO *2nd Fruites* 141 Children, whores, and fugitiues..A man must not beleeue these runagate *earth-planets. **1847** BRETT & LITTLE *Compendium Improvements Electric Telegraphs* 22 An *earth plate..which carries the current back by the conducting powers of the earth. **1872** Earth-plate [see *earth-current*]. **1585** J. HIGINS tr. *Junius Nomenclator* (N.) Mushrooms, tadstooles, earthturfes, *earthpuffes. **1871** *Eng. Mech.* 8 Sept. 627/1 *Earth return currents are not practical. **1902** *Encycl. Brit.* XXXIII. 227/2 Steinheil of Munich..discovered the use of the earth return. **1940** *Chambers's Techn. Dict.* 277/2 *Earth return circuit*, a telegraphic current using one transmission wire, the return current passing through the earth and thereby encountering a low resistance. **1962** F. I. ORDWAY et al. *Basic Astronautics* v. 191 Later, when Earth-return vehicles become feasible, samples can be brought back. **1968** *Times* 23 Dec. 6/4 There is no reason in logic why it should not..eject them into an earth-return orbit. *c* **1200** ORMIN 12132 Nan eorþliȝ kinedom Here upponn *eorþeriche. **1850** CARLYLE *Latter-d. Pamphl.* iv. 8 On what a bottomless volcano..separated from us by a thin *earth-rind, Society..in the present epoch, rests! **1871** HARTWIG *Subterr. W.* i. 5 The history of the earth-rind opens to us a vista into time. **1708** *Lond. Gaz.* No. 4471/2 We began..to fill the Fosse..with Fascines and *Earth-Sacks. **1949** *Rocket Jet Flying* Spring 6 The '*earth satellite vehicle program'..is the most imagination-firing news we've heard in quite a while. **1950** *Jrnl. Brit. Interplanetary Soc.* IX. 155 As performances improve, so we may expect to see the appearance of the close-orbit Earth satellite vehicle. **1956** *Collier's Year-Bk.* 48/2 Plans to launch an earth satellite were announced in the middle of 1955. **1959** DAVIES & PALMER *Radio Studies of Universe* x. 180 A most spectacular and ambitious project..has been the launching of earth satellites by Russia and the U.S.A. **1883** MRS. PRESTWICH in *Gd. Words* 643/2 Glaciers and other agents of *earth-sculpture. **1647** R. STAPYLTON *Juvenal* 184 Th' *earth-shaker Neptune. **1846** GROTE *Greece* (1869) I. 55 The mighty Poseidon, the earth-shaker and the ruler of the sea. **1387** TREVISA *Higden* (Rolls) V. 299 Mammertus.. ordeyned Rogacious aȝenst *erþe schakynge. *Ibid.* VII. xv. (1527) 280 b, In ytalye was an erth-sakynge that dured xl dayes. **1634** MILTON *Comus* 869 By the earth-shaking Neptune's mace. **1807** J. BARLOW *Columbiad* IV. 10 p. 135 Earth-shaking storms and constellated skies. **1875** LONGF. *Masq. Pandora* III. sp. 8 The earth-shaking trident of Poseidon. **1948** E. SITWELL *Notebk. on Shakes.* viii. 104 With the exception of two earth-shaking sentences, and one speech of great beauty..Iago never speaks 'above a mortal mouth'. **1966** OGILVY & ANDERSON *Excurs. Number Theory* xi. 144 Besides, what if a study is not of earth-shaking importance? **1834** *Nat. Philos.* (U.K.S.) III. *Astron.* iii. 77/2 That part of the moon which receives no light directly from the sun, may, by indirectly receiving it from the earth, become..faintly visible. The appearance..has received the name of *earth-shine. **1876** G. CHAMBERS *Astron.* 87 The Earth-shine is more luminous before the New Moon than after it. **1946** *Nature* 21 Dec. 907/1 The portion of the moon's surface that is lighted up by earthshine. **1963** *Daily Tel.* 20 May 26 (*heading*) Space man slept well... Kept out 'earthshine'. *c* **1315** SHOREHAM 124 Altha was an *erthe-schoke. **1816** BYRON *Siege Cor.* xxxiii, All the living things that heard That deadly earth-shock disappear'd. **1693** in *Phil. Trans.* XVII. 851 The Shrew-mouse or Erd, i.e. *Earth-shrew. **1858** SEARS *Athan.* II. ix. 226 On this dark or *earth-side of his [Christ's] nature. **1865** DICKENS *Mut. Fr.* I. xiv, The earth-side of the grave. **1949** R. HEINLEIN *Red Planet* (1963) iv. 53 Many's the time he's told me stories about the school he went to back Earth-side. **1956** *Galaxy Sci. Fiction* XLIII. 11/2 Some Earth-side official of the Interstellar Prison Service. **1851** H. MELVILLE *Moby Dick* 79 It smells like another world, more strangely than the moon would to an *Earthsman. **1871** SWINBURNE *Songs bef. Sunrise* 149 The *earth-soul Freedom, that only Lives, and that only is God. **1905** W. JAMES *Ess. Rad. Emp.* (1912) iv. 136 Speculations like Fechner's, of an Earth-soul, of wider spans of consciousness enveloping narrower ones throughout the cosmos, are..philosophically quite in order. **1948** C. DAY LEWIS *Poems 1943–47* 64 You might well surmise They are earth-souls. **1883** *Chamb. Jrnl.* 1 Dec. 760/2 A common *earth-spider, the tarantula. **1881** MAXWELL *Electr. & Magn.* I. 299 When P moves away from the *earth-spring it carries this charge with it. **1816** BYRON *Siege Cor.* v, Its *earth-stars melted into heaven. **1839** BAILEY *Festus* xxviii. (1848) 335 Is the earth-star struggling still with death? **1885** W. H. GIBSON in *Harper's Mag.* May 912/1 The fungus called the earth-star, *Geaster hygrometricus*, a plant of the puff-ball tribe. **1880** *Times* 2 Nov. 4/5 There are huntsmen, whips, and grooms, kennel attendants, smiths, and *earth-stoppers to be employed. **1875** GWILT *Archit.* Gloss., **Earth Table*..the plinth of a wall..or lowest course of projecting stones immediately above the ground. **1869** PHILLIPS *Vesuv.* ix. 261 Heat in some way generates the force of the *earth-wave. **1878** HUXLEY *Physiogr.* 188 [In earthquakes] near the sea the water waves may be far more destructive than the earth waves. **1884** *Earth-wax [see OZOCERITE]. **1958** W. T. O'DEA *Social Hist. Lighting* 216 Ozokerit, or 'earth-wax', found in the region of the Roumanian oil wells, later proved.. superior, at a price, to paraffin wax candles. **1908** F. MAIRE *Mod. Pigments* iv. 40 **Earth whites* are so named to distinguish that class of pigments which owe their origin to mother earth in contradistinction to those which are derived from a metallic origin. **1868** E. ATKINSON tr. *Ganot's Physics* (ed. 3) 650 Into the other hole of the fuse a wire is placed which serves as *earth wire. **1876** PREECE & SIVEWRIGHT *Telegraphy* 258 It is always advisable to earth-wire at least the last five supports on each side of every office, as a protection against the effects of lightning. **1911** *Encycl. Brit.* XXVI. 512/1 For protection from lightning each pole has an 'earth wire' running from the top, down to the base. **1966** Earth wire [see EARTH *v.* 8]. **1876** PREECE & SIVEWRIGHT *Telegraphy* 215 *Earth-wiring... The object of the earth-wires is to prevent contact from arising through the leakage of currents from one wire at its point of support into another. *Ibid.* 216 In dry sandy soil or in rock the earth-wiring is therefore to be avoided. **1904** *Earth-woman [see *earth-man*]. **1955** 'J. WYNDHAM' in 'E. Crispin' *Best S.F.* 72 He greeted Lellie [*sc.* a Martian] just as if she were an Earth woman.

†**earth**, *sb.*² *Obs.* or *dial.* Forms: 1 ierþ, irþ, yrþ, earþ, ærþ, 4–5 erþe, 6 earthe, 6– earth. [OE. **ęrþ*, WS. *ierþ* str. fem. (OTeut. type **arþi-z*) f. **ar-*, root of OE. *ęrian*, EAR *v.*¹ to plough + suffix as in BIRTH.]

1. The action of ploughing; a ploughing. In OE. also 'ploughed land' and 'produce of arable land, a crop' (Bosw.-Toller).

c **890** K. ÆLFRED *Bæda* IV. xxviii. (Bosw.) Ða ȝeorn ðær sona up ȝenihtsumlic yrþ and wæstm. *a* **1000** *Rect. Sing. Pers.* in Thorpe *Laws* (1840) 189 Feola syndan folcȝerihtu.. ben-feorm for ripe, ȝyt-feorm for yrðe. **1398** TREVISA *Barth. De P.R.* XVII. xviii (MS.) þe more gardyne was of twenty days erþe oþer eryngе [**1495** erthe ar eryenge]. **1552** HULOET, Earth or earynge of Lande in some place taken for tyllage of lande, as the first earth..first plowynge styrringe. **1573** TUSSER *Husb* xxxv. (1878) 84 Such lande as ye breake vp for barlie to sowe, two earthes at the least er ye sowe it bestowe. *a* **1813** VANCOUVER in A. Young *Agric. Essex* I. 203 One or two deep clean ploughings is all that can..be required..and one or both of these earths, under certain circumstances, had better be dispensed with.

2. The soil turned up by the plough on the edge of the furrow.

1765 A. DICKSON *Treat. Agric.* 275 If the earths of the furrows are set on their edge, the harrows turn them back.

earth (ɜːθ), *v.* Forms: α. *Sc.* and *north. dial.* 4–6 erde, 6 eird, 9 eard, yird. β. 6– earth. [f. EARTH *sb.*¹; until 16th c. app. only *Sc.*]

†**1.** *trans.* To commit (a corpse) to the earth; to bury. (In *Sc.* formerly the usual word for this sense; in Eng. writers only *poet.* or *rhet.*, with a reference to the etymology.) Now only *dial.*

1375 BARBOUR *Bruce* XIII. 666 And the laiff..In-to gret pittes erdit war. *c* **1425** WYNTOUN *Cron.* IX. xii. 7 Robert oure secound Kyng..Wes erdyde in Skone, quhare he lyes. **1513** DOUGLAS *Æneis* V. ii. 12 The reliquies and bonis in feir Of my divyne fadir we erdit heir. **1557** *Tottell's Misc.* (Arb.) 142 Though earthed be his corps, yet florish shall his fame.

1591 GREENE *Maiden's Dr.* Wks. (1881–3) XIV. 316 His liuelesse bodie..Let that be earthed..in gorgeous wise. **1626** DK. BUCKHM. *Sp. Ho. Lords* in Rushw. *Hist. Coll.* (1659) I. 377 If my Posterity should not inherit the same fidelity, I should..be glad to see them earthed before me. **1742** R. BLAIR *Grave* 169 Why thy ado in earthing up a carcase? **1808** *Poet. Register* 73 We'll earth her tomorrow, 'Tis the only wise method to bury one's sorrow. **1832–53** *Whistle-Binkie* (Sc. Songs) Ser. II. 100 But Lauchie did dee, and was welcomely yirdet. **1875** *Whitby Gloss.* (E.D.S.) *Earded*, consigned to the earth; buried.

2. To plunge or hide in the earth; to cover with earth. Also *intr.* (for *refl.*) Only *poet.* or *rhetorical.* Also *fig.*

1648 BP. HALL *Select Th.* §25 Let a man strictly examine his own affections, he shall find them so deeply earthed. **1652** BENLOWES *Theoph.* XI. xliii, Seeds thrive When earth't. **1742** YOUNG *Nt. Th.* IX. 948 The miser earths his treasure. **1839** BAILEY *Festus* (1848) 16 Could I, like Heaven's bolt, earthing quench myself, This moment would I, etc.

3. *Gardening.* To heap the earth over (roots and stems of plants). Usually with *up.*

1693 SIR R. BULKLEY, *Maize*, in *Phil. Trans.* XVII. 939 It must be earth'd up with the Howe twice or thrice in growing. **1719** LONDON & WISE *Compl. Gard.* 299 In dry Soils, you must Earth up a little our Artichoaks. **1796** C. MARSHALL *Garden.* xv. (1813) 231 Earth up the plants frequently..a little at a time, in order to blanch them. **1881** WHITEHEAD *Hops* 8 The plant centres being 'earthed' or covered over with a few shovels of earth.

4. a. *trans.* To conceal in a hole or burrow.

1619 J. KING *Serm.* 40 Beasts..earthed in their thickets and bogges. *a* **1635** CORBET *Iter Bor.* 127 The cunning men, like moles, Dwelt not in howses, but were earth't in holes.

b. *refl.* (In 17th c. often *transf.* and *fig.*)

1609 BP. BARLOW *Answ. Nameless Cath.* 335 This wily Creature, fearing lest hee should bee taken by the..sent, hath earth'd himselfe backe againe into the 92 page. **1656** *Artif. Handsomeness* 137 He then retreats to this [stronghold] of Scandal, and earths himself in this burrough. **1719** D'URFEY *Pills* IV. 56 He Earths himself in Cellars deep.

c. *intr.* for *refl.* of the fox, etc.: To run to his earth; to hide in the earth.

1622 FLETCHER *Span. Curate* II. i, They wil not die here, They will not Earth. **1634** HEYWOOD *Witches of Lanc.* I. i. Wks. 1874 IV. 172 Perhaps some Foxe had earth'd there. **1713** *Guardian* No. 125 (1756) II. 163 Hence foxes earth'd, and wolves abhorr'd the day. *c* **1820** S ROGERS *Italy* (1852) 188 Once again he earths, Slipping away to house with them beneath. **1882** *Echo* 20 Feb. 4/2 The vulp earthed at last, and had to be left for another day.

5. *trans.* To drive (a fox, etc.) to his earth. Also *fig.*

1575 TURBERV. *Bk. Venerie* 239 We earth and digge a Badgerd. **1719** D'URFEY *Pills* II. 270 The vixen's just now Earth'd. **1742** YOUNG *Nt. Th.* IV. 96 The circling hunt, of noisy men..Pursuing, and pursu'd, each other's prey..Till death, that mighty hunter, earths them all. **1827** *Blackw. Mag.* XXI. 272 The consciousness of having now fairly..earthed the objects of this arduous search.

6. *intr.* (See quot.) *dial.*

1875 PARISH *Sussex Gloss.*, *Earth*, to turn up the ground as a mole does.

7. In *Sugar-making.* See quot., and cf. CLAYED.

1727–52 CHAMBERS *Cycl.* II. s.v. *Sugar*, Earthed Sugar is that which is whitened by means of earth laid on the top of the forms it is put in to purge itself.

8. *Electr.* To connect (a conductor) with the earth.

1885 *Jrnl. Soc. Telegraph Engineers* XIV. 454, I have myself seen a circuit 'earthed' at an intermediate station in the middle of a message. **1888** *Science* 13 July 18/1 In dry weather they [*sc.* conductors] are not earthed at all well. **1902** *Encycl. Brit.* XXV. 773/1 Let a conductor—say, a metallic sphere—be supported by a metal rod of negligible capacity whose other end is earthed. **1966** *Buying Secondhand* (Consumers' Assoc.) 72 If the appliance is intended to be earthed, make sure there is an earth wire fitted.

Hence **earthed** *ppl. a.* and **'earthing** *vbl. sb.* (also *attrib.*).

1727–52 [see sense 7 above]. **1889** *Daily News* 25 Dec. 6/7 A piece of mechanism known as an 'earthing device', the invention of Major Cardew, which infallibly cuts off the current if a condition of danger occurs. **1898** *Ibid.* 3 May 5/3 The swaying to and fro of the earthed line in the field due to terrestrial magnetism. **1906** A. F. COLLINS *Man. Wireless Telegr.* 212 Earthed terminal. The wire connecting the plate buried in the earth and the aerial wire. **1909** *Install. News* III. 80/1 Mr. Leckie recommended earthing through a resistance. **1966** *Buying Secondhand* (Consumers' Assoc.) 72 With earthed appliances the continuity of the earth wire ought to be checked.

† **'earth-apple.** *Obs.* [f. EARTH *sb.*¹]

1. In OE. ? A cucumber; also = glossarial L. *mandragora.*

c **1000** ÆLFRIC *Num.* xi. 5 Cucumeres þæt synd eorþæppla. *c* **1000** —— *Gloss.* in Wr.-Wülcker 136 *Mandragora*, eorðæppel.

2. = SOW-BREAD (? *Cyclamen europæum*).

1601 HOLLAND *Pliny* II. 300 Cankerous sores are cured with the root of Sowbread, which we call the earth-apple.

3. ? The potato [transl. Fr. *pomme de terre*]. In mod. Dicts.

'earth-board. [f. EARTH *sb.*¹ (or perh. *sb.*²) + BOARD.] The mould-board of a plough.

1649 BLITHE *Eng. Improv. Impr.* (1653) 190 The Shield-board, some call Breast-board, or Earth-board, or Furrow-board. **1765** *Univ. Mag.* XXXVII. 33/2 The plat, or earth-board, turned most of the carrots out of the ground. **1884** *Longm. Mag.* Feb. 403 The 'hardy rustic' still goes into the woods and seeks for an elm..for the earth-boards.

'earth-born, *ppl. a. poet.* or rhetorical.

1. Born by emerging from the earth: applied e.g. to the Titans, to the offspring of the dragon's teeth of Cadmus, etc. Also = AUTOCHTHONOUS.

1603 KNOLLES *Hist. Turks* (1638) 231 They had like the earth-borne brethren, wrought one anothers destruction. **1774** GOLDSM. *Nat. Hist.* (1776) VI. 403 Young turtles..are seen bursting from the sand, as if earth-born. **1831** CARLYLE *Misc.* (1857) II. 324 Lessing still towers in the distance like an Earth-born Atlas. **1875** JOWETT *Plato* (ed. 2) III. 41 Cadmus and his earth-born men.

2. Born on the earth; of earthly or mortal race, as opposed to angelic or divine.

1667 MILTON *P.L.* IV. 360 Creatures of other mould, earth-born perhaps, Not Spirits. **1738** WESLEY *Psalms* cxlvii. II. vi, By all the Earth-born Race His Honours be express'd.

b. *transf.* Of humble, as opposed to royal birth.

1709 EDM. SMITH *Phædra & Hippol.* I. ii. (1793) 594 Earth-born Lycon may ascend the throne.

3. Of things: Produced by the earth; arising from the earth.

1702 ROWE *Tamerl.* v. i, Behold the vain Effects of Earth-born Pride. **1810** SCOTT *Lady of L.* I. xi, Nor were these earth-born Castles bare. **1864** PUSEY *Lect. Daniel* ix. 563 The serene depth of heaven..undimmed..by the black earth-born clouds, which roll so far below.

† **'earth-din.** *Obs.* For forms see EARTH *sb.*¹, DIN; in 4 *Sc.* erdine, erdinge. An earthquake.

a **1079** *O.E. Chron.* an. 1060 On þisan ȝere wæs micel eorð-dyne. *c* **1250** *Gen. & Ex.* 1108 Oc siðen loth wente ut of hine, brende it ðhunder, sanc it erðe-dine. *a* **1300** *Cursor M.* 20499 An erth-din þar com þat scok All thinges. *c* **1375** BARBOUR *Troy-bk.* I. 455 Scho walde horribile erdinge ger be, Ande hydwisly wp raise the see. *c* **1375** —— *St. Margarete* 590 Sone wes herde a fellone bere Of thonir and of erdine. *c* **1440** *Promp. Parv.* 141 Erthe qwake, or erþe dene [*K.* erdyn, or erde qwave, *P.* erthdyn]. **1483** *Cath. Angl.* 117 An Erthe dyne, or an Erthe qwake.

earthen ('ɜːθ(ə)n), *a.* Forms: 3 eorðen, erthin, 4–5 erþen, 5 erþyn, (6 erdyn), 6– earthen. Also EARTHERN. [app. not recorded in OE.; the normal form would be *erþen, WS. *ierþen, yrþen = OHG. *irdîn*, Goth. *airþeins*:—OTeut. **irþîno-z*, f. *erþâ* EARTH; see -EN.]

1. Made or composed of earth.

a **1225** *Ancr. R.* 388 A lefdi was þet was mid hire uoan biset al abuten..wiðinnen one eorðene castle. *a* **1300** *Cursor M.* 27646 þou man þat es in erth stad þat es noght bot an erthin gadd. *c* **1440** *Promp. Parv.* 141 Erþyn [*written* eryyn] or of the earth, *terrenus.* **1719** DE FOE *Crusoe* (1840) II. xiv. 286 The earthen floors we have in use in several parts of England..as hard as stone. **1807** G. CHALMERS *Caledonia* I. II. ii. 243 A high earthen rampart..running off, from a British fort. **1871** PALGRAVE *Lyr. Poems* 16 Pacing the earthen floor with solemn feet.

b. Made of baked clay.

1382 WYCLIF *Jer.* xix. 1 Go and tac the erthene litil wyne vessel of the crockere. **1481–90** *Howard Househ. Bks.* (1841) 150 Item, for ij. erthen panys ijd. **1527** *MS. Acc. R. Gibson Master of Revels*, Itm, dew for iiij dosyn erdyn dishes, yᵉ dosyn, iiijd. **1697** DRYDEN *Virg. Georg.* II. 536 The God of Wine, Whose Earthen Images adorn the Pine. **1725** DE FOE *Voy. round W.* (1840) 102 Two hundred large earthen jars. **1800** tr. *Lagrange's Chem.* I. 233 A tubulated earthen or iron retort. **1875** JOWETT *Plato* (ed. 2) I. 66 The three measures of wine, or the earthen vessel which contains them.

2. Said disparagingly of the human body, or of the world. Sometimes *transf.* and *fig.* of conditions, qualities, etc.: Characteristic of the earth, merely material. Also in comb., as ***earthen-hearted.***

16.. LEVER *Prayer* in Farr's *S.P.* 523 Let thy holy eyes reflect Their influence upon my earthen state. **1633** EARL MANCH. *Al Mondo* (1636) 174 Nor will he care who shuts up his earthen eyes, when death it selfe opens his soules eyes. *a* **1656** BP. HALL *Rem. Wks.* (1660) 68 The best part of this Earthen World is man. **1855** BROWNING *Grammarian's Funeral*, To make the heavenly period Perfect the earthen. **1870** LOWELL *Among my Bks.* Ser. I. (1873) 211 We know who is to be the guest of this earthen hospitality,—how much beauty, love, and heartbreak, are to be covered in that pit of clay. **1876** *Ibid.* Ser. II. 15 Far from a man..be so rash and earthen-hearted a humility.

'earthen, *v. rare*⁻¹. [f. EARTH *sb.*¹ + -EN.] *intr.* To turn into earth.

1839 BAILEY *Festus* v. (1848) 39 While one so beautiful lies earthening here.

earthenware ('ɜːθ(ə)nwɛə(r)). [f. EARTHEN *a.* + WARE; until 19th c. often written as two words.]

1. Vessels or other objects made of baked clay.

1673 RAY *Journ. Low C.* 29 The Town [Delft] is noted for good earthen Ware, as Stone-jugs, Pots, etc. **1727** DE FOE *Eng. Tradesm.* xxvi. (1841) I. 267 Earthenware from Stafford, Nottingham, and Kent. **1792** *Phil. Trans.* LXXXII. 270 When earthen ware is mentioned in this paper, the cream-coloured or queen's ware is meant. **1879** J. J. YOUNG *Ceram. Art* 30 The manufacture of earthen-ware.

b. In *pl.* Kinds of earthenware.

1832 G. PORTER *Porcelain* i. 19 Efforts..for improving the quality of common earthenwares made in Staffordshire.

2. The material of which such vessels are made.

1799 *Med. Jrnl.* I. 295 Pour it into a jar of stone or earthen-ware. **1811** A. T. THOMSON *Lond. Disp.* (1818) Introd. 40 A trough of earthen-ware, divided in its length by numerous partitions of the same material. **1873** WATTS *Fownes' Chem.* 388 Earthenware is made from a white secondary clay.

3. *attrib.* and in *comb.*, as ***earthenware vessel, -dealer, -man.***

1812 J. & H. SMITH *Rej. Addr.* v. (1873) 41 England is a large earthenware pipkin. **1813** *Examiner* 24 May 329/1 J. Downes, High Holborn, earthenwareman. **1868** GEO. ELIOT *F. Holt* 53 The light by which the minister was reading was a wax-candle in a white earthenware candlestick.

earthern *a.*, corrupt form of EARTHEN.

1726 SWIFT *Corr.* Wks. 1841 II. 591 Your earthern vessel, provided it is close stopped, I allow to be a good succedaneum. **1775** ADAIR *Amer. Ind.* 407 Beating also with a stick..on the top of an earthern pot covered with a wet and well-stretched deer-skin.

earthfast ('ɜːθfɑːst, -fæst), *a.* [f. EARTH *sb.*¹ + FAST *a.*] Fixed in the ground; cf. quot. 1869.

c **1000** ÆLFRIC *Saints' Lives* xvii. (1885) I. 130 Sume men synd swa ablende þæt hi bringað heora lac to eorðfæstum stane. **1868** G. STEPHENS *Runic Mon.* I. 199 No runic earthfast monument of any kind..has ever been found in any Saxon or German territory. **1869** R. B. PEACOCK *Gloss. Lonsdale Dial.*, *Earthfast*, said of a stone appearing on the surface but fast in the earth. **1881** tr. *Nordenskiöld's Voy. Vega* I. ii. 97 A box..fixed to the ground with earthfast stakes and cross-bars.

† **'earth-grine, -grith.** *Obs. rare.* [f. EARTH *sb.*¹; the correct form and the etymology of the second element are unknown.] An earthquake.

1297 R. GLOUC. (1810) 414 þoru out al Engelond so gret erþgryþe [*v.r.* erþgrine, erþgrene, erþe dene, erþe den] þer com. *Ibid.* 530 Erthgrine strong inou aboute Leinte.

† **'earth-horn.** ? *nonce-wd.* A contrivance said by Langtoft and his translator Robert of Brunne to have been used by the English at the battle of the Standard, in order to discomfit the Scots by terrifying their cattle with a subterraneous noise.

Langtoft's words are 'Homme dist, tymmers Englays suz terre avayent.' The original source seems to be the following: 'Idem archiepiscopus [Thurstinus]..fieri jussit in viis subterraneis quaedam instrumenta sonos horribiles reddentia, quae Anglice dicuntur *Petronces*' (*Life of Abp. Thurstan* in Raine *Historians of Church of York* II. 266).

1330 R. BRUNNE *Chron.* (1810) 118 Yn ilk strete & way þei ordeynd an erþe horn. *Ibid.* þis was at Kouton more, þat þe erþe hornes blewe þer þe Scottis misfore.

earthiness ('ɜːθɪnɪs). [f. EARTHY *a.* + -NESS.]

1. The quality of being earthy; the properties characteristic of earth as a substance or as an 'element'.

1398 TREVISA *Barth. De P.R.* XVII. cxxiv. (1495) 685 Tame peres grene..be soure: but in sethynge..wyth hony..the erthynesse..therof maye be somwhat tempryd. **1678** R. R[USSELL] *Geber* II. II. I. x. 166 We find Bodies of more Earthiness of more easie Calcination. **1750** tr. *Leonardus' Mirr. Stones* 18 There is no stone but will, by reason of its earthiness, sink in water. **1870** READE *Put yourself in his Pl.* III. 275 The water had a foul and appalling odour, a compound of earthiness and putrescence.

† **b.** *concr.* Earthy matter. *Obs.*

1528 PAYNELL *Salerne Regim.* B iij b, The moystnes therof [of fleme] is conieyled and some what altered to erthynes. **1641** FRENCH *Distill.* i. (1651) 19 The Spirit..ariseth..without any earthinesse mixed with it. **1693** EVELYN *De la Quint. Compl. Gard.* I. 124 Having a juice extremely sweet and sugred, leaving no Earthiness or Lees behind it.

2. *fig.* = EARTHLINESS I.

1670 WALTON *Lives* IV. 340 This dignity hath no such earthiness in it, but it may very well be joined with Heaven. **1849** RUSKIN *Sev. Lamps* v. §24. 161 There is dreaming enough, and earthiness enough..in human existence. **1864** D. MITCHELL *Sev. Stor.* 265 The eyes are living eyes, but with no touch of earthiness.

earthing ('ɜːθɪŋ), *vbl. sb.* [f. EARTH *v.* + -ING¹.] Occas. *attrib.*

† **1.** Burial. *northern* and *Sc.*

a **1300** *Cursor M.* 1190 [Abel had] at his erthing [*Gött.* birijng, *Trin.* buryinge] all lede. *c* **1375** BARBOUR *Troy-bk.* II. 2054 Nocht lange eftir his erdinge..Egistus tuke to wyf Cletemistra. **1535** STEWART *Cron. Scot.* (1858) I. 86 Euerilk clan had..ane commoun erding place.

† **b.** The state of being buried. *Obs.*

a **1300** *Cursor M.* 18041 þat stinkand lazarun fra vs Of his erding þe thridd dai He losed him.

2. The action of heaping (*up*) earth round a plant.

1664 EVELYN *Kal. Hort.* (1729) 195 Several of which [vegetables]..are most of them to be blanch'd by laying them under Littier, and earthing up. **1721–1800** BAILEY, *Earthing* is the covering of Trees, Plants, and Herbs with Earth. **1862** DELAMER *Kitch. Gard.* 117 All that will be required after, besides these earthings, is a regular supply of air.

† **3.** Anchorage. *Obs. rare.*

1646 H. LAWRENCE *Comm. Angels* 171 Our anchor casts deepe in heaven, where there is good earthing.

4. a. The action of taking refuge in an 'earth' or burrow: *concr.* the earth or burrow itself. **b.** Driving an animal to its earth; perh. also used for UNEARTHING.

1597 *2nd Pt. Return Parnass.* II. v. 830 Do you meane at the vnkennelling, vntapezing, or earthing of the Fox? **1706** PHILLIPS, *Earthing*, among Hunters, a Term us'd for a Badger's lodging. **1741** *Compl. Fam.-Piece* II. i. 295 Having found a Fox's Earth, cause all his Holes you can find to be stopt..in order to prevent his Earthing. **1854** H. MILLER *Sch. & Schm.* (1858) 335 Our party..had its dog..and my companions were desirous of getting his earthing ability tested upon the badger of the establishment.

†**'earthish,** *a. nonce-wd.* [f. EARTH *sb.*[1] + -ISH.] = EARTHLY.

1536 TINDALE *Exp. Matt.* Wks. 1849 II. 87 But an if thou wilt not come within the covenant of God..thou art bound by these words so fast that none..can loose thee; no, though our earthish god whisper all his absolutions over thee.

'earthite. *nonce-wd.* [f. EARTH *sb.*[1] + -ITE.] An inhabitant of earth.

1825 R. AYTON *Ess. & Sk. Char.* 210 We loyal earthites may be pleased to think so; but what may the moonites..say to such a notion?

'earthland. [f. EARTH *sb.*[2] + LAND.] Arable land.

826 *Chart. Ecgberht* in *Cod. Dipl.* V. 84 Ðonon wæst for ðonæ sealstub oð ðæt yrðland. *c* **1000** *Voc.* in Wr.-Wülcker 279 *Arua*, yrþland. **1885** *Archæol. Jrnl.* XLII. 271 That slight deposit of mud from the river which is at present imperceptibly converting them from earthland into marsh.

'earthless, *a. nonce-wd.* [f. EARTH *sb.*[1] + -LESS.] Unencumbered by earth (by the body).

1817 BYRON *Manfred* III. iv. 152 He's gone—his soul has ta'en his earthless flight.

'earth-light. *Astron.* The partial illumination of the dark portion of the moon's surface by light reflected from the earth; = *earth-shine*, q.v. in EARTH *sb.*[1] B. II.

1833 SIR J. HERSCHEL *Astron.* vi. 223 It [the earth] then illuminates its [the moon's] dark half by strong earth-light. **1874** MOSELEY *Astron.* xlvii. 150 In the conical shadow there is absolutely no light (except, perhaps, some little reflected from the earth called earthlight).

earthliness ('ɜːθlɪnɪs). [f. EARTHLY *a.* + -NESS.]

1. The quality of being earthly; the distinctive properties of terrestrial things; worldliness as opposed to *heavenliness*.

1583 GOLDING *Calvin on Deut.* cxcvi. 1215 When we.. worship him [God], wee imagine not any earthlinesse in him. **1611** COTGR., *Terresterrité*..earthlinesse, worldlinesse. **1665** WITHER *Lord's Prayer* 107 They in whom the first natural Earthlyness and will, are predominant. **1813** SHELLEY *Q. Mab* i. (1853) 4 Each stain of earthliness Had passed away. **1851** HAWTHORNE *Twice-told T.* II. xiii. 211 For often there was an earthliness in his conceptions.

†**2.** = EARTHINESS 1. *Obs.*

c **1535** DEWES *Introd. Fr.* in *Palsgr.* 920 The one is pure, separate of erthlynesse. **1594** *Mirr. Pol.* (1599) 178 If of an earthly substance wee would make fire, we must first purge and purifie it from the earthlinesse. **1641** FRENCH *Distill.* v. (1651) 144 It is..the earthlinesse that is so nauseous. **1642** FULLER *Holy & Prof. St.* v. iv. 371 Vulturs are said to smell the earthlinesse of a dying corps.

†**'earthling,** *sb.*[1] *Obs.* Forms: 1 yrþling, 2 urþling, 8 earthling. [f. EARTH *sb.*[2] + -LING.] A ploughman, cultivator of the soil. Perh. only in OE.; quots. 1200 and 1714 merely give the OE. word in later spelling.

c **1000** ÆLFRIC *Colloq.* in Wr.-Wülcker 99 Se yrþling us ealle fett. *a* **1200** *Fragm. Ælfric's Gloss.* (1838) 2 Urþling. **1714** FORTESCUE-ALAND *Fortescue's Abs. & Lim. Mon.* 79 [The Anglo-Saxon] Eorthling, is a Husbandman, or Earthling.

earthling ('ɜːθlɪŋ), *sb.*[2] [f. EARTH *sb.*[1] + -LING.]

1. An inhabitant of the earth.

1593 NASHE *Christ's T.* (1613) 124 Wee (of all earthlings) are Gods vtmost subiects. *c* **1630** DRUMM. OF HAWTH. *Poems* Wks. (1711) 31 Nature gaz'd on with such a curious eye, That earthlings oft her deem'd a deity. **1819** H. BUSK *Vestriad* III. 176 Shall we..in absence be betray'd, Like puny earthlings by a faithless maid? **1839** BAILEY *Festus* xxiii. (1848) 297 Behold this earthling standing by my side. **1949** R. HEINLEIN *Red Planet* (1963) viii. 125 An Earthling has no good way to estimate the age of a Martian. **1965** J. BLISH *Mission to Heart Stars* vi. 77 The Earthlings are now deep into the Heart Stars. **1967** *Ampleforth Jrnl.* Summer 163 To receive the overspill by immigration..the planets might come to the rescue of the Earthlings.

2. One who is earthly in mind or disposition.

1615 ROWLANDS *Melanch. Knt.* 35, I haue interiour excellence that shines Beyond your earthlings gold and siluer mines. *a* **1652** J. SMITH *Sel. Disc.* v. 148 It is not gold or silver that the earthlings of this world seek after. **1866** ALGER *Solit. Nat. & Man* II. 59 The cold earthlings who form the various embodiments of selfishness.

earthly ('ɜːθlɪ), *a.* For forms see EARTH *sb.*[1] [f. EARTH *sb.*[1] + -LY[1].]

1. a. Pertaining to the earth, terrestrial. Chiefly and now almost exclusively with implied opposition to *heavenly*.

971 *Blickl. Hom.* 43 þæm wiþerweardan beoþ þæs mannes synna ȝecwemran þonne eal eorþlic goldhord. *c* **1000** *Ags. Gosp.* Matt. xxvi. 29 Witodlice ic secȝe eow þæt ic ne drince heonunforð of þysum eorþlican wine. *c* **1175** *Lamb. Hom.* 39 þet þu luuie þine drihten ofer..alle eorðliche þing. *a* **1200** *Moral Ode* 155 in *Trin. Coll. Hom.* 224 Eðlate him ware al wele and erðeliche blisse. *a* **1300** *Cursor M.* 1157 Hou suld ani erdli fless Duelle wid þe in sikirness. *c* **1320** *Sir Beues* 3344 Erþliche man semeþ he nouȝt..Boute a fend stolen out of helle. **1413** LYDG. *Pylgr. Sowle* I. xxx. (1859) 33 Man, of heuenly nature and erdely very partyner, knytteth to geders bothe heuen and erthe. **1526** *Pilgr. Perf.* (W. de W. 1531) 1 A pilgrym that entendeth to go to the erthly Jerusalem. **1600** SHAKS. *A.Y.L.* v. iv. 115 Then is there mirth in heauen, When earthly things made euen attone together. **1732** BERKELEY *Alciphr.* iv. §23 Wks. 1871 II. 171 This earthly globe is but a point in respect of the whole system of God's creation. **1810** SCOTT *Lady of L.* II. xxxv, The pageant pomp of earthly man. **1847** MOZLEY *Univ. Serm.* i. 1 [The Church] has taken her own way in claiming earthly sovereignty.

b. Of or belonging to the material or lower elements of human nature.

1850 TENNYSON *In Mem.* cxiv, For she [knowledge] is earthly of the mind. **1858** ROBERTSON *Lect.* ii. 191 This influence of the religious element of the imagination on the earthlier feeling.

c. As an emphatic expletive; = 'on earth'. Colloq. phr. ***no earthly, not an earthly***, (*a*) with *sb.*, no — whatever, (*b*) *ellipt.*, no conceivable (chance, hope, use, etc.).

1753 *Stewart's Trial* in *Scots Mag.* Mar. 132/2 What earthly purpose could the pannel serve by such a..piece of villany? **1838** DICKENS *Let.* 25 Jan. (1965) I. 359 The fifty pounds..makes no earthly difference. **1868** ROGERS *Pol. Econ.* iv. 37 If a man were alone on an island..the precious metals would be of no earthly use. **1899** *Referee* 22 Oct. (Ware, s.v. *No*), The actors who have not booked their seats via Mr. Henry Dana, are hereby notified that they have now no earthly, as all seats have been allotted. **1907** *Hockey* 13 Dec. 101/2 The poor goal-keeper had not an 'earthly'. **1910** WODEHOUSE *Psmith in City* xxvii. 239 There's no earthly need to get out. **1911** W. J. LOCKE *Clementina Wing* xii. 134 Just an extra fiver on Punchinello. He's got no earthly—you know that as well as I do. **1912** GALSWORTHY *Eldest Son* III, *Christine.* Let's go and beg him, Ronny! *Keith.* No earthly! The only hope is in the girl. **1922** —— *Loyalties* I. ii, The Inspector's no earthly. **1936** J. CURTIS *Gilt Kid* xxix. 279 'Going to get away with it?' 'Not a hope, mate. Not a bleeding earthly.' **1965** *Listener* 11 Nov. 765/3 Received standard, like the Liberals, won't stand an earthly.

d. Like or resembling the earth. *rare.*

1836 LYTTON *Athens* (1837) I. 304 Thales..maintained the stars and sun to be earthly.

e. As quasi-*sb.* with pl.: A terrestrial being. *rare.*

1850 MRS. BROWNING *Poems* II. 177 Let all earthlies and celestials wait Upon thy royal state.

†**2.** Existing or living in or on the ground. *Obs.*

1593 SHAKS. *3 Hen. VI*, I. iii. 17 Richard cry'de..A Scepter, or an Earthly Sepulchre. **1658** ROWLAND *Moufet's Theat. Ins.* 1103 Some earthly Insects..are bred in the earth, some in living creatures.

†**3. a.** Partaking of the nature of earth, resembling earth as a substance, consisting of earth as an element; = EARTHY. *arch.* or *Obs.*

1398 TREVISA *Barth. De P.R.* IV. xi. 96 Yf unkind melancoly hath maystry..soure sauour and sharpe and erthly is felt in the mouth. **1562** TURNER *Herbal* (1568) 107 b, Penny ryall..is made of a fyrie substance with som burnt erthly part. **1578** LYTE *Dodoens* III. xiv. 335 The roote is..covered with a thicke rinde or barke, of a browne earthly colour without. **1614** W. B. *Philos. Banquet* (ed. 2) 15 The gristles are..more earthly, drie, and hard, then Liguaments. **1644** PRYNNE & WALKER *Fiennes Trial* App. 11 He said the mount..was of an earthly substance for a certaine depth. **1660** STANLEY *Hist. Philos.* (1701) 64/2 The Creatures were first generated of Humidity, Calidity and Earthly Matter. **1770** PRIESTLEY in *Phil. Trans.* LX. 222 Metals and charcoal agree in consisting of phlogiston united to an earthly base. **1771** N. NICHOLLS *Corr. w. Gray* (1843) 131 An earthly smell..exhaled by the sun from the loose and fermenting mould. **1853** KANE *Grinnell Exp.* xlvi. (1856) 423 No earthly covering masks the grinning rocks of Proven.

†**b.** Pale or lifeless as earth. *Obs.*

1588 SHAKS. *Tit. A.* II. iii. 229 A precious Ring..Doth shine vpon the dead mans earthly cheekes.

†**c.** *fig.* Stolid, dull; cf *airy, fiery.* ? *nonce-use.*

1662 FULLER *Worthies* (1840) III. 394 Nor so airy [English horses] as the Spanish gennets..nor so earthly as those in the Low Countries.

†**4.** Made of earth or baked clay; = EARTHEN. *rare* and *doubtful.*

1440 *Promp. Parv.* 143 Erthly [*P.* or of erthe made], *terrenus, terrestris.* **1533** FRITH *Anoth. Bk. agst. Rastell* 333 We have this..treasure in frail, brittle, and earthly vessels.

5. *Comb.* **earthly-minded** *a.*, having the affections fixed on the earth, worldly-minded; whence **earthly-mindedness; earthly paradise**: see PARADISE *sb.* 1; **earthly-wise** *adv.* (*nonce-wd.*), in an earthly manner.

1593 HOOKER *Eccl. Pol.* I. xi. (1611) 35 To be earthly minded men. *a* **1665** J. GOODWIN *Filled w. Spirit* (1867) 7 An earthly fulness, which..the children of this world, or earthly-minded men, do affect and set their hearts upon. **1670** EACHARD *Cont. Clergy* 93 A very earthly-minded man, and too much sighted into this lower world. **1608** HIERON *Wks.* I. 749 Suppresse within me all earthly-mindednesse. **1691** NORRIS *Pract. Disc.* 258 That particular sort of Earthly-mindedness which we call Covetousness. **1874** TENNYSON *Holy Grail* 627, I speak too earthlywise, Seeing I never strayed beyond the cell.

'earthly, *adv. rare.* [f. prec. adj.] = 'In any way on earth', at all.

1829 SCOTT *Rob Roy* Introd. 36, I do not know earthly where to go or what to do.

†**'earth-mad.** *Obs. rare.* [OE. *eorþmata* 'vermis' in Corpus Gloss. for *eorþmaþa*, f. *eorþe*, EARTH *sb.*[1] + *maþa* MATHE.] An earthworm.

1601 HOLLAND *Pliny* I. 334 The earth-mads and all the sort of worms & grubs, are without eies.

'earth-nut. Also 6 ernut(e.

1. The roundish tuber of an umbelliferous plant (*Bunium flexuosum*, including *B. Bulbocastanum*), called also *earth-chestnut* and *pig-nut*.

875 *Charter* in *Cod. Dipl.* III. 399 (Bosw.) Of ðam cumbe in eorþnutena þorn. **1551** TURNER *Herbal* I. D iij b, Apios is called also Chamebalanos in greke..and the same semeth to me to be called in Englishe, an ernut, or an erthnut. **1597** GERARD *Herbal* II. ccccxxxi. (1633) 1064 Earth nut, Earth chest nut, or Kipper nut. **1725** BRADLEY *Fam. Dict.* II. s.v. *Sallet*, Earth-Nuts, when the Rind is pared off, are eaten raw by Country People. **1784** COWPER *Task* v. 90 Daws forsake the fields, Where neither grub..nor earth-nut..Repays their labour. **1879** JEFFERIES *Wild Life in S.C.* 331 The earth-nut, pig-nut, or ground-nut, as it is variously called.

2. Applied variously to other plants, as the truffle (*Tuber*), the ARACHIS, the *Œnanthe pimpinelloides*, and the Heath Pea (*Lathyrus macrorrhizus*).

1548 TURNER *Names of Herbes* (1881) 17 Astragalus..may be called in english peaserthnut. **1644** EVELYN *Mem.* (1857) I. 83 A dish of Truffles, which is a certain earth-nut. **1713** PETIVER in *Phil. Trans.* XXVIII. 62 Four leaved Earth-Nut. **1725** BRADLEY *Fam. Dict.*, *Gesse*, a plant of which there are two sorts, one..cultivated..and the other the wild one in Latin Chamælalanus, called by some *Earth-Nut.* *a* **1854** *Phytologist* III. 260 (Britten) *Œnanthe pimpinelloides*, L. The children eat the tubercles under the name of earth-nuts.

earthquake ('ɜːθkweɪk). [f. EARTH *sb.*[1] + QUAKE *sb.*]

1. A shaking of the ground; usually *spec.* a convulsion of the earth's surface produced by volcanic or similar forces within the crust.

c **1340** *Cursor M.* 20499 (Trin.) An erþequake [*v.r.* erthdin] coom þat shoke alle þinge. **1382** *Pol. Poems* (1859) I. 252 The pestilens, and the eorthe-qwake, Theose..things Beoth tokenes. **1432–50** tr. *Higden* (Rolls) III. 305 As thro an erthe qwake. **1513** DOUGLAS *Æneis* VIII. iv. 131 By fors of thunder or erdquayk wyth a clap. **1583** STANYHURST *Æneis* III. (Arb.) 73 Thee doors, thee laurel, thee mount with terribil earth quake Doo totter shiuering. **1635** N. CARPENTER *Geog. Del.* II. ix. 156 After an Earth-quake many new springs..discouered themselues. **1719** DE FOE *Crusoe* I. 91, I plainly saw it was a terrible Earthquake, for the Ground I stood on shook three times at about eight Minutes distance. **1821** SHELLEY *Hellas* 5 All its banded anarchs fled, Like vultures frighted..Before an earthquake's tread. **1864** *Q. Jrnl. Science* I. 57 An Earthquake..is the transit of a wave or waves of elastic compression in any direction.. through the substance and surface of the Earth, from any centre of impulse.

b. *fig.*

1641 MILTON *Animadv.* (1851) 188 Whosoever..so earnestly labours to keep such an incumbring surcharge of earthly things, cannot but have an earth-quake still in his bones. **1662** FULLER *Worthies* (1840) III. 310 In this age, wherein there is an earthquake of ancient hospitals. **1835** L. HUNT *Capt. Sword* II. lviii. See where comes the horse-tempest again, Visible earthquake. **1868** BRIGHT in *Star* 14 Mar., This social and political earthquake under which Ireland is heaving.

attrib. **1814** BYRON *Ode Napoleon* 30 The earthquake voice of Victory.

2. *Comb.* **a.** *attrib.*, as ***earthquake-fiend, -gown, -pendulum-microphone, -shock, -voice, -wave***.

1821 SHELLEY *Prometh. Unb.* I. 38 The *Earthquake-fiends are charged To wrench the rivets from my quivering wounds. **1750** H. WALPOLE *Let. Sir H. Mann* 2 Apr., Several women have made *earthquake gowns, that is, warm gowns to sit out of doors all to-night [an earthquake having been predicted]. **1882** *Nature* XXVI. 220 For the study of ..seismological movements of the earth's crust as revealed by the microphone..Dr. A. V. G. Mocenigo..has devised an *earthquake-pendulum-microphone. **1878** HUXLEY *Physiogr.* 188 *Earthquake-shocks are happily of rare occurrence in this country. *Ibid.* An *earthquake-wave is a vibration of the solid crust of the earth.

b. *instrumental*, as ***earthquake-rifted, -ruined, -shaken, -swallowed*** adjs.

1819 SHELLEY *Prometh. Unb.* I, New fire From *earthquake-rifted mountains of bright snow Shook its portentous hair. *Ibid.* II. iv, The lurid smoke Of *earthquake-ruined cities. **1860** RUSKIN *Mod. Paint.* V. IX. iv. 240 Silent villages, *earthquake-shaken, gleam in white ruin. **1839** BAILEY *Festus* ix. (1848) 102 *Earthquake-swallowed cities.

'earth-quakes. *dial.* [f. EARTH *sb.*[1] + stem of QUAKE *v.*] 'A species of quaking-grass common in England' (*Treas. Bot.*).

1884 MILLER *Plant-N.*, Earthquakes, *Briza media.*

'earthquaking, *vbl. sb.* [f. EARTHQUAKE + -ING[1]; in first quot. f. EARTH *sb.*[1] + QUAKING.]

†**a.** = EARTHQUAKE (*obs.*). **b.** The occurrence of earthquakes. **c.** *attrib.*

c **1400** MAUNDEV. viii. 84 When the Jewes hadden made the Temple, com an Erthe quakeng, and caste it doun. **1883** *Pall Mall G.* 6 Apr. 31/2 The constant earthquaking has ceased.

'earthquaking, *ppl. a.* [f. EARTH *sb.*[1] + QUAKING; also f. EARTHQUAKE + -ING[2].]

a. Causing the earth to shake. Also *fig.* ¶**b.** Subject to earthquakes.

1589 GREENE *Menaphon* (Arb.) 72 Jove shaking his earth-quaking haire. **1820** SHELLEY *Witch Atl.* xlii, The earth-quaking cataracts which shiver Their snow-like waters into golden air. **1881** *Contemp. Rev.* Apr. 570 But here amid earthquaking shocks Whirlwinds rave around the rocks. **1881** *Athenæum* 27 Aug., That..earth-quaking spot which was selected by the Spanish leader for the site of his capital (Lima). **1887** *Illust. Lond. News* 19 Mar. 306/3, I have travelled a good deal in earthquaking lands.

earthquaky ('ɜːθkweɪkɪ), *a.* [f. EARTHQUAKE + -Y[1].] Resembling the effect of or suggesting the motion of an earthquake.

1837 DICKENS *Pickw.* xlv, Legs shaky—head queer—round and round—earthquaky sort of feeling—very. **1846**

THACKERAY *Cornhill to Cairo* ii. 15 Many churches..had a dry, uncomfortable, earthquaky look, to my idea.

†**ˈearthquave.** *Obs.* [f. EARTH *sb.*¹ + QUAVE *sb.*] = EARTHQUAKE.

1382 WYCLIF *Esther* xi. 5 There semeden voisis..and thundris, and erthe quaues, and disturbing up on the erthe. *c* **1430** LYDG. *Bochas* I. iii. (1558) 5 God..may confounde it with an erth quaue. **1540–1** ELYOT *Image Gov.* (1549) 67 Where diuerse citees by earthe quaues had ben frushed, and therewith defourmed.

ˈearth-ridge. [f. EARTH *sb.*² or *sb.*¹] See quot.

1796 MARSHALL *Rural Econ. W. Eng.* 158 Earth-ridges are formed in the field, either with mold hacked from the borders of it, or with the soil of the area raised with the plow. **1848** HALLIWELL, *Earth-ridge*, a few feet of earth round a field which is ploughed up close to the hedges.

†**ˈearth-tiller.** *Obs.* [f. EARTH *sb.*¹ + TILLER.] A cultivator of the soil. So in OE. and ME. **erthe-tilie, -tilye** [see TILIE].

c **1000** ÆLFRIC *Gen.* iv. 2 Abel was sceaphyrde, and Cain eorþtilia. *c* **1205** LAY. 22107 He hæhte..þa eorðe-tilien [**1250** erþe-tilies] teon to heore cræften. *c* **1325** *Chron. Eng.* 93 in Ritson *Metr. Nom.* II. 274 Bruyt hade muche folk with him..That were erthe-tilyes gode. **1382** WYCLIF *Matt.* xxi. 34 He sente his seruantis to the erthe tiliers, that they token fruytis of it. **1612** DAVIES *Why Ireland, &c.* (1747) 190 Over that 4*d.* or 6*d.* daily to every one of them to be had and paid of the poore earth-tillers. **1674** N. FAIRFAX *Bulk & Selv.* To Rdr., Off-cast words in the mouths of Handy-crafts-men and Earth-tillers.

†**ˈearth-tilth.** *Obs.* [f. EARTH *sb.*¹ + TILTH.] Cultivation of the soil, agriculture. Hence †**earth-tilther** = EARTH-TILLER.

c **1000** ÆLFRIC *Colloq.* in Wr.-Wülcker 99 Eorþtilþ, *agricultura*. **1388** WYCLIF *Ecclus.* vii. 16 Haate thou not trauelouse werkis, and erthetilthe maad of the hiȝeste. **1398** TREVISA *Barth. De P.R.* XVII. clxxx. (1495) 720 Erthe tylthers and kepers of vynes.

earthward (ˈɜːθwəd), *adv.* and *adj.*

A. *adv.* Towards the earth. Also *fig.*

c **1440** *Gesta Rom.* xc. 413 (Add. MS.) The Fadre loked to the Erthward, and fownde a peny. **1646** JENKYN *Remora* 28 Shall we run with the swiftnes of the Roe earthward, and go a dull Asses trot heavenward? **1880** *Daily Tel.* 4 Nov., The ..outpourings of smoke..sink earthward.

B. as *adj.*

1870 M. D. CONWAY (*title*), The Earthward Pilgrimage.

†**ˈearth-ware,** *sb. pl. Obs.* [OE. *eorþware*, f. *eorþe*, EARTH *sb.*¹ + *-ware*, as in *heofonware* heaven-dwellers, *burhware*, etc.] Earth-dwellers.

c **893** K. ÆLFRED *Oros.* III. v. §5 Crist..sibb is heofonwara and eorðwara. *c* **1175** *Lamb. Hom.* 139 Sunne dei blisseð togederes houeneware and horðe ware. *a* **1225** *Ancr. R.* 322 Al þe wide worlde—eorðe ware and heouene ware.

earthwork (ˈɜːθwɜːk). [f. EARTH *sb.*¹ + WORK *sb.*] **1.** A bank or mound of earth used as a rampart or fortification. Not in 18th c. Dicts.

1633 T. STAFFORD *Pac. Hib.* xv. (1821) 385 The Enemy had ground sufficient..to cast up new Earth workes. **1830** LYELL *Princ. Geol.* I. 278 The remains of an ancient entrenchment..This earth-work was evidently once of considerable extent. **1863** KINGLAKE *Crimea* (1877) III. iii. 340 The Russians had thrown up strong earthworks on the banks of the river.

2. The action or process of excavating (the bed of a canal, line of a railway, or other civil engineering work); the soil so cast up; EMBANKMENT 3.

1831–3 *Encycl. Metropol.* (1845) VIII. 247/1 The earthwork for a complete line of communication between Liverpool and Manchester. **1842** FRANCIS *Dict. Arts, Earthwork*, a term applied to cuttings, embankments, and all other works where earth is to be removed or collected together. *a* **1854** C. TOMLINSON *Cycl. Useful Arts* II. 448/2 The inclination of the earth-works, whether for excavations or embankments, must be determined mainly by their height. **1862** *Chambers's Encycl.* IV. 27/2 In the formation of canals, railways, and other roads, embankment and excavation go hand in hand, and, under the name of earthwork, form..a vast branch of industry. **1899** *Daily News* 8 Mar. 7/1 The wretched earthwork labourers..would be earning from 2½ to 4 piastres per day near their own homes. **1911** *Daily Colonist* (Victoria, B.C.) 30 Apr. 1/7 Considerable heavy rock work here presents itself, as well as a fair amount of medium earthwork. **1955** *Times* 30 June 13/5 It is easy to forget that the gigantic earthworks of the railway age..were performed in the main by spade and barrow, horse and cart.

earthworm (ˈɜːθwɜːm). [f. EARTH *sb.*¹ + WORM.]

1. A worm that lives in the ground, *esp.* an individual of the genus *Lumbricus*.

1591 PERCIVALL *Sp. Dict.*, *Lombriz*, an easse, an earth worme, *lumbricus*. **1594**? GREENE *Selinus* Wks. 1881–3 XIV. 220 We, like earth wormes lurking in the weeds, Do liue inglorious in all mens eyes. **1718** QUINCY *Compl. Disp.* 148 Earth-Worms, are often us'd in compositions for cooling and cleansing the Viscera. **1855** OWEN *Comp. Anat.* (ed. 2) xi. 228 The second order [of annelids] includes the earthworms.

2. *fig.* **a.** As a disparaging designation for a human being, *esp.* a mean or grovelling person. **b.** With allusion to the 'worm' in the grave.

1594 T. B. *La Primaud. Fr. Acad.* II. Ep. Ded. 2 This generation of earth-wormes, which place nature..in the roome of the Creatour. **1625** BURGES *Pers. Tithes* 39 The Couetous Earth-worme would laugh in his sleeue to see his elbow vnderlaid with such a Cushion. **1684** CHARNOCK *Attrib. God* (1834) II. 606 How should such an earth-worm ..be afraid to speak irreverently of so great a king? **1869** GOULBURN *Purs. Holiness* viii. 73 Apt to be smitten by the earthworm of death.

attrib. **1626** W. SCLATER *Expos. 2 Thess.* (1629) 22 God so ordering the state of his earth-worme Children.

earthy (ˈɜːθɪ), *a.* [f. EARTH *sb.*¹ + -Y.]

I. 1. a. Of material substances: That is of the nature of earth or soil; having the characteristic properties of earth; resembling earth in some specific property. Of minerals: Without lustre, friable, and rough to the touch; also, containing impurities of the nature of earth, as in ***earthy cobalt, hæmatite, manganese***, etc.

1667 BOYLE *Orig. Formes & Qual.*, The Earthy powder, I obtain'd from already distill'd Rain water. **1695** WOODWARD *Nat. Hist. Earth* (J.) All water..is..stored with matter, light in comparison of the common mineral earthy matter. **1797** M. BAILLIE *Morb. Anat.* (1807) 284 The kidneys have been said to be converted into an earthy substance. **1843** PORTLOCK *Geol.* 225 Earthy Hæmatite is found at Bardahessigh. **1846** J. BAXTER *Libr. Pract. Agric.* II. 293 An excess of vegetable matter is..to be remedied by the application of earthy materials. **1863–82** WATTS *Dict. Chem.* III. 814 Earthy Cobalt is a wad in which oxide of cobalt sometimes occurs to the amount of 33 per cent. **1877** GREEN *Phys. Geol.* ii. §5. 46 Crystalline rocks occasionally put on a loose friable form and are then said to be earthy.

b. Of qualities, etc.: Characteristic of earth. So ***earthy taste, smell, colour. earthy fracture***: see quot. 1817.

1555 EDEN *Decades W. Ind.* II. ix. (Arb.) 131 The skyn is of earthy coloure. **1626** BACON *Sylva* §387 All sweet Smells have joyned with them some Earthy or Crude Odors. **1817** R. JAMESON *Char. Min.* 235 When the fracture surface shews a great number of very small elevations and depressions, which make it appear rough, it is called earthy. **1839** T. THOMSON *Chem. Org. Bodies* 508 An earthy fracture. **1840** R. DANA *Bef. Mast* xxxv. 133 The crispness of the raw onion, with the earthy taste.

c. Consisting of earth (said of the ground; cf. *sandy*), or of material resembling earth. Said *fig.* of the human body, *esp.* of a dead body.

a **1586** SIDNEY *Ps.* xcvi, Starry roofe, and earthy floore. **1593** SHAKS. *Rich. II*, IV. i. 219 And soone lye Richard in an Earthie Pit. **1593** —— *2 Hen. VI*, III. ii. 147 His dead and earthy Image. *a* **1652** J. SMITH *Sel. Disc.* viii. 380 The soul must be wholly dissolved from this earthy body in which it is so deeply immersed. **1854** HOOKER *Himal. Jrnls.* I. ii. 46 The..egg-like earthy chrysalis of the Sphynx Atropos.

d. *Electr.* (See quot. 1940.)

1876 PREECE & SIVEWRIGHT *Telegr.* 257 If an underground wire becomes earthy, owing to the insulating covering being partly removed, and the conductor being thus laid bare, [etc.]. **1940** *Chambers's Techn. Dict.* 278/1 *Earthy*, said of (1) circuits when they are connected to earth, either directly.. or through a condenser; (2) any point in a communicating system..which is at earth potential, although not actually connected to earth, through zero impedance. **1945** *Electronic Engin.* XVII. 735 The 'earthy' terminal is a shrouded insulated terminal which is connected to the earth terminal of the case. **1949** *Ibid.* XXI. 359 The feedback may be very conveniently taken from the earthy end of the cathode load resistor.

¶ *humorously*.

1836 DICKENS *Sk. Boz* (1877) 69 A damp earthy child.

†**2. a.** Having the properties of the 'element' earth, as distinguished from those of fire, air, or water; heavy, gross. So ***earthy vapour***. *Obs.*

1626 BACON *Sylva* §390 When they [flowers] are Crushed, the Grosser and more Earthy Spirit cometh out with the Finer and troubleth it. **1641** WILKINS *Math. Magic* (J.) Lamps are inflamed by the admission of new air, when the sepulchres are opened, as we see in fat earthy vapours. **1677** HALE *Prim. Orig. Man.* 76 The Clouds are attracted out of moist and watry, and also earthy Vapours.

b. *fig.* Grossly material, coarse, dull, unrefined. Sometimes with mixture of 1.

1594 T. B. *La Primaud. Fr. Acad.* II. 65 The sense of touching..is most earthy of all the rest. **1610** SHAKS. *Temp.* I. ii. 273 Thou wast a Spirit too delicate To act her earthy, and abhor'd commands. **1665** BOYLE *Occas. Refl.* IV. ii. (1675) 176 Men whom..he was wont to undervalue, as being far more Earthy than himself. **1856** EMERSON *Eng. Traits* xiv. *Literature* Wks. (Bohn) II. 103 They [the English] delight in strong earthy expressions..coarsely true to the human body. **1868** NETTLESHIP *Browning* ii. 74 The dumb striving of a humanity prisoned in too earthy a chamber.

3. *Chem.* Pertaining to the class of substances technically called 'earths', or to one of those substances; in mod. use, pertaining to the class of metallic oxides so designated. †Also quasi-*sb.*

1718 QUINCY *Compl. Disp.* 10 The Particles of Sal Alcali do consist of earthy and acid united together. **1794** SULLIVAN *View Nat.* I. 135 Bodies have been divided into six classes, saline, inflammable, metallic, earthy, watery, and aerial. **1805** W. SAUNDERS *Min. Waters* 40 Sulphat of Lime ..is one of the commonest of all the earthy salts that are found in natural springs. **1809** *Med. Jrnl.* XXI. 475 Earthy carbonates. **1863–82** WATTS *Dict. Chem.* II. 360 Baryta, strontia, and lime..are sometimes designated earthy alkalis. **1883** *Syd. Soc. Lex., Eastbourne*. There is an earthy spring here of little moment.

4. Pertaining to the ground, or to what is below the ground; dwelling inside the earth; resembling a place underground.

1665 DRYDEN *Indian Emp.* II. i. Wks. (1821) II. 313 Those earthy spirits black and envious are. **1794** SULLIVAN *View Nat.* II. 106 Beneath the earthy surface of the globe, we shall be able to trace its levelling and its dreadful energy. **1848** DICKENS *Dombey* (C.D. ed.) 36 Little Paul might have asked with Hamlet 'into my grave?' so chill and earthy was the place.

†**5.** Pertaining to the earth in its geographical or astronomical aspect. *Obs.*

1398 TREVISA *Barth. De P.R.* XIII. v. (1495) 443 The ryuer Gyon hyghte Nilus..and is callyd the joynynge of the erthe, other erthy. **1640** WILKINS *New Planet* II. (1684) 115 The gravity and magnitude of this Earthy Globe, do make it altogether unfit for so swift a Motion. **1721–1800** BAILEY, Earthy Triplicity [in Astrology], the Signs Taurus, Virgo and Capricorn.

6. Dwelling or existing on the earth; characteristic of earthly as opposed to heavenly existence. Now only with a mixture of sense 1, 1 c, or 2 b, as in the Biblical phrase ***of the earth, earthy***.

1595 SHAKS. *John* III. i. 147 What earthie name to Interrogatories, Can task the free breath of a sacred King? **1609** CHAPMAN *End of Learn.* in Farr's *S.P.* (1848) 253 Let a scholar all earthy volumes carrie, He will be but a walking dicionarie. **1615** —— *Odyss.* VII. 290 The impious race Of earthy giants, that would heaven outface. **1667** MILTON *P.L.* IV. 583 If Spirit of other sort..have oreleapt these earthie bounds. **1682** NORRIS *Hierocles* 19 As apt to dwell and converse upon the Earth, and inform earthy bodies. **1829** H. NEELE *Lit. Rem.* 45 The latter [Shakspeare] is of the earth, earthy. **1869** *Sat. Rev.* 13 Feb. 219 The..muse Urania is almost his only patroness; from her eight earthier sisters he gets hardly any assistance.

7. *Comb.*

a **1658** CLEVELAND *Gen. Poems* (1677) 167 O that in this case we were Earthy-minded. **1923** W. DEEPING *Secret Sanctuary* vi. 62 A lean, peevish, earthy-faced man in a hard felt hat. **1922** D. H. LAWRENCE *England, My England* 240 Then he removed her saturated, earthy-smelling clothing.

ˈear-ˌtrumpet. An apparatus in the form of a straight or convoluted conoidal tube, used by persons somewhat deaf, to enable them to hear more distinctly.

1776 BURNEY *Hist. Mus.* I. 184 Perhaps Asclepiades was the inventor of the acousticon, or ear-trumpet. **1823** BYRON *Juan* X. xxxiv, The ear-trumpet of my good old aunt.

eartu, obs. f. *art thou*: see BE *v.*, and THOU.

earun, obs. form of *are*: see BE *v.*

ˈear-wax. [f. EAR *sb.*¹] A viscid secretion which collects in the external meatus of the ear.

1398 TREVISA *Barth. De P.R.* XVII. v. (1495) 606 Eere wexe is put thereto to make it [aloes wood] somdeale bytter and redde. **1519** HORMAN *Vulg.* 27 b, Earewaxe doth stop the entrynge from small bestis. **1573** *Art of Limming* 2 If there stand any belles uppon the sise, put in eare waxe, for it ys a remedy therefore. **1614** T. ADAMS in Spurgeon *Treas. Dav.* Ps. xxvi. 10 Far be from our souls..that the ear..should be stopped with the earwax of partiality. **1791** E. DARWIN *Bot. Gard.* II. 20 *note*, The ear-wax in animals seems to be in part designed to prevent insects from getting into their ears. **1876** QUAIN *Anat.* (ed. 8) II. 631 The cerumen or ear-wax is secreted by these glands.

earwig (ˈɪəwɪg). Forms: 1, 2 **earwicga**, (1 **eorwicga**), 5 **erwyge**, **ȝerwigge**, **erewygge**, 6 **erwygge**, (**herewigge**), 6–7 **earwigge**, 7 **earwick**, **earewig**, 6– **earwig**. [OE. *éarwicga*, f. *éar-e*, EAR *sb.*¹ + OE. *wicga* earwig; cf. WIGGLE *v.* to wriggle. See also ARWYGYLL. Cf. Fr. *perce-oreille*, Ger. *ohr-wurm*.]

1. An insect, *Forficula auricularia*, so called from the notion that it penetrates into the head through the ear.

c **1000** ÆLFRIC *Gloss.* in Wr.-Wülcker 122 *Blatta*, erowicga. *c* **1000** *Sax. Leechd.* II. 44 Wiþ earwicgan, ȝenim þæt micle greate windel streaw twyecȝe..ceop on þæt eare he bið of sona. **14..** *Voc. Harl. MS.* 1002 in *Promp. Parv.* 143 *note*, *Auriolus*, a ȝerwigge. *c* **1450** *MS. Sloane* 4. 80 in *N. & Q.* III. VI. 4 Yᵉ blacke flye, yᵉ erwyge, yᵉ old waspys. **1547** SALESBURY *Welsh Dict.*, *Pryf klustioc*, an erwygge. **1601** HOLLAND *Pliny* II. 300 If an earwig..be gotten into the eare ..spit into the same, and it will come forth anon. *a* **1643** W. CARTWRIGHT *Poems* (1651) (N.) I'm afraid 'Tis with one worm, one earwick overlaid. **1727** SWIFT *To Young Lady*, To fall into fits at the sight of a spider, an earwig or a frog. *a* **1845** HOOD *Tale of Trumpet* ix, No verbal message was worth a pin, Though you hired an earwig to carry it in!

¶ Perhaps with a pun on *heretic*.

1563 FOXE *A. & M.* (1631) III. xii. 988/2 He was once at the burning of an Herewigge (for so hee termed it) at Uxbridge.

†**2.** *fig.* An ear whisperer, flatterer, parasite.

1633 FORD *Broken H.* II. i, That gawdy earwig, or my lord your patron, Whose pensioner you are. **1688** *Pol. Ballads* (1860) I. 260 Court earwigs banish from your ears. **1758** *Herald* II. 46 The earwigs of royalty..will not hereafter be suffered to mislead majesty by whispering, etc.

3. *Comb.*, as †**earwig-brain**, one who has a 'maggot' or craze in his brain.

1599 NASHE *Lent. Stuffe* 74 Eight score more galliard cross-points, and kickshiwinshes, of giddy ear-wig brains.

earwig (ˈɪəwɪg), *v.* [f. the sb.]

1. a. To pester with private importunities or admonitions. **b.** To influence, bias (a person) by secret communications; to insinuate oneself into the confidence of (a person).

1837 MARRYAT *Dog-fiend* (L.), He was so sure to be earwigged in private that what he heard or said openly went for little. **1839** DICKENS *O. Twist* (1850) 251/2 Suppose he was to do all this..not grabbed, trapped, tried, earwigged by the parson..but off his own fancy. **1839** *Blackw. Mag.* XLV. 767 Each secretary of state is earwigged by a knot of sturdy beggars. **1867** SMYTH *Sailor's Word-bk.*, *Earwigging*, feeding an officer's ear with scandal against an absent individual.

2. in *pa. pple.* ? Having a 'maggot' or craze in one's brain. *nonce-use.*

1880 BROWNING *Pietro* 340 The people clamour, Hold their peace, now fight, now fondle, earwigged through the brains.

earwiggy ('ɪəwɪgɪ), *a.* [f. EARWIG *sb.* + -Y.]

a. Infested by earwigs. **b.** Resembling an earwig. Hence 'ear,wigginess.

1870 MISS BROUGHTON *Red as Rose* I. 82 A seat..'I don't fancy it..it looks earwiggy'. **1865** MASSON *Rec. Brit. Philos.* iv. 388 There was an inherent dogginess or earwigginess in the given kind of associable feelings.

earwise ('ɪəwaɪz), *adv. rare.* [See -WISE.]

1. After the manner of an ear of corn. [EAR *sb.*¹]

1723 BRADLEY *Fam. Dict.* II. s.v. *Mint*, The Great Mint.. has leaves like Sage..with a good Number of Stems at the End of which it produces Flowers growing Ear-wise.

2. By means of the ear; auricularly. [EAR *sb.*²]

1835 T. HOOK *G. Gurney* (1850) I. vii. 123 Although I took the advice earwise, I did not act upon it.

ear-witness. [f. EAR *sb.*¹] A person who testifies, or is able to testify, to something on the evidence of his own hearing.

1594 HOOKER *Eccl. Pol.* v. 257 All which are present being made eare-witnesses. **1636** HEALEY *Epictetus' Man.* lxix. 89 Let not..the vulgar bee eare-witnesses of thy words, but eye-witnesses of thy workes. **1734** tr. *Rollin's Anc. Hist.* (1827) I. I. §1. 181 Strabo himself was an ear-witness of this. **1850** GROTE *Greece* II. lxiv. VIII. 269 The last words of these drowning men reported by an ear-witness. **1870** BOWEN *Logic* xiii. 433 The Testimony of eye- and ear-witnesses.

†'eary, *a. Obs.* In 6 earie. [f. EAR *sb.*² + -Y.] Of the nature or appearance of an ear (of corn).

1578 LYTE *Dodoens* II. xviii. 168 His spikie tuftes, or earie floures are greater, longer and fuller.

easalon, var. of ESALON, a small buzzard.

ease (iːz), *sb.* Forms: 3 eaise, ays, esse, (4 hess, hayse), 3-4 eise, ais, 3-6 es(e, 4 ess, eyss, 4-5 eyse, ayse, 5 aiese, (hesse), 6 eas, (*Sc.*) eais, eis, 4- ease. [a. OF. *eise, aise* (mod. *aise*) fem., cogn. w. Pr. *ais*, It. *agio* (formerly also *asio*), Pg. *azo* masc.; late L. type **asia*, **asium*, of uncertain origin.

The earliest senses of Fr. *aise* appear to be: 1. elbow-room ('espace libre aux côtés de quelqu'un', A. Darmesteter, from Heb.-Fr. gloss 11th c.); 2. opportunity. It has been suggested by Bugge that **asia*, **asium* may be f. *āsa*, a recorded vulgar form of L. *ansa* handle, used fig. in sense 'opportunity, occasion'. With reference to the sense 'elbow-room' it is remarked that *ansātus* 'furnished with handles' is used in Lat. for 'having the arms a-kimbo'. This is not very satisfactory, but it does not appear that any equally plausible alternative has yet been proposed. Connexion with EATH is impossible.]

†I. 1. Opportunity, means or ability to do something (cf. EASY *a.* 1).

a **1225** *Ancr. R.* 288 ȝif þer were eise uorto fulfullen þe dede. *c* **1230** *Hali Meid.* 17 Man seið þat eise makeð þeof. *a* **1500** *Life St. Katherine* (Halliwell 1848) 2 The riche come ..and broghte with them ryches moche, And the pore come also And after there ese broght tho.

II. Comfort, absence of pain or trouble.

2. Comfort, convenience; *formerly* also, advantage, profit, and in stronger sense, pleasure, enjoyment. *to take one's ease*: to make oneself comfortable. *† to do (a person) ease*: to give pleasure or assistance to. *†to be (a person's) ease*: to be pleasing, convenient, advantageous.

a **1225** *Ancr. R.* 114 Gruccheð ȝif heo naueð nout oðer mete oðer drunch efter hire eaise. *c* **1230** *Hali Meid.* 28 I-se swote eise wiðute swuch trubuil. *a* **1300** *Cursor M.* 22773 Werldis worschip..siluer and gold and esse [*F.* ese, *C.* es, *Edinb.* ais] of lijf. **1375** BARBOUR *Bruce* III. 623 Bot mycht nane eyss let him to think On the king, that sa sar wes stad. **1393** GOWER *Conf.* III. 35 The woundes of his malady They [*i.e.* the hounds] licken for to done him ese. **1398** TREVISA *Barth. De P.R.* XVIII. xlvi. (1495) 807 Them that liue delycately and in ease and reste. *c* **1400** *Cato's Mor.* 199 in *Cursor M.* p. 1672 Quen þou art in gode ese . þou þink on misese. *c* **1400** *Rom. Rose* 7500 We wolden, if it were your ese..A short sermon unto you seyne. *c* **1440** *Gesta Rom.* lxx. 386 (Add. MS.), I wil neþer selle it..for the aiese that it dothe me. **1503-4** *Act 19 Hen. VII*, xxviii. Preamb., His Highnes is not mynded for the eas of his subgiectes..of longe tyme to calle..a newe parliament. **1523** LD. BERNERS *Froiss.* I. cccxcvii. 686 It was nat his ease to come to Tourney as at that tyme. **1535** STEWART *Cron. Scot.* II. 653 He levis weill that levis into eis. *a* **1555** LATIMER *Wks.* 1845 II. 479 *Latimer*:—'Good master Prolocutor, do not exact that of me which is not in me.' *Prolocutor*:—'Take your ease.' *Latimer*:—'I thank you, sir, I am well.' **1602** SHAKS. *Ham.* I. i. 131 Any good thing..That may to thee do ease; and grace to me. **1651** HOBBES *Leviath.* II. xxx. 184 The ease, and benefit the Subjects may enjoy. **1762-71** H. WALPOLE *Vertue's Anecd. Paint.* (1786) IV. 234 The General could not live in it to his ease. **1825** T. JEFFERSON *Autobiog.* Wks. 1859 I. 4 The portion which came..to Mrs. Jefferson..doubled the ease of our circumstances. **1841-4** EMERSON *Ess. Manners* Wks. (Bohn) I. 205 The popular notion [of a gentleman] certainly adds a condition of ease and fortune. **1870** HAWTHORNE *Eng. Note-bks.* (1879) II. 217 The occasional ease of rustic seats.

†b. *concr.* A convenience, gratification, luxury.

1393 GOWER *Conf.* II. 38 Idelnesse..secheth eses many folde. **1484-5** CAXTON *Curial* 3 b, Noman preyseth ynough the ayses that he hath in hys pryuate and propre hous. **1526** *Pilgr. Perf.* (W. de W. 1531) 81 She can cause her prelate to dispence with her to haue suche pleasures & eases. **1629** PARKINSON *Paradisi in sole* (1656) 5 A Fountain in the midst ..to serve as an ease to water the nearest parts thereunto. *a* **1631** DONNE *Serm.* xxxix. 384 Uriah..refused to take the Eases of his own house.

3. Absence of pain or discomfort; freedom from annoyance.

a **1225** *Ancr. R.* 358 Nis he a kang knit þet secheð reste iðe nihte, and eise iðe place? *a* **1300** *Havelok* 59 þanne was engelond at hayse. **1597** MORLEY *Introd. Mus.* 55, I wish you such contentment of minde, and ease of bodie. **1657** S. PURCHAS *Pol. Flying Ins.* 276 There were more ease in a nest of Hornets, then under this one torture. **1711** STEELE *Spect.* No. 80 ¶1 They now no longer enjoyed the Ease of Mind and pleasing Indolence in which they were formerly happy. **1750** JOHNSON *Rambl.* No. 85 ¶4 Ease, a neutral state between pain & pleasure. **1792** BURKE *Corr.* (1844) IV. 1 The horrid scenes..hardly leave one ease enough of heart or clearness of head to put down any thing..on paper to you. **1863** GEO. ELIOT *Romola* II. ii. (1880) II. 16 He wanted a little ease..after the agitation and exertions of the day.

4. Absence of painful effort; freedom from the burden of toil; leisure; in bad sense, idleness, sloth.

1393 GOWER *Conf.* III. 110 He loveth ese, he loveth rest, So he is nought the worthiest. *c* **1440** *Promp. Parv.* 143 Ese, or reste, *quies.* **1577** tr. *Bullinger's Decades* (1592) 138 Ease breedeth vice. **1697** DRYDEN *Virg. George.* I. 184 The Sire of Gods and Men..Forbids our Plenty to be bought with Ease. **1871** R. ELLIS *Catullus* li. 15 Ease hath entomb'd princes of old renown and Cities of honour.

b. Facility as opposed to difficulty. Chiefly in phrase, *with ease.*

1610 SHAKS. *Temp.* III. i. 30, I should do it With much more ease. **1697** DRYDEN *Virg. Georg.* IV. 137 With ease distinguish'd is the Regal Race. **1737** POPE *Horace' Epist.* II. i. 108 The mob of gentlemen who wrote with ease. **1856** RUSKIN *Mod. Paint.* III. IV. xvi. §27 Another..test of greatness is..the appearance of Ease with which the thing is done. **1868** TENNYSON *Lucretius* 174 Seeing with how great ease Nature can smile.

c. Indifference, unconcern; absence of hesitation or scruple.

1808 BENTHAM *Sc. Reform* 2 In your lordship it beholds its patron and introducer; the author, it is matter of ease to me not to know. **1818** JAS. MILL *Brit. India* II. v. viii. 661 Where the Governor-General spoke of pensions with so much ease, he well knew, that in the circumstances..a pension..little or nothing differed from a name.

5. Freedom from constraint; an unconstrained position or attitude; *esp.* in *Mil.* phrase, *to stand at ease*: see quot.

1802 C. JAMES *Mil. Dict., Ease*..signifies a prescribed relaxation of the frame from the erect and firm position which every well-dressed soldier should assume..*To stand at ease* is to draw the right foot back about six inches, and to bring the greatest part of the weight of the body upon it. **1830** MARRYAT *King's Own* xli, His usual 'stand at ease' position. **1833** *Regul. Instr. Cavalry* I. 43 Stand at Ease. *Ibid.* 61 Sit at Ease. **1853** STOCQUELER *Milit. Encycl.* s.v. *Stand*, To stand at ease is to be allowed..a certain indulgence with regard to bodily position, with or without arms.

6. Freedom from embarrassment or awkwardness in social behaviour.

1750 JOHNSON *Rambl.* No. 157 ¶8 Enabled me to discourse with ease and volubility. *a* **1764** LLOYD *Whim*, Wears his own mirth with native ease. **1832** HT. MARTINEAU *Hill & Vall.* iv. 65 Mrs. Wallace envied Mrs. Sydney the ease and kindness with which she conversed. **1855** MACAULAY *Hist. Eng.* III. 469 A certain graceful ease marks him as a man who knows the world. **1863** FROUDE *Hist. Eng.* VIII. 91 She..moved about among the dignitaries of the University, with combined authority and ease.

7. Phrases (senses 1-6). **a.** *at ease, at one's ease, †well at ease*: in comfort, without anxiety or annoyance, unconstrained, unembarrassed; formerly also, in comfortable circumstances, well-to-do. **b.** *ill (†evil) at ease*: uncomfortable, uneasy. **†c.** *little ease*: used as a name for a prison-cell too small to permit the person occupying it to assume a comfortable position.

a. *a* **1300** *Cursor M.* 13136 All war sett and ete at esse. *Ibid.* 17651 He was gestind ful wele at ais. **1375** BARBOUR *Bruce* I. 228 He levys at ess that frely levys. *c* **1450** *Merlin* xxii. 397 Galashin was not all at his ese, ffor he was yet a-monge the horse feet. **1535** COVERDALE *Hosea* ii. 7, I will go turne agayne to my first huszbonde, for at yᵗ tyme was I better at ease, then now. **1668-9** MARVELL *Corr.* cix. Wks. 1872-5 II. 268 If..you have given us a rule to walke by, our discretion will be more at ease. **1670** COTTON *Espernon* II. v. 210 Monied men..amongst whom his Majesty conceiving the Duke of Espernon to be one the most at his ease, etc. **1711** ADDISON *Spect.* No. 106 ¶2, I am the more at Ease in Sir Roger's Family, because it consists of sober and staid Persons. **1821** SYD. SMITH *Lett.* cc, An old Aunt has..left me an estate..this puts me a little at my ease. **1860** TYNDALL *Glac.* I. §27. 202 We all felt more at ease when a safe footing was secured. **1868** E. EDWARDS *Ralegh* I. xxiv. 564 He felt much more at his ease in the saddle than afoot.

b. *a* **1300** *Cursor M.* 16119 Mi wyf es sumquat iuel at ess [*v.r.* ese]. *a* **1450** *Knt. de la Tour* (1868) 59 She..was of euelle atte ease in this worlde. **1483** *Vulg. abs Terentio* 2 a, Iii. or .iiii. days ȝitt j was euyll att ese in my hede. **1642** T. TAYLOR *God's Judgem.* I. I. xx. 70 He feigned himselfe to be evill at ease. **1832** TENNYSON *Miller's Dau.* xix, You were ill at ease..Too fearful that you should not please.

c. **1690** W. WALKER *Idiomat. Anglo-Lat.* 156 A little ease (i.e. a prison). **1829** HEATH *Grocer's Comp.* (1869) 92 *note*, Little Ease was a place of confinement for unruly apprentices; it was situated in the Guildhall.

III. Relief, alleviation. [Somewhat influenced by the verb.]

8. Relief or mitigation of pain or discomfort; release from an annoyance. Const. *from, of.*

1542-3 *Act 34 & 35 Hen. VIII*, viii. §1 Surgions.. mindinge onely their owne lucres, & nothing the profit or ease of the disesed or pacient. **1588** ALLEN *Admon.* 17 Sum little ease and release of the intolerable feares and miseries. **1702** J. PURCELL *Cholick* (1714) 103 The Patient breaks much Wind upwards and downwards, and finds Ease thereby. **1729** BUTLER *Serm.* Wks. 1874 II. 61 That positive enjoyment, which sudden ease from pain..affords. **1775** JOHNSON *Tax. no Tyr.* 61 That a great man may get ease from importunity. **1841** LANE *Arab. Nts.* I. 112 Liberate him, said the King, and give us ease.

b. *† to do one's ease*: to relieve the bowels. So *seat, † house of ease.*

c **1645** HOWELL *Lett.* (1655) I. §1. xviii. 28 It happen'd the King was come from doing his Ease. **1731** SWIFT *Strephen & C.* Wks. 1755 IV. I. 157 Had you but through a cranny spied, On house of ease your future bride. *c* **1850** *Rudim. Navig.* (Weale) 143 Round-house at the Head. Conveniences or seats of ease for the officers.

c. *chapel of ease*: see CHAPEL. So also (humorously) *court of ease, theatre of ease*: one provided to relieve the crowding in a larger building.

1779 SHERIDAN *Critic* I. i, Make the stage a court of ease to the old Bailey. **1796** J. OWEN *Trav. Europe* II. 429 It seems a sort of theatre of ease to that called the National.

9. Relief from constraint or pressure; abrogation or alleviation of a burden or obligation; †redress of grievances. *† writ of ease*: a certificate of discharge from employment; *transf.* a 'bill of divorcement'.

1576 LAMBARDE *Peramb. Kent* (1826) 107 Hastings, Dover, Hithe [etc.]..were the first Ports of priviledge.. although..divers other places also (for the ease of their charge) be crept in. **1587** FLEMING *Contn. Holinshed* III. 1345/2 Thus was justice ministred, and that execution to Gods glorie, & the ease of the common wealths greefe dispatched. **1643** MILTON *Divorce* II. xvi. (1851) 103 Salomith..sent a writ of ease to..her husband; which, as Josephus there attests, was lawfull only to men. **1647-8** COTTERELL *Davila's Hist. Fr.* (1678) 18 Having..tried gentle measures, and..found no Ease. **1679-1714** BURNET *Hist. Ref.*, Mischiefs..might follow, if princes get not..ease from the apostolic see. **1693** W. ROBERTSON *Phraseol. Gen.* 519 He hath a writ of ease given him; *rude donatus est.*

†10. *concr.* (from 8, 9): An act or means of relieving pain or discomfort, of giving relaxation from burdens, an easement, relief. *Obs.*

c **1440** *Promp. Parv.* 143 Ese, or cowmfort, *levamen, consolamen.* **1603** FLORIO *Montaigne* II. xii. (1632) 275 Eases of griefes he reposeth..in calling from the thought of offence. **1606** SHAKS. *Tr. & Cr.* v. x. 56 Till then, Ile sweate, and seeke about for eases. **1701** J. LAW *Counc. Trade* (1751) 172 This ease..of the industry, would chiefly and principally fall on the lands by two several ways. *a* **1718** PENN *Life* in Wks. 1726 I. 129 Dissenters receiv'd a General Ease, and enjoy'd their Meetings peaceably. **1737** WHISTON *Josephus' Antiq.* III. iii, That [discovery of springs] was an ease to them [the Israelites suffering thirst]. **1747** in *Col. Rec. Penn.* V. 141 Required by His Majesty from those Colonies to be done in ease of the National Expence.

IV. 11. *Comb.*, as *†ease-bred, -loving* adjs.; **ease-and-comfort**, a leg-rest, consisting of two boards fixed in the shape of a **T**; *†* **ease-room**, a comfortable lodging-room; cf. EASEMENT 1 d.

1591 *Troubl. Raigne K. John* (1611) 62 The ease-bred Abbots, and the bare-foot Friars..Are all in health. **1629** RUTHERFORD *Let* v. (1862) I. 47 In your house there are fair ease-rooms and pleasant lights. **1847** C'TESS BLESSINGTON *M. Herbert* (Tauchn.) I. 126 A bergère in each of the rooms, with abundant pillows to prop up her weak frame, and an ease-and-comfort to each, to support her legs. **1878** BOSW. SMITH *Carthage* 175 Around Hanno gathered all that was ease-loving, all that was shortsighted.

ease, obs. and dial. var of EAVES.

ease (iːz), *v.* Forms: 4 eysy, eyse, (heise), eyss, (*Sc.*) eiss, eese, ayse(n, 4-5 esy(n, 4-6 ese(n, 5- ease. [Prob. originally ad. OF. *aaisier* = It. *adagiare*, f. L. *ad* to, at + late L. **asiu-m* EASE *sb.*¹; but virtually f. the sb.]

1. a. *trans.* To give ease (physically) to; to render more comfortable, relieve from pain, etc. Also with *out of* and (*U.S.*) with *up.*

1340 *Ayenb.* 82 þo þet byeþ zuo wyse to loky þet body and to eysy and to delyty. **1398** TREVISA *Barth. De P.R.* XVII. liii. (1495) 635 Iuy hathe vertue of rypynge, of clensynge and of easynge. ? *a* **1400** *Chester Pl.* II. (1847) 5 This woman..That esead me this hasse. **1413** LYDG. *Pylgr. Sowle* IV. xxxii. (1483) 81 Oftimes these armes wil bleden to esen and comforten the hede. **1535** COVERDALE *1 Sam.* xvi. 23 So was Saul refreszshed, & eased. **1588** J. UDALL *Diotrephes* (Arb.) 7 Though it grieue mee to thinke vpon it, yet it easeth my stomacke to tell it. **1809** *Med. Jrnl.* XXI. 56 He drank it because it 'broke the wind, and eased' him. **1847** EMERSON *Poems, Dæmonic Love*, Even the fell Furies are appeased, The good applaud, the lost are eased. **1916** 'BOYD CABLE' *Action Front* 148 There is nothing we can do for him.. except morphia again, to ease him out of his pain. **1923** R. D. PAINE *Comr. Rolling Ocean* v. 83 The doctor is down there easing up the guys that got the hide burned off 'em.

†b. To refresh with repose or food: to entertain, accommodate hospitably. Also *refl. Obs.*

1330 R. BRUNNE *Chron.* (1810) 96 Toward Wynchestre þam dight, his folk forto eyse. *Ibid.* 192 Seke were þer heised, heled þam of wound. **1375** BARBOUR *Bruce* XIV. 387 Thai esyt thame, and maid gud cher. *c* **1386** CHAUCER *Knts. T.* 1336 Theseus..festeth hem, and doth so gret labour To esen hem. *c* **1400** *Ywaine & Gaw.* 232 That night had i..mi stede esed of the best. *c* **1430** *Syr Gener.* (Roxb.) 2816 Anazaree..into a feire chambre him ladd, And eased him as a fre prisovn. *c* **1450** LONELICH *Grail* xlii. 543 [Se] that..

they ben esed with the beste. *c* **1440** *Gesta Rom.* lxi. 257 (Harl. MS.) His squier soȝte an host, for swiche a worthi knyȝt to be eside ynne. **1650** Row[son] *Hist. Kirk* (1842) 513 To harbour more souldiers nor conuenientlie they can lodge & ease. **1695** Blackmore *Pr. Arth.* vi. 457 Boldly fall on, before their Troops are eas'd.

c. *to ease nature, ease oneself*: to relieve the bowels.

c **1440** *Promp. Parv.* 143 Esyn, *stercoriso, merdo, egero.* **1581** Mulcaster *Positions* vi. (1887) 47 Passage to dismisse excrements which easeth. **1611** Bible *Deut.* xxiii. 13 If thou wilt ease thyself. **1697** Potter *Antiq. Greece* i. xxvi. (1715) 145 Whosoever easeth Nature in Apollo's Temple shall be Indicted. **1877** E. Peacock *N.-W. Linc. Gloss.* (E.D.S.), *Ease one's self*, to relieve the bowels. **1926** T. E. Lawrence *Seven Pillars* (1935) xliv. 256 Gasim explained that he had dismounted to ease nature.

2. To give ease of mind to; to comfort, disburden, relieve (the mind or heart). Also *refl.*

c **1340** *Cursor M.* 13868 (Trin.) He esed him wiþ wordes hende. *c* **1385** Chaucer *L.G.W.* 1700 And with oure speche lat us ese oure herte. **1483** *Vulg. abs Terentio* 6 b, I shall ese my mynde or hertt, *animo meo morem gessero.* **1526** Tindale *Matt.* xi. 28 Come unto me . . and I will ese you. **1631** Gouge *God's Arrows* iv. viii. 385 Torment [may prove] an occasion of easing the mind. **1732** Pope *Ep. Bathurst* 365 Some scruple rose, but thus he eas'd his thought. **1807** Crabbe *Hall of Just.* i. 29 Give me to ease my tortured mind. **1820** Keats *Hyper.* i. 112 And all those acts which Deity supreme Doth ease its heart of love in. **1848** Macaulay *Hist. Eng.* II. 294 The Chancellor . . could not well ease himself by cursing and swearing at Ormond.

†**3.** To give relief to (any one suffering from oppression, or burdened with expenses or laborious duties) in wider sense; to benefit, help, assist. Also (rarely) *absol. Obs.* or *arch.*

1330 R. Brunne *Chron.* Prol. 84, I made it not forto be praysed, Bot [þ]at þe lewed menne were aysed. **1389** in *Eng. Gilds* (1870) 8 So þat þe somme be nat so moche þ^t on may be esed as wel as an oþer. **1553** Eden *Treat. New Ind.* (Arb.) 16 As though they would ease you with a sterope. **1587** Fleming *Contn. Holinshed* III. 1541/2 They were afterwards eased by purueiors appointed for those and other purposes. *a* **1619** Donne *Biathan.* (1644) 100 If that rule . . be . . a good guide in all perplexities, it will ease very much. **1647** *Protests Lords* I. 15 The kingdom eased . . by the discharging of all unnecessary forces. **1653** Urquhart *Rabelais* i. xlv, He . . gave unto each of them a horse to ease them upon the way. **1697** *Phil. Trans.* XIX. 746 Towards the latter end of Summer . . they constantly eased the Country, and retired of themselves. **1761–2** Hume *Hist. Eng.* (1806) IV. lxiii. 713 The declared intention of easing the dissenters.

4. a. To relieve, lighten, set free (a person, etc.) *of* (†*from*) a burden, pain, anxiety, or trouble.

1393 Gower *Conf.* III. 354 Thou shalt be esed er thou go Of thilke unsely jolif wo. *c* **1460** Fortescue *Abs. & Lim. Mon.* (1714) 75 His Son, King Roboham, would not ease them thereoff. **1526** *Pilgr. Perf.* (W. de W. 1531) 13 b, In maner easynge them of theyr labour. **1535** Coverdale *Ps.* lxxx.[lxxxi.] 6 He eased his shulder from the burthen. **1575–85** Abp. Sandys *Serm.* (1841) 227 If this law were observed, the people should be eased of great expences, judges and justices of great travail. **1630** J. Taylor (Water P.) *Trav. Prague* Wks. III. 90, I am no sooner eased of him, but Gregory Gandergoose . . catches me by the goll. **1663** Charleton *Chor. Gigant.* 9 Nor, indeed, can I ease you of that wonder. **1697** Dryden *Virg. Georg.* iii. 486 The Pastor . . eases of their Hair, the loaden Herds. **1725** Pope *Odyss.* xxi. 342 Ease your bosoms of a fear so vain. **1748** Anson *Voy.* i. vi. 63 To ease the expedition of all unnecessary expence. **1833** Ht. Martineau *Brooke F.* vi. 76 To ease my mind of all worldly concerns. **1862** Borrow *Wales* I. 34 A powerful priest . . has . . eased me of my sins.

b. in *pass.* with prep. omitted. *poet. rare.*

1667 Milton *P.L.* iv. 739 [Adam & Eve] eas'd the putting off These troublesom disguises which wee wear, Strait side by side were laid.

c. *humorously.* To deprive, despoil *of.*

1609 Holland *Livy* xxxvii. xiii. 952 Having eased them [*exutos*] of a great part of their prey . . he chased themselves to the sea unto their ships. *a* **1639** Massinger *Unnat. Combat* iii. ii. (R.) He is sure to be eased of his office, though perhaps he bought it. **1832** J. P. Kennedy *Swallow Barn* II. i. 4 He became notorious for picking up stragglers . . and now and then, for easing a prisoner of his valuables. **1882** *Sydney Slang Dict.* 4/1 *Ease*, to rob. To Ease a Bloak, to rob a gentleman.

d. *to ease in* or *into*: to 'break in' gently (to work, etc.); to move or manœuvre into (a place, appointment, etc.). Similarly, *to ease out.*

1892 *Leisure Hour* May 462/1 He is gradually eased in to his work. **1951** *N.Y. Times* 28 Nov. 1/6 There have been many precedents in the Soviet satellites for easing prominent Communist leaders into jail by incessive steps. **1955** *Times* 10 May 8/7 It is being suggested that the Russians are easing him out of office because of the resistance he is said to have shown towards some of their demands. **1968** *Listener* 1 Aug. 133/3 A fair number . . have either been pensioned off or eased into some job which gives them a living.

e. *Dressmaking.* To join two pieces of material whose edges are of unequal length in such a way that the extra fullness of the larger section is distributed evenly along the join. Freq. with *in.*

1932 D. C. Minter *Mod. Needlecraft* 108/2 Allow sufficient width at armhole to allow for easing in. **1967** *Simplicity 7391* (Simplicity Pattern Co. Inc.), To ease top of sleeve, stitch along seam line and ¼" *inside* seam line between notches, using a long machine-stitch. *Ibid.*, Slip-stitch, easing in fullness. **1968** J. Ironside *Fashion Alphabet* 82 *Ease*, v. When one section of a garment is fuller than another to which it is to be joined, the excess material is distributed evenly without gathers or pleats and usually pressed away.

5. a. To lighten (a burden, etc.); to lessen (an inconvenience); to assuage, relieve (pain, distress).

a **1374** Chaucer *Troylus* iii. 950 And ech of ȝow eseth otheres sorwes smerte. **1586** J. Hooker *Girald. Irel.* in *Holinsh.* II. 152/2 And for easing whereof he . . in verie deed had also promised, and deuised how and by what means these charges might be answered. **1590** Shaks. *Mids. N.* v. i. 35 Is there no play To ease the anguish of a torturing houre? **1601** R. Johnson *Kingd. & Commw.* (1603) 112 The haven is not very large nor safe, but that inconvenience is somewhat eased by an artificiall key. **1633** G. Herbert *Temple, Crosse* vi, Ah my deare Father, ease my smart. **1701** *Col. Rec. Penn.* II. 109 'Tis resolved that it cannot be eased or remitted. **1774** Goldsm. *Nat. Hist.* (1776) IV. 355 The horse and the ass . . contribute to ease his fatigues. **1834** Ht. Martineau *Moral* i. 3 Machinery, which easeth man's labour. **1846** McCulloch *Acc. Brit. Empire* (1854) II. 133 This conduct is found conducive to easing the rates.

b. *poet.* To rest from, relax (labour).

1715–20 Pope *Iliad* x. 543 Eased in sleep the labours of the day. **1871** R. Ellis *Catullus* lxiii. 36 The rest which easeth long toil.

6. To render easy, facilitate. *rare.*

1632 Mass. & Field *Fatal Dow.* ii. i, My miracle is eased. **1667** Milton *P.L.* vii. 430 [Storks] with mutual wing Easing thir flight. **1795** Anderson *Narr. Embassy China* in Morse *Amer. Geog* (1796) II. 516 But with this aid in easing the passage, the beginning of the ascent has a very fearful appearance.

7. a. To relax slightly (anything that is too tight); to move gently; to lift slightly; to shift a little, make to fit.

Mod. Tell the carpenter to ease the door a little.

b. To move, lift, or shift *down* gradually or gently; or spec. *into* a person's pocket.

1688 S. Sewall *Diary* 31 Oct. in *Mass. Hist. Soc. Coll.* (1878) 5th Ser. V. 234, I help'd to ease the Corps into the Grave. **1850** N. Kingsley *Diary* 154 The road is very steep . . so bad in some places that a rope is necessary to ease them down with. *a* **1875** 'Mark Twain' *Works* (1900) XIX. 246 The widow caught the limp form and eased it to the earth. *Ibid.* 252 'Ease this down for a fellow, will you?' I eased the gravestone down till it rested on the ground. **1926** J. Black *You can't Win* iv. 41 The only thing to do is to blow back his money. Either the lawyer or one of the girls eased in into his coat pocket.

8. a. *intr.* To cease, slacken. Cf. 10 b.

1583 *Exec. for Justice* (1675) 46 The remnant of the wicked flock . . would ease from their . . libellings. **1875** Robinson *Whitby Gloss.* (E.D.S.), *Ease*, to cease operations, abate. T'rains boun to ease a bit. **1937** *New Statesman* 25 Dec. 1089/1 The fighting in northern China has eased a little since the fall of Nanking.

b. To relax or cease one's efforts, *spec.* in rowing; also with *up*; *to ease all*, to stop rowing (cf. easy *v.*).

1863 *Rowing & Sailing* 55 This spurt should be continued till the boat begins to rock, when it is better to 'ease all' than to attempt altering the stroke into a milder one. **1882** *Daily Tel.* 2 Mar. (Cassell), They also row right through to Iffley without easing. **1883** 'Mark Twain' *Life on Miss.* 44, I eased up and went slow and cautious. *Ibid.* xii. 115 When the measurements indicate that the yawl is approaching the shoalest part of the reef, the command is given to 'Ease all!' **1889** J. K. Jerome *Three Men in Boat* v. 73 On catching sight of Harris and me . . , he eased up and stared. **1915** 'Boyd Cable' *Between Lines* 25 'Can't you keep on belting 'em for a bit?' asked the Platoon officer. 'Might make 'em ease up on us.' **1945** E. Waugh *Brideshead Revisited* ii. iv. 262 She's playing up the religious stuff at the moment for all it's worth. I daresay she'll ease up a bit when she's settled.

c. *to ease up* intr. To become less burdensome.

1939 M. Spring Rice *Working-Class Wives* iv. 79 Things will ease up a bit soon when the children get older.

9. *Naut.* Often with *away, down, off*: to slacken (a rope, sail, etc.). *to ease up*: to come up handsomely with a tackle-fall. Also in forms of command, as *ease away! ease off!*: slacken out a rope or tackle. *ease her!* (in a steam vessel): reduce the speed of the engine. *ease the helm!*: put the helm down a few spokes in a head sea. (Adm. Smyth.)

1627 Capt. Smith *Seaman's Gram.* v. 20 When the Shrouds are too stiffe, we say, ease them. **1692** *ibid.* xvi. 76 To make her go *more large*, they say, *Ease the Helm.* **1769** Falconer *Dict. Marine* (1789), *Larguer . . l'Ecoute*, to ease off the sheet. **1833** Marryat *P. Simple* (1863) 101 Ease the ship with a spoke or two when she scuds. **1841** *Punch* I. 35 The dirty lad below, whose exclamation of 'Ease her—stop her—one turn ahead'—may one day be destined to give the word of command on the quarter deck. **1859** Gen. P. Thompson *Audi Alt.* II. xcv. 78 The present government might have stood its ground, if it had known how to ease off the rope handsomely. **1860** H. Stuart *Seaman's Catech.* 8 Luff and ease off the fore-sheet. **1881** *Daily Tel.* 5 July 2/2 She ratched like a phantom to windward of us, and . . eased away her sheets fore and aft. **1882** Nares *Seamanship* (ed. 6) 132 The earings are eased down.

10. ease off. a. *trans.* To get rid of with the view of giving or obtaining relief. **b.** *intr.* To become less burdensome.

1884 S. Dowell *Hist. Taxation* I. 177 It was an object with the king to ease off the business. **1884** *Manchester Exam.* 11 Oct. 4/1 To-morrow . . the rates are likely to again ease off. **1887** *Spectator* 30 July 1012/1 Every effort to ease off the immediate pressure of the agrarian difficulty.

c. *intr.* To fall away with a gentle slope.

1880 'Mark Twain' *Tramp Abroad* xli. 477 The slope eased off, . . and Croz and I, dashing away, ran a neck-and-neck race. **1925** E. F. Norton *Fight for Everest, 1924* 79 The slope began to ease off towards the edge of the shelf above.

d. *trans.* To fire off.

1916 'Taffrail' *Carry On* 93 What I do want is a nice little cruiser or a destroyer; something, at any rate, to ease off the guns at. **1962** W. Granville *Dict. Sailors' Slang* 44/1 *Ease off a fish*, fire a torpedo (Submariners).

e. *intr.* To take things easily.

1925 E. F. Norton *Fight for Everest, 1924* 35 It enabled us to . . have a welcome bath, and generally ease off after our first taste of high-level marching.

11. *intr.* Of shares: to become easier, fall in value.

1900 *Daily News* 5 Mar. 10/7 There is no easing in the prices for coal. **1904** *Financial Times* 23 Nov. 1/7 Sewing Cottons eased off to 12*s.* 3*d.* **1927** *Daily Tel.* 22 Nov. 2 Marconi eased 3*d.* and Eastern Telegraph declined 3.

Hence **eased** *ppl. a.*

1851 *Ord. & Regul. R. Engineers* §27. 124 The Arms to be carefully deposited in the Rack, with eased springs. **1877** M. Arnold *Heine's Grave*, Poems II. 257 Cool drinks, and an eased Posture and opium.

easeful (ˈiːzfʊl), *a.* Also 4 eisfull, 5 esful. [f. ease *sb.* + -ful.]

1. That gives ease, comfort, or relief; comfortable, soothing.

1375 Barbour *Bruce* v. 70 Myne auenture heir tak will I, Quhethir it be eisfull or angry. *c* **1425** Wyntoun *Cron.* vi. xx. 46 Wyth oþire thyng Ðat esful ware to þare lykyng. **1580** Sidney *Arcadia* iii. 377 Wishing easeful rest to Philoclea. **1577** Holinshed *Chron.* I. 58/2 How pleasant and easefull the good lucke of those princes. **1607** C. Lever in Farr's *S.P.* 168 To make his burthen Easeful as hee may. **1625** tr. *Gonsalvio's Sp. Inquis.* 123 A bed of flags which serued them both to couch on, more painefull a great deale then easefull. **1641** Milton *Ch. Govt.* Wks. 1738 I. 67 It is neither easeful, profitable, nor praiseworthy in this Life to do evil. **1820** Keats *Ode Nightingale* 52 For many a time I have been half in love with easeful Death. **1886** T. Hardy in *Macm. Mag.* 70 That easeful sense of accomplishment which follows work done that has been a hard struggle in the doing.

2. Unoccupied, at rest; addicted to ease or indolence, slothful, careless.

1611 Cotgr., *Aiser*, to be lazie, easefull. *a* **1618** Raleigh *Seat of Govt.* (1651) 66 Giving the best of their grain to the easefull and idle. **1628** Wither *Brit. Rememb.* iii. 18 The faire smooth way, of easefull Pleasure tends. **1686** J. Crook *Ep. Yng. People prof. Truth* 4 Rest no longer in an easeful mind . . but sink down in deep Humility. **1855** Singleton *Virgil* I. 88 Winter is easeful for the husbandman.

Hence ˈ**easefully** *adv.*, in an easeful manner; comfortably; idly. ˈ**easefulness**, the condition of being easeful.

1611 Cotgr., *Estre en la paille iusques au ventre*, to be fully accommodated, easefully lodged. *a* **1639** W. Whateley *Prototypes* i. xix. (1640) 235 The diligent man takes as much content in his moderate labour, as the sluggard in somnolency and easefulnesse. **1883** *Brit. Q. Rev.* July 15 The exceeding sense of comfort and easefulness. **1886** *Graphic* 27 Feb. 242/1 Standing with her hands on her hips, easefully looking at the preparations on her behalf.

easel (ˈiːzəl, ˈiːz(ə)l). Also 7–8 easle, 8 ezel. [ad. Du *ezel* = Ger. *esel* ass. Cf. the similar use of horse.] A wooden frame to support a picture while the painter is at work upon it; a similar frame used to support a blackboard, etc. (In quot. 1791 a blunder for *palette.*)

1634 J. B[ate] *Myst. Nat.* 119 Provide a frame or Easel called by Artists. **1688** R. Holme *Armoury* iii. 193/1 St. Luke, the Patron of Painters . . is drawn at his Easle working. **1733** Belchier in *Phil. Trans.* XXXVIII. 196 The Trunk of a Skeleton fix'd to a Painter's Ezel. **1791** E. Darwin *Bot. Gard.* i. 7 Many of the unexpected changes in mixing colours on a painter's easle . . may depend on these principles. **1859** Gullick & Timbs *Paint.* 199 The Easel is a frame which supports the painting during its progress.

b. as the typical instrument of a painter.

1838–9 Hallam *Hist. Lit.* I. i. iii. 223 *note*, Some productions of his easel vie with those of Raphael.

Hence ˈ**easeldom** (*nonce-wd.*), painting as a profession; the whole body of painters. **easel-picture, easel-piece**, a picture painted at the easel, or small enough to stand upon it.

1706 *Art of Painting* (1744) 308 He continued working on his easel-pieces. **1841** W. Spalding *Italy & It. Isl.* II. 396 His easel-pictures are perfect models of colouring. **1860** Sala in *Cornh. Mag.* I. 578 This grandee of easeldom.

easeless (ˈiːzlɪs), *a.* [f. ease *sb.* + -less.]

1. Of persons: Having no ease or rest. *rare.*

1632 Vicars *Æneid* ii. 915 Thus as I ceaselesse, easelesse pri'd about, In every nook, furious to finde her out.

2. Of pain or distress: Having no abatement, admitting of no relief.

a **1593** H. Smith *Wks.* (1867) II. 169 It will take from them all pleasure, and bring them to easeless, and yet endless, pain. **1633** Drumm. of Hawth. *Speeches K. Chas.*, Thou becalm'st Mind's easeless anguish. *a* **1770** Whitefield *Serm.* xxxii. Wks. 1772 VI. 10 Easeless and endless misery.

3. Destitute of ease in bearing or manner. *rare.*

1811 *Monthly Mag.* XXXI. 5 It is often accompanied with a punctilious easeless behaviour.

easement (ˈiːzmənt). Also 4 eyse-, 4–5 esement, 5 esmint, -ment, aysyament, (6 hesement), 6–8 eas-, 7 aisment. [a. OF. *aisement*, f. *ais-ier*, ease *v.*: see -ment; cf. Anglo-Lat. *aisiamentum.*]

1. The process or means of giving or obtaining ease or relief from pain, discomfort, or anything annoying or burdensome; relief, alleviation; †redress of grievances. Now somewhat *rare.*

c **1386** Chaucer *Reeve's T.* 259 Some esement has lawe yshapen us. *c* **1400** *Destr. Troy* 7988 We exiled for euermore

our easement to laite. **1583** GOLDING *Calvin on Deut.* xviii. 105 In sted of easement he findeth himself tormented dubble. **1640–9** SIR B. RUDYARD in Rushw. *Hist. Coll.* III. (1692) I. 24 They must..be eased in their Goods, from the exactions..of Pursevants [etc.]..And if the People have all these easements, yet if, etc. **1796** BURKE *Let. noble Ld.* Wks. 1842 II. 260, I certainly stand in need of every kind of relief and easement. **1840** W. HOWITT *Visits Remark. Places* 200 Seeking a little easement of their swollen purses. **1876** BANCROFT *Hist. U.S.* III. ix. 405 He promised its reduction to three shillings in the pound, an easement to the landed interest of five hundred thousand pounds.

†**b.** ***dogs of easement***: dogs employed to take up the chase in place of those that are spent. *Obs.*

1616 SURFL. & MARKH. *Countr. Farm* 692 Then also you must let slip some of your fresh dogs, or dogs of easement.

†**c.** *spec.* The relieving of the body by evacuation of excrement; *concr.*, a privy. Phrases, ***house, stool of easement; to do one's easement.*** *Obs.*

c **1430** *Life St. Kath.* (1884) 43 Schal þey [children] not..make me foule wyth her kyndely esement. **1513** *Bk. Keruynge* in *Babees Bk.* (1868) 283 And se the hous of hesement be swete and clene. **1555** *Fardle Facions* I. v. 51 In the easemente of vrine, the men rowked doune. **1580** HOLLYBAND *Treas. Fr. Tong, Aller à la selle*, to go to the stoole of easement. **1634** HARINGTON *Salernes Regim.* 3 Doing his easement. **1712** DIGBY *Epicurus' Morals* 124 The soldiers..found him in a House of Easement.

†**d.** *spec.* Refreshment by food and repose; hence, comfortable accommodation, food and lodging; 'entertainment for man or beast'. *Obs.*

c **1400** *Ywaine & Gaw.* 3384 He had ful nobil rest, With alkins esment of the best. **1480** CAXTON *Chron. Eng.* clxx. 155 He wold not abyde in scotland in wynter season for esement of his peple. **15..** *Eger & Gr.* 235 in Furniv. *Percy Folio* I. 361 Easment for me and my hackney. **1523** FITZHERB. *Surv.* i. (1539) 5 A place of easement to put in cattel. **1535** STEWART *Cron. Scot.* I. 93 Meit and drink, fyre, claithis and easment. **1820** SCOTT *Monast.* xvi, He might have had less to complain of in respect of easements.

2. Advantage, convenience, comfort; furtherance, assistance; formerly also, gratification, enjoyment. †***common easement***: something done for the public benefit. *arch.* or *Obs.*

c **1400** *Destr. Troy* 3338 A place onestly ordainit for esmint of hir. *c* **1425** WYNTOUN *Cron.* VII. viii. 772 Wyth þare possessyounys and þare Rentis Wyth wont Fredomys and Aysyamentis. *c* **1449** PECOCK *Repr.* I. xx. 120 Into esement of him silf and also of his neiȝbour, a man mai singe, pleie, and lauȝe vertuoseli. **1581** W. STAFFORD *Exam. Compl.* i. (1876) 16 The reparation of such wayes, brydges, and other common easements. **1601** R. JOHNSON *Kingd. & Commw.* (1603) 212 Nature unwilling that humane life should want any easement, hath provided..the labour of cammels. **1791** SMEATON *Edystone L.* §283 To leave our..loose materials, stowed away in the store-room,..was indeed a great easement to us. **1818** SCOTT *Hrt. Midl.* xxxvii, I had the cast of a horse from Ferrybridge—and divers other easements.

b. *concr.* Something that serves for an assistance or convenience; *e.g.* accommodation in or about a house, as rooms, sheds, or farm buildings.

c **1400** MAUNDEV. xix. 214 Schippes..made with Halles & Chambres and other eysementes. **1502** ARNOLDE *Chron.* (1811) 138 Easmentis fixed vnto houses or to soile. **1609** SKENE *Reg. Maj., Act Robt. I*, 26 That nane of them [our subjects] sall..carie..anie kind of armour: or horse, or other aismentis, to the comon enemies of our Realme. **1703** MAUNDRELL *Journ. Jerus.* (1721) 28 Without the assistance of such easements. **1771** SMOLLETT *Humph. Cl.* II. 48 The bills in their houses [in Scotland] say they have different easements to let.

3. The right or privilege of using something not one's own; esp. in *Law.* (See quot.)

1463 *Bury Wills* (1850) 22, I wille the seid Jenete terme of hire lyff haue esement of the kechene to make in hire mete, and esement of the welle in yᵉ yeerd. **1598** KITCHIN *Courts Leet* (1675) 210 A Way or other thing of easement. **1607** COWELL, *Easement*, esamentum, is a seruice that one neighbour hath of another by charter or prescription, without profite, as a way through his ground, or such like. **1876** DIGBY *Real Prop.* iii. 154 If the purposes for which the land of another are used merely tend to the more convenient enjoyment of another piece of land, the right is called an easement.

easer ('iːzə(r)). [f. EASE *v.* + -ER.] One who or that which gives ease or relief. Hence **'easeress.**

1599 GREENE *Alphons.* (1861) 235 Farewell, Medea, easer of my heart. **1610** MARKHAM *Masterp.* I. xcii. 179 This is lenitiue and a great easer of paine. **1631** *Celestina* xii. 136 Easeresse of my paine, and my hearts joy! **1779** JOHNSON *Lett.* (1788) II. ccxxi. 82 The depository of her troubles, and easer of her bosom.

†**'easierly**, *adv. Obs. rare.* Used for *easilier*, comparative degree of EASILY.

1494 FABYAN VI. clxxxvi. 187 He myght the more easyerly optayne the possession. **1661** LOVELL *Hist. Anim. & Min.* 146 The lesser are more moist, easierly concocted.

easily ('iːzɪlɪ), *adv.* Formerly compared **easilier, -est**; also EASIERLY. Forms: 4 aisieliche, eseliche, eesely, eesili, 4–5 esely, esili, esyly, 5–6 easely, 6 easly, easilie, 6– easily. [f. EASY *a.* + -LY².]

1. Comfortably; without pain, discomfort, or anxiety, luxuriously, self-indulgently.

c **1300** *St. Brandan* 395 Ȝe schulle wende, Al eseliche withoute anuy [*MS. Laud* 108, 106 (Halliw.) *has* aisieliche]. *c* **1380** WYCLIF *Wks.* (1880) 20 To disceyue men in gostly goodis and worldly, and norischen hem esily in synne. *c* **1386** CHAUCER *Prol.* 471 Vp on an Amblere esily [*v.r.* esely] she sat. *c* **1440** *York Myst.* xlviii. 298 Belyve ȝe brought me of þe beste And made my bedde full esyly. **1562** *Act 5 Eliz.* xii. §3 Persons seeking only to live easily, and to leave their honest Labour. **1600** SHAKS. *A.Y.L.* III. ii. 339 The one sleepes easily because he cannot study. *Mod.* The patient rested much more easily last night.

2. Without constraint or stiffness; smoothly, freely.

1398 TREVISA *Barth. De P.R.* v. iii, Þis puppis [the hinder part of the brain] is harde þat þe synewis of meuynge meue þe eseloker [**1535** easelier] and þe soner. **1535** COVERDALE *2 Sam.* xx. 8 A swerde..which wente easely out and in. **1599** SHAKS. *Much Ado* v. i. 159 Sir, your wit ambles well; it goes easily. *Mod.* The window-frame fits quite easily.

†**3.** Without hurry; deliberately, gradually. Also, calmly, quietly. *Obs.*

1384 CHAUCER *H. Fame* 1675 That through the worlde her fame goo Esely and not to faste. *c* **1400** *Destr. Troy* 2208 When Priam hade his prologe preched to ende, Ector hym answarede esely and faire. *c* **1440** *Anc. Cookery* in *Househ. Ord.* (1790) 473 Let hit renne thorugh esiliche. **1483** *Vulg. abs Terentio* 7 b, Bere esily thy harme & it shall greue the the lesse. **1611** TOURNEUR *Ath. Trag.* II. iv, I am acquainted with the way..Lets easily walke. **1695** LD. PRESTON *Boeth.* I. 9 She reach'd her Hand easily towards my Breast.

4. a. With little exertion, labour, or difficulty.

c **1384** CHAUCER *H. Fame* 1929 So great a noyse..Men myght hyt have herd esily to Rome. *c* **1400** MAUNDEV. xiv. 160 The poyntes [of these contrefetes] wil breken lightly, and men may esily pollische hem. *c* **1449** PECOCK *Repr.* I. ix. 46 Withoute the clerkis..lay persoones schulen not esili liȝtli and anoon haue the dew vndirstonding of Holi Scripture. **1538** STARKEY *England* II. ii. §12 (1871) 190 By thys mean..the controuersys..schold easelyar be pacyfyd. **1550** VERON *Godly Saiyngs* (1846) 9 Whyche thing we may easly se in the historyes of the olde auncyent Jewes. **1651** HOBBES *Leviath.* I. xiv. 65 Nothing is more easily broken than a mans word. **1718** MOTTEUX *Quix.* (1733) II. 178 Who might easiliest get out of the City. **1878** JEVONS *Prim. Pol. Econ.* 29 It is a..better rule not to put off till tomorrow what we can do more easily to-day.

b. In phrases like ***easily possible, it may easily happen.*** Also ***easily first*** (= beyond question) after L. *facile princeps.*

1590 SWINBURN *Testaments* 145 They are more straung, nor easilie like to happen. **1599** SHAKS. *Much Ado* I. i. 75. **1674** N. FAIRFAX *Bulk & Selv.* 96 We name..things according to what they oftenest or easiliest do seem to us to be. **1871** R. ELLIS *Catullus* xlix. 6 He as easily last among the poets As thou surely the first among the pleaders. **1883** W. BLAIKIE in *Harper's Mag.* Nov. 907/1 Harvard has..easily the finest gymnasium in the world.

5. With little resistance or reluctance.

1649 MILTON *Eikon.* Wks. 1738 I. 392 The House of Peers..gave..easily [their consent]. **1656** RIDGLEY *Pract. Physic* 56 If it come from the Brain it [a Catarrh] afflicteth easily, long and continually. **1711** STEELE *Spect.* No. 153 ¶4 Youth catches Distempers more easily [than Age]. **1715** DESAGULIERS *Fires Impr.* 38 They easily bear with the smothering Heat of Stoves. **1725** DE FOE *Voy. round W.* (1840) 24, I had too easily, and, I may say, too weakly, put that to the vote. **1871** TENNYSON *Last Tourn.* 401 [He] had thought He loved her..wedded easily But left her all as easily.

†**6.** Preceded by *but*: In a listless or indifferent manner; hence, in a trifling degree; with poor success; indifferently, meanly, poorly. *Obs.*

1475 *Bk. Noblesse* 29 Some peple endowed with worldly goodes,..can not depart but easily withe finaunce. **1476** SIR J. PASTON in *Lett.* 776 III. 162 The Frenshe Kynge cheryssheth hyr [Queen Margaret] butt easelye. **1519** HORMAN *Vulg.* 16 Some nonnys kepe theyr virginite but easely. *Ibid.* 34 For lacke of tethe I cham my meate but easily. **1536** *Remed. Sedition* 16 Can they here goddis lawes, ye though they be but easily preached, and not abhorre sedition..?

7. (Made) in such a manner as to be easy.

1599 HAKLUYT *Voy.* II. II. 75 The staires..are so easily made, that one may go them vp and downe a hors-backe.

8. *colloq.* At least (a specified number or time); more than.

1947 *Library Jrnl.* Aug. 1097/2 Easily, a million cards were handled in the process and the difference between that and 100,000 destroyed.

easiness ('iːzɪnɪs). [f. EASY + -NESS.] The state or quality of being EASY (in any of its senses).

1. Freedom from discomfort or anxiety.

1691 RAY *Creation*, The rest and easiness we enjoy when asleep.

2. The quality of being easy in attitude, behaviour, style, etc.

1567 DRANT *Horace's De Arte Poet.* A j, I followe flowinge easynes, my style is clearely marde. **1742** RICHARDSON *Pamela* III. 343 Her Easiness of Behaviour makes him secure of acceptance. *a* **1791** WESLEY *Wks.* (1830) XIII. 378 Perspicuity, purity, propriety, strength and easiness, constitute a good style. **1841** D'ISRAELI *Amen. Lit.* (1867) 551 Virgil..wanting much of that natural easiness of wit that Ovid had.

3. Indolence, carelessness, indifference.

1581 SIDNEY *Def. Poesie* (Arb.) 49 They are full of very idle easines. **1602** SHAKS. *Ham.* v. i. 75. **1699** T. C[OCKMAN] *Tully's Offices* (1706) 207 Ruin'd by his Easiness and Neglect. **1825** *Houlston Tracts* I. xxx. 3 There was no reason for deferring it, but only just his easiness.

4. The quality of not being difficult or burdensome; facility.

1398 TREVISA *Barth. De P.R.* v. lvii. (1495) 172 Many and dyuerse boones ben in the body and that for..easynesse of mouynge. **1581** MARBECK *Bk. of Notes* 727 No man..should with too much easinesse be promoted without witnesses. **1602** SHAKS. *Ham.* III. iv. 166 Refraine to night And that shall lend a kinde of easinesse To the next abstinence. **1616** SURFL. & MARKH. *Countr. Farm* 320 The easinesse of the purchase makes the profit so much the greater. **1800** STUART in *Wellington's Disp.* (1877) 575 Besides easiness of conquest, they would find wealth.

5. The quality of not being harsh or exacting; gentleness, indulgence, kindness.

1483 *Vulg. abs Terentio* 20 a, To holde chylder vndir wyth shame & gentillnes sofnes or esynes. **1611** BEAUM. & FL. *Maid's Trag.* IV. i, Do you raise mirth out of my easiness? **1651** HOBBES *Leviath.* IV. xliv. 347 The Easinesse of our Saviour, in bearing with offences, etc. **1748** BUTLER *Serm.* Wks. 1874 II. 304 That easiness of temper, which..is expressed by the word good-humour. **1862** TRENCH *Mirac.* xxiii. 344 Behind a seeming severity lurks the real love, while under the mask of greater easiness selfishness lies hid.

†**6.** The quality of being easily influenced; in bad sense, credulity; want of firmness, fickleness.

a **1619** DANIEL *Coll. Hist. Eng.* (1626) 35 The King..working vpon the easinesse of his youth, and ambition. **1674** *Ch. & Court of Rome* 12 Persons..who practised upon their easiness. **1705** STANHOPE *Paraphr.* II. 496 The Envy and Spight of the Chief Priests and Pharisees, The Easiness and Fury of the Common People. *a* **1797** H. WALPOLE *Mem. Geo. II*, (1847) III. vii. 174 All made advantage of English easiness and dissipation.

easing ('iːzɪŋ), *vbl. sb.*¹ [f. EASE *v.* + -ING¹.] The action of the verb EASE. Mostly gerundial. Also †***easing-chair***, a nightstool.

1580 HOLLYBAND *Treas. Fr. Tong, Allegeance*, an easing or succouring. **1598** SHAKS. *Merry W.* II. ii. 179 For easing me of the carriage. **1626** BACON *Sylva* §757 The Staying and Easing of the Tooth-ach. **1627** CAPT. SMITH *Seaman's Gram.* xi. 54 The easing of her Masts and Shrouds, for some ships will saile much better when they are slacke. **1718** HICKES & NELSON *J. Kettlewell* II. §40. 149 The Easing and Pleasing many of his Poor Subjects. **1771** SMOLLETT *Humph. Cl.* III. 3 Oct., The doctor..found Frogmore enthroned on an easing-chair. **1823** P. NICHOLSON *Pract. Build.* 195 The taking away of an angle..of the rail..is called by workmen the easings of the rail. **1875** 'STONEHENGE' *Brit. Sports* II. VIII. ii. §1. 649 Easing and starting are of course the exact opposites of each other.

easing ('iːzɪŋ), *vbl. sb.*² *Obs.* exc. *dial.* Forms: 5 esyng, 9 *dial.* yeazin, 6– easing. [contracted form of EAVESING.] = EAVESING 2. Also in *comb.*, as ***easing-drops, -sparrow.***

a **1400–50** *Alexander* 1522 Euen als þe esynges ȝode ouer be þe costez. **1483** *Cath. Angl.* 117 An Esynge, *domicilium, tectum.* **1580** NORTH *Plutarch* 597 He..lay without doors, under the easing of the House. **1611** *Manchester Court Leet Rec.* (1885) II. 267 Anoyed by the water wᶜʰ cometh from the easinge of the howse. **1781** J. HUTTON *Tour Caves* Gloss. (E.D.S.), *Easings*, eaves. **1857** J. SCHOLES *Jaunt* 31 in *Lanc. Gloss.* (E.D.S.), See yo, Tim, hoo sed to me, iv ther is nah o felley peeorcht on th' yeazin's wi' o choilt in his arms. **1881** *Leicestersh. Gloss.* (E.D.S.), *Easings*, eaves, more particularly the eaves of a stack or rick.

easing ('iːzɪŋ), *ppl. a.* [f. EASE *v.* + -ING².] That eases.

a **1665** J. GOODWIN *Filled w. Spirit* (1867) 39 He did it upon lightening and easing circumstances.

easki, early variant of ASK.

†**'easle.** *dial.* Also 1 ysle, 4 his-, huysseles, 5 iselle, isyl, ysyle, 6 *Sc.* isill, 8–9 *Sc.* aizle. [OE. *ysle* (app. wk. fem.), cogn. w. ON. *usli* wk. masc., embers, perh. f. Aryan root *eus to burn, whence L. *ūr-ĕre.* The mod. forms *easle* (17th c. eːz(ə)l), *aizle*, are phonetically anomalous.] Hot ashes or cinders; see quot.

a **1000** *Cædmon's Gen.* 2553 (Gr.) Bearwas wurdon to ascan and to yslan. *a* **1000** ÆLFRIC *Voc.* in Wr.-Wülcker 146 *Fauilla*, ysle. *c* **1325** *Gloss. W. de Biblesw.* in Wright *Voc.* 171 *De falemetches*, from hiseles [*v.r.* huysseles]. *c* **1440** *Promp. Parv.* 266 Isyl of fyre, *fauilla.* *c* **1483** *Cath. Angl.*, Aiselle, *favilla*, or a sperke. **1513** DOUGLAS *Æneis* x. i. 125 Had sytten still, amang the assys cauld And lattyr isillys of thar kynd cuntre. **1691** RAY *N.C. Wds.* Pref. 4 (E.D.S.) We in Essex use Easles for the hot embers (or as it were burning coals) of straw only. **1785** BURNS *Halloween* xiii, She fuff't her pipe wi' sic a lunt..An aizle brunt Her braw new worset apron. **1874** *N. & Q.* 10 Oct. 290 So as to receive and enclose the falling aizle, as well as the wax or tallow of the candle.

Hence †**easle-cake**, a cake baked in the ashes.

c **1440** *Promp. Parv.* 261 Isylkake, or chesekake, or eykake bakyne vndyr askys.

†**easse.** *Obs.* exc. *dial.* Also 9 ease. An earthworm.

1591 PERCIVALL *Sp. Dict.*, *Lombriz*, an easse, an earth worme. **1598** FLORIO, *Lumbrici*, little easses or earth-wormes. *Mod. Devonsh. Dial.*, *Eases*, worms.

'eassel, *adv. Sc.* Also easel, eissel. [f. EAST; the mode of formation is obscure.] Eastward, easterly. Hence **eassel-gate, -ward.**

1810 HOGG *Brownie of Bodsb.* I. 12 (Jam.) The wind being eissel. **1815** SCOTT *Guy M.* i, 'O, if ye get to eassel and wessel again, I am undone.' **1816** —— *Antiq.* I. vii. 162 'Weize yoursell a wee easel-ward.' **1829** —— *Guy M. note* v, Dandie Eassil-gate, Dandie Wassail-gate..had their names from living eastward and westward in the street of the village.

'eassin, *v. Sc.* Also easten, eicen, -sen. [? repr. OE. **œxnian*, **œhsnian*, f. *oxan-*, **ohsan-*, OX; cf. ON. *kýr yxna* 'a cow in heat' (Vigf.).] **a.** Of a cow: To desire the male. **b.** *fig.* To desire strongly. Hence **'eisning** *vbl. sb.*

1661 *Act Chas. II*, vii. 183 (Jam.) Fiftie sex calves, which within three years..would have eicened. **1715** PENNECUIK

Tweeddale 15 (Jam.) The country people call this plant.. Eastning wort, which they affirm makes cows come to bulling. *a* **1774** FERGUSSON *Poems* (1789) II. 42 (Jam.) Ye'll weet mony a drouthy mou', That's lang a eisning gane for you, Withouten fill, O' dribles frae the gude brown cow.

east (iːst), *adv.*, *sb.* and *a.* Forms: α. 1 **éastan** (*Northumb.* **éasta**), 3-4 **esten**. β. 1-2 **éast**, 2-5 **est**, 3 **æst**, (4 **yeast**), 4-5 **este**, 4-6 **easte**, **eest**, 6 *Sc.* **eist**, 3- **east**. [repr. two distinct forms in OE., both of which occur only as adv. or in composition. (1) OE. *éastan* = OS. *ôstan*(*a* (Du. *oost*), OHG. *ôstana*, (MHG. *ôsten*(*e*, mod.G. *osten*), ON. *austan*:—OTeut. **aus-to-nô* 'from the east', f. base **aus-* dawn (found in L. *aurōra*:—**ausōsa*, Lith. *auszrà*, Skr. *ushās* dawn, Gr. *αὔριον*:—**αὔσριον* morning) + double suffix, as in OE. *hin-da-n* from behind. (2) OE. *éast*, in compounds repr. OTeut. **aus-to-* (see above), but as adv. perh. shortened from **éaster* 'toward the east' = OS., OHG. *ôstar* (Du. *ooster-* in compounds), ON. *austr* advbs.:—OTeut. **aus-tr-*, f. **aus-* + suffix, as in OE. *hinder* backwards; cf. ON. *austr* sb. masc. (gen. *austrs*), Goth. **Austragutôs* Ostrogoths. A trace of the lost OE. **éaster* appears in the adj. (compar.) *éasterra* more easterly; also in certain place-names, as *Eastoreȝe*, Eastry; cf. 'Alduulfus rex Estranglorum' Bæda *H.E.* IV. xvii.

As a nautical term the Eng. word has been adopted into Romanic langs.: Fr., It. *est*, Sp., Pg. *este*, Pg. also *leste*.]

A. *adv.*

†**I. 1.** [repr. OE. *éastan*.] From the east. Also in OE. *bi éastan*, ME. *bi esten* eastward; sometimes as prep. with dat. = eastward *of*. Comb. **eastan-wind**: see EAST-WIND.

c **893** K. ÆLFRED *Oros.* I. i. §12 Be eastan Rine sindon Eastfrancan. *a* **1000** *Cædmon's Gen.* 806 (Gr.) Ȝif wind cymþ westan oððe eastan. *a* **1225** *Ancr. R.* 232 'Bihold,' cweð [he] bi esten. *c* **1330** R. BRUNNE *Chron. Langt.* (1725) 5 Grete taliage laid he þeron bi Esten.

II. [repr. OE. *éast*.]

2. a. With reference to motion or position: In the direction of the part of the horizon where the sun rises. More definitely: In the direction of that point of the horizon which is 90° to the right of the north point; also *due* (†*full*) *east*.

c **890** K. ÆLFRED *Bæda* I. iii. (Bosw.) Ðæt ealond on Wiht is þrittiȝes mila lang east and west. *a* **1000** *Boeth. Metr.* xiii. 59 (Gr.) Sio sunne.. norð eft and east Eldum oðeweð. *c* **1200** ORMIN 7270 We sæȝhenn æst in ure lond þiss newe kingess sterrne. **1250** LAY. 23223 Ferden heo æst ferden heo west. **1473** WARKW. *Chron.* (1839) 22 It [a comet] arose ester and ester, till it arose full este. **1526** *Pilgr. Perf.* (W. de W. 1531) 35 b, Where it weneth to go est, it gothe west. **1562** J. HEYWOOD *Prov. & Epigr.* (1867) 41 Alwaie the longe east the shorter west. **1611** BIBLE *Gen.* xiii. 11 Lot iourneyed East. **1828** J. H. MOORE *Pract. Navig.* (ed. 20) 144 If the place be any distance east or west of Greenwich. **1832** *Act 2 & 3 Will. IV*, lxiv. Sched. O. 38 A straight line drawn due east to a point one hundred yards distant.

b. *about east*: in U.S. slang 'regularly', in proper style, as it should be.

a **1860** H. BIGELOW *Lett.* in *Family Comp.* (Bartlett), I did walk into the beef and 'taters and things about east. **1864** LOWELL *Biglow P.* Wks. (1879) 231 To find out what was about east and to shape his course accordingly.

3. quasi-*sb.* Preceded by prep. *from*, *on*, etc.

c **1200** ORMIN 11258 All þiss middellærd iss ec O fowwre daless dæledd Onn Est, o Wesst, o Suþ, o Norþ. *a* **1240** *Sawles Warde* in *Cott. Hom.* 265 As swifte as þe sunne gleam þe scheot from est into west. *a* **1300** *Cursor M.* 2212 Fra est he broght a felauscap vnto þe feld of sennar.

B. *sb.*

1. a. subst. use of A. 2. The portion of the horizon or of the sky near the place of the sun's rising. More definitely, that one of the cardinal points near which the sun rises.

c **1180** *Newminster Cartul.* (1878) 118 Versus le Est. *c* **1200** *St. Brandan* 35 Towards than Est so fur we wende. **1340** *Ayenb.* 124 Sleȝþe: hit wereþ wyþ þet yeast be poruenynge aye þe perils. *c* **1440** *Promp. Parv.* 143 Est, *oriens*. **1535** COVERDALE *Ezek.* viii. 16 Fyue and twenty men.. turned.. their faces towarde the easte. **1599** SHAKS. *Much Ado* v. iii. 27 The gentle day.. Dapples the drowsie East with spots of grey. **1655** H. VAUGHAN *Silex Scint.* I. 65 Herbs sleep unto the East. **1732** POPE *Ep. Cobham* 64 The Wind just shifted from the East. **1850** TENNYSON *In Mem.* xcv, And East and West.. Mixt their dim lights.. To broaden into boundless day.

b. *to the east* (*of*): (situated) in an eastward direction (from).

1778 ROBERTSON *Hist. Amer.* I. 431 If the countries.. had been situate to the east of those whose longitude mariners had ascertained. *Mod.* Barking is 7 miles to the east of London.

2. a. The eastern part of the world, the orient; the eastern part of a country, district, or town.

a **1300** *Cursor M.* 3384 Þai held.. þe landes þat war tilward þe est. *c* **1380** WYCLIF *Serm.* Sel. Wks. I. 339 Þre kingis camen afer out of þe eest. **1482** CAXTON *Chron. Eng.* xxii. 21 The real wey from the eest in to the west was called watling strete. **1535** COVERDALE *Ezek.* xxv. 4, I will delyuer yᵉ to the people of the east. **1667** MILTON *P.L.* II. 3 Where the gorgeous East.. Showrs on her Kings Barbaric Pearl. **1732** BERKELEY *Alciphr.* vi. §27 There was a general expectation in the east of a Messiah. **1853** ROBERTSON *Serm.* Ser. III. iii. (1872) 38 In the same East, men take off their sandals in devotion.

b. The states of eastern Europe; the Communist powers. Freq. *attrib.* and appositively with *west* (or *West*).

1951 *Ann. Reg. 1950* III. 188 There were more 'espionage' convictions.. and the closing of the Czech Consulate-General in New York. These incidents, significant of the growing estrangement of East and West, were also.. evidence that neither party wished to push its claims to the limit. **1959** *Daily Tel.* 10 Mar. 1/5 Russia had been told her proposals could not be accepted because there was no trust between East and West. **1959** *News Chron.* 5 Aug. 4/2 The harsh reality of the cold war, of East-West tension. **1959** *Manch. Guardian* 11 Aug. 7/4 East-West experts agreed.. on the feasibility of detecting tests in the outer orbit. **1968** K. MARTIN *Editor* xv. 318 It would be very difficult to maintain an objective view of East/West relations.

3. = EAST-WIND.

a **1763** SHENSTONE *Elegies* xx. 12 Where the sharp east for ever.. blows. **1785** COWPER *Task* IV. 363 The unhealthful East, That.. searches every bone Of the infirm. **1864** BRYANT *Return of Birds* iv, The blustering East shall blow.

4. *Bridge.* (With capital initial.) The player sitting opposite 'West'.

1926 *Auction Bridge Mag.* Aug. 126/2 West and North passed, and East doubled. *Ibid.*, East's top cards are all sure tricks. *Ibid.*, East is justified in expecting to set South at least one trick. **1929** *Bridge World* Oct. 7/1 The Five Spade bid by East is very good. **1958** *Listener* 2 Oct. 541/2 East had been able to recognise his plan.

C. as *adj.* That is situated in or adjacent to the eastern part of anything; that is towards the east; oriental, easterly. Formerly often used where *eastern* would now generally be preferred.

The adjectival use of the word arises from the analysis of compounds like OE. *éast-dǽl* (see D. 1), the first element of which, having a virtually adjectival force, came to be regarded as a separable word.

c **1175** *Lamb. Hom.* 5 [Christ] rad in et þan est ȝete þere burh. **1297** R. GLOUC. (1810) 2 Temese by the Est syde. *a* **1300** *Cursor M.* 11395 A folk.. Wonnand be þe est occean. *c* **1400** MAUNDEV. xiv. 156 Ethiope is departed.. in the Est partie, and in the Meridionelle partie. **1413** LYDG. *Pylgr. Sowle* v. xiv. 81 The sonne.. hastyd hym vpward toward the eest oryson. **1593** HOOKER *Eccl. Pol.* IV. xi, The East and West Churches. **1642** FULLER *Holy & Prof. St.* III. vii. 167 An East window welcomes the infant beams of the Sun. **1693** EVELYN *Compl. Gard.* I. 30 There are four sorts of Expositions, the East, the West, the South and the North.

D. In Combination.

1. a. Combined with sb., as in †**east-deal**, eastern part; †**east-half** [cf. ON. *austr-halfr*], eastern or easterly side; †**east-man** (see quot.); **east-sea**, a sea on the east side of a country, or in an eastern region of the world; formerly also as the proper name of the Baltic [= Ger. *Ostsee*]. See also EAST-COUNTRY, -END, -LAND, -WIND, ESTRICHE. (The combs. of this class still in use are now commonly written without hyphen, and *east* regarded as an adj.)

c **1000** *Ags. Gosp.* Matt. ii. 2 We ȝe-sawon hys steorran on *east-dæle. *c* **1200** ORMIN 16400 Æstdale off all þiss werelld iss Anatole ȝehatenn. *a* **1300** *E.E. Psalter* cii[i]. 12 How mikle estdel stand westdel fra. **898** *O.E. Chron.* an. 894 Ðæm monnum þe on *east healfe þære e wicodon. *c* **1200** ORMIN 3430 He sette a steorrne upp o þe lifft.. Onn æst hallf off þiss middellærd. *c* **1400** *Destr. Troy* 10581 He grauntid þo grete a graunt for to haue In the entre of the est halfe. **1610** HOLLAND *Camden's Brit.* II. 68 The Oustmans, as one would say Esterlings or *Eastmen, came out of.. Germanie into Ireland. *c* **890** K. ÆLFRED *Bæda* I. xii, Fram *east sæ oþ wæst sæ. *c* **1305** *St. Kenelm* 18 in *E.E.P.* (1862) 48 Temese [goþ] into þe est see. **1710** *Lond. Gaz.* No. 4669/3 A Danish Frigot arrived from the East-Sea.

b. Prefixed to names of countries or districts, usually with sense 'eastern portion of...', as in *East Germany*, *East London*; often forming the recognized name of a political or administrative division, as *East Prussia*, *East Derbyshire*. Also prefixed to adjs. of territorial signification, as *East-midland*, *East-central*; and to names of peoples, as *East-Goths* (= *Ostrogoths*), *East-Franks*. ***East Coast fever***, in East and South Africa, a disease of cattle caused by a protozoan organism (*Theileria*) and transmitted by ticks.

898 *O.E. Chron.* an. 894 Norþhymbre and Eastengle hæfdon aþas ȝesealde. **1513–75** *Diurn. Occurr.* (1833) 40 Vpoun the xxvj day of September, the Homes wan eist-Nisbet. **1561** DAUS tr. *Bullinger on Apoc.* (1573) 196 The Eastgothes & Lumbardes, obtained Italy. **1817** *Edin. Rev.* XXIX. 49 The East-insular tribes have a chivalrous abhorrence of.. personal abuse. **1841** W. SPALDING *Italy & It. Isl.* II. 55 The East-Goths had a strongly monarchical constitution. **1904** A. THEILER in *Rep. S. Afr. Assoc. Advancem. Sci.* 203 The disease was originally called Rhodesian Redwater... An improvement in the nomenclature was the words Rhodesian Tick Fever: a still better name is East Coast Fever. **1955** J. H. WELLINGTON *Southern Africa* II. I. v. 79 *East Coast fever*, or 'African Coast fever', a very virulent and highly fatal form of piroplasmosis.

2. With ppl. adj., as †***east-surprised***; **east-bound**, eastward bound (chiefly in America of railway traffic); also *ellipt.*

1599 NASHE *Lent. Stuffe* (1871) 29 By the proportion of the east-surprised Gades.. diuers have tried.. to configurate a twin-like image of it. **1881** *Chicago Times* 12 Mar., The east-bound express was held at North Platte. **1882** *Times* 22 Mar. 5/3 East bound freight rates. **1909** R. A. WASON *Happy Hawkins* 222 This time the west-bound had to take a sidin' and wait twenty minutes for the east-bound. **1948** H. DRAKE-BROCKMAN in B. James *Austral. Short Stories* (1963) 111 The east-bound was on the way towards Wallu.

3. ***east-south-east***, ***east-north-east***: the points of the compass distant $22\frac{1}{2}°$ from due East; ***east-by-south***, ***east-by-north***: the points distant $11\frac{1}{4}°$ from due East. Used as sb., adj., and adv.

1555 EDEN *Decades W. Ind.* I. VI. (Arb.) 87 An Eastsoutheaste wynde arose. **1594** DAVIS *Seaman's Secr.* (1607) 14 East and by north raiseth a degree in sailing 102 leagues and a mile. **1713** *Lond. Gaz.* No. 5141/3 A Sand lies almost East and by South, half Southerly from the Spurn Light. **1725** DE FOE *Voy. round W.* (1840) 84 We.. then stood away east, and east-by-north. *Ibid.* 302 [We] stood away.. east-north-east. *Ibid.* 335 A much larger river.. which.. ran east-by-south towards the sea. **1742** WOODROOFE in Hanway *Trav.* (1762) I. II. xxiii. 98 A light breeze springing up at east south east, we weighed. **1849** DANA *Geol.* ix. (1850) 489 The course of a fissure is east-by-north.

east (iːst), *v.* [f. prec.] **a.** *intr.* To move, turn, or veer towards the east. Cf. EASTING *vbl. sb.* **b.** *refl.* To orientate, find out one's true position.

1858 O. BROWNSON *Wks.* V. 202 He must make many a turning.. before he can east himself.

east-about, *adv. U.S.* [Cf. *west-about*, WEST *adv.* E. b.] In an easterly direction.

1886 *Sci. Amer.* 2 Jan. 7/1 The cause, whatever it was, gradually spread, moving east-about.

'East-ˌcountry. An eastern country: in 18th c. applied *spec.* to the region of the Baltic; cf. EASTLAND, ESTRICHE. Also *attrib.*

1701 J. LAW *Counc. Trade* (1751) 141 Since by them they will be capable of receiving corn in the east-countrys. **1709** *Lond. Gaz.* No. 4604/4 Will be exposed to publick Sale.. about 730 Quarters of East-Country Wheat. **1710** *Ibid.* No. 4708/4 Inquire at the Works, or Royal Exchange East Country-Walk in Exchange Time. **1719** W. WOOD *Surv. Trade* 120 Our Trade to the East Indies and East Country is as free to us as ever.

†**eastee-man.**

1681 E. WHITAKER *Ignoramus Just.* 18 To turn Informer, Promoter, or Eastee-man, unless in case of a Riot, or such like, the Constable can do no such thing but at his own Peril.

†**'easten**, *a. Obs.* Forms: 3 **æsten**, 6 *Sc.* **estin**. [f. EAST + -EN; cf. NORTHEN. In quot. 1205 the reading *æsterne* (EASTERN) has been suggested; in quot. 1549 the word may possibly represent OE. *éastan*: see EAST.] **a.** Belonging to Eastern countries: **b.** Coming from the east; easterly.

c **1205** LAY. 27393 Eorles and dukes eke of æstene weorlde. **1549** *Compl. Scot.* vi. (1872) 61 The.. cardinal vynd callit subsolanus.. quhilk the vulgaris callis estin vynd.

'East-'end. The easterly extremity of anything. In mod. use often *spec.* the eastern part of London. Hence **ˌEast-'ender**, an inhabitant of the East End.

O.E. Chron. an. 893 Se muþa is.. æt þæs miclan wuda east ende þe we Andred hatað. *c* **1205** LAY. 28305 Þæ wind him gon wende, & stod of þan æst ende. *a* **1300** *Cursor M.* 1251 Toward þe est end of þis dale. **1846** R. FORD *Gatherings from Spain* xxi. 297 Our East end tailors' pattern-book of the last new fashion. **1867** *Punch* 23 Nov. 216 In the regions of sport and of money, In the circles of East-end and West. **1883** BLACK *Shandon Bells* xxix, What we are doing in the East-end. **1884** *Pall Mall G.* 14 Aug. 11/1 The stereotyped East-ender of London. **1886** *Ibid.* 28 Apr. 1/1 The East-enders have several advantages.. over the West-enders.

Easter ('iːstə(r)), *sb.*[1] Forms: 1 (as pl.) **éastron**, **-un**, **-an**, **-u**, **-o**, *Northumb.* **éastro**, **éostro**, **éostru**; (as sing.) **éastre**, *Northumb.* **éostro**; genit. (as pl.) **eastreno**, **-ana**, **eastra**; (as sing.) **éastran**, *Northumb.* **éastres**, **éostres**; 2 **eastran**, **eastren**, 3, 5 **eastre**, 3-6 **esterne**, 4-6 **ester**, (4 **hestern**), 5 **aster**(**e**, **estren**(**e**, **eesterne**, **estryn**, 6 **estur**, 6- **easter**. [OE. *éastre* wk. fem. = OHG. *ôstara*; more freq. in plural *éastron*, corresponding to OHG. *ôstoron* (MHG., mod.G. *ostern* pl.); the strong forms occas. appearing seem to have been derived from the combining form *éastor-*. Bæda *Temp. Rat.* xv. derives the word from *Eostre* (Northumb. spelling of *Éastre*), the name of a goddess whose festival was celebrated at the vernal equinox; her name (:—OTeut. **austrôn*- cogn. w. Skr. *usrā* dawn; see EAST) shows that she was originally the dawn-goddess.]

1. a. One of the great festivals of the Christian Church, commemorating the resurrection of Christ, and corresponding to the Jewish passover, the name of which it bears in most of the European langs. (Gr. *πασχά*, ad. Heb. *pésaḥ*, L. *pascha*, Fr. *Pâques*, It. *Pasqua*, Sp. *Pascua*, Du. *pask*). According to the modern rule it is observed on the first Sunday after the calendar full moon—i.e. 'not the actual full moon, but the 14th day of the calendar moon' (Bp. Butcher)—which happens on or next after 21 March. In ordinary language *Easter* is often applied to the entire week commencing with Easter Sunday.

c **890** K. ÆLFRED *Bæda* v. xxi. Ic ðas tide Eastrena ecelice healdan wille. *c* **1050** *Ags. Gloss.* in Wr.-Wülcker 471 *Phase*, eastran. *a* **1123** *O.E. Chron.* an. 1101 Heold se cyng Heanrig

his hired..to Eastran on Winceastre. *c* **1200** *Trin. Coll. Hom.* 101 þe þre dage biforen estre [ben] cleped swidages. *c* **1250** *Gen. & Ex.* 3288 Ðor-of in esterne be we wunen Seuene siðes to funt cumen. *c* **1300** *St. Brandan* 148 Ther ȝe shulle this Ester beo. **1389** in *Eng. Gilds* (1870) 35 þe soneday fourtnythe after esterne. *c* **1420** *Chron. Vilod.* 785 þis miracle was þus..y do, In þe Astere nexste after hurre body dyenge. *c* **1440** *Promp. Parv.* 143 Esterne, *Pascha.* **1450–1530** *Myrr. Our Ladye* 278 From passyon Sonday tyl Esterne. **1480** CAXTON *Chron. Eng.* ccxxxiii. 254 The clergye..wold not graunte vnto Estre next comyng. **1593** HOOKER *Eccl. Pol.* IV. xi, Keeping the feast of Easter on the same day the Jews kept theirs. **1655** FULLER *Ch. Hist.* II. 55 The Springtime, wherein the Feast of Easter..was celebrated. **1782** PRIESTLEY *Corrupt. Chr.* II. VIII. 129 The first..festival..that was observed..was Easter. **1837** HOWITT *Rur. Life* VI. iv. (1862) 432 Easter was the great festival of the Church.

b. R.C. Ch. *to make* (†*do*) *one's Easter* (see MAKE *v.* 57 e): to perform one's Easter duties (see below). Hence *Easter* is used for an individual performance of these.

1700 T. MARWOOD *Diary* 8 Apr. in *Cath. Rec. Soc. Publ.* (1909) VII. 62, I was at St Gomars & Saw ye Quire do their Easter. *Ibid.* 11 Apr., I was at my Easter at St Gomars. **1885** E. H. DERING *Lady of Raven's Combe* I. ii. 20 Mick..is..very happy about everything, when he has made his Easter. **1892** *Month* May 37 Taking in those who have made their Easters at Melior St...we may count the Easters as 2000.

†**2.** The Jewish passover. *Obs.*

971 *Blickl. Hom.* 67 Hælend cwom syx daʒum ær Iudea eastron. *c* **1000** *Ags. Gosp.* Mark xiv. 1 Æfter twam daʒum wæron eastron. **1398** TREVISA *Barth. De P.R.* IX. xxxi. (1495) 366 Ester is callyd in Ebrewe Phase, that is passynge other passage. **1535** COVERDALE *Ezek.* xlv. 21 Vpon ye xiiij. daye of the first moneth ye shal kepe Easter. **1563** *Homilies* II. *Whitsunday* I. (1859) 453 Easter, a great, and solemne feast among the Jews. **1611** BIBLE *Acts* xii. 4 Intending after Easter to bring him foorth.

3. *Comb.* and *attrib.*

a. Obvious combinations: in sense 1, as ***easter-festival, -gambols, -holidays, -lamb*** (see also b), ***-morning,*** †***-morrow,*** †***-pence, -Sunday*** (***-Monday, -Tuesday***, etc.).

c **1380** WYCLIF *Serm.* Sel. Wks. II. 133 On Eester monedai. **1460** in *Pol. Rel. & L. Poems* (1866) 249 He ros on estryn morwe. **1517** TORKINGTON *Pilgr.* (1884) 66 Ther we a bode..Ester evyn, Ester Day, And also Ester munday..Ester Tewysday..we Departyd. **1676** MARVELL *Mr. Smirke* Wks. 1875 IV. 11 [Some] would..have ventur'd their coffer-farthing, yea their Easter-pence by advance. **1722** *Lond. Gaz.* No. 6052/1 The Easter-Holidays having passed. **1815** SCOTT *Ld. of Isles* III. xxviii, How there the Easter gambols pass. **1826** in Cobbett *Rur. Rides* II. 193 The house-lambs and the early Easter-lambs.

b. Special combs., as **Easter-book**, an account-book for recording easter-dues; **Easter bunny** chiefly *U.S.*: in popular folklore, a rabbit (symbolizing fertility) said to bring gifts of Easter eggs to children at Easter; a representation of this; **Easter-dues**, money payable at Easter to the parson of a parish by the parishioners; **Easter duty** (or **duties**), the religious duties (viz. of confession and communion) obligatory at Eastertide; **Easter-eggs**, eggs painted in bright colours, which it was (and, by a partial revival, still is) customary to present to friends at Easter (= PACE-EGGS); now chiefly, egg-shaped forms of confectionery presented at Easter; **Easter-eve**, †**-even**, the evening, and hence the day, before Easter-Sunday; †**Easter-lamb**, the paschal lamb; **Easter lily**, any of several species of (white) lily, or other spring-flowering plant (chiefly *U.S.*); **Easter-offering** = *Easter-dues*; formerly also used for the paschal sacrifice; **Easter Parade**: see PARADE *sb.* 3 c; **Easter sitting(s** = *Easter term* (a); †**Easter-supper**, the passover; **Easter-taper** [L. *cereus paschalis*], a taper used in church ceremonies at Easter; **Easter term**, (*a*) a term in the law-courts formerly movable and falling between Easter and Whitsuntide, now fixed within a certain period each year; (*b*) in the older universities, a term which was kept formerly between Easter and Whitsuntide, but which is now included in the Trinity term; in some universities and schools, the term between Christmas and Easter; **Eastertide, time**, the church season of Easter, either Easter Sunday, or the Sunday with the following days until Ascensiontide; **Easter week**, the week beginning with Easter Sunday. Also EASTER-DAY.

1546 *Mem. Ripon* (Surtees) III. 10 Item the *Easter Booke communibus Annis, lxvjs. viijd. **1642** FULLER *Holy & Prof. St.* III. xxv. 229 Necessity will..make him study his Easter-book more then all other Writers. **1909** *St. Nicholas* Apr. 548 (*title*) The *Easter bunny. **1922** *Child Life* Apr. 225/1 It was Easter Eve. The Easter Bunny with his basket of eggs, was on his way home across the fields to wherever he lives, singing to himself. **1957** T. STURGEON *Thunder & Roses* 206 A child's implicit belief in Santa Claus and the Easter Bunny. **1983** *Times* 26 Aug. 1/3 The last time he recalled seeing Miss Honegger was when she was dressed up as an Easter bunny in the White House Easter egg roll. **1720** in *Jrnl. Derbysh. Archæol. Soc.* (1905) XXVII. 215 *Easter dues I. 11. 0. **1848** in J. T. Bunce *Old St. Martin's, B'ham* (1875) 35 Easter dues 4*d.* for a man and his wife, and 4*d.* for each single person above the age of 16, and 2*d.* from each housekeeper. **1723** S. LL. *Gen. Instruct. Hist. & Tenets Relig.* II. v. 256 What Punishments hath the Church decreed against those who have not perform'd their *Easter Duty? **1809** J. MILNER in F. C. Husenbeth *Life* (1862) viii. 166 To be particularly anxious that all should make their Easter duty. **1804** M. WILMOT *Let.* 11 May in *Russian Jrnls.* (1934) I. 97, I must not forget Easter Sunday..the service is the same, and after it is over *Easter Eggs are presented painted and carv'd and decorated in a variety of ways. **1825** HONE *Every-day Bk.* I. 426 *Easter Eggs*..pass about at Easter week under the name of *pask, paste*, or *pace* eggs. **1894** G. DU MAURIER *Trilby* I. I. 34 They would..marvel at the beautiful assortment of bonbons..especially, at this particular time of the year, the monstrous Easter-egg, of enchanting hue. **1949** A. HUXLEY *Let.* 6 Mar. (1969) 594, I am enclosing an Easter egg. *c* **1200** *Trin. Coll. Hom.* 95 On *estereuen gon abuten þe fantston. **1594** HOOKER *Eccl. Pol.* v. (1617) 391 That one Sabboth or Saturday which falleth out to bee the Easter-eue. **1598** HAKLUYT *Voy.* I. 66 Vpon Easter even we were called vnto the tent. **1535** COVERDALE *1 Esdr.* vii. 10 They that came out of captiuyte, kylled the *easter lambe. **1587** GOLDING *De Mornay* xxx. 481 Jesus the true Easterlamb. **1877** BARTLETT *Dict. Amer.* (ed. 4) The Calla is frequently called the *Easter Lily. **1894** *Jrnl. Amer. Folk-Lore* VII. 101 *Zephyranthes Atamasco*,..Easter lily. **1896** T. W. SANDERS *Encycl. Gardening* (ed. 2) 206 Lilium..Bermuda Easter Lily. **1909** WEBSTER 693/2 *Easter lily. a.* The Annunciation lily (*Lilium candidum*). *b.* A large-flowered and early forcing variety..of the common trumpet lily (*Lilium longiflorum*). **1932** *Discovery* Aug. 256/2 The Easter lily,..the royal lily, and the leopard or tiger lily of California. **1387** TREVISA *Higden* (Rolls) II. 339 Iosue offrede þe *Ester offrynge. **1818** BENTHAM *Ch. Eng.* 422 Were it only by Easter-offerings. **1875** *Act 38 & 39 Vict.* c. 77. Sched. I. Order lxi, The *Easter sittings shall commence on the Tuesday after Easter week and terminate on the Friday before Whitsunday. **1910** *Law Times* 9 Apr. 509/2 On Tuesday last the Easter Sittings commenced with 145 appeals and 1514 causes awaiting hearing. **1913** HALSBURY et al. *Laws Eng.* XXVII. 436 The third, Easter sitting. **1548** UDALL, etc. *Erasm. Par. Mark* xiv. 15 There prepare you for vs our *easter souper. **1848** *Secret Soc. Mid. Ages* 361 The bone..he had filled with the wax of an *Easter-taper, and with incense. **1603** J. STOW *Survey of London* (ed. 2), *Of towers & castles*, *Easter tearme beginneth not afore xvii. dayes after Easter. **1641** G. CAVENDISH *Negotiations Cdl. Woolsey* xi. 30 Untill such time as the Cardinall resorted thither to him, where after Easter terme was ended, he kept his feast of Whitsontide. **1672** COWELL *Interpr.* s.v. *Terme, Terminus Paschae*, Easter term, which begins the Wednesday fortnight after Easter-day, and ends the Monday next after Ascension-day. **1728** CHAMBERS *Cycl.* s.v. *Term*, Oxford Terms... Easter-term begins the 10th day after Easter, and ends the Thursday before Whitsunday. Cambridge Terms... Easter-term begins the Wednesday after Easter-week, and ends the week before Whitsunday. **1818** CRUISE *Digest* II. 477 The fine levied..in Easter term 1697. **1905** H. A. VACHELL *Hill* viii, Racquets, the chief game in the Easter term. **1930** *Law Times* 26 Apr. 373 The Easter Law Term will commence on ..the 29th April, and will end on..the 26th May. *c* **1000** ÆLFRIC *Hom.* I. 312 Nu is his ðrowung and his ærist ure *Easter-tid. *c* **1440** *Prose St. Brandan* (Percy) 39 A place lyke Paradyse wherein they shold kepe theyr Eestertyde. **1856** SMYTTAN *Hymn*, '*Forty days*' vi, That with thee we may appear At the eternal Eastertide. **1868** MORRIS *Earthly Par.* II. 213 If one chanced to fare Into that place at Easter-tide. **1885** *Manch. Exam.* 6 Apr. 5/2 The weather this Eastertide is bright. **14..** *Gesta Rom.* lxii. 266 (Add. MS.) Our Lord Jhesu Crist, the whiche many desire for to norisshe, and namly in *Esterne tyme. **1579** L. VAUX *Catech.* f. 77 Euery man and woman..should receiue the blessed Sacrament at Easter time. **1849** M. ARNOLD *Strayed Reveller* 104 'Twill be Easter-time in the world. *c* **1000** *Ags. Gosp.* John xx. i. *rubric*, Ðys sceal on sæternes dæʒ on þære *easter wucan. *c* **1406** in G. R. OWST *Preaching Med. Eng.* (1926) i. 23 At Seint Marie Spitel, in Estir Weke. **1549** *Bk. Com. Prayer* 54 b, Tewesdaye in Easter weke. *a* **1558** G. CAVENDISH *Wolsey* (1959) 133 The thursday in Ester weke. *a* **1670** S. COLLINS *Pres. State Russia* (1671) 18 In the Easter week all his Majesties Servants and Nobility kiss the Patriarchs Hand, and receive either gilded, or red Eggs. **1728** [see *Easter term*]. *a* **1773** A. BUTLER *Moveable Feasts & Fasts Cath. Ch.* (1839) viii. 233 Every day during Easter week. **1884** ADDIS & ARNOLD *Cath. Dict.* 285/1 Down to the twelfth century each day in Easter week was a holiday of obligation.

easter, *sb.*² *dial.* Forms: 6 **astire**, 9 **ester**, 7– **easter.** See also ASTRE. [a. OF. *aistre, astre* (mod.F. *âtre*) hearth.] (See quot.)

1541 *Schole-house of Women* in Hazlitt *E.P.P.* IV. 129 Bad her take the pot..set it abooue upon the astire. **1674** RAY *N.C. Wds.*, *Easter*, the back of the chimney or chimney stock. **1848** A. B. *Leicestershire Wds.*, *Ester*, back of the fire-place. 'My hay..is as black as the Ester.'

†**'easter**, *a. Obs.* Also 4 **ester**, 6 *Sc.* **eister.** [perh. comparative of EAST *a.* (OE. had *éasterra*); possibly suggested by Du. *ooster-* in compounds.] Nearest the east; eastern (part of a country, a building, etc.). Also in comb., as ***easter-board.***

1387 TREVISA *Higden* (1865) I. 257 Boemya is þe firste prouince of þat ester Germania. **1513–75** *Diurn. Occurr.* (1833) 29 James Colvillis sone [was restoirit] to his landis of eister Weymes. **1591** HARINGTON tr. *Ariosto's Orl. Fur.* XXIII. vi, The dawning brake, and all the Easter parts were full of light. **1622** R. HAWKINS *Voy. S. Sea* (1847) 117 This bay is all sandie and cleane ground on the easter part. *Ibid.* 135 One evening, being calme, and a goodly cleare in the easter-boord, I willed our anchor to be weyed. **1708** *Lond. Gaz.* No. 4430/4 The Town of Anstruther-Easter. **1777** WATSON *Philip II* (1793) I. x. 448 Covering it from north to south, that is, from the Easter to the Wester Scheld, with water. **1816** SCOTT *Old Mort.* x, He's keeping guard o'er Milnwood in the easter round of the tower.

'Easter-'day. For forms see EASTER. [OE. *éastor-dæʒ*, f. *éastor-* combining form of *éastron*, EASTER; some of the ME. and early mod. forms are f. the genit. or nom.] Easter Sunday.

c **1175** *Lamb. Hom.* 45 Uwilc sunne-dei is to locan alswa ester dei. *c* **1200** *Trin. Coll. Hom.* 61 Forte þene þuresdai biforen estrene dai. *Ibid.* 99 þis dai is cleped estre dai. **1398** TREVISA *Barth. De P.R.* IX. xxxi. (1495) 367 Eester daye is tyme of gladnesse. **1447** BOKENHAM *Seyntys* (1835) 180 On esterne day next folwyng. **1480** CAXTON *Descr. Brit.* 29 He helde vnlawfully esterday. **1517** TORKINGTON *Pilgr.* (1884) 53 He sawe..Criste rysen vpon Estern Day. *a* **1641** SUCKLING *Ballad Wedding* Poems (1648) 38 No sun upon an Easter day Is half so fine a sight.

'eastering, *ppl. a. rare.* [? f. EASTER *a.* + -ING²; cf. *westering.*] Shifting eastward.

1876 MORRIS *Sigurd* III. 202 As the eastering wind shall lead.

easterliness ('iːstəlɪnɪs). [f. EASTERLY *a.*² + -NESS.] Easterly quality or condition.

1927 J. ADAMS *Errors in School* 222 Each of them has acquired an absolute quality; Edinburgh of easterliness and Liverpool of westerliness.

†**'easterling.** *Obs.* exc. *Hist.* [app. f. EASTER *a.* + -LING, prob. after Du. *oosterling.*

The word seems not to have been found as Eng. before 16th c. In Anglo-French and Anglo-Lat. *sterling(us, esterling(us* appear in the 13th c., but only in the sense of 'sterling penny' or 'pennyweight' (cf. *libræ sterilensium, sterilensis monetæ* in Ordericus Vitalis, *a* 1142); in Matt. Paris *moneta esterlingorum* seems to mean 'the coinage of sterling pennies', not 'the coin of the easterlings'; nor do AF. phrases like 'vint soutz desterlings', 'cinkaunte mars desterlings' show that *esterlings* was understood to be the name of a people. The antiquaries of the 16th and 17th c., however, assumed that the 'esterling' was so called as having been coined by the Easterlings or Hanse merchants; hence they use *easterling money* as a transl. of *moneta esterlingorum*, etc. See STERLING.]

A native of the east.

1. *spec.* A native of eastern Germany or the Baltic coasts; chiefly applied to the citizens of the Hanse towns.

1534 WRIOTHESLEY *Chron.* (1875) I. 24 Alis Gray, and Wolfe, an Esterlinge. **1538** LELAND *Itin.* VI. 57 Many Esterlinges were buried there. **1598** HAKLUYT *Voy.* I. 6 Witland is apperteining to the Easterlings. **1611** SPEED *Hist. Gt. Brit.* IX. xvii. (1632) 878. **1668** CHILD *Disc. Trade* (ed. 4) 127 The Danes, Swedes, Holsteiners, and all Easterlings, who..import..Eastern Commodities. **1662** FULLER *Worthies* I. xxiii. 67 The High-Dutch of the Hans Towns ..(known by the name of Easterlings). **1771** GOLDSM. *Hist. Eng.* I. 251 The city of Wexford, and the two adjoining districts..were then in possession of the Easterlings.

b. attrib. ***easterling money***: see etymology.

1605 CAMDEN *Rem.* (1657) 184 Money coined in the East parts of Germany..was called Easterling money. **1641** *Termes de la Ley* 176 Guilhalda Teutonicorum is used for the fraternity of Easterling Merchants in London called the Stilyard. **1677** YARRANTON *Eng. Improv.* 145 A Tax being laid upon these Easterling Clothes. **1871** J. C. ADAMS in C. Davies *Metr. Syst.* III. 112 The Rochelle and easterling pound was therefore the same.

c. A ship of Germany or the Baltic countries.

1563 *Mirr. Mag.*, *Hastings* xxi. 3 At hand whole fleet of easterlynges. **1633** T. STAFFORD *Pac. Hib.* xi. (1821) 593 The ships that were descryed being a Fleet of Easterlings.

d. [transl. Anglo-L. *esterlingus.*] The weight of the easterling or sterling penny; a penny-weight, $\frac{1}{20}$ of an ounce.

1605 CAMDEN *Rem.* (1637) 185 In a pound there ought to be eleven ounces, two Easterlings and one ferling, and the other allay.

2. *gen.* An inhabitant of an eastern country or district; also, a member of the Eastern Church. *arch.*

1561 DAUS tr. *Bullinger on Apoc.* (1573) 279 b, In..1215 he [Pope Innocent III] helde a generall counsell in Laterane, wherin warre was declared agaynst the Easterlinges. **1565** CALFHILL *Answ. Treat. Crosse* (1846) 156 John, the legate of the Easterlings, brought forth another reason. **1577** EDEN & WILLES *Hist. Trav.* 230 b, The farre South asterlynges doe know this parte of Europe by no other name then Portugall. **1609** HOLLAND *Amm. Marcell.* XXXI. xvi. 431 The..regiment of Easterlings [*Orientalis turma* i.e. *Saracenorum*] got the upper hand. **1649** JER. TAYLOR *Gt. Exemp.* III. xv. 84 It was a custome of the Easterlings, and of the Roman Empire generally. **1688** BP. PARKER *Reasons Abrog. Test* 107 Mahomet gives them that name of Zabii, because they lay Eastward from Arabia, for so the Word signifies Easterlings. **1816** SOUTHEY *Lett.* (1856) III. 19 Of all the Easterlings, the Persians are the worst. **1855** KINGSLEY *Westw. Ho.* (1861) 4 One west country man can fight two easterlings. **1870** MORRIS *Earthly Par.* II. III. 124 With Easterlings and his own country-folk they dealt.

3. See quot.

1802 G. MONTAGU *Ornith. Dict.* (1833) 161 *Easterling*, a name for the Smew.

†**'Easterly**, *a.*¹ *Obs.* [f. EASTER *sb.*¹ + -LY¹.] Pertaining to Easter or to the passover.

c **1000** *Ags. Gosp.* Luke ii. 42 Hy foron to hierusalem to þam easterlican freolse. *c* **1175** *Lamb. Hom.* 89 Ðas fifti daʒes fram þan esterliche deie beoð alle ihalʒode to ane herunge. **1450–1530** *Myrr. Our Ladye* 135 Pryncypally amongest these estirnly solempnytes.

easterly ('iːstəlɪ), *a.*², *adv.*, and *sb.* [? f. EASTER *a.* + -LY; cf. Du. *oosterlijk* in same sense.]

A. *adj.* **1.** Situated towards the east.

1548 THOMAS *Ital. Gram.*, *Orientale*, easterlie. **1609** DOULAND *Ornith. Microl.* 87, I would have the Easterly Franci to follow the best manner. **1655** MOUFET & BENNET *Health's Improv.* (1746) 85 Easterly Towns..are more wholesome than the westerly. **1751** PERCIVAL in *Phil. Trans.*

XLVII. 218 Condate being placed in the road to Mediolanum shews it to be easterly of Chester. **1869** DUNKIN *Midn. Sky* 43 The most easterly part of this constellation.

2. Coming from the east: chiefly of the wind, rarely of merchandise.

1559 MORWYNG *Evonym.* 399 Then kepe by itself an unce of easterly saffron well beaten. **1626** BACON *Sylva* §662 Cold and Easterly Winds. **1772** DK. RICHMOND in *Burke's Corr.* (1844) I. 399 Going to Uppark in this easterly wind, has made me quite ill. **1816** J. SMITH *Panorama Sc. & Art* II. 43 The wind in the Atlantic..is almost always easterly.

B. *adv.* In an eastern position or direction. Of the wind: From the east, or a point nearly east.

1635 BRERETON *Trav.* (1844) 77 During this time the wind stood most easterly. **1691** *Lond. Gaz.* 2640/3 It blew hard Easterly. **1691** RAY *Creation* II. 1701 195 To them that live more easterly. **1820** SCOTT *Monast.* iii, To get into the little valley of Glendearg he had to proceed easterly.

C. *sb.* An easterly wind.

1901 F. T. BULLEN *Sack of Shakings* 265 The brave west wind..being succeeded by baffling easterlies. **1955** A. L. ROWSE *Expansion Elizabethan England* xi. 416 The English often had to wait for weeks for a favouring easterly.

easter-'magiant, 'mangiant. *dial.* In Cumberland, the green tops of Bistort (L. *Polygonum Bistorta*) which are eaten (Britten and H.).

†**'eastermost,** *a. Obs.* [f. EASTER *a.* + -MOST, in place of the earlier EASTMOST; cf. *bettermost, uppermost,* etc. Now superseded by EASTERNMOST.] Most easterly; situated farthest to the east.

1555 EDEN *Decades W. Ind.* (Arb.) 381 The eastermost tree is the hyghest. **1614** RALEIGH *Hist. World* II. 287 The.. Easter-most Hils of Tyre. **1704** *Collect. Voy. & Trav.* III. 51/2 The bigger Island..is the Eastermost. **1832** J. C. HARE in *Philological Museum* I. 175 The eastermost Pelasgian country on the Propontis.

eastern ('i:stən), *a.* and *sb.* Forms: 1 éasterne, 3 estrin, 4 estren, estern(e, 6–7 easterne, 7– eastern. [OE. *éasterne* = OS. *ôstroni*, OHG. *ôstrôni* (wind), ON. *austrœnn*:—OTeut. **austrônjo-*, f. **austr-* EAST; for the suffix *ônjo-* (? = L. *-āneus*) cf. *northern, southern, western.*]

A. *adj.*

1. a. Of or pertaining to the east side of the world, to countries in the East, or to the empire of the East; dwelling in the East; Oriental. ***Eastern Church***: the great communion otherwise called the Greek Church. ***Eastern question***: a general term for the political problems relating to Eastern Europe.

a **1000** *Ags. Gloss.* in Wr.-Wülcker 228 *Eoi magi*, easterne tungelwitegan. *a* **1300** *Cursor M.* 11388 A prophet of estrinland, hight balaam, crafti and bald. **1593** HOOKER *Eccl. Pol.* IV. xi, His desire was that of the two the Easterne Church should rather yield. **1606** SHAKS. *Ant. & Cl.* v. ii. 311 Oh Easterne Starre. **1732** POPE *Ess. Man* II. 27 As Eastern priests in giddy circles run. **1872** MORLEY *Voltaire* (1886) 82 The simple political conception of an eastern tale, a good-tempered despot with a sage vizier.

b. Situated in, of or pertaining to, the (north-)eastern parts of the United States.

1776 *Jrnl. Cont. Congress* 24 Dec. VI. 1039 That the delegates of the eastern states confer together, and also those of the southern states. **1831** J. M. PECK *Guide for Emigrants* 250 Notice of their plans..was inserted in an Eastern periodical. **1837** *Southern Lit. Messenger* III. 373, I set out to make a tour of the Eastern States. **1885** *Century Mag.* Nov. 33/1 Mr. Tully..admitted willingly that he was an Eastern man—a Down East lumberman and boat builder. **1908** C. E. MULFORD *Orphan* xiii. 153 At one time an Eastern woman had tried to live there, but..New York regained and kept its own. **1943** J. D. HICKS *Short Hist. Amer. Democracy* 334 Eastern farmers were unable to meet in full the needs of their new industrial centers for foodstuffs.

c. ***the Eastern Shore***: that part of Maryland and Virginia lying between Chesapeake Bay and the ocean. Also *attrib.*

1624 CAPT. J. SMITH *Virginia* IV. 141 To plant the Secretaries land on the Easterne shore neere Acomack. **1777** *Maryland Jrnl.* 5 Aug. (Th.), [He] now has a family living near Choptank, on the Eastern Shore. **1785** WASHINGTON *Diary* 31 Dec. (1925) II. 461 Landed 230 Bushels of Oats to day from an Eastern Shore vessel. **1786** *Ibid.* 8 Apr. III. 39 Afterwards I sowed..the common Oat of the Eastern Shore. **1854** W. G. SIMMS *Southward Ho!* 179 In approaching the 'Eastern Shore' of Virginia..you find yourself gliding toward.. scenes of repose, delicacy, and quiet beauty. **1948** MENCKEN *Amer. Lang., Suppl.* II. VII. iv. 128 On the Eastern Shore [of Maryland], south of the Choptank river, the dialect shows the influence of Tidewater Virginia... It is often difficult to say of a strange Eastern Shoreman..whether he comes from below the Choptank or above.

2. Lying towards the east; having a position relatively east; facing eastward.

1593 SHAKS. *Rich. II*, III. ii. 42 He [the sun] fires the prowd tops of the Easterne Pines. **1667** MILTON *P.L.* IV. 541 The eastern Gate of Paradise. *a* **1719** ADDISON (J.), The eastern end of the isle rises up in precipices. **1841** W. SPALDING *Italy & It. Isl.* II. 18 The greatest names of the church continued to be found in the eastern quarter of the empire. **1860** TYNDALL *Glac.* I. §11. 74 A pale light now overspread the eastern sky.

b. Having an eastward direction. *rare.*

a **1719** ADDISON (J.), A ship at sea has no certain method in either her eastern or western voyages.

3. Of the wind: Blowing from the east. *poet.*

a **1000** *Cædmon's Gen.* 315 (Gr.) Đonne cymð on uhtan easterne wind. **1590** SHAKS. *Mids. N.* III. ii. 142 Fan'd with the Easterne winde. **1762** FALCONER *Shipwr.* I. (R.) When eastern breezes yet enervate rise. **1842** TENNYSON *Audley Crt.* 52 She was sharper than an eastern wind.

B. *sb.* **a.** An inhabitant of the East; an oriental. **b.** A member of the Eastern Church.

c **1000** ÆLFRIC *Job* (Thwaite) 167 (Bosw.) Se wer wæs swiðe mære betwux eallum easternum. **1862** J. GADSBY in Spurgeon *Treas. Dav.* Ps. cxix. 136 Most of the easterns shed tears much more copiously than the people of Europe. **1865** PUSEY *Truth Eng. Ch.* 60 S. Meletius remained in the communion of the Easterns. **1884** *Graphic* 4 Oct. 360/2 These degenerate Easterns, who..rush at and devour French novels of the lowest type.

Hence **'Easterner** (U.S.), an inhabitant of one of the eastern or New England states.

1864 LOWELL *Biglow P.* Wks. (1879) 246 One hears such not seldom among us Easterners.

Easternism ('i:stənɪz(ə)m). [f. EASTERN + -ISM.] Eastern characteristics, practices, etc.; tendency to make Eastern in character.

1916 S. GRAHAM *Through Russian Central Asia* i. 8 This year I go into the depths of the Russian East and..continue my study of Easternism and Westernism in the Tsar's Empire. **1921** *Glasgow Herald* 23 June 4 A new Easternism which shall enable the Eastern races to stand on a level with the other races of mankind. **1921** *Chambers's Jrnl.* 819/1 Cairo can show nothing more oriental than this; its [*sc.* Tetuan's] easternism..is nearly complete.

easternly ('i:stənlɪ), *a.* and *adv.* [f. EASTERN *a.* + -LY.]

†**A.** *adj.* Situated to the eastward, or on the east side; of the wind, blowing from the east; = EASTERLY. *Obs.*

1594 BLUNDEVIL *Exerc.* viii. (ed. 7) 790 You shall easily draw the Easternly Meridians. **1614** RALEIGH *Hist. World* I. 39 These hottest regions of the world..are refreshed with a daily gale of Easternely wind. **1688** *Lond. Gaz.* No. 2325/1 Volhinia, the most Easternly Province of Lithuania.

B. *adv.* †**a.** In an eastern position (*obs.*). **b.** In an eastern manner; after the fashion of the Easterns (*rare*).

1765 MICHELL in *Phil. Trans.* LV. 76 Somewhere about the place D, a little less easternly than the point of the sand. **1883** *Athenæum* 9 June 724/1 Men who know nothing of the East..and cannot think easternly.

easternmost ('i:stənməst, -məʊst), *a.* [f. EASTERN *a.* + -MOST; cf. EASTERMOST, EASTMOST.]

Situated farthest to the east; also (*nonce-use*), of a character most essentially oriental.

1830 LYELL *Princ. Geol.* (1875) II. III. xli. 418 The species are most numerous in the Easternmost islands. **1859** SMILES *Stephenson* 51 The railway..crosses this road close by the easternmost end of the cottage. **1861** STANLEY *East. Ch.* i. (1869) 5 Easternmost of all the Eastern Churches, easternmost in thought and custom always, and easternmost in situation also. **1884** *Law Rep.* XIII. *Queen's B.* 675 The defendants' colliery is the easternmost in the group.

†**,East 'India.** *Obs.* exc. *attrib.* Formerly used = (*the*) EAST INDIES. ***East India Company***: a company formed for carrying on an East Indian trade, especially the English company incorporated in 1600, and described in its charter as 'The Company of Merchants of London trading to the East Indies', which from 1773 exercised political power in the East, and had the chief part in the administration of the affairs of Hindustan, till 1858, when the government was assumed by the Crown. ***East India fly***, an East Indian species of Cantharis or blister-fly; ***East Indiaman***, a ship of large tonnage engaged in the East India trade.

1634 SIR T. HERBERT *Trav.* 187, I account so farre of East India, as is from eighteene degrees north..to..Cape Comrein. **1655** E. TERRY (*title*), A Voyage to East India. *a* **1691** BOYLE *Wks.* VI. 192 (R.) Our own eight East India ships..are all safe in our harbours. **1703** *Lond. Gaz.* No. 3980/4 Lost a New East-India Company's Bond..for 150*l.* **1709** STEELE *Tatler* No. 31 ¶2 A Boatswain of an East-India Man. **1809** R. LANGFORD *Introd. Trade* 49 The East India Company was incorporated about..1600. **1844** LD. BROUGHAM *Brit. Const.* xx. (1862) 395 The crew of a West Indiaman or an East Indiaman.

b. In Anglo-Indian use sometimes *attrib.* = EURASIAN.

1831 *Asiatic Jrnl.* New Ser. VI. II. 106 Some elaborate speeches..were delivered by members of the East-India community.

,East 'Indian, *a.* and *sb.* [f. as prec. + -AN.]

A. as *adj.* **1.** Of or pertaining to the East Indies.

1553 EDEN *Treat. New Ind.* (Arb.) 8 The Ilandes of *Molucca* situate in the mayne Easte Indian Sea. **1601** HOLLAND *Pliny* I. 105 From the coast of the East Indian sea. **1951** R. MAYER *Artist's Handbk. of Materials & Techniques* xii. 415 *East Indian Laurel*, a dark, reddish-brown wood with a wavy grain, strong and elastic. **1961** *B.S.I. News* Sept. 13/2 Specifications for oil of East Indian lemongrass.

2. In Anglo-Indian use; = EURASIAN *a.*

1831 *Asiatic Jrnl.* New Ser. VI. II. 106 The Calcutta East-Indian petition. **1849** *Calcutta Rev.* XI. 74 The present situation and prospects of the East-Indian body.

B. as *sb.* **1.** A Eurasian.

1801 JANE AUSTEN *Let.* 8 Jan. (1952) 106 Mrs. Laurel is going to be married to a Mr. Hinchman, a rich East Indian. **1817** M. EDGEWORTH *Harrington* I. vii. 147 'Who is she?' 'An East Indian, I should guess, by her dark complexion.' **1831** *Asiatic Jrnl.* New Ser. VI. II. 106 A meeting of East-Indians took place at the Town Hall. **1849** *Calcutta Rev.* XI. 74 The East-Indians obtained the privilege of sitting on the ..Juries.

2. A man descended from one of the indigenous peoples of the Indian sub-continent, esp. if resident in the West Indies.

1931 *Everyman Encycl.* (ed. 2) III. 23/1 In 1928 the pop. [of British Guiana] was 307,784, which includes E. Indian immigrants. **1961** *Outlook* Feb. 214 East Indians is the name given to the descendants of those who came to British Guiana from India as indentured labourers between 1838 and 1917; the name also includes the few who themselves came from India. East Indians make up the largest group in British Guiana's total population of 540,000.

,East 'Indies. A geographical term, orig. including Hindustan, Further India, and the islands beyond. Opposed to the *West Indies* or Central American islands, and now usu. restricted to the Malay archipelago.

1598 SHAKS. *Merry W.* I. iii. 79 They shall be my East and West Indies, and I will trade to them both. *a* **1667** COWLEY *Mistr.* (1710) I. 82 Mine her fair East-Indies were above. **1837** *Penny Cycl.* IX. 252 The East Indies include also the islands of the Indian Ocean.

easting ('i:stɪŋ), *vbl. sb.* [f. EAST + -ING[1].]

1. *Naut.* 'The course made good, or gained to the eastward' (Adm. Smyth).

1628 DIGBY *Voy. Medit.* (1868) 91 For easting and westing, great diligence is required not to fall into error. **1684** *Bucaniers Amer.* II. (1698) 169 My whole easting I reckoned to be now 677 Leagues and ½ of a league. **1748** ANSON *Voy.* II. iv. (ed. 4) 233 Without hailing in for the main to secure our easting. **1781** BLAGDEN in *Phil. Trans.* LXXI. 339 We..made some easting to keep clear of the dangerous shoals. **1802** PLAYFAIR *Illustr. Hutton. The.* 230 To compute from the observed bearings the amount of all the..easting or westing. **1860** L. BILTON in *Merc. Mar. Mag.* VII. 289, I ran down my easting in 38° S.

2. An approach to an easterly direction; a sloping or veering eastwards. Of a wind or ocean current: A shifting eastward of the point of origin; easterly direction.

1855 MAURY *Phys. Geog. Sea* vii. §344 That diurnal rotation does impart easting to these winds there is no doubt. **1862** DANA *Man. Geol.* 539 In Maine the courses [of the rock-groovings] have an unusual amount of easting. **1865** *Pall Mall G.* 25 Aug. 11/1 This very *gregale*..has there [at Malta] decided easting in it, and may well have blown St. Paul from Crete thither.

3. Of a heavenly body: The reaching the eastern point of its apparent daily path.

1883 PROCTOR *Gt. Pyramid* iii. 139 The easting, southing, westing, and northing of heavenly bodies.

Eastlake ('i:stleɪk). The name of Charles Locke *Eastlake* (1836–1906), English designer, used *attrib.* and *ellipt.* to denote furniture associated with his book *Hints on Household Taste* (see quot. 1878).

1878 C. L. EASTLAKE *Hints on Household Taste in Furniture* (ed. 4) p. viii, I find American tradesmen continually advertising what they are pleased to call 'Eastlake' furniture, with the production of which I have had nothing whatever to do, and for the taste of which I should be very sorry to be considered responsible. **1881** C. C. HARRISON *Woman's Handiwork* III. 141 There is lovely Queen Anne furniture, successor to the more ponderous 'Eastlake'. **1967** *Boston* (Mass.) *Sunday Herald* 9 Apr. (Show Guide) 15/1 Eastlake furniture..was and still is second-rate—a mixture of shoddy workmanship, and a debased Gothic style which was not true to Charles L. Eastlake's ideas.

eastland ('i:stlənd). [f. EAST + LAND.]

1. a. *gen.* An eastern country or district. Now only *poet.* †**b.** *spec.* (in 14th–17th c.): The lands bordering on the Baltic.

c **1000** ÆLFRIC *Gen.* xxix. 1 Witodlice þa he [Jacob] com to þæm eastlande. *a* **1225** *Leg. Kath.* 534 Wittiest ha weren of alle þe meistres þæt weren in estlonde. *c* **1325** *St. Kenelm* 43 Of westsex & of humberlond; & of estlond. **1382** WYCLIF *Gen.* xxix. 1 Jacob thanne forth goon, cam into the est loond. **15..** LINDESAY (Pitscottie) *Chron. Scot.* (1814) 357 Mr. Normand Galloway..was in the eastland. [**1870** MORRIS *Earthly Par.* III. IV. 185 And emeralds from far east lands brought.]

2. *attrib.*

1379 *Mem. Ripon* (Surtees) III. 102 Et in iiij Estlandborde [*i.e.* planks from Norway] emp. ad ponend. subtus le Table ..12*d.* **1580** *Invent.* (1815) 301 (Jam.) Item, in the chalmer of deis ane stand bed of eistland tymmer with ruf and pannell of the same. *a* **1618** RALEIGH *Inv. Shipping* 10 South part of the Baltick, or Eastland Sea. **1668** CHILD *Disc. Trade* (ed. 4) 127 The Eastland and Norway Merchants, who affirm..their Trade is much declined since the passing the Act of Navigation. **1691** T. H[ALE] *Acc. New Invent.* p. xix, Would..send a great deal of Money for Eastland Firr. **1703** *Lond. Gaz.* No. 3880/4 Two of the Convoys to our homeward-bound Eastland Fleet. **1727** W. MATHER *Yng. Man's Comp.* 410 The Eastland Company..enjoying by their charter..the Trade of..Norway, Sweedland, Poland. **1734** WATTS *Reliq. Juv.* (1789) 184 Phronimus, a considerable east-land merchant. **1870** MORRIS *Earthly Par.* III. 408 How goes it then, With him—thy kinsman, mid the Eastland men?

Hence †**'eastlandish** *a.*, *obs.*

1605 VERSTEGAN *Dec. Intell.* Ep. Ded., High, Low, and Eastlandish Teutonicke.

ˈeastling, *a.*, **-lings**, *adv. Sc.* In 8 eastlin, -lins. [f. EAST + -LING, with adverbial genitive *-s*. Cf. BACKLINGS.]

A. *adj.* Of the wind: Easterly. B. *adv.* In an easterly direction.

1725 RAMSAY *Gentle Sheph.* I. ii, This [elm] shields the other frae the eastlin blast. **1768** ROSS *Helenore* 58 (Jam.) Ay hading eastlins, as the ground did fa'. **1789** BURNS *Let. J. Tennant* 7 This blae eastlin wind.

eastmost (ˈiːstməst, -məʊst), *a.* Also 6 *Sc.* eistmest. [OE. had *éastmest* adj., superl. f. EAST *adv.* + *-m-*, *-st*, suffixes (see -MOST); but continuity is not proved, and the word was prob. formed afresh at a later period.] That is most easterly in position. Now *poet.*; see EASTERNMOST.

1535 STEWART *Cron. Scot.* II. 201 The eistmest part of Britane to the se. **1587** *Wills & Inv. N.C.* (1860) II. 306 The eastmoste bed, next to the windowe, in the hye chamber. **1727** A. HAMILTON *New Acc. E. Ind.* I. viii. 75 Bassora is the eastmost City..in the Turkish Dominions. **1825** LD. COCKBURN *Mem.* i. 2 My father purchased the eastmost house on the south side of the Meadows. **1870** MORRIS *Earthly Par.* II. III. 12 Up the eastmost of the beech-slopes brown He turned.

Eastre, varr. EASTER *sb.*[1], EASTER *sb.*[2]; also of ESTRE, *Obs.*

East Side. *U.S.* [f. EAST D. 1 b + SIDE *sb.*[1] 11.] That section of New York City which lies on the east side of Manhattan (to the east of Fifth Avenue). Also *attrib.* Hence **ˈEast-ˈsider**, one who lives on the East side.

1882 J. D. McCABE *New York* iii. 79 This immense volume of travel is now being absorbed by the East Side Elevated Railroad. *Ibid.* li. 642 The original 'Bowery Girl'..passed at a quick gait peculiar to herself along the Bowery, or through Chatham square—it was the perfection of East Side poetry. **1894** C. D. WARNER *Golden House* v, She was so full of sympathy with the East-Side work. **1898** *Westm. Gaz.* 28 Apr. 8/2 The Bowery brigade, recruited from..patrons of the eastside dime hotels and doss-houses. **1899** J. L. WILLIAMS *Stolen Story* 4 The busiest bank presidents..opened their mouths to him [*sc.* a reporter] quite as readily as East Side saloon-keepers. **1903** *N.Y. Even. Post* 21 Aug., The Health Commissioner to-day made a tour of the East Side. **1903** *N.Y. Tribune* 25 Oct., 15,000 East Siders attended the final dedication ceremonies at William H. Seward Park. **1957** *Times Lit. Suppl.* 11 Oct. 603/2 He was born to Italian parents, who brought him in infancy to New York, where he had the usual East Side immigrant upbringing.

eastward (ˈiːstwəd), *adv.* and *a.* [f. EAST + -WARD; OE. had *éasteweard(e* adv., *éastanweard* adj., but the mod. adj. is probably merely a use of the adv.] A. *adv.*

1. Towards the east; in an eastern direction: a. of motion.

959 *Chart. Edgar* in *Cod. Dipl.* VI. 8 Ðonon to holan dic eastwærde. **1297** R. GLOUC. 41 Þis Picardes þenne wende forþ Estward euer faste. **1393** LANGL. *P. Pl.* C. II. 133 Alle þat han wel y-wroght wenden þey shulle Estwarde to heuene. *c* **1440** *York Myst.* xxviii. 18 Whedir is he walked, Estewarde or weste? **1553** EDEN *Treat. New Ind.* (Arb.) 9 Sayling Eastward by the coastes of Aphrica. **1611** BIBLE *1 Kings* xvii. 3 Get thee hence, and turne thee Eastward. **1722** DE FOE *Plague* (1840) 16 The plague..began now to come eastward. **1816** PLAYFAIR *Nat. Phil.* II. 155 Ten of the stars have motions eastward, peculiar to themselves.

b. of position, bearing, or aspect. Also in *comb.*, as ***eastward-flowing***, ***-looking***, etc.

a **1000** *Boeth. Metr.* xvi. 18 (Gr.) Þonan Oð Indeas eastewearde. **1393** LANGL. *P. Pl.* C. I. 14 Esteward ich byhulde after þe sonne. **1535** COVERDALE *Ezek.* xl. 10 The chambers of the dore eastwarde, were thre on euery side. **1611** BIBLE *Gen.* xiii. 14 Looke..Northward, and Southward, and Eastward, and Westward. **1878** BLACK *Green Past.* ii. 11 The eastward-looking branches of the great elms. **1911** M. NEWBIGIN *Mod. Geogr.* iv. 90 The long, eastward-stretching, inland sea. **1914** G. A. J. COLE *Growth of Europe* viii. 157 The eastward-running rivers. **1915** E. POUND *Cathay* 14 And evening drives them on the eastward-flowing waters.

2. quasi-*sb.*

1695 *Lond. Gaz.* No. 3099/3 The 17th arrived the *Smirna* Factor..from the Eastward. **1725** DE FOE *Voy. round W.* (1840) 318 It might..empty itself to the Eastward. **1828** J. H. MOORE *Pract. Navig.* 230 If a ship has been sailing to the eastward.

B. *adj.* That moves or looks eastward. ***eastward position***: the position of the celebrant standing on the west side of the altar (and so facing east) in the Communion Service.

824 *Chart. Ecgberht* in *Cod. Dipl.* V. 71 Ðonan on rihscmere eastanweardne. *c* **1440** *Promp. Parv.* 143 Estwarde, *orientalis*. **1873** J. B. DYKES *Let.* 5 July (1897) 306 The eastward position of the Celebrant. **1876** J. HARRISON *Eastward Position* 9 The phrase 'eastward position' as descriptive of the posture claimed by some for the minister at the Communion Table is inaccurate, misleading, and deceptive. **1882-3** SCHAFF *Relig. Encycl.* II. 903 The..eastward posture in prayer. **1885** *L'pool Daily Post* 27 Mar. 4/7 The Russians on their side are quietly prosecuting an eastward concentration. **1890** *Times* 5 Feb. 3/2 The third charge [against the Bishop of Lincoln]—relating to the eastward position—was contained in article 5. **1921** M. BARING *Passing By* 256 She said that the local clergyman was so low—no eastward position.

ˈeastwardly, *adv.* and *a.* [f. prec. + -LY[1], [2].]

A. *adv.* a. In an eastern direction. b. Of wind: From an eastern quarter.

1667 H. OLDENBURG in *Phil. Trans.* II. 421 Another people, not far from these, Eastwardly, of a Dwarfish Stature. **1747** DOBBS in *Phil. Trans.* XLIV. 474 Behring sailed..to the Isles of Japon, and from thence Eastwardly 50 German miles. **1791** SMEATON *Edystone L.* §100 There is a breeze eastwardly. **1807** VANCOUVER *Agric. Devon* (1813) 46 Continuing eastwardly along the coast.

B. *adj.* a. That has an eastern direction. Also, facing the east. b. Of the wind: That blows from the east.

1703 *Essex Inst. Hist. Coll.* XLII. 360 Thence on a Straigh[t] lien to a heap of Stones on the Eastwardly sied of a hill. **1768** WASHINGTON *Diary* 2 Aug. (1925) I. 286 Wind Eastwardly—with appearances of Rain. **1791** SMEATON *Edystone L.* §68 The wind was eastwardly. **1805** FLINDERS in *Phil. Trans.* XCVI. 258 The eastwardly winds appearing to have set in. **1870** PROCTOR *Other Worlds* iv. 108 *note*, Higher latitudes where the earth's eastwardly motion is less. **1883** —— in *Knowledge* 20 July 41/2 The body at P is carried eastward by the eastwardly motion of G.

eastwards (ˈiːstwədz), *adv.* [f. EASTWARD + *-s*; cf. *backwards*, *upwards*.] = EASTWARD *adv.*

1517 TORKINGTON *Pilgr.* (1884) 38 The londe..marcheth Estwardis to the kyngdom of Araby. **1877** R. J. MORE *Under Balkans*, The corpse..was..laid feet eastwards.

ˈeast ˈwind, ˈeast-ˈwind. [OE. *éastanwind*: see EAST A. 1.] a. The wind blowing from the east. In England and in New England proverbially bleak, unpleasant, and injurious to health; hence often *fig.* In quots. from or allusions to the Bible the fig. sense refers to the scorching and destructive east wind of Palestine. Hence **east-winded** *adj.*

c **1000** ÆLFRIC *Gloss.* in Wr.-Wülcker 143 *Subsolanus*, eastenwind. **1398** TREVISA *Barth. De P.R.* XI. iii. (1495) 386 The Este wynde that hight Subsolanus. **1483** *Cath. Angl.* 118 þe Estewynde, *eurus*. **1535** COVERDALE *Ezek.* xvii. 10 Withered..as soone as yᵉ east wynde bloweth. **1649** R. HODGES *Plain. Direct.* 4 An East-winde may spoil a nest of yong birds. **1722** DE FOE *Plague* 262 It was to no more purpose to talk to them than to an East-wind. **1860** PUSEY *Min. Proph.* 75 The east wind in Palestine..is parching, scorching, destructive to vegetation, oppressive to man. **1864** LOWELL *Fireside Trav.* 53 [A nature] so steeped..in sunshine that the east winds (physical or intellectual) of Boston..assailed it in vain.

1873 MISS THACKERAY *Old Kensington* ii. 9 One bitter east-winded morning.

b. In the game of mah jong the name given to one of the four tiles called winds, and to a disc representing this tile; hence, the player drawing this disc, who is the first to play.

1922 R. E. LINDSELL *Ma-cheuk* 9 Four players make up a table, and seats are usually determined by chance, the four discs ('East', 'South', 'West', and 'North') being placed face-down on the table and each player drawing one in turn. The player who draws 'East' has choice of seats. *Ibid.* 25 In the East round, South has originally one East wind. **1923** *Daily Mail* 3 Mar. 7 Why 'East Wind' should have played his 'Red Dragon'. **1924** *Mah Jong Rules of Queen's Club* 9 'Jong' is always East Wind, the player on his right South. **1960** R. C. BELL *Board & Table Games* vi. 152 The tiles are grouped into..The East, South, West, and North Winds. *Ibid.* 153 The person drawing East Wind takes the seat in front of the tong and drops his disc into it. *Ibid.* 156 The first round is East Wind's, and continues until each player in turn has been East.

ˈeast-wise, *adv.* (*nonce-wd.*) [f. EAST + -WISE.] = EASTWARD.

1882 E. C. BABER in *Roy. Geog. Soc. Suppl. Pap.* I. I. 115 The elegant northward meander with the graceful turn eastwise provided for it by cartographers.

easy (ˈiːzɪ), *a.* and *adv.* Forms: 3-4 aisie, -y, ? eise, 3-5 eese, -i, -y, 4-6 esee, -i(e, -y(e, (4 eisy, 5 eyse, ȝeesy, hesy), 6-8 easie, -ye, (9 *dial.* yezzy, yeasy) 4- easy. [a. OF. *aisié* (mod. *aisé*), pa. pple. of OF. *aiser*, *aisier* to put at ease, whence EASE *v.* The development of the Eng. senses has been affected by EASE *sb.*; the mod.Fr. uses of *aise* may also have had some influence.]

A. *adj.* I. At ease; characterized by ease or freedom from pain or constraint.

†1. At liberty, having opportunity or means (to do something). Cf. EASE *sb.* 1.

[Possibly *eise* in quot. 1225 may be a distinct word, a. Fr. *aise* at ease.]

c **1200** *Trin. Coll. Hom.* 47 Offredde loc for him . alse hie aisie was; gif hie was riche wimman . a lomb . gif hie was poure two duue briddes. *a* **1225** *Ancr. R.* 20 Et te one psalme ȝe schulen stonden, ȝif ȝe beoð eise, [*v.r.* aise] & et te oðer sitten.

2. Of conditions or state: Characterized by ease or rest; comfortable, luxurious, quiet.

c **1380** WYCLIF *Wks.* (1880) 166 Worldly honour & aisy lif. **1483** *Cath. Angl.* 117 Esy; *ediosus*, *secundus*. **1664** EVELYN *Kal. Hort.* (1729) 185 You vie Happiness in a thousand easy and sweet Diversions. *c* **1680** BEVERIDGE *Serm.* (1729) I. 123 In the full enjoyment of all things that can make their life easy, pleasant and happy. **1719** DE FOE *Crusoe* I. 114 My Condition began now to be..much easier to my mind. **18..** MRS. BROWNING *Lit. Mattie* v, 'Twas a green and easy world As she took it.

3. Of persons: Free from physical pain or discomfort, or from outward annoyance or burden.

c **1440** *Promp. Parv.* 143 Esy, *Quietus*. **1695** BLACKMORE *Pr. Arth.* II. 741 The sick grow easie, and the feeble strong. *a* **1791** WESLEY *Wks.* (1830) XII. 131 Mr. W's radical cure I shall hardly try, I am very easy, and that is enough. **1803** *Med. Jrnl.* X. 256 Head easy, thirst and general indisposition continued. **1809** *Ibid.* XXI. 487 After an opiate he became easier. **1902** O. WISTER *Virginian* iv. 44 'She's easier this morning, since the medicine.' This was the engineer, whose sick wife had brought a hush over Medicine Bow's rioting.

4. a. Free from constraint or stiffness; chiefly of or with reference to bodily posture or movements. Also *transf.* of manners or behaviour: Free from embarrassment or awkwardness. Also in phrase, ***free and easy*** (see FREE).

1483 *Cath. Angl.* 117 Esy of gate; *gracilis*. **1656** H. MORE *Antid. Ath.* (1712) Gen. Pref. 17 That I might the more undisturbedly write the easie Emanations of mine own Mind. **1680** BURNET *Rochester* 7 His conversation was easie and obliging. **1704** ROWE *Ulyss.* I. i. 77 Be easie, affable, familiar, friendly. **1750** EARL SHAFTESB. in *Priv. Lett. 1st Ld. Malmesbury* I. 77 Handel..is quite easy in his behaviour. **1821** SCOTT *Kenilw.* xvi, Leicester, bowing to his rival with the easiest and most graceful courtesy. **1837** HT. MARTINEAU *Soc. Amer.* III. 142 He was a most friendly personage, as willing as he was free and easy. **1850** MRS. JAMESON *Leg. Monast. Ord.* (1863) 279 To an easy graceful carriage..he added..great skill in argument.

b. of written compositions: Showing no trace of effort; smooth, flowing. Also *transf.* Of a writer or thinker.

1711 STEELE *Spect.* No. 109 ¶5 He sits with one Hand on a Desk writing and looking as it were another way, like an easy Writer. **1713** *Guardian* No. 15 (1756) I. 69 As there is an easy mien, and easy dress..so there is an easy sort of poetry. **1832** tr. *Sismond's Ital. Rep.* vii. 153 The light, elegant, and easy prose of his novels. **1880** L. STEPHEN *Pope* iv. 90 He could seldom lay aside his self-consciousness sufficiently to write an easy letter. **1884** CHURCH *Bacon* ix. 220 Easy and unstudied as his writing seems, it was..the result of unintermitted trouble and varied modes of working.

5. a. Not hard pressed: not hurried, gentle; said of motion, a breeze, a fire, etc. Also *Naut.*, as ***easy sail***.

c **1385** CHAUCER *L.G.W.* 284, I saugh comyng of ladyes nientene In..a ful esy paas. **1398** TREVISA *Barth. De P.R.* III. xvii. (Tollem. MS.), To make þe syȝte perfit þis þingis beþ nedful; þe cause efficient..and takynge hede, and esy meuynge [L. *motus mediocris*]. *Ibid.* XIX. lx. (1495) 897 Oximell is sodde on easy fyre and softe vnto it be thycke. *c* **1440** *Promp. Parv.* 143 Esy, or softe, yn sterynge, *lentus*. **1607** TOPSELL *Serpents* 795 They have a very slow and easie pace. **1671** MILTON *P.R.* I. 120 So to the Coast of Jordan he directs His easie steps. **1704** J. CUNINGHAM in *Phil. Trans.* XXV. 1659 Fair and serene weather..with easie Gales at S. **1716** *Lond. Gaz.* No. 5450/2 We made an easie sail for the Maese. **1834** CAUNTER *Orient. Ann.* i. 2 We coasted within four leagues of the land, under easy sail, with light breezes. **1852** G. W. CURTIS *Wand. in Syria* I. i. 8 The donkeys are like large dogs, and of easy motion. **1867** SMYTH *Sailor's Word-bk*, *Easy draught*. The same as light draught of water. *Easy roll*. A vessel is said to roll deep but easy, when she moves slowly, and not with quick jerks.

b. ***be easy!*** do not hurry, don't be so eager. Now considered an 'Irishism'.

1746 W. THOMPSON *R.N. Advoc.* (1757) 26 That Gentleman..advised the said *William Thompson* to be easy for a little Time. **1838** J. GRANT *Sk. Lond.* 41 'Be aisy, be aisy!..and don't be after killin' him quite.'

6. Free from mental anxiety, care, or apprehension. Phrase, ***to make*** (a person) ***easy***.

1692 E. WALKER *Epictetus' Mor.* xx, Manage the rest of your affairs of Life With easie Conversation, void of Strife. **1719** DE FOE *Crusoe* (1840) I. xx. 363, I was perfectly easy as to the security of my effects. **1722** —— *Col. Jack* (1840) 208, I made her easy on that point. **1818** JAS. MILL *Brit. India* II. IV. v. 187 Meer Causim was not easy upon the prospect of a connexion between the Emperor and the English. **1885** SIR J. HANNEN in *Law Rep.* 10 *P.D.* 88 A sensitive girl, whose conscience was not easy on the subject.

7. Fond of ease, averse to taking pains or thought; not strenuous, indolent; careless, thoughtless, unconcerned; = EASY-GOING.

1649 JER. TAYLOR *Gt. Exemp.* II. §10. 3 The easie softnesses of religious affections. **1650** —— *Holy Living* ii. (1727) § 79 For no easie, healthful and idle person was ever chaste. **1697** DRYDEN *Virg. Georg.* II. 604 Easy Sloath. **1724** WATTS *Logic* IV. i. (1802) 371 In this easy view of things. **1798** WORDSW. *Old Cumb. Beggar* 108 The easy man Who sits at his own door,—and..Feeds in the sunshine. **1862** STANLEY *Jew. Ch.* (1877) I. xiii. 251 They mark out for their prey the easy colonists. **1871** ROSSETTI *Dante at Ver.* xvi, He'd meet them flushed with easy youth.

8. a. (With mixed notion of 2, 3, 6.) In comfortable circumstances, well off. Also of 'circumstances', fortune.

1701 *Col. Rec. Penn.* II. 41 To make them and their Posterity easie in all times to come. **1708** SWIFT *Abol. Chr.* Wks. 1755 II. I. 86 Such a rent as, in the modern form of speech, would make them easy. **1721** BERKELEY *Prev. Ruin Gt. Brit.* Wks. III. 206 Men easy in their fortunes, and unprovoked by hardships of any sort. **1726** BUTLER *Serm.* vi. 108 One in easie Circumstances. **1783** BURKE *Sp. E. Ind. Bill* Wks. IV. 59 These plots and rebellions..are the offspring of an easy condition, and hoarded riches. **1796** MORSE *Amer. Geog.* II. 46 Easy farmers display a variety of plate. **1857** *Edin. Rev.* July, The 'easy' classes will contrive to furnish the governing classes of the country. **1879** B. TAYLOR *Stud. Germ. Lit.* 160 He was in easy circumstances.

b. ***easy street***: comfortable circumstances, affluence. Esp. preceded by *on*. *colloq.* (orig. *U.S.*).

1901 G. W. Peck *Peck's Red-Headed Boy* iii. 18 This rich old Jew..who has been economical until he has got a million and is residing on easy street, will forget the traditions of two thousand years. **1902** G. V. Hobart *It's up to You* 31 A young man who could walk up and down Easy Street. **1903** A. H. Lewis *Boss* 205 Just as a sport finds himself on easy street. **1923** Wodehouse *Adv. Sally* xiv. 180 Honestly,..it's the chance of a lifetime. It would put you right on easy street. **1932** M. de la Roche *Master of Jalna* v. ix. 101 'Are you sure you can spare it?' 'Good Lord! I hope so—after the sale! I'm in Easy Street.' **1938** F. Scott Fitzgerald *Let.* 25 Nov. (1964) 44 There will have to be a period of tough sledding before you come to Easy Street. **1957** L. P. Hartley *Hireling* viii. 60 He knew that she lived in Easy Street, but then so did most, if not all, of his customers.

II. 9. a. Conducive to ease or comfort: chiefly of appliances for repose. See also easy-chair.

138. *Antecrist* in Todd *3 Treat. Wyclif* 129 Þei slepyn ful soft in ful eesi beddis. *c* **1400** *Rom. Rose* 5609 Though he have lytel worldis goode, Mete & drynke, & esy foode. **1525** Ld. Berners *Froiss.* II. lxxviii. [lxxiv.] 234 Theyr lodgynge ..was not so easye nor large as thoughe they had ben at Parys. **1855** Bain *Senses & Int.* ii. i. §19 (1864) 104 Driven along at a moderate speed, in an easy carriage. **1879** Walford *Londoniana* II. 105 An office much sought after as one of those 'easy cushions' reserved for the repose of men of merit or favourites of the great.

†**b.** Advantageous, affording convenience, satisfactory. *Obs.*

c **1485** *Digby Myst.* (1882) ii. 126 [A horse is] esy and prophetabyll. **1673** Temple *Observ. United Prov.* Wks. 1731 I. 34 Having all one common End of publick Good, they come after full Debates to easie Resolutions.

c. In phrs. ***easy to look at***, ***easy on the eye(s)***, affording pleasure to the beholder; esp. of women: comely, beautiful. *colloq.* (orig. *U.S.*). Also in various combs., as ***easy-to-make***, ***easy-to-operate***, ***easy-to-use***, ***easy-to-wear***, etc.

1902 Ade *Girl Proposition* 141 He put his Tag on a blonde Canary 17 Years of Age who spelled Sure with an H and had from 7 to 9 Thoughts every 24 Hours. But she was very Easy to Look at. **1922** Wodehouse *Clicking of Cuthbert* x. 253 Her Highness is the easiest thing to look at these eyes have ever seen. **1937** C. Beaton *Diary* 3 June in *Wandering Years* (1961) 310 A pliable, easy-to-pose subject. **1937** *Punch* 8 Sept. 260/1 The same incorrigibly cheerful creature, very easy to look at, very pleasant to listen to. **1938** *Amer. Speech* XIII. 205 [The dictionary] is a substantial compilation, easy on the eyes, comparatively rich in idiomatic expressions. **1939** *Vogue's Cookery Bk.* i. 15 This is an easy-to-make soup for a hot day. **1943** D. E. Stevenson *Two Mrs. Abbotts* v. 35 Miss Walters was certainly easy on the eye. **1949** *Consumer Reports* Feb. 68/2 Many prospective purchasers want an easy-to-operate device. **1951** in M. McLuhan *Mech. Bride* 153/1 The same easy-to-follow lessons. **1958** *Oxf. Mail* 1 July 6/5 One of the good Westerns, east on the eye and mind, and pretty tough on the pulses. **1959** *Times* 9 Mar. Suppl. p. x/3 Easy-to-serve packed foods. **1959** Easy-to-use [see applicator]. **1959** *News Chron.* 10 Aug. 6/5 This hat has the soft easy-to-wear line. **1960** *Farmer & Stockbreeder* 15 Mar. 122/1 This tough, easy-to-use, real wood building panel. **1960** *Guardian* 25 Apr. 4/1 Easy-to-follow recipes.

III. Causing little discomfort or obstruction.

10. a. Of the means, method, or object of an action: Presenting few difficulties; offering little resistance. Const. *inf.* (act., less freq. pass.) or *of* followed by sb. denoting the action; also with the nature of the action contextually implied: of books, language; = easy to read, understand; of the soil; = easy to cultivate, etc.

c **1340** *Cursor M.* 16357 (Trin.) Þei..cut þis tre in two; þei fond hit good and esy to dele wiþ. *c* **1380** Wyclif *Wks.* (1880) 202 Þis pater noster þat is best & most hesy of alle. **15..** *Frere & Boye* 76 in Ritson *Anc. Pop. P.* 38 The olde man was easy to please. **1578** Lyte *Dodoens* iii. xlviii. 385 Vitalba..hath long branches ful of ioyntes, easie to ploy. **1581** Charke in *Confer.* iv. (1584) Cc iij, The place is easie Greeke. **1609** Holland *Livy* xxiii. xiii. 481 Nothing..is more eise and easie [*facilius*] to be knowne. **1651** Hobbes *Leviath.* ii. xviii. 89 From want of understanding this easie truth. **1674** Brevint *Saul at Endor* 240 Two ready and easie waies of procuring Atonement. **1697** Dryden *Virg. Georg.* ii. 283 Ploughing is an imitative Toil, Resembling Nature in an easie Soil. **1712** Addison *Spect.* No. 291 ¶6 This part of a critick is very easie to succeed in. **1762–71** H. Walpole *Vertue's Anecd. Paint.* (1786) II. 163 *note*, Those, which being in great collections are most easy of access. **1776** Adam Smith *W.N.* I. i. 11 Men are much more likely to discover easier..methods of attaining any object. **1823** Lamb *Elia* Ser. ii. xii. (1865) 314 The writings of Temple are, in general, after this easy copy. **1879** Lubbock *Sci. Lect.* ii. 31 The colors and scents are useful in making the flowers more easy to find.

b. Of a road: That may be travelled without discomfort or difficulty. Of a slope: Gradual, not steep.

1340 Hampole *Pr. Consc.* 1402 Þe way of dede semes large and eesy. **1523** Ld. Berners *Froiss.* I. ccxxxiv. 328 And all the other of the Companyons..had more easy passage thanne those that passed the day before. **1563** *Homilies* ii. *Repentance* ii. (1859) 536 An easie and short ladder, whereby we may climbe. **1596** Spenser *State Irel.* 3 Subdued the people unto him, & made easie way to the settling of his will. **1613** Shaks. *Hen. VIII*, iv. ii. 17 At last, with easie Rodes he [Wolsey] came to Leicester. **1709** Steele *Tatler* No. 179 ¶6 You mount by six easy steps. **1801** Southey *Thalaba* vii. xx, Children of Earth,..Whom I have guided here By easier passage.

c. Of water, etc.: not rapid, swift, or turbulent.

1875 'Mark Twain' *Old Times Mississippi* iii. 52 Follow along close under the reef—easy water there—not much current.

d. ***easy listening***, designating a category of (recorded) music which is popular without being loud, abrasive, or otherwise demanding; also *transf.*

1965 *Billboard* 5 June 1/3 Billboard this week introduces the 'Top 40 Easy Listening' chart. **1974** C. James in *New Rev.* Aug. 20/2 We found out how to write from talking *Scouse*... That's what makes our poems easy listening. **1976** *National Observer* (U.S.) 25 Sept. 9/1 All the plants can groove to continuous music. 'I stick with easy-listening or classical,' said Blakeley, pointing to mounted speakers. **1979** *Farmington* (New Mexico) *Daily Times* 27 May (Entertainment Suppl.) 6/2 (Advt.), All of yesterday's and today's sounds! Country & Western, Easy Listening, Contemporary and Disco. **1986** W. Safire in *N.Y. Times Mag.* 7 Sept. 16/3 You can also get easy listening, which until recently meant the music of the 60's played in the 80's with the style of the 40's.

11. Of actions: Not difficult; to be accomplished with little effort. Frequently as complement when the subject is a vb. in the inf.; = eath 1.

c **1380** Wyclif *Wks.* (1880) 245 For drede of lettyng of bettre occupacion þat is more liȝt or eisy. **1398** Trevisa *Barth. De P.R.* vi. xx. (1495) 208 In olde men abstynence of meete is softe and easy. **1538** Starkey *England* iii. 69 Much easyar to spy ij fautys then amend one. **1578** T. Procter *Gorg. Gallery* in *Heliconia* I. 81 As eese a broken Syve Should holde the dropping rayne. **1626** Bacon *Sylva* §57 After taking of somewhat of easie Digestion. **1650** Hubbert *Pill Formality* 144 You must live after the spirit..and thats no easie thing to do. **1729** Butler *Serm.* Wks. 1874 II. 128 It is as easy to close the eyes of the mind as those of the body. **1842** A. Combe *Physiol. Digestion* (ed. 4) 144 The easier digestibility of animal food in man. **1876** Mozley *Univ. Serm.* vii. 151 It is of the nature of habit to make acts easier and easier. **1878** Morley *Carlyle, Crit. Misc.* 196 It is easy to make a solitude and call it peace.

12. a. Of persons and their dispositions: Moved without difficulty to action or belief; soon yielding, compliant; credulous. ***lady of easy virtue***: euphemistically for an unchaste woman. ***easy game***, ***mark***, ***meat***: see sense 13 b.

1611 Shaks. *Cymb.* ii. iv. 47 Not a whit, Your lady being so easy. **1643** Denham *Poems* 169 An easy ear deceives, and is deceiv'd. **1672** Dryden *Conq. Granada* iii. i, An easie King deserves no better Fate. **1697** —— *Virg. Æneid* ii. 261 With such Deceits he gain'd their easie hearts. **1752** Young *Brothers* iii. i, To which his easy nature, soon appeas'd, Invited me. **1809** W. Irving *Knickerb.* v. i. (1849) 263 The great city..seemed, like some fair lady of easy virtue, to lie open to attack, and ready to yield to the first invader. **1848** Macaulay *Hist. Eng.* I. 258 Juries were no longer so easy of belief.

†**b.** Not unwilling, ready. Const. *inf.* Now only with passive, as ***easy to be entreated***; cf. 10. *Obs.*

1653 Holcroft *Procopius* iii. 83 When men ignorantly.. do wrong, the wronged are to be easie to grant pardon. **1665** Mrs. Hutchinson *Mem. Col. Hutchinson* (1848) 55 Hutchinson was neither easy to believe it, nor frighted at the example. **1715** Burnet *Own Times* (1823) I. 529 He was too easy to enter into any employment that might bring him into favour. **1738** Wesley *Psalm* cxvi. 5 How easy to forgive!

c. Esp. in colloq. phr. ***I'm easy***, I'm ready to comply (with whatever is proposed), without having any strong feelings (about the proposal); I don't mind one way or the other.

1941 in Baker *Dict. Austral. Slang* 27. **1945** in C. H. Ward-Jackson *Piece of Cake* (ed. 2) 26. **1948** D. Ballantyne *Cunninghams* (1963) ii. xviii. 80 'How about you, honey?' 'I'm easy.' **1968** 'L. Marshall' *Blood on Blotter* xii. 84 You can believe 'em or not. I'm easy. *Ibid.* xxi. 145 You'll have to make up your own mind. I'm easy.

13. a. That is obtained with ease, with little effort or sacrifice. ***easy money***: money obtained without effort, and, often, illegally; also with an amount specified (***easy dollar***, etc.) (orig. *U.S.*).

1697 Dryden *Virg. Georg.* ii. 641 The Swain..Receives his easy Food from Nature's Hand. *Ibid.* iv. 704 A Fault which easie Pardon might receive, Were Lovers Judges. **1785** Cowper *Tiroc.* 766 Disease or comes not, or finds easy cure. **1856** Trevelyan *Macaulay* (1876) II. xiv. 463 He obtained an easy pardon. **1882** *Sydney Slang Dict.* 5/1 The money earned by a prostitute is said to be 'honest', as distinguished from that earned by a thief. Probably from the story of the converted burglar who determined to sin no more himself and who lectured against dishonesty, but sent his wife out every night to earn an *honest shilling*. '*Easy shilling*' is synonymous in the foregoing sense. **1896** Ade *Artie* x. 79, I guess it's easy money too from the way he lets go of it. **1909** 'O. Henry' *Roads of Destiny* vi. 88 The boarding houses were corralling the easy dollars of the gamesome law-breakers. **1914** G. Atherton *Perch of Devil* i. i. 15 It may be this..spirit that inspires the midnight burglar.., not merely the desire for 'easy money'. **1923** Wodehouse *Adv. Sally* vi. 79 If you want to make a little easy money, you go and bet somebody ten seeds that I'm going to interrupt it again. **1935** *Discovery* Feb. 50/1 It is not to be assumed..that fox farming is a short cut to easy money. **1956** 'J. Wyndham' *Seeds of Time* 100 To enable quick-turnover spivs to make easy money out of suckers. **1967** *Observer* 26 Mar. 9 Here the pursuit of happiness fuses with the pursuit of the easy dollar.

b. ***easy meat*** (colloq.): someone or something overcome, mastered, or persuaded without difficulty; anything compassed with ease. Similarly ***easy game***, ***mark***.

1896 W. C. Gore in *Inlander* Jan. 147 *Easy mark*, an easy prey to a joke. *Ibid.*, *Easy meat*, one easily duped. **1899** 'Mark Twain' in *Harper's* Dec. 49/1 So I disguised myself and came back and studied you. You were easy game. **1927** T. E. Lawrence *Let.* 8 Dec. (1938) 557 That..made him easy meat for all the politicians. *a* **1928** in C. F. S. Gamble *North Sea Air Station* (1928) ix. 143 Had the Zeppelin been picked up by a searchlight, it would..have been easy meat. **1929** Wodehouse *Gent. of Leisure* i. 9 If a man's fool enough to be an easy mark ——. *a* **1935** T. E. Lawrence *Mint* (1955) i. xix. 66 The driver is an old sweat, not a rookie's easy meat. **1935** *Evening News* 29 June 3/1 An immense number of names has been invented for the victims [of confidence men] —..suckers, easy marks, wise guys, come-ons. **1943** *Archit. Rev.* XCIII. 23 All are easy meat, because a civilization is disintegrating and has lost its standards. **1944** W. E. Harney *Taboo* (ed. 4) 92 He had a gentle nature, ever out to please. He was the type that is known both to white and black as 'an easy mark'. **1955** *Sci. News Let.* 28 May 342/1 American pipelines are easy game for an enemy. **1958** *Times* 29 Oct. 3/2 The play was chosen, no doubt, on the principle that comedy is easy meat for the inexperienced. **1967** Partridge *Dict. Slang* Suppl. 1105/1 *Easy mark*, a girl easy to persuade into sexual intercourse: since ca. 1920.

14. a. Of burdens or penalties: Not oppressive or painful. Of prices or conditions: Moderate, not burdensome.

1382 Wyclif *Matt.* xi. 30 My 3oc is swete, or softe, and my charge liȝt, or eisy. **1413** Lydg. *Pylgr. Sowle* iii. vi. (1483) 54 That hath..graunted the to be purged with more esy peynes. **1426** Audelay *Poems* 47 Curators Engeyne ȝe not to ȝeesy penans, ne to strayt algat. **1488–9** *Act 4 Hen. VII*, ix, They woll sell theym at none eisier price. **1557** N. T. (Genev.) *Matt.* xi. 22 It shalbe easier for Tyre and Sidon at the day of iudgement, then for you. **1663** Gerbier *Counsel* C ij b, Where Marble is to be had at easy rate, but where Copper is very dear. **1696** Pepys *Diary* VI. 187 Secure it for me on the easiest terms you can. **1766** Entick *London* IV. 31 An easy fee of one shilling. *a* **1771** Smollett *Love Elegy* 18 And bid the turf lie easy on my breast. **1855** Macaulay *Hist. Eng.* IV. 251 He remained there in easy confinement. **1879** Froude *Cæsar* iv. 34 Peace was granted to him on the easy conditions of a nominal fine.

†**b.** Of persons: Not oppressive or severe; not exacting; lenient, gentle; cf. 12. In 18th c. also: Not difficult to 'get on' with [cf. Fr. *aisé à vivre*].

c **1325** *Body & Soul* (Laud MS.) in Wright *Mapes' Poems* 336 For I [the body] the [the soul] so eise fond the[r]fore couthe I nevere blinne. *c* **1386** Chaucer *Prol.* 223 He was an esy man to yeue penaunce. **1460** Capgrave *Chron.* (1858) 70 Sche mad hir son more esy, and sesed mech his persecucion. **1483** *Vulg. abs Terentio* 30 b, Faders shuld be esy ande tendyr anemste theire chyldere. **1699** Bentley *Phal.* 310 Pisistratus,..a generous and easie Governour. **1714** Swift *Pres. St. Affairs* Wks. 1755 II. i. 221 Supposing..that the elector should refuse to be..easy with the queen herself. **1727** —— *To very yng. Lady* Wks. II. ii. 42 A shrew from Billingsgate would be a more easy and eligible companion.

c. ***easy rider*** (*U.S. slang*): (*a*) a sexually satisfying lover (see also quot. 1926); (*b*) a guitar.

1912–13 W. C. Handy *Memphis Blues*, Mr. Crump don't 'low no easy riders here. **1926** in R. de Toledano *Frontiers Jazz* (1947) iii. 37 'Rider', 'easy rider', which term means both lover and (not either, or) procurer... Fidelity to his woman is expected of the easy rider. **1927** *Jrnl. Abnormal & Social Psychol.* XXII. 16 'Easy rider'. This apt expression is used to describe a man whose movements in coitus are easy and satisfying. It is frequently met both in Negro folk songs and in formal songs. 'I wonder where my easy rider's gone', is a sort of by-word with Southern negroes. **1949** R. Blesh *Shining Trumpets* vi. 128 In rural Negro parlance..*easy rider* meant the guitar..carried suspended by its cord. In the double meaning of Negro imagery, the femininely formed guitar..typifies also a woman companion. In Negro 'city talk', the term *easy rider* has come to mean either a sexually satisfying woman or a male lover who lives off a woman's earnings. **1958** P. Oliver in P. Gammond *Decca Bk. Jazz* i. 24 For the blues singer, the most valuable instrument was the guitar,..and, as his 'easy rider', could be slung across his back when he wished to travel.

†**15.** Of small 'weight' or importance, insignificant, slight; not very good, indifferent. So ***easy birth***, ***easy capacity***; cf. dial. '*Easy*, idiotic' (East Cornw. Gloss.). *Obs.*

1468 Sir J. Paston in *Lett.* (1874) II. 321 Thow..I.. have govyn yow bot easy cause to remembyr me..yet..let me not be forgotyn. **1475** *Bk. Noblesse* 78 Holden vertuous ..though he were descendid but of esie birthe. **1481** Caxton *Tulle's Old Age* H j, Of so grete age that he..shold be of easy power of bodily strength to make werre ayenst Carthage. **1491** *Will of Cliff* (Somerset Ho.), I shall leue but Esy good. **1519** Horman *Vulg.* 147 b, Easy agrement foloweth..where thou be maried not for loue but for good. **1542** Udall *Erasm. Apophth.* (1877) 348 Wine that was but easie and so-so. **1642** R. Carpenter *Experiences* ii. vii. 171 Shall one of us dirty creatures..frowne and be troubled..moved by every small and easie occasion. **1648** Symmons *Vind. Charles I*, 191 Though an easie capacity might foresee that they could do nothing by such an enterprize.

16. Not pressing hardly; loosely fitting; opposed to *tight*.

1594 Shaks. *Rich. III*, v. iii. 50 Is my beaver easier? **1601** —— *All's Well* v. iii. 278 This womans an easie gloue my Lord, She goes off and on at pleasure. *Mod.* The coat is an easy fit. An easy pair of slippers. The nut of the screw is a little too easy.

17. *Comm.* (opposed to *tight*.) Of a commodity: Not much in demand; hardly maintaining its price. Of the state of the market: Not characterized by eager demand; showing little firmness in prices.

1836 D. Webster *Private Corr.* (1856) II. 21 The deposit and distribution bill has become a law, and money is already getting to be much easier, as the phrase is. **1848** Bartlett *Dict. Amer.* s.v., 'The money market is easy'; i.e. loans of money may easily be procured. **1870** J. K. Medbery *Men & Myst. Wall St.* 69 The lender seeks the borrower. Money becomes a drug. Technically it is 'easy' or 'inactive'. **1873** *Money Market* (ed. 3) 4 When the total supply of surplus money, unemployed in a reproductive manner, is abundant, the market is said to be 'easy'; when it is scarce, the market is 'tight'. **1875** *Economist* 2 Jan. 18/2 The prevailing anticipation of an easy money market. **1888** *Standard* 7 Apr. 2/8 (Trade report) Bacon is easier. *a* **1891** *Mod.* The money-

market is easy. **1957** *Economist* 7 Dec. 867/2 The objective expert inquiry which Mr Eisenhower sought was swamped in the House when the advocates of easy money climbed aboard.

18. In Whist. ***honours easy***: said when the 'honours' are evenly divided. (Merely *colloq.*: the technical phrase is 'honours divided'.)

1884 *Sat. Rev.* 26 July 103 If we have the worst of that, honours are easy.

B. *adv.* In an easy manner.

1. Without difficulty. Chiefly in compar. or superl.; now *colloq.* or *vulgar*.

1400 in *Pol. Rel. & L. Poems* (1866) 239 For esye he comun al esye ho ssuln wende. **1564** *Brief Exam.* ***b, This thyng is easyer.. saide of you, then proued. **1596** SPENSER *F.Q.* I. viii. 4 Three miles it might be easie heard. **1600** SHAKS. *Sonn.* cix, As easie might I from my selfe depart, As, etc. **1680** SIR R. FILMER *Patriarcha* iii. §12 The voice of a multitude is easier heard. **1768–74** TUCKER *Lt. Nat.* (1852) II. 279 The good man can easiest persuade himself that God is good. **1823** BYRON *Juan* XIV. lxxxv, A wavering spirit may be easier wreck'd. **1871** SMILES *Charac.* v. (1876) 134 All the easier led away by bad example.

†2. In a very moderate degree. *Obs.*

1475 *Bk. Noblesse* 72 Many of the officers have be but esy vaileable to the defense of youre countre.

3. Not tightly, with freedom of movement.

1710 STEELE *Tatler* No. 204 ¶2 Fit as easie as any Piece of Work. **1820** KEATS *St. Agnes* xli, The bolts full easy slide.

4. a. *colloq.* At a leisurely pace, comfortably, without much trouble; in a comfortable position (also *transf.* of a ship). In phr. ***to take it easy***, to make oneself comfortable, to do no more than one must; also, ***to let one off easy***, i.e. with a light penalty; ***to go easy (on or with)***, to use sparingly; to act cautiously, to proceed with caution; also *absol.* (cf. quot. 1885); ***easy does it***, go carefully, take your time.

1779 FORREST *Voy. N. Guinea* 13 Which kept the vessel's head to the sea, and made her lie easy. **1821** BYRON *Lett.* civ. in Moore *Life* 1833 III. 139 'The two dozen' were with the cat-o'-nine tails;—the 'let you off easy' was rather his own opinion than that of the patient. **1850** MRS. STOWE *Uncle Tom's C.* xii. 103 Everything was going on quite easy and comfortable. **1867** SMYTH *Sailor's Word-bk.* s.v., Taking it easy. Neglecting the duty. **1885** *Illust. Lond. News* 23 May 539/2 Take my advice, and go easy for a bit. **1891** FARMER *Slang* II. 352/1 *Easy does it!* (popular). An exclamation of encouragement and counsel = 'Take your time and keep your coat on.' **1900** C. W. WINCHESTER *Victories of Wesley Castle* vii. 143 You will have to go easy on that subject. **1928** J. P. MCEVOY *Showgirl* 21 No high pressure stuff, sis. Easy does it with Dick. **1934** R. MACAULAY *Going Abroad* xxx. 279 I've more or less gone easy on the powder and lipstick. **1935** 'A. BRIDGE' *Illyrian Spring* xi. 143 Easy does it—to be easy was the thing. **1947** D. M. DAVIN *For Rest of Lives* xxii. 108 Go easy with that torch. **1955** L. P. HARTLEY *Perfect Woman* xxx. 272, I won't ask her yet what's the matter he decided. Easy does it. **1965** *Times Lit. Suppl.* 22 Apr. 317/1 A couple of foreign translations of my works should have warned me to go easy.

b. *colloq.* As word of command. ***easy!***: (move) gently! Also ***easy ahead!***: (steam) at a moderate speed!; ***easy on***: steady on! go easy! In Boating, ***easy all!***: stop (rowing)! Hence as *sb.* A short rest.

1865 'A DON' *Sketches fr. Cambr.* 119 Hallo! easy all! Hard word there, Smith! what does it mean? **1867** SMYTH *Sailor's Word-bk.*, *Easy*, lower gently. **1883** MRS. BISHOP *Sk. in Malay Pen.* v. in *Leisure Hour* 193/2 'Easy ahead', shouts the.. captain. **1885** *Standard* 6 Mar. 3/7 They reached Iffley lock without an easy. **1892** G. R. LOWNDES *Camping Sk.* v. 161 We took a day's easy at Tyn-y-groes,.. by the salmon pool. **1922** T. E. LAWRENCE *Let.* 7 Sept. (1938) 365, I.. read it in an easy, as we sat on the stye roof. **1928** *Observer* 19 Feb. 14 In the fourth [movement], being unable to switch off, I took an easy by thinking of something else. **1929** M. DE LA ROCHE *Whiteoaks* x. 490 'What's the to-do?'.. 'Easy on, Mama... It's nothing but young Finch. We've found out where he is.' **1941** BAKER *Dict. Austral. Slang* 27 *Easy on!*, go easy! desist! be sensible!

c. ***stand easy***: an order in military use allowing a greater freedom of posture than 'stand at ease'.

1859 *Field Exerc. Infantry* 5 If the command to Stand-at-Ease is followed by the word Stand Easy, the men will be permitted to move their limbs, but without quitting their ground. **1883** *Ibid.* I. 6 On the word *Squad* being given to men standing easy, every soldier will at once assume the position of standing at ease. **1914** *Recruit Training (Infantry)* 5 Stand at Ease. Feet sufficiently apart. Easy position. Dressing maintained. Men perfectly still till 'Stand easy' given. **1920** GALSWORTHY *Foundations* III. 62 Form fours—by your right—quick march!.. Left turn!.. Stand easy!

C. *Comb.* **a.** parasynthetic, as ***easy-hearted, -humoured, -priced, -spirited, -tempered***; **b.** adverbial, as ***easy-borrowed, -flowing, -handled, -held, -rising, -spoken, -yielding***. Also EASY-GOING.

1605 SHAKS. *Lear* II. iv. 187 A Slaue whose *easie borrowed pride Dwels in the fickle grace of her he followes. **1839** J. DARLEY *Introd. Beaum. & Fl.* Wks. 1839 I. 25 Fletcher's liveliness, bustle, his *easy-flowing language.. are sure to titillate a mixed audience. **1876** GEO. ELIOT *Dan. Der.* II. xxv. 142 One of those *easy-handled personages. **1634** MILTON *Comus* 164, I.. wind me into the *easy-hearted man, And hug him into snares. **1591** SHAKS. *1 Hen. VI*, v. iii. 139 Her *easie held imprisonment. *a* **1720** SHEFFIELD (Dk. Buckhm.) *Wks.* (1753) II. 177 Tully, the most *easy-humoured and facetious man in the world. **1876** GEO. ELIOT *Dan. Der.* II. xxv. 147 The easiest-humoured amateur of luxury. **1593** SHAKS. *3 Hen. VI*, II. i. 171 Haue wrought the *easie-melting King, like Wax. **1625** K. LONG tr. *Barclay's Argenis* II. xi. 98 There were small hillocks upon an *easie-rising plain. **1633** FORD *Love's Sacrif.* II. iv, I was a good, cold, *easy-spirited man. **1865** M. ARNOLD *Ess. Crit.* i. 10 A world, where most of us are plain *easy-spoken people. **1822** W. IRVING *Braceb. Hall* iv. 38 Her ladyship is one of those *easy-tempered beings. *a* **1680** BUTLER *Rem.* (1759) XIV. 65 For what does vast Wealth bring, but Cheat.. An *easy-troubled Life, and short? **1597** DANIEL *Civ. Wares* I. clxi, And *easie-yeelding zeale was quickly caught.

c. Special collocations. **easy-care**, used *attrib.* of (the properties of) man-made and other fabrics: convenient, serviceable (implying rapid drying after laundering, and crease-resistance); **easy-clean**, used *attrib.* of a fabric, etc., that is easy to clean; **easy-paced** *a. Cricket* and *Golf*, said of the ground or pitch when the ball comes at an easy pace off or along it.

1960 *Farmer & Stockbreeder* 12 Jan. Suppl. 2/1 The easy-care properties common to all synthetic fibre or man-made fabrics. **1962** J. T. MARSH *Self-Smoothing Fabrics* ii. 11 The production of 'easy-care' goods. **1963** *New Yorker* 8 June 88 Walking shorts, made expressly for us in cool, easy-care cotton-and-acetate seersucker. **1937** *Times* 5 Oct. 6/5 The easy-clean wheels have large hubs—a break from Daimler tradition. **1966** *Daily Tel.* 26 Oct. 13/2 Easy-clean fabrics for chair covers are not yet all available by the yard in shops. **1905** *Westm. Gaz.* 25 July 8/2 Cotter, though he made the ball bump considerably at times, was scarcely suited by the easy-paced wicket. **1928** *Observer* 1 July 28/1 Batting first on an easy-paced pitch, Leicestershire began well against Warwickshire. **1959** *Times* 12 Sept. 3/4 Easy-paced greens.

D. as *sb.*; see B. 4 b.

'easy, *v.* [f. prec. adj.] **†a.** To make easy; to facilitate. *Obs.* **†b.** To relieve, assist. *Obs.*

1567 MAPLET *Gr. Forest* 68 Their [cranes'] flight is like a Triangle, sharpe at the ende, and broade aboue, and easied therewithall by one another his helping. **1551** RECORDE *Cast. Knowl.* (1556) 51 If I myght see their forme I shoulde be muche easyed in framynge it.

c. *intr.* Of an oarsman or crew: to cease rowing. **d.** *trans.* To give (an oarsman or crew) the order to stop rowing.

1852 J. F. BATEMAN *Aquatic Notes* iii. 32 The University steerer, supposing he had bumped them there, 'easied all', but his Crew, perceiving their mistake, pulled on again. **1881** *Rowing, Steering & Coaching on Cam* 25 All boats going down are supposed to give way to boats coming up —*i.e.*, to easy and pull in their oars. *Ibid.*, You must always easy for the 'Varsity trials in the October term. *Ibid.* 26 You must take care to easy some distance from where you want to stop. **1882** *Daily Tel.* 2 Mar. (Cassell), They.. were not easied until reaching Iffley Lasher. **1890** S. LANE-POOLE *Barbary Corsairs* II. xvi. 213 She.. 'easies' with every blade suspended motionless above the waves. **1959** *Times* 13 Mar. 18/1 King's easied opposite the Doves.

'easy 'chair, ˌeasy-'chair. A chair adapted for sitting or half reclining in in an easy posture, often furnished with arms and padded back.

1707 FARQUHAR *Beaux' Strat.* IV. i, Get my easie chair down stairs, put the gentleman in it. **1713** *Guardian* No. 131 (1756) II. 188 Immersed in the luxury of an easy-chair. **1855** MACAULAY *Hist. Eng.* IV. 371 His host was confined by gout to an easy chair. **1881** MRS. A. ELLIS *Sylvestra* II. 65 He sunk.. into an easy-chair, pipe-and-bottle life.

'easy-'going, *ppl. a.* **a.** Of a horse: Having an easy gait or step. **b.** *fig.* That takes things easily; comfort-loving; inactive, indolent.

1674 *Ch. & Court of Rome* 7 Let us suppose an easie-going, good-natur'd man. **1837** THACKERAY *Ravenswing* iii, That easy-going cream-coloured 'oss. **1862** BURTON *Bk.-hunter* I. 3 Antiquarianism, which used to be an easy-going slipshod sort of pursuit. **1879** BEERBOHM *Patagonia* iii. 36 He is a careless, easy-going vagabond, always cheerful.

Hence **ˌeasy'goingness.**

1879 MRS. HOUSTON *Wild West* 34 The temptation to cheat.. owing to the easy-goingness of his master. **1881** *N.Y. Nation* XXXII. 164 The good-natured easygoingness of the then leader of the House of Commons.

eat (iːt), *v.* *Pa. t.* ate, eat (eɪt, ɛt, iːt). *Pa. pple.* eaten ('iːt(ə)n). Forms: *Inf.* 1–2 et-, eat-, eatt-, eotan, 2–4 eat-, eoten, ete(n, (2–3 aeten, 4 ethen, 3–4 hete, heyt), 4–6 ete, ette, (4 eete, ehyt, 4–5 eyt(e), 3–7 eate, 6 *Sc.* eait, eit, 6– eat. *Pa. t.* 1–3 æt, (2 æat), 2–4 et(t, 4–6 ete, 3–4 at, (4 hete), 4–5 eet(te, 6–7 eate, 7–9 eat, 6– ate. *Pa. pple.* 1–5 eten, 4–5 ete, eete(n, 4–6 etin(e, -un, -yn, ettyn, 6 *Sc.* eatin, eittin, 7–9 eat, 8–9 ate, 7– eaten. [Common Teut. and OE. *etan* str. vb. (3rd sing. pr. *ytt, ieteþ*, pa. t. 1st, 3rd sing. *ǽt, æt*, pl. *ǽton*, pa. pple. *eten*) = OFris. *ita, eta*, OS. *etan* (MDu., Du. *eten*), OHG. *ezan, ezzan* (MHG. *ezzen*, mod.G. *essen*), ON. *eta* (Sw. *äta*, Da. *äde*), Goth. *itan*:—OTeut. *etan* = L. *ed-ĕre*, Gr. *ἔδ-ειν*, Ir., Gael. *ith*, Lith. *ed-*, Skr. *ad-*. The accentuation of OE. MSS. shows that this verb differed, as in Goth. and ON., from other verbs of the same conjugation in having a long vowel in the pa. t. sing. *ǽt*, whence the mod. *eat* (iːt); but a form *æt*, with short vowel, must also have existed, as is proved by the ME. form *at*, mod. *ate*. The pronunc. (ɛt) is commonly associated with the written form *ate*, but perh. belongs rather to *eat*, with shortened vowel after analogy of wk. vbs. *read, lead*, etc.; cf. dial. (bɛt) pa. t. of *beat*.]

I. To consume for nutriment.

1. a. *trans.* To take into the mouth piecemeal, and masticate and swallow as food; to consume as food. Usually of solids only.

c **825** *Vesp. Psalter* xlix. [l.] 13 Ah ic eotu flesc ferra. *c* **1000** *Ags. Gosp.* John vi. 54 Se hæfð ece lif þe ytt [**1160** *Hatton et*] min flæsc. *c* **1200** *Trin. Coll. Hom.* 181 For þat þu ete þat ich þe forboden hadde. *c* **1250** *Gen. & Ex.* 337 Sum ȝhe ðer at, and sum ȝhe nam, And bar it to her fere adam. *a* **1300** *Cursor M.* (Cott.) 922 þou sal wit.. suinc Win þat þou sal ete and drinc. *Ibid.* 11111 He hete na bred ne dranc na win. **1382** WYCLIF *Isa.* xxxvii. 30 Et this ȝer that freeli ben sprunge, and in the secunde ȝer et appelis. *c* **1400** MAUNDEV. ii. (1839) 11 That Tree that Adam ete the appulle of. *c* **1420** *Liber Cocorum* 29 Tho heroun is rosted.. And eton with gynger. *c* **1449** PECOCK *Repr.* 498 The Tacianys.. helden that fleisch schulde not be ete. **1508** FISHER *Wks.* I. (1876) 56 Ete vnholsome metes, and anone cometh sekenes. **1526** *Pilgr. Perf.* (W. de W. 1531) 174 A synner is not worthy the breed that he eateth. **1557** NORTH *Gueuara's Diall Pr.* (1619) 700/1 In that golden age.. they.. eate rootes for breade and fruites for flesh. **1667** MILTON *P.L.* IX. 724 Whoso eats thereof forthwith attains Wisdom. **1763** *Priv. Lett. Ld. Malmesbury* I. 93 Whitebait.. are only to be eat at Greenwich. **1860** TYNDALL *Glac.* I. §22. 155 Up to this point I had eaten nothing.

b. Of liquid or semifluid food. Now chiefly with reference to soup, or other similar food for which a spoon is used.

1644 EVELYN *Mem.* (1857) I. 75 We eat excellent cream. **1691** RAY *Creation* II. (1704) 405, I observed it afterwards not only to eat Milk. **1789** WOLCOTT (P. Pindar) *Ep. falling Minis.* Wks. 1812 II. 127 He might have eat his soup. **1885** SINNETT *Karma* II. 36 He began to eat the soup.

c. In phrases, ***to have something, enough, little,*** etc. ***to eat***; formerly also ***to have to eat, to give (a person) to eat***. Cf. F. *donner à manger*.

In some dialects 'something to eat' is the common expression for food: 'The something to eat at the hotel was very good' (Sheffield).

c **893** K. ÆLFRED *Oros.* III. xi. §3 Seo leo bringð his hungreȝum hwelpum hwæt to etanne. *c* **1175** *Lamb. Hom.* 147 Mon.. leuseð his fleis, hwenne he him ȝefeð lutel to etene. *a* **1300** *Cursor M.* 13501 All þai had i-nogh at ette. **1340** HAMPOLE *Pr. Consc.* 6191 Yhe wald noght gyfe me at ete. *c* **1380** WYCLIF *Serm.* Sel. Wks. I. 17 þei hadden not to ete. **1611** BIBLE *2 Chron.* xxxi. 10 Wee haue had enough to eate. **1887** *Pall Mall G.* 13 Oct. 2/2 We had hardly anything to eat all the while we were prisoners.

†d. *fig.* To submit to, 'swallow' (an insult, an injury). Also, To treasure up, 'feed upon' (thoughts, words, etc.); orig. a Biblical idiom.

1382 WYCLIF *Jer.* xv. 16 Found ben thi wrdys, and Y eet hem [1611 I did eate them]. **1607** DEKKER *Sir T. Wyatt* Wks. 1873 III. 119 Ile eate no wrongs, lets all die, and Ile dye. **1611** SHAKS. *Wint. T.* IV. iv. 185 Hee vtters them as he had eaten ballads, and all mens eares grew to his Tunes.

e. *absol.* with *of* in partitive sense. In early ME. sometimes with *genitive*.

c **1000** ÆLFRIC *Gen.* iii. 17 For ðan.. ðu æte of ðam treowe. *c* **1175** *Lamb. Hom.* 11 Moyses.. þes daȝes.. nefre ne ete mennisses metes. *c* **1175** *Cott. Hom.* 241 Se þe of þese brad ett, ne sterfeð he nefer. *c* **1205** LAY. 18858 Of his breosten scullen æten aðele scopes. *a* **1300** *Cursor M.* 3944 O sinnu etes [*v.r.* etis] neuer juu. *c* **1380** *Sir Ferumb.* 5258 Hymself dronke whit wyn & eten of hure vytaile. **1581** MARBECK *Bk. of Notes* 108 Finding him eating of an Albrew. **1611** BIBLE *Ex.* xxxiv. 15 Lest.. thou eate of his sacrifice. **1835** WILLIS *Pencillings* I. ii. 19 But the rest eat very voraciously of a loaf of coarse bread.

f. *colloq. fig.* To receive (esp. a stage performance) with gusto; to acclaim. Also ***eat up***. (Cf. DEVOUR *v.* 6.)

1911 L. MERRICK *Peggy Harper* iv. 197 They *ate* the piece —it was only Galbraith they were guying. **1917** WODEHOUSE *Uneasy Money* iv. 23 I'm an English countess, doing barefoot dancing to work off the mortgage on the ancestral castle, and they eat me. **1919** F. HURST *Humoresque* 195 You wait until you see the way they're going to eat me up in the court scene in 'Saint Elba'. **1928** 'IAN HAY' *Poor Gentleman* iii. 58 The highbrow and pacifist reviewers there simply ate it [*sc.* the book] up, and said that if this was war, war ought to be stopped. **1949** N. MITFORD *Love in Cold Climate* 261 London society.. simply ate Cedric up, occasional echoes of his great success even reaching Oxford. **1958** K. AMIS *I like it Here* 158 He held forth instead in a series of essays... The *Sunday Times* would absolutely eat this chap.

g. *U.S. slang.* To practise fellatio or cunnilingus on (a person). Cf. *to eat pussy* s.v. PUSSY *sb.* 6. Also used *absol.*

1927 *Immortalia* 167 He tried at her dent But when his thing bent, He got down on his knees and he ate 'er. **1951** S. LONGSTREET *Pedlocks* IV. x. 249 'I could eat you with a spoon.' 'Never mind the dirty remarks.' **1975** L. ALTHER *Kinflicks* v. 133 '*Eat me*,' he said, seizing my head with his hands and fitting my mouth around his cock and moving my head back and forth. **1976** N. THORNBURG *Cutter & Bone* xii. 276 Cutter winked lasciviously at the girl. 'Well, I don't know,' he said. 'I already did quite a bit of eating this morning.' Monk, turning scarlet, closed her eyes.

2. Phrases, chiefly *transf.* and *fig.*

a. ***to eat one's terms***: a colloquial phrase for 'to be studying for the Bar'; students being required to have dined in the Hall of an Inn of Court three or more times during each of twelve terms before they can be 'called'. Also, ***to eat dinners***.

1834 MACAULAY *Pitt* Misc. (1860) II. 312 He had already begun to eat his terms. **1850** THACKERAY *Pendennis* xxix, In term time, Mr. Pen showed a most praiseworthy regularity in performing one part of the law-student's course of duty, and eating his dinners in Hall. **1856** H. MAYHEW *Gt. World*

of London I. 72 Lawyerlings 'qualify' for the bar by eating so many dinners. **1861** Lever *One of Them* 159 He had eaten his terms in Gray's Inn. [**1867** *Cassell's Mag.* I. 287/2 These dinners he must eat in hall in his own person.] **1879** *Chamber's Jrnl.* 23 Aug. 539/2 No student shall be called to the Bar until he has eaten a certain number of dinners at his Inn. **1929** A. Waugh *Three Score & Ten* 71 The eating of dinners in the Temple, and the attendance of lectures.

†**b.** ***to eat the air***: to be 'fed upon promises', tantalized. *Obs.*

1597 Shaks. *2 Hen. IV*, I. iii. 28 Who lin'd himself with hope, Eating the ayre, on promise of Supply.

c. ***to eat one's words***: to retract in a humiliating manner. See also humble pie.

1571 Golding *Calvin on Ps.* lxii. 12 God eateth not his word when he hath once spoken. *a* **1618** Raleigh *Rem.* (1644) 73 Nay wee'le make you confesse that you were deceived in your projects, and eat your own words. **1679** *Hist. Jetzer* 35 He..began to boggle, and would fain have eaten his words. **1725** Ramsay *Gentle Sheph.* IV. i, Ye lied auld roudes,—and, in faith, had best Eat in your words. **1806–7** J. Beresford *Miseries Hum. Life* (1826) VII. xli, Unguarded words, which, as soon as you have uttered them, you would die to eat. **1837** Sir F. Palgrave *Merch. & Friar* (1844) Ded. 7 Quoting one's own books is next worst to eating one's own words.

d. † ***to eat iron, a sword***: to be stabbed (*obs.*). ***to eat stick***: a mod. orientalism for 'to be beaten'.

15.. *Hickscorner* in Hazl. *Dodsley* I. 168 The whoreson shall eat him [*i.e.* the dagger], as far as he shall wade. **1594** *Contention betw. Lancaster & York* I. (1843) 63 Ile make thee eate yron like an Astridge. **1862** W. M. Thomson *Land & Bk.* 319, I frequently hear them say of one who has been bastinadoed on the soles of his feet, that he has eaten fifty or five hundred sticks. **1865** *Spectator* 4 Feb. 122 The uncivilized freedom in which they could do as they liked, 'eating stick' included.

e. In certain Biblical Hebraisms; ***to eat the fruit of one's own doings***: to receive the reward of one's actions; ***to eat the good of the land***, etc.

1611 Bible *Prov.* xiii. 2 A man shall eate good by the fruit of his mouth. —— *Isa.* iii. 10 They shall eate the fruit of their doings.

f. ***to eat earth***: a colonial expression for 'to possess oneself of land'; cf. *earth-hunger*.

1882 *Times* 8 Apr. 9/5 A man [in Australia] can eat as much earth as he likes for 5*s.* to 10*s.* a square mile.

g. ***to eat dirt***: see dirt *sb.* 6 c.

h. ***to eat one's hat***: see hat *sb.* 5 c.

3. a. *intr.* To consume food, take a meal.

c **825** *Vesp. Psalter* xxi[i]. 26 Eatað ðearfan and bið ʒefylled. *c* **1000** *Ags. Ps.* lxxvii[i]. 29 Swiðe ætan and sade wurdan. *c* **1175** *Cott. Hom.* 223 [Hio] æat and ȝiaf hire were, and he æt. *c* **1205** Lay. 13456 For alle heo sculden aeten [**1275** heote] ther. *c* **1250** *Gen. & Ex.* 1779 Ðor-on he eten bliðe and glað. *c* **1325** *Coer de L.* 3497 Whenne they hadde eeten, the cloth was folde. *a* **1340** Hampole *Psalter* xxi. 27 Þe pore sall ete & þai sall be fild. *c* **1400** *Apol. Loll.* 93 Weþer het ȝe or drynk..do all þingis in þe name of our Lord. **1483** *Cath. Angl.* 118 To Ete, *epulari.* **1526** Tindale *Acts* xi. 3 Thou wentest in unto men uncircumcised and atest with them. **1563** Foxe *A. & M.* (1684) III. 905 Now we cannot eat, unless we gnaw with our Teeth. *a* **1678** Marvell *Wks.* III. 457 He had not eat since the day before at noon. **1687** Shadwell *Juvenal* 23 He does forget..his Friends Face, with whom last Night he Eat. **1774** Goldsm. *Nat. Hist.* (1776) IV. 46 They eat and sleep at proper intervals like all other quadrupedes. **1856** Emerson *Eng. Traits, Wealth* Wks. (Bohn) II. 74 There should be temperance..in eating.

b. ***to eat well***: to have a good appetite; also, to keep a good table, be an epicure. So also † ***to eat ill***: to be badly fed.

1677 Earl Orrery *Art of War* 16 The Peasant..eats and lodges worse than the Citizen. **1709** Addison *Tatler* No. 148 ¶9 Who is a great Admirer of the French Cookery, and (as the Phrase is) eats well.

c. Const. †*on*, *upon* (a kind of food). Cf. *to dine on, feed on*; also 1 e. Also const. *from*, *off*, †*in* (gold, china, etc.).

1605 Shaks. *Macb.* I. iii. 84 Have we eaten on the insane Root, That takes the Reason Prisoner? **1607** Topsell *Four-f. Beasts* 361 [He] did eat upon Cakes made with meal and hony. **1625** Purchas *Pilgrimes* II. 1474 Hee alwayes eates in priuate among his women vpon great varietie of excellent dishes. **1642** C'tess Sussex in *7th Rep. Comm. Hist. MSS.* (1879), I am loth..to eat in pewter yet, but truly I have put up most of my plate. **1735** Pope *Ep. Lady* 82 Yet on plain pudding deign'd at home to eat.

d. ***to eat out of another's hand***: to be completely submissive to a person, to be under another person's control.

1915 Conrad *Victory* II. vii. 139 He's like that—sometimes that familiar you might think he would eat out of your hand, and at others he would snub you sharper than a devil. **1921** H. S. Walpole *Young Enchanted* II. v. 185, I won a glorious victory and Victoria has eaten out of my hand ever since. **1957** J. Masters *Far, far the Mountain Peak* xxiii. 236 This reconnaissance would have him eating out of his hand before it was done. **1968** M. Carroll *Dead Trouble* iii. 53 Shaun won't turn me out now. I've got him eating out of my hand.

4. quasi-*trans.* uses of 3.

a. with obj. followed by adj. or prep.: To affect in a certain way by eating: e.g. ***to eat oneself sick, into a sickness***; ***to eat*** (a person) ***out of house and home*** (i.e. to ruin him by eating up his resources); of animals: ***to eat the ground bare.***

a **1300** *Cursor M.* 4574 In þat medu sa lang þai war þat etten þai had it erthe bare. **1597** Shaks. *2 Hen. IV*, II. i. 80 All I haue, he hath eaten me out of house and home. **1712** Arbuthnot *John Bull* (1755) 53 John's family was like to be eat out of house and home. **1807** Anna Porter *Hungar. Bro.* v, You would not deny me my dinner, because I might eat myself into an apoplexy. **1832** Ht. Martineau *Life in Wilds* iv. 54 They would soon eat us out of house and home.

b. ***to eat its head off***: said of an animal that costs more for food than it will sell for.

1736 Byrom *Jrnl. & Lit. Rem.* (1856) II. I. 35 The eating his head off means that he would eat as much hay and corn as he was worth. **1860** Trollope *Framley P.* xiv. 277 A gentleman..does not like to leave him [a good horse] eating his head off. **1877** E. Peacock *N.-W. Linc. Gloss.* (E.D.S.), Cattle which have been bought at a loss are said to eat their heads off.

c. ***to eat one's fill***: to eat until satisfied.

c **1175** *Lamb. Hom.* 53 þe tadde..neure ne mei itimien to eten hire fulle. *a* **1300** *Cursor M.* 12947 Bidd þir stanes be bred to will, And siþen mai þou ete þi fill. **1611** Bible *Lev.* xxv. 19 Ye shall eat your fill, and dwell therein in safetie. **1737** Pope *Hor. Epist.* II. ii. 323 You've play'd, and lov'd, and eat, and drunk, your fill.

5. *intr.* with pass. force (chiefly with *adj.* or *adv.*): To have a certain consistence of flavour when eaten.

1601 Shaks. *All's Well* I. i. 175 Like one of our French wither'd peares..it eates drily. **1607** Topsell *Four-f. Beasts* 36 Being dressed they eat like Barbles. **1682** J. Collins *Making Salt Eng.* 6 A Chine of this Beef..Eat with a savour like Marrow. **1766** Goldsm. *Vicar W.* xvi. (1857) 96 If the cakes at tea eat short and crisp.

6. To cause to be eaten.

†**a.** (See quot.)

1784 Twamley *Dairying* 71 Cheese..that will spend well, or according to the common Phrase, will eat Bread well.

b. To have (a crop, etc.) eaten; to give up (to animals) to be eaten. Const. *with*.

1601 Weever *Mirr. Mart.* F iij, Their dead with dogs Hircanians do eate. **1799** J. Robertson *Agric. Perth* 218 A custom of eating his hay, sometimes, with sheep, close to the ground. **1868** *Perthshire Jrnl.* 18 June, The pasture..he intended to eat with sheep.

¶**7.** *U.S. slang.* To provide with food.

1837 *Crockett Almanac* 17 Well, Capting, do you ate us, or do we ate ourselves? **1842** *Spirit of Times* (Philad.) 4 Mar. (Th.), [The *Bay State Democrat* says that Mr. Dickens] has declined the invitation of the Philadelphians to eat him. **1855** M. Thomson *Doesticks* vii. 53, I resolved..to quit the premises of the Emerald Islander who agreed to 'lodge and eat' us. *a* **1860** *Pickings fr. Picayune* 47 (Bartlett), I was told you'd give us two dollars a day and eat us. **1889** Farmer *Americanisms* s.v., A steamer is alleged to be able to eat 400 passengers and sleep about half that number. **1928** S. V. Benét *John Brown's Body* 367 You ought to be et. We'll eat you up to the house when it's mealin' time.

II. To destroy by devouring.

8. a. *trans.* To devour, consume (as a beast of prey); to prey upon; to feed destructively upon (crops, vegetation); *transf.* to ravage, devastate. *lit.* and *fig.*

c **950** *Lindisf. Gosp.* John x. 10 Ðeaf ne cymes buta þæt te ʒestele & eteð [V. *mactet*] & losað. *a* **1300** *E.E. Psalter* (Mätz.), Þei ete [V. *comederunt*] Jacob, ilka lim, And unroned þe stede of him. *a* **1300** *Cursor M.* 22862 Men.. Wit hundes eten þe mast parti. *a* **1340** Hampole *Psalter* xxi. 21 Saf me þat þe deuel ete me noght. **1594** Shaks. *Rich. III*, I. ii. 65 Or Earth gape open wide, and eate him quicke. **1611** Bible *Ex.* x. 12 That they may..eate every herbe of the land. **1730** Pope *Ep. Bathurst* 196 The gaunt mastiff.. Affrights the beggar whom he longs to eat. **1863** Kingsley *Water-bab.* 8 Monsters who were in the habit of eating children. *Mod.* He went to Africa, and got eaten by a lion.

†**b.** To absorb (time) wastefully. *Obs.*

1598 Marston *Pigmal.* iii. 147 His ruffe did eate more time in neatest setting Then Woodstocks worke in painfull perfecting.

c. ***to eat one's (own) heart***: to suffer from silent grief or vexation. Also in Biblical phrase, ***to eat one's own flesh***: said of an indolent person.

1596 Spenser *F.Q.* I. ii. 6 He could not rest; but did his stout heart eat. **1611** Bible *Eccles.* iv. 5 The foole foldeth his hands together, and eateth his owne flesh. **1850** Tennyson *In Mem.* cviii. 3, I will not eat my heart alone. **1879** Farrar *St. Paul* I. 333 Eating away their own hearts in the consciousness of an ineffectual protest.

d. Colloq. phr. ***he won't eat you***, and varr.: he (we, they) will not injure or harm (the person addressed): an exhortation not to be alarmed.

1738 Swift *Polite Conv.* II. 126 Why, we won't eat you, Sir *John*. **1848** Trollope *Kellys & O'Kellys* III. vii. 161 Why, man alive, the ogre can't eat you! **1904** A. Bennett *Great Man* xxiv. 261 Don't be afraid. She won't eat you. **1949** F. Swinnerton *Doctor's Wife comes to Stay* 96 Don't be afraid. We shan't eat her, much as we should like to. You'll have her safe home again, with plenty dollars and the hearts of all our people over there. **1965** J. Symons *Belting Inheritance* ii. 23 You don't want to let Mamma worry you. She won't eat you, though she may look as if she will.

e. To disturb, vex. Also *intr.* in *to eat at.* (Cf. bite *v.* 13 b.) orig. *U.S.*

1893 S. Crane *Maggie* (1896) 90 'Well,' he growled, 'what's eatin' yehs?' **1904** W. H. Smith *Promoters* xvi. 238 What's eatin' 'em? Are they trying to hog the whole game? **1910** C. E. Mulford *H. Cassidy* xi. 74 'What's eating him, anyhow?' 'I don't know. I never saw him act that way before.' **1929** S. Anderson in *Mercury Story Bk.* 235 There was something else eating at me. **1934** R. Stout *Fer-de-Lance* xi. 158 You can answer my simple question without running a temperature. Was that what was eating you? **1938** E. Bowen *Death of Heart* II. iii. 232 'Now, what's eating him?' said Mr. Bursley. **1957** I. Cross *God Boy* (1958) xv. 118 'What's eating you?' asked Joe. 'Nothing,' I said.

9. *trans.* Of small animals: To gnaw, pierce, wear away by gnawing.

1611 Bible *Acts* xii. 23 Hee was eaten of wormes and gave up the ghost. **1793** Smeaton *Edystone L.* §61 *note*, It is not uncommon for the timber of ships to be eat by the worm under the copper sheathing. *c* **1822** Beddoes *Alfarabi* Poems 137 Many a wrinkled sun Ate to the core by worms.

10. *transf.* **a.** Of slow and gradual action, as of frost, rust, cancerous or similar disease, chemical corrosives, the waves, etc. Const. *into* (the result).

1555 Eden *Decades W. Ind.* III. IX. (Arb.) 177 It is eaten & indented with two goulfes. **1579** Lyly *Euphues* (Arb.) 100 The Rose though a lyttle it be eaten with the canker. **1691** T. H[ale] *Acc. New Invent.* 12 The Dreadnought's Rudder-Irons being..so eaten, as not to be fit for her being adventured to Sea again with them. **1796** Coleridge *Destiny of Nat.* Wks. I. 199 His limbs The silent frost had eat, scathing like fire. **1819** J. Hodgson in J. Raine *Mem.* (1857) I. 265 The cliffs chalky and stratified, like those of Marsden, eaten into caves.

b. *absol.*

1610 Markham *Masterp.* II. clxxiii. 484 Arsnick.. bindeth, eateth, and fretteth, being a very strong corrosiue. **1677** Moxon *Mech. Exerc.* (1703) 242 Being washed three or four times, it Bites or Eats not, but dries quickly. **1693** W. Robertson *Phraseol. Gen.* 520 To eat as rust doth, *rodere.* To eat as a canker doth, *corrodere.* **1823** Lamb *Elia* Ser. II. vii. (1865) 280 His disease was a scrofula, which appeared to have eaten all over him.

†**c.** *fig.* Of passions, grief, etc.: To 'devour', torment. Cf. *eat up* 18. *Obs.*

c **1000** *Ags. Gosp.* John ii. 17 Þines huses anda me et [*c* **1160** *Hatton* ett]. *a* **1225** *St. Marher.* 17 For onde that et ever ant aa ure heorte. *a* **1300** *Cursor M.* 23280 Enst and hete, þat iþenli þair hertes ete.

11. To make (a hole, a passage) by fretting or corrosion. With cognate obj. ***to eat one's (its) way.*** *lit.* and *fig.*

1697 Dryden *Virg. Georg.* III. 843 The slow creeping Evil eats his way, Consumes the parching Limbs, and makes the Life his Prey. **1762–71** H. Walpole *Vertue's Anecd. Paint.* V. 138 Something like a figure eaten into the barril. **1856** Kane *Arct. Expl.* I. xxvi. 344 The long canal which the running waters have eaten into the otherwise unchanged ice. **1878** Huxley *Physiogr.* 138 Little water-courses may be eaten out of solid rock by a running stream.

12. *intr.* To make a way by gnawing or corrosion; *lit.* and *fig.* Const. *into, through.*

1606 Shaks. *Tr. & Cr.* III. iii. 136 How one man eates into anothers pride. *a* **1656** Bp. Hall *Rem. Wks.* (1660) 189 The canker..eats through the cheek. **1697** Dryden *Virg. Georg.* III. 674 Searching Frosts have eaten thro' the Skin. **1780** Cowper *Table Talk* 8 Strange doctrine this! that..eats into his [the warrior's] bloody sword like rust. **1837** J. H. Newman *Par. Serm.* (ed. 2) III. xxii. 365 Has not the desire of wealth so eaten into our hearts? **1861** Bright *India, Sp.* 19 Mar. (1876) 61 Anticipation..more likely to eat into the heart of any man.

13. *Naut. trans.* and *intr.* (See quots.)

1769 Falconer *Dict. Marine* (1789), *Sourdre au vent*, to hold a good wind; to claw or eat to windward. **1867** Smyth *Sailor's Word-bk.*, *Eating* the wind out of a vessel, applies to very keen seamanship, by which the vessel..steals to windward of her opponent.

III. Combined with adverbs. (*trans.* unless marked.)

14. eat away. To remove, destroy by gradual erosion or corrosion. *lit.* and *fig.*

1538 Starkey *England* ii. 46 They be as hyt were etyn away. **1815** Elphinstone *Acc. Caubul* (1842) I. 147 The river..frequently eats away its banks. **1853** Phillips *Rivers Yorksh.* i. 8 Carbonic acid eats away the limestone. **1858** Hawthorne *Fr. & It. Jrnls.* II. 286 The sun still eats away the shadow inch by inch.

15. eat in. †**a.** To take into the mouth and eat; *fig.* to consider, 'inwardly digest'. Also, to consume, waste away (*obs.*). **b.** To 'bite in' with acid, etch.

c **1340** *Cursor M.* App. ii. 20527 þe appel of a tre that adam toke & ete it Inne. **1603** Florio *Montaigne* (1632) 133 That their very skin, and quicke flesh is eaten in and consumed to the bones. *c* **1620** Z. Boyd *Zion's Flowers* (1855) 125 What I have said, I'le neither lesse nor more, Nowe eate it in.

16. a. eat off. To take off or remove by eating.

1640 Fuller *Joseph's Coat* viii. (1867) 182 Some thieves have eat off their irons..with mercury water.

b. To clear off (a crop) by feeding it to cattle: said also of the cattle. Also *intr.* (for *pass.*) of a crop.

1733 W. Ellis *Chiltern & Vale Farm.* 28 One of our best Farmers..eat off his Turneps early, and chalked his Ground well. **1764** *Museum Rust.* II. xxv. 79 We eat it [*sc.* coleseed] off with sheep..to make them fit for the butcher. **1841** *Jrnl. R. Agric. Soc.* II. I. 126 Nitrate of soda may be sown..on pasture that does not eat off regularly. **1921** W. E. Heitland *Agricola* 266 Stock must be kept on the farm, partly to eat off your own fodder-crops.

17. eat out. a. = *to bite out.*

1858 Trollope *Dr. Thorne* I. 267, I suppose I ought to eat my tongue out, before I should say such a thing.

b. To exhaust eatables or pasture in (a place).

1865 Carlyle *Fredk. Gt.* VI. xv. xi. 71 But, in the mean while, he is eating-out these Bohemian vicinages. **1887** *Pall Mall G.* 30 Mar. 6/1 Wyoming is a natural grazing country ..and to suppose that it can be 'eaten out' in ten years or a generation is to suppose an impossibility.

c. To destroy as a parasite or a corrosive. Also *fig.*, esp. in phrases with *heart.*

1616 [see 18 b]. *a* **1656** Bp. Hall *Breath. Devout Soul* (1851) 165 Yet, when we have all done, time eats us out at the last. **1656** Dugard *Gate Lat. Unl.* ¶103. 33 Yvie clambering over trees, eateth them out. **1664** Power *Exp. Philos.* I. 74 A little of the said oyl..presently eats out the Colour. **1677** Yarranton *Engl. Improv.* 146 The cheapness of these Threds will eat out the very Spinning in most parts of England. **1886** G. T. Stokes *Ireland of Celtic Ch.* xi. 212 Image worship..which had largely eaten out the heart of religion among them. **1890** [see heart *sb.* 47]. **1890** *Review of Reviews* II. 323/1 General Boulanger is not eating out his heart in vain regrets. **1919** M. K. Bradby *Psychoanalysis* 70

Commonsense says that it is better .. 'to let off steam' than to 'eat your heart out'.

d. To encroach upon (space, formerly also time) belonging to something else.

a **1716** SOUTH *Serm.* (1717) V. 67 No.. Business of State ate out his times of Attendance in the Church. **1865** DICKENS *Mut. Fr.* II. iv. I. 197 A certain handsome room on the ground floor, eating out a back-yard.

e. *Mining.* (See quot.)

1851 *Coal-tr. Terms Northumbld. & Durh.* 25 *Eat out*, this expression is applied when a level coal drift is turned to the dip, in order to take advantage of (or 'eat out') a rise hitch.

f. *intr.* To take a meal elsewhere than at one's residence.

1933 *Maclean's Mag.* 1 Aug. 35/1 They had planned to 'eat out', but presently Norma's chances of being 'discovered' in some smart café became completely nil. **1945** 'L. LEWIS' *Birthday Murder* (1951) iv. 47 Why don't we eat out tonight?. **1954** R. MACAULAY *Let.* 8 July (1962) 159 Women.. stay at home while the men eat out in cafés and restaurants.

18. eat up. a. To consume completely, eat without leaving any; to devour greedily. Also *fig.*

1535 COVERDALE *Bel* 22 Ate vp soch thinges as were vpon yᵉ altare. **1583** STUBBES *Anat. Abus.* II. 27 By this meanes rich men eate vp poore men, as beasts eate vp grasse. **1816** JANE AUSTEN *Emma* ii, The wedding-cake was all ate up. **1873** BROWNING *Red Cott. N-Cap C.* 1472 Monsieur Leonci Miranda ate her up with eye-devouring.

b. To devastate, consume all the food in (a country); to consume all (a person's) provisions or resources; to ruin (a person) for one's own benefit. Also (in mod. use) of nations: To absorb, annex rapaciously (neighbouring territories).

1616 HIERON *Wks.* I. 589 Goe not from the church, to eate out & to eate vp one another in the market, by fraud & cruelty. **1715** BURNET *Own Times* (1823) I. 413 He set as many soldiers upon him, as should eat him up in a night. **1721** DE FOE *Mem. Cavalier* (1840) 158 The Scots were sent home, after having eaten up two counties. **1722** WOLLASTON *Relig. Nat.* vii. 146 Others.. would not fail to make themselves greater or stronger by eating up their neighbours. **1879** FROUDE *Cæsar* v. 42 On they swept eating up the country. **1884** *Graphic* 4 Oct. 342/2 The Boers.. will gradually 'eat-up' all the surrounding territories, as they are now 'eating-up' Zululand.

c. *fig.* To absorb wastefully; to have a destructive effect upon; to consume (time, money, etc.).

1680 ALLEN *Peace & Unity* Pref. 54 Hath eaten up the comfort of love in a great measure. **1711** STEELE *Spect.* No. 6 ¶4 The Affectation of being Gay and in Fashion, has very near eaten up our good Sense and our Religion. **1776** ADAM SMITH *W.N.* (1869) II. v. ii. 416 Whose salaries may eat up the greater part of the produce of the tax. **1840** MARRYAT *Poor Jack* xxxv, The sun had so much power.. that it eat up the wind. **1856** MISS YONGE *Daisy Chain* I. xviii. (1879) 179, I got a bit of Sophocles that was so horridly hard, it ate up all my time.

d. To absorb, assimilate the ideas of (a writer).

1561 DAUS tr. *Bullinger on Apoc.* (1573) 138 We say in Dutch, He hath eaten Galen or Priscian quyte vp, that is to say, he hath learned them by hart. **1865** MASSON *Rec. Brit. Philos.* 281 Kant ate up all Hume, and redigested him.

e. Of passions: To 'consume', absorb (a person). Of diseases, troubles, etc.: To wear out the life of (a person). Chiefly in *pass.*; const. *with* (pride, selfishness, etc.; a disease, debts, etc.).

1604 SHAKS. *Oth.* III. iii. 391, I see, you are eaten vp with Passion. **1712** ADDISON *Spect.* No. 494 ¶1 The saint was.. generally eaten up with spleen and melancholy. **1751** JORTIN *Serm.* (1771) I. vi. 109 Nehemiah found the people.. eaten up with debts. **1799** in Nicolas *Disp. Nelson* (1845) III. 316 The garrison is.. eat up with the scurvy. **1813** JANE AUSTEN *Pride & Prej.* v. 15 He is eat up with pride.

†**f.** To elide or slur over (syllables) in pronunciation. *Obs. rare.* [So. Fr. *manger.*]

1585 JAS. I *Ess. Poesie* (Arb.) 57 Sa is the hinmest lang syllabe the hinmest fute, suppose there be vther short syllabis behind it, quhilkis are eatin vp in the pronounceing, and na wayis comptit as fete.

g. *fig.* To traverse (a distance, ground) rapidly.

1898 H. S. CANFIELD *Maid of Frontier* 111 If I don't put my spurs into him an' make him eat up the groun'. **1905** R. T. SLOSS *Bk. Automobile* 179 One of the keenest pleasures in possessing a car is being able to annihilate a hill or 'eat it up'. **1919** WODEHOUSE *Damsel in Distress* x, Ten minutes in the gray car ate up the distance between the links and George's cottage.

IV. The verb-stem in comb. with obj.: **eat-all**, a glutton; †**eat-flesh**, transl. L. *sarcophagus*, Gr. σαρκοφάγος the name of a kind of stone which had the property of consuming the flesh of corpses laid in it (see SARCOPHAGUS).

1598 FLORIO, *Pamphago*, the name of a dogge, as one would saie a rauener, an eate-all. **1884** C. POWER in *Gentl. Mag.* Feb. 121 Idle people in the community-do nothings and eat-alls. **1632** SHERWOOD, An eate-flesh, *sarcophago.*

eat, *sb.* Forms: 1–3 æt, 2–4 ete, (2 hete), 3 at, 4 ethe, 7 eat. [Com. Teut.: OE. *æt* = OFris. *êt*, OS. *ât*, OHG. *âz*, ON. *át*:—OTeut. **ǣto-m*, f. ablaut-stem of **etan* to EAT. In later use perh. the vb. stem used subst.]

1. That which is eaten, food. Now freq., esp. in *pl.* (*colloq.*).

a **1000** *Guthlac* 708 (Gr.) Oft he him æte heold. *c* **1000** ÆLFRIC *On O.T.* in Sweet *Ags. Reader* 60 Moyses.. ætes ne gimde on eallum ðam fyrste. *c* **1175** *Lamb. Hom.* 109 On monie wisen mon mei wurchen elmessan, on ete and on wete. *c* **1200** ORMIN 11640 Adam.. Biswikenn wass þurrh æte. **1340** *Ayenb.* 248 Vor be to moche drinke and ethe sterfþ moche volk. **1609** BEAUM. & FL. *Scornf. Lady* II. 70 Thou art cold of constitution, thy eat unhealthful. **1782** MME. D'ARBLAY *Diary* 26 Oct. (1842) II. 158, I was too much tired to choose appearing at dinner, and therefore eat my eat upstairs. **1889** *Kansas Times & Star* 7 May, A majority.. adjourned to the Coates House for 'eats' and refreshment. **1897** KIPLING *Captains Courageous* ix. 213 How shall I take money when I make so easy my eats and smokes? **1912** W. OWEN *Let.* 23 Apr. (1967) 130, I suppose I must thank you for the eats too. **1918** 'IAN HAY' *Last Million* p. xiii, There is no ice-water, no ice-cream, no soda-fountains, no pie. It is hard to get the old familiar eats in our restaurants. **1955** J. P. DONLEAVY *Ginger Man* (1962) xxi. 214 On the tables were eats the like of which I'm sure have never been seen on this isle.

2. The action of eating; a meal.

c **1000** *Ags. Ps.* lvi i[ix]. 15 (Gr.) Hi to æte ut ȝewitað. *a* **1200** *Moral Ode* 258 in *Cott. Hom.* 175 þo þe sungede muchel a drunke and an ete. *c* **1200** *Trin. Coll. Hom.* 63 þe lichames festing is wiðtiging of estmetes.. and untimliche etes. **1844** J. T. HEWLETT *Parsons & Widows* III. liv. 269 What was he to do 'between the eats'? **1904** *Westm. Gaz.* 20 May 10/1 One Tennessee innkeeper described his establishment as.. 25 cents a sleep, 25 cents an eat. **1951** J. FRAME *Lagoon* 60 Goodbye and thank you for the little eat.

eat, Sc. variant of OAT.

eatable ('iːtəb(ə)l), *a.* and *sb.* [f. EAT *v.* + -ABLE.]

A. *adj.* That may be eaten, suitable for food; edible, esculent.

1483 *Cath. Angl.* 118 Eteabylle, *comessibilis.* **1551** TURNER *Herbal* I. (1568) M v b, The eatable cucumbre pepon that is to saye rype, is of a fyne substance. **1579** FULKE *Heskins' Parl.* 306 The crosse maketh our Lordes fleshe layde vpon it eatable of men. ?**1690** *Consid. Raising Money* 15 To lay a Home-Excise upon things eatable and drinkable. **1756–7** tr. *Keysler's Trav.* (1760) IV. 8 Bread mixed with sea-water.. in time becomes so bitter as not to be eatable. **1863** LYELL *Antiq. Man* 13 The common eatable oyster.

B. *sb.* That which may be eaten; an article of food. Chiefly in *pl.*

1672 PETTY *Pol. Anat.* 362 More eatables were exported anno 1664, than 1641. **1719** DE FOE *Crusoe* (1840) II. ii. 46 Bread or other eatables. **1726** BERKELEY in Fraser *Life* iv. (1871) 137 Whether a minor be not chargeable for eatables and wearables. **18..** LANDOR *Wks.* (1868) II. 82 We had brought no eatable with us but fruit and thin *marzopane.* **1879** BEERBOHM *Patagonia* xvi. 242 Till.. all the drinkables and eatables in Pedro's shop had disappeared.

Hence **'eatableness**; also **eata'bility**, *nonce-wd.*

1795 SOUTHEY *Letters fr. Spain* (1799) 113 P.'s theory of the eatability of cats. **1813** *Ann. Reg.* 1812 Chron. 518 Water-cresses, of the eatableness of which the Persians appeared totally ignorant.

eatage ('iːtɪdʒ). *north. dial.* [f. EAT *v.* + -AGE; cf. EDDISH, which may have been confused.]

1. Grass available only for grazing; *esp.* the aftermath, or growth after the hay is cut. Also with some defining word, as *after-*, *spring*, *winter.*

1641 BEST *Farm. Bks.* (1856) 129 Three landes in the Carre at 16*s.* 8*d.* a lande without the eatage. **1723** *Lond. Gaz.* No. 6209/4 The Winter Eatage.. arising from.. West Inggs. **1784–1815** A. YOUNG *Ann. Agric.* XIX. 313 in *Old Country Wds.* (E.D.S.) There is no grass that will bring so heavy a crop of hay [as clover and rye-grass] and that after an early spring eatage. **1797** BURNS *Eccl. Law* III. 469 The after-mowth or after-eatage. *Ibid.* 477 Cattle.. put and kept upon the same land.. for the spring eatage. **1863** MRS. TOOGOOD *Yorksh. Dial.*, The eatage of the Lanes of the Township will be let by ticket. **1877** JUSTICE LUSH in *Law Rep. Queen's B.* II. 449 The winter eatage of the tenement.

2. The right of using for pasture.

1843 [see EDDISH 2 b]. **1857** C. B. ROBINSON *Gloss. Best's Farm. Bks.* (1856) 184 An increased charge being made for eatage of the fogge. **1869** *Pall Mall G.* 6 Sept. 5 It is the eatage of the straw rather than the straw itself which belongs to the off-going tenant. **1885** *East Cumbrld. News* 18 July, To be sold, eatage of fog.

†**'eat-bee.** *Obs.* An English name for the *Merops apiaster*, (sometimes wrongly identified with the Wood-pecker.) Cf. BEE-EATER.

[**1573** COOPER *Thesaur.*, Apiastra Avicula est, Seruius, Eadem quæ merops, auis Germaniæ ignota. Longe enim errant, quæ picum viridem interpretantur.] **1608** TOPSELL *Serpents* 646 Divers living creatures are nourished by.. honey; as the bear.. the woodpecker or eat-bee. **1611** COTGR., *Guespier*, a Woodwall, Wood-pecker, Eat-bee (a little bird). **1693** W. ROBERTSON *Phraseol. Gen.* 520 An eat-bee, a bird; *apiaster, merops.*

†**eat-bill.** ? Blundered form of prec. *Obs.*

1598 FLORIO, *Grallo*, a woodpecker, or eate-bill, or wit-wall.

eatche. Also 7 eitch. Sc. form of ADZE.

1611 *Rates* (Jam.) Eitches for cowpers, the dozen iii*l.* xiis. **1818** SCOTT *Br. Lamm.* xxv, 'Let me hae a whample at him wi' mine eatche—that's a'.'

eatelich, var. of ATELICH *a.*, *Obs.* frightful.

eaten ('iːt(ə)n), *ppl. a.* [pa. pple. of EAT *v.*]

1. Consumed as food; devoured.

1599 MINSHEU *Span. Gram.* 80 Eaten bread is forgotten. **1656** DUGARD *Gate Lat. Unl.* ¶862. 271 Half-eaten morsels, and other scraps. **1864** SWINBURNE *Atalanta* Thou whose mouth Looks red from the eaten fruits of thine own womb.

2. Gnawed, corroded, ulcerated. Cf. MOTH-, WORM-EATEN.

1581 SIDNEY *Apol. Poetrie* (Arb.) 31 Old Mouse-eaten records. **1607** TOPSELL *Four-f. Beasts* 401 The aforesaid eaten or lanced wounds.

eater ('iːtə(r)). Also 1–5 eter(e, 5 etar. [f. EAT *v.* + -ER.] **1. a.** One who eats; also with *up*, a consumer, devourer, and with object sb. prefixed, as *bread-*, *flesh-eater.*

a **1000** *Prov.* 18 (Bosw.) Eteras, *commessatores.* **1340** *Ayenb.* 47 Ase byeþ þe mochele drinkeres and eteres. **1483** CAXTON *Gold. Leg.* 267/2 Thou etar of porrete wene thou to take me out of myn hows? **1483** *Cath. Angl.* 118 An Eter, *comestor.* **1535** COVERDALE *Ezek.* xxxvi. 13 Thou art an eater vp of men, and a waister of thy people. **1625–6** SHIRLEY *Maids' Rev.* III. ii, Do I look like a spider-catcher, or toad-eater? **1710** FULLER *Tatler* No. 205 ¶2, [I] always speak of them with the Distinction of the Eaters, and the Swallowers. **1807** SIR R. WILSON *Jrnl.* 7 June *Life* (1862) II. viii. 253 We slept like pudding-eaters. **1837** J. H. NEWMAN *Par. Serm.* (1842) VI. vii. 95 It severs the fruit from the eater.

fig. **1829** E. ELLIOTT *Vill. Patriarch* Notes 179 Unless the bread-tax-eaters can be induced to convene.

b. with adj. prefixed, as *great*, *moderate*, etc.

1796 MORSE *Amer. Geog.* II. 37 They are great eaters. **1809** JAS. MOORE *Camp. Spain* 62 He [Sir John Moore] was a very plain and moderate eater. **1865** CARLYLE *Fredk. Gt.* III. VIII. v. 43 He is no great eater.

c. *transf.* Of chemical corrosives.

1610 MARKHAM *Masterp.* II. cxxx. 432 Litergie, or lime, in lye.. are likewise very violent and strong eaters.

2. A fruit that eats well, or is intended to be eaten uncooked (cf. COOKER 2).

1906 *N. & Q.* V. 156/1 The apples with none, or only small pips, were not so good as eaters or cookers. **1930** *Observer* 11 May 13/2 The blossom is as thick.. on the hardy 'cooker' as on the shy and delicate 'eater'. **1953** E. HYAMS *Vineyards in England* ix. 78 This [grape] is quite a good eater.

Hence **'eatress** [see -ESS], a woman who eats.

1834 BECKFORD *Italy* II. 244, I never beheld eaters or eateresses lay about them with greater intrepidity. **1840** *New Month. Mag.* LIX. 312 In a salon filled with the insatiable eaters and eatresses of macaroni.

eatery ('iːtərɪ). *colloq.* (orig. *U.S.*). [f. EAT + -ERY 2 b.] An eating-house.

1901 'H. MCHUGH' *Down the Line* 52 Muttheimer's is one of those eateries where the waiters look wise. **1923** WODEHOUSE *Inimit. Jeeves* i. 11 Why, then, was he lunching the girl at this God-forsaken eatery? **1927** *Daily Express* 30 Nov. 10/5, I think you served me with tea and toast at one of those cheap, colossal eating-houses in the West-End... No doubt you think that that clattering eatery.. is 'life' and independence. **1938** M. ALLINGHAM *Fashion in Shrouds* xx. 366 Lugg and I have been round every fishy club and suspicious eatery in London. **1959** *Times* 26 May 8/1 His inability to make contact with a really good hunk of beefsteak in the eateries of Germany, Italy and France. **1959** *Vogue* June 124 Pull in at one of the curb-service eateries.

eath, eith (iːð, iːθ), *a.* and *adv.* *Obs.* exc. *Sc.* Forms: 1–3 **eað(e, eð(e**, 1–4 **eþ(e**, 3–6 **eth(e**, 3 **æþ, eið, eitht, ith, ieþe, yþe**, 4–5 **eyth**, (4 **eeþ, eeth, eȝathe**), 6 **eathe**, 6– **eath**, *Sc.* **eith.** [OE. *éaþe* adv. = OS. *ôðo* easily, perhaps, OHG. *ôdo* perhaps (also in *un-ôdo* 'with difficulty'):—OTeut. **auþô*; the combining form *éaþ-* = ON. *auð-*, as in *auð-gǫrr* easy to do. Of the adj. the normal OE. form is *íeþe*, *ýþe* (also used as adv.) = OS. *ôði* easy, OHG. *ôdi* easy, possible:—WGer. **auþjo-z*; perh. the word was orig. an *-u* stem, which would account for the existence of the form *éaþ(e* without umlaut. The OE. compar. degree of the adv. was *íeþ*, *éþ*, but there is no distinct evidence of its survival into ME.

It has been disputed whether the present word is related to OHG. *ôdi*, MHG. *ôde*, *œde*, mod.G. *öde*, ON. *auðr*, Goth. *auþs* (? or *aupeis*, *aupus*), desert, uninhabited, empty. The sense offers no valid objection to the connexion of the words, as the notion of 'empty' might give rise both to that of 'desert' and to that of 'free from difficulties'.]

A. *adj.*

1. Of an action: Easy, not difficult.

c **1200** ORMIN 19673 And Crist wass æþ to witenn þatt Forr Crist wat alle þingess. *a* **1300** *Cursor M.* 18385 Of eldrin men þai mette wit tuin, þat þai war ald was eth [*v.r.* ith] to se. *c* **1340** *Gaw. & Gr. Knt.* 676 To fynde hys fere vpon folde, in fayth is not eþe. **1375** BARBOUR *Bruce* XVII. 454 It wes nocht eyth till ta the toune. **1398** TREVISA *Barth. De P.R.* VI. xxi, In olde men abstinence of mete is eth and esy. **1513** DOUGLAS *Æneis* Exclamatioun 28 Far eithar is.. Ane othir sayaris faltis to spy and note, Than but offence or falt thame self to wryte. *c* **1579** MONTGOMERIE *Navigation* 200 To the Porte of Leith: To come right in, we thoght it very eith. **1647** H. MORE *Cupid's Confl.* xiii, And eath it was, since they're so near a kin. **1748** THOMSON *Cast. Indol.* I. lxxiv, To stir him from his traunce it was not eath. **1821** MRS. WHEELER *App. Cumbrld. Dial.* 10 E'en yet its eith to trace A guilty conscience in my blushing feace. **1862** HISLOP *Prov. Scotl.* 55 Eith working when will's at hame.

b. Of a passage, etc.: That may be travelled with ease, not rough.

Beowulf 228 (Gr.) Wedera leode.. ȝode þancedon þæs þe him yþlade eaðe wurdon. **1579** SPENSER *Sheph. Cal.* July 90 Hereto, the hilles bene nigher heauen, and thence the passage ethe. **1627** P. FLETCHER *Locusts* I. ix, Hels yron gates to every guilty soule yeelds entrance eath.

2. Of the object, means, or method of an action: Making slight resistance; presenting few difficulties; = EASY. Const. *inf.*, usually active in form but passive in sense.

a **1225** *Juliana* 57 Wenest tu þat we beon se eð to biwihelin? *a* **1240** *Wohunge* in *Cott. Hom.* 279 Pouerte wið menske is eað for to þolien. **1297** R. GLOUC. (1810) 327 He was symple & myldore, & eþ to ouercome. *c* **1374** CHAUCER *Troylus* v. 849 He was ethe ynough to maken dwelle. *c* **1400** *Rom. Rose* 3955 A foole is eyth to bigyle. *c* **1450** HENRYSON

Mor. Fab. 58 The Bairne is eith to buske that is vnborne. **1532** MORE *Confut. Tindale* Wks. 382/1, I woulde euery other thinge wer as ethe to mend as thys is. *a* **1535** —— *Wks.* 83 For as saint Poule saith, ye fleshly sinnes be eth to perceiue. **1632** SANDERSON *Serm.* 323 A great mountaine is eath to be seene. **1691** RAY *N.C. Words* Coll. 23 It is eath to do, i. e. Easie. **1847-8** H. MILLER *First Impr.* xiv. (1857) 235 One of our old Scotch proverbs [says] God's bairns are eath to lear, i. e. easily instructed.

†**b.** Of a person: Easy to be entreated, gentle; in ME. with genit, ***eði modes*** gentle of mood. Also, Ready, susceptible; const. *inf. Obs.*

c **1250** *Gen. & Ex.* 2249 God hunne him eði-modes ben. **1596** SPENSER *F.Q.* IV. vi. 40 Her gentle hart..More eath was new impression to receive.

†**3.** Comfortable, at ease, free from pain.

c **1205** LAY. 2234 Eð him wes on heorten. *Ibid.* 8178 þa wes his hurte æðe. *Ibid.* 1250 þo was he þe eþere.

B. *adv.* Easily, without difficulty.

a **1000** *Boeth. Metr.* ix. 54 He wel meahte þæt unriht him eðe forbiodan. *a* **1000** *Andreas* 425 (Gr.) God eaðe mæᵹ heaðoliðendum helpe ᵹefremman. *c* **1175** *Cott. Hom.* 219 He wolde and eaðe mihte bien his sceoppinde ᵹelic. *a* **1200** *Moral Ode* 284 in *Cott. Hom.* 177 Ieþe he muwen ben of-drad þe hine sculled bi-helde. *a* **1225** *Ancr. R.* 62 Ablinde þe heorte, heo is eð ouercumen, & ibrouht sone mid sunne to grunde. *a* **1300** *K. Horn* 61 So fele miȝten yþe Bringe hem þre to diþe. *a* **1300** *Cursor M.* 11219 Moght he not þan..Be born vte of a maiden eth At þe time o nine moneth? *c* **1315** SHOREHAM 7 Wel eȝathe, God thorwe miracles ketheth hit A-lyve and eke a-dethe. *c* **1460** *Towneley Myst.* 193 Oone worde myght thou speke ethe. **1538** STARKEY *England* I. ii. §6 (1871) 32 We may the..ether also avoyd thys ignorance. **1600** FAIRFAX *Tasso* x. xlii. 187 Who thinkes him most secure is eathest shamed. *a* **1774** FERGUSSON *Rising of Sess.* Poems (1845) 28 Eith can the pleugh-stilts gar a chiel Be unco vogie Clean to lick aff his crowdie-meal. **1862** HISLOP *Prov. Scotl.* 54 Eith learned, soon forgotten.

C. **eath-** in *Comb.*

1. Forming adjs. (which did not survive beyond 14th c.), the final element being f. the stem of a verb: **eðbete** [see BEET *v.*], easy to amend; **eðfele** [see FEEL *v.*], easily felt; **eþgete** [see GET *v.*], easily obtained; **eðlete** [see LET *v.*¹, and cf. OE. *earfoðlæte* emitted with difficulty], easily dismissed, lightly esteemed; **eðluke** [see LOUK *v.*], easily pulled; **eðsene** [see SENE *a.*, SEE *v.*], easy to see; **eþwinne** [see WIN *v.*], easy to win.

c **1200** *Trin. Coll. Hom.* 63 þat we hauen agilt her biforen ..buð *eðbete gif hie us sore rieweð. *c* **1225** *Ancr. R.* 194 Uorði þet heo beoð *eð fele. *c* **1000** ÆLFRIC on *O. & N. Test.* 32 (Bosw.) Him wæs *eaþgete ele to ðam baþe. *c* **1275** *Sinners Beware* 19 in *O.E. Misc.* 74 þy vs is eþ-gete Helle þat is unlede. *a* **1200** *Moral Ode* 38 in *E.E. Poems* (1862) 24 *Eðlete [is] muchel gyue ðenne ðe heorte is ille. *a* **1225** *Juliana* 70 Me ledde hire & hleac forð ant heo wes *eðluke. *a* **1000** CYNEWULF *Crist* 1235 Ðær biþ *eþᵹesyne þreo tacen. *a* **1200** *Moral Ode* 338 in *O.E. Misc.* 70 þat is wel eþ-sene. *a* **1225** *Leg. Kath.* 381 Sutel is and eðsene.. þæt tu were iset ȝung to leaf and to lare. *a* **1225** *Ancr. R.* 116 Wiðuten writunge, þe fulðe is to eð-cene. *c* **1200** *Trin. Coll. Hom.* 49 Nime we þe turtles bitocninge þat is *eðwinne.

2. With final element f. a sb.: see EDMOD, -MEDE.

†**eathe,** *v. Obs. rare.* In 3 *pa. t.* **eððede.** [f. EATH *a.*] *trans.* To lighten, alleviate, assuage.

c **1250** *Gen. & Ex.* 1439 Eliezer him cam a-gon, Eððede his sorȝe, broȝt him a wif Of faiȝer waspene.

eather, dial. form of EDDER, osier.

†**'eathly,** *a.* and *adv. Obs.* Forms: see EATH. [f. EATH *a.* + -LY.]

A. *adj.*

1. Easy, not difficult.

c **1000** *Ags. Gosp.* Matt. xix. 26 Ealle þing synt mid Gode eaðelice [*c* **1160** *Hatton* æðelice]. *c* **1160** *Hatton Gosp.* Matt. xix. 24 Æþelicor beoð þam olfende to ganne þurh nædle eaȝe. *c* **1175** *Lamb. Hom.* 135 Of ane eðeliche dede.

2. Inconsiderable, slight, trifling. Often in antithesis to *eche* (= eternal): Of short duration.

c **890** K. ÆLFRED *Bæda* II. v. (Bosw.) Gif ðu ne wilt us ᵹeþafian in swa æðelicum þingo. *c* **1176** *Cott. Hom.* 221 Mid þare aeðelice hyrsumnesse þu ȝearnest hefen rices merhðe. *a* **1225** *Ancr. R.* 282 On eðelich stiche, oðer on eðelich eche makeð uorte understonden hwu lutel wurð is prude.

3. a. Of a person: Low in station; mean in character. **b.** Of a thing: Of small value.

c **1200** *Trin. Coll. Hom.* 35 Ne was þe engel isend ne to kinge..ac to loȝe and eðeliche men alse heordes buð. *a* **1300** *Floriz & Bl.* 274 Abute þe orchard is a wal; þe eþelikeste ston is cristal.

B. *adv.* Easily, without difficulty.

c **1000** *Ags. Gosp.* Luke xviii. 25 Eaðelicor mæᵹ se olfend gan þurh are nædle eaᵹe. *c* **1200** ORMIN 12532 Soþ Godd.. mihhte standenn æþeliȝ ȝæn himm. **1513-75** *Diurn. Occurr.* (1833) 249 His lyik eithlie culd not heirtofoir be fundin. **1737** RAMSAY *Scot. Prov.* Ded., You may eithly make yoursells master of the hale ware. **1813** HOGG *Queen's Wake* 73 The rein deir dun can eithly run, Quhan the houndis and the hornis pursue. **1872** BLACKIE *Lays Highl.* 71 This only lore my beggar wit Could eathly understand.

b. At an easy price, cheaply.

c **1225** *Ancr. R.* 290 Ne sule þu neuer so eðeliche..his deorewurðe spuse.

†**eaths,** *adv. Obs.* [f. EATH *a.* with genitival *-s*; cf. UNEATHS.] Easily.

1594 *Cornelia* in Hazl. *Dodsley* V. 209 Which eaths appear in sad and strange disguises To pensive minds.

'eat-in, *attrib. phr.* Chiefly *N. Amer.* [f. EAT *v.* + IN *prep.*] ***eat-in kitchen***, a kitchen designed for eating as well as cooking in; a kitchen-diner. (Estate agents' jargon.)

1955 *N.Y. Times* 3 Apr. VIII. 12R/6 (Advt.), An oversized living-dining master room combination with fireplace, eat-in kitchen, 3 master sized bedrooms, 2 tiled baths. **1968** *Globe & Mail* (Toronto) 13 Feb. 30/4 (Advt.), 5 bedrooms and den, 'eat-in' kitchen, rec. room with bar and fireplace. **1969** *Sydney Morning Herald* 24 May 39/8 (Advt.), Huge loungerm., eat-in kit., ultra mod. bathroom. **1979** *Arizona Daily Star* 5 Aug. (Advt. Section) 17/2 Eat-in kitchen with adjacent family rm. **1984** *Real Estate Buyer* (St. Augustine, Florida) Mar. 3/3 (Advt.), Heated, screened pool, brick BBQ, equipped eat-in kitchen.

eating ('iːtɪŋ), *vbl. sb.* [f. EAT *v.* + -ING¹.]

1. The action or habit of taking food.

c **1175** *Lamb. Hom.* 19 þe licome luuað muchele slauðe and muchele etinge and drunkunge. *c* **1200** *Trin. Coll. Hom.* 37 Sume men ladeð here lif on etinge and on drinkinge alse swin. *c* **1380** WYCLIF *Serm.* Sel. Wks. I. 66 Hous of etynge. *Ibid.* III. 410 Ffor gostily eetynge of Cristis owne body. *a* **1450** *Knt. de la Tour* 22 Ther was gret noyse betwene the man and hys wiff for etinge of the ele. **1528** PAYNELL *Salerne Regim.* E., They that haue a putrified feuer, are forbyden eatynge of mylke. **1601** SHAKS. *Jul. C.* I. ii. 296. **1651** HOBBES *Leviath.* III. xli. 264 By eating at Christ's table, is meant the eating of the Tree of Life. **1755** SMOLLETT *Quix.* (1803) II. 133 The proof of the pudding is in the eating of it. **1884** RUSKIN in *Pall Mall G.* 27 Oct. 6/1 You have..kickshaws instead of beef for your eating.

b. An act of taking food; a meal. Also a way or manner of feeding. *arch.*

1483 *Cath. Angl.* 118 An Etynge, *commestio, edilis.* **1535** COVERDALE *Ecclus.* xxxvii. 29 Be not gredy in euery eatynge. **1608** HIERON *Wks.* I. 691 Taking heed to our selues in our eatings, in our apparrell, in our companie, in our recreations. **1847** L. HUNT *Men, Wom. & B.* I. iv. 77 Marvelling at their eatings, their faces, and at the prodigious jumps they took. **1873** LYTTON *K. Chillingly* III. v. (1878) 118 Epochs are signalised by their eatings.

c. *good,* etc., ***eating***: said of an article of food.

1763 MRS. HARRIS in *Priv. Lett. 1st Ld. Malmesbury* I. 93 Whitebait..are really very good eating. **1781** *Phil. Trans.* LXXI. 169 *note,* White Ants..are most delicious and delicate eating. **1871** *Gd. Words* 720 A..fish, weighing from half-a-pound to two pounds, and excellent eating.

2. Corrosion; disintegration by a chemical agent.

1691 T. H[ALE] *Acc. New Invent.* 1 The extraordinary Eating and Corroding of their Rudder-Irons and Bolts.

3. *attrib.* and *Comb.*, as ***eating-apple, -parlour***, etc. Also EATING-HOUSE, -ROOM.

c **1440** *Promp. Parv.* 143 Etynge appulle tre, *esculus.* **1483** *Cath. Angl.* 118 An Etynge place, *pransorium.* **1509** FISHER *Fun. Serm. Marg. C'tesse Richmonde* (1708) 12 The hour of dyner..of the Etynge day was ten of the Cloke, and upon the fastynge day, Eleven. **1535** COVERDALE *Ruth* ii. 12 Whan it is eatinge tyme, come hither, and eate of the bred. **1622** MASSINGER, etc. *Old Law* III. i, I shall have but six weeks of Lent..& then comes eating-tide. **1630** J. TAYLOR (Water P.) *Gt. Eater Kent* 12 Nothing comes amisse. Let any come in the shape of fodder or eating-stuffe, it is welcome. **1719** DE FOE *Crusoe* (1840) I. xv. 256 The said man-eating occasions. **1823** F. COOPER *Pioneer* vii. (1869) 35/2 The remainder of the party withdrew to an eating parlour. **1845** DARWIN *Voy. Nat.* viii. (1873) 172 The elevatory movement, and the eating-back power of the sea. **1853** ROCK *Ch. of Fathers* III. II. 86 They went in procession to the eating-hall.

eating ('iːtɪŋ), *ppl. a.* [f. EAT + -ING².]

1. That eats; chiefly in comb. with prefixed obj. Formerly also, Greedy, voracious.

1483 *Cath. Angl.* 118 Etynge, *edax, edaculus.* **1712** ADDISON *Spect.* No. 446 ¶6 An eating Parasite, or a vain-glorious Soldier. *Mod.* He has killed a man-eating tiger.

†**b.** quasi-*sb.* = EATER. *Obs.*

c **1340** *Cursor M.* 7125 (Trin.) Of þe etyng þe mete out sprong. **1382** WYCLIF *Nahum* iii. 12 His vnripe fijgis..shuln falle in to the mouth of the etynge [**1388** etere].

2. That consumes or eats away; gnawing, corroding, fretting: of sores, chemical corrosives, etc.

1621 BURTON *Anat. Mel.* II. iv. III. (1651) 383 Plaisters to raise blisters, eating medicines of pich, mustard-seed and the like. **1702** ROWE *Tamerl.* IV. i. 1774 Drops of eating Water on the Marble. **1835** BROWNING *Paracels.* 130 Festering blotches, eating poisoning blains.

fig. *c* **1602** FR. DAVISON *Ps.* lxxiii. in Farr's *S.P.* (1845) 322 From sweatting toyle, and eating care. **1632** MILTON *L'Allegro* 135 And ever against eating cares, Lap me in soft Lydian airs. **1702** ROWE *Ambit. Step-Moth.* I. i. 278 That eating canker, Grief. **1876** BLACKIE *Songs Relig. & Life* 186 From eating care thy heart to free.

'eating-house. A house for eating, *esp.* one in which meals are supplied ready dressed; a cook's shop, restaurant.

c **1440** *Promp. Parv.* 143 Etynge howse, *pransorium.* **1673** DRYDEN *Marr. à la Mode* IV. iv, An eating house. Bottles of wine on the table. **1748** SMOLLETT *Rod. Random* xiii, To dine at an eating-house. **1805** N. NICHOLLS *Let.* in *Corr. Gray* (1843) 49 He dined generally alone, and was served from an eating-house..in Jermyn Street. **1848** MACAULAY *Hist. Eng.* I. 237 A third had stepped into an eating house in Covent Garden.

'eating-room. *Obs.* exc. *arch.* A room appropriated for eating; a dining-room.

1613 in *Northern N. & Q.* I. 74 Chalmeirs to be ordinaire eitting roomes. **1751** SMOLLETT *Per. Pic.* (1779) III. lxxvi. 27 He handed her down stairs into the eating-room. **1849** H. MAYO *Pop. Superst.* vi. 87 He went to the hotel of M. Lafargue..and entered the eating room.

†**'eatnell.** *Obs.*⁻¹ [obscurely f. EAT *v.*]

1611 COTGR., *Croqueteur,* an eatnell, a greedie, and lickorous feeder.

eaton, obs. form of ETIN, giant.

‖**eau** (o), French for 'water', occurring in the names of several liquids, used as scents or in medicine, as **eau-de-Cologne**, a perfume consisting of alcohol and various essential oils, originally (and still very largely) made at Cologne; also (*nonce-use*) as a *vb.*; **eau de Javelle**, see JAVELLE; **eau-de-Luce**, a medicinal preparation of alcohol, ammonia, and oil of amber, used in India as an antidote to snake-bites, and in England sometimes as smelling salts; **eau-de-nil** (erron. **-du-**), **eau-de-Nil** [lit. 'water of (the) Nile'], a pale green colour supposed to resemble that of the Nile; **eau de Portugal**, a perfume comprising an essential oil known as essence of Portugal; **eau de toilette** = *toilet-water* s.v. TOILET *sb.* 9b; **eau-de-vie** [lit. 'water of life'], the Fr. name for brandy; **eau sucrée** (o sukre), water with sugar in it. See also EWE ARDAUNT, EWROSE.

1802 C. WILMOT *Let.* 19 June in *Irish Peer* (1920) 72 The Ladies most frequently have their Baths perfum'd with *Eau de Cologne, Rose Water, or some perfume of that kind. **1823** BYRON *To Ld. Blessington* 14 Apr., Neither lemon-juice nor eau de Cologne, nor any other eau. **1845** *Tait's Mag.* XII. 803 Her maid..comforted and eau-de-cologned her. **1854** MRS. GASKELL *North & S.* xxii, Mrs. Thornton bathed Margaret's temples with eau de Cologne. **1756** *Gentl. Mag.* XXVI. 33 This gives you the genuine *Eau de luce. **1808** *Med. Jrnl.* XIX. 492 The wounds were deeply scarified, and filled with eau de luce. **1852** TH. ROSS tr. *Humboldt's Trav.* II. xxiv. 447 In vain have ammonia and eau-de-luce been tried against the Curare. **1870** *Young Ladies' Jrnl.* VII. 482 A pretty toilette of *eau-du-nil. **1890** [see CREVETTE]. **1891** *Truth* 10 Dec. 1240/2 A row of begonia leaves in eau-de-Nil velvet. **1905** E. F. BENSON *Image in Sand* ix, Four greens—*eau-de-nil, vert-doré,* aquamarine, and emerald—shone and shimmered together. **1928** *Times* 9 May 11/5 A robe de style of eau-de-nil tulle. **1960** *Times* 30 Jan. 7/4 *Eau-de-nil* and *tilleul* green. **1825** H. WILSON *Mem.* 43 'A little *Eau de Portugal would do no harm..' I remarked,..alluding to his dislike of perfumery. **1848** MRS. GASKELL *Mary Barton* I. vi. 104 Did not I get you that eau de Portugal from town. **1938** L. MACNEICE *Zoo* xiv. 229 We poured a bottle of eau-de-Portugal over our heads. **1963** 'M. ALBRAND' *Call from Austria* vii. 64 He smelled of Eau de Portugal, the lotion he used on his hair; he smelled a little like an orange. **1907** *Yesterday's Shopping* (1969) 537/3 Houbigant's *Eau de Toilette..bot. 4/6. **1985** *Times* 23 Jan. 10/5 The continental man has never had any reservations about buying eau de toilette rather than aftershave. **1748** SMOLLETT *R. Random* II. xlii. 54 We..were treated at breakfast with chocolate and **l'eau de vie* by our paramours. **1804** M. WILMOT *Let.* 24 Jan. in *Russ. Jrnls.* (1934) I. 78 The desert was in another room, dry'd fruits, Cakes, and *eau de vie.* **1840** BARHAM *Ingol. Leg.* 1st Ser. 168 Many a flaggon Of double ale..and *eau-de-vie.* **1846** DICKENS *Pict. fr. Italy* 86 He..produces a jorum of hot brandy and water; for that bottle..now holds nothing but the purest *eau de vie.* **1911** E. M. CLOWES *On Wallaby* vii. 184 Delicately burning his spoonful of eau-de-vie over his coffee. **1825** H. WILSON *Mem.* III. 69 The Frenchman..drank *eau sucré, and studied in his dictionary. **1844** THACKERAY *Misc. Ess.* (1885) 61 There was *eau sucrée* in the dining-room if the stalwart descendants of Du Guesclin were athirst. *a* **1845** BARHAM *Ingol. Leg.* 3rd Ser. (1847) 189 Lemonade, *eau sucrée*—and drinkables mild. **1872** E. BRADDON *Life in India* viii. 314 Playing dominoes and drinking *eau sucrée.*

eau, erroneous form of EA, canal.

†**'eaubruche,** *sb.*¹ *Obs.* Forms: 1 **ǽwbryce,** 2–3 **eu-, ewe, ewue, eaubruche.** [OE. *ǽwbryce,* f. OE. *ǽw, æ sb.*² marriage + *bryce,* BRUCHE, a breaking.] Adultery.

a **1000** in Thorpe *Laws* I. 374 (Bosw.) Wið æᵹhwylcne æwbryce. *c* **1175** *Lamb. Hom.* 49 Alse þeos men doð þe liggeð inne eubruche. *c* **1200** *Trin. Coll. Hom.* 137 Alle þo..don ewuebruche on here agene spuse. *Ibid.* 213 Ollende word and idele lehtres..beð bispeke ewebruche. *a* **1225** *Ancr. R.* 204 Heo beoth..Hordom, Eaubruche, etc.

†**'eaubruche,** *sb.*² *Obs.* Forms: 1 **ǽwbryca,** 2 **eubruche.** [OE. *ǽwbryca,* f. prec.]

Also **'eaubrekere.** *Obs.* In 2 **eawbrekere.** [f. ME. *brekere* BREAKER.] An adulterer.

a **1000** in Thorpe *Laws* II. 268 (Bosw.) Se ðe his æwe forlæt, and nimð oðer wif, he biþ æwbryca. *c* **1175** *Lamb. Hom.* 13 Ne beo þu eubruche. Ne do þu þeofðe. *Ibid.* 29 Rubberes..and þa eawbrekeres..habbeð an þonc fulneh.

‖**eau forte** [*lit.* 'strong water'], French for 'nitric acid'; hence, for an etching.

Hence **eau fortiste**, an etcher.

1882 *Society* 11 Nov. 22/1 The etching being by the well-known *eaufortiste,* Mr. J. L. Steele.

eave (iːv). [Back-formation from EAVES, treated as pl.] Used as the sing. of EAVES. Hence **eave** *v.*, to provide with shelter under eaves; **eaved** *ppl. a.*, provided with eaves; **'eaving** *sb.* (usually pl.) = EAVES.

1580 NORTH *Plutarch* 378 He hid the Money he had stolne under the house eavings. **1611** COTGR., *Agouttis,* the eauings of a house. **1710** T. WARD *Eng. Ref.* i. (1716) 102 (D.) His hat..With narrow rim scarce wide enough To eave from rain the staring ruff. *a* **1722** LISLE *Husb.* (1757) 445 On these walls..is a large eaving to his house. **1823** P.

NICHOLSON *Pract. Build.* 402 *Eave.*—The skirt or lower part of the slating hanging over the naked of the wall. **1851** RUSKIN *Stones Ven.* (1874) I. xiv. 151 The Eaved Cornice.. as represented in the simplest form by cottage eaves. **1871** TYNDALL *Forms Water* §37. 258 The water trickles to the eave and then drops down.

eaver[1] ('i:və(r)). *Obs.* exc. *dial.* Also **ever.** [Of unknown origin; some have suggested adoption of F. *ivraie* darnel, *Lolium temulentum*; the forms of the Eng. word, however, seem to forbid this.] Rye grass (*Lolium perenne*).

1732 DE FOE *Tour Gt. Brit.* (1769) I. 359 Clover, Eaver, and Trefoil Grass. **1796** W. MARSHALL *West of Eng.* Gloss. Eaver, *lolium perenne*, ray-grass. **1880** *East Cornwall Gloss.* (E.D.S.) *Eaver*, in some parts pronounced *Hayver*. The grass, *Lolium perenne*.

eaver[2] ('i:və(r)). *dial.* Also 7 **eever,** 9 **ether.** A provincial term for the direction of the wind; a quarter of the heavens. (Adm. Smyth.)

1867 SMYTH *Sailor's Word-bk.* **1875** *Lanc. Gloss.* (E.D.S.) *Eaver* (sometimes *Ether*).. The wind is in a rainy eaver.

eaver, obs. Sc. var. of AVER.

1609 SKENE *Reg. Maj.* 72 Great number of eavers or beasts.

eaver, var. of EVER, *Obs.*, wild boar.

eaves (i:vz). Forms: 1 **efes,** 3-5 **eouesen** (*pl.*), **ouese, -ise,** 4 **euez, euese,** 4-8 **eves(e,** (4 **hevese**), (6 **ease,** 6 *pl.* **esen**), 7 **eaues,** (**eeves, heaves**), *dial.* **eize,** 7- **eaves.** [OE. *efes*, fem. = OFris. *ose*, Flem. (Kilian) *oose*, OHG. *obasa* (MHG. *obse*, mod. dial.G. *obsen*) eaves, porch (:—WGer. **obis(w)a*, **obas(w)a*) = ON. *ups* (Sw. dial. *uffs*), Goth. *ubizwa* porch; prob. f. same root as OVER. The final *-s* has been mistaken for the sign of the pl., and in mod. Eng. the word is commonly treated as pl., EAVE being occas. used as the sing. The forms ME. *ovese*, WSomerset *office* (Elworthy), point to an OE. form **ofes*:—WGer. **obas(w)a*.]

1. a. The edge of the roof of a building, or of the thatch of a stack, which overhangs the side.

a **1000** *Lamb. Psalter* ci[i]. 7 (Bosw.) Geworden ic eom swa swa spearwa.. anwuniende on efese. *c* **1205** LAY. 29279, I þan euesen he [þa sparwen] grupen. *c* **1220** *Bestiary* 462 Ðe spinnere.. festeð atte hus rof hire fodredes o rof er on ouese. *c* **1440** *Promp. Parv.* 144 Evese, or evesynge of a house, *stillicidium*. *c* **1500** *Partenay* 5504 Allso thys chambre well depeynted was Ffro foote of wallure the ouise vnto. **1570** LEVINS *Manip.* 211 Y^e ease or eues of a house. **1579** LYLY *Euphues* (Arb.) 91 The Swallow which in the summer creepeth under the eues of euery house. **1610** SHAKS. *Temp.* v. i. 17 His teares runs downe his beard like winters drops From eaues of reeds. **1611** CORYAT *Crudities* 323 The pentices or eauisses of their houses. **1629** *S'hertogenbosh* 48 It.. ruined some houses; of some the heaues and tops were damnified very much. **1632** MILTON *Il Penser.* 130 Ushered with a shower still.. With minute-drops from off the eaves. **1663** COWLEY *Verses & Ess.* (1669) 104 The Birds under the Eeves of his Window call him up in the morning. **1751** W. HALFPENNY *New Designs Farm Ho.* 5 Thence to the Eves of the Roofs one Brick and half. **1799** J. ROBERTSON *Agric. Perth* 161 The best form of corn stacks is circular, with.. a conical top, diverging a little towards the eaves. **1819** SHELLEY *Ros. & Helen* 367 Like twinkling rain-drops from the eaves. **1849** FREEMAN *Archit.* 178 The eaves.. rest commonly on small arcades or corbel-tables.

fig. **1675** CROWNE *City Polit.* II. i, I hang on the eves of life, like a trembling drop, ready every minute to fall.

†**b.** Of a wood: The edge, margin. *Obs.*

898 *O.E. Chron.* an. 894 þa foron hie.. bi swa hwaþerre efes swa hit þonne fierldas wæs. *c* **1325** *Gloss. W. de Biblesw.* in Wright *Voc.* 159 *Desouz l'overayl*, under the wode-side wode-hevese. *c* **1340** *Gaw. & Gr. Knt.* 1178 þus laykez þis lorde by lynde wodez euez.

2. *transf.* Anything that projects or overhangs slightly, as †the brow of a hill, †the flaps of a saddle, the edge of a cloud or precipice, the brim of a hat; also *poet.* the eyelids.

1382 WYCLIF *Job* xi. 5 Anne forsothe sat beside the weye eche dai in the euese [**1388** cop; Vulg. *supercilio*] of the hil. **1663** BUTLER *Hud.* I. I. 412 He got up to the saddle eaves, From whence he vaulted into th' seat. **1850** TENNYSON *In Mem.* lxvi, Closing eaves of wearied eyes I sleep. **1855** MAURY *Phys. Geog. Sea* xi. §511 The southern eaves of the cloud plane. **1860** TYNDALL *Glac.* I. ii. 21 Overhanging eaves of snow. **1862** BORROW *Wales* I. 4 A leather hat.. with the side eaves turned up.

3. *attrib.* and *Comb.* as *eave(s)-shoot, -spout, -trough* (designating various forms of gutter or spout to catch the drip from eaves); also *eaves-troughing*; **eaves-board** (also *eave-board*; see EAVE), **eaves-catch, -lath** (see quot. 1875); †**eaves-knife,** a knife for cutting thatch at the eaves; **eaves-martin,** the House Martin (*Hirundo urbica*). Also EAVES-DROP *sb.* and *v.*, -DROPPER, -DROPPING.

1399 *Mem. Ripon* (Surtees) III. 131 Tabulas quæ vocantur *Esborde. *c* **1505** *Church-w. Acc. St. Dunstan's Canterb.*, For xlv fote of *evys borde xvd. **1627** *MS. Acc. St. John's Hosp. Canterb.*, To the Sawyers for cutting of evesboord. **1809** R. LANGFORD *Introd. Trade* 88 The eave-boards project.. 16 inches. **1875** GWILT *Archit.*, *Arris fillet*. When.. used to raise the slates, at the eaves of a building, it is then called the eaves' board, eaves' lath, or *eaves' catch. **1641** BEST *Farm. Bks.* (1856) 139 A thatchers tooles are.. an *eize-knife for cutting the eize. **1422-3** *Archives Christ Ch. Canterb.* in *Archæol. Cantiana* XIII. 561 Item payd for Caryyng of the Schretherris *Evys-lathe, lathe, and tyle.. iiis. iiijd. **1833** J. HODGSON in J. Raine *Mem.* (1858) II. 307 The *eaves-martin very plentiful. **1889** 'HERRING' & 'ROSS' *Irish Cousin* II. III. iv. 207 The noisy splashing of the water that fell from a broken *eaveshoot on to the gravel. **1899** SOMERVILLE & 'ROSS' *Exper. Irish R.M.* i, The rain sluiced upon me from a broken eaveshoot. **1846** in N. Eliason *Tarheel Talk* (1956) 270 Put up smart of the *eve spout. **1865** H. B. STOWE *House & Home P.* 103 The water-barrel which stood under the eaves-spout. **1889** R. T. COOKE *Steadfast* xxxv. 369 A wild November storm shrieked and wailed in the eave-spout. **1851** H. MELVILLE *Moby Dick* III. xxxv. 211 Same with cocked hats; the cocks form gable-end *eave-troughs. **1878** B. F. TAYLOR *Between Gates* 176 Every day a wooden spout, a great eaves-trough was laid from the top of the steps. **1968** *Globe & Mail* (Toronto) 17 Feb. 53/3 (Advt.), Roofing & Eavestroughing. Chimney, eavestrough, roof repairs, free estimates, guaranteed.

'eavesdrip, -drop, *sb.* [OE. *yfesdrype*, f. EAVES + DRIP, afterwards refashioned after DROP; cf. ON. *upsar-dropi* of same meaning; the Flem. *oosdrup*, according to Kilian, meant simply 'eaves'.] The dripping of water from the eaves of a house; the space of ground which is liable to receive the rain-water thrown off by the eaves of a building.

Chiefly used with reference to the ancient custom or law which prohibited a proprietor from building at a less distance than two feet from the boundary of his land, lest he should injure his neighbour's land by 'eavesdrop.'

868 *Kentish Charter* in *Brit. Museum Fac-Sim.* II. plate xxxviii, An folcæs folcryht to lefænne rumæs butan twiȝen fyt to yfæs drypæ. **1837** CARLYLE *Fr. Rev.* (1872) III. I. ii. 15 The lean demigod.. had.. to wait under eavesdrops. **1880** MUIRHEAD *Gaius* Digest 590 Rights of light, prospect, gutter, and eaves-drop.

eavesdrop ('i:vzdrɒp), *v.* Also 7 **eave-drop.** [f. prec.; or perhaps back-formation from EAVESDROPPER.] *intr.* To stand within the 'eavesdrop' of a house in order to listen to secrets; hence, to listen secretly to private conversation. Also *trans.* To listen secretly to (conversation); formerly also, to listen within the 'eavesdrop' of (a house); to listen to the secrets of (a person).

1606 *Sir G. Goosecappe* v. i. in Bullen *O. Pl.* (1884) III. 82 We will be bold to evesdroppe. **1611** S. W. BAKER in Coryat *Crudities* Panegyr. Verses, That evesdrops a word. **1611** COTGR. s.v. *Escoute, Estre aux escoutes*.. to eaue-drop, to prie into men's actions or courses. **1619** DALTON *Countr. Just.* lxxv. (1630) 189 Against such as by night shall eves-drop mens houses. **1632** SHIRLEY *Hyde Park* I. ii, It is not civil to eavesdrop him. **1820** SCOTT *Abbot* xxi, Art thou already eaves-dropping? **1860** EMERSON *Cond. Life* v. *Behaviour* Wks. (Bohn) II. 386 We must not peep and eaves-drop at palace-doors. **1872** HOWELLS *Wedd. Journ.* 176 What we eavesdropped so shamefully in the hotel parlor.

eavesdropper ('i:vzdrɒpə(r)). For forms see EAVES. [f. EAVESDROP *v.* (or perhaps *sb.*) + -ER.]

a. In English Law: see quot. 1641. **b.** *gen.* One who listens secretly to conversation.

1487 *Nottingham Borough Rec.* III. 10 Juratores.. dicunt.. quod Henricus Rowley.. est communis evys-dropper et vagator in noctibus. *c* **1515** *Modus tenedi Cur. Baron.* (Pynson) A v b, Euesdroppers vnder mennes walles or wyndowes.. to bere tales. **1561** AWDELAY *Frat. Vocab.* 15 Esen Droppers. **1584** R. SCOT *Discov. Witchcr.* III. viii. 24 There must be some eves-dropers with pen and inke behind the wall. **1641** *Termes de la Ley* 153 Evesdroppers are such as stand under wals or windowes.. to heare news. **1748** RICHARDSON *Clarissa* (1811) II. xii. 72 Like a thief, or eves-dropper, he is forced to dodge about in hopes of a letter. **1851** W. W. COLLINS *Ramb. by Railways* xv. (1852) 290 The expertest eaves-droppers, who had listened at the door, brought away no information.

Hence **'eavesdropping** *vbl. sb.* and *ppl. a.*

1601 YARINGTON *Two Lament. Traj.* IV. vi. in Bullen *O. Pl.* IV, Your close eaves-dropping pollicies Have hindred him of greater benefits. **1641** MILTON *Animadv.* (1851) 191 To stand to the courtesy of a night-walking cudgeller for eaves dropping. **1672-3** *Roxb. Ballads* VI. (1887) 440 Where they need fear No.. eves-dropping ear. **1775** SHERIDAN *Rivals* III. iii, A beggarly, strolling, eavesdropping ensign. **1850** CLOUGH *Dipsychus* II. iii. 46 An eaves-dropping menial. **1853** WHARTON *Pa. Digest* 473 Eavesdropping consists in privily listening.

†**'eavesing.** *Obs.* Forms: 1 **oefsung, efesung,** 5 **evesung,** 4-6 **evyss-, evys-, evesyng, -ing,** 6 **eusing, eavesinge.** See also EASING *sb.*[2] [repr. OE. *efesung*, vbl. sb. f. *efes-ian*, EVESE *v.*; in sense 2 directly f. EAVES.]

†**1.** The action of trimming the edges of anything; clipping, polling, shearing. Also *concr.* What is cut off: the clippings of hair. *Obs.*

a **800** *Corpus Gloss.* 474 *Circinatio*, oefsung. *c* **1050** *Ags. Gloss.* in Wr.-Wülcker 364 *Circinnatio*, efesung. *a* **1225** *Ancr. R.* 398 Absalomes schene white, þet ase oft ase me euesede him me solde his euesunge vor two hundred sicles.

2. The eaves of a house or stack; formerly also used for 'roof', and hence *transf.* for 'dwelling'.

a **1225** *Ancr. R.* 142 Þe niht fuel iðen euesunge bitocneð recluses, þet wunieð.. under chirche euesunge. **1393** LANGL. *P. Pl.* C. xx. 193 As we may seo a wynter, Isykles in euesynges · thorgh hete of þe sonne Melteþ in a mynt-while · to myst and to water. *c* **1440** *Promp. Parv.* 144 Evese, or evesynge of a howse. **1547** SALESBURY *Welsh Dict.*, *Bargawt tuy*, house eusing. **1572** *Schole house Wom.* 912 in Hazl. *E.P.P.* IV. 140 King Salomon.. A woman dooth assimilate Unto a dropping euesing guise, Distilling down after rain late. **1572** BOSSEWELL *Armorie* II. 88 A righte little parte of water.. is called Gutta, when it.. hangeth on eavesinges.

eawiht, obs. form of AUGHT.

eax, obs. form of AXE.

eaxl, eaxle: see AXLE[1].

eban(e, -y, obs. forms of EBON, EBONY.

†**eban stone.** *Obs. rare*$^{-1}$.

1621 BURTON *Anat. Mel.* II. iv. I. iv. (1651) 370 The Eban stone which Goldsmiths use to sleeken their gold with.

†**ebapti'zation.** *Obs. rare*$^{-1}$. ? Declaring a person not to have been validly baptized.

1659 GAUDEN *Tears of Ch.* Δενδρολ. **2 f, Ebaptizations, Correptions, Abstentions, Excommunications.

†**e'bate.** *Obs.* [a. Fr. *ébat*.] Sport, diversion.

c **1515** *Compl. to late maryed* (1862) 14 For to blame women was all his ebate.

‖**ébauche** (eboʃ). [Fr., sketch.] **1.** *Painting* and *Sculpture.* A sketch, an outline drawing; a maquette, a rough-hewn version. Also *fig.*, a first draft or attempt.

1722 J. RICHARDSON *Statues in Italy* 310 The Work is extremely Good; not highly Finish'd, but rather a sort of *Ebauche*. **1841** J. S. MILL *Let.* Aug. in *Wks.* (1963) XIII. 483 Its deficiencies, as is usually the case with an *ébauche*, are chiefly in the introductory part. **1844** —— *Ess. Pol. Econ.* v. 126 As a mere anticipation or *ébauche* of a definition,.. we do not quarrel with the received formula. **1873** C. M. YONGE *Pillars of House* III. xxviii. 107 His sketch.. the hastily-designed and partly-coloured *ébauche*. **1958** *Times* 1 Feb. 8/5 A Deposition in our Sketch Club.. would not have been out of place among the *ébauches* of.. Tintoretto.

2. *Horology.* An unfinished watch movement, consisting of plates, bridges, etc.

1929 G. H. BAILLIE *Watches* xii. 251 In England, the *movement in grey* consisted of an *ébauche* with train of wheels and pinions, all more or less in the rough. **1965** *Economist* 18 Dec. 1348/1 These [Swiss] firms make their own *ébauches* (the top and bottom plates of the movement and the train of gears and pinions within).

‖**ebauchoir.** [F. *ébauchoir*, f. *ébaucher* to sketch in outline.] **a.** A large chisel used by sculptors to rough-hew their work. **b.** A large hatchel or comb used by ropemakers.

ebb (ɛb), *sb.* Forms: 1 **ebba,** 4-6 **ebbe,** 7 **eb,** 7- **ebb.** [OE. *ebba* = OFris. *ebba*, Du. *ebbe*, *eb*: the mod.G. *ebbe*, Da. *ebbe*, Sw. *ebb*, are not native in those langs., and Fr. *èbe* is, like other nautical terms, adopted from Eng. The ultimate etymology is uncertain: the OTeut. type might be **abjon-*, f. the prep. *ab* off; or **ebjon-*, connected with Goth. *ibuks* backwards.]

1. The reflux of the tide; the return of tide-water towards the sea. Often in phrase ***ebb and flow***; also ***tide of ebb, half-quarter-ebb.***

a **1000** *Byrhtnoth* 65 (Gr.) Þar com flowende flod æfter ebban. *a* **1123** *O.E. Chron.* an. 1114 On þis ȝeare wæs swa mycel ebba. **1330** R. BRUNNE *Chron. Langt.* (1810) 106 Þe bodies.. wer costen vpon þe sond, After an ebbe of þe flode. *c* **1440** *Promp. Parv.* 135 Ebbe of the see, *refluxus, salaria*. **1561** EDEN *Art. Navig.* II. xviii. 50 Whiche the Mariners call nepe tydes, lowe ebbs.. or lowe fluddes. **1603** DRAYTON *Bar. Warres* I. xxxix, As Seuerne lately in her Ebbes that sanke. **1665** in *Phil. Trans.* I. 54 The Flood runs East.. and the Ebb West. **1762** BORLASE *ibid.* LII. 418 The sea advancing the first time to a quarter ebb; but the second advance was but as far as the sea reaches at half ebb. **1832** DE LA BECHE *Geol. Man* 69 During the freshets the ebb and flow are little felt. **1840** MARRYAT *Poor Jack* xxvii, We.. made sail, stemming the last of the ebb.

2. *transf.* and *fig.* A flowing away backward or downward; decline, decay; a change from a better to a worse state.

c **1400** *Test. Love* I. (1560) 273/1 That sight.. might all my welling sorrowes voide, and of the flood make an ebbe. **1555** *Fardle Facions* Ded. 1 Not coueting to make of my flouḍde, another manes ebbe. **1652** J. HALL *Height Eloquence* Introd. 20 This.. was the Ebbe of his greatnesse. **1713** ADDISON *Cato* II. v. 80 To shed the slow remains, His last poor ebb of blood, in your defence. **1823** BYRON *Island* III. iv, His faintness came.. from.. nature's ebb. **1870** SWINBURNE *Ess. & Stud.* (1875) 279 Her ebbs and flows of passion.

b. A point or condition of decline or depression, *esp.* in phrases ***to be at an ebb, at a low, lowest ebb.*** Also *poet.* of the eyes, *at ebb*: dry.

1610 SHAKS. *Temp.* I. ii. 435 Mine eyes (neuer since at ebbe) beheld.. my Father wrack't. **1631** T. POWELL *Tom All Trades* 142 The low water ebbe of the evill day. **1654** WARREN *Unbelievers* 134 To make the Apostle reason at a very low ebbe. **1763** J. BROWN *Poetry & Mus.* vii. 154 Private and public Virtue were at the lowest Ebb. **1798** in Bay *Amer. Law Rep.* (1809) I. 36 In 1780 money was at its lowest ebb. **1876** GREEN *Short Hist.* ix. (1878) 698 The fortunes of France reached their lowest ebb.

3. *attrib.* and *Comb.*, as *ebb-tide*, etc. Also **ebb-sleeper,** a bird; = DUNLIN.

1699 B. E. *Dict. Cant. Crew*, *Ebb-water*, when there's but little Money in the Pocket. **1837** R. DUNN *Ornith. Ork. & Shet.* 87 *Tringa Variabilis*, Meyer. Ebb-sleeper, Dunlin. **1837** MARRYAT *Dog-Fiend* xxix, They were.. swept out of the harbour by the strong ebb tide. **1849** GROTE *Greece* (1862) V. II. lxiii. 448 They began to feel as if the ebb-tide had reached its lowest point. **1854** H. MILLER *Sch. & Schm.* (1858) 65, I was introduced also, in our ebb excursions, to the cuttle-fish.

†**4.** [? f. the adj.] *pl.* Shallows.

1577 HOLINSHED *Chron.* I. 41/2 Brigantines with flat keeles to serve for the ebbes.

5. [? a distinct word.] The Common Bunting, *Emberiza miliaria. dial.*

1802 G. MONTAGU *Ornith. Dict.* (1833) 61.

† **ebb**, *a. Obs.* exc. *dial.* Forms: 5–7 eb, 6–7 ebbe, 6– ebb. [app. evolved from the attrib. use of the sb., as in *ebb-tide*.]

1. Of water, wells, etc: Shallow, not deep. With *of*: Having a small supply, short. Also *fig.*

c **1425** WYNTOUN *Cron.* IX. iii. 47 Swlway was at þare passyng all Eb. **1523** FITZHERB. *Surv.* xi. 57 The ebber the water is, the swyfter it is. *c* **1581** J. FALKNER in *Eng. Mech.* (1870) 4 Feb. 500/2 The water of Trent [was] dried up, and sodenly fallen so ebb. **1637** RUTHERFORD *Lett.* xciv. I. 243 O, how ebb a soul have I to take in Christ's love! **1665–6** *Phil. Trans.* I. 165 When the water is drawn ebb from Fishes. **1693** LEIGHTON *Comm. 1 Peter* v. 8 This Apostle..drew from too full a spring to be ebb of matter. **1747** *Scheme Equip. Men of War* 23 Their Tide of Learning..is always ebb.

b. *transf.* of a furrow; the sides of a vessel, etc.

1523 FITZHERB. *Husb.* §33 A meane forowe, not to depe nor to ebbe. **1688** R. HOLME *Armoury* II. 185/1 A Greyhound [is] Ebb, or Shallow chested..[when he hath] his breast & body all of a thickness. *Ibid.* III. 320/1 It is a cooling Vessel..with ebb sides. **1733** P. LINDSAY *Interest Scotl.* 149 Plowed with an ebb Furrow. **1880** MISS JACKSON *Shropsh. Word-bk.*, Will this dish do to make the fitchock pie in? No; it's too ebb.

2. Near the surface; **a.** of the sea; **b.** of the land; also as quasi-*adv.*

1601 HOLLAND *Pliny* I. 40 A multitude of fishes floted ebbs about it. *Ibid.* II. 29 Cumin..hath a qualitie to grow with the root very eb. **1608–11** BP. HALL *Medit. & Vowes* II. xiii. Whether I be drowned in the ebber shore or in the midst of the deepe sea. **1679** PLOT *Staffordsh.* (1686) 119 Sometimes it [marl] lyes so ebb..that they plow up the head of it. **1747** HOOSON *Miner's Dict.* M iv b, If Ore be once discovered, and it lie Ebb and Soft. **1794** *Bailiff's Diary* in *Shropsh. Word-bk.*, I am convinced that it is too ebb plow'd.

ebb (ɛb), *v.* Forms: 1 ebbian, 2–5 ebben, 5–6 ebbe, 7– ebb. [OE. *ebbian*, f. EBB *sb.*; cf. OE. *a-ebbian, be-ebbian* to strand a ship; also OHG. *fir-ebbita* 'deferbuerat', and MHG. (*rare*$^{-1}$) *eppen* to ebb.]

1. *intr.* To flow back or recede, as the water of the sea or a tidal river: frequent in phrase, *to ebb and flow*. Also with *away, down, off, out*.

a **1000** *Cædmon's Gen.* (Gr.) 1413 Lago ebbade sweart under sweȝle. *c* **1200** *Trin. Coll. Hom.* 161 Þe sæ floweð and ebbeð. **1340** HAMPOLE *Pr. Consc.* 1216 The se, aftir the tydes certayn, Ebbes and flowes. **1375** BARBOUR *Bruce* XVII. 425 The se wes ebbit sa. *c* **1435** *Torr. Portugal* 223 The see wase ebbyd. **1588** SHAKS. *L.L.L.* IV. iii. 216 The will ebbe and flow. **1635** N. CARPENTER *Geog. Del.* II. vi. 86 In some narrow seas the sea seauen times a day ebbs and flowes. **1721** PERRY *Daggenh. Breach* 121 Ships..may lie afloat, and not have the Water ebb'd away from them. **1835** SIR J. ROSS *N.-W. Passage* v. 59 The water might ebb another fathom. **1855** MAURY *Phys. Geog.* ix. (1860) §429 The tides ebbed and flowed in it.

b. *transf.* Of a ship: To sink with the tide. Of water: To sink lower. Of blood: To flow away.

c **1374** CHAUCER *Troylus* IV. 1145 Ebben gan the well Of hir teares. **1375** BARBOUR *Bruce* XVII. 421 Quhill that scho [the ship] ebbit on the ground. **1655** MRQ. WORCESTER *Cent. Inv.* lvii, The water standing at a level, if a Globe be cast in ..it presently Ebbeth. **1810** SCOTT *Lady of L.* III. viii, [He] eyed The life-blood ebb in crimson tide.

2. *fig.* To take a backward or downward course; to decay, decline; to fade or waste away. Also with *away, down, off, out*.

a **1420** OCCLEVE *De Reg. Princ.* 4828 When that richesses ebben and abate. **1566** DRANT *Horace's Med. Morall* To Rdr. 3 Helpyng hym to ebbe, and helpyng hym to rise. **1633** T. JAMES *Voy.* 12 After full sea, our hopes ebde too. **1681** DRYDEN *Abs. & Achit.* 226 Kingly power, thus ebbing out. **1713** YOUNG *Last Day* II. 325 My passions ebb and flow At Thy command. **1720** DE FOE *Capt. Singleton* x. (1840) 170 As my money declined, their respect would ebb with it. **1833** HT. MARTINEAU *Vanderput & S.* ix. 137 As his strength ebbed away. **1875** B. TAYLOR *Faust* I. i. 29 My spirit's flood tide ebbeth more and more.

3. *trans.* **a.** To hem in (fish) with stakes and nets so that they cannot go back to sea with the ebb-tide; see EBBING *vbl. sb.* 2. **b.** To hem in (the tide) with sandbanks. **c.** (See quot. 1877.)

1827 HARDMAN *Waterloo* 12 Driving that sand along towards the sea shore, To ebb the tide fast in. **1877** *Holderness Gloss.* (E.D.S.), *Ebb*, to gather fish-bait. So termed on account of its being done whilst the tide is ebbing.

ebbed (ɛbd), *ppl. a.* [f. EBB *v.* + -ED.]

a. That has flowed back. **b.** That has been left dry by the falling tide.

1858 HOGG *Shelley* II. 204 A fresh flood of the ebbed waters of a wide sea of troubles. **1859** A. SMITH in *Macm. Mag.* I. 121, I can wander on the ebbed beach.

† ˈ**ebberman.** *Obs.* Also 6–8 hebberman. [f. *ebber*, agent-noun f. EBB *v.* (sense 3) + MAN.] (See quot. 1715.)

1715 KERSEY, *Hebberman*, one that fishes below Bridge, commonly at ebbing Water, etc. **1720** *Stow's Surv.* (ed. Strype 1754) I. I. vii. 35/1 A number of fishermen belonging to the..Thames some stiled..hebbermen. *Ibid.* II. v. xxvii. 480/2 No..Hebberman shall..fish for smelts, between Good Friday and, etc. **1721–90** in BAILEY.

ebbing (ˈɛbɪŋ), *vbl. sb.* [f. EBB *v.* + -ING[1].]

1. The action of flowing back or retiring: of the sea or a tidal river; also, of springs.

c **1000** ÆLFRIC *Voc.* in Wr.-Wülcker 154 *Sinus*, sæ æbbung. **1398** TREVISA *Barth. De P.R.* XIX. cxxvii. (1495) 929 Ebbynge and flowyng of the see comyth and gooth. *c* **1430** *Life St. Katherine* (Gibbs MS.) 52 The ebbyng and þe flowyng of þe see. **1695** WOODWARD *Nat. Hist. Earth* III. i. (1723) 173 The Ebbing and Flowing..of certain Springs. **1870** BOWEN *Logic* xii. 377 Sea-weed..left there by the ebbing of the tide.

b. *transf.* and *fig.*

c **1200** *Trin. Coll. Hom.* 177 For swich ebbinge. **1647** J. BERKENHEAD in *Beaum. & Fl. Wks.* Pref. Verses, Brave Shakespeare flow'd, yet had his Ebbings too. **1660** BOYLE *New. Exp. Phys.-Mech.* xviii. 136 There may be strange Ebbings and Flowings..in the Atmosphere. **1715** BURNET *Own Time* (1766) II. 141 Popular heats, which have their ebbings and flowings. **1863** J. BROWN *Horæ Subs.* (ed. 3) 109 Slow ebbing of life.

2. *Comb.*, as **ebbing-lock, -weir**, a lock or weir for detaining fish at the ebb-tide.

1472 *Act 12 Edw. IV*, vii, Ascuns..tielx..milledammez estankez de molyns lokkez hebbyngwerez, etc. **1531–2** *Act 23 Hen. VIII*, v. §2 Myldammes lokkes hebbynge weres heckes and fludgates. **1539** *Will of Samson, Eryth* (Somerset Ho.) My Tyde bote..my Hebbing locke. **1622** CALLIS *Stat. Sewers* (1647) 211 Locks and Hebbing-weres. **1715** KERSEY, *Hebbing-wears*, nets or devices laid for fish at ebbing water. **1721–90** in BAILEY.

ebbing, *ppl. a.* [f. EBB *v.* + -ING[2].] That ebbs.

1530 *Hist. Jacob & 12 Sonnes* (Collier) 19 Layed him on the fome..But..it was ebbing water. **1820** SHELLEY *Prometh. Unb.* III. ii. 28 Borne down the rapid sunset's ebbing sea. **1837** MARRYAT *Dog-Fiend* xii, They watch'd the ebbing tide. **1845** DARWIN *Voy. Nat.* xx. (1873) 458 These ebbing wells.

b. *transf.* and *fig.*

1597 DANIEL *Civ. Wars* VII. 10 For all this ebbing chance, remains The spring that feeds that hope. **1607** WALKINGTON *Opt. Glass* 53 Since after wine the ebbing'st wit doth flow. **1610** SHAKS. *Temp.* II. i. 226 Ebbing men..do so neere the bottome run. **1750** tr. *Leonardus' Mirr. Stones* 90 Crisoprasius is a stone..of an ebbing and confused colour. **1786** BURNS *Ded. to G. Hamilton* xii, When ebbing life nae mair shall flow. **1807** CRABBE *Par. Reg.* I. 295 My ebbing purse, no more the foe shall fill. **1840** G. S. FABER *Regen.* 263 Mr. Newton's ebbing and flowing religious impressions. **1866** G. MACDONALD *Ann. Q. Neighb.* xxi. (1878) 388 These tide-marks indicated ebbing strength.

† ˈ**ebble.** *Obs.* or *dial.* Also 5 awbel, ebel(le. [app. a var. of ABELE, though the form is not easy to explain.] The Aspen (*Populus tremula*); perhaps also the White Poplar (*Populus alba*).

c **1440** *Promp. Parv.* 17/2 Awbel or ebelle tre [*K, P,* ebeltre]. **1830** FORBY *E.-Angl. Glossary*, *Ebble*, the asp tree ..*populus tremula.*

ebbless (ˈɛblɪs), *a.* [f. EBB *sb.* + -LESS.] Not liable to, or susceptible of, an ebb.

1827 LYTTON *Falkland* 217 An ebbless and frozen substance. *a* **1849** J. C. MANGAN *Poems* (1859) 405 One ebbless flood of many Waves.

ˈ**ebbness.** *Obs.* or *dial.* [f. EBB *a.* + -NESS.] Shallowness.

1637 RUTHERFORD *Lett.* clxxv. I. 413 Their ebbness could never take up His depth.

† ˈ**ebby,** *a. Obs.* [f. EBB *sb.* + -Y.] Having an ebb or receding direction.

1645 DIGBY *Nat. Bodies* xxxv. (1658) 371 The current.. can make a contrary ebby water in the sam channell.

EBCDIC (ˈɛbsɪdɪk). *Computing.* Also Ebcdic. [Acronym f. the initial letters of *E*xtended *B*inary *C*oded *D*ecimal *I*nterchange *C*ode.] A standard eight-bit character code by which information is stored and transmitted in a computer or a data transmission system. Cf. ASCII.

1967 COX & GROSE *Organiz. Bibl. Rec. by Computer* IV. 84 The document control number has an upper limit in excess of two billion and may be recorded in binary, packed digits or EBCDIC in the input document. **1981** *Electronics* 21 Apr. 296 It can handle most standard protocols..and ASCII, EBCDIC, BCD, and Baudot codes. **1982** *Computerworld* 1 Feb. 40/1 A choice of Ascii-B or Ebcdic character sets is offered.

ebdomade, -ary, obs. ff. HEBDOMAD, -ARY.

eben(e, obs. form of EBON.

e'beneous. [f. L. *ebene-us* + -OUS.] Of the nature of ebony.

In mod. Dicts.

Ebenezer (ɛbəˈniːzə(r)). [Heb. *eben hā-ʿezer* 'the stone of help': see *1 Sam.* vii. 12.]

1. a. The name of the memorial stone set up by Samuel after the victory of Mizpeh: see *1 Sam.* vii. 12. Used appellatively in religious literature in fig. phrases, alluding to the sentiment 'Hitherto hath the Lord helped us', associated with the origin of the name. Chiefly *U.S.*

1693 C. MATHER *Wond. Invis. World* 14 Many an Ebenezer has been Erected unto the Praise of God by his Poor People here. **1745** *Essex Inst. Hist. Coll.* VI. 181/2, I can..here set up my Ebenezer, & say that hitherto God has preserved me. **1758** R. ROBINSON *Hymn*, '*Come Thou fount*', Here I raise my Ebenezer, Hither by Thy help I'm come. **1840** *Knickerbocker* XV. 184 These things..were only inducements to him to set up his Ebenezer in this place. **1870** J. H. B. NOWLAND *Early Reminisc. Indianapolis* 86 At a love-feast, the old man said..he was able to raise his Ebenezer, and that the cloud had passed away.

b. Temper, passion. *U.S. slang.*

Evidently by a misunderstanding of 'raise'.

1836 *Public Ledger* (Philad.) 27 July (Th.), Says I, Deb,.. I'll send you wool enough to make a wig. That ris Deb's ebenezer. **1838** T. C. HALIBURTON *Clockm.* 2nd Ser. xxii. 333 If you go for to raise your voice at him,..his Ebenezer is up in a minit. **1849** D. NASON *Jrnl.* 14 Our Steward is under the constant necessity of a check-rein upon his ebenezer.

2. Occasionally (like Bethel, Zoar, Zion, etc.) adopted by Methodists, Baptists, Independents, etc. as the name of a particular chapel or meeting-house. Hence used contemptuously as a synonym for 'dissenting chapel'.

1849 THACKERAY *Pendennis* I. xv. 133 Clavering New Church prospered... Their efforts had thinned the very Ebenezer hard by them. **1856** *Sat. Rev.* II. 318 Such low resorts as public-houses and Ebenezers. **1871** [see ZION].

‖ **ébéniste** (ebenist). [Fr., a furniture-worker who makes use of ebony, f. *ébène* ebony.] An EBONIST, *spec.* a French cabinet-maker who veneers furniture (orig. with ebony).

1906 R. GLAZIER *Man. Hist. Ornament* (ed. 2) 133 The famous master *ébénistes* of the Renascence, of whom the best known is André Boule. **1934** *Burlington Mag.* Oct. 157/1 The first maîtres ébénistes in Paris are mentioned in 1638, and from about that date ebony became one of the most appreciated kinds of 'bois des Indes' for furniture in Europe. **1955** *Times* 11 July 3/4 The French furniture..will include many fine pieces signed by the noted *ébénistes* M. Carlin, N. Petit, R. Lacroix, and C. C. Saunier.

Hence **ébénisterie** (ebenistri), cabinet-making in the manner of the *ébénistes*.

1910 *Encycl. Brit.* IV. 322/1 Boulle..had not only inherited the rather flamboyant Italian traditions of the late Renaissance, but had *ébénisterie* in his blood. **1945** *Burlington Mag.* Oct. 260/2 The bulk of the ébénisterie was carried out by a certain George.

† ˈ**eber,** *a. Obs.* Also 1–2 æbére, æbǽre, 3 ebare, ebure, 4 ebber. [OE. *ǽbére*, (? *æbere*), of obscure origin; = OFris. *âber, âuber*, used as a law term in same sense.]

1. Manifest, unconcealed. The phrase ***ebere morþ*** (open murder) is retained in the Latin Laws of Henry I, and is quoted by the legal antiquaries of 17th c. as a technical term; see also ABERE. (Occasionally *absol.* ? = 'manifest fool' or 'villain'.)

a **975** *Laws of Eadgar* II. vii, Se æbera þeof. *a* **1035** *Laws of Cnut* (Secular) lxv, Husbryce & bærnet & open þyfð and æbere morþ..is botleas. *c* **1200** ORMIN 7189 All þeȝȝre æbære unnþankness. *c* **1205** LAY. 2271 Saie me þu ebure [**1275** ebare] sot. *a* **1300** *Cursor M.* 13662 He wald lere vs her vr lai, þat ebber þat in sine was gotin. *Ibid.* 15921 'Ful eber thuert [*read* thu ert] nai' coth he. *c* **1340** *Ibid.* 13041 (Trin.) She þat was an ebber [*G.* obber] fol.

Hence † ˈ**eberly** *adv.*, manifestly, flagrantly.

a **1300** *Cursor M.* 8680 þou lies..Ful eberli.

† **e'bibe,** *a. Obs. rare*$^{-1}$. [ad. L. *ēbibĕre*, f. *ē* out + *bib-ĕre* to drink.] *trans.* To drink to the dregs, swallow completely. In quot. *fig.*

1689 *Apol. Fail. Walker's Acc.* 13 Having long before ebib'd the Doctrine of Passive Obedience.

Ebionite (ˈiːbɪənaɪt). [ad. L. *ebionita*, f. Heb. *ebyōn* poor; see -ITE. The original signification is prob. 'one who is poor in spirit'.]

One of a body of Christians in the 1st c., who held that Jesus was a mere man, and that the Mosaic Law was binding upon Christians. In the 2nd c. they became a distinct sect. Also *attrib.*

1650 GELL *Serm.* 11 Ebionites, who denied the Deitie of Christ. **1879** FARRAR *St. Paul* II. 103 Ebionite hatred [was] still burning against St. Paul in the second century. **1882** —— *Early Chr.* II. 343.

Hence ˌ**Ebioˈnitic** *a.*, pertaining to the Ebionites, or their doctrines; ˈ**Ebioˌnitism** = EBIONISM.

1780 N. LARDNER *Hist. Heretics* I. 20 Epiphanius's Introduction to his Account of Ebionitism must be allowed to be a remarkable instance of harshness, not to say railing. **1833** G. S. FABER *Recapitulated Apostasy* 18 The early Gnostic and Ebionitic Heresies. **1856** BAGEHOT *Coll. Works* (1965) I. 388 Strange confused beliefs, Millenarianism, Gnosticism, Ebionitism, were accepted. **1882** SCHAFF *Relig. Encycl.* 106 It..shows traces of Ebionitic origin. **1882** FARRAR *Early Chr.* II. 44 The so-called Ebionitism of St. James.

Ebionize (ˈiːbɪənaɪz), *v.* [f. EBION-ITE + -IZE; see -IZE.] *intr.* To adopt or imitate the doctrines or practices of the Ebionites. Hence ˈ**Ebioˌnizing** *ppl. a.* So also ˈ**Ebionism**, the tenets of the Ebionites; tendency towards the tenets or practices of the Ebionites.

1879 FARRAR *St. Paul* II. 168 The liberal Gentiles far more than the Ebionising Jews. *Ibid.* 173 The Ebionism of this section of the Church. **1880** CHAMBERS *Encycl.* s.v. *Ebionites*, Essenism modified Ebionism greatly.

Eblaite (ˈɛblaɪt, ˈiːblaɪt), *sb.* and *a.* [f. *Ebla*, the ancient name of the city of Tell Mardikh in

northern Syria + -ITE[1].] **A.** *sb.* **a.** An ancient inhabitant of Ebla. **b.** A pre-Phoenician Semitic language examples of which were first discovered by Paolo Matthiae (b. 1940), Italian archaeologist and scholar, at the site of Ebla in 1974. **B.** *adj.* Of or pertaining to these people or their language.

1976 *Biblical Archeologist* XXXIX. 47/2 Only under Naram-Sîn did Akkad recover well enough to defeat the Eblaites and finally to destroy Ebla itself. *Ibid.* 49/1 The presence in the Eblaite pantheon of some Sumerian deities. **1976** *N.Y. Post* 9 June 60 Scholars have been electrified by the parallels between the language of the tablets and the language of ancient Hebrews. Eblaite.. seems to be a West Semitic form unlike Sumerian, Akkadian or any of the other ancient languages known to modern science. **1976** *Sci. News* 21 Aug. 118 One of the most important tablets is one containing a vocabulary of Eblaite and Sumeric words. **1978** BERMANT & WEITZMAN *Ebla* (1979) vii. 160 A number of tablets have been discovered with a bearing on Eblaite law. *Ibid.* 161 Other Eblaites followed him on the throne of Mari. **1980** C. HOLME tr. *P. Matthiae's Ebla* vii. 220 (*heading*) Value and originality of the Eblaite culture of the third millennium. **1981** [see UGARITIC *sb.* and *a.*].

ebland, var. of IBLAND, *obs.* among.

†**'eblandish**, *v. Obs. rare*$^{-0}$. [as if f. F. **éblandiss-*, lengthened form of **éblandir*:—L. *ēblandīri* to obtain by coaxing.] (See quot.)

1623 COCKERAM II, To get by Flattery.. *Eblandish*.

†**e'blaze, e'blazon**, *v. Obs. rare.* [f. E-[3] (after words of Lat. etymology) + BLAZE, BLAZON *v.*] *intr.* To shine forth in bright colours.

1610 G. FLETCHER *Christ's Tri.* ii, Th' engladded Spring .. Began to eblazon from her leauie bed. —— *Christ's Vict.* in Farr's *S.P.* (1848) 61 There pinks eblazed wide, And damaskt all the earth.

E-boat. Used, esp. in the war of 1939–45, as an abbreviation for an enemy torpedo-boat.

The view, frequently expressed, that *E* represents G. *Eile* 'speed' is purely speculative. The usual G. word for a speedboat is *Schnellboot*.

1940 *Hutchinson's Pict. Hist. of War* 7 Aug.—1 Oct. 16 One of our motor torpedo-boats, thinking that the enemy ahead was an E-boat, and being too close to take action, rammed the enemy. **1941** *Times Weekly* 30 July 7/3 One ship of the convoy received damage from an E-boat attack. **1958** *Listener* 30 Oct. 691/1 E-boat scares on the convoy routes.

Eboe ('i:bəʊ). A name applied in the W. Indies and U.S. to the Negroes from Benin. The same term as IBO in West Africa, but used with wider application in the W. Indies. Hence *attrib.* **eboe-tree** (*Dipteryx eboensis*), a tree of Central America, yielding **eboe oil**, a name also given to the oil of a different tree; see quot.

1732, 1774 [see IBO *a.*]. **1834** M. LEWIS *Jrnl. W. Ind.* 126 Immediately after the christening the Eboe drums were produced. *Ibid.* 190 The mortification of the Eboes. **1866** *Treas. Bot.* 476 *Aleurites triloba* [candleberry-tree] yields eboe oil.

ebolition, obs. var. EBULLITION.

ebon ('ɛbən), *sb.* and *a.* Forms: (4 **ebenus**), 5–7 **eban(e, heban**, 6–7 **eben(e, heben(e, ebone**, (9 *arch.* **heben**), 6– **ebon**. Some of the forms in *-e* may belong to EBONY. [ad. L. *hebenus, ebenus*, ad. Gr. ἔβενος, perh. of oriental origin: the Heb. *hobnīm* (Ezek. xxvii. 15) is supposed to be the same word. In med.L. *(h)ebanus*, whence some of the Eng. forms; cf. It., Sp., Pg. *ebano*.]

A. *sb.*

1. A hard black wood, the product of a tree belonging to the N.O. *Ebenaceæ*, mentioned in very early times as an article of import from the East; = EBONY. Now only *poet.*

[**1398** TREVISA *Barth. De P.R.* XVII. lii. (1495) 633 Ebenus is a tree growynge in Ethiopia wyth blacke coloure.] *c* **1440** *Promp. Parv.* 135 Eban, tre, *ebanus*. **1558** WARDE tr. *Alexis' Secr.* 96 a, It is very good.. also to make tables and coffers of .. Hebene. **1580** HOLLYBAND *Treas. Fr. Tong, De l' Hebene*, a wood called Heben. **1627** MAY *Lucan* x. 139 Pillars there Not covered with Ægyptian Eben were. **1697** DRYDEN *Virgil* (1806) I. 207 India black ebon and white iv'ry bears. **1846** LYTTON *Lucretia* (1853) 301 Dark as ebon, spreads the one wing.

†**2.** The tree itself, *Diospyros Ebenus*, a native of Ceylon, Madagascar, and the Mauritius. *Obs.*

1555 EDEN *Decades W. Ind.* (Arb.) 284 Wodde of Heben. **1601** HOLLAND *Pliny* I. 148 Great woods of Ebene.. alwaies greene. **1623** COCKERAM III, *Ebone*, a blacke tree, bearing not leafes nor fruit, being burnt, it yeelds a sweet smell.

B. *attrib.* and *adj.* (chiefly *poet.* or *rhet.*)

1. simple *attrib.*

a **1599** SPENSER *Ruines of Time* Wks. (1678) 139 A curious Coffer made of Heben wood. **1613** PURCHAS *Pilgr.* I. VII. xi. 595 They found excellent Eben Trees. **1813** SCOTT *Trierm.* III. xiii, A weighty curtal-axe.. the tough shaft of heben wood.

2. *attrib.* or quasi-*adj.* Consisting or made of ebony; often *fig.* for 'black, dark'.

1592 SHAKS. *Ven. & Ad.* 948 Deaths ebon dart. **1633** P. FLETCHER *Pisc. Ecl.* VII. xvii, Her eye-brow black, like to an ebon bow. **1737** WEST *Let.* in *Gray's Poems* (1775) 20 Fate, whose ebon sceptre rules The Stygian deserts. **1742** YOUNG *Nt. Th.* I. 18 Night, sable goddess! from her ebon throne. **1772** SIR W. JONES *Arcadia* Poems (1777) 102 With ebon knots, and studs of silver, wrought. **1818** SHELLEY *Rev. Islam* I. xxx, But when in ebon Mirror, Nightmare fell. **1863** LONGF. *Wayside Inn, 2nd Day*, Interl. III. 19 From out its ebon case his violin the minstrel drew.

3. *adj.* Of the colour of ebony; black, dark, sombre.

1607 HEYWOOD *Fair M. of Exchange* i. Wks. 1874 II. 16 As blind as Ebon night. **1632** MILTON *L'Allegro* 5 There under ebon shades.. In dark Cimmerian desert ever dwell. *a* **1703** POMFRET *Poet. Wks.* (1833) 116 Night.. spreads her ebon curtains round. **1802** COLERIDGE *Sibyl. Leaves* II. 196 Deep in the air and dark, substantial, black, An ebon mass. **1843** PRESCOTT *Mexico* III. vi. (1864) 168 The image of the mystic deity.. with ebon features.

¶**4.** Erroneously used for 'ivory'.

1593 G. FLETCHER *Licia* Sonn. xxix. (1872) 109 Her Ebon thighes. *Ibid.* xxxix. (1872) 109 Those Ebon hands.

C. *Comb.* **a.** similative, as *ebon-black, -coloured*; **b.** instrumental and parasynthetic, as *ebon-faced, -masted, -sceptred, -tipped*, etc.

1592 GREENE *Poems* 85 How bright-eyed his Phillis was.. When fro th' arches *ebon-black flew looks as a lightning. **1588** SHAKS. *L.L.L.* I. i. 246 The *ebon coloured Inke. **1835–6** TODD *Cycl. Anat.* I. 621/1 Melanosis may be found in the form of brown or ebon-coloured fluid. **1601** *Death Earl Huntington* II. i. in Hazl. *Dodsley* VIII. 256 Pitch-colour'd, *ebon-fac'd, blacker than black. **1845** HIRST *Poems* 66 Royal vessels.. *ebon masted. **1745** T. WARTON *Pleas. Melanch.* 113 Night.. Sister of *ebon-sceptred Hecat, hail! **1818** KEATS *Endym.* I. 147 With *ebon-tipped flutes.

Hence '**ebonine** *a.*, dark, sombre.

1881 PALGRAVE *Visions of Eng.* 292 Through that ebonine gate of doom The thrice five thousand are flown.

ebonist ('ɛbənɪst). [f. EBON-Y + -IST. Cf. F. *ébéniste*.] A worker or dealer in ebony or other ornamental woods.

1706 PHILLIPS, *Ebonist*, one that works or deals in Ebony. **1721–1800** in BAILEY. **1871** *Athenæum* 24 June 783 A great hubbub of glaziers, carpenters, ebonists, iron and tile workers.

ebonite ('ɛbənaɪt). [f. EBON-Y + -ITE.] A hard compound of india-rubber and sulphur, united by the action of heat. Another name for it is VULCANITE. Also *attrib.*

1861 *Chem. News* Oct. 221 The material known as hard india rubber, vulcanite,.. or in its most perfect condition as ebonite. **1879** in *Cassel's Techn. Educ.* IV. 288/1 Hard or horny caoutchouc, such as will come under the designation of ebonite.

ebonize ('ɛbənaɪz), *v.* [f. EBON-Y + -IZE.] *trans.* To make (furniture, etc.) look like ebony.

Hence '**ebonized** *ppl. a.*

1880 *Daily Tel.* 27 Oct., Since black and gold is so fashionable in furniture, he might be agreeably ebonised and gilded. **1879** MISS BRADDON *Vixen* III. 313 Ebonised chairs.

ebony ('ɛbənɪ). Forms: 4 **hebenyf**, 6 **hebeny, ebonie**, (7 **ebany, ebeny, ibony**), 7– **ebony**. [Of somewhat obscure formation: ME. *hebenyf* is app. ad. L. *hebeninus* (? misread as *hebeniuus*), ad. Gr. ἐβένινος made of ebony, f. *hebenus* ebony. Cf. EBON.]

1. a. A hard black wood, obtained from various species of the N.O. *Ebenaceæ*, especially that mentioned under EBON *sb.* 2, and *Diospyros Melanoxylon*, a native of Coromandel. **b.** The wood of *Brya Ebenus* (quot. 1725), a native of Jamaica.

1382 WYCLIF *Ezek.* xxvii. 15 Teeth of.. hebenyf [Vulg. *dentes hebeninos*], *that is a tree that after that it is kit waxith hard as a stoon.* **1573** *Art Limning* 9 The saide vernishe maketh tables.. of.. hebeny to glister. **1597** GREENE *Poems* (1861) 312 In a coach of ebony she went. **1608** NORDEN *Surv. Dial.*, I saw pales made of an Oke.. blacke as Ibony. **1682** WHELER *Journ. Greece* VI. 448 Here grows some Ebany. *a* **1748** THOMSON *Sickness* I. (R.) Affliction, hail!.. open wide thy gates, Thy gates of ebony. **1816** J. SMITH *Panorama Sci. & Art* I. 84 Hard woods, such as box, lignum-vitæ, or ebony. **1837** WHEWELL *Hist. Induct. Sc.* (1857) II. 50 A ball of ebony sinks in the water. **1878** BOSW. SMITH *Carthage* 434 Real downright negroes, half-naked, black as ebony.

2. One of the trees above-mentioned.

1810 *Charac.* in *Ann. Reg.* 614/2 There are entire woods of cedars and ebonies. **1859** TENNENT *Ceylon* II. IX. v. 494 Ebony is the most important of the trees which they are in the habit of felling.

3. *attrib.*

1598 W. PHILLIPS *Linschoten's Trav. Ind.* in Arb. *Garner* III. 28 They carry into India, gold.. ebony wood. **1633** G. HERBERT *Temple, Even-song*, Thus in thy Ebony box Thou dost inclose us. **1681** R. KNOX *Hist. Ceylon* 86 Ebeny pestels about four foot long. **1756–7** tr. *Keysler's Trav.* (1760) I. 378 A large nasso, or ebony-tree, which much resembles the fir-tree. **1861** DU CHAILLU *Equat. Afr.* xvi. 277 Quengueza and I.. started up river for the ebony country.

4. a. As the type of intense blackness. *son of ebony*: humorously = Negro. Also *attrib.*, as in *ebony complexion, skin*, etc.

1823 C. MATHEWS *Let.* 23 Feb. in *Memoirs* (1839) III. 388 A Hottentot Adonis appeared, with.. an effluvia arising from his ebony skin. **1834** MRS. SOMERVILLE *Connex. Phys. Sc.* xxvii. (1849) 308 The different tribes of mankind, from the ebony skin of the torrid zone to, etc. **1850** MRS. STOWE *Uncle Tom's C.* vi. 35 Black Sam.. about three shades blacker than any other son of ebony on the place. **1878** BOSW. SMITH *Carthage* 39 A race of savages.. the ebony negroes of the Soudan.

b. A Negro. *U.S.*

1851 H. MELVILLE *Moby Dick* II. xxii. 165 The old black .. came shambling along from his galley;.. this old Ebony floundered along. **1863** 'E. KIRKE' *My Southern Friends* iv. 69 The scented ebony roared. **1889** FARMER *Americanisms* s.v., An *ebony* is a negro in common parlance.

‖**eboulement.** [F. *éboulement*, f. *ébouler* to crumble (said of earthworks).]

1. *Fortification.* The crumbling or falling of the wall of a fortification.

2. *Geology.* A sudden rock-fall and earthslip in a mountainous region.

ebracteate, -ated (i:'bræktiːət, -eɪtɪd). *Bot.* [ad. mod.L. *ēbracteātus*, f. *ē-* out of + *bractea* BRACT; see -ATE, -ED.] Destitute of bracts.

1830 LINDLEY *Nat. Syst. Bot.* 167 Apetalous dicotyledons, with.. herbaceous ebracteate calyxes. **1870** BENTLEY *Bot.* 181 When bracts are absent altogether, such plants are said to be ebracteated. **1882** VINES *Sachs' Bot.* 621 The ebracteate flowers stand on the rachis of the inflorescence.

e'bracteolate, *a. Bot.* [ad. mod.L. *ēbracteolātus*; cf. prec. and BRACTEOLATE.] Not furnished with bracteoles.

1870 HOOKER *Stud. Flora* 201 Receptacle ebracteolate.

Ebraick, Ebrew: see HEBRAIC, HEBREW.

1721–1800 in BAILEY, *Ebraick*.

†**e'brangle**, *v. Obs. rare*$^{-1}$. [ad. F. *ébranler*, after BRANGLE.] *trans.* To shake violently.

a **1693** URQUHART *Rabelais* III. xxxii. (1708) 452 Their whole body is shaken and ebrangled.

ebriate ('i:brɪət), *a. humorous.* [ad. L. *ēbriāt-us*, pa. pple. of *ēbriāre* to make drunk.] Intoxicated; *fig.* Hence '**ebriating** *ppl. a.*, intoxicating.

1847 *Blackw. Mag.* LXI. 704 Acme.. Kissed her sweet youth's ebriate eyes. **1872** M. COLLINS *Plunges for Pearl* II. vii. 120 He.. solaced himself with something ebriating.

†'**ebrie,tating**, *ppl. a. Obs. rare*$^{-1}$. [f. **ebrietate* vb. (f. EBRIETY + -ATE; cf. *capacitate, habilitate*, etc.) + -ING[2].] Intoxicating.

1711 *Brit. Apollo* IV. No. 18. 2/1 Things.. of an ebrietating Quality.

ebriety (ɪ'braɪɪtɪ). [ad. F. *ébriété*, f. L. *ēbrietāt-em*, f. *ēbrius* drunk.]

1. The state or habit of being intoxicated, drunkenness. †Also *pl.* instances of intoxication.

1582 *N.T.* (Rhem.) *Gal.* v. 21 The workes of the flesh.. are, fornication.. ebrieties, commessations, and such like. **1614** T. ADAMS *Devil's Banq.* 42 The Satietie of Epicurisme, the gallantnesse of Ebrietie. **1670** MAYNWARING *Vita Sana* vi. 73 Ebriety may properly be said to be a Disease or sickness. **1758** *Monthly Rev.* 185 Some under the most extreme exigencies of poverty, will indulge in ebriety. **1785** W. F. MARTYN *Geog. Mag.* II. 144 His father's unconquerable ebriety. **1859** JEPHSON *Brittany* xvi. 273 Our guide to the garrulity of age added that of partial ebriety.

2. *fig.* Excitement, an excited condition.

1751 JOHNSON *Rambl.* No. 167 ¶6, The ebriety of constant amusement.

‖**ebrillade.** [Fr.] *Manège.* A check of the bridle which the horseman gives to the horse, by a jerk of one rein, when he refuses to turn.

1753 CHAMBERS *Cycl. Supp.* **1755** JOHNSON; and mod. Dicts.

ebriose (ˌi:brɪ'əʊs), *a. humourous.* [ad. L. *ēbriōsus*.] Drunk.

1871 *Atlantic Monthly* Jan., A.. cabman 'copiously ebriose'. *a* **1882** J. BROWN *John Leech* in *Horæ Subs.* Ser. III. (1882) 17 Returning home.. copiously ebriose from Epsom.

ebriosity (i:brɪ'ɒsɪtɪ). *rare.* [ad. F. *ebriosité*, L. *ēbriōsitāt-em*, f. *ēbriōsus* habitually drunk.]

a. Habitual intoxication. **b.** Exhilaration; physical excitement.

1646 SIR T. BROWNE *Pseud. Ep.* 270 Will neither acquit ebriosity nor ebriety, in their known and intended perversions. **1859** THOREAU *Walden* xi. 237 Of all ebriosity, who does not prefer to be intoxicated by the air he breathes.

ebrious ('i:brɪəs), *a.* [f. L. *ēbri-us* + -OUS.]

a. Addicted to drink; tipsy. **b.** Characteristic of the intoxicated state. Hence '**ebriously** *adv.*

1569 NEWTON *Cicero's Old Age* 33 Not ebriously swilled but moderatlye tasted. **1630** PRYNNE *Anti-Armin.* 268 The second was but a dissolute, ebrious, prophane, luxurious English-Dutchman. **1656** BLOUNT *Glossogr.*, *Ebrious*, drunken, or that causeth drunkenness. **1858** *Cassell's Art Treas. Exhib.* 412 Those young sots with the ebrious faces.

†**E'britian.** *Obs. rare*$^{-1}$. [irreg. f. *Ebr-ew* HEBREW, to match *Grecian*.] A Hebraist.

1691 WOOD *Ath. Oxon.* I. 97 He was a very good Grecian and Ebritian.

†'**ebryson**, *a. Obs. rare*$^{-1}$. [prob. corrupted form of late Gr. ὄβρυζον (χρυσίον) pure gold, Cf. Chambers *Cycl. Supp.* (1753), '*Ebrizius color*, a

term used by some of the old writers to express a very fine yellow'.]
*c*1485 *Digby Myst.* (1882) I. 14 Of Ierico the sote rose ffloure, Gold Ebryson callid in pictur.

†**e'buccinate**, *v. Obs.* [f. E- + BUCCINATE.] *trans.* To trumpet forth. Hence **e'buccinator**.
1541 BECON *News out of Heav.* Wks. (1843) 43 The ebuccinator, shewer, and declarer of these news, I have made Gabriel. **1588** NEWTON in Farr's *S.P.* (1845) II. 553 The troupes seraphicall.. Ebuccinate Gods power. **1666** tr. *Horace 2 Odes* xix, He fill'd with Bacchus power assayes To ebuccinate his fame and praise.

†**'ebull.** *Obs. rare*⁻¹. [ad. L. *ebulus*.] The Dwarf Elder (*Sambucus Ebulus*).
1398 TREVISA *Barth. De P.R.* XVII. lx. (1495) 636 Ebulus is a wede moost lyke to Elerne tree bothe in leuys and in stalkys. **1589** FLEMING *Virg. Eclog.* x. 23 Pan..we saw [colourd] red With bloudie berries of ebull tree.

†**'ebullate**, *v. Obs. rare.* Also 8 **ebulate**. [f. late L. *ebullāre*, var. of *ebullīre*; see -ATE.] *intr.* To boil, be in a state of ebullition.
1623 COCKERAM I I, To Boyle, Elixate, Ebullate. **1656** BLOUNT *Glossogr.*, *Ebullate*, to bubble or burst out. **1738** [G. SMITH] *Cur. Relations* II. 195 Continually boiling and ebulating over a great Fire.

e'bulliate. *rare.* [badly f. L. *ēbullīre*; see next and -ATE³.] *trans.* and *intr.* To boil; to bubble out.
1599 A. M. tr. *Gabelhouer's Bk. Physicke* 38/2 The vineger wherin the pepper was ebulliated. **1633** PRYNNE *Histrio-M.* I. vi. iii. (R.) Whence this 29. play-oppugning argument will ebulliate. **1710** *Brit. Apollo* III. 77 The Blood..ebulliates. **1853** LANDOR *Wks.* (1868) II. 259 A heart too contracted.. to let what it holds ebulliate very freely.

ebullience (ɪ'bʌlɪəns). [f. L. *ēbullient-em*, pr. pple. of *ēbullīre*, f. *ē* out + *bullīre*, to BOIL. See -ENCE.] An issuing forth in agitation, like boiling water; overflow; enthusiasm, extravagance.
1749 FIELDING *Tom Jones* Wks. 1775 II. 170 The extravagance, or rather ebullience of his passion. **1825** CARLYLE *Schiller* II (1845) 79 The ebullience of youth is now chastened into the stedfast energy of manhood. **1885** SWINBURNE in *19th Cent.* Jan. 67 The danger of an overflow into gushing ebullience.

ebulliency (ɪ'bʌlɪənsɪ). [f. prec. + -Y.]
1. The quality of being ebullient: readiness to boil or bubble forth or overflow. *lit.* and *fig.*
1676 R. DIXON *Two Test.* 228 Mistaking..the ebulliency of their Fancies..for a supernatural Inspiration. **1817** COLERIDGE *Biog. Lit.* 68 The simple, whom.. an original ebulliency of spirit, had urged to the investigation of the ground of all things. **1885** *Athenæum* 19 Sept. 379/2 Neville acts with his customary ebulliency and manliness.
2. *pl.* = EBULLITION 4.
1667 H. MORE *Div. Dial.* i. §12 (1713) 24 In the.. ferments and ebulliencies of the Spirits of Men in this Age.

ebullient (ɪ'bʌlɪənt). [ad. L. *ēbullient-em*, pr. pple. of *ēbullīre*; see prec.]
1. That boils; boiling; agitated, as if boiling.
1599 A. M. tr. *Gabelhouer's Bk. Physicke* 4/1 Let this bottle remayne one hower in hot ebullient water. **1814** CARY *Dante* (1871) 304 Every cirque Ebullient shot forth scintillating fires. **1842** G. P. SCROPE *Volcanos* 14 Lava in a liquid and ebullient state.
2. a. Of the humours of the body: Agitated, hot, effervescent. **b.** Of drugs and diseases: Causing heat and agitation.
1620 VENNER *Via Recta* iv. 79 The same is of an hot and ebullient nature. *Ibid.* (1650) 161 They engender ebullient humors. **1684** tr. *Bonet's Merc. Compit.* VI. 226 The body is affected..as if some part were put in boiling water, wherefore some have called this the Ebullient Ague. **1727** SWIFT *Gulliver* III. vi. 216 Great counsels are often troubled with..ebullient..humours. **1742** YOUNG *Nt. Th.* VIII. 1320 They scarce can swallow their ebullient spleen.
3. *fig.* Of energy, feelings, influences: Gushing forth like boiling water; bubbling over, overflowing, enthusiastic. Constr. *with*.
1664 H. MORE *Myst. Iniq.* vii. 126 That fountain of life which ought to be ebullient in every Regenerate Christian. **1828** SOUTHEY *Ess.* (1832) I. 352 The general and ebullient feeling with which all Britain overflowed imposed silence upon the lying lips. **1844** *Blackw. Mag.* LVI. 532 His commentaries on the past are ebullient with subtlety. **1876** G. P. LATHROP in *N. Amer. Rev.* CXXIII. 429 The ebullient undulating prose style of the poet.
Hence **e'bulliently** *adv.*
1887 *Punch* 10 Sept. 110 Ebulliently sentimental novelist.

ebullioscope (ɪ'bʌlɪəʊskəʊp). [mod.f. in Fr.; hybrid formation on L. *ēbullīre* + Gr. -σκοπος an observer.] (See quot.)
1880 *Chamber's Cycl.*, *Ebullioscope*, an instrument for ascertaining the strength of distilled liquors by observing the boiling point and the atmospheric pressure. **1882** *Nature* No. 636. 236 [M. Malligand's] ebullioscope..which the French Syndical Chambers adopted in 1878.

ebullioscopic (ɪ,bʌlɪəʊ'skɒpɪk), *a.* [f. EBULLIOSCOPE + -IC.] Of or pertaining to the ebullioscope or ebullioscopy. So **ebullioscopy** (ɪbʌlɪ'ɒskəpɪ), the study and use of the ebullioscope.
1902 *Nature* 4 Sept. 436/2 Molecular weight determinations in liquid nitrogen peroxide by the ebullioscopic method. **1914** *Jrnl. Chem. Soc.* CVI. II. 170 Of the following five formulæ for calculation of the ebullioscopic constant. **1914** *Jrnl. Amer. Chem. Soc.* XXXVI. II. 1411 The Constants of Ebullioscopy and Cryoscopy. **1922** *Jrnl. Chem. Soc.* Abstr. II. 117 Extension of ebullioscopy and its application to binary mixtures. **1948** GLASSTONE *Physical Chem.* (ed. 2) ix. 636 The proportionality constant K_e is called the molal elevation constant, or the ebullioscopic constant, and..it can be seen to be equivalent to the boiling point elevation for a solution of unit molality. *Ibid.* 637 The experimental procedure is often described as the ebullioscopic method for the determination of molecular weights, and the whole subject is referred to as ebullioscopy. **1956** *Nature* 21 Jan. 128/1 Molecular weight determination (by ebullioscopic method in methanol) gave 445.

ebullism ('ɛbəlɪz(ə)m). [f. L. *ēbullīre* (see EBULLIENCE): see -ISM.] The formation of bubbles in body fluids as a result of reduced environmental pressure.
1956 J. E. WARD in *Jrnl. Aviation Med.* XXVII. 439/1 The term 'ebullism' is introduced to describe the phenomenon of vaporization of body fluids at low atmospheric pressures and at body temperatures. **1962** F. I. ORDWAY et al. *Basic Astronautics* xii. 460 At 12 miles there is another functional border. Here the atmospheric pressure is so low, 47 mm Hg, that it equals the water vapor pressure of the body's fluids at body temperature and ebullism occurs. **1974** *Encycl. Brit. Macropædia* I. 143/1 Ebullism, or boiling of body fluids, occurs immediately after exposure to altitudes above 63,000 feet and may significantly increase hypoxic effects.

ebullition (ɛbʌ'lɪʃən). Forms: 6 **ebullycion**, **ebulicion**, **-ition**, 6–7 **ebolition**, 7 **ebulliction**, 7– **ebullition**. [ad. L. *ēbullītiōn-em*, f. *ēbullīre* (see EBULLIOSCOPE), whence OF. *ebullicion*, Sp. *ebulicion*, It. *ebullizione*, *ebollizione*. The earlier Eng. forms are prob. from Fr.]
1. The process of boiling, or keeping a liquid at the boiling point by the application of heat; the state of bubbling agitation into which a liquid is thrown by being heated to the boiling point. In first quot. perh. (etymologically) the process of extracting by boiling.
1594 PLAT *Jewell-ho* III. 16 When you haue gotten out by ebulition the full strength & vertue. *a* **1681** tr. *Willis' Rem. Med. Wks.* (1681) Voc., Ebullition, a boiling up. **1791** HAMILTON *Berthollet's Dyeing* I. I. I. v. 76 Galls are almost totally soluble in water by long ebullition. **1792** *Phil. Trans.* LXXXII. 403 Ebullition is that state of a liquid in which steam is continually formed within itself. **1831** BREWSTER *Nat. Magic* xii. (1833) 302 Fluids of easy ebullition. **1842** G. P. SCROPE *Volcanos* (1862) 30 This body of lava is evidently at such times in igneous ebullition.
†**b.** *Pathol.* A state of agitation in the blood or 'humours' due to heat; formerly supposed to be the cause of the action of the heart, and when morbid to give rise to febrile and inflammatory disorders. *Obs.*
1547 BOORDE *Brev. Health* lxxiii. 21 b, It maye come of.. ebullycion of the lyver. **1623** HART *Arraignm. Ur.* ii. 7 The ebullition or concoction of blood. **1647** LILLY *Chr. Astrol.* xliv. 263 [Mars] being the cause of a Feaver..shewes ebolition or a boyling of the humours. **1710** T. FULLER *Pharm. Extemp.* 20 Scorbutick Ale..restraineth the Ebullition..of the Vapourous Blood. **1753** CHAMBERS *Cycl. Supp.*, Ebullition of the Blood..in medicine a term used by some of the old writers.
2. *transf.* A state of agitation in a liquid resembling that produced by boiling heat; rapid formation of bubbles, effervescence.
1646 SIR T. BROWNE *Pseud. Ep.* 197 Copper, which is dissolved with lesse ebullition. **1686** W. HARRIS *Lemery's Course Chym.* II. xxi. 602 The ebullition which happens between acid and alkali. **1727** BRADLEY *Fam. Dict.* I. s.v. *Euphorbium*, Spirit of Nitre and that of Vitriol, penetrate the same, without Ebullition. **1822** IMISON *Sc. & Art.* II. 109 Muriatic acid does not act upon copper except in a state of ebullition.
3. The action of rushing forth in a state of agitation or boiling; said of water, and *transf.* of fire, lava, etc. (In quot. 1599 *humorously* of tobacco-smoke.)
1599 B. JONSON *Ev. Man out Hum.* III. iii. 44 The practice of the Cuban ebullition, Euripus, and Whiffe. **1660** STANLEY *Hist. Philos.* (1701) 166 The fiery ebullitions of Ætna. **1683** PETTUS *Fleta Min.* II. s.v. *Boyling*, This ebolition or plawing [of a spring]. **1692** RAY *Discourses* II. v. (1732) 269 The Ebullition and Volutation of the melted Materials. **1759** B. MARTIN *Nat. Hist. Eng.* I. 381 The ebullitions of this Spring are very remarkable. **1830** LYELL *Princ. Geol.* (1875) I. II. xix. 448 A great ebullition of gas took place. **1860** TYNDALL *Glac.* II. xxiv. 356 Ebullition is converted into explosion.
4. *fig.* A sudden outburst or boiling or bubbling over: **a.** of war or civil commotion.
1534 LD. BERNERS *Gold. Bk. M. Aurel.* (1546) B viij, The ebulicion and mouyng of cyuyll warres. **1665** MANLEY *Grotius's Low-C. Warrs* 11 The Law, which kept under the violent ebullitions of their power. **1878** W. F. NAPIER *Penins. War* I. 31 After the first ebullition at Manresa, the insurrection of Catalonia lingered awhile.
b. of passion; also, of fancy, sentiment, etc.
1638 SANDERSON *Serm.* II. 109 The ebullitions of those lusts that war in our members. **1655** H. VAUGHAN *Silex Scint.* I. (1858) Pref. 9 The obvious ebullitions of that light humour which takes the pen in hand..to be seen in print. **1758** JOHNSON *Idler* No. 79 ¶5 Such faults may be said to be ebullitions of genius. **1796** MORSE *Amer. Geog.* I. 339 These ebullitions of jealousy. **1816** J. SCOTT *Vis. Paris* App. 293 A slight ebullition of French flattery. **1841** D'ISRAELI *Amen. Lit.* (1867) 325 A revolutionary reform breaks out with an ebullition of popular feelings.

Hence **ebu'llitionary** *a.*, of the nature of an ebullition.
1830 BLACK in *Fraser's Mag.* I. 287 The saline particles have been added to the ebullitionary agitation.

†**'ebulum.** *Obs.* [a. L. *ebulum* the dwarf elder-tree] A name for elderberry wine.
1713 *Lond. & Country Brew.* III. (1743) 195 Make a white Ebulum with pale Malt and white Elder-berries. **1750** E. SMITH *Compl. Housewife* 245 To make Ebulum.

ebure, obs. form of IVORY.

†**eburgese.** *Obs. rare*⁻¹. Some silken stuff.
1558 *Wills & Inv. N.C.* I. (1835) 182 One other teaster of yellowe and blewe satten eburgese.

eburin ('iːbjʊərɪn). [f. L. *ebur* ivory + -IN.] 'A substance obtained by subjecting a mixture of ivory or bone dust with albumen or ox blood to great pressure at a high temperature. It is very hard, and is a non-conductor of electricity' (*Syd. Soc. Lex.*).

eburnation (ɪbɜː'neɪʃən). *Pathol.* [f. L. *eburnus* made of ivory + -ATION.] 'The act or process of becoming hard and dense like ivory' (*Syd. Soc. Lex.*). So also **eburnated** *ppl. a.*
1840 LISTON *Surgery* 83 Eburnation of the surfaces of the Bones. **1861** BUMSTEAD *Ven. Dis.* (1879) 616 This tendency to eburnation and thickening of the osseous tissue is not confined to the part first affected. **1870** HOLMES *Surgery* (ed. 2) III. 712 A fractured rachitic 'eburnated' bone.

eburnean, -ian (ɪ'bɜːnɪən), *a.* [f. L. *eburneus* made of ivory + -(I)AN.] Made of or resembling ivory.
1656 BLOUNT *Glossogr.*, *Eburnean*, of Ivory, or white like Ivory. **1721–1800** in BAILEY. **1866** J. ROSE *Virg. Ecl. & Georg.* 97 Of Pelops and far-famed eburnian limb.

eburneoid (ɪ'bɜːniːɔɪd), *a.* [f. as prec. + -OID.] Showing a resemblance to ivory.
1847–9 TODD *Cycl. Anat.* IV. 705/2 Parts of bone acquire that degree of hardness, which has been termed eburneoid induration.

e,burnifi'cation. *rare.* = EBURNATION.
1878 BARTLEY tr. *Topinard's Anthrop.* iv. 135 Another [characteristic] drawn from the eburnification..of the teeth.

eburnine (ɪ'bɜːnaɪn), *a. rare*⁻¹. [f. L. *eburnus* + -INE.] Ivory-like, ivory-coloured.
1822 *Blackw. Mag.* XII. 669 Arms and bosom eburnine.

ecad ('iːkæd). *Ecology.* [f. Gr. οἶκ-ος house + -AD.] An organism modified by its environment.
1905 F. E. CLEMENTS *Res. Methods Ecol.* iii. 148 On the basis of their..behavior in the production of new forms, species may be distinguished as variable, mutable, or adaptable. The new form which results from variation is a *variant*; the product of mutation is a *mutant*, and that of adaptation, an *ecad*. **1920** *Nature* CIV. 708/1 The so-called species of the mycologist is comparable with the 'ecad' of the ecologist, and is the resultant of the organism and its environment. 'Ecads' indistinguishable from each other may be produced from two distinct organisms interacting with one and the same environment, or with two different environments. **1964** V. J. CHAPMAN *Coastal Veget.* ii. 47 Another free-living fucoid, *Ascophyllum nodosum* ecad *scorpioides* is to be found..on the salt marshes of the western Scottish lochs. **1970** *Watsonia* VIII. 26 It is concluded that *P. pseudodistans* and *P. fasciculata* are ecads of one species.

ecalcarate (ɪ'kælkəreɪt), *a. Bot.* [f. E-³ + L. *calcar* spur + -ATE.] Without a spur.
1819 *Pantologia*, *Ecalcarate*, in botany, a corol, without any spur, or spur-shaped nectary. As in Wolfenia. **1866** in *Treas. Bot.* **1883** in *Syd. Soc. Lex.*

ecardine (ɪ'kɑːdaɪn). [f. E-³ + L. *cardin-em* hinge.] A mollusc whose shell has no hinge.
1878 BELL *Gegenbauer's Comp. Anat.* 308 In the Ecardines the two valves..have pretty much the same form.

ecarinate (ɪ'kærɪnət), *a. Bot.* [f. E-³ + L. *carina* keel + -ATE.] That has no carina.

‖**écarté** (ekarte). [F. *écarté*, *écarter* to discard, to throw out cards.] **1.** A game of cards for two persons, in playing which the cards from 2 to 6 are excluded. One feature is that a player may ask leave to discard, or throw out certain cards from his hand, and replace them with fresh ones from the pack. Also *attrib.*
1824 (*title*) A Treatise on the Game of Écarté, as played in the first circles of London and Paris. **1848** THACKERAY *Van. Fair* xxv, She watched over him kindly at Écarté of a night. **1848** W. H. KELLY tr. *L. Blanc's Hist. Ten Y.* I. 355 M. Cavaignac threw on an écarté-table in the Louvre a packet of cartridges. **1878** 'CAVENDISH' [Hy. Jones] *Ecarté* 21 The game of écarté in some of its features, namely the discard (from which its name is derived) and the score for the king, is of modern origin.
2. *Ballet.* (See quot. 1957.)
1922 BEAUMONT & IDZIKOWSKI *Man. Theory & Pract. Class. Theatr. Dancing* I. 29 (*caption*) Position of the body in the direction of the body termed écarté. **1957** G. B. L. WILSON *Dict. Ballet* 109 *Écarté*,..a position of the body, oblique to the audience, in which the arm and the leg, on the ground or raised nearest to the audience, are extended on the same vertical and diagonal plane as the rest of the body. **1960** J. LAWSON *Classical Ballet* vi. 148 This *écarté* position for the commencement of a turn is extremely important when the dancer has to circle the stage.

‖**ecartelé**, *a.* [F. *écartelé*, pa. pple. of *écarteler* to divide into quarters.] *Her.* Of a shield: Divided into quarters by an horizontal and a vertical line 'quarterly'. (Bailey.)

1731–6 in BAILEY. **1775** in ASH.

†**ecarts.** *Obs. rare*⁻¹.

1714 *Fr. Bk. of Rates* 383 A List of Merchandizes coming from the Levant.. Buff called Ecarts.

†**e'casterly**, *adv. Obs.*⁻⁰ [f. L. *ecastor* 'by Castor' + -LY².] (See quot.)

1623 COCKERAM II, By my Faith, *ecasterly*.

ecaudate (iːˈkɔːdeɪt), *a.* [ad. mod.L. *ēcaudāt-us*, f. *ē* (see E-³) + L. *cauda* tail: see -ATE.]

1. *Zool.* That has no tail, or a very short one.

1847–9 TODD *Cycl. Anat.* IV. 4/1 Animals.. changing their form to caudate or ecaudate at pleasure. **1856–8** W. CLARK *Van der Hoeven's Zool.* I. 52 Astusice. Body not loricated, caudate or ecaudate, form mutable.

2. *Bot.* 'Spikeless, without a stem' (Paxton, *Bot. Dict.* 1840).

‖**'ecbasis.** [Gr. ἔκβασις, f. stem of ἐκβαίνειν to go out, digress.] See quot. (Craig's explanation, copied in later Dicts., appears to be merely a guess. In sense 'digression' the word appears in late Lat.)

1706 PHILLIPS, *Ecbasis*, a going out, an Event; also a Rhetorical Figure call'd Digression. **1847** CRAIG, *Ecbasis*, in Rhetoric, a figure in which the orator treats of things according to their events or consequences.

ecbatic (ɛkˈbætɪk), *a. Gram.* [ad. Gr. ἐκβατικός, implied in the adv. ἐκβατικῶς, used by late grammarians; f. ἐκβαίνειν to result, issue; cf. ἔκβασις a result, consequence.] Of a clause or a conjuntion: Denoting a mere result or consequence, as distinguished from a purpose or intention.

1836 E. ROBINSON *Greek Lex. N.T.* (1869) 376 [The use of ἵνα is sometimes] ecbatic. **1866** E. MASSON tr. *Winer's Gram. N.T.* (ed. 6) 479 Others.. are for admitting the ecbatic import of ἵνα.

‖**ecblastesis** (ɛkblæˈstiːsɪs). *Bot.* [mod.L., a. Gr. ἐκβλάστησις 'shooting or budding forth' (Liddell and Scott).] (See quot.)

1866 *Treas. Bot.*, *Ecblastesis*, the production of buds within flowers, in consequence of monstrous developement, or in inflorescences.

‖**ecbole** (ˈɛkbəliː). [mod.L., a. Gr. ἐκβολή, f. ἐκβάλλ-ειν to throw out.]

1. *Rhet.* A digression, in which a person is introduced speaking his own words. (Webster.)

1753 CHAMBERS *Cycl. Supp.*, *Ecbole* in rhetoric is used for a digression.

2. In ancient Music: see quot.

1819 *Pantologia*, *Ecbole*, a.. change in the enharmonic genus, by the accidental elevation of a chord, or string, five dieses above its ordinary pitch.

ecbolic (ɛkˈbɒlɪk), *a.* and *sb. Med.* [as if ad. Gr. ἐκβολικός, f. ἐκβολή expulsion.]

A. *adj.* That promotes the expulsion of the fœtus.

1877 WOODMAN & TIDY *Forensic Med.* 756 The ecbolic properties of ergot are too well known.

B. *sb.* A drug that possesses this property.

1753 CHAMBERS *Cycl. Supp.*, *Ecbolics*.. a term used to express such medicines as were given to promote delivery in child-birth. **1875** H. WOOD *Therap.* (1879) 549 Cases must be rare in which the latter [obstetric instruments] are not preferable to the ecbolic.

ecca, var. EKKA.

eˌccaleo'bion. [Gr. sentence ἐκκαλέω βίον (intended to mean 'I evoke life') written as one word.] The name given to an egg-hatching apparatus invented by W. Bucknell about 1839.

1839 BUCKNELL (*title*), Eccaleobion: a Treatise on Artificial Incubation. **1847** CRAIG, *Eccaleobion*, a contrivance for hatching eggs by artificial heat. **1880** *Harper's Mag.* 787 Willis's *Home Journal* was at one time a very eccaleöbion for young writers.

†**ecca'thartic**, *a. Obs.* [as if ad. Gr. *ἐκκαθαρτικός, f. ἐκκαθαίρειν to cleanse out.] = CATHARTIC; erroneously taken by Willis in the contrary sense.

1681 tr. *Willis' Rem. Med. Wks.* Voc., Eccathartic, not purging.

‖**ecce** (ˈɛksɪ, ˈɛkeɪ, ˈɛtʃeɪ). Latin for 'lo!' or 'behold!' Used in phrases like ***Ecce signum!*** behold a sign! Also **Ecce Homo**, 'behold the Man' (*John* xix. 5); hence used subst. for a picture representing Christ wearing the crown of thorns.

1596 SHAKS. *1 Hen. IV*, II. iv. 187 Ecce signum. **1665** J. SPENCER *Prophecies* 46 The many Ecce's and Selah's they affix to their prophetic Speeches.

Hence †**ec'ceity** [ad. med.L. *ecceitas*; see -ITY], the quality of being present.

1549 CHALONER *Erasm. Moriæ Enc.* M j a, Innumerable such fine toyes have they.. of Instantes.. and ecceitees. **1581** J. BELL *Haddon's Answ. Osor.* 56 In Distinctions, eccyties and quiddities, they [the Schoolemen] could many time easely see that thing which was no where at all. **1711** tr. *Werenfelsius' Discov. Logomachys* 101 Hæcceitys, ecceitys, petreitys, etc.

eccentric (ɛkˈsɛntrɪk), *a.* and *sb.* Forms: 6 eccentrike, 6–9 excentric(k(e, 7–8 eccentrick, 7 ec-, excentrique, 7– eccentric. [ad. late L. *eccentricus*, f. Gr. ἔκκεντρος eccentric as opposed to concentric (f. ἐκ out of + κέντρον centre); see -IC; the word is found in all the Romanic langs.: Fr. *excentrique* (14th c. in Littré), Pr. *excentric*, It. *eccentrico*, Sp. *excéntrico*.] **A.** *adj.*

1. Of a circle: Not concentric with another circle (const. *to*). Of two or more circles: Not mutually concentric. Chiefly used of circles of which one is within the other. † ***eccentric orb***: in the Ptolemaic astronomy, an orbit not having the earth precisely in its centre (afterwards sometimes used in a Copernican sense: an orbit not having the sun precisely in its centre).

1551 RECORDE *Cast. Knowl.* (1556) 247 These two circles.. are eccentrike, for that they haue not one common centre. **1621** BURTON *Anat. Mel.* II. ii. III. (1651) 159/2 Which howsoever Ptolemy, &c., maintaine to be reall Orbs, excentrick, concentricke. **1656** tr. *Hobbes' Elem. Philos.* (1839) 431 This annual orb [of the earth] is eccentric to the sun.

†**b.** *fig.* Not agreeing, having little in common. Const. *from*, *to*. *Obs.*

1607–12 BACON *Wisdom, Ess.* (Arb.) 184 His owne endes, which must needes be often eccentrique to the endes of his Master or State. **1666** COLLINS in Rigaud *Corr. Sci. Men* (1841) II. 463 My book of Accounts.. is so eccentric to your studies as I thought it unworthy your acceptance. **1670** SANDERSON in Ussher *Power Princes* (1683) Pref., A task.. altogether excentrick from their function and calling.

2. That has its axis, its point of support, etc., otherwise than centrally placed. Cf. B. 2.

1647 WARD *Simp. Cobler* 45 Else the world will be Eccentrick, and then it will whirle. **1743** SAVERY in *Phil. Trans.* XLVIII. 177 Large object-glasses for telescopes are not commonly well center'd.. I.. return'd [two faulty ones] and had two sent me again, as eccentric well nigh as the former ones. **1825** WOOD *Railroads* 148 This eccentric circle is loose upon the axle.. a circular hoop.. fits the circumference of the eccentric motion. **1831** J. HOLLAND *Manuf. Metals* I. 92 That ingenious but simple contrivance the eccentric wheel.

3. Not centrally placed. Of an axis, etc.: Not passing through the centre.

1849 SIR J. HERSCHEL *Outlines Astron.* iii. §141 (1858) 83 If the axis be excentric. **1882** VINES *Sachs' Bot.* 203 The organic centre of the transverse section does not usually coincide with the geometrical centre, as is easily seen in the transverse sections of most petioles and horizontal branches with an 'eccentric' pith. **1884** BOWER & SCOTT *De Bary's Phaner. & Ferns* 365 The position of the bundle in the root is from the first slightly eccentric.

†**b.** Of a locality: Remote from the centre; out of the way. [So Fr. *quartier excentrique*.] *Obs.*

1800 T. JEFFERSON *Writ.* (1859) IV. 312 [The College] is.. eccentric in its position, exposed to all bilious diseases abandoned by the public care.

c. *Phys.* (See quot.)

1876 BERNSTEIN *Five Senses* 20 The sensation of sight can only take place.. in the brain.. and yet we transfer the object seen to the external world surrounding us. This fact is called the law of eccentric sensation.

†**4.** Misused for: Having no centre. *Obs.*

1633 T. ADAMS *Exp. 2 Peter* iii. 7 Only that is eccentric, which was never made. **1652** BENLOWES *Theoph.* II. xli. 28 Deaths hell deaths Self out-deaths, Vindictive Place!.. Excentrick Space! **1681** tr. *Willis' Rem. Med. Wks.* Voc., *Eccentric*, without centre.

5. Of orbital motion: Not referable to a fixed centre of revolution; not circular. Of a curve, an elliptic, parabolic, or hyperbolic orbit: Deviating (in greater or less degree) from a circular form.

1642 HOWELL *For. Trav.* 77 Let these Lights.. be kept from irregular and eccentrique motions. **1692** BENTLEY *Boyle Lect.* vii. 247 They could not acquire such Revolutions in Ellipses very little Eccentric. **1796** MORSE *Amer. Geog.* I. 32 Like other planets moving about the sun in very eccentric ellipses. **1866** SIR J. HERSCHEL *Fam. Lect. Sc.*, *Comets* 104 A comet moves round the sun.. in an immensely elongated, or as it is termed a very eccentric, ellipse.

b. *transf.* Of a heavenly body: Moving in an orbit deviating (more or less) from a circle.

a **1721** KEILL *Maupertuis Diss.* (1734) 63 The Comets are no more.. than very excentric Planets. *a* **1791** WESLEY *Serm.* lxix. 8 Wks. 1811 IX. 249 Those horrid, eccentric orbs. **1816** J. SMITH *Panorama Sc. & Art* I. 581 When very eccentric planets or comets go round any flat star, in orbits much inclined to its equator.

c. ***eccentric anomaly***: the true anomaly of a planet moving in an eccentric orbit (opposed to the mean anomaly). ***eccentric equation***: see EQUATION.

6. *fig.* Regulated by no central control.

a. Of actions, movements, and things in general: Irregular, anomalous, proceeding by no known method, capricious.

c **1630** DRUMM. OF HAWTH. *Poems* 195 Finding all eccentrick in our times. **1792** BURKE *Pres. St. Aff.* Wks. I. 586 The eccentrick aberration of Charles the Second. **1848** MACAULAY *Hist. Eng.* I. 657 This eccentric clemency has perplexed some writers.

b. Of persons and personal attributes: Deviating from usual methods, odd, whimsical.

1685 *86 Loyal Poems, Shaftesbury's Farew.* 6 The brightest, yet the most excentrick Soul. **1695** LD. PRESTON *Boeth.* II. 68 The Extravagance of Excentrick and irregular Desires. **1771** MACKENZIE *Man Feel.* xxxiv. (1803) 61 His motives were rather excentric. **1802** MAR. EDGEWORTH *Moral T.* (1816) I. Pref. 7 [Forester is the picture of] an eccentric character. **1836** H. ROGERS *J. Howe* ii. (1863) 19 That great, though unequal and eccentric genius.

7. a. quasi-*adv.* **b.** *absol.* quasi-*sb.*

1672 DRYDEN *Conq. Granada* I. v. i, He moves excentrique, like a wand'ring Star. **1870** LOWELL *Among my Bks.* Ser. I. (1873) 203 Wordsworth never quite saw the distinction between the eccentric and the original.

B. *sb.*

†**1.** [= *eccentric circle*, *orb*; see A. 1.] In Ptolemaic astronomy: A circle or orbit not having the earth precisely in its centre. *Obs.* exc. *Hist.*

[**1398** TREVISA *Barth. De P.R.* VIII. xi. (1495) 317 The fyrste meuynge of a planete.. is a cercle that hyghte Ecentricus.] **1561** EDEN *Art Navig.* I. xx. 22 *Eccentricke*, is a circle which hath his center distant.. from the center of the worlde. **1646** SIR T. BROWNE *Pseud. Ep.* 293 The Perigeum or lowest part of the eccentric. **1724** WATTS *Logic* (1736) 225 Excentricks and Epicycles of Ptolomy. **1783** W. F. MARTYN *Geog. Mag.* I. Introd. 14 A number of circles called eccentrics and epicycles.

fig. a **1660** HAMMOND *Wks.* IV. 551 Reserving.. somewhat for common calamities, somewhat as it were for the universal motion of the whole body, somewhat for eccentricks.

2. *Mech.* A circular disc fixed on a revolving shaft, some distance out of centre, working freely in a ring (the *eccentric strap*), which is attached to a rod called an *eccentric rod*, by means of which the rotating motion of the shaft is converted into a backward-and-forward motion. Its most frequent use is for working the slide-valve of a steam-engine. (Earlier *eccentric circle*, *motion*; see A. 2).

1827 *Specif. Mandelay's Patent* No. 5531 It consists.. in the application of an eccentric to work the slide [valve]. **1838** *Public Wks. Gt. Brit.* 69 The slides are worked by four fast eccentrics.. instead of two loose ones. **1881** *Mechanic* §657. 302 The set screw in the eccentric shall be downwards.

3. [Cf. A. 6 b.] A person whose conduct is irregular, odd, or whimsical.

1832 SCOTT *St. Ronan's* Introd., Men of every country playing the eccentric. **1850** KINGSLEY *Alt. Locke* vi. (1879) 65, I have given no description of the old eccentric's abode.

C. *Attrib. and Comb.* **a.** In various parts connected with the eccentric that works the slide-valve in a steam-engine, as ***eccentric-catch***, ***-hook***, ***-rod***. Also **eccentric-hoop**, **-ring**, or **-strap**, the ring in which the eccentric revolves.

b. In various machines or parts of machines, whose distinctive feature is that they are worked by an eccentric wheel or depend upon an eccentric arrangement; as ***eccentric-arbor***, ***-chuck***, ***-cutter*** (in Turning), ***-engraving***, ***-fan***, ***-gear***, ***-pump***.

1859 *Handbk. Turning* 57 Eccentric turning.. includes all the various.. work for which the powers of a lathe are.. celebrated. *Ibid.* 87 Eccentric chuck. **1884** F. BRITTEN *Watch & Clockm.* 100 When the three screws are loosened the two parts of the eccentric arbor may be shifted.

ec'centrical. [f. as prec. + -ICAL.]

†**1. a.** = ECCENTRIC A. 1. Also *fig.* **b.** Pertaining to an eccentric orbit. *Obs.*

1640 WILKINS *New Planet* x. (1707) 262 Supposing the Earth to move in an Eccentrical Orb about the Sun. **1641** MILTON *Ch. Govt.* i. (1851) 98 With a kind of eccentricall equation. **1646** W. DELL *Right Reformation* *Whose.. interest is eccentricall from the.. interest of the kingdoms. **1658** SIR T. BROWNE *Gard. Cyrus* iv. 62 Why in the knotts of Deal.. the Circles are often eccentrical. **1669** W. SIMPSON *Hydrol. Chym.* 208 For want of some pregnant Principles.. they [Physicians].. are mostwhat eccentrical to the truth.

2. Out of the regular track; exceptional, irregular.

a **1652** J. SMITH *Sel. Disc.* IX. ix. (1859) 445 An all-seeing eye.. governs the most eccentrical motions of creatures. *a* **1674** CLARENDON *Hist. Reb.* (1704) III. xv. 490 There were.. many illegal and eccentrical Proceedings. **1768** BLACKSTONE *Comm.* II. 3 There is allowed in those cases an extrajudicial or eccentrical kind of remedy. **1827** POLLOK *Course T.* II, Vanity to be Renowned for creed eccentrical. **1845** PETRIE *Round Towers Irel.* 29 Tops either pointed, or truncated at the summit, and ornamented with something eccentrical.

ec'centrically, *adv.* [f. prec. + -LY².] In an eccentric direction or manner.

1. Not concentrically; not symmetrically with respect to the centre.

a **1687** PETTY *Pol. Arith.* (1690) 93 A Wheel.. excentrically hung neither moves so easily nor performs its work so truely. **1703** *Brit. Apollo, Supern. Paper* No. 1, 2/1 [The Moon] moves Eccentrically with Respect to Us. **1849–52** TODD *Cycl. Anat.* IV. 1206/1 The liver cells in Boltenia are.. arranged in eccentrically radiated groups. **1875** LASLETT *Timber Trees* 8 The pith is excentrically placed.

2. Out of one's proper sphere; irregularly; in mod. use, oddly, whimsically, strangely.

1678 *Yng. Man's Call.* 55 Prudence is herein very sollicitous.. That nothing be done excentrically. **1737**

Common Sense 10 Sept., Women..are confined within the narrow Limits of Domestic Offices, and when they stray beyond them, they move excentrically, and consequently without Grace. **1861** DICKENS *Gt. Expect.* II. 4 The skylight eccentrically patched like a broken head.

†**ec'centricate,** *v. Obs. rare.* [f. ECCENTRIC *a.* + -ATE.]

1. *trans.* Used bombastically for: To disclose. **1708** MOTTEUX *Rabelais* v. xx, My design is to.. excentricate to you my Cogitations.

2. *intr.* To go out of one's proper sphere. **1643** *Mercurius Britannicus* 3 Oct. No. 6. 42 We can discuss our differences in our own seates and no man go out nor excentricate.

eccentricity (ɛksɛn'trɪsɪtɪ). [f. as prec. + -ITY.] The state or quality of being ECCENTRIC, q.v.

1. The quality of being abnormally centred; of not being concentric; of not having the axis in the centre. †Orig. of planetary orbits: The fact of having the earth at a distance from the centre (*Obs.* exc. *Hist.*). In mod. astronomy of a circle or arc in the celestial sphere: The fact of not being concentric with the sphere.

1551 RECORDE *Cast. Knowl.* (1556) 247 Sith the centre of the greater circle is by A, and the centre of the lesser circle is by B, the distaunce betweene A and B is the quantitie of their eccentricitye. **1594** DAVIS *Seaman's Secr.* (1607) 5 All which differences are caused by the excentricity of her Orbe wherein she moueth. **1646** SIR T. BROWNE *Pseud. Ep.* 325 Yet by reason of his Excentricity, his [the sun's] motion is unequall. **1839** R. S. ROBINSON *Naut. Steam Eng.* 107 *o r*, being the whole motion caused by the eccentricity..a portion of *o r* must be cut off by the eccentric pulley. **1849** SIR J. HERSCHEL *Outlines Astron.* iii. §141 (1858) 83 The effect of excentricity is..to increase the arc representing the angle in question on one side of the circle.

†**2.** The condition of not being centrally situated; distance from the centre. *Obs.*

1825 T. JEFFERSON *Autobiog.* Wks. 1859 I. 48 Its local eccentricity..lessened the general inclination towards it. **1836–7** SIR W. HAMILTON *Metaph.* xxxii. (1870) II. 241 The agitation of one place of a sheet of water expands itself, in wider and wider circles..although, in proportion to its eccentricity, it is always becoming fainter.

3. Of a curve: Deviation from circular form. **1696** WHISTON *The. Earth* I. (1722) 18 All degrees of Eccentricity make Ellipses of all species. **1868** LOCKYER *Heavens* (ed. 3) 72 The orbit of Mercury is very elongated, or, in astronomical language, its excentricity is considerable.

b. as a measurable quantity.

The eccentricity of an ellipse was formerly defined as the distance between the centre and one of the foci; it is now represented as an abstract number, *e.g.* as the ratio of the focal distance of the centre to the semi-major-axis. The more modern expression, however, for the eccentricity of all conic sections is the ratio of the focal distance (of any point in the curve) to the distance from the directrix. In the case of the ellipse this is numerically identical with the ratio previously mentioned.

1726 tr. *Gregory's Astron.* I. 71 The right Line *AP*, connecting the Apsides..the line of the Apsides; the Part *CS* of it, the Excentricity. **1787** BONNYCASTLE *Astron.* vi. 90 The distance between the centre of the ellipse O, and one of its foci F, is called its eccentricity. **1874** MOSELEY *Astron.* lxxiii. (ed. 4) 210 Ellipses whose foci..are near one another ..are called ellipses of small eccentricity. **1881** C. TAYLOR *Conics* 164 Having given four points and the eccentricity of a hyperbola..shew how to construct a curve.

4. The quality or habit of deviating from what is usual or regular; irregularity, oddity, whimsicality.

1794 SULLIVAN *View Nat.* V. 187, An excursion, for the eccentricity of which I shall..be condemned. **1859** MILL *Liberty* iii. (1865) 39/2 Eccentricity has always abounded when and where strength of character has abounded. **1886** *Pall Mall G.* 29 Apr. 4/1 What in some persons is called eccentricity, in others would be called insanity.

b. *concr.* An instance of deviation from what is usual, an extravagance. Also *pl.*

1657 COLVIL *Whigs Supplic.* (1751) 49 The like uncertainty he sees In change of Excentricities. **1818** MRS. SHELLEY *Frankenst.* i. (1865) 10 To render their seeming eccentricities consistent for ever. **1856** EMERSON *Eng. Traits* vi. *Manners* Wks. (Bohn) II. 47, I know not where any personal eccentricity is so freely allowed. **1870** HAWTHORNE *Eng. Note-bks.* (1879) II. 196 Miscellaneous eccentricities of sculpture.

ec'centrize, *v. nonce-wd.* [f. ECCENTR-IC + -IZE.] To play the eccentric (quasi-*refl.* in quot.).

1836 *New Monthly Mag.* XLVIII. 461 It has been the fashion..to take up any scribbler who has libelled, fought, or eccentrized himself into notice.

eccheness, variant of ECHENESS, *Obs.*

eccho, obs. var. ECHO.

ecchondroma (ɛkɒn'drəʊmə). *Path.* [mod.L., f. Gr. ἐκ out + CHONDROMA.] A chondroma growing outwards from the surface of a bone or cartilage.

1890 in BILLINGS *Med. Dict.* **1897** *Allbutt's Syst. Med.* IV. 826 Ecchondromas are usually firmly attached, hard, sessile growths. **1929** WAKELEY & BUXTON *Surg. Path.* xv. 124 Chondroma..may burst through the shaft and become pedunculated (*ecchondroma*). **1954** G. P. WRIGHT *Introd. Path.* (ed. 2) xxix. 537 Chondromas arise most frequently in bony structures, and are termed enchondromas or ecchondromas according to their internal or external situation.

ecchondrosis (ɛkɒn'drəʊsɪs). *Pathol.* [a. assumed Gr. ἐκχόνδρωσις, f. ἐκ out + χόνδρος cartilage; after words like *ecchymosis*.]

1874 JONES & SIEV. *Phys. Anat.* 141 Outgrowths of cartilage, known as ecchondrosis.

‖**ecchymoma** (ɛkɪ'məʊmə). *Pathol.* [mod.L., a. Gr. ἐκχύμωμα; see next.] A tumour formed by an effusion of blood under the skin.

1541 R. COPLAND *Galyen's Terap.* 2 H iij, Such rupcyons be with ecchymosis or ecchymonia [*sic*]. **1684** tr. *Bonet's Merc. Compit.* v. 139 When the Ecchymoma..was just turning to an Abscess, I opened it. **1876** DUHRING *Dis. Skin* 329 Ecchymomata consist of extensive extravasations, which appear in the form of tumors.

ecchymosed (ˌɛkɪ'məʊst, -'məʊzd), *ppl. a. Pathol.* [ad. Fr. *ecchymosé*. f. *ecchymose*, Fr. form of next.] Affected with ecchymosis.

1834 J. FORBES *Laennec's Dis. Chest*, There was an ecchymosed spot..on the inner surface of the pericardium. **1878** T. BRYANT *Pract. Surg.* I. 49 The..lymphatic glands ..are usually swollen, red, and ecchymosed on section.

‖**ecchymosis** (ɛkɪ'məʊsɪs). *Pathol.* [mod.L., a. Gr. ἐκχύμωσις, f. ἐκχυμόεσθαι to extravasate blood, f. ἐκ out + χυμός juice.]

'A blotch caused by extravasation of blood below the skin' (*Syd. Soc. Lex.*).

1541 R. COPLAND *Galyen's Terap.* 2 Hiijb, All acchymosis or ecchymonia indycateth vacuacyon for remedy of yᵉ cure. **1612** WOODALL *Surg. Mate* Wks. (1653) 385 Blood is forced into the Muscles confusedly, as by the Echymosis may appear. **1758** J. S. *Le Dran's Observ. Surg.* (1771) 163, I..found a little Ecchymosis towards the Elbow. **1866** A. FLINT *Princ. Med.* (1880) 27 When the hemorrhages are minute, they are called punctate or ecchymoses.

ecchymotic (ɛkɪ'mɒtɪk), *a. Pathol.* [f. Gr. ἐκχυμόεσθαι; see prec.] 'Of the nature or appearance of an ecchymosis' (*Syd. Soc. Lex.*).

1857 BULLOCK *Cazeaux' Midwif.* 67 The surface is.. covered..sometimes with ecchymotic spots.

'eccle, *v. dial.* Also eckle. [app. var. of ETTLE.] *intr.* To aim or intend.

1721–1800 in BAILEY. **1847–78** HALLIW., *Eckle*, to aim; to intend; to design. *North.*

'eccle-grass. (See quot.)

1806 P. NEILL *Tour Orkney* (Jam.) Pinguicula vulgaris, or common butter-wort—in Orkney is known by the name of Ecclegrass.

Eccles ('ɛk(ə)lz). [Name of a town in Lancashire.] ***Eccles cake***, a kind of fancy cake.

1872 *Young Englishwoman* Nov. 620/1 Can you tell me how to make Bride Cake and Eccles' Cakes? **1881** E. SKUSE *Confect. Hand-Bk.* (ed. 3) 155 Eccles Cake. Roll out a sheet of paste..about a quarter of an inch thick, then roll out another sheet same size,..spread on the first sheet some Banbury meat..then cover it with the second sheet. **1889** *Manch. Sch. Board Cookery Classes* 38 Eccles Cakes. 2 oz. brown sugar, 1 oz. butter, ½ lb. currants, 1 oz. candied peel, a little grated nutmeg and lemon rind. **1908** J. KIRKLAND *Mod. Baker* III. 354 Eccles cakes are made in nearly the same manner and with the same ingredients as Banburys, only the usual shape is round. **1957** *Encycl. Brit.* VII. 881/1 Eccles cakes, made of pastry with currants, have a wide reputation.

‖**ecclesia** (ɛ'kliːzɪə, -sɪə). *Hist.* [med.L., a. Gr. ἐκκλησία, f. ἔκκλητος called out, f. ἐκκαλεῖν to call out.] A Greek word for a regularly convoked assembly; chiefly applied to the general assembly of Athenian citizens. On the introduction of Christianity it became the regular word for CHURCH, q.v.

1577 tr. *Bullinger's Decades* (1592) 79 Ecclesia, which worde wee vse for the Church, is properly an assembly. **1820** T. MITCHELL *Aristoph.* I. 227 The ecclesia consisted of all such as were freemen of Athens. **1849** GROTE *Hist. Greece* (1862) II. lxiv. V. 533 That misguided vote, both of the Senate and of the Ekklesia.

e'cclesial, *a.* [a. OF. *ecclésial*, f. L. *ecclēsia*; see prec.] Of or pertaining to the church; = ECCLESIASTICAL. Freq. in Milton.

1649 MILTON *Eikon.* iii. (1851) 443 It is not the part of a King..to meddle with Ecclesial Government. **1961** B. R. WILSON *Sects & Society* III. xii. 250 The significant charismatic element at work at the ecclesial level. **1966** J. D. CRICHTON in *Studia Patristica* (Internat. Conf. Patr. Stud.) VIII. 208 The pleas for liturgical reform..achieved an ecclesial dimension.

ecclesialogy, bad form of ECCLESIOLOGY.

ecclesiarch (ɛ'kliːzɪɑːk). [f. Gr. ἐκκλησία church + -αρχος ruler.] A ruler of the church. Hence **e'cclesiarchy.**

1781 GIBBON *Decl. & F.* III. lxvi. 671 The great ecclesiarch poorly excuses his submission to the emperor. **1878** E. JENKINS *Haverholme* 92 He..was..a sort of lay ecclesiarch in the county. *Ibid.* 167 Emancipation of Christianity from tradition and ecclesiarchy.

Ecclesiast (ɛ'kliːzɪæst). [(? a Fr. *ecclesiaste*), ad. (through L.) Gr. ἐκκλησιαστής one who takes part in an ECCLESIA (= sense 3 below); used by the LXX. to render Heb. *qōhéleth* one who addresses a public assembly.]

1. 'The Preacher', i.e. Solomon considered as the author of the Book of Ecclesiastes. In first quot. applied to the author of Ecclesiasticus, the reference being to xxxiii. 19.

c **1386** CHAUCER *Wyfs Prol.* 651 Thanne wolde he, vp-on his Bible seke That ilke prouerbe, of Ecclesiaste Where he comandeth, and forbedeth faste Man shal nat suffre his wyf go roule aboute. **1873** *Contemp. Rev.* XXII. 536 The happiness that allures me, says the Ecclesiast, is a mockery.

2. †**a.** [suggested by 1.] One who performs public functions in church (*obs*). **b.** [Suggested by ECCLESIASTIC.] A church administrator.

c **1386** CHAUCER *Prol.* 708 He [the Pardonere] was in churche a noble ecclesiaste. **1866** F. W. NEWMAN *Relig. Weakness Prot.* 40 We see a great ecclesiast.

3. A member of the Athenian Ecclesia.

1849 GROTE *Greece* II. I. VI. 382 Present to the mind of every citizen in his character of dikast or Ekklesiast. **1872** SYMONDS *Grk. Poets* Ser. I. i. (1877) 30 The whole Athenian nation as dikasts and ecclesiasts were interested in Rhetoric.

Ecclesiastes (ɛˌkliːzɪ'æstiːz). [a. Gr. ἐκκλησιαστής; see prec.] The title of a book of the Old Testament, written in the person of Solomon, and traditionally ascribed to his authorship.

(Properly the Gr. title is the designation of Solomon considered as the author of the book, and is occas. so used by Eng. writers, though in the text of the book the Eng. versions render the corresponding Heb. word as 'The Preacher'.)

a **1300** *Cursor M.* 8464 [Of Salamon] þe first boke Man it clepes ecclesiastes. **1382** WYCLIF *Eccles.* Prol. *note*, Here gynneth the prologe in the boc of Ecclesiastes. **1579** W. FULKE *Heskins' Parl.* 9 Salomon in his Ecclesiastes pleaseth not M. Heskins. **1641** HINDE *J. Bruen* Ded. 1 [Salomon] was both an Ecclesiastes, and a King.

ecclesiastic (ɛˌkliːzɪ'æstɪk), *a.* and *sb.* Forms: 5 ecclesyastyke, 6–7 -iastique, 7 -tick(e, -tik, 7– ecclesiastic. [ad. (through Fr. and L.) Gr. ἐκκλησιαστικός, ultimately f. ἐκκλησία church.]

A. *adj.* (Now *rare*; see ECCLESIASTICAL.)

1. Of or pertaining to the church; concerned with the affairs of the church; opposed to *civil* or *secular*.

1483 CAXTON *Cato* G j b, The benefyces and the thynges ecclesyastyke. **1588** A. KING *Canisius' Catech.* 42 b, Jesus Christ..commandit thais thingis quhilk perteins to obedience to be geuin to the Apostolique and Ecclesiastique commandimentis. **1678** CUDWORTH *Intell. Syst.* I. §iv. xiii. 213 Some ecclesiastick writers..impute a Trinity of gods to Marcion. **1695** KENNETT *Par. Antiq.* vii. 30 The disposition of the Ecclesiastick state depending always on the revolutions of the civil government. **1766** COLE in Ellis *Orig. Lett.* II. 510 IV. 487 To unloose all ties both civil and ecclesiastic. **1856** EMERSON *Eng. Traits* x. *Wealth* Wks. (Bohn) II. 73 Whatever is excellent..in civil, rural, or ecclesiastic architecture.

†**b.** Of language (*esp.* Gr. or L.), words, or senses of words: Characteristic of ecclesiastical writers; opposed to *classical* or *secular*. *Obs.*

1651 HOBBES *Leviath.* I. vii. 31 This singularity of the Ecclesiastique use of the word [*credo*] hath raised many dissenters. *a* **1638** MEDE *Wks.* II. iv. (1672) 360 [In] S. John's Writings..we find two Ecclesiastick terms of Λόγος, and Κυριακὴ ἡμέρα.

2. Of persons: Belonging to the church viewed as consisting of the clergy; clerical (= older sense of *spiritual*) as opposed to *lay*. Also of attire, functions, etc.: Pertaining to the clergy.

1603 KNOLLES *Hist. Turks* (1638) 81 He caused the Priests in their ecclesiastick attire and ornaments, to march forth in the army. **1610** DONNE *Pseudo-Mart.* 26 Nor deale they onely with temporall punishments upon Ecclesiastique persons. **1820** COMBE (Dr. Syntax) *Consol.* III. 182 A gay ecclesiastic Beau.

B. *sb.*

1. [See A. 2.] A clergyman, person in orders, a 'churchman' as distinguished from a 'layman'. App. not before 17th c., the earlier term being 'spiritual man'. Chiefly *techn.* and *Hist.*

1651 HOBBES *Leviath.* II. xxix. 168 The subjection of Ecclesiastiques to the Common-wealth. **1707** ADDISON *State of War* 254 And at the same time such vast numbers of Ecclesiasticks, secular and religious. **1870** F. WILSON *Ch. Lindisf.* 93 A fragment of an effigy of an ecclesiastic. **1880** MCCARTHY *Own Times* IV. lxiii. 427 He had in him much of the taste and the temper of the ecclesiastic.

†**2.** *pl.* **a.** Matters ecclesiastical. **b.** The science of church government. (*rare*). *Obs.*

a **1619** FOTHERBY *Atheom.* II. xiv. §2 (1622) 356 For Morall Philosophie..hath three parts: Ecclesiastickes, Oeconomickes, and Politickes. **1672** CHAS. II. in Gutch *Coll. Cur.* I. 311 He is much troubled, that that Declaration ..should have..given an occasion to the questioning of his power in ecclesiasticks. **1738** NEAL *Hist. Purit.* IV. 455.

eccles'astical *a.* [f. prec. + -AL¹.]

1. = ECCLESIASTIC A. 1.

1538 COVERDALE *N.T.* Ded., Jurisdiction ecclesiastical. **1593** HOOKER *Eccl. Pol.* I. xvi. 47 Our whole question concerneth the qualitie of ecclesiasticall lawes. **1635** N. CARPENTER *Geog. Del.* II. xiv. 235 Their Churches haue no perfect platforme of Ecclesiasticall gouernment. **1704** NELSON *Fest. & Fasts* (1739) 1 Festivals..are of Ecclesiastical Institution. **1865** MAFFEI *Brigand Life* II. 15 Both the ecclesiastical and civil tribunals.

b. ***ecclesiastical commission, commissioners***: a body of commissioners, acting in subordination to the Privy Council, for

administering certain portions of the revenues of the Established Church of England. *ecclesiastical corporations*: corporations consisting solely of ecclesiastical persons. *ecclesiastical courts*: courts for administering ecclesiastical law and maintaining the discipline of the Established Church. *ecclesiastical law*: the law, derived from Canon and Civil law, administered by such courts. *ecclesiastical judge*: a judge of an ecclesiastical court.

1649 BP. HALL *Cases Consc.* II. v. (1654) 113, I see not why the Ecclesiastical Judge may not convent the person accused. **1651** HOBBES *Govt. & Soc.* xiv. §5. 215 The humane Lawes (which are also called Ecclesiasticall) concerning things sacred. **1681** NEVILE *Plato Rediv.* 176 The Clergy..had and will have..inferior Courts in their own Power, called Ecclesiastical. **1827** HALLAM *Const. Hist.* (1876) III. xiv. 63 No legal defence could be made for the Ecclesiastical commission of 1686. **1836** H. ROGERS *J. Howe* viii. (1863) 195 Dignitaries of the Church..put into motion all the..machinery of the ecclesiastical courts. **1846** MCCULLOCH *Acc. Brit. Emp.* (1854) II. 259 All bishops have chancellors to assist them in..matters of ecclesiastical law.

2. Of or pertaining to the church viewed as consisting of the clergy; pertaining to or characteristic of an ecclesiastic or ecclesiastics.

1538 STARKEY *England* iv. 138 Are gyuen to the Church and Ecclesyastycal personys. **1576** LAMBARDE *Peramb. Kent* (1826) 137 How hee might..without offence to the Ecclesiasticall estate..conteine that treasure within the Realme. **1841** MIALL *Nonconf.* I. 2 A final grapple with ecclesiastical tyranny. **1845** S. AUSTEN *Ranke's Hist. Ref.* I. 17 To maintain the ecclesiastical rights and privileges.

†**b.** spec. *Ecclesiastical State(s*, the provinces formerly ruled by the Pope as Head of the Roman Church; = *States of the Church, Papal States. Obs.*

1689 LUTTRELL *Brief Rel.* (1857) I. 543 The pope has published a bull, excommunicating all persons..that shal hinder the commerce..of the ecclesiastical state. **1815** WELLINGTON *Let.* in Gurw. *Disp.* XII. 238 This officer says that he already in fact governs the Ecclesiastical States.

3. quasi-*sb.* **a.** = ECCLESIASTIC B. 2, a. *pl.* Matters concerning the church.

1641 C. BURGES *Serm.* 26 To adhere to the Pope as supreme in all Spiritualls and Ecclesiasticalls. **1649** JER. TAYLOR *Gt. Exemp.* I. Add. ix. 143 Their..greater ministeries in Ecclesiasticals. **1710** W. HUME *Sacr. Success.* 249 What is said to vindicate pope Joan's negotiation in Ecclesiasticals, may be apply'd to any sort of hypocrites.

b. = ECCLESIASTIC B. 1. *rare.*

1882–3 SCHAFF *Relig. Encycl.* II. 911/2 Nor could any ecclesiastical receive his office from a layman.

ecclesi'astically, *adv.* [f. prec. + -LY².] In an ecclesiastical manner or fashion; in an ecclesiastical sense or relation.

1588 J. UDALL *Demonstr. Discip.* (Arb.) 60 To gouerne the Church by the rules of his worde, and that ecclesiastically. **1877** MRS. OLIPHANT *Makers Flor.* v. 124 The noble group of buildings which form ecclesiastically the centre of Florence.

†**ecclesi'asticalness.** *Obs. rare*⁻¹. [f. as prec. + -NESS.] Ecclesiastical character.

1659 FULLER *App. Inj. Innoc.* (1840) 334 Wills..are proved in the Court-Christian, which evidenceth something of ecclesiasticalness in them.

ecclesiasticism (ɛˌkliːzɪˈæstɪsɪz(ə)m). [f. ECCLESIASTIC + -ISM.] The spirit and temper, or the principles of action, which are distinctively ecclesiastical.

1862 SHIRLEY *Nug. Crit.* vii. 297 There are..certain anomalies of mediæval ecclesiasticism..which are utterly repugnant to his intellect. **1876** A. M. FAIRBAIRN *Strauss* II. in *Contemp. Rev.* June 139 The struggle between.. Ecclesiasticism and Humanism. **1882** FARRAR *Early Chr.* II. xxxvi. 506 A character extremely familiar in the annals of ecclesiasticism.

b. *concr.* An ecclesiastical system.

1868 *Fortn. Rev.* May 498 Those organisations..contrast ..with the older ecclesiasticisms.

ˌecclesi'asticize, *v. nonce-wd.* [f. as prec. + -IZE.] *trans.* To render ecclesiastical.

1865 *Lond. Rev.* 241/2 He would lose all caste if he did not appear ecclesiasticized from head to foot.

ecclesiastico-, combining form of Gr. ἐκκλησιαστικός, as in **ecclesiastico-conservative** *a.*, advocating a conservative policy in church affairs; **ecclesiastico-military** *a.*, combining an ecclesiastical with a military organization.

1685 H. MORE *Para. Proph.* 269 Hieratico-Political or Ecclesiastico-Secular Sovereignties. **1753** BP. WARBURTON *Lett. late Prelate* (1809) To consider it in..an ecclesiastico-political light. **1817** BENTHAM *Church-of-Englandism* 308 Ecclesiastico-statistical information. **1845** S. AUSTIN *Ranke's Hist. Ref.* I. 23 The German empire..extended the ecclesiastico-military State of which the Church was an integral part. **1854** H. MILLER *Sch. & Schm.* xxiv. (1857) 536 The ecclesiastico-Conservative journal..patronized.. by the Scottish Church.

e'cclesiastry. *nonce-wd.* [f. ECCLESIAST + -RY.] Ecclesiastical pomp or business.

1865 CARLYLE *Fredk. Gt.* VII. XVIII. xii. 19 Olmütz..has much to do with artillery, much with ecclesiastry.

ecclesi'ography. [f. *ecclesio-*, combining form of ECCLESIA + Gr. -γραφία writing, description.] A descriptive treatise on the church.

1881 J. G. MANLEY (*title*), Ecclesiography or the Biblical Church analytically delineated.

ecclesiolatry (ɛˌkliːzɪˈɒlətrɪ). [f. as prec. + Gr. λατρεία worship.] Worship of the church; excessive reverence for church forms and traditions. So **ecclesi'olater** [cf. *idolater*], one who is guilty of 'ecclesiolatry'.

1847 J. W. DONALDSON *Vindication of Protestant Princ.* 26 The Anglican Ecclesiolatry of the Archbishop. *Ibid.* Pref. p. vii, With regard to the Ecclesiolaters. **1853** CONYBEARE *Ess. Eccles. & Soc.* (1855) 161 If a champion of ecclesiolatry is qualified..to render good service to his partisans, etc. **1881** CRAWFORD in *Ch. Bells* 25 June 477/2 The uncompromising ecclesiolatry which many goodmen have..adopted as part of their religion.

ecclesiologic, -ical (ɛˌkliːzɪəʊˈlɒdʒɪk, -ɪkəl). [f. ECCLESIOLOGY + -IC, -ICAL.] Of or pertaining to ecclesiology; devoted to ecclesiology. Hence **eˌcclesio'logically** *adv.*, from an ecclesiological point of view.

1847 *Handbk. Eng. Ecclesiology* 1 Church Schemes published by the Ecclesiological late Cambridge Camden Society. **1853** CDL. WISEMAN *Ess.* III. 391 The ecclesiological movement in the Anglican Church. **1869** MRS. OLIPHANT *Perpet. Curate* xlv. 387 Buller..is too ecclesiological for my taste. **1882** F. HARRISON *Choice Bks.* (1886) 286 The church..pranked out with staring ecclesiological trumpery, is..of rare antiquity. **1883** B. H. BECKER in *Eng. Illust. Mag.* Nov. 88 The more correct ecclesiological taste developed by Pugin.

ecclesiologist (ɛˌkliːzɪˈɒlədʒɪst). [f. next; see -IST.] A student of ecclesiology.

1841 (*title*) The Ecclesiologist, published by the Cambridge Camden Society. **1847** LADY G. FULLERTON *Grantley Manor* II. ix. 7 My uncle..is not much of an ecclesiologist. **1884** G. ALLEN in *Eng. Illust. Mag.* Feb. 309/1 The swift is the better ecclesiologist, loving to perch his nest under the tall pinnacles of some cathedral steeple.

ecclesiology (ɛˌkliːzɪˈɒlədʒɪ). Also 9 (incorrectly) ecclesialogy. [f. *ecclesio-* (see ECCLESIOGRAPHY) + Gr. -λογία discoursing: see -LOGY.] **a.** The science relating to the church or to churches; now usually, The science of church building and decoration. **b.** A treatise on churches.

1837 *British Critic* xxi. 220 We mean then by Ecclesialogy, a science which may treat of the proper construction and operations of the Church. **1847** (*title*) Handbook of English Ecclesiology. **1849** FREEMAN *Archit.* 4 The first phase of ecclesiology was simple antiquarianism. **1851** D. WILSON *Preh. Ann.* (1863) II. IV. i. 249 The..characteristics of Irish ecclesiology. **1865** W. WHITE *E. Eng.* I. 47 To say but a few words about each church..in Norfolk would be to compose an ecclesiology.

eˌcclesio'phobia. *nonce-wd.* [f. as prec., after *hydrophobia.*] A morbid dread of ecclesiasticism.

1877 *Daily News* 25 Oct. 5/7 That..form of ecclesiophobia which consists in seeing the finger of Jesuitry everywhere.

ecclyptic, obs. form of ECLIPTIC.

eccoprotic (ɛkəʊˈprɒtɪk), *a.* and *sb.* [ad. Gr. ἐκκοπρωτικός, f. ἐκκοπρόω, f. ἐκ out + κόπρος dung.]

A. *adj.* Producing evacuation of the bowels; mildly purgative. **B.** *sb.* A mild aperient.

1656 RIDGLEY *Pract. Physic* 231 It must be brought forth with diureticks..or with Eccoproticks. **1782** W. HEBERDEN *Comm.* xx. (1806) 106 Eccoprotics used occasionally, so as just to prevent costiveness. **1827** ABERNETHY *Surg. Wks.* I. 107 He prescribes purgative medicines to act as eccoprotics, to excite but not to stimulate the bowels.

eccrinology (ɛkrɪˈnɒlədʒɪ). *Phys.* [a. F. *eccrinologie*, f. Gr. ἐκκρίν-ειν to secrete + -λογία discoursing (see -LOGY).] 'Term for the doctrine of, or a treatise on, the secretions' (*Syd. Soc. Lex.*).

‖**eccrisis** (ˈɛkrɪsɪs). *Med.* [mod.L. a. Gr. ἔκκρισις secretion, f. ἐκκρίν-ειν to secrete.] Old term for an excretion or expulsion, whether a normal secretion or a product of disease; also the thing excreted. (*Syd. Soc. Lex.*)

1706 PHILLIPS, *Eccrisis*, a voiding of Humours, Excrements, or Ordure. **1721–1800** in BAILEY.

eccritic (ɛˈkrɪtɪk), *a. Med.* [ad. Gr. ἐκκριτικός having the power of secretion or excretion; cf. ECCATHARTIC.] (See quot.)

1681 tr. *Willis' Rem. Med. Wks.* Voc., *Eccritic*, not critical [app. a mere blunder]. **1883** WEBSTER, *Eccritic*, a remedy which promotes discharges, as an emetic, or a cathartic.

eccyty, obs. var. ECCEITY.

ecdemite, var. EKDEMITE.

ecderon (ˈɛkdərɒn). [irregularly f. Gr. ἐκ out + δέρ-ος, δέρ-μα skin.] A term introduced by Prof. Huxley to denote the outer part of the skin and skin-like structures, including the epidermis, the epithelium, and all structures homologous with these. Opposed to ENDERON.

Hence **ecde'ronic** *a.*

1859 HUXLEY in Todd *Cycl. Anat.* V. 476/1 The whole external area of metamorphosis, I call the Ecderon. *Ibid.* The ecderonic area of metamorphosis.

ecdysiast (ɛkˈdɪzɪæst). [f. Gr. ἔκδυσις (see ECDYSIS) + -αστής, after type ἐνθουσιαστής.] A strip-teaser. Hence **ec'dysiasm**, the activity or occupation of strip-teasing. Also *fig.*

1940 MENCKEN *Let.* 5 Apr. in *Amer. Lang.* Suppl. I. (1945) VI. vi. 585 It might be a good idea to relate strip-teasing in some way..to the associated zoölogical phenomenon of molting... A resort to the scientific name for molting, which is *ecdysis*, produces both *ecdysist* and *ecdysiast*. **1947** I. BROWN *Say the Word* 50 And there we can leave the problems and pride of ecdysiasm. **1957** *Times Lit. Suppl.* 11 Oct. 611/2 As happily sustained a piece of autobiographical ecdysiasm as we remember. **1958** *Time* 7 July 44/1 Is it possible for a nightclub to lose money with famed Ecdysiast Sherry Britton stripping to bugle beads and pearls?

‖**ecdysis** (ˈɛkdɪsɪs). [mod.L., a. Gr. ἔκδυσις, f. ἐκδύειν to put off.] The action of stripping or casting off, *esp.* of slough or dead skin in serpents and caterpillars, or of the chitinous integument in Crustacea. Also *concr.* that which is cast off, slough.

1854 J. HOGG *Microsc.* II. iv. (1867) 581 The change consisting in what is termed 'ecdysis', a casting off, or moulting only. **1881** *Nature* XXIII. 380 There has not been observed any inert stage before the transformations or ecdysis.

fig. **1863** HUXLEY *Man's Place Nat.* ii. 58 A skin of some dimension was cast [by 'the human larva'] in the 16th century..a new ecdysis seems imminent. **1876** M. & F. COLLINS *Blacksmith & Sch.* (1883) 191 There is to be an ecdysis.

ecdysone (ˈɛkdɪsəʊn). Also ecdyson. [ad. G. *ecdyson* (P. Karlson 1956, in *Ann. des Sci. naturelles* (*Zool.*) XVIII. 133), f. Gr. ἔκδυσις: see ECDYSIS.] A steroid, present as a hormone in the young forms of insects and some other arthropods, that controls moulting.

1956 *Vitamins & Hormones* XIV. 234 The name ecdysone,..pointing to the significance of the active substance for all molting processes, was proposed..for the pure, chemically defined, substance after isolation of the prothoracic gland hormone. **1961** *New Scientist* 2 Nov. 279/3 The moulting hormone (ecdyson) is produced at intervals by the thoracic glands under the influence of another hormone secreted by certain cells in the brain. *Ibid.*, Adults do not normally produce any ecdyson, but if this is provided artificially they can be induced to moult again. **1968** *Nature* 9 Nov. 601/2 The ecdysones control moulting in three diverse classes of arthropods besides insects.

ece, OE. and early ME. f. ECHE, *a. Obs.* eternal.

ecesis (ɛˈkiːsɪs). [f. Gr. οἴκησις act of inhabiting.] Of plants: the entry into, or establishment in, another habitat.

1904 F. E. CLEMENTS in *Bot. Surv. Nebraska* VII. 50 (*Cent. Dict.* Suppl.), In a word, Ecesis is the adjustment of a plant to a new habitat. It comprises the whole process covered more or less incompletely by acclimatisation, naturalisation, accommodation, etc. **1938** WEAVER & CLEMENTS *Plant Ecology* (ed. 2) i. 3 Migration alone, however, cannot produce vegetation... The migrants must make themselves at home, an idea that is expressed in a single term *ecesis*. *Ibid.* vi. 131 Ecesis is the adjustment of the plant to a new home. **1952** P. W. RICHARDS *Tropical Rain Forest* xvii. 383 The ecesis of secondary species is always effected by seeds or fruits.

Hence **ecesic** (ɛˈkiːsɪk) *a.*, of, or belonging to, ecesis.

1916 F. E. CLEMENTS *Plant Succession* 63 (*title*) Ecesic Causes.

ecgonine (ˈɛkgɒnɪn). *Chem.* [ad. G. *ecgonin* (F. Wöhler 1862, in *Ann. d. Chemie u. Pharm.* CXXI. 372), f. Gr. ἔκγονος, f. ἐκ out of, from + γον-, γεν- to produce + -INE⁵.] An alkaloid base, $C_9H_{15}NO_3$, obtained by the decomposition of cocaine. Hence **ecgonic** (ɛkˈgɒnɪk) *a.*, defining an acid obtained from ecgonine; **'ecgonate**, a salt of this.

1864 WATTS tr. *Gmelin's Hand-Bk. Chem.* XVI. 304 Chloroplatinate of Ecgonine. A mixture of hydrochlorate of ecgonine with chloride of platinum and strong alcohol. **1885** *Jrnl. Chem. Soc.* XLVIII. II. 913 It would seem that cocaine, ecgonine, and isotropine are derivatives of ethyl tetrahydropyridine. **1891** *Jrnl. Chem. Soc.* LX. I. 749 The acid $C_7H_{11}NO_3$, obtained by the oxidation of lævo-ecgonine, is termed ecgonic acid. *Ibid.*, Ethyl ecgonate, $C_7H_{10}EtNO_3$, is a colourless, viscid liquid. **1901** *Ibid.* LXXX. I. 291 Ecgonic acid..crystallizes from ethyl acetate or benzene in colourless needles. **1920** [see DIAMORPHINE]. **1957** *Encycl. Brit.* V. 908/2 On hydrolysis with mineral acids or baryta, cocaine breaks up into *ecgonine* (tropine carboxylic acid), benzoic acid and methyl alcohol... All the 'cocaines' are found to be derivatives of a simple base, ecgonine, which contains both a hydroxyl (.OH) and a carboxyl (.COOH) group.

echap(e, -appe, obs. var. ESCAPE *v.*.

echard (ˈɛkɑːd). *Ecology.* [f. Gr. ἔχειν to hold, withhold + ἀρδεία irrigation.] Water in the soil which is not available to plant roots.

1905 F. E. CLEMENTS *Res. Methods Ecol.* ii. 32 The terms, physiological water-content, and physical water-content, are awkward... It is here proposed to replace them by short words which will refer directly to the availability of the soil water for absorption... The terms suggested..are respectively, *holard..chresard..echard* (ἔχω, to withhold). *Ibid.* 32 This is the non-available water, or the echard. **1926** TANSLEY & CHIPP *Study of Vegetation* vii. 127 When the plants show signs of permanent wilting..the amount [of water] which the soil then contains is called the *echard* (water held back by the soil from the plant). **1938** WEAVER & CLEMENTS *Plant Ecology* (ed. 2) viii. 203 The water retained in the soil at the time of permanent wilting is nonavailable for growth or the *echard* (to withhold). **1960** N. POLUNIN *Introd. Plant Geogr.* x. 301 It is often necessary to distinguish between water which is available to plants..and that which is so strongly held as to be unavailable (*echard*).

‖**echarpe.** A Fr. word for a scarf or sash worn across the breast from shoulder to waist. ***en écharpe*** (Mil.): see quot.

1772 SIMES *Mil. Guide* s.v., To batter *an* [? read *en*] *echarpe* is to batter obliquely or side ways.

†**eche,** *sb.*[1] *Obs. rare.* [? var. of EKE addition; or f. ECHE *v.*] A piece added (*e.g.* to a bellrope). Cf. EKE *sb.*

1525 *Churchw. Acc. St. Dunstan's, Canterb.*, For ij ropes for eches for the bell ropys. For a eche to the gret bell *jd.*

†**eche,** *sb.*[2] *Obs. rare.* [app. ad. OF. *esche, aiche* tinder:—L. *esca* bait.] A taper.

1546 BALE *Eng. Votaries* II. (1550) 52 [Women] that gaue aultre clothes and towels, waxe candels and eches, masse grotes and trentals. *Ibid.* 84 b, They toke of these sea crabbes, and tyed eches vnto them light.

†**eche,** *a. Obs.* Forms 1 ǽce, 1–2 éce, 2 ech, ache, 2–3 eche. [OE. *ǽce, éce*, repr. OTeut. **aiwokjo-*, f. **aiwo*(*m* = L. *ævum* age (see A *adv.*, AY); cf. Goth. *ajuk* (:—**aiwoko-*) in *ajukdups* eternity.] Everlasting, eternal. Also quasi-*sb.* in phrase ***in eche.***

c **825** *Vesp. Psalter* cxi[i]. 7[6] In ʒemynde æcre bið se rehtwisa. **837** *Kentish Charter* in Sweet *O.E. Texts* (1885) 449 Ðæt mon agefe ðæt lond inn hiʒum to heora beode him to brucanne on ece ærfe. *a* **1000** *Riddles* (Gr.) xli. 1 Ece is se scyppend. *c* **1175** *Cott. Hom.* 239 Witeð into ece fer. *a* **1200** *Moral Ode* 364 in *Trin. Coll. Hom.* 231 God one sal ben ache lif, and blisse..and ache reste. *a* **1225** *Juliana* 79 Iheiet beo he him ane as he wes and is eauer in eche. *a* **1250** *Owl & Night.* 1277 Ah eavreeuh thing that eche nis A-gon schal and al this worldes blis.

†**eche,** *v. Obs.* Forms: 1 íecan, ícan, ýcan, écan (also with prefix ʒe-), 2–3 echen, 4–7 eche, eech(e, 6 etche, eatch, 7 each, ich. See also EKE *v.* [repr. OE. *écan*, in WS. *íecan* wk. vb. = OS. *ôkian*:—OTeut. **aukjan* (cf. OHG. *auhhôn* :—**aukôjan*), f. **auk-an* str. vb. (ON. *auka*, Goth. *aukan*; elsewhere only in pa. pple. OE. *éacen*, OS. *ôkan*) to increase, cogn. w. L. *augēre*, Gr. αὐξάνειν to increase.]

1. *trans.* To enlarge, augment, increase.

a **1000** *Andreas* 1386 (Gr.) Ðu scealt ecan ðine yrmþu. *c* **1000** *Sax. Leechd.* II. 208 Gif him fefer ne sie, yc þæt mid wine. *c* **1175** *Lamb. Hom.* 103 He..his sunnen echeð. *a* **1225** *Ancr. R.* 44 God ou echeð furðre his deorewurðe grace. *a* **1374** CHAUCER *Troylus* III. 1460 God might not oo poynt of my joyes eche. **1530** PALSGR. 531/1, I etche, I increase a thynge, *Je augmente.* **1596** SHAKS. *Merch. V.* III. ii. 23 To peize the time, To ich [Qo. 2, 3, 4 ech *and* eech] and to draw it out in length. **1608** —— *Per.* III. Prol. 13 Time..with your fine fancies quaintly eche [*rime-wd.* speech].

b. with *out* = *eke out.*

1599 SHAKS. *Hen. V*, III. Prol. 35 Still be kind, And eech out our performance with your mind. **1655** *Francion* I. iii. 63 He had such a full Character eech'd out with long Cloak-bag-string dashes, etc.

2. To add (something) *to.*

c **1000** *Ags. Gosp.* Luke xii. 25 Hwylc eower mæʒ þencende ican [*c* **950** *Lindisf.* and *c* **975** *Rushw.* ʒe-ece; *c* **1160** *Hatton* echan] ane elne to his anlicnesse? **1382** WYCLIF *Lev.* ix. 17 He made brent sacrifice, echynge into the sacrifyce offrynges of licours. *c* **1420** *Pallad. on Husb.* I. 1122 Hardde pitche and wex, take even weight, And herdde with pix liquide herto eche An halven dele.

b. ? To increase (one's) stature. [But possibly a different word; cf. ICCHE.]

1640 A. HARSNET *God's Summ.* 413 Riches cannot..each us one haires breadth neerer heaven.

3. *intr.* To grow.

1565 GOLDING *Ovid's Met.* x. (1593) 249 Her bellie big The eatching [L. *crescens*] tree had overgrowne.

b. Of a 'pace': To increase, be quickened.

1644 QUARLES *Sheph. Orac.* ix, How each envious pace Vies to be first, and eches for the place.

†ˈ**echelich,** *a. Obs.* [f. ECHE *a.* + *-lich*, -LY[1].] Everlasting, eternal.

Hence †ˈ**echeliche** *adv.*, eternally.

c **825** *Vesp. Psalter* xxiii[i]. 7 Bioð upahefene geatu ecelice. *c* **1175** *Lamb. Hom.* 139 Ðeo echeliche riche þet he haueð iʒarwed. *c* **1200** *Trin. Coll. Hom.* 23 Alle men shullen cume to libben echeliche. *a* **1225** *St. Marher.* 19 Healunge on & leome of echelich heale.

‖**e'chelle.** *Obs. rare*[−1]. [Fr. *échelle* ladder.] ? An arrangement of ribbons in the form of a ladder; a lacing of ribbons in front of the stomacher.

1690 *Songs Costume* (1849) 188 Of ribbon, various echelles, Gloves trimm'd, and lac'd as fine as Nells.

echelon (eʃlɔ̃, ˈɛʃəlɒn). Also **echellon.** [a. F. *échelon*, f. *échelle* ladder.]

1. a. 'A formation of troops in which the successive divisions are placed parallel to one another, but no two on the same alignement, each division having its front clear of that in advance' (Stocqueler). Also *attrib.* ***in echelon*** (also Fr. *en échelon*): drawn up in this manner. ***direct, oblique echelon***: see quot. 1832. ***echelon-lens***: see LENS *sb.*

1796 *Instr. & Reg. Cavalry* (1813) 55 The Echellon (or diagonal) changes of position. **1803** WELLINGTON *Mem.* in Gurw. *Disp.* II. 332 The 74th was not in an echellon. **1812** *Examiner* 24 Aug. 531/2 The..rear-guard..was perceived drawn up *en echellon.* **1832** *Regul. Instr. Cavalry* III. 46 Direct Echellon—Is when the Line is broken into several parts, moving direct to the front or rear in succession. Oblique Echellon—Is when the Line is broken into several parts by wheels from Line, or Column, less than the quarter circle, so as to be oblique to the former front, and parallel with each other. *Ibid.* 69 The..Troops..advance in echellon. **1834** MUDIE *Brit. Birds* (1841) I. 167 If you do not stir, he [raven] will drop down..and begin to hop in an echellon fashion.

b. Each of the subdivisions in the rear of the main supply service for troops in warfare.

1922 *Encycl. Brit.* XXXII. 493/2 One corps..was subdivided at all échelons into telephone units, wireless units, and visual units. **1924** L. E. VINING *Held by Bolsheviks* 88 People are coming to me in numbers asking me to get their trains and echelons away. *Ibid.* 104 Each echelon commander is demanding to have his train put on the west-bound track. **1948** A. BARON *From City, from Plough* xvii. 155 There was a clutter of signboards..with the emblems of battalions and brigades blazing a trail for their rear echelons to follow. **1955** *Times* 7 June 6/5 Their transport echelon, supplying them from the comparative comfort of the reserve, is now known as 'the passive wing'.

c. *N.Z.* (See quot. 1941.)

1941 BAKER *N.Z. Slang* iii. 24 The New Zealand application, dating from 1939, of *echelon* to a division of an Expeditionary Force..represents a new meaning applied to an old term. **1947** C. V. SMITH in J. Reid *Kiwi Laughs* (1961) 152 They are only a few short of the number that went overseas with the first Echelon.

2. Used for: One of the divisions of an army marching in echelon.

1808 J. BARLOW *Columb.* VII. 324 Disposed..all his ardent train, To charge, change front, each echelon sustain. **1862** *Guardian* 23 Apr. 400/2 Each échelon..deployed into line.

3. *transf.* A grade or rank in any (esp. civil) administration or profession. orig. *U.S.*

1950 in M. McLuhan *Mech. Bride* (1951) 2/3 'The catalogue will be confined to posts in the higher echelons,' said Mr. Ross. **1951** *Here & Now* (N.Z.) May 20/2 The United States delegation on any one day may, on the other hand, amount to as many as 100 people (with reserve echelons of advisers, experts, consultants and translators in Washington). **1957** P. FRANKAU *Bridge* 203 Do educationalists get as drunk when they convene as the lower echelons do? **1958** *Times* 12 Jan. 5/3 The higher echelons of the law and politics have become almost an Oxford preserve. **1969** *Daily Tel.* 8 Feb. 15/1 A security leak in the top echelon of the Civil Service.

echelon (ˈɛʃəlɒn), *v.* [f. prec., or ad. Fr. *échelonner.*] *trans.* To arrange (troops) in the form of an echelon; to dispose in divisions at successive intervals. Mostly in *pa. pple.*; also *absol.*

1864 *Sat. Rev.* 380/2, 150,000 troops echelonned over the country. **1879** *Daily News* 1 Mar. 5/7 To echelon the flanks of the attacking force somewhat to the rear.

b. *transf.* and *fig.*

c **1860** WRAXALL tr. *R. Houdin* xv. 213 Miseries we had to undergo, like so many pinpricks echeloned on our passage. **1886** *Pall Mall G.* 10 June 5/1 Along the infinite ascending spiral which leads from earth to heaven..the whole human race is echeloned at irregular intervals.

Hence ˈ**echeloned** *ppl. a.*

1857 C. ADAMS *Gt. Campaigns* 76 The echeloned formation of his divisions. **1924** SKERL tr. *Wegener's Orig. Cont. & Oceans* iv. 65 The Cordilleras..run from south to north along the coast, and terminate in echeloned folds which retreat successively westwards.

†**eche'neis.** *Obs. rare.* Also echineis. [Gr. ἐχενηΐς, f. ἔχ-ειν to hold + ναῦς (dat. νηΐ) ship, from its supposed power of holding back a ship.] The Remora, or Sucking-fish, which has on the crown of its head an oblong flat disk, or sucker, by means of which it can adhere to foreign bodies.

1594 ? GREENE *Selimus* Wks. (1881–3) XIV. 209 The Echinæis swimmes against the streames. **1651** J. F[REAKE] *Agrippa's Occ. Philos.* 29 The litle fish Echeneis stops the Ships. **1774** GOLDSMITH *Nat. Hist.* (1862) II. III. i. 300 The Echineis, or Sucking-fish.

†ˈ**echeness.** *Obs.* Also 1–3 ecness, -nyss, 2–3 ech-, eccheness. [f. ECHE *a.*; see -NESS.] Eternity; only in phrase ***on*** or ***in echeness.***

c **825** *Vesp. Psalter* ix. 8[7] Dryhten in ecnesse ðorhwunað. *c* **1175** *Lamb. Hom.* 109 Vniseli bið þe ȝitsere þe..þurh his ahȝene ehte forwurð a on echnesse. *a* **1225** *Ancr. R.* 430 From worlde to worlde, euer on ecchenesse!

echeveria (ɛkiːˈvɪərɪə). ['In honour of M. Echeveri, author of the splendid drawings of the *Flora Mexicana*' (Paxton).] A handsome genus of succulent plants allied to the house-leek (N.O. *Crassulaceæ*), extensively used in carpet gardening.

1840 PAXTON *Bot. Dict.* **1883** *Pall Mall G.* 17 Sept. 3/2 My Londoner, who..likes old friends among the flowers whose names he has got well into his head better than all the Alternantheras and Echeverias. **1883** G. ALLEN in *Colin Clout's Calendar* 147 It will not away with your modern gloxinias and echeverias.

‖**echevin** (eʃəvɛ̃). [F. *échevin*, OF. *eschevin* = It. *schiavino*:—med.L. *scabinus*; of Teut. origin; cf. OLG. *scepeno* (Schade), OHG. *sceffeno, sceffen* (Ger. *schöffe*(*n, schöppen*).] A municipal functionary in French and Belgian towns, corresponding nearly to an English alderman.

1766 SMOLLETT *Trav.* (1797) 17 The civil magistracy of Boulogne consists of a mayor and echevins. **1881** *Edin. Rev.* Jan. 81 A highly connected echevin or alderman of Ghent.

‖**Echidna** (ɪˈkɪdnə). *Zool.* [mod.L., a. Gr. ἔχιδνα viper.] A genus of Australian toothless burrowing monotremate mammals (family *Echidnidæ*), resembling hedgehogs in size and external appearance. In several points their structure is allied to that of birds. The best known species is *E. Hystrix*, the Porcupine Ant-eater.

1847 CARPENTER *Zool.* §320 The Echidna, or Porcupine Ant-eater..is about the size and form of a Hedgehog.

echidnine (ɪˈkɪdnaɪn). *Chem.* [f. Gr. ἔχιδνα viper + -INE.] (See quot.)

1861 HULME tr. *Moquin-Tandon* II. v. ii. 284 Prince Lucien Bonaparte has shown that the poison of the Viper consists essentially of a principle to which he has given the name Echidnine or Viperine.

echinal (ɪˈkaɪnəl, ˈɛkɪnal), *a.* [f. ECHIN-US + -AL[1].] Of or belonging to a sea-urchin.

1830 LYELL *Princ. Geol.* I. 129 A saurian vertebra together with patellæ and echinal spines.

echinate (ˈɛkɪneɪt), *a.* [ad. L. *echinātus*, f. *echīnus* hedgehog.]

1. *Bot.* 'Furnished with numerous rigid hairs, or straight prickles; as the fruit of *Castanea vesca*' (*Treas. Bot.*).

1668 WILKINS *Real Char.* 116 Whose outward husk is Echinate and prickly. **1835** LINDLEY *Introd. Bot.* (1848) I. 344 Each grain is echinate.

2. *Zool.* Resembling an echinus or sea-urchin.

1846 DANA *Zooph.* (1848) 230 The spiniform teeth which give the echinate character to this species.

Hence **echinato-'dentate,** *a. Zool.*, having toothlike prickles or spines.

1846 DANA *Zooph.* (1848) 173 Exterior..echinato-dentate.

echinate (ˈɛkɪneɪt), *v.* [f. prec.] **a.** *intr.* To set up one's prickles like a hedgehog; in quot. *fig. nonce use.*

1788 J. WILLIAMS (A. Pasquin) *Childr. Thespis* (1792) 243 When merit exhibits his guinea gorged purse, They'll echinate, redden and tacitly curse.

b. *trans.* Of a sponge spicule: to project from (the fibre) at an acute angle. So ˈ**echinating** *ppl. a.*

1882 *Cassell's Nat. Hist.* VI. 328 The skeleton is..composed of chief spicules lying parallel to form a fibre, which is spined by other (echinating) spicules projecting from it. **1900** E. R. LANKESTER *Treat. Zool.* II. 140 The spicules so placed are said to 'echinate' the fibre. **1940** L. H. HYMAN *Invertebrates* I. vi. 347 Spongin fibers may have both enclosed ('*coring*') and echinating spicules.

echinated (ˈɛkɪneɪtɪd), *ppl. a.* [f. as prec. + -ED.] = ECHINATE *a.*

1657 TOMLINSON *Renou's Disp.* 346 Bearing..crasse, spinous and echinated Apples. **1756** P. BROWNE *Jamaica* 233 Half the capsule is echinated, the other smooth. **1881** MACDONALD in *Jrnl. Linn. Soc.* XV. No. 85. 281 Lobes of apertures finely echinated.

†ˈ**eching,** *vbl. sb. Obs.* [f. ECHE *v.* + -ING[1].] The action of increasing, enlarging, supplementing; *concr.* an addition.

1382 WYCLIF *Isa.* xv. 9, I shal putte vpon Dibon ecchingus [**1388** encreessyngis; Vulg. *additamenta*]. **1502** *Priv. Purse Exp. Eliz. York* (1830) 34 Item for mending and eching of iiij. hopys to the said whelys ijd.

†ˈ**eching,** *ppl. a. Obs.* [f. ECHE *v.* + -ING[2].] That increases. In quot., that increases speed, is quickened; cf. ECHE *v.* 3 b.

1644 QUARLES *Sheph. Orac.* ii. (1646) 13 Lord, how my Lambs divide Their eching paces to the farther side.

echinid (ɪˈkaɪnɪd). *Zool.* [mod. f. Gr. ἐχῖν-ος sea-urchin + -ID; cf. F. *échinide.*] Any member of the *Echinus* family. As pl. mod.L. **e'chinida** is often used; also **e'chinidans** in same sense.

1835 KIRBY *Hab. & Inst. Anim.* I. vi. 209 The most powerful..organs with which the Creator has gifted the Echinidans are their jaws and teeth. **1851** RICHARDSON *Geol.* 225 Echinida have a globular ovoid or depressed body without rays. **1887** *Athenæum* 5 Feb. 194/2 The echinids,

asterids, and holothurids have sprung from a common primitive form.

echinite (ˈɛkɪnaɪt). [ad. mod.L. *echinita*; see ECHINUS and -ITE.] A fossil echinoderm; a fossil sea-urchin. Hence **echiˈnital** *a.*, pertaining to or resembling echinites.

[**1695** WOODWARD *Nat. Hist. Earth* IV. (1723) 203 The Bodyes which are call'd, by Naturalists, *Echinitæ.*] **1750** G. HUGHES *Barbadoes* II. 55, I have likewise a middle-sized petrified Echinite. **1851** RICHARDSON *Geol.* 24 The echinites.

echino- (ɪˈkaɪnəʊ, ˈɛkɪnəʊ), combining form of Gr. ἐχῖνος, used (either in its original sense of 'hedgehog', denoting something prickly, or in that of 'sea-urchin', ECHINUS) to form compounds in scientific use. **eˈchinochrome**, a brown or yellowish brown pigment found in some echinoderms; **eˌchinococˈcosis** *Path.*, disease caused by infection with tapeworms of the genus *Echinococcus*; hydatid disease; **echinococcus** (-ˈkɒkəs) *Zool.* [Gr. κόκκος seed-grain], a former genus of ACEPHALOCYSTS or hydatids, now known to be the scolex or higher larval form of a species of tapeworm, hence called *Tænia Echinococcus* (formerly *T. nana*); †**eˈchinod**, *Obs.*, in 8 **ekinod** [Gr. ὀδ-ούς tooth], (see quot.); **eˌchino-ˈencrinite**: see ENCRINITE; **eˌchinoˈpluteus** *Zool.*, the free-swimming larval form of an echinoid.

1883 C. A. MACMUNN in *Proc. Birmingham Philos. Soc.* III. 380 **Echinochrome.*—It is unfortunate that as one meets with new colouring-matters long names have to be invented to distinguish them from other colouring matters. This has been the case with the pigment which I have now to mention, and for which I propose the name of *echinochrome*. **1886** *Jrnl. R. Microsc. Soc.* 48 Dr. C. A. MacMunn describes the spectroscopic or chemical characters of the blood of various worms and molluscs; one of the most interesting pigments which he has detected is that which he calls echinochrome..obtained from the perivisceral cavity of *Strongylocentrotus lividus*. **1912** *Jrnl. Chem. Soc.* CII. I. 520 Echinochrome is probably held in the same way as chlorophyll is held in the plant cell. **1959** *Chambers's Encycl.* III. 763/1 They [*sc.* naphthoquinones]..are apparently limited to sea-urchins. Many such species display conspicuous amounts of naphthoquinoid echinochromes in their thin skin and in the calcareous material of spines and shells, which thus assume red, purple, pink or greenish colours. **1836–9** TODD *Cycl. Anat.* II. 126 *note*, These may be considered rather as the Parasites of the *Echinococcus. **1878** BELL *Gegenbauer's Comp. Anat.* 131 When the youngest of these can again bud off tænia-heads on its inner wall, we get the Echinococcus-form. **1900** *Veterinarian* Dec. 655 The liver was an interesting specimen of echinococcosis. **1961** CHANDLER & READ *Introd. Parasitol.* (ed. 10) xv. 362 The malignant alveolar form of echinococcosis known from North and Central Europe..is caused by a distinct species, *E. multilocularis*. **1708** in *Phil. Trans.* XXVI. 78 The *Ekinod or Fossil Tooth of the Sea-Urchin. **1850** DANA *Geol.* App. i. 713 Encrinites, particularly the *echino-encrinites. **1909** *Cent. Dict.* Suppl., **Echinopluteus*, the pluteus, or free-swimming larva, of a sea-urchin. **1913** T. MORTENSEN in *Jrnl. Marine Biol. Assoc.* X. 16 (*caption*) Part of the skeleton of the *Echinopluteus* of *Spatangus purpureus*. **1932** L. A. BORRADAILE et al. *Invertebrata* xviii. 556 The 'posterolateral arms'..if they are present in the *Echinopluteus*, are there small. **1955** L. H. HYMAN *Invertebrates* IV. xv. 490 The echinopluteus occurs in an infinite variety of shape and structure. **1967** P. A. MEGLITSCH *Invert. Zool.* xi. 409/1 The echinopluteus develops as the gastrula becomes flattened on the future oral surface.

echinoderm (ɪˈkaɪnəʊ-, ˈɛkɪnəʊdɜːm). [f. *echinodermata*, by shortening], a member of the class *Echinodermata*; hence **echinoˈdermal** *a.* [see -AL] = ECHINODERMATOUS. ‖**echinodermata** (-ˈdɜːmətə), *sb. pl.* [mod.L., f. Gr. δέρματ- stem of δέρμα skin], a class of animals formerly included in the *Radiata*, but now placed in the sub-kingdom *Annuloida*, including Sea-urchins, Sea-cucumbers. etc.; the name refers to the sharp-pointed spines with which the skin of the typical species is studded. **echinoˈdermatous** *a.*, belonging to or resembling the echinodermata.

1835 KIRBY *Hab. & Inst. Anim.* I. vi. 201 The *Echinoderms form the second order of the Radiaries. **1886** *Athenæum* 18 Dec. 828/2 The blastoids form an extinct group of stalked echinoderms. **1845** WHEWELL *Indic. Creator* 39 The higher types of *Echinodermal, Articulate, and Molluscous, Animals. **1835–6** TODD *Cycl. Anat.* I. 109/2 Some marine animals without an *echinodermatous covering.

echinoid (ˈɛkɪnɔɪd), *a.* and *sb.* [mod. f. ECHIN-US + -OID.]

A. *adj.* Bearing a resemblance to, or having the characteristics of, an Echinus or Sea-urchin.

1851 RICHARDSON *Geol.* viii. 208 The fossil species of Crinoid, Asteroid, and Echinoid radiata.

B. *sb.* An individual of the Order *Echinoidea* (Class *Echinodermata*), the characteristics of which are a shell composed of calcareous plates, and locomotion by suckers and spines.

1864 *Reader* No. 85. 204/2 Starfishes, echinoids, or ophiurans.

echinology (ɛkɪˈnɒlədʒɪ). [f. Gr. ἐχῖνο-ς ECHINUS + -λογία discourse.] The study of Echinoids. Hence **echiˈnologist** [see -IST], a student of echinology.

1881 H. W. MACINTOSH in *Nature* No. 628. 41 Zoologists in general, and echinologists in particular.

echinulate (ɪˈkɪnjʊlət), *a.* [f. on the analogy of ACICULATE, as if ad. mod.L. *echīnulātus*, f. **echīnulus*, dim. of ECHINUS.] Having or covered with small prickles.

1846 DANA *Zooph.* (1848) 157 Calicles small, nearly hemispherical and echinulate. **1874** COOKE *Fungi* 29 The spores are in many instances..beautifully echinulate.

Hence **eˈchinulately** *adv.*, with small prickles. **echinulato-striate** *a.*, streaked with rows of small prickles.

1846 DANA *Zooph.* (1848) 157 Surface finely echinulato-striate. *Ibid.* 450 The calicles..are striate, though not echinulately so.

echinuliform (ɪˈkɪnjʊlɪˌfɔːm), *a.* [mod. f. L. **echīnul-us*, dim. of ECHINUS + -FORM.] In the form of, or resembling, small prickles.

1846 DANA *Zooph.* (1848) 707 Delicate echinuliform points.

echinus (iːˈkaɪnəs). *Zool.* Also 4 **echynnys**, 6 **echynus**. [a. L. *echīnus*, Gr. ἐχῖνος hedgehog, sea-urchin.] The Sea-urchin; a genus of animals (Order *Echinoidea*, Class *Echinodermata*), inhabiting a spheroidal shell built up from polygonal plates, and covered with rows of sharp spines. (The sense 'hedgehog' given in Bailey and some mod. Dicts. seems to be merely Gr. and Lat.)

c **1374** CHAUCER *Boeth.* II. ix. (1868) 82 Sharpe fisshes þat hyȝten echynnys. *c* **1520** ANDREWE *Noble Lyfe* in *Babees Bk.* (1868) 234 Echynus is a lytell fysshe of half a fote longe, & hath sharpe prykeles vnder his bely in stede of fete. **1695** WOODWARD *Nat. Hist. Earth* (1723) 33 In Chalk..there are only found Echini, and the other lighter Sorts of Shells. **1791** E. DARWIN *Bot. Gard.* I. 120 Yon round Echinus ray his arrowy mail. **1877** W. DALL *Tribes N.W.* 51 The echinus ..is furnished with ovaries on the inner side of the dome of the test.

†**2.** See quot. *Obs.* or *doubtful*; cf. ECHINATE.

1721–1800 BAILEY, *Echinus*, [among Botanists] is the prickly Head, Cover of the Seed or Top of any Plant, so called from its likeness to a Hedg-hog.

3. *Anat.* 'The rough stomach of a ruminant; also, the rough and muscular gizzard of graminivorous and gallinaceous birds' (*Syd. Soc. Lex.*).

1716 G. CHEYNE *Philos. Princ. Relig.* II. 360 In all granivorous birds, the Crop, the Echinus, and the Gizzard.

4. *Archit.* The ovolo moulding next below the abacus of the capital of a column. [So in Gr. and L.; the reason for this use of the word has been variously conjectured.]

1563 SHUTE *Archit.* D ij a, The Antiques in diuers of their edifices, hath made Echinus, to be in Proiecture like vnto Abacus. **1664** EVELYN tr. *Freart's Archit.* 127 *Echinus*, a Bottle cut with an edg. **1789** P. SMYTH tr. *Aldrich's Archit.* (1818) 90 This part is called an echinus, because of its resemblance to the prickly coat of chestnut. **1876** GWILT *Archit.* Gloss., *Echinus*, the same as the ovolo or quarter round, though..only properly so called when carved with eggs and anchors.

†**echiquette**, *a. Obs. Her.* [a. Fr. *échiqueté*, connected with *échiquier* chess-board.] = CHECKY.

1727–51 CHAMBERS *Cycl.*, *Echiquette*. See CHECKY. **1775** ASH, *Echiquette* (adj. in heraldry), checky.

†**eˈchiquier**. *Mil. Obs. rare*⁻¹. [F. *échiquier* chess-board.] In phrase, ***to retire in échiquier*** [so Fr. *en échiquier* (Littré)], i.e. by alternate squares.

1812 *Examiner* 21 Dec. 812/1 They retired in echiquier, under a very heavy fire.

echitamine (ɛˈkɪtəmɪn). *Chem.* [ad. G. *echitamin* (O. Hesse 1878, in *Ber. d. Deut. Chem. Ges.* XI. 1548), f. mod.L. *echītēs* generic plant-name + AMINE.] An alkaloid found in the bark of *Echites scholaris* and other species of *Echites*. So **echiˈtamidine**, **eˈchiteine**, **eˈchitenine**, **ˈechitine** (see quots.).

1876 *Jrnl. Chem. Soc.* XXIX. 277 Echitein crystallizes from hot strong alcohol in light needles. *Ibid.*, Echitin, $C_{32}H_{52}O_2$, forms white scales. **1879** *Ibid.* XXXVI. 71 Dita bark (the bark of *Alstonia scholaris* or *Echites scholaris*) contains two alkaloïds, ditamine and echitamine. **1881** *Ibid.* XL. 185 The action of hydrochloric acid on echitamine hydrochloride. **1886** *Buck's Handbk. Med. Sci.* II. 519/2 Three alkaloids, ditamine, echitamine, and echitenine. **1906** *Watts' Dict. Chem.* II. 413/1 Echitin..accompanies echicerin, from which it differs in being less soluble in ligroïn. **1932** *Jrnl. Chem. Soc.* II. 2626 (*title*) *Echitamine in* Alstonia *Barks*. Barks of various species of *Alstonia* have been examined in the hope of finding a source of echitamine richer in that alkaloid than is the bark of *A. congensis*. *Ibid.*, A new crystalline alkaloid, $C_{20}H_{26}O_3N_2$, which it is proposed to call *echitamidine*, has been obtained..from the mother-liquors from echitamine hydrochloride.

eˈchites. Also 7 **echite**. [a. Gr. ἐχίτης, f. ἔχις viper.]

†**1.** A precious stone, dark-green, red, or violet, with fabulous properties, found in India and Persia; cf. AETITES. *Obs.*

1398 TREVISA *Barth. De P.R.* XVI. xxxviii. (1495) 565 Echites conteyneth and bredyth a nother stone wythin. **1567** MAPLET *Gr. Forest* 6 Echites is a stone..without the which the Eagle can not bring forth her yong. **1688** R. HOLME *Armoury* II. 40/1 The Echite is a stone..of a violet colour. **1731** BAILEY vol. II, *Echites*, a precious stone, of a darkish-green colour, somewhat resembling a viper.

2. *Bot.* A genus of climbing plants (N.O. *Apocynaceæ*), 'so called from its twisting habits'.

1731 BAILEY vol. II, *Echites*, an herb, a kind of Clivers. **1858** GLENNY *Gard. Everyday Bk.* 138/1 Echites are beautiful climbers.

echium (ˈɛkɪəm). [mod.L. (J. P. de Tournefort in C. Linnæus *Genera Plantarum* (1737) 38), f. Gr. ἔχιον the name used by Dioscorides, f. ἔχις viper, in allusion to the spotted stem.] A plant of the genus of shrubs or herbs so called, belonging to the family Boraginaceæ and native to Europe; cf. *viper's bugloss* (VIPER 6 b).

1883 W. ROBINSON *Eng. Flower Garden* 118/2 These five species..are representative of the annual and biennial Echiums. **1924** W. DEEPING *Three Rooms* v. 40 Later, the spikes of the echium would make a wonderful and rich blueness. **1963** W. BLUNT *Of Flowers & Village* 267 There were some splendid echiums on Teide.

echiuroid (ɛkɪˈjʊərɔɪd), *a.* and *sb.* [f. mod.L. *Echiurus*, generic name, f. Gr. ἔχις adder + οὐρά tail + -OID.] **A.** *adj.* Of or pertaining to marine worms of the phylum *Echiuroidea* or genus *Echiurus*. **B.** *sb.* A member of this phylum or genus. So **echiˈurian**, **echiˈurid**.

1886 *Jrnl. R. Microsc. Soc.* Dec. 984 The armed Gephyrea or Echiuroids. *Ibid.* 985 The nerve-trunk has in adult Echiurians lost all trace of segmentation. **1897** *Q. Jrnl. Microsc. Sci.* Dec. 367 A new British Echiuroid Gephyrean. **1902** *Encycl. Brit.* XXVII. 625/2 The female [of *Bonellia*] has the normal Echiuroid structure. **1909** *Jrnl. R. Microsc. Soc.* 50 New Deep-sea Echiurid. **1941** J. STEINBECK *Log from Sea of Cortez* (1958) 273 *Echiuroid*, a worm-like animal related to the sipunculids. **1967** P. A. MEGLITSCH *Invertebrate Zool.* xv. 646/2 Echiuroid nephridia are much like the nephridia of sipunculids. *Ibid.* 648/1 The sedentary life of the echiuroids is reflected in the simplicity of the neuro-sensory equipment.

echo (ˈɛkəʊ), *sb.* Pl. **echoes**, rarely **echos**. Also 4 **ecko**, 5–7 **ecco**, 6–8 **eccho**. [a. L. *ēchō*, a. Gr. ἠχώ, related to ἠχή sound.

The termination -ώ was common in Gr. female names, and perh. (as in the similar case of πειθώ persuasion) the form may be due to personification, although in Gr. literature it is used in an appellative sense much earlier than the mention of Echo as a distinct mythological person.]

1. a. A repetition of sounds, which is produced by the reflexion of the sound-waves due to their incidence on something denser than the aerial medium in which they are propagated; hence *concr.* a secondary or imitative sound produced by reflected waves, as distinguished from the original sound caused by the direct waves.

1340 *Ayenb.* 60 *Ecko*, þet is þe rearde þet ine þe heȝe helles comþ ayen and acordeþ to al þet me him sayþ. **1388** WYCLIF *Wisdom* xvi. 16 Ecco sownynge aȝen fro hiȝeste hillis. **1485** CAXTON *Trevisa's Higden* I. xxii, Ecco is reboundynge of noyse. **1571** GOLDING *Calvin on Ps.* xxvii. 8 The voyce of God must resound..as it were an Eccho in holow places. **1601** HOLLAND *Pliny* II. 581 This miraculous rebounding of the voice, the Greekes haue a pretty name for, and call it Echo. **1678** CUDWORTH *Intell. Syst.* 581 Which if considered in Audibles, then will the Second Hypostasis be look'd upon, as the Eccho of an Original Voice; and the Third as the Repeated Eccho, or Eccho of that Eccho. **1810** SCOTT *Lady of L.* I. x, Round and around the sounds were cast, Till echo seemed an answering blast. **1877** BRYANT *Lit. People of Snow* 313 Like echoes softly flung from rock and hill.

b. ***to applaud to the echo***: i.e. so vociferously as to produce echoes.

1605 SHAKS. *Macb.* v. iii. 53, I would applaud thee to the very Eccho That should applaud againe. **1840** DICKENS *Old C. Shop* (C. D. ed.) 77 The performance was applauded to the echo.

c. *Telephone Engineering*. (See quots.) Also *attrib.*

1925 *Electr. Commun.* IV. 40/1 Echo effects are caused by reflections of voice waves which take place whenever electrical irregularities are encountered in telephone circuits. **1959** *Post Office Electr. Engineers' Jrnl.* LII. 69/1 A problem which continually confronts the communication engineer is the avoidance of echoes. *Ibid.*, These echoes arise from reflections occurring at unavoidable electrical discontinuities.

d. In full ***radio echo***. A radio wave which has been reflected or otherwise returned with sufficient magnitude and delay to be perceived as a wave distinct from that transmitted (see also quot. 1941). Also *attrib.* and *fig.*

1928 C. STØRMER in *Nature* 3 Nov. 681/1 (*heading*) Short wave echoes and the Aurora Borealis. *Ibid.*, On Feb. 29 of this year I received a letter from Engineer Jørgen Hals..in which he says: '..I repeatedly heard signals from the Dutch short-wave transmitter station... At the same time as I heard the telegraph-signals I also heard echoes.' *Ibid.* 17 Nov. 768/1 (*heading*) Radio echoes and magnetic storms. **1930** *Times* 25 Mar. 11/4 Neither..appear to attach very much importance to these 'echo' effects... The effect of

these 'echoes' at the receiving station can .. be overcome by a directive aerial system which does not accept radiation from the backward direction. Echo signals may .. also be produced by radiation leaving the transmitter .. and travelling more than once round the world. **1941** *B.B.C. Gloss. Broadc. Terms* 10 *Echo*, (1) Repetition of a sound after an interval of time, caused for example by reflection of sound waves, or occurring as a result of propagation of electro-magnetic waves over more than one path. (2) Reverberation artificially added to the output from a studio or hall. **1965** *New Statesman* 11 June 904/3 The hire-purchase controls just introduced, small enough not to induce substantial 'echo' effects in the future.

e. A radar wave which has been reflected from an object; also, the representation of it on a radar screen.

1944 [see ECHOLOCATION]. **1945** *Electronic Engin.* XVII. 719/2 The measurement of interval between pulse and echo on the time base of the C.R. tube. **1947** etc. [see ANGEL *sb.* 10]. **1953** R. CHISHOLM *Cover of Darkness* iii. 36 In the air the 'noise' (interference) was usually worse and often the echo was less clear. On the elevation (left-hand) tube there is slightly more of the echo above than below the horizontal trace.

2. The cause of this phenomenon personified.
(In Greek mythology, Echo was regarded as an 'Oread' or mountain nymph.)

1592 SHAKS. *Rom. & Jul.* II. ii. 162 Else would I teare the Caue where Eccho lies And make her ayrie tongue more hoarse. **1795** WOLCOTT (P. Pindar) *Pindariana* Wks. 1812 IV. 161 And Echo, long banish'd, sweet Maid, Return'd with her stories of love. **1860** TYNDALL *Glac.* I. §2. 15 The echoes talked down to me from the mountain walls.

3. An artifice in verse, by which one line is made to consist of a repetition (such as might be given by a literal echo) of the concluding syllables of the preceding line, so as to supply an answer to the question contained in it, or otherwise to give a continuous sense. Hence, the name of the species of verse in which this was done. Also *attrib.*, as in *echo verse*.

The most perfect modern example of this once fashionable device is Hugo's *Chasse du Burgrave*, where every alternate line throughout a long poem is an 'echo' of the preceding line.

1633 G. HERBERT *Temple, Heaven*, But are there cares and businesse with the pleasure? *Echo*, Leisure. **1663** BUTLER *Hud.* I. iii. 199 Quoth he, O whither, wicked Bruin? Art thou fled to my—Eccho, Ruin! **1711** ADDISON *Spect.* No. 62 ¶3 False wit chiefly consists in the resemblance and congruity ..sometimes of Syllables, as in Echos and Doggerel Rhymes. **1791-1824** D'ISRAELI *Cur. Lit.* (1866) 263/2 A similar contrivance, that of Echo Verses, may here be noticed.

†**4.** A response received or expected as a matter of course from the nature of the address. *Obs.*

1642 R. CARPENTER *Experience* v. xx. 333 Give out, from the inwards of his heart and Soule, with an Eccho, Amen. **1711** SHAFTESB. *Charac.* (1737) III. 300 Now the eccho or antiphony which these elegant exclaimers hope .. to draw necessarily from their audience, is that, etc.

5. *fig.* A repetition or close imitation, chiefly of things that can be compared to speech, voice, or sound (*e.g.* a writer's thoughts or style), but occas. with wider meaning; an enfeebled reproduction; an effect that continues after its cause has ceased; and the like.

1622 SPARROW *Bk. Com. Prayer* (1661) 221 Their Services are, as it were, so many Eccho's and Reflexions upon the Mystery of Pentecost. **1632** SANDERSON *12 Serm.* 465 God .. also causeth the Eccho of that word to sound in our hearts. **1701** SWIFT *Contests Nobles & Com.* Wks. 1755 II. I. 50 His folly, and his wisdom .. are all of his own growth, not the eccho or infusion of other men. **1749** *Power Numbers Poet. Comp.* 60 The Sound is still an Eccho to the Sense. **1860** FARRAR *Orig. Lang.* i. 28 A feeble echo of splendours. **1878** B. TAYLOR *Deukalion* II. ii. 60 Was it some last echo blown From ended struggles?

6. *transf.* A person who reflects or imitates the language, sentiments, or conduct of others; one who assents obsequiously to the opinions of another.

a **1631** DONNE *Poems* (1650) 168 Then write, that I may follow, and so bee Thy debtor, thy eccho, thy foyle, thy zanee. **1691** *Saytr agst. French* 3 These Apes, these Echo's ..of Men, Shall be the present Subject of my Pen. **1732** SWIFT *Corr.* Wks. 1841 II. 672 Clarendon, whom they reckoned the faithful echo of their master's intentions. **1841-4** EMERSON *Ess.* vi. Wks. (Bohn) I. 88 Better be a nettle in the side of your friend than his echo.

7. *Music.* (See quot.)

1711 *Lond. Gaz.* No. 4797/3 The lesser Organ .. has in it 10 Stops and 4 Eccho's. **1876** HILES *Catech. Organ* i. (1878) 4 The Echo consisted of duplicates of some of the Treble stops of the other Manuals. **1878** E. J. HOPKINS in Grove *Dict. Mus.* I. 21 The resources for .. accompaniment were extended .. by the insertion of an additional short manual organ called the Echo.

8. *Whist.* (See quot. 1876.) Also in *Bridge*, a signal to one's partner, esp. by the playing of a higher card of a suit followed by a lower, indicating how many cards of a suit are held, or requesting a specific lead.

1862 'CAVENDISH' *Whist.* (1879) 268 The advantages of the echo are manifold. **1876** A. CAMPBELL-WALKER *Correct Card* (1880) Gloss. 11 *Echo*, asking for trumps in response to your partner's ask, when but for his demand you would not have called. **1899** A. DUNN *Bridge* 51 The plain suit echo. **1902** —— *New Ideas on Bridge* 80 A player must have either led or 'called for' trumps before his partner gives the 'three-trump echo'. **1939** N. DE V. HART *Bridge Players' Bedside Bk.* 140 High-low play as a signal to the partner is termed a peter if it occurs in a suit contract and an echo at No-Trumps. *Ibid.* 141 There is .. no longer any difference between a peter and an echo. **1960** T. REESE *Play Bridge with Reese* iii. 20, I should imagine that West has led from four hearts and the diamonds may well be 3-3 since no one began an echo.

9. *Comb.*, as ***echo-detection, device, mixture, -phrase, -question, -ranging, -reflex, -word; echo-echoing, -giving*** ppl. adjs., ***-wise*** adv., **echo box** (see quot.); **echo chamber** orig. *U.S.*, a confined space where sound reverberates; also *attrib.* and *fig.*; **echo organ**, a set of pipes in an organ, enclosed in a wooden box to give a distant sound effect; **echo-plummet** [ECHO *sb.* 1 d], a radio sounder for measuring height above ground level or the depth of water in the sea; **echo room** = *echo chamber*; †**echo-sound**, a certain artifice in verse (see quot.).

1950 *Gloss. Terms Radar* (*B.S.I.*) 7 *Echo box*, a cavity resonator, having small damping, energized by pulses of energy radiated from a nearby aerial or by a probe in a waveguide. **1937** *Variety Radio Directory 1937/38* 341 *Echo chamber*, a reverberant room used to add hollow effects and actual echoes. **1953** *New Yorker* 4 Apr. 6/3 There's free-wheeling music in the echo-chamber grill. **1955** *N.Y. Times* 16 Jan. VI. 26/4 New York, an echo chamber of squeezed apartment buildings, is even more in need of a honking ban than .. Paris. **1958** *Punch* 22 Jan. 152/1, I was going to write about echo-chambers, which are currently giving such pleasure to all listeners by piping the broadcast voice into an empty, thirty-foot room and piping it out again with sonorous accretions of overtones. **1947** CROWTHER & WHIDDINGTON *Science at War* iv. 156 The numerous break-downs in service almost caused the use of the echo-detection to be dropped by the Navy. **1933** *Discovery* June 174/1 Use will also be made of an 'echo' device which measures the depth of the sea by the time which the echo takes to return from the bed. **1839** BAILEY *Festus* xx. (1848) 259 Its echo-echoing walls at a whisper fall. *a* **1856** LONGF. *Sunrise Hills* 25 The echo-giving hills. **1962** A. NISBETT *Technique Sound Studio* xi. 192 When echo is wanted on only one voice, as .. in a conversation between two people, one of whom is at the bottom of a well, control over this can be exercised with the echo-mixture switch. **1855** E. J. HOPKINS *Organ* xv. 66 The Echo organ consists of a duplication of the treble portion of some of the stops found on the other manual organs, closed in a wooden box, to render their tone soft and more distant-sounding. **1884** *Encycl. Brit.* XVII. 830/1 The fifth manual, where it occurs, is the echo organ. **1938** *Oxf. Compan. Mus.* 659/1 In certain very large instruments there is a manual devoted to delicate stops, with a far-away sound, and this is called the Echo Organ. **1962** Y. OLSSON in F. Behre *Contrib. Eng. Syntax* 90 The echo-phrase 'We have'. **1931** *Flight* 27 Mar. 274/2 The echo-plummet used extensively for maritime navigation seems to encounter certain difficulties in aeroplanes. **1933** *Discovery* Oct. 307/1 The well known acoustic echo plummet which is employed in measuring ocean depths. **1956** *Kenyon Rev.* XVIII. 433 Rising juncture .. signals an 'echo question'. **1961** *New Scientist* 11 May 304 To point the beam out from the side of the ship (echo-ranging) and tilt it down a few degrees below the horizontal. **1957** D. L. BOLINGER in *Publ. Amer. Dial. Soc.* xxviii. 26 The difference between yes-no echo-reflex and how-why echo-reflex. **1933** 'R. STRANGER' *Dict. Wireless Terms* 59 *Echo Room*, a term used in broadcasting to indicate the place where echoes are produced artificially in order to give a more life-like effect to broadcasting. **1589** PUTTENHAM *Eng. Poesie* (Arb.) 210 Ye make one worde both beginne and end your verse, which therefore I call the slow retourne, otherwise the Eccho sound. *a* **1626** BP. ANDREWES *Serm.* xix. (1661) 385 If it come .. from Him to us first, and from us then to you (echo-wise). **1922** O. JESPERSEN *Lang.* xvi. 313 Fr. *pisser*—an echo-word if ever there was one. **1938** *Michigan Daily* 14 July 1/1 In general, an 'echo-word', Dr. Emeneau elucidated, is formed by the reduplication of a part of the word after an inserted pattern syllable that has no meaning of its own.

Hence **'echoism**, the formation of words imitative of natural sounds; **echoist**, one who repeats like an echo; **'echoize** *v.*, †to repeat as does an echo (*obs.*); to form words imitative of sounds.

1600 TOURNEUR *Transf. Met.* Prol. Wks. 1878 II. 187 The ecchoized sounds of horrorie. **1880** J. A. H. MURRAY *Addr. Philol. Soc.* 20 Onomatopœia .. I prefer to call echoism. *Ibid. note*, Echoism suggests the echoing of a sound heard, and has the useful derivatives echoist, echoize, and echoic.

echo ('ɛkəʊ), *v.* [f. the sb.]

1. a. *intr.* Of places: To resound with an echo. Also *fig.*

1596 SHAKS. *Tam. Shr.* III. ii. 181 Kist her lips with such a clamorous smacke That .. all the Church did eccho. **1684** BUNYAN *Pilgr.* 105 And at every Roar it gave, it made all the Valley Eccho. **1747** HERVEY *Medit. & Contempl.* (1818) 163 All eternity [will] echo to their triumphant acclamations. **1870** YEATS *Nat. Hist. Comm.* 93 Larks and nightingales make the sky echo with song.

b. Of a sound: To be repeated by echoes, give rise to echoes, reverberate, resound; hence *fig.* of rumours, fame, etc.

a **1559** SACKVILLE in *Mirr. Mag.* Induct. xiii. (1563) 116 b, With dolefull shrikes, that eckoed in the skye. **1690** *Lond. Gaz.* No. 2532/2 This was followed by *Long Live King Joseph*, which quickly eccho'd all over the City. **1725** DE FOE *Voy. round W.* (1840) 253 That sound echoed and reverberated from innumerable cavities among the rocks. **1801** SOUTHEY *Thalaba* V. xxxii, Now the deaden'd roar Echoed beneath.

2. *trans.* Of places or material objects: to repeat (a sound) by echo.

1855 BAIN *Senses & Int.* II. ii. §7 (1864) 215 A sound echoed from many sides is made voluminous.

¶ Used for: To reflect (light).

1822 BEDDOES *Rom. Lily, Poems* 145 Fair as .. The last dim star, with doubtful ray .. Echoed to the eye on water.

3. *fig.* **a.** Of persons: To repeat (sounds, words) in the manner of an echo; to repeat the words of, imitate the style or sentiments of (another person); to play the echo to, flatter with servile assent. Of language, compositions, etc.: To imitate, resemble (an earlier model).

1604 SHAKS. *Oth.* III. iii. 107 *Othel.* What do'st thou thinke? *Iago* Thinke, my Lord? *Othel.* Thinke, my Lord? Alas, thou eccho'st me. **1649** BLITHE *Eng. Improv. Impr.* (1653) 111 All which I Eccho with thee that possibly it may be so. **1759** FRANKLIN *Ess.* Wks. 1840 III. 254 This language was never echoed at home. **1839** KEIGHTLEY *Hist. Eng.* II. 32 Posterity have echoed these censures. **1876** GREEN *Short Hist.* vi. §6 (1882) 333 In England Colet and More echoed, with greater reserve, the scorn and invective of their friends.

b. *absol.* To repeat words like an echo.

1880 MRS. FORRESTER *Roy. & Viola* I. 7 Dreams, indeed, my dear, echoes Netta lightly.

c. *intr.* To play the echo *to*.

1637 HEYWOOD *Dialogues* II. 29 Now echo vnto me, and sing, Thou myne. **1702** ROWE *Tamerl.* IV. i. 1705, I will Eccho to thee, thou Adulterer, Thou dost profane the name of King and Soldier. **1767** HUGH KELLY *Babler* II. 209 She constantly echoed to his groans.

4. a. In *Whist.*

1862 'CAVENDISH' *Whist* (1879) 268 You should not echo a call unless you have at least four trumps.

b. *absol.* Also in *Bridge* (cf. ECHO *sb.* 8), to indicate how many cards of a suit are held, or to request a specific lead.

1885 R. A. PROCTOR *How to Play Whist* 96 You cannot readily echo, as you can signal, by the discard. **1900** A. DUNN *Bridge* (ed. 3) 53 The 'trump suit echo' is played to inform a partner that the player who 'echoes' originally held four, or more, trumps. *Ibid.* 54 He should take the first opportunity of echoing in a plain suit, which will inform the leader that he has still one trump remaining. **1959** REESE & DORMER *Bridge Player's Dict.* 77 It is possible to echo by playing a three followed by a two. *Ibid.* 78 In the next example a defender echoes with four cards. *Ibid.* 236 If East had held a slightly different hand .. he would not have echoed in trump.

echoed ('ɛkəʊd), *ppl. a.* [f. ECHO *v.* + -ED.]

1. Repeated by an echo.

1596 SPENSER *F.Q.* I. xii. 4 Then gan triumphant trompets sownd on hye That sent to heven the ecchoed report. *a* **1704** T. BROWN *On Ormond's Recov.* Wks. 1730 I. 48 The clifts and hills my echo'd thoughts rehearse. **1860** TYNDALL *Glac.* I. §23. 168 The echoed voices mingled strangely with the gusts of the wind.

2. *fig.* Imitated, unoriginal.

1853 LYNCH *Self-Impr.* iii. 66 Books of vapid, echoed talk.

echoer ('ɛkəʊə(r)). [f. as prec. + -ER.] One who echoes or repeats.

1823 *Monthly Review* CI. 353 We shall be but .. the echoers of a mock-bird's song. **1837** *Fraser's Mag.* XV. 169 The borrower, the echoer, the copier, cannot do it.

echogram ('ɛkəʊgræm). [ECHO *sb.* 1 + -GRAM.] The record made by an echo-sounder.

1936 *Discovery* Dec. 388/1 Some of the motor skiffs were fitted out with the necessary apparatus, and directly they came in contact with a shoal of 'invisible' herring the echogram or recorded echo gave evidence of their presence. **1947** *Times* 3 Sept. 5/6 The bottom is so hilly that the record dissolves into three or more intersecting convexities, which appear simultaneously on the echogram, as if the ship were moving over numerous hills or hummocks. **1958** *New Scientist* 2 Oct. 947 Tracings of echograms of some leveed channels found off the California coast.

echograph ('ɛkəʊgrɑːf, -græf). [ECHO *sb.* 1 + -GRAPH.] A device which automatically records echograms.

1947 *Times* 3 Sept. 5/6 The ship is equipped with a powerful echograph specially constructed for us. **1950** *Ann. Reg. 1949* 428 A continuous record of the bottom profile .. registered by an ultrasonic echograph specially constructed in London. **1959** *Oceanogr. & Marine Biol.* I. 84 (*caption*) Echo-graphs and cathode ray tube records.

echoic (ɛ'kəʊɪk), *a.* [f. ECHO *sb.* + -IC.] Of the nature of an echo: a term proposed by J. A. H. Murray and used in this Dictionary to describe formations which echo the sound which they are intended to denote or symbolize.

1880 J. A. H. MURRAY *Addr. Philol. Soc.* 20 *note*, Echoism ..has the useful derivatives echoist, echoize, and echoic. **1886** *N.E.D.* s.v. *Botch* v.¹, App. related to Du. *botsen* to knock, dash, Ger. dial. *butschen, butzen* to strike, knock; according to Franck an onomatopœic word of echoic origin. **1950** PARTRIDGE *Here, There & Everywhere* 182 *Grurmstipth*, an omnibus: obviously an echoic term.

echoing ('ɛkəʊɪŋ), *vbl. sb.* [f. ECHO *v.* + -ING¹.] The action of the vb. ECHO, *lit.* and *fig. Poet.* occas. in pl.

1638 DRUMM. OF HAWTH. *Irene* Wks. (1711) 164 The alarms of trumpets and drums are not heard .. save by the ecchoing of the perplexed continent. **1810** SCOTT *Lady of L.* I. Introd., Some feeble echoing of thine earlier lay. **1850** MRS. BROWNING *Poems* II. 263 All echoings from out the hills.

echoing ('ɛkəʊɪŋ), *ppl. a.* [f. as prec. + -ING².]

1. Of places or material objects: That reverberates sounds; characterized by or resounding with echoes.

1667 MILTON *P.L.* IX. 1107 A Pillard shade High over-arch'd and echoing walks between. **1683** BOYLE *Effects of*

Mot. v. 65 The better sort of our Echoing places. **1829** SOUTHEY *All for Love* VII. xxxiii, The echoing ground repeated the sound. **1842** LONGF. *Slave in Dism. Swamp* v, Wild birds filled the echoing air with songs.

2. Of sounds or sound-producing agencies: That causes echoes. *lit.* and *fig.*

1702 ROWE *Ambit. Step-Moth.* IV. iii. 1958 This way the Ecchoing Accents seem to come. **1725** POPE *Odyss.* XIX. 603 My echoing griefs the starry vault invade. **1817** J. SCOTT *Paris Revisit.* 111 The echoing Bugle sounded through the streets of Brussels. **1856** EMERSON *Eng. Traits* xiv. Wks. (Bohn) II. 108 His countrymen forsook..Parnassus, on which they had once walked with echoing steps.

3. That gives or constitutes an expected response.

a **1764** LLOYD *Actor* Wks. 1774 I. 13 Equipoised he stands Till praise dismiss him with her echoing hands. **1862** 'CAVENDISH' *Whist* (1879) 268 Here your partner cannot tell whether your card is an original or an echoing one.

Hence **'echoingly** *adv.*

1854 *Chamb. Jrnl.* I. 395 The first chords..wandered echoingly round the church.

echolalia (ɛkəʊ'leɪlɪə). [mod.L., f. Gr. ἠχώ ECHO + λαλιά talk.] **1. a.** *Path.* The meaningless repetition of words and phrases. **b.** *Educational Psychol.* The repetition of words and phrases by a child that is learning to speak.

1885 *Buck's Handbk. Med. Sci.* I. 290/1 Periphrastic forms of speech and the recurring or barrel-organ utterances, constituting what is known as *echolalia.* **1890** W. JAMES *Princ. Psychol.* II. xxiv. 407 His condition is that of 'Echolalia',—instead of answering the question, he simply reiterates it. **1924** R. M. OGDEN tr. *Koffka's Growth of Mind* v. 311 At the time when speech is being learned, there begins a period of echolalia in which the child repeats with tireless continuation all the words or sentences it hears. **1924** [see ECHOPRAXIA]. **1930** *Times Lit. Suppl.* 27 Mar. 264/2 *Echolalia* or imitation of definite phonetic patterns. **1943** *Mind* LII. 317 The uttering of a tautology may be a natural sign-function which..truly mediates in a particular context many useful inferences, such as, that the person is an unconscious metaphysician, is subject to echolalia, [etc.]. **1948** [see ECHOPRAXIA]. **1955** T. MORROW in G. Caplan *Emotional Probl. Early Childhood* III. 343 He displayed, and displays, classical echolalia and delayed echolalia. **1964** B. RIMLAND *Infantile Autism* (1965) III. 180 There are numerous instances of affirmation by repetition and echolalia in the literature on autism.

2. A depreciatory term for a succession of sounds in poetry which subordinates sense to sound.

1895 *Westm. Gaz.* 3 Dec. 2/1 Our suspect poets, with.. their liking for echolalia. **1897** R. VALLANCE *William Morris* iii. 31 The 'Eve of Crecy' contains two magnificent examples of that mode of poetic expression, dubbed 'echolalia' by Max Nordau, and as such condemned by him.

Hence **echo'laliac, echo'lalian, echo'lalic** *adjs.*

1927 C. GRAY in H. J. Foss *Heritage of Music* 181 Von Bülow..was at least constant in his echolalian obsessions. **1931** E. WILSON *Axel's Castle* vii. 252 Most of us balk at her soporific rigmaroles, her echolaliac incantations. **1938** J. EISENSON *Psychol. Speech* iii. 47 When the infant reaches the echolalic and voluntary utterance levels, he has reached a developmental stage where rather finely differentiated muscular responses can be made. **1959** S. SITWELL *Bridge of Brocade Sash* viii. 170 The priest..who with echolalic persistence reiterated the same name over and over again.

echoless ('ɛkəʊlɪs), *a.* [f. ECHO + -LESS.] That has no echo; chiefly *poet.* or *rhet.* in the sense 'silent, noiseless'.

1728 *Monthly Review* XXVI. 503 An aerial telegraph..by means of which the voyagers [in balloons] can talk with each other in the echoless space. **1816** BYRON *Prometh.* 14 The suffocating sense of woe, Which speaks but in its loneliness ..nor will sigh Until its voice is echoless. **1825** *Blackw. Mag.* XVIII. 440 No unfit haunting place for things of echoless footstep. **1868** A. J. MENKEN *Infelicia* 3 That far off, echoless promise.

b. *fig.* That gives no echo; unresponsive.

1868 BROWNING *Ring & Bk.* x. 553 Father and mother stunned, and echoless To the blow.

,echolo'cation. [f. ECHO *sb.* 1 + LOCATION *sb.* 7.] The location of objects by means of the echo reflected from them by a sound-signal, as of ultrasonic sounds emitted by bats or by man-made devices. Hence **'echolocate** *v.*, **,echolo'cating** *vbl. sb.* and *ppl. a.*

1944 D. R. GRIFFIN in *Science* C. 589 (*title*) Echolocation by Blind Men, Bats and Radar. *Ibid.*, To describe this process of locating obstacles by means of echoes, I suggest the word *echolocation. Ibid.* 590/1 A radio signal is sent out from the airplane and electronic devices measure the time required for this signal to be reflected back... Finally we have radar, a refinement of the radio altimeter so beautifully perfected that it can echolocate airplanes at great distances by sending out radio waves and picking up the reflected energy returning from the distant aircraft. **1957** *New Biol.* XXIII. 43 Another theory about moth behaviour, in which sound acts as an aid to navigation, suggests that they use a system of echo-location analogous with that of bats. **1958** *Observer* 3 Aug. 5/5 The Harvard scientists estimate that the bat's echo-location system is incomparably more efficient for its size, weight and power, than the most modern radar system. **1959** *Observer* 14 June 5/4 Asdic, another wartime device used for echolocating underwater objects by ultrasonic vibrations, has given us more knowledge about whales. **1964** *Oceanogr. & Marine Biol.* II. 438 The conversational squeals and echolocating clicks of porpoises.

e'chometer. Also 8 echometre. [f. Gr. ἦχο-ς sound + μέτρον measure; in Fr. *échomètre* (Littré).] (See quot. 1875.) Also, a type of echo-sounder.

1736 BAILEY, *Echometre.* **1875** BRANDE *Dict. Science* 749 In Music, a sort of scale or rule, marked with lines which serve to measure the duration of sounds, and to ascertain their intervals and ratios. **1881** in WORCESTER. **1937** *Nature* 18 Sept. 499/1 An 'echometer' depth sounder. *Ibid.* 25 Sept. 553/2 Another exhibit..shows how one type of echometer can indicate to a trawler the depth of the sea-bed and also that at which a shoal of fish may be passing. **1961** *Times* 2 June 14/7 Dry-paper recording echometer.

† e'chometry. ? *Obs.* [mod. f. Gr. ἠχώ ECHO, or ἦχος sound + -μετρία measuring. Littré has Fr. *échométrie* 'art de calculer, de combiner la réflexion des sons', = sense 1 below.]

1. 'The art of making vaults or arches so as to produce an artificial echo.'

1818 in TODD.

2. The art of measuring the duration of sound.

1847 in CRAIG.

echopraxia (ɛkəʊ'præksɪə). *Path.* Also echopraxis. [mod.L., fr. Gr. ἠχώ ECHO + πρᾶξις action.] The meaningless repetition or imitation of the movements of others. Hence **echo'practic** *a.*

1904 T. JOHNSTONE tr. *Kraebelin's Lect. Clin. Psychiatry* iii. 25 All his movements showed a certain constraint and want of freedom. His limbs remained for some time in the position in which you placed them. If you raised your arms quickly in front of him, he imitated the movement, and he also clapped his hands when it was done before him. These phenomena, called respectively *flexibilitas cerea*, 'waxen flexibility', or catalepsy and *echopraxis*, are familiar to us from experiments in hypnotism. **1905** A. J. ROSANOFF tr. *Rogues de Fursac's Man. Psychiatry* I. iv. 92 Some [patients] repeat exactly the words (*echolalia*) or the gestures (*echopraxia*) of the persons around them. **1924** A. A. BRILL tr. *Bleuler's Textbk. Psychiatry* ii. 152 The impulse for such an action can also be given by means of example alone, as in *echopraxia* and *echolalia. Ibid.* 153 The echopractic patients imitate whatever strikes them in the actions or words of their surroundings... It is partly a question of hysteria-like mechanism..and partly a matter of an incapacity to get away from a conceived idea, so that instead of giving an answer the question is repeated, or instead of a new action the preceding act is imitated (organic echolalias and echopraxias). **1948** *Brit. Jrnl. Psychol.* Dec. 89 Mutism.. echolalia, echopraxia, negativism..were the most common symptoms of this group [of schizophrenics].

'echo-sounding, *vbl. sb.* [f. ECHO *sb.* + SOUNDING *vbl. sb.*[2]] The action or process of sounding or ascertaining the depth of water or of an object below a ship by meauring the time taken for a transmitted sound-signal to return as an echo. Also in extended uses, e.g. of the flight of bats. Also *attrib.* or as *adj.* Hence **echo-sounder**, a device used for this purpose; (as back-formations) **echo-sound** *v.* and *sb.*

1923 *Hydrographic Rev.* I. 72 (*title*) Echo Sounding. Test carried out by the U.S.S. 'Stewart' 20th to 29th June 1922. **1927** S. H. LONG *Navigational Wireless* xi. 148 Admiralty Type Echo Sounder. A second type of echo depth sounder ..developed by the Admiralty Research Department. **1928** *Marine Observer* June 115/2 This vessel is fitted with the Admiralty Echo Sounding machine.., a wonderful aid to navigation, as one is able to get soundings up to 135 fathoms with accuracy. **1933** *Jrnl. R. Aeronaut. Soc.* XXXVII. 343 A very efficient 'height over the ground' indicator is installed in the 'Graf Zeppelin'. This is the 'Behm' echo sounding device. **1935** *Nature* 1 June 898/1 For navigation the echo sounder was employed originally to delineate the 100 fathom line. **1936** *Discovery* Dec. 388/1 The electrical echo-sounder is to be used for the detection of shoals of fish. **1947** *Times* 3 Sept. 5/6 Thanks to echo-sounding, one of the most marvellous inventions of our days, belief in the perfect smoothness of the deep-sea bottom has been much revised, especially in regard to the Atlantic. **1953** J. Y. COUSTEAU *Silent World* vi. 63 We were passing the same area in the research ship *Élie Monnier* when the echo-sound tape recorded another massive object on the floor. *Ibid.* x. 97 Our echo sounder located the wreck of a French submarine. **1958** *Observer* 3 Aug. 5/4 Scientists at Harvard University have been studying the 'echo-sounding' behaviour of bats. **1959** A. HARDY *Fish & Fisheries* iii. 51 His having previously echo-sounded herring shoals in the same area. **1968** *Times* 18 Oct. 16/7 By a combination of echo-sounding from the air and rapid sampling it was found possible to determine in only 20 minutes the main features of any lake.

ECHO virus ('ɛkəʊ ,vaɪərəs). *Path.* Also echovirus. [f. the initials of *e*nteric *c*ytopathogenic *h*uman *o*rphan: 'orphan' because when first discovered there was no disease of which they were known to be the cause.] Any of a group of enteroviruses infection with which is usually asymptomatic but which may produce symptoms resembling those of the common cold, mild meningitis, or (rarely) poliomyelitis. So ***ECHO group***, etc.

1955 *Science* 16 Dec. 1188/1 These viruses—some of which have been referred to in previous literature as 'orphan viruses' and others as 'human enteric viruses'—are now classified as the 'enteric cytopathogenic human orphan (ECHO) group'. *Ibid.* 1188/2 Kidney cells of different monkey species vary in their susceptibility to the ECHO viruses. **1957** [see *enterovirus*]. **1961** M. HYNES *Med. Bacteriol.* (ed. 7) xxv. 378 Three groups of viruses—polioviruses, Coxsackie viruses and ECHO viruses—are primarily invaders of the human intestinal tract. All are small, 25–35 mμ in diameter, and survive well outside the body. *Ibid.* 384 ECHO viruses can often be isolated from the fæces or nasopharynx of healthy individuals, but they can probably cause aseptic meningitis, acute diarrhœa in children, and mild respiratory infections. **1965** *Times* 3 Sept. 14/5 The echoviruses, of which over 30 types are known,..are closely related to the poliovirus, and produce a form of meningitis, but they have also been isolated from children with an upper respiratory infection resembling the common cold.

echoy ('ɛkəʊɪ), *a. rare.* [f. ECHO *sb.* + -Y.] Of the nature of an echo. Also, liable to resound with an echo.

1841 *Blackw. Mag.* I. 587 The very beams and rafters.. throwing off their ἔπεα πτερόεντα in echoy sounds. **1906** J. JOYCE *Let.* 7 Aug. (1966) II. 147 When he goes into an 'echoy' place he shouts: in the Colisseum [*sic*] and in S. Peter's. **1967** *Listener* 18 May 652/3 There are three tiers of galleries..it's very echoey.

‖**echt** (ɛçt), *a.* [G., real, true, genuine.] Authentic, genuine, typical. Also as *adv.*

1916 G. B. SHAW in *New Age* 25 May, Many Englishmen who know Germany, and whose social opinions are *echt* Junker opinions, hail this war as a means of forcing England to adopt the Prussian system. **1917** E. POUND 19 Dec. in *Lett. J. Joyce* (1966) II. 414 The opening is echt Joice [*sic*]. **1934** C. LAMBERT *Music Ho!* iii. 173 England has never produced an artist so 'echt-English' as Mussorgsky is 'echt-Russian', or Renoir 'echt-French'. **1950** D. GASCOYNE *Vagrant* 56 His endlessly varied *echt*-lyrical lute-ditties. **1956** *Essays & Studies* IX. 14 Those passages in his letters which are *echt*-Coleridge do not belong at all to letter-writing. **1962** N. FREELING *Love in Amsterdam* II. 70 'Are you married?' he asked.., 'I see your ring, but is that camouflage or *echt*?'

ecize ('iːsaɪz), *v. intr. Ecology.* [f. Gr. οἰκίζειν to colonize; cf. ECESIS.] Of plants: to become established in a new habitat; to COLONIZE (sense 3).

1916 F. E. CLEMENTS *Plant Succession* iv. 69 Ecesis..has proved so definite and convenient in use that it seems desirable to employ a corresponding verb, *ecize*, from οἰκίζω, to make a home, colonize. *Ibid.* 71 The plants which can ecize in such extremes are necessarily restricted in number and specialized in character. **1938** WEAVER & CLEMENTS *Plant Ecology* (ed. 2) iii. 72 A habitat in which the seeds.. may germinate and the seedlings successfully ecize (i.e. make a home).

ecka, var. EKKA.

ecko, obs. form of ECHO.

éclair (eɪ'klɛə(r)). [Fr., lit. lightning.] A small finger-shaped cake made of choux-pastry, and filled with any of various kinds of cream.

1861 *Vanity Fair* 2 Feb. 50/1 A waiter, whereon stood.. a plate of macaroons, éclairs and sponge cake. **1870** *London Society* XVIII. 506/2 You get..meringue à la crême, eclairs. **1889** R. WELLS *Pastrycook & Confect. Guide* 103 Eclairs.. after baking fill with cream. **1902** *Daily Chron.* 15 Feb. 8/4 Chocolate éclairs are not difficult to make at home. **1925** A. HUXLEY *Those Barren Leaves* IV. iii. 291 At one of the little tea-tables..Miss Elver..was eating chocolate éclairs and meringues, messily, with an expression of rapture on her cream-smeared face. **1927** C. MACKENZIE *Vestal Fire* I. iii, You knew that the éclairs of the Villa Amabile would effuse authentic cream and not discharge stale custard like those dreadful waistless middle-aged éclairs you had met in some houses. **1956** *C. Spry Cookery Bk.* xxix. 866 Pipe out in finger or éclair shapes on to lightly greased baking-sheets. **1969** H. MACINNES *Salzburg Connection* xi. 154 Have a chocolate éclair.

eclaircise, *v. rare.* [Back-formation from ÉCLAIRCISSEMENT; as if ad. Fr. *éclairciss-*, *éclaircir.*] *trans.* To clear up.

1754 NEWTON *Proph.* (1832) 668 Till time shall accomplish and eclaircise all the particulars. **1872** *Chr. World Pulpit* I. 309/1 Till the enigma is solved; till the mystery is eclaircised. **1884** *Ibid.* XXV. 238/3 If men.. listen to preaching that stimulates them, eclaircises their imagination.

‖**éclaircissement.** Forms: 7–8 ec(c)lercisment, -clarcis(e)ment. [F. *éclaircissement* (eklɛrsismɑ̃) clearing up, f. *éclairciss-*, *éclaircir* to clear up. Very common in 18th c.]

1. A clearing up or revelation of what is obscure or unknown; an explanation.

1673 DRYDEN *Marr. à la Mode* v. i, This éclaircissement, which is made this day of your quality. **1716** POPE *Let.* in *Lady M. W. Montague's Lett.* xxxiii. I. 117 You could give me great eclaircissements upon many passages in Homer. **1751** SMOLLETT *Per. Pic.* (1779) III. lxxxiii. 294 Their mutual astonishment was unspeakable at the eclaircissement. **1792** PITT in *Academy* No. 616. 132/2 His readiness to give me any *eclaircissement.* **1848** THACKERAY *Van. Fair* xv, When the éclaircissement comes there will be a scene.

2. A mutual explanation of equivocal conduct; *esp.* in phrase, ***to come to an éclaircissement.***

a **1674** CLARENDON *Hist. Reb.* XII. III. 243 Till the first interview and eclarcisements were passed between the King & Queen. **1676** ETHEREDGE *Man of Mode* III. iii, To get me to meet Loveit here in order to an ecclaircissement. **1741** RICHARDSON *Pamela* (1824) I. lxxiii. 419 As soon as you are prepared to speak all that is upon your mind..then we may come to an eclaircissement. **1815** SCOTT *Guy M.* xx, Such.. restraints as might prevent any engagement or eclaircissement taking place.

eclampsia, eclampsy (ɛ'klæmpsɪə, -sɪ). *Pathol.* [a. and ad. mod.L. *eclampsia*, as if a. Gr. *ἐκλαμψία, regularly f. ἐκλάμπειν to shine forth. Cf. Fr. *éclampsie.*] 'Epileptiform convulsions

dependent on some actual disturbance of the nervous centres caused by anatomical lesion' (*Syd. Soc. Lex.*). So also **e'clamptic** *a.*, affected with, or characteristic of eclampsia; (the less correct form *eclampsic* has been also used).

1866 A. FLINT *Princ. Med.* (1880) 823 Epileptiform convulsions, or eclampsia..are to be discriminated by means of the..symptoms. **1857** BULLOCK tr. *Cazeaux' Midwif.* 295 Eclamptic patients. **1886** *Syd. Soc. Lex.*, *Idiocy*, eclampsic..One of Ireland's divisions, including those cases that have followed infantile convulsions.

‖**éclat** (ekla). [Fr. *éclat*, OF. *esclat*, related to *éclater*, OF. *esclater* to burst, burst out. The senses occuring in Eng. use are taken (with more or less accuracy) directly from Fr. In 18th c. and first half of the 19th c. the word was in much more frequent use than it has been subsequently. (Sometimes ignorantly written *éclât*.)

The OF. *esclater* = Pr., Cat. *esclatar* is usually believed to be ad. WGer. **slait-an*, causative of **slītan*; see SLIT. The Teutonic *sl-* became in Romanic *scl-*, to which the usual euphonic *e-* before initial *s* + cons. was afterwards prefixed. The Fr. sb. has also the sense of 'splinter', and its early form, or a synonymous fem. (*e*)*sclate*, is the source of Eng. SLATE.]

†**1.** Brilliancy, radiance, dazzling effect (in lit. sense or with conscious metaphor). *Obs.*

1676 ETHEREDGE *Man of Mode* III. ii (1684) 36 The Eclat of so much beauty..ought To have charm'd me sooner. **1749** UDAL RHYS *Tour Spain & Port.* (1760) 5 There was the greatest Eclat of Beauty and Finery imaginable. **1784** J. BARRY *Lect. Art* v. (1848) 180 The sun is so concealed by clouds as to give no particular eclat to that part of the hemisphere. **1835** KIRBY *Hab. & Inst. Anim.* I. v. 183 They [the polypes] strike the beholder by the eclat of petal-like animals with which their branches are covered.

†**2.** Public display, ostentation; notoriety, publicity; *concr.* a public exposure, scandal, 'scene'. ***to make an éclat***: to 'make a noise in the world', create a sensation.

a **1674** CLARENDON *Hist. Reb.* III. XII. 223 He was then a man of eclat, had many servants. **1753** HANWAY *Trav.* (1762) II. II. i. 68 A disposition inclined to the submissive, is not that which makes the greatest eclat. **1795** T. JEFFERSON *Writ.* (1859) IV. 114 Not to commit the honor..of your college, by an useless act of eclat. **1823** BYRON *Juan* XIV. lx, With the kind view of saving an éclat.

3. 'Lustre' of reputation; social distinction; celebrity, renown. In 19th c. often in disparaging sense: 'false glitter', showy brilliancy.

1742 MIDDLETON *Cicero* II. vi. 70 Cæsar..by the eclat of his victories, seemed to rival the fame of Pompey. **1807** G. GREGORY *Dict. Arts & Sc.* I. 330/1 He..gave chemistry an eclat which it did not before possess. **1823** BYRON *Age of Bronze* xvi, Montmorenci..Turns a diplomatist of great éclat. **1847** MRS. SHERWOOD *Lady of Manor* II. x. 44 The glitter and eclat of foreign levity.

b. Conspicuous success; universal applause, acclamation. Chiefly in phr. ***with*** (***great***) ***éclat***.

1741 WARBURTON *Div. Legat.* II. 37 *note*, Professed with the greatest eclat. **1787** 'G. GAMBADO' *Acad. Horsem.* 41 Thus..you go off with eclat. **1798** T. JEFFERSON *Writ.* (1859) IV. 250 Marshall was received here with the utmost eclat. **1810** BYRON *To H. Drury* 3 May, We get on with great éclat.

‖**eclat**, *v. rare.* [f. prec.] **a.** *intr.* To burst forth, become known. **b.** *trans.* To make notorious, bring into publicity.

1736 HERVEY *Mem.* I. 11 The superior enmity they bore to men in power hindered that which they felt to one another from eclating. **1835** W. H. MAXWELL *Capt. Blake* I. xv, A love affair which his blundering management had *eclated*. *Ibid.* III. i, Your being *eclated* in the newspapers.

eclect (ɛ'klɛkt), *a. rare.* [ad. Gr. ἐκλεκτός, f. ἐκλέγ-ειν to select.] Chosen, select.

1839 BAILEY *Festus* xix. (1848) 205 Exists This class eclect in all things. **1855** —— *Mystic* 66 A band eclect.

eclectic (ɛ'klɛktɪk), *a.* and *sb.* [ad. Gr. ἐκλεκτικός selective, f. ἐκλέγ-ειν to select.] **A.** *adj.*

1. In ancient use, the distinguishing epithet of a class of philosophers who neither attached themselves to any recognized school, nor constructed independent systems, but 'selected such doctrines as pleased them in every school' (Liddell and Scott); Diogenes Laertius speaks of an 'eclectic sect' founded by Potamon of Alexandria in the second century after Christ. In mod. times this designation has been for similar reasons given to or assumed by various philosophers, notably V. Cousin; and it is also applied to those who combine elements derived from diverse systems of opinion or practice in any science or art. So also ***eclectic method***, ***system***, etc.

1683 DRYDEN *Life Plutarch* 37 The Eclectick sect, which was begun by Potamon. **1702** tr. *Le Clerc's Prim. Fathers* 11 Clemens..followed that manner of Philosophising which was then call'd Eclectick. **1796** *Monthly Mag.* II. 466 To endeavour at preparing..some eclectic system of belief. **1828** KIRBY & SP. *Entomol.* xlviii. IV. 465 Era of Latreille, or of the Eclectic System. **1859** GULLICK & TIMBS *Paint.* 181 The Eclectic, or..the Academic style was developed..by..the Caracci school. **1878** MORLEY *J. De Maistre* Crit. Misc. 101/1 There were three chief schools of thought, the Sensational, the Catholic, and the Eclectic.

2. More vaguely: That borrows or is borrowed from diverse sources. Also, of persons or personal attributes: Unfettered by narrow system in matters of opinion or practice; broad, not exclusive, in matters of taste.

1847 DISRAELI *Tancred* II. xiv. (1871) 141 With..an eclectic turn of mind, Mr. Vavasour saw something good in everybody. **1865** LECKY *Ration.* (1878) I. 301 The higher virtue, which binds men..to endeavour to pursue an eclectic course. **1876** FREEMAN *Norm. Conq.* V. xxiii. 208 The strangely eclectic character of Scottish royal nomenclature. **1876** M. DAVIES *Unorth. Lond.* 8 The hymn-book in use is a tremendously eclectic one. **1879** CHURCH *Spenser* 45 When allowance is made for an eclectic..phraseology..the Shepherd's Calendar is..of great interest.

3. In etymological nonce-uses. **a.** Made up of 'selections'. **b.** That selects, does not receive indiscriminately.

1814 *Monthly Rev.* LXXIII. 462 The..volumes are wholly eclectic; they contain no original matter. **1876** GLADSTONE *Homeric Synchr.* 67 His mind was in the best sense eclectic, and he had a strong..repugnance to the debased.

B. *sb.* **a.** An adherent of the Eclectic school of philosophy. **b.** One who follows the eclectic method; one who finds points of agreement with diverse parties or schools.

1817 COLERIDGE *Biog. Lit.* I. xii. 281 By certain..Eclectics, who..choose whatever is most plausible. **1856** R. VAUGHAN *Mystics* (1860) I. 56 The Alexandrians were eclectics. **1857** W. SMITH *Thorndale* 400 He has added to his title of Utopian that of Eclectic. **1886** *Syd. Soc. Lex.*, *Eclectics*, a term applied to certain medical practitioners in America.

eclectical (ɛ'klɛktɪkəl), *a.* [f. prec. + -AL[1].] = ECLECTIC *a.*

1862 R. PATTERSON *Ess. Hist. & Art* 82 The Eclectical system [in Art]—that of choosing the best points out of a multitude of fine forms.

Hence **e'clectically** *adv.*, in an eclectic manner.

1844 *Blackw. Mag.* LV. 236 Others..voted arbitrarily or eclectically, that is, by no law generally recognised. **1856** KINGSLEY *Misc.* II. 27 They reverence..a few..facts eclectically picked out of the past.

eclecticism (ɛ'klɛktɪsɪz(ə)m). [f. ECLECTIC + -ISM.] **a.** The eclectic philosophy; the eclectic method applied to speculation or practice.

1798 WILLICH *Elem. Crit. Philos.* 1 There arose a sort of *Eclecticism*, which discouraged party-spirit, and recommended philosophical discretion. **1835** I. TAYLOR *Spir. Despot.* iv. 124 Abstracted selfishness..in its modern guise of philosophic eclecticism. **1836–7** SIR W. HAMILTON *Metaph.* (1877) I. vi. 107 Eclecticism, conciliation, union were..the grand aim of the Alexandrian school. **1838** EMERSON *Lit. Ethics* Wks. (Bohn) II. 212 The French Eclecticism, which Cousin esteems so conclusive. **1881** WESTCOTT & HORT *N.T. Grk.* II. 246 The eclecticism of the Syrian revisers.

b. *concr.* The product of an eclectic method.

1841–4 EMERSON *Ess.* Ser. I. xii. (1876) 278 What is a man but a finer..landscape than the horizon figures,—nature's eclecticism?

eclecticize (ɛ'klɛktɪsaɪz), *v.* [f. ECLECTIC + -IZE.] *trans.* To treat in an eclectic method; to make selections from.

1854 MAURICE *Mor. & Met. Philos.* (ed. 2) 135 Proclus, who was to eclecticise and harmonise all mythologies.

eclectism (ɛ'klɛktɪz(ə)m). [ad. Fr. *eclectisme.*] = ECLECTICISM. So also **e'clectist**.

1867 *Contemp. Rev.* VI. 379 After these come Domenichino and the Caracci, eclectism and polish. **1882** *Blackw. Mag.* May 645 An eclectist like the Caracci in painting.

†**e'clegme.** *Med. Obs.* Also 7 eclegm, eclegmat. [a. (directly or through Fr. *eclègme*) med.L. *eclegma* (gen. *eclegmat-is*) for *ecligma*, a. Gr. ἔκλειγμα, f. ἐκλείχειν to lick out.]

'Old term for a linctus, or form of medicine of a semifluid consistence, which is licked off the spoon' (*Syd. Soc. Lex.*).

1605 DANIEL *Queene's Arcadia* III. i. (1623) Eclegmats Embrochs, Lixiues, Cataplasmes. **1621** BURTON *Anat. Mel.* II. iv. I. v. (1676) 233/2 Confections, Treacle, Mithridate, Eclegmes or Linctures. **1710** T. FULLER *Pharm. Extemp.* 271 No Eclegme..can be sent directly..into the Lungs.

eclipsable (ɪ'klɪpsəb(ə)l), *a.* [f. ECLIPSE *v.* + -ABLE.] Capable of being eclipsed.

1845 J. O'DONOVAN *Irish Gram.* 63 After the interrogative particle 'an'..all verbs beginning with eclipsable consonants are eclipsed.

†**eclip'sareon.** *Obs.* [f. ECLIPSE.] (See quot.)

1794 G. ADAMS *Nat. & Exp. Philos.* IV. 179 A globe to show the phenomena of solar and lunar eclipses on all places of the terrestrial globe, called an eclipsareon. **1867–77** G. CHAMBERS *Astron.* Voc. 915 *Eclipsareon*, an astronomical toy invented by Ferguson.

†**eclip'sation.** [f. ECLIPSE *v.* + -ATION; in med.L. *eclipsatio* (Du Cange).] The action of eclipsing or state of being eclipsed. Also *fig.*

1471 RIPLEY *Comp. Alch.* in Ashm. (1652) 187 Obscuratyon..callyd Eclypsation. **1575** G. HARVEY *Letter-bk.* (1884) 93 That..owtelandish word, Eclipsation of my absence. **1584** *Almanack*, She [the moon] wyll..continue in her totall Eclipsation one houre and .xx. minutes.

eclipse (ɪ'klɪps), *sb.* Forms: 4 esclepis, (enclips), 4–7 eclips, 5–6 eclypse, (5 ecleps, -ypce, 6 eclip(s)is, 7 eeclipse), 4– eclipse. [a. OF. *eclipse*, *esclipse*, ad. L. *eclīpsis*, Gr. ἔκλειψις, noun of action f. ἐκλείπειν to be eclipsed, literally to forsake its accustomed place, fail to appear.]

1. a. *Astron.* An interception or obscuration of the light of the sun, moon, or other luminous body, by the intervention of some other body, either between it and the eye, or between the luminous body and that illuminated by it; as of the moon, by passing through the earth's shadow; of the sun, by the moon coming between it and the observer; or of a satellite, by entering the shadow of its primary. Also in phrase, ***in eclipse***. For ***annular***, ***partial***, ***total eclipse***, see those adjs. Cf. OCCULTATION.

a **1300** *Cursor M.* 16814 Oft siths haue we sene..esclepis [*v.r.* clipes, clyppes, clippis] of sun and mone. *c* **1374** CHAUCER *Boeth.* (1868) 133 Whan þe moone is in the eclips. **1393** LANGL. *P. Pl.* C. XXI. 140 þis eclipse . þat ouer-closeþ now þe sonne. **1494** FABYAN VII. ccxlvi. 289 In yᵉ yere of our Lord .xii.c.xxii...apered a great eclypce of the sone. **1549** *Compl. Scot.* vi. (1872) 55 In the tyme of the eclipis, the eird is betuix the mune and the soune. **1605** SHAKS. *Lear* I. ii. 112 These late Eclipses in the Sun and Moone portend no good to vs. **1637** MILTON *Lycidas* 100 That fatal..bark Built in the eclipse. **1750** HARRIS *Hermes* (1841) 119 Often had mankind seen the sun in eclipse. **1868** LOCKYER *Heavens* 258 An eclipse of Titan. **1871** PALGRAVE *Lyr. Poems* 33 The Sun cloak'd himself in wan eclipse.

b. *transf.* Absence, cessation, or deprivation of light, temporary or permanent; *techn.* the periodical obscuration of the light from a light-house.

1526 *Pilgr. Perf.* (W. de W. 1531) 305 A vniuersall derknes & eclipse was ouer all the worlde. **1563** *Mirr. Mag.*, *Buckhm.* xciii, With fowle eclypse had reft my syght away. **1671** MILTON *Samson* 80 Blind among enemies..Irrecoverably dark, total eclipse. **1784** COWPER *Task* III. 736 The eclipse That metropolitan volcanoes make. **1830** TENNYSON *Burial of Love*, His eyes in eclipse. **1858** *Merc. Mar. Mag.* V. 186 A Fixed Red Light, varied by *flashes* preceded and followed by short *eclipses*.

2. *fig.* **a.** Obscuration, obscurity; dimness; loss of brilliance or splendour.

1598 BARCKLEY *Felic. Man* (1631) 645 This..eclipse of Christian manners, doth presage the destruction of the world to be at hand. **1642** FULLER *Holy & Prof. St.* II. xxi. 140 God oftentimes leaves the brightest men in an eclipse. **1650** *Bounds Publ. Obed.* (ed. 2) 18 How knowes he..that the..Power is..in an Ecclipse? *a* **1711** KEN *Serm.* Wks. (1838) 114 Goodness has an inseparable splendour, which can never suffer a total eclipse. **1878** BROWNING *La Saisiaz* 31 When I..declare the soul's eclipse Not the soul's extinction.

b. (See quot. 1838.) Hence ***eclipse-dress***, ***-feathers***, ***-plumage***.

1838 C. WATERTON *Ess. Nat. Hist.* 202 At the close of the breeding season, the drake undergoes a very remarkable change of plumage..and..is..so completely clothed in the raiment of the female, that it requires a keen..eye to distinguish the one from the other... Thus we may say that once every year..the drake goes, as it were, into an eclipse. **1906** C. W. BEEBE *Bird* 48 The invisible cloak of his brooding mate is dropped over him for a while—his colours vanish, and by a partial moult..the hues of his plumage change to an inconspicuous mottling of brown, hardly distinguishable from the female... This has been happily termed the 'eclipse' plumage. **1913** *Brit. Birds* VII. 2 The short eclipse-feathers..differ so little in general tint from the feathers of the winter- and breeding-plumage..that it is difficult to see what advantage the bird derives from the change. *Ibid.* 74 The second eclipse is for the most part similar in colouring to the first eclipse,..but these second eclipse Eiders can always be distinguished..from the first eclipse..birds. **1914** *Bull. Brit. Ornith. Club* XXXIII. 67 The pigment for the coloration of the eclipse-dress was beginning to form. **1930** KIRKMAN & JOURDAIN *Brit. Birds* 159 Gadwall..In eclipse much like duck. **1958** BANNERMAN *Birds Brit. Isles* VII. 1 The male [*sc.* mallard] in eclipse resembles the female closely. *Ibid.* 31 The adult drake [of the teal] begins to assume eclipse plumage in June..by August the eclipse is complete.

†**3.** A fraudulent device in dice-playing; (see quot.). *Obs.*

1711 J. PUCKLE *Club* (1817) 19 Gamesters have the Top, the Peep, Eclipse [*note*, securing with the little Finger, a Die on the outside of the Box], Thumbing, etc.

eclipse (ɪ'klɪps), *v.* Forms: see prec. 5 *pa. pple.* eclippid. [f. prec. Cf. Fr. *éclipser*, late L. *eclipsare.*]

†**1.** *intr.* To suffer eclipse; to be eclipsed. *Obs.*

1393 GOWER *Conf.* II. 153 The sonne and mone eclipsen both. *a* **1593** T. WATSON *Poems* (Arb.) 206 Thou neuer doest eclips..thy glorie still doth waxe. **1667** MILTON *P.L.* II. 666 The night-hag..comes..to dance With Lapland witches while the labouring moon Eclipses at their charms.

†**b.** *fig. Obs.*

c **1430** LYDG. *Bochas* I. ii. 5 a, God..can..maken princes eclipsen in theyr glory. **1590** GREENE *Poems* (1861) 296 Starry eyes, whereat my sight Did eclipse with much delight.

2. *trans.* Of one of the heavenly bodies: To cause an obscuration of some other heavenly body, by passing between it and the spectator, or between it and the source from which it derives its light.

c **1485** *Digby Myst.* (1882) iv. 356 The son had lost his sight; Eclippid was hee. **1596** DRAYTON *Legends* I. 928 The blessed Sunne..Eclips'd to me, eternally appeares. **1726** tr.

Gregory's Astron. I. 34 The Duration of some Eclipses is.. so long..as to let the Moon go the Length of three of its Diameters in the Shadow totally eclipsed. **1832** *Nat. Philos.* II. *Introd. Astron.* p. lii. (Usef. Knowl. Ser.) When the moon eclipses the sun to us, the earth is eclipsed to the moon.

b. *transf.* To intercept (light); used *techn.* with reference to an intermittent light in a lighthouse.

1858 *Merc. Mar. Mag.* V. 60 It is a White Revolving Light, eclipsed once a minute.

3. *fig.* To cast a shadow upon, throw into the shade; to obscure, deprive of lustre.

1581 R. GOADE in *Confer.* II. (1584) Hiiij b, The glorie of it was..eclipsed. **1650** B. *Discollim.* 30 A toleration of errours eclipsing and accosting Gods Truths. **1662** DRYDEN *Wild Gall.* Wks. 1725 I. 164, I confess I was a little eclips'd; but I'll chear up. **1774** J. BRYANT *Mythol.* II. 525 The ancient name was eclipsed by a later title. **1855** MACAULAY *Hist. Eng.* III. 351 The splendour of the House of Argyle had been eclipsed.

†**b.** To hide, screen *from.* Also, to extinguish (life). *Obs.*

1591 SHAKS. *1 Hen. IV*, IV. v. 53 Here I take my leaue of thee..Borne to eclipse thy Life this afternoone. **1642** G. ENGLISHAM *Forerunner of Rev.* 3 How easily I may eclipse myself from his power to do me harm. **1653** *Cloria & Narcissus* I. 243 He was not to be ecclipsed from the eyes of the multitude.

4. To render dim by comparison; to outshine, surpass. Chiefly *fig.*

1717 LADY M. W. MONTAGUE *Lett.* II. xliv. 18 Her earrings eclipsed all the rest. **1761** HUME *Hist. Eng.* II. xxvii. 127 The Earl of Surrey had totally eclipsed him in favour. **1812** S. ROGERS *Columbus* XII. 61 A spark is thrown that shall eclipse the sun. **1831** BREWSTER *Newton* (1855) I. xiii. 381 A discovery which is the glory of one age is eclipsed by the extension of it in another. **1870** DISRAELI *Lothair* xxxi. 159 One must sing in a room or the nightingales would eclipse us.

5. †**a.** To elide or omit (sounds) in pronunciation (*obs.*). **b.** In Irish (Gaelic, etc.) Grammar: To change the sound of an initial consonant according to euphonic laws. (In writing, the letter expressing the new sound is prefixed to the original initial which becomes silent.) See ECLIPSIS.

1589 PUTTENHAM *Eng. Poesie* II. xii. (Arb.) 127 If he [a word] goe before another word commencing with a vowell not letting him to be eclipsed, his vtterance is easie. **1602** CAREW *Cornwall* 56 a, The English which they speake is good..but they disgrace it..eclipsing (somewhat like the Somersetshire men) specially in pronouncing the names.

eclipsed (ɪˈklɪpst), *ppl. a.* [f. prec. + -ED.]

1. Suffering from eclipse, darkened.

1633 G. HERBERT *Temple, Parodie* iii, No stormie night Can so afflict..As thy eclipsed light. **1673** R. HEAD *Canting Acad.* 130 An eclipsed Moon. **1884** *Athenæum* 11 Oct. 469/1 The absence of red colour in the eclipsed moon.

2. *transf.* and *fig.* Obscured, 'in the shade'.

1577 HOLINSHED *Chron.* I. 177/1 The eclipsed state of England after his [king Edmund's] death. **1666** DRYDEN *Ann. Mirab.* xc, Mine shall sing of his eclipsed estate.

†**b.** Enfeebled; labouring under infirmity. (In quot. 1667 perhaps = *blind*). *Obs.*

1607 TOPSELL *Four-f. Beasts* 431 Those which are effeminate or defective, and eclipsed in their minde or courage. **1667** *Carte Papers* (*MS.*) CLIV. fol. 132 b (Bodl. Libr.), The humble petition of William Walsh eclipsed.

†**3.** = ECLIPTIC *a. Obs.*

1627 in Rushw. *Hist. Coll.* (1659) I. 484 Who..would make a new Zodiack, and draw his eclipsed lines through the East and West Indies.

eclipser (ɪˈklɪpsə(r)). [f. ECLIPSE *v.* + -ER.] One who eclipses, darkens, obscures, or outshines.

1594 BARNFIELD *Affect. Sheph.* II. xxix, Oh foule Eclipser of that fayre sun-shine. **1748** RICHARDSON *Clarissa* (1811) IV. xvi. 79 They confessed themselves eclipsed, without envying the eclipser.

eclipsing (ɪˈklɪpsɪŋ), *vbl. sb.* [f. ECLIPSE *v.* + -ING[1].] **a.** The action of causing an eclipse. **b.** The condition of being in an eclipse. Also *fig.*

1430 LYDG. *Chron. Troy* III. xxv, The name of whom shall ..ever yliche without eclipsing shine. *a* **1541** WYATT *Wks.* (1861) 49 He..gives the moon her horns their eclipsing. **1650** HUBBERT *Pill Formality* 61 An eclipsing..of the shinings of grace.

e'clipsing, *ppl. a.* [f. as prec. + -ING[2].]

1. That is suffering eclipse; that is being eclipsed.

1748 A. PHILIPS *Pastorals* vi. 114 His Voice had power To free the 'clipsing Moon at Midnight Hour. **1923** *Discovery* Sept. 245/2 Mr. F. C. Jordan..announces the discovery of a remarkable eclipsing variable star.

2. That causes eclipse; that darkens, or causes darkness or obscurity. In quots. *fig.* only.

1635 QUARLES *Embl.* III. vii. (1718) 153 O why Does thy eclipsing hand so long deny The sunshine of thy soul-enliv'ning eye? **1821** SHELLEY *Adonais* liv, That Benediction which the eclipsing Curse Of birth can quench not. **1876** GEO. ELIOT *Dan. Der.* III. xl. 183 Despondency ..had floated in and hovered above him with eclipsing wings.

3. That outshines or surpasses others.

1660 BOYLE *Seraph. Love* §2 Their greatest Accomplishments..are in that Eclipsing company, as inconspicuous as the faint Qualities of more ordinary persons. **1891** HARDY *Tess* I. ii. 25 The name of the eclipsing girl..has not been handed down.

e'clipsis. *Gram.* [ad. Gr. ἔκλειψις, noun of action f. ἐκλείπειν to leave out; in sense 1 perh. confused with *ellipsis*; in sense 2 app. suggested by ECLIPSE in fig. sense 'to obscure'.]

†**1.** An omission of words needful fully to express the sense. *Obs.*

1538 COVERDALE *Prol. N.T.*, The cause..is partly the figure called eclipsis. **1589** PUTTENHAM *Eng. Poesie* III. xii. (Arb.) 175 Eclipsis or the Figure of default.

†**b.** (See quot.) *Obs.*

1727 W. MATHER *Yng. Man's Comp.* 38 *Eclipsis*, is a piece of a Line drawn to denote that some part of a Verse or Sentence cited, is left out..As, —— 'Tis still the Miser's Lot. The young Fool spends all that the old Knave got.

2. In Irish (Sc. Gaelic, Manx) Grammar: see quot.

1845 J. O'DONOVAN *Irish Gram.* 58 *Eclipsis* in Irish Grammar may be defined the suppression of the sounds of certain radical consonants, by prefixing others of the same organ.

eclipt, obs. form of YCLEPT.

ecliptic (ɪˈklɪptɪk), *a.* and *sb.* Forms: 4–8 eclipticк(e, -tik(e, -que, (4, 7 ecc-, eclyptic(k, 7 æcliptique, 8 eccliptic), 7- ecliptic. [ad. (directly or through F. *écliptique*) L. *eclīptic-us*, Gr. ἐκλειπτικός in same sense.]

A. *adj.* Of or pertaining to an eclipse. ***ecliptic limits***: the limits within which an eclipse is possible. ***ecliptic conjunction***: a conjunction of sun and moon which results in a solar eclipse.

1609 HOLLAND *Amm. Marcell.* XX. iii. 145 When [the Sunne] himselfe and the roundle of the Moone..are come to those dimensions which they usually tearme..eclipticke or defective [*defectivas*] conjunctions ascending and descending. **1755** B. MARTIN *Mag. Arts & Sci.* II. vi. 153 These ecliptic Nights last but a little Time. **1771** MASKELYNE in *Phil. Trans.* LXI. 544 The time of the ecliptic conjunction may be deduced. **1834** *Nat. Philos.* III. *Astron.* 93/2 (Usef. Knowl. Ser.) The solar ecliptic limits exceed the lunar.

fig. **1678** SIR T. HERBERT *Mem. Chas. I*, 88 (T.) In this ecliptick condition was the king..sequestered in a manner from the comfort earth and air affords.

†**b.** ***ecliptic circle, line, way***: = ECLIPTIC *sb.*

c **1391** CHAUCER *Astrol.* Prol. 3 To knowe in owre orizonte ..the arising of any planete aftur his latitude fro the Ecliptik lyne. **1594** BLUNDEVIL *Exerc.* III. I. xiv. (ed. 7) 305 You must have respect only to the Ecliptique line. **1662** HOBBES *Seven Prob.* Wks. 1845 VII. 10 Does not the earth move..in the ecliptic circle once a year? **1712** BLACKMORE *Creation* II. (1736) 52 The sun revolving thro' th' ecclyptic way.

fig. **1649** SELDEN *Laws Eng.* II. xxx. (1739) 137 He would therefore have his way like that of the Zodiack, broad enough for Planetary motion of any one that could not contain himself within the Ecliptick Line of the Law.

¶ Used by mistake for ELLIPTIC.

1634–46 ROW *Hist. Kirk* (1842) 53 The Exercise of Prophesieing, or, in ecliptick expression, the Exercise of the Ministers.

B. *sb.*

1. The great circle of the celestial sphere which is the apparent orbit of the sun. So called because eclipses can happen only when the moon is on or very near this line. Sometimes put for the plane of the ecliptic.

1635 N. CARPENTER *Geog. Del.* I. ix. 208 The distance of the Pole circles from the Pole is iust so much as the declination of the Eclipticke from the Equatour. **1646** SIR T. BROWNE *Pseud. Ep.* 291 If we imagine the Sun to make his course out of the Eclyptick, and upon a line without any obliquity. **1698** KEILL *Exam. The. Earth* (1734) 225 It [is].. impossible to conceive how a Sphere can be inclin'd to a Plane, passing thro' its Center as the Ecliptick does thro' the Center of the Earth. **1774** GOLDSMITH *Nat. Hist.* (1862) I. iv. 13 Its equator was in the plane of the ecliptic. **1854** KELLY & TOMLINSON tr. *Arago's Astron.* 121 The inclination of the orbit of this comet to the ecliptic is 12° 34′.

2. The great circle on the terrestrial sphere which at any given moment lies in the plane of the celestial ecliptic.

1819 *Pantologia, Ecliptic*, in geography, an imaginary great circle on the terrestrial globe..falling upon the plane of the celestial ecliptic.

ecliptical (ɪˈklɪptɪkəl), *a.* [f. ECLIPTIC + -AL[1].] Pertaining to the ecliptic; situated on the ecliptic.

1556 RECORDE *Cast. Knowl.* (1556) 281 The Eclipticall pointes, whiche be commonly called the Headde and the Tayle of the Dragon. **1885** CLERKE *Pop. Hist. Astron.* 429 In carrying out the work of ecliptical charting..M. M. Henry ..resolved..to have recourse to the Camera.

¶ Used in error for ELLIPTICAL.

1583 FULKE *Defence* (1843) 402 When the sentence is ecliptical or defective. **1642** FULLER *Holy & Prof. St.* IV. xii. 299 He conceives this word, On mine Honour, wraps up a great deal in it..and no lesse then an eclipticall oath, calling God to witnesse, who hath bestowed that Honour upon him.

Hence **e'cliptically** *adv.*, in the direction of the sun's (apparent) annual motion in the ecliptic.

1658 SIR T. BROWNE *Gard. Cyrus*, The flower twists Aequinoctionally from the left hand to the right..the stalk twineth ecliptically from the right to the left.

†**eclip'ticity.** *Obs. rare*$^{-1}$.

1747 CARTE *Hist. Eng.* I. 68 Discoveries, with regard to the eclipticity of the Zodiac.

eclogite (ˈɛklədʒaɪt). *Min.* Also 9 eclogyte, eklogite. [f. Gr. ἐκλογή selection; see quot. 1822.] A metamorphic rock, consisting of granular garnet and hornblende, with grass-green smaragdite (Dana *Man. Geol.* (1880) 74).

[**1822** HAÜY *Minéralogie* IV. 548 Diallage, Espèce unique: Eclogite, d' ἐκλογη choix, parce que les composans de cette roche n'étant pas de ceux qui existent plusieurs ensemble dans les roches primitives..semblent s'être choisis pour faire bande à part.] **1852** TH. ROSS tr. *Humboldt's Trav.* III. xxix. 169 Feldspar with a basis of souda..forms..with garnet, eclogyte. **1866** LAWRENCE tr. *Cotta's Rocks Class.*, This rock, to which Haüy gave the name of eklogite, is usually very firm and coherent.

eclogue (ˈɛklɒg). Forms: 6–8 eglog(ue, (6, 9 æglogue, -ge), 6- eclogue. [ad. L. *ecloga*, a. Gr. ἐκλογή selection, f. ἐκλέγειν to select.

The spelling *æglogue* (med.L. *ægloga*, Fr. *églogue*) was associated with a fanciful derivation from αἴξ, αἰγ-ός goat (as if 'discourse of goatherds').]

1. A short poem of any kind, *esp.* a pastoral dialogue, such as Virgil's Bucolics.

1514 BARCLAY *Cyt. & Uplondyshm.* (*heading*), The fyfte Eglog of Alexandre Barclay of the Cytizen & Uplondyshman. **1579** E. K. in *Spenser's Sheph. Cal.* Gen. Arg. §2 They be not termed *Eclogues.* **1591** FLORIO *2nd Fruites* Ep. Ded. 1, Some..deuising how to..blanche their passions with æglogues, songs and sonnets. **1605** CAMDEN *Rem.* 172 His meaning might be perceyved out of the last Eglogue of Virgill. **1704** POPE *Disc. Past. Poetry* 55 It is not sufficient that the sentences only be brief, the whole Eclogue should be so too. **1876** GREEN *Short Hist.* i. §4 (1882) 37 A little eclogue descriptive of the approach of spring.

¶**2.** Erroneously for: Conversation, discourse.

1613 R. C. *Table Alph.* (ed. 3), *Eglogue*, a talking together. *a* **1670** HACKET *Cent. Serm.* (1675) 288 The Shepherds in the Eclogue which they had together about going to Bethlem to find Christ, use this Speech.

3. *attrib.*, also ***eclogue-wise*** adv., as in an eclogue.

1580 SIDNEY *Arcadia* (1613) 219 Which gaue occasion to Histor and Damon..to present Basilius with some other of their complaints Eclogue-wise. *Ibid.* 388 In eclogue wise.

Hence **'eclogue**y *a. nonce-wd.*, pertaining to, or of the nature of, an eclogue or pastoral poem.

18.. BARNES *Poems Dorset Dial.*, They poems..fill my heart wi'..The most ecloguey thoughts they do!

eclosion (ɪˈkləʊʒən). [a. F. *éclosion*, n. of action of *éclore*, f. *é-* = EX- + *clore*:—L. *claudĕre* to shut.] Emergence from concealment; *spec.* in *Ent.*, the emerging of an insect from the pupa case, or of a larva from the egg.

1889 in *Cent. Dict.* [**1906** W. JAMES *Let.* 7 Apr. (1920) II. 246 It is queer to be assisting at the *éclosion* of a great new mental epoch, life, religion, and philosophy in one.] **1925** A. D. IMMS *Gen. Textbk. Entomol.* 186 As the time for the eclosion of the imago approaches the pupa noticeably darkens in colour. **1928** S. THOMPSON *Battle of the Horizons* v. vii, Her speculation vaguely pursued the fate of that simper—the man waiting for the savour of its rehearsed eclosion. **1953** H. MILLER *Plexus* (1963) vii. 282 What intrigues me to this day, is the glory and the wonder of eclosion.

eclude, erron. form of EXCLUDE *v.*

1681 R. KNOX *Hist. Ceylon* 66 He is utterly ecluded from his family.

ecmnesia (ɛkmˈniːzɪə, -sɪə). *Psychol.* [mod.L., f. Gr. ἐκ out + μνῆσις memory.] Loss of memory with regard to the events of a particular period.

1890 BILLINGS *Med. Dict.*, *Ecmnesia*, a form of amnesia in which there is normal memory of occurrences prior to a certain date, with loss of memory of what happened for a certain time after that date. **1967** BRUSSEL & CANTZLAAR *Chambers's Dict. Psychiatry* 77 *Ecmnesia*, amnesia with poor memory for recent events, but with relatively intact memory for events in the remote past.

ecness, -nyss, var. of ECHENESS, *Obs.*

eco- (iːkəʊ), shortening of ECOLOGICAL, ECOLOGY, as in **eco-'activist**, one who actively opposes the pollution, or destruction by other means, of the environment; **ecoca'tastrophe**, major damage to the environment, esp. when caused by human activity; **eco'cidal** *a.*, designed or tending to destroy the environment; **'ecocide**, destruction or damage of the environment, esp. intentionally; **'ecofreak** *colloq.*, a fanatical conservationist or environmentalist. See also ECOCLIMATE, ECOPHENE, etc.

1969 *Time* 10 Oct. 70/1 Last week *eco-activists staged a 'Damn DDT Day' in San Francisco's Union Square. **1975** *Weekend Mag.* (Montreal) 6 Dec. 28/3 The Greenpeace eco-activists, noted for their campaigns against nuclear testing and the slaughter of whales, are by no means alone in expounding the new planetary morality. **1969** *New Scientist* 2 Oct. 18/2 Some major *eco-catastrophes seem bound to occur in the coming decades. **1973** *Science* 12 Oct. 173/2 An ecocatastrophe of serious magnitude to the seaward fringe of the Everglades National Park and adjacent areas appears to be in progress. **1970** *Guardian Weekly* 15 Aug. 18 Beyond that lie the use of *ecocidal weapons—herbicides in Vietnam—and 'humane incapacitants'. **1973** *Bull. Peace Proposals* IV. I. 84/2 It is also important to distinguish between specific occasions of environmental warfare and persistent patterns of warfare that produce cumulative effects on ecosystems that can be properly called 'ecocide' or policies that can be designated 'ecocidal'. **1969** *Encycl. Sci. Suppl.* (Grolier) 159 Discarded automobiles, old newspapers and telephone books, tin cans, nonreturnable bottles—all add to

the growing problems of solid-waste disposal... *Ecocide—the murder of the environment—is everybody's business. **1972** *Punch* 1 Mar. 298/2 The new word for bravado is custerism. Wilful destruction of the environment is now ecocide. **1982** *New Scientist* 3 June 663/1 Olof Palme denounced the Americans for ecocide in Vietnam. **1970** *Natural Hist.* Oct. 22/3 I've been an *ecofreak for 30 years. **1980** *Guardian Weekly* 11 May 14 Alexandre Hebert,..a staunch anarchist trade unionist, has nothing but disdain for 'those eco-freaks who want to turn back the wheels of history'.

ecoclimate ('iːkəʊˌklaɪmət). [f. *eco-* as in ECOLOGY + CLIMATE *sb.* 3.] The climate as an ecological factor; the climate of a habitat; cf. MICROCLIMATE. So **ˌecoclima'tology**.

1931 B. P. UVAROV in *Trans. Entomol. Soc.* LXXIX. I. 128 In the study of insect ecology we must, therefore, pay special attention to the climate of the actual habitat of the insect, or to the *ecoclimate*, as I would suggest that the sum-total of meteorological factors within a habitat should be called. **1937** *Nature* 16 Oct. 664/1 Another weak point is the lack of discussion on ecoclimates of the actual animal habitats, which very often enable an animal to survive in a region the general climate of which is wholly unsuitable for it. **1966** R. L. SMITH *Ecology & Field Biology* i. 6 Early investigation of the physical environment of organisms..led to ecoclimatology.

†**e'cod**, *int. Obs.* [var. of EGAD, *egod*, AGAD, q.v.] Used as a mild oath.

1733 FIELDING *Don Quix.* I. viii, 'Ecod! it runs in my head. **1777** SHERIDAN *Trip Scarb.* III. iv, It's well I have a husband acoming, or ecod I'd marry the baker. **1865** DICKENS *Mut. Fr.* xiv. 371 Ecod, when I say to him..

ecology (iː'kɒlədʒɪ). Also œcology. [mod. f. Gr. οἶκ-ος house, dwelling + -(O)LOGY; after *œconomy*.]

1. The science of the economy of animals and plants; that branch of biology which deals with the relations of living organisms to their surroundings, their habits and modes of life, etc.

A supposed use of *ecology* in Thoreau's letters represents a misreading of *geology*: see *Science* (1965) 13 Aug. 707 and *Bull. Thoreau Soc.* (1973) No. 123.6.

1873 tr. *Haeckel's Hist. Creat.* Pref., The great series of phenomena of comparative anatomy and ontogeny,.. chorology and œcology. **1879** tr. *Haeckel's Evol. Man* I. 114 All the various relations of animals and plants to one another and to the outer world, with which the Oekology of organisms has to do..admit of simple and natural explanation only on the Doctrine of Adaptation and Heredity. **1893** *Brit. Med. Jrnl.* 16 Sept. 613/1 Œcology, which uses all the knowledge it can obtain from the other two [physiology and morphology], but chiefly rests on the exploration of the endless varied phenomena of animal and plant life as they manifest themselves under natural conditions. **1894** *Proc. Madison Bot. Congr.* 36 The separation of..vegetable physiology into two departments: physiology proper and ecology. **1896** *Pop. Sci. Monthly* Dec. 185 Botany..especially with reference to the physiology and ecology of plants. **1902** *Nature* 17 Apr. 574/1 The ecology of a glacial lake. **1904** C. L. LAURIE *Flowering Plants* 6 The study of plants that grow together, forming plant associations, in some respects the most interesting part of Ecology. **1916** F. E. CLEMENTS *Plant Succession* 73 It is one of the most important tasks of ecology to determine the root and shoot relations of communal plants. **1928** R. S. TROUP *Silvicultural Syst.* xix. 183 The development of ecology as a science has given a special impetus to the study of the physical and physiological conditions bearing on natural regeneration. **1931** H. G. WELLS *Work, Wealth & Happiness of Mankind* (1932) i. 29 Economics..is spoken of in the *Science of Life* as a branch of ecology; it is the ecology of the human species. **1933** —— *Shape of Things to Come* I. §12. 111 Of human ecology he betrays no knowledge. **1935** *Nature* 2 Feb. 168/1 The study of such interactions under the given conditions of habitat is the most important part of what is called plant ecology. **1941** AUDEN *New Year Letter* I. 23 And grasped in its complexity The Catholic ecology. **1967** *Listener* 6 Apr. 459/3 In different ecologies territorial systems will vary or even be absent altogether.

2. Used *attrib.* (and *absol.*) with reference to ecological issues such as industrial pollution considered in a political context; *spec.* applied to various political movements (esp. in western Europe) which represent the environmental or 'green' interest.

[**1963** A. HUXLEY (*title*) The politics of ecology.] **1970** *Environmental Quality Mag.* I. I. 30/2 Write to Granny.. and tell her about your ecology activities and ideas... Wear your ecology symbol [*sc.* a pin] to promote a better environment. **1973** *Antioch Rev.* XXXII. III. 449 Ecologists as scientists may or may not share the perspectives of the ecology movement. **1974** RATHER & GATES *Palace Guard* i. 6 Some of the leaders wound up in jail..still others, buckling under pressure, turned their attention to less threatening issues, like ecology. **1979** Ecology-conscious [see GREEN *sb.* 17]. **1980** J. F. PILAT *Ecological Politics* 73 The United Kingdom has no significant ecological parties; the Ecology party recently had only 600 members. **1985** *Observer* 22 Sept. 2/8 The Ecology Party changed its name to the Green Party at is annual conference in Dover. **1986** *New Socialist* Sept. 36/1 The strongest organised hesitation before socialism is perhaps the diverse movement variously identified as 'ecology' or the 'the greens'.

Hence **eco'logical**, **eco'logic** *a.*, pertaining to ecology; **eco'logically** *adv.*, **e'cologist**.

1893 J. S. BURDON-SANDERSON in *Nature* 14 Sept. 465/1 Whether with the œcologist we regard the organism in relation to the world, or with the physiologist as a wonderful complex of vital energies, the two branches have this in common. **1896** *Pop. Sci. Monthly* May 72 These ecologic color adaptations. **1899** *Natural Sci.* July 11 One of the most important oecological studies which has yet appeared in the United States. **1904** C. L. LAURIE *Flowering Plants* 8 Ecological classification of plants. **1909** WEBSTER, Ecologically. **1909** E. WARMING *Oecol. Plants* p. v, I have given my views on oecological classification in a more comprehensive and detailed manner. **1926** *Spectator* 25 Sept. 492/1 Part of the distinctively modern progress in palaeontology has just been this ecological outlook. **1930** C. ELTON *Anim. Ecol. & Evolution* 7 Evolution..is not at all a popular subject among animal ecologists to-day. **1935** *Times* 6 Mar. 10/3 We know that in some cases ecologically related trees can well gain the freedom of another country. **1936** H. G. WELLS *Anat. Frustration* ix. 86, I assume the world community..subject to general ecological laws. **1955** M. GLUCKMAN *Custom & Conflict in Africa* i. 7 The ecological needs for this friendship and peace lessen as the distance grows greater. **1959** A. HARDY *Fish & Fisheries* xvi. 302 The work of the marine ecologists is only in its infancy.

†**eco'nomacy.** *Obs. rare.* In 7 œconomacy. [f. L. *œconom-us* (ad. Gr. οἰκονόμος steward) + -ACY.] The position or office of being 'spiritual œconomus' or controller of ecclesiastical affairs.

1651 C. CARTWRIGHT *Cert. Relig.* I. 45 That Objection of Protestants against the œconomacy of the Bishop of Rome.

econometric (iːkɒnəʊ'mɛtrɪk), *a.* and *sb. Econ.* [f. ECONO(MY + METRIC *a.*[1] 2.] **A.** *adj.* Of, or relating to, or characterized by, the application of mathematics to economic data or theories.

1933 (*title*) Econometrica: Journal of the Econometric Society, vol. I. **1956** R. F. HARROD in A. Pryce-Jones *New Outl. Mod. Knowl.* 490 Trade Cycle study appeared an especially good field for the use of econometric methods. **1959** *Economist* 28 Feb. 809/2 The econometric model.. represents the actual workings of the economy by a system of mathematical equations.

B. *sb.* (*pl.*) The branch of economics concerned with the application of mathematical economics to economic data by the use of statistical methods.

1933 *Econometrica* I. 5 (*heading*) The Common Sense of Econometrics. **1951** *Univ. Birmingham Faculty of Commerce & Social Sci.* Regs. 63 Econometrics..deals mainly with the difficulties encountered in applying statistical technique to economic data. **1954** *Times Lit. Suppl.* 26 Mar., Econometrics now vies with mathematical philosophy..as an exercise in formal logic. **1970** *Daily Tel.* 23 Feb. 9/7 American research economists have pioneered the science of 'econometrics', in which factors affecting the economy are written as mathematical symbols.

econometrician (iːˌkɒn-, ɪˌkɒnəʊmɛ'trɪʃən). *Econ.* [f. prec. + -IAN.] A student of, or specialist in, econometrics.

1947 J. TINBERGEN in S. E. Harris *New Economics* 219 It seems worth while to consider the many-sided contributions made to economic thought by John Maynard Keynes from the angle of the econometrician. **1956** R. F. HARROD in A. Pryce-Jones *New Outl. Mod. Knowl.* 490 It was the ambition of the econometricians..to formulate economic laws in terms which could be statistically verified. **1968** *Listener* 18 July 68/2 It is mere playing with words to call management consultants specialists in the same sense as chemical engineers or econometricians.

economic (iːkə-, ɛkə'nɒmɪk), *a.* and *sb.* For forms cf. ECONOMY. [ad. L. *œconomicus*, ad. Gr. οἰκονομικός, f. οἰκονόμος; see ECONOMY and -IC. The Fr. *économique* is of earlier date, and may have been the first source of the Eng. word.]

A. *adj.* **1.** †**a.** Pertaining to the management of a household, or to the ordering of private affairs (*obs.*). **b.** Relating to private income and expenditure.

1592 SIR JOHN DAVIES *Immort. Soul* xii. (1697) 52 Doth employ her Oeconomick Art..her Household to preserve. **1603** FLORIO *Montaigne* (1634) 111 In this Oeconomicke or houshold order. **1627** DRAYTON *Agincourt* 212 A man of naturall goodness..whose courses..serue me for Oeconomike booke. **1650** ROW *Hist. Kirk* (1842) 193 Imploying them in oeconomick & naturall morall duties. **1669** GALE *Crt. Gentiles* I. III. i. 17 Oeconomic Poesie..also ..Politic Poesie..had their Original from Moses's Oeconomics, and Politics. **1791** COWPER *Odyss.* XIX. 408 That I in wisdom œconomic aught Pass other women. **1831** CARLYLE *Sart. Res.* (1858) 77 Landlords' Bills, and other economic Documents. —— *Sterling* I. ix. (1872) 55 His outlooks into the future, whether for his spiritual or economic fortunes, were confused.

2. a. Relating to the science of economics; relating to the development and regulation of the material resources of a community or nation.

1835 I. TAYLOR *Spir. Despot.* ii. 70 The economic experiment. **1863** FAWCETT *Pol. Econ.* I. iv. 35 Principles which will enable us to investigate economic problems. **1883** *Manch. Exam.* 22 Nov. 5/3 M. Leroy-Beaulieu..one of the ablest writers on economic subjects.

b. Maintained for the sake of profit. Also, Connected with the industrial arts. (The former title of the 'Museum of Practical Geology' was 'Museum of Economic Geology'.)

1854 BADHAM *Halieut.* 36 The advantages to be derived from economic fish-ponds. *Mod.* The many economic applications of electricity.

c. Practical or utilitarian in application or use, e.g. ***economic botany, geography***, etc.

1861 *Jrnl. Soc. Arts* 22 Mar. 295 (*heading*) The Economic History of Paraffine. **1882** W. CUNNINGHAM *Growth Eng. Ind. & Comm.* 5 Economic History is not so much the study of a special class of facts, as the study of all the facts of a nation's history from a special point of view. **1882** B. D. JACKSON (*title*) Vegetable technology; a contribution towards a bibliography of economic botany. **1914** J. MCFARLANE *Economic Geography* 1 Economic Geography may be defined as the study of the influence exerted upon the economic activities of man by his physical environment. **1922** C. K. LEITH *Econ. Aspects Geol.* i. 1 The application of geology to practical uses, resulting in the development of the science generally known as *economic geology*. **1959** *N.Z. Timber Jrnl.* Apr. 52/2 Economic Forestry..is directed mainly towards marketing and utilization of forest products.

d. economic man, a convenient abstraction used by some economists for one who manages his private income and expenditure strictly and consistently in accordance with his own material interests. Cf. *economical man.*

1889 G. B. SHAW *Fabian Essays in Socialism* 25 There is no such person as the celebrated 'economic man'. **1890** A. MARSHALL *Princ. Econ.* I. vi. 78 When the older economists spoke of the 'economic man' as governed by selfish, or self-regarding motives, they did not express their meaning exactly. **1929** A. HUXLEY *Do what you Will* 217 Historical materialists, who deal..with abstract 'Economic Men'. **1930** *Economist* 19 July 115/2 There is the danger..that the State..may prove to be a mechanism..so forgetful of human personality in its concentration on the barren concept of 'economic man' that ordinary men, hungry for individual well-being, may revolt against it. **1965** SELDON & PENNANCE *Everyman's Dict. Econ.* 138 *Economic Man*, concerned with the immediate aim of obtaining the largest possible command over resources with the minimum of sacrifice.

e. economic rent, a rent that brings a fair return on capital and current expenditure (see also quots. 1965 and 1966).

1889 G. B. SHAW *Fabian Essays in Socialism* 6 Here is a clear advantage of £500 a year to the first comer. This £500 is economic rent. **1894** —— in *Fortn. Rev.* Apr. 480 The difference between the worst acre and the best (otherwise the 'economic rent') can be reduced finally by equality of cultivation. **1950** G. BRENAN *Face of Spain* v. 103 On their present wages, no working-class family can pay an economic rent. **1965** SELDON & PENNANCE *Everyman's Dict. Econ.* 142 *Economic rent*,..the earnings of a factor of production in excess of the minimum sum necessary to keep it in existing use. **1966** A. GILPIN *Dict. Econ. Terms* (1967) 60 *Economic rent*, a payment to a unit of a factor of production which is in excess of the minimum amount necessary to keep that unit in its present occupation. A firm may pay a wage sufficient to retain its present staff. In attempting to increase its staff, however, the firm may find it necessary to raise wages and attract workers from other employment. The increase in wage now enjoyed by the original staff is economic rent.

f. economic system, the sum of the economic institutions and arrangements of a society.

1898 A. P. ATTERBURY tr. *Sombart's Socialism & Social Movement* i. 4 By a 'social class' I understand..men who are interested in a specific system of production and distribution. We must, in understanding any social class, go back to this economic system. **1909** M. EPSTEIN tr. *Sombart's Socialism & Social Movement* (ed. 6) 1 In using the words 'economic system' I mean a given social order, or an economic condition of things, which is characterized by one or more prominent economic principles. **1929** W. SOMBART in *Econ. Hist. Rev.* II. 13 The general conception which I employ in order to distinguish, describe and correlate economic phenomena is that of *the economic system*. *Ibid.* 14 By an economic system I understand a mode of satisfying and making provision for material wants, which can be comprehended as a unit, wherein each constituent element of the economic process displays some given characteristic. **1937** R. L. HALL (*title*) The economic system in a socialist state. **1951** R. FIRTH *Elem. Soc. Org.* iv. 127 The role of the anthropologist here is rather that of a watch-dog—to see that no one takes away the reality of the economic systems of primitive peoples by default.

g. economic war(fare), the use of economic measures as a means of bringing pressure to bear on another country, or in retaliation for such measures taken against the user.

1916 G. L. DICKINSON (*title*) Economic war after the war. **1939** W. S. CHURCHILL in *War Illustr.* 2 Dec. 374/3 Nazi Germany is all the time under the grip of our economic warfare falling back in oil and other essential war supplies. **1949** E. POUND *Pisan Cantos* lxxviii. 64 And the economic war has begun.

h. economic growth, the growth per head of the population in the production of goods and services over a stated period of time; the rate of expansion of the national income. Cf. GROWTH[1] 1 c.

1940 C. G. CLARK *Conditions of Economic Progress* x. 337 (*heading*) The morphology of economic growth. **1948** *Proc. Amer. Philos. Soc.* XCII. 229/2 The economic growth of the United States can thus be defined. **1953** J. VINER *Internat. Trade & Econ. Devel.* vi. 103 It is not necessary to look for other factors..to explain pervasive poverty and slow economic growth. **1965** *Times* 17 Feb. 19/6 Economic growth is no longer regarded as the cure-all for the nation's ills.

†**3.** Thrifty, careful, saving, sparing. *Obs.*

1755 H. WALPOLE *Mem. Geo. II*, II. 96 We should be economic. **1801** MAR. EDGEWORTH *Belinda* vi. (1832) I. 112, I never saw any one so economic of her smiles.

†**4. economic rat**: a transl. of *Mus œconomicus*, a name given by Linnæus to a burrowing rodent found in Siberia and Kamtchatka (now called *Arvicola œconomus*). *Obs.*

1802 BINGLEY *Anim. Biog.* (1813) I. 378 The migrations of the Economic Rats, are not less extraordinary.

5. Pertaining to 'economy' in religious teaching, or to 'economy of truth'. Cf. ECONOMY 6.

[**1815** J. C. HOBHOUSE *Substance of some Letters* (1816) I. 11 That species of writing called by Voltaire, the œconomic style, or an expedient falsification of facts.] **1851** ROBERTSON *Serm.* Ser. IV. vi. (1863) I. 34 His economic management of Truth. I use this word though it may seem pedantic.

6. Pertaining to a dispensation, or method of the Divine government. Cf. ECONOMY 5 b.

1817 G. S. FABER *Eight Dissertations* (1845) I. 31 Jacob gives to this agent the.. economic title of The Angel.

B. *sb.*

†1. The art or science of managing a house; housekeeping. *Obs.*

1393 GOWER *Conf.* III. 141 That othir point, which to practique Belongith, is economique. **1609** C. BUTLER *Fem. Mon.* v. (1623) K iv, As well in Musick as Oeconomick there must sometime be Discords.

2. *pl.* (after L. *œconomica*, Gr. τὰ οἰκονομικά).

†a. The science or art of managing a household; a treatise on that subject. *Obs.*

1586 COGAN *Haven Health* (1636) 16 Aristotle.. in his Œconomikes.. biddeth us to rise before day. *a* **1619** FOTHERBY *Atheom.* II. xiv. §2 (1622) 356 Morall Philosophie .. hath three parts: Ecclesiastickes, Oeconomickes, and Politickes. [**1621** *Bk. Discip. Ch. Scot.* 43 Ethica, Oeconomica & Politica.] **1665** GLANVILL *Sceps. Sci.* xix. 123 The more practical ones of Politicks and Œconomicks. **1770** LANGHORNE *Plutarch* (1879) II. 586/2 Economics, so far as they regard only inanimate things, serve only the low purposes of gain; but where they regard human beings they rise higher.

b. The art of regulating income and expenditure; also, pecuniary position.

1851 CARLYLE *Sterling* I. iv. (1872) 27 The family economics getting yearly more propitious and flourishing. *Ibid.* II. vi. 140 The Original Regulations.. a very solid lucid piece of economics.

c. The science relating to the production and distribution of material wealth; sometimes used as equivalent to *political economy*, but more frequently with reference to practical and specific applications. Sometimes qualified by an adj. prefixed, as in ***rural economics***. Also, the condition of a country with regard to material prosperity.

1792 A. YOUNG *Trav. France* 176 He.. engaged to go with me.. to Tour D'Aigues to wait on The baron.. whose essays are among the most valuable on rural œconomics. **1839** CARLYLE *Chartism* iv. (1858) 17 The oppression has gone far farther than into the economics of Ireland. **1841–4** EMERSON *Ess.* Ser. I. vii. (1876) 181 Chemistry, natural history, and economics. **1844** DISRAELI *Coningsby* III. iii. 100 Those moral attributes.. are independent of economics. **1863** MARY HOWITT tr. *F. Bremer's Greece* I. v. 138 The improvement of Greece in economics. **1881** P. GEDDES in *Nature* XXIV. 526 Those sections.. were devoted to.. physical economics.

†3. One who understands the art of housekeeping. *Obs.*

1656 TRAPP *Comm. Eph.* i. 10 God is the best economic; his house is exactly ordered for matter of good husbandry.

†4. *Eccl. Hist.* An administrator of the revenues of a vacant benefice [= med.L. *œconomus*]. *Obs.*

1616 N. BRENT *Hist. Counc. Trent* (1676) 611 There being a suit for a benefice, an Oiconomick may be created. *Ibid.* 735 The Episcopal See being void, the Chapter shall elect one or two economicks.

economical (iːkəˈnɒmɪkəl, ɛ-), *a.* Forms: see ECONOMY. Also 6 oiconomical. [f. as prec. + -AL[1].]

1. a. Pertaining to a household or its management; resembling what prevails in a household. *arch.*

1579 G. HARVEY *Lett.-bk* (1884) 61 The other œconomical matter you wotte of. **1586** T. B. *La Primaud. Fr. Acad.* I. 493 Oeconomicall science, that is.. the art of ruling a house well. **1612** T. TAYLOR *Comm. Titus* i. 6 Those priuate vertues.. concerne his economicall administration. **1680** SIR R. FILMER *Patriarcha* ii. §2 Adam had only economical power, but not political. **1748** HARTLEY *Observ. Man* I. iv. §1. 425 Œconomical Convenience first determined the Ratio's of Doors, Windows, etc.

b. Pertaining to pecuniary position.

1825–45 CARLYLE *Schiller* App. (ed. 2) 270 My economical circumstances render it impossible for me to travel much.

2. a. Pertaining to, or concerned with, the development of material resources; relating to political economy. Cf. ECONOMY 3.

1781 GIBBON *Decl. & F.* II. xxxi. 173 The economical writers of antiquity.. recommend the former method. **1790** BURKE *Fr. Rev.* 117 Commerce.. and manufacture, the gods of our œconomical politicians, are themselves perhaps but creatures. **1878** MORLEY *Condorcet* 43 Why did not France sink under her economical disorders?

b. = ECONOMIC 2 b.

1792 A. YOUNG *Trav. France* 210 He had the direction.. of the œconomical garden. **1822** IMISON *Sc. & Art* II. 28 Many very important applications of this principle have been made by Count Rumford to œconomical purposes. **1856** EMERSON *Eng. Traits* v. 99 Bakewell created.. breeds in which every thing is omitted but what is economical.

3. a. Characterized by, or tending to economy; of persons; saving, thrifty; opposed to *wasteful*. Cf. ECONOMY 4.

1780 BURKE *Sp. on Œconomical Reform* 17 An œconomical constitution is a necessary basis for an œconomical administration. **1837** THIRLWALL *Greece* IV. xxxii. 228 The more economical application of the public revenue. **1851** CARPENTER *Man. Phys.* (ed. 2) 259 The use of animal flesh .. as a principal article of diet.. is very far from being economical. **1878** JEVONS *Prim. Pol. Econ.* 89 He will not work in an economical way. **1880** L. STEPHEN *Pope* iv. 92 Illustrative of his economical habits.

b. ***economical man*** = *economic man* (ECONOMIC *a.* 2 d).

1858 H. C. CAREY *Princ. Social Sci.* I. i. 29 We have the politico-economical man, on one hand influenced solely by the thirst for wealth, and on the other.. under the control of the sexual passion. **1880** BAGEHOT *Econ. Studies* ii. 83 The nature of the 'man' who first occupied new countries did not 'conform' to the standard of economical man; the being of reality was not the being of the hypothesis. The first men.. nearly approached in nature to the present savage man... They could not make any of the articles which we now call 'wealth'.

4. = ECONOMIC 5.

1833 J. H. NEWMAN *Arians* 80 Careful ever to maintain substantial truth in our use of the economical method. **1864** —— *Apol.* 386 She observes no half-measures, no economical reserve.

5. a. Pertaining to a dispensation; cf. ECONOMY 5 b. b. Pertaining to an organization; cf. ECONOMY 8.

1577 tr. *Bullinger's Decades* (1592) 631 The Trinity.. doth defende the Oiconomical state, that is, the mistery of the dispensation. **1646** *Burd. Issachar* in *Phenix* (1708) II. 265 This Sanhedrim is Christ's Vicegerent in his oeconomical Kingdom. **1670** MAYNWARING *Vita Sacra* iii. 40 The Oeconomical harmony is disturbed. *a* **1726** W. REEVE *Serm.* (1729) 171 When the.. Son of God had served the prophetic and priestly parts of his œconomical charge. **1817** G. S. FABER *Eight Dissertations* (1845) I. 37 The economical office of the Word.. is to declare the Father to his creatures.

economically (iːkəˈnɒmɪkəlɪ), *adv.* [f. prec. + -LY[2].] In an economical manner.

1. With reference to, or from the point of view of, economic science.

1856 OLMSTED *Slave States* 172 The best examples of the application of science, economically to agriculture, can.. be found in Virginia. **1868** ROGERS *Pol. Econ.* v. (ed. 3) 49 Economically considered, the existence of mankind is conditioned by some sort of saving.

2. In a thrifty or saving, as opposed to a wasteful, manner.

1812 *Examiner* 28 Sept. 620/1 Those resources the kingdom should economically apply. **1844** H. H. WILSON *Brit. India* (1845–8) III. 549 The object might be attained.. more economically, by the appointment of a Lieutenant-Governor. **1879** *Cassell's Techn. Educ.* IV. 415/2 Labour can be more.. economically carried out.

3. *Theol.* According to the method or subject to the conditions of the divine economy.

1696 LORIMER *Goodwin's Disc.* vii. 71 The Sin of Man.. disabled the Law of Works that it could not give that Eternal Life which after the Fall it promised only œconomically. **1817** G. S. FABER *Eight Dissertations* (1845) I. 36 God the Father.. economically declares his high behests through the medium of the Word. **1864** J. H. NEWMAN *Apol.* 67 The system which is of less importance is economically or sacramentally connected with the more momentous system.

economism (iːˈkɒnəmɪz(ə)m). [f. Fr. *économisme*, f. *économ(ie* economy + *-isme* -ism.]

A belief in the primacy of economic causes or factors (see also quots. 1949, 1967).

1919 W. R. INGE *Outspoken Essays* i. 23 Ruskin.. saw.. the danger to which spiritual values were exposed at the hands of the dominant economism. **1940** *Mind* XLIX. 423 Marx's economism—his emphasis on the economic background as being the ultimate basis of any sort of development—is exaggerated. **1948** J. L. ADAMS tr. *Tillich's Protestant Era* (1951) p. xxxiii, Religious socialism was always interested in human life as a whole and never in its economic basis exclusively. In this it was sharply distinguished from economic materialism, as well as from all forms of 'economism'. **1949** I. DEUTSCHER *Stalin* ii. 31 The first strikes.. stimulated a new trend called 'Economism'. This peculiar label was used by Russian socialists to describe what the French called Syndicalism, that is non-political Trade Unionism. **1967** *Times* 19 Jan. 7/2 The past week has seen the coining [in China] of a new derogatory term, 'economism', which was linked today with the parallel errors of better wages and conditions.

economist (ɪˈkɒnəmɪst, ɛ-). [f. Gr. οἰκονόμος (see ECONOMY) + -IST. Cf. Fr. *économiste*.]

†1. One who manages a household; a housekeeper. *Obs.* or *arch.*

1586 T. B. *La Primaud. Fr. Acad.* I. (1594) 100 A prudent man.. may first become a good oeconomist, that is, a governor & father of a familie. *c* **1645** HOWELL *Lett.* (1650) I. 99 Mr. Penry.. will prove a good husband, and a great œconomist. **1765** WILKES *Corr.* (1805) II. 219, I am got into lodgings of my own, and will endeavour to be as good an œconomist as my villainous nature will let me. **1857** RUSKIN *Pol. Econ. Art* 11 The perfect economist or mistress of a household.

2. A manager in general; one who attends to the sparing and effective use of anything, *esp.* of money. Const. *of.*

1710 SHAFTESB. *Charac.* III. §1. (1737) II. 372 O wise Oeconomist.. whom all the Elements and Powers of Nature serve! **1711** STEELE *Spect.* No. 64 ¶2 He is a good Oeconomist in his extravagance. **1725** BRADLEY *Fam. Dict.* II. s.v. *Lime*, Every good Oeconomist will purchase as.. cheap as he can. **1824** J. JOHNSON *Typogr.* I. 553 He appears to have been but an indifferent œconomist. **1841** D'ISRAELI *Amen. Lit.* (1867) 47 [He] was such a rigid economist of time, that every hour was allotted to its separate work.

3. One who practises or advocates saving.

1758 *Herald* II. 199 No. 27 He is an œconomist in his expences. **1771** H. MACKENZIE *Man Feel.* xxxvi. (1803) 72 His aunt was an economist. **1796** MORSE *Amer. Geog.* II. 420 An Italian.. must be a rigid economist. **1868** FREEMAN *Norm. Conq.* (1876) II. vii. 115 Economists who pressed for the reduction of the public expenditure.

4. a. A student of, or writer upon, economics or political economy.

1804 EARL LAUDERD. *Publ. Wealth* (1819) 354 To the economists commerce ought to have appeared a direct means of increasing wealth. **1827** WHATELEY *Logic* (1836) 393 The great defect of.. our own economists in general, is the want of definitions. **1866** ROGERS *Agric. & Prices* I. Pref., Those facts which form the special study of the economist.

b. More fully, **political economist**.

1825 MISS MITFORD in L'Estrange *Life* II. x. 197 He [Mr. Monck] is a great Grecian and a great political economist. **1855** MACAULAY *Hist. Eng.* IV. 326 David Hume.. one of the most profound political economists of his time.

c. One of the school of 'Economistes' (who flourished) in France in the 18th c.

1776 ADAM SMITH *W.N.* IV. ix, A.. considerable sect, distinguished in the French republic of letters by the name of 'The Economists'. **1869** BUCKLE *Civilis.* II. vii. 328 Soon after 1755 the economists effected a schism between the nation and the government. **1878** MORLEY *Condorcet* 33 As a thinker he is roughly classed as an Economist.

d. One who practises or advocates economism.

1949 I. DEUTSCHER *Stalin* ii. 31 The 'Economists' wanted to confine their activities to supporting workers' claims for higher wages and better conditions of work, without bothering about politics. **1955** H. HODGKINSON *Doubletalk* 46 An Economist is one who accepts a Marxist analysis of society and believes in the inevitable rise of socialism, but maintains that 'the unaided evolution of inevitable economic changes can bring about the desired revolution without theoretical guidance'.

economization (ɪˌkɒnəmɪˈzeɪʃən). [f. next + -ATION.] The action or process of economizing (force, material, etc.).

1866 *Even. Standard* 13 July 3 The economisation of the elements of electricity. **1885** *Manch. Exam.* 26 May 4/5 A great economisation of the commercial processes.

economize (ɪˈkɒnəmaɪz), *v.* [f. Gr. οἰκονόμ-ος (see ECONOMY) + -IZE.]

†1. *intr.* To act as the governor of a household.

1648 MILTON *Tenure Kings* (1650) 41 The power.. to .. œconomize in the Land which God hath given them, as Masters of Families in their Houses.

†2. *trans.* To arrange, constitute, organize. *Obs.*

1691 BEVERLEY *Thous. Years Kingd. Christ* 12 So shall the Divine Person.. Oeconomize.. the Lustre of its Glory. *Ibid.* 18 The Throne of God.. is so Oeconomiz'd as to be distinct.

3. To use sparingly; to effect a saving in.

1820 W. IRVING *Sketch Bk.* I. 122 He is calculating how he shall economize time. **1847** EMERSON *Repr. Men* vi. *Napol.* Wks. (Bohn) I. 371 He never economized his ammunition but.. rained a torrent of iron.. to annihilate all defence.

b. To procure the funds for anything by economy or saving. Somewhat *rare.*

1849–50 ALISON *Hist. Europe* I. iii. §82. 341 Her.. charities.. were economised from her own personal revenue.

4. *intr.* To practise economy; to spend money more sparingly than before.

1790 BURKE *Fr. Rev.* Wks. V. 219 Œconomising on principles of justice and mercy. **1843** MRS. CARLYLE *Lett.* xl. (1883) I. 217 Light is one of the things I do not like to economise in. **1845** MCCULLOCH *Taxation* I. iii. (1852) 95 When wages fall.. the poor.. are obliged to economise.

5. *trans.* To turn to account, turn to the best account; to apply to industrial purposes.

1832 HT. MARTINEAU *Life in Wilds* ix. 117 It must be for man's advantage to economize this power. **1857** RUSKIN *Pol. Econ. Art* i. (1868) 6 How this labour may.. be.. economized, so as to produce the richest results. **1863** A. RAMSAY *Phys. Geol.* (1878) 606 Who knows.. what motive powers may.. be economised other than those that result from the direct application of heat. **1872** YEATS *Techn. Hist. Comm.* 366 [Machinery's] object is to economise force supplied from without.

Hence eˈconomized *ppl. a.*

1875 WHITNEY *Life Lang.* vi. 106 These are already economized alterations of something still more primitive.

economizer (ɪˈkɒnəˌmaɪzə(r)). [f. prec. + -ER[1].] One who or that which economizes.

1. One who makes money go a long way; one who effects saving in expenditure.

1840 DICKENS *Old C. Shop* (1867) 281 Sarah is as good an economiser as any going. **1886** *Pall Mall Budget* 7 Jan. 4/2 He was a most rigid economizer who spent a halfpenny in tar, but when the ship foundered his economy was not much appreciated even by himself.

2. One who practises 'economy of truth'.

1874 MORLEY *Compromise* (1886) 86 The modern economiser keeps back his opinions or dissembles the grounds of them.

3. *Mech.* An appliance of any kind intended to effect a saving, *esp.* of heat or fuel. Also *attrib.*

18.. *Chambers' Encycl.* s.v. *Caloric Engine*, [Economy of fuel] is effected by a 'regenerator,' or more properly, 'economizer'. **1884** *Health Exhib. Catal.* 64/2 Fire Economiser for ordinary grates. **1885** *Manch. Exam.* 3 Jan. 85/1 A boiler in the economiser house exploded.

economizing (ɪˈkɒnəˌmaɪzɪŋ), *vbl. sb.* [f. as prec. + -ING[1].] The action or process: a. of turning to account for industrial purposes; b. of using with reserve and to the best effect.

1879 *Cassell's Techn. Educ.* IV. 214/2 The appliances for the economising of water. **1881** *Athenæum* 17 Sept. 364/2 Work, which a slight economizing of his boundless materials might.. expedite.

economy (ɪˈkɒnəmɪ, ɛ-). Forms: 6 econ-, yconomie, 7 œconomie, (7, 8 æconomy), 7–9 œconomy, 7– economy. [ad. L. *œconomia*, ad. Gr. οἰκονομία, f. οἰκονόμος one who manages a household (usu. *spec.* a steward), f. οἶκο-ς house + -νόμος, f. νέμειν to manage, control. The Gr. οἰκονόμος was adopted in classical Lat. as *œconomus*, but seems to have been re-introduced into med.L. from contemporary Gr. (in an ecclesiastical sense) with the phonetic spelling *yconomus*, whence the early Fr. and Eng. *yconomie* as forms of this word.

In Christian Latin the accepted transl. of οἰκονομία was *dispensatio* (cf. L. *dispensator* = Gr. οἰκονόμος steward); hence in certain *Theol.* senses *economy* and *dispensation* are used convertibly.]

I. Management of a house; management generally.

†**1. a.** The art or science of managing a household, *esp.* with regard to household expenses. *Obs.* exc. in phrase ***domestic economy***.

c **1530** *Pol. Rel. & L. Poems* (1866) 29 The Doctrynal Princyplis and Proverbys Yconomie, or Howsolde keepyng. [**1580** North *Plutarch* 303 A part whereof is Oeconomia, commonly called House-rule.] **1673** Marvell *Reh. Transp.* II. 255 You have contrary to.. good œconomy made a snow-house in your upper Roome.

b. The manner in which a household, or a person's private expenditure, is ordered. *arch.*

1710 Steele *Tatler* No. 50 ¶3 His Equipage and Oeconomy had something in them.. sumptuous. *a* **1723** Mrs. Centlivre *Artifice* iv. (D.) He ought to be very rich, whose œconomy is so profuse. **1727** Pope *Th. Var. Subj.* in *Swift's Wks.* 1755 II. i. 229 Three great ministers, who could exactly compute.. the accompts of a kingdom, but were wholly ignorant of their own œconomy. **1788** Priestley *Lect. Hist.* v. xlix. 372 Impertinence.. to watch over the œconomy of private people. **1825–45** Carlyle *Schiller* ii. (ed. 2) 70 If you could find me any person that would undertake my small economy.

†**c.** *concr.* A society ordered after the manner of a family. *Obs.*

1751 Wesley *Wks.* (1872) II. 249 At Holbeck we.. had an economy of young men.

†**d.** The rules which control a person's mode of living; regimen, diet. *Obs. rare.*

1735 Barber in *Swift's Lett.* (1768) IV. 85 The œconomy you are under must necessarily preserve your life many years.

2. a. In a wider sense: The administration of the concerns and resources of any community or establishment with a view to orderly conduct and productiveness; the art or science of such administration. Frequently specialized by the use of adjectives, as *Domestic*, *Naval*, *Rural*, etc. So †***charitable economy*** [in Fr. *économie charitable*]: the management of charitable institutions.

1651 Hobbes *Leviath.* ii. xxiii. 124 Special Administration.. at home, for the Oeconomy of a Common-wealth. **1691** T. H[ale], *Acc. New Invent.* 117 Of Naval Oeconomy or Husbandry. **1730** A. Gordon *Maffei's Amphith.* 344 'Twould have been bad Oeconomy to make such an use of them [Cushions]. **1772** Pennant *Tours Scotl.* (1774) 194 Rural æconomy is but at a low ebb here. **1778** Robertson *Hist. Amer.* I. iv. 320 The functions in domestic œconomy are many, which fall to the share of women. **1801** Mrs. Trimmer (*title*), Oeconomy of Charity, or an address to Ladies adapted to the present state of charitable institutions. **1863** P. Barry (*title*), Dockyard Economy and Naval Power. **1866** Rogers *Agric. & Prices* I. xix. 455 Articles.. employed in the.. economy of agricultural operations.

b. *esp.* Management of money, or of the finances.

1741 Betterton in Oldys *Eng. Stage* II. 7 It was not the only erroneous Instance of his Oeconomy. **1796** Burke *Let. Noble Ld.* Wks. VIII. 23 A system of œconomy which would make a random expence.. not easily practicable.

3. political economy [transl. Fr. *économie politique*]: originally the art or practical science of managing the resources of a nation so as to increase its material prosperity; in more recent use, the theoretical science dealing with the laws that regulate the production and distribution of wealth.

1767 Sir J. Stewart (*title*), An Inquiry into the Principles of Political Economy. **1776** Adam Smith *W.N.* iv. Introd. II. 3 Political œconomy.. proposes two distinct objects.. to provide a plentiful revenue or subsistence for the people.. and.. to supply the state.. with a revenue sufficient for the publick services. **1825** McCulloch *Pol. Econ.* i. §1. 1 Political Economy is the science of the laws which regulate the production, distribution, and consumption of those articles or products which have exchangeable value, and are either necessary, useful, or agreeable to man. *a* **1830** Sir J. Sinclair *Corr.* (1831) II. 125 The French have long distinguished themselves by their knowledge of political economy. **1868** Rogers *Pol. Econ.* i. (ed. 3) 2 The subject of a treatise on political economy is, the services which men render to each other; but those services only on which a price can be put.

4. Careful management of resources, so as to make them go as far as possible.

a. with reference to money and material wealth: Frugality, thrift, saving. Sometimes euphemistically for: Parsimony, niggardliness.

1670 Cotton *Espernon* i. ii. 62 Men have.. been very liberal in their censure of the Duke's Oeconomy. *a* **1674** Clarendon *Hist. Reb.* x. (1704) III. 88 Nor was this Oeconomy well liked even in France. **1762–71** H. Walpole *Vertue's Anecd. Paint.* (1786) I. 162 The luxury of Britain did not teach him [Holbein] more oeconomy than he had practised in his own country. **1770** Jas. Harris in *Priv. Lett. 1st Ld. Malmesbury* I. 196 There can be no independence without economy. **1863** Froude *Hist. Eng.* VII. 5 The economy with which [Q.] Mary had commenced her reign had been sacrificed to superstition.

b. *concr.* An instance or a means of saving or thrift; a saving.

1788 T. Jefferson *Writ.* (1859) II. 389 The suppression of the packets is one of the economies in contemplation. **1868** Rogers *Pol. Econ.* xiii. (1876) 10 Improved breeds of horses, cattle.. are really economies. **1876** *Times* 4 Oct., [The Railway Company] has only been saved from utter bankruptcy by economies.

c. with reference to immaterial things, as time, personal ability, labour, etc.

1862 Darwin *Fertil. Orchids* vi. 275 The economy shown by nature in her resources is striking. **1875** Hamerton *Intell. Life* iii. vii. 107 To read a language that has been very imperfectly mastered is felt to be a bad economy of time.

II. 5. *Theol.* **a.** The method of the divine government of the world, or of a specific department or portion of that government.

1660 Jer. Taylor *Worthy Commun.* i. §1. 28 All this is the method and Oeconomy of heaven. **1725** tr. *Dupin's Eccl. Hist.* I. v. 127 The whole Oeconomy of our Salvation might be the better represented. **1814** Chalmers *Evid. Chr. Revel.* i. 15 That particular scheme of the divine economy which is revealed to us in the New Testament. **1879** Farrar *St. Paul* II. 226 The true theological position of the Law—its true position, that is, in the Divine œconomy of salvation.

b. *esp.* A 'dispensation', a method or system of the divine government suited to the needs of a particular nation or period of time, as the ***Mosaic, Jewish, Christian economy***.

1664 H. More *Myst. Iniq.* 516 Apol., Tending to the greater ornament and completeness of the Christian Oeconomy. **1698** Norris *Pract. Disc.* (1707) IV. 256 The Oeconomy of Faith should go before that of Vision. **1710** Prideaux *Orig. Tithes* ii. 58 The Mosaical Oeconomy. **1841** Myers *Cath. Th.* iii. §4. 13 This Egyptian influence in the Mosaic Economy has been largely over-rated. **1862** Goulburn *Pers. Relig.* 97 The Economy of Grace. **1871** Macduff *Mem. Patmos* viii. 100 The twofold song descriptive of both economies.

III. 6. a. *Theol.* [after Gr. οἰκονομία in the late sense 'politic administration'.] The judicious handling of doctrine, *i.e.* the presentation of it in such a manner as to suit the needs or to conciliate the prejudices of the persons addressed. **b.** This sense has been (by misapprehension or word-play) often treated as an application of 4. Hence the phrase ***economy of truth*** (as if 'cautious or sparing use').

Newman's history of the Arians (1833) contained a section on the use of 'the Economy' by the Fathers. The word was eagerly caught up by popular writers and used contemptuously, as if it were a euphemistic name for dishonest evasion; in this sense it is still freq. met with. The sense of οἰκονομία to which Newman referred occurs freq. in Chrysostom and Gregory Nazianzen; *e.g.* the former, commenting on the words 'vain deceit' (*Col.* ii. 8) says that some deceits are good, *e.g.* that practised by Jacob, which was οὐκ ἀπάτη ἀλλ' οἰκονομία not a fraud but an 'economy'. The ecclesiastical use of the word occurs in Fr. writers of the 17th and 18th c., and was ridiculed by Voltaire; hence the appearance of b so early as 1796. See also economic *a.* 5.

a. **1833** J. H. Newman *Arians* i. §3 (1876) 65 The Economy is certainly sanctioned by St. Paul in his own conduct. To the Jews he became as a Jew, etc. **1841** —— *Tracts for Times* xc. (ed. 4) 83 What was an economy in the reformers, is a protection to us. **1885** E. S. Ffoulkes *Prim. Consecration* iv. 93 Whether S. Cyril pushed his economy—or, as it would now be called, his diplomacy—too far.

b. **1796** Burke *Regic. Peace* i. Wks. VIII. 208 Falsehood and delusion are allowed in no case whatever. But.. there is an œconomy of truth.. a sort of temperance, by which a man speaks truth with reason that he may continue to speak it the longer. *Mod.* 'I do not impute falsehood to the Government, but I think there has been considerable economy of truth'.

IV. Organization, like that of a household.

7. The structure, arrangement, or proportion of parts, of any product of human design.

†**a.** *spec.* of a poem, play, etc. [Immediately from Gr. and Lat.] *Obs.*

1671 Milton *Samson* Introd., Such œconomy or disposition of the fable as may stand best with.. decorum. **1697** Dryden *Virg. Past.* Pref. (1721) I. 91 In this.. Œconomy of a Poem, Virgil much excells Theocritus.

b. *gen.*

1734 Watts *Reliq. Juv.* (1789) 217 An odd sort of elegance in the oeconomy of her table. **1730** A. Gordon *Maffei's Amphith.* 311 The Crossings of Stairs.. would confound the Oeconomy of the Building. **1751** Smollett *Per. Pic.* (1779) II. xxxvii. 21 The œconomy of the table was recomposed. **1756** Colman & Thornton *Connoisseur* No. 103 That the oeconomy of the beaufait.. may not be disarranged.

8. In wider sense: The organization, internal constitution, apportionment of functions, of any complex unity.

†**a.** of the Trinity. *Obs.*

1592 tr. *Junius on Rev.* iv. 2 According to the œconomie or dispensation thereof [of the divine essence]. **1660** Jer. Taylor *Worthy Commun.* i. §3. 46 For now we are to consider how his natural body enters into this œconomy and dispensation. **1720** Waterland *Eight Serm.* 268 This Order and Oeconomy, observable in the Persons of the Sacred Trinity.

b. of an individual body or mind. Sometimes *concr.* (like 'system') for the body as an organized whole.

1660 Boyle *New Exp. Phys. Mech.* (1682) 176 The whole Oeconomy of the body. *a* **1704** T. Brown *Praise of Pov.* Wks. 1730 I. 95 The whole oeconomy of their brain is corrupted. **1752** Hume *Ess. & Treat.* (1777) I. 192 With regard to the œconomy of the mind.. all vice is indeed pernicious. **1880** J. W. Legg *Bile* 193 An effort of the œconomy to eject the poison.

c. of the material creation or its subdivisions, as in phrases, ***animal, vegetable economy, economy of nature***.

1658 R. White tr. *Digby's Powd. Symp.* (1660) 53 Within the course and œconomy of nature. **1710** Shaftesb. *Charac.* ii. §1 (1737) II. i. 19 An Animal-Order or Oeconomy, according to which the Animal Affairs are regulated and dispos'd. **1794** Martyn *Rousseau's Bot.* Introd. 2 They.. had no idea.. of the vegetable oeconomy. **1813** Sir H. Davy *Agric. Chem.* v. (1814) 209 Water is absolutely necessary to the economy of vegetation. **1825** Waterton *Wand. S. Amer.* ii. ii. 174 We will retire to its forests to collect and examine the economy of its most rare and beautiful birds.

d. of human society as a whole, or of any particular community.

1643 Sir T. Browne *Relig. Med.* (1682) 16 Nor will [heads that are disposed unto schism] be ever confined unto the order or œconomy of one body. **1651** Hobbes *Govt. & Soc.* v. §2. 75 In old time there was a manner of living, and as it were a certain œconomy.. living by Rapine. **1712** *Spect.* No. 404 ¶1 In the Dispositions of Society, the civil Œconomy is formed in a chain as well as the natural. **1815** Dk. York *Let.* in Gurw. *Disp. Wellington* X. 4 Your.. attention must.. be directed to.. the interior economy of the different corps. **1879** *Cassell's Techn. Educ.* IV. 67/2 This real value in the economy of society is not disparaged.

9. economy-size, applied *attrib.*, esp. in *Advertising*, to objects which are sold in a size that is said to be economically advantageous to the customer; also ***economy-sized*** adj.; also in extended uses. orig. *U.S.*

In practice freq. but not always the largest packet, etc., in a series.

1950 R. P. Bissell *Stretch on River* xix. 185 The only trouble with the economy size tube of shaving cream is that it takes up more room in the valise than a pair of rubber boots. **1953** *Harper's Mag.* Mar. 100 [His] mother.. treats him as something between a lapel ornament, a trained marmoset, and an economy-sized male escort. **1955** *N.Y. Herald-Tribune* 12 Nov., Lou Gehrig had just hit a large economy-size home run into the right-field bleachers. *Ibid.* 1 Dec. ii. 1/5 The investigators managed to arrange 'economy sized package deals which included a little bit of everything'. **1957** Wodehouse *Over Seventy* v. 65 It was a bear. And not a small bear either. One of the large economy size. **1958** *Times Lit. Suppl.* 23 May 281/3 Another giant, economy-size book about the hard lot of Scandinavian females in the bad old days! **1962** L. Deighton *Ipcress File* vi. 36 Economy-sized cafés. **1962** *Times* 17 Oct. 13/3 'Economy' sized cars. **1966** H. Yoxall *Fashion of Life* xiv. 134 The small tube [of shaving cream] is called 'large', .. we have a medium tube called 'king size', and a large tube called 'economy size'.

10. *attrib.* or as *adj.* Designating consumer products, services, etc., which are designed to be cheaper or more efficient for the customer, as *economy car, fare*, etc.; also, that enables one to make economies.

1821 M. Wilmot *Let.* 21 Dec. (1935) 149 One of the œconomy Leghorn hats, intended to be cut in two on arriving in England. **1908** *Sears, Roebuck Catal.* 19 The Economy cream separator saves $15⁰⁰ yearly on each cow. **1944** A. Thirkell *Headmistress* xi. 237 She.. licked the so-called economy label that was to take the envelope back to its sender. **1959** *ASTA Travel News* Feb. 140 (Advt.), Full tourist savings 30% to 50% under lowest Economy Fares! **1959** *World Air Transport Statistics* iii. 38/1 Scheduled Operations.. First.. Tourist.. Economy. **1963** *Daily Tel.* 13 May 12/2 A five per cent. increase in the cost of 'economy-class' travel across the Atlantic. **1967** *Gloss. Terms Gas Industry (B.S.I.)* 93 *Economy valve*, a valve which enables hot water to be stored either in part or the whole of the storage vessel. **1970** *Times* 3 Nov. 8/3 America's domestic airlines.. are competing to see which can carry the fewest possible economy class passengers in the greatest possible comfort. **1976** *Milton Keynes Express* 28 May 49/1 (Advt.), *Peugeot 104 Saloon 4-door*, economy car in white, folding rear seat. **1984** *Which?* Jan. 19/3 E is an economy programme. Cost savings may result from reduced wash temperature.

†**eˈcontrary**, *adv. Obs. rare*$^{-1}$. [f. L. *e contrario* in same sense.] Contrariwise, vice versâ.

1512 *Act 4 Hen. VIII*, xix. §11 That no persone that ys rated for landes.. be sette or taxed for his goode and catelles moveables neythere econtrary.

†**eˈconverse**, *adv. Obs. rare*$^{-1}$. [f. L. *e converso* of same meaning.] Conversely.

1547 Boorde *Brev. Health* ccviii. 71 b, That reason may knowe the truth from the falshod and so econverse.

ecophene (ˈiːkəʊfiːn). *Ecology.* [f. *eco-* as in ecology + phen(otype + *-e*.] (See quots.)

1922 G. Turesson in *Hereditas* III. 346 The reaction-types of the ecotypes called forth by the modificatory influences of extreme habitat factors may appropriately be termed *ecophenes*. *Ibid.* 347 The term *ecophene* is proposed to cover each of the reaction-types of the ecotypes arising through the modificatory influences of the combinations of extreme habitat factors given in nature. **1949** Darlington & Mather *Elem. Genetics* 389 *Ecophene*, the range of phenotypes produced by one genotype within the limits of habitat under which it is found in nature. **1957** *Encycl. Brit.* XXI. 177/2 Ecophenes are illustrated by climatic modifications at the tree line, by shade types of plants that

normally range through a variety of light conditions, and by temperature influences on growth at different latitudes. **1968** R. DAUBENMIRE *Plant Communities* i. 33 Whether these variations represent ecotypes or ecophenes, the habitat type is the best indicator of the extent of each type of variance.

‖**écorché** (ekɔrʃe). *Painting* and *Sculpture*. [Fr., pa. pple. of *écorcher* to flay.] A subject so treated as to expose the muscular system.

1854 THACKERAY *Newcomes* lxxviii, If you will have the kindness to look by the *ecorché* there, you will see that little packet which I have left for you. **1862** *Chamber's Encycl.* III. 761/2 It is not uncommon to represent the ecorché in action, in the form of the Fighting Gladiator. **1883** J. W. MOLLETT *Illustr. Dict. Art & Archæol.* 120/2. **1891** 'L. MALET' *Wages of Sin* IV. v, Try to put the bones into this upper figure and make an *écorché* of the lower one. **1963** *Encycl. World Art* VII. 662 One of the earliest examples is ascribed to Baccio Bandinelli and, because of its peculiar dancing movement, is usually called the 'dancing *écorché*'. *fig.* **1891** HARDY *Group of Noble Dames* 85 Lifting her eyes as bidden she regarded this human remnant, this *ecorché*, a second time. But the sight was too much. **1908** —— *Dynasts* III. II. iv. 376 The contorted and attenuated écorché of the Continent appearing as in an earlier scene, but now obscure under the summer stars.

ecospecies ('iːkəʊˌspiːʃiːz). *Ecology*. [f. *eco-* as in ECOLOGY + SPECIES.] A subdivision of a species of which the individual members are interfertile.

1922 G. TURESSON in *Hereditas* III. 102 In the efforts made by the writer to arrive at an understanding of the Linnean species from an ecological point of view—of the ecospecies, as I prefer to say in the following—studies have been made of a number of plant species. *Ibid.* 344 The term ecospecies has been proposed.. to cover the Linnean species or genotype compounds as they are realised in nature. *Ibid.* 347 The Linnean species represents an ecological unit.. narrowed down to the ecological combination-limit. A genotype compound of this order is here termed an ecospecies. **1957** M. ABERCROMBIE et al. *Dict. Biol.* 76 *Ecospecies*, group of plants comprising one or more ecotypes within a coenospecies whose members can reproduce amongst themselves without loss of fertility in offspring. Approximates to conventional 'species'.

'**ecosphere.** [f. *eco-* as in ECOLOGY + SPHERE *sb.*] The region of space including planets whose conditions are not incompatible with the existence of living things.

1953 H. STRUGHOLD *Green & Red Planet* (1954) iv. 36 Only a small zone about 75 million miles wide—out of the 4,300 million that stretch between the sun and Pluto at its farthest point—provides a planetary environment well-suited to the existence of life. We might call this zone the thermal ecosphere of the sun. Other stars may have such ecospheres of their own. **1965** DOLE & ASIMOV *Planets for Man* iv. 109 To be habitable, a planet must be inside the ecosphere.

‖**écossaise.** Also 9 ecossaise. [F. *écossaise* fem. adj. 'Scotch'. Cf. SCHOTTISCHE.] **a.** (See quot.)

1863 E. PAUER *Programme* 27 Apr., A lively dance tune in 2/4 time. In older music the Ecossaise was in 3/4 slow time, and was sometimes used for the Andante.

b. A dance to such a tune.

1841 MRS. GASKELL *Let.* (1966) 43 A very fashionable waltz step came up while we were at Heidelberg the ecossaise,—and the little girls with their empty milk pails went dancing it along the road. **1954** *Grove's Dict. Mus.* (ed. 5) II. 881/2 Authorities differ about the question whether the Écossaise and the Schottisch are.. one and the same kind of dance... The modern view is that the dance has nothing to do with Scotland, but was.. originally a French dance.

ecostate (ɪ'kɒstət), *a.* [f. E- *pref.*³ + L. *costa* rib + -ATE.] (See quot.)

1866 *Treas. Bot.*, *Ecostate*, not having a central or strongly-marked rib or costa.

'**ecosystem.** *Ecology*. [f. *eco-* as in ECOLOGY + SYSTEM.] (See quots.)

1935 A. G. TANSLEY in *Ecology* XVI. 299 There is constant interchange.. within each system, not only between the organisms but between the organic and the inorganic. These *ecosystems*, as we may call them, are of the most various kinds and sizes. They form one category of the multitudinous physical systems of the universe. *Ibid.* 306 The fundamental concept appropriate to the biome considered together with all the effective inorganic factors of its environment is the *ecosystem*, which is a particular category among the physical systems that make up the universe. **1939** —— *Brit. Islands* III. x. 228 A unit of vegetation.. includes not only the plants.. but the animals habitually associated with them, and also all the physical and chemical components... Such a system may be called an *ecosystem*. **1952** P. W. RICHARDS *Tropical Rain Forest* v. 111 Certain animals.. which play an important part in the rain-forest ecosystem. **1963** *New Scientist* 28 Mar. 684/2 The unit of ecology is the ecosystem, which includes the plants and animals occurring together plus that part of their environment over which they have an influence.

ecotone ('iːkəʊtəʊn). *Ecology*. [f. *eco-* as in ECOLOGY + Gr. τόν-ος tension, TONE.] A transitional area between two ecological communities. Hence '**ecotonal** *a.*

1904 F. E. CLEMENTS in *Bot. Surv. Nebraska* VII. 153 Zonation in a habitat... The line that connects the points of accumulated or abrupt change in the symmetry is a stress line or *ecotone*... Ecotones are well marked between formations, particularly where the medium changes: they are less distinct within formations. It is obvious that an ecotone separates two different series of zones in the one case, and merely two distinct zones in the other. **1926** TANSLEY & CHIPP *Study of Vegetation* iv. 53 Transitional belts between well-marked communities are called *ecotones* or 'tension belts'. **1950** *Jrnl. Ecology* XXXVIII. 70 Apart from interdigitation of typical stands, ecotonal communities are to be found. **1952** P. W. RICHARDS *Tropical Rain Forest* xv. 338 Within the Closed forest there is manifestly a transition or ecotone from the.. evergreen forests of the wettest areas to the.. deciduous forests bordering the savannas. **1967** *Oceanogr. & Marine Biol.* V. xi. 265 Mixing along the boundaries of two water masses may result in nature in an increase of the diversity of frontier or ecotone populations.

ecotype ('iːkəʊtaɪp). *Ecology*. [f. *eco-* as in ECOLOGY + TYPE *sb.*¹] A subdivision of an ecospecies the members of which are the product of genotypical adaptation to a particular habitat.

1922 G. TURESSON in *Hereditas* III. 112 The term *ecotype* is proposed here as ecological unit to cover the product arising as a result of the genotypical response of an ecospecies to a particular habitat. The ecotypes are then the ecological sub-units of the ecospecies. **1949** W. C. ALLEE et al. *Princ. Animal Ecol.* v. xxxiv. 674/2 The interbreeding population would indicate either a hybridization between the river and cave forms, or that the cave form is an ecotype (ecological sub-species) of the river form. **1949** *Q. Jrnl. Forestry* XLIII. 88 The new concept of ecotypes—races of species adapted to various environments—which the ecologists claim to distinguish although taxonomists cannot discern any constant structural differences between them. **1959** E. P. ODUM *Fund. Ecol.* (ed. 2) I. iv. 144 If marked ecotypes exist, the occurrence of the same series of taxa in different localities does not necessarily mean that the same conditions exist.

‖**ecoute** (ekut). *Mil.* [F. *écoute* (f. *écouter* to listen) an excavation, in which a miner can listen for the working of the enemy's miners.] (See quot.)

1815 HUTTON *Phil. & Math. Dict.* I. 282 *Catacoustics*,.. are écoutes or small galleries.. in front of the glacis of a fortified place, all of which communicate with a gallery that is carried parallel to the covert-way.

‖'**ecphasis.** [Gr. ἔκφασις declaration, f. stem either of ἐκφαίνειν to show forth, or of ἐκφάναι to tell forth. Cf. ECPHRASIS.] (See quot.)

1706 PHILLIPS, *Ecphasis* (in Rhet.) a plain declaration or interpretation of a thing. **1775** in ASH; and in mod. Dicts.

‖**ecphonema** (ɛkfəʊ'niːmə). *Rhet.* [Gr. ἐκφώνημα, f. ἐκφωνέ-ειν to cry out.] (See quot.)

1736–1800 BAILEY, *Ecphonema*, a rhetorical figure, a breaking out of the voice, with some interjectional particle. **1775** in ASH; and in mod. Dicts.

‖**eccpho'nesis.** *Rhet.* Also 6 **ecphonisis.** [Gr. ἐκφώνησις, f. as prec.] Exclamation, an exclamatory phrase.

1589 PUTTENHAM *Eng. Poesie* (Arb.) 221 Ecphonisis, the figure of exclamation.. it vtters our minde by all such words as do shew any extreme passion. **1642** JOHN EATON *Honeycombe of free Justif.* 318 The Ecphonesis or acclamation of Chrysostome upon this plea. **1711** J. GREENWOOD *Eng. Gram.* 226 Ecphonesis, Admiration or Wonder and Exclamation.. is marked thus (!). **1715** in KERSEY. **1721–1800** in BAILEY. **1775** in ASH; and in mod. Dicts.

‖**ecphora** ('ɛkfərə). *Archit.* [Gr. ἐκφορά, f. ἐκφέρειν, f. ἐκ out + φέρειν to bear.] (See quot.)

1715 KERSEY, *Ecphora*, a jutting or bearing out in a building. **1736** in BAILEY. **1775** in ASH. **1842–76** GWILT *Archit.* Gloss, *Ecphora*, a word used by Vitruvius to signify the projecture of a member or moulding of a column.

ecphore ('ɛkfɔə(r)), *v.* *Psychol.* Also **ek-**. [ad. G. *ekphorieren* (R. Semon *Die Mneme* (ed. 3, 1912) iii. 93), f. Gr. ἐκφορεῖν, f. ἔκφορος (to be) made known (cf. ἐκφέρειν to carry or bring forth, produce, disclose).] *trans.* To evoke or revive (an emotion, a memory, or the like) by means of a stimulus. So **ecphoric** (ɛk'fɒrɪk) *a.*, pertaining to or characterized by ecphory; whence **ec'phorically** *adv.* Also **ecphorize** ('ɛkfəraɪz) *v.*; whence '**ecphorizable** *a.*; **ecphory** ('ɛkfərɪ) [ad. G. *ekphorie* (R. Semon *ibid.* 25)], the evocation of a disposition from a latent to a manifest state.

1917 *Brit. Jrnl. Psychol.* June 429 An 'ekphored' feeling is always a new state of feeling and never the memory image of a previous one. *Ibid.* 453 If we look at.. a red rose and perceive it, and after a little while ekphore its memory-image, we note immediately how unlike.. this memory-image is to the original perception. *Ibid.* 456 The ekphory of the memory-image of a pain. **1921** L. SIMON tr. *Semon's Mneme* 39 Groups of influences may act ecphorically on an engram. *Ibid.* 73 The diurnal periodic leaf movements of plants are ecphorised chronogeneously for some time after the cessation of the light-stimulus that normally liberates them. *Ibid.* 138 The ecphory of an engram. *Ibid.*, The ecphoric factor.. consists of the partial or entire repetition of that energetic condition which formerly acted engraphically. **1921** B. RUSSELL *Analysis of Mind* iv. 84 The second mnemic principle, or 'Law of Ekphory'. *Ibid.*, When two stimuli occur together, one of them, occurring afterwards, may call out the reaction for the other also. We call this an 'ekphoric influence', and stimuli having this character are called 'ekphoric stimuli'. **1923** B. DUFFY tr. *Semon's Mnemic Psychol.* 155 An engram which, when evoked into life (*ecphorized*), will produce a mnemic sensation in consciousness. *Ibid.* 314 Homophonously ecphorizable engrams. **1925** C. FOX *Educat. Psychol.* 10 The process by which future stimuli touch off the engrams is known as ecphory. *Ibid.*, The partial recurrence of the excitation-complex which left behind it a simultaneous engram-complex acts ecphorically on the latter. **1937** G. W. ALLPORT *Personality* (1946) v. xix. 525 One variation of the associational theory is the doctrine of redintegration, or as it is sometimes called, *ecphory*. **1958** H. B. & A. C. ENGLISH *Dict. Psychol. Terms* 169 Ecphory, the activation of a memory trace, or engram.

†**ec'phractic,** *a.* *Med. Obs.* [ad. late Gr. ἐκφρακτικός, f. ἐκφράσσειν to remove obstructions.] Adapted to clear away obstructions; aperient, deobstruent. Also as quasi-*sb.* Hence †**ec'phractical** *a.*, of same meaning.

1657 TOMLINSON *Renou's Disp.* 30 Must be dissolved by a ..cutting Ecphracticke. *Ibid.* 124 Ecphractical, as it were purging fractures. **1665** G. HARVEY *Advice agst. Plague* 16 It is of great concernment.. to procure the bloud and spirits a free course.. by sutable purges and Ecphractick Medicines. **1775** ASH, *Ecphractic*, attenuating, dissolving tough humours. **1883** *Syd. Soc. Lex.*, *Ecphractic*, aperient, also the same as deobstruent.

‖**ecphrasis** ('ɛkfrəsɪs). [Gr. ἔκφρασις, f. ἐκφράζειν, f. ἐκ out + φράζειν to speak.] (See quot.)

1715 KERSEY, *Ecphrasis* (in Rhet.) a plain declaration or interpretation of a thing. **1814** *Edin. Rev.* XXIV. 65 The same florid effeminacies of style.. in.. an ecphrasis of Libanius, are harmless.

‖**ecraseur** (ekrazœr). *Surg.* [F. *écraseur* crusher, f. *écraser* to crush.] A blunt chain-saw, tightened by a screw or by a rack and pinion, for removing piles, polypi, etc. (*Syd. Soc. Lex.*)

1859 *Dubl. Hosp. Gaz.* 15 Jan., On the use of the Ecraseur in the operation for Anal Fistula.

‖**écrevisse** (ekrəvis). [Fr.] A freshwater lobster.

1854 THACKERAY *Newcomes* I. xxviii. 266 Pass me the écrévisses [*sic*], they are most succulent. **1930** E. WAUGH *Labels* viii. 188 There were heaps of rather dangerous-looking lobsters and *écrevisses*. **1966** *Punch* 14 Sept. 384/2 We import frozen fragments of dogfish tail and call them *scampi*, while not bothering to gather the écrevisses.. in our ..chalk-streams.

†**ecrhythmous** (ɛ'krɪθməs). [f. Gr. ἔκρυθμος out of tune, f. ἐκ out + ῥυθμός rhythm; see -OUS.]

[**1715** KERSEY, *Ecrhythmus*, a Pulse that observes no Method.] **1883** *Syd. Soc. Lex.*, *Ecrhythmous*, old term applied by Galen to the pulse, and meaning irregular or unrhythmical.

‖**écrin** (ekrɛ̃). [Fr.] A casket for jewellery.

1854 THACKERAY *Newcomes* II. xxi. 203 The cigar-boxes given over to this friend, the *écrin* of diamonds to that, et cætera. **1910** S. R. CROCKETT *Dew of their Youth* xxxviii, A hoop of rubies.. was placed in a lined box of morocco leather, called an 'ecrin'.

‖**ecroulement.** [Fr.] The fall of a mass of rock, a building, etc. Used *fig.*; also *spec.* in *Geol.*

1820 H. MATTHEWS *Diary of an Invalid* (1835) 288 Napoleon has so catamaranned the foundations, that more than one écroulement has already taken place. **1839** MURCHISON *Silurian System* I. xiii. 163 The great ecroulement of rocks round Daren. *Ibid.* I. xxxii. 435, I found the phenomena to be similar to many ecroulemens of Alpine tracts.

‖**ecru** (ekry, 'eɪkruː), *a.* [F. *écru* raw, unbleached.] The name of a colour; the colour of unbleached linen. Also quasi-*sb.*

1869 *Latest News* 5 Sept. 7 White écru or maize are the shades preferred. **1884** *Pall Mall G.* 24 Sept. 9/1 The bridesmaids.. wore dresses of pink satin and écru muslin.

ec'stasiate, *v.* *rare.* [f. ECSTASY + -ATE, after F. (*s'*)*extasier*, f. *extasie*, early form of *extase* ECSTASY.]

a. *trans.* = ECSTASIZE *v.* 1. **b.** *intr.* and *refl.* To go into an ecstasy.

1823 *New Month. Mag.* VIII. 278 The singer.. may extasiate his audience. **1838** J. PARDOE *River & Desert* I. 10 He extasiated on the Emperor, and shrugged his shoulders at all other crowned heads. **1889** *Sat. Rev.* 7 Dec. 662/2 What we admit that we cannot sincerely extasiate ourselves before or admire is M. Huysmans's idea of style. **1923** A. HUXLEY *Antic Hay* xv. 213 The holy Teresa's quivering and ecstasiated flank. **1957** *Observer* 8 Dec. 14/3 The appearance of the Chimp Father Christmas, scattering soot, is so ecstatiating [*sic*] that [etc.].

ecstasied ('ɛkstəsɪd), *ppl. a.* [f. ECSTASY *v.* + -ED.] **a.** Exalted in contemplation. **b.** Enraptured.

1649 JER. TAYLOR *Gt. Exemp.* II. iv, Seraphims and the most ecstasied order of intelligence. **1661** K. W. *Conf. Charac.* (1860) To Rdr. 9 Those.. whose extasied souls ravished with joy of his condigne punishment, by excesse of exalted spirits did themselves injuries. **1787** tr. *Klopstock's Messiah* III. 115 Thus ecstasied, sang the youthful spirits of Heaven.

‖**ecstasis** ('ɛkstəsɪs). Also 7 **extasis.** [mod.L., a. Gr. ἔκστασις; see ECSTASY.]

= ECSTASY *sb.* 2, 3.

1621 BURTON *Anat. Mel.* II. v. I. v. (1651) 392 Another.. like in effect to Opium, Which puts them.. into a kind of Extasis. **1656** RIDGLEY *Pract. Physick* 109 Ecstasis is either true, as when the mind is drawn away to contemplate heavenly things, or etc. **1874** H. REYNOLDS *John Bapt.* iii. §3. 201 Vision, dream, trance, ecstasis, were common incidents in the history of the Hebrew prophets.

ecstasize (ˈɛkstəsaɪz), *v.* [f. ECSTAS-Y + -IZE. Cf. ECSTASY *v.*]

1. *trans.* To throw into an ecstasy or transport of rapturous feeling; to give pleasurable excitement to. Also *refl.*

1835 *New Month. Mag.* XLV. 469 The auditors were delighted, enraptured, ecstacized. **1853** MISS SHEPPARD *Ch. Auchester* I. 54, I should have ecstasised myself ill. **1879** G. MACDONALD *Sir Gibbie* III. xvi. 251 Read passages from Byron..ecstasizing the lawyer's lady.

2. *intr.* To 'go into ecstasies'.

1854 T. GWYNNE *Nanette* (1864) 18 The merry old woman was ecstasizing over the size and beauty of the..fish.

ecstasy (ˈɛkstəsɪ). Forms: 4–5 exstasie, -cye, 6–9 extasie, -y, ecstacy, exstacy, -ie, 6–8 exstasy, 6 extascie, 7 extase, ecs-, estasie, 8, 9 ectasy, ecstasie, 7–9 extacy, 6– ecstasy. See also ECSTASIS. [a. OF. *extasie*, (after words in *-sie*, ad. L. *-sia*) f. med.L. *extasis*, a. Gr. ἔκστασις, f. ἐκστα- stem of ἐξιστάναι to put out of place (in phrase ἐξιστάναι φρενῶν 'to drive a person out of his wits'), f. ἐκ out + ἱστάναι to place. The mod. Eng. spelling shows direct recourse to Gr. The Fr. *extase* is ad. med.L. or Gr.

The classical senses of ἔκστασις are 'insanity' and 'bewilderment'; but in late Gr. the etymological meaning received another application, viz., 'withdrawal of the soul from the body, mystic or prophetic trance'; hence in later medical writers the word is used for trance, etc., generally. Both the classical and post-classical senses came into the mod. langs., and in the present fig. uses they seem to be blended.]

1. The state of being 'beside oneself', thrown into a frenzy or a stupor, with anxiety, astonishment, fear, or passion.

1382 WYCLIF *Acts* iii. 10 Thei weren fulfillid with wondryng, and exstasie, that is, leesyng of mynde of resoun and lettyng of tunge. ?*a* **1400** *Chester Pl.* II. (1847) 113 I knowe.. That you be in greate exstacye. **1592** MARLOWE *Jew Malta* I. ii. 217 Our words will but increase his ecstasy. **1605** SHAKS. *Macb.* III. ii. 19 To lye In restlesse extasie. **1634** SIR T. HERBERT *Trav.* 201 With a great and sudden Army he entered..In which extasie the English Factours fled to Bantam. **1834** DISRAELI *Rev. Epick* I. ii, The crouching beasts Cling to the earth in pallid ecstasy.

2. *Pathol.* † a. By early writers applied vaguely, or with conflicting attempts at precise definition, to all morbid states characterized by unconsciousness, as swoon, trance, catalepsy, etc.

1598 MARSTON *Pygmal.* v. 124 Beames..shoote from out the fairenes of her eye: At which he stands as in an extasie. **1600** HOLLAND *Livy* XLIIII. xv. 179 The principall person of the embassage..fell downe flat before them in a swowne and extasie. **1604** SHAKS. *Oth.* IV. i. 80, I..layd good scuses vpon your extasie [*Stage direction to line* 40: Falls into a trance]. **1647** CLARENDON *Hist. Reb.* III. (1702) I. 160 The Ministers of the State..like men in an Extasy..had no Speech or Motion.

b. In modern scientific use. (See quot.)

1866 A. FLINT *Princ. Med.* (1880) 840 Ecstasy. In this condition, the mind, absorbed in a dominant idea, becomes insensible to surrounding objects. **1882** QUAIN *Dict. Med.*, s.v., The term ecstasy has been applied to certain morbid states of the nervous system, in which the attention is occupied exclusively by one idea, and the cerebral control is in part withdrawn from the lower cerebral and certain reflex functions. These latter centres may be in a condition of inertia, or of insubordinate activity, presenting various disordered phenomena, for the most part motor.

3. a. Used by mystical writers as the technical name for the state of rapture in which the body was supposed to become incapable of sensation, while the soul was engaged in the contemplation of divine things. Now only *Hist.* or *allusive*.

a **1652** J. SMITH *Sel. Disc.* iv. 107 In such sober kind of ecstacies did Plotinus find his own soul separated from his body. **1656** H. MORE *Antid. Ath.* III. ix. (1712) 171 The Emigration of humane Souls from the bodie by Ecstasy. **1690** LOCKE *Hum. Und.* II. xix. (1695) 119 Whether that which we call Extasie, be not dreaming with the Eyes open, I leave to be examined. **1696** AUBREY *Misc.* (1721) 181/2 Things seen in an Extacy are more certain than those we behold in dreams. **1842** EMERSON *Transcend.* Wks. 1875 II. 282 He [the Transcendentalist] believes in inspiration and in ecstasy. **1856** R. VAUGHAN *Mystics* (1860) I. III. ii. 65 Ecstasy..is the liberation of your mind from its finite consciousness. **1879** LEFEVRE *Philos.* i. 29 The Chaldæans and the Semites let loose on the West these wanton rites, the intoxication of the senses, and by a natural transposition, mystic ecstasy.

b. The state of trance supposed to be a concomitant of prophetic inspiration; hence, Poetic frenzy or rapture. Now with some notion of 4.

1670 MILTON *Hist. Eng.* II. Wks. (1851) 59 Certaine women in a kind of ecstasie foretold of calamities to come. **1682** BURNET *Rights Princes* iv. 125 Eucherius, Bishop of Orleans..being in an Extasy, saw him in Hell. **1751** GRAY *Elegy* xii, Hands..waked to ecstasy the living lyre. **1755** —— *Progr. Poesy* (R.), He that rode sublime Upon the seraph wings of ecstacy. **1813** SCOTT *Trierm.* III. xxxv, He leant upon a harp, in mood Of minstrel ecstasy.

4. An exalted state of feeling which engrosses the mind to the exclusion of thought; rapture, transport. Now chiefly, Intense or rapturous delight: the expressions ***ecstasy of woe, sorrow, despair***, etc., still occur, but are usually felt as *transferred*. Phrase, *to be in, dissolve* (trans. and intr.), ***be thrown into ecstasies***, etc.

1526 *Pilgr. Perf.* (W. de W. 1531) 162 After they come downe agayn to themselfe from suche excessyue eleuacyon or extasy. **1583** STUBBES *Anat. Abus.* (1877) Ep. Ded. 6 In extasie of despaire. **1601** WEEVER *Mirr. Mart.* D iv b, In a sorrow-sighing extasie, Henry tooke leaue. **1620** MELTON *Astrolog.* 4 This extasie of my admiration was broken off by the occasion of a noyse. **1632** MILTON *Il Penser.* 165 As may with sweetness, through mine ear, Dissolve me into ecstasies. *a* **1704** T. BROWN *Pleas. Love* Wks. 1730 I. 112 In exstasies I wou'd dissolving lie. **1723** DE FOE *Col. Jack* (1840) 26 Boyish tricks that I played in the ecstacy of my joy. **1820** SCOTT *Monast.* v, The ecstasy of the monk's terror. **1831** MACAULAY *Moore's Byron, Ess.* (1854) I. 165 What somebody calls the 'ecstasy of woe'. **1848** —— *Hist. Eng.* I. 627 The crowd was wrought up to such an ecstasy of rage that, etc. **1866** GEO. ELIOT *F. Holt* (1868) 19 There had been no ecstasy, no gladness even. **1879** M. ARNOLD *Fr. Critic on Milton* Ess. 242 When he hears it he is in ecstasies.

b. An outburst, a tumultuous utterance (of feeling, etc.) *Obs.*

1695 LD. PRESTON *Boeth.* I. 32 The Fury and Extasies of a giddy and passionate Multitude. **1725** POPE *Odyss.* IV. 1013 Shrill extasies of joy declare The fav'ring goddess present to the pray'r.

5. *Comb.*

1850 MRS. BROWNING *Poems* II. 169 A poet! know him by The ecstasy-dilated eye.

'ecstasy, *v.* [f. the sb. Cf. ECSTASIZE *v.*]

† 1. *trans.* To throw into a state of frenzy or stupor. Only in *pass. Obs.*

1627 FELTHAM *Resolves* II. i. Wks. (1677) 159 They us'd to be so extasi'd..as..to tear their garments. **1646** G. DANIEL *Poems* Wks. (1878) I. 12 My Blood was Corral, and my Breath was Ice, Extasied from all Sence, to thinke, etc. **1670** *Conclave wherein Clem. VIII elected Pope* 2 They were extasied with distractions.

† 2. *intr.* To behave as in an ecstasy. *Obs.*

1636 W. DENNY *in Ann. Dubrensia* (1877) 15 With seeming seeing, yet not seeing eyes..he extasies.

3. *trans.* To raise to a high state of feeling; to fill with transport; now *esp.* to delight intensely, enrapture. Chiefly in *pass.*; see ECSTASIED.

1624 HEYWOOD *Captives* v. i. in Bullen *O. Pl.* IV, Thou with these woordes hast extasyde my sowle. **1631** —— *Fair M. of West* I. II. i. Wks. 1874 II. 281, I cannot but wonder why any fortune should make a man ecstasied. **1660** *Character Italy* 89 She would extasy a foreiner with the sight of her stately fabricks. **1864** NEALE *Seaton. Poems* 251 Breathless with haste and ecstasied with joy. **1874** T. HARDY *Madding Crowd* II. xx. 232 The crowd was again ecstasied.

ecstatic (ɛkˈstætɪk), *a.* and *sb.* [ad. Gr. ἐκστατικός, f. stem ἐκστα-. See ECSTASY *sb.* and -IC.]

A. *adj.*

1. Of the nature of trance, catalepsy, mystical absorption, stupor, or frenzy (see ECSTASY *sb.* 1, 2, 3); accompanied by or producing these conditions. Of persons: Subject to experiences of this kind.

c **1630** MILTON *Passion* 42 There doth my soul..sit In pensive trance..and ecstatic fit. **1697** C. LESLIE *Snake in Grass* (ed. 2) 286 The Quakers..during these Extatick years ..were not in a Solid Condition. **1718** POPE *Eloisa* 339 In trance extatic may thy pangs be drowned. **1814** SCOTT *Ld. of Isles* II. xxx, Convulsions of extatic trance. **1821** JOANNA BAILLIE *Metr. Leg., Colum.* xxvii. 27 The banded Priest's ecstatic art. **1856** R. VAUGHAN *Mystics* (1860) I. 62 In the ecstatic state, individuality, memory, time, space..all vanish.

2. Of the nature of ecstasy or exalted feeling; characterized by, or producing intense emotion (now chiefly pleasurable emotion). Of persons: Subject to rapturous emotion. (See ECSTASY *sb.* 4.)

1664 H. MORE *Apology* 503 Carried quite away in an Ecstatick fit of Love and Joy and transporting Admiration. **1749** FIELDING *Tom Jones* XVIII. xi, Mrs. Miller..burst forth into the most ecstatic thanksgivings to Heaven. **1762** FALCONER *Shipwr.* I. 260 He quivers in extatic pain. **1813** H. & J. SMITH *Horace in Lond.* 42 Thy Newgate thefts impart ecstatic pleasure. **1870** DISRAELI *Lothair* vii. 24 She had thrown herself in ecstatic idolatry at the feet of the hero of Caprera. **1878** TAIT & STEWART *Unseen Univ.* i. §27. 45 Minds of a visionary and ecstatic nature.

3. *absol.* quasi-*sb. rare.*

1748 RICHARDSON *Clarissa* (1811) III. 25 The man indeed at times is all upon the ecstatic.

B. *sb.* 1. One who is subject to fits of ecstasy (see ECSTASY *sb.* 2, 3).

1659 GAUDEN *Tears of Ch.* 201 (D.) Old Hereticks and idle Ecstaticks. **1879** BARING-GOULD *Germany* II. 190 A swarm of..ecstatics..spread over the country. **18..** PROCTOR in *Cycl. Sc.* I. 433 The childhood and youth of an ecstatic.

2. *pl.* Sarcastically used for: Utterances in a state of ecstasy or transport; transports.

1819 BYRON *Juan* III. xi, Dante's more abstruse ecstatics Meant to personify the mathematics. **1865** *Sat. Rev.* 11 Nov. 616 Ecstatics again, might be spared.

‖ **ec'statica.** [mod.L., f. as prec.] (See quot.)

1879 CARPENTER *Ment. Phys.* II. xix. 689 'Ecstaticas,' i.e. females of strongly Emotional temperament, who fell into a state of profound Reverie. **1883** SALMON in *Contemp. Rev.* Oct. 521 Abbé Clocquet was able to consult an ecstatica of his acquaintance.

ec'statical, *a. arch.* [f. ECSTATIC + -AL¹.] = ECSTATIC.

1600 O. E. *Repl. Libel* I. ii. 43 Let this lunaticall or extaticall frier..forebeare to bragge. **1613** PURCHAS *Pilgr.* III. xv. 320 At the solemne Feasts of Bellona those sacred seruants wounded each other in an extaticall furie. **1612–5** BP. HALL *Contempl. N.T.* IV. xii. (1796) III. 297 This was not Abraham's or Elihu's extatical sleep. *a* **1656** BP. HALL in Spurgeon *Treas. Dav.* Ps. cxliv. 3 David's rapture, expressed in an ecstatical question of sudden wonder. *a* **1678** WOODHEAD *Holy Living* (1881) 186 Graces..which some saints of God enjoy in extatical..raptures. **1678** NORRIS *Coll. Misc.* (1699) 239 Extatical love..continually carries me out to Good without myself. **1682** *News fr. France* 5 If he thinks what he sayes will be reported in the Kings hearing ..he grows almost Ecstatical.

Hence **ec'statically** *adv.*, in an ecstatic manner; in a state of ecstasy. Also † **ec'staticalness**, ecstatic condition.

1664 H. MORE *Synopsis Proph.* 293 Spoken rapturously and ecstatically. **1667** —— *Div. Dial.* ii. §14 (1713) 131 Madness is nothing else but an Ecstaticalness of the Soul. **1809** W. IRVING *Knickerb.* (1861) 63 The Dutch discoverers ..made certain of the natives most ecstatically drunk. **1824–9** LANDOR *Imag. Conv.* (1846) II. 6, I would.. extatically shed the last drop of my blood for His Holiness. **1885** *Spectator* 8 Aug. 1047 *Blackwood*..rejoices ecstatically over the downfall of the Gladstone Government.

† **'ecstatize**, *v. Obs. rare.* [f. ECSTAT-IC + -IZE.] *trans.* To throw into an ecstasy, ecstasize.

1654 GAYTON *Fest. Notes* IV. viii. 222 He stood extatiz'd at that Picture.

ectad (ˈɛktæd), *adv. Anat.* [f. Gr. ἐκτός outside + -AD.] On the outward side of, external to. Const. *of. rare.*

1882 WILDER & GAGE *Anat. Technol.* 27 The dura (mater) may be described as *ectad* of the brain, but *entad* of the cranium. **1900** DORLAND *Med. Dict.* 220/1. **1953** *Faber Med. Dict.* 133/1 *Ectad*, on or towards the outer part.

ectal (ˈɛktəl), *a. Anat.* [f. Gr. ἐκτός outside + -AL.] External, superficial. *rare.*

1881 B. G. WILDER in *Science* (N.Y.) 19 Mar. 125/1 *Ental*, and *ectal* are here first proposed as substitutes for the more or less ambiguous words *inner* and *outer*, *interior* and *exterior* [etc.]. **1940** *Chambers's Techn. Dict.* 280/1 *Ectal layer*, a thin membrane at the extreme edge of an excipulum.

‖ **ectasia** (ɛkˈteɪzɪə). *Pathol.* [mod.L., as if a Gr. *ἐκτασία, f. as next, on the analogy of ἀναισθησία, etc.] A dilatation. A synonym of ANEURISM. (*Syd. Soc. Lex.*)

1876 tr. *Wagner's Gen. Pathol.* 599 Bronchial ectasias with intact or ulcerated mucous membrane.

‖ **'ectasis.** [mod.L., a. Gr. ἔκτασις, f. ἐκτείνειν, f. ἐκ out + τείνειν to stretch.]

1. (See quot.)

1706 PHILLIPS, *Ectasis*, Extension or Stretching out. In *Grammar* a Figure whereby a short Syllable is extended or made long. **1715** in KERSEY. **1721–1800** in BAILEY; and in mod. Dicts.

2. *Pathol.* Any morbid condition characterized by a state of dilatation. (*Syd. Soc. Lex.*)

ectene (ˈɛktɪniː). *Gr. Church.* Also **ektene.** [eccl. Gr., f. ἐκτενής extended.] A litany recited by a deacon and choir.

1850 J. M. NEALE *Holy East. Ch.* I. III. ii. 361 The Ectene for the first Sunday in Lent. **1882** *Encycl. Brit.* XIV. 707/1 A series of short intercessions resembling the Greek 'Ektene', or deacon's litany. **1916** N. F. ROBINSON *Monasticism Orthodox Ch.* 89 Then followeth the customary Ectene. **1957** *Oxf. Dict. Chr. Ch.* 437/2 *Ectene*..In the E. Church, a prayer constructed like a Litany for use in the Liturgy. It consists of short petitions said by the deacon to which choir or congregation respond with Kyrie Eleison.

ectenic (ɛkˈtɛnɪk), *a.* [f. Gr. ἐκτεν-ής strained, f. ἐκτείνειν to stretch out + -IC.] Epithet applied to the phenomena, otherwise called 'mesmeric' or hypnotic, considered as produced by a state of strained attention.

1882 *Ch. Times* 17 Feb. 104 Manifestations..psychic, biological, odylic, ectenic.

ecteron, -onic, bad forms of ECDERON, -ONIC.

1873 MIVART *Elem. Anat.* vii. 237 The common term Ecteron is applied to both structures. **1881** —— *Cat* 27 The teeth..in part are ecteronic.

ectethmoid (ɛkˈtɛθmɔɪd), *a.* [f. ECTO- + ETHMOID.] 'A term for the prefrontal of the fish, or of the lateral ethmoidal mass, with upper and middle turbinals in man' (*Syd. Soc. Lex.*).

1882 PARKER in *Trans. Linn. Soc.* II. III. 171 This is the prefrontal or ectethmoid [bone].

ecthesis (ˈɛkθəsɪs). [ad. Gr. ἔκθεσις exposition, f. ἐκτιθέναι to put forth.] An edict of the Emperor Heraclius promulgated A.D. 638, maintaining the doctrine that Christ has only one will.

1728 CHAMBERS *Cycl.* s.v., The *Ecthesis* favour'd the error of the *Monothelites.* **1850** J. MILEY *Hist. Papal States* I. I. i. 225 Meddlers in theology, attempting by *ectheses* and *types* ..to dictate what the vicars of Christ were to teach the Church. **1854, 1902** [see TYPE *sb.*¹ 5 b]. **1902** H. K. MANN *Lives of Popes* I. I. 365 Monothelism and the *Ecthesis* were condemned. **1956** J. HUSSEY tr. *Ostrogorsky's Hist. Byzantine State* ii. 97 He [*sc.* the Patriarch Sergius] relegated the single energy to the background, and now propounded the doctrine of a single will (θέλημα) in Christ. This new monothelete formula..was promulgated by the Emperor [*sc.* Heraclius] in 638 under the name of the *Ecthesis*.

‖**ecthlipsis** (ɛkθ'lɪpsɪs). *Prosody.* [mod.L., a. Gr. ἔκθλιψις, f. ἐκθλίβειν, f. ἐκ out + θλίβειν to rub, squeeze.] (See quot. 1880.)

1657 J. Smith *Myst. Rhet.* 175 Ecthlipsis..a striking out. It is a figure of Prosodia, especially when (M) with his vowel is taken away, the next word beginning with a vowel. **1678** in Phillips. **1715** in Kersey. **1880** Roby *School Lat. Gr.* §941 *Ecthlipsis*, crushing out, in verse, of a syllable ending in *m* before an ensuing vowel.

‖**ecthyma** (ɛk'θaɪmə). *Pathol.* [mod.L., a. Gr. ἔκθυμα, f. ἐκθύειν 'to break out as heat or humours' (Liddell & Scott).] 'By some it is looked upon as the same as *Impetigo*' (*Syd. Soc. Lex.*).

1834 M. Good *Study of Med.* (ed. 4) IV. 497 In Ecthyma the pustules are seldom numerous.

Hence **ec'thymatous** *a.*

1861 Bumstead *Ven. Dis.* (1879) 359 The ecthymatous form is nothing more than a chancroid.

ecto- ('ɛktəʊ), repr. Gr. ἐκτο, -stem of ἐκτός *adv.*, outside; employed as comb. form in many compounds of mod. formation, as **'ecto-blast** [Gr. βλαστός sprout], see quot.; **ecto'blastic** *a.*, of or belonging to an ectoblast; **ˌecto-cal'caneal** *a.*, see quot. and calcaneal; **ecto'chondral** *a. Anat.*, situated or occurring outside cartilage; **'ectochone** *Zool.*, the outermost structure of a chone; **ˌecto-'condyloid** [Gr. κόνδυλος knuckle + -oid], see quot.; **ˌecto-'cuneiform** *a.*, see quot. and cuneiform; **'ectocyst** [Gr. κύστ-ις bag], see quot. and cyst; **'ectoderm** [Gr. δέρμα skin], the outer layer of the blastoderm, also called *epiblast*; also, a term applied to the outer layer of the body of the Cœlenterata; hence **ecto'dermal** *a.*, **ecto'dermic** *a.*; **ˌectodynamo'morphic** *a.* (see quots.); **ecto-'ethmoid** *Zool.*, the prefrontal bone of the skull; **ecto'lecithal** *a. Embryol.*, having the food yolk situated outside the formative yolk; **'ectoloph** *Zool.*, the outer ridge on the crown of a lophodont tooth; **'ectomere** *Embryol.*, each of the cells produced by the segmentation of the ovum; **ˌecto-'metatarse** [mod.L. *metatarsus* the bones between the tarsus and the toes], see quot. for *ecto-calcaneal*; **ecto'neural** *a. Zool.*, of or pertaining to nerves situated superficially in an echinoderm; **ˌecto-'parasite**, see quot. 1861; hence **ˌecto-para'sitic** *a.*; **'ectophyte**, an external vegetable parasite; hence **ecto'phytic** *a.*; **ˌecto-'proctous** *a.* [Gr. πρωκτός anus, rump], belonging to the *Ectoprocta*, an order of Polyzoa having the anus outside the mouth-tentacles; **ˌecto-'pterygoid** *a.* [see pterygoid], see quot.; **ecto'rhinal** *a.*, situated on the outer side of the nose; **'ecto-sarc** *Zool.* [Gr. σάρξ, σαρκ-ός flesh], the outer transparent sarcode-layer of certain rhizopods, such as the Amœba; **'ectosome**, the outer layer of the body wall of certain sponges; hence **ecto'somal** *a.*; **ec'tosteal** *a. Anat.*, of, pertaining to, or situated on the exterior surface of a bone; hence **ec'tosteally** *adv.*; **ecto'stosis** [on the analogy of Gr. ἐξόστωσις, f. ὀστέον bone], an external growth of bone; **ecto'zoon** (*pl.* **-a**) [Gr. ζῷον animal], see quot.

1864 Webster, *Ecto-blast, the Membrane composing the walls of a cell. **1889** *Cent. Dict.*, *Ectoblastic. **1902** *Daily Chron.* 16 Sept. 5/2 A pair of ectoblastic invaginations. **1910** *Practitioner* Jan. 40 The core of the chorionic villus is mesoblastic in origin,..whereas the trophoblast is ectoblastic. **1854** Owen in *Circ. Sc.* (c. 1865) II. 74/2 There are three calcaneal processes..the third, called '*ectocalcaneal', from behind the ectocondyloid cavity and the ectometatarse. **1889** A. Macalister *Text-bk. Hum. Anat.* 38 The mesoblastic tissue..is replaced by bone in either of two ways, which are called respectively *ectochondral and entochondral ossification. **1913** *Cunningham's Text-bk. Anat.* (ed. 4) 86 Cartilage bones are those which are preformed in cartilage, and include most of the bones of the skeleton. Their growth is often described as endochondral and ectochondral, the former term implying the deposition of membrane bone in the centre of the cartilage, while the latter signifies a deposit of membrane bone on the surface of the cartilage. **1887** Sollas in *Encycl. Brit.* XXII. 415/1 A transverse muscular sphincter, which defines an outer division or *ectochone from an inner or endochone. **1888** Rolleston & Jackson *Forms Anim. Life* 795 The..chonae..are divided into an outer part, the ectochone, long and cylindrical, and an inner part, the endochone. **1854** Owen in *Circ. Sc.* (c. 1865) II. 74/1 The '*ectocondyloid' surface. *Ibid.* 68/2 A smaller ossicle..is the '*ectocuneiform'. **1873** Mivart *Elem. Anat.* v. 208 The ecto-cuneiform may enormously preponderate over the other cuneiforms as in the Horse. **1880** *Athenæum* 23 Oct. 536/1 Each individual of a colony of Polyzoa is encased in a cell known as the *ectocyst. **1861** J. R. Greene *Man. Anim. Kingd., Cœlent.* 11 The *ectoderm growing from within outwards. **1879** tr. *Haeckel's Evol. Man* I. iii. 67 The upper germ-layer, from which the outer skin and the flesh proceed, Huxley named Ecto-derm, or Outer layer. **1877** Huxley *Anat. Inv. An.* i. 55 The *ectodermal cells constitute the epidermis (ecderon). **1877** Foster *Text-bk. Physiol.* iii. 74 The junction of the *ectodermic muscular process [in *Hydra*] with the body of its cell. **1927** C. F. Marbut tr. *Glinka's Great Soil Groups* 34 We propose to designate them as endo-dynamomorphic soils to distinguish them from the *ekto-dynamomorphic soils in which external factors predominate over the internal. **1930** *Nature* 19 July 89 Ektodynamomorphic soils, that is, those in which climatic and other external factors in soil formation predominate over internal ones. **1888** Rolleston & Jackson *Forms Anim. Life* 91 Anteriorly to the septum is a large bone, the *ecto-ethmoid..(= the pre-frontal of Huxley). **1928** C. F. Cooper *Parker & Haswell's Text-Bk. Zool.* (ed. 4) II. 78 The outer walls of the olfactory capsules may be ossified by paired ecto-ethmoids. **1884** Sedgwick & Heathcote tr. *Claus' Zool.* I. 112 The first processes of segmentation in these at first *ectolecithal ova are withdrawn from observation, since they take place in the centre of an egg covered by a superficial layer of food yolk. **1905** *Amer. Geol.* Apr. 244 The outer border (*ectoloph) rises higher than the cross crests. **1966** A. S. Romer *Vert. Paleont.* (ed. 3) xx. 239 An ectoloph, forming the outer wall of the tooth, connecting paracone and metacone and often..with a W-shaped contour. **1889** *Cent. Dict.*, *Ectomere. **1890** Billings *Med. Dict.*, *Ectomere*, the larger of the two primitive cells produced by the segmentation of the mammalian ovum after impregnation. **1924** E. V. Cowdry *Gen. Cytology* 584 The subdivisions of these ectomeres are much more numerous in large eggs than in small ones. **1909** A. Sedgwick *Student's Text-Bk. Zool.* III. iii. 123 The ectodermal part of this plexus, which is continuous with the endodermal and may be called the *ectoneural, is especially concentrated in an annular tract round the mouth. **1962** D. Nichols *Echinoderms* ii. 28 The main sensory part lies orally, and has been called the superficial oral or ectoneural system. **1861** Hulme tr. *Moquin-Tandon* II. vi. 291 Those Parasites which derive their nourishment from the skin..have..been named..*Ectoparasites. **1877** Huxley *Anat. Inv. An.* iv. 192 Balatro [is] an ectoparasite, upon oligochætous Annelids. **1870** Rolleston *Anim. Life* Introd. 42 The Myxinoids..are..*ecto-parasitic. **1883** D. Macalister tr. *Ziegler's Path. Anat.* I. 354 *Ectophyte. **1902** *Encycl. Brit.* XXV. 439/1 There is a reciprocal symbiosis between the Angiosperm and the fungus which is endophytic, only rarely *ectophytic. *Ibid.*, More or fewer of their rootlets have their extremities invested by a weft of hyphal mycelium as an ectophytic mycorhiza. **1877** Huxley *Anat. Inv. An.* viii. 460 The characteristic polypide of the *ectoproctous Polyzoa is a structure developed from the cystid. **1872** Mivart *Elem. Anat.* 131 The bony palate may be enriched by the addition..of two extra bones, the *ecto-pterygoid and the ento-pterygoid. **1890** *Jrnl. Anat.* XXV. 106 The demarcation between these two parts is due to the presence of a fissure, more or less distinctly defined in different animals, which has been named the rhinal or *ectorhinal fissure. **1904** A. Keith *Hum. Embryol.* (ed. 2) 258 Hippocampal and Ectorhinal Fissures. **1877** Huxley *Anat. Inv. An.* ii. 94 Beneath this lies a thick cortical layer (*ectosarc) distinguished by its clearness and firmness from the semifluid central substance (endosarc). **1888** Sollas in *Challenger Rep.* XXV. p. xvi, This cleavage occurs parallel to the outer surface, dividing the sponge at once into a choanosomal and *ectosomal portion. **1887** *Encycl. Brit.* XXII. 415/1 An outer or *ectosome and an inner or choanosome. **1959** *Chambers's Encycl.* XIII. 101/2 The ectosome consists of a single-layered epithelium which may become several layers thick. **1868** W. K. Parker *Monogr. Struct. & Devel. Shoulder-Girdle Vertebrata* 66 In all the known Urodela the endosteal deposits are entirely ruled by the much earlier and more potent *ectosteal sheath. **1870** W. H. Flower *Introd. Osteol. Mamm.* vii. 74 They ossify, according to Parker, *ectosteally, or from without inwards. **1860** Mayne *Exp. Lex.*, *Ectozoon, a general term for those parasitic insects..that infest the surface, or external part of the body, in distinction from the Entozoa.

ectocrine ('ɛktəʊkraɪn, -ɪn). [f. ecto- + *-crine* as in endocrine.] An external metabolite which on release to the external world influences the vital processes of members of the same or other species. Also *attrib.*

1947 C. E. Lucas in *Biol. Reviews* XXII. 291 Many organisms have adapted themselves to tolerate or take advantage of the external metabolites of their neighbours... Ecological relationships appear to have arisen in this way, both stimulating or inhibiting..community integration, competition and succession, and probably symbiosis. The term 'ectocrine' is suggested for a substance mediating such processes. **1961** —— in M. Sears *Oceanography* 508 The production of a very small number of specific algae..may depend on..particular harmful ectocrines not reaching dangerous concentrations. *Ibid.* 509 Ectocrine processes may also be relevant in any attempts which may yet be made to culture 'food' algae on a commercial scale. **1963** Henderson *Dict. Biol. Terms* (ed. 8) 162/1 *Ectocrine*, organic substances or decomposition products in the external medium which inhibit or stimulate plant life. **1967** *Oceanogr. & Marine Biol.* V. iii. 104 The fertility of the English Channel during the following winter much depends on the partition of nutrients and ectocrines which occurs at these several discontinuities.

ectogenesis (ɛktəʊ'dʒɛnɪsɪs). *Biol.* [mod.L.: see ecto- and genesis.] The production of structures or bodies outside the organism. So **ectogenetic** (ɛktəʊdʒɪ'nɛtɪk), **ectogenic** (ɛktəʊ'dʒɛnɪk), **ectogenous** (ɛk'tɒdʒɪnəs) *adjs.*, pertaining to ectogenesis, producing or produced from without.

1883 D. Macalister tr. *Ziegler's Path. Anat.* I. 291 Some of the pathogenous bacteria are accustomed to develope and multiply without the body, while others only do so within it. The former kind we may describe as ectogenous, the latter as endogenous. *Ibid.*, Sometimes the ectogenous bacteria proceed to multiply within the body. **1900** B. D. Jackson *Gloss. Bot. Terms* 83/2 Ectogenic. **1909** *Cent. Dict.* Suppl., *Ectogenesis*, the production of or the giving rise to structures from without. **1923** Haldane *Daedalus* (1924) 63 It was in 1951 that Dupont and Schwarz produced the first ectogenetic child. *Ibid.* 64 France was the first country to adopt ectogenesis officially, and by 1968 was producing 60,000 children annually by this method. **1926** *Times Lit. Suppl.* 21 Oct. 710/4 Mr. Shaw's affinities..are with the biological school, whose most startling forecast, so far, is Mr. Haldane's ectogenetic baby. **1930** *Ibid.* 24 Apr. 11 By the twenty-first century science will have solved the problem of ectogenesis, will be able, that is to say, to develop a human infant from a fertilized cell by laboratory methods. **1957** I. Asimov *Naked Sun* (1958) xviii. 223 Dr. Delamarre himself was planning a future in which ectogenesis would be possible and marriage unnecessary.

ectomorph ('ɛktəʊmɔːf). *Anthropometry.* [f. ecto- + Gr. μορφ-ή form.] A person with the lean body-build in which the physical structures developed from the ectodermal layer of the embryo, i.e. the skin and the nervous system, predominate: one of W. H. Sheldon's three constitutional types (cf. endomorph 2, mesomorph). Hence **'ectomorphic** *a.*, **'ectomorphy**.

1940 W. H. Sheldon *Varieties Human Physique* i. 5 In proportion to his mass, the ectomorph has the greatest surface area and hence relatively the greatest sensory exposure to the outside world. *Ibid.*, Ectomorphy means relative predominance of linearity and fragility. *Ibid.* iii. 45 Hair of ectomorphic people is of nearly the same abundance as in the case of endomorphy. **1954** R. Fuller *Fantasy & Fugue* iv. 75 Now you..unfortunately incline to the cerebrotonic ectomorph—you worry too much, you're too good looking, and you can't abandon yourself happily to booze. **1956** C. P. Snow *Homecomings* li. 367 His profile confronted hers, each of them firm and beautiful in their ectomorphic lines. **1961** *New Scientist* 6 Apr. 854/1 The ectomorph is much more of an introvert and more shrewd and calculating. **1962** *Listener* 24 May 905/2 A sort of parlour game, deciding how many points he scores for endomorphy, mesomorphy, and ectomorphy. **1963** Auden *Dyer's Hand* 345 The chirpy social endomorph will give a different picture of it from that of the melancholic withdrawn ectomorph.

-ectomy, a combining form representing Gr. ἐκτομή excision, used to form words denoting a surgical operation for the removal of a part, as *appendicectomy*, *colectomy*, *hysterectomy*, *lobectomy*.

‖**ec'topia.** *Pathol.* [mod.L. *ectopia*, f. Gr. ἔκτοπ-ος, adj. f. ἐκ out + τόπ-ος place.] 'Displacement; anomaly of situation or relation' (*Syd. Soc. Lex.*).

1847 in Craig; and in mod. Dicts.

ectopic (ɛk'tɒpɪk), *a. Path.* [f. ectopia + -ic.] Characterized by ectopia: said esp. of pregnancy and gestation. Hence **ec'topically** *adv.*

1873 R. Barnes *Clin. Hist. Dis. Women* 424 The gestation is ectopic, that is, proceeding in an abnormal locality. **1893** *Brit. Med. Jrnl.* 1 Apr. 50/1 Ectopic gestation with ruptured sac. **1929** G. S. Dodds *Essent. Hum. Embryol.* 78 In ectopic pregnancy the uterus hypertrophies. **1938** *Proc. Prehistoric Soc.* IV. 61 It is unknown outside Wessex, save in one or two obviously ectopic grave-groups. **1961** *Lancet* 26 Aug. 454/2 One or both of the following conditions must exist to produce ectopic calcification. **1962** *Ibid.* 5 May 937/1 Very rarely, a single kidney may be drained by an ectopically opening ureter.

ectoplasm ('ɛktəʊplæz(ə)m). [Gr. πλάσμα something moulded or formed.]

1. (See quot.)

1883 J. E. Ady in *Knowl.* 15 June 355/2 Its [Amœba's] jelly-like body becomes faintly parcelled out into an outer firm (ectoplasm) and an inner soft (endoplasm) layer.

2. A viscous substance which is supposed to emanate from the body of a spiritualistic medium, and to develop into a human form or face.

a **1901** F. W. H. Myers *Human Personality* (1903) II. 548 In describing..imperfectly aggregated ectoplasms we have already touched on the next class, that of quasi-organic detached ectoplasms. **1922** *Daily Mail* 2 Dec. 13 Frederick Munnings-Gaulton..prominent as a medium..appears to have been an adept at producing 'ectoplasm'. **1923** *Ibid.* 5 Mar. 5 Ectoplasm..is described as being to the touch 'a cold and viscous mass comparable to contact with a reptile'. **1926** A. Conan Doyle *Hist. Spiritualism* I. v. 114 The ectoplasm pictures photographed by Madame Bisson and Dr. Schrenck Notzing..may in their first forms be ascribed to the medium's thoughts or memories taking visible shape in ectoplasm. **1926** J. Laird *Our Minds & their Bodies* I Those hearers look for photographic evidence of 'auras' and 'ectoplasms'. **1953** A. W. Fielding *Stronghold* II. i. 105 Each bearded *pallikari*..glared angrily from his frame as though emerging from an ocean of ectoplasm.

So **ecto'plasmic**, **ecto'plastic** *adjs.*; **ecto'plasmically** *adv.* Also *fig.*

1882 Vines *Sachs' Bot.* 583 Two cells..separated..by an ectoplasmic layer..of protoplasm. **1885** *Encycl. Brit.* XIX. 834/1 Ectoplastic products in which the material produced by the protoplasm is separated from it. **1900** G. C. Bourne *Introd. Comp. Anat. Anim.* 109 The cell-protoplasm..has given rise to substances which..are formed on the outside of the cell as a sort of envelope..in which case they are called ectoplastic products. *a* **1901** F. W. H. Myers *Human Personality* (1903) II. 549 Utterance may be referable to an ectoplastic throat as distinctly as grip to ectoplastic fingers. **1923** S. De Brath tr. *Richet's Thirty Years Psychical Research* I. ii. 12 In this book..will be found two chapters on each variety of phenomena,..whether the matter in hand concerns..the movement of objects (telekinesis), or materializations (ectoplasmic forms). **1926** A. Conan Doyle *Hist. Spiritualism* I. xii. 259 The mediumship of the Eddy brothers..has probably never been excelled in the matter of materialization, or, as we may now call them, ectoplasmic forms. **1926** C. E. M. Joad *Babbitt Warren* 116 Ectoplastic mediums, quack doctors and inspired clairvoyants. **1927** S. De Brath tr. *Geley's Clairvoy. & Material.* 175 It seems to me desirable to substitute for 'materialization' the term 'ectoplasmic form'. **1952** M. McCarthy *Groves of Academe* (1953) v. 84 Mulcahy's

rather ectoplasmic voice effused itself into Furness's ear. **1954** KOESTLER *Invisible Writing* IV. xxxvii. 400 As I read on, I had the impression of meeting the *Doppelgaenger*, the spectral doubles of Rubashov and Ivanov—a ghostly, ectoplastic regurgitation by reality of the characters and events of my imagination. **1960** *Spectator* 29 July 176 He had always evaporated, ectoplasmically, and swirled on.

ectotrophic (ˈɛktəʊtrɒfɪk), *a. Bot.* [ad. G. *ectotrophisch* (A. B. Frank *Lehrb. d. Pflanzenphysiologie* (1890) II. 135), f. ECTO- + TROPHIC *a.*] Chiefly of Mycorrhiza: forming a tissue on the surface of roots. Opp. to ENDOTROPHIC *a.*

1899 [see ENDOTROPHIC *a.*]. [**1903** H. C. PORTER tr. *Strasburger's Text-bk. Bot.* (ed. 2) I. ii. 209 The fungal hyphæ are sometimes present.. within the cells... In other cases the fungus surrounds the young roots with a dense investment of interwoven hyphæ. The former arrangement is spoken of as endotrophic, the latter as exotrophic [later edd. ectotrophic] mycorhiza.] **1926** TANSLEY & CHIPP *Study of Vegetation* ix. 158 Ectotrophic [fungi].. are found .. mainly as a mantle around the rootlets of trees. **1938** WEAVER & CLEMENTS *Plant Ecology* (ed. 2) xi. 329 If the fungal mycelium occurs on the outside of the root and between its cells.. the mycorrhiza is ectotrophic (i.e., nourished outside). **1959** *New Scientist* 24 Sept. 528/2 The well-defined ectotrophic mycorrhizas of certain forest trees, and the more variable endotrophic condition of the majority of plants.

ectrodactyly (ɛktrəʊˈdæktɪlɪ). *Anat.* Also **ectrodactylia**. [ad. mod.L. *ectrodactylia*, f. Gr. ἔκτρω-μα, -τρω-σις, etc. (f. ἐκ- + τρω- to damage) + δάκτυλος finger.] Congenital absence of digits. Also **ectroˈdactylism**.

1848 DUNGLISON *Med. Lex.* (ed. 7) 296/2 *Ectrodactylia*, a malformation in which one or more fingers or toes are wanting. **1883** *Index-Catal. Libr. Surg.-Gen. U.S.* IV. 51/1 Ectrodactylism. **1893** *Jrnl. Anat.* XXVII. 422 Schæfar gives an account of five cases of ectrodactyly. **1894** W. BATESON *Study of Variation* 358 Absence of Digits (Ectrodactylism). **1899** *Jrnl. Anat.* XXXIII. 524 A case in which ectrodactyly and syndactyly of the right hand co-existed with double ectrodactyly of the feet. **1909** W. BATESON *Mendel's Princ. Heredity* xii. 228 Several pedigrees of ectrodactylism.. are recorded in medical literature. **1946** R. R. GATES *Human Genetics* I. xi. 434 Lobster claw appears to be an extreme form of syndactyly (i.e., combined with ectrodactyly).

ectromelia (ɛktrəʊˈmiːlɪə). [mod.L., f. Gr. ἔκτρω-σις miscarriage + *-melia* f. Gr. μέλ-ος limb + -IA¹.] **1.** The congenital absence of a limb or limbs.

1908 *Jrnl. Amer. Med. Assoc.* LI. 2002/2 (*title*) Case of Ectromelia. Associated with Other Deformities. G. W. Kosmak... Ectromelia. Kosmak reports, with an illustration, a case showing entire absence of the upper extremities... There is.. not a dimple indicating where the arms ought to appear on the shoulder-girdle.

2. A virus disease of mice often causing loss of limbs. Also *attrib.*

1930 J. MARCHAL in *Jrnl. Path. & Bacteriol.* XXXIII. III. 713 (*title*) Infectious Ectromelia. A hitherto undescribed virus disease of mice. *Ibid.* 726 As regards the proposed name of this condition, for which I have to thank Mr. Clifford Dobell who proposed it, I hope that any suggestion of a congenital abnormality in the word 'ectromelia' may be dissipated by the adjective 'infectious'. **1946** *Nature* 27 July 119/1 Ectromelia virus in mice.. agglutinated the same limited range of fowl cells as were agglutinated by vaccinia virus preparations. **1963** *New Scientist* 12 Sept. 540 Ectromelia, a killing disease of mice, is produced by a pox virus.

‖**ecˈtropion, -um.** *Pathol.* [mod.L. *ectropium*, Gr. ἐκτρόπιον, f. ἐκ out + τρέπειν to turn.] 'An outward bending; especially applied to the condition in which the eyelid folds on itself, so that the conjunctival surface becomes external; eversion of the eyelid' (*Syd. Soc. Lex.*).

1685 COOKE *Marrow of Chirurg.* (ed. 4) II. §iii. 154 Ectropion is when the lower eyelid is fallen down. **1736** in BAILEY. **1751** in CHAMBERS *Cycl.* **1875** H. WALTON *Dis. Eye* 697 Ectropium is common in the under, and very uncommon in the upper eyelid. **1878** T. BRYANT *Pract. Surg.* I. 345 Ectropion signifies an everted condition of the lid.

ectrotic (ɛkˈtrɒtɪk), *a. Med.* [ad. Gr. ἐκτρωτικός pertaining to abortion, ἐκτιτρώσκειν to miscarry.] 'Term formerly applied to medicines and agents which cause abortion of the fœtus. Also applied to medicines or modes of treatment which tend to produce the abortion or sudden cutting short of a disease' (*Syd. Soc. Lex.*).

1866 A. FLINT *Princ. Med.* (1880) 1039 The local treatment [in small pox] embraces measures to render the eruption abortive on the face, or to prevent the disfiguration caused by pitting. The treatment for this end is called ectrotic.

ectylotic (ɛktɪˈlɒtɪk), *a.* and *sb. Med.* [ad. Gr. ἐκτυλωτικός, f. ἐκτυλό-ειν, recorded in sense of 'swell out into a callus', but here taken as meaning 'to remove warts', f. ἐκ out + τύλος wart.] (See quots.)

1736 BAILEY, *Ectyloticks*, remedies proper to consume and eat off callus's, warts and other excrescences found on the flesh. **1753** CHAMBERS *Cycl. Supp.* **1847** CRAIG *Ectylotic*, having a tendency to remove callosities or indurations of the skin. **1864** in WEBSTER.

ectypal (ˈɛktɪpəl), *a.* [f. next + -AL¹.] Of or pertaining to an ectype; of the nature of an ectype or copy; opposed to *archetypal*.

1642 R. C. *Union of Christ & Ch.* 3 Materiall things are but Ectypall Resemblances and Imitations of spirituall things. *a* **1711** KEN *Hymnoth.* Wks. 1721 III. 232 Ectypal Salem here is in their Eye, The Model of Archetypal on high. **1845** CORRIE *Theol.* in *Encycl. Metrop.* 857/1 A common division [of Theology].. used to be.. 1, Archetypal Theology,.. 2, Ectypal,.. derived from the former.

ectype (ˈɛktaɪp). [ad. Gr. ἔκτυπον, neut. of ἔκτυπος worked in relief, f. ἐκ out + τύπος figure.]

†**1.** An impression (in wax, clay, etc.) of a seal or medal. ? *Obs.* in *lit.* sense.

1662 PHILLIPS Pref., *Ectype*, a thing taken out of another Copy. **1697** EVELYN *Numism.* v. 196 Sent the Ectype of a Medal to Sir Robt. Cotton. **1751** in CHAMBERS *Cycl.*

b. *fig.* A copy, reproduction; *esp.* as opposed to *archetype* or *prototype*.

1646 J. HALL *Poems* I. 48 Thine own ectype Brownrigge. **1692** BEVERLEY *Disc. Dr. Crisp* 10 It is an Ectype or Exemplification of the Everlasting Covenant. **1690** LOCKE *Hum. Und.* II. xxxi. (1695) 212 The Complex Ideas of Substances are Ectypes, Copies too; but not perfect ones. **1722** WOLLASTON *Relig. Nat.* iii. 53 The true ectypes of their originals. **1846** SIR W. HAMILTON in *Reid's Wks.* 771 To subordinate.. the prototype to the ectype.

2. *Archit.* An object in relievo or embossed.

1876 GWILT *Archit.* Gloss.

ectypography (ɛktɪˈpɒgrəfɪ). [f. Gr. ἔκτυπο-ς (see ECTYPE) + -γραφία a writing.] (See quot.)

1870 FAIRHOLT *Dict. Terms Art* s.v., A mode of etching by which the lines are raised on the plate instead of sunk in. *Ibid.* 179 [In ectypography] the lights are etched-in and the lines of the design left standing in relief, similar to the letters of type-founders.

‖**écu** (eky). [Fr.: originally 'shield':—L. *scutum*; according to Littré so called because it bore on one face 3 fleurs-de-lis, like a heraldic shield.]

A French silver coin; commonly regarded as equivalent to the English 'crown'. Now used in France as a name for the five-franc piece.

The relation of the *écu* to the *livre*, and its actual value, varied greatly at different periods. There was also a gold écu, similarly variable in nominal and actual value.

1704 *Royal Proclam.* 18 June in *Lond. Gaz.* No. 4029/1 Ecu's of France, or Silver Lewis.. Four Shillings and Six Pence. **1875** JEVONS *Money* xii. 145 The coinage of écus.. had been left unrestricted.

Ecuadorian (ɛkwəˈdɔərɪən), *a.* and *sb.* Also **-ean.** [f. *Ecuador* name of country in S. America + -IAN.] **A.** *adj.* Of, belonging to, or characteristic of Ecuador. **B.** *sb.* A native or inhabitant of Ecuador.

1860 *Jrnl. R. Geogr. Soc.* XXX. 70 The Pailon of San Pedro, or St. Peter's Cauldron, was surveyed by Captain Kellett, of H.M.S. *Herald*. A copy of the Survey was presented to the Equatorian Government. **1861** *Ibid.* XXXI. 181 It is known to every one that gold exists at a short distance,.. if the Ecuatoreans would only take the trouble to search for it. **1877** *Encycl. Brit.* VII. 645/1 The only real glacier known to exist in the Ecuadorian Andes. **1886** A. SIMSON *Trav. Ecuador* ii. 27 The dinner, in an Ecuadorian sense, was capital. **1892** E. WHYMPER *Trav. Gt. Andes* 179 Ecuadorian Hand-Made Lace. *Ibid.* 421 The head-coverings worn by Ecuadorians shew that the sun's rays are seldom so powerful as to be dangerous. **1927** *Glasgow Herald* 24 Oct. 7 Ecuadorian Hats [commonly called 'Panama' hats]. **1936** *Discovery* Aug. 249/2 The Ecuadorean Government. **1959** *Chambers's Encycl.* IV. 788/1 The territory in dispute between Ecuador and Peru consisted of.. a small.. area around Túmbez.. and practically the whole of the Ecuadorian Oriente.

ecuelle (eɪkˈwɛl). Also **écuelle.** [ad. F. *écuelle*:—pop.L. **scūtella*, altered from *scŭtella*.]

1. A two-handled porringer used for soup.

1856 J. C. ROBINSON *Inv. Mus. Ornamental Art* 19 'Ecuelle' or Shell Tazza, ornamented with interlaced arabesque ornament in ruby and yellow lustre. **1872** W. CHAFFERS *Keramic Gallery* I. p. xi, Ecuelle and Dish, painted with Carnival figures. **1956** G. TAYLOR *Silver* vi. 129 The écuelle, a similar French vessel with two opposed flat handles, somewhat resembling the Scottish quaich, but with a domed cover, was introduced early in the [eighteenth] century. **1963** *Times* 15 May 8/7 A Meissen chinoiserie ecuelle and cover.

2. The process or apparatus by which oils are extracted from the peel of citrus fruit. Also **ecuˈelling.**

1884 *Encycl. Brit.* XVII. 812/1 The process known as *écuelle*, in which the skin of the ripe fruit is scraped against a series of points or ridges arranged upon the surface of a peculiarly-shaped dish or broad funnel. **1891** *Bull. R. Bot. Gardens Kew* May–June 120 From the rind of the fruit, by a process known as 'ecuelling', which consists of gently rubbing the fruit on rounded projections arranged inside a brass basin, a very fine essence of limes is obtained. **1949** J. B. S. BRAVERMAN *Citrus Products* v. 184 The écuelle.. can be regarded as the prototype of all machines rasping whole fruit. It is a very old process.

†**eculee.** *Obs. rare*⁻¹. [OF. *eculee*, ad. L. *equuleus* rack, dim. of *equus* horse.] (See quot.)

1483 CAXTON *Gold. Leg.* 152/1 An instrument named eculee of which two endes stonde on the ground and ii upward lyke Saynt Andrews crosse.

ecumaniac (ˌiːk(j)uːˈmeɪnɪæk, ɛ-). *joc.* and *derog.* [f. ECU(MENIC *a.*, etc., + MANIAC *sb.*] A zealous supporter of the ecumenical movement.

1963 *Maclean's Mag.* 6 July 26/3 The 'ecumaniacs'—as hostile religious separatists like to call them—have come to believe that it is their religious duty to break down the barriers between denominations. **1966** *Glasgow Herald* 29 July 4/3 Ecumaniacs favour a policy of unprincipled surrender all along the line. **1976** *Church Times* 31 Dec. 10/5 Those who had not previously had a genuine desire for unity with fellow-Christians.. would not overnight have become ecumaniacs. **1986** *Christian Order* Feb. 75 They would be ecumaniacs, not ecumenists.

ecumenacy, -ic: see ŒCUMEN-.

ecumenic, œcumenic (iːkjuːˈmɛnɪk, ɛ-), *a.* Also 7 *erron.* œco-. [ad. L. *œcūmenic-us*, a. Gr. οἰκουμενικ-ός of or belonging to ἡ οἰκουμένη 'the inhabited (earth)', the whole world. Cf. F. *œcuménique* (16th c. in Hatz.-Darm.).]

= ECUMENICAL *a.*

1588 A. KING tr. *Canisius' Catech.* 215 The decree and doctrin of the Haly, Œcumenik and General Counsel of Trent. **1652** ROW *Let.* in *Hist. Kirk* (1842) 537 That eldership and breithren can know the cace better nor ane Œcumenick Synod. **1715** M. DAVIES *Athen. Brit.* I. Pref. 76 The only Author—that is universally Read—to a far more Œcumenick Intent than ever any of the Jesuit Pamphlets. **1835** I. TAYLOR *Spir. Despot.* VI. 263 That great economy of provincial government and of œcumenic relationship. **1840** *Penny Cycl.* XVI. 400/2 Councils called Œcumenic or Œcumenical.

ecumenical, œcumenical (iːkjuːˈmɛnɪkəl, ɛ-), *a.* Also 7 *erron.* œco-. [f. as ECUMENIC *a.* + -AL¹.]

1. *Eccl.* Belonging to or representing the whole (Christian) world, or the universal church; general, universal, catholic; *spec.* applied to the general councils of the early church, and (in mod. use) of the Roman Catholic Church (and hence occas. to a general assembly of some other ecclesiastical body); also assumed as a title by the Patriarch of Constantinople; formerly sometimes applied to the Pope of Rome.

1563–87 FOXE *A. & M.* (1596) 8 That anie one bishop aboue the rest had the name of œcumenicall, or uniuersall, or head.. that is not to be found. **1624** HAYWARD *Suprem. Relig.* 53 John Bishop of Constantinople.. assumed the title of Oecumenicall, or universal Bishop. **1633** PRYNNE *1st Pt. Histrio-M.* VII. iii. 643 By the expresse resolution of all these severall Councels, whereof one is œcumenicall. **1673** MARVELL *Reh. Transp.* II. 409 You imagined the whole world had been of that mind, and 'twould pass for œcumenical Doctrine. **1845** *Encycl. Metrop.* XVIII. 387/2 Ecumenical. **1861** STANLEY *East. Ch.* i. (1869) 19 These Oriental Councils were 'general'—were 'Oecumenical' in a sense which fairly belonged to none besides. **1864** J. H. NEWMAN *Apol.* 396 It is to the Pope in Ecumenical Council that we look, as to the normal seat of Infallibility. **1881** (*title*) Proceedings of the Œcumenical Methodist Conference. **1887** HEARD *Russian Ch.* iv. 63 That the first œcumenical prelate of the Church was the patriarch of Constantinople, the second the patriarch of Alexandria. **1941** W. TEMPLE *Citizen & Churchman* v. 87 What is known as the Ecumenical Movement represents a movement of the spirit.

2. *gen.* Belonging to the whole world; universal, general, world-wide.

1607 J. KING *Serm. Novemb.* 13 This epidemical and œcumenical contagion. *a* **1638** MEDE *Wks.* (1672) 627 This was the Oecumenical Philosophy of the Apostles times and of the times long before them. **1681** H. MORE *Exp. Dan.* iv. Notes 123 That Oecumenical Tax appointed by Augustus. **1869** LECKY *Europ. Mor.* I. i. 160 No other literature exhibits so expansive and œcumenical a genius [as the French]. **1882** W. H. MALLOCK *Soc. Equal.* viii. 213 Our œcumenical commerce.

Hence **ecuˈmenicalism**, the theological system or doctrine of the ecumenical councils; **ecumeniˈcality** = ECUMENICITY; **ecuˈmenically** *adv.*, in an ecumenical way, in relation to the whole world, universally.

1888 *Chicago Advance* 10 May 290 Three strata, Œcumenicalism, Augustinianism, Evangelicalism. **1949** *Theology* LII. 15 To endeavour along the lines of a misconceived ecumenicalism to smooth out these differences. **1869** in *Echo* 29 July, It will not be an Œcumenical Council... The primary essence of Œcumenicality is wanting to it—viz., a delegation from all Churches. Half Christendom will hold aloof from it. *a* **1751** BOLINGBROKE *Ess., Author. Relig.* Wks. 1754 IV. 349 The church oecumenically assembled. **1876** DRAPER *Confl. Relig. & Sc.* xii. 341 The papacy is administered not œcumenically, not as a universal Church, for all nations.

ecumenicity, œcumenicity (iːkjuːmɪˈnɪsɪtɪ, ɛ-). [ad. eccles. med.L. *œcūmenicitās*, f. *œcūmenic-us*: see prec. and -ITY. Cf. F. *œcuménicité* (1752 in *Dict. Trévoux*).] Ecumenical character; universality, catholicity.

1840 GLADSTONE *Ch. Princ.* 510 It is.. the supposed ecumenicity of the council, which renders it binding on their conscience. **1867** *Contemp. Rev.* V. 454 He destroyed the œcumenicity and authority of Trent. **1882–3** SCHAFF *Encycl. Rel. Kn.* III. 2448/2 The disputed oecumenicity of the reformatory councils of Pisa, Constance, and Basel. **1963** T. WARE *Orthodox Church* xii. 257 The ecumenicity of a council cannot be decided by outward criteria alone.

ecumenics (ˌiːk(j)uːˈmɛnɪks, ɛ-). [Pl. of ECUMENIC *a.* used subst., construed as sing.]

The study of the Christian Church as a unity; ecumenic activity.

1961 in WEBSTER. **1971** *Month* May 147 (*title*) The Irish school of ecumenics. **1975** *Church Times* 18 July 7/3 It contains the record of an international consultation on the subject of mixed marriages organized in Dublin last year by the Irish School of Ecumenics. **1982** *Sunday Times* 6 June 5/7 Ecumenics, the drive for inter-church unity, was where the change in the Pope was most remarked.

ecumenism ('iːkjuːmɪnɪz(ə)m, ɛ-). [f. Gr. οἰκουμένη (see ŒCUMENIC *a.*) + -ISM.]The doctrine, or quality, of universality (esp. of the Christian church). Hence **'ecumenist**.

1948 W. A. VISSER 'T HOOFT in *Univ. Church in God's Design* IV. iv. 183 There is still in much of our present ecumenism a strong element of relativism. **1964** *Economist* 25 Jan. 315/2 Monsignor Cardinale is a noted ecumenist. **1970** *Daily Tel.* 19 May 18 The cause of ecumenism has received no setback. It might indeed be enhanced, if the Archbishop [of Canterbury] were to receive and accept an invitation to be present in Rome at the canonisation ceremony.

eczema ('ɛkzɪmə). *Pathol.* [Gr. ἔκζεμα, f. ἐκζέ-ειν, f. ἐκ out + ζέ-ειν to boil.] 'An acute, or chronic, non-contagious, simple inflammation of the skin, characterized by the presence of itching papules and vesicles which discharge a serous fluid, or dry up' (*Syd. Soc. Lex.*). There are many kinds of eczema; a form occurring in cattle (*E. epizooticum*), is known as 'the foot and mouth disease'.

1753 CHAMBERS *Cycl. Supp.*, *Eczema*, a name given by the antient physicians, to any fiery pustule on the skin. **1884** *St. James's Gaz.* 24 Apr. 5 Animals..may communicate disease ..though..not suffering from..eczema themselves.

Hence **ec'zematous** *a.*, **ec'zematously** *adv.*

1869 *Pall Mall G.* 19 Oct. 4 A family drank the milk [from a cow having the foot and mouth disease] undiluted, and are now suffering from an eczematous condition of the lips, tongue, and palate. **1876** DUHRING *Dis. Skin* 165 The eczematously diseased tissues.

†**ed**, *a. Obs. rare.* Only in *superl.* **edist** or **eddist**. [Of uncertain origin; it has been identified with the OE. *éad* happy (cf. EADI, EADNESS), but the latter appears to be a spurious word evolved from corrupt readings. Perh. *ed(d)ist* may be a scribal error for *oddist*, which occurs elsewhere in the poem.] ? Distinguished in war.

c **1400** *Destr. Troy* 5324 Ercules, þat honerable, edist of my knightes. *Ibid.* 5950 Ector..eddist of knightes.

Ed. or **ed.**, abbrev. of *edited (by)*, *edition*, *editor*.

1843 *Ladies' Companion* (N.Y.) Feb. 167/1 Mr. Poe's article concludes with the following words.—*Eds.* **1878** S. G. C. MIDDLEMORE tr. *Burckhardt's Civilisation Renaissance in Italy* II. IV. iv. 38 Roscoe, *Leone X.*, ed. Bossi, viii. 174. **1892** K. E. DIGBY *Introd. Hist. Law Real Property* (ed. 4) i. II. 39 Camden, Britannia, ed. 1610, p. 348. **1934** 'N. BELL' *Winding Road* ix. 180 He..said the ed. fellow was an old rascal. **1953** F. SHEBAB *Progressive Taxation* ii. 11 Adam Smith, The Wealth of Nations (ed. Cannan). *Ibid.*, Sir John Sinclair, The History of Public Revenue of the British Empire (3rd ed., 1803). **1957** S. N. SEN *Eighteen Fifty-Seven* 421 Forrest, G.W., ed. Selections from the Letters, Despatches and other state papers..of the Government of India. **1969** D. WALEY *Italian City-Republics* 245 Giovanni Villani, Cronica, ed. F.G. Dragomanni.

†**ed-**, *prefix*, OE. *ed-* = OHG. *it(a, id-* (MHG. *ite-, it-*, mod.G. dial. *it-*), ON. *ið-*, Goth. *id-*, again, backwards (= L. *re-*). Frequent in OE.; a few examples survived into ME.; see EDBOTE, EDGREW, EDHALDE.

-ed, *suffix*[1], the formative of the pa. pple. of wk. vbs., had in OE. the forms *-ed, -ad, -od (-ud)*, where the vowel represents (though not with uniform consistency) the thematic suffix characteristic of the class to which the vb. belongs; the ppl. suffix proper being *-d*:—OTeut. *-do-*:—OAryan *-tó-*; cf. Gr. vbl. adjs. in -τός, and L. pples. in *-tus*. In some OE. vbs. the suffix is added immediately to the root-syllable, and therefore appears without preceding vowel as *-d*, or after a voiceless cons. as *-t*; e.g. in *seald* SOLD, f. *sęllan* to SELL, *boht* BOUGHT, f. *byczan* to BUY. In ME. the several vowelled forms of the suffix (where they were not contracted) were levelled to *-ed (-id, -yd)*, and this *-ed* is in most cases still retained in writing, although the pronunc. is now normally vowelless (d), or after voiceless cons. (t), as in *robed* (rəʊbd), *hoped* (həʊpt). The full pronunc. (ɪd) regularly occurs in ordinary speech only in the endings *-ted*, *-ded*; but it is frequently required by the metre of verse, and is still often used in the public reading of the Bible and the Liturgy. A few words, such as *blessed, cursed, beloved*, which are familiar chiefly in religious use, have escaped the general tendency to contraction when used as adjs.; and the adjectival use of *learned* is distinguished by its pronunc. ('lɜːnɪd) from its use as simple pple. (lɜːnd). From 16th to 18th c. the suffix, when following a voiceless cons. (preceded by a cons. or a short vowel), was often written *-t*, in accordance with the pronunc., as in *jumpt, whipt, stept*. This is still practised by some writers, but is not now in general use. Where, however, a long vowel in the vb.-stem is shortened in the pple., as in *crept, slept*, the spelling with *-t* is universal. Some pples. have a twofold spelling, according as the vowel is shortened or not in pronunc.; e.g. *leapt* (lɛpt), and *leaped* (liːpt).

In several other classes of instances the *-ed* of early ME. has undergone subsequent contraction (in the inflected forms, however, this process had already begun in OE.): e.g. the endings *-ded*, *-ted* became *-d(d, -t(t*, as in *bled(d*, mod. *bled*, for OE. *blēded* (see BLEED *v.*), *set(t*, mod. *set*, for OE. *sęted* (see SET *v.*[1]); after *l, n, r*, the ending *-ded* has often become *-t*, as in *gilt, sent, girt*; and in certain cases *l, m, n* at the end of a verb-stem cause the suffix *-ed* to become *-t*, as in *spilt, unkempt, burnt*. These contractions occur only in the older words of the language, and many of the words in which they are found have parallel forms without contraction, in most cases with some difference of meaning or use. The Sc. form of *-ed* is *-it*, with which cf. such early ME. forms as *i-nempnet* named, *i-crunet* crowned, though these belong chiefly to extreme southern dialects.

2. The suffix was (chiefly in 15th, 16th, and 17th c.) added to adapted forms of L. pples., the intention being to assimilate these words in form to the native words which they resembled in function; e.g. *acquisited, situated, versed (sine)*. Similarly, the ppl. adjs. in *-ate*, ad. L. *-ātus*, common in mod. scientific nomenclature, have usually parallel forms in *-ated*, without difference in meaning; e.g. *bipinnate(d), dentate(d)*.

3. It is possible that some of the adjs. formed by the addition of *-ed* to sbs. may be examples of this suffix rather than of -ED[2]. The apparent instances of this which can be traced back to OE., however, are found to belong to the latter.

-ed, *suffix*[2], OE. *-ede* = OS. *-ôdi* (not represented elsewhere in Teut., though ON. had adjs. similarly f. sbs., with ppl. form and *i*-umlaut, as *eygðr* eyed, *hynrdr* horned):—OTeut. type *-ôðjo-*, is appended to sbs. in order to form adjs. connoting the possession or the presence of the attribute or thing expressed by the sb. The function of the suffix is thus identical with that of the Lat. ppl. suffix *-tus* as used in *caudātus* tailed, *aurītus* eared, etc.; and it is possible that the Teut. *-ôðjo-* may originally have been f. *-ôðo-* (see -ED[1]), the suffix of pa. pples. of vbs. in *-ôjan* formed upon sbs. In mod.Eng., and even in ME., the form affords no means of distinguishing between the genuine examples of this suffix and those ppl. adjs. in -ED[1] which are ultimately f. sbs. through unrecorded vbs. Examples that have come down from OE. are *ringed*:—OE. *hringede*, *hooked*:—OE. *hócede*, etc. The suffix is now added without restriction to any sb. from which it is desired to form an adj. with the sense 'possessing, provided with, characterized by' (something); e.g. in *toothed, booted, wooded, moneyed, cultured, diseased, jaundiced*, etc., and in parasynthetic derivatives, as *dark-eyed, seven-hilled, leather-aproned*, etc. In *bigoted, crabbed, dogged*, the suffix has a vaguer meaning. (Groundless objections have been made to the use of such words by writers ignorant of the history of the language: see quot.) In pronunciation this suffix follows the same rules as -ED[1].

1779 JOHNSON *Gray* Wks. IV. 302 There has of late arisen a practice of giving to adjectives derived from substantives, the termination of participles: such as the 'cultured' plain.. but I was sorry to see in the lines of a scholar like Gray, the 'honied' spring. **1832** COLERIDGE *Table-T.* (1836) 171, I regret to see that vile and barbarous vocable *talented*..The formation of a participle passive from a noun is a licence that nothing but a very peculiar felicity can excuse.

edacious (ɪ'deɪʃəs), *a.* [f. L. *edāci-* (nom. *edax*), f. *edĕre* to eat + -OUS.]

1. Of or relating to eating; devoted to eating, voracious. Now chiefly *humorous*.

1829 I. TAYLOR *Enthus.* viii. 199 Our..high-toned irritability, edacious appetites, and pampered constitutions. **1865** CARLYLE *Fredk. Gt.* III. IX. viii. 135 Who shall judge him?—transcendent King of edacious Flunkies. **1866** R. CHAMBERS *Ess.* Ser. II. 182 His edacious peculiarities—whether..he was..most partial to lamb or turkey.

b. *fig.* Greedy, eager.

1865 CARLYLE *Fredk. Gt.* V. XIII. v. 62 These words Hyndford listened to with an edacious solid countenance. **1866** —— *Remin.* (1881) I. 259 A hardy little figure, of edacious energetic physiognomy.

2. Said of time. (After L. *tempus edax rerum.*)

1819 H. BUSK *Banquet* I. 372 Edacious Time has all his works consumed. **1862** LOWELL *Biglow P.* Ser. II. 31 Concord Bridge had long since yielded to the edacious tooth of Time. **1865** *Pall Mall G.* 8 Apr. 4 Edacious Time too visibly devours her last charm.

edacity (ɪ'dæsɪtɪ). [f. as prec. + -TY.]

1. The quality of being edacious; capacity for eating; good appetite. Now chiefly *humorous*.

1626 BACON *Sylva* §972 The Wolf is a Beast of great Edacitie and Disgestion. **1633** P. FLETCHER *Purple Isl.* II. xxxix, If those pipes windings..Should not refrain too much edacitie. **1684** tr. *Bonet's Merc. Compit.* XVIII. 613 Edacity in the Small Pox is usually an ill Sign. **1823** *New Month. Mag.* VII. 335 He has vivacity, edacity, and bibacity. **1854** BADHAM *Halieut.* 516 Ulysses' edacity is competently attested in the Odyssey.

†**2.** Corrosive quality, destructive power. *Obs.*

1657 TOMLINSON *Renou's Disp.* 146 Lest the noxious quality of the air or edacity of heat spoyl their qualities.

†**e'dad**, *int. Obs.* [Cf. ADAD, ADOD, EDOD, EGAD, ECOD.]

1710 *Brit. Apollo* III. 28 1/1 *Add* and *edad* is only a mincing of *by G—d*.

Edam ('iːdæm). In full *Edam cheese*: a cheese of a type originally made at Edam, near Amsterdam.

1836 J. MURRAY *Handbk. Trav. Continent* 52/1 A vast quantity of these cheeses (called here Edam cheeses, but known all over the world as Dutch cheeses). **1885** *Times* 8 Oct. 6/6 Specimens of Gorgonzola, Roquefort, Gruyere, Parmesan, Edam and Gouda cheese. **1890** J. MACDONALD *Stephen's Bk. Farm* (ed. 4) IV. 515 The two important cheeses made in Holland, both of which are sold in the English markets in very large quantities, are known as round or Edam, and flat or Gouda Cheese. **1902** *Encycl. Brit.* XXVII. 355/2 The Edam and Gouda are the common cheeses of Holland. **1951** *Good Housek. Home Encycl.* 449/1 To serve Edam cheese, the top is sliced off and used as a cover, and the cheese is scooped out from the centre with a spoon. **1955** J. G. DAVIS *Dict. Dairying* (ed. 2) 191 The real Edam has at least 40 per cent. fat in the dry matter and the skimmed milk cheese at least 20 per cent.

edaphic (ɪ'dæfɪk), *a. Ecology.* [ad. G. *edaphisch* (A. F. W. Schimper *Pflanzen-Geogr.* (1898) I. i. 5), f. Gr. ἔδαφος floor + -IC.] Pertaining to, produced or influenced by, the soil.

1900 JACKSON *Gloss. Bot. Terms* Additions. **1902** *Encycl. Brit.* XXV. 430/1 The varying climatic or environmental conditions to which Angiosperms may be exposed in their wide distribution, including those of the soil, edaphic, those of the atmosphere, epedaphic, and those of water, aquatic. *Ibid.*, Geophytes are..subject to the influence of both edaphic and epedaphic factors of environment. **1906** CHAMBERLIN & SALISBURY *Geol.* II. 343 Adaptation to the immediate physical environment, particularly the nature and depth of the sea-bottom (edaphic adaptation). **1930** *Nature* 25 Jan. 120 Wherever domesticated animals come upon the scene the biotic factor undoubtedly ranks with the edaphic and climatic as of supreme importance. **1930** *Forestry* IV. 29 The term edaphic association is used by Tansley and other British ecologists for relatively permanent communities which do not reach the climatic climax owning to soil conditions. **1936** *Geogr. Jrnl.* LXXXVIII. 566 'Social ecology' in relation to the edaphic factor. **1938** *Nature* 7 May 815/1 The sand dune..can be aptly described as an edaphic desert—a desert that is due, not to climatic but to soil conditions, since the coarse texture and very low organic content render sand a very poor retainer of water. **1949** *New Biology* VI. 54 Thus under semi-arid conditions, the 'natural' vegetation type may be open grassland, without trees of any kind... Such grasslands..may provide an example of an edaphic climax, seral development being arrested because of soil influences.

edaphodont ('ɛdəfəʊdɒnt), *a. Palæont.* [ad. mod.L. *edaphodus* (*-odont-*), f. Gr. ἔδαφος floor + ὀδούς, ὀδόντ-ος tooth; the name was given by Buckland on account of the shape of the teeth.] A fish of the fossil genus *Edaphodus*, remains of which are found in deposits ranging from the Cretaceous to the Eocene.

1854 OWEN in *Circ. Sc.* (*c* 1865) II. 97/1 The cylindrical dental masses of the..edaphodont fishes.

edaphon ('ɛdəfɒn). *Ecology.* [G. (R. Francé *Das Edaphon* (1913)), f. Gr. ἔδαφ-ος floor + *-on* as in *plankton*.] The community of microflora and microfauna in the soil.

1927 S. A. WAKSMAN *Princ. Soil Microbiol.* xxiv. 642 We are..justified in speaking of a soil population and may even accept the idea of an Edaphon as suggested by Francé, although his conclusion that the edaphon is an indicator of soil fertility may not be fully justified. **1932** FULLER & CONARD tr. *Braun-Blanquet's Plant Sociol.* iv. 76 The quantitative investigation of the edaphon and aeroplankton ..the soil and air floras. **1960** N. POLUNIN *Introd. Plant Geogr.* xi. 316 Mention should also be made..of the 'edaphon', the flora and fauna of the soil.

†**'edbote.** *Obs. rare.* [f. ED- + BOOT *sb.*[1]] Restitution, amends, satisfaction.

c **1315** SHOREHAM 31 Penaunce heth maneres thre, Thorȝ sorȝe, schryfte, and edbote. *Ibid.* 36 Wanne man hys repentaunt i-schrive, He schold don edbote.

‖**Edda** ('ɛdə). [ON.; usually identified with *Edda* the name of the great-grandmother in the ON. poem 'Rigsþul' (see Vigf. and Powell *Corpus Poet. Bor.* II. 514); others consider it to be f. *óðr* poetry.] The name given to two distinct Icelandic books:

a. By Icelandic poets of 15th c. applied to a miscellaneous handbook to Icel. poetry, containing prosodic and grammatical treatises, with quotations and prose paraphrases of myths from old poems. This work (partly written by

the Icelandic historian Snorre Sturluson *c* 1230) has since 1642 been commonly called Snorre's Edda, or the Younger or Prose Edda.

b. A collection (made *c* 1200) of ancient ON. poems on mythical and traditional subjects. The names 'Elder or Poetic Edda', 'Edda of Sæmund', were applied to this work by Biorn of Skardsá, who erroneously ascribed its compilation to the Icelandic historian Sæmund (*d.* 1133).

1771 MACPHERSON *Introd. Hist. Gt. Brit.* 180 Neither does the Islandic Edda..supply that defect. **1840** CARLYLE *Heroes* (1858) 196 Edda, a word of uncertain etymology, is thought to signify Ancestress. **1866** *Reader* 3 Mar. 221/2 The Elder (or Poetic) Edda is a volume of very old mythological and heroic lays. **1875** WHITNEY *Life Lang.* x. 181 The Edda is the purest and most abundant source of knowledge for primitive Germanic conditions.

Hence **E'ddaic, 'Eddic** *a.*, of or pertaining to the Eddas; resembling the contents of the Eddas.

1868 G. STEPHENS *Runic Mon.* I. Introd. 41 No Eddic or other Manuscripts..are older than..the 13th century. **1884** *Athenæum* 30 Aug. 267/1 African and Australian myths almost as Eddaic..may be quoted. **1883** VIGF. & POWELL *Corp. Poet. Bor.* I. 101 There are not one but many mythologies in the Eddic poems.

eddas, var. of EDDOES.

edder ('ɛdə(r)), *sb. Obs.* exc. *dial.* Also 8–9 **eather**. [Of doubtful etymology; some have identified it with OE. *eodor, eder* enclosure = OHG. *etar*, ON. *jaðarr* edge, border.] Osiers, hazelrods, or other light flexible wood, used for interlacing the stakes of a hedge at the top. Also in ***stake and edder (eather) fence***. Hence **'edder** *v.*; also **ether**, *trans.* to interlace or bind (a hedge) at the top with osiers, etc. **'eddering** *vbl. sb.*, (*a*) the action of the verb; (*b*) *concr.* the materials used in the operation.

[*Beowulf* 1038 Mearas..on flet teon in under ederas. *a* **1000** *Wanderer* (Gr.-Wülcker) 77 Stondaþ..hryðge ða ederas.] **1523** FITZHERB. *Husb.* §126 Whan thou haste made thy hedge and eddered it well, than take thy mall agayne and dryue downe thy edderinges. **1577** TUSSER *Husb.* xxxiii. (1878) 73 Save edder and stake, strong hedge to make. **1664** SPELMAN *Gloss.* s.v. *Etarchartea*, Angli..hoc ipsum the edar and ethar appellantes. **1725** BRADLEY *Fam. Dict.* II. s.v. *Quickset*, Edder..is to bind the Top of the Stakes in with some small long Poles, or Sticks on each Side. **1784–1815** A. YOUNG *Ann. Agric.* VII. 25 The stake and eather fence, for new made fences, is the cheapest. **1805** R. W. DICKSON *Pract. Agric.* (1807) II. 626 Hurdles, fagots, stakes and edders. **1863** MORTON *Cycl. Agric.* Gloss. (E.D.S.) *Ethering* is running a line of hazel, or other flexible rods, intertwiningly along the top of a hedge.

edder, obs. and dial. var. of ADDER *sb.*[1], EIDER.

edders, var. of EDDOES.

eddish ('ɛdɪʃ). Forms: (? 1 edisc, -esc), 6–7 edysche, -ysshe, -ish, 6–8 etch(e, 7–8 eadish (7 esh), (9 *dial.* eddige, hedditch), 7– eddish. See also EARSH, ARRISH. [Of obscure etymology.

Usually identified with OE. *edisc* park or enclosed pasture (glossed *vivarium*), with which cf. OE. *yddisc*, rendering L. *supellex, supellectile*, ? household stuff. It is difficult to see how the meaning of the OE. word could have given rise to the mod. sense of *eddish*, which, though widely diffused in dialects, has not been traced further back than the 15th c.; and the assumption that 'aftergrowth' is the unrecorded primary sense of OE. *edisc* 'park' appears too hazardous. The current derivation from OE. *ed-* 'again' suits the modern sense, but (even if this sense were demonstrated for OE.) involves difficulties with regard to form.]

†**1.** OE. *edisc*: A park or enclosed pasture for cattle.

a **700** *Epinal Gloss.* 147 Broel, edisc [*Corpus* 324 *Broel*, edisc, deortuun]. **778** *Ags. Charter* in Sweet *O.E. Texts* 427 *Agellum qui dicitur* tatan edisc. **822** *Ibid.* 458 Greotan edesces lond. *a* **1000** *Ags. Ps.* xcix. [c.] 3 We his folc syndan and his fæle sceap, þa he on his edisce ealle afedde.

2. a. Grass (also clover, etc.) which grows again; an aftergrowth of grass after mowing (in first quot. perhaps 'brushwood'). **b.** Stubble; a stubble-field.

1468 *Medulla Gram.* in *Promp. Parv.* 136 *Frutex*, a styke, a yerde, and buske, vnderwode, or eddysche. **1523** FITZHERBERT *Surv.* 2 Yet hath the lorde the Edysshe and the aftermathe. **1573** TUSSER *Husb.* xviii. (1878) 43 Soile perfectly knowe, er edish ye sowe. **1634** W. WOOD *New Eng. Prosp.* I. iv, There is little edish or after-pasture. **1669** WORLIDGE *Syst. Agric.* (1681) 325 Eddish, Eadish, Etch, Ersh or Eegrass, the latter Pasture, or Grass that comes after Mowing or Reaping. *a* **1728** BP. KENNETT *Lansdowne MS.* 1033 in *Promp. Parv.* 135 *note*, Eddish, roughings or aftermath in meadows, but more properly the stubble or gratten in corn-fields. **1744–50** W. ELLIS *Mod. Husbandm.* v. i. 101 Eddishes, stubble-fields. **1795** VANCOUVER *Agric. Survey Essex* 50 The bean etche well cleaned in the autumn and sown again with wheat; a small portion of these etches are occasionally sown with tares. **1830** *Boston* (Linc.) *Gazette* 19 Oct., Pastures have been abundant and the eddishes luxuriant. **1863** *Lanc. Fents* 23 Owd Ned had gone ..a-helpen..t' heawse ther hedditch. **1880** MISS JACKSON *Shropsh. Word-bk.* s.v., The young beäs han broke into the clover eddish.

c. = EATAGE.

1843 LD. ABINGER 12 *Meeson & Welsby's Rep.* LXII, The action is brought..for the eddish or eatage of a field.

3. *attrib.*, as in ***eddish-grass***; **eddish-cheese**, cheese made from the milk of cows fed on the aftermath; **eddish-crop** (see quot. 1863); †**eddish-hen** [f. OE. *edisc*; see 1], a quail.

c **825** *Vesp. Psalter* civ. [cv.] 40 Bedun flæsc & cwom him edeschen. *a* **1300** *E.E. Psalter* civ. [cv.] 40 Þai asked, and come þe edissehenne. **1610** MARKHAM *Masterp.* I. xxxv. 68 Eddish grasse..in some countries is called after-maths. **1615** —— *Eng. Housew.* II. vi. (1668) 152 Touching your Eddish cheese, or Winter cheese. **1861** WHYTE-MELVILLE *Mkt. Harb.* 267 A ham..an Eddish cheese, and a few other trifles. **1863** MORTON *Cycl. Agric.* (E.D.S.) *Eddish-crop* (Ess.) is a grain crop after grain.

eddit, var. of ADIT, a watercourse.

1807 VANCOUVER *Agric. Devon* (1813) 79 The eddits that are taken up from the several streams.

eddoes ('ɛdəʊz). Also edoes, eddas, edders, eddy (in *eddy-root*). [An African word, from the language of the Gold Coast.] 'The tuberous stems of various araceous plants, as *Colocasia esculenta..Caladium bicolor*, etc.' (*Treas. Bot.*). ***eddy-root***: the root of the taro (*Colocasia macrorhiza*).

1685 BURTON *Engl. Empire America* x. 142 Carrots, Potatoes, and Edoes, a substantial wholesome nourishing Root. **1750** G. HUGHES *Barbados* 227 The different species of Eddas are distinguished into the blue Eddas, the scratching Eddas, and the roasting Eddas. **1772–84** COOK *Voy.* (1790) VI. 2022 Extensive plantations, consisting of the taro or eddy root, and sweet potatoes. **1803** T. WINTERBOTTOM *Sierra Leone* I. iv. 64 *note*, Eddoes, arum sagittæ folium, have been introduced by the Nova Scotian settlers. **1841** ORDERSON *Creol.* ii. 10 Yams, potatoes, and eddoes.

†**'eddre.** *Obs.* Forms: 1 ǽdre, édre, ædre, 3 eddre. [OE. *ǽdre* = OFris. *eddere, eddre*, OHG. *âdara, âdra* (Du., Ger. *ader*), OSw. *áþra* (Sw. *ådra*):—OTeut. ***ǣðrôn-***; cogn. w. ON. *ǽð-r* (repr. OTeut. type **ǣði-z*), of same meaning; the Gr. ἦτορ heart, ἦτρον belly, may be ultimately connected.] A bloodvessel, vein.

Beowulf 2967 (Gr.) Swat ædrum sprong forð under fexe. *c* **1000** *Ags. Ps.* lxxii[i]. 17 (Gr.) Wærun mine ædra ealle tolysde. *a* **1225** *Ancr. R.* 258 Men..hudeð ham hwon heo beoð ileten blod on one erm eddre. *a* **1300** *Vox & Wolf* 45 Ich have hem leten eddre blod.

eddy ('ɛdɪ), *sb.* Also 5 *Sc.* **ydy**, 6–7 **edie**, **eddee**, **-ie**. [Of unknown history; app. first recorded in 15th c.; if of Eng. origin, the sense seems to point to connexion with ED-; cf. ON. *iða* of same meaning.]

1. 'The water that by some interruption in its course, runs contrary to the direction of the tide or current' (Adm. Smyth); a circular motion in water, a small whirlpool.

a **1455** *Houlate* lxiv, The barde..socht wattir to wesche him thar out in ane ydy. **1553** BRENDE *Q. Curtius* 245 (R.) Suche as..escaped theire enemies, were..drowned wyth.. the eddies of the streame. **1665** MANLEY *Grotius' Low-C. Warrs* 251 The strong eddy or Whirlepoole of the River.. brought it into the Trench. **1684** T. BURNET *Th. Earth* I. 131 Those great eddees..that suck into them..whatever comes within their reach. **1727** THOMSON *Spring* 816 The madness of the straiten'd stream Turns in black eddies round. **1810** SCOTT *Lady of L.* III. vii, The wheeling eddies boil. **1882** WHITE *Naval Archit.* 449 It is blunt tails rather than blunt noses that cause eddies.

2. *transf.* Wind, fog, dust, etc. moving in a similar way; a circular movement of wind, etc.

1815 ELPHINSTONE *Acc. Caubul* (1842) I. 173 Rain.. brought..by the eddy in the winds. **1865** DICKENS *Mut. Fr.* III. i. 269 Indicated through circling eddies of fog. **1878** M. A. BROWN *Nadeschda* 22 A dustcloud rolls in eddies forth.

3. *fig.*

1791 G. MORRIS in Sparks *Corr. Amer. Rev.* (1853) IV. 413 There is in the current of their affairs a strong eddy or counter tide. **1817** COLERIDGE *Biog. Lit.* 147 An eddy of criticism. **1850** TENNYSON *In Mem.* xlviii, The lightest wave of thought shall lisp, The fancy's tenderest eddy wreathe. **1868** STANLEY *Westm. Ab.* iii. 139 These are but the eddies of the royal history. **1875** FARRAR *Seekers* II. iv. 231 In the mighty eddies of an unseen, mysterious agency.

4. *Comb.*, as ***eddy-breeze, -stream, -tide***; **eddy-chamber**, a chamber in which a current of fluid is compelled to whirl in eddies; **eddy-current**, a current of electricity induced in places where such currents are undesirable and cause waste of energy; also ***eddy-current brake, loss***; **eddy-rock** (see quot.); **eddy-water** (also *eddy*, Adm. Smyth), the dead water under a ship's counter. Also EDDY-WIND.

1799 *Naval Chron.* I. 250 *Eddy breezes from a hilly shore. **1899** *Yearbk. U.S. Dept. Agric.* 153 W. S. Barnard, working under the direction of Riley, invented the admirable *eddy chamber, or 'cyclone system' of nozzles. **1600** HAKLUYT *Voy.* III 291 (R.) From the Cape to Virginia ..are none but *eddie currents. **1887** *Soc. Telegr. Engin. Jrnl.* XVI. 65 The coil is surrounded..by a circular pole piece, cut away at one point to hinder eddy-currents. **1892** W. P. MAYCOCK *Electr. Lighting* I. vi. 158 Most armatures of direct current machines have iron cores, and the revolution of the cores in the magnetic field would..cause currents to be induced in the core... These currents [are] called *foucault* or *eddy currents*. **1930** *Engineering* 6 June 724/3 Three systems were in use, operated, respectively, by hydraulic, pneumatic and electro-magnetic (eddy currents in the wheels) means. **1934** WEBSTER, *Eddy-current brake. **1940** *Chambers's Techn. Dict.* 281/1 *Eddy-current loss. **1943** *Electronic Engin.* XVI. 194 If a solid conductor is replaced by a number of insulated strands..it appears obvious at first sight that the eddy current losses must be reduced. **1877** A. GREEN *Phys. Geol.* iv. §1. 124 Rock possessing this [Current-Bedding] structure is sometimes called **Eddy-Rock* by quarrymen and well-sinkers. **1725** DE FOE *Voy. round W.* (1840) 352 They would rather have an *eddy stream against them. **1627** CAPT. SMITH *Seaman's Gram.* x. 48 An *Eddie tide is where the water doth runne backe contrary to the tide. **1887** *Pall Mall G.* 23 Aug. 8/2 Owing to the eddy tide these operations were not attended with success.

eddy ('ɛdɪ), *v.* [f. prec. sb.]

1. *intr.* To move in an eddy or eddies: said properly of water and objects borne on water; also of air, vapour, etc., and *transf.* of birds on the wing. Also *fig.*

1810 SCOTT *Lady of L.* I. xvii, Eddying in almost viewless wave, The weeping willow twig to lave. **1813** —— *Trierm.* III. vii, The unwonted sound, Eddying in echoes round and round. **1833** MARRYAT *P. Simple* (1863) 158 The wind was high..sweeping in the rain in every direction as it eddyed to and fro. **1844** *Mem. Babylonian P'cess* II. 91 Large hungry eagles..eddying far above into the regions of air. **1856** KANE *Arct. Expl.* II. xxviii. 285 A flat cake of ice eddied round near the floe we were upon. **1860** TYNDALL *Glac.* I. §14. 97 The vapour..eddying wildly in the air.

2. *trans.* To whirl round in eddies. Also with *in*: to collect as into an eddy (*rare*).

1730 THOMSON *Autumn* 322 The circling mountains eddy in From the bare wild the dissipated storm. **1858** *Sat. Rev.* VI. 113/1 How are we to tell that a comet..may not get eddyed (so to speak) by some great planet? **1878** SMILES *Robt. Dick* iv. 28 The water is churned and eddied about.

eddying ('ɛdɪɪŋ), *vbl. sb.* [f. prec. + -ING[1].] The action of the vb. EDDY: moving in circles, whirling. In quots. *transf.* and *fig.*

1817 COLERIDGE *Biog. Lit.* 220 An eddying instead of progression of thought. **1830** TENNYSON *Ode to Mem.* ii, The eddying of her garments caught from thee The light of thy great presence. **1886** *Athenæum* 10 July 39/1 The twistings and eddyings of the political current.

'eddying, *ppl. a.* [f. as prec. + ING[2].] Moving in eddies; full of eddies.

1837 HAWTHORNE *Twice-told T.* (1851) II. ix. 127 The eddying wind has kept them [the roofs] bare at the bleak corners. **1870** BRYANT *Iliad* I. v. 158 From Lycia where the eddying Xanthus runs. **1873** H. SPENCER *Stud. Sociol.* i. 16 The eddying vapours..had been mingling..in endless ways.

eddyless ('ɛdɪlɪs), *a.* [f. EDDY *sb.* + -LESS.] Without eddies, tranquil; also *fig.*

1621 G. SANDYS *Ovid's Met.* v. (1626) 104 A silent streame I found, All eddilesse, perspicuous to the ground. **1862** R. PATTERSON *Ess. Hist. & Art* 485 To mortify the body, and still the mind into eddyless meditation.

eddy-root: see s.v. EDDOES.

'eddy-wind. A wind that moves in an eddy.

1626 CAPT. SMITH *Accid. Yng. Seamen* 17 A gust, a storme ..an eddy wind. **1647** WARD *Simp. Cobler* 20 Men..that are weather-waft up and down with every eddy-wind of every new doctrine. **1697** DRYDEN *Virg. Georg.* I. 505 Chaff with eddy Winds is whirl'd around. **1715** DESAGULIERS *Fires Impr.* 152 Such Eddy-Winds blow from the South when we have them here at London. **1772–84** COOK *Voy.* (1790) IV. 1218 There is..an eddy wind at S.W. **1867** SMYTH *Sailor's Word-bk.* s.v., The eddy-wind of a sail escaping in a curve makes the sail abaft shiver.

ede, ME. f. of *eode*, OE. pa. t. of GO.

†**edeci'mation.** *Obs.* *rare*$^{-1}$. [a. L. *ēdecimātiōn-em*, f. *ēdecimā-re*, f. *ē* out + *decimus* tenth.] The action or process of taking a tithe or tenth.

a **1693** URQUHART *Rabelais* III. xlviii. 386 The Edecimation and Tith-haling of their Goods.

‖**edelweiss** ('eːdəlvaɪs). [f. Ger. *edel* noble + *weiss* white.] An Alpine plant, *Gnaphalium Leontopodium* or *Leontopodium alpinum*, remarkable for its white flower, growing in rocky places, often scarcely accessible, on the Swiss mountains. Also *attrib.*, as in ***edelweiss-lace***.

1862 EMERSON *Thoreau* Wks. (Bohn) III. 339 It is called by..the Swiss Edelweiss, which signifies Noble Purity. **1878** BROWNING *La Saisiaz* 21, I knew an Alpine-rose which all beside named Edelweiss. **1882** *Charles Lowder* 356 A.. cross of edelweis had been placed on the coffin. **1884** *Daily News* 10 Nov. 2/7 Perhaps the most successful rival of Nottingham goods is the German-Swiss Edelweiss lace.

edematose, -ous, var. ff. ŒDEMATOSE, -OUS.

Eden ('iːd(ə)n). [a. Heb. *ēden*; etymologically 'pleasure, delight'.]

1. The abode of Adam and Eve at their creation, Paradise; also more fully, ***the garden of Eden***.

1382 WYCLIF *Gen.* iv. 16 Caym..dwellide at the eest plage of Eden. **1535** COVERDALE *Gen.* ii. 8 The Lorde God also planted a garden of pleasure in Eden. *Ibid.* iii. 23 Then the Lorde God put him out of the garden of Eden. **1667** MILTON *P.L.* v. 143 Discovering..all the East Of Paradise and Edens happie Plains. **1796–7** COLERIDGE *Poems* (1862) 14 Ah flowers! which joy from Eden stole While innocence stood smiling by. **1860** HAWTHORNE *Marb. Faun*, II. x. 108 What the flaming sword was to the first Eden, such is the malaria to these sweet gardens and groves.

2. *transf.* and *fig.* A delightful abode or resting-place, a paradise; a state of supreme happiness.

a **1225** *Juliana* 79 He [the translator] mote beon a corn i godes guldene edene. **1593** SHAKS. *Rich. II*, II. i. 42 This sceptred Isle This other Eden, demy paradise. **1665–9** BOYLE *Occas. Refl.* (1675) 320 He inherits..a gay and priviledg'd Plot of his Eden. **1792** S. ROGERS *Pleas. Mem.* II. 128 Who acts thus wisely mark the moral Muse A blooming Eden in his life reviews. **1830** MRS. BRAY *Fitz of F.* i. (1884) 9 Mount Edgcombe, that Eden of Devon. **1842** TENNYSON *Gardener's Dau.* 187 Henceforward squall nor storm Could keep me from the Eden where she dwelt.

Hence **Edenic** (iːˈdɛnɪk), *a.*, of or pertaining to Eden; **ˈEdenize** *v. trans.*, to make like Eden; to admit into Eden or Paradise; **ˈEdenized** *ppl. a.*, **ˌEdeniˈzation**.

a **1618** J. DAVIES *Wit's Pilgrim.* N iv. (T.) For pure saints edeniz'd unfit. **1850** MRS. BROWNING *Poems* I. 75 By the memory of Edenic joys Forfeit and lost. **1862** D. WILSON *Preh. Man* iii. (1865) 22 The moral contrast which the savage presents to our conceptions of Edenic life. **1877** WRAXALL tr. *V. Hugo's Miserables* IV. v. 4 The Edenization of the world.

edenite (ˈiːdənaɪt). *Min.* [ad. G. *edenit* (E. F. Glocker *Grundriss d. Min.* (1839) 410), f. *Eden*ville, Orange County, New York: see -ITE[1].] A light-coloured sodian variety of hornblende containing relatively little iron.

1842 L. C. BECK *Mineral. New York* II. vi. 302 About a mile north of Edenville is another locality, at which the crystals [of hornblende] are of a hair-brown or grey color, associated with..mica and chondrodite, in white limestone. They vary in size from very small to an inch in diameter. From the peculiarity of its colour, it has sometimes been called *Edenite*. **1868** J. D. DANA *Syst. Min.* (ed. 5) 235 Aluminous Magnesia-Lime Amphibole. (*a*) Edenite... (*b*) Smaragdite. **1886** *Jrnl. Chem. Soc.* L. 519 Edenite (Hornblende). Colour green..or greyish-yellow. **1932** W. E. FORD *Dana's Textbk. Mineral.* (ed. 4) 575 The varieties of hornblende here included range from the light-colored edenite, containing but little iron..to the dark-colored or black hornblende.

edental (iːˈdɛntəl), *a.* [f. E- + L. *dent-em* tooth + -AL[1].] = next.

1845 DARWIN *Voy. Nat.* v. (1873) 82 Another gigantic edental quadruped. **1883** in *Syd. Soc. Lex.*

‖**Edenˈtata**, *sb. pl.* [mod.L., f. *ēdentātus*, f. *ēdentāre* to render toothless, knock a person's teeth out, f. *ē* out + *dent-em* tooth.] An order of Mammalia characterized by the absence of front teeth; represented by the Ant-eater, Armadillo, Sloth, etc.

1834 MᶜMURTRIE *Cuvier's Anim. Kingd.* 92 The Edentata, or quadrupeds without front teeth. **1859** DARWIN *Orig. Spec.* iv. (1878) 99 The three lowest orders of mammals, namely, marsupials, edentata, and rodents.

edentate (iːˈdɛnteɪt), *a.* and *sb.* [ad. L. *ēdentātus*; see prec.]

A. *adj.* Characterized by the absence of incisor and canine teeth; belonging to the order *Edentata*; see B. Sometimes = 'toothless'.

1828 STARK *Elem. Nat. Hist.* I. 406 Mouth not entirely furnished with teeth, and often edentate. **1835–6** TODD *Cycl. Anat.* I. 245/2 The mouth..consists of two..edentate mandibles sheathed with horn. **1885** PARKER *Mammalian Desc.* iv. 96 He is not truly edentate, but has teeth.

B. *sb.* **1.** in *pl.* = EDENTATA.

1835 KIRBY *Hab. & Inst. Anim.* II. xvii. 208 Like most of the other Edentates, they [the Sloths] can roll themselves up and take a long and reckless sleep. **1880** HAUGHTON *Phys. Geog.* vi. 269 The Edentates are among the lowest forms of placental Mammals.

2. *humorously.* One who has lost his teeth.

1850 KINGSLEY *Alt. Locke* xxxvi. (1874) 270 How could a poor edentate like myself articulate a word?

†**eˈdentate**, *v. Obs.*⁻⁰ [f. as prec.] *trans.* To strike out, or draw out (a person's) teeth.

1656 in BLOUNT *Glossogr.* **1721–1800** in BAILEY.

Hence †**edenˈtation**, the extraction of teeth.

1623 in COCKERAM.

edention, erroneous form of EDENTATION.

1623 COCKERAM II, A Pulling out of teeth, *edention* [but *edentation* in pt. I].

edentulous (iːˈdɛntjʊləs), *a.* [f. L. *edentulus* toothless, f. *ē* out + *dent-em* tooth + -OUS.] Having no teeth, toothless.

1782 MONRO *Compar. Anat.* 110 The chin and nose of edentulous people are much nearer. **1784** *Phil. Trans.* LXXIV. 281 Fishes..[are] apparently utter strangers to edentulous old age. **1839–47** TODD *Cycl. Anat.* III. 367/1 The jaws [of echidna] are edentulous. **1859** J. TOMES *Dental Surg.* 39 Instances..in which the jaws have been entirely edentulous.

†**ˈeder, ˈedera.** *Obs. rare.* [ad. and a. L. (*h*)*edera*.] Ivy. (The L. word was prob. retained by Wyclif in the version of 1382 from ignorance of its meaning. In *Jonah* the A.V. has 'gourd'.)

1382 WYCLIF *Jonah* iv. 6 The Lord God made redy an eder [**1388** an yuy], and it styede vp on the hed of Jonas. —— *2 Macc.* vi. 7 Crownyd with edera [**1388** with yuy].

ederling. ? Mistake for **elderling* ancestor [f. *elder*, ALDER *sb.*[2] + -LING.]

c **1300** *K. Alis.* 1711 Darie, the kyng of alle kynges, The godis..hath to ederlyng.

edestin (ɪˈdɛstɪn). *Chem.* [f. Gr. ἐδεστός eatable + -IN[1].] A globulin occurring in hempseed; also, any of several globulins in wheat, rye, etc.

1894 OSBORNE & VOORHEES in *Rep. Connecticut Agric. Exper. Station 1893* 216 This substance agrees in composition with the vitellin which exists in the seeds of wheat, maize... For this body we adopt the name *Edestin.* **1896** *Jrnl. Chem. Soc.* LXX. I. 400 The proteid which is soluble in saline solutions the author shows to be edestin, or vegetable vitellin. **1926** J. S. HUXLEY *Essays Pop. Sci.* viii. 88 Many others [*sc.* proteins], such as edestin from hemp-seed. **1947** *New Biol.* III. 121 Edestin (molecular weight 300,000) and other protein particles have also been photographed.

edge (ɛdʒ), *sb.* Forms: 1 ecg(g, 3–7 egge, (3 agge, hegge, 5–6 eg(e, 6–7 edg), 5– edge. [OE. *ęcg* str. fem. = OS. *eggia* (MDu. *egghe*, Du. *egge*) edge, corner, point, OHG. *ekka* edge, point (MHG. *ecke* edge, point, corner, mod.Ger. *ecke* fem., *eck* neut., corner), ON. *egg* edge:—OTeut. **agjâ*, f. OAryan root **ak*, whence many words of cognate sense, e.g. L. *acies*, Gr. ἀκίς point; cf. AIL *sb.*, AWN, EAR *sb.*[2] (The sense 'corner', which has been developed in Ger. and Du., is wanting in Eng.)]

I. A cutting edge.

1. a. The thin sharpened side of the blade of a cutting instrument or weapon; opposed to the 'back' or blunt side; or to the 'flat' or broad surface of the blade. Often associated with *point* (OE. *ord*). ***the edge of the sword***: used rhetorically for 'the sword' as the typical instrument of slaughter or of conquest.

Beowulf 1549 (Gr.) Breost net..wið ord and wið ecge ingang forstod. *c* **1000** *Ags. Gosp.* Luke xxi. 24 Hi3 feallað on swurdes ecge [*c* **1160** egge]. *c* **1200** *Trin. Coll. Hom.* 61 He wile smite..mid egge and cleuen..oðer mid orde and pilten. *c* **1374** CHAUCER *Troylus* IV. 899 Beth rather to hym cause of flat than egge. *c* **1450** *Voc.* in Wr.-Wülcker 735 *Hoc acumen, Hec acies*, a neg. **1594** PLAT *Jewell-ho.* I. 20 Some kindes of salt..doe giue such temper to the edges of weapons. **1605** SHAKS. *Macb.* IV. i. 150, I will..giue to th' edge o' th' Sword his Wife. **1611** BIBLE *Gen.* xxxiv. 26 They slew Hamor and Shechem..with the edge of the sword. —— *Hebr.* xi. 34 [They] escaped the edge of the sword. **1648** MILTON *Tenure Kings* Wks. 1738 I. 317 And what restraint the Sword comes to at length, having both edge and point, if any Sceptic will needs doubt, let him feel. **1797** GODWIN *Enquirer* I. ii. 9 A tool with a fine edge may do mischief. **1828** SCOTT *F.M. Perth* II. 20 When it was steel coat to frieze mantle, the thieves knew..whether swords had edges or no. **1871** FREEMAN *Norm. Conq.* (1876) IV. xvii. 54 The King by the edge of the sword changed himself..into a King according to the laws of England.

¶ humorously misused.

1596 SHAKS. *Merch. V.* II. ii. 173 To be in perill of my life with the edge of a featherbed. **1599** —— *Hen. V*, III. vi. 50 And let not Bardolphs vitall thred bee cut With edge of Penny-Cord.

b. *poet.* A cutting weapon or tool; in ME. also a lance.

Beowulf 2876 (Gr.) þæt he hyne sylfne 3ewræc ana mid ecge. *c* **1205** LAY. 5605 He hauede monie Alemains: mid agge [**1275** hegge] to-heowen. *c* **1300** *K. Alis.* 1271 He griputh in hond a spere..Thoroghout the bruny creopeth the egge. *c* **1325** *E.E. Allit. P.* B. 1104 Nauþer to cout ne to kerue, with knyf ne wyth egge. *c* **1374** CHAUCER *Former Age* 19 No flessh ne wyste offence of egge or spere. **1607** SHAKS. *Cor.* v. v. 113 Men and lads Stain all your edges on me. **1791** COWPER *Iliad* XXI. 25 On all sides Down came his edge.

c. The sharpness given to a blade by whetting.

c **1430** *Syr Gener.* (Roxb.) 5147 His naked swerd in hond he bare, The egge was mich wered a-wey. **1517** TORKINGTON *Pilgr.* (1884) 21 Tooles made of Iron that never lese ther egge by myracle of Seynt Nicholas. **1850** BLACKIE *Æschylus* I. Pref. 10 It is for lack of skill in the workman, not from want of edge in the tool. *Mod.* The knife has no edge. Put an edge on this knife.

2. *fig.* **a.** With direct reference to 1, 1 c. Power to 'cut' or wound; keen effectiveness. of language: Trenchant Force (cf. *point*). Of appetite, passion, desires, enjoyment, etc.: Keenness. Phrases (used also *lit.* in 1, 1 c), †*to add an edge to*; *to put, set an edge upon*; *to dull, blunt the edge of*, etc. ***not to put too fine an edge upon it***: to use 'blunt', outspoken language. *to give* (a person) ***the rough edge of one's tongue***, to abuse, revile.

a **1593** H. SMITH *Serm.* (1866) II. 88 To add an edge unto our prayers. **1594** SHAKS. *Rich. III*, v. v. 35 Abate the edge of Traitors, Gracious Lord. **1596** —— *Tam. Shr.* I. ii. 73 She moues me not, or not remoues, at least, Affections edge in me. **1603** FLORIO *Montaigne* (1634) 503 Faults and contrary successes give it [love] edge and grace. **1610** SHAKS. *Temp.* IV. i. 29 To take away The edge of that dayes celebration. **1625** DONNE *Serm.* 195 The apostle there changes the edge of his argument. **1642** FULLER *Holy & Prof. St.* III. xi. 179 Take not too much at once, lest thy brain turn edge. **1661** BRAMHALL *Just Vind.* iv. 87 The edge and validity of it [ecclesiastical law] did proceed from authority royal. **1704** *Col. Rec. Penn.* II. 142 Pleads reasons yᵉ Edge of which..has wore off. **1775** SHERIDAN *Rivals* 1st Prol., No tricking here, to blunt the edge of law. **1830** T. HAMILTON *C. Thornton* (1845) 79 Exercise..had given more than its wonted edge to my appetite. **1846** PRESCOTT *Ferd. & Is.* II. vii. 416 Several circumstances operated to sharpen the edge of intolerance. **1870** SWINBURNE *Ess. & Stud.* (1875) 286 The marble majesty of Calantha [in Ford's 'Broken Heart']..gives force and edge to the lofty passion of the catastrophe. **1879** LOWELL *Poet. Wks.* 375 Yet knows to put an edge upon his speech. *a* **1891** *Mod.* He is, not to put too fine an edge upon it, a thoroughpaced scoundrel. **1915** WODEHOUSE *Psmith, Journalist* (1923) xiii. 90 It will give our output precisely the edge it requires. **1932** H. CRANE *Let.* 31 Mar. (1965) 405 Dangers that give the same edge to life here that the mountains give to the horizon. **1936** W. HOLTBY *South Riding* III. iii. 175 That girl gives them the rough edge of her tongue. **1939** W. H. BAUMER *Sports as taught and played at West Point* 348 Often talk by the trainer on any other subject than the game will take off the 'edge'. **1939** F. THOMPSON *Lark Rise* i. 14 It took the edge off the appetite. **1946** *Penguin Music Mag.* Dec. 103 The tone is full and incisive, with a distinct edge to it—perhaps rather too distinct. **1957** *Essays & Studies* X. 42 'Then came still Evening on.' The stately order takes the edge off the homely expression 'Evening came on'.

†**b.** Of persons: Ardour, keenness in pursuit of an object; in weaker sense, inclination, liking.

1581 SAVILE *Tacitus' Hist.* II. xlii. (1591) 78 The Othonians, laying aside all edge to fight. **1605** BACON *Adv. Learning* II. 112 He must take heed he shew..some sparkles of liberty, spirit, and edge. *a* **1638** MEDE *Ep. Hayn* xii. Wks. 752, I have little or no edge to contend with one I think perswaded. **1642** ROGERS *Naaman* 183, I have so small hope to prevaile with men, because I goe against their edge. *Ibid.* 390 As for others, their edge is not so much toward them. **1868** W. COLLINS *Moonstone* I. v. 55 'Betteredge, your edge is better than ever...' 'He's a wonderful man for his age.'

†**c.** ***to give an edge to, set an edge upon*** (a person): to stimulate, incite. *Obs.* (Cf. EDGE, EGG *vbs.*)

1602 SHAKS. *Ham.* III. i. 27 Giue him a further edge. **1609** HOLLAND *Livy* VI. xxviii. 237 The memoriall of that late..losse sustained might rather stirre them up and set an edge upon them. **1626** W. SCLATER *Expos. 2 Thess.* (1629) 274 What is wanting to give us an edge to the duty.

d. Of temper (cf. EDGY *a.* 4).

1916 'BOYD CABLE' *Action Front* 224 The company commanders found him with rather a sharp edge to his temper.

e. ***to have an*** (or ***the***) ***edge on, to get the edge on*** (and similar phrases with *over*): to have a grudge against (quot. 1896); to have (or acquire) an advantage over. Also used without a following *on* or *over* in sense 'advantage, superiority'. orig. *U.S.*

1896 *Daily News* 18 Mar. 7/5, I expect that when I am gone, especially from your own people, who always had an edge on me, and for no reason. **1911** C. E. MULFORD *Bar-20 Days* (1921) xiv. 147 I'll do anything to get th'edge on that thief. **1914** JOYCE *Dubliners* 48 She had always had an edge on her, especially whenever there were people listening. **1929** *Publishers' Weekly* 14 Sept. 1060 Here we have the edge on our rivals, not only because of our superior location, but also because we are reputedly reckless about reducing prices. **1932** *Latimer Co. News-Democrat* (Wilburton, Okla.) 19 Feb. 1/6 Ray Tucker of the Scripps-Howard Newspaper Alliance gives Murray the edge over Roosevelt in the North Dakota primary. **1932** *N.Y. Herald-Tribune* 2 May 1/4 (*heading*) Herriot's party obtains edge and is held sure to win. **1936** M. MITCHELL *Gone with Wind* liv. 943 Belle's got the edge on you..because she's a kind-hearted, good-natured soul. **1946** WODEHOUSE *Money in Bank* xxiv. 214 Jeff..thought he saw now where she had the edge on Myrtle Shoesmith. She was a quicker starter. **1949** M. MEAD *Male & Female* xv. 316 He has to compete..with girls who have an edge in almost all the activities for which reward is given. **1952** *Times* 19 Dec., Scottish schools also had the edge on the English and Welsh in the matter of pullovers and sweaters. **1953** G. S. COFFIN *Acol & New Point Count* 11 If you hold an average hand..it has no edge over other hands around the table. **1957** *New Yorker* 12 Jan. 79 The Cincinnati Daily Enquirer is solid No. 1 right down the line. Including a 21,000 edge in City Zone circulation..a healthy lead in Retail Display Linage. **1958** *Daily Express* 15 July 6/6 Nancy Mitford's great edge is that she never went to school. **1959** *Listener* 23 Apr. 738/3 The edge was with Mrs. Durran who goes through to the final. **1959** *Spectator* 8 May 654/2 Goat's milk..makes a yoghourt which, therapeutically speaking, has the edge over any made from cow's milk. **1960** *Times* 14 June 16/1 They still hold the edge, especially with Statham in his present form. **1966** *Listener* 3 Mar. 299/2 Labour's special relationship with the working classes..was supposed to give it an edge over the tories.

f. The state of being drunk. *U.S. colloq.*

1920 F. S. FITZGERALD *This Side Paradise* (1921) I. iii. 117 We'll drink to Fred Sloane, who has a fine, distinguished edge. **1925** E. HEMINGWAY *In our Time* iv. 60 'How do you feel?'..'Swell. I've just got a good edge on.'

†**3.** *fig.* Phrases (with direct reference to sense 1), ***back and edge***: adjoining, close by. ***fall back, fall edge***: 'come what may', in any case. ***on edge*** (said of *ears, heart, teeth*; also, *to set*): full of eagerness, all agog, ready.

1580 T. M. *Pref. Verses* in Baret *Alv.* viii, Learned Athens did..set his teeth on edge, such floures to pull As best him likte, to store his skilfull brest. **1590** SPENSER *F.Q.* I. iv. 43 With harts on edg To be aveng'd each on his enimy. **1591** LYLY *Sapho* IV. iv, You will set mine eares on edge with sweet words. **1641–2** HOTHAM in Rushw. *Hist. Coll.* III. (1721) I. 496 Fall back! fall edge! I will go doun. **1699** B. E. *Dict. Cant. Crew* s.v., *Fall back fall edge*, or come what will. **1748** RICHARDSON *Clarissa* (1811) VII. 135 The people who live back and edge.

4. a. ***to set*** (*a person's*) ***teeth on edge***: 'to cause an unpleasant tingling in the teeth' (J.). Also *fig.* Also (rarely) ***out of edge***, in same sense.

It is not quite clear what is the precise notion originally expressed in this phrase. The earlier expression was *to edge the teeth* (see EDGE *v.* 3); in the passage *Ezek.* xviii. 2 the Vulgate has *obstupescere* to be benumbed.

1382 WYCLIF *Ezek.* xviii. 2 And the teeth of sones wexen on egge. **1398** TREVISA *Barth. De P.R.* XVII. clxxxii. (1495) 723 A grene grape greueth the rotes and synewes of the teeth wyth colde soo that they make the teeth an egge. **1535** COVERDALE *Jer.* xxxi. 29 Ye fathers haue eaten a sower grape, and the childrens teth are set on edge. **1578** LYTE *Dodoens* v. xx. 576 The same eaten rawe are good against the teeth being set on edge. **1585** J. HIGINS tr. *Junius' Nomenclator* 428 *Dentium stupor*, a bluntnesse of the teeth, when with eating of ..sowre things they be out of edge. **1596** SHAKS. *1 Hen. IV*, III. i. 133 That would set my teeth nothing an edge, Nothing so much as mincing Poetrie. **1741** MONRO *Anat.* (ed. 3) 162 How come they..to be set on Edge by Acids. **1839** CARLYLE *Chartism* iv. (1858) 20 The strong have eaten sour grapes, and the teeth of the weak are set on edge.

b. *to be on* (occas. *upon* or *on the*) *edge*: to be excited or irritable (cf. 2 d).

1872 MINTO *Man. Eng. Prose Lit.* II. ii. 261 Whitgift's strenuous hostility and unsparing rigour of argument set his opponent on edge. **1900** *Daily News* 4 Oct. 6/1 For me there was to be no sleep far into that night, for my nerves were upon edge. **1908** R. W. CHAMBERS *Firing Line* v. 56 I'm all on edge over this landscape scheme. **1924** J. BUCHAN *Three Hostages* xvi. 227 His manner had not the ease it used to have. He seemed on the edge about something. **1932** *Daily Express* 29 June 6/2 Her nerves were plainly on edge. **1938** S. V. BENÉT *Thirteen o'Clock* 290 He felt fagged and on the edge already. **1951** J. B. PRIESTLEY *Festival at Farbridge* III. i. 394 Laura had in fact worked much too hard, and now she was altogether too fine-drawn and too much on edge.

c. *over the edge*: insane.

1929 E. BOWEN *Last September* III. xvii. 217 He would go over the edge, quite mad.

†**5.** As rendering of L. *acies*: **a.** Line of battle. **b.** Keenness of eyesight. *Obs.*

1535 COVERDALE *1 Sam.* iv. 2 In the Edge in the felde they slewe aboute a foure thousande men. **1682** SIR T. BROWNE *Chr. Mor.* 61 The wise Contriver hath drawn the pictures and outsides of things softly and amiably unto the natural edge of our eyes.

II. Things resembling a cutting edge.

* *with regard to sharpness.*

6. a. The crest of a sharply pointed ridge; freq. in topographical names, as Swirrel Edge, Striding Edge). (More frequently, however, names of this kind denote escarpments terminating a plateau, and therefore are to be referred to sense 11; *e.g.* Millstone Edge, Bamford Edge; in Sc. *edge* usually denotes merely a ridge, watershed.)

c **1325** *E.E. Allit. P.* B. 451 Bot þe hyȝest of þe eggez vnhuled wern a lyttel. **1513** DOUGLAS *Æneis* VIII. viii. 55 The worthy peple Lydiane..remane apoune the edge of the Hetruscane hyllis. **1535** STEWART *Cron. Scot.* III. 371 At Sowtra ege thair merchis than tha maid.

b. A perilous path on a narrow ridge; *fig.* a sharp dividing line; a critical position or moment. (Sometimes with notion of 1; cf. 'to walk on a razor's edge', Gr. ἐπὶ ξυροῦ ἀκμῆς. See also RAZOR *sb.* 1 b.)

1597 SHAKS. *2 Hen. IV*, I. i. 170 You knew he walk'd..on an edge More likely to fall in, then to get o're. **1667** MILTON *P.L.* I. 276 That voyce..heard so oft..on the perilous edge Of battel when it rag'd. **1718** POPE *Iliad* x. 197 Each..Greek ..Stands on the sharpest edge of death or life.

7. a. The line in which two surfaces of a solid object meet abruptly; *spec.* in Geometry, the line of meeting of two faces of a polyhedron.

1823 H. J. BROOKE *Introd. Crystallogr.* 149 Terminal solid angles replaced by two planes, resting on the obtuse edges of the pyramids. **1878** GURNEY *Crystallogr.* 30 The edges formed by the intersections of pairs of adjacent faces.

b. Skating. (*to cut, do*) *the inside* or *outside edge*: a particular form of fancy skating on the inner *or* outer edge of the skate-iron.

1772 JONES *Skating* 22 The inside edge is sometimes required in performing some of the more difficult manœuvres. *Ibid.* 37 [The Dutch] travel on the outside edge. **1806–7** J. BERESFORD *Miseries Hum. Life* (1826) III. i, Learning to cut the outside edge on skaits that have no edge to cut with. **1880** VANDERVELL & WITHAM *Figure-Skating* 137 The inside edge backwards..may be taken up from the turn on both feet by continuing backwards. *Mod.* Can you do the outside edge?

c. *edge of regression*: see REGRESSION 3 b.

** *as contrasted with a broad surface.*

8. a. Of a thin flat object: One of the narrow surfaces showing the 'thickness' or smallest dimension, as distinguished from the broad surfaces. *on edge* (formerly often written *an edge*): resting upon the edge, placed 'edgewise'. † *to plough the soil up on an edge*: to plough it into ridges.

1677 MOXON *Mech. Exerc.* (1703) 72 The Board is set an edge with one end in the Bench-screw. **1708** MORTIMER *Husb.* 50 Harrow it as you plow it up, but then..you must speedily plow it up an edge again. **1784** DE LOLME *Eng. Const.* II. xvii. 276 Ran the edge of his hand with great quickness along his neck. **1878** BROWNING *La Saisiaz* 14 Fangs of crystal set on edge in his demesne. *Mod.* A plate set up on edge. The shilling has a milled edge.

†**b.** *fig.* Phrase, *to get by the edges*: to get (information) indirectly or imperfectly. *Obs.*

1702 C. MATHER *Magn. Chr.* II. 45 They had got by the Edges a little Intimation of the then Prince of Orange's undertaking.

c. *spec.* Of a book: One of the three surfaces left uncovered by the binding; called severally *top*, *bottom*, and *fore edge*.

Mod. The top edge of the book is gilt; the others are left white.

9. The rim (of a hollow vessel).

c **1400** *Beryn* 587 The egge of the panne met with his shyn. **1459** *Inv.* in *Paston Lett.* 335 I. 468 Vj bolles with oon coverede of silver, the egges gilt.

III. The boundary of a surface.

10. a. The line which forms the boundary of any surface; a border, verge. By extension, that portion of the surface of any object, or of a country, district, etc., adjacent to its boundary. (Cf. BORDER.)

In geographical sense formerly often used where *frontier* or *boundary* would now be preferred.

c **1391** CHAUCER *Astrol.* II. §46 And sett þou þere þe degree of þe mone according wiþ þe egge of þe label. *c* **1460** J. RUSSELL *Bk. Nurture* in *Babees Bk.* (1868) 129 Ley þe bouȝt on þe vttur egge of þe table. **1494** FABYAN VI. cxcvi. 202 The abbey of Leof, besyde Hereforde, in the egge of Walys. **1535** COVERDALE *Ezek.* xl. 12 The edge before the chambres was one cubite brode. **1588** SHAKS. *L.L.L.* IV. i. 9 Hereby vpon the edge of yonder Coppice. **1606** —— *Ant. & Cl.* II. ii. 117 From edge to edge A th' world. **1664** EVELYN *Kal. Hort.* (1729) 228 Many of their Leaves parch'd about their Edges. **1732** DE FOE *Tour Gt. Brit.* (1769) II. 181 Elestre, is a Village on the Roman Watling-street, on the very Edge of Middlesex. **1823** LAMB *Elia* Ser. II. vii. (1865) 280 All this time sat upon the edge of the deck quite a different character. **1833** N. ARNOTT *Physics* II. 210 The image will be more perfect..at its middle than towards its edges. **1836** THIRLWALL *Greece* III. xxii. 238 He..drew up his men at the water's edge. **1879** HARLAN *Eyesight* ii. 21 The edges of the orbit are comparatively dense and strong.

b. *fig.* of portions of time, seasons, etc.

1638 FEATLY *Transubst.* 229 Win the day in the edge of the evening. **1782** JOHNSON *Let.* 20 Mar. in *Boswell*, I made a journey to Staffordshire on the edge of winter. **1868** E. WAUGH *Sneck-Bant* iv. 72 in *Lanc. Gloss.* (E.D.S.) We's be back again abeawt th' edge-o'-dark.

c. That which is placed on the border of a garment, etc.; = EDGING.

1502 *Priv. Purse Exp. Eliz. York* (1830) 68 Blake velvet for an edge and cuffes for the same gowne. **1552** HULOET, Edge of a fillet or roll..*Tænia*. **1611** BIBLE *Ex.* xxvi. 10 Fiftie loopes on the edge of the curtaine. **1856** MRS. GASKELL *Let.* ? 22 July (1966) 397 The white..& the lavender edge—did you look after black, (imitation,—Cambray, or Maltese) lace.

†**d.** *Archit.* In first quot. rendering L. *regula* 'the shank of a Doric triglyph' (Lewis and Short). In second quot. app. = FILLET. *Obs.*

1563 SHUTE *Archit.* C ij b, The edge which Vitruuius calleth Regula. *Ibid.* D j a, The lowest edge that standeth vppon Plinthus shalbe in height half a part.

11. a. The brink or verge (of a bank or precipice).

c **1325** *E.E. Allit. P.* B. 383 Er vch boþom watz brurd-ful to þe bonkez eggez. **1480** CAXTON *Descr. Brit.* 3 The edge of the frenssh clif shold be the ende of the world yf the ylonde of brytayn ne were not. **1827** POLLOK *Course T.* v, Toppling upon the perilous edge of Hell. **1865** *Reader* 3 June 619/3 In Derbyshire it nests in the rocks and 'Edges,' as the precipices are called.

b. fig. *on the edge of*: on the point of (doing something).

1606 SHAKS. *Tr. & Cr.* IV. v. 68 Will you, the Knights Shall to the edge of all extremitie Pursue each other? **1884** CHURCH *Bacon* v. 114 He was now on the very edge of losing his office.

c. *fig.* Often with defining word, as *absolute*, *outside*: the 'limit', the very extreme. Phr. *over the edge* (see quot. 1945).

1911 'IAN HAY' *Safety Match* i. 8 Cheating again! My word, Nicky, you are the absolute *edge!* **1925** WODEHOUSE *Carry on, Jeeves* ix. 218, I am still blushing all over at the recollection of something she says in paragraph two... You can take it from me that it's the edge. **1945** BAKER *Austral. Lang.* vi. 134 *Over the edge* (or *fence*), unreasonable, beyond the pale of fairness or decency.

IV. 12. *attrib.* and *Comb.* **a.** locative, as *edge-hummock*, *-moulding*, *-plate*, *-teeth*, *-way*; *edge-gilt* adj.; also *edge-to-edge*, attrib.; **b.** objective, as *edge-cutting*, *nailing*; **c.** adverbial, as *edge-view*. Also **edge-coals**, coals from an edge-seam; **edge-joint** (see quot.); † **edge-leam, -lome** [OE. *lóma*], an edge-tool; **edge-metal** (see quots.); **edge-mill, edge-rail, edge-roll** (see quots.); **edge-runner**, an apparatus for crushing stone, fibrous matter, etc.; **edge-seam**, a layer or seam of coal that has been tilted into a nearly vertical position; **edge-shot** *a.*, (see quot.); **edge-tone** *Mus.*, a sound-wave produced when a stream of air is deflected by an edge; **edge-wheel** (see quot.); **edge-zone** (see quot. 1902). Also EDGE-TOOL, -WAYS.

1854 MILLER *Sch. & Schm.* xiv. (1860) 153 *'Edge-coals'—those steep seams of the Mid-Lothian Coal-basin. **1843** CARLYLE *Past & Pr.* (1858) 91 Do honour to any *edge-gilt vacuity in man's shape. **1853** KANE *Grinnell Exp.* xxix. (1856) 241 *Edge-hummocks, that is to say, hummocks formed at the margin of floes and afterward cemented there. **1874** KNIGHT *Dict. Mech.*, **Edge-joint* (Carpentry), a joint formed by two edges, forming a corner. **1781** J. HUTTON *Tour Caves* (E.D.S.) **Edgeleams*, sb. pl., edge tools. **1570** LEVINS *Manip.* 161 An *Edgelome, *culter*. **1839** URE *Dict. Arts* 961 The coal-seams thus upheaved [*sc.* at a high angle], are called *edge-metals by the miners. **1883** GRESLEY *Gloss. Coal-m.* 95 *Edge coals, edge metals, edge seams* (Sc.), highly inclined seams of coal. **1874** KNIGHT *Dict. Mech.*, **Edge-mill*, an ore-grinding or oil-mill in which the stones travel on their edges. **1762** BORLASE in *Phil. Trans.* LII. 509 All the *edge-mouldings of the canopy were tore to pieces. **1876** *Encycl. Brit.* IV. 493/1 For side or *edge nailing..clasp-nails..are used. **1879** in *Cassell's Techn. Educ.* IV. 175/1 All along each bottom side of the body should be plated with iron..The *edge-plate, as this is technically called. **1874** KNIGHT *Dict. Mech.*, **Edge-rail* (Railroad). *a.* One form of rail-road-rail, which bears the rolling stock on its edge. *b.* A rail placed by the side of the main rail at a switch to prevent the train from running off the track when the direction is changed. *Ibid.* **Edge-roll*, A brass wheel used hot, in running an edge ornament, on a book cover. **1871** *Cassell's Techn. Educator* II. 267/1 The clay..is conveyed to the *edge-runners or other machinery used to pulverise it. **1883** H. G. HARRIS in H. J. Powell *Princ. Glass-Making* 46 The pieces of limestone are further crushed under a pair of 'edge-runners'. **1883** *Encycl. Brit.* XVI. 463/2 Edge-runners (Chilian mills). **1891** *Engineer* 9 Jan. 36 Edge runner grinding mill. **1963** R. R. A. HIGHAM *Handbk. Papermaking* ii. 24 Kollergang or edge-runner. This machine consists of two large circular stones, driven by a central shaft, which revolve in a metal or stone pan. **1802** PLAYFAIR *Illustr. Hutton. The.* 236 We obtain the same information from inspecting the *edge-seams. **1805** FORSYTH *Beauties Scotl.* I. 269 The strata..receive the appellation of edge seams, from their descending, or almost upright position in the earth. **1874** KNIGHT *Dict. Mech.*, **Edge-shot*, a board with its edge planed is said to be edge-shot. **1854** WOODWARD *Mollusca* II. 162 *Edge-teeth dentated. **1952** C. W. CUNNINGTON *Eng. Women's Clothing* vii. 259 Lined '*edge-to-edge' coat in wool georgette. **1961** F. H. BURGESS *Dict. Sailing* 81 *Edge to edge*, descriptive of the planking of a carvel-built boat. **1963** C. R. COWELL et al. *Inlays, Crowns & Bridges* vii. 70 (*caption*) For an edge-to-edge bite the tip is prepared horizontally. **1931** G. JACOB *Orchestral Technique* ix. 95 The contrast between the '*edge-tone' of the trumpets and the rounder tone of the horns. **1962** A. NISBETT *Technique Sound Studio* iii. 67 The breathy edge tone that we hear with the flute. **1857** W. BINNS *Orthographic Project.* iii. (1862) 22 If the paper be now turned..we shall have an *edge-view..of the plane on which the lines are drawn. **1880** MRS. WHITNEY *Odd or Even* x. 83 Trudging along on the opposite *edgeways of the soft brown, deep-rutted road. **1874** KNIGHT *Dict. Mech.* 774 **Edge-wheel*, a wheel travelling on its edge in a circular or annular bed. **1902** *Encycl. Brit.* XXV. 459/2 A fold of soft tissue extending to a greater or less distance over the theca, and containing..a cavity continuous over the lip of the calicle with the cœlenteron. This fold of tissue is known as the *edge-zone. **1904** *Ann. & Mag. Nat. Hist.* XIII. 22 The epitheca is that part of the skeleton secreted by the edge-zone.

edge, dial. var. of ADZE.

edge (ɛdʒ), *v.*[1] Also 3–4 egge(n, 5 eggyn. [f. EDGE *sb.*

The older forms of this word coincide graphically with those of EGG *v.*, which is ultimately of identical etymology. The forms with *gg* are for convenience treated under EGG, exc. where used in senses now peculiar to this word.]

1. a. *trans.* To give an edge, impart sharpness, to (a weapon, etc. or tool); chiefly in fig. sentences.

1297 R. GLOUC. *Chron.* (1810) 274, I-egged yt [the sword] ys in on alf. **1609** BP. BARLOW *Answ. Nameless Cath.* 364 Not blunting the sword of Iustice, but rather edging it. **1621–31** LAUD *Sev. Serm.* (1847) 55 Will God..edge the sword upon the common enemy of Christ? **1718** POPE *Odyss.* xx. 62 Thy sure divinity shall..edge thy sword to reap the glorious field. **1719** YOUNG *Busiris* IV. i, One dear embrace; 'twill edge my sword. **1808** J. BARLOW *Columb.* VI. 336 Fame fired their courage, freedom edged their swords.

b. *transf.* and *fig.* To give keenness or incisive force to (appetite, wit, endeavours, etc.).

1599 SHAKS. *Hen. V*, III. v. 38 With spirit of Honor edged More sharper then your Swords, high to the field. **1643** T. GOODWIN *Child of Light* 39 These doe edge and sharpen the wit. **1647** FULLER *Good Th. in Worse T.* (1841) 156 O that this would edge the endeavours of our generation. **1673** *Lady's Call.* I. ii. §10. 16 All the torments there being edged and sharpned by the woful remembrance. **1742** R. BLAIR *Grave* 644 Some intervals of abstinence are sought To edge the appetite. **1855** BRIMLEY *Ess.* 36 The piercing cold of the night-wind edged with sea-salt. **1885** R. BRIDGES *Nero* II. i. 6/1 But now to hear how she hath edged her practice.

†**2. a.** To urge on, incite, provoke, encourage (a person); = EGG *v.* (but usu. with more direct reference to the sb.); also, to stimulate, give activity to (an industry, etc.). *Obs.* exc. as in b.

1575 J. HOOKER *Carew* 116 He..would..edge, procure and cause others to do the like [bestow money]. **1577** HOLINSHED *Chron.* III. 1239/2 He accused the moonks of manie things, and did therewith so edge the king against them. **1613** in *Harl. Misc.* (Malh.) III. 141 The Duke edged his soldiers, by declaring unto them the noble works of their ancestors. **1625** BACON *Usury, Ess.* (Arb.) 545 This..will Encourage and edge, Industrious and Profitable Improuements. **1648** GAGE *West. Ind.* xiii. (1655) 76 Which edgeth the Spaniards to a constant and continuall war with the Inhabitants.

b. with *on*: = *egg on* (see EGG *v.* 2).

1580 NORTH *Plutarch* 613 Cassius..did..edge him [Brutus] on the more, for a private quarrell he had conceived against Cæsar. **1609** HOLLAND *Livy* XLII. liv. 1147 b, It envenomed the enemies and edged them on [*infestiores fecisset*]. **1652** H. L'ESTRANGE *Americans no Jewes* 61 [Cannibalism is] a national helluonisme..Whetted and edged on by..Revenge. **1725** *New Cant. Dict.*, To *Edge*, or as 'tis vulgarly call'd, to *Egg* one on. **1842** PUSEY *Crisis Eng. Ch.* 36 To this they will ever be edged on by those, who are watching to take advantage of our perplexities. **1867** BUSHNELL *Mor. Uses Dark Th.* 41 To be cornered and pressed and edged on..into the best ways and noblest endeavors.

†**3. a.** To set (the teeth) on edge. *Obs.* exc. *dial.* [Cf. Flem. *eggen de tanden* (Kilian).]

a **1300** *Cursor M.* 796 Þair suns tethe are eggeid yitt. *c* **1440** *Promp. Parv.* 136 Eggyd, as teethe for sowre frute, *acidus*. *a* **1555** LATIMER *Serm. & Rem.* (1845) 347 Lest peradventure we take chalk for cheese, which will edge our teeth, and hinder digestion. **1604** T. WRIGHT *Passions* VI. 318 That bitter Apple which edged all mens teeth. **1634** HEYWOOD *Maidenh. well lost* IV. Wks. 1874 IV. 147 If youle

eate grapes vnripe, edge your owne teeth. **1865** B. Brierley *Irkdale* I. 26 It edges my teeth wurr nor a railroad whistle.

†**b.** ? *transf.* ? To irritate.

c **1450** Lydg. *Min. Poems* 115 How shrewly he was egged For to here hys dyrge do, and se hys pet deggyd.

4. a. To furnish with a border or edging; to border; also, to colour or ornament on the edge.

1555 Eden *Decades W. Ind.* (Arb.) 197 One of these is edged with belles. *c* **1570** Thynne *Pride & Lowl.* (1841) 20 Of golde and silver and such trumperie, To welte, to edge, to garde. **1629** Milton *Ode Nativity* 185 From haunted spring and dale Edged with poplar pale. **1684** Wilding in *Collect.* (Oxf. Hist. Soc.) I. 259 For edging my Hatt, 4*d.* **1728** Pope *Dunc.* III. 248 Whose sarcenet skirts are edged with..gold. **1746–7** Hervey *Medit. & Contempl.* (1818) 133 The glittering fringes which edge the pink. **1870** Hooker *Stud. Flora* 202 Matricaria inodora..bracts edged with brown.

b. Of a range of hills, etc.: To form a border or enclosure to; to enclose.

1644 Evelyn *Mem.* (1857) I. 126 On the top of all, runs a balustrade which edges it quite round. **1717** Berkeley in Fraser *Life* (1871) 569 The 2 first miles of this post close along the Dea, being edged on the left by mountains. **1725** Pope *Odyss.* x. 102 A bay there lies, Edg'd round with cliffs. **1886** *Manch. Exam.* 2 Jan. 5/3 Except where it is edged by the border lands of China and Thibet, Burmah is surrounded by British territory.

5. *intr.* To move edgeways; to advance (esp. obliquely) by repeated almost imperceptible movements. Also with advs. *aside, away, down, in,* etc. Chiefly *Naut.* (see quot. 1867).

1624 Capt. Smith *Virginia* IV. 128 We descried a ship.. we edged towards her to see what she was. **1627** —— *Seaman's Gram.* xiii. 60 Be yare at the helme, edge in with him. *a* **1628** F. Greville *Sidney* (1652) 60 Publiquely edging nearer the holy mother Church. **1630** J. Taylor (Water P.) *Wks.* III. 41 The James..then edged vp in the winde. **1650** Cromwell *Let.* 4 Sept. Causing their right wing of horse to edge down towards the sea. **1712** Arbuthnot *John Bull* (1727) 72 He observed Frog and old Lewis edging towards one another to whisper. **1720** De Foe *Capt. Singleton* xvi. (1840) 269 They..stood edging in for the shore. **1777** Cook *2nd Voy.* III. vii. (R.) On edging off from the shore, we soon got out of sounding. **1790** Beatson *Nav. & Mil. Mem.* I. 382 Rear-Admiral Knowles..kept edging down on the enemy. **1832** Marryat *N. Forster* xli, The..admiral edged away with his squadron. **1853** Kane *Grinnell Exp.* xxxiii. (1856) 283 The wind edged round a little more to the northward. **1863** Mrs. Oliphant *Salem Ch.* xv. 275 He edged past the table in the back-parlour to the window. **1867** Smyth *Sailor's Word-bk.*, *Edge away*, to decline gradually from the course which the ship formerly steered, by sailing larger or more off, or more away from before the wind than she had done before. *To edge down*, to approach any object in an oblique direction.

fig. **1859** *Sat. Rev.* VIII. 5/1 A disposition, on the part of a youth, to edge into a different station from that in which he was born.

6. a. *trans.* To move by insensible degrees; to insinuate (something, oneself) *into* a place. With advs.: To force (something) by imperceptible degrees *away, in, off, out.* Also *fig.*

1677 Earl Orrery *Art of War* 161 During the motion of your advanced Wing, to edge it, by degrees, and insensibly, towards, etc. **1690** Locke *Educ.* Wks. 1714 III. 67 Edging by Degrees their Chairs forwards. **1704** Davenant in Ellis *Orig. Lett.* II. 397 IV. 245 If you believe him obstinate.. advise me of it, for I can edge it [a wager] off. **1708** Mrs. Centlivre *Busie Body* II. i, A Son of One and Twenty, who wants..to edge himself into the Estate! **1824** W. Irving *T. Trav.* I. 14 Every one edging his chair a little nearer. **1812** L. Hunt in *Examiner* 31 Aug. 545/2 An opportunity..of edging himself into the paper. **1829** I. Taylor *Enthus.* vii. (1867) 143 Christianity..is seen constantly at work edging away oppressions. **1883** *Manch. Exam.* 30 Nov. 5/5 The products of the Continent are gradually edging those of England out of the [Turkish] market.

b. *to edge in* (a word, etc.): to push in, as if with the edge first.

1683 D. A. *Art Converse* 9 Without giving them so much time as to edge in a word. **1806–7** J. Beresford *Miseries Hum. Life* (1826) xii. Concl., Andromache..contrived to edge in a smile.

c. To defeat by a small margin. *N. Amer.*

1953 *Springfield* (Mass.) *Sunday Republican* 20 Sept. 8B (*heading*) Bellows Falls edges Windsor eleven, 12–6. **1966** *N.Y. Times* (Internat. ed.) 22 Apr. 12/1 The Los Angeles Dodgers edged the Houston Astros, 3–2. **1968** *Globe & Mail* (Toronto) 17 Feb. 41/8 Malvern edged Parkdale 4–3 in the first game.

7. *Cricket.* To deflect (the ball) with the edge of the bat.

1904 P. F. Warner *How we recovered Ashes* xi. 215 The only blemish in his display was that he once edged a ball from Rhodes between the wicket-keeper and slip. **1906** *Daily Chron.* 28 July 7/4 Seeing his first ball edged by Rhodes over the slips. **1927** *Observer* 7 Aug. 18/2 Being inclined to edge the ball. **1970** *Times* 19 Aug. 6/2 He was fortunate now to edge Wilson only just wide of Fletcher in the gully.

edge (ɛdʒ), *v.*² Also 4 hegge-n. [OE. *ęcȝan* (pa. t. *ęȝide*), = MDu., Du. *eggen*, OHG. *ecken* (pa. pple. *gi-egit*), MHG. *egen*, mod.G. (from LG.) *eggen* to harrow:—OTeut. **agjan*, whence OE. *ęȝiðe, ēȝðe* = MLG. *egede*, MDu. *ēghede* (Du. *eegd*), OHG. *egida* a harrow. Outside Teut. cf. L. *occa*, Welsh *oged* (:—**ocet*), Lith. *akėczos* a harrow, *akiti* to harrow. The root may possibly be identical with that of edge *sb.*] To harrow.

a **800** *Corpus Gloss.* 1430 *Occabat*, eȝide. **1393** Langl. *P. Pl.* C. VI. 19 Canstow..Heggen oþer harwen · oþer swyn oþer gees dryue. **1669** Worlidge *Syst. Agric.* (1681) 325 *To Edge*, to Harrow. **1726** *Dict. Rusticum* (ed. 3) To *Edge*..a Country-word for to harrow.

edge-bone, corruption of aitch-bone, q.v.

edged (ɛdʒd), *ppl. a.* [f. edge *sb.* and *v.* + -ed.]

1. Furnished with a cutting edge; sharpened, trenchant. Also *fig.* Cf. two-edged. For *edged tool* see edge-tool.

1591 Shaks. *1 Hen. VI*, III. iii. 52 O turne thy edged Sword another way. *a* **1593** Marlowe *Dido* IV. i, With the sharpness of my edged sting. *a* **1639** T. Carew *Wks.* (1824) 102 Justice hath to the sword of your edg'd eyes His equall balance joyn'd. **1677** Moxon *Mech. Exerc.* (1703) 213 Afterwards with edg'd Grooving Tools..they cut down.. the Extuberances. **1833** Lardner *Manuf. Metal* II. 2 (Cabinet Cycl.) Nor are the edged stones..so defectively formed..as might be imagined.

2. Having an edge or lateral boundary: only with defining prefix, indicative of colour, number, etc.

1776 Withering *Bot. Arrangem.* (1796) I. 255 Anthers 3-edged. **1884** Black *Jud. Shaks.* vi, The red-edged leaves. *Mod.* Black-edged note-paper.

†**3.** Having a border (of ornamental work). *Obs.*

1697 *Lond. Gaz.* No. 3304/4 A Gold Watch..having an Edged Case. **1722** De Foe *Col. Jack* (1840) 80 An edged hat. **1727** Bradley *Fam. Dict.* I. s.v. *Clear Starching*, To order the edged heads; when you find they are clapp'd sufficiently, pin it down to the board.

†'**edgeful**, *a. Obs. rare*⁻¹. [f. edge *sb.* + -ful.] Having abundance of edge; keen, cutting.

1614 T. White *Martyrd. St. George* A iij, Hee..Against the Empires enemies did set His warlicke brow, and edge-full humor whet.

†**edge-growth**, corruption of **edgrowth* = edgrew.

1610 W. Folkingham *Art of Survey* II. x. 63 The second is of Mastage, Edge-grouth, Winter-Herbage, etc.

edgeless ('ɛdʒlɪs), *a.* [f. edge *sb.* + -less.] That has no edge. *lit.* and *fig.*

1617 Collins *Def. Bp. Ely* II. ix. 400 His sword, which he carried neither edgeles, nor in vaine. **1661** J. Fountain *Rewards Virtue* 2 To save her sheers, Which else had sure been edgeless long ago. **1869** Ruskin *Q. of Air* §143 The dumb and edgeless shore of darkened sand. **1884** H. D. Traill in *Macm. Mag.* Oct. 444/2 As lustreless and edgeless as an old shilling.

†'**edgeling, -long**, *adv.* Also 4 egge-, eghelynge(s. [f. edge *sb.* + -ling, as in backling(s *adv.* (OE. *bæcling*); for the corrupt form *-long* cf. *sidelong, headlong.*]

a. With the edge. **b.** On the edge; edgeways.

? *a* **1400** *Morte Arth.* 3675 Upcynes eghelynge þay ochene þare aftyre. **1489** Caxton *Faytes of A.* I. ix. 24 They scorned them that smote edgelyng. **1580** Hollyband *Treas. Fr. Tong, Fraper d'estoc & de taille*, to strike both foyning and edgeling. **1603** Florio *Montaigne* II. xii. (1632) 330 It is hard, be it flat-long, side-long, or edge-long, but an ingenious..wit shal..meet with some aire that wil fit his turn. **1611** Cotgr., s.v. *Az*, A dye that stands edgeling, so as tis doubtfull what chance it will yeeld.

edger ('ɛdʒə(r)). [f. edge *sb.* and *v.* + -er¹.]

1. One who edges or puts an edge on anything.

1591 Percivall *Sp. Dict.*, *Bordador*, an imbroderer, an edger.

†**2.** Of flowers and leaves: (see quot.)

1688 R. Holme *Armoury* II. 115/1 Edgers are the spring or first ripe Tulipa's. **1725** Bradley *Fam. Dict.*, *Edger*, a plant whose leaves are edged with white or yellow.

3. *Mech.* (See quot.)

1874 Knight *Dict. Mech.*, *Edger*, a circular saw..by which the bark [etc.] are ripped from slab-boards.

4. An operative in various crafts.

1909 *Daily Chron.* 26 June 8/5 Optician's Edger wanted. **1921** *Dict. Occup. Terms* (1927) §105 *Edger*, a fettler who smoothes edges and joints of clay ware articles with a knife, leather or sponge before firing. *Ibid.* §429 *Black edger* (gloves);..stains, with a blackened pad, as received from machinist, the white edge left on black kid gloves.

edge-tool, edged tool. In early use, Any implement with a sharp cutting edge, as a knife or sword; now (in lit. sense) restricted to industrial tools, and technically denoting chiefly chisels, gouges, planes, etc., also (with defining adj. *heavy*) axes, hatchets, etc. Also *attrib.* (The form *edged tools* is now used only in fig. sense.)

c **1350** *Will. Palerne* 3755 And ȝif any egge tol wol entre in-to his bodi I wol do him to þe deth. *c* **1430** Lydg. *Bochas* II. v. (1554) 47 b/1 Leuer I haue, with some edge tole Too slea my selfe, than liue in slaundre and dole. **1548** *Act 2 & 3 Edw. VI*, xxvii, The greatest part of edged Tools, Weapons, and other necessary things having Edges. **1677** Moxon *Mech. Exerc.* (1703) 167 An Edge-Tool..will..cut off all the parts. **1719** De Foe *Crusoe* (1840) II. v. 108 Nor had they any edged tool. **1723** *Lond. Gaz.* No. 6175/6 Robert Wilkins ..Edge Tool maker. **1732** Berkeley *Alciphr.* vi. §8 Edged tools are in general designed to cut. **1825** J. Nicholson *Operat. Mechanic* App. 771 To make Edge-tools with cast Steel and Iron. **1886** *Daily News* 18 Oct. 5/5 The saw and edge-tool houses are doing moderately well.

2. *fig.* and in proverbial use. esp. in phrase ***play*** or ***jest with edge tools.***

1579 Gosson *Sch. Abuse* (Arb.) 57 Some say that it is not good iesting with edge toles. **1622** Massinger, etc. *Old Law* v. i, If you move the duke's patience, 'tis an edge-tool. **1767** Wesley *Jrnl.* 4 May, They find it is playing with edged tools. **1798** Hutton *Autobiogr.* 27 The man who plays with edge-tools, may, by chance, cut his fingers. **1815** Scott *Guy M.* v, I begin to think..I have been rather jesting with edge-tools. **1866** Mill in *Edin. Rev.* CXXIII. 337 He came to think that the Sokratic cross-examination is a dangerous edge-tool.

'**edge-ways, -wise,** (rarely) **-way.**

1. a. Of position: With the edge (instead of the broad surface) uppermost, foremost, or turned towards the spectator.

1566 in Peacock *Eng. Ch. Furniture* (1866) 73 Alter stones ij—one is broke..thother yet standeth edgewaie in the grownd. **1641** Best *Farm. Bks.* (1856) 126 They layd them [fir deals] edg-wayes. **1715** Desaguliers *Fires Impr.* 160 The Partition Plates must be..fix'd edgewise to the great Plate. **1723** *Lond. Gaz.* No. 6156/4 One of his fore Teeth.. standing edgeway. **1775** Sheridan *Rivals* v. iii, I'll stand edge-ways. **1857** Birch *Anc. Pottery* (1858) II. 303 Curved bricks set edgeways in a thick slip of the material. **1879** Newcomb & Holden *Astron.* 358 At certain times the rings of Saturn are seen edgeways. **1885** H. J. Stonor in *Law Times* LXXX. 119/1 The ladder..standing edgeways.

fig. **1664** H. More *Myst. Iniq.* Apol. 538 This Objection is set edge-wise, and seems to stand..in a very dangerous posture. **1677** Gilpin *Dæmonol.* (1867) 409 Sometime a scripture will be set so cross or edgeway to their good and comfort.

b. Edge to edge.

c **1850** *Rudim. Navig.* (Weale) 121 Each is composed of.. deals..bolted together edgewise.

2. a. Of motion: With the edge foremost.

1794 Vince in *Phil. Trans.* LXXXV. 44 When they [the planes] move edge-ways. **1828** Scott *F.M. Perth* II. 156 The savage raised the axe..and brought it down again edge-ways.

b. *fig.* in ***to get a word,*** etc. ***in edgeways,*** etc.

1777 Sheridan *Sch. Scand.* II. ii, All her words appear to slide out edgewise. **1824** Miss Mitford *Village* Ser. I. (1863) 156 As if it were possible for any of us to slide in a word edgewise. **1854** S. Hale *Lett.* (1918) i. 9 Mrs. Otis herself talked all the time, so there was no room for me to get in a word edgewise. **1870** Morris *Earthly Par.* III. IV. 206 At the last [he] pushed in his word Edgewise, as 'twere.

3. On the edge (instead of the broad side).

1791 Smeaton *Edystone L.* §239 The sea acting edgewise upon the joint would exert the same power to lift it up.

edgily ('ɛdʒɪlɪ), *adv.* [f. edgy *a.* + -ly².] In an edgy manner; irritably, testily.

1837 H. E. Manning *Let.* 8 Mar. in S. Leslie *Life* (1921) xvi. 269 Newman did not like my joking letter. He answered rather edgily and defensively. **1922** M. Arlen *Piracy* III. ix. §3 'You are making a butt of me, Virginia,' he complained edgily.

edginess ('ɛdʒɪnɪs). [f. edgy + -ness.] **a.** The condition of having the outlines too clearly marked; angularity, hardness of outline. Also *fig.* **b.** Irritability.

1822 *Blackw. Mag.* XI. 427 It would supply an excellent study for a painter; all edginess..is gone. **1877** Morley *Crit. Misc.* Ser. II. 391 To be clear, acute, and definite, without that edginess and inelasticity. **1962** *Listener* 7 June 991/1 This edginess in the presence of the actual world characterizes a great deal of transcendent metaphysics. **1963** *Times* 8 June 5/2 Her tone sometimes acquired an edginess out of character. **1965** M. Morse *Unattached* iv. 131 There was a certain amount of edginess..between the groups.

edging ('ɛdʒɪŋ), *vbl. sb.* [f. edge *v.* + -ing¹.]

†**1.** The setting on edge (of the teeth). *Obs.*

1382 Wyclif *Amos* iv. 6 Y ȝaue to ȝou eggyng of teeth.

2. a. The putting of an edge or border to anything. Also *attrib.*, as in *edging-lace, -stroke, -tile.*

1580 Hollyband *Treas. Fr. Tong, Canetille*, an edging lace. **1607** Topsell *Four-f. Beasts* 446 Very much used for the edging of the best garments. **1664** Evelyn tr. *Freart's Archit.* (R.), The edging strokes, by some called outlines, and contours only. *c* **1850** *Rudim. Navig.* (Weale) 116 *Edging of plank*, sawing or hewing it narrower. *a* **1877** Knight *Dict. Mech.* I. 774/1 *Edging-machine*, a machine for edging boards to a given pattern. An edger. *a* **1884** Knight *Dict. Mech.* Suppl. 293/1 *Edging and dividing bench*, a circular saw of special adaption for sawing blocks into voussoir shapes. **1957** *N.Z. Timber Jrnl.* Feb. 45 *Edging strips*, pieces fixed on the edges of flush doors to cover and secure the edges of the plywood.

b. The trimming of the edges (of a lawn or grassplat); also *attrib.*, as in ***edging-iron, -shears.***

1858 Glenny *Gard. Everyd. Bk.* 236/1 The edging-iron must be used instead of the shears. **1880** *G. Turner's Catal. Tool Wks. Sheffield* 24 Common Grass Plot Edging Knives.

3. *concr.* **a.** That which forms an edge to anything; a border, fringe, etc. sewn on the edge of a garment; a border (of box or other plants) surrounding a flower-bed; and the like.

1664 Evelyn *Kal. Hort.* (1729) 199 Adorn the outward Verge with an Edging of Pink, Limon Thyme, etc. *a* **1700** Dryden (T.), The garland which I..border'd with a rosy edging round. **1699** Garth *Dispens.* IV. (1706) 66 The Clouds aloft with golden Edgings glow. **1741** *Compl. Fam.-Piece* II. iii. 366 After Rain, clip your Edgings of Box. **1807** Crabbe *Library* 148 The dull red edging of the well fill'd page. **1841** Mrs. J. W. Loudon *Ladies' Comp. Flower Garden* 117/2 *Gentiana acaulis* is frequently used as an edging plant. **1873** Tristram *Moab* xvi. 302 The old road.. marked by its bold edging of stones. **1907** *Macm. Mag.* 825 Lepidoptera seek out this sunny retreat and suck the edging plants.

b. A trimming on a seam.

1664 Pepys *Diary* 10 Feb., A close-bodied..coat, with a gold edgeing in each seam. **1717** Addison *Ovid's Met.* II. (R.) To show The golden edging on the seam below.

4. Lace made to be sewn on to the edge of some article of dress. Shorter form of *edging-lace*.

1558 *Richmond. Wills* (1853) 127 Vj yeards of edgine xxd. **1716** *Lond. Gaz.* No. 5438/4 Two Quarter Boxes of Lace and Edgings. **1750** MRS. DELANY *Life & Corr.* (1861) II. 555, I have got your harp shell, and will send it you, and the Elizabeth edging. **1851** MAYHEW *Lond. Labour* I. 387 'Edgings', or the several kinds of cheap lace used for the bordering of caps and other female requirements.

5. The action of moving by insensible degrees; *attrib.*, as in ***edging movement.***

1879 A. FORBES *Daily News* 16 Apr. 3/2 A kind of sidelong edging movement.

edging ('ɛdʒɪŋ), *ppl. a.* [f. EDGE *v.* + -ING².] That moves by imperceptible degrees. Hence **'edgingly** *adv.*

1748 RICHARDSON *Clarissa* (1811) II. 220 The new-made beau awkwardly followed, but more edgingly.

'edgrew, -grow. *Obs.* exc. *dial.* Also 9 *dial.* etgro. [f. ED- + stem of OE. *grów-an*; cf. OE. *edgrówung*, Ælfric *Gloss.* in Wr.-Wülcker 149.] The aftergrowth of grass; aftermath, eddish.

c **1440** *Promp. Parv.* 135 Edgrow, greese [*K*, etc. edgraw, herbe, *H.P.* growe, greese], *bigermen, regermen.* **1688** R. HOLME *Armoury* III. 72/2 Edgrewe is the Grass left growing after Mowing, some term it the Latter grass, or latter growing. **1726** *Dict. Rusticum* (ed. 3), *Edgrew*, some term it Latter-grass or Latter-math. **1875** *Lanc. Gloss.* (E.D.S.) s.v., So mitch for t'gress and soa mitch for t'etgro.

edgy ('ɛdʒɪ), *a.* [f. EDGE *sb.* + -Y.]

1. Having an edge or edges; sharp, cutting.

1775 C. DAVY *Bourrit's Glac. Savoy* (1776) 99 Constantly walking over broken rocks, either ragged, or cleft, or edgy. **1820** L. HUNT *Indicator* No. 15 (1822) I. 118 Lastly, think of the razor itself..how cold, how edgy, how hard! **1849** RUSKIN *Sev. Lamps* iii. §11. 75 Binding the dusty remnants and edgy splinters into springing vaults.

2. Of a painting: Having the outlines too hard.

1825 *Blackw. Mag.* XVII. 438 There were two Holbeins, flat, shadowless, edgy compositions. **1868** *Illust. Lond. News* 11 Apr. 362 Less edgy and more softly sweet in colour than previous works.

3. *fig.* Full of edge or keenness; eager. *dial.*

1858 A. B. EVANS *Leicestersh. Wds., Edgy*, eager. 'He's very edgy to go there': also 'pert' and 'forward'.

4. Having one's nerves on edge; irritable; testy.

1837 [implied in EDGILY *adv.*]. **1864** in WEBSTER. **1914** KIPLING *Divers. Creatures* (1917) 149 'I say,' he began hurriedly, 'do you mind if I come in here for a little? I'm a bit edgy.' **1915** J. BUCHAN *39 Steps* i. 33 Then I could see that he began to get edgy again. He listened for little noises. **1924** *Chambers's Jrnl.* 555/1 The horses were very nervous and edgy for the rest of the day. **1929** S. AUMONIER *Ups & Downs* 514 That its mood was tense and 'edgy' was evident from the way in which the members spoke and behaved. **1958** *Times Lit. Suppl.* 23 May 280/3 An American family of harassed father, edgy mother and irritated crop-headed boys.

edh (ɛð). Also **eth.** Name of the Anglo-Saxon and Old Icelandic letter, or the phonetic symbol, ð ('crossed d').

1846 E. J. VERNON *Guide Anglo-Saxon Tongue* i. 4 đ (*eth*) our soft *th*, as in *other.* **1875** *Encycl. Brit.* I. 612/2 In order to express the corresponding sonant (heard in '*that*', and confusedly denoted by the same compound *th*) a stroke was drawn across the simple d (ð), and the new letter was called *edh.* **1965** C. BARBER *Flux of Language* vii. 130 The Old English scribes confused matters a little by using two symbols,..'thorn', and..'eth'..indiscriminately. **1969** *English Studies* Suppl. p. ii, Conybeare..made no use of thorn, Thk [*i.e.* Thorkelin] none of eth in transcription, though both sometimes wrote *th* as in modern English.

ed'halde, var. ATHOLD, *v. Obs.*

c **1175** *Lamb. Hom.* 149 Edhalde þet brihte ikunde; þet god haueð in ow ibroht of saule and of likame.

edi, var. of EADI *a. Obs.*

edi'bilatory, *a.* [badly f. *edibilis* EDIBLE, after adjs. in *-atory*; see -ORY.] Relating to edibles or eating.

1828 LYTTON *Pelham* I. 216 Edibilatory Epicurism holds the key to all morality.

edibility (ɛdɪ'bɪlɪtɪ). [f. next; see -ITY.] The quality of being edible, capability of being eaten.

1849 *Fraser's Mag.* XL. 130 To convert, so far as edibility ..is concerned, an old fowl into a young capon.

edible ('ɛdɪb(ə)l), *a.* and *sb.* [ad. late L. *edibilis*, f. *ed-ĕre* to eat.]

A. *adj.* Eatable, fit to be eaten.

1611 COTGR., *Ouë*, the paunch, and intralls of edible creatures. **1661** LOVELL *Hist. Anim. & Min.* Introd., The head is edible..of the cow, calfe, etc. **1802** BINGLEY *Anim. Biog.* (1813) II. 395 The edible frog. **1837** M. DONOVAN *Dom. Econ.* II. 219 The Edible Snail or *Helix pomatia.* **1884** J. COLBORNE *Hicks Pasha* 104 Everything edible was brought up.

B. *sb.* An eatable substance, an article of food. (chiefly in *pl.*)

1661 LOVELL *Hist. Anim. & Min.* Introd., Birds, fishes, and other edibles. **1670** G. H. *Hist. Cardinals* II. I. 114 Impositions upon Edibles. **1859** SALA *Tw. round Clock* (1861) 357 The delightful hampers of edibles and drinkables. **1864** *Daily Tel.* 23 Dec., What will be the effect of the introduction of this new edible?

Hence **edibleness**; = EDIBILITY.

1772 in SCOTT *Bailey's Dict.* **1775** in ASH; and in mod. Dicts.

edict ('iːdɪkt). Also 3 edit, 5 edycte, 6 *Sc.* edik. [ad. L. *edictum* (the earliest form a. OFr. *edit*), f. *ēdīcĕre*, f. *ē* out + *dīcĕre* to say. In 16th and 17th c. accented on the last syllable.]

1. That which is proclaimed by authority as a rule of action; an order issued by a sovereign to his subjects; an ordinance or proclamation having the force of law; *esp.* the edicts of the Roman prætors, and subsequently of the emperors, and of the French monarchs. ***Edict of Nantes***, an edict issued by Henry IV of France, granting toleration to the Protestants; revoked by Louis XIV.

1297 R. GLOUC. (Rolls) 11966 þe edit ywis. þat was þe ban of kenigwurþe. **1483** CAXTON *Cato* A iij, He dyd doo make an edycte or decree. **1535** STEWART *Cron. Scot.* II. 12 With ane consent [they] contempnit that edik. **1541** ELYOT *Image Gov.* 114 The Creditours to be compelled by an Edict of your maiestee, to holde them content with repaiement of the summe..of the thyng that they lende. **1651** HOBBES *Leviath.* II. xxvi. 147 The Edicts of Prætors, and of the Ædiles. **1683** *Brit. Speculum* 60 Monarchs at first governed ..by immediate Edicts. **1711** STEELE *Spect.* No. 97 ¶4 By Our Royal Resolutions declared in this Edict as follow. **1752** JOHNSON *Rambl.* No. 204 ¶9 He therefore fixed upon the gate of the palace an edict. **1845** GRAVES *Rom. Law* in *Encycl. Metrop.* 777/1 Constitutions of Justinian, improperly called edicts. **1875** POSTE *Gaius* I. (ed. 2) 34 Edicts were legislative ordinances issued by the emperor.. and were analogous to the edicts of the prætors and ediles.

fig. **1590** SHAKS. *Mids. N.* I. i. 151 If then true Louers haue beene euer crost, It stands as an edict in destinie. **1597** HOOKER *Eccl. Pol.* v. lxvii, The generall Edicts of nature. **1878** BROWNING *La Saisiaz* 68 Law, Now styled God's, now Nature's edict?

2. *Sc.* 'The name of a writ whereby all concerned were called by proclamation at the market cross or church-door, to appear for their interest in some cause... The term is used in ecclesiastical law for certain notices made to a congregation from the pulpit' (Barclay *Digest Laws Scotl.* s.v.).

1876 GRANT *Burgh Sch. Scot.* II. vi. 214 In 1636 the Council of Aberdeen ordain a public edict to be served at both the Kirk doors and at the College gate.

†e'dict, *v. Obs. rare*⁻¹. [ad. OF. *édicter.*] *trans.* To publish (a law); to decree.

1652 GAULE *Magastrom.* 362 Some of them [Lycurgus' laws] were such that old wives and slaves might easily have both predicted and edicted.

edictal (iː'dɪktəl), *a.* [ad. late L. *ēdictālis.*] **a.** Of or pertaining to an edict or edicts; consisting of edicts. **b.** In Scotch Law: That is done by means of an 'edict' or public proclamation. ***edictal citation***: a citation (formerly) made by public announcement in cases where personal citation was impossible, *e.g.* when the person cited was resident outside the kingdom. The term is still retained, though the procedure which it strictly denotes is no longer used: see quot. 1880.

1814 SCOTT in *Lockhart* (1839) IV. 215 All edictal citations are made at Scalloway. **1854** *Blackw. Mag.* LXXVI. 565 That reservoir of equity, the prætorian or edictal law of Rome. **1868** *Act 31 & 32 Vict.* c. 100 §95 The Lord Ordinary shall also appoint edictal intimation thereof to be made by publication in the record of edictal citations. **1875** POSTE *Gaius* III. (ed. 2) 327 Patrona mother of two children had..the edictal rights of patronus. **1880** BARCLAY *Digest Law Scotl.* (ed. 4) 334 Edictal Citations or Intimations. In the case of foreigners, these were formerly given at the market cross of Edinburgh, and pier and shore of Leith. This is now more judiciously done by leaving the copies at the Office of Edictal Citations.

Hence **e'dictally** *adv.*, in an edictal manner; by public proclamation.

1868 *Act 31 & 32 Vict.* ci. §30 Publication has been made edictally in Edinburgh. **1887** *Scotsman* 31 Jan. 10/2 On 19th November she charged him edictally to make payment.

†e'diction. *Obs.* Also 5 ediccion. [ad. L. *ēdictiōn-em*, f. as EDICT.] Edict, command.

c **1470** HARDING *Chron.* lxxxix. i, To Bedes dayes yᵉ Scottes..obeyed his ediccion. **1581** MARBECK *Bk. Notes* 231 In the former edition of the Councell.

†'edi,fiable. *Obs. rare*⁻¹. [f. EDIFY + -ABLE, in trans. sense: see -ABLE.] Fitted to edify; edifying, profitable.

1612 T. TAYLOR *Comm. Titus* iii. 2 And with these all opportunitie of good and edifiable speach perisheth.

†e'dificant, *a. Obs.* [ad. L. *ædificant-em*, pr. pple. of *ædificāre* to build.] Edifying.

1642 BP. OF DURHAM *Presentm. Schismatic* 11 The Apostle hath prescribed rules for regulating the Ceremonies of the Church, one whereof is Edification, and what is edificant, the same as also significant. **1655** T. DUGARD *Verses on Gataker* 73 Edificant It [his pen] also was, like those bless'd builders, who Stood on their guard, and stoutly builded too.

†e'dificate, *a. Obs.* [ad. L. *ædificātus*, pa. pple. of *ædificāre* to build.] Built up, constructed, instituted, arranged.

c **1470** HARDING *Chron.* xxxiii. iii, There were in his tyme ouer all, With other so afore edificate, X viij flamynes. **1530** LYNDESAY *Test. Papyngo* 110 The erth be Nature so edificate With holsum herbis. *a* **1560** ROLLAND *Crt. Venus* II. 582 That proper place sa weill edificate.

So **e'dificate** *v. rare*⁻⁰. *trans.*

1623 COCKERAM II, To *Build*, Fabricate, Edificate.

edification (,ɛdɪfɪ'keɪʃən). [ad. L. *ædificātiōn-em*, f. *ædificāre* to build, EDIFY.]

1. Building. *rare* in mod. use.

1549 W. THOMAS *Hist. Ital.* 10 b About 700 yeres after the edificacion of Rome. **1599** HAKLUYT *Voy.* II. 111 The castle ..is not onely of situation the strongest I have seene, but also of edification. **1669** GALE *Crt. Gentiles* I. III. ii. 27 Cadmus..is said to have written 4 Books, touching the Edification of his own Citie. **1705** STANHOPE *Paraphr.* I. 80 The Edification whereof would be best promoted by attributing to those Workmen neither more nor less than their Due. **1721–33** STRYPE *Eccl. Mem.* II. I. II. ii. 261 Officers to make all manner of provision for the edification of the said fortresses. **1805** *Ann. Rev.* III. 236 The exhibition of games, the edification of palaces. **1859** JEPHSON *Brittany* xviii. 293 Church-edification is everywhere the order of the day.

†b. *concr.* A building. *Obs.*

1432–50 tr. *Higden* (1865) I. 405 To make edificacions in cites. **1584** R. SCOT *Discov. Witchcr.* XV. ii. 320 He throweth down also the enimies edifications. **1656** in BLOUNT *Glossogr.* and in mod. Dicts; not in BAILEY, JOHNSON, or ASH.

c. *fig.* Building up of character, etc.

1856 RUSKIN *Mod. Paint.* IV. v. App. iii, The whole period of youth is one essentially of formation, edification, instruction. **1870** SWINBURNE *Ess. & Stud.* (1875) 165 The religious idea, as opposed to Philistine demolition or to Philistine edification.

2. *fig.* In religious use, after Gr. οἰκοδομή in *1 Cor.* xiv: The building up of the church, of the soul, in faith and holiness; the imparting of moral and spiritual stability and strength by suitable instruction and exhortation.

1382 WYCLIF *Rom.* xiv. 19 And kepe we tho thingis to gidere that ben of edificacioun, that is, to bylde soulis to heuene. *c* **1440** *Gesta. Rom.* lxiv. 276 (Harl. MS.) Noble and profitable wordis, to edificacion of þe peple. **1548** LATIMER *Serm. Ploughers* i. 67 Devilish ploughing, the which worketh to have things in Latin, and letteth the fruitful edification. **1611** BIBLE *2 Cor.* x. 8. **1651** HOBBES *Leviath.* III. xxxvii. 236 To the edification of God's people. **1710** NORRIS *Chr. Prud.* v. 202 To build up men in Faith and Holiness of Life, that which we properly mean by Edification. *a* **1876** J. H. NEWMAN *Hist. Sk.* II. IV. xi. 417 In providing for the religious necessities of posterity, they were directly serving their own edification.

b. Mental or moral improvement, intellectual profit; instruction. (Now often *ironical.*)

1660 W. SECKER *Nonsuch Prof.* Pref. 16 The design of this Peece is not the ostentation of the Author, but the edification of the Reader. **1691** T. H[ALE] *Acc. New Invent.* p. lxxvii, For the Edification of the Citizens of our Metropolis in Loyalty. **1772** PRIESTLEY *Inst. Relig.* (1782) II. 199 Promote ..mutual edification by every proper means. **1777** SHERIDAN *Sch. Scand.* v. ii, It certainly is edification to hear him talk. **1826** SCOTT *Woodst.* iii, Where was the edification of all this? **1857** DE QUINCEY *Whiggism* Wks. VI. 39 That he might distribute his edification in equal proportions. **1875** JOWETT *Plato* (ed. 2) III. 206 Kindly answer, for the edification of the company and myself.

†e'dificative, *a. ? Obs.* [f. L. *ædificāt-* ppl. stem of *ædificāre* + -IVE.] Edifying; adapted to promote spiritual improvement.

c **1410** LOVE *Bonavent. Mirr.* xxxviii. 78 (Gibbs MS.) Gostly comforte of hem by hys edyfycatyf [W. de W. **1530** edificacyon] and holy wordes. **1491** CAXTON *Vitas Patr.* (W. de W.) I. xxvi. 24 a/1 His worde was edyfycatyff that they whom he endoctryned put in effecte..all his doctryne. **1530** R. WHITFORD *Worke for Household* (1533) A, So that..it sholde be..edificatyve and profitable. **1634–46** ROW *Hist. Kirk* (1842) 328 Whilk exercises..proved verie edificative to those who were partakers of them.

Hence **†'edifi,catively** *adv.*, in an edifying manner.

?*c* **1530** (*title*) The Dialogues of Creatures moralysed, applyably and edificatyfly to euery mery and iocunde Mater.

edificatory ('ɛdɪfɪkeɪtərɪ). [ad. L. *ædificātōrius*; see prec. and -ORY.] Intended or suited for purposes of religious edification.

1649 BP. HALL *Cases Consc.* x. (R.) An exercise so beneficially edificatory to the church of God. **1678** *Lively Oracles* viii. §31. 316 Some parts of it..are not so.. edificatory to us. **1882–3** SCHAFF *Relig. Encycl.* II. 1613 The edificatory character of Neander's history.

edifice ('ɛdɪfɪs). Also 6–8 ædifice, 7 edifyce. [a. F. *édifice*, ad. L. *ædificium*, f. *ædis* temple, house + *-ficium* making.]

1. A building, usually a large and stately building, as a church, palace, temple, or fortress; a fabric, structure.

c **1386** CHAUCER *Melib.* ¶367 Castelles and othere manere edifices. **1475** CAXTON *Jason* (1477) 71 And with this they shal ordeyn solempne edifices and houses for the cite. **1538** LELAND *Itin.* IV. 72 The ædifices of the Abbey have beene made by many men in continuance. **1598** SHAKS. *Merry W.* II. ii. 225, I haue lost my edifice, by mistaking the place, where I erected it. **1605** HARRINGTON *View State Irel.* (1880), Hee cold not preach to edifye the Church, yet hee will bee famows to all posterytye for edifyces in the Church. **1621** BURTON *Anat. Mel.* II. ii. IV. (1651) 270 The inner roomes of a fair-built and sumptuous ædifice. **1711** *Dissenting Teachers Addr. agst. Bill for 50 new Churches* 10 Shall this be done for a few ungodly steepled Ædifices? **1796** H. HUNTER tr. *St. Pierre's Stud. Nat.* (1799) I. 128 For you will see under water..the ruins of many edifices. **1849**

FREEMAN *Archit.* 14 A moist and a dry climate require different kinds of edifices.

b. *transf.* and *fig.*

1711 ADDISON *Spect.* No. 98 ¶1, I am not for adding to the beautiful Edifices of Nature. **1845** S. AUSTIN *Ranke's Hist. Ref.* II. 485 The edifice of a new church must have been raised on a purely democratical basis. **1868** M. PATTISON *Academ. Org.* §5. 223 Upon the integrity and judgment of these Quinqueviri will depend really the whole edifice of the University. **1878** MORLEY *Carlyle, Crit. Misc.* Ser. I. 197 The corner-stone of Comte's edifice.

†**2. a.** The action or process of building or construction. **b.** Style of building, architecture.

1580 NORTH *Plutarch* 394 The Arsenall and Armory.. being of a strange and wonderfull edifice. **1663** GERBIER *Counsel* 2 How.. Princes and Magistrates have proceeded in their Edifices.

edificial (ɛdɪˈfɪʃəl), *a. rare.* [ad. late L. *ædificiālis*, f. *ædificium*; see prec. and -AL¹.]

a. Of or pertaining to building, architectural. **b.** That is of the nature of an edifice.

1658 SIR T. BROWNE *Gard. Cyrus* 63 The edificial Palaces of Bees and Monarchical spirits. **1794** *Hist. Rivers Gt. Brit.* I. 232 (R.) Mansions.. without any striking edificial attraction. **1830** GALT *Lawrie T.* VI. ii. (1849) 255 Long surpassed by many other edificial structures.

edifier (ˈɛdɪfaɪə(r)). [f. next + -ER¹.] **a.** A builder. *rare.* **b.** One who edifies.

1460 CAPGRAVE *Chron.* 21 Certeyn strong men and rich.. edifieres of citees. **1678** BUTLER *Hud.* (R.) They scorn their edifiers to own who taught them all their sprinkling lessons. **1832** CARLYLE *Crit. & Misc. Ess.* (1872) IV. 117 The true Spiritual Edifier and Soul's-Father of all England. **1909** *Westm. Gaz.* 22 Jan. 3/1 The real edifiers. **1921** *Glasgow Herald* 19 Feb. 6 The professional edifiers of British youth.

edify (ˈɛdɪfaɪ), *v.* Also 4 ede-, edifien, 4–7 edifie, 4–6 ede-, edy(f)fy, edifye, 6 ædefie, 6–7 ædify. [a. F. *édifie-r*, ad. L. *ædificā-re*, f. *ædes, ædis* dwelling + *-ficāre* to make; see -FY.]

1. *trans.* To build; to construct (a dwelling, edifice) of the usual building materials. *rare* in mod. use.

a **1340** HAMPOLE *Psalter* l. 19 Þat edified be þe waghes of ierusalem. **1393** LANGL. *P. Pl.* C. XXI. 42 To for-don hit on a day, and in þre dayes after Edefien hit efte newe. **1462** J. PASTON in *Lett.* 461. II. 113 A plase late be the seid Sir John edified at Caster. *c* **1534** tr. *Pol. Verg. Eng. Hist.* (1846) I. x. 46 He did.. ædefie a gate on the bancke of the river Thames. **1641** *Termes de la Ley* 117 To take timber to edifie the house againe. **1704** HEARNE *Duct. Hist.* (ed. 3) I. 187 Babylon.. was largely edified by the Assyrian Monarchs. **1851** LONGF. *Gold. Leg.* II. 118 The names of all who had died in the convent since it was edified.

†**b.** *absol.*

c **1400** *Test. Love* I. (1560) 276b/2 Lo this man began to edifie, but for his foundement is bad, to the ende may he it nat bring. *c* **1420** *Pallad. on Husb.* I. 364 The see gravel is lattest for to drie, And lattest may thou therwith edifie. **1531** ELYOT *Gov.* I. viii, A man, whiche intendeth to edifie. **1655** L'ESTRANGE *Chas. I*, 124 To edifie at pleasure upon the Convent Garden.

†**c.** To furnish with buildings.

c **1432–50** tr. *Higden* (1865) I. 199 Apulia is a coste of the see of Ytaly.. byldede and edifiede firste by Grekes. **1596** SPENSER *F.Q.* III. i. 14 Through countries waste, and eke well edifyde.

†**2.** To construct, set up, irrespective of the object, or kind of materials. *Obs.* or *arch.*

1460 CAPGRAVE *Chron.* 21 The puple edified ymages to her liknes. **1546** LANGLEY *Pol. Verg. De Invent.* III. v. 70 Some beganne to edify cotages of boughes of trees. **1591** SPENSER *Virg. Gnat* 661 And thereupon did raise full busily A little mount, of greene turffs edifide. **1643** SIR T. BROWNE *Relig. Med.* (1682) 51 She was edified out of the Rib of Adam. **1850** NEALE *Med. Hymns* 155 The brazen sea That Solomon had edified.

†**b.** To work up or fashion (materials) *into* a building or structure. Cf. BUILD 5. *Obs.*

1382 WYCLIF *Gen.* ii. 22 And the Lord God edified the rib, the whiche he toke of Adam, into a woman.

†**c.** *fig.* To build up, establish, organize (a system, institution, or law, a moral quality, etc.), to establish or strengthen (a person).

a **1340** HAMPOLE *Psalter* xxvii[i]. 7[5] Þou sall distroy þaim & noght edifye þaim. *c* **1374** CHAUCER *Boeth.* IV. vi. 140 Þere þat uertues han edified þe bodie of þe holy man. **1425** *Ord. Whittington's Alms-house* in Entick *London* (1766) IV. 354 Inforcing himself to edifie and nourish charity.. among his felawes. **1461–83** *Ord. R. Househ.* 61 The Clerkys of Greneclothe.. to helpe kepe in course the Statutes.. edyfyed before-tyme. **1534** WHITTYNTON *Tullyes Offices* I. (1540) 34 Solon fyrste edifyed the schole called Areopagus in Athenes. **1704** SWIFT *T. Tub* i. (1710) 28 To edify a name and reputation. **1781** GIBBON *Decl. & F.* III. xlix. 95 He secretly edified the throne of his successors.

†**d.** To frame a notion; 'make out', imagine.

1645 MILTON *Tetrach.* Wks. 1738 I. 238, I cannot edify how, or by what rule of proportion that man's virtue calculates.

†**e.** *intr.* To take form, grow; also *fig.* to prosper, achieve success. Cf. 4. *Obs.*

a **1400** *Cov. Myst.* 252 Mannys sowle in blys now xal edyfy. **1622** BACON *Henry VII*, 160 Perkins Proclamation did little edifie with the people of England. **1646** SIR T. BROWNE *Pseud. Ep.* 147 It [the seed] then beginneth to edifie in chiefe. *a* **1662** HEYLIN *Laud* I. 142 But all this did not edifie with the House of Commons.

3. *trans.* In religious use: To build up (the church, the soul) in faith and holiness; to benefit spiritually; to strengthen, support. Also *absol.*

In early use sometimes with distinct allusion to sense 1; rarely in bad sense as in quot. 1440.

1340 *Ayenb.* 197 Þe uelaȝrede of poure men, þet byeþ poure uor God.. hise moȝe wel edefie be uorbisnes. *c* **1380** WYCLIF *Sel. Wks.* III. 354 Petre and Poul.. token power of Crist.. but for to edifie þe Chirche. *c* **1440** *Gesta Rom.* xvi. 58 (Add. MS.) All that is done agayn conscience edefieth to helle. **1521** MORE *Heresyes* I. Wks. (1557) 108/2 In whose deuout sermons the people were greatly edified. **1542** BRINKLOW *Compl.* xxiv. (1874) 62 Thei were edifyed to walke in the amendment of lyfe. **1604** DRAYTON *Owle* 908 To edifie the conscience that is weake. **1719** SWIFT *To Yng. Clergym.* Wks. 1755 II. II. 9 A plain convincing reason.. will edify a thousand times more than the art of wetting the handkerchiefs of a whole congregation. **1776** GIBBON *Decl. & F.* xxi, The complaints and mutual accusations which assailed the throne of Constantine.. were ill adapted to edify an imperfect proselyte. **1876** FREEMAN *Norm. Conq.* I. App. 751 He was much edified by the king's prayers and almsdeeds.

b. To inform, instruct; to improve in a moral sense; sometimes *ironical.*

1534 LD. BERNERS *Gold. Bk. M. Aurel.* (1546) G v b, His saiynges thus ended, the Senate was greatly edified therwith. **1601** SHAKS. *Twel. N.* v. i. 298 Looke then to be well edified when the Foole deliuers the Madman. **1606** —— *Tr. & Cr.* v. iii. 112 My loue with words and errors still she feedes But edifies another with her deedes. **1705** STANHOPE *Paraphr.* I. 3, I shall endeavour to edifie my Reader in the Virtues proper to these Purposes. **1845** B'NESS BUNSEN in Hare *Life* (1879) II. iii. 84, I have been much edified by seeing how your father and sister take the privation.

†**4.** *intr.* To profit in a spiritual sense. *Obs.*

1636 W. SAMPSON *Vow-Breaker* I ij, Is there any man here desires to edyfie? I am in the humour of converting. **1657** J. GOODWIN *Triers Tried* 6 A Minister, whom they can cordially.. affect, or by whom they can edifie. *a* **1670** HACKET *Abp. Williams* I. (1692) 188 And few will captivate their understanding to edify by a sacrilegious reformer.

†**b.** To gain instruction generally. *Obs.*

1610 B. JONSON *Alch.* III. i, I haue not edified more truely, by man.. since the beautifull light first shone on me. **1675** WYCHERLEY *Country Wife* v. (1735) 104, I edify so much by example, I will never be one [a husband]. *a* **1726** VANBR. & CIB. *Prov. Husb.* I. i, This is like to be a warm Debate! I shall edify. **1800** T. JEFFERSON *Writ.* (1859) IV. 311 The great mass of our nation will edify and thank you.

†**ˈedify**, *sb. Obs.* Erroneous form of EDIFICE.

1555 EDEN *Decades W. Ind.* III. (Arb.) 153 The houses & other edifyes of this prouynce. **1555** —— *Moscouia & Cathay* 279 The rouffes of whose edefies are gylted & embowed.

ˈedifying, *vbl. sb.* [f. EDIFY *v.* + -ING¹.]

†**1.** The action or process of building; also *concr.* a building. *Obs.*

1432–50 tr. *Higden* (1865) I. 411 At Brehenoc is a water.. where a man may see in clere tymes meruellous edifienges. **1513** *Test. Ebor.* v. (Surtees) 49 To the edifying of a portche to the church of Est Drayton xxs. **1517** TORKINGTON *Pilgr.* (1884) 32 Ther [the Sarrazins'] edifying wold not stonde in no wyse. **1602** FULBECKE *2nd Pt. Parall.* 13 The foundation, the edifying, and the endowment [of a church].

2. Spiritual instruction and improvement.

1509 FISHER *Fun. Serm. Marg. C'tess Richmond* (1708) 10 To the edifyinge of other, by the example of her. **1542–3** *Act 34 & 35 Hen. VIII*, i, Al maner of persons.. may reade.. the bible.. for their owne edifieng. **1611** BIBLE *Pref.* 5 For the.. edifying of the vnlearned. **1705** STANHOPE *Paraphr.* (1709) IV. 542 My.. End is Godly Edifying.

ˈedifying, *ppl. a.* [f. as prec. + -ING².]

†**1.** That builds. *Obs.*

1662 FULLER *Worthies* (1840) II. 499 One demolishing hammer can undo more in a day than ten edifying axes can advance in a month.

2. Tending to produce moral and spiritual improvement; instructive. In mod. use often *ironical.*

1526 *Pilgr. Perf.* (W. de W. 1531) 1 b, What so euer ye fynde therin, good and edifyenge, gyue laude and praysynge to god therfore. **1651** HOBBES *Leviath.* IV. xlv. 361 Their Conversation.. might.. be.. Edifying to others. **1767** FORDYCE *Serm. Yng. Wom.* I. v. 186 How edifying to the soul is this generous sensibility! **1813** SYD. SMITH *Wks.* (1867) I. 224 The humiliating and disgusting, but at the same time most edifying spectacle. **1872** MORLEY *Voltaire* (1886) 41 Voltaire's spirit may be little edifying to us.

Hence **ˈedifyingly** *adv.*, in an instructive or improving manner; in mod. use often *ironical.*

1662 SPARROW tr. *Behme's Theosoph. Lett.* 3 He.. might thereby.. edifyingly.. quicken himself in a Christian brotherly Union. **1702** ECHARD *Eccl. Hist.* (1710) 305 Not so well or edifyingly instructed. **1876** *Contemp. Rev.* XXVII. 969 The sermon was edifyingly platitudinarian.

edile, variant of ÆDILE.

1820 MAIR *Tyro's Dict.* (ed. 10) 2 Aedilis, an edile or officer who took care of the repair of temples and other buildings.

ediness, var. of EADINESS, *Obs.*, s.v. EADI.

edingtonite (ˈɛdɪŋtɒnaɪt). *Min.* [f. the surname *Edington* (see quot. 1825) + -ITE.] A greyish white translucent mineral, consisting chiefly of the silicates of alumina, baryta, etc.

1825 HAIDINGER in *Edin. Jrnl. Sci.* III. 317 It is in compliment to that gentleman [Mr. Edington, in whose collection Haidinger first saw the mineral] that the name of Edingtonite is here proposed. **1868** DANA *Min.* 417 Edingtonite occurs in the Kilpatrick Hills, near Glasgow, Scotland, associated with harmotome, another baryta mineral.

†**edipol.** *Obs. rare.* [miswritten for L. *edepol* by Pollux. (Erroneously connected with *ædis* temple.)] Any common asseveration.

c **1450** *Voc.* in Wr.-Wülcker 579 *Edepol*, by the house of edepol. **1600** DEKKER *Gentle Craft* Wks. 1873 I. 14 Away with your pishery pashery, your pols and your edipolls.

edisonite (ˈɛdɪsənaɪt). *Min.* [f. name of Thomas Alva *Edison*, American inventor (1847–1931) + -ITE¹.] A name formerly given to a supposed variety of rutile. *Disused.*

1888 W. E. HIDDEN in *Amer. Jrnl. Sci.* 3rd Ser. XXXVI. 274, I therefore propose for it the name *Edisonite*, after Mr. Thomas Alva Edison. **1889** *Jrnl. Chem. Soc.* LVI. 354 Edisonite, a fourth form of Titanic Anhydride. **1944** C. PALACHE et al. *Dana's Syst. Min.* (ed. 7) I. 560 Edisonite, a supposed orthorhombic polymorph of TiO_2.

edit (ˈɛdɪt), *v.* [(1) f. L. *ēdit-us*, pa. pple. of *ēdĕre* to put forth, f. *ē* out + *dăre* to put, give; (2) back-formation from EDITOR *sb.*]

†**1.** To publish, give to the world (a literary work by an earlier author, previously existing in MS.). Chiefly in pa. pple., after L. *ēditus*. *Obs.*

1791 ENFIELD tr. *Brucker's Hist. Philos.* II. 367 [Abelard] wrote many philosophical treatises which have never been edited.

2. a. To prepare an edition of (a literary work or works by an earlier author); so with the name of the author as obj., *e.g.* 'to edit Horace, Shakspere', etc. **b.** To prepare, set in order for publication (literary material which is wholly or in part the work of others). Sometimes euphemistically for: To garble, 'cook' (*e.g.* a war-correspondent's dispatch, etc.). **c.** To be or act as the EDITOR of (a newspaper or other periodical).

1793 V. KNOX *Lett. to Yng. Nobleman* (R.), Read.. the few orations of Demosthenes, which Monteney has edited. **1835** DICKENS *Lett.* (1880) I. 3 To write and edit a new publication. **1880** E. WHITE *Cert. Relig.* 72 The progress of science and art in editing from ancient manuscripts. **1885** *Harper's Mag.* Mar. 647/2 It has not been guilty of the.. folly of attempting to 'edit' the news.

d. To prepare a film for the cinema or recordings for broadcasting, etc. (by eliminating unwanted material, etc.); = CUT *v.* 21 e. Also with *in* and *out.*

1917 *Sci. Amer.* 8 Dec. 441/3 Editing a film is perhaps the most interesting phase of laboratory work. **1933** A. BRUNEL *Filmcraft* 94, I have myself edited.. 35 mm. films with just a bench, scissors.. winder, film cement, a brush to put it on with, and a bin to unroll my film into. **1938** *Encycl. Brit. Bk. of Yr.* 122/1 Mobile recording vans with a new method of editing records. **1961** *Encounter* XVI. 49 Her [*sc.* Ada Leverson's] frequent use of film scenario devices.. 'editing in' scenes and themes apparently unrelated to the one that, in realistic terms, she is just then evoking. **1962** A. NISBETT *Technique Sound Studio* 265 *Pot-cut*, editing a short segment of unwanted material out of a programme.. by quickly fading out and fading in again. **1969** J. ELLIOT *Duel* III. v. 312 Keep running... We can edit this out.

Hence **ˈedited** *ppl. a.*

Mod. A carefully edited work.

edit (ˈɛdɪt), *sb.* [f. the vb.] **a.** An act or spell of editing, esp. a recording; the action or process of editing; also, edited material. **b.** A feature or facility that allows for or performs editing.

1960 *Jrnl. Soc. Motion Picture & Television Engineers* Mar. 164/3 Edit sync is applied to the cue track of the videotape recorder. **1961** *Cinemeditor* Oct. 3/2 The edit point lies somewhere within the ninety frames encompassed by the four images. **1962** A. NISBETT *Technique Sound Studio* vii. 126 Fluffs, where the speaker has gone back on himself. Again an edit will generally improve intelligibility. **1964** *AFIPS Conf. Proc.* XXVI. 354/2 At completion of the edit, all subroutines within an area are sequentially assigned. **1968** *N.Y. Times* 1 July 51 New York Magazine has been running so light on ads recently that a friend of the ad director said, 'It's just like Channel 13, just uninterrupted good edit.' **1970** *New Yorker* 7 Mar. 96 At times the movie feels like a travelogue... Luckily, the fast edit keeps the action from sagging. **1976** *Gramophone* Oct. 627/1 A clumsy edit at bar 18 in No. 13 is also apparent. **1984** E. P. DEGARMO et al. *Materials & Processes in Manuf.* (ed. 6) xxxviii. 968 Features such as program edit.. are common on today's CNC [*sc.* computerized numerical control] machines. **1984** *Which Micro?* Dec. 96 (Advt.), TEXT mode with.. continuous screen edit. **1986** *Keyboard Player* Apr. 3/3 The sophisticated edit facilities allow complicated musical forms to be created.

editing (ˈɛdɪtɪŋ), *vbl. sb.* [f. EDIT *v.* + -ING¹.]

a. The action of the vb. EDIT.

1840 J. S. MILL *Let.* 16 Apr. in *Wks.* (1963) XIII. 427 There, I think, is a full account of all the world has got by my editing and reviews. **1885** *Athenæum* 15 Aug. 198/1 The 'Letters..' have had the advantage of careful editing.

b. = CUTTING *vbl. sb.* 1 d.

1921 A. C. LESCARBOURA *Cinema Handbk.* (1922) v. 236 With the positive films printed up.. a very necessary operation in the preparation of motion picture films is the editing and cutting. **1944** S. COLE (*title*) Film editing. **1944** R. MANVELL *Film* iv. 37 Editing is the art of putting the film together shot by shot from the celluloid strips themselves. **1962** A. NISBETT *Technique Sound Studio* vii. 117 'Editing' can mean various things: cutting and rejoining a tape..; *copy editing*, in which selected sections.. are copied.. on to a make-up tape; *mixing*, where the combined output of two tapes are fed to a third recorder. **1963** *Movie* Apr. 32/2 A director shouldn't use his camera and editing bench to

impose something which he hasn't been able to put into the action.

edition (ɪˈdɪʃən), *sb.* [a. F. *édition*, ad. L. *ēditiōn-em*, f. *ēdĕre* to put forth, publish; see EDIT.]

†**1.** The action of putting forth, or making public; publication. *Obs.*

1551 RECORDE *Pathw. Knowl.* Ep. to King, Desiring your grace not so muche to beholde the simplenes of the woorke ..as to fauour the edition thereof. **1577** tr. *Bullinger's Decades* (1592) 111 Touching yᵉ proclamation or first edition of the ten Commaundements. **1611** SPEED *Hist. Gt. Brit.* IX. xix. (1632) 929 The said pretensed marriage was made..without edition of banes. **1659** A. LOVEDAY in *R. Loveday's Lett.* To Rdr., So tender was I of his honour in edition of his labours. **1663** J. SPENCER *Prodigies* (1665) Pref., God never saw it necessary..to correct and amend any thing in this great Volume of the Creation, since the first edition thereof.

†**2. a.** The action of producing, or bringing into existence; hence, birth, creation (of orders of knighthood, etc.), extraction, origin. *Obs.*

1599 SANDYS *Europæ Spec.* (1632) 147 The great States of Italy..are loth to have their Pope of a Spanish edition. **1607** CHAPMAN *Bussy D'Amb.* Plays 1873 II. 17 The Duke mistakes him (on my life) for some knight of the new edition. **1615** CROOKE *Body of Man* 332 The Birth..we define to be an Edition or bringing into the world of an infant. **1656** EARL MONM. *Advt. fr. Parnass.* 211 Barons of late edition. **1677** HALE *Prim. Orig. Man* II. iv. 151 Consequently the World..is of a far later Edition than Eternity.

†**b.** Kind, species; fashion, 'stamp'. *Obs.*

*a*1625 FLETCHER *Nice Val.* I. i, It kisses the forefinger still: which is the last edition. **1632** BROME *North Lasse* II. iv. Wks. 1873 III. 33 A large window, one of the last Edition. **1640** J. LEY *Patterne of Pietie* 155 The Saints of the old edition. **1646** H. LAWRENCE *Communion with Angels* 93 His condition, his spirit and his worke were all of a lowe and humble edition.

3. *concr.* **a.** One of the differing forms in which a literary work (or a collection of works) is published, either by the author himself, or by subsequent editors. **b.** An impression, or issue in print, of a book, pamphlet, etc.; the whole number of copies printed from the same set of types and issued at the same time.

In the case of printed works the meanings a and b are often coincident; but an 'edition' (sense a) of a classic or the like, with a corrected text and critical or illustrative matter, being in a sense an independent work, may go through several 'editions' (sense b). It is awkward to speak of, *e.g.* 'the second edition of Campbell's edition of Plato's *Theætetus*'; but existing usage affords no satisfactory substitute for this inconvenient mode of expression. To say 'the second impression' would now imply an unaltered reprint. The word is sometimes used in a narrower sense than that of the definition of b: thus a 'large paper edition' may be printed from the same type as, and issued simultaneously with, an 'edition' on small paper; but it is also usual to say '100 copies of this edition are on large paper'.

[**1555** ROBINSON tr. *More's Utop.* (ed. 2) A iij b, I haue now in this seconde edition taken about it such paines.] **1570** FOXE *A. & M.* (ed. 2) 1885 Although sufficient relation be made before in our former edition to be seene, pag. 1277. **1607** SIR W. VAUGHAN *Directions for Health* (title page), The third Edition. **1624** GATAKER *Transubst.* 104 Their severall Editions..so chopped and changed. **1662** STILLINGFL. *Orig. Sacr.* I. vi. §1 He might make use of the Edition of Causinus. **1703** DE FOE *True-born Eng.* Expl. Pref., I have mended some faults in this Edition. **1712** ADDISON *Spect.* No. 470 ¶1 Upon examining the new Edition of a Classick Author. **1782** PRIESTLEY *Corrupt Chr.* I. Pref. 21 There are different editions of many of the authors..I have quoted. **1807** M. BAILLIE *Morb. Anat.* Pref. 22 In preparing this Third Edition for the press. **1838–9** HALLAM *Hist. Lit.* I. I. iv. §63 Above 60 editions of the Orlando Furioso were published in the 16th century. **1845** STEPHEN *Laws Eng.* I. 185 [King John's] charter was finally altered, in its last edition, by Henry the third. *Mod.* The latest edition of this evening's paper.

c. *fig.*

1612 DONNE *Sec. Anniv.* 309 All the vertuous Actions they expresse, Are but a new, and worse edition Of her some one thought. **1802** C. WILMOT *Let.* 30 Aug. in *Irish Peer* (1920) 83 Mr. Richard Trench..is..so beautiful that if I was to describe him, you'd fancy it was the Apollo Belvedere in a Second Edition. **1823** CARLYLE *Let.* 22 Oct. in *Early Lett.* (1886) II. 232 A kind of theological braggadocio, an enlarged edition of the Rev. Rowland Hill. **1828** STEUART *Planter's G.* 51 Boutcher had another plan..for removing Trees..it is a better edition of Lord Fitzharding's system. **1856** in *Century Mag.* (1887) May 95/2 We cannot hazard a second edition of imbecility. **1892** *Daily News* 18 Oct., The exhilarating ballet of 'Don Juan'..seems likely to run into many 'editions', as the phrase goes, before it exhausts its popularity. **1920** H. CRANE *Let.* 24 Sept. (1965) 43 About every other person..are [*sic*] enlarged editions of Lord Douglas. **1943** J. S. HUXLEY *TVA* x. 74 The slightly younger edition of the architect.

†**e'dition,** *v. Obs. rare*⁻¹. [f. the sb.] *trans.* To make an edition of; to issue, publish.

1716 M. DAVIES *Athen. Brit.* III. 4 The Jesuit Petavius's Chronological Tables were edition'd.

Hence †**e'ditioner.** *Obs. rare.* = EDITOR *sb.*

*a*1646 J. G[REGORY] *Maps & Charts, Posth.* (1650) 321 That necessarie Guide, added to a little, but not much augmented, by the late Editioner. **1658** W. BURTON *Itin. Anton.* 18 You have there Βουβονίαν, which the dexterity of the Editioner, or Interpreter hath turned into Βορβονίαν.

édition de luxe: see LUXE 2.

e'ditionizing, *vbl. sb.* [f. EDITION *sb.* + -IZE + -ING¹.] The production of several editions of a newspaper. Also **e'ditionized** *ppl. a.*

1972 *Oxford Times* 4 Aug. 1/8 The size and editionising of The Oxford Times have had to be restricted this week. **1979** *Times* 20 Nov. 4/4 If I could wire up pages like Hickey to Manchester, it would give their composing room capacity to do more editionizing for the *Daily Star* and *Daily Express* in the North of England. **1982** *Daily Tel.* 10 Aug. 17 (Advt.), From November an editionised newspaper..will be produced centrally.

‖**editio princeps** (ɪˈdɪʃɪəʊ ˈprɪnsɛps). Pl. **editiones principes** (ɪdɪʃɪˈəʊniːz ˈprɪnsɪpiːz). [mod.L.] The first printed edition of a book.

1802 T. F. DIBDIN *Introd. Knowl. Rare & Val. Ed.* 4 This editio princeps contains but nine comedies. **1815** J. SCOTT *Visit to Paris* xv. 294 The room of the *Editiones principes*, contains every thing to gratify the taste of the bibliographer. **1875** *Encycl. Brit.* III. 656/2 Azzoguidi's *editio princeps* of Ovid. **1885** J. B. LIGHTFOOT *Apostolic Fathers* I. 113 A misprint of the editio princeps. **1930** *Times Lit. Suppl.* 6 Feb. 85/4 Laid down the plan of the *editio princeps*. **1955** *Times* 9 May 13/2 He published..an *editio princeps* of several minor works.

Editola (ɛdɪˈtəʊlə). Also **editola.** [Proprietary name.] A machine used for editing films (see quots.).

1935 *Trade Marks Jrnl.* 31 July 952/2 Editola, apparatus included in Class 8 for reproducing motion picture films and sounds simultaneously. Photographic Electrical Co. Ltd., 80/2 Wardour Street, London, W. 1, Manufacturers. **1939** *Times* 18 Nov. 10 The 'editola' on which the picture film and sound track are synchronized and checked. **1967** *Listener* 14 Sept. 326/3 The rattling chipmunk chatter of the Editola.

editor (ˈɛdɪtə(r)), *sb.* [a. L. *ēditor*: see EDIT, EDITION *sb.*] One who edits.

†**1.** The publisher of a book (cf. Fr. *éditeur*).

1649 BP. HALL *Cases Consc.* I. v. (1650) 33 Otherwise some Interloper may perhaps underhand fall upon the work at a lower rate, and undoe the first editor.

2. One who prepares the literary work of another person, or number of persons for publication, by selecting, revising, and arranging the material; also, one who prepares an edition of any literary work.

1712 ADDISON *Spect.* No. 470 ¶1 When a different Reading gives us..a new Elegance in an Author, the Editor does very well in taking Notice of it. **1725** POPE *Notes on Shaks.* (J.), This nonsense got into all the editions by a mistake of the stage editors. **1748** ANSON *Voy.* Introd., The Editors of a new variation-chart..have..been misled by an erroneous analogy. **1831** J. DAVIES *Manual Nat. Med.* Introd., The Editor conceives that the plan laid down here is, etc. **1863** BURTON *Bk. Hunter* 302 The editors of club books are not mere dreary drudges.

3. a. *esp.* One who conducts a newspaper or periodical publication.

1803 G. ROSE *Diaries* (1860) II. 111 The Editor of the *True Briton*. **1823** COBBETT *Rur. Rides* 146 This blunder-headed editor of *Bell's Messenger*. **1874** MORLEY *Compromise* (1886) 248 The editor of the daily newspaper.

b. A person in charge of a particular section of a newspaper, e.g. of the financial news (*City editor*: see CITY 9).

1843 *Knickerbocker* XXII. 494 We cannot permit the young associate-editor of that print..to misrepresent us. **1894** E. L. SHUMAN *Steps into Journalism* 19 On the larger papers the work of the managing editor is divided, giving him an assistant, the managing news editor. **1936** *S.P.E. Tract* XLV. 188 In American newspaper offices, a member of the staff who is in charge of a single feature or department is dignified by the title of *editor*. This practice is being introduced into English journalism, but not without protest. **1954** *Manch. Guardian Weekly* 14 Oct. 7/1 'Say,' said the American photographer... 'My editor's hopping mad for pictures.'

c. The literary manager of a publishing house, or head of one of its publishing departments. orig. *U.S.*

1915 *Bookman* XLI. 306/2 You now find erstwhile stonewall editors wax in your hands. **1930** *Publishers' Weekly* 5 Apr. 2096 Far more attention might well be given the West's peculiar needs by Eastern editors. **1958** *Oxford Books* (catal.) 3 *Oxford Progressive English*..was founded by E. C. Parnwell, while oversea editor of the Oxford University Press.

d. *attrib.* (appos.), as ***editor-author, -manager, -proprietor, -publisher***; also **editor-in-chief,** the chief editor of a publication, in a publishing-house, etc.

1952 M. LOWRY *Let.* Mar. (1967) 292, I had a right..and the aim..to achieve an editor-author relationship. **1873** J. M. BAILEY *Life in Danbury* 287 Our highest ambition has been to be the editor-in-chief of a large New York daily, and help do up the mail. **1913** E. C. BENTLEY *Trent's Last Case* ii. 19 He was..editor-in-chief of the *Record*. **1955** *Times* 2 July 4/3 The editor-in-chief was Mr. Humphry House, Fellow of Wadham College, Oxford. **1959** *Encounter* July 67/1 He..is now editor-in-chief of Stanford University Press. **1959** *Manch. Guardian* 21 July 6/7 Sir William [Haley] had then been for one year editor-in-chief [at the B.B.C.]. **1961** (*title*) Webster's Third New International Dictionary. Editor in Chief Philip Babcock Gove, Ph.D. **1899** *Westm. Gaz.* 20 May 1/3 Editor-manager of the *Oxford Chronicle*. **1906** *Ibid.* 20 Sept. 10/2 The editor-proprietor of the 'Studio'. **1907** *Ibid.* 8 Nov. 12/1 The staff, from the editor-publisher downward.

4. *Antiq.* [L. *editor ludorum*.] The exhibitor (of Roman public games).

1880 L. WALLACE *Ben-hur* v. x. (1884) 283, I have here the notice of the editor of the games, just issued.

5. One who cuts and edits a film.

1917 *Sci. Amer.* 8 Dec. 441/3 The editor, usually the director himself in dramatic productions, directs the cutting and assembling of the various strips of film into the complete production; and just as the editor of a magazine..makes his corrections, so does the film editor view the assembled film on the screen and make corrections and changes. **1933** A. BRUNEL *Filmcraft* 158 *Editor*, one who cuts, assembles, edits and titles a film. **1937** H. G. WELLS *Brynhild* v. 61 The brightest and best producers, directors, scenarists, cameramen, special effects men, editors.

6. *Computing.* A program that permits the user to alter programs or to alter or rearrange data or text held in a computer.

1959 *Jrnl. Assoc. Computing Machinery* VI. 153 The input data for the program are..converted to binary by the system input editor. **1963** *Compatible Time-Sharing System* (M.I.T. Computation Center) iii. 26 The user can also by appropriate commands or supervisor calls generate other disk editor control cards to be entered into the disk editing process. **1967** *Communications of ACM* X. 793/2 The present paper is built around a description of the editor in the Berkeley time sharing system for the SDS-930..which is called QED. **1976** *Sci. Amer.* Nov. 120/2 APL/3000's editor has greater flexibility and power than the typical APL editor, with modes for both line editing of simple problems and complete text editing. **1980** S. HOCKEY *Guide to Computer Applications in Humanities* ii. 31 More sophisticated editors allow the user to jump about the file making corrections at random. **1986** *What Micro?* Apr. 6/2 A full-screen editor is now incorporated which also carries out extensive syntax checking.

Hence **'editor** *v. trans.* (*rare*), to edit (a work). **'editored** *ppl. a.*, provided or furnished with an editor. **'edito,ress** = EDITRESS. **'editorless** *a.*, without an editor.

1826 *Blackw. Mag.* XIX. 335 Some laggardly editorless, or ten editor'd periodical. **1836** *Ibid.* XL. 766 Lady Blessington is registered..editoress of half-a-score of books. **1961** *Amer. Speech* XXXVI. 138 The Britannica is now editored by Walter Yust.

editorial (ɛdɪˈtɔːrɪəl), *a.* and *sb.* [f. EDITOR *sb.* + -(I)AL.]

A. *adj.* **a.** Of or pertaining to an editor; proper to, or characteristic of, an editor.

1744 AKENSIDE *Let.* in *Poems* (1845) 30 He has intirely dedicated himself to..editorial criticism. **1794** PARR in *Brit. Critic* Feb. (T.), Lambin..and Heyne also..seem to have considered it as part of their editorial duty, etc. **1850** CARLYLE *Latter-d. Pamph.* iv. (1872) 117 In spite of editorial prophecy. **1837** DICKENS *Pickw.* (1847) 234/2 Bless our editorial heart.

b. *spec.* Written, or ostensibly written, by the editor of a newspaper, as distinct from news items.

1802 *Deb. Congress U.S.* 25 Feb. (1851) 796 The editorial part of the paper..was supposed to come from the pen of Mr. Hobby. **1816** *Niles' Weekly Register* X. Index, Editorial articles. **1849** *Knickerbocker* XXXIV. 9 We shall set forth in this editorial leader, that our friends may know exactly where we are. **1877** *Harper's Mag.* Dec. 109/1 [He] thoroughly worked an idea into an editorial leader. **1920** P. C. BING *Country Weekly* 145 [They minimized] the importance of the editorial page.

c. ***editorial we*** [WE *pron.* 2], the pronoun *we* used by a single person to denote himself, as in an editorial.

1841 DICKENS *Let.* 24 Aug. (1969) II. 368 Every rotten-hearted pander who..struts it in the Editorial We once a week. **1888** KIPLING *Phantom 'Rickshaw* (1890) 137 Under special patronage of the editorial We. **1964** E. A. NIDA *Toward Sci. Transl.* ix. 204 Such 'editorial we's' must be shifted to 'I' if they are to be intelligible in some languages. **1964** R. H. ROBINS *Gen. Ling.* vii. 287 A different anomaly in relation to number in pronouns is seen in what is often called the 'editorial *we*'.

B. *sb.* A newspaper article written by, or under the responsibility of, the editor; a 'leader'.

1830 *Collegian* (Cambridge, Mass.) 44 The great green table in the centre groaning under the weight of editorials, and friendly correspondence. **1864** *Spectator* 539 Mr. Bennett..thinks that 'an editorial' is the highest style of composition known. **1866** MRS. STOWE *Lit. Foxes* 14 To set up the editorial of a morning paper. **1883** *Harper's Mag.* Mar. 601/1 The *Daily Proteus* sent Jack twenty dollars..for two editorials. **1887** *Pall Mall G.* 15 Oct. 12/1 Finely worded editorials.

Hence **edi'torially** *adv.*, in an editorial manner or capacity; as an editor does. †**edi'torialship** = EDITORSHIP.

1818 *Blackw. Mag.* III. 142 You are editorially exonerated. **1826** J. GILCHRIST *Lecture* 34 During his Editorialship he must have been a kind of Consul or Dictator in the Republic of Letters. **1883** *Harper's Mag.* Oct. 789/2 She wrote editorially for a London paper. **1885** *Manch. Exam.* 14 Apr. 8/6 The anticipations which..you ventured editorially to give expression to.

edi'torialist. [f. EDITORIAL *sb.* + -IST 2.] One who writes editorials. Also *transf.*

1901 *N.Y. Even. Post*, The syndicator..talks to the would-be 'editorialist'. **1941** KOESTLER *Scum of Earth* 26 It seemed impossible that the editorialist of the paper had dared to write this off his own bat. **1964** *Spectator* 28 Feb. 270 Its education comes from street gossip and the exhortations of radio editorialists. **1965** H. KAHN *On Escalation* xi. 223 An editorialist or commentator may be invited to express a strong view of the matter.

edi'torialize, *v.* orig. *U.S.* Also **-ise.** [f. EDITORIAL + -IZE.] *intr.* To write editorials; to make editorial comment; to introduce editorial comments or an editorial slant into a factual account, etc. Also *trans.*

1856 G. D. BREWERTON *War in Kansas* 75 As Mrs. Partington feelingly remarked, when Ike tumbled into a barrel of soft soap: 'Isn't it a blessed thing to editorialize for an appreciative public?' **1928** *Nation* (N.Y.) 24 Oct. 416

The Italian press is free..to editorialize with the utmost braggadocio about Italy's plans for world domination. **1960** *New Left Rev.* May–June 3/1 'A clear statement that the party remains committed..'—the *New Statesman* editorialises (5 March 1960). **1961** *Sunday Times* 12 Nov. 48/5 The only 'editorialising' slip that I spotted was Bill Grundy's remark, while anonymous and unseen square-squatters spoke: 'Listen to the voices of progress.' Bernard Braden editorialises almost nonstop in *The Time, The Place and the Camera.* **1963** *Economist* 26 Oct. 353/1 That feeling that led him..to editorialise too much.

Hence **edi'torialized** *ppl. a.*; **edi'torializing** *vbl. sb.*, the action of the verb; also *concr.*, editorial comment.

1917 M. L. Spencer *News Writing* 87 The necessity of presenting news from an unbiased standpoint,..of avoiding 'editorializing'. **1958** Blesh & Janis *They all played Ragtime* i. 34 Prissily Victorian as these editorializings are, they were the trivia of a new age. **1961** *Guardian* 30 Mar. 13/3 The newspapers..rushed into print with editorialised reports of President Kennedy's press conference. **1967** R. J. Sterling *President's Plane is Missing* (1968) ii. 20 Stories that were.. hard-hitting with no tinge of biased editorializing.

'editorship. [f. editor *sb.* + -ship.] **a.** The duties, functions, and office of an editor. **b.** The tenure of that office. **c.** Editorial superintendence.

1782 Tyers *Hist. Rhaps. on Pope* 14 (T.) The editorship of Shakespeare..Pope afterward undertook. **1812** *Examiner* 28 Dec. 831/1 Captain Benjafield, who was formerly Editor of the *Morning Post*, has been charged..with obtaining, during that editorship, an annuity. **1813–40** W. Gifford *Massinger's Wks.* (1840) 447/1 If such portentous lines as these may be introduced without reason, and without authority, there is an end of all editorship. **1882** Pebody *Eng. Journalism* xix. 144 The *Daily Telegraph*, under the editorship of Mr. Edwin Arnold.

editress ('ɛdɪtrɪs). [f. editor *sb.* + -ess.] A female editor.

1799 W. Taylor in Robberds *Mem.* I. 286 The editress.. has inserted the French letter to Anquetil du Perron. **1826** *Gentl. Mag.* Sept. 244/1 The fair Editress has got up this work judiciously and tastefully. **1884** *Bazaar* 17 Dec. 648/1 The editress of this volume..is herself an authoress.

†**e'dituate** *v. Obs. nonce-wd.* [f. L. *ædituāt-*, ppl. stem of *ædituāri*, f. *æditu-us*, transl. νεωκόρος 'temple-keeper' in *Acts* xix. 35, where the 'town-clerk' of Ephesus speaks of that city as 'temple-keeper' (A.V. 'worshipper') of Diana.] (See quot.)

1646 J. G[regory] *Notes & Obs.* x. (1684) 49 The Devotion whereof could not but move the City [Ephesus].. to affect the Dignity and Title of the Νεωκόρος, to ædituate such a piece of Divine Office. **1732** in Coles. **1775** in Ash. **1818** in Todd; and in mod. Dicts.

†**'edlen.** *Obs.* [OE. *edléan*, f. ed- + OE. *léan* reward; cf. OHG. *itlôn* of same meaning.] Reward.

c **888** K. Ælfred *Boeth.* iii. §4 þæt edlean þe ðu..ȝehete. *c* **1175** *Lamb. Hom.* 103 Forðon bið þe lesse his edlen þere dede.

†**edmede**, *sb. Obs.* Forms: 1 éadmédu, 3 æd-, að-, æðmede. [OE. *éad-*, *éaþmédu*, abstr. f. *éad-*, *éaþmód*, edmod. (OE. *éadmédu* = OS. *ôdmôdi*, OHG. *ôtmuotî*; OE. *éaþmédu* = OS. *ôðmuodi*, OHG. *ôdmuotî*.)] Gentleness, humility.

c **1000** *Ags. Ps.* cxviii[xix]. 92 þæt ic on minum eadmedum eall forwurde. *c* **1205** Lay. 21866 Ʒeornden Arðures grið & his aðmeden. *Ibid.* 10013 þurh his æðmeden.

†**'edmede**, *a. Obs.* [OE. *éadméde*, *éaþméde*, f. edmod *a.* (OE. *éadméde* = OS. *ôdmôdi*, OHG. *ôtmuoti*; OE. *éaþméde* = OHG. *ôdhmôti*.)] Humble.

c **1000** *Ags. Ps.* cxv. 1 [cxvi. 10] (Gr.) Ic eom eadmede swiþe. *c* **1175** *Lamb. Hom.* 115 þe edmeda riche..mei beon godes wrecche.

†**'edmod**, *a. Obs.* Also eadmod, edmeod, æddmod, admod, aðmod. [OE. *éadmód*, phonetic variant of *éaþmód*, f. *éaþe*, eath + *mód* mood; the exact equivalent (type **aupu-môdo-*) does not occur in continental Teutonic, but the derivatives in *-môdjo-* (= edmede *a.*) and in *-môdîn-* (= edmede *sb.*) are found with forms parallel to the OE. *éaþ-*, *éad-*; see edmede *sb.* and *a.*] Gentle, humble, meek.

c **1000** *Ags. Gosp.* Matt. xi. 29 Ic eom bilwite and eadmod on heortan. *c* **1175** *Lamb. Hom.* 5 þes we ahte to beon þe edmoddre. *Ibid.* 113 Drihten..ȝeueð þan edmeodan streinþe. *c* **1200** Ormin 10837 Æddmod allse cullfre. *c* **1200** *Trin. Coll. Hom.* 89 Ich am milde and admod on herte. *c* **1205** Lay. 25571 þurh þine aðmode [*c* **1275** edmode] will.. let þu mi sweuen to selþen iturnen. *a* **1225** *Ancr. R.* 276 ȝif þu wilt beon edmod, þenc euer hwat þe wonteð of holinesse. *c* **1275** Lay. 23255 Woweyn was edmod.

Hence **'edmodi** *a.* [cf. OHG. *ôtmuatig*; see -y] = edmod. **edmodien** *v. trans.*, to humble. **edmoded** *ppl. a.*, meek. **'edmodleȝc** [see -lock], humility, gentleness. **'edmodliche** *adv.* [see -ly[2]], humbly, meekly. **'edmodness** [see -ness], gentleness, humility, meekness.

c **888** K. Ælfred *Boeth.* xii, Crist eardað on þære dene eadmodnesse. *a* **1175** *Cott. Hom.* 221 Mid ælra ædmodnisse ..ȝearnian mid admodnisse. *Ibid.* 237 His edmodnisse deað ofer com. and fordede ure soriȝe and ȝelice deað. *c* **1175** *Lamb. Hom.* 17 Crist..eadmode hine seolfne þet he wes iboren of ure lefdi. *Ibid.* 89 Cristes apostles weren wuniende edmodliche on heore ibeoden on ane upflore. *c* **1200** Ormin 17649 Forr to berrȝhen æddmodliȝ þe werelld þurrh hiss are. *Ibid.* 19297 Full off baþe, off millce, off are, off æddmodleȝȝc. *a* **1225** *Ancr. R.* 94 þe anui þet heo her uor his luue edmodliche polieð. *Ibid.* 130 Heo holdeð..þet heaued lowe þuruh milde edmodnesse. *Ibid.* 246 þe edmodies monnes bonen þurleð þe weolcne. *Ibid.* 278 Makieð edmod [*T. C.* eadmodieð] our heorte.

†**edmondsonite** ('ɛdmənsənaɪt). *Min. Obs.* [f. name of George *Edmondson* (1798–1863), headmaster of Queenwood College, Hampshire + -ite[1].] = tænite 2.

1882 W. Flight in *Proc. R. Soc.* XXXIII. 344 Lying on the plates of meteoric iron..were found thin metallic plates ..of a flexible mineral, which had the composition Fe_5Ni_2. .. I propose to call this compound Edmondsonite.

edness, variant form of eadness, *Obs.*

Edo ('ɛdəʊ), *sb.* (and *a.*) [Native name.] A language or group of languages of the Kwa family spoken by peoples inhabiting the district of Benin in Nigeria. Also *attrib.* or as *adj.*

1890 *Proc. R. Geogr. Soc.* XII. 606 The following have been named to me as countries or provinces..of the kingdom of Benin, within which the Eddo language, or some dialect thereof, is spoken. **1910** N. W. Thomas *Anthropol. Rep. Edo-Speaking Peoples Nigeria* I. i. 6 Certain words appear to be common to the Edo and other families of languages. **1937** H. Melzian *Conc. Dict. Bini Lang. S. Nigeria* p. vii, The Bini or Edo..language, together with the Ishan..dialect,..forms the central group of the cluster of languages generally known under the same name and belonging to the Kwa group of Western Sudan languages. **1957** *Encycl. Brit.* III. 410/2 They speak a homogeneous language, Edo (Bini), a name which is extended to include the more or less closely related dialects of Ishan and Kukuruku, [etc.]. **1976** *Nigerian Herald* 21 May 2/2, 4.45 News in Edo, Efik and Fulfulde. **1977** *Language* LIII. 861 These two sounds in Abua sound like the plain and tapped laterals of the Ẹdo languages. **1983** *English World-Wide* IV. 17 All are classified as Kwa and fall into four groups, viz. Edo, Igbo, Ijo, and Yoruba.

†**e'doceate**, *v. Obs.*[−0] [incorrectly f. L. *ēdocēre* + -ate[3].] *trans.* To teach.

1623 Cockeram ii, To teach, *Edoceate.*

†**'edocke.** *Obs.* [OE. *éa-docca*, f. ea water, river + dock.] Some broad-leaved water-plant; ? the Clote or Yellow Water-lily (*Nuphar lutea*).

c **1000** Ælfric *Gloss.* in Wr.-Wülcker 136 *Nimphea*, eadocca. *a* **1387** *Sinon. Barthol.* (Anecd. Oxon.) 28 *Lilium aquaticum*, an edocke; flos ejus nenufar. *a* **1450** *Alphita* (Anecd. Oxon.) 94 *Lappacium Aquaticum*..angl. waterdokke uel edokke. [**1884** Holland *Cheshire Gloss.* (E.D.S.) *Eddick*, the bur or burdock (*Ardium Lappa*); also *Errick.*]

†**e'doctrinate**, *v. Obs. rare*[−1]. [f. e- + doctrinate.] *trans.* To teach thoroughly, train.

1625 Shirley *Love-tricks* iii. v, In what kind of complement please you, venerable sir, to be edoctrinated?

†**e'dod**, *int. Obs. rare*[−1]. Variant of adod.

1694 Echard *Plautus* 92 Edod, I thought the remembrance o' your last wife had frighted you from matrimony.

edoes, variant of eddoes.

†**E'domic**, *a. Obs. rare*[−1]. In 7 -ique. [f. *Edom*, another name for Esau + -ic.] (See quot.)

1659 R. Gell *Amendm. Last Eng. Bible* 296 Even the Edomique nature, the animalis homo who wrongs his brother the spiritual & heavenly man.

'Edomitish, *a.* [f. *Edomite* inhabitant of Edom + -ish.] Pertaining to Edom; characteristic of the Edomites. In 17th c. sometimes used allusively with reference to Ps. cxxxvii. 7.

1641 W. Hooke *New Eng. Tears* 6 A right Edomitish quality; for Edom rejoiced over the children of Judah, etc. **1641** Milton *Animadv.* Wks. (1851) 240 This is a more Edomitish conceit than the former. **1645** —— *Colast.* ibid. 349 [Job's] Edomitish Freins.

edrioph'thalmate, *a.* [See next.] Of or pertaining to the Edriophthalma. Also **edrioph'thalmatous, -mic** *adjs.*

1889 *Cent. Dict.*, Edriophthalmatous, edriophthalmic. **1904** *Ann. & Mag. Nat. Hist.* Feb. 154 In the Edriophthalmate orders no similar arrangement is known.

edriophthalmian (ˌɛdrɪɒf'θælmɪən), *a.* and *sb.* [f. mod.L. *edriophthalma* sb. pl. (irregularly f. Gr. ἕδρα seat + ὀφθαλμ-ός eye) + -ian.]

A. *adj.* Belonging to or resembling the *Edriophthalma*, or 'sessile-eyed' Crustacea (including the Prawns, Shrimps, etc.). **B.** *sb.* An individual of that order.

1877 Huxley *Anat. Inv. An.* vi. 369 The organisation of the Stomatopoda is more Edriophthalmian..than Podophthalmian. **1835–6** Todd *Cycl. Anat.* I. 787/1 Several Edriophthalmians are also born before they have acquired the whole of their extremities.

So ˌ**edrioph'thalmous**, *a.* [see -ous.]

1877 Huxley *Anat. Inv. An.* vi. 285 The head..of an Insect, or Edriophthalmous Crustacean.

edropic, Sc. var. of hydropic.

†**e'droppit**, *ppl. a. Sc. Obs.* Affected with dropsy.

1536 Bellenden *Cron. Scot.* ix. xxi. (Jam.) His wambe throw immoderat voracitie was swolin as he had bene edroppit [*instar hydropici inflatus*].

educability (ˌɛdjʊkə'bɪlɪtɪ). [f. educable *a.*; see -ity.] The quality of being educable; capability of being educated.

1842 *Chamb. Jrnl.* 16 Apr. 97 Educability of Animals. *a* **1866** J. Grote *Exam. Utilit. Philos.* x. (1870) 169 The moral educability of man. **1874** Carpenter *Ment. Phys.* i. ii. §83 (1879) 89 Birds of the Parrot tribe are pre-eminent for their educability.

educable ('ɛdjʊkəb(ə)l), *a.* [as if ad. L. **ēducābilis*, f. *ēducā-re* to educate.] Capable of being educated.

1845 R. Hamilton *Pop. Educ.* viii. (ed. 2) 178 Of educable age. **1879** Bain *Education as Sci.* iii. 24 In old age, when we cease to be educable in any fresh endowment. **1886** *Sat. Rev.* 1 May 590/1 Tories will prove educable.

educand ('ɛdjʊkænd). [ad. L. *ēducandus*, gerundive of *ēducāre* to educate.] One who is to be or is being educated.

a **1909** Petty (Cent. D. Suppl.), We wish therefore that the educands be taught to observe. **1917** J. Adams *Student's Guide* 6 We have a case where the teacher is all educator, and the pupil all educand. **1927** —— *Errors in School* 44 Preparing the educand to take his place in his surroundings.

educatable ('ɛdjʊkeɪtəb(ə)l), *a.* [f. educate *v.* + -able.] = educable *a.* Hence ˌ**educata'bility.**

1868 A. B. Alcott *Tablets* 105 Not letters but life chiefly educate if we are educatable. **1894** C. C. Stopes *Brit. Free Women* 153 A constantly expanding view of the educatability even of ordinary girls. **1926** *Glasgow Herald* 21 July 10 Some fishes are 'more intelligent', or, as Dr. Longley puts it, 'have a greater degree of educatability' than others.

†**'educate**, obs. and Sc. pa. pple. of next.

1536 *Act 27 Hen. VIII*, xlii. in *Oxf. & Camb. Enactm.* 11 Where yowth and good wyttes be educate and norysshed. **1861** Ramsay *Remin.* v. (ed. 18) 118 The hospital where Eppie was educate.

educate ('ɛdjʊkeɪt), *v.* [f. L. *ēducāt-* ppl. stem of *ēducāre* to rear, bring up (children, young animals), related to *ēdūcĕre* to lead forth (see educe), which is sometimes used nearly in the same sense.] *trans.* or *absol.*

†**1.** To rear, bring up (children, animals) by supply of food and attention to physical wants. *Obs.*

1607 Topsell *Four-f. Beasts* 229 The Epirotan & Sicilian horses are not to be despised, if they were well bred & educated. **1651** Wittie tr. *Primrose's Pop. Err.* 292 A boy of a good habit of body, with large veines, well and freely educated. **1690** [see educated]. **1818** [see 2].

2. To bring up (young persons) from childhood, so as to form (their) habits, manners, intellectual and physical aptitudes.

1618 Bolton *Florus* i. i. 3 Himselfe delighting in the Rivers and Mountaines, among which he had beene educated. **1818** Cruise *Digest* VI. 336 A devise..to the intent that with the profits he should educate his daughter. **1839** tr. *Lamartine's Trav. East* 168/1 The principal amongst them [Greeks] have their children educated in Hungary. **1875** Jowett *Plato* (ed. 2) V. 40 The youth of a people should be educated in forms and strains of virtue.

b. To instruct, provide schooling for (young persons).

1588 Shaks. *L.L.L.* v. i. 84 Do you not educate youth at the Charg-house on the top of the Mountaine? **1863** Mary Howitt tr. *F. Bremer's Greece* I. i. 13 It has educated, and it educates to this day, a great portion of the Athenian female youth of all classes. **1863** A. Tylor *Educ. & Manuf.* 40 It costs 8*d.* per week to educate a child.

3. To train (any person) so as to develop the intellectual and moral powers generally.

1849 Kingsley *Lett.* (1878) I. 198 In my eyes the question is not what to teach, but how to Educate. **1875** Jowett *Plato* (ed. 2) V. 120 Elder men, if they want to educate others, should begin by educating themselves. **1886** *Pall Mall G.* 10 July 4/2 Our artists are not educated at all, they are only trained.

4. To train, discipline (a person, a class of persons, a particular mental or physical faculty or organ), so as to develop some special aptitude, taste, or disposition. Const. *to*, also *inf.*

1841–4 Emerson *Ess. Hist.* Wks. (Bohn) I. 11 And the habit of supplying his own needs educates the body to wonderful performances. **1847** —— *Repr. Men.* v. *Shaks.* ibid. I. 359 Our ears are educated to music by his rhythm. **1867** Disraeli in *Scotsman* 30 Oct., I had to prepare the mind of the country, and to educate,—if not too arrogant to use such a phrase,—our party. *Mod.* He is educating himself to eat tomatoes.

b. To train (animals).

1850 Lang *Wand. India* 2 No horses, except those educated in India, would crawl into these holes cut out of the earth and rock. **1856** Kane *Arct. Expl.* I. xxix. 389 The dogs of Smith's Sound are educated more thoroughly than any of their more southern brethren.

educated (ˈɛdjʊkeɪtɪd), *ppl. a.* (and *sb.*) [f. EDUCATE *v.* + -ED.] **A.** *ppl. a.* **a.** That has received education, mental or physical; instructed, trained, etc.; see the vb. Often with an adverb prefixed, as *half-*, *over-*, *well-*. Phr. ***educated guess***, a guess based upon a background of experience of the matter in hand.

1670 R. COKE *Disc. Trade* 60 A Merchant better educated, and more conversant in Trade, may better understand it, than a Privy Counsellor, who is not so educated, and less conversant in it. **1690** B. E. *Dict. Cant. Crew, Tender-parnel*, a very nicely Educated creature, apt to catch Cold upon the least blast of Wind. **1845** DISRAELI *Sybil* (1863) 67 He was over-educated for his intellect. **1855** MACAULAY *Hist. Eng.* III. 320 Lochiel..might indeed have seemed ignorant to educated and travelled Englishmen. **1882** J. H. BLUNT *Ref. Ch. Eng.* II. 411 But the Puritans were neither educated nor reverent. **1887** E. BERDOE *St. Bernard's* 168 Every half-educated..young man. **1954** J. C. INGRAHAM *Mod. Traffic Control* 58 A lot of 'educated guesses', based on experience coupled with study, must go into answering questions like that. **1958** *Wall St. Jrnl.* 15 Dec. 14/1 It's an educated guess of top canners, for example, that more than half of the chain's tinned fruit is sold under its private labels (Iona and others). **1962** A. BATTERSBY *Guide to Stock Control* iv. 37 'An educated guess,' said General Patton, 'is just as accurate and quicker than compiled error.' **1966** M. CATTO *Bird on Wing* vi. 94 'What's happened to her?' 'I wouldn't be sure. I could make an educated guess. I think she's gone home.'

b. *transf.* Carefully tended, trained into shape.

1842 TENNYSON *E. Morris* 131 Slight Sir Robert with his watery smile And educated whisker.

†**B.** as *sb.* The person educated.

1673 O. WALKER *Education* 213 It concerns..Parents and Educators to see that the educated converse as much as may be with his..superior. *Ibid.* 107 It will be the Teachers care and Educateds endeavour.

ˌeducaˈtee. *nonce-wd.* [f. EDUCATE *v.* + -EE.] One who is subjected to the process of education.

1815 T. PEACOCK *Nightmare Ab.* 144 It is the only piece of academical learning that the finished educatee retains. **1857** *Sat. Review* III. 53/2 It is not enough for the educator to pour fact after fact into the educatee.

ˈeducating, *ppl. a.* [f. EDUCATE + -ING[2].] That educates.

1856 MASSON *Chatterton* II. iii. (1874) 166 O month of June, 1770! and is this the kind of educating circumstance you provide for Chatterton?

education (ɛdjuːˈkeɪʃən). [ad. L. *ēducātiōn-em*, f. *ēducāre*; see EDUCATE *v.* and -TION.]

†**1.** The process of nourishing or rearing a child or young person, an animal. *Obs.*

1540 T. RAYNALDE *Birth Mankynde* C iij, The education ..of infantes at this tyme [1 year old]. **1542** BOORDE *Dyetary* xvi. (1870) 271 Beefe..doth make an Englysshe man stronge, the educacion of hym with it consyderyd. **1651** WITTIE tr. *Primrose's Pop. Err.* 185 The people doe erre much about the education of children..I have seen some frequently give to their children..strong Beere. **1661** LOVELL *Hist. Anim. & Min.* 72 They [harts] delight in woods, and places of their first education.

b. *spec.* [after Fr.] The rearing of silkworms; *concr.*, a number of silkworms reared at one time.

1888 E. A. BUTLER *Silkworms* 56 For large 'educations' a room is fitted with shelves.

2. The process of 'bringing up' (young persons); the manner in which a person has been 'brought up'; with reference to social station, kind of manners and habits acquired, calling or employment prepared for, etc. *Obs.* exc. with notion of 3.

1531 ELYOT *Gov.* I. ii. (1883) I. 24 In the fyrste [volume] shall be comprehended the beste forme of education or bringing up of noble children. **1593** HOOKER *Eccl. Pol.* I. vi, Education and instruction are the meanes..to make our naturall faculty of reason..better. **1596** SHAKS. *Tam. Shr.* Induct. ii. 20, I Christopher Slie..by education a Cardmaker. **1624** CAPT. SMITH *Virginia* I. 10 Their..handy crafts, and educations, are much like them in that part of Virginia we now inhabite. **1644** MILTON *Educ.* Wks. (1847) 99/2 A complete and generous education..fits a man to perform..all the offices..of peace and war.

fig. **1647** CLARENDON *Hist. Reb.* VII. (1703) II. 206 He Begot many opinions, and motions, the Education whereof he committed to other Men.

3. The systematic instruction, schooling or training given to the young in preparation for the work of life; by extension, similar instruction or training obtained in adult age. Also, the whole course of scholastic instruction which a person has received. Often with limiting words denoting the nature or the predominant subject of the instruction or kind of life for which it prepares, as ***classical, legal, medical, technical, commercial, art education.***

1616 BRINSLEY *Lud. Lit.* 10 It much concerneth every parent to see their children to have the best education and instruction. **1670** R. COKE *Disc. Trade* 71 Education in Geometry and Numbers. **1748** GRAY *Comment Educ. & Govt.* Wks. 1836 I. 152 The principal drift of education should be to make men think in the northern climates, and act in the southern. **1795** BURKE *Corr.* (1844) IV. 299 If you consent to put your clerical education, or any other part of your education, under their direction or control. **1801** STRUTT *Sports & Past.* I. i. 3 As early as the ninth century ..hunting constituted an essential part of the education of a young nobleman. **1809** SYD. SMITH *Wks.* (1859) I. 183/2 Education gives fecundity of thought..quickness, vigour, fancy, words, images, and illustrations. **1812** J. HENRY *Camp. agst. Quebec* 123 Many of our sergeants were, with good educations, substantial freeholders in our own country. **1862** SIR B. BRODIE *Psychol. Inq.* II. ii. 73 Hours of relaxation truly [are] as necessary a part of education as hours of study.

b. The training of animals.

1538 STARKEY *England* 189 Theyr haukys and theyr houndys, of whose educatyon they have grete care. **1618** LATHAM *2nd Bk. Falconry* (1633) 147 By which means with her naturall education together, she wil be as perfect in knowledge of the countrey, as the wilde Haggard her naturall damme that bred her.

c. *fig.*

1832 HT. MARTINEAU *Ireland* iii. 52 There is another kind of education always going forwards..the education of circumstances. **1860** TEMPLE in *Essays & Reviews* 1 The education of the world.

4. [From sense 3, influenced by sense 2 and sometimes by the quasi-etymological notion 'drawing out'.] Culture or development of powers, formation of character, as contrasted with the imparting of mere knowledge or skill. Often with limiting word, as *intellectual, moral, physical.*

1860 MILL *Repr. Govt.* (1865) 66/2 Among the foremost benefits of free government is that education of the intelligence and of the sentiments. **1868** ROGERS *Pol. Econ.* x. (ed. 3) 116 It confounds education with the knowledge of facts, whereas it really is the possession of method. **1871** *Figure Training* 37 The..training and education of the figure. **1872** MORLEY *Voltaire* (1886) 45 The Jesuits' devotion to intellectual education. **1875** H. E. MANNING *Mission H. Ghost* xiii. 377 Education is the formation of the whole man—intellect..character, mind, and soul.

5. *attrib.* and *Comb.*

1662 GLANVILL *Lux Orient.* (1682) Pref. 22 These prepossest discerners presently conclude everything that is ..of another stamp from their Education-receptions, false and ridiculous. **1794** MATHIAS *Purs. Lit.* (1798) 218 The unfortunate Education Sermon, which Bishop Hurd happened to dislike. **1824** MISS MITFORD *Village* I. (1863) 151 The young ladies..who..had trodden the education-mill till they..had lost sense in sound, and ideas in words. **1858** HOLLAND *Titcomb's Lett.* i. 17 The Education Society, and kindred organizations. **1872** RUSKIN *Fors* II. xvii. 5 Listen to this, you cheap education-mongers.

eduˈcationable, *a. rare.* [f. prec. + -ABLE.] Capable of receiving education.

1859 I. TAYLOR *Essays* 248 The educationable classes of our Indian subjects.

educational (ɛdjuːˈkeɪʃənəl), *a.* [f. prec. + -AL[1].]

†**1.** Due to, or arising from, education. *Obs.*

1652 GAULE *Magastrom.* 30 The educationall and professionall are to be.. accounted for nationall sinnes. **1790** CATH. GRAHAM *Lett. Educ.* 212 Every love intrigue.. must naturally tend to debase the female mind, from its violence to educational impressions. **1815** ASHBEL GREEN *Report* 287 Opinions which interfered with his educational creed.

2. Of or pertaining to education; concerned with education. Also in Special Combs.: **educational psychology** (see quot. 1961); so ***educational psychologist***; **educational sociology**, the study of educational methods or systems from a sociological standpoint.

1831 CARLYLE *Sart. Res.* II. xi, Is there not an everlasting demand for Intellect in the..political, or religious, educational, commercial departments. **1837** BULWER *Athens* II. 413 Much of his [Pythagoras] educational discipline.. bear[s] an evident affinity to the old Cretan..institutions. **1840** MILL *Diss. & Disc.* (1859) II. 192 The regeneration.. of our educational institutions is an object of more urgency. **1876** GRANT *Burgh Sch. Scotl.* Pref. 5 The history of educational progress in any country, can hardly fail to be interesting to the historian. **1917** W. R. SMITH (*title*) Introduction to educational sociology. **1923** D. SNEDDEN *Educational Sociology* I. iii. 33 Educational sociology has as its chief province the scientific determination of educational objectives. It constitutes an *applied* or *linking* science between the fields of sociology (as a pure science) and social economy (as the science of all phases of human well-being) on the one hand, and the practice of education on the other. **1928** W. R. SMITH *Princ. Educational Sociology* I. i. 6 Educational sociology may be defined as the application of the methods, principles, and data of sociology to the study and practice of education. Its interests center about the socializing process, as those of educational psychology center about the learning process. **1936** *Discovery* May 147/1 More books on educational films. **1959** *Chambers's Encycl.* IV. 814/2 The experience of the forces educational broadcasts. *Ibid.* 815/1 'Further educational' broadcasting includes all types of serious broadcasting. *Ibid.* 816/1 *Educational psychology*..includes observation of human beings in action and inquiry into all the means by which their behaviour is modified through their contact with other human beings either directly or indirectly. **1960** *Where?* III. 13/2 *Educational psychologist*, a man or woman who studies human behaviour and the human mind in order to deal with the problems of children, and, sometimes, their teachers. **1961** WEBSTER, *Educational psychology*, a field of study that deals with the application of objective psychological methods and esp. of standardized tests to such problems as the selection of students for advanced or specialized training, the assessment of a student's progress, and the development of more effective methods of instruction.

Hence **eduˈcationally** *adv.*, with reference to education; from an educational point of view. ***educationally subnormal*** *adj. phr.*, applied to children who are mentally backward and cannot be taught in ordinary schools.

1845 R. HAMILTON *Pop. Educ.* viii. (ed. 2) 196 Educationally considered, the sister isle is not an ignorant country. **1881** *Atlantic Monthly* XLVII. 296 Educationally he has been of service to us, and merits our thanks. **1886** *Durham Univ. Jrnl.* 20 Feb. 3 The Durham course is educationally better than what a Theological College is able to offer. **1953** C. BURT *Causes & Treatm. Backwardness* (ed. 2) 5 Special arrangements for those children..who appeared to be educationally subnormal. **1960** [see E.S.N. *s.v.* E III].

eduˈcationalist. [f. prec. + -IST.] One who makes a study of the science or methods of education; an advocate of education.

1857 TOULM. SMITH *Parish* 498 The real philanthropist and educationalist of our day. **1869** A. J. ELLIS *E.E. Pronunc.* I. iv. §3. 314 *note*, T. W. Hill..a well-known orthoepist and educationalist.

eduˈcationary, *a.* [f. EDUCATION + -ARY.] Concerned with education.

1879 C. R. SMITH *Addr. Strood Elocut. Class* 5 Founders of educationary Clubs..have overlooked Literature.

educationese (ɛdjuːkeɪʃəˈniːz). [f. EDUCATION + -ESE.] A dismissive term for the jargon-ridden language supposedly characteristic of educationalists and educational administrators.

1966 *PMLA* LXXXI. II. 8/2 (To coin a term, which is probably already embalmed in educationese) curriculologists. **1978** *Jrnl. Technical Writing & Communication* VIII. 303 Some textbooks, unfortunately, are painfully dull and poorly written, composed of condescendingly simplistic sentences or laden with aseptic educationese. **1985** *U.S. News & World Rep.* 18 Feb. 57/2 For many schools, what was the library is now a learning-resource center. These are just a few examples of a language disorder known as..'educationese'.

eduˈcationist. [f. EDUCATION + -IST.] = EDUCATIONALIST.

1829 *Blackw. Mag.* XXV. 130 The sensitive educationists of this thin-skinned age. **1876** GRANT *Burgh Sch. Scotl.* II. v. 209 Educationists have written for and against the system of giving school prizes.

ˈeducationize, *v. rare.* [f. as prec. + -IZE.] To subject to education. *absol.* in quot. Hence **ˈeducationized** *ppl. a.*

1835 *Tait's Mag.* II. 405 Lord Brougham's attempts to educationize, without teaching religion or morals. *Ibid.* 406 The..religiously educationized portions of the public.

educative (ˈɛdjʊkətɪv), *a.* [f. L. *ēducāt-* ppl. stem of *ēducāre* (see EDUCATE) + -IVE.]

1. Of or pertaining to education.

1856 FROUDE *Hist. Eng.* (1858) I. i. 52 The educative theory..was simple but effective. **1885** *Manch. Exam.* 10 Sept. 4/7 During the educative process.

2. That has the power of educating; bearing upon or conducive to education.

1844 EMERSON *Ess. Experience*, The plays of children are nonsense, but very educative nonsense. **1869** M. PATTISON *Serm.* (1885) 192 Theology affords the materials of a true and a truly educative knowledge. **1872** M. COLLINS *2 Plunges for Pearl* I. ix. 198 Educative endowments.. designed for both sexes. **1881** *Nature* XXIV. 161 Suggestions..towards making our schools healthy..and educative centres.

educator (ˈɛdjʊkeɪtə(r)). [a. L. *ēducātor*, agent-noun f. *ēducāre*; see EDUCATE *v.*]

†**1.** He who or that which nourishes or rears physically. *Obs.*

1566 PAINTER *Pal. Pleas.* I. 43 [The female breast] that most sacred fountaine of the body, the educatour of mankinde.

2. One who or that which educates, trains, or instructs.

1673 [see EDUCATED B]. **1735** BERKELEY *Querist* §203 Wks. 1871 III. 372 Modern educators of youth. **1859** C. BARKER *Assoc. Princ. Mid. Ages* i. 9 They were..educators of the poor in their schools. **1875** JOWETT *Plato* (ed. 2) IV. 276 Language..is the greatest educator of mankind. **1885** *Manch. Exam.* 10 Sept. 5/4 Lord Randolph Churchill, who is the guide and educator of his party.

educatory (ˈɛdjʊkeɪtərɪ), *a.* [f. *ēducāt-* ppl. stem of *ēducāre* + -ORY.] That has an educating influence.

1845 R. HAMILTON *Pop. Educ.* vi. (ed. 2) 137 That educatory regimen of which Scripture is the rule and end. **1878** MOZLEY *Rul. Ideas* ii. 53 The ideas which His own educatory providence has since instilled.

educatress (ˈɛdjʊkeɪtrɪs). [f. EDUCATOR + -ESS.] A female educator.

1805 *Ann. Rev.* III. 544 This supposedly exemplary mother too was the educatress of Caligula. **1815** *Monthly Rev.* LXXVI. 500 Hospitality will become the educatress of the human race.

educe (ɪˈdjuːs). [ad. L. *ēdūcĕre*, f. *ē* out + *dūcĕre* to lead.]

†**1.** *pass.* To be led forth, branch out (said of a river, a blood-vessel). *Obs.*

1432-50 tr. *Higden* (1865) I. 69 The firste floode..the invndacion of whom is educede in to Ynde. **1578** BANISTER *Hist. Man* VII. 93 Where the vessels are inserted and educed.

†**2.** *Med.* To draw forth so as to remove. *Obs.*

a **1617** BAYNE *On Eph.* (1658) 140 Medicine will..work on the sickenesse, and educe it. **1658** J. ROBINSON *Eudoxa* ix. 50 Warm Water..doth, as an emetick vehicle, often educe superfluous and putrid humours.

3. To bring out, elicit, develop, from a condition of latent, rudimentary, or merely potential existence.

1603 SIR C. HEYDON *Jud. Astrol.* vii. 187 The Heauens are efficients, which educe the forme out of the matter of the corne. **1612-5** BP. HALL *Contempl.* XIX. vii, He educeth warmth out of that corps. *a* **1652** J. SMITH *Sel. Disc.* x. iii. (1856) 475 Hell is not so much induced, as educed out of men's filthy lusts and passions. **1669** GALE *Crt. Gentiles* I. III. iii. 42 Chaos was that ancient slime, out of which al things were educed. **1781** COWPER *Hope* 155 [Hope] has the wondrous virtue to educe From emptiness itself a real use. **1816** COLERIDGE *Lay Serm.* 328 Education—consists in educing the faculties and forming the habits. **1840** CARLYLE *Heroes* (1858) 356 Given a world of Knaves, to educe an Honesty from their united action. **1836-7** SIR W. HAMILTON *Metaph.* (1877) I. vi. 105 Anaximenes found the original Element in air, from which, by rarefaction and condensation he educed existences.

b. *Chem.* To disengage (a substance) from a compound in which it already existed ready formed; contrasted with *produce.* Cf. EDUCT *sb.*

1805 HATCHETT in *Phil. Trans.* XCV. 312 *note*, Educed by the action of the nitric acid on the original principles of the dragon's blood.

c. To draw forth, elicit (a principle, the result of a calculation, etc.) *from* the data.

1836-7 SIR W. HAMILTON *Metaph.* xxxviii. (1870) II. 353 Notions..which we educe from experience, and build up through generalisation. **1871** BLACKIE *Four Phases* I. 101 From the careful comparison of facts to educe laws. **1880** KINGLAKE *Crimea* VI. viii. 181 A Statist will quickly educe what he calls the 'percentages'.

4. To evoke, give rise to (actions, manifestations, etc.).

1879 FARRAR *St. Paul* I. Introd. 8 The circumstances which educed his statements of doctrine.

Hence **e'ducement**, the action or process of drawing out or developing. **e'ducible** *a.*, that can or may be educed. **e'ducing** *vbl. sb.*, the action of the verb EDUCE; a bringing out or drawing forth.

1665 GLANVILL *Sceps. Sci.* xviii, By educing, the affirmers only mean a producing. **1677** GALE *Crt. Gentiles* II. IV. 157 Faith is natural, i.e. educible out of the potence of corrupt nature. **1678** CUDWORTH *Intell. Syst.* I. iii. §31. 137 All manner of life..is..educible out of nothing and reducible to nothing again. **1842** H. E. MANNING *Serm.* (1848) I. xvi. 237 The educing of a new creation out of the old. **1868** *Contemp. Rev.* VIII. 612 The new impulses it ministered to the educement of the individual consciousness.

educrat ('ɛdjuːkræt). *N. Amer.* [f. EDU(CATION + -CRAT.] An educational administrator or theorist; one who forms or directs educational policy. (Usu. *derog.*)

1968 *Sat. Rev.* (U.S.) 20 Apr. 64/2 He [*sc.* C. R. Kirk, Governor of Florida] early exhibited..a remarkable talent for flamboyant invective (education leaders are referred to as 'educrats' or wielders of 'blackboard power'). **1973** *Globe & Mail* (Toronto) 19 Dec. 7/2 By creating and then pushing the foolish Hall-Dennis Report, our educrats taught the people of Ontario to expect flashy results from fashionable illusions and limitless expenditure. **1982** *Underground Grammarian* Mar. 4/2 There *are*, of course, some villains. There are agency-spawned educrats and grant-hustlers who really *do* profit from 'increased spending'.

educt ('iːdʌkt). [ad. L. *ēductum*, neut. pa. pple. of *ēdūcĕre* to EDUCE.] That which is educed.

1. *Chem.* 'A body separated by the decomposition of another in which it previously existed as such, in contradistinction to product, which denotes a compound not previously existing, but formed during the decomposition' (Watts *Dict. Chem.*).

1799 KIRWAN *Geol. Ess.* 197 To form an idea of the composition of this stone..we must consider the educts of its analysis. **1805** HATCHETT in *Phil. Trans.* XCV. 299 In the first experiment it was obtained as a product, and not as an educt. *Ibid.* 312 *note*, Consequently the latter..is considered as an original ingredient or educt. **1875** H. WOOD *Therap.* (1879) 628 The black coloring-matter of such urine is in all probability an educt from carbolic acid.

2. A result of inference or of development.

1816 COLERIDGE *Lay Serm.* 321 In the Scriptures, they are the living educts of the imagination. **1857** SIR W. HAMILTON *Reid* 784 All our Knowledge is an Educt from Experience. **1865** *Reader* 22 July 86/3 Throw revelation overboard, and its educt, natural theology..must bear it company.

†**e'duct**, *v. Obs. rare*⁻¹. [f. L. *ēduct-* ppl. stem of *ēdūcĕre*; see prec.] *trans.* = EDUCE.

1683 E. HOOKER *Pref. Pordage's Mystic Div.* 105 Educted, or brought forth out of the Womb of pure Nature.

eduction (ɪ'dʌkʃən). [ad. L. *ēductiōn-em*, noun of action f. *ēdūcĕre* to lead forth.]

†**1. a.** A leading forth or out. **b.** A putting forth (of the tongue). *Obs.*

1649 BULWER *Pathomyot.* II. x. 233 This ironicall eduction of the Tongue. **1654** TRAPP *Comm. Job* i. 13 Israel's eduction out of Egypt. **1659** T. WALL *Char. Enemies of Ch.* 19 God ascribes their eduction from Ægypt..unto Moses.

†**2.** *Med.* Removal by drawing forth. *Obs.*

1657 TOMLINSON *Renou's Disp.* 139 We need not suspect any harme by the eduction of some of them. **1684** tr. *Bonet's Merc. Compit.* XIV. 493 The eduction of the Matter is hindred. **1710** T. FULLER *Pharm. Extemp.* 180 The true cure ..consists in the..Eduction of..Phlegm.

3. The action of drawing forth, eliciting, or developing from a state of latent, rudimentary, or potential existence; the action of educing (principles, results of calculation) from the data. Also *concr.* = EDUCT.

1655 D. CAPEL *Tentation* 78 But the work [of sin] must begin at the inward eductions and motions of the will. **1677** HALE *Prim. Orig. Man.* IV. ii. 295 This eduction..of the Light should begin and be continued..for the first three Days of the World. **1678** *Phil. Trans.* XII. 938 The most ancient Atheistick Hypothesis was the Eduction of all things ..out of Matter. **1686** GOAD *Celest. Bodies* I. IX. 35 The Power of Matter, and Eduction therefrom, are meer Words. *c* **1840** SIR W. HAMILTON *Logic* App. (1866) II. 257 The logicians have..limited reasoning..to a mediate eduction of one proposition out of the correlation of two others. **1865** MASSON *Rec. Brit. Philos.* 70 [Sensible objects] are not the actual existences out of us, but only..eductions by our physiology out of a 'something'.

4. The bringing on or occasioning (an event). Cf. EDUCE *v.* 4. *rare.*

a **1806** K. WHITE *Rem.* (1811) II. 280 We see..men sedulously employed in the eduction of their own ruin.

5. *Steam-engine.* **a.** The exit of waste steam from the cylinder either to the condenser or into the atmosphere; chiefly *attrib.*, as in ***eduction-pipe, -side, -steam, -valve***; but now almost entirely superseded by EXHAUST. **b.** Short for *eduction-valve.*

1782 WATT *Specif. of Patent* No. 1321 The steam rushes into the eduction-pipe. **1829** R. STUART *Anecd. Steam Engines* II. 374 g.g., Exhausting or eduction valves. **1835** SIR J. ROSS *N.-W. Pass.* ii. 14 Having led the steam from the eduction pipe. **1839** R. S. ROBINSON *Naut. Steam Eng.* 102 The steam will be cut off..but the eduction will remain open. **1841** SCOTT RUSSELL *Steam Engine* 201 The eduction valves, ports, and passages by which the steam enters the condenser. **1859** W. RANKINE *Steam Eng.* (1861) 486 An eduction valve..to let the steam escape to the condenser.

eductive (iː'dʌktɪv), *a.* [f. L. *ēduct-* ppl. stem of *ēdūcĕre* to EDUCE + -IVE.]

†**a.** *Med.* Tending to draw out (*obs.*). **b.** Having the function of eliciting or developing.

1657 TOMLINSON *Renou's Disp.* 165 Every humour..hath its proper eductive Cathartick. **1667** BOYLE *Orig. Formes & Qual.*, The power of Matter in reference to Forms is partly Eductive.

eductor (ɪ'dʌktə(r)). [a. L. *ēductor*, agent-noun f. *ēdūcĕre.*] He who, or that which, educes.

1794-6 E. DARWIN *Zoon.* (1801) I. 84 A stimulus must be called an eductor of vital ether.

edulcorate (ɪ'dʌlkərət), *ppl. a. rare.* [ad. L. *ēdulcorāt-us*; see next.] Softened, sweetened.

1810 BENTHAM *Packing* (1821) 112 An excuse such as might have been expected to..call forth sympathy and edulcorate feelings in the bosom even of the most obdurate Judge. **1819** H. BUSK *Dessert* 459 Edulcorate juice from every clustering vine.

edulcorate (ɪ'dʌlkəreɪt), *v.* [f. L. *ēdulcorāt-* ppl. stem of *ēdulcorāre*, f. *ē* out + *dulc-or* sweetness.]

†**1.** To sweeten, make sweet. *Obs.*

1661 LOVELL *Hist. Anim. & Min.* 415 Giving to the infants..water of succory, endive, and violets edulcorated. **1675** EVELYN *Terra* (1729) 31 Dung of Swine..is said..to edulcorate..fruit so sensibly as to convert the bitterest Almond into sweet. **1710** T. FULLER *Pharm. Extemp.* 60 Strain off, and edulcorate with Sugar to make it palatable.

2. To free from harsh and acrid properties; to purify, soften.

1641 FRENCH *Distill.* iii. (1651) 75 Edulcorate it..by boiling it in spirit of Vinegar. **1684** tr. *Bonet's Merc. Compit.* III. 108 This Vinegar impregnated and edulcorated with the Lead. **1762** *Gentl. Mag.* 225 Experiments for edulcorating vicious train-oil.

3. *Chem.* To free from soluble particles by agitation or trituration in water, or by washing on a filter.

1669 W. SIMPSON *Hydrol. Chem.* 14 By evaporating the corrosive Menstruum, then edultorating [sic]. **1683** SALMON *Dom. Med.* lxi. 320 Which you may edulcorate by many washings. **1754** HUXHAM in *Phil. Trans.* XLVIII. 858 Let the salt be well washed off, and the mass well edulcorated. **1832** G. PORTER *Porcelain & Gl.* 218 The silex which is precipitated by this means must then be edulcorated and dried. **1844** *North Brit. Rev.* II. 72 He might..edulcorate the muriatic and fluoric radicals.

Hence **e'dulcorated** *ppl. a.* **e'dulcorating** *vbl. sb., ppl. a.*, softening, sweetening, purifying. **e,dulco'ration**, the action or process of washing away particles soluble in water.

1660 *Character of Italy* 83 We will allay the bitterness of this potion with the edulcorating ingredients of their virtues. **1718** CHAMBERLAYNE *Relig. Philos.* (1730) II. xxi. §27 This the Chymists call Edulcorating, that is to say, making sweet or fresh. **1758** *Elaboratory laid Open* 241 The edulcoration may be sufficiently perfected by such an ablution. **1776** *Phil. Trans.* LXVI. 609 A precipitation.. after edulcoration and exsiccation, weighed forty-two grains. **1782** WITHERING in *Phil. Trans.* LXXII. 332 The edulcorated powder was now perfectly white. **1805** GREGOR *ibid.* XCV. 336 The last portion of edulcorating water dropped through the filter of an opalish hue. **1866** GRIFFIN *Chem. Handicraft* (Heading of Chapter), Filtration, Percolation, Edulcoration.

edulcorator (ɪ'dʌlkɒreɪtə(r)). [f. as prec. + -OR.] **a.** One who, or that which, edulcorates. **b.** 'A term for a dropping-bottle or a wash-bottle' (*Syd. Soc. Lex.*).

1669 WORLIDGE *Syst. Agric.* (1681) 135 Swines Dung..is supposed to be a great Edulcorator of Fruit.

†**'edule,** *a.* and *sb. Obs. rare.* [ad. L. *edūlis*, f. *edĕre* to eat.] = EDIBLE A and B.

1699 EVELYN *Acetaria* 1 Sallets..are a Composition of Edule Plants and Roots of several kinds. *Ibid.* (1729) 168 So many rare Edules unknown to the Ancients.

So also **e'dulious** *a.*, in same sense.

a **1682** SIR T. BROWNE *Tracts* (1684) 13 Pease, beans, or such edulious pulses. *Ibid.* 63 And so, producing an edulious or esculent Fruit, is properly named Esculus.

Edward ('ɛdwəd). [f. the proper name.] A coin of one of the Edwards: **a.** The 'angel' of Edward IV, or the 'noble' of Edward III. **b.** ***Edward shovelboard***, a broad shilling of Edward VI, frequently used in the game of Shovel-board.

1598 SHAKS. *Merry W.* I. i. 158 Two Edward Shouel-boords, that cost me two shilling and two pence a peece. *c* **1817** HOGG *Tales & Sk.* IV. 49 The golden Edward, with three holes in it, with which I presented my Mary.

Edwardian (ɛd'wɔːdɪən; also ɛd'wɑːdɪən), *a.* and *sb.* [f. as prec. + -IAN.]

A. *adj.* **1.** *Archit.* Belonging to, or characteristic of, the reigns of the first three Edwards.

1861 A. B. HOPE *Eng. Cathedr. 19th C.* ii. 65 A style.. transcendent in the combination of grace and majesty—the style of Edwardian England. **1884** *Athenæum* 16 Aug. 216/2 A..splendid specimen of the concentric type of shell keeps typical of the Edwardian period.

2. Belonging to the reign of Edward VI. In this sense also **Ed'wardine.**

1866 LITTLEDALE *Cath. Ritual Ch. Eng.* 11 This enactment of the Edwardine ornament was renewed in 1662. **1879** *Dublin Rev.* Jan. 92 He [*sc.* R. Edgeworth] had also denounced..the pulling down of altars and the Edwardian communion service. **1882-3** SCHAFF *Relig. Encycl.* I. 748 The Edwardian reformers compiled the First Book of Edward.

3. Belonging to or characteristic of the reign of Edward VII.

The spelling *Edvardian* is occasionally found.

1908 *Westm. Gaz.* 28 Sept. 2/2 That the Edwardian age is more placidly disposed towards such a threat [*viz.* 'your beer will cost you more'] than the times of the King's great-grandfather, George III. **1909** BEERBOHM *Yet Again* 199 Let special suburbs be founded for Edvardian buildings. **1911** —— *Zuleika Dobson* ii. 10 Miss Dobson now, in the midst of the Edvardian Era, was the toast of two hemispheres. **1926** *Chambers's Jrnl.* 462/1 He sleeked his Edwardian moustache. **1927** M. SADLEIR *Trollope* 3 To the critical eye of Edwardian and Georgian enlightenment the mid-Victorians have appeared smug and hypocritical and selfish. **1930** *Birmingham Post* 24 Apr. 15/2 Most Edwardian little girls enjoyed a foretaste of the permanent wave—but without the permanence—suffering the infliction of tightly-twisted 'curl rags' at night. **1968** *Woman's Own* 28 Sept. 28/1 Can you tell me what is the difference between a veteran car and a vintage car? A veteran is a car built before 1905 and a vintage car is one manufactured between the beginning of 1919 and the end of 1930. The period in between is covered by the category 'Edwardian car'.

4. Designating or characteristic of the clothes worn by Edwardians (senses 2 and 3).

1934 D. C. CALTHROP *Eng. Dress* v. 108 Let our pious prayer be that we shall not see our men and women in Edwardian clothes with a few exceptions, and those..are the grey frock coat and top hat and white waistcoat. **1954** 'N. BLAKE' *Whisper in Gloom* I. iv. 55 A..young man, in Norfolk jacket and tight Edwardian trousers. **1959** *Cath. Times* 23 Oct. 11/1 Any boy turning up in 'this exaggerated form of Edwardian-style dress' will be sent home.

B. *sb.* **1.** An alumnus of a school of King Edward VI's or VII's foundation, of St. Edward's School, Oxford, or of King Edward VII School, Sheffield.

1873 *S. Edward's Sch. Chron.* Apr. 15/2 Then with a kick S. Edward's chief raises the ball on high; And above their adversaries' heads the Edwardians see it fly. **1875** *Ibid.* July 154/2 The captain of the Old Edwardians. **1920** *Serv. Rec. K. Edw. Sch., B'ham* p. vii, [His] unrivalled knowledge and memory of Old Edwardians. **1933** *Birmingham Post* 16 Feb. 6/3 (*heading*) Distinction for an Old Edwardian. **1967** *King Edward VII School* (Sheffield) *Mag.* Spring 352 The Headmaster opened his report by expressing gratitude to.. the Old Edwardians.

2. A person belonging to the period of Edward VII. Also *transf.*

1920 *Times Lit. Suppl.* 23 Sept. 617/2 Beguiled to sleep towards the end of last century..and suddenly awoken in a world of earnest Edwardians. **1929** S. AUMONIER *Ups & Downs* 147 He was an Edwardian of Edwardians.. surprisingly gracious, tactful and charming. **1930** V. SACKVILLE-WEST (*title*) The Edwardians. **1963** BIRD & HUTTON-STOTT *Veteran Motor Car* 238 They were splendid cars with the beautiful balance and road-holding of the best Edwardians.

3. A person wearing clothes of Edwardian style; a 'Teddy boy'.

1954 *Newsweek* 17 May 47/1 They are the Edwardians —the dead-end kids of London. The Edwardians take their name from the costume that is, with variations, their uniform... Tightly buttoned, knee-length 'Milord' coat with soft, black-velvet collar; double-breasted, pearl-gray waistcoat; and tight, drainpipe trousers.

Ed,wardi'ana, *sb. pl.* [f. EDWARDIAN: see ANA *suff.*] **1.** Matter relating to a school of King Edward VI's foundation, St. Edward's School, Oxford, or King Edward VII School, Sheffield.

1902 *S. Edward's Sch. Chron.* June 231/2 A very interesting collection of what I may perhaps term 'Edwardiana', that is 1st, all printed matter designed for the use of the School.

2. Objects made in the reign of Edward VII, or imitations thereof.

1951 N. Marsh *Opening Night* iii. 62 There was a tarnished looking-glass, upon the surface of which someone had..painted a number of water-lilies and leaves. Among this growth, as if drowned in Edwardiana, Jacko's and Martyn's faces were reflected. **1961** *Times* 9 June 15/4 The old wafer-thin genteel affairs..have gone the way of most Edwardiana. **1966** *Guardian* 1 Dec. 6/5 All sorts of modish Victoriana and Edwardiana including parasols with elaborate handles re-covered to make umbrellas.

Ed'wardianism. [f. Edwardian *a.* 3 + -ism 3.] The collective characteristics of the reign of Edward VII; an Edwardian sentiment or expression.

1935 N. Marsh *Enter a Murderer* i. 18 'Has Gardener cut me out?' 'My sweet, *what* an Edwardianism.' **1936** J. Beith *Sand Castle* ii. i. 230 Edwardianism, that brief ten-years' flower, was ready to burst into bloom, and..life surged forward gay and hopeful. **1963** *Punch* 16 Jan. 101/3 The prissy mannerisms of hangover Edwardianism.

Edwardine ('ɛdwədi:n), *a.* and *sb.* [f. Edward + -ine[1].] **A.** *adj.* **1.** Belonging to the reign of Edward VI.

1866 [see Edwardian *a.* 2]. **1936** M. V. Ronan in *European Civilization* IV. 589 The proclamation of the Edwardine Liturgy.

2. Belonging to or characteristic of the reign of Edward VII.

1910 *Tablet* 14 May Suppl. 792/2 One event of the Edwardine reign afforded to the Catholics of this country satisfactions that were all their own, the union of the King of Spain and the Princess Ena.

B. *sb.* An adherent of the religious principles of Edward VI.

1942 P. Hughes *Rome & Counter-Reformation* iv. 67 The French ambassador..was initiated into the anti-Catholic publicity campaign which the Edwardines were preparing.

†**'edwit.** *Obs.* Also 3 **ædwit, edwyte.** [OE. *edwit* + OS. *edwît*, Lips. Gloss. OHG. *itawîz* (MHG. *itewîz*), Goth. *idweit*:—OTeut. **eduwîto-m*, f. **eduwît-an* to reproach; see edwite *v.*] Reproach, rebuke, taunt; taunting speech.

c **825** *Vesp. Psalter* lxviii[ix]. 8 Forðon fore ðe ic aber edwit. *c* **1000** *Ags. Ps.* lxviii[ix]. 9 Me eac fela þinra edwita on ʒefeollon. *c* **1205** Lay. 5827 Heorten we haueden sare and ure cun ædwit auere mare. **1297** R. Glouc. 379 He made hym somdel wroþ, Vor edwyt of hys grete wombe. *c* **1430** *Hymns Virg.* 124 (Mätz.) Hytt was full grett dispyte So offte to make me edwyte.

†**ed'wite,** *v.* *Obs.* Also 1 **edwítan,** 3 **eadwiten.** [OE. *edwítan* str. vb.:—OTeut. **edo-, eduwîtan*, not represented exc. in Eng.; the OHG. *itawîzian* (MHG. *itewîzen*), Goth. *idweitjan* wk. vbs., are f. the derived sb. **edowîto(m* edwit), f. *edo-, edu-*, ed- + *wîtan* (OE. *wítan*) to impute, blame. Cf. atwit.]

1. *trans.* To taunt, blame, reproach.

c **825** *Vesp. Psalter* lxviii[ix]. 10 Edwit edwitendra ðe ʒefeollun ofer mee. *a* **1225** *Ancr. R.* 212, & ʒif þer is out to eadwiten. *a* **1300** *Commandm.* in *E.E.P.* (1862) 16 þat we ssold edwite is worþi wound. **1388** Wyclif *Ecclus.* xx. 15 He schal edwite many thingis. *c* **1430** *Hymns Virg.* (1867) 70 To Conscience þei adwiten me.

2. To make (a thing) a subject of reproach *to* a person. Const. *dat.* or *to*. (Sometimes with obj. sentence instead of acc.)

c **1230** *Hali Meid.* 37 We ne edwiten nawt wiues hare weanen. *a* **1240** *Sawles Warde* in *Cott. Hom.* 253 Ha wið hokeres edwiteð ant up breideð euch an his sunnen. **1377** Langl. *P. Pl.* B. v. 368 His [wif] gan edwite hym þo How wikkedlich he lyued. **1388** Wyclif *Wisd.* ii. 12 He vpbreidith [*C.* edwiteth] to vs the synnes of lawe. *c* **1430** *Stans Puer* 28 in *Babees Bk.* (1868) 29 Be not to hasti upon breed to bite Lest men þerof Do þee edwite.

Hence **ed'witing** *vbl. sb.*, the action of reproaching or rebuking; a rebuke, reproach.

1388 Wyclif *Wisd.* v. 3 These..we hadden..into licnesse of vpbreidyng [*C.* ether edwiting]. —— *Ecclus.* xviii. 18 *marg.*, The resseyuere..aschamed of edwitingis doon to him.

ee, *north.* and esp. *Sc.* form of eye, q.v. for the word and its compounds, *ee-bree, ee-list*, etc.

'ee. Colloq. contraction for ye.

1775 Sheridan *St. Patr. Day* i. i, Hark'ee lads, I must have no grumbling.

-ee, *suffix*[1], used in technical terms of Eng. law, was orig. an adaptation of the *-é* of certain AF. pa. pples., which were used as sbs. The existence in legal AF. of pairs of correlative words like *apelour* appellor, *apelé* appellee, seems to have led in the first place to the invention of words in *-ee* parallel to those agent-nouns in *-or* which had been adapted in legal use from AF.; and subsequently the terminations *-or* and *-ee* were freely added to Eng. vb.-stems to form sbs., those in *-or* denoting the agent, and those in *-ee* the passive party, in such transactions as are the object of legislative provision. The derivatives in *-ee*, however, unlike the AF. participial sbs. after which they were modelled, have not usually a grammatically passive sense, but denote the 'indirect object' of the vbs. from which they are derived. Thus *vendee* is the person to whom a sale is made, *indorsee* the person in whose favour a draft, etc. is indorsed, *lessee* the person to whom property is let. With still greater departure from the original function of the suffix, *payee* denotes the person who is entitled to be paid, whether he be actually paid or not. In a few cases the suffix has been appended, not to a verb-stem in Eng. or AF., but to a Latin ppl. stem etymologically related to an Eng. sb., as in *legatee*, a person to whom a *legacy* has been bequeathed.

2. The use of this suffix in law terms has been freq. imitated in the formation of humorous (chiefly) nonce-words, as *iestee, cuttee, educatee, laughee, sendee*, denoting the personal object of the verbs from which they are formed.

3. In a few words, as *bargee, devotee*, the suffix is employed app. arbitrarily.

4. *-ee* also appears in the English spelling of certain sbs. adopted from mod. F. ppl. sbs. in *-é*, as *debauchee, refugee*.

-ee, *suffix*[2], of vague meaning and obscure origin. In *bootee, coatee*, where it has a diminutive force, it may (though not very probably) be an altered form of -y (in Sc. *-ie*). In other words, as *goatee, settee*, the analogies that may have given rise to the suffix are uncertain.

†**eefe,** *a.* *Obs.* [Corrupt f. eath *a.*] Easy.

1578 T. Proctor *Gorg. Gallery* G, It is as eefe a broken syve Should holde the dropping rayne.

eegrass ('i:grɑ:s, -æ-). *dial.* Also 8 **eagrass.** [Of unknown etymology; cf. WSom. *eargrass* (jə:grɑ:s) 'the annual or biennial grasses sown upon arable land' (Elworthy).] = eddish, edgrew.

1669 Worlidge *Syst. Agric.* (1681) 325 Eddish..or Eegrass, the..Grass that comes after Mowing. **1725** Bradley *Fam. Dict.*, *Eddish*, otherwise called..Eagrass. **1844** W. Barnes *Poems Rural Life* 256 An' we've a-trod the sheenen bliade Ov eegrass in the zummer shiade.

eel (i:l), *sb.* Forms: 1 **ǽl, eol,** 1–6 **ele,** 5–7 **eele,** 6 *Sc.* **eill,** (5 **ʒele,** 6 **ye(e)le,** 7 **yeel),** 6– **eel.** [Com. Teut.: OE. *ǽl* = MDu. *ael* (Du. *aal*), OHG. *âl* (Ger. *aal*), ON. *áll* (Da. *aal*, Sw. *ål*):—OTeut. **ǽlo-z*. The ultimate etymology is unknown; the hypothesis that the word is cogn. with the synonymous L. *anguilla*, Gr. ἔγχελυς, is untenable.]

1. a. The name of a genus (*Anguilla*) of soft-finned osseous fishes, strongly resembling snakes in external appearance. The best known species are the Common or Sharp-nosed Eel (*A. anguilla*) found both in Europe and in America, and the Broad-nosed Eel or grig (*A. latirostris*). The true eels are fresh-water fishes, but migrate to the sea to spawn. **b.** Used (both in popular and in scientific language) as the name of the entire family *Murænidæ*, comprising the true eels with several other genera, notably the conger.

c **1000** Ælfric *Colloq.* in Wr.-Wülcker 94 Hwilce fixas ʒefehst þu? Ælas and hacodas, etc. *c* **1000** *Sax. Leechd.* II. 308 Hrefnes geallan..& eles, & feld beon huniʒ meng to somne. **1052–67** *Chart. Eadweard* in *Cod. Dipl.* IV. 242 Foure þousend eol in lenton to carite to ðe abbot. *a* **1300** *Havelok* 897 A carte lode..Of grete laumprees, and of eles. *c* **1420** *Liber Cocorum* (1862) 50 Fyrst flyghe þyn elys, in pese hom smyte. **1528** More *Heresyes* i. Wks. (1557) 165/2 A blynde bagge full of snakes and eles together. **1528** Paynell *Salerne Regim.* O iij b, The yele is an vnholsome fyshe. **1586** Cogan *Haven Health* clxxvi. (1612) 140 An old yeele is wholsomer than a yong. **1671** Salmon *Syn. Med.* iii. lxxxi. 707 The fat..of a mole, eele, or serpent. **1712** Addison *Spect.* No. 538 ¶3 They passed to eels, then to parsnips, and so from one aversion to another. **1802** Bingley *Anim. Biog.* (1813) III. 2 The Common Eel..forms a connecting link..between the serpents and the fishes. **1866** Geo. Eliot *F. Holt* (1868) 27 It is a lucky eel that escapes skinning. **1883** G. C. Davies *Norfolk Broads* xxxi. 237 The silver-bellied eel or bed-eel..corresponds to the sharp-nosed eel.

c. In fig. phrases, as the type of something 'slippery'.

1524 Dk. Norfolk in *St. Papers Hen. VIII*, IV. 224 Whosoever have hym best, is no more sure of hym, than he that hath an ele by the tayle. ? *c* **1600** *Distracted Emp.* v. iv. in Bullen *O. Pl.* III. 258 They have sweete eeles to hould by. **1791** Newte *Tour Eng. & Scot.* 374 He may possibly take an eel by the tail in marrying a wife.

†**d.** *salt eel*: a rope's end used for flogging. *Obs.* [From the use of an eel skin as a whip.]

1663 Pepys *Diary* 24 Apr., With my salt eele went down in the parler and there got my boy and did beat him. **1699** B. E. *Dict. Cant. Crew*, *Salt-eel*, a Rope's end used to Drub the Boies and Sailors on board of Ship.

2. Applied popularly to various other fishes resembling eels in their snake-like form. *electric eel*: = gymnotus. *nine-eyed eel*: the River Lamprey. *sand eel*: the Launce of Ammodyte.

a **1705** Ray. *Syn. Piscium* (1713) 154 *Sand-eel* [Given as a synonym for the launce]. **1810** P. Neill *Fishes in Forth* 30 (Jam.) Lesser Lamprey..The popular name Nine-eyed-eel arises from the spiracles being taken for eyes.

3. The popular name for the minute animals (resembling an eel in shape) found in vinegar (*Anguillula aceti*) and in sour paste (*A. glutinis*). They are *Entozoa* of the order *Nematoidea*.

1746 Sherwood in *Phil. Trans.* XLIV. 67 The Eels in sour Paste are the Animalcules in Question. **1753** Chambers *Cycl. Supp.* s.v., The long bodied animalcules, discovered by the microscope in vinegar, sour paste, etc...have been generally distinguished..by the name of eels. **1881** Carpenter *Microscope* (ed. 6) 695 *Anguillulæ* or 'Eels' of the microscopist.

4. *U.S.* A nickname for a New Englander.

1837–40 Haliburton *Clockm.* (1862) 318 The eels of New England and the corncrakers of Virginia.

5. General comb.: **a.** attributive, as ***eel-boat, -freak, -fry, -line, -man, -net, -oil, -pie, -river, -trap, -weir***, and ***eel-like*** adj. and adv.; **b.** objective, as ***eel-catching, -fisher, -netting***.

1883 G. C. Davies *Norfolk Broads* vi. 43 These *eel-boats are precisely like the Noah's ark of childhood. *Ibid.* xxxi. 237 Naturalists can only rely upon the observations of those whose occupation is connected with *eel-catching. *Ibid.* vi. 43 Through the night the *eel-fisher sits in his cabin..waiting for the eels the stream will bring to his net. *Ibid.* xxxi. 235 The *eel fisheries are nearly as valuable as the salmon fisheries. **1882** *Blackw. Mag.* Jan. 101 This singular *eel-freak. *Ibid.*, Thousands and thousands of *eel-fry all alive in the bodies of eels. **1685** Boyle *Effect of Mot.* iv. 41 The *Eel-like particles of water. **1838** Dickens *O. Twist* vii, Eel-like positions. **1871** B. Taylor *Faust* i. iii. 27 Eel-like gliding, Skipping and hiding. **1883** G. C. Davies *Norfolk Broads* xix. 137 Formerly *eel-lines, with a thousand hooks strung on at intervals..used to be set. *Ibid.* xxxii. 251 The *eelmen, living so much on the water..become very observant. *Ibid.* xix. 145 The *eel-net is set across the dyke to catch them [eels] in its long 'poke'. **1769** Mrs. Raffald *Eng. Housekpr.* (1778) 155 An *Eel Pye. **1849** Southey *Comm.-Pl. Bk.* Ser. ii. 340 Monstrellet mentions horseloads of eel-pies brought from Mantes to the market of Paris. **1883** G. C. Davies *Norfolk Broads* xxxii. 249 The Yare is the best *eel-river of all. **1879** Lubbock *Sci. Lect.* i. 5 The bladders are on the principle of an *eel-trap, having a closed entrance with a flap which permits an easy entrance, but effectually prevents the unfortunate victim from getting out again. **1868** Peard *Water-farm.* xvii. 180 At various points in the course of the rivers *eel-weirs are placed.

6. Special comb.: **eel-babber, -bobber,** = bobber[2] 2; **eel-basket,** a trap of basket-work with funnel-shaped entrance, allowing the eels to enter, but preventing their escape; **eel-backed** *a.* (see quot.); **eel-bob** (see bob *sb.*[1] 7); **eel-buck** (see buck *sb.*[4]); **eel-cake** (see quots.); **eel-crow** (see quot.); **eel-fork** = eel-spear; **eel-hut,** the hut occupied by an eel-fisher when engaged in fishing; **eel-leap,** *dial.* [leap basket] = *eel-basket*; **eel-pick** = eel-spear; **eel-picker,** one who fishes with an eel-pick; so ***eel-picking*** vbl. sb.; **eel-pot** = *eel-buck*; also *fig.*; **eel-putchon,** (see quot.); **eel-schuit,** an eel-boat; **eel-set, -setter, -setting, -trunk** (see quots.); **eel-ware,** *Ranunculus fluitans* (Britten and Holland); **eel-weel** (misspelt *-wheel*) = *eel-buck*. Also eel-grass.

1883 G. C. Davies *Norfolk Broads* xxxi. 237 The bunch of worms strung on worsted with which the *eel-babber works. **1726** *Dict. Rusticum*, **Eel-Back'd Horses*, such as have black Lists along their Backs. **1883** *Fisheries Exhib. Catal.* 196 Hand-lines..snares and *eel-bobs; Indian fishing lines. **1883** G. C. Davies *Norfolk Broads* v. 40 An eel-fisher..treading lob-worms on to worsted for the purpose of making an *eel-bob. **1866** *Sat. Rev.* 21 Apr. 471/1 The present alleged fishery rights for netting and *eel-bucks are to be revised. **1883** G. C. Davies *Norfolk Broads* xxxi. 235 On the Thames..the eels are intercepted in their descent by weirs or frameworks holding basket-work traps, called 'eel-bucks'. **1885** *Sat. Rev.* 21 Nov. 673/1 Snigs are only taken in the eel-bucks if they are set *with* the stream. **1653** Walton *Angler* x. 189 Small Eeles..The poorer sort..make a kind of *Eele-cake of them, and eat it like as bread. **1796** Morse *Amer. Geog.* I. 213 *Eel crow [given as the popular name of *Columbus migratorius*]. **1883** G. C. Davies *Norfolk Broads* xxxii. 250 In these lonely *eel-huts..the eel fishers sat watching their nets. **1877** E. Peacock *N.-W. Linc. Gloss.* (E.D.S.) **Eel-leap*, an eel-trap made of wickerwork. **1883** G. C. Davies *Norfolk Broads* xxxi. 238 They [eels] work down into the soft mud, far beyond the reach of *eel-picks and darts. *Ibid.* xxvi. 203 The *eel-picker in his little punt..is a common object on the flats. *Ibid.* xix. 143 *Eel-picking is an art in which some men attain considerable skill. Sometimes an eel-picking match takes place on the Broad. **1631** in T. Hutchinson *Coll. Orig. Papers Massachusetts-Bay* (1769) 51 The *yeele potts you sent for are made. **1647** J. Eliot *Let.* 24 Sept. in T. Shepard *Clear Sunshine* (1648) 28 All winter they sell Brooms, Staves, Elepots, Baskets. **1838** Dickens *Nickleby* xvi. 143 Manchester Buildings is an eel-pot, which has no outlet but its awkward mouth. **1883** *Fisheries Exhib. Catal.* 8 Eel Pot, for use in salt water. *Ibid.* (ed. 4) 125 *Eel Putchons..are the ordinary eel baskets that are baited and placed in the river during the spring and summer months for eels. *a* **1865** Smyth *Sailor's Word-bk.* (1867) 269 *Dutch* **eel-skuyt*, a flat-bottomed somewhat cutter-rigged sea-boat. **1899** Eel schuyt [see schuit]. **1905** M. A. Wyllie *London to the Nore* iv. 42 Gaily painted and varnished Dutch eel-schuits. **157..** H. Manship *Gt. Yarmouth* in G. C. Davies *Norfolk Broads* xxvii, Certen *ele settes..all soch fishe as usually are tacon in the seid settes. **1882** *Blackw. Mag.* Jan. 97 Eelsets..are nets set athwart the stream for the purpose of catching a..species of eel. *Ibid.* 98 The oldest Norfolk *eel-setters. **1883** G. C. Davies *Norfolk Broads* xxxii. 250 This [ebb and flow of the tide] militates against *eel-setting. **1877** E.

PEACOCK *N.-W. Linc. Gloss.* (E.D.S.) **Eel-trunk*, a box with holes in the sides, in which eels are kept alive till wanted for the table. **1883** *Fisheries Exhib. Catal.* 57 *Eel Wheels or Traps. Lampern Spurts.

eel (iːl), *v.* [f. the sb.] *intr.* **a.** To fish for eels. **b.** To move or progress sinuously like an eel. Also (with *way*) *trans.* Cf. EELING *gerund* and *vbl. sb.*

1922 JOYCE *Ulysses* 226 Five..sandwichmen..eeled themselves. ?**1953** DYLAN THOMAS *Lett.* (1966) 416, I must ..ooze and eel up wheezily. **1962** M. DRABBLE *Summer Bird-Cage* xi. 185, I..use a small red plastic colander, and everything eels into the sink as often as not. **1969** *Daily Tel.* (Colour Suppl.) 17 Jan. 6 (Advt.), The Herald 13/60.. simply eels its way through town traffic.

'eel-bed. **1.** **a.** A pond or preserve for eels. **b.** *transf.* A bivouac on swampy ground.

1483 *Cath. Angl.* 113 An Ele bed, *anguillarium*. **1813** SIR R. WILSON *Diary* II. 430 The pains of an eel-bed.

2. *pl.* A plant (*Ranunculus fluitans*).

eeler ('iːlə(r)). [f. EEL *sb.* + -ER¹.] An eel-catcher.

1851 *Fraser's Mag.* XLIII. 254 The artful eeler..lets down a hank some cubits long of the intestines of a sheep.

eelery ('iːlərɪ). [f. EEL *sb.* + -ERY.] A place where eels are caught.

1854 BADHAM *Halieut.* xvii. 371 The moderns, like the ancients, have their favourite eeleries. **1864** *Q. Rev.* Jan. 190 We must not suppose there are no valuable eeleries in the British Isles.

eel-fare ('iːlfɛə(r)). **a.** The passage of young eels up a river. **b.** A brood of young eels (see ELVER).

1533 *Act 25 Hen. VIII*, c. vii, Any frye, spaume, or brode of yeles, called yele fares, or Ell vares. **1721–1800** BAILEY, *Eel-fares, -vares*, a Fry or Brood of Eels. **1836** YARRELL *Brit. Fishes* (1859) I. 54 This passage of young Eels is called Eel-fare on the banks of the Thames. **1883** G. C. DAVIES *Norfolk Broads* xxxi. 235 This 'eel-fare' lasts several days.

'eel-grass. Chiefly *U.S.* [See EEL *sb.* 6.] A plant with long narrow leaves: (*a*) = *grass-wrack* (GRASS *sb.*¹ 14); (*b*) = *tape-grass* (TAPE *sb.*¹ 4); (*c*) *fig.*

1790 S. DEANE *New-England Farmer* 19/1 The farmer.. may cart into it [stock-yard]..marsh-mud, eel-grass, flats, or even sand and loam [for making manure]. **1806** *Baltimore Even. Post* 19 Feb. 3/3 (Th.), A young man at Sullivan [Maine] saw a Fox go down to some eel-grass, and roll himself up in it. **1838** *Rep. Agric. Mass. 1837* 58 The eel-grass is of little value except as litter. **1864** LOWELL *Fireside Trav.* 45 The kelp and eel-grass left by higher floods. **1867** *Amer. Naturalist* May 164 Go to the nearest brook, gather.. a root of the Eel grass, [etc.]. **1880** C. E. BESSEY *Botany* 473 Order Hydrocharideæ.—This contains the Eel Grass, *Vallisneria spiralis*. **1884** MILLER *Plant-n.* 58/1 Tape, or eel grass, *Vallisneria spiralis*. **1888** GOODE *Amer. Fishes* 65 Jungles of eel-grass and meadows of lily pads. **1893** B. TORREY *Foot-path Way* 39 The beach was strewn with sea-weeds and eel-grass. **1901** 'H. MCHUGH' *John Henry* 53 He's running his fingers through the eel-grass on his topknot and looking wise. **1951** *Dict. Gardening* (R. Hort. Soc.) IV. 2192/2 *V*[allisneria] *spiralis*, eelgrass, tapegrass. **1956** *Ibid.* Suppl. 200/2 *Eel-grass*,..a name also used for species of Zostera but these are of no horticultural importance.

eelhood ('iːlhʊd). *nonce-wd.* [f. EEL *sb.* + -HOOD.] The rank or condition of a full-grown eel.

1864 *Q. Rev.* Jan. 185 Of the myriads that ascend our rivers few..ever arrive at eelhood.

eeling ('iːlɪŋ), *gerund* and *vbl. sb.* [f. the vb.] Fishing for eels.

1780 in *Narragansett Hist. Reg.* (1882) I. 104 Made an eel spear. Went eeling. *Ibid.*, Went an eeling. **1843** *Knickerbocker* XXII. 426 No clammin', no eelin', and no pastur to feed your cows onto. **1895** *Outing* (U.S.) XXVI. 406/2 When he couldn't go eeling. **1955** E. S. DUCKETT *St. Dunstan* v. 135 In later years the fowling, eeling, and fisheries of the Fens..were to provide ample maintenance.. for the abbeys.

'eel-pout. [OE. *ǽle-puta*, f. EEL *sb.* + POUT.] **1.** A marine fish of the family Zoarcidæ, esp. the viviparous blenny, *Zoarces viviparus*; also formerly applied to the BURBOT.

c **1000** ÆLFRIC *Colloq.* in Wr.-Wülcker 94 Hwilce fixas ʒefehst þu?..mynas and æleputan. **1598** FLORIO, *Agufeo*, an eelepout. **1601** HOLLAND *Pliny* I. 246 A kind of Lamprels or Elepouts like to sea Lampreis. **1740** R. BROOKES *Art of Angling* I. xli. 87 The Eel-Pout or Burbot..has a smooth, soft, slippery Body like an Eel. **1772** in P. L. Phillips *Notes B. Romans* (1924) 124 There are three species of Eel Ponts [*sic*], but these are in every Sea or River on the Earth besides. **1810** P. NEILL *Fishes in Forth* 8 (Jam.) *B. viviparus*. Viviparous Blenny; Green bone. Here this species sometimes gets the name of Eelpout and Guffer. **1842** *Nat. Hist. N.Y., Zoology* IV. 155 The thick-lipped Eel-pout..is caught on the coast. **1863** COUCH *Brit. Fishes* III. 93 The Burbolt is..distinguished by exhibiting some of the manners of the eel, by which it has obtained in some places the name of Eelpout. **1885** [see LAMPER-EEL 2]. **1905** D. S. JORDAN *Guide to Study of Fishes* II. xxix. 518 The Zoarcidæ, or eel-pouts, have the body elongate. **1969** A. WHEELER *Fishes Brit. Isles & N.W. Europe* 448 Eelpouts often lie under stones or buried in mud.

†**2.** A yellow flower. ? = *eel-ware* (see EEL *sb.* 6).

1736 BAILEY *Househ. Dict.* 141 Butter..As for that which is tinged with eel pouts, it not only deceives the sight, but is very often disagreeable to the taste.

'eel-skin. [f. EEL *sb.* + SKIN.] The skin of an eel. †*merchant of eel-skins* = ? rag and bone collector. Also *attrib.*, as in **eelskin-dress**, a tight-fitting dress; **eelskin-queue**, ? a pig-tail.

1562 J. HEYWOOD *Prov. & Epigr.* (1867) 54 A marchaunt of eele skins. A marchaunt without either money or ware. **1595** SHAKS. *John* I. i. 141 My armes, such eele-skins stuft. *a* **1613** OVERBURY *Charac., Drunken Dutchm.*, When he's drunke, you may thrust your hand into him like an eele-skin. **1809** W. IRVING *Knickerb.* (1849) 308 He directed that he should be carried to the grave with his eelskin queue sticking out of a hole in his coffin. **1881** MISS BRADDON *Asph.* II. 226 Jersey jackets and eel-skin dresses. **1884** *Pall Mall G.* 15 Mar. 4/1 A smooth-faced, vicious-looking fellow, dressed in a close cap and eelskin neckcloth.

'eel-spear. [f. EEL *sb.* + SPEAR.] A forked or pronged instrument for catching eels by transfixing them as they lie in the mud. (See quots.)

1555 EDEN *Decades W. Ind.* (Arb.) 197 Speares..lyke vnto troute speares or yele speares. **1610** GUILLIM *Heraldry* (1679) 235 He beareth..3 Eel-spears argent. **1785** *Sportsman's Dict., Eel-spear*; this instrument is made for the most part with three forks or teeth, jagged on the sides. **1867** SMYTH *Sailor's Word-Bk., Eel-spear*, a sort of trident with ten points for catching eels, called in Lincolnshire an eel-stang.

Hence **eel-spearer**, **eel-spearing** *vbl. sb.*

1883 G. C. DAVIES *Norfolk Broads* v. 40 Here and there was an eel-spearer in his punt. *Ibid.* xxxi. 244 Eel-spearing is quite an athletic occupation.

'eel-worm. [f. EEL + WORM *sb.* 4.] A nematode worm, esp. one parasitic on plants.

1888 E. A. ORMEROD *Notes of Observations of Injurious Insects* XI. 8 If the Eelworms are once established in land there is difficulty in clearing them. **1897** *Yearbk. U.S. Dept. Agric.* 568 What appeared to be eel worms, or nematodes, were observed in potato stalks, causing the foliage to turn yellow. **1901** *Dundee Advertiser* 15 Jan. 4/3 'Tulip-root', a disease [of oats] caused by a minute eelworm. **1935** *Discovery* Sept. 266/1 Eelworms that live in vinegar barrels and the many species which inhabit the soil and by their effects upon it influence the work of agriculturists. **1946** *Nature* 14 Dec. 882/1 Bud-rot in the eastern tropics, hitherto fortunately never confused with eelworm attack, is due to *Phytophthora*. **1970** *Times* 14 July 10/6 Maris Piper is resistant to eel worm.

eely ('iːlɪ), *a.* [f. EEL *sb.* + -Y.] Eel-like.

†**a.** Resembling the flesh of an eel. **b.** Resembling an eel in movement; wriggling, writhing.

1655 MOUFET & BENNET *Health's Improv.* (1746) 124 A Conger..is..of a moist, soft, and Eely Substance. **1862** CALVERLEY *Verses & Tr.* 16, I..See you sit with that composure On the eeliest of hacks. **1871** *Cassell's Mag.* 22 July 336/1 We have the pleasure of seeing the snaky, eely monster whisking about in the water.

eem. *dial.* [repr. OE. *efnan*, ON. *efna* to perform (Da. *evne* to have ability, Sw. *ämna* to form, shape. Cf. ME. *em-cristen* for *even-*.] To spare time; to find an opportunity; to 'afford'; to succeed (in doing a thing), 'get' (to do).

1674 RAY *N. Country Wds.* Coll. 16 Chesh...I cannot Eem, I have no leisure, I cannot spare time. **1745** BYROM *Misc. Poems* (1773) I. 157 in *Lanc. Gloss.* (E.D.S.) We worken hard..An cannot eem to be so feert. **1750** J. COLLIER *Wks.* (1819) 71 in *Lanc. Gloss.* (E.D.S.) Aw've tried mony a time but aw could never eem to do it.

een, obs. and dial. pl. of EYE.

-een (iːn), *suffix*¹, ultimately derived from L. *-īnus*, *-īna* adj. suffix, through F. *-in*, *-ine*, as in †*damaskeen* (1551), *canteen* (1737), *tureen* (1706), *bombazeen* (18th–19th century variant of *bombasine*). *Bombazeen* apparently furnished the model for *velveteen* (1795, *velvatean* 1776), on which followed *sateen* (an alteration of *satin*).

-een (iːn), *suffix*², ad. Ir. dim. suffix *-ín*, as in *buckeen* (1793), *colleen* (1828), *dudeen* (1841), *girleen* (1836), *jackeen* (1840), *poteen* (1812), *spalpeen* (1780), *squireen* (1809).

e'en, var. form of EVEN *adv.*

e'enamost ('iːnəməʊst), *adv. Eng.* and *U.S. dial.* Also α. **e'en a most**, **a'most**; β. **enymost**, **eeny(-)most**, **enermost**. [f. *e'en* EVEN *adv.* + *a'most* ALMOST *adv.*] Almost; nearly.

α. **1735–6** PEGGE *Alphabet of Kenticisms* (1876), *E'en a'most*, almost. **1781** *Pennsylvania Jrnl.* (Philadelphia) 20 June, I once heard a man say, another 'swore terribly; he swore *e'en amost like a wood pile*'. **1839** *Havana* (N.Y.) *Republ.* 21 Aug. (Th.), [The whale's head] was e'en a most off. **1843** T. C. HALIBURTON *Attaché* I. xiv. 253 The repudiation of debts has lowered us down e'en a'most to the bottom of the shaft. **1844** 'J. SLICK' *High Life in N.Y.* I. iv. 43 He looked eenamost tuckered out. **1891** H. FREDERIC *Copperhead* (1894) 208 'I could e'en a'most 'a' thought it was Alvy talkin',' was what he said. **1911** in *Dialect Notes* III. 543.

β. **1813** JANE AUSTEN *Let.* 18 Oct. (1932) II. 356 Poor Will Amos..said the fleas were so starved..that they..*eenermost* eat him up. **1833** C. A. DAVIS *Major Downing* 168 It was made so long ago he has enymost forgot it. **1840** *Crockett Almanac* 2 The sun will be enermost hid. **1845** S. JUDD *Margaret* I. xiv. 113 He..has got the whole Bible eeny most by heart. **1870** STOWE *Oldtown Fireside Stories* (1871) 189 Then he'd jaw and scold so that she was eenymost beat out.

eeny ('iːnɪ). A nonsense word (also *eny*, *eenee*, *eena*) used in the first line of the most popular counting-out rhymes among children in Britain and the U.S.

1855 *N. & Q.* 1st Ser. XI. 113/2 The Schoolboy Formula. .. Eeny, meeny, moany, mite... Eeny, meeny, tipty, te. **1883** W. W. NEWELL *Games & Songs Amer. Children* xiv. 199 Eny, meny, mony, mite. **1923** KIPLING *Land & Sea Tales* 279 Eenee, Meenee, Mainee, Mo! Catch a nigger by the toe! **1944** H. G. WELLS *'42 to '44* 199 However counting began, it is evident that from the first it produced a profound effect of mystery and magic upon the human mind. 'Eena, meena, mina, mo'—they counted men out for definite purposes. **1958** A. HACKNEY *Private Life* xiii. 123 'It'll cost your government a bit more, about sixty thousand nicker more, which is a nice easy amount to divide into three. Eeny, meany, miney.' He pointed daintily round the table.

eer, obs. form of ERE, before.

-eer, *suffix*¹, is an anglicized form of the Fr. suffix *-ier* (repr. normally L. *-iārius*, and in many words replacing *-air*:—L. *-ārius*; see -ARY¹), used to form sbs. denoting persons, as in *canonnier* CANNONEER, *muletier* MULETEER; the usual sense is 'one who is concerned with', or 'one who deals in'. (Where the sb. from which the F. word was formed never became familiar in Eng. use, the original spelling *-ier* is retained, as in *bombardier*, *grenadier*). In imitation of these words (perh. in some instances rather in imitation of Sp. sbs. in *-ero*, of similar origin) the suffix is added to Eng. sbs. to form designations of persons, as *auctioneer*, *charioteer*, *mountaineer* (earlier *-er*). In many of the words so formed there is a more or less contemptuous implication, as in *crotcheteer*, *garreteer*, *pamphleteer*, *pulpiteer*, *sonneteer*.

The spelling *-eer*, replacing the older *-ier*, became frequent in new words in the early 17th century. *Mountaineer* and *waistcoateer* (a prostitute) afford early instances, and are also exceptional examples, of the use of this suffix. A few formations denote inanimate objects, as *gazetteer* (1704), *muffineer* (1806–7).

In the latter part of the 17th century gerundial and (to a less extent) participial formations on agent-nouns in *-eer* appeared, and increased in the course of the following century, as *auctioneering* (1733), *buccaneering* (1703), *electioneering* (1774), *engineering* (1720), *parliamenteering* (1711), *privateering* (1664), *volunteering* (1691). These, being formed directly on the sbs. in *-eer*, do not necessarily imply the existence of a corresponding infinitive or finite verbal form, though an early example actually appears in *mutineered* (1682). Some of these formations, e.g. *parliamenteering*, were in commoner use than the original sb.; occasionally, as in *revolutioneering*, no sb. exists, *-eering* itself being used as a suffix.

-eer, *suffix*², representing Du. *-eren*, ad. F. infinitive ending *-er*; as in *domineer* (Shakespeare), ad. Du. †*domineren*, ad. F. *dominer* to DOMINATE; *commandeer* (1881), ad. Cape Du. *commanderen*, ad. F. *commander* to COMMAND.

e'er, variant of EVER.

eerie, eery ('iːrɪ), *a.* Forms: 4 eri, hery, 4–6 ery, 6 erie, 9 eirie, -y (Anglo-Irish airy), 8– eery, -ie. [ME. *eri*, ? var. of *erʒ*, ARGH; or ? f. that word + -Y.

The word occurs in the northern (not in the midland) version of the *Cursor Mundi*. It has recently been often used in general literature, but is still regarded as properly Scotch.]

1. Fearful, timid. In mod. use, expressing the notion of a vague superstitious uneasiness.

a **1300** *Cursor M.* 17685 (Gött.) Ioseph be noght eri. *c* **1375** ? BARBOUR *S. Cosmas & D.* 321, & scho..wes for hyme hery. **1501** DOUGLAS *Pal. Hon.* Prol. xii, With ery courage. **1513** —— *Æneis* VII. iv. 91 He fled..and to his cave hym sped wyth ery spreyt. **1572** *Sempill Ballates* (1872) 159 We pure sall cry with eirie hartis..To the, O God. *a* **1774** FERGUSSON *Drink Ecl.* Poems (1845) 50 They glower eery at a friend's disgrace. **1807–10** TANNAHILL *Poems* (1846) 98 The watch-dog's howling..makes the nightly wanderer eerie. **1876** MRS. WHITNEY *Sights & Ins.* II. ii. 357 Do you feel eerie? **1878** H. M. STANLEY *Dark Cont.* I. xiv. 353 This eerie feeling..might be causeless.

2. Fear-inspiring; gloomy, strange, weird.

1792 BURNS *Wks.* (1800) II. 403 Be thou a bogle by the eerie side of an auld thorn. **1795** MACNEILL *Waes o' War* in Poems (1801) 5 Night comes dark and eerie. **1828** J. WILSON in *Blackw. Mag.* XXIII. 116 Hae ye walked..fra Bawhannan Lodge, in sic an eerie night. **1875** MISS BRADDON *Str. World* II. i. 10 The..sheep bell had an eerie sound.

Hence **'eerily** *adv.*, in an eerie manner; weirdly. **'eeriness**, an undefined sense of fear; superstitious dread. **'eerisome** *a.*, weird, gloomy.

c 1375 BARBOUR *Bruce* II. 295 Sum man for erynes will trymbill. 1724 RAMSAY *Vision* vi, Debar then..All eiryness or feir. 1848 C. BRONTË *J. Eyre*, It spoke in pain and woe.. eerily. 1863 *Gd. Words* 522 A weird unhappy sound! what could it be That through the wan night wailed so eerily. 1839 DE QUINCEY *Recoll. Lakes* Wks. II. 13 Feeling the sensation of eeriness as twilight came on. 1865 *Jrnl. Horticulture* Christm. No. 16/2 From that night I have never known eeriness. 1818 *Edin. Mag.* Dec. 503 (Jam.) The kye ..gied a dowf an' eerisome crune. 1832–53 *Whistlebinkie* (Sc. Songs) Ser. III. 49 The objects sae dear..Turn eerisome hame thoughts.

e'ery, contraction for EVERY.

†**ees.** *Obs.* [possibly repr. OE. *ǣs* 'food, meat, carrion' (Bosw.); possibly a. corresponding MDu. *aes* food, bait (mod.Du., Ger. *aas*).] (See quot.)

c 1440 *Promp. Parv.* 143 Ees, fysch mete on a hoke [*P.* boyght for fisshes], *esca, escarium.*

eese, eesily, eesy, obs. ff. of EASE, etc.

eesome ('iːsəm). [f. *ee*, Sc. form of EYE + -SOME.] Attractive or gratifying to the eye.

1823 LOCKHART *Reg. Dalton* III. 159 (Jam.) Look at them now,—Will ony body deny that that's an eesome couple?

eete(n, eete, obs. forms of pres. t., pa. t. and pa. pple. of EAT.

eeþ, eeth, obs. forms of EATH.

eever, var. of EAVER *sb.*² *dial.*

ef (ɛf). Name of the letter F, q.v.

ef- *pref.*, the form of the L. pref. *ex-* used before words beginning with *f.*

efacks, efackins, efags, efecks, efeclings: see I'FEGS, *Obs.*

†**e'fact,** *int. Obs.* [perh. var. of *efaks*, I'FEGS, influenced by *in fact.*] Used as a mild oath.

1680 *Revenge* IV. i. 34 We'll have tother Dance, efact we will.

efen, obs. form of EVEN.

efendee, var. of EFFENDI.

efere, var. of IFERE, *adv. Obs.* together.

†**efestide(s.** *Obs.* [corruption of L. *hephæstitis*, a. Gr. *ἡφαιστῖτις, f. Ἥφαιστος the name of the God of Fire.] A jewel described by Pliny.

1567 MAPLET *Gr. Forest* 7 [Of Stones] Efestides is in colour..shamefast and childish. 1688 R. HOLME *Armoury* II. 40/1 Efestide..held against the Sun is Fiery coloured.

eff (ɛf), *v.* [Variant of EF, name of the letter F, euphemistically representing FUCK *v.* 2, 3.]

1. (Used as an expletive on its own account, as a milder alternative to the full form of the word *fuck*, or else as a euphemistic report of an actual use of the full word.)

1950 HEMINGWAY *Across River & into Trees* ix. 78 'Eff Florence,' the Colonel said. 1958 K. AMIS *I like it Here* xiii. 164 You young people eff off. 1958 D. SANDERSON *Night of Horns* xxv. 165 You sure effed things up. 1963 L. MEYNELL *Virgin Luck* viii. 191 'Eff off,' Johnny told Antonio. Antonio effed off to the other end of the bar. 1967 K. GILES *Death & Mr. Prettyman* ii. 62 'What did he matter?' 'Effed if I know.'

2. To utter the word *fuck* or some equivalent word. Also ***to eff and blind***, to use strong expletives, to swear continuously.

1943 M. HARRISON *Reported Safe Arrival* 31 They'd eff and blind till yer ear-'oles started ter frizzle. 1959 A. WESKER *Chicken Soup & Barley* I. ii, He started effing and blinding and threw their books on the floor. 1965 J. GASKELL *Fabulous Heroine* 50 He would argue and eff in an intellectual ecstasy all afternoon.

Hence **'effer; 'effing** *vbl. sb.* and *ppl. a.*; also as *adv.*

1944 J. AGATE *Red Letter Nights* 45 (Carrying a sandbag.) 'Arf of effing France, and 'ad to walk the other 'arf to fetch it. 1945 *Penguin New Writing* XXV. 186 He's a bastard, but I'll effing well get him. 1950 E. PARTRIDGE *Here, There & Everywhere* 28 The British workman's exclusive preference for *bloody*... A preference shared with 'effing'. 1961 S. PRICE *Just for Record* vi. 56 You're effing right. 1963 P. WEST *Mod. Novel* II. i. 142 On it goes, the livid effing-and-blinding. 1964 S. BELLOW *Herzog* 81 What good are those effing eggheads! 1967 C. DRUMMOND *Death at Furlong Post* ii. 16, I had an argument with that effer, Joe Fryer. 1969 *Observer* 2 Feb. 5/1 Mary felt the situation was 'diabolical' and there was plenty of effing and blinding. 1969 *Private Eye* 24 Oct. 14 The relatives get effing tough. 1970 K. GILES *Death in Church* i. 11 I'm a tolerant effer myself, but blasphemy I can't come at.

eff, var. of EFT, EVET.

effable ('ɛfəb(ə)l), *a.* [a. F. *effable* (Cotgr.), ad. L. *effābilis*, f. *ef-fāri* to utter, f. *ex* out + *fāri* to speak.] †**a.** Of sounds, letters, etc.: That can be pronounced (*obs.*). **b.** That can be, or may lawfully be, expressed or described in words. Now only *arch.* in antithesis to *ineffable.*

1637 BASTWICK *Litany* I. 1 Paules notions..were such as could not be expressed..mine were..easily effable. 1668 WILKINS *Philos. Lang.* 414 How this Universal Character may be made effable in a distinct Language. 1755 JOHNSON *Effable.* Expressive, utterable. *Dict.* 1872 LONGF. *Div. Trag.* II. ii, These effable and ineffable impressions of the mysterious world.

†**e'ffabule,** *v. Obs. rare*⁻¹. [as if ad. L. **effābulāri*, f. *ex-* out + *fābulāri* to fable.] To fable.

c 1600 NORDEN *Spec. Brit., Cornw.* (1728) 82 The graue will fitt eueryе stature, as is effabuled.

efface (ɛ'feɪs). [ad. F. *effacer* (= Pr. *esfassar*), f. L. *ex* out + *facies* face.]

1. To rub out, obliterate (writing, painted or sculptured figures, a mark or stain) from the surface of anything, so as to leave no distinct traces.

1611 COTGR., *Effacer*, to efface, deface, raze, blot, rub out, wipe away; to abolish. 1780 COWPER *Progr. Err.* 279 So coin grows smooth..Till Cæsar's image is effaced at last. 1863 GEO. ELIOT *Romola* II. xxi, The ignominious images, painted on the public buildings..were effaced.

b. In wider sense: To cause to disappear entirely, do away with (a visible feature or object).

1843 PRESCOTT *Mexico* (1850) I. 105 The close of a cycle, when the sun was to be effaced from the heavens, the human race from the earth. 1853 KANE *Grinnell Exp.* xxiv. (1856) 192 Pools of water, which would be effaced again, soon after they were formed. 1870 F. WILSON *Ch. Lindisf.* 83 The entrance through the tower has been effaced.

c. *Crystallography.*

1823 H. J. BROOKE *Introd. Crystallogr.* 214 A right square prism..may result from..an octahedron with a square base, by the concurrence..of the modifications *a* and *e*..when those modifications efface the primary planes.

2. To expunge, erase (words or sentences) from a written composition or document. Now only in fig. sentences.

1737 POPE *Hor. Epist.* II. i. 279 Fluent Shakspeare scarce effac'd a line. 1805 N. NICHOLLS *Let.* in *Corr. w. Gray* (1843) 40 The lines of Mason which were effaced and replaced by these. 1848 MACAULAY *Hist. Eng.* II. 440 Perhaps the passions excited by the tyranny of James might make it impossible to efface the penal laws from the statute book.

3. *fig.* To obliterate, wipe out (a memory, a mental impression); to 'blot out', pardon, obtain oblivion for (an offence); to abolish, destroy (distinctive characteristics, etc.).

1490 CAXTON *How to Die* 21 That effacest..the synnes of theym that ben repentaunt. *a* 1626 BACON in Webster, Efface from his mind the theories and notions vulgarly received. 1703 POPE *Thebais* 822 'Tis thine t' efface With virtuous acts thy ancestor's disgrace. 1738 WESLEY *Psalms* li. i, In tender Mercy look on me, And all my Sins efface. 1857 BUCKLE *Civilis.* viii. (1873) 456 An impression had been made upon the popular mind which it was hardly possible to efface. 1874 MORLEY *Compromise* (1886) 194 If such a proposition is true, the world must efface its habit of admiration for the..heroes of the past.

4. *fig.* To cast utterly into the shade, reduce to virtual nonentity. **b.** *refl.* [after Fr. *s'effacer*]. To reduce oneself to insignificance; to abandon or forfeit one's claim to consideration.

1716–8 LADY M. W. MONTAGUE *Lett.* I. xxxvii. 143 Her beauty effaced everything I have seen. 1871 M. COLLINS *Mrq. & Merch.* II. ii. 30 Amy Gray was..quite effaced. *Mod.* As a politician he has completely effaced himself by this act of imprudence.

effaceable (ɛ'feɪsəb(ə)l). [f. prec. + -ABLE.] Capable of being effaced.

1839 DICKENS *Nich. Nick.* vi, Washed off all effaceable marks of the late accident. 1881 MIVART *Cat* 27 Mucous membrane, when not stretched, is thrown into effaceable folds or rugæ.

effacement (ɛ'feɪsmənt). [f. as prec. + -MENT.] The process of effacing; the fact of being effaced.

1797 *Monthly Rev.* XXIII. 572 A state of simplicity.. subsequent to the effacement of the vices of barbarism. 1866 WEDGWOOD *Origin of Lang.* 7 Effacement of a sense from want of practice. 1876 MOZLEY *Univ. Serm.* v. 99 The effacement of the national sentiment is an artificial and violent evasion of a fact of nature.

effacing (ɛ'feɪsɪŋ), *ppl. a.* [f. EFFACE *v.* + -ING².] That effaces or obliterates.

1813 BYRON *Giaour* 73 Decay's effacing fingers. 1883 *Pall Mall G.* 12 Nov. 4/1 The effacing fingers of death were.. shockingly apparent on the Cardinal's visage.

effacive (ɛ'feɪsɪv). *nonce-wd.* [f. EFFACE *v.* + -IVE.] Disposed or tending to efface. *self-effacive*: modest, retiring.

1883 CAIRD *Edinbro' Lect. Hume* 23 Nov., In society he was the most self-effacive of men.

effald, -ly, obs. ff. AFALD, AFALDLY.

†**e'ffamish,** *v. Obs. rare.* [f. OF. *effamer* (cf. AFFAMISH, f. *affamer*), f. L. *ex-* out + *fam-es* hunger.] = FAMISH, *v.*

a 1603 T. CARTWRIGHT *Confut. Rhem. N.T.* (1618) Pref. 3 Being effamished, [they] are content..to eate it. 1634–46 ROW *Hist. Kirk* (1842) 137 Ministers shamefullie abused, they and their families effamished.

‖**effaré** (ɛ'fɑːreɪ), *a. Her.* [a. F. *effaré*, pa. pple. of *effarer* to agitate.] (See quot.)

1738 CHAMBERS *Cycl.* (ed. 2), *Effaré*, in heraldry, a term applied to a beast when rearing on its hind legs, as if it were affrighted. 1828 BERRY *Encycl. Her.* I. s.v. *Effeaé* or *Effaré*, a French term for a beast in the attitude which English Heralds call 'salient' or 'springing'.

†**e'ffascinable,** *a. Obs. rare*⁻¹. [as if ad. L. **effascinābilis*, f. *effascināre*: see next.] Susceptible to enchantment.

1660 H. MORE *Myst. Godl.* VII. xvii. 359 A strangely-impure and effascinable passivity of Phancie.

†**e'ffascinate,** *v. Obs.* Also 7 **effacinate.** [f. L. *effascināt-* ppl. stem of *effascināre*: see -ATE³.] = FASCINATE.

Hence **e'ffascinating** *ppl. a.*

1616 HOLYDAY *Persius* in Halliwell's *Shaks.* V. 330 Skilfull to depell the harmes Of an effascinating eye. 1624 HEYWOOD *Gunaik.* VIII. 399 Of force to effacinate the gods. 1670 G. H. *Hist. Cardinals* II. II. 143 He has..effascinated the hearts of the Court. 1678 H. MORE in Glanvill *Sadduc. Triumph.* (ed. 1727) 63.

†**e,ffasci'nation.** *Obs.* [ad. L. *ef-fascinātiōn-em*, f. *effascināre* to bewitch.] = FASCINATION.

1624 HEYWOOD *Gunaik.* VIII. 402 There are others whom their effascinations can keepe from eiecting their Vrine. 1650 CHARLETON *Paradoxes* 59 The effascination by the optick emission of the eyes. 1660 H. MORE *Myst. Godl.* VI. xiv. 255 Hood-winked and held down with an over-bearing effascination and witchcraft.

†**e'ffate.** *Obs.* [ad. L. *effātum*, f. *ef-fāri* to speak out.] A saying, dictum, maxim. Also ‖**e'ffatum** (pl. effata).

1650 ELDERFIELD *Tythes* 154 Their effata or most reverenced contents equalled by parliament to the oracles of the common law. 1678 GALE *Crt. Gentiles* III. 177 The effates of Scripture seem to contradict themselves. 1685 BOYLE *Enq. Notion Nat.* 294 The Effatum, That Nature abhors a Vacuum. 1690 NORRIS *Beatitudes* (1694) I. 118 That common Theological Effate, Grace is Glory begun.

†**e'ffatuate,** *ppl. a. Obs.* [as if ad. L. **effatuātus*, f. *ex-* out + *fatu-us* stupid, foolish: cf. AFFATUATED.] Infatuated.

1600 *Dr. Dodypoll* II. i. in Bullen *O. Pl.* (1884) III. 112 Had I not beene effatuate even by Fate.

†**e'ffatuate,** *v. Obs.* [f. prec.] *trans.* To besot, render dull or stupid.

1630 BRATHWAIT *Eng. Gentl.* (1641) 16 Nothing effatuates the understanding of man more than excesse in meat.

†**e'ffaut.** *Obs. Music.* Also (corruptly) **effauz.** The fuller name (F *fa ut*) of the note F, which was sung to the syllable *fa* or *ut* according as it occurred in one or other of the Hexachords (imperfect scales) to which it could belong.

a 1327 *Learn. Music* in *Rel. Ant.* I. 292 Of effauz and elami ne coud y nevere are. 1671 DK. BUCKHM. *Rehearsal* II. v, A certain note..in Effaut flat.

effect (ɛ'fɛkt), *sb.* Also 6 *Sc.* effeck. [a. OF. *effect* (F. *effet*), ad. L. *effectus*, n. of action f. *efficĕre* to work out, accomplish, f. *ex-* out + *făcĕre* to make.]

1. a. Something accomplished, caused, or produced; a result, consequence. Correlative with CAUSE.

c 1391 CHAUCER *Astrol.* I. §21 The planetes..causen us by hir influence..effectes lik to the operaciouns of bestes. 1485 CAXTON *Paris & V.* (1868) 6 Thy enterpryse came to none effect. 1572 JONES *Bathes of Bathes Ayde* III. 22 a, Cause of sicknesse is that unto which any thing followeth, which is named effecte. 1657 J. SMITH *Myst. Rhet.*, The Effect, is that which is brought to passe by the Cause. 1715 DESAGULIERS *Fires Impr.* 4 Contrivances..that are the Effect of a great deal of Study. 1736 BUTLER *Anal.* I. i. Wks. 1874 I. 16 We know not at all what death is in itself; but only some of its effects. 1751 HARRIS *Hermes* (1841) 119 Nature begins from causes, and thence descends to effects. 1831 BLAKEY *Free Will* 198 We..give the name of cause to that event which precedes, and the name of effect to that event which follows in the order of time. 1844 H. H. WILSON *Brit. India* III. 485 The beneficial effects of their interposition had given shelter and security to private trade.

b. *collective* and *abstr.* Results in general; the quality of producing a result, efficacy. Phrases, ***with effect, of no*** (†***none***) ***effect.***

c 1385 CHAUCER *L.G.W.* 620 Thing that beryth more effect. 1480 CAXTON *Chron. Eng.* ccxxv. 30 This ordynaunce ..was of lytell effect. 1538 STARKEY *England* 15 Thys law [*i.e.* civil law] takyth effecte of the opynyon of man. 1555 EDEN *Decades W. Ind.* I. IX. (Arb.) 99 Whose perfume is of most excellent effect to heale the reumes. 1611 BIBLE *Mark* vii. 13 Making the word of God of none effect through your tradition. 1667 MILTON *P.L.* IX. 865 This Tree is..of Divine effect To open Eyes. 1782 PRIESTLEY *Corrupt. Chr.* I. IV. 341 A law was made..but it had little effect. 1809 ROLAND *Fencing* 115 You may..throw his foil at a sufficient distance..to enable you to deliver a thrust with effect. 1865 CARLYLE *Fredk. Gt.* III. x. viii. 288 Respectful message to his Majesty was of no effect.

c. *Mechanics.* The amount of work done in a given time. ***useful effect***: the net result, after making deductions for loss from friction, etc.

1812–6 PLAYFAIR *Nat. Phil.* (1819) I. 111 The effect of animal force, then, or the quantity of work done in a given time will be proportional. 1871 B. STEWART *Heat* §389 An agent for generating mechanical effect.

d. Any of various phenomena of physical science, e.g. those connected with electric currents, usually named after the first

discoverer or describer of the appearance. See also DOPPLER, EINSTEIN, FARADAY, ZEEMAN.

1881 S. P. THOMPSON *Elem. Less. Electr. & Magn.* 343 This phenomenon of heating (or cooling) by a current, where it crosses the junction of two dissimilar metals (known as the 'Peltier effect', to distinguish it from the ordinary heating of a circuit where it offers a resistance to the current, which is sometimes called the 'Joule effect'). *Ibid.* 346 This effect, known as the Thomson effect from its discoverer Sir W. Thomson, is opposite in iron to what it is in copper or zinc. **1894** *Ibid.* 563 Kerr's Effect. Dr. Kerr showed in 1877 that a ray of polarized light is also rotated when reflected at the surface of a magnet or electromagnet.

e. *Psychol.* (See quots.)

1905 E. L. THORNDIKE *Elem. Psychol.* (1907) x. 166 This law..[of acquired connections] might be stated..as follows. (1) The line of least resistance is,..that resulting in the greatest satisfaction to the animal... We may call (1) the Law of Effect. **1922** R. S. WOODWORTH *Psychol.* 392 The law of effect, stated as objectively as possible, is simply that the successful or unsuccessful outcome or effect of a reaction determines whether it shall become firmly linked with the stimulus, or detached from the stimulus and thus eliminated. **1929** *Encycl. Brit.* XVIII. 683/1 The so-called 'Law of Effect',..which refers..more particularly to the acquisition of skill, and to the formation of habit. **1951** J. C. FLUGEL *Hundred Years Psychol.* (ed. 2) II. ii. 83 Thorndike and others owe to Bain the first clear formulation of what later became known as the 'law of effect' (the 'stamping in' of movements under the influence of pleasure).

2. †**a.** A contemplated result, a purpose; chiefly in phrases, ***to this*** or ***that effect, to the effect that*** (*obs.*). **b.** In the same phrases: Purport; drift, tenor, essential significance.

c **1386** CHAUCER *Merch. T.* 153 And for hise freendes on a day he sente To tellen hem theffect of his entente. **14..** *Pol. Rel. & L. Poems* (1866) 50 Theffect of whych was thus in dede. **1513** DOUGLAS *Æneis* VI. ii. 131 Ane othir goldin grane to the ilk effect Thow sall nocht mis. **1601** SHAKS. *Jul. C.* I. ii. 283 *Cask.* He spoke Greeke. *Cassi.* To what effect? **1652** WADSWORTH tr. *Sandoval's Civ. Wars Spain* 287 Hee incharged the same Don Pedro..to go and surprise the said Souldiers, giving him two hundred hors and five hundred Foot to that effect. **1818** CRUISE *Digest* II. 17 A subsequent proviso was added to that effect. **1872** MORLEY *Voltaire* (1886) 157 The famous reviewer's sentence..to the effect that, etc.

†**3. a.** An outward manifestation, sign, token, symptom; an appearance, phenomenon. *Obs.*

c **1450** *Why can't be Nun* 67 in *E.E.P.* (1862) 140 In a gardyne I sportyd me..to see The swete effecte of aprelle flowres. **1593** HOOKER *Eccl. Pol.* I. ii, His wisdome hath stinted the effects of his power. **1599** SHAKS. *Much Ado* II. iii. 112 What effects of passion shows she? **1656** COWLEY *Pind. Odes* (1669) 22 *note*, No natural effect gives such impressions of Divine fear, as Thunder.

b. A (pleasing or remarkable) combination of colour or form in a picture, a landscape, etc. Also of music (see also quot. 1938). Cf. 6.

1870 *Porcupine* 19 Mar. 492/3 The other perfectly unique 'Spohr effects' produced during the performance of this cantata. **1884** RUSKIN *Art of Eng.* 222 The old water-colour men were wont to obtain their effects of atmosphere by, etc. *a* **1891** *Mod.* The reflexion of the trees in the brook is a very pretty effect. Here's a painter with his sketch-book hunting for 'effects'. **1938** *Oxf. Compan. Mus.* 285/1, *Effects*, a term used in dance-band parlance..for imitative instruments such as various forms of whistle and anvil, baby cry..whip crack, &c. **1955** KEEPNEWS & GRAUER *Pictorial Hist. Jazz* ii. 19 They went in for cowbells and other dubious 'novelty' effects.

c. (Cf. STAGE-*effect*, *sound-effect*.) Now usu. in pl.: the various aids and contrivances (appropriate 'noises off', lighting, etc.) used to accompany and vivify the production of plays, films, or broadcasts. Also *attrib.*, as in ***effects studio, microphone***, etc.

1881 P. FITZGERALD *World behind Scenes* I. 46 Few pieces excited more mysterious interest on its first production than the spectral effect in the drama. *Ibid.* 70 One of the most startling and successful effects was given in a revival of 'Sardanapalus'... In the midst of the banqueting, a thunderbolt descended. **1911** C. N. BENNETT et al. *Handbk. Kinematogr.* ix. 69 We append a table of well-known tinting effects... Moonlight effect,..candle light and lamp light effects,..firelight effect. **1914** E. A. DENCH *Playwriting for Cinema* xviii. 78 Lighting effects often present a difficulty. **1928** *B.B.C. Handbk.* 268/2 *Effects Studio*, a studio in which the noise effects incidental to a transmission are made. **1933** A. BRUNEL *Filmcraft* 217 Salaries..wages..set-building materials..costumes..properties, laboratory charges, trick effects. **1941** *B.B.C. Gloss. Broadc. Terms* 10 *Effects*, sounds characteristic of a scene or incidental to an event, either produced artificially in order to create illusion (e.g. in a dramatic broadcast) or occurring naturally (e.g. in an outside broadcast); sound effects. Hence *effects microphone*, microphone specially placed to pick up such sounds. **1950** T. S. ELIOT *Cocktail Party* 40 She has simply faded—into some other picture—Like a film effect. **1951** N. MARSH *Opening Night* iv. 98 A stage-hand..carried an effects-gun. This was fired at the appropriate moment. **1961** K. REISZ *Technique Film Editing* (ed. 9) 279 *Effects track*, soundtrack of sound effects other than speech and music.

†**4. a.** Something which is attained or acquired by an action. *Obs.*

1602 SHAKS. *Ham.* III. iii. 54, I am still possest Of those effects for which I did the Murther.

b. *pl.* 'Goods and chattels', movable property. ***personal effects***: personal luggage as distinguished from merchandise, etc. Also with wider meaning in phrase ***no effects***: written by bankers on dishonoured cheques when the drawer has no funds in the bank; also, ***to leave no effects***: to leave nothing for one's heirs.

1704 J. LOGAN *Pa. Hist. Soc. Mem.* IX. 290 The effects of their plantations will scarce buy them clothes. **1711–14** ADDISON *Spect.* (J.), The Emperour knew that they could not convey away many of their Effects. **1843** THACKERAY *Ravenswing* v. (1887) 196 The bankers declined to cash the Captain's draft..simply writing the words 'No effects' on the paper. *Mod.* Sale of household effects. The contents of the trunks were insured as 'personal effects'. He died leaving no effects.

5. a. Operative influence; a mode or degree of operation on an object.

1668 *Phil. Trans.* I. 635 What Effects are thereby produced upon the body. **1831** BREWSTER *Nat. Magic.* vi. (1833) 149 It will act like a *concave* lens when the cooling effect has reached the axis. **1875** JOWETT *Plato* (ed. 2) I. 104 Speeches which will have an effect upon the courts. **1883** *Harper's Mag.* Sept. 562/1 The effects which the demand for aboriginality..had upon the race of builders.

b. The state or fact of being operative. ***to give effect to***: to render operative. ***to take effect***: to become operative: to prove successful; (of a law, an agreement, etc.) to come into force (*from* a certain date).

1771 GOLDSMITH *Hist. Eng.* ii. 62 The stratagem took effect; the English..began to fly on all sides. **1844** H. H. WILSON *Brit. India* I. 529 The Administration was willing to give effect..to the arrangements. **1868** FREEMAN *Norm. Conq.* (1876) II. App. 545 Eadward's grant was not to take effect till after the death of Ælfwine.

6. The impression produced on a beholder, hearer, or reader, *esp.* by a work of art or literature; sometimes = ***general effect***, the impression produced by a picture, building, etc., viewed as a whole. ***for effect***: for the sake of creating a telling impression on the minds of spectators or hearers.

1736 BUTLER *Anal.* II. iii. 328 What they call the effect in architecture. **1824** J. S. MILL in *Westm. Rev.* II. 347 He who writes for effect..must address himself to the prevalent feeling. **1868** GLADSTONE *Juv. Mundi* i. (1870) 16 With a view..to poetical effect. **1869** SWINBURNE *Ess. & Stud.* (1875) 219 His [Shelley's] aim is rather to render the effect of a thing than the thing itself. *Mod.* His whole behaviour and conversation are calculated for effect.

7. a. Accomplishment, fulfilment. Now only in phrases, ***to bring to effect, carry into effect***: to accomplish, bring to a successful issue; ***to put into effect***: to accomplish, to realize.

1483 CAXTON *Gold. Leg.* 389/1 Who someuer shal..calle me that he may haue..theffecte of his requeste & prayer. **1538** STARKEY *England* 195, I thynke hyt schold be very hard to bryng thys to effect. **1591** SHAKS. *Two Gent.* I. i. 50 Losing..the faire effects of future hopes. **1603** KNOLLES *Hist. Turks* (1621) 177 What he tooke in hand, he..brought to good effect. **1638** BRATHWAIT *Hist. Surv.* (1651) 403 Never bringing their designes to effect. **1705** *Col. Rec. Penn.* II. 208 The only means to bring all happily to effect. **1709** SWIFT *Adv. Relig.* Wks. 1755 II. I. 111 The proposals are..such as a pious active prince..might soon bring to effect. **1936** *Discovery* Sept. 296/1 A tireless film director who was forever having ideas and would not rest until they were put into effect successfully.

†**b.** Practical reality, fact, as opposed to name or appearance: see 8. *Obs.*

1606 SHAKS. *Tr. & Cr.* V. iii. 109 Meere words..Th' effect doth operate another way. *a* **1674** CLARENDON *Hist. Reb.* (1849) III. 545 He should depart only with a title, the effect whereof he should not be possessed of, before he had very well deserved it.

8. ***in effect***: formerly = in fact, in reality, opposed to *in show, in words*. In mod. use, virtually, substantially, so far as the result is concerned (see senses 1, 2).

1588 R. PARKE tr. *Mendoza's Hist. China* 243 With pretence to depart from thence vnto China, as in effect they did. *a* **1600** HOOKER (J.) In shew, a..senate..was to govern, but in effect one only man should..do all in all. **1626** BACON *Sylva* (J.), No man, in effect, doth accompany, but he learneth, ere he is aware, some gesture, or voice, or fashion. *a* **1668** DENHAM (J.) State and Wealth..is to him..No other in effect than what it seems. *a* **1719** ADDISON (J.) To say of a celebrated piece that there are faults in it, is, in effect, to say that the author of it is a man. **1804** H. T. COLEBROOKE *Husbandry Bengal* (1806) 37 The duties are paid..by the purchaser; but the charge in effect falls upon the importer. *Mod.* The two methods are in effect identical. He was, in effect, accused of falsehood. I cannot tell you what he said, but in effect it was that he, etc.

9. [After Fr. *effet*.] (See quot.)

1738 CHAMBERS *Cycl.*, Effect in the manage, is applied to the movements of the hand which direct the horse. They distinguish four effects,..viz. in using the bridle to put a horse forwards, draw him backwards, and shifting it out of the right hand into the left, and vice versa.

effect (ɛˈfɛkt), *v.* [f. prec. sb.]

1. a. *trans.* To bring about (an event, a result); to accomplish (an intention, a desire).

The existence of obstacles or difficulties is, in mod. use, ordinarily implied in this sense of the vb.

1589 WARNER *Alb. Eng.* VI. xxxi. (1612) 154 And nothing else I did effect but to effect my sute. **1593** SHAKS. *3 Hen. VI*, II. vi. 98 Ile crosse the Sea To effect this marriage. **1635** QUARLES *Embl.* I. vi. (1718) 25 Let wit, and all her studied plots effect The best they can. **1718** *Free-thinker* No. 90. 244 At first they only wish to be secure; that effected, they endeavour to grow Powerful. **1792** *Anec. W. Pitt* III. xliv. 196 Peace..would never be effected. **1833** LARDNER *Manuf. Metal* II. 227 (Cab. Cycl.) This reciprocating movement of the carriage is effected by a pinion fixed upon the end of a vertical spindle. **1837** DISRAELI *Venetia* IV. i. (1871) 203 Just effected his escape as the servant announced a visitor. **1850** BROWNING *Easter-Day* 5 Effecting thus, complete and whole, a purpose of the human soul. **1875** JOWETT *Plato* (ed. 2) I. 13 The cure..has to be effected by the use of certain charms. **1878** HUXLEY *Physiogr.* 105 The most skilful chemists have hitherto failed to effect such decomposition.

†**b.** To produce (a state or condition). *Obs.*

1596 SHAKS. *Tam. Shr.* I. i. 86 Sorrie am I that our goodwill effects Biancas greefe. **1655–60** STANLEY *Hist. Philos.* (1701) 135/1 The concurrence of Pleasures which effecteth Beatitude, is very difficult.

c. To make, construct. *rare. arch.*

1791 SMEATON *Edystone L.* §75 The Lighthouse happily effected by Mr. Rudyerd. **1884** STEVENSON *New Arab. Nts.* 317 An enormous window..had been effected in the wall.

d. Comm. ***to effect a sale, an insurance***; hence, ***to effect a policy*** (of insurance).

1866 ROGERS *Agric. & Prices* I. xxiii. 598 The earliest purchases are effected in immediate proximity to the mines. **1883** *Manch. Guard.* 17 Oct. 5/4 Nominee life policies are often effected which are altogether invalid.

†**2.** To give effect to (a resolution, a feeling); to fulfil (a promise). *Obs.*

c **1590** MARLOWE *Faust.* v. 95 Faustus I swear..To effect all promises between us made. **1606** SHAKS. *Tr. & Cr.* V. x. 6 You heauens, effect your rage with speede. **1660** MARVELL *Corr.* iii. Wks. 1872–5 II. 20 We shall be called upon shortly to effect our vote made the former sitting.

†**3.** *absol.* and *intr.* To have an effect, be effectual; to accomplish its purpose. *Obs.*

1592 WARNER *Alb. Eng.* VII. xxxiv. (1612) 164 But that Cadwalladers Fore-doomes in Tuders should effect Was vnexpected. **1603** KNOLLES *Hist. Turkes* (1621) 1330 The petard having effected as we have said. **1655–60** STANLEY *Hist. Philos.* (1701) 161/2 Elements, of which Air and Fire have a faculty to move and effect. **1817** A. CONSTABLE *Let.* 16 Jan. in *J. Constable's Corr.* (1962) 153, I..hope you will ..endeavour to make all right with the Doctor, even tho' as by this time you know I dare say that your first letter did not effect.

¶**4.** Confused with AFFECT (? and INFECT).

1494 FABYAN VII. 371 The Albygensis..had been effected wt dyuers poyntes of herysy. **1652** WADSWORTH tr. *Sandoval's Civ. Wars Spain* 301 The Abbat of Santa Pia.. whom the earl particularly esteemed and effected. **1729** T. COOKE *Tales, Prop. &c.* 135 His words effected much the Laureat's Mind. **1772–84** COOK *Voy.* (1790) IV. 1279 He effects to preserve an entire silence about Kerguelen.

†**eˈffected,** *ppl. a. Obs. rare.* [f. EFFECT *v.* + -ED; prob. confused with AFFECTED.] With *adv.* (*well*, etc.) prefixed; Affected, disposed.

1604 HIERON *Wks.* (1619–20) I. 503 Holy men..haue.. bin the meanes of much comfort to well effected people. **1640–1** *Kirkcudbr. War-Comm. Min. Bk.* (1855) 61 Thair are sundrie persones..evill effected to the caus.

effecter (ɛˈfɛktə(r)). Also 7 effectour, 7–8 effector. [f. EFFECT *v.* + -ER, or a. L. *effector*.]

1. He who, or that which, brings about an event or result, accomplishes a purpose, etc.

1601 DEACON & WALKER *Spirits & Div.* 202 The howerly effectours of many admirable actions. **1610** HEALEY *St. Aug. City of God* 447 Wee shall make his nature the effecter of his vicious will. **1611** MARKHAM *Countr. Content.* I. xiii. (1668) 66 Baits and inticements..are effecters of our desires in this pastime. **1662** CHANDLER *Van Helmont's Oriat.* 151 They blame the Air as the effecter of all corruptions whatsoever. **1713** DERHAM *Phys.-Theol.* II. vi. 475 That infinite Being, who was the Effector of it [Creation]. **1863** VANCE in *Sat. Rev.* 415 Had the translation of Saintré to be entered on afresh, it is not..certain that I had been the effecter of the same.

†**2.** A maker, creator. *Obs.*

1635 HEYWOOD *Hierarch.* II. 67 One Monarch of the world the great Effector. **1677** GALE *Crt. Gentiles* II. IV. 242 The omnipotent Effector and Productor of al things.

¶ = AFFECTER 1. *Obs.*

1641 BAKER *Chron.* (1679) 179/1 He was indeed a great effecter of glory.

†**eˈffectfull,** *a. Obs.* In 6 *Sc.* effecf-. [f. EFFECT + -FULL.] Effectual.

1555 *Sc. Acts Mary* xviii, Our souerane Lady in her parliament..maid actis..quhilkis as yit hes tane na dew and effecfull execucion. **1669** SIMPSON *Hydrol. Chym.* 78 The effectual cause of direful diseases.

eˈffectible (ɛˈfɛktɪb(ə)l), *a.* [f. EFFECT *v.* + -IBLE.] Capable of being effected.

1646 SIR T. BROWNE *Pseud. Ep.* II. v. 87 Not effectible upon the strictest experiment. **1650** *Descr. Future Hist. Europe* 14 His Decrees most effectible, when we think him the furthest off. **1677** HALE *Prim. Orig. Man.* IV. v. 338 Whatsoever..is effectible by the most congruous and efficacious application of Actives to Passives.

effecting (ɛˈfɛktɪŋ), *vbl. sb.* [f. EFFECT *v.* + -ING[1].] The action of the verb EFFECT.

1581 MULCASTER *Positions* (1887) Ep. Ded. 6 The effecting wherof pretendeth great honour to your Maiesties person. **1609** ROWLANDS *Knaue of Clubbes* 17 Although the plot..by thee was lai'd, Th' effecting of it by me thou didst obtaine. **1671** FLAVEL *Fount. Life* vi. 15 In order to the sure effecting of this Design.

¶Used gerundially with omission of *in*: virtually serving the function of a pr. pple. passive.

1789 GOUV. MORRIS in Sparks *Life & Writ.* (1832) II. 88 Four sentiments on the revolution effecting here. **1818** JAS. MILL *Brit. India* II. v. i. 325 During the time in which this great revolution was effecting in the government of Bengal. **1826** DISRAELI *Viv. Grey* I. ix. 21 Ought you not to congratulate yourself that a great change is effecting?

eˈffecting, *ppl. a.* [f. as prec. + -ING[2].] That effects.

Hence **eˈffectingness** = EFFICACIOUSNESS.

1768–74 TUCKER *Lt. Nat.* (1852) II. 179 If we are instructed to believe the particular effectingness of a

religious discourse proceeds from the workings of the Spirit, etc.

†e'ffection. *Obs.* [ad. L. *effectiōn-em*, f. *efficĕre*: see EFFECT *sb.*]

1. a. Fabrication, formation, production.
1430 LYDG. *Chron. Troy* II. xvii, An ymage..All of brent golde by false effection. **1677** HALE *Prim. Orig. Man.* 290 Attributing the Effection of the Soul unto the Great God. *Ibid.* IV. vii. 350 The primitive Effection of the Humane Nature.

b. Accomplishment, performance.
1652 GAULE *Magastrom.* 53 To invent..their own way for the cognition, acquisition, or effection of any thing. **1656** JEANES *Fuln. Christ* 151 The incarnation..belongs unto all the three Persons *effectivè*, in regard of effection.

†2. *Geom.* A construction; a proposition; a problem or praxis drawn from some general proposition. (Todd.) *Obs.*
1706 in PHILLIPS. **1796** HUTTON *Math. Dict.* **1818** in TODD; and in mod. Dicts.

¶ Confused with AFFECTION and INFECTION.
1398 TREVISA *Barth. De P.R.* v. xxiii. (1495) 131 A swete voyce..chaungith the effeccion of the herers. **1555** EDEN *Decades W. Ind.* II. III. (Arb.) 115 Of such force is education & natural effection. **1544** PHAER *Regim. Lyfe* (1560) N ij, Beware of..fennes, for oftentymes the effection of the aire, ariseth of the corrupte vapoures.

effectism (ɛ'fɛktɪz(ə)m). *rare.* [f. EFFECT + -ISM.] The habit of aiming at 'effect'.
1871 H. B. FORMAN *Living Poets* 472 Any flimsy effectism of plot. **1889** *Harper's Mag.* Nov. 964/1 The vice which has been very graphically called *effectism*, or the itch of awaking at all cost in the reader vivid and violent emotions.

effective (ɛ'fɛktɪv), *a.* and *sb.* [a. F. *effectif, -ive*, ad. L. *effectīvus*: see EFFECT *v.* and -IVE.]

A. *adj.*

†1. a. That is concerned in the production *of* (an event or condition; *rarely*, a material product).
1594 T. B. *La Primaud. Fr. Acad.* II. 379 Powers..are effectiue principles of all actions. **1607** *Schol. Disc. agst. Antichr.* I. ii. 91 The signe of the Crosse is..effectiue of grace. **1677** GALE *Crt. Gentiles* II. IV. 170 Politic Philosophie is defined..a Science effective of Justice in the Citie. **1684** tr. *Bonet's Merc. Compit.* VI. 193 In the Tertian [Ague] the part effective of the bloud is out of its natural temper.

†b. Having the power of acting upon objects.
1646 SIR T. BROWNE *Pseud. Ep.* 214 Time is not effective, nor are bodies destroyed by it, but from the action and passion of their Elements in it. *a* **1652** J. SMITH *Sel. Disc.* v. 139 The more unbodied any thing is, the more unbounded also is it in its effective power.

†2. Concerned with, or having the function of, carrying into effect, executing, or accomplishing.
c **1425** WYNTOUN *Cron.* IX. xxvii. 256 Ðis wes þe Proces causative, Ðat eftyr folowit effective. **1597** MORLEY *Introd. Mus.* Annot., Musicke is diuided into two parts..The second may be called syntactical, Poetical, or effectiue. **1607** *Schol. Disc. agst. Antichr.* I. i. 33 The former was significatiue onely, his effectiue.

3. a. That is attended with result or has an effect.
1760 GOLDSMITH *Cit. W.* I. (1837) 200 There is an effective power superior to the people. **1776** ADAM SMITH *W.N.* I. I. x. 149 The masters alone had an effective voice in the legislation. **1863** BURTON *Bk. Hunter* 90 The honour of the first effective shot.

b. In mechanical and economical science: Said of that portion of an agency or force which is actually brought to bear on a particular object.
1798 MALTHUS *Popul.* III. x. (1806) II. 250 The quantity of effective capital employed in agriculture. **1825** J. NICHOLSON *Operat. Mechanic* 67 This we call the virtual or effective head [of water]. **1879** THOMSON & TAIT *Nat. Phil.* I. I. §228 The Component of a force in any direction, (sometimes called the Effective Component in that direction).

c. Theol. ***effective faith, love***, etc.: that bears fruit in conduct [med.L. *effectivus*].
1854 F. W. FABER *Growth in Holiness* v. (1872) 75 Effective love makes us the living images of Jesus.

d. ***effective range***: the range within which a missile, weapon, or fire-arm is effective.
1859 FROUDE *Hist. Eng.* (1858) I. i. 65 Two hundred and twenty yards..is to be taken as the effective range for fighting purposes of the old archery.

e. ***effective temperature***: see quots. 1929, 1930, 1957.
1915 *Sci. Amer.* 3 Apr. 328/2 Whereas in the case of terrestrial illuminants the actual temperature can be gaged, we must be satisfied with determining the *effective* temperatures of celestial bodies. Supposing the sun to radiate like a 'black' body,..its 'effective' or 'black' temperature can be determined from the sum total of radiation sent to the earth (solar constant). **1924** H. DINGLE *Mod. Astrophysics* ix. 119 The wavelength of maximum energy, from which the effective temperature is determined. **1929** R. A. WARDLE *Princ. Applied Zool.* 197 There would seem to be for each species of insect a range of temperatures between whose maximum and minimum extremes the insect is active... This range of temperatures may be termed the range of Effective Temperatures. **1930** *Engineering* 28 Nov. 671/1 The effective temperature of a room, that is to say, the temperature at which, in still air, a sizeable black body at standard temperature will lose heat at the same rate as it is being lost in its environment. **1957** *Encycl. Brit.* XVII. 847F/2 The term 'effective temperature' was sometimes used to denote what we now call 'colour temperature'. 'Effective temperature' is now used to denote the temperature of a black body for which the total emitted radiation..is the same as the total radiation..emitted from the surface of a star.

f. *Philology.* Denoting the completion or result of an action. Cf. EFFECTIVE *sb.* 3.
1932 *Jrnl. Eng. & Germanic Philol.* XXXI. 251 The latter class may be called the effective aspect: 'His strength *gave out*', i.e., he came to the end of his strength. **1970** *Language* XLVI. 300 The *-t* forms were predominantly selected..for preterits in contexts suggestive of non-durative ('effective') aspect.

g. Optics. ***effective aperture***, the diameter of the widest beam of light incident on an optical system that goes to form an image, whether formed at a principal focus or not.
1893 *Proc. R. Soc.* LII. 412 The effective aperture of one or more of the various stops supplied with the lens is found by a well-known method. **1965** M. J. LANGFORD *Basic Photogr.* iii. 54 As the aperture closes the diameter of this incident light beam or 'Effective Aperture' narrows proportionally.

4. a. Powerful in effect; efficient, effectual.
1398 TREVISA *Barth. De P.R.* XVII. lxxxiv. (1495) 654 Oleum iuniperium is most effectyf ayenst the Quartayn. **1836** *Random Recoll. Ho. Lords* xvi. 402 He does not speak often; nor can he be considered an effective speaker. **1837** HOWITT *Rur. Life* (1862) I. iv. 30 Contributed to make these pursuits effective, elegant, and attractive. **1856** EMERSON *Eng. Traits, Land* Wks. (Bohn) II. 17 Its best admiral could not have..anchored it [England] in a more effective position. **1860** HAWTHORNE *Marb. Faun* xliii. 338 An Italian comedy..effective over everybody's risibilities. **1879** FROUDE *Cæsar* iv. 39 Fewer men, better trained and disciplined, could be made more effective.

b. Of works of art, literary compositions, etc.: Producing a striking impression; picturesque.
1853 G. JOHNSTON *Nat. Hist. E. Bord.* I. 107 The high bank..is..rendered effective by a perpendicular wall of naked sandstone. **1872** FREEMAN *Hist. Ess.* 21 It is not one suited to produce any very effective romantic narrative. **1882** *Garden* 18 Feb. 119/1 Varieties of Amarantus are..effective in the..garden.

5. a. Fit for work or service: chiefly of soldiers or sailors. (Also *absol.*; see B. 2.)
1684 *Scanderbeg Rediv.* v. 105 Being not above 15 or 16000 Men Effective. **1701** *Lond. Gaz.* No. 3733/4 The Imperial Army is said to consist of 44000 Effective Men. **1791** SMEATON *Edystone L.* §295 The copper-smiths..were not likely very soon to be effective. **1865** CARLYLE *Fredk. Gt.* VII. XVIII. i. 93 Army of 60,000 on paper; of effective more than 50,000.

b. ***effective charge***: the expenditure upon effective forces, as distinguished, *e.g.*, from that upon military pensions, retired pay, etc.
1848 MACAULAY *Hist. Eng.* I. 306 The whole effective charge of the army, navy, and ordnance, was about seven hundred and fifty thousand pounds.

6. a. Actual, *de facto*; existing in fact; that is...so far as the effect is concerned; opposed to ***potential, nominal***.
1786 BURKE *Art. W. Hastings* Wks. 1842 II. 113 Afterwards displacing two effective governours..appointed by himself. **1790** —— *Fr. Rev.* 9 The collection of an effective and well-distributed revenue. **17..** BENTHAM *Levelling Syst.* Wks. 1843 I. 361 Those..whose present fortunes are above the mark..would be but a small part of the real and effective losers. **1878** GURNEY *Crystallogr.* 39 Potential and not effective planes of symmetry.

b. ***effective money***; also quasi-*sb.* (see quot.).
1858 SIMMONDS *Dict. Trade, Effective*, a term used in many parts of the Continent to express coin in contradistinction to paper money. Thus bills on Vienna are generally directed to be paid in effective.

B. *sb.* **†1.** An efficient cause. *Obs.* See A. 5.
1610 HEALEY *St. Aug. City of God* XII. xxv. (1620) 442 Had the eye, the apple..their rotundity, not from any externall effectiue. **1686** GOAD *Celest. Bodies* I. i. 1 No less are they the due Effective of the former.

2. *Mil.* **a.** An effective soldier. (See A. 5.) Usually *pl.*
1722 *Lond. Gaz.* No. 6060/1 The Garrisons..consist of 1000 Effectives. **1809** WELLINGTON *Let.* in Gurw. *Disp.* IV. 478 An abstract..which shows the comparative numbers of effectives and total. **1876** BANCROFT *Hist. U.S.* VI. xxiv. 4 They counted nine thousand effectives.

b. *collect. sing.* The effective part of an army.
1885 *Standard* 29 Oct. 5/5 The effective of the Turkish forces in the Balkan Peninsula now reaches 180,000 men.

3. An effective verb or an effective aspect or part of a verb. Cf. A 3 f.
1935 CURME *Gram. Eng. Lang.* II. xii. 237 In duratives, ingressives, effectives..the present participle represents the act as incomplete.

effectively (ɛ'fɛktɪvlɪ), *adv.* [f. prec. + -LY².]

†1. As a means of causing or producing. Cf. quot. 1607 in EFFECTIVE *a.* 1.
1607 *Schol. Disc. agst. Antichr.* I. i. 34 That [the sign of imposing hands] is effectiuely vsed, is out of the question.

†2. a. By a direct exercise of power. **b.** With regard to the effects. (Chiefly *Theol.*) *Obs.*
1644 BP. MAXWELL *Prerog. Chr. Kings* i. 16 This [deposing an emperor] is done by the Pope..not effectively but consecutively. **1652** GAULE *Magastrom.* 85 Whether the planets have (either actually and formally, in themselves, or virtually and effectively upon others) those prime elementary qualities. **1656** JEANES *Fuln. Christ* 211 [God's love to Christ] is said to be in believers..not onely effectively, in regard of its effects, grace, and glory; but also objectively.

3. = *in effect* (see EFFECT *sb.* 8): **†a.** Actually, in fact (*obs.*). **b.** Virtually, substantially.
1659 *Gentl. Call.* (1696) 43 A rectified Will..alone..effectively gives us the preeminence above Beasts. **1671** DRYDEN *Even. Love* IV. i, Don Melchor..is effectively at Madrid. **1844** MACKINTOSH *T. More* Wks. 1846 I. 442 It is not equitable to treat him as effectively..answerable for measures of state. **1884** *Harper's Mag.* Oct. 796/2 Effectively England is a republic and not a monarchy.

4. So as to produce an effect. Often *emphatically*: With powerful effect; decisively, completely.
1825 MᶜCULLOCH *Pol. Econ.* II. ii. 104 Give to any people the power of accumulating, and..they will not be disinclined to use it effectively. **1833** I. TAYLOR *Fanat.* v. 113 Mohammed..effectively cashiered from his system every pure and spiritual conception of virtue. **1858** FROUDE *Hist. Eng.* III. xvi. 374 A parliament composed of other members than those who had sate so long and so effectively. **1878** R. W. DALE *Lect. Preach.* vi. 163 If we can preach without reading, we are likely to preach more effectively.

5. In a manner to be fit for service. Cf. EFFECTIVE A. 5.
1665 PEPYS *Diary* 18 Sept., 10,000 men effectively always in armes. *a* **1667** COWLEY *Anacreont.* (1710) I. 52 The fair Ionian Regiment. And next the Carian Company, Five hundred both effectively.

e'ffectiveness. [f. EFFECTIVE *a.* + -NESS.] The quality of being effective, in various senses.
1607 *Schol. Disc. agst. Antichr.* I. i. 34 We agree in many vses with them [the Papists], but one of their vses (to wit) their effectiuenes we forbeare. **1678** CUDWORTH *Intell. Syst.* 583 Infinite self-activity or effectiveness. **1830** ARNOLD *Jrnl.* in *Life* (1858) II. 336 The comforts and effectiveness of society. **1836** *Random Recoll. Ho. Lords* x. 227 Effectiveness in debate. **1879** ROGERS in *Cassell's Techn. Educ.* IV. 53/2 The labour is average in point of effectiveness.

effectless (ɛ'fɛktlɪs), *a.* [f. EFFECT *sb.* + -LESS.] Without effect, fruitless: also quasi-*adv.*
1588 SHAKS. *Tit. A.* III. i. 76 Ile chop off my hands..they haue seru'd me to effectlesse vse. **1673** O. WALKER *Education* 8 Both Capacity and Instruction are effectles without practise and exercise. **1755** T. H. CROKER *Orl. Furioso* XIV. lxxiii, Nor were his fervent prayers effectless said. **1815** W. TAYLOR in Robberds *Mem.* II. 459 Silence alike improbable and effectless. **1851** RUSKIN *Mod. Paint.* II. III. I. v. §5 The sun itself at noonday is effectless upon the feelings.

effector (ɛ'fɛktər). **1.** As a variant of EFFECTER.

2. *Biol.* In attrib. use or as adj., or sb., applied to an organ which shows the specific effect of a nervous reaction.
1906 C. S. SHERRINGTON *Integrative Action Nerv. Syst.* i. 7 An *effector* organ, e.g., gland cells or muscle cells. *Ibid.* ix. 309 The conductor mediating between receptor and effector. *Ibid.*, At the deep, i.e. effector, end the branching of the conductive stem places it in touch not with one effective cell but with many. **1920** T. P. NUNN *Education: its Data & First Princ.* 166 Connector-axons which make their way to effector-neurones entirely outside the cord. **1927** W. SHUMWAY *Vert. Embryol.* 186 The sense organs (receptors) from the nerves (transmittors) by which stimuli are passed on to the muscles or glands (effectors). **1927** S. W. RANSON *Anat. Nerv. Syst.* (ed. 3) 18 A sensitive mechanism for receiving stimuli and conducting them to the appropriate organs of response. These organs..are known as effectors. **1952** *Brit. Jrnl. Psychol.* Feb. 18 To keep his attention one step ahead of his effector performance, or any decrease of effector accuracy. **1962** *Gray's Anat.* (ed. 33) 943 (*caption*) Effector neurones. Effector organs. *Ibid.*, Specialized receptors are differentiated at the surface of the body for the receipt of the stimulus and specialised effectors, either muscle or secretory cells, are differentiated for the response. **1968** *Lebende Sprachen* XIII. 39/1 Such an adaptive system requires..an effector mechanism for adaptively seeking that goal condition.

†effectress (ɛ'fɛktrɪs). *Obs.* [f. EFFECTER + -ESS.] A female effecter. (Cf. next.)
1601 CORNWALLYES *Ess.* II. xxxviii. (1631) 152 It is so certaine an effectresse of things prosperity. **1615** G. SANDYS *Trav.* 8 The Virgin Marie..reputed an effectresse of miracles. **1662** J. CHANDLER *Van Helmont's Oriat.* 143 The effectress of a thingliness or essence.

‖e'ffectrix. [L.; fem. of *effector* EFFECTER: see -TRIX. (In mod philosophical L. used in apposition with *causa, vis.*)] An efficient cause or power.
1610 BARROUGH *Meth. Physick* III. i. (1639) 100 Weaknesse of the stomack is sometime caused through distemper of the effectrix or working quality.

†e'ffectuable, *a.* *Obs.* *rare*⁻¹. [f. Fr. *effectu-er* + -ABLE.] That can be effectuated.
1611 SPEED *Hist. Gt. Brit.* IX. xvi, It was a worke worthy of his labour..and not easily effectuable.

effectual (ɛ'fɛktjuəl), *a.* Also 4–5 **effectuell.** [a. OF. *effectuel*:—late L. *effectuālis*, f. *effect-us* EFFECT *sb.*: see -AL¹.]

1. That produces its intended effect, or adequately answers its purpose. Of legal documents or convenants: Valid, binding.
c **1386** CHAUCER *Sompn. T.* 162 Our orisouns ben more effectuel. **1485** *Act 1 Hen. VII, Annex. Ducat. Lanc.* Ruffhead IX. App. 106 Every such Lese..be as good effectual and available in the Law. *c* **1489** CAXTON *Sonnes of Aymon* vi. 151 To bryng the matere to a conclusion effectuell. **1664** EVELYN *Kal. Hort.* (1729) 232 One single Pipe of competent bore, would be as effectual as three our four. *a* **1687** PETTY *Pol. Arith.* (1690) 73 The Charge of the Government..would be more..effectual. **1794** BURKE *Corr.* (1844) IV. 205 We must endeavour to make our complaints rather effectual than loud. **1884** EARL SELBORNE in *Law Times Rep.* 1 Mar., Registration does not make effectual a document which was..inoperative and of no effect.

b. Theol. *effectual calling* (see quot.). So also *effectual grace*: the special grace given to those elected to salvation.

1609 BIBLE (Douay) Index, Grace sufficient is geven to every one, effectual of Gods especial mercie to some. **1648** *Shorter Catech.*, Effectual calling is the work of God's Spirit, whereby..he doth persuade and enable us to embrace Jesus Christ. **1662** STILLINGFL. *Orig. Sacr.* III. iii. §7 If God withdrew not any effectuall grace from man.

c. *effectual demand*: in Political Economy.

1776 ADAM SMITH *W.N.* I. I. vii. 58 Such people may be called effectual demanders, and their demand the effectual demand; since it may be sufficient to effectuate the bringing of the commodity to market. **1798** MALTHUS *Popul.* III. x. (1806) II. 250 The sole cause which would determine the quantity of effective capital employed in agriculture would be the extent of the effectual demand for corn. **1868** ROGERS *Pol. Econ.* iii. (ed. 3) 21 And this demand must be effectual, that is, must be accompanied with the power of proffering some other object in exchange.

†**2.** = EFFECTIVE in various senses. *Obs.*

1398 TREVISA *Barth. De P.R.* XIII. xxvi. (1495) 462 The more whyte..a perle is, the more effectuell and vertuous it is holde. **1586** BRIGHT *Melanch.* x. 44, I take it..to be an effectuall & pregnant substance. **1662** MARVELL *Corr.* xxxv. Wks. 1872–5 II. 79 My Lord of Bath, who is..as effectuall an hand as can be chosen in the whole Court. **1674** PLAYFORD *Skill Mus.* I. 60 With his Harp he expressed such effectual melody and Harmony. **1689** BP. G. WALKER *Siege Derry* 37 We also got into our Garrison some Effectual Men out of their number.

†**3.** *effectual cause*: = efficient cause. *Obs.*

1581 W. STAFFORD *Exam. Compl.* iii. (1876) 83, I must.. try out the effectuall cause of these inclosures.

4. Of prayers, entreaties: earnest, urgent (see also 1).

Cf. Anglo-Lat. *effectuose supplicantes* 'earnestly entreating', A.D. 1229 in Rymer I. 308. Perhaps this use was originally due to confusion with AFFECTUAL; but the translators of the A.V. ingeniously availed themselves of it in *James* v. 16 to render Gr. ἐνεργουμένη (R.V. 'in its working').

[cf. **1386** in 1.] **1440** [see EFFECTUALLY 2]. **1547** *Bidding Prayer*, Ye shall also make your harty and effectual prayer to Almighty God for the peace of all Christian regions. **1611** BIBLE *James* v. 16 The effectual fervent prayer of a righteous man availeth much. **1616** N. BRENT tr. *Sarpi's Hist. Counc. Trent* (1676) 505 Letters came..with most effectual exhortations, in the Popes name, to accommodate the differences.

†**5.** ? Actual, now existing. *Obs.*

1598 J. HEYWOOD (*title*), Workes, namelie a Dialogue, where-in are pleasantlie contrived the number of all the effectual Proverbs in our English tongue. **1655** FULLER *Ch. Hist.* II. 116 The Danes had London..and Alfred onely three effectuall Shires.

†**6.** 'To the point', pertinent, conclusive. *Obs.*

1593 SHAKS. *2 Hen. VI*, III. i. 41 Reprove my allegation.. Or else conclude my words effectuall. **1608** *Yorksh. Trag.* I. iv. 207 'Tis..my fashion..to be plain and effectual. **1625** MEADE in Ellis *Orig. Lett.* I. 315 III. 203 He would give a speedy and effectual answer. **1677** MARVELL *Corr.* cccviii. Wks. 1872–5 II. 552 There will be no mony given this sitting, but upon very visible and effectuall termes.

effectu'ality. [f. prec. + -ITY.] The quality of being effectual.

a **1641** MOUNTAGU *Acts & Mon.* (1642) 132 The nature, condition, force, and effectuality of grace. **1758** *Herald* II. 46 No. 18 The simplicity, facility, and effectuality of my scheme is undeniably a proof, etc. **1865** CARLYLE *Fredk. Gt.* VI. xv. ix. 52 Solidity, brilliant effectuality, shining through all he does.

effectually (ɛ'fɛktjʊəlɪ), *adv.* [f. as prec. + -LY².]

1. a. So as adequately to answer the purpose.

c **1375** WYCLIF *Wks.* (1880) 385 ȝif a man schuld do effectualy almes. **1466** SIR J. FELBRIGGE in *Paston Lett.* 538 II. 255 Yff yt please your gentylnesse to be effectualy my frend. **1576** LAMBARDE *Peramb. Kent* (1826) Introd. 8, I know not how I may more fitly and effectually commend it than to say, etc. **1662** FULLER *Worthies* (1840) III. 119 Doing his charity effectually, but with a possible privacy. **1699** BENTLEY *Phal.* 159, I have already effectually confuted Pausanias's date of Anaxilas. **1711** ADDISON *Spect.* No. 98 ¶4 An excessive Head-dress may be attacked the most effectually when the Fashion is against it. **1818** CRUISE *Digest* II. 359 Any conveyance by the covenantor..will effectually destroy all contingent uses. **1880** HAUGHTON *Phys. Geog.* v. 205 The equatorial meridian chain has so effectually robbed the eastern Trade Winds of their vapour.

b. *Theol.* See EFFECTUAL 1 b.

1634 CANNE *Necess. Separ.* (1849) 225 We have been partakers of the true word and sacraments, and many of us effectually called thereby.

†**2.** Of entreaties, prayers, etc. (cf. AFFECTUALLY): Earnestly, ardently. *Obs.*

c **1440** *Gesta Rom.* xxxiii. 352 (Add. MS.) We pray the effectually of one counsaile..and help. **1478** C. REYNFORTH in *Paston Lett.* 813 III. 221 Effectually desyryng to here of yowr welfare. **1528** MORE *Heresyes* I. Wks. (1557) 167/2 He meruaylous effectually besecheth christen people to agre. **1578** *Chr. Prayers* in *Priv. Prayers* (1851) 457 Grace to pray effectually.

†**3.** Pertinently, to the purpose, explicitly. *Obs.*

1583 T. WATSON *Poems* (Arb.) 78 Plainely and effectually set downe, albeit in fewe wordes. **1633** T. STAFFORD *Pac. Hib.* xiii. 146 Write to me effectually your Lordships mind.

†**4.** As the effect of a cause. *Obs.*

1398 TREVISA *Barth. De P.R.* XIX. cxvi. 921 Of him that is one god in substaunce comyth all creatures effectually.

†**5.** In effect; in fact, in reality. *Obs.*

c **1600** SHAKS. *Sonn.* cxiii, Mine eye..Seemes seeing, but effectually is out. **1662** J. BARGRAVE *Pope Alex. VII* (1867) 18 There arrived..a gentleman traveller..but effectually he was the Pope's nuntio. **1768** STERNE *Sent. Journ.* (1778) I. 35 Something darken'd the passage..it was effectually Mons. Dessein.

effectualness (ɛ'fɛktjʊəlnɪs). Now *rare.* [f. as prec. + -NESS.] The quality of being effectual; the power of producing effects; efficacy.

1545 *Pref. Hen. VIII's Primer* in Wilkins *Concilia* III. 873 The pith or effectualnes [Lat. *vim*] of the talke. **1587** GOLDING *De Mornay* xxx. (1617) 523 The effectualnesse of his doctrine in the curing of mens soules. **1621** AINSWORTH *Annot. Pentat.* Ex. iv. 7 A thing done in the bosome signifieth secresie and effectualnesse. **1696** STILLINGFL. *Serm.* I. IV. (R.) From the effectualness of it in order to that end, it is the power of God to salvation. **1877** M. ARNOLD *Last Ess. Ch.* 91 Has the advantage of a far greater effectualness than Butler's way.

†**e'ffectuate,** *pple. Obs.* [as if ad. L. **effectuāt-us*, pa. pple. of **effectuā-re*; see next and -ATE².] Used as pa. pple. of next.

1609 W. BARLOW *Answ. Nameless Cath.* 291 A mans death may bee effectuate by two meanes. **1646** Z. BOYD in *Zion's Flowers* (1855) App. 31/1 That he see the premisses well effectuate.

effectuate (ɛ'fɛktjuːeɪt), *v.* Also 6–7 effectuat. [f. (on the analogy of ACTUATE) F. *effectu-er*, f. L. *effectu-s*; see EFFECT *sb.* and -ATE³.]

trans. To bring to pass (an event); to carry into effect, accomplish (an intention, desire).

1580 SIDNEY *Arcadia* II. 127 He found him a most fit instrument to effectuate his desire. **1587** FLEMING *Contn. Holinshed* III. 1577/2 A deed of great honour..and easie to effectuat. **1588** D. ROGERS in Ellis *Orig. Lett.* II. 233 III. 146 Gentlemen, against whom the kinge can lyttle effectuate. **1638** *Relat. State Kirk Scotl.* 5 To the end they might effectuat this point the more easily. **1733** CHEYNE *Eng. Malady* II. iii. §1 (1734) 138 The only Means that can effectuate a Palliative Cure. **1773** JOHNSON in *Boswell* II. 113, I should probably be put to death without effectuating my purpose. **1818** CRUISE *Digest* VI. 167 Courts of justice have been always anxious to effectuate the intentions of testators. **1870** BOWEN *Logic* viii. 229 If the Premises precede, and, as it were, effectuate the conclusion.

effectuating (ɛ'fɛktjuːeɪtɪŋ), *vbl. sb.* [f. prec. + -ING¹.] The action of the verb EFFECTUATE.

1619 in *Eng. & Ger.* (1865) 47 For the disguising and effectuating of their designes. **1630** LORD *Banians* 85 They make as few instruments serve for the effectuating of divers workes as may bee. **1685** J. SCOTT *Chr. Life* (1747) III. 65 In order to the effectuating this his Mediation. **1812** *Examiner* 28 Sept. 619/2 The effectuating such a plan.

e'ffectuating, *ppl. a.* [f. as prec. + -ING².] That effectuates; efficient, operative.

1615 CROOKE *Body of Man.* 87 The effectuating cause of sensation. **1851** W. HANNA *Mem. Chalmers* (1854) II. 158 The effectuating influence.

effectuation (ɛ,fɛktjuː'eɪʃən). [noun of action f. EFFECTUATE: see -ATION.] A carrying out, or carrying into effect; accomplishment, fulfilment.

1611 SPEED *Hist. Gt. Brit.* IX. xx, Charles King of France ..resolued to breake thorow all respects,..rather then to faile in effectuation. **1818** BENTHAM *Ch. Eng.* 135 In the effectuation of which..the exclusionary system is the main instrument employed. **1818** DWIGHT *Theol.* xiii. (1830) I. 233 To publish laws for..the effectuation of the common duties. **1865** W. PALGRAVE *Arabia* I. 375 The effectuation of his great scheme.

†**e'ffectuous,** *a. Obs.* Also 4 effectuos, 5 -wis, -uis, -eous, 6 -us. [ad. OF. *effectueux*, ad. med.L. *effectuōsus*, f. *effectu-s*: see EFFECT *sb.* and -OUS.]

1. = EFFECTUAL *a.* 1.

c **1400** *Apol. Loll.* 55 þe word of dede is more effectuos in werkyng þen þe word of þe mouþ. **1495** *Act 2 Hen. VII*, c. 61 §7 The same graunt..[shall be] advaillable, good and effectuous. **1548** G. WISHART in *Misc. Wodr. Soc.* (1844) 12 This fayth is effectuous through charitie. **1562** TURNER *Herbal* II. 96 b, The lesse kynde [of Poly] is..more effectuous or stronger in workyng. **1563** *Homilies* II. *Right Use Ch.* I. (1859) 154 The effectuous presence of his heavenly Grace. **1567** MAPLET *Gr. Forest* 4 b, Ceraunium..is..effectuous to bring a man in sweete sleepe. **1610** BARROUGH *Meth. Physick* III. lx. (1639) 197 You must come to more effectuous remedies.

2. Of prayer, etc.: Urgent, earnest; = EFFECTUAL 4.

1535 *Goodly Primer* (1834) 226 An effectuous prayer, very needful in these last..days. **1536** BEDYL in Strype *Eccl. Mem.* I. I. xxxv. 269 Two brethren..have given their bills inclosed to me, very effectuous. **1655** FULLER *Ch. Hist.* IX. 203 By our most effectuous and earnest Letter.

†**e'ffectuously,** *adv. Obs.* [f. prec. + -LY².]

1. Effectually, with powerful effect.

a **1400** *Cov. Myst.* (1841) 380 Whiche in this cas Thou lykyst to chesyn effectuously To ocapye the lott of Judas plas. *c* **1425** WYNTOUN *Cron.* VII. xxxviii. 260 To þe Pope þai wrat for-þi All þe more effectwysly. **1526** *Pilgr. Perf.* (1531) 61 To thynke..not superficially..but..effectuously. **1543** TRAHERON *Vigo's Chirurg.* IV. 154 Oyle of lyneseed.. swageth payne effecteouslye. *a* **1555** RIDLEY *Wks.* 274 Whosoever receiveth worthily that bread and wine, receiveth effectuously Christs body..he is made effectually partaker of his passion.

2. Urgently, earnestly: cf. AFFECTUOUSLY.

1533 BELLENDEN *Livy* v. (1822) 441 Thay..desirit him effectuislie to lede thame..to the tentis of inemyis. **1582–8** *Hist. Jas. VI* (1804) 3 Praying effectuouslie to graunt hir constancie.

†**e'ffectuousness.** *Obs. rare*⁻¹. [f. as prec. + -NESS.] The quality of being effectuous; efficacy.

1686 GOAD *Celest. Bodies* I. xii. 48 The effectuousness of the Semisextile..must be referred..to that efficacy, which ..is not yet extinct in the Oblique Line.

†**e'ffeeble,** *v. Obs.* [variant of AFFEEBLE or ENFEEBLE; the prefix being assimilated to EF-.] *trans.* To enfeeble.

1571 GOLDING *Calvin on Ps.* xlviii. 8 The welfare of the Church..may..be sore shaken, but yit not so effeebled that it shuld fal. **1581** MARBECK *Bk. of Notes* 326 That foule [Eagle] is..not effeebled by yeeres, nor subject to diseases.

†**e'ffeeblish,** *v. Obs.* [var. of AFFEEBLISH *v.*; see prec.] *trans.* To enfeeble. Hence **e'ffeeblishing** *vbl. sb.* **e'ffeeblishment** *sb.*, weakening.

1570–80 T. HACKET *Amadis of Gaule* 305 The brave Lyons..shall be brought under, and the strength of their clawes effeeblished. **1540** RAYNALD *Byrth Man.* (1634) 123 To the great effeeblishing of the woman. *Ibid.* (1634) 49 For in some they linger upon five, sixe, seven, yea eight dayes at each Terme, to their great effeeblishment.

†**e'ffeir,** *sb. Obs.* or *arch.* Also 4–5 effer(e, 6 effeer, -air. [Sc. var. of AFFAIR, q.v.]

1. = AFFAIR 1; a 'cause'.

1375 BARBOUR *Bruce* x. 305 He sped him to the were, Till help his Eym and his effere. **1501** DOUGLAS *Pal. Hon.* I. lxviii, For greit effeir me thocht na pane to die. *a* **1605** MONTGOMERIE *Oppos. Court to Consc.* 22 No furtherer of thair effairs.

2. = AFFAIR 6; appearance, bearing; show, 'pomp and circumstance'; ceremony.

1375 BARBOUR *Bruce* v. 608 The king persauit be thair effeir, That all wes suth men till hym tald. *Ibid.* VII. 30 Iohn of lorn, with gret effere. *Ibid.* 126 Thai persauit be his spekyng, And his effer, he wes the kyng. *c* **1425** WYNTOUN *Cron.* IX. xxii. 69 Dame Anabil Qwene of Scotland.. Cunnand, curtas in her efferis. *c* **1500** *Lancelot* 2357 Sche gart bryng..With grete effere this knycht to hir presens. **1535** STEWART *Cron. Scot.* (1858) I. 299 Thair forwardnes and eik thair fresche effeir. **1818** SCOTT *Hrt. Midl.* xii, This rising in effeir of war.

b. *pl.* Phenomena, properties.

1500–20 DUNBAR *Thistle & Rose* 128 Discirnyng all thair [flouris] fassionis and effeiris.

effeir, effere (in Sc. ə'fir), *v.*¹ *north. dial.* Also 7 effeer. [Usual spelling of AFFEIR, AFFERE.]

1. *impers. intr.* To fall by right, appertain, become, be proper or meet. Obs. exc. in Sc. law phrase 'as effeirs'.

c **1375** BARBOUR *Troy-bk.* II. 3020 And þai In Achaia hime erde With kyngis honour, as efferde. *c* **1375** ? BARBOUR *St. Philippus* 90, & al þe remaynyne to do þat efferyte þare ordyr to. *c* **1430** HENRYSON *Mor. Fab.*, *Tale of Dog* 23 The Ravin, as to his office weill effeird, Indorsat hes the write. *Ibid.* (1832) 25, I drewe a little by, For it effeirs nether to heare nor spye. **1535** STEWART *Cron. Scot.* III. 326 Or to his stait effeirit for to haif. **1657** COLVIL *Whigs Supplic.* (1751) 95 It effeers That I be judged by my Peers. **1833** *Act 3 & 4 Will. IV*, c. 46 §128 All competent diligence may pass and be directed hereon in form as effeirs.

†**2.** As *personal* vb. To be becoming, pertain properly. Const. *to* or dat.

a **1550** *Christis Kirke Gr.* viii, He cheist a Flane as did affeir him. *a* **1600** *Maitland Poems* 328 (Jam.) Honest weidis, To thair estait doand effeir [= effeirand]. *a* **1605** MONTGOMERIE *Flyting* 573 All his fousome forme thereto effeirs. **1820** SCOTT *Monast.* xxxiii, In all that effeirs to war.

†**e'ffeir,** *v.*² *Sc. Obs. rare.* [var. AFEAR, q.v.]

1. *trans.* To frighten.

1513 DOUGLAS *Æneis* XI. xii. 102 Na wound nor wapyn mycht hym anis effeir. **1553** (ed. 1) *Ibid.* VIII. iv. 88 The first time that ony..persauit Cacus efferde [*v.r.* afferd].

2. *trans.* To fear, be afraid of.

1552 LYNDESAY *Monarche* 2576 Effeir ȝe nocht Diuine punytione?

†**e'ffeiring,** *ppl. a. Sc. Obs.* Also 6 efferand. See also AFFEIRING. [pr. pple. of EFFEIR *v.*¹] Properly appertaining, suitable, proportionate.

1549 *Compl. Scot.* vi. (1872) 56 God almychty..mittigatis ..bayth the gude..and euil operations of the planetis, efferand for the vertu and vice that ringis amang the pepil. **1536** BELLENDEN *Cron. Scot.* I. (1821) Introd. 34 Litill Johne..hes bene fourtene feet of hicht, with square membris effering thairto. **1816** SCOTT *Antiq.* xli, With annual rent and expenses effeiring.

Hence **e'ffeirandly** *adv.*, suitably.

1551 *Sc. Acts Mary* (1814) 485 (Jam.) Efter thair qualite foirsaid to be punischit effeirandlie.

effeminacy (ɛ'fɛmɪnəsɪ). Also 6 effeminaty. [f. EFFEMINATE *a.*: see -ACY.]

1. Effeminate quality; Unmanly weakness, softness, or delicacy.

1602 WARNER *Alb. Eng.* Epit. (1612) 360 Finding..the Britons alienated from themselues through ease and effeminacie. **1626** T. H. *Caussin's Holy Crt.* 13 A spirit soothed with its owne Effeminaty. **1711** STEELE *Spect.* No. 104 ¶2 His Features, Complexion, and Habit had a remarkable Effeminacy. **1763** J. BROWN *Poetry & Mus.* §7. 153 Their coarse manners melted gradually into false Politeness and Effeminacy. *a* **1876** J. H. NEWMAN *Hist. Sk.* I. I. iv. 172 A barbarous people, possessed of a beautiful country, may be relaxed in luxury and effeminacy.

†**2.** (Cf. EFFEMINATE *a.* 3.) *Obs.*

1642 CHAS. I. *Declar. Soldiers at Southamp.* 21 Oct. 6 Avoid..excessive drinking and effeminacy (by some esteemed the property of a souldier). **1671** MILTON *Samson* 410 But foul effeminacy held me yok't Her Bond-Slave.

effeminate (ɛˈfɛmɪnət), *a.* and *sb.* [ad. L. *effēmināt-us*, f. *effēminā-re*, f. *ex* out + *fēmina* woman.] A. *adj.*

1. Of persons: That has become like a woman: a. Womanish, unmanly, enervated, feeble; self-indulgent, voluptuous; unbecomingly delicate or over-refined. Also (*Obs.*) *absol.* (cf. quot. 1609 in B.)

(The two first quots. may possibly belong to 3).
c **1430** LYDG. *Bochas* III. v. (1554) 77 a, It is..the most perilous thyng A prince to been of his condicion Effeminate. **1534** LD. BERNERS *Gold. Bk. M. Aurel.* (1546) E viij, An effeminate persone neuer hathe spirite to any hie or noble dedes. **1549** *Compl. Scot.* xi. (1873) 25 Effemenet men sal be ther dominatours. **1555** EDEN *Decades W. Ind.* (Arb.) 50 The sclendernesse of theyr capacitie and effeminate hartes. **1625** K. LONG tr. *Barclay's Argenis* IV. xxii. 319 But a Souldier's death shall make amends for thy effeminate life. **1748** ANSON *Voy.* II. xiv. (ed. 4) 386 A Luxurious and effeminate race. **1841** W. SPALDING *Italy & It. Isl.* I. 107 This step..enabled the Germanic soldiers to compare themselves with the effeminate troops of the south.
absol. quasi-*sb.* **1609** BIBLE (Douay) *Prov.* xviii. 8 The soules of the effeminate shal be hungrie. **1692** DRYDEN tr. *St. Evremont's Ess.* 162 A softness, wherein for the most part languish the Effeminate.

b. Of things: Characterized by, or proceeding from, unmanly weakness, softness, or delicacy.
1579 GOSSON *Sch. Abuse* (Arb.) 32 Effeminate gesture to rauish the sence. **1591** SHAKS. *1 Hen. VI*, v. iv. 107 Shall we at last conclude effeminate peace? **1685** CROWNE *Sir C. Nice* v. 49, I scorn those effeminate revenges. If I hurt any man it shall be with my sword. **1776** GIBBON *Decl. & Fall* I. 148 Rome was..humbled beneath the effeminate luxury of Oriental despotism. **1839** H. ROGERS *Ess.* (1874) II. iii. 149 They would sooner employ..the most effeminate circumlocution than resort to a..homely term or phrase.

†c. Without implying reproach: Gentle, tender, compassionate. *Obs.*
1594 NASHE *Unfort. Trav.* 26 Their handes had no leasure to aske counsell of their effeminate eyes. **1594** SHAKS. *Rich. III*, III. vii. 211 We know your tenderness of heart, And gentle kinde effeminate remorse.

†d. Of music, odours, etc.: Soft, voluptuous. *Obs.*
1674 PLAYFORD *Skill Mus.* I. 61 The Ionick Mood was more light and effeminate Musick. **1692** O. WALKER *Hist. Illustrated* 77 The Myrtle..because of its Effeminate smell, etc.

¶ Used for: Feminine, characteristic of women.
1549 OLDE *Erasm. Par. 1 Timothy* ii. 9 Nowe let the women also praye after thexample of the men. Yf there be any effemynate affection [Lat. '*Si quid est in animo muliebrium affectuum*'] in their stomakes, let them caste it out.

†2. Physically weak, 'delicate'. *Obs.*
1652 FRENCH *Yorksh. Spa* x. 91, I..advise those that have effeminate stomachs to take off the cold from the water before they drink it.

†3. The notion 'self-indulgent, voluptuous' (see 1) seems sometimes to have received a special colouring from a pseudo-etymological rendering of the word as 'devoted to women'. Unequivocal instances are rare; cf. quot. 1430 in 1; also EFFEMINACY 2; EFFEMINATENESS 2. *Obs.*
1490 CAXTON *Eneydos* xvi. 55 Man effemynate [Virgil *uxorius*] wythout honour rauysshed in to dileectation femynyne. **1589** PUTTENHAM *Eng. Poesie* II. (Arb.) 146 The king was supposed to be..very amorous and effeminate.

†4. Used as pa. pple. of EFFEMINATE, *v. Sc. Obs.*
1536 BELLENDEN *Cron. Scot.*, How strang..pepill grew in our regioun afore they were effeminat with lust. *a* **1560** ROLLAND *Crt. Venus* III. 619 How mony men hes it effeminate.

B. *sb.* An effeminate person. b. *spec.* (see quot. 1609).
1597 DANIEL *Civ. Wars* I. 70 This wanton young effeminate [Richard II]. **1609** BIBLE (Douay) *1 Kings* xiv. 24 Effeminates [Vulg. *effeminati*, **1611** Sodomites] were in the land. **1784** COWPER *Task* II. 223 With a just disdain Frown at effeminates. **1860** W. WEBB in *Medical Times* 15 Sept. 266/2 Soft-handed effeminates.

effeminate (ɛˈfɛmɪneɪt), *v.* [ad. L. *effēminātus*, pa. pple. of *effēmināre* (see EFFEMINATE *a.*). Cf. F. *efféminer*.]

†1. *trans.* To make into a woman; to represent as a woman. *Obs. rare.*
1678 CUDWORTH *Intell. Syst.* 493 They effeminated the Air and attributed it to Juno. **1739** CIBBER *Apol.* (1756) I. 90 Till the male Queen cou'd be effeminated [*i.e.* till the actor playing that part could be shaved].

2. To make womanish or unmanly; to enervate.
1551-6 ROBINSON tr. *More's Utop.* (Arb.) 40 It is not to be feared lest they shoulde be effeminated, if thei were brought vp in good craftes. **1577** HANMER *Anc. Eccl. Hist.* (1585) 155 He effeminated his souldiers with all kind of delicacy and lasciuiousnesse. **1579** GOSSON *Sch. Abuse* (1841) 19 Bringing sweet comfortes into Theaters which rather effeminate the minde. **1676** SHADWELL *Libertine* IV. ii, Luxurious living..Effeminates fools in body. **1699** T. C[OCKMAN] *Tully's Offices* (1706) 61 *note*, A Stream which was said to..effeminate those that washed in it. **1758** *Herald* II. 252 If the too free admission of wealth..could..effeminate their manners. **1829** SOUTHEY *Sir T. More* II. 236 Luxury has not effeminated them.

3. *intr.* To become womanish; to grow weak, languish.
1393 GOWER *Conf.* III. 236 To seen a man from his estate Through his soty effeminate And leve that a man shall do. **1612** BACON *Greatness Kingd., Ess.* 239 In a slothfull peace both courages will effeminate, and manners corrupt.

effeminated (ɛˈfɛmɪneɪtɪd), *ppl. a.* [f. prec. + -ED.] a. Rendered womanish or unmanly. b. Reduced to the employments of a woman. †c. ? Degraded by subjection to a woman.
1611 SPEED *Hist. Gt. Brit.* IX. iii §38 His chiefest Consorts were Effeminated persons, Ruffians and the like. **1619** H. HUTTON *Follie's Anat.* 24 See Omphale, her effeminated king Basely captive, make him doe any thing. **1726** DE FOE *Hist. Devil* I. iv, The effeminated Male Apple eater [Adam].

effeminately (ɛˈfɛmɪnətlɪ), *adv.* [f. EFFEMINATE *a.* + -LY².]

1. In an effeminate or unmanly manner or style.
1528 TINDALE *Obed. Chr. Man.* in Wks. (1573) 143 That white rocherte that the Byshops..weare so like a Nunne, and so effeminatly. **1555** EDEN *Decades W. Ind.* III. I. (Arb.) 138 Effeminately decked. **1611** COTGR., *Laschement*..coldly, faintly, effeminately. **1638** BRATHWAIT *Hist. Surv.* (1651) 306 A youth too curiously and effeminately drest. **1697** POTTER *Antiq. Greece* (1715) I. I. xxvi. 172 If any one ..take hire for him [a Boy] to be effeminately embraced. **1701** W. WOTTON *Hist. Rome* 359 The Roman Soldiers had lived too effeminately to fight well. **1836** MARRYAT *Olla Podr.* xxv, They..are..a..very effeminately built race. **1881** J. HAWTHORNE *Fort. Fool* I. xix, He's not effeminately lovely.

†2. ? Through degrading passion for a woman.
1671 MILTON *Samson* 562 To let in the foe, Effeminately vanquished.

eˈffeminateness. [f. as prec. + -NESS.]

1. The quality or condition of being effeminate or womanish; unmanly softness or weakness.
1581 SIDNEY *Apol. Poetrie* (Arb.) 59 An Art..not of effeminatenes, but of..stirring of courage. **1639** FULLER *Holy War* II. xxvii. (1840) 84 They sent a distaff and a spindle..as upbraiding their effeminateness. **1670** LASSELS *Voy. Italy* (1698) Pref. 19 My young traveller should leave behind him..all effeminateness. **1812** H. C. ROBINSON *Diary 17 June* in Earle *Philol. Eng. Tong.* §322 His sensibility ..is in danger of being mistaken for effeminateness.

†2. (Cf. EFFEMINATE *a.* 3.) *Obs.*
1648 HEXHAM *Dutch Dict.* (1660) *Verwijvinge*, effeminatenesse, or given to women.

eˈffeminating, *vbl. sb.* [f. EFFEMINATE *v.* + -ING¹.] The action or process of rendering effeminate; unmanly softening or weakening.
1555 EDEN *Decades W. Ind.* (Arb.) 190 They make rather to theffeminatynge of the myndes of men. **1710** LADY M. W. MONTAGUE *Lett.* lxvii. II. 110 We are permitted no books but such as tend to the..effeminating of the mind.

eˈffeminating, *ppl. a.* [f. as prec. + -ING².] Making effeminate or unmanly; enervating.
1676 WYCHERLEY *Pl. Dealer* III. i, Thou art as hard to shake off as that..effeminating mischief, love. **1757** *Herald* (1758) I. 91 Effeminating luxury. **1860** EMERSON *Cond. Life* (1861) 121, I..find the religions of men..unmanly and effeminating.

effemination (ɛˌfɛmɪˈneɪʃən). [ad. L. *effēminātiōn-em*, f. *effēmināre* to EFFEMINATE.] The process of rendering or of becoming effeminate.
1650 SIR T. BROWNE *Pseud. Ep.* (ed. 2) 120 [The hare] figured..degenerous effemination. **1684** tr. *Bonet's Merc. Compit.* I. 36, I know a place in the Belly..which, if burnt [with moxa], a certain Effemination follows, without hope of recovering a man's Virility.

†eˈffeminator. *Obs. rare*⁻¹. [f. as prec. + -OR.] He who, or that which, renders effeminate.
1630 BRATHWAIT *Eng. Gentlew.* (1641) 279 That Effeminatour both of youth and age, Delicacy of apparell.

effeminize (ɛˈfɛmɪnaɪz), *v.* Now *rare.* [f. EFFEMIN-ATE *a.* + -IZE.] *trans.* To render effeminate or womanish in character or appearance.
c **1612** SYLVESTER *Du Bartas* (1621) 1083 His braue Knights effeminiz'd by Sloath. **1616** R. C. *Times' Whis.* iii. 970 A lovelocke..Doth the lewd wearer quite effeminize. **1836** DONALDSON *Theat. Greeks* (ed. 4) 376 The tragic poets ..effeminized them. **1863** *Blackw. Mag.* Sept. 269 [Pope] is considered..to have..effeminised Dryden's style.

Hence **eˈffeminized** *ppl. a.*, **eˈffeminizing** *ppl. a.*
1824 *Blackw. Mag.* XVI. 162 Enthusiasm..inspired..by the effeminizing sensuality of Moore. **1881** LD. LYTTON in *19th C.* Nov. 769 Our present somewhat effeminised civilisation. *Ibid.* 774 It tends to encourage..an effeminising influence in English poetry.

‖**effendi** (ɛˈfɛndɪ). Also 7 **aphendis**, 9 **efendee**. [Turkish *efendī*, a corruption of Gr. αὐθέντης (pronounced afˈθendis) lord, master.] A Turkish title of respect, chiefly applied to government officials and to members of the learned professions.
1614 SELDEN *Titles Hon.* 381 Their aphendis written also by the later Greeks ἀφένδης is corrupted from Αυθεντης, *i.* Lord. **1688** *Lond. Gaz.* No. 2313/2 Nachis Effendi (who is the chief of those that wear a Green Turbant, as being descended from Mahomet). **1716** LADY M. W. MONTAGUE *Lett.* (1825) 207 He assembled the chief effendis or heads of the law. **1732** EAMES in *Phil. Trans.* XXXVII. 340 It has the Imprimatur..of a Turkish Divine, and three Effendies. **1814** W. BROWN *Hist. Propag. Chr.* II. 535 The Effendis or doctors frankly confessed that they were unable to answer the arguments of the missionaries.

†eˈffer, *v. Obs. rare.* Also 7 **efferre**. [ad. L. *efferre*, f. *ex* out + *ferre* to bear.] *trans.* To bring forth; to give off.
1606 WARNER *Alb. Eng.* lxxxv. 352 But Insolencie hath a time as well to fall as erre..To which no Opportunities but doe Effects efferre. **1657** TOMLINSON *Renou's Disp.* 526 Honey must be cocted till it effer no more spume.

effer: see EFF *v.*

†ˈefferate, *ppl. a. Obs. rare.* [ad. L. *efferāt-us*; see next.] Fierce, harsh, morose.
1684 H. MORE *Answ.* 112 Either heedlesness or an efferate religious Melancholy.

†ˈefferate, *v. Obs.* [f. L. *efferāt-* ppl. stem of *efferāre*, f. *effer-us* EFFERE *a.*] *trans.* To render fierce, exasperate.
1658 USSHER *Ann.* VI. 243 The fœdity of such an act might ..efferate their minds more. **1653** MANTON *Exp. James* ii. 6 Riches exalt the mind and efferate it.

Hence **†effeˈration.** *Obs. rare.* Irritating action.
1684 tr. *Bonet's Merc. Compit.* VIII. 295 Spirits..by their efferation often hurt the Bowels.

†eˈffere, *a. Obs. rare*⁻¹. [ad. L. *effer-us*, f. *ex* out + *ferus* fierce.] Excessively wild or fierce.
1586 J. HOOKER *Girald. Hist. Irel.* in *Holinshed* II. 144/1 Let us returne to the historie of this effere..nation.

†eˈffere, *sb. Sc. Obs. rare.* Also **afeir, affeir.** [Used *metr. gr.* for FEAR *sb.*¹; the prefix vaguely after AFEAR *v.*, EFFRAY: see EFFEIR *v.*²] Fear.
1553 DOUGLAS *Æneis* II. v. [iv.] 21. (ed. 1) 34 a, We fled away al bludles for effere [*v.r.* afeir]. *Ibid.* III. i. 57 And for effere [*ed.* **1874** affeir] my blude togiddir fresit.

effere, var. of EFFEIR, *v. Sc.*, to suit.

efferent (ˈɛfərənt), *a.* and *sb. Phys.* [ad. L. *efferent-em*, pr. pple. of *efferre*: see EFFER.]

A. *adj.* Conveying outwards, discharging.
1856 TODD & BOWMAN *Phys. Anat.* II. 487 A minute venous radicle, efferent vessel [may be seen] to emerge..in close proximity to the artery. **1870** ROLLESTON *Anim. Life* Introd. 34 The efferent arteries are..connected with afferent veins. **1879** H. SPENCER *Data of Ethics* vii. 108 An impression made on an afferent nerve causes by discharge through an efferent nerve a contraction.

B. *sb.* That which carries outwards.
1876 *Contemp. Rev.* XXVII. 541 Look upon..the ethereal waves as the afferents and efferents of Omniscient Thought.

Hence **effeˈrential.**
1836-9 TODD *Cycl. Anat.* II. 992/2 In Athalia..the efferential vessel is entirely absent.

†ˈefferous, *a. Obs. rare.* [f. L. *effer-us* (see EFFERE *a.* + -OUS.] Fierce, violent.
1614 BP. J. KING *Vine Palat.* 34 From the teeth of that efferous beaste..preserue our roote. **1657** TOMLINSON *Renou's Disp.* 167* To correct the efferous nature of the purgatives.

†eˈffervency. *Obs.* [f. L. *effervent-em*, pr. pple. of *effervēre* to boil up or over: see -ENCY.] The condition of being overheated, of issuing forth in a heated state.
1670 E. R. *Ne Plus Ultra* 105 Effervency of that [blood] in the heart. **1670** J. CLARIDGE *Sheph. Banbury's Rules* (1744) 33 When they [fulminating matters] are burst forth and floating in the air, they [cold winds] hinder their effervency [in thunderstorms]. **1681** [see EFFERVESCENCY].

effervesce (ɛfəˈvɛs), *v.* [ad. L. *effervesc-ĕre*, f. *ex* out + *fervesc-ĕre* to begin to boil, inceptive vb. f. *fervēre* to be hot.]

†1. *intr.* 'To generate heat by intestine motion' (J.); to break into violent chemical action.
1702 MEAD *Mech. Acc. Poisons* (J.), The compound spirit of nitre, put to oil of cloves will effervesce even to a flame. **1748** HARTLEY *Observ. Man* I. iii. §2. 364 If these Corpuscles effervesce together..repulsive Powers may arise.

2. To give off bubbles of gas, *esp.* as the result of chemical action; to bubble.
1784 KIRWAN *Min.* 43 [Calcareous Grit] effervesces with acids. **1792** A. YOUNG *Trav. France* 94 A vein of earth.. which..did not effervesce with acids. **1805** W. SAUNDERS *Min. Wat.* 166 Which, when mixed up with soda.. effervesced and fused into a perfect glass. **1816** ACCUM *Chem. Tests* (1818) 281 The residue will..effervesce with dilute acids. **1846** G. DAY tr. *Simon's Anim. Chem.* II. 28 Human gastric juice..effervesces on the addition of alkalies.

b. Of the gas itself: To issue forth in bubbles.
1830 M. DONOVAN *Dom. Econ.* I. 173 As the carbonic acid effervesces away, the particles of yest..begin to sink. **1874** LYELL *Elem. Geol.* ii. 13 The carbonic acid..froths up or 'effervesces'..in small bubbles through the drop of liquid.

3. *fig.*
1850 MRS. STOWE *Uncle Tom's C.* ix. 65 A number of.. juveniles..were effervescing in all those modes of..gambol and mischief. **1871** R. H. HUTTON *Ess.* II. 337 No period could be found when mingling faith and culture effervesced with more curious results.

4. *trans. rare.* To stir up, excite, exhilarate.
1866 *Harvard Mem. Biog., G. W. Batchelder* II. 6 The steady, regular tramp of the marching thousands effervesced our spirits.

effervescence (ɛfəˈvɛsəns). [f. L. *effervescent-em*, pr. pple. of *effervescĕre*; see prec. and -ENCE. Cf. F. *effervescence*.]

†**1.** The action of boiling up; heated agitation of the particles of a fluid. *Obs.*

1651 BIGGS *New Disp.* 164 Black blood..or lurid, green, &c. do not signifie the corruption of it, but are symbolizations of only..its effervescence, or fermentall turbulency. **1676** GREW *Lect. Luctation* i. §4 Effervescence; then and only properly so called, when they [the bodies mixed] produce some degree of heat. **1684** tr. *Bonet's Merc. Compit.* VI. 160 The effervescence of the Fever must be permitted. **1710** T. FULLER *Pharm. Extemp.* 44 By proper Internals..allay the Effervescence of the Blood.

2. (Without necessarily implying heat.) The action of bubbling up as if boiling; the tumultuous rise of bubbles of gas from a fluid; *esp.* as the result of chemical action.

1684-5 BOYLE *Min. Waters* 87 An effervescence..with some potent Acid. **1695** *New Light Chirurg. put out* 63 'Tis an Acid, because of its Effervescence with Volatile Salts. **1744** BERKELEY *Siris* §132 That effervescence observed in the mixture of acids and alkalies. **1834** MRS. SOMERVILLE *Connex. Phys. Sc.* xvi. (1849) 151 A tall glass half full of champagne cannot be made to ring as long as the effervescence lasts. **1844-57** G. BIRD *Urin. Deposits* 22 If brisk effervescence follows..the urea has been converted into carbonate of ammonia.

3. *fig.*

1748 JOHNSON *L.P.* Wks. 1816 X. 310 The effervescence of invention had subsided. **1791** *Heroic Ep. to J. Priestley* in *Poet. Regist.* (1808) 397 The weekly burthen of their drowsy din Is..Mere effervescence of an acid soul. *c* **1800** K. WHITE *Rem.* (1837) 400 An effervescence of the sublimer affections. **1848** MACAULAY *Hist. Eng.* I 167 The first effervescence of boyish passions. **1876** GEO. ELIOT *Dan. Der.* IV. lii. 55 A fellow..who was in an effervescence of surprise.

effervescency (ɛfəˈvɛsənsɪ). [f. as prec. + -ENCY.] Effervescent state or condition; also loosely = prec.

1681 tr. *Willis's Rem. Med. Wks.* Voc., Effervency, effervescency, a being very hot or inflamed. **1686** W. HARRIS tr. *Lemery's Course Chym.* (ed. 3) Introd. 49 Effervescency is the Ebullition of a liquid without the separation of its parts. **1767** STERNE *Tr. Shandy* IX. i. 5 Nor did she superinduce the least heat..from the manual effervescencies of devotional tracts.

effervescent (ɛfəˈvɛsənt), *a.* [ad. L. *effervescent-em*, f. *effervescĕre* to EFFERVESCE.]

†**1.** That is in a state of bubbling heat. *Obs.*

1684 tr. *Bonet's Merc. Compit.* VI. 180 While the bloud is too effervescent, evacuation is not very proper.

2. That has the property of rising in bubbles.

1875 tr. *Ziemssen's Cycl. Med.* I. 459 Administer effervescent powders. *Mod.* The mixture is slightly effervescent. The abuse of effervescent beverages.

3. *fig.*

1833 MACAULAY *Walpole's Lett. H. Mann, Essays* (1851) I. 285 It was nonsense effervescent with animal spirits and impertinence. **1837** CARLYLE *Fr. Rev.* II. III. ii, The old Gaulish and Gaelic Celthood, with its..effervescent promptitude. **1867** HOWELLS *Ital. Journ.* 67 He had been in that State during its effervescent days.

effervescible (ɛfəˈvɛsɪb(ə)l), *a.* [f. as next + -IBLE.] **a.** Capable of producing effervescence. **b.** *fig.* Ready to effervesce; heated, excited.

a **1812** KIRWAN (W.) A small quantity of effervescible matter. **1866** *Morning Star* 16 Mar. 5/4 The effervescible imagination of the extravagant fair.

effervescing (ɛfəˈvɛsɪŋ), *ppl. a.* [f. EFFERVESCE + -ING².] That effervesces; *lit.* and *fig.*

1793 T. BEDDOES *Consumpt.* 128 Effervescing mixture of chalk and vinegar. **1837** CARLYLE *Fr. Rev.* III. I. vi, He..was ..conducted along the streets, amid effervescing multitudes. **1858** HOLLAND *Titcomb's Lett.* vi. 222 Life's first effervescing hopes.

efferˈvescingly, *adv.* [f. EFFERVESCING *ppl. a.* + -LY².] In an effervescing manner, sparklingly.

1898 *Westm. Gaz.* 15 June 3/1 He speaks briskly and effervescingly.

effervescive (ɛfəˈvɛsɪv), *a.* [f. EFFERVESCE *v.* + -IVE.] Tending to or characterized by effervescence.

1854 HICKOK *Mental Philos.* 77 An effervescive force.

effet, obs. form of EFT *sb.*

effete (ɛˈfiːt), *a.* Also 7 effœte. [ad. L. *effēt-us* that has brought forth young, hence worn out by bearing, exhausted, f. *ex* out + *fētus* breeding.]

†**1.** Of animals: That has ceased to bring forth offspring. *Obs.*

1660 H. MORE *Myst. Godl.* II. vi. 39 The Earth..grown effete and old Hardly bears small ones [*i.e.* men] now. **1691** RAY *Creation* I. (1704) 134 The Animal becomes barren and effete. **1774** GOLDSM. *Nat. Hist.* (1776) V. 165 Hens..after three years become effete and barren.

fig. **1621** BURTON *Anat. Mel.* II. iv. I. §5 (1651) 374 Nature is not effœte..to bestow all her gifts upon an age. **1796** BURKE *Regic. Peace* Wks. 1842 II. 289 Even she [France], the mother of monsters..shews symptoms of being almost effete. **1830** *Blackw. Mag.* XXVII. 410 Wonder-producers in youth generally become in manhood effete even of common births. **1840** CARLYLE *Heroes* (1858) 337 Nature..was as if effete now; could not any longer produce Great Men.

2. *transf.* Of material substances: That has lost its special quality or virtue; exhausted, worn out.

1662 H. STUBBE *Ind. Nectar* v. 100 The [Chocolata] Paste alone grows effœte, and insipid. **1664** EVELYN *Kal. Hort.* (1729) 228 That imprison'd and Effœte Air, within the Green-house. **1756** C. LUCAS *Ess. Waters* II. 106 It..grows more effete or less smart to taste. **1828** STEUART *Planter's G.* 187 The Lime is rendered nearly effete and powerless. **1845** TODD & BOWMAN *Phys. Anat.* I. 12 Animals and plants are ever throwing off effete particles from their organisms.

¶ Of strength, vital power: Spent, worn out.

1765 WARBURTON *Lett. late Prelate* (1809) 359 Till all the vigour..of that monarch of the grove [the oak] be effete and near exhausted.

3. *fig.* Of persons in an intellectual sense, of systems, etc.: That has exhausted its vigour and energy; incapable of efficient action. Also, of persons: weak, ineffectual; degenerate. More recently, effeminate.

1790 BURKE *Fr. Rev.* 228 They find the old governments effete, worn out. **1844** EMERSON *Lect. Yng. Amer.* Wks. (Bohn) II. 295 It [gardening] is the fine art which is left for us, now that sculpture, painting..have become effete. **1857** KINGSLEY *Two Y. Ago* I. 226 Pray accept your effete English aristocrat. **1869** GOULBURN *Purs. Holiness* xv. 143 But the monastic system..is now effete altogether. **1905** BARONESS ORCZY *Scarlet Pimpernel* (1906) xvi. 147 Those happy days of courtship, before he had become the lazy nincompoop, the effete fop, whose life seemed spent in card and supper rooms. **1958** 'A. BURGESS' *Enemy in Blanket* i, in *Malayan Trilogy* (1964) 176 The intrepid British of the past... Ah, they were becoming an effete race. The least thing upset them now. **1964** A. WYKES *Gambling* vii. 158 The king's appearance has also changed from that of a black man with a fierce expression..to a somewhat effete white fellow with sensual nostrils. **1981** *Economist* 6 June 18 Cool, practical and macho in the open air, indoors the uniform tends to trip the wearer up, needs gathering up like a skirt, and looks a trifle effete.

eˈffeteness, exhaustion, worn-out condition.

1862 R. PATTERSON *Ess. Hist. & Art* 274 The effeteness of this Mantchoo dynasty. **1876** GLADSTONE in *Contemp. Rev.* 6 June, The mummy-like effeteness..of Ultramontanism.

†**ˈefficable**, *a. Obs. rare*⁻¹. [f. L. *effic-ĕre* + -ABLE.] Efficacious, effective.

1607 TOPSELL *Four-f. Beasts* 582 The fat of a wolf is no less efficable then the flesh.

†**ˈefficace**, *sb. Obs.* [a. OF. *efficace*, ad. L. *efficācia*, f. *efficax*; see next.] **a.** Efficacy. **b.** Effect. **c.** Active duty.

a **1225** *Ancr. R.* 246 Ich habbe iseid of ham [tears] her uour muchel efficaces. *a* **1491** CAXTON *Vitas Patr.* (W. de W.) I. Prol., Vertues, In the whiche was all efficace of verytee. **1606** SYLVESTER *Du Bartas* (1621) 327 By the touch of their liue efficace. **1678** BUTLER *Hud.* III. II. 602 Saints That fine, like Aldermen, for grace To be excused the efficace. **1712** G. WHELER *Liturgy* 94 All-holy Spirit, his Life-giveing Efficace.

†**effiˈcace**, *a. Obs.* [a. F. *efficace*, ad. L. *efficax*, (stem *efficāci-*), f. *efficĕre* to accomplish.] = next.

15.. T. HACKET *Treas. Amadis de Gaule* (Bynneman) 259 To drawe them..by efficace promises and perswasions.

efficacious (ɛfɪˈkeɪʃəs), *a.* [f. L. *efficāci-* (see prec.) + -OUS: see -ACIOUS.] That produces, or is certain to produce, the intended or appropriate effect; effective. (Said of instruments, methods, or actions; not, in prose, of personal agents.)

1528 ROY *Sat.* (1845) Goddis worde is so efficacious. **1651** BIGGS *New Disp.* 35 Lesse efficacious, that is, in plain English ineffectual. **1669** GALE *Crt. Gentiles* I. III. iii. 39 He saies it is the first efficacious cause of the Being of althings. *a* **1679** T. GOODWIN *Wks.* (1863) VII. 510 God..vouchsafeth..efficacious grace to overcome temptation. **1744** BERKELEY *Siris* §58 Soap, therefore, is justly esteemed a most efficacious medicine. **1830** LYELL *Princ. Geol.* (1875) II. III. xli. 421 Variation and Natural Selection will be efficacious in forming distinct races in separate islands. **1860** MILL *Repr. Govt.* (1865) 51/2 To provide efficacious securities against this evil. **1873** BROWNING *Red. Cott. Nt.-Cap* 497 Be efficacious at the Council there.

effiˈcaciously, *adv.* [f. prec. + -LY².] In an efficacious manner; effectively.

1647 CLARENDON *Hist. Reb.* VI. II. 152 No man delivered himself more..efficaciously with the hearers. **1725** BRADLEY *Fam. Dict.* II. s.v. *Watering*, They..act efficatiously, and yield what is expected from them. **1836** SIR H. TAYLOR *Statesman* xii. 84 Objects on which men are..efficaciously employed. **1879** CHR. ROSSETTI *Seek & F.* 181.

effiˈcaciousness. [f. as prec. + -NESS.] The quality of being efficacious; effectiveness.

1630 J. PRESTON *Sermons bef. his Majesty* 44 As that which hath sinewes and efficatiousnesse in it [differs] from that which is..powerlesse. **1650** WEEKES *Truth's Confl.* ii. 42 The efficaciousness of the death of Christ. **1669** BUNYAN *Holy Citie* 265, I come to speak to this Tree touching..the efficaciousness of its leaves. **1756** BLAKE in *Phil. Trans.* LI. 2 Which multiplied by the lever *a* gives *ma*—*nb* for the efficaciousness of that force. *c* **1860** WRAXALL tr. *R. Houdin* ii. 11 The Vermifuge Balsam, whose sovereign efficaciousness is indisputable.

efficacity (ɛfɪˈkæsɪtɪ). Also 5-6 efficacite, 6-7 -itie. [ad. L. *efficācitāt-em* (cf. F. *efficacité*, but this may be of later origin), f. *efficax*: see EFFICACE *a.*] = prec. and next.

1430-50 tr. *Higden* (1865) I. 61 [The occean] felethe by more efficacite the strenghte of ye moone then a see coartate. **1528** ROY *Sat.* (1845) Yf their paynted efficacite Is but as it semeth to be. **1543** TRAHERON *Vigo's Chirurg.* v. v. 170 The oyle of..saint Jhons wort is of singuler efficacitie, in all paynes of..the knee. **1624** F. WHITE *Repl. Fisher* 540, I could bring Testimonies..of the efficacitie thereof to expiate sinne. **1678** GALE *Crt. Gentiles* III. 3 We may firmly assert..the efficacitie of Divine Concurse. **1775** ASH, *Efficacity* (from Efficacy, but not much used) Efficacy. **1868** BROWNING *Ring & Bk.* IX. 150 Better estimate exorbitantly, than disparage Aught of the efficacity of the act. **1874** LEWES *Probl. Life & Mind* I. 114 The efficacity of Intelligence depends on the organs which cooperate. **1886** *Sat. Rev.* 21 Aug. 251/1 The National Liberal Federation..a monument of the efficacity..of programmes and delegacy.

efficacy (ˈɛfɪkəsɪ). Also 6 effecacy. [ad. L. *efficācia*, f. *efficax*; see EFFICACE *a.* and -ACY.]

1. Power or capacity to produce effects; power to effect the object intended. (Not used as an attribute of personal agents: cf. EFFICACIOUS.)

1527 ANDREW *Brunswyke's Distyll. Waters* Prol., Charmes of eficacye unnaturall by the devyll envented. **1532** MORE *Confut. Barnes* VIII. Wks. (1557) 740/2 Theffect and effecacy of al these thynges, commeth of God. **1563** HYLL *Art Garden.* (1593) 165 The seedes may well be kept for three yeares in good efficacie. **1646** SIR T. BROWNE *Pseud. Ep.* I. x. 40 An act, not..beyond the efficacy of the Sun. **1744** BERKELEY *Siris* §4 A medicine of such efficacy in a distemper. **1750** JOHNSON *Rambl.* No. 47 ⁋11 The efficacy of mirth it is not always easy to try. **1792** in Chipman *Amer. Law Rep.* (1871) 55 The division was not taken to have any legal efficacy. **1844** H. H. WILSON *Brit. India* II. 553 To maintain the village institutions of the country in entireness and efficacy. **1856** FROUDE *Hist. Eng.* (1858) I. ii. 103 No measures would be of efficacy which spared the religious houses.

†**2.** A process or mode of effecting a result. *Obs.*

1690 LOCKE *Hum. Und.* II. xxiii. (1695) 156 The Efficacy whereby the new Substance or Idea is produced, is called, in the subject exerting that Power, Action; but in the subject, wherein any simple Idea is changed or produced, it is called Passion. *Ibid.* IV. iii. §24 We are ignorant of the several Powers, Efficacies, and Ways of Operation, whereby the Effects..are produc'd.

†**3. a.** Effect. **b.** ? Actual event. *Obs.*

1549 LATIMER *Serm. bef. Edw. VI*, v. O iiij, You by youre prayer can worcke greate efficacye. *a* **1613** OVERBURY *Characters* (1638) *A Puritane*, His arguing is but the efficacy of his eating. **1633** BP. HALL *Hard Texts* 350 In the efficacy of his appearance, he shall be so glorious.

eˈfficiat, *ppl. a.* ? Mistake for EFFICIENT.

1594 GREENE *Fr. Bacon* xiii. 76 The poniard that did end the fatal liues, Shall breake the cause efficiat of their woes.

†**eˈfficiate**, *v. Obs. rare*⁻¹. Only in vbl. sb. efficiating. [incorrectly f. L. *efficĕre*; cf. EFFICIENT, and see -ATE³.] *trans.* To effect, bring to pass.

1612 WOODALL *Surg. Mate* Wks. (1653) 406 A few instruments or medicaments for the efficiating thereof.

efficience (ɛˈfɪʃəns). *Obs.* or *arch.* [ad. L. *efficientia*, noun of quality f. *efficiens*: see EFFICIENT and -ENCE.]

1. The exercise of efficient power; causative or productive activity.

1669 GALE *Crt. Gentiles* I. III. iii. 37 The first piece of this Divine efficience is..referred to the Divine Ideas. *a* **1680** J. CORBET *Free Actions* I. §1 God's Efficience is concern'd in the Event decreed. **1794** MRS. PIOZZI *Synon.* I. 319 The surprising efficience of two bodies..to produce a third unknown before.

2. Effectiveness, efficacy.

1865 SIR K. JAMES *Tasso* XII. xxviii, Do thou for her with such efficience pray.

†**effiˈciˈenciary**, *a. Obs. rare*⁻¹. [f. L. *efficientia*: see prec. + -ARY.] Pertaining to executive action.

1649 SELDEN *Laws Eng.* I. xiv. (1739) 26 [They] exercised not only a Judiciary power..but challenged an Efficienciary power in the Marriage-making.

efficiency (ɛˈfɪʃənsɪ). [ad. L. *efficientia*; see EFFICIENCE and -ENCY.]

1. a. The fact of being an operative agent or efficient cause. Now only in philosophical use.

1593 HOOKER *Eccl. Pol.* I. i, The manner of this deuine effeciencie being farre above us. **1628** T. SPENCER *Logick* 31 God is sayd to be the Efficient Cause of man: the office of this efficiency, is placed in ioyning the forme vnto the matter. **1676** HALE *Contempl.* I. 365 The Efficiency..of the Principal Cause is that which gives efficacy to the Means and makes it effectual. **1695** WOODWARD *Nat. Hist. Earth* I. (1723) 56 [Gravity of bodies] does not proceed from the Efficiency of any such Contingent and unstable Agents. **1870** BOWEN *Logic* xii. 417 Constancy of sequence is no certain indication of causal efficiency.

†**b.** The action of an operative agent or efficient cause; production, causation, creation. *Obs.*

1663 J. SPENCER *Prodigies* (1665) 221 These Prodigies are of Diabolical efficiency. **1677** HALE *Prim. Orig. Man.* IV. vii. 350 That Power and Wisdom..were equal to the formation and efficiency of the Sun. **1678** CUDWORTH *Intel. Syst.* 576 These ancient pagans..used it [*creare*] generally for all manner of production or efficiency.

2. a. Fitness or power to accomplish, or success in accomplishing, the purpose intended; adequate power, effectiveness, efficacy.

1633 AMES *Agst. Cerem.* I. 49 The very frame of it..had an efficiency..to cary up the heart to God. **1818-60** WHATELY *Com.-pl. Bk.* (1864) 76 The penalty annexed to any law is an instance, not of its efficiency, but..of its failure. **1858** BUCKLE *Civiliz.* (1873) II. viii. 556 The navy was..more than doubled in efficiency. **1859** MILL *Liberty* v. (1865) 67/2 The greatest dissemination of power consistent with efficiency. **1863** FAWCETT *Pol. Econ.* II. v. 193 That nothing more powerfully promotes the efficiency of labour than an abundance of fertile land.

b. *pl.* Efficient powers or capacities.

1646 SIR T. BROWNE *Pseud. Ep.* 46 The production of effects beyond their created efficiencies.

c. *spec.* in *Economics*, as ***economic***, ***marginal***, ***technical efficiency*** (see quots.).

1906 A. SHADWELL (*title*) Industrial efficiency. A comparative study of industrial life in England, Germany and America. **1916** A. MARSHALL *Princ. Econ.* (ed. 7) IV. v. 193 Health and strength, physical, mental and moral..are the basis of industrial efficiency, on which the production of material wealth depends. **1926** *Industrial Management* Jan. 4/1 The choice is restricted to a definitely established range of sizes and types, outside of which the designer of the average car would venture with considerable trepidation, and at the sacrifice of manufacturing efficiency. *Ibid.* 34 (Advt.), Sure and efficient power drives make for higher overall plant efficiency. **1936** J. M. KEYNES *Gen. Theory Employment, Interest & Money* IV. ii. 135 The relation between the prospective yield of a capital-asset and its supply price or replacement cost, *i.e.* the relation between the prospective yield of one more unit of that type of capital and the cost of producing that unit, furnishes us with the *marginal efficiency of capital* of that type. **1953** G. HUTTON *We too can Prosper* i. 13 Productivity is the efficiency..of production. **1965** J. L. HANSON *Dict. Econ. & Commerce* 133/1 *Economic efficiency*, the maximum average output per employee. *Ibid.*, Economic efficiency is a much wider term than technical efficiency, which applies only to the efficiency of one factor of production, namely capital. **1965** SELDON & PENNANCE *Everyman's Dict. Econ.* 137 *Economic efficiency*, relates to output per unit cost of the resources employed; contrasted with *technical* efficiency, which measures output of energy per unit of energy applied. **1966** A. GILPIN *Dict. Econ. Terms* 57 *Economic efficiency*, the efficiency with which scarce resources are used and organised to achieve stipulated economic ends. In competitive conditions, the lower the cost per unit of output, without sacrifice of quality, in relation to the value or price of the finished article, the greater the economic efficiency of the productive organisation.

3. *Mech.* and *Physics.* †**a.** The work done by a force in operating a machine or engine; the total energy expended by a machine. *Obs.*

1827 D. GILBERT in *Phil. Trans. R. Soc.* CXVII. 27 Since therefore a machine is efficient in producing duty, or effect, in proportion to the force applied, multiplied into the space through which it acts, I propose to denominate this function ($f \times s$) *efficiency*; retaining the word *duty* for a similar function indicative of the work performed... By a comparison of these two quantities, the *efficiency* expended on any machine, and the *duty* performed by it, an exact measure will be ascertained of its intrinsic worth. *Ibid.* 31 The received efficiency of a water wheel being represented by the pounds of water passing over it × by the fall in feet, less the height due to the velocity with which the periphery moves in its rotation. **1832** W. WHEWELL *First Princ. Mech.* iv. 54 It has been proposed by Mr Davies Gilbert..to call the product $f \times s$ the Efficiency of the force f. *Ibid.* 55 The work done by any machine is always equal to the Efficiency of the moving force... But machinery may very much increase the convenience of application of the force. *Ibid.* 64 To find the theoretical Efficiency of a Steam Engine working for one minute.

b. The ratio of useful work performed to the total energy expended or heat taken in.

radiant or ***luminous efficiency***, the ratio of the total luminous flux produced to the total power consumed.

1855 W. J. M. RANKINE in *Proc. Philos. Soc. Glasgow* III. VI. 398 Efficiency of engines. An engine is a contrivance for transforming energy by means of the periodical repetition of a cycle of variations of the accidents of a substance. The *efficiency* of an engine is the proportion which the energy permanently transformed to a useful form by it bears to the whole energy communicated to the working substance. **1858** —— *Man. Appl. Mech.* VI. 610 The object of improvements in machines is to bring their efficiency as near to unity as possible. **1879** G. B. PRESCOTT *Speaking Telephone* xiv. 465 The true comparative measure of the efficiency of dynamo-electric machines. **1887** *Encycl. Brit.* XXII. 496/1 The efficiency of furnace and boiler is the ratio which the amount of heat taken up by the water bears to the whole potential energy of the fuel. In good boilers this efficiency is about 0·7. **1902** *Ibid.* XXXIII. 418/1 The ratio between the power given out by a transformer and the power taken up by it is called its efficiency. **1929** *Ibid.* VIII. 290/1 The 'efficiency' of a lamp is measured in lumens per watt. **1958** *Van Nostrand's Sci. Encycl.* (ed. 3) 561/1 Usually there is a load for which the efficiency is a maximum. **1960** R. W. MARKS *Dymaxion World of B. Fuller* 51/1 In engineering, the term 'efficiency' means the ratio of foot-pounds of work realized to the foot-pounds of energy consumed by a given mechanical system. **1967** CONDON & ODISHAW *Handbk. Physics* (ed. 2) v. 6/1 Of all engines working between two heat reservoirs of temperature τ_1 and τ_2 ($\tau_2 > \tau_1$), the reversible engine is the one of maximum efficiency.

4. An efficiency apartment; a room with limited facilities for washing and cooking. *N. Amer.*

1952 *Times-Picayune* (New Orleans) 11 May v. 8 (Advt.), Modern, furnished efficiency. Living room, bedroom combined, kitchen and bath. **1959** H. GARDNER *So what else is New?* 70 Irving Hoffman..spotted this room-for-rent sign down in Greenwich Village: 'One room efficiency, no bath, suitable for artist.' **1959** *Times Lit. Suppl.* 6 Nov. p. xiii/2 Even in..the motel, you will find..a curiously abrupt sign labelled 'Efficiencies', by which token you will learn that your expensive quarters are furnished with..an up-to-date kitchenette. **1968** *Globe & Mail* (Toronto) 17 Feb. 34 (Advt.), Efficiencies 67.50 per week.

5. *attrib.* **efficiency apartment** *N. Amer.*, one with limited facilities for washing and cooking; **efficiency audit**, an examination of a business organization, etc., for the purpose of establishing the efficiency of its procedures; **efficiency bar**, a restriction of salary to a maximum figure which may be increased only when satisfactory evidence of efficiency has been produced; **efficiency engineer** *U.S.*, = *efficiency expert*; **efficiency expert**, one who examines the efficiency of industrial or commercial organization or production.

1930 *San Antonio* (Texas) *Light* 31 Jan. 14/8 (Advt.), 641 N. Flores..*Efficiency Apts.* **1965** L. H. WHITTEN *Progeny of Adder* (1966) 25 The efficiency apartment he really couldn't afford in southwest Washington. **1952** *Public Administration* XXX. 77/2 Accountancy is developing the technique of standard costs; and the new science of business management is devising techniques of 'efficiency audit'. **1965** J. L. HANSON *Dict. Econ. & Commerce* 133/1 If a nationalised industry is to be run deliberately at a loss 'as a service' it loses the economic test of its efficiency. In such a case the profit test would have to be replaced by some kind of 'efficiency audit'. **1897** *Daily News* 16 Mar. 2/2 (*heading*) An efficiency bar. No officer whose salary had reached 112 *l.* is to be allowed to pass that figure without a satisfactory certificate of the excellence of his conduct and of his ability to perform the highest duties of his class. **1964** *New Statesman* 10 Apr. 580/1 (Advt.), Lecturer £1,250..-£2,150 with an efficiency bar at £1,750. **1913** *Engineering Mag.* Aug. 715/1 Whenever an efficiency engineer is engaged to study a business or a manufactory, he must of necessity deal to a great extent with the rank and file in obtaining the vital data upon which to base his recommendations. **1954** J. A. C. BROWN *Social Psychol. Industry* x. 276 The efficiency engineers Taylor and Gilbreth and the early industrial psychologists. **1913** *Engineering Mag.* Aug. 717/2 So important is the work of this latest class of engineers, the efficiency experts, that no factor should be passed lightly over that has a bearing on their success. **1924** E. SHEPHARD *P. Bunyan* 184 Paul hired a kind of efficiency expert..and Gerber used to walk around..and keep tab on the men and count up how they spent their time. **1959** D. EWEN *Compl. Bk. Amer. Mus. Theater* 295 This musical spoofs an efficiency expert.

efficient (ɛˈfɪʃənt), *a.* and *sb.* [a. F. *efficient*, ad. L. *efficient-em*, pr. pple. of *efficĕre*, f. *ex* out + *facĕre* to make.] **A.** *adj.*

1. Making, causing to be; that makes (a thing) to be what it is; chiefly in connexion with *cause*.

1398 TREVISA *Barth. De P.R.* III. xvii. (1495) 61 The cause efficient. **1477** NORTON *Ord. Alch.* i. in Ashm. (1652) 19 For cause efficient of Mettalls finde ye shall Only to be the vertue Minerall. *a***1560** ROLLAND *Crt. Venus* III. 505 Of this slauchter he was caus efficient. **1577** tr. *Bullinger's Decades* (1592) 614 By members are shewed the efficient powers of God. **1635** SWAN *Spec. M.* v. ii. (1643) 149 The efficient cause [of dew] is the temperate cold of the night. **1656** STANLEY *Hist. Philos.* II. I. 54 Præexistent..in the Intellect of the efficient God. **1756** BURKE *Subl. & B.* Wks. 1842 I. 58 The common efficient cause of beauty. **1829** I. TAYLOR *Enthus.* ii. (1867) 55 The efficient will of the First Cause. **1866** ARGYLL *Reign Law* vi. (1871) 321 This change in mind is the efficient cause of a whole cycle of other changes.

2. Productive of effects; effective; adequately operative. Of persons: Adequately skilled.

1787 J. BARLOW *Oration* 4 July 8 Without an efficient government our Independence will cease to be a blessing. **1801** SOUTHEY *Thalaba* XI. xxxii, Soon his hand Shall strike the efficient blow. **1833** I. TAYLOR *Fanat.* v. 114 The belief of their efficient intercession in the court of heaven. **1850** MRS. STOWE *Uncle Tom's C.* xxxiii. 297 He was an expert and efficient workman.

B. *sb.*

†**1.** 'The cause which makes effects to be what they are' (J.). *Obs.*, but in 17th c. very common.

[**1579** GOSSON *Sch. Abuse* (Arb.) 37 There are more..causes in nature than efficientes.] **1594** HOOKER *Eccl. Pol.* I. (1632) 76 To take away the first efficient of our being, were to annihilate vtterly our persons. **1611** SPEED *Hist. Gt. Brit.* IX. xx. 68 The abuse of Sanctuaries had beene an efficient of many troubles. **1646** SIR T. BROWNE *Pseud. Ep.* VII. iv. 345 Beside the solary Iris..there is another Lunary, whose efficient is the Moone. **1649** ROBERTS *Clavis Bibl.* 511 The Efficient or Author of it, is..God himselfe. **1722** WOLLASTON *Relig. Nat.* v. 67 An infinite succession of effects will require an infinite efficient, or a cause infinitely effective. **1754** EDWARDS *Freed. Will* IV. ix. 259 The Motion of the Sun..is not the proper cause, Efficient or Producer of them. **1774** MITFORD *Harmony of Lang.*, Ignorance concerning the efficients of the harmony of language. **1804** —— *Inq. Principles Harm. Lang.*

2. *Mil.* An efficient soldier; *esp.* a volunteer adequately qualified for service.

1864 MRQ. HARTINGTON *Sp. Ho. Commons* 4 May, The number of 'efficients' under the new system was 112,165. **1884** *Manch. Exam.* 17 Mar. 5/1 The number of efficients..present at inspection..[was] higher than ever before.

efficiently (ɛˈfɪʃəntlɪ), *adv.* [f. prec. + -LY².]

†**1.** As by an efficient cause; in the relation of an efficient cause; by the operation of an agent.

1628 T. SPENCER *Logic* 158 Created effects are Necessary..When the next cause is determined to one..Naturally, [or] Efficiently. **1651** BAXTER *Inf. Bapt.* 291 All men believed, that faith was confirmed by signes (that is efficiently). **1678** CUDWORTH *Intell. Syst.* 739 It is Impossible..For a thing to be Efficiently Caused, by that which hath not..a Sufficient Productive Power.

2. In an efficient manner; so as to produce an effect; with adequate success; effectively.

1828 FOSTER in *Life & Corr.* (1846) II. 139 Means to act efficiently as his advocates. **1851** SIR F. PALGRAVE *Norm. & Eng.* I. 403 None so efficiently protect the weak. **1856** FROUDE *Hist. Eng.* (1858) I. i. 19 There is a fair evidence that the system worked efficiently and well.

†**eˈffiction.** *Obs. rare*⁻⁰. [ad. L. *effictiōn-em*, noun of action f. *effingĕre* to fashion.]

1656 BLOUNT *Glossogr.*, *Effiction*, an expressing or representing. **1775** in ASH.

†**eˈffierce,** *v. Obs. rare.* [f. EF- + FIERCE.] *trans.* To render fierce, madden.

1596 SPENSER *F.Q.* III. xi. 27 With fell woodness he effierced was.

effigial (ɛˈfɪdʒɪəl), *a. rare.* [f. L. *effigi-es* + -AL¹.] Of the nature of an effigy.

1715 M. DAVIES *Athen. Brit.* 6 The three first Volumes contain chiefly Effigial Cuts.

effigiate (ɛˈfɪdʒɪeɪt), *v.* Now *rare.* [f. late L. *effigiāt-* ppl. stem of *effigiāre*, f. *effigies*: see EFFIGIES.] *trans.* To present a likeness of; to portray, represent by a picture or sculpture. Also *fig.*

1608 BP. J. KING *Serm.* 5 Nov. 5 Reasonable soules, effigiated to God's image. **1627** HAKEWILL *Apol.* III. iv. §1 A Roman amphora..is exquisitely effigiated by Villapandus. **1628** J. WALL *Serm.* Ded., It was the design of Seneca to effigiat the Emperour Nero. **1809** *Monthly Mag.* XXVII. 160 Two-headed eagles..were effigiated in many houses..in Peru.

†**b.** To fashion *into* a likeness. *Obs.*

1660 JER. TAYLOR *Duct. Dubit.* II. ii. vi. §17 A light or fire effigiated into such a resemblance. **1700** J. BROME *Trav. Eng. & Scot.* III. (1707) 297 Some [stones] we observed whose lower Parts seem to be effigiated into divers little Feet.

Hence **eˈffigiating** *ppl. a.*

1616 HOLYDAY *Persius* (1618) 310 Like the potters clay, now thou must feel Sharp discipline's effigiating wheel.

eˌffigiˈation. [f. as prec.: see -ATION.] The action of fashioning or of representing; chiefly *concr.* a likeness, representation.

*c***1535** DEWES *Introd. Fr.* in *Palsgr.* 1057 In the whiche all..effigiation doth shyne clerely. **1655** FULLER *Ch. Hist.* x. 41 No such effigiation was therein discovered. **1741** tr. *Cicero's Nat. Gods* I. 66 Philosophers call every such Effigiation of the Mind vain Motion. **1876** MRS. WHITNEY *Sights & Ins.* xv. 163 The effigiation shocked me with its rude literalness.

‖**effigies** (ɛˈfɪdʒiːz). *arch.* [L. *effigies.*] A likeness, image, portrait, whether drawn, painted, or sculptured, or of any other kind. (Now superseded by EFFIGY, exc. as humorously pedantic.)

1600 SHAKS. *A.Y.L.* II. vii. 193. **1615** G. SANDYS *Trav.* 181 The effigies of Saint Ierome, miraculous framed by the naturall veines of the stone. **1676** *Lond. Gaz.* No. 1123/4 Which Sentences were..Executed upon them in Effigies, they being fled. **1702** W. J. *Bruyn's Voy. Levant* vi. 17 The Statue which we saw at this Castle is the Effigies of Queen Semiramis. **1820** SCOTT *Monast.* xxiii. *note*, A gold coin of James V..the effigies of the sovereign is represented wearing a bonnet. **1831** CARLYLE *Sart. Res.* (1858) 178 A Signpost, whereon..stood painted the Effigies of a Pair of Leather Breeches.

fig. **1653** S. FAIRCLOUGH *Fun. Serm.* 11 To delineate..the effigies and beauty of his like and conversation.

†**eˈffigies,** *v. nonce-wd.* [f. prec.] *trans.* To portray, picture.

1652 SPARKE *Prim. Devot.* (1663) 223 Sorrows inexpressible..fitter here to be effigiessed like sacrificed Iphigenia, with Agamemnon's veil of silence.

†**eˈffigium.** *Obs. rare.* [med.L. (see Du Cange).] Corrupt var. of EFFIGIES *sb.*

1564 BULLEIN *Dialogue* (1888) 81 It was the picture or Effigium of a noble man.

effigurate (ɛˈfɪgjʊəreɪt), *a. Bot.* [f. EF- (= *ec-*, *ex-*) + FIGURATE.] Having a definite outline.

1872 W. A. LEIGHTON *Lichen-Flora* (ed. 2) p. xxiv, *Effigurate*, having a distinct form or fringe. **1886** HOLMES & GRAY *Brit. Fungi, Lichens* 6 When its [*sc.* of the thallus] circumference is radiate or stellate, it is effigurate. **1921** A. L. SMITH *Lichens* iii. 80 A frequent type of squamulose thallus is that termed 'placodioid', or 'effigurate', in which the squamulose character is chiefly apparent at the circumference.

†**eˈffigure,** *v. Obs. rare*⁻¹. [f. EF- + FIGURE *v.*] *trans.* To put into shape.

1486 *Bk. St. Albans, Heraldry* A ij b, The law of armys..the whiche was effygured..before ony lawe of the worlde.

effigy (ˈɛfɪdʒɪ). [a. F. *effigie*, ad. L. *effigiēs* in same sense, f. *effingĕre* to fashion. Our examples before 18th c. are either pl. or in the phrase *in effigie* (see 2), so that they may belong to L. EFFIGIES.]

1. A likeness, portrait, or image. Now chiefly applied to a sculptured representation, or to a habited image, as in 2; also to a portrait on a coin; in wider sense somewhat *arch.*

1539 N. WOTTON in Ellis *Orig. Lett.* I. cxliv. II. 122 Hanze Albein hath taken th'effigies of my Ladye Anne and the ladye Amelye. **1611** CORYAT *Crudities* 211 Their pictures or effigies (for I doubt whether picture be a proper word..

because it is not done with the pensill) are made of this worke [mosaic]. **1673** CAVE *Prim. Chr.* III. ii. 282 The Effigies & Representations of Martyrs. **1713** STEELE *Englishm.* No. 55 ¶1 The burning the Effigy of the Pretender. **1727** A. HAMILTON *New Acc. E. Ind.* I. xxxi. 384 But his Effigie is often carried abroad in Procession, mounted on a Coach four Stories high. **1847** EMERSON *Repr. Men* iv. Wks. (Bohn) I. 343, I look at his effigy opposite the title-page. **1853** PHILLIPS *Rivers Yorksh.* viii. 195 Coins, bearing the effigy of the Horse. **1870** F. WILSON *Ch. Lindisf.* 29 An ancient cross-legged effigy clad in mail.

2. Phrases. ***in effigy***: under the form, or by means of, a portrait or image; also *fig.* ***to execute, hang, burn in effigy***: to inflict upon an image the semblance of the punishment which the original is considered to have deserved; formerly done by way of carrying out a judicial sentence on a criminal who had escaped; now only as an expression of popular indignation or hatred.

In the early examples the phrase *in effigie* was prob. always intended as Latin; in poetry of the 17th c. the pronunc. with 4 syllables is usually indicated.

1617 DONNE *Serm.* (1661) III. 14 In those that are damned before, we are damned in Effigie. *a* **1652** BROME *Queene's Exch.* II. i. (1657) C j b, Marvel not..when this but in Effigy [*sic*, though metre requires L. *in effigie*] Was but plac'd by her. **1666** *3rd Advice Painter* 31 Gibson, farewell, till next we put to sea, Faith thou hast drawn her in Effigie. **1678** BUTLER *Hud.* III. II. 1528 Some, on the Sign-post of an Ale-house Hang in Effigy on the Gallows. **1707** *Lond. Gaz.* No. 4367/1 A Third, nam'd Piaget, was executed in Effigie, he had fled from Justice. **1711** ADDISON *Spect.* No. 69 ¶7 One of our old Kings..is represented in Effigy. **1724** SWIFT *Wood's Exec.* Wks. 1755 V. II. 157 The people..appointed certain commissioners to hang him in effigie. **1833** HT. MARTINEAU *Manch. Strike* iii. 32 Who proposed to burn them in effigy?

3. **effigy-mound**, a prehistoric earth mound in the shape of an animal.

1885 *Science* V. 131/2 So few earthworks resembling animals in their shape are known beyond the limits of Wisconsin, that I send you an account..of the most interesting..Minnesota effigy mounds. **1929** *Encycl. Brit.* (ed. 14) XV. 928/2 In Wisconsin the most interesting mounds are the effigy mounds—earthen forms of mammals, birds and reptiles. *Ibid.*, The purpose of these effigy mounds is probably totemic. **1948** A. L. KROEBER *Anthropology* (ed. 2) xviii. 820 Some early Woodland cultures..Proto-Effigy Mound or Old Copper, Wisconsin... Some middle-period cultures..Effigy Mound, Wisconsin.

Hence **'effigy** *v. trans.*, to serve as a picture of, to 'body forth'.

1816 J. SCOTT *Vis. Paris* 52 Paris..is..rich in what is calculated..to suggest reflection..by effigying the events of a far distant date.

†**e'ffiner.** *Obs. rare*$^{-1}$. [f. **effine*, var. of AFFINE *v.* (cf. EFFIRM *v.*) + -ER.] A refiner (of silver or gold).

1591 SIR A. NAPIER *Let.* in *Mem. J. Napier* (1834) 230 The said effyneris may mak mair nor xl^{m} [£40,000] of profeitt.

effing: see EFF *v.*

†**e'ffinge,** *v. Obs.* [ad. L. *effingĕre*, f. *ex* out + *fingĕre* to fashion.] *trans.* To fashion, shape.

1657 TOMLINSON *Renou's Disp.* 592 Each Medicament is ..effinged into a form proper for the diseased.

†**e'ffirm,** *v. Sc. Obs.* [var. of AFFIRM.] *trans.* To assert (the existence of).

1549 *Compl. Scot.* vi. 51 Lactantius firmien..scornis the mathematiciens that effirmis antipodos.

†**e'fflagitate,** *v. Obs. rare.* [f. L. *efflāgitāt-* ppl. stem of *efflāgitāre*, f. *ex* out + *flāgitāre* to demand.] *trans.* To demand eagerly; to desire eagerly. Hence **efflagitated** *ppl. a.*

1641 PRYNNE *Antip. Ded.* 5 Which long efflagitated difficult worke..the publishing of this Antipathy will much facilitate. **1676** SHADWELL *Virtuoso* II. i, The noble enterprize..devoutly to be efflagitated by all ingenious persons.

efflagration (ɛflə'greɪʃən). *rare.* [as if ad. L. *efflagrātiōn-em*, f. *efflagrāre*, f. *ex* out + *flagrāre* to blaze.] Emission of flames.

1811 PINKERTON *Petral.* II. 271 This mountain was formerly in a state of efflagration. *Ibid.* 304 The efflagration ceased.

†**e'fflate,** *v. Obs. rare.* [f. L. *efflāt-* ppl. stem of *efflāre*, f. *ex* out + *flāre* to blow.] *trans.* To puff out.

1634 SIR T. HERBERT *Trav.* 78 Efflated with pride and high opinions of his worth. **1656** in BLOUNT *Glossogr.* **1775** in ASH. **1864** in WEBSTER; and in mod. Dicts.

efflation (ɛ'fleɪʃən). [as if ad. L. **efflātiōn-em*, noun of action f. *efflā-re*: see prec.]

1. Blowing out, strong expulsion of breath.

1578 BANISTER *Hist. Man* I. 19 Efflation, which is the immediate matter of voyce, is the action of the same Arterie. **1661** LOVELL *Hist. Anim. & Min.* 359 The cough..is a vehement, frequent, and sounding efflation of much breath. **1772** in SCOTT *Bailey's Dict.* (Ash).

2. *concr.* That which is blown or breathed forth; an emanation.

1862 F. HALL *Hindu Philos. Syst.* 65 The *Rig-veda* is the efflation of that great being.

‖**effleurage** (eflœraʒ), *sb. Massage.* [Fr., f. *effleurer* to touch or stroke lightly.] A centripetal stroking movement made with the flat or the heel of the hand. So **effleurage** *v. intr.*, to massage a part or a limb with this movement.

1886 MURRELL *Massage* iii. 10 *Effleurage*..is a stroking movement made with the palm of the hand passing with various degrees of force over the surface centripetally. **1890** A. KELLGREN *Man. Treatment* 9 The effleurage may be very superficial or deep. **1893** A. C. HALE *Massage* 133 Separate the fingers and effleurage throughly over and round the malleoli. **1961** I. FLEMING *Thunderball* iv. 36 Two hands, clad in..fur, were rhythmically passing..up and down the whole length of his body... Presently he said sleepily, 'Is that what they call effleurage?'

effloresce (ɛflɒ'rɛs). [ad. L. *efflōrescĕre*, f. *ex* out + *flōrescĕre* to blossom, f. *flōs, flōr-is* a flower.]

1. †**a.** To bloom, burst forth into flowers (*obs.*). **b.** To burst forth into something resembling a flower. **c.** To burst forth as a plant when flowering; const. *into.*

1775 SIR E. BARRY *Observ. Wines* 25 They will..begin to effloresce and shoot out into Flowers. **1807** VANCOUVER *Agric. Devon* (1813) 432 Fungi germinate, effloresce, disseminate, and die, during the evolutions of the seasons. **1826** GOOD *Bk. Nat.* (1834) II. 18 Zoophytes, or Plant-animals, so denominated from their efflorescing like plants. **1870** ROLLESTON *Anim. Life* 144 Efflorescing into two or three coecal ampullæ.

2. *Chem.* **a.** Of a crystalline substance: To change over the surface, or throughout, to 'flowers' or fine powder, owing to the loss of the water of crystallization on exposure to the air.

1788 W. NICHOLSON tr. *Fourcroy's Nat. Hist. & Chem.* II. 305 Some salts..readily effloresce, and continue to fall in pieces, till the whole becomes a fine white powder. **1791** HAMILTON tr. *Berthollet's Dyeing* I. I. III. i. 214 It effloresces, that is, it parts with its water of crystallization in the air, and assumes the appearance of flour. **1860** H. W. REVELEY in *Jrnl. Soc. Arts* VIII. 323/2 Tufo, a volcanic production, never effloresces.

b. Of a salt: To come (in solution) to the surface (of the ground, etc.) and there crystallize. Also, To form a crust (by capillary attraction and evaporation) on the sides of a vessel containing a solution.

1820 T. CROMWELL *Excurs. Ireland* vii. 61 The vitriolic particles..are seen to effloresce in various places. **1868** DANA *Min.* (1880) 636 Mirabilite..effloresces with other salts on the limestone below the Genesee Falls.

c. Of the ground, a wall, etc.: To become covered with a powdery crust of saline particles left by evaporation from a solution which has been drawn to the surface by capillary attraction.

18.. DANA (W.) The walls of limestone caverns sometimes effloresce with nitrate of lime.

3. *fig.* **a.** (after 1) To 'blossom out', break out into brilliant display. **b.** (after 2 c) Of hidden agencies, etc.: To come to the surface, become manifest.

1834 FOSTER *Pop. Ignorance* Knowledge..has seemed at last beginning to effloresce through the surface of the ground. **1837** CARLYLE *Fr. Rev.* (1872) III. III. i. 101 The secret courses of civic business..effervescing & efflorescing ..as a concrete Phenomenon. **1864** *Sat. Rev.* 31 Dec. 812/1 A disposition..to effloresce into extremely tall talk. **1865** *Pall Mall G.* 13 Apr. 10 The man who effloresces in later life into the full-blown social science orator.

effloresced (ɛflɒ'rɛst), *ppl. a.* [f. prec. + -ED.] That has crystallized on the surface; also, that has crumbled to powder. (See the vb.)

1809 *Naval Chron.* XXI. 230 Effloresced matter thrown down from the rocks. **1854** HOOKER *Himal. Jrnls.* I. i. 13 They were frequently white with effloresced salts. **1884** *Athenæum* 15 Nov. 628/2 The heat of dissolution of effloresced sodium sulphate.

efflorescence (ɛflɒ'rɛsəns). [a. F. *efflorescence*, as if ad. L. **efflōrescentia*, f. *efflōrescent-em*, pr. pple. of *efflōrescĕre* to EFFLORESCE: see -ENCE.]

1. The process of producing flowers, or bursting into flower; the period of flowering.

1626 BACON *Sylva* §389 The Spirit of the Plant is.. severed from the grosser Juyce in the Efflorescence. **1869** GOULBURN *Purs. Holiness* ii. 15 They are the blossom on the fruit-tree, an efflorescence which shows the tree's vitality. **1870** YEATS *Nat. Hist. Comm.* 117 The tendency to efflorescence in the trees of America..has encouraged their diffusion through Europe.

2. *fig.* A development like that of blossom; an abundant or ostentatious growth; the 'flower' of age, etc.

1672 MARVELL *Reh. Transp.* I. 40 His impertinent efflorescence of Rhetorick upon so mean Topicks. **1675** EVELYN *Terra* (1729) 14 The pared-off Turf is the very fat, and Efflorescence of the Earth. *a* **1711** KEN *Hymns Evang.* Poet. Wks. 1721 I. 187 Lord, who in Efflorescence of thy Age Wouldst from the World thy Spirit disengage. **1751** JOHNSON *Rambl.* No. 141 ¶11 Mirth can never please, but as the efflorescence of a mind loved for its luxuriance. **1831** CARLYLE *Misc.* (1857) II. 284 Of Fable Literature this was the summer-tide and highest efflorescence. **1865** LECKY *Ration.* II. vi. 265 That noble efflorescence of charity which marked the first ages of Christianity.

†**3.** Colour developed on the skin, either in the ordinary course of nature, or as the result of disease. *Obs.* in gen. sense.

1646 SIR T. BROWNE *Pseud. Ep.* VI. x. 330 A shadow or darke efflorescence in the outside. **1782** V. KNOX *Ess.* (1819) III. cxxxiii. 69 The hectic efflorescence on the countenance of an invalid.

b. *Pathol.* 'A morbid redness, or rash of the skin' (*Syd. Soc. Lex.*).

1684 tr. *Bonet's Merc. Compit.* v. 152 There is a threefold difference of Efflorescences in the skin. **1783** J. C. SMYTH in *Med. Commun.* I. 149 The efflorescence on her arms [is] entirely gone. **1876** tr. *Wagner's Gen. Pathol.* 135 In measles, infection reaches its greatest power during the eruptive stage and the stage of efflorescence.

4. *Chem.* The process of efflorescing, in various senses (see EFFLORESCE 2 a, b, c); also *concr.* the powdery deposit which is the result of this process.

1667 BOYLE *Orig. Formes & Qual.* 326 To afford an efflorescence which..appear'd to be Vitriol. **1671** KIRKBY in *Phil. Trans.* (1672) VII. 4070 It [an inland sea, near Danzick] becomes..green in the midle with an hairy efflorescence. **1677** PLOT *Nat. Hist. Oxfordsh.* 62 Pyrites are ..the efflorescence of Minerals. **1703** MAUNDRELL *Journ. Jerus.* (1721) Add. 10 We found under it Efflorescences of pure Salt. **1828** STEUART *Planter's Guide* 189 The sulphate of iron is..distinguished by an efflorescence of small white crystals. **1858** O. W. HOLMES *De Sauty*, Whitened round his feet the dust of efflorescence. **1886** ROSCOE *Elem. Chem.* 183 [Nitrate of potassium] occurs as an efflorescence on the soil.

†**efflo'rescency.** *Obs. rare.* [f. as prec.: see -ENCY.] Efflorescent condition; an abundant display. *fig.* Also = prec. (sense 4).

1649 J. H. *Motion Parl.* 14 Such persons, as shall discover the greatest luxury and efflorescency of Vertue. **1701** BEVERLEY *Glory of Grace* 4 Highest Efflorescency of glory. **1703** MAUNDRELL *Journ. Jerus.* 81 These Saline efflorescencies I found at some leagues distance from the Dead Sea.

efflorescent (ɛflɒ'rɛsənt), *a.* [ad. L. *efflōrescent-em*, pr. pple. of *efflōrescere*: see EFFLORESCE.]

1. *Bot.* That is efflorescing or blooming.

2. a. Resembling an efflorescence. **b.** Forming an efflorescence; appearing on the surface in a powdery deposit; also *fig.*

1818 FARADAY *Res.* vii. (1848) 18 A slight efflorescent appearance was seen on the broken edge. **1876** HARLEY *Mat. Med.* 69 In combination..it is found efflorescent on the soil in some countries. **1878** BATES *Centr. Amer.* vi. 81 Gold..is found mostly efflorescent or disseminated in the mines of La Luz and S. Bernabé. **1879** G. MACDONALD *P. Faber* I. x. 117 Deadening his touch with the efflorescent crusts..upon the dry bones of theology.

efflo'rescing, *ppl. a.* [f. EFFLORESCE + -ING.] That effloresces; that resembles an efflorescence.

1853 KANE *Grinnell Exp.* xxxvi. (1856) 331 A tideless river, margined by new ice and crusted with efflorescing snow. *Ibid* xxxvii. 343 Great efflorescing knobs.

†**e'fflower,** *v.*[1] *Obs. rare*$^{-1}$. In 5 efflour. [f. EF- + FLOWER *v.*] *intr.* Of a plant: To go out of bloom.

c **1420** *Pallad. on Husb.* III. 82 This meene [kynde] effloureth [L. *deflorescit*] sone.

efflower (ɛ'flaʊə(r)), *v.*[2] *rare.* [ad. F. *effleurer* in same sense (after FLOWER).] (See quot.)

1875 URE *Dict. Arts* III. 87 Chamois, or Shamoy leather. The skins are first washed, limed, fleeced, and branned as above described. They are next efflowered, that is deprived of their epidermis, by a blunt knife.

effluction, obs. form of EFFLUXION.

effluence ('ɛfl(j)uːəns). [as if ad. L. **effluentia*, f. *effluent-em* flowing out (see EFFLUENT); cf. earlier AFFLUENCE, ad. L. *affluentia*.]

1. A flowing out (*esp.* of light, electricity, magnetism, etc.); also *transf.* a (tumultuous) streaming forth (of men).

1635 N. CARPENTER *Geog. Del.* I. iii. 54 Electricall bodies draw other bodies vnto them by reason of a moist effluence of vapours. **1646** SIR T. BROWNE *Pseud. Ep.* II. ii. 64 Where the greater continents are joyned, the action and effluence [of magnetism] is also greater. **1759** *Phil. Trans.* LI. 386 The cohesion cannot be owing to an effluence and affluence of one and the same electrical fluid. **1837** CARLYLE *Fr. Rev.* III. I. i. 6 That stormful effluence towards the Frontiers. **1877** L. MORRIS *Epic Hades* III. 233 Gladdened by that broad effluence of light.

b. *fig.*

1628 T. SPENCER *Logick* 196 Truth, not of constitution.. But, of emanation, effluence, and consecution. *a* **1716** SOUTH *Serm.* in *Daily Tel.* (1883) 10 July 5/4 The fulness and effluence of man's enjoyments. **1836** *New Monthly Mag.* XLVIII. 203 In this effluence of words..the genuine art of dramatic writing consists.

2. *concr.* That which flows forth; an emanation.

1603 HOLLAND *Plutarch's Mor.* 1301 All water and moisture..they call the effluence of Osiris. **1718** PRIOR *Poems* 311 Heav'n's fuller Effluence mocks our dazl'd Sight. **1862** F. HALL *Hindu Philos. Syst.* 225 When the jar is seen, an effluence of the internal organ..takes its form. **1875** JOWETT *Plato* (ed. 2) I. 276 Colour is an effluence of form.

b. *fig.*

1625 GILL *Sacr. Philos.* i. 30 We speake of goodnesse, of power, &c., as of the effluences..thereof. *a* **1711** KEN *Edmund* Poet. Wks. 1721 II. 371 And to support the Martyr, on his Head Consolatory Effluences shed. **1860** MOTLEY *Netherl.* (1868) I. v. 148 The effluence which came so naturally from the tranquil eyes of William the Silent. **1865** MERIVALE *Rom. Emp.* VIII. lxiv. 70 They were persuaded that the empire itself..was an effluence from the divine regimen of the world.

†'**effluenced**, *ppl. a. Obs. rare*$^{-1}$. [f. prec. + -ED.] That is borne out in an effluence or outflow; outpoured.

1691 E. TAYLOR tr. *Behmen's Theos. Philos.* 56 The effluenced spoken Matter of the third.

†'**effluency.** *Obs. rare.* [See EFFLUENCE and -ENCY.] = EFFLUENCE.

1646 SIR T. BROWNE *Pseud. Ep.* II. i. 52 These scintillations are..the inflamable effluencies discharged from the bodies collided.

effluent ('ɛfl(j)uːənt), *a.* and *sb.* [ad. L. *effluent-em* pr. pple of *efflŭere* to flow out, f. *ex* out + *flŭere* to flow.]

A. *adj.* That flows forth or outwards.

1726 MONRO *Anat. Nerves* (1741) 21 Arterious or effluent. **1738** KEILL *Anim. Œcon.* 90 The Motion of the effluent Water will be alike in both cases. **1828** *Blackw. Mag.* XXIII. 590 The pure, hot, effluent gravy of your steak. **1880** *Daily News* 9 Jan., An effluent drain into the Thames.

fig. **1803** *Monthly Mag.* XV. 151 The Acts of Peter form a..narrative, so widely different in character from the Acts of Paul, that it is hardly possible to conceive them effluent from the same pen. **1839** BAILEY *Festus* (1848) 60/1 Born Of effluent or influent Deity.

B. *sb.* **a.** A stream flowing from a larger stream, lake, or reservoir. **b.** The outflow from a sewage tank, or from land after irrigation or earth-filtration of sewage.

1859 R. BURTON *Centr. Afr.* in *Jrnl. Geog. Soc.* XXIX. Geographers will doubt that such a mass..can maintain its level without an effluent. **1879** JEFFERIES *Wild Life in S.C.* 344 This old hatch..is situate..on the effluent. **1883** *Pall Mall G.* 20 Oct. 4/1 The clear effluent has been drawn off from each tank.

c. Waste discharged from an industrial works.

1930 *Jrnl. Iron & Steel Inst.* CXL. 159 A The effluent is very clear..and is not harmful to human or fish life. **1959** *Listener* 8 Jan. 48/2 The nuisances of smoke and factory effluent. **1969** MORSE *Fur Trade* II. vi. 85 This is the result of industrial effluent from the two paper mills.

d. Radioactive waste discharged from an atomic plant.

1955 *Rep. U.K. Atomic Energy Auth.* I. ix. 24 The Authority are required to analyse samples of all liquid effluent discharged.

Hence '**effluentness.** *rare*$^{-0}$.

1772 in SCOTT *Bailey's Dict.* (Ash).

†'**effluous,** *a. Obs.*$^{-0}$ [f. late L. *efflu-us* of same meaning + -OUS.] That runs or flows out.

1656 in BLOUNT *Glossogr.*

effluve (ɛ'fl(j)uːv). *Electr.* [a. F. *effluve* in same sense, ad. L. *effluv-ium*, f. *ex* out + *flu-ĕre* to flow.

The Fr. word was first employed in this sense as a translation of EFFLUVIUM, used in English by Hauksbee 1767.]

The diffusion of electricity from an electrified body by radiation or atmospheric conduction.

1881 in *Nature* XXV. 168 Combination of hydrogen with oxygen under the influence of electric effluves.

†e'**ffluviable,** *a. Obs. rare*$^{-1}$. [f. EFFLUVIUM + -ABLE.] That can pass off in effluvia.

a **1691** BOYLE *Electricity* Wks. 1772 IV. 354 A great degree of heat..[in a diamond being ground] may force it to spend its effluviable matter.

†e'**ffluviate,** *v. Obs.* [f. EFFLUVI-UM + -ATE³.] **a.** *trans.* To throw off (in a stream) small particles or corpuscles; also *absol.* **b.** *intr.* Of the corpuscles themselves: To pass off in a stream. Hence **e'ffluviating** *ppl. a.*

1664 POWER *Exp. Philos.* I. 57 Camphire which spends itself by continually effluviating its own Component Particles. *Ibid.* II. 103 The Stars and Planets with their Luminous and Vaporous Sphæres continually effluviating from them. *Ibid.* III. 159 Bodies that effluviate intrinsecally from themselves. **1685** BOYLE *Salub. Air* 53 The various effluviating Bodies. **1693** SIR T. BLOUNT *Nat. Hist.* 186.

e'ffluvient, *a. nonce-wd.* Extremely fluent.

1835 BECKFORD *Recoll.* 169 To say truth, they were not only intolerably effluvient but inveterately prosy.

effluvious (ɛ'fluːvɪəs), *a.* [f. EFFLUVI-UM + -OUS.] Of the nature of an effluvium, passing off like an effluvium.

1668 HOWE *Bless. Righteous* (1825) 125 The soul should covet a re-union with every effluvious particle of its former body. **1678** CUDWORTH *Intell. Syst.* 851 They supposing Humane Volitions..to be Mechanically Caused..from those Effluvious Images of Bodies.

effluvium (ɛ'fluːvɪəm). *Pl.* **effluvia,** 7-8 **effluviums.** [a. late L. *effluvium*, f. *efflu-ĕre*, f. *ex* out + *flŭere* to flow.]

†**1.** A flowing out, an issuing forth; a process or manner of issuing forth. *Obs.*

1651 BIGGS *New Disp.* 156 The effluvium of bloud. **1676** MARVELL *Mr. Smirke* Wks. 1875 IV. 8 [The bishops]..cannot transmit it [wit] by breathing, touching, or any other natural effluvium. **1704** SWIFT *T. Tub* (1768) I. 123 Owing to certain subteraneous effluviums of wind.

2. Chiefly applied to the (real or supposed) outflow of material particles too subtle to be perceived by touch or sight; *concr.* a stream of such outflowing particles. †**a.** *gen.* (*obs.*).

1651 BIGGS *New Disp.* 114 A continual steame of most subtle effluviums. **1677** PLOT *Oxfordsh.* 89 A spirituous, yet corporeal effluvium..flowing from it. **1711** SHAFTESB. *Charac. Enthus.* (1749) I. 33 Epicurus..thinks to solve 'em by his Effluvia, and aerial looking-glasses. **1732** POPE *Ess. Man* I. 191 Quick effluvia darting through the brain.

b. A stream of minute particles, formerly supposed to be emitted by a magnet, electrified body, or other attracting or repelling agent, and to be the means by which it produces its effects. Chiefly *pl.* (Now only *Hist.*; but it probably survived the theory which it strictly implies.) Also *fig.*

1646 SIR T. BROWNE *Pseud. Ep.* 86 So will a Diamond or Saphire emit an effluvium sufficient to move the needle or a straw without diminution of weight. **1658** J. ROBINSON *Eudoxa* II. 121 The Load-stone doth..so freely send forth its effluviums. **1660** BOYLE *New Exp. Phys.-Mech.* xvii. 120 The Effluvia of the Load-stone. **1701** BEVERLEY *Glory of Grace* 23 He as the Sovereign Magnet..Attracts every Living Stone by the Effluviums, the Flowings out of Life into, and upon, it. **1788** COWPER *Let.* 9 Aug., Mr. Rose a valuable young man..attracted by the effluvia of my genius. **1837** BREWSTER *Magnet.* 152 A plane or circle held east and west..divides the north from the south magnetic effluvia. **1863** DRAPER *Intell. Devel. Europe* xix. (1865) 449 The doctrine..that magnetism is an effluvium issuing forth from the root of the tail of the Little Bear.

c. An 'exhalation' affecting the sense of smell, or producing effects by being received into the lungs. In mod. popular use chiefly a noxious or disgusting exhalation or odour.

1656 tr. *Hobbes' Elem. Philos.* (1839) 503 They that say, there goes something out of the odorous body, call it an effluvium. **1663** BOYLE *Usef. Exp. Philos.* II. 244 Infectious Diseases..conveyed by insensible Effluvia. **1712** ADDISON *Spect.* No. 538 ⁋3 The miraculous Powers which the Effluviums of cheese have. **1821** CRAIG *Lect. Drawing* ii. 132 The effluvium proceeding from the colours..is extremely injurious to..health. **1845** DARWIN *Voy. Nat.* iii. (1852) 49 At the distance of half a mile..I have perceived the whole air tainted with the effluvium. **1867** J. MARTINEAU *Ess.* II. 260 [They] know nothing of the effluvia of the orange.

¶**3.** The pl. *effluvia* has often been ignorantly or carelessly treated as a sing. (in senses 2 a, b, c), with a new pl. *effluvias* or *effluviæ.*

1652 FRENCH *Yorksh. Spa* xvii. 120 Subtile insensible spirits, or rather atomes and effluvia's. **1692** NORRIS *Curs. Refl.* 24 Tell me how these corporeal effluvias..enter the eye. **1796** C. MARSHALL *Garden.* ii. (1813) 20 Pieces of a different flavour and effluvia in the bark, wood, leaves, etc. **1806** T. THOMAS *To W. Hanbury* 14 The fam'd Perfumes of Summer..Men to Rapture with Effluvias move. **1806** T. PAINE *Yellow Fev.* Misc. Wks. II. 180 An impure effluvia, arising from..the ground. **1822** IMISON *Sc. & Art* II. 64 The putrid effluviæ in prisons. **1834** BECKFORD *Italy* II. 85 A strong effluvia of the stable.

efflux ('ɛflʌks), *sb.* [ad. L. *efflux-us*, f. *efflŭere*: see EFFLUENT.]

1. A flowing outwards of water or other liquid; a stream, river. Also, of air, gases, volatile particles, magnetic or electric currents, etc.; opposed to *afflux* or *influx*. Also *attrib.* Hence, a channel of outflow.

1649 JER. TAYLOR *Gt. Exemp.* xiv. §21 A pool was made from the frequent effluxes. **1656** tr. *Hobbes' Elem. Philos.* (1839) 504 The cause of smelling must consist in the simple motion of the parts of odorous bodies without any efflux or diminution of their whole substance. **1660** BOYLE *New Exp.* ii. (1682) 81 The Reciever did afford some efflux to the air. **1747** FRANKLIN *Wks.* (1840) V. 184 We had even discovered ..its [electrical fire's] afflux to the electrical sphere, as well as its efflux. **1846** GROTE *Greece* (1862) I. xvi. 329 The narrow defile of Tempê, forming..the efflux of all the waters from the Thessalian basin. **1867** W. W. SMYTH *Coal & Coal-mining* 187 The efflux point of the water. **1870** R. FERGUSON *Electr.* 55 It seems unlikely that efflux of – E.. should be immediately succeeded by an influx of + E.

b. *fig.*

1641 SANDERSON *Serm.* II. 186 His..providential acts.. by reason of that their efflux and emanation are made better known to us. **1651** JER. TAYLOR *Course Serm.* I. ii. 17, I have described the effluxes of the Holy Spirit upon us in his great chanels. **1827** C. BRIDGES *Exp. Ps.* cxix. (1830) 183 The acts of God are nothing else but the effluxes of his goodness. **1882** PEBODY *Eng. Journalism* xvii. 129 Prestige with a newspaper..is..an invisible efflux of personal power.

†**2.** *Pathol.* (See quot.) *Obs.*

1754-64 SMELLIE *Midwif.* I. 124 A miscarriage that happens before the tenth day was formerly called an efflux.

3. The lapse, passing away (of time, or of a particular period); hence, expiry, end.

1647 N. BACON *Hist. Disc.* v. 21 Austin..left it to successors to work out by degrees in efflux of time. *a* **1677** MANTON *Serm. Ps.* cxix. 100 All that efflux of time which was between Christ's ascension and his second coming, is called 'the latter days'. **1768-74** TUCKER *Lt. Nat.* II. 322 The workings of mechanical causes in the efflux of rolling years. **1884** SIR J. DAY in *Law Reports 13 Queen's B.* 631 The efflux in 1877 of the time within which the turnpike trust was limited.

4. *concr.* That which flows out; an emanation.

1647 H. MORE *Psychozoia* Pref., All our souls are free effluxes from his essence. **1677** HALE *Prim. Orig. Man.* IV. iii. 310 The natural production of Insects out of the finest parts and effluxes of most Vegetable Natures. *a* **1711** KEN *Christophil* Poet. Wks. 1721 I. 500 Such Graces, O co-effluent Dove, Are the Effluxes of thy Love. **1880** GLADSTONE in *Scotsman* 23 Mar., The Established Church of Scotland..was the efflux of the mind of the people.

†**e'fflux,** *v. Obs. rare.* [f. prec. sb.]

a. *trans.* To subject to efflux; to cause to flow forth. **b.** *intr.* To flow forth; (of time) to elapse. Hence **e'ffluxing** *ppl. a.*, outflowing.

1660 BOYLE *Seraph. Love* xi. (1700) 61 Some odd Centuries of years, (efflux'd since the Creation). **1669** —— *Contn. New Exp.* Wks. 1772 III. 222 As much mercury as will of itself flow out is effluxed. **1674** R. GODFREY *Inj. & Ab. Physick* 147 From his own effluxing goodness of Charity, he alwayes took care of me.

effluxion (ɛ'flʌkʃən). Also 7-9 **effluction.** [f. prec. + -ION¹.]

1. The action or process of flowing out; an outflow (of fluids or currents of any kind). Also *fig.*

1646 SIR T. BROWNE *Pseud. Ep.* 80 We might perhaps beleeve that..by this effluxion bodies tended to the earth. **1651** tr. *Bacon's Life & Death* 53 An abundant and continual Effluxion of blood causeth suddain death. **1670** G. H. *Hist. Cardinals* II. III. 209 Would he but endeavour to suppress certain passionate effluctions from his youth. **1874** *Wiltsh. Times* 3 Apr. 5/2 Death occurred from a sudden effluxion of the blood to the brain.

b. *concr.* An abortion. Cf. EFFLUX *sb.* 2.

1643 R. O. *Man's Mort.* vi. 48 The Soule of that Effluction ..must needs continue its immortallitie. **1696** in PHILLIPS. **1721-1800** in BAILEY.

2. The lapse or passing away (of time); the expiry or completion (of a certain period).

1621 MOLLE *Camerar. Liv. Libr.* V. xii. 362 Till friendship may be consolidated by effluxion of time. **1633** EARL MANCH. *Al Mondo* (1636) 9 The glasse then runnes most faintly when it [the hour] draws nearest to effluxion. **1807** G. CHALMERS *Caledonia* I. Pref. 6 The effluxion of a century. **1868** *Times* 12 June 10 The partnership..having expired by effluxion of time.

3. *concr.* = EFFLUVIUM, EFFLUX 3.

1626 BACON *Sylva* §941 There are..some Light Effluxions from spirit to spirit. *c* **1630** JACKSON *Creed* V. cxiii, Some..deny all effluxions from objects sensible. **1852** SIR W. HAMILTON *Discuss.* 69 Dr. Brown confounds the matterless species of the Peripatetics with the corporeal effluxions of Democritus and Epicurus.

†**e'ffluxive,** *a. Obs. rare.* [as if ad. L. **effluxīvus*, f. *efflux-*, ppl. stem of *efflŭere*: see prec. and -IVE.] Outflowing.

a **1657** R. LOVEDAY *Lett.* (1663) 24 The kindred of our.. souls is called friendship, when their effluxive beams.. meet, embrace, and weave themselves into a constellation.

†'**effocate.** *rare*$^{-0}$. [ad. L. *effōcāt-* ppl. stem of *effōcāre*, f. *ex* out + *faux* throat. Cf. SUFFOCATE.] To choke, strangle.

1656 in BLOUNT.

†**e'ffode,** *v. Obs. rare.* [ad. L. *effodĕre*, f. *ex* out + *fodĕre* to dig.] To dig out (of the ground), dig up.

1657 TOMLINSON *Renou's Disp.* 41 Some may be effoded and gathered. **1657** *Phys. Dict.*, *Effoded*, digged up.

†**e'ffodiate,** *v. Obs. rare.* [irreg. f. L. *effodĕre*: see prec. and -ATE³.] = prec.

1612 W. PARKES *Curtaine-Dr.* 73 Trenches that it [this little Spade] hath efodiated.

†**e'ffodicate,** *v. Obs. rare*$^{-1}$. [f. EF- + L. *fodicāt-*, ppl. stem of *fodicāre* to dig.] = prec.

1599 A. M. tr. *Gabelhouer's Bk. Physicke* 34/1 Roote of Buglosse..effodicated in the end & last quarter of the Moone.

e'ffodient, *a. rare*$^{-0}$. [ad. L. *effodient-em*, pr. pple. of *effodĕre*: see EFFODE.] Digging; accustomed to dig.

1847 in CRAIG. **1864** in WEBSTER; and in mod. Dicts.

†**e'ffoliate,** *v. Obs. rare.* [f. EF- + FOLIATE *v.*] To open into leaf. Hence **e'ffoliated** *ppl. a.*, that has opened into leaf. Also (with different sense) **effoli'ation,** removal of leaves (*Treas. Bot.*).

1671 GREW *Anat. Plants* i. §44 That which here befalls the now effoliated Lobes.

†**e'fforce,** *sb. Obs. rare*$^{-1}$. [a. OF. *efforce, -se*, f. *efforcer*; see next.] A violent means.

1549 SIR T. CHALONER *Erasm. Moriæ Enc.* P j a, Woulde they so manfully defende and kepe it, both with swoorde, with poyson, and with all other efforce.

efforce (ɛ'fɔəs), *v.* Also 6 **efforse.** [ad. F. *efforcer* (OF. *esforcer*) = Pr. *esforsar, -zar*, It. *sforzare* :—med.L. *exfortiāre*, f. *ex* out + *forti-s* strong.]

†**1.** *refl.* To force oneself, to make an effort (transl. F. *s'efforcer*). *Obs.*

1512 *Helyas* in Thoms *Prose Rom.* III. 31 Eveniche of the company efforced them to doo honour. **1543** TRAHERON *Vigo's Chirurg.* III. I. xv. 105 b, Manye efforce themselves to make argumentes to be contrarye.

2. *trans.* In Spenser's use: To force open, to gain by force, to compel; also, *to efforce it.*

1596 SPENSER *F.Q.* (J.) Iron chests and coffers..Them to efforce by violence or wrong. *Ibid.* III. ix. 9 Affray with cruell threat, Ere that we to efforce it do begin. *Ibid.* xii. 43 Th' enchaunter..all that fraud did frame To have efforst the love of that faire lasse.

3. To force out, tear out by force. *rare.*

1855 SINGLETON *Virgil* I. 91 Standing corn, From lowest roots aloft efforced.

Hence **e'fforced** *ppl. a.*, uttered with effort.

1596 SPENSER *F.Q.* II. viii. 4 Againe he heard a more efforced voyce.

e'ffore, *prep.* var. of AFORE. *Obs.*
1535 *Sc. Acts Jas. V* (1814) 336 (Jam.).

efform (ɛ'fɔːm). Also 6 effourm. [f. EF- + FORM *v.*] *trans.* To make into a certain form; to shape, fashion.
1578 BANISTER *Hist. Man* I. 16 Nature (as I haue sayd) effourmed in such sorte this bone Hyoides. 1647 H. MORE *Poems* 10 Of warlike instruments they plow-shares shall And pruning-hooks efform. 1805 J. BERESFORD *Song of Sun* 31 Stains on themselves they bring, tho' first efform'd Of purest mold, by God. 1862 M. HOPKINS *Hawaii* 211 And efforming the government to some model.

†**effor'mation.** *Obs.* [f. prec. + -ATION.] Formation, framing, shaping.
1578 BANISTER *Hist. Man* IV. 61 We haue noted the noble vse and effourmation of this member. 1662 EVELYN *Chalcogr.* (1769) 16 As the protypus was of wax for efformation. 1691 RAY *Creation* (1714) 40 To give an account of the Production and Efformation of the Universe.

†**e'fformative**, *a. Obs.* [f. as prec.: see -IVE.] Formative, tending to form.
1647 H. MORE *Song of Soul* Notes 163/2 Δύναμις πλαστική, is that efformative might in the seed that shapes the body in its growth. 1669 GALE *Crt. Gentiles* I. III. iii. 43 A plastic and efformative virtue.

e'fformer. [f. EFFORM *v.* + -ER.] One who, or that which, forms, moulds, or fashions.
1662 H. MORE *Immort. Soul* 195 If the Mother's Soul could be the Efformer of the Foetus, etc.

effort ('ɛfət), *sb.* [a. F. *effort*, noun of action, f. *efforcer*: see EFFORCE *v.*; in OF. and Pr. *esfort*, It. *sforzo*. In 17th and 18th c. accented *e'ffort*; see quots. in 2.]
†**1.** Power: also, *pl.* powers, properties. *Obs.*
1490 CAXTON *Eneydos* I. 14 The yate..passed alle other in efforte and strengthe. *a* 1680 BUTLER *Rem.* (1759) II. 15 The same Efforts, she does confer Upon the same Productions here.
2. a. A strenuous putting forth of power, physical or mental; a laborious attempt; a struggle.
c 1489 CAXTON *Sonnes of Aymon* 527 Thadmyrall sawe the grete efforte of armes that Reynawde made agenste his folke. *c* 1636 DENHAM *Passion of Dido* 248 Life's last efforts yet striving with her wound. 1682 SHADWELL *Medal* 121 In Cromwels Court, Where first your Muse did make her great effort. 1735 SOMERVILLE *Chase* III. 113 The panting Courser..Makes many a faint Effort. 1769 FALCONER *Dict. Marine* (1789) Hh iv, The rope-bands are sufficient to sustain the effort of the sail. 1809-10 COLERIDGE *Friend* (1865) 7 On whatever subject the mind feels a lively interest, attention, though always an effort, becomes a delightful effort. 1860 TYNDALL *Glac.* I. §27. 202 It required a considerable effort to escape.
b. In the fine arts, oratory, etc.: A display of power, an achievement. Often used somewhat trivially for any kind of achievement, artefact, or result of activity.
1857 BUCKLE *Civilis.* I. xiii. 728 There is..in some of his [Bossuet's] greatest efforts..much..majesty of genius. 1871 L. W. M. LOCKHART *Fair to See* xxiii, His first attempt [*sc.* the letter itself] ran thus..and he tried again... This effort was also torn up in despair. 1924 A. D. SEDGWICK *Little French Girl* I. vii. 59 The Venus is an effort of Ruth's. 1945 C. H. WARD-JACKSON *Piece of Cake* (ed. 2) 26 *Effort*, applied to anything that has been made, especially mechanical. 1967 *Lebende Sprachen* XII. 161/1 Companies who have extensive development efforts under way. *Ibid.*, The research effort will be carried out by the development of laboratories already in operation. *Ibid.*, The government recognizes the benefits of a broadbased space effort.
c. *Mech.* (See quots. 1842, 1875.)
1842 FRANCIS *Dict. Arts, Effort*, the force with which a body in motion tends to produce an effect, whether the effect be really produced or impeded. 1875 RANKINE & BAMBER *Mech. Text-Bk.* (ed. 2) 205 A direct force is..distinguished, according as it acts with or against the motion of the point..by the name of effort, or of resistance, as the case may be. 1883 *Encycl. Brit.* XV. 764/2 If the component along the direction of motion acts with the motion, it is called an effort. 1959 *Chambers's Encycl.* IX. 200/2 The ratio of the load to the effort is the mechanical advantage of the machine, and the ratio of the distance moved by the effort to the distance moved by the load is the velocity ratio.

†**e'ffort**, *v. Obs.* [f. EF- + L. *fortis* strong.] *trans.* To strengthen, fortify.
1662 FULLER *Worthies* (1840) I. 276 He efforted his spirits with the remembrance..of what formerly he had been.

effortful ('ɛfətfʊl), *a.* [f. EFFORT *sb.* + -FUL.] Exhibiting, full of, or requiring effort.
1900 *Academy* 1 June 473/1 At its most effortful it is strained and excited—a painfully obvious striving beyond the poet's power. 1926 *Brit. Weekly* 4 Nov. 120/4 A life of value is always a strenuous and effortful life. 1927 C. C. MARTINDALE *Christ is King* ii. 34 It is usually more effortful to do right than to do wrong. 1927 *Manch. Guardian Weekly* Sept. 169/2 The effortful conscious striving towards an æsthetic and philosophical ideal. 1964 *Economist* 31 Oct. 469/1 The effortful field of the Government's attempts.

effortless ('ɛfətlɪs), *a.* and quasi-*adv.* [f. EFFORT *sb.* + -LESS.] Making no effort.
1. Abstaining from effort, passive, tame.
1801 SOUTHEY *Thalaba* IV. xix, Idly to remain Were yielding effortless. 1880 H. JAMES *Madonna* 37 You have lost time in effortless contemplation.
2. Acting without effort; unstrained, easy.
1831 *Blackw. Mag.* XXIX. 683 The effortless sublimity of Homer. 1861 *Wheat & Tares* 37 He delighted in their [children's] easy, unconscious, effortless, condition.
Hence **'effortlessly** *adv.*, without exertion.
1865 *Pall Mall G.* 31 July 10/2 Effecting all our object painlessly and effortlessly.

'effortlessness. [f. EFFORTLESS *a.* + -NESS.] The character or quality of being effortless.
1889 W. B. CARPENTER *Perm. Elem. Relig.* vii. 253 He passed from the effortless stage, through the stage of pain and effort, and on again to the stage of effortlessness. 1904 *Daily Chron.* 18 Apr. 3/2 And, in spite of its effortlessness, how splendid in technique. 1923 *Public Opinion* 28 Dec. 643/2 He gave an impression of effortlessness in the calm ease of his manner. 1928 *Observer* 8 Jan. 21/4 That effortlessness and comparative noiselessness of the engine.

†**e'ffossion.** *Obs. rare.* [ad. L. *effossiōn-em*, f. *effoss-us*, pa. pple. of *effodĕre*: see EFFODE.] The action of digging out (of the ground).
1657 TOMLINSON *Renou's Disp.* 271 Its roots..after their effossion are cut and dryed. *c* 1714 ARBUTHNOT, etc. *Mar. Scriblerus* I. i. in *Pope's Wks.* (1886) X. 279 He..set apart several annual sums for..the effossion of coins. 1755 in JOHNSON; and in mod. Dicts.

†**e'ffracted**, *ppl. a. Obs. rare*$^{-1}$. [f. L. *effract-* ppl. stem of *effringĕre*, f. *ex* out + *frang-ĕre* to break + -ED^{1}.] Broken off.
1657 TOMLINSON *Renou's Disp.* 259 Manna, is collected from its effracted boughs.

effraction (ɛ'frækʃən). [a. Fr. *effraction*, as if ad. L. **effractiōn-em*, f. as prec.] Breaking open (a house); burglary.
1840 *New Monthly Mag.* LVIII. 277 The dwelling-place where the effraction was perpetrated. 1868 MILMAN *St. Paul's* iv. 80 A riot, with effraction and murder. 1881 J. PAYNE *Villon's Poems* Introd. 54 Such efficient instruments of effraction that no bolts or locks could resist them.

†**e'ffracture.** *Obs. rare.* [ad. L. *effractūra*, f. as prec.] (See quot.)
1634 T. JOHNSON tr. *Parey's Chirurg.* x. vi. (1678) 232 An Effracture [of the Skull] is when the bone falls down, and is broken by a most violent blow.

effrajable, *a.* Perhaps a misprint for EFFROYABLE, which Harvey elsewhere uses. The Dicts. have *effraiable* with this example.
1665 G. HARVEY *Advice agst. Plague* 5 Pestilential symptoms declare nothing a proportionate efficient of their effrajable and miscreant nature. 1755 JOHNSON, *Effraiable.* So 1775 in ASH. 1782-1800 in BAILEY; and in mod. Dicts.

effranchise (ɛ'frɑːntʃaɪz, -æ-), *v.* [corresp. formally to OF. *effranchiss-*, *effranchir*, f. *es-* (:—L. *ex-*) out + *franc* free; but perh. the Eng. word may be a recent formation from the same elements. Cf. AFFRANCHISE, ENFRANCHISE.] To invest with franchises or privileges.
1864 in WEBSTER; and in mod. Dicts.
Hence **e'ffranchisement**, the action of effranchising; the state of being effranchised.
1795 tr. *Mercier's Fragm. Pol. & Hist.* II. 436 The subsidies they [the Romans] demanded from them [the provinces] were on the condition of effranchisement.

effray, obs. var. AFFRAY *sb.*
1375 BARBOUR *Bruce* V. 113 In sic effray thai baid that nycht. 1483 CAXTON *G. de la Tour* Biij, For no gentil wymmen ought to make none effrayes in them. 1553 (ed. 1) DOUGLAS *Æneis* XI. xvii. 67 Acca schawis to him and all his feris The huge effray [*ed. Small* affray].

†**e'ffray**, *v. Obs.* [a. F. *effraye-r*: see AFFRAY.]
1. *trans.* To frighten; to affect with fear; to alarm, startle.
1375 BARBOUR *Bruce* VII. 610 Thai effrayit war suddanly. 1480 CAXTON *Chron. Eng.* ccxiv. 201 Moche other folke were sore effrayed. 1500-20 DUNBAR *This. & Rose* 68 And that no schouris nor blastis cawld Effray suld flouris nor fowles on the fold. 1596 SPENSER *F.Q.* I. i. 16 Their dam upstart out of her den effraide.
2. To keep off by frightening; to scare.
1588 A. KING tr. *Canisius' Catech.* 58 Fra y^{is} profane noueltie..effrayis vs ye Apostolique..doctrine.
3. To feel fear of; to fear.
1485 CAXTON *Trevisa's Higden* (1527) III. xxx. 122, I lyue in grete drede and effray myne owne wardyens.
Hence **effrayed** *ppl. a.*, frightened, shaking with fear. **e'ffrayedly** *adv.*, in an alarmed manner, as men do who are alarmed. **e'ffraying** *vbl. sb.*, the state of being afraid; fright. All *Obs.*
1375 BARBOUR *Bruce* V. 110 The men..full effraytly gat thair ger. *Ibid.* IX. 599 The Inglis..war stonayit for effrayng. 1533 BELLENDEN *Livy* II. (1822) 150 The senate effrayetlie convenit to this counsell, and wes mair effrayetlie consultit. 1553 DOUGLAS *Æneis* IX. iii. (ed. 1) 170 Wyth pikkis brekand doun Zone forteres, and now..wyth me Assailzeant this effrayit strenth.

†**e'ffrenable**, *a. Obs. rare*$^{-1}$. [f. L. *effrēn-us* unbridled (f. *ex* out + *frēn-um* bridle) + -ABLE.] Incapable of restraint, violently rebellious.
1621 BOLTON *Stat. Irel.* 313 (an. 11 Eliz.) The saide traytor having by this effrenable meanes growen to great power.

†**'effrenate.** *a. Obs.* [ad. L. *effrēnāt-us*, f. *effrēnāre*, f. *ex* out + *frēn-um* bridle. Cf. F. *effréné.*] **a.** Of passions: Unbridled, ungovernable. **b.** Of drugs: Violent in action.
1561 ABP. PARKER *Corr.* (1852) 157 Men of effrenate intemperancy. 1657 TOMLINSON *Renou's Disp.* 143 Nothing doth so much dehort from..any medicament as its effrenate, prepotent and malign quality.
Hence **'effrenated** *ppl. a.*, unbridled, unruly.
1586 J. HOOKER *Girald. Irel.* in *Holinshed* II. 144/1 Let vs returne to the historie of this effere and effrenated nation.

†**effre'nation.** *Obs.*$^{-0}$. [ad. L. *effrēnātiōn-em*, f. *effrēnāre*: see prec.] (See quot.)
1623 COCKERAM, *Effrenation*, unruliness. 1656 in BLOUNT *Glossogr.* 1818 in TODD; and in mod. Dicts.

†**e'ffrenous**, *a. Obs. rare*$^{-1}$. [f. L. *effrēn-us*; see EFFRENABLE and -OUS.] = EFFRENATE b.
1657 TOMLINSON *Renou's Disp.* 164 Stibium also..though it be immite and effrenous.

†**e'ffringe**, *v. Obs. rare*$^{-1}$. [ad. L. *effringĕre*, f. *ex* out + *frangĕre* to break.] *trans.* To break or pound out; to make by pounding.
1657 TOMLINSON *Renou's Disp.* 195 Medicaments from which..Powders can be efringed.

†**e'ffront**, *v. Obs. rare.* [(1) back-formation from next; (2) ad. OF. *effronter* to break the forehead of; see next.]
1. *trans.* To free from bashfulness.
1643 SIR T. BROWNE *Relig. Med.* I. §40, I am naturally bashfull, nor hath..age..been able to effront..me.
2. To put to confusion.
1649 G. DANIEL *Trinarch., Rich. II*, cclvi, Least Glocester's Credit and Relations might Effront his storye.

†**e'ffronted**, *ppl. a. Obs.* [f. F. *effronté*, OF. *esfronté* (= It. *sfrontato*):—late L. **ex-* (*ef-*) *frontātus*, f. (**ex-*) *ef-frons*, f. *ex* out, without + *frons* forehead + -ED. (The L. *frons* occurs in the sense of 'ability to blush', so that *effrons* prob. meant 'unblushing'; cf. *browless*, *frontless*. Some, however, suppose the lit. sense to be 'putting forth the forehead'.)]
Shameless, barefaced, unblushingly insolent.
1598 E. GILPIN *Skial.* (1878) 41 Yet their effronted thoughts adulterate, Think the blind world holds them legitimate. 1612 J. TAYLOR (Water P.) *Sculler* Wks. III. 17/2 He..with his effrontit shamelesse face, Seemes to command the diuell. 1614 SIR W. ALEXANDER *Doomesday* II. (R.) Th' effronted whore prophetically showne By holy John in his mysterious scrouls. 1641 *Relat. Answ. Earl Strafford* 97 Others..imputed this to his effronted boldnesse.
Hence †**e'ffrontedly** *adv.*, in a barefaced manner; shamelessly.
1628 LE GRYS tr. *Barclay's Argenis* 216 Lest my Vncle..should the more effrontedly execute vpon mee the remainder [of his treachery]. 1680 HICKES *Spir. Popery* 40 To shew..how effrontedly this Antiepiscoparian speaks.

effrontery (ɛ'frʌntərɪ). Also 8 **effronterie, -ary.** [ad. F. *effronterie*, f. *effronté*: see EFFRONTED.] Shameless audacity, unblushing insolence. Also *concr.*
1715 M. DAVIES *Ath. Brit.* I. Pref. 28 By Printing those Orthodox Letters he gain'd the Point of making his own Effrontaries to sell the better. 1720 WELTON *Suffer. Son of God* I. v. 100, I express my Resentment..by the superficial Effrontery..of my Brows. 1751 SMOLLETT *Per. Pic.* (1779) III. lxxx. 65 The happy inheritance of impregnable effrontery. 1814 D'ISRAELI *Quarrels Auth.* (1867) 362 Both as modest in their youth as afterwards remarkable for their effrontery. 1858 ROBERTSON *Lect.* ii. 58 With blasphemy and unscrupulous effrontery.
Hence †**e'ffronterist** [see -IST], *nonce-wd*, one who displays effrontery.
1776 *Adv. Corkscrew* ii. 18 He was now become a perfect effronterist.

†**e'ffrontuous**, *a. Obs. rare.* [irreg. f. EFFRONTED, after words like *affectuous*, *fatuous*.] Characterized by effrontery.
a 1734 NORTH *Exam.* III. vii. 543 That a Government should appear so weak as to suffer such an effrontuous proceeding to run on to this height.
Hence **e'ffrontuously**, *adv.*
a 1734 NORTH *Lives* II. 127 To hear his decrees most brutishly and effrontuously arraigned. —— *Exam.* I. i. 23.

†**e'ffroyable**, *a. Obs. rare.* [a. F. *effroyable*, f. *effroi* fright.] Frightful.
1689 G. HARVEY *Curing Dis. by Expect.* iv. 23 The first..upon the sight of such an effroyable symptom..might mistake it for an Apoplexy.

†**e'ffude**, *v. Obs.* [incorr. ad. L. *effundĕre* (see EFFUND *v.*), the perfect stem *effūd-* being taken instead of the pres. stem.] *trans.* To pour out.
1634 SIR T. HERBERT *Trav.* 7 This hidious cataract..effudes it selfe altogether..into the ocean. 1657 TOMLINSON *Renou's Disp.* 79 Whereby part of it will be effuded.

effulge (ɛ'fʌldʒ), *v. poet.* (but now mainly in humorously pedantic use). [ad. L. *effulg-ēre*, f. *ex* out + *fulgēre* to shine.]
1. *intr.* To shine forth brilliantly.
1735 THOMSON *Liberty* V. 361 As on pure winter's eve, Gradual the stars effulge. 1744 AKENSIDE *Pleas. Imag.* I. 479 Like rays effulging from the parent sun. 1865 ALEX. SMITH *Summ. Skye* I. 38 Each effulging like Phoebus.
b. *fig.*

1828 J. WILSON in *Blackw. Mag.* XXIV. 277 He effulges with the sun in velveteen jacket and breeches. **1852** D. MOIR *Contadina* i, The eloquence of purest truth effulges in thy smile.

2. *trans.* To flash forth. *lit.* and *fig.*

1729 SAVAGE *Wanderer* v. 20 The topaz charms the sight, Like these, effulging yellow streams of light. **1729** THOMSON *Britannia*, His eyes effulging a peculiar fire.

effulgence (ɛˈfʌldʒəns). [f. next: see -ENCE.] The quality of being effulgent, splendid radiance. *lit.* and *fig.*

1667 MILTON *P.L.* III. 388 On thee Impresst the effulgence of his Glorie abides. **1774** GOLDSM. *Nat. Hist.* (1862) I. xxi. 135 In the first half of its visible course, it emitted a prodigious effulgence. **1821** CRAIG *Lect. Drawing* ii. 103 The splendour of rich colour is to be found only in the effulgence of light.

effulgent (ɛˈfʌldʒənt), *a.* [ad. L. *effulgēnt-em*, f. as prec.] Shining forth brilliantly; sending forth intense light; resplendent, radiant. Hence **eˈfulgently** *adv.*

1738 GLOVER *Leonidas* II. 89 Whose spacious orb collects th' effulgent beams. **1852** MRS. JAMESON *Leg. Madonna* (1857) 178 He is upborne by an effulgent cloud. **1860** TYNDALL *Glac.* I. §27. 218 The fiery light of the sinking sun . . mottled the mountains with effulgent spaces.

fig. **1744** AKENSIDE *Pleas. Imag.* I. 330 Venus . . stood Effulgent on the pearly car. **1831** BREWSTER *Newton* (1855) II. xxiv. 358 Others . . resist the effulgent evidence which sustains the strongholds of our faith. **1868** J. T. NETTLESHIP *Ess. Browning* vi. 219 Its beauty might be more effulgent by reason of the . . dulness of the rest.

† **eˌffulmiˈnation.** *Obs.* *rare*⁻¹. [f. EF- + FULMINATION.] The launching of thunderbolts; *concr.* a thunderbolt launched. *fig.*

a **1670** HACKET *Abp. Williams* I. (1692) 32 The Popes . . attempting to send out effulminations against Christian kings in all countries.

† **eˌffumaˈbility.** *nonce-wd.* *Obs.* [f. L. *effumāre* + *-bility*: see EFFUME and -ITY.] Capability of being converted into vapour.

1680 BOYLE *Scept. Chem.* IV. 271 Paracelsus . . seems to define Mercury by Volatility, or (if I may coyne such a Word) Effumability.

† **effuˈmation.** *rare.* [a. OF. *effumation*, as if ad. L. **effūmātiōn-em*, f. *effūmāre*: see next.] The action of converting into 'fumes' or vapour; *concr.* a vapour emitted.

1666 G. HARVEY *Morb. Angl.* iv. 47 Swelling ebullition, whence afterwards those hot effumations . . arise. **1684** tr. *Bonet's Merc. Compit.* XIV. 494 Instruments fit for Effumation and Vaporation.

† **eˈffume,** *v.* *Obs.* *rare*⁻¹. [ad. F. *effumer*, f. L. *effūmāre*, f. *ex* out + *fūm-us* smoke.] *trans.* To puff out (smoke).

1599 B. JONSON *Ev. Man out Hum.* III. i, I can make this dog take as many whiffes as I list, and he shall retain, or effume them, at my pleasure.

effund (ɛˈfʌnd), *v.* [ad. L. *effund-ĕre*, f. *ex* out + *fund-ĕre* to pour.]

trans. To pour out (*lit.* and *fig.*); to shed (blood); to pour out the contents of (a vessel).

c **1420** *Pallad. on Husb.* IV. 107 Oyldregges salt effunde uppon the roote [of olives]. *a* **1500** *Cuckow & Night.* Lenvoye, Suspires whiche I effunde in silence! **1550** BALE *Image Both Ch.* II. Iij b (T.), After this went forth the seconde angel . . effundinge his vial upon the sea. **1578** BANISTER *Hist. Man* v. 70 The Arterie being from that deriued, which is effunded into the liuer. **1647** H. MORE *Poems* 51 If he his life effund To utmost death. **1719** D'URFEY *Pills* (1872) III. 322 Much Blood they effund. **1776** tr. *Da Costa's Conchol.* 60 Several [kinds of shells] . . effund this purple juice. **1866** J. ROSE tr. *Ovid's Fasti* II. 146 Now doth the Idæan boy appear Effunding . . nectar rare.

† **effuˈscation.** *Obs.* *rare*⁻¹. [as if ad. L. **effuscātiōn-em*, f. *ex* out + *fuscā-re* to darken.] The action of making obscure; a beclouding.

1624 DONNE *Devotions* Wks. 1839 III. 497 These eclipses, sudden Effuscations and darkening of his Senses.

† **eˈffuse,** *sb.* *Obs.* *rare.* [f. the vb.] A pouring out, effusion.

1593 SHAKS. *3 Hen. VI*, II. vi. 28 Much effuse of blood doth make me faint. **1631** HEYWOOD *Maid of W.* II. II. Wks. 1874 II. 369 Such a small effuse of blood.

effuse (ɛˈfjuːs), *a.* [ad. L. *effūs-us*, pa. pple. of *effundĕre* to pour: see EFFUND.]

1. Poured out freely; chiefly *transf.* and *fig.* wide-spreading, overflowing, unrestrained, extravagant. *Obs.* or *arch.*

c **1530** H. RHODES *Bk. Nurture* in *Babees Bk.* (1868) 105 If lyke a chylde, it [laughing] is effuse and wanton. **1650** BULWER *Anthropomet.* viii. (1653) 141 A Nation . . whose Eares are dilated to so effuse a magnitude, that they cover the rest of their bodies with them. **1655** BP. RICHARDSON *On O. Test.* 321 (T.) Wherever the body is, yet the heart of fools is in effuse mirth. **1742** YOUNG *Nt. Th.* IX. 1086 No wanton waste amidst effuse expence.

2. a. *Bot.* Of an inflorescence: Spreading loosely, especially on one side. **b.** *Conch.* Having the lips separated by a groove.

1842 JOHNSTON in *Proc. Berw. Nat. Club* II. 31 *Bulla Pectinata*, aperture ampullaceous, effuse above. **1870** HOOKER *Stud. Flora* 388 *Iuncus glaucus* . . cymes effuse.

effuse (ɛˈfjuːz), *v.* [f. L. *effūs-* ppl. stem of *effundĕre*: see EFFUND.]

1. *trans.* To pour forth or out (a liquid); †to shed (blood); in *pass.* to be extravasated. Also *refl.*

1526 *Pilgr. Perf.* (W. de W. 1531) 253 That moost precyous blode effused & shedde. **1591** SHAKS. *1 Hen. VI*, V. iv. 52 Maiden-blood thus rigorously effus'd Will cry for Vengeance. **1682** *Disc. Addr. or Presentm. agst. Association* 7 The Cup out of which they were to effuse Wine . . in Honour of the Gods . . broke into pieces. **1725** POPE *Odyss.* XIX. 633 My pitying eye . . effus'd a plenteous stream. **1759** DA COSTA in *Phil. Trans.* LI. 33 The marble finely powdered, and aqua fortis effused over it, the marble particles were nigh destroyed. **1804** ABERNETHY *Surg. Observ.* 174 A little blood was supposed to be effused upon the dura mater. **1835–6** TODD *Cycl. Anat.* I. 229/1 Lymph is effused from the wound in the vessel. **1859** HAWTHORNE *Fr. & It. Jrnls.* II. 287 The same gentle shower . . had been effusing itself all the morning.

2. *transf.* **a.** To pour out, shed, send forth (air, heat, light, odours, etc.).

1398 TREVISA *Barth. De P.R.* VI. xx. (1495) 208 In somer kynde heete drawyth oute . . and is effusyd . . and departed and is lesse in the body wythin. **1758** JOHNSON *Idler* No. 3 ¶4 The sun, by shining too long, will effuse all its light. **1821** *New Monthly Mag.* I. 291 The scented pulvilio, which the untwisted hairs reproachfully effused. **1847** J. WILSON *Chr. North* (1857) I. 259 From his disc . . is effused now a gentle crimson light.

b. *poet. nonce-uses* of pa. pple. By Thomson, of the horse: Rushing unchecked (cf. L. *effusis habenis* and EFFUSED *ppl. a.*). By Cowper, of a crowd: Poured forth.

1727 THOMSON *Summer* 509 The horse . . o'er the field effus'd Darts on the gloomy flood. **1791** COWPER *Odyss.* VIII. 632 From the horse effused the Greeks Left their capacious ambush.

3. *fig.* Also *absol.*

1633 T. ADAMS *Exp. 2 Peter* ii. 1, God must infuse, before we effuse. **1652** BENLOWES *Theoph.* I. xcv, Good words effus'd Thou dost me give. *c* **1750** SHENSTONE *Elegy* i. 22 'Twas his fond heart effus'd the melting theme. **1813** H. & J. SMITH *Rej. Addr.* 58 Professions lavishly effused and parsimoniously verified. **1830** GALT *Laurie T.* III. viii. (1849) 110 A palpable tranquillity had been effused abroad.

†**4.** *Phys.* To throw off (a branch).

1578 BANISTER *Hist. Man* VII. 96 After that these Arteries haue effused forth these braunches to the palate . . they rise vp into the Scull.

effused (ɛˈfjuːzd), *ppl. a.* [f. EFFUSE *v.* + -ED.]

1. Poured out, shed; also (of blood, etc. within the system) extravasated.

1621 G. SANDYS *Ovid's Met.* III. (1626) 59 Thy Mother, and her sisters shall imbrue Their furious hands in thy effused bloud. **1845** G. DAY tr. *Simon's Anim. Chem.* I. 315 Blood-corpuscles being found in the effused fluid.

2. Stretched at full length, with limbs relaxed. [cf. L. *effusus.*]

1870 SWINBURNE *Ess. & Stud.* (1875) 323 The goddess languid and effused like a broad-blown flower.

Hence **eˈffusedly** *adv.* *rare*⁻¹, in an overflowing manner, unrestrainedly.

1594 *2nd Report Faustus* in Thoms' *Prose Rom.* III. 331 Therewith laughing effusedly vanished away.

effusion (ɛˈfjuːʒən). Also 4 **effuscion**, 5–6 **effucion**. [ad. (directly or through Fr. *effusion*, 14th c. in Littré) L. *effūsiōn-em*, n. of action f. *effund-ĕre*: see EFFUND.]

1. A pouring out, a spilling (of liquid); †shedding (of tears). ***effusion of blood***: bloodshed, slaughter; also in general sense, the pouring out of blood by a wound, etc. (and see 1 e).

c **14..** *Tundale's Vis., Circumcision* 8 Cryst in his manhode Sched his blode by effusyon. *c* **1440** *Gesta Rom.* xl. 164 (Harl. MS.) In holy writte Effucion of bloode is not elles but trespas in synnyng. **1526** TINDALE *Hebr.* ix. 22 With out effusion of bloud is no remission. **1595** SHAKS. *John* v. II. 49 This effusion of such manly drops . . Startles mine eyes. **1603** HOLLAND *Plutarch's Morals* 1295 The effusions and funerall libaments. **1660** JER. TAYLOR *Worthy Commun.* i. §4. 76 By breaking bread and effusion of wine. **1660** JER. TAYLOR *Duct. Dubit.* II. iii. 19 For the danger of effusion of the holy wine, they in some places chose that expedient. **1767** GOOCH *Treat. Wounds* I. 162 The effusion of blood . . may bring the patient's life into danger. **1850** MERIVALE *Rom. Emp.* (1865) I. i. 9 Every new conquest required a fresh effusion from her veins. **1867** SIR J. HERSCHEL *Fam. Lect. Sc.* 43 The effusion of lava.

concr. **1603** SHAKS. *Meas. for M.* III. i. 30 Thine owne bowels . . the meere effusion of thy proper loines. **1734** tr. *Rollin's Anc. Hist.* (1827) VII. XVII. iv. 149 Shed a constant effusion of wine.

¶ Used for AFFUSION.

1687 G. TOWERSON *Baptism* 54 To baptize by a bare Effusion, or sprinkling of water. **1726** AYLIFFE *Parerg.* 103 Baptism . . may be performed . . by Effusion or Sprinkling.

†**b.** ***effusion of spirits*** (see ANIMAL SPIRITS): supposed to be the cause of fainting. *Obs.*

1651 SIR H. WOTTON in Ellis *Orig. Lett.* I. 340 III. 255 *note*, On a sudden effusion of spirits, he sunk under the table. **1656** RIDGLEY *Pract. Physic* 15 A wound of the brain, and from thence an effusion or troubling of the spirits.

†**c.** A copious emission of smoke, 'effluvia' (see EFFLUVIUM), etc. Also *concr.* *Obs.*

? **1477** NORTON *Ord. Alch.* in Ashm. vii. (1652) 104 Magnetia is Fier of Effusion. **1664** POWER *Exp. Philos.* I. 58 Besides the Magnetical One of the Earth, several Effusions there may be from divers other Bodies. **1667** MILTON *P.L.* VI. 766 From about him fierce Effusion rowld Of smoak.

d. *Physics.* (See quot.)

1850 T. GRAHAM *Chem.* (ed. 2) I. 78 Effusion of gases . . by which I express their passage into a vacuum by a small aperture in a thin plate.

e. *Pathol.* The escape of any fluid out of its natural vessel, and its lodgment elsewhere; 'the separation of fluid from the vessels in a morbid state of the parts' (*Syd. Soc. Lex.*).

1732 ARBUTHNOT *Rules of Diet* 364 The Effusions . . of any . . Blood upon the Ventricles of the Brain. **1813** J. THOMSON *Lect. Inflam.* 122 The effect of inflammation termed effusion. **1856** KANE *Arct. Expl.* I. xix. 232 The immovability of my limbs was due to dropsical effusion.

2. *transf.* and *fig.* †**a.** Of persons: Dispersion, rout. Also *poet.* of things: Confused downfall.

? *a* **1400** *Chester Pl.* (Shaks. Soc.) 92 Godes people were put to effuscion. **1725** POPE *Odyss.* XXII. 99 In mix'd effusion roll, Th' untasted viands.

†**b.** 'Bounteous donation' (J.). *Obs.*

1514 PACE in Fiddes *Wolsey* II. 203 He doithe seke nothynge but favors, and procurithe the same bi effusion off mony. **1614** RALEIGH *Hist. World* IV. v. §3 Antigonus sped so well by large effusion of his treasure. **1654** HAMMOND *Fundamentals* 68 The great force that the gospel . . had . . upon men's souls, melting them into that liberal effusion of all that they had.

c. A 'pouring' forth of any influence or agency; often of the Holy Ghost.

1550 CROWLEY *Inform. & Petit.* 324 You shall not be forgotten in the effucion of thys plage. **1658** BAXTER *Saving Faith* §4. 27 The Promise of Infusion and Effusion [*I will pour out my Spirit to you*]. **1741** tr. *Cicero's Nat. Gods* I. 28 The World, with an universal Effusion of its [Reason's] Spirit, is God. **1879** FARRAR *St. Paul* (1883) 66 The fulfilment of Christ's promise in the effusion of His Spirit.

3. *fig.* A pouring forth, unrestrained utterance (of words, sounds, etc.); frank and eager expression (of emotions).

1659 HAMMOND *On Ps.* Pref. 4 It was a new hymne of Christ's effusion. **1778** ROBERTSON *Hist. Amer.* I. II. 108 The effusion of joy was general. *c* **1812** JANE AUSTEN *Sense & Sens.*, An involuntary confidence, an irrepressible effusion to a soothing friend. **1848** MACAULAY *Hist. Eng.* II. 606 William talked to them [Dykvelt and Witsen] with . . an effusion of heart, which seldom appeared in his conversations with Englishmen. **1870** SWINBURNE *Ess. & Stud.* (1875) 266 The other's [song] . . warmer in effusion of sound.

b. *abstr.* Effusiveness, enthusiastic demeanour. [So in Fr.]

1878 H. S. WILSON *Alp. Ascents* ii. 61 Talking cheerily, I dine with effusion.

4. *concr.* Applied to a literary composition, to a speech (formerly also to any work of art), considered as an 'outpouring' of the author's feelings, genius, etc. Now often *contemptuous.*

1779 JOHNSON *L.P., Pope* Wks. IV. 71 Queen Caroline had declared her intention to visit him [Pope]. This may have been only a careless effusion. *c* **1811** FUSELI *Lect. Art.* v. (1848) 462 The effusions of Lanfranco and Pietro da Cortona. **1826** SCOTT *Woodst.* i, Here ended this wild effusion. **1839** THIRLWALL *Greece* I. 247 The extemporaneous effusions . . of a Phemius and a Demodocus. **1873** H. ROGERS *Orig. Bible* viii. (1875) 346 That book . . was the effusion of one master mind.

Hence **eˈffusionist**, a writer of 'effusions'.

1842 *Fraser's Mag.* XXVI. 449 All great novelists . . were men of genius and learning. The popular monthly effusionists nowadays are neither.

effusive (ɛˈfjuːsɪv), *a.* (and *sb.*) [f. L. *effūs-* (see EFFUSE *a.*) + -IVE as if ad. L. *effūsīvus.*]

†**1. a.** That proceeds from a pouring out. *Obs.*

1725 POPE *Odyss.* XXII. 490 The floor Wash'd with th' effusive wave. **1791** E. DARWIN *Bot. Gard.* I. III. 1781 With fine films . . Of oil effusive lull the waves to sleep.

b. *Geol.* [G. (H. Rosenbusch *Mikrosk. Physiographie d. Massigen Gesteine* (ed. 2, 1887) 6).] Of an igneous rock: poured out on the earth's surface in a state of fusion and afterwards solidified; so ***effusive period***, the period in which effusive rocks were formed. Also *sb.*, an effusive rock.

1888 F. H. HATCH in J. J. H. Teall *Brit. Petrogr.* 429 *Effusive*, a term lately used abroad for those rocks which have been poured out at the surface, the word *eruptive* now being generally used for the whole group of massive rocks. **1895** A. HARKER *Petrol.* 128 The two periods of consolidation were styled by Rosenbusch the 'intratelluric' and the 'effusive'. **1897** G. P. MERRILL *Treat. Rocks* II. i. 60 To divide the eruptive rocks into two general groups: first, the intrusive or plutonic rocks; and second, the effusive or volcanic rocks. **1903** *Amer. Jrnl. Sci.* XVI. 121 An origin contemporaneous with that of the Rossland effusives. **1903** A. GEIKIE *Text-bk. Geol.* (ed. 4) 197 The effusive or volcanic rocks (Erguss-gesteine). **1905** J. GEIKIE *Struct. & Field Geol.* 206 Effusive rocks . . are of two types, crystalline and fragmental. **1915** W. LINDGREN in W. N. Rice et al. *Probl. Amer. Geol.* v. 273 Basalt is probably the most widely spread of the Tertiary effusives. **1939** A. JOHANNSEN *Descr. Petrogr.* (ed. 2) I. i. 5 The effusive or extrusive rocks (vulcanites of Scheerer) are those which were poured out upon the surface of the earth; for example, our modern lavas. . . In this group are also included certain other rocks which, strictly speaking, are not extrusives, namely, the pyroclastics.

2. Of emotions, affections, etc.: Overflowing, irrepressible; in mod. use, demonstratively expressed.

1662 H. MORE *Enthus. Tri.*, Scholia (1712) 52 The innocence of his private Life, and his most effusive Charity and Humanity. **1863** GEO. ELIOT *Romola* in *Cornh. Mag.*

VII. 304 Tito could only be saved from alienation by..a recovery of her effusive tenderness.

3. That expresses feeling demonstratively.

1863 Mrs. Oliphant *Salem Ch.* xxi. 12 A very effusive hymn..an utterance of unmitigated thanksgiving. **1879** McCarthy *Own Times* I. 358 Peel..was not effusive; he did not pour out his emotions.

4. That has the function of giving outlet to emotion. *rare.*

1855 Bain *Senses & Int.* iii. iv. §27 (1864) 622 The purely effusive arts, such as music or the dance.

Hence **e'ffusively** *adv.*, in an effusive manner. **e'ffusiveness**, the quality of being effusive.

1870 *Daily News* 22 July 3 You came upon damsels..who giggled and talked effusively by the wayside. **1877** H. Page *De Quincy* I. iii. 46 The enthusiastic effusiveness of these lines. **1880** Mrs. Forrester *Roy & Viola* I. 40 Netta embraced her effusively. **1879** Farrar *St. Paul* (1883) 529 None of the tender effusiveness and earnest praise which we have been hearing.

effuti'ation. *nonce-wd.* [f. L. *effutī-re* to prate + -ation.] Twaddle, balderdash.

1823 J. Lacy [G. Darley] in *Lond. Mag.* VIII. 648 The plotlessness, still-life, puling effutiation..of modern plays.

Efik ('ɛfɪk), *sb.* and *a.* [Native name.]

A. *sb.* **a.** A southern Nigerian language of the Benue-Congo family. **b.** (A member of) a people of southern Nigeria, closely related to the Ibibio. **B.** *adj.* Of or pertaining to the Efik or their language.

1849 H. M. Waddell (*title*) Vocabulary of the Efik or Old Calabar language. **1862** H. Goldie *Dict. Efik Lang.* p. xi, In the language cultivated by this mission, the Efik, the following works have been produced. **1876** *Encycl. Brit.* IV. 649/2 It was not till the early part of the 18th century that the Efik, owing to civil war with their kindred the Ibibio, migrated from the neighbourhood of the Niger to the shores of the Old Calabar. **1883** [see Kwa]. **1888** *Proc. R. Geogr. Soc.* X. 633 The Efik people..are dotted here and there among the Bantu tribes, beyond the Rio del Rey. **1932** *Africa* V. 504 An examination of Efik, a river-dialect of Ibibio, reveals..the fact that from English has been taken a considerable number of words. **1934** Webster, *Efik*... 2 One of a Negro people of Nigeria. **1950** D. Jones *Phoneme* viii. 32 In the Efik language of Nigeria there exists an i (similar to the English vowel in *eat*) and an ə (similar to the sound of *a* in *along*). **1963** G. I. Jones *Trading States of Oil Rivers* iii. 36 Dapper..tells us nothing about the Efiks or why they should be called Old Calabar. **1976** [see Edo]. **1984** *Washington Post* 19 Nov. c6/2, 30 candidates from 21 to 60 years in age were..cast by Deal in a revival of his 'Efik-Ibibio Suite'.

†**efisc**, *v.* *Obs. rare*$^{-1}$. [Corruptly ad. Fr. *offusqu-er* = obfuscate.] *trans.* To obfuscate, dim.

1656 *Sheph. Kal.* viii, Wrath efisceth and leeseth [Fr. *ofusque et pert*] the eye of reason.

‖**efreet** ('ɛfriːt). Another form of afreet.

1841 Lane *Arab. Nts.* I. 8 Come down, and fear not this Efreet. **1862** Fairholt *Up Nile* 133 The lady..asserted that the father was an efreet or evil spirit.

eft (ɛft), *sb.*[1] Forms: 1 efeta, -e, 2-4 euete, 2-7 evete, 4 auete, 4-6 ewt(e, (5 eefte, 6 ewft, euit), 6-8 euet, (8 eff, 9 *dial.* effet, evvet), 7- eft. See also newt. [OE. *efeta*, of unknown origin. The form newt (*a newt* corruptly for *an ewt*) is more frequent in literary use, and in some dialects has superseded the older form.]

A small lizard or lizard-like animal. Now (like newt) chiefly applied to the Greater Water-Newt (*Triton cristatus*) and to the Smooth Newt (*Lophinus punctatus*), of the order *Salamandridæ*.

c **1000** Ælfric *Gloss.* in Wr.-Wülcker 122 *Lacerta* uel *stilio*, efete. *a* **1100** *Voc.* ibid. 321 *Lacerta*, efeta. *a* **1200** *Moral Ode* 273 in *Cott. Hom.* 177 Þeor beð naddren and snaken, eueten and frude. *c* **1300** *K. Alis.* 6126 Evetis, and snakes, and paddokes brode. **1388** Wyclif *Prov.* xxx. 28 An euete enforsith with hondis, and dwelleth in the housis of kingis. **1398** Trevisa *Barth. De P.R.* xii. xxix. (Tollem. MS.), Venimouse bestes and auetes [**1535** lisardes]. *c* **1400** Maundev. v. 61 In that Abbeye ne entrethe not no Flye ne Todes ne Ewtes. **1480** Caxton *Descr. Brit.* 48 Eeftes that doon none harme. **1572** Bossewell *Armorie* ii. 52 b, [The Cameleon] beyng like to ye Ewte in the bodye. **1580** Lyly *Euphues* (Arb.) 315 All things that breede in the mudde are not Euets. **1613** W. Browne *Brit. Past.* i. ii, May never euet, nor the toade, Within thy banks make their abode. **1679** Plot *Staffordsh.* (1686) 251 Animals somewhat like Evets or Newts. **1750** W. Ellis *Mod. Husbandman* iii. ii. 79 (E.D.S.) *Eff*, an eft. **1763** Churchill *Proph. Fam.* Poems I. 112 In quest of food, Efts strove in vain to crawl. **1800** Hurdis *Favorite Vill.* 153 Wriggles the viper and the basking eft. **1875** Parish *Sussex Gloss.*, *Effet*, a newt or eft. **1876** A. B. Buckley *Short Hist. Nat. Sc.* xxiv. 201 Aquatic salamanders, which resemble our newts or efts. **1878** Besant & Rice *Celia's Arbour* I. xiv. 195 We used to hunt as boys for..the little evvet, the alligator of Great Britain.

†**eft**, *sb.*[2] *Obs. rare.* [Of obscure origin; cf. OE. *æfest*, *æfst*, malice, which freq. occurs in connexion with *nīð*.] ? Malice.

c **1325** *Metr. Hom.* 35 Jowes havis eft and nithe At me for the ferlikes that I kithe. *Ibid.* 125 Eft and nythe and felonny.

†**eft**, *a.* *Obs. rare*$^{-1}$. In 6 *superl.* eftest. [? A blunder ascribed to Dogberry; but it is not clear what word is alluded to.] ? Ready, convenient.

1599 Shaks. *Much Ado* iv. ii. 38 Yea, marry, that's the eftest way.

†**eft** (ɛft), *adv.* *Obs.* or *arch.* Also 3-5 efte, (3 heft, *Orm.* efft). [OE. *ęft* = OS., OFris. *eft*, ON. *eptir*, *eftir*, *eft*:—OTeut. **aftiz* adv. compar. deg., f. stem *aft*: see aft. Cf. OE. *lęng*, compar. deg. of *lang*, long *adv.*]

1. A second time, again; back.

c **825** *Vesp. Psalter* lxx[i]. 20 Of neolnisse eorðan eft ðu alædes mec. *c* **1000** Ælfric *Gen.* viii. 10 Noe..asende ut eft culfran. *c* **1200** Ormin 16638 Hu maȝȝ ald mann ben borenn efft. *c* **1205** Lay. 15081 Nu was Vortigerne æft [*c* **1275** heft] king. *a* **1300** *Cursor M.* 24403 He cried ans and eft. **1330** R. Brunne *Chron.* (1810) 105 Ontille Inglond eft he turned ouer þe se. *c* **1386** Chaucer *Man Lawes T.* 694 Eft were his lettres stolen everichon. *c* **1420** *Pallad. on Husb.* xii. 267 Again the goode [chestnuts] under gravel be do, and tried efte and thries preve hem so. **1589** Puttenham *Eng. Poesie* (Arb.) 160 Many a word yfalne shall eft arise. **1607** Walkington *Opt. Glass* 145 Hee..vanished eft away.

b. *eft and eft*: again and again. *eft...eft*: first...then.

1393 Langl. *P. Pl.* C. xvi. 145 ȝif hym eft and eft euere at his neede. *c* **1420** *Pallad. on Husb.* i. 416 And as it drieth, efte and efte it dight. **1583** Golding *Calvin on Deut.* clxxviii. 1108 Eft at one side and eft a tother.

2. Indicating sequence or transition in discourse: Again, moreover, likewise.

c **1000** *Ags. Gosp.* Matt. xviii. 19 Eft [*c* **950** *Lindisf.* eft sona] ic eow secȝe. *c* **1175** *Lamb. Hom.* 107 Ne eft he ne mei on his welan..modegian. **1340** *Ayenb.* 133 Yet eft þer is a stape huerinne is þe uolle of perfection of þise uirtue. **1432-50** tr. *Higden* (1865) I. 327 Meny nyȝtes in þe somer..þe sonne goþ nouȝt doun..and eft as many dayes in þe wynter..the sonne ariseþ nouȝt. **1533** *Act 25 Hen. VIII*, c. 13 §12 It is efte declared by this presente acte, that, etc. **1651** Gataker *Ridley* in Fuller *Abel Rediv.* 195 It pleasing God eft..to imprint in the face..a living portraiture of those endowments.

3. Afterwards.

O.E. Chron. an. 685 (Parker MS.) Þone [*sc.* Mul] mon eft on Cent forbærnde. *c* **1200** *Trin. Coll. Hom.* 85 Sume men leden erest iuel liflode, and turnen eft to god. *c* **1325** *E.E. Allit. P.* A. 332 He hit schal efte with tenez tyne. **1430** Lydg. *Chron. Troy* i. vii, First with right make our selfe strong; And efte our force manly for to shewe, Of knyghtes chose taken out a fewe. **1528** More *Heresyes* iv. Wks. 269/2 Dauid fell..fyrst in aduoutrie & eft in manslaughter. *a* **1559** Cavill in *Mir. Mag.* (1563) B 2 b, Whom fortune brought to boote and efte to bale.

b. with *never*, *if ever*.

c **1175** *Lamb. Hom.* 49 He ualleð in to helle pine þer neuer eft ne cumeð of bote. *c* **1230** *Hali Meid.* 11 Beo ha eanes fulliche forcoruen ne spruteð ha neauer eft. *c* **1314** *Guy Warw.* (A.) 2776 ȝif þou haue euer eft nede to me. *c* **1325** *Seven Sag.* (P.) 302 Hys hert scholde to-breke, Ne schold he never eft more speke. **1513** Douglas *Æneis* ii. xii. [xi.] 99 Neuir syne with ene saw I hir eft.

4. *Comb.* **eft-sithe** *v.* (in 2 *eftsīðian*) to return; **eft-sith, -sithes** *adv.*, another time, once more; also, from time to time, often (cf. oftesithes). Also eftsoon(s.

c **1175** *Lamb. Hom.* 119 þet ure saule moten eft-siðian to him. *a* **1300** *Cursor M.* 1901 Noe..sent þe dofe eftsith. *a* **1547** Earl Surrey *Æneid* ii. 588 Which way eft-sithes..Andromache alone Resorted to the parents of her make. **1875** *Whitby Gloss.* (E.D.S.), *Eftsith*, often.

†**eft-**, obs. Sc. form of aft (see aft 4); only in **eft castle, eft ship**, the after part of a ship, the poop: cf. after *a.*, and forecastle.

1513 Douglas *Æneis* iii. viii. 26 Furth of his eft schip a bekyn gart he stent. *Ibid.* v. iii. 58 The patrouns in eft castellis, fresche and gay, Stude.

Efta ('ɛftə). Also **E.F.T.A., EFTA.** [f. the initials of *E*uropean *F*ree *T*rade *A*ssociation.] An economic alliance, on free trade principles, comprising the United Kingdom and several other European countries.

The United Kingdom ceased to be a member of Efta in 1972.

1959 *Cmnd.* 906 5 in *Parl. Papers 1959-60* XXIV. 21 The individual freedom of action of E.F.T.A. members in their external tariffs. **1960** *Times Rev. Industry* Dec. 4/2 European Free Trade Association (Efta). **1961** *Economist* 17 June 1252/3 Markets in which a decisive majority felt prospects were improving were EFTA, North America, the Common Market and the Communist block. **1963** *Times* 1 Feb. 13/5 Commercially we can mark our sense of unity with Europe by urging the Efta countries to join with us in inviting the E.E.C. to join the European Free Trade Area.

eften, app. spurious f. eft *adv.*, after often.

1623 Cockeram ii. A. ⁋b, Againe, *eften.*

efter, efter-, obs. Sc. var. after, after-.

†'**efter-char.** *Obs. rare.* [f. *efter*, var. of after + char:—OE. *cerr*, *cyrr* a turn.] Return.

a **1300** *Cursor M.* 21922 He sal find þan nan efter-char.

efters, early misreading for estres.

1532 *Rom. Rose* iv. 61 in *Chaucer's Wks.* (ed. Thynne), It was not left Till I had all the garden been In the efters [*ed. Bell-Skeat* l. 1448 estres] that men might seene. **1715** Kersey, *Efters*, Walks, Galleries, Entries, Hedges. **1721-1800** in Bailey.

†'**eftersoons**, *adv.* *Obs.* Also 1 efter sóna, 3-4 eftir-, -tur-, -son(e, -sons. [f. OE. *ęfter*, var. of *æfter*, after + soon, with advbl. *-s*. Cf. eftsoons.] **a.** Again. **b.** Soon after, presently.

c **950** *Lindisf. Gosp.* Mark x. 1 Gesomnadon efter sona meniȝo to him and eftersona [he] lærde hia. *a* **1300** *Cursor M.* 4241 Vn-til egipte þai haue him [Joseph] broght, þar he was efturson saald. *c* **1400** *Destr. Troy* 7424 Ector eftirsons ettlyt on Achilles.

efther, efther-, dial. f. after, after-.

†**eft'soon, -soons**, *adv.* *Obs.* or *arch.* Forms: 1 eftsóna, 3-5 eft-, efsone, 4-7 eft(e)soone, (6 eft sonne), 3-6 eft(e)sons, -nes, -nis, (4 efsoins, 5 eftones, aftsounes, 6 eftsens, 7 eftsonce, 8 effesons), 4-7 eft(e)soones, (6 effsoones), 6- eftsoons, 7- eftsoon. In several of the forms sometimes written as two words. [f. eft *adv.* + soon; in the later forms with *-s* after the analogy of advbs. from genitive cases.]

1. A second time, again.

c **1000** *Ags. Gosp.* Mark x. 1 Þa comon eft meniȝu to him and..he hi lærde eft sona. *c* **1300** *St. Brandan* 231 Gret travayl ȝou is to come er ȝe eftsone lond i-seo. *c* **1400** Maundev. v. 51 The Sarazines countrefeten it [Bawme] be sotyltee of Craft..the Apotecaries countrefeten it eftsones. *c* **1449** Pecock *Repr.* 540 It is no nede forto write the same proof of resoun eftsoone here. **1576** Lambarde *Peramb. Kent* (1826) 303 It therefore needeth not now eftsoones to be rehearsed. **1637** R. Ashley tr. *Malvezzi's David Persecuted* 166 Those other are seldom delivered out of their dangers but they returne eftsoones to their misdoings.

b. quasi-*adj.* with vbl. sb.

1571 [see 3]. **1611** Cotgr., *Iteration*..repetition..eftsoones-doing.

2. Indicating sequence or transition in discourse: Again, moreover, likewise.

950 [see eft *adv.* 2]. *c* **1175** *Lamb. Hom.* 133 Eft-sone godes word is icleped sed. *c* **1200** *Trin. Coll. Hom.* 7 Eftsone ure helendes on tocume þincð dieliche and grisliche all manne. *c* **1340** *Gaw. & Gr. Knt.* 2417 So watz Adam in erde with one bygyled..& Samson eft sonez. *c* **1400** *Destr. Troy* 2478 Then Elinus, eftesones, he drest hym to say. **1601** Holland *Pliny* II. 217 Vnlesse the party do eat some garlick before, and eftsoones in the gathering [of the white Ellebore] sup off some wine..it wil..offend the head.

3. Afterwards, soon afterwards. (The notion of 'soon', though app. implied in the etymology, is not distinctly evidenced in early examples, and down to 17th c. is sometimes absent; but in mod. archaistic use the sense is commonly 'forthwith, immediately'.)

1297 R. Glouc. *Chron.* (1724) 397 Anoþer gret mayster he slou, & efsone þe þrydde. **1330** R. Brunne *Chron.* (1810) 81 Hacon..praied him ȝit eftsonne To com tille Inglond. **14..** *E.E. Misc.* (1855) 78 Eft sone set hit one the fyre to hit boyle. **1530-1** *Act 22 Hen. VIII*, c. 12 If he do not accomplishe the order..to be eftsones taken and whipped. **1571** *Act 13 Eliz.* c. 12 If any Person Ecclesiastical shall not reuoke his errour, or after such reuocation eftsoones affirms such untrue doctrine..such eftsoones affirming shalbe iust cause to deprive such person, etc. **1598** *Ord. Prayer* in *Liturg. Serv. Q. Eliz.* (1847) 680 Those disloyal defections in Ireland..turned eftsoons into violent commotions. **1608** Shaks. *Per.* v. i. 256 Toward Ephesus Turn our blown sails; eftsoons I'll tell thee why. **1610** Holland tr. *Camden's Brit.* i. 558 Henry the fourth Earle, efts-once honorably employed. **1748** Thomson *Cast. Indol.* i. xxix, Not one eftsoons in view was to be found. *a* **1764** Lloyd *Progr. Envy* Wks. 1774 I. 136 She wav'd it round: Eftsoons there did appear Spirits and witches. *a* **1856** Longf. *Elected Knight* vii, Sir Oluf questioned the knight eftsoon. **1871** *Sunday Mag.* 118 They eftsoons fell down, as men very nigh dead.

4. From time to time, occasionally, repeatedly.

1398 Trevisa *Barth. De P.R.* xvii. cxliii. (1495) 700 They [wylowes] mowe efte sones be shred and paryd without a ladder. **1540** Raynald *Byrth Man.* (1614) 153 Infirmities, which eft-soones happen to Infants in their infancy. **1605** Camden *Rem.* (1636) 81 Maugre, a name eftsoones vsed in the worshipfull family of Vavasors, Malgerius, in old histories. **1609** Holland *Livy* ix. xxxiii. 338 He eftsoons [*identidem*] rehearsed and reiterated the law Æmylia. **1632** Sherwood, Eftsoone, *souvent.* **1720** *Stow's Surv.* (ed. Strype 1754) I. i. vi. 31/2 Both these do happen eftsoons.

5. *eftsoons as*: as soon as.

c **1555** in *Ridley's Wks.* (1841) 256 Dr. Ridley..eftsoons as he had heard the cardinal named..put on his cap. *c* **1555** Latimer *Serm. & Rem.* (1845) 278 The other prisoner..eftsoons as he was placed, said to the lords.

†**eft-white**, *v.* *Obs.*$^{-1}$ [? f. eft *adv.* + *white*, var. of *quite*, quit.] *trans.* (*absol.*) To repay.

c **1469** *Towneley Myst.* 106 A fatt shep I dar say A good flese dar I lay, Eft whyte when I may, Bot this wille I borow.

efulcrate (ɪ'fʌlkrət), *a.* *Bot.* [f. E- *pref.*[3] + L. *fulcr-um* + -ate.] 'Said of buds from below which the customary leaf has fallen' (*Treas. Bot.*). Cf. fulcrate.

egad (ɪ'gæd), *int.* Also 7 igad, 8 egod. [prob. representing earlier *A God!* from *a* interjection: but in later times perhaps associated with asseverations, like *i'faith*, or possibly with *by God*: cf. agad, adad, adod, ecod, etc.] Used as a softened oath.

1673 [R. Leigh] *Transp. Reh.* 4 Which is very civil I gad. **1751** Smollett *Per. Pic.* (1779) III. lxxxv. 323 An exclamation of 'Humbugged egad!' **1791** 'G. Gambado' *Ann. Horsem.* xviii. (1809) 140 Egod, off we set, and never stopt till I got to the bottom. **1823** Byron *Island* ii. xxi, Egad! she seem'd a wicked-looking craft. **1868-9** Miss Braddon *Charlotte's Inher.* iv. ii. 93 Yes, egad, and such a fortune as few girls drop into now-a-days.

†**e'gagropile.** *Obs.* [a. Fr. *égagropile* f. Gr. αἴγαγρο-ς wild goat + πῖλος felted hair.] See quot.

1811 W. WALTON *Peruvian Sheep* 97 The egagropiles, or hairballs, taken from the inside of horned cattle. *Ibid.* 99 In the Llama they [concretions] rather become egagropiles.

egalitarian (ɪgælɪ'tɛərɪən), *a.* and *sb.* [After F. *égalitaire*: see -ARY and -AN.]

A. *adj.* That asserts the equality of mankind.

1885 G. MURRAY *Under Lens* II. 103 Will not hear of the egalitarian doctrine. **1894** *Daily News* 21 July 5/2 The Scot ..is, of course, the most 'egalitarian' of mankind. **1898** J. E. C. BODLEY *France* I. 162 In warlike but egalitarian France. **1909** BELLOC *Marie Antoinette* 377 The violent egalitarian mood which had now for a year and more driven the military fury of the Republic. **1930** W. K. HANCOCK *Australia* iii. 67 The economic and social foundations of the homogeneous egalitarian society.

B. *sb.* One who asserts the equality of mankind.

1920 *19th Cent.* July 10 A variant of the superman as noxious as the mediocrity or the egalitarian. **1931** A. HUXLEY *Music at Night* II. 123 The theatres in which the egalitarians will enjoy the talkies, tasties, smellies, and feelies.

Hence **egali'tarianism**, the doctrine or condition of such equality.

1932 *Nation* (N.Y.) 6 July 16/1 There is apparently a further identification of egalitarianism, communism, and materialism. **1937** *Times* 8 June 22/5 With an eye to the growing egalitarianism of social life..the ceremonial side of the monarchy should be scrutinized afresh. **1955** M. GLUCKMAN *Custom & Conflict in Africa* ii. 31 Not even the first introduction of..European trade-goods broke up this egalitarianism.

e'gality. *Obs.* [ME. *egalite*, a. F. *égalité*: see EGALL *a.* and -ITY.] = EQUALITY (in 14th c. with sense 'equanimity').

(Re-formed as a nonce-wd. by Tennyson, to convey the modern associations connected with the Fr. word.)

c **1374** CHAUCER *Boeth.* II. iv. 42 Al fortune is blisful to a man by þe agreablete or by þe egalite of hym þat suffreþ it. *c* **1386** —— *Pers. T.* ¶875 She is as thise martirs in egalitee. **1628** COKE *On Litt.* 170 a, A rent may be granted for egality of partition. **1864** TENNYSON *Aylmer's F.* 265 That cursed France with her egalities!

†**'egall,** *a. Obs.* Also 5–6 **egalle,** 6 **eguall,** 6 **egal.** [a. OF. *egal* (*esgal*, *igal*, mod.F. *égal*):—L. *æquālem* EQUAL.] = EQUAL. Also quasi-*sb.*

c **1374** CHAUCER *Troylus* III. 88 To have right as you list comfort, Under your yerde egall to mine offence. *c* **1450** *Crt. of Love* 1041 Thy birth and hers they be nothing egall. **1553** T. WILSON *Rhetorique* 109 Eguall members [of a sentence] are such, when, etc. **1555** *Instit. Gentleman* D, Makyng those their egalles whyche ought to be their inferiors. **1588** SHAKS. *Tit. A.* IV. iv. 4 An Emperour.. Confronted thus, and for the extent Of egall [*Ff.* 2. 3. 4 equal] iustice, vs'd in such contempt? **1594** WEST *Symbol* II. *Chancerie* §28 Ministers of Justice..frame their judgments after the square and rule of good and egall. **1596** SHAKS. *Merch. V.* III. iv. 13 Companions Whose soules doe beare an egal [*Q.* equal] yoke of loue.

Hence †**'egally** *adv.*, equally, evenly; with even judgement or temper; **'egalness,** equality.

c **1374** CHAUCER *Boeth.* II. iv. 43 Wiþ hem þat every fortune receyuen agreablely or egaly. *c* **1450** *Crt. of Love* 365 Egally to discerne Betwene the lady and thine ability. **1526** TINDALE *2 Cor.* viii. 14 That ther be egalnes now at this tyme, that youre aboundaunce sucker their lacke. **1561** NORTON *Gorboduc* (1590) I. ii. And such an egalnes hath nature made Betweene the brethren of one fathers seede. **1594** SHAKS. *Rich. III*, III. vii. 213 Your tendernes..to your Kindred And egally indeede to all Estates. **1621** BOLTON *Stat. Irel.* 157 (28 Hen. VIII.) The other part thereof egally to be devided amongst them.

†**'egall,** *v. Obs. rare.* [f. prec.; cf. Fr. *égaler.*] *trans.* To equal, be equal to.

1591 LODGE *Catharos* E iv b, The surplusage should not egall the principal.

†**e'gar,** *v. Obs. rare.* [ad. F. *égarer* to mislead, and *refl.* to stray.] *trans.* To put aside, dispense with; *intr.* To stray, wander. Hence **e'garring** *vbl. sb.*

1544 *St. Papers Hen. VIII*, I. 765 Item, to know the Kinges Majestes pleasur..for egarring of certeyn fotemen. **1584** SOUTHERNE *Pandora* 3 But if I will thus like Pindar, In many discourses Egar.

†**egede,** *a. Obs.* [Of unknown etymology, but app. related to *ægæde*, *ægede* (? folly), which occurs in the Ormulum.] Foolish.

a **1225** *Ancr. R.* 282 Hwu egede þing is horel. *c* **1230** *Hali Meid.* 39 Þah hit be egede sahe; hit ah meiden to eggi þe swiðre þer framward.

†**e'gelidate,** *v. Obs. rare*⁻¹. [f. late L. *ēgelidāt-* ppl. stem of *ēgelidāre* to thaw, f. *ē* out + *gelid-us* frozen.] *trans.* To render fluid (what is congealed).

1609 J. DAVIES *Holy Roode* 20 Then should my teares egelidate his gore.

'egence. *rare.* [as if ad. L. **egēntia*, f. *egēnt-em*, pr. pple. of *egēre* to be in need.] Need, the existence of needs.

1865 J. GROTE *Moral Ideas* ii. (1876) 31 Egence is the life of the universe.

†**'egency.** *Obs.* [f. as prec.: see -ENCY.] Neediness, poverty.

1600 TOURNEUR *Transf. Met.* xviii, So plac'd, hir ground might feed hir egencie.

†**e'gene,** *a. Obs. rare*⁻¹. [ad. L. *egēnus*, f. *egēre*: see prec.] Needy, poor.

1631 R. H. *Arraignm. Whole Creature* xiii. §3. 210 The perverse will of man..must needs it selfe alwayes be hungry and lancke, egene and leane.

†**'egepy.** *Obs. rare*⁻¹. [ad. (? through mod.L.) Gr. αἰγυπιός.] A kind of vulture.

1651 J. F[REAKE] *Agrippa's Occ. Philos.* 42 Egepis and Eagles.

[**'eger,** app. a misreading of EDGER in R. Holme: see EDGER 2.

1706 PHILLIPS, *Egers*, [country-word], the Spring or first blown tulips. **1715** in KERSEY. **1721–1800** in BAILEY. **1864** in WEBSTER; and in mod. Dicts.]

eger, obs. form of EAGER *a.*, EAGRE.

Egeria (ɪ'dʒɪərɪə). In *Roman Mythology*, the name of a goddess, supposed to be the instructress of Numa Pompilius, and regarded as the giver of life; *transf.* a tutelary divinity; a patroness and adviser.

1621 BURTON *Anat. Mel.* (1624) To Rdr. b, My Mistris Melancholy, my Ægeria, or my *malus Genius.* **1818** LADY MORGAN *Fl. Macarthy* III. ii. 82 Why may not I have my Egeria or my dæmon, as well as another? **1826** DISRAELI *Viv. Grey* III. vi, It is in these moments, that Nature becomes our Egeria. **1890** *Athenæum* 24 May 670/2 With the help and counsel of Beatrice, who turns his Egeria, he wins fame in law and politics. **1932** H. NICOLSON *Diary* 9 Dec. (1966) 124 She has a sort of *Egeria* look which must be put on. **1934** E. POUND *Eleven New Cantos* xxxv. 23 His Wife now acts as his model and the Egeria Has, let us say, married a realtor.

egerminate (ɪ'dʒɜːmɪneɪt), *v.* [ad. L. *ēgermināt-* ppl. stem of *ēgermināre*, f. *ē* out + *germināre* to sprout.] *intr.* Of a plant: To shoot forth.

1623 COCKERAM, *Egerminate*, to spring or bud out. **1721–1800** in BAILEY. **1846** in WORCESTER; and in mod. Dicts.

Hence **e,germi'nation.**

1736 in BAILEY.

†**'egerne,** *a. Obs.* [of obscure etymology; cf. ON. *ágiarn*]. Greedy.

c **1200** *Trin. Coll. Hom.* 37 Ðis oref is swiðe egerne, and fecheð his leswe hwile uppen trewes and hwil uppen cliues and hwile in þe dales.

egest (ɪ'dʒɛst), *v.* [f. L. *ēgest-* ppl. stem of *ēgerĕre*, f. *ē* out + *gerĕre* carry.] *trans.* To pass off, expel; *esp.* from within the body, *e.g.* by evacuation of the bowels, perspiration, etc.

1607 TOPSELL *Four-f. Beasts* 65 When one is troubled with a desire of going often to the stool, and can egest nothing. **1626** BACON *Sylva* §899 The Beare, the Hedge-hog ..all wax Fat when they Sleepe, and egest not. **1631** BRATHWAIT *Whimzies* To Rdr. 11 Ill drest meat..to be egested long before it come to bee digested. **1633** T. ADAMS *Exp. 2 Peter* ii. 13 What [is] rich apparel, which man takes up in pride, but that the worm hath egested in scorn? **1685** MANTON *Christ's Transfig.* iii. Wks. 1870 I. 362 The grave was like a woman ready to be delivered; it suffered throes till this blessed burden was egested. **1884** *Health Exhib. Catal.* 5 Alcohol..undergoes no..change when taken into the stomach, but is egested from the lungs and skin.

‖**egesta** (ɪ'dʒɛstə), *sb. pl.* [L. *ēgesta*, neut. pl. of *ēgestus*, pa. pple. of *ēgerĕre*: see prec.] Waste matters passed off from the body; excreta.

1787 E. FORD in *Med. Commun.* II. 128 An exact attention to the ingesta and egesta would be conducive to recovery. **1833** J. RENNIE *Alph. Angling* 36 It feeds..if we may judge from its egesta, upon..slime or moistened clay. **1862** SIR H. HOLLAND *Ess. Mod. Chem.* 448.

egestion (ɪ'dʒɛstʃən). [ad. L. *ēgestiōn-em*, noun of action f. *ēgerĕre*: see prec.]

†**1.** *gen.* The action of discharging or emptying out. In quot. *concr. Obs.*

c **1420** *Pallad. on Husb.* XI. 449 Now thai condite her must egestion [L. *primo amne musti spumantis egesto*] That wol with gipse her wynes medicyne.

2. *Phys.* The passing off of excreta from within the body; opposed to *ingestion.*

1670 RAY *Proverbs* (1768) 8 Why the naming of some Excrements of the body, or the egestion of them is condemned. **1677** HALE *Prim. Orig. Man.* I. i. 32 These natural or involuntary exertions of Digestion, Egestion, Circulation. **1847–9** TODD *Cycl. Anat.* IV. 459/1 The functions of egestion are more necessary to the maintainance of life than those of ingestion. **1878** BELL tr. *Gegenbauer's Comp. Anat.* 84 The form of which is very varied, and which at times contains the orifice of egestion also.

†**b.** *spec.* Evacuation of the bowels. *Obs.*

1547 BOORDE *Brev. Health* xv. 12 They do defyle them selfe other by uryn, or by egestion, or both at once. **1578** BANISTER *Hist. Man* v. 64 The Muscles..are vnto egestion seruiceable. **1608** TOPSELL *Serpents* 756 He which is stung by a scorpion..is..affected with..a continual desire to egestion. **1711** *Last Distemp. Tom Whigg* I. 5 Sliced, a.. Term in Hawking to signifie Egestion.

†**c.** Occasionally used for 'vomiting'. *Obs.*

1633 T. ADAMS *Exp. 2 Peter* i. 20 The true history of Jonah, his swallowing and egestion by the whale. **1633** BP. HALL *Hard Texts* 383 By luke-warme water..the stomack is made apt to egestion.

d. *concr.* Excrement, †vomit.

1607 TOPSELL *Four-f. Beasts* 482 The excrements of his [the ox's] belly and egestion or dung, for the amending and enriching of plowed lands. **1609** BP. BARLOW *Answ. Nameless Cath.* 100 The vnsauorie egestion of a filthy strong stomake. **1610** BARROUGH *Meth. Physick* I. xvi. (1639) 25 For the most part their egestions be liquid. **1656** HOBBES *Six Less.* Wks. 1845 VII. 324 To take wing..like beetles from my egestions. **1671** SALMON *Syn. Med.* II. xlvi. 309 The Egestion, soft, equal, yellow, is well digested.

†**3.** The expulsion of a product of digestion, secretion, etc., from the organ producing it. Also *concr. Obs.*

1643 DIGBY *Nat. Bodies* xxxv. (1658) 367 The arteries which lie fittest to receive these sudden egestions of blood. **1696** PHILLIPS, *Egestion*, the Expulsion of Meat, digested through the Pylorus or gate of the Stomach, to the rest of the Intestines. **1715** in KERSEY. **1721–1800** in BAILEY.

egestive (ɪ'dʒɛstɪv), *a.* [f. L. *ēgest-* (see EGEST *v.*) + -IVE.] Pertaining to, or connected with, the process of egestion.

1677 HALE *Prim. Orig. Man.* III. vi. 276 They have the digestive, egestive, and other parts of the Nutritive Faculty. **1835–6** TODD *Cycl. Anat.* I. 69/1 Less activity is indicated in the egestive than in the ingestive system. **1877** HUXLEY *Anat. Inv. An.* i. 50 In the Porifera, the terminal aperture of the gastræa becomes the egestive opening of the adult.

†**e,gestu'ose,** *a. Obs.*⁻⁰ [ad. late L. *egestuōsus*, irreg. f. *egestas* poverty.] = EGESTUOUS.

1775 ASH, *Egestuose*, poor, needy.

†**e,gestu'osity.** *Obs. rare.* [as if ad. L. **egestuōsitāt-em*, f. as prec.] Meagreness, poverty.

1656 BLOUNT *Glossogr.* **1709** *Brit. Apollo* II. No. 64. 2/2 Clothing the Egestuosity of your Matter with pompous Epithets.

†**e'gestuous,** *a. Obs.*⁻⁰ [see EGESTUOSE.] Very poor and needy.

1656 BLOUNT *Glossogr.* **1721–1800** in BAILEY. **1775** in ASH.

egg (ɛg), *sb.* Forms: α. 1 **ǽȝ,** (**ǽiȝ**), 2 **aiȝ,** 3–5 **ey(e,** 4–6 **ay(e,** 5 **ȝey;** *pl.* 1 **ǽȝ(e)ru,** 4 **eyer,** 3–5 **ay-, ei-, eyren(e,** 5 **eyron, -oun.** β. 4–7 **eg, egge,** (5 **eeg, ege, hegge**), 6– **egg.** [Com. Teut.: OE. *ǽȝ*, pl. *ǽȝru* (whence the α. forms) = OS. *ei* (MDu., Du. *ei*), OHG. *ei*, pl. *eigir* (MHG. *ei*, mod.G. *ei*, pl. *eier*), ON. *egg*, Goth. **addjis* (Crim.-Goth. 16th c. *ada*):—OTeut. **ajjoz-* neut. The β. forms are from the ON. *egg.*

The connexion of the Teut. word with its WAryan synonyms, Gr. ᾠόν, L. *ōvum*, OSl. *jaje*, Ir. *og*, is probable, but has not yet been demonstrated.]

I. 1. a. The (more or less) spheroidial body produced by the female of birds and other animal species, and containing the germ of a new individual, enclosed within a shell or firm membrane. ***addle, wind egg***: see those words.

a **1000** *Boeth. Metr.* xx. 169 On æȝe bið ȝioleca on middan. *c* **1000** *Sax. Leechd.* II. 156 Wiþ þon þe hær ne weaxe æmettan æȝru ȝenim. *a* **1225** *Ancr. R.* 66 Kumeð þe coue ..& reueð hire hire eiren. *c* **1300** *K. Alis.* 568 A faukon..An ay he laide..That feol the kyng Phelip nygh. **1377** LANGL. *P. Pl.* B. XI. 343 Many other briddes Hudden..her egges.. In mareys. **1382** WYCLIF *Isa.* lix. 5 The eiren of edderes thei to-breeken. *c* **1440** *Gesta Rom.* xxviii. 106 (Harl. MS.) Anoþere birde..laborithe..to infecte hir nest or hir eyren. **1486** *Bk. St. Albans* A ij a, To speke of hawkis fro an eg to thei be habull to be takene. **1535** COVERDALE *Job* xxxix. 13 The Estrich..when he hath layed his egges vpon the grounde, he bredeth them in the dust. **1601** SHAKS. *Jul. C.* II. i. 32 Thinke him as a Serpents egge. **1657** S. PURCHAS *Pol. Flying-Ins.* 48 Improperly that is an egg out of the whole whereof a living creature is bred, as the eggs of Spiders, Ants, Flies. **1747** GOULD *Eng. Ants* 32 A Queen..in a Box ..will in a few Days deposit some Eggs, unless she had laid before you took her. **1774** GOLDSM. *Nat. Hist.* (1776) II. 339 The numerous brood of [turtles'] eggs are..buried in the warm sands of the shore. **1851** CARPENTER *Man. Phys.* 95 The eggs of the Slug, when dried up by the sun or by artificial heat..are found not to have lost their fertility.

b. *spec.* An egg of a domestic fowl as an article of food.

805–31 *Chart. Oswulf* in Sweet *O.E. Texts* 444 ȝif hit ðonne festendæȝ sie, selle mon uneȝe cæsu and fisces and butran and æȝera. *c* **1000** *Sax. Leechd.* II. 103 Smire mid æȝes ȝeolcan. *c* **1000** *Ags. Gosp.* Luke xi. 12 ȝif he bit æȝ [*c* **1160** *Hatton* aiȝ] segst þu ræcð he him scorpionem. **1297** R. GLOUC. *Chron.* (Rolls) 8334 Vor aney tueie ssillinges wel vawc þo hii boȝte. *c* **1300** *K. Alis.* 4719 Men to heom threowe drit and donge, With foule ayren. *c* **1400** MAUNDEV. v. 49 Thidre bryngen Wommen..here Eyren of Hennes, of Gees & of Dokes. *c* **1400** *Rowland & O.* 222 The lawes of Cristyante ne are noghte worthe ane aye. *c* **1420** *Pallad. on Husb.* I. 582 Wol thou..eyron grete thai legge? **1490** CAXTON *Eneydos* Prol., What sholde a man in thyse dayes now wryte, egges or eyren, certaynly it is harde to playse every man. **1530** *Proper Dyaloge* (1863) 9 So is it not worthe a rotten aye. **1596** SHAKS. *1 Hen. IV*, II. i. 64 They are vp already, and call for Egges and Butter. **1614** W. B. *Philosopher's Banquet* (ed. 2) 52 Goose-egges are loathing. **1670** G. H. *Hist. Cardinals* II. II. 148 Constrain'd to..keep Lent with Bisket and hard Eggs only. **1732** ARBUTHNOT *Rules of Diet* 255 Eggs are perhaps the..most nourishing.. of all animal Food. **1850** MRS. STOWE *Uncle Tom's C.* xv. 137 Give them to this fellow; he'll put them down as if they were eggs, now. **1879** FARRAR *St. Paul* (1883) 46 Was it.. worth..discussion..whether an egg laid on a festival might or might not be eaten?

2. *fig.* **a.** That which contains the germ of anything; generally in a bad sense. Also in phrase, ***to crush in the egg.***

1645 TOMBES *Anthropol.* 8 This was the egge out of which their contentions were hatched. **1649** G. DANIEL *Trinarch. Hen. IV*, ccexlviii, Soe Power of Warre From the first Egge of Libertie, out-Creepes A fatall Serpent. **1689** *Apol. Fail. Walker's Acc.* 91 The Rebellion..had not been either prevented or crush'd in the Egg.

b. Applied contemptuously to a young person.

1605 SHAKS. *Macb.* IV. ii. 83 What you Egge? Yong fry of Treachery. **1835** E. ELLIOTT *Taurassdes* IV. iv. Wks. III. 272 Who would suspect a boy? Who hir'd thee? Egg!

3. a. Applied to anything that resembles an egg in shape or appearance. So † *to turn up the eggs* (i.e. the whites) *of one's eyes.*

1589 PUTTENHAM *Eng. Poesie* (Arb.) 105 The egge or figure ouall. **1635** A. STAFFORD *Fem. Glory* (1869) 89 The eggs of their eies are at their highest elevation. *a* **1637** B. JONSON (R.) A puritan poacht, That used to turn up the eggs of his eyes. *a* **1691** BOYLE (J.) There was taken a great glass-bubble wih a long neck, such as chemists are wont to call a philosophical egg.

b. In full *egg coal*: see quots. orig. *U.S.*

1855 *Santa Barbara* (Calif.) *Gaz.* 22 Nov. 1/5 The attempt to make omelets out of 'egg' coal has been abandoned. **1880** *Bradstreet's* 2 Oct. 5/4 The sizes used are 'lump', 'steamboat', 'broken', and 'pea'; while for family use the sizes are 'egg', 'stove' and 'nut'. **1881** RAYMOND *Mining Gloss. Egg-Coal*, Pennsylvania. **1900** *Coal & Metal Miners' Pocketbk.* (ed. 6) 434 Egg passes over 2" mesh, and through 2¾" mesh. *Ibid.* 585 Egg coal, anthracite coal that will pass through a 2¾" square mesh and over a 2" square mesh. **1924** A. T. SHURICK *Coal Industry* 144 The broken coal..is again screened into egg, stove, and nut coal. **1970** F. MCKENNA *Gloss. Railwaymen's Talk* 35 *Eggs*, ovoid briquettes, made of coal dust and cement dust, used during coal shortage.

c. *Cricket.* = DUCK'S EGG b.

1861 *Bell's Life* 25 Aug. (Suppl.) 2/1 Dowson 'laid an egg'; R. D. Walker made 10 in an hour and a quarter. **1898** K. S. RANJITSINHJI *With Stoddart's Team in Australia* x. 195 Gregory..was yorked first ball... Iredale also secured an 'egg'.

d. A bomb, a mine. *slang.*

1917 *War Illustr.* 13 Jan. 524/2 That seaplane..having some explosive 'eggs' to drop. **1918** E. M. ROBERTS *Flying Fighter* 335 *Eggs*, bombs weighing twenty pounds and upward filled with high explosives and 'laid' in Hunland. **1929** F. C. BOWEN *Sea Slang* 44 *Eggs*, submarine mines, a war-time phrase. **1939** *War Illustr.* 9 Dec. 399/1 The Germans are thought to be using relays of U-boats. Even the smallest of these can carry up to a dozen 'eggs'... A fast surface layer can put down more than 200 mines 'at a sitting'. **1947** AUDEN *Age of Anxiety* (1948) i. 18 But we laid our eggs Neatly in their nest.

4. a. Phrases: *a bad egg* (colloq.): a person or a scheme that disappoints expectation. Similarly *good egg* (slang): (*a*) an excellent person or object; (*b*) an exclamation of enthusiastic approbation; also with other preceding adjs., esp. *tough.* † *egg and bird*: in youth and maturity, from beginning to end, first and last. *to break the egg in anybody's pocket*: to spoil his plan. † *to take eggs for money*: to be put off with something worthless. *to have eggs on the spit*: to have business in hand. *to tread upon eggs*: to walk warily, as on delicate ground. † (*to be*) *with egg*: (to be) ready to lay; also *fig.* † *to come in with five eggs*: to break in fussily with an idle story; more fully, *five eggs a penny, and four of them addle. to have* (*get*, etc.) *egg on one's face*: to be made to look foolish; to be embarrassed or humiliated by the turn of events.

1542 UDALL *Erasm. Apoph.* 272 Persones comyng in with their fiue egges, how that Sylla had geuen ouer his office of Dictature. **1551** ROBINSON tr. *More's Utop.* (Arb.) 56 An other commeth in with his fiue egges. **1598** B. JONSON *Ev. Man in Hum.* III. iii, I have eggs on the spit; I cannot go yet, sir. **1611** SHAKS. *Wint. T.* I. ii. 161 Mine honest Friend Will you take Egges for Money? **1670** G. H. *Hist. Cardinals* II. I. 130 Contented to take Eggs (as it were) for their money. **1711** *Vind. Sacheverell* A iiij, I have been such a profligate Liver, Egg, and Bird. **1733** P. DRAKE *Grotto* (*title-page*), Apollo's..Grotto makes them [Witts] all with egg. *a* **1734** NORTH *Exam.* 324 This very circumstance..broke the egg ..in the Pockets of the Whigs. *a* **1734** —— *Ld. Guilford* (1808) I. 245 (D.) This gave him occasion..to find if any slip had been made (for he all along trod upon eggs). **1747** GOULD *Eng. Ants* 57 Very like that of a Female Bee, Wasp, or Queen Ant, when not with Egg. **1855** 'P. PAXTON' *Capt. Priest* 319 In the language of his class, the Perfect Bird generally turns out to be 'a bad egg'. **1864** *Athenæum* 559/1 'A bad egg',..a fellow who had not proved to be as good as his promise. **1884** BLACK *Jud. Shaks.* xiii. in *Harper's Mag.* May 954/2, I have other eggs on the spit. **1903** KIPLING *Traffics & Discoveries* (1904) 138 'Us'll find they ships!' ..'Good egg!' quoth Moorshed. **1910** GALSWORTHY *Justice* I, A real bad egg. **1914** C. MACKENZIE *Sinister St.* II. III. x. 711 It doesn't look a hundred quid to a tanner on his blue. Bad luck. He's a very good egg. *Ibid.* xii. 739 Oxford was divided into Bad Men and Good Eggs. **1915** D. O. BARNETT *Lett.* 56 We are going to do this regularly, and I think it is a very good egg. **1915** WODEHOUSE *Something Fresh* x. §3 'She isn't going to sue me for breach?' 'She never had any intention of doing so.' The Hon. Frederick sank back on the pillows. 'Good egg!' he said with fervour. **1920** GALSWORTHY *In Chancery* I. xii. 100 He was a rotten egg. **1929** S. AUMONIER *Ups & Downs* 418 Hullo, Pan! Good egg! **1930** E. H. LAVINE *Third Degree* (1931) iii. 30 Occasionally, a really tough egg is trained to be a killer. **1938** WODEHOUSE *Summer Moonshine* i. 18 She's a tough egg. **1964** *Saturday Night* (Toronto) July 17/1 The move left many critics with egg on their faces. **1972** *Times* 19 Feb. 7/1 There is something reassuringly changeless about the capacity of the highest military authorities for getting egg on their faces. **1977** *Times Educ. Suppl.* 21 Oct. 11/2 The most immediate need is to decide why the physical measurements of the ages of the East African rocks appear to suggest such different patterns of hominid evolution from that provided by the evolution of the wild pig. In the process, many people will be discovered to have egg on their faces. **1983** 'J. LE CARRÉ' *Little Drummer Girl* x. 186 I'm just stuck there, am I, with egg on my face. **1984** *Listener* 15 Mar. 16/3 'Canadian Far East Trade Corporation', 'H and H Enterprises' and 'CMI Investments' led the trustee to conclude that the CIA must have 'egg on its face' for associating with a swindler. **1985** *Times* 3 Jan. 13/1 BAT..succeeded in constantly getting egg on its face.

b. In many proverbial phrases of obvious meaning; also, *as sure as eggs is eggs*; hence, *as safe as eggs* (in same sense). *teach your grandmother to suck eggs*: said to those who presume to offer advice to others who are more experienced. *to have all your eggs in one basket*: to risk all one's property on a single venture; also *to put* (†*venture*) *all one's eggs in one basket*, etc.

1592 SHAKS. *Rom. & Jul.* III. i. 26 Thy head is as full of quarrels, as an egge is full of meat. **1606** BRYSKETT *Civ. Life* 5 Critiques that spend their eyes to find a haire vpon an egge. **1620** SHELTON *Quix.* III. vii, The Hen lays as well upon one Egg as many. *a* **1610** BABINGTON *Wks.* (1622) 51 To be wonne with the egg and lost with the shell, is a great inconstancie. **1611** SHAKS. *Wint. T.* I. ii. 130 We are Almost as like as Egges. **1638** CHILLINGW. *Relig. Prot.* I. ii. §160. 117 They are as like your own, as an egge to an egge. *a* **1632** G. HERBERT *Jacula Prud.* (1640) 291 He that steals an egg, will steal an ox. **1666** G. TORRIANO *Second Alphabet of Proverbial Phrases* 125/2 To put all ones Eggs in a Paniard, *viz.* to hazard all in one bottom. **1699** B. E. *Dict. Cant. Crew*, As sure as Eggs be Eggs. **1707** J. STEVENS tr. *Quevedo's Com. Wks.* (1709) 348 You would have me teach my Grandame to suck Eggs. **1710** S. PALMER *Proverbs* cxxiii. 344 (*heading*) A Mouse that has but one Hole, is soon Catch'd: or, Don't venture all your Eggs in One Basket. **1777** SHERIDAN *Trip. Scarb.* iii. iv, As full of good-nature as an egg's full of meat. **1857** HUGHES *Tom Brown* II. vi, I shall come out bottom of the form as sure as eggs is eggs. **1871** M. COLLINS *Mrq. & Merch.* III. iv. 114 We've got the Derby and Leger this next year as safe as eggs. **1874** WHYTE MELVILLE *Uncle John* III. xxvii. 140 'Annie, my own darling, may I carry your basket all my life?' 'If you'll put all your eggs in it, yes,' answered Annie boldly. **1925** D. H. LAWRENCE *Refl. Death Porcupine* 179 It is a pity that we have insisted on putting all our eggs in one basket: calling love the basket, and ourselves the eggs. **1955** *Times* 3 May 3/6 An area which had all its eggs in one basket. **1969** *Times* 5 Nov. 23/3 The earl is evidently feeling a little uncomfortable that all his family eggs are in one basket.

c. *old egg*: a familiar form of address = old chap, old fellow, old sport.

1919 *Punch* 5 Mar. 190/2 Cheerio, old egg. **1927** 'A. ARMSTRONG' *Patrick Engaged* ix. §3 'You'd be arrested.. and spoil the whole show,' replied Patrick tersely. 'Sorry, old egg, sorry!'

II. *Comb.*

5. In Plant-names: *eggs and bacon, eggs and butter, eggs and collops*; popular names for several plants, esp. *Linaria vulgaris*, the Field Snap-dragon or Toad-flax.

1878 BRITTEN & HOLL. *Plant-n. Eggs and Bacon.* From the two shades of yellow in the flower. 1 *Linaria vulgaris*, Mill.; 2 *Lotus corniculatus.* Eggs and Butter, *Linaria vulgaris*, Mill. Eggs and Collops, *Linaria vulgaris*, Mill.; 2 *Ranunculus acris*, L.

6. General comb.: **a.** attributive, as *egg-ball, -basket, -coloration, -mass, -pie, -sauce, -season, -spoon, -stage, -stall, -state, -tongs, -yelk* or *-yolk.*

1869 *Beeton's Househ. Management* 201 *Egg-balls for Soups and Made Dishes. **1773** J. WEDGWOOD *Let.* 21 Nov. (1965) 156 *Egg Baskets; Egg Cups, with covers and without. **1867** G. W. HARRIS *Sut Lovingood* 132 He wer histin aig-baskets. **1911** J. A. THOMSON *Biol. Seasons* II. 177 A stereotyped kind of *egg-coloration. **1869** *Beeton's Househ. Management* 858 Silver or plated *egg-dishes are now very much used. **1889** M. E. BAMFORD *Up & Down Brooks* 45 The bright-yellow *egg-mass. **1921** *Brit. Museum Return* 119 An exceedingly fine egg-mass of *Natica sp.* from Scotia Bay, South Orkneys. **1956** *Nature* 10 Mar. 489/2 Fifteen days after sowing, second-generation larvæ were hatching within the egg-masses. *a* **1592** GREENE *Fr. Bacon* (1861) 174 When *egg-pies grow on apple-trees, then will thy grey mare prove a bag-piper. **1634** J. TAYLOR (Water-P.) *Gt. Eater Kent* 12 It is welcome, whether it bee sawsedge or custard or egge-pye. *c* **1685** in *Dk. Buckhm's Wks.* (1705) II. 48 She..neatly dish'd it up with *Egg-sauce. **1828** MACAULAY *Hallam, Ess.* (1865) I. 80/2 Judgments only to be averted by salt-fish and egg-sauce. **1953** N. TINBERGEN *Herring Gull's World* x. 94 Once I saw the results of repeated raids by a fox in the *egg-season. **1883** F. DAY *Indian Fish* 26 They have their enemies in the *egg stage.. and during their maturity. **1824-9** LANDOR *Imag. Conv.* (1846) I. 273 Those who kept *egg-stalls and fish-stalls cursed him and removed them. **1747** GOULD *Eng. Ants* 38 The Continuance of Ants in the *Egg State is somewhat precarious. **1868** *Q. Rev.* 354 These 'colifichets' are made principally of the *egg-yelk.

b. objective, as *egg-collecting, -eating, -hunting, -laying* vbl. sb. and ppl. adj.; *egg-gatherer, -hunter, -monger, -robber*; also, *egg-boiler, -detector, -poacher, -slicer, -tester, -timer*, appliances and implements used for or in boiling, poaching, etc., eggs. Also EGG-BEATER.

1936 *Discovery* Feb. 56/2 What branch of science can *egg collecting now advance? **1836** T. HOOK *G. Gurney* I. iii. 85 *Egg-eating and prawn-picking are not delicate peformances. **1882** A. HEPBURN in *Proc. Berw. Nat. Club* IX. No. 3. 505 The egg-eating birds kept the wood pigeon within very moderate bounds. **1855** *Knickerbocker* XLVI. 223 Upon the approach of the *egg-gatherers, with little or no dissenting clamor, they rise up in one vast, dangling-legged body. **1936** *Discovery* Jan. 12/1 Saddlebags are strapped to horses, and egg-gatherers fill these bags in no time. **1856** KANE *Arct. Expl.* II. xxvi. 265 Our *egg-hunters found it difficult to keep their feet. **1855** *Knickerbocker* XLVI. 223 As *egg-hunting is viewed by our country people as a species of 'picnicking', lovers and their mistresses..are the principal actors in these excursions. **1751** SMOLLETT *Per. Pic.* (1779) II. lxi. 186 Like a goose in the agonies of *egg-laying. **1676** SHADWELL *Virtuoso* III, All oviparous or egg-laying creatures. **1884** *Health Exhib. Catal.* 110/2 *Egg Poachers. **1953** N. TINBERGEN *Herring Gull's World* xvi. 133 Potential *egg-robbers. **1951** *Catal. Exhibits, South Bank Exhib., Festival of Britain* 63/1 'Skyline' *Egg Slicer. **1884** *Health Exhib. Catal.* 25/1 Microscopes, *Egg Testers, Lamps, etc. *Ibid.* 112/2 An assortment of *Egg..Timers, etc.

c. similative, as *egg-bald, -ended, -eyed, -faced, -like, -oblong, -shaped*, adjs.; *egg-fashion* adv.

1877 TENNYSON *Harold* v. i, But If thou [the monk] blurt thy curse among our folk..I may give that *egg-bald head The tap that silences. **1859** W. J. M. RANKINE *Man. Steam Engine* §63 The ends of '*egg-ended' cylindrical boilers. **1875** *Plain Needlework* 10 Abel Morrell's '*egg-eyed' needles. **1921** *Glasgow Herald* 26 Sept. 6 He will find the *egg-faced man there. **1702** *Lond. Gaz.* No. 3819/8 Three Diamonds..two of them pretty large cut *Egg-fashion. **1599** T. M[OUFET] *Silkwormes* 18 *Egg-like [marginal gloss or *oval*]. **1835-6** TODD *Cycl. Anat.* I. 742/2 The bones of the cranium..concur in the production of an egg-like cavity. **1857** WOOD *Com. Objects Sea Shore* 50 Some of them have anything but an egg-like aspect. **1859** GEO. ELIOT *A. Bede* 16 A small oval face..with an egg-like line of cheek and chin. **1776** WITHERING *Bot. Arrangem.* (1796) I. 155 Seed single, *egg-oblong. **1766** BAKER in *Phil. Trans.* LVI. 186 The seeds *egg-shaped, one or two strongly adhering to the calyx. **1845** STOCQUELER *Handbk. Brit. India* (1854) 370 Ceylon is egg shaped.

7. Special comb.: **egg albumin**, albumin obtained from the white of an egg, esp. ovalbumin; also = ALBUMEN 1; **egg and anchor, egg and dart, egg and tongue (mouldings)**, varieties of the ECHINUS, produced by the alternation of vertical with egg-shaped ornaments: see ECHINUS 3 and quots. there given; **egg-and-spoon race**, a foot race during which the competitors are required to carry an egg in a spoon (see also quot. 1894); **egg-apparatus** *Bot.*, the group of three cells at the micropylar end of the embryo-sac in seed plants, only one of which is fertile; **egg-apple**, the fruit of the Egg-plant (*Solanum Melongena*); **egg-bag**, (*a*) the ovary; (*b*) = *egg-case*; **egg-binding**, the condition or disease of a fowl that is egg-bound; **egg-bird**, a species of tern (*Hydrochelidon fuliginosum*) common in the West Indies, where its eggs are collected for use as food; **egg-born** *a.*, produced from an egg; **egg-bound** *ppl. a.*, said of fowls suffering from weakness or disease, so that they are unable to expel their eggs; **egg-bread** *U.S.*, bread made of the meal of Indian corn, eggs, etc.; **egg-breaker** (see quot.); **egg-burster**, a thickened area on an embryonic insect helping it to burst the egg membranes when hatching; **egg-capsule**, a natural envelope containing eggs; **egg-case** (see quot.); **egg-cell**, the cell or germ from which an egg or a living animal is subsequently developed; **egg-cheese** (see quot.); **egg-chinned** *ppl. a.*, ? double-chinned, or having an egg-shaped chin; **egg-cluster** = *egg-case*; **egg-cosy** [COSY *sb.* 2], a cover to keep a boiled egg warm; **egg-covering**, the external membrane of an insect's egg; **egg-dance**, a dance blindfold among eggs; *fig.* an intricate and difficult task; **egg-eater** *S. Afr.*, a snake of the genus *Dasypeltis*, capable of crushing eggs with internal projections from its vertebrae; **egg-eating snake** = prec.; **egg-flip** = EGG-NOG; **egg-form**, an ellipse; † **egg-fraise**, a pancake; **egg-fruit**, the fruit of the egg-plant; † **egg-fry**, zoosperms, semen of the male; cf. FRY; **egg-full** *a.*, as full as an egg is of meat; **egg-glass**, (*a*) a glass for holding an egg; (*b*) a sand-glass in which the running of the sand indicates the time during which an egg should be boiled; **egg-hole** (see quot.); **egg-hot**, 'a hot drink made of beer, eggs, sugar, and nutmeg' (Berks. Gloss. E.D.S.); **egg-life** (see quot.); **egg-membrane**, a membrane surrounding an egg; = *vitelline membrane*; † **egg-nest** = *egg-case*; † **egg-pea**, an old variety of garden pea; **egg-peg**, the sloe; **egg-plum**, an egg-shaped plum, generally of a light yellow colour; **egg-pop** (*U.S.*), ?; **egg-posset** = *egg-flip*; **egg-pouch, egg-sac** = *egg-case*; **egg powder**, an artificially prepared substitute for eggs in cookery; **egg-purse** = *egg-capsule*; **egg-raft, -rope, -string**, a connected series of eggs laid by various insects; **Egg-Saturday**, the Saturday before Shrove Tuesday (Nares); **eggs Benedict** *Cookery* (orig. *U.S.*), a dish consisting of poached eggs placed on a slice of ham on toast, with a covering of

hollandaise sauce; **egg-slice**, a kitchen utensil for removing omelets or fried eggs from the pan; **egg(s)-man**, a collector of (wild fowls') eggs; **egg-spoon**, (*a*) a spoon used in eating eggs; (*b*) (see quot.); **egg-stand**, a stand or frame for holding a set of egg-cups; †**egg-starch** *a.*, ?; **egg-stone** = OOLITE; **egg-sucker** (see quot.); **Egg-Sunday**, the Sunday before Shrove-Tuesday; **egg tempera**, a medium of painting consisting of tempera colours mixed with egg in various forms, usu. the yolk; **egg-timer**, (*a*) a device for timing the cooking of an egg; (*b*) a device for boiling an egg; **egg-tooth**, a small, hard, white protuberance developed in the embryo bird and reptile which is used to crack the egg and is cast off after hatching; **egg-trot** = *egg-wife's trot*; **egg-tube**, an oviduct, esp. of an insect; **egg-urchin**, the popular name of one or more species of ECHINUS; **egg-whip**, an egg-whisk; **egg-whisk**, an utensil for beating eggs to a froth; †**egg-wife**, a woman who offers eggs for sale; hence **egg-wife's trot**, the pace at which an egg-wife would ride to market.

1871 *Jrnl. Chem. Soc.* XXIV. 572 Some properties of *Egg Albumin. **1919** J. B. COHEN *Class-Bk. Chem.* II. 94 Of the albumins, egg- and serum-albumin are the most important. **1956** *Nature* 18 Feb. 330/1 The cells were smeared on microscopical slides coated with egg-albumin or human serum. **1751** CHAMBERS *Cycl.* s.v., The profile or contour of the echinus, is enriched with *eggs and anchors, alternately placed. **1871** MISS BRADDON *Lovels* xxxii. 257 A house glorified within by *egg-and-dart mouldings. **1894** *Daily News* 8 Sept. 5/3 The gentlemen had a turn in the *egg-and-spoon race, in which the competitors had to punt with one hand and balance an egg on a spoon with the other. **1936** *Punch* 12 Aug. 187 (*caption*), I would like you to meet Mr. Scooter, the winner of our Parents' Egg-and-Spoon race. **1902** *Encycl. Brit.* XXV. 434/2 Of the three energids of the *egg-apparatus, one alone is normally functional as the egg. **1774** GOLDSM. *Nat. Hist.* VI. 253 From this ovary, or *eggbag, as it is vulgarly called, the fish's eggs drop one by one into the womb. **1822** *Edin. Rev.* XXXVII. 127 Thus also spiders carry out about their nest or egg-bag. **1882** *Bazaar* 15 Feb. 175 My queries as to *egg-binding .. my hen budgerigar died *egg-bound. **1697** DAMPIER *Voy.* (1729) I 54 Small grey Fowls no bigger than a Black-bird, yet lay Eggs bigger than a Magpy's; and they are therefore by Privateers called *Egg-birds. **1772–84** COOK *Voy.* (1790) IV. 1362 Upon the shore were .. some egg birds. *a* **1631** DRAYTON *Elegies, Lady Aston's Departure*, Leda's brood, Jove's *egg-born issue smile upon the flood! **1854** M. J. HOLMES *Tempest & Sunshine* vii. 118 *Egg-bread which Southern cooks know so well how to make. **1862** in *Southern Hist. Soc. Papers* (1884) XII. 26 The table was spread with rich egg-bread, fried ham, and pure coffee. **1911** R. D. SAUNDERS *Col. Todhunter* ii. 29 The Missouri supper of fried chicken, egg-bread, butterbeans and corn on the ear. **1772** FORSTER in *Phil Trans.* LXII. 422 A sort of Gull, called *Egg-breakers, by the natives. **1920** *Brit. Museum Return* 121 The *Egg-burster of Encephalous Fly-larvæ. **1953** *New Biology* XIV. 116 There are three larval stages in most species [of fleas], two in a few, very alike except in size and in the presence of a conical egg-burster on the top of the head of those of the first stage. **1959** SOUTHWOOD & LESTON *Land & Water Bugs* 411 *Egg-burster*, a thickened, often sclerotized, usually Y- or T-shaped area on the vertex of the embryonic cuticle; it bears a tooth and its movement is considered to help in rupturing the chorion and egg membranes. **1883** *Encycl. Brit.* XVI. 653/2 When *egg-capsules are formed they are often of large size, have tough walls, and in each capsule are several eggs floating in a viscid fluid. **1921** *Brit. Museum Return* 119 A string of egg-capsules containing young examples of *Buscyon perversum*. **1936** RUSSELL & YONGE *Seas* (ed. 2) ii. 50 Common on the under side of rocks are the egg-capsules of the dog-whelk. **1847** CARPENTER *Zool.* 755 The females [Spiders] lay their eggs in these tubes; inclosing them in a silken cocoon, or *egg-case, which they carry about with them when they go to hunt. **1880** LANKESTER *Degen.* 20 A structureless particle .. thrown off from its parent .. known as the *egg-cell. **1879** tr. *Haeckel's Evol. Man* I. vi. 121 The human egg-cell is .. not essentially different from those of other Mammals. **1784–1815** A. YOUNG *Ann. Agric.* XXXVIII. 504 (E.D.S.) Farmers .. make *egg cheeses .. by putting five yolks of eggs to every pound of curd. **1625** B. JONSON *Staple of N.* IV. i, My *egg-chin'd laureate here. **1692** RAY *Phys.-Theol. Disc.* iv. (1732) 49 Ovary or *Egg-cluster. **1857** WOOD *Com. Objects Sea Shore* 52 The egg-cluster from which the sketch was taken. **1894** SOMERVILLE & 'ROSS' *Real Charlotte* III. xxxv. 23 The *egg-cosy that his wife had crocheted for him. **1906** *Westm. Gaz.* 3 Nov. 6/2 The sale of pin-cushions, d'oyleys, and knitted egg-cosies was unprecedented. **1909** *Lady's World* Dec. 284 The egg cosy made in the form of a cock's head and comb. **1967** A. WILSON *No Laughing Matter* III. 352 Journalism and worked up righteous anger, that's all she'd written. Egg cosies and cloaks! **1835–6** TODD *Cycl. Anat.* I. 270/1 The young .. swim about .. the instant that they are liberated from the *egg-coverings. **1801** STRUTT *Sports & Past.* III. v. 172 The *egg-dance .. was common enough about thirty years back. **1882** *Society* 18 Nov. 29/2 The slip is very excusable, for it is an egg-dance. **1887** *Encycl. Brit.* XXII. 194/2 A .. genus of snakes, *Dasypeltis*... In Cape Colony these snakes are well known under the name of 'eyer-vreter', i.e. '*egg-eaters'. **1911** *East London Dispatch* 1 Sept. 7 (Pettman), The Egg-eater lives almost entirely on eggs, which it eats in a curious fashion. **1969** A. BELLAIRS *Life of Reptiles* I. iv. 183 An egg-eater is able to demolish all the eggs of a clutch in rapid succession. **1897** *Daily News* 19 July 3/1 Natal .. now claims to possess an *egg-eating snake of phenomenal abilities. **1931** *Times Educ. Suppl.* 27 June p. iv/3 A very young egg-eating snake from Africa. **1965** R. & D. MORRIS *Men & Snakes* viii. 174 The egg-eating snake eats nothing but eggs and it is not surprising to find that many African birds have evolved elaborate anti-snake devices. **1832** J. ROMILLY *Diary* 23 June (1967) 16 *Egg-flip & sack in Sen[ate] H[ouse] at 11. **1871** NAPHEYS *Prev. & Cure Dis.* II. iii. 487 Some concentrated liquid nourishment, as a few spoonsful of egg-flip or beef-tea. **1551** RECORDE *Pathw. Knowl.* I. Def., It is lyke a circle that were brused .. whiche forme Geometricians dooe call an *egge forme. **1693** W. ROBERTSON *Phraseol. Gen.* 323 An *egg-fraise. **1811** W. J. TITFORD *Sks. Hortus Bot. Amer.* 53 (*heading*) *Egg fruit or Mad Apple, *Solanum Melongena*... It is called in India, Branjaw, in Jamaica, Garden Egg and Valanghanna, Brown Jolly or Bolangena. **1817** W. DARBY *Geogr. Descr. Louisiana* (ed. 2) 222 All the solanums (Irish potatoe, peppers, and egg-fruit,) whose leaves are easily killed by the slightest degree of freezing. **1887** *Harper's Mag.* Jan. 310/1 A dozen well-grown plants will supply a large family with egg-fruit. **1674** N. FAIRFAX *Bulk & Selv.* 124 An egg .. that sprang from the impetus of the tread, the Harvey-antang, or contagion and *egg-fry of Kerckring and de Graaf. **1839** BAILEY *Festus* xxvii. (1848) 324, I am *egg-full of life. **1867** EMERSON *Lett. & Soc. Aims, Culture* Wks. (Bohn) III. 227 No more a measure of time than an hour-glass or an *egg-glass. **1881** RAYMOND *Mining Gloss.*, **Egg-hole* (Derby), a notch cut in the wall of a lode to hold the end of a stempel. **1796** LAMB in *Lett.* (1849) 25, I have been drinking *egg-hot and smoking Oronooko. **1850** DICKENS *Dav. Copp.* xi. 119 She .. made a little jug of egg-hot afterwards to console us. **1886** *Folk-Lore Jrnl.* IV. 116 At the plentiful supper always provided on this night [*sc.* Christmas Eve], egg-hot, or eggy-hot, was the principal drink. It was made with eggs, hot beer, sugar, and rum, and was poured from one jug into another until .. covered with froth. **1879** tr. *Haeckel's Evol. Man* I. i. 12 *Egg-life or embryo-life within the egg-membranes. **1879** *Egg membrane [see *egg-life* above]. **1885** *Science* V. 425/1 In the Scombresocidae the entire egg-membrane is covered with strong filaments, which intertwine with those of contiguous eggs. **1893** J. TUCKEY tr. *Hatschek's Amphioxus* 74 The movement of the embryos inside the egg membrane .. is a quite peculiar one. **1704** A. VAN LEEUWENHOEK in *Phil. Trans.* XXV. 1620, I saw exceeding small ones still remaining in the Ovarium or *Egg-nest. **1744** *Notes & Observ. Tusser's Husb.* 19 Runcival Pease .. in their room are got the *Egg-pea, the Sugar-pea, etc. **1878** BRITTEN & HOLL. *Plant-n.*, *Egg-peg Bushes, *Prunus spinosa* L. **1859** *All Y. Round* No. 1. 17 The persiman is like a large *egg-plum. **1860** O. W. HOLMES *Prof. Breakf.-t.* i. (Paterson) 6 Water to make *egg-pop with. **1832** HONE *Year-bk.* 9 Jan. 61 *Egg-posset, alias Egg-flip, otherwise .. 'rum booze'. **1826** KIRBY & SP. *Entomol.* III. 72 The only insects .. known to spin an *egg-pouch like the spiders are the hydrophili, a kind of water beetle. **1862** *Englishwoman's Dom. Mag.* Sept 239/2 With the mysteries of making *egg-powder we are quite unacquainted. **1864** *Chemist & Druggist* 193 It seems that certain cooks .. are in the habit of buying and using egg powders. **1907** H. W. WILEY *Foods & their Adulteration* II. 115 The egg powder .. formed is almost devoid of moisture and .. may be kept for a long time without deterioration. **1921** *Chambers's Jrnl.* 375/2 The cockroach .. is very careful in the selection of a suitable site to place her *egg-purse. *Ibid.*, Each egg-purse [of a cockroach] contains sixteen eggs, arranged in two rows, with the ends from which the larvæ will emerge pointing towards the top. **1927** *Observer* 18 Sept. 8 The *egg-raft is laid by the many species of that group of mosquitoes, the *Culicine*, represented by our common gnat. **1891** *Nature* 10 Sept. 457 Each *egg-rope is moored to the bank by a thread. **1857** WOOD *Com. Objects Sea Shore* 50 All the *egg-sacs would have been found empty. **1867** J. HOGG *Microsc.* II. ii. 368 They [the Gregarinæ] have been described under a variety of titles, such as worm-nodules, egg-sacs, etc. **1607** *Chr. Prince* in *Misc. Ant. Angl.* (1816) 68 On the sixt of february, beeing *egge satterday, it pleased some gentlemen schollers in the towne to make a dauncing night of it .. the next Tuesday following beeing shrovetuesday. **1670** SIR R. BAKER *Theatr. Tri.* 37 One trick which he .. seems to have learned .. from Egge-Saturday in Oxford, to make diversity of meats with diversity of dressing. **1898** A. MEYER *Eggs, & how to use Them* 43 *Poached *eggs .. Benedict*, split and toast some small muffins; put on each a nice round slice of broiled ham, and on the ham the poached egg; pour over some Hollandaise sauce. **1907** S. T. RORER *Many Ways for cooking Eggs* 46 *Eggs Bénédict*. Separate two eggs [etc.]. **1971** A. HAILEY *Wheels* v. 72 Brett .. coerced them into preparing Eggs Benedict, which was never on the standard menu. **1986** *Washington Post* 16 Feb. E4/2 Eggs Benedict go for $5.95, omelets for $4.95, and the view is priceless. **1796** MRS. GLASSE *Cookery* xiv. 238 Fry them brown in fresh butter; then take them out with an *egg slice. **1886** E. C. DAWSON *Bp. Hannington* viii. (1887) 107 The enthusiastic *eggsman .. scrambled up again with the contents of three nests in his pockets. *Ibid.* The egg hunter arms himself with an instrument called an *egg-spoon, like a tiny landing-net, at the end of a long, light rod. **1839** *Rep. Constabulary Force Commissioners* 25 in *Parl. Papers* [169] XIX, P— slipped into the parlour and brought out a watch and a silver *egg-stand. **1909** BENNETT *Old Wives' Tale* II. i. §3 The resplendent egg-stand holding twelve silver-gilt egg-cups and twelve chased spoons to match. **1969** E. H. PINTO *Treen* 136 Double-decker egg stands .. made to hold 12, 24 or 48 eggs, were to be found in all Victorian and Edwardian larders. **1630** TAYLOR *Workes* (N.) Whose calves *eg-starch may in some sort be taken As if they had been hang'd to smoake like bacon. **1822** G. YOUNG *Geol. Surv. Yorksh. Coast* (1828) 68 This rock is called oolite, or *egg-stone. **1888** ROLLESTON & JACKSON *Forms Anim. Life* (ed. 2) 222 In *Nephelis* and *Clepsine* .. '*egg-strings', produced by the continuous division of a cell, lie free in the capsular cavity. *c* **1865** LD. BROUGHAM in *Circ. Sc.* I. *Introd. Disc.* 22 A bird called the Toucan, or *Egg-sucker, which chiefly feeds on the eggs found in .. nests. **1899** C. J. HERRINGHAM *Bk. of Art of Cennino Cennini* 207 For Pacheco *egg-tempera meant the whole egg with fig-milk. **1922** R. FRY *Let.* 12 Apr. (1972) II. 525 [Picasso]'s doing wonderful little pictures of nudes .. in egg tempera, like some highly finished miniatures by Giulio Romano or Sebastiano del Piombo. **1974** *Encycl. Brit. Micropædia* IX. 877/2 The earliest European forerunners of a controlled egg-tempera medium are found among the religious paintings of the Byzantine era. **1884** *Egg-timer [see EGG *sb.* 6b]. **1909** *Cent. Dict.* Suppl., *Egg-timer*, an apparatus for the automatic cooking of eggs. It consists of a vessel containing boiling water and a series of .. baskets... When the time has elapsed the basket automatically rises out of the water. **1962** *TV Times* 28 Dec. 6/2 An egg-timer, I repeated with the assurance of a man who knew which way the sand trickled. **1893** A. NEWTON *Dict. Birds* 36 The '*egg-tooth' .. is developed in the embryos of all birds as a small whitish protuberance or conglomeration of salts of calcareous matter, deposited in the middle layers of the epidermis of the tip of the upper bill. **1959** *New Biology* XXX. 87 In viviparous reptiles the eggshell is reduced to a thin, soft membrane or lost entirely, and the egg-tooth, which assists the young of oviparous forms to break out of their eggs, is sometimes rudimentary. **1960** M. BURTON *Wild Animals* 145 The young grass snakes .. make their way out of the egg by tearing several rents in it with a special egg-tooth projecting from the front of the jaws. **1826** KIRBY & SPENCE *Entomol.* IV. xlii. 148 The ovaries, or *egg-tubes as they are sometimes called. **1895** D. SHARP in *Cambr. Nat. Hist.* V. 137 The number of egg-tubes varies greatly in different Insects. **1843** EMBLETON in *Proc. Berw. Nat. Club* II. No. 11. 51 E. Sphæra. —— *Common *Egg Urchin.* E. miliaris. —— *Purple-tipped Egg Urchin.* **1909** *Cent. Dict.* Suppl., *Egg-whip. **1910** *Daily Chron.* 23 Apr. 7/5 Beat with an egg whip until smooth and glossy. **1868** M. JEWRY *Warne's Model Cookery* 36/1 *Egg whisk, for beating eggs. **1882** [see WHISK *sb.*[1] 3]. **1924** *Week-end Bk.* 261 A large jug, and an egg-whisk .. efficiently replace the [cocktail] shaker. **1659** H. H. BURNEL *Plutus* C ij b, A Bawd, a scolding *Eggwife.

egg (ɛg), *v.*[1] [a. ON. *eggja* (Da. *egge*), = EDGE *v.*[1]]

1. *trans.* To incite, encourage, urge on; to provoke, tempt. Cf. EDGE *v.*[1] Const. (†*til*), *to*, *unto* (an action, enterprise, etc.). *Obs.* exc. as in 2.

c **1200** *Trin Coll. Hom.* 195 Alse þe deuel him to eggede. *c* **1230** *Hali Meid.* 3, & eggeð þe to brudlac. **1330** R. BRUNNE *Chron.* (1810) 278 Þe clergi of Scotland egged þer kyng Jon. *c* **1350** *Will. Palerne* 1130 He sent enuiously to þemperour and egged him swiþe bi a certayne day bataile to a bide. *c* **1386** CHAUCER *Pers. T.* ¶894 Þei þat eggen or consenten to þe sinne bien partiners of þe sinne. *c* **1440** *Promp. Parv.* 136 Eggyn, or entycyn to doon well or yvele [*P.* eggen, or styre to gode or yll], *incito, provoco.* **1508** BARCLAY *Shyp of Folys* 141 b, He shall haue frendes and felawys at honde, To egge him forwarde vnto vnhappynes. **1513** DOUGLAS *Æneis* v. viii. 17 Thai foyne at vthir, and eggis to bargane. **1563–87** FOXE *A. & M.* (1596) 299/1 Especiallie being egged .. by his brethren taking it to stomach. *a* **1593** H. SMITH *Wks.* (1866–7) I. 379 A man which sharpens his enemy with taunts, when he would egg him to fight. **1598** GRENEWEY *Tacitus' Ann.* I. xi. (1622) 21 The like occasion egged him to the like cruelty against Semp. Gracchus. **1665** MANLEY *Grotius' Low-C. Warrs* 93 Their suspicions egged them to cruelty.

2. with *on*. Const. *to*, etc.

1566 DRANT *Horace' Sat.* v. D b, Ile egge them on to speake some thyng, whiche spoken may repent them. **1594** CAREW *Huarte's Exam. Wits* iv. (1596) 45 Sibils and Bacchants .. men think are egged on by some diuine inspiration. **1642** H. MORE *Song of Soul* I. III. xxxii, That foregoing light That egs us on 'cording to what we have liven. **1691** WOOD *Ath. Oxon.* II. 328 Mathew Hazard [was] a main Incendiary in the Rebellion, violently egged on by his wife. **1705** STANHOPE *Paraphr.* II. 257 Thus they egg Men on to old Age .. till they learn too late. **1747** CARTE *Hist. Eng.* I. 21 Everything conspired to .. egg them on to the undertaking. **1852** THACKERAY *Esmond* II. x. (1876) 207 Schemers and flatterers would egg him on.

egg (ɛg), *v.*[2] [f. the sb.] *trans.* **a.** In comb. *to egg and crumb*: to cover with yolk of egg and crumbs. **b.** To pelt with (rotten) eggs. **c.** *intr.* To collect (wild fowls') eggs.

1833 MARRYAT *P. Simple* i, 'They be all hegged and crumbed.' **1857** *Baltimore Sun* 1 Aug. (Bartlett) The abolition editor of the Newport News, was egged out of Alexandria .. on Monday. **1864** MRS. H. WOOD *Trev. Hold* III. ix. 131 To see a sweetbread egged and crumbed. **1883** *Harper's Mag.* Oct. 806/1 An Iowa poet has been egged by the populace. **1887** E. C. DAWSON *Bp. Hannington* viii. 106 They .. fished, egged .. and explored to their heart's content.

egg-beater. **1.** An implement or appliance used for beating eggs.

1828 E. LESLIE *Receipts* 49 Beat the eggs in a broad shallow pan with a wooden-egg-beater or whisk. **1884** *Health Exhib. Catal.* 110/2 Patent Egg Beaters.

2. = HELICOPTER (see also quot. 1946). *U.S. slang.*

1937 *Atlantic Monthly* Jan. 26/1 Pilots of airplanes contemptuously termed autogiros 'egg beaters', and the whole idea appeared to be a colossal flop. **1946** *Amer. Speech* XXI. 310/1 *Egg-beater*, a twin-engine training plane, so termed because of the small size of the engines. **1948** *Canadian Alpine Jrnl.* June 178 One of those strange contraptions known as a helicopter or 'egg-beater'. **1962** L. DEIGHTON *Ipcress File* xxiv. 156 [Amer. loq.] 'Egg beaters.' The two helicopters came in.

egg-box. A box in which eggs are packed. Also *attrib.* and *transf.* (= EGG-CRATE).

1854 DICKENS *Hard T.* I. iv. 20 That was the cot of *my* infancy; an old egg-box. **1937** *Discovery* May 134/2 The men [*sc.* egg-stealers] .. were equipped with egg-boxes, coils of rope, climbing irons. **1952** *Archit. Rev.* CXI. 17/2 'Eggbox' screens may be designed across roof openings to obscure views of the sky for all normal angles of vision.

egg-crate. A crate in which eggs are packed; also *transf.* and *attrib.*, esp. in *egg-crate ceiling*, etc., denoting a construction which diffuses light.

1943 *Newsweek* 16 Aug. 54 The rickety 'egg crate' plane was shunned by all but true pioneers and thrill seekers. **1949** *Archit. Rev.* CVI. 307 The upper gallery at this point has an 'egg-crate' ceiling of steel sheeting to preserve a human scale. **1959** *Engineering* 13 Feb. 198/3 To meet the need for improved lamp screening appearance, translucent opal plastics egg-crate louvres are made.

egg-cup (ˈɛgkʌp). A cup-shaped vessel to hold an egg. Also *transf.* Hence **ˈeggcupful** (usually *egg-cupful*), as much as will fill an egg-cup.

1773 [see *egg-basket* (EGG *sb.* 6 a)]. **1837** DICKENS *Pickw.* xvi. 160 There's nothin' so refreshin' as sleep, Sir, as the servant-girl said afore she drank the egg-cup-full o' laudanum. **1848** H. R. FORSTER *Stowe Catal.* 117, 6 egg-cups. **1870** F. WILSON *Ch. Lindisf.* 108 The font..is of an egg-cup form. **1871** *City-Road Mag.* I. 263 We drank all but boiling coffee at half a piastre an egg-cupful. **1905** H. G. WELLS *Kipps* I. v. 88 An egg-cupful of brandy. **1936** G. POLLETT *Song for Sixpence* x. 82 But the oak-trees shower their 'egg-cups' everywhere. **1962** E. O'BRIEN *Lonely Girl* xix. 237 Egg-cupfuls of Joanna's home-made Advocaat. **1969** E. H. PINTO *Treen* 73/2 The early Victorian revolving egg cup stand..is of mahogany, with ebony egg cups.

egge, obs. var. of EDGE *sb.* and *v.*[1]

egged (ɛgd), *ppl. a.* [f. EGG *sb.* + -ED.] Mixed with egg.

1835 T. HOOK *G. Gurney* (1850) I. v. 107 Directions about egged-wine.

†**ˈegger**, *sb.*[1] *Obs.* Also 6 eggar. [f. EGG *v.*[1] + -ER.] One who urges on or incites; an instigator. Also *egger on*.

1598 BARRET *Theor. Warres* IV. i. 120, I wish the ill yeare to his Eggars and setters on. **1605** *Answ. Supposed Discov. Romish Doctr.* 37 The eggers and instruments of all those slaughters. **1693** W. ROBERTSON *Phraseol. Gen.* 524 An egger on, *impulsor*.

egger (ˈɛgə(r)), *sb.*[2] [f. EGG *v.*[2] + -ER.] One who collects (wild fowls') eggs.

1834 AUDUBON *Ornith. Biogr.* II. 370 Turtles..deposit their eggs in the burning sand, and clouds of sea-fowl arrive every spring for the same purpose. These are followed by persons called 'Eggers'. **1849** D. J. BROWNE *Amer. Poultry Yd.* (1855) 310 A class of persons called 'eggers', who follow ..the avocation of procuring the eggs of wild birds. **1875** BP. HANNINGTON in Dawson *Life* (1887) viii. 109 And to the eggers of this isle The emu's egg she shows. **1908** *Daily Chron.* 16 Apr. 3/7 Driven out of Cornwall by the 'Eggers' a few pairs for a time managed to breed..in South Wales.

egger (ˈɛgə(r)), *sb.*[3] Also **eggar**. [app. f. EGG *sb.* + -ER; see quot. 1720.] A collector's name for various species of moths, *esp.* the Oak Egger-moth (*Bombyx quercus*).

?**1705** B. WILKES BOWLES *New Collection Engl. Moths* Plate I, The Great Egger Moth. **1720** ALBIN *Nat. Hist. Insects*, Descr. Pl. xviii, It spun itself..a brittle brown Case *b*, in form of an Egg, like Caterpillar *a* in the next plate; for which reason they are called by some the great and small Egger. **1775** M. HARRIS *Eng. Lepid.* 21. **1859** W. COLEMAN *Woodlands* (1862) 89 The caterpillar of that fine large insect, the Oak Egger-moth, is said to feed on the leaves of the Heath. **1869** E. NEWMAN *Nat. Hist. Brit. Moths* 41 The Pale Oak Eggar (*Trichiura cratægi*); the Small Eggar (*Eriogaster lanestris*); the Oak Eggar (*Bombyx quercus*); the Grass Eggar (*Bombyx trifolii*). **1884** *Pall Mall G.* 12 Aug. 3/2 An oak-egger has been seen in Hyde Park.

eggery (ˈɛgərɪ). [f. EGG *sb.* + -ERY.] A collection of eggs; an establishment for producing eggs.

1846 WORCESTER, *Eggery*, a nest of eggs. **1910** *Daily Chron.* 21 Mar. 4/7 A Western Canadian paper declares that next to the discovery of a gold-mine the most profitable investment is the 'importation of a batch of well-disposed hens and the establishment of an up-to-date eggery'. **1938** *Reader's Digest* Mar. 93/1 An Arndt eggery consisting of four sections.

ˈegg-head, egghead. *colloq.* (orig. *U.S.*). [f. EGG *sb.* + HEAD *sb.*] An intellectual, a 'highbrow'. Also *attrib.* So **eggheadish** *a.*; **eggheadery, eggheadism.**

1907 O. JOHNSON in *Sat. Even. Post* 16 Nov. 9/1 His genius lived in the nicknames of the Egghead,..Morning Glory, [etc.]. *c* **1918** C. SANDBURG *Let.* (deposited in Toledo-Lucas County Public Library, Toledo, Ohio), Dear N. D...'Egg heads' is the slang here for editorial writers. **1952** *Cleveland* (Ohio) *Plain Dealer* 27 Sept. 10/3 A good many intelligent people..obviously admired Stevenson. 'Sure,' was the reply, 'all the egg heads love Stevenson.' **1952** *N.Y. Times* 19 Oct. E1/7 Writers of letters to editors tend to be in the intellectual or 'egg-head' category where Stevenson sentiment is strong. **1953** R. CHANDLER *Long Good-Bye* xlvii. 289, I told him I didn't think it would do Springer any harm. 'Only with the eggheads.' **1954** *Daily Tel.* 23 Mar., Mr. Stevenson..said..'Eggheads of the world, unite—you have nothing to lose but your yolks.' 'Eggheads' is a derogatory description for intellectuals in America. **1955** *Sci. Amer.* Apr. 2/3, I fear that, while publicly unspoken, anti-intellectualism and suspicion of 'eggheads' may have been a factor. **1956** *N.Y. Times Mag.* 9 Sept. 68/3 People said it was 'eggheadism' or 'moderation'. **1957** *Listener* 2 May 725/2 A former American ambassador to India and one of the Democratic Party's leading egg-heads. **1960** *Ibid.* 13 Oct. 627/1 This autumn six British firms are trying out one special kind of paper-back—the 'egghead' or quality or highbrow paper-back. **1962** *Punch* 30 May 827/1 The theatre (alas for would-be eggheadery) is nowadays scarcely noticed at all. **1963** *Times* 25 Feb. (Canada Suppl.) p. xiv/4 Often excessively eggheadish in their choice of material, these little dramatic islands have still proved [etc.]. **1963** *New Society* 26 Sept. 4/1 There is a reaction against eggheadery in America. **1965** *Spectator* 22 Jan. 98/1 Not all American egg-heads are equally self satisfied about the standard of their own criticism.

ˈegg-headed, *a.* [cf. HEADED *a.* 1 c.] With a head shaped like an egg; also *transf.* (see prec.). So **egg-ˈheadedness.**

1919 W. DEEPING *Second Youth* iv. 37 A little egg-headed pedant. **1938** *Time* 27 June 31/1 That man was starchy, six-foot-six Sir John Charles Walsham Reith, a dour, egg-headed, ascetical Aberdonian. **1957** H. CROOME *Forgotten Place* xiii. 163 Howard's own Old Intellectual tie had always been so conspicuous and Howard's views..so uncompromisingly egg-headed. **1959** V. PACKARD *Status Seekers* (1960) xv. 216 The four factors thus far cited—money, ancestry, distance of home from center of the city, and eggheadedness. **1965** *Economist* 10 July 154/1 More eggheaded discussion of these matters brings in the concepts of 'social rates of discount' and a 'shadow price' for capital. *Ibid.* 25 Sept. 1226/1 The Department of Economic Affairs was at pains..to underplay economic eggheadedness.

egging (ˈɛgɪŋ), *vbl. sb.*[1] [f. EGG *v.*[1] + -ING[1].] An urging forward, incitement, instigation. Also ***egging forward*** or ***on***.

c **1200** *Trin. Coll. Hom.* 197 Þat heued þat Iob helede wið þe deules egginge was his rihte bileue. *a* **1300** *Cursor M.* 7206 His [Samson's] wijf wald noght fin Thoru egging of his wiþerwin. *a* **1400** *Octouian* 688 Selle hem noght For no eggenges. **1521** *Old City Acc. Bk. Archæol.* XLIII, A fyne lost by John Stone for eggyng of an other mannes apprentice from his maistre xxd. **1564** HAWARD *Eutropius* VII. 63 Antonius began a greate ciuill warre through the..egging forward of his wife Cleopatra. **1598** R. BERNARD tr. *Terence's Hecyra* II. i, They have married by your egging on. *a* **1659** CLEVELAND *Wks.* (1687) 370 How curst an egging..do these unwily Dances bring. **1875** A. R. HOPE *Schoolboy Fr.* 90 He needed very little egging on, to talk nonsense.

ˈegging, *vbl. sb.*[2] [f. EGG *v.*[2] + -ING[1].] **1.** The action of collecting (wild fowls') eggs; also *attrib.*

1883 G. C. DAVIES *Norfolk Broads* II. 15 The unholy trade of egging and bird-destroying. **1886** E. C. DAWSON *Bp. Hannington* viii. (1887) 107 They had arrived in the height of the egging season.

2. The laying or production of eggs, as in ***egging season, time.***

1905 *Westm. Gaz.* 4 May 4/1 Among the risks which attend the breeding of game birds, frost at the 'egging' time is not the least serious. **1909** *Ibid.* 14 May 5/1 This is the 'egging' season, and outlying nests of pheasants and partridges may be disturbed.

eggler (ˈɛglə(r)). *dial.* [f. EGG *sb.*, ? after *pedlar* or *higgler*.] An egg-dealer and poulterer.

1791 *Census* (*Mertoun*) in *Stat. Acc. Sc.* (1795) XIV. 589 Weavers 4, Clothier 1, Egglers 2. **1869** *Daily News* 6 Jan., But his chief profession is that of an 'eggler,' that is, he used to buy eggs and forward them in large quantities to England. **1880** *Daily News* 11 Nov. 6/6 They do not even eat the eggs, but sell them to an 'eggler'. **1881** *Supp. Oxford Gloss.*, *Eggler*, a poulterer.

eggless (ˈɛglɪs), *a.* [f. EGG *sb.* + -LESS.] Without eggs.

1904 H. G. WELLS *Food of Gods* I. iv. 92 The two surviving hens..spent their remaining years in eggless celebrity. **1909** *Daily Chron.* 2 Feb. 4/7 The recipe for an eggless omelette. **1915** *Evening News* 20 Jan. 7 Eggless and Less Egg Cookery. **1967** A. WILSON *No Laughing Matter* II. 73 Sukey..was trying out a new eggless recipe.

egglet (ˈɛglɛt). *nonce-wd.* [f. EGG *sb.* + -LET.] A small egg.

1883 *Cornh. Mag.*, *On being 'Pilled'*, The sight of those addled egglets [pills] lying in their cardboard nest.

ˈeggling, *vbl. sb. Sc.* [f. EGG *sb.* after EGGLER.] The business of an eggler.

1881 J. YOUNGER *Autobiog.* ix. 90 Try the eggling or cadgering.

†**ˈeggment.** *Obs.* [f. EGG *v.* + -MENT; an early example of the addition of -MENT to an Eng. vb.] Incitement, instigation.

c **1340** *Cursor M.* 25733 (Fairf.) We synne þorou egment of þer þre. *c* **1386** CHAUCER *Man of Lawes T.* 744 Thurgh wommannes eggement Mankynde was lorn. *c* **1440** *Promp. Parv.* 136 Egment, or sterynge, *incitamentum*.

egg-nog(g (ˈɛg-ˈnɒg). Also (*rarely*) egg-noggy. [f. EGG + NOG strong ale.] A drink in which the white and yolk of eggs are stirred up with hot beer, cider, wine, or spirits.

1825 *Bro. Jonathan* I. 256 The egg-nog..had gone about rather freely. **1844** MRS. HOUSTON *Yacht Voy. Texas* II. 179 Followed by the production of a tumbler of egg-noggy. **1853** KANE *Grinnell Exp.* xlvi. (1856) 428 And made an egg-nogg of eider eggs. **1872** COHEN *Dis. Throat* 91, I would rely chiefly on egg-nog, beef essence, and quinine.

ˈegg-plant. A popular name for the *Solanum esculentum*, originally given to the white-fruited variety, but afterwards extended to that which bears the purple fruit or Aubergine.

1767 J. ABERCROMBIE *Ev. Man own Gard.* (1803) 102 The choicest kinds [of tender annuals] are the double balsams.. ice-plant, egg-plant, etc. **1794** MARTYN *Rousseau's Bot.* xvi. 202 When this [its fruit] is white it has the name of Egg-Plant. **1847** MRS. SHERWOOD *Life* xv. 273 Soup made of a glutinous vegetable, and the egg-plant roasted before the fire. **1861** DELAMER *Kitch. Gard.* 125 There is the purple-fruited egg-plant, and the white-fruited egg-plant.

eggritte, obs. form of EGRET.

ˈegg-shell. Also **eggshell**. [f. EGG *sb.* + SHELL.] **a.** The shell or external calcareous covering of an egg; often as a type of worthlessness or of fragility.

c **1300** *K. Alis* 577 He fondith to creope..Ageyn into the ay-schelle. **1471** RIPLEY *Compl. Alch.* VIII. in Ashm. (1652) 171 Fro Eggshells calcynyd. **1562** J. HEYWOOD *Prov. & Epigr.* (1867) 36, I gat not so muche..As..a poore eggshell. **1599** H. BUTTES *Diet's Dry Din.* To Rdr., I haue put into a by-dish (like Eg-shelles in a Saucer) what worthily may breed offence. *a* **1618** RALEIGH *Prerog. Parl.* 57 Without the Kings acceptation, both the publicke and priuate aduices be but as emptie Egg-shels. **1799** HATCHETT in *Phil. Trans.* LXXXIX. 328 The carbonate of lime exceeds in quantity the phosphate..in the egg shells of birds. **1859** TODD *Cycl. Anat.* V. 63/1 The pores of the egg-shell may be easily stopped by any..oily matter. **1859** TENNYSON *Enid* 1213 He ..babbled..How Enid never..cared a broken egg-shell for her lord.

b. *attrib.*, chiefly *similative.* ***egg-shell china:*** a porcelain ware of extreme thinness and delicacy.

1835 WILLIS *Pencillings* II. xlv. 52 We..stepping into an egg-shell caique, crossed the Golden Horn. **1860** EMERSON *Cond. Life* vii. Wks. (Bohn) II. 424 We come out of our egg-shell existence. **1861** C. P. HODGSON *Resid. Japan* 31 Fragile and sweetly pretty little egg-shell porcelain cups. **1887** *Times* 11 Aug. 13/2 The egg-shell sides of the Mercury.

c. Used *attrib.* or as *adj.* as a term of colour or of a paint finish intermediate between flat and glossy, e.g. ***eggshell enamel, finish, glaze.*** (See also quot. 1929).

1894 F. B. GARDNER *Painters' Encycl.* 119 *Egg-shell gloss*, a term frequently used by painters. **1898** *Westm. Gaz.* 3 June 8/3 A costume of egg-shell blue cheque silk. **1908** *Daily Chron.* 12 Mar. 3/3 The sun is reflected by its front of dull white terra-cotta stone with egg-shell glaze. **1909** *Westm. Gaz.* 27 Apr. 5/2 People argue of paints, and enamels, and varnishes, and..whether the true 'egg-shell gloss' has been obtained or not. **1909** *Chambers's Jrnl.* 25 Sept. 684/1 That beautiful, characteristic, velvety, egg-shell enamel is highly artistic. **1925** *Arts & Decoration* Mar. 82/2 The egg-shell finish of the freshly laid egg..is the dull finish the decorators now prefer. **1929** A. E. OWEN-JONES *Retail Stationer's Handbk.* 193 *Eggshell Finish*, a finish imparted to notepapers by omitting the calendering; the surface is dull, and is covered with pin-point pores. **1936** C. DAY LEWIS *Friendly Tree* vii. 96 A sky of egg-shell blue. **1943** W. WILCOX in 55 *Short Stories from N. Yorker* (1949) 139 She was wearing dark blue..and a neat little eggshell blouse. **1953** *Gloss. Paint Terms* (*B.S.I.*) 27 The following stages in increasing order of gloss are normally recognized:—Flat (or matt)...Eggshell flat. Eggshell gloss. **1955** E. BOWEN *World of Love* v. 88 Electric candelabra..round all the eggshell walls. **1958** *Woman* 22 Feb 2/1 Gloss, matt, flat, eggshell paints go over themselves or each other.

Hence **eggshell-ful**, as a measure of quantity.

1460-70 *Bk. Quintessence* 29 An eye-schelle ful of good brennynge water. **1579** LANGHAM *Gard. Health* (1633) 73 Drink an eggshelfull of the iuice of Betony. **1746** BERKELEY *Sec. Let. Tar-water* §14 An egg-shell full of tar. **1758** J. S. *Le Dran's Observ. Surg.* (1771) 247, I found about an Egg-Shell full of purulent Serosity.

egg-white. [WHITE *sb.* 1.] The white of an egg, the albumen. Also *attrib.*, esp. in ***egg-white injury***, a disease caused by eating an excess of raw egg-white.

1898 *Jrnl. Physiology* XXIII. 130 Fresh egg-white is thoroughly whipped into a froth. **1916** E. POUND *Lustra* 52 Green arsenic smeared on an egg-white cloth. **1936** *Discovery* Dec. 388/2 A preparation from egg-white, which reduces the clotting time of blood, provides new hope for haemophiliacs. **1937** H. T. PARSONS et al. in *Biochemical Jrnl.* XXXI. I. 425 (*heading*) Egg white injury and protective factor. **1959** *Chambers's Encycl.* XI. 260/1 Albumins and globulins..are frequently found together as in..milk and egg white. *Ibid.* XIV. 350/2 *Biotin* is a..factor..identified with the so-called vitamin H..or anti-egg-white-injury factor.

eggy (ˈɛgɪ), *a.*[1] [f. EGG + -Y.] **a.** Full of eggs, abounding in eggs. Also *spec.*, as in quot. 1901. **b.** Marked with stains of egg.

1709 *Rambl. Fuddle-Caps* 7 So Eggy withal, that a man would have Sworn, He had just in the Pill'ry been taking a Turn. **1901** *Farm, Field & Fireside* 13 Dec. 357/3 If it has laid eggs, or is within a short time of laying, it is also detected. These birds are called 'eggy'. **1924** *Blackw. Mag.* Feb. 249/2 Abdul brought his most welcome offering an eggy rice pudding. **1929** E. BOWEN *Last September* III. xix. 238 The sponge cake..was moist and eggy. **1951** J. B. PRIESTLEY *Festival at Farbridge* II. ii. 263 You might push that eggy plate away then with your foot.

eggy (ˈɛgɪ), *a.*[2] *colloq.* and *dial.* [f. EGG *v.*[1] + -Y[1].] Annoyed, irritated.

1935 J. T. FARRELL *Judgment Day* vi. 131 That's why I feel so eggy. They probably saved this afternoon to give us the works. **1966** F. SHAW et al. *Lern Yerself Scouse* 73 Don get eggy.

eȝathe, obs. form of EATH.

eghe, obs. form of EYE.

eȝe, obs. f. of AWE, EYE.

egir, obs. form of EAGER, *a.*

egistment, var. of AGISTMENT.

1681 J. W. *Syst. Agric.* 325, *Egistments*, cattle taken in to graze or be fed by the week or month.

eglandular (ɪˈglændjʊlə(r)), *a. Bot.* [f. E- *pref.*[3] + GLANDULAR.] That has no glands.

1870 J. D. HOOKER *Student's Flora* 21 Matthiola incana.. pod eglandular.

eglandulose (ɪˈglændjʊləʊs), *a. Bot.* [f. E- *pref.*[3] + GLANDULOSE.] = prec.

1878 HULME *Wild Flowers* I. Summary 15 Leaves pinnate, eglandulose, slightly hairy.

eglantine[1] (ˈɛgləntaɪn, -tɪn). Forms: 4-6 eglentine, (6 eggletyne), 7- eglantine. [a. F. *églantine* (= Pr. *aiglentina*), f. OF. *aiglent* of

same meaning, prob. repr. Lat. type **aculentus* prickly, f. *acu-s* needle + *-lentus* suffix, as in *viru-lentus, lucu-lentus*; cf. *aculeus* sting, prickle.]

1. The Sweet-briar; also *attrib.*

c **1400** MAUNDEV. ii. 14 There he was crouned with Eglantier [*v.r.* Eglentine]. **1551** TURNER *Herbal* I. N vj a, The eglentine is much like the common brere but the leues are swete and pleasant to smel to. **1590** SHAKS. *Mids. N.* II. i. 152 Quite ouer-cannoped with..Eglantine. **1688** R. HOLME *Armoury* II. 62/2 The Eglantine Rose is the Sweet brier Rose. *a* **1763** SHENSTONE *Odes* (1765) 122 Nor spare the sweet-leaft eglantine. **1820** KEATS *Isabella* xxiv, Ere the hot sun count His dewy rosary on the eglantine. **1882** MISS BRADDON *Mount-Royal* II. iv. 82 Hedges filled with honey-suckle and eglantine.

¶ **2.** By Milton possibly taken for: The honeysuckle.

1632 MILTON *L'Allegro* 48 Through the sweetbriar or the vine, Or the twisted eglantine.

'eglantine². (See quot.)

1774 GOLDSM. *Nat. Hist.* (1862) I. vi. 31 Eglantine, a stone of the hardness and grain of marble.

eglatere (ɛglə'tɪə(r)). *Obs.* exc. *poet.* Forms: 5 **eglantere**, 4–5 **eglenter**, **-ier**. [a. OF. *esglantier*, *aiglantier* (mod.F. *églantier*), f. *aiglant* (see EGLANTINE¹) + *-ier*, as in *ros-ier* rose-tree, etc.] = EGLANTINE¹.

a **1387** *Sinon. Barthol.* (Anecd. Oxon.) 12 Bedegar est nodus rosæ albæ silvestris, vulgari nomine, eglenter. **1459** *Test. Ebor.* (1855) II. 226 Ij gilt peces with ij coverkills with treiles of eglenters. *a* **1500** *Flower & Leaf* viii, The hegge.. With sicamour was set and eglatere. *Ibid.* xii, I..Thought suddenly I felt so swete an air Of the Eglantère. **1830** TENNYSON *Dirge* 23 The woodbine and eglatere Drip sweeter dews than traitor's tear.

egle, obs. form of EAGLE.

† **e'gleche**, *a. Obs.* [app. repr. or f. OE. *aglæca*, *aglæcea*, sb., cruel person, fierce warrior, f. *aglác* misery, sharp conflict; of uncertain origin.] ? Valiant.

a **1250** *Prov. Ælfred* in *O.E. Misc.* 102 Knyhtes egleche. *a* **1300** *Magdalena* in *Saints' Lives* (1887) 462 Sleiȝe men and egleche.. Lustniez nouþe to mi speche. *c* **1300** in R. GLOUC. (Rolls) Append. XX. 125 þe lefdi [the empress Matilda] was egleche.

eglenter, obs. form of EGLATERE.

eglestonite ('ɛg(ə)lztənaɪt). *Min.* [f. name of Thomas *Egleston*, an American mineralogist (1832–1900) + -ITE¹.] A native oxychloride of mercury, occurring in brownish-yellow isometric crystals.

1903 A. J. MOSES in *Amer. Jrnl. Sci.* 4th Ser. XVI. 258 The eglestonite crystals are usually easily recognized. **1912** *Brit. Museum Return* 196 Eglestonite and calomel from Palo Alto, California. **1933** *Amer. Mineralogist* XVIII. 7 Descending acid solutions altered the cinnabar, producing the secondary quicksilver minerals, metacinnabar, calomel, and eglestonite. **1968** EMBREY & PHEMESTER tr. *Kostov's Mineralogy* 204 Eglestonite is isostructural with garnet.

eglogue, obs. form of ECLOGUE.

† **eglomerate** (ɪ'glɒməreɪt), *v. Obs.*—⁰ [as if f. L. **ēglomerāt-* ppl. stem of **ēglomerā-re*, f. *ē* out + *glomerāre* to wind or gather into a ball; f. *glomus*, *-ěr-is* clew, or ball.] *trans.* and *intr.*

1656 BLOUNT *Glossogr.*, *Eglomerace* [sic], to unwinde. **1775** ASH, *Eglomerate*, to unwind itself. In mod. Dicts.

‖ **églomisé** (eglɒmize), *a.* and *sb.* [Fr., f. name of *Glomy*, a Parisian picture-framer of the 18th cent. So It. *agglomizzato*, G. *eglomisiert*.] Applied to glass painted on the back, and used by Glomy for frames.

1877 LADY C. SCHREIBER *Jrnls.* (1911) II. 19 His Eglomisé Glass is also lent on view. **1897** A. HARTSHORNE *Old Eng. Glasses* 343 To the last quarter of the eighteenth century belong also those florid painted panels—'églomisés'—inserted in the bottoms. **1912** *Catal. Wks. Art J. E. Taylor sold at Christie's* Lot 85 A portable altar of eglomisé and silver-gilt. The base is further enriched with two eglomisé plaques. **1967** *Times* 21 Feb. 21/7 (Advt.), A Louis XVI gold and verre eglomisé snuff-box by Joseph-Etienne Blerzy, Paris, 1798.

eglotte, obs. var. of AGLET.

1570 LEVINS *Manip.* 176 An Eglotte, *bracteolum*.

'egma. A 'stage rustic's' blunder for ENIGMA.

1588 SHAKS. *L.L.L.* III. i. 73 No egma, no riddle, no lenuoy.

ego ('ɛgəʊ, 'iːgəʊ). Orig. *Metaph.* [L. *ego* I.]

1. That which is symbolized by the pronoun I; the conscious thinking subject, as opposed to the *non-ego* or object. Also *humorously*, for 'self'.

[**1789** COWPER *Letter* 6 June, To thee both Ego and all that Ego does is interesting.] **1824** GALT *Rothelan* II. 201 He plainly regarded Ego as one of the most captivating of the human race. **1829** *Edin. Rev.* L. 200 In every act of consciousness we distinguish a self or ego. **1847** LEWES *Hist. Philos.* (1867) II. 514 The Ego is essentially an Activity; consequently free. **1870** GLADSTONE *Prim. Homer* (1878) 142 The harmonious laws of his mind are everywhere visibly at work—but the ego—the mere personality—is nowhere to be traced. **1871** TYNDALL *Fragm. Sc.* (ed. 6) II. iv. 51 While the Non-ego shifts, the Ego remains the same.

2. In speech: I, the speaker. Hence **'ego** *v. trans.*, to say 'ego' when claiming an object, in response to 'quis?'. *Schoolboy slang.*

1913 C. MACKENZIE *Sinister Street* I. I. vii. 103 He was often first with the claimant 'ego', when someone shouted 'quis?' over a broken pocket-knife found. **1959** I. & P. OPIE *Lore & Lang. Schoolch.* viii. 134 In private schools a child who wishes to dispose of something..calling out ' Quis?' and the boy or girl who first replies 'Ego' receives the object and may say (to the horror of the classicist) 'I egoed it'.

3. Self-esteem, egotism, self-importance.

Some examples are influenced by sense 4.

1891 KIPLING *Light that Failed* v. 59 I've made a discovery. Torp, there's too much Ego in my Cosmos. **1907** *Daily Chron.* 13 Feb. 7/4 By 'exaggerated ego',..he meant a disproportionate idea of the importance of oneself and a belief that one was clothed with powers, capacities, and ability far above the normal or above those actually possessed. **1952** S. KAUFFMANN *Philanderer* (1953) vi. 97 The quarrels—which had begun between him and his wife simply because his ego could not possibly be satiated even when fortune was good—increased terribly now. **1962** J. D. SALINGER *Franny & Zooey* 166 You keep talking about *ego*. My God, it would take Christ himself to decide what's ego and what isn't.

4. *Psychol.* That part of the mind which is most conscious of self; *spec.* in the work of Freud that part which, acted upon by both the id and the super-ego (ego-ideal), mediates with the environment.

1894 *Brain* XVII. 130 By reason of the clouding over of the *ego* produced in one case by hypnotism, in another by nervous shock, an idea once installed..will further develop and acquire sufficient force for objective realisation. **1910** H. W. CHASE (tr. Freud) in *Amer. Jrnl. Psychol.* XXI. 193 The incompatibility of the idea in question with the 'ego' of the patient was the motive of the repression. **1922** [see EGO-IDEAL]. **1927** J. RIVIERE tr. *Freud's Ego & Id* v. 83 Like the dweller in a borderland that it is, the ego tries to mediate between the world and the id, to make the id comply with the world's demands and, by means of muscular activity, to accommodate the world to the id's desires. **1943** *Psychol. Rev.* L. 454 In a semi-doze we lose all sense of our egos though we may be conscious enough of impersonal items. **1943** H. READ *Education through Art* vi. 197 The super-ego is the direct representative of the unconscious, of the id, and hence the possibility, indeed, the inevitability of a conflict with the ego, a conflict between what is perceptual and real and what is imaginative and ideal.

5. *attrib.* and *Comb.* (senses 3 and 4), as ***ego-attitude***, ***-complex***, ***-consciousness***, ***-instinct***, ***-satisfaction***; *ego-altruistic*, *-bound*, *-less*, (also *egolessness*), adjs.; **ego-hood**, individuality, personality; **ego-identity** *Psychol.*, the sense of one's identity or self gained from the results of self-perception and external perceptions of oneself; **ego-trip**, an activity, period of time, etc., devoted entirely to indulging in one's own interests or in self-expression; also as *v. intr.*, to indulge in an 'ego-trip' (chiefly as *pr. pple.*); hence **ego-tripper**; **ego-tripping** *vbl. sb.* and *ppl. a.*

1855 H. SPENCER *Princ. Psychol.* II. VIII. vii. 595 The ego-altruistic sentiments..sentiments which while implying self-gratification, also imply gratification in others. **1937** *Brit. Jrnl. Psychol.* Jan. 265 When the object is encountered in a new environment with a different Ego-attitude, then the communication takes place between object-process and object-trace. **1929** D. H. LAWRENCE *Pansies* 67 As a plant becomes pot-bound Man becomes ego-bound Enclosed in his own limited mental consciousness. **1916** C. E. LONG tr. *Jung's Coll. Papers Analyt. Psychol.* i. 80 They are disturbances which only belong to the superficial, and none reaches so deep as to attack the strong-knit foundation of the ego-complex. **1922** *Brit. Jrnl. Psychol.* Oct. 115 Jung then goes on to describe the 'ego complex' (*Ichkomplex*) which in the normal mind is the dominant psychic instance. **1926** W. MCDOUGALL *Introd. Soc. Psychol.* (ed. 20) Suppl. iv. 404 The Freudians have recognised the importance of this rôle [*sc.* self-regard] in all that they have written of the function of the 'ego-complex', and the 'ego instincts' in inhibiting, controlling, conflicting with, and repressing the sexual tendencies. **1917** GLUECK & LIND tr. *Adler's Neurotic Constitution* (1921) ii. 21 Consciousness of guilt and conscience are fictitious guiding principles of caution, like religiosity and subserve the craving for security. Their object is to prevent a lowering of the ego-consciousness when the irritated aggressiveness impels immoderately to selfish deeds. **1963** AUDEN *Dyer's Hand* 96 An ego-consciousness which paints himself painting himself. **1873** *Brit. Q. Rev.* LVII. 79 We must face..the reality of our own ego-hood. **1906** S. S. LAURIE *Synthetica* II. 241 This is his return to God, from Whom his negating Egohood for a time separates him. **1951** E. H. ERIKSON *Childhood & Society* III. vii. 228 The sense of ego identity, then, is the accrued confidence that the inner sameness and continuity are matched by the sameness and continuity of one's meaning for others, as evidenced in the tangible promise of a 'career'. **1964** M. ARGYLE *Psychol. & Social Probl.* x. 129 A very important kind of cognitive learning is that in which a person comes to look at himself in a different way—his self-perception or 'ego-identity' is changed. **1977** A. GIDDENS *Stud. in Social & Polit. Theory* ix. 311 Frustration generated by disjunction between ego-ideal and ego provides the basis for aggression turned against the 'inadequate' ego-identity. **1917** C. R. PAYNE tr. *Hirschmann's Freud's Theories of Neuroses* x. 241 Freud is perfectly clear on the point of the decisive rôle played in life and also in the neurosis by the egotistic or ego instincts alongside of the sexual instinct. **1922** C. J. M. HUBBACK tr. *Freud's Beyond Pleasure Principle* iii. 54 Our discussion so far results in the establishing of a sharp antithesis between the 'ego-instincts' and the sexual instincts, the former impelling towards death and the latter towards the preservation of life. **1937** *Sunday Times* 12 Dec. 5/2 Those subconscious ego-less depths of it [*sc.* the consciousness] from which..only the greatest things in art can come. **1972** T. RAVENSCROFT *Spear of Destiny* xxii. 297 The egoless zombie. **1984** *Byte* May 420/3 What I suggest is..working toward the 'egoless programming' model. **1972** CHÖGYAM TRUNGPA *Mudra* 68 From the action one develops the transcendental knowledge of egolessness. **1982** *Financial Times* 13 Mar. 19/3 You hold sway, if you do, by egolessness. **1954** J. A. C. BROWN *Soc. Psychol. Industry* vii. 189 Work becomes an avenue for securing ego satisfactions. **1969** *It* 13–28 June 11/2 They're using the music as a vehicle for character and personality building. I don't think they're half as much a musical ego-trip as people imagine. **1970** *Observer* 20 Sept. 26/1 His was no musical ego-trip, no money-grubbing Tin-Pan Alley beano feast. **1970** *Melody Maker* 12 Sept. 29 Ego tripper... That's me, folks! **1970** *New York* 16 Nov. 6/2 Father ego-tripping on his children's academic and other achievements. **1972** *Atlantic Monthly* Oct. 80 What is overlooked in the inevitable discussion of the alleged ego-tripping in Mailer's writing is that these more 'modest' selves are often at work in the sounds and turns of his sentences. **1972** *N.Y. Times Bk. Rev.* 12 Nov. 63 Tate's poems are not..bardic, political, populist, confessional, ego-tripping, hash-inspired or full of fine sentiments and derivative techniques. **1977** *Time* 7 Mar. 2/3 Sadly for Ireland, O'Brien is but one of the ego-tripping ministers in the present coalition government. **1984** D. LODGE *Small World* IV. iii. 308 All that travelling away from home and duty, staying in swanky hotels, ego-tripping, partying, generally overindulging.

egocentric (ɛgəʊ'sɛntrɪk), *a.* [f. EGO + CENTRE *sb.*, after *geocentric*, *heliocentric*.] Centred in the ego; in vague or popular use: self-centred, egoistic.

1900 in *Ann. Rep. Bur. Amer. Ethnol.* *1897–8* 831 An earlier ethnocentric system born of the primeval egocentric cosmos of inchoate thinking. **1901** J. M. BALDWIN *Dict. Philos. & Psychol.* II. 194/2 For the ego-centric point of view is substituted the homocentric. **1919** in B. H. Streeter *Spirit* iii. 97 The instincts, the radical fault in most of which is their selfish and egocentric character. **1926** *19th Cent.* July 83 The girl of to-day absorbs a freedom-loving and egocentric conception of life. **1943** H. READ *Education through Art* v. 140 When an attempt is made, not merely to express egocentric sensation..but also to represent an external object as it presents itself to the sensations of the artist..then some control is exercised by other than tactual and somatic sensations. **1953** R. NIEBUHR *Christian Realism & Political Problems* (1954) i. 22 It might be noted that, without a sense of the universality of an egocentric corruption, the passion for a universal humanity quickly degenerates. **1964** M. CRITCHLEY *Developmental Dyslexia* xii. 70 The age at which a child..turns from an autistic, egocentric individual, to a societal, ethnocentric being.

b. Philos. ***egocentric predicament***, the supposed impossibility of knowing anything outside one's own mind.

1910 R. B. PERRY in *Jrnl. Philos.* VII. 5 (*title*) The Ego-Centric Predicament. *Ibid.*, I shall seek to discover whether a certain circumstance, which has never been disputed, does or does not constitute evidence for a theory that has been much disputed. The circumstance I shall call *the ego-centric predicament*, and the theory, *ontological idealism*. **1917** A. S. PRINGLE-PATTISON *Idea of God* x. 192 This is what an American Realist, in a phrase worthy of Kant, in its full-flavoured technicality, has dubbed 'the ego-centric predicament'. The Ego is..the pre-supposition of all its knowledge.

Also as *sb.*, one who is self-centred. So **,egocen'tricity**, **ego'centrism**, the state or quality of being egocentric; self-centredness; **ego'centrically** *adv.*

1903 *Amer. Jrnl. Psychol.* July–Oct. 100 Ziehen limits the hysterical constitution to emotional instability, egocentricity, craving for attention. **1918** E. JONES *Psycho-analysis* (ed. 2) 632 Its ruthless and absolute egocentricity. **1926** M. WARDEN tr. *Piaget's Lang. & Thought of Child* v. 238 All ego-centrism is designed by its structure to stand half-way between autistic thought which is 'undirected'.. and ' directed' intelligence. Ego-centrism is therefore obedient to the self's good pleasure and not to the dictates of impersonal logic. **1928** *Brit. Weekly* 22 Mar. 593/2 In this book the first personal pronoun occurs with a frequent and monotonous ego-centricity. **1932** D. H. LAWRENCE *Last Poems* 179 The hordes of the ego-centric, the robots. **1934** *Mind* XLIII. 87 Egocentrism, in so far as it means confusion of the ego and the external world, and egocentrism in so far as it means lack of co-operation, constitutes one and the same phenomenon. **1943** H. READ *Education through Art* viii. 276 Then by stages the player grows out of his egocentrism, observes other players, gradually begins to co-operate with others, and finally in conjunction with a group arrives at a reciprocal agreement embodying definite rules. **1957** *Times Lit. Suppl.* 25 Oct. 637/1 The..complete ruthlessness and egocentricity of the very young female person. *a* **1963** L. MACNEICE *Astrol.* (1964) iii. 86 Gemini is the patron not only of intellectuals but of egocentrics. **1969** *Daily Tel.* 5 May 19/2 They hang on every word of the actorly actor, just as the actors themselves are egocentrically absorbed by anything but the truth. **1970** *Ibid.* 13 Mar. 17 Behind their sham chivalry, I contend, lurk some nasty tendencies to sadism, egocentricity, rebellion and neurosis. **1981** *Word* *1980* XXXI. 122 Parametric structuring is applied to Tolkien's representation of the specific effects of uncontrolled and egocentrically wielded power.

egoical (ɛ'gəʊɪkəl), *a.* [f. EGO + -ICAL.] Of or pertaining to egotism.

ego-ideal ('ɛgəʊaɪ,diːəl). *Psychol.* [f. EGO + IDEAL *sb.*; tr. G. *Ichideal*.] **a.** That part of the mind which, in Freudian theory, is evolved from the ego as it becomes aware of parental and social standards, and imposes upon it concepts of ideal behaviour with which it should conform. **b.** = SUPEREGO. **c.** In vague or popular

use: a conception of oneself as one would like to be.

1922 J. STRACHEY tr. *Freud's Group Psychol.* vii. 69 We have been driven to the hypothesis that some such faculty develops in our ego which may cut itself off from the rest of the ego and come into conflict with it. We have called it the 'ego ideal', and by way of functions we have ascribed to it self-observation, the moral conscience, the censorship of dreams, and the chief influence in repression. 1943 H. READ *Education through Art* vi. 176 A spearhead.. passes through the pre-conscious and conscious levels of the ego, and emerges above everything as the ego-ideal or super-ego. 1949 J. I. M. STEWART *Character & Motive in Shakes.* 109 If we regard the Othello-figure on the stage as.. Othello's ego-ideal or self-exemplar, then Bradley is really right in point of dramatic feeling. 1951 E. C. TOLMAN in Parsons & Shils *Toward Gen. Theory of Action* III. iii. 311 The ego-ideal consists of acquired positive values and valences for those types of behavior in which one *should* engage. 1952 W. SPROTT *Social Psychol.* ix. 185 The recipients of praise are their [*sc.* children's] models and bit by bit what has conveniently been called an 'ego-ideal' is elaborated. 1964 GOULD & KOLB *Dict. Soc. Sci.* 593/2 The repressing force derives from cultural standards which have been incorporated by the individual to serve as his 'ego-ideal' or 'super-ego'.

'ego-in'volvement. *Psychol.* [f. EGO + INVOLVEMENT.] The process or fact of the ego being identified with various aims, attitudes, values, etc., so that behaviour defending and furthering these is strongly reinforced, and affects one's self-esteem. Hence **'ego-in'volved** *a.*, having one's self-esteem dependent on something external.

1936 M. SHERIF *Psychol. Soc. Norms* ix. 179 As the social values.. include positive values.. the ego involvement does not appear only as a checking or inhibiting factor, but also as a positive indicator of certain lines of action and striving. 1940 *Jrnl. Abnormal & Soc. Psychol.* XXXV. 500 One might expect different levels of aspiration for a given task in ego-involved subjects who have.. experienced different amounts of success or failure with that task. 1955 T. H. PEAR *Eng. Social Differences* i. 15 In studying social stratification, it is necessary to free oneself.. from ego-involvement. 1963 *Daily Tel.* 14 Feb. 11/5 Some enjoy it even though its barbs threaten their own ego-involved concepts.

egoism ('ɛg-, 'iːgəʊɪz(ə)m). [ad. F. *egoïsme*, ad. mod.L. *egoismus*, f. L. *ego* I: see -ISM. Cf. EGOMISM.]

1. *Metaph.* The belief, on the part of an individual, that there is no proof that anything exists but his own mind; chiefly applied to philosophical systems supposed by their adversaries logically to imply this conclusion.

[1722 C. M. PFAFF (*title*), De Egoismo, nova philosophica hæresi.] 1785 REID *Int. Powers* II. x. 285, I am left alone in that forlorn state of egoism. 1803 *Edin. Rev.* I. 279 The egoism of Berkeley and Hume is largely incorporated in his system.

2. *Ethics.* The theory which regards self-interest as the foundation of morality. Also, in practical sense: Regard to one's own interest, as the supreme guiding principle of action; systematic selfishness. (In recent use opposed to *altruism.*)

1800 *Hist. Europe* in *Ann. Reg.* 234/1 Affection.. was lost in selfishness or according to their new word Egoism. 1825 T. JEFFERSON *Autobiog.* Wks. 1859 I. 103 A contrast of his egoism (for he was beneficed on them) with the generous abandonment of rights by the other members of the Assembly. 1840 GLADSTONE *Ch. Princ.* 463 Egoism.. is sure to prevail whenever the pressure of high Christian motives is removed. 1850 CARLYLE *Latter-day Pamph.* i. 9 The mature man, hardened into sceptical egoism, knows no monition but that of his own frigid cautions. 1860 MILL *Repr. Govt.* (1865) 19/2 Religion in this shape is quite consistent with the most selfish and contracted egoism. 1873 H. SPENCER *Stud. Sociol.* viii. 198 The promptings of egoism are duly restrained by regard for others.

b. (See quot.)

1882 HAECKEL in *Nature* XXVI. 540 The natural instinct of self-preservation, Egoism.

c. *pl.* Selfish aims or purposes; instances of selfishness.

1795 T. JEFFERSON *Writ.* Wks. 1859 IV. 115 It must be so extensive as that local egoisms may never reach its greater part. 1843 CARLYLE *Past & Pr.* (1858) 90 Hearsays, egoisms, purblind dilettantisms. 1870 J. STIRLING *Mill on Trades Un.* in *Recess Stud.* viii. 309 The internecine strife of anarchical egoisms.

3. In matters of opinion: **a.** The habit of looking upon all questions chiefly in their relations to oneself. **b.** Excessive exaltation of one's own opinion; self-opinionatedness.

1840 GLADSTONE *Ch. Princ.* 134 He is deprived of every shadow of a plea to impute fanaticism or any form of egoism. 1852 ROBERTSON *Lect.* 169 That egoism of man.. can.. read in the planets only prophecies of himself. 1870 LOWELL *Among my Bks.* Ser. I. (1873) 177 Every narrow provincialism whether of egoism or tradition.

4. = EGOTISM I.

1807 T. JEFFERSON *Writ.* (1830) IV. 69 Pardon me these egoisms. 1870 GLADSTONE *Prim. Hom.* (1878) 148 Never once.. does Odusseus indulge in the slightest egoism. 1870 SPURGEON *Treas. Dav.* Ps. xxxiv. 4 Note the egoism of this verse and of those preceding it.

5. *Hindu Philosophy.* Used as transl. of Skr. *abhimâna*, by some rendered 'self-consciousness'.

1862 F. HALL *Hindu Philos. Syst.* 45 The organ of egoism. 1878 COWELL *Aphorisms of Sandila* 110 The Sán-khya considers 'intellect' 'egoism', and 'mind' as quite distinct from each other.

egoist ('ɛg-, 'iːgəʊɪst). [f. as prec. + -IST.]

1. (See quot.)

1785 REID *Int. Powers* 640 A sect.. called Egoists, who maintained that we have no evidence of the existence of anything but ourselves. 1860 MANSEL *Proleg. Logica* App. 313 It would not add one tittle to the evidence of the fact.. in the eyes of anyone but an Egoist.

2. One who makes regard to his own interest the guiding principle of his conduct.

1879 *Sat. Rev.* 15 Nov., He is.. thoroughly selfish, an 'egoist,' as Mr. Meredith, adopting current slang, writes the word which used to be 'egotist'.

3. One who talks much about himself; = EGOTIST. Also quasi-*adj.*

1794 LD. AUCKLAND *Corr.* (1862) III. 217 My next letter shall be less egoist. 1831 LYTTON *Godolph.* xix. (1877) 102, I will turn egoist, and tell you *my* adventures.

egoistic (ɛg-, iːgəʊ'ɪstɪk), *a.* [f. prec. + -IC.]

1. Pertaining to, or of the nature of, metaphysical or ethical egoism.

a 1834 COLERIDGE *On Faith* in *Lit. Rem.* IV. (1839) 434 The thirst and pride of power, despotism, egoistic ambition. 1839 SIR W. HAMILTON *Discuss.* (1853) 194 Of Absolute Idealism only two principal species are possible.. the Theistic and the Egoistic. 1862 F. HALL *Hindu Philos. Syst.* 18 The egoistic conceit that the soul energizes, enjoys, and suffers, is the foundation of desire, aversion, virtue, etc. 1874 SIDGWICK *Meth. Ethics* i. 9 Egoistic and Universalistic Hedonism.

2. Of feelings, desires, actions: Self-regarding, prompted by self-interest; in bad sense, selfish.

1840 CARLYLE *Heroes* (1858) 255 His very pity will be cowardly, egoistic,—sentimentality, or little better.

3. Given to talk about oneself; = EGOTISTIC.

1852 ROBERTSON *Lect.* 170 Among.. the egoistic class of first-rate poets, severe justice compels me.. to place Lord Byron.

egoistical (ɛg-, iːgəʊ'ɪstɪkəl), *a.* [f. prec. + -AL¹.] = prec. Hence **ego'istically** *adv.*, from an egoistical point of view.

1842 SIR W. HAMILTON in *Reid's Wks.* II. 817/1 If the Idea be regarded as a mode of the human mind itself, we have a scheme of Egoistical Idealism. 1836 SIR H. TAYLOR *Statesman* xxxi. 235 There is a dignity in the desire to be right.. which will not fail to supersede what is egoistical and frivolous in a man's personal feelings in society. 1847 LEWES *Hist. Philos.* (1867) I. 57 He had learned to despise the splendours of rank and fortune, without being misanthropical or egoistical. 1879 H. SPENCER *Data Ethics* xii. 207 Each profits egoistically from the growth of an altruism.

'egoistry. *nonce-wd.* [f. EGOIST + -RY.] = EGOISM.

1841 LD. SHAFTESBURY in *Life* ix. (1887) 184 His love of expediency, his perpetual egoistry.

egoity (ɛgəʊɪtɪ). [f. EGO + -ITY.] **a.** Selfhood; that which forms the essence of personal identity. **b.** (See quot. 1867.)

1651 BIGGS *New Disp.* ¶290 Our individual singularity and egoity. 1667 H. MORE *Div. Dial.* II. xvii. (1713) 139 Those mysterious depths of Satan which the Theosophers so diligently discover, such as are Ipseity, Egoity, or Selfishness. 1722 WOLLASTON *Relig. Nat.* ix. 198 If you would permit me to use a school term, I would say the egoity remains. 1867 J. H. STIRLING tr. *Schwegler's Hist. Philos.* (ed. 8) 261 We are to understand.. not the particular individual, but the universal ego, universal reason.. Egoity and individuality, the pure and the empirical ego, are entirely different ideas.

egoizer ('ɛgəʊaɪzə(r)). *rare.* [f. **egoize* v. (f. L. *ego* + -IZE) + -ER.] Used as trans. of Skr. *ahaṁkâra* (*lit.* 'ego-maker') a term in Hindu philosophy. See quot. and cf. EGOISM 5.

1862 F. HALL *Hindu Philos. Syst.* 57 That internal organ which has egoism for its characteristic affection is the egoizer.

egomania (ɛgəʊ'meɪnɪə). . [f. Gr. ἐγώ I + μανία madness; after *monomania*, *bibliomania*, etc.] Morbid egotism.

1825 W. S. WALKER *Poet. Wks.* (1852) Introd. 88 Would I could get rid of this egomania! 1895 tr. *Nordau's Degeneration* 241. 1895 *Times* 21 Nov. 11/2 He panders either to the morbid egomania of the sitter or to the snobbism of his readers. 1901 *Academy* 18 May 427 There is not much reasoning with nerves and temperament; and as for 'egomania', was she not shut up with a mirror all her life? 1924 W. B. SELBIE *Psych. Relig.* 140 Instances abound of religious individualism degenerating into egoism and producing even egomania. 1957 *New Yorker* 26 Oct. 50/2 A profession that has more than its share of artists given to displays of egomania and other irritating forms of temperament.

egomaniac (ɛgəʊ'meɪnɪæk). [f. EGOMANIA, after *monomaniac*, etc.] One who suffers from egomania. Also *attrib.* and *transf.*

1890 *Daily News* 8 July 6/1 To the end she is an egomaniac, and her religion is but another expression of the sensuousness that is the active principle of her being. 1895 *Westm. Gaz.* 25 Feb. 2/1 The Ego-maniac—the degenerate who is too feeble of will to control his thoughts by a regard to the welfare of society. 1914 *Daily Express* 17 Nov. 4 The crazy egomaniac who has deluged Europe with blood. 1915 C. S. JONES *Hohenzollern* 199 So ruthless and imperious as to become that most dangerous of lunatics—a confirmed egomaniac! 1920 *Glasgow Herald* 20 Nov. 5 Pretensions that had grown to egomaniac heights. 1921 GALSWORTHY *To Let* II. ii, I know those enthusiastic egomaniac gentry. 1963 *Punch* 30 Oct. 640/2 And cats, egomaniacs.

‖**'egomen.** *rare*⁻¹. [ad. Gr. ἡγούμενος, pr. pple. of ἡγέεσθαι to lead.] A monastic functionary in the Greek Church.

1591 HORSEY *Trav.* (1857) 174 The principall.. archiemanders and egomens of the.. religious houses of his kingdom.

†**'egomism.** *Obs. rare.* [a. Fr. *égomisme*: see EGO and -ISM. The inserted *m* Littré conjectures to be derived from the pronoun *me*. More probably the word was a parody of some older term, such as *atomisme*.] The belief of one who considers himself the only being in existence.

[1727 RAMSAY *Disc. sur la Mythol.* 90 Une espèce de Pyrrhonisme nommé l'Egomisme, ou chacun se croit le seul être existent.] *c* 1730 A. BAXTER *Eng. Nat. Soul* (1745) XI. 21 That kind of Scepticism called Egomism. 1856 W. H. THOMPSON in A. Butler *Hist. Anc. Philos.* I. 80 *note*, It [egoism] is not more barbarous than its homonym 'egotism', and much less so than 'egomism', which occurs in 'Baxter On the Soul', where it is attributed to certain Cartesians.

egophony, var. of ÆGOPHONY.

egotheism (ɛgəʊ'θiːɪz(ə)m). *rare.* [f. Gr. ἐγώ + θε-ός God + -ISM.] The (mystical) identification of oneself with the Deity.

1856 R. VAUGHAN *Mystics* (1860) II. VII. i. 7 The arrogant egotheism of some passages they took in another sense. 1882 J. NICHOL *Amer. Lit.* viii. 267 He approaches the Egotheism of the Sufis.

egotism ('ɛg-, iːgətɪz(ə)m). [f. EGO + -ISM, with intrusive *t* as in AGIOTAGE.

If the statement of Addison (quot. 1714) can be trusted, the word seems to have been invented by some of the Port-Royalists to range with the terms of rhetoric denoting 'figures of speech' and the like. (In accordance with this, Lord Chesterfield speaks of '*the* egotism' as one might say 'the aposiopesis', 'the chiasmus'.) It seems probable that *egotism* was formed on the pattern of some older word in *-otism*; cf. for example Fr. *idiotisme*.]

1. The obtrusive or too frequent use of the pronoun of the first person singular: hence the practice of talking about oneself or one's doings.

1714 ADDISON *Spect.* No. 562 ¶3 The Gentlemen of Port-Royal.. branded this Form of Writing [in the First Person] with the Name of an Egotism. 1747 CHESTERF. *Lett.* I. cxxix. 344 Banish the egotism out of your conversation. 17.. *Ibid.* II. 238 Though I do not recommend the egotism to you with regard to any body else, I desire that you will use it with me. 1753 HANWAY *Trav.* (1762) I. Introd. 16 The nature of journals renders egotisms unavoidable. 1775 MASON *Mem. Gray* Poems (1775) 173 The Reader.. will excuse this short piece of egotism. 1856 KANE *Arct. Expl.* I. xxx. 407 The egotism of personal narrative.

2. The vice of thinking too much of oneself; self-conceit, boastfulness; also, selfishness.

1800 *Med. Jrnl.* IV. 503 My readers will pardon any appearance of egotism.. since it is not easy to talk of oneself without giving offence. 1830 COLERIDGE *Lect. Shaks.* II. 116 The intense selfishness, the alcohol of egotism, which would rather reign in hell than serve in heaven. 1847 EMERSON *Repr. Men, Napoleon* Wks. (Bohn) I. 381 His absorbing egotism was deadly to all other men. 1853 ROBERTSON *Serm.* Ser. III. vii. 101 Sin is the withdrawing into self and egotism out of the vivifying life of God. 1858 GREENER *Gunnery* 232 Without egotism, I can safely offer to make a gun or guns against any maker in the world. 1878 LECKY *Eng. in 18th C.* II. vii. 257 An intense class and national egotism then dominated all politics.

egotist ('ɛg-, 'iːgətɪst). [f. as prec. + -IST.] One who makes too frequent use of the pronoun I; one who thinks or talks too much of himself; a selfish person. Also *attrib.*

1714 ADDISON *Spect.* No. 562 ¶4 The most eminent Egotist.. was Montaigne, the author of the.. Essays. 1806 R. JAMIESON *Pop. Ball. & Songs* I. Pref. 4 A man, that acknowledges favours may be allowed to be an egotist. 1830 MACINTOSH *Eth. Philos.* Wks. 1846 I. 175 As much an egotist as Montaigne; but not so agreeably so. 1848 W. H. KELLY tr. *L. Blanc's Hist. Ten Y.* II. 452 Such is, in the egotist and vulgar meaning of the phrase, the genius of the ambitious. 1853 ROBERTSON *Lect.* 240 The egotist is ever speaking and thinking of that which belongs to himself alone. 1860 READE *Cloister & H.* lvii, The sailors were preparing to desert the sinking ship in the little boat.. then there was a rush of egotists; and thirty souls crowded into it.

egotistic (ɛg-, iːgəʊ'tɪstɪk), *a.* [f. prec. + -IC.] Pertaining to, or characterized by, egotism.

c 1860 WRAXALL tr. *R. Houdin* iv. 36, I began to lose the egotistic indifference which a lengthened illness usually produces. 1865 *Reader* 8 July 30 His diction is entirely his own, avowedly egotistic. 1877 MOZLEY *Univ. Serm.* iii. 70 The Christian hope of immortality cannot be an egotistic hope.

ego'tistical, *a.* [f. as prec. + -ICAL.] = prec.

1825 MACAULAY *Milton, Ess.* (1851) I. 14 The character of a writer from the passages directly egotistical. 1841 D'ISRAELI *Amen. Lit.* (1867) 321 Patriotism has often covered the most egotistical motives. 1859 THACKERAY *Virgin.* lxxxvi. (1878) 697, I have a right to be garrulous and egotistical. 1870 DISRAELI *Lothair* xlix. 268, I am talking in an.. egotistical.. manner.

Hence **ego'tistically** *adv.*, in an egotistical manner, as a result of egotism.

1809–12 MAR. EDGEWORTH *Vivian* iii. (1832) 195 Egotistically secured from the pains of sympathy. 1848 DICKENS *Dombey* (C.D. ed.) 66 An old black cat.. lay.. upon the centre foot of the fender purring egotistically. 1880 H.

JAMES *Benvolio* I. 344 A man..who assumes, a trifle egotistically, that the rest of the world was equally at leisure.

egotize (ˈɛg-, ˈiːgətaɪz), *v.* [f. EGOT-ISM: see IZE.] *intr.* To talk or write in an egotistic way.

Hence ˈ**egotizing** *vbl. sb.* and *ppl. a.*

1789 COWPER *Lett.* 6 June, I egotize in my letters to thee. **1791** *2nd Ep. J. Priestley* in *Poet. Register* (1808) 406 E'en the first egotizing sentence flags. **1811** L. HAWKINS *C'tess & Gertr.* 75, I am involving myself in the sins of preaching and egotising. **1865** R. PAUL *Let.* in *Mem.* xix. (1872) 328, I am not going to egotise.

egranulose (ɪˌgrænjʊˈləʊs), *a. Bot.* [f. E- *pref.*³ + GRANULOSE.] Without granules.

1884 in *Syd. Soc. Lex.*

egre, obs. form of EAGER.

†**eˈgredient**, *a. Obs. rare*⁻¹. [ad. L. *ēgredient-em*, pr. pple. of *ēgredi* to go out, f. *ē* out + *gradi* to step.] That goes out or issues forth.

1635 PERSON *Varieties* II. 74 The one is as ingredient, the other as egredient.

egregious (ɪˈgriːdʒ(ɪ)əs, -dʒɪəs), *a.* Also 6 æ-, egregius. [f. L. *ēgregi-us*, f. *ē* out + *grex, greg-is* flock + -OUS: hence *lit.*, towering above the flock.]

†**1.** Prominent, projecting.

1578 BANISTER *Hist. Man* VII. 92 All the poynt, and egregious portion of the right side of this inuolucre.

2. Remarkable in a good sense:

a. Of persons and personal qualities: Distinguished, eminent, excellent, renowned. *Obs.* (exc. in humorously pedantic use).

*c***1534** tr. *Pol. Verg. Eng. Hist.* (1846) I. 172 Peda, the sonne of Penda, an ægregius yonge gentilmanne. **1590** MARLOWE *2nd Pt. Tamburl.* I. i, Egregious viceroys of these eastern parts. **1609** BIBLE (Douay) *Ex.* xxxviii. 23 Ooliab.. was himself also an egregious artificer in wood. **1656** HOBBES *Six Less.* Wks. 1845 VII. 283, I am not so egregious a mathematician as you are. **1738** BIRCH *Milton* in *Milton's Wks.* (1738) I. App. 84 Egregious was their Loyalty and Veneration of Majesty. **1820** L. HUNT *Indicator* No. 53 There is a school book by the Egregious John Amos Comenius. **1855** THACKERAY *Newcomes* I. 122 When he wanted to draw..some one splendid and egregious, it was Clive he took for a model.

b. Of things: Remarkably good or great. Of events and utterances: Striking, significant. ? *Obs.*

1547–64 BAULDWIN *Mor. Philos.* II. (Palfr.) Prol., Certain reserved sentences very egregious lively and excellent. **1599** SHAKS. *Hen. V*, IV. iv. 11 Except..thou doe giue to me egregious Ransome. **1645** MILTON *Tetrach.* (1851) 220 This is egregious doctrine, and for which one day charity will much thanke them. **1710** T. FULLER *Pharm. Extemp.* 147 It [emulsion] is especially of egregious use in Fevers.

3. Remarkable in a bad sense; gross, flagrant, outrageous. [This sense does not belong to L. *egregius* or to It. *egregio*; prob. it arose from an ironical use of 2, though our earliest quotations afford no evidence of this.]

a. of persons and personal attributes.

1573 G. HARVEY *Letter-bk.* (1884) 33 Thai them selvs cannot dissemble it without egregius impudenci. **1593** NASHE *Four Lett. Confut.* 67 Egregious is neuer used in english but in the extreame ill part. **1611** SHAKS. *Cymb.* V. v. 211 Italian Fiend..Egregious murtherer. **1648** MILTON *Observ. Art. Peace* (1851) 576 Egregious Liars and Impostors. **1734** FIELDING *Univ. Gallant* v. i, He would be an egregious ass who wou'd venture to lay out his money in them [jewels]. **1839** JAMES *Louis XIV*, I. 50 The egregious superstition of the higher orders. **1864** *Morning Star* 13 Sept., Every tradesman..with egregious bonhomie tries to cheat you.

b. of things, actions, etc.

1630 BRATHWAIT *Eng. Gentl.* (1641) 88 He toucheth severity towards servants, as a hainous and egregious offence. **1709** STEELE *Tatler* No. 47 ⁋2 People that want Sense, do always in an egregious Manner want Modesty. **1761–2** HUME *Hist. Eng.* (1806) IV. li. 48 An egregious exercise of tyranny. **1816** KIRBY & SP. *Entomol.* ii. (1828) I. 21 An egregious waste of time. **1878** LECKY *Eng. in 18th C.* II. vii. 426 No blunder could have been more egregious.

4. *nonce-use.* Wandering from the flock.

1873 BROWNING *Red Cott. Night-C.* 1203 An egregious sheep..Unearthed the image in good Mailleville's time.

Hence **eˈgregiousness**, the quality of being egregious; the possession of uncommon qualities.

1632 SHERWOOD, Egregiousness, *excellence.* **1877** *Times* Feb. 19. 12/1 Professor Guthrie pointed out that water..is unusual, and shows egregiousness in its properties.

eˈgregiously, *adv.* [f. prec. + -LY².] In an egregious manner, remarkably; in 17th c. occasionally in a good sense, remarkably well, excellently; now exclusively in bad or ironical sense, grossly, monstrously, shamefully.

*a***1555** LATIMER in Foxe *A. & M.* (1684) III. 368 Here have I blotted your Paper vainly, and played the fool egregiously. **1635** N. R. tr. *Camden's Hist. Eliz.* I. an. 2. 25 The French egregiously dissembled a desire of peace. *a***1693** URQUHART *Rabelais* III. xix. 156 Whom he had seen to act his part most egregiously upon the Stage. **1866** TROLLOPE *Belton Est.* II. xiv. 267 Well aware..that he was trespassing egregiously.

egremoigne, -moyn, obs. ff. AGRIMONY.

*a***1387** *Sinon. Barthol.* (Anecd. Oxon.) 9 *Agrimonia*, egremoyn. *a***1450** *Alphita* (Anecd. Oxon.) 3 *Agimonia uel agrimonia*..gall. et angl. egremoigne.

egress (ˈiːgrɛs), *sb.* [ad. L. *ēgressus*, n. of action f. *ēgredi-*, f. *ē* out + *gradi* to step.]

1. A going out, or issuing forth, from an enclosed or confined place; the right or liberty of going out, *esp.* in phrase originally legal, *Ingress, egress*, and *regress*. Also *attrib.*

1538 tr. *Lyttleton's Tenures* viii. fol. 15 b, Free entre, egresse, and regresse. **1543–4** *Act 35 Hen. VIII*, c. 10 To haue free ingresse egresse and regresse into all suche places. **1601** DEACON & WALKER *Answ. Darel* 84, I have..obserued ..in sundrie Demoniakes, a vomiting immediatly before the egresse of the Spirit. **1667** MILTON *P.L.* II. 437 Gates of burning Adamant..prohibit all egress. **1724** T. RICHERS *Hist. Royal Geneal. Spain* 400 The French Fleet..enter'd the Bay of Cadiz, to prevent all Egress and Regress of that Harbour. **1870** E. PEACOCK *Ralf Skirl.* I. 13 The other door which afforded egress into the small court. **1886** *Pall Mall G.* 22 Dec. 5/2 Another improvement is the egress chamber.

b. *Astron.* The emergence of a heavenly body from an eclipse or occultation; also, the passing of a planet off the sun's disc in a transit; the end of an eclipse or transit. Also *attrib.*

1706 HEARNE *Collect.* 2 May (1885) I. 239 They plainly perceiv'd the Ingress and Egress. **1867–77** G. CHAMBERS *Astron.* Voc. 915 *Egress*, the passage of a satellite from the disc of its primary, at the end of the phenomenon known as a 'transit'. **1882** *Daily News* 30 Dec. 5/4 The Transit of Venus..the egress observations in the West Indies.

2. *Anat.* Of nerves and vessels: An issuing forth, or branching out.

1578 BANISTER *Hist. Man* VIII. 110 After the egresse or goyng out therof [of the nerve] it cleaueth into two braunches. **1668** CULPEPPER & COLE tr. *Barthol. Anat.* I. xvii. 46 That the Ingress and Egress of the Vessels might be discerned. **1830** R. KNOX *Béclard's Anat.* 359 The nervous fasciculi..are collected together at their egress from the ganglion.

3. A channel of exit, an outlet.

1677 HALE *Contempl.* II. 229 God..as a wise Artist..stops all other egresses but that which fits his design. **1817** J. SCOTT *Paris Revisit.* 142 A lane..an egress from which was shut up. **1863** WHYTE MELVILLE *Gladiators* III. 163 The door..was a private egress opening on the wide terrace.

4. *fig.*

1604 T. WRIGHT *Passions* v. §4. 264 Ingresse into this world..Progresse of Life..Egresse or death. **1612** WOODALL *Surg. Mate* Wks. 1653 Pref. 11 This present Work..the Authour entreats..may receive a charitable Construction upon the egresse thereof. **1640** BP. REYNOLDS *Passions* ix. 74 Love then consists in a kind of expansion or egresse of the heat and spirits to the object loved. **1874** HELPS *Soc. Press.* iii. 43 What should prevent the ingress.. of noxious trades, or facilitate their egress.

egress (ɪˈgrɛs), *v.* [f. the sb.] *intr.* To issue, to go forth. (Perfect tenses sometimes conjugated with *be.*)

1578 BANISTER *Hist. Man* VIII. 111 b, Two other payre of sinewes..which after they are egressed or gone forth, beget also, by together knittyng, one notable nerue. **1765** W. LAW tr. *Behmen's Myst. Magnum* i. (1772) 11 That which is egressed is called the Lubet of the Deity. **1866** J. ROSE *Ovid's Fasti* II. 203 Forth from the camp egress'd their bands.

egression (ɪˈgrɛʃən). [ad. L. *ēgressiōn-em*, f. *ēgress-* ppl. stem of *ēgredi*: see EGRESS *sb.*]

1. The action of issuing forth or going out from any enclosed place or specified limits.

*a***1529** SKELTON *Image Hypocr.* III. 272 To send a man.. To his egression. **1607** TOPSELL *Serpents* 753 Scorpions, which at their first egression do kill their Dam that hatched them. **1650** H. BROOKE *Conserv. Health* 117 The Cold hinders the egression of Vapors. **1660** JER. TAYLOR *Duct. Dubit.* IV. i, Mævius..in the instant of its [the arrow's] egression..repents of the intended evil. **1767** HEBERDEN in *Phil. Trans.* LVII. 461 The accession of strangers and the egression of the natives being so equally inconsiderable. **1862** R. PATTERSON *Ess. Hist. & Art* 448 The Indian peninsula is a huge cul-de-sac, into which race after race.. has poured..without the possibility of any egression.

†**b.** *spec.* The exodus of the Israelites from Egypt. *Obs.* (freq. in 18th c.).

1614 RALEIGH *Hist. World* II. 352 The times from the egression to the building of Solomon's Temple. **1738–41** WARBURTON *Div. Legat.* II. 256 The Egression of the Israelites.

†**c.** *transf.* The issuing as a branch, etc. *Obs.*

1578 BANISTER *Hist. Man* IV. 59 Sinewy and sharpe is the egression of this muscle at the first.

†**2.** Emergence *from, out of* (obscurity, etc.); a deviation from accustomed rules; an outburst of feeling, poetic fervour, etc. *Obs.*

1509 BARCLAY *Shyp of Folys* Argt. Aj, Leuynge the egressyons poetyques and fabulous obscurytees. **1651** JER. TAYLOR *Course Serm.* I. iv. 50 Extraordinary egressions and transvolations beyond the ordinary course of an even Piety. *Ibid.* (1678) 85 The Gospel..requiring the heart of man did stop every egression of disorders. **1654** TRAPP *Comm. Ps.* lxiii. 1 Egressions of affection unto God. **1738–41** WARBURTON *Div. Legat.* II. 31 All Countries on their first Egression out of Barbarity. **1753** *Ess. Celibacy* 80 Such egressions from her laws are degeneracies from the connate standard of human perfection.

eˈgressive, *a.* [as if ad. L. **ēgressīv-us*; cf. prec. and -IVE.] Tending to issue forth.

1691 ED. TAYLOR tr. *Behmen's Theos. Phil.* 356 The desire is egressive, and the Egress is the Spirit of the Will.

egret (ˈɛgrɪt, ˈiːgrɪt). Forms: 5 egrete, -ette, 6–7 eggret, 7 (egript), 8 eggritte, eigrette, 5- egret. See also AIGRETTE. [var. of AIGRETTE: a. Fr. *aigrette*, dim. of **aigr-*, a. OHG. *heigir*: see HERON.]

1. The Lesser White Heron: cf. AIGRETTE 1. Also *attrib.*, as in ***egret-heron.***

1411 ROGERS *Agric. & Prices* III. 129/2 Egrets 4 @ 1/2. *c***1535** DEWES *Introd. Fr.* in *Palsgr.* 911 Theggret, *laigret.* **1600** HAKLUYT *Voy.* III. 520 An egript..is all white as the swanne, with legs like to an hearnshaw. **1766** PENNANT *Zool.* (1768) II. 513 Egrets, a species of Heron now scarce known in this island. **1849** C. BRONTË *Shirley* III. viii. 178 As quiet poultry might look on an egret. **1859** TENNENT *Ceylon* II. IX. iv. 455 Snowy egrets..station themselves lower down to watch the fish.

2. The feathery pappus of the seeds of the dandelion, thistle, and other plants; = AIGRETTE 3.

1794 MARTYN *Rousseau's Bot.* vi. 70 Seeds in which the down or egret..is sessile. **1800** J. HURDIS *Favourite Vill.* 110 Egret from the head Of thistle ravished. **1851** S. JUDD *Margaret* VI. (1871) 29 The egret of a thistle.

3. *attrib.*, as †**egret-monkey** [Fr. *aigrette*; so called by Buffon from the tuft on the top of its head], an assumed species of ape called by Linnæus *Simia Aygula*; it is now supposed that the female of some species of *Macacus* was meant.

1802 BINGLEY *Anim. Biog.* (1813) I. 81 The egret monkey. **1829** *Tower Menagerie*, Contents.

egrimonie, -y, obs. ff. AGRIMONY.

†ˈ**egrimony.** *rare*⁻⁰. [ad. L. *ægrimonia*, f. *æger* sick.] Deep sorrow.

1626 in COCKERAM. **1656** BLOUNT *Glossogr.* **1818** in TODD. **1847** in WEBSTER and mod. Dicts.

egriot, var. of AGRIOT, *Obs.*, a sort of cherry.

egritude, var. of ÆGRITUDE, *Obs.*

egromancy, obs. var. NECROMANCY. Also **egromantic** adj.

[Cf. note s.v. NECROMANCY. Sir R. Burton believed that he had found the words in some Eng. writer of 17th c.]

*c***1450** *Merlin* (1899) 375, 508 Egramauncye. *a***1469** *Gregory's Chron.* (Camden Soc. 1876) 183 Egremauncey. *arch.* **1885** R. BURTON *Arab. Nights* I. 76 By virtue of my egromancy become thou half stone and half man. *Ibid.* I. 133 An hundred and seventy chapters of egromantic formulas.

†**eˈgrote**, *v. Obs.*⁻⁰ [ad. L. *ægrōtāre*, f. *ægrōtus* sick.] *intr.* To be sick; to feign oneself sick.

1721–61 in BAILEY.

Hence **eˈgroting** *vbl. sb.*, a feigned sickness.

1732 in COLE. **1775** in ASH.

egrymon, obs. variant of AGRIMONY.

egte, obs. form of EIGHT.

eguall, var. of EGALL *a. Obs.* equal.

egurgitate (ɪˈgɜːdʒɪteɪt), *v. rare.* [ad. L. *ēgurgitāt-* ppl. stem of *ēgurgitāre*, f. *ē* out + *gurgit-em* whirlpool, gulf.] *trans.* To vomit forth; *humorously*, to utter (phrases).

1656 BLOUNT *Glossogr.* **1709** *Brit. Apollo* II. No. 64. 2/2 Horisonant Phrases..which..with..Facility you Egurgitate. **1862** *Q. Rev.* July 192 The most purposeless crystallo-chalybeate bubbles which earth has yet egurgitated.

egyl(le, obs. ff. EAGLE.

†**Eˈgyptiac**, *a. Obs. rare.* [ad. late L. *Ægyptiăcus.*] = EGYPTIAN.

1635 PAGITT *Christianogr.* I. ii. (1636) 48 Groning under their Egyptiack bondage.

†**Egypˈtiacal**, *a. Obs.* [f. as prec. + -AL¹.] = EGYPTIAN.

1556 ABP. PARKER *Psalter* lxxx. 14 Egiptiacall bondage. **1586** J. HOOKER *Girald. Irel.* in *Holinshed* II. 134/1 Suffering no glibes..nor the Egyptiacal rolles vpon womens heads.

Egyptian (ɪˈdʒɪpʃən), *a.* and *sb.* Forms: 4 egi-, egypcian, -ien, -yan, 6 egiptian, egypcy-, (sy-)an, 7 æg-, 7- egyptian. [f. *Egypt* + -IAN.]

A. *adj.*

1. a. Belonging or relating to Egypt.

1646 CRASHAW *Delights of the Muse* 129 Th' Egyptian Pyramids themselves must live. **1726** tr. *Gregory's Astron.* I. 245 The Egyptian, Julian, and Gregorian [year]. **1885** RAWLINSON *Egypt & Bab.* 223 No trace has been found of camels in the Egyptian monuments. *Mod.* The recent Egyptian campaign. He speculated in Egyptian bonds.

b. *fig.* In Biblical allusions, as ***Egyptian bondage***: bondage like that of the Israelites in Egypt; ***Egyptian darkness***: intense darkness (see *Exod.* x. 22); also, †***Egyptian days***: the two days in each month which were believed to be unlucky.

1398 TREVISA *Barth. De P.R.* IX. xxi. (1495) 358 For there ben xxiiij Egypcyans dayes it folowyth that god sente mo wreches vpon the Egypcyens than ten. *c***1400** *Apol. Loll.* 93 A waytiþ not þeis Egipcian daies, (þat we call dysmal). **1641** R. BROOKE *Eng. Episc.* II. iv. 76 A Glympse that might Enlighten them in the midst of Egyptian darknesse. **1659**

MILTON *Rupt. Commw.* Wks. (1851) 401 A part of the Nation were desperately conspir'd to call back again thir Egyptian Bondage. **1854** J. ABBOTT *Napoleon* II. viii. 133 It was a night of Egyptian darkness.

2. *Bot.* **Egyptian bean**: perh. the fruit of *Nelumbium speciosum*; **Egyptian lily**, the white arum, or trumpet lily, *Zantedeschia æthiopica*; = CALLA 2; **Egyptian lotus** = *Nymphæa Lotus*; **Egyptian millet**, *Pennisetum spicatum*; **Egyptian onion**, a form of the common onion, *Allium cepa aggregatum*; **Egyptian pea**: see PEA[1] 3; **Egyptian privet**, henna; **Egyptian rose**: (*a*) *Scabiosa arvensis* L. (*b*) *Scabiosa atropurpurea* L.; **Egyptian thorn**: *Cratægus Pyracantha*.

1847 A. H. LINCOLN *Lect. Bot.* (ed. 2) xxxvi. 191 The elegant exotic, Calla ethiopica, or Egyptian lily. **1959** R. M. CARLETON *Index Common Names Herbaceous Plants* 41/2 *Egyptian-lily*, Agapanthus africanus (A. umbellatus); Zantedeschia (Richardia). **1829** *Virginia Herald* (Fredericksburg, Va.) 25 Apr. 2/4 The leaves are of a beautiful green—long, narrow, dagger shaped, not unlike those of the Egyptian millet [see MILLET[1] 2]. **1907** L. H. BAILEY *Cycl. Amer. Agric.* II. 471/1 Various other names have been applied to this plant, such as penicillaria, cat-tail millet, Egyptian millet. **1880** *Encycl. Brit.* XII. 285/1 The Tree Onion or Egyptian Onion.. produces small bulbs instead of flowers. **1959** R. M. CARLETON *Index Common Names Herbaceous Plants* 41/2 *Egyptian onion*, Allium cepa. **1825** LOUDON *Encycl. Agric.* §1057 The henné or Egyptian privet. **1956** *Colour Index* (ed. 2) I. 1751 The powdered dried leaves of the Egyptian privet.

3. *Min.* **Egyptian jasper**, † **Egyptian pebble**: a brown mottled jasper from Egypt.

1771 HILL *Fossils* 226 Egyptian Pebble. **1804** JAMESON *Mineralogy* I. 230 Egyptian Jasper. **1884** DANA *Mineralogy* 195 Egyptian Jasper.

4. = GIPSY. *humorous.*

1749 FIELDING *Tom Jones* XII. xiii. IV. 295 Mr. Jones.. took leave of his Egyptian majesty.

5. In Printing. ***Egyptian type*** (***letters, figures***): a particular kind of type distinguished by the thickness of the stems; also as quasi-*sb.*

1855 J. GORDON *Interest Tables* Pref. 7 The introduction of Egyptian figures at the tens.. will.. give increased facility to the eye in running over the columns. **1859** H. BEADNELL *Guide Typography* II. 35 Types are.. distinguished according to the information.. of the letter.. [as].. Roman, Italic.. Egyptian.

6. **Egyptian binding** (see quot. 1728); **Egyptian cotton**, a cotton of fine quality developed in Egypt; **Egyptian pound** (see POUND *sb.*[1] 3 d); **Egyptian wheel** (see quots.).

1728 CHAMBERS *Cycl.* s.v. *Bookbinding*, The Manner of binding Books in Volumes, *i.e.* of sewing the leaves together, to roll 'em on round Pieces or Cylinders of Wood, appears the most Ancient.. which we may call *Egyptian binding*. **1877** *Encycl. Brit.* VI. 485/1 The new description of Egyptian cotton has since been known by the name 'Jumel' in France. **1957** Egyptian cotton [see BACK-DOOR 2]. **1793** *Descr. Estate of Culross* 9 Sir George Bruce erected machinery, consisting of the Egyptian wheel, commonly called chain and bucket, to drain the Coal to the dip of the old workings. **1867** M. E. HERBERT *Cradle Lands* vii. 196 A well of water worked by a thoroughly Egyptian wheel. **1880** *Encycl. Brit.* XII. 435/1 The Egyptian Wheel or Noria.

7. *Zool.* **Egyptian cobra**: see COBRA.

B. *sb.*

1. A native of Egypt. Often *fig.* with allusion to the aspect in which the Egyptians appear in the Bible. ***to spoil the Egyptians***: cf. *Exod.* xii. 36.

1388 WYCLIF *Isa.* xix. 21 Egipcions schulen knowe the Lord. **1398** TREVISA *Barth. De P.R.* IX. iii. (1495) 347 Amonge the Egypcyens the yere was tokenyd by a dragon paynted bytynge his owne taylle. *c* **1400** *Apol. Loll.* 73 Decretistis, as to þat part of wysdam þat þei haue of þe worldis wisdam, are Egipciens. **1658** CLEVELAND *Rustic Ramp.* Wks. (1687) 422 All without the Fold of the Godly were Ægyptians. **1828** *Blackw. Mag.* XXIV. 323 The.. abhorrence of the Ægyptians for these barbarous Iconoclasts. *Mod.* The manners of the ancient Egyptians.

2. = GIPSY.

1514 FITZHERB. *Just. Peas* 98 b, It is ordayned agaynste people callynge themselves Egypcyans, that no such persons be suffred to come within this realme. **1609** SKENE *Reg. Maj.* 179 For the better triall of.. masterfull beggers, fenȝeit foolis, counterfit Egyptians. **1697** *View of Penal Laws* 310 If any Transports into England or Wales, any lewd People, calling themselves Egyptians, they forfeit 40*l.* **1749** FIELDING *Tom Jones* xii, A company of Egyptians, or as they are vulgarly called, gipsies.

3. *pl.* In late 19th-c. use = ***Egyptian stocks***: securities issued by the Egyptian government.

4. The Hamitic language of Egypt.

1556 A. VELE in R. Robynson tr. *More's Utopia* (ed. 2) Printer to Reader, It is a tongue to vs muche straunger then the Indian, the Persian,.. the Arabicke, the Egyptian, the Macedonian. **1646** J. GREGORY *Notes & Obs.* (1650) To Rdr., This Booke of ours.. may be read in.. Coptick or Ægyptian. **1842** *Visitor or Monthly Instructor* 409/1 It ain't Greek at all: except, perhaps a few words. What ain't Greek is Egyptian; and what ain't Egyptian is Greek. **1857** S. BIRCH in J. G. Wilkinson *Egyptians* 182 Enlightened rulers prided themselves in speaking foreign tongues... Cleopatra spoke seven, Egyptian among the number. **1875** W. D. WHITNEY *Life Lang.* 254 In this [*sc.* 'Hamitic'] family, the Egyptian occupies the same commanding position as the Chinese. **1877** *Encycl. Brit.* VII. 721/2 The inscribed and written character of Egyptian was the hieroglyphic. **1960** S. POTTER *Lang. in Mod. World* viii. 112 It is customary to divide the history of Egyptian into three periods; Old or hieroglyphic, Middle or hieratic, and New or demotic.

5. a. A mother-of-pearl shell from Egypt. **b.** An Egyptian cigarette.

1885 *Encycl. Brit.* XVIII. 447/2 The Arabs still obtain from this district [*sc.* Jiddah and Koseir] a quantity of mother-of-pearl shells, which are shipped from Alexandria, and come into the market as 'Egyptians'. **1892** *Whitehall Rev.* 22 Oct. 8/1 She could tell Russians from Egyptians, and sometimes took a mild Havannah with her B and S in the smoking-room. **1905** *Westm. Gaz.* 28 Oct. 10/2 A box of Egyptians. **1965** P. ROBINSON *Pakistani Agent* viii. 107, I only smoke Egyptians, thank you.

Hence **E'gyptianize** *v.* (*a*) *intr.*, to act like an Egyptian; to adopt Egyptian practices; (*b*) *trans.*, to make like an Egyptian or the Egyptians; (*c*) to develop a country or district according to the methods adopted in Egypt; in later use, see quot. 1958; **E'gyptianized** *ppl. a.* **E'gyptianism**, Egyptian characteristics, inclination to Egyptian customs.

1664 H. MORE *Myst. Iniq.* vi. 17 It was.. wickedness.. to Ægyptianize in the adoration of the God of Israel. **1827** G. S. FABER *Expiat. Sacrif.* 268 God's condescension to the Egyptianism of the Israelites. **1847** GROTE *Greece* II. xx. III. 442 This dynasty [Psammetichus's] had too little of pure Egyptianism in them to find favour with the priests. **1851** H. TORRENS in *Jrnl. Asiat. Soc. Bengal* 9 The existence of an Egyptianised race. **1899** *Westm. Gaz.* 4 Aug. 9/1 Were we prepared to.. begin the work of Egyptianising the Yangtse Valley? **1958** *Britannica Bk. of Year 1957* 519/1 *Egyptianize*, meaning to nationalize foreign holdings in the manner of the Egyptian government in 1956. **1959** *Daily Tel.* 3 Mar. 16/3 The U.A.R. government is paying to the British Government a lump sum of £27,500,000 in compensation for British private property Egyptianised, that is nationalised or compulsorily acquired. **1959** *Times* 24 Mar. 15/4 The 4,500 registered owners of sequestrated or Egyptianized property will wish to go to Egypt to recover their property or assess their loss. **1962** *Listener* 1 Mar. 366/2 The new 'Egyptianized' middle class which the regime has put into power.

E,gyptiani'zation. [f. EGYPTIAN *a.* + -IZATION.] **a.** The compulsory acquisition by the Egyptian government of foreigners' property and interests in Egypt. **b.** The rendering Egyptian in character or organization; the placing of a country under Egyptian officials.

1957 *Times* 22 Feb., It is since reported that 'verbal assurance' has been given that the Egyptianization of Greek business interests will not occur 'for at least five years'. **1961** *Daily Tel.* 29 Sept. 1/1 Syria.. is seething with discontent over the Egyptianisation of the country. **1962** *Listener* 1 Mar. 365/2 Then there is the gradual, but all-pervasive Egyptianization. Tens of thousands of foreigners have left Egypt. **1967** *Ibid.* 25 May 674/1 The expulsion of thousands of Britons.. the removal of all foreign doctors, dentists, accountants.. from professional organizations; those were all part of Nasser's Egyptianization process.

E'gyptianizing, *vbl. sb.* Making Egyptian or like the Egyptians.

1921 G. A. F. Knight *Nile & Jordan* xv. 193 To promote the Egyptianizing of the province, Amenhotep III built at Soleb.. a gigantic temple.

E'gyptianizing, *ppl. a.* = EGYPTIZING *ppl. a.*

1949 W. F. ALBRIGHT *Archaeol. of Palestine* viii. 185 A small Egyptianizing statue dating about the eighteenth century B.C.

Egypticity (iːdʒɪp'tɪsɪtɪ). [f. *Egypt* + -ICITY.] The character or quality of being Egyptian (see quot. 1895).

1888 *Expositor* Sept. 219 The Pentateuch—Egypticity and Authenticity. **1895** W. H. TURTON *Truth of Christianity* x. 147 The Egypticity of the narrative. By this is meant that the part of the Pentateuch in which reference is made to Egyptian customs, seasons, and names appears to be written with correct details throughout. **1921** G. A. F. KNIGHT *Nile & Jordan* xxviii. 384 The reference.. is thoroughly Egyptian, and testifies to the 'Egypticity' of the book.

'Egyptize, *v. nonce-wd.* [f. *Egypt* + -IZE.] *intr.* To refer things to Egyptian sources.

1854 KEIGHTLEY *Mythol. Anc. Greece & It.* (ed. 3) 408 Little given as we are to Egyptising.

Egyptizing ('iːdʒɪptaɪzɪŋ), *ppl. a.* [f. *Egypt* + -IZE + -ING[2].] Becoming Egyptian in character; adopting Egyptian characteristics.

1847 J. LEITCH tr. *Müller's Anc. Art* §240 The Egyptising image of the god of Heliopolis. **1923** *Weekly Westm. Gaz.* 24 Mar. 16/2 The art of two great and widely different empires knew its Egyptising phases. **1934** *Discovery* Oct. 278/1 The Egyptizing and Phoenicizing character of much of the art of South Eastern Cyprus in the early archaic period must not be allowed to disguise the fact of its Cypriote origin.

Egypto-, repr. stem of Gr. Αἴγυπτος Egypt, in comb. (= Egyptian and...), as ***Egypto-Abyssinian***, ***-Arab***, ***-Arabic***, ***-Caucasian***, ***-Semitic***, ***-Syrian***, ***-Turk***.

1831 *Athenæum* 3 Dec. 787/3 All.. were obviously of Arabian or Egypto-Caucasian extraction. **1870** P. B. RANDOLPH *Seership!* (1884) 73 Nor do I see any reason why the white women of Western Europe.. should not be as.. successful.. as their Arabian and Egypto-Syriac sisters. **1879** *Chambers's Jrnl.* 174/2 The Egypto-Syrian forces. **1884** *Illustr. Lond. News* 9 Feb. 130/1 Peace had been completely restored on the Egypto-Abyssinian frontier. **1893** F. ADAMS *New Egypt* 16 Even these fanatical Egypto-Turks,.. even these degraded Egypto-Arabs. **1909** WEBSTER s.v. *Saracenic*, The square or polygonal minarets in diminishing stories of the Arabic or Egypto-Arabic style. **1937** J. R. FIRTH *Tongues of Men* iv. 52 The diffusion of the Egypto-Semitic wordcraft.

E'gyptologue. *rare.* [a. Fr. *Égyptologue*; cf. next.] = EGYPTOLOGIST.

1856 *Sat. Rev.* II. 419/1 The famous Egyptologue, the Vicomte de Rougé. **1859** *Ibid.* VIII. 401/2 Many writers on Greek mythology, to say nothing of professed Egyptologues.

Egyptology (iːdʒɪp'tɒlədʒɪ). [f. as if ad. Gr. *αἰγυπτολογία, f. Αἴγυπτος Egypt + -λογία discoursing (see -LOGY).] The study of Egyptian antiquities, of the ancient Egyptian language and history. Hence **Egyp'tologer** = EGYPTOLOGIST. **Egypto'logical** *a.*, pertaining to, concerned with, or devoted to Egyptology. **Egyp'tologist**, one versed in the study of Egyptian antiquities.

1859 GREGORY *Egypt* I. 37 The name Sesortesen.. recent Egyptologists are.. unanimous in maintaining. **1862** *Sat. Rev.* 8 Feb. 162 Egyptology, he [Sir George Lewis] says, has an historical method of its own. **1864** PIAZZI SMYTH *Our Inher. Gt. Pyramid* v. xxii. (1874) 418 By the sadly Egyptological Baron Bunsen. **1873** GEIKIE *Gt. Ice Age* ii. 14 Hieroglyphics are to the Ægyptologist—the silent.. records of an age long passed away. **1876** GLADSTONE *Homeric Synchr.* 210 The key afforded by the researches of Egyptology. **1876** *Trans. Victoria Inst.* 22 The historical discoveries of the earlier Egyptologers were for a time arrayed against Revelation. **1882** *Academy* No. 513. 150 Mr. O. modestly disclaims all Egyptological pretensions.

egyr, obs. form of EAGER.

egyrmonye, obs. var. of AGRIMONY.

eh (eː, eɪ), *int.* [repr. an exclamation of instinctive origin; ME. had EY; the mod. spelling may be after Fr. *eh*, though it might have suggested itself independently.]

1. An ejaculation of sorrow. Cf. AH 1.

1567 *Triall Treas.* in Hazl. *Dodsley* III. 281 Eh, they have used me with too much villainy.

2. An interjectional interrogative particle; often inviting assent to the sentiment expressed.

1773 GOLDSM. *Stoops to Conq.* II. i, Wasn't it lucky, eh? **1816** 'QUIZ' *Grand Master* VI. 132 What have I brought you here for—eh? **1859** CAPERN *Ball. & Songs* 68 You are joking, Jesse, eh? **1867** E. WAUGH *Owd Blanket* iii. 61 (*Lanc. Gloss.*) Eh, iv that blanket could talk, Ailse, it could oather make folk laugh or cry! **1870** B. BRIERLEY *Bundle o' Fents* i. 31 (*Lanc. Gloss.*) 'Eh, whatever is ther' t' do?' hoo shrikt eawt.

3. Used interrogatively, as a request for the repetition or explanation of something that has just been said: = What do you say? *colloq.* or *vulgar*.

1837 T. BACON *Impressions in Hindostan* II. 149 Eh? What's that, Sackville? *a* **1845** HOOD *Hood's Own* 2nd Ser. (1861) 26 'The mail bags are on board—and it's more than my post is worth to put back.' 'Eh? What? How?' exclaimed the Oddity. **1869** *Chambers's Jrnl.* 595/2 'Eh?' said the old clerk, at last detecting my intrusion. I repeated my business. **1903** C. MARRIOTT *House on Sands* xvi, 'Ass!' muttered Lanyon, with a diabolical grin. 'Jelly-belly!' 'Eh?' said Sir Peter, blankly. 'Your health,' replied Lanyon, gravely, raising his glass. **1905** H. G. WELLS *Kipps* III. i. 321 'I'm going to build a house, Ann.' 'Eh?' said Ann suddenly, as if awake. 'Build a house.' **1969** *Listener* 27 Feb. 280/2 Most of what we think characteristically modern already existed by 1914: aircraft, radio-telegraphy, psychoanalysis, Post-Impressionism, motion-picture palaces, and the Labour Party (eh?).

Hence **eh** *v. intr.*, to say 'Eh!'

1824 SCOTT *Redgauntlet* vii, The former ha'd, eh'd.

ehe, ehelid, ehsihðo, ehthurl, obs. forms of EYE, EYE-.

ehlite ('eɪlaɪt). *Min.* [f. *Ehl*, local name (see quot.) + -ITE.] A variety of Pseudomalachite.

1868 DANA *Min.* s.v. *Pseudomalachite*, Ehlite of Breithaupt. Occurs in veins at Ehl near Lenz on the Rhine.

ehrenbergite (ɛərən'bɛəgaɪt). *Min.* [f. the surname *Ehrenberg* + -ITE.] A species of CIMOLITE.

1868 DANA *Min.* s.v. *Cimolite*, Ehrenbergite occurs in clefts in trachyte at the quarries of Steinchen.

ehte, obs. form of AUGHT, property.

ehyt, obs. form of EAT *v.*

ei, ME. contracted form of ANY.

†**ei'castic,** *a. Obs. rare.* [ad. Gr. εἰκαστικός, f. εἰκάζ-ειν to liken, portray.] Imitative.

1669 GALE *Crt. Gentiles* I. III. i. 295 Eicastick Art or Skill in Imitation: whence also Eicastik Poesie receeved its origination.. because its main use lies in framing Images, and pleasing representations of persons or Things.

eich(e, obs. var. of EACH.

eiconic, var. of ICONIC.

eicos-, eicosa-, eikos-, varr. ICOS-, etc.

1909 WEBSTER, *Eikosane*, Chem., a solid hydrocarbon, $C_{20}H_{42}$, of the methane series, of artificial production, and also occurring in petroleum. **1958** *Jrnl. Brit. Interplanetary Soc.* XVI. 442 Values of specific impulse for heptane, octane, decane and eicosane oxidized by WFNA have been calculated. **1964** J. A. LOVERN in *Oceanogr. & Marine Biol.* II. 188 Lipids from fish mitochondria are, like fish depot lipids, low in arachidonic acid but rich in eicosapentaenoic and docosahexaenoic acids. **1968** *New Scientist* 18 July 142/1 This eicosanucleotide (a string of 20 nucleoside beads)

..is the longest that needs to be synthesized by purely chemical methods.

eicosihedron, obs. form of ICOSAHEDRON.

eident (ˈaɪdənt), *a. Sc.* Also 6 ydant, 8 eydent. [Variant of IDENT, Sc. form of ITHAND, which is an altered form of northern ME. *iþen*, *iþin* (a. ON. *iðinn* assiduous, diligent) assimilated to pr. pples. in *-and.*] Diligent, industrious, busy; attentive *to*. Cf. YTHAND.

1591 R. BRUCE *Serm.* vi. O iij, The soules of the Sanctes departed ar mair ydant in this exercise [of praise] then when they wer aliue. *a* **1774** FERGUSSON *Farmer's Ingle* Poems (1845) 36 Wad they [gentler gabs] to labouring lend an eident hand. **1807–10** TANNAHILL *Poems* (1846) 12 The lad ..Was eident ay, and deftly hel' the plough. **1816** SCOTT *Old Mort.* iv, 'Be eident and civil to them baith.'

eider (ˈaɪdə(r)), *sb.* Also 8–9 edder. [Ultimately a. Icel. *æðar* pron. (aiðar), genit. of *æð-r* eider-duck, in the comb. *æðar-dún* eider-down. The continental forms, Sw. †*eider*, now *ejder* (*-gås*), Da. *eder*(*-fugl*), Ger. *eider*(*-ente*), are similarly adopted from. Icel. The present Eng. spelling is probably from the Sw. used by Von Troil.]

1. A species of duck, *Somateria mollissima*, abundant in the Arctic regions, that lines its nest with EIDER-DOWN; also, ***king-eider*** (*Somateria spectabilis*). Chiefly *attrib.*, as in ***eider-bird***, ***-duck***, EIDER-DOWN.

1743 in *Phil. Trans.* XLII. 612 Amongst the Sea-birds are the Edder, Ducks of Three Kinds. **1780** VON TROIL *Iceland* 143 The eider-bird is yet more useful to the natives. **1852** D. MOIR *Fowler* viii, The eider ducks, With their wild eyes, and necks of changeful blue. **1863** KINGSLEY *Water-Bab.* 269 Swans and brantgeese, harlequins and eiders. **1863** *Spring Lapl.* 384 The king eider and Barrow's Iceland duck are only occasionally seen in the autumn.

2. The down itself.

1766 PENNANT *Zool.* (1812) II. 243 The down known by the name of Eider or Edder which these birds furnish.

3. *attrib.* or *adj.* Resembling eider-down.

1791 E. DARWIN *Bot. Gard.* II. 18 Sleep protects him with his eider wings. **1848** KINGSLEY *Saint's Trag.* III. ii. 259 Beneath her eider robe the..earth Watches..for the sun.

ˈeider-down. Also eiderdown. [ultimately a. Icel. *æðar-dún*: see EIDER and DOWN *sb.*²; the Icel. word has been adopted as Sw. *ejder-dun*, Da. *eder-duun*, Ger. *eiderdon*, Fr. *édredon*.]

1. The small soft feathers from the breast of the eider duck. Also *attrib.*

1774 GOLDSM. *Nat. Hist.* (1776) VI. 125 In this number we may reckon the Eider-down. **1804** CT. RUMFORD in *Phil. Trans.* XCIV. 85 Having its two ends well covered up with eider-down. **1856** KANE *Arct. Expl.* II. xvi. 167 All who could work, even at picking over eider-down. **1859** W. COLLINS *Q. of Hearts* (1875) 17 You top up with a sweet little eider-down quilt, as light as roses.

2. A quilt filled with eider-down or any similar soft material.

1950 *Times* 26 Apr. 7/7, I ask you..to lend your pen to scotching the unwarrantable..term 'eiderdown' when applied to the ordinary goose-down quilt. **1955** *Oxf. Jun. Encycl.* XI. 20/2 In the 20th century, eiderdowns, stuffed with down or flock and covered in silk or chintz, became popular. **1970** J. PRIOR *Soft Furnishing* vii. 80 An eiderdown is made like a very large cushion, with a design stitched right through the cover to keep the feathers in fixed pockets.

3. A heavily napped wool or cotton or man-made fabric of thick texture, in plain and fancy colours, used for petticoats, cloaks, bath-robes, etc. Freq. *attrib.*

1872 A. MERCIER *Our Mother Church* xvi. 360 For more elaborate texts..letters may be made of cotton wool, of the fluffy calico called eiderdown, [etc.]. **1873** *Young Englishwoman* Nov. 572/2 Could the kind Editor..give directions..for making an eider-down petticoat. **1890** *Amer. Mail Order Catal.* (1961) 11 Handsome Eider-down short cloak, with astrachan shoulder cap. **1905** *Smart Set* Sept. 155/2 A red eiderdown bath-robe.

eidetic (aɪˈdɛtɪk), *a. Psychol.* [ad. G. *eidetisch* (E. R. Jaensch), f. Gr. εἰδητικός, f. εἶδος form.] Applied to an image that revives an optical impression with hallucinatory clearness, or to the faculty of seeing such images, or to a person having this faculty. Also *sb.*, **a.** one who sees eidetic images; **b.** *pl.* (see quot. 1930). Hence **eiˈdetically** *adv.*, by an eidetic image.

1924 G. W. ALLPORT in *Brit. Jrnl. Psychol.* Oct 100 The true eidetic image, in distinction to the visual memory-image, revives the earlier optical impression when the eyes are closed, in a dark room, and sometimes when the eyes are normally open, with hallucinatory clearness. *Ibid.* 101 Children with less eidetic ability frequently need to be instructed regarding the nature of the phenomenon. *Ibid.* 120 Eidetic imagery is a common possession of children. **1925** C. FOX *Educat. Psychol.* 81 The inability to discriminate between hallucinations and normal mental imagery and the mental confusion thereby entailed is responsible for a psychological abortion called the ' eidetic image'. **1929** *Encycl. Brit.* VIII. 112/1 An object may be eidetically seen either immediately after it has been removed from sight or after a considerable period of time..has elapsed. **1930** O. OESER tr. *Jaensch's Eidetic Imagery* 1 Eidetics—the theory of eidetic or perceptual images. **1931** *Brit. Jrnl. Psychol.* July 95 The most vivid and original fantasias were produced by eidetic children. **1939** J. D. S. PENDLEBURY *Archaeol. of Crete* v. 275 Snijder has produced some remarkable parallels between Minoan art and that of a class of people known as 'eidetics'. **1943** H. READ *Education through Art* iv. 83 But generally Jaensch's attempt to force racial distinctions..contradicts the whole genetic theory of eidetics. **1949** KOESTLER *Insight & Outlook* xxvi. 361 There are people endowed with the faculty of eidetic imagery. **1970** *Nature* 17 Jan. 227/1 Many people may wish for a 'photographic memory', an ability which has been referred to by psychologists as eidetic imagery. *Ibid.* 227/2 Only thirty-five of the children were classified as eidetic. *Ibid.*, The eidetics claimed that they were not simply remembering what had been in the picture. *Ibid.* 27 June 1268/1 Can a purely binocular pattern..be stored eidetically?

eidograph (ˈaɪdəgrɑːf, -æ-). [f. Gr. εἶδο-ς form + γράφειν to sketch.] (See quot.)

1801 HUTTON *Course Math.* (1828) II. 81 Professor Wallace's eidograph may be advantageously employed. **1869** *Eng. Mech.* 3 Dec. 288/1 The eidograph is a correct instrument for enlarging or reducing drawings.

‖**eidolon** (aɪˈdəʊlən). *Pl.* sometimes **-a.** [a. Gr. εἴδωλον (see IDOL, IDOLUM) image, spectre, phantom.] An unsubstantial image, spectre, phantom.

1828 CARLYLE *Misc.* (1857) I. 137 Flying through the air, and living..with mere Eidolons. **1830** SCOTT *Demonol.* i. 36 Calling up his eidolon in the hall of his former greatness. *a* **1849** POE *Dreamland*, An Eidolon named Night On a black throne reigns upright. **1850** MRS. BROWNING *Poems* II. 155 How Ulysses left the sunlight For the pale eidola race. **1875** B. TAYLOR *Faust* I. xxi. 193 It is a magic shape, a lifeless eidolon. **1876** LOWELL *Among my Bks.* Ser. II. (1873) 174 No real giant, but a pure eidolon of the mind.

b. *Optics.*

1881 G. R. PIGGOTT in *Nature* No. 622. 515 If [the objects are] transparent..strange eidola are generated difficult of interpretation and dispersion.

Hence **eiˈdolic** *a.*, of the nature of an eidolon. **eiˈdoloclast** [f. Gr. κλάστης breaker; cf. *iconoclast*], one who demolishes idols.

1881 G. R. PIGGOTT in *Nature* No. 622. 515 The earlier.. plates..teem with eidolic varieties of form. **1824** DE QUINCEY *Goethe* Wks. 1863 XII. 191 Let the object of the false worship..be made his own eidoloclast.

Eidophusikon (aɪdəˈfjuːzɪkɒn). Also -con. [f. Gr. εἶδο-ς form + φυσικόν natural, f. φύσις nature.] A kind of magic lantern showing a series of pictures illustrative of some occurrence, invented by Philip de Loutherbourg *c* 1780.

a **1800** S. PEGGE *Anecdotes* (1803) 252 How otherwise is the next generation to understand what is meant by the *Lyceum*, the *Eidophusicon*, Sir Ashton Lever's *Holophusicon*, Walker's *Eidouranion*? **1866** *Nature & Art* I. 162/2 In 1782 De Loutherbourg took the theatre for the exhibition of his *Eidophusikon*... He confined the Eidophusikon for the most part to the exhibition of English landscapes under different conditions of light and shadow. **1934** *Burlington Mag.* Feb. p. xv/1 De Loutherbourg's 'Eidophusikon' of movable representations of natural effects which caused the world to wonder when displayed in 1782.

†**eidouˈranion.** [f. Gr. εἶδ-ος form + οὐραν-ός heaven.] The name given to a mechanical contrivance for representing the motions of the heavenly bodies; cf. ORRERY.

a **1800** [see EIDOPHUSIKON]. **1825** MAR. EDGEWORTH *Frank* (Sequel) (ed. 2) II. 243 He saw in large letters.. Orrery and Eidouranion. **1829** PEACOCK *Misfort. Elphin* 82 Astronomy..elevating the mind, as the eidouranion lecturers have it, to sublime contemplations.

eidyll, -ic, var. of IDYLL, -IC.

eie, obs. form of ANY, AWE, EYE.

Eifel (ˈaɪfəl). The name of a plateau in Western Germany, used *attrib.* to designate a subdivision of Middle Devonian in the region so named, and the rocks. Hence **Eifelian** (aɪˈfiːlɪən) *a.* and *sb.* [ad. F. *eifélien* (A. H. Dumont 1848, in *Mém. de l'Acad. R. des Sciences*, etc., *de Belgique XXII.* 67)].

1853 *Q. Jrnl. Geol. Soc.* IX. 20 The Eifelian limestone and schists of Belgium and the Rhenish provinces. *Ibid.* 23 The *Système eifelien* of M. Dumont is formed of three distinct groups,—the Eifel limestone, Eifel fossiliferous schists, and the red sandstones and conglomerates. **1879** *Encycl. Brit.* X. 341/2 Stringocephalus group, consisting of the great Eifel limestone with underlying crinoidal beds. **1895** J. D. DANA *Man. Geol.* (ed. 4) 626 The Lower, Middle, and Upper divisions are named (1) the Rhénan, (2) the Eifelian, and (3) the Famennian. **1912** A. J. JUKES-BROWNE *Strat. Geol.* (ed. 2) 217 Middle Devonian. This also comprises two divisions, the Eifelian and the Givetian. **1957** *Encycl. Brit.* VII. 289/2 The Eifelian (Couvinian in Belgium) consists of limestones and shales abounding in corals and brachiopods. **1963** D. W. & E. E. HUMPHRIES tr. *Termier's Erosion & Sedimentation* xiii. 290 Most of the others are Eifelian, and the reef barrier seems to have persisted almost to the Late Devonian.

eiffule, obs. form of AWFUL.

eigen- (ˈaɪgən). G. *eigen* OWN, proper, peculiar, characteristic, used in adoptions or partial translations of G. compounds in *Math.* and *Physics*, as EIGENTON, EIGENFUNCTION; hence employed as comb. form in many scientific compounds, as ***eigenload***, ***-period***, ***-solution***, ***-state***, ***-vector***, ***-vibration*** (see quots.).

1930 Eigenstate [see EIGENVALUE]. **1940** *Chambers's Techn. Dict.* 283/1 *Eigenperiod, eigenton*, frequencies at which acoustic resonance is experienced in rectangular chambers, because of continued reflections between opposite walls. **1947** *Jrnl. R. Aeronaut. Soc.* LI. 204 A complete theory of the conditions for the existence, and the form of the self-equilibrating orthogonal and load systems (eigenloads).. which vary similarly along all generators, is given. **1951** *Rev. Mod. Physics* 1 (*title*) Approximate eigen-solutions. **1955** *Electronic Engin.* XXVII. 200 An infinite line of similar quadripoles each with matrix A connected in cascade.. must be a vector such that the effect of operating on it with A is to leave it unaltered except for a change in magnitude. .. Any vector..fulfilling this condition is called an eigen-vector of the operator matrix H. **1955** W. PAULI *Niels Bohr* 39 The transformation..can be interpreted as replacing every emission operator by an absorption operator of the same eigen-vibration *without* interchange of particle and anti-particle. **1955** H. B. G. CASIMIR in W. Pauli *Niels Bohr* 131 The remarkable feature of Bose-Einstein condensation is that a sizable fraction of the particles is forced into the very lowest eigenstate, a state which should have curious and essentially non-classical properties. **1957** L. FOX *Two-point Boundary Probl.* vii. 162 Third, if the vector y is an approximation to any eigenvector y_k, so that, in 18, a_k is much greater than any other a_r, then first-order changes in y give rise to second-order changes in λ, and the eigenvalue is determined more accurately than its eigenvector. **1968** C. G. KUPER *Introd. Theory Superconductivity* ix. 150 Likewise, $b\phi_n$ is either zero or an eigenstate with energy $E_n - \hbar\omega$.

ˈeigenfrequency. *Physics.* [tr. G. *eigenfrequenz.*] One of the frequencies that cause a given system to vibrate; a resonant frequency.

1955 W. HEISENBERG in W. Pauli *Niels Bohr* 14 Schrödinger attempted..to resolve quantum theory into a simple classical wave theory. The motive for this attempt was the discovery that the discrete eigenvalues appeared in wave mechanics not as energies, but as the eigenfrequencies of waves.

ˈeigenfunction. *Physics.* [tr. G. *eigenfunktion.*] A solution of a differential equation possessing solutions only for special values of a parameter.

1926 *Proc. R. Soc.* A. CXII. 661 A set of independent solutions, which may be called eigenfunctions. **1927** [see EIGENVALUE]. **1938** *Nature* 16 Apr. 668/1 The homopolar or bond eigenfunction method associated with the names of Heitler, London, Slater and Pauling. **1946** E. C. TITCHMARSH (*title*) Eigenfunction expansions associated with second-order differential equations. **1951** *Rev. Mod. Physics* XXIII. 1/2 The eigenfunction of a bound state.

eigenton, -tone (ˈaɪgəntəʊn). *Acoustics.* [a. and tr. G. *eigenton.*] A frequency at which acoustic resonance characteristically occurs in an enclosure.

1940 [see EIGEN-]. **1962** A. NISBETT *Technique Sound Studio* iii. 57 The even harmonics of the eigentones—the basic resonances of the room—will be missing. **1968** CHOMSKY & HALLE *Sound Pattern Eng.* 352 The feature of 'proper pitch' (*Eigenton*)..subsumes the phonetically quite different features of rounding and backness.

ˈeigenvalue. *Physics.* [tr. G. *eigenwert.*] One of those special values of a parameter in an equation for which the equation has a solution (see quot. 1938).

1927 *Nature* 23 July 117/1 Among those..trying to acquire a general acquaintance with Schrödinger's wave mechanics there must be many who find their mathematical equipment insufficient to follow his first great problem—to determine the eigenvalues and eigenfunctions for the hydrogen atom. **1930** P. A. M. DIRAC *Princ. Quantum Mech.* iii. 35 The physical meaning of an eigenvalue is that there exists a state, namely, the eigenstate belonging to it, such that a measurement of the observable when the system is in this state will certainly give for result just this eigenvalue. **1938** R. W. LAWSON tr. *Hevesy & Paneth's Man. Radioactivity* (ed. 2) viii. 93 A single-valued, finite, and continuous solution of the differential equation is found only for particular values of the parameter E which occurs in the equation, and these are the 'proper'- or 'eigen'-values of the differential equation. **1939** A. S. EDDINGTON *Philos. Phys. Sci.* 162 In mathematical language [existence is represented by] a symbol J with two eigenvalues, which are most conveniently taken to be 1, standing for existence, and 0, standing for non-existence. **1951** *Rev. Mod. Physics* XXIII. 1/2 The reason why we choose a as the known parameter and b as the eigen-value. **1955** [see EIGENFREQUENCY]. **1958** P. A. M. DIRAC *Princ. Quantum Mech.* (ed. 4) ii. 36 The set of eigenvalues of a real dynamical variable are just the possible results of measurements of that dynamical variable and the calculation of eigenvalues is for this reason an important problem.

eigh (eɪ), *int. dial.* [cf. EH, EY.] An exclamation expressing wonder or asseveration.

1750 J. COLLIER (Tim Bobbin) *Wks.* (1819) 54 *Mary.* Is Serots o' Rutchots so honsome? *Tim.* Eigh, hoos meeterly. **1755** JOHNSON, *Eigh*, an expression of sudden delight. **1775** in ASH. **1812** W. TENNANT *Anster F.* v. i, Eigh! I would kiss them. **1867** J. P. MORRIS *Selby Beck Dobby* 5 (*Lanc. Gloss.*) Eigh, ther's many a million on 'em.

eighe, obs. form of AWE.

eight (eɪt), *a.* and *sb.* Forms: α. 1 ahta, eahta, æhte, 2 ehte, (*Orm.*) ehhte, 3 æhte, eahte, 3–5 eyȝt(e, eiȝ-, eih-, eyhte, (3 eȝte, eyth), 4–6 eyght(e, (4 eheit, heyt, eyt, ȝit(t, 5 eght, eyȝthe), 6– eight. β. 3–5 acht, aght, aȝt(e, aht(e, *Sc.* auht(e, 5 *Sc.* awcht, 4– *Sc.* aucht, 6– *Sc.* aught. [Com. Teut.

and Aryan: OE. *ahta*, *eahta*, *æhte*, Northumb. *æhto*, = OFris. *achta*, *achte*, *acht*, OS. *ahto* (Du. *acht*), OHG. *ahto* (MHG. *ahte*, mod.G. *acht*), ON. (**ahta*) *átta* (Sw. *åtta*, Da. *otte*), Goth. *ahtau*; cf. L. *octo*, Gr. *ὀκτώ*, OIr. *ocht*, Lith. *asztûni*, Skr. *ashtáu*.]

The cardinal numeral next after seven, represented by the symbols 8 or viii.

A. as *adj.*

1. a. In concord with sb. expressed.

Beowulf 2075 (Th.) Heht ða..eahta mearas..on flet teon. *a* **1000** *Menologium* 95 (Gr.) þæs emb ahta and nigon Dogera rimes. **1070** *O.E. Chron.* (Laud MS.) Turold abbot and æhte siþe twenti Frencisce men mid him. *c* **1200** ORMIN 4327 Rihht ehhte siþe an hunndredd. *a* **1225** *Ancr. R.* Pref. 23 This an Boc is todealet in eahte lesse Boke. **1297** R. GLOUC. (1810) 385 As in þe ȝer of grace a þousend ȝer yt was And four score & eyȝte. *a* **1300** *Cursor M.* 188 He heled on al vnfere þat seke was thritte and aht yeir. **1375** BARBOUR *Bruce* XI. 523 Aucht hundreth armyt, I trow, thai weir. *c* **1425** WYNTOUN *Cron.* VI. viii. 104 Aucht hundyr wynter and seventy. *c* **1489** CAXTON *Sonnes of Aymon* 210, I shall make them to be accompanyed of eyghte erles. **1513–75** *Diurn. Occurr.* (1833) 10 In the year of God j^m. v^c. twantie aucht yeiris. **1541** ELYOT *Image Gov.* (1549) 80 In eight the first yeeres of his empire. **1631** MILTON *Epit. Mchness. Winchester* 7 Summers three times eight save one She had told. *a* **1758** RAMSAY *Poems* (1844) 83 Twa times aught bannacks in a heap. **1735** POPE *Prol. Sat.* 182 The Bard.. strains from hard-bound brains, eight lines a year. **1885** BALL *Story of the Heavens* 146 An interval of eight years.

b. (*an*) *eight days* = a week.

c **1160** *Hatton Gosp.* John xx. 26 Efter ehte [*c* **1000** eahta] daȝen hys leorning-cnihtes wæren inne. **1340** *Ayenb.* 45 Naȝt uor ane monþe ne to eȝte dayes: ac ine one zelue day. **1611** BIBLE *Luke* ix. 28 About an eight dayes after these sayings. **1664** EVELYN *Kal. Hort.* (1729) 194 Eight Days after, prick them forth at distances.

2. a. With ellipsis of sb., which may usually be supplied from context.

c **1205** LAY. 26502 þer achte þer niȝene. *a* **1225** *Ancr. R.* 334 Al þene world, bute eihte i þen arche. *c* **1325** *E.E. Allit. P.* B. 331 þis meyny of aȝte I schal saue of monnez saulez. *c* **1330** R. BRUNNE *Chron.* (1810) 84 þe date was a þousand & fourscore & auhte. *c* **1340** *Cursor M.* 1927 ȝou ȝitt haue I forborn..My brode benesoun I ȝou ȝyue. *c* **1425** WYNTOUN *Cron.* VII. x. 521 For awcht or ten In comowne prys sawld wes þen. *c* **1460** *Towneley Myst.* 13 We, acht, acht, and neyn, and ten is this. **1588** A. KING tr. *Canisius' Catech.* 161 b, Our Lords beatitudes.. ar rakened aught in number as follouis. **1864** TENNYSON *Aylmer's F.* 638 Eight that were left to make a purer world.

b. *esp.* With omission of *hours*; as *eight o'clock*, etc.

1598 SHAKS. *Merry W.* III. iii. 210 Let him be sent for tomorrow, eight a clock to haue amends. **1601** —— *Twel. N.* V. i. 205 His eyes were set at eight i'th' morning. **1710** STEELE *Tatler* No. 263 ¶1, I went to see him..about Eight a Clock in the Evening. *Mod.* We breakfast at eight.

c. Prosody. *in eight and six* (*four*, etc.): in lines alternately consisting of those numbers of syllables. See B. 2 d.

1590 SHAKS. *Mids. N.* III. i. 25 It shall be written in eight and sixe.

†**d.** *piece of eight* (*reals*): the Spanish 'dollar' or 'piastre' (Sp. *pieza de á ocho*). *Obs.* exc. *Hist.*

1699 TEMPLE *Ess. Constit. & Int. Empire* Wks. 1731 I. 111 Crying up the Pieces of Eight. **1727** A. HAMILTON *New Acc. E. Ind.* (1744) II. 129 At Rambang I bought a cow..for two Pieces of Eight. **1790** BEATSON *Nav. & Mil. Mem.* I. 163 The Salisbury..took a Spanish ship, with one hundred and fifty thousand pieces of eight on board. **1883** R. L. STEVENSON *Treasure Isl.* 225 Pieces of eight.

3. Coupled with a higher cardinal or ordinal numeral following, so as to form a compound (cardinal or ordinal) numeral.

1579 FULKE *Heskins' Parl.* 485 The eight and fortieth Chapter abideth in the exposition of the same text. **1607** TOPSELL *Four-f. Beasts* 259 Every year, upon the eight and twenty day of August, they observe a solemn feast. **1832** MARRYAT *N. Foster* xxii, D—n your eight-and-twenties!

B. as *sb.*

1. The abstract number eight.

1398 TREVISA *Barth. De P.R.* XIX. cxxi. (1495) 922 One doo to seuen makyth the nombre of eyghte. **1808** WILFORD in *Asiat. Res.* VIII. 289 Seven is a fortunate number among the Hindus: eight among the Baudd'hists.

2. A set of eight persons or things.

a. *Card-playing.* A card marked with eight pips.

1598 FLORIO, *Otto*, the number of eight, an eight vpon the cards. **1680** COTTON *Compl. Gamester* in Singer *Hist. Cards* 341 Then he plays his eight of hearts.

b. The crew of a rowing boat, consisting of eight oarsmen; a boat for eight oarsmen. *the Eights*: boat-races at the University of Oxford and elsewhere between the boats of the different colleges, which take place in the Summer Term. Hence *Eights Week*.

1847 *Illust. Lond. News* 28 Aug. 142/1, I rowed in a fairish 'eight'. **1871** M. COLLINS *Mrq. & Merch.* I. i. 6 He..could not be persuaded to be one of the University eight. **1890** *Pall Mall Gaz.* 27 May 6/1 (Oxf. Notes), Tomorrow the eights week will come to an end. **1898** S. LE BLANC-SMITH in W. A. Morgan *The 'House' on Sport* 302 It is more difficult to obtain eight such men than to obtain four, added to which the eight being the heavier boat..greater rigidity is necessitated in the thowl-pin. **1908** *Daily Chron.* 21 May 4/6 Oxford has every right to distinguish her annual inter-college races..as 'The Eights'. **1911** BEERBOHM *Zuleika D.* vi. 81 Isn't it a lovely day for the Eights? **1955** *Times* 6 June 7/7, I noticed in your issue of May 30 your Eights Week chart... You record a double overbump... I should like to know whether this feat has ever been accomplished before in Eights? *Ibid.* 25 July 3/6 Beaumont College, who won their juniors at Molesey a week ago, followed it up by winning the junior-senior eights. **1962** *Ibid.* 13 Feb. 4/6 They have offered to build a racing eight by the hot-moulded effort.

c. Bibliography. *in eights*: an expression indicating the number of leaves in a sheet of an early printed book.

1858 LOWNDES *Bibliogr.* s.v. *Caxton*, It [the Cronicles] terminates on the recto of Y 6 in eights. **1883** GREGOR in *Rolland's Crt. Venus* Introd. 31 It is a quarto, and consists of A to I in eights. *c* **1884** *Brit. Mus. Cat., Sarum Primer* (1538) Register: sigs. A–T, in eights, except T which has four leaves.

d. Metre. *in eights*: in lines of eight syllables. So *in eights and sixes* (*fours*, etc.): in alternate lines of those lengths. Chiefly said of hymns.

3. The figure (8) representing this number; hence anything in the form of an 8; *esp.* a figure made on the ice in skating. Also *figure* (*of*) *eight*; sometimes *attrib.*

1607 DEKKER *Knts. Conjur.* (1842) 15 All our courses are but figures of eight. **1842** TENNYSON *Epic* 10 Cutting eights that day upon the pond. **1851** SIR F. PALGRAVE *Norm. & Eng.* I. 626 The thrice-repeated eight, the eight hundred and eighty and eight. *c* **1860** H. STUART *Seaman's Catech.* 1 What is a figure of eight knot used for? **1876** A. ARNOLD *Persia* in *Contemp. Rev.* June 42 One is surprised to see a European cutting figures of eight upon frozen pools. **1887** *Cornh. Mag.* Mar. 255 They danced a figure 8 chain.

4. Slang phr. *one over the eight*: one alcoholic drink too many. (Cf. ONE *numeral a.*, etc., 1 d.)

1925 FRASER & GIBBONS *Soldier & Sailor Words* 88 *One over the eight*, one drink too many. Slightly intoxicated, the presumption being that an average 'moderate' man can safely drink eight glasses of beer. **1928** *Daily Express* 3 Aug. 7/4 Luton magistrate: What does he mean by 'one over the eight'? ('A glass too many'?)

C. *Comb.*, as *eight-angled*, *-celled*, *-manned*, *-oared*, *-rowed*, *-sided*, *-spoked*, *threaded*, *-wheeled* adjs.; combined with sbs. forming adjs. of dimension, etc., as *eight-bore*, *-inch*, *-line*, *-ounce*, *-penny*; *eight-bearer*, *-company*, *-dog*; *eight-pointer* [POINTER 10], *-wheeler*, *-yarder*; *eight-day* adj.; **eight-coupled** *a.*, having eight coupled wheels; **eight-day clock**, a clock that goes for eight days without winding up; **eight-foil** *Her.* (see quot.); **eight-oar** *a.* (of a boat), manned by eight rowers; also as sb.; **eight-shaft**, a kind of corded fabric; **eightsman**, one of the crew of an eight-oar. (*Eight pence* is almost always written as one word, usu. without hyphen.)

1656 DUGARD *Gate Lat. Unl.* 155 A Dye, four-square though six-sided, and *eight angled. **1908** *Westm. Gaz.* 17 Dec. 7/2 An *eight-bearer yellow chair. **1874** J. W. LONG *Amer. Wild-Fowl Shooting* 23 For flight-shooting, an *8-bore [gun] is as large as is advantageous, and a 10 is sufficiently small. **1882** VINES *Sachs' Bot.* 521 The neck appears to form..an *eight-celled rosette. **1900** *Daily News* 26 June 3/5 An *eight-company battalion. **1893** *English Mechanic* 14 Apr. 181/1 (*heading*) *Eight-coupled goods engines. **1903** *Westm. Gaz.* 3 Oct. 7/3 One of the standard eight-coupled goods engines. **1904** C. S. LAKE *Locomotive* 60 Goods engines with eight-coupled wheels. **1741** RICHARDSON *Pamela* IV. xiii. 77 Being wound up..once a Week, like a good *Eight-day Clock. **1836** DICKENS *Sk. Boz* ii, He took to pieces the eight-day clock. **1850** MRS. BROWNING *Poems* I. 293 An eight-day watch had watchëd she. **1866** HOWELLS *Venet. Life* xviii. 278 Little eight-day-old Venetians. **1876** *Coursing Calendar* 56 An *eight-dog stake was added to the card in the evening. **1825** J. NICHOLSON *Operat. Mechanic* 660 His patent locomotive engine, with two *eight-inch cylinders, weighs five tons. **1860** *All Y. Round* No. 73. 548 The cost of an eight-inch cast-iron gun..is about a hundred pounds. **1847** *Gloss. Terms Brit. Her.*, *Huit-foil*, *Eight-foil*, or *Double quatrefoil*, an *eight leaved flower used as a mark of cadency for the ninth son. **1864** HAZLITT *Early Pop. Poetry* IV. 19 In four *eight-line stanzas. **1874** KNIGHT *Dict. Mech.*, Eight-line Pica. A type whose face has eight times the length of pica. **1897** *Daily News* 3 Feb. 6/4 A woman riding one among seven men on an *eight-manned wheel. **1850** KINGSLEY *Alt. Locke* xii. (1874) 105 An *eight-oar lay under the bank. **1862** *Sat. Rev.* 15 Mar. 300 If Mr. Urquhart could persuade the Universities to substitute Turkish baths for eight-oars. **1874** K. H. DIGBY *Temple of Memory* iii. 40 Their *eight oar'd races. *Ibid.* 41 Their eight-oar'd crew felt quite in Heav'n. **1886** *Outing* (U.S.) VIII. 161/1 On one side an *eight-ounce rod, a thread of silk [etc.]. **1596** SHAKS. *1 Hen. IV*, III. iii. 119 A Trifle, some *eight-penny matter. **1678** *Lond. Gaz.* No. 1348/4 Eight pieces of Eight-peny taffaty Ribon. *c* **1850** *Rudim. Navig.* (Weale) 135 Nails of sorts..8, 10, 24, 30, and 40-penny nails. **1909** *Daily Chron.* 28 Sept. 4/5 A good *eight-pointer, weighing over 15 stone. **1838** *Mass. Agric. Rep. 1837* 24 The Pickwacket corn, an early *eight-rowed variety. **1869** *Rep. Comm. Agric. 1868* (U.S.) 431 A small variety of eight-rowed corn. **1944** *Burpee's Seeds* 26 If you want the best and sweetest for your table, it's true 8-rowed Golden Bantam. **1840** *L'pool Jrnl.* 4 July 1/2 A great Stock of Fustians, in Beaverteens..*Eightshaft, Constitution, and other excellent Cords. **1823** H. J. BROOKE *Introd. Crystallogr.* 133 A series of double *eight-sided pyramids might result from class *h*, *i*, and *k*. **1882** *Standard* 16 Mar. 2, I am, Sir, your obedient servant, An *Eightsman. **1884** F. KROHN tr. *Glaser de Cew's Magn. & Dyn.-electr. Mach.* 33 The armature consists of an *eight-spoked wheel. **1696** BP. PATRICK *Comm. Ex.* xxviii. (1697) 536 Some will have it that [*Maschzar*]..signifies *eighthtredded Linen. **1906** *Daily Chron.* 1 Mar. 7/2 *Eight-wheeled first and third-class carriages. **1904** *Westm. Gaz.* 28 Dec. 3/1 A special mail train consisting of twelve *eight-wheelers. **1930** *Morning Post* 17 June 14/7 He holed an *eight-yarder for a 2 at the sixth.

eight, obs. form of AIT.

1664 EVELYN *Sylva* 42 Some do also plant Oziers in their Eights like Quick-sets, thick, and neer the water.

eight ball, eight-ball, eightball (ˈeɪtbɔːl). *U.S.* [f. EIGHT *a.* and *sb.* + BALL *sb.*[1]] **a.** The black ball, numbered eight, in the North American variety of pool (POOL *sb.*[3] 3); this variety of pool. **b.** Phr. *behind the eight ball*, at a disadvantage; 'snookered'. **c.** *slang.* A Negro. **d.** *slang.* A stupid person. **e.** (See quot. 1937.).

1932 J. T. FARRELL in *This Quarter* Dec. 379 Well, after this, you walk in yere own neighbourhood, eight-ball, or else you can be the guest to yere own funeral. **1932** *World's Work* Feb. 26/1 Mr. Ells, the wizard of the cue, in a position he expertly diagnosed as squarely behind the 8-ball. **1934** J. O'HARA *Appointment in Samarra* (1935) 12 You get signing checks for prospects down at the country club, and you wind up behind the eight-ball. **1937** *Printers' Ink Monthly* Apr. 53/1 *Eight ball*, an astatic microphone characterized by non-directional pick-ups and having a 360-degree beam. **1944** *N.Y. Herald* (Bk. Rev.) 24 Sept. 12/4 An attempt to describe what makes the drawings funny lands you behind the eight ball. **1945** L. SHELLY *Jive Talk Dict.* 11/1 *Eightball*, colored man or obstacle. **1964** D. G. WISBESKI *Otter in House* (1965) x. 157 Okee..broke up a pool game by climbing on the table and taking off with the eight ball.

eighte, eiȝte, obs. ff. AUGHT, property.

eighteen (eɪˈtiːn, ˈeɪtiːn), *a.* and *sb.* Forms: 1 **ehta-týne**, 2 **ehte-tyna**, 3 **æh-**, **ah-**, **ehte-**, **eyȝtetene**, 4–5 **eyȝ-**, **eyghtene**, *Sc.* **auh-**, **auchtene**, 6 **eightene**, 6– **eighteen**. [OE. *e*(*a*)*htatýne*, *-téne*, corresponds to OFris. *achtatîne*, OS. *ahtotian*, *ahtetehan* (Du. *achttien*), OHG. *ahtozehan* (MHG. *ahtzehen*, mod.G. *achtzehn*), ON. *átján* (*átján*, Sw. *adertån*, Da. *atten*), Goth. **ahtau-taihun*; f. OTeut. **ahtau*, *ahtô*, EIGHT + **tehun* TEN; for the divergent Eng. form of the second element, see -TEEN.]

1. The cardinal number next after seventeen; represented by the symbols 18 or xviii.

c **1000** *Ags. Gosp.* Luke xiii. 4 Swa þa ehta-tyne [**1160** *Hatton* ehte-tyna] ofer þa feoll se stypel on siloa. **1205** LAY. 18014 Ohtere cnihten ahtene [*c* **1275** ehtetene] þusen. **1297** R. GLOUC. (1810) 407 In þe ȝer of grace a þousend & four score & eyȝtetene. *c* **1330** R. BRUNNE *Chron.* (1810) 48 þe date of Criste a þousand & mo bi auhtene. **1398** TREVISA *Barth De P.R.* XIX. cxxvi. (1495) 928 Syxe and twelue makyth eyghtene. *c* **1425** WYNTOUN *Cron.* (Mätz), Hundyr byschapis and awchtene. *c* **1440** *Promp. Parv.* 137 Eyȝtene [*P.* eyghtene], *octodecim*. **1559** *Mirr. Mag.*, *Dk. Suffolk* xi. 3 For eightene monthes we dyd conclude a truce. *a* **1641** SUCKLING *Fragm. Aurea* (1646) 35 For your eighteen pence you sit The Lord and Judge of all fresh wit. **1777** ROBERTSON *Hist. Amer.* (1783) II. 356 He appointed Sandoval to command..eight hundred and eighteen foot soldiers. **1828** SCOTT *F.M. Perth* xxvi, About eighteen years since..it chanced, etc.

2. a. quasi-*sb.* = *eighteen-pounder* (see 3).

1833 MARRYAT *P. Simple* xvii, We took a seat upon the long eighteen.

b. *sb. pl.* A sheet of eighteen pages; a book in 18mo.

1683 MOXON *Mech. Exerc.*, *Printing* II. 55 When a Twelves, Eighteens, etc. is wrought. **1795** *Hull Advertiser* 19 Dec. 4/3 A purposely manufactured wove paper, in Octodecimo or Eighteens. **1808** C. STOWER *Printers' Gram.* 199 A plan for imposing a half sheet of eighteens. **1839** T. C. HANSARD *Print. & Type-Founding* 168 Works done in sixteens, eighteens, twenty-fours, or thirty-twos. **1937** E. J. LABARRE *Dict. Paper* 139 *Eighteenmo*, or *eighteens*, are other terms for *decimo-octavo*.

3. a. Comb. *eighteen-headed*, *-hole*(*s* (golf-course), *-tailed*, adjs.; *-tonner*; **eighteen-knot** *a.*, (a vessel) capable of going eighteen knots in an hour; **eighteen-penny** *a.*, that is worth or costs eighteen-pence; also quasi-*sb.*; **eighteen-pounder**, a gun throwing a shot that weighs eighteen pounds. (*Eighteen pence* is often written as one word, with or without hyphen.)

1766 SHARP in *Phil. Trans.* LVII. 84 This has been used many years in St. Bartholomew's hospital, instead of the old *eighteen-headed bandage. **1907** *Westm. Gaz.* 21 Sept. 9/1 The opening of Matlock's new *eighteen-holes golf course. **1944** *Mod. Lang. Notes* Dec. 515, 18-hole golf course. **1884** *Pall Mall G.* 13 Nov. 4/2 Exposed to any hostile Power with an *18-knot cruiser. **1817** COBBETT *Pol. Reg.* 8 Feb. 168 Having an *eighteen-penny-piece put into his hand. **1859** SALA *Tw. round Clock* (1861) 14 Simpson's..eighteenpenny fish ordinary. **1883** H. R. HAWEIS in *Gentl. Mag.* July 47, I proceeded to elicit from the red eighteenpenny [fiddle] all it had to give. **1876** BANCROFT *Hist. U.S.* V. x. 443 The vessel of war suffered severely from two *eighteen-pounders on the Jersey shore. **1748** SMOLLETT *Rod. Rand.* xxviii. (1804) 191 We dressed the wound, and applied the *eighteen-tailed bandage. **1888** (*title*) To Gibraltar and back in an *eighteen-tonner.

b. As in *eighteen-twenties*, the years between 1819 and 1830.

1906 *Daily Chron.* 16 Oct. 4/4 A collection of poems by Frances Ridley Havergal, belonging to the eighteen-seventies. **1909** *Westm. Gaz.* 24 Mar. 2/1 She has abundance of 'sensibility', as that word was understood in the eighteen-twenties. **1924** GALSWORTHY *White Monkey* II. ix, The Hotch-potch Club went back to the eighteen-sixties. **1929** S. ERTZ *Galaxy* x, The eighteen-nineties came, with their revival of interest in literature and painting. **1929** (*title*) The eighteen-seventies: essays by Fellows of the Royal Society of Literature. Ed. H. G. Granville-Barker. **1930** (*title*) The eighteen-eighties. Ed. W. de la Mare.

eighteener (eɪˈtiːnə(r)). [f. EIGHTEEN + -ER.] A cask holding 18 gallons.
1870 E. PEACOCK *Ralf Skirl* II. 117 He finds..our Steven wi' two eighteeners.

eighˈteenmo. [English reading of the symbol 18mo for OCTODECIMO; cf. *twelvemo, sixteenmo*.] Used colloq. in the book trades for OCTODECIMO.
1858 in SIMMONDS *Dict. Trade.*

eighteenth (eɪˈtiːnθ, ˈeɪtiːnθ), *a.* Forms (see EIGHT) + 1 **-tuða, -teða, -téoða** (*fem. neut.* **-ðe**), 3 **-teþe, -tenthe,** 4 **-teoþe,** 6 **-tenth,** 6– **-teenth;** from 6– the *t* of *eight* has been dropped, though some dialects still retain it in pronunciation. [OE. *eahtatéoða*, f. *eahta*, EIGHT + *téoða* tenth; cf. ON. *áttjándi*; in the other OldTeut. langs. this numeral is not recorded. The mod. form is f. EIGHTEEN + -TH[1] (after FOURTH) which has become the ordinal suffix for all numerals above 3.]
Next in order after the seventeenth. Hence **eighˈteenthly** *adv.*, in the eighteenth place.
c **893** K. ÆLFRED *Oros.* VI. ii. §3 On þæm eahteteoþan ȝeare his [Tiberius'] rices..wearð micel þeosternes ofer ealne middangeard. **1258** *Procl. Hen. III* (ed. Ellis 1868) Witnesse vs seluen æt Lundæn þane eȝtetenþe day on the Monþe of Octobr. **1297** R. GLOUC. (1810) 436 Þo deyde Mold þys god quene, enlene hondred ȝer And eyȝteþe after þat God anerþe alyȝte her. *c* **1305** *St. Swithin* 5 in *E.E.P.* (1862) 43 Þe eiȝteteoþe king. **1530** PALSGR. 372 *Dixhuitiesme*, eyghtenth. **1579** FULKE *Heskins' Parl.* 192 The eighteenth Chapter beginneth the exposition. **1611** BIBLE *1 Kings* xv. 1 In the eighteenth yeere of king Ieroboam. **1872** MORLEY *Voltaire* (1886) 4 Voltairism may stand for the name of the Renaissance of the eighteenth century.
1642 SIR W. MONSON *Naval Tracts* III. (1704) 322/2 Eighteenthly, That One of the Three Officers do..reside at Chatham. **1681** H. MORE *Exp. Dan.* App. iii. 303 Eighteenthly, why..should the name..be said to be written?

eightfold (ˈeɪtfəʊld), *a.* (and *adv.*) [f. EIGHT + -FOLD.] **1. a.** Consisting of eight things. **b.** Eight times as great or numerous. Also *adv.*, in eightfold proportion; by eight times.
1557 RECORDE *Whetst.* B ij, Octupla..eightfolde. **1848** MACAULAY *Hist. Eng.* I. 344 The customs had multiplied eightfold within sixteen years.
2. a. *the Eightfold Path*: the Buddhist path to enlightenment or nirvana, comprising eight stages which the aspirant must achieve (see quots.).
[**1845** *Jrnl. Ceylon Branch R. Asiatic Soc.* (1859) 25 The path leading to the cessation from sorrow..is this eminent eight-sectioned path: that is to say, correct views, correct thoughts, correct words, correct conduct, correct modes of obtaining a livelihood, correct efforts, correct meditation and correct tranquillity.] **1871** ALABASTER *Wheel of Law* Introd. 42 The paths of the saints, or the eightfold path of purity. **1877** T. W. R. DAVIDS *Buddhism* ii. 48 The Middle Path..This middle course of a virtuous life, resulted from four fundamental truths..as the path is called 'the Noble Eightfold Path'. **1951** C. HUMPHREYS *Buddhism* viii. 110 The Eightfold Path consists of..*Samma Ditthi*, or Right Understanding..*Samma Sankappa*, or Right Attitude of Mind..*Samma Vacha*, or Right Speech..*Samma Kammanta*, or Right Action..*Samma Ajiva*, or Right Livelihood..*Samma Vayama*, or Right Effort..*Samma Sati*, or Right Recollection..*Samma Samadhi* in its lowest stages..Right Meditation..its highest..the threshold of Nirvana. **1976** H. DUMOULIN *Buddhism in Mod. World* xvii. 248 The ethical contents of the Eightfold Path and of the perfect virtues (pāramitā) are fully appreciated.
b. ***eightfold way*** (Particle Physics): the grouping of hadrons into supermultiplets by means of SU(3).
1961 M. GELL-MANN in Gell-Mann & Ne'eman *Eightfold Way* (1964) 11 (*title*) The eightfold way: a theory of strong interaction symmetry. **1973** L. J. TASSIE *Physics Elem. Particles* xi. 136 The prediction of the Ω^-..was one of the early successes of the eightfold way. **1975** *Sci. Amer.* Oct. 40/2 The eightfold way is only an approximation,..and within the families [of particles] there are significant differences in mass.

eighth (eɪtθ), *a.* and *sb.* Forms: **eahtoða, eah-, ehteða-** (late WS. also **eahteoða**), 1–3 **eah-, ehtuða, -ðe,** 3 **eihteoðe, -tuðe, eg-, ehteðe,** 3–4 **eiȝteðe, -iþe, aȝtþe,** 5 **eghtid, eyted,** 7– **eighth:** from 3– the forms are often identical with those of the cardinal, 3 **eiȝt,** 4 **eȝte, heyt, aght,** 5 **eght,** 5–6 **eyght,** 6 **awght, ayghte,** 5–9 **eight,** *Sc.* **aucht.** [OE. *eahtoða* = OHG. *ahtodo* (MHG. *ahtode, ahtede, ahte,* mod.G. *achte*) repr. OTeut. type *ahˈtoþon-*, f. **ahtau, *ahtô* EIGHT (The OS. *ahtodo*, Goth. *ahtuda* represent a type **ˈahtoðon-*, the result of accent-shifting or of analogy; for the OFris. and ON. forms see EIGHTIN.]
A. *adj.*
1. a. That comes next in order to the seventh.
a **1000** *Menologium* 3 (Gr.) Crist wæs..on þy eahteoðan dæȝ Hælend ȝehaten. *c* **1000** *Sax. Leechd.* II. 298 Eahtoþe is þæs stanes mæȝen, þæt, etc. *c* **1175** *Lamb. Hom.* 81 Þet me sculde in þe ehtuþe dei þet knaue child embsniþen. *a* **1225** *Ancr. R.* 144 Þe eihtuðe þinc is hu muchel is þe mede iðe blisse of heouene. *a* **1300** *Signs before Judgm.* 113 in *E.E.P.* (1862) 10 Þe eiȝt dai so is dotus and þat ful wel þou salt se. *a* **1300** *Cursor M.* 29310 Þe aght case falles all þa in þat any witchecraft gers bigyn. **138.** WYCLIF *Serm.* Sel. Wks. II. 267 Þe eiȝtiþe condicioun. *c* **1400** *Destr. Troy* 6222 The Eghtid Batell in the burgh [was] Vnder Serces..the souerain of Perce. **1477** NORTON *Ord. Alch.* vi. in Ashm. (1652) 100 The vertue of the Eight sphere. **1535** COVERDALE *1 Kings* viii. 66 And on the eight daye he let the people go. **1552** ABP. HAMILTON *Catech.* (1884) 11 The rycht keping of the aucht command. **1605** HEYWOOD *If you know not me* Wks. 1874 I. 207 If it be treason To be the daughter to th' eight Henry, I am a traitor. **1609** BP. HALL *Disswas. Poperie* (1627) 635 Let him heare Origen, what he answers, in the eight volume of his Explanations of Esay. **1664** EVELYN *Kal. Hort.* (1729) 194 The sixth, eighth or tenth day. **1788** GIBBON *Decl. & F.* liii. (1838) V. 266 But the seventh and eighth centuries were a period of discord and darkness. **1887** *Gray's Anat.* (ed. 11) 667 The eighth or auditory nerve.
b. With ellipsis of sb., to be supplied from context. Also in dates, with ellipsis of *day* (of the month).
a **1000** *Guthlac* 1010 (Gr.) Min feorh heonan On þisse eahteðan [nihte] ende ȝeseceð. **1297** R. GLOUC. (1810) 473 The eiȝteþe was, that..citacion non nere Thoru bulle of the pope. *c* **1325** *E.E. Allit. P.* A. 1010 Þe aȝtþe þe beryl cler & quyt. *a* **1400** *Cov. Myst.* (1841) 83 The eyted is contempt of veyn glory in us. *c* **1400** *Apol. Loll.* 77 Þe heyt. Crist biddiþ in þe gospel to His vicar, turn þe swerd in to þe scheþ. **1526** TINDALE *Rev.* xxi. 20 The ayghte berall. **1588** A. KING tr. *Canisius' Catech.* 183 The awght is meiknes quhilk assuages and mitigats al angrie motions of ire. **1642** CHAS. I. *Answ. Petit. Pres. at York* 18 Apr. 1 Our Message of the eighth of April. **1647** LILLY *Chr. Astrol.* xliv. 257 When the Lord of the Ascendant is..in the Antiscion of the Lord of the eighth. **1667** MILTON *P.L.* IX. 67 The space of seven continu'd Nights he [Satan] rode With darkness..On the eighth return'd. **1861** RAMSAY *Remin.* Ser. II. 181 She answered them..'The tongue no man can tame..James Third and Aucht', and drank off her glass.
2. ***eighth part***: one of eight equal parts into which a quantity may be divided.
1523 LD. BERNERS *Froiss.* I. cxxvii. 154 He had nat the eyght part in nombre of men as the frenche kynge had. **1571** DIGGES *Pantom.* III. ix. R ij, An eight part of the great Pyramis HIK. **1660** BLOOME *Archit.* A. c, One eight part of the thicknesse.
3. ***eighth note*** = QUAVER *sb.*[1] *U.S.*
1889 in *Cent. Dict.* **1958** BLESH & JANIS *They all played Ragtime* iv. 77 Unaccented eighth notes alternating with accented quarter notes.
B. *sb.* **1. a.** = *eighth part.* See A. 2.
1557 RECORDE *Whetst.* B ij b, An eight more. **1747** J. LIND *Lett. Navy* i. (1757) 23 The commander in chief is to have one half of the eight. **1842** PRICHARD *Nat. Hist. Man* 391 The Muskhoyees from seven eighths of what is termed the Creek Confederacy.
b. *Mil.* ***eighth-wheel***, when a body of troops revolves upon its centre or one of its ends to the extent of one-eighth part of a circle.
1796 *Instr. & Reg. Cavalry* (1813) 110 The eighth wheel is toward the flank which is to be the head of the column.. Advantage will arise if the eighth wheel is made on the center of each body. *Ibid.* 130 According to the degree ordered, whether half, quarter, or eighth wheel.
2. †**a.** *Music.* = OCTAVE. *Obs.* An interval of seven notes of the diatonic scale.
1597 MORLEY *Introd. Mus.* 70 A third, a Fift, a Sixt, and an eight. **1652** *News fr. Lowe-Countr.* 8 He..Knows Thirds, Fifths, Eights, Rests, Moods, and Time. **1694** *Phil. Trans.* XVIII. 73 He next Observes, that all Progressions by Concords, except by Eighths, produce Discord. **1706** A. BEDFORD *Temple Mus.* iii. 54 They sang the..Part an Eighth, or Seven Notes higher than the Men.
b. The note separated from any given one above or below by an interval of an eighth.
1609 DOULAND *Ornith. Microl.* 15 In b fa ♯ mi, and his eight, you may not sing mi for fa. **1674** PLAYFORD *Skill Mus.* I. i. 3 Which will be the same, and only eights to those above. **1685** BOYLE *Effects of Mot.* vii. 88, I made him raise his Voice to an Eighth.
c. = *eighth note.*
1956 M. STEARNS *Story of Jazz* (1957) xxi. 273 Iturbi produces the feeling that he is playing straight (not dotted) eighths.

eighthly (ˈeɪtθlɪ), *adv.* Also 6–7 **eightly.** [f. EIGHTH + -LY[2].] In the eighth place.
1579 FULKE *Refut. Rastel* 770 Eightly, that images were not set vp to be worshiped. **1607** TOPSELL *Four-f. Beasts* 21 Eightly, a woman dissembling her pregnancy. **1648** D. JENKINS *Wks.* 38 Eightly, We maintaine that the King is King by an inherent birth-right. **1681** H. MORE *Exp. Dan.* App. iii. 298 Eighthly, If any demand why it is said to, etc.

eight hours. A period of time regarded as a fair working-day; freq. *attrib.* (or with possessive apostrophe) and in form *eight-hour* (esp. in phr. ***eight-hour day***).
1845 DISRAELI *Sybil* VI. vi. 430 We have a right to four shillings a day wages, eight hours' work and two pots of ale. —A fair day's wage for a fair day's work. **1865** *Nation* (N.Y.) I. 517/2 It is enough to condemn the scheme of this eight-hour labor league to say that..it would diminish production. **1867** in S. & B. Webb *Hist. Trade Un.* (1920) 309 Such a measure of legislative restriction as shall secure a uniform Eight Hours Bill in factories, exclusive of meal-times. **1869** C. L. BRACE *New West* v. 60 The effort to gain a larger share of the profits of capital by means of an Eight-Hour Law. *Ibid.* 61 From all we can hear, the eight hour movement will soon fall to the ground. **1891** S. WEBB & H. COX (*title*) The eight hours day. **1895** in *Encycl. Brit.* (1902) XXXII. 668/1 Higher wages and eight hours for Government workmen—all these things were in the direction of helping the unemployed. **1899** *Daily News* 6 Mar. 7/1 It should never be forgotten that Alfred was the inventor of the eight hour day. **1902** *Encycl. Brit.* XXXII. 668/1 English public opinion was sceptical when the Trades Union Congresses declared themselves powerless to establish an eight hours' working day without the help of the State. **1910** J. F. FRASER *Australia* 202 The eight hours' day is operative throughout the Commonwealth. **1948** J. BETJEMAN *Coll. Poems* (1958) 227 An eight-hour day for all.

eightieth (ˈeɪtɪɪθ), *a.* (*sb.*) Also 4 **eiȝtithe,** 6 **eyghteth.** [f. EIGHTY: see -TH[1].] The ordinal numeral answering to the cardinal eighty.
1382 WYCLIF *2 Macc.* i. 10 In the hundred ȝeer and eiȝte and eiȝtithe. **1530** PALSGR. 372 *Octantiesme*, eyghteth. **1867** DENISON *Astron. without Math.* 176 Our moon is nearly one eightieth of the earth.

†**ˈeightin,** *a. Obs.* Forms: 3 **eȝten(e)de, ehtende,** (*Orm.*) **ehhtennde,** 4 **eyh-, eytand, -end, aighteden, agt-, aghtand(e, -end, aghten, achtande, aughtene,** 5 **heghten, auchtand,** 6 **egh-, eyȝ-, eyhtyn(e, eighytyn, auchtane, -in.** [The northern form of EIGHTH; perh. of Scandinavian origin; cf. ON. (**ahtundi*) *áttundi*; the intrusive *n*, due to the analogy of *seventh* (cf. ONorthumb. *seofunða*), occurs in OFris. *achtunda*.] = EIGHTH.
c **1200** *Trin. Coll. Hom.* 87 On þe ehtende dai after þe childes burde, þ e frend shopen þe child name. *c* **1250** *Gen. & Ex.* 2543 Ðe eȝtenede king amonaphis, Agenes ðis folc hatel is. *a* **1300** *Cursor M.* 9169 Þe eyhtand sibile bigan to rise. *Ibid.* 10573 Of decembre þe aghten dai Was sco geten. *c* **1340** HAMPOLE *Prose Tr.* (1866) 11 The aughtene commandement es that 'thou sall noghte bere false wyttnes agaynes thi neghteboure'. *c* **1440** *Melayne* 828 All solde come..By the heghten day at none. **1522** *Test. Ebor.* (Surtees) V. 150, I will that my executrix..make an eghtyn day honestly for me. **1558** LYNDESAY *Dreme* 531 The sewint [is callit] Thronus, the auchtin, Cherubin.
b. *Comb.* †**eightin-dele, -dole** [*lit.* eighth part]: an obsolete measure of capacity.
(Wey in *Promp. Parv.* says '⅛ of a coom' = 16 quarts; the *haughendo, aghendole* of Lancashire may be the same word, though identified with HALVENDEAL by the editors of *Lanc. Gloss.* (E.D.S.), who quote conflicting explanations of it as '7 quarts', '8 pounds'.)
1440 *Promp. Parv.* 137 Eyȝtyndele, mesure. **1887** ROGERS *Agric. & Prices* V. 323 At Gawthorp..Shuttleworth pays 6*d.* for an eightendole.

eightsome (ˈeɪtsəm), *a.* Now chiefly *Sc.* Also 4 **aȝt-sum.** [f. on the analogy of OE. phrases like *syxa sum* one of six, where the numeral is in genit. pl. See EIGHT and SOME, and cf. Sc. *twasome, threesome*; -SOME[2].]
Eight together. **eightsome-reel** (after *foursome*), a kind of dance in which eight persons take part. Also *sb.* = an eightsome reel.
c **1325** *E.E. Allit. P.* B. 411 Hym aȝt-sum in þat ark as aþel god lyked. **1745** A. MURRAY *Let.* 3 July in J. J. Murray *Chrons. Atholl & Tullibardine Families* II. 481, I am to be in the 'Eightsome Minuet' if I be at the Ball. **1843** *Blackw. Mag.* LIII. 615 The eightsome-reel of the heptarchy became the pas-seul of the kingdom of England. **1875** W. ALEXANDER *Sks. Life amang Ain Folk* 246 They..caper through the 'eightsome' figure with louder 'hooch-hoochs!' than before. **1899** *Daily Mail* 1 June 4/5 After two o'clock reels and eightsomes were indulged in. **1905** *Westm. Gaz.* 15 Sept. 7/2 A host of charming young Highland girls, with the tartans and badges of their clans, danced the eightsomes and the Reel of Tulloch. **1926** *Glasgow Herald* 7 June 8 The dancing of Scottish reels, foursomes, eightsomes, and sometimes even a sixteensome. **1952** 'J. TEY' *Singing Sands* vii. 109 There was room, with some squeezing, for three eightsomes.

ˈeight-ˈsquare, *a. Obs.* exc. *Naut.* [f. EIGHT + SQUARE, after the logically correct *four-square*; cf. *three-square*.] Having eight equal sides; in the form of a regular octagon, octagonal.
1538 LELAND *Itin.* II. 53 The work is 8-square. **1598** HAKLUYT *Voy.* II. I. 104 It was eight square and very thicke. **1680** *Lond. Gaz.* No. 1499/4 A small eight-square Watch. **1710** *Ibid.* No. 4748/4 Two Silver polished Candlesticks eight square. *c* **1860** H. STUART *Seaman's Catech.* 75 All yards are made eight-square in the centre. **1907** S. E. WHITE *Arizona Nights* I. i. 4 He..carried across his saddle a heavy 'eight square' rifle.
quasi-*adv.* **1679** PLOT *Staffordsh.* (1686) 369 The tower of the Church of Dilhorn..is somewhat remarkable, it being built eight square. **1682** WHELER *Journ. Greece* v. 395 He built a Tower eight square of Marble. *c* **1850** *Rudim. Navig.* (Weale) 114 A short beam..trimmed eight-square.
Hence **eight-square** *sb.*, an octagonal figure; **eight-square** *v.*, to fashion into octagonal shape.
1794 *Rigging & Seamansh.* I. 21 A straight line is then struck..and the eight-square lined from it. *Ibid.* 20 The..side is then canted up and eight-squared.

eighty (ˈeɪtɪ), *a.* (*sb.*) Forms: 1 **(hund)eahtatiȝ, -æhtatiȝ, -ehtatiȝ, -eahtiȝ,** 3–4 **eiȝteti,** 5 **eyȝty,** 6 **eyghty, eightie,** 6– **eighty.** [OE. *hundeahtatiȝ*, f. *hund-* (prefix to the denary numerals: see HUNDRED) + *eahta* EIGHT + *-tiȝ*:—OTeut. **tigiwiz* plur. of **tegu-z* decade (see -TY).]
1. The cardinal number equal to eight tens, represented by 80 or lxxx. Also with omission of sb. and in comb. with numbers below ten (ordinal and cardinal), as *eighty-one, eighty-first,* etc.
c **825** *Vesp. Psalter* lxxxix. [xc.] 10 In mæhtum hundæhtatiȝes ȝera. —— *O.E. Chron.* (Laud MS.) Introd., Gaius Iulius Romana Kasero mid hund ehtatiȝum scipum ȝesohte Brytene. **1297** R. GLOUC. (1810) 478 Endleue hundred ȝer of grace, & eiȝteti & thre. **1375** BARBOUR *Bruce* XVIII. 349 Auchty thousand he wes and ma. **1382** WYCLIF *Isa.* xxxvii. 36 The aungil of the Lord smot in the tentus of Assiries an hundrid and fyue and eiȝteti thousend. *c* **1440**

Promp. Parv. 137 Eyȝty, *octoginta.* **1530** Palsgr. 367 *Octante*, eyghty, lxxx. **1594** Shaks. *Rich. III*, iv. i. 96 Eightie odde yeeres of sorrow haue I seene. **1655** Fuller *Ch. Hist.* ix. 187 Mr. Fox fore-told the ruine and destruction of the Invincible (so called) Armado in the eighty eight. **1771** Raper in *Phil. Trans.* LXI. 533 When the Romans began to coin gold, it did not exceed the eighty-fourth part of their Pound. **1777** Robertson *Hist. Amer.* (1783) II. 217 In the year one thousand four hundred and eighty-five. **1872** Morley *Voltaire* (1886) 47 Aspasia, now over eighty.

2. quasi-*sb.* **a.** The age of eighty years. **b.** ***the eighties***: the years between eighty and ninety in a particular century.

1835 E. Elliot *Poems* 221 He stoop'd no more, like toothless eighty. **1883** Seeley *Expansion of Eng.* 260 Adam Smith, writing in the eighties.

c. Eighty acres of land. *U.S.*

1842 C. M. Kirkland *Forest Life* II. 207 Happy he whose far reaching 'eighties' enclose a sugar-bush. **1872** *Amer. Naturalist* VI. 77 The whole surface of the plains is sere and brown save some 'eighties' or larger tracts that are fenced. **1936** M. H. Bradley *Five-Minute Girl* v. 74 So his ax had set to work on the maples and hemlocks in his north eighty.

3. *Comb.*, as in ***eighty-gun ship, eighty-ton (gun)***.

1747 J. Lind *Lett. Navy* i. (1757) 30, I have known some gentlemen captains of eighty gun ships, who..were not old enough to be lieutenants. **1769** Falconer *Dict. Marine* (1789) Hhijb, The 80-gun ships..begin to grow out of repute. **1874** *Porcupine* 18 Apr. 37/1 The construction of an 80-ton gun at Woolwich is stated to be decided upon. **1880** *Encycl. Brit.* XI. 292/2 In the 80-ton gun powder cubes of 1¼ in. edge are used. **1888** A. C. Gunter *Mr. Potter of Texas* iii, That was the first eighty-ton gun fired in war.

eighty-six. *U.S. slang.* [See eighty *a.* (*sb.*); perh. rhyming slang for nix[1] i.] In restaurants and bars, an expression indicating that the supply of an item is exhausted, or that a customer is not to be served; also, a customer to be refused service. Also *transf.*

1936 *Amer. Speech* XI. 43/1 *Eighty-six*, item on the menu not on hand. **1941** J. Smiley *Hash House Lingo* 58, *86*, sold out. **1944** G. Fowler *Good Night, Sweet Prince* iii. i. 227 There was a bar in the Belasco building,..but Barrymore was known in that cubby as an 'eighty-six'. An 'eighty-six', in the patois of western dispensers, means: 'Don't serve him.' **1971** P. Tamony *Americanisms* (typescript) No. 28. 16 *Eighty-six.* Bar and restaurant usage, 'nix', i.e., customer has had enough to drink or house is out of comestible ordered. Basically, simple rhyming slang but among habitues has as many [e]tymons as Homer had home-places, such probably being boozed up ex cathedra. **1977** *Washington Post* 17 May b1/5, 86 means you're all out of something or you cut some guy off. **1981** W. Safire in *N.Y. Times Mag.* 15 Mar. 10/2 Eighty-six on etymologies for "cocktail".

Hence as *v. trans.*, to eject or debar (a person) from premises; to reject or abandon.

1959 *Observer* 1 Nov. 7/6 'Eighty-sixed some square bankers from the temple'..eighty-sixed means evicted. **1963** J. Rechy *City of Night* ii. 186 I'll have you eighty-sixed out of this bar. **1968** *N.Y. Times* 31 July 29 On the evening of July 22, Mr. Mailer was filming a dream sequence at the house of Alfonso Ossorio in East Hampton, when Mr. Smith came into the house. 'He told me, "You're 86'd",' Mr. Smith recalled yesterday. This is a barroom phrase that means 'you're banned in here'. **1980** *New Yorker* 30 June 67 Most of the program was devoted to the lessons in campaign management that could be learned from Presidential races, real and fictional (A scene was shown from the movie 'The Candidate', in which the media adviser said to Robert Redford, 'O.K., now, for starters, we got to cut your hair and eighty-six the sideburns').

eigne (eɪn), *a. Law.* [corrupt spelling of ayne, ad. Fr. *aîné.*] First-born, eldest; see ayne.

1586 Ferne *Blaz. Gentrie* 286 Hee hath issue a sonne naturall by a concubine and after marryeth the same concubine, him the lawyers of Englande, call a Bastarde eigne. **1613** Sir. H. Finch *Law* (1636) 253 Where there be many of one name, diuersitie of the names must be put by addition of eigne, puisne, etc. **1677** Wycherley *Pl. Dealer* iv. i, Thou art not so much as Bastard eigne. **1809** Tomlins *Law Dict.*, *Eigne*, eldest or first-born; as bastard eigne.

b. ***eigne title***: a prior, superior title. ***eigne estate***: one that is entailed.

1619 Dalton *Countr. Just.* lxxxiii. (1630) 213 By reason of the eigne title of the disseisee. *c* **1640** J. Smyth *Hundred of Berkeley* (1885) 264 Hee was remitted to his eigne estate taile, to him and to the heires males of his body.

eigrette, obs. var. of aigrette 2.

1765 Foote *Commissary* i. i, Take care of the eigrette, leave the watch upon the table.

eik (iːk). *Sc.*

1. 'The liniment used for greasing sheep' (Jam.).

2. 'A sort of unctuous perspiration that oozes through the pores of the skin of sheep in warm weather (Roxb.); often called ***sheep-eik***' (Jam.).

1641 *Parl. Proc.* 8 Sept. in *Scotch Acts* (1870) V. 598 Bicaus the eik and filthines of the samene [wooll] is a great prejudice to the workeris thairof.

eik, Sc. form of eke *sb.* and *v.*

eikon, var. of icon.

eil, obs. form of ail *a.* and *v.*

eild (iːld), *a. Sc.* [? var. of yeld *a.*] Of a cow: Not giving milk, from being in calf, or from age.

1822 W. J. Napier *Pract. Store-farming* 252 The gimmers giving milk will consume more grass than when eild. **1837** Lockhart *Scott* (1839) VI. 21 No man could guess at how large a price Constable had estimated his eild kye.

eild, var. eld, *Obs.*, old age, eld *v.* to grow old.

'eild, var. of yield *v.*, to requite.

eildin(g, var. ff. elding, fuel.

eildritch, var. of eldritch.

†**eileber.** *Obs.* [App. a corrupt form of OE. *éalifer* (? f. *éa* river + liver), a plant used as a remedy for liver disease and lumbago; ? Water Liverwort (*Ranunculus aquatilis*).] Some plant; in Gerard's 'List of names gathered out of antient, written and printed copies' identified with *Alliaria* (*i.e.* Sauce-alone, *A. officinalis*).

[*c* **1000** *Sax. Leechd.* II. 64 Ealifer hatte wyrt.] **1597** Gerard *Herbal* App. to Table. **1847** in Halliwell. **1878** in Britten & Holl.

eilet, obs. form of eyelet.

eilich, *a. Obs.*, dreadful, terrible: see awly.

†**ei'lland.** *Obs. rare.* Also eillond. [OE. *ęlland*, f. *ęl-* (:—OTeut. *aljo- other) + land; cf. OS. *elilendi* adj. foreign, OHG. *ali-*, *elilanti* foreign, of another country, hence wretched (mod.G. *elena*). (The spelling is perh. due to confusion with *eiland* island.)] A foreign land.

Beowulf 3020 (Gr.) Eorl..sceal..el land tredan. *a* **1300** *Cursor M.* 2189 Til eillandes þir þam drou.

eilond, obs. form of island.

-ein, -eine, variants of -in[1] and -ine[5] used as suffixes in the names of certain chemical compounds containing anhydrides, esp. phthalic anhydride. In bases the ending is usually *-eine*, and in non-bases *-ein*.

1871 *Jrnl. Chem. Soc.* XXIV. 834 (*heading*) Fluorescein and Fluorescin. *Ibid.*, By heating together phthalic anhydride and resorcin, Baeyer has obtained a body which he calls fluorescein. **1884**, etc. [see cysteine]. **1889** *Jrnl. Chem. Soc.* LVI. 1153 Catecholphthaleïn..is obtained when phthalic anhydride (3 parts) is heated with catechol and zinc chloride. **1932** *Chem. Abstr.* 1388 One of the alleged secondary alkaloids, nicoteine, isolated by Pictet, is shown to have no existence. **1949** *Blakiston's New Gould Med. Dict.*, *Narceine*, an alkaloid contained in morphine.

eine, obs. pl. of eye.

‖**einfühlung** ('aɪnfyːlʊŋ). *Psychol.* Also Ein-. [G., see empathy.] = empathy.

1904, etc. [see empathy]. **1925** I. A. Richards *Princ. Lit. Crit.* xv. 108 The work done by Lipps, Groos and others on *einfühlung*, or empathy. **1929** C. I. Lewis *Mind & World-Order* ii. 41 'Real duration'..is something which is immediate, in his own case, and is to be apprehended in its other manifestations only by empathy or *einfühlung.* **1936** *Times Lit. Suppl.* 2 May 374/2 If..a doctrine of Einfühlung could be established. **1966** *English Studies* XLVII. 311 Some of the elements which have caused Vernon Lee..to be almost forgotten by a later age, to the point of not even crediting her with the introduction of the idea of *Einfühlung* or empathy.

einkorn ('aɪnkɔːn). [G., f. *ein* one + *korn* seed.] An inferior species of wheat, *Triticum monococcum.*

[**1884** tr. *De Candolle's Orig. Cultivated Plants* v. 365 The one-grained wheat, or little spelt, *Einkorn* in German, is distinguished..by a single seed in the little ear.] **1904** T. F. Hunt *Cereals in America* iv. 48 Einkorn never..gives rise to a fertile cross with common wheat. **1924** J. A. Thomson *Science Old & New* xliii. 250 Inferior cultivated wheats like Emmer, Spelt, and Einkorn. **1965** *Jrnl. R. Hort. Soc.* XC. 284 The basic crops of neolithic agriculture were the wheats einkorn..and emmer.

einsent, obs. form of enceinte *a.*

einsiȝt, obs. var. of eyesight.

Einstein ('aɪnʃtaɪn, -staɪn). The name of Albert *Einstein* (1879–1955), German physicist and mathematician, used *attrib.* or in the possessive to designate certain theories and principles enunciated by him or arising out of his work.

1922 Glazebrook *Dict. Appl. Physics* II. 359/2 According to Einstein's theory all energy possesses mass. *Ibid.* 595/1 Richardson has shown that Einstein's equation may be derived by thermodynamic and statistical methods. **1923** J. M. Murry *Pencillings* 68 To some the Einstein theory may show the way of reconciliation. **1927** A. S. Eddington *Stars & Atoms* 52 The Einstein effect is proportional to the mass divided by the radius of the star. **1934** Webster, *Einstein shift*, the difference in wave-length..between light emitted by a source of a definite nature in the sun..and that emitted by a like source on the earth. **1958** *Listener* 11 Dec. 973/1 Eddington remained faithful to this idea that the universe evolved from the static but unstable Einstein universe. **1967** *Handbk. Chem. & Physics* (Chem. Rubber Co.) (ed. 48) F-69, *Einstein theory for mass-energy equivalence*, the equivalence of a quantity of mass *m* and a quantity of energy *E* by the formula $E = mc^2$. The conversion factor c^2 is the square of the velocity of light.

Einstein-Bose ('aɪnʃtaɪn'bəʊs, -'bəʊz, -st-). *Physics.* [The names of Albert *Einstein* (see prec.) and S.N. *Bose* (see boson).] A designation used as an alternative to Bose-Einstein, as ***Einstein-Bose particle, statistics***, etc.

[**1929** Dirac in *Proc. Cambr. Philos. Soc.* XXV. 62 The so-called 'statistics' of Einstein-Bose or Fermi applies only to an assembly of actual systems which could interact with each other.] **1931** *Physical Rev.* XXXVII. 333 We..justify the assumption that the clusters satisfy the Einstein-Bose or Fermi-Dirac statistics according to whether the number of particles in each cluster is even or odd. **1938** *Proc. R. Soc.* A. CLXVI. 127 (*heading*) Quantum theory of Einstein-Bose particles and nuclear interaction. **1955** R. D. Evans *Atomic Nucleus* iv. 178 Photons and α particles obey Einstein-Bose statistics.

Einsteinian (aɪnʃ'taɪnɪən, -st-), *a.* [f. the name of Albert *Einstein* + -ian.] Pertaining to or characteristic of Einstein or his theories.

1925 C. E. M. Joad *Mind & Matter* 46 In an Einsteinian universe the velocity of light is the greatest velocity possible. **1928** *Observer* 25 Mar. 9/4 Einsteinian physics. **1937** *Mind* XLVI. 101 He rejects the view which would confine the importance of the Einsteinian relativity theory to scientific method. **1941** D. L. Sayers *Mind of Maker* iii. 33 We may say..that Einsteinian physics has superseded Newtonian physics. **1959** *Encounter* Dec. 64/2, I confused Bergsonian time with Einsteinian time. **1968** E. McGirr *Lead-Lined Coffin* ii. 55 Once in every few years one of these thousands of men shows he has a brain of Einsteinian capacity.

einsteinium (aɪnʃ'taɪnɪəm, -st-). *Chem.* [f. the name of Albert *Einstein* + -ium.] An artificially produced radioactive element. Symbol Es. Atomic number 99. Atomic mass of isotope 253 (1967) 253·0847.

1955 [see fermium]. **1958** *Times* 29 Aug. 6/3 The following 10 [transuranic elements] were known.. einsteinium (99), fermium (100). **1967** *New Scientist* 6 July 22/2 Oak Ridge National Laboratory says it has succeeded in separating roughly one ten millionth of an ounce of einsteinium, the transuranic element first discovered in 1954.

eir(e, obs. form of air, eyre, heir.

eirack ('ɛːrək, 'ɪərək). *Sc.* Also earack, ea-, ee-, erock. [a. Gael. *eireag* = Ir. *eireog.*] A hen of the first year.

1791 A. Wilson *Laurel Disput.* Wks. (1846) 123 Three fat eerocks fastened by the legs. **1795** *Statist. Acc.* XX. 8 (Jam.) *Eirack*, a chicken. **1831** J. Wilson in *Blackw. Mag.* XXIX. 306 A simultaneous charge of cocks, hens, and earocks!

[**'eirant,** erroneous form of haurient, *Obs.*

1587 Fleming *Contn. Holinshed* III. 1370/1 A fesse indented sable charged with foure leuses heads eirant.]

eird, obs. form of earth; var. erd, *Obs.*, dwelling.

eirdly, Sc. form of earthly.

eirede, var. erede *a.*, *Obs.*, lacking counsel: cf. *Æ- prefix.*

eirenarch ('aɪrɪnɑːk). [ad. Gr. εἰρηνάρχης, f. εἰρήνη peace + ἄρχειν to rule. (In English Latin *eirenarcha* is used for 'justice of the peace'.)] An officer charged with preserving the public peace. Hence **eire'narchical** *a.*, having the function of an eirenarch. **'eirenarchy** (see quot.).

1641 J. Jackson *True Evang. T.* iii. 173 The Messias..is also Eirenarchicall, and atones. **1656** Blount *Glossogr.*, *Eirenarchy*, the office or Government of a Constable, or a Iustice of the Peace. **1721–1801** Bailey, *Eirenarch*, a Justice of the Peace. **1775** in Ash. **1867** Pearson *Early & Mid. Ages Eng.* I. 48 Under these, probably, were eirenarchs, or village bailiffs.

eirenic, (aɪ'riːnɪk), *a.* [ad. Gr. εἰρηνικός, f. εἰρήνη peace.] Tending to or productive of peace. (See also irenic *a.* and *sb.*)

1885 *Ch. Q. Rev.* Jan. 283 The 'eirenic' efforts or aspirations of such divines. **1938** *Sunday Times* 13 Feb. 14/3 In view of the eirenic purpose of the Commission, this omission is the more regrettable. **1964** P. F. Anson *Bishops at Large* i. 37 The Bishop of Iona made good speed on his eirenic journey.

eirenical, var. irenical *a.*

1890 Gasquet & Bishop *Edw. VI & Bk. Com. Prayer* 28 The choice of Quignon's work for a model had an aspect almost eirenical. **1891** *Tablet* 3 Jan. 11 The whole Pastoral ..is decidedly eirenical. **1958** *Spectator* 30 May 702/3 The scholarly writer and preacher and most eirenical divine, Richard Baxter.

‖**eirenicon** (aɪ'riːnɪkɒn). [ad. Gr. εἰρηνικόν, neut. of εἰρηνικός: see eirenic *a.*] A proposal tending to make peace; an attempt to reconcile differences.

[**1656** (*title*) Εἰρηνικόν, a Poeme, wherein is persuaded the composing of the differences of all the faithfull.] **1865** Pusey *Truth Eng. Ch.* (title-page), The Church of England a Portion of Christ's One Holy Catholic Church, and a Means of restoring visible Unity: An Eirenicon. **1886** *Pall Mall G.* 19 June 1/2 We wait with interest to see Mr. Chamberlain's response to the new Eirenicon.

†**'eires.** *Obs. rare*$^{-1}$. Some kind of hawk. (? Mistake for *eyas.*)

1655 Walton *Angler* (ed. 2) 19 The Eires, the Brancher, the Ramish Hawk, the Haggard and the two sorts of Lentners.

ˈeirmonger. *Obs.* [f. *eir-en*, ME. pl. of EGG + MONGER.] A dealer in eggs.

c**1305** *St. Swithin* 69 in *E.E.P.* (1862) 45 Miȝte eirmongers nou fare so, þe baldelikere hi miȝte Huppe ouer diches.

eirn, obs. form of YEARN.

eiry, var. of AERY, EERIE, *a.*

eise, ? obs. var. of EASY.

eisegesis (aɪsɪˈdʒiːsɪs). [f. Gr. εἰς in, into + *-egesis* of EXEGESIS.] The interpretation of a word or passage (of the Scriptures) by reading into it one's own ideas. Hence **eiseˈgetical** *a.*

1878 P. SCHAFF *Through Bible Lands* I. v. 53 The eisegetical manner of those allegorical and typological exegetes who make the Scriptures responsible for their own pious thoughts and fancies. **1892** *N.Y. Evangelist* 3 Mar. 4/4 (Funk), Dr. Elliot..held firmly to the doctrine that exegesis, and not 'eisegesis', is the province of the student of the Scriptures. **1924** H. E. FOSDICK *Mod. Use Bible* iii. 87 The reformers..could use eisegesis instead of exegesis on many a passage which they thought they were literally interpreting. **1958** *Times Lit. Suppl.* 3 Jan. 10/1 Fully aware of the perils of *eisegesis*, Dr. Grant pronounces quite firmly against any such reverence for philosophy or theology as would empty history of meaning.

†**ˈeisell.** *Obs.* Forms: 2–3 aisille, 2–4 eisil, 3–5 aysel(l, -il, -ylle, (4 aycel, -zell), 4–6 aisel, -il, -ylle, (4 aissil, 5 ascill, ass-, asell(e), 4–7 eisel(l, -ill, eysell(e, -seel, -sil, -syl, -zell, 5 esylle, -zyl, (4 heysyl, 6 esile). [a. OF. *aisil*, *aissil*:—late L. **acētillum*, dim. of *acētum* vinegar.] Vinegar.

c**1160** *Hatton Gosp.* Mark xv. 36 Fylde ane spunge mid eisile. *Ibid.* John xix. 29 Ða stod an fet full aisiles. a**1225** *Ancr. R.* 404 þis eisil..þuruh fulleð mine pine. a**1240** *Wohunge* in *Cott. Hom.* 283 Nu beden ha mi leof..aisille. a**1300** *E.E. Psalter* lxviii. 22 [lxix. 21] In mi thriste with aysile dranke þai me. **138.** *Antecrist* in Todd 3 *Treat. Wyclif* 133 Crist tasted eysel; and þei nolden non but goode wynes. c**1420** *Pallad. on Husb.* VIII. 134 In this moone is made Aisel squillyne. c**1450** MYRC 1884 Loke thy wyn be not eysel. **1557** *Primer, XV Oos* F iv, I beseche thee for the bitternesse of the Aisell and Galle. **1602** SHAKS. *Ham.* V. i. 299 Woo't drinke vp Esile, eate a Crocodile? **1620** VENNER *Via Recta* vi. 94 Eisell..is also a good sauce. **1634** HARINGTON *Salerne Regim.* 67 Summer-sauce should be verjuyce, eyzell or vinegar.

†**ˈeisful,** *a. Obs.* Forms: 1 eȝesfull, 3 æiȝesful, 2–3 eisful. [OE. *eȝesfull*, f. *eȝes-a* (= OS. *egiso*, OHG. *ekiso*:—OTeut. **agison-*, f. **agis-*: see AWE) + -FUL.] Fearful, terrible.

a**1000** *Judith* 21 Ðæs se rica ne wende, Eȝesfull eorla dryhten. c**1175** *Lamb. Hom.* 111 Ðe lauerd scal beon liðe þan godan and eisful þan dusian. c**1205** LAY. 17972 þæt is an æiȝes-ful sune? þæt of þine licame scal cume. a**1225** *St. Marher.* 9 Aȝein þis eisful wiht..help me mi lauerd.

†**ˈeisie,** *v. Obs.* In 2 eisian. [OE. *eȝ(e)sian* = OS. *egisôn*, OHG. *ekisôn*:—OTeut. **agisôjan*, f. **agis-* terror: see AWE *sb.*] *trans.* To frighten.

Beowulf 6 (Gr.) Oft Scyld..eȝsode eorl[as]. c**1175** *Lamb. Hom.* 111 Swa mihtles..þet he his men eisian ne der.

†**ˈeislich,** *a. Obs.* Forms: 1 eȝeslíc, 2 eislic, 3 eiselich, 4 aisliche. [OE. *eȝeslíc*, f. *eȝes-a* terror (see EISFUL) + *-líc*, -LY[1]; cf. OS. *egislîc*, *eislîc*, OHG. *ekislîh*.] Fearful, terrible.

c**888** K. ÆLFRED *Boeth.* xxxv. §6 Ða wæs ðær eac swiðe eȝeslic geatweard, ðæs nama sceolde bion Caron. c**1000** WULFSTAN *Addr. Engl.* in Sweet *Reader* 108 Eall ðæt sindon micle and eȝeslice dæda. c**1175** *Lamb. Hom.* 87 Eislic swei and blawende beman. c**1200** *Trin. Coll. Hom.* 67 To beregen us..wið þe eiseliche shame.

Hence **ˈeisliche** *adv.* (*a*) Fearfully; (*b*) Timidly.

c**1175** *Lamb. Hom.* 41 Heȝe treon eisliche beorninde etforen helle ȝete. c**1394** *P. Pl. Crede* 341 þere y auntrede me in & ai[s]liche y seide.

eissel, Sc. form of EASSEL.

eist, var. of ESTE *a. Obs.* dainty.

Eisteddfod (‖əisˈtɛðvod, aɪsˈtɛdfɒd). [Welsh; lit. 'session', f. *eistedd* to sit.] A congress of (Welsh) bards.

1822 *Ann. Reg.* I. *Chron.* 428 An Eisteddfodd, or Congress of Bards, was held..last week. **1847** *National Cycl.* II. 858 Since the time of Queen Elizabeth no royal commission has been issued for holding an eisteddfod.

Hence **eiˈsteddfodism.**

1868 *Lond. Q. Rev.* Oct. 53 That eisteddfodism by which Mr. M. Arnold seems to have been bitten.

Eisteddfodic (ˌaɪstɛdˈfɒdɪk), *a.* [f. EISTEDDFOD + -IC.] Of or belonging to the Eisteddfod.

1877 J. RHYS *Lect. Welsh Philol.* vi. 314 *Ofydd*..is defined to be an Eisteddfodic graduate who is neither bard nor druid, and translated into ovate. **1894** *Daily News* 31 May 5/4 One of the Eisteddfodic conductors. a**1922** H. JONES *Old Mem.* (1923) i. 29, I pass over the Eistedfodic prizes we won.

eister, obs. Sc. var. of EASTER *a.*

†**eiˈstricion.** *Obs. rare*[−1]. ? Erroneous form of EXTRACTION (OFr. *estracion*).

c**1460** *Pol. Rel. & L. Poems* (1866) 2 Growinge be eistricion, that worthi and wis is, Concayued in wedlocke.

eis wool (aɪs). [G. *eis* ice.] (See quots. 1882, 1957.)

1882 CAULFEILD & SAWARD *Dict. Needlework*, *Eis wool* (sometimes written 'Ice Wool'), a very fine glossy description of worsted wool, made of two-thread thickness, and employed double for making shawls. **1891** *Queen* 17 Oct. 639/3 Twelve balls of eis wool are required. **1957** M. B. PICKEN *Fashion Dict.* 110/1 *Eis wool*, fine, glossy, wiry woolen yarn. Used for clouds, scarfs, etc.

eisy, obs. var. of EASY.

eitch, obs. var. of EATCHE, *Sc.*, adze.

eith, Sc. form of EATH.

either (ˈiːðə(r), ˈaɪðə(r)), *a.* (*pron.*) and *adv.* (*conj.*). Forms: 1 **ǽȝ-**, **ǽȝ-**, **éȝhwæðer**, 1–2 **ǽȝðer**, 2 **eiȝðer**, (3 *Orm.* **eȝȝðer**), 3 **æiðer**, **aieþer**, 2–4 **eiðer**, **eiþer**, 3–5 **aiþer**, **aither**, **ayther**, (**ayder**, 5 **eyder**), 3–6 **ether**, (? 4–6 **aþer**, **ather**, **-ir**, 4 **euther**, **ewther**), 3–7 **eyther**, **-thir**, (5 **eithar**), 6 **eather**, 4– **either**. See also ER. [OE. *ǽȝhwæðer* (contracted *ǽȝðer*) = OHG. *eogihwedar* (MHG. *iegeweder*), f. WGer. **aiwo(n* (in OE. *á*, *ó*) AY, always + **gihwaþaro-z* (in OE. *ȝehwæðer*: see Y- and WHETHER) each of two.

In OE. and early ME. the word appears only in its original sense 'each of two', or as adv. = 'both'; but about the beginning of 14th c. it assumed the disjunctive sense 'one or the other of two' (and the corresponding adverbial use), which properly belonged to OE. *áhwæðer*, *áwðer*, ME. *owþer*, *oþer* (see OUTHER). This disjunctive sense has so far prevailed that in mod.Eng. such expressions as *on either side* = 'on both sides' are felt to be somewhat *arch.*, and must often be avoided on account of their ambiguity. The word OUTHER became obs. in literary use in 16th c.; its mod. dial. forms (pronounced ɔːðə(r)) are popularly regarded as belonging to *either*. (It is not quite clear whether the forms *aþer athir* in Sc. from 14th to 16th c. should not be referred to OUTHER; cf. OE. *áðor*.)

The pronunciation (ˈaɪðə(r)), though not in accordance with the analogies of standard Eng., is in London somewhat more prevalent in educated speech than (ˈiːðə(r)). The orthoepists of 17th c. seem to give (ˈɛːðər, ˈeːðər); Jones 1701 has (ˈeːðər) and (ˈaɪðər), Buchanan (1766) has (ˈaɪðə(r)) without alternative (see Ellis, *Early Eng. Pron.* ix, x.). Walker (1791) says that (ˈiːðə(r)) and (ˈaɪðə(r)) are both very common, but gives the preference to the former on the ground of analogy and the authority of Garrick. Smart (1849) says that 'there is little in point of good usage to choose' between the two pronunciations, though in the body of his dictionary he, like earlier orthoepists, gives (ˈiːðə(r)) without alternative.]

A. *adj.* (*pron.*)

I. Each of the two.

1. a. As adj. used *attrib.*

c**893** K. ÆLFRED *Oros.* I. ix. §1 Hwa is þætte ariman mæȝe hwæt þær moncynnes forwearð on æȝðere hand. **1297** R. GLOUC. (Rolls) 1439 Muche folc in eiþer half to gronde me slou. a**1300** *Cursor M.* 12881 þe holi strem of flum iordane On aeiþer side stude still as stane. **1340** HAMPOLE *Pr. Consc.* 1274 Bot with þe world comes dam fortone, þat ayther hand may chaung sone. **1375** BARBOUR *Bruce* II. 346 On athir syd thus war thai yhar. c**1420** *Anturs of Arth.* xxxix, Aythire freke appoune fold has fastned his spere. **1535** COVERDALE *Ezek.* xl. 48 By the walles also were pilers, on either syde one. **1628** HOBBES *Thucyd.* (1822) 25 The standard being on either side lift up, they joind battle. **1762** FALCONER *Shipwr.* Proem 40 The fierce extremes of either zone. **1820** SCOTT *Ivanhoe* iii, There was a huge fireplace at either end of the hall. **1842** TENNYSON *E. Morris* 37 Either twilight and the day between.

†**b.** With plural sb.: = 'both'. Also (rarely), ***either both***, in same sense. *Obs.*

1561 T. NORTON *Calvin's Inst.* I. Pref., They all endeuor ..to kepe still eyther bothe kingdome safe. **1586** *Let. Earle Leycester* 20 The Lords and Commons in either houses assembled. **1608** TOPSELL *Serpents* 694 Upon either feet they [skinks] have five distinct fingers or claws.

†**c.** With possessive pron. interposed before the sb. *Obs. rare.*

c**1305** *St. Kenelm* 355 in *E.E.P.* (1862) 57 Out berste aiþere hire [the queen's] eȝe & fulle adoun vpe hire sautere.

†**d.** ***either other***: each of the two. (In quot. with pl. vb. as if = 'both'.) *Obs.*

1526 TINDALE *Lev.* Prol., For which cause either other of them were ordained.

†**2. a.** *absol.* as *pron.*; used both of persons and things. Often followed by *of* with pl. sb. or pron. (In ME. with genit. pl. in same sense; in the case of pronouns this survived until 17th c., *e.g.* ***your either*** = 'either of you'.) *Obs.* or *arch.*

c**1000** *Ags. Gosp.* Matt. ix. 17 Hiȝ doð niwe win on niwe bytta, and æȝðer byð ȝehealden. c**1175** *Lamb. Hom.* 15 Eour eyþer sunegað bi-foran drihten. c**1200** *Trin. Coll. Hom.* 141 Hur eiðer alumð þe se. c**1200** ORMIN 119 Forr eȝȝþer hete ȝede swa Rihht affterr Godess lare. c**1205** LAY. 15982 Æiðer [c**1275** aiþer] wende to his hole. a**1300** *Cursor M.* 8360 And did þair ether dun for to sitt. c**1420** *Pallad. on Husb.* I. 808 So shall her eitheres werke been oblowe With colde or hoote. **1479** *Bury Wills* (1850) 54, I beqwethe to eyther of myn executors xls. **1535** COVERDALE *Ruth* I. 9 Ye maie fynde reste ether of you in hir huszbandes house. **1591** SPENSER *M. Hubberd* 551 So parted they, as eithers way them led. **1615** CHAPMAN *Odyss.* IV. 79 The portraiture of Jove-sustain'd and sceptre-bearing kings Your either person in his presence brings. **1676** in Picton *L'pool Munic. Rec.* (1883) I. 268 The Serjeant and Water Baylive shall have either a cloak. **1759** GOLDSM. *Misc. Wks.* (1837) III. 219 Fontenelle and Voltaire were men of unequal merit; yet how different has been the fate of either.

†**b.** With plural concord. *Obs.*

1542 UDALL *Erasm. Apoph.* 53 b, Either of them as naked as ever they wer born. **1647** W. BROWNE tr. *Polex.* II. 90 Either of them have treated me as the scandall..of my Sex.

c. Sometimes = each (of more than two things).

1588 R. PARKE tr. *Mendoza's Hist. China* 76 The other thirteene prouinces that do remaine haue eyther of them a vizroy or governor. **1867** HOWELLS *Ital. Journ.* 228 Just above the feet, at either of the three corners, is an exquisite ..female bust.

†**d.** ***either other***: = 'each other': cf. EACH. *Obs.* exc. in form ***either..the other.***

Usually the two words were in different grammatical relations, one of them (in most cases the former) being the subj., and the other governed in acc., genit., or dat. by a vb., sb., or prep. Sometimes, however, *either other* became a compound (cf. *each other*, and might be governed by a prep.

a**1000** *Andreas* 1053 (Gr.) Æȝðer þara eorla oðrum trymede Heofonrices hyht. c**1200** *Trin. Coll. Hom.* 213 þesse wise biswikeð her aiðer oðer. c**1205** LAY. 3932 Eiþer hateden oþer. a**1300** *Floriz & Bl.* 509 Eiþer oþer sone ikneu. a**1300** *Cursor M.* 799 Quen ayder biheld oþer naked, For scham þay stode bath and quakid. c**1320** *Sir Beues* 1991 Ather askede of otheres stat. **1393** LANGLAND *P. Pl.* C. XXI. 127 Ayþer axed of oþ er of þis grete wonder. **1398** TREVISA *Barth. De P.R.* v. i. (1495) 99 Membres helpen eyther other. **1439** *E.E. Wills* (1882) 124 Aither aftir othir in the taile. **1471** *Hist. Arrivall Edw. IV* (1838) 19 There was a greet myste and letted the syght of eithar othar. **15..** *Kyng to Hermyt* 513 in Hazl. *E.P.P.* I. 33 Ather betauȝt other gode dey. **1552** LYNDESAY *Monarche* 4023 Atheris deand in vtheris armis. **1593** SHAKS. *Lucr.* 66 Beauties red and Vertues white, Of eithers colour was the other Queene. **1677** HALE *Prim. Orig. Man.* 297 There seems to be a more connatural Transmutation of either into other. **1874** MORLEY *Compromise* (1886) 103 The rights of either to disturb the other.

II. One or other of the two.

3. a. As adj. used *attrib.*

c**1300** *Beket* 2247 He miȝte..wende up aither side. c**1320** *Sir Tristr.* (1886) 356 Chese onaiþer hand. **1667** MILTON *P.L.* I. 424 Spirits when they please Can either Sex assume, or both. **1740** CHESTERF. *Lett.* I. lx. 170 When the sun shines on either side of us (as it does mornings and evenings) the shadows are very long. **1788** GIBBON *Decl. & F.* (1846) VI. 190 The artificial thunder, in the hands of either nation, must have turned the fortune of the day.

¶ Incorrectly with plural vb.

1874 RUSKIN *Val d' Arno* 119, I don't mean that either of the writers I name are absolutely thus narrow in their own views.

†**b.** ***either other***: one or the other of two. *Obs.*

1532 MORE *Confut. Tindale* Wks. (1557) 707/2 Wythoute anye chaunge of beliefe on eyther other syde. **1567** JEWEL *Def. Apol.* (1611) 100 Let him take whether he liketh best, if either other of these words shall serue his turne.

4. a. *absol.* as *pron.* (Formerly sometimes inflected in genit.)

1548 COVERDALE *Erasm. Par.* 1 *Cor.* iii. 15 If eythers worke be with fyre destroyed, the workeman shall lose his labour. **1593** HOOKER *Eccl. Pol.* I. x. (1611) 25 If wee bee both or eyther of these. **1802** *Med. Jrnl.* VIII. 188 It is by no means necessary to determine a preference between the two..since either of them may be resorted to. **1848** MACAULAY *Hist. Eng.* I. 164 Whatever was ridiculous or odious in either increased the scorn and aversion which the multitude felt for both. **1866** CRUMP *Banking* viii. 167 Either causes a loss to the community.

¶ Incorrectly with plural vb.

1833 BP. THIRWALL *Philolog. Museum* II. 656 Religious rites by which either Thebes or Eleusis were afterwards distinguished.

†**b.** ***either of both***: = 'either of the two'. *Obs.*

a**1575** ABP. PARKER *Corr.* 396, I never heard of either of them both till your honour had sent me your last letters. **1621** AINSWORTH *Annot. Pentat.* (1639) 86 Wives were taken in Israel by bils of Dowry, and solemne espousals; but concubines without either of both.

c. Sometimes = any one (of more than two).

1616 HIERON *Wks.* (1624) II. 11 That doctrine which tends to the furtherance of all or either of these three. **1796** *Encycl. Brit.* XVII. 566 Rubens, Jordens, and Snyders, used to co-operate in each other's..pictures..and thus they became more valuable than if finished by either of them singly. **1845** STEPHEN *Laws Eng.* II. 31 If either of them [several methods] be found to fail.

B. as *adv.* (*conj.*)

I. Adverbial uses of A. I.

†**1.** In OE. and early ME. = BOTH. In the oldest use followed by *ȝe..ȝe*, or *ȝe..and*; afterwards *ȝe* was omitted, *and* being retained in the second place. *Obs.*

c**893** K. ÆLFRED *Oros.* II. v. §8 Æȝþer ȝe of Sciþþium ȝe of Crecum. a**1067** *Chart. Eadweard* in *Cod. Dipl.* IV. 227 Æȝðer ȝe binnan burh and butan. a**1175** *Cott. Hom.* 223 [3e] imugan ȝecnowen eiȝðer god and euyl. c**1175** *Lamb. Hom.* 23 Bute þu heo alle for-lete eiðer ȝe þa ane ȝe þa oðer. a**1200** *Moral Ode* 32 in *E.E.P.* (1862) 24 Ayþer to lutel & to muchel. c**1205** LAY. 30887 Aiðer [c**1275** boþe] bi worden and by writen.

†**2.** Used to connect more than two terms. *Obs.*

c**1175** *Lamb. Hom.* 115 Eiðer ȝe on herȝunge ȝe on hungre ȝe on cwalme ȝe on uniwidere ȝe on wilde deoran.

II. Adverbial uses of A. II.

3. Introducing the mention of alternatives.

a. ***either..or***, †***either..o(u)ther.*** (Formerly *either* might be preceded by an adj.; see quot. 1594.)

138. WYCLIF *Sel. Wks.* III. 297 Eþer to kyng..oþer to deukis. c**1385** CHAUCER *L.G.W.* Prol. 5 Non..that eythir hath in heuyn or in hell I-be. c**1420** *Pallad. on Husb.* I. 25 Eyther springing there Or elles thider brought from elles where. **1540** CROMWELL in Ellis *Orig. Lett.* II. 142 II. 168, I never thought treson to your Highnes..ayther in woorde

or dede. **1563** *Homilies* II. *Rogation Wk.* IV. (1859) 498 They either quite ear them up..or else, etc. **1593** HOOKER *Eccl. Pol.* I. ii, How should either men or Angels be able perfectly to behold? **1594** BP. J. KING *Jonas, &c.* (1618) 623 The mutable and transitory either pleasures or profits of this life. **1713** BERKELEY *Hylas & P.* I. Wks. 1871 I. 291 Either, Hylas, you are jesting, or have a very bad memory. **1875** JOWETT *Plato* (ed. 2) III. 266 A narration of events, either past, present, or to come.

†**b.** *either..either*: = either..or. *Obs.*

1551 RECORDE *Pathw. Knowl.* Pref., Knowledge..that maye appertaine either to good gouernance in time of peace, eyther wittye pollicies in time of warre. **1574** HELLOWES *Gueuara's Ep.* (1584) 20 In those golden times either philosophers did governe, either else governours did use philosophie. **1588** A. KING tr. *Canisius' Catech.* G viij b, Ather on ye day self of y^e æquinoxe, ather ellis on ye day nixt yairefter.

c. *either-or, either/or* [in some examples reflecting Da. *enten-eller* (title of book by the Danish philosopher Kierkegaard, 1843)], used as *sb.*, a necessary or unavoidable choice between alternatives. Also *attrib.* or as *adj.*, black and white, susceptible of only one of two (often extreme) solutions, responses, etc.

1931 *Times Lit. Suppl.* 10 Sept. 672/3 Dr. Harris is a philosopher and a logician with a little too much of the 'either-or' in his mental make-up. **1931** *Church Times* 9 Oct. 388/2 Catholicism..provides..a check upon humanism, which any 'either/or' theology cannot give. **1941** AUDEN *New Year Let.* II. 44 The either-ors, the mongrel halves Who find truth in a mirror. **1942** 'G. ORWELL' in *Partisan Rev.* IX. 498 One can predict the future in the form of an 'either-or': either we introduce Socialism, or we lose the war. **1944** W. LOWRIE tr. *Kierkegaard's Either/or* II. 134 Although my life now has to a certain degree its either/or behind it, yet I know well that it may still encounter many a situation when the either/or will have its full significance. **1951** C. S. LEWIS *Let.* 23 Apr. (1966) 228, I have no use for mere *either-or* people. **1953** *Economist* 10 Jan. 58/1 Too much rigid logic of the black-and-white either-or variety. **1958** *Spectator* 30 May 709/1 An 'either-or' attitude, leading to..the Cawnpore Well and the hanging-parties at Benares. **1965** *Language* XLI. 258 Either-or questions.

†**4.** = Or. Also, *either else* = or else. *Obs.*

138. WYCLIF *Antecr.* in Todd *3 Treat. Wyclif* 118 Who ever clepiþ himself unyversal prest eiþer desireþ to be clepid. **1395** PURVEY *Remonstr.* (1851) 8 The cruelte of all thevis eithir robberis. **1483** CAXTON *G. de la Tour* K vij b, She was brente eyther stoned with stones. **1546** COVERDALE *Lord's Supper* Wks. 1844 I. 462 Perhaps men would have forgotten themselves, either else the mercy of God should not have been so much known as it ought to be. **1583** STUBBES *Anat. Abus.* II. 10 Either else they would neuer be so desirous of reuenge. **1611** BIBLE *Luke* vi. 42 Either [**1881** *Revised*, Or] how canst thou say to thy brother.

5. a. As an alternative, 'which way you please'. **b.** In negative or interrogative sentences: Any more than the other.

c **1400** *Destr. Troy* 1479 Or Alisaunder ewther was his other name. **1601** SHAKS. *Twel. N.* II. v. 206 *To.* Wilt thou set thy foote o' my necke? *An.* Or o' mine either? **1828** SCOTT *F.M. Perth* xxxii, Thy sex cannot help that either. *Mod.* If you do not go I will not go either. If John had said so, or William either, I could believe it.

eittin, obs. Sc. pa. pple. of EAT.

-eity [cf. Fr. *-éité*], termination of nouns of quality or condition corresp. to adjs. in -EOUS, on the model of L. *idoneus* IDONEOUS, late L. *idoneĭtās* IDONEITY (1617), scholastic L. *homogeneus* HOMOGENEOUS, *homogeneitās* HOMOGENEITY (1625). Among other early examples are *spontaneity* (1651), *subterraneity* (1686), *consentaneity* (1798). Two exceptional mod.L. formations *ecceitās* (f. *ecce* lo, behold), *velleitās* (f. *velle* to will) gave ECCEITY (1549), VELLEITY (1618).

ejaculate (ɪˈdʒækjʊleɪt), *v.* [f. L. *ējaculāt-* ppl. stem of *ējaculārī*, f. *ē* out + *jaculārī* to dart, f. *jaculum* javelin.]

†**1.** *trans.* To dart or shoot forth; to throw out suddenly and swiftly, eject. *Obs.* in general sense.

1613 R. C. *Table Alph.* (ed. 3) *Ejaculate*, cast out. **1661** LOVELL *Hist. Anim. & Min.* 102 They [Porcupines] have..prickles..which they ejaculate. **1762** tr. *Busching's Syst. Geog.* III. 179 The stones thus ejaculated have been found to contain all kinds of minerals.

b. *spec.* To eject fluids, etc. from the body.

1578 BANISTER *Hist. Man* VI. 88 To eiaculate seede into the matrice. **1638** T. WHITAKER *Blood of Grape* 35 So doth the heart eiaculate the influent spirit. **1693** URQUHART *Rabelais* III. xxxi, The cavernous nerve, whose office is to ejaculate the moisture. **1807** *Ann. Reg.* 823 The spider..ejaculates..several threads. **1816** KIRBY & SP. *Entomol.* (1828) II. xvii. 68 To ejaculate its venom into the wound. **1836-9** TODD *Cycl. Anat.* II. 422/1 A..tube through which the seminal liquor is..ejaculated. **1878** tr. *Ziemssen's Cycl. Med.* VIII. 905 A man who could never ejaculate.

†**c.** *transf.* and *fig. Obs.*

c **1630** JACKSON *Creed* V. xxv, The sun..can..ejaculate his beams upon any body capable of heat and illumination. **1679** BP. OF HEREFORD *Let. Popish Idol.* 22 [They] groan and sigh, as if they would breath forth and ejaculate their very Hearts unto it. **1704** SWIFT *Mech. Operat. Spirit* (1711) 280 There are three general ways of ejaculating the Soul. **1712** BLACKMORE *Creation* 13 The mighty magnet..Its active rays ejaculated then Irradiate all the wide circumference. **1853** KANE *Grinnell Exp.* xli. (1856) 374 A hissing sound, ejaculated by sudden impulse.

2. To utter suddenly (a short prayer; now in wider sense, any brief expression of emotion). Also *absol.*

1666 PEPYS *Diary* 23 July (1879) IV. 22, I could not but with hearty thanks to Almighty God ejaculate my thanks to him. **1791** MRS. INCHBALD *Simp. Story* I. iv. 38 Miss Woodley ejaculated a short prayer to herself. **1865** CARLYLE *Fredk. Gt.* II. VII. vi. 314 But where can the Prince be? he kept ejaculating. **1872** LIDDON *Elem. Relig.* vi. 184 We may of course ejaculate to such a thing if we like.

Hence **e'jaculated** *ppl. a.*

1711 KEN *Christophil* Poet. Wks. 1721 I. 524 Each Moment by ejaculated Pray'r We keep Possession of our Mansion there. **1865** FARRAR *Chapters on Lang.* 100 We may condense into a single ejaculated monosyllable, all, and more than all, of a whole sentence.

ejaculate (ɪˈdʒækjʊlət), *sb.* [f. the vb.] Ejaculated seminal fluid.

1927 *Jrnl. Amer. Med. Assoc.* LXXXVIII. 901/2 Since the diagnostic vasostomy, the patient has not had sperms in his ejaculate. **1938** *Amer. Jrnl. Med. Sci.* CXCVI. 369 A determination of the number of sperm in the total ejaculate is obtained by multiplying the count per cc. by the volume of the entire ejaculate. **1966** *Biol. Abstr.* XLVII. 5708/1 Spermatozoa were observed in coagulated spontaneous ejaculates of isolated male guinea pigs.

ejaculation (ɪˌdʒækjuːˈleɪʃən). [as if a. L. **ējaculātiōn-em*, f. as EJACULATE *v.*: see -ATION.]

†**1.** The action of hurling (missiles); the spouting out (of water); the throwing up (stones, etc. by subterranean forces). *Obs.*

1610 GUILLIM *Heraldry* IV. xiv. (1660) 332 Man..furnished himself to the full..with Instruments of ejaculation. **1625** K. LONG tr. *Barclay's Argenis* II. xxii. 143 Ashes..carried many miles..with their own violent ejaculation. **1633** BP. HALL *Hard Texts* 238 A sling..should be altogether for ejaculations. **1762** tr. *Busching's Syst. Geog.* III. 61 When the ejaculation is strong and brisk, the petroleous wells are observed to become very turbid. **1818** *Ann. Reg., Chron.* 495 [He] spouted out of his mouth..several tuns of water..This ejaculation was received with the highest applause.

2. The sudden ejection or emission (of seed, fluids, etc.) from the animal or vegetable system. *spec.* the discharging of the male sperm.

1603 HOLLAND *Plutarch's Mor.* 1301 The ejaculation or casting foorth of naturall seed. **1646** SIR T. BROWNE *Pseud. Ep.* III. iv. 113 The vessels of ejaculations. **1677** GREW *Anat. Fruits* V. §19 That violent and surprising Ejaculation of the Seeds. **1727** BRADLEY *Fam. Dict.* I. s.v. *Bee*, The Bees..are generated..by the Ejaculation of a little Crystalline Water into the Bottom of the small Cells in the Combs. **1807** *Ann. Reg.* 823 The ejaculation or darting of the [spider's] threads is doubted. **1865** *Reader* No. 151. 576/3 Ejaculation of aqueous fluid from leaves. **1888** E. L. KEYES *Surg. Dis. Genito-Urinary Organs* I. xxvi. 442 Ejaculation of semen may be produced by a variety of causes. **1928** [see EJACULATIO PRÆCOX]. **1966** R. D. AMELAR *Infertility in Men* ii. 32 The semen is ejaculated in a liquid form and becomes a gel or coagulation, immediately after ejaculation, only to liquefy again within 5 to 20 minutes.

3. *transf.* and *fig.* **a.** The emission of rays (by a luminary), of occult or magical influence, etc. **b.** The putting up of short earnest prayers in moments of emergency; the hasty utterance of words expressing emotion.

1625 BACON *Envy, Ess.* (Arb.) 511 There seemeth to be acknowledged, in the Act of Enuy an Eiaculation..of the Eye. *a* **1635** NAUNTON *Fragm. Reg.* (Arb.) 20 In the ejaculation of her prayers on her people. *a* **1657** SIR J. BALFOUR *Ann. Scotl.* (1824-5) II. 73 The suns eiaculatione of his beames wpone the earthe, more then 6,900,000 myles. **1866** G. MACDONALD *Ann. Q. Neighb.* vii. (1878) 101 An ejaculation of love is not likely to offend Him.

4. *concr.* Also *fig.* **a.** *gen.*

1708 MOTTEUX *Rabelais* IV. xviii. (1737) 77 Lightnings, fiery Vapours, and other aerial Ejaculations. **1841-4** EMERSON *Ess. Poet* Wks. (Bohn) I. 168 The religions of the world are the ejaculations of a few imaginative men.

b. *spec.* A short prayer 'darted up to God' (Fuller) in an emergency. In wider sense: A short hasty emotional utterance.

1624 T. GOKINS *Hallowed be Thy Name* in Farr's *S.P.* (1847) 325 Thou takest recreation In..one eiaculation. **1656** FINETT *For. Ambass.* 237, I found by his ejaculations that they repented of their punctillios. **1684-5** in Ellis *Orig. Lett.* I. 382 III. 338 The other Bishops giving their assistance..with very good ejaculations. **1790** BURKE *Fr. Rev.* 24 He makes the lords and commons fall to a pious, legislative ejaculation. **1863** FR. KEMBLE *Resid. Georgia* 133 The usual chorus of..ejaculations of welcome.

‖**ejaculatio præcox** (ɪdʒækjʊˈleɪʃɪəʊ ˈpriːkɒks). [mod.L.: see EJACULATION, PRÆCOCIAL *a.*] (See quot. 1925.)

1892 C. G. CHADDOCK tr. *Krafft-Ebing's Psychopathia Sexualis* iii. 196 He became neurasthenic, being afflicted with weakness of erection and ejaculatio præcox. **1921** E. J. KEMPF *Psychopath.* vii. 326 During his marriage, he was virtually impotent, and only at times was he able to perform as much as ejaculatio præcox. **1925** STEDMAN *Med. Dict.* (ed. 8) 307/2 *E[jaculatio] praecox*, premature ejaculation, rapid termination of the sexual act on the part of the male. **1928** EISENDRATH & ROLNICK *Text-Bk. Urology* xxviii. 441 The term impotence conveys a relative meaning, varying in degree from premature ejaculation (ejaculatio praecox) to total inability to have erection. **1959** L. P. WERSHUB *Sexual Impotence in Male* viii. 102 Some forms of *ejaculatio praecox* can often be due to *physical* causes.

ejaculative (ɪˈdʒækjʊlətɪv), *a.* [f. as EJACULATE + -IVE.] **a.** Of the nature of an ejaculation. †**b.** Pertaining to the emission of occult influence (*obs.*).

1660 Z. CROFTON *Fasten. St. Peter's Fett.* 58 [It] can be no warrant for such premeditated, ejaculative expressions, to be prescribed in set and publick prayer. **1603** FLORIO *Montaigne* I. xx. (1632) 44 The Tortoises and the Estriges hatch their egges with their looks only, a signe that they have some ejaculative vertue. **1841** DISRAELI *Amen. Lit.* (1859) I. 35 An Anglo-Saxon poem has the appearance of a collection of short hints..curt and ejaculative.

‖**e'jaculator.** *Phys.* [mod.L. f. *ējaculā-ri* to EJACULATE.] (See quot.)

1727-51 CHAMBERS *Cycl.*, *Ejaculator* in anatomy, a name applied to two muscles of the genitals, from their office in the ejaculation of the seed.

ejaculatory (ɪˈdʒækjʊlətərɪ), *a.* [f. as prec. + -ORY.]

1. †**a.** Adapted for ejecting (a missile, or the like). **b.** *Phys.* That is concerned in the ejection of semen, etc.

1655 EVELYN *Mem.* (1857) I. 322 The bullet's falling on the ejaculatory spring. **1666** J. SMITH *Old Age* (ed. 2) 117 Seminary vessels both preparatory, and ejaculatory. **1751** CHAMBERS *Cycl.*, *Ejaculatory*..ducts, or canals, arising from the *vesiculæ seminales.* **1860** SIR H. THOMPSON *Dis. Prostate* (1868) 7 Two slight lines of depression..indicate the tracks of the ejaculatory ducts. **1861** HULME tr. *Moquin-Tandon* II. I. 47 The excretory canal of the gland, called Ejaculatory Duct.

†**2.** Inclined to ejaculate; given to abrupt, impulsive expression. *Obs.*

1644 QUARLES *Barnabas & B.* To Rdr., This small Essay (the epitome of his ejaculatory soul).

3. Of the nature of or resembling an ejaculation or sudden utterance. (Originally of prayers: see EJACULATION 4 b; now in wider sense.)

1644 SIR E. DERING *Prop. Sacr.* C iij b, In hymns and Psalms ejaculatory passages..are warranted. **1698** W. CHILCOT *Evil Thoughts* vi. (1851) 65 Not only in ejaculatory, but in our set prayers. **1748** SMOLLETT *Rod. Rand.* lxv. (1804) 472 Strap..venting ejaculatory petitions to Heaven for our safety. **1851** LONGF. *Gold. Leg. Convent of Hirschau*, To breathe an ejaculatory prayer.

4. quasi-*sb.* = EJACULATION 4 b. *rare.*

1883 *Harper's Mag.* Mar. 575/1 'Indeed, I have reason to know it,' was the severe ejaculatory.

eject (ˈiːdʒɛkt), *sb.* [ad. L. *ēject-um*, neut. of *ējectus* thrown out; see next. The term was coined by Prof. Clifford on analogy of *subject*, *object*.]

Something (*viz.* a sensation or mental state other than our own) which is neither an actual nor a conceivable object of *our* consciousness, but which is inferred to be a real existence analogous in kind to our own sensations or mental states.

1878 CLIFFORD *Things-in-thems., Lect. & Ess.* (1886) 275, I propose..to call these inferred existences *ejects*, things thrown out of my consciousness, to distinguish them from *objects*, things presented in my consciousness, phenomena. **1883** ROMANES *Ment. Evol. Anim.* i. 22 The evidence derived from ejects is practically regarded as good in the case of mental organizations inferred to be closely analogous to our own. **1884** —— in *Nature* XXIX. No. 747. 380 The eject of my contemplation is the mind of a dog. **1885** C. L. MORGAN *Springs of Cond.* III. ii. 267 My neighbour's mind, feelings, motions are ejects to me; they can never be objects.

†**e'ject,** *pple. Obs.* [ad. L. *ēject-us*, f. *ējicĕre*, f. *ē* out + *jacĕre* to throw.] Used as pa. pple. of next.

1432-50 tr. *Higden* (1865) I. 123 The inhabitatores of whom somme tyme eiecte and put in captiuite. **1526** *Pilgr. Perf.* (W. de W. 1531) 208 b, Now is the prynce of ye worlde eiecte & casten out.

eject (ɪˈdʒɛkt), *v.* [ad. L. *ēject-āre*, freq. of *ējicĕre* to throw out, f. *ē* out + *jacĕre* to throw; or directly f. *ēject-* ppl. stem of *ējicĕre*. As in many other Eng. vbs. identical in form with L. ppl. stems, the precise formation is somewhat doubtful; the senses are derived partly from *ējicĕre*, partly from *ējectāre*.]

1. *trans.* To throw out from within.

1607 TOPSELL *Four-f. Beasts* 197 Seethe the same till all the scum or earthy substance thereof be ejected. **1644** EVELYN *Mem.* (1857) I. 62 In the Queen's Garden is a Diana ejecting a fountain. **1646** SIR T. BROWNE *Pseud. Ep.* III. xxii. 165 To reduce that indigestible substance [gold] into such a forme as may not be ejected by seidge. **1807** *Med. Jrnl.* XVII. 221 He died..while endeavouring to eject saliva. **1830** LYELL *Princ. Geol.* (1875) II. II. xxxiii. 217 If stones are thrown into the Crater they are instantly ejected.

b. *transf.* and *fig.*; esp. To dart forth, emit (flames, light, etc.).

1598 B. JONSON *Ev. Man in Hum.* II. iii, Every look or glance mine eyes ejects [**1601** mine eye objects]. **1630** DRAYTON *Muses Elyz. Nym.* 78 The Carbunckle..a flaming light And radiency eiecteth. **1620** QUARLES *Jonah* (1638) 35 His home-bred stomack's curb'd or quite ejected. **1738** BROOKE *Jerusalem Deliv.* iii. 10 His arms and eager eyes ejecting flame..Tancred came. **1742** YOUNG *Nt. Th.* I. 258 How groaning hospitals eject their dead!

2. To expel, drive out (by force or with indignity) *from* any place or position.

1555 EDEN *Decades W. Ind.* III. VI. (Arb.) 162 Al the barbarous Kynges & Idolatours beinge eiected. **1607** SHAKS. *Cor.* III. i. 287 To dispatch This Viporous Traitor; to eject him hence Were but one danger. **1671** MILTON *P.R.* I. 414

Ejected, emptyed, gazed, unpityed, shun'd, A spectacle of ruin or of scorn. **1726** Swift *Bec's Birthday* Wks. 1819 XIV. 542 If the gout should seize the head, Doctors pronounce the patient dead; But if they can.. eject it to th' extremest parts, etc. **1828** D'Israeli *Chas. I*, I. viii. 270 Those inferior minds, who had ejected the master-spirit from their councils. **1863** Fr. Kemble *Resid. Georgia* 57 They [two free black preachers] have lately been ejected from the place.

†**b.** In pass. with omission of *from*. *Obs.* (Cf. *to be banished the country*.)

1657 J. Smith *Myst. Rhet.* 64 And for that they would be justified by the works of the law, were ejected the house of God. **1660** T. Watson in Spurgeon *Treas. Dav.* Ps. xvi. 11 Austin saith 'Lord.. if I might see thy face one day; but alas! were it only a day, then to be ejected heaven'.

3. To expel from a dignity or office. Also, To turn out, evict (a person) *from* property or possessions; *esp.* in *Law*.

1570–6 Lambarde *Peramb. Kent* (1826) 229 The Abbat.. eiected the Kings Clarke. **1623** Bingham *Xenophon* 127 That I might be reuenged vpon them, that had eiected vs out of our patrimony. **1653** Baxter *Chr. Concord* 117 If they can prove their Ministers fit to be ejected, let them there prove it. **1794** S. Williams *Vermont* 217 When the executive officers came to eject the inhabitants from their houses and lands. **1836** H. Rogers *J. Howe* ii. (1863) 18 [The elder Howe] was not the man for Loughborough, and he was consequently ejected. **1879** Froude *Cæsar* iii. 20 He had ejected disreputable senators from the Curia.

ejecta (ɪˈdʒɛktə), *sb. pl.* [neut. pl. of pa. pple. of L. *eicĕre*, f. *e-* out, forth + *iacĕre* to cast.]

1. The matter ejected from a volcano.

1886 *Amer. Meteor. Jrnl.* III. III. 109 Dust and other ejecta played but a secondary part in the production of the phenomena. **1890** *Nature* 16 Oct. 601/2 It may be thought that any volcanic ejecta would speedily melt the snow upon which they fell. **1902** *Daily Chron.* 11 Sept. 6/2 On the afternoon of the 3rd the ejecta was of the colour of sulphur. **1957** G. E. Hutchinson *Treat. Limnol.* I. i. 25 The summit of the volcano usually has a well-defined crater from which ejecta escape to continue the building of the cone.

2. *Path.* That which is ejected from the body.

1890 Billings *Med. Dict.* I. 433/1 *Ejecta*, matters thrown out. **1908** *Practitioner* Oct. 601 Frequent vomiting,.. the ejecta being often blood-stained and sometimes faecal. **1953** *Faber Med. Dict.* 134/2 *Ejecta*, matter thrown out; excretions.

‖**ejectamenta** (ɪˌdʒɛktəˈmɛntə), *sb. pl.* [pl. of L. *ējectāmentum*, f. *ējectāre*: see EJECT *v.*] Substances ejected by eruptive forces.

1863 Lyell *Antiq. Man* x. (ed. 3) 192 Yet the cone, an incoherent heap of scoriæ and spongy ejectamenta, stands unmolested. **1879** Rutley *Stud. Rocks* iv. 32 These fragmentary ejectamenta are often thrown high into the air.

†**ejec'tation.** *Obs.*$^{-0}$ [f. as prec.: see -ATION.]

1736 Bailey, *Ejectation*, a casting or throwing out. **1775** Ash, *Ejectation* (not much used, from *eject*), the act of casting out.

ejected (ɪˈdʒɛktɪd), *ppl. a.* [f. EJECT *v.* + -ED.]

1. Thrown out from the interior of anything.

1756 C. Lucas *Ess. Waters* II. 165 If the water be.. upon the fire.. these ejected bubbles will be more apparent. **1799** Kirwan *Geol. Ess.* 269 The low heat of the ejected lava. **1853** Kane *Grinnell Exp.* xlviii. (1856) 445 That singular ejected rock, the Devil's Thumb. **1856** —— *Arct. Expl.* I. xxiv. 320 The young gulls were feeding on the ejected morsel.

2. Expelled from a country, or from an office; evicted, turned out from a possession, tenancy, etc.

1649 Milton *Eikon.* Wks. 1738 I. 408 True policy will teach them to find a safer interest in the common friendship of England, than in the ruins of one ejected Family. **1665** Marvell *Corr.* xlviii. Wks. 1872 II. 183 Non-conformist ejected Ministers. **1836** H. Rogers *J. Howe* iv. (1863) 116 But though Howe was an ejected minister, he could not consent to be a silenced one.

ejecting (ɪˈdʒɛktɪŋ), *vbl. sb.* [f. EJECT *v.* + -ING¹.] Casting out, expulsion.

1602 Fulbecke *1st Pt. Parall.* 100 Our law punisheth.. the immature eiecting of any of these out of the wombe. **1692** Bentley *Boyle Lect.* 26 The miracles of our Lord.. were.. for the real benefit and advantage of men, by.. ejecting of devils.

ejection (ɪˈdʒɛkʃən). [ad. L. *ējectiōn-em*, n. of action f. *ējicĕre*: see EJECT *v.*]

1. a. The action of casting out from within. Formerly applied *spec.* in *Physiology* (see quot. 1751).

1613 R. C. *Table Alph.* (ed. 3) *Eiection*, a casting forth. **1636** Healey *Epictetus' Man., Cebes* 135 Her owne receipt.. which purgeth out all their ingulphed evils, as by vomit or ejection. **1652** French *Yorksh. Spa* viii. 74 There is no ejection of their excrements by stool for two or three dayes. **1751** Chambers *Cycl., Ejection*, the act of throwing out or discharging anything at some of the emunctories; as by stool, vomiting or the like. **1813** Eustace *Tour Italy* i. (R.) The vast ejection of ashes.. must have left a large void in its [Vesuvius'] centre. **1862** Darwin *Fertil. Orchids* vi. 260, I pricked deeply the column.. without causing the ejection of this pollinium. **1881** Stokes in *Nature* No. 625. 597 The ejection of gas from the body of the sun.

b. *concr.* Something ejected; *spec.* by a volcano.

1654 Gayton *Fest. Notes* 158 The Apothecary sware he smelt him [the mouse] comming by the scent of the ejection. **1794** Sullivan *View Nat.* II. 197 One unclassed volcanic ejection.. the *roche rouge* in Velay, in France. **1833** Lyell *Princ. Geol.* III. 197 The ejections in this place entirely conceal from view the stratified rocks of the country.

†**c.** *fig.* An outgoing of emotion. *Obs.*

1655 H. Vaughan *Silex Scint.* I. 36 What thin Ejections, Cold affections.

d. *Aeronaut.* The mechanically contrived 'baling out' of a pilot from an aeroplane or space-craft. Also *attrib.*, as ***ejection seat***, on which this is effected. Cf. EJECTOR 2.

1945 *Aeroplane* 16 Nov. 569/1 It was the first German aeroplane to employ a pilot-ejection seat... The single-seat cockpit is positioned well forward and the pilot ejection seat is of the explosive cartridge type. **1946** *Aeroplane Spotter* 10 Aug. 182/1 The first automatic high-speed 'baling-out' ejection by Mr. Bernard Lynch.. on.. July 24. **1956** W. A. Heflin *U.S. Air Force Dict.* 184/2 Ejection chute, cockpit capsule, seat, seat-trainer. **1967** *New Scientist* 27 Apr. 195/1 Ejection seats were omitted from the multi-man *Voskhod* spacecraft.

2. a. A casting out or expulsion from a particular place or position; also from office or possessions.

1566 Knox *Hist. Ref.* Wks. 1846 I. 349 He.. did entreat of the ejectioun of the byaris and the sellaris furth of the Tempill of Jerusalem. **1627** Hakewill *Apol.* I. i. §1 [Adam and Eve's] Creation and Ejection. **1651** Hobbes *Leviath.* IV. xlv. 356 Exorcisme (that is to say, of ejection of Devills by Conjuration). **1704** Hearne *Duct. Hist.* (1714) I. 417 To the Syracusians he gave Laws upon the ejection of their King. **1765** Johnson *Pref. Shaks.* (R.) Some of these alterations are only the ejection of a word for one that appeared to him more elegant. **1853** Marsden *Early Purit.* 48 The ejection of many good men immediately followed.

†**b.** The state of being banished, exile. *rare.*

1655–60 Stanley *Hist. Philos.* (1701) 49/1 The People with whom he [the son of Periander] lived in his ejection.

c. In Scotch Law. ***action of ejection***: = EJECTMENT 2. ***letters of ejection***: see quot.

1764 Erskine *Princ. Sc. Law* 427 Actions of spuilzie, ejection and intrusion are penal. *Ibid.* 464 If one be condemned.. to quit the possession of lands, and refuses.. letters of ejection are granted.. ordaining the Sheriff to eject him.

†**3.** = ECBOLE 2. *Obs.*

1603 Holland *Plutarch's Mor.* 1257 Polymnestus.. first made the drawing out of the note longer, and the.. ejection thereof much greater than before.

†**ejec'titious,** *a. Obs.*$^{-0}$ [f. L. *ējectīci-us*, f. ppl. stem of *ējicĕre*: see prec. + -ITIOUS.] (See quot.)

1736 Bailey, *Ejectitious*, cast out. **1775** in Ash.

ejective (ɪˈdʒɛktɪv), *a.* (and *sb.*) [as if ad. L. **ējectivus*: see EJECT *v.* and -IVE.]

1. That has the function or the power of ejecting.

1657 Tomlinson *Renou's Disp.* 45 The one a vomiting or ejective medicament. *c* **1720** W. Gibson *Farriers Dispens.* II. i. (1734) 57 The Ancients thought there was some ejective Property in all purging Medicines. **1858** Greener *Gunnery* 301 Each shot carries with it its own share of ejective force. **1886** *Cornh. Mag.* Oct. 428 The giant planets must have possessed corresponding ejective energies.

2. Pertaining to an eject.

1883 Romanes *Ment. Evol. Anim.* i. 16 This necessarily ejective method of enquiry. **1884** —— in *Nature* XXIX. No. 747. 380 Our ejective inferences can only be founded on the observable activities of organisms.

3. *Philol.* Of voiceless consonants: articulated by means of non-pulmonic air-pressure, created by closing and raising the glottis. Also as *sb.*

1932 D. Jones *Outl. Eng. Phonetics* (ed. 3) xvii. 141 Consonants.. in which the necessary air pressure is produced by some other means than by the lungs. Sounds in which the air is forced outwards by these means are called *ejective* consonants. **1939** L. H. Gray *Found. Lang.* iii. 57 Ejectives (plosives with a simultaneous glottal stop). **1964** R. H. Robins *Gen. Ling.* iii. 103 Three non-pulmonic types of consonant articulations are used in some languages: ejectives, implosives, and clicks. *Ibid.*, Ejective consonants, which are sometimes also called glottalized consonants, are most commonly found with plosive or affricate release. **1968** Chomsky & Halle *Sound Pattern Eng.* 323 Ejectives have a transition with a somewhat higher termination frequency than the corresponding nonejectives.

Hence **e'jectively** *adv.* (*a*) By means of ejection. (*b*) With reference to ejects. **ejec'tivity**, the fact of being an eject.

1883 Romanes *Ment. Evol. Anim.* i. 17 Ejectively some such criterion is required. **1886** —— in *Contemp. Rev.* July 48 Both subjectivity and ejectivity are only known under the condition of being isolated from objectivity.

ejectment (ɪˈdʒɛktmənt). [f. EJECT *v.* + -MENT; app. first used in legal Anglo-French.]

1. a. *Law.* The act or process of ejecting a person from his holding. **b.** In wider sense, = EJECTION 2 (but chiefly with allusion to a.).

1567 Rastell *Termes of Law* 68 b, A writ of eiectement of warde lieth wher, etc. [Fr. *briefe deiectment de gard gist*, etc.]. **1602** Warner *Alb. Eng.* Epit. (1612) 359 This Eiectment of the Britons. **1672** H. Stubbe *Justif. Dutch War* 60 Continued after their [the Danes'] ejectment, by our English Kings. **1851** Ht. Martineau *Hist. Peace* (1877) III. v. xiii. 468 Forcible ejectments of the negroes from their habitations. **1869** Spurgeon *Treas. Dav.* Ps. xxiv. 1 [Man] is but a tenant at will.. liable to instantaneous ejectment. **1869** *Pall Mall G.* 4 Aug., The Irish land question divides itself naturally into three great points—improvements, tenant right, and ejectment.

2. (More fully, ***action, writ of ejectment***): 'An action at law whereby a person ousted or amoved from an estate for years may recover possession thereof' (Tomlins *Law Dict.*); the writ (otherwise *de ejectione firmæ*) by which this action is commenced.

An action of this kind, under which damages were claimed for a fictitious ejectment by an imaginary person, was formerly the recognized mode of trying the title to landed property.

1697 Prideaux *Lett.* (1875) 188 An ejectment hath been left at Sr H. Hobarts house for 800*l.* **1715** *Act Reg. Papists 2 Geo. I*, in *Lond. Gaz.* (1716) No. 5455/2 He may bring an Ejectment upon his own Demise. **1755** Young *Centaur* vi. Wks. 1757 IV. 253 But will not be at the trouble of bringing a writ of ejectment. **1768** Blackstone *Comm.* III. 199 A writ then of *ejectione firmae*, or action of trespass in ejectment. **1788** J. Powell *Devises* (1827) II. 45 He might bring his ejectment. **1794** S. Williams *Vermont* 216 Actions of ejectment were commenced in the courts at Albany. **1886** Stephen *Comm.* (ed. 10) III. 415.

†**3.** *pl.* [after L. *ejectamenta*]. Things cast up or out. *Obs. rare.*

1658 Sir T. Browne *Gard. Cyrus* II. 514 Ejectments of the Sea.

ejector (ɪˈdʒɛktə(r)). [f. as prec. + -OR, upon the analogy of L. agent-nouns in -OR.]

1. a. *gen.* One who ejects. *lit.* and *fig.* See EJECT *v.* 1, 2.

1640 Bp. Hall *Episc.* I. §17. 70 The ejectors should show better proofe than the ancient possessours. **1645** J. Bond *Occasus Occid.* 25, I find that sin branded as an Ejector, as an Exiler, not only of Persons, but of whole Churches. **1657** J. Goodwin *Triers Tried* To Rdr. 2 Two Apocryphall Orders of Commissioned Officers.. known by the names of Triers, and Ejectors. **1831** Syd. Smith *Speeches* Wks. 1859 II. 218/1 The merciless ejector.. will be restrained within the limits of decency and humanity. **1834** *Tait's Mag.* I. 494 The venomous slaver.. must be carried back to the face of the foul-breathed ejector.

b. *Law.* The person who ejects another from his holding. ***casual ejector***: see CASUAL.

1651 W. G. tr. *Cowel's Inst.* 191 If a third person eject him against Right, he shall recover damages against the Ejector. **1768** Blackstone *Comm.* III. 200 The lessee had no other remedy against the ejector but in damages. **1817** W. Selwyn *Law Nisi Prius* II. 680 The parties, viz. the plaintiff, and the defendant, the ejector, usually termed the casual ejector, are fictitious persons. **1880** Muirhead *Gaius* IV. §154 The result of violent, clandestine, or precarious taking from the ejector himself.

2. Applied to various portions of machinery, etc. serving the purpose of ejecting; *e.g.* an appliance for discharging empty cartridge cases from a breech-loader; a contrivance for ejecting the ashes from the stoke-hole of a marine engine; an apparatus for discharging the contents of sewers by means of compressed air, etc. Also *attrib.*, as in ***ejector-condenser, ejector gun, rifle, -sewer***; **ejector seat** *Aeronaut.* = *ejection seat*.

1874 Knight *Dict. Mech.*, *Ejector-condenser* (steam-engine), a form of condenser worked by the exhaust steam from the cylinder. **1881** Greener *Gun* 128 The ejector is acted upon through its rear claw, that nearest its pivot. **1884** *Health Exhib. Catal.* 57/2 Egg-shaped Isaac Shone's House Ejector Sewers. **1887** *Daily News* 25 Oct. 5/2 Of these ejectors there are eight, placed in pairs in different parts of the town. **1892** W. W. Greener *Breech-loader* 42 Fine guns and ejector guns cannot be purchased under £35. **1907** *Yesterday's Shopping* (1969) 636 The Society's hammerless ejector rook rifle. **1920** G. Burrard *Notes on Sporting Rifles* 68 Spare fore sights, extractors in the case of ejector-rifles. **1945** *Flight* 15 Nov. 524/1 Two types of German pilot-ejector seats. **1948** *Flight* 22 July 100/1 There are no known reports of a pilot getting out of the Vampire. To fit an ejector seat now would be a major operation. **1955** *Times* 6 July 10/6 Lieutenant-Commander Rickell used his ejector seat to bale out.

‖**ejido** (eˈxiðo, eɪˈhiːðəʊ). [Mexican Sp., f. Sp. *ejido* common land, f. L. *exitus* departure, f. *exīre* to go out.] In Mexico, land farmed communally; a co-operative farm; land to which communal title is held. Also *attrib.*

1889 in *Cent. Dict.* **1931** C. Beals *Mexican Maze* ii. 37 Their *ejidos* (village commons).. were again menaced. **1938** *New Statesman* 12 Feb. 241/1 To facilitate the harvesting of profitable crops, the lands are in some places worked collectively, the members of each neighbourhood or 'ejido' helping each other in co-operative fashion. **1946** H. F. Infield *Co-operative Living in Palestine* 4 The Russian Kolkhoz, the Palestinian Kvutza, the Mexican Ejido.. have made effective use of comprehensive co-operation. **1964** *New Statesman* 28 Feb. 327/3 Zapata stressed the return of the lost communal holdings to the rural Indian villages. Thus he proposed the '*ejido*' system in which title to lands was to be vested in the landholding village.

†**eju'lation.** *Obs.* [ad. L. *ējulātiōn-em*, noun of action f. *ējulāre* to wail.] Wailing, lamentation.

a **1619** Fotherby *Atheom.* I. xv. §2 (1622) 156 It should be lamented, with this pitifull eiulation. **1659** *Gentl. Call.* §7 Pref. 3 What ejulations can be bitter or loud enough. **1708** J. Philips *Cyder* II. 85 With dismal groans and Ejulations in the pangs of death. **1721–1800** in Bailey. **1755** in Johnson; and in mod. Dicts.

†**'ejurate,** *v. Obs.* [f. L. *ējūrāt-* ppl. stem of *ējūrāre* to abjure.] *trans.* To abjure, renounce. Hence **eju'ration** (see quot.).

1622–62 Heylin *Cosmogr.* I. (1682) 209 The Faith of Christ.. was defiled with Arrianism; not ejurated till the year 588. **1626** Cockeram, *Ejurate*, to forsweare, or resigne ones place. **1656** Blount *Glossogr.*, *Ejuration*, a renouncing or resignation. **1678–96** in Phillips. **1721–1800** in Bailey.

†**e'jure**, *v. Obs. rare.* [ad. L. *ējūr-āre*: see prec.] = prec.

1642 ROGERS *Naaman* 855 To be a close client of his for ever, ejuring all former false and idolatrous service.

eka- ('iːkə), *pref. Chem.* [a. Skr. *eka* one.] Used 1872 in *Ann. d. Chemie u. Pharmacie*, VIII. Supplementband 196 by D. I. Mendeléeff (1834–1907), Russian chemist, to denote a predicted element that should occupy the next lower position to that so qualified in the same group in the periodic system.

1889 *Jrnl. Chem. Soc.* LV. 648 *Gallium*, which proved to correspond to eka-aluminium of the periodic law ..*scandium*, corresponding to eka-boron..and ..*germanium*, which proved to correspond in all respects to eka-silicum. **1931** *Observer* 18 Oct. 22/4 Eight years ago there were six [atomic] numbers corresponding to unknown elements... Both 43 and 75 were known before their discovery as eka-manganeses, from their anticipated similarity to manganese... 85 should be chemically akin to iodine, and so is provisionally called eka-iodine... On Friday the news came from America that eka-caesium had been discovered. **1938** *Ann. Reg. 1937* 355 Curie & Savitich ..obtained three new series of short period radioactive elements ending possibly in eka-gold, eka-iridium, and eka-rhenium. **1955** *Ann. Reg. 1954* 398 It was announced in February that physicists of the University of California had produced element No. 99 provisionally called eka-holmium. **1969** *Daily Tel.* 5 May 13/7 Russian scientists at Dubna and Leningrad are looking for element 114, eka-lead, in old mirrors made from lead glass.

ekdemite ('ɛkdɪmaɪt, ɛk'diːmaɪt). *Min.* Also ecdemite. [ad. Sw. *ekdemit* (A. E. Nordenskiöld 1877, in *Geol. För. Förh.* III. 379), f. Gr. ἔκδημος unusual + -ITE[1].] A yellow oxychloride of lead and arsenic, of uncertain formula, found in Sweden and the U.S.A.

1879 *Jrnl. Chem. Soc.* XXXVI. 22 Ekdemite.., a new mineral, coarse-crystalline, foliated, monoaxial, with a distinct basal cleavage. **1882** J. D. DANA *Man. Min.* (ed. 4) 152 Ecdemite, a lead chloro-arsenite. **1951** C. PALACHE et al. *Dana's Syst. Min.* (ed. 7) II. 1036 Found as crystals and masses associated with heliophyllite in manganoan calcite at Långban, Wermland, Sweden. Ecdemite apparently also constitutes the uniaxial parts of the intergrowths with heliophyllite found..in Wermland. **1968** EMBREY & PHEMESTER tr. *Kostov's Mineralogy* 467 Ekdemite is tetragonal, dimorphous with heliophyllite.

†**eke** (iːk), *sb.*[1] *Obs.* exc. *dial.* Forms: 1 éaca, 3, 6, 9 eke, *Sc.* (6 eik, 7 eeke). See also ECHE *sb.* [OE. *éaca* = ON. *auke*:—OTeut. **aukon-*, f. same root as ECHE *v.*]

1. An addition, increase; a piece added on; a supplement. In OE., A reinforcement (of troops).

894 *O.E. Chron.* (Parker MS.) Him com micel eaca to. *a* **1000** *Sal. & Sat.* 460 (Gr.) Forþon is witena ȝehwam wopes eaca. **1786** GEDDES *Prosp. New Trans. Bible* 95 The words in Italics..are generally ill-assorted and clumsy ekes. *Mod. Sc.* It would be too short without an eke.

2. *spec.* **a.** A tag to a bell-rope; also *attrib.*, as in *bell-eke*. Also ECHE. **b.** A short straw or wooden cylinder on which a beehive is placed to increase its capacity.

1549 in Miss T. Smith *Rotherham Acc.* (1878) 12 Paid to Robt. Machon for a neke to our gret Bell. **1566** ROGERS *Agric. & Prices* III. 577/2, 6 ekes for bell ropes 1/4. **1594** in Miss T. Smith *Rotherham Acc.* (1878) 12 Payd unto Robert Okes for 10 payre of bell ekes 10s. **1857** C. B. ROBINSON *Gloss. Best's Farm. Bks.* 184 Underlay. Now called ekes; additional bands of straw placed beneath the hive.

3. *Sc.* (16th and 17th c.) A supplement, postscript, appendix to a formal document.

1568 *Declar. Murray, &c.* in H. Campbell *Love-lett. Mary Q. Scots* 11 The eik or additioun to our answer. *a* **1651** CALDERWOOD *Hist. Kirk* (1843) II. 451 The other partie had givin in an eeke or additioun to their former answere.

4. In advb. phrase, *to eken* (OE. *tó éacan*) in addition, besides, contracted in ME. into TEKE(N, q.v. Also, in same sense, *on eke*.

c **888** K. ÆLFRED *Boeth.* i, þæt wæs to eacan oþrum unarimeðum yflum. *c* **1200** *Trin. Coll. Hom.* 51 To eken oþer þo gremeden hem sore. *a* **1225** *Ancr. R.* 174 þe nome of Hester ne seið nout one 'abscondita'..auh deð þer teken 'eleuata in populis'. *a* **1310** in Wright *Lyric P.* 34 Hire chyn ys chosen, ant eyther cheke Whit ynoh ant rode on eke.

eke, *sb.*[2] *dial.* A male salmon.

1887 *Pall Mall. G.* 22 Aug. 10/2 It [a salmon] was a male fish, or what is known in the north of England amongst fishermen as an 'eke'.

eke (iːk), *v.* Forms: 1 (see ECHE *v.*), 2–3 eken, 4–6 ek, (4 ayke, ȝeke(n), 5–8 eek(e, 6–7 eak(e, (7 eck, eyk), 4– eke, 5– *Sc.* eik. [partly f. EKE *sb.*[1]; partly dial. (northern) form of ECHE *v.*]

1. *trans.* To increase, add to, lengthen. Also *absol.* †*neither to eke nor to pair* (*Sc.*): neither to add to nor take from. Proverb, ***every little ekes.*** *arch.* or *dial.*

c **1200** *Trin. Coll. Hom.* 57 þe holie man fasteð forto..eken his holinesse. *a* **1300** *E.E. Psalter* civ. [cv.] 24 He ayked his folk swith mikel on an. *c* **1400** *Apol. Loll.* 13 Nowe..þe pricis are ekid. *Ibid.* 26 þey..ȝekun þer synnis. *c* **1430** LYDG. *Min. Poems* (1840) 133 Theyr bounté for to eeke. **1530** PALSGR. 531/2, I eke..my gowne is to shorte for me, but I wyll eke it. **1566** KNOX *Hist. Ref.* Wks. (1846) I. 130 This miserie..which the malice of man cane neyther eak nor paire. **1599** HARSNET *Agst. Darell* 193 As they say, Every thing Eiketh. **1609** SKENE *Reg. Maj.* 96 Quhen the partie hes named ane certaine number of witnes, he may not thereafter eike, nor pair the number of the witnes. **1639** J. CLARKE *Parœmiol.* 10 A litle eekes. **1650** FULLER *Pisgah* 372 It not being princely to..eek the same [the vail of the tabernacle] another was contrived. **1731** POPE *Ep. Burlington* 32 Some patch'd dog-hole ek'd with ends of wall. **1755** SMOLLETT *Quix.* (1803) II. 258 Without eking or curtailing God's precious truth. **1829** CLARE *Ode Autumn, Anniversary* 76 The moaning brook, that ekes its weary speed.

†**b.** *intr.* To increase, grow. *Obs.*

1535 STEWART *Chron. Scot.* III. 162 His power eikit so and grew.

†**2.** To add. Const. †*til*, *to*. Also *absol. Obs.*

c **1200** ORMIN 16352 ȝiff þ u takesst twiȝȝes an And ekesst itt till fowwre. *a* **1300** *Cursor M.* 21194 þar-til þai eked mar and mare. *c* **1425** WYNTOUN *Cron.* VIII. xxvi. 190 Sal I ek til Goddis wengeance? **1549** *Compl. Scot.* xv. 123 Ther can na thing be eikkyt to my parsecutione bot cruel dede. **1634–46** Row *Hist. Kirk* (1842) 17 We..conforme..to the notes and additions thereto eiked. **1733** NEAL *Hist. Purit.* II. 14 His Majesty..eked others that I had omitted.

3. ***to eke out***: **a.** to supplement, supply the deficiencies of anything (const. *with*); *esp.* to make (resources, materials, articles of consumption, etc.) last the required time by additions, by partial use of a substitute, or by economy.

1596 BP. BARLOW *Three Serm.* iii. 133 Not to bee so.. giuen to spending..but eeke it out to the vtmost. **1600** SHAKS. *A. Y. L.* I. ii. 209 *Ros.* The little strength that I haue, I would it vvere with you. *Cel.* And mine to eeke out hers. **1623** LISLE *Ælfric on O. & N.T.* To Rdr. 6 Best is he that inuents, the next he that followes forth and eekes out a good inuention. **1719** DE FOE *Crusoe* (1858) 140 My ink..had been gone..all but a very little, which I eked out with water. **1788** BURNS *Extempore 2 Lawyers*, But what his common sense came short, He eked out wi' law, man. **1872** BAKER *Nile Tribut.* xx. 353, I determined to start..to eke out our scanty supply of water. **1874** SAYCE *Compar. Philol.* i. 25 The meaning of their [savage races'] words has to be eked out by gesture. **1878** H. S. WILSON *Alp. Ascents* ii. 57 After a glass apiece we eke out the remainder with snow.

b. To prolong (a speech or composition, an action) by expedients devised for that purpose; to contrive to fill up (a certain amount of space in writing, etc.).

1641 MILTON *Animadv.* (1851) 245 Your reverence to eek out your sermonings shall need repaire to Postills, or Polianthea's. *a* **1656** USSHER *Ann.* VI. (1658) 551 As for his ecking out..the Siege, it was done upon good grounds. **1747** JOHNSON *Plan Eng. Dict.* Wks. IX. 186 To eke out any thing, signifies to lengthen it beyond its just dimensions, by some low artifice. **1847** BARHAM *Ingol. Leg.* (1877) 289 Enough to have eked out a decent-sized volume. **1865** LIVINGSTONE *Zambesi* xi. 236 He..eked out the measure with a peculiar musical sound.

c. To contrive to make (a livelihood), or to support (existence) by various makeshifts.

1825 T. JEFFERSON *Autobiog.* Wks. 1859 I. 89 To eke out the existence of the people, every person..was called on for a weekly subscription. **1845** DARWIN *Voy. Nat.* ii. (1879) 19 Some runaway slaves..contrived to eke out a subsistence. **1875** FARRAR *Seekers* I. i. 12 To eke out a scanty livelihood.

†**4.** ***to eke up***: to supply, repair (a loss). *Obs.*

1633 D. ROGERS *Treat. Sacr.* ii. 53 What meanes are so like to eike up..spiritual losses, as the Supper of the Lord?

eke (iːk), *adv. arch.* Forms: 1–2 éac, (1 ǽc, éc), 3–4 ec, ek, 3 æac, ok, 4–6 eek(e, (4 heke, yke), 6–7 eake, *Sc.* 6 eik(e, 8 eek, 3– eke. [Com. Teut.:—OE. *éac* = OFris. *âk*, OS. *ôk* (Du. *ook*), OHG. *ouh* (MHG. *ouch*, mod.G. *auch*), ON. *auk* 'also' (Da. *og*. Sw. *och* 'and'), Goth. *auk* for, but. The ultimate origin is uncertain; some connect the word with the root of EKE *v.*, while others consider it f. Aryan **au* again + **ge* particle of emphasis; cf. Gr. αὖ γε. The form *ok* in 13th c. is app. a. ON.] Also, too, moreover; in addition.

Beowulf 3131 (Gr.) Dracan ec scufun Wyrm ofer weall clif. *a* **700** *Epinal Gloss.* 846 *Quinetiam*, æc þan..æc don. *c* **1000** *Ags. Gosp.* Matt. xi. 9 Ic eow secȝe, eac maran þonne witeȝan. **1154** *O.E. Chron.* an. 1118 Eac on þison ȝeare wæs unȝemetliche mycel wind. *c* **1175** *Lamb. Hom.* 3 Mid his apostles and ec mid oðere floc manna. *c* **1175** *Cott. Hom.* 221 Swa mihte æac þe oðre. *a* **1225** *Ancr. R.* 56 Vor þæt ec þæt he dude hire was iðe frumðe sore hire unðonckes. *a* **1300** *Havelok* 200 þe beste, fayreste, the strangest ok. *c* **1325** *E.E. Allit. P.* A. 210 Her here heke al hyr vmbe-gon. **1362** LANGL. *P. Pl.* A. I. 88 And eke I-liknet to vr lord. *c* **1386** CHAUCER *Prol.* 757 Eke therto he was right a mery man. *a* **1420** OCCLEVE *De Reg. Princ.* 565 The ende is dethe of male and eke femele. **1500–20** DUNBAR *How Dunbar ane Freir* 38 In it haif I in pulpet gon and preichit In Derntoun kirk, and eik in Canterberry. **1580** SIDNEY *Arcadia* II. 219 These forrests eke, made wretched by our music. **1616** R. C. *Times' Whis.* v. 1658 But eke doth comprehend That base vnmanly sinne of drunkennesse. **1759** STERNE *Tr. Shandy* II. ii. 39 Supposing the wax good, and eke the thimble. *a* **1856** LONGF. *Childr. Lord's Supper* 122 Answered the young men Yes! and Yes! with lips softly breathing answered the maidens eke.

ekebergite. *Min.* [f. name of the Swedish traveller *Ekeberg* + -ITE.] An important member of the scapolite family occurring in square prisms of a white, greyish, greenish, or reddish colour.

1822 CLEVELAND *Min.* 359 [Ekebergite of Thomson] is probably a variety of scapolite. **1884** DANA *Min.* 325 It is probable that the mineral is an altered ekebergite.

†**'ekement.** *Obs. rare*[−1]. [f. EKE *v.* + -MENT.] An increase, extension, enlargement.

a **1603** T. CARTWRIGHT *Confut. Rhem. N.T.* (1618) 586 There is no ekement or inlargement in matter.

†**'eke-name.** *Obs.* [f. EKE *sb.* + NAME; cf. ON. *aukanafn.*] An additional name, a nickname.

Now superseded by the corrupt form NICKNAME: *a nekename* (*Promp. Parv.*) for *an ekename*.

1303 BRUNNE *Handl. Synne* 1530 As moche þan he ys to blame þat ȝeueþ a man a vyle ekename. **1483** *Cath. Angl.* 112 An Ekname, *agnomen*. **1885** CLODD *Myths & Dr.* I. vi. 109 Nicknames (*i.e.* ekename or the added name).

†**'eker**[1]. *Obs.*[−0] [f. EKE *v.* + -ER.] One who increases.

1483 *Cath. Angl.* 112 An eker, *auctor, augmentator*.

†**'eker**[2]. *Obs. rare.* Also **iker.** [Origin and meaning unknown; possibly a corruption of *niker*, NICKER, water-sprite. Cf. also EAGRE.]

c **1300** *K. Alis.* 6175 They woneth in water, y-wis, With eker [*v.r.* Iker] and fysch. *Ibid.* 6202 He say the ekeris wonynge And the fysches lotynge.

eking ('iːkɪŋ), *vbl. sb.* [f. EKE *v.* + -ING[1].]

1. The action of adding or making an addition; the action of putting an 'eke' to (a bell-rope).

c **1425** WYNTOUN *Cron.* VIII. viii. 53 In ekyng als of Goddis serwyce Scho fowndyt..twa chapellanyis. **1576** in Miss T. Smith *Rotherham Acc.* (1878) 12 For ekeing of a bell-rope. **1579** SPENSER *Sheph. Cal.* Sept. 31 But such eeking hath made my hart sore.

2. An augmentation, increase.

1393 GOWER *Conf.* II. 22 And make an ekynge of my peine. **1483** *Cath. Angl.* 112 An Ekynge, *augmentum*. **1611** COTGR. s.v. *Accrue*, a growth, eeking, augmentation.

3. (See quot.)

1819 J. ROSS *Voy. Discovery* p. xviii, Hooks and ekeings were placed in the bows above the lower-deck hook. **1867** SMYTH *Sailor's Word-bk.*, *Ekeing*, a piece of wood fitted, by scarphing or butting, to make good a deficiency in length, as the end of a knee and the like. The ekeing is also the carved work under the lower part of the quarter-piece, at the aft part of the gallery.

eking ('iːkɪŋ), *ppl. a.* [f. as prec. + -ING[2].] That serves to eke out.

1653 B[ARNABAS] O[LEY] *Account of Wks.* in *Jackson's Wks.*, His stile..is more short than other Authours in Relatives, in Eeking and helping particles. **1814** D'ISRAELI *Quarrels Auth.* (1867) 346 Suppressed invectives and eking rhymes could but ill appease so fierce a mastiff.

ekistics (ɪ'kɪstɪks). [f. mod.Gr. ἡ οἰκιστική, f. Gr. οἰκιστικός relating to settlement, f. οἰκίζ-ειν to settle (a colony), f. οἶκος house, dwelling.] A name given by C. A. Doxiadis to the study of human settlements and the way they develop and adapt themselves to changing circumstances. Hence **e'kistic** *a.*, relating to ekistics; **eki'stician** (-ʃən), one who studies or is versed in ekistics.

1959 C. A. DOXIADIS in *Rep. Proc. Town & Country Plan. Summer Sch.* (Town Plan. Inst.) 119 Ekistics, as a scientific discipline, can be divided into Ekistic geography, Ekistic economy, social Ekistics, and the other branches which.. make up its whole and..relate it to the neighbour sciences of geography, economics, sociology, etc. **1968** *New Society* 26 Sept. 456/1 Only the new science of ekistics can embrace the whole study of human settlements and their planning, in all their manifold elements. **1968** C. A. DOXIADIS *Ekistics* ii. 75 Among all the experts who deal with the problems of human settlements, the Ekistician should be the one who has the most inter-disciplinary approach. *Ibid.* 516 *Ekistics*, science of human settlements. Term coined by the author..; first used in his lectures of 1942 at the Athens Technical University.

ekka[1] ('ɛkə). *Anglo-Ind.* Also ecca, ecka. [a. Hindi *ekkā* lit. unit, f. Skr. *eka* one.] A small one-horsed vehicle used in India. Also *attrib.*

1811 F. B. SOLVYNS *Les Hindous* III. XXXI. pl. 4 Ekka.. perhaps the simplest carriage that can be imagined, being nothing more than a chair covered with red cloth, and fixed upon an axle-tree between two small wheels. The Ekka is drawn by one horse. **1848** J. H. STOCQUELER *Oriental Interpreter*, *Ecka*, a light pony gig on two wheels, with crimson cloth cushions on the top, on which the natives of India (who alone use them) sit cross-legged. **1887** KIPLING *Departm. Ditties* (1888) 21 The Waler jumped an *ekka* just above the City Drain. **1888** —— *Plain Tales* iii. 21 The *ekka*-pony..had gone home. **1892** *Pall Mall Gaz.* 21 Dec. 3/2, I am going to take an ecka. **1895** B. M. CROKER *Village Tales* 148 His wife had real silver tyres to the wheels of her ekka! **1899** *Westm. Gaz.* 25 Oct. 3/1 Ekka bells. **1922** *19th Cent.* Oct. 592 The bullock carts, the loaded camels, the eccas, the elephants, of typical India. **1966** E. NEWBY *Slowly down Ganges* 101 The only vehicle..was an ekka, a small pony cart with a canopy over it and side curtains.

Ekka[2] ('ɛkə). *Austral. colloq.* [Altered abbrev. of EXHIBITION.] The annual Royal National Agricultural and Industrial Association of Queensland Show or 'Brisbane Exhibition'.

1967 *Telegraph* (Brisbane) 5 Aug. 2/2 Brisbane's 'Ekka'.. is the focal point of months of planning, organisation and discussions. **1978** *Courier-Mail* (Brisbane) 21 Aug. 4/10, I think the 'Ekka' should be shifted to a new site on the periphery of Brisbane. **1984** *Ibid.* 17 Aug. 10/5 In 1982, Sir Ninian Stephen broke a 50-year tradition by refusing to open the Ekka.

ekker ('ɛkə(r)). *University* or *School slang.* [See -ER[6].] = EXERCISE *sb.* 7.

1891 S. J. DUNCAN *Amer. Girl in London* xxiii. 254 Walking for what in the vulgar tongue might be called exercise, but here [*sc.* in Oxford] was 'ekker'. **1901** *Winchester Coll. Notions* 40 Most houses have Ekker Rolls, the amount of compulsory exercise varying from four to six hours a week. **1970** *Wykehamist* 21 Mar. 447/1 Whatever the supposed range of activities that qualify as ekker, the demands of the major games.. usually over-ride all others.

ekmannite ('ɛkmænaɪt). *Min.* [so called by Igelström 1865, after G. Ekmann, the proprietor of the mine where found; see -ITE.] A hydrous silicate of iron and manganese, resembling chlorite in appearance.

1868 DANA *Min.* 490 Ekmannite.. on heating yields water.

ekphore, etc.: see ECPHORE *v.*, etc.

ektene, var. ECTENE.

ektodynamomorphic, var. *ectodynamomorphic* (ECTO-).

El, el (ɛl), colloq. U.S. abbrev. of *elevated railroad*; **el train** = *elevated train* (ELEVATED *ppl. a.* 1).

a **1906** 'O. HENRY' *Trimmed Lamp* (1916) 120 Behold Ikey as he ambles up the street beneath the roaring 'El' between the rows of reeking sweatshops. **1932** E. WILSON *Devil take Hindmost* xii. 126 Irma Meyer lives under the El [in Brooklyn]. **1936** J. DOS PASSOS *Big Money* ii. 9 An el train clattered raspingly through the.. streets. **1959** *Times Lit. Suppl.* 6 Nov. p. xvii/4 John Frederick Nims has a poem 'Penny Arcade', set in Chicago, which begins with a description of 'This pale and dusty palace under the El'.

el, obs. form of AWL.

-el, *suffix*[1], repr. OE. *-el*, *-ela*, *-ele* (OTeut. **-ilo-*, *-ilon-*, *-ilôn-*), has in mod.Eng. usually become -LE, q.v., though the older form is retained after *v*, *th*, *ch*, *n*, as in *hovel*, *brothel*, *hatchel*, *kernel*.

OE. *-el* is added to vbl. stems to form agent-nouns, instrumental sbs., and adjs., and to sbs. to form diminutives; *-ela*, *-ele*, are chiefly used to form diminutives from sbs. and object-nouns from vbl. stems. See further under -LE.

-el, *suffix*[2], a. OF. *-el* (mod.F. usu. *-eau*), *-elle*, repr. L. *-ello-*, *-ella-*. This suffix is in classical Latin used to form diminutives from sbs. or adjs. in *-er* and *-ra*, as *libellus*, *libella*, from *liber* book, *libra* balance; it is also substituted for *-ulo-*, *-ula-*, to form diminutives of nouns of that termination, where the latter had lost its original diminutive force, as in *porcellus* little pig, dim. of *porculus*, f. *porc-us* pig. In Romanic it was much more widely used in the formation of diminutives. Examples in Eng. (with the spelling *-el*) are (from the masc. *-el*), *tunnel*, *bowel*, *carnel*; (from the fem. *-elle*) *chapel*, *novel*, *pimpernel*, etc.

2. It should be noted that the ending *-el* in Eng. words adapted from Fr. frequently represents other L. suffixes than *-ello-*, *-ella-*; e.g. in *jewel*, *vowel*, it stands for Fr. *-el*:—L. *-āli-* (see -AL[1]); in *apparel* for Fr. *-eil*:—L. *-iculo-* (see -CULE); in *kennel* for Fr. *-il*:—L. *-īle*, as in *ovīle* sheepfold.

† **ela** ('eː'lɑː). *Mus. Obs.* exc. *Hist.* Also 7 **eela**. [f. E + LA; denoting the particular note E which occurred only in the seventh Hexachord, in which it was sung to the syllable *la*. Cf. E-LA-MI.]

The highest note in the Gamut, or the highest note of the 7th Hexachord of Guido, answering to the upper E in the treble. Often *fig.* as a type of something 'high-flown'. Also *attrib.*

1580 LYLY *Euphues* (1609) A ij, The Musitions, who being intreated, will scarse sing Sol Fa, but not desired, straine aboue Ela. **1593** NASHE *Christ's T.* 64 a, You must straine your wits an Ela oboue theyrs. **1607** WALKINGTON *Opt. Glass* 168 Vntill our wit can reach an Ela straine. **1649** BULWER *Pathomyot.* II. ii. 111 Although it [laughter] be at the highest pitch and scrued up to the very Eela of mirth, it vanisheth away. **1675** J. SMITH *Chr. Relig. Appeal* I. 50 An Age elevated above the Ela of common Humanity. **1820** SCOTT *Abbot* II. IV. 121 'Why God-a-mercy.. this is a note above E La.'

elaat, obs. form of ELATE *a.*

elaate ('ɛlaeɪt). *Chem.* [f. ELA-IC + -ATE.] A salt of elaic acid.

1845 TODD & BOWMAN *Phys. Anat.* I. 82 An elaate of glycerine.

e'labe, *v. rare*[−1]. [ad. L. *ēlābi*, f. *ē* out + *lābi* to glide.] *intr.* To slip away.

1837 S. B. HARPER *Bertrand* I. ii. 15 She.. to a convent hied Whence she will ne'er emerge till he's no more.. With him elabes the anchor of her vow.

elaborate (ɪ'læbərət), *ppl.* and *a.* [ad. L. *ēlabōrāt-us*, pa. pple. of *ēlabōrāre* to ELABORATE.]

† **A.** as *pple.* = ELABORATED: see ELABORATE *v.*

1581 NOWELL & DAY in *Confer.* I. (1584) G b, It was elaborate before, by the.. studie of all the best learned Iesuites.

B. as *adj.*

1. Produced or accomplished by labour. Also, that has been subjected to processes of art; = ELABORATED. *Obs.* or *arch.*

1592 NASHE *P. Penilesse* (ed. 2) 19 a, Some elaborate pollished Poems. **1607** TOPSELL *Four-f. Beasts* 27 The Gray .. leaveth her elaborate house to the Fox. **1725** POPE *Odyss.* XIV. 360 The vast unnumber'd store Of steel elab'rate, and refulgent ore. **1779** JOHNSON *L.P.*, *Cowley*, Wks. II. 65 He has no elegances either lucky or elaborate. **1814** SOUTHEY *Roderick* xxv. 152 Eyeing the elaborate steel.

2. Worked out in much detail; highly finished.

1621 BURTON *Anat. Mel.* II. ii. IV. (1676) 176/1 Those elaborate Maps of Ortelius. **1687** *Penal Laws* 22 A.. veneration for his Learned and Elabourate Works. **1704** DAVENANT in Ellis *Orig. Lett.* II. 397 IV. 244, I had prepared a very elaborate letter to Her Royal Highness. **1862** DARWIN *Fertil. Orchids* ii. 71 In the same flower we apparently have elaborate contrivances for directly opposed objects. **1875** HAMERTON *Intell. Life* x. v. 393 In scientific pursuits the preparations are usually elaborate. **1875** JOWETT *Plato* (ed. 2) I. 112 He then proceeds to give another and more elaborate explanation of the whole passage.

b. Of an investigation, a study, an operation, etc.: Conducted with great minuteness. Hence *transf.* applied to personal agents or their attributes: Minutely careful, painstaking.

1649 MILTON *Eikon.* iv. (1851) 362 The King was emphatical and elaborate on this Theam against Tumults. **1669** GALE *Crt. Gentiles* I. III. ii. 28 Amongst the Ancients, none have spent more elaborate studies herein than Eusebius. **1728** MORGAN *Algiers* I. iii. 37 He was a most curious and elaborate Collector of valuable Histories. **1782** V. KNOX *Ess.* (1819) III. cxxxvii. 89 From the annals of the elaborate Maittaire. *a* **1836** W. GODWIN *Essays* (1873) 193 The world is busy and elaborate to tear him from my recollection. **1871** MORLEY *Voltaire* (1886) 86 He read Shakespeare, and made an elaborate study of his method.

elaborate (ɪ'læbəreɪt), *v.* [f. L. *ēlabōrāt-* ppl. stem of *ēlabōrāre* to work out, produce by labour, f. *ē* out + *labōrāre* to LABOUR.

Sense 2 may probably be the earliest in Eng. from the use of the L. word by writers on alchemy or medicine. Cf. Fr. *élaborer*, 16th c. (Littré) = sense 2.]

1. To produce or develop by the application of labour; to fashion (a product of art or industry) from the raw material; to work out in detail, give finish or completeness to (an invention, a theory, literary or artistic work, etc.).

1611 COTGR., *Elabourer*, to elaborate. **1626** COCKERAM, *Elaborate*, to do a thing with great paines. **1726** YOUNG *Love Fame* Wks. (1866) II. 96 Attend, and you discern it [ambition] in the fair Conduct a finger, Or, in full joy, elaborate a sigh. **1846** RUSKIN *Mod. Paint.* (1848) I. II. I. vii. §12 85 The objects of landscape may be either elaborated or suggested according to their place and claim. **1850** GLADSTONE *Glean.* V. cx. 238 The constitutional system which was in course of being gradually elaborated and matured. **1865** LECKY *Ration.* (1878) II. v. 199 He elaborates his theory from his own reason. **1875** JOWETT *Plato* (ed. 2) III. 390 Little things are elaborated with an infinity of pains.

2. *transf.* Of nature or natural agencies: To produce (a chemical substance) from (its) elements or sources; to fashion or develop (an animal or vegetable tissue, etc.); also, to transmute (crude materials) *into* a developed product.

1607 WALKINGTON *Opt. Glass.* 54 Nothing elaborates our concoction more then sleepe. **1665–9** BOYLE *Occas. Refl.* (1675) 65 Honey.. is elaborated by the Bee. **1671** J. WEBSTER *Metallogr.* iv. 81 If the waters be saltish, pure and clear,.. then a pure Metal is generated; but in defect of purity an Impure Metal, in elaborating of which, Nature spreadeth.. a thousand years. **1744** BERKELEY *Siris* §87 The animal spirits are elaborated from the blood. **1828** STEUART *Planter's G.* 211 As well might it be imagined, that the roots elaborate it [the sap] in the leaves. **1834** SOUTHEY *Doctor* lxxvi. (1862) 161 The Sun, under whose influence one plant elaborates nutriment for man and another poison. **1870** H. MACMILLAN *Bible Teach.* x. 194 Year after year.. the leaf is elaborating from air and rain and sunshine.. those solid structures which are destined to outlive it.

3. *intr.* To become elaborate.

1876 H. SPENCER *Princ. Sociol.* I. §103 This custom elaborates as social development goes through its earlier stages. **1903** R. LANGBRIDGE *Flame & Flood* xx, These [*sc.* preparations] she discovered had augmented and elaborated to a considerable extent.

elaborated (ɪ'læbəreɪtɪd), *ppl. a.* [f. prec. + -ED[1].] That has been worked up, has undergone preparation or development; worked out in detail, finely wrought, etc. (see the vb.).

1602 WARNER *Alb. Eng.* XII. lxx. (1612) 295 One elaborated Pen compendiously doth floe. *a* **1649** DRUMM. OF HAWTH. *Fam. Ep.* Wks. (1711) 162 He doth it so finely as if he found such purposes in his way, and went not astray with a search too curiously elaborated. **1824** DIBDIN *Libr. Comp.* 740 It is the most perfect and highly elaborated of all the author's pieces. **1879** STAINER *Music of Bible* 23 An instrument of a more elaborated character.

elaborately (ɪ'læbərətlɪ), *adv.* [f. ELABORATE *a.* + -LY[1].] In an elaborate manner.

1633 EARLE *Microcosm.* (Arb.) 104 He is so elaborately excessive, that none will believe him. **1724** SWIFT *Drapier's Lett.* Wks. 1755 V. II. 48 It is.. elaborately shewn, that former patents have passed in the same manner. **1823** SCOTT *Peveril* xlviii, I see you are elaborately dressed.

elaborateness (ɪ'læbərətnɪs). [f. as prec. + -NESS.] The quality of being elaborate.

1694 ECHARD *Plautus* Pref., His [Terence's] extream Closeness and great Elaborateness. **1779** JOHNSON *L.P.* Wks. 1816 X. 167 The 'Old Bachelor'.. is.. composed with great elaborateness of dialogue. **1874** CARPENTER *Ment. Phys.* I. ii. §3 (1879) 99 For they are further remarkable for the elaborateness of their internal structure.

elaboration (ɪˌlæbɒ'reɪʃən). [ad. late L. *ēlabōrātiōn-em*, noun of action f. *ēlabōrāre*: see ELABORATE *v.*]

1. The process of producing or developing from crude materials; †*spec.* in Chemistry (see quot. 1612). Also, the process of working out in detail, developing, perfecting (an invention, a theory, a literary work, etc.).

1612 WOODALL *Surg. Mate* (*Chemistry*) (1617) 304 Where distillations doe preuaile Distraction takes the head, Then by Elaboration Wise men may be misled. **1858** GLADSTONE *Homer* III. 531 The first thought of Virgil was his Emperor .. the second the elaboration of his verse.

b. The state of being elaborated; elaborateness.

1824 DIBDIN *Libr. Comp.* 770 Intermediate editions of.. less elaboration. **1861** W. COLLINS *Dead Secr.* 149 The housekeeper cleared her throat with extraordinary loudness and elaboration, and read on thus. **1877** MRS. OLIPHANT *Makers Flor.* xiii. 319 Various copies exist in various stages of elaboration.

2. The production by natural agencies of chemical substances from their elements or sources; *spec.* (in Physiology) the formation of animal or vegetable tissues, or the changes undergone by alimentary substances from their reception into the body to their complete assimilation.

1578 BANISTER *Hist. Man* v. 81 b, Arteries.. by their heat helpyng to the exact elaboration of his bloud. **1677** W. HARRIS tr. *Lemery's Course Chym.* I. xx. (1686) 442 Milk is a chyle which.. has received but a light Elaboration. **1725** BRADLEY *Fam. Dict.* II. s.v. *Vegetables*, There happen different Fermentations and other Elaborations amongst the sensible parts. **1858** CARPENTER *Veg. Phys.* §220 In this process of Elaboration.. the most important change is the concentration of the fluid.

3. *concr.* in various senses.

1765 *Univ. Mag.* XXXVII. 235/1 This spirit is a last elaboration. **1856** DOVE *Logic Chr. Faith* IV. ii. §1. 177 Science is an elaboration. **1879** *Cassell's Techn. Educ.* I. 200/1 Fig. 138 is a further elaboration of the same design, the lines being doubled.

elaborative (ɪ'læbərətɪv), *a.* [f. L. *ēlabōrāt-* ppl. stem of *ēlabōrāre* + -IVE.] That has the property of elaborating.

1836–7 SIR W. HAMILTON *Metaph.* (1859) II. xx. 14 The Elaborative or Discursive Faculty. **1845** *Florist Jrnl.* 45 The elaborative organs of the plants. **1876** A. M. FAIRBAIRN in *Contemp. Rev.* June 135 Ancient heresies were elaborative, modern disintegrative of dogma.

e'laborator. [as if L. **ēlabōrātor*: see ELABORATE *v.* and -OR.] One who or that which elaborates.

In mod. Dicts.

elaboratory (ɪ'læbərətərɪ). [as if ad. L. **ēlabōrātōrium*, f. *ēlabōrāre* to ELABORATE.]

1. A place where chemical operations are performed, or where medicines are compounded; = LABORATORY. *Obs.* exc. *Hist.*

1652 EVELYN *St. France* Misc. (1805) 81 Every great person.. pretends to his elaboratory and library. **1676** COLES, *Elaboratory*.. a (chymist's) workhouse or shop. **1759** B. MARTIN *Nat. Hist. Eng.* I. 258 Two Elaboratories; one for Chymical, and the other for Galenical Preparations. **1801** *Med. Jrnl.* V. 200 Dr. Pearson's Lectures.. will recommence in the Elaboratory. **1873** M. COLLINS *Sq. Silchester's* I. v. 71 Parlour, bedroom, elaboratory, kitchen.

2. A natural apparatus for elaborating any product of vital action. (Formerly *transf.* from 1.)

1667 *Phil. Trans.* II. 578 The Sanguification is performed in any one part of the Animal, as the peculiar Shop or Elaboratory of it. **1684** tr. *Bonet's Merc. Compit.* IX. 325 Obstruction of the passages, by which the Aliment passes to its elaboratories. **1708** *Brit. Apollo* No. 86. 2/1 The Elaboratory of the Nervous Juice. **1845** *Florist's Jrnl.* 11 The functions of leaves are to.. act as elaboratories.

† **e'labour**, *v. Obs.* [ad. F. *elabour-er* (Cotgr.) or L. *ēlabōrāre* to ELABORATE.]

1. *trans.* = ELABORATE *v.* 2.

1543 TRAHERON *Vigo's Chirurg.*, *Straunge Wds.*, More parfectly digested and elaboured. **1606** BIRNIE *Kirkburiall* x. (Jam. Suppl.) A sepulchrall Pyramide elabored by the panefull taske of God's people. **1653** URQUHART *Rabelais* Prol., The marrow is a nourishment most perfectly elaboured by nature.

2. *intr.* To struggle to make one's way.

1606 WARNER *Alb. Eng.* cii. 403 Flesh so proudlie stout That but as in a Labyrinth elaboureth about.

† **e'lacrymate**, *v. Obs. rare*[−1]. [f. L. **ēlacrimāt-* ppl. stem of **ēlacrimāre*, f. *ē* out + *lacrimāre* to

shed tears, weep: cf. LACRYMAL, etc.] *trans.* To shed in the form of tears.
1657 TOMLINSON *Renou's Disp.* 403 The trunk.. elacrymates a certain Gummeous Succe.

†**e'lact**, *v. Obs. rare.* [as if ad. L. **ēlactāre*, f. *ē* out + *lactāre* to suckle.] *trans.* To suckle.
a **1521** *Helyas* in Thoms *Prose Rom.* (1828) 116 She found in her bed three fayre children The which she elacted and gave to souke of her owne milke.

elæo-, comb. form of Gr. ἔλαιο-ν oil (properly olive-oil), used in technical, chiefly chemical, words, as **elæocerate** (ˌɛliːəʊˈsɪəreɪt) [cf. CERATE], same as CERATE. **elæomargaric** (*acid*) (ˌɛliːəʊmɑːˈgærɪk), *a.* [cf. MARGARIC], an acid found in the oil extracted from the seeds of some species of *Elæococca*. **elæometer** (ɛliːˈɒmɪtə(r)); also **elaio-** [see METER], 'an instrument for determining the specific weight of oils, and so their purity' (*Syd. Soc. Lex.*). **elæopten(e** (ɛliːˈɒptiːn), also **ela-**; [Gr. πτην-ός winged, volatile: cf. Fr. *éléoptène*], the liquid part of a volatile oil, as distinguished from the crystallizable portion called 'stearoptene' or 'camphor'. **elæostearic** (*acid*) (ˌɛliːəʊstiːˈærɪk), *a.* [cf. STEARIC], a solid acid separated by the action of alcohol upon the solid fat obtained from the oil of *Elæococca*.

elæodic (ɛliːˈəʊdɪk), *a. Chem.* [f. Gr. ἐλαιώδ-ης oily (f. ἔλαι-ον oil) + -IC.] A synonym for RICINOLEIC (acid).
1882 WATTS *Dict. Chem.*

elæolate (ɪˈliːələt). *Med.* [obscurely f. Gr. ἔλαι-ον oil.] 'A medicament which has a volatile oil for its base' (*Syd. Soc. Lex.*).

elæolite (ɪˈliːəlaɪt). *Min.* Also elao-. [f. Gr. ἔλαι-ον oil, olive oil + -LITE.] A variety of nephelite occurring massive, or in large crystals, and having a greasy lustre.
1816 R. JAMESON *Char. Min.* II. 43 It is named Elaolite.. on account of its resinous lustre. **1846** *Penny Cycl. 1st Supp.* II. 305/1 Elæolite..occurs in amorphous masses. **1877** WATTS *Dict. Chem.* IV. 30 Before the blow-pipe, nephelin melts with difficulty to a vesicular glass; elæolite easily. **1879** RUTLEY *Stud. Rocks* x. 108 Elæolite is a greenish, brownish, sometimes reddish variety of nepheline.

elaic (ɪˈleɪk), *a. Chem.* [irreg. f. Gr. ἔλαι-ον oil + -IC: cf. ELAIN.] = OLEIC (acid).
1845 TODD & BOWMAN *Phys. Anat.* I. 82 The acids are, the stearic, margaric, and elaic.

elaidic (ɛleɪˈɪdɪk), *a. Chem.* [f. as prec. + *-idic*: cf. *caffeidic*, *glycidic*, etc.] The designation of an acid $C_{18}H_{34}O_2$, a solid isomeric modification of elaic (oleic) acid, produced by the action of nitrous acid. Also *elaidic ethers*: a name for two oily liquids, *elaidate of ethyl* ($C_{18}H_{33}O_2 \cdot C_2H_5$) and *elaidate of methyl* ($C_{16}H_{33}O_2 \cdot CH_3$), prepared from elaidic acid and alcohol. So **e'laidate** [see -ATE[4]], a salt of elaidic acid. **e'laidin** [see -IN], a solid isomeric modification of olein, produced by the action of nitrous acid on olein.
c **1865** LETHEBY in *Circ. Sc.* I. 97/1 The conversion of the liquid oleic acid into solid elaidic. **1838** T. THOMSON *Chem. Org. Bodies* 345 Elaidic ether. *Ibid.* 436 Elaidates of potash .. Elaidate of magnesia is not sensibly soluble in water. **1869** ROSCOE *Elem. Chem.* 390 Oleic acid when acted upon by nitrous acid forms..elaidic acid. *c* **1865** LETHEBY in *Circ. Sc.* I. 102/1 The oleine of the oil being converted into a semi-transparent jelly-like mass, named *elaidine*. **1884** *Syd. Soc. Lex.*, Elaidin.

elain (ɪˈleɪɪn). [irreg. f. Gr. ἔλαι-ον oil + -IN: cf. F. *élaïne*.] A synonym of OLEIN.
(As a trade term commonly pronounced ɪˈleɪn.)
1810 HENRY *Elem. Chem.* (1840) II. 409 An oil which is.. called by Chevreul elaïn (from ἔλαιον, oil). **1819** CHILDREN *Chem. Anal.* 310 Elain..is the name given to the other substance contained in fat. **1835–6** TODD *Cycl. Anat. & Phys.* I. 59/1 Fat consists essentially of two proximate principles, stearine and elaine. *c* **1865** LETHEBY in *Circ. Sc.* I. 105/1 The elaine or oleine of palm oil. **1875** URE *Dict. Arts* III. 431 The particles consist of a strong membranous skin, enclosing stearine and elaine, or solid and liquid fat.

elaioplast (ɪˈlaɪəplæst). *Cytology.* Also elæo-. [a. Du. *elaioplast* (J. H. Wakker 1887, in *Maandblad voor Natuurwetenschappen* XIII. 110), f. Gr. ἔλαιον oil + -PLAST.] A type of plastid, found esp. in some angiosperms, that contains or secretes oil.
1888 *Jrnl. Microsc. Soc.* 443 Elaioplast.—Under this term Herr J. H. Wakker describes nearly globular strongly refringent yellow bodies which he finds..in epidermal cells of the leaves of *Vanilla planifolia*. *Ibid.*, The elaioplasts are formed gradually in the epidermal cells during the development of the leaf. **1969** BROWN & BERTKE *Textbk. Cytol.* xiii. 244/1 Leukoplasts containing one or more large starch grains are often called amyloplasts;..or if droplets of oil, they are called elaioplasts.

elam. var. of HELM, *dial.*, handful of thatch.

†**eˌlambi'cation.** *Obs.*$^{-0}$ [ad. med.L. *ēlambicātiōn-em*: see ALEMBICATION.] 'Old term for a mode of analysing mineral waters, for the purpose of investigating their qualities, either by the sand bath, or by heat in a glass vessel' (Mayne).

†**e-la-mi.** *Mus. Obs.* Also 6 ellamy. The note E, sung to the syllable *la* or *mi* according as it occurred in one or the other of the Hexachords to which it belonged.
c **1550** *Armonye of Byrdes* in Hazl. *E.P.P.* III. 187 Then sang the..mavys The trebble in ellamy. **1596** SHAKS. *Tam. Shr.* III. i. 78 E la mi. **1721** CIBBER *Double Gall.* I, One laughs in Gamut, another sneeres in Elami Alt.

Elamite (ˈiːləmaɪt), *sb.* and *a.* Also 4–6 Elamyt. [f. *Elam*, the name of an ancient country in Mesopotamia + -ITE[1].] **A.** *sb.* An inhabitant of Elam; the language of its people. **B.** *adj.* Of or pertaining to Elam, its inhabitants, or their language.
[*c* **1000** *Genesis* (Junius MS., 1931) l. 2081 Fleonde wæron Elamitarna aldordugoðe dome bedrorene.] *c* **1384** WYCLIF *Bible* (1850) IV. 511/1 Party, and Medy, and Elamyte, and thei that dwellen in Mesopotamye. **1526** TINDALE *Acts* ii. 9 Parthians, Medes and Elamyts, and the inhabiters of Mesopotamia. **1614** RALEIGH *Hist. World* (caption of map between pp. 178 and 179), Elam. The eldest sonn of Sem possest the regions of Persia and therfore were those nations first called Elamites. **1874** [see AKKADIAN *a.* and *sb.*]. **1880** *Encycl. Brit.* XI. 155/1 It [*sc.* Nestorian Christianity] was successfully preached to the Bactrians, the Huns, the Persians, the Indians, the Persarmenians, the Medes, the Elamites. **1894** A. H. SAYCE '*Higher Criticism' & Verdict of Monuments* iii. 164 Chedor-laomer..would have been written in Elamite Kudur-Lagamar. *Ibid.*, Eri-Aku..bore a Sumerian and not an Elamite name. *Ibid.* xi. 516 The Elamite kings..entitle themselves lords 'of the kingdom of Anzan, kings of Shushan'. **1928** C. DAWSON *Age of Gods* iv. 83 Resemblances certainly exist between the Dravidian Brahvi and the ancient Elamite tongue, and it is possible that all three languages are early representatives of the Caucasian linguistic group. **1937** *Discovery* Sept. 287/1 Many of them resemble certain seal-amulets of early Elamite date. **1970** *Ashmolean Mus., Rep. Visitors 1969* 15 Three cylinder seals, Mitannian, Cappadocian and Elamite.

†**e'lamp**, *v. Obs. rare.* [? f. E- *pref.*[3] + LAMP *v.*; perh. suggested by Gr. ἐκλάμπ-ειν to shine forth.] *intr.* To shine forth.
1610 G. FLETCHER *Christ's Vict.* in Farr's *S.P. Jas. I*, 42 The cheerfull sunne, elamping wide Glads all the world with his uprising ray.

‖**élan.** [Fr.; believed to be f. *élancer* (see next).] **a.** An impetuous rush (*e.g.* of troops). **b.** In Eng. use chiefly *abstr.*: Ardour, impetuousness, vivacity.
1880 BURTON *Reign Q. Anne* III. xiv. 22 With the first charge—the élan as they like to call it, the French seemed to carry all before them. **1880** *Fraser's Mag.* May 651 The unquenchable *élan* of boyhood.

elance (ɪˈlɑːns, -æ-), *v. Obs.* or *arch.* [ad. F. *élancer* = It. *slanciare*, Pr. *eslansar*, f. L. *ex* out + late L. *lanceāre*, f. *lancea* LANCE.]
1. *trans.* To launch; to cast or throw (a lance or dart). Also *fig.*
1718 PRIOR *2nd Hymn Callim. to Apollo*, Thy unerring Hand elanc'd..another Dart. —— *Poems* 436 The Word obscene, Or harsh, which once elanc'd must ever fly Irrevocable. **1742** YOUNG *Nt. Th.* IX. 628 Elance thy thought, and think of more than man. *c* **1800** K. WHITE *Time* 444 The Holy One..elanced The rolling world along its airy way. **1839** BAILEY *Festus* (1848) 9/2 A thousand worlds..were elanced Each minute into life.
2. *intr.* for *refl.* To shoot, dart, glance.
1729 SAVAGE *Wanderer* iii. 85 We behold..'Cross ether swift elance, the vivid fires!

eland (ˈiːlənd). [a. Du. *eland* elk.
The Du. word is a. Ger. *elend* (*elentier*), believed to be ad. Lith. *élnis* elk. See ELLAN, ELLEND, which are earlier adoptions of the word from sources other than Du.]
The largest member (*Taurotragus oryx*) of the Antelope tribe, belonging to S. Africa, E. Africa (*T. derbianus*, giant eland) W. Africa and the Sudan, standing five feet high at the shoulders, of a heavy build, for the most part very fat, and much prized for its flesh. Also *attrib.*
1786 tr. *Sparrman's Voy. Cape G. Hope* II. 204 Eland..is a name given by the colonists to a species of gazel. **1834** *Penny Cycl.* II. 89/1 Elands..are now rarely met with except in the most distant and retired parts of the colony [Cape Colony]. **1857** LIVINGSTONE *Trav.* ii. 43 The eland.. would grace the parks of our nobility more than deer. **1866** —— *Jrnl.* ix. (1873) I. 227 A piece of eland meat.

eland, obs. var. of ISLAND.

elanet (ˈɛlənɪt). [app. f. mod.L. *elān-us* (by some writers conjectured to be ad. Fr. *élan* darting motion) + -ET[1].] A species of kite, the *Elanus melanopterus* or Black-winged Swallow-hawk.
1880 *Libr. Univ. Knowl.* VIII. 538 Kite..a genus of falconidæ, or a sub-family including elanets, etc.

‖**élan vital** (elɑ̃ vital). [Fr. (H. Bergson *L'Évolution créatrice* (1907) iii. 276); see ÉLAN.] In the philosophy of Henri Bergson (1859–1941), a vital impulse or life force, of which we are aware intuitively; *spec.*, an original impetus of life supposed to have brought about the variations which during the course of evolution produced new species; a creative principle found in all living beings. Hence *gen.*, any mysterious vital principle.
1907 W. JAMES *Let.* to Bergson 13 June (1920) II. 292 The *élan vital*, all contentless and vague as you are obliged to leave it, will be an easy substitute to make fun of. **1912** G. B. SHAW *Let.* 8 Dec. (1952) 61 Your illness..is a trap of the Life Force—the *Élan Vital*. **1926** J. S. HUXLEY *Ess. Biologist* i. 33 Bergson..ascribes it [*sc.* biological progress] to his *élan vital*... But to say that biological progress is explained by the *élan vital* is to say that the movement of a train is 'explained' by an *élan locomotif* of the engine. **1938** L. MACNEICE *Mod. Poetry* i. 18 The *élan vital* of Whitman or of Lawrence. **1959** *Listener* 28 May 937/1 No other theory as to the basic mechanism of evolution (Lamarckism, orthogenesis, *élan vital*, etc.) is consonant with the facts of general biology. **1962** *Ibid.* 20 Dec. 1062/2 The *élan vital*? A complete red herring, Dr. Crick asserted; biologists just didn't ask questions like that any more.

elaolite, etc.: see ELÆOLITE, etc.

elaopten(e, var. of ELÆOPTEN(E: see ELÆO-.

elaphine (ˈɛləfaɪn), *a.* [f. L. *elaph-us*, a. Gr. ἔλαφ-ος stag, deer + -INE.] Belonging to or resembling the stag.
1835 SWAINSON *Quadrupeds* 292 The elaphine group. **1857** *Fraser's Mag.* LVI. 209 The elaphine group..is principally represented in India by the..Axis or Ganges Stag.

elaphure (ˈɛləfjʊə(r)). [ad. mod.L. *Elaphurus* (A. Milne-Edwards 1866, in *Comptes rendus Acad. Sci.* LXII. 1091), f. Gr. ἔλαφος stag + οὐρά tail] A species of reddish-tawny deer, Père David's deer (*Elaphurus davidianus*), discovered in northern China, and introduced into England in captivity. So **'elaphurine** *a.*
1872 *Trans. Zool. Soc.* VII. 336 The Elaphure is..very distinct in the form of its horns from every other described species of the genus [*Cervus*]. **1891** FLOWER & LYDEKKER *Mammals* ix. 320 The Elaphurine group is represented..by *Cervus davidianus*.

elapid (ˈɛləpɪd), *a.* and *sb. Zool.* Also **elapide**, **elapine**, **elapoid**. [ad. mod.L. *Elapidæ* or *Elapinæ*.] **A.** *adj.* Of, pertaining to, or resembling a venomous colubrid snake of the family Elapidæ or subfamily Elapinæ. **B.** *sb.* A member of this family.
1885 H. C. BUMPUS in J. S. Kingsley *Standard Nat. Hist.* III. 379 The *Elapides* are characterized by having the head rounded and depressed. **1895** *Athenæum* 14 Dec. 838/2 *Boulangerina stormsi* an elapoid snake from Lake Tanganyika. **1910** R. DITMARS *Reptiles of World* IV. 196 The Elapine snakes swarm in Australia. **1926** T. BARBOUR *Reptiles & Amphibians* iii. 22 The mambas or tree cobras are the most widespread and prominent Elapine types. *Ibid.* 35 The venom of the Elapid types is much more neurotoxic than is that of the vipers. *Ibid.*, The venom of the Old World Elapids..causes a paralysis of the phrenic nerve. **1969** A. BELLAIRS *Life of Reptiles* I. iv. 121 The elapid and back-fanged snakes..tend to hold on to their prey.

†**e'lapidate**, *v. Obs.*$^{-0}$ [f. L. *ēlapidāt-* ppl. stem of **ēlapidāre* to clear from stones, f. *ē* out, away + *lapid-em* stone.] *trans.* To rid or clear (a place) of stones.
1623 in COCKERAM. **1656** in BLOUNT *Glossogr.* **1721–1800** in BAILEY.
Hence †**e'lapiˌdated**, *ppl. a.* †**eˌlapi'dation**.
1721–1800 in BAILEY; **1847** in CRAIG; and in mod. Dicts.

‖**Elaps** (ˈiːlæps). [mod.L. a. Gr. ἔλαψ corrupt var. of ἔλλοψ: see ELLOPS.] A genus of venomous colubrine snakes, chiefly found in the tropical countries both of the Old and New World.

elapse (ɪˈlæps), *v.* [f. L. *ēlaps-* ppl. stem of *ēlābi* to slip or glide away: see LAPSE.]
1. *intr.* Of time, a period of time: To slip by, pass away, expire. (Perfect tenses occas. with *be.*)
1644 [see ELAPSED *ppl. a.* 1]. **1657** BURTON *Diary* (1828) II. 114 The Act was to commence at the 1st of February last, which time was elapsed. **1758** JOHNSON *Idler* No. 10 ¶9 The time elapses without a revolution. **1792** T. JEFFERSON *Writ.* (1859) III. 390 Fourteen months were now elapsed. **1848** MACAULAY *Hist. Eng.* II. 229 Twenty-seven years had elapsed since the Restoration. **1876** GREEN *Short Hist.* viii. §10 (1882) 568 Three years..were to elapse between the assembling of one Parliament and another.
†**2.** *trans.* To suffer (time) to pass by. *Obs.*
1654 CROMWELL *Sp.* 22 Jan., You have wholly elapsed your time. **1705** *Lond. Gaz.* 4105/1 Fulke Emes Gent. and others, who had Elapsed their times..for paying their Money. **1709** *Tatler* No. 109 ¶6 Dead Persons, who have.. elaps'd the proper Time of their Interrment.
†**3.** *intr.* **a.** To lapse, sink insensibly *into* (a condition). **b.** To slip away (from memory).
1742 JOHNSON Wks. IV. 484 Others..have elapsed into idleness and security. **1762–9** FALCONER *Shipwr.* III. 544 Swift from their minds elapsed all dangers past.
4. *nonce-use.* To flow gently *from*.
1839 BAILEY *Festus* (1848) 66/1 One there was From whose sweet lips elapsed as from a well, Continuously truths which made my soul..fertile with rich thoughts.

Hence **e'lapsing** *vbl. sb.* and *ppl. a.*

1720 WODROW *Corr.* (1843) II. 514 To take the oaths before the elapsing of the day. **1830** ALFORD in *Life* (1873) 59 The world is a channel into which God lets a partial and elapsing stream of the great deep of eternity.

e'lapse, *sb. arch.* [f. prec. vb.: cf. LAPSE *sb.*]

†**1.** A flowing out or away; *fig.* an emanation, effluence (of divine grace, etc.).

a **1677** BARROW *Serm.* (1686) III. 426 The sweet elapses of spiritual consolation in devotion. *a* **1703** POMFRET *Rem.* (1724) 9 Some nobler Bard, O Sacred Power.. th' Elapses to receive. **1811** PINKERTON *Petral.* II. 370 The under current continues to flow; so that upon its complete elapse, the space remains void.

2. Expiration, lapse, passing away (of time).

1793 ANNA SEWARD in *Parr's Wks.* (1828) VIII. 464 The distinctions of Whig and Tory.. have lost their force during the elapse of many years. **1800** *Essay on Ramsay* in *Ramsay's Wks.* (1848) I. 70 The elapse of a few months justified the poet's foresight. *c* **1800** K. WHITE *Time* 275 The past is.. an elapse Which hath no mensuration. **1823** *Monthly Mag.* LV. 517 They considered Daniel's seventy weeks of years on the brink of elapse. **1883** F. W. POTTER *French Celeb.* II. 109 After an elapse of two decades. **1988** *Mod. document,* References to people, institutions, nations,.. and so on, which have been invalidated by the elapse of time since the Dictionary was edited.

elapsed (ɪ'læpst), *ppl. a.* [f. as prec. + -ED.]

1. Lapsed, past, gone by.

1644 QUARLES *Sheph. Orac.* I, Such may have pardons for elapsed crimes. *a* **1774** GOLDSM. *Grecian Hist.* I. 223 The first campaign being elapsed. **1790** MARSDEN in *Phil. Trans.* LXXX. 573 The Hindoos compute from the elapsed year. **1805** FOSTER *Ess.* I. I. 6 The elapsed periods of life. **1854** H. MILLER *Sch. & Schm.* xvi. (1857) 366 The elapsed half of the present century.

†**2.** Suffered to slip by, neglected. *Obs.*

1649 JER. TAYLOR *Gt. Exemp.* II. viii. 86 Such great acts.. comprise the elapsed duty of many moneths.

†**3.** Of angels: Fallen. *Obs.*

1665 WITHER *Lord's Prayer* 27 The Prince of the Spirits elapsed began to Usurp a part of God's Kingdom.

†**e'lapsion.** *Obs. rare.* [as if ad. L. **ēlapsiōn-em*, f. *ēlābi*: see ELAPSE *v.* and -ION[1].] The action of elapsing or slipping away, the state of having elapsed; (in quot.) subsidence.

1656 BLOUNT *Glossogr.* **1678–1706** in PHILLIPS. **1721–1782** in BAILEY. **1799** KIRWAN *Geol. Ess.* 37 The dissolution, elapsion, or different compression of some of these strata.

†**e'lapsive,** *a. Obs. rare.* [f. L. *ēlaps-* (see ELAPSE *v.*) + -IVE.] Apt to let slip.

1652 SPARKE *Prim. Devot.* (ed. 3) 191 Our memories are so elapsive.

e'laqueate, *v. rare*—0. [f. L. *ēlaqueāt-* ppl. stem of *ēlaqueāre*, f. *ē* out + *laque-us* noose, snare.] *trans.* To set free from a noose: to disentangle.

1656 BLOUNT *Glossogr.* **1721–61** in BAILEY. **1775** in ASH. **1847** in CRAIG; and in mod. Dicts.

Hence **e,laque'ation**.

1730–6 in BAILEY. **1775** in ASH. **1847** in CRAIG.

†**e'largement.** *Obs. rare.* [? mistake for *enlargement*; but cf. Fr. *élargir* to widen, enlarge.] = ENLARGEMENT.

1680 H. MORE *Apocal. Apol.* 152 That elargement which God intends for the Kingdom of his Son Christ.

†**elar'gition.** *Obs.*—0 [f. L. *ēlargī-ri* to distribute, bestow: cf. L. *largītio* LARGITION.] Free or liberal impartation or bestowal.

1730–6 in BAILEY.

elasmobranch (ɪ'læzməbræŋk). *Zool.* [Shortened f. mod.L. *elasmobranchii*, f. Gr. ἐλασμό-ς metal beaten out, metal-plate + βράγχ-ια gills.] An individual of the *Elasmobranchii* or *Chondropterygii*, a class of fishes marked by the cartilaginous nature of the bones, and the absence of sutures in the cranium, as the Shark, Sturgeon, Ray, etc. Also *attrib.* or *adj.*

1872 MIVART *Elem. Anat.* 38 The neural arches may be made up of two separate pieces on each side, as in Elasmobranch fishes. **1878** BELL tr. *Gegenbauer's Comp. Anat.* Introd. 11 Two pairs of fins such as we find in the Elasmobranchs. **1881** *Nature* XXV. 61 Mr. F. M. Balfour's ..work on the development of the elasmobranch fishes. **1887** *Sci. American* 26 Feb. 130 The true fishes form one class, the elasmobranchs, sharks and rays, another class.

elasmobranchian (ɪ,læzməʊ'bræŋkɪən), *a.* and *sb. Zool.* = ELASMOBRANCH.

1889 in *Cent. Dict.*

e,lasmo'branchiate, *a.* and *sb.* [f. as prec. + -ATE.] = prec.

elasmosaurus (ɪ,læzməʊ'sɔːrəs). *Palæont.* Also anglicized **-saur.** [mod.L. (E. D. Cope 1868, in *Proc. Acad. Nat. Sci. Phila.* 93), f. Gr. ἐλασμός metal plate + σαῦρος lizard.] An extinct marine reptile.

1879 *Encycl. Brit.* X. 359/2 One of the most extraordinary of these reptilian forms was the *Elasmosaurus*—a huge snake-like form 40 feet long, with slim arrow-shaped head on a swan-like neck rising 20 feet out of the water. **1889** *Cent. Dict.*, Elasmosaur. **1924** *Glasgow Herald* 5 July 4 One of them, Elasmosaurus, seems to have been 45 feet in length, half consisting of neck. **1961** *Observer* 28 May 30/5 Loch Ness contains the answer to the sea-serpent problem..a relict population of Elasmosaurs.

e'lasmose (ɪ'læzməʊz). [f. Gr. ἐλασμ-ός plate of metal + -OSE.]

1. 'An obsolete synonym of Altaite' (Dana).

2. Same as ELASMOSINE.

1844 ALGER *Phillips' Min.* 520 Black tellurium.. Elasmose.

elasmosine (ɪ'læzməʊsiːn). [f. prec. + -INE.] A tellurid of lead and gold with an easy cleavage into thin metallic flexible laminæ; nagyagite.

elasmotherium (ɪ,læzməʊ'θɪərɪəm). *Palæont.* Also **elasmothere.** [mod.L. (G. Fischer de Waldheim 1808, in *Mém. Soc. Imp. Nat. Moscou* II. 250), f. Gr. ἐλασμός metal plate + θηρίον beast.] A large extinct rhinoceros of the genus so named, the remains of which are found in the Pleistocene of Eurasia.

1879 H. A. NICHOLSON *Man. Palæont.* (ed. 2) II. xlii. 329 We may mention here the singular *Elasmotherium* of the Post-Pliocene. **1905** E. R. LANKESTER *Extinct Animals* iii. 144 One great extinct beast (the Elasmotherium), allied to the rhinoceroses, had a great horn. **1927** PEAKE & FLEURE *Hunters & Artists* iii. 32 Another grass-eating rhinoceros from Siberia, usually known as the Elasmothere. **1932** J. S. HUXLEY *Probl. Rel. Growth* v. ii. 151 The extinct Elasmotherium possessed a horn in the shape of a flattened cone. **1966** A. S. ROMER *Vertebrate Paleont.* (ed. 3) xxx. 345/2 Some of the contrasting types, such as the woolly rhinoceros and the giant tundra-dwelling *Elasmotherium* of Eurasia, were cold-climate forms.

elastance (ɪ'læstəns). *Electr.* [irreg. f. ELASTIC + -ANCE.] The capacity of a dielectric for opposing an electric charge or displacement.

1885 O. HEAVISIDE in *Electrician* 9 Oct. 408/2 (*bb*). If in the final state (*b*), we unite P to Q by a second dielectric wire also of infinite capacity, we make a closed dielectric circuit which has no elastance (or elastic resistance to displacement). **1890** W. P. MAYCOCK *Pract. Electr. Notes* (ed. 2) 48 Elastance is the reciprocal (or reverse) of Permittance; the comparative elastance of a dielectric is called its elastivity. For instance, a dielectric of great permittance has little elastance and *vice versâ.* **1890** *Electrician* 14 Nov. 41 The use of the words decalescence, reluctancy, reluctivity, elastance, elastivity, permittivity, might be well deferred till they are more generally adopted. **1893** O. HEAVISIDE *Electromagn. Theory* I. ii. §31. 29 The formal relation of reluctance to reluctivity with magnetic force and induction, is the same as that..of elastance to elastivity with electric force and displacement.

elastase (ɪ'læsteɪs, -z). [f. ELAST(IC *a.* + -ASE.] An enzyme, usu. isolated from the pancreas, which decomposes elastin. Also *Comb.*, as ***elastase-inhibitor***; ***elastase-inhibiting*** ppl. a.

1949 BALÓ & BANGA in *Nature* 17 Sept. 491/1 (*title*) Elastase and Elastase-Inhibitor. *Ibid.*, The extract of fresh pancreas as well as that of acetone-dried pancreas powder contains a specific enzyme which we called 'elastase'. **1950** —— in *Biochem. Jrnl.* XLVI. 387/2 Pancreatic extract contains an enzyme which dissolves the elastic fibres of the aorta wall and which is called elastolytic enzyme or elastase. **1956** *Nature* 10 Mar. 468/1 The elastase-inhibiting effect of the serum of Ehlers Danlos patients was found to be quantitatively increased over that of normal serum... It would not seem too unlikely to suggest that the elastase inhibitor can be an essential factor in the formation of elastic fibre. **1969** *Times* 21 Jan. 5/6 The structure of two other protein splitting enzymes, known as ox chymotrypsin and pig elastase, were also announced. **1970** *Nature* 28 Feb. 802/1 The proteolytic enzyme elastase.

elastic (ɪ'læstɪk), *a.* and *sb.* [ad. mod.L. *elasticus*, a. Gr. ἐλαστικός that drives, propulsive, impulsive, f. ἐλα- stem of ἐλαύνειν to drive.

The L. word, together with the related ELATER, occurs, app. as a novelty, in Pecquet's *Dissertatio Anatomica* (1651), where *elastica virtus* denotes the 'impulsive force' of the atmosphere, which the Torricellian experiment (1643) had shown to be the cause of the phenomena previously ascribed to 'Nature's horror of a vacuum'.]

A. *adj.*

†**1.** Pertaining to or causing the 'spontaneous' expansion of air or gases; in phrase *elastic force* (***virtue, faculty, power***, etc.). Now merged in 3.

1653 tr. *Pecquet's Anatomical Exper.* 122 The Spontaneous dilatation [of the air] enerveth the power of the Elastick (impulsive) faculty [Orig. **1651** *virtutis Elasticæ*].. But the other, which is extraneous to the Air, *viz.*, from the accession of heat, will make it firm. **1656** MORE *Antid. Ath.* II. ii. (1712) 45 There is an Elastick power in the Air. **1669** W. SIMPSON *Hydrol. Chym.* 129 The air of the convex part must of necessity have a strong pressure or elastick force to return into the concave thereof.

†**2.** Of air or gas: Possessing the property of spontaneous expansion. Now merged in 3.

The ultimate particles of air were by some supposed to act like a coiled spring; hence the word came to express the characteristic property of a spring, as in the early instances of sense 3.

1681 tr. *Willis's Rem. Med. Wks.* Voc., *Elastick*, that goeth off with a force like gunpowder, or spreads forcibly forth with a jerk. **1732** ARBUTHNOT *Rules of Diet* 279 Wind is elastick and rarify'd [? air] pent up in some vessel of the body.

3. a. Of material substances, whether solid, liquid, or gaseous: That spontaneously resumes (after a longer or shorter interval) its normal bulk or shape after having been contracted, dilated, or distorted by external force. (In this sense ELASTICAL appears to be somewhat older.) Also of motions, forces, etc.: Characteristic of an elastic body. Also ***elastic collision*** (G. *elastisch* used in this sense, e.g. by Franck and Hertz 1913, in *Verh. d. Deut. Physik. Ges.* XV), a collision between two particles in which the total kinetic energy is conserved; ***elastic constant***, a constant that expresses the reaction of a material to stress; ***elastic fluids***: still often used specifically for gases (cf. 2), though liquids are now known to be perfectly elastic according to the mod. definition; ***elastic hysteresis*** = HYSTERESIS 2; ***elastic limit***: (see quot. 1864); ***elastic modulus*** = *modulus of elasticity*; ***elastic scattering***, the scattering of particles without loss of kinetic energy; ***elastic strain***, a temporary deformation of a material under strain; ***elastic wave***, a wave consisting of elastic deformations propagated through a medium.

'Elasticity of shape' belongs to solids only; 'elasticity of bulk' to bodies of all kinds. In the case of gases the 'normal bulk' to which they tend is indefinitely great. The strict modern use as applied to solids dates from James Bernouilli's memoir of 1694; respecting the earlier instances see note to sense 2.

1674 PETTY *Dupl. Proportion* 3 An Appendix, to what is said of Springs and other Elastique bodies. **1692** BENTLEY *Boyle Lect.* vii. 224 The Air is now certainly known to consist of elastic or springy Particles. **1774** GOLDSM. *Nat. Hist.* (1776) II. 162 Every body that strikes against another produces a sound..simple, and but one in bodies which are not elastic. **1791** COWPER *Iliad* v. 117 At once he bent Against Tydides his elastic bow. **1794** SCHMEISSER *Min.* I. 290 Elastic Bitumen..is of a brown color, has no lustre, and is very elastic. **1800** VINCE *Hydrostat.* (1806) Def. 1 An elastic fluid is one, whose dimensions are diminished by increasing the pressure. **1847** EMERSON *Repr. Men, Montaigne* Wks. (Bohn) I. 340 We want some coat woven of elastic steel. **1848** R. MALLET in *Trans. R. Irish Acad.* XXI. 97 The determination of the time of transit of the elastic wave through the earth's crust. **1864** *Q. Jrnl. Sc.* I. 63 The elastic limit, that is the extent to which their particles may be relatively displaced without fracture or other permanent alteration. **1871** TYNDALL *Fragm. Sc.* I. i. 11 The atoms recoil, in virtue of the elastic force. **1872** BAKER *Nile Tribut.* xi. 197 The elastic boughs sprang back with dangerous force. **1884** EVERETT tr. *Deschanel's Nat. Philos.* 138 The name of elastic fluids is often given to gases. **1886** J. MILNE *Earthquakes* III. 44 An earthquake consists of elastic waves of compression and distortion. **1909** *Cent. Dict.* Suppl., *Elastic hysteresis*, an effect, analogous to magnetic hysteresis in iron, observed in the relation of strain to stress when the stress to which an elastic body is subjected is alternately increased and diminished. **1913** *Proc. R. Soc.* A. LXXXVIII. 299 We shall suppose for the sake of generality that the collision of ion and molecule is not perfectly elastic, an assumption which allows roughly for a possible loss of energy on collision. **1925** *Jrnl. Iron & Steel Inst.* CXI. 589 Ultimately the whole question of the tensile strength of metals and of the elastic limit resolves itself into an investigation of variation with temperature. **1927** H. N. RUSSELL et al. *Astronomy* II. xvii. 551 After colliding with the far more massive atom the electron may be found moving at the same speed as before; such a collision is called *elastic.* **1930** *Engineering* 14 Feb. 231/3 This must not be so high as to cause heating of the piece by elastic hysteresis. **1930** A. W. JUDGE *Engineering Materials* III. i. 12 It will be seen, then, that the elastic strains occurring in engineering work are very small indeed. **1930** RUTHERFORD et al. *Radiations from Radioactive Substances* v. 134 The difficulties..may be illustrated by the distinction made to-day between an 'elastic', and 'non-elastic' collision of an electron with an atom. **1931** *Discovery* Apr. 123/1 Elastic waves travel through different rocks at different velocities. **1933** *Physical Rev.* XLIII. 112 (*heading*) Elastic scattering of electrons by mercury atoms. **1936** F. FOSTER *Mech. Testing Metals & Alloys* i. 2 If, after the application and removal of the load, the strain disappears completely, the material is said to be perfectly elastic and the strain is then referred to as *elastic strain.* **1940** *Chambers's Techn. Dict.* 284/1 Elastic modulus. **1941** in M. Gowing *Brit. & Atomic Energy 1939–1945* (1964) App. II. 403 The diffraction effect (elastic scattering) is confined mainly to small angles. **1948** *Sci. News* VII. 14 For rubber, firmness therefore depends on the nearly constant ratio of pressure to amount of deformation, which is called an 'elastic modulus'. **1950** *Engineering* CLXX. 97/2 The links..will break before the elastic limit of..the guide apparatus is reached. **1955** H. B. G. CASIMIR in W. Pauli *Niels Bohr* 122 The elastic constants in the superconducting state are not appreciably different from those in the normal state. **1955** *Gloss. Terms Radiology (B.S.I.)* 14 *Elastic scattering*, in which the scattered radiation has the same quantum energy as the incident radiation. **1958** W. K. MANSFIELD *Elem. Nuclear Phys.* iv. 30 When the neutrons are deflected the collisions are called *elastic*, since the kinetic energy is conserved and the collisions can be treated by the normal dynamics of billiard ball collisions. **1966** *New Scientist* 5 May 296/3 An electromagnetic interaction between the electron and the nucleus can cause the electron to veer off in its path at some angle while the interacting nucleus recoils in a different direction. This phenomenon is called 'elastic scattering'.

b. *transf.* Of motion: Resembling that of an elastic body; springy.

1848 B'NESS BUNSEN in Hare *Life* (1879) II. iii. 116 Her light, elastic, continually lively motions.

c. *fig.* Of feelings, temperaments, etc., hence, also, of persons: Not permanently or easily depressed; buoyant.

1778 HAN. MORE *Florio* II. 193 Th' elastic spirits nimbly bound. **1816** J. SCOTT *Vis. Paris* (ed. 5) 3 An elastic spirit, anxious to overleap distance. **1822** CARLYLE *Misc.* (1857) I. 145 This elastic little urchin. **1848** MACAULAY *Hist. Eng.* I. 429 Those elastic spirits..had borne up against defeat. **1870** E. PEACOCK *Ralf Skirl.* III. 116 The elastic temperament of Mr. Skirlaugh.

4. a. (Partly attrib. use of the sb.) In popular language, *esp.*: That can be stretched without permanent alteration of size or shape. Applied to fabrics, or articles made of them, containing threads or thin strips of rubber usually covered by a woven material. †*elastic gum* [= Fr. *gomme élastique*]: india-rubber; *elastic web*: cloth woven with india-rubber threads so as to stretch; *elastic boots*: boots with elastic web at the sides. So *elastic sides*, of elastic boots; also *attrib.*, as *elastic side boots*, and *ellipt.* = such boots; *elastic-sided* adj. Also *elastic band* (BAND *sb.*² 2); *elastic stocking*, a remedial stocking made partly of rubber.

1781 CAVALLO in *Phil. Trans.* LXXI. 519 Common vitriolic ether..could not affect elastic gum. **1793** SCHMEISSER *Ibid.* LXXXIII. 165, I have..fixed the tube into the stopper by means of a thin piece of elastic gum. **1802** HENRY *Ibid.* XCIII. 31 A transfer bottle of elastic gum. **1835** DICKENS *Sk. Boz* 1st Ser. (1836) I. ii. 15 Elastic waistcoats, bosom friends, and warm stockings, poured in upon the curate. *c* **1835** in A. Adburgham *Shops & Shopping* (1964) iii. 27 Madame L. begs also to recommend her highly approved *elastic Parisian corsets.* **1839** URE *Dict. Arts* s.v., *Elastic bands.* The manufacture of braces and garters, with threads of caoutchouc..seems to have originated..in Vienna. **1846** A. BAIN *Brit. Pat. 11,480* 5 In order to support ..the paper I employ elastic bands of india rubber. **1851** *Great Exhib. Catal.* II. III. xvi. 525/1 Elastic side, dress, and other boots. *Ibid.* xx. 579/2 Corset..made to fasten in the front with patent spring clasp, and gauze elastic sides... Boots and shoes, with elastic sides, made by sewing pieces of India-rubber to the upper leather and then to the sole. **1855** J. H. NEWMAN *Let.* in M. Trevor *Newman: Light in Winter* (1962) 63 My accident of the autumn not being well I had just been obliged to put on my elastic stocking again. **1856** R. GARDINER *Handbk. Foot* 48 The introduction of elastic-web for the sides of boots, is a very important improvement. **1858** SIMMONDS *Dict. Trade, Elastic-bands*, belts, braces, gaiters, &c., made with threads of caoutchouc, either naked or covered. **1859** JEPHSON *Brittany* i. 5 A pair of moderately strong French elastic boots. *a* **1877** KNIGHT *Dict. Mech.* I. 776/2 *Elastic-fabric loom*, one having mechanical devices for stretching the rubber threads or shirrs, and holding them at a positive tension while the fabric is woven. **1880** *Encycl. Brit.* XII. 842/1 The threads used in making elastic webbing are usually cut from spread sheets. **1899** SOMERVILLE & 'Ross' *Irish R.M.* 295 Narrow feet in elastic-sided cloth boots. **1902** M. BARNES-GRUNDY *Thames Camp* 30 A man with a soft felt hat and elastic-sided boots. **1922** V. WOOLF *Jacob's Room* vii. 136 One pair of elastic stockings for Mrs. Page, widow, aged sixty-three. **1928** GALSWORTHY *Swan Song* II. vi. 157 He's made millions..out of the elastic band —has some patent for making them last only just long enough. **1937** F. STARK *Diary* 25 Nov. in *Winter in Arabia* (1940) 29 The cook, who, in elastic-sided boots, announces dinner. **1970** *Focus* June 10/2 *Elastic waistband* means ordinary elastic is sewn on at the waist.

b. *fig.* Of immaterial things: That can be 'stretched' or expanded to suit circumstances; flexible, accommodating.

1859 BRIGHT *Sp. India* 1 Aug., The revenue of India is not elastic. **1864** LD. POLLOCK in *Morning Star* 12 Jan., A lax or elastic interpretation of a criminal statute. **1866** CRUMP *Banking* viii. 164 Currency laws..will never make capital so elastic..any more than, etc. **1874** MORLEY *Compromise* (1886) 150 A certain elastic relativity of dogma. **1884** CHURCH *Bacon* ix. 212 The new ideas..would want a much more elastic..instrument than Latin. *Mod.* He seems to have a very elastic conscience.

c. Anat. *elastic tissue*: one of the varieties of areolar or connective tissue. *elastic fibre*, a fibre of a kind present in certain types of connective tissue and cartilage, characterized by being branched, easily stretched, and giving tissue a yellow colour when present in bulk.

1849 A. H. HASSALL *Microsc. Anat. Human Body* I. xvii. 331 Acetic acid applied to a portion of mixed cellular tissue, at once allows the elastic fibres to be clearly seen. **1861** HULME tr. *Moquin-Tandon* II. I. 41 Elastic Tissue is composed of homogeneous fibres. **1876** QUAIN *Anat.* (ed. 8) II. 67 Yellow or Elastic Tissue. **1968** PASSMORE & ROBSON *Compan. Med. Stud.* I. xxix. 10 The lung's elastic fibres form a system of branching springs.

†**5.** In etymological sense: Propulsive. *Obs.* (*nonce use*).

1712 BLACKMORE *Creation* IV, By what elastic engines did she rear The starry roof, and roll the orbs in air?

B. *sb.* Elastic cord or string, usually woven with india-rubber.

1847 in H. Howe *Hist. Collect. Ohio* 48 With the *elastics* supplied by the ladies, for a halter..the young dog passed from the shores of time. **1863** E. B. *Drifting Clouds* 140 Adèle had been enquiring for a piece of elastic for her hat. **1886** W. HOOPER *Sk. Academic Life* 13 The thorough-going prim man will always place a circle of elastic round his hair previous to putting on his college cap.

†**e'lastical**, *a. Obs.* = ELASTIC.

1660 BOYLE *New Exp. Phys. Mech.* i. 22 There is a Spring or Elastical power in the Air in which we live. *Ibid.* 26 Elastical bodies (if I may so call them). **1664** POWER *Exp. Philos.* II. 141 The Elastical pressure of the external Ayr upon the surface of the Quicksilver in the vessel. **1685** BOYLE *Effects of Mot.* viii. 99 By the Elastical force of the bent Bow the string is brought into a violent state of Tension. **1694** SLARE in *Phil. Trans.* XVIII. 213 Suffers no Elastical Air to lye concealed in any Liquors. **1718** J. CHAMBERLAYNE *Relig. Philos.* (1730) II. xvii. §19 An inherent Elastical Power..like the Steel Springs of Watches.

fig. **1662** STILLINGFL. *Orig. Sacr.* III. i. §2. 364 There is an elastical power in conscience. **1664** POWER *Exp. Philos.* III. 163 The Noble and Elastical Soul of Des-Cartes.

elastically (ɪˈlæstɪkəlɪ). [f. prec. + -LY².] In an elastic manner.

1830 LINDLEY *Nat. Syst. Bot.* 234 The cells..bursting elastically with 2 valves. **1882** VINES *Sachs' Bot.* 804 The cell-walls which were previously in a state of tension evidently contract elastically.

b. *transf.* and *fig.*

1816 J. SCOTT *Vis. Paris* 272 The visitor..feels his existence sit as..elastically as if he were just born in the full possession of the powers of manhood. **1883** SYMONDS *Ital. Byways* 224 Their bodies are elastically supple.

e'lasticated, *pa. pple.* and *ppl. a.* [f. ELASTIC *a.* + -ATE³ + -(E)D¹.] Of cloth, etc.: woven or stitched with indiarubber thread and so made stretchable. Also *fig.*, rendered flexible.

1925 *Chambers's Jrnl.* Feb. 130/1 A sense of the joy of power silkened and elasticated. **1931** *News Chron.* 26 Mar., Let the whole matter be considered..by the League Council so that this instrument may be so elasticated as to start a movement for the general lowering of tariff walls. **1959** *Observer* 5 Apr. 13/3 The fitted slacks are elasticated. **1959** *Manch. Guardian* 3 July 5/6 Elasticated sides and reinforced bra top. **1963** *Times* 10 June 15/6 The laziest boy in the group asked for a swivelling head and elasticated arms so that he could turn around and reach for things without moving. **1969** *Daily Tel.* 17 Nov. 12/6 Trousers which do have an elasticated nylon lining.

elastician (iː-, ɛlæˈstɪʃ(ɪ)ən). [f. ELASTIC + -IAN.] One who is conversant with the science of elasticity.

1885 KARL PEARSON in *Nature* XXXI. 457 It would be extremely valuable to have the opinion of some of our leading elasticians.

elasticin (ɪˈlæstɪsɪn). [f. ELASTIC + -IN.] 'The substance composing the elastic fibres of connective tissue' (*Syd. Soc. Lex.*).

1878 KINGZETT *Anim. Chem.* 385 Elasticin is the special principle of yellow elastic tissues.

elasticity (iː-, ɛlæˈstɪsɪtɪ). [f. as prec. + -ITY: cf. Fr. *élasticité*.] The quality of being elastic.

1. In literal sense. Cf. ELASTIC 2, 3.

1664 POWER *Exp. Philos.* III. 175 The External and Internal Ayr were come to the same..Elasticity. **1674** PETTY *Dis. Royal Soc.* 119 Elasticity is the power of recovering the Figure, upon removal of such Force. **1685** BOYLE *Effects of Mot.* 111 The Elasticity that Iron, Silver and Brass acquire by hammering. **1721** in BAILEY. **1802** PALEY *Nat. Theol.* iii. §3 (1819) 32 By its own elasticity returning..to its former position. **1834** MRS. SOMERVILLE *Connex. Phys. Sc.* xxv. (1849) 262 The elasticity or tension of steam..varies inversely as its volume. **1845** DARWIN *Voy. Nat.* ii. (1879) 31 Sufficient stress does not appear to have been laid on the elasticity of the spine. **1860** TYNDALL *Glac.* II. §16. 312 The substance, after stretching, being..devoid of that elasticity which would restore it to its original form.

2. *fig.* **a.** Energy, vigour, buoyancy of mind or character; capacity for resisting or overcoming depression. Cf. ELASTIC A. 2b.

1678 NORRIS *Coll. Misc.* (1699) 232 This spring of my soul (my Appetitive Faculty)..presses and endeavours with its whole Elasticity. **1728** POPE *Dunc.* I. 182 Me emptiness and dulness could inspire, And were my elasticity and fire. **1815** SCOTT *Guy M.* xxi, Nature had given him that elasticity of mind which rises higher from the rebound. **1829** I. TAYLOR *Enthus.* iv. (1867) 72 To break the elasticity of the inventive faculty. **1875** JOWETT *Plato* (ed. 2) V. 41 Our old men have lost the elasticity of youth.

b. Capacity for being 'stretched'; expansiveness, flexibility, accommodatingness. Cf. ELASTIC A. 3b.

1801 JANE AUSTEN *Let.* 8 Jan. (1952) 106 Appleshaw, that village of wonderful Elasticity, which stretches itself out for the reception of everybody who does not wish for a house on Speen Hill. **1858** O. W. HOLMES *Aut. Breakf. T.* iii. 21 There is no elasticity in a mathematical fact. **1863** J. MURPHY *Comm. Gen.* iii. 23 Good, evil, life, and death are striking specimens of this elasticity of signification. **1865** *Pall Mall G.* 17 Oct. 1 'Elasticity', that is to say, a discretionary issue of bank-notes. **1874** MORLEY *Compromise* (1886) 3 There are some common rules..but their application is a matter of..the widest elasticity.

c. *Econ.* Flexibility in supply or demand in response to variations in other factors.

1925 S. E. THOMAS *Elem. Econ.* iv. 37 The Elasticity and Inelasticity of Demand. **1959** *Oxf. Univ. Gaz.* 16 Mar. 797/1 Analysis of the interaction of beef, milk and feed prices and the elasticities in livestock production within the United Kingdom. **1966** A. BATTERSBY *Math. in Management* ix. 232 The quantity 'e' is related to the economists' 'elasticity of demand'.

e'lasticized, *pa. pple.* and *ppl. a.* [f. ELASTIC *a.* + -IZE + -(E)D¹.] = ELASTICATED *pa. pple.* and *ppl. a.*

1909 in WEBSTER. **1957** *New Yorker* 16 Nov. 164/2 A dog ski suit..elasticized at all four ankles. **1958** *Times* 1 Dec. 13/6 The washable velvet shorts..have an elasticized waist. **1970** *Daily Tel.* 6 July 13 A battle-dress jacket, elasticised at the waist.

elastin (ɪˈlæstɪn). = ELASTICIN (*Syd. Soc. Lex.*).

1875 GAMGEE tr. *Hermann's Hum. Physiol.* 35 Elastin..is insoluble in all agents which do not decompose it.

elastivity (iːlæˈstɪvɪtɪ). *Electr.* [irreg. f. ELASTIC + -IVITY.] The property of a dielectric by virtue of which the flow of current between points having difference of potential is restrained.

1890, **1893** [see ELASTANCE].

elastomer (ɪˈlæstəmə(r)). [f. ELAST(IC *a.* + *-omer* as in ISOMER.] Any of various rubbers (esp. synthetic ones) or plastic substances resembling rubber. Hence **elasto'meric** *a.*

1939 *Ind. & Engin. Chem.* (*Ind. ed.*) XXXI. 944/2 The writer [*sc.* H. L. Fisher] also comes into the discussion with new suggestions, the first of which is 'elastomer'. This word is reminiscent of isomer, electromer, metamer, and polymer... The writer presents elastomer to cover the elastic or rubberlike substances. **1940** *Ibid.* (*News ed.*) XVIII. 757 (*title*) Chemigum—a new elastomer. *Ibid.* 757/2 Out of the study of more than 300 elastomers developed on a laboratory scale, the decision to study further..ten of these was arrived at. **1951** *Engineering* CLXXI. 480/3 Brochure entitled 'Elastomeric Engineering Examples'. **1954** *Sci. News* XXXII. 52 Rubbers, for which the appropriate name 'elastomers' has been coined and is used in the United States, are chain polymers which have been cross-linked to form a widely meshed network. **1958** *New Scientist* 17 Apr. 22/2 Flexible silicone elastomer tape. **1963** *Economist* 16 Nov. 700/3 The new elastomeric synthetic fibres. **1965** *New Scientist* 24 June 857/1 Although very expensive to produce, the elastomer yarns are finer and so the amount used is less than in the case of rubber. **1970** *Guardian* 5 Sept. 4/4 Nylon/elastomeric support tights.

Elastoplast (ɪˈlɑːstəplɑːst, ɪˈlæstəplæst). Also with small initial. [f. ELAST(IC + -O + PLAST(ER.] A proprietary name for a type of sticking-plaster, orig. made of stretchable fabric and subsequently also of other materials. Also loosely, any adhesive dressing.

1928 *Trade Marks Jrnl.* 29 Aug. 1378 Elastoplast.. Bandages (medical and surgical). Luscher & Bomper Aktiengesellschaft..Fahr, Rheinland, Germany; Manufacturers. **1939–40** *Army & Navy Stores Catal.* 412/2 Elastoplast Bandage..1/2 in. × 1 yd. [to] 4 in. × 3 yds. **1948** G. GREENE *Heart of Matter* I. I. i. 36 Now iodine... Now the elastoplast. **1959** I. JEFFERIES *Thirteen Days* ix. 142 There were no bandages but there was Elastoplast. **1964** S. DUKE-ELDER *Parson's Dis. Eye* (ed. 14) XXX. 481 Complete occlusion, effected by a patch of Elastoplast or similar material, shaped to cover the better eye. **1977** *Spare Rib* July 48 The ladies fit in his waiting room With elastoplast on their frames.

‖**elatcha.** *Obs.* Also alleja(r, alajah, allajar (Yule), alliza, allacha. [a. Turki *alchah*, *alāchah*, any kind of corded stuff.] A silk fabric from Turkestan: 'a silk cloth 5 yards long, which has a sort of wavy line pattern running in the length on one side' (Baden-Powell, in Yule s.v. *Alleja*). Also *attrib.*

c **1613** DOWNTON in *Purchas* I. 504 (Y.) The Nabob bestowed on him..30 allizaes. **1696** J. F. *Merchant's Wareho.* 14 Elatchis..an Indian Silk strip'd with variety of colours..is usually for Gowns. **1712** *Lond. Gaz.* No. 5051/3 Damasks, Elatches, Guiney Stuffs. **1712** *Advt.* In *Spect.* (Y.) An Allejah petticoat. **1757** *New Hist. E. Ind.* II. 145, 400 pieces Elatchas. **1813** MILBURN *Oriental Comm.* II. 221 (Y.) Allachas (pieces to the ton) 1200.

elate (ɪˈleɪt), *a.* Also 4 elaat, elat, elayt. [ad. L. *ēlāt-us*, pa. pple. of *efferre* to bring or carry out; to elevate, raise. Cf. OF. *elat* proud.]

†**1.** Lifted, raised. *Obs. rare.*

a **1730** FENTON *Let. Knight Sable Shield* in Anderson *Poets* VII. 663 With upper lip elate, he grins.

2. *fig.* Of condition, and of persons with regard to their condition: Exalted, lofty. Of feelings, etc.: Lofty, proud.

c **1386** CHAUCER *Monk's T.* 177 This kyng of kynges proud was and elaat [*v.r.* elat(e, elayt]. **1430** LYDG. *Chron. Troy* I. vi, Whom than he fonde..With sceptre in hande ful pompous and elate. **14..** *Epiph.* in *Tundale's Vis.* 113 O pompe elate with thy cheres bold. **1610** *Histriom.* IV. 117 Thy high fate Shall not discerne a fortune more Elate. **1626** T. H. tr. *Caussin's Holy Crt.* 58 This Courage..is powerfully elate. **1649** SELDEN *Laws Eng.* II. xxxiii. (1739) 148 Two Kings we have at once in view, both of them of an elate spirit. **1755** T. H. CROKER *Ariosto's Orl. Fur.* XLIII. lxi. II. 339 Shall this little burgh grow up to make A city ample, pompous and elate? **1833** CHALMERS *Const. Man* (1835) I. ii. 117 There is an elate independence of soul.

b. Of persons: Inspired (as with joy or hope), in high spirits, exultant, flushed (as with success or victory).

1647 CLARENDON *Hist. Reb.* II. I. 116 An Army elate with victory. **1725** POPE *Odyss.* I. 176 A brutal crowd, With insolence, and wine, elate and lowd. **1839** KEIGHTLEY *Hist. Eng.* II. 67 The Romish party in England were elate. **1870** DISRAELI *Lothair* xlvi. 244 The ladies returned with elate and animated faces.

e'late, *v.* [f. L. *ēlāt-* ppl. stem of *efferre*: see prec.]

†**1.** *trans.* To lift on high, raise, elevate. *Obs.*

1578 BANISTER *Hist. Man* I. 37 The superiour part [of the bone] is..in the middest most elated, and vpwardes heaued. *c* **1611** CHAPMAN *Iliad* XXII. 416 Placus doth elate His shady forehead. **1634** SIR T. HERBERT *Trav.* 25 The eighteenth of October, wee found by observation, the North pole elated seventeene degrees. *Ibid.* 168 Sometimes they elate a finger, smile and pray to Mahomet. **1772** PENNANT *Tours Scotl.* (1774) 235 Two of his fingers elated, in the attitude of benediction.

b. *fig.*

1635 NAUNTON *Fragm. Reg.* (Arb.) 14 The House..was suddenly elated into the best Families of England and Ireland. **1641** SIR E. DERING *Sp. on Relig.* ix. 33 This Bishop..elates himself up into usurped titles.

2. To raise the spirits of (a person), inspirit, encourage; to stimulate, excite; also, to puff up, make proud. Also *absol.* and (rarely) *refl.*

a **1619** DONNE *Biathan.* (1644) 186 But Sapritius elated with the glory of Martyredome, refused him. **1636** R. BRAITHWAIT *Lives Rom. Emperors* 354 This Emperour.. elated himselfe with self-conceite and pride. **1725** POPE *Odyss.* XVII. 33 Schemes of revenge his pondering breast elate. **1751** JOHNSON *Rambl.* No. 91 ⁋5 Ready..to elate each other with reciprocal applause. **1851** LONGF. *Gold. Leg., Village School,* The wine..elateth me. **1863** FR. KEMBLE *Resid. Georgia* 108, I was elated with my own part of this performance.

elated (ɪˈleɪtɪd), *ppl. a.* [f. prec. + -ED.] Uplifted, raised; proud, exalted. Cf. senses of vb.

1615 G. SANDYS *Trav.* 31 The Talismanni with elated voyces do congregate the people. *a* **1658** OSBORNE *Characters, &c.* (1673) 617 The Rabble, for want of a more elated Prudence, imagining their Governours to proceed.. from some Diviner Extraction than their Own. **1757** DYER *Fleece* I. 674 Elated man, forgetful of his charge.

¶ With a word-play on the musical term ELA.

a **1653** G. DANIEL *Idyll, Cerem.* 10 Accents ela-ted to the Sharpe Clangor of Warre.

elatedly (ɪˈleɪtɪdlɪ), *adv.* [f. prec. + -LY².] With elation; haughtily, pompously.

1661 FELTHAM *Disc. Luke* xiv. 20 (R.) Where do we find any so elatedly proud, or so unjustly rapacious as he [Nero]?

eˈlatedness. [f. as prec. + -NESS.] Elated state or condition; elation.

1731–1800 in BAILEY. **1791** tr. *Swedenborg's Apoc. Rev.* xviii. (1875) 578 In proportion to their elatedness of heart from dominion..they experience internal grief after Death. **1805** KNOX & JEBB *Corr.* I. 222 We may be in danger of presumptuous elatedness. **1850** D. KING *Geol. & Relig.* 152 A poor ground for elatedness.

elatement (ɪˈleɪtmənt). [f. as prec. + -MENT.] Elation, elatedness.

1746–7 HERVEY *Medit. & Contempl.* (1818) 272 We reflect upon some inconsiderable..superiority over others, and a sudden elatement swells our minds. **1799** CORN. WINTER *Let.* in W. Jay *Mem.* (1843) 67 Such an elatement of mind as imaginary painted prospects often occasion. **1894** *Leisure Hour* Jan. 146/2 Impossible to describe the child's elatement. **1922** C. SIDGWICK *Victorian* xv. 117 A note of elatement in his voice.

elater¹ (ˈɛlətə(r)). [a. (through mod.L.) Gr. ἐλατήρ one who or that which drives.

The adoption of the Gr. word into mod.Lat. (in sense 1) seems to be due to Pecquet (1651), whose English translator, however, usually rendered it by ELATERY.]

†**1.** The expansive or 'elastic' property inherent in air or gases; hence, more widely, = 'spring', 'elasticity'. Also *fig.*

1653 tr. *Pecquet's Anatomical Exper.* 90 By its [the Atmosphere's] Spontaneous dilatation (which I call Elater) [orig. *quem Elaterem nuncupo*]. **1660** BOYLE *New Exp. Phys.-Mech.* xxii. 162 The swelling..and the springing up..were not the effects of any internal Elater of the Water. **1682** SIR T. BROWNE *Chr. Mor.* (1756) 117 Persons..having the elater and spring of their own natures to facilitate their iniquities. **1711** F. FULLER *Med. Gymn.* (1718) 30 Gives 'em a better Tone, or Elater. **1730** STUART in *Phil. Trans.* XXXVI. 349 The Elater of the Guts.

2. *Zool.* Linnæus' name for a genus of beetles (now the family *Elateridæ*) possessing the power of springing upward from a supine position for the purpose of falling upon their feet; also, a member of this family, a skip-jack.

1802 BINGLEY *Anim. Biog.* (1813) 142 The Elater or Skipper Tribe. The Elaters fly with great facility. **1845** DARWIN *Voy. Nat.* ii. (1879) 31 At Bahia, an elater or beetle ..seemed the most common luminous insect. **1873** BLACKMORE *Cradock Now.* xxx. (1883) 168 She didn't know an elater from a tipula.

3. *Bot.* An elastic spiral filament, or elongated cell, attached to the sporangium or sporecase in certain Liverworts (*Hepaticæ*), to the spore of Horse-tails (*Equisetaceæ*), etc., and serving to discharge and disperse the sporules when ripe.

1830 LINDLEY *Nat. Syst. Bot.* 324 Spiral fibres, called Elateres, within which the sporules are intermixed. **1866** *Treas. Bot.* II. 641/2 The elaters which accompany the spores are distinct spiral vessels. **1870** HOOKER *Stud. Flora* 472 Equisetaceæ..spores of one kind, attached to 4 clubbed elastic threads (elaters).

elater², **elator** (ɪˈleɪtə(r)). [f. ELATE *v.* + -ER, -OR.] He who or that which elates.

1818 RICHARDSON, *Elater* [with example for ELATER¹]. **1847** CRAIG, *Elator.* In mod. Dicts.

†**elaˈterical,** *a. Obs. rare*⁻¹. [f. ELATER + -IC + -AL¹.] Pertaining to the theory of elasticity.

1674 *Phil. Trans.* IX. 82 What his Reasons and Evidences are to evince the mistake..of this Elaterical supposition.

elaterin (ɪˈlætərɪn). *Chem.* Also elatine. [f. ELATER-IUM + -IN: cf. F. *élatérine.*] The active principle of elaterium ($C_{20}H_{28}O_5$).

1830 LINDLEY *Nat. Syst. Bot.* 193 An extremely active poisonous principle, called Elatine, has..been found in the placenta of this plant. **1866** *Treas. Bot.* I. 437/2 The active principle of elaterium is a crystalline substance called elaterin. **1887** BRUNTON *Pharmacol.* 929 Elaterin is the most powerful hydragogue we possess.

†**eˈlaterist.** *Obs.* [f. ELATER¹ + -IST.] One who explains certain phenomena as due to the 'elatery' or elasticity of the air.

1661 BOYLE *Spring of Air* I. ii. (1682) 3 His Adversaries (whom for brevities sake we will venture to call Elaterists). **1674** [M. HALE] *Difficiles Nugæ* 237 The Gravitation and Elasticity of the Air, invented by the modern Elaterists. **1708** in KERSEY. **1721–1800** in BAILEY.

elaterite (ɪˈlætəraɪt). *Min.* [f. ELATER¹ elasticity + -ITE.] A brown hydrocarbon, usually soft and elastic like india-rubber; elastic bitumen.

1826 EMMONS *Min.* 215 Elaterite, see Bitumen, elastic. **1876** PAGE *Adv. Text-bk. Geol.* xiv. 244 Masses of elaterite, and slaggy mineral pitch.

‖**elaterium** (ɛləˈtɪərɪʌm). [a. L. *elatērium*, ad. Gr. ἐλατήριον an opening medicine, f. ἐλα- stem of ἐλαύνειν to drive. Senses 3 and 4 are due to ELATER¹.]

†**1.** A purgative medicine. *Obs.*⁻⁰

1721–1800 in BAILEY.

2. A sediment or precipitate from the juice of the Squirting Cucumber (*Ecballium agreste, Momordica Elaterium*), having a bitter acrid taste, and acting as a drastic purgative and emetic. Also called ***English Elaterium***, to distinguish it from ***French Elaterium***, a much less active preparation, produced by evaporation of the juice.

1578 LYTE *Dodoens* III. xl. 373 Elaterium..drieth foorth by siege grosse fleme. **1657** *Phys. Dict., Elaterium*..is good against the dropsie. **1684** tr. *Willis' Pharmaceutice Rat.* 41 Other purging Medicins, as Jalap, Colycinthis, Elaterium.. consist of sharp particles. **1790** BUCHAN *Dom. Med.* 551 If two grains of white vitriol, and the same quantity of elaterium, be dissolved in half an ounce of marjoram-water, etc. **1831** J. DAVIES *Manual Mat. Med.* 22 The elaterium.. contains a principle *sui generis*, and a bitter substance almost inert by itself. **1866** *Treas. Bot.* I. 437/1 So powerful is pure elaterium, that one eighth part of a grain is sufficient to produce strong cathartic effects.

†**3.** Elasticity, springiness (*spec.* of the air): = ELATER¹, ELATERY. *Obs.*

1708 in KERSEY. **1721–1800** in BAILEY. **1775** in ASH.

4. Used by Richard for the fruit of the *Euphorbiaceæ*, which opens elastically when ripe.

elaterometer (ɪˌlætəˈrɒmɪtə(r)). [ad. F. *élatéromètre*: cf. ELATER¹ and METER.] An instrument for indicating the pressure of confined air or steam.

1874 KNIGHT *Amer. Mech. Dict.*

†**ˈelaˌtery.** *Obs.* [f. ELATER + -Y; cf. ELATERIUM 3.] The elastic force, elasticity of the air; = ELATER¹.

1653 tr. *Pecquet's Anat. Exper.* 91 The superficie of the Earth-Watrish Orb is pressed of the same [the Atmosphere] not by its weight alone, but also by vertue of his Elatery [orig. *non solo pondere, sed et Elateris..virtute*]. **1664** POWER *Exp. Philos.* 103 The ayr hath..a strong elatery of its own. **1676** *Phil. Trans.* X. 534 Corrosions of bodies may further bend the springy particles of the Air, giving it a greater Elatery. **1847** in CRAIG; and in mod. Dicts.

elatine, obs. var. of ELATERIN.

elation (ɪˈleɪʃən). Also 4–5 **elacion,** 5 **elacyoun,** 5–6 **elacyon,** 6 **elatioun.** [In ME. ad. OF. *elacion*, ad. L. *ēlātiōn-em*, n. of action f. ppl. stem of *efferre*: see ELATE *a.*]

†**1.** (after Lat.) **a.** Lifting, elevation. **b.** Carrying out (e.g. of a dead body). *Obs. rare.*

1578 BANISTER *Hist. Man* I. 25 The brest bones..yeeld to the elation and depression of the ribbes. **1697** POTTER *Antiq. Greece* IV. iv. (1715) 189 Its [the body's] Elation from the House wherein it was prepar'd for Burial.

2. Elevation of mind arising from success or self-approbation, pride of prosperity; pride, vainglory.

c **1386** CHAUCER *Pers. T.* ⁋326 Elacion is whan he ne may neither suffre to haue maister ne felawe. *c* **1410** N. LOVE *Bonavent. Mirr.* xxv. 56 (Gibbs MS.), We haue no mater of elacyoun or veyn ioye of oure selfe. *c* **1522** SKELTON *Why not to Court* 479 He is in such elacyon Of his exaltation. **1678** OWEN *Mind of God* viii. 231 A noysome elation of mind. **1712** ADDISON *Spect.* No. 464 ⁋3 Riches exposes a Man to ..a foolish Elation of Heart.

†**b.** *concr.* A proud or vain-glorious action.

c **1630** JACKSON *Creed* IV. II. i. Wks. 1844 III. 202 Their next elation..was to elect him for their King.

3. Elevation of spirits (in neutral or good sense); buoyancy, joyousness, pleasurable self-satisfaction. (The usual current sense.)

1750 JOHNSON *Rambler* No. 184 ⁋5 Their time is past between elation and despondency. **1804–8** FOSTER in *Life & Corr.* (1846) I. 278 These praises give me but very little Elation. **1841** D'ISRAELI *Amen. Lit.* (1867) 619 In the elation of youth, he astounded the..fellows of his college. **1863** GEO. ELIOT *Romola* I. II. xxvii. (1880) 332 She saw her father..sink from elation into new disappointment.

b. *concr.* An 'outburst' of high spirits. *rare.*

1870 LOWELL *Among my Bks.* Ser. II. (1873) 243 These are the natural jets and elations of a mind energized by the rapidity of its own motion.

†**4.** *concr.* Growth. *Obs. rare.*

c **1420** *Pallad. on Husb.* III. 859 Thai be apte unto putacion Of bowes drie or foule elacion [L. *arida aut male nata*].

eˈlative, *a.* (and *sb.*) [as if ad. L. **ēlātīvus*: see ELATE *v.* and -IVE.]

†**a.** That raises, elevates. (*obs. rare*). **b.** That elates, causes elation. *rare.* **c.** *Gram.* Having a superlative or intensive force. Also *absol.* **d.** *Gram.* Denoting the case used in some languages to express motion away from. Also *absol.*

1595 LODGE *Fig for Momus* I, By their attracted moyst humiditie, Drawne from a certain vertue elative..Seeke more than their accustom'd nutriment Whence raine his generation doth derive. **1838** STRUTHERS *Poetic Tales* 125 Thither shall gratitude's feelings elative wend. **1860** *Trans. Philol. Soc.* 1857 34 The declension of the personal pronouns [in the Tushi language] is as follows..Elative.. Comitative..Terminative. **1906** J. H. MOULTON *Gram. N.T. Greek* I. v. 78 In the NT the obsolescence of the superlative, except in the elative sense, is most marked. *Ibid.* 79 Mt 11²⁰ may show the elative—'those very numerous mighty works'. *Ibid.* 97 The repetition of an adjective produces an elative. **1915** A. H. MCNEILE *St. Matt.* 59/2 'Ελάχιστος..may be elative, 'very small'. **1922** FOAKES-JACKSON & LAKE *Beginnings Christianity* II. 505 This is what the grammarians call an elative superlative. **1951** *Archivum Linguisticum* III. I. 60 An elative-ablative type of case suffix. **1959** J. C. CATFORD in Quirk & Smith *Teaching of English* vi. 186 Roughly the same field is covered by the system of 'local cases' in Finnish.. 'illative' ..'ablative'..'elative'.

†**elatrate,** *v. Obs.*⁻⁰ [f. L. *ēlātrāt-* ppl. stem of *ēlātrāre*, f. *ē* out + *lātrāre* to bark; see -ATE³.] 'To bark out or speak aloud' (Bailey).

1623 in COCKERAM. **1721–61** in BAILEY. **1820** in JODRELL.

Hence †**elaˈtration.**

1730–6 in BAILEY. **1775** in ASH. **1820** in JODRELL.

†**elavate,** *v. Obs. rare*⁻¹. [f. L. *ēlavāt-* ppl. stem of *ēlavāre* to wash out, wash away: cf. OF. *eslaver, elaver*.] *trans.* To wash clean.

1599 A. M. tr. *Gabelhouer's Bk. Physicke* 142/2 First elavate them with water wherin hath decoctede chickweede.

†**elaxate,** *v. Obs.*⁻⁰ [f. E- *pref.*³ + L. *laxāt-* ppl. stem of *laxāre* to unloose, relax: see LAX.] To loosen; to widen.

1656 BLOUNT *Glossogr.* **1721–1800** in BAILEY. **1775** in ASH. **1847** in CRAIG.

Hence †**elaˈxation.**

1731–6 in BAILEY. **1775** in ASH. **1847** in CRAIG.

†**eˈlay,** *v. Obs. rare*⁻¹. [? var. of ALLAY *v.*¹ or²; cf. Fr. *délayer* to dilute.] *trans.* ? To mix, dilute.

1573 *Art of Limming* 5 Orpyment may be elayed with Chalke, and dimmed..with Oker de Luke.

†**elayl** (ˈɛleɪl). *Chem. Obs.* [f. Gr. ἐλα-ίς an olive-tree (cf. ἔλαιον olive-oil) + ὕλη substance, material.] Same as ETHYLENE. In quot. in *comb.*

1865 MANSFIELD *Salts* 509 We see..why the base.. should differ so greatly in its behaviour from..Elayl-Stannethyl.

elayt, obs. var. of ELATE *a.*

elboic, var. of ELBOWIC.

elbow (ˈɛlbəʊ), *sb.* Forms: 1 **elnboȝa, eleboȝa, elboȝa,** 2–6 **elbowe,** 3 **elbou,** 7 **elboe,** 7– **elbow;** also (*Sc.*) 6 **elbok,** 8 **elbuck.** [A Com. Teut. compound: OE. *ęlnboȝa* = Du. *elleboog*, OHG. *elinbogo* (MHG. *ellenboge*, mod.G. *ellen-, ellbogen*), ON. *ǫlnboge* (Icel. *ölnbogi, ölbogi*, Da. *albue*):—OTeut. **alino-bogon-*, f. **alinâ* arm (see ELL) + **bogon-* bending = BOW *sb.*¹]

1. a. The outer part of the joint between the fore and the upper arm.

c **1000** ÆLFRIC *Voc.* in Wr.-Wülcker 158 *Cubitum*, fædm betwux elboȝa and handwyrste. *c* **1150** *Voc.* ibid. 536 *Ulna*, elbowe. *a* **1300** *Cursor M.* 8086 Þair armes hari wit hirpild hid War sette til elbous in þair side. *a* **1300** *Fragm.* 322 in *Popular Treat. on Sc.* 139 Thelbowes to the schare. *c* **1340** *Gaw. & Gr. Knt.* 184 A much berd..Watz euesed al vmbe-torne, abof his elbowes. *c* **1440** *Promp. Parv.* 137 Elbowe, *cubitus.* **1588** A. KING tr. *Canisius' Catech.* 138 Wae be vnto thame..quha sewis soft kods to putt vnder euerie Elbok. *a* **1613** OVERBURY *A Wife* (1638) 101 Turnes..from one Elbow to another. **1676** ETHEREDGE *Man of Mode* I. i. (1684) 11 He was yesterday at the Play, with a pair of Gloves Up to his Elbows. **1714** LADY M. W. MONTAGUE *Lett.* lxxxv. 140 In..a great crowd..people..knock others with their elbows. **1786** BURNS *The Ordination* vii, To see our elbucks wheep And a' like lamb-tails flyin. **1797** COLERIDGE *Christabel* I, She..on her elbow did recline To look at the lady Geraldine. **1879** STAINER *Music of Bible* 122 Irish bagpipes are inflated by the elbow, Scotch by the mouth.

b. The point resembling an elbow in the shoulder or hock of quadrupeds.

1607 TOPSELL *Four-f. Beasts* 317 The Curb..is a long swelling beneath the elbow of the hough. **1789** W. MARSHALL *Gloucester* (E.D.S.), *Elbows*, the shoulder-points of cattle. **1908** *Animal Managem.* 330 For the horse, a small sausage-shaped pillow, long enough to surround the pastern ..will be found to prevent the elbow touching the ground when lying down. *Ibid.* [see *elbow-brushing* in 5].

2. *transf.* Anything resembling an elbow.

a. A sharp bend in the course of a river, road, etc.

1591 PERCIVALL *Sp. Dict., Ahocinarse el rio*..to run with turnings or elbows. **1618** BP. HALL *Serm.* V. 117 The current..speeds forward from one elbow of earth unto another. **1762–71** H. WALPOLE *Vertue's Anecd. Paint.* (1786) IV. 297 The elbows of serpentine rivers. **1792** A. YOUNG *Trav. France* 99 The road..presents from an elbow the finest view of a town I have ever seen. **1861** MISS BEAUFORT *Egypt. Sepul.* II. xxiii. 311 The ravine..turns with a sudden elbow round the end of mount Silpius.

b. A forward or outward projection; a corner.

1626 BACON *Sylva* §472 Fruit-trees or Vines, set upon a Wall against the Sun, between Elbows and Buttresses of Stone, ripen more than upon a plain Wall. **1691** T. H[ALE] *Acc. New Invent.* p. cvii, Some Elbows of Wharfs..being taken away. **1756** NUGENT *Gr. Tour* III. 206 Ancona..The name of this city is said to be owing to its situation, because of the elbow (ἀγκών)..which the shore makes in that place. **1829** SOUTHEY *Sir T. More* (1831) I. 120 You cross a wall and the elbow of a large tree that covers it. **1830** W. PHILLIPS *Mt. Sinai* IV. 504 Departing day Behind the mountain's elbow disappear'd. **1876** BLACKMORE *Cripps* II. xiv. 217 The elbow of a hedge jutted forth upon the common.

c. *Mechanics.* An angle in a tube, etc.; a short piece of pipe bent at an angle to join two long straight pieces.

1777 *Phil. Trans.* LXVII. 643 As the elbow made a right angle, the tube itself was of course horizontal. **1874** KNIGHT *Amer. Dict. Mech.*, *Elbow*, 1. The junction of two parts having a bent joint. 2. A knee or toggle joint. 3. A bend, as of a stove-pipe. **1880** MACCORMAC *Antisept. Surg.* 147 The tube should..have no elbows.

d. *Arch.* (see quot.)

1823 P. NICHOLSON *Pract. Builder* 584 *Elbows of a Window*, the two flanks of panelled work, one under each shutter. **1875** PARKER *Gloss. Archit.*, *Elbows*, the projections on the side of stalls. **1876** GWILT *Archit.* Gloss., *Elbow*, the upright side which flanks any panelled work, as in windows below the shutters, etc.

e. *Naut.* (see quot.)

1769 FALCONER *Dict. Marine* (1789) *Cable tourné*..a foul hawse; a cross or elbow in hawse. **1867** SMYTH *Sailor's Word-bk.* s.v., *Elbow in the hawse.* When a ship, being moored in a tideway, swings twice the wrong way, thereby causing the cables to take half a round turn on each other.

f. *dial.* (see quot., and cf. *elbow-health* in 5).

1877 E. PEACOCK *N.-W. Linc. Gloss.* (E.D.S.), *Elbow*, the conical hollow in the bottom of a wine-bottle.

†**3.** *transf.* An arm of a chair, made to support the elbow. *Obs.* exc. in *comb.* ELBOW-CHAIR.

1611 COTGR. s.v. *Accoudoir*, *Vne chaire à accoudoirs*, a chaire with elbowes. **1679** *Marriage of Charles II*, 3 A great Chair with elbows. **1750** CARTE *Hist. Eng.* II. 14 Elbows (as the sides of chairs are now called). **1784** COWPER *Task* I. 60 But elbows still were wanting; these, some say, An alderman of Cripplegate contriv'd.

4. Phrases: **a.** *at the, one's elbow(s*: close by, very near; in close attendance; also *fig.*; so *from the, one's elbow*: away from one's side. **b.** *up to the elbows*: *lit.*; also *fig.* engrossed in work, excessively busy. **c.** *to be out at elbow(s*: to have a coat worn out at the elbows, to be ragged, poor, in bad condition; hence, in same sense, *out-at-elbowed* adj. (*nonce-wd.*). So, in contrary sense, *in at elbows* (rare). **d.** † *to scratch, rub the elbow*: to show oneself pleased, to chuckle. **e.** *to shake the elbow*: to play at dice (*arch*). † *knight of the elbow*: a gambler. **f.** † *to suck at* (*one's*) elbow: ? to play the parasite, sponge upon (one). **g.** *more power to one's elbow*: may you (he, etc.) succeed (in a laudable enterprise). **h.** *to lift one's* (or *the*) *elbow*: to drink immoderately. Similarly *to bend the elbow*; *to crook the elbow*: see CROOK *v.*^{1} 1 d.

a. 1548 LD. SOMERSET *Epist. Scots* 243 Ye haue youre enemies..at your elbowe. **1581** MULCASTER *Positions* vi. (1887) 47 In the elder yeares, reason at the elbow must serue the student. *Ibid.* xxxvii. 143 You are not able to spare him from your elbow. **1698** VANBRUGH *Æsop* II. i. (1730) 230 Talk of the Devil and he's at your elbow. **1840–1** DICKENS *Old C. Shop* i, I found at my elbow a pretty little girl.

b. 1601 SHAKS. *Jul. C.* III. i. 107 Let vs bathe our hands in Caesars blood Vp to the Elbowes. **1883** A. ROBSON *Dead Letter* II. v, Up to our Elbows making Damson Jam.

c. 1623 SHAKS. *Meas. for M.* II. i. 61 He cannot [speak] Sir; he's out at Elbow. **1771** SMOLLETT *Humph. Cl.* (1815) 55 Sir Ulic Mackilligut..is said to be much out at elbows. **1841** THACKERAY *Sec. Fun. Nap.* i, Seedy out-at-elbowed coats. *a* **1847** MRS. SHERWOOD *Lady of Manor* I. vi. 244 He was himself just now so terribly out at elbows, that he could not command a hundred pounds. **1865** CARLYLE *Fred. Gt.* III. VIII. iv. 17 Several things known to be out-at-elbows in that Country. **1872** G. ELIOT *Middlemarch* xxxviii. (D.) Pay that hardly keeps him in at elbows. **1885** *Times* 28 May, There is an out-at-elbows look about some quarters of Dublin.

d. 1588 SHAKS. *L.L.L.* v. ii. 109 One rub'd his elboe thus, and fleer'd, and swore, A better speech was neuer heard before. **1598** E. GILPIN *Skial.* (1878) 25 He'le..scratch the elbow too To see two butchers curres fight.

e. 1705 HEARNE *Collect.* 26 Nov. (1885–6) I. 100 Money which..he squander'd away in shaking his Elbow. **1760** T. BROWN Wks. II. 46 (D.) Knight of the elbow. **1826** J. WILSON *Noct. Ambr.* Wks. 1855 I. 127 Many good and great men have shook the elbow.

f. 1548 HALL *Chron.* (1809) 312 He had many..that daily sucked at his Elbowe.

g. 1832 LOVER *Leg. Ireland* 1st Ser. (ed. 2) 133 More power to your honour's elbow. **1860** [see POWER *sb.*^{1} 2]. **1928** F. M. FORD *Let.* 5 Mar. (1965) 177 Anyhow more power to your elbow! **1956** A. WILSON *Anglo-Saxon Attitudes* II. i. 196 Some Members of Parliament..are to ask questions..about the unfortunate mishandling of Mr. Cressett's market-garden. More power to their elbow, I say.

h. 1823 GROSE *Dict. Vulgar T.* s.v. *lift*, To lift one's hand to one's head; to drink to excess, or to drink drams. To lift or raise one's elbow; the same. **1915** CONRAD *Victory* I. vi. 130, I would watch them lifting their elbows at my expense. **1928** *Daily Express* 7 Mar. 15/4 Many a young man who has been lifting his elbow too frequently in Dublin is packed off to Melleray for a cure. **1938** D. RUNYON *Take it Easy* xiii. 247 A great change comes over Haystack Duggeler. He stops bending his elbow and helps Hattie cook and wash the dishes. **1939** J. B. PRIESTLEY *Let People Sing* iv. 86, I only hope to goodness this couple we're picking up this afternoon don't lift the elbow too much. **1967** *Coast to Coast 1965–6* 145 He's not much chop. Too fond of bending the elbow.

5. *attrib.* and *Comb.*, as *elbow-cushion*, *-guard*, *-point*; also **elbow-bombard** [transl. It. *bombardo cubito*], a kind of cannon in which the breech was at right angles with the bore; **elbow-brushing** (see quot.); **elbow-cloak**, ? a cloak reaching down to the elbows only; **elbow-deep** *a.* (see quot.; cf. 2 f. and *elbow-health*); **elbow-health**, *fig.*, a bumper; **elbow-length** *a.*, reaching to the elbow; **elbow-piece**, (*a*) in plate armour, a covering for the juncture of the plates meeting at the elbow; (*b*) a piece of tubing forming an elbow; **elbow-pipe**, a pipe having a bend resembling an elbow; cf. 2 c; **elbow-polish** = ELBOW-GREASE; **elbow-shaker** (see quot.); **elbow-shaking** *vbl. sb.* and *ppl. a.*, playing at dice; **elbow-sleeve**, a sleeve reaching only to the elbow; **elbow-wind**, a wind blowing sideways. Also ELBOW-CHAIR, GREASE, -JOINT, -ROOM.

1881 GREENER *Gun* 20 It was called the *elbow bombard. **1908** *Animal Managem.* 330 *Elbow brushing in the camel is a serious condition resulting from the friction of the elbow pad against the side in animals which are tied in at the elbow and whose toes are turned out. *c* **1612** ROWLANDS *Spy Knaves*, An *elbow cloake, because wide hose and garters May be apparent in the lower quarters. **1653** MILTON *Hirelings* Wks. (1851) 366 A pulpited Divine..a lollard..over his *elbow-cushion. **1642** T. TAYLOR *God's Judgem.* II. vii. 102 No man was able to contend with him in his ..*Elbow-deep Healths. **1874** BOUTELL *Arms & Arm.* 190 *Elbow-guards, or *coudières*..were rarely adopted till after the year 1300. **1622** MIDDLETON, &c. *Old Law* v. i, The nimble fencer..that..gave me Those *elbow-healths. [**1897** *Sears, Roebuck Catal.* 231/2 This length is very stylish, and known as the *elbow length.] **1904** *Westm. Gaz.* 26 May 10/1 Fashion launched on us the mandate that all sleeves must be elbow length. **1908** *Ibid.* 9 Jan. 4/1, I find for everyday wear the elbow-length cream 'Viyella' gloves hard to beat. **1932** D. C. MINTER *Mod. Needlecraft* 148/2 An elbow-length sleeve. **1967** E. SHORT *Embroidery & Fabric Collage* ii. 54 Gloves..elbow length with more elaborate decoration for evening wear. **1777** *Phil. Trans.* LXVII. 643 This tube was connected to the receiver of the air-pump by means of an *elbow-piece of brass. **1861** W. FAIRBAIRN *Iron* viii. 166 An *elbow-pipe..establishes a communication.. between the blast-pipe and the tuyere. **1883** *Specif. Alnwick & Cornhill Rlwy.* 22 Proper elbow pipes and connections to be made with existing drains. **1859** G. ELIOT *A. Bede* I. vi. (D.) Genuine *elbow-polish, as Mrs. Poyser called it. **1785** COWPER *Task* IV. 44 Bored with *elbow-points through both his sides. **1725** *New Cant. Dict.*, **Elbow-shaker*, a Gamester or Sharper. **1700** *Prol. to Farquhar's Const. Couple* (D.), Your *elbow-shaking fool that lives by's wits. **1849** THACKERAY *Pendennis* (1875) 594 'It's been cut into by your master, with his helbow-shakin' and his bill discountin'.' **1875** L. TROUBRIDGE *Life amongst Troubridges* (1966) 117 A pretty white muslin with..*elbow sleeves, plissées with lace. **1899** *Daily News* 24 June 4/6 Some of the smart people compromise by adopting elbow sleeves with very long gloves rucked up the whole length of the fore-arm. *Ibid.* 22 July 4/3 Elbow sleeves have come in with the heat. **1908** L. M. MONTGOMERY *Anne of Green Gables* xiii. 130 Diana is having a new dress made with elbow sleeves. *a* **1722** LISLE *Husb.* (1752) 113 A face or back-wind signifies little, nor the *elbow-wind neither to peas and vetches.

elbow ('ɛlbəʊ), *v.* [f. prec. sb.]

1. *trans.* To thrust with the elbow; to jostle; also *fig.*

1605 SHAKS. *Lear* IV. iii. 44 (Globe ed.) A sovereign shame so elbows him. **1673** DRYDEN *Conq. Granada* I. i, Grown more strong, it..Elbows all the Kingdoms round about. **1691–8** NORRIS *Pract. Disc.* (1711) III. 138 They have scarce room to pass in without elbowing..one another. **1710** STEELE & ADD. *Tatler* No. 253 ¶8 Must our Sides be elbowed, our Shins broken? **1876** GREEN *Stray Stud.* 190 The trader elbowing the noble and the artisan the trader.

2. To thrust aside with the elbow; also, *to elbow off, out of* (*anything*). Chiefly *fig.*

1712 STEELE *Spect.* No. 484 ¶5 It is ever want of breeding ..to be..elbow'd out of his honest ambition. **1712** ARBUTHNOT *John Bull* (1727) 74 He used to..elbow his fellow-servants to get near his mistress. **1855** MACAULAY *Hist. Eng.* IV. 485 They would elbow our own Aldermen off the Royal Exchange. **1884** *Manch. Exam.* 13 Nov. 5/2 The small farming class have been gradually elbowed out of their holdings.

†**3.** *absol.* and *intr.* To push right and left with the elbows; also *fig.* So also, † *to elbow it.*

1636 HEYWOOD *Challenge* v. i. Wks. 1874 V. 68 That Picke-devant that elbowes next the Queene. **1681** MANNINGHAM *Disc. Truth* 50 (T.) He..grows hot and turbid..elbows in all his philosophick disputes. **1767** *Babler* II. 195 To be elbowing it among people of fashion. **1885** L. WINGFIELD *Barbara Philpot* III. xii. 291 Beaux elbowed for a place.

4. a. quasi-*refl.* To force one's way by elbowing; const. *into*, *through*. **b.** quasi-*trans.* To make (one's way) by elbowing.

1833 HT. MARTINEAU *Berkeley* I. vii. 132 A carrier had left the market early to elbow his way into the bank. **1863** MRS. C. CLARKE *Shaks. Char.* vi. 162 She..elbows herself in wherever she sees business going on.

5. *intr.* To make an 'elbow' in one's path, go out of the direct way.

1804 SOUTHEY in Robberds *Mem. W. Taylor* I. 503, I would elbow out of my way to Norwich. **1839–40** W. IRVING *Wolfert's R.* (1855) 149 Elbowing along, zig-zag.

6. (See quot.)

1755 JOHNSON, *Elbow* To jut out in angles. *Dict.* **1775** in ASH. **1832** in WEBSTER; and in mod. Dicts.

ˌ**elbow-'chair.** A chair with elbows: see ELBOW *sb.* 3.

1655 tr. *Sorel's Comical Hist. Francian* x. 9 He.. permitted that the two men should put him in an Elbow chair. *a* **1704** T. BROWN *Praise Drunk.* Wks. 1730 I. 36 A drunkard seated in an elbow chair. **1822** W. IRVING *Braceb. Hall* ii. 9 Very eloquent in praise of an ancient elbow chair. **1887** R. N. CAREY *Uncle Max* xiv. 278, I fetched father's big elbow-chair with a cushion or two.

elbowed ('ɛlbəʊd), *ppl. a.* [f. ELBOW *sb.* + -ED^2.] **a.** Having elbows or bends. *elbowit grass*, Sc. (see quot.). **b.** Of a seat: Provided with elbow-rests. **c.** Formed into the shape of an elbow, bent, curved.

1825 HONE *Every-day Bk.* I. 784 An elbowed seat had been introduced. **1825–80** JAMIESON *Scot. Dict.*, *Elbowit Grass*, Flote Fox-tail Grass. Alopecurus Geniculatus.

'elbow-grease. *humorous.* Vigorous rubbing, proverbially referred to as the best unguent for polishing furniture. Hence *allusively*, energetic labour of any kind.

1672 MARVELL *Reh. Transp.* I. 5 Two or three brawny Fellows in a Corner, with meer Ink and Elbow-grease, do more Harm than an Hundred systematical Divines with their sweaty Preaching. **1699** B. E. *Dict. Cant. Crew*, *Elbow-grease*, a derisory Term for Sweat. **1735** LITTLETON *Lat. Dict.*, It had no elbow-grease bestowed on't. *Nec demorsos sapit ungues.* **1879** TROLLOPE *Thackeray* 122 Forethought is the elbow-grease which a novelist,—or poet, or dramatist, —requires.

†**el'bowic,** *a. humorous. Obs.* In Dicts. **elboic(k.** [f. ELBOW *sb.* + -IC.] (See quot.)

1654 GAYTON *Fest. Notes* I. iii, Verses, which being above Hexameters, full sometimes, and sometimes over-makes, that rather sounding verse, we call Elbowick. **1727** BAILEY II, *Elboick*, a sentence or verse of a rude or ruffling quality, as it were hunching or pushing with the elbow. **1734** LITTLETON *Lat. Dict.*, Elboick verse, *carmen hypermetrum* or *redundans*. **1775** in ASH.

elbowing ('ɛlbəʊɪŋ), *vbl. sb.* [f. ELBOW *v.* + -ING^1.] The action of thrusting with the elbow; *concr.* a thrust with the elbow.

1820 T. MITCHELL *Aristophanes* I. 17 What crowding then and elbowing among them! **1846** W. S. LANDOR *Imag. Conv.* I. 17, I received on the stairs many shoves and elbowings. **1863** GEO. ELIOT *Romola* I. I. xiv. (1880) 188 He pushed his way..with a sort of pleasure in the..elbowing.

elbowing ('ɛlbəʊɪŋ), *ppl. a.* [f. ELBOW *v.* + -ING^2.] That thrusts with the elbow; also *fig.*

1767 GRAINGER *Solitude* (T.), Purse proud, elbowing Insolence. **1871** LOWELL *Study Wind.* (1886) 23 The elbowing self-conceit of youth.

'elbow-joint. [f. ELBOW *sb.* + JOINT.]

a. *Anat.* 'The hinge-joint formed by the connexion of the lower end of the humerus with the upper ends of the radius and ulna by means of ligaments' (*Syd. Soc. Lex.*). **b.** *Mech.*: = ELBOW *sb.* 2 c.

1831 R. KNOX *Cloquet's Anat.* 310 This muscle is deeply seated at the lower and fore part of the arm, before the elbow-joint. **1881** *Mechanic* §1101 In fig. 556 an illustration is given of an elbow-joint.

'elbow-room. [f. ELBOW *sb.* + ROOM.] Room to move one's elbows; hence, freedom from constraint; space sufficient to move or work in at one's ease. Also *fig.*

c **1540** BOORDE *The Boke for to Lerne* A ij b, He..whiche wyll dwell at pleasure..must dwell at elbowe rome. **1670** BROOKS *Wks.* (1867) VI. 331 Give faith scope, give it elbow-room to work. **1758** CHESTERFIELD *Lett.* No. 348 (1792) IV. 155 Which would give him more elbow-room to act against France. **1868** M. PATTISON *Academ. Org.* §5. 315 The improvement..in its [teaching] quality by the..elbow-room which the teacher would obtain.

elbuck, Sc. var. of ELBOW *sb.*

elc(h, obs. form of EACH.

elcampane, obs. var. ELECAMPANE.

‖**elchee** ('ɛltʃiː). Also elchi, eltchi. [Turk. *īlchī*, 'from *īl* a (nomad) tribe, hence the representative of the *īl*' (Y.).] An ambassador.

1824 J. MORIER *Adv. Hajji Baba* III. xiii. 148 Ignorant of what is due to the character of *Elchi*, or ambassador. **1828** *Blackw. Mag.* XXIII. 64 So well described by an English Elchee. **1863** KINGLAKE *Crimea* I. viii. 113 The great Eltchi [Sir Stratford Canning].

†**'elchur,** *adv. Obs.* Forms: 1 elcor, -ur, 2 elchur. [OE. *ęlcor* = OS. *elkor*, *-kur*, OFris. *elker*, OHG. *elichôr*; app. the comparative deg. of an adv. related to OTeut. **aljo-* other.] Elsewhere, otherwise, besides.

c **890** K. ÆLFRED *Bæda* IV. xxviii. (Bosw.) Gif hit hwæt elcor biþ. *c* **1175** *Lamb. Hom.* 105 þet þe mon beo iþuldi.. and lete elchur his iwit weldre þene his wreðôe.

†**'elcrook.** *Obs. rare*$^{-1}$. [? f. *el*, name of the letter L + CROOK; but cf. ELLRAKE.] ? An L-shaped hook.

1606 BIRNIE *Kirk-Burial* (1833) 35 Lyke Hophnees with elcrookes to minche..the offerings of God.

† **eld**, *sb.*[1] *Obs. rare*$^{-1}$. [app. repr. OE. *ǣled* (genit. *ǣldes*) fire; cf. synonymous OS. *eld*, ON. *eld-r* (Sw. *eld*, Da. *ild*).] Fire.

c **1200** *Trin. Coll. Hom.* 258 þu sscope eld & wind & water.

eld (ɛld), *sb.*[2] *arch.* and *north.* Forms: 1 ǣld(u, eldo, eld, (WS. ieldu, ild(u, yld(u), 2–6 elde, 2–3 ulde (y), 3 ælde, ealde, (4 *north.* heild, held, ellde), 4–5 eelde, (helde), 5 *Sc.* eylde, 3 (6–9 *Sc.*) eild, (elth), 4– eld. See also ALD, OLD, *sbs.* [OE. *ęldo* (abstr. sb. f. *ald*, in WS. *eald*, OLD *a.*), corresp. to OS. *eldî*, OHG. *altî*, *eltî*, ON. *elli* (Da. *ælde*).

Synonymous derivatives from the same root are ON. *ǫld* (:—**aldâ*) and Goth. *alþs* (:—**alþi-z*).]

1. The age, period of life, at which a person has arrived. *Obs.* exc. *dial.*

a **1000** *Guthlac* (Gr.) 80 Se halȝa wer In þa ærestan ældu ȝelufade Frecnessa fela. c **1000** ÆLFRIC *Hom.* in Sweet (1879) 90 Eadiȝ is heora [the innocents'] yld. c **1000** *Sax. Leechd.* III. 162 He leng ne leofað þonn on miðre ilde. a **1225** *Ancr. R.* 318 Ich was of swuche elde. a **1300** *Cursor M.* 22814 Old and ying, At þat fortald vprising sal be of eild, als þai suld here, Haue deide of eild of thritti ȝere. c **1300** *Beket* 159 This child was bot in elde of tuo and twenti ȝer. **1340** HAMPOLE *Pr. Consc.* 742 Bot swa grete elde may nane now bere. c **1350** *Will. Palerne* 403 William & ȝhe were of on held. c **1400** *Gamelyn* 643 Gamelyn, that yong was of elde. **1513** DOUGLAS *Æneis* VIII. ix. 41 In sic strenthis and eyld. **1559** *Mirr. Mag.*, *Edward IV*, vii. 2 Ye wote well all I was of no great elde. **1600** TOURNEUR *Transf. Metamorph.* (1878) 200 Erinnis purveyor, young elth I meane. **1691** RAY *N.C. Wds.* s.v. *Eald*, He is tall of his Eald. **1724** RAMSAY *Tea-t. Misc.* (1733) I. 63 His eild and my eild can never agree. **1860** RAMSAY *Remin.* Ser. I. (ed. 7) 177, 'I am just ae eild wi' the auld king' [George III].

†**2.** Conventional or legal age; full age; majority. ***of eld*** = of age; ***within eld*** = under age; also (quot. 1400) of military age. *Obs.*

a **1300** *Havelok* 128 Sho were comen intil helde. a **1300** *Cursor M.* 29444 (*Cott.* Galba), Childer within elde, of cursed man may haue þaire belde. **1357** *Lay-Folks Mass-Bk.* App. II. 118 Ilke man and woman that of eld is. c **1400** *Rowland & O.* 682 And alle that are with-in elde loke that thay to batayle helde. **1450** MYRC 236 Alle that ben of warde and elde. **1529** LYNDESAY *Complaynt* 115, I prayit, daylie.. My ȝoung maister that I mycht see Off eild.

3. Old age, advanced period of life; usually with regard to its effects upon man. Also *personified*. *arch.* & *poet.*

971 *Blickl. Hom.* 59 Se wlite eft ȝewiteþ & to ylde ȝecyrreþ. a **1200** *Moral Ode* 373 in *Cott. Hom.* 181 Þer is ȝeoȝeðe bute ulde. c **1205** LAY. 11546 Vnhæle & ælde hæueð þene king vnbalded. c **1250** *Gen. & Ex.* 1197 Sarra.. wurd wið child, on elde wac. **1340** HAMPOLE *Pr. Consc.* 801 Alle thir.. That clerkes propertes of eld calles. **1388** WYCLIF *Prov.* xvi. 31 A coroun of dignyte is eelde. c **1449** PECOCK *Repr.* III. v. 303 A staffe forto go by in his eelde for sijkenes. **1549** *Compl. Scot.* i. 20 Tha begyn to decresse ande declinis til eild ande to the dede. **1599** MARSTON *Sco. Villanie* I. iv. (1764) 187 Cold, writhled Eld, his liues-wet almost spent. **1600** FAIRFAX *Tasso* XVII. xi. (1726) 297 His eies (not yet made dim with eild) Sparkled his former worth and vigor braue. **1637** B. JONSON *Sad Sheph.* II. ii, Who scorns at eld, peels off his own young hairs. **1748** THOMSON *Cast. Indol.* II. xxxi, The whitening snows Of venerable eld. **1800–24** CAMPBELL *Pilgr. Glencoe* 478 Hale and unburden'd by the woes of eild. **1858** KINGSLEY *Weird Lady* 17 His beard was white with eld.

†**b.** People of advanced age; old men; senate or aristocracy. (In quot. 1592 perhaps the adj. used *absol.*) *Obs.*

c **1000** ÆLFRIC *Hom.* (Thorpe) II. 506 (Bosw.), Seo yld hi ȝebæd and seo iuȝuþ wrat. a **1075** *O.E. Chron.* (Laud MS.) an. 1004 Ðær wærð East Engla folces seo yld ofslaȝen. **1592** WYRLEY *Armorie* 147 That pleasant sweet content That diuers eld haue found within a wall.

c. *poet.* An old man. (But perh. an absol. use of the adj.) Rarely in pl. *elds*.

1796 COLERIDGE *Dest. Nations*, To the tottering eld Still as a daughter would she run. **1830** W. PHILLIPS *Mt. Sinai* II. 364 That eld august Came out from Israel. *Ibid.* III. 165 To the expectant host In solemn order did these elds descend.

†**4.** Antiquity, duration of existence; time considered as a destroying or wearing agency. *Obs.*

c **1374** CHAUCER *Anel. & Arc.* 12 That eeld which that all can frete and bite. **1602** R. T. *Five Godlie Serm.* 64 Eld eateth al things. a **1667** JER. TAYLOR *Serm.* Suppl. (1678) 148 An old sore.. by its eld almost habituate. **1740** SHENSTONE *Schoolmistress* 137 In elbow-chair.. By the sharp tooth of cankering Eld defaced.

5. Antiquity, the olden time. ***men, times,*** etc. ***of eld*** = men, etc. of old. *poet.* and *arch.*

c **1400** *Destr. Troy* 11881 Hit is said oftsythes with sere men of elde, The last Ioy of ioly men Ioynys with sorow. **1640** J. GOWER *Ovid's Fest.* I. 11 In times of eld men pleased the powers of heaven. **1812** BYRON *Ch. Har.* I. xciii, Lands that contain the monuments of Eld. **1834** LD. HOUGHTON *The Eld*, Blessed by the Eld, Its echoes and its shades. **1847** LONGF. *Ev.* Prel. 3 The murmuring pines and the hemlocks .. Stand like Druids of eld.

b. People of the olden time, antiquity (personified). *poet.* and *arch.*

Chiefly in Shakspere's phrase 'superstitious eld'.

1598 SHAKS. *Merry W.* IV. iv. 36 The superstitious.. Eld Receiu'd.. This tale of Herne the Hunter, for a truth. **1820** SCOTT *Monast.* Introd., Superstitious eld.. has tenanted the deserted groves with aerial beings. **1823** —— *Peveril* II. i. 5 Tradition and superstitious eld.. had filled up the long blank of accurate information.

†**6.** An age of the world, a secular period. *Obs.*

a **1000** *Guthlac* (Gr.) 807 In þam leohtan ham þurh ælda tid ende ȝebidan. c **1000** ÆLFRIC *Hom.* in Sweet (1879) 60 Seo þridde yld wæs ða wuniende oð David. c **1250** *Gen. & Ex.* 705 Ðis oðer werldes elde is so A ðhusent ȝer seuenti and two. a **1300** *Cursor M.* 9230 Blissed be sco þat us has spedd þat we þe elds four has redd. *Ibid.* 21847 Sex eildes ha we broght in place. c **1425** WYNTOUN *Cron.* II. ix. 77 Wytht-in þe ferd Eylde Yrland Was to þe Scottis obeyssande. **1513** DOUGLAS *Æneis* VII. xii. 99 Ceculus.. all eildis.. schawis ws Engenerit was by the God Vulcanus.

7. *Comb.*, as ***eld-time***.

1839 BAILEY *Festus* x. (1848) 110 In the eld-time.

† **eld**, *sb.*[3]: ME. *ane eld* = *a neld*, a NEEDLE.

a **1400–50** *Alexander* 1370 So nere, vnethes at ane eld miȝt narowly betwene.

eld (ɛld), *a. poet.* and *arch.* [repr. ME. *eld(e*, OE. (WS.) *eald* (see OLD); the mod. word may however be newly f. ELD *sb.*] Occas. used in poetry for OLD (q.v. for earlier instances).

[c **1440** *Promp. Parv.* 137 Elde, or olde, for-weryde [**1499** eeld, or worne], *vetustus, detritus, inveteratus*.] **1619** H. HUTTON *Follies Anat.* (1842) 42 Steward.. To serue their commons as eld servants use. **1854** DOBELL *Balder* xxv. 185 Ye eld And sager Gods.

b. quasi-*sb.*

1592 [see ELD *sb.*[2] 3 b]. **1796–1830** [see ELD *sb.*[2] 3 c].

† **eld**, *v.*[1] *Obs.* Forms: 1 WSax. eald-ian, 2 eald-ien, 3 æld-en, 3–5 eld-en, eld-e (4 *Kent* yeald-y), 4–5 eeld-en, eelde, 6 eld, *Sc.* eild. See also OLD(E *v.* [In southern dialects repr. OE. (WS.) *ealdian* (:—type **aldōjan*, not represented in any other language), f. *eald*, OLD; the equivalent Mercian from **aldian* survived in ME. as OLD(E *v.* The midland and northern instances of *eld(en*, *eeld(en*, *eild*, probably belong formally to ELD *v.*[2] (type **alðjan*).]

1. *intr.* To grow old.

c **1000** *Ags. Gosp.* John xxi. 18 þonne þu ealdast [c **1160** *Hatton* ealdest]. c **1200** ORMIN 18830, All iss itt whilwend-like þing þatt eldeþþ annd forrwurrþeþþ. c **1205** LAY. 2937 Þa ældede [c **1275** holdede] þe king. a **1300** *E.E. Psalter* ci. 27 (M.) As kleþinge elde sal alle þai. **1340** *Ayenb.* 97 Hi ne mo-naȝt yealdy, ase dede þe yealde laȝe. **1382** WYCLIF *Josh.* xii. 1 Thou hast eeldid, and art of loong age. c **1440** *Promp. Parv.* 137 Eelden, agyn. **1496** *Dives & Paup.* (W. de W.) I. viii. 39 They be paynted lyke yong men.. in token that they .. elden not. **1536** BELLENDEN *Cron. Scot.* (1821) I. 200 This Valeriane.. eildit in miserabill servitude.

2. *trans.* To make old.

c **1400** *Rom. Rose* 392 Tyme.. eldith our auncessours And eldith kynges and emperours.

† **eld**, *v.*[2] *Obs.* Also 1 eld-an, (WS. ield-an, yld-an), 2 eld-en. [OE. *ęldan* (in WS. *ieldan*, *yldan*) = OHG. *alten* to delay (also more literally to make or become old):—OTeut. **alðjan*, f. **aldo-* OLD.] *trans.* and *intr.* To put off to a later time, defer, delay.

c **897** K. ÆLFRED *Gregory's Past.* xxi. 152 Se lareow ieldende secð ðone timan. a **1121** *O.E. Chron.* (Laud MS.) ann. 1100 þeah þe ic hit læng ylde. c **1175** *Lamb. Hom.* 21 Þe wrecche sunfulle ne elde nawiht þet he ne ga to bote þe wile he mei.

† **eld**, *v.*[3] *Obs.* exc. *dial.* = AIL.

156. *Thersites* in Hazlitt *Dodsley* I. 414 My son, what thing eldeth thee? **1880** MISS JACKSON *Shropsh. Word-bk.* s.v., Doctor.. didna seem to know whad elded 'im. Molly's.. bin eldin' a lung wilde.

elde, obs. var. of YIELD *v.*

† **'elded**, *ppl. a. Obs.* [f. ELD *v.*[1] + -ED.] That has grown old, inveterate.

a **1300** *Cursor M.* (Cott. MS.) 26654 Of eilded [*F.* eldid] thing.. better [*F.* hard] it es to change þe state.

elder ('ɛldə(r)), *sb.*[1] Forms: α. ellærn, ellæn, ellen, 2–4 ellarne, 4 ellerne, elrene, (5 elerne, elorne, ellern, elnerene 5, 9 *dial.* ellen), 4–7 eller, 4–6 eldre, 5 eldyr, (6 ellore), 6–7 eldren, eldern, 5 eller; β. 5 helren, hilder (-tre), hyldyr, hyllor, hillar, hillerne (-tre), hyl (-tre). [With OE. *ellærn* (of which *ellen* is app. a reduced form, as *isen* of *isern*) cf. MLG. *ellern*, *elderne*, *alhorn*, *elhorn* (Schiller & Lübben), Flem. *elhoren*, *alhoren* (Kilian). Possibly an originally adjectival formation; cf. Ger. *ahorn* maple = L. *acernus* adj. (For the euphonic change of *elr-* to *eldr-* cf. ALDER[1].) The forms with initial *h* seem to belong to a wholly different word, prob. of ON. origin; cf. Da. *hyld*, *hyldetræ*, Sw. *hyll*, app. related to the synonymous OHG. *holuntar*, MHG. *holander*, *holder*, mod.G. *holunder*, *holder*; in which a connexion of some kind with HOLE, HOLLOW, is plausible, as the tree might naturally have been named from its tubular stems.]

1. A low tree or shrub, *Sambucus nigra* (N.O. *Caprifoliaceæ*), called, for distinction, the Common or Black-berried Elder; bearing umbel-like corymbs of white flowers; the young branches are remarkable for their abundance of pith.

a **700** *Epinal Gloss.* 893 *Sambucus*, ellaen. a **800** *Corpus Gloss.* 1175 *Sambucus*, ellaern. c **1000** *Sax. Leechd.* II. 68 Wiþ fotece ȝenim ellenes leaf. c **1150** *Voc.* in Wr.-Wülcker 556 *Sambucus*, suew, ellarne. c **1325** *Gloss. W. de Biblesw.* in Wright *Voc.* 163 *De suhen* (hildertre, helren) *font les souheaus*. **1362** LANGL. *P. Pl.* A. I. 66 Iudas he Iapede with þe Iewes seluer And on an Ellerne treo [*v.r.* eldir; **1377** B. I. 68 eller] hongede him after. c **1425** in *Voc.* Wr.-Wülcker 646 *Hec sambuca*, hyllortre. c **1440** *Promp. Parv.*, Eldyr or hyldyr, or hillerne tre [*v.r.* hillar; hyltre, or elerne; elder, or hyltre, or elorne]. a **1450** *Alphita* 161 *Sambucus*.. ellen. **1471** RIPLEY *Comp. Alch.* v. xlii. in Ashm. (1652) 158 Wene they.. to have.. of an Elder an Apple swete? **1523** FITZHERB. *Husb.* §126 The stakes of the.. ellore be good. **1598** SHAKS. *Merry W.* II. iii. 30 My heart of Elder. **1608** PLAT *Gard. Eden* (1653) 100 Every plant of an Eldern will grow. **1615** W. LAWSON *Orch. & Gard.* (1648) 3 Some thinke the.. eller [would have] a waterish marish. **1728** THOMSON *Spring* 443 Then seek the bank where flowering elders crowd. **1876** HARLEY *Mat. Med.* 576 The Elder, indigenous in Europe, was known to the Greeks.

2. Extended to other species of the genus *Sambucus*; in N. America applied chiefly to *S. canadensis*. With distinguishing epithets: **dwarf elder, ground elder, dog elder** (*S. Ebulus*) = DANEWORT; **wild elder**, used by Lyte for *S. racemosa*.

1578 LYTE *Dodoens* III. xliv. 379 The nature and vertues of the wilde Eldren are as yet unknowen.

b. In popular names of other plants bearing a superficial resemblance to the elder: **bishop's elder, dog elder, dwarf elder, ground elder, wild elder** (cf. 2), names for Goutweed (*Ægopodium Podagraria*); **ground elder**, *Angelica silvestris*; **marsh** or **marish elder, water elder, white elder** = GUELDER ROSE (*Viburnum Opulus*).

3. *Attrib.*, as ***elder-blossom, -branch, -bud, -bush, -flower, -pith, -stick, -tree, -vinegar, -wine, -wood***; ***elder-leaved***, adj.; **elder-blow**, elder-blossom; **elder-gun**, a pop-gun made of a hollow shoot of elder; **elder-moth**, *Uropteryx Sambucata*. Also ELDER-BERRY, etc.

1862 BARNES *Rhymes Dorset Dial.* I. 76 A vield.. Where *elder-blossoms be a-spread. **1875** EMERSON *Lett. & Soc. Aims*, *Poet. & Imag.* Wks. (Bohn) III. 154 The scent of an *elder-blow.. is event enough for him. **1579** SPENSER *Shep. Cal.* Nov. 147 The Muses.. Now bringen bitter *Eldre braunches seare. **1642** FULLER *Holy & Prof. St.* I. v. 12 In the beginning of the spring.. sallads are made of *eldern-buds. **1815** SCOTT *Guy M.* i, A hut, or farmhouse.. surrounded by large *elder-bushes. **1626** BACON *Sylva* §692 Of this kind are *Elder-flowers, which therefore are proper for the Stone. **1718** QUINCY *Compl. Disp.* 133 Elder-flowers .. Flowers from May to July. **1599** SHAKS. *Hen. V*, IV. i. 210 That's a perilous shot out of an *Elder Gunne. a **1613** OVERBURY *A Wife* (1638) 201 As boyes doe Pellets in Elderne Guns. **1882** *Garden* 23 Sept. 273/1 The *Elder-leaved or black Ash.. the leaves of which.. are serrated. c **1600** J. DAY *Begg. Bednall Gr.* IV. ii, Thou wither'd *Elder-pith. **1532** MORE *Confut. Tindale* Wks. 425/1 No more then .. thys greke woorde *presbyteros* signifyeth an *elder sticke. **1398** TREVISA *Barth. De P.R.* XVII. cxliv. (1495) 700 The *Ellern tree hath vertue Duretica. **1566** WARDE tr. *Alexis' Secr.* III. I. 11 b, Foure vnces of the water of Elderne tree. **1712** tr. *Pomet's Hist. Drugs* I. 32 The Arabian Costus is the Root of a Shrub very like an Elder Tree. **1709** STEELE *Tatler* No. 150 ¶6 They had dissented.. about the Preference of *Elder to Wine-Vinegar. **1735** BERKELEY *Querist* §151 Men of nice palates have been imposed on, by *elder wine for French claret. **1760** T. HUTCHINSON *Hist. Col. Mass.* v. (1765) 464 A young stick of *elder wood.

¶**4.** Misused for ALDER[1].

c **1535** DEWES *Introd. Fr.* in Palsgr. 914 Thelder, *aulne*. **1611** FLORIO *Alno negro*, the blacke Elder-tree.

'elder, *sb.*[2] *dial.* [cf. MDu. *elder* of same meaning; perh. repr. OTeut. **aliþro(m*, f. **alan* to nourish. (Not etymologically connected with UDDER.)] The udder of a cow or mare.

1674 RAY *N.C. Wds.* 17 The Elder: the Udder. **1679** PLOT *Staffordsh.* (1686) 262 Which was a yard and an inch high at 2 days old, and had.. milk in its elder. **1797** J. DOWNING *Disord. Horned Cattle* 87 The beast should be.. milked quite clean out of the elder. **1875** *Lanc. Gloss.* s.v. (E.D.S.) Hur [the cow's] elder's a bit sore. **1880** MISS JACKSON *Shropsh. Gloss.* s.v. (E.D.S.) The mar'.. wuz glad to see the cowt for 'er elder wuz as 'ard as a stwun.

elder ('ɛldə(r)), *a.* and *sb.*[3] Forms: 1 (*Mercian, Kent.*) eldra, (*Northumbrian, Mercian*) ǣldra, (*WSax.*) ieldra, yldra, 2–3 eldere, eldre, ealdre, 3 eældre, ældre, elldre, eldore, ælder, 3–4 (heldre), uldre, ildre, 4 eilder, eldir, 5 elther, yelder, eelder, (*Sc.* 6 eldar, 8 ellar), 3– elder. See also ALDER, OLDER, *adjs.* [OE. *ęldra* (fem. and neut. *ęldre*) = OS. *aldira*, OFris. *alder*, *elder*, OHG. *altiro*, *eltiro* (mod.Ger. *älter*), ON. *eldre*, *ellre* (Da. *ældre*), Goth. *alþiza*:—OTeut. **alþizon-*, regularly f. **aldo-*, OE. *ald* (WS. *eald*), OLD.

The late WS. form *yldra* survived in the south as *uldre* (*ü*), *ildre* until the 13th c.]

A. *adj.* The comparative degree of OLD *a.*; formerly equivalent to the mod. OLDER, but now restricted to certain special uses.

1. That has lived or existed longer; senior, more advanced in age.

†**a.** Formerly used (both of persons and things) as a *predicate*; also as an *attribute* followed by *than*. Now superseded by OLDER.

c **1000** *Riddles* xli. 42 (Gr.) Ic eom micle yldra, þonne ymbhwyrft þes. c **1175** *Lamb. Hom.* 23 A þet ic beo ealdre. c **1200** *Moral Ode* (Egerton MS.) 1 Ic æm elder þænne ic wæs, a winter and a lore. a **1240** *Wohunge* in *Cott. Hom.* 277 Swa þu eldere wex, swa þu pouerer. **1541** ELYOT *Image Gov.* 93 If she shall be as olde, or elder than I am. **1593**

BILSON *Govt. Christ's Ch.* 364 The lawes of forren countries are farre elder then ours. **1596** SHAKS. *Merch. V.* IV. i. 251 How much more elder art thou then thy lookes? *a* **1639** W. WHATELEY *Prototypes* II. xxxiv. (1640) 161 Friendship is like wine, the elder the better. **1673** CAVE *Prim. Chr.* I. vii. 203 A custom probably not much elder than his time.

b. as *attribute* without *than*. Not now used of things, except with quasi-personification. Now chiefly with sbs. denoting family relationship, or as denoting the senior of two indicated persons; otherwise somewhat *arch.* Often with omission of sb. implied in the context.

Beowulf 469 (Gr.) Wæs hereȝar dead min yldra mæȝ. *c* **888** K. ÆLFRED *Boeth.* viii, Ic ðe ȝeongne ȝelærde swelce snytro swylce maneȝum oþrum ieldran ȝewittum oftoȝen is. *c* **975** *Durh. Gosp.* Luke xv. 25 Wæs ða sunu his ældra on lond. **1279** R. GLOUC. (1724) 367 Margarete.. þe eldore of þe tuo, in spoushod he nome. *a* **1300** *Cursor M.* 3861 þe eilder sister he for-sok. **1382** WYCLIF *Luke* xv. 25 Forsothe his eldere sone was in the feeld. *c* **1450** *Merlin* i. 5 The elther suster vndirstode hym wele. *c* **1478** *Plumpton Corr.* 38 The said Wil. Rycroft yelder. **1717** LADY M. W. MONTAGUE *Lett.* II. xliv. 22 It is a great part of the work of the elder slaves to take care of these young girls. **1745** WESLEY *Wks.* (1872) VIII. 217 These are too young; send elder men. **1815** SCOTT *Ld. of Isles* VI. xvi, Elder brother's care And elder brother's love were there. **1876** FREEMAN *Norm. Conq.* (1876) IV. xvii. 47 The Cathedral Church of the bishoprick whose throne is now hidden in the elder minster of Saint Fritheswyth.

c. ***elder statesman***, in Japan, a member of the GENRO; *transf.*, a person of ripe years and experience whose counsel is therefore sought and valued.

1921 *Contemp. Rev.* July 8 Prince Yamagata.. continues the most influential member of the *Genro*, or Elder Statesmen. **1923** *19th Cent.* Jan. 138 The exclusive powers of the *genro*, or elder statesmen, are passing with the men themselves. **1932** *Fortune* Sept. 100 This choice was exercised by the last of the *genro*, or 'Elder Statesmen', Prince Saionji, aged eighty-three. **1934** WEBSTER, *Elder statesmen.* a In Japan, an informal body (*genro*)... b Any similar class of persons. **1935** G. GREENE *Bear fell Free*, One should have made some prescient elder-statesman pronouncement. **1937** *John o' London's* 15 Jan. 667 (*heading*) Balfour, the Elder Statesman. **1955** H. SPRING *These Lovers fled Away* ii. 61 When you are twelve, a boy of fifteen.. seems almost an elder statesman. **1958** *Observer* 19 Oct. 22/4 Professor Tawney is the elder statesman of English economic history. **1959** T. S. ELIOT *Elder Statesman* II. 56 The difference between being an elder statesman And posing successfully as an elder statesman Is practically negligible.

†**2. a.** Of an obligation, right, or title: Of longer standing, prior, that has superior validity. **b.** Of officials, etc.: That ranks before others by virtue of longer service; senior. *Obs.* (*Elder Brethren*: see BROTHER 4 b.)

1642 tr. *Perkins' Prof. Bk.* iv. §285 If the possession bee not devested out of them by an elder title. **1594** WEST *Symbol.* II. *Chancerie* §139 It cannot be intended that.. he would have left the elder bond.. unsued for. **1721–1800** BAILEY, *Elder Battalion*, that Battalion which was first raised, and has the post of honour according to its standing. *Elder Officers*, such officers whose Commissions bear the eldest Date.

†**3.** ***elder man***: = *elder* sb., in senses B. 2, 3. Sometimes written as one word *elderman*. *Obs.*

a **1300** *Cursor M.* 5784 (Cotton MS.) Ga gedir samen þin eldir men. **1387** TREVISA *Higden* (Rolls) I. 41 þe senatoures and elder men of Rome. *c* **1400** *Apol. Loll.* 2 Jerom, & Gregor take a wey þe name of þe bischop, or heldarman. **1530** *Compend. Treat.* (1863) 51 The prophet Moses hadde chosen seuenty eldermen. **1708** MOTTEUX *Rabelais* IV. xxv, So they call'd their eldest Elderman.

4. In Card-playing. ***elder hand***: the first player. Cf. ELDEST 5.

1589 *Pappe w. Hatchet* C iiij, The poore Church should play at vnequal game, for it should loose al by the Elder hand. **1746** HOYLE *Whist* (ed. 6) 22 You are elder Hand. **1873** CAVENDISH [H. Jones] *Piquet* 29 The pack is then cut by the non-dealer, or *elder hand*.

†**5.** Of or pertaining to a more advanced period of life; later. *Obs.*

(In this sense *elder days* are the opposite of the *elder days* of sense 6, just as an *older* portrait has a *younger* face.)

1593 SHAKS. *Rich. II*, II. iii. 43, I tender you my seruice raw and young; Which elder dayes shall ripen. **1611** —— *Cymb.* V. i. 14 To second illes with illes, each elder worse. **1737** WHISTON *Josephus' Ant.* XVI. xi. 8 He also was guilty of.. a crime in his elder age.

6. a. That existed at a previous time; ancient, earlier, former. **b.** Of or pertaining to ancient times or to an earlier period.

c **1340** *Cursor M.* App. i. p. 1636. 23876 We.. in eldern men vr mirur se. *c* **1449** PECOCK *Repr.* II. x. 202 In eeldir daies, whanne processioun was mad. **1587** *Mirr. Mag., Induction* xii. 7 What thinges were done, in elder times of olde. **1668** HALE *Pref. Rolle's Abridgm.* 8 Many of the Elder Year-Books are Filled with Law, now not so much in use. **1801** SOUTHEY *Thalaba* IX. ix, Huge as the giant race of elder times. **1823** LAMB *Elia* Ser. II. i. (1865) 242 Curiosity prevailing over elder devotion. **1852** MISS YONGE *Cameos* I. Introd. 2 The elder England has been so fully written of. **1867** MACFARREN *Harmony* ii. 35 Modern writers.. may produce compositions in the elder style.

7. *Comb.* as **elder-born** adj.; **elder-brotherhood**, the state or dignity of an elder brother; **elder-brotherly**, **-sisterly** *a.*, pertaining or proper to an elder brother or sister.

1870 BRYANT *Iliad* II. xv. 81 *Elder-born am I. **1884** in *Littell's Living Age* No. 2077. 66 Its *elder-brotherhood Writ on the face of its perfected plan. **1823** BENTHAM *Not Paul* 370 *note*, This.. assumed fatherly affection, under the name of *elder-brotherly.. what was it? **1870** MISS BRIDGMAN *R. Lynne* II. viii. 163 'So I told them', said Fanny, with a demure, *elder-sisterly air.

B. *sb.* An elder person, *lit.* and *fig.*

†**1. a.** A parent [cf. mod.G. *eltern* pl.]; an ancestor, forefather; hence, in wider sense, a predecessor, one who lived in former days. Almost exclusively in *pl. Obs.*

971 *Blickl. Hom.* 195 Ure yldran swultan and swiþe oft us from wendan. *a* **1000** *Elene* 462 (Gr.) þa me yldra min ageaf andsware. *a* **1067** *Chart. Eadweard* in *Cod. Dipl.* IV. 167 For mines fader and for allra minra yldrena sawlan. *c* **1175** *Lamb. Hom.* 123 Helle.. we weren in bifolen þurh ure eldra gult. *c* **1205** LAY. 7290 þet me mine ældre [**1275** eldre] dude scome. *c* **1230** *Hali Meid.* 27 Feire children.. gladien muchel þe ealdren. **1297** R. GLOUC. (1724) 11 Here elderne.. were y nome in ostage Fram the bataile of Troie. *c* **1325** *Metr. Hom.* 109 Underlout till thaim was he, Als god child au til elderes be. **1393** LANGL. *P. Pl.* C. IV. 419 þat agag of amalek · and al hus lyge puple Sholde deye delfulliche · for dedes of here eldren. *c* **1440** *York Myst.* XXVII. 14 That with oure elthers euer has bene. **1513** DOUGLAS *Æneis* VII. iv. 44 And sett himselfe amyde his elderis trone. **1535** COVERDALE *John* ix. 18 They called the elders of him that had receaued his sight. **1557** *N. T.* (Genev.) *2 Tim.* i. 3, I thanke God, whome I serue from myne elders with pure conscience.

†**b.** *transf.* (see quot.) *Obs.*

1719 LONDON & WISE *Compl. Gard.* vi. 115 Some [branches] shoot directly out of the main Body.. and may be called Elders, or Mothers.

2. a. (A person's) superior in age, senior. Almost exclusively in *pl.*

c **1000** ORMIN 13215 He þatt iss þin elldre. *c* **1340** *Cursor M.* 12092 To his eldre worship drawe. *c* **1420** *Pallad. on Husb.* I. 125 That yonger men obeye unto thaire eldron. **1552** ABP. HAMILTON *Catech.* (1884) 36 Ic haif had.. understanding aboue my eldaris. **1596** SHAKS. *Tam. Shr.* II. 7 So well I know my duty to my elders. **1737** POPE *Hor. Epist.* II. i. 117 If our elders break all reason's laws. **1801** *Med. Jrnl.* V. 411, I.. leave my elders to judge of them. **1848** MACAULAY *Hist. Eng.* I. 47 The child.. undoubtingly listens to.. his elders. **1864** TENNYSON *Enoch Ard.* 375.

b. A person advanced in life.

1597 SHAKS. *2 Hen. IV*, II. iv. 281 The wither'd Elder hath his Poll claw'd like a Parrot. *a* **1643** G. SANDYS (J.) From their seats the reverend elders rose. **1884** *Illust. Lond. News* 20 Sept. 268/12 The three elders, his companions in this terrible adventure, are now brought home.

3. A member of a 'senate', governing body or class, consisting of men venerable for age, or conventionally supposed to be so. Now chiefly *Hist.*

Orig. as transl. of the *seniores* of the Vulgate, rendering the Heb. *z'qēnīm* (lit. 'old men'). Cf. the equivalent Gr. *γέροντες*.

1382 WYCLIF *Deut.* xix. 12 The aldren [*MS.* C. elderes; **1388** eldere men] of that citee shulen seende. **1535** COVERDALE *Susanna* 50 The elders (that is the principall heades) sayde. —— *1 Macc.* xi. 31 The lettre which we dyd wryte vnto oure elder Lasthenus. **1607** SHAKS. *Cor.* I. i. 230 See our best Elders: **1611** BIBLE *Ruth* iv. 9 Boaz saide vnto the Elders, and vnto all the people. **1715–20** POPE *Iliad* XVIII. 586 The reverend elders nodded o'er the case. **1815** ELPHINSTONE *Acc. Caubul* (1842) I. 221 To which the chief and elders always lend their weight. **1870** GLADSTONE *Prim. Homer* (1878) 116 They bear the general appellation of *gerontes*, elders, as well as kings.

4. a. In ecclesiastical use. A literal rendering of Gr. *πρεσβύτερος*, the title given to a certain order or class of office-bearers in the early Christian Church. The Gr. word was adopted in ecclesiastical Latin as *presbyter*, and its historical representative in Eng. is PRIEST. In certain Protestant churches, chiefly those called Presbyterian, the Eng. word *elder* (with *presbyter* as an occasional synonym) is used as the designation of a class of officers intended to correspond in function to the 'elders' of the apostolic church.

In the Presbyterian churches the term *elders* includes the clergy (for distinction called '*teaching* elders'), but in ordinary language it is restricted to the *lay* or *ruling elders*, who are chosen in each parish or congregation to act with the minister in the management of church affairs.

[**1382** WYCLIF *Acts* xv. 6 And apostlis and eldre men camen to gidere.] **1526** TINDALE *Titus* i. 5 That thou.. shuldest ordeyne elders [WYCLIF, preestis] in every citie. **1579** TOMSON *Calvin's Serm. Tim.* 237/2 Seing yᵉ Church is compared to a flocke.. the word shepeherde signifieth an Elder, not by age, but by office. **1651** HOBBES *Leviath.* III. xlii. 289 Timothy was an Elder. **1719** D'URFEY *Pills* (1872) II. 288 When their Bishops are pulled down, Our Elders shall be sainted. **1760** T. HUTCHINSON *Hist. Col. Mass.* iv. (1765) 426 Most of the churches.. had one or more ruling elder. **1794** BURNS, *Robin shure in hairst*, Robin.. Play'd me sic a trick, And me the eller's dochter. **1846** MᶜCULLOCH *Acc. Brit. Empire* (1854) II. 285 The Kirk Session is.. composed of the minister of the parish and of lay-elders. New elders are chosen by the Session. **1858** LONGF. *M. Standish* 31 The excellent Elder of Plymouth.

b. An order of priests in the Catholic Apostolic Church.

1828 E. IRVING *Sermons* I. p. xxiii, These Sermons on the Incarnation.. you received with all acceptation; and the Elders whom God hath set over you made choice of them to stand first in these volumes. **1876** *Encycl. Brit.* V. 238/1 Four-and-twenty priests, divided into the four ministries of 'elders, prophets, evangelists, and pastors'... The understanding is that each elder, with his co-presbyters and deacons, shall have charge of 500 adult communicants in his district.

c. A minister of any denomination. *U.S. local.*

1792 in *Mass. Hist. Soc. Coll.* II. 30 In the year 1673 settlers.. employed one Elder Jones as their preacher. **1851** *Advent Rev. & Sabbath Herald* 21 July 3/3 Elder Jesse Thompson and his companion [wife], (at whose table we are now writing,) were of this number. **1874** B. F. TAYLOR *World on Wheels* I. xix. 140 Take a young fellow from Hamilton or Rochester.. and call him Elder, as his country brethren and sisters always will. **1921** R. M. JONES *Later Periods Quakerism* I. iv. 120 Even now in the rural districts of New England a minister of any denomination is called 'Elder'. **1925** Z. A. TILGHMAN *Dugout* 7, I can remember some of the elder's sermon that day.

d. *Quakerism.* An officer of the Society of Friends appointed by a monthly meeting and responsible for the organization and proper conduct of meetings held within the jurisdiction of the monthly meeting.

1703 *Yearly Meeting Epistle* (Friends House) I We.. tenderly Recommend unto Faithful Friends, and Elders especially, to Watch over the Flock of Christ. **1789** *Yearly Meeting Minutes* (Friends House) XVIII. 527 This Committee is of the Judgment that the offices of Elder & Overseer are distinct. *a* **1847** in W. & T. Evans *Friends' Library* XI. 425/2 This Epistle [of 31 Mar. 1672] seems to be specially addressed to Ministers, and those filling the responsible station of overseers of the flock; the duties subsequently assigned to *Elders*, probably devolved at this time, on the faithful, perhaps in both the stations above mentioned, but.. especially on overseers. **1917** E. GRUBB *What is Quakerism?* v. 99 The principal offices in the Society of Friends are those of *Overseer* and *Elder*. These officers are appointed, triennially, by the Monthly Meetings... The main work of the Elders is to foster more directly the spiritual life of the congregations, specially in regard to the vocal ministry. **1921**, etc. [see OVERSEER *sb.* 1 e]. **1974** G. HUBBARD *Quaker by Convincement* IV. iii. 209 The whole concept of Elders and Overseers is that the functions of spiritual and material caring which would elsewhere devolve on a professional pastor should be carried by lay members. **1983** MILLIGAN & THOMAS *My Ancestors were Quakers* 14 The word 'elder' appears in Quaker documents from commonwealth days.. here it means a seasoned Friend... The specific appointment by monthly meetings of elders 'to counsel ministers' belongs to the first half of the 18th century.

5. *Comb.*, as ***elder-like*** adv.

1640 *Witt's Recreat.* in Southey *Comm.-Pl. Bk.* Ser. II. 314 Now most Elder-like he can Behave himself. **1795** SOUTHEY *Joan of Arc* III. 542 Fathers of the church.. what! elder-like Would ye this fairer than Susannah eye?

'elder, *v.* [f. prec.] **1.** *trans. to elder it*: to play the elder (brother or sister). *nonce-wd.*

1855 *Chamb. Jrnl.* III. 243 She elders it with such tender protection over the little sister.

2. *intr.* To become older, to begin to show age. So **'eldering** *ppl. a. poet.* and *colloq.*

1876 G. M. HOPKINS *Wr. Deutschland* (1918) st. 18 Never-eldering revel and river of youth. **1885** S. W. MITCHELL *In War Time* xii. 186 Before she went away she was what my nurse used to call 'eldering'. **1949** O. NASH *Versus* 121 In my eldering age.

elder, dial. form of HELDER, rather.

1857 E. WAUGH *Lanc. Sk.* 26 in *Lanc. Gloss.* (E.D.S.) One could elther manage we't at th' for-end o' their days. **1874** *Manch. Critic* 21 Feb. *ibid.*, I'd elder see 'em wortchin for th' next to nought nor see 'em doin nought.

'elder-berry. [f. ELDER *sb.*¹ + BERRY.] The fruit of the elder. Also *attrib.* in *elderberry-wine*.

Hence **elderberriness** (*nonce-wd.*), used as a mock title, after *highness*, etc.

1589 *Pappe w. Hatchet* (1844) 27 His Elderberines.. is.. like an elderberrie. **1625** *Althorp MS.* in Simpkinson *Washingtons* Introd. 62 Surrop of elderberries. **1766** PENNANT *Zool.* (1777) IV. 12 (Jod.) The ova become.. almost as large as ripe elder berries. **1840–1** S. WARREN *Ten Thous. a Year* 84/1 Cowslip, currant, ginger, or elderberry wine.

elderhood ('ɛldəhʊd). [f. ELDER *sb.*³ + -HOOD.] **a.** The position or estate of an elder, seniority. **b.** The estate of the elders or rulers; the body of elders.

1597 DANIEL *Civ. Wares* VII. lxxvi, No elderhood, Rufus and Henrie stayes The imperial Crowne.. t'undertake. **1860** ELLICOTT *Life our Lord* vii. 346 The Nazarene was.. a blasphemer in the face of the elderhood of Israel.

'elderling. *rare.* [f. ELDER *sb.*³ + -LING.]

†**1.** Contemptuously for ELDER *sb.*³ 4. *Obs.*

1606 BP. W. BARLOW *Serm.* (1607) A 3 b, Euery.. Ceremonie which, in the Cockpit of Elderlings, is concluded to be Poperie, is not so.

2. An elderly person.

1863 MARK LEMON *Wait for End* xix. (1866) 237 The two elderlings began to lament their situation.

elderly ('ɛldəlɪ), *a.* [f. ELDER *a.* + -LY¹.]

1. Of persons or of things quasi-personified: Somewhat old, verging towards old age. Also in comb., ***elderly-looking*** adj.

1611 COTGR., *Vieillot*, elderlie, somewhat old. **1660** R. COKE *Power & Subj.* 107 Let.. twelve elderly men of free condition, together with the Sheriff be sworne. **1712** BUDGELL *Spect.* No. 301 ¶1 Elderly Fops, and superannuated Coquets. **1773** PRIESTLEY *Inst. Relig.* (1872) II. 353 The more elderly.. members presided. **1848** MACAULAY *Hist. Eng.* I. 341 The elderly inhabitants [of Leeds] could still remember the time when the first brick house.. was built. **1867** FREEMAN *Norm. Conq.* (1876) I. vi. 529 An elderly man at the time of his marriage. **1871** TYNDALL *Fragm. Sc.* I. vi. 198 The 'Urgent' is an elderly ship. **1876** GEO. ELIOT *Dan. Der.* III. xxxv. 30 You had need hire men to.. chip it all over artistically, to give it an elderly-looking surface.

2. Of or pertaining to one in later life.

1674 N. FAIRFAX *Bulk & Selv.* 152 In our own elderly doings..we are set on work after higher scantlings of wisdom. **1863** GEO. ELIOT *Romola* (1880) I. Introd. 8 The Frate carried his doctrine rather too far for elderly ears. **1866** —— *F. Holt* (1868) 19 No elderly face can be handsome, looked at in that way.

3. quasi-*sb.*

1865 *N. & Q.* Ser. III. VIII. 82 Fifty years ago a common exclamation among the elderlies was 'my eye Kitty Fisher'.

Hence **'elderliness.** [see -NESS.]

1876 MISS YONGE *Womankind* xxxv. 322 The trials of elderliness have either been unfelt or safely weathered. **1883** W. M. BAKER *Roll of Waves* in *Chicago Advance* 27 Sept., A certain reserve and elderliness of manner.

elderman, see ELDER *a.* 3.

eldern ('ɛldən), *a.* Also 3 (*Orm.*) elldern, eldrin, 7–8 *Sc.* eldren, 8 elderin. [f. ELDER *a.* + -EN. In quot. 1839 prob. a new formation.]

†1. Elderly. *Obs.* exc. *Sc.*

c **1200** ORMIN 1213 ȝiff þu..hafesst ȝet..tohh þu be ȝung, Elldernemanness late. *Ibid.* 1235. **1611** HUDSON *Judith* 49 (Jam.) The tree bends his eldren braunch That way where first the stroke hath made him launch. **1739** A. NICOL *Poems* 73 (Jam.) The eldern men sat down their lane, To wet their throats within. **1768** ROSS *Helenore* 68 (Jam.) Colin and Lindy..The ane an elderin man, the niest a lad. **1790** A. WILSON *To E. Picken*, Aneath some spreading eldren thorn. **1818** SCOTT *Rob Roy* xxxiv, His Excellency is a thought eldern.

2. Old, belonging to earlier times. *arch.*

a **1300** *Cursor M.* (Gött. MS.) 18016 Mine eldrin folk of iuen lede Haue i [Satan] done rise againes him. *a* **1400** [implied in ELDERNLY *adv.*]. **1839** DARLEY *Introd. Beaum. & Fletch. Wks.* I. 26 Our eldern dramatist was a decided poet, which our modern was not.

Hence †**'eldernly,** *adv.* [see -LY²], of old time.

a **1400** in *Eng. Gilds.* (1870) 352 þat þe chalouns þat eldernlyche hadde y-set, so halde here a-syse.

eldern ('ɛldən), *a.*² [f. ELDER *sb.*¹ + -EN.]

For apparent examples in 17th c. (probably to be referred to the attrib. use of *eldern* = ELDER *sb.*¹) see ELDER *sb.*¹ 3.

Made of elder.

1842 AKERMAN *Wiltsh. Gloss.* (E.D.S.). **1847** in HALLIW. **1875** PARISH *Dict. Sussex Dial.* s.v., An eldern stake and blackthorn ether Will make a hedge to last for ever.

eldership ('ɛldəʃɪp). [f. ELDER *a.* and *sb.*³ + -SHIP.]

1. The position of being elder or senior; seniority, precedence of birth, primogeniture.

1549 R. PARSONS *Confer. Success.* I. vi. 128 Primogenitura or eldership of birth..was greatly respected by God. **1667** DRYDEN *Ind. Emperor* I. ii, My claim to her by Eldership I prove. **1754** RICHARDSON *Grandison* I. v. 19 Her sister addressed her always by the word Child, with an air of eldership. **1838** ARNOLD *Hist. Rome* I. 274 [By Roman law] all children..inherited their father's estate in equal portions, without distinction of sex or eldership.

2. *nonce-use.* As a mock title of honour (after *lordship*): The personality of an elderly person.

1748 RICHARDSON *Clarissa* (1811) IV. 90 So irresistible to their elderships to be flattered.

3. The office or position of elder in a church.

1577 HARRISON *England* II. v. (1877) I. 109 The office of eldership is equallie distributed betweene the bishop and the minister. **1655** FULLER *Ch. Hist.* IX. vi. §52 He was deposed from his Eldership.

4. The collective body of (ecclesiastical) elders; a body or court of elders, a presbytery.

1557 *N. T.* (Genev.) *1 Tim.* iv. 14 That gyft..which was geuen thee by prophecie with the laying on of the handes, by the Eldership. **1634–46** ROW *Hist. Kirk* (1824) 66 They that tyrannize not over, but be subject to their particulare elderships. **1721** WODROW *Corr.* (1843) II. 568 Do you not lay in one scale the minister against the whole eldership in the other? **1828** E. IRVING *Last Days* 151 As office-bearers in the church we are an unholy and an unworthy eldership. **1885** EDGAR *Old Ch. Life Scotl.* 189 All the courts of the Church might be called either Presbyteries or Elderships.

eldest ('ɛldɪst), *a. superl.* Forms: 1 eldest(a, ældest(a, (WS. ieldest(a, yldest(a), yltst, 2 ylste, 2–3 ealdeste, eldeste, 3 eldast, -ost, -ust, (heldest, 5 eeldist), 3– eldest, *north.* eildest. [OE. *ęldest(a*, superl. of OE. *ald* (WS. *eald*) OLD; cf. OFris. *eldest(a*, OHG. *altist(o* (mod.G. *ältest(e*), Goth. *alþist(a*:—OTeut. **aldisto-* (*-on-*). See ELDER *a.*]

The original form of the superlative of OLD; now superseded by OLDEST exc. in special uses.

†1. Of persons or things: Most aged, farthest advanced in age. Also *absol.* (quasi-*sb.*). *Obs.* in general sense: replaced by OLDEST.

It is, however, still not unusual to speak of 'the (two or three) eldest members of a family,' 'the eldest of the company,' etc.; but this is due either to some slight notion of precedence or superior rank conferred by seniority, or to the wish to avoid the implication that the persons are, absolutely, *old*.

c **1000** *Ags. Gosp.* Matt. xxiii. 11 Seðe eower yltst [*c* **1160** *Hatton G.* yldest] sy beo se eower þen. *c* **1205** LAY. 2721 Gloigin hehte þa alre elduste [**1250** heldeste]. *a* **1300** *Cursor M.* 5847 Wid the eldest folk of israel. **1523** LD. BERNERS *Froiss.* I. liii. [lii.] 190 The eldest man that lyuyng neuer saw nor herde of the lyke. **1559** MORWYNG *Evonym.* 323 A sexta or xx unces of the eldest wine. **1607–12** BACON *Parents & Childr., Ess.* (Arb.) 274/1 A man shall see where there is a howsefull of Children, one or two of the eldest respected. **1611** BIBLE *John* viii. 9 They..went out..beginning at the eldest, euen vnto the last [so **1881** in *R.V.*].

2. The first-born, or the oldest surviving (member of a family, son, daughter, etc.). Also quasi-*sb.*

c **1000** ÆLFRIC *Gen.* xliv. 12 He sohte fram þam yldestan oþ þone ȝingestan. *c* **1175** *Cott. Hom.* 227 Se asprang of Noes ylste sune. *c* **1205** LAY. 2930 þa ældeste dohter haihte Gornoille [**1275** eldeste]. *c* **1230** *Hali Meid.* 41 Heo of alle unþeawes is his ealdeste dohter. **1297** R. GLOUC. (1724) 381 Normandye hys erytage he ȝef hys eldoste sone Roberd þe Courtese. *a* **1300** *Cursor M.* 4119 An was eildest o þe elleuen ..ruben. **1398** TREVISA *Barth. De P.R.* VI. xiv. 199 Lawe woll that the eldest sone haue the more parte of therytage. **1536** WRIOTHESLEY *Chron.* (1875) I. 50 The Erle of Ruttlandes eldyste daughter. **1595** SHAKS. *John* I. 159 Good old sir Roberts wiues eldest sonne. **1715** DE FOE *Fam. Instruct.* I. iv. (1841) I. 86 Why not..with you as well as with your eldest sister. **1788** J. POWELL *Devises* (1827) II. 365 A testator..desired that the first annuity..might devolve upon the eldest child. **1818** CRUISE *Digest* VI. 320 The eldest son had but an estate for life. **1887** R. GARNETT *Carlyle* 12 Carlyle was the eldest of nine children.

3. Earliest, first produced; first, most ancient. *arch.* Also quasi-*sb.*

c **897** K. ÆLFRED *Gregory's Past.* xliii. 313 Ðæt we ȝemyndȝiað ðære scylde þe ure ieldesta mæȝ us on forworhte. **1340** *Ayenb.* 104 He [God] is þe eldeste and þe meste yknawe. *c* **1449** PECOCK *Repr.* III. xix. 406 In the eeldist tyme. **1593** HOOKER *Eccl. Pol.* IV. vii, Neither is the example of the eldest Churches a whit more auailable. **1602** SHAKS. *Ham.* III. iii. 37 My offence..hath the primall eldest curse vpon't. **1649** SELDEN *Laws Eng.* I. xxxix. (1739) 59 Of Imprisonment there was little use in the eldest times. **1681** DRYDEN *Abs. & Achit.* 458 And Self-defence is Nature's Eldest Law. **1773** MONBODDO *Language* (1774) I. I. vii. 87 Matter must be the eldest of things. **1801** SOUTHEY *Thalaba* XI. xii, Thou the eldest, thou the wisest, Guide me. **1819** SHELLEY *Cenci* V. iv. 101 Plead with the swift frost That it should spare the eldest flower of spring.

†4. *Mil.* Senior in rank or standing. *Obs.*

1721 *Lond. Gaz.* No. 5930/1 The eldest Battallion of Foot-Guards.

5. In Card-playing. ***eldest hand***, the first player; the right of playing first.

1599 MINSHEU *Dialogues Sp. & Eng.* (1623) 26/2, I did lift an ace..I a fower..I a sixe, whereby I am the eldest hand. **1680** COTTON *Compl. Gamester* in Singer *Hist. Cards* (1816) 342 If there be three kings, &c. turned up, the eldest hand wins it. **1719** D'URFEY *Pills* I. 99 The 'tothers eldest Hand Gave Hopes to make a Jest on 't. **1876** A. CAMPBELL-WALKER *Correct Card* (1880) Gloss. 11 *Eldest hand*, the player on the dealer's left hand.

†6. Law. ***eldest part***: (see quot.) *Obs.*

1641 *Termes de la Ley* 137 The eldest part. Enitia pars is that part that upon partition amongst coparceners falls unto the eldest sister or auncientest coparcener.

7. *Comb.*, as ***eldest-born***, ***-hearted***.

1605 SHAKS. *Lear* I. i. 55 Gonerill Our eldest borne speak first. **1840** CARLYLE *Heroes* i. 7 Man..the eldest born of a certain genealogy. **1853** KINGSLEY *Hypatia* i. 7 They had elected Pambo for their abbot..eldest-hearted of them.

†**'eldfather.** *Obs.* Forms: 1 ealdfæder, 3 aldevader, 4 aldfader, eldefader, edl(e-, eeldefadir, 5 eldfader, -fadyre, elfadyr, 6 elfader, eldefather. [OE. (WS.) *ealdfæder*, f. *eald*, ELD *a.*, OLD, + FATHER; cf. OS., OFris. *aldfader*, OHG. *altfater*, mod.G. *altvater* patriarch, ancestor. The occurrence in northern dialects of the forms with *eld-* (as if from WS. *eald*) has not been accounted for. Cf. ELDMOTHER.

Sense 2 does not occur in the other Teut. langs.; the form *elfadyr* has given rise to a suggestion that it is a distinct word, f. OE. *ęl-* other; but this is against the evidence of the older forms.]

1. A grandfather; a forefather in general.

Beowulf 373 (Gr.) Wæs his ealdfæder Ecgþeo haten. *c* **1000** ÆLFRIC *Gen.* xv. 15 þu soþlice forþfærst..to þinum ealdfæderum. *c* **1205** LAY. 31009 He wes Mærwales fader; Mildburȝe aldeuader. *c* **1325** *Metr. Hom.* 122 Hir aldfader cal I Adam. *c* **1374** CHAUCER *Boeth.* II. iv. 40 þer shineþ þe lyknesse of þe witte of hir fadir and of hir eldefadir. **1375** BARBOUR *Bruce* XIII. 694 Eftir his gude eld-fadir [he] was Callit robert. *c* **1425** WYNTOUN *Cron.* VII. viii. 230 Oure Kyng of Scotland, Dawy..Wes eld-fadyre til oure kyng Willame. **1460** CAPGRAVE *Chron.* 24 Sarugh, whech was eld-fader to Abraham.

2. A father-in-law.

c **1200** *Trin. Coll. Hom.* 165 Nis þe gist siker of þe husebonde. ne þe aldefader of his oðem. *a* **1300** *Cursor M.* 5730 Moyses..was sett to kepe All his eildfader scepe. *c* **1440** *Promp. Parv.* 137 Elfadyr, *socer*. **1510** *Will of Bakeber* (Somerset Ho.) To be bestowed at the mind of myn elfader. **1634** *Will* in *Acts Durham High Commiss. Crt.* (1857) 17 *note*, In the parish Church of St. Nicholas as neare my eld-father, Charles Slingsbye..as possible may be.

'eldin. *dial.* Also elgins, eldin-docken. [Of unknown etymology: identified with next by Jamieson, who alleges that the plant was used for fuel.] The Butter-bur (*Petasites vulgaris*); by Jamieson erroneously said to be *Rumex aquaticus*.

1562 TURNER *Herbal* II. 83 a, Petasites..is called in Northumbreland an Eldin, in Cambridgeshire a Butterbur. **1808** JAMIESON *Eldin-docken*, Roxb.—*Elgins*, Loth.

elding¹. ('ɛldɪŋ). *Obs.* exc. *dial.* Also eilding, eyldynge, eldin, elden(e, eldinge. [a. ON. *elding*, f. *eldr* fire. Cf. Da. *ilding*.] Fuel.

a **1300** *Cursor M.* 3164 Ysaac þe elding broght. *c* **1440** *Promp. Parv.* 136 Eyldynge, or fowayle, *focale*. **1580** *Kirton-in-Lindsey Ch. Acc.* in *Proc. Soc. Antiq.* Ser. II. II. 387 Item for Eldene xiid. **1648** *Ibid.* in Peacock *N.-W. Linc. Gloss.* (E.D.S.) To blind Sutton wife for elding. **1705** *Inv.* ibid., Eldin..and stocks and blocks 10s. **1790** A. WILSON *Elegy on Unfort. Tailor*, He'd sit, And ilka wee the eldin hit, And gab fu' trimly. **1816** SCOTT *Antiq.* xi, 'Wadna ye be glad to buy a dram wi't, to be eilding and claise?' **1857** E. WAUGH *Lanc. Life* 140 Up blazed the inflammable eilding with a crackling sound.

'elding.² *Sc. Obs. rare.* [f. ELD *v.* + -ING².] Old age.

a **1600** *Maitland Poems* 193 (Jam.) Elding is end of erthlie glie.

†**'eldmother.** *Obs.* exc. *dial.* Forms: 1 (WS.) ealdmódor, 3–6 eldmoder, 5–9 elmother, 6– eldmother. [OE. (WS.) *ealdmódor*, f. *eald*, ELD *a.*, OLD + MOTHER. Cf. OFris. *aldmóder*, *aldemóder*; and see ELDFATHER.]

1. A grandmother.

c **1000** ÆLFRIC *Gloss.* in Wr.-Wülcker 173 *Auia*, ealde modor. *a* **1300** *Cursor M.* 1189 Abel..had his eldmoder maiden-hede. *c* **1425** *Voc.* in Wr.-Wülcker 672 *Hec auia*, eldmoder.

2. a. A mother-in-law. b. A stepmother.

c **1440** *Promp. Parv.* 137 Eld modyr [*K* elmoder], *socrus*. **1513** DOUGLAS *Æneis* II. ix. (viii.) 112 Eldmoder to ane hundreth thair saw I Hecuba. **1519** *Will of R. Payne* (Somerset Ho.) To Margaret Shelle myne Elmother, a melche neete. **1571** *Wills & Inv. N.C.* (1835) I. 352, I gyue vnto my eldmother his wyffe my wyffes froke. **1674** RAY *N.C. Words* 16 An Elmother. Cumb. A Step Mother. **1864** *Whitby Gloss.*, *Elmother*, step-mother.

†**'eldness.** *Obs.* [repr. OE. (WS.) *ealdnyss*, f. *eald*, ELD, OLD *a.* + -NESS: see OLDNESS.]

a. Oldness, old age. b. A former state of things, antiquity.

c **1000** ÆLFRIC *Hom.* I. 194 (Bosw.) We awur-þon ða deri-ȝendlican ealdnysse. **1387** TREVISA *Higden* (Rolls) I. 7 Storie is..messager of eldnesse. **1388** WYCLIF *Isa.* xxiii. 18 Thei be ..clothid to eldnesse. —— *Ezek.* xvi. 55 Thi sister Sodom and her doȝtris shulen turne aȝen to her eldnesse.

†**'eldnyng.** *Obs. rare.* [possibly repr. OE. *ęlnung*, f. *ęlnian* to envy, be jealous: see EYNDILL.] ? Jealousy, suspicion.

1500–20 DUNBAR *Twa Maryit Wem. & Wedo* 119 That carll mangit, That full of eldnyng is, et anger, et all euill thewis. *Ibid.* 126, I dar nought keik to the knaip that the cop fillis For eldnyng of that ald schrew that euer on euill thynkis.

Eldonian (ɛl'dəʊnɪən), *a.* [f. the name of John Scott, Earl of *Eldon* (1751–1838) + -IAN.] Belonging to or characteristic of Lord Eldon, regarded as typical of 'diehard' toryism. Also **Eldonine** ('ɛldənaɪn) *a.*

1855 *National Rev.* Oct. 257 Those years were the commencement of what is called the Eldonine period. **1876** W. CORY *Lett. & Jrnls.* (1897) 419 A fusion of Benthamic legislation with Eldonine evolution. **1898** *Daily News* 8 July 4/7 His Toryism is Eldonian and antediluvian. **1900** *Ibid.* 31 Dec. 4/7 The century, considered from a political point of view, may be divided into the Eldonian, the Peelite, the Palmerstonian, and the Gladstonian eras. **1926** *London Merc.* May 104 An Eldonian Tory still describes a type peculiar to the English temperament, and never, perhaps for that reason, personally unpopular.

‖**El Dorado** (ˌɛldɒr'ɑːdəʊ). [Sp. *el* the, *dorado* gilded, pa. pple. of *dorar* to gild.] The name of a fictitious country (according to others a city) abounding in gold, believed by the Spaniards and by Sir W. Raleigh to exist upon the Amazon within the jurisdiction of the governor of Guiana.

1596 RALEIGH (*title*) Discoverie of Guiana, with a relation of the Great and Golden Citie of Manoa (which the Spaniards call El Dorado). **1622–62** HEYLIN *Cosmogr.* IV. (1682) 142 Letting pass these dreams of an El Dorado, let us descend. etc. **1667** MILTON *P.L.* XI. 411 Unspoil'd Guiana, whose great Citie Geryon's Sons Call El Dorado.

b. *fig.*

1827 F. COOPER *Prairie* I. i. 15 A band of emigrants seeking for the Eldorado of their desires. *c* **1860** WRAXALL tr. *R. Houdin* i. 2 How often, in my infantile dreams, did a benevolent fairy open before me the door of a mysterious El Dorado.

eldress ('ɛldrɪs). [f. ELDER *sb.*³ + -ESS.] A female elder, a woman ordained to rule or teach in a church.

1640 BP. HALL *Episc.* III. iv. 237, I suppose no man will think S. Paul meant to ordain Eldresses in the Church. **1753** WHITEFIELD *Let. to Zinzendorf* Wks. 1771 IV. 255 Over the head of the general Eldress, was placed her own picture. **1880** HOWELLS *Undisc. Country* xii. 172 The office sisters consulted with the eldress.

†**'eldring.**¹ *Obs.* [f. ELDER *a.* + -ING³.] In *pl.*, Elders, parents, ancestors.

c **1300** *K. Alis.* 4948 Her eldrynges beth elde. *c* **1315** SHOREHAM 97 ȝyf thou rewardest thyne eldrynges nauȝt A-lyve and eke a-dethe. **1340** *Ayenb.* 118 þe..yefþes þet he broȝte mid him uor to yeue..to his eldringes.

†**'eldring.**² *Obs. rare.* Also 4 elringe, 7 elldring, 8 eldriene. [app. = OHG. *erlinc*, 'escaurus', prob. cognate and synonymous with mod.Ger. *elritze* minnow, which Kluge connects with *eller* (OHG. *elira*, *erila*), ALDER, as if 'fish that lives under the shade of alders'.]

A fish; perh. properly the minnow (*Leuciscus phoxinus*), though this does not suit quot. 1618.

c 1325 *Metr. Hom.* 136 Wit pouer men fares the king Riht als the quale fars wit the elringe. 1618 in *Naworth Househ. Bks.* 83, 3 elldrings vd. 1753 CHAMBERS *Cycl. Supp.*, *Eldriene* . . a name by which some call the . . minnow.

eldritch ('ɛldrɪtʃ, 'ɛlrɪtʃ), *a. Sc.* Forms: 6 elrich(e, elritch(e, -risch(e, -rish, elraige, -rage, alriche, 8–9 eldrich, (9 eltrich), 8– eldritch. [Of obscure origin; connexion with ELF, conjectured by Jamieson, would be suitable for the sense, and is supported by the form *elphrish*, app. the same word.]

Weird, ghostly, unnatural, frightful, hideous. 1508 DUNBAR *Gold. Targe* 125 Thare was Pluto the elrich incubus. 1513 DOUGLAS *Æneis* VII. 108 Vgsum to heir was hir wyld elriche screik. 1535 STEWART *Cron. Scot.* II. 636 Thair cleithing quhilk wes of elritche hew. 1536 BELLENDEN *Cron. Scot.* I. 217 Mony haly and relligious men . . fled in desertis and elraige placis. 1585 JAS. I. *Ess. Poesie* (Arb.) 68 The king of Fary . . With many elrage Incubus rydant. 1598 J. MELVILL *Diary* 25 Feb. 320 The amazfull, ugly alriche darkness. 1789 BURNS *On Capt. Grose*, Ye'll find him snug in Some eldritch part. 1834 PRINGLE *Afr. Sk.* ii. 144 Loud bursts of wild and eldrich laughter. 1850 HAWTHORNE *Scarlet Let.* vii. (1879) 122 Pearl . . gave an eldritch scream. 1860 LD. LYTTON *Lucile* I. iii. §1. 87 Truth is appalling and eltrich, as seen By this world's artificial lamplights. 1866 HOWELLS *Venet. Life* iii. 40 Joy that had something eldritch and unearthly in it.

†**'eldship.** *Obs. rare*⁻¹. [f. ELD *a.* + -SHIP.] Old age.

1647 H. MORE *Song of Soul* I. ii. xxxi, Like winter-morn bedight with snow . . so did his goodly Eldship shine.

†**ele**, *sb. Obs.* Forms: 1 œle, 1–4 ele, 3 eli, ely, eoli. [OE. *œle* = OHG. *oli* (mod.G. *öl*) :—WGer. *oli*, ad. late L. *oli-um* (L. *oleum*). Afterwards replaced by the Fr. form of the same word, now represented by OIL, q.v. for the forms *oli, eoile*.] = OIL.

c 950 *Lindisf. Gosp.* Matt. xxv. 4 Hogofæste uutetlice onfengon œle in fetelsum hiora mið leht-fatum. *c* 1000 *Sax. Leechd.* II. 230 Wiþ wambe coþe, seoð rudan on ele. *c* 1200 ORMIN 13252 Forr þatt te33 . . Onnfon þurrh hall3hedd ele att Crist Hiss Hall3he Gastess frofre. *a* 1225 *Ancr. R.* 428 Me schal helden eoli and win beoðe ine wunden.

†**ele**, *v.*¹ *Obs.* [f. prec. sb.] *trans.* To anoint.

c 1205 LAY. 31941 He wes icruned and ieled [*c* 1275 iheled]. *c* 1315 SHOREHAM 41 He schel elye hym wyth ele. *Ibid.* 42 This children eleth me nau3t.

Hence **'eling** *vbl. sb.* **last eling**: extreme unction.

c 1315 SHOREHAM 42 For the sygne of thys sacrement the elyngys boute. *c* 1450 MYRC 533 And the laste elynge wyth-owte fayle.

†**ele**, *v.*² *Obs.* [f. OF. *ele, eele* (mod.F. *aile*) wing.] To carve (certain birds).

c 1500 *For serve Lord* in *Babees Bk.* (1868) 375 To tyre or to ele a partorich or a quayle y-whyngged: rere uppe whynge and legge, as of an henne; cowche them aboute the carcas; no sawse save salte, or mustard and sugar.

ele, obs. form of AISLE, AWL, EEL *sb.*

Eleatic (ɛliː'ætɪk), *a.* and *sb.* [f. L. *Eleātic-us*, from *Elea*, name of an ancient Greek city in S.W. Italy: cf. -ATIC.]

A. *adj.* Pertaining to Elea or its inhabitants; *spec.* used of the philosophy of Xenophanes, Parmenides, and Zeno, who lived or were born there. **B.** *sb.* An Eleatic philosopher.

1695 LD. PRESTON *Boeth.* I. 5 Brought up in Eleatique & Academique Studies. 1837 WHEWELL *Hist. Induct. Sc.* (1857) I. 342 Parmenides must be regarded as an Eleatic [dialogue]. 1849 GROTE *Greece* (1862) VI. lxvii. 44 The dialectical movement emanated . . from the Eleatic school. 1870 BOWEN *Logic* ix. 312 The famous argument, called the Achilles, proposed by Zeno the Eleatic.

Hence **Ele'aticism**, the doctrine or system of the Eleatics.

1867 J. H. STIRLING tr. *Schwegler's Hist. Philos.* (ed. 8) 15 Eleaticism is consequently monism, so far as it endeavours to reduce the manifold of existence to a single ultimate principle.

elebore, -bory, -bre, -bur, obs. forms of HELLEBORE.

elecampane (ˌɛlɪkæm'peɪn). Forms: 6 ely-, (alecampane, alacompane, heli-, hilicampana), 6–7 elicampane, 7 elecampana, elecompane, elecampany, elicumpany, helicampane, elcampane, 8 elecampain, (9 elicampene, alycompaine, alicompayne, allicampane), 6– elecampane. Also 7 enulacampane. [corruptly ad. med.L. *enula compāna*. The sb. *enula* is a late form of the classical *inula*. The pseudo-Apuleius (4th c.) and later writers identify the plant with the *helenium* described by Pliny; hence Linnæus adopted *helenium* as the specific name. In OE. *inula* was (corruptly) adopted as *eolone* (:—earlier **iluna*). The adj. *campana* may mean 'Campanian', or it may have the late sense 'of the fields'; the latter interpretation was current in 14th c., as Glanvil distinguishes two species, *hortulana* and *campana*.]

1. A perennial composite plant, Horse-heal (*Inula Helenium*), with very large yellow radiate flowers and bitter aromatic leaves and root; formerly used as a tonic and stimulant.

[1398 TREVISA *Barth. De P.R.* XVII. lviii. (1495) 636 Enula is an herbe and is oft callyd Enula campana. ? 1540 *Treas. of Poore Men* 62 Elena campana.] 1533 ELYOT *Cast. Helth* (1541) 91 Drinke therof . . with the water of wilde carettes, or elycampane. 1562 BULLEYN *Bk. Simples* 15 (Britten & Holl.), *Enula campana*, which we common plain people call Alacompane. 1562 TURNER *Herbal* II. 21 Innula is called . . in Englishe Elecampane or Alecampane. 1599 *Life Sir T. More* in Wordsworth *Eccl. Biog.* (1853) II. 47 The fume of hilicampana is very pleasing. 1601 HOLLAND *Pliny* II. 91 Elecampane . . sprang first (as men say) from the teares of Ladie Helena. 1616 SURFL. & MARKH. *Countr. Farm* 198 The Wine wherein the root of Elicampane hath steept . . is singular good against the colicke. 1657 RUMSEY *Org. Salutis* v. (1659) 29 Afterwards eat of the said Cordial made of Enulacampane, etc. 1718 QUINCY *Compl. Disp.* 141 Elecampain grows in many Places of England. 1794 W. F. MARTYN *Rousseau's Bot.* xxvi. 393 The true Elecampane is distinguished by its large . . wrinkled leaves, downy underneath. 1876 HARLEY *Mat. Med.* 532 Elecampane has been prescribed since the time of Hippocrates.

2. A species of sweetmeat flavoured with a preparation from the root of this plant.

1806–7 J. BERESFORD *Miseries Hum. Life* (1826) Post. Groans xxix, Some long-forgotten bonbon of your boyhood (treacle, elecampane, stick liquorice). 1855 THACKERAY *Newcomes* I. 244, I don't know how he spent it except in hard-bake and alycompaine. 1875 F. I. SCUDAMORE *Day Dreams* 128, I have admired Napoleon in marble, I have eaten him in elecampane.

b. *attrib.*

1610 MARKHAM *Masterp.* II. lii. 298 Powders of brimstone and elecampany roots. 1752 CHAMBERS *Cycl.* II. s.v. *Wine*, Elecampane Wine, *vinum enulatum*, is an infusion of the root of that plant, with sugar and currans, in white port. 1838 T. THOMSON *Chem. Org. Bodies* 498 Its [Helenin] taste and smell are similar to those of elecampane root.

eleccion, -ioun, -youn, obs. ff. ELECTION.

†**e'lect**, *sb.*¹ *Obs.* [? f. the vb.; or ? ad. L. *ēlect-us*, f. *ēligĕre*; see next.] = ELECTION.

1398 TREVISA *Barth De P.R.* II. xix. (1495) 44 By electes and choys [L. *electione*] of his owne free aduysement he . . wolde be rebell agaynst god. *c* 1425 WYNTOUN *Cron.* IX. xxvii. 141 Schire Henry . . Wald þis Elect had beene undone Sua þat his son mycht be Promovit to þat Dignite.

elect (ɪ'lɛkt), *a.* and *sb.*² Also 4–5 elekte, eleckte, 5–6 electe. [ad. L. *ēlect-us*, pa. pple. of *ēligĕre* to pick out, choose.]

A. *adj.*

1. Picked out, chosen; also, chosen for excellence or by preference; select, choice. Also *absol.* a person or persons chosen.

? *a* 1400 *Chester Pl.* I. (1843) 212 Man . . which is his owne eleckte. 1477 NORTON *Ord. Alch.* in Ashm. (1652) Introd. 3 A Booke of secrets given by God; To men Elect, a Beaten-Trod. 1480 CAXTON *Chron. Eng.* I. (1520) 8/1 Saul . . was a good man and elect of God. 1558 W. WARDE tr. *Alessio's Secrets* I. II. 48 b Take Iris electe, what quantitie you will. 1538 STARKEY *England* II. i. §19 To be prestys . . such only schold be admyttyd as haue electe wyttys. 1609 HOLLAND *Livy* XXIV. xl. 537 Hee . . shipped a thousand elect and choise souldiours . . in gallies. 1613 SHAKS. *Hen. VIII*, II. iv. 60 You haue heere Lady . . the elect o' th' Land, who are assembled To pleade your Cause. 1667 MILTON *P.L.* XII. 214 The Race elect . . advance Through the wilde Desert. 1863 FR. KEMBLE *Resid. Georgia* 10 This country . . the land elect of liberty. 1870 LOWELL *Among my Bks.* Ser. II. (1873) 310 He saw . . that small procession of the elder poets to which only elect centuries can add another laurelled head. 1876 G. BRADFORD in *N. Amer. Rev.* CXXIII. 4 The executive, the elect of the whole state, has . . no . . medium of communication with his constituents.

2. a. *spec.* in *Theol.* Chosen by God, *esp.* for salvation or eternal life. Opposed to *reprobate*. Often *absol.* with plural sense, *the elect*.

1526 *Pilgr. Perf.* (W. de W. 1531) 4 b, His owne electe and chosen chyldren. 1535 JOYE *Apol. Tindale* 41 The electe shal be there with their bodyes. 1582 *N.T.* (Rhem.) Rom. viii. 33 Who shal accuse against the elect of God? 1593 HOOKER *Eccl. Pol.* I. iv, The elect Angels are without possibilitie of falling. 1630 PRYNNE *Anti-Armin.* 122 It makes, the Elect and Reprobate, all alike. 1667 MILTON *P.L.* III. 136 In the blessed Spirits elect Sense of new joy ineffable diffus'd. 1719 D'URFEY *Pills* (1872) V. 105, I mean the Sect of those Elect, That loath to live by Merit. *a* 1763 BYROM *Predestination, etc.* (R.), While others . . Are mercy's vessels, precious and elect. 1837 *Penny Cycl.* IX. 333/2 All the elect are effectually called at some point of time in life.

b. *allusively*. (Cf. *Matt.* xxiv. 24.)

1885 J. J. MANLEY *Brit. Almanac Comp.* 29 The street was a miracle in lath and plaster, which might almost deceive the very elect.

3. Chosen to an office or dignity. Now usually, Chosen, elected, but not installed in office (in this sense almost always following the sb.). Similarly, in mod. use, **bride, bridegroom elect**, said of betrothed persons. See also BRIDE *sb.*¹ 1.

1643 PRYNNE *Open. Gt. Seal* 21 And that the Warden of Yarmouth so elect and sworne, shall, etc. 1726 AYLIFFE *Parerg.* 128 The Bishop elect takes the Oaths of Supremacy. 1742 MIDDLETON *Cicero* I. v. 393 Sextius was one of the Tribunes elect. 1751 CHAMBERS *Cycl.* I. s.v., A lord mayor is elect, before his predecessor's mayoralty is expired. 1761 HUME *Hist. Eng.* I. xi. 221 The elect bishop of Cambray was taken prisoner. 1806 C. WILMOT *Let.* 21 Oct. in *Russ. Jrnls.* (1934) II. 239 The Bride elect dissolved in tears. 1829 MARRYAT *F. Mildmay* xvi, My captain elect.

B. *sb.* †**1.** One 'chosen' by God, *esp.* one chosen for eternal salvation; one of 'the elect' (cf. A. 2).

1532 MORE *Confut. Tindale* Wks. 525/2 Yet are there also in thys churche of electes, manye that neuer came to the fayth. 1546 BALE *Eng. Votaries* II. (1550) 42 b, A forewarnynge to hys electes. 1584 R. SCOT *Discov. Witchcr.* VII. ix. 113 Saule . . was an elect. 1646 H. LAWRENCE *Comm. Angels* 20 It is probable that every elect hath his proper and peculiar Angell.

†**2.** One that has been chosen for an office or function; often *spec.* = *bishop elect* (see A. 3). *Obs.*

c 1425 WYNTOUN *Cron.* IX. xxvii. 121 Comfermyt he wes Elect of Legis Ðat Bischoprike in þe Impire is. 1490–1 *Ld. Treas. Acc. Scotl.* I. 197 Item for a compositioun maid with Master Johne Guthre, elect of Ross, for the anna of the temporalite. 1570–6 LAMBARDE *Peramb. Kent* (1826) 149 Afterward he [the Pope] refuseth both the elects, and preferreth Stephan Langton. 1709 STRYPE *Ann. Ref.* I. vi. 98 Parker and the other four Elects . . did offer to give unto her yearly a thousand marks.

†**3.** = ELECTO. *Obs.*

1783 WATSON *Philip III* (1793) I. II. 139 Having chosen an elect or leader.

4. In the Royal College of Physicians: One of the eight officers (abolished in 1860) who had formerly the function of granting licences, and the right of electing the President of the College from their own number.

1523 *Act 14–15 Hen. VIII*, c. 5 §3 That the sixe persons beforesaid . . chusing to them two moe . . be called and cleaped Elects. 1697 *View Penal Laws* 8 Apothecaries faulty Wares, to be destroyed by the President and Elects of the College of Physicians in London. 1840 *Penny Cycl.* XVIII. 133/2 The constituted officers then of this corporation are the eight elects.

elect (ɪ'lɛkt), *v.* Also 6 electe. *Sc.* eleck. *Pa. t.* and *pple.* elected, 6 elect(e. [f. *ēlect-* ppl. stem of *ēligĕre* (see prec.).]

†**1.** *trans.* To pick out, choose (usually, for a particular purpose or function). Also *absol. Obs.* in general sense.

1513 BRADSHAW *St. Werburge* (1848) 164 A noble gentilman . . Elected a spouses at his owne deuice. 1557 PAYNEL *Barclay's Jugurth.* 28 b, He had elect and assembled such compani as him thought competent for an army. 1571 DIGGES *Pantom.* I. xxxiv. L, Hauing elected a loftie seate. 1591 SHAKS. *1 Hen. VI*, IV. i. 4. 1603 —— *Meas. for M.* I. i. 19 We haue with speciall soule Elected him our absence to supply. 1607 ROWLANDS *Diog. Lanth.* 28 A heedefull care wee ought to haue, When we doe frends elect. 1681 CHETHAM *Angler's Vade-m.* ii. §1 (1689) 7 Elect your Hair not from lean, poor, or diseased jades. 1802 PALEY *Nat. Theol.* xxv. (1819) 399 The magnetic needle elects its position.

2. To make deliberate choice of (a course of action, an opinion, etc.) in preference to an alternative. In legal use often *absol.*

1509 HAWES *Past. Pleas.* VIII. i, Comyn wytte doothe full well electe What it shoulde take, and what it shall abjecte. 1677 HALE *Prim. Orig. Man.* I. ii. 59 It can suspend its own acting, either of electing or rejecting. 1818 CRUISE *Digest* VI. 26 He must therefore elect. 1837 *Penny Cycl.* IX. 334/1 They are seldom called to adjudicate upon it, except where the party has already elected. 1847 EMERSON *Repr. Men* iii. *Swedenborg* Wks. (Bohn) I. 334 He elected goodness as the clue to which the soul must cling in all this labyrinth of nature. 1874 CARPENTER *Ment. Phys.* I. i. §25 The Motives which we determinately elect as our guiding principles of action.

b. with infinitive as obj. (Now common, but formerly chiefly in legal use).

a 1626 BACON *Max. Com. Law* ix. 38 If there bee an overplus of goods . . then ought he . . to determine what goods hee doth elect to have in value. 1661 BOYLE *Style of Script.* 182, I would not have Christians . . elect to read God's word, rather in any book than his own. 1788 J. POWELL *Devises* (1827) II. 65 The daughter . . was a lunatic, and therefore incompetent to elect to take the estate as land or money. 1817 W. SELWYN *Law Nisi Prius* II. 905 The assured may elect to abandon to the underwriter all right to such part of the property as may be saved. 1868 HELPS *Realmah* xvi. (1876) 447 She was secretly delighted that the jester had elected to live with her.

3. To choose (a person) by vote for appointment to an office or position of any kind. Used in three different constructions: *to elect* (a person) *to* (an office, etc.); *to elect* (an officer, etc.) ; and with complement, as 'they elected him their chief'. Also *absol.*

1494 FABYAN VI. ccii. 212 Gerbres . . was electe pope of Rome. 1513 BRADSHAW *St. Werburge* 79 Sexburge was electe To be abbesse. 1588 SHAKS. *Tit. A.* I. i. 228 If you will elect by my aduise, Crowne him, and say: Long liue our Emperour. 1743 TINDAL tr. *Rapin's Hist. Eng.* II. XVII. 94 They resolved to elect an Inter-Rex. 1785 BURNS *Twa Herds* iv, Ye wha were . . by the brutes themselves eleckit, To be their guide. 1777 WATSON *Philip II* (1839) 159 They elected for their king Don Ferdinand de Valor. 1867 BUCKLE *Civilis.* (1873) III. i. 32 Few of the Scotch towns ventured to elect their chief magistrate from among their own people.

4. *Theol.* Of God: To choose (certain of His creatures) in preference to others, as the recipients of temporal or spiritual blessings; *esp.* to choose as the objects of eternal salvation. Also *absol.*

a 1617 BAYNE *On Eph.* (1658) 42 Antecedency of faith before the act of electing. 1626 W. SCLATER *Expos. 2 Thess.* (1629) 68 To induce the Lord to elect or predestinate. 1837

Penny Cycl. IX. 333/1 Particular persons, without any regard whatever to their merits or demerits, are elected, or rejected for ever.

electable (ɪˈlɛktəb(ə)l), *a.* [f. prec. + -ABLE.] Able to be elected, qualified for election.
1879 *Echo* 6 Mar. 2/4 The electorate has been widened, but the electable class has been narrowed.

†**eˈlectancy.** *Obs. rare.* [f. as next; see -ANCY.] The power of choosing.
1768 TUCKER (Todd, s.v. *Electant*).

†**eˈlectant.** *Obs. rare.* [ad. L. *ēlectant-em*, pr. pple. of *ēlectāre*, freq. of *ēligĕre* to choose: cf. ELECT *a.*, and -ANT.] One who has power of choosing.
1768 TUCKER *Lt. Nat.* (1852) I. 552 Man is a free agent, and a free volent..but you cannot go on further to entitle him a free electant too. **1847** in CRAIG.

electar, var. form of ELECTRE, *Obs.*

electary, variant of ELECTUARY.

elected (ɪˈlɛktɪd), *ppl. a.* [f. ELECT *v.* + -ED.]
1. Chosen; chosen for office, etc.; see the vb.
1559 *Form Consecr. Bishops* in *Liturg. Serv. Q. Eliz.* (1847) 293 The elected Bishop shall be presented..unto the Archbishop of that Province. **1611** SHAKS. *Cymb.* III. iv. 12 Why hast thou gone so farre To be vn-bent? when thou hast 'tane thy stand, Th' elected Deere before thee? **1673** PENN *Chr. Quaker* vi. 538 Some Parents..do frequently bestow their Favours upon an Elected Darling. **1851** LONGF. *Gold. Leg.*, *Farm in Odenw.*, Thou art my elected bride.
†**b.** *absol.* with plural sense. *Obs. rare.*
1548 tr. *Erasm. Paraph.*, *Acts*, 23 a Iesus..the defendour of his owne elected. **1550** CRANMER *Defence* Pref. *2 a To..geue pardon..to al his elected.
2. Chosen by vote as distinguished from other modes of selection.
Mod. The elected members of the council command more confidence than the nominated members.

electee (ɪ͵lɛkˈtiː). [f. as prec. + -EE.] One chosen or elected.
1593 BILSON *Govt. Christ's Ch.* 357 They could witnesse the behauiour of the electees to be sincere.

†**eˈlectic**, bad form of ECLECTIC, after ELECT *v.*
1636 FEATLY *Clavis Myst.* xxxii. 448, I will rather be an Electicke than a Criticke.

electing (ɪˈlɛktɪŋ), *vbl. sb.* [f. ELECT *v.* + -ING[1].] The action of the verb ELECT.
1611 in Picton *L'pool Munic. Rec.* (1883) I. 160 The ellecting of a Towne Clarke. **1687** in *Magd. Coll. & Jas. II* (Oxf. Hist. Soc.) 88 The Electing of the Bishop of Oxford.

eˈlecting, *ppl. a.* [f. as prec. + -ING[2].] Choosing, etc.: cf. senses of vb.
1674 HICKMAN *Hist. Quinquart.* (ed. 2) 181 They say, that Electing love makes men willing, and that Holiness is an effect of Election.

election (ɪˈlɛkʃən). Forms: 4 eleccioun, -ciown, -cyoun(e, 4–6 -cion, 5–6 -cyon, (5 alexcion), 5 electyown, 6 -tyon, -tioune, -ttyon, 6- election, 9 (*U.S.*) 'lection. [a. OF. *election*, ad. L. *ēlectiōn-em*, n. of action f. *ēligĕre*: see ELECT *v.*]
The action of choosing: in various specific applications.
1. a. The formal choosing of a person for an office, dignity, or position of any kind; usually by the votes of a constituent body.
c **1270** *St. Edmund* in *Saints' Lives* (1887) 443 Þe Eleccioun was i-maud in þe chapitle at Caunterburi. *c* **1330** R. BRUNNE *Chron.* (1810) 208 To mak eleccion, To chese þe suld cheue aman of gode renoun. **1419** BP. CLIFFORD in Ellis *Orig. Lett.* II. 29 I. 91, I..confermed the eleccion of dame Jhone North abbesse. *c* **1450** *Erle Tolous* 1202 Be alexcion of the lordys free The erle toke they thoo, They made hym ther emperoure. **1535** COVERDALE *Acts* xiv. 23 Whan they had ordeyned them Elders by eleccion thorow all the congregacions. **1583** STUBBES *Anat. Abus.* II. 99 The churches haue no further power in the election of their pastor. **1614** RALEIGH *Hist. World* II. 365 Abimelech practised with the inhabitants of Sechem, to make election of himselfe. **1776** GIBBON *Decl. & Fall* vii. I. 172 In a large society the election of a monarch can never devolve to the wisest. **1845** S. AUSTIN *Ranke's Hist. Ref.* I. 39 The empire ..had waived the right..to interfere in the election of the pope. **1867** BRIGHT *Sp. Amer.* 29 June (1876) 146 They found that the presidential election was adverse to the cause of slavery.
b. *spec.* The choice by popular vote of members of a representative body (in the United Kingdom, chiefly of members of the House of Commons); the whole proceedings accompanying such a choice. ***general election***: an election of representatives throughout an entire country, to fill vacancies simultaneously created; opposed to BY-ELECTION.
1648 *Eikon Bas.* 2, I was..sorry to heare with what partiality..Elections were carried in many places. **1705** LUTTRELL *Brief Rel.* (1857) V. 612 A writt ordered for a new election at Castle Rising. **1789** BELSHAM *Ess.* II. xli. 533 It is not infamous to be incapable of voting at a county election. **1853** LYTTON *My Novel* II. xxii. 379 The election.. suddenly grew into vivid interest. **1874** MORLEY *Compromise* (1886) 20 At elections the national candidate has not often a chance against the local candidate.
†**c.** A vote. *Obs. rare.*
1543–4 *Act 35 Hen. VIII*, c. 11 §3 The burgesses..shal.. come and giue their elections.
†**d.** *concr.* An electoral body. *Obs. rare.*
1529 RASTELL *Pastyme, Hist. Pap.* (1811) 55 But parte of the eleccyon did chose one Victor.
2. a. The exercise of deliberate choice or preference; choice between alternatives, *esp.* in matters of conduct. † ***at*** or ***in*** ***(one's) election***: at (one's) option or discretion.
1393 GOWER *Conf.* III. 86 Which stant in disposicion Of mannes fre election. **1483** CAXTON *Gold. Leg.* 321/4 Where he now resteth by his election and by the purueaunce of god. *c* **1510** MORE *Picus* Wks. 8/1 Which he wold chose, if he should of necessitie be driuen to that one, and at his election. **1526** *Pilgr. Perf.* (W. de W. 1531) 94 b, Vsed to chose by eleccyon & full deliberacyon ye thynge that is of lesse goodnes. **1602** FULBECKE *1st Pt. Parall.* 26 Where the tenant is outlawed of felony, it is in the Lords election to haue a Writ of Escheate. **1670** CLARENDON *Ess.* in *Tracts* (1727) 191 True virtue presupposeth an election. **1685** PETTY *Last Will* 11 As for beggars by trade and election I give them nothing. **1754** EDWARDS *Freed. Will* I. iv. (1762) 26 A man has a Thing in his Power, if he has it in his Choice, or at his Election. **1788** J. POWELL *Devises* (1827) II. 71 The enquiry, who are personally competent to make, and what amounts to such an election. **1818** CRUISE *Digest* III. 312 Disseisins of incorporeal hereditaments are only at the election and choice of the party injured. **1859** MILL *Liberty* v. (1865) 59/1 So ordering matters that persons shall make their election.. on their own prompting. **1873** BROWNING *Red Cott. Night-C.* 120 On such a lady if election light..If henceforth 'all the world' she constitute For any lover.
†**b.** Judicious selection; the faculty of choosing with taste or nice discrimination. *Obs.*
1531 ELYOT *Gov.* (1580) 76 Election is of an excellent power and authoritie..is part and as it were a member of Prudence. **1597** BACON *Coulers Good & Evill* Pref., The discouering..of these coulers..cleareth mans iudgement and election. **1602** FULBECKE *Pandectes* 63, I know not whether Ouid his inuention, or Sir Phillippes election be more to be commended.
3. *Theol.* **a.** The exercise of God's sovereign will in choosing some of His creatures in preference to others for blessings temporal or spiritual, *esp.* for eternal salvation. ***doctrine of election***: the doctrine that God actually exercises this prerogative with regard to mankind; in popular language often identified with the (Calvinistic) doctrine of 'unconditional election', *i.e.* election not conditioned by the conduct or disposition of the individual.
1382 WYCLIF *Rom.* ix. 11 That the purpos of God schulde dwelle vp the eleccioun [**1526** TINDALE, election], not of workis, but of God clepinge. **1554–9** in *Songs & Ball.* (1860) 3 The redemptyon and ryghte to owr fyrst electtyon. **1605** BACON *Adv. Learn.* I. vi. §7 The..election of God went to the shepherd, and not to the tiller of the ground. **1611** BIBLE *Rom.* xi. 5. **1630** DONNE *Serm.* xiii. 136 Prove thine Election by thy Sanctification for that is the right method. **1645** USSHER *Body Div.* 91 Election..is the everlasting predestination, or foreappointing of certain Angels and Men unto everlasting life. **1702** tr. *Le Clerc's Prim. Fathers* 354 As to Election..Pelagius believed Two sorts of it; the one to Grace and the other to Glory. **1841** MYERS *Cath. Th.* III. §11. 41 This process was founded upon the election and peculiar training of a single people. **1865** CARLYLE *Fredk. Gt.* II. VII. ix. 338 The doctrine of Election..that a man's good or ill conduct is foredoomed upon him by decree of God. **1871** MORLEY *Voltaire* (1886) 2 They realised life as a long wrestling with..forces of grace, election, and fore-destiny.
†**b.** *concr.* The body of the elect. *Obs. rare.*
1611 BIBLE *Rom.* xi. 7 The election hath obtained it.
†**4.** *Astrol.* The choice on astrological grounds of the fit time for undertaking any particular business; *concr.* a time so selected. *Obs.* exc. *Hist.*
c **1386** CHAUCER *Man Lawes T.* 214 Of viage is ther noon eleccioun. **14..** *Epiph.* (*Tundale's Vis.* 103) Sowght and chosen owt by eleccion. **1621** BURTON *Anat. Mel.* I. ii. IV. vii, What is Astrology but vain elections, predictions? **1721** BAILEY, *Elections* (among Astrologers) are certain Times pitched upon as fittest for the undertaking a particular business. **1831** LYTTON *Godolph.* xxvii, In spite of..your ephemeris and your election of happy moments.
†**5.** The choosing of things for special purposes; *spec.* in Pharmacy (see quot.). Chiefly in 17th c.
1612 WOODALL *Surg. Mate* Wks. (1653) 270 Election is of simples according to time and season wherein they are gathered. **1614** MARKHAM *Cheap Husb.* (1623) 137 Doe not in the election of your Egges chuse those which are monstrous great. **1667** DRYDEN *Ess. Dram. Poesie* Dram. Wks. 1725 I. 72 An election of apt words, and a right disposition of them. **1667** PRIMATT *City & C. Builder* 51 Let the builder make election of bricks that are, etc. **1695** WESTMACOT *Script. Herb.* 49 In the Election of it [the herb Elaterium] the oldest is accounted the best. **1727–51** CHAMBERS *Cycl.*, *Election*..teaches how to chuse the medicinal simples, drugs, etc.
†**6.** *Arith.* (See quot.) *Obs.*
1721 BAILEY, *Election* (in Numbers) is the several ways of taking any Number of Quantities given, without having respect to their places. **1727–51** CHAMBERS *Cycl.* s.v.
7. *Law.* **a.** In AFr. phr. ***Election de Clerk*** (rarely in Eng. form ***election of clerk***).
1607 COWEL *Interpr.*, *Election de Clerke.* **1721** BAILEY, *Election de Clerk*, is a writ that lyeth for the choice of a Clerk, assigned to take and make Bonds, called Statute Merchant. **1835** TOMLINS *Law Dict.* (ed. 4) *Election of Clerk.*
b. The choosing between two rights by a person who derives one of them under an instrument in which a clear intention appears that he should not enjoy both.
1628 COKE *On Litt.* II. xii. ccxix. 145a If a man granteth a Rent..or a robe to one and to his heires, the Grantor shall haue the election, for he is the first Agent, by payment of the one, or deliuerie of the other. **1891** G. SERRELL *Equitable Doctrine Election* 6 Election is often said to rest on an implied condition. **1959** JOWITT *Dict. Eng. Law* I. 699/2 The equitable doctrine of election is founded on the principle that there is an implied condition that he who accepts a benefit under an instrument must adopt the whole of it, conforming with all its provisions and renouncing every right inconsistent with them.
8. *attrib.* and *Comb.*, as ***election-address***, ***-ale***, ***-cry***, ***-day***, ***dinner***, ***expenses***, ***-monger***, ***-vote***; ***election-mad*** adj.; also **election bun, cake** *U.S.*, varieties of fancy bread; **election commissioner**, one of a body of men appointed to inquire into corrupt practices during an election or (*U.S.*) to take charge of an election; **election-committee**, a committee formed to promote the election of a particular candidate; also (before the Election Petitions Act of 1868) a committee of the House of Commons appointed to inquire into the validity of controverted elections; **election district** *U.S.*, a district created for the purposes of elections; **election-dust**, the commotion of an election; **election petition**, a petition brought against a member of parliament for illegal practices during his election campaign.
1874 MORLEY *Compromise* (1886) 124 Proper for the hustings, or expedient in an *election address. **1768–74** TUCKER *Lt. Nat.* (1852) II. 571 By his elder brother's death he comes into possession of the fox hounds and the tubs of *election ale. **1860** O. W. HOLMES *Prof. Breakf.-t.* ii. 52 [He] recollects he had a glazed *'lection bun, and sat eating it, and looking down on the Common. **1805** *Pocumtuc Housewife* (1906) 30 *Elections Cake. **1832** L. M. CHILD *Amer. Frugal Housewife* 71 Old-fashioned election cake is made of four pounds of flour [etc.]. **1947** R. BEROLZHEIMER et al. *U.S. Regional Cook Bk.* 53 Election Cake was always served on Election Day. **1899** *Kansas City Star* 17 Feb. 1/3 He said that Julius Wurzberger, an *election commissioner of St. Louis,..had spent $10 getting him drunk. **1902** *Encycl. Brit.* XXVI. 369/1 A prosecution for any of the above offences cannot be instituted more than a year after the offence was committed, unless an inquiry by Election Commissioners takes place. **1864** *Times* 22 Mar. 9/6 An *election committee must sit from day to day until they complete the inquiry. **1861** DICKENS *Gt. Expect.* xviii, I doubt if the words ['Pip' and 'Property'] had more in them than an *election cry. **1651** *Narrative late Parlt.* in *Select. fr. Harl. Misc.* (1793) 400 Meetings..to agree and make choice before-hand..and then promote their choice against the *election-day. **1648** OLDHAM *Poems* 161 (Jod.) That vile wretch..Whose works must serve the next election day For making squibs. **1751** G. STONE *Let.* 18 May in *9th Rep. Hist. MSS. Comm.* App. III. (1884) 40/2 Of the two sorts of champagne that sealed with yellow wax might go off at balls. .. The red wax is too bad for an *election dinner at Dover. **1839** R. PEEL *Let.* 8 Dec. in *Corr. C. Arbuthnot* (1941) 212 May not a half-pay captain stand a contested election—or may not he be present at his brother's election dinner? **1799** in *Deb. Congress U.S.* (1851) 7th Congr. 2nd Sess. App. 1411 In every *election district in the country. **1835** *Southern Lit. Messenger* I. 218 One or two..get a resolution passed for a general caucus of the whole party, in the town, or election district. **1902** E. C. MEYER *Nominating Systems* 19 The township or ward, is included in a number of different election districts, each of which has its own convention. **1815** SCOTT *Guy M.* xxxvi, 'There's been nae *election-dusts lately.' **1859** J. S. MILL *Parl. Reform* 19 Let law and opinion conspire to the end that *election expenses be suppressed. **1869** W. F. COLLIER *Let.* 28 Mar. in B. & P. Russell *Amberley Papers* (1937) II. 159 You are fully aware that my views with respect to Election expenses are very nearly identical with your own. **1768** TUCKER *Lt. Nat.* (1852) I. 493 Had I run opera-mad..or *election-mad, I might have found companions enow. **1881** *Daily News* 12 Feb. 6/5 This disadvantage *election-mongers would seek to remedy by running bogus candidates. **1835** J. A. ROEBUCK *Short Rev. of Long Session* 9/1 Connected with this matter of elections was one peculiar and distinguishing work of this Parliament—I mean *Election Petitions. **1839** *Act 2 & 3 Vict.* c. 38 (*title*) An Act to amend the Jurisdiction for the Trial of Election Petitions. **1840** *Penny Cycl.* XVII. 278/2 In 1741, Sir Robert Walpole..was..driven from office by a vote upon the Chippenham election petition. **1885** *Encycl. Brit.* XVII. 705/1 By the Act of 1879 the trial of an election petition is conducted before two judges instead of one, as before. *a* **1743** SAVAGE *Wks.* (1775) II. 174 (Jod.), I have no power *election votes to gain.

electional (ɪˈlɛkʃənəl), *a. rare.* [f. prec. + -AL[1].] Relating to (astrological) election.
1652 GAULE *Magastrom.* 239 If you would know on what ..electional hour to enter your suit.

electionary (ɪˈlɛkʃənərɪ), *a. rare.* [f. ELECTION + -ARY.] Pertaining to election, electoral.
1837 *Fraser's Mag.* XVI. 291 The more publicly electionary suffrages are given, the less chance there is of bribery.

electioneer (ɪ͵lɛkʃəˈnɪə(r)), *v.* [f. ELECTION + -EER[1], prob. after *auctioneer-ing.*] *intr.* To busy oneself in (political) elections.
1789 T. JEFFERSON *Writ.* (1859) II. 580 All the world here is occupied in electioneering, in choosing or being chosen. **1802** MAR. EDGEWORTH *Rosanna* iii, Those underlings delight in galloping round the country to electioneer. **1836** R. P. SMITH *Col. Crockett's Exploits & Adv.* 11 For this reason he came out openly to electioneer against me. **1843** 'R. CARLTON' *New Purchase* xviii. 139 Numbers go to see their neighbours, or to hear the news, and not a few to

electioneer. *a* **1922** C. C. ANDREWS *Recoll.* (1928) 185 Soldiers have electioneered to some extent for different candidates.

electioneer (ɪlɛkʃə'nɪə(r)), *sb.* [f. ELECTION + -EER, after *auctioneer*, etc.] = ELECTIONEERER.

1848 J. R. LOWELL *Biglow P.* 1st Ser. vi. 77, I du believe hard coin the stuff Fer 'lectioneers to spout on. **1895** *Pall Mall Gaz.* 26 July 8/1 In the Yorkshire Constituencies. The Champion Electioneer. **1905** *Jrnl. Educ.* Apr. 272/2 To secure that the professorship shall not necessarily go to the most successful electioneer. **1928** *Daily Express* 11 Oct. 11/1 The Liberal electioneers at once denounced it as a 'Tory trick'.

electioneerer (ɪˌlɛkʃə'nɪərə(r)). [f. ELECTIONEER *v.* + -ER.] One who manages elections, who uses arts or influence to secure the return of a candidate; one skilled in such arts.

1800 M. EDGEWORTH *Parent's Assistant* (ed. 3) VI. 150 A damn'd bad electioneerer!.. Why, unless he bought a vote, he'd never win one. **1809–12** —— *Vivian* viii, Loud-tongued electioneerers. **1824** BYRON *Juan* XVI. lxx, Lord Henry was a great electioneerer, Burrowing for boroughs like a rat or rabbit. **1865** *Sat. Rev.* 18 Feb. 186/2 The proverbially sanguine temperament of electioneerers.

electioneering (ɪˌlɛkʃə'nɪərɪŋ), *vbl. sb.* [f. as prec. + -ING[1].] The art or practice of managing elections; canvassing on behalf of candidates for membership in representative assemblies. Also *attrib.*

1760 E. PYLE *Let.* 22 Nov. (1905) 330 He will never give them any more trouble on the article of electioneering. **1785** G. A. BELLAMY *Apology for Life* III. 89 A solicitor, who was a very bustling man, and well versed in electioneering affairs. **1790** BURKE *Fr. Rev.* 315 Officers.. are to manage their troops by electioneering arts. **1796** MORSE *Amer. Geog.* I. 472 That base business of electioneering. *a* **1859** MACAULAY *Biog.* (1867) 17 He busied himself in electioneering, especially at Westminster. **1878** BLACK *Green Past.* xvi. 129 Deeply interested in this electioneering plot.

eˌlectio'neering, *ppl. a.* [f. as prec. + -ING[2].] That takes an active part in elections.

a **1845** HOOD *Tale Trumpet* xliv, As yellow and blue, As any electioneering crew Wearing the colours of Whigs and Tories.

†**elec'titious**, *a. Obs. rare*[−1]. [as if ad. L. **ēlectīcius*, regularly f. *ēlect-*: see ELECT *v.*] Arbitrarily chosen.

1631 J. BURGES *Answ. Rejoined* 167 Will-worship, even that electitius worship, which we fansie, out of our owne seeming and pleasure of our selues.

elective (ɪ'lɛktɪv), *a.* and *sb.* Also 6–7 electif. [a. Fr. *électif* (cf. It. *elettivo*, Sp. *electivo*), on L. type **ēlectīvus*: see ELECT *v.* and -IVE.

In English, as app. in Romanic, the active sense (normally belonging to words similarly formed) is of later origin than the passive sense.]

A. *adj.*

I. Connected with election to office or dignity.

1. a. In passive sense. Of the holder of an office, dignity, etc.: Appointed by election. Of an office, etc.: Filled up by election. Of authority: Derived from election.

1530–1 *Act 22 Hen. VIII*, c. 12 Every.. baylye electif and elected. **1563** FOXE *A. & M.* (1596) 3/2 Abbasies, priories conuentuall, and other benefices electiue. **1614** RALEIGH *Hist. World* II. 325 It may be that those Kings were elective, as the Edumæans anciently were. **1641** MILTON *Prel. Episc.* (1851) 82 A Temporary, and elective sway. **1735–8** BOLINGBROKE *On Parties* 167 The Gothick Kings were at first elective, and always limited. **1772–84** COOK *Voy.* (1790) I. 78 A regent being necessary, that office, though elective, generally falls upon the father. **1867** FREEMAN *Norm. Conq.* (1876) I. iii. 81 The hereditary prince may be exchanged for an elective chief magistrate.

†**b.** Subject to election (at specified intervals).

1659 J. HARRINGTON *Lawgiving* I. iv. (1700) 394 Annually elective of the People, as in the.. Archons of Athens. **1759** B. MARTIN *Nat. Hist. Eng.* II. 86 He is elective every three years.

2. In active sense: Having the power of electing officers or representatives by vote.

1632 *Star Chamb. Cases* (1886) 155 At the reading of the said letters he had the greater number of elective voices. **1844** LD. BROUGHAM *Brit. Const.* iv. (1862) 61 Elective body, a body whose functions are confined to the choice of representatives. **1862** ANSTED *Channel Isl.* IV. xxiii. 527 The business of the Elective States [in Guernsey] is limited to the election of the jurats and the sheriff.

3. a. Pertaining to the election of officers or representatives; (of a system of government, etc.) based upon the principle of election.

1642 BRIDGE *Wound. Consc. Cured* iv. 27 When the government is elective and pactionall, are not the Princes the Ministers? **1791** MACKINTOSH *Vind. Gallicæ* Wks. 1846 III. 68 The elective constitution of the new clergy of France. **1831** CARLYLE *Sart. Res.* (1858) 152 He appears to make little even of the Elective Franchise. **1862** MERIVALE *Rom. Emp.* (1865) IV. xxxix. 373 A preference of the elective to the hereditary principle in every department of government.

b. Of college or high-school studies: subject to the student's choice; optional. So ***elective system***. orig. *U.S.*

1847 in *Ann. Rep. Harvard Coll. 1883–4* 14 The elective system is now given up in this department. **1868** C. W. DILKE *Greater Brit.* I. vii. 89 The system of elective studies pursued at Michigan [University] is one to which we are year by year tending in the English universities. **1880** *Harper's Mag.* July 254/1 In the German Universities the studies are all elective and optional; in the colleges of the United States compulsory. **1890** J. G. FITCH *Notes Amer. Schools* 59 In the high schools and universities the practice of prescribing 'elective' subjects is very common. **1957** G. G. READER in R. K. Merton *Student-Physician* 84 Two months of elective work. **1969** *Brit. Jrnl. Med. Educ.* III. 102 There should be an elective period of, say, 10 weeks, in which the student should be able to choose from a wide variety of elective topics.

II. Pertaining to choice in general.

4. Pertaining to the action of choosing. Of actions: Proceeding from free choice, optional, voluntary. Formerly *Obs.*, but now revived in medical use: optional, not urgent (see quot. 1941).

1643 MILTON *Divorce* Wks. 1738 I. 208 God delights not to make a drudge of Virtue, whose Actions must be all elective and unconstrained. **1656** HOBBES *Liberty, Necess. & Ch.* (1841) 409 All elective actions are free from absolute necessity. **1668** HOWE *Bless. Righteous* (1825) 4 To apply at last his intellectual and elective powers. **1775** JOHNSON *Tax. no Tyr.* 14 A duty temporary, occasional, and elective. **1941** *Dorland's Med. Dict.* (ed. 19) 476/2 *Elective*, subject to the choice or decision of the patient or physician.., applied to procedures that are only advantageous to the patient but not necessary to save his life. **1963** *Lancet* 19 Jan. 132/1 A self-contained, thirty-bed hospital which catered solely for elective surgical cases. *Ibid.*, The theatre was used twice weekly for elective operating sessions. **1964** G. L. COHEN *What's Wrong with Hospitals?* iv. 65 An elective operation such as tonsillectomy. **1966** *Lancet* 24 Dec. 1394/1 A reversed intestinal segment was inserted as an elective procedure after massive resection for a mesenteric embolus.

†**5.** Preferentially selected according to circumstances. *Obs. rare.*

1643 T. GOODWIN *Child of Light* 117 There are to be peculiar elective plaisters to heale these wounds, because these wounds are often differing.

†**6.** Proper according to astrological election. *Obs. rare.*

1681 CHETHAM *Angler's Vade-m.* ix. §21 (1689) 96 Elective Times most propitious to Anglers.

†**7.** = ECLECTIC. *Obs. rare.*

1681 H. MORE *Exp. Dan.* Pref. 20 Like a Philosopher of the Elective Sect, addicting my self to no persons.

8. a. Of physical forces and agencies: Having a tendency to operate on certain objects in preference to others. ***elective affinity*** (Chem.): the tendency of a substance to combine with certain particular substances in preference to others; formerly ***elective attraction***, which is still used, but chiefly in a wider sense.

1766 *Phil. Trans.* LVI. 100 There seems.. to have been a double elective attraction in the fourteenth Experiment. **1794** J. HUTTON *Philos. Light* 50 The elective affections of this irradiated influence. **1800** HENRY *Epit. Chem.* (1808) 18 Tables of elective affinity have been formed. **1802** PALEY *Nat. Theol.* xxi. (1819) 330 It is owing to this original elective power in the air that we can effect the separation which we wish. **1869** TYNDALL *Light* §257 Light.. which has been sifted.. by elective absorption. **1876** tr. *Schutzenberger's Ferment.* 32 Dubrunfant has given this phenomenon the name of elective fermentation.

b. *fig.*

1796 BURKE *Regic. Peace* iii. Wks. VIII. 285 Sympathetick attraction discovers.. our elective affections. **1827** CARLYLE *German Romance* IV. 12 In the Romance department, Goethe has written.. *Wilhelm Meister's Apprenticeship*, and *Die Wahlverwandtschaften* (The Elective Affinities). **1853** DE QUINCEY *Autobiog. Sk.* Wks. I. 203 The effect of the music is to place the mind in a state of elective attraction for everything in harmony with its own prevailing key. **1860** *Harper's Mag.* July 205/1 We hear much of *passional attraction*, of *elective affinity*, etc. **1872** O. W. HOLMES *Poet Breakf. T.* v. 151 A chance for the elective affinities. **1926** M. BARING *Daphne Adeane* xvii. 212 These things happen: 'elective affinities', you know.

B. *sb.* †**1.** An elected representative. *Obs. rare.*

1701 *Answ. to Black-List* i, The Just and Prudent Proceedings of their Electives.

2. A subject of study specially selected by the student in a college or university; an optional subject or course of study. orig. *U.S.*

1850 *Docs. City Boston* (Mass.) Doc. No. 38, 45 Making some studies electives and giving to the members of the first class some liberty of choice. **1876** J. D. WHITNEY in E. T. Brewster *Life J.D.W.* (1909) 330, I shall have an elective this winter in economical geology. **1901** *Westm. Gaz.* 30 May 12/1 At Yale, where the study of this language had been neglected for many years, more than a hundred students have chosen it as one of their 'electives'. **1902** J. CORBIN *American at Oxford* 167 The idea of grouping electives is the fundamental difference between English and American education. **1926** *Amer. Oxonian* July 100 Oxford is a school for specialists. There are no minors, no electives, nothing but majors. **1930** *Lambeth Conference Rep.* 174 For the Priesthood he [*sc.* a candidate] must pass a further examination in.. The Bible.. Pastoral Care and one of a long list of Electives. **1957** G. G. READER in R. K. Merton *Student-Physician* 84 The student.. would divide his time between pediatric and psychiatric clinics and part-time electives. **1962** B. LENNOX *Rep. Visit to U.S.A. & Canada* ix. 25 Once we have broken ground with the new curriculum [at Glasgow], I think we should next consider the introduction of electives. **1969** *Brit. Jrnl. Med. Educ.* III. 182 An exciting range of electives in community medicine.

electively (ɪ'lɛktɪvlɪ), *adv.* [f. prec. + -LY[2].] In an elective manner; by choice or preference.

1643 T. GOODWIN *Child of Light* 105 Humours in the body.. he can electively work upon. **1677** GALE *Crt. Gentiles* II. IV. 137 Electively to espouse evil is the worst of evils. **1684** tr. *Bonet's Merc. Compit.* XIV. 489 Medicines that purge electively. **1802** PALEY *Nat. Theol.* xviii. (1819) 272 In the cabbage, not by chance, but studiously and electively, she lays her eggs.

e'lectiveness. *nonce-word.* [f. ELECTIVE *a.* + -NESS.] The fact of (a government's) being elective.

1850 L. HUNT *Autobiog.* xi. (1860) 209 French mutability, and American electiveness.

electivity (iːlɛk'tɪvɪtɪ). [f. ELECTIVE + -ITY.] 'The property by which some substances attach themselves to certain anatomical tissues and not to others; as when carmine stains growing tissue and avoids formed substance. The act or property of selection.' (*Syd. Soc. Lex.*)

‖**e'lecto.** *Obs.* [Sp.; pa. pple. of *elegir* to ELECT.] A leader or commander chosen by mutineers. (Also adapted as ELECT.)

1609 BIBLE (Douay) *Numb.* xiv. *comm.*, Verie mutiners themselves do ever choose such a one, & cal him, the Electo. **1614** RALEIGH *Hist. World* II. v. §3. 175 The Israelites.. consulted to choose them a captain (or as they call it nowadays an Electo). **1650** R. STAPYLTON *Strada's Low-C. Warres* VIII. 5 The old souldiers, after the manner of seditions, created a Generall, whom they called the Electo.

elector (ɪ'lɛktə(r)). Also 5–6 electour. [a. L. *ēlector* chooser, f. *ēligĕre* to ELECT.]

1. a. *gen.* One who has the right to vote in election to any office or dignity. **b.** *spec.* In Great Britain and Ireland, one legally qualified to vote in the election of members of parliament; in U.S., a member of the Electoral College chosen by the several States to elect the President and Vice-President.

1467 in *Eng. Gilds* (1870) 409 þe electors to go to a new elleccioun. **1474** CAXTON *Chesse* II. ii. B iij b, For often tymes the electours and chosers can not ne wylle not accorde. **1660** R. COKE *Power & Subj.* 54 The Electors are the Instruments by which the Elected King or Monarch receives his power. **1756–7** tr. *Keysler's Trav.* (1760) IV. 25 The nine who draw these golden balls chuse forty other electors, all of different families. **1789** *Constit. U.S.* I. ii, The electors in each state shall have the qualifications requisite for electors of the most numerous branch of the state legislature. **1827** SCOTT *Surg. Dau.* i, A score or two of quiet electors, who settle the business over a table. **1861** MAY *Const. Hist.* I. 298 The representation of this capital city [Edinburgh].. was returned by thirty-three electors. **1874** BANCROFT *Footpr. Time* xliii. 374 An Elector.. is one who has been appointed to choose or elect the President of the United States.

†**2.** ***Knights Electors***: the four gentlemen appointed by the sheriff to serve as members of the jury, and to elect the remaining members, in the process of trial by 'Grand Assize'.

1628 COKE *On Litt.* 294 a, The foure Knights Electors of the grand Assise are not to be challenged.

3. One of the Princes of Germany formerly entitled to take part in the election of the Emperor.

1529 RASTELL *Pastyme* E iv. b, [The Emperor] dyd assocyate with hym Maximilyan his son by the consent of the electours. **1591** L. LLOYD *Triplicitie* E iii. b, The seuen Electors hattes of Germany. **1603** KNOLLES *Hist. Turks* (1638) 73 Conradus, Archbishop of Mogunsia, another of the Electors. **1647** CLARENDON *Hist. Reb.* I. (1702) I. 14 The Prince Electour, who had.. incurr'd the Ban of the Empire. **1756–7** tr. *Keysler's Trav.* (1760) IV. 216 The elector of Saxony. **1872** FREEMAN *Gen. Sketch* xvi. §4 (1874) 333 A new electorate of Hessen-Cassel was made, whose Elector, as it turned out, never had any one to elect.

electoral (ɪ'lɛktərəl), *a.* and *sb.* [f. prec. + -AL[1].]

A. *adj.* **1.** Relating to or composed of electors: see ELECTOR 1. ***electoral college***: see COLLEGE *sb.* 1 b; *spec.* in *U.S.* (see quot. 1889).

1790 BURKE *Fr. Rev.* Wks. V. 327, I only consider this constitution as electoral. *a* **1691**, **1790** [see COLLEGE *sb.* 1 b]. **1800** *Deb. Congress U.S.* 23 Jan. (1851) 31 If this body of the Electors of all the States had been directed by the Constitution to assemble in one place, instead.. of being formed into different Electoral colleges [etc.]. **1812** W. BOYLAN *Let.* 5 Sept. in J. Steele *Papers* (1924) II. 689 The sense of each district may then be pretty generally represented in the Electoral College. **1827** HALLAM *Const. Hist.* (1876) III. xv. 148 Control of the electoral over the representative body. **1845** S. AUSTIN *Ranke's Hist. Ref.* I. 413 Austria had.. friends in the electoral college. **1851** GALLENGA tr. *Mariotti's Italy* 197 Bozzelli followed up his scheme by an electoral law. **1852** GLADSTONE *Glean.* IV. lxxviii. 120 Extension of the electoral franchise. **1889** *Cent. Dict.*, *Electoral College*, a name informally given to the electors of a single State, when met to vote for President and Vice-President of the United States, and sometimes to the whole body of electors. **1903** R. L. ASHLEY *Amer. Govt.* 274 The work of the Electoral College. **1949** *Pacific Discovery* Jan.–Feb. 3/2 Once we even elected a president of the United States through open and brazen corruption of the electoral college. **1969** *Pioneer* (Lucknow) 13 Aug. 1/1 The Congress has a clear majority in the Presidential electoral college.

2. Holding rank as, or belonging to, a German Elector.

1675 *Lond. Gaz.* No. 978/3 His Electoral Highness has convoked the States. **1788** H. WALPOLE *Remin.* ii. 16 George the first, while electoral prince, had married his cousin. **1834** MACAULAY *Chatham, Ess.* (1854) I. 301 Frederick.. had set his heart on the Electoral dominions of his uncle.

¶**3.** = ELECTIVE 1. *rare.*

1849 SIR J. STEPHEN *Eccl. Biog.* (1850) I. 88 He found the Papacy electoral by the Roman people and clergy. **1866** C.

W. HOSKYNS *Essays* 223 Harold was the favourite of the people, and their electoral king.

†**B.** *sb.* = ELECTOR (cf. A. 2). *Obs.*

1692 *Lond. Gaz.* No. 2816/3 The Electoral of Saxony. **1693** *Ibid.* 2893/2 The Electoral gave Orders to march immediately. **1707** *Ibid.* No. 4358/3 His..Majesty having written to the Electoral of Hanover.

†**electo'rality.** *Obs. rare*⁻¹. [f. ELECTOR + -ALITY.] = ELECTORATE.

1620 tr. *Accord of Ulm* in *Reliq. Wotton.* (1685) 534 The Electoralities, Principalities, and Estates within the Empire.

electorally (ɪ'lɛktərəlɪ). [f. ELECTORAL + -LY².] With reference to electors or elections.

1881 *Daily News* 19 May 4 France would be in some danger of being electorally absorbed into Paris. **1884** *Pall Mall G.* 7 July 1/1 Nothing is electorally more certain.

electorate (ɪ'lɛktərət). [f. ELECTOR + -ATE¹.]

1. a. The state or dignity of a German Elector. **b.** The dominions of an Elector.

1675 *Lond. Gaz.* No. 983/3 Imperialists have now quite cleared the Electorate of Cologne. **1721** SWIFT *Corr.* Wks. 1841 II. 654 It was a Whiggish action to honour duke Schomberg, who was..in the service of that electorate. **1827** HALLAM *Const. Hist.* (1876) III. xvi. 241 The abdication of the electorate. **1834** MACAULAY *Chatham, Ess.* (1854) I. 308 The whole electorate was in the hands of the French.

2. The whole body of electors.

1879 O'CONNOR *Beaconsfield* 534 The entire urban electorate of England. **1885** *Manch. Exam.* 15 May 5/1 The arguments..are such as will tell upon the new electorate.

electoress, obs. form of ELECTRESS.

electorial (i:lɛk'toərɪəl). [f. ELECTOR + -IAL.] = ELECTORAL in its various senses.

1790 BURKE *Fr. Rev.* Wks. V. 48 Erect themselves into an electorial college. **1822** *New Monthly Mag.* V. 271 Disentangling themselves at once from their electorial perplexities. **1829** K. DIGBY *Broadst. Hon.* I. 232 The first class of the nobility of Venice is of the electorial families.

electorship (ɪ'lɛktəʃɪp). [f. ELECTOR + -SHIP.]

1. The state or dignity, or the dominions, of a German Elector.

1624 *Aphor. State* in *Harl. Misc.* (Malh.) III. 501 Revoke the electorship from the Duke of Bavaria. **1678** WANLEY *Wond. Lit. World* v. i. §102 The King..of Bohemia..is proscribed and put out of his Electorship. **1762** tr. *Busching's Syst. Geog.* V. 632 Neumark remained still to the electorship.

2. The state or condition **a.** of a voter; **b.** of a member of the (U.S.) Electoral College.

1870 *Daily News* 16 Feb., If appearances are any test of electorship, there were not a score of voters amongst them. **1871** FREEMAN *Hist. Ess.* Ser. I. xii. 393 Candidate for the electorship of the President.

†**e'lectory,** *a. Obs. rare*⁻¹. [as if ad. L. **ēlectōrius*, f. *ēlector*: see ELECTOR.] Capable of being filled by election, elective; = ELECTIVE I.

1660 R. COKE *Power & Subj.* 204 The free election of all Archbishops..and all other dignities and benefices electory.

Electra (ɪ'lɛktrə). Name in Greek tragedy of the daughter of Agamemnon and Clytemnestra, responsible for the murder of the latter, used *attrib.*, esp. in ***Electra complex***, a term used by psychoanalysts to denote a daughter's feelings of attraction towards her father and hostility towards her mother.

1913 [see COMPLEX *sb.* 3]. **1927** B. MALINOWSKI *Sex & Repression in Savage Society* I. viii. 65 This is the configuration of the Electra complex; it is therefore of an entirely different nature from the Oedipus complex. **1963** A. HERON *Towards Quaker View of Sex* 58 This is the Oedipus situation... Its female counterpart is called the Electra situation, but this appears a rather less powerful and significant event in the life of the girl.

†**e'lectral,** *a. Obs.* [as if a. L. **ēlectrālis*, f. *ēlectrum* amber.] = ELECTRICAL *a.*, in various senses.

1673 GREW *Anat. Roots* II. §36 From the Electral nature of divers other Bodies. **1708** in *Phil. Trans.* XXVI. 72 Amber directed me to that of a Diamond, from its being Electral.

b. *fig.*

a **1763** SHENSTONE *Wks.* (1764) I. 290 And what electral fire Shall solve the frosty gripe, and bid it flow?

†**e'lectre.** *Obs.* Also electar. [ad. L. *ēlectr-um* (cf. Pr. *electre*, OF. *eleutre*), ad. Gr. ἤλεκτρον amber, also = sense I: cf. ELECTRON¹, ELECTRUM. (In OE. the L. word was adapted as *elehtre.*)]

1. An alloy of gold and silver, bright and precious; also *attrib.*

1382 WYCLIF *Ezek.* i. 4 Electre..a metal of gold and siluer, cleerere than gold. **1585** JAS. I *Ess. Poesie* (Arb.) 25 Pale Electre light. *Ibid.* 76 *Electre*, a metal, fowre parts gold and fift part siluer. *a* **1626** BACON *Physiol. Rem.* (1679) 98 Change Silver Plate or Vessel into the Compound Stuff, being a kind of Silver Electre. **1656** H. MORE *Antid. Ath.* III. ix. (1712) 168 The Bell made of Paracelsus's Electre.

2. Amber; also elixir, healing gum (cf. AMBER 7). Also *attrib.*

1595 B. BARNES *Spir. Sonn.* in Farr's *S.P. Eliz.* I. 41 O blessed sweet wounds! fountains of electre! **1632** RANDOLPH *Jealous Lov.* III, Sweet gumms that from Electar trees Distill.

electress (ɪ'lɛktrɪs). Also: 7–8 **electoress.** See also ELECTRICE, ELECTRIX. [f. ELECTOR + -ESS.]

1. The wife of a German Elector of the Empire.

1618 *Barnevelt's Apol.* D iv, The Electoresse, and Countesse Palatine. **1703** *Ibid.* No. 3896/2 The Electress of Bavaria..is removed..to Ingolstad. **1798** EDGEWORTH *Pract. Educ.* (1822) I. 375 The electoress came in with one of her daughters. **1870** CURTIS *Hist. Eng.* 412 George I was the son of the electress Sophia, granddaughter of James I.

2. A female elector; a woman having a vote.

1869 *Spectator* 6 Nov. 1295 The electresses evidently think, even more earnestly than the electors, that, etc.

electret (ɪ'lɛktrɪt). [f. ELECTR(ICITY + MAGN)ET.] A permanently polarized piece of dielectric material, the electric counterpart of the permanent magnet.

1885 *Electrician* 7 Aug. 230/1 Solid insulating substances may be made electrets artificially, with a greater or less amount of permanency. **1936** *Nature* 18 July 130/1 An 'electret' is produced by solidifying certain types of wax, for example, carnauba wax, in a strong electric field... It is known that electrets can retain their original charge for a considerable period. **1960** *New Scientist* 7 Apr. 884/3 An electret which tends to depolarize when exposed to light. **1968** *Ibid.* 4 July 30/1 The advantages of using electrets in telephony are economy and performance.

electric (ɪ'lɛktrɪk), *a.* and *sb.* [ad. mod.L. *ēlectric-us*, f. L. *ēlectr-um*, Gr. ἤλεκτρον amber: see ELECTR-UM and -IC. The mod.L. word seems to have been first used by W. Gilbert in his treatise *De Magnete*, 1600.] **A.** *adj.*

1. a. Possessing the property (first observed in amber) of developing electricity when excited by friction or by other means.

Originally the word had reference only to the property of attracting light bodies, even the phenomenon of electrical repulsion being a later discovery (Gilbert indeed mentions the non-existence of such a phenomenon as an evidence of a distinction between magnetism and electricity).

1646 SIR T. BROWNE *Pseud. Ep.* II. iv. 78 By Electrick bodies, I conceive..such as conveniently placed unto their objects attract all bodies palpable.

b. Charged with electricity, excited to electrical action. ***positively*** or ***negatively electric***: charged with positive or negative electricity.

2. a. Of the nature of, or pertaining to, electricity; producing, caused by, or operating by means of, electricity.

Except in the phrases in b, ELECTRICAL *a.* is now more usual in this sense. In some cases the choice between the two adjs. is somewhat arbitrarily restricted by usage: thus we usually say 'an *electrical* machine', but 'an *electric* battery'.

1675 NEWTON in Rigaud *Corr. Sci. Men* (1841) II. 377 The electric virtue of the glass. **1752** FRANKLIN *Lett.* Wks. 1840 V. 296 From electric fire..spirits may be kindled. **1803** *Med. Jrnl.* IX. 286 The electric power has efficacy sufficient to cure diseases. **1839** G. BIRD *Nat. Phil.* Introd. 28 The effects of chemical affinity and electric action being connected. **1851** CARPENTER *Man. Phys.* 464 A lady..who was for many months in an electric state so different from that of surrounding bodies, that, etc.

b. Forming phraseological comb. with sbs., esp. in many names of instruments for developing, measuring, illustrating, or applying electricity, and of machines, etc. in which electricity serves as the motive or controlling power, as in ***electric alarm, annunciator, clock, escapement, furnace, fuse, governor, heater, lamp, pendulum, railway, regulator, steam-gauge, telegraph, telegrapher*** (see these sbs.); **electric action** *Mus.*, the action of an organ in which the mechanical parts are operated by electricity; **electric arc**, the luminous electrified space between the points of two electrodes through which a powerful electric current is passing; also *attrib.*, as *electric-arc welding* (see also ARC WELDING); **electric atmosphere**, the space round electrical bodies within which they manifest their special properties; **electric balance**, an instrument for measuring the attractive or repulsive force of electrified bodies; **electric battery** (see BATTERY 10); **electric bell**, a bell operated by electricity; **electric blanket**, an electrically warmed blanket; **electric brake**, (in electrically driven vehicles) a brake operated by the temporary use of the driving motor as a generator, the resulting current being either returned to the supply line or dissipated as heat in a resistance; hence *electric braking*; **electric bridge**, an arrangement of electrical circuits used for measuring the resistance of an element of the circuit; **electric calamine** *Min.* (*U.S.*) = HEMIMORPHITE; **electric candle**, a form of electric-light apparatus in which the carbon pencils are parallel and separated by a layer of plaster of Paris; **electric car**, (*a*) *N. Amer.* a trolley car, (*b*) a motor car propelled by electrical power; **electric chair** *U.S.*, an instrument of capital punishment by electrocution; **electric charge**, the accumulation or condensation of electricity in a Leyden jar or the like; **electric chimes**, three bells suspended on a metal rod, rung by electricity; **electric circuit**, the passage of electricity from a body in one electric state to one in another through a conductor, also the conductor; **electric column**, a form of the voltaic pile; **electric conflict** (see quot.); **electric convulsive therapy** = *electro-convulsive therapy*; **electric cooker**, an electrically operated cooker; also *electric cooking*; **electric current**, the flow of electricity through a conducting body from the positive to the negative pole, or from a high to a low potential; **electric density** or **thickness**, the quantity of electricity found at any moment on a given surface; **electric discharge**, the escape of electricity from a Leyden jar or similar apparatus; also *attrib.*; **electric displacement**, see DISPLACEMENT 2 d; **electric eel** = GYMNOTUS; cf. *electrical eel* (ELECTRICAL *a.* 2); **electric egg**, an ellipsoidal glass egg, with metallic caps at either end, which, when exhausted of air, may by the action of an electrical machine be filled with faint violet light; **electric eye**, = *magic eye*, (*a*) a photo-electric cell on which a beam of light is directed, the interruption of which acts as a trigger for the operation of electric relays; (*b*) a miniature cathode-ray tube used as a tuning indicator in a radio receiver, etc.; **electric fan**, a fan driven by an electric motor; **electric fence**, a fence, often consisting of a single strand of wire, charged with electricity; hence *electric fencing*; also *fig.*; **electric field** (see FIELD *sb.* 17, quot. 1881); **electric fire**, (*a*) used by Franklin as = *electric fluid*; (*b*) an electric heater (mainly for domestic use); **electric fishes**, certain fishes that can give electric shocks; **electric fluid**, Franklin's term for a (supposed) subtle, imponderable, all-pervading fluid, the cause of electrical phenomena; **electric flux** (see quots.); **electric force**, the force with which electricity tends to move matter; **electric generator** (see GENERATOR 2, quot. 1879); **electric guitar**, a guitar in which the sound from the plucked strings is picked up electromagnetically or by means of a form of condenser microphone and then amplified; hence **electric guitarist**, one who plays the electric guitar; **electric hare**, a dummy hare made to run by electricity, used in greyhound racing; also *transf.* (quot. 1941); **electric harpoon**, one in which a bursting charge is exploded by electricity; **electric hedge** *nonce-wd.*, an invisible barrier charged with electricity (see *N. & Q.* (1959) CCIV. 338); **electric helix**, a screw-shaped coil of copper wire, used in forming an electro-magnet; **electric indicator**, indicating electro-magnetic currents; **electric iron**, an iron (sense 5) heated by an electric element; **electric kettle**, a kettle heated by electric power; **electric kite**, that devised by Franklin to attract electricity from the air; **electric lobe** (see quot. 1849); **electric locomotive**, an electrically driven railway locomotive engine, powered either by diesel-driven motors or from a contact wire or rail; cf. DIESEL-*electric* adj.; **electric log**, a ship's log registering by electricity; **electric machine**, usu. *spec.* a machine for developing frictional electricity; **electric mixer**, an electrically driven machine or mechanical contrivance for mixing food (cf. MIXER 2); **electric motor**, a motor (MOTOR *sb.* 3) for transforming electric energy into mechanical energy; **electric nerve** *Zool.* (see quot. 1940); **electric organ**, (*a*) *Zool.*: (see ORGAN *sb.*¹ 5, quot. 1773; also quot. 1851 s.v. ELECTRICAL *a.* 2); (*b*) *Mus.*, an organ [ORGAN *sb.*¹ 2] with an electric action; **electric piano**, a piano, or an instrument resembling this, in which the mechanism is worked or the sounds are produced electronically; **electric potential** [POTENTIAL B. 4], see quots. 1941 and 1962; **electric power** (cf. POWER *sb.*¹ 14); **electric precipitation** = *electrical precipitation*; **electric range** [RANGE *sb.*¹ 12], an electric cooker; **electric ray** (*a*) = TORPEDO; (*b*) = *electric wave*; **electric razor**, a razor operated by electricity; **electric recording** = *electrical recording*; so *electric record*; **electric regulator**, for stopping or starting a machine by electro-magnetic circuit; **electric residue**, a second charge that tends to arise in a discharged Leyden jar; **electric resistance**, the opposition offered by a body to the passage of an electric current through it (the reverse of conductivity); **electric shaver** = *electric razor*; **electric shock**, the

effect on the animal body of a sudden discharge from a Leyden jar, etc.; also *attrib.*, esp. of medical treatment by means of an electric shock (cf. *shock therapy*, *treatment*; *electro-shock*); **electric sign**, a sign illuminated by electricity; **electric signal**, a signal conveyed by electric influence; **electric spark**, the luminous discharge from the conductor of an electrical machine to a pointed body presented to it; **electric steel** (see quot. 1919); **electric storm** *Meteorol.*, a violent disturbance of the electrical condition of the atmosphere, often causing interference with electrical transmissions; **electric strength**, the stress, usually expressed in kilovolts per millimetre, which an insulating material can withstand without breakdown; dielectric strength; also, the property of withstanding such stress (cf. STRENGTH *sb.* 1 j, esp. quot. 1873); **electric stress** (see quot. 1943); **electric switch**, a device for interrupting or dividing one circuit and transferring it or part of it to another circuit, a commutator; **electric tension**, the strain or pressure exerted upon a dielectric in the neighbourhood of an electrified body; **electric timeball**, a large hollow globe dropped at a particular time by an electric circuit; **electric toaster**, a toaster operated by electricity; **electric toothbrush**, a toothbrush which is controlled by electricity; **electric torch**, (*a*) a gas-lighter operated by electricity (Knight *Dict. Mech. a* 1877); (*b*) a contrivance consisting essentially of an electric lamp enclosed in a portable case containing a battery; **electric traction** (see quot. 1940); **electric train**, a train operated by electricity; **electric tramway**, a tramway operated by electricity; **electric typewriter**, a typewriter operated by electricity (*Funk's Stand. Dict.*, 1893); **electric wand**, a baton-shaped electrophorus; **electric wave**, an electrical wave (see WAVE *sb.* 5 a, esp. quot. 1889); **electric welding** = *electric-arc welding*; **electric wind** = AURA 3 b; **electric wires**, those of the electric telegraph.

1889 *Cent. Dict.*, *Electric action. **1948** *Penguin Music Mag.* VII. 25 Electric action..and similar delights enable modern organists to gambol through Bach fugues at a hair-raising speed. **1885** *Electrician* 31 July p. iv. (Advt.), *Electric Arc Lamps. **1893** *Operator & Electrical World* XXII. 14 (*title*) *Electric arc welding and metal working. **1936** *Economist* 18 Jan. 150/2 Its business in electrodes, a natural consequence of the development of electric-arc welding. **1879** G. PRESCOTT *Sp. Telephone* 104 A wire bearing an electric current seems to be for the time surrounded by an *electric atmosphere. **1887** *Nature* 29 Sept. 522/1 New *electric balances. These balances are founded on the mutual forces, discovered by Ampère, between the fixed and movable portions of an electric circuit. **1795** *Gentl. Mag.* LXV. 141/2 Perhaps the *electric batteries..may be realized. **1946** *Whittaker's Electr. Engin. Pocket-Bk.* (ed. 7) 859 (*heading*) Commercial electric battery vehicles. **1877** *Telegraphic Jrnl.* V. 7/2 The *Manchester Evening News* says that the *electric bell system has been carried out..at the Manchester City Hall. **1891** A. E. KENNEDY in *Electr. in Daily Life* 239 The first application of electricity to household purposes was presented by the electric bell early in the [19th] century. **1930** *Punch* 16 Apr. 425/1 Had a rotten night. My *electric blanket fused and I had to get up to mend it. **1938** S. R. ROGET *Dict. Electr. Terms* (ed. 3) 34/1 *Electric blanket*, a blanket having woven into it resistance wires by which a certain amount of warming effect can be procured by a current. **1959** *B.S.I. News* Feb. 6/2 The Home Secretary was asked recently in the Commons if he was aware of the number of fires and accidents caused by electric blankets. **1885** *Electrician* 3 July 147/2 Arrangements are being made to render this *electric brake automatic, so that the main circuit will be broken and the brake circuit with the motors closed automatically. **1910** *Stand. Handbk. Electr. Engin.* (ed. 3) 986 An efficiency of 60 per cent could be obtained during retardation by *electric braking. **1836** W. T. BRANDE *Man. Chem.* (ed. 4) II. 860 Silicate of Zinc occurs native under the name of *electric calamine. **1946** J. R. PARTINGTON *Gen. & Inorg. Chem.* xv. 383 The hydrated silicate..is electric calamine or hemimorphite. **1888** F. M. A. ROE *Army Lett.* (1909) 366 Most of my outings are on the *electric cars. **1899** 'MARK TWAIN' in *Cosmopolitan* XXVII. 592 The merry electric car replaced the melancholy bus. **1901** *Daily Colonist* (Victoria, B.C.) 27 Oct. 1/4 An electric car ran into a cow last night near Cedar Cottage. **1947** *Newsweek* 8 Sept. 85/3 Electric cars would do in town. **1966** *Economist* 17 Dec. 1246/3 The motor car companies are working hard to improve the battery—the main block in the way of an electric car. **1889** *Peel City Guardian* 8 June 6/2 The preparations, which are to consist of taking a seat in an *electric chair. **1903** *N.Y. Even. Post.* 28 Oct. 12 Two men were sentenced to die in the electric chair. **1948** *Chicago Daily News* 18 Sept. 3/6 A 24-year-old former convict..must die in the electric chair. **1767** J. PRIESTLEY *Hist. Electr.* VIII. 651 The conductors which form an *electric circuit. **1782** *Brit. Pat. 1318* 3 Making the part..a portion of that electric circuit. **1879** G. PRESCOTT *Sp. Telephone* 5 The telephone is a device for transmitting..over an electric circuit..various kinds of sound. **1845** *Brit. Pat. 10,838* 1 Improvements in *Electric Clocks. **1884** F. BRITTEN *Watch & Clockm.* 100 Electric clocks may be divided into three classes. **1922** JOYCE *Ulysses* 109 They ought to have..an electric clock or a telephone in the coffin. **1814** G. J. SINGER *Elem. Electr.* I. i. 27 The *electric column (invented by J. A. De Luc, esq.)..consists of 800 or 1000 small discs, of silver, zinc, and paper. **1840** *Ann. Electr. Magn. & Chem.* IV. 43 The dry electric column ..will emit sparks and charge coated glass. **1823** J. BADCOCK *Dom. Amusem.* 126 A zinc plate..was immersed in the liquid, and a wire united the extremities of the pile: the effect produced hereby, was termed the *electric conflict. **1953** HINSIE & SHATZKY *Psychiatric Dict.* (ed. 2) 767/1 *Electric convulsive therapy, or E.C.T., is indicated in mania, depressions, and certain cases of schizophrenia. **1963** H. BURN *Drugs, Med. & Man* (ed. 2) xi. 122 Treatment by taking a certain number of tablets each day is much pleasanter than electric convulsion therapy, but electric convulsion therapy is still retained for those patients in whom the drugs are ineffective. **1907** *Electr. Bull.* Jan. 5/1 Tell your husband it was that wretched gas stove and by and bye he will send home an *electric cooker. **1933** *Archit. Rev.* LXXIV. p. xlii, What is the outstanding fact about an ordinary electric cooker? Its capacity for being switched on and off. **1907** *Electr. Bull.* May 9/1 The..most promising field for the introduction of *electric cooking methods is the first-class hotel. *Ibid.* 9/2 Electric cooking will not appreciably increase the room temperature. **1837** BREWSTER *Magnet.* 307 The influence of *electric currents. **1863** TYNDALL *Heat* i. 19 The existence and direction of an electric current are shown by its action upon a freely suspended magnetic needle. **1935** *Economist* 23 Mar. 690/2 There is no doubt that the electric lighting of streets has made a very big step forward by the use of the *electric discharge lamp, which..illuminates roads without any dark patches. **1794** R. J. THORNTON *Med. Extracts* (1796) I. II. xii. 121 Vandelott makes two species of the *electric eel, the black and reddish. **1881** *Encycl. Brit.* XII. 650/1 The electric eel is the most powerful of electric fishes. **1954** G. DURRELL *3 Singles to Adv.* ix. 205 The rare specimen turned out to be a baby electric eel, some two feet long. **1868** *Q. Jrnl. Sci.* V. 117 Electric discharge in vacuo, such as..an *electric egg. **1877** *Phil. Mag.* III. 176 P. Thiess attempts to derive the action of the electric egg from the fact that the air which surrounds the electrode is charged with the electricity. **1930** *Electronics* Aug. 216/2 '*Electric Eye' for Glass Industry..a photo-electric cell for determining weak spots in glass construction. **1933** *Ibid.* Apr. 103/1 (*heading*) Bar and rod heating controlled by an electric eye. *Ibid.*, Valve-stem heaters are also available with electric-eye control. **1937** *Daily Express* 3 Mar. 5/2 Take this 'electric eye', for example. We're installing it in the hotel driveway to warn people in the street whenever a car's coming out. **1966** *Punch* 23 Nov. 784/1 The period is obviously some time in the future..: electric eyes open the average door. **1883** *Electr. Light* 1 Mar. 173/1 *Electric fans. The small electric motors..have been ingeniously applied, under a patent recently taken out, to the working of fans for drawing-room use. **1905** A. BENNETT *Sacred & Profane Love* II. iv. 168 The electric fans revolved ceaselessly. **1901** L. G. BROWN *Among Tuaregs* in D. Ker *Knight of Honour* 46 'It is my *electric fence,' he replied. **1944** G. HENDERSON *Farming Ladder* xv. 174 The calves..are confined with a single, thin strand of wire, electrically charged, and which they graze up to, but do not touch. We are great believers in electric fences. **1952** M. MCCARTHY *Groves of Academe* (1953) vi. 98 Her personality was posted with all sorts of No Trespassing signs and criss-crossed with electric fences, which repelled the intruder with a smart shock. **1958** *Times* 26 May 9/7 Electric fences are used everywhere and the grass so saved conserved as silage or hay. **1942** *Farming Handbk.* 41 Considerable success has been reported from several quarters with *electric fencing. **1943** *Gloss. Terms Telecomm.* (*B.S.I.*) 4 In contradistinction [to electric circuit], an *electric field implies action which can only be specified uniquely in terms of time and two or three dimensions. **1962** CORSON & LORRAIN *Introd. Electromagn. Fields* ii. 29 We define the electric field intensity E to be the force per unit charge exerted on a test charge in a field. **1921** *Spectator* 9 Apr. 455/1 A 'Magicoal' *electric fire, a device which..deceives our short-sighted friends into believing that we are burning an unconscionable amount of the best coal. **1933** *Sunday Referee* 2 July 16/2 In the living-room is ..a ply-wood built-in book-case, at one end of which is an electric fire. *c* **1790** IMISON *Sch. Arts* I, The *electric fluid with which the conductor is overloaded, repels the electric fluid from those parts of the threads, &c. which are next to it. **1854** LARDNER *Mus. Sc. & Art* III. 119 The electric fluid is deposited in a latent state in unlimited quantity in the earth, the waters, the atmosphere. [**1904** GOODCHILD & TWENEY *Technol. & Sci. Dict.* 230/2 *Flux* (Elect.), the total number of lines of force which pass through any given space or cross any given area.] **1904** *Electr. Rev.* (N.Y.) 24 Dec. 1040/1 (*title*) A hydrodynamic model of *electric flux. **1934** WEBSTER, *Electric flux*, the flux existing in the space between charged bodies. **1885** *Electrician* 9 Oct. 411/2 A dynamo electric machine..will permit of the establishment of the *electric furnace on a larger scale. **1937** *Discovery* May 153/2 There is an increasing tonnage of high speed steel being melted in the high frequency electric furnace. **1938** *Oxf. Compan. Mus.* 288/1 *Electric Guitars, Mandolins, &c., were by 1936 on the market. **1940** *Sears, Roebuck Spring & Summer Catal.* 561 Give your guitar the volume and tone of an electric guitar. **1959** H. HOBSON *Mission House Murder* ii. 13 A nice, clean, unusual noise from vibraharp, electric guitar, a piano and a..bass-viol. **1957** *Observer* 1 Dec. 14/2 The Negro *electric-guitarist Charlie Christian, who died in 1942 [etc.]. **1927** *Punch* 27 July 85/3 A greyhound race at the White City had to be re-run last week because the *electric hare ran too fast. **1941** *Hutchinson's Pict. Hist. War* 19 Mar.–13 May 219 An ingenious device now in operation for the training of air gunners is an 'electric hare' plane. Mounted on a truck, it is run at high speed round the track while the gunner works from a mobile turret. *a* **1877** KNIGHT *Dict. Mech.* I. 780/2 **Electric heater*, a device in which a fine platinum wire heated by a passing electric current is made to communicate sensible heat as a means of warming or burning, as the case may be. **1935** *Discovery* May 145/1 A small electric heater is placed under the table. **1921** G. B. SHAW *Back to Methuselah* IV. I. 169 *The Elderly Gentleman*:.. When I tried to step off the pier on to the road, I received a shock, followed by an attack of pins and needles which ceased only when I stepped back on to the stones. *Zoo*: Yes: there is an *electric hedge there. It is a very old and very crude method of keeping animals from straying. **1907** *Electr. Bull.* Aug. 32/2 (*heading*) *Electric Irons. *Ibid.*, Ironing benches, each equipped with an electric iron. **1920** *Whittaker's Electr. Engin. Pocket-Bk.* (ed. 4) 491 The average loading of an electric iron is 70 to 80 watts per lb. [**1907** *Yesterday's Shopping* (1969) 270 Electric Copper Kettle.] **1910** H. G. WELLS *New Machiavelli* II. iv. 252 Everything was put ready for me to make tea..*electric kettle, infuser, biscuits. **1965** M. ERSKINE *Take Dark Journey* vi. 68 The electric kettle was plugged in..but not turned on. **1856** *Brit. Pat. 2456* 1 We, Joseph Lacassagne, Chemist, and Rodolphe Thiers, Manufacturer,..do hereby declare the nature of the said Invention for 'An Improved *Electric Lamp', to be as follows [etc.]. **1882** *Electric Light* 1 June 21/1 Incandescent lamps, in which a carbon thread is enclosed in a glass bulb..form the safest kind of electric lamp. **1849** NOAD *Electricity* (ed. 3) 461 Of the four lobes of the brain, the fourth only is found to actuate the electric current; it is hence called the *electric lobe. **1935** *Discovery* Nov. 327/2 A special brain-centre [in the Electric torpedo fish] known as the electric lobe. The organ as a whole resembles a beehive, for the electrogenic units or elements are grouped in batteries of prismatic form. **1884** *Pop. Sci. Monthly* XXIV. 745 This motor is connected with the driving-wheels by gearing, belting, [etc.]..so that its revolution produces..a consequent progressive motion of the *electric locomotive. **1760** WESLEY *Desideratum: Electr. Made Plain* 35 That the *Electric Machine may as properly be term'd a Fire-Pump, as Mr. Boyle's Machine, an Air Pump? **1933** *Pop. Sci.* Jan. 50/1 *Electric Mixer... Driven by a small motor, this new kitchen utensil..is said to cause no radio interference. **1959** *Which?* June 44/1 Many women who have long ago accepted every other kind of electric domestic gadget seem to be still vehemently divided about the merits of the electric mixer. **1886** *Electrician* 15 Jan 194/1 With *electric motors..one has to be contented with a much lower efficiency. **1936** *Discovery* Aug. 238/1 Each of the shutters for the nine lenses is actuated by an individual electric motor. **1935** *Ibid.* Nov. 329/2 (*caption*) Cross section of *Malopterurus electricus*. Nfe, *electric nerve; oe, electric organ. **1940** *Chambers's Techn. Dict.* 285/2 *Electric nerve*, a modified motor nerve, serving an electric tissue. **1870** ROLLESTON *Anim. Life* Introd. 128 *Electric organs of Fishes. **1944** J. S. HUXLEY *On Living in Rev.* iv. 50 The eel's electric organs. **1885** *Electr. Engin.* Mar. 149/1 We are enabled to imagine in our houses..*electric pianos and organs. **1886** *Telegraphic Jrnl.* 17 Sept. 294/2 (*caption*) An electric organ. **1936** *Discovery* July 223/2 This cupboard full of valves replaces, in the Coupleux electric organ, the pipe-chest of the ordinary organ. **1885** *Electric piano [see *electric organ*]. **1927** A. HUXLEY *Let.* 17 May (1969) 286 Everything happening to the strains of the steam organs and electric pianos of the inevitable Flemish kermesse. **1938** A. E. WIER *Macmillan Encycl. Mus.* 519 *Electric piano*, an instrument to which the principle of electric amplification is applied; the sound-board and tri-chord strings are dispensed with, and a microphone picks up the sound from the strings in groups of five. **1969** *It* 13–28 June 12/2 Eclection were seen for the first time with new member John Palmer, who plays excellent flute and vibes but rather erratic electric piano. **1871** *English Mechanic* 12 May 193/1 With *electric potentials of less amount than sufficient to decompose water, they can be charged and discharged like condensers. **1902** Electric potential [see POTENTIAL B. 4]. **1902** *Encycl. Brit.* XXX. 449/1 A transverse difference of electric potential (Hall effect). **1941** S. R. ROGET *Dict. Electr. Terms* (ed. 4) 282/2 *Electric potential*, the quality, analogous to pressure, which tends to cause a flow of electricity from a point where it is higher to a point where it is lower. **1962** S. HANDEL *Dict. Electronics* 112 *Electric potential*, of a point, the potential difference between the point and some equipotential surface, usually that of the earth which is chosen to have zero potential. **1883** *Encycl. Brit.* XX. 249/2 The first attempt to apply *electric power for propulsion on railways was made ..in 1842. **1922** *Ibid.* XXX. 955/2 A Departmental Committee..on electric power supply was formed. *Ibid.* 958/1 The latest statistics available for Canada..show 795 central electric power stations. **1956** A. H. COMPTON *Atomic Quest* v. 340 Electric power came from curiosity about the relation between electricity and magnetism. **1920** *Whittaker's Electr. Engin. Pocket-Bk.* (ed. 4) 651 The *Electric Precipitation of Smoke and Fumes... The precipitation of dust and fume suspended in gases, by means of the electrostatic field..has only been applied to industrial purposes within the last six years. **1882** *Proc. R. Inst. Gt. Brit.* X. 69 Siemens' Lichterfelde *Electric Railway, now running at Berlin. **1902** *Encycl. Brit.* XXVI. 228/1 An overhead electric railway runs from the Zoologischer Garten to the Schlesisches Thor. **1921** *Daily Colonist* (Victoria, B.C.) 26 Mar. 3/1 A complete little home, 4-room, modern and almost new..hot water heating system and *very good *electric range*. **1922** *Encycl. Brit.* XXX. 957/2 Another activity curtailed by the war was the organized sale of electric ranges. **1774** J. WALSH in *Philos. Trans. R. Soc.* LXIV. 464 The Torpedo, or *Electric Ray, frequents the shores of this island, contrary to a received opinion among Naturalists. **1862** COUCH *Brit. Fishes* I. 119. **1880** *Encycl. Brit.* XII. 649/2 The electric rays (*Torpedinidæ*). **1896** *Pearson's Mag.* II. 754/2 A solid wall..is very transparent to the electric ray. **1897** *Strand Mag.* Mar. 273/1 Electric rays or waves..will penetrate all substances at all distances. **1958** G. DURRELL *Encounters with Animals* II. 88 The electric-ray or torpedo-fish, a curious creature that looks rather like a frying-pan run over by a steam-roller. **1933** *Chambers's Jrnl.* Dec. 1007/1 (*caption*) A Vibrating *Electric Razor. **1945** S. LEWIS *Cass Timberlane* (1946) xxi. 126 She made coffee for them, and she lent them an electric razor. **1926** *Glasgow Herald* 16 Dec. 13/6 Columbia introduced *Electric Recording into Great Britain... This is the first Christmas that a..programme of *Electric Records has been available for the gramophone. **1940** F. & R. LOCKRIDGE *Norths meet Murder* iii. 55 He..had recently bought an *electric shaver. **1959** *Listener* 30 July 161/1 Infra-red cookers, electric shavers, sterophonic amplifiers. **1767** J. PRIESTLEY *Hist. Electr.* p. xiii, The *electric shock itself..will appear almost as surprising, as any discovery that he [*sc.* Sir Isaac Newton] made. **1779** J. WEDGWOOD *Let.* 8 Nov. (1965) 244 The Doctor gives us great hopes of our poor little girl's limbs being restored, even without the assistance of the electric shocks. **1802** PALEY *Nat. Theol.* xix. (1817) 166 Power of giving the electric shock. **1839** G. BIRD *Nat. Phil.* 230 Electricity..will discharge itself through his arms, producing an electric shock. **1881** [see COLLOQUIALISM 2]. **1934** H. C. WARREN *Dict. Psychol.* 90/2 *Electric shock method*, a variety of the method of punishment in animal training, whereby a habit is broken or a new habit formed by applying an electric shock at some point in the behavior series. **1947** P. L. HARRIMAN *Dict. Psychol.* 118 *Electric-shock therapy*, treatment of mental disorders by electric shocks to the head of the patient. **1958** *Listener* 13 Nov.

799/1 The inventor of electric shock treatment. **1907** *Electr. Bull.* Jan. 31 (Advt.), Art Fittings, Lamps..*Electric Signs and Letters. **1937** *Discovery* July 217/1 Electric signs, posters, magazines, catalogues, all use the appeal of colour to enhance their commercial value. **1812** SIR H. DAVY *Chem. Philos.* 105 When two in volume of this gas, and one in volume of oxygene, are acted upon by an *electric spark, over mercury, they inflame. **1909** *Cent. Dict.* Suppl. I. 415/1 *Electric steel process. **1919** E. HENDRICK *Chem. Everyday Life* xi. 99 Electric steel is the latest method whereby the steel is heated, and the required ingredients added in an electric furnace. **1872** F. M. A. ROE *Army Lett.* (1909) 52 There was a terrific rain and *electric storm last evening. **1906** *Springfield Weekly Republ.* 14 June 16 A severe electric storm, accompanied by a high wind, swept over Springfield. **1944** 'G. GRAHAM' *Earth & High Heaven* 277 'Must have been a bad electric storm lately,' he remarked. **1934** WEBSTER, *Electric strength. **1886** *Electrician* 15 Jan. 187/1 U_1 is the intensity of the *electric stress. **1935** *Discovery* July 213/2 The behaviour of air, solids, liquids and the vacuum respectively as dielectrics when under high electric stress. **1943** *Gloss. Terms Electr. Engin. (B.S.I.)* 12 *Electric stress*, the stress occurring in an insulating material when subjected to an electric force. **1913** *Technical World Mag.* 152 (Advt.), The economy *electric toaster. **1926** *Daily Colonist* (Victoria, B.C.) 3 July 10/2 (Advt.), Upright Electric Toasters. Will toast two pieces at the one time. Heavy nickelplated finish. **1951** *Catal. of Exhibits, S. Bank Exhib., Festival of Britain* 133/2 Automatic electric toaster. **1936** *Punch* 20 Apr. 478/2 The latest invention is an *electric toothbrush. **1963** *Which?* Dec. 374/2 An electric toothbrush is not very different in principle from an ordinary toothbrush. You still have a stick with a brush on the end, but instead of moving the brush by hand, the brush is driven by a small electric motor. **1875** *English Mechanic* 9 July 441/3 (*title*) Frictional *electric torch. **1902** *Windsor Mag.* June p. xxv/2 (Advt.), The 'Ever-Ready' Portable Electric Torch. **1925** E. F. NORTON *Fight for Everest, 1924* v. 102 Somervell and I had to carry..a light rucksack apiece, with compass, electric torch, [etc.]. **1888** *Encycl. Brit.* XXIII. 495/2 Another method of effecting *electric traction is to carry a store of energy on the car or on a special locomotive. **1940** *Chambers's Techn. Dict.* 286/1 *Electric traction*, the operation of a railway or road vehicle by means of electric motors, which obtain their power from an overhead contact wire or from generators or batteries mounted on the vehicle. **1901** *Trans. Amer. Inst. Electr. Engin. 1900* XVII. 90 In the future there may be a..tendency to reduce the weight of *electric trains. **1908** A. BENNETT *Buried Alive* vi. 139 The roar of an electric train. **1939** 'R. CROMPTON' *William & A.R.P.* vii. 185 'Steal that electric train of his he's always swankin' about,' suggested Ginger. **1885** *Electrician* 3 July 146/2 With *electric tramways the energy (electricity) is conveyed from the generating station to the rails. **1958** *Oxf. Mail* 30 Sept. 10/5 Apart from the fact that an *electric typewriter makes typing easier and faster, many more clear carbon copies can be obtained than on an ordinary typewriter. **1964** T. L. KINSEY *Audio-Typing & Electric Typewriters* iv. 35 It takes twenty-two times more mechanical energy to operate a manual typewriter than it does to operate an IBM electric typewriter. **1871** *Leisure Hour* 18 Nov. 720/2 The *electric wave, produced by a few pieces of copper and zinc. **1895** S. P. THOMPSON *Electr. & Magn.* (new ed.) II. xiv. §516 In the case of true electric waves, portions of the energy of the current..are thrown off. **1902** *Encycl. Brit.* XXVIII. 55/2 Electric waves must be passing through the dielectric surrounding a condenser in the act of discharging. **1890** *Times* 17 Jan. 3/3 *Electric Welding..is the invention of Professor Elihu Thomson, of Lynn, United States... The development of electric welding in America has been rapid. **1907** [see WELDING *vbl. sb.*[1] 3]. **1930** *Engineering* 8 Aug. 164/1 The chapter..giving ..information on..electric and gas welding. **1899** *Phil. Mag.* XLVIII. 401 (*title*) On the velocity and mass of the ions in the *electric wind in air. **1854** DICKENS *Hard T.* II. vi. (C.D. ed.) 115 The *electric wires..ruled a colossal strip of music-paper out of the evening sky.

3. *fig.* Chiefly with reference to the swiftness of electricity, or to the thrilling effect of the electric shock; also in obvious metaphorical uses of the phrases in 2 b.

1793 COLERIDGE *Songs of Pixies* v, The electric flash, that from the melting eye Darts the fond question or the soft reply. **1819** L. HUNT *Indicator* No. 6 We..feel the electric virtue of his [Shakspere's] hand. **1830** SIR J. HERSCHEL *Stud. Nat. Phil.* I. ii. (1851) 29 The effect on all on board might well be conceived to have been electric. **1831** CARLYLE *Sart. Res.* (1858) 175 Wait a little, till the entire nation is in an electric state. **1871** PALGRAVE *Lyr. Poems* 133 A thrill of electric pain Smote through each English breast.

4. electric blue: a trade name for a steely-blue colour used for textile fabrics; also, a brilliant light blue; also in extended use and *ellipt.* **electric green** = *electric blue.*

1873 *Young Englishwoman* Feb. 77/1 One model..is of bronze velvet and electric green silk. **1882** *Queen* 23 Dec. (Advt.), Opera hood..Black, Brown, Cream, Pale Blue, and Electric. **1893** *Ladies' Home Jrnl.* Oct. 2/2 Her preference is for subdued tints, her favorite color being a soft shade of electric blue. **1912** *Queen* 4 May 750/2 Lady Mary C. in electric-blue cloth with black and white hat. **1955** *Times* 9 July 3/3 A huge black fish with a brilliant electric blue tail.

5. *Comb.*, as †*electric-magnetic* = ELECTRO-MAGNETIC.

1823 J. BADCOCK *Dom. Amusem.* 71 Ascribing to the influence of electric magnetic causes the accuracy with which he succeeds in all his experiments.

B. *sb.*

1. A substance in which the electric force can be excited and accumulated by friction. See A. I.

1646 SIR T. BROWNE *Pseud. Ep.* 81 Our other discourse of Electricks concerneth a generall opinion touching Jet and Amber. **1664** POWER *Exp. Philos.* II. 133 The effluviums of an Electrick upon its retreat, pluck up Straws. **1748** FRANKLIN *Lett.* Wks. 1840 V. 211 Air is an electric *per se.* **1832** *Nat. Phil.* II. *Electric* iii. §56. 14 (Usef. Knowl. Soc.) The essential parts of..an electrical machine..are the electric, the rubber, etc. **1870** R. FERGUSON *Electr.* 51 The term electrics is applied to those substances which, when held in the hands and rubbed, become electric.

2. ***positive* (*negative*) *electrics***: = electro-positive (-negative) substances.

1842 TURNER *Chem.* (ed. 7) 130 *Negative Electrics*—Oxygen, Sulphur, Nitrogen..*Positive Electrics*—Potassium-Sodium, Lithium, etc.

3. Short for (*a*) ***electric lamp, light***; (*b*) ***electric motor car, railway, tramcar***, etc.; (*c*) ***electric circuit***; (*d*) ***electric company shares.***

1886 *Harper's Mag.* July 314/1 The light of common day ..is preferable to any manner of..alabaster lamps, or even the latest improvement in electrics. **1890** *Boston* (Mass.) *Jrnl.* 3 Mar. 1/7 Do the electrics travel too fast for the public safety? **1892** S. HALE *Lett.* (1919) 269 There are cables, and electrics, but these haven't entirely driven out the horse. **1896** *New Peterson Mag.* Jan. 65/2 [They] would no more enter an 'electric' than they would give up wearing mitts all day. **1897** KIPLING *Capt. Cour.* 215 Harvey..was asleep before his father could shade the electrics. **1905** E. GLYN *Viciss. Evangeline* 166 In the twinkle of an eye we were rolling in the electric to Willis's. **1909** *Westm. Gaz.* 2 Sept. 9/1 Underground electrics. **1916** E. WALLACE *Clue Twisted Candle* (1917) xiii. 149 He felt for the switch of the electric. **1924** S. GLASPELL *Fidelity* iv. 33 She told him..that Mrs. Blair had come for Mrs. Franklin in her 'electric' and they had gone to a tea. **1931** *Economist* 10 Jan. 78/2 Rates, especially for electrics, potash and stores, were far below the level of the beginning of December. **1946** A. PHELPS *I couldn't care Less* xiv. 118 Checking some of the other electrics and finding them working I realized..there must be a break in that circuit somewhere. **1947** *Jrnl. R. Aeronaut. Soc.* LI. 92/2 Electrics in the small and medium aircraft may absorb only a small fraction of the auxiliary power load. **1959** *Engineering* 16 Jan. 86/2 Booklets on glass fibre, yacht electrics, sail rigs. **1961** *Countryman* LVIII. 435 Last summer I returned, glad to find so much the same, except for 'the electric' which stretches its ugly spider poles to every croft. **1963** *Sunday Times* (Colour Suppl.) 7/1 He tried to lower his flaps part way—forgetting, in the anxiety of the moment, that without electrics his flap position indicator would not work. **1970** *Which?* May 143/1 The electrics are described as 'solid state', which means they use printed circuits instead of wires.

electrical (ɪ'lɛktrɪkəl), *a.* [f. prec. + -AL[1].]

†**1.** = ELECTRIC A. 1 a. *Obs.*

1635 N. CARPENTER *Geog. Del.* I. iii. 54 Electricall bodies drawe and attract not without rubbing and stirring vp of the matter first. **1646** SIR T. BROWNE *Pseud. Ep.* 86 Bodies electricall, whose emissions are lesse subtile. **1744** BERKELEY *Siris* §243 The phænomena of electrical bodies, the laws and variations of magnetism.

b. = ELECTRIC A. 1 b.

1813 SIR H. DAVY *Agric. Chem.* ii. (1814) 39 When a piece of sealing wax..gains the power of attracting light bodies.. it is said to be electrical. **1813** BAKEWELL *Introd. Geol.* (1815) 313 The smoke and vapour of volcanoes are highly electrical. *c*1860 FARADAY *Forces Nat.* v. 129 It is so electrical that it will scarcely leave my hand unless to go to the other.

2. (The usual modern sense.) Relating to or connected with electricity; also, of the nature of electricity. Sometimes used in the combinations mentioned under ELECTRIC A. 2 b, in most of which, however, *electric* is more usual; exceptions are ***electrical machine, electrical eel***; **electrical engineer**, an engineer devoting himself to electrical aspects of engineering; **electrical engineering**, the work done by, or the profession of, an electrical engineer; **electrical precipitation**, precipitation of a substance, esp. in a gas, by the action of a uni-directional electric field; cf. *electric precipitation*; **electrical recording** (see quot. 1940).

1746 W. WATSON *Sequel to Experiments in Electr.* 32 If the electrical machine is placed upon originally-electrics, the man..gives no sign of being electrified. **1747** WESLEY *Wks.* (1872) II. 73, I went..to see..the Electrical experiments. **1747** FRANKLIN *Lett.* Wks. 1840 V. 182 Draw off the electrical fire. **1748** *Ibid.* 210 A turkey is to be killed for our dinner by the electrical shock. **1775** *Phil. Trans. R. Soc.* LXV. I. 102 An Account of the *Gymnotus Electricus*, or Electrical Eel. **1793** SMEATON *Edystone L.* Cont. 14 No damage, except to a part of the Electrical Strap. **1802** BINGLEY *Anim. Biog.* (1813) III. 7 The electrical gymnotus or eel. **1803** *Edin. Rev.* I. 195 The electrical pile. **1812** SIR H. DAVY *Chem. Philos.* 104 Wires for passing the electrical spark. *Ibid.* 129 The electrical balance of Coulomb. *Ibid.* 169 The electrical column, formed of zinc, Dutch leaf, and paper. **1818** MRS. SHELLEY *Frankenst.* i. (1865) 42 He constructed a small electrical machine. **1822** IMISON *Sc. & Art* I. 463 When many of these..jars are connected together, it is called an electrical battery. **1836** MACGILLIVRAY tr. *Humboldt's Trav.* xv. 196 Electrical eels ..abound in the..confluents of the Orinoco. **1842** *Brit. Pat. 9465* 40 For connecting any number of distant clocks together in the manner of what are called electrical clocks, so that they will all move with an exact uniformity. **1845** DARWIN *Voy. Nat.* iii. (1879) 62 Is it not possible that the mixture of large bodies of fresh and salt water may disturb the electrical equilibrium? **1851** CARPENTER *Man. Phys.* 462 In..Electrical fishes, the electric organs are supplied with nerves of very great size. **1883** (*title*) The Electrical Engineer, a Journal of Electrical Engineering. *Ibid.* 1 May 3/1 In view of the larger extension of electrical interests..we have deemed it advisable to alter the title ['Electric Light'] to 'The Electrical Engineer'. **1883** *Pop. Sci. Monthly* XXIV. 255 Electrical engineering..embraces a knowledge of cables, telegraphy, electric lighting, electrical measurement. *a*1891 *Mod.* Are there any electrical books in the library? **1912** *Metall. & Chem. Engin.* X. 686/2 Electrical precipitation of suspended particles... Review of the processes of condensing dust and fume by means of high-tension electric current. These processes are the invention of Dr. F. G. Cottrell. **1925** *'His Master's Voice' Album Ser.* No. 3 The Rose Cavalier..Electrical Recording. **1930** *Engineering* 27 June 833/3 Considerable progressive development could be recorded in the use of electrical precipitation plants. **1935** *Discovery* Apr. 111/2 This new and valuable testing instrument..put into its hands by the electrical engineer. **1940** *Chambers's Techn. Dict.* 286/1 *Electrical recording*, the use of amplified currents from microphones for operating electromagnetic or electrodynamic drives for the cutting stylus in wax recording. **1965** M. MORSE *Unattached* i. 18 A large electrical-engineering firm.

3. *fig.* Cf. ELECTRIC 3.

1775 SHERIDAN *Rivals* II. i, The atmosphere becomes electrical. **1814** SCOTT *Wav.* I. iv. 59 The electrical shock caused by the discovery. **1873** LOWELL *Among my Bks.* Ser. II. 315 The leaves..seem to thrill our fingers with..the flutter of his electrical nerves.

†**4.** Skilled in the science of electricity. *Obs. rare.*

1757 E. DARWIN in *Phil. Trans.* L. 240 The author, having no electrical friend whose sagacity he could confide in.

electrically (ɪ'lɛktrɪkəlɪ), *adv.* [f. ELECTRICAL *a.* + -LY[2].] In an electrical manner.

1. In the manner of, by means of, or in relation to electricity.

1812 SIR H. DAVY *Chem. Philos.* 307 Points of platina are electrically ignited. **1854** SCOFFERN in *Orr's Circ. Sc.* Chem. 212 Glass and flannel have been electrically excited. **1861** SIR W. FAIRBAIRN *Addr. Brit. Assoc.*, Electrically, india-rubber possesses high advantages. **1873** B. STEWART *Conserv. Force* iii. 67 Metallic coatings..not electrically connected. **1883** *Daily News* 18 Sept. 3/7 The electrically-lighted marquee in Carlton-road.

2. *fig.* With suddenness, rapidity, or force as of electricity.

1842 LYTTON *Zanoni* 25 The orchestra—electrically sensitive to the impression of the audience. **1865** CARLYLE *Fredk. Gt.* V. xv. iii. 284 This electrically sudden operation on Prag. **1869** MRS. WHITNEY *Hitherto* xviii. 250 Why? she demanded electrically, like a thunder-clap.

†**e'lectricalness.** *Obs.*[—0] [f. as prec. + -NESS.] The state or quality of being electrical.

1736 BAILEY, *Electricalness*, attracting quality. Hence in mod. Dicts.

†**e'lectrice.** *Obs.* [a. F. *électrice*, fem. of *électeur* ELECTOR.] = ELECTRESS 1.

1695 *Lond. Gaz.* No. 3105/3 The Electrice of Bavaria.. has Miscarried. **1710** *Ibid.* No. 4742/2 He brought with him a Letter from the Electrice.

electrician (iːlɛk-, ɛlɛk'trɪʃən). [f. ELECTRIC + -IAN.] One who studies, or is versed in, the science of electricity; one who works with electrical instruments.

1751 FRANKLIN in *Phil. Trans.* XLVII. xliv. 291, I have not heard that any of your European electricians have been able to..do it. **1829** E. JESSE *Jrnl. Nat.* 368, I am no electrician. **1869** *Pall Mall G.* 31 Aug. 4 The electrician had gone to Brest to repair a fault in the French cable.

electricity (iːlɛk-, ɛlɛk'trɪsɪtɪ). [f. ELECTRIC + -ITY.]

1. In early use, the distinctive property of 'electric bodies', like amber, glass, etc., *i.e.*, their power when excited by friction to attract light bodies placed near them; also, the state of excitation produced in such bodies by friction. Subsequently the name was given to the cause of this phenomenon and of many others which were discovered to be of common origin with it, *e.g.* the electric spark, lightning, the galvanic current, etc. Franklin considered electric phenomena to be due to a subtle fluid diffused through all bodies, the excess of which above its normal quantity constituted 'positive electricity', and its deficiency below the normal quantity 'negative electricity'; but he also used 'electricity' as a name for the fluid itself. Others believed 'positive' and 'negative' electricity to be two distinct fluids, which when combined neutralized each other. Before the formulation of the present theory of atomic structure (see note to ATOM *sb.* 1), the prevailing view was that electricity is 'a peculiar condition either of the molecules of the electrified body or of the ether which surrounds them' (*Syd. Soc. Lex.*). The term 'electric fluid' survived for some time in popular language, and the names 'positive' and 'negative' electricity (also an inheritance from Franklin's theory) are still retained in scientific use.

Electricity may be developed by any means that produces disturbance of the molecular condition of bodies: by friction (*frictional electricity*), by chemical action (*galvanic electricity*), by heat (*thermal electricity*), by magnetism (*magnetic electricity*). Occasionally *electricity* and its related adjs. are used in a narrower sense with reference to the electricity produced by friction, as distinguished from galvanism or from magnetic or thermal electricity.

1646 SIR T. BROWNE *Pseud. Ep.* II. i. 51 Crystal will calefy into electricity; that is, a power to attract strawes or light bodies, and convert the needle freely placed. *Ibid.* 79 Saltes ..if gently warmed..will better discover their Electricities. **1668** *Phil. Trans.* III. 850 Observations about the Electricity of Bodies. **1736** BUTLER *Anal.* II. ii, Such powers in nature as magnetism and electricity. **1747** FRANKLIN *Lett.*

Wks. 1840 V. 195 Restoring the equilibrium in the bottle does not at all affect the electricity in the man. **1770** PRIESTLEY in *Phil. Trans.* LX. 209 The difference of the two electricities. **1794** J. HUTTON *Philos. Light, &c.* 232 Electricity..is distinctly different from both light and heat. **1803** *Med. Jrnl.* IX. 569, I began to use electricity, by small shocks. **1834** MRS. SOMERVILLE *Connex. Phys. Sc.* xxviii. (1849) 310 Electricity may be called into activity by mechanical power, by chemical action, by heat, and by magnetic influence. **1837** BREWSTER *Magnet.* 273 Feebler electricities will..produce the sheets of summer lightning. **1885** S. P. THOMPSON *Electr. & Magn.* 9 Electricity may either reside upon the surface of bodies as a charge, or flow through their substance as a current.

b. Preceded by adjs. denoting (*a*) the source or mode of production, as ***frictional, galvanic, induced, magnetic, thermal, vital, voltaic***; (*b*) the place of development, as ***animal, atmospheric, organic***; (*c*) the quality, as ***active, constant, free, negative, positive. vitreous, resinous electricity***: older synonyms for positive and negative electricity, which were first observed as resulting from the friction of glass and of resinous bodies respectively.

1755 FRANKLIN *Let.* 14 Mar. Wks. 1882 V. 341 Their negative electricity [is] increased. **1799** E. DARWIN *Phytol.* 310 (T.) Two electrick fluids diffused together, and strongly attracting each other; one..vitreous, the other resinous, electricity. **1832** *Nat. Phil.* II. *Galvan.* iv. §30. 12 (Usef. Knowl. Soc.) The circulation of voltaic electricity produces an elevation of temperature. *Ibid. Electr.* ii. §49. 13 The body is said to be negatively electrified, or to have negative electricity. *Ibid.* Positively electrified, or to have positive electricity. **1850** tr. *Humboldt's Cosmos* III. 189 Transitions of atmospheric electricity to an opposite condition.

2. *fig.*

1791 BURKE *Regic. Peace* i. Wks. VIII. 110 They [ambassadors] will become true conductors of contagion to every country which has had the misfortune to send them to the source of that electricity. **1831** CARLYLE *Sart. Res.* (1858) 175 Wait a little, till the entire nation is in an electric state; till your whole vital Electricity..is cut into two isolated portions of Positive and Negative (of Money and of Hunger). **1858** HAWTHORNE *Fr. & It. Jrnls.* II. 24 The electricity of human brotherhood. **1864** LOWELL *Fireside Trav.* 73 The natural electricity of youth.

3. The branch of physical science which deals with the nature and phenomena of electrical action.

1734 DESAGULIERS *Course Exper. Philos.* 450 Gray has found out several new Phenomena in Electricity. **1796** HUNTER tr. *St. Pierre's Stud. Nat.* (1799) I. 107 That new..wonderful art of electricity, which screens their hotels from the thunder. **1885** S. P. THOMPSON (*title*) Lessons in Electricity and Magnetism.

4. *Comb.*, as ***electricity-laden*** adj.

1884 *Century Mag.* XXVII. 922 The electricity-laden raindrops.

electricize (ɪˌlɛktrɪˈsaɪz). *rare.* [f. as prec. + -IZE.] To charge with electricity, make electric. = ELECTRIFY *v.* 1.

1872 FOX *Ozone* 16 Ozone has been considered..to be produced only when Oxygen is positively electricized.

eˈlectric ˈlight. **a.** *gen.* Light produced by electrical action. **b.** *spec.* The same as applied to purposes of illumination. It is ordinarily produced either by the incandescence of a filament of metal or carbon, or by the electric arc formed by the passing of electricity between two carbon points. Also *attrib.*, as in ***electric-light apparatus***.

1767 J. PRIESTLEY *Hist. Electr.* I. 9 A much finer appearance of electric light..was observed by Dr. Wall. **1777** T. CAVALLO *Compl. Treat. Electr.* p. v, He [*sc.* Mr. Hawkesbee] first remarked various appearances of the electric light. **1843** *Mech. Mag.* XXXIX. 352 Electric light—Substitute for Gas [*heading of paragraph*]. **1849** WALKER in *Circ. Sc.* (*c* 1865) I. 138/2 We..saw the electric light outshining all the other..lights. **1871** TYNDALL *Fragm. Sc.* (ed. 6) II. xvi. 430 The electric light was afterwards established at Cape Grisnez. **1878** *Boston Transcript* 16 Nov. 4 The electric-light patents he [*sc.* Edison] has applied for are already antiquated. **1893** *Outing* (U.S.) XXII. 132/2 The famous Spokane Falls..furnish abundant power for..electric-light plants. **1936** *Discovery* June 189/2 The natives [in Kano, Nigeria] run their own electric light plant and water services.

fig. **1870** MAX MÜLLER *Sc. Relig.* (1873) 3 The electric light of Comparative Philology.

Hence **electric-lighted** *ppl. a.*, lighted by electricity; **electric lighting** *vbl. sb.*, illumination by the electric light; also *attrib.*

1881 *Daily News* 3 Sept. 2/4 Beautiful electric-lighted clock. **1887** *Whitaker's Almanack* 141 advt., Electric-lighting engineers.

electriˈcology. *rare.* [See -LOGY.] (See quot.)

1746 R. TURNER (*title*) Electricology, or a Discourse upon Electricity.

eˈlectrico-ˌmeteoroˈlogical, *a.* Relating to electrical meteorology, or to electricity and meteorology.

1787 BENNET in *Phil. Trans.* LXXVII. 289 An electrico-meteorological diary.

†**elecˈtriferous,** *a. Obs.* [see ELECTRUM and -FEROUS.] Bearing or producing amber.

1656 in BLOUNT *Glossogr.* **1721–1800** in BAILEY.

electrifiable (ɛˈlɛktrɪfaɪəb(ə)l), *a.* [f. ELECTRIFY + -ABLE.] Capable of being electrified.

1828–32 WEBSTER.

electrification (ɪˌlɛktrɪfɪˈkeɪʃən). [f. ELECTRIFY *v.* after L. nouns of action in *-ficātio*.]

1. a. The action or process of electrifying; subjection to the electric current.

1748 *Phil. Trans.* XLV. 194 An Electrification of five or six Hours. **1750** *Ibid.* XLVI. 385 The Prelate was not cured; and since the Electrification..had been as he was before. **1881** A. MACFARLANE in *Nature* XXIV. 465 After a few electrifications..particles collect to form a chain.

b. The action or process of converting (a railway system, factory, etc.) to the use of electricity.

Earlier attempts to provide a term for this were *electrolisation* and *electrilisation*, with a verb *electralise* [sic] = ELECTRIFY *v.* 1 b.

[**1900** *Westm. Gaz.* 15 Feb. 4/1 The electrolisation of the inner circle, with its twenty-six stations. *Ibid.* 15 Aug. 3/1 The complete electrolisation of London tramways. **1901** J. BURNS in *Standard* 4 Mar., If Londoners had only done in 1895 what they did on Saturday, three-fourths of the tramways would have been electralised. **1901** *Westm. Gaz.* 28 Aug. 4/3 Americanised companies which go in for the 'standard' system of electrilisation.]

1901 *Westm. Gaz.* 2 Jan. 8/3 The character of the coal consumed..has altered the position for the worse... The one possible remedy is electrification. *Ibid.* 6 June, District Railway Electrification. **1904** *Daily Chron.* 26 Aug. 7/4 Electrification Perils. Risk Entailed by the Transformation of the 'Underground'. **1921** *Dict. Occup. Terms* (1927) §561 Electrification ganger. **1963** M. GOLDSTEIN *Dict. Mod. Acronyms* 123 REA, Rural Electrification Administration. **1967** [see ELECTRIFIER].

2. The state or condition of a body charged with electricity.

1787 *Phil. Trans.* LXXVII. 29 The electrification of fogs and rain. **1878** GURNEY *Crystallogr.* 114 The electrifications of the glass and the resin are of opposite kinds. **1881** MAXWELL *Electr. & Magn.* I. 32 It is the..practice..to call the vitreous electrification positive, and the resinous electrification negative.

3. *fig.* The condition or state of being electrified or excited. (Cf. ELECTRIFY *v.* 2.)

1878 F. A. KEMBLE *Rec. Girlhood* I. iv. 113 The tragedy was ended, and I had electrified the audience, my companions, and, still more, myself; and so, to avert any ill effects from this general electrification, Mrs. Rowden thought it wise and well to say to me [etc.]. **1892** *Leisure Hour* Aug. 657/1 Her electrification by Mr. Belport's proposal.

electrified (ɪˈlɛktrɪfaɪd), *ppl. a.* [f. ELECTRIFY *v.* + -ED.] Charged with electricity by the passage of an electric current.

1745 W. WATSON in *Phil. Trans.* XLIII. 485 In electrified Bodies you see a perpetual Endeavour to get rid of their Electricity. *Ibid.* 491 The Finger of the electrified Person is brought near thereto. **1751** —— in *Ibid.* XLVII. 203 Stream of electrified effluvia. **1834** MRS. SOMERVILLE *Connex. Phys. Sc.* xxviii. (1849) 314 Attraction between electrified and un-electrified substances. **1881** MAXWELL *Electr. & Magn.* I. 32 No force, either of attraction or of repulsion, can be observed between an electrified body and a body not electrified.

electrifier (ɪˈlɛktrɪˌfaɪə(r)). [f. next + -ER.] He who or that which electrifies or (*fig.*) startles or shocks violently.

1860 RUSSELL *Diary India* I. 210 There is nothing to rouse one like the sound of a cannonade: it's a tremendous electrifier. **1906** *Chambers's Jrnl.* Sept. 703/2 Then it [*sc.* peat] falls into the electrifier. **1967** *Listener* 26 Jan. 122/2 Now that electrification from Euston to Manchester and Liverpool is finished, the British Railways Board have become eager electrifiers again.

electrify (ɪˈlɛktrɪfaɪ), *v.* [f. ELECTR-IC + -(I)FY.]

1. *trans.* **a.** To charge a body with electricity, or pass the electric current through it; to subject (a person) to an electric shock or current.

1745 W. WATSON in *Phil. Trans.* XLIII. 490, I procur'd an iron Bar..; this I electrified lying on Cakes of Wax and Resin. *Ibid.* 498, I was desirous to know if I was able to electrify a Drop of cold Water. **1747** FRANKLIN *Lett.* Wks. 1840 V. 188 We electrify..a book that has a double line of gold round upon the covers. **1765** WESLEY *Jrnl.* 26 Dec. (1827) III. 233 Being electrified morning and evening, my lameness mended. *c* **1796** IMISON *Sch. Arts* I. 41 The body is said to be electrified, and is capable of exhibiting appearances which are ascribed to the power of electricity. **1830** SIR J. HERSCHEL *Stud. Nat. Phil.* II. vi. (1851) 150 Quicksilver electrified under a conducting fluid. **1885** WATSON & BURBURY *Math. Th. Electr. & Magn.* I. 76 The inside will be resinously electrified.

b. To introduce electric power into (a system of railways, a farm, factory, etc.).

1900 *Westm. Gaz.* 17 Oct. 9/3 It is not very astonishing that the directors of the District Railway should be in no violent hurry to start upon the electrifying of their line. **1970** *Yankee* (Dublin, New Hampshire) Aug. 140 You can electrify a flat wick oil lamp with a Gyro Queen Converter. **1970** *Railway Mag.* Oct. 574/2 The electric locomotive was supplied to the East Sussex County Council when the hospital railway was electrified in 1903.

2. *fig.* To startle, rouse, excite, as though with the shock of electricity.

1752 CHESTERF. *Lett.* 285 III. 308 You will not be so agreeably electrified..as you were at Manheim. *c* **1794** BURKE *Addr. Brissot to Constit.* (R.), Those heights of courage which electrify an army and ensure victory. **1870** EMERSON *Soc. & Solit., Eloq.* Wks. (Bohn) III. 37 An audience is electrified.

3. *intr.* To become charged with electricity.

1745 W. WATSON in *Phil. Trans.* XLIII. 490 Whilst the Bar was at one End electrifying, a Spoon lay upon the other.

electrifying (ɪˈlɛktrɪfaɪɪŋ), *vbl. sb.* [f. ELECTRIFY *v.* + -ING[1].] The action or process of charging with electricity, or of passing the electric current through a body. Also *attrib.*

1747 W. WATSON in *Phil. Trans.* XLV. 58 The Room where the electrifying Machine was placed. **1752** —— in *Ibid.* XLVII. 373 The electrifying machine. **1764** WESLEY *Jrnl.* 13 July, I advised electrifying.

eˈlectrifying, *ppl. a.* [f. as prec. + -ING[2].] That electrifies.

1820 J. SCOTT in *Lond. Mag.* Jan., Vivid, searching, electrifying language. **1834** CAMPBELL *Mrs. Siddons* II. xiii. 393 A manner so electrifying as to make the poor shopman start back.

†**electrine,** *a. Obs.* [ad. L. *ēlectrīnus*, or Gr. ἠλέκτρινος: see ELECTRUM and -INE.]

1. Resembling what exists in amber, electric.

a **1687** H. MORE in *Div. Dial.* (1713) 560 They supposed it to contain an Electrine Principle in it.

2. Made of the metal ELECTRUM.

1677 PLOT *Oxfordsh.* 311 It was no matter in a Legacy of Electrine vessels, how much Silver or Electrum was in them.

†**eˈlectrix.** *Obs.* [a. L. *ēlectrix*, fem. of *ēlector*.] = ELECTRESS 1.

1665 *Lond. Gaz.* No. 11/1 The Emperor and his Mother ..are going into Mourning for..the Electrix of Bavaria.

†**elecˈtrizable,** *a. Obs.* [f. ELECTRIZE *v.* + -ABLE.] Capable of being electrized.

1753 WATSON in *Phil. Trans.* XLVIII. 205 Electrisable bodies..were sometimes electrised under thick clouds, but without..lightning, or even without rain.

electrization (ɪˌlɛktrɪˈzeɪʃən). [f. ELECTRIZE *v.* + -ATION; so Fr. *électrisation*.]

1. The process of subjecting (a person or thing) to the action of electricity; the state or condition of being subjected to electrical action.

1752 *Phil. Trans.* XLVII. 403 The washing of the boy's feet..immediately preceded his electrisation. **1812** SIR H. DAVY *Chem. Philos.* I. 355 Alumina cannot be decomposed by the electrization of mercury. **1871** NAPHEYS *Prev. & Cure Dis.* III. iii. 677 Persistent electrization has been known to cure obstinate cases. **1880** HOWELLS *Undisc. Country* iii. 49 Electrization of persons in the vicinity of a point struck by lightning.

b. Decomposition by electro-chemical action.

1807 SIR H. DAVY in *Phil. Trans.* XCVIII. 38 The process of the electrization of ammonia.

2. *fig.* The stirring of the soul mightily, as by electric shock. [after Fr.]

1870 *Echo* 9 Nov., The *levée en masse*, that electrisation of all souls.

electrize (ɪˈlɛktraɪz). Also 8 electerize. [f. ELECTR-IC + -IZE; cf. Fr. *électriser*.]

trans. To charge with electricity; to subject to the action of electricity; = ELECTRIFY *v.*

1746 BROWNING in *Phil. Trans.* XLIV. 373, I was desirous to electrise a Tree. **1747** FRANKLIN *Lett.* Wks. 1840 V. 187 We electrize a person twenty or more times running, with a touch of the finger on the wire. **1748** *Lond. Mag.* 255 All animal bodies..being constantly electeriz'd..by the earth. **1808** J. WEBSTER *Nat. Phil.* 141 The prime conductor is electrized with the negative. **1869** MRS. SOMERVILLE *Molec. Sc.* I. I. ii. 90 A spiral wire electrized by the great battery.. at the London Institution.

Hence **eˈlectrized** *ppl. a.*

1753 WATSON in *Phil. Trans.* XLVIII. 207 An electrised phial of water. **1757** E. DARWIN *ibid.* L. 252 Electrised down of the juncus bombycinus. **1837** WHEWELL *Hist. Induct. Sc.* (1857) III. 13 Decanting the water out of an electrized into another bottle.

electrizing (ɪˈlɛktraɪzɪŋ), *vbl. sb.* [f. ELECTRIZE *v.* + -ING[1].] The action or process of charging with electricity. Also *attrib.*

1763 WATSON in *Phil. Trans.* LIII. 26 The electrising has been discontinued. **1809** HENRY *ibid.* XCIX. 433 *note*, Transferring the..gas..into the electrizing tube.

electro (ɪˈlɛktrəʊ), *sb.* and *v.* Used colloq. as an abbreviation for: **a.** ELECTRO-PLATE *v.*, ELECTRO-PLATING *vbl. sb.*; **b.** ELECTROTYPE *sb.* and *v.*

1864 SALA in *Daily Tel.* 14 Dec., Intrinsically base metal might have passed current until the electro wore off. *Mod.* They allowed him to take electros of all their woodcuts. It would save expense to electro the illustrations. The spoons ought to be electro'd afresh.

electro- (ɪˈlɛktrəʊ), formally repr. Gr. ἠλεκτρο- combining form of ἤλεκτρον, which, after the analogy of its derivative ELECTRIC, is treated as if meaning 'electricity'; first occurring in quasi-Greek derivatives like ELECTROMETER, and now used without restriction to form combinations (chiefly written with hyphen) denoting processes carried on by electrical means, or the application of electricity to particular departments of art or industry, as in ***electro-blasting, -cautery, -dentistry, -engraving,***

-etching, *-horticulture*, *-lithotrity*, *-otiatrics*. Also in the following:

eˌlectro-aˈcoustics, acoustics investigated by electrical methods; hence **eˌlectro-aˈcoustic**, **-aˈcoustical** *adjs.*; **eˌlectro-aˈnalysis** *Chem.*, electrolytic analysis; so **eˌlectro-anaˈlytical** *a.*; **eˌlectrobaˈllistic** *a.*, relating to the art of timing by electricity the flight of projectiles; **eˌlectro-biˈoscopy** [+ *-bioscopy*, f. BIO- + *-scopy*, after *microscopy*, etc.], the examination of an animal body by means of a galvanic current, to discover muscular contractions as evidence of life; **eˌlectro-ˈbrasser** (see quot. 1921); † **eˈlectrobus** *Obs.*, an omnibus propelled by electricity; also *attrib.*; **eˌlectro-ˈcapillary** *a.*, having reference to the influence of electricity on capillary tubes under certain conditions; **eˌlectroˈcardiogram** *Med.* [ad. G. *electrocardiogramm* (W. Einthoven 1894, in *Arch. Ges. Physiol.* LVI. 541)], a record of the electric currents produced in the body by the heart-beats of a patient; **eˌlectroˈcardiograph**, the apparatus used in registering electrocardiograms; hence **eˌlectrocardioˈgraphic** *a.*, **-graphy**; **eˌlectro-ˈcautery** *Med.*, cautery by means of an electrically heated instrument; **eˌlectro-ˈchemic**, **-ˈchemical** *adjs.*, pertaining to electricity and chemistry jointly; hence ***electro-chemical equivalent***, the weight of a substance deposited during electrolysis by the passage of a specified quantity of electricity, usu. expressed in grams per coulomb; ***electro-chemical series*** (see quot. 1943); **eˌlectro-ˈchemically** *adv.*, in accordance with the laws of electro-chemistry; **eˌlectro-ˈchemist**, one who practises electro-chemistry; **eˌlectro-ˈchemistry**, the science of the application of electricity to chemistry; **eˌlectrochroˈmatogram**, a chromatogram produced by electrochromatography; **eˌlectrochromaˈtography** [ad. F. *électro-chromatographie* (H. Lecoq 1944, in *Bull. de la Soc. R. des Sciences de Liége* XIII. 21)], chromatography in which the migration and separation of the constituents of a mixture take place under the influence of a constant electric field; zone electrophoresis; so **eˌlectrochromatoˈgraphic** *a.*; **eˌlectro-ˈchronograph**, an instrument for electrically recording exact instants of time; **eˌlectro-coaguˈlation** [a. F. *électro-coagulation* (Doyen)], the hardening and destruction of tissue or the control of bleeding by the direct application of an electrically heated surgical instrument (= *electro-cautery*) or by means of a high-frequency electric current; **eˌlectro-ˈcoating** *vbl. sb.*, the process of coating a body over with metal by the galvanic battery; **eˌlectro-ˈcontact**, used *attrib.* of a submarine mine which is exploded by means of electricity; **eˌlectro-conˈvulsive** *a.*, of or pertaining to a convulsive response to electric shock treatment, spec. ***electro-convulsive therapy*** (abbrev. *E.C.T.*), ***treatment***, the treatment of mental disease by the application of an electric shock to the central nervous system; **eˌlectro-ˈcopper**, iron coated with copper by means of the galvanic battery; hence as *v. trans.*, to coat with copper by electrolysis; **eˌlectroˈcortin** *Biochem.* [CORTIN], = ALDOSTERONE; **eˌlectro-ˈculture**, the use of electricity in the growing of crops; **eˌlectroˈcyclic** *a. Chem.*, of a chemical change, characterized either by the formation of a single bond between the two ends of a linear conjugated organic molecule, or by the converse process of breaking such a bond; **eˌlectro-deˈposit** *v.*, to deposit (a coating of metal, etc.) by means of electricity: hence **eˌlectro-deˈposit**, **-depoˈsition**, the process of depositing by electricity; **eˌlectro-deˈpositor**, one who conducts this process; **eˌlectro-desiˈccation**, the drying and consequent destruction of tissue or the control of bleeding by the local application of a high-frequency electric current; **eˌlectro-diagˈnosis**, the application of electricity to purposes of medical diagnosis; **eˌlectro-diˈalysis**, dialysis accelerated by the passage of an electric current; **eˌlectro-enˈcephalogram** (occas. **electrencephalogram**) [ad. G. *elektrenkephalogramm* (H. Berger 1929, in *Arch. f. Psychiatrie u. Nervenkrankheit* LXXXVII. 527 ff.)], the record made by an electro-encephalograph; abbrev. *E.E.G.*; **eˌlectro-enˈcephalograph**, an instrument for recording the electrical activity of the brain; hence **eˌlectro-encephaˈlographer**, **eˌlectro-encephaˈlographist**, **eˌlectro-encephaˈlography** *sbs.*, **eˌlectro-encephaloˈgraphic** *a.*; **eˌlectro-erˈgometer**, an instrument for measuring the work done by an electric machine; **eˌlectro-exˈtraction** [EXTRACTION 3], the electrolytic recovery of a metal from a solution of its salts (Webster 1934); **eˌlectroˈforming** *vbl. sb.*, the production of metallic objects by a process of electro-deposition; hence (as a back-formation) **eˈlectroform** *v. trans.*; also **eˈlectroform**, an electroformed metallic object; **eˈlectroformed** *ppl. a.*; **eˌlectro-ˈfusion**, the fusion of metals by means of the electric current; **eˌlectro-galˈvanic** *a.*, pertaining to the galvanic form of electricity; also, pertaining to electricity as including galvanism; **eˌlectro-ˈgalvanizing** *vbl. sb.* (see quot. 1940); **eˌlectro-ˈgenesis** [see GENESIS], the state of tetanoid spasm that supervenes in the muscles highly stimulated by galvanism, when the current is withdrawn: so **eˌlectroˈgenic** *a.* [see -GENIC], pertaining to electrogenesis; **eˌlectro-ˈgild** *v.*, to gild by means of an electric current: hence ***eˌlectro-ˈgilding*** vbl. sb., ***electro-gilt*** ppl. adj.; **eˌlectrograˈvitics** (see quot. 1960); so **eˌlectro-graˈvitic** *a.*; **eˌlectro-hyˈdraulic** *a.*, (*a*) pertaining to a hydraulic system that is powered or controlled electrically; (*b*) pertaining to electro-hydraulics; hence **eˌlectro-hyˈdraulically** *adv.*; **eˌlectro-hyˈdraulics**, the use of high-voltage electrical discharges in liquids; **eˈlectrojet**, an intense electric current that occurs in a narrow belt in the lower ionosphere, esp. in regions of strong auroral displays and near the magnetic equator; **eˌlectro-kiˈnetic** *a.* [see KINETIC], having reference to electricity in motion; **eˌlectro-lumiˈnescence**, electrical luminescence, as created in a gas-filled tube or by the excitation of a layer of phosphor (cf. LUMINESCENCE, quot. 1896); hence **eˌlectrolumiˈnescent** *a.*; **eˌlectro-ˈmassage**, kneading the body or a limb with a combined roller and small galvanic machine; **eˌlectro-meˈchanical** *a.*, of or pertaining to the application of electricity to a mechanical process, device, etc.; **eˌlectro-ˈmedical** *a.*, pertaining to the application of galvanism to medical purposes; **eˌlectro-meˈtallurgy**, the application of electrolysis to the deposition of thin coatings from metallic solutions: hence ***eˌlectro-metaˈllurgic***, ***-metaˈllurgical*** adjs; **eˌlectroˈmotograph**, see MOTOGRAPH; **eˌlectro-ˈmuscular** *a.*, having reference to the mutual influence of the electric current and muscular contraction; **eˌlectroˈmyogram**, a graphical record of the variations in electric potential in a muscle; **eˌlectroˈmyograph**, an instrument for making electromyograms; so **eˌlectromyoˈgraphic** *a.*, **eˌlectromyo-ˈgraphically** *adv.*; **eˌlectromyˈography**; **eˌlectronarˈcosis**, the production of a narcotic state by the passage of an electric current through the brain; hence **eˌlectronarˈcotic** *a.*; **eˌlectro-ˈnegative** *a.*, (*a*) pertaining to, or producing, negative electricity; (*b*) a term used by Berzelius to describe atoms that go to the anode in electrolysis; hence, having a tendency to form negative ions; so **eˌlectro-ˈnegatively** *adv.*; **eˌlectro-negaˈtivity**, the degree to which atoms or radicals attract electrons; the state of being electro-negative; **eˌlectro-nervous** *a.*, relating to the affinity between electric and nervous action; **eˌlectro-ˈoculogram**, the record produced by an electro-oculograph; **eˌlectro-ˈoculograph**, an instrument for studying the eye by registering the varying electric potentials of the skin around it; hence **eˌlectro-oculoˈgraphic** *a.*, **eˌlectro-oculoˈgraphically** *adv.*; **eˌlectro-ocuˈlography**, the technique of using the electro-oculograph; **eˌlectro-ˈoptic**, **eˌlectro-ˈoptical** *adjs.*, of or pertaining to electro-optics; **eˌlectro-ˈoptics** the science of the relations between electricity and optics; **eˌlectro-osˈmosis**, osmosis under the influence of an electric field; also called ***electro-endosmosis***, ***electrosmosis***; hence **eˌlectro-osˈmotic** *a.*, **eˌlectro-osˈmotically** *adv.*; **eˌlectro-paˈthology**, the science of morbid conditions as they are revealed by electrical means; **eˌlectroˈphilic** *a.*, having an affinity for electrons; **eˌlectro-phoˈtography**, the production of photographic prints by electronic means (see also quot. 1894); so **eˌlectro-photoˈgraphic** *a.*; **eˌlectro-phoˈtometer**, an instrument for comparing the intensity of lights by referring them to the standard of the electric spark; **eˌlectro-ˈphrenic** (-ˈfrɛnɪk, -ˈfriːnɪk) *a.*, of or pertaining to electrical stimulation of the phrenic nerves; **eˌlectro-physiˈology**, the science of the electrical conditions of the physiological processes; the testing by electricity of the bodily functions: hence ***eˈlectro-ˌphysioˈlogical*** adj. also, ***eˌlectro-physiˈologist***; **eˈlectroˌplexy** *Psychiatry* [after APOPLEXY], electro-shock or electro-convulsive therapy; **eˌlectro-pneuˈmatic** *a.*, pertaining to a combination of electrical and pneumatic power; **eˌlectro-ˈpoion** [f. Gr. -ποιόν, neut. of -ποιός that makes], a name for Bunsen's carbon battery; **eˌlectro-ˈpolar** *a.*, an epithet applied to the condition of a cylindrical conductor when, on being electrified by induction, the ends become polar; **eˌlectro-ˈpolish** *v. trans.*, to polish the surface of a metal by electrolysis; hence ***eˌlectroˈpolished*** ppl. a.; **eˌlectro-ˈpositive** *a.*, (*a*) pertaining to, or producing, positive electricity; (*b*) a term used by Berzelius to describe atoms that go to the cathode in electrolysis; hence, having a tendency to form positive ions; so **eˌlectro-ˈpositively** *adv.*; **eˌlectro-posiˈtivity**, the degree to which atoms or radicals tend to form positive ions; the state of being electro-positive; **eˌlectro-ˈprocess** = *electrotyping process*; **eˌlectroˈpuncture** = GALVANO-PUNCTURE; **eˌlectro-pyˈrometer** = electric PYROMETER; **eˌlectro-reˈduction**, the reduction which takes place in an electrolytic cell (cf. REDUCTION 10); **eˌlectro-ˈretinogram**, a graphic record of the electrical activity of the retina; hence **eˌlectro-retiˈnography**, the study of, or the technique of obtaining, such records; **eˌlectro-ˈshock**, an electric shock, used esp. *attrib.*, as ***electro-shock treatment***, medical treatment by means of an electric shock (cf. *electric shock*, *electro-convulsive therapy*); **eˌlectro-ˈsilver** *v.* = ELECTROPLATE, hence as *sb.*; also *ellipt.* **electro**; **eˈlectro-slag**, a name given to a process for refining or welding metal in which an electric current is passed through a layer of slag in contact with it and into the metal itself; **eˌlectrostimuˈlation** *Med.*, electrical treatment sometimes used in the therapy of impaired nerves or muscles; in *Psychiatry*, a form of electro-shock therapy; **eˌlectroˈstriction** [STRICTION] (see quot. 1942); hence **eˌlectroˈstrictive** *a.*; **eˌlectro-ˈsynthesis**, chemical synthesis effected by electricity; **eˌlectrosynˈthetic** *a.*, causing chemical composition by means of the galvanic current; hence **eˌlectrosynˈthetically** *adv.*; **eˌlectroˈtaxis** *Biol.* [TAXIS 6], the response of an organism to an electric current; so **eˌlectroˈtactic** *a.*; **eˌlectro-techˈnology**, the science of the application of electricity to the arts; **eˌlectro-teleˈgraphic** *a.*, pertaining to **eˌlectro-teˈlegraphy** = electric telegraphy; **eˌlectro-theraˈpeutics**, the treatment of disease by electricity; so **eˌlectro-theraˈpeutical** *a.*, of or pertaining to electro-therapeutics; **eˌlectro-ˈtherapist**, **-theraˈpeutist**, one who practises electro-therapy; **eˌlectroˈtherapy** [+ *-therapy*, ad. Gr. θεραπεία healing] = *electro-therapeutics*; **eˌlectro-ˈthermal**, **-ˈthermic** *adjs.*, relating to heat derived from electricity; **eˌlectro-ˈthermancy** [cf. DIATHERMANCY], and **eˈlectroˌthermy** [as if ad. Gr. -θερμία, f. θερμός hot], the science of the electricity developed by heat; **eˌlectro-ˈtin** *v. trans.*, hence **eˌlectro-ˈtinning**, tinning (sense 1) by electrolysis; so **eˈlectro-tinned** *ppl. a.*, **eˌlectro-ˈtinˈplate**, electrolytic tinplate; also ***electro-tin plating*** vbl. sb.; **eˈlectroˌtint** [cf. AQUATINT], a mode of engraving, the design being drawn on copper-plate and transferred by means of an electric bath; **eˈlectro-ˈtropic** *a.*, of, pertaining to, or exhibiting electrotropism; **elecˈtrotropism**, curvature of growth in plants due to slight electric currents; **eˌlectro-ˈvalence**, **-ˈvalency**, a chemical bond in which two oppositely charged ions are linked by the electrostatic attraction between them; an ionic bond; so **eˌlectro-ˈvalent** *a.*; **eˌlectro-viˈscosity**, the property of being electroviscous, the component of the viscosity of a substance that is due to the electroviscous effect; **eˌlectroˈviscous** [ad. G. *elektroviskos* (A. Passynski 1935, in *Kolloid Zeitschr.* LXX. 182/2)], (of a liquid or dispersion) having a viscosity that depends on the applied electric field; of or pertaining to electroviscosity; **eˌlectro-ˈvital** *a.*, having

reference to the connexion of electricity and the vital actions: hence **e,lectro-'vitalism**; **e'lectro-win** *v.*, hence **e,lectro-'winning** *vbl. sb.*, the process of extracting a metal from a solution of its salts or from its ore by electrolysis (cf. WINNING *vbl. sb.*[1] 5).

1935 *Amer. Speech* X. 72/2 An *electro-acoustic determination of the factors of voice quality which distinguishes one voice from another. **1956** *Nature* 10 Mar. 464/2 Electro-acoustic measuring techniques. **1959** *Times* 11 Mar. 3/1 Important Position with small American Company open for electro-acoustic technical man. **1970** *Sci. Jrnl.* May 45/2 The obvious first use for the electro-acoustic strip is as a store for signals. **1934** *Amer. Speech* IX. 309/2 A method for measuring small intensities by means of *electro-acoustical apparatus. **1955** *Gloss. Acoust. Terms (B.S.I.)* 17 *Electro-acoustical transducer*, a transducer which is actuated by energy from an electrical system and supplies energy to an acoustical system or vice versa. **1927** *Electro Acoustics [see ABSTRACTOR]. **1943** *Endeavour* II. 123/2 The term 'electro-acoustics', which not only indicates the combination of electrical and mechanical apparatus but also the methods by which masses, restoring forces represented by springs and the like, and mechanical resistance find their analogies in electrical terms. **1903** *Electr. World & Engin.* 28 Mar. 530/2 The difference observed in the *electro-analysis of mercury from a potassium cyanide solution are due to an attack of the platinum disc serving as cathode and to the solubility of platinum in potassium cyanide. **1903** *Electr. World & Engin.* 21 Nov. 853/2 *Electro-analytical methods. **1964** R. JOHNSTON in *Oceanogr. & Marine Biol.* II. 112 The modern electro-analytical techniques. **1890** *Nature* 18 Sept. 502/2 In 1860..I carried on for the Government the first *electro-ballistic experiments made in this country. **1921** *Dict. Occup. Terms* (1927) §278 **Electro-brasser*..effects electrolytic deposition of brass on better types of finished screws. **1960** *Classification of Occupations* (General Register Office) 30/2 Electro-brasser (screws). **1906** *Westm. Gaz.* 20 Apr. 11/1 The London *Electrobus Company. *Ibid.* 4 Dec. 6/3 About January..the first of the electrobuses will be placed in regular running. **1879** G. PRESCOTT *Sp. Telephone* 287 Lipmann's *electro-capillary electrometer. **1904** *Sci. Amer.* 5 Mar. 197/3 The human *electrocardiogram discovered by A. D. Waller. **1927** A. V. HILL *Living Machinery* iii. 117 The second record is a normal 'electro-cardiogram' accompanied by a 'phono-cardiogram'. **1952** *Electronic Engin.* XXIV. 102 The electrical output of the heart, which when recorded is termed the electrocardiogram or E.C.G. **1913** *Q. Jrnl. Med.* VI. 442 The two installations, electro-phonograph and *electro-cardiograph, are arranged side by side. **1927** A. V. HILL *Living Machinery* iii. Pl. xii *(caption)*, String galvanometer ('electrocardiograph') as used for recording currents produced by the human heart. **1958** *Observer* 9 Nov. 17/5 With the electrocardiograph one records the electrical activity of the hearts of both child and mother, superimposed on one another. **1910** *Canad. Jrnl. Med. & Surg.* XXVII. 276 As a result of *electrocardiographic work, we can for the first time be perfectly sure that the nature of excitation..in an extra-systole is wholly different from that of the normal heart beat. **1913** *Lancet* 21 June 1784/1 The advances made in the application of electrical methods to the study of the heart are well illustrated in a catalogue..of electro-cardiographic apparatus. **1961** *Ibid.* 22 July 183/2 Electrocardiographic changes often suggest or confirm the presence of an aneurysm, but they do not always agree..with the radiological..evidence. **1910** *Canad. Jrnl. Med. & Surg.* XXVII. 273 *(title)* *Electrocardiography and electro-phonography as aids in clinical diagnosis. **1957** *Electronic Engin.* XXIX. 132 The striking advances which have been made in electrocardiography in recent years. *a* **1884** KNIGHT *Dict. Mech.* Suppl. 305/2 *Electro-cautery. **1931** *Times Lit. Suppl.* 27 Aug. 650/4 His view that electro-cautery..affords permanent relief. **1953** *Jrnl. Brit. Interplanet. Soc.* XII. 235 The behaviour of a normal mouse was contrasted with that of a labyrinthinectomized mouse (i.e., an electrocautery needle had been applied to the horizontal semi-circular canals in the membranous labyrinth of the middle ear). **1807** DAVY in *Phil. Trans.* XCVIII. 2 Application of the powers of *electro-chemical analysis. **1848** H. WATTS tr. *Gmelin's Hand-bk. Chem.* I. 155 The elements succeed one another in the electro-chemical series of Berzelius. **1857** [see *absolute unit*]. *c* **1865** J. WYLDE in *Circ. Sc.* I. 193/2 Laws of..electro-chemical decomposition. **1883** E. ATKINSON tr. *Mascart & Joubert's Treat. Electr.* I. iii. 247 The electromotive force of an electrolyte is equal to the mechanical equivalent of the heat of combination of its electro-chemical equivalent. **1922** GLAZEBROOK *Dict. Appl. Physics.* II. 354/1 Since the ratio of the mass to the charge for a hydrogen ion in solution, *i.e.* the electro-chemical equivalent of hydrogen, is $1{\cdot}04 \times 10^{-4}$ e.m.u., the mass of the hydrogen atom is given [etc.]. **1943** *Gloss. Terms Electr. Engin. (B.S.I.)* 94 *Electro-chemical series*, a tabular arrangement of the elements in the order of the electrode potential developed when an element is immersed in a solution of normal ionic concentration. **1834** [see ELECTROLYZED *ppl. a.*]. **1881** MAXWELL *Electr. & Magn.* I. 330 The quantities of these ions being *electrochemically equivalent. **1946** *Nature* 19 Oct. 548/1 These advances led to the 'ground' mine, laid on the sea-bed, operated either magnetically, electro-chemically or acoustically. **1837** *Ann. Electr., Magnet., & Chem.* I. iii, I shall shortly take an opportunity of calling the attention of *electro-chemists to two points. **1885** *Jrnl. Franklin Inst.* Feb. 81 The man skilled in its science [*sc.* electro-metallurgy] and art may appropriately be styled an electro-chemist. **1814** G. J. SINGER *(title)* Elements of electricity and *electro-chemistry. **1829** *Nat. Philos.* II. *Electr.* i. §2. 1 (Usef. Knowl. Soc.) Electro-Chemistry..one of the connecting branches between remote divisions of the Philosophy of Nature. **1956** *Nature* 28 Jan. 181/2 *(heading)* Electro-chemistry of stainless steel in sulphuric acid. **1951** *Analytical Chem.* XXIII. 27/2 *(caption)* Arrangement for formation of *electrochromatogram in paper strip, *P*, between glass plates. **1951** *Analytical Chem.* XXIII. 30/1 For ions of identical sign, chromatographic sequences are usually identical with *electrochromatographic sequences. **1948** *Chem. Abstr.* XLII. 6703 A new analytical technique, *electrochromatography, in which the adsorption is effected with the aid of an e.m.f., is described. **1966** *McGraw-Hill Encycl. Sci. & Technol.* III. 97/2 Electrochromatography is especially useful for the examination of ionized substances such as acids, bases, and salts. **1851** C. CIST *Sk. Cincinnati* 302 The invention of the *electro-chronograph by Professor Locke of our city. **1878** NEWCOMB *Pop. Astron.* II. ii. 157 The electro-chronograph on which his laps are recorded. **1913** *Jrnl. Advanced Therapeutics* XXXI. 29 *Electro-coagulation is used to destroy the neoplasms of the skin and of the mucous orifices. **1960** *Surg. Forum* X. 439 Positive electrocoagulation is very effective in creating hemostasis in tissues not usually amenable to suture, using currents up to 100 ma. *c* **1865** G. GORE in *Circ. Sc.* I. 239/2 *Electro-coating with zinc. **1888** *Encycl. Brit.* XXIII. 449/2 This is done..in *electro-contact mines by a circuit closer in the mine. **1903** *Daily Chron.* 25 June 4/3 The relative merits of electro-contact and observation mines. **1952** *Brit. Jrnl. Psychol.* Feb. 38 A course of *electroconvulsive therapy..the weakening or breaking up of certain behaviour patterns promoted by affective disturbances. *Ibid.*, If E.C.T. blots out or breaks up the depressive pattern. **1958** A. WILSON *Middle Age of Mrs. Eliot* II. 251, I hope they don't give your friend E.C.T. If it's a very expensive place they probably won't. But at the hospitals they do. **1965** *Nursing Times* 5 Feb. 188/2 Electroconvulsive therapy (ECT) is used in the treatment of both depressive and manic states. **1968** *Times* 8 Nov. 5/8 A new legitimate opportunity for studying human brain function has recently been afforded by the use of electroconvulsive shock treatment, or ECT as a therapy for depressive illness. **1852** JOUBERT in *Jrnl. Soc. Arts* 26 Nov., One *electro-copper plate has yielded more than 12,000 impressions. **1873** E. SPON *Workshop Rec.* 1st Ser. 212/2 Steel, iron, zinc, lead, and tin which have been previously *electro-coppered. **1954** *Electrocortin [see ALDOSTERONE]. **1955** *Sci. News Let.* 5 Feb. 82/1 At the Mayo Clinic, Rochester, Minn., Dr. Philip S. Hench, co-discoverer of cortisone and Nobel Prize winner, and a number of his associates have been trying out two of the new anti-arthritis drugs. These two are aldosterone, also called electrocortin, and fluorohydrocortisone. **1902** WEBSTER Suppl., *Electro-culture. **1917** *Electrical Rev.* 6 July 21/1 Though only just beginning to attract public attention, electro-culture is by no means a new idea. **1932** *Times* 13 May 9/3 Even if electroculture in the vegetable garden were to become common, [etc.]. **1965** WOODWARD & HOFFMANN in *Jrnl. Amer. Chem. Soc.* 20 Jan. 395/1 We define as **electrocyclic* transformations the formation of a single bond between the termini of a linear system containing *k* π-electrons.., and the converse process. *Ibid.* 5 May 2045/1 The stereochemical course of an electrocyclic ring closure is determined by the symmetry of the highest occupied molecular orbital of the open-chain reactant. **1864** *Reader* 5 Oct. 483/3 For *electro-deposit a large series of depositing cells is required. **1882** *Nature* XXV. 360 An *electro-deposited coating. *c* **1865** G. GORE in *Circ. Sc.* I. 239/2 Coating metals..by *electro-deposition. *Ibid.* 215/2 Some *electro-depositors use vats..of wrought iron. **1919** W. L. CLARK in *Amer. Jrnl. Electrotherapeutics & Radiology* XXXVII. 211 *(title)* The treatment of some lesions of the skin and mucous membranes by *electrodesiccation. **1926** *Arch. Dermatol. & Syphilol.* XIII. 344 Electrodesiccation..should be evaluated as an additional therapeutic weapon in the hands of the dermatologist. *Ibid.* 345 Electrodesiccation produces a dehydration of the tissue, with shrinking of the cellular elements. **1962** *Southern Med. Jrnl.* LV. 391/1 Postoperative bleeding was controlled by electrodesiccation under halothane anesthesia. **1921** *Chem. Abstr.* XV. 3983 The Ca is removed by '*electrodialysis'. **1959** *Observer* 7 June 10/6 With brackish water it is cheaper to remove the salt from the water. The most promising method of doing this is electro-dialysis, which uses an electric charge across sets of special membranes to separate out the salt. **1965** *New Scientist* 4 Nov. 341/1 Electro-dialysis can reduce the acidity of citrus fruits by at least 50 per cent. **1934** *Arch. Neurol. & Psychiatry* (Chicago) XXXI. 469 *Electroencephalogram of the cortex in stimulation of the labyrinth. **1936** W. G. WALTER in *Lancet* 8 Aug. 305 He [*sc.* Hans Berger] called the record of this activity..the Electrenkephalogram, abbreviated as 'EEG' by analogy with the electrocardiogram—ECG. In English-speaking countries the term has come to be 'electroencephalogram'. **1969** *Times* 15 Apr. 9/3 Recording the pattern of brain waves, or electroencephalogram..emitted. **1939** *Times* 9 Mar. 11/5 The exhibits included an *electrencephalograph, lately brought from the United States by Dr. Denis Williams. The apparatus is an amplifying device for recording on paper the minute electrical waves from the human brain. **1968** *Sunday Tel.* 28 Jan. 4/4 The donor, Miss Denise Darvell, a motor accident victim, was then given electrocardiograph and electroencephalograph tests on heart and brain. **1951** *Sci. News Let.* 17 Feb. 106/2 The Eastern Association of *Electroencephalographers. **1936** W. G. WALTER in *Lancet* 8 Aug. 307/2 This confirmed the *electro-encephalographic diagnosis. **1958** *Observer* 21 Sept. 13/4 Electro-encephalographic recordings of the brain of the unborn child. **1958** *New Yorker* 5 Apr. 74/3 Here was the *electroencephalographist's summary of his findings. **1936** W. G. WALTER in *Lancet* 8 Aug. 305 *(title)* Location of cerebral tumours by *electroencephalography. **1941** BEAUMONT & DODDS *Rec. Adv. Med.* (ed. 10) xiii. 317 Electro-encephalography..is now accepted as a genuine method of studying electrical changes in the cerebral cortex. **1934** WEBSTER, *Electroform, v., *electroforming, n. **1950** *Jrnl. Iron & Steel Inst.* CLXV. 245/1 The bending fatigue properties were determined for electroformed sheets of iron-nickel. **1954** *Electronic Engin.* XXVI. 325/2 Electroforming..is particularly suited to the production of waveguides and micro-wave equipment. *Ibid.* 325/3 Copper is the metal most commonly deposited, but *electroforms can be produced with an initial deposit of ·003/·005 in. silver or nickel. **1881** C. W. SIEMENS in *Nature* XXIII. 353 *Electro-fusion of..iron or platinum. **1837** J. S. COYNE *Queer Subject* I. iii, You shall see me make this subject more by the action of the *Electro-Galvanic Battery. **1847** BRETT & LITTLE *Impr. Electr. Telegr.* 13 The nature of electro-galvanic action. **1922** *Encycl. Brit.* XXX. 966/1 **Electrogalvanizing*, the electrolytic deposition of a coating of zinc, from sulphate solutions, upon iron articles is now a well-established industry in all the leading manufacturing countries. **1940** *Chambers's Techn. Dict.* 287/1 *Electro-galvanising*, the electro-deposition of a protective coating of zinc on metal objects. **1935** *Discovery* Nov. 327/2 The organ as a whole resembles a beehive, for the *electrogenic units or elements are grouped in batteries of prismatic form. **1970** *Nature* 28 Feb. 820/1 Electrogenic explanations of ionic pumps have been proposed. **1858** O. W. HOLMES *Aut. Breakf. T.* (1865) 14 Men of letters..will not disturb the popular fallacy respecting this or that *electro-gilded celebrity. *c* **1865** G. GORE in *Circ. Sc.* I. 227/2 Liquid..for..*electro-gilding. **1871** tr. *Schellen's Spectr. Anal.* §28. 98 Delicate steel parts..have been *electro-gilt. **1956** *Interavia* XI. 373 An *electro-gravitic field acting on all parts simultaneously. *Ibid.* 374/1 The communication possibilities of *electro-gravitics, as the new science is called, confound the imagination. **1956** *Jrnl. Brit. Interplan. Soc.* XV. 387 'Electrogravitics' may revolutionize methods of transport by control of gravity fields. **1960** C. H. GIBBS-SMITH *Aeroplane* 296 *Electrogravitics*, a popular, but increasingly used, term for the general study of gravity and the force it exerts. **1880** in *Nature* XXI. 457 The expense of *electro-horticulture depends mainly upon the cost of mechanical energy. **1922** J. W. M. SOTHERN *Marine Diesel Oil Engines* xi. 359 In the *electro-hydraulic gear the power unit is placed directly beside the steering gear, and consists of a constant speed, non-reversing electric motor E driving a pump unit. **1966** *Science* 7 Oct. 155/1 Electrohydraulics is a new process for converting electrical energy directly to other forms of energy. It depends upon the discharge of a high-voltage arc under the surface of a liquid medium. *Ibid.* 157/2 Electrohydraulic treatment is an extremely effective..way to sterilize water and sewage. **1967** *Jane's Surface Skimmer Systems* 18/1 Similar electro-hydraulic signalling and feed-back systems are used to control propeller pitches. *Ibid.* 117 *(caption)* Power is provided by four 850 hp M-50 diesels,..controlled *electro-hydraulically from the forward wheelhouse. **1955** E. BURGESS *Frontier to Space* v. 99 This experiment appears to confirm that the equatorial *electrojet does in fact exist..and that it occurs in the E layer. **1956** *Jrnl. Brit. Interplan. Soc.* XV. 276 At 100 km. is the E layer in which electrojets flow and which were detected by early Aerobee rockets penetrating into this region. **1881** MAXWELL *Electr. & Magn.* II. 207 The *Electrokinetic Energy of the system. **1889** Electroluminescence [see PHOTOLUMINESCENCE]. **1902** MANN & MILLIKAN tr. *Drude's Theory of Optics* III. iii. 540 The sodium light is produced by an electric discharge in a vacuum tube. In this *electro-luminescence the temperature is..lower. **1936** *Times Lit. Suppl.* 15 Feb. 125/3 Electroluminescence, such as is exhibited in neon signs, perhaps shows the way to greater efficiency. **1956** *Sat. Rev.* 6 Oct. 55/1 This new form of light is called electroluminescence. The glow comes from a powdered phosphor..sprayed on the surface of a glass plate... On the side that emits the light the glass is coated..with a transparent stuff that conducts electricity. **1909** *Cent. Dict.* Suppl., Electroluminescence, *electroluminescent. **1956** *Nature* 4 Feb. 240/2 The electro-luminescent properties of some zinc sulphide phosphors have been tentatively ascribed to a partial transformation from hexagonal to cubic. **1888** *Encycl. Brit.* XXIII. 450/1 *Electro-mechanical mines can be made by placing a voltaic battery inside the mine itself. **1927** *Observer* 22 May 13/1 The national exhibit of hydro-electricity..consists principally of drawings, graphs..which will give an idea..of the electro-mechanical constructions..in Italy. **1943** *Gloss. Terms Electr. Engin. (B.S.I.)* 135 *Electromechanical brake*, a brake consisting of friction shoes applied..and released electrically. **1963** B. FOZARD *Instrumentation Nucl. Reactors* vii. 72 Where an electro-mechanical register is used..care must be taken to ensure that this does not lead to lost counts. **1967** *Jane's Surface Skimmer Systems* 12/1 The craft..is balanced prior to moving off by an electro-mechanical weight shifting arrangement. **1909** R. B. MATTHEWS *Electr. for Everybody* I. ix. 87 *(heading)* *Electro-medical apparatus. **1961** *Engineering* 2 June 753 The large number of electro-medical appliances now in use. **1854** SCOFFERN in *Orr's Circ. Sc.* Chem. 117 Covering it with a thin layer of gold by the *electrometallurgic process. *c* **1865** J. WYLDE in *Circ. Sc.* I. 302/1 *Electro-metallurgical processes require certain temperatures. **1840** SMEE *(title)* Elements of *Electro-metallurgy. **1846** JOYCE *Sc. Dialog.* iii. *Electr.* 412 The whole art of electro-metallurgy..consists in making a good selection of solutions. **1879** DU MONCEL *Telephone* 11 The *electro-musical telephones. **1870** HOLMES *Surg.* (ed. 2) IV. A peculiar pain, which is called *electro-muscular sensibility. **1917** *Amer. Jrnl. Physiol.* XLII. 229 The undulations seen in the *electromyogram of human muscles in voluntary contraction. **1963** *Lancet* 19 Jan. 152/2 A 'myopathic' pattern in the electromyogram can be obtained from a high proportion of carrier females. **1964** *Amer. Speech* XXXIX. 231 Electromyograms of muscular activity are similar for all positions of [f]. **1958** *IRE Trans. Med. Electronics* XI. 45 *(heading)* A new six-channel *electromyograph for studies on muscle. **1923** *Amer. Jrnl. Physiol.* LXV. 234 *(heading)* *Electro-myographic studies of muscular fatigue in man. **1951** *Sci. News* XXII. 7 The great advantage of the electromyographic method..is that the activity of the muscles can be studied in the intact individual, practically without any interference whatsoever with the normal modes of posture or movement. **1970** *Language* XLVI. 315 We will present some new electro-myographic data obtained from the laryngeal and supra-laryngeal muscles during speech. **1928** *Brain* LI. 517 It is possible that the evidence of physiological fatigue could be demonstrated *electromyographically. **1926** *Jrnl. Amer. Med. Assoc.* 16 Oct. 1300/1 Work in *electromyography is complicated by variations in the resistance of the body in different individuals. **1949** J. F. FULTON *Textbk. Physiol.* (ed. 16) v. 133 Electromyography, as a convenient method for detection and measurement of neuromuscular disorders, can be used only on the basis of deviation from the known normal patterns of muscular activity. **1950** *Electronic Engin.* XXIV. 43/1 The measurement of phenomena associated with the nervous, cardio-vascular and respiratory systems. This includes..electromyography (E.M.G.). **1951** *Sci. News* XXII. 7 Electrical potentials can be recorded from contracting muscles... This technique is called electromyography. **1956** *Nature* 18 Feb. 340/2 Electromyography of the internal laryngeal muscles has been applied in the diagnosis of laryngeal palsy. **1949** POLATIN & PHILTINE *How Psychiatry Helps* (1951) vi. 168 *Electronarcosis..is a new form of shock therapy for mental diseases. *Ibid.*, The term electronarcosis means, literally, coma or sleep induced by electrical current. *Ibid.* 169 Results of Electronarcosis Therapy. **1961** *Times* 17 Mar. 19/6 Electrical anaesthesia, or electronarcosis. **1952** *Brit. Jrnl. Psychol.* May 92 Bernberg showed that lengthy *electronarcotic treatment of young rats..impedes their

later learning. **1810** HENRY *Elem. Chem.* (1826) I. 202 Bodies..attracted by positively electrified surfaces, and repelled by negative ones..may be termed..*electro-negative bodies. **1813** BERZELIUS in *Ann. Philos.* II. 453 If.. an acid or electro-negative oxide is neutralized by a quantity of base or electro-positive oxide. **1834** FARADAY in *Phil. Trans.* CXXIV. 79 Substances are frequently spoken of as being *electro-negative*, or *electro-positive*, according as they go under the supposed influence of a direct attraction to the positive or negative pole. **1881** MAXWELL *Electr. & Magn.* I. 343 The Anion, or the electronegative component. **1968** *New Scientist* 30 May 460/1 Oxygen is one of the most electronegative of elements, having a greater 'acquisitiveness' for electrons than most other elements. **1905** W. SIMON *Man. Chem.* (ed. 8) II. viii. 94 Each element in the table below behaves *electro-negatively toward those following, and electro-positively toward those preceding. **1926** *Jrnl. Amer. Chem. Soc.* XLVIII. 3130 A study of the *electronegativity of organic radicals is of much importance from the standpoint of the electronic conception of valence. **1843** GRAVES *Clinical Med.* xxi. 429 The *electro-nervous theory received a great accession of probability. **1947** CARMICHAEL & DEARBORN *Reading & Visual Fatigue* (1948) viii. 266 The term *electro-oculogram..is used to apply to the records traced in ink upon the recording paper... These records are made..by an ink-writing oscillograph which is actuated by amplified currents originating in electrodes placed about the orbits of the eyes. **1951** *Arch. Ophthalmology* XLV. 185 There remains much that could be investigated using the *electro-oculograph as an instrument of research. **1955** *Brit. Jrnl. Ophthalmology* XXXIX. 398 This recorded *electro-oculographic response (EOG) depends on the angle and speed at which the globe rotates. **1958** *Amer. Jrnl. Ophthalmology* XLV. 158/2 In 25 subjects with unilateral amblyopia there was uncertain fixation which is..*electrooculographically demonstrable. **1951** *Arch. Ophthalmology* XLV. 184 Many optimistic predictions or suggestions have been made for the future of *electro-oculography in visual research. **1879** *Telegr. Jrnl.* VII. 306/2 (*title*) *Electro-optic properties of liquids. **1906** *Westm. Gaz.* 20 Sept. 2/1 Lorentz made an *electro-optical model which led Zeeman to recognise the action of a magnetic field on the lines of the spectrum. **1963** G. TROUP *Masers & Lasers* (ed. 2) ix. 162 Optical modulation techniques, using electro- and magneto-optical methods. **1906** *Jrnl. Soc. Chem. Industry* 15 Feb. 127/2 (*heading*) Water and juices from mineral, animal and vegetable substances; continuous process for extracting—by *electro-osmosis. **1944** S. FIELD *Princ. Electro-deposition* xx. 279 This motion of the dispersion medium is known as electro-osmosis. **1962** *New Scientist* 15 Mar. 630 Electro-osmosis.. is the flow of liquid through the pores in a membrane under the influence of an electric field. **1907** *Chem. Abstr.* I. 2206 The solid constituents remain as separate as in mixtures such as sand, clay, and lime, the *electrosmotic components separating readily while the non-electrosmotic components remain in the liquid. **1946** *Nature* 10 Aug. 205/1 The variations of speed [of colloidal particles]..are due to electro-osmotic currents. **1969** *Times* 30 July 10/6 The electrical method of damp-proofing is known as electro-osmotic damp-proofing. **1907** *Chem. Abstr.* I. 2651 Any substances that do not wander *electro-osmotically remain in the liquid. **1942** S. GLASSTONE *Introd. Electrochem.* xvi. 527 The volume *v* of liquid transported electro-osmotically per second. **1941** E. D. HUGHES in *Trans. Faraday Soc.* XXXVII. 605 The substituting agent uses its electrons to attack the nucleus..or..its nucleus to combine with the electrons... The latter [type of substituting agent is termed] '*electrophilic', and we name the substitution processes accordingly. **1964** J. W. LINNETT *Electronic Struct. Molecules* vi. 92 The most common type of reagent that attacks an aromatic system is an electrophilic one. **1959** HALAS & MANVELL *Technique Film Animation* 338 **Electro-photographic transfer*, the photographic recording of pictures projected electrically, as through the cathode ray tube of television. **1967** E. CHAMBERS *Photolitho-Offset* xiv. 205 The electro-photographic system..is described. **1894** E. L. WILSON *Cycl. Photogr.* 138/1 *Electro-Photography, the production of photographs by means of electricity, or electric light. **1944** *Electronic Engin.* XVII. 145/2 (*title*) Electro-photography..a new system of producing photographic prints by electronic action. **1948** *Science* 29 Oct. 482/1 (*heading*) *Electrophrenic Respiration.... A new type of artificial respiration has been developed which uses electrical stimulation of one or both phrenic nerves. **1939** *Brit. Jrnl. Psychol.* Jan. 260 Hartline's *electrophysiological studies of nerve impulses in the vertebrate eye. **1962** *Oxf. Univ. Gaz.* 9 Mar. 786/1 An electro-physiological study of the way in which the bee discriminates the visual patterns which are known to be of importance in its normal life. **1889** *Cent. Dict.*, *Electro-physiologist. **1948** *Mind* LVII. 245 In the book before us [by Adrian] we have renewed proof of the debt owed by the modern student of nerve and brain to the electro-physiologist. **1838** *Ann. Electr., Magn., & Chem.* II. 228 Mr. Leithead's late work on *electro-physiology. **1881** W. SPOTTISWOODE in *Nature* XXV. 118 The..prospects of electro-physiology. **1945** *Electronic Engin.* XVII. 564 In electrophysiology it is becoming increasingly important for workers to familiarise themselves with quantitative procedures such as wave analysis. **1950** *Jrnl. Mental Sci.* XCVI. 514 (*title*) 'Regressive' *electroplexy in schizophrenics. *Ibid.* 520 In the light of our experiences we have discontinued the use of 'regressive' electroplexy. **1958** *Sunday Times* 6 July 10/5 Before the days of Electro-plexy (electrical shock treatment). **1965** J. POLLITT *Depression & its Treatment* iv. 50 Electro-convulsive treatment (E.C.T.) also referred to as electro-shock treatment (E.S.T.) or electroplexy is still the most rapid and effective treatment. **1899** *Daily News* 1 July 4/5 This Westinghouse *electro-pneumatic signalling plant. **1933** *Discovery* Feb. 65/2 A novel electro-pneumatic system of synchronizing the changing of the two gears has been evolved in the latest models with outstanding success. **1870** F. POPE *Electr. Tel.* i. (1872) 17 This modification of the Grove battery is sometimes called the *Electropoion battery. **1956** *Electronic Engin.* XXVIII. 484/2 The losses produced by *electropolished copper wires left out-of-doors for several months increased by 40 per cent. **1813, 1834** *Electro-positive [see *electro-negative*]. **1850** DAUBENY *Atom. The.* vii. (ed. 2) 205 Chlorine, an electro-negative body, takes the place of hydrogen, an electro-positive one. **1883** *Chamb. Jrnl.* 1 Dec. 765/1 Tin is..electro-positive to iron. **1967** C. W. DAVIES *Electrochemistry* xii. 139 Metals like cadmium, zinc or sodium, which tend to liberate hydrogen from acids, are often called electro-positive... The term 'electro-positive' implies that the metal has a relatively strong tendency to ionize as a positive ion. **1905** *Electro-positively [see *electro-negatively*]. **1955** *Chem. Abstr.* 7303 (*heading*) *Electropositivities of iodine. *c* **1865** G. GORE in *Circ. Sc.* I. 233/2 Taking copies..by the *electro-process. **1871** HOLMES *Surg.* (ed. 2) V. 528 *Electro-puncture is nothing more than the application of a galvanic current to the tissues included between two acupuncture needles. **1927** *Chem. Absr.* 57 (*heading*) The preparation of amino acids by *electroreduction of oximino esters. **1946** *Nature* 16 Nov. 706/1 The irreversible electro-reduction of each compound involves two electrons per molecule. **1936** *Amer. Jrnl. Physiology* CXVII. 338 Certain visual phenomena can be recorded not only from the eyeball itself in the usual *electro-retinogram, but from other stations in the optic pathway such as the optic nerve. **1951** *Electronic Engin.* May 170/1 An electro-retinogram is the voltage change generated by the retina in response to a flash of light falling on the eye. *Ibid.*, The amplifier..has been used..for recording human and animal electro-retinograms. **1964** J. Z. YOUNG *Model of Brain* vii. 118 The electro-retinogram produced by a moving spot of light changes with the direction of movement. **1948** *Brit. Jrnl. Psychol.* Dec. 80 Experiments on the *electro-retinography of various animals. **1944** *Dorland's Med. Dict.* 486/2 **Electroshock*, shock treatment by applying electric current to the brain. **1955** *Sci. News Let.* 29 Jan. 73/1 Electroshock treatment of the mentally ill can be 'softened'..by a new drug, succinyl-choline chloride. **1879** F. W. ROBINSON *Coward Conscience* II. II. xxi. 160 Dish-covers..radiant with *electro-silver. **1884** R. JEFFERIES *Dewy Morn* I. xxv. 282 For all their silver and electro 'the family' went to London. **1959** *Metalworking Production* 29 May 950 (*heading*) *Electro-slag welding comes to UK. *Ibid.* 950/1 A molten pool of highly-ionized and consequently electrically conductive slag which transfers the heat instead of the arc itself—therein lies the secret of the 'electro-slag' welding technique. **1966** *New Scientist* 7 July 6/2 Electro-slag refining..is what the steelmaker calls a secondary refining process—one, that is, which refines an ingot of steel to higher standard of purity and structural perfection. **1953** *Confinia Neurologica* XIII. 300 (*title*) Physiodynamic differentiation with non-convulsive *electrostimulation. *Ibid.* 301 My preference as to order of therapeutic priority based on safety, psychodynamic productivity and economy is as follows: carbon dioxide therapy has first priority unless there are specific contraindications, then non-convulsive electrostimulation (E.S., nc.), then convulsive electrostimulation (E.C.T.). **1969** *Nature* 9 Aug. 645/2 It is difficult to compare precisely the various forces produced by electrostimulation with those obtained when the subject volitionally tried to isolate and drive the same muscle groups. **1909** *Cent. Dict. Suppl.*, *Electrostriction. **1942** E. B. UVAROV *Dict. Sci.* 66 *Electrostriction*, state caused in a solution of an electrolyte by forces of attraction and repulsion between charged ions, giving rise to decreased mobility. **1956** *Electronic Engin.* XXVIII. 132/3 The distinction between piezostrictive (linear) and *electrostrictive (square-law, etc.) response to applied field. **1957** *Sci. News* XLIV. 98 For ultrasonic vibrations magnetostrictive, piezo-electric, and electrostrictive vibration generators are used. These convert electrical energy into mechanical energy and vice versa. **1898** H. W. F. LORENZ tr. W. Löb (*title*) Electrolysis and *electro-synthesis of organic compounds. **1965** *New Scientist* 23 Dec. 877/1 The application of large scale potentiostats in.. electrosynthesis and electrorefining,—particularly in organic and molten salt solvents. **1843** W. GROVE *Contrib. Sc.* in *Corr. Phys. Forces* (1874) 273 *Electro-synthetic absorption of nitrogen..Capable of *electro-synthetically combining. **1900** R. PEARL in *Amer. Jrnl. Physiol.* IV. 122 He [*sc.* Carlgren] does not attempt to make the cataphoric action the cause of all *electrotactic phenomena. **1900** R. PEARL in *Amer. Jrnl. Physiol.* IV. 96 Nearly all of the work on *electrotaxis among the Protozoa has been done either to determine the sense of reaction..or to analyze the effect of the current on protoplasm. **1968** *Biol. Abstr.* XLIX. 2347/2 The collection of the active zoospore by electrotaxis was not successful. **1885** *Pall Mall G.* 18 June 11/2 The recent developments of practical electricity and *electro-technology. **1843** *Chamb. Jrnl.* XII. 128 Communications may be transmitted with *electro-telegraphic speed. *c* **1865** J. WYLDE in *Circ. Sc.* I. 258/2 The voltaic battery in *electro-telegraphy. **1908** *Practitioner* Oct. 609 The other sections, namely, Dermatological, *Electro-therapeutical, Epidemiological. **1909** *Ibid.* Dec. 870 The Electro-therapeutical Department, West London Hospital. **1868** W. JAMES in *N. Amer. Rev.* CVII. 326 The 'laws' of nerve and muscle electricity..have not..furnished a single hint even towards *electro-therapeutics. **1887** J. BUTLER (*title*) Text-book of Electro-Therapeutics, etc. **1899** *Westm. Gaz.* 19 July 10/1 Oculists, and *electro-therapeutists. **1928** *Sunday Dispatch* 23 Dec. 5/6 Even Grosvenor-street having a dressmaker and an electro-therapeutist. **1928** *Daily Express* 16 May 7 An electro-therapist. **1881** *Nature* XXIV. 351 A new and effective method of treating disease—*electrotherapy. **1884** W. THOMSON in *Pract. Applications Electr.* 174 Joule's *electro-thermal method. **1902** *Encycl. Brit.* XXVIII. 123/2 In 1885 the brothers Cowles patented a process for the electrothermal reduction of oxidized ores. **1961** *Engineering* 10 Nov. 611 A new non-explosive process for breaking rock has been studied by the United States General Electric Company. The process is known as electrothermal forcing. **1899** *Engineering Mag.* June 495/1 *Electrothermic methods have been in use for a number of years in connection with the production of aluminium, sodium, [etc.]. **1959** *Jrnl. Iron & Steel Inst.* CXCI. 197/2 Results of electro-thermic smelting tests carried out on these ores. **1889** *Cent. Dict.*, *Electrotin v. **1944** *Jrnl. Iron & Steel Inst.* CXLIX. 152 P, It was understood from results of American experience in the use of *electro-tinned strip that steel electroplated with 6–8 oz. of tin per basis box..could be made into cans..without difficulty. **1937** *Jrnl. Iron & Steel Inst.* CXXXVI. 27 A, It appeared that in the acid bath, speeds of *electro-tinning comparable with those used for hot-tinning are feasible. **1945** HOARE & HEDGES *Tinplate* xii. 256 *Electro-tinplate is a new material, the full scope of which is as yet untried. **1942** *Iron & Steel Engineer* Feb. 90/1 The importance of the matter of *electro-tin plating of steel strip stems from the magnitude of the tin plate industry. **1842** J. SAMPSON (*title*) *Electro-tint, or the Art of making paintings in such a manner that copper Plates and 'Blocks' can be taken from them by Voltaic Electricity. [**1898** H. C. PORTER tr. *Strasburger's Text-bk. Bot.* 263 The existence of electropism in plants shows clearly that an irritability may be present, from which no direct benefit is ordinarily derived.] **1907** R. J. H. GIBSON tr. *Jost's Lect. Plant Physiol.* xxxi. 481 Hegler..established negative *electrotropism in *Phycomyces*. **1965** BELL & COOMBE tr. *Strasburger's Textbk. Bot.* III. 374 Roots and shoots behave inversely.., roots bending towards the side which becomes positively charged, and shoots away from it (electrotropism). **1921** I. LANGMUIR in *Science* LIV. 61/1 We shall see that the positive and negative valence differ from one another fundamentally only in algebraic sign, so that we shall find it convenient to include both positive and negative valence under the term **electrovalence*, which we may designate by the symbol v_e. *Ibid.* 61/2 The *electrovalence* of an atom in any compound may thus be defined as the number of electrons which the neutral atom must give up in forming that compound. **1923** *Jrnl. Chem. Soc.* CXXIII. 822 Whilst a single bond may be either a covalency or an *electrovalency, a double bond in organic chemistry usually reacts as if it contained one covalency and one electrovalency. **1927** N. V. SIDGWICK *Electronic Theory Valency* 84 Covalencies, unlike electrovalencies, are directed forces. **1964** N. G. CLARK *Mod. Org. Chem.* ii. 23 Atoms bound by this type of valency must remain in close proximity..and there is no question of their leading separate existences, as do the ions in electrovalency. **1927** N. V. SIDGWICK *Electronic Theory Valency* 83 The electronic structure which we assign to an atom in a molecule depends on whether we regard its attachments to other atoms as *electrovalent or covalent. **1947** *Nature* 18 Jan. 100/2 The long-chain molecules of which collagen fibres are composed are mainly held together by lateral bondings of an electro-valent character. **1950** *Sci. News* XV. 58 The whole thing is held together by the fact that it is made up of mutually attracting particles..the ionic or electrovalent link, as it is called. **1936** *Chem. Abstr.* XXX. 6621 (*heading*) The theory of *electroviscosity. **1941** *Jrnl. Phys. Chem.* XLV. 953 The electroviscosity accounts for 59 per cent of the specific viscosity in a 1 per cent calcium caseinate system. **1935** *Chem. Abstr.* XXIX. 4236 (*heading*) The effect of an electric field on the viscosity of colloidal solutions. I. The external *electroviscous effect. **1967** *New Scientist* 30 Mar. 666/1 (*caption*) Apparent viscosity of a typical electroviscous dispersion varies directly with the strength of the applied electric field, and inversely with the shear rate. **1843** GRAVES *Clinical Med.* xxi. 432 *Electro-vital or neuro-electric currents. **1934** WEBSTER, *Electrowin, v. **1940** *Chambers's Techn. Dict.* 291/1 *Electro-winning. **1961** *Times* 13 Apr. 2/4 The fields of mining..electrowinning and refining. **1967** *New Scientist* 5 Oct. 21/1 If we extend the generally understood meaning of the term 'electro-winning' to include the electrochemical recovery not only of metals, but of all elemental substances from aluminium to chlorine. *Ibid.* 23/1 Aqueous electrowinning processes mostly take place in acid electrolytes.

electro-biology (ɪˌlɛktrəʊbaɪˈɒlədʒɪ). [f. prec. + BIOLOGY.]

1. The branch of electricity which deals with the electrical phenomena of living beings; = *electro-physiology* (see ELECTRO-).

1849 SMEE (*title*) Elements of Electro-biology. **1881** in *Nature* XXIV. 39 The first number of *L'Electricien* contains] an interesting article on electrobiology.

2. The name given about 1845 to a form of 'animal magnetism' or hypnotism, in which unconsciousness was induced by causing the patient to gaze steadily at a small bright object.

Originally the object used was a disc of zinc and copper, the galvanic action of which was supposed to be concerned in producing the result; hence perhaps the name, which however was employed by some writers as a synonym for 'animal magnetism' in general, with reference to its imagined relation to vital electricity.

1850 W. GREGORY *Anim. Magn.* 74 All the phenomena of the conscious state in..electro biology..can be produced.. by the older mesmeric or magnetic..methods. **1874** CARPENTER *Ment. Phys.* II. xiv. (1879) 550 Who styled themselves 'professors' of a new art which they termed Electro-Biology.

Hence **eˌlectrobioˈlogical** *a.* [see -ICAL], relating to electrobiology. **eˌlectrobiˈologist** [see -IST], a practiser of electrobiology.

1849 MACAULAY *Jrnl.* 13 May, I fought a mesmeric and electro-biological battle. **1856** R. VAUGHAN *Mystics* (1860) II. 109 The real combat was one of spirit against spirit.. what would now be called electro-biological. **1860** JEAFFRESON *Bk. about Doctors* II. 38 Electro-biologists, spirit-rappers, and table-turners. **1862** LYTTON *Str. Story* II. 220 This sage anticipated our modern electro-biologists.

electrocute (ɪˈlɛktrəkjuːt), *v.* [f. ELECTRO-, after EXECUTE *v.*] *trans.* To put to death by means of a powerful electric current.

1889 *Voice* (N.Y.) 1 Aug., Kemmler, the murderer sentenced to be 'electrocuted'. **1890** *Boston* (Mass.) *Jrnl.* 3 May 5/6 The important thing to consider is that the State has a large number of murderers which it can neither hang nor 'electrocute'—as the new phrase hath it. **1890** *Congress. Rec.* 8375/1 That the gentleman..should be 'electrocuted' by the Kemmler process recently adopted in the state of New York. **1920** A. HUXLEY *Limbo* x. 84 It was as though he were about to be electrocuted. **1970** *Capital Times* (Madison, Wis.) 16 Sept. 27/4 In 1890 the court cleared the way for William Kemmler of Buffalo, N.Y. to be the first person to be electrocuted in the United States.

b. *transf.* To kill in any way by electricity.

1909 *Yorkshire Post* 4 Aug. 4/5 [A boy] who was electrocuted on the Mersey Railway last Saturday. **1913** *Daily Mail* 13 Jan. 3/2 The horse..was struck by the wire and instantly electrocuted. **1970** *N.Y. Times* 18 Sept. 24/4 A girl electrocuted herself..when she got into a bath wearing electric hair curlers.

electrocution (ɪlɛktrəˈkjuːʃən). [f. prec.: see -TION.] Execution by electricity.

1890 *Evening News* 6 May 4/1 The Supreme Court of the United States has refused to grant a writ of habeas corpus in the case of the wife murderer under sentence of electrocution. **1890** *Columbus* (Ohio) *Dispatch* 4 Aug., Buffalo parties invited to witness the Kemmler electrocution. **1902** *Encycl. Brit.* XXVI. 579/1 Sentence of death is executed by hanging by the neck except in New York and Ohio, where it is carried out by 'electrocution', or by passing through the body of the convict a current of electricity of sufficient intensity to cause death and until death is caused.

b. Death caused in any way by electricity.

1940 in *Chambers's Techn. Dict.* **1948** *Nat. Geogr. Mag.* Mar. 395/1 A few whiffs of gas or chloroform are sometimes used, but most ranchers prefer electrocution.

electrode (ɪˈlɛktrəʊd). [f. ELECTRO- + *-ode* (as in ANODE), ad. Gr. ὁδός way.]

1. a. A conductor by means of which electricity enters or leaves an electrolyte, gas, or other medium, or a vacuum. See ANODE and CATHODE.

1834 FARADAY *Res. Electr.* (1839) §662 In place of the term pole I propose . . *Electrode*, and I mean thereby that surface . . which bounds the extent of the decomposing matter in the direction of the electric current. **1850** DAUBENY *Atom. The.* vii. (ed. 2) 207 The same wire, if made the positive electrode of the galvanic battery, is not acted upon by the acid. **1878** HUXLEY *Physiogr.* 102 This plate forms one of the electrodes or entrances by which the electricity reaches the liquid (otherwise called the poles).

b. *spec.* A welding-rod, a filler-rod.

1930 *Engineering* 14 Mar. 353/2 About 75 per cent. of his work was with bare wire electrodes. **1940** *Chambers's Techn. Dict.* 194/1 *Continuous electrode*, a type of carbon electrode used in electric furnaces; the electrode is gradually fed forward as the lower part burns away, and the upper part is renewed by adding fresh material. **1958** *Engineering* 11 Apr. 478/2 Automatic machines utilising . . continuous electrodes were employed for the automatic welding of the vessel.

2. *attrib.* and *Comb.*, as ***electrode efficiency, holder, material***; **electrode potential**, the difference of potential between an electrode and the electrolyte with which it is in contact (*Gloss. Terms Electr. Engin., B.S.I.*, 1943).

1940 *Chambers's Techn. Dict.* 287/1 *Electrode efficiency*, the ratio of the quantity of metal deposited in an electrolytic cell to the quantity which should theoretically be deposited according to Faraday's laws. **1944** S. FIELD *Princ. Electrodeposition* iii. 26 Another convenient term is 'electrode efficiency', representing the relative efficiencies at anode and cathode. **1909** *Cent. Dict.* Suppl. s.v. *Arc*, (*caption*) Electrode-holder. **1936** *Discovery* July 221/1 A ferruled electrode holder of the clamp type. **1940** *Chambers's Techn. Dict.* 287/1 *Electrode-holder*, in electric arc-welding, a device used for holding the electrode and leading the current to it. **1902** *Encycl. Brit.* XXVIII. 123/2 Ordinarily carbon is used as the electrode material. **1907** *Trans. Faraday Soc.* July 70 Electrode potentials in liquid ammonia. **1931** *Jrnl. Iron & Steel Inst.* CXXIII. 742 The electrode potentials of pearlitic steels of various carbon contents . . were also measured. **1944** S. FIELD *Princ. Electrodeposition* xiii. 167 Two of these electrode potentials, or 'single' potentials as they are sometimes called, contribute to the e.m.f. of the Daniell cell.

Hence **eˈlectrodeless** *a.*, destitute of electrodes.

1893 *Athenæum* 13 May 609/2 Mr. E. C. Rimington read a paper 'On Luminous Discharges in Electrodeless Vacuum Tubes'. **1899** *Daily News* 29 June 6/5 The electrode-less or ring discharge in various gases. **1966** *McGraw-Hill Encycl. Sci. & Technol.* XII. 589/1 A simple and extremely useful light source has been developed since 1946. . . It consists of an electrodeless glass or quartz tube containing a minute amount of volatile metal or compound plus a trace of argon gas excited in alternating electro-magnetic fields of ultra-high frequency.

electrodynamic (ɪˌlɛktrəʊdaɪˈnæmɪk), *a.* [f. ELECTRO- + DYNAMIC; cf. *hydrodynamic*.] Pertaining to the force excited by one magnetic current upon another. Also, of a loudspeaker, microphone, etc.: = *moving-coil* (*loudspeaker, microphone*). Hence **eˌlectrodyˈnamical** *a.*, **eˌlectrodyˈnamics**, the dynamics of electricity; the science of the mutual influence of electric currents. **eˌlectroˈdynamism** [see DYNAMISM] = *electrodynamics*. **eˌlectro-dynaˈmometer** [see DYNAMOMETER], an instrument for measuring electrodynamic force.

1827 H. DAVY in *Phil. Mag.* I. 197 What may be called the electro-dynamic relations. **1832** *Nat. Phil.* II. *Electro-Magnet* xii. §291. 90 (Usef. Knowl. Soc.) An electro-dynamic ring. **1881** SIR W. ARMSTRONG in *Nature* No. 619. 451 Electrodynamic machine. **1934** *Discovery* Oct. 301/2 Electro-dynamic sound producer. **1940** *Chambers's Techn. Dict.* 287/1 Electrodynamic loudspeaker . . electrodynamic microphone. **1907** *Nature* 11 Apr. 554/1 In spite of the fact that the word 'electrodynamical' has gone out of fashion, and that it is more proper nowadays to say 'electromagnetic', the old word is here retained. **1827** J. CUMMING *Man. Electro Dynamics* p. vi, A new science . . treating of the effects of electricity in motion through a continued system of conductors, has been termed Electro-dynamics. **1830** SIR J. HERSCHEL *Stud. Nat. Phil.* 324 Theory . . developed by M. Ampere, under the name of Electro-dynamics. **1870** R. FERGUSON *Electr.* 171 Electrodynamics treats of the mutual attractions and repulsions of currents on currents, and currents on magnets. **1876** *Catal. Sci. App. S. Kens.* 200 Electro-dynamometer, for measuring electric currents which are constantly being reversed in direction.

electrograph (ɪˈlɛktrəʊgrɑːf, -æ-). [f. ELECTRO- + Gr. -γράφος that writes.]

†**1.** (See quot.) *Obs.*

1840 SPENCER *Multipl. Wks. of Art by Electr.* Pref. 8 The instruments themselves [for producing electrotypes] should be called 'electrographs'.

2. An instrument for registering electrical conditions; the automatic record of an electrometer.

1881 G. M. WHIPPLE in *Nature* XXIII. 349 This want of accordance between the electrograph and magnetographs was, etc.

Hence **electroˈgraphic** *a.*

1868 LOSSING *Hudson* 191 From his study he has electrographic communication with all parts of the United States.

electrography (iː-, ɛlɛkˈtrɒgrəfɪ). [f. as prec. + Gr. -γραφία writing.] The process of copying an engraving on an electro-copper plate.

1840 SPENCER *Mutipl. Wks. of Art by Electr.* Pref. 8 The whole art of applying electricity to the production of such works of art should be termed 'electrography'.

electrolier (ɪˌlɛktrəˈlɪə(r)). [f. ELECTRO-, with ending arbitrarily adopted from *chandelier*; cf. *gaselier*.] A cluster of electric lamps.

1882 *Standard* 27 Mar. 5 Gigantic gilt-brass electrolier. **1884** *Health Exhib. Catal.* p. lxii/1 One large Metal Electrolier. **1923** A. HUXLEY *Antic Hay* xiii. 192 The convex reflections of the electroliers. **1942** *Times* 21 Mar. 2/4 'Look at all these lights!' he exclaimed, with a motion of the arm towards the numerous ornate electroliers with their dazzling brilliance.

electrology (iː-, ɛlɛkˈtrɒlədʒɪ). [f. ELECTRO- + -LOGY.] The science of electricity. Also occasionally used in other senses (see quots. 1896, 1940, and 1970). Hence **electroˈlogic, -ical** *adjs.*

1840 W. WHEWELL *Philos. Induct. Sci.* I. p. lxxii, Electricity is in the same condition as heat; having only one word to express the property and the science. M. Le Comte proposes Electrology: for the same reason as before, I should conceive Electrics more agreeable to analogy. **1896** *Daily News* 13 Feb. 2/1 The newly-elected president [*sc.* Capt. Abney] avowed his preference for 'electrology' as against 'photography'. **1940** *Chambers's Techn. Dict.* 290/2 *Electro-therapy* . . , the treatment of diseases by electric currents, or by electrically produced radiations. Also called *electrology*. **1970** *Daily Hampshire Gaz.* (Northampton, Mass.) 1 Oct. 2/1 (Advt.), Electrology. Permanent Hair Removal.

electrolysis (iːlɛk-, ɛlɛkˈtrɒlɪsɪs). [f. ELECTRO- + Gr. λύσις unbinding; after ANALYSIS.]

1. a. Chemical decomposition by galvanic action.

1834 W. WHEWELL *Let.* 5 May (1876) II. 182 If you take anode and cathode, I would propose for the two elements resulting from electrolysis the terms anion and cation. **1839–47** TODD *Cycl. Anat.* III. 720/1 The organ generates electricity . . and can effect electrolysis. **1873** H. SPENCER *Stud. Sociol.* ix. 224 The great contributions of Faraday—magneto-electricity, the quantitative law of electrolysis.

b. as the name of a branch of science.

1870 R. FERGUSON *Electr.* 161 Electrolysis is generally understood to treat of the changes effected in a substance subjected to, but not giving rise to, the current.

2. a. *Surgery.* The breaking up of tumours, also of calculi, by electric agency.

1867 ALTHAUS in *Brit. Med. Journ.* 11 May, Tumours . . treated by electrolysis. **1871** SIR T. WATSON *Princ. Med.* (ed. 5) II. 634 Dr. Hilton Fagge . . [has] treated light cases of hydatid disease of the Liver by electrolysis.

b. (See quots.)

1909 *Daily Mirror* 4 Oct. 10/3 (Advt.), Electrolysis. Superfluous hair permanently removed; ladies only; consultations free. **1934** WEBSTER, *Electrolysis*, surgical destruction, as of hair roots . . with an electric current. **1959** *Woman* 5 Sept. 18/1 The only permanent way of getting rid of superfluous hair is by electrolysis.

electrolyte (ɪˈlɛktrəlaɪt). [f. ELECTRO- + Gr. λυτός loosed, f. λύειν to loose.] **a.** A substance which dissolves in water or another suitable medium to give a solution capable of conducting an electric current; also, such a solution. **b.** The ionized or ionizable constituents of a biological system.

1834 FARADAY *Res. Electr.* (1839) §664 Many bodies are decomposed directly by the electric current, . . these I propose to call electrolytes. **1842** W. GROVE *Corr. Phys. Forces* (1874) 143 All liquids capable of being decomposed by the voltaic electrical force, thence called Electrolytes. **1885** WATSON & BURBURY *Math. Th. Electr. & Magn.* I. 231 The same constituent which in one electrolyte becomes an anion, may in another electrolyte become a cation. **1950** J. OSBORNE *Dental Mech.* (ed. 3) xxiii. 384 Care must be taken to maintain the electrolyte solution in its correct condition, otherwise satisfactory plating cannot be achieved. **1960** *Times* 11 Apr. 1/4 Neuro-physiology, electrolyte regulation, hormone assay. **1962** *Lancet* 6 Jan. 32/1 Awareness of impaired function of the distal tubule . . alerts the surgeon to the possible need for electrolyte replacement in patients who do badly after prostatectomy. **1966** *McGraw-Hill Encycl. Sci. & Technol.* XII. 426/2 The pH of acid soils varies between 3 and 7, the reaction depending on the ion saturation and the soluble electrolyte content. **1968** *Practical Motorist* Nov. 333/1 *Electrolyte.* In a car battery, the liquid filling the cells, in which the plates are immersed. It is a mixture of sulphuric acid and distilled water.

eˌlectroˈlytic, *a.* and *sb.* [f. ELECTROLYTE: see -IC.] Pertaining to, or capable of, electrolysis. Also as *sb.* = electrolytic copper (shares).

1842 W. GROVE *Corr. Phys. Forces* (1874) 153 Electrolytic power of water. **1861** MILLER in *Circ. Sc.* I. 167/2 Decomposition . . by electrolytic action. **1872** COHEN *Dis. Throat* 208 The improvement began with the institution of the electrolytic treatment. **1892** *Daily News* 7 Dec. 5/6 The united production of all the electrolytic copper works in the world is estimated . . at between thirty and forty thousand tons of copper every year. **1897** *Ibid.* 4 Jan. 2/6 The electrolytic refinery at Anaconda has now the capacity of treating the other half of the Company's product. **1909** WEBSTER, *Electrolytic dissociation theory*, the theory that the molecules of electrolytes in solution dissociate into ions. **1912** *Times* 19 Dec. 20/3 The level of prices in this market [is] considered favourable to buyers in comparison with those at present ruling in New York for electrolytic. **1923** U. R. EVANS *Metals & Metallic Cpds.* I. 55 Electrolytic Dissociation or Ionization: a splitting into electrically charged ions, of which the 'positive ion' consists of the most characteristic metal present, bereft of some or all of its valency electrons. **1929** *Bell System Techn. Jrnl.* VIII. 41 The aluminum electrolytic condenser . . utilises the dielectric property of the film to provide electrostatic capacity. **1930** *Engineering* 11 Apr. 475/2 Precautions are necessary to ensure that only electrolytic copper is used. **1930** *Economist* 20 Sept. 538/2 Some of the smaller independent producers in America are now offering electrolytic at only 10½ c. per lb. **1931** S. R. ROGET *Dict. Electr. Terms* (ed. 2) 105/2 *Electrolytic rectifier* or *valve*, an apparatus in which alternate half waves of an alternating current are suppressed . . so that a unidirectional current is produced. **1937** *Jrnl. Iron & Steel Inst.* CXXXVI. 42 A, Electrolytic polishing—really a type of etching—allows the properties of the crystal faces to be studied. **1940** *Chambers's Techn. Dict.* 287/2 *Electrolytic capacitor*, a capacitor in which the dielectric between the plates is an electrolyte, instead of the more usual solid insulating material. *Ibid.*, *Electrolytic cell*, a vessel in which electrolysis is carried out. *Ibid.*, *Electrolytic refining*, the method of producing pure metals, by making the impure metal the anode in an electrolytic cell and depositing a pure cathode. **1958** *Chambers's Techn. Dict.* Suppl. 976/1 *Electrolytic polishing*, forming an apparently polished surface on metal by making it an anode in an electrolytic bath. **1958** *Newnes Compl. Amat. Photogr.* 113 A 22.5 V. hearing aid battery is used to charge an electrolytic capacitor through the flashbulb.

Hence **eˌlectroˈlytical** *a.* = prec. **eˌlectroˈlytically** *adv.*, by means of electrolysis.

1834 FARADAY *Res. Electr.* (1839) §664 The term electrolytical will be understood at once. Muriatic acid is electrolytical, boracic acid is not. **1843** W. GROVE *Contrib. Sc.* in *Corr. Phys. Forces* (1874) 279 Completion of the circuit and the electrolytical action are synchronous. **187.** *Chamb. Encycl.* s.v. *Galvanism*, Gold . . can be deposited electrolytically.

electrolyze (ɪˈlɛktrəlaɪz), *v.* [f. ELECTROLYTE, after analogy of *analyze*, etc.] *trans.* **a.** To decompose by electrical means. **b.** To break up (a tumour, calculus) by means of galvanism.

1834 FARADAY *Res. Electr.* (1839) §665 Chloride of lead . . when electrolyzed evolves the two ions, chlorine and lead. **1881** S. P. THOMPSON in *Proc. Soc. Arts* 24 Dec. 454 Electrolysing water with small platinum points.

Hence **eˌlectroˈlyzable** *a.* [see -ABLE], capable of being electrolyzed. **eˌlectrolyˈzation** [see -ATION], the process of electrolyzing. **eˈlectroˌlyzed** *ppl. a.*, decomposed by galvanic action.

1834 FARADAY *Res. Electr.* §664 For electro-chemically decomposed I shall often use the term electrolyzed. **1834** —— in *Phil. Trans.* CXXIV. 117 When it has performed its full work of electrolyzation, it has only separated the elements of a single grain of water. **1876** DUHRING *Dis. Skin* 95 Electrolyzation is of value in the treatment of . . tumors. **1881** *Athenæum* 12 Nov. 635/1 The electrolyzed liquid is sulphuric acid.

electromagnet (ɪˌlɛktrəʊˈmægnɪt). Also with hyphen. [f. ELECTRO- + MAGNET.] A piece of soft iron surrounded by a coil of wire, through which a current of electricity may be passed, rendering the iron temporarily magnetic.

1831 *Amer. Jrnl. Sci.* XX. 201 Account of a large Electro-magnet. **1832** W. STURGEON in *Phil. Mag.* XI. 194 On Electro-magnets. *c* **1865** J. WYLDE in *Circ. Sc.* I. 250/2 A horse-shoe electro-magnet. **1879** G. PRESCOTT *Sp. Telephone* Introd. 2 The first simple electro-magnet was made by Sturgeon [of Manchester].

Hence **eˌlectromagˈnetic, -magˈnetical** *adjs.*, pertaining to electromagnetism. **eˌlectromagˈnetically** *adv.*, by means of electromagnetism. **eˌlectromagˈnetics**, the science of electromagnetism. **eˌlectroˈmagnetism**, the phenomena of the production of magnetism by the electric current; also, the influence of a magnet on the electric current.

1821 FARADAY *Diary* 3 Sept. (1932) I. 49 Electro-magnetic expts. with Hare's Calorimotor. **1823** J. BADCOCK *Dom. Amusem.* 126 The electro-magnetic influence always increased with the number of the plates. **1837** *Ann. Electr., Magn., & Chem.* I. 387 We need scarcely despair of seeing the electro-magnetic telegraph established for regular communication from one town to another. **1879** G. PRESCOTT *Sp. Telephone* Introd. 2 An electro-magnetic telegraph. **1905** *Harmsworth Encycl.* III. 2174/3 It was shown by Clerk Maxwell that a repeated electrical or magnetic disturbance or change would set up and radiate waves of an electro-magnetic nature in the ether, and that, with certain assumptions concerning the ether, these waves would travel with the velocity of light. Upon this is based his electro-magnetic theory of light. **1908** *Chem. Abstr.* 372

Calculation of the resistance of a wire when reflecting electro-magnetic waves. **1929** E. MALLETT *Telegr. & Teleph.* xi. 281 Whenever an electric current changes in a circuit, energy in the form of electromagnetic waves is radiated away from the circuit. **1937** J. E. SHRADER *Physics for Students* lv. 539 (*caption*) The electromagnetic spectrum. **1955** *Gloss. Terms Radiology* (*B.S.I.*) 10 *Electromagnetic radiation*, radiation associated with a periodically varying electric and magnetic field. **1957** *Technology* Mar. 13/1 The common feature of these new electromagnetic pumps is that, instead of using electromagnetic forces to cause solid metal to rotate, they use these forces to drive liquid metal under pressure along a pipe. **1965** M. GARBUNY *Optical Physics* i. 2 Altogether, it is now known that the electromagnetic spectrum..encompasses radio- and microwaves, infrared, visible, and ultraviolet light, *x* (or Roentgen-) rays, gamma, and cosmic radiation. **1823** J. BADCOCK *Dom. Amusem.* 126 Electro-magnetical effects. **1881** SIR W. THOMSON in *Nature* XXIV. 435 To transmit electro-magnetically the work of waterfalls. **1828** F. WATKINS (*title*) Popular Sketches of Electro-Magnetism. **1830** SIR J. HERSCHEL *Stud. Nat. Phil.* 94 Oërsted's great discovery of electro-magnetism. **1879** G. PRESCOTT *Sp. Telephone* 5 Reproducing tones by electro-magnetism.

electromatic (ɪˌlɛktrəˈmætɪk), *a.* [f. ELECTRO- + AUTO)MATIC *a.*] Of, pertaining to, or designating electrical equipment operated automatically, particularly road traffic light signals.

Electromatic was registered as a trade mark for a particular kind of telephone by Messrs. Gent & Co. Ltd., Leicester, in 1912; and (in the form *Electro-Matic*) for 'street traffic visual signalling apparatus' by the Automatic Electric Company Ltd., Liverpool, in 1932.

1933 *Boys' Mag.* XLVII. 170/1 The greatest advance [in traffic signals]..has been the introduction of the 'Vehicle Operated' or Electromatic System. **1937** *Times* 13 Apr. p. viii/1 With the wide adoption of electromatic vehicle-actuated traffic lights of recent years, complaints of unnecessary delay at signal-controlled crossings have been much dispelled. **1960** *Times* 13 Jan. 17/7 Electromatic washing machines.

electromeric (ɪˌlɛktrəˈmɛrɪk), *a.* [f. ELECTRO- + *-meric* as in ISOMERIC *a.*] Of, pertaining to, or characterized by a displacement of electrons in a molecule postulated to occur during some chemical reactions. Also **eˈlectromer**, one of two or more hypothetical forms of a compound that differ only in the distribution of the electrons between the constituent atoms.

1923 G. N. LEWIS *Valence* xi. 132 We no longer..see any justification for the assumption that nitrogen trichloride must be either $N^{+++}Cl_3^-$, or $N^{---}Cl_3^+$. Such a pair of hypothetical substances have become known in the modern dualistic theory as electromers. *Ibid.*, It is hardly to be expected that we shall be able to segregate and isolate the several species of molecules so as to obtain electromeric *substances*. **1941** *Nature* 28 June 813/2 The effect depends on the possibility of the electromeric displacement..in the transition state. **1964** N. G. CLARK *Mod. Org. Chem.* xxv. 529 This temporary electronic displacement is known as the electromeric effect, and it operates in the same sense as the mesomeric effect.

electrometer (iːlɛk-, ɛlɛkˈtrɒmɪtə(r)). [f. ELECTRO- + METER.] An instrument for ascertaining the quality and quantity of electricity in an electrified body. Cf. also BINANT.

1749 *Gentl. Mag.* 352 A true and exact electrometer. **1766** LANE in *Phil. Trans.* LVII. 451 An instrument which I have contrived for this purpose may not improperly be called an electrometer. **1787** A. YOUNG in *Glasg. Weekly Her.* (1883) 7 July 2/7 An electrometer—a small, fine pith ball. **1812** SIR H. DAVY *Chem. Philos.* 128 The electrometer..consists of two gold leaves attached to a metal-plate. **1881** MAXWELL *Electr. & Magn.* I. 300. **1946** *Electronic Engin.* XVIII. 277/3 The two control grids are both highly insulated in accordance with electrometer valve requirements. **1958** *Chambers's Techn. Dict.* Suppl. 976/1 *Electrometer tube or valve*, one with high grid insulation, specially designed for measuring minute currents or voltages.

Hence **eˌlectroˈmetric, -ical**, *adjs.*, pertaining to electrometry. **elecˈtrometry**, the measurement of electricity by the electrometer.

1779 VISCT. MAHON *Princ. Electr.* I. 8 The electrometrical Balls may thereby be made to divaricate. **1814** G. J. SINGER *Elem. Electr. & Electro-Chem.* III. iv. 312 Some difficulty attends the demonstration of the electro-metrical effects. **1868** *Brit. Assoc. Rep.* 1867 489 The first step towards accurate electrometry in every case is to deduce from the scale-readings numbers which shall be in simple proportion to the difference of potentials to be determined. **1956** *Nature* 14 Jan. 57/2 Aviation medicine research depends on a detailed application of electrometrical recording techniques.

electromobile (ɪˌlɛktrəməʊˈbiːl). (Disused.) [f. ELECTRO- after *automobile.*] A motor vehicle driven by electricity. Also *attrib.*

1899 *Automotor* Nov., Accumulators for Electro-mobiles. **1900** G. ILES *Flame, Electr. & Camera* 148 An electromobile cab. **1906** (*title*) Steam car and electro-mobile review. **1907** *Daily Chron.* 12 Nov. 7/4 The new electromobile garage, the largest in the world.

electromotion (ɪˌlɛktrəʊˈməʊʃən). [f. ELECTRO- + MOTION.] The motion of a galvanic current. Also, in recent use, mechanical motion produced by electrical means.

1803 *Edin. Rev.* III. 195 The ingenious hypothesis of Volta concerning electro-motion. **1806** DAVY in *Phil. Trans.* XCVII. 46 There is no exhibition..of electromotion.

electromotive (ɪˌlɛktrəʊˈməʊtɪv), *a.* and *sb.* [f. as prec. + MOTIVE *a.*]

A. *adj.* Pertaining to electromotion. *electromotive force*: originally, the force exhibited in the voltaic battery; in mod. use, the difference of potential which is the cause of electric currents. Also, *electromotive series* (see quot. 1940).

1806 DAVY in *Phil. Trans.* XCVII. 46 Permanent electromotive power. **1810** HENRY *Elem. Chem.* (1826) I. 187 Zinc and copper plates..by their electromotive power. **1827** J. CUMMING *Man. Electro Dynamics* I. 1 To the power which certain agents possess, of separating the two electricities, Volta has given the name of electro-motive force. **1833** N. ARNOTT *Physics* II. (1865) 624 The electrical excitement, called also the electromotive force, produced in voltaic arrangements. **1878** FOSTER *Phys.* I. ii. §2. 49 The electromotive force of the sciatic nerve of a frog. **1882** MINCHIN *Unipl. Kinemat.* 220 The sum of the sudden changes of potential, $\Delta_1 + \Delta_2$..is called the Electromotive Force between *A* and *B*. **1889** *Cent. Dict.*, Electromotive series. **1940** *Chambers's Techn. Dict.* 288/2 *Electromotive series*, the chemical elements arranged in order of their standard electrode potentials.

B. *sb.* [after *locomotive.*] A locomotive engine of which the motive power is electricity.

1887 *Engineer* 29 July 95 The electro-motive consists of an angle iron frame supporting three platforms.

electromotor (ɪˌlɛktrəʊˈməʊtə(r)), *sb.* (*a.*) [f. ELECTRO- + MOTOR.]

A. *sb.* Originally, a metal serving as a voltaic element. In mod. use, a machine for applying electricity as a motive power. **B.** *attrib.* or *adj.* = ELECTROMOTIVE, as in *electromotor force*.

1827 FARADAY *Chem. Manip.* xxiii. 570 Plate or sheet zinc is a powerful electromotor. **1879** G. PRESCOTT *Sp. Telephone* 260 During this year (1855)..Henry M. Paine was then trying to construct a successful electromotor. **1881** MAXWELL *Electr. & Magn.* I. 452 No current will flow through the electromotor.

‖**electron**[1] (ɪˈlɛktrən). [a. Gr. ἤλεκτρον: see ELECTRUM.] = ELECTRUM 2.

1856 GROTE *Greece* II. xcviii. XII. 659 Precious metals (gold, silver, and electron). **1877** W. JONES *Finger-ring L.* 459 Mediæval ring..formed of electron, or gold much alloyed with silver.

electron[2] (ɪˈlɛktrɒn). [f. ELECTR(IC *a.* + *-on* as in *anion, cation, ion.*] A stable elementary particle which has an indivisible charge of negative electricity, is a constituent of all atoms, and is the carrier of electric current in solids; also, the anti-particle of this, having a positive instead of a negative charge (see POSITRON). Orig. the name of the magnitude of the electronic charge.

1891 G. J. STONEY in *Trans. R. Dublin Soc.* 2nd Ser. IV. 583 A charge of this amount is associated in the chemical atom with each bond... These charges, which it will be convenient to call *electrons*, cannot be removed from the atom; but they become disguised when atoms chemically unite. **1902** *Fortn. Rev.* June 1023 Larmor's hypothesis of electrons, which supposes a kind of an electric atom, a charge not associated with ordinary matter. **1902** *Nature* 18 Sept. 488 The conception..that the ultimate atoms of matter involve positive and negative electrons. **1902** [see CORPUSCLE 2c]. **1927** A. S. EDDINGTON *Stars & Atoms* 16 The electron is the lightest thing known, weighing no more than 1/1,840 of the lightest atom. **1933** *Discovery* Mar. 69/2 Experimentally there is now a case for the existence of a positive electron, and..this particle is apparently one of several pieces which can result from impact of matter in the atmosphere with the cosmic or pentrating radiation. **1955** *Sci. News Let.* 30 Apr. 274/3 Electrons are light-weight, fundamental particles of the atom having a negative charge. **1958** [see CORPUSCLE 2c]. **1968** M. LIVINGSTON *Particle Physics* iv. 62 This has the effect of producing, out of energy, a pair of electrons, one with negative and one with positive charge.

b. *fig.*

1904 *Sat. Rev.* 30 Jan. 138/1 Mr. Hardy's puppets are infinitesimal—mere 'electrons', shifted hither and thither, for no reason, by some impalpable agency. **1913** *Empire Rev.* Dec. 1336 The imponderable electrons of sentiment and feeling which allow our far-away peoples and clans to cohere. **1929** D. H. LAWRENCE *Pansies* 26 The swan within vast chaos, within the electron.

2. a. *attrib.*

1903 *Science* 26 June 1001/2 The electron theory.. explains Ampère's idea that magnetism is due to a rotating current of electricity round each atom of iron. **1921** *Discovery* Sept. 226/2 The corresponding electron velocities are so small that it is difficult to measure them. *Ibid.*, We must recognise that wave radiation and electron radiation are in a sense mutually convertible. **1923** J. S. HUXLEY *Essays of Biologist* vii. 252 From this state there evolved one in which the various electron-systems that we call atoms first appeared. **1926** *Atlantic Monthly* Apr. 377/2 The study of electron-emisssion has given us..radio broadcasting. **1926** R. W. LAWSON tr. *Hevesy & Paneth's Man. Radioactivity* iii. 42 The electron shells of the atoms. **1938** *Ibid.* (ed. 2) iv. 90 The energy levels of atoms as established by experiments on electron collisions. **1955** *Bull. Atomic Sci.* Mar. 94/3 The basic methods of operation of the synchrocyclotron, the electron synchrotron, the linear accelerator, and the proton synchrotron. **1955** H. B. G. CASIMIR in W. Pauli *Niels Bohr* 120 In many metals the electron bands may well have a complicated structure. **1956** *Nature* 10 Mar. 483/2 Straightforward hydrogen atom transfer, and electron transfer..followed by proton expulsion. **1962** *Listener* 10 May 810/1 The living muscle is made up of atomic nuclei, mostly of carbon, linked together by fixed electron bonds. **1967** *New Scientist* 21 Dec. 707/2 To understand the electron-transfer process in detail has proved to be a stiff test for the theoreticians.

b. *Comb.* **electron beam**, a beam or stream of electrons, a cathode-ray beam; **electron camera** *Television* (see quot. 1940); **electron cloud**, a cloud-like mass of electrons; **electron diffraction** [DIFFRACTION 1], the diffraction of a beam of electrons; **electron gas**, a system of free electrons; **electron gun**, a device in which electrons obtained by thermionic emission from a heated cathode are emitted as a narrow beam; **electron lens** (see quot. 1960); **electron microgram** = next; **electron micrograph**, a micrograph produced by an electron microscope; hence **electron micrography**; also *electron micrographic*; **electron microscope** [ad. G. *elektronenmikroskop* (E. Brüche 1932, in *Naturwissensch.* 15 Jan. 49)], a microscope in which the resolution and magnification of minute objects is obtained by the passage of a stream of electrons through a system of electron lenses (cf. MICROSCOPE *sb.* 1); hence **electron microscopy**; also *electron microscopic, microscopical, microscopist*; **electron multiplier** [MULTIPLIER 4], an instrument used for amplifying the intensity of a current of electrons; **electron optics** [ad. G. *elektronenoptik* (Knoll & Ruska 1932, in *Ann. d. Physik* XII. 607)], a branch of physics concerned with the influence of electric and magnetic fields on the movement of electrons (quot. 1916 represents a different sense); hence **eˌlectron-ˈoptical** *a.*; **electron pair**, (*a*) = DUPLET 2; (*b*) (see quot. 1955[1]); **electron spin**, the intrinsic angular momentum of an electron, described by the quantum number *s*; the property of an electron by virtue of which it possesses this momentum; *electron spin resonance*, resonance (sense 1 d(iii)) in which the transition involved is that of electrons between states of different spin, esp. unpaired bound electrons in a paramagnetic ion; **electron telescope**, a telescope of electron-optical type in which the image is obtained by the use of infra-red rays; **electron tube**, a vacuum tube in which a current of electrons passes between electrodes; **electron volt** (abbrev. eV, e.V.), a unit of energy used in nuclear physics (see quot. 1962); **electron wave**, a (hypothetical) wave associated with the movement of an electron and held to account for its various wave-like properties; a de Broglie wave of an electron.

1927 *Physical Rev.* Dec. 705 Electron beams resulting from diffraction by a nickel crystal. **1956** *Nature* 3 Mar. 419/2 A series of remarkable electron micrographs.. obtained by..using a new fine electron-beam technique. **1958** O. R. FRISCH *Nuclear Handbk.* vii. 5 The electron beam takes the place of the current in the secondary coil. **1937** *Discovery* Nov. 329/1 The electron camera at the transmitter, with a cathode-ray tube at the receiving end. **1940** *Chambers's Techn. Dict.*, *Electron camera*, a generic term for any device which converts an optical image into a corresponding electric current directly by electronic means, without the intervention of mechanical scanning. **1926** R. W. LAWSON tr. *Hevesy & Paneth's Man. Radioactivity* vii. 62 Atomic sphere..at the disposal of the electrons... The dimensions of this electron cloud [etc.]. **1946** *Nature* 16 Nov. 717/1 The electron-cloud in the outer incomplete shells of the atom or the molecule react on the nucleus. **1927** *Physical Rev.* Dec. 705 The spacing factor concerned in electron diffraction by a nickel crystal. *Ibid.* 731 At sufficiently high voltages there is no difference between the occurrence of x-ray and electron diffraction beams. **1939** *Nature* 25 Feb. 372/2 Messrs. W. Edwards and Co... have recently published details of their Finch electron diffraction camera intended for industrial research. **1958** *Jrnl. Iron & Steel Inst.* CLXXXIX. 56/2 The marked thinness of the blades and prisms..resulted in electron diffraction patterns being observed. **1955** H. B. G. CASIMIR in W. Pauli *Niels Bohr* 129 There is something rather tempting in the idea that due to some sort of interaction the electron gas 'coagulates' into blocks. **1962** *Listener* 10 May 809/2 A few free electrons, drifting about hither and thither and forming an electron-gas in the metal. **1924** *Brass World* Feb. 52/1 The electron gun is not swung about, but its stream of projectiles is deflected by means of electric or magnetic forces. **1930** *Chem. Abstr.* 2044 The electron gun..consists of a hot filament near the small hole in a diaphragm and on the axis of a hollow cylinder at a pos. potential, which produces a 'visible' beam of electrons. **1953** AMOS & BIRKINSHAW *Television Engin.* I. iv. 52 The electron gun is an electrode assembly designed to produce a narrow beam of electrons. **1957** R. W. G. HUNT *Reprod. Colour* iii. 31 Three electron guns are used in the [mosaic colour television] tube and they fire from the three positions R, G and B. **1931** *Physical Rev.* 1 Aug. 585 (*heading*) Electron lenses. **1960** *Gloss. Terms Telecommunic.* (*B.S.I.*) 61 *Electron lens*, a device producing a system of electric and/or magnetic fields capable of controlling the convergence or divergence of a beam of electrons or ions. **1943** *Jrnl. Amer. Med. Assoc.* 16 Oct. 400/2 Figure 1 shows an electronmicrogram (1 × 14,500) of a sample of purified SK murine virus. **1934** *Sci. Abstr.* A. XXXVII. 203 The electron micrographs, taken with a kathode temperature of 1000° C., showed the crystalline surface structure of the nickel. **1956** *Sci. News* XXXIX. 114 Electron micrographs..showed the partial splitting of nucleic acid and protein [from tobacco mosaic virus]. **1959** *New Biol.* XXX. 61 Electron micrographs can

now be made of sections of cells in much the same way as light micrographs were previously made and the result looks more familiar although larger and sharper in detail. **1944** *Jrnl. Biol. Chem.* CLVI. 598 The difference probably was related to the measurement of the images irrespective of orientation on the electron micrographic plates. **1941** *Amer. Jrnl. Path.* XVII. 576 (*heading*) The electron micrography of purified viruses. **1932** *Brit. Chem. Abstr.* A. 209/1 (*title*) Electron microscope. **1941** *Ann. Reg.* *1940* 345 An important advance during the year was the construction of an electron microscope with about twenty times the resolving power of the best light microscope with oil immersion. **1955** *Bull. Atomic Sci.* Mar. 75/1 The electron microscope.. permitted us to observe objects measured in hundred thousandths of a millimeter. **1968** *Times* 13 Nov. 16/1 Scanning electron microscopes.. have a much greater depth of focus than electron microscopes have. **1933** *Chem. Abstr.* XXVII. 5631 (*heading*) Electron microscopic images from secondary electrons. **1961** *Lancet* 12 Aug. 380/2 Electron-microscopic appearances in pinocytosis. **1945** *Jrnl. Appl. Physics* XVI. 731/2 Thin replicas suitable for electron microscopical studies. **1948** *Ibid.* XIX. 119 (*heading*) The training of technical electron microscopists. **1960** *New Biol.* XXXI. 30 A complicated intracellular system of double membranes.. which is known to the electron-microscopists as the 'endoplasmic reticulum'. **1934** *Nature* 16 June 911/2 It seems that the osmium impregnation method can be applied.. to electron microscopy. **1946** *Nature* 14 Sept. 363/2 The size and approximate shape of bacteriophage particles has been investigated by electron-microscopy. **1940** *Chambers's Techn. Dict.* 289/1 Electron multiplier. **1953** AMOS & BIRKINSHAW *Television Engin.* I. v. 107 If the return beam is directed into an electron multiplier the tube output can be increased until it is well above the noise level of conventional vision-frequency amplifiers. **1955** *Gloss. Terms Radiology (B.S.I.)* 22 *Electron multiplier*, a device, generally in the form of a vacuum tube.. in which small electron currents are amplified in several stages by a cascade process employing secondary emission. **1933** *Sci. Abstr.* A. XXXVI. 199 A combined electric and magnetic deflection method which gives electron-optical enlargements of emitting surfaces. **1951** *Engineering* 13 July 40/2 A tube with sufficiently good electron-optical focus for high-definition pictures was made. **1916** *Chem. Abstr.* 299 Electron optics of the hydrogen molecule. **1932** *Sci. Abstr.* A. XXXV. 645 Application of geometric electron optics makes it possible to explain the behaviour of the beam in an electron tube. **1938** *Nature* (Suppl.) 20 Aug. 331/1 A system of 'electron optics' has been elaborated which shows how a beam of cathode rays issuing from a point can be reassembled into an image by passing through a localized electrostatic or magnetic field having axial symmetry. **1934** WEBSTER, *Electron pair*, a group of two electrons, as called for in certain atomic theories. If the pair acts as a bond between atoms, it is called a *sharing pair*, otherwise a *lone pair*. **1940** *Chambers's Techn. Dict.* 289/1 Electron pair (equated with *duplet*). **1955** *Gloss. Terms Radiology (B.S.I.)* 15 *Electron pair*, an electron and a positron arising from pair production. **1955** H. B. G. CASIMIR in W. Pauli *Niels Bohr* 131 There does not seem any possibility to reconcile the idea of electron pairs with the thermodynamics of superconductors. **1958** O. R. FRISCH *Nuclear Handbk.* viii. 12 Electron pairs can be created by other processes including: (*a*) Passage of a heavy particle through matter.. (*b*) Passage of a fast electron through the field of a nucleus.. (*c*) Collision between two electrons. **1964** J. W. LINNETT *Electronic Struct. Molecules* ii. 28 This difficulty of solving the Schrödinger equation for systems containing two or more electrons means that the development of the electron-pair bond has to be based, to a large extent, on empirical reasoning. [**1926** *Nature* 20 Feb. 264/2 The dotted lines represent the position of the energy levels to be expected in the absence of the spin of the electron.] **1930** RUARK & UREY *Atoms, Molecules & Quanta* iii. 96 It is not surprising that the discovery of the electron spin was delayed until 1926. **1941** *Mind* L. 279 Although we cannot pretend to describe the nature of electron-spin as an activity or a condition in the external world, we may say this much about it: spins can be differentiated from one another by specifying their components in a set of mutually orthogonal planes. **1952** *Physical Rev.* 15 Nov. 951/1 We have observed conduction electron spin resonance absorption in fine particles of metallic sodium.. at a frequency of 9240 Mc/sec. **1955** [see *ESR* s.v. E III]. **1972** R. A. JACKSON *Mechanism* iv. 61 Electron spin resonance spectroscopy, which is very sensitive and will detect radical concentrations down to about 10^{-9}M, is extremely useful. **1978** *Jrnl. R. Soc. Arts* CXXVI. 660/1 There were also groups dealing with thermochemistry, crystallography and x-ray diffraction, and with newer techniques involving physical properties such as electron spin resonance. **1948** *Jrnl. Brit. Interplan. Soc.* Nov. 250 The 'electron telescope' has been used to make visible stars which could not otherwise be detected. **1923** *Chem. Abstr.* 2801 The positive pole and the auxiliary positive plate in an electron tube consist of a hollow tube and a spiral. **1930** *Electronics* Apr. 25/2 The electron-tube control of the stage lighting in the.. Chicago Civic Opera House. **1932** *Iron & Steel Engineer* Mar. 124 (*title*) The application of electron tubes in the steel industry. **1930** RUTHERFORD et al. *Radiations from Radioactive Subst.* xvii. 530 In dealing with the changes of energy in atomic nuclei, it is convenient to express the energy in terms of the kinetic energy gained by an electron .. in volts. The energy per atom associated with a change of mass 1 on the atomic mass scale can be shown to be 933 million electron volts. **1938** R. W. LAWSON tr. *Hevesy & Paneth's Man. Radioactivity* (ed. 2) iii. 48 Energies of less than 100 e.V.. **1962** *Gloss. Terms Nuclear Sci. (B.S.I.)* 41 *Electronvolt*, a unit of energy (abbreviation: eV) equal to the kinetic energy acquired by an electron when accelerated through a potential difference of one volt (1 eV = $1{\cdot}60 \times 10^{-12}$erg). **1927** *Proc. Nat. Acad. Sci.* XIII. 460 A single plane of atoms reflects a very appreciable fraction of the electron wave, whereas the same plane would reflect only an inappreciable part of an X-ray wave. **1930** G. P. THOMSON *Wave Mechanics of Free Electrons* ii. 36 On de Broglieo's theory the space round a nucleus has a refraction index for electron waves which varies with the distance from the nucleus. **1942** J. D. STRANATHAN *Particles Mod. Physics* xiv. 540 These electron waves travel with a velocity greater than that of light.

electronic (iːlɛk-, ɛlɛk'trɒnɪk), *a.* [f. ELECTRON² + -IC.] **1.** Of or pertaining to an electron or electrons.

1902 J. A. FLEMING (*title*) The electronic theory of electricity. **1905** A. M. CLERKE *Mod. Cosmogonies* x. 175 An electronic theory of gravitation. **1906** J. B. BURKE *Orig. Life* xi. 191 Three states of electronic aggregation. **1922** J. MILLS *Within the Atom* xi. 147 Whenever electronic impacts give rise to radiation, the energy associated therewith is always proportional to the frequency. *Ibid.* xii. 159 Only in a highly evacuated tube would there be the possibility of large electronic orbits. **1923** *Times Lit. Suppl.* 15 Nov. 763/2 The earth's atmospheric circulation is.. dependent upon the sun's electronic emissions. **1927** N. V. SIDGWICK (*title*) The electronic theory of valency. **1928** *Phil. Mag.* VI. 1254 (*title*) Electronic waves and the electron. **1937** *Discovery* July 226/2 Ideas concerning electronic energy and electron levels in atoms *in vacuo*. **1955** C. G. DARWIN in W. Pauli *Niels Bohr* 4 He [*sc.* Planck].. derived the electronic charge as $4{\cdot}69 \times 10^{-10}$ e.s.u.

2. Of or pertaining to electronics; esp. of something operated by the methods, principles, etc., of electronics. *Spec.* of music: produced electronically, without pipes, strings, etc. Also applied to devices producing such music.

1930 *Electronics* Dec. 435 Electronic Musical Instruments .. Examples of such instruments are the electronic organ of M. Coupleaux of Paris. **1931** *Ibid.* July 18/1 All recent developments in electronic music in Europe have used the same principle.. that of the beat note produced by the interference of two tube-oscillators. **1939** *Nature* 25 June 1119/2 Electronic organs are making us acquainted with the synthesis of musical sounds. **1951** *Times* 23 Oct. 6/3 The electronic camera claims many advantages over its optical counterpart. **1952** KOESTLER *Arrow in Blue* xxix. 271 The final conclusion was suddenly present in my mind—like the result which appears on the dial of electronic calculators. **1953** *Sci. News* XXX. 70 The problem of electronic computing is basically simple, for the fundamental requirement is electrical manipulation of information. **1959** *Observer* 23 Aug. 7/3 Electronic music.. makes use of electrically generated sounds recorded on tape and then rearranged into patterns. **1962** *Gloss. Terms Autom. Data Processing (B.S.I.)* 7 Electronic data processing (e.d.p.) is a term widely used in the U.S.A. for data processing largely performed by electronic means. **1962** M. MCLUHAN *Gutenberg Galaxy* 275 As we experience the new electronic and organic age with ever stronger indications of its main outlines, the preceding mechanical age becomes quite intelligible.

3. Special Combs. as **electronic brain** *colloq.*, = *electronic computer* (see also quot. 1945); **electronic computer**, a computer operated electronically; **electronic flash**, a flash produced by an electrical discharge through a gas-filled tube and used for high-speed photography; **electronic heating**, dielectric heating (cf. DIELECTRIC B. 1); **electronic mail**, the sending of non-spoken information between individuals over a telecommunication network to a selected location or locations where it is stored for subsequent retrieval, *spec.* in a computer; information sent in this way; so **electronic mailbox**, an individual facility for receiving and storing such information for retrieval by a recipient; **electronic typewriter**, an electric typewriter in which solid-state circuitry is used to provide additional facilities such as storing typed characters.

1945 *Aero Products* Jan. 22 An 'electronic brain', which helps pilots test-fly new airplanes, has been invented by flight research engineers of Consolidated Vultee Aircraft Corporation. Technically, the device is known as a 'flight recorder'. **1946** *Aircraft Yearbk.* 165 Electronic 'brains' will guide the counter-missile with precision. **1958** *Listener* 11 Dec. 983/1 Automatic digital calculators, sometimes called 'electronic brains', are just over a decade old. **1946** *Electronics* Aug. 110/1 The servomechanism is part of the computer, and.. computers of this type have become known as electronic computers. **1962** *Mod. Lang. Rev.* LVII. 162 An electronic computer [has] been used to index the *Summa Theologiae* of St. Thomas Aquinas. **1947** *Americana Ann.* 561 The Electronic Flash Gun, made by the Abrams Instrument Corporation. **1949** *British Birds* XLII. 240 The photographs shown.. were taken by high-speed electronic flash. **1962** *Listener* 22 Feb. 337/2 The invention of the electronic flash camera has permitted photographs to be taken at much higher speeds than ever before. **1968** *Gloss. Terms Offset Lithogr. Printing (B.S.I.)* 12 *Electronic flash lamp*, a discharge lamp giving a high light output for a very brief period. **1946** *Sci. News Let.* 26 Jan. 53 The drying and curing of rubber by electronic heating is six times faster than conventional processes. **1959** *Gloss. Packaging Terms (B.S.I.)* 82 *Electronic heating*, heating produced by dielectric loss. **1977** *Science* 18 Mar. 1161/1 An electronic mail system is becoming practical today, because of the wide availability.. of electronic communication channels. *Ibid.*, Electronic mail can be originated by conventional means (typewriter, handwriting, printing). **1982** A. J. MEADOWS et al. *Dict. New Information Technol.* 63/1 A combination of facsimile transmission and telex or teletex makes possible electronic mail systems able to handle both text and graphics. **1982** *Sci. Amer.* Sept. 126/3 Many of the users of terminals and small computers can communicate with one another and with their home offices through one of the half-dozen 'electronic mail' networks now in existence in the U.S. **1984** *Daily Tel.* 3 Dec. 3/3 A major security alert involving the hacking of electronic mail. **1981** *Computerworld* 28 Dec. ETC/EM features electronic mailboxes, automatic message routing and broadcasting, correspondence archiving, [etc.]. **1983** *Observer* 9 Oct. 12/2 (Advt.), Services such as British Telecom.. allow computer terminals to dial up over the telephone network to consult personal electronic mailboxes. **1984** *New Scientist* 4 Oct. 4/3 A value added network.. includes services not normally available from the telephone system—services such as code conversion, electronic mailboxes and speed matching. **1975** *Economist* 20 Sept. 79/2 Rank-Xerox launched a new *electronic typewriter, said to handle 350 words a minute. **1978** *Business Week* 13 Feb. 80/1 Its new line of electronic typewriters will bridge the gap between standard electric typewriters and low-priced word processors. **1984** *Austral. Personal Computer* May 171/1 An electronic typewriter.. is capable of simple formatting, storing small amounts of often-typed text.., and will normally have a 'type-ahead' buffer.

elec'tronically, *adv.* [f. ELECTRONIC *a.*; see -LY *suffix*².] By electronic means.

1923 *Science* 31 Aug. 164/2 A vibrationless, but electronically excited molecule. **1943** *Times* 21 Sept. 4/5 Details of 'one of America's best kept military secrets', an electronically-controlled auto pilot for bombing aeroplanes, were disclosed here to-day. **1954** E. E. CUMMINGS *Let.* 8 Dec. (1969) 238 With a flexible (electronically) instrument I could have roared as softly as a seashell. **1954** *Economist* 13 Mar. 791/1 A machine that calculates electronically.

electronics (iːlɛk-, ɛlɛk'trɒnɪks). [Plural of ELECTRONIC *a.* used *subst.* and construed as a singular; cf. *dynamics*, *physics*, etc.] That branch of physics and technology which is concerned with the study and application of phenomena associated with the movement of electrons in a vacuum, a gas, a semi-conductor, etc., as in thermionic valves, X-ray tubes, etc.

1910 *Chem. Abstr.* IV. 2767 Radio activity and electronics. **1945** *Times* 15 Oct. 3/2 The committee's report said.. that 'knowledge of electronics promises the ability to detonate atomic bombs at great distances by radio'. **1954** *Economist* 30 Oct. 412/2 The stream-lining of operations that.. electronics engineers believe to be the main.. attraction of computers. **1958** *Listener* 23 Oct. 632/1 The three industries in the American economy where employment is likely to grow the fastest are education, electronics, and chemistry.

electronographic (ɪˌlɛktrənə'græfɪk), *a.* [f. ELECTRON² + -O + -GRAPHIC.]

1. Employing or being a printing process in which ink is transferred without pressure by utilizing electrostatic attraction between the printing surface and that to be printed.

1948 *Business Week* 13 Mar. 24/1 If Huebner makes his Electronographic press work, he will revolutionize printing press design. **1949** *Amer. Printer* Dec. 106/2 The electronographic press prints without pressure, utilizing controlled polarities of static charges. **1971** R. W. & E. W. POLK *Pract. Printing* (ed. 7) xli. 318 A process of electronographic printing known as Onset can produce matter by any printing method through the application of electronic principles instead of pressure of a form on a sheet.

2. Pertaining to or being an image tube in which photoelectrons are accelerated and focused on to a sensitive emulsion to form an image.

1964 *Astron. Jrnl.* LXIX. 534/2 (*heading*) Transfer efficiency and storage capacity of electronographic image tubes. **1970** *Sci. Jrnl.* Mar. 14/1 The Spectracon electronographic image intensifier was developed for astronomers. **1977** *New Scientist* 24 Mar. 712/2 At present one of the most sensitive devices for recording astronomical pictures is the electronographic camera. **1985** *Astron. & Astrophysics* CXLIV. 343/1 High resolution electronographic plates were used to study three extreme Population II stars.

Hence (as back-formations) **e'lectronograph**, an image obtained by electronography; **electro'nography**, electronographic techniques or their use.

1955 M. REIFER *Dict. New Words* 72/1 Graphic Arts... Electronography. **1967** *Publ. Astron. Soc. Pacific* LXXIX. 567 It will be possible, using electronography, to measure the magnitudes of such objects as.. extremely faint gravitationally contracting stars embedded in the Orion Nebula. **1970** *Sci. Jrnl.* Mar. 14/1 Because the electron beam is focused, an 'electron picture' (electronograph) results. **1975** *Physics Bull.* Oct. 446/2 The paper includes an interesting comparison of pictures of a human pelvis made by conventional radiography and by electronography. *Ibid.*, The sensitivity so far obtained is about the same as that of a medium speed film-screen combination but the resolution of the electronograph is distinctly better and there is a marked absence of background fog and noise.

electronome (ɪ'lɛktrəʊnəʊm). [f. ELECTRO-; cf. *metronome*.] = ELECTROMETER.

electropathy (iː-, ɛlɛk'trɒpəθɪ). [f. ELECTRO-, in imitation of *homœopathy*; cf *hydropathy*.] The treatment of disease by electrical remedies. Hence **electro'pathic** *a.*, pertaining to electropathy.

1882 *Society* 11 Nov. 24/1 Electropathic socks.

electrophone (ɪ'lɛktrəfəʊn). [f. ELECTRO- + -PHONE.] An instrument for transmitting sounds by means of electric currents. Hence **e'lectrophone** *v. trans.*, to transmit (a speech, etc.) by this instrument; **electro'phonic** *a.*, of or pertaining to an electrophone; also, (of music, sound) produced electronically; **elec-tro'phonically** *adv.*

1864 *Trans. R. Scottish Soc. Arts* 185 (*title*) On the electrophone and some of its applications. By T. S. Wright. *Ibid.*, The best form for a sonorous condenser or electrophone for the production of audible sounds by.. induction currents. *Ibid.*, The electrophonic relay had a further advantage also, that the most delicate apparatus

might be used for the working of the relay. **1868** *Chambers's Encycl.* X. 510/2 The electrophone may be adapted to the telephone. **1898** *Westm. Gaz.* 22 July 5/1 People who could hear Melba, Jean de Reszke, and the rest through the electrophone. **1900** *Ibid.* 13 Feb. 10/2 An electrophonically-heard sermon. **1904** *Ibid.* 20 Jan. 8/2 The rapidity with which the words spoken by Mr. Chamberlain in the Guildhall were electrophoned to Langham-place. **1921** *Glasgow Herald* 30 Mar. 9 By means of wireless and an electrophone device British troops on the Rhine are to be entertained at bi-weekly concerts. **1922** *Ibid.* 22 Dec. 9 The Radio Association anticipates a popularity for wireless telephony far exceeding that of the electrophone. **1958** *Times Lit. Suppl.* 4 July 372/5 The problems of structure, of rhythmic debility and of such future complications as electrophonic glissandi, which have been thrown up by the abandonment of key and the adoption of dodecaphony. **1960** *20th Cent.* Nov. 459 Electrophonic music has already threatened the performer of serious music.

e'lectrophore. Anglicized form of ELECTROPHORUS, which is more freq. used.

1778 INGENHOUSZ in *Phil. Trans.* LXVIII. 1045, I will now explain the nature of an electrophore. **1860** *All Y. Round* No. 69. 451 The ball is repulsed..according to the size of the electrophore or the lightness of the ball.

electrophoresis (ɪˌlɛktrəʊfə'ri:sɪs). [f. ELECTRO- + Gr. φόρησις being carried.] The migration of colloidal particles suspended in a liquid under the influence of an electric field (cf. CATAPHORESIS). Hence **eˌlectropho'retic** *a.*, **eˌlectropho'retically** *adv.*

1911 *Chem. Abstr.* 641 Electrophoresis of Lampblack. **1925** *Ibid.* 1376 An examn. of the electrophoretic migration velocities. **1938** *Nature* 4 June 1000/2 The study of molecular migrations in the electric field has been facilitated by the development of an improved electrophoresis apparatus by Tiselius in Svedberg's laboratory. **1942** *Jrnl. Gen. Physiol.* XXV. 507 This material was electrophoretically homogeneous, *i.e.* gave a single sharp peak..in the electrophoretic pattern. **1944** [see CATAPHORESIS]. **1946** *Nature* 28 Sept. 447/1 The clinical properties of the electrophoretically homogeneous fibrinogen obtained by these authors have not yet been examined. **1957** *Sci. News* XLVI. 21 When a charged particle of colloidal dimensions is suspended in a liquid between two charged electrodes, it moves towards the electrode with a charge opposite to its own... This is known as electrophoresis. **1960** *Times* 8 Apr. 2/3 The successful applicant..should have experience in chemical chromatographic and electrophoretic methods of analysis. **1962** *Lancet* 8 Dec. 1185/1 The abnormal haemoglobin was identified by paper electrophoresis. **1962** M. RABAEY in A. Pirie *Lens Metabolism Rel. Cataract* 312 It was not possible to demonstrate α-crystallin electrophoretically in embryos of less than 10 days incubation.

electrophorus (i:lɛk-, ɛlɛk'trɒfərəs). [mod.Lat. f. ELECTRO- + Gr. -φόρος that bears or produces. Cf. It. *elettroforo*, Fr. *électrophore*, and ELECTROPHORE] A simple instrument, invented by Volta, for generating statical electricity by induction.

1778 INGENHOUSZ *On Electrophorus* in *Phil. Trans.* LXVIII. 1027 To explain how far the *electrophorus perpetuus* may be accounted for on the..theory of Dr. Franklin. **1782** tr. Volta *ibid.* LXII. App. vii, My electrophorus..is a machine well known to electricians. **1880** *Gentl. Mag.* Dec. 751 A cat's skin..is an admirable rubber for an electrophorus.

electro-plate (ɪ'lɛktrəʊpleɪt), *v.* [f. ELECTRO- + PLATE.] *trans.* To coat with silver by electrolysis. Hence, **e'lectro-ˌplater**, one who electroplates. **e'lectro-ˌplating** *vbl. sb.*

1870 *Eng. Mech.* 25 Feb. 590/1, I electro-plated many articles. *c* **1865** G. GORE in *Circ. Sc.* I. 215/1 The kind chiefly in use by electro-platers, is the German or Liège Zinc. **1865** *Reader* 23 Sept. 351/1 Elkington founded the first establishment in this country, for carrying out the processes of electro-plating. **1879** *Cassell's Techn. Educ.* I. 93 The electro-plating process began at Birmingham.

electro-plate (ɪ'lɛktrəʊpleɪt), *sb.* [f. prec. vb.] The ware produced by electro-plating.

1844 *Penny Mag.* XIII. 417 (*title*) A day at an electro-plate factory. **1866** J. MARTINEAU *Ess.* I. 30 Our breakfast-table displays our electro-plate. **1868** HOLME LEE *B. Godfrey* xxviii. 149 This is an age of stucco and electroplate.

e'lectro-plated, electroplated, *ppl. a.* [f. the vb.] Coated with a metal by electrolysis.

1851 *Art-Jrnl. Illustr. Catal.* (1970) 38/2 A bridle, contributed by Mr. Penny,..a metal chaser, who has executed the whole of the ornamental work in electro-plated silver. **1861** MRS. BEETON *Bk. Househ. Managem.* 174 Where silver fish-carvers are considered too dear to be bought, good electro-plated ones answer very well. **1875** G. H. LEWES *Problems* 1st Ser. II. 135 On the bleached damask stand the silver teapot and electro-plated toast rack. **1967** *Times Rev. Industry* June 71/2 Significant inroads are being made into this market by the use of electro-plated plastics.

eˌlectro-psy'chology. [f. ELECTRO- + PSYCHOLOGY.] A proposed name for 'animal magnetism' or 'electro-biology'.

1850 W. GREGORY *Anim. Magn.* 73 Electro-psychology and other similar names in which..the theory that electricity is identical with the vital force is kept in view.

electroscope (ɪ'lɛktrəʊskəʊp). [f. ELECTRO- + Gr. -σκόπος looker.] An instrument for ascertaining the presence of electricity, and its quality if present. Hence **eˌlectro'scopic** *a.* [see -IC], measured by the electroscope.

1810 J. A. DE LUC in *Jrnl. Nat. Philos.*, etc. XXVII. 83 The pile produces the same effects with so small a quantity of the [electric] fluid, as to be often hardly sufficient to move the gold leaf electroscope. **1824** *Mech. Mag.* No. 66. 150 The aerial electroscope is an instrument for determining the electric state of the atmosphere. **1842** TURNER *Chem.* (ed. 7) 85 Several simple electroscopic methods. **1844** H. M. NOAD *Lect. Electr.* (ed. 2) 448/1 Condensing Electroscope. **1870** R. FERGUSON *Electr.* 53 A gold leaf electroscope. **1879** *Encycl. Brit.* VIII. 34/1 Advantage of this principle has been taken in the condensing electroscope of Volta, which is an ordinary gold-leaf apparatus, except that the knob is replaced by a circular disc. **1879** G. PRESCOTT *Sp. Telephone* 285 The electroscopic delicacy of the telephone. **1881** MAXWELL *Electr. & Magn.* I. 300 Instruments by means of which the existence of electric charges..may be indicated, but which are not capable of affording numerical measures, are called Electroscopes. **1908** *Practitioner* Sept. 364 By means of the electroscope the passage of the tube can be controlled, if it should meet with any obstruction from pathological displacements of the oesophagus. **1955** *Gloss. Terms Radiology (B.S.I.)* 21 *Electroscope*, an instrument for indicating a potential difference by electrostatic means.

electrostatic (ɪˌlɛktrəʊ'stætɪk), *a.* [f. ELECTRO- + STATIC; cf. *hydrostatic*.] Pertaining to statical electricity. Also Special Combs., as ***electrostatic field*** (cf. FIELD *sb.* 17, quot. 1881), ***generator***, ***induction*** (cf. INDUCTION 10), ***lens*** (= *electron lens*), ***precipitation*** (= *electrical precipitation*), ***voltmeter***; **electrostatic unit**, an electrical unit based on the C.G.S. system (1893 in *Funk's Stand. Dict.*), abbrev. **E.S.U., e.s.u.** Hence **eˌlectro'statical** *a.*, of same meaning. **eˌlectro'statically** *adv.* **electrostatics**, the science dealing with statical electricity.

1827 J. CUMMING *Man. Electro Dynamics* 4 M. Ampère has proposed to apply the term electro-statics to all the effects of electricity in its state of tension. **1853** W. THOMSON in *Phil. Mag.* June 403 Results..enable us to determine the numerical relation between electro-statical and electro-magnetic units. *Ibid.*, Resistance measured as above in terms of the electro-statical unit. **1860** —— *Ibid.* Sept. 233 In..June 1853, I described a method for measuring differences of electric potential in absolute electrostatic units. **1863** *Brit. Assoc. Comm. Electr. Standards Rep.* 26 Aug. IV. 34 *Electrostatic System of Units.* This new measurement of quantity forms the foundation of a distinct system or series of units, which may be called the electrostatic units. *Ibid.* 39 Electric resistance in electrostatic units is measured by the reciprocal of an absolute velocity. **1867** SIR W. THOMSON in *Athenæum* No. 2084. 428 Self-acting electro-static accumulator. **1880** *Jrnl. Soc. Telegr. Engin.* IX. 430 These examples are perhaps sufficiently elucidative of the part that electro-static induction plays during the establishment of a current in a wire. **1881** MAXWELL *Electr. & Magn.* I. 453 The.. electromotive force of an electromotor may be measured.. electrostatically by means of the electrometer. **1882** MINCHIN *Unipl. Kinemat.* 248 An electrostatical distribution. **1885** *Athenæum* 3 Jan. 21/2 The action of the air felt in front of an electrostatic machine in action. **1885** WATSON & BURBURY *Math. Th. Electr. & Magn.* I. 208 The ..two-fluid theory of electricity in its application to Electrostatics. **1906** GOODCHILD & TWENEY *Technol. & Sci. Dict.* 829/2 *Electrostatic voltmeters.* These depend on the principle of the Electrometer. **1912** *Metall. & Chem. Engin.* X. 173/2 (*caption*) Cross-section through one of the electrostatic precipitation chambers. **1916** *Chem. Abstr.* 562 At present the differences between the electrostatic units and the electromagnetic units of measurement are the cause of much confusion. **1920** *Whittaker's Electr. Engin. Pocket-Bk.* (ed. 4) 651 The precipitation of dust..by means of the electrostatic field..has only been applied to industrial purposes within the last six years. **1931** S. R. ROGET *Dict. Electr. Terms* (ed. 2) 109/2 *Electrostatic Generator*, a machine which produces charges at high potentials when driven mechanically, by an electrostatic process. **1938** R. W. LAWSON tr. *Hevesy & Paneth's Man. Radioactivity* (ed. 2) I. iv. 7 Since 1 coulomb = 3 × 10^9 electrostatic units, it follows that the charge borne by a monovalent ion is 1·6 × 10^{-19} × 3 × 10^9 = 4·8 × 10^{-10} e.s.u. **1953** AMOS & BIRKINSHAW *Television Engin.* I. x. 237 A practical electrostatic lens of the type used in cathode-ray tubes has an optical equivalent containing several convex and concave elements. **1958** O. R. FRISCH *Nuclear Handbk.* xvi. 1. 14 In such a system of electrostatic lenses, the ideal sought is one having fixed optical properties independent of the mass number and initial energy of the ions. **1962** *Gloss. Terms Nuclear Sci. (B.S.I.)* 6 The electrostatic generator (first designed by Van de Graaff), in which a conveyor belt is used to charge an insulated electrode to the desired potential.

electrotechnic (ɪˌlɛktrəʊ'tɛknɪk). [f. ELECTRO- + TECHNIC B. 3.] *pl.* The technics of electricity. Hence **eˌlectro-'technical** *a.*; **eˌlectro-tech'nician**, one who is versed in electrotechnics.

1884 S. P. THOMPSON (*title*) Dynamo-electric machinery: a manual for students of electrotechnics. **1885** *Electrician* XVI. 3/2 The following synopsis..in electro-technics at the various high schools in Germany. **1896** *Daily News* 1 Dec. 5/5 A commercial as well as an electro-technical success. **1902** *Encycl. Brit.* XXXII. p. xxxii, In close touch with the Engineering Laboratory should be a Laboratory for Electro-Technical Industries. **1927** *Daily Express* 21 Dec. 11/7 Engineers who are to take charge of large machines, locomotive drivers and electro-technicians, where instant and accurate response to any change in conditions is essential, are tested by another machine. **1945** *Archit. Rev.* XCVII. 103 (*title*) Electro-technical industry and Highlands. **1952** *Electronic Engin.* XXIV. 382 M.K.S. units ..are now the internationally agreed system for electrotechnics.

‖**electrotonus** (i:lɛk-, ɛlɛk'trɒtənəs). [mod.Lat., f. ELECTRO- + Gr. τόνος tension: see TONE.] The modified condition of a motor nerve under the influence of a constant galvanic current. Also in anglicized form **e'lectrotone**.

1860 *New Syd. Soc. Yr. Bk.* 52, *Title*, Contributions to the Physiology of Electrotone. **1878** FOSTER *Phys.* I. ii. 2. 59 The nerve, both between and beyond the electrodes, is..in a peculiar condition known as 'electrotonus'.

So **eˌlectro'tonic** *a.* [see -IC], relating to or characterized by electrotonus; also (in Faraday's use), the epithet of the peculiar electrical state characteristic of a secondary circuit in the electromagnetic field. **eˌlectroto'nicity** [see -ITY], the condition produced by electrotonizing. **elec'trotonize** *v.* [see -IZE], to produce electrotonus. **elec'trotonizing** *vbl. sb.*

1832 FARADAY *Res. Electr.* §60, I..have ventured to designate it as the Electro-tonic state. **1873** A. FLINT *Nerv. Syst.* iii. 116 The electrotonic condition. **1881** MAXWELL *Electr. & Magn.* II. 174 The Electrotonic State.

electrotype (ɪ'lɛktrəʊtaɪp). [f. ELECTRO- + TYPE.]

1. A model or copy of a thing formed by the deposition of copper on a mould by galvanic action: also *attrib.*

1840 *Athenæum* 11 Apr., 324 We have received from Mr. Barclay what he calls an electrotype seal. **1857** WHEWELL *Hist. Induct. Sc.* (ed. 3) III. 537 The Electrotype Process is now one of the great powers which manufacturing art employs. **1880** *Print. Trades Jrnl.* xxx. 13 Stock of electrotype cuts.

2. The process of electrotyping.

1840 *Mech. Mag.* 15 Aug. XXXIII. 224 (*heading of paragraph*) The Electrotype in America. **1842** *Proc. Amer. Phil. Soc.* II. 198 Treatise on the Electrotype. **1859** SIR W. HARRIS *Electr.* 190 The useful arts..namely, electro-metallurgy, electrotype, etc.

e'lectrotype, *v.* [f. prec. sb.] *trans.* To copy in electrotype. Also *fig.*

1847 LADY G. FULLERTON *Grantley M.* I. viii. 273 We are only electrotyped. **1858** O. W. HOLMES *Aut. Breakf. T.* xi. 105 Electrotyped..in the medallions that hang round the walls of your memory's chamber.

Hence **e'lectroˌtyper** [see -ER]. **e'lectroˌtypist** [see -IST]. **e'lectroˌtyping** *vbl. sb.*

1870 *Pall Mall G.* 2 Sept. 4 Engravers and electrotypers. **1884** *Ibid.* 7 May 8/2 The firm are type-founders, stereotypers, and electrotypers. **1845** H. DIRKS in *Athenæum* 11 Jan. 42 Copying for the electrotypist. *c* **1865** in *Circ. Sc.* I. 234/1 Advantages of electrotyping over stereotyping.

electroweak (ɪˌlɛktrəʊ'wi:k), *a. Particle Physics.* [f. ELECTRO(-MAGNETIC *a.* + WEAK *a.*] Of, pertaining to, or designating the unified weak and electromagnetic interactions as proposed in certain unified field theories, according to which these interactions are different low-energy manifestations of a single interaction.

1978 *Sci. News* 11 Nov. 327/2 Abdus Salam, one of the people who started the work on the unified field theory, has been going around calling it 'electroweak'. **1981** A. SALAM in J. H. Mulvey *Nature of Matter* v. 124 Unification of the electro-weak and the strong nuclear force leads to the prediction of an unstable proton. **1982** V. I. KISIN tr. *Okun's Leptons & Quarks* xxii. 199 The prediction of neutral currents constituted the main contribution of the unified electroweak model to the domain of weak interactions at low energies, that is energies of the existing accelerators. **1984** D. G. GIANCOLI *Gen. Physics* xliii. 857 The electroweak theory has had many successes, including the prediction of the $W^{\pm}$ particles. **1986** *Sci. Amer.* July 35/3 About 10^{-35} second after the big bang the strong force separated from the electroweak force.

electrum (ɪ'lɛktrəm). [a. L. *ēlectrum*, ad. Gr. ἤλεκτρον, in same senses. See also ELECTRE.]

†**1.** Amber. *Obs.*

1398 TREVISA *Barth. De P.R.* XVII. cxxi. (1495) 683 Of the pyne appyll tree cometh droppyng and woosynge whyche is made harde..and soo tornyth in to a precyous stone that hyghte Electrum. **1602** *Metamorph. Tobacco* (Collier) 17 Eridanus his pearl'd Electrum gaue. **1794** SULLIVAN *View Nat.* II. 58 These fishes..are unable to attract, or to repel the lightest substances, which even the electrum can affect.

†**b.** *fig.* of tears. *Obs.*

1591 GREENE *Maidens Dreame* v. 4 It was her masters death That drew electrum from her weeping eyes.

2. a. An alloy of silver and gold (of pale yellow colour) in use among the ancients; = ELECTRE 1. Also *attrib.* **b.** *Min.* Native argentiferous gold containing from 20 to 50 per cent of silver.

1398 TREVISA *Barth. De P.R.* XVI. xxxvii. (1495) 565 Electrum is a metall..it shyneth more clere than gold or syluer. **1555** EDEN *Decades W. Ind.* I. IV. (Arb.) 83 *marg. note*, Electrum is a metall naturally mixt of one portion of golde & an other of siluer. **1626** BACON *Sylva* §798 The Ancient Electrum had in it a fifth of Silver to the Gold. **1674** EARL SANDWICH tr. *Barba's Art Metals* (1740) 72 Electrum ..which is a natural mixture of Gold and Silver. **1868** DANA *Min.* (1880) 5 A mass of electrum..consisting of large crystals, containing 25 p.c. of silver. **1876** HUMPHREYS *Coin Coll. Man.* xvi. 186 The coins of Lydia were frequently of electrum.

3. An alloy of copper, zinc, and nickel.

1875 URE *Dict. Arts* II. 252 A base metal in modern use has received the name of electrum. It is an alloy of copper, zinc, and tin, with sometimes nickel.

†**electu'arious**, *a.* *Obs. rare.* In 6 electuarius. [f. ELECTUARY + -OUS.] Of the nature of an electuary; wholesome, beneficial.

1562 BULLEYN *Bk. Compounds* 17b, This oile is electuarius to the teeth.

electuary (ɪ'lɛktjʊərɪ). Forms: 6 electuarye, -ie, (*Sc.* electuar), 8 electary, 4- electuary. See also LECTUARY. [ad. late L. *ēlectuārium*, *ēlectārium* (5th c.), perh. a corrupt derivative of the synonymous Gr. ἐκλεικτόν, f. ἐκλείχειν to lick out.]

1. A medicinal conserve or paste, consisting of a powder or other ingredient mixed with honey, preserve, or syrup of some kind.

1398 TREVISA *Barth. De P.R.* VII. xxxv. (1495) 250 The Etyk is holpe..by an electuary that hight Electuarium patris. **1527** ANDREW tr. *Brunswyke's Distyll. Waters* A j, With waters dy[styl]lyd, all maner of..electuaryes be myxced. **1549** *Compl. Scot.* xvii. (1872) 145 Spicis..for to mak exquisit electuars. **1636** FEATLY *Clavis Myst.* xii. 148 Many simples goe to the making of a soveraigne Electuary. **1758** BROOKES *Pract. Physic* (ed. 3) II. 134 The antiscorbutic Electary..is very efficacious in this Disease. **1791** BOSWELL *Johnson* (1816) II. 372 Make them an electuary with honey and treacle. **1853** KANE *Grinnell Exp.* xxxvi. (1856) 326 Raw potato and saur-kraut, pounded with molasses into a damnable electuary.

b. *fig.*

1526 *Pilgr. Perf.* (W. de W. 1531) 85 Electuaryes to preserue them from spirytuall diseases. **1641** MILTON *Ch. Govt.* II. (1851) 139 Some eye-brightning electuary of knowledge, and foresight. **1878** EMERSON *Sov. Ethics* Wks. (Bohn) III. 385 Innocence is a wonderful electuary for purging the eyes.

¶**2.** ? Confused with *electar*, ELECTRE 1 and 2.

1536 BELLENDEN *Cron. Scot.* (1821) I. Introd. 52 Ane maner of electuar..hewit like gold, and sa attractive of nature, that it drawis stra. **1638** PENKETHMAN *Artach.* D, This weight serveth to weigh..Gold, Silver, Pearles, and other precious things, as Electuaries and Amber.

‖**Eledone** (ɛlɪ'dəʊniː). [mod.L., a. Gr. ἐλεδώνη a kind of polypus.] A cephalopod of the tribe *Octopoda.*

1835-6 TODD *Cycl. Anat.* I. 528/2 In the..Eledone the suckers are soft and unarmed. **1854** WOODWARD *Mollusca* (1856) 35 The *eledone* makes twenty respirations per minute, when resting quietly in a basin of water. **1878** BELL tr. *Gegenbauer's Comp. Anat.* 327 The modified end of the arm in Eledone and Octopus.

†ˌ**elee'mosynar.** *Sc. Obs.* exc. *Hist.* Also 7 elymosinar. [ad. med.L. *eleēmosynārius*: see next. Cf. OF. *elemosinaire*, which may be the immediate source.] = ALMONER.

a **1639** SPOTTISWOOD *Hist. Ch. Scotl.* I. (1677) 22 Alcuin, commonly held to be Charles the Great his Master, was made his Eleemosynar. **1663** SPALDING *Troub. Chas. I* (1829) 16 The bishop of Murray was made lord Elymosinar. **1884** C. ROGERS *Soc. Life Scotl.* I. ii. 53 Other officials were the carver, the cupbearer, the eleemosynar.

eleemosynary (ˌɛliːɪ'mɒsɪnərɪ), *a.* and *sb.* Also 7-8 elemo-, eleemo-, -sin-, -sn-, -sunary. [ad. med.L. *eleēmosynārius*, f. *eleēmosyna*: see ALMS.]

A. *adj.*

1. Of or pertaining to alms or almsgiving; charitable. ***eleemosynary house, corporation,*** one established for the distribution of alms, etc.

c **1630** RISDON *Surv. Devon* §293 (1810) 302 These her eleemosinary acts..are almost vanished. **1695** KENNETT *Par. Antiq.* ix. 659 The Elemosinary House or Hospital for the maintenance of two Capellanes. **1702** in *Lond. Gaz.* No. 3812/1 Divers Persons to whom Eleemosinary Protections were granted. **1827** HALLAM *Const. Hist.* (1876) I. ii. 80 The blind eleemosynary spirit inculcated by the Romish church is notoriously the cause..of beggary. **1865** H. STAUNTON *Grt. Schools Eng., Dulwich* 502 Three [portions] are assigned to the Educational and one to the Eleemosynary branch.

2. Dependent on or supported by alms.

1654 G. GODDARD in Burton *Diary* (1828) I. Introd. 65 If we be a mere elemosynary Parliament we are bound to do his drudgery. **1667** H. MORE *Div. Dial.* III. xxxii. (1713) 264 Is not the whole World the Alms-house of God-Almighty ..[in] which he had a right..to place us his eleemosynary Creatures? **1707** J. STEVENS tr. *Quevedo's Com. Wks.* (1709) 353 There is a sort of Spunging, elemosinary Travellers. **1860** HAWTHORNE *Marb. Faun* (1879) I. vi. 62 Threw forth ..food, for the flock of eleemosynary doves.

3. Of the nature of alms; given or done as an act of charity; gratuitous.

a **1620** JER. DYKE *Sel. Serm.* (1640) 348 God will not have the Ministery of the Word eleemosynary, to be matter of meere almes. **1791** BOSWELL *Johnson* (1831) 46 An eleemosynary supply of shoes. **1849** C. BRONTË *Shirley* II. v. 121 Eleemosynary relief never yet tranquillized the working classes. **1859** I. TAYLOR *Logic in Theol.* 246 We have nothing..to do..with eleemosynary..education.

b. *Law.* Given in 'free alms'. See ALMOIGN.

1671 F. PHILIPPS *Reg. Necess.* 440 Baronies..given in Frank Almoigne and as Elemosinary.

†**B.** *sb. Obs.*

1. One who lives upon alms; a beggar. Also *fig.*

1643 SIR T. BROWNE *Relig. Med.* 141 Those professed Eleemosynaries..direct..their petitions on a few and selected persons. **1665** GLANVILL *Sceps. Sci.* xviii. 112 That the cause should be an Eleemosynary for its subsistence to its effect. **1673** H. STUBBE *Vind. Dutch War* To Rdr. 3 The Parliamentarians were their Eleemosynaries.

2. = ALMONER. *rare.*

1656 BLOUNT *Glossogr.*, *Eleemosynary*, an almoner, or one that gives alms. **1678** in PHILLIPS. **1809** BAWDWEN *Domesday Bk.* 458 Robert the Priest had one carucate of land of the King's Eleemosinary.

3. = ALMONRY [ad. med.L. *eleēmosynārium*].

1688 R. HOLME *Armoury* III. 43/1 [In] the Almonry, or Eleemosinary..[are] 4 Yeomen. **1775** in ASH.

Hence **elee'mosynarily** *adv.*, in an eleemosynary manner; charitably, by way of charity.

†**elee'mosynate**, *v.* *Obs.*⁻⁰ [f. L. *eleēmosyna*, Gr. ἐλεημοσύνη + -ATE.] *intr.* To give alms.

1656 in BLOUNT *Glossogr.* **1775** in ASH.

†**elee'mosynous**, *a.* *Obs. rare*⁻¹. In 6 elemosinus. [f. as prec. + -OUS.] Compassionate, merciful.

c **1590** BUREL *2nd Pass. Pilgrimer* Poems (1596) P ij a, Ane pepill..na ways Elimosinus.

‖**eleeson** (ɛlɪ'iːsɒn). *nonce-wd.* [A use of Gr. ἐλέησον 'have mercy!'] = KYRIE ELEISON.

1822 W. L. BOWLES in *Blackw. Mag.* XII. 72, I hear far off Faint eleesons swell.

e'legal, bad form of ILLEGAL.

1647 *16 Quæres to Prælates* Ded. 2 These Quæres will proove fatall to your..elegall Ecclesiasticall Iurisdictions.

elegance ('ɛlɪgəns). [a. Fr. *élégance*, ad. L. *ēlegāntia*, f. *ēlegānt-em*: see ELEGANT.] The quality or state of being elegant.

1. Refined grace of form and movement, tastefulness of adornment, refined luxury, etc. See ELEGANT 1, 2, 3.

1797 BEWICK *Brit. Birds* (1847) I. Introd. 7 The.. elegance discoverable in their outward appearance. **1807** CRABBE *Par. Reg.* II. 140 With untutored elegance she dressed. **1821** CRAIG *Lect. Drawing* iv. 224 Elegance, I take to signify that intricate combination and contrast of lines in the form of a figure which constitute an essential part of beauty. **1880** MRS. FORRESTER *Roy & Viola* I. 1 Nowhere else in the world could you see such a display of luxury and elegance.

2. Of spoken or written compositions, literary style, etc.: Tasteful correctness, harmonious simplicity, in the choice and arrangement of words. See ELEGANT 4.

c **1510** BARCLAY *Mirr. Good Mann.* (1570) G. vj, In eligance of meter and speeche. **1589** NASHE *Pref. Greene's Menaph.* (Arb.) 10 Sir Thomas Eliots elegance did seuer it selfe from all equales. **1616** *Pasquil & Kath.* IV. 270, I.. Detest thy purest elegance of speech. **1751** JOHNSON *Rambl.* No. 157 ¶11 Nothing to say of elegance..equal to my wishes. **1824** LANDOR *Imag. Conv.* xxvii. Wks. 1846 I. 165 Elegance, by which I always mean precision and correctness. **1882** HINSDALE *Garfield & Educ.* II. 402 The elegance of her translations.

3. a. Of scientific processes, demonstrations, inventions, etc.: 'Neatness', ingenious simplicity, convenience, and effectiveness; so of a prescription, etc. See ELEGANT 5. **b.** Roman Law: transl. L. *elegantia juris*: see quot. 1864.

1756 P. BROWNE *Jamaica* 285, I doubt not but they might be used, with as much elegance, in emulsions. **1812** WOODHOUSE *Astron.* xi. 84 This formula, undoubtedly of great elegance, probably was not derived by a direct mathematical process. **1864** MAINE *Anc. Law* iv. (1876) 79 To this sense of simplicity and harmony..significantly termed 'elegance'..the Roman jurisconsults..surrendered themselves. **1965** *Encounter* Aug. 57/1 The elegance of the solution and the economy of the thought and work that went into it are qualities scientists give some weight to.

4. †**a.** Correctness of taste: cf. ELEGANT 6. *Obs.*

1660 STANLEY *Hist. Philos.* (1701) 116/1 Ælian argued the Elegance of the Person, in choosing such things as were fair.

b. Of manners, etc.: Refined propriety.

1816 MISS AUSTEN *Emma* I. xvi. 114 With all the gentleness of his address, true elegance was sometimes wanting.

5. *concr.* Something which is elegant; a particular instance or kind of elegance.

1676 EVELYN *Diary* (1827) II. 417 A nice contriver of all elegances. **1779** JOHNSON *L.P., Pope* Wks. IV. 126 He has left in his Homer a treasure of poetical elegances to posterity. **1824-9** LANDOR *Imag. Conv.* (1846) 88 What your father and grandfather used as an elegance in conversation is now abandoned to the populace. **1837** J. H. NEWMAN *Par. Serm.* (ed. 3) I. xxvi. 396 The measure of this world's elegances. **1863** EMERSON *Thoreau* Wks. (Bohn) III. 337 He had many elegances of his own.

elegancy ('ɛlɪgənsɪ). [ad. L. *ēlegāntia*: see -ANCY.] = ELEGANCE in its various senses.

1. = ELEGANCE 1. *rare* in mod. use.

1552 HULOET, Elegancye, *elegantia.* **1622** PEACHAM *Compl. Gent.* xii. (1634) 107 Most of them venerable for their antiquitie and elegancy. **1674** GREW *Anat. Plants* I. §15 31 Two general advantages to the Leaves, Elegancy and Security. **1741** RICHARDSON *Pamela* (1824) I. 218 An elegancy ran through..persons as well as furniture. **1768** A. CALCOTT *Deluge* 407 Neither do the fossil reliquiæ..yield in elegancy..to the medalic insignatures. **1838** EMERSON *Milton* Wks. (Bohn) III. 301 He threw himself, the flower of elegancy, on the side of the reeking conventicle.

b. *humorously*, in a form of address or title.

1824 SOUTHEY *Lett.* (1856) III. 435 Your Elegancy will be looking for some news.

†**2.** Of language and style; = ELEGANCE 2. *Obs.*

1531 ELYOT *Gov.* (1834) 38 The elegancy of poets. **1572** J. JONES *Bathes of Bath* I. 1 b, Tullie cheefe of all latyne elegancy. **1665** EVELYN *Mem.* (1857) III. 162 Some judgment might be made concerning the elegancy of the style. **1746** CHESTERF. *Lett.* I. cv. 288 The purity, and the elegancy of his language.

3. *concr.* Something which is elegant; an instance or a kind of elegance; = ELEGANCE 5.

1587 GOLDING *De Mornay* xxxiv. 547 They count Greek phrases for an elegancie. **1673** DRYDEN *Marr. à la Mode* IV. ii. 305 Instruct your wife's woman in these elegancies. **1746-7** HERVEY *Medit. & Contempl.* (1818) 157 Art never attempts to equal their incomparable elegancies. **1823** LAMB *Elia* Ser. I. xxii. (1865) 170 Palates not uninstructed in dietetical elegancies. **1874** PUSEY *Lent. Serm.* 41 We must.. have this or that elegancy..according to our condition of life.

elegant ('ɛlɪgənt), *a.* Forms: 5 ileȝant, 6 eligant, -aunt, elygant, 6- elegant. [a. F. *élégant*, ad. L. *ēlegānt-em*, usually regarded as pr. pple. of **ēlegāre* (f. **ēleg-us* adj.), related to *ēligĕre* to select.

The etymological sense is thus 'choosing carefully or skilfully.' In early Lat. *elegans* was a term of reproach, 'dainty, fastidious, foppish', but in classical times it expressed the notions of refined luxury, graceful propriety, which are reproduced in the mod.Eng. use.]

1. Tastefully ornate in attire; sometimes in unfavourable sense: Dainty, foppish.

c **1485** *Digby Myst.* (1882) III. 505, I woll, or even, be shavyn, for to seme ȝyng..that makyt me Ileȝant and lusty in lykyng. **1509** BARCLAY *Ship of Fooles* (1570) 113 It is..not for man to be so elegant, To such toyes wanton women may encline. **1552** HULOET, Elegant person, *philocalus.* **1621** BURTON *Anat. Mel.* I. ii. III. vii, A woman if she see her neighbour more neat or elegant..is enraged. **1801** MAR. EDGEWORTH *Good Fr. Gov.* (1832) 124 She is the elegantest dresser about town. **1882** tr. *Challamet Hist. Fashion in France* i, An elegant town lady would..adorn herself with a mantle that half covered her.

2. a. Characterized by refined grace of form (usually as the result of art or culture); tastefully ornamental. Of physical movements: Graceful, free from awkwardness.

1658 W. BURTON *Itin. Anton.* 117 The Sixth Legion..left behind them here a remembrance..yet to be seen, in large and elegant Characters. **1684** RAY *Corr.* (1848) 138 The *Polypodium plumosum* is an elegant plant. **1760** GOLDSM. *Cit. W.* xiv. (1837) 53 Nothing is truly elegant but what unites use with beauty. **1774** T. WARTON *Hist. Eng. Poetry* (1840) II. 272 A most splendid and elegant manuscript on vellum. **1809** ROLAND *Fencing* 137 The passing of the sword to the left side..has..a more..elegant appearance.

†**b.** Of stature: in 16th c. with sense 'tall'.

1513 DOUGLAS *Æneis* VII. xiv. 10 Turnus..Enarmit walkis ..Wyth corps of statur eligant [*præstanti*]. **1450-1530** *Mirr. Our Ladye* 7 That the sayd blessyd virgyne Katheryn because she was of an Eligant stature wold gather them of the sayd grapes.

3. Of modes of life, dwellings and their appointments, etc.: Characterized by refined luxury.

a **1687** PETTY *Pol. Arith.* ii. (1691) 38 Beautifying the Country..by elegant Dyet, Apparel, Furniture. **1806** *Gazetteer Scotl.* 141 Dumfries-shire contains many elegant seats. **1822** DE QUINCEY *Confess.* (1862) 137 What he considered a really elegant dinner. **1835** SIR J. ROSS *N.-West Pass.* v. 66 An elegant repast of venison. **1859** W. COLLINS *Q. of Hearts* (1873) 2 He felt languid pulses in elegant bedrooms.

4. a. Of composition, literary style, etc.; also of words or phrases: Characterized by grace and refinement; 'pleasing by minuter beauties' (J.).

Formerly used somewhat vaguely as a term of praise for literary style; from 18th c. it has tended more and more to exclude any notion of intensity or grandeur, and, when applied to compositions in which these qualities might be looked for, has a depreciatory sense.

1528 MORE *Heresyes* I. Wks. (1557) 174/2 The bokes neither lesse eligaunt nor lesse true. **1529** RASTELL *Pastyme, Hist. Brit.* (1811) 292 In a longe oracyon..with elygant wordes. **1649** JER. TAYLOR *Gt. Exemp.* III. xiv. 51 A most elegant and perswasive parable. **1672-5** COMBER *Comp. Temple* (1702) 23 Arnobius, an African, writ his elegant books against the Gentiles. **1756** J. WARTON *Ess. Pope* (1782) I. vi. 302 Addison has inserted..an elegant character of this poetess. **1791** BURKE *Corr.* (1844) III. 207, I thank you, too, for the elegant poem. **1841-4** EMERSON *Ess.* xx. Wks. (Bohn) I. 250 Pope's Odyssey..is correct and elegant. **1876** FREEMAN *Norm. Conq.* V. xxv. 545 The love of hard words, of words which are thought to sound learned or elegant, that is..which are not thoroughly understood.

b. Of a speaker or author: Characterized by refinement and polish of style. (Formerly in wider use: see above.)

1641 MILTON *Animadv.* (1851) 189 They did no more then the elegantest Authors among the Greeks. **1672-5** COMBER *Comp. Temple* (1702) 44 The learned volumes of this Elegant Father [Chrysostom]. **1887** *Spectator* 6 Aug. 1057/2 Rogers belongs to the elegant order of poets.

5. a. Of scientific processes, contrivances, etc.: 'Neat', pleasing by ingenious simplicity and effectiveness.

1668 CULPEPPER & COLE *Barthol. Anat.* IV. ix. 166 An elegant Workmanship of Nature. **1803** *Med. Jrnl.* X. 336 Profound discoveries and elegant improvements in every branch of medical science. **1823** J. BADCOCK *Dom. Amusem.* 198 An elegant cement may also be made from rice-flour. **1844-57** G. BIRD *Urin. Deposits* 146 An elegant mode of showing the composition of the deposit. *a* **1891** *Mod.* An elegant chess problem. An elegant method of solving equations. **1952** G. MANLEY *Climate & Brit. Scene* iii. 32 We owe to Sir Geoffrey Taylor of Cambridge one of the most elegant discussions of the factors governing the depth and density of such fogs. **1966** 'A. HALL' *9th Directive* viii. 74 This operation..was sensitive and it was elegant. **1966** *Listener* 1 Sept. 304/1 MacNeish's demonstration is particularly elegant because he could trace the whole processes in a small, almost self-contained area.

b. Of medicinal preparations: see quot.

1710 T. FULLER *Pharm. Extemp.* 127 It [the Electuary] is an elegant Composition for a troublesome..Cough. **1788** V. KNOX *Winter Even.* I. vi. 67 The physicians call a medicine which contains efficient ingredients in a small volume, and of a pleasant or tolerable taste, an elegant medicine. **1868** ROYLE & HEADLAND *Mat. Medica* (ed. 5) 172 This elegant chalybeate has been long in use.

6. a. Of persons: Correct and delicate in taste. Now only in the phrase ***elegant scholar***, which is influenced in meaning by 7.

1667 MILTON *P.L.* IX. 1018 Thou art exact of taste, And elegant. **1774** T. WARTON *Hist. Eng. Poetry* (1840) I. Diss. i. 19 A very..elegant enquirer into the genius..of the northern nations. **1788** V. KNOX *Winter Even.* II. ii. 118 An elegant spectator of the vegetable world. **1856** EMERSON *Eng. Traits* xiv. Wks. (Bohn) II. 109 Mr. Hallam, a learned and elegant scholar.

b. Refined in manners and habits (formerly also, in feeling).

1712 STEELE *Spect.* No. 491 ¶2 An utter Stranger to the.. Delicacies that attend the Passion..in elegant Minds. **1797** MRS. RADCLIFFE *Italian* i. (1824) 533 Her features.. expressed the tranquillity of an elegant mind. **1841-4** EMERSON *Ess.* xvi. Wks. (Bohn) I. 209 A sainted soul is always elegant. **1866** GEO. ELIOT *F. Holt* (1868) 26 Such a stock of ideas may be made to tell in elegant society.

7. Of pursuits, studies (formerly also, of sentiments): Graceful, polite, appropriate to persons of refinement and cultivated taste. ***elegant arts***: those pertaining to the adornment of life; nearly = 'fine arts'.

1705 POPE *To Yng. Lady* 4 Trifles themselves are elegant in him. **1712** STEELE *Spect.* No. 466 ¶7 Every thing in Nature that can pretend to give elegant Delight. **1752** HUME *Ess. & Treat.* (1777) I. 7 The ardours of a youthful appetite become an elegant passion. **1779** JOHNSON *L.P.*, *Shenstone* Wks. IV. 215 Eminent for English poetry, and elegant literature. **1821** CRAIG *Lect. Drawing* i. 1 A high state of the elegant arts..is indicative of great advancement in civilization.

¶**8.** Vulgarly used for 'excellent, first-rate'. Cf. ILIGANT *a.*

1764 J. BLAIR *Acct. Coll. New-Jersey* 12 The college had ..'an elegant hall of genteel workmanship'. **1817** M. BIRKBECK *Notes Journey America* 152 You hear of an *elegant* mill, an *elegant* orchard, an *elegant* tan-yard, &c. and familiarly of *elegant* roads, meaning such as you may pass without extreme peril. The word implies eligibility or usefulness in America, but has nothing to do with taste. **1822** J. WOODS *Engl. Prairie Illinois* 203 This negro said, some very *elegant* potatoes grew on this land last year. **1848** BARTLETT *Dict. Amer.*, *Elegant* for *excellent* applied to articles of food and drink, is very common: as elegant water, elegant beef, elegant butter. **1931** O. T. BARCK *New York City* iv. 83 The most elegant of these homes were occupied by officers.

9. *Comb.*

1799 MALTHUS *Jrnl.* 3 July (1966) 117 We had met with many pretty elegant looking women. **1809** HANNAH MORE *Coelebs* I. 38 (Jod.) Sir John is a valuable elegant-minded man.

Hence **'elegan,tize** *v. trans.* [see -IZE], to make elegant. **'elegant,ish** *a.* [see -ISH], rather elegant.

1798 LAMB *Lett. to Southey* iv. 35 You might..elegantise this supersedeas. **1830** *Fraser's Mag.* I. 568 What criticisms ..have been put forth..in that elegantish..periodical!

†**elegante.** *Obs.* [Cf. *alegant*, var. of ALICANT.] Some kind of dried fruit; ? Alicante raisins.

1579 in Rogers *Agric. & Pr.* III. 543 Elegantes ¾ *c* 14/3.

‖**élégante** (elegɑ̃t). Also 9 **elegante.** [Fr. *élégante*, fem. of *élégant*, ELEGANT *a.*] A fashionable lady.

1806 MAR. EDGEWORTH *Leonora* (1832) 32 Would you know the fashionable dress of a Parisian élégante? **1814** SCOTT *Wav.* i, The elegantes of Queen Anne Street East. **1922** E. SITWELL *Façade* 8 And Madame A..the élégante, With Madame X..the elephant. **1927** —— *Rustic Elegies* 79 Our élégantes favouring bonnets of blond. **1965** *Harper's Bazaar* Nov. 80 Gamine turns into élégante when the clock strikes six.

elegantly ('ɛlɪgəntlɪ), *adv.* [f. ELEGANT + -LY².] In an elegant manner; see senses of the adj. Also in comb. with adjs.

1552 HULOET, *Elegantlye*, eleganter, rotunde. **1571** GOLDING *Calvin on Ps.* lix. 17. 228 Hee elegantly putteth the doubtfull speeche in a diverse mening. **1728** YOUNG *Love Fame* vi. (1757) 146 She's elegantly pain'd from morn till night. **1753** HANWAY *Trav.* (1762) II. I. x. 54 Many hollanders..live elegantly. **1783** LD. HAILES *Antiq. Chr. Ch.* vi. 178 *note*, The latter part of the passage in Lampridius is elegantly paraphrased. **1858** W. ELLIS *Vis. Madagascar* viii. 212 A number of elegantly-bound volumes lay on the table. **1879** O. W. HOLMES *Motley* ii. 14 Elegantly brutal onslaughts.

elegiac (ɛlɪ'dʒaɪæk), *a.* and *sb.* Also 6 **eligiack.** [ad. L. *elegīac-us*, ad. Gr. ἐλεγειακός, f. ἐλεγεῖον ELEGY.]

A. *adj.*

1. *Prosody.* Appropriate to elegies. *spec.* Usually applied to the metre so called in Greek and Latin, which consists of a (dactylic) hexameter and pentameter, forming the ***elegiac distich***. Sometimes the term ***elegiac verse*** has been applied to the pentameter of the couplet separately.

1586 WEBBE *Eng. Poetrie* (Arb.) 86 The most vsuall kindes [of verse] are foure, the Heroic, Elegiac, Iambick, and Lyric. **1603** HOLLAND *Plutarch's Mor.* 1246 A chronicler penning the historie of these affaires in elegiack verses. **1741** WATTS *Improv. Mind* (1801) 62 He has turned the same psalms.. into elegiac verse. **1779** JOHNSON *L.P.*, *Hammond* Wks. III. 240 Why Hammond or other writers have thought the quatrain of ten syllables elegiac, it is difficult to tell. **1846** GROTE *Greece* (1862) I. xx. 503 The iambic and elegiac metres..do not reach up to the year 700 B.C. **1873** SYMONDS *Grk. Poets* i. 15 The pathetic melody of the Elegiac metre.

2. Of the nature of an elegy; pertaining to elegies; hence, mournful, melancholy, plaintive; also (rarely) of a person, melancholy, pensive.

1644 BULWER *Chiron.* 20 An ingenious friend..in his Elegiack knell. **1720** GAY *Poems* (1745) II. 18 He..Might sweetly mourn in Elegiac verse. **1752** GRAY *Wks.* (1825) II. 169 Mr. Lyttleton is a gentle elegiac person. *c* **1800** K. WHITE *Rem.* (1837) 383 Its elegiac delicacy and querimonious plaintiveness. **1808** SCOTT *Marm.* III. Introd., Hast thou no elegiac verse For Brunswick's venerable hearse? **1856** MRS. BROWNING *Aur. Leigh* I. 994 Elegiac griefs, and songs of love.

3. ***elegiac poet***: one who writes **a.** in elegiac metre; **b.** in a mournful or pensive strain.

1581 SIDNEY *Def. Poesie* (Arb.) 28 The most notable [denominations of poets] bee the Heroicke, Tragicke.. Iambic, Elegiacke. Some of these being termed..by the sortes of verses they liked best to write in. **1589** PUTTENHAM *Eng. Poesie* I. xi. (Arb.) 40. **1855** H. REED *Lect. Eng. Lit.* x. (1878) 319 It is the theme of the elegiac poet, to show the virtues of sorrow. **1888** *Spectator* 30 June 875/2 Matthew Arnold..the greatest elegiac poet of our generation.

B. *sb.* †**a.** An elegiac poet (*obs.*). **b.** *pl.* Elegiac verses (sense A. 1).

1581 SIDNEY *Def. Poesie* (1622) 515 The lamenting Elegiacke..who bewayleth..the weakenesse of mankinde. **1774** T. WARTON *Hist. Eng. Poetry* (1840) II. 508 His Latin elegiacs are pure. **1886** F. H. DOYLE *Reminiscences* 30, I soon acquired ease..in rattling over my elegiacs.

Hence as combining form **ele'giaco-.**

1832 CARLYLE in *Fraser's Mag.* V. 255 We named Rousseau's Confessions an elegiaco-didactic Poem.

ele'giacal, *a.* [f. prec. + -AL¹.]

†**1.** Of metre: = ELEGIAC 1. *Obs.*

1546 LANGLEY *Pol. Verg. De Invent.* I. viii. 17 a, Of Meters there bee..that hath their name..of the nomber of the fete, as Exameter and Pentameter which is also called Elegiacal. **1583** STANYHURST *Poems* (Arb.) 125 The heroical and the elegiacal enterlaced one with the oother.

2. Of the nature of an elegy, pertaining to elegies. *arch.* Cf. ELEGIAC 2.

1631 WEEVER *Anc. Fun. Mon.* 769 An Elegiacall or sorrowfull Epitaph. **1640** T. CAREW *Poems* Wks. (1824) 92 An elegiacall letter upon the death of the king of Sweden. **1846** LANDOR *Exam. Shaks.* Wks. II. 294 Study this higher elegiacal strain.

elegiambic (,ɛlɪdʒaɪ'æmbɪk), *a.* [f. L. *elegīa* + IAMBIC.] Of a metre: Consisting of half an elegiac pentameter, followed by an iambic dimeter.

1721-1800 BAILEY *Elegiambick Verse.*

e'legiast. *rare.* [f. ELEGY, after the analogy of *ecclesiast*, etc.] A writer of elegies.

1766 GOLDSMITH *Vic. W.* xvii. 47 These Elegiasts..are in despair for griefs that give the sensible part of mankind very little pain. **1969** *Daily Tel.* 3 July 20/2 She is the elegiast of bleakness and decay, an original artist of major attainment.

†**e'legic,** *a. Obs.*—⁰ [f. ELEGY + -IC.] = ELEGIAC. In some modern Dicts.

,elegi'ographer. *rare*—⁰. [f. ELEGY, on the analogy of *biographer*.] A writer of elegies.

1623 in COCKERAM. **1656** in BLOUNT *Glossogr.* **1721-61** in BAILEY. **1864** in WEBSTER; and in mod. Dicts.

†**e'legious,** *a. Obs. rare.* [f. ELEGY + -OUS.] Resembling an elegy; hence, lugubrious, melancholy, mournful.

1632 QUARLES *Div. Fancies* IV. x, Th'affrighted heav'ns sent down elegious Thunder. **1635** —— *Embl.* v. i. (1818) 259 If your elegious breath should hap to rouse A happy tear.

elegist ('ɛlɪdʒɪst). [f. ELEGY + -IST.] The writer of an elegy.

1774 WARTON *Eng. Poetry* (1840) I. 95 Our elegist, and the chroniclers, impute the crime..to the advice of the king of France.

elegit (ɪ'li:dʒɪt). *Law.* [f. L. *ēlēgit* 'he has chosen', 3rd pers. sing. perfect tense of *ēligĕre* to choose; see quot. 1809.] A writ of execution, by which a creditor is put in possession of (formerly half) the goods and lands of a debtor, until his claim is satisfied.

1503-4 *Act 19 Hen. VII*, c. 36 §1 To sue execucion..by write or wryttes of Elegit. **1632** *Star Chamb. Cases* (1886) 124 He tooke forth an Elegit for the rest of the Judgment. **1796** J. ANSTEY *Pleaders G.* (1803) 70 Quare clausum fregit May breed a monster called Elegit. **1809** TOMLINS *Law. Dict.*, *Elegit* from the words in the writ, *elegit sibi liberari*, because the plaintiff hath chosen this writ of execution. **1876** DIGBY *Real Prop.* v. §5. 247 The writ..has ever since the Statute of Westminster II been called the writ of elegit.

b. The right secured by this writ.

1715 M. DAVIES *Ath. Brit.* I. 309 As for Tenancy of Elegit, Statute-merchant and Staple, etc. **1809** TOMLINS *Law Dict.* s.v., The creditor..during that term..is tenant by *elegit*.

elegize ('ɛlɪdʒaɪz), *v.* [f. ELEGY + -IZE.]

1. *intr.* **a.** To write an elegy; also const. *upon*; **b.** To write in a mournful strain.

1702 C. MATHER *Magn. Chr.* III. I. iii. (1852) 313 His death gave the same gentleman occasion thus to elegize upon him. **1754** H. WALPOLE *Lett.* I. 329 (D.), I..should have elegized on for a page or two farther. **1886** *Edin. Rev.* July 155 Propertius and Tibullus elegised.

2. *trans.* To write an elegy upon.

1809 BYRON *Eng. Bards* 266 The bard who soars to elegise an ass. *a* **1845** HOOD *Poems* (1846) II. 66 Whose late, last voice must elegise the whole. **1858** CARLYLE *Fredk. Gt.* II. x. ii. 590 He elegises poor Adrienne Lecouvreur, the Actress.

elegug, var. of ELIGUG.

elegy ('ɛlɪdʒɪ). [ad. Fr. *élégie*, ad. L. *elegīa*, ad. Gr. ἐλεγεία, f. ἔλεγος a mournful poem.]

1. A song of lamentation, *esp.* a funeral song or lament for the dead.

1514 BARCLAY *Cyt. & Uplondyshm.* Introd. 69, I tell mine elegy. **1594** DRAYTON *Idea* 749 My Lives complaint in dolefull Elegies. **1649** JER. TAYLOR *Gt. Exemp.* I. ix. 140 The Church's song is most of it Elegy. **1750** GRAY *Elegy* xxi, Their name, their years..The place of fame and elegy supply. **1762** GOLDSM. *Nash* 180 The public papers were filled with elegies. —— (*title*) Elegy of a Mad Dog. **1812** SCOTT *Rokeby* v. xvii, Thy strings mine elegy shall thrill, My Harp alone. **1871** R. ELLIS *Catullus* lxv. 12 Death's dark elegy.

2. Vaguely used in wider sense, app. originally including all the species of poetry for which Gr. and Lat. poets adopted the elegiac metre. See also quots. 1755 and 1833.

1600 SHAKS. *A.Y.L.* III. ii. 379 There is a man..hangs.. Elegies on brambles..defying the name of Rosalinde. **1716-8** LADY M. W. MONTAGUE *Lett.* I. xxxiv. 120 A subject affording many poetical turns..in an heroic elegy. **1755** JOHNSON, *Elegy*, a short poem without points or turns. *a* **1763** SHENSTONE *Wks. & Lett.* (1768) I. 17 They gave the name of elegy to their pleasantries as well as lamentations. **1833** COLERIDGE *Table-T.* 23 Oct., Elegy..may treat of any subject, but..of no subject for itself..always and exclusively with reference to the poet. **1859** KINGSLEY *Burns* Misc. I. 379 The poet descends from the..dramatic domain of song, into the subjective and reflective one of elegy.

3. a. Poetry, or a poem, written in elegiac metre. †**b.** [after Gr. ἐλεγεῖον] An elegiac distich (*obs.*).

1589 PUTTENHAM *Eng. Poesie* (Arb.) 64 Long lamentation in Elegie. **1794** T. TAYLOR *Pausanias' Greece* II. 369 An elegy on one of these bases..signifies that the statue..was that of Philopœmen. **1839** THIRLWALL *Greece* II. 126 The elegy, which [Mimnermus] adopted as the organ of his voluptuous melancholy..had been invented by another Ionian poet, Callinus. **1862** MERIVALE *Rom. Emp.* (1871) V. xli. 124 Ovid was the successor in elegy of Propertius and Tibullus.

elekte, obs. variant of ELECT.

†**elelendish,** *a. Obs.* Forms: 1 elelendisc, 2 -is, helelendis, (helendis). [OE. *ęlelęndisc*, f. *ęle-land* (see EILLAND) + *-isc*, -ISH.] Of another land, foreign.

a **1000** *Lamb. Ps.* xxxviii[ix]. 13 (Bosw.) Elelendisc ic eom mid ðe. *c* **1175** *Lamb. Hom.* 81 Nu kumeð þes helendisse Mon..elelendis he is icleped for he is of unkuþe þode.

eleme ('ɛlɪmɪ). *Comm.* Also 9 **elemi.** [a. Turk. *eleme* something sifted or selected.] *attrib.* in ***eleme figs***, a kind of dried figs from Turkey.

1879 *Encycl. Brit.* IX. 154 The best kind, known as elemi, are shipped at Smyrna. **1888** *Grocer's Price List*, Fine Eleme Figs.

element ('ɛlɪmənt), *sb.* Forms: 3-4, 7 **elemens** (*pl.*), 4 **ela-, elemente,** 5 **elymente,** 6 **elyment, elemente,** 4- **element.** [a. OF. *element*, ad. L. *elementum*, a word of which the etymology and primary meaning are uncertain, but which was employed as transl. of Gr. στοιχεῖον in the various senses:—a component unit of a series; a constituent part of a complex whole (hence the 'four elements'); a member of the planetary system; a letter of the alphabet; a fundamental principle of a science.]

I. A component part of a complex whole.

* *of material things.*

1. One of the simple substances of which all material bodies are compounded.

†**a.** In ancient and mediæval philosophy these were believed to be: Earth, water, air, and fire. See examples in 9. *Obs.* exc. *Hist.*

†**b.** In pre-scientific chemistry the supposed 'elements' were variously enumerated, the usual number being about five or six. (See quots.)

1724 WATTS *Logic* I. ii. §2 (1822) 17 The chemist makes spirit, salt, sulphur, water, and earth, to be their five elements. **1765** *Dict. Art & Sc.* II. s.v. *Element* [enumerate Water, Air, Oil, Salt, Earth].

c. In modern chemistry applied to those substances (of which more than seventy are now known) which have hitherto resisted analysis, and which are provisionally supposed to be simple bodies.

1813 SIR H. DAVY *Agric. Chem.* i. (1814) 8 Bodies..not capable of being decompounded are considered..as elements. **1830** M. DONOVAN *Dom. Econ.* I. 111 Sugar is composed of three elements, carbon, hydrogen, and oxygen. **1841** EMERSON *Ess. Hist.* Wks. (Bohn) I. 17 Fifty or sixty chemical elements. **1854** BUSHNAN in *Circ. Sc.* (*c* 1865) II. 6/1 The proximate elements are formed by the union of

several ultimate elements. **1881** WILLIAMSON in *Nature* No. 618. 414 The foundation of..chemistry was laid by the discovery of chemical elements.

2. In wider sense: One of the relatively simple substances of which a complex substance is composed; in *pl.* the 'raw material' of which a thing is made.

c **1386** CHAUCER *Freres T.* 206 Make ye yow newe bodies alway Of elementz. **1593** HOOKER *Eccl. Pol.* I. iii, If those principall & mother elements of the world, whereof all things in this lower world are made, should loose the qualities which now they haue. **1610** SHAKS. *Temp.* III. iii. 61 The Elements Of whom your swords are temper'd may as well Wound the loud windes. **1851** CARPENTER *Man. Phys.* 319 The two elements [Fibrine and the Red Corpuscles] separating from each other laterally.

3. The bread and wine used in the Sacrament of the Eucharist. Chiefly *pl.*

[The word *elementa* is used in late L. in the sense of 'articles of food and drink, the solid and liquid portions of a meal' (see Du Cange); but in the ecclesiastical use there is probably a reference to the philosophic sense of mere 'matter' as apart from 'form'; the 'form', by virtue of which the 'elements' became Christ's body and blood, being believed to be imparted by the act of consecration.]

1593 HOOKER *Eccl. Pol.* IV. i. (1611) 128 Vnto the element let the word bee added, and they two make a Sacrament. *a* **1600** tr. *Calvin's Comm. Prayer-bk.* in *Phenix* (1708) II. 245 As if these Elements were turn'd and chang'd into the Substance of his Flesh and Blood. **1607** HIERON *Wks.* I. 256 Such slender & vnlikely elemens of water, bread & wine. **1633** D. ROGERS *Sacraments* 132 They..bring an whole unbroken Element, made of a fine white delicate wafer. **1745** WESLEY *Answ. Ch.* 35 He deliver'd the Elements with his own Hands. **1866** *Direct. Angl.* (ed. 3) 354 Elements, the materials used in the Sacraments.

4. a. *Physiol.* A definite small portion of an animal or vegetable structure.

1841–71 T. R. JONES *Anim. Kingd.* 654 Two elements [of a vertebra] which embrace the spinal marrow. **1884** BOWER & SCOTT *De Bary's Phaner. & Ferns* 182 Small vascular bundles composed of narrow elements. *Ibid.* 459 On the side of the wood, new elements..are constantly added.

b. One of the essential parts of any scientific apparatus; used *esp.* of simple instruments united to form a complex instrument of the same kind. ***voltaic element***: usually = CELL 10, but sometimes = *electrode*.

1831 BREWSTER *Nat. Magic* vi. (1833) 148 We can even reproduce them..with the simplest elements of our optical apparatus. **1871** tr. *Schellen's Spectr. Anal.* ix. 67 An electric battery of 50 Bunsen's or Grove's large elements.

c. The resistance wire carrying the current in an electric heater; (also used of) the bar or collection of pieces of asbestos, etc., in an electric or gas stove.

1906 *Nature* 17 May 60/2 The method exemplified is the use of silicated carbon upon a terra-cotta base, forming an 'element'. **1925** *Jrnl. Iron & Steel Inst.* CXI. 535 The dimensions, temperature..distribution of heating elements ..and various furnace types are considered. **1926** *Gloss. Terms Electr. Engin.* (*B.S.I.*) 153 *Heating element*, the complete resistor, including the element carrier on which it is wound, as used in ovens, electric fires, radiators, etc. **1952** 'N. SHUTE' *Far Country* iii. 75 The girl stared at the hot elements of the fire.

****** *of non-material things.*

5. a. A constituent portion of an immaterial whole, as of a concept, character, state of things, community, etc.

1599 SHAKS. *Much Ado* II. i. 357 There's little of the melancholy element in her, my lord. **1678** CUDWORTH *Intell. Syst.* 7 These simple Elements of Magnitude, Figure, Site and Motion..are all clearly intelligible as different Modes of extended Substance. **1833** BROWNING *Pauline* 21, I strip my mind bare—whose first elements I shall unveil. **1841** EMERSON *Eng. Traits, Character* Wks. (Bohn) II. 61 This [English] race has added new elements to humanity, and has a deeper root in the world. **1845** GRAVES in *Encycl. Metrop.* 783/1 Mixed with bigotry and superstition, it [the canon law] will be found to contain many pure elements. **1867** FREEMAN *Norm. Conq.* (1876) I. iii. 93 In our old constitution we find the elements of feudalism. **1870** E. PEACOCK *Ralf Skirl.* III. 187 Size is certainly one main element of beauty. **1876** GREEN *Short Hist.* vii. §5 (1882) 386 The woollen manufacture had become an important element in the national wealth. *Mod.* The Celtic and Teutonic elements in the population.

b. Often followed by *of* = 'consisting of'.

1851 HELPS *Friends in C.* I. 11 These practices have elements of charity and prudence as well as fear and meanness in them. **1866** KINGSLEY *Herew.* vii. 129 It had its usual element of cant. **1875** JOWETT *Plato* (ed. 2) I. 241 The greatest strength is observed to have an element of limitation. **1869** FREEMAN *Norm. Conq.* (1876) III. xii. 162 Mingled with all this there is a certain element of grim merriment.

c. *Math.* Any of the symbols or quantities which, set out in an array, constitute a determinant or matrix.

[**1859** G. SALMON *Lessons Mod. Higher Algebra* i. 1 The coefficients a_1, b_1, &c., which enter into the expression of a determinant, are called the constituents of that determinant, and the products a_1b_2, &c., are called the elements of the determinant.] **1867** C. L. DODGSON *Elem. Treat. Determinants* ii. 6 If *mn* quantities be so placed as to form *m* rows and *n* columns: they are said to form a Block; and the *mn* quantities are called the Elements of such a Block. **1881** [see CONSTITUENT *a.* and *sb.* B. 4]. **1939** A. C. AITKEN *Determinants & Matrices* i. 4 A matrix may possibly consist of a single row, or of a single column, of elements. **1968** P. A. P. MORAN *Introd. Probability Theory* iii. 109 $p(t)$ is a column vector whose elements are $p_1(t), \ldots, p_n(t)$.

d. *Math.* and *Logic.* [cf. G. *element* in same sense (G. Cantor in *Math. Ann.* (1882) XX. 114, (1883) XXI. 587, (1895) XLVI. 481, etc.).] Any of the (real or conceptual) entities of which a set is composed; an entity that satisfies the criterion or criteria used to define a set.

1857 [see SET *sb.*[2] 10]. **1901** L. E. DICKSON *Linear Groups* i. 5 A set of *s* distinct elements satisfying the above four conditions is said to form a field of order *s*. **1953** A. A. FRAENKEL *Abstract Set Theory* i. 22 In fact '*x* is red' corresponds to the relation '*x* is an element of the set of all red things'. **1965** SHIH-CHÊN HU *Elem. Mod. Algebra* v. 119 The only nilpotent element in an integral domain is the zero element 0.

6. One of the facts or conditions which 'enter into' or determine the result of a process, calculation, deliberation, or inquiry. Also with *of* (cf. 5 b).

1812 WOODHOUSE *Astron.* ix. 66 The length of a sidereal year (an element of little or no importance in Astronomy). **1823** CHALMERS *Serm.* I. 129 His will was reduced to an element of utter insignificancy. **1842** W. GROVE *Corr. Phys. Forces* 32 If the element of quantity be included, this objection will not apply. **1866** CRUMP *Banking* iii. 72 The periodical publication of accounts by the joint-stock banks furnishes a very important element in coming to a decision. **1876** MOZLEY *Univ. Serm.* iv. 88 Everything depends upon one element in the case, which element they cannot get at.

7. *spec.* (*pl.*) **a.** *Astron.* The data necessary to determine the orbit of a heavenly body. **b.** *Crystallography.* Those needed to determine the form of a crystal.

1788–9 HOWARD *Encycl.*, *Elements*, in astronomy, are.. those fundamental numbers, which are employed in the construction of tables of the planetary motions. **1816** PLAYFAIR *Nat. Phil.* II. 197 The elements of their [comets'] orbits..agreed nearly with those of the Comet of 1682. **1834** MRS. SOMERVILLE *Connex. Phys. Sc.* ii. (1849) 12 This depends upon seven quantities called the elements of the orbit. **1878** GURNEY *Crystallogr.* 41 The three angles between the axes and two of the ratios between the parameters, are called the elements of the crystal.

8. *Math.* An infinitesimal part of a magnitude of any kind; a differential.

1727–51 CHAMBERS *Cycl.*, *Element* of an area, called also its differential, is the rectangle..of the semi-ordinate..into the differential of the absciss. **1882** MINCHIN *Unipl. Kinemat.* 112 *P* any point in the lamina at which the element of mass is *dm*. **1885** WATSON & BURBURY *Math. Th. Electr. & Magn.* I. 250 The molecular distributions within the element of volume *dx dy dz*.

II. The 'four elements'.

9. a. Used as a general name for earth, water, air, and fire; originally in sense 1, to which many of the earlier instances have explicit reference; now merely as a matter of traditional custom.

a **1300** *Signs bef. Judgm.* 177 in *E.E.P.* (1862) 12 Þe .xii. dai þe fure elemens sul cri..merci ihsu fiz mari. *c* **1300** *Fragm. Pop. Sc.* (Wright) 120 Bynethe the loweste hevene..Beoth the four elementz, of wham we beoth i-wroȝt. *a* **1340** HAMPOLE *Psalter* ix. 34 Þe erth is þe end of thynges & þe last element. **1393** GOWER *Conf.* III. 97 It [air] is eke the thridde element. **1483** CAXTON *Cato* 4 The foure elementes menace alle men that thanke not god. **1535** COVERDALE *Wisd.* xix. 18 The elementes turned in to them selues, like as whan one tune is chaunged vpon an instrument of musick. **1645** DIGBY *Nat. Bodies* iv. (1658) 37 There are but four simple bodies: and these are rightly named Elements. **1656** H. MORE *Antid. Ath.* (1712) Gen. Pref. 15 Regions of looser particles of the third Element. **1711** POPE *Temp. Fame* 447 Thro' undulating air the sounds are sent, And spread o'er all the fluid element. **1723** *Briton* No. iii, Rich wines and high-season'd Ragouts supply the place of Vegetables and meer Element. **1787** G. WHITE *Selborne* i. 3 Fine limpid water.. much commended by those who drink the pure element. **1816** BYRON *Ch. Har.* III. lxxiv, When elements to elements conform, And dust is as it should be. **1886** T. K. OLIPHANT *New Eng.* II. 219 If the great authors named were set up as models..we should never hear of fire as 'the devouring element'.

b. *fig.*

1813 WELLINGTON *Lett.* in Gurw. *Disp.* XI. 12 A British minister cannot have too often under his view the element by which he is surrounded. **1850** KINGSLEY *Alt. Locke* i. (1876) 2 Italy..where natural beauty would have become the very element which I breathed.

†10. a. The sky; ? also, the atmosphere. *Obs.*

[This sense is app. due to med.L. '*elementum ignis*' as a name of the starry sphere; but there may be a mixture of the sense 'air'.]

c **1485** *Digby Myst.* (1882) II. 371 A meruelous lyȝt fro thelement dyd glyde. **1509** HAWES *Past. Pleas.* 15, I..sawe a craggy rocke..neare to the element. **1534** MORE *Treat. Passion* Wks. 1307/1 The moone & the sterres appere in the element. **1580** SIDNEY *Arcadia* v. (1590) 458 Morning had taken full possession of the element. **1634** MILTON *Comus* 299, I took them for a faery vision Of some gay creatures of the element. **1676** HOBBES *Iliad* XIX. 331 A thick Snow, Which Boreas bloweth through the Element. **1714** GAY *Shepherd's Week* VI. 3 *note*, Welkin..is frequently taken for the Element or Sky.

†b. ? One of the 'heavens' or celestial spheres of ancient astronomy (see SPHERE); also (rarely) one of the heavenly bodies themselves. *Obs.*

[Cf. med.L. *elementa* 'planets' and 'signs of the zodiac'; but neither of these senses is clearly evidenced in our quots.]

a **1300** *Cursor M.* 395 Þe sterres gret and smale þat we may se..In þe ouermast element of alle. *c* **1384** CHAUCER *H. Fame* 975 Wyth fetheris of Philosophye To passen everyche element. **1534** LD. BERNERS *Gold. Bk. M. Aurel.* (1546) B b, These were the fyrste that wold serche the trouthe of the elementes of the heuen. **1593** HOOKER *Eccl. Pol.* I. ix, The Sunne, the Moone, any one of the heauens or elements. **1604** SHAKS. *Oth.* III. iii. 464 Witnesse you euer-burning Lights aboue, You Elements, that clip vs round about.

11. *pl.* Atmospheric agencies or powers.

1555 EDEN *Decades W. Ind.* I. IV. (Arb.) 81 Owre nation hadde trowbled the elementes. **1605** SHAKS. *Lear* III. ii. 16, I taxe not you, you Elements with vnkindnesse. **1813** BAKEWELL *Introd. Geol.* (1815) 239 Diminution of rocks.. by the incessant operation of the elements. **1855** PRESCOTT *Philip II*, I. iv. (1857) 61 Too gallant a cavalier to be daunted by the elements. **1866** NEALE *Sequences & H.* 102 The war of elements above.

12. That one of the 'four elements' which is the natural abode of any particular class of living beings; said chiefly of air and water. Hence *transf.* and *fig.* (a person's) ordinary range of activity, the surroundings in which one feels at home; the appropriate sphere of operation of any agency. Phrases, ***in, out of*** (***one's***) ***element***.

1598 SHAKS. *Merry W.* IV. ii. 186 She workes by Charmes ..beyond our element. **1599** *Broughton's Lett.* viii. 26 You are in for all day..it is your element. **1667** MILTON *P.L.* II. 275 Our torments also may in length of time Become our Elements. **1673** TEMPLE *Observ. United Prov.* Wks. 1731 I. 69 It seems to be with Trade, as with the Sea (its Element). **1719** DE FOE *Crusoe* (1840) II. iv. 73 When they came to make boards..they were quite out of their element. **1784** JOHNSON in *Boswell* III. 629 The town is my element; there are my friends, there are my books. **1823** LAMB *Elia* Ser. I. xii. (1865) 104 My proper element of prose. **1848** MACAULAY *Hist. Eng.* I. 534 Ferguson was in his element. **1874** MAURICE *Friendship Bks.* iii. 69 Englishmen were to be taught that..the sea was to be their element. *Mod.* Some fishes can live a long time after removal from their element.

III. 13. Primordial principle, source of origin. *rare.*

1655–60 STANLEY *Hist. Philos.* (1701) 61/1 Infinity is..the principle and Element of things. **1850** TENNYSON *In Mem.* Concl., That God, which ever lives and loves, One God, one law, one element.

IV. 14. a. *pl.* †The letters of the alphabet (*obs.*). Hence, the rudiments of learning, the 'A, B, C'; also, the first principles of an art or science.

1382 WYCLIF *Gal.* iv. 9 Hou ben ȝe turned..to syke, or freel, and nedy elementis. **1552** HULOET *Elementes* or principles of grammer—*Elementes* letters wherof be made sillables. **1612** BRINSLEY *Lud. Lit.* i. (1627) 7 Beginning at the very first Elements, even at the A, B, C. **1644** MILTON *Educ.* (1738) 137 At the same time..might be taught..the Elements of Geometry. **1649** JER. TAYLOR *Gt. Exemp.* II. viii. 60 Man knows first by elements & after long study learns a syllable, & in good time gets a word. **1799** MACKINTOSH *Stud. Law Nat., &c.* Wks. 1846 I. 342 Public lectures..have been used..to teach the elements of almost every part of learning. **1833** CRUSE *Eusebius* IV. xxiv. 161 Books containing elements of the faith. **1875** JOWETT *Plato* (ed. 2) III. 425 Calculation and geometry and all the other elements of instruction.

b. ***Euclid's Elements***: the title of a treatise on the rudiments of Geometry.

1655–60 STANLEY *Hist. Philos.* (1701) 8/2 Those [propositions] which Euclid hath reduced into his Elements. **1793** T. BEDDOES *Math. Evid.* 47 As if the elements of Euclid were not already tedious enough. **1828** LARDNER *Euclid* Pref., Euclid's Elements were first used in the school of Alexandria.

ˈelement, *v.* Also 6 ellement. [f. prec. sb.]

†1. *trans.* To compound of elements. *Obs.*

1400 [see ELEMENTED *ppl. a.*]. **1477** NORTON *Ord. Alch.* v. in Ashm. 86 The third thinge elemented of them all. *c* **1535** [see ELEMENTED *ppl. a.*]. **1582** BATMAN *On Barthol.* XI. XVI. 165 Foure elements..of the which all things ellemented.. are made. *a* **1631** DONNE *Poems* (1650) 194 As of this all, though many parts decay, The pure which elemented them shall stay. **1647** FARINGDON *Serm.* (1672) I. 135 Man thus created, thus elemented and composed.

2. *fig.* Now *rare.*

1628 DONNE *Serm.* xlviii. 487 Elemented and composed of Heresies. **1640** WALTON *Donne* 38 His very soul was elemented of nothing but sadness. **1670** —— *Lives* I. 33 Absence..doth remove Those things that Elemented it [sublunary love]. **1654** WHITLOCK *Zootomia* 32 A world elemented with Sinne and Misery. **1905** F. GREENSLET *J. R. Lowell* i. 2 When we endeavor to add to our portrait of his personality some analysis of the things that elemented it.

†3. To instruct in the rudiments of learning; cf. ELEMENT *sb.* 14. *Obs.*

1651 *Reliq. Wotton.* 489, I thought he had been better element at Eton. **1662** [see ELEMENTED *ppl. a.* 2].

elemental (ɛlɪˈmɛntəl), *a.* and *sb.* [f. prec. + -AL[1].]

A. *adj.* **1.** Of or pertaining to the 'four elements', earth, air, fire, and water, or to any one of them.

1519 *Interl. Four Elements* in Hazl. *Dodsley* I. 11 The lower region, called the elemental. **1561** EDEN *Art Nauig.* I. iv, The worlde is deuided into two regions: Celestiall, and Elementall. **1635** SWAN *Spec. M.* (1670) 465 The.. purifying both of the Elements and Heavens in their Elemental qualities. **1732** POPE *Ess. Man* I. 169 All subsists by elemental strife. **1824** MISS MITFORD *Village* Ser. I. (1863) 73 Mixing the deep note of love with the elemental music. **1831** CARLYLE *Sartor Res.* II. vi. 98 With no prospect of breakfast beyond elemental liquor. **1851** —— *Sterling* III. ii. (1872) 174 Elemental tumults, and blustering wars of sea and sky.

†2. a. Composed of, or produced by, the elements; material as opposed to spiritual; inorganic as opposed to vital; 'material' as opposed to 'formal'; also, in the condition of raw material. *Obs.*

1574 WHITGIFT *Def. Aunsw.* II. Wks. 1851 I. 255 An external thing and elemental, but not indifferent. **1577** DEE *Relat. Spir.* I. (1659) 391 All Elemental Creatures. **1602** FULBECKE *1st Pt. Parall.* 80 The Law considereth not bare and elementall bodies, but bodies apparelled. **1605** TIMME *Quersit.* Ded. 2 Without the which [the spirit] the elemental

and material character..profiteth not. **1610** *Histrio-m.* vi. 131 This elementall bodie (thus compact) Is but a scattred Chaos of revenge. **1644** MILTON *Areop.* (Arb.) 35 A kind of massacre whereof the execution ends not in the slaying of an elementall life. **1646** SIR T. BROWNE *Pseud. Ep.* 121 Nor is onely an animall heate required hereto [for hatching eggs], but an elementall and artificiall warmth will suffice.

†**b.** *absol.* (quasi-*sb.* in *pl.*) The bread and wine of the Eucharist considered apart from their consecration. *Obs.*

a **1655** VINES *Lord's Supp.* (1677) 298 The elementals of bread and wine.

†**3.** Applied to fire, in two different senses (cf. ELEMENTARY 3). **a.** Material, physical, literal, as opposed to 'spiritual' or figurative; also, such as exists in this lower world. **b.** In its (hypothetical) pure condition, as opposed to the impure form in which it is actually known. *Obs.*

1533 *Hylton's Scala Perf.*, God is not fyre elementall [**1494** elementare]. **1627** F. E. *Hist. Edw. II*, (1680) 6 Majestick thoughts, like Elemental fire, should tend still upwards. **1751** JOHNSON *Rambl.* No. 99 ¶4 Vanish like elemental fire. **1755** YOUNG *Centaur* i. Wks. 1757 IV. 129 A fire elemental is diffused through all nature.

4. a. Pertaining to the powers or agencies of physical nature. ***elemental spirits, gods***, etc.: those which are personifications of natural phenomena, or are associated with particular departments of nature. So ***elemental worship, religion***.

1821 SHELLEY *Prometh. Unb.* IV. i, Elemental Genii.. From Heaven's star-fretted domes. **1850** MERIVALE *Rom. Emp.* (1865) I. v. 231 Elemental worship of the grossest kind. **1865** LECKY *Ration.* (1878) I. 42 To rise to intercourse with these elemental spirits of nature was the highest aim of the philosopher. **1875** MERIVALE *Gen. Hist. Rome* lxviii. (1877) 554 He continued to serve his elemental fetiche, and introduced the rude black stone which represented the Sun. **1876** GLADSTONE *Homeric Synchr.* 109 Amphitrite appears in the Odyssey only as an elemental power.

b. *fig.* Comparable to the great forces of nature.

1820 L. HUNT *Indicator* No. 42 (1822) I. 336 A bold elemental imagination. **1860** EMERSON *Cond. Life* i. 21 All great force is real and elemental. There is no manufacturing a strong will. **1873** LOWELL *Among my Bks.* Ser. II. 287 With an elemental movement like the shifting of mighty winds. **1878** MORLEY *Carlyle* 175 The freedom and elemental grandeur of Byron.

†**5.** Pertaining to the sky; also, governed by celestial influences. (Cf. ELEMENT *sb.* 10.) *Obs.*

1527 ANDREW *Brunswyke's Distyl. Waters* Aj, Dystyllacyon is an elementall thyng. **1583** STUBBES *Anat. Abus.* II. 57 They observed..the elemental signes and tokens in the firmament. **1627** FELTHAM *Resolves* I. xlvii, An elemental and ascentive soul.

6. Of the nature of an ultimate constituent, whether of material or non-material things; *esp.* of physical substances, simple, uncompounded.

1555 EDEN *Decades W. Ind.* (Arb.) 362 Elementall substances. **1651** BIGGS *New Disp.* 113 Without the elementall, true..entity. **1773** MONBODDO *Language* (1774) I. III. v. 482 The division of elemental sounds into Vowels and Consonants. **1821** SHELLEY *Epipsych.* 437 As clear as elemental diamond. **1851** BRIMLEY *Ess.* 115 Elemental passions and affections. **1859** DARWIN *Orig. Spec.* xiv. (1878) 364 Minerals and the elemental substances. **1863** E. NEALE *Anal. Th. & Nat.* 207 The primitive elemental operations of thought.

7. That is an essential or integrant part of any unity; constituent.

1639 FULLER *Holy War* I. xiii. (1840) 21 The four elemental nations whereof this army was compounded. **1805** *Ann. Rev.* III. 254 Mere seasonings in the cauldron of public opinion, not its elemental ingredients. **1874** MOTLEY *Barneveld* I. vii. 311 The few simple but elemental fibers which make up the tissue of most human destinies.

8. Relating to the beginnings or first principles of learning; rudimentary; = ELEMENTARY 6. *rare* in mod. use.

1577 HANMER *Anc. Eccl. Hist.* 30 Them [Epistles] that haue need of an elemental introduction. **1589** GREENE *Menaph.* (Arb.) 68 Everie elementall worde of arte. **1624** WOTTON *Archit.* in *Reliq.* (1672) 5 Some..Method.. shortest and most Elemental. **1790** BURKE *Fr. Rev.* Wks. V. 353 Elemental training to those higher and more large regards. **1841** HOR. SMITH *Moneyed Man* II. x. 328 An elemental work upon astronomy. **1855** H. REED *Lect. Eng. Lit.* x. (1878) 334 Elemental truths, which have been assailed by some of the heresies of the day.

B. *sb.* An entity or a force which is regarded by occultists as capable of producing physical manifestations.

1877 H. P. BLAVATSKY *Isis* p. xxx, These elementals are the principal agents of disembodied but never visible spirits. **1894** H. NISBET *Bush Girl's Rom.* 235 So that we may not be horrified or shy aside at the sight of the strange beings and elementals that surround us. **1923** *Westm. Gaz.* 7 Apr., Did they suppose that God Almighty would permit a Pharaoh.. thousands of years after his own death..to loose what spiritualists called an Elemental? **1965** *Listener* 27 May 792/2 He said gently..'there is an Elemental out there.'..I said, 'No, there isn't.' His reaction was..something between disappointment in me and extreme elation that I should have denied the apparition.

Hence †**ele'mentalish** *a.* (*Alchemy.*) Pure, uncompounded, lying at the base of other substances. *Obs. rare*$^{-1}$.

1671 J. WEBSTER *Metallogr.* viii. 120 The Elementalish Gold..lies hid in many Earths.

elementalism (ɛlɪˈmɛntəlɪz(ə)m). [f. ELEMENTAL *a.* + -ISM.]

1. A method or theory which divinizes the elemental powers of nature.

1863 DUFF in *Chr. Work* July 273 Elementalism, if I may coin a word, the worship chiefly of the Fire, the Air, the Water and the Sun. **1882** OGILVIE Suppl., *Elementalism*, the theory which identifies the divinities of the ancients with the elemental powers. *Gladstone.*

2. A system based upon elemental forces or characters.

1921 *Glasgow Herald* 8 Jan. 4 An incompetent charlatan, performing in public under the guise of 'sublime elementalism' his worthless exercises. **1921** *Times Lit. Suppl.* 17 Feb. 106/4 To reduce two women, one the embodiment of inherited fastidiousness, the other touched with intellectual greatness, to a common level of elementalism.

3. The verbal separation into separate concepts or entities of things which cannot be separated empirically or physically, e.g. space and time, mind and body. So **elementa'listic** *a.*

1933 A. KORZYBSKI *Science & Sanity* i. 24 Meanings, and the meanings of meanings, with their inseparable affective components, give us..the *non-elementalistic* foundation on which all civilization and culture depends...The psychological mechanism is extremely simple and necessitates a breaking away from the older elementalism. But it is usually very difficult for any given individual to break away from this older elementalism, as it involves the established *s.r.*...the *semantic reaction.* **1946** S. A. HAYAKAWA in W. S. Knickerbocker *20th Cent. Eng.* I. 50 We have been defining man in non-functional and elementalistic terms.

†**ˌelemen'tality.** *Obs.* [f. ELEMENTAL *a.* + -ITY.] The fact of being an element.

1654 WHITLOCK *Mann. Eng.* 456 [Essay, 'The Fifth Element, or, Of Detraction'] By this I hope the Elementality (that is the universality) of Detraction..is out of Dispute.

†**ele'mentally,** *adv. Obs.* [f. as prec. + -LY^{2}.] In an elemental manner or sense.

1643 MILTON *Divorce* II. xv. (1851) 101 Those words.. elementally understood, are against nature.

elementaloid (ɛlɪˈmɛntəlɔɪd), *a.* [f. ELEMENTAL + -OID.] *Chem.* Like an element; having the appearance of, or behaving like, an element.

1885 in OGILVIE *Supp.*

elementarian (ˌɛlɪmɛnˈtɛərɪən). *rare*$^{-1}$. [f. ELEMENTARY + -IAN.] One who has not advanced beyond the rudiments of his studies.

1876 GRANT *Burgh Sch. Scotl.* II. xiii. 355 Elementarians who are not sufficiently qualified to be advanced.

elementarily (ɛlɪˈmɛntərɪlɪ), *adv.* [f. ELEMENTARY + -LY^{2}.] In a simple or rudimentary manner; also, †by purely physical causes (*obs.*).

1643 R. O. *Man's Mort.* v. 21 The Rationall Facultie in Man..may as well be produced elementarily by Man. **1849** RUSKIN *Sev. Lamps* ii. (1855) 52 Explaining elementarily.

elementariness (ɛlɪˈmɛntərɪnɪs). [f. as prec. + -NESS.] The quality of being elementary.

1669 W. SIMPSON *Hydrol. Chym.* 250 The material elementaryness of concrets. **1862** C. J. VAUGHAN *Bk. & Life* 64 Things almost puerile in their elementariness. **1881** *N.Y. Nation* 386 The elementariness of 'the things of the mind'.

†**ele'mentarist.** *Obs. rare*$^{-1}$. [f. ELEMENTARY + -IST.] One who treats of the 'four elements'.

1651 BIGGS *New Disp.* 159 Putrefaction, according to that great Elementarist, Aristotle, is, etc.

†**ˌelemen'tarity.** *Obs. rare*$^{-1}$. [f. ELEMENTARY + -TY.] = ELEMENTARINESS.

1650 SIR T. BROWNE *Pseud. Ep.* (ed. 2) 42 Creatures.. farre above the condition of elementarity.

elementary (ɛlɪˈmɛntərɪ), *a.* Forms: 5-6 elementar(e, -air, -arie (7-8 elimentarie, -y). [ad. L. *elementārius*, f. *elementum*: see ELEMENT and -AR, -ARY. Cf. F. *élémentaire.*]

1. Of or pertaining to the four elements or any one of them; = ELEMENTAL 1. *rare* in mod. use.

1549 *Compl. Scot.* vi. (1872) 47 The fyrst part [of the varld] is the regione elementair. **1605** TIMME *Quersit.* I. v. 21 The elementary qualities passiue. *c* **1645** HOWELL *Lett.* (1650) III. 19 A species of living Creatures in the Orb of the Moon, which may bear som analogie with those of this Elementary world. **1669** GALE *Crt. Gentiles* I. III. iii. 46 If our Light be a Substance, its either Heavenly, or Elementarie. *a* **1761** LAW *Comf. Weary Pilgr.* (1809) 90 This elementary world. **1856** *Tait's Mag.* XXIII. 763 This year of peace has been distinguished by 'elementary' war—by deluges and earthquakes.

†**2. a.** Composed of, or produced by, the (four) elements; material, physical; opposed to *spiritual, celestial*, etc.; = ELEMENTAL 2. *Obs.*

c **1440** [see 3]. **1612** WOODALL *Surg. Mate* Wks. (1653) 239 A Mineral is an elementarie body that is of it self firm and fixed. **1635** SWAN *Spec. M.* iii. §2 (1643) 48 The uncreated Light (viz. God) commanded this elementarie light to be. *a* **1656** BP. HALL *Occas. Med.* (1851) 9 A false and elementary apparition. **1727** DE FOE *Syst. Magic* I. iii. (1840) 88 The Devil..set his human and elementary instruments at work. **1750** tr. *Leonardus' Mirr. Stones* 48 Others..say, there is only an elementary virtue in stones.

†**b.** That is in the condition of raw material.

1799 tr. *Meister's Lett. on Eng.* 145 There is more gross and elementary matter in the English diet.

†**3.** Applied to air, fire, water, earth (cf. ELEMENTAL 3): **a.** Physical, material, literal, as opposed to *figurative* or '*spiritual*'; also, such as they exist in this lower world. **b.** In their state of pure elements, as opposed to the impure state in which they are cognizable by the senses.

c **1440** HYLTON *Scala Perf.* (W. de W. 1494) II. xxxiii, God is not fyre elementare. **1610** HEALEY *St. Aug. City of God* 438 Some..held the Christalline heavens composed of waters..of a farre other nature then the Elementary. **1652** FRENCH *Yorksh. Spa* ii. 7 The whole Elementary air being of its owne nature most subtile. **1658** *Torments of Hell* in *Phenix* (1708) II. 438 Corporal elementary Fire is light..the Fire of Hell is not corporal Fire. **1782** KIRWAN in *Phil. Trans.* LXXII. 230 Fixed air..when stripped of phlogiston, and impregnated with..elementary fire, becomes again dephlogisticated air. **1794** SULLIVAN *View Nat.* I. 56 Glass appears to be the true elementary earth, and all mixed bodies are only glass in disguise.

4. a. Pertaining to the great forces of nature. ***elementary gods***: the gods of the elements. Cf. ELEMENTAL 4, which is now in more frequent use.

1739 H. WALPOLE *Corr.* (1820) I. 23 The elementary god of fire. **1841** ELPHINSTONE *Hist. India* I. 173 The worship of the old elementary gods.

b. *fig.* Comparable to the great forces of nature.

1865 M. ARNOLD *Ess. Crit.* v. 185 Byron..the greatest elementary power..in our literature since Shakespeare.

†**5.** Like one's 'native element'; congenial. *Obs.*

1760 H. BROOKE *Fool of Quality* (1792) v. 5 He found their manners congenial and elementary to his own natural turn and disposition.

6. a. Of the nature of an (absolutely or relatively) ultimate constituent. Of chemical substances: Simple, not decomposable. ***elementary particle***: now used in *Physics* spec. for any of a number of particles smaller than an atom (the leptons, mesons, and baryons) which are not known to be composed of any simpler particles and which are characterized by having a definite mass, a lifetime that is long compared with the interaction time, and well-defined electromagnetic properties, and are capable of an independent existence.

1622 PEACHAM *Compl. Gent.* xv. 161 As if light were a quality resulting of an elementary composition, it being created before all mixed bodies. **1736** BUTLER *Anal.* I. i. 18 The solid elementary Particles of Matter. **1751** HARRIS *Hermes* (1841) 210 To about twenty plain elementary sounds..we owe that variety of articulate voices. **1813** BAKEWELL *Introd. Geol.* (1815) 33 The elementary substances of which [rocks] are composed are very few. **1876** GEO. ELIOT *Dan. Der.* II. xxxiii. 339 What one may call the elementary expressions of the face. **1934** *Chem. Abstr.* 2258 Theory of elementary particles...A relativistic wave equation of the Dirac type for a particle of given rest mass will allow only a spin of ½ in the usual units. **1937** F. RASETTI *Elem. Nuclear Physics* 8 If the elementary particles are to be kept together in a stably bound nucleus, we must expect energy to be released in the formation process. **1949** GAMOW & CRITCHFIELD *Theory Atomic Nucleus* i. 8 It is possble to develop the theory of the fundamental nuclear properties and the various nuclear reactions..on the basis of.. interaction-laws between the nucleons from which the composite nuclei are built. Here lies a convenient,..though not sharply defined, boundary between nuclear physics proper, and the next, as yet rather unexplored, division of the science of matter which can be called tentatively the physics of elementary particles. **1963** K. W. FORD *World of Elementary Particles* i. 2 The elementary particles represent the deepest-lying sub-structure of matter to which man has been able to probe. *Ibid.* 17 The heaviest known 'elementary' particle, the xi particle..has not yet been explained as a composite of any of the lighter particles. That *all* of these particles are built up from some more primordial material remains..a strong possibility. **1963** *Oxf. Univ. Gaz.* 9 May 1183/2 The University has established a Professorship of Elementary Particle Physics.

b. *Math.* Of the nature of an element or infinitesimal part (see ELEMENT 8).

1882 MINCHIN *Unipl. Kinemat.* 83 Elementary polar area of the curve C. **1885** WATSON & BURBURY *Math. Th. Electr. & Magn.* I. 98 An elementary area of that surface.

7. a. Of the nature of elements or rudiments; rudimentary, introductory. ***elementary book, writer***, one that deals with first principles. ***elementary school***, one in which primary instruction is given. Also ***elementary education, schoolmaster***.

1542 RECORDE *Gr. Artes* (1575) 429, I would not wishe you to cleaue still to these elementarie aydes. **1597** MORLEY *Introd. Mus.* Annot., Musicke is diuided into two parts, the first may be called Elementarie or rudimental. **1793** T. BEDDOES *Math. Evid.* 17 The same thing must..be..true of every other elementary author. **1812** SIR H. DAVY *Chem. Philos.* 24 Elementary books on the science. **1841** SPALDING *Italy & It. Isl.* III. 341 In 1835, the elementary schools were 4422. **1860** MILL *Repr. Govt.* (1865) 22/2 Elementary maxims of prudence. **1863** LYELL *Antiq. Man* 5 These innovations have been treated of in my..Manual of Elementary Geology. **1870** *Act 33 & 34 Vict.* c. 75 §1 This Act may be cited as 'The Elementary Education Act, 1870'. **1912** W. OWEN *Let.* 2 July (1967) 148 By him sat an Elementary School-master, of Elementary Education. **1944** H. C. DENT *Education Act, 1944* 12 Under Clause 7 of the Act the category 'elementary' disappears from the English educational system, and *ipso facto* local education authorities for elementary education only disappear also.

†**b.** That has not advanced beyond the rudiments. *Obs.*

1599 B. JONSON *Cynthia's Rev.* (T.) Your courtier elementary is one but newly entered, or as it were in the alphabet.

†**ele'mentate,** *ppl. a. Obs. rare.* [ad. mod.L. *elementāt-us*, pass. pple. of *element-āre*: see next.] = ELEMENTATED.

1471 RIPLEY *Comp. Alch.* IX. in Ashm. 177 Erth ys Gold, so ys the Sowle also, Not Comyn but Owers thus Elementate. **1561** EDEN *Art Navig.* I. iv, Elementate, is euerie body compounded of the foure elementes.

†**'elementate,** *v. Obs. rare.* [f. mod.L. *elementāt-* ppl. stem of *elementāre*, f. *elementum* ELEMENT.

The vb. *elementare* occurs in the Latin versions of Paracelsus; the original German has *elementieren.*]

trans. **a.** To impregnate with an element; to compound out of elements. **b.** To be (one or more of) the elements of (a substance).

1650 ASHMOLE *Chym. Coll.* 113 Fermented Ferment, equally elementated with every Element.. is Gold. **1660** tr. *Paracelsus' Archid.* I. II. 15 The substance.. is not from that element which.. elementateth the substance.

†**'elemen,tated,** *ppl. a. Obs.* [f. prec. + -ED.] Compounded of the four elements; = ELEMENTED; hence, material, physical; impregnated with an element. ***elementated degrees***: the 'degrees' (of 'hot' or 'cold' quality) in medicinal substances, resulting from the proportions of their 'elements'. Hence **,elemen'tatedness.**

1605 TIMME *Quersit.* I. xiii. 67 Bodyes elementated, as wel of minerals as of vegetables. *c*1650 WHARTON *Soul of World* Wks. (1683) 657 Physicians should.. segregate the Medicinal vertues of things from the Body, and the Elementated Impurities thereof. **1660** tr. *Paracelsus' Archid.* II. 101 The Sum or Number which respects the Elementated Degrees is.. to be noted. **1662** J. CHANDLER *Van Helmont's Oriat.* 43 A Body above an Elementated one, and heavenly. **1675** EVELYN *Terra* (1729) 26 Salt.. the first and last of Elementated Bodies. **1660** tr. *Paracelsus' Archid.* II. 109 The External Elementatedness.. corrupts and breaks the former Nature.

†**ele'mentative,** *a. Obs. rare*$^{-1}$. [f. ELEMENTATE *ppl. a.* + -IVE.] Of the nature of mere passive matter, inorganic.

1477 NORTON *Ordin. Alch.* i. in Ashm. 20 Mettalls be only Elementative, Having noe seede, nether feeling of life.

†**'elemented,** *ppl. a.* [f. ELEMENT *v.* + -ED.]

1. Composed of or produced by (any or all of) the four elements.

*c*1400 *Test. Love* II. (1560) 288 b/2 Of hem all governments in this elemented world proceden. *c*1535 DEWES *Introd.* in Palsgr. (1852) 1053 All thynges ben elemented [Fr. ellementées] onely, as.. metals or be elemented and vegetables, as herbes. **1605** TIMME *Quersit.* III. 142 Three distinct substances in euery natural elemented body. **1650** ASHMOLE *Chym. Coll.*, Mercury in all Elemented substances is one and the same. **1680** BOYLE *Scept. Chem.* v. 350 That all Elemented bodies be compounded of the same number of Elements. **1771** *Muse in Min.* 77 Now rushing cataracts descend To calm the elemented fray.

b. Impregnated with various elements; *fig.*

1650 ASHMOLE *Chym. Coll.* 24 Collecting into Books this Elemented Water falling from Heaven.

2. Instructed, well-grounded in one's art.

1662 FULLER *Worthies* I. 23 The Fishery did breed the natural and best elemented seamen.

†**'elementing,** *vbl. sb. Obs. rare*$^{-1}$. [f. as prec. + -ING¹.] Calling into existence, origination.

1638 BAKER tr. *Balzac's Lett.* (1654) II. 20 The first elementing and foundation of love.

†**ele'mentish,** *a. Obs.* [f. ELEMENT + -ISH.] Of the nature of (any of) the four elements; material, physical.

1580 SIDNEY *Arcadia* III. Wks. 264 Elementish and ethereal parts. **1585-7** ROGERS *39 Art.* (1607) 177 Scornfully terming the.. water at baptism, elementish water. **1646** F[ISHER] *Mod. Divinity* 222 God at first gave man an elementish body.

†**'elemently,** *a. Obs. rare*$^{-1}$. [f. ELEMENT *sb.* + -LY¹.] Pertaining to the four elements.

1398 TREVISA *Barth. De P.R.* x. ii. (1495) 372 Elemently and heuenly fourme.

elemi ('ɛlɪmɪ). Forms: 6 (gumme) elimi, (gummi) elennij, 8 (gum) elimy, (elemni), 7- elemi. [In Fr. *élémi*, It., Sp. *elemi*, Pg. *gumileme*; of unknown (perhaps oriental) etymology; the Arab. name *lāmī*, cited by some writers, appears, according to Devic, to be known only as a very modern word. The name (*gumi elimi*) occurs in Vigo's Latin *Pratica* (Rome 1517).]

A stimulant resin obtained from various trees, as *Canarium commune* (Manilla), *Icica Icicariba* (Brazil), *Elaphrium elemiferum* (Mexico), used in plaisters, ointments, and the manufacture of varnish. More fully GUM ELEMI. Also *attrib.* in ***elemi oil*** (= ELEMIN), ***elemi resin, elemi tree.***

1543 TRAHERON *Vigo's Chirurg.* III. xiv. 104 b/1 Of mastike .ʒ. vi. of gumme elimi, armoniake dissolued wᵗ wyne ʒ.i. & .ʒ. **1699** *Descr. Isthmus of Darian* 4 The Tree likewise that affords *Gummi Elemi* grows here in great Aboundance. **1703** *Lond. Gaz.* No. 3898/3 The Cargo of the Galeon.. consisting of.. Jollop, Gum Elemni,.. etc. **1714** *Fr. Bk. Rates* 93 Gum Elimy per 100 weight 05 *li.* 00 *so.* **1751** CHAMBERS *Cycl.*, *Elemi* is usually called gum elemi, though very improperly, inasmuch as it takes fire readily enough. **1831** T. P. JONES *Convers. Chem.* xxviii. 287 The principal resins are common rosin, copal, lac.. and elemi. **1851-9** HOOKER in *Adm. Man. Sci. Enq.* 427 Elemi is also produced in Mexico, where it is known as Copal. **1876** HARLEY *Mat. Med.* 664 Elemi tree is imported from Manilla.

elemin ('ɛlɪmɪn). *Chem.* [f. prec. + -IN.]

1868 ROYLE & HEAD *Mat. Med.* (ed. 5) 391 The Elemi analysed.. yielded.. a peculiar crystalline body, Elemine. **1882** WATTS *Dict. Chem.* s.v., Oil of Elemi.—Elemin. Elemi resin distilled with water yields a transparent colourless oil, having the composition of a camphene.

†**elench** (ɪ'lɛŋk). *Obs.* Also 6 elenke, -cke, 6-7 elenche. [ad. (either directly or through OF. *elenche*) L. *elench-us*, a. Gr. ἔλεγχος ELENCHUS.]

1. *Logic.* A syllogism in refutation of a proposition that has been syllogistically defended (see quot. 1860 in ELENCHUS 1); hence, in wider sense, a logical refutation. ***ignorance of the elenche***: = IGNORATIO ELENCHI (*rare*).

*a*1529 SKELTON *Col. Cloute* 820 Nor knoweth his elenkes Nor his predicamens. **1597** BACON *Coulers Good & Evill* 139 Their seuerall fallaxes and the elenches of them. **1610** J. DOVE *Advt. Seminaries* 47 A fallacy called the ignorance of the Elenche. **1614** JACKSON *Creed* III. Pref., The second.. contains.. an elench of those vulgar fallacies. **1631** MASSINGER *Emp. of East* II. i, She will have her elenchs To cut off any fallacy I can hope To put upon her.

b. *Aristotle's Elenchs*: his treatise περὶ σοφιστικῶν ἐλέγχων 'concerning sophistical elenchs' or sophisms. (The title does not mean, as is implied in quot. 1837, 'concerning the *refutation* of sophisms'.) Hence *elench* was often used for: A sophistical argument, a fallacy.

1565 JEWEL *Repl. Harding* (1611) 5 Your Elenchs, your Fallacies, your sillie Syllogismes. **1571** ASCHAM *Scholem.* (Arb.) 132 Aristotle.. in his.. Elenches, should be.. fruitfull. **1588** FRAUNCE *Lawiers Log.* I. vi. 36 A double Elench lurketh in this place, one of composition, an other of division. **1605** BACON *Adv. Learn.* II. 54 This part concerning Elenches is excellently handled by Aristotle. **1667** *Decay Chr. Piety* ix. §20. 308 Our common adversary, that old sophister.. puts the most abusive elenchs on us. **1689** SELDEN *Table T.* 59 All your Elenchs in Logick come within the compass of Juggling. [**1837** HALLAM *Hist. Lit.* III. iii. §55 A similar doubt might be suggested with respect to the elenchs, or refutations, of rhetorical sophisms.]

2. An index, analytical table of contents. [So Gr. ἔλεγχος; cf. It., Sp. *elenco* in same sense.]

1563-87 FOXE *A. & M.* (1596) 195/1 Certeine notes or elenchs upon this epistle. **1715** in KERSEY. **1721-1800** in BAILEY. **1775** in ASH.

elenchic (ɪ'lɛŋkɪk), *a.* [f. L. *elench-us* (see prec.) + -IC.] = ELENCTIC.

1850 GROTE *Greece* II. lxviii. VIII. 634 History presents to us only one man who ever devoted his life to prosecute this duty of an elenchic or cross-examining missionary.

elenchical (ɪ'lɛŋkɪkəl), *a. rare.* [f. prec. + -AL¹.] = prec.

1641 J. JACKSON *True Evang. T.* I. 53 Elenchicall, or Confutative against Error. **1721-1800** in BAILEY. **1832** in WEBSTER. **1847** in CRAIG; and in mod. Dicts.

e'lenchically, *adv. rare.* [f. prec. + -LY².] In an elenchical manner, by means of an elenchus.

1646 SIR T. BROWNE *Pseud. Ep.* Pref., Any Penne, that shall Elenchically refute us.

†**e'lenchize,** *v. Obs. rare*$^{-1}$. [f. ELENCH + -IZE.] *intr.* To make use of the elenchus; to argue.

1631 B. JONSON *New Inn* II. vi, Hear him problematize.. Or syllogize, elenchize.

‖**elenchus** (ɪ'lɛŋkəs). *pl.* **elenchi.** [L. *elench-us*, a. Gr. ἔλεγχος cross-examination. (Sense 3 appears to be only Lat.; perh. another word.]

1. a. *Logic.* = ELENCH 1. **b.** *Socratic elenchus*: the method pursued by Socrates of eliciting truth by means of short question and answer.

1663 BUTLER *Hud.* I. III. 1258, I shall bring you, with your pack Of fallacies, t' Elenchi back. **1721-1800** in BAILEY. **1850** MAURICE *Mor. & Met. Philos.* (ed. 2) 116 My [Socrates'] elenchus is nothing better in itself than the logic.. of any other professor. **1860** ABP. THOMSON *Laws Th.* §127. 271 Admitting the apparent correctness of the opposing argument, we may prove the contradictory of its conclusion by an unassailable argument of our own, which is then called an Elenchus (ἔλεγχος). **1874** MAHAFFY *Soc. Life Greece* xi. 340 Such people.. cared little about even the Socratic elenchus. **1878** GEO. ELIOT *Coll. Breakf. P.* 713 No dull elenchus makes a yoke for her.

2. = ELENCH 2. *Obs.*

1721-1800 in BAILEY.

†**3.** *Antiq.* (See quot.)

1727-51 CHAMBERS *Cycl.*, *Elenchus* in antiquity, a kind of ear-ring set with pearls. In mod. Dicts.

elenctic (ɪ'lɛŋktɪk), *a.* Also (incorrectly) **elenchtic.** [ad. Gr. ἐλεγκτικ-ός, f. ἐλέγχ-ειν to refute; cf. prec.] Of or pertaining to refutation; concerned with refutation; that occupies himself with cross-examination.

1833 *Blackw. Mag.* XXXIII. 627 His duty is elenchtic. **1850** GROTE *Greece* II. lxviii. VIII. 566 An elenchtic or cross-examining god. **1866** MILL in *Edin. Rev.* CXXIII. 335 The dogmatic Plato seems a different person from the elenctic Plato.

†**e'lenctical,** *a. Obs.* Also 7 (incorrectly) **elenchtical.** [f. prec. + -AL¹.] Pertaining to elenchus, concerned with logical refutation.

1615 *Curry-C. for Coxe-C.* i. 70 His next Chapter is wholy Elenchticall. **1646** WILKINS *Ecclesiastes* §2 (T.) Elenchtical.. which is usually called an use of confutation. **1699** BURNET *39 Art.* vi. (1700) 87 In these Writings some parts are.. Elenchtical or Argumentative. **1721-1800** in BAILEY. **1847** in CRAIG; and in mod. Dicts.

†**'elende.** *Obs. rare*$^{-1}$. [a. Ger. *elend*, Du. *eland*: cf. ELAND.] An elk.

1697 *Phil. Trans.* XIX. 502 That sort of Animal call'd the Alche, Elche, or Elende.

'elenge, *a. Obs.* exc. *dial.* Forms: 1-3 **ǽlenge,** 3 **elinge,** (4 **eling, elyng(e, helynge, eleynge,** 7-8, 9 *dial.* **ellinge**), 2-6, 9 *dial.* **elenge.** Also ALANGE, q.v. [OE. *ǽlęnge*, f. Æ- *pref.* + **lęnge*:—OTeut. **langjo-* f. **lango-* LONG *a.* The two etymological senses of 'very long, tedious' and 'remote, lonely', seem to blend in the later uses. Chaucer abnormally accents *e'lenge* (riming with *cha'lenge*.)]

†**1.** Very long, tedious. *Obs.*

*c*897 ÆLFRED *Gregory's Past.* v. 40 þæt hie bioð on ælengum ðingum.. ȝeðyldiȝe. *c*1430 *ABC Aristotle* in *Babees Bk.* (1868) 11 E to elenge, ne to excellent, ne to eernesful.

2. Remote, lonely; dreary, miserable. *Obs.* exc. *dial.*

*c*1205 LAY. 15190 þe stude wes Ælenge [**1275** Elinge]: nu hatte hit Stanhenge [**1275** Stonhenge]. *a*1300 *Cursor M.* 3075 An elenge lijf þare þai ledd. *c*1300 *St. Brandan* 637 Eling ich ȝeode her alone. **1377** LANGL. *P. Pl.* B. x. 94 Elyng is þe halle.. þer þe lorde ne þe lady liketh nouȝte to sytte. *c*1386 CHAUCER *Wyf Bathes T.* 343 Povert is this, although it seme elenge [*v.r.* alange, alenge, alinge]. **1387** TREVISA *Higden* (Rolls) VII. 341 Lanfrank leet neuere a man goo from hym helynge and sory. *c*1400 *Beryn* 967 Why do yee thus? this is an elyng fare. *a*1420 OCCLEVE *De Reg. Princ.* 1008 His labour to hym is the elengere. **1481** *Reynard* (1844) 65 We goo not into another foreste, where we sholde be strange, and elenge. **1674** RAY *S. & E. Country Wds.* 65 Ellinge. **1858** *Murray's Hand-bk. Kent* Introd. 32 The fairies.. may still be.. heard of in the more 'elenge' (lonely) places of the Downs. **1875** PARISH *Sussex Gloss.* s.v. *Ellynge*, 'Tis a terrible ellynge, lonesome old house.

¶**3.** Explained in Dicts. as 'strange, foreign'.

1678-96 in PHILLIPS. **1721** in BAILEY; and in mod. Dicts.

†**'elengely,** *a.* and *adv. Obs.* In 4 **elenge-, eling-, elyngelich(e,** 8 **elengelick.** [f. ELENGE + -LY¹ and ².]

A. *adj.* Solitary, cheerless, miserable. **B.** *adv.* Drearily, miserably.

*c*1305 *Land Cokayne* 15 Elinglich.. may hi go, Whar þer woniþ men no mo. **1377** LANGL. *P. Pl.* B. XII. 45 Alisaundre, that al wan Elengeliche ended. **1393** *Ibid.* C. XXIII. 38 Filosofres.. wonede wel elyngeliche and wolden nat be riche. **1721-61** BAILEY, *Elengelick*, strangely or miserably. *Old.*

†**'elengenesse.** *Obs.* Also 4 **elangenes,** 6 **ellingness.** [f. ELENGE + -NESS.] Loneliness, dreariness, misery.

*c*1320 *Seuyn Sag.* (W.) 1735 His seriaunts.. of alangenes him undernome. **1398** TREVISA *Barth. De P.R.* XVI. liv. (Tollem. MS.) Jacinctus haþ virtu of comforte, and doþ awey elengenesse. *c*1400 *Rom. Rose* 7408 She had a.. scrippe of faint distresse, That full was of elengenesse. *a*1536 HEN. VIII *Let.* in *Select. fr. Harl. Misc.* (1793) 147 The great ellingness that I find here since your departing.

eleolite, -lith, var. forms of ELÆOLITE.

eleonorite (,ɛlɪə'nɔəraɪt). *Min.* [ad. G. *eleonorit* (A. Nies 1880, in *Ber. d. Oberhessischen Ges. f. Natur- u. Heilkunde* XIX. 111), f. *Eleonore*, woman's name used as the name of a mine near Giessen.] A name formerly given to a supposed variety of beraunite.

1881 *Jrnl. Chem. Soc.* XL. 525 New Minerals from the Eleonora Mine in the Dünsberg near Giessen... 1. Eleonorite... This mineral occurs, together with strengite, in an isolated block of brown hæmatite. **1923** *Nature* 24 Nov. 779/1 A very well-defined specimen of the variety of beraunite known as eleonorite, found at the iron and manganese mine of Roury Glen, Glandore, Co. Cork, consists of a mass of diverging fibrous crystals of a reddish-brown colour, between walls of limonite. The fibres are elongated in the direction of the *b* axis and show very strong pleochroism.

eleot. ? *Obs.* A kind of apple.

1676 WORLIDGE *Cyder* (1691) 208 Eleots are apples much in request in those Cider-countries for their excellent liquor. **1731-1800** in BAILEY. **1755** in JOHNSON. **1775** in ASH; and in mod. Dicts.

†**'elephancy.** *Obs.* [ad. L. *elephantia*, f. *elephas*, *elephant-is*, ELEPHANT.] = ELEPHANTIASIS.

[**1398** TREVISA *Barth. De P.R.* VII. lxiv. (1495) 279 One manere Lepra comyth of pure Melancoly, and hyght Elephancia. **1494** FABYAN VII. 651 Peynfull sykenesse, which of myne auctoure is callyd in Latyne Morbus Elephancie.] **1547** BOORDE *Brev. Health* cxiv. 43 In Englyshe it is named the Elephancy, or the Olyphant sicknesse. **1601** HOLLAND *Pliny* II. 318 For the leprosie, elephansie, and all gouts or diseases of the ioynts. **1657** W.

COLES *Adam in Eden* clvi, Cancer, Elephancy and foul diseases of the Skin.

elephant ('ɛlɪfənt). Forms: α. 4–6 oli-, olyfaunte, (4 *pl.* olifauns, -fauntz), 4 olyfont, -funt, 5–6 olifant(e, 4 olephaunte, 5–6 olyphaunt, 4–7 oli-, olyphant(e. β. 4 elifans, 4–5 ele-, elyphaunt(e, 5 elefaunte, 6 eliphant, 5–6 elephante, 6– elephant. [ME. *olifaunt*, a. OF. *olifant*, repr. a popular L. **olifantu-m* (whence Pr. *olifan*; cf. MDu. *olfant*, Bret. *olifant*, Welsh *oliffant*, Corn. *oliphans*, which may be all from ME. or OFr.), corrupt form of L. *elephantum*, *elephantem* (nom. *elephantus*, *-phas*, *-phans*), ad. and a. Gr. ἐλέφας (gen. ἐλέφαντος). The refashioning of the word after Lat. seems to have taken place earlier in Eng. than in Fr., the Fr. forms with *el-* being cited only from 15th c.

Of the ultimate etymology nothing is really known. As the Gr. word is found (though only in sense 'ivory') in Homer and Hesiod, it seems unlikely that it can be, as some have supposed, of Indian origin. The resemblance in sound to Heb. *eleph* 'ox' has given rise to a suggestion of derivation from some Phœnician or Punic compound of that word; others have conjectured that the word may be African. See Yule *Hobson-Jobson* Suppl., s.v. For the possible relation to this word of the Teut. and Slavonic name for 'camel', see OLFEND. The origin of the corrupt Romanic forms with *ol-* is unknown, but they may be compared with L. *oleum*, *olīva*, ad. Gr. ἔλαιον, ἐλαία.]

1. a. A huge quadruped of the Pachydermate order, having long curving ivory tusks, and a prehensile trunk or proboscis. Of several species once distributed over the world, including Britain, only two now exist, the African and Indian; the former is the largest of extant land animals, and the latter is often used as a beast of burden, and in war.

c **1300** *K. Alis.* 854 Olifauns, and camelis, Weoren y-charged with vitailes. **1340** *Ayenb.* 84 Virtue makeþ man.. strang ase olyfont. *Ibid.* 224 Þe elifans nele naȝt wonye mid his wyue, þerhuyle þet hi is mid childe. *c* **1374** CHAUCER *Boeth.* III. viii. 80 Mayst þou sourmounten þise olifuntz in gretnesse. **1398** TREVISA *Barth. De P.R.* v. xxviii. (1495) 138 The elyphaunt hath a longe nose lyke a trompe. *c* **1400** MAUNDEV. xxii. 238 Olifauntz, tame and othere. **1430** LYDG. *Chron. Troy* II. xi, Elyphauntes and large Unicornes.. Forged of brasse. **1481** CAXTON *Myrr.* II. vi. 75 An olyphaunt bereth wel a tour of woode vpon his backe. **15..** *Proph. on State of Eng.* in Furniv. *Ballads fr. MSS.* I. 316 ffor the Sklaunderyng of the Olyfaunte with the long nose. **1555** EDEN *Decades W. Ind.* (Arb.) 383 The elephante (which sum caule an oliphant) is the biggest of all foure footed beastes. **1570** B. GOOGE *Pop. Kingd.* II. (1880) 24 b, Of Flyes they able are to make, great Eliphants in sight. **1606** SHAKS. *Tr. & Cr.* II. iii. 113 The Elephant hath ioynts, but none for curtesie. **1667** MILTON *P.L.* IV. 345 Th' unwieldy Elephant To make them Mirth..wreath'd His Lithe Proboscis. **1727** THOMSON *Summer* 721 The huge Elephant, wisest of brutes. **1857** LIVINGSTONE *Trav.* xxviii. 563 Full-grown male elephants..ranged in height at the withers from 9 feet 9 inches to 9 feet 10 inches.

b. *fig.* of a man of huge stature.

1606 SHAKS. *Tr. & Cr.* II. iii. 2 Shall the Elephant Aiax carry it thus?

c. ***elephant's teeth*** (i.e. tusks): ivory.

1398 TREVISA *Barth. De P.R.* XIV. xxxiii. (1495) 480 Salomons seruauntes broughte..elephauntes teeth. **1483** CAXTON *Gold. Leg.* 73/3 The nauye of the kynge..brouht.. teeth of Olyphauntes and grete richesses. **1562** *Lanc. Wills* I. (1857) 183 A sett of chest men of oliphants teeth. **1657** R. LIGON *Barbadoes* (1673) 2 A Frigot..her Lading Gold and Elephants teeth.

d. ***to see the elephant*** (U.S. slang): to see life, the world, or the sights (as of a large city); to get experience of life, to gain knowledge by experience. Also ***to show*** or ***get a look at the elephant***. (Cf. LION *sb.* 4.)

[**1835** A. B. LONGSTREET *Georgia Scenes* 10 (Th.), That's sufficient, as Tom Haynes said when he saw the elephant.] **1844** G. W. KENDALL *Narr. Santa Fé Exped.* I. 108 There is a cant expression, 'I've seen the elephant' in very common use in Texas. *a* **1847** W. T. PORTER *Quarter Race Kentucky* (1847) 87 (Th.), I axed him if he'd ever seen the elephant. **1849** N. KINGSLEY *Diary* (1914) 86 [I] went up town and saw the Elephant, and it almost baffles description. **1849** T. T. JOHNSON *Sights in Gold Region* 324 (Th.), If you think we have not shown you enough of the elephant..please to mount him and take a view for yourself. **1857** *Quinland* II. II. xviii. 126 The 'Fox and Crow' is one of the famous sights in New York. It is never missed by the countryman or the foreigner, who is searching after the 'elephant'. **1878** J. H. BEADLE *Western Wilds* iii. 45 My friend Will Wylie, who had seen the elephant in its entirety, from trunk to tail. **1906** 'O. HENRY' *Four Million* 87 He makes his rounds every evening, while you and I see the elephant once a week. **1960** T. V. OLSEN *High Lawless* (1961) iii. 30 Saturdays some of the boys from the three big outfits come in to see the elephant.

e. As the emblem of the Republican party in the United States.

[**1860** *Railsplitter* in Sperber & Trittschuh *Amer. Pol. Terms* (1962) 141/2 Woodcut: elephant..announcing a Lincoln demonstration. **1874** *Harper's Weekly* XVIII. 912 (*caption under an elephant*) The Republican Vote.] **1876** *Ibid.* 28 Oct. 868 (*caption*) 'The elephant walks around'—and the 'still hunt' is nearly over. **1904** *Chicago Tribune* 20 June 6 The selection..will..handicap the republic elephant in the coming race. **1952** *Economist* 12 July 89/1 It would now take some sort of a miracle for Mr. Taft to catch the Republican elephant.

f. In full ***elephant-colour***: a fashion shade simulating the grey colour of the elephant. Cf. *elephant-grey* below.

1875 *All Year Round* 278/1 So admirably is elephant-colour copied. **1894** *Queen* 6 Oct. 574/1 The shade of cloth used..being known as 'Elephant'. **1923** *Daily Mail* 7 June 6 In Almond Green,..Mole, Elephant, Honey.

2. ***white elephant***. **a.** A rare albino variety of elephant which is highly venerated in some Asian countries. **b.** *fig.* A burdensome or costly possession (from the story that the kings of Siam were accustomed to make a present of one of these animals to courtiers who had rendered themselves obnoxious, in order to ruin the recipient by the cost of its maintenance). Also, an object, scheme, etc., considered to be without use or value.

1607 TOPSELL *Four-f. Beasts* 208 An Indian, who had brought vp from a Foale a white Elephant. **1663** H. C[OGAN] tr. *Pinto's Travels* xlviii. 274 The white elephant whereon he [the King of Siam] was mounted. **1841** *Penny Cycl.* XXI. 451/2 White elephants..are kept in the stables of the king [of Siam], and treated with a kind of veneration. **1851** G. E. JEWSBURY *Let.* 23 July (1892) 414 His services are like so many white elephants, of which nobody can make use, and yet that drain one's gratitude, if indeed one does not feel bankrupt. **1883** CROFT in *Elyot's Governor* I. Life 60 Elyot regarded this new dignity much as the gift of a white elephant. **1928** GALSWORTHY *Swan Song* II. ii. 113 'You look so well in that hat, Uncle.' Soames took it off again. 'White elephant,' he said. 'Can't think what made Fleur get me the thing!' **1931** 'R. CROMPTON' *William's Crowded Hours* viii. 182 Let's have it a sort of second-hand stall—what they call a White Elephant Stall. **1950** G. J. RENIER *History* III. iii. 203 The miser often has a white elephant upon which he lavishes money: a house, or an unworthy friend. **1963** *Times* 4 Mar. 11/4 The original white elephant was presumably an elephant, but he or she might well have been a poor man's mediocre racehorse. **1970** *Daily Mail* 27 Oct. 2/8 The new rail link may prove to be ideologically satisfying, but in financial terms it looks like becoming the biggest white elephant in all Africa.

3. As the sign of an inn; the modern 'Elephant and Castle'.

1601 SHAKS. *Twel. N.* III. iii. 39 In the South Suburbes, at the Elephant, Is best to lodge. **1852** DICKENS *Bleak Ho.*, (C.D. ed.) xxvii. 235 The far-famed Elephant who has lost his castle.

†**4. a.** Ivory [after L. *elephantus*]. **b.** A horn or trumpet of ivory [after OFr. *olifant*]. *Obs.*

c **1300** *K. Alis.* 1182 To mouth he set his olifaunt. **1615** CHAPMAN *Odyss.* XIX. 77 A chair..The substance silver and rich elephant. **1698** DRYDEN *Virg. Æneid* III. 595 Heavy Gold, and polished Elephant. **1725** POPE *Odyss.* XXI. 10 The handle..With steel and polish'd elephant adorn'd.

5. A Danish Order of Knighthood.

1703 *Lond. Gaz.* No. 3895/2 The King of Denmark conferred the Order of the Elephant upon the Duke of Mecklembourg. **1751** CHAMBERS *Cycl.*, Its badge..is an elephant, with a castle on its back, set with diamonds, and hung on a watered sky-coloured ribband, like the George in England...In 1189..a gentleman among the Danish croisees killed an elephant; in memory of which..the order was erected. **1837** *Penny Cycl.* VIII. 401/1 The orders of knighthood [in Denmark] are the order of the Elephant, etc.

6. sea elephant: a species of Seal (*Macrorhinus proboscideus*), the males of which have the snout somewhat prolonged.

1798 *Naval Chron.* (1799) I. 254 The sea elephant..has been rather scarce. **1841** *Penny Cycl.* XXI. 165 *Macrorhinus proboscideus*..Sea-Elephant and Elephant-Seal of the English.

†**7.** A species of lizard mentioned by Pliny. *Obs.*

1601 HOLLAND *Pliny* II. 451 Black Elephants..which be the black kind of the Lizards. **1608** TOPSELL *Serpents* 718 There be..serpents called 'Elephants', because whomsoever they bite they infect with a kinde of leprosie.

†**8.** [after Pg. *elephante*: see ELEPHANTA.] 'A name given originally by the Portuguese to violent storms occuring at the termination, though some travellers describe it as at the setting in, of the Monsoon' (Yule). *Obs.*

[**1554** *Sidi' Ali* 75 (Y.) The kind of storm is known under the name of the Elephant; it blows from the west.] **1616** SIR T. ROE in Purchas *Pilgr.* I. 549 (Y.) The 20th day (August), the night past fell a storme of raine called the Oliphant, vsuall at going out of the raines. **1703** *Art's Improv.* Introd. 26 Eighthly, Of Winds, and storms at Sea; as Trades-Winds, Huricanes.. Elephants, Monsoons.

9. *Bot.* A species of Scabious.

1847 in HALLIW. **1878** BRITTEN & HOLL. *Plant-n.*

10. a. (more fully **elephant-paper**): A size of drawing and cartridge paper measuring 28 × 23 inches. ***double elephant***: a similar paper measuring 40 × 26½ inches.

1702 *Lond. Gaz.* No. 3814/4 On two large sheets of Elephant Paper. **1716** *Ibid.* No. 5493/4 The fine Imperial will not be sold under 7*l*...and the Elephant 3*l*. *c* **1790** IMISON *Sch. Art.* I. 238 A sheet of the largest elephant paper. **1807** OPIE *Lect. Art* iv. (1848) 323 Writing..upon.. double elephant..paper. **1870** JEVONS *Elem. Logic* iv. 35 Elephant in a stationer's..shop means a large kind of paper. **1880** *Daily Tel.* 3 Dec., 'Elephant folio'..that is to say, of the fullest portfolio size.

b. *Army slang.* (See quots. 1925 and 1943.)

1917 A. G. EMPEY *From Fire Step* 152 One gun..had the exact range of our 'elephant' dug-out entrance. **1919** *War Terms* in *Athenæum* 15 Aug. 759/1 Elephant, corrugated iron shelter. Baby elephant, small corrugated iron shelter. **1919** G. K. ROSE *2/4th Oxf. & Bucks Lt. Infty.* 10 Battalion Headquarters..were comfortable enough with many 'elephant' dug-outs and half a farm-house for a mess. **1925** FRASER & GIBBONS *Soldier & Sailor Words*, *Elephant* (*and Baby Elephant*) *Dug-Out*: a dug-out made with semi-circular linings of heavy corrugated iron. The two names refer to the two sizes issued. **1943** HUNT & PRINGLE *Service Slang* 30 *Elephant hut*, a Nissen hut (shaped somewhat like the beast).

11. a. *attrib.* and *Comb.*, as ***elephant bell***, ***-horn***, ***house***, ***-keeper***, ***-killer***, ***-shed***; ***elephant-headed***, ***-like*** adjs. Also **elephant-bed** (see quot.); **elephant-beetle**, some South American beetle, prob. *Dynastes Neptunus*; the name has also been applied to the African species *Goliathus giganteus* and *G. cacicus*; **elephant bird**, a large fossil bird of the genus *Æpyornis*, found in Madagascar; **elephant's breath**, a shade of colour, light steel grey; **elephant-fish** (see quot.); **elephant-gravel**, gravel containing remains of elephants; **elephant-grey** = 1 f; **elephant hawk-moth** (see quot.); **elephant joke**, a child's nonsense riddle of which an elephant (usu. in a ridiculous situation) is the subject: (see quot. 1984); **elephant-leg** = ELEPHANTIASIS; **elephant-paper** (see 10); **elephant-path**, a path trodden by elephants; **elephant-rain** (see quot.); **elephant-seal** = *sea-elephant* (see 6); **elephant-shrew** (see quot.); **elephant-trumpet** (see 4); **elephant('s) trunk** *rhyming slang*, drunk, also *ellipt.*; **elephant's-tusks**, a genus of gasteropodous molluscs belonging to the family *Dentalidæ* or tooth-shells.

1887 WOODWARD *Geol. Eng. & Wales* 519 The *Elephant Bed [at Brighton] first described by Dr. Mantell is provincially termed Combe rock..it contains remains of *Elephas primigenius*, etc. **1774** GOLDSMITH *Nat. Hist.* (1776) VIII. 139 The *Elephant-beetle..is found in..Guiana and Surinam. **1777** HENLY in *Phil. Trans.* LXVII. 123 Thigh of the elephant beetle. **1923** D. H. LAWRENCE *Birds, Beasts & Flowers* 170 The *elephant bells striking slow, tong-tong, tong-tong. **1889** *Cent. Dict.*, *Elephant-bird. **1933** A. S. ROMER *Vert. Paleont.* x. 214 In Madagascar lived a number of species of 'elephant-birds'. **1969** *New Scientist* 13 Mar. 20/1 The peculiar and often bizarre forms evolved in isolation: species such as..the elephant-bird in Madagascar. **1884** *Cassell's Fam. Mag.* Mar. 246/2 Dressed in grey, the shade known as '*elephant's breath'. **1772–84** COOK *Voy.* (1790) IV. 1283 Fish..known to seamen by the name of *elephant fish. **1867** SMYTH *Sailor's Word-bk.*, *Elephant-fish*, the *Chimæra callorhynchus* named from the proboscis-like process on its nose. **1852** E. FORBES *Let.* in *Life Forbes* xiv. 505 The newer *elephant-gravel of these parts. **1896** *Daily News* 12 Sept. 6/2 '*Elephant' grey is another favourite. **1906** *Westm. Gaz.* 7 Apr. 18/2 A tailor suit of elephant-grey facecloth. **1921** G. JEKYLL *Colour Schemes Flower Garden* 2 The trunks of the Spanish Chestnuts are elephant-grey. **1922** JOYCE *Ulysses* 153 Molly had that elephantgrey dress with the braided frogs. **1879** LUBBOCK *Sci. Lect.* ii. 52 *Chærocampa elpenor*, the *elephant hawk-moth. **1854** F. HALL *Rája-níti* Notes 1 *Elephant-headed..Ganesa, fulfil my desires. **1884** *19th Cent.* Feb. 252 A dozen *elephant-horns heralded forth that the royal party were in motion. **1895** C. J. CORNISH *Life at Zoo* 7 The *Elephant and Antelope Houses. **1922** JOYCE *Ulysses* 92 A tall blackbearded figure..stumping round the corner of Elvery's elephant house. **1943** HUNT & PRINGLE *Service Slang* 30 *Elephant houses*, old forts at Dunkirk. **1966** C. WILLIAMS *Don't just stand There* (1967) 148 Well, hell, do isometric exercises, tell *elephant jokes, write postcards. **1976** *Daily Mirror* 11 Mar. 12/2 They should chew gum and tell elephant jokes and experiment with lipstick and play their transistor radios very loudly indeed. **1984** T. AUGARDE *Oxf. Guide Word Games* i. 13 How can you tell if an elephant has been in your fridge? Footprints in the butter. The last of these [riddles] is obviously modern—and a typical example of the craze for 'elephant' jokes which existed in the 1970s. **1799** CORSE in *Phil. Trans.* LXXXIX. 210 Besides these, the *elephant-keepers notice other varieties, which are less distinct. **1607** TOPSELL *Serpents* 703 Neither have they any other name for those Dragons but *Elephant-killers. *a* **1603** T. CARTWRIGHT *Confut. Rhem. N.T.* (1618) 500 Your knees..are ioyntlesse and *Elephant-like in your obedience unto his precepts. **1853** *Edin. New Philos. Jrnl.* LV. 79 Passages made formerly by the gigantic elephant, which are well adapted for bridle-paths... The knowledge of these various *elephant-paths forms the resource of the marauding Caffre. **1895** KIPLING *2nd Jungle Bk.* 215 A light spring rain—*elephant-rain they call it—drove across the Jungle. **1859** J. LANG *Wand. India* 261 Her tomb..had been taken away bodily, to pave the *elephant shed. **1868** WOOD *Homes without H.* i. 15 The *Elephant Shrew of Southern Africa (*Macroscelides typicus*) a thick-furred, long-snouted, short-eared burrower. **1859** HOTTEN *Dict. Slang* 143 *Elephant's trunk, drunk. **1909** J. R. WARE *Passing Eng.* 123/2 *Elephant's trunk*: drunk. The phrase became incomprehensible by the dropping of the rhyming. 'Oh he's elephants' (*i.e.*, intoxicated) will, in time to come, exercise many an etymologist. **1931** *Evening Standard* 19 Aug. 10/1 He came home and he found the artful dodger elephant trunk in the bread and butter (He found the lodger drunk in the gutter).

b. Also in the names of various plants, as **elephant-apple** (see quot.); **elephant-creeper**, (*Argyreia speciosa*); **elephant grass**, any of various kinds of grass or grasslike plants, esp. *Pennisetum purpureum* (also **elephant's-grass**); **elephant's ear**, the Begonia; **elephant's foot**, (*a*) a species of Yam (*Testudinaria elephantipes*); (*b*) a plant belonging to the genus *Elephantopus*; **elephant's-trunk-plant**, **elephant's-vine** (see quot.).

1866 *Treas. Bot.*, *Feronia.* The Wood-apple or Elephant-apple tree of India, *F. elephantum*, is the only species belonging to this genus of Aurantiaceae. **1832** W. ROXBURGH *Flora Indica* III. 566 Elephant grass... Elephants are fond of it. **1895** MRS. CROKER *Village Tales* 15 We marched two and two,..glancing askance at every bush, at every big tuft of elephant grass. **1906** *Westm. Gaz.* 28

Dec. 2/1 Long grass in Uganda, 'elephant grass', grows from fifteen feet to twenty feet high. **1968** J. W. PURSEGLOVE *Tropical Crops* II. 472 Elephant grass. *Pennisetum purpureum* Schum., is the common mulch. **1866** *Treas. Bot.*, *Feronia*. Elephant's-ear, the common name for *Begonia*. **1884** MILLER *Plant-n.*, Elephant's-ear. The genus begonia. **1789** W. AITON *Hortus Kewensis* III. 280 *Elephantopus scaber*. Rough-leav'd Elephant's foot. Nat. of the East Indies. Cult. 1695, in Chelsea Garden. **1845–50** MRS. LINCOLN *Lect. Bot.* 186 The elephant's-foot (*Elephantopus*), a low, hairy-leaved plant, with purple, ligulate florets. **1872** OLIVER *Elem. Bot.* II. 271 *Testudinaria elephantipes* .. From the appearance of the rhizome it is called 'Elephant's foot' at the Cape of Good Hope. **1901** C. T. MOHR *Plant Life Alabama* 759 Carolina Elephant's-Foot .. [grows in] open dry woods, borders of fields, pastures. **1966** H. W. RICKETT *Wild Flowers of U.S.* I. 508 The genus *Elephantopus*—elephant's foot— is mainly tropical. **1884** MILLER *Plant-n.*, Elephant's-trunk-plant, *Martynia proboscidea*. *Ibid.* Elephant's Vine, *Cissus latifolia*.

ele'phanta. Also (corruptly) elephanter. [a. Pg. *elephante*: see quot. 1698.] = ELEPHANT 8.

[**1698** FRYER *Acc. E. India & P.* 48 (Yule) We are now winding about the South-West part of Ceilon; where we have the Tail of the Elephant full in our mouth; a constellation by the Portugals called Rabo del Elephanto, known for the breaking up of the Munsoons, which is the last Flory this season makes.] **1725** J. REYNOLDS *View Death* (1735) 24 Till .. Enters th' elephanta with thundring noise. **1772** GROSE *Voy. E. Indies* I. 33 (Y.) The setting in of the rains is commonly ushered in by a violent thunderstorm, generally called the Elephanta. **1852** *Life in Bombay* 194 A tremendous burst of thunder and lightning, termed the Elephanta .. The heavy thunderclouds .. apparently form directly over the Island of Elephanta. **1867** SMYTH *Sailor's Word-bk.*, *Elephanter*, a heavy periodical rain of Bombay.

elephantiac (ɛlɪ'fæntɪæk). [ad. L. *elephantiacus*, f. *elephantia*: see ELEPHANCY.] One who is affected with elephantiasis.

1868 KINGSLEY *Hermits* 103 Thou elephantiac .. wilt thou not stop shouting blasphemies?

‖**elephantiasis** (ˌɛlɪfən'taɪəsɪs). [L. *elephantiasis*, a. Gr. ἐλεφαντίασις, f. ἐλέφας, ELEPHANT.]

1. The name given to various kinds of cutaneous disease, which produce in the part affected a resemblance to an elephant's hide. The best known are: **a.** *E. Græcorum*, a tubercular disease, often identified with Eastern leprosy; **b.** *E. Arabum*, called also Elephant Leg, and in the W. Indies Barbadoes Leg, which produces an induration and darkening of the skin, chiefly on the leg.

1581 MULCASTER *Positions* x. (1887) 57 Egyptian lepre, called Elephantiasis. **1656** RIDGLEY *Pract. Physick* 111 Elephantiasis of the Arabians, is a swelling of the Foot, wan, and looks like an Elephants Foot. **1807** SOUTHEY *Espriella's Lett.* (1814) III. 275 Those [letters] which should be thin look as if they had the elephantiasis. **1869** W. M. ROSSETTI *Mem. Shelley* Introd. 45 Shelley had a fancy .. that he was about to be visited with elephantiasis.

2. *fig.* A great or undue expansion or enlargement.

1866 G. MEREDITH *Let.* 22 Dec. (1970) I. 349 You have become the victim of a kind of mental elephantiasis—you fancy all things as immensities. **1928** R. CAMPBELL *Wayzgoose* ii. 53 But ah! her Soul's dimensions to report —Elephantiasis comes far too short! **1955** *Bull. Atomic Sci.* Oct. 276/1 It is a tremendous building, saved from elephantiasis by the skill of its architects in blending classical and modern. **1969** *Daily Tel.* (Colour Suppl.) 27 June 5/3 The Monopolies Commission itself no longer acts. .. Even if it *is* asked to investigate, the managements later have almost complete freedom to develop corporate elephantiasis.

elephantic (ɛlɪ'fæntɪk), *a.* and *sb.* [ad. L. *elephanticus*, f. *elephas* ELEPHANT.]

A. *adj.* Pertaining to or resembling an elephant; huge, ponderous; = ELEPHANTINE. Now *rare.*

1598 E. GILPIN *Skial.* (1878) 31 And speaking painters excuse Titian, For his Ioues loves; and Elephanticke vaine. **1766** G. CANNING *Anti-Lucretius* III. 194 Give those a sting, or elephantic snout. **1835** *New Monthly Mag.* XLIII. 85 The fervent lightness of Lewis, the elephantic ponderosity of Cooke.

†**B.** *sb.* = ELEPHANTIASIS. *Obs. rare.*

1491 CAXTON *Vitas Patr.* (W. de W.) IV. 332 b/1 A man .. was seke of a maladye called elephantyke.

ele'phanticide. *nonce-wd.* [See -CIDE.] The killing of an elephant.

1855 *Illust. Lond. News* 28 July 126/2 Elephanticide seems the order of the day.

elephantide. *rare.* [irreg. f. ELEPHANT.] A person affected with elephantiasis.

1843 BORROW *Bible in Spain* xxvii. 161 Lawsuits .. from .. elephantides having been buried with other dead.

elephantine (ɛlɪ'fæntaɪn, -tɪn), *a.* [ad. L. *elephantin-us*, a. Gr. ἐλεφάντινος, f. ἐλέφας ELEPHANT.]

1. Of or pertaining to an elephant, or elephants. ***elephantine epoch*** (*Geol.*): the period marked by the abundance of large pachydermata.

1675 HOBBES *Odyssey* (1677) 239 Find a word of truth you never will In those that come through th' elephantine tooth. *a* **1711** KEN *Edmund* Poet. Wks. 1721 II. 26 Their Garment was an Elephantine Hide. **1767** HUNTER *Fossil Bones* in *Phil. Trans.* LVIII. 46 It was true elephantine ivory. *a* **1794** SIR W. JONES *Tales* (1807) 180 Chaste elephantine bone By min'rals ting'd. **1862** HUXLEY *Lect. Wrkg. Men* 145 An elephantine mammal. **1875** *Wonders Phys. World* II. IV. 300 Fossil elephantine remains.

2. Elephant-like, resembling an elephant in action or manner; clumsy, unwieldy.

1845 HOOD *Remonst. Ode* ii, While poor elephantine I pick up a sixpence. **1860** HOLLAND *Miss Gilbert* ix. 146 Cattle .. frisked in ungraceful, elephantine play. **1881** *Macm. Mag.* XLIV. 478/2 The good-humour and somewhat elephantine spirits of the others were quite inexhaustible.

3. Resembling an elephant in size or strength; (of a task) requiring the strength of an elephant.

1630 BRATHWAIT *Eng. Gentlew.* (1641) 279 Wearing great sleeves, mishapen elephantine bodies, trains sweeping the earth. **1662** FULLER *Worthies* (1840) II. 286 This elephantine birth [a book of seven volumes]. **1788** WESLEY *Wks.* (1872) VII. 24 Let there be .. no elephantine hats or bonnets. **1849** STOVEL *Canne's Necess.* Introd. 81 Elephantine as its strength appeared .. its back was broken. **1880** *Sat. Rev.* 20 Mar. 387 The task of reviewing a dictionary must needs be elephantine.

4. ***elephantine leprosy***: = ELEPHANTIASIS. *rare.*

1843 BORROW *Bible in Spain* xxvii. 161 Sad is leprosy in all its forms, but most so when elephantine.

5. *Rom. Antiq.* (see quot. 1751). Also *allusive.*

1695 LD. PRESTON *Boeth.* III. 99 My Eye into each page shall look Of the Elephantine Book [*note*, the Book of Nature]. **1751** CHAMBERS *Cycl.*, *Elephantine* .. applied to certain books of the ancient Romans, wherein were recorded the transactions of the emperors, and the proceedings, acts, etc. of the senate. They were called elephantine, because composed of ivory leaves, or tablets.

elephantoid (ɛlɪ'fæntɔɪd), *a.* [f. Gr. ἐλέφας, ἐλέφαντο-ς ELEPHANT + -ειδής like (cf. Gr. ἐλεφαντώδης): see -OID.] **a.** Elephant-like. **b.** Of or belonging to elephant-like animals. So **elephantoidal**, *a.*

1841 TRIMMER *Pract. Geol.* 407 No elephantoid remains. **1856** PAGE *Adv. Text-bk. Geol.* xix. (1876) 371 True elephantoid genera, as the .. mammoth. **1857** H. MILLER *Test. Rocks* ii. 89 The Mastodon, an elephantoid animal.

elephantry ('ɛlɪfəntrɪ). [f. ELEPHANT + -RY, after *cavalry*.] Troops mounted on elephants.

1747 W. HORSLEY *Fool* (1748) II. No. 83. 258 Before we took the Field, we demolished our Elephantry. **1858** F. HALL in *Journ. Amer. Orient. Soc.* (1861) VII. 40 That is to say, elephantry, cavalry, and infantry.

'elephantship. *humorous.* [f. ELEPHANT + -SHIP.] The personality of an elephant.

1882 *Daily News* 23 Mar. 5/5 Her elephantship [Alice] was not found in hysterics.

Elers ware ('ɛləz wɛə(r)). Also Elers' ware. A kind of red stoneware made in Staffordshire about 1690–1700 by the two Elers brothers, David (1656–1742) and John Philip (1664–1738). (See also quot. 1903).

[**1691** *Newcastle-under-Lyme Corp. Minutes* in *Evening Sentinel* 2 Feb. 1944, 3/4 At an Assembly in the Gildhall, 18 August, 3 William and Mary, 1691, William Burslem, Mayor .. Ordered that a present be made to my Lord Cheife Justice Holt .. of some of Mr. David Elers earthen ware to the vallew of three pounds or thereabouts.] **1869** LADY C. SCHREIBER *Jrnl.* (1911) I. 8 Elers ware teapot with effigies of King and Queen. *Ibid.* 32 An Elers ware coffee pot. **1870** W. CHAFFERS *Marks & Monograms on Pottery* 508 The sharply moulded ornaments on Elers' red Staffordshire ware was but a continuance of the moulded enscrollments of the stone ware of Germany. **1903** R. L. HOBSON *Catal. Eng. Pott. in Brit. Mus.* 168 The term 'Elers ware' has passed into general use as the name for all the red stoneware made in Staffordshire during the eighteenth century. **1924** RACKHAM & READ *Eng. Pott.* vi. 95 Lacework ornament of the kind associated with Elers ware.

†**'elesæw.** *Obs.* [f. OE. *ele* oil + *séaw*, SEW *sb.*, juice.] Oil.

c **1200** ORMIN 924 Bræd .. smeredd wel wiþþ elesæw. *Ibid.* 8667 Drihhtinn seȝȝþ .. tatt te shall þin elesæw Lasstenn.

†**elescophe.** *Obs.* [Corruptly ad. Gr. ἡλιοσκόπιος, -ον.] Some medicinal plant, ? Sun Spurge (*Euphorbia Helioscopium*).

1621 BURTON *Anat. Mel.* II. iv. II. iii. (1676) 237/2 Rubarbe, Agaricke, Elescophe, &c .. are not so proper to this humour.

elest, var. of *ee-list*, EYE-LIST: see EYE.

†**'elet.** *Obs.* exc. *dial.* [app. identical with OE. *æled*, also *alet* (Grein) fire: see ELD *sb.*[1]] Fuel.

c **1200** *Trin. Coll. Hom.* 119 Fir haueð on him þre mihtes on to giuende hete, oðer to giuende liht, þridde to weldende elet to none þinge. *c* **1320** *Sir Beues* 3264 Wiþ oute þe toun hii piȝte a stake þar þe fur was i-make .. þai fette wode and elet. **1847–78** HALLIW. *Elet*, fuel; ollit. *Wilts.*

eleusine (ɛlju:'si:n). *Bot.* [mod.L. (J. Gaertner *De Fructibus et Seminibus Plantarum* (1788) I. 7), f. the name of the Attic town *Eleusis*, site of a temple to the corn-goddess Demeter + -INE[4].] A member of the genus of annual tropical grasses so named, some of which are grown for grain in Africa and Asia; also called RAGI, finger millet, or birdsfoot millet.

1829 LOUDON *Encyl. Plants* 1089. **1914** H. KRAEMER *Applied & Economic Bot.* v. 467 The fruit is a grain .. the seed being always firmly united with the thin pericarp (except in Sporobolus, Eleusine, etc.). **1932** *Antiquity* VI. 337 The usual method of planting [among the Nandi] is to have a little of everything in the same patch—eleusine, millet, maize, beans, and sweet potatoes. **1938** *Nature* 6 Aug. 259/1 The staple food [of the Ciga of Uganda] is eleusine, eked out by peas, beans, corn and wild greens. **1969** F. R. ALLCHIN in Ucko & Dimbleby *Domestication & Exploitation of Plants & Animals* 327 The probability that certain of the millets, notably *Eleusine* and *Pennisetum*, were first domesticated in Africa.

Eleusinian (ɛlju:'sɪnɪən). [f. L. *eleusīni-us* (Gr. ἐλευσίνιος) belonging to Eleusis + -AN.] Belonging to Eleusis in Attica. ***Eleusinian mysteries***: the mysteries of Demeter there celebrated; also *fig.* Hence **Eleu'sinianism** (*nonce-wd.*).

1643 MILTON *Divorce* Wks. 1738 I. 190 Eleusinian Mysteries, that no man can utter what they mean. **1841–4** EMERSON *Ess.* xx. Wks. (Bohn) I. 250 The Eleusinian mysteries .. show that there always were seeing and knowing men in the planet. **1857** *Chamb. Jrnl.* VII. 226 The eleusinianism of bonnetdom.

E'leutherarch. *rare.* [f. Gr. ἐλεύθερος free + -αρχης ruler.] The chief of an (imaginary) secret society called 'the Eleutheri'.

1813 T. J. HOGG *Alexy Haimatoff* 178, The Eleutherarch .. asked if they had any objection to my being initiated in the mysteries of the Eleutheri. **1813** SHELLEY *Let.* 26 Nov. in *Contemp. Rev.* (1884) 387 The Swans and the Eleutherarchs are proofs that you were a little sleepy. **1817** T. PEACOCK *Nightmare Ab.* 97 He slept .. and dreamed of venerable eleutherarchs.

Eleu'therian, *a. rare.* [f. Gr. ἐλευθέρι-ος of same meaning (f. ἐλεύθερ-ος free) + -AN.] The title of Zeus as protector of political freedom.

1623 COCKERAM, *Eleutherian*, a deliverer. **1801** SOUTHEY *Thalaba* I. xii, Where the family of Greece Hymn'd Eleutherian Jove.

eleutherism (ɪ'lju:θərɪz(ə)m). [f. Gr. ἐλεύθερ-ος free + -ISM.] Zeal for freedom.

1802 W. TAYLOR in Robberds *Mem.* I. 435 A Miltonic swell of diction and eleutherism of sentiment. **1803** *Ann. Rev.* I. 360 Ever since the American war, eleutherism had been the fashion of Europe.

eleuthero- (ɪ'lju:θərəʊ), combining form of Gr. ἐλεύθερος free: **eˌleuthero'mania** [see MANIA], mad zeal for freedom. **eˌleuthero'maniac** *a.* [see MANIAC], one possessed by a mad zeal for freedom. Also in botanical compounds, as **eˌleuthero'petalous** [Gr. πέταλον leaf], **eˌleuthero'phyllous** [Gr. φύλλον leaf], **eˌleuthero'sepalous** [see SEPAL] *adjs.*, having the petals, leaves, sepals, free, *i.e.* distinct, not cohering.

1837 CARLYLE *Fr. Rev.* I. III. iv. Nothing but insubordination, eleutheromania, confused, unlimited opposition in their heads. *Ibid.* I. II. v, Eleutheromaniac philosophedom grows ever more clamorous. **1880** GRAY *Struct. Bot.* vi. §5. 245 Eleutheropetalous .. has .. been used for polypetalous.

†**'elevable,** *a. Obs. rare*[−1]. [a. Fr. *élévable*, f. *élever*, (see next).] That can be elevated.

1676 H. MORE *Remarks upon two Ingen. Disc.* 164 The Embolus .. being elevable near to the top of the Laton Syringe or pump. **1691** ED. TAYLOR *Behmen's Aurora* xxiii. 256 Not accessible nor elevable.

elevate ('ɛlɪveɪt), *pa. pple.* and *ppl. a.* Also 4–5 eleuat(e, (5 eliuate), 6 elevat. [ad. L. *ēlevāt-us*, pa. pple. of *ēlevā-re* to elevate.] Used as pa. pple. of ELEVATE; also = ELEVATED *ppl. a.*; in various senses. From 18th c. only *poet.*

c **1391** CHAUCER *Astrol.* II. §23 This is to seyn, as many degrees as thy pool is eleuat, so michel is the latitude of the Regioun. **1432–50** tr. *Higden* (Rolls) I. 227 If that ston be oon say .. by what arte hit was elevate. **1509** HAWES *Examp. Virt.* vii. 134 He in rychesse shall be so eleuate. **1513** BRADSHAW *St. Werburge* (1848) 125 The graue was, opened, eleuat was the chest. **1598** STOW *Surv.* xxix. (1603) 259 A Tombe eleuate and arched. **1667** MILTON *P.L.* II. 559 In thoughts more elevate. **1673** R. LEIGH *Transp. Reh.* 22 This is elevate, this is the new way of writing. **1676** HALLEY in Rigaud *Corr. Sci. Men* (1841) I. 228 St. Helena .. where the south pole is considerably elevate. **1742** YOUNG *Nt. Th.* II. 350 Souls elevate, angelic, wing'd with fire. **1814** SOUTHEY *Roderick* VI, Elevate Amid the thousands .. above their heads upraised. **1873** BROWNING *Red Cott. Night-C.* 1638 There had been shaggy eyebrows elevate.

elevate ('ɛlɪveɪt), *v.* Also 6 ellevate, eleuate. [f. L. *ēlevāt-* ppl. stem of *ēlevāre*, f. *ē* out + *levā-re* (related to *levis* light) to render light, lighten, hence, to lift, raise.]

†**I. 1.** *trans.* To lighten, lessen the weight of; to depreciate, extenuate. *Obs.*

1533 ELYOT *Cast. Helth* (1541) 35 a, Custome from chyldhode doth eleuate the power of meates and drynkes. *c* **1570** THYNNE *Pride & Lowl.* (1841) 5 Cato .. dooth their credit ellevate, As thing whereof but small regard he tooke. **1609** HOLLAND *Livy* XLIV. xliv. 1199 b, [The Consul] forgat not to elevate as much as he could, the fame of the first fortunate unhappie field. **1624** BP. MOUNTAGU *Gagg* 94 To avoide or elevate the censure of the church .. [they] procured letters deprecatory. **1788** V. KNOX *Winter Even.* II. v. xii. 195 Instead of exalting our idea of the Deity they elevate or lower it.

II. To raise, lift up.

2. a. To raise above the usual position, or above the level of surrounding objects. Also *fig.*

1497 J. ALKOK *Mons Perfectionis* Cj 20/2 Obedyence.. openeth heuens it eleuatith a man fro the erth dweller with angels. **1607** TOPSELL *Four-f. Beasts* 350 This first picture of the Ichneumon was taken by Bellonius, except the back be too much elevated. **1797** M. BAILLIE *Morb. Anat.* (1807) 61 Unless the head..be more or less elevated from the horizontal posture. **1830** J. G. STRUTT *Sylva Brit.* 4 The character..of the Oak is rather to extend its arms, than elevate its head. **1858** LARDNER *Handbk. Nat. Phil.* 109 The rope by which the bucket is elevated. **1878** HUXLEY *Physiogr.* 186 The land in the Bay of Concepcion had been elevated to the extent of four or five feet.

b. To hold up to view. Now only with reference to the Mass: To lift up (the Host) for the adoration of the people.

1637 GILLESPIE *Eng. Pop. Cerem.* III. ii. 32 When the hoste is elevated in the celebration of the Masse. **1649** J. KENT in Ellis *Orig. Lett.* II. 295 III. 342 A rogue of a minister, after his head was severed from his sacred body, elevated it publicly to the people. **1660** R. COKE *Power & Subj.* 243 She [the Queen] had forbidden the Archbishop..to elevate the Host for adoration.

†**c.** To rear or raise (by building). *Obs.*

1798 FERRIAR *Eng. Historians* 243 On the northern side of the choir, was elevated one of those lofty, conical towers.

†**d.** Of the action of heat: To raise in the form of vapour; to evaporate or sublime. *Obs.*

1607 WALKINGTON *Opt. Glass* 28 The damping fumes that the Sun elevates from bogges. **1665–9** BOYLE *Occas. Refl.* IV. xii. (1675) 240 The Sun has by its..Beams elevated this Water in the form of Vapours. **1667** —— *Orig. Formes & Qual.*, These volatile particles of Gold, with the Salts wherewith they were elevated. **1715** [see ELEVATED 1 b].

3. *transf.* To raise (the voice).

1618 ROWLANDS *Sacred Mem.* 30 But they the more do eleuate their voyce. **1816** [See ELEVATED *ppl. a.* 2.] *Mod.* It is unnecessary to elevate your voice.

4. To raise in direction, direct upwards.

a. To raise (one's eyes), direct (glances) upwards; *fig.* to 'lift up' (one's hopes, thoughts) to a higher object.

c **1611** SHAKS. *Wint. T.* v. ii. 82 One Eye declin'd for the losse of her Husband, another eleuated, that the Oracle was fulfill'd. **1818** JAS. MILL *Brit. India* II. IV. iv. 143 The English now elevated their hopes to the recovery of the province.

b. *Gunnery.* To raise the axis of (a gun, etc.) to an angle with the horizon.

1692 in *Capt. Smith's Seaman's Gram.* II. xxi. 134 Put in your Bullet with a Wad after it, if the Piece be not elevated. **1769** FALCONER *Dict. Marine* (1789) Hh b, The mortar must be more elevated. **1859** F. GRIFFITHS *Artil. Man* (1862) 112 No. 2 searches, sponges, rams home, elevates.

5. a. To raise, exalt in rank or status.

1509 HAWES *Past. Pleas.* XXVII. xix, For riche mennes goodes I muste ofte translate, Unto the poore, them for to elevate. **1606** WARNER *Alb. Eng.* XIV. lxxxv. (1612) 351 Nathak, who, eleuated, altered from vertuous to most vaine. **1709** STEELE *Tatler* No. 56 ¶2 Footmen, Fiddlers, and Lacqueys, are elevated into Companions in this present Age. **1713** —— *Englishman* No. 2. 10 We like nothing but what will..elevate us above our Neighbours. **1835** LYTTON *Rienzi* I. i, See what liberty exists in Rome, when we, the patricians, thus elevate a plebeian.

†**b.** To extol or magnify (in praise). *Obs.*

1513 BRADSHAW *St. Werburge* (1848) 48 With reverence hym elevate.

6. a. To raise in a moral or intellectual sense.

1624 GATAKER *Transubst.* 89 To elevate our minde by faith. **1711** STEELE *Spect.* No. 79 ¶9 Choose Books which elevate the Mind above the World. **1850** MRS. STOWE *Uncle Tom's C.* xxiii. 229 You might as well set Mount Ætna on them flat, and tell them to stand up under it, as tell me to elevate my servants with all the superincumbent mass of society upon them. *a* **1867** BUCKLE *Misc. Wks.* (1872) I. 63 There is hardly any virtue which so elevates our character, as moral courage. **1883** H. DRUMMOND *Nat. Law in Spir. W.* iii. (1884) 98 The attempt to elevate the race has been mysteriously thwarted.

b. *absol.*

1886 'M. GRAY' *Silence of D. Maitland* III. III. vi. 154 It was the kind of sorrow that purifies and elevates. **1967** *Listener* 5 Oct. 448/2 The first step is to brainwash the pop audience of its pirate-induced distrust of the Corporation.. then, slyly and imperceptibly, *elevate*.

7. a. To elate, exhilarate. Somewhat *rare* in mod. use.

1634 *Malory's Arthur* (1816) I. 173, I was so elevated..in my heart. **1709** LUTTRELL *Brief Rel.* (1857) VI. 483 Being elevated by the terror he had struck into the enemy..[he] resolved to advance and fight them. **1725** DE FOE *Voy. round W.* (1840) 34 He seemed extremely pleased at this, and even elevated. **1818** JAS. MILL *Brit. India* II. IV. ii. 77 The French, elevated by this advantage, reinforced their victorious party.

b. *spec.* of the effects of liquor. Now *humorous* or *slang.*

a **1704** T. BROWN *Wks.* (1760) II. 194 (D.) We were all elevated above the use of our legs as well as our reason. **1763** *Brit. Mag.* IV. 372, I, being elevated with liquor. **1816** 'QUIZ' *Grand Master* VIII. 230 But with the jumping-powder heated, He got completely—elevated. **1844** DICKENS *Mart. Chuz.* ix. (C.D. ed.) 94 His depth of feeling is misunderstood. He is supposed to be a little elevated; and nobody heeds him.

elevated ('ɛlɪveɪtɪd), *ppl. a.* (and *sb.*) [f. ELEVATE *v.*]

1. a. Raised up; (of buildings, etc.) reared aloft; (of the hands) uplifted; (*Geog.*) situated at a high level. ***elevated pole*** (see quot.). ***elevated railway***: a railway supported on pillars above the street-level; also (*U.S.*) ***elevated highway, railroad, road***; so ***elevated station, train***; *ellipt.* as *sb.* = elevated railway, etc.

1553 EDEN *Treat. New Ind.* (Arb.) 32 The south pole is there eleuated fortie & syxe degrees. **1615** CROOKE *Body of Man* 434 The intelligible faculty of the Soule, as the Queene and Princesse of the rest should sit in an eleuated Tribunall. **1651** HOBBES *Leviath.* III. xlii. 290 To elect..by plurality of elevated hands. **1674** *Ch. & Court of Rome* 7 The idolatrous Worship of the elevated Wafer. **1774** GOLDSM. *Nat. Hist.* (1776) I. 200 Rivers have their source either in mountains, or elevated lakes. **1856** STANLEY *Sinai & Pal.* i. (1858) 11 Um Shaumer, the most elevated summit of the whole range. **1867** SMYTH *Sailor's Word-bk.*, *Elevated Pole*, that..pole which is above the horizon. **1868** *N.Y. Tribune* 1 July 8/2 The remarkable work of constructing an elevated railway.. was again on trial yesterday. **1868** *Ibid.* 8/6 The elevated railroad through Greenwich street has 'gone up' higher than was contemplated in the charter of the company. **1868** *Comm. & Financ. Chron.* VI. 361/1 Three tiers of roads could be constructed; a basement road..a surface road.. and an elevated road. **1880** *Harper's Mag.* Sept. 563 The buzzing which vibrates in the air comes from an elevated railway. **1881** *Scribner's Mag.* May 159/2 The clatter and roar and groaning wail of the Elevated train. **1881** W. G. MARSHALL *Through Amer.* 24 The effect of the 'elevated'—the 'L', as New Yorkers generally call it—is, to my mind, anything but beautiful. **1884** *N.Y. Herald* 27 Oct. 2/2 Commodious First Flat; Rent $37; Elevated Station 86th st. **1890** *Century Mag.* Nov. 45 In those days there were no elevated roads. **1901** *Scribner's Mag.* XXIX. 454/1 In the street the Ninth Avenue Elevated train roared by... The cobble-stones on Sixth Avenue were shining under the Elevated. **1906** 'O. HENRY' *Four Million* 8 Standing under a gas-light and looking over the elevated road at the moon. **1945** W. MAXWELL *Folded Leaf* 257 They rode on the elevated railway. **1947** *Harper's Mag.* May 453/2 The remaining eighty per cent [of the population] cling to the greasy straps of the antiquated, unsanitary, dilapidated, and dangerous Elevated. **1963** *P.M.L.A.* Dec. p. vii/2 (*list*) U.K. flyover: U.S. elevated highway.

†**b.** Of vapours: Raised by heat. *Obs.*

1715 tr. *Pancirollus' Rerum Mem.* II. viii. 322 Distillation ..whereby elevated Fumes..are resolv'd into Waters, Oils.

c. *fig.* Exalted in rank.

1665–9 BOYLE *Occas. Refl.*, So elevated a station is apt to make men giddy. **1855** MACAULAY *Hist. Eng.* IV. 545 The most elevated position among English subjects.

2. *transf.* Of the voice, of temperature.

1816 SCOTT *Antiq.* i, With an elevated voice. **1878** HUXLEY *Physiogr.* 76 If the liquid metal be kept..at an elevated temperature.

3. *Math.* Of an equation: Involving high powers of the unknown quantity.

1841 J. R. YOUNG *Math. Dissert.* III. 138 Whenever..the proposed equation is of an elevated order. **1854** BOOLE *Laws Thought* i. 17 When that equation is of an elevated degree.

4. a. *Astrol.* **b.** *Her.* (see quots.).

1721–1800 BAILEY, *Elevated*, a Planet is said to be elevated above another, when being stronger it weakens the Influence of the other. **1731** *Ibid.* vol. II, *Elevated* in Heraldry..signifies the points of them [wings] turned upwards, which is the true flying posture.

5. Exalted in character, style, and tone; lofty, sublime; dignified.

1604 T. WRIGHT *Pass.* IV. i. 117 Among..eleuated spirits it will often chance that there will arise in conuersation, a certaine diuersitie of opinion. **1713** BERKELEY *Ess.* Wks. III. 183 The most elevated notions of theology and morality. **1834** MRS. SOMERVILLE *Connex. Phys. Sc.* (1849) Introd. 1 Science..must ever afford..subject of elevated meditation. **1875** JOWETT *Plato* (ed. 2) V. 120 One of the most elevated passages in Plato.

6. a. Elated, exhilarated. **b.** Slightly intoxicated (*humorous* or *slang*).

1624 MASSINGER *Parl. of Love* II. i, A little elevated With the assurance of my future fortune. **1800** BLOOMFIELD *Farmer's Boy, Winter* 384 Sunshine, Health, and Joy... cheer the elevated Boy! **1827** J. WIGHT *More Mornings at Bow St.* 51 A *leetle* elevated in liquor. **1859** JEPHSON *Brittany* v. 64 Some of the men were a little elevated. **1863** MRS. OLIPHANT *Salem Ch.* xi. 189 This elevated frame of mind. **1898** C. M. YONGE *Founded on Paper* xviii. 211 Though the landlord declared him to have been fairly sober, he was what one awe-stricken youth termed 'a little elevated'.

Hence **'elevatedly** *adv.*, in an elevated manner; with exaltation. **'elevatedness**, the quality or condition of being elevated.

1593 NASHE *Christ's T.* (1613) 27 So penetrating and eleuatedly haue I praid for you. **1731** BAILEY, vol. II, *Elevatedness*, exaltedness, a being lift up, etc. **1799** W. GODWIN *St. Leon* (L.), The elevatedness and generosity of my station.

elevating ('ɛlɪveɪtɪŋ), *vbl. sb.* [f. ELEVATE *v.* + -ING[1].] The action of the verb ELEVATE.

1641 WILKINS *Math. Magick* I. ix. (1648) 58 It is likewise used for the elevating or lifting up of weights. **1692** in *Capt. Smith's Seaman's Gram.* II. xxiv. 129 A Gunner's Ruler, for the Elevating of any Piece of Ordnance to any degree of Mounture. **1870** MISS BRIDGMAN *R. Lynne* I. ix. 138 Elevatings of the eyebrows.

attrib. **1859** F. GRIFFITHS *Artil. Man.* (1862) 122 The elevating screw must..be clamped. **1881** *Times* 28 Jan. 3/6 The elevating gear of this gun.

elevating ('ɛlɪveɪtɪŋ), *ppl. a.* [f. ELEVATE *v.* + -ING[2].] That elevates; chiefly *fig.*

1817 COLERIDGE *To a Lady*, The elevating thought of suffered pains. **1853** ROBERTSON *Serm.* Ser. IV. xvii. (1876) 229 The elevating power of faith. **1875** HAMERTON *Intell. Life* I. iv. 24 Elevating influences of literature.

elevation (ɛlɪ'veɪʃən). [ad. L. *ēlevātiōn-em*, n. of action f. *ēlevāre*: see ELEVATE *v.*]

I. Process or result of elevating.

1. a. The action or process of lifting up or raising aloft; also, the giving of an upward direction to anything. ***valley of elevation*** (see quot. 1887).

1526 *Pilgr. Perf.* (1531) 15 b, The eleuacyons or wawes of the see ben meruaylous. **1607** TOPSELL *Four-f. Beasts* 8 A Bull..can toss into the air very great..beasts, which he receiveth again as they fall down, doubling their elevation with renewed strength and rage. **1663** W. CHARLETON *Chor. Gigant.* 32 At first elevation of their eyes. **1676** GREW *Lect.* II. i. §6 Elevation; when, like Paste in baking..they [the bodies mixed] swell and huff up. **1695** WOODWARD *Nat. Hist. Earth* (J.) The disruption of the strata, the elevation of some, and depression of others. **1863** A. RAMSAY *Phys. Geog.* i. (1878) 11 Volcanic regions subject to earthquakes are often areas of elevation. **1878** HUXLEY *Physiogr.* 205 But the land is subject also to local elevations and depressions. **1887** WOODWARD *Geol. Engl. & Wales* (ed. 2) 586 We sometimes find the higher tracts to be formed by what was ..a depression, while tracts originally elevated have been converted into..'Valleys of Elevation'.

†**b.** *spec.* = *erection. Obs.*

1543 TRAHERON *Vigo's Chirurg.* I. xi. 10 b, The yarde..is full of ventosite..by which the eleuation of the same commeth.

c. *spec.* The lifting up of the Host for the adoration of the people.

1563–87 FOXE *A. & M.* (1684) III. 666 Before the Elevation..he turned him to the People in a great Rage. **1637** GILLESPIE *Eng. Pop. Cerem.* III. ii. 28 The elevation of the bread *materialiter*, is not Idolatrous. **1699** BURNET *39 Art.* xxviii. (1700) 342 The Elevation of the Sacrament began to be practised in the Sixth Century. **1884** F. M. CRAWFORD *Rom. Singer* I. 9 And only takes it off when he sings the Gloria Patri, or at the Elevation.

†**d.** *fig.* The lifting up of the soul (in adoration); a devout exaltation of feeling. *Obs.*

a **1600** HOOKER (J.) All which different elevations of spirit unto God, are contained in the name of prayer. **1643** SIR T. BROWNE *Relig. Med.* I. §3, I could never heare the Ave Maria Bell without an elevation. **1674** OWEN *Holy Spirit* (1693) 185 The Elevation of Faith to apprehend Divine Power. **1687** BURNET *Death prim. Persecutors*, Let us then Celebrate Gods Triumph over his Enemies with all the Elevations of Joy. **1711** NORRIS (J.) We are..to love him with all possible ..elevation of spirit.

e. *Ballet.* A dancer's leap or jump (steps of elevation) off the ground; the point attained in such a leap; in modern dance, an act or the action of tightening the muscles and improving the general lift of the body in a dancer's stance. (Also in Fr. form *élévation.*)

1830 R. BARTON tr. *Blasis's Code of Terpsichore* II. vi. 77 In all your high caperings, develope a manly vigour, and let your *steps of elevation* be agreeably contrasted, by the rapidity of your *terre-à-terre* steps. **1889** G. B. SHAW *London Mus. 1888–89* (1937) 223 The *entrechats, battements, ronds de jambes, arabesques, élévations*, that are the stock-in-trade of the art of theatrical dancing. **1934** A. HASKELL *Balletomania* xi. 223 She has gained an elevation that allows her to do thirty-six consecutive *entrechats six*! **1948** *Ballet Ann.* II. 36 A magnificent soaring elevation. *Ibid.* 126 A slender dancer of exceptional elevation. **1949** SHURR & YOCUM *Mod. Dance* i. 14 Elevation refers not only to 'inches off the floor'—as in running, jumping, and leaping—but also to the body lift. **1961** [see À TERRE].

2. *concr.* A rising or swelling (on the skin or surface of the ground); a rising ground, an eminence.

1543 TRAHERON *Vigo's Chirurg.* II. x. 23 a, Pruna hath not so great eleuation as ignis persicus. **1599** A. M. *Gabelhouer's Bk. Physicke* 288/2 If..the Patient hath no externalle disease, nor anye eleuatione. **1799** KIRWAN *Geol. Ess.* 285 Secondary strata present..elevations, from an original elevation in the fundamental stone. **1825** MACAULAY *Milton, Ess.* (1854) I. 14/1 Nooks and dells, beautiful as fairyland, are embosomed in its most rugged and gigantic elevations. **1848** W. BARTLETT *Egypt to Pal.* x. (1879) 221 The remaining part of the elevation seemed like a small hill placed upon a terrace.

†**3.** Sublimation; vaporization by heat. *Obs.*

1605 TIMME *Quersit.* II. i. 103 The elevations and sublimations of the spirits of the said salt. **1612** WOODALL *Surg. Mate* Wks. (1653) 270 Elevation is subtiliation, when spiritual parts from the corporal..by the force of fire are elevated. **1641** FRENCH *Distill.* i. (1651) 10 *Elevation*, is the rising of any matter in manner of fume, or vapour by vertue of heat. **1677** HALE *Prim. Orig. Man.* IV. ii. 301 An elevation or rectification of some parts of that Matter.

4. *transf.* **a.** A raising or increase (of temperature). **b.** A quickening (of the pulse); a raising of the animal spirits. Hence (*dial.* or *vulgar*) that which raises the spirits, a 'pick-me-up'.

1725 N. ROBINSON *The. Physick* 88 Elevation or Depression of the Pulse. **1850** KINGSLEY *Alt. Locke* xii, What's elevation? Opium, bor' alive, opium. **1882** VINES *Sachs' Bot.* 825 The slight elevation of temperature in the forenoon.

5. a. The raising (of the voice) in loudness (? also in pitch). †**b.** *concr.* The stressed syllable of a metrical foot; = ARSIS (*rare*).

1605 BACON *Adv. Learn.* II. 60 The consideration of the Accedents of Wordes, which are Measure, Sound, and Eleuation, or Accent. **1668** WILKINS *Real Char.* 45 Prolongation of Vowels, or Elevation of voice in the pronouncing of any syllable, Accent. *a* **1789** BURNEY *Hist. Mus.* (ed. 2) I. vi. 64 They [feet] were divided into two parts ..the first of which was called elevation.

†**6.** *Music.* One of the 'graces' in old English music. *Obs.*

1659 CHR. SIMPSON *Division Viol* 9 Sometimes a Note is graced by sliding it from the Third below, called an Elevation, now something obsolete.

†**7.** The raising or rearing (of plants). *Obs.*

1658 EVELYN *Fr. Gard.* (1675) 38 The elevation and raising of trees.

8. The action of raising in rank or dignity; the state or fact of being elevated in rank.

16.. LOCKE (J.) Angels, in their several degrees of elevation above us. **1701** LUTTRELL *Brief Rel.* (1857) V. 4 The duke of Berwick was gone..to compliment the pope upon his elevation. **1827** HARE *Guesses* Ser. II. (1873) 541 A sudden elevation in life..smells us out, and often perniciously. **1856** FROUDE *Hist. Eng.* (1858) II. viii. 270 The many men of talent who owed their elevation to Wolsey.

II. The height to which anything is elevated.

9. Of angular magnitude: **a.** *Astron.* The altitude or angular height of the pole, or of any heavenly body, above the horizon. †Of a place: The elevation of the pole at that place; the latitude (*obs.*). Also in *Dialling*, the angle made by the gnomon with the horizon (which is equal to the latitude of the place).

c **1391** CHAUCER *Astrol.* II. §23 Tak ther the elevacioun of thi pool. **1549** *Compl. Scot.* vi. (1872) 47 Cosmaghraphie..sal declair the..eleuation..of the sone, mune, and of the sternis. **1593** FALE *Dialling* 10 Before Sunne rising and after Sunne setting in our Elevation. **1642** HOWELL *For. Trav.* (Arb.) 87 The distance between places may be known by the elevation of the pole. **1683** TRYON *Way to Health* 471 Under the Elivation of oure Pole. **1686** tr. *Chardin's Trav.* 247 The Elevation of Erivan is in 40 Deg. 15 Min. **1706** PHILLIPS, *Elevation* of the Pole (in Dialling) is the Angle which the Style..makes with the Substylar Line. **1726** tr. *Gregory's Astron.* I. II. 373 The Elevation of the Pole in that place therefore is also given. **1867–77** G. CHAMBERS *Astron.* Vocab. Def. 915 Elevation of the Pole.

b. The angle made with the horizontal by any line of direction; *spec.* the angle at which a gun is elevated.

1692 in *Capt. Smith's Seaman's Gram.* II. iv. 93 If his Piece be mounted to any Elevation, he need not put a Wad after the shot. **1769** FALCONER *Dict. Marine* (1789) Hh b. The shell being fired at an elevation of 45°. **1798** CAPT. MILLAR in Nicolas *Disp. Nelson* (1846) VII. Introd. 155, I observed their shot..and knowing that..they would not have coolness enough to change their elevation, I closed them suddenly.

10. a. A particular height or altitude above a given level; as the height of a locality above the level of the sea; of a building, etc., above the level of the ground.

1732 BERKELEY *Alciphr.* iii. §9 The particular distance, position, elevation, or dimension of the fabric. **1830** J. G. STRUTT *Sylva Brit.* 4 In sheltered groups they will reach an elevation of eighty or a hundred feet. **1856** STANLEY *Sinai & Pal.* ii. (1858) 129 Jerusalem is of nearly the same elevation as the highest ground in England. **1860** TYNDALL *Glac.* I. §2. 19 What was snow at the higher elevations changed to rain lower down.

b. *fig.*

1822 IMISON *Sc. & Art* II. 391 He will perceive to what an elevation the excellence of the art can raise him.

11. *concr.* A drawing of a building or other object made in projection on a vertical plane, as distinguished from a ground plan.

1731 BAILEY vol. II, *Elevation* (in Architect.) a draught or description of the face or principal side of a building, called also the *Upright*. **1762–71** H. WALPOLE *Vertue's Anecd. Paint.* (1786) IV. 244 The plan and elevations of the late earl of Leicester's house. **1833** BREWSTER *Nat. Magic* xi. 281 An elevation of the automaton, as seen from behind. **1847** S. BROOKS (*title*) City, Town and Country Architecture, designs for Street Elevations, Shop Fronts, etc. **1874** R. TYRWHITT *Sk. Club* 28 That's the front of your block which faces you,—the 'elevation' they call it.

12. As an abstract quality: Height, loftiness. **a.** *lit.* Of a building, etc. **b.** *fig.* Of literary style: Grandeur, dignity; formerly also in *pl.*, instances of elevation. **c.** *fig.* Of character and sentiments: Nobleness, loftiness of tone.

a. *Mod.* A building of imposing elevation.

b. *a* **1639** WOTTON (J.) His style..wanted a little elevation. **1716–8** LADY M. W. MONTAGUE *Lett.* I. xxxiv. 126 The elevation of an expression in an ancient author. **1750** JOHNSON *Rambl.* No. 1 ¶6 Some [epic poets] that imagined themselves intitled..to elevations not allowed in common life. **1871** MORLEY *Voltaire* (1886) 134 A return to..the classic form, its dignity, elevation, and severity.

c. *a* **1680** GLANVILL *Serm.* iii. (R.) They..pitied the poor and carnal world..all that were not of their conceited pitch and elevation. **1751** JOHNSON *Rambl.* No. 87 ¶7 When nothing is necessary to elevation but detection of the follies of others. **1868** LECKY *Europ. Mor.* II. i. 72 Elevation of character constituted the Roman ideal of perfection. **1880** MCCARTHY *Own Times* III. xlvi. 407 His character was somewhat wanting in the dignity of moral elevation.

elevational (ɛlɪˈveɪʃənəl), *a.* [f. ELEVATION + -AL[1].] Of or pertaining to elevation. Cf. ELEVATION 11.

1928 *Daily Tel.* 13 Nov. 10/6 The use of a model for an intended building was, he considered, far superior to any plan or elevational drawing. **1948** *Archit. Rev.* CIV. 238 (*caption*) The illustration shows an elevational view. **1970** H. BRAUN *Parish Churches* i. 16 In the same way that elevational architecture had been examined from the pictorial aspect, the plan came to be investigated from the point of view of its accommodation.

elevator (ˈɛlɪveɪtə(r)). [a. L. *ēlevātor*, f. *ēlevā-re* to ELEVATE.] One who or that which elevates.

1. *Anat.* **a.** A muscle which raises or moves a limb or an organ.

1646 SIR T. BROWNE *Pseud. Ep.* IV. vii. 196 Being destitute of any motion, they conferre no reliefe unto the Agents or Elevators. **1746** PARSONS *Human Phys.* i. 17 The Elevator arises tendinous and fleshy from the Edge of the Foramen lacerum. **1748** HARTLEY *Observ. Man* I. ii. §1. 148 The Elevators of the lower Jaw. **1870** ROLLESTON *Anim. Life* 13 The main elevator of the humerus and the wing.

b. In insects, one of the two flat joints of the maxillary or labial feelers.

1826 KIRBY & SPENCE *Entomol.* III. 448 Thus in the hive bee and the humble bee the labials including the two flat joints or elevators have four joints.

2. *Surg.* 'An instrument for raising any depressed portions of bone, particularly of the skull. Also, an instrument used in Dentistry for the removal of stumps of teeth' (*Syd. Soc. Lex.*).

3. a. A machine used for raising corn or flour to an upper storey. **b.** *U.S.* A large building (containing one or more of these machines) used for the storage of grain. **c.** A machine used for raising hay or straw to the top of the stack. Also, an appendage to a thrashing machine. **d.** chiefly *N. Amer.* A lift, hoist, ascending chamber. Also *attrib.*

1787 in *Rep. Comm. Pat. 1848* (U.S.) (1849) 574 One of which [machines], denominated by the said Oliver Evans an elevator, is calculated by its own motion to hoist the wheat or grain from the lower floor..to the upper loft of such mill. **1799** I. WELD *Trav. N. Amer.* iii. 21 The elevators are inclosed in square wooden tubes. **1825** J. NICHOLSON *Operat. Mech.* 100 These elevators consist of a chain of buckets, or concave vessels..fixed at proper distances upon a leathern band, which goes round two wheels. **1853** *Harper's Mag.* VII. 130/2 The introduction of a steam elevator, by which an indolent, or fatigued, or aristocratic person may..be borne up..to the third, fourth, or fifth floor. **1862** TROLLOPE *N. Amer.* I. 248 An elevator is as ugly a monster as has been yet produced. **1862** J. WILSON *Farming* 161 A larger set of elevators is usually employed to carry up the roughs to the feeding board [in a thrashing machine]. **1872** M. E. HOLLEY *Betsy Bobbet* (1891) 295 She spoke up and says she, 'Here is the elevater, be carried up.' **1879** *Chicago Tribune* 8 May 8/4 As is the custom with elevator-boys— a reprehensible one it is too—the lad in charge of the elevator started it before closing the door. **1879** JEFFERIES *Wild Life in S.C.* 114 The new-fangled elevator carries up the hay by machinery from the waggon to the top. **1883** *Harper's Mag.* Jan. 275/1 He did not trust the elevator, but almost flew down the stairs. **1884** HOWELLS *ibid.* Dec. 118/1 The Elevator boy, pulling at the rope [says] 'We're not there yet'. **1884** *Lisbon* (Dakota) *Star* 10 Oct., A. H. Laughlin..has bought the store building..near the elevator. **1885** *Century Mag.* XXX. 579/1 With staircases and elevator-shafts which must remain open, [etc.]. **1887** *Contemp. Rev.* May 699 Extensive elevator Companies. **1890** *Congress. Rec.* 8123/2 On this list there are firemen, watchmen, elevator men. **1902** *Encycl. Brit.* XXVIII. 129/1 A..plunger, which..carries the elevator-cage on its upper end. *Ibid.* 130/2 The walls..of the elevator shaft. **1945** *Chicago Tribune* 26 Jan. 27/1 (Advt.), Elevator operator for office building. **1947** AUDEN *Age of Anxiety* (1948) ii. 47 When elevators raise blondes aloft to bachelor suites.

4. *Aeronautics.* **a.** An elevating screw. **b.** A control surface of an aeroplane (now always on the tailplane) used to change its angle of pitch.

1871 *English Mechanic* 27 Jan. 448/2 The side elevators would not only raise but poise the car. **1910** R. FERRIS *How it Flies* v. 83 The large elevator planes in front have been a distinctive feature of the Wright machine. *Ibid.* xx. 460 *Elevator*, a shorter name for the elevating planes or elevating rudder, used for directing the aeroplane upward or downward. **1911** *Reports & Mem.* (Adv. Comm. Aeronaut.) No. 59, 103 The most convenient arrangement of controls of elevator..might be investigated. **1915** G. BACON *All about Flying* 3 In monoplanes, of course, the elevator has always been in the tail. **1934** J. A. SINCLAIR *Airships in Peace & War* iv. 84, I had remained inside the control car with only the elevator-man and we both left the ship [*sc.* a zeppelin]. **1969** *Listener* 1 May 596/1 An elevator bracket broke.

5. ***Elevators***, a proprietary name for a make of shoe with a raised insole intended to make the wearer appear taller. Also (now generically) ***elevator shoe***. *U.S.*

1940 *Official Gaz.* (U.S. Patent Off.) 5 Mar. 28/1 Stone-Tarlow Co., Inc., Brockton, Mass... *Elevators*. For leather shoes. Claims use since Dec. 13, 1939. **1953** WODEHOUSE *Performing Flea* 165 Some are wearing elevator shoes. **1969** *Wall St. Jrnl.* 30 Sept. 1/1 He used to wear elevator shoes to increase his height. **1976** W. ALLEN *Without Feathers* 10 His ..elevator shoes, curiously enough, made him two inches shorter. **1984** *New Yorker* 9 Apr. 76/1 There are a lot of midgets in politics who run around in elevator shoes.

elevatory (ˈɛlɪveɪtərɪ), *a.* and *sb.* [f. ELEVATOR: see -ORY.]

A. *adj.* Of or pertaining to elevation, that tends to elevate.

1. *Geol.* Concerned in raising or tending to raise the crust of the earth.

1833 LYELL *Princ. Geol.* III. 117 The disturbing and dislocating force of the elevatory movements. **1847** H. MILLER *First Impr.* xi. (1861) 140 Should the time ever arrive when the elevatory agencies motionless and chill shall sleep within their profound depths. **1878** HUXLEY *Physiogr.* 205 Elevatory forces must have been at work.

2. In a non-material sense.

1851 RUSKIN *Mod. Paint.* II. III. I. xiv. §5 The moral feelings are thus elevatory of the mental faculties.

B. *sb.* = ELEVATOR 2 [as if ad. L. **ēlevātōrium*; so Fr. *élévatoire*, It. *elevatorio*].

1612 WOODALL *Surg. Mate* Wks. (1653) 91 If a depression of the Cranium be, strive with the elevatorie to raise it. **1758** J. S. tr. *Le Dran's Observ. Surg.* (1771) D d iij, *Vectis*, an Elevatory used to raise depress'd Bones. **1832** in WEBSTER; and in mod. Dicts.

†**e'leve.** *Obs.* as Eng. [a. Fr. *élève*, f. *élever* to bring up.] A pupil.

The Fr. word is occas. used when Fr. subjects are spoken of: e.g. 'He was an *élève* of the *Ecole Normale*.'

1736 BAILEY, An *Eleve*, a pupil or scholar educated under any one. **1769** HOPE in *Phil. Trans.* LIX. 241 *note*, Mr. James Robertson is an eleve of mine. **1807** J. HALL *Trav. Scotl.* I. 146 Dr. Hunter..the eleve of Lord Monboddo. **1829** *Gentl. Mag.* XCVII. II. 527 Their Eleves should have ..an excellent classical education.

eleven (ɪˈlɛv(ə)n), *a.* and *sb.* Forms: 1 endleofan, -lufon, -lyfon, -an, ellefne (*Northumb.* ællefne), 3–4 endlevene, -leve, -luve, 3–5 enleve(n(e, -levyn, (3 enlovene, 4 onlevene), elleve(n(e, -evin, -yven, (3 ællevene, eolleve), 5–7 elevyn, (5 eleivan), aleven, -eaven, -euyn, 5– eleven, (6 *Sc.* allevin, alewin, 9 *dial.* ellebn, eleeben, lebn). [Common Teutonic: OE. *ęndleofon* corresponds to OFris. *andlova*, *elleva*, OS. *elleban* (MDu. *elleven*, Du. *elf*), OHG. *einlif* (MHG. *eilf*, Ger. *elf*), ON. *ellifu* (Sw. *ellifva*, *elfva*, Da. *elleve*), Goth. *ainlif*:—OTeut. **ainlif-* f. **ain-* (shortened from **aino-*) ONE + *-lif-* of uncertain origin. Outside Teutonic the only analogous form is the Lith. *vënó-lika*, where *-lika* (answering in function to Eng. *-teen*) is the terminal element of all the numerals from 11 to 19.

The OE., OFris., OS., and ON. forms represent a type **ainlifun*, app. assimilated to **tehun* TEN. The theory that the ending is a variant of OTeut. **tehun*, Aryan **dekm* TEN, is now abandoned; some would derive it from the Aryan root **leiq* or from **leip* (both meaning to leave, to remain) so that *eleven* would mean 'one left' (after counting ten).]

The cardinal number next after ten, represented by the symbols 11 and xi.

A. *adj.*

1. In concord with a sb. expressed.

c **890** K. ÆLFRED *Bæda* v. xviii. (Bosw.) Osred ðæt rice hæfde endleofan wintra. *a* **1000** *Andreas* (Gr.) 664 Næs þær folces ma..Nemne ellefne orettmæcgas. *c* **1000** ÆLFRIC *Gen.* xxxii. 22 [Jacob] nam his wif mid hira endlufon sunum. *c* **1325** *Coer de L.* 2725 Onlevene thousand of our meyné. **1382** WYCLIF *Acts* i. 26 Mathi..was noumbrid to gidere with enlevene apostlis. **1393** LANGL. *P. Pl.* C. IV. 227 Thou hast hanged on myn hals elleuen tymes. *c* **1400** *Pol. Rel. & L. Poems* 216, I have had ther-to lechys aleven, and they gave me medysins all. *a* **1440** *Sir Degrev.* 342 More then enleve mele. **1480** CAXTON *Chron. Eng.* cii. 82 And this mysauenture dured enleuen yere and moo. **1552** LYNDESAY *Monarche* 4509 The ȝeir of oure Saluatioun Alewin hundreth and sax and fyftie. **1591** HORSEY *Trav.* (1857) 188 Aleaven of his..servants. **1594** SHAKS. *Rich. III*, III. vi. 6 Eleuen houres I haue spent to write it ouer. **1664** EVELYN *Kal. Hort.* (1729) 229 Nor the Height above ten or eleven [Feet] at most. **1796** BURKE *Regic. Peace* iii. Wks. VIII. 301 Eleven days they had the full use of Bantry Bay. **1887** RUSKIN in *Pall Mall G.* 2 Sept. 3/2 Humanity..had reduced itself to see no more than eleven eyes in a peacock's tail.

2. a. With ellipsis of sb., which may usually be supplied from the context. ***the Eleven***: *sc.* disciples; also, a body of executive officers at Athens.

c **1205** LAY. 14531 Bi tene & bi ælleuene [*c* **1275** enlouene]. *c* **1275** *O.E. Misc.* 55 He seyde to his apostles . hi weren elleouene. **1297** R. GLOUC. (1724) 298 In þe þousend ȝer of grace, and endleuene þerto. *a* **1300** *Cursor M.* 4119 An was eildest o þe elleuen. **1387** TREVISA *Higden* (Rolls) I. 343 Sex score and enleuene. **1591** GARRARD *Art Warre* 130 When they passe a leven or twelve they are not to be accompted an aray. **1611** BIBLE *Luke* xxiv. 33 And found the eleuen gathered together. **1814** BYRON *Juan* I. xlix, At six a charming child, and at eleven With all the promise of as fine a face. **1849** GROTE *Hist. Greece* V. II. lxii. 427 They were handed over to the magistrates called the Eleven.

b. *esp.* sc. *hours*: as *eleven o'clock*, etc.

1548 UDALL, etc., *Erasm. Par. Matt.* xx. 6 About a leuen of the clocke. **1602** SHAKS. *Ham.* I. ii. 252 Vpon the Platforme twixt eleuen and twelue Ile visit you. **1759** *Compl. Letter-Writer* (ed. 6) 227 The Ball continued its Briskness and vivacity..'till about Eleven. **1803** R. ANDERSON *Cumbrld. Ball.* 67 When the clock strack eleeben.

c. ***eleven o'clock*** (dial. and formerly in U.S.A.), ***eleven hours*** (Sc.), a refreshment or slight repast taken at about eleven o'clock.

1805 A. SCOTT *Poems* (1808) 120 At length, 'le'en hour's time brought the dame. **1808** JAMIESON, *Eleven-hours*, a luncheon; so called from the time that labourers or children get their meridian. **1845** S. JUDD *Margaret* II. i. 214 Men and boys were seen going to the tavern for their eleven o'clock. **1898** 'S. TYTLER' *Mrs. Carmichael's Goddesses* xv. 183, I was trying my 'prentice hand at sawing and hammering and polishing till my 'leven hours'. **1900** *Eng. Dial. Dict.* II. 247/2 *Eleven hours*,—*o'clock* or *o'clocks*.

B. as *sb.*

1. The abstract number eleven.

1398 TREVISA *Barth. De P.R.* IX. iv. (1495) 349 Thryes enleuen makyth thre and thyrty. **1547** BOORDE *Introd. Knowl.* 123 Nyne, ten, aleuyn, twelue.

2. A set of eleven persons; *esp.* a set of eleven players forming 'a side' at cricket or football.

1743 in T. Waghorn *Cricket Scores* (1899) 30 The above match was played in the Artillery Ground between the above elevens. *c* **1800** in *Etoniana* v. 95 The eleven of football and the eleven of cricket. **1885** *Truth* 28 May 836/2 Such a county should..produce a few bowlers to maintain the credit of its eleven.

†**3.** In phrase, ***by the elevens!*** (of uncertain origin). *Obs.*

1773 GOLDSM. *Stoops to Conq.* II. i, By the Elevens, my place is gone quite out of my head.

C. *Comb.*, as ***elevenfold*** adj. and adv.; **elevenpenny**, comb. form of *eleven pence*, as in **elevenpenny bit**, formerly, in the *U.S.*, a coin of the value of twelve and a half cents; = LEVY *sb.*²; **eleven-plus**, the age (between 11 and 12) at which pupils leave primary schools; also, an examination taken at the same stage before entering one of the various types of secondary schools; **eleven-pointer**, a stag whose horns show eleven points. Also **eleven-o'-clock** (see A. 2 b) used *attrib.* or as *adj.* in **eleven-o'-clock lady, eleven-o'-clock wind** (see quots.).

1557 RECORDE *Whetst.* B ij, Vndecupla 11 to 1: 22 to 2: 33 to 3, aleuenfolde. **1803** E. L. PEEL in *Longm. Mag.* Nov. 74 A grand eleven-pointer..standing out alone. **1807** C. W. JANSON *Stranger in Amer.* xiv. 186 Beggars will also stipulate with you as to the sum they expect to be given them—they will name a quarter of a dollar, a nine-penny or eleven penny bit. **1826** *New-Harmony Gaz.* 3 May 256/2 (Th.), There were many poor people that would have made the shirts for three elevenpenny bits apiece. **1859** [see LEVY *sb.*²]. **1879** PRIOR *Plant-n.*, Eleven o'clock lady, Fr. *dame d'onze heures*, from its waking up and opening its eyes so late in the day; the star of Bethlehem (*Ornithogalum umbellatum*, L.). **1888** *Pall Mall G.* 9 July 8/2 A..stiff breeze..called 'eleven o'clock wind'..that is to say, supposing the target to be marked like the dial of a clock, the wind would blow..in the direction of the figure 11. **1891** KIPLING *Light that Failed* ix. 182 The one-and-elevenpenny umbrella. **1937** E. GARNETT *Family from One End Street* iii. 27 The age known in state educational circles as 'eleven-plus' (that year of destiny for all elementary school children with any ambition). **1945** *Lancet* 30 June 823/1 A universal age of entry at 11+ and a leaving age of 16 will go far. **1957** *Listener* 21 Nov. 853/2 The so-called eleven plus examination. *Ibid.*, The most helpful book that has so far appeared on 'eleven plus'. **1958** *Economist* 12 Apr. 99/1 Labour..turns to the Rent Act, the block grant, the 'iniquitous eleven-plus'. **1959** I. & P. OPIE *Lore & Lang. Schoolch.* xi. 227 They [*sc.* children] are particularly conscientious about bringing charms to the 11-plus examination, the 'scholarship' as they call it, which determines whether they shall go on to a grammar school or to a secondary modern.

Hence **e'levens** (*dial.*), an eleven-o'-clock meal, a luncheon.

1849 W. & H. RAYNBIRD *Agric. Suffolk* vi. 296 The name 'fourzes' and 'elevens', given to these short periods of rest and refreshment, show when taken. **1865** W. WHITE *E. Eng.* II. 197, 'I commonly has a drop [of ale] for my elevens; but I can manage a pint o' a'ternoons besides.'

elevener (ɪ'lɛvənə(r)). [f. ELEVEN + -ER¹.]

1. An eleven-o'-clock meal, a luncheon.

1823 E. MOOR *Suffolk Words & Phr.* s.v. *Bever*, the *'levener*—this..is the interstitial *snack* between the *prime* and the next. **1875** PARISH *Sussex Dial*, *Elevener*, a luncheon.

2. One who takes a drink at 11 a.m. *rare*⁻¹. *U.S.*

1807 C. W. JANSON *Stranger in Amer.* xxii. 299, I know of no custom more destructive than that which is practised by slingers and eleveners.

elevenses (ɪ'lɛvənzɪz), *sb. pl.* [orig. *dial.* form of *elevens* s.v. ELEVEN *a.*] Elevens; light refreshment about 11 a.m.

1887 PARISH & SHAW *Dict. Kent. Dial.* 51 Elevenses. **1895** C. J. CORNISH *Wild Eng. Today* 243 The workmen rest for their 'elevenses' and 'fourses'. **1923** *Daily Mail* 30 July 6 The men at work with bare chests or enjoying their drink in the shade of the hedge at 'elevenses' or 'fourses' according to the hour. **1927** WODEHOUSE *Meet Mr. Mulliner* ii. 56 At eleven o'clock he has his 'elevenses', consisting of coffee, cream, more bread and more butter. **1930** T. THURSTON *Man in Black Hat* viii. 143 Charwomen..consuming what I am told they call their 'elevenses'. **1933** *Punch* 2 Aug. 124/2, I came upon him drinking his elevenses (these functions usually lasted from eleven-thirty to twelve—the time of his dinner-hour). **1947** I. BROWN *Say the Word* 17 'Elevenses' is middle-class and particularized, usually coffee and a biscuit at the hour named. **1951** *Lilliput* Sept.-Oct. 111/2 On the desk in front of him was a cup of coffee and some sandwiches. 'Elevenses,' he said.

†**e'leventeen.** *Obs. nonce-wd.* [f. ELEVEN + -TEEN.] Twenty-one.

16.. WITHER *Weakness*, Many giglets I have married seen Ere they forsooth could reach eleventeen.

eleventh (ɪ'lɛv(ə)nθ), *a.* and *sb.* Forms: α. 1 endlyfta, *Northumb.* ællefta, 3–4 enlefte, *north.* elleft. β. 1 endleofeða, 4 ellevefþe, 4–5 enleuenþ, -the, ellevend, -ent, -enþe, -ynd, -ynt, (4 allevenþe, elned, 5 aleffant), 6 elleventh, (ellewint, elevynth, aleventh, eleven, leventh, *Sc.* levint, 7 eleventh, 9 *dial.* elevent), 7– eleventh. [OE. *ęndlyfta, ællefta*, correspond to OFris. *andlofta, ellefta*, OS. *ellifto*, OHG. *einlifto* (MHG. *einlifte, eilfte*, mod.G. *elfte*), ON. *ellifte* (not recorded in Goth.):—OTeut. **ainlifton-* f. **ainlif-* ELEVEN + ordinal suffix f. OAryan *-to-*. As in the case of other numerals, the original word has been superseded (since 14th c.) by a new formation on the cardinal numeral + *-th* (after FOURTH), which is now the universal ordinal suffix. Certain forms in ME. and mod.Eng., following other analogies, have *-t* or *-d* instead of *-th*.]

A. *adj.*

1. a. That comes next in order to the tenth. ***eleventh hour***: the latest possible time, in allusion to the parable of the labourers (*Matt.* xx.); also ***eleventh-hour*** used attrib. or as adj.

971 *Blickl. Hom.* 93 Eall eorþe bið mid þeostrum oforþeaht æt þa endlyftan tid þæs dæges. *c* **1000** *Ags. Gosp.* Matt. xx. 6 Ða embe þa endlyftan tide he uteode. **1297** R. GLOUC. (1724) 414 Þe enlefte day of heruest. *a* **1300** *Cursor M.* 22627 Þe signe o þe dai elleft, It es na skil þat it be left. **1340** HAMPOLE *Pr. Consc.* 4798 Þe ellevend day men sal com out Of caves. **1398** TREVISA *Barth. De P.R.* IX. xix. (1495) 357 The enleuenth month is Nouembre. **1489** *Plumpton Corr.* 78 Aleffant day of moneth of March. **1513–75** *Diurn. Occurr.* (1833) 10 Wpoun the ellewint day of July, &c. **1551** RECORDE *Pathw. Knowl.* I. xvii, According vnto the eleuen conclusion. **1599** SHAKS. *Hen. V*, I. i. 2 In th' eleuenth yere of yᵉ last Kings reign. **1663** COWLEY *Verses & Ess.* (1669) 60 Come the eleventh Plague, rather than this should be. **1829** SOUTHEY *All for Love* I. xxiv, Though at the eleventh hour Thou hast come to serve our Prince of Power. **1870** ROSSETTI *Let.* 17 Mar. (1965) II. 820 But I am getting into that mistrustful state which 11th hour work is sure to engender. **1897** C. M. FLANDRAU *Harvard Episodes* 230 So, in response to John's eleventh-hour prayers, he did what he could. **1904** *Daily Chron.* 24 Oct. 5/4 An eleventh-hour alteration in the arrangements for the return of Queen Alexandra from Copenhagen. **1966** *Listener* 1 Dec. 810/2 To commit a boy to preparing for *either*..examination..deprives the eleventh-hour developer of a chance of an award.

b. with ellipsis of sb.

c **1325** *E.E. Allit. P.* B. 1013 Þe Iacyngh þe enleuenþe gent. **1340** *Ayenb.* 14 Þe enlefte is to leve þe lesnesse of zenne. *c* **1380** *Sir Ferumb.* 2845 Basyn was þe elleuefþe þat ȝe han slawe there. *c* **1400** *Apoll. Loll.* 78 Þe elleuynt. **1552** ABP. HAMILTON *Catech.* (1884) 51 The levint, quha presumis of thame self ony thing. **1588** A. KING tr. *Canisius' Catech.* 183 The ellewint is continence quhairby we abstein nocht only from meats, bot also from al vickednes. **1632** SANDERSON *12 Serm.* 101 At the eleventh.

2. ***eleventh part***: one of eleven equal parts into which a quantity may be divided.

1797 BURKE *Regic. Peace* Wks. VIII. 402 An increase.. from an eleventh to a twentieth part of the whole duty.

†**3.** quasi-*adv.* in the eleventh place, ELEVENTHLY.

1526 *Pilgr. Perf.* (W. de W.) 292 b, Elleuenth, they be mortifyed from all feares, scrupules, and euyll dedes.

B. *sb.* **1.** = *eleventh part*; see A. 2.

1557 RECORDE *Whetst.* B ij b, Sesquiundecima. 12 to 11: 24 to 22..|1 1/11| a leuenth more.

2. *Mus.* A note eleven diatonic degrees above or below a given note; also (usually) the interval between this and the given note, equivalent to an octave and a fourth; a chord containing two such notes.

1597 MORLEY *Introd. Mus.* 70 From Gam vt to D la sol re is a twelfe, although it seeme in common sence but an aleuenth. **1811** T. BUSBY *Dict. Mus.*, Eleventh, an interval consisting of ten conjunct degrees, or eleven diatonic sounds. **1880** GROVE *Dict. Mus.* I. 437 The chord of the dominant eleventh, when complete..is hardly likely to be found unabridged. *Ibid.* 438 [Some] theorists..repudiate the chords of the eleventh and thirteenth. **1934** C. LAMBERT *Music Ho!* i. 26 The ninths and elevenths and whole-tone chords that form the stock-in-trade of Debussy's early mannered style.

eleventhly (ɪ'lɛv(ə)nθlɪ), *adv.* [f. ELEVENTH *a.* + -LY².] In the eleventh place. Also quasi-*sb.*

1609 R. BARNERD *Faithf. Sheph.* 55 Eleventhly & lastly. **1648** D. JENKINS *Wks.* 39 Eleventhly, wee maintaine, etc. **1711** *Vind. Sacheverell* 85 We are now come to *Eleventhly*, these *Eleventhly's* and *Twelfthly's*, these false Stories.

elevi'ation, bad form of ALLEVIATION.

1543–4 *Act 35 Hen. VIII*, c. 12 To the eleuiation of parte of his great and inestimable charges.

elevon ('ɛlɪvɒn). *Aeronaut.* [f. ELEV(ATOR (sense 4 b) + AILER)ON.] The movable section of the trailing edge of a delta wing, so called because it fulfils the function of both aileron and elevator on the wing and tailplane of an aeroplane so equipped.

1945 *Sphere* 22 Sept. 358 (*caption*) Elevons. **1946** *Aircraft Recognition Jrnl.* Dec. 65/2 It is not absolutely necessary to have sweep-back in the flying wing's plan form, but it is useful because otherwise the 'elevons'..would have such poor leverage about the centre of gravity. **1948** *Jane's Aircraft* 21c/1 Longitudinal and lateral control by 'controllers' or 'elevons' which are hinged on each outer wing to serve as both elevators and ailerons. **1953** 'N. SHUTE' *In the Wet* ix. 301 He could see the four engines, the elevons, the flaps, the long line of the fuselage.

elf (ɛlf), *sb.*¹ Forms: 1 ælf, ylf (app. recorded only in pl. ylfe), 3 alve, 5 alfe, 5–7 elfe, 4– elf. *Plural* elves: 1 ylfe, 3 alven, 6–7 elfes, *Sc.* elvis, 8 elfs, 6– elves. See also ELVEN, AUF, OAF¹. [OE. *ælf* str. masc. = OHG. *alp* (MHG., mod.G. *alp* nightmare, ON. *álfr* (Da. *alf*) elf:—OTeut. **albo-z*; a parallel type **albi-z* (cf. Sw. *elf*, Da. *elv*) appears in late WSax. **ylf* (found in pl. *ylfe*:—**ięlfe*) = Mercian, Kent. **ęlf*, Northumb. **ælf*, one or other of which is represented in the mod. word. (The mod.G. *elf* is believed to be adopted from Eng.; MHG. had *elbe* a female elf.)

Some have compared the Teut. word with the Skr. *ṛbhu*, the name given to the three genii of the seasons in Hindu mythology.]

1. *Mythol.* **a.** The name of a class of supernatural beings, in early Teutonic belief supposed to possess formidable magical powers, exercised variously for the benefit or the injury of mankind.

They were believed to be of dwarfish form, to produce diseases of various kinds, to act as *incubi* and *succubi*, to cause nightmares, and to steal children, substituting changelings in their place. The Teutonic belief in elves is probably the main source of the mediæval superstition respecting fairies, which, however, includes elements not of Teutonic origin; in general the Romanic word denotes a being of less terrible and more playful character than the 'elf' as originally conceived. In mod. literature, *elf* is a mere synonym of FAIRY, which has to a great extent superseded it even in dialects. Originally *elf* was masculine, ELVEN feminine; but in 13th and 14th c. the two seem to have been used indifferently of both sexes. In mod. use *elf* chiefly, though not always, denotes a male fairy.

Beowulf 112 (Gr.) Fram þanon untydras ealle onwocon eotenas and ylfe. *c* **1000** *Sax. Leechd.* II. 296 Wið ælfe and wiþ uncuþum fidsan gnið myrran on win. *c* **1205** LAY. 19256 Sone swa he com an eorðe: aluen hine iuengen. *c* **1386** CHAUCER *Man Lawes T.* 656 The mooder was an elf by aventure. **1426** AUDELAY *Poems* 77 (Mätz.) Alfe Rofyn begon to rug. *c* **1460** *Towneley Myst.* (Mätz.) He was takyn with an elfe. **1513** DOUGLAS *Æneis* VIII. vi. 7 Wyth Nymphis and Favnis apoun euery syde, Quhilk fairfolkis, or than elvis, clepyng we. **1579** E. K. in *Spenser's Sheph. Cal.* June 25 *Gloss.*, For Guelfes and Gibelines, we say Elfes & Goblins. **1610** SHAKS. *Temp.* v. i. 33 Ye Elves of hils, brooks, standing lakes and groues. **1635** HERRICK *Hesper.* (1869) II. App. 477 Come follow, follow me You fairie elves that be. **1700** DRYDEN *Wife Bath's T.* 3 The King of elfs.. Gamboll'd on heaths. **1712–4** POPE *Rape Lock* I. 33 Airy elves by moonlight shadow seen. **1866** KINGSLEY *Herew.* xv. 193 You are an elf and a goddess. **1875** B. TAYLOR *Faust* I. i, Then the craft of elves propitious Hastes to help where help it can.

†**b.** Sometimes distinguished from a 'fairy': (*a*) as an inferior or subject species; (*b*) as a more malignant being, an 'imp', 'demon'; also *fig.* *Obs.*

1587 M. GROVE *Pelops & Hipp.* (1878) 75 To exercise your selfe In feates of armes, thereby to shun of loytring loue the elfe. *a* **1593** H. SMITH *Wks.* 1867 II. 483 Frenzies, furies (wayward elves): What need ye call for whip or scourge? **1623** J. ABBOTT *Force Contrition* in Farr's *S.P. Jas. I* (1848) 353 The raine which this detested elfe must drowne Must from aboue..come downe. *a* **1628** F. GREVILLE *Mustapha, 3rd Chorus*, What means..This finite Elfe of mans vaine acts and errors? **1651** HOBBES *Leviath.* (1839) 699 When the fairies are displeased with any body, they are said to send their elves, to pinch them. *a* **1700** DRYDEN (J.) That we may angels seem, we paint them elves.

2. *transf.* **a.** (See quot.)

1651 HOBBES *Leviath.* (1839) 699 The fairies..are said to take young children..and to change them into natural fools, which common people do therefore call elves, and are apt to mischief.

b. A tricksy, mischievous, sometimes a spiteful and malicious creature. ***to play the elf***: to act elfishly, maliciously.

a **1553** UDALL *Royster D.* III. iii. (1869) 46 Women be all such madde pieuishe elues. **1613** *Uncasing of Machiav.* 25 For never it was Ape but plaide the Elfe. **1740** SOMERVILLE *Hobbinol* III. (1749) 174 This other Elf, in ev'ry Art Of smiling Fraud, in ev'ry treach'rous Leer, The very Hobbinol! **1800** BLOOMFIELD *Farmer's Boy, Summer* 243 Happy the man that foils an envious elf, Using the darts of spleen to serve himself. **1820** SCOTT *Abbot* iv, Stray elf of a page.

3. *transf.* A diminutive being. **a.** A dwarf, mannikin; hence as *adj.* (quots. 1710, 1725).

1530 PALSGR. 216/2 Elfe or dwarf, *nain.* **1547** SALESBURY *Welsh Dict.*, *Nar*, an elfe. **1710** *Street Robberies Consid.* *Elf*, little. **1725** *New Cant. Dict.*, *Elf*, little. *a* **1763** SHENSTONE (J.), He..Wisheth, poor starving elf, his paper-kite may fly. **17..** *Seven Wise Men* in R. Bell *Hist. Eng.* (1840) X. vii. 143 *note*, The prince..Laughed at the merry elf; Rejoiced to see within his court One shorter than himself. **1840–5** BARHAM *Ingol. Leg.* (1877) 102 As a muscular Giant would handle an elf.

b. Applied to a child (chiefly with some notion of 2 b), to a small animal or insect.

1573 TUSSER *Husb.* (1878) 59 Looke to thy cattle, Serue yoong poore elues alone by themselues. **1660** J. M[ILTON] in H. Morley *King and Commons* (1868) So the little wanton elf [a bee] Most gloriously enshrined itself [in amber]. **1786** BURNS *Despondency*, Ye tiny elves that guiltless sport. **1824** MISS MITFORD *Village* Ser. I. (1863) 15 His own pretty little boys, and two or three other four-year-old elves. **1886** G. ALLEN *Kalee's Shrine* xii. 128 Herons..intent on the quick pursuit of the elusive elves in the stream below.

†**4.** By Spenser applied to the knights of his allegorical 'faerie land'.

1596 SPENSER *F.Q.* I. i. 17 Which when the valiant Elfe perceiu'd. *Ibid.* I. v. 11 Goe, caytive Elfe.

5. In a vague depreciatory sense, 'a (poor) creature', 'a (poor, pious) soul', 'a (poor) devil'.

1573 TUSSER *Husb.* (1878) 208 Like worldly elfe, to moile and toile. **1703** DE FOE *Ref. Mann.* Misc. 69 Magistrates, like Pious Elves, Let none be Drunk a Sundays but themselves. *a* **1849** HOR. SMITH *Addr. Mummy* viii, Still silent, uncommunicative elf.

6. *Comb.* **a.** appositive, as *elf-child, -girl, -knight, -lady, -woman*; **b.** attributive, as *elf-castle, -craft, -dance, -flame, -flower, -folk, -friend, -horn, -house, -key, -kingdom, -land, -light, -rod, -speech, -wing*; *elf-like* adj. Also **elf-arrow, -bolt**, a flint arrowhead (see ELF-SHOT); also, a belemnite; **elf-bore**, a hole in a piece of wood, out of which a knot has dropped or been driven; †**elf-cake**, an enlargement of the spleen attributed to the agency of elves (cf. AGUE-CAKE); **elf-cup**, a small stone perforated by friction at a waterfall; **elf-dart** = ELF-SHOT 1; **elf-dock**, a

name of the Elecampane; **elf-fire**, *ignis fatuus*, Will o' the wisp; **elf-god**, Cupid; **elf-knot** = ELF-LOCK; **elf-queen**, queen of the fairies; †**elf-skin**, a man of shrivelled and shrunken form; **elf-stone** = ELF-SHOT 2; **elf-stricken, -struck** *ppl. a.*, bewitched; also **elf-striking** *vbl. sb.*; **elf-taken** *ppl. a.* (in quot. *elfe y-take*), bewitched by elves; **elf-twisted** *ppl. a.*, twisted or gnarled by elves; **elf-wort** = *elf-dock*. Also ELF-LOCK, -SHOOT, -SHOT.

1590 in Pitcairn *Crim. Trials* I. 198 Thow directit George Cuik to twa wemen..for ane *elf-arrow-heid. **1679** PLOT *Staffordsh.* (1686) 396 These..they there [at Aberdeen] call Elf-Arrows. **1796** MORSE *Amer. Geog.* II. 151 The stones which the country people call elf-arrow heads. **1855** SMEDLEY *Occult Sc.* 31 The triangular flints, Belemnites, so numerous in Scotland..are popularly termed Elf arrows. **1773** JOHNSON *Journ. West. Isl.* Wks. 1806 IX. 208 The stone heads of arrows..The people call them *elf-bolts. **1883** G. ALLEN *Col. Clout's Gard.* xxxix. 223 The neolithic arrows came to be regarded as elf-bolts. **1814** *Northern Antiq.* 404 (Jam.) If you were to look through an *elf-bore in wood. **1579** LANGHAM *Gard. Health* (1633) 2 To heale the *elfe cake and hardnesse of the side. **1586** LUPTON *1000 Notable Th.* (1675) 157 The hardness of the side called the Elfcake. **1884** CHILD *Ballads* II. §37. 321/2 After some description of the life at the *elf-castle. **1856** R. VAUGHAN *Mystics* (1860) II. 74 When the *Elf-children scatter gold-dust on the ground. **1919** W. DE LA MARE *Flora* 5 Lovely as *elf-craft. **1810** CROMEK *Rem. Nithsdale Song* 290 (Jam.) *Elf-cups were placed under stabledoors..as a safeguard against witchcraft. **1884** CHILD *Ballads* II. §42. 375/1 Why are you so pale, as if you had been in an *elf-dance? **1879** PRIOR *Plant-n.*, **Elf-Dock*, the elecampane, from its broad leaves called a dock. **1855** SMEDLEY *Occult Sc.* 31 The 'Ignis fatuus' has been named '*Elf fire'. **1884** CHILD *Ballads* II. §42. 375/2 Olaf..has to make his way through the *elf-flame. **1919** W. DE LA MARE *Crossings* 47 A steeple hat bound round with *Elf flowers. **1922** —— *Down-adown-derry* 12, I saw from concealment a company of *elf-folk. **1937** TOLKIEN *Hobbit* iii. 62 The master of the house was an *elf-friend. **1871** ROSSETTI *Poems* 9 Poets' fancies all are there: There the *Elf-girls flood with wings Valleys full of plaintive air. **1859** TENNYSON *Vivien* 98, I saw the little *elf-god eyeless once In Arthur's arras hall at Camelot. **1884** CHILD *Ballads* II. §41. 360/1 Lady Isabel..hears an *elf-horn. *Ibid.* §42. 375/1 He rides to the hills and comes to an *elf-house. **1924** R. GRAVES *Mock Beggar Hall* 78 The *elf-key at the rainbow's rise. **1954** TOLKIEN *Fellowship of Ring* I. xi. 203 A story of the *Elf-kingdoms. **1884** CHILD *Ballads* I. §4. 23/1 An *elf-knight, by blowing his horn, inspires Lady Isabel with love-longing. **1824** HEBER *Jrnl.* II. xxii. 416 Ghastly Yogis, with their hair in *elf knots. **1884** CHILD *Ballads* II. §37. 320/1 The *elf-lady's costume and equipment. **1483** *Cath. Angl.* 113 *Elfe lande. **1847** TENNYSON *Princ.* III. 357 O sweet and far from cliff and scar, The horns of elfland faintly blowing. **1913** W. DE LA MARE *Peacock Pie* 172 *Elf-light, bat-light, Touchwood-light and toad-light. **1583** STANYHURST *Aeneis* III. (Arb.) 80 Shee swowns, and after long pausing thus she sayd *elflyke. **1841** LYTTON *Night & Morn.* I. vi. I. 65 His..hair hung elf-like and matted down his cheeks. *c* **1386** CHAUCER *Wyf Bathes T.* 860 The *elf-queen, with hir joly compaignye. **1884** CHILD *Ballads* II. §41. 362/2 He strikes her with an *elf-rod. **1596** SHAKS. *1 Hen. IV*, II. iv. 270 Away..you *Elfe-skin. **1955** TOLKIEN *Return of King* App. F 409 Fragments of *Elf-speech. **1778** *Phil. Surv. S. Irel.* 281, I have seen one of those *elf-stones. **1825** SCOTT *Betrothed* (1860) 290 He looks as if he were *elf-stricken. **1699** E. LHWYD in *Phil. Trans.* XXVIII. 99 Some on May Day put them into a Tub of Water, and besprinkle all their Cattle with that Water, to prevent being *Elf-struck, bewitch'd, &c. *Ibid.*, As to this *Elf-stricking, their Opinion is, that the Fairies..do sometimes carry away Men in the Air. *a* **1500** *MS.* in *Promp. Parv.* 138 *note*, A chylde that ys *elfe y-take..may nat broke hys mete. **1885** *Chamb. Jrnl.* 371 Lo—instead of the Hunter in Green, there was only a brown withered twig, so *elf-twisted and dry. **1929** BLUNDEN *Near & Far* 49 *Elf-wings set out on visit and patrol. **1884** CHILD *Ballads* II. §29. 259/1 Three *elf-women had been not less than fifteen years in weaving it. **1878** BRITTEN & HOLL., *Elfwort, *Inula Helenium*.

elf, *sb.*[2] *S. Afr.* Also elft. [Afrikaans, f. Du. *elft* shad.] The spiny-finned sea-fish *Pomatomus saltator*.

1731 G. MEDLEY tr. *Kolben's Pres. State Cape G. Hope* II. 190 In the Table-Bay, and in Bay-Falzo, is caught a Sort of Fish the Dutch call Elft. The Elft is Three Quarters of a Yard long or more; and is scal'd much like a Herring. **1902** *Trans. S. Afr. Philos. Soc.* XI. 215 The Elf (*Temnodon saltator*), which somewhat resembles the Elft (*Clupea alosa*) of Holland, though the two are by no means scientifically related. **1947** K. H. BARNARD *Pict. Guide S. Afr. Fishes* III. 108 The Elf (*Pomatomus saltator*)..known in Natal as the Shad (quite different, of course, from the true Shad of the Herring family), and in other parts of the world as the Bluefish, Skipjack, Tailer, etc. **1949** *Cape Times* 22 Nov. 13/6 Three elft..have been landed by..anglers.

†**elf**, *v. Obs. rare*[−1]. [f. ELF *sb.*[1]] *trans.* To tangle or twist (hair) as an elf might do.

1605 SHAKS. *Lear* II. iii. 10 Ile..elfe all my haires in knots. **1721–1800** BAILEY, To Elfe the Hair, to tie it up in Knots or Ringlets.

†**elfayde.** *Obs.* Some kind of animal.

?*a* **1400** *Morte Arth.* 2288 Elfaydes, and Arrabys, and olyfauntez noble.

elfhood ('ɛlfhʊd). [f. ELF + -HOOD.] The state of being an elf.

1837 CARLYLE *Fr. Rev.* (1857) I. I. II. vi. 39 Little elf, or imp..with its withered air of..completed elf-hood.

'elfic, *a. rare.* [f. ELF + -IC.] Pertaining to an elf.

1872 HARDWICK *Trad. Lanc.* 231 They find it impossible to leave their husbands and resume their elfic nature. **1886** C. ROGERS *Soc. Life in Scotl.* III. 263 Fire had a potent influence against all elfic arts.

elfin ('ɛlfɪn), *a.* and *sb.* Also 6–7 elphyne, -in, ? 8 *Sc.* elfan. [Obscurely f. ELF *sb.*[1]; app. first used by Spenser, and perh. suggested to him by the phrase *elvene land* 'land of elves' (see ELVEN); the proper name Elphin in the Arthurian romances may possibly have influenced the form.]

A. *adj.*

1. Pertaining to elves; of elfish nature or origin.

1596 SPENSER *F.Q.* I. iv. 42 Him litle answerd th' angry Elfin knight. *Ibid.* I. x. 65 A Faery..her base Elfin brood there for thee left; Such, men do Chaungelings call. **1673** *Elphin Knight* i. in Child *Ballads* I. 15/1 The elphin knight sits on yon hill. **1742** COLLINS *Ode* iv. 4 His loveliest Elfin queen has blest. **1792** S. ROGERS *Pleas. Mem.* I. 117 Heroes ..Whose elfin prowess scaled the orchard-wall. **1808** SCOTT *Marm.* III. xxiv, The Elfin knight fell. **1820** KEATS *St. Agnes* xxxix, Hark! 'tis an elfin storm from faery land. **1828** CARLYLE *Misc.* (1857) I. 145 Elfin bells, when the Queen of Faery rides by moonlight.

2. *transf.* a. Diminutive, dwarfish. b. Fairy-like, full of strange charm.

1796–7 COLERIDGE *Poems* (1862) 28 The elfin tribe.. Released from school. **1873** DIXON *Two Queens* III. XVI. ii. 191 From childhood she had been a bright and elfin creature.

B. *sb.* 1. = ELF; also *attrib.*

1596 SPENSER *F.Q.* I. x. 60 And thou, faire ymp.. accompted Elfins sonne. **1807** CRABBE *Birth Flattery* 128 A wicked elphin, roved this land around. **1840** HOOD *Up Rhine* 69 Elfins..swarm in their romantic mythology. **1864** SKEAT *Uhland's Poems* 307 Darling, join the elfin-dance 'Neath the stars' and moonlight's glance.

†2. *Sc.* ? Elf-land.

1567–83 *Simpill Ballades* 210 Ane carling of the Quene of Phareis The ewill win geir to elphyne careis. *a* **1800** *Q. of Elfan's Nourice* iii. in Child *Ballads* II. 359/1 Waken, Queen of Elfan, An hear your nourice moan. *a* **1802** *Young Tamlane* vi. *ibid.* 508/1 The Queen o Elfin will gie a cry.

3. *transf.* A child.

1741 SHENSTONE *Schoolmistress* (1794), In those elfins' ears [she] would oft deplore The times. **1804** J. GRAHAME *Sabbath* (1839) 19/1 Then would he teach the elfins how to plait The rushy cap.

4. **elfin-tree**, a dwarfed tree found commonly in alpine regions; **elfin-wood**, a wood composed of such trees. Hence ***elfin timber, woodland.***

1903 W. R. FISHER tr. *Schimper's Plant-Geogr.* III. ii. 704 We contrast alpine grassland, alpine shrubland, and alpine desert with those of the lowlands, and retain for alpine forest merely the title elfin-wood. *Note*, 'Elfin-wood' and 'elfin-tree' are the terms introduced here as the equivalents of 'Krummholz'. *Ibid.* 705 Elfin-tree..is characterized by a short, gnarled, often oblique or horizontal stem, and long serpentine branches, which are bent in all directions. **1929** WEAVER & CLEMENTS *Plant Ecol.* xi. 257 The gnarled, sprawling, much-branched, elfin timber grows through the short summer of high altitudes. **1952** P. W. RICHARDS *Trop. Rain Forest* xvi. 346 In many places..the Montane Rain forest consists of dwarf crooked trees smothered with.. mosses; this very characteristic type of vegetation is often called..Elfin woodland.

Hence **'elfindom**, *nonce-wd.*, the estate of the elves.

1886 *Harper's Mag.* May 838 The traditional type of elfindom.

elfish ('ɛlfɪʃ), *a.* [f. ELF + -ISH.] Pertaining to elves; weird, spectral; of the nature of an elf, resembling an elf; tricksy, mischievous; formerly also of inanimate things, unmanageable, intractable. See ELVISH.

The older form ELVISH is still the more usual; but in some connexions *elfish* might be preferred on account of its more obvious relation to the primitive sb.

1542 UDALL *Erasm. Apoph.* 296 b, The Cypres tree..is elfishe and frowarde to spryng vp. **1583** STANYHURST *Aeneis* II. (Arb.) 68 The goast of verye Creüsa..mad her elfish aparance. *a* **1791** *Yng. Tom Line* xv. in Child *Ballads* II. 343/2 If my lord were an earthly knight, As he's an elfish grey. **1798** COLERIDGE *Anc. Mariner* IV. xii, The elfish light Fell off in hoary flakes. *a* **1802** *Yng. Tamlane* xxxii. in Child *Ballads* II. 354/2 Then would I never tire..In Elfish land to dwell. **1856** KANE *Arct. Expl.* I. xxviii. 372 Three men, Ootuniak, our elfish rogue Myouk, and a stranger. **1876** FREEMAN *Norm. Conq.* I. App. 770 The elfish names are mainly English.

elf-lock ('ɛlflɒk). In 6, 9 *pl.* elves-locks. [f. ELF + LOCK (of hair).] A tangled mass of hair, superstitiously attributed to the agency of elves, *esp.* Queen Mab: 'which it was not fortunate to disentangle' (Nares).

1592 SHAKS. *Rom. & Jul.* I. iv. 90 Elf-locks [**1623** elk-locks]. **1596** LODGE *Wits Miserie* (Halliw.), Curl'd and full of elves-locks. **1637** HEYWOOD *Dialogues* xvii. Wks. 1874 VI. 241 What though my thin and unkemb'd scattered haire Fell in long Elfe-locks from my scalpe, now bare? **1810** *Gentl. Mag.* LXXXVI. I. 214 Their hair remains matted and wreathed in elves-locks. **1848** KINGSLEY *Saint's Trag.* II. iv. 84 The listless craftsmen through their elf-locks scowled.

Hence **'elf-locked** *ppl. a.*, having elf-locks or tangled hair.

1647 R. STAPYLTON *Juvenal* VII. 83 The elfe-lockt fury all her snakes had shed. **1946** W. DE LA MARE *Traveller* 23 Plaiting cramped fingers in the elf-locked mane.

elfship ('ɛlfʃɪp). *nonce-wd.* [f. ELF + -SHIP; cf. *his lordship.*] The personality of an elf.

1812 W. TENNANT *Anster F.* VI. xxxix, The gown in which her elf-ship was arrayed.

'elf-shoot, *v. north. dial.* [f. ELF + SHOOT (after ELF-SHOT *sb.*).] *trans.* 'To shoot, as the vulgar suppose, with an elf-arrow.' (Jam.)

a **1758** RAMSAY *Poems* (1800) II. 66 Nine braw nowt were smoor'd, Three elf-shot were. **1778** *Phil. Surv. S. Irel.* 281 When these animals are seized with a certain disorder..they say they are elf-shot. **1806** *Falls of Clyde* 120 (Jam.) You'll a warlock turn..Elfshoot our Ky. **1872** HARDWICK *Trad. Lanc.* 138 It secures their cattle..from being elfshot by fairies, etc.

'elf-shot. [f. ELF *sb.*[1] + SHOT.]

1. 'Disease, supposed to be produced by the immediate agency of evil spirits' (Jam.).

[*c* **1000** *Ags. Leechd.* III. 54 Ylfa ȝescot.] **1681** GLANVILL *Sadducismus* (1726) 398 The sickness of William Black was an Elf-shot. **1841** BORROW *Zincali* (1843) I. I. viii. 148 Shepherds and cowherds are most exposed to the effects of the elf-shot.

2. *Sc.* A flint arrow-head; see quot.

1769 PENNANT *Tour Scotl.* (1774) 101 Elf-shots..are supposed to be weapons shot by fairies at cattle.

Elgarian (ɛl'gɑːrɪən, ɛl'gɛə-), *a.* and *sb.* [f. the name of the English composer Sir Edward William *Elgar* (1857–1934) + -IAN.]

A. *adj.* Of, pertaining to, or characteristic of Elgar or his works.

1906 E. NEWMAN *Elgar* i. 8 Those mannerisms of vocabulary and rhythm that so often enable us to mark a tune of his as being typically Elgarian. **1914** *Everyman* 13 Mar. 717/1 Taking Elgarian works at unauthorised *tempi*. **1942** *Scrutiny* X. 219 The noisy Elgarian climaxes. **1953** C. DAY LEWIS *Italian Visit* i. 21 A great Elgarian clash and bray of sunshine.

B. *sb.* One who admires or plays the music of Elgar.

1972 *Times* 23 Sept. 11/4 Elgarians will also note how he achieves flexibility. **1976** *Gramophone* Nov. 791/1 My disappointment..lies in the variation which for most Elgarians presents the core of the experience, 'Nimrod'. **1985** *Financial Times* 27 June 25/4 Throughout the concert Previn bore himself as a natural Elgarian.

†**'elger.** *Obs.* [? f. OE. *ǽl* eel + *gár* spear. Cf. Flem. *aalgeer, elger*, an eel-spear, of which the Eng. word may possibly be an adoption.] An eel-spear: see ALGERE.

c **1440** *Promp. Parv.* 138 Elyer, or elger, fyscharis instrument; *anguillaris, fuscina, fragidica, dentata*. *Ibid.* 186 Garfangyl, or elger: *anguillaria, anguillare*.

Elgin Marbles ('ɛlgɪn 'mɑːb(ə)lz). A collection of sculptures and architectural fragments from Athenian buildings, chiefly from the frieze and pediment of the Parthenon, which were collected, transported to England, and sold in 1816 to the British Government by Thomas Bruce, 7th Earl of *Elgin* (1766–1841).

1809 B. R. HAYDON *Diary* Nov. (1960) I. 95 Mengs said fifty years ago, that perhaps the statues they then possessed were not the works the Ancients accounted their best, and had Mengs been happy enough to see the Elgin Marbles, he would have been convinced of the truth of his conjecture. **1816** *Rep. Sel. Comm. Earl of Elgin's Collection* (*Parl. Papers* III) 14 In what proportion the state of mutilation in which the *Elgin* marbles are left, and above all the corrosion of much of the surface by weather reduce their value, it is difficult precisely to ascertain. **1817** KEATS (*title*) On seeing the Elgin Marbles for the first time. **1926** S. T. WARNER *Lolly Willowes* II. 93 He admitted that there were no wigs in the Elgin Marbles. **1967** W. ST.CLAIR *Lord Elgin & Marbles* xxiv. 272 Ever since Mr. Hugh Hammersley's motion in the House of Commons in 1816 that the Elgin Marbles should be held in trust and returned to Greece, the question of their possible return has been a political issue.

elhi ('ɛlhaɪ, ɛl'haɪ), *a. N. Amer. Educ.* [f. EL(EMENTARY *a.* + HI(GH SCHOOL.] Of or pertaining to educational publishing for students of elementary to high-school level; also of a student, etc., for which such material is intended.

1959 *Publisher's Weekly* 18 May 17/2 In moves to meet economic and ideological threats to textbooks, each section of the Institute—elhi (elementary and high school), college and reference—voted expanded budgets for public relations and other projects. **1970** *Wall St. Transcript* 28 Sept. 21839/1, I would also avoid making new commitments in the El-hi school publishing area at this time. **1975** *Publishers Weekly* 8 Sept. 40/2 [A book] designed for the adult general reader and the elhi student. **1984** *Defining Curriculum* (Amer. Educ. Research Assoc.) 2 The most reliable set of figures on Canadian elhi publishing has been provided by Pepperwood Consultants.

eli, var. of ELE oil. *Obs.*

eliad, obs. var. of OEILLADE, glance.

Elian ('iːlɪən), *a.* Pertaining to or characteristic of the *Essays of Elia* (1823), or their author, Charles Lamb (1775–1834). So **'Elian** *sb.*, an admirer of 'Elia'. Also **Eliaism** ('iːlɪəɪz(ə)m), a characteristically Elian essay.

1854 PATMORE *Friends & Acq.* I. 99 Lamb, in his exquisite Eliaism, 'Blakesmoor in H—— shire'. **1903** in *Dobell's Catal.* June 31/2 It is a comfort to think that there are so

many good and true Elians in the world. **1905** *Athenæum* 3 June 681/1 Many of the new letters are of no literary account; perhaps a score have the true Elian *cachet*. **1923** *Times Lit. Suppl.* 23 Aug. 555/2 Mr. Tillyard renounces all claims to satisfying 'every Elian'. **1929** *Daily Express* 3 Jan. 8/5 The Elian Chinaman's device for roasting pork.

eliasite (ɪ'laɪəsaɪt). *Min.* [f. *Elias*, name of a mine at Joachimsthal.] Hydrous oxide of uranium, of a brown colour and resin-like appearance.

1852 SHEPARD *Min.* 266 Eliasite occurs in flattened pieces half an inch thick. **1880** DANA *Min.* §209 Eliasite. In amorphous masses more or less resinlike in aspect, or like gum.

†**eli'bation.** *Obs.*—⁰ [as if ad. L. **ēlībātiōnem* f. *ē* out + *lībāre* to pour out a libation.] A tasting or offering sacrifices.

1656 in BLOUNT. **1721–1731** in BAILEY.

†**e'liciate,** *v. Obs. rare*—¹. [irreg. f. L. *ēlic-ĕre* to ELICIT + -ATE; cf. next.] *trans.* To draw out.

1651 BIGGS *New Disp.* 147 To eliciate all the purulent matter at once out of an Aposteme, is not good.

†**e'licient,** *a. Obs. rare*—¹. [ad. L. *ēlicient-em*, pr. pple. of *ēlic-ĕre* to ELICIT.] That performs an 'elicit act'. Cf. ELICIT *a.*

1617 COLLINS *Def. Bp. Ely* II. ix. 359 It springs from the vertue of religion in the mind of him that yeilds it, as the original of his act, & yet imperant only, not elicient; dirigent, not exequent, as your School-men loue to speak.

†**elicit** (ɪ'lɪsɪt), *a. Philos. Obs.* [ad. L. *ēlicitus*, pa. pple. of *ēlicĕre* to draw forth.]

Of an act: Evolved immediately from an active power or quality; opposed to *imperate*.

The '*elicit acts*' of the will are its internal acts (i.e. the volitions themselves); its 'imperate acts' are the external acts 'commanded' by it. In *Ethics*, the 'elicit acts' of a particular virtue are those essentially implied in its definition; its 'imperate acts' are those which it may under peculiar circumstances require.

1624 F. WHITE *Repl. Fisher* 544 Satisfaction sometimes importeth all the actions elicite or imperate, which a sinner must performe. **1646** S. BOLTON *Arraignm. Err.* 314 Not.. the..elicite acts of conscience, but the imperate, commanded and externall acts. **1660** JER. TAYLOR *Duct. Dubit.* II. iii. §6 I. 411 The imperate acts..of the Vertue of one Commandment must not contradict the elicite acts of another. **1665** GLANVILL *Sceps. Sci.* 26 Experience..attests that our Wills determine..our corporeal motions..What else means the distinction of the Schools of actions imperate and elicit? **1693** G. FIRMIN *Rev. Mr. Davis' Vind.* i. 9 Can the Elicite Act of the Will be forced, and yet the Essence of the Will be preserved? **1751** CHAMBERS *Cycl.* s.v. *Will.*

elicit (ɪ'lɪsɪt), *v.* Also 7–8 elicite. [f. L. *ēlicit-* ppl. stem of *ēlicĕre*: see prec.]

1. *trans.* To draw forth (what is latent or potential) into sensible existence. Also *fig.*

1641 J. JACKSON *True Evang. T.* III. 178 The former method, of shewing how to elicite..the five-fold profit of Doctrine, Redargution, Correction, Instruction, and Consolation. **1647** H. MORE *Poems* 138 And when he hath that life elicited. **1677** HALE *Prim. Orig. Man.* I. iii. 76 Which seminal Principle is..derived and elicited from the Plant or Animal. **1791** COWPER *Iliad* XIII. 503 Elicited a tinkling sound. **1837** J. H. NEWMAN *Proph. Office Ch.* 157 They elicit..the innate sense of right and wrong. **1853** ROBERTSON *Serm.* Ser. III. x. 127 A corrupt heart elicits in an hour all that is bad in us. **1860** ADLER *Fauriel's Prov. Poetry* xii. 251 Having elicited sparks from two flints he lighted a large fire. **1877** L. MORRIS *Epic Hades* II. 92 Only suffering ..can elicit The perfumes of the soul.

2. To bring out, educe (principles, truths, etc.) *from* the data in which they are implied. Also, to extract, draw out (information) *from* a person by interrogation; sometimes with object clause introduced by *that*.

1677 HALE *Prim. Orig. Man.* I. i. 25 Although..the very same truths may be elicited. **1795** BURKE *Scarcity* Wks. VII. 382 Legislative acts..require the exactest detail..in order ..to elicit principles. **1845** J. H. NEWMAN *Ess. Develop.* 402 The pressure of the controversy elicited..a truth. **1875** JOWETT *Plato* (ed. 2) V. 88 The matter in dispute should be clearly elicited from the contending parties. *Mod.* It was at length elicited that a bribe had been offered.

3. To draw forth, evoke (a response, manifestation, etc.) *from* a person.

1822 *Q. Rev.* XXVII. 92 He could not elicit a syllable from him on the subject. **1847** DISRAELI *Tancred* I. vi. (1871) 33 The exploits..elicited frequent bursts of laughter. **1860** TYNDALL *Glac.* I. §25. 188 The edge of one [fissure] which elicited other sentiments than those of admiration.

elicit, obs. pa. pple. of prec.

1671 *True Non-Conf.* 493 A..scant act of justice, elicit by a visible State-conveniency.

†**e'licitate,** *v. Obs.* [f. L. *ēlicit-* (see ELICIT *v.*) + -ATE.] = ELICIT.

1647 H. MORE *Poems* 239 Thus may a skilful man hid truth elicitate.

elicitation (ɪˌlɪsɪ'teɪʃən). [f. as prec. + -ATION.] The action of eliciting or drawing forth. (See quots. and cf. ELICIT *a.*)

1656 HOBBES *Liberty, Necess. & Ch.* (1841) 283 By elicitation, he understands a persuading or enticing with flattering words..That elicitation which the Schools intend, is a deducing of the power of the will into act. **1874** O. BROWNSON *Wks.* V. 573 That the elicitation of the act is not necessary..to salvation.

†**elicitive** (ɪ'lɪsɪtɪv), *a. Obs.* [as if ad. L. *ēlicitīvus*, f. *ēlicĕre*: see ELICIT and -IVE.] Pertaining to, of the nature of, 'elicit acts'; cf. ELICIT *a.*

1624 F. WHITE *Repl. Fisher* 323 None of these actions are the formall or elicitiue actions of Religion. **1660** STILLINGFL. *Iren.* I. ii. (1662) 41 The internal, formal, elicitive power of Order, concerning things in the Church.

elicitor (ɪ'lɪsɪtə(r)). [f. ELICIT *v.* + -OR.] One who elicits or draws forth.

1839 BAILEY *Festus* (1854) 137 The death dispeller, life elicitor. **1860** TRISTRAM *Gt. Sahara* xix. 320 The most skilful elicitor of statistics and traditions I ever met with.

elicumpany, obs. form of ELECAMPANE.

elide (ɪ'laɪd), *v.* Also 7 *Sc.* elid. [ad. L. *ēlīd-ĕre* to crush out, f. *ē* out + *lædĕre* to dash.]

†**1.** *trans.* To destroy, annihilate (the force of evidence). *Obs.*

1593 HOOKER *Eccl. Pol.* IV. iv, The force and strength of their arguments is elided. **1637** GILLESPIE *Eng. Pop. Cerem.* III. vii. 117 Which doth elude and elide all that which they alleadge. **1688** *Ess. Magistracy* in *Harl. Misc.* I. 9 They transfer a necessity of eliding them by clearer evidences.

b. *Law*, esp. *Sc.* To annul, do away with, quash, rebut. [So *elidere* in Roman Law.]

1597 *Acts Jas. VI.* (1816) 126 They wald haue elidit and stayit the samyn to haue bene put to ony probatioun. **1609** SKENE *Reg. Maj.* 115 He may..take away, elid, and exclude his [the persewer's] action, clame, and petition. **1754** ERSKINE *Princ. Sc. Law* (1809) 109 The concurring testimony of the husband and wife..is sufficient to elide this legal presumption. **1828** SCOTT *Hrt. Midl.* xii, Whilk uncertainty is sufficient to elide the conclusions of the libel. **1880** MUIRHEAD *Gaius* IV. §124 He may..elide the exception.

2. To strike out, suppress, pass over in silence.

1847 GROTE *Greece* II. xxx. IV. 153 Many of them made the still greater historical mistake of eliding these last four years altogether. **1851** SIR F. PALGRAVE *Norm. & Eng.* I. 750 Gibbon and Sismondi have elided these monarchs. **1870** BOWEN *Logic* (ed. 2) 133 The predesignations of quantity.. belonging to the Predicate are usually elided in expression.

3. *Gram.* To omit (a vowel, or syllable) in pronunciation. Hence **e'lided** *ppl. a.*

1796 *Brit. Crit.* (T.), The consonant belonging to the elided syllable. **1851** SIR F. PALGRAVE *Norm. & Eng.* I. 47 Some sounds elided, others exaggerated. **1867** A. J. ELLIS *E.E. Pronunc.* I. iv. 342 It must remain an undecided question whether Chaucer would or would not have elided the vowel.

elidible (ɪ'laɪdɪb(ə)l), *a.* [f. ELIDE *v.* + -IBLE.] That may be elided.

1878 G. CONWAY *Versification* 67 Theoretically, there is no interval between the elidible vowels of separate phrases.

†**'eligent.** *Obs.* [ad. L. *ēligent-em*, pr. pple. of *ēligĕre* to choose.] One who chooses; also, one who elects (to an office); = ELECTOR.

a **1670** HACKET *Abp. Williams* II. (1692) 201 In Polonia.. the eligents who make the King by their vote, are tyed fast by their oaths. **1688** NORRIS *Theory Love* (1694) 198 That which determines the Choice of the Eligent.

†**elight,** *v. Obs.* var. (? misprint) of ALIGHT.

1542 UDALL *Erasm. Apoph.* 200 a He had brought the horse backe again and had elighted down.

eligibility (ˌɛlɪdʒɪ'bɪlɪtɪ). [f. next; see -ITY.]

1. Fitness to be chosen or preferred.

1650 JER. TAYLOR *Holy Dying* VI. iii. (T.) Sickness hath some degrees of eligibility, at least by an after-choice. **1688** NORRIS *Theory Love* I. v. 57 Evill..must in order to eligibility be considered under the formality of good.

2. The condition of being eligible to an office.

1715 *Lond. Gaz.* No. 5387/1 The Imperial Ambassador solicited the Pope for a Brief of Eligibility to the Church of Munster. **1771** BURKE *Sp. Middx. Election* Wks. X. 69 The eligibility of persons to serve in Parliament. **1815** *Hist. Univ. Cambridge* I. 130 The eligibility to which [fellowships] is not subject to any..limitations. **1844** LD. BROUGHAM *Brit. Const.* vii. (1862) 95 Without any restriction whatever upon eligibility, except the period of infancy.

3. *concr.* in *pl.* Eligible courses of action; also, qualities that render (a man) eligible.

1660 JER. TAYLOR *Duct. Dubit.* IV. i. §1 II. 440 [God] hath set before us eligibilities in order to several ends which must either be wholly to no purpose, or..to evil purpose, or else ..to a very good purpose. **1865** CARLYLE *Fredk. Gt.* II. VII. i. 237 These are his eligibilities, recommending him at Berlin.

eligible ('ɛlɪdʒɪb(ə)l), *a.* Also 6 elygyble, 8 elegible. [a. Fr. *éligible*, as if ad. L. **ēligibilis* f. *ēligĕre* to choose.]

1. Fit or proper to be chosen (for an office or position). Const. *for*, †*of*, *to* (an office), *into* (a corporation).

1561 in W. H. TURNER *Select Rec. Oxford* 283 The Mayre shold be elygyble. **1604** EDMONDS *Observ. Cæsar's Comm.* 2 These foureteene were such as had serued fiue yeares in the warres, whereby they became eligible of that dignitie. **1655** FULLER *Ch. Hist.* III. 116 Four Essentials are requisite in the Persons Eligible into this Order. **1712** PRIDEAUX *Direct. Ch.-Wardens* (ed. 4) 44 All others are Elegible. **1789** *Constit. U.S.* ii. §1 No person except a natural born citizen..shall be eligible to the office of president. **1832** tr. *Sismondi's Ital. Rep.* vi. 135 They ordained that a general list of all the eligible citizens..should be formed. **1853** BRIGHT *Sp. India* 3 June, The natives of India were declared to be eligible to any office. **1863** H. COX *Instit.* I. viii. 124 A member of Parliament cannot, without vacation of his seat, be eligible for any other place.

2. †**a.** Subject to appointment by election. (*obs.*) **b.** (*nonce-use*). That can be elected (in a certain manner).

1660 R. COKE *Power & Subj.* 108 King Henry the First being requested by the Bishop of Rome to make them [the Bishops] eligible. **1739** *Selden's Laws Eng.* II. iv. 24 *note*, Both the Chancellor and other Great Officers of State were originally eligible by the Parliament. **1843** CARLYLE *Past & Pr.* (1858) 267 Elected and eligible by bribery.

3. Fit or deserving to be chosen or adopted.

1603 HOLLAND *Plutarch's Mor.* 1067 What greater contrariety can there be, as touching things eligible or refusable, than to say that, etc. **1655–60** STANLEY *Hist. Philos.* (1701) 192/1 That he conceiveth the Vertues to be eligible in theselves, is manifest. **1748** ANSON *Voy.* I. ix. (ed. 4) 120 The most eligible manner of doubling Cape Horn. **1851** CARLYLE *Sterling* I. xi, It was fixed upon as the eligiblest course. **1856** STANLEY *Sinai & Pal.* ii. (1858) 133 In this equality of mountains, all were alike eligible.

b. That is a matter of choice or preference.

1769 BURKE *Corr.* (1844) I. 181, I never looked upon this method of petition to the Crown as a thing eligible, but as a matter of urgent and disagreeable necessity. **1856** FERRIER *Inst. Metaph.* Introd. 71 Our selection of a new question, as our starting point, is not simply convenient, it is constraining: it is not eligible, but inevitable.

4. (A weakening of sense 3:) That one would choose or like: Desirable, acceptable, suitable.

1761 HUME *Hist. Eng.* II. xxiii. 75 The condition of the commons was nowise eligible. **1802** MAR. EDGEWORTH *Mor. T.* (1816) I. x. 82 He resolved..to seek some other more eligible situation. **1854** THACKERAY *Newcomes* 222 Not a very eligible admirer for darling Rosey. **1863** FAWCETT *Pol. Econ.* II. x. 282 It provides them with the most eligible investment for their savings. **1871** NAPHEYS *Prev. & Cure Dis.* I. v. 164 Eligible property.

5. quasi-*sb.* in *pl.* Eligible persons or things.

1844 *Calcutta Rev.* I. 10 There is no scarcity of brides; and merchants' clerks and Ensigns are eligibles. **1850** MRS. STOWE *Uncle Tom's C.* xv. 131 She had, of course, all the eligibles and non-eligibles of the other sex sighing at her feet. **1881** *Athenæum* 23 July 107/3 A choice of preference of eligibles.

Hence **'eligibly** *adv.*, in an eligible manner.

1815 JANE AUSTEN *Emma* II. ii. 138 Eligibly and happily settled.

eligibleness ('ɛlɪdʒɪb(ə)lnɪs). [f. ELIGIBLE *a.* + -NESS.] Eligibility.

1692 LOCKE *Third Letter for Toleration* i. 45 You leave the Matter very perplex'd, when you defend the Eligibleness of vesting a power in the Magistrates Hands. **1877** G. P. FISHER *Begin. Christ.* ii. 49 The right of suffrage, and eligibleness to office.

'eligug. *dial.* Also 7 elegug, helegug, 9 eligoog. [Derivation unknown: Prof. Rhys and the Rev. Silvan Evans do not know it as Welsh.] A local name (in South Pembrokeshire) applied to certain sea-birds, the Common Guillemot, the Puffin, and the Razor-bill.

1662 RAY *Three Itin.* III. 176 This name, elegug, some attribute to the puffin, and some to the guillem. **1676** WILLUGHBY *Ornithologia* 244 *Anas Artica* [i.e. the Puffin] Wallis meridionalibus circa Tenby oppidum Guldenhead, Bottle-nose & helegug. **1867** SMYTH *Sailor's Word-bk.*, *Eligugs*..called also razor-bills. **1883** *Harper's Mag.* Feb. 350/1 Gulls, razor-bills, and puffins—the birds called locally [in Pembroke] 'eligoogs'.

†**e'like,** *a.* and *adv. Obs.* Also 4–6 **elik, -yk, -yche.** A variant form of ALIKE q.v.

A. *adj.* Alike, equal.

1513 DOUGLAS *Æneis* VI. xiv. 50 Schynand with elyk [*v.r.* elik] armes paregate. **1555** *Scotch Acts, Mary* (1814) 507 That the elike lettre of naturalitie be grantit..to all..the said King of Frances subiectis..in the realme of Scotland.

b. Comb. **elike-dele** *adv.*, similarly; elikwis *adv.* = ALIKEWISE.

a **1400** *Alexander* 4157 þe entring of þe equinox it euire elike-dele kyndils. **1488** *Act. Audit* 113 (Jam.) The said Laurence is elik wiss bundin. **1495** *Acc. Ld. High Treas. Scot.* I. 268 Item to the portaris, elikwis..x. li.

B. *adv.*

a **1300** *Cursor M.* 9984 (Gött.) þat lasteþ euer elike [*v.r.* ilik, iliche, elyke] new. *Ibid.* 25106 þi will in erd be wroght elik. *a* **1400** *Ibid.* 18446 (Laud) There lyf is lastyng euyr elyche.

†**'elimate,** *v. Obs.*—⁰ [f. L. *ēlīmāt-* ppl. stem of *ēlīmāre*, f. *ē* out + *līma* a file.] *trans.* To file up; to polish.

1656 in BLOUNT *Glossogr.* **1736** in BAILEY. **1775** in ASH. **1847** in CRAIG; and in mod. Dicts.

†**eli'mation.** *Obs.*—⁰ [ad. L. *ēlīmātiōn-em*, f. *ēlīmāre*: see prec.] Filing up or polishing.

1678 in PHILLIPS. **1715** in KERSEY. **1721–1800** in BAILEY.

eliminability (ɪˌlɪmɪnə'bɪlɪtɪ). The property or quality of being eliminable.

1947 H. REICHENBACH *Elem. Symb. Logic* §13. 63 How is this statement compatible with the eliminability of the rule of replacement? **1957** P. SUPPES *Introd. Logic* viii. 154 We may now formalize the concept of eliminability. **1967** S. C. KLEENE *Math. Logic* §39. 219 The application of the eliminability theorem.

eliminable (ɪ'lɪmɪnəb(ə)l), *a.* [see ELIMINATE and -ABLE.] Capable of being eliminated.

1862 F. HALL *Hindu Philos. Syst.* 258 Its being eliminable by right apprehension, on the ground of its falseness, is thus established.

eliminant (ɪˈlɪmɪnənt), *a.* and *sb.* [ad. L. *ēlīminānt-em*, pr. pple. of *ēlīmināre*: see next.]

A. *adj.* Expulsive; having power to throw off by the excretions (*Syd. Soc. Lex.*).

1876 BARTHOLOW *Mat. Med.* (1879) 262 The curative power..is..due to its eliminant action on the mucous and cutaneous surfaces.

B. *sb.* **1.** The result of eliminating *n* variables between *n* homogeneous equations of any degree.

1881 BURNSIDE & PANTON *Theor. Equations* xiii. 140 The quantity R is..called their Resultant or Eliminant. **1885** *Athenæum* 11 Apr. 477/3 Eliminants and Associated Roots.

2. *Med.* An agent which eliminates deleterious matter from the system.

1887 C. A. MOLONEY *Sk. Forestry W. Afr.* 417 Recommended as an eliminant in malignant cholera. **1907** *Practitioner* Oct. 557 Stoeltzner states that the intestinal mucosa acts both as absorbent and eliminant of lime-salts. **1922** *Daily Mail* 15 Nov. 12 (Advt.), It consists of uric acid solvents and eliminants which exert an irresistible solvent action upon uric acid.

eliminate (ɪˈlɪmɪneɪt), *v.* [f. L. *ēlīmināt-* ppl. stem of *ēlīmināre* to thrust out of doors, expel, f. *ē* out of + *līmen*, *līmin-is*, threshold.]

1. *trans.* To thrust out of doors, expel. Now somewhat ***humorous***.

1568 ABP. PARKER *Lett.* (1852) 314 To help eliminate out of his [God's] house this offendicle. **1610** G. FLETCHER *Christ's Vict.* To Rdr., The secound sorte thearfore, that eliminate Poets out of their citie gates. **1848** THACKERAY *Van. Fair* xiv, From which [room], with the most engaging politeness, she eliminated poor Ferkin.

†**b.** To carry out of doors, divulge (secrets). *Obs.* [Cf. Hor. *Ep.* I. v. 5.]

1608 TUVIL *Essayes* 115. *a* **1619** FOTHERBY *Atheom.* I. x. §4 (1622) 100 He did eliminate, and divulge the mysteries of their gods. **1618** HALES *Gold. Rem.* (1673) II. 64 Whatsoever ..we do, is..presently eliminated and carried to them.

†**c.** To release, set at liberty. *Obs. rare*⁻¹.

1742 YOUNG *Nt. Th.* IX. 588 Eliminate my spirit, give it range Through provinces of thought yet unexplor'd.

†**2.** To pass the threshold of, come out of. *rare*⁻¹.

a **1658** LOVELACE *Snail* in *Poems* (1864) 209 Th'art hood all ore, And ne'r eliminat'st thy dore.

3. a. *Phys.* To expel from the body; *esp.* to get rid of (waste matter, foreign substances, etc.) from the tissues by excretion. **b.** *Chem.* To disengage, expel (a constituent) from a compound.

1794–6 E. DARWIN *Zoon.* (1801) I. 496 A week or two are required to eliminate the mercury from the constitution. **1835–6** TODD *Cycl. Anat.* I. 66/1 The infant just eliminated from the uterus. **1859** DARWIN *Orig. Spec.* iv. (1878) 73 Certain plants excrete sweet juice..for the sake of eliminating something injurious from the sap. **1877** ROSENTHAL *Muscles & Nerves* 87 An acid is formed, which is..again eliminated and carried away by the blood.

4. *gen.* To expel, exclude, remove, get rid of. Used both with reference to material and non-material objects.

1714 LOWTH *Comm. Isa.* Prel. Diss. 62 To be able to discharge and eliminate the errors. **1846** GROTE *Greece* I. xvi. I. 533 The..tendency of Herodotus to eliminate from the myths the idea of special aid from the gods. **1861** GOSCHEN *For. Exch.* 19 Eliminating middle men and intermediate profits. **1871** R. H. HUTTON *Ess.* II. 306 Miss Brontë finds it needful to eliminate the supernatural. **1877** W. THOMSON *Voy. Challenger* I. i. 30 Which enables the potash to be eliminated from the apparatus. **1877** J. E. CARPENTER tr. *Tiele's Hist. Relig.* 32 All mythological expressions have probably been eliminated.

b. *fig.* To ignore, treat as non-existent, set aside as irrelevant (certain elements of a question or concept).

1850 KINGSLEY *Alt. Locke* ii. (1879) 30, I forgot the Corsair's sinful trade..I honestly eliminated the bad element. **1859** THACKERAY *Virgin.* vi. (1878) 47 Eliminating him from the argument. **1870** LUBBOCK *Orig. Civiliz.* i. (1875) 3 We must eliminate these customs from our conception of that condition.

5. *Algebra.* To get rid of (one or more quantities) from an equation or set of equations; *esp.* to get rid of (one or more of the unknown quantities) in simultaneous equations by combining two or more of the equations; also, to get rid of (one or more of the variables) from an analytical equation.

1845 *Penny Cycl. 1st Suppl.* I. s.v., If by means of one of these we eliminate *p* from the rest, the process..would allow of our eliminating both *x* and *y* by one equation only. **1875** TODHUNTER *Algebra* 89 By this process we are said to eliminate the unknown quantity which does not appear in the single equation. **1882** MINCHIN *Unipl. Kinemat.* 237 Eliminate *x* between the given relations.

fig. **1844** GLADSTONE *Glean.* V. ii. 82 The Church..might be eliminated like a constant quantity from among those fluent materials with which history is conversant.

¶**6.** Incorrectly used for: To disengage, isolate, extract (particular elements) from a compound; to disentangle (a fact, a principle) from a mass of confused details; hence, to elicit, deduce.

1843 *For. & Col. Q. Rev.* II. 337 It being..impossible that such infinite ideas as God, eternity, etc...could ever be eliminated by either the will, the reason, or the finite evidence of the finite senses. **1850** MCCOSH *Div. Govt.* IV. i. §2. 455 We have sought to eliminate the truth by exhibiting nature in its full and living action. **1855** BAIN *Senses & Int.* III. ii. §33 (1864) 523 He would..eliminate the main fact from all the confusing circumstantials. **1872** H. MACMILLAN *True Vine* iii. 97 The roots, indeed, eliminate nourishment from the soil. **1877** E. CONDER *Bas. Faith* iv. 183 The corrupt use of 'eliminate' for 'educe'.

eliminating (ɪˈlɪmɪneɪtɪŋ), *ppl. a.* [f. ELIMINATE *v.* + -ING².] That eliminates.

1888 *Pall Mall Gaz.* 13 Sept. 4/1 The eliminating influence of the battle-field. **1909** *Westm. Gaz.* 9 June 14/3 To face the ordeal of the eliminating competition.

elimination (ɪˌlɪmɪˈneɪʃən). [n. of action f. L. *ēlīmināre*: see ELIMINATE and -ATION.]

†**1. a.** The action of turning persons out of doors, or expelling them from their country; the fact of being thus expelled. **b.** Divulgation of secrets (cf. ELIMINATE *v.* 1 b.). **c.** (See quot. 1809.)

1601 BP. W. BARLOW *Defense* 175 Fabulous eliminations of hels secrets. **1624–47** BP. HALL *Rem. Wks.* (1660) 201 The Jews..after all their disgracefull eliminations. **1809** *Edin. Rev.* XIV. Apr. 20 The process of excluding this proportion [of the French Legislative Assembly] is entitled elimination.

2. *gen.* Expulsion, casting out, getting rid of anything, whether material or immaterial.

1627 DONNE *Serm.* 221 This difference gives no occasion to an Elimination to an extermination of those books which we call Apocryphall. **1833** SIR W. HAMILTON in *Edin. Rev.* Apr. 205 An elimination of those less precise and appropriate significations, which, etc. **1862** H. SPENCER *First Princ.* I. i. §1 (1875) 4 The elimination of individual errors of thought. **1878** A. GREEN *Coal* 171 The gradual elimination of the oxygen and the concentration of the carbon still go forward. **1883** H. DRUMMOND *Nat. Law in Spir. W.* i. (1884) 28 The elimination of mystery from the universe is the elimination of Religion.

3. *Phys.* The process of throwing off (effete and waste matter) from the tissues.

1855 BAIN *Senses & Int.* II. i. §11 (1864) 94 The elimination of waste matter from the skin is promoted by exercise. **1877** ROSENTHAL *Muscles & Nerves* 87 In the death-stiffening this elimination cannot occur.

b. *transf.* and *fig.*

1859 DARWIN *Orig. Spec.* xv. (1873) 405 This elimination of sterility apparently follows from the same cause. **1871** —— *Desc. Man* I. v. 172 Some elimination of the worst dispositions is always in progress. **1873** H. SPENCER *Study Sociol.* xiv. 346 That natural process of elimination by which society continually purifies itself.

4. *Algebra.* (See ELIMINATE *v.* 5.)

1845 *Penny Cycl. 1st Suppl.* I. s.v., As to equations which are not purely algebraical..we cannot..say that there is any organized method of elimination existing, except that of solution. **1881** BURNSIDE & PANTON *Theor. Equations* xiii. (1866) 140 We now proceed to show how the elimination may be performed so as to obtain the quantity *R*.

¶**5.** *catachr.* The process of selecting and abstracting some special element; also, the process of disentangling an essential fact or principle from a mass of confused details. Cf. ELIMINATE 6.

1869 G. C. WALLICH in *Sci. Opin.* 10 Feb. 271/2 The elimination from the surrounding waters of the elements entering into the composition of body-substance. **1850** MAURICE *Mor. & Met. Philos.* (ed. 2) I. 159 He [Plato] was not able to apply his dialectic to the elimination of this idea from the names or facts in which it was imbedded. **1854** FARADAY in *Lect. on Educ.* 68 [Hypotheses] of the utmost value in the elimination of truth.

eliminative (ɪˈlɪmɪnətɪv), *a. rare.* [f. L. *ēlīmināt-* ppl. stem of *ēlīminā-re* (see ELIMINATE *v.*) + -IVE.] That eliminates or tends to eliminate; concerned or employed in eliminating. Const. *of.* (See senses of the vb.)

1861 WYNTER *Soc. Bees* 278 There can be no congestion of the internal eliminative organs. **1861** *Sat. Rev.* 18 May 511 Baxter's habit of mind might be called essentially eliminative. **1883** T. M. POST *Serm., Anniv. Exerc. Jacksonville, Ill.* 51 [Protestant principles] are naturally..curative or eliminative of the poison of despotism or intolerance. **1883** *Harper's Mag.* June 123/2 Diarrhœa presents itself under two chief forms—*irritative* and *eliminative*.

eliminator (ɪˈlɪmɪneɪtə(r)). [as if a. L. **ēlīminātor*, agent-noun f. *ēlīmināre* to ELIMINATE.] **a.** He who or that which eliminates.

1883 *Fortn. Rev.* Feb. 197 The sarcastic..get rid of it [malice] by its proper eliminator—the tongue.

b. Any apparatus which eliminates the need for a battery (high or low tension or grid bias) by enabling a wireless set to be worked from any electricity supply.

1928 *Morn. Post* 9 July, The rectifier intended for inclusion in high tension battery eliminators.

eliminatory (ɪˈlɪmɪnəˌtərɪ), *a. rare.* [f. L. *ēlīmināt-* (see prec.) + -ORY.] Of or pertaining to elimination; esp. in *Phys.*

1847–9 *Cycl. Anat.* IV. 103/2 Deposits..tend to produce eliminatory action. **1883** G. H. TAYLOR *Health by Exerc.* 380 Fails..sensibly to promote the eliminatory processes.

eling(e, var. EYLING, *Obs.*, 'wing' of a building.

elinge, var. form of ELENGE. *Obs.*

†**e'linguate**, *v. Obs. rare*⁻¹. [f. L. *ēlinguāt-* ppl. stem of *ēlinguā-re*, f. *ē* out + *lingua* tongue.] *trans.* To deprive of the tongue.

1609 J. DAVIES *Holy Roode* D 4 b, The Diu'll that Diu'll elinguate for his doome.

Hence **elin'guation**. *Obs.*⁻⁰ The cutting out of the tongue.

1731 and **1736** in BAILEY. **1775** in ASH; and in mod. Dicts.

†**e'lingued**, *a. Obs. rare*⁻¹. [as if f. a vb. **elingue*, ad. L. *ēlinguāre* (see prec.) + -ED.] Deprived of the tongue; hence *fig.* tongue-tied, speechless, dumb.

1627 FELTHAM *Resolves* II. §37 Wks. (1677) 234 Fear.. often leaves him..quite elingued. **1656** in BLOUNT *Gloss.* [**1775** ASH has *Elinguid*, citing COLES, who has only *Elingued*. So **1847** in CRAIG; and in mod. Dicts.]

Elint (ˈiːlɪnt). orig. *U.S.* Also **ELINT**. Abbrev. of *electronic* (also *electromagnetic*) *intelligence*, and applied to covert intelligence-gathering by such methods. Freq. *attrib.*, as ***Elint ship***, etc.

1961 *Britannica Bk. of Year* 537/2 *United States*... New words from initials included ELINT, electronic intelligence warning system. **1968** *N.Y. Times* 28 Jan. IV. 1/1 In the intelligence business they call them 'elint' ships. Elint stands for electronic intelligence. **1970** *Dict. Naval Abbrev.* 78/2 *Elint*, electronic intelligence. *Ibid.*, *Elint*, *elmint*, electromagnetic intelligence. **1977** BREYER & POLMAR *Guide to Soviet Navy* (ed. 2) 396 A surprising feature of these new ELINT ships is that the electronic gear is scarcely visible. **1979** N. POLMAR *Mod. Soviet Navy* iv. 38 The ELINT and radar satellites can provide almost real-time detection. **1983** —— *Guide to Soviet Navy* (ed. 3) 46/2 Sometimes the satellites are operated in pairs.., to enhance coverage or to permit the passive ELINT satellite to 'key' the RORSAT to areas of interest. **1984** *Sunday Tel.* 5 Feb. 17/1 One reason for the Cabinet's decision finally to clamp down on union activity at Elint establishments..was the increased sensitivity of the material they handle.

elinvar (ˈɛlɪnvɑː(r)). [f. Fr. *élinvar* (C. E. Guillaume 1920, in *Compt. Rend. Acad. Sci.* CLXXI. 83), f. *élasticité invariable* invariable elasticity.] (See quot. 1923.)

1922 *Raw Material* V. 434/2 Elinvar permits of its application in the very good watches and even to chronometers of the non-metallic pendulum. **1923** GLAZEBROOK *Dict. Appl. Physics* V. 320/1 *Elinvar* (short for *el*asticity *invar*iable) is an alloy of iron and nickel, with a considerable admixture of other metals or metalloids, possessing an invariable modulus of elasticity (Young's modulus). **1929** *Daily Tel.* 8 Jan. 8/6 Dr. Charles Edouard Guillaume..is the inventor of three metallic alloys of great importance, invar, elinvar, and platinite. **1934** *Nature* 1 Sept. 318/1 (*heading*) Elinvar hairsprings in watches. **1950** *Electronic Engin.* XXII. 2 Tuning forks made from elinvar are available.

†**e'liquament.** *Obs.* [as if ad. L. **ēliquāmentum*, f. *ēliquā-re* to clarify, strain.] 'A fat juice squeezed out of flesh' (Phillips 1678).

1623 COCKERAM, *Eliquament*, fatnesse of fish, or flesh. **1656** in BLOUNT *Glossogr.* **1721–1800** in BAILEY. **1775** in ASH; and mod. Dicts.

eliquate (ˈɛlɪkweɪt), *v.* Also 7 eliquat. [f. L. *ēliquāt-* ppl. stem of *ēliquāre*, f. *ē* out + *liquāre* to melt.]

†**1.** *trans.* **a.** To melt (by heat), fuse. **b.** To liquefy. **c.** To cause to flow freely. *Obs.*

1621 VENNER *Tobacco* (1650) 416 It eliquateth the pinguie substance of the kidnies. **1638** A. READ *Chirurg.* iv. 28 Immoderat heat doth eliquat or melt the humours. **1684** tr. *Bonet's Merc. Compit.* xix. 742 Such [Diureticks] as..only plentifully eliquate the Urine. **1710** T. FULLER *Pharm. Extemp.* 244 It eliquates the Blood, dilutes the Juices.

2. To separate by fusion; to smelt (an ore).

1879 G. GLADSTONE *Antimony*, The ore to be eliquated.

eliquation (ɛlɪˈkweɪʃən). [ad. L. *ēliquātiōn-em*, n. of action f. as prec.]

1. The action or process of converting into a liquid; liquefaction. *Obs.*

1651 BIGGS *New Disp.* 72 A meer putrefactive eliquation of the bloud. **1710** T. FULLER *Pharm. Extemp.* 180 The Eliquation..of..obstructing Phlegm. **1757** *Phil. Trans.* L. 136 Its eliquation indeed could not be so remarkable as in pure alum.

2. (See quots.) Cf. ELIQUATE 2.

1753 CHAMBERS *Cycl. Supp.*, *Eliquation* in metallurgy is a separation of the different parts of mixed bodies by the different degrees of fire required to melt them. **1822** IMISON *Sc. & Art* II. 224 To separate..a small quantity of silver from much copper..the process called eliquation is resorted to. **1881** RAYMOND *Mining Gloss.*, *Eliquation*, separating an alloy by heating it so as to melt the more fusible of its ingredients, but not the less fusible.

†**e'liquidate**, *v. Obs. rare*⁻¹. [f. E- *pref.*³ + LIQUIDATE.] *trans.* To make clear, explain.

1596 HARINGTON (*title*) Metamorphosis of Ajax, Wherein ..is plainly, openly, & demonstratively declared, explaned, & eliquidated..how vnsauerie places may be made sweet.

elision (ɪˈlɪʒən). [ad. L. *ēlīsiōn-em*, f. *ēlīdĕre*: see ELIDE.]

1. The action of dropping out or suppressing: **a.** a letter or syllable in pronunciation; **b.** a passage in a book or connecting links in discourse. Also, an instance of either of these. Also *fig.*

1581 SIDNEY *Apol. Poetrie* (Arb.) 70 The Italian is so full of Vowels, that it must euer be cumbred with *Elisions.* **1589** PUTTENHAM *Eng. Poesie* II. xii[i]. (Arb.) 129 If there were no cause of elision. **1710** STEELE *Tatler* No. 230. ¶6 The.. Elisions, by which Consonants of most obdurate Sound are

joined together. **1836** Hor. Smith *Tin Trump.* I. 2 Standard words..are arbitrarily cut off by elision. **1870** Bowen *Logic* iii. 57 The science claims, therefore, to fill up the gaps and elisions of ordinary discourse. **1893** in *Funk's Stand. Dict.* **1936** R. Campbell *Mithraic Emblems* 20 Seven hues in white elision. **1962** *Sunday Times* 28 Jan. 12/2 The elision of pay pause into pay restraint has at this stage scarcely been attempted. **1964** M. Critchley *Developmental Dyslexia* viii. 52 The process of learning to read entails the elision from the focus of attention of the confusing memory-images of the non-dominant hemisphere.

†**2.** ***elision of the air***: formerly assigned as the cause of sound (see quot.). *Obs.*

1626 Bacon *Sylva* §124 The Cause given of Sound, that it should be an Elision of the Air (whereby, if they mean anything, they mean Cutting or Dividing, or else an Attenuating of the Air) is but a Terme of Ignorance. **1660** Boyle *New Exp. Phys.-Mech.* Digress. 346 The Production and Modulation of the Voice by the Elision of the Air.

3. A breaking (so as to make a gap) by mechanical force. (Scarcely a recognised Eng. use.)

1760 tr. *Juan & Ulloa, Voyage to S. Amer.* (1772) II. 98 The sea formed these large cavities..by its continual elisions. **1881** *Times* 12 Mar., It [Casamicciola] is now half in ruins, and even those houses which have stood are crippled by elisions.

e'lisionable, *a. rare.* [f. elision + -able.] That may be elided.

1877 G. M. Hopkins *Let.* 3 Apr. (1935) 40, I treat *ng* as elisionable, like a Latin *m*.

elisional (ɪ'lɪʒənəl), *a. rare.* [f. elision + -al¹.] Of or pertaining to elision.

1866 *Reader* 2 June 536 *Prado* may be pronounced *Pra'o* ..but it need not be spelt with the elisional apostrophe.

elisor ('ɛlɪzə(r)), *sb.* Also 5 ellyser, 6 ely-, elizour, -zar, -zor, 6–8 eslisor, 6 eslior. [a. OF. *elisour*, f. *elis-* stem of *elire* to choose.] One who elects.

†**1.** = elector 1–3. *Obs.*

14.. Caxton tr. *Higden* (Rolls) VII. 524 [see elite *sb.*¹]. **1529** Rastell *Pastyme, Hist. Rom.* (1811) 33 Made emperour..by the vii. elyzours of Almayne. —— *Fr. Hist.* 71 The markes Brandonburgh one of the elizours of the emperour.

2. *Law.* One of two persons appointed in certain cases to select a jury.

1628 Coke *On Litt.* 158 a, The court shall appoint certain elisors or esliors. **1768** Blackstone *Comm.* III. 355. **1863** H. Cox *Instit.* II. iii. 352 Where the sheriff is not an indifferent person..the precept may be directed..to two elisors or electors, who shall indifferently name the jury.

elist, var. of eye-list, *Obs.*, a defect.

†**e'lite**, *sb.*¹ *Obs.* In 4 ellite, 5 elyte. [a. OF. *elit* (in same use), pa. pple. of *elire*: see elite *v.*] A person chosen; *spec.* a bishop elect; = elect B. 2.

1387 Trevisa tr. *Higden* (Rolls) VII. 155 þe pope see of Rome was fer fro þe elites [Harl. MS. 2261 men electe; Harl. MS. 1900 ellites; Caxton ellysers; Lat. *ab ipsis electis*]. *c* **1425** Wyntoun *Cron.* VII. vii. 300 Rychard Byschape in his stede Chosyn he wes concorditer And elyte twa yhere bad eftyr.

†**e'lite**, *sb.*² *Obs. rare*⁻¹. [a. OFr. *elite* = next.] Election.

c **1330** R. Brunne *Chron.* (1810) 209 þe pape wild not consent, he quassed þer elite.

élite (eɪ'liːt), *sb.*³ [F. *élite* (in OFr. *eslite*, *elite*; see prec.) selection, choice; in mod. use *concr.* that which is chosen:—med.L. *ēlecta* choice, f. L. *ēligĕre*: see elect *v.*] **1.** The choice part or flower (of society, or of any body or class of persons). Also *attrib.* and *Comb.*; **élite stand, tree** (see quot. 1953).

1823 Byron *Juan* XIII. lxxx, With other Countesses of Blank—but rank; At once the 'lie' and the 'élite' of crowds. **1848** W. H. Kelly tr. *L. Blanc's Hist. Ten Y.* I. 439 The élite of the Russian nobility. **1852** C. M. Yonge *Two Guardians* viii. 143 She did not belong to those élite circles. **1880** Goldw. Smith in *Atl. Monthly* No. 268 If we take into consideration..the élite of a comparatively civilized generation. **1912** J. H. Moore *Ethics & Educ.* xiv. 111 The fighting instinct persists so strongly, even in élite peoples, that all our games nearly..are arranged on the plan of a battle. **1922** Joyce *Ulysses* 644 The élite society of oilskin and company. **1936** *Forestry* X. 35 By this process, in every fifth row of trees *élite* trees were selected, roughly every fifth stem when suitable. **1948** T. S. Eliot *Notes towards Def. Culture* ii. 36 An élite-governed society. **1953** *Brit. Commonw. For. Terminol.* I. 128 *Elite stand*, one selected for seed collection on account of its specially good quality. *Ibid.* 139 *Elite tree*, a tree selected for seed collection or for vegetative propagation on account of some specially good quality it may possess [etc.]. **1955** Koestler *Trail of Dinosaur* 209 The proposal aims at the creation of an élite force, within the framework of the Atlantic Pact. **1958** *Listener* 30 Oct. 685/1 Formal schooling which a generation ago was still confined to a small élite group. **1968** *Ibid.* 4 Apr. 445/2 The *New Statesman* was, and remains, an élite paper, a 'quality' paper.

2. (Normally without accent.) A standard size for letters used in typewriting, measuring horizontally twelve letters to the inch.

1920 H. Etheridge *Dict. Typewr.* 103 Elite Type. **1923** *Amer. Type Founders Co., Specimen Bk.*, Popular Typewriter Faces..10 Point Elite Underwood. **1927** F. Heelis *Advanced Typewriting* 52 'Elite' type, which is most suitable for private correspondence, measures twelve [letters or spaces] to the inch. **1928** *Big Six (Remington Typewriter Co. Ltd.)*, Type Styles..Elite. **1951** J. Steinbeck *Log f. Sea of Cortez* (1958) p. liv, The neat page full of small elite type.

†'**elite**, *v. Obs.* Also 5 elyte; *pa. t.* elit. [f. OF. (*eslit*) *elit*, obs. pa. pple. of the verb *elire* to elect.] *trans.* To choose; to elect to office.

c **1400** *Destr. Troy* 1491 Of his Deghter..One Creusa was cald..þat Eneas afterward elit to wed. **1461** T. Denyes in *Paston Letters*, No. 397 (1874) II. 22 He may not of reson do so largely..be cause he is elyted, as the Comons myght.

élitism (eɪ'liːtɪz(ə)m). [f. élite *sb.*³ + -ism.] Advocacy of or reliance on the leadership and dominance of an *élite* (in a society, or in any body or class of persons). Hence **é'litist** *sb.* and *a.*

1950 D. Riesman in *Psychiatry* XIII. 303/1 He [*sc.* Freud] shared with..Nietzsche and Carlyle elements of an elitist position. **1951** —— *Individualism Reconsidered* (1954) 30 In Elton Mayo and in other recent writers, one can find a similar elitism and..concern with the formation of group consensus through strong leadership. **1957** C. Hunt *Guide to Communist Jargon* xlix. 161 His [*sc.* Lenin's] conception of the 'narrow' party consisting of an *élite*, whose more highly developed class consciousness enables it to see further than those among whom it works... But this *élitism* is anti-democratic. **1960** *New Left Rev.* Nov.–Dec. 30/1 The élitist manipulation..of the Communist Party. **1961** *Ibid.* Jan.–Feb. 59/2 Thompson doesn't know what to do with..us..condemn us as quotation mongers? class us with elitists? **1968** *New Scientist* 30 May 446/2 The theme of his speech was 'Elitism and Excellence', the excellence being that of the mathematically gifted, and the elitism being the varying degrees of regard paid to this talent.

†'**elitrope**. *Obs. rare*⁻¹. [var. of heliotrope.] Some kind of precious stone. Cf. elutropia.

1609 *Will of Sir R. Lee* (Som. Ho.) Cheyne of elitrope. [**1750** tr. *Leonardus' Mirror of Stones* 97 Elitropia, or Elitropus, is a green gem..sprinkled with bloody spots.]

elixate (ɪ'lɪk-, 'ɛlɪkseɪt), *v.* [f. L. *ēlixāt-* ppl. stem of *ēlixāre* to boil, stew.]

1. *trans.* To boil, seethe; to extract by boiling.

1623 in Cockeram. **1631** Brathwait *Whimzies* 62 Elixate your antimonie. **1657** Tomlinson *Renou's Disp.* 162 Its enough to elixate a few simples in water on a slow fire. **1884** in *Syd. Soc. Lex.*

2. To steep (in water); to macerate.

1657 G. Starkey *Helmont's Vind.* 310 The Caput mortuum being elixated by warm water will give an Alcali. **1805** Gregor in *Phil. Trans.* XCV. 345 The brownish-gray mass was elixated with distilled water, which dissolved nearly the whole of it.

Hence **elixated** *ppl. a.*

1823 P. Nicholson *Pract. Build.* 334 The elixated ashes of divers vegetables.

elixation ('iːlɪk-, ɛlɪk'seɪʃən). [as if ad. L. **ēlixātiōnem*, f. *ēlixāre*: see elixate *v.* and -ation.]

1. The action of boiling or stewing.

1605 Timme *Quersit.* III. 190 Elixation..is a concoction made by a moyst heate of a thing indifinitely existing in a humour. **1615** Crooke *Body of Man* 113 Finally they serue to moysten the guts, that their concoction may be celebrated by elixation or boyling. **1757** Walker in *Phil. Trans.* L. 122 After elixation the water became of a turbid yellow colour with ochre.

2. Concoction in the stomach; digestion.

1621 Burton *Anat. Mel.* I. i. II. v, Elixation, is the boyling of meat in the stomacke, by the said naturall heat. **1651** Biggs *New Disp.* 96 The rest of the pouder, as it is not overcome by elixation, so it continues in a permanency of indigestion in the stomack.

†**e'lixed**, *ppl. a. Obs. rare.* [f. L. *ēlix-us* (cf. elixate) + -ed.]

a. Boiled; hence, refined by boiling, distilled; also *fig.* **b.** Macerated or steeped in water.

1602 Marston *Antonio & Mel.* I. Prol., The pur'st elixed juyce of rich conceipt. **1665–6** *Phil. Trans.* I. 46 Being laid in a heap, are covered with other elixed or dramed Ashes.

elixir (ɪ'lɪksə(r)), *sb.* Forms: 4 elixir, 5–7 elixar, -er, (6 alixer). [a. med.L. *elixir* (cf. Fr. *élixir*, It. *elissire*, Sp. *elixir*, Pg. *elexir*), ad. Arab. *al-iksīr* (= sense 1), prob. ad. late Gr. ξήριον 'desiccative powder for wounds'.]

1. *Alchemy.* A preparation by the use of which it was sought to change metals into gold. Sometimes identified with 'the philosopher's stone'; but perh. of wider meaning, including powders, liquids, or vapours used for the same purpose. Also ***elixir-stone***.

c **1386** Chaucer *Chan. Yem. Prol. & T.* 310 The philosophre stoon, Elixir clept, we sechen fast echoon. **1471** Ripley *Comp. Alch.* in Ashm. 188 Thow must devyde thy Elixer whyte into partyes two. **1584** R. Scot *Discov. Witchcr.* XIV. ii. 295 The philosophers stone, called Alixer. **1614** Rowlands *Fooles Bolt* 9 Fryer-Bacon..could teach Kelley the Elixar stone. **1667** Milton *P.L.* III. 607 What wonder then if fields and regions here Breathe forth elixir pure, and Rivers run Potable Gold. **1676** Hale *Contempl.* I. 297 A Good Man is like the Elixir, it turns Iron into Gold. **1855** Milman *Lat. Chr.* (1864) IX. XIV. iii. 159 Roger Bacon sought..a transmuting Elixir with unlimited powers.

b. *transf.* and *fig.*

1635 Quarles *Embl.* IV. iv. (1718) 202 True fear's the Elixir, which in days of old Turn'd leaden crosses into crowns of gold. **1663** Cowley *Verses & Ess.* (1669) 130 She taught him Loves Elixar, by which Art, His Godhead into Gold he did convert. **1878** Browning *La Saisiaz* 51, I shall bless the kindly wrench that..left all grace Ashes in death's stern alembic, loosed elixir in its place.

2. A supposed drug or essence with the property of indefinitely prolonging life; imagined by the alchemists to be either identical with, or closely related to, the 'elixir' of sense 1. More fully, ***elixir of life*** (tr. med.L. *elixir vitæ*).

[**1266** Roger Bacon *Opus Minus* (Rolls Ser.) 314 Medicinam..quam philosophi vocant Elixir..Si libra medicinæ projiciatur super mille plumbi fiet..aurum..Et hoc est quod corpora infirma reducet ad sanitatem..et vitam..ultra contenarios annorum prolongabit.] **1605** Timme *Quersit.* I. xiii. [Mercury, sulphur, and salt]..brought into one bodie (which the Arabians call elixir)..wil be..a medicine, etc. **1799** Godwin *St. Leon* IV. 324 The..secrets of alchemy and the elixir vitæ. **1815** Moore *Lalla R.* (1824) 136, I know too where the Genii hid The jewell'd cup of their king Jamshid With Life's elixir sparkling high. **1826** Miss Mitford *Village* Ser. II. (1863) 318 Honey..was, in her mind..the true elixir vitæ. **1831** Brewster *Nat. Magic* xii. (1833) 299 Though the elixir of life has never been distilled. **1873** Dixon *Two Queens* I. II. i. 75 Carillo had been glad to toy with magic, and pursue the elixir of life.

b. A sovereign remedy for disease. Hence adopted as a name for quack medicines, as ***Daffy's elixir***, etc.

1631 Massinger *Emp. of East* IV. iv, A little cyath or quantity of my potable elixir. **1633** P. Fletcher *Purple Isl.* XII. li, The best Elixar for souls drooping pain. **1681** Ashmole *Diary* 11 Apr., I took early in the morning a good dose of elixer. **1681** *Lond. Gaz.* No. 1679/4 Anthony Daffy, Author of the Famous Elixir Salutis. **1713** *Guardian* No. 11 (R.) The grand elixir, to support the spirits of human nature. **1724** Ramsay *Tea-T. Misc.* (1733) I. 79 Take your glass to clear your een, 'Tis the elixir heals the spleen. **1753** Chambers *Cycl. Supp.*, An universal medicine..called by way of excellence, the grand elixir. **1768–74** Tucker *Lt. Nat.* (1852) II. 234 A sip of Daffy's elixir..has proved a powerful means of grace. **1830** Scott *Demonol.* v. 144 Before he established the reputation of his..elixir, or pill.

†**3.** A strong extract or tincture. *Obs.* exc. *Hist.*

1597 Bp. Hall *Sat.* II. iv. 43 And bring quintessence of elixir pale Out of sublimed spirits minerall. **1673** Grew *Anat. Roots* II. §60 The remainder, is..an Oleous Elixyr, or extract, in the form of a Milk. **1677** W. Harris tr. *Lemery's Chym.* (ed. 3) 630 The name Elixir has been given to many Infusions or Tinctures of spirituous bodies prepared in spirituous Menstruums. **1820** Scott *Abbot* xxvii, That elixir being in truth a curious distillation of rectified acetum.

b. *fig.* The quintessence or soul of a thing; its kernel or secret principle.

1638 Chillingw. *Relig. Prot.* I. Pref. §1 The Spirit and Elixir of all that can be said in defence of your Church and Doctrine. **1641** Milton *Ch. Govt.* II. (1851) 181 A distill'd quintessence, a pure elixar of mischief, pestilent alike to all. **1675** Traherne *Chr. Ethics* xxiv. 366 The chief elixir of its [love's] nature is founded in the excellency of a spirit that suffers for another's sake. **1860** Emerson *Cond. Life, Fate* Wks. (Bohn) II. 311 Sometimes the rank unmitigated elixir, the family vice, is drawn off in a separate individual.

4. *Pharmacy.* (See quot.) ***elixir of vitriol***: aromatic sulphuric acid. ***paregoric elixir***: see paregoric.

1736 Bailey s.v., An Elixir is a compound magistery, i.e. a composition of various bodies chang'd after the same manner as a single body. **1783** F. Michaelis in *Med. Commun.* I. 350 He ordered her..a gargle of decoction of bark, with elixir of vitriol. **1871** Napheys *Prev. & Cure Dis.* I. viii. 203 Elixir of calisaya bark. **1884** *Syd. Soc. Lex.*, *Elixir*, a preparation similar to a compound tincture. Also applied in a compound of many drugs with syrup and spirit.

5. *Bot.* **elixir of love**: an orchid (*Grammatophyllum speciosum*), a native of Java. Also a decoction made from the seeds of this plant.

6. *Comb.*, as ***elixir-like*** adj.

a **1631** Drayton *Poems* I. (1753) 201 O tears! Elixir-like turn all to tears you touch. *a* **1631** Donne *Poems* (1650) 165 Soft dispositions which ductill be, Elixar-like, shee makes not cleane, but new.

†**e'lixir**, *v. Obs. rare.* [f. prec. sb.] *trans.* To distil as an elixir; to work upon as by an elixir. Also *absol.* Hence **e'lixired** *ppl. a.*, concentrated, refined. Also *fig.*

a **1658** Lovelace *To J. Hall* Wks. (1864) 252 Thou hast so spirited, elixir'd, we Conceive there is a noble alchymie. —— *Toad & Spider* 200 Then in his self the lymbeck turns, And his elixir'd poyson urns. **1660** Ognell *Elegy* in *Lovelace's Wks.* (1864) 289 This elixir'd medecine, For greatest grief a soveraign anodyne. **1687** *Elegy on Cleveland* in Wks. 277 Rich in Elixar'd Measures, and in all That could breath Sense in Airs Emphatical.

†**e'lixirate**, *v. Obs.* [f. elixir + -ate³.]

a. *trans.* To distil; to refine by distillation. Also *absol.* **b.** To cleanse in general, to purify.

1605 Timme *Quersit.* Pref. 7 Every meane Apothecarie..should wel understand how to elixerate. **1694** Westmacott *Script. Herb.* 27 Every chymical and rational brain can elixyrate such domestic wines. *Ibid.* 216 The volatile parts..ascend to the brain and heart..elixirating the animal spirits. **1733** *Phil. Trans.* XXXVIII. 64 By the Means of these Salts..the Fæces Alvinæ are the better elixirated.

Hence **e'lixirated** *ppl. a.*

1657 Starkey *Helmont's Vind.* 321 Imagining your self to be Master of these elixerated Oyls, and essencificated Salts. **1670** W. Simpson *Hydrol. Ess.* 125 Graduated to so high an elixerated liquor.

†**eli'xiviate**, *v. Chem. Obs. rare.* [f. e- *pref.*³ + lixiviate to clear of lye.] *trans.* To clear from lixivium or lye; to refine thoroughly. Hence

eli'xiviate, eli'xiviated *ppl. a.*, that has lost its lye, that has lost its essential properties. **eli͵xivi'ation**, steeping in water for the sake of extracting the lye.

1674 *Phil. Trans.* IX. 70 Several Minerals..are to the taste altogether insipid and elixiviated. **1675** EVELYN *Terra* (1729) 42 By the Air, the most efflete and elixiviated Mould comes to be repair'd. **1684** tr. *Bonet's Merc. Compit.* XIX. 852 Salt of Vitriol is prescribed to be made..of an elixiviate Colcothar. **1684-5** BOYLE *Min. Waters* 23 Examining these substances by..elixiviation. **1748** *Phil. Trans.* XLV. 542 The Art of converting..Wood-ashes into Pot-ash, without the..Process of Elixiviation. **1756** C. LUCAS *Ess. Waters* I. 6 The artificial, are those that are extracted..by..elixiviation.

†**E'lizabeth.** *Obs.* A coin of Queen Elizabeth.

1710 STEELE *Tatler* No. 245 ¶2 An Elizabeth and Four Jacobus's.

Elizabethan (ɪ͵lɪzə'biːθən), *a.* and *sb.* Also 9 Elizabethian. [f. ELIZABETH + -AN.]

A. *adj.* **1.** Belonging to the period of Queen Elizabeth I (1558-1603). Also, belonging to the period of Queen Elizabeth II (1952-).

1807 I. D'ISRAELI *Curiosities of Lit.* (ed. 5) I. 388 The fashions of the Elizabethean age have been chronicled by honest John Stowe. **1817** COLERIDGE *Biog. Lit.* II. xxii. 166 Daniel, one of the golden writers of our golden Elizabethian age. **1840** CARLYLE *Heroes* (1858) 261 This glorious Elizabethan Era. **1887** J. W. HALES *3 Elizab. Comedies* in *Macm. Mag.* May 61/2 He is..never to flog him the [pupil] when he cannot say his lesson—a peculiar hardship to an Elizabethan teacher. **1957** D. J. ENRIGHT *Apothecary's Shop* 235 The 'New Elizabethan' theme, cooking in the minds of statesmen, leads to nothing more glorious than the devastation of an Arab quarter.

2. Of dress, furniture, architecture: In the style in vogue during the period of Queen Elizabeth I. Also of language, literary form, etc.

1823 LAMB *Elia* 190 What a collegiate aspect has that fine Elizabethan hall. **1840** HOOD *Up Rhine* 307 A large Elizabethan ruff. **1869** *Daily News* 15 Mar., In the drama 'Lady Grace,' the contrast between modern manners and Elizabethan language is rather incongruous. **1874** PARKER *Goth. Archit.* I. ii. 20 The Elizabethan style..is a mixture of the old English and the ruder Italian of the Renaissance.

B. *sb.* A person (*esp.* a poet or dramatist) of the period of Queen Elizabeth I. Chiefly *pl.* Also, a person of the period of Queen Elizabeth II

1859 D. MASSON *Life Milton* I. 69 The..literature of England would be represented to Milton, in the year 1624, by that cluster of..men..who had been already named 'the Elizabethans'. **1881** *Athenæum* 12 Nov. 623/3 The murders and adulteries that..had pleased the Elizabethans. **1882** GROSART *Spenser's Wks.* III. Introd. 62 Our Elizabethans, Lodge and Greene especially. **1884** *Athenæum* 22 Mar. 386/2 The savage sublimity of the Elizabethans. **1953** F. E. HALLIDAY in R. Carew *Surv. Cornwall* 11 It still remains..one of the best accounts that we possess of life in Elizabethan England, a quality that should appeal to Elizabethans of the new age.

Elizabethanism (ɪlɪzə'biːθənɪz(ə)m). [f. ELIZABETHAN *a.* and *sb.*: see -ISM.] A manner or style, or a (literary, etc.) work, or a particular feature of these, characteristic or imitative of the style, language, etc., of the reign of Queen Elizabeth I (1558-1603).

1895 S. BUTLER in H. F. Jones *Mem.* (1919) II. xxxiii. 207 He who would write a translation like those of the Elizabethans must above all things avoid Elizabethanisms. **1897** *Daily News* 10 May 9/1 Complaint is heard of his 'affected Elizabethanisms'. **1909** G. K. CHESTERTON in D. Figgis *Vis. Life* p. vii, The latest Elizabethanism has differed not only from the actual Elizabethan work, but from other revivals of it. **1938** *Times* 16 Feb. 10/3 The small string orchestra..provided a pleasant Elizabethanism in a consort of recorders.

Elizabethanize (ɪ͵lɪzə'biːθənaɪz). [f. ELIZABETHAN *a.* and *sb.* + -IZE.] *trans.* To give an Elizabethan character to. Hence **Eliza'bethanized** *ppl. a.*

1841 *Fraser's Mag.* XXIII. 335 A man who built himself a residence Elizabethanised upon a moderate scale.

elk[1] (ɛlk). Forms: 5-7 elke, (6 alke), 6 elcke, 7- elk. See also ALCE. [Of obscure history: the existing word is not the normal phonetic representative of OE. *elch*, *elh* (*eolh*), and is probably ad. MHG. *elch* (:— OHG. *elaho*). The relation of the ON. *elg-r* (Sw. *elg*):— type **algi-z* to the OE. and German words (:— types **elho-*, **elhon-*) is uncertain. The Eng. form *alke* was influenced by L. *alces*, Gr. ἄλκη (cf. ALCE), which appear only as the name of an animal living in northern Europe (app. the elk), and are probably adopted from Teut. or some other northern lang.]

1. a. The largest existing animal of the deer kind (*Alces malchis*), inhabiting large portions of Northern Europe and of North America. The American variety is also called the MOOSE. (In quot. 1541 the name seems to be applied to some English species of deer.)

[*a* **700** *Epinal Gloss.* 233 *Cer[v]us*, elch. *a* **800** *Corpus Gloss.* 443 *Cer[v]us*, elh. *Ibid.* 2054 *Tragelaphus*, elch. *a* **900** *Leiden Gloss.*, *Damma*, elha.] **1486** *Bk. St. Albans* D iij b, The symplest of theis iij will slee an Hynde calfe, a Fawn, a Roo, an Elke. **1541** *Act 33 Hen. VIII*, c. 6 It shall be lawfull..to have, exercise, and vse their handgounnes..so that it be at no maner of deere..or wild elke. [**1555** EDEN *Decades W. Ind.* (Arb.) 305 Bisontes which in theyr toonge [Swedish] they caule Elg (that is) wild asses.] **1577** HARRISON *Descr. Eng.* III. v. (1877) II. 29 Plowing with vres..and alkes a thing commonlie vsed in the east countries. **1607** TOPSELL *Four-f. Beasts* 169 The Elk on the contrary is most impatient of all heat. **1629** CAPT. SMITH *Trav. & Adv.* xv. 28 These Tartars possesse many..plaines, wherein feed Elkes, Bisones, Horses..and divers others. **1682** MILTON *Hist. Mosc.* ii. (1851) 482 Those Messengers..made report of..people riding on Elks. **1774** GOLDSM. *Nat. Hist.* II. 82 It is known in Europe by the name of the *elk*, and in America by that of the *Moose-deer*. **1836** W. IRVING *Astoria* (1849) 196 They saw..frequent gangs of stately elks. **1853** KINGSLEY *Hypatia* xxii. 281 Followed by..elks from beyond the Danube.

b. *pl.* (With capital initial.) In full: the Benevolent and Protective Order of Elks, formed in New York City in 1868, orig. a society of actors and writers, later a social and charitable organization; *sing.* a member of this organization.

1879 *Chicago Tribune* 14 Mar. 5/4 The second annual benefit of Chicago Lodge, No. 4, 'D.', Protective Order of Elks, was given yesterday afternoon. **1922** L. MUMFORD in H. Stearns *Civiliz. U.S.* 6 In every American city, small or big, Odd Fellows,..Elks,..and other orders without number..found for themselves a prominent place. **1950** W. STEVENS *Let.* 27 Feb. (1967) 670 The other hotels are full of Elks. **1957** W. H. WHYTE *Organization Man* VII. xxi. 268 He can move upward (from the Elks, say, to the Rotary) only by sanction of the next upper group.

2. a. Applied to certain species of deer: e.g. to the 'Irish Elk', an extinct animal (*Cervus megaceros*), which inhabited Ireland in prehistoric times; and to the Canadian Deer or Wapiti (*Cervus canadensis*).

1884 MISS HICKSON *Irel. in 17th C.* I. Introd. 11 Celts and Saxons being as extinct in Ireland as the ancient elk.

b. In Anglo-Indian use, the SAMBUR.

1884 W. RICE *Indian Game* vi. 95 The deer in the foreground..are the samber stag, beautiful animals one sometimes hears miscalled the 'elk'. **1890** S. BAKER *Wild Beasts* XXV. 306 Sambur deer, (miscalled elk in Ceylon).

3. A species of antelope: the ELAND or Cape-elk.

1731 MEDLEY *Kolben's Cape G. Hope* II. 110 The haunts of the African Elks are generally on high mountains, on good pasture grounds, and near good springs. **1786** tr. *Sparrman's Voy. Cape G.H.* II. 264 The Cape elk, or more properly the elk-antilope, is a name given by the colonists to a species of gazel.

4. *Comb.* as *elk-skin*; also **elk-bark**, *Magnolia glauca*; **elk-hound**, a dog of Scandinavian origin specially adapted for hunting the elk, having a thick and weather-resisting coat of a grey colour with black tips, and a thick tail curled over the back; **elk('s)-horn**, a kind of fern, *Platycerium alcicorne*; **elk-horse**, a horse employed in hunting the elk; **elk-nut**, *Hamiltonia oleifera*; **elk-tree**, *Andromeda arborea*; **elk-wood** *Andromeda arborea* and *Magnolia macrophylla*; **elk-yard**, a kind of habitation made by the elk.

1865 GOSSE *Land & Sea* (1874) 330 *note*, The *Elk-horn fern. **1882** J. HARDY in *Proc. Brew. Nat. Club* IX. 434 The Elk's-horn fern. **1888** *Century Mag.* Jan. 451/2 The '*elk' horses received three-quarters forage at night and a quarter forage in the morning. [**1835** C. F. HOFFMAN *Winter in West* II. 12 A very successful experiment has been made here in crossing the greyhound and Newfoundland... If the race be continued, they ought to be dubbed elkhounds.] **1878** *Kennel Club Stud Bk.* 213 Norwegian *Elbehound [*sic*]. **1889** *Kennel Gaz.*, Swedish Elk Hound. **1907** R. LEIGHTON *New Bk. Dog* XVI. 491 The Elk-hound..may be termed the Scandinavian Pointer, for, as well as for elk and bear-hunting, it is used as a gun-dog for blackcock. **1908** *Kennel Encycl.* II. 588 The true Elk or Bear hound is distinctly by nature a hunting dog, hailing originally from Swedish Lapland or Jemtland... The dogs are designated by their owners 'Svenske Hunder'. **1945** C. L. B. HUBBARD *Observer's Bk. Dogs* 62 In 1923..the British Elkhound Society was formed. **1759** HARTE *Gust. Adolphus* II. 321 He wore..an *elkskin buff-waistcoat. **1807** F. PURSH *Jrnl. Bot. Excursion* (1923) 27 Acer montanum, very common throughout these woods, called *Elkwood. **1834** *Southern Lit. Messenger* I. 97 The underwood is mostly streaked maple or elkwood (the *Acer Striatum* of Michaux). **1880** *Harper's Mag.* July 182/2 Vines and elk-wood cover both sides (of the rock). **1868** WOOD *Homes without H.* xxxi. 612 That curious temporary habitation..popularly termed an *Elk-yard.

†**elk**[2]. *Obs. rare.* Also 6 elke (see quots.).

1541 *Act 33 Hen. VIII*, c. 9 §6 No bowyer shall sell..any bowe of ewe of the taxe called elke, aboue the price of .iii.*s.* iiii.*d.* **1607** COWEL *Interpr.*, *Elk*, a kind of ewe to make bowes of.

†**elk**[3] (ɛlk). Forms: 6-7 elke, 7 *pl.* elkys, 7- elk. The Wild Swan or Hooper (*Cygnus ferus*). Also the Wild Goose (*Anas anser*).

1552 HULOET s.v. *Swanne*, Some take thys to be the elke, or wild swanne. **1621** MARKHAM *Fowling* (1655) 6 Such as liue of the water and on the water, are wild Swannes or Elkes. **1674** RAY *Water Fowl* 95 The Elk, Hooper, or wild Swan. **1691** —— *Local Wds.* 129 Elkys, Wild Geese. **1709** DERHAM in *Phil. Trans.* XXVI. 466 *Cygnus ferus*, the Elk, or Hooper, or Wild Swan. **1839** *Proc. Berw. Nat. Club.* I. 189 Both of these were of the common or elk species.

†**'elken,** *v. Obs. rare.*[−1] [? var. of OLUHNEN to flatter.] ? To flatter, propitiate.

a **1400-50** *Alexander* 163 Þai..Honourd him with offryngs & elkend him fayre.

ell[1] (ɛl). Forms: 1-7 eln, 2-7 elne, 3-6 ellen (3 a nellen for *an ellen*), (4 ellyn, 6 eline), 6 el, 5-7 elle, 6- ell. [Com. Teut.: OE. *ęln*, str. fem. = MDu. *elne*, *elle* (Du. *el*), OHG. *elina* (MHG. *elne*, mod.G. *elle*), ON. *ǫln*, *alin* (Sw. *aln*, Da. *alen*), Goth. *aleina* (? scribal error for **alina*) cubit:— OTeut. **alinâ*, whence med.L. *alena*, It., OSp., OPg. *alna*, F. *aune*. The OTeut. word (a compound of which is ELBOW *sb.*) meant originally arm or fore-arm, and is cogn. with Gr. ὠλένη, L. *ulna*, of same meaning.

The diversity of meanings (see below) is common to all words denoting linear measures derived from the length of the arm; cf. CUBIT and L. *ulna*. The word *ell* seems to have been variously taken to represent the distance from the elbow or from the shoulder to the wrist or to the finger-tips, while in some cases a 'double ell' has superseded the original measure, and has taken its name.]

1. a. A measure of length varying in different countries. The English ell = 45 in.; the Scotch = 37·2; the Flemish = 27 in. Now only *Hist.* or with reference to foreign countries, the Eng. measure being obsolete.

In early use often in sing. when preceded by numerals.

c **1000** *Ags. Gosp.* Matt. vi. 27 Hwylc eower mæȝ..ȝeþencan þæt he ȝe-eacniȝe ane elne [**950** *Lindisf.* elne an *vel* enne; **1160** *Hatton* enne elne] to hys anlicnesse. *c* **1000** ÆLFRIC *Gloss.* in Wr.-Wülcker 158 *Ulna*, eln. *c* **1250** *Gen. & Ex.* 586 So wunderlike it wex and get Ðat fiftene elne it ouer-flet. **1297** R. GLOUC. (1724) 429 False elnen & mesures he broȝte al clene adoun. *a* **1300** *Cursor M.* 1675 A schippe..Seuen score ellen lang and ten. *Ibid.* 1838 Þe flod ouer raght seuen eln and mare. **1487** *Act 3 Hen. VII*, c. 7 All merchandises..used to be measured with Eln or Yard. **1502** ARNOLDE *Chron.* (1811) 204 Item a Fll ell conteyneth iii q't's of an Eng. yarde, and v. q't's of yᵉ Fll ell makith an Eng. ell. **1520** *Test. Ebor.* (Surtees) V. 119 A ellen of yolow velvett. **1542** RECORDE *Gr. Artes* (1575) 207, 3 Foote and 9 Ynches make an Elle. **1597** SHAKS. *Rom. & Jul.* II. iv. 88 O, here's a wit of Cheuerel, that stretches from an ynch narrow to an ell broad! **1609** SKENE *Reg. Maj.* 57 King Davids common elne conteines threttie seven measured inches. **1625-8** N. R. tr. *Camden's Hist. Eliz.* II. an. 17 (1635) 180 A monstrous Whale..whose length was..twenty of our Elnes. **1633** EARL MANCH. *Al Mondo* (1636) 138 Ere long two ells of earth shall serve, whom scarce a world could satisfie. **1753** HANWAY *Trav.* (1762) I. VII. lxxxviii. 408, 102 Ells dantzig make 50 ells english. **1805** FORSYTH *Beauties Scotl.* II. 275 The ell by which their acres have been measured (called the barony ell) contains 42 inches, whereas the common ell made use of in the country is only 38 inches. **1837** CARLYLE *Fr. Rev.* II. I. ix. 58 Tearful women wetting whole ells of cambric in concert.

b. *fig.* Contrasted with *inch*, *span*, etc.; *esp.* in proverbial phrase, ***give him an inch and he'll take an ell***: meaning that undue advantage will be taken of a slight concession.

1562 J. HEYWOOD *Prov. & Epigr.* (1867) 78 Ye liked..better an Ynche of your Wyll, Than an ell of your thrift. **1580** H. GIFFORD *Gilloflowers* (1875) 57 Whereas shee tooke an inche of liberty before, tooke an ell afterwardes. **1633** G. HERBERT *Temple, Ch.-porch* ad fin., Lifes poore span Make not an ell by trifling in thy wo. **1643** *Myst. Iniq.* 40 That gave but a Yard, they took an Ell. **1653** BOGAN *Mirth Chr. Life* 305 Have a care of taking an ell, when you have but an inch allowed you. **1798** CANNING *Ballynahinch* v, in *Anti-Jacobin* 9 July, Tho' they still took an ell when we gave them an inch.

c. As a fluid measure.

[Several correspondents inform us that they remember seeing the announcement 'Beer sold by the yard', on the signboards of country taverns, the reference being to the long narrow glasses about a yard high.]

1649 LOVELACE *Poems* 99 For Elles of Beere, Flutes of Canary Thankes freest, freshest, Faire Ellinda.

†**2. a.** A measuring rod; = ELL-WAND. Phrase, ***to measure with the long ell, with the short ell***: to measure unfairly as buyer or seller respectively.

1474 CAXTON *Chesse* 119 In hys right hand an elle for to mesure wyth. **1580** SIDNEY *Arcadia* (1622) 62 The night measured by the short ell of sleepe. **1637** R. MONRO *Exped.* II. 46 Sometimes the Souldiers (the worst sort of them) measured the packes belonging to the Marchants with the long ell. *a* **1656** BP. HALL *Soliloquies* 78 Thus spake a true Idol's Priest that knew no ell, whereby to measure religion, but profit. **1768** TUCKER *Lt. Nat.* (1852) I. 85 The mercer..upon seeing the ladies gown..can cut off her quantity by guess, without..taking his ell to measure it.

†**b.** *Sc.* ***King's ell***: 'Orion's belt': = ELL-WAND 3. *Obs.*

a **1605** MONTGOMERIE *Flyting* Wks. (1821) 118 Be the hornes, the handstaff and the King's ell.

†**3.** ***long ell***: a particular kind of cloth. *Obs.*

1725 DE FOE *Voy. round World* (1840) 198 Baize, long ells, druggets, broadcloth. **1735** BERKELEY *Querist* §520 Fine cloths in Somersetshire, long ells at Exeter.

†**4.** As a rendering of L. *ulna*: The larger bone of the fore-arm. *Obs.*

1615 CROOKE *Body of Man* 903 The other externall branch at the middle of the Ell shooteth out a propagation from his outside. **1634** T. JOHNSON tr. *Parey's Chirurg.* VI. xxvi. 147 The Ell, or bone of the cubit..hath..two appendices.

5. *Comb.*, as *ell-broad*, *-long*, *-wide* adjs.; **ell coal** *Sc.*, a type of coal normally found in seams one ell or more in thickness; †**ell-glass** (see 1 c.); †**ell-ridge**, an old land-measure; †**ell-yard**, an ell-measure. Also ELL-WAND.

1476 *Plumpton Corr.* 37 The bredth of it is *elme broade. 1696 J. F. *Merchant's Wareho.* 20 This being the last sort of Ellbroad Gentish that I shall treat of at present. 1794 J. NAISMITH *Agric. Clydesdale* 36 About 16 or 17 fathoms under this, lies the *ell coal, so called, because it was first found of this thickness, but it is frequently from 4 to 6 feet thick. 1845 *New Statistical Acct. Sc.* V. 813 Seven other workable seams, in the following ascending order, viz. the stone-coal 2¼ feet; ell coal, 2½. 1931 *Econ. Geol. Fife* (Geol. Survey) I. 82 The *Ell Coal* lies 1 to 7 fms. above the Upper Eight Foot... Sometimes it is a single seam of 3 to 4 ft... The Ell is a steam coal. 1931 *Times* 16 Mar. 19/7 Lanarkshire.—Ell best, 15s. 6d. 1682 *Way to make Rum* in *Harl. Misc.* I. 541 The Germans commonly drink whole tankards, and *ell-glasses, at a draught. 1832 *Tour German Prince* III. II. 36, I ate a good dinner, and then added to this *ell-long letter. 1756 *Extract fr. MS. Let.*, Peter Guffin (aged 82 in 1756) was unacquainted with such an old measure of land as an *Ell Ridge, but had heard it contained 60 Luggs. 1652 COLLINGES *Caveat for Prof.* iv. (1653) 25 Your *ell-wide opinion. 1826 MISS MITFORD *Village* Ser. II. (1863) 425 A pretty quaker.. did persuade me that ell-wide muslin would go as far as a yard and a half. *c* 1340 *Gaw. & Gr. Knt.* 210 þe hede of an *eln-ȝerde þe large lenkþe hade. *c* 1450 MYRC 713 False ellen yerdes, wetyngly other than the lawe of the lond.

ell[2] (ɛl). *U.S.* = L 2a. Also *attrib.*

1773 *Rec. Early Hist. Boston* (1887) XVIII. 198 A Major part of the Selectmen of said Town.. [have] Established a New Street.. beginning at the North Easterly Corner of the Brick Tenement, (or Ell, so called) belonging to [etc.]. 1875 J. G. HOLLAND *Sevenoaks* xii. 157 Can't we put on an ell when we want it? 1876 'MARK TWAIN' *Tom Sawyer* ix. 81 A single minute later he was.. creeping along the roof of the 'ell' on all fours. 1888 *Pall Mall G.* 6 June 6/1, I had occasion to rebuild the ell of a dwelling-house. On removing the old ell.. a rat's nest was found when it was joined to the main structure. 1892 W. D. HOWELLS *Mercy* xix. 367 Matt could see a light in the ell-chamber. 1904 T. WATSON *Bethany* (1920) 9 So it came to pass that two handsome rooms were built in the front of the west end of the old house, forming an 'ell' thereto. 1924 H. CROY *R.F.D. No. 3* 60 Higbee's house.. was dirty white in color, with a series of ells and lean-tos fastened to it.

ellagate ('ɛləgət). [f. ELLAGIC: see -ATE[4].] A salt of ellagic acid.

1819 CHILDREN *Chem. Anal.* 276 Ellagate of potassa forms brilliant pearly scales like talc. 1882 WATTS *Dict. Chem.* s.v. *Ellagic*, The ellagates are little known; many of them appear to be basic salts.

ellagic (ɛ'lædʒɪk), *a.* [ad. Fr. *ellagique*, f. *ellag*, anagram of *galle* gall-nut: see -IC. The name GALLIC had been pre-occupied by another acid obtained from galls.]

ellagic acid: $C_{14}H_8O_9$ (Watts *Dict. Chem.* 3rd Suppl.); originally obtained from oak-galls; found also in bezoar, whence the synonym *bezoartic acid.*

1810 HENRY *Elem. Chem.* (1840) II. 243 Ellagic acid.. is a tasteless white powder, with a shade of buff. 1819 CHILDREN *Chem. Anal.* 277 Ellagic acid dissolves in concentrated sulphuric acid. 1882 WATTS *Dict. Chem.* s.v.

ellagitannin (ɛlədʒɪ'tænɪn). *Chem.* Also ellago-. [f. ELLAGI(C *a.* + TANNIN.] Any tannin that on hydrolysis gives ellagic acid and a sugar.

1895 *Naturalist* 25 Ellagotannin $C_{14}H_{10}O_{10}$, which is the most highly oxidised of vegetable astringents. 1898 *Proc. Chem. Soc.* 104 The presence of ellagic acid has also been detected, and thus besides gallotannin, ellagitannin is also present. 1956 HICKINBOTTOM & GARWOOD in E. H. Rodd *Chem. Carbon Compounds* IIIB. xii. 806 The hydrolysable tannins are usually divided into gallotannins which on hydrolysis give gallic acid, and ellagitannins which give ellagic acid. 1966 E. HASLAM *Chem. Vegetable Tannins* iv. 122 The most important sources of ellagitannins are.. Valonea, Myrobalans, Divi-divi and Algarobilla.

ellamy, var. of E-LA-MI, *Obs.*

†'**ellan.** *Obs.* [a. Fr. *élan*, a. Ger. *elend*; the Ger. word has been adopted through Du. in different sense as ELAND.] The Elk (*Alces malchis*).

1613 PURCHAS *Pilgr.* I. VIII. iv. 630 [Newfoundland and Nova Francia] The Ellan, Deare, Stagge, and Beare, are their game. *c* 1682 J. COLLINS *Making Salt in Eng.* 99 Deer called Ellans as big as Oxen.

ellar, dial. form of ELDER *sb.*[1], ALDER[1].

ellarn(e, obs. form of ELDER *sb.*[1]

elle, obs. rare var. of ILL; ? also of ELSE.

ellebore, -bory, obs. forms of HELLEBORE.

elleck ('ɛlɪk). A kind of fish: the Red Gurnard, *Trigla cuculus.*

1862 COUCH *Brit. Fishes* II. 19 The Elleck is caught on the west coast of England and Ireland at all seasons. 1867 SMYTH *Sailor's Word-bk.*, *Elleck*, the trivial name of the *Trigla cuculus.*

elle-maid, -maiden. A half-adoption, half-transl. of Da. *elle-pige* elf-girl.

1850 KEIGHTLEY *Fairy Mythol.* 234 The.. Wild-women of Germany bear a very strong resemblance to the Elle-maids of Scandinavia. *a* 1859 L. HUNT *Shewe Faire Seem.* xxv, Like trunk of dread Elle-maiden, haunting Germany.

ellen, obs. and dial. form of ELDER *sb.*[1]

†'**ellend.** *Obs.* [a. Ger. *elend*: cf. ELAND, ELLAN.] An elk.

1616 SURFLET *Country Farm* 150 The Ellend hath eares like unto an Asse.

†'**Ellenmas.** *Obs.* [f. *Ellen* = *Helena* + MASS; cf. *Christmas, Martinmas*, etc.] St. Helena's day; but the date intended is uncertain.

Two saints of the name were commemorated in England: 'St. Helen the virgin,' perhaps the one whose day is May 22; and Helena the mother of Constantine. The latter is probably intended here; her festival is Aug. 18, but the Sarum Martyrology assigns 'Saynt Elene' to May 18, the date of her translation.

1597 *Vestry Bks.* (Surtees) 41 About St Ellenmas Mr Deane keepinge Court here att Pittington. 1621 in *Naworth Househ. Bks.* (Surtees) 141 [A payment made June 8] due at the last St. Ellenmas Court, 1621.

eller, obs. or dial. form of ELDER *sb.*[1], ALDER[1].

ellestadite (ɛlɪ'stædaɪt). *Min.* [f. the name of R. B. *Ellestad* (b. 1900), American analytical chemist + -ITE[1].] A halogen-containing mineral of the apatite group in which phosphorus is largely replaced by sulphur and silicon.

1937 D. MCCONNELL in *Amer. Mineralogist* XXII. 977 The name ellestadite is proposed for the end-member of the apatite group which contains SiO_4- and SO_4-groups substituting for PO_4-groups. 1959 P. F. KERR *Optical Min.* (ed. 3) xii. 230 Fermorite, strontian apatite, and ellestadite are similar to apatite in physical properties.

ellinge, var. of ELENGE *a.*, *Obs.*

Ellingtonian (ɛlɪŋ'təʊnɪən), *a.* and *sb.* [f. the name of the American musician, Edward ('Duke') *Ellington* (b. 1899) + -IAN.]

A. *adj.* Of, pertaining to, or characteristic of 'Duke' Ellington, or his musical productions. **B.** *sb.* A devotee or follower of Ellington. So **Elling'tonia** *sb. pl.*, music written by, or in the style of, Ellington.

1933 *Fortune* (U.S.) Aug. 93/1 By the time the orchestra plays them they are Ellingtonian. 1952 B. ULANOV *Hist. Jazz Amer.* (1958) xv. 180 His shaking of the maracas, the rattling gourds which several other Ellingtonians quickly picked up. 1958 in P. Gammond *Decca Bk. Jazz* viii. 103 From this solid root of Ellingtonian music.. grew.. mainstream jazz. *Ibid.* xxi. 262 Some of these.. were mere adaptations of pop tunes, bop tunes and Ellingtonia. 1961 *John o' London's* 6 July 55/1 Duke and his faithful esquire.. take five numbers from Grieg and turn them into authentic Ellingtonia.

ellipse (ɛ'lɪps). [ad. Gr. ἔλλειψις, n. of action f. ἐλλείπειν to come short. (In the case of the ellipse regarded as a conic section the inclination of the cutting plane to the base 'comes short of', as in the case of the hyperbola it exceeds, the inclination of the side of the cone.)

Not in Johnson, Todd, or Richardson (1836); for early examples of the pl. *ellipses* see ELLIPSIS.]

1. A plane closed curve (in popular language a regular oval), which may be defined in various ways: **a.** Considered as a conic section; the figure produced when a cone is cut obliquely by a plane making a smaller angle with the base than the side of the cone makes with the base. **b.** A curve in which the sum of the distances of any point from the two foci is a constant quantity. **c.** A curve in which the focal distance of any point bears to its distance from the directrix a constant ratio smaller than unity.

The planetary orbits being (approximately) elliptical, *ellipse* is sometimes used for 'orbit' (of a planet).

1753 CHAMBERS *Cycl. Supp.* s.v. *Ellipsis*, [The form *ellipse* is used throughout; the *Cycl.* 1751 has only *ellipsis*]. 1815 HUTTON *Math. Dict.*, Ellipse or Ellipsis. 1842 TENNYSON *Gold. Year* 24 The dark Earth follows wheel'd in her ellipse. 1868 LOCKYER *Heavens* (ed. 3) 120 A circle seen obliquely or perspectively shows the form of an ellipse. 1880 C. & F. DARWIN *Movem. Pl.* 1 Other irregular ellipses.. are successively described.

2. *transf.* An object or figure bounded by an ellipse. Also *fig.*

1857 BULLOCK tr. *Cazeaux's Midwif.* 29 The abdominal strait has been.. compared to an ellipse. 1869 DUNKIN *Midn. Sky* 163 An ellipse of small stars.

3. *Gram.* = ELLIPSIS 2. Somewhat *rare.*

1843–83 LIDDELL & SCOTT *Gr. Lex.* s.v. Ἔλλειψις. 1886 ROBY *Lat. Gram.* II (ed. 5) 511 (Index).

†**e'llipsed,** *ppl. a. nonce-wd.* [f. ELLIPS-IS + -ED.] Characterized by ellipsis.

1607 S. HIERON *Defence* I. 148 M. H. cannot show us one place in all the Bible so ellipsed or ecclipsed as to need, etc.

†**e'llipsical,** *a. Obs. rare.* In 6 ellepseycal. [f. ELLIPSE + -IC + -AL[1].] = ELLIPTICAL.

1571 DIGGES *Pantom.* IV. Pref., Ellepseycal circumscribed & inscribed bodies.

ellipsing (ɛ'lɪpsɪŋ), *ppl. a. rare.* [as if f. vb. **ellipse*; cf. *circling.*] Revolving in ellipses.

1878 T. SINCLAIR *Mount* 173 The whole well-balanced ellipsing solar system.

‖**ellipsis** (ɛ'lɪpsɪs). Pl. ellipses (-siːz). Also 7 elipsis, 8 elleipsis, *pl.* ellipsises. [a. L. *ellipsis*, ad. Gr. ἔλλειψις: see ELLIPSE.]

1. = ELLIPSE. Now *rare.*

1570 BILLINGSLEY *Euclid* XII. xv. 376 This section is a Conicall section, which is called Ellipsis. 1656 HOBBES *Six Less.* Wks. 1845 VII. 316 If the section be an ellipsis.. you may use the same method. 1677 MOXON *Mech. Exerc.* (1703) 272 The Ellipsis or Oval ABCD. 1692 BENTLEY *Boyle Lect.* 229 The planets.. could not possibly acquire such revolutions.. in ellipses very little eccentric. 1696 WHISTON *Th. Earth* I. (1722) 14 Comets' Ellipses come near to Parabola's. 1705–30 S. GALE in *Bibl. Topogr. Brit.* III. 47 A fine bowling-green cut into an ellipsis. 1854 TOMLINSON tr. *Arago's Astron.* 119 It had traversed.. an ellipsis.

†**b.** *attrib. Obs.*

1677 MOXON *Mech. Exerc.* (1703) 273 These Ellipsis, or Semi-Oval Arches.. are sometimes made over Gate-ways.

2. *Gram.* The omission of one or more words in a sentence, which would be needed to complete the grammatical construction or fully to express the sense; *concr.* an instance of such omission.

1612 BRINSLEY *Pos. Parts* (1669) 67 The first of the Substantives is oft understood by a figure called Ellipsis. *a* 1667 COWLEY *Davideis* I. Notes (1710) I. 368 It is an Elleipsis, or leaving something to be understood by the Reader. 1727 POPE, &c. *Art Sinking* 115 The ellipsis, or speech by half-words [is the peculiar talent] of ministers and politicians. 1789 BELSHAM *Ess.* I. ii. 25 Violent ellipses and inversions of language. 1789 BENTHAM *Princ. Legisl.* xviii. §27 *note.* The ancient lawyers in the construction of their appellatives have indulged themselves in much harsher ellipsises without scruple. 1848 MACAULAY *Hist. Eng.* II. 476 The ellipsis was now filled up with words of high import. 1874 H. REYNOLDS *John Bapt.* ii. 112 Grammatical roughnesses or ellipses.

†**3.** Formerly used as the name of the dash (—) employed in writing or printing to indicate the omission of letters in a word. *Obs.*

1824 L. MURRAY *Eng. Gram.* I. 413 An Ellipsis.. is used, when some letters in a word, or some words in a verse, are omitted: as 'The k—g' for 'the king'.

ellipsist (ɛ'lɪpsɪst). *nonce-wd.* [f. ELLIPS-IS + -IST.] One addicted to the use of the figure Ellipsis in argument or discourse.

1859 I. TAYLOR *Logic in Theol.* 42 These.. would hold in contempt the timidity of the ellipsists.

ellipsograph (ɛ'lɪpsəgrɑːf, -græf). Cf. ELLIPTOGRAPH. [f. ELLIPSE + -GRAPH, f. Gr. γράφειν to write.] An instrument for describing ellipses.

ellipsoid (ɛ'lɪpsɔɪd). [f. ELLIPSE + -OID.]

A. *sb.*

1. A solid of which all the plane sections through one of the axes are ellipses, and all other sections ellipses or circles. Formerly in narrower sense: A solid generated by the revolution of an ellipse round one of its axes; now called *ellipsoid of revolution.*

a 1721 KEILL tr. *Maupertuis' Diss.* (1734) 7 The Earth must be an Ellipsoid whose Equatorial Diameter is to its Axis as $\sqrt{289}$ to $\sqrt{288}$. 1787 *Phil. Trans.* LXXVII 202 Ellipsoids of different degrees of oblateness. 1831 BREWSTER *Optics* vi. 55 A meniscus whose convex surface is part of an ellipsoid. 1871 B. STEWART *Heat* §281 The isothermal surfaces are ellipsoids. 1879 C. NIVEN (*title*) On the Conduction of Heat in Ellipsoids of Revolution.

2. ? A figure approximately elliptical.

1837 WHEWELL *Hist. Induc. Sc.* (1857) II. 59 An eccentric ellipsoid; that is a figure resembling an ellipse.

B. *adj.* = next.

1861 HULME tr. *Moquin-Tandon* II. VI. i. 313 The eggs.. are ellipsoid or oval. 1870 HOOKER *Stud. Flora* 142 Styles erect or spreading, pollen ellipsoid.

ellipsoidal (ɛlɪp'sɔɪdəl), *a.* [f. prec. + -AL[1].] Having the nature or shape of an ellipsoid.

1831 BREWSTER *Optics* xli. §201. 344 A concave ellipsoidal reflector. 1845 TODD & BOWMAN *Phys. Anat.* I. 213 Some vesicles are.. ovoidal, or ellipsoidal. 1849 MURCHISON *Siluria* iii. (1867) 58 The Llandillo formation.. rises to the surface in the form of a rugged ellipsoidal mass. 1884 *Law Times* 9 Feb. 267/1 The proper shape for a ceiling of a room used for public speaking [is] ellipsoidal or coved.

ellipsone (ɛ'lɪpsəʊn). *nonce-wd.* [f. ELLIPSE, on the analogy of CYCLONE.] A revolving storm following an elliptical instead of a circular path.

1860 ADM. FITZ ROY in *Merc. Mar. Mag.* VII. 354 The smaller cyclonic motions (*ellipsones?*).

elliptic (ɛ'lɪptɪk), *a.* [ad. Gr. ἐλλειπτικός elliptic, defective, f. ἐλλείπειν to come short: cf. ELLIPSE.]

1. That has the form of an ellipse; pertaining to ellipses.

1726 tr. *Gregory's Astron.* I. 380 If the whole Area.. of the Elliptic Orbit be imagined to be divided into 360 equal Parts. 1776 GIBBON *Decl. & F.* I. xii. 262 A building of an elliptic figure. 1808 A. PARSONS *Trav. Afr.* iii. 36 All others [arches] which I had hitherto observed being elliptick. 1830 SIR J. HERSCHEL *Stud. Nat. Phil.* 11 These are the steps by which we have risen to a knowledge of the elliptic motions of the planets. 1877 B. WILLIAMSON *Int. Calculus* vii. 190 The area of any elliptic sector. 1888 W. W. ROUSE BALL *Hist. Math.* 292 The rectification of an elliptic arc.

¶ That has an elliptic (as opposed to a circular orbit): in quot. = 'eccentric'.

1806 MOORE *Epist.* II. i. 42 Every wild, elliptic star.

b. ***elliptic chuck***: a chuck for oval or elliptic turning; ***elliptic compass(es***, an instrument for drawing ellipses; ***elliptic spring*** (for carriages), a spring formed by two sets of curved plates, forming two elliptic arcs united at the ends.

c. *Comb.* In definitions of form: (*Bot.*) ***elliptic-lanceolate***, ***-oblong***, ***-obovate***, ***-ovate***, ***-ovoid*** adjs., having a form intermediate between elliptic and lanceolate, etc.

1845 LINDLEY *Sch. Bot.* vi. (1858) 88 Radical [leaves] *elliptic-lanceolate. 1870 HOOKER *Stud. Flora* 54 Lower leaves petioled *elliptic-oblong. *Ibid.* 417 Rhombic or *elliptic-obovate. *Ibid.* 234 Leaves *elliptic-ovate. *Ibid.* 410 Perigynia *elliptic-ovoid.

2. ***elliptic integrals***: a class of integrals discovered by Legendre in 1786, so named because their discovery was the result of the investigation of elliptic arcs. ***elliptic functions***: certain specific functions of these integrals. (Formerly the term *elliptic functions* was applied to what are now called *elliptic integrals*.)

1845 *Penny Cycl. 1st Supp.* s.v., A large class of integrals closely related to and containing among them the expression for the arc of an ellipse have received the name of Elliptic functions. 1876 CAYLEY *Elliptic Functions* 8 sn *u* is a sort of sine function, and cn *u*, dn *u* are sorts of cosine-functions of *u*; these are called Elliptic Functions. 1881 WILLIAMSON in *Encycl. Brit.* XIII. 63 The epithet 'elliptic' applied to these integrals is purely conventional, arising from the connexion of one of them with the arc of an ellipse.

3. *Gram.* Of sentences, phrases, or style: Characterized by ellipsis; = ELLIPTICAL 2.

4. quasi-*sb.* (*nonce-use.*)

1807 SOUTHEY *Espriella's Lett.* (1814) II. 79 They were talking of parabolics and ellipticals, and describing diagrams on the table with a wet finger.

Hence as combining form **e'lliptico-**.

1876 HARLEY *Mat. Med.* 389 Leaves..elliptico-lanceolate. 1883 *St. James's Gaz.* 3 Feb. 6 His style..is of the elliptico-interjectional sort.

elliptical (ɛ'lɪptɪkəl), *a.* [f. prec. + -AL¹.]

1. That has the form of an ellipse; pertaining to ellipses.

1656 HOBBES *Six Less.* Wks. 1845 VII. 305 The cone described by the subtense of the..elliptical line. 1755 B. MARTIN *Mag. Arts & Sc.* I. v. 23 They all move in Orbits, which are more or less oval, or (as the Astronomers call it) Elliptical. 1812–6 J. PLAYFAIR *Nat. Phil.* II. 185 The orbit of the fourth satellite is sensibly elliptical. 1831 BREWSTER *Optics* xxvii. 225, I have been enabled to refer all the phenomena of the action of metals to a new species of polarisation, which I have called elliptical polarisation. 1878 HUXLEY *Physiogr.* xx. 354 In the great elliptical path of the earth the sun occupies one of these foci.

b. ***elliptical compasses***: = elliptic compasses. †***elliptical dial***, a small pocket-dial (Kersey). Also in Bailey 1721–1790, Chambers 1751.

c. *Comb.*

1845 LINDLEY *Sch. Bot.* v. (1858) 53 Leaves *elliptical-lanceolate.

2. *Gram.* Of sentences and phrases: Defective, lacking a word or words which must be supplied to complete the sense. Of style, etc.: Characterized by ellipsis.

1778 BP. LOWTH *Isaiah* (ed. 12) 313 *note*, It was necessary to add a word or two in the version to supply the elliptical expression of the Hebrew. 1828 WHATELY *Rhetoric* in *Encycl. Metrop.* 284/1 Aristotle's Style..is frequently so elliptical as to be dry and obscure. 1848 MILL *Pol. Econ.* I. iii. §1 (1876) 29 Production and productive, are..elliptical expressions, involving the idea of a something produced. 1884 TRAILL in *Macm. Mag.* Oct. 441/1 Carlyle's violently elliptical manner.

3. Omitted by ellipsis. ? *nonce-use.*

1829 W. DUNCAN *Greek Test.* Pref., He has given at the foot of the page..many of the principal elliptical words.

elliptically (ɛ'lɪptɪkəlɪ), *adv.* [f. prec. + -LY².] In an elliptical manner.

1. *Gram.* With use of ellipsis.

1816 J. GILCHRIST *Philos. Etym.* Introd. 21 Almost every word is put elliptically. 1856 DOVE *Logic Chr. Faith* I. i. §2. 39 [Certain sciences] use..elliptically, the Syllogism.

2. In the form or after the manner of an ellipse.

1831 BREWSTER *Optics* xxvii. 229 Light polarised + 45° is elliptically polarised.

e'llipticalness. *rare.* [f. ELLIPTICAL *a.* + -NESS.] The quality of being elliptical.

1681 H. MORE *Exp. Dan.* App. iii. 300 According to the Ellipticalness of the Apocalyptick style.

ellipticity (ɛlɪp'tɪsɪtɪ). [f. ELLIPTIC + -ITY.] Elliptic form; degree of deviation (of an orbit, etc.) from circularity, (of a spheroid) from sphericity.

1753 *Phil. Trans.* XLVIII. 84 [In] the case of beds supposed of the same ellipticity..I have taken greater care. 1833 SIR J. HERSCHEL *Astron.* iii. 109 Its deviation from the circular form, arising from so very slight an ellipticity. 1864 *Athenæum* No. 1926. 402/2 The ellipticity of Mars. 1870 JEVONS *Elem. Log.* xxxiii. (1880) 291 An orbit of slight ellipticity.

b. as a measurable quantity.

The ellipticity of a spheroid (e.g. of the figure of a planet) is expressed by some mathematicians as the ratio of the difference of the axes to the major axis, and by others as the ratio of this difference to the minor axis. (With reference to orbits this mode of expressing ellipticity is not used; see ECCENTRICITY 3 b.)

1753 *Phil. Trans.* XLVIII. 77 The diminution of the gravity having been found greater than $\frac{1}{230}$, the ellipticity or difference of diameters ought to be less than that fraction. 1831 BREWSTER *Newton* (1855) I. xiii. 361 The ellipticity of the earth..has been found to be $\frac{1}{299}$. 1867 DENISON *Astron. without Math.* 7 Its ellipticity..means the proportion between the difference of the two axes..of an ellipse, and the greater of them.

elliptograph. = ELLIPSOGRAPH.

1855 *Encycl. Brit.* (ed. 8) s.v. [A description of the instrument].

†**ellip'toides.** *Obs.* Also 8 **elliptoide.** [Badly f. *ellipt-* (cf. ELLIPTIC) + mod.L. *-oides*: see -OID.] An infinite ellipse.

1731 BAILEY, Elliptoides. 1796 HUTTON *Math. Dict.*, Elliptoide, an infinite or indefinite Ellipsis, defined by the indefinite equation $ay^{m+n} = bx^m. a-x^n$ when *m* or *n* are greater than 1.

‖**ellops** ('ɛlɒps). *Obs.* in actual use. [a. Gr. ἔλλοψ or ἔλοψ, the name of a fish and of a serpent.

(The variants ELAPS and ELOPS are used in mod. zoological Latin in different senses).]

1. A kind of serpent.

1667 MILTON *P.L.* x. 526 Cerastes hornd, Hydrus, and Ellops drear.

2. A kind of fish mentioned by ancient writers.

1601 HOLLAND *Pliny* I. 266 The Lamprey in Sicilie: the Elops at Rhodes, and so forth of other sorts of fishes. 1774 GOLDSM. *Nat. Hist.* (1862) II. I. iii. 299 The Elops or Sea-serpent. 1775 ASH, *Ellops*, a fish affording delicious food which some think to be the sturgeon of the moderns. 1875 BROWNING *Aristoph. Apol.* 110 Spends all his substance on stewed ellops-fish.

ellore, obs. f. ELDER *sb.*¹ (the tree).

ell-rake. *dial.* Also **eld-**, **eller-rake.** [Derivation uncertain; cf. ELCROOK; the writers of the Chesh. and Shropsh. glossaries suggest *heel-rake*. Halliwell gives also '*Ellock-rake*, a small rake for breaking up ant-hills. *Salop.*'] A large rake with curved iron teeth, drawn behind the raker.

1879 *Shropsh. Word-bk.* (E.D.S.) Ellrake, eldrake. 1884 *Chesh. Gloss.* (E.D.S.) Ell-rake, eller-rake.

ell-wand ('ɛlwɒnd). Chiefly *Sc.* and *north. dial.* Also 5 **elenwand**, **ellewande**, **elwonde**, *Sc.* **elnewande**, 7–9 **elwand.** [f. ELL + WAND.]

1. A measuring rod, an ell-measure: sometimes used for 'yard-measure'.

[1403 *Nottingham Borough Rec.* II. 34 Ipse Johannes cepit quendam elenwand, et ipsam percussit super capud.] ?*a* 1500 tr. *Leges Burgorum Scociæ* xlviii. in *Sc. Acts* (1844) I. 342 Ilk burges may hafe in his hous..ane elnewand. 1609 SKENE *Reg. Maj.* 36 The heire of ane burges, is of perfite age, quhen he..can..measure claith (with ane elwand). 1725 RAMSAY *Gentle Sheph.* III. i, An elwand fills his hand, his habit mean. 1834 H. MILLER *Scenes & Leg.* xxi. (1857) 304 Beating time with his ellwand on the point of his shoe.

†**2.** The larger of the bones of the fore-arm; = ULNA. *Obs.*

c 1440 *Promp. Parv.* 139 Elle wande [*P.* elwonde,] *ulna.*

3. *Sc.* The group of stars called Orion's Belt.

1513 DOUGLAS *Æneis* VIII. Prol. 153 The son, the sevin sternis, and the Charll wane, The elwand, the elementis, and Arthuris hufe. *c* 1817 HOGG *Tales & Sk.* IV. 29 King's Elwand (now foolishly termed the Belt of Orion).

elm (ɛlm), *sb.* Forms: 1 **elm**, 5–7 **elme**, 9 *dial.* **elem**, **ellum**, 4– **elm.** Also 4 **ulm**, 6 **ulme.** [OE. *elm* str. masc. = OHG. *elm* str. masc. (whence the derivatives MHG. *elme*, *ilme*, *ilmene* wk. fem.) :—WGer. **elmo-z*; the same word with difference of ablaut appears as ON. *álmr* (Sw. *alm*, Da. *alm*, *ælm*) etymologically = L. *ulmus*. The mod.Ger. *ulme*, Du. *olm*, and the Eng. form *ulm(e*, are due to the influence of the Lat. word.]

1. The name of well-known trees belonging to the genus *Ulmus*, esp., in England, the Common or Small-leaved Elm (*Ulmus campestris*), a tree having rough, doubly serrated leaves, flowers nearly sessile, the fruit oblong, deeply cloven and glabrous; in Scotland, the Witch or Wych Elm (*Ulmus montana*) or the Cork-barked Elm (*Ulmus suberosa*); in U.S. the White Elm (*Ulmus americana*).

c 1000 *Sax. Leechd.* II. 52 Eft ȝenim elmes rinde, ȝebærn to ahsan. 1382 WYCLIF *Isa.* xli. 19, I shal sette in desert fyrr tree and vlm and box togidere. *c* 1440 *Promp. Parv.* 138 Elm, tre, *ulmus.* 1541 *Act. 33 Hen. VIII.* c. 9 §5 Two other bowes..of ashe, elme, wyche, hasyll or other wood mete for the same. 1567 DRANT *Horace Epist.* I. vii. D vj, Our cittizen is now a Corridon. He trimmes his ulmes. 1664 EVELYN *Sylva* iv. §6 The Elm delights in a sound, sweet and fertile Land. 1750 GRAY *Elegy* iv, Beneath those rugged elms, that yew tree's shade. 1794 MARTYN *Rousseau's Bot.* xvii. 224 Few persons know that the Elm has any flower. 1830 LINDLEY *Nat. Syst. Bot.* 94 The inner bark of the Elm is slightly bitter and astringent. 1850 TENNYSON *In Mem.* xciv. 58 Rock'd the full foliaged elms. 1858 O. W. HOLMES *One-hoss Shay*, Logs from the 'Settler's ellum'. 1877 E. PEACOCK *N.W. Linc. Gloss.* (E.D.S.) *Elem*, the elm. 1881 *Isle Wight Gloss.* (E.D.S.) *Ellum*, an elm.

2. With distinguishing epithets, denoting the above-named and other species of the genus *Ulmus*: **broad-leaved elm**, *Ulmus latifolia* or *montana*; **Chichester elm**, also called **American elm**, *Ulmus americana*; **Dutch elm**: see DUTCH A. *adj.* 3 c. **witch** or **wych elm**, *Ulmus montana*. Also **yoke elm**, the HORNBEAM (*Carpinus Betulus*).

1876 HARLEY *Mat. Med.* 423 The Broad-Leaved Elm.. 60–80 feet high, with rugged bark. 1882 *Garden* 11 Nov. 419/3 The Chichester Elm..is variously known as the Huntingdon, Scampston, or unfortunately as the American Elm.

3. *fig.* with reference to the practice of training vines on elms.

1590 SHAKS. *Com. Err.* II. ii. 179 Thou art an Elme my husband, I a Vine. 1643 *Myst. Iniq.* 2 Subverting the Protestant Religion, together with the Subjects Liberty, (the Elme of that Vine).

4. The wood of these trees.

1823 P. NICHOLSON *Pract. Build.* 261 Elm is another tough and strong species of wood.

5. *Comb.*, chiefly *attrib.*, as ***elm-dresser***, ***-plank***, ***-shadow***, ***-tree***, ***-wood***; ***elm-arched***, ***-bordered***, ***-embosomed***, ***-encircled***, ***-fringed***, ***-grey*** adjs.; **elm-balm**, the fluid contained in elm-galls; **elm bark beetle**, **elm (leaf) beetle**, (see quots); **elm butterfly**, a butterfly whose larva feeds on the leaves of the elm, as the comma-butterfly (*Grapta comma-album*); **Elm City** (also *City of Elms*) *U.S.* (see quots.); **elm-gall**, the gall produced on the different species of elm by the puncture of *Aphis ulmi*; **elm-pipe**, the trunk of an elm hollowed for use as a drain or water-pipe.

1860 *Harper's Mag.* June 4/1, I wandered through the *elm-arched streets [of New Haven] in solitude as absolute as though I trod the aisles of a primeval forest. 1868 J. R. LOWELL *Al Fresco* (1896) 61 Upon these elm-arched solitudes No hum of neighbor toil intrudes. 1861 MISS PRATT *Flower. Pl.* V. 42 Galls are also produced on the leaves by the puncture of a cynips, and each gall contains some drops of liquid, which has been called *Elm balm. 1909 *Cent. Dict.* Suppl., **Elm bark-beetle*, a scolytid beetle, *Phlæophthorus liminaris*, which bores the bark of elm-trees. 1936 *Discovery* Feb. 41/2 The Elm-Bark Beetle (*Eccoptogaster scotylus* Fab.) has increased remarkably in recent years and as it carries the fungus of elm disease, its increase is a serious economic problem of the future. 1961 *New Scientist* 16 Mar. 665/1 DDT..is used to control the elm-bark beetle. 1876 *Field & Forest* II. 12 One [insect] found destroying the foliage of the elm, pronounced..to be *Galeruca calmariensis*, the *elm beetle. 1902 C. J. CORNISH *Naturalist on Thames* xxxvi. 224 The *elm-bordered meadows of the Vale of White Horse. 1872 A. S. PACKARD *Study Insects* Index 692/1 *Elm butterfly. 1843 *Yale Lit. Mag.* VIII. 328 Some inconsiderate hard-hearted beauty, that was supposed to reside somewhere in the '*City of Elms'. 1871 SCHELE DE VERE *Americanisms* (1872) 664 New Haven in Connecticut, is known throughout the United States as Elm City, from the number and magnificent size of the elm-trees that adorn the public squares and most of the principal streets. 1596 in Rogers *Agric. & Prices* III. 578 *Elm dresser 20/. 1839 CLOUGH *Poems* II. 11 Field and wood And *elm-embosomed spire. 1777 T. WARTON *Poems* Ode vii, Or grange, or *elm-encircled farm. 1909 *Westm. Gaz.* 14 Apr. 5/1 The *elm-fringed arm of the Tyburn stream. 1935 E. BOWEN *House in Paris* I. v. 70 The *elm-grey autumn park. 1881 *Amer. Naturalist* XV. 242 Inquiries about the imported *elm leaf-beetle. 1731 S. HALES *Stat. Ess.* II. App., Where *elm-pipes lay underground. 1677 MOXON *Mech. Exerc.* (1703) 173 An Oaken plank, or *Elm plank. 1835 MRS. HEMANS *Haunted House*, Where the deep *elm shadows fall. 1562 TURNER *Herbal* II. 169 b, The leues, the boughes, and the barck of the *elm tre, haue a binding vertue. 1688 R. HOLME *Armoury* II. 52/1 The Elme Tree is of some called All-Heart. 1771 GOLDSM. *Hist. Engl.* II. 387 Her body was..thrown into a common chest of elm tree. 1832 TENNYSON *Dream Fair Wom.* 57 Enormous elmtree-boles did stoop and lean Upon the dusky brushwood underneath Their broad curved branches.

elm, var. of HELM *sb.* and *v.* *dial.*

†**elmawes.** *Obs. rare*⁻¹.

a 1500 *Voc.* in Wr.-Wülcker 591 *Lameres*, *anglice* elmawes.

elmen ('ɛlmən), *a.* Now *dial.* or *arch.* Forms: 5 **elmyn**, (6–7 **elming**), 5–9 **elmin**, 5– **elmen.** [f. ELM + -EN.]

1. Of or pertaining to an elm-tree.

1494 FABYAN VII. 585 They were hanged vpon an elmyn tree. 1599 T. M[OUFET] *Silkwormes* 56 Tender Elming bud May..be giuen in steede of foode. 1607 TOPSELL *Four-f. Beasts* 301 Let him feed upon..Elming boughs. 1676 HOBBES *Iliad* VI. 402 Planted about it many Elmen-trees. 1807 CRABBE *Hall Justice*, We slept beneath the elmin tree. 1813 SCOTT *Rokeby* II. xxvii, Leaning against the elmin tree. 1881 PALGRAVE *Visions Eng.* 21 The elmen leaf Thinn'd into gold, and fell.

2. Made of the wood of the elm-tree.

1466 *Mann. & Househ. Exp.* 323 Item, for lx. fete of elmen borde, xx.*d.* 1648 *Bury Wills* (1850) 209 A great chest of elming borde.

3. Composed of elm-trees.

1876 *World* No. 106. 19 The elmen bowers are in their prime of foliage.

Elmenteitan (ɛlmɛn'teɪtən), *a.* [f. *Elmenteita*, a lake in Central Kenya + -AN.] Of, or relating to, the mesolithic culture which belongs to the Makalian wet phase, and which was found in deposits of the East African lake Elmenteita by

Dr. L. S. B. Leakey in 1927. Also as *sb.*, a member of this culture; the culture itself.

1929 L. S. B. LEAKEY in *S. Afr. Jrnl. Sci.* XXVI. 754 The Elmenteitan. This is a localised development from the Upper Kenyan Aurignacian in Makalian times. It has no exact parallel in Europe, but has close affinities with the Magdalenian. **1931** —— *Stone Age Cultures Kenya Colony* viii. 172 The Elmenteitan culture certainly represents a very late and aberrant development of the upper Kenya Aurignacian culture. **1939** C. S. COON *Races of Europe* iv. 85 The East African Elmenteitans represent.. a gerontomorphic or sexually differentiated Mediterranean or Galley Hill form, and in cranial features [are] closer to Galley Hill itself than any other branch. **1964** K. P. OAKLEY *Framework for dating Fossil Man* II. 268 The Elmenteitan was named after Lake Elmenteita, for the typical occurrence is in Gamble's Cave which is close to the lake.

elmes, elmisse, elmys, obs. ff. ALMS, q.v.

elmy ('ɛlmɪ). [f. ELM *sb.* + -Y.] Consisting of, characterized by, or abounding in elms.

1757 DYER *Fleece* I. 206 The sandy soil Of elmy Ross. **1795** SOUTHEY *Joan of Arc* x. 5 The summer breeze Moves o'er the elmy vale. **1799** COLERIDGE in *New Monthly Mag.* (1835) XLV. 225 We have elmy hedges. **1873** MISS THACKERAY *Old Kensington* i. 4 The old palace that stands blinking its sleepy windows across elmy vistas.

eln(e, obs. var. of ELL.

†**elne, 'ellen**, *sb. Obs.* [Com. Teut.: OE. *ęllen* (gen. *ęlnes*) corresponds to OS. *ellen, ellien*, OHG. *ellan, ellen, ellin*, Goth. *aljan* str. neut.; ON. *eljan, eljun* str. fem. (Icel. *elja* wk. fem.):—OTeut. types **aljano(m*, **aljanâ*.]

Strength, courage (also, in OE., zeal); in *Theol.* strength vouchsafed, comfort, grace.

Beowulf 602 Ac ic him ȝeata sceal Eafoð and ellen unȝeara nu guþe ȝebeodan. **888** K. ÆLFRED *Boeth.* xxvii. §2 (Bosw.) Feower cræftas, þara is an wærscipe, oðer metȝung, þridde is ellen. *a* **1000** *Guthlac* 264 Wæs Guþlac on elne strong. *a* **1225** *Ancr. R.* 106 Vor ȝe schulden wenen þet God, uor ouwer holi liue, sende ou his grace and his elne. *c* **1230** *Hali Meid.* 27 Ah monnes elne is muche wurð. *a* **1240** *Ureisun* in *Cott. Hom.* 185 We.. buggeþ worldles froure. wiþ moni sori teone. and elne of monnes speche. *Ibid.* Hwa se euer haueð longe wone of gastliche elne.

Hence **'ellenlæs** *a.* [see -LESS], powerless.

a **1000** *Juliana* 393 (Gr.) Ic ȝeomor sceal secan oðerne ellenleasran cempan. *c* **1200** *Ormin* 10908 Illc meocnesse iss ellenlæs Wiþþutenn herrsummnesse.

†**'elne**, *v. Obs.* [OE. *ęlnian* = OHG. *ellinôn*, ON. *elna*, Goth. *aljanôn*:—OTeut. **aljanôjan*, f. **aljano-m*: see prec.] *trans.* To strengthen, hearten, comfort.

a **1225** *Ancr. R.* 10 Gon & iseon swuch & elnen ham & helpen mid fode of holi lore. *a* **1225** *Leg. Kath.* 1374 As men droh ham to hare deað, þa.. elnede þe oðre. *a* **1240** *Lofsong* in *Cott. Hom.* 215 Ich wot þet þu wult senden me þene holi gost to elnen me.

†**'elning.** *Obs.* [OE. *ęlnung*, f. *ęlnian*, ELNE *v.*: see -ING[1].] Comfort, grace.

a **1240** *Ureisun* in *Cott. Hom.* 185 Min ihesu liues louerd þu beodest us þin elning [*printed* elming]. *Ibid.* 201 þu beodest þin elning.

†**elo'cation.** *Obs. rare.* [as if ad. L. **ēlocātiōn-em*, n. of action f. *ēlocāre*, lit. to place out, f. *ē* out + *-locāre* to place.]

1. Removal from a person's control.

1649 BP. HALL *Cases Consc.* (1650) 294 When the child by.. former elocation shall be out of the Parents disposing.

2. *fig.* Alienation (of mind), ecstasy.

a **1619** FOTHERBY *Atheom.* I. v. §1 (1622) 30 In all Poesie.. there must be.. an elocation, and emotion of the minde.

elocular (ɪ'lɒkjʊlə(r)), *a. Bot.* [f. *ē* out + *locul-us* small cell + -AR.] Without partitions or loculi.

1864 in WEBSTER.

elocute ('ɛləkjuːt), *v.* [Playful back-formation f. ELOCUTION.] To practise elocution; to declaim in an elocutionary manner.

1884 'MARK TWAIN' *Huck. Finn* 315 They didn't yellocute long till the audience got up. **1896** *Idler* Mar. 183/1 'Elocute' as he might, his reputation was always overshadowed by that of a 'past' boy. **1908** *Dialect Notes* III. IV. 308 *Elocute, v.i.*, to recite in elocutionary style. **1920** S. LEWIS *Main Street* x. 121 That was fine. I don't know but what you can elocute just as good as Ella. *Ibid.* iv. 47 Ella is our shark at elocuting. **1963** *Times* 14 May 15/4 Dorothy Reynolds's Oenone, flutingly elocuted.

elocution (ɛlə'kjuːʃən). Forms: 6 elocucion, -sion, -syon, eloquution, 6– elocution. [ad. L. *ēlocūtiōn-em*, n. of action f. *ēloqui* to speak out: cf. ELOQUENCE.

Sense 1 is identical with the meaning of *elocutio* as used by Roman rhetoricians. Sense 4, which has been evolved from the etymology without regard to Latin usage, corresponds to what the Romans expressed by *pronuntiatio*.]

†**1. a.** Oratorical or literary expression of thought; literary 'style' as distinguished from 'matter'; the power or art of appropriate and effective expression. *Obs.*

1509 HAWES *Past. Pleas.* XI. i, Elocusion with the powre of Mercury, The matir enorneth right well facundyously. **1553** T. WILSON *Rhet.* 4 Elocucion is an applying of apte wordes and sentences to the matter founde out to confirme the cause. **1586** WEBBE *Eng. Poetrie* (Arb.) 19 Why should we think so basely of this? rather then of her sister, I meane Rhetoricall Eloquution. **1634** HABINGTON *Castara* (Arb.) 11 How unhappie soever I may be in the elocution, I am sure the Theame is worthy enough. **1681** NEVILE *Plato Rediv.* 167 A Person of good Learning and Elocution. **1731** BAILEY vol. II, *Elocution* (with Rhetoricians) consists in apt expressing, and a beautiful order of placing of words. **1844** LINGARD *Hist. Anglo-Sax. Ch.* (1858) II. xi. 171 Your.. acquaintance with those forms of elocution in which it is expressed.

†**b.** *concr.* A mode of expression. *Obs.*

a **1679** HOBBES *Rhet.* (1840) 492 Elocutions are made decent: 1. By speaking feelingly.. 2. By speaking as becomes the person of the speaker, etc.

†**2.** Eloquence, oratory; *concr.* in *pl.* harangues.

1593 NASHE *Christ's T.* 39 a, How shall I arme myne elocution. **1631** MASSINGER *Emp. East* II. i, She'll tire me with Her tedious elocutions. **1635** NAUNTON *Fragm. Reg.* (Arb.) 49 She began to be taken with his elocution. **1649** MILTON *Eikon.* 241 To stirr the constancie of any wise man is.. above the genius of his cleric elocution. **1715–20** POPE *Iliad* III. 283 When he speaks, what elocution flows! **1791** COWPER *Iliad* IX. 549 Both elocution and address in arms.

3. Oral utterance; way or manner of speaking. Now only with some notion of 4.

1623 COCKERAM, *Elocution*, vtterance. **1667** MILTON *P.L.* IX. 747 Whose taste.. Gave elocution to the mute. **1754** RICHARDSON *Grandison* (1781) II. xxix. 274 He had a lively and easy elocution. **1794** GODWIN *Cal. Williams* 18 For this Mr. Tyrrel was indebted to a boisterous and overbearing elocution. **1795** BURKE *Let.* Wks. VII. 371 You have a natural, fluent, and unforced elocution. **1846** RUSKIN *Mod. Paint.* I. I. I. ii. §7 The clear and vigorous elocution of useless and senseless words.

4. The art of public speaking so far as it regards delivery, pronunciation, tones, and gestures; manner or style of oral delivery. Also *attrib.*

1613 R. C. *Table Alph.* (ed. 3), *Elocution*, good vtterance of speech. **1678** PHILLIPS, *Elocution*, proper Speech, handsome utterance. **1739** CIBBER *Apol.* (1756) I. 87 True theatrical elocution. **1815** SCOTT *Guy M.* xxxvii, It.. served to give zest and peculiarity to the style of elocution. **1864** *Sat. Rev.* 13 Dec. 819/1 The worst of the other system, that of boarding-schools and 'elocution-masters', is that, etc.

Hence **elo'cutional** *a.*, **elo'cutionally** *adv.*

1933 *Times Lit. Suppl.* 30 Mar. 220/3 Sentence-form being in the main elocutional, there may be sentences without locutional sentence-form. **1932** A. H. GARDINER *Theory Speech & Lang.* v. 322 No sentence can be really elocutionally formless, since utterance itself imposes a certain minimum of form.

elocutionary (ɛlə'kjuːʃənərɪ), *a.* [f. prec. + -ARY.] Of or pertaining to elocution.

1846 POE *Wks.* (1864) III. 40 The elocutionary.. value of her programmes. **1882** *Daily News* 7 Mar. 5/4 Mr. Newdegate, with great.. elocutionary effect, read the letter. **1884** *Manch. Exam.* 14 May 5/4 Dr. Parker's elocutionary gifts added to the strong impression which it made.

elocutionist (ɛlə'kjuːʃənɪst). [f. ELOCUTION + -IST.] One who practises the art of elocution; a proficient in the art of elocution.

1847 in CRAIG. **1860** *Daily News* 17 Dec., Mr. Bengough is a good elocutionist. **1875** WHITNEY *Life Lang.* xiv. 283 The.. variations of tone which the skilled elocutionist uses.

elocutionize (ɛlə'kjuːʃənaɪz), *v.* [f. ELOCUTION + -IZE.] *intr.* **a.** To make use of florid or eloquent language. **b.** To speak or read in public.

a **1849** POE *Wks.* (1864) III. 250 The author proceeds.. to elocutionize. **1883** *Homiletic Monthly* Aug. 661 The two tasks [of a preacher].. writing and elocutionizing.

elocutive (ɪ'lɒkjʊtɪv), *a.* and *sb. rare.* [as if ad. L. **ēlocūtīv-us*, f. *ēloqui*: see ELOCUTION.]

A. *adj.* That is concerned with utterance or eloquence. **B.** *sb.* An utterance.

1627 FELTHAM *Resolves* II. xlviii. (1677) 254 Though Preaching in it's elocutive part be but the conception of Man. **1821** *New Monthly Mag.* II. 41 Mr. Manager.. went through the appeasing elocutives of dumb show.

e'locutory, *a. rare*[−1]. [ad. L. *ēlocūtōri-us* pertaining to oratorical expression.] That pertains to elocution; elocutionary.

1817 *Monthly Mag.* XLIV. 448 Dr. Carey has.. in forwardness, an elocutory edition of Thomson's Seasons.

elodea (ɛ'ləʊdɪə, ɛləʊ'diːə). *Bot.* [mod.L. (A. Michaux *Flora Boreali-Americana* (1803) I. 20), f. Gr. ἑλώδης marshy.] A member of a small genus of aquatic plants, belonging to the family Hydrocharidaceæ and native to temperate America; cultivated in aquaria and pools. (Cf. WATER-THYME 2.)

1894 DARWIN & ACTON *Pract. Physiol. Plants* i. 16 An Elodea leaf is mounted in water. **1937** E. C. B. WRIGHT *Gen. Plant Physiol.* viii. 226 The main study was made of the chloroplasts of the aquatic Elodea. **1955** *Sci. News Let.* 16 July 46/1 Elodea, the moss-like weed in most American goldfish bowls, yielded from 12 to 14 tons green weight to the acre in a Kansas pond. **1960** *Times* 9 July 9/5 Soft weed (such as Elodea, Hornwort).

e'loge. [a. Fr. *éloge*, ad. L. *ēlogium* (see ELOGIUM). Now treated as Fr.: pronounced (elɔʒ).]

†**1.** An expression of praise or commendation; an encomium. *Obs.*

c **1566** NUCE tr. *Seneca's Octavia* I. iii, That woman wight shal have alwaye This eloge yet. **1693** J. BEAUMONT *On Burnet's Th. Earth* I. 55 The Author here gives us an Eloge on Mountains. **1764** WILKES *Corr.* (1805) III. 128 The eloge which the noblest of poets gives me. *a* **1789** BURNEY *Hist. Mus.* III. iv. 287 Pere Mersenne.. has given us an.. eloge of him. **1802** *Edin. Rev.* I. 23 The latter member of this eloge would now be wholly unintelligible, if applied to a spirited coach-horse.

2. A funeral oration; a discourse in honour of a deceased person, *e.g.* that pronounced by a newly-elected member of the French Academy upon his predecessor.

c **1725** ATTERBURY *Epist. Corr.* I. (1783) 179, I return you, Sir, the two eloges, which I have perused with pleasure. I borrow that word from your language. **1753** CHAMBERS *Cycl. Supp.*, The secretary of the royal academy of sciences in Paris composes the eloges of such members as die. **1861** G. WILSON & GEIKIE *E. Forbes* xv. 553 Pronouncing the Eloge of his old master into whose place he now ascends!

†**'elogist.** *Obs.* [f. ELOGE + -IST.] 'One who pronounces a panegyric' (Todd).

a **1639** WOTTON *Rem.* (1685) 366 She did not want a passionate Elogist, as well as an excellent Preacher [for her funeral sermon].

‖**e'logium.** *Obs.* [L. *ēlogium* a short saying, an inscription on a tombstone; this word and its mod. forms seem to have been confused with EULOGIUM, EULOGY.]

1. An explanatory inscription.

a **1699** STILLINGFL. *Serm.* I. viii. (R.) The elogium of his cross, Jesus of Nazareth, King of the Jews.

2. = ELOGY 2–4.

1570–6 LAMBARDE *Peramb. Kent* (1826) 251 Where he bestoweth this honourable Elogium upon him. **1683** D. A. *Art Converse* 54 Let your Elogium's be alwaies within the circumference of common sense. *a* **1764** DODSLEY *Art Preach.* 99 In elogiums, 'tis the art, With plain simplicity to win the heart. *a* **1789** BURNEY *Hist. Mus.* (ed. 2) I. lx. 166 Posterity.. will.. meet with their names and elogiums.

†**'elogy.** *Obs.* Also 7–8 elogie. [Anglicized form of prec.]

1. An explanatory inscription, *esp.* on a monument or a portrait. Cf. ELOGIUM 1.

1605 BACON *Adv. Learn.* II. 13 Many personages.. deserue better than dispersed report, or barren Elogies. **1645** EVELYN *Mem.* (1857) I. 209 The effigies of the several Dukes, with their Elogies. **1658** J. BURBERY *Hist. Christina Q. Swedland* 422 In several pastboords hung their elogies. **1663** COWLEY *Verses & Ess.* (1669) 47 His Statue or Picture, with an Elogy under it, shall be placed in the Galery.

2. A brief summary of a person's character; a characterization; usually in favourable sense, a eulogy, expression of praise.

1612 DRAYTON *Poly-olb.* iv. *Notes* 70 But for Arthur you shall best know him in this elogie. This is that Arthur, etc. **1629** EARLE *Microcosm.* lxii. (Arb.) 87 No man.. comes off more with the elogie of a kind Gentleman. **1638** EVELYN *Mem.* (1857) I. 12 One Stokes.. did.. set forth a pretty book, which was published, with many witty elogies before it. **1681** tr. *Willis' Rem. Med. Wks.* Voc., Elogie, a report in praise or dispraise of a thing. **1704** EARL CROMARTY *Sp.* in *Lond. Gaz.* No. 4037/5 An Elogie or Panegerick on Her Majesty. **1740** JOHNSON *Blake* Wks. IV. 369 We must then admit, amidst our elogies and applauses.

3. A biographical notice (usually of a deceased person).

1644 MILTON *Judgm. Bucer* (1851) 291 Jacobus Verheiden.. in his Elogies of famous Divines. **1646** SIR T. BROWNE *Pseud. Ep.* IV. xii. 217 As Paulus Jovius hath delivered in his Elogie of learned men. **1652** C. STAPYLTON *Herodian* 74 Of such before as writ his Acts or Elogie, Some Records doe unto this day remain.

4. A funeral oration.

1677 *Govt. Venice* 197 His Funerals are kept in the Church of St. Mark; and his Elogy pronounced in presence of the Senat. **1689** EVELYN *Mem.* (1857) III. 296 She.. had her obsequies celebrated.. by a solemn procession, and elogy of all the witness of that renowned city.

‖**Elohim** (ɛ'ləʊhɪm, -hiːm). Also 7 elohym. [Heb. *ĕlōhīm*, pl. of *ĕlôah* god, but often construed as sing. with sense 'God' or 'a god'.] **a.** One of the Hebrew names of God, or of the gods.

1605 TIMME *Quersit.* I. ii. 7 That Elohym.. Who moved upon the waters. **1715** KERSEY, *Elohim*, one of the names of God in the bible. **1862** STANLEY *Jew. Ch.* (1877) I. i. 19 Abraham saw that all the Elohim were meant for God.

†**b.** *transf.* in allusion to the supposed use of the word in certain passages of the Bible to denote earthly potentates. (This interpretation is now abandoned, exc. in the ironical passage *Ps.* lxxxii. 6.)

1682 SIR T. BROWNE *Chr. Mor.* 19 He who.. sways the scepter of himself, not envying the glory of.. elohims of the earth.

c. *attrib.* = ELOHIMIC *a.*

1875 *Encycl. Brit.* III. 637/1 It is still possible to reconstruct at least the Elohim document. **1886** *Ibid.* XX. 30/1 The Elohim psalms.. have undergone a common editorial treatment distinguishing them from the rest of the Psalter. **1936** J. E. CARPENTER in A. S. Peake *Commentary on Bible* 122/1 He [*sc.* Jean Astruc] noticed that in different narratives the Deity was designated by different names... On this basis he distributed the contents of Genesis into two main documents, an Elohim narrative A and a Yahweh story B. **1963** S. SANDMEL *Hebrew Scriptures* xxvi. 330 There was a source additional to the Yahve and Elohim source, which could be called the Deuteronomic code.

Elohimic (ɛləʊˈhɪmɪk), *a. rare.* [f. prec. + -IC.] Of passages in the Hebrew scriptures: Characterized by the use of the word *Elohim* instead of the word *Yahveh*. See ELOHIST.

1871 F. BOLTON *Delitzsch on Ps.* III. 172 Two Elohimic fragments brought together. **1882-3** SCHAFF *Relig. Encycl.* III. 1954 The Elohimic psalms.

Elohism (ɛˈləʊhɪz(ə)m). [f. ELOH(IM) + -ISM.] The worship of Elohim.

1888 *Edin. Rev.* Apr. 502 It was the task of the great prophets..to bring Israel back to the primitive Elohism of the patriarchs.

Elohist (ɛˈləʊhɪst). [f. ELOH(IM) + -IST.] The name given by Hebraists to the author (or authors) of those parts of the Hexateuch which are marked by the use of *Elohim* as the name of God instead of *Yahveh* (popularly written *Jehovah*). See JEHOVIST, YAHVIST.

1862 H. J. ROSE *Bunsen* 77 Ilgen imagined two Elohists, and one Jehovist. **1882-3** SCHAFF *Relig. Encycl.* II. 1043/1 Amended by a younger Elohist and a Jehovistic editor.

Elohistic (ɛləʊˈhɪstɪk), *a.* [f. prec. + -IC.] Of or pertaining to the ELOHIST; characterized by the use of ELOHIM instead of *Yahveh*: see prec.

1841 RYLAND *Hengstenberg on Pentat.* (1847) 331 In some passages of the Elohistic part..Elohim must stand under all circumstances. **1863** JOHANNES LAICUS *Anti-Colenso* I, The Jehovistic passages taken by themselves require the Elohistic story to connect them. **1881** W. R. SMITH *Old Test. in Jew. Ch.* vii. 197 The Elohistic collection [of psalms]..was formed after the time of Ezra.

eloin, eloign (ɪˈlɔɪn), *v.* Forms: 6 eloine, eloygn, 6-7 esloyn(e, eloyn, 7 esloign, elloigne, 7-9 eloigne, 6- eloin, 8- eloign. [a. AF., OF. *esloignier* (Fr. *éloigner*) to remove to a distance:—late L. *exlongāre*, *ēlongāre* to remove to a distance (see ELONG *v.*). In English law-Latin *ēlongāre* is used in the various senses defined below.]

I. *gen.* (Sometimes *transf.* from the legal use.)

†**1.** To remove to a distance, *lit.* and *fig. Obs.*

1535 *Goodly Primer*, O bone Jesu wipe clean away that eloineth me from thee. **1575** *Brieff Disc. Troub. Franckford* 158 They shall be eloigned from us that would gladly succor the poore. **1624** FISHER in F. White *Repl. Fisher* 448 Their spirit being eloyned..from the contagion of the bodie. **1636** ABP. J. WILLIAMS *Holy Table* (1637) 205 If the Table be so far esloigned from the people. **1653** COGAN tr. *Pinto's Voy.* xxix. (1663) 115 Leastwise labour to esloign thy minde from the vanities of the Earth. **1692** *Christ Exalted* § 127. 98 Thou hast eloyned, or cast me far away.

b. *refl.* To take oneself off, abscond; to retire to a distance, seclude oneself (*from*). Now *rare.*

1539 *Act 31 Hen. VIII*, c. 8 If any person..eloine..himselfe within any parte of this realme. **1575** TURBERV. *Bk. Venerie* 35 The harte..eloygning him self from the houndes. **1596** SPENSER *F.Q.* I. iv. 20 From worldly cares himselfe he did esloyne. **1662** FULLER *Worthies Linc.* II. 162 If..you should elloigne your self by residence there from those imployments. **1818** COLERIDGE *Rem.* (1836) I. 223 The artist must..eloign himself from nature. **1858** HOGG *Shelley* II. 402 He eloigned himself, and evaded pursuit.

II. *spec.* in *Law.*

2. *trans.* To convey or remove out of the jurisdiction of the court or of the sheriff.

1558 *Act 1 Eliz.* c. 21. §25 If..his goods or chattels be so eloyned. **1682** LUTTRELL *Brief Rel.* (1857) I. 234 His lordship had eloigned the body of..Henrietta. **1768** BLACKSTONE *Comm.* III. 129 The sheriff may return that he is eloigned. **1796** J. ANSTEY *Pleader's Guide* (1803) 48 Content his person to eloign. **1809** TOMLINS *Law Dict.* s.v., If such as are within age be eloined.

3. To remove, carry off, send away (property).

1622 CALLIS *Stat. Sewers* (1647) 151 If such best beast should be esloyned. **1714** SIR W. SCROGGS *Courts Leet* (ed. 3) 78 If one eloign my Goods that are not distrainable by Law. **1823** *New Monthly Mag.* VII. 518 Many a tale of plundered flocks..and eloigned cattle.

4. To divert (money) from its proper use.

1640 *Prerog. Parl.* in *Sel. Harl. Misc.* (1793) 239 The rents, profits, and revenues of this realm..are so much..eloined.

†**eˈloinate, eˈloignate.** *Obs. rare.* [f. Fr. *éloigner* (see prec.) + -ATE.] *trans.* = prec.

1642 HOWELL *For. Trav.* (Arb.) 56 Nor is some vulgar Greek so farre adulterated, and eloignated from the true Greek, as Italian is from the Latin. **1847** CRAIG, *Eloinate*, to remove.

eloiner (ɪˈlɔɪnə(r)). *Law.* [f. ELOIN + -ER; after AF. *esloigneour.*] One who eloins.

1865 NICHOLS *Britton* I. 67 Our Justices can convict the eloiners of malice.

†**eˈloinment, eˈloignment.** *Obs.* Also 7 esloinment, 8 eloignement. [a. AF. *esloignement*, Fr. *éloignement*: see ELOIN and -MENT.]

1. Removal to a distance.

1678-96 PHILLIPS, *Eloinment*, a removing a great way off. **1847** in CRAIG; and in mod. Dicts.

2. a. The space or distance between one object and another. **b.** Distance, in the sense of the distant part or background of a scene or of a picture.

a **1670** HACKET *Abp. Williams* I. (1692) 92 The sun..appears to us no bigger than a platter..because of that esloinment..between our eyes and the object. **1715-20** POPE *Iliad* I. 291 In the eloignement we behold Jupiter in golden armour.

3. *fig.* Remoteness in feeling or taste (*from*).

a **1763** SHENSTONE *Ess.* 146 He discovers an eloignment from vulgar phrases.

†**elome.** *Obs. rare*—⁰. (See quot.)

1753 CHAMBERS *Cycl. Suppl.*, *Elome*, a name given by some authors to orpiment.

†**eˈlong.** *Obs.* Forms: 5 eslonge, 5-7 elonge, 6-7 elong. [ad. late L. *ēlongā-re* to remove to a distance, f. *ē* out + *longē* far away.

Sense 1 of this word, and the ordinary modern sense of ELONGATE, show that the L. word was sometimes taken as f. *ē* + *long-us* long. The form *eslonge* is due to the influence of the equivalent Romanic form: see ELOIN.]

1. *trans.* To make longer, lengthen.

c **1420** *Pallad. on Husb.* II. 79 Elonge eke as the liketh best thi lande.

b. To retard, delay; to retard the growth of.

c **1420** *Pallad. on Husb.* IV. 632 Premature yf that the list elonge [*maturam ficum vis serotinam facere*]. **1610** G. FLETCHER *Christ's Vict.* in Farr's *S.P. Jas. I.* 57 Upon the roof the bird of sorrow sat, Elonging joyfull day with her sad note.

2. To remove, separate, cause to wander away *from. lit.* and *fig.* Also *fig.* To set free (from trouble or grief).

1475 CAXTON *Jason* 135 b, I haue found and felte my self eslonged..of all my sorowes. *a* **1541** WYATT *Wks.* (1861) 55 By seas, and hills elonged from thy sight. **1603** FLORIO *Montaigne* III. ix. (1632) 539 Doth not too much elonge..us from our..principles. **1609** SKENE *Reg. Maj.* 108 Ane beast that is elonged, and wavered away from his maister.

3. *intr.* To go far away. *rare*—⁰.

1598 FLORIO, *Allontanare*, to elonge, to go farre off.

elongate (ˈiːlɒŋgeɪt, ɪˈlɒŋgeɪt), *v.* [f. late L. *ēlongāt-* ppl. stem of *ēlongāre*: see prec.]

†**1.** *trans.* To remove, set at a distance (*from*).

c **1540** BOORDE *The boke for to Lerne* B j a, Let the common howse of esement be..elongatyd from the howse. **1656** BLOUNT *Glossogr.*, *Elongate*, to remove afar off. **1721-1800** BAILEY, *Elongate*, to remove or carry a great way off.

2. *intr.* †**a.** *gen.* To depart, move away or recede *from* (*obs.*). **b.** *spec.* in *Astronomy*: To recede apparently from the sun or a fixed point in the celestial sphere; said, *e.g.*, of a star or a planet.

1646 SIR T. BROWNE *Pseud. Ep.* II. ii. 63 But elongating from the coast of Brasilia toward the shore of Africa it [the south point] varyeth Eastward. **1775** ASH, *Elongate*, to go off to a distance.

3. *trans.* To lengthen, draw out, prolong.

1578 BANISTER *Hist. Man* VIII. 107 It [spinal marrow] is..a portion of the brayne elongated. **1656** BLOUNT *Glossogr.*, *Elongate*, to prolong. **1793** M. BAILLIE *Morb. Anat.* (1807) 9 Time has been given for the adhesions to be elongated by the motion of the heart. **1830** SCOTT *Demonol.* vii. 217 The mode of elongating a goat's back by means of a spit. **1865** DICKENS *Mut. Fr.* vii, Having thus elongated and emphasised the word.

4. *Bot.* (*intr.*) To grow or increase in length; to be lengthy; to have a slender or tapering form.

1801 KNIGHT in *Phil. Trans.* XCI. 340 The wood between the bunch and the next leaf below, has ceased to elongate. **1828** STEUART *Planter's G.* 128 The minutest Fibres both expand and elongate with facility. **1870** HOOKER *Stud. Flora* 263 Linaria repens..Racemes elongating.

Hence ˈ**elongating** *ppl. a.*, that elongates.

1858 GREENER *Gunnery* 422 The patent elongating socket.

elongate (ɪˈlɒŋgeɪt), *a.* [formed as prec.] Lengthened, prolonged, extended; esp. in *Bot.* and *Zool.* that is long in proportion to its breadth; that has a lengthened, slender, or tapering form.

1828 STARK *Elem. Nat. Hist.* II. 196 Lip elongate..narrowing towards the point. **1847** HARDY in *Proc. Berw. Nat. Club* II. No. 5. 235 The remaining five forming an elongate club. **1860** GOSSE *Rom. Nat. Hist.* 336 Immense unrecognised creatures of elongate form roam the ocean. **1870** HOOKER *Stud. Flora* 103 Peduncles elongate.

Hence as combining form ˈ**elongato-**, in various zoological terms, as **elongato-conical, -ovate, -triangular** *adjs.*, that has the form or outline of a lengthened cone, egg, triangle.

1846 DANA *Zooph.* (1848) 276 Ridges small, acute, sometimes elongato-conical. **1852** —— *Crust.* II. 932 Hand..elongato-ovate. *Ibid.* I. 483 Beak lamellar, elongato-triangular.

elongated (ˈiːlɒŋgeɪtɪd, ɪˈlɒŋgeɪtɪd), *ppl. a.* [pa. pple. of ELONGATE *v.*]

1. Made longer; drawn out or extended to an unusual or unnatural length.

1751 R. CAMBRIDGE *Scribbleriad* III. 83 O'er all her Limbs were seen Th' elongated papillæ of the skin. **1859** HELPS *Friends in C.* Ser. II. I. vi. 217 An elongated maxim of Rochefoucault's. **1861** READE *Cloister & H.* I. 251 He stood transfixed..sudden horror in his elongated countenance. **1870** F. HALL in Wilson tr. *Vishnu-purāṇa* V. 68 [Bhishmaka is] the elongated form of Bhíshma. **1884** *Times* (weekly ed.) 26 Sept. 6/3 The lover of elongated farces.

2. That is excessively long in proportion to its breadth, as if drawn out or extended.

1831 R. KNOX *Cloquet's Anat.* 51 Two of these edges..present anteriorly an elongated surface. **1836** MACGILLIVRAY tr. *Humboldt's Trav.* xxi. 305 One..has an elongated snout. **1863** BERKELEY *Brit. Mosses* iii. 13 The stem..consists more or less of elongated cells. **1877** W. THOMSON *Voy. Challenger* I. ii. 131 The heart, an elongated tube.

elongation (iːlɒŋˈgeɪʃən). Also 4 elongacioun. [ad. late L. *ēlongātiōn-em*, n. of action f. *ēlongāre*: see ELONGATE.]

1. *Astr.* **a.** The angular distance of a heavenly body from some relatively fixed point; in mod. usage, the angular distance of a planet from the sun, or of a satellite from its primary.

c **1391** CHAUCER *Astrol.* II. §25 Take the heiest altitude..of any sterre fix..& tak his nethere elongacioun. ? **1540** *Dyfference of Astron.* A ii b, Of sygnes, and of theyr elongations. **1647** LILLY *Chr. Astrol.* 31 ☿ is in his greatest elongation or distance from the ☉. **1662** FULLER *Worthies* II. 237 The star Venus was visible all day long, as sometime it falls out neer her greatest Elongation. **1841** BREWSTER *Mart. Sc.* iii. (1856) 35 We saw her [Venus] in the form of a crescent, resembling exactly the moon at the same elongation. **1868** LOCKYER *Heavens* (ed. 3) 76 In the morning..its maximum western elongation attains the same value.

†**b.** The difference in motion between the swifter and the slower of two planets, or the quantity of space whereby the one has overgone the other.

1727-51 in CHAMBERS.

†**c.** The difference between the true place and the geocentric place of a planet. *Obs.*

1796 in HUTTON.

†**2. a.** Removal to a distance, departure, recession; hence, remoteness; also *fig. Obs.*

1616 BULLOKAR, *Elongation*, a putting far off. **1639** J. SYMONDS in Spurgeon *Treas. Dav.* Ps. xxxviii. 9 Ofttimes there is a frustration of our desires, or an elongation of the things. **1654** tr. *Scudery's Curia Politiæ*, Those who designed his elongation and further removal from Court. **1661** HICKERINGILL *Jamaica* 5 That vulgar errour, that it's [the Sun's] elongation [is] the reason of extremity of cold. **1672** *Phil. Trans.* VII. 5126 The Dis-appearance of those Stars may be ascribed to their Elongation from..our Eyes. **1694** R. BURTHOGGE *Essay on Reason* 140 In its utmost Elongation or Removal from him.

†**b.** *Astron.* The removal of a planet to its furthest distance from the sun; aphelion.

1715 in KERSEY. **1721-1800** in BAILEY. **1787** SMEATON in *Phil. Trans.* LXXVII. 319 The same disappointment..with respect to the approaching elongation in September.

3. The action or process of elongating, lengthening out, or extending.

1731 ARBUTHNOT *Aliments* 42 This Motion of Elongation of the Fibres. **1793** T. BEDDOES *Math. Evid.* 142 What overturns this whole system of analogical elongation..is a discovery..to which Lennep contributed an hint. **1828** STEUART *Planter's G.* 277 This decided tendency to elongation of the boughs on the lee-side. **1831** BREWSTER *Nat. Magic* iv. (1833) 80 The figure will undergo most curious elongations and contractions. **1878** L. P. MEREDITH *Teeth* 47 There is also an elongation of the anterior portion of the jaws.

†**4.** *Surgery.* **a.** 'An imperfect luxation, when the ligaments are only relaxed and lengthened, but the bone is not out of place' (*Syd. Soc. Lex.*).

1676 WISEMAN *Surg.* 480 Those Elongations which are the effect of an Humour soaking upon a Ligament..making it liable to be stretcht. **1715** in KERSEY. **1847** in CRAIG.

b. 'The extension of a limb for the purpose of reducing a dislocation or setting fractured bones' (*Syd. Soc. Lex.*).

1847 in CRAIG.

5. The state of being elongated or lengthened. *concr.* That which is elongated; an extended space, a continuation, a part produced.

1751 R. CAMBRIDGE *Scribbleriad* III. 83 *note*, His skin was..grown over with an horny excrescence called by the Naturalists the Elongation of the papillæ. **1796** H. HUNTER tr. *St. Pierre's Stud. Nat.* (1799) III. 29 To prove the truth of my theory respecting their [the poles'] elongation. **1797** M. BAILLIE *Morb. Anat.* (1807) 299 If these elongations were to be situated at a distance from the neck of the bladder. **1813** H. & J. SMITH *Rej. Addr.* 61 But when on this boarded elongation it falls to my lot to say a good thing. **1837** WHEWELL *Hist. Induct. Sc.* (1857) II. 282 The elongation of the image. **1869** J. MARTINEAU *Ess.* II. 76 His morality..is a mere elongation of law.

6. *Mech.* In mechanical testing, the amount of extension of a test piece when stressed, usu. expressed as a percentage of the original length; also *attrib.*

1866 *Engineering* 19 Jan. 33/2 The elongation of homogeneous metal and steel is only $\frac{1}{16600}$th part of its length for every ton of direct tensile strength per square inch. **1877** *Encycl. Brit.* VII. 818/1 Eight different specimens..bore from $43\frac{1}{2}$ to 46 lb. (average 45·2) just before breaking, with elongations of from 17 per cent to 22 per cent. *a* **1884** KNIGHT *Dict. Mech.* Suppl. 868/2 The index needle also moves two slides which show the maximum of elongation or compression. **1909** *Cent. Dict. Suppl.*, *Elongation strain*, the percentage of elongation of a piece of material being tested in a testing-machine. **1922** GLAZEBROOK *Dict. Appl. Physics* I. 144/1 The elongation and contraction of area are required in order to obtain a measure of the ductility of the material. **1930** *Engineering* 3 Jan. 31/2 The percentage elongation observed for arsenical copper was 58 per cent.

elongative (ˈiːlɒŋˌgeɪtɪv), *a. nonce-wd.* [f. ELONGATE + -IVE.] That tends to elongate or lengthen out: see quot.

1836 *Fraser's Mag.* XIII. 591 A hope, that the expedient..adopted by the elongative class of commentators, ancient and modern..may never more be resorted to.

e'longe, var. of ALLONGE *v.* and *sb.*[1]
1699 B. E. *Dict. Cant. Crew, Elonge*, to stretch forward the right Arm and Leg, and to keep a close Left-foot. **1707** SIR W. HOPE *New Meth. Fencing* (1796) 95 Other Masters.. maintain..that he will Elonge or Stretch, as far as this Way, as when his Foot is couched to one side. *Ibid.*, Which certainly shortens his Elonge.

†**e'longing**, *vbl. sb. Obs. rare*⁻¹. [f. ELONG *v.* + -ING[1].] (See quot.)
1611 FLORIO, *Allontananza*, an elonging or farre distance.

elope (ɪ'ləʊp), *v.* Also 6 ellope. [In AF. (14th c.) *aloper*, perh. f. ME. **alope(n*, pa. pple. of **aleapen* (f. A- *pref.* 4 + LEAP) = MDu. *ontlōpen*, Ger. *entlaufen* to run away; cf. OE. *úthléapan*, the technical word for the 'escaping' of a thief. The assumed ME. **alope* however might stand for *ilope*, pa. pple. of *leapen* in same sense; cf. 'þe wicke giv [was] a wei i-lope' (*Childh. Jes.* 972).
The current hypothesis of derivation from MDu. *ontlōpen* seems improbable on account of the early appearance of the word in AF.]
1. a. *Law.* Of a wife: To run away from her husband in the company of a paramour. **b.** In popular language also (and more frequently) said of a woman running away from home with a lover for the purpose of being married.
[**1338** in *Year-bks 11-12 Edw. III* (Horw.) 587 En bref de dower plede fut qil alopa de soun baroun. **1538** *Nottingham Borough Rec.* III. 214 Ipsam Katherinam ad elopandum de viro suo..tentavit.] **1628** COKE *On Litt.* 32a, If the wife elope from her husband she shall lose her dower. **1697** LUTTRELL *Brief Rel.* (1857) IV. 323 He sets forth divers accusations against his lady, who is elop'd from him. **1768** GOLDSM. *Good-n. Man* IV, We..must elope methodically, madam. **1818** CRUISE *Digest* I. 204 A man by deed granted his wife to another, with whom she eloped and lived in adultery. **1837** W. IRVING *Capt. Bonneville* III. 230 He endeavoured to prevail upon his quondam mistress to elope with him. **1884** *Law Reports Chanc. Div.* XXV. 483 On the following day Captain Sampson and Miss Wall eloped.
2. *gen.* To run away, escape, abscond.
1596 SPENSER *F.Q.* V. iv. 9 She left me quight, And to my brother did elope streightway. **1664** BUTLER *Hud.* II. i. 260 In close catasta shut, past hope Of wit or valour to elope. **1727** A. HAMILTON *New Acc. E. Ind.* II. xlvii. 188 When the Term of Payment came, they eloped. **1840** DICKENS *Barn. Rudge* lxxxii, The..valet..eloped with all the cash and moveables he could lay his hands on.
3. *transf.* and *fig.* (Chiefly in *nonce-uses.*)
1726 SWIFT *To a Lady*, But with raillery to nettle..Never lets your mind elope. **1785** COWPER *Tiroc.* 876 Since thy strength must with thy years elope. **1817** KEATS *Ep. C.C. Clarke*, Spenserian vowels that elope with ease.

elopement (ɪ'ləʊpmənt). [In AF. (14th c.) *alopement*: see prec. and -MENT.] The action of eloping, in various senses. See the vb.
[**1338** in *Year-bks. 11-12 Edw. III* (Horw.) 587 Lalopement fut alegge en autre counte qe le dower ne fut demande.] **1641** *Termes de la Ley* 133 Elopement is when a married woman departeth from her husband with an adulterer. **1698** LUTTRELL *Brief Rel.* (1857) IV. 346 She had 3 children since her elopement. **1719** DE FOE *Crusoe* (1869) 5 Without any Purpose of making an Elopement that time. *a* **1763** SHENSTONE *Ess.* 2 The accidental elopements..of a composition. **1819** BYRON *Juan* I. cciii, Myself, and several now in Seville, Saw Juan's last elopement with the devil. **1822** J. FLINT *Lett. Amer.* 115 The indolence and disorderly conduct of slaves, together with their frequent elopements. **1853** DE QUINCEY *Wks.* XIV. 460 My elopement from school.

eloper (ɪ'ləʊpə(r)). [f. ELOPE.] One who elopes.
1748 RICHARDSON *Clarissa* (1811) IV. 212 To be..an eloper from my friends to him. **1782** MISS BURNEY *Cecilia* ii. (D.) By making you an eloper with a duellist. **1830** MARRYAT *King's Own* xviii, Seizing what was left, and cursing the elopers. **1856** KANE *Arct. Expl.* II. xii. 126 The report.. makes the lady a willing eloper. **1879** ESCOTT *England* II. 198 He is taken into a room where..he recognises the eloper.

elopine ('eləpaɪn), *a. Zool.* [f. mod.L. *elop-s* + -INE.] Resembling the genus *Elops* of fishes.
1887 *Athenæum* 9 July 58/3 He considered it [the genus *Rhacolepis*] an elopine clupeoid.

eloping (ɪ'ləʊpɪŋ), *vbl. sb.* [f. ELOPE + -ING[1].] The action of the verb ELOPE.
1783 BLACKSTONE *Comm.* II. viii (ed. 9), If a woman voluntarily leaves (which the law calls eloping from) her husband.

eloping (ɪ'ləʊpɪŋ), *ppl. a.* [f. ELOPE + -ING[2].] That elopes, in various senses.
1700 BLACKMORE *Job* 24 The eloping flood did from its channel stray. **1703** ROWE *Fair Penitent* Epil., There's dreadful dealing with Eloping Wives.

‖**Elops** ('i:lɒps). *Zool.* [mod.L. a. Gr. ἔλοψ: see ELLOPS.] A genus of fishes of the Herring family; 'spread over all tropical and sub-tropical seas' (Günther).

elops, var. of ELLOPS.

eloquence ('eləkwəns). Forms: 5 eloquens, elloquence, 4- eloquence. [a. Fr. *éloquence*, ad. L. *ēloquentia*, f. *ēloquent-em* ELOQUENT.]
1. The action, practice, or art of expressing thought with fluency, force, and appropriateness, so as to appeal to the reason or move the feelings. Also *concr.* eloquent language.
Primarily of oral utterance, and hence applied to writing that has the characteristics of good oratory. In mod. use the notion of *impassioned* utterance is more prominent than in the early examples.
1382 WYCLIF *Cor.* Prol., Summe [were overturned] of wordy eloquence of philosofie. *c* **1440** *Gesta Rom.* I. xxi. 71 (Harl. MS.) Wise men..by deceyuable eloquence and takyng of money deceyueth. **1591** SHAKS. *Two Gent.* III. i. 83 And naught esteemes my aged eloquence. **1665-9** BOYLE *Occas. Refl.* Ded., Those Celebrated Ladies..by their.. Eloquence..taught their Children to sway those Rulers of the World. **1709** *Tatler* No. 70 ¶2 Eloquence, set off with the proper Ornaments of Voice and Gesture. **1840** H. ROGERS *Ess.* (1874) II. v. 224 To give a brief definition of.. this truest style of eloquence..it was 'practical reasoning,' animated by strong emotion. **1847** GROTE *Greece* (1862) IV. II. xlvi. 108 His eloquence was irresistibly impressive.
b. *fig.*
1593 HOOKER *Eccl. Pol.* I. ii, Our safest eloquence concerning him [God] is our silence. **1713** YOUNG *Last Day* III. 129 The dreadful eloquence of pain, Our only song. **1715-20** POPE *Iliad* XIV. 252 Silence that spoke and eloquence of eyes. **1814** S. ROGERS *Jacquel.* 56 Her tears her only eloquence. **1822** HAZLITT *Table-t.* II. iii. 37 That undisturbed silence of the heart which alone is perfect eloquence.
c. in *pl. arch.*
1534 LD. BERNERS *Gold. Bk. M. Aurel.* (1546) Biiij, People came to Rome to se the eloquences of the bokes. **1865** CARLYLE *Fredk. Gt.* V. XIX. v. 495 Suasive eloquences and advices.
†**2.** Speech or verbal expression in general. *Obs.*
c **1400** *Rom. Rose* 7541 Your wikked thought..That mooveth your foule eloquence. **1658-9** N. ST. NICHOLAS in Burton's *Diary* (1828) III. 119, I wish we do not draw God's judgment by such light eloquence.
3. The quality of being eloquent, as an attribute of speakers or writers, their utterances or style.
c **1430** LYDG. *Min. Poems* (1840) 5 Alle to declare I have noone eloquence. *c* **1450** *Crt. Love* 2 Of cunning naked, bare of eloquence. **1526** *Pilgr. Perf.* (W. de W. 1531) 1b, My insuffycyency and ignoraunce..lacke bothe lernynge and eloquence. **1662** STILLINGFL. *Orig. Sacr.* III. i. §15 This particular argument..is managed with a great deal of eloquence. **1704** SWIFT *T. Tub* xi. 129 This I have produced as a Scantling of Jacks great eloquence. **1831** LYTTON *Godolph.* 6 Her father's eloquence had descended to her. *Mod.* A passage of unsurpassed eloquence.
4. = RHETORIC.
1623 COCKERAM, *Eloquence*, the Art of Rhetoricke. **1796** MORSE *Amer. Geog.* I. 525 Professor of..eloquence. **1852** SIR W. HAMILTON *Discuss.* 6 Abraham Remi..Professor Royal of Eloquence.
†**5.** An alleged technical term denoting a company of lawyers. *Obs. rare*⁻¹.
1486 *Bk. St. Albans* F vij a, An Eloquens of laweyeris.

†'**eloquency.** *Obs. rare.* [f. as prec.; see -ENCY.] = ELOQUENCE 3.
1545 TH. RAYNALD *Womans booke* B 8 Witty Mercury with his doulce & sugred eloquency. **1546** LANGLEY *Pol. Verg. De Invent.* I. ix. 19a, The latin tong is not so fyt to receiue the ornamentes of Eloquencie as the Greke tong is. **1683** CAVE *Ecclesiastici* App. 27 The wisdom, clearness, and eloquency of his discourses.

eloquent ('eləkwənt), *a.* [a. Fr. *éloquent*, ad. L. *ēloquent-em*, pr. pple., f. *ēloqui* to speak out.]
1. a. Of persons: Possessing or exercising the power of fluent, forcible, and appropriate expression.
1393 GOWER *Conf.* II. 288 In his speche Of wordes he was eloquent. **1480** CAXTON *Chron. Eng.* ccxxxvii. 261 A wyse knyȝt and a trewe and an eloquent man. **1586** T. B. *La Primaud. Fr. Acad.* I. (1589) 249 The eloquentest orator in the world. **1651** HOBBES *Leviath.* I. xi. 49 Eloquent speakers are enclined to Ambition. *a* **1714** BURNET *Own Time* (1766) I. 172 The eloquentest man of that time. **1874** MORLEY *Compromise* (1886) 48 The school of which M. Renan is the most eloquent representative.
b. *transf.* and *fig.*
1599 SHAKS. *Hen. V*, III. vii. 37 Turne the Sands into eloquent tongues. **1781** GIBBON *Decl. & F.* III. lxx. 774 His pen was not less eloquent than his tongue. **1814** S. ROGERS *Jacquel.* I. 81 Her dark eyes—how eloquent! **1862** TROLLOPE *Orley F.* xxxix, There is a silence which may be more eloquent than the sounds which it follows.
2. Of utterances or style: Characterized by forcible and appropriate expression.
1393 GOWER *Conf.* III. 85 Rhetorique, whose facounde Above all other is eloquent. **1509** HAWES *Past. Pleas.* XVIII. xxi, Your payne and wordes eloquent. *a* **1593** H. SMITH *Wks.* (1866-7) I. 79 To the godly it seemeth the wisest, and eloquentest, and sweetest, and easiest book of all others. **1627** DONNE *Serm.* 49 As powerfull as the Eloquentest Sermon. **1806** *Med. Jrnl.* XV. 81 The author of this eloquent little pamphlet. **1841** LANE *Arab. Nts.* I. 105 Well-shaped, and of eloquent speech.
†**3.** *humorously.* That inspires eloquence.
1599 PORTER *Angry Wom. Abingd.* (1841) 22 You have the most eloquent ale in all the world.
4. *fig.* Effectively expressive *of*.
1870 ROSSETTI *Poems* 191 Close kissed and eloquent of still replies. **1873** R. A. PROCTOR *Expanse of Heaven* xi. 123 To the Almighty every atom in infinite space is eloquent of the universe itself. **1885** A. FORBES *Souvenirs of some Continents* ix. 208 His whole attitude eloquent of discouragement.

eloquential (elə'kwenʃəl), *a. rare.* [f. L. *ēloquenti-a* ELOQUENCE + -AL[1].] Pertaining to eloquence; rhetorical.
a **1711** KEN *Hymnotheo* Poet. Wks. 1721 III. 351 Orators, who with Eloquential Might, Black'ned bright Day, to guild infernal Night. **1839-48** BAILEY *Festus* (ed. 3) 73/2, I Was waiting for an eloquential pause In this..odd story. **1867** LD. STRANGFORD *Sel. Writings* II. 54 Eloquential gush. *Ibid.* 308 In his eloquential aspect.

eloquently ('eləkwəntlɪ), *adv.* [f. ELOQUENT + -LY[2].] In an eloquent manner. Also *fig.*
1471 RIPLEY *Comp. Alch.* V. xxiv. in Ashm. (1652) 154 How eloquently..they clape. **1570** ASCHAM *Scholem.* (Arb.) 140 Carolus Sigonius hath written of late, both learnedlie and eloquentlie. **1651** HOBBES *Leviath.* III. xxxiii. 204 Written by them eloquently in Greek. **1850** W. IRVING *Goldsm.* i. 20 Pictures, rural and domestic..appeal so eloquently to the fancy.
¶**b.** *humorously.*
1853 BRIMLEY *Ess.* 276 Eloquently drunk.

eloquentness ('eləkwəntnɪs). *rare*⁻⁰. [f. ELOQUENT + -NESS.] = ELOQUENCE 3.
1727-31 in BAILEY II. **1775** in ASH.

†**e'loquious**, *a. Obs. rare.* [f. L. *ēloqui-um* eloquence + -OUS.] Eloquent.
1599 NASHE *Lent. Stuffe* Harl. Misc. VI. 162 Eloquious hoarie beard, father Nestor, you were one of them. **1607** HEYWOOD *Fayre Mayde Exchange* Wks. 1874 II. 54 Heer's a most eloquious alure for the memory.

†**e'lozable**, *a. Obs. rare*⁻¹. [as if a. OF. **eslosable*, f. *esloser* to praise.] Amenable to flattery.
1537 *Machiavel's Vind.* in *Harl. Misc.* I. 61 The execution of the laws would reach them..who in the time of Tarquin it seems found the prince more elozable.

†**elp.** *Obs.* Also 1 ylp, 3 alp. [shortened form of OE. *elpend*, ad. L. *elephant-em.*] = ELEPHANT. Hence **alpes bon**, ivory.
c **1000** *Ags. Gloss.* in Wr.-Wülcker 320 Elefans, ylp. *c* **1220** *Bestiary* 604 Elpes arn in Inde riche, on bodi borlic berges ilike. *Ibid.* 646 Ðanne cumeð ðis elp unride. *c* **1325** *St. Katherine* (Auchinl. MS.) 282 in Horstmann *Alteng. Leg.* II. 248 Hir body white as alpes bon.

elpasolite (el'pæsəlaɪt). *Min.* [f. *El Paso Cocolo*, where first found.] A fluoride of potassium, aluminium, and sodium, occurring in pachnolite, in small colourless nodules.
1885 *U.S. Geol. Surv.* III. 275 We wish to propose the name elpasolite for it.

elpi, var. of ONELEPY *a. Obs.* sole, single.
c **1200** *Trin. Coll. Hom.* 258 Ihesu crist, þin elpi sune. *a* **1225** *Ancr. R.* 324 þu waschest þine honden in one elpi deie twies oðer þries.

†**El'pistic**, *a. Obs. rare*⁻¹. [ad. Gr. ἐλπιστικός, f. ἐλπίζειν to hope.] The distinctive epithet of a sect of Greek philosophers (see quot.).
1586 T. B. *La Primaud. Fr. Acad.* I. (1589) 286 The Elpisticke Philosophers affirmed, that nothing better maintained and preserved the life of man, than Hope.

elrage, -aige, -ich, -ische, -itch, var. ff. ELDRITCH.

elren, elren, obs. ff. ELDER *sb.*[1]

elroquite (el'rɒkaɪt). *Min.* [f. *El Roque*, name of an island in the Caribbean Sea: see -ITE.] A silicate of aluminium and iron, coloured green by chromium.
1882 DANA *Min.* App. iii. 41 Elroquite..an apple green to grey, massive substance.

-els, *suffix*, in OE. *-els*, repr. OTeut. *-islo-z*, *-islo(m*, *-isljo(m*, forming instrumental sbs. or verbal abstracts, chiefly from vbs. in (OTeut.) *-jan*. The suffix was very common in OE., as in *ȝyrdels* (in Epinal Glossary *ȝyrdisl*, *-ils*) girdle, *byrȝels* (BURIELS) tomb, *græfels* quarry, *riecels* (REKELS) incense, *rædels* RIDDLE. The few words of this type that have survived into mod. English have lost their final *s*, owing to the original forms having been mistaken for plurals: see -LE.

Elsan ('elsæn). [App. f. initials of *E*phraim *L*ouis Jackson, a chemical manufacturer, + SAN(ITATION.] The trade name of the Elsan Manufacturing Co. (1924 *Trade Marks Jrnl.* 9 Jan., 47) for a type of lavatory in which the sludge is rendered inoffensive by chemical means.
1939-40 *Army & Navy Stores Catal.* 248/2 *Elsan chemical closet*... No drains, no water-flush..Elsan model '33'. **1943** HUNT & PRINGLE *Service Slang* 30 *Elsan gen*, news which cannot be relied upon. Literally, 'news invented in the gentlemen's toilet', Elsan being the trade name of the excellent chemical lavatories with which bombers are equipped. **1959** *Now & Then* No. 103 17, I..loaded all my belongings, the old beds and chairs and tables, the paraffin lamps and stoves, even the Elsan, into a turf lorry. **1961** J. B. PRIESTLEY *Saturn over Water* xii. 159 In a recess..were two pails of water and an Elsan kind of lav.

else (els), *adv.* Forms: 1-6 elles, (2 helles, *Orm.* elless, 3-4 ? el(le, 4 eles), 4 ellez, 4-5 ellus, 4-6

ellis, -ys, (4 hellis), 4–7 ells, els, 6- else. [OE. *elles* = OHG. *elles, alles*, OSw. *äljes* (Sw. *eljest*), adverbial use of the genit. case neuter (= Goth. *aljis*:— OTeut. **aljeso*) of OTeut. **aljo-* other (whence OE. *el-* in compounds: see ELELENDISH) = L. *alius*.

Senses 1 and 2 appear to arise from phrases in which the word retained its original force as an adj. used absol.; senses 3–5 are prob. strictly adverbial genitives.]

1. a. A synonym of *other*, used in connexion with indef., rel., or interrog. pronouns, or with words or phrases equivalent to any of these, such as *anything, nothing, everything, anybody, some one*; also with *all* (absol.), *much, little, a great deal*. (In mod. language *else* follows the pronominal word or phrase.) In this use *else*, like its synonym *other*, admits contextually of two different interpretations: e.g. *something else* may mean 'something in addition' to what is mentioned, or 'something as an alternative or a substitute'. In the former case *else* may be replaced by *besides, further, more*; in the latter case it may sometimes be rendered by *different, instead, with that exception*, etc. Often (like *other*) followed by *but* (see BUT 5 b.) or *than*.

In OE. *elles*, as thus used, admits of being construed, in accordance with its etymology, as a neut. adj. in gen. case; e.g. *áwiht elles* (aught else) is lit. 'aught of other', cf. *áwuht gódes* (*Metr. Boeth.* xxv. 59) lit. 'anything of good'; also Lat. *quid novi, amari aliquid*, Fr. *quelquechose de bon*. The extension of this construction seen in phrases like *anyone else, who else*, etc., and in the examples under 1 b, may be compared with Fr. *il n'y a personne de blessé; voilà trois hommes de mort*, etc. It is however probable that even in OE. the consciousness of the genitival character of *else* was already obscured; and from the standpoint of mod. usage, it is hard to say whether the word should be regarded as an adj. in concord with the words that from the point of view of historical grammar would be said to 'govern' it, or whether it should be classed as an adverb.

a **1000** *Seafarer* (Gr.) 46 Ne biþ him to hearpan hyge.. ne ymbe owiht elles nefne, etc. *c* **1200** ORMIN 9304 Nohht elless ne nohht mare þann þatt tatt ȝuw iss sett. *c* **1250** *Gen. & Ex.* 4096 Alle elles he driuen in deades weph. *a* **1300** *Cursor M.* 13471 (Cott.) þis he said.. To fand him and nathing elles. *c* **1340** *Gaw. & Gr. Knt.* 1550 For to haf wonnen hym to woȝe, what-so scho þoȝt ellez. **1340** HAMPOLE *Pr. Consc.* 1072 þe world.. es noght elles, Bot þe maners of men þat þar-in dwelles. **1532** HERVET tr. *Xenophon's Househ.* (1768) 55 Shall he nede any thynge elles. **1535** COVERDALE *Zeph.* ii. 15, I am, and there is els none. **1662** STILLINGFL. *Orig. Sacr.* Ded. 6 Were there nothing else to commend Religion to the minds of men. *a* **1677** BARROW *Serm.* Wks. 1716 II. 38 What do they else, but scrape and scramble.. for these things? **1705** ADDISON *Italy* Pref., Antiquities that no Body else has spoken of. **1842** TENNYSON *Audley Court*, Emilia, fairer than all else but thou, For thou art fairer than all else that is. **1879** STAINER *Music of Bible* 2 Singing is little else than a highly beautiful speaking.

b. In the same sense, referring to a sb., chiefly preceded by an adj. correlative with one of the pronouns, etc. mentioned in 1. Formerly common; now only *poet.* or *arch.*

Modern usage permits us to say 'Have you seen anybody else?' 'have you read anything else?' because *body* and *thing* have lost their substantival force; but not 'Have you seen any soldier else?' 'have you read any book else?'

971 *Blickl. Hom.* 39 Hwylc beren mænde he þonne elles buton heofona rice? **1340–70** *Alex. & Dind.* 1017 þo bostful dedeus.. Schal ȝou procre to pryde & to no profit ellus. **1538** BALE *God's Promises* in *Dodsley* (1780) I. 25 The adders ded stynge other wycked persones els In wonderfull numbre. **1577** VAUTROULLIER *Luther on Ep. Gal.* 92 Sharpe chidings and bitter wordes are as necessary.. as any other vertue els. **1613** PURCHAS *Pilgr., Descr. India* (1864) 19 Hee is Lord of all nor hath any else possession of any thing, but at the will of the King. **1615** CHAPMAN *Odyss.* XVII. 186 By force She kept his person from all else recourse. **1803** WORDSWORTH *Airey-Force Valley* Wks. VI. 33 Where all things else are still and motionless. **1827** POLLOK *Course T.* x, This silence .. Was now forgot, and every silence else.

†**c.** *elliptically.* Something, anything else; 'otherwise'. *Obs.*

1525 *Tale of the Basyn* 2 in Hazl. *E.P.P.* III. 44 Summe byn trew and sum byn ellis. **1571** in W. H. Turner *Select Rec. Oxford* 339 Noe freman of the Cytie, beyng baker or els. **1595** SHAKS. *John* II. i. 276 Bastards, and else.

d. Forming a quasi-compound *sb.* with inflected genitive: ***somebody*** (***anybody, everybody, some one, any one, every one***) ***else's***. Very common *colloq.*

1668 PEPYS *Diary* 9 Dec., My.. pleasure was just the same as yesterday, and no more, nor anybody else's about us. **1860** *Sat. Rev.* IX. 12/1 A clergyman who is inclined to misconduct himself will prefer to do so in somebody else's parish. *Mod.* If it be not my business, it is nobody else's.

2. Subjoined to one of the advbs. or adverbial expressions correlative with the pronouns, etc. mentioned in 1: = 'in (some, any, what, etc.) other manner, place, or time'.

c **1200** ORMIN 8471 Seldenn owwhær elless. *c* **1449** PECOCK *Repr.* I. vii. 32 Groundid sumwhere ellis. **1512** *Act 4 Hen. VIII*, c. 19. §11 Wher he then shalbe most conversaunte.. & no wher elles. **1548** UDALL *Erasm. Par.* Pref. 2 Are than and neuer els. **1827** POLLOK *Course T.* III, Sinks—where could he else?—to endless woe. **1878** MORLEY *Crit. Misc.* Ser. I. 199 Here more than anywhere else.

†**3. a.** In a different manner, by other means. *Obs.*

Beowulf 2520 (Gr.) Gif ic wiste hu wið ðam aȝlæcean elles ic meahte ȝylpe wið gripan. *c* **1000** ÆLFRIC *Gram.* 38 *Aliter*, elles. *c* **1200** ORMIN Ded. 107 He ne maȝȝ nohht elless Onn Ennglish writtenn rihht te word. **1393** LANGL. *P. Pl.* C. II. 174 þe same mesure þat ȝe meteþ amys oþer ellys. **1471** RIPLEY *Comp. Alch.* v. in Ashm. 148 For Bodies ells may not be alterat naturally.

†**b.** In another direction; = *elsewhither*. *Obs.*

c **1320** *Sir Tristr.* 2139 Of lond ichil elles fare. **1591** SHAKS. *Two Gent.* IV. ii. 125 Since the substance of your perfect selfe is else deuoted, I am but a shadow.

†**c.** At another time, or at other times. Hence, Already, formerly. *Obs.* exc. *dial.*

1393 LANGL. *P. Pl.* C. I. 89 In lentene, and elles. *c* **1400** MAUNDEV. xi. 125 On the Saturday, hyt renneth faste; and alle the Wooke elles, hyt stondeth stylle. **1513** DOUGLAS *Æneis* XI. vi. 136 Contrar hys kene dartis ellis stand haue we. **1597** MONTGOMERIE *Cherrie & Slae* 1491 Did he not els, quod he, consent the cherrie for to pow? **1691** RAY *N.C. Words* 24, I have done that else, *i.e.* already. *Mod. Sc.* Have you come back else?

4. a. In another case, under other circumstances; otherwise, on any other supposition; if not.

c **1000** *Ags. Gosp.* Matt. vi. 1 Elles næbbe ȝe mede mid eowrum Fæder þe on heofenum ys. *c* **1175** *Lamb. Hom.* 111 Elles ne bið his rixlunge ne fest ne lonsum. *c* **1250** *Gen. & Ex.* 3072 Beter ist laten hem vt-pharen, Al sal egipte elles for-faren. **1297** R. GLOUC. (1724) 451 El [*v.r.* elles] yt were amys. *c* **1400** MAUNDEV. XXII. 241 And elle he rytt in a Charett with 4 Wheles. **1596** SPENSER *F.Q.* I. i. 19 Strangle her, els she sure will strangle thee. **1642** ROGERS *Naaman* 89 The land certainly had.. vomited them out else. **1765** H. WALPOLE *Otranto* v. (1798) 80 It comes to warn your highness; why should it appear to me else? **1837** J. H. NEWMAN *Par. Serm.* (ed. 3) I. v. 115 Else how should any one be saved? **1873** BROWNING *Red Cott. Night-C.* 115 Boughs above, Darken, deform the path, else sun would streak.

b. preceded by *or*. Also ***or else***, with aposiopesis (the alternative to be imagined), as a *colloq.* form of warning or threat.

a **1300** *Cursor M.* 9715 Or ells agh dom be cald a-gain. *c* **1325** *E.E. Allit. P.* A. 723 Bot he com þyder ryȝt as a chylde, Oþer ellez neuer more com þer-inne. *c* **1394** *P. Pl. Crede* 480 Oþers elles Satan him-self sente hem fro hell. *c* **1440** *Generydes* 2732 The helm was sure, or ellys he had hym slayn. **1555** *Tract* in Strype *Eccl. Mem.* III. App. xliv. 126 Make your hearts pure or els your prayers are sin. **1592** SHAKS. *Ven. & Ad.* 208 Speak fair words, or else be mute. **1659** HAMMOND *On Ps.* xlviii. 13 Annot. 249 Or els it will be impossible to number them exactly. **1820** KEATS *St. Agnes* xii, Follow me, child, or else these stones will be thy bier. **1833** *Examiner* 6 Jan. 1/2 The *Chronicle* puts a case in strict analogy:—Suppose a landlord were to say to his tenant, 'I have got a cause coming on at Chelmsford Assizes; you must give me your pledge to be there as a witness, and swear to such and such a falsehood, or else..' **1872** RAYMOND *Statist. Mines & Mining* 323 The tunnel should be owned by the mines.. or else it should be constructed upon some agreement. **1879** J. MCCARTHY *Hist. our own Times* II. 275 Correspondence.. between two Irish chieftains. 'Pay me my tribute,' wrote the one, 'or else!' **1940** HARRISSON & MADGE *War begins at Home* viii. 205 Air-Raid Wardens.. could knock on your door and tell you that your lights must be properly masked or else. **1958** M. DICKENS *Man Overboard* xiii. 196 You've been engaged to make this small-boys' penitentiary show a profit, or else. **1959** J. VERNEY *Friday's Tunnel* vi. 61 If I do.. have children.. they'll jolly well obey me and no argument. Or else.

c. *idiomatically.* = 'If it is not believed'. Now *rare* or *dial.*

1590 GREENE *Orl. Fur.* (1599) 28, I am Orgalio, Aske all these people else. **1595** SHAKS. *John* IV. i. 108 The fire is dead with griefe, See else your selfe. **1741** RICHARDSON *Pamela* II. 108 Shew her else, Madam. **1809** PARKINS *Culpepper's Eng. Physic. Enl.* 245 St. Peter being the greater Apostle, ask the Pope else.

d. qualifying an adj. *rhetorical.*

1800–24 CAMPBELL *Ode Burns* iii, Love.. The choicest sweet of Paradise, In life's else bitter cup distill'd. **1839** DE QUINCEY *Recoll. Lakes* Wks. II. 222 Carrying the reader fluently along the else monotonous recurrences. **1871** HAWTHORNE *Sept. Felton* (1879) 191 To wander with her through places else so desolate.

†**5.** quasi-*conj.* If only, provided that, so long as. *Obs.* (Cf. Ger. *anders* in same sense.)

c **1325** *E.E. Allit. P.* B. 466 þe rauen.. reches ful lyttel How alle fodez þer fare, ellez he fynde mete. *c* **1340** *Gaw. & Gr. Knt.* 215 Ellez þou wyl diȝt me þe dom to dele hym an oþer. *c* **1375** *Sc. Leg. Saints, St. Paulus* 903 Ellis þat till our saweoure þe will of þe mane knawyne be.

†**elsehow**, *adv. Obs.* exc. *dial.* [f. ELSE + HOW.

In this and the following compounds of *else* (exc. ELSEWISE) the stress is variable.]

In some, or any, other way.

1666 J. SMITH *Old Age* (ed. 2) 64 Immoderate sweatings in hot houses, or elsehow, do cause the same distemper. *Ibid.* (1752) 146 The sap stirs, though it be not elsehow perceived. **1848** A. B. EVANS *Leicestersh. Gloss.* s.v., I can't do it elsehow.

elsewards ('ɛlswədz, 'ɛlswɔːdz), *adv. rare*⁻¹. [f. ELSE + -WARDS.] In the direction of, towards some other place.

a **1882** TROLLOPE *Autobiogr.* (1883) II. xviii. 173 These earthly sufferers know that they are making their way heavenwards,—and their oppressors their way elsewards.

†**elsewhat**, *pron. Obs.* [f. ELSE + WHAT.] Something or anything else.

c **890** K. ÆLFRED *Bæda* IV. iii. (Smith) 569 Gif he æt leornunge sæt, oþþe elles hwæt dyde. *a* **1240** *Lofsong* in *Cott. Hom.* 215 Of þet ase of helles hwat iwurðe þi wille euer. *a* **1400–50** *Alexander* 4556 Queþir þai here or elsquat it hurtis ay þe saule. **1586** SIDNEY *Sonn.* (1622) 489 For why should I, whom free choise slaue doth make, Elsewhat in face, then in my fancie beare? **1602** WARNER *Alb. Eng.* lxxiii. 300 With jewels.. and else-what of great worth.

†**elsewhen**, *adv. Obs.* [f. ELSE + WHEN.] At another time, at other times.

1418 *E.E. Wills* (1882) 43 Or ellys whan quan hem lest to remeve þens. **1563** FOXE *A. & M.* (1641) III. 795 Her husband willed her to go to the church, which she both then and elsewhen refused to do. **1570** ASCHAM *Scholem.* (Arb.) 86 More els when, if occasion so require.

elsewhence, *adv. arch.* [f. ELSE + WHENCE.] From some other place or quarter.

1603 FLORIO *Montaigne* I. xxxv. (1632) 112 All things being exactly furnished else whence. **1855** W. SMITH *Lat.-Eng. Dict.* 51 *Aliundē*, adv. (ali unde), lit. else-whence. **1892** *Pall Mall Gaz.* 9 Dec. 1/2 He has learnt.. not only the lesson of reticence from his Chief, but a certain lesson in vivacity to boot elsewhence.

elsewhere (ɛls'hwɛə(r)), *adv.* [f. ELSE + WHERE, q.v. for forms.]

1. At some other point; in some other place.

Beowulf 138 Elles hwær. *a* **1200** *Moral Ode* 331 in *Trin. Coll. Hom.* 230 Hwu litle hwile we bieð her. hwu longe elles hware. *c* **1340** *Cursor M.* 12485 (Fairf.) Lere him quare þou wil ellis-quare. **1393** LANGL. *P. Pl.* C. XXII. 189 To bynde and vnbynde · both here and elleswher. **1495** *Act 2 Hen. VII*, c. 37 Preamb., In the Countie of Lancaster or elliswhere in England. **1513** DOUGLAS *Æneis* VII. ix. 93 The dyne was hard eik ellis quhair full far. **1587** GOLDING *De Mornay* xxiv. 408 God was not knowne and worshipped elswhere than among the people of Israell. **1621** BURTON *Anat. Mel.* I. i. III. ii, The parties, which shall be more opportunely spoken of els-where. **1711** ADDISON *Spect.* No. 261 ¶8, As I have elsewhere observed. **1790** PALEY *Horæ Paul.* Rom. i. 9 Inquire whether we can find these circumstances elsewhere. **1828** SCOTT *F.M. Perth* xxxii, I can speak with you here as well as elsewhere. **1872** FREEMAN *Gen. Sketch* xiii. §2 (1874) 238 In England and elsewhere many men had been burned as heretics.

2. To some other point; = ELSEWHITHER.

1513 DOUGLAS *Æneis* XI. vii. 68 Bot gif so be that thai lyst ellisquhair To othir costis or pepill for to wend. **1766** GOLDSM. *Vic. W.* xxvi, If used ill in our dealings with one man we.. go elsewhere. **1863** G. MACDONALD *Ann. Q. Neighb.* xxv. (1878) 436 Many of them went elsewhere to church.

elsewhither, *adv.* Somewhat *arch.* [f. ELSE + WHITHER.] To some other place, in some other direction. Formerly also = 'whithersoever'.

c **1000** ÆLFRIC *Gram.* 38 Elleshwider, *aliorsum*. **1297** R. GLOUC. (1724) 103 To Yrlond heo flowe aȝeyn, & elles wyder heo myȝte. **1480** CAXTON *Chron. Eng.* liv. 38 He.. sayd he must gone elles whyder. **1571** GOLDING *Calvin on Ps.* xxxi. 23 That they bee not haried elsewhither. **1616** SURFL. & MARKH. *Countr. Farm* 570 Send to the towne or elsewhither to buy bread. **1837** CARLYLE *Fr. Rev.* (1872) III. I. i. 11 The dusty fugitives must shrink elsewhither.

†**elsewho**, *pron. Obs.* [f. ELSE + WHO.] Anyone else.

c **1542** UDALL in Ellis *Orig. Lett. Lit.* (1843) 4, I cannot persuad myself that your maistershipp hateth in me or elswhom any thyng excepte vices.

elsewise ('ɛlswaɪz), *adv.* [f. ELSE + -WISE.] In some other manner; in other circumstances, otherwise.

1548 UDALL, etc. *Erasm. Par. 1 Cor.* iii. 3 This matter.. would elswise haue caused much spyte. **1549** COVERDALE *Erasm. Par. Rom.* i. 29 Whiche wer elswyse ful of al naughtynes. **1865** DICKENS *Mut. Fr.* I. 97 Elsewise the world got up at eight. **1888** *N. Amer. Rev.* Feb. 214 The leaders elsewise.. have declared themselves.. as his enthusiastic supporters.

†**Elsibeth players.** *Obs. rare*⁻¹. [app. f. the name *Elizabeth*.] A kind of strolling actors.

1672 MARVELL *Reh. Transp.* I. 318 A set of Elsibeth Players, that in the Country having worn out.. all the Playes they brought with them from London, etc.

elsin ('ɛlsɪn). *Obs.* exc. north *dial.* Forms: 5 elsyn(g, 6–9 elsen, 5- elson, 8- elshin, 9- elsin. [app. a. MDu. *elssene* (later *elzen(e*, mod.Du. *els*):—**alisna*:—OTeut. **alasnâ* (whence by transposition OHG. *alansa, alunsa*); f. the same root as AWL + suffix as in OTeut. **segasnâ* (-*isnâ*), Ger. *sense* scythe. (The Teut. word was adopted into Romanic: cf. Sp. *alesna, lesna*, It. *lésina*, Fr. *alêne*, Pr. *alena*.)] An awl.

c **1440** *Promp. Parv.* 138 Elsyn [*v.r.* elsyng], *sibula*. **1530** PALSGR. 216/2 Elson for cordwayners, *alesne*. **1681** COLVIL *Whigs Supplic.* (1751) 107 There lyes his elson and his lingle. *a* **1774** FERGUSSON *Election*, Syne wi' a muckle elshin lang He brogit Maggie's hurdies. **1830** GALT *Laurie T.* III. ix. (1849) 114, I never bored a hole with an elsin in my life. **1864** ATKINSON *Whitby Gloss.*, *Elsin*, an awl. 'As sharp as a cobler's elsin,' acute.

2. *Comb.*: **elsin-blade**, the blade of an awl, or the awl itself; **elsin-box**, a box for holding awls; **elsin-haft**, the haft or handle of an awl; also, 'the old designation for a jargonelle pear from its resemblance to the haft of an awl' (Jam.).

1571 *Wills & Inv. N.C.* (1835) I. 261 Vj doss' elsen heftes ..elsonblades viijs. viijd. **1805** A. SCOTT *Poems* 57 (Jam.) Ane ca's a thing like elsin-box, That drools like corn-pipes Fu' queer that day.

elt (ɛlt), *sb. dial.* Also hilt. [? var. of YELT.] (See quots.)
1842 AKERMAN *Wilts. Gloss.* (E.D.S.) *Hilt*, a young sow kept for breeding. **1864** BARNES *Dorset Gloss.* in *Philol. Soc. Trans.* 55 *Elt*, a young sow or pig.

† **elt** (ɛlt), *v. Obs.* or *dial.* [ad. ON. *elta* to knead, work.] To knead.
c **1250** *Gen. & Ex.* 2892 And ðoȝ holden ðe tiȝeles tale, And elten and eilden, grete and smale. **1691** in Ray *N.C. Wds.* 24. **1721–1800** in BAILEY. **1875** *Lanc. Gloss.* s.v. Hoos eltin t' doff an canno' come. **1854** in A. E. BAKER *Northamptonsh. Gloss.*

? Hence **'elting**, *vbl. sb.*; used *attrib.* or as adj. in ***elting-moulds***, 'the soft ridges of fresh-ploughed land' (Clare).
1821 CLARE *Vill. Minstr.* I. 74, I took my rounds O'er elting moulds of fallow grounds. *Ibid.* I. 91 He scampers over the elting soil. **1854** in A. E. BAKER *Northamptonsh. Gloss.*

eltchi, var. of ELCHEE (*Turk.*) ambassador.

eltrich, var. of ELDRITCH.

eltrot ('ɛltrɒt). *dial.* [Etymology doubtful: ? f. ELT *sb.* + ROOT.] **a.** A name for the stalk of several plants; *esp.* Wild Parsley (*Chœrophyllum sylvestre*). **b.** The plant itself. Also *attrib.*
1878 BRITTEN & HOLL. *Plant-n.*, Eltrot 1. *Heracleum Sphondylium*. 2. *Anthriscus sylvestris*. 3. Stalk of wild barley. **1880** *Gd. Words* 150 I used to make trumpets of..elder sticks, eltrot stems, and even stinging nettle stalks.

eluate ('ɛljuːət). *Chem.* [f. L. *ēlu-ĕre* + -ATE¹ c.] The solution resulting from elution. Also *attrib.*
1934 in WEBSTER. **1939** *Ann. Reg. 1938* 371 In the vitamin B complex..factors..accepted by many workers were.. Macrae's yeast-filtrate and yeast eluate factors. **1949** H. W. FLOREY et al. *Antibiotics* I. IV. vii. 283 Foster (1944) who adsorbed the active substance..eluted it with methanol, and concentrated the eluate *in vacuo*. **1962** WALEY & VAN HEYNINGEN in A. Pirie *Lens Metabolism Rel. Cataract* 343 Fractions of the eluate were assayed..for peptidase.

† **e'lucid**, *a. Obs. rare*⁻¹. [f. E- *pref.*³ + LUCID.] That gives out light.
1660 BOYLE *New Exp. Phys.-Mech.* xxxvii. 309 Surfaces, which..confusedly represent..Images of the elucid Body.

† **e'lucidary.** *Obs. rare.* [ad. late L. *ēlūcidārium* an introductory treatise explanatory of a book or subject: cf. next.] An explanatory treatise or commentary; an explanation.
1603 HOLLAND *Plutarch's Mor.* 1253 Anticles and Hister in their Commentaries, and *Elucidaries*, of these things doe quote and alledge as much. **1692** COLES, *Elucidaries*, expositions of obscure things. **1775** in ASH.

† **e'lucidate**, *a. Obs.* [f. late L. *ēlūcidāt-us*, pa. pple. of *ēlūcidāre*: see next.] Clear, plain, intelligible.
a **1670** HACKET *Abp. Williams* I. (1692) 137 There was not a greater master of perspicuity and elucidate distinctions.

elucidate (ɪ'l(j)uːsɪdeɪt), *v.* [f. late L. *ēlūcidāt-* ppl. stem of *ēlūcidā-re*, f. *ē* out + *lūcidus* bright.] *trans.* To render lucid; now only *fig.* to throw light upon, clear up, explain. Also *absol.*
a **1568** COVERDALE *Let.* Wks. II. 492 Such annotations.. elucidate and clear [the text]. **1675** BAXTER *Cath. Theol.* II. v. 88 Your own conceptions..tend to elucidate. **1676** BULLOKAR, *Elucidate*, to make bright or shining. **1685** EVELYN *Mem.* (1857) II. 256 This..was made out of human blood and urine, elucidating the vital flame, or heat, in animal bodies. **1748** J. MASON *Elocut.* 33 The great End of Pronunciation is to elucidate and heighten the Sense. **1789** GIBBON *Autobiog.* (1854) 85 Sir William Hamilton..has elucidated a country of such inestimable value to the naturalist. **1804** WELLINGTON *Let.* in Gurw. *Disp.* III. 127, I mention these circumstances only because they tend to elucidate the foreign policy of this Prince. **1825** MACAULAY *Milton, Ess.* (1851) I. 1 His notes have the rare merit of really elucidating the text. **1840** MILL *Diss. & Disc.* (1873) I. 408 This language..serves not to elucidate. **1872** DARWIN *Emotions* Introd. 5 Elucidating the physiology of the muscles of the hand.

elucidation (ɪˌl(j)uːsɪ'deɪʃən). [f. as prec.: see -ATION.]
1. The action or process of elucidating, throwing light upon, making plain or intelligible.
1570 BILLINGSLEY *Euclid* v. iii. 128 Somewhat will I now say for the elucidation of the first kinde. **1774** J. BRYANT *Mythol.* II. 62 The person alluded to stands too manifest to need any farther elucidation. **1818** JAS. MILL *Brit. India* II. v. viii. 688 Zeal for the elucidation of Indian delinquency. **1843** CARLYLE *Past & Pr.* (1858) 101 Shall disclose itself, to mutual elucidation. **1858** FROUDE *Hist. Eng.* III. Pref. 8 Documents..and the notes..added for their elucidation.
2. That which serves to elucidate or clear up; an explanation, demonstration, or illustration.
1667 *Phil. Trans.* II. 568 There being no further Elucidation of the said Theoreme since publisht. **1772** PENNANT *Tours Scotl.* (1774) 293 We may expect further elucidations from a skillful antiquary. **1813** SIR H. DAVY *Agric. Chem.* viii. (1814) 344, I trust I shall be able to offer you satisfactory elucidations on the subject. **1840** CARLYLE *Heroes* (1858) 265 The latest generations of men will find new meanings in Shakspeare, new elucidations of their own human being.

elucidative (ɪ'l(j)uːsɪdətɪv), *a.* [f. L. *ēlūcidāt-* (see ELUCIDATE) + -IVE.] That tends to elucidate, throw light upon, make plain or intelligible.
1822 *Blackw. Mag.* XI. 207, I send you a few Notes, elucidative of the letter. **1878** BAYNE *Purit. Rev.* ii. 54 Bold caricature sketches..with elucidative comments.

elucidator (ɪ'l(j)uːsɪdeɪtə(r)). [f. as prec. + -OR.] One who elucidates.
? *a* **1633** ABBOT (J.) Obscurity is brought over them..by their pedantical elucidators. **1787–91** 'G. GAMBADO' *Acad. Horsem.* (1809) 41 As my ingenious elucidator shews you. **1846** HAWTHORNE *Mosses* II. viii. (1864) 180 The works of his own elucidators were flung upon him.

elucidatory (ɪ'l(j)uːsɪdəˌtərɪ), *a.* [f. prec. + -Y.] That elucidates, or tends to elucidate. Const. *of.*
1774 W. HUTCHINSON (*title*) Freemasonry.—The Spirit of Masonry in Moral and Elucidatory Lectures. **1814** *Q. Rev.* XI. 74 These various letters are any thing but elucidatory. **1861** CRAIK *Hist. Eng. Lit.* I. 588 His works..are..not simply demonstrative or elucidatory of mere matters of fact.

† **e'luctate**, *v. Obs. rare*⁻¹. [f. L. *ēluctāt-*, ppl. stem of *ēluctāri* to struggle out.] *intr.* To struggle forth.
a **1670** HACKET *Abp. Williams* I. (1692) 36 They did eluctate out of their injuries with credit to themselves.

† **eluc'tation.** *Obs.* [ad. L. *ēluctātiōn-em* a struggling, n. of action f. *ēluctāri*: see prec.]
1. The action of bursting or struggling forth. *fig.*
1633 T. ADAMS *Exp. 2nd Peter* ii. 3 (1865) 268 The breath being gathered into those straits, with a forcible eluctation opens the artery. **1682** SIR T. BROWNE *Chr. Mor.* (1756) 61 There is nothing more acceptable unto the ingenious world, than this noble eluctation of truth.
2. *fig.* Escape through struggle; release.
1627 DONNE *Serm.* clvii. 257, I shall be with him in his Eluctations, in his Victory. *a* **1656** BP. HALL *Rem. Wks.* (1660) 268 At last we..find our selves freed by a comfortable and joyful eluctation.

† **e'lucubrate**, *v. Obs.* [f. L. *ēlūcubrāt-* ppl. stem of *ēlūcubrā-re* to compose by lamplight.] *trans.* To produce (a literary work) by the expenditure of 'midnight oil'.
1623 COCKERAM, *Elucubrate*, to doe a thing by candlelight. **1651** *Erasm.* in Fuller's *Abel Rediv.* (1867) I. 89 Many of his noblest works he elucubrated at Basil. **1656** BLOUNT *Glossogr.*, *Elucubrate*, to watch and write by candle-light.

elucubration (ɪˌl(j)uːkjuː'breɪʃən). [f. as prec.: see -ATION.]
† **1.** The action of studying or composing by candle-light; expenditure of 'midnight oil'. *Obs.*
1643 *Sober Sadness* 6 After so many monethes elucubrations. **1697** EVELYN *Numism.* ix. 305 Macerating Studies and Elucubrations. **1775** in ASH.
2. *concr.* The product or result of studying or composing by candle-light: hence *gen.* any literary composition. Cf. LUCUBRATION.
1664 H. MORE *Synop. Proph.* To Rdr. 185 Those worthily-magnified elucubrations of Mr. Joseph Mede. **1716** M. DAVIES *Athen. Brit.* II. 272 S. Cyrillus..whose most Erudite Elucubrations were printed at Paris. **1859** F. MAHONEY *Rel. Father Prout.* 168 Such is the perfume that breathes from thy chest of posthumous elucubrations.
Hence **elucubrationary** *a.*
1716 MYLES DAVIES *Athen. Brit.* II. 383 Those corrupt Elucubrationary mixtures of Orthodoxy and inoculated Heterodoxy.

† **e'lucubrator.** *Obs. rare.* [agent-n. f. as prec.: see -OR.] One who elucubrates; an historian or investigator.
1566 PAINTER *Pal. Pleas.* I. 3 Histories, chronicles and monumentes, by the first authors and elucubrators.

elude (ɪl(j)uːd), *v.* [ad. L. *ēlūdĕ-re*, f. *ē* out + *lūdĕre* to play.]
† **1. a.** To befool, delude. (Partly confused with ILLUDE.) **b.** To baffle, disappoint. *Obs.*
1538 WRIOTHESLEY *Chron.* (1875) I. 75 The people had bene eluded and caused to doe great idolatrie. **1594** WEST *Symbol.* II. § 173 A witch or hagg is she which being eluded by a league made with the devil..thinketh, etc. **1656** MILTON *Lett. State* Wks. 1738 II. 196 If that hope fail 'em, eluded and frustrated..where at length to find a resting-place they know not.
† **c.** To wile away (tedium). *Obs.*
1660 R. COKE *Justice Vind.* 12 Men.. seek company to divert themselves, so to elude the length of time.
2. To escape by dexterity or stratagem (a blow, attack, danger, or difficulty).
1634–46 ROW *Hist. Kirk* (1842) 141 Murderers, adulterers, &c., labours to elude discipline by fleeing from place to place. *a* **1677** BARROW *Serm.* II. xxxiii. (R.) The stroke of humane law may..often be..eluded by slight, by gift, by favour. **1715–20** POPE *Iliad* III. 444 The wary Trojan, bending from the blow Eludes the death. **1790** BURKE *Fr. Rev.* Wks. V. 302 Difficulties which they rather had eluded than escaped, meet them again in their course. **1809** W. IRVING *Knickerb.* (1861) 161 A thousand devices.. prepared him to elude the wound. **1828** SCOTT *F.M. Perth* I. 250 It was..agreed, that, to elude the bad omen, the new King should assume the name of Robert.
b. To evade the force of (an argument).
1612 T. TAYLOR *Comm. Titus* i. 6. (1619) 102 Others seeking to elude this text say, etc. **1665** BOYLE *Occas. Refl.* (1675) 342 Men..elude what they cannot despise. **1696** WHISTON *Th. Earth* (1722) 27 The Holy Books ought not to be tormented or eluded. **1710** LUTTRELL *Brief Rel.* (1857) VI. 625 All which the Paris letters of the 1st seem to elude. **1841** D'ISRAELI *Amen. Lit.* (1867) 415 He thus adroitly eludes an argument which, etc.
3. To evade compliance with or fulfilment of (a law, order, demand, request, obligation, etc.).
1651 HOBBES *Govt. & Soc.* xviii. § 13. 360 He would.. elude that obedience which he hath contracted to yeeld. **1698** SIDNEY *Disc. Govt.* iii. § 27 (1704) 344 He that dos by art obliquely elude, confesses he has not a right absolutely to refuse. **1709** STEELE *Tatler* No. 6 ¶ 13 The Pope uses all imaginable shifts to elude the Treaty. **1769** ROBERTSON *Chas. V*, III. x. 192 He wished..to have eluded the obligation of his oath. **1837** THIRLWALL *Greece* VIII. 381 A cavil was now devised to elude this title. **1878** BROWNING *La Saisias* 69 How comes law to bear eluding?
4. To slip away from, escape adroitly from (a person's grasp or pursuit, *lit.* and *fig.*); to evade (curiosity, vigilance, etc.).
1667 MILTON *P.L.* IX. 158 Of these..the vigilance I dread, and to elude, thus wrapt in mist..glide obscure. **1766** GOLDSMITH *Vic. W.* xxix. (1857) 210 Providence has thought fit to elude our curiosity. **1859** JEPHSON *Brittany* iv. 42 The glittering gem of the Arabian tale ever eludes the grasp. **1879** HARLAN *Eyesight* iii. 35 The something..that evolves thought and reason—like an ignis fatuus, eludes the grasp of science.
b. Hence, ***to elude a person***: to escape his embrace, grasp, pursuit.
1791 COWPER *Iliad* x. 411 Lest he elude us, and escape to Troy. **1813** H. & J. SMITH *Horace in Lond.* 156 The jilt [wit] in spite Eludes the man of letters. **1843** CARLYLE *Past & Pr.* (1858) 297 He eludes thee like a Spirit. **1879** FROUDE *Cæsar* xvii. 286 Ambiorix..had as yet eluded him.
5. Of things: ***to elude enquiry, notice, observation***, etc.: to remain undiscovered or unexplained.
1791 BOSWELL *Johnson* (1816) II. 358 *note*, This celebrated Epitaph..has eluded a very diligent enquiry. **1860** TYNDALL *Glac.* II. § 3. 243 The total absorption being so small as to elude even Melloni's delicate tests. **1878** TAIT & STEWART *Unseen Univ.* vi. § 177. 181 So infinitesimally small as to elude our observation.
Hence **e'luded** *ppl. a.*, **e'luding** *vbl. sb.*
1703 POPE *Thebais* 303 Th' eluded rage of Jove. **1725** —— *Odyss.* XVI. 495 Th' eluded suitors stem the wat'ry way. **1737** JOHNSON in Boswell (1816) I. 87 A feeble government, eluded laws. **1872** GEO. ELIOT *Middlem.* v. 121 A triumphant eluding of his purpose.

e'ludent, *a. nonce-wd.* [ad. L. *ēlūdent-em*, f. *ēlūd-ĕre*: see prec.] That eludes (the gaze).
1848 CLOUGH *Bothie* III. 21 Unseen by turns, now here, now in ether eludent.

e'luder. [f. ELUDE + -ER.] One who eludes.
1642 ROGERS *Naaman* 529 Eluders and shifters with Gods Commands.

eludible (ɪ'l(j)uːdɪb(ə)l), *a.* [f. ELUDE + -(I)BLE.] That may be eluded, evaded, or set at nought.
1724 SWIFT *Drapier's Lett.* Wks. 1755 V. II. 132 If this blessed part of our law be eludible at pleasure..we shall have little reason to boast.

eluent ('ɛljuːənt). *Chem.* Also **eluant**. [f. L. *ēluent-em*, pres. pple. of *ēluĕre* to wash out: see -ENT, -ANT¹.] A fluid used to elute adsorbed material.
1941 BACHARACH & ROBINSON tr. *Zechmeister & Cholnoky's Princ. & Pract. Chromatography* ii. 75 The individual homogeneous portions of the column are coarsely broken up..and then immediately dropped into the eluent ..and stirred round. **1942** H. H. STRAIN *Chromatographic Adsorption Anal.* v. 65 Eluants, as a rule, are chosen with the object of obtaining rapid and complete liberation of adsorbed compounds. **1966** E. HASLAM *Chem. Vegetable Tannins* iv. 100 The tannin may then be isolated using acetone or methyl ethyl ketone as eluant. **1969** J. A. DEAN *Chem. Separation Methods* iv. 68 Assuming a fixed flow rate for the eluent, the time..at which each component in the sample will emerge from the column depends on the individual partition coefficients.

Elul ('iːlʌl). [a. Heb. *ĕlūl.*] The name of one of the Jewish months, being the twelfth of the civil and sixth of the ecclesiastical year.
1535 COVERDALE *Neh.* vi. 15 The wall was fynished on the fyue & twentyeth daye of the moneth Elul. **1611** BIBLE *1 Macc.* xiv. 27 The eighteenth day of the moneth Elul, in the hundred threescore and twelft yeere. **1753** in CHAMBERS *Cycl.* Suppl. **1886** *Encycl. Brit.* XXI. 126/2 What we do know from a calendar of the intercalary month Elul II. is that in that month the 7th, 14th, 19th, 21st, and 28th days had a peculiar character. **1907** *Daily Chron.* 10 Aug. 4/6 With the advent of the Jewish month of Ellul, of which tomorrow is the first day, a religious revival annually takes place in Jewry. **1962** C. ROTH *Standard Jewish Encycl.* 617 Elul..has become the traditional month of penitence and spiritual preparation for the Day of Judgment, and the *shophar* is sounded after morning service on weekdays throughout Elul.

elumbated (ɪ'lʌmbeɪtɪd), *ppl. a.* Now only *humorous.* [f. L. *ēlumb-is* (f. *ē* out + *lumb-us* loin) + -ATE³ + -ED¹.] Weakened in the loins.
1731–1800 BAILEY vol. II, *Elumbated*, made lame in his Loins. **1882** *Confess. of Medwin* xiii. 133 Our elumbated tailor came forward.

† **e'luminate**, *v. Obs. rare*⁻¹. [as if f. L. **ēlūmināt-* ppl. stem of *ēlūmināre*; see next.] = ILLUMINATE.
1580 H. GIFFORD *Gilloflowers* (1875) 77 Remember not my sinnes forepast, Eluminate my wayes.

†**e'lumine**, *v. Obs. rare*⁻¹. [ad. med.L. *ēlūmināre* (implied in *ēlūminātio* enlightenment), f. *ē* out + *lūmen, lūmin-is* light.] = ILLUMINATE.

1532 MORE *Confut. Tindale* Wks. 635/1 Thys lyghtsome elect of Tindall..is elumined by Luther.

†**e'luscate**, *v. Obs.*⁻⁰. [f. L. *ēluscāt-* ppl. stem of *ēluscā-re*, f. *ē* out + *lusc-us* blind of one eye.] To make blind of one eye. Hence **elu'scation**, purblindness.

1623 in COCKERAM.

elusion (ɪ'l(j)uːʒən). [as if ad. L. **ēlūsiōn-em*, n. of action f. *ēlūdě-re* to ELUDE.]

†**1.** The action of deluding or befooling a person; *concr.* an illusion, deceptive appearance. Cf. ELUDE *v.* 1.

1550 CRANMER *Defence* 22b, Than is the sensible sacrament nothyng else but an elusion of our senses. **1683** SALMON *Doron Med.* II. 294 Strengthens the Brain, takes away Elusions and Phantasms of the Mind. **1695** WOODWARD *Nat. Hist. Earth* IV. (1723) 239 The Impostures and Elusions of those who have pretended to it [i.e. transmutation of metals].

2. The action of escaping dexterously from (danger, pursuit, etc.), of evading (an argument, a command, law, or obligation): cf. ELUDE 2, 3. *rare* in mod. use. Const. *of*.

1624-47 BP. HALL *Rem. Wks.* (1660) 272 The place is so choakingly convictive, that there can be no probable elusion of it. **1633** T. ADAMS *Comm. 2 Peter* i. 3 Yet shall there be no elusion of God's will. **1681** H. MORE *Exp. Dan.* Pref. 94 Interposals of humane invention are..wicked elusions of the power..of the Gospel. **1726** AMHERST *Terræ Fil.* App. 278 The trouble of writing..a book upon the..elusion of one particular statute. **1874** T. HARDY *Madding Crowd* II. xvi. 197 The planting of flowers on Fanny's grave had been ..but a species of elusion of the primary grief.

†**b.** *absol.* An evasion, subterfuge; *abstr.* evasiveness. *Obs.*

1617 BP. HALL *Recoll. Treat.* 498 I heare your answer.. An elusion fit for children. **1628** —— *Old Relig.* (1686) 168 Cardinal Bellarmine's elusion is not a little prejudicial to his own cause. **1651** JER. TAYLOR *Serm.* I. xxiii. 296 Laws are not to be cosened and abused by..phantastick elusions. **1688** *Vox Cleri Pro R.* 7 He hath writ with all the..Elusion, to which the Capacity of his Wit could extend.

elusive (ɪ'l(j)uːsɪv), *a.* [f. L. *ēlūs-* ppl. stem of *ēlūděre* to ELUDE.]

1. That eludes or seeks to elude. Const. *of*.

1725 POPE *Odyss.* II. 99 Elusive of the bridal day she gives Fond hopes to all. **1736** GRAY *Transl. Statius* Then grasped its [the ball's] weight elusive of his hold. **1737** SAVAGE *Publ. Spirit* 56 The grot, elusive of the noontide ray.

†**b.** Of an argument: Evasive, of the nature of a subterfuge. *Obs.*

1719 WATERLAND *Vind. Christ's Div.* 121 An elusive, equivocating Answer to the Objection.

2. a. That eludes the grasp or pursuit; chiefly *fig.* **b.** That eludes distinct perception or precise definition; evanescent.

1751 *Student* II. 364 Pleasures..insubstantial, elusive, and transitory. **1762** FALCONER *Shipwr.* II. 731 They.. groaning, cling upon the elusive weed. **1830** CUNNINGHAM *Brit. Paint.* II. 142 It presents us with images so vivid and yet elusive. **1863** HAWTHORNE *Old Home* (1879) 138 A faint, elusive smell. **1865** M. ARNOLD *Ess. Crit.* iii. (1875) 111 Guérin's elusive, undulating, impalpable nature. **1883** *Harper's Mag.* July 177/2 Striving..after the elusive spirit of the general landscape.

elusively (ɪ'l(j)uːsɪvlɪ), *adv.* [f. prec. + -LY².] In an elusive manner.

1885 CRADOCK *Prophet Gt. S. Mount.* vi, A tawny streak elusively appearing upon a hilltop or skirting a rocky spur.

elusiveness (ɪ'l(j)uːsɪvnɪs). [f. ELUSIVE *a.* + -NESS.] The quality of being ELUSIVE.

1873 MASSON *Drumm. of Hawth.* vi. 104 Shakespeare's elusiveness of publicity. **1881** —— *De Quincey* x. 124 His [De Quincey's] elusiveness of all ordinary social gatherings had increased. **1884** *Pall Mall G.* 14 May, 5/1 Von Hartmann is..Protean in his elusiveness. **1884** ROE *Nat. Ser. Story* vii, Her..reserve and elusiveness.

elusory (ɪ'l(j)uːsərɪ), *a.* [ad. late L. *ēlūsōrius*, f. *ēlūs-* ppl. stem of *ēlūděre* to ELUDE.]

1. Tending to elude (a danger, argument, law, etc.); of the nature of an evasion or subterfuge.

1646 SIR T. BROWNE *Pseud. Ep.* I. x. 42 They are..elusory tergiversations. **1676** TEMPLE *Let.* Wks. 1731 II. 401 They had delayed the Exchange..and at length offered it with Conditions that I esteemed wholly elusory. **1758** SIR J. DALRYMPLE *Ess. Feudal Prop.* 37 People..took directly an elusory duty, as a rose, a pair of spurs, etc. **1849-50** ALISON *Hist. Europe* III. xiv. §63. 199 Security..which proved in the end almost elusory.

b. *nonce-use.* Characterized by eluding.

1825 SCOTT *Talism.* i, The Christian knight, desirous to terminate this elusory warfare..seized the mace.

2. Of an object of thought: That eludes the mental grasp; that one cannot 'get hold of'.

1856 FERRIER *Inst. Metaph.* Introd. 68 This..is a most elusory..problem.

Hence **e'lusoriness**. *rare*⁻⁰.

1731 in BAILEY; **1775** in ASH; and in mod. Dicts.

e'lute, *v.* [f. L. *ēlūt-* ppl. stem of *ēluě-re* to wash out.] *trans.* To wash out, cleanse. Now *spec.* [after G. *eluieren*, in same sense] to wash (adsorbed matter) away from the substance that has adsorbed it. Hence **e'luted** *ppl. a.*

1731 ARBUTHNOT *Aliments* 116 The more oily any Spirit is, the more pernicious, because it is harder to be eluted by the Blood. **1782-90** in BAILEY. **1847** in CRAIG. [**1925** FODOR & REIFENBERG in *Biochem. Jrnl.* XIX. 189 With a view to separating the proteins from other nitrogenous substances, we have tried to adsorb them by suitable adsorption media and afterwards to eluate [*sic*] them. [*Note*] We are adopting the terminology of Willstätter.] **1934** *Nature* 14 Apr. 554/1 From the adsorption on fuller's earth..the pigments were eluted by mixtures of pyridine and water. **1934** *Jrnl. Biol. Chem.* CV. 527 The solution of the eluted carotene was evaporated and the β-carotene recrystallized from *n*-heptane. **1946** *Nature* 20 July 96/1 By varying the nature and concentration of the solution used in eluting the adsorbed cations, it should be possible to isolate them in successive fractions of eluate. **1951** W. G. BERL *Physical Methods in Chem. Anal.* II. 593 It is not necessary in this case to elute until the solutes appear in the effluent. **1966** *Lancet* 31 Dec. 1432/1 Iron-solubility tests were carried out on the eluted fractions of unlabelled gastric juice.

elution (ɪ'l(j)uːʃən). *Chem.* [f. L. *ēlūtiōn-em* n. of action f. *ēluě-re*: see prec.] Washing from impurity; in early Chemistry (see quot.). In later use [G. *elution*, in same sense], the removal of adsorbed matter. (Cf. ELUTE *v.*)

1612 WOODALL *Surg. Mate* Wks. (1653) 270 Elution is the preparation of common Bole, Talcum, Crocus Martis, Terra Lemnia, etc., by pulverization, calcination, lotion, etc. **1870** H. E. GODFREY in *Eng. Mech.* 28 Jan. 484/2 All these starches are prepared by elution. **1922** *Chem. Abstr.* XVI. 2338 (*heading*) Remarks on the 'elution' of saccharase and maltase from their adsorption compounds. **1934** *Nature* 1 Sept. 307/2 Experiments dealing with the inactivation of enzymes on adsorption and their reactivation by elution. **1966** *Lancet* 31 Dec. 1432/1 When gastric juice of controls was resolved by molecular sieving, a consistent elution pattern was found.

elutriate (ɪ'l(j)uːtrɪeɪt), *v.* [f. L. *ēlutriāt-* ppl. stem of *ēlutriā-re* to wash out.] *trans.* To decant; to strain out; to purify by straining: in *Chem.* to separate the lighter from the heavier particles of a pulverulent mixture by washing.

1731 BAILEY vol. II, *Elutriated*, poured out of one vessel into another. **1733** ARBUTHNOT *Air* The alteration..must produce some difference in elutriating the blood as it passes through the lungs. **1775** in ASH. **1855** GARROD *Mat. Med.* (ed. 6) 76 Chalk reduced to a very fine powder and elutriated.

elutriation (ɪ,l(j)uːtrɪ'eɪʃən). [f. L. *ēlutriāt-*: see prec. and -ATION.] The action of elutriating.

1661 *Origen's Opin.* in *Phœnix* (1721) I. 44 Matter—which after all its..Elutriations..in the Body, is not purged from the coarse Tincture it had from its Earthly Original. **1756** C. LUCAS *Ess. Waters* III. 107, I repeted this elutriation or washing..till I found the water was no longer affected. **1770-4** A. HUNTER *Georg. Ess.* (1803) I. 231 Twenty grains ..gave, by elutriation, five grains of sand. **1876** HARLEY *Mat. Med.* 17 The simple process of elutriation.

elutriator (ɪ'ljuːtrɪeɪtə(r)). [f. ELUTRIATE *v.* + -OR.] An apparatus for sorting finely divided material according to mass and size by means of a stream of liquid or gas.

1904 *Econ. Proc. R. Dublin Soc.* I. 278 The residue now left in the elutriator consists of particles from 0·1 to 1 mm. diameter. **1957** R. A. SCOTT in H. W. Cremer et al. *Chem. Engin. Pract.* III. 352 Air elutriators are commonly employed in certain branches of the food industry..for the separation of husk and of small foreign seeds from grain.

†**elu'tropia.** *Obs.* [bad form of med.L. *eliotropia*, f. Gr. ἡλιοτρόπιον: see HELIOTROPE.]

a. A gem supposed to possess optical virtues and properties. **b.** A herb supposed to have been used in witchcraft.

1567 MAPLET *Gr. Forest* 7 Elutropia is a Gemme, in colour greene, or grassie, in part coloured and bespotted with Purple speckes & bloud coloured vaines..Also a certaine Hearbe which Enchaunters & Witches haue oftentimes vsed, and doe vse. **1688** R. HOLME *Armoury* II. 40/1 The Elutropia..will cause things a farr off to be presented to your Eyes.

eluvial (ɪ'l(j)uːvɪəl), *a.* [f. ELUVI-UM + -AL¹.]

1. *Geol.* Pertaining to, or of the nature of, eluvium.

1862 G. P. SCROPE *Volcanos* 172 There is another not unfrequent cause of such 'eluvial' debacles. **1881** GEIKIE in *Nature* XXIII. 225 The superficial weathering of rocks, and the formation of 'eluvial' accumulations.

2. *Soil Sci.* Pertaining to a layer of soil which has undergone ELUVIATION, as in *eluvial horizon*.

1924 *Geol. Mag.* LXI. 451 Three main horizons are generally recognized,..the A or eluvial horizon, the B or illuvial horizon, and the C horizon, which consists of the parent material. **1934** *Forestry* VIII. 26 The leached layer above being known as the eluvial horizon. **1952** P. W. RICHARDS *Tropical Rain Forest* ix. 208 All soils of the rain-forest region..are therefore strongly leached and have an eluvial horizon, or leached zone, above the illuvial horizon. **1963** D. W. & E. E. HUMPHRIES tr. *Termier's Erosion & Sedimentation* vi. 138 A soil is composed of an impoverished zone, the *eluvial horizon*, and also a zone of enrichment or accumulation, the *illuvial horizon*.

eluviate (iː'ljuːvɪeɪt), *v. Soil Sci.* To undergo eluviation. Usually in pa. pple. or as **e'luviated** ppl. a.

1926 TANSLEY & CHIPP *Study of Vegetation* vii. 116 With lapse of time not only are calcium carbonate and other soluble salts leached from the surface soil..but the finer *insoluble* particles tend also to be mechanically carried down, so that the coarser particles alone remain in the surface layers, which are then said to be 'eluviated' as well as 'leached'. **1963** S. R. EYRE *Vegetation & Soils* ii. 36 In most soils which are subject to leaching, it is possible to distinguish two quite distinct sets of horizons... The upper set are referred to as '*eluviated horizons*'.

eluviation (ɪljuːvɪ'eɪʃən). *Soil Sci.* [as if ad. L. **ēluviātiōn-em*, noun of action f. *ēluěre* to wash off.] The lateral or vertical movement of material in solution or suspension through the soil.

1924 *Geol. Mag.* LXI. 450 Situations where surface erosion is sufficiently rapid to predominate over eluviation. **1928** in B. D. JACKSON *Gloss. Bot. Terms* (ed. 4) Suppl. **1930** L. A. WOLFANGER *Major Soil Divisions of U.S.* ii. 45 The extraction and concentration are brought about in part through eluviation. **1932** G. W. ROBINSON *Soils* iii. 53 We may refer to the translocation of material either mechanically or in solution, as eluviation, and two main types of eluviation may be distinguished..mechanical eluviation, in which..the finer fractions of the mineral portions of the soil are washed down to lower levels, and.. chemical eluviation in which decomposition occurs and certain products thus liberated are translocated in true or colloidal solution. **1952** L. M. THOMPSON *Soils & Soil Fertility* vi. 73 The term eluviation designates the movement or shifting of the materials through the soil body. **1957** *Gloss. Geol.* (Amer. Geol. Inst.) 94/2 Eluviation may take place downward or sidewise according to the direction of water movement. **1968** R. W. FAIRBRIDGE *Encycl. Geomorphol.* 1001/1 Infiltrating precipitation passes through the slope prism, exiting by the lower boundary and carrying down ions, colloids and perhaps even mineral particles of clay and silt grades, a process generally termed *eluviation*, or simple *leaching*.

‖**eluvies** (ɪ'l(j)uːvɪiːz). [L. *ēluvies* a washing away of impurities, f. *ēluě-re* to wash off.]

a. 'Old term for the humour discharged in leucorrhœa; an inordinate discharge of any kind' (*Syd. Soc. Lex.*). **b.** 'The effluvium from a swampy place' (Hooper *Med. Dict.*).

1710 T. FULLER *Pharm. Extemp.* 316 This Medicament.. extirpates..the..Eluvies of depraved Humours out of the whole Body.

eluvium (ɪ'l(j)uːvɪəm). *Geol.* [mod.Lat., f. *ē* out + *luěre* to wash, on the analogy of ALLUVIUM.] A term proposed for accumulations of débris either produced *in situ* by atmospheric agencies, or carried by wind-drift.

1882 GEIKIE *Text-bk. Geol.* III. II. i. §1. 322 For atmospheric accumulations of this nature Traufschold has proposed the name eluvium.

eluxate (ɪ'lʌkseɪt), *v.* [f. E- *pref.*³ + *luxāt-* ppl. stem of *luxā-re* to put out of joint.] *trans.* 'To dislocate or put out of joint' (*Syd. Soc. Lex.*).

1731-1800 BAILEY, *Eluxated*, wrenched, strained, sprained, put out of joint. **1775** in ASH.

Hence **elu'xation**.

1847 CRAIG, *Eluxation*: see Luxation. In mod. Dicts.

elvan ('ɛlvən). Also 8 elvin. [In the West Cornwall Gloss. (E.D.S.) referred to Corn. *elven* spark, 'the rock being so hard as to strike fire'.]

1. The name given in Cornwall to intrusive rocks of igneous origin, so hard as to resist the pick, as quartz-porphyry, whinstone, etc. Also *attrib.*

1791 BEDDOES in *Phil. Trans.* LXXXI. 65 Whether the basaltes proceeds southward by such interruptions till it join the Elvin or Whinstone. **1864** LYELL in *Reader* 17 Sept. 358 One wall consisting of elvan or porphyritic granite. **1865** J. T. TURNER *Slate Quarries* 22 Elvan (or slate whose cleavage was destroyed by internal heat) of unknown thickness. **1879** RUTLEY *Stud. Rocks* iv. 33 The quartz-porphyries or elvans.

2. A broad vein or dike of this rock.

1849 MURCHISON *Siluria* xvii. 417 Limestone pierced by elvans, or granite dykes.

Hence **'elvanite.** *Min.* = ELVAN. **elva'nitic** *a.*, containing or characterized by elvanite.

1882 GEIKIE *Text-bk. Geol.* II. II. §6. 136 Elvan or elvanite ..is a Cornish term for a crystalline-granular mixture of quartz and orthoclase. **1883** *Standard* 28 July 1/6 Granulite is an elvanitic or fine-grained granite.

†**'elvat.** Also 1 elefæt, 5 elevat. [OE. *elefæt*, f. ELE, oil + *fæt* vessel: see VAT.] An oil-vessel, an ampulla: see AMPULLA 2.

c **1000** ÆLFRIC *Voc.* in Wr.-Wülcker 123 *Emicadium*, elefæt. *c* **1050** *Ibid.* 437 *Legithum*, ampellan, oððe elefæt. *c* **1450** *Ibid.* 593 *Lechitus*, an elevat. *c* **1450** *Ibid.* 592 *Lenticula*, a crismatorye or an Elvat. *c* **1450** *Ibid.* 621 *Xrismatorium*, the Eluat.

elve, obs. var. of ELF.

'elven. Forms: 1 ælfen, elfen, 3 *pl.* alfene, alvene, elvene. [OE. *ælfen, ęlfen*, repr. a WGer. type **albinjā* fem., f. **albi-z* ELF.

Although the OE. word glosses plural sbs. in the Latin, it is grammatically necessary to regard it as a fem. sing.]

†**1.** *Obs.* Originally, a female elf, but in later use applied to both sexes.

a **1100** *Ags. Voc.* in Wr.-Wülcker 189 *Oreades*, muntælfen. *Dryades*, wuduelfen. *Moides*, feldelfen. *Hamadryades*, wylde elfen. *Naiades*, sæelfen. *Castalides*, dunelfen. *c* **1205** LAY 21998 Alfene [**1275** aluene] hine dulfen. **1297** R. GLOUC. 130 þer beþ in þe eir an hey.. wyȝtes.. þat men clepuþ eluene. *c* **1314** *Guy Warw.* (A.) 3862 A brond þat was y-made in Eluene lond.

2. *Comb.* (referring to a kind of imaginary being in the works of J. R. R. Tolkien). **a.** appositive, as ***elven-kin***; **b.** attributive, as ***elven-king***, ***-tongue***; ***elven-wise*** adj.

1937 TOLKIEN *Hobbit* xvii. 285 But the Elvenking said: Long will I tarry. **1954** —— *Fellowship of Ring* I. iii. 88 It was singing in the fair Elven-tongue. *Ibid.* II. i. 248 Words unheard were spoken then of folk of Men and Elven-kin. **1955** —— *Return of King* 341 He was elven-wise.

elver (ˈɛlvə(r)). [var. of EELFARE.] A young eel, *esp.* a young conger or sea-eel. Also *attrib.*, as in **elver-cake**, a cake made of elvers.

c **1640** J. SMYTH *Hundred Berkeley* (1885) 319 Elvers, supposed by some to bee the younge eele. **1679** LOCKE in Lord King *Life* (1858) 134 At Bristol.. taste.. elvers. **1748** DE FOE, etc. *Tour Gt. Brit.* II. 306 [Little eels] they make.. into small Cakes.. These Elver-cakes they dispose of at Bath and Bristol. **1726** *Dict. Rust.*, *Elvers*, a sort of Griggs, or small Eels. **1863** H. C. PENNELL *Angler-nat.* 394 The Eelets, or Elvers, are at first very small and transparent.

Hence ˈ**elverhood.** *nonce-wd.*

1886 *Fishing* 18 Sept. 414 Eels of the size caught.. at the New Mills.. must have passed all their lives since elverhood above the mills.

elves, pl. of ELF.

elvet (ˈɛlvɪt). [f. ELF + -ET¹.] A tiny elf.

1885 T. P. BATTERSBY *Elf Land* 73 'He is an elf', Psyche answered, 'but he is one of those we call elvets'.

elvish (ˈɛlvɪʃ), *a.* Also 4 alvisch, elvisch, -yssh, 6 -yshe. See also ELFISH. [f. ELF + -ISH.]

1. Of or pertaining to elves; having the nature of an elf; supernatural, weird.

c **1340** *Gaw. & Gr. Knt.* 681 Wyth an aluisch mon. *c* **1386** CHAUCER *Chan. Yem. Prol. & T.* 198 Whan we been there as we shul exercise Oure Eluysshe craft. **1597** BP. HALL *Sat.*, *Defiance Envie* 49 Scour the rusted swords of elvish knights. **1814** SCOTT *Ld. of Isles* I. xxi, Wild sparkles.. the vessel's side With elvish lustre lave. **1834** BECKFORD *Italy* II. 77 These oracular little elvish beings. **1840** LYTTON *Pilgr. Rhine* xxx, Elvish spells.

2. Like an elf in behaviour: †**a.** Spiteful, cross-grained, peevish; also *transf.* of diseases, Irritating, troublesome (*obs.*). **b.** Now in a milder sense: Tricksy, mischievous (cf. ELFISH).

c **1386** CHAUCER *Sir Thopas* Prol. 13 He semeth eluyssh by his contenance. **1529** MORE *Comf. agst. Trib.* II. Wks. 1182/2 Eye, what eyleth this gyrle? that eluish vrchin weneth I wer a diuell I trow. **1549** CHEKE *Hurt. Sedit.* (1641) 14 Where.. prating is judged wisdome, and the elvishest is most meet to rule. **1566** STUDLEY *Seneca's Agam.* (1581) Ab, Thou malipert and witlesse wench, thyne elvishe prating stay. **1601** DENT *Pathw. Heaven* 389 Hee regardeth not our infirmities, though we be often times waiward and eluish. **1601** HOLLAND *Pliny* II. 258 Sow-bread sodden in water, cureth the eluish & angry kibes.. vpon the heels. **1607** TOPSELL *Four-f. Beasts* 321 The crown-scab [in horses].. is an elvish and painful disease. **1623** COCKERAM, II, Froward, *Eluish*. **1678–96** PHILLIPS, *Elvish*, froward. **1721–1800** in BAILEY.

3. *Comb.*, as ***elvish-marked***.

1597 SHAKS. *Rich.* I. iii. 228 Thou eluish mark'd, abortiue rooting Hogge.

ˈ**ely**, *v. Sc.*

1. *intr.* To disappear gradually from sight.

1813 HOGG *Queen's Wake* 174 Quhan the sun and the world haif elyit awaye. **1818** —— *Brownie of Bodsb.* II. 36 It elyed away o'er the brow, an' I saw nae mair o't.

2. To drop off one by one, as a company does that disperses imperceptibly. (Jam.)

†**eˈlychnious**, *a. Obs. rare*⁻¹. [f. Gr. ἐλλύχνιον lamp-wick, f. ἐν in + λύχνος lamp.] Of the nature of a wick. (Erroneously explained by Blount.)

1646 SIR T. BROWNE *Pseud. Ep.* III. xiv. 140 Men practise to make long Snasts or Elychnious parts for lampes, out of Alumen plumosum. **1656** BLOUNT *Glossogr.*, *Elychnious*, that hath no match or light, without a wick. **1775** in ASH.

elydoric (ɛlɪˈdɒrɪk), *a.* [ad. F. *éludorique*, badly f. Gr. ἔλαιον oil + ὕδωρ water.] The distinctive epithet of a mode of painting invented by Vincent, of Montpetit, in which both oil and water were used.

1826 ELMES *Dict. Fine Arts*, *Elydoric Painting* [The process is fully described]. **1847** in CRAIG; and in mod. Dicts.

†**elyne**, *adv. Obs.*, var. of ALINE *adv.*, q.v.

c **1375** *Sc. Leg. Saints, VII Sleperis* 417 þai enteryt al þat mycht elyne.

†**elynel.** *Her. Obs. rare*⁻¹.

1486 *Bk. St. Albans, Her.* B iv b, Elynellis be calde in armys iiij quadrantis truncholis.

elynge, var. of ELENGE, *Obs.*

elyot, obs. form of HELOT.

Elysée (eɪˈliːzeɪ). In full *Elysée Palace*: a building in Paris, on the Champs Elysées, the official residence of the French head of state: hence used as a synonym for the head of state and his advisers, or the Government, of the day.

1851 *Observer* 7 Dec. 4/1 The President.. had proclamations printed at a private printing press in the Elysée. **1870** E. G. E. WARD *Jrnl.* 7 Oct. in *Outside Paris* (1871) 26, I had seen William of Prussia enter the Château of Francis the First as a conqueror. When will he enter the Tuileries or the Elysée? **1934** A. THIRKELL *Wild Strawberries* xiii. 297 Alas for the lilies of France!.. The tricolore still flew over the Elysée. **1966** *Guardian* 11 Nov. 13/3 The new direct communication link between the Elysée Palace and the Kremlin. **1967** *Ibid.* 9 Oct. 7/7 The phrase.. has been the Elysée's line since Mr Wilson's first advances.

Elysian (ɪˈlɪzɪən, -ʒɪən), *a.* Forms: 6–7 elis-, elizian, 6– elysian. [f. ELYSI-UM + -AN.]

1. Of or pertaining to Elysium.

1622 MASSINGER, etc. *Virgin Mart.* IV. iii, The remembrance Of the Elysian joys thou might'st have tasted. **1667** MILTON *P.L.* III. 358 The river of Bliss.. Rowls o're Elisian Flours her amber stream. **1831** CARLYLE *Sart. Res.* (1858) 42 Is that a real Elysian brightness? **1882** OUIDA *Maremma* I. 149 Vast grasslands.. covered in spring with the elysian asphodel.

b. ***Elysian fields*** = ELYSIUM 1 and 2; also *fig.*

1579 SPENSER *Sheph. Cal.* Nov. 179, I see thee blessed soule, I see, Walk in Elisian fieldes so free. **1641** MAISTERTON *Serm.* 23 Orchards of delight, surpassing the Elysian fields. **1716** LADY M. W. MONTAGUE *Lett.* xl. I. 162 This place.. perfectly answers the description of the Elysian fields. **1843** CARLYLE *Past & Pr.* (1858) 102 The Elysian-Fields of Memory.

2. *fig.* Of the nature of, or resembling, what is in Elysium; beatific, glorious.

1750 JOHNSON *Rambl.* No. 36 ¶1 We.. suffer ourselves.. to be transported to elysian regions. **1813** BYRON *Br. Abydos* I. vi, Too transcendent vision, When heart meets heart again in dreams Elysian. **1850** MRS. JAMESON *Leg. Monast. Ord.* (1863) 277 Nothing can be imagined more.. bright and elysian than these figures.

B. as *sb.* = ELYSIUM. *Obs. rare.*

1586 MARLOWE *1st Pt. Tamburl.* v. ii, To get a passage to Elisian. *Ibid.* Hell and Elisian swarme with Ghosts of men.

Hence **eˈlysianize** *v. intr.*, to speak in terms of rapturous or extravagant approbation.

1868 BUSHNELL *Serm. Living Subj.* 413 They.. fall into a strain of elysianizing.

Elysium (ɪˈlɪzɪəm, -ʒɪəm). Forms: 7–8 elizeum, -ium, elyzium, 8 elisium, 6– elysium. [a. L. *ēlysium*, ad. Gr. Ἠλύσιον (πεδίον) the abode of the blessed.]

1. The supposed state or abode of the blessed after death in Greek mythology.

1599 BROUGHTON *Lett.* xiii. 44 Two passages one leading into Elysium, the other into Tartarus. **1646** J. HALL *Horæ Vac.* 29 There is more in that Elizium of the Poets then a meere flowrish. **1702** ROWE *Amb. Step-Moth.* IV. ii. 1845 That Lethe and Elisium Which Priests and Poets tell. **1768–74** TUCKER *Lt. Nat.* (1852) II. 321 The enjoyments of Elysium and punishments of Tartarus.

2. *transf.* Any similarly-conceived abode or state of the departed.

1603 H. PETOWE in Farr's *S.P. Jas. I*, 105 Shee's hence, For sweet Eliza in Elizium lives. **1667** MILTON *P.L.* III. 472 Thee who to enjoy Plato's Elysium, leap'd into the Sea. **1796** MORSE *Amer. Geog.* I. 511 The departed spirit is ten days in its passage to their happy elysium. **1847** LYTTON *Lucretia* (1853) 220 The son of the East [placed].. his elysium by cooling streams.

3. *fig.* A place or state of ideal or perfect happiness.

1599 SHAKS. *Hen. V*, IV. i. 291 The wretched Slaue all Night sleepes in Elizium. **1640** T. CAREW *Poems* Wks. (1824) 60 Flye with me to love's Elizium. **1702** ROWE *Tamerl.* IV. i. 1831 Injur'd Lovers find Elizium there. **1836** HOR. SMITH *Tin Trump.* (1876) 179 Holidays.. the Elysium of our boyhood, perhaps the only one of our life.

†**4.** *attrib. Obs.*

1616 *Pasquil & Kath.* III. 278 Why do'st thou forsake Elizeum pleasures. *c* **1685** *Roxb. Ball.* (1886) VI. 223 To th' Elizium Shades I post. *c* **1740** MRS. PENDARVES *Autobiog.* I. 12, I.. thought the poet's description of the Elysium fields nothing to the delights of those entertainments.

elyte, var. of ELITE, *Obs.*

elytral (ˈɛlɪtrəl), *a. Entom.* [f. ELYTR-ON + -AL¹.] Of or pertaining to the elytra of a beetle.

1880 *Athenæum* 18 Dec. 819/3 Mr. Pascoe exhibited a large series of *Arescus histrio* from Peru, to show the extreme variability of the elytral markings in this species.

elytriform (ɛˈlɪtrɪfɔːm), *a.* [f. as next + -FORM.] That has the form of elytra.

1835 KIRBY *Hab. & Inst. Anim.* II. xx. 318 The Strepsiptera have.. two elytriform subspiral organs.

elytrigerous (ɛlɪˈtrɪdʒərəs), *a.* [f. *elytri-*, comb. f. ELYTRUM + L. *-ger-* bearing + -OUS.] That has or bears elytra.

1877 HUXLEY *Anat. Inv. An.* v. 234 The order of arrangement of the elytrigerous.. somites is very curious.

elytrin (ˈɛlɪtrɪn). [f. ELYTR-ON + -IN.] 'The form of chitin which composes the elytra of insects' (*Syd. Soc. Lex.*).

elytro-, comb. form of Gr. ἔλυτρον sheath, used = VAGINA in various medical terms, as †**elytroˈcele**, vaginal hernia. **elytroˈplasty**, the operation of closing a vesico-vaginal fistulous opening by borrowing a flap from the labia or nates: hence **elytroˈplastic** *a.* **elyˈtrorrhaphy**, the operation of closing the orifice of the vagina by suture in order to support the uterus when prolapsed; the suturing of a ruptured vagina.

1872 F. THOMAS *Dis. Women* 195 Elytroplasty is still employed sometimes where great destruction of tissue has taken place at the base of the bladder. *Ibid.* 169 The operation of elytrorrhaphy.

elytroid (ˈɛlɪtrɔɪd) *a.* [ad. Gr. ἐλυτροειδής, f. ἔλυτρον sheath + εἶδος form.] Resembling an elytron or sheath, sheath-like.

1864 in WEBSTER; and in mod. Dicts.

elytron (ˈɛlɪtrɒn). *Pl.* **elytra**; also 8 elitra. [a. Gr. ἔλυτρον a sheath.] A sheath or covering.

†**1.** (See quot.) *Obs.*⁻⁰.

1753 CHAMBERS *Cycl. Supp.*, *Elytron*.. Hippocrates has appropriated the word to signify the membranes, which involve the spinal marrow. **1882** in *Syd. Soc. Lex.*

2. The outer hard wing-case of a coleopterous insect, pl. *elytra*. Also *Comb.*, as ***elytra-like*** adj.

1774 GOLDSMITH *Nat. Hist.* (1862) II. IV. vi. 548 The elytron, or case for the wings [of the beetle]. **1777** HENLY in *Phil. Trans.* LXVII. 123 Elitra of the stag-beetle. **1802** BINGLEY *Anim. Biog.* (1813) III. 151 The larvæ of the Earwigs.. have neither wings nor elytra. **1852** DANA *Crust.* II. 1370 The two elytra-like prolongations of the shell. **1871** DARWIN *Desc. Man* I. x. 343 The females of some water beetles have their elytra deeply grooved.

3. 'A term applied to the shield-like plates or notopodial appendages on the back of some polychætous annelids' (*Syd. Soc. Lex.*).

1841–71 T. R. JONES *Anim. Kingd.* 274 In *Aphrodite aculeata* the tale of the real uses of the elytra or scales is plainly told. **1878** BELL tr. *Gegenbauer's Comp. Anat.* 134 The elytra are special appendages of the parapodia.

4. 'A term for the vagina' (*Syd. Soc. Lex.*).

elytrous (ˈɛlɪtrəs), *a.* [f. ELYTR-ON + -OUS.] That resembles or has the nature of elytra.

1848 JOHNSTON in *Proc. Berw. Nat. Club.* II. VI. 302 The back.. partially covered with an elytrous.. ovate skin.

ˈ**elytrum.** [mod.L. ad. Gr. ἔλυτρον.] = ELYTRON.

1816 KIRBY & SP. *Entomol.* (1820) II. xxiii. 347 In Blatta the left elytrum laps over the right.

Elzevir (ˈɛlzɪvə(r)). Also 8 elzever, 9 elziver.

1. The name (properly *Elzevier*, latinized *Elzevirius*) of a family of printers at Amsterdam, The Hague, Leyden, and Utrecht (1592–1680), famous chiefly for their editions of the classics, many of which are still valued by collectors. Used *attrib.* or as *adj.*, e.g. in ***Elzevir edition***, an edition published by one of the Elzeviers; formerly applied also to editions printed in the small neat form and with the kind of type adopted by them. Also *absol.* a book printed by one of the Elzeviers.

17.. POPE *Let.* Wks. VI. 19, I gave the boy a small bagg, containing three shirts and an elzevir Virgil. **1713** STEELE *Englishm.* No. 52. 335 The Poem I speak of.. is just now published in a little Elzevir Edition. **1842** MRS. GORE *Fascin.* 126 Placing his spectacles in one of his pockets, and.. one of his precious Elzevirs in the other. **1860** J. KENNEDY *Swallow B.* vi. 66 Some famous Elzivirs were picked up.

2. Elzevir letter, type. a. The style of type used by the Elzeviers in their small editions of the classics.

1710 *Lond. Gaz.* No. 4637/3 A neat Edition on an Elzever Letter.

b. Now used as the name of a special form of printing types.

Elzevirian (ɛlzɪˈvɪərɪən), *a.* [f. prec. + -IAN.]

1. Of or pertaining to the Elzeviers; (of books) published by or in the style of the Elzeviers.

1802 DIBDIN *Introd. Classics* 11 The Elzevirian Press.

2. quasi-*sb.* One who collects or fancies the editions of the Elzeviers.

1862 BURTON *Bk. Hunter* 18 He was not a black-letter man.. or an Elzivirian.

em (ɛm). The name of the letter M. In *Printing*, the square, formerly of the type m, used in typography as the unit for measuring and estimating the amount of printed matter in a line, page, etc. The em of pica is the standard. Also *attrib.*, as ***em quad***, ***quadrat***, a square QUADRAT (see also quots. 1927 and 1967). Cf. M 2.

[**1683–1824** see QUADRAT 2.] **1793** in Stower *Printer's Gram.* (1808) xvii. 419 That em and en quadrats.. be included. **1808** STOWER *Printer's Gram.* xvii. 419 The ems and ens at the beginnings and ends of the lines not to be reckoned in the width. **1863** W. BLADES *Life & Typogr. W. Caxton* II. iv. p. xliii, When a 'white' line was wanted under a chapter head or over a colophon, em quadrats were ranged side by side for the purpose. **1864** *Daily Tel.* 3 Oct. [The printers' union] advanced its demands from forty-five cents to sixty cents per thousand 'ems'. **1871** Em quad [see *mutton-quad*]. **1888** *Encycl. Brit.* s.v. *Typography*, The width of.. pages.. is expressed according to the number of 'ems', that is of a pica 'm'—the square of the depth of pica.. A page of 24 ems wide is equal to one of 4 inches. **1927** R. B. MCKERROW *Introd. Bibliogr.* I. ii. 13 Quads were no doubt usually square spaces, as broad as the height of a line.

From the fact that the letter m (or M) used to be cast on a square body, such a square space is called an em-quad. **1967** E. CHAMBERS *Photolitho-Offset* ii. 12 Quads and spaces are the separation material used between letters and words. The em quad is the square of a given body size; the en quad is half the square width.

'em (əm), *pron.* Originally the unstressed form of HEM, dat. and accus. 3rd pers. pl. The emphatic form of the pronoun was early superseded by THEM, but the unstressed form continued to be used, being regarded as an abbreviation of *them*. In literature it is now obs. or arch., but is still common in familiar speech.

In north midland dialects *'em* may have arisen from *them*: cf. South Yorkshire *'at* for *that*. In strictly northern dialects it is never used.

1380 *Sir Ferumb.* 3098 Þer na ascapedem non. **1599** SHAKS. *Hen. V*, IV. iii. 124 These joints.. As I will leave 'em them. **1672** R. WILD *Poet. Licent.* 35 Some men there be that carry all before 'em. **1702** *Eng. Theophrast.* 2 New-cast your poems, purge 'em of their dross. **1750** W. PELHAM *Let.* in Lady Chatterton *Mem. Adm. Gambier* (1861) I. iii. 36 You know my thoughts, I will trouble you therefore no more about 'em. **1832** TENNYSON *Death Old Year*, He gave me a friend, and a true true-love. And the New-Year will take 'em away. **1868** FURNIVALL *Temp. Pref. to Six-Text Cant. Tales* 41 *note*, We can't blame 'em, as we all used to do the same.

em, obs. form of AM: see BE *v.*

em, var. of EME, *Obs.*, uncle.

em-, *prefix*, the form assumed by the prefix EN- (q.v.) before *b*, *p*, and (frequently) *m*. For the reasons stated under EN-, nearly all the Eng. words with this prefix, whether of Romanic or Eng. formation, have (or formerly had) alternative forms with IM-. In this Dictionary the *em-* and the *im-* form, except where usage has introduced a distinction of sense between the two, will be treated as belonging to one and the same word, the article being placed under E or I in accordance with the principles explained under EN-.

The various functions of the prefix, and its use as an Eng. formative, are explained under EN-. Of the many compounds formed by prefixing *em-* to English words, those which have any special importance or require special remark, are inserted in their alphabetical place; the following are examples of those which are nonce-words or of rare occurrence.

1. Transitive vbs. (often found only in vbl. sb., pa. pple., or ppl. adj.).

a. f. *em-* + sb., 'to put (something) into or upon what is denoted by the sb.'; also 'to put what is denoted by the sb. into' (something).

embag, to put into a bag; †**embalance**, to put in the balance (with); †**embare**, to make bare; †**embarrel**, to pack in barrels; †**embill**, to put food into (a bird's) bill; **embirch** (cf. *embark*), to put on board a birch-bark canoe (in quot. *intr.* for *refl.*); †**embottle**, to put into a bottle; †**embrail**, to put (a sail) into a brail, to brail; †**embreech**, to put (a gun) upon a breech or stock; **embronze**, to represent in bronze; †**embusk**, to put on a busk, raise by means of a busk; †**embuskin**, to encase (the leg) in a buskin; †**empall**, to cover with a pall or cloak; **empanoply**, to array in complete armour; **empaper**, to put down on paper; **emparchment**, to put or write on parchment; †**empill** [after *empoison*], to dose as with a pill.

1812 W. TENNANT *Anster F.* i, Mad t' *embag their limbs. **1643** T. GOODWIN *Aggrav. Sin* 4 The least dram of which, the whole world *emballanced with, would be found too light. **1615** A. NICCHOLES *Marriage & Wiv.* vii. in *Harl. Misc.* (1744) II. 152 *Embared Breasts. **1599** NASHE *Lent. Stuffe* in *Harl. Misc.* VI. 179 Our *embarreld white-herrings.. last in long voyages. **1598** FLORIO, *Imbeccare*, to *embill or feede birds. *Imbeccata*, an embilling, a billing or feeding. **1864** LOWELL *Fireside Trav.* 153 We were *embirching.. for our moose-chase. *a* **1693** URQUHART *Rabelais* III. lii. 422 I had *embottled them. **1708** J. PHILIPS *Cyder* II. 352 Firmest Fruit, Embottled long. **1762** FALCONER *Shipwr.* II. 303 He who strives the tempest to disarm, Will never first *embrail the lee yardarm. **1598** FLORIO, *Imbracare*, to *embreech, or put any artillerie vpon a stocke. **1743** FRANCIS *Horace's Satires* II. iii. That you.. in the Capitol *embronz'd may stand. **1593** NASHE *Christ's T.* (1613) 145 Their breasts they *embuske vp on hie. **1596** FITZ-GEFFRAY *Sir F. Drake* (1881) 26 Statelie shanks *embuskind by the Muses. **1599** NASHE *Lent. Stuffe* 22 The red herring.. *empals our sage Senatours.. in princely scarlet. **1581** J. BELL *Haddon's Answ. Osor.* 360 The empalled and Mytred Byshoppes. **1784** W. SPENCER in *Poems* (1811) 60 *Empanoply'd in arms. **1847** TENNYSON *Princ.* v. 472 Empanoplied and plumed We entered in. **1861** READE *Cloister & H.* III. 233 I will *empaper it before your eyes. **1840** CARLYLE *Heroes* (1858) 284, I take your Bull, as an *emparchmented Lie, and burn it. **1605** SYLVESTER *Du Bartas* 428 In the sugar (even) of sacred writ He may *empill us with som banefull bit.

b. f. *em-* + sb. or adj., with general sense 'to bring into a certain condition or state'; also (cf. 3) 'to furnish with something'.

embeggar; †**embloody**; †**embrawn**, to make brawny, harden; †**embulk**, to make bulky, to extend; †**embullion** (cf. BULLION *sb.*[3]) to bestud; †**empeevish**, to make peevish; †**emprelate**, to make a prelate of.

1806 SOUTHEY in C. Southey *Life* III. 54 They have so.. vulgarised, impoverished and *embeggared the language. **16..** T. ADAMS *Wks.* 1861–2 II. 146 Oh the unmatchable cruelty that some men's religion (if I may so call it) hath *embloodied them to! **1599** NASHE *Lent. Stuffe* 38 It will *embrawne and iron crust his flesh. **1775** HARRIS *Philos. Arrangem.* (1841) 273 *note* This (that is, the first matter) being *embulked with three extensions. **1523** SKELTON *Garl. Laurel* Wks. 487 *Embullyoned with sapphires. *a* **1687** H. MORE in Ward *Life* (1710) 207 Pain.. doth ordinarily *empeevish the Spirit of the Afflicted. **1603** FLORIO *Montaigne* III. x. (1632) 571 Who *emprelate themselves even to the heart and entraïles.

2. Verbs f. *em-* + verb, with additional sense of *in*, or simply with more or less intensive force.

†**embias**; †**embribe**; †**embruise**; †**embubble**; †**emplight**; †**empromise**.

1682 MRS. BEHN *Roundheads* II. i, A.. mind *embyass'd in affairs of blood. **1611** SPEED *Hist. Gt. Brit.* IX. ix. 27 Five thousand Markes, with which the Queene Dowager of France had (as he said) *embribed him. *c* **1570** *Treas. Amadis de Gaule* (Bynneman) 279 My *embrused brest. **1652** BENLOWES *Theophila* v. xc. Like diamonds thaw'd to Air, *embubble forth in streams. *c* **1860** S. BAMFORD in Harland *Lanc. Lyrics* 14 She *emplighteth her vow. *c* **1540** tr. *Polyd. Vergil's Eng. Hist.* (Camd.) I. 140 The dowghter of Offa.. was *empromised him to espouse.

3. Participial adjs. f. *em-* + sb. + *-ed*, with the sense 'furnished with':

embastioned, embeadled, empimpled.

1832 E. ROBERTS *Oriental Sc.* 49 Each tower-*embastion'd citadel. **1859** SALA *Tw. round Clock* (1861) 194 Oxford Street, with its *embeadled colonnade. **1839** *Blackw. Mag.* XLV. 354 [A toper's] *empimpled proboscis.

(For words beginning with *em-* not found in their alphabetical place, or included in this article, see IM-.)

†**e'macerate**, *v. Obs. rare.* [f. L. *ēmacerāt-* ppl. stem of *ēmacerāre*, f. *ē-* intensive + *macer-āre* to make lean.] *trans.* = EMACIATE.

1610 [see next]. **1676** BULLOKAR, *Emacerate* or *Emaciate*, to make thin, lean, or poor in flesh. **1669** *Lond. Gaz.* No. 400/4 The Dauphin is weak, and much emacerated by his long distemper. **1731–6** BAILEY vol. II. **1818** in TODD.

†**e'macerated**, *ppl. a. Obs.* [f. prec. + -ED.] Emaciated; also *transf.* of soils, exhausted, impoverished.

1610 W. FOLKINGHAM *Art of Survey* I. x. 26 All Emacerated Soyles are much amended with fatte Ashes. **1704** *Collect. Voy.* (Churchill) III. 598/1 The poor emacerated Soldiers of the Garison.

†**e'macerating**, *ppl. a. Obs.* [f. as prec. + -ING[2].] = EMACIATING.

1681 *Moores Baffled* 5 After some emacerating disease has reduced it. **1709** *Brit. Apollo* II. Extra No. 6. 3/1 Emacerating Liquors.. will make them leaner.

†**e,mace'ration.** *Obs.*[−0] [f. as prec.: see -ATION.]

a. = EMACIATION. **b.** = MACERATION (of drugs).

1656 BLOUNT *Glossogr.*, *Emaceration*, a Pulling down or making lean. **1678** PHILLIPS, *Emaceration*, a soaking or wasting. **1715** in KERSEY. **1721–1800** in BAILEY. **1818** TODD, *Emaceration*, leanness or falling away in flesh.

†**e'maciant**, *a. Obs.* [ad. L. *ēmaciānt-em*, pr. pple. of *ēmaciāre* see next.] That emaciates.

1651 tr. *Bacon's Life & Death* 64 Diet Emaciant, and Renewing.

emaciate (ɪ'meɪʃɪət), *ppl. a.* [ad. L. *ēmaciātus*, pa. pple. of *ēmaciāre* to EMACIATE.] = EMACIATED.

1675 EVELYN *Terra* (1729) 23 Some are so emaciate and lean. **1774** T. WARTON *Oxford Ale* 91 Emaciate steeds. **1795** SOUTHEY *Joan of Arc* II. 313 Pale, hollow-eyed, emaciate, sleepless wretch. **1818** MILMAN *Samor* 14 Ah generous King! That sets the emaciate wolf to dog the flock. **1818** TODD, *Emaciate*, sunk; wasted; deprived of flesh.

emaciate (ɪ'meɪʃɪeɪt), *v.* [f. L. *ēmaciāt-* ppl. stem of *ēmaciāre* + *ē* out + *maci-es* leanness.]

1. *trans.* **a.** To make lean, waste, deprive of flesh. **b.** *transf.* To impoverish (soil).

1650 H. BROOKE *Conserv. Health* 177 Dries and emaciates the Body. **1746** HERVEY *Medit.* (1818) 159 Consumption may emaciate the dimpled cheeks. **1818** MRS. SHELLEY *Frankenst.* iv. (1865) 23 His body was dreadfully emaciated by fatigue and suffering. **1862** *Fraser's Mag.* Nov. 575, I was so emaciated by illness.

2. *intr.* To become lean, dwindle.

1646 SIR T. BROWNE *Pseud. Ep.* VI. xiii. 366 That he emaciated and pined away. **1873** T. H. GREEN *Introd. Pathol.* (ed. 2) 21 When a person emaciates, the fat is gradually removed from the cells. **1934** R. FROST *Let.* 23 Feb. (1964) 237, I have been in bed with a bug.. etiolating and emaciating.

e'maciated, *ppl. a.* [f. prec. + -ED[1].] Made lean, atrophied. Also *fig.*

1665 *Phil. Trans.* I. 87 The whole Body was bloudless, thin and emaciated. **1713** CHESELDEN *Anat.* I. i. (1726) 6 The emaciated bone weighed thirty grains less than half the weight of the other. **1777** HOWARD *Prisons Eng.* (1780) 5 Many who went in healthy, are in a few months changed to emaciated dejected objects. **1855** MACAULAY *Hist. Eng.* III. 403 The emaciated corpse was laid.. next to the corpse of Monmouth. **1880** MAX MÜLLER *Ess.* I. 363 The prose of our traditional and emaciated speech.

e'maciating, *vbl. sb.* [f. EMACIATE *v.* + -ING[1].] Making lean; *fig.* enfeebling.

1717 L. HOWEL *Desiderius* (ed. 3) 125 Without these all other Food tends to the emaciating and imparing our spiritual Strength.

e'maciating, *ppl. a.* [f. as prec. + -ING[2].] That emaciates.

a **1626** BACON (J.) Men, after long emaciating diets, wax plump, fat, and almost new. **1656** BLOUNT *Glossogr.*, *Emaciating* diseases, Consumptions or such like. **1794** S. WILLIAMS *Vermont* 331 Emaciating pains and maladies.

emaciation (ɪ,meɪʃɪ'eɪʃən). [ad. L. *ēmaciātiōn-em*, f. *ēmaciāre* to EMACIATE.] The action of emaciating; the process or state of being emaciated; abnormal leanness. Also *fig.*

1662 GRAUNT *Observ. Bills Mortality* 24 Searchers.. cannot tell whether this emaciation or leanness were from a Phthisis or from an Hectick Fever. **1793** T. BEDDOES *Calcul.* Cont. 13 Acids produce emaciation. **1834** J. FORBES *Laennec's Dis. Chest* (ed. 4) 329 A girl.. died.. without any emaciation. **1872** SPURGEON *Treas. Dav.* Ps. lxix. 10 The emaciation which these exercises wrought.

emacity (ɪ'mæsɪtɪ). *rare.* [f. L. *emācitas*, f. *emāc-em* fond of buying, f. *emĕre* to buy.] Fondness for buying.

1656 in BLOUNT *Glossogr.* **1692** in COLES. **1806** BLAGDON & PREVOST *Flowers of Lit.* 347 The disease of emacity, or itch for buying bargains.

†**e'maculate**, *v. Obs.* [f. L. *ēmaculāt-* ppl. stem of *ēmaculāre* to clear from blots, f. *macula* spot, blot.]

1. *trans.* To free from spots or blemishes, emend.

1623 COCKERAM, *Emaculate*, to make cleane, to take out spots. *a* **1656** HALES *Gold. Rem.* (1688) 348 Lipsius.. and others have taken great pains with him in emaculating the text. **1721–1800** in BAILEY: and in mod. Dicts.

2. To efface (a spot). *fig.*

1649 LD. HERBERT *Autobiog.* (1886) 60 By a serious repentance, to expiate and emaculate those faults.

emagery, obs. var. IMAGERY.

‖**email**[1] (ɛ'meɪl). [Fr., = enamel.] Used *attrib.* in **email ink**, ink used on glass, porcelain, etc.; **email ombrant** *Pottery*, a process in which the impressions of the design appear as shadows (see quots. *a*1877 and 1957).

a **1877** KNIGHT *Dict. Mech.* I. 796/1 *Email-ombrant*, a process which consists in flooding colored but transparent glasses over designs stamped in the body of earthenware or porcelain. **1880** C. A. JANVIER *Pract. Keramics* viii. 95 In these the pattern is.. exactly the opposite of the *émaux ombrants*. *a* **1884** KNIGHT *Dict. Mech.* Suppl., *Email ink*... Colored inks—black, white, red, blue—used with a quill on glass, porcelain, ivory, marble, bone, mother of pearl, or metal. **1957** MANKOWITZ & HAGGAR *Encycl. Eng. Pott. & Porc.* 83/2 *Email ombrant*, an illusionist style of decoration like lithophane but the intaglio decoration was filled with coloured glaze (usually green) which produced a monochrome picture in a variety of tones. Developed at the Rubenes [*sic* = Rubelles] factory by Baron A. du Tremblay in the 1840's.

email[2] ('iːmeɪl). *Computing.* Also **e-mail.** Colloq. shortening of *electronic mail* s.v. ELECTRONIC *a.* 3.

1982 *Computerworld* 5 July 68 ADR/Email is reportedly easy to use and features simple, English verbs and prompt screens. **1983** *Infosystems* Sept. 113/2 Email promotes movement of information through space. **1984** *Listener* 28 June 38/1 E-mail achieves the same as a telex, or teleprinter, but at much lower cost. **1986** *Times* 14 Jan. 27/5 Electronic mail—now known universally as e-mail. The partnership of word processor and e-mail almost eliminate [*sic*] the need for paper. **1986** *Sunday Times* 25 May 69/6 Simple enough for 'email', as it is sometimes called, to be one of the fastest-growing businesses in the world. In Britain, Telecom Gold is doubling its email customer base every year.

†**e'mailed**, *ppl. a. Obs.* In 5 **emaylled.** [? f. F. *émaillé* enamelled, embossed; but cf. OF. *emmailleüre* network.] ? Embossed (with a raised pattern); or perh. arranged in net or open work.

1480 *Wardr. Acc. Edw. IV*, (1830) 146 A longe gowne made of blue clothe of gold upon satyn grounde emaylled.

emakimono, var. MAKIMONO.

emanant ('ɛmənənt), *ppl. a. arch.* [ad. L. *ēmānānt-em*, pr. pple. of *ēmānāre*: see EMANATE *v.*] That emanates or issues from a source.

1614 T. ADAMS *Devil's Banq.* 4 Filling eminent places, with emanant poisons. **1676** HALE *Contempl.* I. 25 The Emanant and Communicative Goodness of God. **1833** *Fraser's Mag.* VIII. 573 A brighter dawning emanant over the horizon. **1839** BAILEY *Festus* (1848) 20/1 Like emanant dew on earth.

emanant ('ɛmənənt), *sb. Math.* [f. the ppl. adj.] The result of operating upon a quantic with the operator $(x'd/dx + y'd/dy + \ldots)$.

1852 J. J. SYLVESTER in *Camb. & Dublin Math. Jrnl.* VII. 56 Every emanant is.. itself a covariant of the function to

which it belongs with respect to each of the related classes of variables which enter into it. **1860** A. CAYLEY *Math. Papers* (1891) IV. 604 The coefficients of the successive terms λ^m, $\lambda^m - {}^1\mu$, etc. are said to be the emanants of the quantic (*) $(x,y)^m$.

emanate ('ɛmənet), *v.* [f. L. *ēmānāt-* ppl. stem of *ēmānāre* f. *ē-* out + *mānāre* to flow.]

1. *intr.* Of immaterial things, qualities, laws, principles, courses of action: To flow forth, issue, originate *from* a person or thing as a source.

1756 *Crit. Rev.* II. 340 The French author is not much oblig'd..to his English translator. We meet with the words, ..misanthropes, tranquilly, emanate, legerity..and many others. **1788** BURKE *Sp. W. Hastings* Wks. XIII. 50 A new dominion, emanated from a learned and enlightened part of the world. **1823** LAMB *Elia* Ser. II. xxiii. (1865) 396 His destruction..emanating from himself. **1868** MILL *England & Irel.*, The feudal idea, which views all rights as emanating from a head landlord.

2. In physical sense: To flow forth, issue, proceed, from a material source; chiefly of intangible things, as light, gases, effluvia, etc. Also, to issue, originate, as a branch from the stem.

1818 BYRON *Ch. Harold* IV. xxxviii, A glory round his furrow'd brow, Which emanated then. **1830** LYELL *Princ. Geol.* (1875) II. III. xxx. 146 Fissures..from which mephitic vapours emanated. **1854** J. HOGG *Microsc.* II. i. (1867) 270 These organs..emanate..from a reddish coloured point. **1859** W. COLEMAN *Woodlands* (1866) 61 This vast vegetable curiosity all emanating from a single stem. **1865** TYLOR *Early Hist. Man.* ix. 229 The sparks emanating from the flint and steel.

¶ **3.** Of persons: To issue, proceed *from* a place, an educational institution, etc. *rare.*

1867 SMILES *Huguenots Eng.* xiii. (1880) 230 A centre of polite learning, from which emanated some of the most distinguished men in Ireland.

4. *trans.* To emit, send out. *lit.* and *fig.*

1797 *Monthly Rev.* XXIII. 584 A magnetism which a more sublime genius is often unable to emanate. **1823** CHALMERS *Serm.* I. 195 He did not emanate the gift. **1832** —— *Pol. Econ.* ii. 49 They emanate nothing but their own peculiar articles. **1929** W. FAULKNER *Sartoris* I. ii. 34 Bookcases..emanating an atmosphere of..meditation. **1939** S. DE MADARIAGA *Columbus* xii. 136 In this land [*sc.* Castille]..the mental-moral soil was broken..by forbidding abysses which emanated all kinds of poisonous gases and murderous flames.

emanated ('ɛmənetɪd), *ppl. a.* [f. prec. + -ED[1].] Produced by emanation.

1874 BLACKIE *Self-Cult.* 5 The essential unity of our divinely emanated human souls.

emanation (ɛmə'neɪʃən). [ad. L. *ēmānātiōn-em*, f. *ēmānāre*: see EMANATE *v.*]

I. 1. a. The process of flowing forth, issuing, or proceeding from anything as a source. *lit.* and *fig.* Often applied to the origination of created beings from God; chiefly with reference to the theories that regard either the universe as a whole, or the spiritual part of it, as deriving its existence from the essence of God, and not from an act of creation out of nothing. Also, in Theology, used to denote the 'generation' of the Son, and the 'procession' of the Holy Ghost, as distinguished from the origination of merely created beings.

1570 DEE *Math. Pref.* 19 It concerneth all Creatures..by Emanation of beames perfourmed. **1647** H. MORE *Poems* 279 Man's soul 's not by Creation..Wherefore let 't be by emanation. *a* **1652** J. SMITH *Sel. Disc.* iv. 92 Those elicit motions..which..have their first emanation from nothing else but the soul itself. **1659** PEARSON *Creed* (1839) 223 Jesus Christ..by the right of emanation of all things from him.. hath an absolute..dominion over all things as God. **1699** BURNET *39 Art.* ii. (1700) 43 Why the Emanation of the Son, and not that of the Holy Ghost likewise is called begetting. **1721–1800** BAILEY, *Emanation* (with Divines) is used to express the Proceeding of the Holy Ghost from the Father and the Son. **1880** *Macm. Mag.* No. 246. 497 Its pantheistic doctrine of emanation.

b. The action of emitting, evolving, producing. Cf. EMANATE *v.* 4.

1742 YOUNG *Nt. Th.* II. 203 The Dread Sire, on emanation bent..Call'd forth creation. **1822** IMISON *Sc. & Art* I. 431 The sun was long considered, from its constant emanation of heat..[a] globe of fire.

†**c.** Logical development from premises; inference. Cf. 3 b. *Obs.*

1628 T. SPENCER *Logick* 199 This truth is necessary by emanation, and consecution.

d. *Math.* The process of finding successive emanants.

1853 J. J. SYLVESTER in *Phil. Trans.* CXLIII. 545 The process of emanation is one of incessant occurrence in the theory of invariants. **1856** A. CAYLEY *Math. Papers* (1889) II. 321 The facients $(X, Y, \ldots)$ may be termed the facients of emanation, or simply the new facients.

II. *concr.* That which emanates; an efflux.

2. a. Something emitted or radiated by a material object; *esp.* applied to impalpable things, as light, a magnetic or electric effluvium, an odour, etc.

1646 SIR T. BROWNE *Pseud. Ep.* 86 Amulets doe worke by Aporrhoias, or emanations from their bodies. **1692** NORRIS *Curs. Refl.* 24 Corporeal Emanations from sensible Objects. **1763** *Nat. Hist.* in *Ann. Reg.* 70/2 Emanations of Vesuvius, especially the Lava. **1774** GOLDSM. *Nat. Hist.* I. 191 The powerful emanations of the loadstone. **1836** MACGILLIVRAY tr. *Humboldt's Trav.* v. 74 Gaseous emanations occasionally escape in places considerably remote from unextinguished volcanoes. **1871** B. STEWART *Heat* §174 This heating emanation..we term radiant heat.

b. *spec.* A beam, flash, ray of light.

1699 GARTH *Dispens.* I. (1700) 3 Dart in emanations through the eyes. **1726** DE FOE *Hist. Devil* I. ix. (1840) 106 Over him..a bright emanation shone. **1855** BAIN *Senses & Int.* II. ii. §11 (1864) 245 White emanations occurring on the retina together.

c. *Chem.* A radioactive gas produced by the radioactive decay of a solid; *spec.* any of the three gases radon, actinon, and thoron produced respectively by radium, actinium, and thorium (so ***radium*** etc. ***emanation***); also used as a name for the element radon, of which these gases are now known to be isotopes.

1900 RUTHERFORD in *Phil. Mag.* XLIX. 1, I have found that thorium compounds continuously emit radio-active particles of some kind, which retain their radio-active powers for several minutes. This 'emanation', as it will be termed for shortness, has the power.. of passing through thin layers of metals. **1903, 1907** [see THORIUM]. **1906** RUTHERFORD *Radioactive Transformations* iii. 72 A large quantity of emanation was introduced into a glass tube.. and the ionization due to the issuing rays was measured. **1927** N. V. SIDGWICK *Electronic Theory Valency* iii. 29 The names radon, thoron, and actinon are now accepted for the three isotopic emanations. It is desirable that there should be some name for element no. 86 irrespective of any particular isotope, and I have retained the name emanation (with the symbol Em) for this purpose. **1940** GLASSTONE *Physical Chem.* ii. 125 The emanations, particularly that from actinium, lost their activity relatively rapidly. **1950** —— *Sourcebk. Atomic Energy* v. 116/2 The production of a gaseous emanation provides a convenient means of separating this radioactive species from those which precede it in the disintegration series. **1957** *Encycl. Brit.* XVII. 882 B/1 There are six elements collectively known as the inert gases... Their atomic numbers and their names are: 2 Helium, 10 Neon, 18 Argon, 36 Krypton, 54 Xenon, 86 Emanation. **1964** J. R. PARTINGTON *Hist. Chem.* IV. xxvii. 941 Some doubts about the existence of radium emanation were removed by Rutherford and Soddy, who liquefied it by cooling in liquid air.

3. *transf.* and *fig.* **a.** Applied to immaterial things, moral and spiritual powers, virtues, qualities, emanating from or emitted by a source.

1577 DEE *Relat. Spir.* I. (1659) 58 The Emanations from God, to, and into his Creatures..are established. **1656** H. MORE *Antid. Ath.* (1712) Pref. 1 The easie Emanations of mine own Mind. *a* **1698** TEMPLE *Ess. Poetry* Wks. 1731 I. 234 So is Prophecy the greatest Emanation of Divine Spirit in the World. **1775** JOHNSON *Tax. no Tyr.* 25 From this all legal rights are emanations. **1829** I. TAYLOR *Enthus.* iii. (1867) 56 Virtue and happiness are emanations of the divine blessedness and purity.

b. A necessary consequence or result.

1710 STEELE *Tatler* No. 74 ¶11 The Emanation or Consequence of good and evil Actions. **1861** MILL *Utilit.* v. 92 A direct emanation from the first principle of morals.

4. A person or thing produced by emanation from the Divine Essence.

1650 R. GELL *Serm.* 12 She is the emanation of the power of God. **1658** SIR T. BROWNE *Gard. Cyrus* 196 The whole Sephiroth, or divine emanations. **1777** PRIESTLEY *Matt. & Spir.* (1782) I. vi. 71 Christ was..considered..a peculiar emanation of the divine essence. **1826** GOOD *Bk. Nat.* (1834) I. 11 According to this hypothesis, the universe is an emanation..of the essence of the Creator. **1875** MAINE *Hist. Inst.* ii. 51 The first teacher..was a direct emanation from God.

emanational (ɛmə'neɪʃənəl), *a.* [f. prec. + -AL[1].] Pertaining to the theory of the origin of existence by emanation as distinguished from creation.

1843 *For. & Q. Col. Rev.* II. 346 Emanational ideas.

emanationism (ɛmə'neɪʃənɪz(ə)m). [f. EMANATION + -ISM.] = EMANATISM.

1881 G. S. HALL *Aspects German Culture* 315 It [superstition] settled very thickly again in the first Christian centuries, as cabalism, emanationism, neo-platonism..with their hierarchies of spirit-hosts. **1951** N. ANNAN *Leslie Stephen* v. 163 These two conceptions of God, though logically opposed, were united by Plato in the *Timaeus* by the device of emanationism: the Transcendental God, the goal of all desires, is perfect Good and therefore envious of nothing; hence He will wish everything to be as He, and He accordingly overflows into the imperfect and projects Himself into the universe. **1956** E. L. MASCALL *Chr. Theol. & Nat. Sci.* iii. 92 Emanationism, according to which the existence of the universe follows with *physical* necessity from the existence of God.

ema'nationist, *a.* [f. as prec. + -IST.]

1. In sociology, relating to the theory that behaviour is conditioned exclusively by environment.

1937 T. PARSONS *Struct. Social Action* xiv. 536 A naive 'emanationist' view of the mechanisms of the influence of nonscientific ideas.

2. Relating to the philosophical theory of the origin of the world by emanation.

1941 G. G. SCHOLEM *Major Trends in Jewish Mysticism* vii. 256 The emanationist doctrine of Neoplatonism.

Emanatism ('ɛmənətɪz(ə)m). [f. L. *ēmānāt-* (see EMANATE *v.*) + -ISM; cf. *conservatism.*] The philosophical doctrine of emanation.

1864 CORKRAN tr. *Pressense's Reply Renan* 21 Nor does he tell us that his idea of the Word bore the impress of Emanatism.

'Emanatist. [f. as prec. + -IST.] A believer in EMANATION; *Theol.* (see quot.) also *attrib.*

1838 J. H. NEWMAN *Arians* i. §5 The Emanatist, if he may so be called, denied that He [Christ] was a *Person*, or more than an extraordinary manifestation of Divine Power. **1867** H. P. LIDDON *Divinity of Lord* vii. 646 These Emanatist doctrines. *Ibid.* 647 The Nicene Fathers..were able..to vindicate for the word its Catholic sense, unaffected by any Emanatist gloss.

emanatistic (ˌɛmənə'tɪstɪk), *a.* [f. EMANATIST + -IC.] Relating or pertaining to EMANATISM.

1852 BP. FORBES *Nicene Cr.* 46 Or, by another division, into emanatistic, idealistic, and realistic (Pantheism).

emanative ('ɛmənetɪv), *a.* [as if ad. L. **ēmānātīvus*: see EMANATE and -IVE.]

1. Tending to issue forth; of the nature of an emanation; due to emanation.

1661 tr. *Origen's Opin.* in *Phœnix* (1721) I. 13 All Effects and Productions whatever, whether voluntary or emanative. **1685** H. MORE *Para. Proph.* 471 The Holy Ghost proceedeth..by an Emanative procession. **1842** G. S. FABER *Prov. Lett.* (1844) II. 213 The Father..is superior to the emanative or derivative Persons of the Son and the Holy Spirit.

2. With transitive force: Tending to produce, emit, bring forth.

1651 BIGGS *New Disp.* 220 Emit their vertues by an emanative and influential manner. **1678** CUDWORTH *Intell. Syst.* 739 No Imperfect Being..hath a sufficient Emanative Power to Create any other Substance. **1829** I. TAYLOR *Enthus.* ix. 233 True wisdom is an emanative principle. **1855** MILMAN *Lat. Chr.* (1864) IX. XIV. ii. 55 A concentered and emanative power of imparting..spiritual influences.

3. Relating to or connected with the philosophical or the theological theory of emanation.

1838–9 HALLAM *Hist. Lit.* I. I. vii. §21. 399 That fundamental theorem of the emanative philosophy. **1838** J. H. NEWMAN *Arians* i. §5 They advocated the Emanative, as it may be called, or in-dwelling theory.

emanatively ('ɛmənetɪvlɪ), *adv.* [f. prec. + -LY[2].] In an emanative manner, by process of emanation.

1678 CUDWORTH *Intell. Syst.* 745 No..Created Being, can Create, or Emanatively Produce, a New Substance.

emanatory ('ɛmənəˌtərɪ), *a.* [as if ad. L. **ēmānātōrius*, f. *ēmānāre* to EMANATE.] **a.** Of the nature of an emanation, derivative. **b.** Pertaining or referable to the philosophical theory of emanation.

1659 H. MORE *Immort. of Soul* (1662) 28 Something which we may in some sense call Substance, though but Secondary or Emanatory. **1882–3** SCHAFF *Relig. Encycl.* I. 162/1 The old emanatory views of God.

emancipate (ɪ'mænsɪpət), *ppl. a.* Now chiefly *poet.* [ad. L. *ēmancipāt-us*, pa. pple. of *ēmancipāre*: see next.] = EMANCIPATED.

1605 BACON *Adv. Learn.* II. 36, I doe take the Consideration..of Humane Nature to be fit to be emancipate, & made a knowledge by it self. **1785** COWPER *Task* II. 39 Slaves..themselves once ferried o'er the wave.. are emancipate and loos'd. *c* **1800** COLERIDGE *Picture* 119 Emancipate From passion's dreams. **1880** *Daily Tel.* 19 Feb., He is..conspicuously emancipate from musical prejudices.

emancipate (ɪ'mænsɪpeɪt), *v.* [f. L. *ēmancipāt-* ppl. stem of *ēmancipāre* of same meaning.]

1. *trans.* In Roman Law: To release or set free (a child or wife) from the *patria potestas*, the power of the *pater familias*, thus making the person so set free *sui juris*.

1651 HOBBES *Leviath.* II. xxiv. 131 Requires no more of them, then Fathers require of the Children, whom they emancipate. **1741** T. ROBINSON *Gavelkind* ii. 11 In case a Son was dead or emancipated. **1875** MAINE *Hist. Inst.* vii. 217 The Son discharged from Paternal Power is emancipated.

2. *gen.* **a.** To set free from control; to release from legal, social, or political restraint.

In mod. lang. the word suggests primarily the liberation of slaves, the other uses being often felt as *transf.* from this.

1625 DONNE *Serm.* 27 To emancipate them from the Tyrant. **1768–74** TUCKER *Lt. Nat.* (1852) II. 123 As an apprentice is emancipated by running away. *a* **1832** BENTHAM *Wks.* 1843 II. 502 Individuals who have been emancipated, or have emancipated themselves from governments. **1832** HT. MARTINEAU *Irel.* 117 The law has.. emancipated us from our civil disabilities. **1848** MACAULAY *Hist. Eng.* I. 651 That the convicts should be carried beyond sea as slaves, that they should not be emancipated for ten years. **1851** GLADSTONE *Glean.* VI. lxviii. 44 Suppose the Colonial Churches emancipated. *a* **1876** J. H. NEWMAN *Hist. Sk.* I. I. ii. 84 Workmen emancipating themselves from their employer.

b. *absol.*

1775 DK. RICHMOND *Let.* in *Burke's Corr.* (1844) II. 29 If our [colonies] emancipate, it will..be some good to humanity.

c. *transf.* and *fig.* To set free from intellectual or moral restraint. Also *refl.*

1646 SIR T. BROWNE *Pseud. Ep.* 25 We become emancipated from testimoniall engagements. **1699** EVELYN *Acetaria* 152 From many troublesome and slavish Impertinencies..he had Emancipated and freed himself. **1710** BERKELEY *Princ. Hum. Knowl.* §14 To emancipate our thoughts from particular objects. **1848** MACAULAY *Hist. Eng.* II. 558 Those evil passions..were on a sudden emancipated from control. **1850** KINGSLEY *Alt. Locke* iii. (1876) 41, I was emancipated from modern Puritanism. **1875** JOWETT *Plato* (ed. 2) V. 126 Plato has not emancipated himself from the limitations of ancient politics.

†**3.** To deliver into servitude or subjection; to enslave; (because emancipation in Roman Law was effected by fictitious sale). *Obs.*

1629 H. BURTON *Babel no Beth.* 71 Emancipate..is, to captiuate ones selfe to another, as well as to free. **1629** CHOLMLEY *ibid.* 70 A wiues Emancipating herselfe to another husband. **1752** SMART *Hop Garden* I. 195 To dalliance vile and sloth Emancipated.

e'mancipated, *ppl. a.* [f. prec. + -ED.]

1. Set free, released:

a. from the *patria potestas.* (Roman Law.)

1726 AYLIFFE *Parerg.* 33 Emancipated children. **1870** LUBBOCK *Orig. Civiliz.* iv. (1875) 152 An emancipated son ceased to be one of the family.

b. from a state of slavery or imprisonment.

1776 ADAM SMITH *W.N.* I. III. iii. 402 A parcel of emancipated slaves. **1837** J. LANG *New S. Wales* II. 38 The writer was an emancipated convict. **1878** BROWNING *Poets Croisic* xli, Erect, Triumphant, an emancipated slave.

2. *fig.* Freed from prejudices, moral or customary restraints, conventional rules, etc. Esp. of or relating to women.

1850 G. E. JEWSBURY *Let.* 29 Aug. (1892) 365, I don't think he knew what an 'emancipated woman' he was showing off to. **1887** *Pall Mall G.* 25 Oct. 4/2 These emancipated compositions..fail to sound as they did beneath Liszt's own magic touch. **1888** MRS. H. WARD *R. Elsmere* III. v. xxxi. 7 His wife..was..in all matters of religious or political opinion 'emancipated' to an extreme. **1904** CONRAD *Nostromo* II. iii. 129 The tall Antonia..offered him her hand (in her emancipated way). **1970** *Guardian* 16 Sept. 11/5 As emancipated as the Lebanese are educated Palestinian women, who are influential in many Middle East countries.

e'mancipating (ɪˈmænsɪpeɪtɪŋ), *ppl. a.* [f. as prec. + -ING².] Setting free, liberating. *fig.*

1874 MORLEY *Compromise* (1886) 8 Strong in their hold of great emancipating principles.

emancipation (ɪˌmænsɪˈpeɪʃən). [a. F. *émancipation*, f. L. *ēmancipātiōn-em*, n. of action f. *ēmancipāre* to EMANCIPATE.]

1. *Roman Law.* The action or process of setting children free from the *patria potestas.*

1651 W. G. tr. *Cowel's Inst.* 29 Paternall Jurisdiction is dissolved also by Emancipation. **1696** PHILLIPS, *Emancipation* hath the same reference to Children, as manumission to Servants. **1880** MUIRHEAD *Gaius Dig.* 486.

2. a. The action or process of setting free or delivering from slavery; and hence, generally, from restraints imposed by superior physical force or legal obligation; liberation. Often used with reference to the freeing of Roman Catholics from the civil disabilities imposed on them by English law. ***Catholic Emancipation Act***: the popular designation of the Act 10 Geo. IV. c. 7 (1829), by which those disabilities were removed.

1785 JEFFERSON *Let.* 7 Aug. (1853) I. 377 Emancipation is put in such a train that in a few years there will be no slaves northward of Maryland. **1797** BURKE *Affairs Irel.* Wks. (1812) IX. 454 The Opposition..connects the emancipation of the Catholicks with these schemes of reformation. **1835** THIRLWALL *Greece* I. viii. 312 Emancipation of Helots was not unfrequent. **1860** MOTLEY *Netherl.* (1868) I. i. 6 A harvest of civil and religious emancipation. **1872** YEATS *Growth Comm.* 254 The royal monopoly..was for the age an emancipation rather than a restriction of labour.

b. *transf.* and *fig.* Setting free, delivering from intellectual, moral, or spiritual fetters.

a **1631** DONNE *Serm.* 27 Redeeming Emancipation, a delivering from the chaines of Satan. **1774** T. WARTON *Hist. Eng. Poetry* (1840) III. 403 A certain freedom and activity of mind..followed the national emancipation from superstition. **1841-4** EMERSON *Ess. Poet* Wks. (Bohn) I. 166 The use of symbols has a certain power of emancipation and exhilaration for all men. **1855** MACAULAY *Hist. Eng.* IV. 607 The day on which the emancipation of our literature was accomplished. **1874** MORLEY *Compromise* (1886) 105 The great spiritual emancipation of the sixteenth and seventeenth centuries.

emancipationist (ɪˌmænsɪˈpeɪʃənɪst). [f. prec. + -IST.] An advocate for the setting free of slaves, and the abolition of slavery. Also, an advocate of the emancipation of any class from legal disabilities or the like. (First applied to the advocates of 'Catholic Emancipation': see EMANCIPATION 2 a.)

1822 SOUTHEY in *Life* (1850) V. 112 The Emancipationists ..and the Dissenters will not be pleased. **1828** *Q. Rev.* XXXVIII. 557 To this point the emancipationists have.. brought their vessel. **1859** GEN. P. THOMPSON *Audi Alt.* II. xcviii. 87 Now is the time for the Emancipationists..to be up and doing. **1882** T. MOZLEY *Remin.* I. iv, The..son of the great emancipationist [Wilberforce].

emancipatist (ɪˈmænsɪpeɪtɪst). [f. EMANCIPATE + -IST.] = EMANCIPIST.

1852 *Fraser's Mag.* XLVI. 135 The convict obtained his ticket of leave..became an emancipatist..and found transportation no punishment.

emancipative (ɪˈmænsɪpətɪv), *a.* [f. L. *ēmancipāt-* (see EMANCIPATE *v.*) + -IVE.] That has the property of emancipating.

1862 F. HALL *Hindu Philos. Syst.* 195 In order to gaining emancipative knowledge, the practice of devotion likewise is prescribed.

emancipator (ɪˈmænsɪpeɪtə(r)). Also 8 emancipater. [a. L. *ēmancipātor*, f. *ēmancipā-re* to EMANCIPATE.] One who emancipates. *lit.* and *fig.*

1782 SIR W. JONES tr. *Mahomedan Law Success.* Wks. 1799 III. 492 Those who inherit among males are..The son, and the son's son..and the husband, and the emancipator nearly connected. **1828** *Blackw. Mag.* XXIV. 5 Such is our classification..of the heads of the Catholic Emancipators. **1830** MACKINTOSH *Ethical Philos.* Wks. 1846 I. 38 The emancipators of Reason. **1878** STANFORD *Symb. Christ* ii. 45 They waited for Him as their Emancipator from the Roman yoke.

emancipatory (ɪˈmænsɪpəˌtərɪ), *a.* Also 7 -orie. [f. EMANCIPATE *v.* + -ORY.] That has the function or the effect of emancipating.

1652 URQUHART *Jewel* Wks. (1834) 232 He [Crichtoun] did..undergo that emancipatorie task..to give a demonstration. **1836** *Fraser's Mag.* XIII. 182 The emancipatory bill of twenty-nine. **1887** *Pall Mall G.* 30 June 4/2 Describing the Crimes Bill as an emancipatory measure.

emancipatress (ɪˈmænsɪpeɪtrɪs). *nonce-wd.* [f. EMANCIPATOR + -ESS.] A female emancipator; one who advocates the 'emancipation' of her sex.

1882 *Standard* 26 Dec. 3/1 The masculine..coiffure..of a London emancipatress.

emancipist (ɪˈmænsɪpɪst). *Australian.* [f. EMANCIP-ATE + -IST.] An ex-convict, who has served his term of punishment. Also *attrib.*

1827 P. CUNNINGHAM *Two Years in N.S.W.* II. xxiv. 118 The grand division..of the free classes..is into that of emigrants, who have come out free from England, and emancipists, who have arrived here as convicts, and have either been pardoned or completed their term of servitude. **1834** *Tait's Mag.* I. 405 Emancipists, as the felons who have suffered out their terms of imprisonment are named. **1837** J. LANG *New S. Wales* I. 141 Crosley, the emancipist attorney. **1868** DILKE *Greater Brit.* II. III. xiii. 129 Ticket-of-leave men and 'emancipists'.

emandibulate (ˌiːmænˈdɪbjʊlət), *ppl. a. Entom.* [f. E- *pref.*³ + L. *mandibul-um* + -ATE²: cf. MANDIBULATE.] Destitute of mandibles.

1826 KIRBY & SP. *Entomol.* xlvii, Mouth emandibulate.

†**e'mane,** *v. Obs.* [ad. F. *émane-r*, (or) ad. L. *ēmānāre* to flow out: see EMANATE *v.*] = EMANATE in its various senses.

1. *intr.* To flow out, issue from a source or fountain head; *lit.* and *fig.*; *esp.* of the Second Person of the Trinity.

1656 tr. *White's Peripateticall Institutions* 296 Nature actually emanes and flows out from Him. **1657** TOMLINSON *Renou's Disp.* 282 Out of which scarification emanes a crass juice. **1720** WATERLAND *Eight Serm.* Pref. 20 Wherein the Son is affirmed to have emaned, or been emitted by Necessity of Nature. **1795-8** T. MAURICE *Hindostan* (1820) I. I. i. 50 The Deity..caused to emane from himself 'an immeasurable torrent of water'. **1817** BENTHAM *Ch.-Engl.* (1818) 129 The several authorities from which..acts..are spoken of as having emaned.

2. *trans.* To give forth as an emanation. *rare.*

1708 MOTTEUX *Rabelais* v. xx, Pythagoras, from whom the venerable Antiquity of my Progenitors..was eman'd. **1800** MOORE *Ode Anacreon* xvii, Her eyes..Emaning fire..e'en in anger sweet!

Hence **e'maning,** *ppl. a.*

1658 J. ROBINSON *Calm Vent* I. 118 All mens Souls are alwaies alike; though their emaning beams be either brighter or duller.

emang(e, obs. variant of AMONG, EMONG.

emanu'ensis, erron. form of AMANUENSIS.

1692 COLES, *Emanuensis* (for *Ama*), one that writes for another, a secretary. **1709** KENNETT tr. *Erasm. Moriæ Enc.* (ed. 8) 129 (D.) Clerks, emanuenses, notaries. **1736** in BAILEY.

emarcid (ɪˈmɑːsɪd), *a.* [as if ad. L. **ēmarcidus*, f. *ē-* intensive + *marcidus* withered.]

†**1.** Drooping, limp. *Obs. rare*⁻¹.

1661 LOVELL *Hist. Anim. & Min.* Introd., The eares..in horses..shew their spirits, being emarcid in those that are weary.

2. *Bot.* Withered, flaccid, wilted.

In mod. Dicts.

emarginate (ɪˈmɑːdʒɪnət), *a.* [ad. L. *ēmarginātus*, pa. pple. of *ēmargināre*: see next.]

1. Notched at the margin: said of portions of animal or vegetable organisms. In *Bot.* chiefly of leaves or petals: Having a notch at the apex.

1794 MARTYN *Rousseau's Bot.* v. 52 The end..is emarginate or slightly notched. **1830** LINDLEY *Nat. Syst. Bot.* 58 Stigma emarginate. **1835** KIRBY *Hab. & Inst. Anim.* I. viii. 244 The valves of the shells..are emarginate. **1882** VINES *Sachs' Bot.* 510 The leaves are flat and broader..with a deeply emarginate apex.

2. *Crystallography.* Having the edges of the primitive form cut off.

emarginate (ɪˈmɑːdʒɪneɪt), *v.* [f. L. *ēmargināt-* ppl. stem of *ēmarginā-re* to remove the edge.]

†**1.** *trans.* To remove the morbid matter from the edges of wounds, etc. *Obs.*⁻⁰

1656 BLOUNT *Glossogr.*, *Emarginate*, to take away the scurf about the brims of wounds or soars.

2. *Crystallography.* (See quot. 1817 under EMARGINATED.)

3. *Optics.* Of the effects of unequal refraction: To emphasize or double the contour lines of (an object embedded, e.g., in a jelly).

1881 LANKESTER in *Jrnl. Microsc. Sc.* Jan. 127 These groups..are strongly emarginated by the difference of refractive index between their substance and that of the material in which they are deposited.

emarginated (ɪˈmɑːdʒɪneɪtɪd), *ppl. a.* [f. prec. + -ED.] = EMARGINATE *a.*

1731 BAILEY, *Emarginated* (with Botanists), cut in and indented. **1770** ELLIS in *Phil. Trans.* LX. 529 Antheræ.. oblong, and emarginated. **1817** R. JAMESON *Char. Min.* 198 A crystal is named emarginated, when every edge of the primitive form is intercepted by a plane. **1870** ROLLESTON *Anim. Life* 19 The neural arches..are..emarginated.

emargination (ɪˌmɑːdʒɪˈneɪʃən). [as if ad. L. **ēmarginātiōn-em*, n. of action f. *ēmargināre* to EMARGINATE.]

1. The process of cleansing wounds or sores by removing the morbid matter on the edges.

1676 in BULLOKAR. **1678-96** in PHILLIPS. **1721** in BAILEY. **1882** in *Syd. Soc. Lex.*

2. Notching or indentation of the margin.

1834 MCMURTRIE *Cuvier's Anim. Kingd.* 251 They all have a widely opened..shell, with neither operculum, emargination, nor syphon. **1870** ROLLESTON *Anim. Life* 21 The sternum has a wide lateral emargination.

emasculate (ɪˈmæskjʊlət), *a.* [ad. L. *ēmasculāt-us*, pa. pple. of *ēmasculāre*: see next.] = EMASCULATED. **a.** Castrated, deprived of virility. In lit. sense chiefly quasi-*sb.*

1886 *Homilet. Rev.* Nov. 403 The *kadeshim* or emasculates.

b. *fig.* Unmanly, deprived of vigour; weak, effeminate.

1622 H. SYDENHAM *Serm. Sol. Occ.* (1637) 259 Of Spirits emasculate and sick. **1752** SMART *Hop Garden* With love Emasculate, and wine. **1849** ROBERTSON *Serm.* Ser. I. vi. 90 Too emasculate to trudge through cold and rain. **1867** *Contemp. Rev.* VI. 169 German architecture is at once eclectic, scholarly, and emasculate.

emasculate (ɪˈmæskjʊleɪt), *v.* [f. L. *ēmasculāt-*, ppl. stem of *ēmasculā-re* to castrate, f. *ē* out + *mascul-us*, dim. of *mas* male.]

1. *trans.* To deprive of virility, to castrate (a male person or animal).

1623 COCKERAM, *Emasculate*, to geld. **1662** GRAUNT *Observ. Bills Mortality* 48 If you emasculate fewer [lambs]. **1744** J. BRYANT *Mythol.* II. 104 Another invention..was that of emasculating men. **1846** J. BAXTER *Libr. Pract. Agric.* II. 221 Young cocks should be emasculated at three months old.

2. *transf.* and *fig.* To deprive of strength and vigour; to weaken, make effeminate and cowardly; to enfeeble, impoverish (language).

1607 TOPSELL *Serpents* 79 Drones..lacking their sting, and by that defect being as it were ema[s]culated. **1652** BP. PATRICK *Serm.* in *J. Smith's Sel. Disc.* 555 Do not..enervate your souls..do not emasculate them. **1675** EVELYN *Terra* (1729) 26 'Tis the want of Salt, which emasculates the Virtue of Seeds. **1775** T. SHERIDAN *Art Reading* 88 The French have emasculated their tongue. **1848** DE QUINCEY *Protestantism* Wks. VIII. 125 Is the lightning dimmed or emasculated? **1876** M. DAVIES *Unorth. Lond.* 296 A religion without thought is emasculated.

b. *esp.* To take the force out of (literary compositions) by removing what is supposed to be indecorous or offensive.

1756-82 J. WARTON *Ess. Pope* I. v. 274 Pieces that are not emasculated with this epidemical effeminacy. **1815** SOUTHEY *Lett.* (1856) II. 395 How Gifford mutilates and emasculates my reviews. **1850** KINGSLEY *Alt. Locke* xviii. (1879) 200, I..consented to emasculate my poems.

†**3.** *intr.* (See quot.) *Obs. rare*⁻¹.

1646 SIR T. BROWNE *Pseud. Ep.* III. xvii. 147 Mutation of sexes..[is] observable in man..though very few..have emasculated or turned women.

e'masculated, *ppl. a.* [f. prec. + -ED.]

1. Deprived of virility; castrated.

1837 M. DONOVAN *Dom. Econ.* II. 309 The flesh of the emasculated animal is universally preferred. **1871** DARWIN *Desc. Man* II. xviii. 289 The emasculated bull reverts to the colour of the female.

2. *fig.* Unmanly, effeminate.

1701 COLLIER *M. Anton.* (1726) 97 The Legions.. Vectilianus found perfectly emasculated. **1850** MAURICE *Mor. & Met. Philos.* (ed. 2) 215 The impression of a wretched emasculated age. **1877** MORLEY *Crit. Misc.* Ser. II. 19 That emasculated caste, who shewed their quality..by flying.

e'masculating, *ppl. a.* [f. as prec. + -ING¹.] *fig.* That deprives of vigour or manliness; weakening, enfeebling.

1741 BETTERTON in Oldys *Eng. Stage* ii. 26 Opera..with its emasculating sounds. **1803** WORDSW. *Sonn. Lib., England! the time is come,* Wean Thy heart from its emasculating food. **1860** SMILES *Self-Help.* xi. 284 The habit of intellectual dissipation..cannot fail..to produce a thoroughly emasculating effect.

emasculation (ɪˌmæskjuːˈleɪʃən). [as if ad. L. *ēmasculātiōn-em*, noun of action f. *ēmasculā-re* to EMASCULATE.]

1. The action or process of depriving of virility; the state of impotence.

1623 COCKERAM II, A Gelding of a man, *emasculation.* **1721–1800** BAILEY, *Emasculation,* a Gelding, Unmanning, or making Effeminate. **1849** GROTE *Greece* (1862) V. II. lxii. 367 Tying down the patient while the process of emasculation was being consummated.

2. *fig.* The depriving of force, vigour, or manliness; making weak or effeminate; prudish expurgation of a literary work.

1654 GAYTON *Fest. Notes* 22 The emasculations were some Scotch mans. **1815** SOUTHEY *Lett.* (1856) II. 393 As for his emasculations, they must be submitted to. **1865** *Pall Mall G.* 12 Oct. 1 Centuries of emasculation and oppression under foreign and domestic tyranny. **1886** J. EBSWORTH in *Roxb. Ball.* (1886) VI. 198 This emasculation looks like the notorious Lady Wardlaw's handiwork.

emasculative (ɪˈmæskjʊlətɪv), *a.* [f. EMASCULATE *v.* + -IVE.] That tends to emasculate.

1876 *World* No. 112. 12 The emasculative tendency of the Papacy.

emasculator (ɪˈmæskjʊleɪtə(r)). [a. L. *ēmasculātor,* agent-n. f. *ēmasculāre* to EMASCULATE.] He who or that which emasculates.

In mod. Dicts.

emasculatory (ɪˈmæskjʊləˌtərɪ), *a.* [f. prec.; see -ORY.] That tends to or has the effect of emasculating.

1885 E. P. GOODWIN *Serm.* in *Pulpit Treas.* Dec. 469 Teachings emasculatory of the Gospel.

†**emastyce.** *Obs. rare*⁻¹. [? corruption of HÆMATITE, bloodstone.] Some precious stone.

c **14..** *Tundale's Vis.* 2109 Emastyce and charbokull.

emathites, ematite: obs. ff. HÆMATITE.

ematte, obs. form of EMMET.

‖**e'maunché,** *a. Obs. rare*⁻¹. *Her.* [a. Fr. *emmanché.*] Of a shield: Divided into portions, having the form of a long narrow triangle.

1586 FERNE *Blaz. Gentrie* 199 He beareth Emaunche, of arg. and Gewles.

emaung, obs. form of AMONG.

emayle, var. of ESMAYLE *Obs.*, enamel.

†**emba'buinized,** *ppl. a. nonce-wd.* [f. F. *embabouiner* + -IZE + -ED¹.] Infatuated (with).

1603 FLORIO *Montaigne* I. xxxix. (1632) 126 Doting youth, embabuinized [Fr. *embabouiné*] with this farie.

embace, -ing, var. ff. EMBASE, -ING. *Obs.*

†**emba'dometry.** *Obs. rare.* [f. Gr. ἐμβαδόν by land + -μετρία: see -METRY. Cf. Gr. ἐμβαδομετρικός.] Land-measurement.

1570 DEE *Math. Pref.* 16 To be certified of the content of any plaine Superficies..which measuring, is named Embadometrie.

†**em'bail,** *v. Obs.* [f. EN- + BAIL *sb.*² (? or *sb.*³).] *trans.* To enclose in a ring. Hence **em'bailing** *vbl. sb.*

1593 NASHE *Christ's T.* 276 A blacke inckie hood embayling her [the Moones] bright head. **1599** —— *Lent. Stuffe* (1871) 22 The procerous stature of it, so embailing and girdling in this mount. **1623** COCKERAM *Eng. Dict.* II, A Compassing about, *circuition..Embayling.*

†**em'bain,** *v. Obs.* [ad. Fr. *embaign-er* (Godef.), f. *en-* in + *baigner* to bathe. (See BAIN *v.*)] *trans.* To bathe, steep.

1593 NASHE *Christ's T.* 13 b, I washed and embained thy filth. **1623** COCKERAM, *Embayned,* soaked.

†**em'bait,** *v. Obs.* [f. EN- + BAIT *v.*¹]

a. ? To attract by a bait; also *fig.* **b.** To feed, glut (one's malice).

1567 DRANT *Horace's Epist.* I. xiii. E iiij, Such geare, As will embaite our Cesars eye. **1611** FLORIO, *Adescaménto,* an embaiting. *Adescáre,* to embait. *a* **1620** T. ROBINSON *Mary Magd.* 531 The Crocodile can sorrowe to yᵉ sight, And vnder sighes embaite his venom'd spight.

embalance: *see* EM- *prefix.*

embale (ɛmˈbeɪl), *v.* [f. EN- + BALE *sb.*³ Cf. F. *emballer* to pack up.] *trans.* To do up (goods) into bales or packages; also *fig.*

1727 A. HAMILTON *New Acc. E. Ind.* II. xxxiii. 17 Gunnies..in use in Persia for embaling Goods. **1739** in *Hanway's Trav.* (1762) I. I. viii. 39 There are conveniencies for..the embaling a thousand cloths. **1827** CARLYLE *Richter Misc.* (1869) 10 Embaled in some fantastic wrappage.

†**em'ball,** *v.*¹ *Obs.* [a. F. *emballe-r* to pack up.] *trans.* To pack up, do up into packages.

1599 HAKLUYT *Voy.* II. I. 227 The marchandize..they emball it well with Oxe hides.

emball (ɛmˈbɔːl), *v.*² [f. EN- + BALL *sb.*]

1. *trans.* To encompass with a sphere.

1580 *Sidney & Lady Pembroke* in Farr's *S.P. Eliz.* (1845) I. 84 Thou spheare, within whose bosom play The rest that earth emball. **1875** BROWNING *Aristoph. Apol.* 129 As lark emballed by its own crystal song.

2. (See EMBALLING *vbl. sb.*)

‖**em'ballage.** *Obs. rare.* Also 8 **embalage.** [a. F. *emballage.*] **a.** That in which anything is packed. **b.** The action or process of packing up.

1714 *Fr. Bk. of Rates* 62 Wrappers, or other Embalage. **1815** SIR W. GRANT in G. Rose *Diaries* (1860) II. 522 At the time of the general *emballage.*

†**em'balling,** *vbl. sb.* [f. EMBALL *v.*² + -ING¹.] (Prob. used in indelicate sense; explained by commentators as 'investing with the ball as the emblem of royalty'.)

1613 SHAKS. *Hen. VIII,* II. iii. 47 For little England You'ld venture an emballing.

†**em'balm,** *sb. Obs. rare.* [f. next.] Spice for embalming.

1642 G. HUGHES *Art of Embalming Dead Saints* 8 The proposition of the confection of Embalme it selfe, together with its force or vertue.

embalm (ɛmˈbɑːm), *v.* Forms: 4 **enbaume, -bawme,** 5 **-bame,** 6 **en-, embaulme, -baum, -balme,** 6– **embalm.** Also 6 **inbau(l)me,** 7 **imbalm(e.** [ME. *enbaume,* a. F. *embaume-r,* f. *en-* (see EN-) + *baume* BALM *sb.*]

I. 1. To impregnate (a dead body) with spices, to preserve it from decay.

c **1340** *Cursor M.* 16873 They..wyth oynementes the body enbawmyd. *c* **1385** CHAUCER *L.G.W.* 676 Let the corse enbaume. *a* **1400–50** *Alexander* 3319 Þan was his body enbawmed · &, as he bede, graven. **1483** CAXTON *Gold. Leg.* 136/3 The body enbamed wythin the tombe. **1570–6** LAMBARDE *Peramb. Kent* (1826) 313 They had before his buriall embaulmed his body. **1611** BIBLE *Gen.* I. 26 They imbalmed him and he was put in a coffin in Egypt. **1613** SHAKS. *Hen. VIII,* IV. ii. 170, I was a chaste Wife to my Grave: Embalme me, Then lay me forth. **1615** G. SANDYS *Trav.* 170 They brought it to the place where they say he was imbalmed. **1644** MILTON *Areop.* (Arb.) 35 A good Booke is the pretious life-blood of a master spirit imbalm'd and treasur'd up on purpose to a life beyond life. **1685** JAS. COOKE *Marrow of Chirurgery* (ed. 4) VI. iii. ii, The Heart, which may be embalm'd with the body. **1744** BERKELEY *Siris* §15 In Egypt they embalmed dead bodies with it [tar]. **1875** JOWETT *Plato* (ed. 2) I. 457 The body when shrunk and embalmed, as is the custom in Egypt.

2. *transf.* To preserve (a corpse) from decay by other means, as by cold, etc. *rare.*

1856 KANE *Arct. Expl.* I. xix. 240 The frost has embalmed their remains.

3. *fig.* **a.** To preserve from oblivion; chiefly in good sense, to keep in sweet and honoured remembrance.

1675 TRAHERNE *Chr. Eth.* xxi. 343 Being embalmed as it were by eternity. **1722** WOLLASTON *Relig. Nat.* v. 118 Some second Homer, in whose sheets his [Alexander's] name might be imbalmed for ages to come. **1791** BOSWELL *Johnson* (1816) I. Introd. 1 That..elegance of language in which he has embalmed so many. **1820** HAZLITT *Lect. Dram. Lit.* 23 The lines ought to embalm his memory. **1850** TENNYSON *In Mem.* Concl. iv, To embalm In dying songs a dead regret. **1864** KIRK *Chas. Bold* I. iii. 166 That universal dread of poison which had embalmed itself in one of the commonest ceremonies of the feudal household.

b. *nonce-use.*

18.. (H. or J.?) SMITH *Address to a Mummy in Belzoni's Exhibition* (last verse), Oh! let us keep the soul, embalmed and pure in living virtue.

II. 4. †**a.** To salve or anoint with aromatic spices, oil, etc. (*obs.*) **b.** To endue with balmy fragrance.

1393 LANGL. *P. Pl.* C. XIV. 107 Þe bisshop þat blessed ȝow and embaumede ȝoure fyngeres. *Ibid.* xx. 86 With þe blod of that barn embaumed and baptized. **1447** BOKENHAM *Seyntys* 79 For wyth heuynly deu she enbalmyd was. **1511** BARCLAY *Cyt. & Uplondyshm.* 36 With fragrant savour inbaumeth all the house. **1563** *Homilies* II. *Excess Appar.* (1859) 315 In painting our faces..in embalming our bodies. **1667** MILTON *P.L.* II. 842 The buxom air, imbalm'd With odours. **1746–7** HERVEY *Medit. & Contempl.* (1818) 139 They reserve their richest exhalations to embalm his morning and evening walks. **1877** BRYANT *May Even.* vi, Among the opening buds thy breathings pass, And come embalmed away.

†**5.** To steep (e.g. in poison). *Obs. rare*⁻¹.

1623 FAVINE *Theat. Hon.* II. v. 90 Let flie their darts and arrowes embalmed in venemous hearbs.

embalmed (ɛmˈbɑːmd), *ppl. a.* [f. prec. + -ED¹.] In senses of the verb; also, perfumed, fragrant.

1526 SKELTON *Magnyf.* 1574 Her mouthe embawmed, delectable & mery. **1744** *The Travels of the late Charles Thompson* III. 286 Various small Instruments and Utensils denoting the Trade or Occupation of the embalmed person, when he was alive.

†**em'balment.** *Obs.* [f. EMBALL *v.*¹ + -MENT.] A package; an envelope, wrappage.

1697 EVELYN *Numism.* v. 186 Cipher..our Merchants use to mark their..Embalments.

embalmer (ɛmˈbɑːmə(r)). Also 6–7 **im-.** [f. EMBALM *v.* + -ER.] He who or that which embalms.

1. One whose occupation it is to embalm dead bodies.

1587 GOLDING *De Mornay* viii. 95 Imbalmers..of deade bodies. **1626** BACON *Sylva* § 771 The Romans..were not so good Embalmers as the Egyptians. **1700** *Bickerst. detected* in *Swift's Wks.* (1755) II. I. 165 Undertakers, imbalmers, etc. **1744** *The Travels of the late Charles Thompson* III. 289 The Embalmers having done their part, the body was delivered to the relations. **1775** SHERIDAN *Duenna* I. iii, As.. embalmers serve mummies. **1861** ALL *Y. Round* V. 14 The embalmer's work from all decay Had kept his royal person. **1877** A. B. EDWARDS *Up Nile* xxii. 690 A straggling suburb inhabited by the embalmers.

2. *fig.* That which sweetly preserves from decay.

1838 EMERSON *Wks.* (Bohn) II. 192 The religious sentiment is a mountain air. It is the embalmer of the world.

embalming (ɛmˈbɑːmɪŋ), *vbl. sb.* [f. EMBALM + -ING¹.] The action of the verb EMBALM. Also *attrib.*

1530 *Calisto & Mel.* in Hazl. *Dodsley* I. 60 Their embalming and their unshamefacedness. **1626** BACON *Sylva* §771 The Embalming..no doubt was of the best. **1647** H. MORE *Poems* Ded., The embalming of his name to Immortality. **1685** JAS. COOKE *Marrow of Chirurgery* (ed. 4) VI. iii. ii, For Embalming having all things in readiness, etc. **1744** *Travels late Chas. Thompson* III. 287 It seems natural before I leave this subject to say something of the Egyptian manner of embalming human bodies. **1867** TROLLOPE *Chron. Barset* I. xliii. 381 The embalming of her dear remains. **1883** *Harper's Mag.* Mar. 539/2 Oh, that embalming smell!

embalmment (ɛmˈbɑːmmənt). Also 7–9 **em-, imbalment,** (7 **embaulment**). [f. EMBALM *v.* + -MENT.]

1. Impregnation of a corpse with aromatic spices, to prevent putrefaction.

1661 MORGAN *Sph. Gentry* III. viii. 81 The Egyptians were doctors in imbalment. **1819** SOUTHEY in *Q. Rev.* XXI. 376 The Abazas..have a strange way of procuring a natural embalment for their beys. **1864** CARLYLE *Fredk. Gt.* IV. 259 An odour of embalmment.

2. A preparation used for embalming.

1620 *Jrnl. of Pilgrims* (1848) 38 The red powder was a kind of Embaulment. **1658** SIR T. BROWNE *Hydriot.* I. 3 The Ægyptians..by precious Embalments..contrived the notablest wayes of integrall conservation. **1832** *Blackw. Mag.* XXXII. 966 The people..have..torn away the embalments of the Idol Mummy.

fig. **1834** *Fraser's Mag.* X. 40 The art of clear and strong language..has, like an embalmment, preserved the memory of Denham.

†**embamma** (ɛmˈbæmə). *Med. Obs.* [a. Gr. ἔμβαμμα, f. ἐμβάπτειν to dip in.] An appetizing sauce in which articles of food were dipped (before administration to an invalid).

1623 COCKERAM, *Embamma,* any sort of medicament or sauce good to create appetite. **1715** in KERSEY. **1731** in BAILEY. **1775** in ASH. **1884** in *Syd. Soc. Lex.*

emband, var. IMBAND obs., to form into a band.

†**em'bandown** *v. Obs. rare. Sc.* [f. OF. phrase *en bandon* synon. with *a bandon* (see BANDON *sb.*, ABANDON *v.*).] = ABANDON.

1375 BARBOUR *Bruce* I. 244 All that he has enbandownyt [*v.r.* embandownyt] is Till hys lord.

†**em'bane,** *v. Obs. rare.* In 6 **enbane.** [f. EN- + BANE.] *trans.* To poison.

1587 *Mirr. Magistr.* 20 b, Beauty is the bait enbaneth many a bower, A meate two sweete in taste, that sauced is two sower.

embank (ɛmˈbæŋk), *v.* Also 7 **imbank,** *v.* [f. EN- + BANK *sb.*¹; cf. Fr. *embanquer.*]

1. *trans.* To enclose, shut in, confine, or protect by banks; *esp.* to confine the course of (a river) by a mound, dyke, or raised structure of stone or other material.

1576 FLEMING *Panopl. Epist.* 351 Or what should become of the water, if it were not imbancked with the earth? **1700** TYRRELL *Hist. Eng.* II. 814 No River..shall be imbanked. **1770** *Monthly Rev.* 490 Embank the north side of the Thames. **1796** MORSE *Amer. Geog.* II. 526 A..lofty.. mound..embanked one side of the river. **1808** J. BARLOW *Columb.* I. 517 York leads his wave, imbank'd in flowery pride. **1853** KANE *Grinnell Exp.* xl. (1856) 363 This hole was critically circular..symmetrically embanked.

b. *to embank out*: to exclude (the sea) by embankments.

1822 in Picton *L'pool Munic. Rec.* (1886) II. 353 To embank out the sea at that place.

†**2.** *intr.* Of a ship: To run aground. *Obs.* [Cf. F. *embanquer* in this sense.]

1649 DRUMM. OF HAWTH. *Hist. Jas. IV* Wks. (1711) 64 The English ships..embanked, and stuck moor'd upon the shelves.

3. To cover with embankments; to cut into embankments.

1872 J. RUSKIN *Fors Clavig.* II. xix. 13 The operation of embanking hill-sides, so as to stay the rain-flow, is a work of enormous cost and difficulty.

em'banked (ɛm'bæŋkt), *ppl. a.* [f. EMBANK *v.* + -ED[1].] Shut in or confined by banks.
1810 J. T. in *Risdon's Surv. Devon* Introd. 32 An embanked navigation.

embanker (ɛm'bæŋkə(r)). [f. EMBANK *v.* + -ER[1].] One who makes an embankment.
1852 J. WIGGINS *Pract. Embanking Lands* ii. 80 The embanker may..always test the time it will take to freshen and to admit the growth of clover. **1896** *Contemp. Rev.* Aug. 203 Barrowers,..embankers,..and bricklayers.

embanking (ɛm'bæŋkɪŋ), *vbl. sb.* [f. as EMBANKED *ppl. a.* + -ING[2].] The action or process of enclosing or protecting by banks.
1662 DUGDALE (*title*), History of Imbanking and Drayning of divers Fenns. **1856** OLMSTED *Slave States* 467 This embanking has been going on. **1864** H. SPENCER *Illust. Univ. Progr.* 54 Cuttings, embankings, tunnellings.

embankment[1] (ɛm'bæŋkmənt). [f. EMBANK *v.* + -MENT.]
1. The action or process of embanking.
1874 HELPS *Social Pressure* iii. 50 For instance the embankment of the Thames.
2. A mound, bank, or other structure for confining a river, etc. within fixed limits.
1786 BURKE *Art. W. Hastings* Wks. 1842 II. 159 To make ..new and additional embankments in aid of the old ones. *a* **1806** S. HORSLEY *Serm.* xxix. (1810) II. 404 To him Babylon owed..the embankments which confined the river. **1832** G. DOWNES *Lett. Cont. Countries* I. 490 The islets are defended from the water by earthen embankments. *Mod.* Cleopatra's Needle is on the Thames Embankment.
fig. **1875** HAMERTON *Intell. Life* x. ix. 384 Some solid embankment of unshakable rule and resolution.
3. A long earthen bank or mound, *esp.* one raised for the purpose of carrying a road or a railway across a valley.
1810 J. T. in *Risdon's Surv. Devon* Introd. 33 A vast embankment, over which the canal is carried. **1846** J. BAXTER *Libr. Pract. Agric.* II. 194 Early crops may..be protected by..embankments of earth..at the north side. **1862** *Rep. E. Ind. Railw. Comp.* 19 The embankments, nevertheless, have not suffered more than was expected. **1872** J. RUSKIN *Fors Clavig.* II. xix. 13 Spend annually one-tenth of the sum you now give to build embankments against imaginary enemies in building embankments for the help of people whom you may easily make your real friends.

†**em'bankment**[2]. *rare.* [f. EM- + BANK *sb.*[3] + -MENT.] A banking speculation; a bank account. Also *attrib.*
1813 SHELLEY in Hogg *Life* (1858) II. 198 The embankment affairs in which I thoughtlessly engaged. **18..** JEFFREY *Let.* in Cockburn *Life* II. 365, I am sorry your embankment is no larger. *Ibid.* 429 And how does the embankment proceed?

embannered (ɛm'bænəd), *ppl. a.* Also 9 imbannered. [f. **embanner* (f. EN- + BANNER) + -ED[1]; cf. It. *imbandierare.*] Arrayed under banners.
1827 POLLOK *Course T.* v. (1860) 141 Armies of the Saints, embannered. **1847** CRAIG, *Imbannered*, furnished with banners.

‖**embaphium** (ɛm'bæfɪəm). *Med. Obs.* [mod.L., ad. Gr. ἐμβάφιον, f. ἐμβάπτειν to dip in.] A small vessel in which food or medicine is put or measured, or in which it is dipped.
1715 in KERSEY. **1884** in *Syd. Soc. Lex.*

embar (ɛm'bɑː(r)), *v.* Also (6 imber) 6–7 imbar(re. [ad. F. *embarrer*, f. *en-* (see EN-) + *barre* bar; cf. Pr. and Sp. *embarrar*, It. *imbarrare.*]
1. *trans.* To enclose within bars; to enclose, imprison. Also *fig. arch.*
1594 NASHE *Unfort. Trav.* 27 If there bee anie sparke of Adams Paradized perfection yet imberd vp in the breastes of mortall men. **1596** SPENSER *F.Q.* I. vii. 44 Fast embar'd in mighty brazen wall. **1600** FAIRFAX *Tasso* III. lv, Three sides are sure imbard. *Ibid.* XII. i, Now in dark night was all the world embard. **1603** FLORIO *Montaigne* II. xii. (1632) 314 There is great reason why the spirit of man should be so strictly embarred. **1855** SINGLETON *Virgil* I. 42 The ground began..the ocean to embar.
2. To oppose a barrier to; to arrest, stop; to interrupt. Also, to impede (commerce) by an embargo. *arch.* or *Obs.*
1577 HOLINSHED *Chron.* II. 25/1 Not imbard from his posting pase, by reason the towne was not perclosed. **1583** STANYHURST *Aeneis* I. (Arb.) 30 Venus embarring his tale.. sweetlye replyed. **1603** KNOLLES *Hist. Turks* (1621) 290 He ..lay readie to embarre the Turks passage..out of Asia. **1622** BACON *Hen. VII* Wks. (1860) 398 The King.. embarred also all farther trade for the future. *a* **1662** HEYLIN *Laud* I. 160 Embarred their trade.
†**b.** *Law.* To put a stop or end to; to forbid by legislative enactment; to bar (a claim, a title) = BAR *v.* 5 b. *Obs.*
1542–3 *Act 34 & 35 Hen. VIII*, c. 20 (*title*) An act to embarre feined recoueries of landes, wherin the kinges maiestie is in reuercion. **1599** SHAKS. *Hen. V*, I. ii. 94 To imbarre their crooked Titles Vsurpt from you.
†**3.** To exclude, prohibit, debar (a person) *from* an action. Rare const. *to* with *inf. Obs.*
c **1506** *Plumpton Corr.* 201 Ye be aboutward against all right to imbarr & exclud my Chapleyn. **1562** *Apol. Priv. Masse* (1850) 9 Embarring none to communicate with him. **1565** JEWEL *Repl. Harding* (1611) 11 To imbarre the people from reading and vnderstanding of the Scriptures. **1582** *N.T.* (Rhem.) Pref., The Church doth it..not to embarre them from the true knowledge of Christ. **1583** STANYHURST *Aeneis* IV. (Arb.) 107 What reason embars theym, soom forreyn countrye to ferret? **1603** KNOLLES *Hist. Turks* (1621) 107 So embarring them from all government in the common wealth.
†**b.** To refuse, deny (something) *to* a person.
1611 SPEED *Hist. Gt. Brit.* IX. xvi. (1632) 837 The French made choise of the Burgundian to protect them, which could not be embarred to them.
†**4.** To lay (persons or property) under embargo.
1647 MAY *Hist. Parl.* I. i. 9 The English, whose goods were thereupon imbarr'd, and confiscate. **1649** MILTON *Eikon.* 79 The imbarring of all our Merchants in that kingdom.
†**5.** To break inwards the bars of (a helmet). *Obs.*
1480 CAXTON *Ovid's Met.* XII. x, But Achylles brake hys targe & his helme he embarred.

†**embarcadere.** *Obs.* [a. Fr. *embarcadère*, ad. Sp.: see next.] See quot.
1731 BAILEY vol. II, *Embarcadere*, a term used in America, signifying a place which serves as a port to some considerable place farther within land.

‖**embarca'dero.** *rare.* [Sp. f. *embarcar* to EMBARK.] A wharf, quay.
1850 B. TAYLOR *Eldorado* xxi. 219 The forest of masts along the embarcadero.

embarcation, var. of EMBARKATION.

embare: see EM- *prefix.*

†**em'barge,** *sb. Obs.* Also 7 imbarge, em-, imbargue; corruptly -barque, -bark. [ad. Sp. *embargo*: see EMBARGO.] = EMBARGO.
1574 HELLOWES *Gueuara's Ep.* 53, I cannot tel what imbarge or stay..you had. **1614** RALEIGH *Hist. W.* II. v. iii. 362 In the great Imbarge he tooke all our Ships and goods in his Ports. **1651** *Reliq. Wotton.* 104 After an Embark [*ed.* **1672** embarque, **1685** imbarque] of our ships in the river of Bourdeaux. **1656** BRAMHALL *Replic.* iii. 133 All Nations have their Imbargues, and prohibited goods.

†**em'barge,** *v. Obs.* Also 7 imbarge, embargue, -barque. [f. prec. sb.] *trans.* To lay an embargo upon (ships or goods); to sequestrate, confiscate; to arrest (persons). Hence **em'barging** *vbl. sb.*
1600 HAKLUYT *Voy.* III. 555 (R.) Our merchants with their goods were embarged or arrested. **1617** MORYSON *Itin.* II. II. ii. 140 The twelue ships..were..embarged (or arested) to serue the King. **1618–29** *Duke's Acc. of Fleet* in Rushw. *Hist. Coll.* (1659) I. 187 Spain being the Enemy, our Merchant goods would be imbarged. **1624** [SCOTT] *Vox Cœli* 35 The Duke..embarg'd and confisk'd a world of Goods and Ships. **1657** REEVE *God's Plea for Niniveh* 165 To embarque our own Nation, to build Blockhouses against our selves.
Hence **em'barging,** *vbl. sb.*
a **1618** RALEIGH *Invention of Shipping* 37 The imbarging.. of their Ships in Spaine.

embarge, var. of IMBARGE, *obs.* to go on board a barge.

†**em'bargement.** *Obs.* Also 6 imbargment, 7 embarquement. [f. EMBARGE *v.*[1] + -MENT.] A placing under embargo.
1591 HORSEY *Trav.* (1857) 236 Had made a great imbargment and stay of the English merchants. **1599** HAKLUYT *Voy.* II. Index ad fin., The king of Spaines Commission for the generall imbargment or arrest of the English, etc. **1607** SHAKS. *Cor.* I. x. 22 Embarquements all of fury.

embargo (ɛm'bɑːgəʊ), *sb.* Also 7 imbargo. See also EMBARGE. [a. Sp. *embargo*, n. of action f. *embargar* to arrest, impede, repr. a late L. type **imbarricāre*, f. *in-* (see IN-) + *barra* BAR. (Florio has *imbargo* as Italian.)]
1. A prohibitory order, forbidding the ships of a foreign power to enter or leave the ports of a country, or native ships to proceed thither, generally issued in anticipation of war. An embargo may also be laid on particular branches of commerce, for fiscal purposes.
1602 CAREW *Cornwall* 19 b Had not the Imbargo with Spaine..foreclosed this trade. **1758** J. BLAKE *Plan Mar. Syst.* 33 An embargo..is daily expected. **1808** T. JEFFERSON *Writ.* (1830) IV. 111 The embargo appears to be approved. **1860** MOTLEY *Netherl.* (1868) II. x. 71 The embargo was intended to injure the obedient Provinces and their Sovereign.
2. A suspension of commerce, either general or of some particular branch, imposed by municipal law. Also in phrases: *to be under, to lay* (*on*), *to take off an embargo.*
1658–9 in Burton *Diary* (1828) IV. 235 And lay an embargo of all..ships in the river of Thames. **1722** DE FOE *Plague* (Rtldg. 1884) 276 Trade was..under a general Embargo. **1803** WELLINGTON in Gurw. *Disp.* I. 398 In order that they may take off the embargo. **1861** MAY *Const. Hist.* (1863) II. xvi. 522 An embargo on the export of provisions. **1868** ROGERS *Pol. Econ.* xxiii. (1876) 25 Unless it place an embargo on the exportation of capital.
3. *transf.* and *fig.* A stoppage, prohibition, impediment.
1692 E. WALKER tr. *Epictetus' Mor.* (1737) xiii, Thou on thy Feet may'st an Embargo lay. **1691–8** NORRIS *Pract. Disc.* IV. 8 As if Religion had a kind of Imbargo laid upon it. **1824** MISS FERRIER *Inher.* xxxvii, G. complied with this embargo. **1865** TROLLOPE *Belton Est.* xiii. 143 An embargo on his prosperity.

embargo (ɛm'bɑːgəʊ), *v.* Also 7–8 imbargo. See also EMBARGE. [f. EMBARGO *sb.*]
1. To forbid (a vessel) to leave or enter a port; to lay (vessels, trade) under an embargo.
1755 MAGENS *Insurances* II. 31 They may be arrested or embargoed. **1851** CARLYLE *Sterling* I. x. (1872) 64 Ship seized and embargoed in the King's name. **1886** *Sat. Rev.* 22 May 697/2 To have your ships embargoed.
b. *fig.* To prohibit.
1824 BYRON *Juan* XV. 310 When Rapp the Harmonists embargoed marriage.
2. To seize, 'requisition' (ships or other means of transport, goods) for the service of the state.
1755 MAGENS *Insurances* I. 68 If a Ship be embargo'd for the Service of the Potentate in whose Port she is. **1810** WELLINGTON in Gurw. *Disp.* VI. 529 They must embargo means of transport. **1879** DOWDEN *Southey* iii. 48 Every carriage..being embargoed for the royal service.
3. To seize, impound, confiscate.
1650 R. STAPYLTON *Strada's Low C. Warres* VI. 34 Merchants..weere clapt up prisoners, and their Goods.. imbargoed. **1798** SOUTHEY *Lett.* (1856) I. 50, I embargoed the likeness for you.

†**em'bark,** *sb. Obs. rare.* In 7 embarque. [f. next vb.: cf. Sp. *embarco.*] = EMBARKATION.
1654 L'ESTRANGE *Chas. I*, 136 Being after his embarque, twice driven back by tempest.

embark (ɛm'bɑːk), *v.* Forms: 6–8 embarque, (6 enbarque), 6–7 imbarke, 7–8 imbark, -que, 6– embark. [ad. F. *embarquer*, a com. Romanic word = It. *imbarcare*, Pr., Sp., Pg. *embarcar* :—late L. *imbarcāre*, f. *in-* (see IN-) + *barca* BARK *sb.*[2]]
I. *trans.* **1. a.** To put on board ship, make to go on board. **b.** Of the ship: To receive on board. †**c.** *refl.* = 3 a.
1550 NICOLLS *Thucyd.* 20 The Corinthians who..had thair people embarqued. *Ibid.* 52 b, One part of them embarqued themself. **1599** SHAKS. *Hen. V*, III Prol. 5 You haue seene The well-appointed King at Douer Peer, Embarke his Royaltie. **1603** KNOLLES *Hist. Turks* (1638) 89 And therupon imbarking themselues with all things necessary. **1621** If any master doe permit..any person..to imbarque..any parcell. **1705** OTWAY *Orphan* v. vii. 2103 The Vessel..Where all the Treasure of my Soul's embarqu'd. **1781** GIBBON *Decl. & F.* II. xxxvi. 329 They always embarked a sufficient number of horses. **1843** PRESCOTT *Mexico* (1850) I. 235 Then embarking..his troops, Cortés crossed the river. **1885** *Manch. Exam.* 25 Mar. 4/7 The Osborne will..embark the Prince.
2. *transf.* and *fig.*; *esp.* To invest (money) in a commercial undertaking; to involve (a person) in an enterprise. †Also *refl.* = 3 b, 4.
1584 R. SCOT *Discov. Witchcr.* x. vi. 147 Such would be imbarked in the Ship of fooles. **1642** ROGERS *Naaman* 31 The soule..imbarkes her selfe in this error, by the conceit of her wealth, health, youth. **1647** CLARENDON *Hist. Reb.* III. (1702) I. 206 He..embark'd himself in Publick employments. *a* **1674** —— *Life* (1751) III. 956 Such an Alliance..as might embark them against France. **1742** MIDDLETON *Cicero* III. IX. 2 Age..rendered him wholly unfit..to embark himself in an affair so desperate. **1832** HT. MARTINEAU *Hill & Vall.* ii. 20 A few thousand pounds, which he embarked..in an ironwork.
II. *intr.* for *refl.*
3. To go on board ship; to take ship.
a. *lit.* Const. *for* (the destination).
1580 SIDNEY *Arcadia* v. 448 Forthwith imbarqued for Byzantium. **1602** WARNER *Alb. Eng.* IX. xlix. 227 Our Gallants did imbarke each-wheare. **1693** TEMPLE *Mem.* Wks. 1731 I. 456 Prince and Princess embarqu'd for Holland. **1735** POPE *Donne's Sat.* viii. 27 The ark Where all the Race of Reptiles might embark. **1757** BURKE *Abridgm. Eng. Hist.* Wks. X. 173 Cæsar..accordingly embarked with the infantry. **1816** SHELLEY *Alastor* 304 A restless impulse urged him to embark. **1856** KANE *Arct. Expl.* II. xxviii. 282 We..joyously embarked again upon a free lead.
b. *transf.* and *fig.*
1635 QUARLES *Embl.* Introd. (1718) 3 Blest soul, that here embark'st: thou sail'st apace. *a* **1667** COWLEY *Bk. at Oxford* Wks. 1710 II. 548 The sacred Ark, Where all the World of Science does imbark. **1745** *De Foe's Eng. Tradesm.* (1841) I. vii. 55 The same Creditors will embark with you again.
4. To engage *in* a business or undertaking, as in war, commerce, or the like.
1649 SELDEN *Laws Eng.* I. lxiii. (1739) 128 [He] imbarqued together with the Laity against the growing power of the Clergy. **1787** PITT in G. Rose *Diaries* (1860) I. 67 Prussia being completely embarked. **1858** CARLYLE *Fredk. Gt.* (1865) I. III. xviii. 249 Friedrich Wilhelm..had been forced..to embark in that big game. **1869** ROGERS *Adam Smith's W.N.* I. Pref. 23 Had he not suffered himself ..to embark in the..most disastrous of..wars.

embark, var. IMBARK, *Obs.*, to enclose in bark.

†**em'barkage.** *Obs. rare*[−1]. Also 6 imbarkage. [f. EMBARK *v.*[1] + -AGE.] = EMBARKATION.
1577 HELLOWES *Gueuara's Chron.* 54 Traiane was constrained..to hasten his imbarkage.

embarkation (ɛmbɑːˈkeɪʃən). Also 6–9 **-cation,** 8 **imbarkation, -cation.** [a. F. *embarcation,* f. *embarquer* EMBARK *v.*[1]]

1. The action or process of embarking. *lit.* & *fig.*

c **1645** HOWELL *Lett.* (1655) I. III. xviii. 26, I can find no commodity of imbarcation at Saint Malos. **1647** CLARENDON *Hist. Reb.* I. 23 Very sollicitous for the Embarcation of the Army. **1790** BEATSON *Nav. & Mil. Mem.* I. 172 To hasten the embarkation of the troops. **1810** WELLINGTON in Gurw. *Disp.* VI. 6, I shall delay the embarkation. **1869** FREEMAN *Norm. Conq.* (1876) III. xii. 222 The point of embarcation was close by the..abode of Godwine.

attrib. **1884** *Pall Mall G.* 16 Sept. 8/2 The embarkation list..will include twenty-three officers. **1899** *Westm. Gaz.* 9 Nov. 10/2 As the ship was about to sail, investigations were made, and..the embarkation officer went aboard to see the supply. **1904** *Daily Chron.* 6 Sept. 6/7 The embarkation staff at the port. **1923** KIPLING *Irish Guards Gt. War* I. 2 Every one was new to embarkation-duty. **1946** KOESTLER *Thieves in Night* III. 322 And back home in Suffolk on embarkation leave he had listened to a sermon.

†**2.** *concr.* A body of troops embarked, gone or put on board ship. *Obs.*

1720 *Lond. Gaz.* No. 5877/1 The Transports..were taking on Board the third..Imbarkation. **1757** BURKE *Abridgm. Eng. Hist.* Wks. X. 252 Another and much greater embarkation followed.

†**3.** A vessel, boat. *Obs.* [cf. F. *embarcation,* Sp. *embarcacion.*]

1690 *Lond. Gaz.* No. 2525/1 They have..taken divers..small Embarkations. **1705** *Ibid.* 4115/4 Sloops, and other Imbarcations. **1781** RENNELL in *Phil. Trans.* LXXI. 106 Embarkations..traverse the inundation. **1804** H. T. COLEBROOKE *Husb. of Bengal* (1806) 10 The peasants repairing to the market..on embarkations. **1807** SOUTHEY *Espriella's Lett.* (1814) II. 179 A..rotten and crazy embarkation.

embarked (ɛmˈbɑːkt, *poet.* ɛmˈbɑːrkɪd), *ppl. a.* Also 7 **embarqued, imbarked, imbarqued.** [f. EMBARK *v.*[1] + -ED[1].] That has gone or been put on board ship.

1590 SHAKS. *Mids. N.* II. i. 127 Marking th' embarked traders on the flood. **1592** —— *Ven. & Ad.* 818 Gazing upon a late-embarked friend.

embarking (ɛmˈbɑːkɪŋ), *vbl. sb.* Also 6 **imbarquing.** [f. EMBARK *v.*[1] + -ING[1].] The action of the verb EMBARK. Also *attrib.*

1591 PERCIVALL *Sp. Dict., Embarcadura,* embarking. **1633** STAFFORD *Pac. Hib.* (1821) viii. 324 The want of wind hinders them in the imbarquing Ports. **1768** BLACKSTONE *Comm.* IV. 154 The statute 8 Eliz. c. 3. makes the transportation of live sheep, or embarking them on board any ship, for the first offence forfeiture of goods.

embarking (ɛmˈbɑːkɪŋ), *ppl. a.* [f. as prec. + -ING[2].] That embarks.

1856 EMERSON *Eng. Traits, Religion* Wks. (Bohn) II. 100 The noise of embarking emigrants.

emˈbarkment. Now *rare.* Also 6 **embarkement,** 6–7 **imbarkment,** 7 **embarquement.** [f. EMBARK *v.*[1] + -MENT.] = EMBARKATION I.

1596 *Life of Scanderbeg* 407 His embarkement and departure. **1598** BARRET *Theor. Warres* I. ii. 12 Skilfull..at imbarkments. **1614** SELDEN *Titles Hon.* 210 Speaking of Paris..in his embarquement for Helen. **1672** DAVENANT *Play-house to be Let* (1673) 89 We may find this place For our imbarkment free. **1750** BEAWES *Lex Mercat.* (1752) 6 Embarkments were made for the Holy Wars. **1813** SOUTHEY *Nelson* I. 159 The embarkment and removal of British property. **1886** *Times* 6 Jan. 12/3.

†**emˈbarment.** *Obs.* In 7 imb-. [f. EMBAR *v.* + -MENT.] The action of the verb EMBAR; an embargo, prohibition, hindrance.

1606 WARNER *Albion's Engl.* XV. xcvii. 387 But many years twixt them and vs hath been Imbarment. **1620** tr. *Boccaccio's Dream* 33 No imbarment remained but remembrance of the Marquesse. **1623** WHITBOURN *Disc. Newfoundl.* 41 We little feare..the Imbarments of any Prince.

embarn, var. of IMBARN, *obs.,* to garner.

embarque, obs. var. EMBARK.

embarque, -ment, var. ff. EMBARGE, -MENT, *obs.*

emˈbarras, *sb.* Also 7–8 **embarass, embarrass.** [a. F. *embarras* obstacle, embarrassment; cf. It. *imbarrazzo,* Sp. *embarazo,* Pg. *embaraço,* related to F. *embarrer,* f. *en-* (see EN-) + *barre* BAR.]

1. = EMBARRASSMENT, in various senses. *Obs.* exc. as Fr. (ɑ̃bara); now chiefly in phrase ***embarras de richesse*** 'embarrassment of riches' [Abbé d'Allainval (*title*) L'embarras des richesses (1726)], the state of having more wealth than one knows what to do with; usually *fig.*

1664 PEPYS *Diary* (1879) III. 13 The greatest embarras that I have..how to behave myself to Sir H. Bennet. **1677** TEMPLE *Let. Sir J. Williamson* Wks. 1731 II. 434 How great an Embarass Count Kinski is like to bring upon you there. **1710** BERKELEY *Princ. Hum. Knowl.* §25 Clear the First Principles of Knowledge from the embarras and delusion of words. **1751** CHESTERF. *Let.* 29 Mar. (1774) II. 6 Say..you dread *l'embaras des richesses* ever since you have seen what an incumbrance they were to poor Harlequin. **1756** FOOTE *Eng. fr. Paris* II, Aid me to escape this embarras. **1778** APTHORPE *Preval. Chr.* 220, I think it impossible to clear up Cicero's embarras. **1826** M. WILMOT *Let.* 11 July (1935) 243 A too large Stock in trade, proving now and then an *embarras de richesse.* **1864** BURTON *Scot Abr.* II. ii. 157 He received us..with some *embarras.* **1866** LIVINGSTONE *Jrnl.* (1873) I. Introd. 8 He has an *embarras de richesses.* **1932** C. WILLIAMS *Eng. Poetic Mind* iii. 77 Iago..is action incarnate only he cannot find his own reason for it. Othello has wronged him ..; Othello has played him false with Emilia; so has Cassio; he loves Desdemona also—*embarras de richesses.*

2. *Canada* and (local) *U.S.* [N. Amer. Fr.] (See quots. 1814.) ? *Obs.*

1793 A. MACKENZIE *Voy. Montreal* (1801) 226 In passing over one of the embarras, our dog..fell in. **1814** H. M. BRACKENRIDGE *Views Louisiana* 205 At the distance of every mile or two,..there are *embarras,* or rafts, formed by the collection of trees closely matted, and extending from twenty to thirty yards. *Ibid.* 208 Passed an *embarras,* N.E. side, the most difficult since we started. **1867** SMYTH *Sailor's Work-bk., Embarras,* an American term for places where the navigation of rivers..is rendered difficult by the accumulation of driftwood.

embarrass (ɛmˈbærəs), *v.* Also 7–8 **embarass,** 8 **imbarrass.** [ad. F. *embarrasser,* lit. 'to block, obstruct', f. *embarras*: see prec.]

1. *trans.* To encumber, hamper, impede (movements, actions, persons moving or acting).

1683 TEMPLE *Mem.* Wks. 1731 I. 376 The Character of Ambassador, which would delay or embarass me with Preparations of Equipage. **1734** tr. *Rollin's Anc. Hist.* (1827) II. II. §2. 2 Hannibal..ran to the assistance of his troops, who were thus embarrassed. **1803** WELLINGTON in Gurw. *Disp.* II. 53 *note,* The state of the rivers..will embarrass the enemy in a considerable degree. **1856** FROUDE *Hist. Eng.* (1858) II. ix. 402 A general council would..embarrass their movements.

b. *pass.* Of persons: To be 'in difficulties' from want of money; to be encumbered with debts. Cf. EMBARRASSED *ppl. a.,* EMBARRASSMENT.

2. a. To perplex, throw into doubt or difficulty.

1672 VILLIERS (Dk. Buckhm.) *Rehearsal* (1714) 41 The People being embarrast by their equal ties to both. **1673** DRYDEN *Marr. à la Mode* V. i, Pray do not Embarrass me.. Embarrass me! what a delicious French word do you make me lose upon you too! **1724** DE FOE *Mem. Cavalier* (1840) 151 The king embarrassed with these difficulties..calls a great council. **1773** MONBODDO *Language* (1774) I. I. ix. 123 Could not conceive and argue..without imbarrassing his thoughts. **1824** TRAVERS *Dis. Eye* (ed. 3) 332 Such a circumstance may embarrass an operator. **1855** MILMAN *Lat. Chr.* (1864) III. VI. iii. 418 Frederick..embarrassed them with the choice among five prelates.

b. To make (a person) feel awkward or ashamed, esp. by one's speech or actions; to cause (someone) embarrassment.

1828 in WEBSTER. **1897** *Daily News* 26 Nov. 8/3 The senator said: 'Mr. President, may I have the privilege of introducing Mr. Clemens?'.. 'Mr. President, I—I am embarrassed. Are you?' **1929** E. BOWEN *Last Sept.* xv. 182 His unordered moods gave him the churlishness of a schoolboy; his silliness embarrassed her. **1957** J. BRAINE *Room at Top* xxx. 238 He always said and did the correct thing and never embarrassed anyone with an unseemly display of emotion. **1984** F. TUOHY *Coll. Stories* 194 He embarrassed everyone by bursting into tears.

3. To render difficult or intricate; to complicate (a question, etc.).

1736 BUTLER *Anal.* I. iv. Wks. 1874 I. 80 One irregularity after another embarrasses things to such a degree, that, etc. **1771** GOLDSM. *Hist. Eng.* Pref. ii, They have effectually embarrassed that road which they laboured to shorten. **1778** BP. LOWTH *Isaiah* Notes (ed. 12) 206 The word..seems to embarrass the sentence. **1818** CRUISE *Digest* VI. 25, I do not apprehend that this case will be embarrassed by that decision. **1876** E. MELLOR *Priesth.* iv. 154 This designation by their ordinary names..must embarras every theory which involves a substantial change.

embarrassed (ɛmˈbærəst), *ppl. a.* [f. prec.]

1. Of a road, a channel, etc.: Made difficult by obstructions; full of obstructions. Now only *fig.*

1727 A. HAMILTON *New Acc. E. Ind.* I. xxiv. 295 Its [a river's] Passage inward is..embarassed with Rocks. **1796–7** *Instr. & Reg. Cavalry* (1813) 183 If the ground is at all embarrassed, the line cannot incline. **1860** TYNDALL *Glac.* I. §26. 193 A less embarrassed field of operations.

2. Of persons, their movements or actions: Hampered by difficulties, impeded.

b. Involved in money difficulties.

1888 *Spectator* 30 June 877/2 Sums of that kind are not spent by an embarrassed State without the gravest reason, etc.

3. a. Perplexed (in thought). **b.** Confused, constrained (in manner or behaviour).

1683 D. A. *Art Converse* 107 Their utterance is embarass'd and uneasie. **1761** CHURCHILL *Rosciad* (R.) Awkward, embarrass'd, stiff, without the skill Of moving gracefully. **1768** STERNE *Sent. Journ.* (1778) II. 198 As much embarrassed as..the lady could be herself. **1828** SCOTT *F.M. Perth* xxiii, 'Tush, father Glover,' answered the embarrassed victor. **1875** HAMERTON *Intell. Life* VII. ix. 270, I was the embarrassed and unwilling witness.

4. Of expressions, narratives, etc.: Involved, confused.

1760 JORTIN *Erasm.* II. 623 That the periods are rather too long, and embarassed. **1824** L. MURRAY *Eng. Gram.* 517 Embarrassed, obscure, and feeble sentences. **1868** J. H. BLUNT *Ref. Ch. Eng.* I. 391 Subjects have been set aside.. to prevent the narrative from becoming embarrassed.

embarrassedly (ɛmˈbærəstlɪ), *adv.* [f. prec. + -LY[2].] In an embarrassed manner.

1883 BRET HARTE in *Longm. Mag.* July 320 She coughed embarrassedly.

embarrassing (ɛmˈbærəsɪŋ), *ppl. a.* [f. EMBARRASS + -ING[2].] That embarrasses.

1807 *Med. Jrnl.* XVII. 537 The general question of amputation..is found in practice difficult and embarrassing. **1849** PRESCOTT *Peru* (1850) II. 46 This was an embarrassing situation for the Spaniards. **1853** GROTE *Greece* II. lxxxvii. XI. 357 An attack..amidst embarrassing woods and rocks.

embarrassingly (ɛmˈbærəsɪŋlɪ), *adv.* [f. prec. + -LY[2].] In an embarrassing manner or degree.

1881 *Daily News* 5 Feb. 5/5 Randolph Churchill..was embarrassingly cheered. **1882** J. HAWTHORNE *Fort. Fool* I. xxvii, It was embarrassingly conspicuous and oppressive.

embarrassment (ɛmˈbærəsmənt). [f. EMBARRASS + -MENT; cf. obs. Fr. *embarrassement.*]

1. The process of embarrassing (*rare*); embarrassed state or condition:

a. of (or with reference to) affairs, circumstances, etc.; often in pecuniary sense.

1676 COLES, *Embarasment,* a perplexing, intangling, hindering. **1849** COBDEN *Speeches* 62 Difficulty and embarrassment in..the agricultural districts. *c* **1850** *Arab. Nts.* (Rtldg.) 354 The embarrassment of Noureddin's affairs. **1853** BRIGHT *Sp. India* 3 June, A state of embarrassment and threatened bankruptcy. **1872** YEATS *Growth Comm.* 56 Political embarrassment and domestic want provoked attacks upon the dealers in corn. **1880** L. STEPHEN *Pope* vi. 139 He managed to run through a splendid fortune and die in embarrassment.

b. Perplexity, sense of difficulty or hesitation with regard to judgement or action; constrained feeling or manner arising from bashfulness or timidity.

1774 BURKE *Sp. Electors of Bristol,* If my real, unaffected embarrassment prevents me from expressing my gratitude to you as I ought. **1796** C. MARSHALL *Garden.* vii. (1813) 99 Bad weather occasions hurry and embarrassment. **1828** SCOTT *F.M. Perth* vi, There was embarrassment on the maiden's part. **1850** MRS. STOWE *Uncle Tom* v. 26 Noticing a certain embarrassment in her husband's manner. **1863** GEO. ELIOT *Romola* (1880) I. I. viii. 124 Ready speech that prevents a blush from looking like embarrassment. **1874** MORLEY *Compromise* (1886) 84 Any embarrassment in dealing with it..is a weakness that hinders social progress.

c. Confusion of thought or expression.

1751 JOHNSON *Rambler* No. 169 ⁋13 He seldom suspects his thoughts of embarrassment.

2. Something which embarrasses; an impediment, obstruction, encumbrance. In *pl.* often = 'pecuniary difficulties'.

1729 BUTLER *Serm.* Wks. 1874 II. 33 Embarrassments.. hindering us from going the nearest way to our own good. **1751** JOHNSON *Rambl.* No. 159 ⁋6 Diffidence..compensates its embarrassments by more important advantages. **1848** MACAULAY *Hist. Eng.* II. 65 In the hope of extricating himself from his embarrassments. **1862** TRENCH *Mirac.* i. 103 She was evidently distressed at the embarrassments of that humble household. **1876** M. ARNOLD *Lit. & Dogma* 157 To be felt by them as an embarrassment to the cause of Jesus.

embarrel: see EM- *prefix.*

†**emˈbarren,** *v. Obs.* or *arch.* [f. EN- + BARREN.] *trans.* To make or render barren, unfertile, unproductive. *lit.* and *fig.*

1627 FELTHAM *Resolves* II. ix, The Ashes from..Vesuvius ..embarren all the fields about it. *Ibid.* I. xviii, Like salt marshes that lye low..[the poor] are..embarrened with a fretting care. **1662** FULLER *Worthies* (1840) I. 546 The most generous and vigorous land will in time be embarrened. **1807–8** W. IRVING *Salmag.* (1824) 364 Like to Java's drear waste they embarren the heart.

†**ˌembarriˈcado,** *v. Obs.* [f. Sp. *embarricado* a barricade.] = BARRICADE *v.*

1603 FLORIO *Montaigne* III. vi. (1632) 505 In haste..to embarricado..any lodgement or quarter. **1630** J. TAYLOR (Water P.) *Wks.* II. 243/2 Coaches..serued as a wall to embarricado and fortifie their campe.

†**emˈbarring,** *vbl. sb. Obs.* [f. EMBAR *v.* + -ING[1].] The action of the verb EMBAR: **a.** the action of prohibiting, or withholding (*from* a person); **b.** the action of laying an embargo upon (a person).

1563 MAN tr. *Musculus' Common-pl.* 28 b, Some doe define lawe to be..the embarryng of that which is wrong. **1566** T. STAPLETON *Ret. Untr. Jewell* i. 9 The embarring of this holy sacrament from excommunicated persons. **1649** MILTON *Eikon.* Wks. 1738 I. 389 The imbarring of all our Merchants in that Kingdom.

†**embase** (ɛmˈbeɪs), *v. Obs.* or *arch.* Forms: 6–7 **embace** (7 **-bass**), **imbace, -base,** 7– **embase.** [f. EN- + Fr. *bas,* BASE *a.* (OF. had *embaissier*:—late L. type **imbassiāre,* of equivalent formation).]

1. a. To lower (physically). **b.** To give a lower direction to.

1605 SYLVESTER *Du Bartas* I. iii. I. 92 When God.. Embast the Valleys and embost the Hills. **1595** SPENSER *Sonn.* xii, And to the ground her eie-lids low embaseth. **1644** NYE *Gunnery* (1670) 29 The Gunner..must..imbase the mouth [of his gun].

c. *fig.*

a **1564** BECON *Art. Chr. Relig. proved* (1844) 433 At the Lord's table let us not embase ourselves to look upon the bread and cup that be there set forth. **1693** SOUTH *Serm.* 288 Embased the very standard of good and evil.

2. To lower in rank, dignity, office, condition, or character; to humble, humiliate; often with the sense of *degrade, make base*. Also *refl.*

1571 GOLDING *Calvin on Ps.* xxiii. 1 Disdeyneth not to embace himself.. for our sake. **1587** —— *De Mornay* xxiv. 365 To violate or imbace the thing that was helde to be so holy. **1612** DRAYTON *Poly-olb.* ix. 137 With the tearme of Welsh, the English now embase The nobler Britans name. **1642** *Life Dk. Buckhm.* in *Select. fr. Harl. Misc.* (1793) 278 No.. ignoble end.. which may.. embase the freedom of my poor judgment. **1737** L. CLARKE *Hist. Bible* II. (1740) 131 Continual servitude of body had imbased their Spirits. **1820** L. HUNT *Indicator* No 64 (1822) II. 96 It is pure self-revolving selfishness that 'embases and embrutes'. **1844** [see EMBASING *ppl. a.*]

3. To lower (coin or commodities) in price or value. *transf.* and *fig.* To take away the value of, depreciate, discredit, undervalue.

1577 HOLINSHED *Chron.* III. 1192/1 The teston coined for twelue pence, and in the reigne of king Edward embased by proclamation to six pence. **1594** R. PARSONS *Confer. Success* I. v. 120 That no man may think we meane to imbase that which we esteme in so high degree. **1657** REEVE *God's Plea* 41 This is to vilipend greatnesse, or to embase noblenesse. **1668** CHILD *Disc. Trade* (ed. 4) 243 As the high rate of Usury doth imbase lands. **1698** SOUTH *Serm.* ix. (1843) II. 134 A temper of mind which will certainly embase and discommend all our services.

4. To debase (coin) by a mixture of alloy; *lit.* and *fig.* Said also of the alloy.

1551 [see EMBASING *vbl. sb.*] **1594** WEST *Symbol.* II. §216 Embase, shave, file, clippe, wast or empaire the currant coin. **1627** FELTHAM *Resolves* I. xviii. Wks. (1677) 32 It will imbase even the purest metal in man. **1679** BURNET *Hist. Ref.* (1865) I. 16 To raise money, not by embasing the coin, but by embasing the Christian religion. **1701** W. WOTTON *Hist. Rome* 314 He embased the current coin. **1752** [see EMBASING *vbl. sb.*]

b. *transf.* and *fig.* To take away the excellence of; to corrupt, impair, vitiate.

1625 BACON *Ess. Love* (Arb.) 449 Wanton love Corrupteth, and Imbaseth it. *a* **1626** —— *Sylva* §575 The Vertue of the Seed.. in a Tree.. is embased by the Ground, to which it is removed. **1655** GURNALL *Chr. in Arm.* ix. (1669) 56/2 Sever'd from that soil and dross which embassed it. *c* **1660** SOUTH *Serm.* (1715) I. 37 A Pleasure embased with no appendant Sting. **1720** WELTON *Suffer. Son of God* I. ix. 225 Those Vanitys.. Embase my Nature.

† **em'based**, *ppl. a. Obs.* [f. prec. + -ED.] = ABASED, DEBASED, in various senses.

1602 FULBECKE *1st Pt. Parall.* 54 The debtor may pay the det in the coin embased. **1627** SPEED *England Abr.* vi. §4 An earthen Pot hoarded with store of Roman Coines—stamped vpon imbased siluer. **1647** N. BACON *Hist. Disc.* xxii. 63 This was a trick of imbased times. **1649** MILTON *Eikon.* vi. (Bohn) 367 An imbased flexibleness to the.. contrary dictates of any factions.

† **em'basement.** *Obs.* [f. as prec. + -MENT.]

1. A lowering in place, dignity, power, etc.; degradation; = ABASEMENT. *lit.* and *fig.*

1575 FENTON *Golden Epistles* 95 This wonderfull embasement of estate whiche the sonne of God tooke vppon him. **1582** N. T. (Rhem.) *Rom.* iii. 10 They esteemed it a great imbasement for such to be in Gods debt. **1635** BARRIFFE *Milit. Discip.* (1643) iii. 347 Suffering too much imbasement, as being often undervalued. **1656** JEANES *Mixt. Schol. Div.* 60 Earthly mindednesse.. is a great depressure and embasement thereof. **1692** SOUTH *Serm.* VIII. iv. (R.) The pleasures of sin.. receive a further embasement.. from the super-addition of a curse.

2. A debasement of precious metal by mixture of base metal; = ABASEMENT 3. Also *fig.*

1677 HALE *Contempl.* II. 65 The very Soul of Man.. receives a Tincture and an imbasement by them. **1709** STANHOPE *Paraph.* IV. 65 Most of Us have.. Vices, for an Allay and Embasement to our.. Vertues.

embasiate, var. of EMBASSIATE, *obs.*

† **em'basing**, *vbl. sb. Obs.* [f. prec. + -ING.[1]] The action of the verb EMBASE, in various senses.

1551 ROBINSON tr. *More's Utop.* (Arb.) 59 *marg.*, Enhauncynge and imbasyng of coyne. **1581** J. BELL *Haddon's Answ. Osor.* 46 Peruse you ye Psalmes.. you finde in them.. humilitie, knowledge, and embacyng of a mans selfe. **1653** MILTON *Hirelings* (Wks. 1851) 381 The frequent imbasing of his [some Gentleman's] Sons with illiterate and narrow Principles. **1752** CARTE *Hist. Eng.* III. 242 As to the embasing of the coin.

em'basing (ɛm'beɪsɪŋ), *ppl. a. arch.* [f. as prec. + -ING[2].] In senses of the verb.

1652 BENLOWES *Theoph.* II. xxi. 26 Your glorious Nature's by embasing sin brought low. *a* **1665** J. GOODWIN *Filled w. the Spirit* (1867) 423 It is a matter of.. imbasing nature to the creature man. **1844** LD. HOUGHTON *Mem. Many Scenes* 130 And would my spirit from earth's embasing rule Were in this moment riven.

embassade (ɛmbə'seɪd). *Obs.* or *arch.* Also 5 enbassed, enbassade, 7 *Sc.* embassaid. [See AMBASSADE, of which this is a less frequent var.]

1. The mission or function of an ambassador; = AMBASSADE 1.

1593 SHAKS. *3 Hen. VI*, IV. iii. 32 When you disgrac'd me in my Embassade. **1601** HOLLAND *Pliny* 491 P. Iunius, and T. Coruncanus.. were put to death, notwithstanding they came in embassade to her.

2. A body of persons (or a single person) sent on a mission, or as a deputation, to or from a sovereign; an ambassador and his suite; = AMBASSADE 2.

1480 CAXTON *Chron. Eng.* ccliii. 325 Also this same yere cam a grete enbassade in to englond. **1494** FABYAN IV. lxvi. 45 He sente to hym an enbassed. *Ibid.* IV. lxxv. 53 An Embassade shuld be made vnto the Kynge of lytell Brytayne. **1551** in Strype *Eccl. Mem.* II. I. II. ix. 320 Upon coming of great embassades or foreign princes.

3. The message sent or delivered by an ambassador; = AMBASSADE 3.

1508 FISHER *Seven Ps.* Ps. cxliii. II. (1529) R i b They fered to shewe thyne embassade. **1601** R. JOHNSON *Kingd. & Commw.* (1603) 57 In this counsell.. they consult of embassaids.

4. quasi-*adv.* On an embassy. *rare.*

1525 LD. BERNERS *Froiss.* II. ccxix. [ccxv.] 677 Howe the frenche kyng.. had sente a knyght of honour embassade to hym. **1596** SPENSER *Hymne Beautie* 252 But when her words embassade forth she sends.

embassador (ɛm'bæsədə(r)). Variant form of AMBASSADOR; now *obs.* in England, though in frequent use during the early part of the present century. In the U.S. this form, which is recommended by the analogy of EMBASSY, is still preferred. For examples see AMBASSADOR *β*.

embassadorial, var. of AMBASSADORIAL.

1852 *Blackw. Mag.* LXXI. 557 He thought it becoming his embassadorial position.

embassadress, obs. var. of AMBASSADRESS.

embassadry, var. of AMBASSADRY, *Obs.*

embassage ('ɛmbəsɪdʒ). *arch.* Also imb-. [A variant (in mod. archaistic use more frequent) of AMBASSAGE, q.v. In ordinary language superseded by EMBASSY.]

1. The sending or despatch of ambassadors, or of an ambassador.

1561 T. N[ORTON] *Calvin's Inst.* III. ii. (1634) 272 That liberal Embassage by which God reconcileth the world to himselfe. **1839** YEOWELL *Anc. Brit. Ch.* v. (1847) 48 The embassage to Rome may be accounted for. **1881** *Contemp. Rev.* Apr. 569 Thy torrent coursers flee With thunderous embassage to the great Sea.

2. The business confided to, or message conveyed by, an ambassador.

1526 *Pilgr. Perf.* (W. de W. 1531) 179 These wordes were.. gyuen to hym as the embassage of god. **1580** SIDNEY *Arcadia* (1622) 440 Let it embassage beare your grieues to show. **1621** QUARLES *Esther* (1717) 34 Nor did they question whether.. false the Prophet were, that brought th' Embassage. **1821** SCOTT *Kenilw.* xvii, I had settled to send thee thither upon a secret embassage.

3. The position of an ambassador; ambassadorship.

1605 BACON *Adv. Learn.* I. ii. §1 (1873) 11 Carneades the philosopher came in embassage to Rome. **1677** *Govt. Venice* 279 To.. lessen any thing of the Honours of his Embassage. **1863** P. S. WORSLEY *Poems & Transl.* 6 So shall my vast renown of embassage Flash wide conviction.

4. A body of persons sent on a mission, or as a deputation, to or from a sovereign, etc.; the ambassador, his retinue, and surroundings.

1621 G. SANDYS *Ovid's Met.* VII. 139 The Attick ship.. Which Cephalus, and his embassage, bore. **1663** MARVELL *Corr.* xliv. Wks. 1872-5 II. 92 *note*, To make me goe along with him Secretary to those Embassages. **1829** SCOTT *Anne of G.* viii, The members of the embassage.

† **embassa'torial**, *a. Obs.* [f. med.L. *embassator* AMBASSADOR + -IAL.] = AMBASSADORIAL.

a **1734** NORTH *Exam.* III. vii. 40 Embassatorial Letters.

† **em'bassatrix**, var. of AMBASSATRIX. *Obs.* A female ambassador, an ambassador's wife.

a **1734** NORTH *Exam.* 479 Here was.. an Embassatrix resident.

embassed, -et, var. ff. EMBASSADE, -IATE.

† **em'bassiate.** *Obs.* Also 5 inbasset, 6 embasset, embasiate. [var. of AMBASSIATE, q.v.] = EMBASSY.

a **1400** *Cov. Myst.* 112 In thyn hey inbasset, Lord, I xal go. **14..** LYDG. *Thebes* (E.E.T.S.) 1848 With hool thempris of the embassyat. *c* **1470** HENRY *Wallace* VI. 134 An inbasset to bryng ane uncouth queyne. **1513** MORE *Rich. III* Wks. 58/2 He sent ouer in embassiate, the Erle of warwike. *Ibid.* 60 Embasiate. **1530** PALSGR., Embasset, *embassade*.

embassy ('ɛmbəsɪ). Also 6 *pl.* imbases. [A variant (now almost the only current form) of AMBASSY, q.v.]

1. The function or office of an ambassador; also, the sending of ambassadors.

1579 J. JONES *Preserv. Bodie & Soule* I. xxiii. 43 To toyle in imbases. **1588** SHAKS. *L.L.L.* I. i. 35 Here comes in Embassie The French Kings daughter. **1669** TEMPLE *Let.* Wks. 1731 II. 196 Lord Falconbridge, who is going on an Embassy. **1799** WELLINGTON in Gurw. *Disp.* I. 16 Various embassies and military preparations on the part of Tippoo Sultaun. **1848** W. H. KELLY tr. *L. Blanc's Hist. Ten Y.* II. 564 They thought it.. liberal in them to reserve for their former chief some embassy or other.

† **2.** The message committed to or delivered by an ambassador. *Obs.*

1595 SHAKS. *John* I. i. 6 Silence (good mother) heare the Embassie. **1615** HEYWOOD *Foure Prentises* I. i. (1874) II. 218 Didst thou deliver our strict Embassie.

3. The body of persons sent on a mission, or as a deputation, to a sovereign, etc.; the ambassador and his retinue, with their surroundings; also, the official residence of the ambassador.

1671 MILTON *P.R.* IV. 67 Embassies from regions far remote. **1764** GRAY *Corr. w. Nicholls* (1843) 59 A half promise of being declared secretary to the embassy. **1843** PRESCOTT *Mexico* (1851) I. 269 The embassy, consisting of two Aztec nobles, was accompanied by the governor. **1837** LYTTON *E. Maltrav.* (1851) 49 It was a brilliant ball at the Palazzo of the Austrian embassy at Naples. *Mod.* The Englishman inquired at the Embassy. They were married at the English Embassy.

embastardize, modernized spelling of IMBASTARDIZE, *Obs.*

emba'stille, *v. nonce-wd.* [ad. F. *embastiller*, f. *en-* in + *bastille* fort.] *trans.* To surround (a city) with forts, or as with forts.

1848 *Tait's Mag.* XV. 537 The embastilling Paris with camps, government by the sword.

embastioned: see EM- *prefix*.

† **em'basure.** *Obs. rare.* Also imbasure. [f. EMBASE *v.* + -URE.] = EMBASEMENT.

1656 JEANES *Fuln. Christ* 145 This composition will be a great imbasure unto the word. *Ibid.* 165 We may be dehorted from embasure of our natures by sin.

‖ **embat.** [Turk. (a. Pers.) *enbād*.] A northerly wind, that blows in Egypt.

1763 MACKENZIE in *Phil. Trans.* LIV. 77 The plague at Cairo begins to cease.. when the.. Embats or Etesian winds begin to blow.

† **em'bater.** *Obs. rare*$^{-0}$. (See quot.)

1736 BAILEY, *Embater*, the hole or look-through to aim a cross-bow. **1775** in ASH.

embathe, imbathe (ɛm-, ɪm'beɪð), *v. poet.* Also 6 inbathe, 6-7 imbath. [f. EN-, IN- + BATHE: cf. OF. *embaigner*, It. *imbagnare*.] *trans.* To bathe, immerse, dip; to bedew, drench, suffuse.

1593 *Tell-Trothe's N.Y. Gift* 42 Whosoever inbathe themselves therein. **1596** FITZ-GEFFRAY *Sir F. Drake* (1881) 22 Imbath your.. lofty quill In.. amber-dropping Castalie. **1606** CHAPMAN *Cont. Marlowe's Hero & L.* iii, [Her love] that with immortall wine Should be embath'd, and swim in more hearts ease Than there was water in the Sestian seas. **1634** MILTON *Comus* 835 Nereus.. gave her to his daughters to embathe In nectared lavers. **1641** —— *Reform.* 2 The sweet odour of the returning gospel [must] imbathe his soul with the fragrancy of heaven. **1776** MICKLE tr. *Camoen's Lusiad* 454 Embathe with gore Carpella's Cape. **1855** BAILEY *Mystic*, His limbs imbathed Amid immortal nymphs. **1879** FARRAR *St. Paul* I. 425 The perfumes with which Mary of Bethany embathed his feet.

b. *intr.* for *refl.*

1817 COLERIDGE, She dare.. embathe in heavenly light.

Hence **em'bathed**, *ppl. a.*, in quot. elliptical for ***embathed in perfume***, hence fragrant.

1590 SPENSER *Muiopotmos* 194 Embathed Balme.

embattle (ɛm-, ɪm'bæt(ə)l), *v.*[1] Forms: *α.* 4-6 em-, enbataile, 6 embattail(e, -ayl, (9 *arch.* embattail), 6 embatteil, 5-6 enbatel(l, -yl, 6-8 embattel(l, (6 enbattle, 7 embatle), 6- embattle. *β.* 5-6 imbatail, -ttail, 6-7 im-, inbattel, 7-8 imbattle. [ME. *embataile*, a. OF. *embataillier* to prepare for battle, f. *en-* (see EN-) + *bataille* BATTLE *sb.*[1]]

1. *trans.* To set (an army) in battle array. Also (Spenser) to arm, prepare for battle (an individual).

1393 GOWER *Conf.* II. 247 He fonde His enemy full embatailed. *c* **1450** *Merlin* 152 Telleth how thei were inbatailed a-gein the xj kynges. **1494** FABYAN VI. ccxvii. 236 Than the Normans imbateled ye fotemen. **1513** MORE *Rich. III* (1641) 429 When the Earle of Richmond knew.. the King was neere embattailed. **1570-87** HOLINSHED *Scot. Chron.* (1806) I. 329 Hereupon Malcolme imbattelling his people. **1596** SPENSER *F.Q.* II. v. 2 One in bright armes embatteiled full strong. *a* **1677** BARROW *Serm.* (1683) II. xi. 155 As a General.. mustereth and embattaileth his troops. **1755** CARTE *Hist. Eng.* IV. 457 It was three.. before the King's army was embattled. *c* **1840** DE QUINCEY *Autobiog. Sk.* Wks. I. 240 But once embattled, what should hinder them from detecting a flaw in their commission?

fig. **1593** NASHE *Christ's T.* (1613) 133 Embattelling our selues against sin, we must vse the weapons & arts of al Nations. **1636** B. JONSON *Discov.* (1692) 702 With ability to render the one lov'd, the other hated, by his proper embatteling them. **1809-10** COLERIDGE *Friend* (1865) 214 Yet let us not embattle our feelings against our reason.

2. *refl.* To form in order of battle; to take up a position in the field.

c **1450** LONELICH *Grail* XIII. 458 Eualach enbatailled him in the feeld. **1503-4** *Act. 19 Hen. VII*, c. 34 Pream., Dyvers.. inbatelled theymself.. contrarie to the Dutie of their allegeaunce. **1580** NORTH *Plutarch* (1676) 212 He commanded the first Bands.. should embattel themselves. **1844** *Blackw. Mag.* LVI. 531 Another had now slowly reared and embattled itself against the.. Crescent.

† **b.** *intr.* for *refl. Obs.*

1597 DANIEL *Civ. Wares* VII. lix, And near Northampton both Embattelling, Made now the very Heart of England bleed. **1662** (?) DK. ORMONDE *Laws & Ord. Army in Irel.*, Every.. Souldier.. shall keep silence when the Armie is.. marching or imbattailing. **1738** GLOVER *Leonidas* IX. 14 An ample space Where myriads might imbattle.

head

3. To fortify (a building, town, etc). Cf. EMBATTLE *v.*[2]; in many passages it is impossible to say which verb is intended. Also *fig.*

c **1380** *Sir Ferumb.* 1684 Oppon ech pere þar stent a tour: enbataild wyþ queynte engynne. **1598** YONG *Diana* 152 The wals loftie and strongly embattelled. **1622** HEYLIN *Cosmogr.* I. (1682) 183 Embattelled according to the modern Art of Fortifications. **1830** *Blackw. Mag.* XXVIII. 126 Fear builds castles and embattles cities. **1830** TENNYSON *Sonn. to J.M.K.*, To embattail and to wall about thy cause With iron-

embattle (ɛmˈbæt(ə)l), *v.*[2] Forms: 5 **enbatel**, 6 **enbatell, embatel**, 7 **embatle**, 7– **embattle**. [f. EN- + BATTLE *v.*[2]; app. not in OF.] *trans.* To furnish (a building, wall, etc.) with battlements. Also *fig.*

c **1400** [see EMBATTLED *ppl. a.*[2]]. **1463** *Bury Wills* (1850) 37, I wil..that the Rysbygate..be..enbatelyd substancyally to endure. **1530** PALSGR. 532, I enbatell a wall, I make bastylmentes upon it. **1538** LELAND *Itin.* III. 34 Treury.. embateling al the Waulles of the House in a maner made it a Castelle. **1610** HOLLAND *Camden's Brit.* I. 753 To fortifie and Kernel his mansion house, that is, to embatle it. **1627** SPEED *England Abr.* xxvi. §5 To build about and embattle a wall. **1823** RUTTER *Fonthill* 71 Another parapet, pierced and embattled. **1851** TURNER *Dom. Archit.* II. Introd. 23 Licenses to embattle manor-houses.

†**emˈbattle**, *sb. Obs. rare*[−1]. In 6 **embatel**. [f. EMBATTLE *v.*[2]] = BATTLEMENT.

a **1547** SURREY *Aeneid* II. 575 Griped for hold thembatel of the wall.

embattled (ɛmˈbæt(ə)ld), *ppl. a.*[1] [f. EMBATTLE *v.*[1] + -ED.]

1. Drawn up in battle array, marshalled for fight.

1475 *Bk. Noblesse* (1860) 32 He comaunded the oost embatailed not forto breke. **1667** MILTON *P.L.* XII. 213 On their embattelld ranks the waves return. **1677** HOBBES *Homer's Iliad* 137 See your men i' th' morn imbattled. **1790** COWPER *Iliad* II. 536 The chiefs..may range Together, the imbattled multitude. **1816** WORDSW. *Sonn. to Liberty* xlii, Bondage threatened by the embattled East. **1866** FELTON *Anc. & Mod. Gr.* I. vii. 108 The din of embattled squadrons.

b. *transf.* and *fig.*

1745 T. WARTON *Pleas. Melanch.* 294 At her presence mild the embattled clouds Disperse in air. **1837–9** HALLAM *Hist. Lit.* I. I. iv. §53. 297 The embattled legions of ignorance.

2. Filled or covered with troops in battle array. Also *fig.*

1593 NASHE *Christ's T.* (1613) 56 The Element euery night was embattailed with Armed men. **1725** POPE *Odyss.* XI. 369 Castor glorious on th' embattled plain. **1842** ORDERSON *Creol.* xviii. 217 He was..anxious to be at the first brunt of the embattled field.

3. Fortified, made strong or secure against attack. Cf. EMBATTLED *ppl. a.*[2]

1765 BLACKSTONE *Comm.* I. 263 That no subject can build a castle, or house of strength imbatteled..without the licence of the king. **1834** BOWRING *Minor Morals, Perseverance* 146 Every feudal chief was obliged to shut himself up in high and embattled towers. **1879** DIXON *Windsor* I. iii. 28 Each manor was embattled for defence.

4. *fig.* That is under attack or pressure; subject to or characterized by conflict; threatened, assailed.

1961 B. LIPPINCOTT *Indians, Privateers, & High Soc.* iv. 54 One historical authority presents laborious and circuitous testimony..that Massachusetts was behind the clouds settling down on the embattled Gorton. **1971** A. SAMPSON *New Anat. Brit.* xxxvi. 627 In its century of existence the Congress has become as much an embattled institution..as the government or companies it is fighting. **1972** *Observer* 25 June 5/3 He was transferred to Olinda and Recife, the ancient See which is now his embattled base. **1978** *N.Y. Times* 30 Mar. A14/1 Miller, the embattled president of the United Mine Workers, suffered..'a mild stroke' today. **1983** *Times* 18 Feb. 15/2 UDS, the embattled high-street retailing group, has agreed an all-share bid from Hanson Trust. **1984** *Ibid.* 13 Jan. 13/1 Britain's embattled newspaper groups are beginning to see better days.

embattled (ɛmˈbæt(ə)ld), *ppl. a.*[2] [f. EMBATTLE *v.*[2] + -ED[1].]

1. *Arch.* Furnished with battlements, crenellated.

c **1400** *Rom. Rose*, I saugh a gardyn..walled welle, With high walles enbatailled. **1525** LD. BERNERS *Froiss.* II. clvii. [cliii.] 431 The whiche castell was enbatylled. **1538** LELAND *Itin.* II. 40 An embatelid Waulle now sore yn ruine. **1769** GRAY in *Poems & Lett.* (1775) 369 This seat..is an ancient hall-house, with a very large tower embattled. **1867** LADY HERBERT *Cradle L.* vii. 195 The old embattled walls still standing.

2. Having an edge or outline shaped like a battlement; crenellated; *spec.* in *Heraldry*.

c **1386** CHAUCER *Nonne Pr. T.* 40 His comb was.. Enbateled [*other texts* And batayld] as it were a castel wall. **1555** *Fardle Facions* II. vii. 160 A copintancke, embatled aboute like a turrette. **1572** BOSSEWELL *Armorie* II. 29 b, Beareth Sables, & Gules, embatyled..three Fer-de-molyns d'Argente. **1753** CHAMBERS *Cycl. Supp.*, Embattled Line, in heraldry. **1803** REES *Cycl.*, *Bretessed*..a..charge.. embattled on both sides opposite to each other. **1834** PLANCHÉ *Brit. Costume* 222 Hats and caps..with embattled or escalloped edges. **1864** BOUTELL *Heraldry Hist. & Pop.* iii. (ed. 3) 18 A Fesse dancette or embattled. **1884** *Harper's Mag.* Mar. 529/2 The embattled cliffs and the..sea fill the view.

embattlement (ɛmˈbæt(ə)lmənt). Also 6 **embatyl-**. [f. EMBATTLE *v.*[2] + -MENT.] = BATTLEMENT.

1538 LELAND *Itin.* VIII. 107 The Enbatylments of it wer full of Pinacles. **1572** BOSSEWELL *Armorie* II. 77 b, A Crowne murall..was made like embattlementes of a wall. **1886** *Sat. Rev.* 10 July 48 The mighty towers and embattlements..yet rear themselves up proudly.

embattling (ɛmbætlɪŋ), *vbl. sb.*[1] [f. EMBATTLE *v.*[1] + -ING[1].] The action of the verb EMBATTLE[1]; **a.** arraying (troops) in order of battle; **b.** taking up a position for fighting.

1531 ELYOT *Gov.* I. viii. (1557) 21 The..embattaylynge of his enemies. **1598** BARRET *Theor. Warres* III. ii. 47 These sundry sorts of imbattailling of men. **1611** CHAPMAN *Iliad* XVI. 154 Th' embattelling of horse and foot. **1697** POTTER *Antiq. Greece* III. vi. (1715) 58 The Macedonians were the most famous for this Way of Imbattling. **1712** STEELE *Spect.* No. 502 ⁋5 To enumerate..the embattling of armies.. would be to transgress the bounds of this paper.

pl. **1677** EARL ORRERY *Art of War* 8 The Velites..both in Embattellings and Campings..were mixt with the other three [bodies].

embattling (ɛmˈbætlɪŋ), *vbl. sb.*[2] [f. EMBATTLE *v.*[2] + -ING[1].] *concr.* in *Her.*; see quot. and cf. EMBATTLED *ppl. a.*[2] 2.

1753 CHAMBERS *Cycl. Supp.* s.v., The heralds express this embattled line by the term crenellé; and when it has the embattling on both sides..they then call it bretessé.

emˈbattling, *ppl. a.* [f. EMBATTLE *v.*[1] + -ING[2].] That forms in order of battle. *fig.*

1794 COLERIDGE *Relig. Musings* vi, Embattling interests on each other rush.

embay (ɛmˈbeɪ), *v.*[1] Also 6 **imbay**. [f. EM- + BAY *sb.*[2] and [3].]

1. *trans.* To lay (a vessel) within a bay. Also of the action of the wind or tide: To force (a vessel) into a bay; to detain within a bay.

1600 HAKLUYT *Voy.* III. 149 Being immediately embayed in the Grand bay. **1628** DIGBY *Jrnl.* 21 When wee were come with our shippes as near the shore..as wee could, for feare of being embayed. **1702** C. MATHER *Magn. Chr.* I. i. (1852) 44 He found himself embayed within a mighty head of land. **1810** *Edin. Rev.* XVII. 150 Many small whales..are yearly embayed and killed. **1870** *Illust. Lond. News* 29 Oct. 438 The headland before her must be weathered, unless she would be embayed and stranded.

b. *transf.* ? with a reference to BAY *sb.*[3]

1851 RUSKIN *Stones Ven.* (1874) I. xviii. 192 Some of them might miss the real doors, and be driven into the intervals, and embayed there.

2. *pass.* Of a town: To be enclosed within a bay.

1825 WATERTON *Wand. S. Amer.* IV. ii. 313 The town Castries is quite embayed. **1842** STERLING *Let.* in Carlyle *Life* III. iv. (1872) 199 The town..is not at all embayed, though there is some little shelter for shipping within the mole.

3. *refl.* Of the sea: To form a bay. *rare.*

1653 HOLCROFT *Procopius* III. 97 But finding..the sea to embay it self on both sides the Land.

4. To enclose (as in a bay); to shut in; to envelop, surround; also *fig.*

1583 STANYHURST *Aeneis* II. (1880) 50 Laocoon..Is to sone embayed with wrapping girdle y coompast. **1624** CAPT. SMITH *Virginia* I. 16 We found our selues imbayed with a mightie headland. **1772–84** COOK *Voy.* (1790) V. 1860 We were, in some degree, embayed by the ice. **1792** *Fortn. Ramble* xi. 69 Bridder Water..looks as if embayed in mountains. **1862** G. P. SCROPE *Volcanoes* 176 The waters were embayed in eddies or pools. **1876** BANCROFT *Hist. U.S.* II. xxii. 32 He found himself embayed in a labyrinth without end.

†**emˈbay**, *v.*[2] *Obs. poet.* [f. EN- *pref.* + BAY *v.*[5]]

1. *trans.* To plunge (in a liquid); to bathe; hence, to drench, wet; to imbrue, steep.

1590 SPENSER *F.Q.* I. x. 27 Sad repentance used to embay His bodie in salt water. **1594** ?GREENE *Selimus* Wks. (Grosart) XIV. 223 Our mouthes in honie to embay. **1600** FAIRFAX *Tasso* XII. lxii, Their Swords both points and edges sharpe embay In purple bloud, where so they hit or light. **1762** CHURCHILL *Ghost*, His horse, Whose sides, in their own blood embay'd, E'en to the bone were open laid.

2. *fig.* **a.** To bathe (oneself) in sleep, sunshine. **b.** Of sleep: To bedew, steep, suffuse, pervade.

1590 SPENSER *Muiopotmos* 200 In the warme sunne he doth himselfe embay. **1590** —— *F.Q.* I. ix. 13 Whiles every sense the humour sweet embay'd. **1610** G. FLETCHER *Christ's Vict.* in Farr's *S.P.* (1847) 63 And all about, embayed in soft sleep, A herd of charmed beasts aground were spread.

embayed (ɛmˈbeɪd), *ppl. a.* [f. EMBAY *v.*[1]]

1. Enclosed in, or as in, a bay. Also, of a shore: Formed into bays, hollowed out by the sea.

1835 MUDIE *Brit. Birds* (1841) I. 125 A shore, embayed and torn by the sea. **1839** MURCHISON *Silur. Syst.* I. xxxvii. 516 The embayed flats..are good examples of the fertile soil. **1851** RUSKIN *Stones Ven.* (1874) I. i. 17 Embayed fragments of the Roman wreck. **1870** YEATS *Nat. Hist. Comm.* 15 The embayed waters of Mexico. **1882** *Nature* XXVI. 151 Great West Bay..bears..the ugly name of 'Dead Man's Bay' from an embayed vessel caught in a South-west gale seldom escaping shipwreck.

2. Forming a bay or recess. See BAY *sb.*[3]

1824–9 LANDOR *Imag. Conv.* (1846) II. 241 The embayed window.

embayment (ɛmˈbeɪmənt). [f. as prec. + -MENT.]

1. a. The action of forming into a bay. **b.** *concr.* A portion of water or coast forming a bay.

1815 SCOTT *Guy M.* xl, The line of sea-coast, with all its varied curves, indentures, and embayments. **1853** G. JOHNSTON *Nat. Hist. E. Bord.* I. 10 Occasionally lingering in some embayment..to collect their waters. **1879** LE CONTE *Elem. Geol.* 525 The Mississippi probably commenced to run into the Tertiary Embayment. **1884** *St. Nicholas* II. 534 It is a larger embayment than that where the gig came to grief.

2. A bay-like recess (of a window).

1848 *Tait's Mag.* XV. 102 The deep embayment of her favourite window.

†**'embe**, *prep. Obs.* Also 1 **emb**. A variant of OE. *ymbe*, ME. UMBE, q.v., about, around, etc.

a **1000** *Athelstan* 5 (Gr.) Embe Brunanburh. *a* **1000** *Menolog.* (Gr.) 210 Emb eahta niht. *c* **1175** *Lamb. Hom.* 51 Þe bitacninge þe ic habbe embe ispeken. *Ibid.* 219 Ne meȝ nan iscefte..understonden embe god. *c* **1205** LAY. 6563 Æuere he þohte embe uuel. *c* **1315** SHOREHAM 141 Ine thylke songe That ich was embe oure faye.

Hence in OE. and early ME. compounds: **embhuȝa** [OE. *hoȝa* care], anxiety; **embsniðe** *v.* [OE. *sniðan* to cut], to circumcise; **embeþonk** [OE. *þanc* thought], anxiety or thought about; **embe-uten** *adv.* [OE. *úton* without], round about.

c **1000** *Ags. Gosp.* Matt. vi. 34 Æghwylc dæȝ hæfð ȝenoh on hys aȝenum ymbhoȝan [*c* **1160** *Hatton* embhuȝan]. *Ibid.* Mark xiv. 47 Soðlice an of þam þe ðar embe-uton [*c* **1160** *Hatton* embe-uten] stodon his swurde abræed. *Ibid.* Luke ii. 210 Þe ehta daȝas ȝefyllede wæron þæt ðæt cild emsnyden [*c* **1160** *Hatton* embsnyðen] wære. *c* **1175** *Lamb. Hom.* 81 Þet me sculde in þe ehtuþe dei þet knaue child embsniþen. *c* **1200** *Trin. Coll. Hom.* 87 Þe bileffulle mannes heorte..ben wasshen of þe embeþonke of fleshliche lustes.

†**embeam** (ɛmˈbiːm), *v. Obs.* [f. EN- + BEAM *sb.*] *trans.* To cast beams (of light) upon, irradiate; to radiate (light).

1610 G. FLETCHER *Christ's Vict.* in Farr's *S.P.* (1848) 75 But now so lively colours did embeam His sparkling forehead. **1652** BENLOWES *Theoph.* I. xcix. 13 Faith in Thee [may] embeam my Night. **1652** JER. COLLIER in Benlowes *Theoph.* B 4 b, Loves self in her his Flame embeams.

†**emˈbeauty**, *v. Obs. rare*[−1]. In 6 **enbewte**. [f. EN- + BEAUTY *sb.*] *trans.* To put beauty on (a person or thing); to beautify.

1523 SKELTON *Garl. Laurel* 868 Whom dame nature.. Hath fresshly enbewted.

embeazle, obs. f. EMBEZZLE.

embed, imbed (ɛm-, ɪmˈbɛd), *v.* [f. EN-, IN- + BED *sb.* (*Embed* is now the more common form.)]

1. a. *trans.* To fix firmly in a surrounding mass of some solid material. Also *refl.*

α. **1794** SULIVAN *View Nat.* I. viii. 62 Calcareous substances are in general found where flints are embedded. **1861** HULME tr. *Moquin-Tandon* II. III. iv. 147 Leeches.. embed themselves in the earth. **1879** J. TIMBS in *Cassell's Techn. Educ.* IV. 6/2 Iron girders embedded in brickwork and cement. **1882** *Standard* 5 Sept. 6/1 The workman takes one diamond and embeds it in heated cement.

β. **1778** WHITEHURST *Inquiry Earth* xii. 90 Marine exuviæ found imbedded near the tops of mountains. **1793** M. BAILLIE *Morb. Anat.* xxiv. 302 Masses of the same sort of substance, lying as it were imbedded in the brain. **1816** R. JAMESON *Char. Min.* (1817) 130 Crystals are said to be imbedded, when they are completely inclosed in another mineral. **1866** LIVINGSTONE *Jrnl.* (1873) I. i. 29 Thus.. insects are..imbedded in the gum-copal. **1950** C. R. HINE *Machine Tools for Engineers* xii. 240 The fine, sharp abrasive particles become imbedded in the lap and it is ready for use. **1972** *Physics Bull.* May 284/3 Indeed, the liquid crystalline properties inherent in this bilayer structure are almost certainly important for the organization of molecules imbedded in the membrane as well as for controlling transport through it.

b. *fig. spec.* in *Linguistics* and *Sci.*

α. **1835** LYTTON *Rienzi* I. xii, The light..embedded, as it were, in vast masses of shade. **1855** BAIN *Senses & Int.* II. ii. §12 The sensation is embedded in a movement. **1870** LOWELL *Among my Bks.* Ser. I. (1873) 79 The winged seeds of his thought embed themselves in the memory. **1961** [see EMBEDDED *ppl. a.*].

β. **1855** BAIN *Senses & Int.* II. ii. §13 The same optical impression..may..be imbedded in a great many different muscular impressions. **1875** MAINE *Hist. Inst.* i. 14 Parts of these..writings are imbedded in the text of the Book. **1969** *N.Y. Rev. Bks.* 16 Jan. 4/4 Some of the divergences between Freud and Jung are, however, better attributed to the fact that they chose opposed solutions to the problem of how to imbed the idea of the unconscious into already existing traditions of Western thought. **1971** *Nature* 18 June 437/2 It will be noted that the regions of the three brightest sources are further imbedded in very dense areas; in fact, they are close to the centroids of the Coma cluster. **1971** POWELL & HIGMAN *Finite Simple Groups* iii. 174 The process simply imbeds one Chevalley group in another.

c. *transf.* Also in wider senses suggested by the etymology.

1848 CLOUGH *Amours de Voy.* III. 302 Nemi, imbedded in wood, Nemi inurned in the hill! **1849** GROTE *Greece* (1862) V. II. lx. 300 A more considerable stream, flowing deeply imbedded between lofty banks. **1852** M. ARNOLD *Poems, Emped. on Etna* 11, Through whose [Typho's] heart Etna drives her roots of stone To imbed them in the sea.

2. Said of the surrounding mass of material: To enclose firmly. Also *fig.*

1853 KANE *Grinnell Exp.* xxvi. (1856) 210 Fields of new ice..imbedded them in a single night. **1855** I. TAYLOR *Restor. Belief* 215 Those Seven Epistles..imbed our problem. **1887** *Harper's Mag.* May 955 A soft sweetish pulp ..embeds the two beans.

Hence **em'bedded** *ppl. a.*, **em'beddedness, em'bedding** *vbl. sb.* and *ppl. a.*

1830 LYELL *Princ. Geol.* I. 85 Others ascribed the imbedded fossil bodies to some plastic power which resided in the earth in the early ages of the world. **1863** —— *Antiq. Man* 8, I have spoken of the embedding of organic bodies and human remains in peat. **1877** W. THOMSON *Voy. Challenger* I. ii. 113 The elegant forms of the imbedded shells. **1877** E. CONDER *Bas. Faith* vii. 315 Smelting out the pure gold of revealed truth from the imbedding ore. **1922** WHITEHEAD *Princ. Relativ.* ii. 15 Fact..is not the sum of factors; it is rather the concreteness (or, embeddedness) of factors, and the concreteness of an inexhaustible relatedness among inexhaustible relata. **1937** *Mind* XLVI. 83 When we know how to deal with the erst-while novelty, when we have 'got it taped', it falls into embeddedness and becomes, or engenders, a part of ourselves. **1952** T. PARSONS *Social System* 361 Philosophical investigation, as distinguished from the general imbeddedness of philosophical problems.. in any system of action. **1961** C. S. SMITH in *Language* XXXVII. 346 When one sentence contains another, the latter sentence will be said to be 'embedded'. *Ibid.* 348 Together the three embedding rules produce all sentences that contain adjectives and exclude ungrammatical sentences. *Ibid.* 360 An embedded compared adjective has the widest possible scope in any given sentence. **1963** *Economist* 7 Sept. 832/1 Man's social embeddedness. **1966** G. N. LEECH *Eng. in Advertising* ii. 20 The prepositional phrase in 'a pipeful of good tobacco' is an embedded adverbial group. **1968** *Language* XLIV. 32 Any rules that are not concerned with embedded sentences..always treat a constituent sentence as an unanalysable unit.

†**em'bedlam,** *v. Obs.* [f. EN- + BEDLAM.] *trans.* To put into Bedlam; hence to drive mad.

a **1628** F. GREVILLE *Alaham* II. ii. (1633) 28 Furie! then spurre thyself, embedlam wit.

embedment (ɛm'bɛdmənt). [f. EMBED *v.* + -MENT.] **a.** The action of embedding, the state of being embedded. **b.** *concr.* Something which embeds; a 'bed' of stonework, etc.

1828-40 TYTLER *Hist. Scot.* (1864) I. 304 The large oak pillars..rested in an embedment of strong masonwork.

embeggar: see EM- *prefix*.

embel, embelf, erron. forms of next.

1692 COLES, *Embel.* **1775** ASH, *Embel, embelf.*

†'**embelif,** *adv.* and *a. Astron. Obs.* [a. OF. phrase *en belif*: see BELEF.]

A. *adv.* In an oblique direction, obliquely.

c **1391** CHAUCER *Astrol.* II. §28 These same signes..ben cleped tortuos signes or kroked signes for they arisen embelif on oure Orisonte.

B. *adj.* Oblique.

c **1391** CHAUCER *Astrol.* II. §28 *heading*, To knowe the assencions of signes in the embelif cercle in euery regioun, I Mene, in circulo obliquo. *Ibid.*, The embelif orisonte.. ouerkervyth the equinoxial in embelif angles. **1413** LYDG. *Pilgr. Sowle* v. i. (1859) 70, I saw the spyeres tornen.. eueriche within other, by contrarious mouyng, and by embelif.

Hence †**embelif** *v. Obs. intr.*, to be oblique.

1413 LYDG. *Pilgr. Sowle* v. i. (1859) 70 There was a Cercle embelyfyng somwhat.

embellish (ɛm'bɛlɪʃ) *v.* Forms: 4-5 embelyssh, (4 enbelyse, embellis), 5 embellissh, -ysh, (embelese, -yse, -yce, enbelis, -issh, embelsh), 6- embellish. Also 7-8 imbelish, imbellish. [a. OF. *embelliss-* lengthened stem of *embellir*, f. *en-* (see EN-) + *bel* beautiful.]

1. †**a.** To render beautiful (*obs.* in general sense). **b.** To beautify with adventitious adornments; to ornament.

c **1340** *Gaw. & Gr. Knt.* 1033 & enbelyse his burȝ with his bele chere. *c* **1385** CHAUCER *L.G.W.*, *Lucrece*, Teeres ful of hevytee Embelysshed [*v.r.* embelesed, enbelised] hire wifly chastitee. *c* **1440** *Partonope* 5981 Wyth beaute..nature Wold so embelyce ony oo creature. **1474** CAXTON *Chesse* 9 The robes of purpure..enbellissheth the body. **1579** SPENSER *Sheph. Cal.* Feb., It was embellisht with blossomes fayre. **1601** HOLLAND *Pliny* II. 185 The Elm [yields] a waterish humour, which is very proper to imbelish the skin. **1679-88** *Secr. Serv. Money Chas. & Jas.* 49 For writing, flourishing, and embellishing, partly in gold, a letre sent to the Emperor of..Morocco. **1734** tr. *Rollin's Anc. Hist.* (1827) II. IV. §1. 215 His hair embellished with artificial locks. **1801** STRUTT *Sports & Past.* I. iii. 36 Bridles.. embellished with bits of yellow gold. **1872** YEATS *Techn. Hist. Comm.* 248 The objects thus embellished were jewel-cases.

c. *fig.*; now often with sense to 'dress up', heighten (a narration) with fictitious additions.

1447 BOKENHAM *Seyntys* Introd. 3 Hys newe poetrye Enbelshyd wyth colours of rethoryk. **1482** CAXTON (*title*) Higden's Polychronicon..emprynted and sette in forme by me William Caxton and a lytel embelysshed fro tholde makyng. **1649** SELDEN *Laws of Eng.* (1739) II. xvii. 90 To imbellish mens minds with..Learning that may gain them preferment. **1722** WOLLASTON *Relig. Nat.* vii. 154 False notions of glory: imbellishd indeed by servile wits. **1726** SWIFT *To a Lady*, I shall..with books my mind embellish. **1772** SIR W. JONES *Ess.* ii. 205 A simple and agreeable melody, which will..embellish [the words]. **1801** HOME in *Phil. Trans.* XCI. 329 Events..probably..much exaggerated and embellished. **1850** MRS. JAMESON *Leg. Monast. Ord.* (1863) 53 A long life..embellished by elegant pursuits. *Mod.* The story is true in substance, but has been greatly embellished.

†**2.** *fig.* To brighten (in feeling), cheer. *Obs.*

1481 CAXTON *Myrr.* I. v. 17 But they were embelisshid moche of that they sawe the firmament thus torne and so nobly to holde his cours.

embellished (ɛm'bɛlɪʃt), *ppl. a.* [f. prec. + -ED[1].] Beautified, adorned, illustrated.

1598 FLORIO *Dict.* Ep. Ded. 2 Your embellisht grace. **1845** J. PYE *Patron. Brit. Art* ii. 55 Embellished books.

embellisher (ɛm'bɛlɪʃə(r)). [f. as prec. + -ER.] He who or that which beautifies or adorns.

1479 CAXTON *Chaucer's Boeth.* Pref., The..first founder and embelisher of ornate eloquence in our English.. Chaucer. **1712** STEELE *Spect.* No. 521 ⁋4 And may be call'd Embellishers. **1813** BYRON *Giaour* xviii. *note*, Sultan Giamschid, the embellisher of Istakhar. **1871** SMILES *Charac.* ix. (1876) 260 Grace is a sweetener and embellisher of life.

embellishing (ɛm'bɛlɪʃɪŋ), *vbl. sb.* [f. EMBELLISH *v.* + -ING[1].] The action or process of making beautiful; also *concr.* ornamentation.

1641 MILTON *Ch. Govt.* ii. (1851) 103 The devices and imbellishings of mans imagination. **1678** CUDWORTH *Intell. Syst.* 33 For the Adorning and Embellishing of the Corporeal World to us.

embellishing (ɛm'bɛlɪʃɪŋ), *ppl. a.* [f. EMBELLISH *v.* + -ING[2].] That embellishes or beautifies.

1545 T. RAYNOLD *Womans Book* Y 5 The embellisshinge or bellifieing medicines whereof I entende to speke here. **1673** *Lady's Call.* I. ii. 19 Meekness is so..peculiarly embellishing to women.

em'bellishment. [f. as prec. + -MENT.]

1. The action or process of embellishing or beautifying; decoration, ornamentation.

1623 COCKERAM *Eng. Dict.* II, *Beautifying*, Embellishment, Decoration. **1678** *Trans. Crt. Spain* 206 The thing that contributed most to the embellishment of that Festival, was the great abundance of Ladies. **1711** ADDISON *Spect.* No. 1 ⁋8, I am sensible they might not tend to the Embellishment of my paper. **1868** MILMAN *St. Paul's* 340 A Turkish merchant devoted no less a sum than 10,000*l.* to the internal embellishment of St. Paul's.

2. That which embellishes or beautifies, *lit.* and *fig.*; an ornament, decoration, setting off; *esp.* a grace of diction or composition, a poetical image, episode, or hyperbole; also, in pejorative sense, an exaggeration (cf. EMBELLISH *v.* 1 c).

1632 QUARLES *Div. Fancies* IV. lxxx. (1660) 165 But now, has not the least Imbellishment Of Heav'nly knowledge. **1662** FULLER *Worthies* (1840) III. 256 Abatement is made for poetical embellishments. **1664** H. MORE *Myst. Iniq.* 223 A book that has some pleasing embellishments on the back. **1717** LADY M. W. MONTAGUE *Lett.* II. xliv. 22 A relation, that has..received many embellishments from my hand. **1772** PENNANT *Tours Scotl.* (1774) 343 Nor are the lofty headlands a less embellishment. **1830** D'ISRAELI *Chas. I*, III. ii. 18 Formed for peace, and the embellishments of life.

†**em'benched,** *ppl. a. Obs. rare*[−1]. [f. EN- + BENCH *sb.* + -ED.] Formed into 'benches'; cf. BENCH *sb.* 6, 7, and *v.* 2.

1599 NASHE *Lent. Stuffe* 9 Cerdicus..was the first..that on those embenched shelues stampt his footing.

ember[1] ('ɛmbə(r)). Forms: 1 æ̆merȝe, 4 aym-, em, eemer, 5 eymbre, -bery, (6 *pl.* embries, emmers, *Sc.* amer-, ammer-, amyrris,) 6-7 imber, 9 *dial.* yummer. [OE. *ǽmerge* wk. fem., corresponds to OHG. *eimuria* (MHG. *eimere*), ON. *eimyrja* (Da. *emmer*, Sw. *mörja*):— OTeut. **aimuzjôn-*; for the suffix cf. Goth. *jukuzi* (stem *jukuzjâ-*) yoke. The ME. forms with *ay- ey-* point to adoption from ON. rather than to descent from OE. The disappearance of the vowel of the original second syllable occasioned the insertion of the euphonic *b*, normal between *m* and *r*.]

1. A small piece of live coal or wood in a half-extinguished fire. Chiefly in *pl.*: The smouldering ashes of a fire.

c **1000** *Ags. Leechdoms* III. 30 Nim ðu clatan moran..& berec hy on hate æmerȝean. ?*c* **1390** *Form of Cury* in Warner *Antiq. Culin.* 15 Take chyches, and..lay hem in hoot aymers. **1398** TREVISA *Barth. De P.R.* x. ix (Tollem. MS.), Also fyry emeris [**1535** emers; **1582** embers] is rauischid and meuid upwarde by rauischynge of wynde. *c* **1440** *Promp. Parv.* 136 Eymbre, hote aschys [**1499** eymery or synder, hote asshes], *pruna.* **1513** DOUGLAS *Æneis* VI. iii. 137 The reliqueis and the dry ammeris syne Thai slokkin. **1555** *Fardle Facions* I. v. 72 They feede them [children] with.. rootes, rosted in the embries. **1600** HAKLUYT *Voy.* (1810) III. 258 They heat it [flesh] a little upon imbers of coales. **1632** MILTON *Penseroso* 79 Glowing embers..Teach light to counterfeit a gloom. **1719** YOUNG *Busiris* I. i. (1757) 13 Sleeping embers which will rise in flames. **1838-42** ARNOLD *Hist. Rome* II. xxxvii. 475 Only the expiring embers of a great fire. *a* **1849** POE *Raven*, Each separate dying ember Wrought its ghost upon the floor. **1874** SPURGEON *Treas. Dav.* Ps. cii. 3 The last comforting ember is quenched.

2. *fig.*

1513 MORE *Edw. V.* Ep. Ded. 3 To revive that which hath for a long time been raked up in the embers of oblivion. **1650** R. STAPYLTON *Strada's Low C. Warres* I. 20 But the secret lay not long in the Embers. **1787** BENTHAM *Def. Usury* 178 Success does not..arise out of the embers of ill-success. **1874** BANCROFT *Footpr. Time* i. 97 The embers of independence..broke forth in war.

3. *Comb.* **ember-bread** (see quot.; but the statement is app. a fiction to explain EMBER-DAYS.)

1681 WHARTON *Fasts & Fest.* Wks. (1683) 30 A Cake baked under the Embers or Ashes, which was called.. Ember-bread. **1796** PEGGE *Anonym.* (1809) 135.

ember[2] ('ɛmbə(r)). Now only *attrib.* and in *Comb.* Forms: α. 1 ymbren, 6-8 embring, -yng, 6 im-, ymbring, 6-7 imb-, embering. β. in *Comb.* 3 umbri-(*ü*), ymbri-, 4 ymber-, 5 embyr-, ymbre-, 6 embre-, (amber-), 7- ember. [The OE. *ymbren* (app. neut.: pl. *ymbren*), perh. a corruption (due to attrib. use) of OE. *ymbryne* masc., period, revolution of time, f. *ymb* about, round + *ryne* course, running.

It seems however not wholly impossible that the word may have been due to popular etymology working upon some Vulgar Lat. corruption of *quatuor tempora*; cf. Ger. *quatember* Ember-tide; for the possibility of OE. *mb* for L. *mp*, and for the suffix, cf. OE. *ęmbren* from L. *amp(h)ora*. The ON. *imbru(-dagar)*, OSw. *ymber(-dagar)* appear to be ad. Eng.; OSw. had also *tamper-dagar* from *tempora*.]

The English name of the four periods of fasting and prayer (L. *quatuor tempora*) appointed by the Church to be observed respectively in the four seasons of the year. Each of these fasts occupies three days, viz. a Wednesday and the following Friday and Saturday; these are called *Ember days*, and the weeks in which they occur are called *Ember weeks*. Since the Council of Placentia A.D. 1095, the Ember days have been the Wednesday, Friday, and Saturday next following (1) the first Sunday in Lent, (2) Whitsunday, (3) Holy Cross Day, 14 Sept., (4) St. Lucia's Day, 13 Dec. In the Roman Church the Ember-Saturdays, and in the Church of England the Sundays immediately following, are the days on which ordinations usually take place.

†**1.** As an independent *sb.*; = *ember-day* (only in α. forms). *Obs.*

c **1010** *Laws of Æthelred* (Thorpe) VI. xxiii, Ymbren & fæstena. *Ibid.* xxv, Heah-freolsdaȝum & riht-ymbrenum. *c* **1000** *Ags. Gosp.* Rubric to *Luke* viii. 40 Ðis sceal on friȝedæȝ on þære pentecostenes wucan to þam ymbrene. **1547** SALESBURY *Welsh Dict.*, *Katcor* [i.e. cadgor, a fast], Embryng. **1573** TUSSER *Husb.* (1878) 28 Keepe Embrings wel, and fasting daies.

2. *attrib.* and *Comb.*, as **ember** (†**embring**)**-day, -fast, -Friday, -time, -tide, -week**; **ember-eve,** the vigil of an Ember day.

α. *a* **1000** *Laws of Ælfred* xliii, On iiii. ymbren-wican. *a* **1036** *Laws of Cnut* (Eccl.) xvi, Si hit Ymbren-fæsten si hit lengcten-fæsten. *Ibid.* xvii, We forbeodað ordal & aðas freolsdaȝum & ymbren-daȝum. **1502** *Ord. Crysten Men* (W. de Worde) II. xvi. (1506) 125 To faste foure tymes in the yere the ymbrynge tyme. **1548** *Act 2 & 3 Edw. VI*, c. 19 Preamb., Abstinence, which hath been used..upon..the Embring Days, and other Days. **1584** R. SCOT *Discov. Witchcr.* XII. xiv. 200 He..must come to church upon an embering fridaie. **1590** TARLETON *News Purgat.* (1844) 64 [The pope] that made the imbering-weekes in honour of his faire and beautifull curtizan Imbra. **1563-87** FOXE *A. & M.* (1684) II. 30/1 Counselling..the said Roger Dods, upon an Embring day, to sup with Bread and Cheese. **1752** CARTE *Hist. Eng.* III. 227 Abstinence from flesh in Lent, and on.. embring days.

β. *a* **1225** *Ancr. R.* 70 Holdeþ silence..iðe Umbridawes [*v.r.* ymbri wikes]. **138.** WYCLIF *Serm.* Sel. Wks. II. 203 þe Wednesday Gospel in ymber weke in Septembre moneþe. *c* **1440** *Promp. Parv.* 139 Embyrday, *angarium vel quatuor temporum.* **1481** CAXTON *Myrr.* III. x. 155 By the kalender we knowe..the ymbre dayes. *c* **1550** BALE *K. Johan* 41 Bothe amber dayes & lentes. **1550** *Wyll of Deuyll* (Collier) 4, I geue..the Embredays to pope Calixtus. **1608** SHAKS. *Per.* I. Cho. 6 A song of old..sung at festivals, On ember-eves, and holy ales. **1622** MIDDLETON, etc. *Old Law* III. i, Are all fallen into fasting-days and Ember-weeks? **1634** CANNE *Necess. Separ.* (1849) 117 And pope Calixtus in the year 206 ordained Ember fasts. **1704** NELSON *Fest. & Fasts* II. iii. (1739) 469 These Fasts..may..be said to be Ember Days. **1726** AYLIFFE *Parerg.* 281 The four Seasons of the year called the Ember-Weeks. **1844** LINGARD *Anglo-Sax. Ch.* (1858) I. App. 386 The Ember fasts, on Wednesday, Friday, and Saturday, four times in the year. **1849-53** ROCK *Ch. of Fathers* IV. xi. 64 On the ember-days, the deacon and subdeacon wore..the chasuble. **1849** MISS MULOCK *Ogilvies* xii. (1875) 90 How near it is to Ember weeks.

ember.[3] Also imber, immer, emmer, ammer. [a. Norw. *emmer(-gaas)*; Icel. has *himbrimi* older *himbrin*; Faroic *imbrim* (Vigf.).] A kind of sea-fowl (*Colymbus Immer* Linn. Pennant) frequenting the seas about Orkney, a variety of the Northern Diver or Loon (*Colymbus glacialis*) to which the name is sometimes given. Chiefly in Comb. as *ember-goose, -diver.*

1744 PRESTON *Zetland* in *Phil. Trans.* XLIII. 61/2 The Ember-Goose, which is said to hatch her Egg under her Wing. **1802** G. MONTAGU *Ornith. Dict.* (1833) 267 Imber-Diver—a name for the Loon. **1822** SCOTT *Pirate* xxi, Be mine the imber-goose to play. **1885** SWAINSON *Prov. Names Brit. Birds* (E.D.S.) 213 Immer or Ember (Orkney), Imber Diver (Ireland), Ammer or Emmer goose (Aberdeen, E. Lothian).

embered ('ɛmbəd), *ppl. a.* [f. EMBER[1] + -ED[2].] **a.** Strewn with embers; **b.** Burnt to embers.

1796 SOUTHEY *Joan of Arc* II. 468 On the white-ember'd hearth Then heapt up fresh fuel. **1863** W. LANCASTER *Præterita* 26 An old crone leaning at an ember'd fire.

embering, obs., var. of EMBER².

†**emberlucock**, *v. Obs. rare.* [ad. F. *emburelucocquer*, a nonce-wd. of fanciful formation.] To bewilder, confuse.

1653 URQUHART *Rabelais* I. vi, Never emberlucock..your spirits with these vaine thoughts and idle conceits.

†**em'better**, *v. Obs.* Also 7 imbetter [f. EN- + BETTER, *a.*] *trans.* To make better.

a. *c* **1583** PECKHAM in Hakluyt *Voyages* (1600) III. 181 Then..estates of such as now liue in want shall be embettered. **1625** LONG tr. *Barclay's Argenis* (1636) Dedic. A 2 Varietie to please the minde, and Learning to embetter the Iudgement. **1839** RICHARDSON; and in mod. Dicts.

β. **1568** NORTH tr. *Gueuara's Diall Pr.* (1582) 363 To enlarge and imbetter my credite and estate. **1607** DANIEL *Philotas* v. Chorus, Crueltie doth not imbetter men. **1680** SIR W. WALLER *Divine Medit.* (1839) 41 Those that are good are imbettered, even by the illness of those that are bad.

embezzle (ɛmˈbɛz(ə)l), *v.* Forms: *α.* 5 enbesyl, enbesel(l, 5–6 embesell, -sill, -syle, -syll, (6 embecill), 6–8 embezel(l, -zil(l, -zle, -zzel(l, 7 embeasil, -zle, embes(s)el(l, 6- embezzle. *β.* 5–8 imbezel(l, -ill, (6–7 imbeazel(l), 7–8 imbezzel(l, -il, imbezle, 6–8 imbesel(l, -il(l, (6–7 imbeasell, -il, imbecile, -ill, imbesle, ymbessill,) 7 imbezzle. [ad. AF. *enbesiler* (quots. 1397, 1404), 'to make away with, cause to disappear, fraudulently destroy'; f. *en-* + *beseler* (see BEZZLE *v.*), which occurs (with the same sense) in the Year-books of 32–33 Edw. III (1305), and appears to be identical with OF. *besillier* (Pr. *besillar*) to maltreat, ravage, destroy; according to M. Paul Meyer f. L. *bis-*, in late L. used as a pejorative prefix.

In 16th c. the Eng. word appears to have been referred to the L. *imbecillare* to weaken (see IMBECILE), and this notion has possibly in some degree influenced the subsequent development of the sense.]

†**1.** *trans.* To make away with (provisions, money, etc.); *esp.* to carry off secretly (what belongs to another person) for one's own use. *Obs.*

a. [**1397** *Will of John of Gaunt* in Nichols *Royal Wills* 155 Drap enbroudes..et toutes autres pieces de la suit..quels je achatay de..la Duchesse de Northfolk aussi entierement sans riens ent enbeseiller com jes les avoy de ele.] **1469** *Househ. Ord.* 91 See that noe vitaills..ne none other stuffe of the seide householde be enbeselled oute. **1530** PALSGR. 531/2 He that embesylleth a thyng intendeth to steale it. **1552** *Inv. Ch. Surrey* 55 There was embeselyd one auter clothe and two towelles. **1598** *Linschoten's Voy.* in Arb. *Garner* III. 18 But little cometh to the owner's hands, being embezzled and privily made away. **1655** FULLER *Ch. Hist.* VIII. 42 The Utensells thereof had lately been Embezelled. **1750** CARTE *Hist. Eng.* II. 151 One of these [bibles] was to be placed in every parish church, chained so as not to be embezzeled.

β. **1474** *Househ. Ord.* 30 Nor that the porters suffree any stuffe to be imbezelled out of the sayde gates. **1574** HELLOWES *Gueuara's Ep.* 166 Babling and foule mouthed boyes..wil imbesill your apparrell. **1598** STOW *Surv.* xxxiii. (1603) 297 Manie of the Kings Jewels were..imbeseled. **1624** CAPT. SMITH *Virginia* IV. 140 The Sailers..are much to blame for imbesling the prouisions.

fig. **1548** GEST *Pr. Masse* 76 Thee pryvee masse.. embecilleth and taketh out of our hartes Christ.

†**b.** To make away with, fraudulently destroy (a charter, title-deed, etc.). In later use also, To mutilate, tamper with (a document or writing of any kind). *Obs.*

a. [**1404** *Act 5 Hen. IV*, c. 14 (Record ed.), Porce que pleuseurs pies de fins..et les notes de tielx fyns demorantz en le comune Bank, aient este devant ces heures enbesilez, & autres pies & notes de fyns fauxement contreovez & mys en lour lieux.] **1494** FABYAN VII. 293 The sayd boke..was enbesylyd, or loste. **1495** *Act 11 Hen. VII*, c. 51 Preamb., The evydences concernyng the same Maners..ben embeselled by..ill disposed persones. **1509–10** *Act 1 Hen. VIII*, c. 8 The said commissioner or escheatour may nott change nor enbesyll the said offices or inquisiciones. **1581** LAMBARDE *Eiren.* IV. xxi. (1588) 625 If a Justice of the Peace will craftily embesill an Enditement. **1660** H. MORE *Myst. Godl.* VII. xi. 326 The Writings of the Evangelists..were never embeseled. **1662** FULLER *Worthies* (1840) III. 296 The records belonging to this family have been embezzled. **1691** E. TAYLOR *Behmen's Life* 425 A Hieroglyphical Monument..was razed and embezelled by the rude Hands.

β. **1504** *Plumpton Corr.* Introd. 64 How..evydenc' hath bene imbeseled. **1665** STILLINGFL. *Rational Acc. Prot. Relig.* 212 Is it then possible to suppose all those Copy's at once imbezeled. **1671** F. PHILLIPS *Reg. Necess.* Ep. Ded., It is Felony to imbezill or corrupt a Record. **1677–8** MARVELL *Corr.* 326 Wks. 1872–5 II. 586 Upon occasion of imbeziling the Bill sent from the Lords.

†**c.** To entice away (a person) from service, etc. *Obs.*

1579 FENTON *Guicciard.* XIII. (1599) 615 He would be a conuenient instrument to imbeasell from the army of Francisco-maria the bands of Gascons. **1594** LYLY *Moth. Bombie* V. iii. 137, I had rather thou shouldst rob my chest, than imbeasell my sonne.

†**2.** To weaken, impair, diminish. *Obs.*

1566 DRANT *Horace' Sat.* I. v, And so imbecill all theyr strengthe, That they are naught to me. **1580** HOLLYBAND *Treas. Fr. Tong*, *Appetisser*, to diminish, to lessen, to imbesill. **1610** in Picton *L'pool Munic. Rec.* (1883) I. 121 Whereby the Quene's Majesties custome..maye..be.. empayred..or embesellеd. **1622** MALYNES *Anc. Law-Merch.* 307 The Kings or Princes Valuation is effected..by embeasiling the standard of money, by allay. **1636** FEATLY *Clavis Myst.* lxx. 892 Our luxury hath imbezelled us. **1670** BASIL VALENTINE *Last Will & Test.* xxxvii, Have a respect to the upper scaffolds, that they be not imbezled.

†**3.** To impair or diminish by waste or extravagance; to squander, dissipate (property, etc.).

a. **1578** BANISTER *Hist. Man* I. 26 Nature..would not..for the insertion of Muscles..embicill, and wast so much of the bones. **1621** BURTON *Anat. Mel.* III. ii. VI. v. (1651) 577 He hath embeazled his estate. **1658** SIR T. BROWNE *Hydriot.* 24 Fearing to embezzle a great commodity of their Country. **1749** CHESTERF. *Lett.* II. ccxi. 308 It is not the fashion..at Paris, to embezzle at least half of it [the day] at table. **1770** LANGHORNE *Plutarch* (1879) II. 901/1 His fortune, which had been so much embezzled.

β. **1621** BURTON *Anat. Mel.* I. ii. III. xv. (1651) 137 When they have with riot and prodigality imbezelled their estates. **1679** J. GOODMAN *Penitent Pard.* I. iv. (1713) 99 He wastes and imbezils the very talents and abilities God had endowed him with. **1683** CROWNE *City Politiques* II. i. 24, I have imbezell'd all the furniture of my soul and body in vice.

4. (The only current sense.) To divert to one's own use (money, etc.) in violation of trust or official duty. [At first app. a contextual use of 1 and 3; in early examples not distinguishable from one or the other of these.]

a. **1600** HOLLAND *Livy* XXXVIII. i. 1016 The Tribunes.. proceeded to charge him..for embezzeling and averting to his proper use certeine treasure gotten from King Antiochus. **1783** BURKE *Rep. Affairs Ind.* Wks. XI. 318 His fortune..grossly mismanaged and embezzled. **1833** MACAULAY *War Success., Ess.* (1854) I. 249/1 Bellasys, the English General, embezzled the stores. **1855** —— *Hist. Eng.* IV. 363 The rapacious governor had daily opportunities of embezzling and extorting.

β. **1585** FLEETWOOD in Ellis *Orig. Lett.* Ser. I. 216 II. 301 To steale and imbesell any thinge in his charge this is felonye. **1613** SIR H. FINCH *Law* (1636) 211 The seruant that hath any goods..deliuered him to keepe by his Master and..doth..imbezle, or conuert the same to his owne vse, the same, shall be judged a theefe. **1653** H. COGAN tr. *Pinto's Trav.* viii. 24 That Mahometan, who had imbezzled away a great part of the goods committed to his charge.

¶**5.** Used by Shelton to render the like-sounding Sp. *embelesar*, to bewilder, stupefy [cf. BEZZLE *v.*].

1620 SHELTON *Quix.* II. liii. 357 Sancho was astonish't and embeseld with what he heard & saw.

embezzled (ɛmˈbɛz(ə)ld), *ppl. a.* [f. prec. + -ED.] In the senses of the verb.

1603 KNOLLES *Hist. Turks* (1621) 555 Those..expences.. were..supported with the embeseled spoile. **1641** *Vind. Smectymnuus* 24 An imbezel'd book. *c* **1645** HOWELL *Lett.* II. 8 An Italian who had the keeping of their embeazled mony. **1833** HT. MARTINEAU *Berkeley Banker* I. viii. 153 The nature of the embezzled property. **1870** LOWELL *Among my Bks.* Ser. II. (1873) 281 An old gentleman..used the contracted form of the participle in conversation, but..gave it back its embezzled syllable in reading.

embezzlement (ɛmˈbɛz(ə)lmənt). Also 6 embecil-, embasel-, 7 embezzil-, imbezle-. [f. EMBEZZLE *v.* + -MENT; in AF. (1404) *embesilement.*] The action of embezzling. †**a.** In senses of EMBEZZLE 1–3 (*obs.*). **b.** (The mod. sense.) Fraudulent appropriation of entrusted property.

1548 GEST *Pr. Masse* 75 What is sacriledge..but an embecilment and stelthe of an holy thing out of an holy place. **1579** *Wills & Inv. N.C.* (1860) I. 234 *note*, To be restored, withoute anye kinde of embaselmente. **1645** MILTON *Colast.* Wks. (1851) 356 Those weak supposes of.. portions and joyntures likely to incurr imbezlement heerby. **1762–71** H. WALPOLE *Vertue's Anecd. Paint.* (1786) I. 205 The lightness which is remarked in the coins of Edward VI. was owing to the embezzlements of this person. **1786** BURKE *Articles agst. W. Hastings* Wks. 1842 II. 166 Fraud, peculation, and embezzlement. **1813** WELLINGTON in Gurw. *Disp.* X. 152 That punishment which is attached to embezzlement. **1886** *Pall Mall G.* 11 Dec. 6/1 Embezzlement is the appropriation by a clerk or servant of money coming into his hands on his master's account.

embezzler (ɛmˈbɛzlə(r)). [f. EMBEZZLE *v.* + -ER.] One who embezzles.

1667 PEPYS *Diary* 25 July, Hogg is the..most observable embezzler, that ever was known. **1687** *Lond. Gaz.* No. 2300/1 The Detainers, Imbezlers, or Concealers of the said Books. **1702** R. CROSFEILD *Affection of People, etc.* 4 The Embezelers of His Majesties Naval Stores. **1821** *Tait's Mag.* XXI. 376 Embezzlers, burglars and pick-pockets. **1887** *Pall Mall G.* 11 Oct. 7/2.

embezzling (ɛmˈbɛzlɪŋ), *vbl. sb.* [f. EMBEZZLE *v.* + -ING¹.] The action of the verb EMBEZZLE, in various senses.

1540 *Act 32 Hen. VIII*, c. 48 Al..wastes, imbesselinges.. and misusynge of the seyd artilleries, stores. **1577** HARRISON *England* II. xi. (1877) I. 224 Embesilling of goods committed by the master to the seruant. **1581** LAMBARDE *Eiren.* II. vii. (1588) 233 The embezelling of any Record. **1665** MARVELL *Let. Mayor of Hull* Wks. I. 51 Another Bill..to prevent the imbezelling of prize goods. **1658** *Whole Duty Man* xv. §26. 124 By careless embezelling of them.

embibe, obs. form of IMBIBE.

1558 WARDE *Alexis' Secr.* (1568) 2 b, When it is almost waxen drie, embibe or water it again as before.

embill, -ing: see EM- *prefix*.

†**em'billow**, *v. Obs. rare.* In 7 enbyllow. [f. EN- + BILLOW.] *trans.* To raise in billows.

1625 LISLE *Du Bartas, Noe* 1 (R.), And then enbyllowed high doth in his pride disdaine With fome and roaring din all hugeness of the maine.

embind (ɛmˈbaɪnd), *v.* Also 7 imbind. [f. EN- + BIND.] *trans.* To confine, hold fast.

a **1628** F. GREVILLE *Alaham* III. ii. (1633) 44 This secret haste is sure: all is imbound. *c* **1838** WORDSW. *Egyptian Maid*, The Damsel, in that trance embound.

embitter (ɛmˈbɪtə(r)), *v.* Also 7–9 imbitter. [f. EN- + BITTER *a.*]

1. *trans.* To make bitter, impart a bitter taste to. Now *rare* in *lit.* sense.

a **1603** T. CARTWRIGHT *Confut. Rhem. N.T.* (1618) 726 When I had eaten it, my bellie was imbittered. **1675** TRAHERNE *Chr. Ethics* 369 It is like wormwood that imbitters the nipple. **1775** ADAIR *Amer. Ind.* 122 Warm water, highly imbittered with the button-snake-root. **1834** *New Monthly Mag.* XL. 85 Brewers embitter their beer with hops.

2. *fig.* To infuse with bitterness, spoil the sweetness of (existence, pleasures, pursuits, etc.).

a **1677** BARROW in Spurgeon *Treas. David* Ps. cxix. 71 Impiety..doth embitter all the conveniences and comforts of life. **1713** STEELE *Guardian* No. 18 ¶1 It would imbitter all the sweets of life. **1776** GIBBON *Decl. & F.* I. 395 The last moments of Diocletian were embittered by some affronts. **1820** SCOTT *Abbot* i, Two circumstances only had imbittered their union. **1848** MACAULAY *Hist. Eng.* II. 38 His prosperity was embittered by one insupportable recollection. **1868** FREEMAN *Norm. Conq.* (1876) II. vii. 89 An act which embittered the remainder of his days.

3. *fig.* To make more bitter or painful.

1642 FULLER *Holy & Prof. St.* II. xxii. 142 He imbitters not a distastfull message to a forrein Prince by his indiscretion in delivering it. **1781** GIBBON *Decl. & F.* (1869) II. xli. 516 His actual misery was embittered by the recollection of past greatness. **1790** BURKE *Fr. Rev.* Wks. V. 85 To aggravate and imbitter that real inequality. **1876** GREEN *Short Hist.* x. §4. 801 His failure was embittered by heavier disasters elsewhere.

4. *fig.* To render (persons or feelings) virulent, intensely hostile or discontented; to exacerbate, intensify (a quarrel, etc.).

1634 SANDERSON *Serm.* I. 65 The like censurings and despisings have imbittered the spirits. **1682** BURNET *Rights Princes* ii. 31 Peoples minds were embittered one against another. **1748** ANSON *Voy.* II. iii. (ed. 4) 208 The Captain.. had much embittered the people against him. **1777** WATSON *Philip II*, (1793) I. VIII. 317 Putting them to death would only serve to embitter the resentment of the people. **1868** E. EDWARDS *Ralegh* I. vi. 98 Personal ill-feeling of long standing..further embittered the old quarrels.

embittered (ɛmˈbɪtəd), *ppl. a.* [f. prec. + -ED¹.] Made bitter, or more bitter. (Chiefly *fig.*; cf. senses of the vb.)

1655 MILTON *Lett. State* (1851) 333 Their imbitter'd and most implacable Enemies. *a* **1716** SOUTH *12 Serm.* (1717) V. 88 The Remorseless Malice of Imbitter'd Rebels. **1797** GODWIN *Enquirer* I. viii. 69 My temper becomes embittered. **1849** MILL *Ess.* (1859) II. 364 The embittered denunciations against the circulars and proclamations.

Hence †**em'bitteredness**. *Obs.*

1643 TUCKNEY *Balme of G.* 35 If imbitterednesse of spirit against God..can make it..Englands present disease..is grown pestilentially malignant.

embitterer (ɛmˈbɪtərə(r)). [f. EMBITTER + -ER.] One who or that which embitters.

1752 JOHNSON in John Taylor *Serm.* (1789) 224 The fear of death has always been considered as the..embitterer of the cup of joy. **1827** HONE *Every-day Bk.* II. 12 Sitting to drink is..the embitterer of their enjoyments. **1884** ANNIE SWAN *Dor. Kirke* xiv. 127 That old man is..an embitterer of the lives of others.

embittering (ɛmˈbɪtərɪŋ), *vbl. sb.* [f. as prec. + -ING¹.] The action of the verb EMBITTER.

1617 HIERON *Wks.* II. 340 The vsing of euill speech hee [Saint James] likeneth to the imbittering..of the Fountaine.

embittering (ɛmˈbɪtərɪŋ), *ppl. a.* [f. as prec. + -ING².] That embitters or tends to embitter.

1746 HERVEY *Medit.* (1818) 209 This embittering circumstance would spoil their relish. **1872** GEO. ELIOT *Middlem.* III. IV. 356 The suspicion..was embittering. *Ibid.* IV. v. 121 The imbittering discovery that, etc.

embitterment (ɛmˈbɪtəmənt). [f. EMBITTER *v.* + -MENT.] The action of embittering; the state of being embittered.

1645 W. JENKYN *Serm.* 37 Labour for a sanctified use of all embitterments or stoppages. **1809–10** COLERIDGE *Friend* (1818) III. 230 The usual embitterment of controversy. **1864** PUSEY *Lect. Daniel* 320 Two portions contending against each other with extremest embitterment.

†**em'bladder**, *v. Obs. rare.* [f. EN- + BLADDER *sb.*] *trans.* **a.** To cause vesicles to rise on the surface of (anything); to blister. **b.** To confine in a bladder. Hence **em'bladdered** *ppl. a.*

1662 CHANDLER *Van Helmont's Oriat.* 170 It doth not embladder a dead carcasse, even as it doth a living body. **1664** POWER *Exp. Philos.* II. 117 The Elater of the external Ayr..forces the embladder'd Ayr into its former extension.

†**em'blanch**, *v. Obs.* Also 4 enblaunch. [a. OF. *emblanch-ir*, f. *en-* (see EN-) + *blanc* white; cf. BLANCH *v.*] *trans.* To whiten. *fig.*

1393 LANGL. *P. Pl.* C. XVII. 269 Preestes, prechours and prelates, þat beþ enblaunched with bele paroles. *a* **1400-50** *Alexander* 3688 A tabernacle..grauen..of gilden platis, flamband all in filour & fewlis en-blanchid. *a* **1662** HEYLIN *Laud* (1671) 260 It was impossible that a spot of so deep a dye should be emblanched.

emblature. ? Mistake for EMBLAZURE.

1606 G. W[OODCOCKE] *Hist. Ivstine* G g 2 a, For whose honor there were Temples erected..and infinite emblatures of his praises decreed.

emblaze (ɛm'bleɪz), *v.*¹ Also **imblaze.** [f. EN- + BLAZE *sb.*¹]

1. *trans.* To light up, illuminate, cause to glow.

1634 MILTON *Comus* 733 Th' unsought Diamonds.. emblaze the forehead of the Deep. **1718** POPE *Iliad* XIII. 433 Polish'd arms emblazed the flaming fields. **1746** HERVEY *Medit.* (1818) 186 Topaz, emblazed with a golden gleam. **1804** J. GRAHAME *Sabbath* (1839) 18/1 Till..the sun Emblaze, with upward-slanting ray, the breast And wing unquivering of the wheeling lark. **1854** BAILEY *Festus* (ed. 5) 323 The golden pane the setting sun doth just Imblaze.

2. To set in a blaze, kindle. Also *fig.*

1728 POPE *Dunc.* I. 235 Sulphur-tipt, emblaze an alehouse fire. **1747** COLLINS *Ode to Liberty* ii, Where nearer suns emblaze its veins. **1815** *Month. Mag.* XXXVIII. 534 Fires, lightning kindled, the tall oaks imblaze.

emblaze (ɛm'bleɪz), *v.*² Also **imblaze.** [f. EN- + BLAZE *v.*²]

†**1. a.** *trans.* To describe heraldically. **b.** To set forth by means of heraldic devices. Cf. BLAZE *v.*²

1593 SHAKS. *2 Hen. VI*, IV. x. 76 But thou shalt weare it as a Heralds coate, To emblaze the Honor that thy master got. **1611** SPEED *Hist. Gt. Brit.* VII. ii. (1632) 199 As Some of our Heralds have imblazed. **1630** J. TAYLOR (Water P.) *Wks.* II. 157/2 Marke how I will emblaze thee..Within a Quagmire-field, two Toades in Chiefe. **1781** *Westm. Mag.* IX. 386 The Herald touches the bright fee, T' emblaze the brimstone of the *vis-a-vis.* **1782-1800** in BAILEY.

2. To adorn with heraldic devices. Hence (and influenced by EMBLAZE *v.*¹), to adorn magnificently, make resplendent.

1522 SKELTON *Why not to Court*, With crowns of gold emblased They make him so amased. **1667** MILTON *P.L.* I. 533 Th' Imperial Ensign..With Gemms and Golden lustre rich imblaz'd Seraphic arms and Trophies. **1717** POPE *Eloisa* 136 No weeping orphan saw his father's stores Our shrines irradiate, or emblaze the floors. **1818** MILMAN *Samor* 289 An enwoven tapestry of flame..emblaz'd Like hall of old barbaric Potentate.

3. To inscribe or portray conspicuously.

1590 GREENE *Orl. Fur.* Wks. 1831 I. 5 Where stout Hercules Emblaz'd his trophies on two posts of brass. **1667** MILTON *P.L.* V. 592 Or in thir glittering Tissues bear imblaz'd Holy Memorials. **1742** YOUNG *Nt. Th.* IX. 1660 Divine Instructor! Thy first volume..In moon, and stars.. Emblaz'd to seize the sight. **1808** J. BARLOW *Columb.* VI. 246 Here herald glory first emblazed her name.

4. To inscribe (a person) on 'the roll of fame' (or of infamy); to celebrate, render famous or notorious.

1596 FITZ-GEFFRAY *Sir F. Drake* (1881) 65 Drake hath no Homer to emblaze his glorie. **1609** HEYWOOD *Troia Brittanica* in Farr's *S.P. Jas.* (1848) 330 These harsh meeters..but to emblaze you, had yet been vnborne. **1630** J. TAYLOR (Water P.) *Wks.* II. 144/1 A Scritch-owle's quill ..shall emblaze thee basest slaue of men.

emblazer (ɛm'bleɪzə(r)). [f. EMBLAZE *v.*¹, ² + -ER.] He who or that which emblazes or illuminates.

1776 MICKLE *Camoens' Lusiad* 446 Apollo here enthroned in light appears The eye of heaven, emblazer of the spheres.

emblazon (ɛm'bleɪzən), *v.* Also 7 **emblazen, imblazon.** [f. EN- + BLAZON *v.*]

1. *trans.* To inscribe or portray conspicuously, as on a heraldic shield; to adorn or inscribe *with* heraldic devices, words, etc. *lit.* and *fig.* Sometimes influenced by EMBLAZE *v.*¹

1593 NASHE *Christ's T.* (1613) 54 God..emblazond the aire with the tokens of his terror. **1596** SPENSER *F.Q.* IV. x. 55 On which..Cupid with his killing bow And cruell shafts emblazond she beheld. **1735** SOMERVILLE *Chase* II. 385 Th' Imperial Standard waves Emblazon'd rich with Gold. **1820** W. IRVING *Sketch Bk.* I. 205 A carriage emblazoned with arms. **1831** BLAKEY *Free-will* (1848) 155 The orbs which emblazon the canopy of heaven. **1872** MORLEY *Voltaire* (1886) He emblazoned it on a banner.

2. To celebrate, extol, 'blaze abroad'; to render illustrious.

1592 NASHE *P. Penilesse* (ed. 2) 18 b, It is better for a Nobleman..to haue his..deedes emblazond by a Poet, than a Citizen. **1629** GAULE *Pract. The.* 31 Requisite it was our.. King should have..his Prophets as Heraulds to emblazen his Progresse. **1720** WELTON *Suffer. Son of God* I. vii. 138 God emblazon'd..His Servants by joyning their Name to His own. **1761** *New Comp. Festiv. & Fasts* xxiv. 213 Prejudice would have prompted to them to emblazon the least appearence of fraud. **1819-30** LINGARD *Hist. Eng.* VI. 225 Their success..was emblazoned to catch the eye of the public. **1839** LONGF. *Coplas de Manr.*, Heroes emblazoned high to fame.

†**em'blazon,** *sb. Obs.* [f. prec. vb.] The delineation or heraldic description of armorial bearings.

1562 LEIGH *Armorie* (1597) 90 b, Erle Mortimers of March his cote..fully descrieth the same without any further emblason. **1592** WYRLEY *Armorie* 27 Vsing the said French phrases in my emblazons. **1661** MORGAN *Sph. Gentry* 34 This sort of Emblazon is proper for Ecclesiastical Persons.

emblazoned (ɛm'bleɪzənd), *ppl. a.* [f. EMBLAZON *v.* + -ED¹.] Decorated with armorial devices or bearings; gorgeously adorned.

1667 MILTON *P.L.* IX. 34 Emblazon'd Shields. *a* **1791** BLACKLOCK *Elegy, Constantia* The herse Of wealthy guilt emblazoned boasts the pride Of painted heraldry. **1813** BYRON *Br. Abydos* II. v, And many a bright emblazon'd rhyme By Persian scribes redeem'd from time.

emblazoner (ɛm'bleɪzənə(r)). [f. as prec. + -ER.] One who emblazons.

1591 FLORIO *2nd Fruites* A iij b, Such a rare emblazoner of his magnanimitie, as the Meonian Poete. **1642** MILTON *Apol. Smectymn.* Wks. 1738 I. 106 But I step again to this Emblazoner of his Title-page.

emblazoning (ɛm'bleɪzənɪŋ), *vbl. sb.* [f. as prec. + -ING.¹] The action of the vb. EMBLAZON; *concr.* armorial or heraldic decoration.

1775 in ASH. **1820** KEATS *Eve St. Agnes* xxiv, Twilight saints and dim emblazonings.

emblazonment (ɛm'bleɪzənmənt). [f. as prec. + -MENT.] The action of the vb. EMBLAZON; *concr.* an armorial ensign or heraldic device.

1799 COLERIDGE *Ode Duchess Devonsh.* Emblazonments and old ancestral crests. **1818** SCOTT *Let.* in *Lockhart* (1839) VI. 12, I have my quarters and emblazonments free of all stain. **1853** KANE *Grinnell Exp.* xxv. (1856) 203 A flagstaff, with armorial emblazonments at the top.

emblazonry (ɛm'bleɪzənrɪ). Also **imblazonry.** [f. as prec. + -RY.]

1. a. The art of depicting or describing heraldic devices. **b.** *concr.* Heraldic devices collectively; symbolic ornament.

1667 MILTON *P.L.* II. 512 With bright imblazonrie, and horrent Arms. **1774** J. BRYANT *Mythol.* II. 345 The poet is speaking of some emblazonry upon the cuirass of Agamemnon. **1815** WORDSW. *White Doe* III. 91 The Banner in all its dread emblazonry. **1842** H. ROGERS *Introd. Burke's Wks.* I. 3 Burke..could dispense with pedigrees and heralds. His works form his best emblazonry. **1851** TRENCH *Poems* 112 Thine ancient standard's rich emblazonry.

2. a. Display of gorgeous colours; brilliant pictorial representation. **b.** Verbal amplification or embellishment.

1805 WORDSW. *Prelude* III. (1850) 72 If these thoughts Are a gratuitous emblazonry. **1827** POLLOK *Course T.* I, In horrible emblazonry, were limned All shapes..of wretchedness. **1831** CARLYLE *Sart. Res.* (1858) 56 The Sun ..with his gold-purple emblazonry. **1843** *Blackw. Mag.* LIV. 273 It would be injurious to spend words in emblazonry.

†**em'blazure.** *Obs. rare*⁻¹. [f. EMBLAZE *v.*² + -URE.] = EMBLAZONING.

1562 LEIGH *Armorie* (1597) 127 Vse themblazure thereof by heauens, fittest for the cote of so noble a prince. **1606** [see EMBLATURE].

†**'emble.** *Obs. rare*⁻¹. [Derivation unknown: Markham's reference is to OF. *emblaié* (of a field) sown with wheat.] (See quot.)

1631 MARKHAM *Weald of Kent* II. i. (1668) 9 A Worm, called an Emble, which in French signifieth Corn in the ground.

emblem ('ɛmbləm), *sb.* Also 5-7 **embleme.** [ad. L. *emblēma* inlaid work, a raised ornament on a vessel, a. Gr. ἔμβλημα an insertion, f. ἐμβλη- perfect etc. stem of ἐμβάλλειν to throw in.]

†**1.** An ornament of inlaid work. *Obs.*

1656 BLOUNT *Glossogr.*, *Emblem*, any fine work cunningly set in wood or other substance, as we see in chessboards and tables. **1667** MILTON *P.L.* IV. 703 The ground more colour'd then with stone Of costliest Emblem. **1678** in PHILLIPS. **1775** ASH, *Emblem*, an inlay, an enamel, that which is inserted into some other substance.

†**2. a.** A drawing or picture expressing a moral fable or allegory; a fable or allegory such as might be expressed pictorially. *Obs.*

c **1430** LYDG. *Chorle & Byrde* (1818) 1 Emblemes of olde likenes and figures Whiche prouyd hen fructuous of sentence. **1625** BACON *Ess. Seditions & Troubles* (Arb.) 407 Iupiter..sent for Briareus, with his hundred Hands..An Embleme, no doubt, to shew, etc. **1635** QUARLES *Embl.* Introd. (1718) 2 An Emblem is but a silent parable. **1642** FULLER *Holy & Prof. St.* IV. 294, I like that Embleme of Charity..a naked child, giving honey to a Bee without wings. **1654** WHITLOCK *Zootomia* 52 Like the Asse..in the Embleme. **1730-6** BAILEY, *Emblem*, a painted enigma or representation of some moral notion by way of device or picture.

†**b.** *abstr.*

1605 BACON *Adv. Learn.* II. 58 Embleme [one of the two parts of the 'art of memory'] reduceth conceits intellectuall to Images sensible.

3. a. A picture of an object (or the object itself) serving as a symbolical representation of an abstract quality, an action, state of things, class of persons, etc.

1601 SHAKS. *All's Well* II. i. 44 One Captaine Spurio with his sicatrice an Embleme of warre heere on his sinister cheeke. **1613** —— *Hen. VIII*, IV. i. 89 The rod, and bird of peace, and all such Emblemes Laid nobly on her. **1641** J. JACKSON *True Evang. T.* II. 89 Such beasts..are emblemes ..of Christian vertues. **1789** MRS. PIOZZI *Journ. France* I. 159 The short cut coat is the emblem of a military profession. **1837** NEWMAN *Par. Serm.* (ed. 2) III. v. 76 The ox is thought to be the emblem of life or strength. **1872** YEATS *Tech. Hist. Comm.* 69 The spindle or the loom was the emblem of woman.

b. In wider sense: A symbol, typical representation. Sometimes applied to a person: The 'type', personification (of some virtue or quality).

a **1631** DONNE *Hymne to Christ*, What sea soever swallow mee, that flood Shall be to mee an embleme of thy blood. **1683** TEMPLE *Mem.* Wks. 1731 I. 480 For my Lord Treasurer and Lord Chamberlain, I found them two most admirable Emblems of the..Felicity of Ministers of State. **1719** DE FOE *Crusoe* I. 14 And my Father, an Emblem of our blessed Saviour's Parable, had even kill'd the fatted Calf for me. **1758** JOHNSON *Idler* No. 43 ¶ 5 The evening is an emblem of autumn. **1860** MOTLEY *Netherl.* (1868) I. ii. 28 Mary Stuart..the emblem and exponent of all that was most Roman in Europe. **1875** HAMERTON *Intell. Life* IX. vi. (1876) 333 Ocean, stars, and mountains, emblems and evidences of eternity.

4. A figured object used with symbolic meaning, as the distinctive badge of a person, family, nation, etc. Chiefly of heraldic devices, and of the symbolic objects accompanying the images of saints.

1616 J. LANE *Sqrs. Tale* IX. (1888) 479 So after his dead lord was pale and cold, takes off his ensigne, which his emblem bore. *a* **1682** SIR T. BROWNE *Tracts* 78 This tree in after-times became the Emblem of that Country. **1828** SCOTT *F.M. Perth* xxviii, The Blue Falcon, the emblem of the Clan Quhele. **1841-4** EMERSON *Ess., Poet* Wks. (Bohn) I. 160 See the power of national emblems..a crescent, a lion, an eagle, or other figure, on an old rag of bunting. **1864** BOUTELL *Heraldry Hist. & Pop.* ix. 53 The weapon represents the emblem of St. Paul.

†**5.** In *pl.* The evidences of sex. *Obs.*

1621 FLETCHER *Pilgrim* IV. ii, Where are his emblems?

6. *attrib.* **emblem book**, a book containing drawings with accompanying interpretations of their allegorical meaning; so ***emblem poem, writer***, etc.

1870 H. GREEN *Shakesp. & Emblem Writers* ii. 30 (*heading*) Sketch of emblem-book literature previous to A.D. 1616. *Ibid.* iii. 107 Of the Emblem-books in Spanish, German, Flemish, Dutch, and English, only the last would be available for Shakespeare's benefit. **1888** G. E. SEARS (*title*) A collection of emblem books by Andrea Alciati. **1945** D. BUSH *Eng. Lit. in Earlier 17th Cent.* 581 The latest and fullest study of Quarles's emblem imagery is by E. James. **1948** R. FREEMAN *Eng. Emblem Books* App. I. 238, I have taken for my criterion four characteristics commonly agreed to be essential by the emblem writers themselves. These are: 1. An emblem book should be a collection of moral symbols. 2. It should have pictures, or..should postulate the existence of pictures. 3. Attached to each picture should be a motto or brief *sententia*... 4. There should be an explanatory poem or passage of prose in which the picture and motto are interpreted and a moral..is drawn. **1963** *N. & Q.* May 168/1 Some of the illustrated *Arma Christi* verses ..are rudimentary emblem poems. *Ibid.*, The medieval poems are not deliberately collected into 'emblem books'.

emblem ('ɛmbləm), *v.* Also 7 **embleme.** [f. prec.] *trans.* To be the emblem of (something); to express, symbolize, or suggest by means of an emblem. Also, ***to emblem forth.***

1584 G. WHETSTONE *Mirour for Magistr. Epistle, etc.*, ad. fin. *c* **1605** ROWLEY *Birth Merl.* IV. v. 344 Those by-form'd fires..emblem two royal babes. **1636** HENSHAW *Horæ Sub.* 28 Much knowledge, not much speech, emblem's a wise man. **1652** SPARKE *Prim. Devot.* (1663) 314 To emblem forth his variety of operations. **1663** J. SPENCER *Prodigies* (1665) 313 This mystery of Providence was emblemed in the prophetick vision of a wheel. **1840** CARLYLE *Heroes* iii. (1858) 257 All Christianism, as Dante and the Middle Ages had it, is emblemed here. **1845** NEALE *Mirr. Faith* 84 And Holy Church hath Her banners high To emblem her Saviour's Victory.

emblema (ɛm'bliːmə). Pl. **-mata.** [L.: see EMBLEM *sb.*] An ornament in relief, either carved or mounted, on jewellery, vases, etc.

1842 W. SMITH *Dict. Gk. & Rom. Antiq.* **1880** C. T. NEWTON *Ess. Art & Archæol.* vi. 265 Embossed and cut out in outline, like the *emblemata* of later Greek art. **1885** *Encycl. Brit.* XIX. 181/1 A seated figure of Athene—an 'emblema' soldered on, in very high relief. **1957** *Ibid.* 404/1 Small mosaic-pictures isolated in geometrical pavements were called *emblemata*.

emblematic (ɛmblə'mætɪk), *a.* [f. Gr. ἐμβληματ- stem of ἔμβλημα (see EMBLEM *sb.*) + -IC.]

Pertaining to, or of the nature of, or serving as, an emblem; symbolical, typical. Const. *of.*

1645 EVELYN *Mem.* (1857) I. 206 The emblematic tree at the other passage out of the church. **1702** tr. *Le Clerc's Prim. Fathers* 54 Neither Christ nor his Apostles haue proposed any doctrine after an Emblematick manner. **1763** DERRICK *Lett.* (1767) II. 110 A monument..enriched with.. inscriptions, and emblematic sculptures. **1775** SHERIDAN *Rivals* 2nd Prol., View her..primly portray'd on emblematic wood! **1808** SCOTT *Marm.* IV. viii. 10 And on his finger given to shine The emblematic ring. **1831** CARLYLE *Sart. Res.* (1858) 43 Clothes..are Emblematic..of a manifold cunning Victory over Want. **1876** MOZLEY *Univ. Serm.* vi. 130 A process in the mind of man..makes material sights and objects first beautiful and then emblematic.

emble'matical, *a.* [f. prec. + -AL[1].] = prec.
1644 BULWER *Chirol.* 77 A spice of their authority more strong then their emblematicall Mace. **1679** J. GOODMAN *Penitent Pard.* I. ii. (1713) 45 An emblematical representation of God's unspeakable mercy. **1709** STEELE & ADDISON *Tatler* No. 81 ¶6 Gorgons, Chimæra's, and Centaurs, with many other Emblematical Figures. **1726** ADDISON *Dial. Medals* i. 31 Such reverses as are purely emblematical. **1843** PRESCOTT *Mexico* (1850) I. 107 Dances and games were instituted, emblematical of the regeneration of the world. **1850** MRS. JAMESON *Leg. Monast. Ord.* (1863) 485 These large emblematical wings.

Hence †**emble'maticalness**. *Obs.*
1731 in BAILEY. **1775** in ASH.

emble'matically, *adv.* [f. prec. + -LY.[2]] In an emblematical manner; after the manner of, for the purpose of, or by means of an emblem.
1607 TOPSELL *Four-f. Beasts* 8 Baboons..some which abhor fishes..which kind the Egyptians Emblematically use to paint. **1796** MORSE *Amer. Geog.* II. 118 The destruction of the city..is emblematically represented in bass relief. **1886** *Manch. Exam.* 16 Feb. 5/3 Whether this work of art was intended to be taken literally or emblematically.

emblematicize (ɛmblə'mætɪsaɪz), *v. rare.* [f. EMBLEMATIC + -IZE.] *trans.* To impart an emblematic or allegorical character to.
1762–71 H. WALPOLE *Vertue's Anecd. Paint.* (1786) IV. 131 His pictures, which he generally endeavoured to emblematicize by genii and Cupids.

emblematist (ɛm'blɛmətɪst). [f. Gr. ἐμβληματ- stem of ἔμβλημα (see EMBLEM) + -IST.] **a.** One who invents or makes use of pictorial emblems. **b.** One who composes allegories; an emblem-writer.
1646 SIR T. BROWNE *Pseud. Ep.* v. iii. 236 The pictures of Emblematists in the coats of severall families. **1679** PLOT *Staffordsh.* (1686) 262 The Emblematists usually express fecundity by that Animal [the Goat]. **1861** *Sat. Rev.* 7 Dec. 591 Hearts, and darts, and butterflies, and crosses, and crowns have always formed the stock in trade of Emblematists. **1870** LOWELL *Among my Bks.* Ser. I. (1873) 138 Alciato, the famous lawyer and emblematist.

emblematize (ɛm'blɛmətaɪz), *v.* [f. as prec. + -IZE.]
1. *trans.* Of things: To serve as an emblem of; to express or represent mystically, allusively, or allegorically.
1615 W. HULL *Mirrour of Maiestie* 134 The vanity of these fading crownes was emblematized by that solemne ceremonie. *c* **1630** JACKSON *Creed* v. §43 A worse error than can rightly be emblematized by Ixion's fabulous imaginations. **1823** LAMB in *Life & Lett.* (1840) xii. 119 The goose and little goslings should emblematise a Quaker poet that has no children. **1870** GOULBURN *Cathedral Syst.* iii. 37 The tabernacle and temple worship was framed to emblematize the worship of heaven.
2. Of persons: To represent by means of an emblem; to figure.
1830 MOIR in *Fraser's Mag.* II. 408 The American poet, who emblematizes departing man, as folding his mantle round him, and lying down to pleasant dreams. **1854** *Blackw. Mag.* LXXVI. 509, I emblematised civilisation, in the Chinese lady in japan-gilt frame.

Hence **em'blematizing** *ppl. a.*
1751 MRS. MONTAGU *Lett.* III. 173 The good man..to an emblematizing genius would have afforded an ample subject.

emblematology (ˌɛmbləmə'tɒlədʒɪ). [f. as prec. + -(O)LOGY.] The science of the origin and meaning of emblems.
1881 *Oracle* 5 Nov. 294 The student of Christian emblematology.

emblement ('ɛmblɪmənt). *Law.* Forms: 5 inblement, 6 emblemente, 7 embleament, 8– emblement. [a. OF. *emblaement*, f. *emblaer*, (mod.F. *emblaver*) to sow with corn:— med.L. *imbladāre* (It. *imbiadare*), f. *in* in + *bladum* (= F. *blé*) wheat.]
'The profits of sown land: but the word is sometimes used more largely for any products that arise naturally from the ground as grass, fruit, etc.' (Tomlins).
1495 *Act 11 Hen. VII*, c. 61. §3 All fermours..[shall] have suche Inblementis and Cornys as be sowyn theruppon. **1590** H. SWINBURN *Treat. Test.* 218 Emblementes, or corne growing vpon the ground. **1641** *Termes de la Ley* 133 b, Embleaments are the profits of the land which have beene sowed. **1741** T. ROBINSON *Gavelkind* II. ii. 167 The Lessee shall not have the Emblements. **1855** H. BROOM *Comm. Com. Law* 15 The general rule of law concerning emblements.

embleming ('ɛmbləmɪŋ), *vbl. sb.* [f. EMBLEM *v.* + -ING[1].] The action of the vb. EMBLEM.
1840 CARLYLE *Heroes* (1858) 257 How unconscious of any embleming!

†**em'blemish**, *v. Obs.* Forms: 4 enblemisch, emblemysh, -ysch, 6 emblemmissh, -bleamish, 7 imblemish. [f. EN- + BLEMISH; AFr. had *emblemir.*] *trans.* **a.** To damage, injure, maim; **b.** to deface, disfigure.
c **1384** WYCLIF *Sel. Wks.* III. 362 And bi sich blyndenesse in cursing many curseris emblemyshen hemsilf. *c* **1385** CHAUCER *L.G.W.*, *Lucrece* (Camb. MS.) And hire teris.. Emblemyschid [*other texts* embellished] hire wifly chastite. **1548** HALL *Chron.* (1809) 137 I fele my name and fame greatly emblemmisshed. **1575** LANEHAM *Let.* (1871) 36, I.. by my fond tempring afore hand embleamish the beauty. **1671** F. PHILLIPS *Reg. Necess.* 472 The said Richard Chedder was imblemished and maimed to the peril of death.

Hence **em'blemishing** *vbl. sb.*
1563–87 FOXE *A. & M.* (1596) 406/1 The great emblemishing of Christian faith.

†**'emblemist.** *Obs.* [f. EMBLEM + -IST.] A delineator or writer of emblems.
1607 WALKINGTON *Opt. Glass* ¶1 b, Other Emblemists haue limd forth a right student, euer to haue one eye shut, and an other open. **1630** J. TAYLOR (Water P.) *Wks.* II. 120/1 Answer a deprauing Emblemist.

emblemize ('ɛmbləmaɪz), *v.* [f. as prec. + -IZE.]
1. *trans.* To represent emblematically.
1646 J. VICARS (*title*) Sight of the Transactions of these Latter Yeares, Emblemized with Engraven Plates. **1639** BARCLAY *Lost Lady* I. i, in Hazl. *Dodsl.* XII. 548 'Twould emblemize, but not express his grief. **1881** W. C. RUSSELL *Ocean Free-Lance* II. 129 Nothing would better emblemise the happiness she had given me.
2. To make into a sign or badge.
1753 HANWAY *Trav.* (1762) I. Cij b, The arms of the russia company, emblemised.

emblic ('ɛmblɪk). Forms: 6 emblico, 7 emblick. [ad. med.L. *emblica*, *-icus*, ad. Ar. *amlaj* a. Pers. *āmleh*, cf. Skr. *āmalaka* of same meaning.] The fruit of *Emblica officinalis*, a tree of the N.O. *Euphorbiaceæ*, whose flowers are aperient, leaves and bark a remedy against dysentery. Also ***emblic myrobalan.***
1555 EDEN *Decades W. Ind.* iii. IV. (Arb.) 151 Mirobalanes ..which the phisitians caule Emblicos and Chebulos. **1678** SALMON *Lond. Disp.* 136/2 The five sorts of Myrobolans.. the Emblick purge Flegm and Water. **1708** MOTTEUX *Rabelais* II. xiv, A Boxfull of conserves, of round Myrabolan plums, called Emblicks. **1811** HOOPER *Med. Dict.*, The emblic Myrobalan is of a dark blackish grey colour.

†**em'blind**, *v. Obs.* [f. EN- + BLIND *a.*] *trans.* = BLIND.
1630 I. CRAVEN *Serm.* 17 Man may..be..emblinded through affection.

†**em'bliss**, *v. Obs. rare.* Also 5 enblisse. [f. EN- + BLISS.] *trans.* To make happy, bless.
c **1430** LYDG. *Bochas* II. xxvi. (1554) 61 b, Nombre of childre t' enblisse his linage. *c* **1725** FIELDING *Pleas. of Town* Wks. 1775 I. 228 How I'll embliss thee. **1797** T. TOWNSEND *Poems* [*Monthly Rev.* 463 Emblissed is a word peculiar to this author].

†**embloom** (ɛm'bluːm), *v. Obs.* [f. EN- + BLOOM *sb.*[1]] *trans.* To cover with bloom; to impart a fresh or ruddy appearance to.
a **1528** SKELTON *Ph. Sparowe* 1038 Her lyppes soft and mery, Emblomed lyke the chery. **1729** SAVAGE *Wanderer* v, Embloomed his aspect shines.

emblossom, imblossom (ɛm-, ɪm'blɒsəm), *v.* [f. EN- + BLOSSOM *sb.*] *trans.* To load or cover with blossoms. Hence **em'blossomed** *ppl. a.*
1766 J. CUNNINGHAM *Day* 33 The warbling throng, On the white emblossom'd spray! **1821** *Blackw. Mag.* X. 651 The wreaths that would our brows emblossom. **1855** BAILEY *Mystic* 115 The whisperings of imblossomed trees.

†**em'blustricate**, *v. Obs.* [Whimsically formed to render the equally fantastic Fr. *emburelucoquer.*] *trans.* To bewilder.
a **1693** URQUHART *Rabelais* III. xxii, The Romish church, when tottering and emblustricated with the Gibble Gabble Gibberish of this odious Error.

†**em'boast**, *v. Obs.* [cf. EMBOSS *v.*, EMBOSTURE.] *trans.* ? To carve (on a building).
1575 FENTON tr. Guevara in *Golden Epistles* 72 Men beare more honor to the Sepulchres of the vertuous, then to the emboasted Palaices of the wicked. **1579** —— tr. *Guicciardini's Hist. Ital.* 1070 Skootchions..affixed and emboasted to the publike pallaices.

†**em'boat**, *v. Obs.* In 6 enbote [f. EN- + BOAT *sb.*] *trans.* To put on board a boat.
1542 *Stat. 34 & 35 Hen. VIII*, cap. 9 §2 No person shall enbote or lade any Wheate..in any picard bot or other vessell.

†**em'bock**, *v. Obs. rare*[−1]. [ad. It. *imboccāre*, f. *in* in + *bocca* mouth.] *trans.* To stop up the mouth of (a cannon).
1598 BARRET *Theor. Warres*, v. ii. 130 The Cannoneras.. may not bee embocked or stopped vp.

embodied, imbodied (ɛm'bɒdɪd), *ppl. a.* [f. EMBODY *v.* + -ED[1].]
1. Of 'soul' or 'spirit': Having a body, invested with a body.
α. **1652** BENLOWES *Theoph.* VIII. lxxxix. 120 O, could embody'd Soules Sinnes bane view well. **1719** DE FOE *Crusoe* (1840) II. iii. 58 Spirits embodied have converse with ..spirits unembodied. **1783** JOHNSON *Lett.* II. 304 External locality has great effects, at least upon all embodied beings. **1839** BAILEY *Festus* ii. (1848) 12 A spirit, or embodied blast of air. **1870** MAX MÜLLER, *Sc. Relig.* (1873) 365 As men, we only know of embodied spirits. **1880** E. KIRKE *Garfield*, 27 The embodied spirit of treason and slavery.
β. **1691–8** NORRIS *Pract. Disc.* 243 Words that cannot be.. understood by an imbodyed Understanding. **176.** WESLEY *Serm.* Wks. 1811 IX. 148 An imbodied spirit cannot form one thought, but by the mediation of its bodily organs.
2. Of principles, ideas, etc.: **a.** Expressed or exhibited in material or concrete form; **b.** incorporated into a system.
1663 J. SPENCER *Prodigies* (1665) 137 There is a great deal of imbodied Art in Nature. **1799** MACKINTOSH *Stud. Law Nat.* Wks. 1846 I. 364 The embodied experience of mankind. **1875** JOWETT *Plato* (ed. 2) V. 37 The individual follows reason, and the city law, which is embodied reason.
3. Formed or combined into a militant body or company; arrayed, marshalled.
1667 MILTON *P.L.* I. 573 Such imbodied force, as, nam'd with these, Could merit more than that small infantry. **1715** POPE *Iliad* II. 540 Not less their number than the embodied cranes. **1798** MALTHUS *Popul.* (1817) II. 11 The number of embodied troops. **1827** HALLAM *Const. Hist.* (1876) I. iv. 179 The advocates of a simpler ritual had by no means assumed the shape of an embodied faction.

embodier (ɛm'bɒdɪə(r)). [f. EMBODY *v.* + -ER.] One who or that which embodies.
1654 R. WHITLOCK *Zootomia* Sig. a. Those Embodyers of Arts..into the limits of their proper method. **1854** *Blackw. Mag.* LXXV. 752 Claude..the embodier of 'foolish pastoralism'. **1870** LOWELL *Among my Bks.* Ser. I. (1873) 165 His native tongue as the embodier and perpetuator of it.

embodiment, imbodiment (ɛm-, ɪm'bɒdɪmənt). [f. EMBODY *v.* + -MENT.]
1. The action of embodying; the process or state of being embodied. *lit.* and *fig.*
1858 HAWTHORNE *Fr. & It. Jrnl.* II. 19 As long as a beautiful thought shall require physical embodiment. **1862** F. HALL *Hindu Philos. Syst.* 125 Souls..condemned, by reason of sin, to repeated embodiment. **1881** *Athenæum* No. 2811. 348/2 No less admirable is Herr Reichmann's embodiment of Wolfram.
2. *concr.* That in which (something) is embodied.
a. The corporeal 'vesture' or 'habitation' *of* (a soul). Also *fig.*
1850 WHIPPLE *Ess. & Rev.* (ed. 3) I. 311 This fiery spiritual essence was enclosed in a frame sensitive enough to be its fit embodiment. **1862** H. SPENCER *First Princ.* I. i. (1875) 13 The soul of truth contained in erroneous creeds is very unlike most..of its several embodiments.
b. That in which (a principle, an abstract idea, etc.) is embodied, actualized, or concretely expressed. Also applied (with some reference to sense **a.**) to persons: The embodied type, 'incarnation' (of a quality, sentiment, etc.).
1828 CARLYLE *Misc.* (1857) I. 117 The most striking embodiment of a highly remarkable belief. **1835** MISS MITFORD in L'Estrange *Life* (1870) III. iii. 30 Jack and Stephen..are..an embodiment of my notion of an English sailor, and of a..tradesman. **1855** H. REED *Lect. Eng. Hist.* iv. 133 He is the imbodiment of the most genuine national feeling. **1868** E. EDWARDS *Ralegh* I. i. 22 To Ralegh, the Spanish empire and polity became the very types and embodiments of evil. **1875** JOWETT *Plato* (ed. 2) III. 141 Works of art..the visible embodiment of the divine.

embody, imbody (ɛm-, ɪm'bɒdɪ), *v.* [f. EN-, IN- + BODY *sb.* The form *imbody* is the only one recognized in Bailey and Johnson (though the latter uses *embody* s.v. *Incorporate*), but is now less usual.]
1. *trans.* To put into a body; to invest or clothe (a spirit) with a body.
α. **1548** GEST *Pr. Masse* 86 No more then the sayd holy ghost is adjudged embodied or enharted. *a* **1699** BONNELL in W. Hamilton *Life* (1703) II. 134 My Saviour Impregnated the Consecrated Elements, and in a manner Embody'd himself there. **1727** DE FOE *Hist. Appar.* iv. (1840) 26 Whether are there any spirits inhabiting the visible world, which have never yet been embodied. **1729** T. COOKE *Tales, Proposals, etc.* 44 Would She embody'd to thy Arms return? **1858** HAWTHORNE *Fr. & It. Jrnls.* II. 10 A pale, small person, scarcely embodied at all. **1869** J. MARTINEAU *Ess.* II. 291 In him the old scholastic spirit seems embodied again.
β. **1600** HEYWOOD *1 Edw. IV* (1874) I. 27 Such haughtie stomacks..Imbodied in the breasts of Citizens. **1610** HEALEY *St. Aug. Citie of God* 561 Devills beeing imbodyed in ayre can..moove it.
2. To impart a material, corporeal, or sensual character to. *rare.* †Also *intr.* for *refl.*
1634 MILTON *Comus* 468 The sole..Imbodies, and imbrutes, till she quite lose The divine property of her first being. **1652** S. PATRICK *Fun. Serm.* in *J. Smith's Sel. Disc.* 555 Do not imbody and enervate your souls by idleness and base neglect. **1833** *Fraser's Mag.* 575 Spirituality of mind enables them to conceive those mysteries with a pure devotion, without the danger of embodying and imbruting them.
3. To give a concrete form to (what is abstract or ideal); to express (principles, thoughts, intentions) *in* an institution, work of art, action, definite form of words, etc.
α. **1750** JOHNSON *Rambl.* No. 168 ¶5 Poetry, that force.. which embodies sentiment. **1815** WELLINGTON Gurw. *Disp.* XII. 455 I have not yet been able to embody in a treaty the principles of this arrangement. **1847** GROTE *Greece* II. xlviii. (1862) IV. 267 The custom having been embodied in law. **1848** DICKENS *Dombey* i, The blue coat and stiff white cravat which..embodied her idea of a father. **1866** ROGERS *Agric. & Prices* I. xxiv. 615 A popular notion, embodied in a rhyming couplet.
β. **1742** RICHARDSON *Pamela* IV. 111 What Words shall be found to imbody Air? **1846** HAWTHORNE, *Mosses* I. v. 110 One century imbodied it in marble. **1859** HOLLAND *Gold F.* v. 74 When this conception is imbodied in an object of worship.

b. Of institutions, works of art, actions, forms of words, etc: To be an embodiment or expression of (an idea, principle, etc.).

1876 MISS BRADDON *J. Haggard's Dau.* II. 64 This house..was to embody her idea of home.

4. To cause to become part of a body; to unite into one body; to incorporate (a thing) in a mass of material, (particular elements) in a system or complex unity.

1601 SHAKS. *All's Well* V. iii. 173 For I by vow am so embodied yours. **1695** WOODWARD *Nat. Hist. Earth* IV. (1723) 192 We shall meet with the same Metall or Mineral embody'd in Stone. **1724** A. COLLINS *Gr. Chr. Relig.* 190 The apostate Jews, among whom..some of the Samaritans..became embody'd. **1799** MACKINTOSH *Stud. Law Nat.* Wks. 1846 I. 385 Yet so much of these treaties has been embodied into the general law of Europe.

†**b.** *intr.* for *refl. Obs.*

1692 tr. *Sallust* 8 Incredible it is to think how easily they [different tribes] embody'd.

c. *trans.* Of a complex unity: To include, comprise (such or such elements).

1847 MEDWIN *Shelley* I. 29 Blue books..embodied stories of haunted castles, bandits, murderers. **1869** *Daily News* 18 Dec., The measure embodies of course the six points of the League's educational charter. **1876** J. H. NEWMAN *Hist. Sk.* I. I. iv. 198 Mahometanism certainly..embodies in it some ancient and momentous truths.

†**5.** *Chem.* and *Phys.* **a.** *trans.* To form into one body. **b.** *intr.* for *refl.* To coalesce, draw together, solidify. *Obs.*

1660 BOYLE *New Exp. Phys. Mech.* xxxv. 264 The Bubbles..imbodyed themselves..into one. **1662** H. STUBBE *Ind. Nectar* iii. 26 These Corpuscles did never embody into greater quantities. **1677** W. HARRIS tr. *Lemery's Course Chym.* I. xvi. (1686) 376 The spirit of wine being a sulphur does unite and imbody with those that remain. *c* **1682** J. COLLINS *Making of Salt* 54 It will naturally Embody in the Sun, and become a substance like Salt. **1709** *Brit. Apollo* II. No. 12. 2/2 An Alimentary Liquor..doth embody with the Blood. **1710** T. FULLER *Pharm. Extemp.* 27 Heating the Oils a little..adding the oil of Vitriol..and stirring 'till all are embodied together.

6. *trans.* To form into a body or company for military or other purposes; to organize.

1649 SELDEN *Laws Eng.* II. xi. (1739) 63 The Army is ever embodied within the Kingdom. *a* **1655** VINES *Lord's Supp.* (1677) 265 Holy persons might..embody themselves into a Church. **1779** T. JEFFERSON *Corr.* Wks. 1859 I. 218 The troops were never before so healthy since they were embodied. **1838–42** ARNOLD *Hist. Rome* III. xliv. 201 Livius..embodied the population of the town. **1873** BURTON *Hist. Scot.* VI. lxx. 174 The forces..may now be considered as embodied against each other.

b. *intr.* for *refl.* To form or join a body or company for military or other purposes.

1648 CROMWELL *Let.* 20 Aug. (Carlyle), I have..ordered Colonel Scroop with five troops of horse and two troops of dragoons, with two regiments of foot, to embody with them. **1661** *Lond. Allarum* 3 They had secretly entred into a Combination..to meet and imbody at their appointed Rendevouz. **1681** *Moores Baffled* 16 [He] commanded the Horse to Embody within the Lines. **1770** BURKE *Pres. Discont.* Wks. 1842 I. 133 Firmly to embody against this court party. **1796** MORSE *Amer. Geog.* I. 669 The tories..embodied in armed parties.

7. *trans.* To impart 'body' to (painting); to paint with a full body of colour.

1784 J. BARRY *Lect. Art*, vi. (1848) 223 His [Vandyck's] lights are..well embodied with colour.

Hence **em'bodying** *vbl. sb.* and *ppl. a.*

1676 W. ROW *Contn. Blair's Autobiog.* xi. (1848) 291 The embodying of Scotland into one commonwealth with England. **1677** EARL ORRERY *Art of War* 182 To prevent all considerable Imbodyings to resist him. **1784** J. BARRY *Lect. Art* vi. (1848) 223 All that..embodying of colour..may be given as you go on. **1791** *Phil. Trans.* LXXXI. 179 Water is the embodying principle of all elastic fluids.

embog (ɛm'bɒg), *v.* Also 7 embogge, imbog, 9 embogue. [f. EN- + BOG *sb.*] *trans.* To plunge into a bog; to hamper in a bog, *lit.* and *fig.*

1602 BEST in Farr *S.P. Eliz.* (1845) II. 472 Imbogg'd he shall be, where nought he shall see But horror and feare. **1611** SPEED *Hist. Gt. Brit.* IX. xii. 64 He was..constrained..to Embogge himselfe in the Bankers and Vsurers bookes. **1752** WESLEY in *Wks.* 1872 II. 256 Attempting to ride over the common..my mare was quickly imbogged. **1867** *N. Brit. Daily Mail* 30 Sept., The valley was so soft that the big guns would have become embogged. **1888** *Daily Tel.* 1 June 5/2 Embogued in a morass.

†**em'bogue,** *v. Obs.* [? corruptly ad. Sp. *embocar*, f. *em-* + *boca* mouth.] = DISEMBOGUE.

Hence †**em'boguing** *vbl. sb.*, the place where a lake or river discharges itself. *Obs.*

1603 FLORIO *Montaigne* (1634) 113 The emboguing [Fr. *embouch eure*] of the Meotis fennes.

†**em'boil.** *Obs. rare.* Also 6 emboyl. [f. EN- + BOIL.] **a.** *trans.* To cause to boil or to agitate with rage. **b.** *intr.* To be in a boil or agitation.

1590 SPENSER *F.Q.* I. xi. 28 Emboyled, grieued, brent. *Ibid.* II. iv. 9 The Knight emboyling in his haughtie hart.

‖**emboîtement** (ãbwatmã). [Fr.; f. *emboîter* to enclose in a box, f. *en-* in + *boîte* box.]

1. *Anat.* The fitting of a bone into another.

1854 OWEN *Skel. & Teeth* (1855) 32 This kind of 'emboitement' of the occipital in the parietal vertebra.

2. *Biol.* Used by Buffon to describe the hypothesis of the generation of living things, according to which successive generations are produced by the successive development of living germs which lie one within the other (*Syd. Soc. Lex.*).

3. The closing up of a number of men in order to secure the front rank from injury.

In Mod. Dicts.

†**em'bold,** *v. Obs.* Also 5–6 enbold, 7 imbold. [f. EN- + BOLD.] *trans.* To make bold, embolden; to incite, encourage.

c **1400** *Test. Love* I. (1560) 273 b/1 Mine heart began somdeale to be enbolded. **1536** in Strype *Eccl. Mem.* I. App. lxxv. Bee she..examined..who did embold..her therunto. **1556** J. HEYWOOD *Spider & F.* lx. 180 The selfe sight of this force shall you so enbold. **1598** SYLVESTER *Du Bartas* 891 Bind and imbold mee once more to present My humble briefs in form of Parliament.

embolden, imbolden (ɛm-, ɪm'bəʊldən), *v.* Also 6 enbolden, -bowlden, 6–7 emboulden, -bowlden. [f. EN-, IN- + BOLD + -EN.] *trans.* To render bold or more bold; to hearten, encourage.

α. **1571** CAMPION *Hist. Irel.* (1633) 2 Ep. Ded., I am embouldned to present them to your Lordships patronage. **1583** T. STOCKER *Tragicall Hist.* I. 109 b, We..are enboldened to exhibite a certeine supplication. **1597** J. PAYNE *Royal Exch.* 46 He enbowldeneth the erringe hart to suffer for error. **1667** MILTON *P.L.* VIII. 434 Thus I embold'nd spake. **1709** ADDISON *Tatler* No. 100 ¶4 Their Aspects were so..emboldened with Resolution. **1818** JAS. MILL *Brit. India* II. v. iii. 403 The Bombay Presidency were more emboldened in their importunity. **1860** MACAULAY *Biog.* (1867) 88 The affronts which his poverty emboldened..low-minded men to offer to him.

β. **1586** T. B. *La Primaud. Fr. Acad.* I. (1589) 218 Ambition..imboldeneth [the son] to seeke his destruction of whom he holdeth his life. **1626** G. SANDYS *Ovid's Met.* x. 201 Their lookes imboldned, modestie now gone. **1741** RICHARDSON *Pamela* III. 231 Whether..my Look, my Dress, my Appearance..imbolden such an affrontive Insolence. **1854** J. ABBOT *Napoleon* (1855) I. xxv. 406 The..inconvenience of imboldening..the foes of the consular government.

Hence **em'boldener**, one who or that which emboldens. **em'boldening** *vbl. sb.* and *ppl. a.*

1847 CRAIG, *Emboldener.* **1882** STEVENSON *Treasure Isl.* iv, Argument is a great emboldener. **1503** *Act. 19 Hen. VII* c. 10 Small fines have been..set to the..great emboldening of the said Offenders. **1575** in W. H. Turner *Select. Rec. Oxford* 364 Another imboldeninge of evill persons. **1628** WITHER, *Brit. Rememb.* III. 248 But, rather, lesse imboldning then before. **1867** FREEMAN *Norm. Conq.* (ed. 3) I. v. 297 There was nothing..but..emboldening of their foes.

†**em'boldish,** *v. Obs. rare.* In 6 enboldish. [f. EN- + BOLD, after words like *impoverish.*] = EMBOLDEN.

1502 ARNOLDE *Chron.* (1811) 293 They that were disposid to do disobeysance were..enboldishide [*printed* enboldrshide].

Hence †**em'boldishment**, *Obs.*, in 6 inboldishment. [see -MENT.] = EMBOLDENING *vbl. sb.*

1512 *Act 4 Hen. VIII*, c. 20. §2 To the greate inboldisshment of..mysgoverned persons disobeyeng your lawes.

‖**embole** ('ɛmbəliː). *Med.* [mod.L., a. Gr. ἐμβολή a throwing or putting in, f. ἐμβάλλειν to throw in, f. ἐν in + βάλλειν to throw.]

†**1.** The reducing of a dislocated limb. *Obs.*

1811 HOOPER *Med. Dict.*, *Embole*, the reduction or setting of a dislocated bone. **1860** MAYNE *Exp. Lex.*, *Embole*, a term formerly used for the reduction of a dislocation.

2. 'A plug or wedge' (*Syd. Soc. Lex.*).

3. = EMBOLUS (*Syd. Soc. Lex.*).

embolectomy (ɛmbəʊ'lɛktəmɪ). *Path.* [f. EMBOL(US + -ECTOMY.] The surgical removal of an embolus.

1923 *Surgery, Gynecology & Obstetrics* XXXVI. 309 (*heading*) Embolectomy in the treatment of circulatory disturbances in the extremities. **1961** *Lancet* 19 Aug. 402/2 Pulmonary embolism not infrequently complicates a variety of..conditions... Until recently Trendelenburg's operation of pulmonary embolectomy afforded the one hope.

embolic (ɛm'bɒlɪk), *a. Pathol.* [f. EMBOL-US + -IC.] **1.** Relating to or caused by an embolus.

1866 A. FLINT *Princ. Med.* (1880) 33 The multiple abscesses in pyæmia are, for the most part, of embolic origin. **1874** JONES & SIEV. *Pathol. Anat.* 270 Embolic softening is the lesion most frequently discovered.

2. *Embryology.* Characterized by emboly.

1875 E. R. LANKESTER in *Q. Jrnl. Microsc. Sci.* XV. 164 The invaginated cells of embolic Planulæ. **1877** —— *Notes Embryol.* i. 13 Two degrees of this Epibolic mode of Invagination (so called by Selenka, in distinction from the Embolic mode) are distinguished by Haeckel as Amphiblastic and Discoblastic. **1881** F. M. BALFOUR *Compar. Embryol.* II. xiii. 276 One half of the blastosphere may be pushed in towards the opposite half, and a gastrula be thus produced... This process is known as embolic invagination. **1966** *McGraw-Hill Encycl. Sci. & Technol.* VI. 79 In some animals, such as certain coelenterates, no pronounced epibolic or embolic movements of cells seem to occur during gastrulation.

†**emboli'mæal,** *a. Obs. rare*[−1]. [f. Gr. ἐμβολιμαῖ-ος of same meaning (cf. EMBOLISM) + -AL[1].] Intercalary. So †**emboli'mæan** [see -AN], **emboli'mæar** [see -AR].

1677 CARY *Chronol.* I. I. I. iv. 11 Differences of years, some ordinary and common, others Embolimæal. **1726** tr. *Gregory's Astron.* I. 244 To this purpose they us'd Intercalary or Embolimean Months. **1796** HUTTON *Math. Dict.*, *Embolimæan* is chiefly used in speaking of the additional months inserted by chronologists to form the lunar cycle of 19 years. **1677** CARY *Chronol.* I. I. I. xii. 46 They must needs make Embolimæar Months or Days.

†**em'bolimary,** *a. Obs. rare*[−1]. [f. Gr. ἐμβολιμαῖος (see prec.) + -ARY.] = prec.

1696 WHISTON *The. Earth* II. (1722) 178 Each year had in it 12 Lunar Months..no Embolimary Month being taken in.

embolism ('ɛmbəlɪz(ə)m). [ad. L. *embolismus*, a. late Gr. ἐμβολισμός intercalation, f. ἐμβολή, ἔμβολος; cf. EMBOLE, EMBOLUS.]

1. *Chronol.* **a.** The periodical intercalation of a day or days in the calendar to correct the error arising from the difference between the civil and the solar year. *concr.* A period of time so intercalated.

1387 TREVISA *Higden* (Rolls) III. 259 Not þe ȝere of þe sonne, noþer of embolisme. **1596** BELL *Surv. Popery* I. III. iv. 107 To make embolismes and intercalations. *a* **1638** MEDE Wks. III. iv. 589 *marg.*, Count the Embolism of 5 days. **1679** PLOT *Staffordsh.* (1686) 426 An Embolisme of 30 days or a full Month must needs be made somewhere this year. **1788** MARSDEN in *Phil. Trans.* LXXVIII. 417 The year of the Mahometans consists of twelve lunar months..no embolism being employed to adjust it to the solar period. **1796** HUTTON *Math. Dict.* s.v. *Embolismus.* **1847** in CRAIG.

†**b.** *attrib.* (in quot. quasi-*adj.*). *Obs.*

1588 A. KING tr. *Canisius' Catech.* H. vij, Ane moneth..addit to y[at] ȝere..makis y[e] same..to be callit embolisme.

†**2.** (*nonce-use.* See quot.)

1772 NUGENT tr. *Hist. Friar Gerund* I. 435 All he has written is a mere embolism or insertion of foreign and absurd matter.

3. a. *Pathol.* [cf. EMBOLUS.] (See quot.)

1855 H. SPENCER *Princ. Psychol.* (1872) I. I. iv. 73 Embolism..a plugging up of an artery with coagulated blood. **1878** T. BRYANT *Pract. Surg.* I. 431 Embolism is a somewhat common affection and consists in the occlusion of a vessel.

b. *Path.* An obstruction in a blood-vessel; = EMBOLUS 2. *air embolism*: see AIR *sb.*[1] B. II.

1902 *Encycl. Brit.* XXXI. 565/2 The small vessels are sometimes blocked by masses of organisms only, producing minute embolisms.

4. In the liturgies of various rites: a prayer occurring after (with partial repetition of) the Lord's Prayer, and before the Communion; = EMBOLISMUS 2.

1720 T. BRETT *Collect. Princ. Liturgies* xl. 337 What follows the Lord's Prayer has been added since Gregory's Time, and is called by some of the Romanists themselves an Embolism or Interpolation. **1881** WESTCOTT & HORT *N.T. in Orig. Greek* II. App. 9/2 Various embolisms include other ascriptions of praise. **1883** *Encycl. Brit.* XVI. 509/1 The 'canon'..(except in the Nestorian liturgy) concludes with the Lord's Prayer and 'embolism'. **1904** HART & FRERE *Rock's Ch. Fathers* IV. II. xi. 105 The Lord's Prayer was said as at the end of the Canon, with its bidding before it and its embolism after it. **1957** *Oxf. Dict. Chr. Ch.* 449/1 *Embolism*, in the Roman Mass, the name given to the prayer..which begins 'Libera nos quaesumus, Domine, ab omnibus malis'. .. Many E[astern] liturgies have a similar prayer at this point.

†**embolis'mæan,** *a. Obs. rare*[−1]. Incorrect form of EMBOLIMÆAN, after EMBOLISM.

1704 HEARNE *Duct. Hist.* (1714) I. 11 The Embolismæan or Intercalated Years.

†**embo'lismal,** *a. Obs. Chronol.* [f. EMBOLISM + -AL[1].] That pertains to embolism or intercalation. **a.** Of a year: That is lengthened by intercalation. **b.** Of a month: That is intercalated.

1681 WHARTON *Disc. Years etc.* Wks. (1683) 72 This year is two-fold, viz. Commune, containing 12 Synodical Lunations: or Embolismal, which containeth 13. **1679** PLOT *Staffordsh.* (1686) 426 There must needs be 7 Embolismal months.

†**embolis'matical,** *a. Obs.*[−0] [f. Gr. ἐμβολισματ- stem of ἐμβόλισμα + -ICAL.] = prec.

1736 in BAILEY. **1775** in ASH.

embolismic (ɛmbəʊ'lɪzmɪk), *a. Chronol.* [f. EMBOLISM + -IC.] = EMBOLISMAL.

1736 BAILEY, *Embolismic*, intercalary. **1775** ASH, *Embolismic*, belonging to an embolism, intercalary. **1871** J. FOWLER in *Archæol.* XLIV. 146 The signs and symbols of the thirteen months of the Anglo-Saxon embolismic year. **1876** *Prayer-bk. Interleaved* 51 All but one of the additional or embolismic lunations. **1877** BP. S. BUTCHER *Eccles. Cal.* 59.

Hence †**embo'lismical,** *a. Obs.*[−0] = prec.

1736 in BAILEY. **1775** in ASH.

‖**embolismus** (ɛmbəʊ'lɪzməs). [L.; see EMBOLISM.]

†**1.** *Chronol.* **a.** The excess of the solar year above the lunar year of twelve synodical months. **b.** Intercalation. *Obs.*

1398 TREVISA *Barth. De P.R.* IX. iv. (1495) 348 Embolismus is encreasynge and excesse by the whyche the

yere of the sunne passyth the yere of the mone. **1796** HUTTON *Math. Dict.*, *Embolismus*..signifies intercalation.

2. In the Greek liturgy: A prayer inserted after the concluding petitions of the Lord's Prayer.

1872 O. SHIPLEY *Gloss. Eccl. Terms* 476 Said..after the embolismus at Easter-tide.

embolite ('ɛmbəlaɪt). *Min.* [f. Gr. ἐμβόλ-ιον an intermediate + -ITE; 'because between the chlorid and bromid of silver' (Dana).] 'A chlorobromide of silver, $Ag_5Br_2Cl_3$. It is perfectly malleable; has a resinous and somewhat adamantine lustre, and varies in colour from asparagus-green to pistachio, olive, and greyish-green' (Watts *Dict. Chem.*). Also *attrib.*

1850 DANA *Min.* 545 Embolite..crystals are implanted in crystallized calc spar. **1868** *Ibid.* (1880) 116 Varieties of embolite based on the proportion of bromid to chlorid.

embolite, error for EMBELIF.

1560 ed. *Chaucer, Astrolabe* 251/1.

embolium (ɛm'bɒlɪəm). *Ent.* [mod.L., a. Gr. ἐμβόλιον insertion, f. ἐν in + βολ-, var. of root of βάλλειν to throw.] The marginal part of the corium in some heteropterous insects.

1865 DOUGLAS & SCOTT *Brit. Hemiptera* I. 3 In the *Corium* are at least 2 principal longitudinal nerves, and sometimes 1 within the anterior margin separates a narrow portion, forming the *Embolium.* **1895** J. H. & A. COMSTOCK *Man. Study Insects* 125 Classification of the Heteroptera... In certain other cases, a narrow piece on the costal margin of the corium is separated by a suture; this is the *embolium.* **1899** G. H. CARPENTER *Insects* 187 The *corium*..in most families reaches to the costa, but in one is separated from that edge by a narrow *embolium.* **1959** SOUTHWOOD & LESTON *Land & Water Bugs* 411 *Embolium*, used traditionally in the Cimicidae for the area between the costal margin and the anterior furrow; a bad term.

emboli'zation. [f. **embolize* (deduced from EMBOLISM) + -ATION.]

†**1.** *Chronol.* Intercalation. *Obs. rare*⁻¹.

1677 CARY *Chronol.* I. I. I. xii. 46 Which Embolisation must have some Analogy with the Greek Mode.

2. *Med.* [see EMBOLIZE *v.*] The introduction of an embolus; embolism.

1949 *Surgery* XXVI. 709 Using pea seeds for embolization of smaller arteries and a 1:20 starch suspension for embolization of the arterioles and capillaries. **1957** *Amer. Heart Jrnl.* LIV. 483 (*heading*) The cause of death in pulmonary embolization. **1967** *Arch. Path.* LXXXIV. 659/1 A case of fatal systemic embolization of gastric contents associated with rupture of the stomach.

embolize ('ɛmbəlaɪz), *v. Med.* [f. EMBOL(US or EMBOL(ISM + -IZE.] *trans.* To introduce an embolus artificially into, or to cause embolism in (a blood-vessel, etc.). Hence **'embolized, 'embolizing** *ppl. adjs.*

1920 *Q. Jrnl. Med.* XIII. 133 In embolized goats in which the condition of dyspnoea was fully established, samples of blood were withdrawn without an anaesthetic. **1949** *Surgery* XXVI. 710 A local reflex spasm of the pulmonary arterioles initiated by mechanical endovascular irritation by the embolizing particles. **1957** *Amer. Heart Jrnl.* LIV. 486 Frequently, clumps of the small particles embolized visible arteries. *Ibid.* 489 In 1917, Mann embolized awake, locally anesthetized, and anesthetized dogs with paraffin or blood clots.

†**em'bolne,** *v. Obs.* Also 5-6 enbolne. [f. EN- + BOLNE.] *trans.* To cause to swell or rise; *fig.* to puff up. Hence **em'bolning** *vbl. sb.*

1430 LYDG. *Chron. Troy* I. ix, With yrous herte enbolned all with pride. *c* **1525** SKELTON *Replyc.* Wks. 1862 II. 232 Yong scolers nowe a dayes enbolned with the flyblowen blast of the moche vayne glorious pipplyng wynde. **1598** NASHE *Christ's T.* 14 b, Embolning the billowes vppe to the ayre, with roring and howling [they] darte themselues on euery Rocke. **1692** in COLES. **1775** ASH, *Embolned*, swelled.

‖**embolon** ('ɛmbəlɒn). *Pathol.* [f. Gr. ἔμβολον a peg, stopper.] = EMBOLUS 2.

1878 A. HAMILTON *Nerv. Dis.* 138 A large embolon plugs up some such artery as the middle cerebral.

†**em'bolster,** *v. Obs. rare.* Also **imbolster.** [f. EN- + BOLSTER.] *trans.* To bolster out, to pad (see BOLSTER 2 d). Hence **em'bolstering** *vbl. sb.*

1593 NASHE *Christ's T.* (1613) 144 The women..adding more Bauines vnto it [beauty] of lasciuious embolstrings. **1630** BRATHWAIT *Eng. Gentlewom.* (1641) 301 That..embolsters her decayed brests, to purchase a sweetheart. **1632** W. LITHGOW *Totall Discourse* 466 Wherevpon my hunger-clungd bellie waxing great, grew Drum-like imbolstered.

‖**embolus** ('ɛmbələs). [L. *embolus* piston of a pump, a. Gr. ἔμβολος peg, stopper.]

†**1.** *Mech.* Something inserted or moving in another, such as the bar of a door, a wedge; *esp.* the piston of a syringe. *Obs.*

1669 BOYLE *Contn. New Exp.* I. xxxii. (1682) 106 The Embolus or Sucker of a Syringe. **1708** KERSEY, *Embolus*, a bar of a Door, a wedge. **1739** J. HUXHAM *Ess. Fevers* (1750) 182 Too great a Weight on the Embolus of a Syringe hinders its fair play. **1847** in CRAIG.

2. *Pathol.* 'The body which causes EMBOLISM' (*Syd. Soc. Lex.*).

1866 A. FLINT *Princ. Med.* (1880) 30 An embolus is a plug of some material which is transported by the blood-current from one situation to another. **1876** tr. *Wagner's Gen. Pathol.* 202 The embolus is usually arrested at a part where the vessels divide.

3. *Anat.* 'The osseous axis of the horns of the *Ruminantia cavicornia*' (*Syd. Soc. Lex.*).

emboly ('ɛmbəlɪ). [as if ad. Gr. *ἐμβολία, f. stem of ἐμβάλλειν to throw in. Fr. has *embolie* (Littré) = EMBOLISM 3.] = INVAGINATION: **a.** *Surg.* The name of a particular operation for hernia. **b.** *Phys.* The process of formation of the double-layered *gastrula* by involution of the wall of the single-layered segmented ovum.

1877 HUXLEY *Anat. Inv. An.* xii. 682 Modification of the blastosphere by the process of invagination or emboly. *Ibid.* 683 The various processes by which the gastrula or its equivalent are produced, are reducible to epiboly and emboly.

†**em'bondage,** *v. Obs.* Also 7 en-, **imbondage.** [f. EN- + BONDAGE.] *trans.* To bring into a state of bondage or slavery; *lit.* and *fig.*

1607 HIERON *Wks.* I. 331 Let vs not so enthrall & enbondage our selues vnder our own lusts. **1673** CAVE *Prim. Chr.* III. ii. 237 Christians embondaging themselves to redeem others. **1691** HOWGIL in *Quakers Unmasked* 12 He and his Assistants sought to inthral all, and Imbondage all.

‖**embonpoint** (ɑ̃bɔ̃pwɛ̃), *a.* and *sb.* Also **enbonpoint.** [F. *embonpoint*: f. phrase *en bon point* 'in good condition'.]

A. *sb.* Plumpness, well-nourished appearance of body: in complimentary or euphemistic sense.

1751 WARBURTON in Pope *Mor. Ess.* IV. 47 Wks. 1751 III. 272 To take care that the..colours are proportioned to her complexion; the stuff to the embonpoint of her person. **1807** Z. PIKE *Sources Mississ.* III. App. 35 They are all inclining a little to enbonpoint. **1849** C. BRONTË *Shirley* xi. 162 A form decidedly inclined to embonpoint. **1876** BARTHOLOW *Mat. Med.* (1879) 343 An increase in the body-weight and the embonpoint of those who take stimulants.

B. as predicative *adj.* Plump, well-nourished-looking. [In Fr. only as phrase *en bon point.*]

[**1662** EVELYN *Sculptura* I. i. (1755) 18 Plump & (as the French has it) en bon point.] *c* **1806** SIR R. WILSON in *Life* (1862) I. App. 372 Before marriage they are generally light in figure; after they are mothers they become more *embonpoint*. **1818** SCOTT *Hrt. Midl.* xxxvii, Her form, though rather *embonpoint*, was nevertheless graceful.

†**em'border,** *v. Obs.* Also 6 enborder, 7-8 imborder. [f. EN- + BORDER.] **a.** To furnish with an edge or border; to edge. Const. *with* **b.** To place or set as a border.

c **1530** LD. BERNERS *Arth. Lyt. Bryt.* (1814) 139 The crampons [of the bed] were of fyne syluer enbordered wyth golde. **1667** MILTON *P.L.* IX. 436 Among thick-wov'n Arborets and Flours Imbordered [*mod. edd.* embordered] on each Bank. **1736** BAILEY, *Imbordered*, bordered, having borders. **1847** CRAIG, *Emborder, Imborder*, to furnish or enclose with a border; to bound. In mod. Dicts. [in both forms].

embordured, -ing, var. ff. IMBORDURED, -ING.

‖**embo'scata** (*pseudo-arch.*), incorrect spelling of (It.) IMBOSCATA, AMBUSCADE.

1820 SCOTT *Monast.* xxi, Have you purpose to set upon me here as in an emboscata?

embosk, var. of IMBOSK, to shelter in a wood.

embosom, imbosom (ɛm-, ɪm'bʊzəm), *v.* Also 7 enbosome. [f. EN-, IN- + BOSOM.]

1. *trans.* To take or press to one's bosom; to cherish in one's bosom; to embrace. †Also, to implant, plunge (a sting, weapon, etc.) in (another's) bosom (*obs.*). Chiefly *fig. rare* in mod. use.

α. **1590** SPENSER *F.Q.* II. ii. 25 The handmayd..glad t' embosome his affection vile. **1610** G. FLETCHER *Christ's Vict.* in Farr *S.P. Jas.* (1848) 67 Thus sought the dire enchauntresse in his minde Her guilefull bait to have embosomed. *c* **1630** DRUMM. OF HAWTH. *Poems* Wks. (1711) 36/2 Tithon's wife embosom'd by him lies. **1645** QUARLES *Sol. Recant.* vii. 9 Anger rests Embosom'd..in foolish brests. **1729** SAVAGE *Wanderer* I. 380 Why embosom me a viper's sting? *a* **1813** A. WILSON *Tears of Britain* Poet. Wks. 158 Shall..such a monster..By Britons be..embosomed? **1874** PUSEY *Lent. Serm.* 459 All the Father embosometh the Son.

β. **1631** *Celestina* I. 7 Suffering them [Muleteers] to imbosome them between their brests. **1671** FLAVEL *Fount. Life* ii. 4 They lay as it were imbosomed in one another. **1806** MOORE *From High Priest of Apollo* ii. 40 Might he but pass the hours of shade Imbosomed by his Delphic maid.

2. *transf.* **a.** To enclose, conceal, shelter, in the 'bosom'. Often *pass.* to be enclosed, enveloped *in*, closely surrounded *with* (woods, foliage, mountains, etc.); *poet.*, to be 'wrapped' *in* (slumber, happiness, beauty, etc.). †**b.** *refl.* Of a river: To pour itself *into* the bosom of a larger stream (*obs.*).

α. **1685** H. MORE *Para. Proph.* xiii, All sorts of people may safely embosom themselves in her. *c* **1750** SHENSTONE *Elegies* vii. 44 My distant home Which oaks embosom. **1764** GOLDSM. *Trav.* 282 Embosom'd in the deep where Holland lies. **1773** WILKES *Corr.* (1805) IV. 158 The vilages are happily embosomed with trees. **1796** MORSE *Amer. Geog.* I. 501 This state [New York] embosoms vast quantities of iron ore. **18..** CAMPBELL *On Visiting Scene in Argylsh.* i, The wind-shaken weeds that embosom the bower. **1829** SCOTT *Anne of G.* iii, One of those spots in which Nature often embosoms her sweetest charms. **1855** SINGLETON *Virgil* I. 279 Deep sleep embosometh their jaded limbs. **1876** GREEN *Short Hist.* x. §4. 798 What sepulchre embosoms the remains..of so much human excellence and glory? **1879** CHR. ROSSETTI *Seek & F.* 24 The sky..over-arching and embosoming not earth and sea only, but clouds and meteors, planets and stars.

β. **1665** MANLEY *Grotins' Low-C. Warres* 837 The River Vecht..imbosomes it self into the same [the Issell]. **1667** MILTON *P.L.* v. 597 By whom in bliss imbosom'd sat the Son. **1835** WILLIS *Pencillings* II. lx. 167 We walked..to a large old villa, imbosomed in trees. **1839** BAILEY *Festus* (ed. 5) 378 Thy heart imbosomed in all beauteousness.

Hence **em'bosomed,** *ppl. a.*, **em'bosoming** *vbl. sb.* and *ppl. a.*

1622-62 HEYLIN *Cosmogr.* III. (1682) 205 Since their embosoming and reconcilement to the Church of Rome. **1626** SANDYS *Ovid's Metam.* x. 205 She..Flusht with imbosomd flames. **1839** BAILEY *Festus* xviii. (1848) 184 The long imbosomed braid. **1859** FARRAR *J. Home* (1874) 9 The hill with its tall spire and embosoming trees. **1873** BROWNING *Red Cott. Night-c.* 660 Bosses of shrubs, embosomings of flowers.

†**em'boss,** *sb. Obs. rare*⁻¹. [f. EMBOSS *v.*] A boss-like projection; a knob.

1644 EVELYN *Mem.* (1857) I. 124 A round emboss of marble.

emboss (ɛm'bɒs), *v.*¹ Also 4-6 enbos(s, 5 enboce. [prob. a. OF. *emboce-r (app. not recorded before 1530): see EN- and BOSS *sb.*¹]

1. *trans.* To cause to bulge or swell out, make convex or protuberant; to cover with protuberances. In modern use chiefly *transf.* from 2 or 3.

α. *c* **1460** *Stans Puer* 31 in *Babees Bk.* (1868) 28 To enboce thy Iowis withe mete. **1541** R. COPLAND *Guydon's Quest. Chirurg.* Some [bones] are enbossed for to entre. **1598** SYLVESTER *Du Bartas* I. iii. (1641) 25/2 When God..Embas't the Valleys and Embost the Hils. **1683** SALMON *Doron Med.* I. 334 Embossed with fat. **17..** GAY *Story of Arachne* 39 Her trembling hand, embossed with livid veins. **1763** CHURCHILL *Proph. Famine*, Poems I. 117 With boils embossed and overgrown with scurf. **1814** SOUTHEY *Roderick* XXI. 18 Its fretted roots Embossed the bank. **1868** KIRK *Chas. Bold* III. v. iii. 413 It is everywhere unequal, embossed with hill-tops.

β. **1664** POWER *Exp. Philos.* I. 13 Her Body is..imboss'd all over with black knobs. **1667** MILTON *P.L.* XII. 180 Botches and blaines must all his flesh imboss.

†**b.** fig. *to emboss* (*out*): to inflate (style), render tumid; to give exaggerated prominence to.

1564 *Brief Exam.* *iiij b, Ye embosse out your glorious stiles. **1565** JEWEL *Repl. Harding* (1611) 36 It hath pleased M. Harding thus to colour and to embosse out this ancient Father. **1577, 1646** [see EMBOSSED *ppl. a.*¹ 3].

†**c.** *intr.* To bulge, be convex. *Obs. rare.*

c **1430** [see EMBOSSING *vbl. sb.*]. **1576** BAKER *Jewell of Health* 215 a, If the same be made hollowe imbossing towarde the myddle.

2. *spec.* To carve or mould in relief; to cause (figures, part of a wrought surface) to stand out, project, or protrude. Also *fig.* The earliest and the prevailing mod. sense. [So Fr. *imbocer* (Palsgr.).]

α. *c* **1385** CHAUCER *L.G.W.*, *Dido*, Of gold the barris vp enbosede [*v.r.* enbossed]. **1563** *Homilies* II. *Idolatry* II. (1859) 194 Images came into the Church, not now in painted cloths only, but embossed in stone. **1644** EVELYN *Mem.* (1857) I. 76 Fleur-de-lis embossed out of the stone. **1796** BURKE *Regic. Peace* Wks. 1842 II. 322 Such claims..stood embossed, and..forced themselves on the view of common, short-sighted benevolence. **1858** HAWTHORNE *Fr. & It. Jrnls.* II. 37 A gold sword-hilt..being actually embossed on the picture. **1885** *Manch. Exam.* 5 June 5/6 Farmer's apparatus..for chasing, glazing, and embossing cloth.

β. **1612** DRAYTON *Poly-olb.* v. 75 Fish..in Antique worke most curiously imbost. **1676** BOYLE in *Phil. Trans.* XI. 807 The figure of a Star..imbost upon the upper superficies of the Regulus.

b. To adorn with figures or other ornamentation in relief; to represent (a subject) in relief. (Sometimes with reference to embroidery.) Also of the figures, etc.: To stand out as an ornament upon.

1430 LYDG. *Chron. Troy* II. xx, An epythaphe..With letters ryche of golde aboue enboced. **1513** BRADSHAW *St. Werburge* 60 The ten plages of Egypte were well embost. **1601** HOLLAND *Pliny* II. 602 Siluer plate curiously enchased and imbossed. **1659** BP. WALTON *Consid. Considered* 299 How come they [Samaritan letters] to adorn and emboss vessels and coins? **1725** POPE *Odyss.* XIX. 293 Regal robe with figured gold embost. **1781** GIBBON *Decl. & F.* III. lx. 523 The sides were embossed with a variety of picturesque ..scenes. **1832** BABBAGE *Econ. Manuf.* xi. (ed. 3) 89 Calicoes ..embossed all over with raised patterns. **1846** PRESCOTT *Ferd. & Is.* I. viii. 346 The rich bronze which embossed its gates. **1855** MACAULAY *Hist. Eng.* IV. 490 Men who..had made a fair profit by embossing silver bowls and chargers.

3. To ornament with or as with bosses or studs. Hence, To adorn or decorate sumptuously.

α. **1579** SPENSER *Sheph. Cal.* Feb., A girdle of gelt Embost with buegle. **1594** J. DICKENSON *Arisbas* (1878) 38 His house ..he found not gorgeously embost, yet gaily trimmed. *c* **1630** DRUMM. OF HAWTH. *Poems* Wks. (1711) 29/1 Bright portals of the sky Emboss'd with sparkling stars. **1697** POTTER *Antiq. Greece* III. iii. (1715) 14 The Chariots being richly emboss'd with Gold and other Metals. **1710** *Lond. Gaz.* No. 4672/1 The Harness was embossed with Silver Plates. **1784** COWPER *Task* v. 426 The studs, that thick emboss his iron door. **1812** H. & J. SMITH *Rej. Addr.* xi.

(1873) 104 Whose tresses the pearl-drops emboss. **1824-9** LANDOR *Imag. Conv.* (1846) I. 5 Did we not.. Emboss our bosoms with the daffodils.

β. **1578** T. PROCTOR *Gorg. Gallery*, With buyldings brave, imbost of variant hue. **1784** COWPER *Task* I. 121, I fed on.. berries that imboss the bramble.

em'boss, *v.*² *Obs.* exc. *arch.* in sense 4. Also 4 **embose, enbose,** 6-8 **imboss.** [ME. *embose*, perh. f. EN- + OF. *bos, bois* wood; the equivalent OFr. *embuiser* occurs with sense of AMBUSH. If so, the word is ultimately identical with IMBOSK *v.* The development of senses as suggested below is strange, but appears to be in accordance with the existing evidence.]

†**1.** *intr.* Of a hunted animal: To take shelter in, plunge into, a wood or thicket. *Obs.*

c **1369** CHAUCER *Dethe Blaunche* 352 [The hunters recounted] how the hert had vpon lengthe So moche embosed [*v.r.* enbosed, enbosid] I not nowe what. **1680** BUTLER *Rem.* (1759) I. 8 Look quickly, lest the Sight of us Should cause the startled Beast t' imboss.

†**b.** The *pa. pple.* is used by Milton for *imbosked.*

1671 MILTON *Samson* 1697 Like that self-begotten bird, In the Arabian woods imbost.

†**2.** To drive (a hunted animal) to extremity. *Obs.*

(The sense 'drive to a thicket,' required by the etymology above suggested, is not clearly evidenced).

1590 SPENSER *F.Q.* III. i. 21 Curres.. hauing.. The Saluage beast embost in weary chace. **1596** DRAYTON *Leg.* II. 379 Like a Deere, before the Hounds imbost. **1601** SHAKS. *All's Well* III. vi. 107 We have almost imbost him, you shall see his fall to night. **1654** GAYTON *Pleasant Notes on Don Quixot* 210 As Mules and Horses, who are imboss'd, foame and chafe the more. **1680** OTWAY *Caius Marius* IV. ii. (1735) 68 Was ever lion thus by dogs emboss'd? **1768** BUYS *Dict. Terms Art*, To Emboss (in Hunting), to inclose in a Thicket.

†**3.** In *pass.* of a hunted animal: To be exhausted by running; *hence*, to foam at the mouth (as a result of exhaustion in running). Also *transf.* of persons: (*a*) To be exhausted, at the last extremity of fatigue; (*b*) to foam at the mouth (from rage, etc.). *Obs.*

[The sense 'to foam at the mouth' is prob. influenced by EMBOSS *v.*¹, as if an 'embossed stag' were one 'studded' with bubbles of foam. Cf. IMBOST *v.*, to foam at the mouth (Cockaine 1590), IMBOST *sb.*, foam (R. Bradley 1727).]

1523 SKELTON *Garl. Laurell* 24 Where hartis belluyng, embosyd with distres Ran on the raunge. **1575** TURBERV. *Bk. Venerie* 242 When he is foamy at the mouth, we saye that he is embost. **1595** MARKHAM *Sir R. Grinuill* cxxiii, With rage imbost. **1611** —— *Countr. Content* I. iv. (1668) 25 A stag .. imbost, that is, foaming.. about the mouth. **1611** COTGR., *Malmené*.. imbossed, or almost spent, as a Deere by hard pursuit. **1625** GILL *Sacr. Philos.* ii. 191 As a stag embossed takes the soyle. **1651** DAVENANT *Gondibert* II. xlix, He [the stag] is imbos'd, and weary'd to a Bay. **1735** SOMERVILLE *Chase* III. 485 The Huntsman knows him by a thousand Marks, Black, and Imbost.

fig. **1592** WARNER *Albion's Eng.* VII. xxxvi. (1612) 175 My chased Heart imboste and almost spent. **1624** QUARLES *Job* Poems (1717) 227 My spirit's faint.. my soul's imbost.

4. *trans.* To cover with foam (the mouth, the body of an animal). *arch.*

1531 ELYOT *Gov.* II. vi. 120 By furie chaunged into an horrible figure, his mouthe foule and imbosed. **1810** SCOTT *Lady of L.* I. vii, Embossed with foam, and dark with soil, The labouring stag strained full in view. **1829** CUNNINGHAM *Magic Bridle, Anniv.* 148 He saw a wild steed.. White foam his flanks embossing.

†**em'boss**, *v.*³ *Obs.* [app. first in Spenser; perh. f. EN- + BOSS *sb.*³ The Sp. *embozarse* to envelop oneself in a cloak, has also been suggested. Some of the quots. might belong to EMBOSS *v.*¹ in sense 'decorate'.]

trans. To cover, encase (in armour); to plunge (a weapon) *in* an enemy's body. Also *fig.* in *pass.* To be 'wrapped' (in ease).

1590-6 SPENSER *F.Q.* I. iii. 24 A knight her mett in mighty armes embost. *Ibid.* I. xi. 20 The knight his thrillant speare again assayd In his bras-plated body to embosse. *Ibid.* III. i. 64 None of them rashly durst.. in so glorious spoyle themselves embosse. *Ibid.* VI. iv. 40 Vowing, that never he .. would lig in ease embost. **1621** BURTON *Anat. Mel.* I. ii. III. xv. (1651) 133 A souldier embossed all in gold [transl. L. *præcingitur auro*].

†**em'boss** *v.*⁴ *Obs.*⁻⁰ [ad. Fr. *embosser* to attach a 'spring' to a cable, f. *en-* (see EN-) + *bosse* knot at the end of a rope.] (See quot. and etymology: evidence of Eng. use is wanting.)

1768 BUYS *Dict. Terms Art*, To Emboss a Cable (sea Term.)

embossed (ɛm'bɒst), *ppl. a.*¹ [f. EMBOSS *v.*¹]

1. Carved or moulded in relief; ornamented with figures in relief; (of figures or ornament) raised, standing out in relief. ***embossed printing***: printing with raised letters, as for the use of the blind, or for ornament.

1541 ELYOT *Image Gov.* 67 Images.. wrought.. in imbossed worke. **1563** *Homilies* II. *Idolatry* II. (1859) 195 Embossed images began to creepe into Churches. **1591** PERCIVALL *Sp. Dict.*, *Relieve*, embossed works, *Toreumata*. **1803** *Phil. Trans.* XCIII. 153 The.. wear which attends the friction of.. embossed surfaces. **1849** WILMOTT *Jrnl. Summer in Country* 15 July 141 The embossed alphabet for the blind. **1856** EMERSON *Eng. Traits, Lit.* Wks. (Bohn) II. 103 The.. bill of fare engraved on embossed paper. **1859** GULLICK & TIMBS *Paint.* 205 With sufficient body to give an embossed effect to the touch.

2. Covered with ornamental bosses or studs; richly or sumptuously decorated.

1591 LYLY *Sappho* I. ii. 161 Endeavour to be a courtier to live in emboste roofes. **1871** WHYTE-MELVILLE *Sarchedon* I. 21 His master drew the embossed bit carefully from his favourite's mouth.

†**3.** In 15th c.: Humpbacked. *Obs.*

c **1430** tr. *Deguilleville's Pilg. Lyf. Manh.* (1869) 130 Boystows she was and wrong shapen and enbosed [Fr. *bossue*].

†**4.** Bulging, convex, swollen, tumid; *fig.* of style.

1577 HOLINSHED *Chron.* II. 163 Thinking by their embossed speech to tickle the eares and harts of the yoong princes. **1578** LYTE *Dodoens* 645 The.. imbossed heades of the first and right Squilla. **1584** R. SCOT *Discov. Witchcr.* XIII. xix. 258 In diverse kinds of glasses; as in the hollowe the plain, the embossed. **1596** SHAKS. *1 Hen. IV*, III. iii. 177 Why thou horson, impudent, imbost Rascall. **1605** —— *Lear* II. iv. 227 My Daughter, thou art a Byle, a plague sore, or imbossed Carbuncle. **1646** J. HALL *Horæ Vac.* 39 Embossed Language tickles the eares.

5. *Bot.* 'Projecting in the centre like the boss of a shield' (*Syd. Soc. Lex.*).

†**em'bossed**, *ppl. a.*² *Obs.* [f. EMBOSS *v.*² + -ED¹.] Of a hunted animal: Driven to extremity; foaming at the mouth from exhaustion. Also *transf.* of persons.

1641 BP. HALL in *Rem. Wks.* (1660) 91 The embossed heart panteth for the rivers. **1649** SELDEN *Laws Eng.* II. xxvi. (1739) 117 Like an embossed Stag.. he must run and out-run all. *a* **1658** CLEVELAND *Gen. Poems* (1677) 100 Once more to single out my emboss'd Committee-man.

embosser (ɛm'bɒsə(r)). Also 7 **imbosser.** [f. EMBOSS *v.*¹ + -ER.] One who embosses.

1625 in RYMER *Fœdera* XVIII. (1726) 74 Wee doe.. appointe and ordaine to be the Maister Imbosser and Maker of the medales of us our heires and successors. **1819** *P.O. Lond. Direct.* 385 Yeatherd, George, Dyer and Embosser of Woollen-cloth, Deal-street. **1883** B. H. BECKER in *Eng. Illust. Mag.* Nov. 89/2 The stamp and die had superseded the embosser.

embossing (ɛm'bɒsɪŋ), *vbl. sb.* [f. EMBOSS *v.*¹ + -ING¹.] **a.** The action of the verb EMBOSS; also *attrib.*, as in ***embossing-iron, -machine, -press.*** **b.** *concr.* Embossed ornamentation; formerly in wider sense, swelling, protuberance.

c **1430** LYDG. *Bochas* I. xx. (1554) 36 If their brestes up to high them dresse, They can.. thenbosing doun represse. **1541** R. COPLAND *Guydon's Quest. Chirurg.*, Of them [bones] that haue enbossyng. **1580** HOLLYBAND *Treas. Fr. Tong, La Bosse*.. the embossing of a Jewell. **1626** BACON *Sylva* §878 All Engravings and Embossings (afar off) appear plain. *c* **1865** J. WYLDE in *Circ. Sc.* I. 272/1 The.. embossings on the paper are made by the method of reverse currents.

em'bossment (ɛm'bɒsmənt). [f. EMBOSS *v.*¹ + -MENT.]

†**1.** The action or process of embossing. *Obs.*

1801 *Ann. Reg.* 1799 Chron. 399 A method of.. ornamenting by.. embossment.. cloths or stuffs.

2. *concr.* A figure carved or moulded in relief; embossed ornament. Now *rare.* Also *attrib.*, as in *embossment-map*, a map of which the surface is moulded in elevations and depressions.

1620 DEKKER *Dreame* iij. §1 There you see the golden embosments and curious enchasings. **1731** CAPT. POWNALL in *Bibl. Topogr. Brit.* (1790) III. 166 An urn.. of.. clay.. without any inscription or embossement. **1813** HOGG *Queen's Wake* 46 Beneath rose an embossment proud,—A rose beneath a thistle bowed. **1881** *Nature* XXIV. 149 All the necessary data for making an embossment-map.

3. *gen.* A bulging, protuberance.

1610 GUILLIM *Heraldry* II. vi. 63 With a swelling embossment. **1611** COTGR. s.v. *Saillie*, The imbossement of an enchaced pretious stone. **1625** BACON *Ess. Gardens* (Arb.) 560 Perfect circles without any.. Imbosments. **1817** R. JAMESON *Char. Min.* 89 These embossments are not formed by the crystallization of that portion of the salt which has been dissolved.

em'bosture. *arch. rare.* Also 7 **imbosture.** [? f. EMBOSS *v.*¹, after *sculpture.* (But cf. EMBOAST *v.*)] = EMBOSSMENT.

1616 BEAUM. & FL. *Faithf. Fr.* IV. iii, There nor wants Imbosture nor embroidery. **1863** SALA *Capt. Dang.* I. ii. 33 This strange device raised in an embosture of gold.

embottle: see EM- *prefix.*

‖**embouchement** (ãbuʃmã, ɪm'bu:ʃmənt). [Fr.; f. *emboucher*: see next.] **a.** The mouth (of a river). **b.** *Phys.* The point at which one vessel enters or leads into another.

1844 W. H. MAXWELL *Sport. & Adv. Scotl.* x. (1855) 99 A heavy sea is tumbling into the embouchment of the Dee. **1878** FOSTER *Phys.* II. i. §4. 248 The embouchement of the thoracic duct into the venous system.

‖**embouchure** (ãbuʃyr). Also 9 **embouchier,** 8 **ambusheer.** [Fr.; f. *emboucher* to put in or to the mouth; also *refl.* of a river, to discharge itself by a mouth; f. *en-* in + *bouche* mouth.]

1. The mouth of a river or creek. Also *transf.* the opening out of a valley into a plain.

1792 *Fortn. Ramble* xvi. 114 We reached the embouchure of the fall. **1812** *Examiner* 14 Sept. 580/2 Near to the embouchier of Berezina. **1830** LYELL *Princ. Geol.* I. 238 The city Foah.. so late as the beginning of the fifteenth century, was on this embouchure. **1856** STANLEY *Sinai & Pal.* II. i. 71 Huge cones of white clay and sand.. guarding the embouchure of the valleys. **1868** G. DUFF *Pol. Surv.* 100 It lies.. at the embouchure of several rivers.

2. *Music.* 'The part of a musical instrument applied to the mouth' (Grove).

1834 MRS. SOMERVILLE *Connex. Phys. S.* xvii. (1849) 169 The embouchure of a flute. **1873** W. LEES *Acoustics* I. iii. 27 The air.. is made to play upon the thin edge of the pipe at the embouchure C.

3. *Music.* 'The disposition of the lips, tongue and other organs necessary for producing a musical tone' (Grove).

1760 GOLDSM. *Cit. W.* xc, You see.. I have got the ambusheer already [on the German flute]. **1879** GROVE *Dict. Mus.* I. 536 The second octave is produced by a stronger pressure of wind and an alteration of embouchure.

embound, imbound (ɛm-, ɪm'baʊnd), *v. poet. arch.* [f. EN-, IN- + BOUND *sb.*] *trans.* To set bounds to; to confine, contain, hem in.

Hence **em'bounded** *ppl. a.*

1595 SHAKS. *John* IV. iii. 137 That sweete breath Which was embounded in this beauteous clay. **1633** P. FLETCHER *Woman's Lightness*, But never bonds a woman might embound. **1812** W. TENNANT *Anster F.* I. xxii, To.. sleep imbounded by his boisterous arms. **1855-9** SINGLETON *Virgil* II. 16 The voice th' imbounded shores Volley along.

‖**embourgeoisé** (ãburʒwaze), *ppl. a.* [Fr., ppl. adj. of *embourgeoiser* to render or become bourgeois.] = BOURGEOISIFIED *ppl. a.*

1946 *Horizon* May 307 He is writing simultaneously about Scotland *embourgeoisé*—Presbyterian, respectable.., and the Scotland of Braxfield, the repressed.. demoniac Scotland. **1966** *Listener* 29 Sept. 445/1 There was the feeling that the Soviet Union was abandoning Marxism-Leninism, and becoming increasingly *embourgeoisé.* **1969** I. DEUTSCHER in *Marxism in our Time* (1972) 192 The great aristocratic English families assumed some of the functions which on the continent were exercised by the bureaucracy. In a sense, the *embourgeoisé* feudal elements administered the state without becoming a distinct and separate social group.

‖**embourgeoisement** (ãburʒwazmã). [Fr.: see prec.] = BOURGEOISIFICATION; adoption (esp. by the proletariat) of middle-class attitudes or life-style.

1937 F. BORKENAU *Spanish Cockpit* i. 35 It could not have succeeded had the Spanish proletariat ever undergone that process of 'embourgeoisement' which is characteristic of the industrial proletariat all over the world. **1940** E. F. M. DURBIN *Politics of Democratic Socialism* II. iv. 113 It is not possible.. to trace out the detail of this *embourgeoisement* (to coin a horrible term) of the proletariat. **1959** *Guardian* 6 Oct. 8/1 China started from so far back that it will be long before embourgeoisement sets in there too. **1970** *Daily Tel.* 16 Dec. 12 Hence its [*sc.* the Labour party's] reluctance to welcome the *embourgeoisement* of the wage-earners into a house-owning, two-car, fashion-conscious, home-entertaining, overseas-holidaying middle class. **1980** N. ABERCROMBIE et al. *Dominant Ideology Thesis* iv. 106 The reciprocal *embourgeoisement* of the aristocracy is important too, since the landed groups seem to have accepted most of the economic thought and some of the political and social beliefs that made up the dominant bourgeois ideology. **1983** E. GELLNER *Nations & Nationalism* v. 60 So these offspring shared in the eventually growing prosperity and general embourgeoisement of the region.

em̩bour,geoisifi'cation. [Blend of Fr. *embourgeoisement*, etc., and BOURGEOISIFICATION.] = BOURGEOISIFICATION.

1973 *Listener* 8 Mar. 311 They were frightened.. that they would not be able to afford the 'fair rents' which would be charged after conversion, and saw the Trust as yet another agent of creeping, expensive embourgeoisification. **1982** *Times Lit. Suppl.* 8 Oct. 1105/4 A man who.. felt betrayed by the new liberality and the embourgeoisification of the proletarian youths he desired.

†**em'bow**, *sb. Obs. rare*⁻¹. [f. next.] The concave surface of an arch, vault, or dome.

1548 HALL *Chron.* (1809) 723 The.. Embowes were of very strange worke with leaves, balles and other garnishinges.

embow (ɛm'bəʊ), *v.*¹ *Obs.* exc. *arch.* Also 5 **enbow,** 6- **imbow.** [f. EN- + BOW *sb.*¹]

1. *trans.* To bend or curve into a bow (see BOW *sb.*¹).

c **1400** *Destr. Troy* VII. 3034 Browes.. Bright as the brent gold enbowet þai were.

2. *Arch.* To arch, vault.

1481 [see EMBOWED *ppl. a.*] **1555** EDEN *Decades W. Ind.* (Arb.) 309 The rouffes.. are gylted and embowed. **1587** GOLDING *De Mornay* viii. (1617) 101 The heauen, being imbowed about these lower parts, like a vaut. **1641** HEYLIN *Help to Hist.* (1671) 294 The West end.. embowed over head seemeth to be very antient. **1838** WORDSW. *Sonn., Cave of Staffa*, The pillared vestibule.. the roof embowed.

3. To enclose as within a sphere; to englobe, encircle.

1605 SYLVESTER *Du Bartas* I. ii. I. 70 Turn'd Vapour, it have round embow'd Heau'ns highest stage. **1649** G. DANIEL *Trinarch., Hen. V*, cxci, His Rayes Embow'd Wth in a vapor here, and there a Cloud.

†**em'bow**, *v.*² *Obs. rare*⁻¹. In 5 **enbowe.** [f. EN- + BOW *v.*¹] *trans.* ? To bow down.

c **1440** *Gesta Rom.* 204 The sonne of man haþe not wer he may reclyne or enbowe his hede.

†**em'bowdle,** *v.* *Obs. rare*⁻¹. [Cf. BOWDLED *ppl. a.*] *trans.* To wrap round.
1625 W. L'ISLE tr. *Du Bartas' Noe* 10 A claggy night of myst embowdleth round [Fr. *envelope*] his brains.

embowed (ɛm'bəʊd), *ppl. a.* [f. EMBOW *v.*¹]
1. Bent or curved into the form of a bow; convex, bow-like.
1578 LYTE *Dodoens* 707 Long lyke a Peare, with certayne embowed or swelling diuisions. **1591** SPENSER *Vis. Worlds Vanitie* ii. With gilden hornes embowed like the Moone. **1639** HORN & ROBOTHAM *Gate Lang. Unl.* xciv. (1643) §759 A globe is round, being embowed on the out-side, and hollow on the in-side. **1697** POTTER *Antiq. Greece* III. vi. (1715) 61 The Wings are doubled, by bestowing the light-arm'd Men under them in an embow'd Form. **1855–9** SINGLETON *Virgil* II. 473 Th' imbowèd points together met.
b. *Her.* (See quots.)
1610 GUILLIM *Heraldry* III. xxii. (1660) 234 He beareth, Azure, a Dolphin Nasant, Imbowed Argent. **1761** *Brit. Mag.* II. 532 Two arms counter, embowed, and vested, gules. **1830** ROBSON *Brit. Herald*, Glossary, *Embowed* (Fr. *courbé*) bent, or bowed. *Embowed contrary*, bowed in opposite directions. *Embowed dejected*, bowed with the extremity turned downwards. **1864** BOUTELL *Heraldry Hist. & Pop.* x. 56 An Arm..when bent at the elbow is embowed.
2. *Arch.* **a.** Arched, vaulted. **b.** Curved or projecting outward, so as to form a recess (cf. BOW *sb.*¹ 12, BOW-WINDOW).
1481 CAXTON *Orat. P.C. Scipion* D. viii. in *Tulle on Friendsh.* The stone werkes enbowed called the Arches tryumphal. **1580** NORTH *Plutarch* (1676) 36 The fair embowed or vawted roofs. **1617** SIR R. BOYLE *Diary* (1886) I. 169, I agreed with..the carpentere to putt a new compaste imbowed Roof on my Chapple. **1632** MILTON *Penseroso* 157 Love the high embowèd roof. **1823** RUTTER *Fonthill* 50 In the embowed recess are three windows. **1826** SCOTT *Woodst.* i, The ancient embow'd arches of the old chantry. **1864** D. MITCHELL *Sev. Stor.* 205 An embowed window.

embowel (ɛm'baʊɪl), *v.* Also 6–7 em-, enbowell, imbowel(l. [In senses 1–2 ad. OF. *emboweler* (recorded in pa. pple. *enbowelé* = OF. *emboulé*, **emboelé*) an alteration (with substitution of the prefix *em-* for *es-*) of OFr. *esboueler*, f. *es-* repr. L. *ex-* out + *bouel* BOWEL. In senses 3–4 f. EN- + BOWEL.]
I. 1. *trans.* To remove the (abdominal) viscera from (a body), either for the purpose of embalming, or as part of a judicial penalty; = DISEMBOWEL.
1521 *Test. Ebor.* (Surtees) V. 141 Item I will that aftir my deth my body be emboweld. **1596** SHAKS. *1 Hen. IV*, v. iv. 109 Imbowell'd will I see thee by and by. **1640** SLINGSBY *Diary* (1836) 64 Wᶜʰ made me..send for a chirurgeon from York to embowel him. **1734** tr. *Rollin's Anc. Hist.* (1827) III. VI. §3. 124 Having prepared their bodies for the purpose by embowelling them. **1854** *Tait's Mag.* XXI. 488 He is the diviner who must embowel the beasts of sacrifice. **1867** FREEMAN *Norm. Conq.* I. vi. 490 Others he put in prison, others he embowelled.
2. *transf.* and *fig.*
1589 NASHE *Almond for Parrat* 20, I haue not halfe emboweld my register. **1601** SHAKS. *All's Well* I. iii. 247 The Schooles embowel'd of their doctrine. **1667** MILTON *P.L.* VI. 587 Whose roar Emboweld with outragious noise the air And all her entrails tore. **1678** *Lively Orac.* viii. §26. 315 How curiously do men..embowel a text to find a pretence for cavil and objection. **1790** BURKE *Fr. Rev.* Wks. V. 166 In England we have not yet been completely embowelled of our natural entrails.
II. †**3.** To put, convey into the bowels; in quots. *transf.* and *fig. Obs.*
1596 FITZ-GEFFRAY *Sir F. Drake* (1881) 44 On Ulysses Circe did bestow A blather, where the windes imboweld were. **1629** DONNE *Whitsunday Serm.* Wks. 1839 I. 578 All was embowelled and enwombed in the waters. **1633** W. STRUTHER *True Happines* 8 When God and man inhere mutually in other, and are embowelled by mutuall love. **1634** SIR T. HERBERT *Trav.* 26 His bodie was..imbowelled in a spacious coffin, the Ocean. *Ibid.* 105 A streame..arising from Mount Taurus here embowels it selfe into that sea.
†**b.** To fill the bowels of (an animal). *Obs.*
1607 TOPSELL *Four-f. Beasts* (1679) 566 The young whelps of weasels being imbowelled with salt.
†**4.** *intr.* To convey food into the bowels. *Obs.*
1618 LATHAM *2nd Bk. Falconry* (1633) 18 It will oftentimes very much molest her in her putting ouer and imbowelling.

embowelled (ɛm'baʊɪld), *ppl. a.* [f. prec.]
1. = DISEMBOWELLED. *lit.* and *fig.*
1594 SHAKS. *Richard III*, v. ii. 10 The Boare makes his trough In your embowel'd bosomes. **1695** BLACKMORE *Pr. Arth.* I. 261 Exploded Thunder tears th' Embowel'd Sky. **1789** WOLCOTT (P. Pindar) *Subj. Painters* 10 Sweeter than hist'ry of embowell'd saint.
2. *fig.* That lies hid in the bowels or heart of a thing; internal, intestine.
1609 BP. BARLOW *Answ. Nameless Catholike* 236 Hauing such Embowelled enemies within his Realmes. *c* **1750** SHENSTONE *Elegy* xx. 62 For them we drain the mine's embowell'd gold. **1854** S. DOBELL *Balder* xxiv. 169 Like an embowelled earthquake yet unbelched.
†**3.** That has the bowels full. *Obs.*
1486 *Bk. St. Albans* A vij, If..the bowell [be] any thyng stiffid . ye shall say she is embowellid.

emboweller (ɛm'baʊələ(r)). [f. as prec. + -ER.] One who performs the operation of disembowelling.
1705 GREENHILL *Art Embalm.* 283 We shall next proceed to speak of the..Emboweller.

embowelling (ɛm'baʊɪlɪŋ), *vbl. sb.* [f. EMBOWEL *v.* + -ING¹.] = DISEMBOWELLING.
1725 SWIFT *Drapier's Lett.* Wks. 1755 V. II. 79 Sentence of death with..hanging, beheading, quartering, embowelling. **1813** SIR S. ROMILLY in *Examiner* 22 Feb. 117/2 The..infliction of embowelling was at present left to the discretion of the executioner.
†**b.** *nonce-use.*
1654 GAYTON *Pleasant Notes on Don Quixot* 91 These exenterations, embowellings, and disgorgings made Sancho's appetite like a swine.

embowelment (ɛm'baʊɪlmənt). [f. EMBOWEL + -MENT.] **a.** The action of disembowelling.
b. The inward parts or contents of a thing.
1823 LAMB *Elia* I. xviii. (1865) 135 A clock with its ponderous embowelments of lead and brass.

embower, imbower (ɛm-, ɪm'baʊə(r), -'baʊə(r)), *v.* Also 7 imbowr(e. [f. EN-, IN- + BOWER *sb.*¹]
1. *trans.* To shelter, enclose, seclude as in a bower; also *absol.*
1580 SIDNEY in Farr *S.P. Eliz.* (1845) I. 78 Him..Whom Sion holds embowered. *c* **1630** DRUMM OF HAWTH. *Poems* Wks. (1711) 44 Ah destinies, & you whom skies embow'r. **1667** MILTON *P.L.* I. 304 Vallombrosa, where th' Etrurian shades High overarch't imbouer. **1738** WESLEY *Ps.* cxlvii, Ye, whom highest Heaven imbow'rs, Praise the Lord. **1833** TENNYSON *Lady Shalott* I. ii, And the silent isle imbowers The Lady of Shalott. **1873** SYMONDS *Grk. Poets* x. 333 Elms and..vines embower them with..rustling leaves.
†**2.** *intr.* for *refl.* To take shelter, lodge as in a bower. ? *Obs.*
1591 SPENSER *Virg. Gnat* 225 Small Birds in their wide boughs embowring. **1610** G. FLETCHER *Christ's Vict.* xxvii, Gaze but upon the house whear man embow'rs.

embowered (ɛm'baʊəd), *ppl. a.* [f. prec. + -ED¹.] **a)** That is surrounded as with a bower, wreathed with foliage; **b.** lodged in a bower.
1757 DYER *Fleece* I. 119 The little smiling cottage warm embow'r'd. **1824** W. IRVING *T. Trav.* I. 317 Seated in the embowered porch of his small parsonage. **1830** TENNYSON *Recoll. Arab. Nights* iv, Imbower'd vaults of pillar'd palm. **1870** HAWTHORNE *Eng. Note-bks.* (1879) I. 254 There are ranges of embowered windows.

embowering (ɛm'baʊərɪŋ), *vbl. sb.* [f. as prec. + -ING¹.] Enclosing, or sheltering in a bower. *concr.* A bower-like retreat; in quot. *fig.*
1882 HALL CAINE *Recoll. D.G. Rossetti* 110 Whatever embowerings I had in my mind.

embowering (ɛm'baʊərɪŋ), *ppl. a.* [f. as prec. + -ING².] That forms a bower; that surrounds as with a bower.
a **1717** PARNELL *Poet. Wks.* (1833) 32 From Helicon's imbowering height repair. **1792** S. ROGERS *Pleas. Mem.* II. 240 Imbowering shrubs with verdure veiled the sky. **1821** SCOTT *Kenilw.* xxv, Above the embowering and richly shaded woods. **1852** MRS. JAMESON *Leg. Madonna* (1857) 129 A..landscape thick with imbowering trees.

emboweriment (ɛm'baʊəmənt). [f. as prec. + -MENT.] The action of embowering.
1848 DICKENS *Dombey* (C.D. ed.) 63 Plants..of a kind peculiarly adapted to the embowerment of Mrs. Pipchin.

†**em'bowing,** *vbl. sb. Obs.* [f. EMBOW *v.* + -ING¹.] The action of the vb. EMBOW¹; vaulting; arching: in quot. *concr.* Also *attrib.*
1430 LYDG. *Chron. Troy* II. xi, The freshe enbowing wᵗ verges right as lynes. **1571** GOLDING *Calvin on Ps.* lxxiv. 5 By the kervings or imbowings he meeneth the verge fashion. **1576** *Richmond. Wills* (1853) 261 To John Whyt ij playnes..ij chesells, and ij embowing playnes.

†**em'bowing,** *ppl. a. Obs.* [f. as prec. + -ING².] Arching, convex, curved.
1561 EDEN *Arte Nauig.* I. v. 6 b, Conuex or embowyng.

†**em'bowl,** *v. Obs. rare.* [f. EN- + BOWL *sb.* I.] **a.** *trans.* To form or mould into a globe. **b.** *intr.* To take or grow into the form of a globe.
1580 LADY PEMBROKE *Ps.* xc. (1823) 171 Long ere the earth embowl'd by thee Bare the forme it now doth beare. **1886** SIR R. BURTON *Arab. Nts.* (abr. ed.) 332 The citrons shone with fruits embowled.

em'bowment. *arch.* [f. EMBOW *v.* + -MENT.] Vaulting.
1626 BACON *Sylva* §249 The Roofe all open, not so much as any Embowment neere any of the walls left. **1919** T. HARDY *Coll. Poems* 54 O for..Light to gaily See thy daily Iris-hued embowment!

embox (ɛm'bɒks), *v.* Also 7 imboxe. [f. EN- + BOX *sb.*²] *trans.* To set in or as in a box.
1611 COTGR., *Emboister*, to imboxe. **1732** FIELDING *Cov. Gard. Trag.* I. iii, In Goodman's-fields the city dame Emboxed sits. **1828** LAMB *Lett.* in C. and M. C. Clarke (1878) 160 The Watchmen are emboxed in a niche of fame. **1835** KIRBY *Bridgewater Tr.* (1852) II. 211 More than thirty alternate layers of earth and web, emboxed, as it were, in each other.

embrace (ɛm'breɪs), *sb.* [f. EMBRACE *v.*²]
1. The action of folding in the arms, of pressing to the bosom. (Sometimes euphemistically for sexual intercourse.)
1592 SHAKS. *Rom. & Jul.* v. iii. 113 Armes, take your last embrace. **1633** P. FLETCHER *Elisa* II. v, Arms, whose..sweet embraces Could quicken death. **1667** MILTON *P.L.* II. 793 In embraces forcible and foule Ingendring with me. **1750** JOHNSON *Rambl.* No. 91 ¶7 Pride..by whose embraces she had two daughters. **1810** SOUTHEY *Kehama* XVII. ix, She turn'd from him, to meet..The Glendoveer's embrace. **1865** TROLLOPE *Belton Est.* xxiii. 273 The demonstrative affection of an embrace between the two women.
2. *transf.* and *fig.*
a **1628** SIR J. BEAUMONT *Mis. State Man*, The soule perswaded that no fading loue Can equall her imbraces. **1634** HABINGTON *Castara* 75 Their streames thus Rivers joyne, And lose themselves in the embrace. **1665** GLANVILL *Sceps. Sc.*, Offering themselves to its [Truth's] embraces. **1856** STANLEY *Sinai & Pal.* (1858) Introd. 42 Rocks..enclosing, in a still narrower and narrower embrace, a valley. **1855** BAIN *Senses & Int.* II. ii. §12 The most perfect combination of perceiving organs is the embrace of the two hands.

†**em'brace,** *v.*¹ *Obs. rare.* Also 4 enbrase, -ass, -brace, 6 imbrace. [f. EN- + Fr. *bras* arm: see BRACE *sb.*¹] *trans.* To put (a shield) on the arm.
c **1300** *K. Alis.* 6651 His scheld enbraceth Antiocus. **1375** BARBOUR *Bruce* VIII. 295 Enbrasit vith that thar scheldis braid. *c* **1380** *Sir Ferumb.* 5539 With scheldes enbraced. ? *a* **1400** *Morte Arth.* 4111 Whene Bretones boldly enbraces there scheldes. *Ibid.* 2459 With brode scheldes enbrassede. **1592** WYRLEY *Armorie* 50 Did baisse his gleaue and well imbrace his shield.

embrace (ɛm'breɪs), *v.*² Forms: 4–5 enbrace, 4–6 embrase, 4– embrace. Also 5–6 imbrase, 6– 8 imbrace. [ad. OF. *embrace-r* (F. *embrasser*) = Pr. *embrassar*, It. *imbracciare*:—late L. **imbracchiāre*, f. *in-* in + *bracchium* (pl. *bracchia* see BRACE *sb.*²) arm.]
1. *trans.* To clasp in the arms, usually as a sign of fondness or friendship.
c **1386** CHAUCER *Sompn. T.* 95 The frere..her embracith in his armes narwe. *c* **1450** LONELICH *Grail* App. 81 This lady..him embraced al in hire slepe. **1535** STEWART *Cron. Scot.* II. 268 The lordis..Imbrasit thame that tyme full tenderly. **1535** COVERDALE *2 Kings* iv. 16 Aboute this tyme yf yᵉ frute can lyue, thou shalt embrace a sonne. **1678** BUTLER *Hud.* III. i. 950 Lovers, when th' are fast In one another's Arms embrac'd. **1845** FORD *Spain* §1. 46 Many a Sancho..is there fondling and embracing his ass.
fig. *c* **1386** CHAUCER *Pers. T.* ¶193 The riche folk that embraceden and oneden al hire herte to tresor of this world shul slepe in..deeth. **1635** A. STAFFORD *Fem. Glory* (1869) 132 Worship their Messias, and imbrace Him in their hearts. **1698** NORRIS *Pract. Disc.* IV. 216 Let us..Hug and Imbrace them [earthly things] never so dearly.
b. Of sexual embraces.
1599 SHAKS. *Much Ado* IV. i. 50 You will say, she did imbrace me as a husband. **1660** R. COKE *Power & Subj.* 168 On other days they [certain penitents] may eat any meat but flesh, and imbrace their own wedlock.
†**c.** As the typical mode of salutation between friends; to salute as a friend. *Obs.*
1707 FREIND *Peterboro's Cond. Sp.* 174, I hope to embrace you in a few Days. **1747** HOADLEY *Susp. Husb.* I. iii. (1756) 12 Any..Friend of my Frankly's I am proud of embracing.
d. *absol.* (Chiefly with reciprocal sense.)
c **1400** *Rom. Rose* 4820 Disordinat desiryng For to kissen & enbrace. **1483** CAXTON *Gold. Leg.* 407/3 Thenne eche kyssed other and embraced straytelye. **1596** WARNER *Alb. Eng.* II. xvi. 76 When they had imbraced Then Archigallo..in Ebranks Towne was plac'd. **1667** MILTON *P.L.* VIII. 636 Easier then Air with Air, if Spirits embrace, Total they mix. **1719** YOUNG *Revenge* IV. i, Two lovers in each other's arms, Embracing and embrac'd. **1855** KINGSLEY *Heroes* IV. (1868) 252 They loved each other, and embraced.
2. In various figurative uses.
†**a.** To compass, gain (an object of desire).
1475 CAXTON *Jason* 20 b, A lady to sone abandonned and given ouer embraceth not grete honour. **14..** *Legendary Poem* in *Retrosp. Rev.* Nov. (1853) 102 With..penaunce smerte They wene ther blys for to imbrase [*printed* unbrase].
†**b.** To worship (a deity). *Obs. rare.*
1490 CAXTON *Eneydos* viii. 37 Temples and aultres in whiche she embraced and honowred as a goddesse.
†**c.** To accept (a person) as a friend; to welcome the services of (a person).
1607 SHAKS. *Cor.* IV. vii. 10 He beares himselfe more proudlier..then I thought he would When first I did embrace him. *a* **1649** DRUMM. OF HAWTH. *Hist. Jas. V.* Wks. (1711) 83 He wrought himself..to be imbraced as their friend. **1607** TOURNEUR *Rev. Trag.* B 4 Wert thou as secret as thou'rt subtil..I would embrace thee for a neere imployment. **1635** [cf. 1 a. *fig.*].
d. To accept gladly or eagerly; also, in weaker sense, to accept; now chiefly, to avail oneself of (an offer, opportunity, etc.).
c **1399** *Pol. Poems* (1859) II. 12 Y hope of king Henries grace, That he it is which schal the pes embrace. **1531** ELYOT *Gov.* I. ii. (1883) 11 The communes..imbracinge a licence, refuse to be brydled. **1582** EARL ESSEX in Ellis *Orig. Lett.* II. 213 III. 80, I can not but embrace with duty your Lordships good counsell. **1591** SHAKS. *1 Hen. VI*, II. i. 13 Embrace we then this opportunitie. **1646** SIR T. BROWNE *Pseud. Ep.* I. viii. 32 The worke is ever to be embraced, as containing the first description of poysons and their Antidotes. **1647** SPRIGGE *Anglia Rediv.* II. iv. (1854) 119 The general sent the prince word that he would embrace a parley. **1725** DE FOE *Voy. round World* (1840) 189 The captain..embraced this offer. **1818** JAS. MILL *Brit. India* II. IV. iii. 107 One alternative; that of embracing the neutrality. **1839** W. CHAMBERS *Tour Holland* 62/1, I will embrace the opportunity of making a few general remarks.
e. To accept, submit to (death, adverse fortune) with resignation or fortitude.
1591 SHAKS. *Two Gent.* v. iv. 126 Thurio give backe, or else embrace thy death. **1598** —— *Merry W.* v. v. 251 What cannot be eschew'd, must be embrac'd. **1672** CAVE *Prim. Chr.* I. x. 111 They readily embrace death. **1711** SHAFTESB. *Charac.* (1737) II. 106 Even death it-self voluntarily

imbrac'd. **1867** LADY HERBERT *Cradle L.* vi. 137 Embracing with joy all its sufferings and privations.

†**f.** To take to one's heart, cultivate (a virtue, disposition, etc.). *Obs.*

1393 GOWER *Conf.* III. 143 He shulde of trouthe thilke grace With all his hole herte embrace. **1576** in Farr *S.P. Eliz.* (1845) II. 291 Of Christes flock let loue be so embraste. **1623** SIR J. STRADLING in Farr *S.P. Jas.* (1848) 232 What good peace (if we it imbrace) will doe vs.

g. To adopt (a course of action, profession or calling, mode of life). Formerly also, to take (a road or course in travelling).

1639 FULLER *Holy War* xv. (1647) 22 They embraced severall courses through sundry countreys. **1655** —— *Ch. Hist.* VIII. 13 Captain Vaughan..embraced the right-hand way towards Westminster. **1768** GOLDSM. *Good-n. Man* I. i, Being compelled..to embrace a life you disliked. **1823** SCOTT *Quentin D.* xv, What fiend possessed you to..embrace the trade of a damsel adventurous. **1871** FREEMAN *Norm. Conq.* IV. xvii. 89 The..home of those..who embraced the monastic life.

h. To adopt (a doctrine, opinions, religion, etc.); often with the notion 'to accept joyfully'. Also, to attach oneself to (a party, cause, etc.).

1545 BRINKLOW *Lament.* (1874) 120 Repent and beleue the Gospell in embrasynge the same. **1553** EDEN *Treat. New Ind.* (Arb.) 41 Foure of the greatest Ilandes embraced the Christian faith. **1646** E. F[ISHER] *Mod. Divinity* 71 This opinion was..generally imbraced amongst them. **1681-6** J. SCOTT *Chr. Life* (1747) III. 269 By embracing Christ and his Doctrine, the believing Jews did not turn to a new Religion. **1720** OZELL *Vertot's Rom. Rep.* II. XIV. 334 Cæsar gave him the choice either to embrace his Party, or to continue his March. **1743** J. MORRIS *Sermons* viii. 214 So may they..heartily imbrace the truth. **1845** S. AUSTIN tr. *Ranke's Hist. Ref.* I. 75 The two princes embraced..different parties. **1867** SMILES *Huguenots Eng.* iii. (1880) 38 Palissy was not the only man of genius in France who embraced the Reformed faith.

†**i.** To take (a matter) in hand; to undertake.

1393 GOWER *Conf.* Prol. 90 So wol I now this werke embrace. **1552** HULOET Embrace anothers accion or title, *Litem propriam vel suam facere.* **1597** BACON *Ess. Sutes* (Arb.) 40 Some embrace Sutes, which neuer meane to deale effectually in them. **1670-1** MARVELL *Corr.* 183 Wks. (1872-5) II. 374 The Duke..had embraced this matter. **1818** JAS. MILL *Brit. India* II. v. vi. 559 When the wisdom of parliament embraced the subject of the government of India.

3. To entwine, encircle, surround; to clasp, enclose. *lit.* and *fig.*

c **1360** *Song of Mercy* in *E.E.P.* (1862) 122 Wormes blake wol vs enbrace. **14..** *Purif. Marie* (*Tundale's Vis.* 130) The passyng joy that can hys hart enbrace. **1447** BOKENHAM *Seyntys* (1835) 44 b, Here that is of grace the welle Of hyr wombe sche [the mother of the Virgin Mary] dede enbrace. **1535** COVERDALE *Song Sol.* ii. 6 His right hande embraceth me. **1607** SHAKS. *Cor.* v. ii. 7 You'l see your Rome embrac'd with fire. **1704** ADDISON *Italy* (1733) 40 The whole Town redoubled Walls embrace. **1796** WITHERING *Arrangem. Brit. Pl.* III. 56 Leaves arrow-shaped at the base, embracing the stem. **1802** PLAYFAIR *Illustr. Hutton. The.* 298 It is on both sides firmly embraced by the whinstone. **1884** *Times* (weekly ed.) 29 Aug. 14/1 The woods, embracing lawns and sloping corn fields.

†**b.** Of an event: ? To lay hold upon, touch (the heart). *Obs. rare.*

c **1430** LYDGATE *Bochas' Falles of Princes* II. xxvi. (1554) 62 This auenture..The heart of Cyrus gan somewhat enbrace And caused him for to be piteous Ageine Cresus.

†**c.** *intr.* To wrap, circle *about*. *Obs.*

1578 LYTE *Dodoens* 388 The blacke Ivie..groweth upon trees and hedges, about the whiche it embraceth.

4. Of things: To include, contain, comprise. So of persons: To include or comprise *in*.

1697 DRYDEN *Virg. Georg.* II. 60 Not that my Song..So large a Subject fully can embrace. **1825** COBBETT *Rur. Rides* 408 Thus the two classes embrace all legitimate merchants. **1846** PRESCOTT *Ferd. & Is.* II. xix. 181 The other productions of this indefatigable scholar embrace a large circle of topics. **1860** TYNDALL *Glac.* I. §4. 33 The time occupied..embraced about five whole days. **1885** F. TEMPLE *Relat. Relig. & Sc.* vii. 196 Some of these events..are substantive facts embraced in the message delivered. *Mod.* It is impossible to embrace all the cases in a single formula.

5. To take in with the eye or the mind; also with these as subject.

1831 BREWSTER *Newton* (1855) II. xxiv. 356 The..distance..which his eye can embrace on the surface of the earth. **1853** H. ROGERS *Ecl. Faith* 308 Religious truth..is embraced by the understanding. **1877** E. CONDER *Bas. Faith* ii. 69 The infinite..the intellect can seize though not embrace. **1884** *Times* (weekly ed.) 19 Sept. 5/3 You embrace the whole broad panorama of wood and water.

embrace (ɛmˈbreɪs), *v.*³ *Law.* [apparently a back-formation from the agent-noun EMBRACER².] *trans.* To attempt to influence (a juryman, etc.) corruptly and illegally. Also *absol.*

1475 *Bk. Noblesse* 77 Also there to embrace and rule among youre pore. **1591** LAMBARDE *Arch.* (1635) 202 That if any person shall (for his owne gaine) embrace any Jurie or Inquest. **1769** BLACKSTONE *Comm.* IV. 140 The punishment for the person embracing is by fine and imprisonment. **1809** in TOMLINS *Law Dict.*

†**em'brace**, *v.*⁴ *Obs.* Also 4 imbrace, 6 enbrace, -se. [f. EN- + BRACE *sb.*²] *trans.* To fix with a brace or buckle; to fasten, fit close.

[Perh. suggested by a misapprehension of EMBRACE *v.*¹]

? *c* **1475** *Sqr. lowe Degre* 227 in Ritson *Met. Rom.* III. 154 Your plates unto your body shal be embrace. **1509** HAWES *Past. Pleas.* XXVII. lxv, And to his legge he my stede embraced. **1596** SPENSER *F.Q.* II. i. 26 Who..His warlike armes about him gan embrace.

embraceable (ɛmˈbreɪsəb(ə)l), *a.* [f. EMBRACE *v.*² + -ABLE.] Capable of being embraced; inviting an embrace.

1841 HOR. SMITH *Moneyed Man* II. ii. 40 Fortune! instant, tangible, embraceable, Fortune! **1879** W. COLLINS *My Lady's Money* iv, The men..finding it [her figure] essentially embraceable, asked for nothing more.

Hence **em'braceably** *adv.*, in a manner that invites an embrace.

1857 W. COLLINS *Dead Secret* (1861) 31 A little too much inclined to be embraceably plump.

em'braced, *ppl. a.*¹ [f. EMBRACE *v.*² + -ED.] In various senses of the vb.

1596 SHAKS. *Merch. V.* II. viii. 52 And quicken his embraced heauinesse. **1599** THYNNE *Animadv.* Ded., Of that most excellente and yet embraced Custome. **1654** R. CODRINGTON tr. *Hist. Ivstine* 331 With her own body she protected the embraced bodies of her children.

em'braced, *ppl. a.*² *Her.* [f. EMBRACE *v.*⁴ + -ED.] Braced together, tied or bound together.

†**em'bracelet.** *Obs. rare*⁻¹. In 6 **enbracelett.** = BRACELET.

1533-9 T. ST. AUBYN in *Lisle Papers* XIII. 96 Thanks for your token mine enbracelett.

embracement (ɛmˈbreɪsmənt). Also 6-7 im-. [f. EMBRACE *v.* + -MENT; or a. OF. *embracement*, F. *embrassement*: see EMBRACE *v.*²] The action of embracing.

1. An enfolding in the arms = EMBRACE *sb.* 1.

1485 CAXTON *St. Wenefr.* 2, I..desyred the to be ioyned to myn enbracementes. **1591** HARINGTON *Orl. Fur.* XXIII. vii, She..went to him..With words..and with embracements. **1598** YONG *Diana* 138 If thou knewest from whom this imbracement came. **1650** HOWELL *Revolutions in Naples* 93 Masaniello, prostrating himself at the feet of the Viceroy, he kiss'd his knee, after which embracement, etc. **1670** MILTON *Hist. Eng.* I. Wks. (1851) 22 Conuvenna..after imbracements and teares, assails him with..a motherly power. **1720** WELTON *Suffer. Son. of God* I. viii. 176 Since I have shunn'd thy Dear Embracements, O Thou my Soul's Bridegroom. **1829** J. WILSON in *Blackw. Mag.* XXV. 553 Embracements that blended spirit with spirit! *c* **1850** NEALE *Hymns East. Ch.* 52 Embrace me with the last embracement.

b. *fig.*

1599 SANDYS *Europæ Spec.* (1632) 192 To the end that..they might..cast them selves..into the armes and embracements of Spaine for safeguard. **1658** R. FRANCK *North. Mem.* (1821) 21 Him that throws vertue into the embracements of vice. **1677** GILPIN *Dæmonol.* (1867) 96 They..consider not that they have received into their embracement another [temptation].

c. *transf.* in certain occasional uses.

1580 SIDNEY *Arcadia* 70 [The bear] being ready to giue me a shrewd embracement. **1842** *Fraser's Mag.* XXVI. 480 Take a wide embracement of the water towards you, one good armful will bring you round directly.

†**2.** What one takes in hand, an undertaking. Cf. EMBRACE *v.*² 2 h.

1630 NAUNTON *Fragm. Reg.* (Arb.) 37 [Sir Francis Walsingham] was one of the great allayes of the Austerian embracements. *a* **1662** HEYLIN *Laud* II. 506 Some..complained, that his Embracements were too large and general.

3. A clasping, encircling, closely surrounding.

1626 BACON *Sylva* §58 The Parts in Mans body easily reparable, as Spirits, Bloud, and Flesh, die in the Embracement of the Parts hardly reparable, as Bones, Nerues and Membranes. **1622-62** HEYLIN *Cosmogr.* I. (1682) 80 Ravenna, situate in the embracement of two Rivers. **1850** BLACKIE *Æschylus* I. 95 Quick, each hand with sure embracement hold the dagger by the hilt!

b. *fig.* An embracing or taking in with the eye or the mind.

1599 DAVIES *Immort. Soul* 23 Nor can her wide Embracements filled bee. **1837** HOWITT *Rur. Life* v. iii. (1862) 386 Their intellectual vision widened to the embracement of the universe.

4. *fig.* An approving acceptance (of a doctrine, religion, etc.); a cheerful acceptance (of something offered).

1535 in Strype *Eccl. Mem.* I. App. lxiii. 157 Affection towards the favorable embracement of Gods word. **1611** SPEED *Hist. Gt. Brit.* VII. ix. (1632) 242 The Conuersion of the Northumbrians to the imbracement of Christian Religion. **1666** G. ALSOP *Maryland* (1869) 89 What Destiny has ordered I am resolved..to subscribe to, and with a contented imbracement enjoy it. **1713** BEVERIDGE *Priv. Th.* II. 106 Their Wills in the Embracement of the Chiefest Good.

embracement, var. f. EMBRASEMENT, *Obs.*

embracer¹ (ɛmˈbreɪsə(r)). Also 6 imb-. [f. EMBRACE *v.*² + -ER.] One who embraces.

1. One who clasps (a person) in his arms.

a **1794** SIR W. JONES *Songs Jayadeva* (R.), Bashful at first, she smiles at length on her embracer. **1839** DICKENS *Nich. Nick.* xxx, Performed by the embracer's laying his or her chin on the shoulder of the object of affection. **1885** NORRIS *Adrian Vidal* II. 302 Adrian was the embracer whom his wife had seen.

2. One who adopts (a doctrine, religion, etc.), or takes up (a line of conduct, etc.).

1547 BAULDWIN *Mor. Philos.* III. iii, Embracers of their owne aduice. **1598** YONG *Diana* 331 Imbracers of all kinde of vice. **1611** SPEED *Hist. Gt. Brit.* VI. xviii. 100 You persecute to the death all the Embracers of that Profession. **1674** *Consid. Peace & Goodw. Prot.* 13 The afflicted Netherlanders, embracers of the same Religion She professed.

embracer² (ɛmˈbreɪsə(r)). *Law.* Forms: 5 ymbrasour, 6 enbracer, 6-9 embraceor, 6- embracer. [a. AF., OF. *embraceor*, *-aseor* instigator, 'boutefeu, ou qui par male signification duyt autre a mal faire' (Gloss cited by Godef.), f. *embraser* lit. 'to set on fire', EMBRASE *v.*; for the development of meaning cf. ENTICE *v.* The word was used in the statute 38 Edw. III. st. II. cap. 12, which provides penalties for *les embraceours demesner ou procurer tielx enquestes*, i.e. those who instigate to bring about such (fraudulent) inquests as have been previously referred to in the act. The contextual meaning of the word in this passage seems to have become its technical sense; hence, by back-formation, EMBRACE *v.*³]

One who attempts to influence a jury corruptly.

1495 *Act 11 Hen. VII*, c. 24 Preamb., Unlawfull mayntenours, ymbrasours and Jurrours. **1502** ARNOLDE *Chron.* (1811) 90 Enbracer of questis or other comon mysdoers. **1581** LAMBARDE *Eiren.* III. i. (1588) 313 The same Justices shall also certifie the names of the maintainours and embracers. **1598** KITCHIN *Courts Leet* (1675) 411 Embraceor is he which comes to the Bar with the party, and speaks in the matter, or is there to overlook the Jury, or to put them in fear. **1607** COWEL *Interpr.* s.v. *Decies tantum*, It lieth also against embracers that procure such an enquest (by suborning a jury). **1697** *View Penal Laws* 312 If the Juror or Embracer have not whereof to make gree, he shall suffer a years imprisonment. **1809** TOMLINS *Law Dict.* s.v., If the party himself instruct a juror, or promise any reward for his appearance, then the party is likewise an embraceor.

†**em'bracer**³. *Obs.* [f. EMBRACE *v.*⁴] He who or that which braces or fastens; a brace, bond.

1548 HALL *Chron. Hen. VI*, an. 2 (R.) Affinitie is an embracer of amitie.

embracery (ɛmˈbreɪsərɪ). *Law.* Forms: 5 enbraciarie, ymbracery, 6-7 em-, imbracerie, -braserie, 5- embracery. [f. AF. *embraceour* EMBRACER²: see -RY.]

The offence of an embracer; the offence of influencing a jury illegally and corruptly.

1450 J. PASTON *Lett.* I. 145 To enquere, here and determyn all..embraceries. **1487** *Act 3 Hen. VII*, c. 1 §1 By endentur, promyses, othes, writyng or otherwise, enbraciaries of his subgettes. **1598** KITCHIN *Courts Leet* (1675) 409 One skilled in the Law, may give the evidence for his Fee to the Jury, and it is no imbracery. **1617** in Rymer *Fœdera* (1710) XVII. 32 Imbraseries, oppressions. **1670** VAUGHAN in *Phœnix* (1721) I. 423 Unless Imbracery, Subornation, or the like were join'd. **1808** BENTHAM *Sc. Reform* 72 To the same Jury not so well, on account of the danger or suspicion of embracery, and so forth. **1887** *Times* 31 Mar. 3/5 The plaintiff..was charged..with the offence of embracery.

embracing (ɛmˈbreɪsɪŋ), *vbl. sb.*¹ [f. EMBRACE *v.*² + -ING¹.] The action of the vb. EMBRACE in its various senses.

c **1386** CHAUCER *Pers. T.* ¶870 To ben a clene widewe, and to eschiewe the embrasynges of men. **14..** *Epiph.* (*Tundale's Vis.* 113) And all the enbrasyng of the goodly cheyne. **1474** CAXTON *Chesse* II. ii, She shold sitte on the lift side of the kyng for the..enbrasynges of her husbond. **1555** *Fardle Facions* II. i. 112 Thei absteine fro the embrasinges neither of sister ne mother. **1563-87** FOXE *A. & M.* (1596) 130/1 His nobles..he did allure to the imbrasing of good letters. **1566** GASCOIGNE *Supposes* Wks. (1587) 11 Farewell..the kind imbracings. **1643** PRYNNE *Sov. Power Parl.* I. (ed. 2) 7 The embracing of the Protestant Religion. **1719** DE FOE *Crusoe* (1840) I. xiii. 223 Eager embracings of the object. **1827** POLLOK *Course T.* v, The kind embracings of the heart.

embracing (ɛmˈbreɪsɪŋ), *vbl. sb.*² *Law.* [f. EMBRACE *v.*³] = EMBRACERY.

1495 *Act 11 Hen. VII*, c. 25 Pream., Mayntenaunce, embrasyng, champertie and corrupcion.

em'bracing, *ppl. a.* [f. EMBRACE *v.*² + -ING².] That encircles, surrounds, or encloses.

1590 SPENSER *F.Q.* II. xii. 54 A porch..Archt over head with an embracing vine. **1621** G. SANDYS *Ovid's Met.* II. (1626) 21 The Land-imbracing Sea. **1863** E. NEALE *Anal. Th. & Nat.* 98 The all-embracing Divine Being.

Hence **em'bracingly** *adv.*, in an embracing manner: (*a*) as one or as those who embrace; (*b*) with wide comprehension, comprehensively. **em'bracingness**, the quality of that which embraces or comprehends; comprehensiveness.

1825 *Blackw. Mag.* XVIII. 451 'Tween whose soft breasts lie nestling fervent love And maiden modesty embracingly. **1850** LYNCH *Theo. Trin.* v. 78, I knelt before her half embracingly. **1872** *Contemp. Rev.* XX. 823 The absoluteness which means all-embracingness. **1882** MABEL COLLINS *Cobwebs* III. 151 The wide embracingness of his stern cruelty.

embracive (ɛmˈbreɪsɪv), *a.* [irregularly f. EMBRACE *v.* + -IVE.] **1.** Given to or fond of embracing; embracing demonstratively. *nonce-use.*

1855 THACKERAY *Newcomes* (1869) II. xix, Not less kind..though less expansive and embracive, was Madame de Montcontour to my wife.

2. Embracing or tending to embrace all. Hence **em'bracively** *adv.*

1897 *Academy* (Fiction Suppl.) 18 Sept. 70/1 'George Du Maurier in three volumes' would be a fair embracive title. **1899** *Westm. Gaz.* 22 Apr. 7/2 General Sir W. Olpherts, V.C., in replying for 'The Army' embracively spoke of the American Army. **1902** *Academy* 16 Aug. 178/1 The 'characteristics of the time' and the 'natural lineaments of contemporary people' may have found no embracive novelist. **1902** *Edin. Rev.* Oct. 357 Important deities have been omitted from this brief catalogue, which is much more representative than embracive. **1930** *Punch* 18 June 683 Perhaps he is too embracive, for it is doubtful if Mr. William Nicholson should be grouped with purely comic artists. **1937** *Sun* (Baltimore) 9 June 10/8 The two nouns are used embracively, of course, 'the tumult and the shouting', and anybody but a numskull would be able to see the purpose of the use of this type of expression with a singular verb.

†**em'braid**, *v.*¹ *Obs.* Forms: 5 enbrayde, 6 en-, embraid, -brayde. Also 6 imbraid, -braied, -brayd. [f. EN- + BRAID *v.*²; cf. ABRAID *v.*²] *trans.* To upbraid, taunt, mock; const. *of*, with. Also, to reproach one with, 'cast in one's teeth'.

1481 CAXTON *Orat. G. Flamineus* F vii, in *Tully of Old Age* My lytil feelde of the which I am enbrayded by Corneli shal suffise for our dayly lyuelode. **1531** ELYOT *Gov.* (1580) 16 He was of his enimies embrayded, and called a schoole master. **1540** MORYSINE tr. *Vives' Introd. Wysd.* Pref., Never imbraidinge benefites gyven and paste. **1548** HALL *Chron.* (1809) 265 To imbrayd him with the pleasure that he had done for him. **1573** TUSSER *Husb.* (1878) 205 If ye be friends embraid me not. **1582** BENTLEY *Mon. Matrones* II. 13 With..words, which I knowe to be foolish..I imbraided thee.

Hence **em'braiding** *vbl. sb.* Also **em'braider**, one who upbraids, an upbraider.

1542 Imbraydyng [see IMPROPERY]. **1552** HULOET, Imbrayder or caster in teeth with an olde benefite. **1568** GRAFTON *Chron.* II. 680 They fell at such great words with such imbraydings and casting in the teeth of olde benefites shewed.

†**em'braid**, *v.*² *Obs.* Forms: 5 enbrayd, 6 enbraid, -brade, embread. [f. EN- + BRAID *v.*¹] *trans.* **a.** To fasten or sew on like braid. **b.** To plait or braid; to interlace, intertwine.

Hence **em'braiding** *vbl. sb.*

1491 CAXTON *Vitas Patr.* (W. de W.) I. xlix. (1495) 95 b, [He] lyued by enbraydynge and weuynge of cordes of Jonkes. **1523** SKELTON *Garl. Laurel* 789 The saumpler to sow on, the lacis to enbraid. **1545** RAYNOLD *Womans Booke* 18 They [the vessels] begynne to entermyngle, enbrade, and enterlade each other. **1596** SPENSER *F.Q.* III. vi. 18 Her golden lockes..in tresses bright Embreaded were.

†**em'braid**, *v.*³ *Obs. rare*⁻¹. In (? 5) 6 enbrayde. [f. EN- + BRAID *v.*¹; see ABRAID.] *trans.* = ABRAID, to arouse.

1430 LYDG. *Troy* v. xxxvii. (1555) Pelleus..gan..Pirrhus to..enbrayde [**1513** abrayde] out of his deadly thoughte.

embrail: see EM- *prefix*.

†**embrake**, *v. Obs.* Also 6 enbrake, 7 imbrake. [f. EN- + BRAKE *sb.*] *trans.* To lead into a brake or snare, entangle.

1542 UDALL *Erasm. Apoph.* 286 Enbraked in the middes of those mortalle streights. **1599** NASHE *Lent. Stuffe* 65 Hee would..hamper and embrake her in those mortal straights for her disdain. **1613-18** DANIEL *Coll. Hist. Eng.* 108 (D.) John..imbraked the state and himselfe in those miserable incombrances thorow his violences. **1628** tr. *Mathieu's Powerfull Favorite* 50 We haue not leisure to imbrake [*implicare*] our selues in these broiles.

†**em'branched**, *ppl. a. Obs. rare.* [f. EN- + BRANCH *sb.* + -ED; OF. had *embranché* in same sense.] Furnished with branches.

*c*1595 J. DICKENSON *Sheph. Compl.* (1878) 9 Vnder an Arboret embranched wide, This..swaine..did lie.

embranchment (ɛm'brɑːnʃmənt, -æ-). [f. as prec. + -MENT: cf. Fr. *embranchement.*] A branching off or out, as of an arm of a river, a spur of a mountain-range: *concr.* a branch, ramification. Also *fig.*

1830 LYELL *Princ. Geol.* I. 194 The lateral embranchments of the main valley of the Rhone. **1856** DOVE *Logic Chr. Faith* VI. §6. 405 Human life is divided into two embranchments. **1862** G. P. SCROPE *Volcanoes* 365 Several embranchments or strings of conoidal hills. **1876** QUAIN *Elem. Anat.* (ed. 8) II. 157 The sympathetic set of nerves is a mere..embranchment of the cerebro-spinal system. **1877** CLERY *Min. Tact.* xiv. 201 The point of embranchment [of the road] was screened by a ridge.

†**em'brand**, *v. Obs.* Also 7 imbrand; *pa. pple.* embrant. [f. EN- + BRAND *v.*] *trans.* To brand, stigmatize; to impress (a stigma).

1604 DANIEL *Fun. Poem Earl Devonshire* Our own fame.. Will be imbranded with the mark of blame. **1625** W. LISLE *Du Bartas, Noe 2* The Rogues passport embrant between his brows.

embrangle, imbrangle (ɛm-, ɪm'bræŋg(ə)l), *v.* [f. EN-, IN- + BRANGLE *v.*] *trans.* To entangle, confuse, perplex.

1664 BUTLER *Hud.* II. iii. 19 In knotted Law, like Nets.. they are imbrangled. **1689** *Trial, Pritchard v. Papillon* 6 Nov. 1684, 26 These things..imbrangled by our Factions and Divisions. **1710** BERKELEY *Princ. Human Knowl.* I. §98, I am..embrangled in inexplicable difficulties. **1811** COLERIDGE *Lett.* in J. P. Collier's 7 *Lectures* (1856) 57 The perplexities with which..I have been thorned and embrangled. **1872** MORLEY *Voltaire* ii. (ed. 2) 62 Physical explanations..were imbrangled with..metaphysics.

embranglement (ɛm'bræŋg(ə)lmənt). [f. prec. + -MENT.] The action of the vb. EMBRANGLE, or the result of such action; entanglement, complication, confusion.

1806-7 J. BERESFORD *Miseries Hum. Life* (1826) *Post. Groans* No. 9 The entanglements and embranglements of the latter [her feet], in her endless train. **1839** T. HOOK in *New Monthly Mag.* LV. 434 All these embranglements conduced very much to the pleasure which the Duke anticipated. **1861** *Times* 22 Feb. 9 Under the control of Parliament there would be no such embranglement.

embrant, pa. pple. of EMBRAND *v.*, *Obs.*

†**em'brase**, *v. Obs.* Also 5 enbrace, embrass, 6 enbrase, 7 *Sc.* embrayis. [a. F. *embrase-r*, f. *en* in + **brase*, *braise* hot charcoal.]

1. *trans.* To set on fire.

1480 CAXTON *Ovid's Met.* XIV. i, Ethna, the hye montayne Embrased wᵗ fyre of helle. **1579** FENTON *Guicciard.* XIII. (1599) 607 The powder..being embrased of the fire.

2. *fig.* To inflame with passion, etc.

1483 CAXTON *Gold. Leg.* 88/1 Saynt Nicholas embraced with the loue of god sette hym hardyly ayenst the righter. **1490** —— *Eneydos* xiv. 50 Her grete desire embrasid wyth the swete flamme of loue. *a*1605 MONTGOMERIE *Bankis Helicon* 102 Hir birning beawtie dois embrayis My breist.

Hence †**em'brasing** *ppl. a.*

1502 *Ord. Crysten Men* (W. de Worde) IV. xxi. (1506) 242 For fere of theues or of the enbrasynge fyre.

†**em'brasement**. *Obs.* [a. F. *embrasement*: see EMBRASE *v.* and -MENT.] A burning, conflagration; *lit.* and *fig.*

1483 CAXTON *Gold. Leg.* 249/4 He ouercam thembracementes of the fyre of helle.

embra'ssade. *rare*⁻¹. [a. Fr. *embrassade*, f. *embrasser* to EMBRACE.] A process of embracing.

1830 MISS MITFORD *Our Village* Ser. 4 (1863) 269 Miss Laura made a speech in her usual style..at the conclusion of which Miss Barbara underwent an embrassade.

†**em'brasure**, *sb.*¹ *Obs. rare.* [f. EMBRACE *v.*² + -URE.] = EMBRACE.

1606 SHAKS. *Tr. & Cr.* IV. iv. 39 Preuents Our lock't embrasures.

embrasure (ɛm'breɪʒ(j)ʊə(r)), *sb.*² Also embrazure. [a. F. *embrasure* (16th c.), f. *embraser* 'to skue or chamfret off the jaumbes of a door or window' (Cotgr.), synon. with *braser* (Cotgr.) and the mod.F. *ébraser*.]

1. A slanting or bevelling in the sides of an opening to a wall for a window or door, so that the inside profile of the window is larger than that of the outside.

1753 CHAMBERS *Cycl. Suppl.*, *Embrasure*, in architecture, an enlargement of the gap, or aperture of a door, or window, within-side the wall. **1832** in WEBSTER. **1858** CARLYLE *Fredk. Gt.* (1865) II. VII. vii. 329 They put me in a chair in the embrasure of a window. **1879** SIR G. SCOTT *Lect. Archit.* I. 181 The spreading or embrasure of the jambs increases the openings inwards.

2. *Mil.* An opening widening from within made in an epaulement or parapet for the purpose of allowing a gun to be fired through it.

1702 *Milit. Dict.*, *Embrazures*, the Gaps or Loopholes, left open in a Parapet for the Cannon to fire through. **1790** BEATSON *Nav. & Mil. Mem.* I. 47 Setting himself close to the wall under an embrasure. **1813** SCOTT *Rokeby* v. xxxiv, The eye could count each embrazure. **1863** KINGLAKE *Crimea* (1877) III. i. 124 Riding straight at one of the embrasures [he] leapt his grey Arab into the breastwork.

b. A port-hole for the same purpose in a ship.

1759 FALCONER *90-Gun Ship* 43 Guns..From dread embrazures formidably peep. **1881** [see 3].

3. *attrib.*

1809 *Naval Chron.* XXII. 514 An embrasure battery of four guns. **1881** *Daily News* 29 Aug. 3/4, I..jumped down on the embrasure port.

embrasure (ɛm'breɪʒ(j)ʊə(r)), *v. trans.* To furnish with embrasures. Hence **em'brasured** *ppl. a.*

1805 *Naval Chron.* XIII. 500 The Fort..being completely embrazured. **1853** *Blackw. Mag.* LXXIV. 73 He would have rushed to Paris, embrasured the walls. **1877** MRS. H. KING *Disciples Ugo Bassi* iv. (ed. 3) 160 The mud embankments, the embrasured walls.

embrave (ɛm'breɪv), *v.* Also enbrave. [f. EN- + BRAVE *adj.*] *trans.* To make brave.

†**1.** To adorn splendidly; to embellish, beautify. Cf. BRAVE 2. *Obs.*

1579 SPENSER *Sheph. Cal.* Nov. 109 The faded flowres her corse embraue. **1610** G. FLETCHER *Christ's Vict.* III. ii, And with their verdure his white head embraves. **1736** W. THOMPSON *Nat.* xvi. 9 Each with circling gold embraved had his head.

2. To inspire with bravery, render courageous.

1648 JOS. BEAUMONT *Psyche* xvii. Argt. (R.) Psyche, embrav'd by Charis's generous flame. *c*1874 PUNSHON *Wilberforce* 11 Natures..have been embraved into the very heroism of sacrifice when the trial came.

embrawd: see EMBROWD.

embrayis, Sc. form of EMBRASE, *Obs.*

embrazure: see EMBRASURE.

†**em'breach**, *v. Mil. Obs.* Also 6 imbrech. [f. EN- + BREACH *sb.*] **a.** *intr.* To enter a breach. **b.** *trans.*, To make a breach in.

1581 STYWARD *Martial Discipl.* I. 38 Imbrech he with his ensigne advancing with the foremost. **1610** HOLLAND *Camden's Brit.* I. 379 New walles, which..time doth force, and as it were embreach with his assault.

†**em'bread**, *v. nonce-wd.* In 6 enbread. [f. EN- + BREAD.] *trans.* To convert into, or incorporate in, bread.

1548 GESTE *Pr. Masse* 86 Why then shuld it [the godhede] be adjudged enbreaded for hys presence in the breade.

embread, var. of EMBRAID *v.*²

embreastment (ɛm'brɛstmənt). ? *nonce-wd.* [f. EN- + BREAST *sb.* + -MENT.] A breast-like swelling of the ground.

1799 COLERIDGE in *New Monthly Mag.* (1835) XLV. 219 A green plain, which heaved up and down in hillocks and embreastments of earth.

embreathe (ɛm'briːð), *v.* Also 5-6 enbreathe, -brethe. See also IMBREATHE, INBREATHE. [f. EN- + BREATHE *v.*]

1. *trans.* To breathe (something) *into*; to inspire (a person) *with*. Also, to give breath to.

*a*1529 SKELTON *Dethe Erle Northumberl.* 157 Enbrethed with the blast of influence deuyne. **1548** GEST *Pr. Masse* 86 The holy ghost is accompted enbreathed for that he was presented in Christes breathe. **1599** T. M[OUFET] *Silkwormes* I What breth embreath'd these almost thingles things. *a*1612 BROUGHTON *Wks.* III. 728 To embreath into your Mʸ. the speech..condemned.

2. To breathe in, inhale. In quot. *fig.*

18.. M. ARNOLD *Poems, Heine's Grave*, May'st thou the rapture of peace Deep have embreathed at its core.

Hence **em'breathing** *vbl. sb.*

1548 GEST *Pr. Masse* 86 Wrytten by the enbrethinge of the holy ghost.

em'breathement. *rare*⁻¹. [f. prec. + -MENT.] = INSPIRATION.

1854 W. LEE *Inspiration* i. 19 The immediate suggestion, embreathment, and dictation of the Holy Ghost.

embreech: see EM- *prefix*.

†**em'breve**, *v. Obs.* In 3 en-, ambreve. [ad. OF. *embrever*, corresp. to med.L. *imbreviāre* IMBREVE *v.*, f. *in-* in + *breve*: see BREVE, BRIEF *sb.*] *trans.* To make a formal entry of; to inscribe.

*c*1225 *Ancren Riwle* 344 Nis non so lutel þing of þeos þet þe deouel naueþ enbreued [*v.r.* ambreued] on his rolle. *c*1240 *Sawles Warde* in *Cott. Hom.* 249 His boc þat is on euch sunne enbrev.

embrew, obs. form of IMBRUE.

†**em'bridle**, *v. Obs. rare.* In 6 enbridle. [f. EN- + BRIDLE *sb.*] *trans.* To restrain as with a bridle.

1583 GOLDING *Calvin on Deuteron.* lxii. 1003 Threatnings whereby God woulde..holde vs enbridled.

embrigade (ɛmbrɪ'geɪd), *v. rare.* [ad. Fr. *embrigader*, f. *en-* + *brigade*.] To form into a brigade; *fig.*, to form into an organized body.

1884 *Times* 2 Feb. 9 The entire nobility are embrigaded into an official hierarchy.

†**em'bright**, *v. Obs.* [f. EN- + BRIGHT *a.*] *trans.* To render bright. Hence **em'brighted** *ppl. a.*

1598 SYLVESTER *Du Bartas* I. iv. (1641) 37 So doth the glorious lustre Of radiant Titan, with his beams embright Thy gloomy Front. **1766** J. CUNNINGHAM *Death late Maj.* xxx, Mercy..Through the embrighted air ascendant flies.

em'brighten, *v.* Also 7 imbrighten. [f. EN- + BRIGHT *a.* + -EN.] *trans.* = BRIGHTEN.

Hence **em'brightening** *ppl. a.*

1610 G. FLETCHER *Christ's Triumph* xvi, Whose garment imbrightned into heau'nly flame. **1652** E. BENLOWES *Theophila* 22 Embrightning our knowledge. *Ibid.* v. xcvi, Like duskie atoms in the suns embrightning ray. **1855** R. C. SINGLETON tr. *Virgil* II. 315 Even Messapus's embrightening helm.

†**em'bring.** *Obs. rare.* In 4 *pa. t.* embrouȝte. Cf. IMBRING. [f. EN- + BRING *v.*] *trans.* To bring in.

*c*1325 *Floriz & Bl.* (Hauskn.) 863 (Auchinl. MS.) And ȝaf him here malisoun þat so fele floures embrouȝte on honde.

embrithite ('ɛmbrɪθaɪt). *Min.* [a. G. *embrithit* (A. Breithaupt 1837, in *Jrnl. f. prakt. Chem.* X. 443), f. Gr. ἐμβριθ-ής heavy + -ITE¹.] A name formerly given to a supposed variety of boulangerite.

1854 J. D. DANA *Syst. Min.* (ed. 4) II. 81. **1868** [see BOULANGERITE]. **1883** *Encycl. Brit.* XVI. 395/1 Plumbostib or Embrethite [*sic*], from Nertchinsk, is only a variety.

em'brittle, *v.* [f. EM- + BRITTLE *a.*] *trans.* To render brittle. Hence **em'brittling** *vbl. sb.* and *ppl. a.*

1902 *Encycl. Brit.* XXIX. 574/2 Sudden cooling hardens and embrittles steel and cast iron. **1903** H. M. HOWE *Iron, Steel & other Alloys* ix. 257 The coarsening and embrittling of low-carbon steel. **1930** *Engineering* 11 Apr. 494/1 Lead pipes embrittled by the prolonged application of water-hammer. **1960** *New Scientist* 20 Oct. 1067/2 The plasticity of..steels and of molybdenum alloys decreases markedly when subjected to neutron irradiation. This embrittling phenomena [*sic*] is important. **1962** J. T. MARSH *Self-*

Smoothing Fabrics v. 45 As early as 1919, it was found.. that cotton and rayon could be made crease resisting.. although the products were greatly embrittled and commercially valueless.

em'brittlement. [f. prec. + -MENT.] The action of the vb. EMBRITTLE, or the result of such action; loss of ductility.

1920 *Amer. Inst. Mining & Metall. Engin. Trans.* LXIV. 440 It showed no evidence of embrittlement. **1926** *Fuel Economist* II. 115 (*heading*) Treatment of boiler feed water to prevent caustic embrittlement. **1939** *Nature* 11 Mar. 443/2 The full effect of the temper-hardening treatment.. cannot be employed with advantage on account of the accompanying embrittlement. **1962** J. T. MARSH *Self-Smoothing Fabrics* ix. 113 Many investigators appear to have assumed that the embrittlement of cotton in conventional processes was due to the use of an acid catalyst at a high temperature. **1969** *Physics Bull.* Mar. 89/2 The embrittlement of alloy steels containing small amounts of P, As, Sb or Sn. *Ibid.*, Embrittlement occurs after long heating at temperatures between 350 and 550°C, while tempering to remove it is achieved by brief heating to 650°C.

†**embro'cado.** *Obs.* Also 7 imbrocado. [corrupt form of IMBROCCATA, as if Spanish: see -ADO.] A pass or thrust in fencing.

?*c* **1600** *Distracted Emp.* IV. ii, in Bullen *Old Plays* III. 233 Favorytts are not without their steccados, imbrocados, and pun[to]-reversos. **1607** DEKKER *Knts. Conjur.* (1842) 16 Hee .. taught him [Cayn] that embrocado by which he kild his brother. **1613** WITHERS *Abuses Stript & Whipt* I. v, They are for nothing but the Imbrocado.

†**embro'cado,** *v. Obs. rare.* [f. EN- + *brocado* = BROCADE *sb.*, q.v.] *trans.* ? To adorn with brocade work. Hence **embro'cadoing** *vbl. sb.* (*fig.*).

1677 FELTHAM *Resolves* II. lxxxiv. (ed. 10) 339 What are all .. the embellishings, the embrocadoings of Fortune to us.

embrocate ('ɛmbrəkeɪt), *v. Med.* Also 7 embrochate, imbrocate. [f. med.L. *embrocāt-* ppl. stem of *embrocāre*, f. *embrocha*: see EMBROCH.] *trans.* To bathe or foment (a part of the body) with liquid, in order to remove or mitigate disease.

1612 WOODALL *Surg. Mate* Wks. (1653) 303 In Wounds of Gun-shot.. Embrocate often. **1655** CULPEPPER *Riverius* v. i. 125 The Tongue may be embrochated with Oxymel. **1689** MOYLE *Sea Chyrurg.* II. vi. 49 When you have imbrocated all about with Oyl of Roses. **1722** DOUGLAS in *Phil. Trans.* XXXII. 85, I embrocated all the Abdomen.. with warm Ol. Chamæmel. **1815** BYRON *Lett. to Moore* 12 June, He has been embrocated. **1856** KANE *Arct. Expl.* II. xxv. 252.

embrocation (ɛmbrəʊ'keɪʃən). *Med.* Also 7 embrochation. [n. of action f. med.L. *embrocāre*: see prec. and -ATION.]

†**1.** The action of embrocating. *Obs.*

1543 TRAHERON *Vigo's Chirurg.* (1586) 437 It is an embrocation when we drop down liquor from a hyer place upon some part of the bodie. **1634** T. JOHNSON *Parey's Chirurg.* XXVI. xxx. (1678) 650 An Embroche or Embrocation, is a watering.

2. A liquid used for bathing or moistening any diseased part; now usually restricted to those applied by rubbing; a liniment.

1610 BARROUGH *Meth. Physick* I. ii. (1639) 4 Embrocations (that is, decoctions made of certaine things to powre upon any member). **1748** SMOLLETT *Rod. Rand.* xxviii, He bathed the doctor's face with an embrocation. **1831** BREWSTER *Nat. Magic* i. 3 Drugs and soporific embrocations.

†**em'broch(e,** *sb. Obs.* Also 6 embrocha. [ad. med.L. *embrocha*, ad. Gr. ἐμβροχή lotion, related to ἐμβρέχειν to steep, foment, f. ἐν in + βρέχειν to wet (as with rain).] = EMBROCATION 2.

1585 LLOYD *Treas. Health* 5 Embrocha is when the membre is washed gentilly wyth a sponge dypt in the decoction of diuerse herbes. **1605** DANIEL *Queen's Arcadia*, Strange Speech Of.. Embroches, Lixives, Cataplasmes. **1657** TOMLINSON *Renou's Disp.* 192 An Embroche or Irrigation is compounded of Simples.

†**em'broche,** *v.*[1] *Obs. rare*⁻¹. [f. prec.; or ad. OF. *embrochier* or med.L. *embroc(h)āre.*] *trans.* = EMBROCATE.

1575 TURBERV. *Bk. Venerie* 367 Washing and embroching the dogges throate.. with vinegar.

†**em'broche,** *v.*[2] *Obs. rare.* Also 7 embroach. [f. EN- + BROCHE *v.*] *trans.* To stitch on by way of ornament.

1611 SPEED *Hist. Gt. Brit.* VII. vii. (1632) 228 Precious Gemmes, embroched in the Celebrating Vestures. **1697** *Observ. Money & Coin* 5 Besides precious Gems Embroach'd upon the Celebrating Vestments.

†**em'broche,** *v.*[3] *Obs.* In 5 enbroche. [ad. F. *embroche-r*, f. *en-* (see EN-) + *broche* BROACH *sb.*[1] spit.] *trans.* To put on a skewer or spit.

c **1420** *Liber Cocorum* (1862) 34 Kostyf of motone.. Enbrochyd shal be. *Ibid.* 35 Fysshe thou schalle enbroche.

embroglio, bad form of IMBROGLIO.

1826 SCOTT *Woodst.* xx, Out of a cursed embroglio during the attack on Brentford. **1868** *Morn. Star* 2 Jan.

†**em'broid,** *v. Obs. rare.* [f. EN- + BROID *v.*] *trans.* To entwine, braid.

1573 TWYNE *Æneid* x. Dd iij b, Gold embroyding bynds their docks.

†**em'broider,** *sb. Obs. rare*⁻¹. [f. prec. (in sense of next: cf. BROID *v.* and OF. *embroder*) + -ER.] = EMBROIDERER.

1609 HOLLAND *Amm. Marcel.* 12 Close vnto the front of the chariot marcheth all the sort of weavers and embroiders.

embroider (ɛm'brɔɪdə(r)), *v.* Forms: 5 enbrowder, -brouder, (onbrouder), embrawdre, 5–7 embrother, 6 enbroder, enbrauder, embrouder, 7 embroder, embroader, embroyder, 7– embroider. Also 5–6 imbrowder, 6 imbrother, imbrodur, imbroyder, 6–7 imbroder, 7 imbrayder, 7– 8 imbroider. [f. EN- + BROIDER; cf. OF. *embroder.*]

1. *trans.* To ornament with needlework; to work in needlework upon cloth, etc. Also *absol.*

14.. *Epiph.* (*Tundale's Vis.* 114) Yor quene.. Of no devyse enbrowdyrd hath hir wede. *c* **1420** *Chron. Vilod.* 572 þis palle enbroudryd wᵗ gold so rede. **1475** *Inv. Goods* in *Rep. Comm. Hist. MSS.* I. 555 A cloth of blac worstede.. with a whyte crosse imbrowderyd in v placis. **1483** CAXTON *Gold. Leg.* 331/2 A noble woman.. was desyred tembrawdre certayne garmentes. **1494** *Househ. Ord.* 125 Above the opening.. to bee embrothered the Kings and Queens armes. **1521** *Mem. Ripon* (1882) I. 183 With S. George on horsbake uppon the brest of the said abbit inbrowderid. **1552** *Inv. Ch. Goods Norwich* in *Norfolk Archæol.* (1865) VII. 51 Twoo coopes of white damaske embroudered wᵗ Lillypotts. **1555** EDEN *Decades W. Ind.* (Arb.) 197 Buskynnes.. imbrothered with gold. *c* **1595** J. DICKENSON *Sheph. Compl.* (1878) 21 A faire hearse curiouslie embrothered. **1651** W. G. tr. *Cowel's Inst.* 63 If any one.. imbrayder his Purple in my garment. **1680** ANNE MONTAGUE in *Hatton Corr.* (1878) 241 A cheery coulerd satten embroderyed with silver thick. **1735** BERKELEY *Querist* § 111 The women.. embroider.. for the embellishment of their persons. **1848** MACAULAY *Hist. Eng.* II. 476 The motto, embroidered in letters three feet long.

†**b.** *transf.* To ornament or variegate as if with embroidery. Sometimes *ironically*, to besmear with dirt or blood. *Obs.*

1460 in *Pol. Rel. & L. Poems* (1866) 152 þese gloues.. Onbroudrid with blood. **1591** LYLY *Endym.* I. iii. 13 Their braines must as it were imbroder my bolts. **1596** SPENSER *State Irel.* 49 Guilded leather with which they use to imbroyder their Irish Jackets. **1624** CAPT. SMITH *Virginia* II. 30 Breasts and face.. imbrodered with.. beasts, serpents. *c* **1630** DRUMM. OF HAWTH. *Poems* Wks. (1711) 38/1 Meadows Embroyd'ring all the banks. *c* **1640** [SHIRLEY] *Capt. Underwit* III. iii. in *Bullen's Old Pl.* II. 367 To Westminster In our torne gownes, embroiderd with Strand dirt. **1685** R. BURTON *Eng. Emp. Amer.* iv. 68 The Women imbroider their Legs, Hands and other parts with divers works. **1762–71** H. WALPOLE *Vertue's Anecd. Paint.* (1786) III. 155 A whole gallery embroidered in pannels by his hand.

2. In various figurative uses.

†**a.** To make splendid, dignify. *Obs.*

1629 SYMMER *Spir. Posie* II. vi. 39 So by his Humilitie he embroydered the basenesse of his birth. *a* **1667** COWLEY *Obscurity* Wks. (1710) II. 704 Nor let my homely Death embroider'd be With Scutcheon, or with Elegy.

†**b.** To set forth in florid language. Cf. *paint.*

1636 HEALEY *Theophrast.* 20 Embroidering and painting out his praise. **1648** *Hunting of Fox* 3 Hee sang a song.. in which.. he passionatly embroyder's what he had done for his well beloved.

c. To embellish with rhetorical ornament or with fictitious additions or exaggerations.

1614 RALEIGH *Hist. World* II. 367 The Grecian Historians and Poets imbroder and intermixe the tales of ancient times, with a world of fictions. **1638** FEATLEY *Transub.* 23 The Doctor made an eloquent speech, imbroidered with all variety of learning. *a* **1797** WALPOLE *Mem. Geo. II*, (1847) III. iv. 97 He had embroidered his own story with some marvellous legends. **1848** MRS. JAMESON *Sacr. & Leg. Art* (1850) 326 The history of Vincent.. has been extravagantly embroidered. **1884** *Weekly Register* 18 Oct. 503/1 Whether the legend.. was accurate or embroidered, Lord Malmesbury best knows.

embroidered (ɛm'brɔɪdərd), *ppl. a.* [f. EMBROIDER *v.* + -ED[1].]

1. Of textile fabrics, leather, etc: Adorned or variegated with figures of needlework. Also of the needlework itself.

1591 FLORIO *2nd Fruites* 9 That [girdle] of blew veluet, embrothered. **1593** SHAKS. *3 Hen. VI*, II. v. 44 A rich Imbroider'd Canopie. **1609** BIBLE (Douay) *Lev.* viii. comm., A girdle.. of twisted silke and gold, embrodered worke. **1665** BOYLE *Occas. Refl.* v. v. (1675) 314 A Lac'd, or an Imbroider'd suit. **1703** MAUNDRELL *Journ. Jerus.* (1732) 29 His embroyder'd Sacerdotal Robe. **1853** KINGSLEY *Hypatia* vii. 86 An embroidered shoe.

2. *transf.* and *fig.*

1612 DRAYTON *Poly-olb.* A, Through delicate embrodered meadowes. **1657** W. COLES *Adam in Eden* To Rdr., The pleasant Aspects of Nature.. and.. her severall imbroidered Beds. **1672** EVELYN *French Gardiner* II. § 1 (1675) 136 Melons.. white, wrought or Embroidered, Ribb'd, and others. **1868** HELPS *Realmah* xv. (1876) 394 In the embroidered language of the Sheviri.

em'broiderer [f. EMBROIDER *v.* + -ER.]

1. One who embroiders.

1413 LYDG. *Pilgr. Sowle* IV. xxxvii. (1483) 84 More necessary to the land is.. a deluer than a goldsmyth or a embrawderer. **1603** KNOLLES *Hist. Turks* (1621) 1342 A Flemish imbroitherer had.. advertised him. **1723** *Lond. Gaz.* No. 6171/9 Mary Bird.. Imbroiderer. **1786** tr. *Beckford's Vathek* (1868) 39 She collected all the sempstresses and embroiderers of Samarah. **1875** JOWETT *Plato* (ed. 2) III. 244 The arts of the.. embroiderer will have to be set in motion.

2. *fig.*; cf. EMBROIDER *v.* 2c.

16.. NORTH *Life Qvoniambec* (R.), This embroiderer.. has stuffed his writings with.. lies.

embroideress (ɛm'brɔɪdərɪs). Also embroidress. [f. as prec. + -ESS.] A female embroiderer; a woman who embroiders.

1723 *Lond. Gaz.* No. 6171/7 Emma Paine.., Embroideress. **1782** LADY LLANOVER in *Mrs. Delany's Corr.* Ser. II. III. 80 To apologize for his niece's being an embroidress by profession. **1867** FREEMAN *Norm. Conq.* (ed. 3) I. vi. 440 The skilful needles of English embroideresses.

embroidering (ɛm'brɔɪdərɪŋ), *vbl. sb.* [f. EMBROIDER *v.* + -ING[1].] **a.** The action of the vb. EMBROIDER. Also *attrib.*, as in ***embroidering machine.*** **b.** *concr.* Embroidered ornamentation.

1536 STRYPE *Eccl. Mem.* I. I. xxxv. 255 He can.. use.. embrotheryng.. carving, painting or graffing. **1555** EDEN *Decades W. Ind.* (Arb.) 301 Part of them exercise.. imbrotherynge. **1548** UDALL, etc. tr. *Erasm. Paraphrase Matt.* 106 b, They go with brode & gorgiouse imbrouderinges. **1611** BIBLE *Ezek.* xvii. 3 Divers colours [*marg.* embroidering]. *a* **1619** FOTHERBY *Atheom.* II. xiv. (1622) 361 Hee teacheth the Arts, both of Weauing, and Imbroydering. **1886** *Daily News* 6 Sept. 2/4 The embroidering is principally done on the Continent.

embroidery (ɛm'brɔɪdərɪ). Forms: 4 enbrouderie, 6–7 embroyderie, -broiderie, 7– embroidery. Also 6 imbroderie, 7 imbrodry, imbrauthery, imbroidery. [ME. *embrouderie*, f. OF. *embroder* EMBROWD *v.*: see -RY; cf. EMBROIDER and BROIDERY.]

1. The art of ornamenting cloth and other fabrics with figures of needlework; also *attrib.*

1393 GOWER *Conf.* II. 11 Of weving or of embrouderie. **17..** ADDISON in *Spect.*, Their more serious occupations are sewing and embroidery. **1872** YEATS *Techn. Hist. Comm.* 286 The ancient feminine occupation of embroidery.

2. *concr.* Embroidered work or material.

c **1570** THYNNE *Pride & Lowl.* (1841) 12 With silke, and golde, and with imbroderie. **1598** SHAKS. *Merry W.* v. v. 75 Saphire, pearle, and rich embroiderie. **1633** G. HERBERT *Temple, Vanitie*, To whom.. solid work [shines not] as false embroyderies. **1688** R. HOLME *Armoury* III. 94 A waistcoat with Imbrauthery. **1699** EVELYN *Acetaria* Plan, Flowers.. Embroyderies, Carvings. **1716** LADY M. W. MONTAGUE *Lett.* I. vii. 22 Window-curtains.. almost covered with Embroidery. **1836** W. IRVING *Astoria* I. 7 They even sell their embroidery, their lace, and their clothes.

3. a. *fig.* with notion of 'elaborate or showy ornament', 'adventitious adornment', etc.

1640 YORKE *Union Hon.* Pref. Verses, Thats but imbrodry of Fame. **1675** TRAHERNE *Chr. Ethics* xxx. 473 A liberal man .. puts embroideries on religion by the chearfulness of his spirit. **1762** HUME *Hist. Eng.* (1806) IV. liii. 124 Their liturgy was.. a species of mass, though with some less shew and embroidery. **1781** COWPER *Expost.* 234 All the embroidery of poetic dreams. **1848** H. MILLER *First Impr.* xvi. (1857) 277 An embroidery of playful humour. **1858** HAWTHORNE *Fr. & It. Jrnls.* II. 112 Rather more embroidery of courtesy than belongs to an Englishman.

b. *Mus.* Ornamentation either contrapuntal or through variation.

1875 OUSELEY *Mus. Form* ix. 49 Brilliant passages.. form an embroidery thereon.

4. *transf.* Applied to other kinds of ornament or marking compared in appearance to needlework, *esp.* (in poetical or elevated language) to the natural adornment of the ground by flowers. †In 17th c. used *techn.* in landscape gardening.

1644 EVELYN *Mem.* (1857) I. 79 The parterres of excellent embroidery. **1672** —— *French Gardiner* II. § 1 (1675) 150 Those Melons which are full of Embroidery and Characters. *a* **1667** COWLEY *Poverty* Wks. (1711) III. 58 Daisies.. their Embroidery bring. **1820** SCOTT *Monast.* ii, And it was garnished with an embroidery of daisies and wild flowers.

¶**5.** *nonce-use.* A place of embroidering; an embroidery manufactory.

1796 BURKE *Regic. Peace* Wks. VIII. 275 From the embroideries of Babylon or from the loom of the Gobelins.

6. *attrib.* and *Comb.*

1695 *Lond. Gaz.* No. 3118/4 All sorts of Gardens.. in Embroidery work in Grass or Gravil. **1841** LADY WILTON *Art Needlework* xxiv. 392 The Empress Josephine.. exercised.. her needle and embroidery-frame, with beautiful address. **1880** L. HIGGIN *Handbk. Embroidery* i. 1 'Embroidery needles' for ordinary crewel handwork. *Ibid.* v. 59 We give a recipe for embroidery paste. **1882** CAULFEILD & SAWARD *Dict. Needlework* 197/1 Embroidery needles.. for canvas work.. are short, thick, and blunt, and the eye is wide and long. *Ibid.*, Embroidery paste is used for two purposes in needlework: one to make two materials adhere together, the other to strengthen and stiffen Embroidery at the back. **1883** OUIDA *Wanda* I. 80 She sat down to her embroidery frame. **1895** *Montgomery Ward Catal.* 90/3 Embroidery cotton on spools. *Ibid.* 126/3 Embroidery Hoops, 4, 5, and 6 inches in diameter. *Ibid.* 448/3 Embroidery Scissors, polished laid steel. **1899** *Daily News* 28 June 8/4 A gigantic embroidery-like cloth of gold. **1909** *English-woman* Apr. 232 The lace-making and embroidery industry. **1909** *Embroidery* V. 119/1 Amongst the many existing varieties of embroidery stitches some of the prettiest and most attractive are those which bring to mind, more or less directly, natural forms and growth. *Ibid.* 124/1 That book decorations were frequent sources for embroidery designs is beyond doubt. **1938** A. G. I. CHRISTIE *Eng. Medieval Embroidery* 18 With the solitary exception of St. Dunstan.. no name of an English medieval embroidery designer has yet been found. **1967** E. SHORT *Embroidery & Fabric Collage* iv. 99 The invention of sewing and embroidery machines during the Victorian era had its effect mainly on dress and furnishings. *Ibid.* 115 Other

articles which give great scope to the embroidery designer are kneelers, banners and dossal hangings.

†em'broil, *sb. Obs.* Also imbroil(e. [f. EMBROIL *v.*² Cf. Sp. *embrollo*, It. *imbroglio*: see IMBROGLIO.]

1. A state of entanglement or confusion; a disturbance, uproar.

1636 E. DACRES tr. *Machiavel's Disc. Livy* II. 510 Before such imbroiles, few of the citizens of Venice could foresee the danger. **1700** RYCAUT *Hist. Turks* III. 550 Impossible for any Embroils..for ever after to arise in the Lesser Asia. *a* **1734** NORTH *Exam.* I. ii. §14 (1740) 37 Any Imbroil or Concussion of the Public. **1788** *Antiquities* in *Ann. Reg.* 120 During these embroils, the god..stole off.

b. A quarrel.

1742 WALPOLE *Lett. H. Mann* I. xxxiii. (1833) 142 As to your embroil with Richcourt I condemn you excessively.

2. Mental disturbance, 'worry'.

1799 in Nicolas *Disp. Nelson* IV. 107 Never let such a thought come into your head, which was never more wanted to be clear from embroils than at this moment.

†em'broil, *v.*¹ *Obs. rare.* [f. EN- + BROIL *v.*¹] *trans.* To set on fire, burn up. Hence **em'broiling** *ppl. a.*

1664 H. MORE *Decay Chr. Piety* (L.) That knowledge, for which we..rifle God's cabinet, should, like the coal from the altar, serve only to embroil and consume the sacrilegious invaders. **1726** THOMSON *Winter* 247 Wisely regardful of the embroiling sky.

embroil (ɛm'brɔɪl), *v.*² Also 7 enbroile, embroyle, 6–7 imbroyle, 6–8 imbroil. [ad. F. *embrouiller* = Sp. *embrollar*, It. *imbrogliare*; cf. EN- and BROIL *sb.* and *v.*]

1. *trans.* To bring (affairs, etc.) into a state of confusion or disorder; to confuse, render unintelligible (a story).

1603 DANIEL *Defence of Rhime* (1717) 12 These pretended Proportions of Words..embroil our Understanding. **1609** —— *Civ. Wares* v. st. 47 One mans Cause shall all the rest imbroyle. **1656** COWLEY *Pindarique Odes* (1669) 16 *note* 2 The mention of his Brother Iphiclus..would but embroil the story. **1678** DRYDEN *All for Love*, Dedic. Your Enemies had so embroyl'd the management of your Office, that etc. **1704** ADDISON *Italy* (1733) 176 The former..are so embroil'd with Fable and Legend. **1823** SCOTT *Peveril* xxxviii, Having embroiled everything in which you are concerned.

2. To throw into uproar or tumult.

1618 BOLTON *Florus* (1636) 67 The tyranny of the Decemvirs embroyled the City the second time. **1667** MILTON *P.L.* II. 966 Tumult and Confusion all imbroild. **1704** HEARNE *Duct. Hist.* (1714) I. 56 The many Wars wherewith his [David's] Reign was embroiled. **1725** POPE *Odyss.* XII. 242 Tumultuous waves embroil'd the bellowing flood. **1726** THOMSON *Winter* 1019 More to embroil the deep.

3. To involve or entangle in dissension or hostility *with* (any one); to bring into a state of discord or disunion.

1610 G. FLETCHER *Christ's Vict.* (1632) 17 Or had his body been imbroyl'd alone In fierce assault. **1631** GOUGE *God's Arrows* iii. §89. 350 They..with delight enbroile themselves therein [warre]. **1653** HOLCROFT *Procopius* 7 The Emperour ..intending to imbroyle Theodatus and the Goths. **1654** GAYTON *Pleas. Notes* 188 Warres have been wag'd, and Nations embroyl'd in blood one against another. **1680** in Somers *Tracts* II. 84 [They] embroiled him with the House of Commons. **1741** RICHARDSON *Pamela* I. 175 What, and imbroil myself with a Man of Mr. B's Power and Fortune! **1756** J. WARTON *Ess. Pope* (1782) I. 312 To be embroiled in controversy. **1865** DICKENS *Lett.* (1880) II. 240 If the Americans don't embroil us in a war.

embroiled (ɛm'brɔɪld), *ppl. a.* [f. EMBROIL *v.*² + -ED¹.] Confused, disturbed, agitated.

1709 J. REYNOLDS *Death's Vis.* vii, Fate Hangs on the Turns of this Embroyled State! **1871** E. BURR *Ad Fidem* xii. 239 Embroiled Nature sunk into complete hush. **1872** GEO. ELIOT *Middlem.* xxx, Moving with kindred natures in the same embroiled medium.

embroiler (ɛm'brɔɪlə(r)). [f. EMBROIL *v.*² + -ER.] One who or that which embroils.

1668 R. L'ESTRANGE *Vis. Quev.* (1708) 8 The Embroylers of Affairs. **1751** J. BROWN *Shaftesb. Charac.* 70 [Ridicule].. is..no less justly regarded..as an embroiler.

em'broiling, *vbl. sb.* [f. EMBROIL *v.*² + -ING¹.] The action of the vb. EMBROIL.

1644 *Jus Populi* 24 They propose..the people's imbroyling.

embroilment (ɛm'brɔɪlmənt) Also 7 im-. [f. EMBROIL *v.*² + -MENT; cf. Fr. *embrouillement*.]

1. The action or process of embroiling.

1622–62 HEYLIN *Cosmogr.* I. (1682) 136 To the great embroilment of the State. **1837** CARLYLE *Fr. Rev.* I. III. vii, Now..does come discussion..but only for new embroilment.

2. An uproar, tumult.

1609 DANIEL *Civ. Wares* VII. 110 [The Muse]..weary with these embroylements, faine would stay Her farther course. **1646** SIR J. TEMPLE *Irish Rebell.* Pref. 3 The true causes of the imbroilments in that Kingdome. *a* **1714** BURNET *Own Time* (1766) II. 32 He was not apprehensive of a new embroilment. **1819** SCOTT *Leg. Montrose* iii, A cavalier of honour is free to take any part in this civil embroilment.

b. A state of variance or hostility; a quarrel.

1667 G. DIGBY *Elvira* v. in Hazl. *Dodsley* XV. 90 Drawing those advantages From the embroilment. *a* **1711** KEN *Hymnarium* Wks. 1721 II. 37 Embroilments ne'er would cease, Shou'd Rivals share the Realm of Peace. **1845** DISRAELI *Sybil* 314 The lively temperament of the Dandy would here probably have involved him in an inconvenient embroilment. **1872** YEATS *Growth Comm.* 216 A bitter embroilment with England followed this merciless act.

3. *transf.* and *fig.* A perplexed or confused state or condition; confused mixture.

1856 FERRIER *Inst. Metaph.* Introd. §62 The whole embroilment of philosophy is due to the practice, etc. **1859** GULLICK & TIMBS *Painting* 257 The careless embroilment of transparent and opaque tints. **1878** DOWDEN *Stud. Lit.* 238 A tangle and embroilment of evil and good.

4. Complication, entanglement (in a story, etc.).

1884 *Sat. Rev.* 14 June 787 Such details and embroilments as the story contains form the only excuse for its length.

embronze: see EM- *prefix*.

embrothelled: modernized spelling of IMBROTHELED, *Obs.*

embrother, obs. form of EMBROIDER.

†em'browd, em'brawd, *v. Obs.* Also 4–5 em-, enbroude(n, -brode(n, -brawde(n. [f. EN- + BROWD *v.*; cf. OF. *embrodé* pple.; the str. pa. pple. *embrawden*, *embroudin* belongs formally to EMBRAID *v.*², but in sense to this word.] *trans.* To embroider.

c **1340** *Gaw. & Gr. Knt.* 909 A lyȝtli vrysoun.. Enbrawden & bounden wyth þe best gemmez. *c* **1380** *Sir Ferumb.* 553 A cote-armure..embrouded with perlis schene. *c* **1385** CHAUCER *L.G.W.* Prol. 119 That was with floures swote embrouded [*v.r.* enbroudit, enbraudyd, enbrouded, enbrowdid, enbrawdid]. *c* **1423** JAS. I *Kingis Quair* clii, A lusty plane..Enbroudin all with fresche flouris gay. *c* **1440** *Partonope* 1927 A cote..Enbrowded wyth peerle. **1555** *Fardle Facions* I. iv. 46 Pauilions..embrauded with silkes.

embrown (ɛm'braʊn), *v.* Also 7 imbroun. 7–9 imbrown. [f. EN- + BROWN *a.*; cf. Fr. *embrunir*, It. *imbrunire*, which are used in sense 1.]

1. *trans.* To darken, make dusky. Chiefly *poet.*

1667 MILTON *P.L.* IV. 246 The unpierc't shade Imbround the noontide Bowrs. **1742** YOUNG *Nt. Th.* v. 74 Thy dark pencil, midnight..embrowns the whole. **1750** G. HUGHES *Barbados* 23 Deep chasms..are imbrowned with the thick foliage of lofty trees. **1813** SCOTT *Rokeby* III. ix, No deeper clouds the grove embrown'd. **1814** CARY *Dante's Inferno* II. 2 The air, Imbrown'd with shadows.

fig. **1738** WARBURTON *Div. Legat.* I. 430 Greek Philosophy, imbrowned with the Fanaticism of Eastern Cant.

2. To make brown. Also (rarely) *intr.* for *refl.*

1725 POPE *Odyss.* XIV. 93 The ready meal before Ulysses lay'd, With flour imbrown'd. **1757** DYER *Fleece* I. 394 Departing Autumn all embrowns The frequent-bitten fields. **1796** D'ISRAELI *Lit. Recreation* 211 A painting, which is just embrowned and mellowed by the hand of time. **1835** LYTTON *Rienzi* II. i, The suns of Italy had but little embrowned his clear and healthful complexion. **1867** LONGF. *Dante's Purg.* IV. v. 21 What time the grape imbrowns.

fig. a **1824** D'ISRAELI *Cur. Lit.* (1858) III. 499 His own uncourtly style is embrowned with the tint of a century old.

embrowned (ɛm'braʊnd), *ppl. a.* Also imbrowned. [f. prec. + -ED.¹] That has been made brown, *esp.* by the sun.

1726 THOMSON *Winter* 1816 Sables of glossy black, and dark embrowned. **1739** *Grobianus* 121 With skin imbrown'd, and fat, and full of Juice. **1828** SCOTT *F.M. Perth* xxxiv, The Smith's hardy and embrowned countenance. **1875** HELPS *Ess.*, *Convers. Railw. C.* 195 Looking over the imbrowned plain.

embrowning (ɛm'braʊnɪŋ), *ppl. a.* In 9 imbrowning. [f. EMBROWN *v.* + -ING².] That embrowns. In quot. *fig.*

1863 GEO. ELIOT *Romola* I. i, Under the same imbrowning and heating circumstances.

embrownment (ɛm'braʊnmənt). *nonce-wd.* [f. as prec. + -MENT.] Brown colouring.

1839–48 BAILEY *Festus* (ed. 3) 12/2 Go, locks, which have The golden embrownment of a lion's eye.

†em'broyn, *v. Obs. rare*⁻¹. [cf. Picard *embrugner* to cover (Littré s.v. *Embroncher*).] *trans.* To make dirty, befoul.

1574 NEWTON *Health Mag.* 34 And never are embroyned with anye filth or diertie slimishnes.

embrue, variant of IMBRUE.

embruise: see EM- *prefix*.

embrutalize (ɛm,bruːtəlaɪz), *v. nonce-wd.* [f. EN- + BRUTALIZE *v.*] *trans.* To render brutal.

1876 W. CLARK RUSSELL *Is he the Man* II. 190 Her temper may have been embrutalized by her husband's ruffianly treatment.

embrute, variant of IMBRUTE.

†em'brutish, *v. Obs. rare.* [f. EN- + BRUTE + *-ish*, after *impoverish*, etc.; cf. Fr. *abrutiss-*, *abrutir*.] *trans.* = IMBRUTE.

1639 W. SCLATER (2nd) *Wor. Comm. Rew.* 6 A person that is embrutished, and sunke below his species in vile affections.

†em'bryge, *v. Obs. rare.* Also 4 enbryge, 5 enbryke. [f. EN- + *bryge*, BRIGUE; cf. Fr. *embriguer*, It. *imbrigare*.] *trans.* To entrap, entangle.

1387 TREVISA *Higden* (Rolls) VII. 431 þe kyng maked.. enbryge [**1485** CAXTON embryge] hem and snarle hem wiþ sotil sophyms. **1413** LYDG. *Pylg. Sowle* IV. xxxiii. (1483) 81 They have for to sene that..he have no nede to [? be] enbryked by dette to ony of his subgettis.

embryo ('ɛmbrɪəʊ), *sb.* and *a.* Also 6–7 embrio. [med.L. corruption of EMBRYON; the transliterated Gr. word was ignorantly regarded as of the third declension (genit. *-ōnis*), and the nom. case was assimilated to the normal Latin type. Cf. Ger. *embryo*, It. *embrione*.]

A. *sb.*

1. The offspring of an animal before its birth (or its emergence from the egg):

a. of man. In mod. technical language restricted to 'the fœtus in utero before the fourth month of pregnancy' (*Syd. Soc. Lex.*) (now, before the third month).

[*c* **1350** GLANVIL *De Propr. Rer.* VI. iii, Hec materia est pellicula embryonis.] **1590** SWINBURN *Treat. Test.* 284 An vnperfect creature, or confused embrio. *c* **1645** HOWELL *Lett.* I. III. xxix, The ripening of the Embryo in the womb. **1777** *Phil. Trans.* LXVII. 23, I found this liquor absorbed into the embrio. **1841** EMERSON *Meth. Nature* Wks. (Bohn) II. 225 The embryo does not more strive to be a man, than ..a nebula tends to be a ring.

fig. **1874** SAYCE *Compar. Philol.* vii. 293 Lay undeveloped within the embryo of a single monosyllable.

b. of animals.

1638 CHILLINGW. *Relig. Prot.* I. ii. §101. 91 Some yet are Embrio's, yet hatching, and in the shell. **1866** TATE *Brit. Mollusks* ii. 18 The embryos have a triangular shell. **1870** EMERSON *Soc. & Solit.*, *Courage* Wks. (Bohn) III. 105 The little embryo [of the snapping-turtle]..bites fiercely.

transf. **1874** CARPENTER *Ment. Phys.* I. ii. §59 (1879) The larva..may be regarded as a mere active embryo.

2. *Bot.* 'The rudimentary plant contained in the seed' (*Syd. Soc. Lex.*).

1728 THOMSON *Spring* 99 The promised fruit Lies yet a little Embryo..Within its crimson folds. **1842** GRAY *Struct. Bot.* ii. (1880) 9 The Embryo is the initial plant, originated in the seed.

†3. *Chem.* A metal or other chemical substance not disengaged from its native state of combination. Also *attrib. Obs.*

1652 FRENCH *Yorksh. Spa* vi. 55 Metals and Minerals..in their..Embrioes. **1751** CHAMBERS *Cycl.* s.v. *Embryonatum Sulphur*, Sulphur united to metals..in an embryo state.

4. *fig.* A thing in its rudimentary stage or first beginning; a germ; that which is still in idea as opposed to what has become actual in fact.

1601 SIR J. OGLE in Sir F. Vere *Comm.* 146 The project itself was but an Embryo. *a* **1628** F. GREVILLE *Sidney* (1652) 20 He bequeathed no other legacie but the fire, to this unpolished Embrio. *a* **1714** BURNET *Own Time* (1766) II. 218 Embrio's of things, that were never like to have any effect. **1863** KINGLAKE *Crimea* VI. iii. 37 There not being in all Great Britain any embryo of a Commissariat force. **1872** MORLEY *Voltaire* (1886) 10 Pale unshapen embryos of social sympathy.

b. *in embryo*: in an undeveloped stage; 'that is to be'. [? orig. Lat., from EMBRYON.]

1636–7 N. HOBART in *Verney Papers* (1853) 188 There is a great preparation in embrio. **1685** tr. *Gracian's Courtier's Orac.* 215 Let every skilfull Master..have a care not to let his works be seen in embrio. **1742** SHENSTONE *Schoolmistr.* 24 There a chancellor in embryo. **1792** *Anecd. W. Pitt* III. xlii. 144 The indecent attempt to stifle this measure in embrio. **1824** MISS MITFORD *Village* Ser. II. (1863) 395 The honourable Frederic G...was a diplomatist in embryo. **1868** GLADSTONE *Juv. Mundi* i. (1870) 9 The Greek nation, as yet in embryo.

5. *attrib.* and *Comb.*, as ***embryo-chick***, ***-child***, ***-germ***, ***-life***, ***-plant***, ***-stage***, ***-state***; also **embryo-bud**, 'an adventitious bud, when enclosed in the bark, as in the cedar of Lebanon' (*Syd. Soc. Lex.*); **embryo-cell**, the first cell of the fecundated animal ovum; also in *Bot.* the germ in the embryo-sac of ferns, mosses, etc.; **embryo-sac**, *Bot.*, a cavity in the ovule or the archegonium of a plant, within which the embryo is produced.

1835 LINDLEY *Introd. Bot.* (1848) I. 177 *Embryo-buds, certain nodules..in the bark of the Beech. **1859** TODD *Cycl. Anat.* V. 4/1 The *Embryo-cell. **1865** LIVINGSTONE *Zambesi* xv. 308 An egg is eaten here though an *embryo-chick be inside. **1882** *Med. Temp. Jrnl.* I. 184 The *embryo-child is fed upon these intoxicants, before he is fairly in the world. **1859** TODD *Cycl. Anat.* V. 134/2 The primitive.. yolk-substance is employed in the formation of..*embryo-germ. **1879** tr. *Haeckel's Evol. Man* I. i. 12 *Embryo-life within the egg-membranes. **1878** HUXLEY *Physiogr.* 220 Subject to chemical analysis, the *embryo-plant yields certain complex bodies. **1872** OLIVER *Elem. Bot.* I. iii. 24 This enlarged cell is called the *embryo-sac.

B. *adj.* [From the attrib. use of the sb.] That is still in germ; immature, unformed, undeveloped.

1684 T. BURNET *The. Earth* II. 135 In that dark womb usually are the seeds and rudiments of an embryo-world. **1742** YOUNG *Nt. Th.* v. 99 Thou..in whose breast Embryo-creation..dwelt. **1798** *Loves of Triangles* 96 in *Anti-Jacobin* 23 Apr. (1852) 110 Flame embryo lavas, young volcanoes glow. **1821** CRAIG *Lect. Drawing* iii. 146 The embryo connoisseur. **1826** DISRAELI *Viv. Grey* I. iii, Scribbling embryo prize-poems. **1853** C. BRONTË *Villette* xxvii. The

collegians he addressed..as embryo patriots. **1876** M. ARNOLD *Lit. & Dogma* 31 Philosophers dispute whether moral ideas..were not once inchoate, embryo.

embryo ('ɛmbrɪəʊ), *v. nonce-wd.* [f. prec. sb.] *trans.* To represent in embryo.
1837 *Blackw. Mag.* XLII. 539 The fine reasonings they contain were..embryoed..in symbols.

embryo-, combining form of Gr. ἔμβρυον EMBRYON, as in ˌ**embryo'cardia**, a condition of the heart in which its sounds resemble those of the fœtal heart (now *rare*); ˌ**embryo'plastic** *a.*, pertaining to or participating in the formation of the embryo (*Cent. Dict.* 1889); '**embryoscope**, an instrument for examining embryos; so ˌ**embryo'scopic** *a.* (*Cent. Dict.* 1889); **embryo'toxic** *a.*, poisonous to an embryo; hence ˌ**embryoto'xicity**.
1890 GOULD *New Med. Dict.* 142/2 *Embryocardia*,..an affection of the heart, characterized by a heart-beat like that of a foetus. **1908** OSLER & MCCRAE *Syst. Med.* IV. 275 Tachycardia with embryocardia exhibits phenomena which correspond to a prolonged series of extrasystole. **1959** J. R. CHRISTIAN in A. A. Luisada *Cardiology* II. III. 147 The rapid rate and equal intensity of the sounds in the new-born produce a tic-tac type of rhythm or embryocardia, similar to that heard in the fetus. **1889** GEDDES & THOMSON *Evol. Sex* viii. 103 The minute area of formative protoplasm [that] the observers of to-day look down upon through their embryoscopes. **1968** *Nature* 22 June 1164/2 *(heading)* Embryotoxic effect of l-asparaginase. **1972** *Ibid.* 4 Feb. 279/1 Aflatoxin B_1..is embryotoxic to rats and mice, and acutely toxic to guinea-pigs. **1977** *Lancet* 14 May 1049/2 The embryotoxic action attributed to dioxin is impressive: in the Hue district the stillborn index (1969–70) was 48.5%, and congenital malformations have been observed in 7.4% of children born in the same period. **1971** *Nature* 25 June 483/3 Dioxin..when fed to pregnant rats causes embryotoxicity at doses of 0.000125 mg/kg. **1985** *Biochem. Pharmacol.* XXXIV. 529 The embryotoxicity of two ethanol metabolites..have [*sic*] been examined in cultured 10-day Albino Wistar rat embryos.

embryoctony (ɛmbrɪ'ɒktənɪ). [as if ad. Gr. *ἐμβρυοκτονία, f. ἐμβρυοκτόνος that kills the fœtus.] 'The destruction of the fœtus in the womb' (*Syd. Soc. Lex.*).

embryoferous (ɛmbrɪ'ɒfərəs), *a. Biol.* [f. EMBRYO *sb.* + -FEROUS.] That bears or contains an embryo.
1859 TODD *Cycl. Anat.* V. 587/2 The embryoferous tumour.

embryogenesis (ˌɛmbrɪəʊ'dʒɛnɪsɪs). *Biol.* [mod. f. EMBRYO-N + Gr. γένεσις birth, production.] 'The origin and formation of the embryo; and the science therof' (*Syd. Soc. Lex.*).
1830 R. KNOX *Béclard's Anat.* 333 The laws of.. embryogenesis. **1879** *De Quatrefages' Human Species* 109 Haeckel goes back to embryogenesis.

embryogenetic (ˌɛmbrɪəʊdʒɪ'nɛtɪk), *a. Biol.* [mod. f. EMBRYO-N + Gr. *γενετικός producing, f. root of γένεσις: see prec.] = next.
1880 HUXLEY *Times* 25 Dec. 4/1 Their adult and embryogenetic characters.

embryogenic (ˌɛmbrɪəʊ'dʒɛnɪk), *a. Biol.* [f. EMBRYO-N + Gr. γεν- (cf. EMBRYOGENESIS) + -IC.] Of or pertaining to embryogenesis.
1852 DANA *Crust.* I. 45 Regarded in their embryogenic relations. **1876** *Beneden's Anim. Parasites* 46 He arrived..at the same result..by his embryogenic observations.

embryogeny (ɛmbrɪ'ɒdʒənɪ). *Biol.* [f. as prec. + -Y]. = EMBRYOGENESIS.
1835 LINDLEY *Introd. Bot.* (1848) II. 229 The theory of vegetable embryogeny. **1864** BALFOUR in *Edin. Med. Jrnl.* June, This is specially true of the functions of fertilization and embryogeny.

embryogony (ɛmbrɪ'ɒgənɪ). *Biol.* [f. EMBRYO-N + Gr. -γονία production.] The formation of an embryo.
In mod. Dicts.

embryography (ɛmbrɪ'ɒgrəfɪ). [f. EMBRYO-N + Gr. -γραφία writing, description.] 'The description of the fœtus or embryo' (*Syd. Soc. Lex.*).

embryoid ('ɛmbrɪɔɪd), *a.* and *sb.* [f. EMBRYO + -OID.] **A.** *adj. Med.* Resembling an embryo; *rare*$^{-0}$ except in ***embryoid body***, an aggregate of cells that develops when certain mouse tumours are injected into the peritoneal cavity of a mouse or grown in culture, somewhat similar to an early embryo in its structure and its potential for differentiation.
1934 WEBSTER, Embryoid. **1958** *Jrnl. Nat. Cancer Inst.* XX. 1263 These embryoid bodies have not been observed in primary strain 129 [mouse] teratomas. **1964** *Cancer Res.* XXIV. 1544 Small embryoid bodies..were obtained from ascitic conversion of a murine terato-carcinoma. **1975** *Nature* 6 Nov. 12/2 The ascites form of the tumour consists of numerous small 'embryoid bodies' floating in the ascites fluid; the simplest of these aggregates are made up of an outer layer of endoderm cells surrounding a core of embryonal carcinoma cells. **1977** C. F. GRAHAM in M. I. Sherman *Concepts in Mammalian Embryogenesis* vii. 332 The greatest range of differentiated tissue forms after both simple and cystic embryoid bodies are plated out on tissue culture dishes... During the next two weeks..many cell types can be observed..such as neural tissue..and glandular epithelium.
B. *sb. Bot.* An embryonic plant developed in a culture medium from a single cell.
1964 I. K. VASIL et al. in *Plant Physiol.* XXXIX. (Suppl.) p. lxiii/2 The tissue first formed a free suspension of cells and cell groups. Gradually many small round masses of tissue, designated here as embryoids, were formed by further cell division. The embryoids produced roots at one end and then typical..leafy structures at the other end giving rise to normal-looking plantlets. Originating from single cells various stages of embryoid formation were seen in the liquid medium. **1971** *New Scientist* 29 Apr. 263 *(caption)* These cells are then cultured, and from them are grown embryoids and eventually whole 'pomatoes'. **1980** *Nature* 27 Mar. 341/2 We report here a repeatable precocious flowering of embryoids derived from mature ginseng root callus cultured in a chemically defined medium. **1983** *New Scientist* 26 May 555/3 We have been altering the concentrations of growth regulator to try to stimulate the callus to form so-called somatic embryos or embryoids. These embryoids are analogous to the normal embryos in the seed but contain only genetic material from the single parent—that is, they are clonal.

embryoism ('ɛmbrɪəʊˌɪz(ə)m). [f. EMBRYO + -ISM.] The state of being an embryo.
1854 H. MILLER *Footpr. Creat.* xii. (1874) 226 They may exist in their state of embryoism.

embryologic (ˌɛmbrɪəʊ'lɒdʒɪk), *a.* [f. EMBRYOLOGY + -IC.] Of or pertaining to embryology.
1882 ROMANES in *Homiletic Monthly* Mar. 366 Arguments from..embryologic progression.

embryological, *a.* [f. as prec. + -AL[1].] = prec.
1859 LEWES *Sea-side Stud.* 312 The results of embryological research. **1859** TODD *Cycl. Anat.* V. 1/2 Of embryological anatomy. **1871** DARWIN *Desc. Man* II. xvi. 183 Embryological structures.
Hence **embryo'logically** *adv.*, with reference to embryology.
1852 DANA *Crust.* I. 56 This form being of a lower grade embryologically. **1867** KINGSLEY *Life & Lett.* II. 246 With what other birds are they embryologically connected.

embryologist (ɛmbrɪ'ɒlədʒɪst). *Biol.* [f. EMBRYOLOGY + -IST.] One who is concerned with or versed in the science of EMBRYOLOGY.
1849–52 TODD *Cycl. Anat.* IV. 836/1 Embryologists.. find another method. **1879** tr. *Semper's Anim. Life* 31 Forms known to embryologists as the germinal layers.

embryology (ɛmbrɪ'ɒlədʒɪ). *Biol.* [f. EMBRYO-N + -LOGY.] The science relating to the embryo and its development. Also *transf.*
1859 DARWIN *Orig. Spec.* vii. (1873) 203 Against the belief in such abrupt changes, embryology enters a strong protest. **1872** MORLEY *Voltaire* (1886) 20 An undiscovered set of facts in embryology.

embryoma (ɛmbrɪ'əʊmə). *Path.* Pl. **-mata**. [f. EMBRYO + -OMA.] A tumour composed of tissues resembling those of the fœtus or thought to arise from fœtal tissues or fœtal remnants: applied esp. to some malignant tumours seen in childhood.
1903 J. H. TEACHER in *Jrnl. Obstet. & Gynæcol.* July 54 Either at once (congenital tumours) or after an interval (mixed tumours of later life) this develops into an imperfect organism—a teratoma or embryoma. **1954** L. B. AREY *Developmental Anat.* (ed. 6) x. 180 An immature type [of teratoma] with poorly differentiated tissue (embryoma) is highly proliferative and usually malignant. **1968** B. M. PATTEN *Human Embryol.* (ed. 3) viii. 167 To be classed as an embryoma a tumor must exhibit enough of the fundamental parts characteristically present in a normal embryo to suggest that it arose from an aggregation of cells which under other conditions might have produced a complete individual.

embryon ('ɛmbrɪɒn), *sb.* (*a.*) Also 5–8 **embrion**. Pl. **embrya, embryons**. [mod.L., a. Gr. ἔμβρυον, in Homer merely 'young animal', but in later writers 'the fruit of the womb before birth'. Usually believed to be f. ἐν in + βρύ-ειν to swell, grow.] The original form of EMBRYO; now rare even in techn. use; in ordinary language obs.
1. = EMBRYO 1. †**a.** of man. *Obs.*
[**1477** NORTON *Ord. Alch.* v. in Ashm. (1652) 90 Passing the Substance of Embrion.] **1592** H. CHETTLE in Greene *Groatsw. Wit* Pref., Like an Embrion without shape. **1653** A. WILSON *Jas. I.* 77 This was but an Embrion, and became an Abortive. **1721** SOUTHERNE *Loyal Brother* III. Wks. I. 44 Rip this womb That form'd him yet an embrion. **1804** ABERNETHY *Surg. Observ.* 11 The embryon..receives nourishment from the surrounding parts.
b. of animals.
1658 ROWLAND tr. *Moufet's Theat. Ins.* 922 Certain imperfect things like Embryons or little worms. **1672** *Phil. Trans.* VII. 4020 The Sceleton of an Embryon..in an Egg. **1713** WARDER *True Amazons* 19 Which otherwise would incommode the Embrion [of bees]. **1722** WOLLASTON *Relig. Nat.* v. 90 The animalcula and embrya. **1880** GÜNTHER *Fishes* 318 Cantor found in a female, nearly 11 feet long, 37 embryons.
2. *Bot.* = EMBRYO 2. In quot. *fig.*
1816 COLERIDGE *Statesm. Man.* (1817) 355 Looking forward to the green fruits and embryons..of the days to come.
†**3.** *fig.* = EMBRYO 4. ***in (the) embryon***: = in embryo. *Obs.*
1596 DRAYTON *Leg.* iv. 167 To perfect that which in the Embryon was. **1607** BARKSTED *Mirrha* (1876) 37 To bring vices Embrion to a forme. **1639** G. DANIEL *Ecclus.* xxiv. 27, I was, ere yet the world in Embrion lay. **1640** J. LEY *Patt. Pietie* 157 Shee had certaine fits or traunces like the embrions of death. **1676** *Phil. Trans.* XI. 614 The first Beings or Embrions of mineral salts are nothing but vapours. **1788** T. JEFFERSON *Writ.* (1859) II. 431 It is yet, indeed, a mere embryon. **1812** SHELLEY *Let.* in Dowden *Shelley* (1886) I. 230, I perceive in you the embryon of a mighty intellect.
†**4.** *attrib.* or *adj.* Immature, unformed, undeveloped; that is still in germ. *Obs.*
1616 W. BROWNE *Brit. Past.* I. iv, The Embrion Blossome of each spray. **1667** MILTON *P.L.* II. 900 Four Champions fierce..to Battel bring thir embryon Atoms. **1728** VANBRUGH & CIBBER *Provoked Husb.* Prol. 26 If..his Art can to those Embrion Scenes new Life impart. **1813** SIR. H. DAVY *Agric. Chem.* (1814) 140 Nourishment..for the use of the Embryon plant. **1835** GRESWELL *Parables* v. ii. 411 All nature's embryon store.

embryonal ('ɛmbrɪənəl), *a.* [f. med.L. *embryōn-em* + -AL[1].] Of or pertaining to an embryo.
1652 FRENCH *Yorksh. Spa* vi. 55 The embrional conservation of the Nut. **1861** HULME tr. *Moquin-Tandon* II. VII. xiii. 395 The Acephalocysts..are without head..even in the embryonal condition. **1882** VINES *Sachs' Bot.* 529 The so-called 'embryonal tubes'.

embryonary ('ɛmbrɪəˌnərɪ), *a.* [f. as prec. + -ARY.] Relating to an embryo. Also *fig.*
1835 LINDLEY *Introd. Bot.* (1848) I. 404 The embryonary sac. **1860** FARRAR *Orig. Lang.* x. 214 Languages in an ante-historical and embryonary state.

embryonate ('ɛmbrɪəneɪt), *a.* [f. as prec. + -ATE[2].]
†**1.** = EMBRYONATED. *Obs.*
1669 W. SIMMONS *Hydrol. Chym.* 56 Maturated into metals, by the embryonate sulphurs. **1675** EVELYN *Terra* (1776) 45 Salts embryonate or undigested and not specificate.
†**2.** = EMBRYONAL. *Obs.*
1693 J. BEAUMONT *On Burnet's The. Earth* I. 52 Fishes.. in an embrionate imperfect state. **1731** in BAILEY, vol. II.
3. 'Having an embryo or germ' (*Syd. Soc. Lex.*).
Hence in *Bot.* **embryonate plants**, plants which possess seeds.

†'**embryonate**, *v. Obs.* [f. as prec. + -ATE[3].] *trans.* **a.** To give embryonic existence to; in quot. *fig.* **b.** To load or fill as with an embryo or germ; to impregnate.
1671 GLANVILL *Disc. M. Stubbe* 15 The Royal Society [was] as it were embryonated there. **1687** *Ess. Tunbridge Waters* in *Harl. Misc.* I. 587 Divers seminary principles with which they [chalybeate waters] are embryonated.

†'**embryonated**, *ppl. a. Obs.* [f. prec. + -ED[1].] Of chemical and mineral bodies: Found in combination with or embedded (like embryos) in other bodies.
1652 FRENCH *Yorksh. Spa* vi. 54 The embrionated Sulphur of Copper. **1662** J. CHANDLER *Van Helmont's Oriat.* 67 Embryonated or imperfect shaped Sulphur. **1667** BOYLE *Orig. Formes & Qual.*, Unripe..Embrionated Minerals. **1676** *Phil. Trans.* XI. 615 This embrionated salt in limestones is a stony juice.

†'**embryonately**, *adv. Obs. rare*$^{-1}$. [f. EMBRYONATE *a.* + -LY[2].] In an embryonate manner; as an embryo.
1665 G. HARVEY *Advice agst. Plague* 6 That those Pestilential fumes be first embryonately or preparatively formed in a close thick or standing air.

†'**embryoˌnative**, *a. Obs. rare*$^{-1}$. [f. as EMBRYONATE *v.* + -IVE.] = EMBRYONATED.
1669 W. SIMPSON *Hydrol. Chym.* 144 It had lost all its embryonative sulphur.

embryonic (ɛmbrɪ'ɒnɪk), *a.* [f. med.L. *embryōn-em* + -IC.]
1. Pertaining to, or having the character of, an embryo.
1849 MURCHISON *Siberia* xx. 483 The first or embryonic idea of the archetype. **1859** DARWIN *Orig. Spec.* xiv. (1873) 396 Community in embryonic structure reveals community of descent. **1863** BERKELEY *Brit. Mosses* iii. 21 The embryonic cell. **1878** HUXLEY *Physiogr.* 220 Within the.. pea, there is inclosed a perfect, though embryonic plant.
2. *fig.* Immature, undeveloped.
1856 EMERSON *Eng. Traits, Manners* Wks. (Bohn) II. 49 Every Englishman is an embryonic chancellor. **1874** SAYCE *Compar. Philol.* i. 46 The parts of speech lay undeveloped in a kind of embryonic common sound.

embryonically (ɛmbrɪ'ɒnɪkəlɪ), *adv.* [f. EMBRYONIC *a.*: see -ICALLY.] In (the) embryo.
1883 FOSTER & BALFOUR *Elem. Embryol.* (ed. 2) viii. 255 The atrophy of the dorsal section of the embryonically large canal of the spinal cord. **1899** E. GRIFFITH-JONES *Ascent through Christ* III. ii. 377 In prophecy He was as it were embryonically incarnated.

embryoniferous (ɛmbrɪə'nɪfərəs), *a. Bot.* [f. EMBRYO + -(I)FEROUS.] Producing or bearing an embryo.

1819 J. LINDLEY tr. *Richard's Observ. Fruits & Seeds* 29 An examination of the embryoniferous cavity. **1834** R. BROWN *Misc. Bot. Wks.* (1866) I. 570 The remains of the embryoniferous areolæ, from four to six in number, were still visible.

embryotic (ɛmbrɪ'ɒtɪk), *a.* [f. EMBRYO, after *exotic, patriotic*, etc.: cf. *chaotic*.]

1. = EMBRYONIC 1.

1835-6 TODD *Cycl. Anat.* I. 786/1 The term of their embryotic development. **1854** H. MILLER *Sch. & Schm.* iv. (1866) 31 The crab..is less embryotic..than the more ancient lobster.

2. *fig.* = EMBRYONIC 2.

1761 STERNE *Tr. Shandy* (1802) IV. xix. 90 The book of embryotic evils. **1785** BURNS *Vision* II. xi, To mark the embryotic trace Of rustic Bard. **1864** KINGSLEY *Rom. & Teut.* 40 Intellect and virtue remain..embryotic.

embryotomy (ɛmbrɪ'ɒtəmɪ). *Surg.* [ad. Gr. ἐμβρυοτομία, f. ἔμβρυο-ν EMBRYON + -τομία cutting.] 'The cutting up of the *fœtus in utero* into pieces in order to effect its removal' (*Syd. Soc. Lex.*).

1721-1800 in BAILEY. **1876** GROSS *Dis. Bladder* 57 A 6 months' fœtus had to be removed by embryotomy.

†'**embryous**, *a. Obs. rare.* [f. EMBRY-ON *sb.* + -OUS.] Of or pertaining to an embryo; in germ; undeveloped. In quot. *fig.*

1677 FELTHAM *Resolves* I. xiv. (ed. 10) 23 Without the last [action], the first [contemplation] is but abortive and embryous. **1656** BLOUNT *Glossogr.*, *Embryous*, pertaining to an embryon. **1692** in COLES. **1847** in CRAIG; and in mod. Dicts.

embubble: see EM- *prefix*.

†**em'bud**, *v. Obs.* Also 6 enbud, 7 imbud. [f. EN- + BUD *sb.*¹]

1. *trans.* To cover as with buds.

1526 SKELTON *Magnyf.* 1572 Enbudded with beautye.

2. *intr.* To bud, sprout. In quot. *fig.*

1603 DANIEL *Panegyrick* (1717) 327 The Op'ning of the Spring..make[s] our Spirits likewise..imbud.

Hence **em'budded** *ppl. a.*

1523 SKELTON *Garl. Laurel* 883 The enbudded blossoms of rose, rede of hewe.

embue, obs. variant of IMBUE.

†**em'buement**. *Obs. rare*⁻¹. [f. *embue*, var. of IMBUE *v.* + -MENT.] A tincture or infusion.

a **1693** URQUHART *Rabelais* III. xiii, With an embuement from its divine source.

embulk: see EM- *pref.*

†**em'bull**, *v. Obs.* Forms: 5 enbull, 6-7 imbull, 6- embull. [f. EN- + BULL *sb.*²; in AFr. *enbuller*.] *trans.* To insert or publish (a matter or a name) in a Papal bull; to issue a bull against; to affix an official (*esp.* the Papal) seal to (a document).

1480 CAXTON *Chron. Eng.* VII. (1520) 93/1 So he was by letter enbulled. **1563-87** FOXE *A. & M.* (1596) 274/1 He also wrote his letters..embulled with gold. **1589** WARNER *Alb. Eng.* V. xxvi. (1612) 130 The Pope imbulled..England.

emburse, obs. variant of IMBURSE.

embus (ɛm'bʌs), *v.* [f. EM- 1 a + BUS *sb.*², after *embark*.] **a.** *intr.* To mount a bus or transport vehicle. **b.** *trans.* To transport by bus.

1915 [see DEBUS *v.*]. **1927** *Daily Tel.* 13 Sept. 10/3 Using the mechanised transport thus released for embussing the headquarters. **1929** D. RORIE *Medico's Luck* vii. 141 On the 24th July we left Clairmarais for Lederzeele, and 'embussed'..for the XVIII Corps. **1940** *Spectator* 16 Aug. 161/2 Embussing happened in the last war; so did debussing... Archeologists embus when they go on their expeditions, at any rate in Wales. The term occurs in Field Service Regulations. **1955** *Daily Tel.* 20 Oct., Troops..had ..on arrival 'embussed' for an unknown destination.

†**embu'scado**. *Obs.* [var. of AMBUSCADO, in Sp. *embuscada*: see -ADO 2.] An ambuscade.

1686 tr. *Chardin's Trav.* 157 The king of Quiretta having laid considerable Embuscados.

embush, embusshe, etc., obs. ff. AMBUSH, etc.

embusk, *v.*¹: see EM- *prefix*.

†**em'busk**, *v.*² *Obs. rare.* [ad. Fr. *embusquer*, mod. form (orig. *north. dial.*) of OF. *embuscher* AMBUSH *v.*] *trans.* To place in ambush.

1596 *Scanderbeg* 368 Other bands..lay close embusked in the mountaines.

embuskin: see EM- *prefix*.

‖**embusqué** (ɑ̃byske). [subst. use of pa. pple. of F. *embusquer* to ambush.] One who avoids military service (as by securing a post in a government office or the Civil Service). Also *attrib.* and *transf.*

1916 J. BUCHAN *Greenmantle* i. 4 Not some *embusqué* business in an office, but a thing compared to which your fight at Loos was a Sunday-school picnic. **1920** *Blackw. Mag.* May 586/2 These particular *embusqués*, who made Egypt a byword during the War. **1925** R. GRAVES *Welchman's Hose* 51 Brave fellows, no *embusqués* in that class. **1926** *Spectator* 7 Aug. 207/2 The best scenes are those between the poor *embusqué* and his wife. **1932** 'A. BRIDGE' *Peking Picnic* v. 51 Perhaps the real use of the presence of Europeans in Peking was to afford shelter to *embusqués* Chinese. **1955** *Times* 21 May 9/4 A number of idle and ill-disposed *embusqués*, whose principal aim in life is to blight their husbands' military career.

†**em'busy**, *v. Obs.* Forms: α. 5-6 enbesy, 6 embesy, enbusy, -ie, 6-7 embusie, -y. β. 6-7 imbusy. [f. EN- + BUSY *a.*] *trans.* To render busy, occupy assiduously; to give care or anxiety to. Chiefly *refl.*

1484 CAXTON *Ryall Bk.* B v, To occupye and enbesy hym in thre thynges. **1526** *Pilgr. Perf.* (1531) 57 b, Enbusy not thy selfe. **1543** *Necess. Doct. Chr. Man* Introd. in Strype *Eccl. Mem.*, The heads and senses of our people have been imbusied..with the understanding of Free Will. **1603** FLORIO *Montaigne* III. ix. (1632) 535 Nor hawking, nor gardens..can much embusie..me. **1611** SPEED *Hist. Gt. Brit.* IX. ix. §28 The Earle of Pembroke..wholly embusied in the enterprize of Britaine. *a* **1693** URQUHART *Rabelais* III. xiii. 104 Not imbusied with..Soul-disturbing Perturbations.

em'cee. Also (erron.) emsee. The names of the letters M and C, used to denote Master of Ceremonies, the introducer of a show or other form of entertainment. *slang* (orig. *U.S.*).

1933 B. J. CHIPMAN *'Hey, Rube'* 194/1 *Emsee*, Master of Ceremonies. **1938** *Sat. Even. Post* 2 Apr. 8/2 The emcee introduces the guest artists. **1940** *Variety* 24 July 34 Emcee announcer. **1955** L. FEATHER *Encycl. Jazz* vii. 227 He spent three years..in vaudeville as singer, dancer and emcee. **1964** *Listener* 27 Aug. 319/3 Emcee Steve Race knows his subject from the inside..and he gives *Jazz 625* an air of mature authority.

Hence **emcee** *v. trans.* and *intr.*

1937 *Hollywood Citizen* (Los Angeles) 14 Sept., Leon Errol..will emcee for the occasion. **1948** *Variety* 25 Aug. 2/1 George Jessel emceed that event.

emcristen, variant of EVEN-CHRISTIAN, *Obs.*

†**eme**. *Obs.* exc. *dial.* Forms: 1-3 éam, (2 eom), 2-5 em, (3 æem, æm, heam, he(e)m), 4-5 eem(e, 4-6 eme, *Sc.* eym(e, (5 emme, yem), 4-7 eam(e, 8 *dial.* eem, 9 *Sc.* eme, *north. dial.* eam. [Com. WGer.: OE. *éam* = OFris. *êm* (MDu. *oem*, Du. *oom*), OHG. *ôheim* (MHG. *ôheim, œheim, -hein*, mod.Ger. *oheim, ohm*); if the word existed in OTeut. the type would be **auhaimo-z*; presumed to be a compound or derivative of **awo-z* = L. *avus* grandfather (of which the L. *avunculus*, uncle, is a diminutive). It is believed that the original sense of the WGer. word was 'mother's brother' (cf. L. *avunculus*); but in later use it is applied to a father's brother as well.] An uncle; also *dial.* a friend, gossip.

Beowulf 881 He swulces hwæt secȝan wolde eam his nefan. *c* **1000** ÆLFRIC *Gen.* xxviii. 2 Nim þe wif of Labanes dohtrum þinis eames. **1154** *O.E. Chron.* an. 1137 He sculde ben alsuic alse þe eom wes. *c* **1205** LAY. 8142 Androgeus wes his hem. —— 8832 Nu is min eam wel bi-ðoht. —— 11174 Hire æem [*c* **1275** heam] Leonin wes in Rome. —— 111464 His fader wes Ælenen æm. *c* **1250** *Gen. & Ex.* 1758 Ðus meðelike spac ðis em. *c* **1330** *Arth. & Merl.* 4583 Gif min eme be king Arthour. *c* **1340** *Cursor M.* 3789 (Trin.) Laban þin eeme. **1375** BARBOUR *Bruce* x. 305 To help hys eyme. *c* **1425** WYNTOUN *Cron.* IX. xviii. 7 His Eym þan Erle of Fyfe. *c* **1465** *Eng. Chron.* 73, I am thyne eme, thy faderes brother. *c* **1565** LINDESAY (Pitscottie) *Chron. Scot.* (1728) 19 His eames, William, earl of Douglas and David his brother. **1612** DRAYTON *Poly-olb.* xxii, Henry Hotspur and his eame The Earl of Worcester. **1674** RAY *N. Country Wds.* 16 Mine Eam: My Unkle, also generally my Gossip, my Compere. **1724** RAMSAY *Tea-t. Misc.* (1733) II. 182 Rob my eem hecht me a stock. **1818** SCOTT *Hrt. Midl.* xii, 'Didna his eme die ..wi' the name of the Bluidy Mackenyie?' **1855** *Whitby Gloss.*, *Eam* or *Eeam*, 'mine eam', my uncle, friend, gossip.

eme, variant of YEME, *Obs.*, heed.

-eme (iːm), *suffix*, in *Linguistics* the termination of many names of significant or distinctive units of structure of some kind in the lexicon, grammar, and phonology of languages, e.g. *grapheme, lexeme, morpheme, phoneme, sememe, toneme.*

1953 W. J. ENTWISTLE *Aspects of Lang.* iii. 79 A by-product of Linguistic Analysis..has been the sudden burgeoning of the *-eme* family. **1962** H. A. GLEASON in Householder & Saporta *Probl. Lexicogr.* 98 Some kind of -emes;..no satisfactory term is at hand, though 'sememe' has been used.

†**e'meade**, *v. Obs. Her.* [? f. E- *pref.* + late L. *medi-āre* to divide in the middle, f. L. *medius* middle.] *trans.* To halve, divide in half.

1562 LEIGH *Armorie* 62 b, The chiefe may not bee emeaded, or halfed. **1586** FERNE *Blaz. Gentrie* 207 Entier (not emeaded) within the scutcheon.

emecristen, var. of EVEN-CHRISTIAN, *Obs.*

†**e'medull**, *v. Obs.*⁻⁰ [ad. late L. *ēmedullāre* to take out the marrow, f. *ē* out + *medulla* marrow.] *trans.* 'To declare, take out the marrow' (Cockeram 1623).

†**e'medullate**, *v. Obs.*⁻⁰ [f. L. *ēmedullāt-* ppl. stem of *ēmedullāre*: see prec.] *trans.* To take out the marrow or pith.

1731 in BAILEY. **1775** in ASH.

emeer(e, var. ff. EMIR, Saracen prince.

emel(l(e, var. forms of AMELL(E, *Obs.*

†**e'membrate**, *v. Obs.*⁻⁰ [f. L. *ēmembrāt-* ppl. stem of *ēmembrā-re* to cut the limbs off.] *trans.* To castrate, geld.

1731 in BAILEY. **1775** in ASH.

emend (ɪ'mɛnd), *v.* Also 5 **emende**. [ad. L. *ēmendā-re*, f. *ē* out + *menda* fault. (OFr. had *esmender, emender*.) Cf. AMEND.]

†**1.** *trans.* To free (a person) from faults, correct. Also *intr.* for *refl. Obs.*

14.. *MS. St. John's Coll. Oxon.* No. 117. 123 b in Maskell *Mon. Rit.* III. 355 Loue him [God] that he emendith the. *c* **1542** UDALL in *Orig. Lett. Eminent Men* (1843) 6 To hope that I maye ere now bee emended for the tyme to cum. —— *Ibid.* 7 As another besides me maye happen to dooe amys, so maye I as well as another emend.

2. To free (a thing) from faults, correct (what is faulty), rectify. *rare* in mod. use.

c **1485** *Digby Myst.* (1882) I. 23 An-other tyme to emende it if we can. **1659** FELTHAM *Low Countries* II. (R.) The.. force of the sun..hath a little emended them. **1867** DRAPER *Amer. Civ. War* I. xxvi. 447 Universal suffrage has emended the law of the landlord and tenant.

b. *esp.* To remove errors from (the text of a book or document); = EMENDATE *v.*

1768 SWINTON in *Phil. Trans.* LVIII. 258 That writer therefore seems to be emended..by my coin. **1832** SIR G. LEWIS in *Philol. Mus.* I. 282 Tyrwhitt..ingeniously emends some choliambics cited by Apollonius. **1836** LYTTON *Athens* (1837) I. 274 Pisistratus..did..collect, arrange, and emend poems. **1854** BADHAM *Halieut.* 524 Passing whole nights.. not in emending Greek, but, etc.

†**3.** To repair or make good (what is broken or damaged); = MEND. *Obs.*

1411 [see EMENDING.] **1480** *Wardr. Acc. Edw. IV* (1830) 121 A broken chayer emended with small gilt nailles.

e'mendable, *a.* [f. L. *ēmendābilis* that may be amended.] That is capable of being emended.

1731-1800 in BAILEY. **1847** in CRAIG; and in mod. Dicts.

†**e'mendals**, *sb. pl. Obs.* [? f. med.L. *ēmenda* (see EMENDS) + -AL¹.] ? Funds set apart for repairs. (See quot.)

1692 COLES, *Emendal*. **1708-15** in KERSEY. **1721-1800** in BAILEY. **1751** CHAMBERS *Cycl.*, *Emendals*, an old term still used in the accounts of the Inner Temple; where, so much in emendals at the foot of an account signifies so much in the bank, or stock of the house, for reparation of losses, and other occasions. In mod Dicts.

†**emendate**, *a. Obs.* [ad. L. *ēmendāt-us* pa. pple. of *ēmendā-re* to free from fault, correct, improve.] Emended, corrected, restored.

1654 HAMMOND *Answ. Animadv. Ignat.* vi. §1. 153 An emendate copie of these Epistles. **1677** CARY *Chron.* I. II. I. viii. 66 The Form of the Emendate Julian Year.

emendate ('iːmɛndeɪt), *v.* [f. L. *ēmendāt-* (see prec. and EMEND.)] *trans.* To remove errors and corruptions from (a text).

1876 J. H. NEWMAN *Hist. Sk.* II. v. v. 477 He.. emendated..the text of Scripture.

†**emendately**, *adv. Obs. rare.* [f. EMENDATE *a.* + -LY.] In an emendated manner.

1539 TAVERNER *Bible*, Dedic., The printers..were.. desirous to have the..bible com forth..as emendatly, etc.

emendation (iːmən'deɪʃən). [ad. L. *ēmendātiōn-em*, noun of action f. *ēmendāre* to EMEND. (In OF. *esmendacion*).] The action of emending.

†**1.** Correction, reformation, improvement (of life, conduct, etc.). *Obs.*

1536 BELLENDEN *Cron. Scot.* (1821) II. 166 The noblis of Scotland..seand na emendation of his life. **1660** R. COKE *Power & Subj.* 201 The emendation of the Church. *a* **1677** BARROW *Serm.* Wks. 1716 II. 110 Emendation..of nature is produced by his grace.

2. Improvement by alteration and correction; *esp.* of literary or artistic products, methods of procedure, scientific systems, etc.; a particular instance of such improvement.

1586 W. WEBBE *Eng. Poetrie* (Arb.) 95 The emendations of Poemes be very necessary. **1641** MILTON *Ch. Govt.* v. (1851) 116 All this..interpolisht by some second hand with crooks and emendations. **1665** WHARTON *Disc. Observ. Easter* Wks. (1683) 36 A better Emendation of the Calendar. **1736** BUTLER *Anal.* Introd. Wks. 1874 I. 7 What would be the amount of these emendations..upon the system of nature. **1783** MASON *Fresnoy's Art Paint.* Pref. (R.) I hardly left a single line in it without giving it..an emendation. **1830** CUNNINGHAM *Brit. Paint.* I. 156 His friends suggested emendations. **1854** H. ROGERS *Ess.* (1860) II. 52 Leibnitz' emendation of the saying..has passed into epigrammatic notoriety. **1872** O. W. HOLMES *Poet Breakf.-t.* vi. 193 A man's biography with..emendations by his ghost.

b. *esp.* The correction (usually by conjecture or inference) of the text of an author where it is presumed to have been corrupted in transmission; a textual alteration for this purpose.

1622–62 HEYLIN *Cosmogr.* (1674) Introd. 9/2 The emendation of Bochartus coming in to help. **1778** BP. LOWTH *Isaiah* Prelim. Dissert. (ed. 12) 45 Whether the conjectural rendering, or the conjectural emendation, be the more agreeable to the context. **1877** DOWDEN *Shaks. Prim.* iii. 30 The emendations being often more wrong than right.

†**emendative**, *a. Obs. rare*⁻¹. [as if ad. L. **ēmendātīv-us*: see EMENDATE *v.* and -IVE.] That tends to emend.

1642 AMES *Marrow of Div.* 352 Emendative Iustice is either commutative, or corrective.

emendator (ˈiːməndeɪtə(r)). [a. L. *ēmendātor* corrector.] One who emendates; a corrector.

1672 COSIN *Canon Script.* 123 (T.) The Roman emendators..know not how to trust it. **1837** EMERSON *Misc.* (1855) 77 The restorers of readings, the emendators.

emendatory (ɪˈmɛndətərɪ), *a.* [ad. L. *ēmendātōri-us* corrective: see EMENDATE *v.* and -ORY.] Of or pertaining to emending.

†**1.** In moral sense: Corrective, disciplinary.

1660 JER. TAYLOR *Duct. Dubit.* IV. i. iv. §10 Punishments emendatory.

2. Of or pertaining to EMENDATION 2 and 2 b.

1795 R. ANDERSON *Life of Dr. Johnson* 142 The sagacity of his emendatory criticisms. **1870** *Athenæum* 2 Apr. No. 2212. 457 Emendatory editions may be yet in store. **1885** *Spectator* 18 July 952/1 Every page..bristles with the emendatory asterisk.

emended (ɪˈmɛndɪd), *ppl. a.* [f. EMEND *v.* + -ED¹.] Freed from faults, improved, corrected.

1882 *Nature* 199 An emended copy. **1884** MAHAFFY in *Contemp. Rev.* June 902 Scholia in an emended form.

emender (ɪˈmɛndə(r)). [f. EMEND *v.* + -ER.] One who emends.

1885 *Spectator* 18 July 952/1 The wildest emenders almost invariably make..discoveries of permanent value.

†**e'mendicate**, *v. Obs.* [f. L. *ēmendīcāt-* ppl. stem of *ēmendīcā-re* (f. *ē* out + *mendīcus* beggar) to obtain by begging.]

1. *trans.* To obtain by begging.

1611 SPEED *Hist. Gt. Brit.* IX. viii. §38 Nor would [he] any longer emendicate their forraine Justice. **1624** F. WHITE *Repl. Fisher* 554 It must emendicate Vertue..to satisfie the Auarice of the Horse-leaches of Rome. **1681** [see below].

2. *absol.* To beg.

1623 COCKERAM, *Emendicate*, to beg, or craue almes. **1847** in CRAIG; and in mod. Dicts.

Hence **e'mendicated** *ppl. a.*

1681 BURNET *Hist. Ref.* II. 56 Orders are..given, upon the credit of emendicated recommendations.

e'mending, *vbl. sb.* [f. EMEND *v.* + -ING¹.] The action of the vb. EMEND.

1411 *E.E. Wills* (1882) 17 In emendynge of weys lyand about þe manere of Bradfeld. *c* **1542** UDALL in *Orig. Lett. Eminent Men* (1843) 4 Aftir myn emendyng and reformacion.

†**e'mendment**. *Obs. rare*⁻¹. In 6 emendement. [f. EMEND *v.* + -MENT.] = AMENDMENT 1 a.

1569 CROWLEY *Soph. Dr. Watson* ii. 92 Our emendement of life.

†**e'mends**. *Obs. rare*⁻¹. [ad. OF. *esmendes*, pl. of *esmende* reparation (in med.L. *ēmenda*, f. *ēmendāre* to EMEND.)] = AMENDS 2.

1542 UDALL *Erasm. Apoph.* II. §2 The..losse..of one precious stone semed a sufficient..emendes for his felicitie.

emer, var. of YEMER, *Obs.*, guardian.

14.. *Tundale's Vis.* 224 That was the angell to beton is bale The whych was emer of Tundale.

emerald (ˈɛmərəld). Forms: 4–7 emeraud(e, -awd(e, emraud, (4 emeraund, -rad(e, -royde, emmorant, 5 emerant, 6 amerand, emerode, emorade, emrade, -rode,) 7 hemerauld, emrald, -auld, -old, (8 emerant), 6– emerald. [a. OF. *emeraude, esmeraude, esmeralde* (Fr. *émeraude*); cf. Pr. *esmerauda*, Sp., Pg. *esmeralda*, It. *smeraldo*:—Com. Romanic types **smaralda*, **smaraldo*, repr. L. *smaragdus*, a. Gr. σμάραγδος: see SMARAGDUS. The change of *gd* into *ld* in Romanic occurs in other cases, as It. *Baldacca* for *Bagdad*. In Eng. the form with *ld* does not appear in our quots. before 16th c., when it may be due to Sp. influence.]

1. A precious stone of bright green colour; in mod. use exclusively applied to a variety of the Beryl species (see BERYL *sb.* 2), found chiefly in S. America, Siberia, and India.

[In early examples the word, like most other names of precious stones, is of vague meaning; the mediæval references to the stone are often based upon the descriptions given by classical writers of the *smaragdus*, the identity of which with our emerald is doubtful. In the AV. (as previously by Tindale) *emerald* has been adopted as the rendering of Heb. *nōphek* (LXX. ἄνθραξ, Vulg. *carbunculus*), a gem as to the nature of which there is no evidence.]

c **1300** *K. Alis.* 7030 Grete drakis..emeraundis in mouth bare. *a* **1310** in Wright *Lyric P.* v. 26 Ase emeraude a-morewen this may haveth myht. **1481** CAXTON *Myrr.* II. vii. 79 The Emerawde..is..playsaunt to the eye. **1526** TINDALE *Rev.* xxi. 19 The fourth an emeralde. **1527** *Test. Ebor.* (Surtees) V. 244 Unum annulum cum lapide vocato an emorade. **1599** HAKLUYT *Voy.* II. 243 [249] Fine emrauds set in golde. **1601** HOLLAND *Pliny* II. 454 Our cups..must be set out with hemeraulds. **1609** BIBLE (Douay) *Ex.* xxviii. 19 In the first rew shal be..the emeraud. **1634** MILTON *Comus* 894 My chariot thick set with emerald green. **1691** WOOD *Ath. Oxon.* II. 523 A ring..having an emrold set therein between two diamonds. **1751** CHAMBERS *Cycl.* s.v., The emerald is supposed..to arrive at its greenness by slow degrees. **1842** LYTTON *Zanoni* 28 Valleys where the birds build their nests with emeralds to attract the moths. **1861** C. KING *Ant. Gems* (1866) 29 The Bactrian and Scythian Emeralds were considered the best.

2. *Her.* The name given by English heralds to the green colour (ordinarily called *vert*) when it occurs in the arms of the nobility.

1572 BOSSEWELL *Armorie* II. 60 b, The fielde is of the Topaze, a Basiliske displayed, Emeraude, cristed, Saphire.

3. *transf.* as name of its colour; = *emerald-green*.

1712 tr. *Pomet's Hist. Drugs* I. 107 Scales of Brass thrice calcin'd..will make a Sea-green, an Emerald..with many other colours.

4. *Printing.* The name of the size of type larger than nonpareil and smaller than minion.

5. *attrib.* and *Comb.* **a.** Simple *attrib.*

1877 W. JONES *Finger-ring L.* 127 An emerald ring was thought to ensure purity.

b. quasi-*adj.* Brilliantly green like the emerald.

1598 SHAKS. *Merry W.* v. v. 74 Hony Soit Qui Mal-y-Pence, write In Emrold-tuffes. **1722** ROGERS *Pleas. Mem.* I. 145 The glow-worm loves her emerald-light to shed. **1813** HOGG *Kilmeny*, The stillness that lay on the emerant lee. **1855** MACAULAY *Hist. Eng.* III. 158 That vast expanse of emerald meadow. **1855** SINGLETON *Virgil* I. 8 Thou mightest have reposed This night upon the emerald foliage.

c. Similative in adjs., as ***emerald-bright***, ***-green***, ***-like***.

1614 EARL STIRLING *Doomes-Day, Twelfth Houre* (R.), Rivers..emulate the emerauld-like grasse. **1646** SIR T. BROWNE *Pseud. Ep.* III. xxv. 177 A..flame of a circular figure and Emerald green colour. **1860** RUSKIN *Mod. Paint.* V. VI. ix. 84 The glades between emerald-bright. **1879** R. H. ELLIOT *Written on Foreheads* I. 1 The fields..were emerald green.

d. Special combinations or phrases: †**emerald copper** (*Min.*) = DIOPTASE; **emerald cuckoo**, an African cuckoo, *Chrysococcyx cupreus*, with green and gold plumage; **emerald green**, a durable pigment of a vivid light-green colour, prepared from the arseniate of copper; **Emerald Isle**, a name given to Ireland, on account of its prevailing verdure; **emerald moth** (*Entom.*), a name applied to certain moths of the genera *Hipparchus*, *Hemithea*, and *Cleora*, distinguished by their bright green colour; **emerald nickel** (*Min.*), a native hydrocarbonate of nickel.

1815 AIKIN *Min.* 91 *Emerald Copper..occurs crystallized in lengthened dodecahedrons. **1876** H. BROOKS *Natal* iv. 136 Amongst the climbers of the coast bush there is one bird known as the *emerald cuckoo. **1937** *Nature* 3 July 18/1 Among the birds [found in Arabia], three are new to science, namely, a race of the common magpie, a small Scops owl, and an emerald cuckoo. **1953** R. CAMPBELL *Mamba's Precipice* xi. 115 The four-note whistle of an emerald cuckoo. **1964** A. L. THOMSON *New Dict. Birds* 170/1 The Emerald Cuckoo *Chrysococcyx cupreus* has plumage of brilliant golden-green with bright yellow on the body. **1879** ROOD *Mod. Chromatics* ix. 121 The pigment known as *emerald-green. **1795** DR. W. DRENNAN *Erin* in *Notes & Q.* Ser. ii. IX. 199 The men of the *Emerald Isle [Drennan afterwards claimed to have invented the name.] **1842** ORDERSON *Creol.* v. 46 Our friend of the Emerald Isle. **1845** WESTWOOD *Brit. Moths* II. 17 *Hipparchus papilionarius* (the large *emerald). *Hemithea vernaria* (the small emerald). *Hemithea smaragdaria* (the Essex emerald). *Cleora bajularia* (the blotched emerald). **1848** *Amer. Jrnl. Sc.* Ser. II. VI. 248 *Emerald Nickel from Texas.

emeraldine (ˈɛmərəldɪn, -aɪn), *a.* and *sb.* [f. EMERALD + -INE.]

A. *adj.* Like an emerald in colour; emerald-green.

1855 *Chamb. Jrnl.* III. 408 The moat..bears on its emeraldine breast parterres crowded with..lovely flowers. **1859** *All Y. Round* No. 19. 448 Emeraldine sea. **1863** THORNBURY *True as Steel* III. 316 The larch puts forth its emeraldine tufts.

B. *sb.* A dye formed from aniline treated with hydrochloric acid and chlorate of potassium, or from a salt of aniline treated with sesquichloride of iron; aniline-green.

1864 *Pop. Sc. Rev.* III. 437 A green aniline dye called emeraldine.

†**emeras**. *Obs.* (See quot.)

1631 WEEVER *Anc. Fun. Mon.* 856 He lieth in complete Armour, on both his Emerases the Crosse of Saint George. **1847** *Gloss. Brit. Heraldry*, *Emerasses* or *Ailettes*, small escutcheons affixed to the shoulders of an armed knight: sometimes shield-shaped..and sometimes circular.

emeraudes, obs. f. EMEROD.

e'merge, *sb. nonce-wd.* [f. next.] A surface that has emerged.

1878 B. TAYLOR *Deukalion* III. i. 101 The slow ages on her bare emerge Gathered the dust for grass.

emerge (ɪˈmɜːdʒ), *v.* [ad. (directly or through Fr. *émerger*) L. *ēmergĕre*, f. *ē* out + *mergĕre* to dip.]

†**1.** *intr.* To rise by virtue of buoyancy, *from* or *out of* a liquid. *Obs.* exc. as a contextual use of 2.

1667 BOYLE *Orig. Formes & Qual.*, Emerging to the top of a much heavier Liquor. **1721** BAILEY, *Emerge*..when a..Body..lighter than Water, being thrust down..into it, rises again..it is said to immerge [*sic*] out of the Water.

2. To come up out of a liquid in which (the subject) has been immersed. Also *transf.* to rise *from* (under the surface of) the earth.

1640 G. WATTS *Bacon's Adv. Learn.* II. xiii. (R.) From whose [Medusa's] blood gushing out, instantly emerged Pegasus the flying horse. **1684** T. BURNET *The. Earth* (J.), The mountains emerged, and became dry land again. **1692** BENTLEY *Boyle Lect.* v. 168 Great multitudes of Animals did fortuitously emerge out of the Soil. **1700** DRYDEN *Homer* Wks. 1821 XII. 377 Thetis..emerging from the deep. **1765** COWPER *Lett.* 4 July, Just emerged from the Ouse, I sit down to thank you. **1856** EMERSON *Eng. Traits, Result* Wks. (Bohn) II. 137 The Ocean out of which [Great Britain] emerged.

3. a. To come forth into view; to pass out, issue, *from* an enclosed space, area of obscuration, etc.

1700 DRYDEN *Fables* (J.), Darkness, we see, emerges into light. **1751** JOHNSON *Rambl.* No. 144 ⁋3 No sooner can any man emerge from the crowd. **1809–10** COLERIDGE *Friend* I. 5 He emerged from his place of shelter. **1860** TYNDALL *Glac.* I. §22. 157, I..saw the party..emerging from one of the hollows. **1878** HUXLEY *Physiogr.* 141 By the time the stream emerges [from the lake].

¶ quasi-*trans.* (cf. *depart this life*, etc.)

1675 R. BURTHOGGE *Causa Dei* 238 Here..as on a..tumultuous Sea, men are Uncapable of..discerning God..but hereafter, when they have emerged it, they shall, etc.

b. *spec.* in *Optics* of a ray of light after passing through a lens, prism, etc.; in *Astron.* of a heavenly body after occultation or eclipse.

1704 NEWTON *Optics* (T.) The rays emerge more obliquely out of the second refracting surface. **1833** SIR J. HERSCHEL *Astron.* x. §541 (1858) 361/2 The satellite..will emerge..after..occultation. **1839** G. BIRD *Elem. Nat. Phil.* 379 If the glass parallelopiped be sufficiently long, the beam of light will emerge circularly polarized.

4. *fig.* **a.** To rise into notice, come forth from obscurity; also, to issue *from* a state of subjection, suffering, embarrassment, etc. Also said of the production of a type by such a process as evolution.

1664 H. MORE *Myst. Iniq.* 296 The Pope once emerged above the Emperor. **1665** GLANVILL *Sceps. Sci.* 79 The Empire began to emerge from that black night of Ignorance. **1713** BENTLEY *Phil. Lips.* §40 (T.) Children, who must needs have emerged in a secular life. **1790** BURKE *Fr. Rev.* 71 How very soon France..recovered and emerged from the..dreadful civil war. **1856** FROUDE *Hist. Eng.* (1858) II. vi. 13 He emerges into distinct notice..ten years subsequent. **1876** GREEN *Stray Stud.* 185 Florence emerged into communal greatness. **1913** G. E. SMITH in *Rep. Brit. Assoc.* *1912* 582 When the true mammal emerged. **1915** [see EMERGENCE 2 a].

†**b.** Used (like L. *evadere*) for: To 'turn out', become. *Obs.*

1699 EVELYN *Acetaria* (1729) 146 An accomplish'd Sallet-Dresser..to emerge an exact Critic.

5. Of a fact, principle, etc.: To come out as the result of an investigation or discussion. Of a state of things, a question or problem: To 'crop up', arise, present itself for solution (*esp.* suddenly or unexpectedly).

1563–87 FOXE *A. & M.* (1596) 86/2 All difficult questions in all prouinces whatsoeuer emerging. **1680** H. MORE *Apocal. Apoc.* 10 Hence emerges a difficulty. **1702** EVELYN in Pepys *Diary* VI. 254 Instructions naturally emerging from the subject. **1710** PRIDEAUX *Orig. Tithes* ii. 52 So many reasons would continually emerge. **1791** BURKE *Thoughts Fr. Affairs* Wks. VII. 51 The train of things as they successively emerge. **1861** TULLOCH *Eng. Purit.* i. 30 The political difficulty..did not emerge in Elizabeth's reign. **1868** M. PATTISON *Academ. Org.* 249 Here emerges the question as to compulsory attendance.

emerge, bad spelling of IMMERGE *v.*

1644 *Jus Populi* 34 The right of Fathers..is now emerged or made subordinate. **1743** *Humours of Whist* 45, I have been emerged in calculation ever since. **1824** *Mechanic's Mag.* No. 50. 351 Emerge it into a..cistern of cold water.

†**e'mergement**. *Obs. rare.* [f. EMERGE *v.* + -MENT.] = EMERGENCY 4.

a **1734** NORTH *Exam.* II. v. ⁋138 It being usually observed that such Emergements disperse in Rumor unaccountably.

emergence (ɪˈmɜːdʒəns). [ad. late L. *ēmergentia*, f. *ēmergĕre* to EMERGE.]

1. The rising (of a submerged body) out of the water.

1833 LYELL *Princ. Geol.* III. 113 The waves..continue their denuding action during the emergence of these islands. **1860** TYNDALL *Glac.* II. 400 A well-wetted oar..on its first emergence from the water. **1875** CROLL *Climate & T.* xxiii. 368 The..emergence of the land during the glacial epoch.

2. a. The process of coming forth, issuing from concealment, obscurity, or confinement. *lit.* and *fig.* (Cf. EMERGE *v.* 3, 4.) Also said of the result of an evolutionary process: cf. EMERGE *v.* 4 a and EMERGENT B. 3.

1755 BROOKE *Univ. Beauty* I. 10 From the deep thy [Venus'] bright emergence sprung. **1779** JOHNSON *Milton, L.P.* 96 Physiological learning is of..rare emergence. **1817** COLERIDGE *Biog. Lit.* (1817) 39 The emergence of an original poetic genius above the literary horizon. **1835–6** TODD *Cycl. Anat.* I. 68/1 The infant is prepared for a more independent existence by the emergence of teeth. **1853**

KANE *Grinnell Exp.* xviii. (1856) 140 Its [a glacier's] emergence from the valley. **1873** SYMONDS *Grk. Poets* i. 1 The emergence from primitive barbarism of the great races. **1884** *Sat. Rev.* 22 Nov. 657/2 That emergence of the adversary's point at the back might trouble a Neapolitan fencer. **1911** GEDDES & THOMSON *Evolution* 102 It is undeniably difficult to discover the factors in his emergence and ascent. **1913** G. E. SMITH in *Rep. Brit. Assoc. 1912* 577 The gradual emergence of human traits from the uncouth simian features of our ancestors. **1915** *Scientia* XVIII. 255 The emergence of anything new in the world.. If intrinsic structure and external conditions are..strictly similar, nothing new emerges. But if with like intrinsic structure the conditions are different, or *vice versa*, something new may emerge. And if genuinely emergent (as contrasted with resultant in accordance with G. H. Lewes's distinction) it may be unpredictable. **1920** S. ALEXANDER *Space, Time, & Deity* II. III. ii. 45 The emergence of a new quality from any level of existence means that at that level there comes into being a certain constellation or collocation of the motions belonging to that level, and possessing the quality appropriate to it, and this collocation possesses a new quality distinctive of the higher complex.

b. *Astron.* and *Optics.* (Cf. EMERGE *v.* 3 b.)

1704 NEWTON *Optics* (J.) Refracted light, at its very first emergence. **1833** SIR J. HERSCHEL *Astron.* ix. 294 The satellite's emergence. **1863** TYNDALL *Heat* iv. 108 As a thermic agent, the beam..is far more powerful than..after its emergence. **1881** LD. RAYLEIGH in *Nature* XXV. 64 Giving the light a more..grazing emergence.

3. An unforeseen occurrence; a state of things unexpectedly arising, and demanding immediate attention.

Now replaced by EMERGENCY, which Ash in 1775 notes as 'less usual'.

1649 BP. GUTHRIE *Mem.* (1702) 72 The Castle of Dunglass was blown up with Powder..This tragical Emergence, etc. **1788** PRIESTLEY *Lect. Hist.* v. lii. 406 To raise the nominal value of money may serve a particular emergence. **1823** SCOTT *Peveril* vi, The best I can think of in this emergence is, etc. **1849** MRS. CARLYLE *Lett.* II. 69 Nothing came out on the present emergence to alter our opinion.

¶ Pressing need, urgent want: 'a sense not proper' (J.).

1781 COWPER *Charity* 188 Not he but his emergence forced the door. **1846** THACKERAY *Cornhill to Cairo* ix. 106 They call in their emergence upon countless saints and virgins.

4. *Bot.* A term applied by Sachs to those outgrowths on leaves or stems which arise from the sub-epidermic tissue and not merely from the epidermis.

1882 tr. *Sachs's Text-bk. Botany* (ed. 2) 161.

emergency (ɪˈmɜːdʒənsɪ). [ad. late L. *ēmergentia*: see prec. and -ENCY.]

1. The rising of a submerged body above the surface of water; = EMERGENCE 1. Now *rare.*

1646 SIR T. BROWNE *Pseud. Ep.* IV. vi. 194 A Tyrant..to prevent the emergencie of murdered bodies did use to cut off their lungs. **1693** *Phil. Trans.* XVII. 689 They [the Goodwin Sands]..may be of late Emergency. **1880** A. R. WALLACE *Isl. Life* ix. 169 Repeated submergencies and emergencies of the land.

†**2. a.** The process of issuing from concealment, confinement, etc.; = EMERGENCE 2. *Obs.*

c **1645** HOWELL *Fam. Lett.* (1650) II. 4 Congratulat his.. emergency from that course he was plunged in. **1656** H. MORE *Antid. Ath.* Pref. Gen. (1712) 14 The..immediate emergency of Vitality from Spirit. **1663** BOYLE *Colours* (J.), The emergency of colours, upon coalition of the particles of such bodies..is very well worth our attentive observation.

†**b.** *Astron.* = EMERGENCE 2 b. *Obs. rare.*

1762 DUNN in *Phil. Trans.* LII. 579, I had compared it with the fixed stars, and the Moon, after emergency from the aforementioned clouds.

†**3.** The arising, sudden or unexpected occurrence (of a state of things, an event, etc.). *Obs.*

1665 GLANVILL *Sceps. Sci.* xxi, Most of our Rarities have been found out by casual emergency. **1755** MAGENS *Insurances* II. 2 The Emergency of an unexpected Case. **1776** GIBBON *Decl. & F.* I. 383 The emergency of war very frequently required their presence on the frontiers.

4. *concr.* **a.** (the ordinary mod. use): A juncture that arises or 'turns up'; *esp.* a state of things unexpectedly arising, and urgently demanding immediate action.

a **1631** DONNE *Select.* (1840) 107 The Psalms minister instruction..to every man, in every emergency. **1764** BURN *Poor Laws* 196 Relief on sudden emergencies. **1821** BYRON *Mar. Fal.* v. i. 183 On great emergencies The law must be remodell'd or amended. **1856** FROUDE *Hist. Eng.* (1858) I. iv. 342 The bishop, beautifully equal to the emergency, arose. **1867** SMILES *Huguenots Eng.* ii. (1880) 22 On an emergency he would even undertake to measure land.

¶ Hence sometimes used for: Urgency, pressing need. 'A sense not proper' (J.).

1716 ADDISON *Freeholder* (J.), In any case of emergency, he would employ the whole wealth of his empire. *Mod.* It is a case of great emergency.

†**b.** *pl.* Casual or contingent profits. *Obs.*

a **1662** HEYLIN *Laud* I. 151 Rents, Profits and Emergencies belonging to a Bishop of Bath and Wells.

c. *Cricket*, etc. An emergency man, a substitute. (No longer current.)

1851 *Nottingham Rev.* 5 Sept. 3/4 Emergency Williams, Esq., b. Goodrich. **1862** in W. G. Grace *Cricketing Remin.* (1899) i. 12 With this ball (presented by M.C.C. to E. M. Grace), he got every wicket in 2nd innings, in the match played at Canterbury, August 14, 15, 1862, Gentlemen of Kent v. M.C.C. for whom he played as an emergency, and in which, going in first, he scored 192 not out. **1885** J. LILLYWHITE *Cricketers' Compan.* 59 George Alexander.. only played as an emergency.

d. *spec.*, as a political term, to describe a condition approximating to that of war; *occas.* as a synonym or euphemism for war; also ***state of emergency***, wherein the normal constitution is suspended.

1893 C. G. LELAND *Memoirs* 251 The rebels..had penetrated into Pennsylvania, and Philadelphia was threatened. This period was called the 'Emergency'. **1958** *Spectator* 17 Jan. 65/2 He has declared a state of emergency to suppress a strike of African railway workers. **1958** *Oxf. Mag.* 13 Mar. 374/2 The unmentionable word 'war' decently euphemised as 'emergency'.

5. *attrib.* **a.** *spec.*, esp. in ***Emergency man***: (in Ireland) an occasional bailiff's officer, recruited for special service, *esp.* in evictions.

1881 *Let.* 14 Dec. in Reid *Life of W. E. Forster* (1888) II. viii. 377 The Emergency Committee..was a purely Orange emanation. **1883** *Ann. Reg.* I. 1 Three Emergency men [were] attacked by an armed party.

b. In general adj. sense 'used, issued, called upon, or arising in an emergency'.

1896 *Daily Chron.* 15 Aug. 11/6 She had been asked by the medical officer to take charge of the emergency brandy. **1898** *Daily News* 13 May 5/2 The emergency ration is never served out for more than five days consecutively. **1900** *Jrnl. Soc. Arts* 21 Sept. 802/2 The fitting of emergency brakes. **1902** *Young Engineer* I. 47/2 Doors are provided both for regular use and as emergency exits. **1903** *Westm. Gaz.* 11 Sept. 8/1 Directly the current between the Bank Station and the stations as far as the British Museum was cut off, an emergency current was turned on. **1904** F. F. MOORE *Original Woman* xxiv. 265 He was a man who had always at hand an emergency exit opening outward by which he could escape from any situation that was getting too hot for him. **1915** *Lit. Digest* (N.Y.) 21 Aug. 348/1 All of the [beaver-]ponds are equipped with 'emergency exits' in the form of holes in the bank. **1920** *Act 10 Geo. V* c. 5 (*title*) An Act to continue temporarily certain emergency enactments. **1921** *Dict. Occup. Terms* (1927) §729 *Emergency man*..a tramway conductor..who is held in readiness to replace anyone of depot cashier's assistants who may be on leave or sick. **1925** W. DEEPING *Sorrell & Son* xxx. 296 He asked you to do an emergency job for him in the [operating] theatre. **1925** A. S. M. Hutchinson *One Increasing Purpose* I. xx, 'Have you a girl on your staff called Glade?' 'Not on my staff... Miss Glade is one of my emergency-calls. I get her when I want her, if she is available.' **1929** *Star* 21 Aug. 12/1 Glamorgan's emergency bowlers. **1935** *Archit. Rev.* LXXVII. 206 (*caption*) Looking along the outside wall of the lecture hall, and at one of the lecture hall emergency exits. **1940** *Ann. Reg. 1939* 397 Many of whom [*sc.* lawyers] were chosen as chairmen of tribunals and committees under one or other of the Emergency Acts. **1944** *Living off Land* v. 102 Carry an emergency ration in the shape of a tobacco tin of salt and oatmeal, well mixed. **1944** A. THIRKELL *Headmistress* iii. 64 An emergency card for her rations. **1956** A. H. COMPTON *Atomic Quest* 259 The fliers returned to an emergency landing at Okinawa. **1961** *Lancet* 12 Aug. 338/2 Data for the occurrence of disease were derived from the Emergency Bed Service (E.B.S.) of the King Edward Hospital Fund for London. **1970** *Ibid.* 19 Sept. 604/2 The past decade has seen the establishment of emergency call services to supplement practice rota systems.

emergent (ɪˈmɜːdʒənt), *a.* and *sb.* [a. L. *ēmergent-em*: see EMERGENCE.] **A.** *adj.*

1. a. Rising out of a surrounding medium, *e.g.* water.

1627 MAY *Lucan* IV. 141 Emergent hills t'appeare began. **1682** *Weekly Mem. Ingen.* 355 One part is emergent above the water. *a* **1774** FERGUSON *Month of April*, Brittania.. Floating emergent on the frigid zone. **1851** RUSKIN *Stones Ven.* II. vi, The great plain, broken by an emergent rock or clump of trees.

b. *fig.* with direct reference to lit. sense.

1636 B. JONSON *Discov.* (1692) 693 The man that is once hated, both his good and his evil deeds oppress him. He is not easily emergent. **1647** MAY *Hist. Parl.* III. vi. 102 Parliament was..so..sunke..that nothing but an extraordinary providence could make it again emergent. **1763** SHENSTONE *Elegies* v. 27 Hope, still emergent, still contemns the wave. *a* **1797** H. WALPOLE *Mem. Geo. II.* I. 376 The emergent humour of his people.

2. a. That is in process of issuing forth.

1640 SHIRLEY *Opportunity* Ded., This poem..emergent from the press. **1728** THOMSON *Spring* 263 This..emergent from the gloomy wood, The glaring lion saw. **1838** J. STRUTHERS *Poetic Tales* 38 The sun emergent smiled.

b. *spec.* in *Astron.* (see quot.); in *Optics* said of a ray of light after passing through a refracting medium; so also of a ray of heat.

1676 NEWTON in *Phil. Trans.* XI. 558 The incident refractions were..equal to the emergent. **1721** BAILEY s.v., When a Star is getting out of the Sun Beams, and ready to become visible, it is said to be emergent. **1822** IMISON *Sc. & Art* I. 246 The emergent rays will be collected to a focus. **1863** TYNDALL *Heat* ix. (1870) 287 Heat emergent from these respective plates.

c. *Science.* That emerges unpredictably as the result of an evolutionary process, *spec.* in ***emergent evolution***.

1915 [see EMERGENCE 2]. **1923** C. L. MORGAN (*title*) Emergent evolution. *Ibid.* i. 1 Under what I here call emergent evolution stress is laid on this incoming of the new. **1928** *Observer* 1 June 5/3 That growing body of thought called 'Emergent Evolution'. **1932** *Discovery* Apr. 108/2 One of the salient features in recent aetiology (i.e. evolution lore) has been the recognition of the more or less open secret expressed in the term 'emergent evolution'... It has become evident that the Ascent of Life has been a succession of 'emergent' steps, novelties that are creative rather than 'additive', such as birds from ancestral reptiles.

3. *fig.* **a.** That is in process of rising into notice.

1654 H. L'ESTRANGE *Chas. I.* (1655) 8 The self same spirit of contest..was emergent long before that marriage. **1837** CARLYLE *Fr. Rev.* II. VI. vi, Either emergent or else emerged and full-blown. **1851** J. H. NEWMAN *Cath. in Eng.* 189 There are emergent parties in this country.

b. Of a nation: that is newly independent; of a people: that is conscious of its national identity.

1954 *N.Y. Times Mag.* 31 Oct. VI. 13 The ambitions and the unquenchable hope of emergent Africa. **1957** H. THOMAS *World's Game* xv. 191 The chauvinistic young foreign ministers of emergent countries. **1960** *Dialy Tel.* 13 Jan. 10/2 Each of the 'emergent' territories in Africa has different problems, to which each must find its own best solution. **1963** *Listener* 7 Feb. 233/1 They [*sc.* the Fijians] just will not be emergent or emancipated.

4. *fig.* That arises from or out of something prior; consequent, derivative.

c **1619** R. JONES *Serm. Resur.* in *Phenix* II. 488 Declining all emergent controversys. **1650** VENNER *Via Recta Advt.* 370 From whose [blood] losse or want so great hurts are emergent. *a* **1716** SOUTH (J.), A necessity emergent from and inherent in the things themselves. **1833** SIR J. HERSCHEL *Astron.* xiii. §689 (1858) The changes of excentricity emergent..from the action of the normal force.

5. Casually or unexpectedly arising; not specially provided for. *arch.*

1593 BILSON *Govt. Christ's Ch.* 375 To amend all matters emergent. **1628** DIGBY *Voy. Medit.* (1868) 3 That the Admirall may giue directions vpon emergent occasions. **1653** H. COGAN *Diod. Sic.* 238 It is their custome after meate to fall into some emergent discourse. **1726** AYLIFFE *Parerg.* 282 Allowances of Money paid to Persons for emergent Services. **1845–6** TRENCH *Huls. Lect.* Ser. I. ii. 33 Occasional documents called forth by emergent needs.

¶ Used for 'urgent', 'pressing'.

1706 DE FOE *Jure Div.* Pref. 1 To perswade their Princes to burst them in their most emergent Occasions. **1717** LADY M. W. MONTAGUE *Lett.* II. xlvii. 45 The most emergent necessity. **1878** *Macm. Mag.* Jan. 254/1 Certain petty and emergent repairs. **1881** *Spectator* 19 Feb. 245 The provocation was of the most emergent kind. **1882** SIR R. TEMPLE *Men & Events* viii. 182–3 If a matter was politically emergent..he cast away his over-caution.

6. Required for emergencies.

1800 WELLINGTON *Let.* in Gurw. *Disp.* I. 65 I have this day sent a supply of emergent ammunition.

†**7.** ***emergent year***: transl. of med.L. *annus emergens. Obs.*

The term was used by Gervase of Tilbury, who says that the Jews have three modes of reckoning their years: viz., *annum usualem*, which they employ in conformity with the practice of their Christian neighbours, beginning on 1 Jan.; *annum legitimum*, which begins in April; and *annum emergentem*, which is reckoned from their departure from Egypt. In this passage *emergens* has its usual med.L. sense 'arising out of a particular circumstance' (cf. 4, 5); but after the publication of Gervase in Leibnitz *Script. Rer. Brunsv.* (1707–10) the phrase *annus emergens* was taken to mean 'the initial year of an era' (a misconception to which the sentence, apart from its context, easily lends itself). Hence the modern equivalents of the L. phrase, with this incorrect explanation, found their way into 18th c. dictionaries of Fr., Sp., and Eng.; but we have failed to discover any evidence that they actually came into use in those langs. A passage from the same ultimate source as that in Gervase occurs in Higden (see quot. 1450).

c **1450** tr. *Higden's Polychron.* (Harl. MS. 2261) I. 37 Also there is a yere emergente as anendes theyme begynnengs from May when thei wente from Egipte. **1736** BAILEY, *Emergent year* [with erroneous explanation as above]. Hence in mod. Dicts.

B. *sb.* **1.** †**a.** An outcome, incidental result. *Obs.*

1528 *State Lett.* in Burnet *Hist. Ref.* II. 89 In this cause of Matrimony with all the emergents and dependencies upon the same. ?**1656** BRAMHALL *Replic.* vi. 235 The consideration of one or two circumstances or emergents.

b. In wider use: something that emerges.

1920 *Challenge* 15 Oct. 337/2 The growing estrangement [between England and Ireland] which is the mildest emergent from the tragedy.

†**2.** An unforeseen occurrence, a contingency not specially provided for; = EMERGENCY 3 b. *Obs.*

1620 BRENT tr. *Sarpi's Hist. Counc. Trent* 658 To be able to giue a rule for all emergents as the times doe require. **1637–50** ROW *Hist. Kirk* (1842) 47 Maters falling out, new incidents and emergents. *a* **1714** BURNET *Own Time* II. 74 By an unlooked for emergent, the session was broke. **1720** WODROW *Corr.* (1843) II. 491 My behaviour in this emergent.

3. *Science.* An effect produced by a combination of several causes, but not capable of being regarded as the sum of their individual effects. Opposed to *resultant.*

1874 LEWES *Problems Life & Mind* I. 98. **1928** C. E. M. JOAD *Future of Life* vi. 105 The mind is an 'emergent' upon the combination of two constituents—namely the body and what Professor Broad calls the 'psychic factor'. **1936** *Nature* 28 Mar. 522/2 The system of thought which he [*sc.* C. Lloyd Morgan] ultimately propounded was what he called a philosophy of evolution, but evolution as meaning the coming into existence of something in some sense new; and this something new, in a specialised sense, he labelled, adopting G. H. Lewes's term, 'emergent', as contrasted with resultant. **1959** *Listener* 8 Jan. 58/1 When Alexander speaks of 'emergents' he sometimes means qualities which some psychologists nowadays would call the *Gestalt* properties of ordered systems..but sometimes he means something more like the possibility of a new way of *functioning* released through a particular kind of ordered structure.

emergently (ɪˈmɜːdʒəntlɪ), *adv.* [f. prec. + -LY².] In an emergent manner; †by way of incidental consequence (*obs.*).

1660 JER. TAYLOR *Duct. Dubit.* III. iv. ℙ5 §1 Not primely necessary, but emergently and contingently..useful.

†**eˈmergentness.** *Obs. rare*⁻⁰. [f. EMERGENT *a.* + -NESS.] The state of being emergent; 'emergency, casualness' (Bailey).

1736 in BAILEY. **1775** in ASH.

emerging (ɪˈmɜːdʒɪŋ), *vbl. sb.* [f. EMERGE *v.* + -ING¹.] The action of the verb EMERGE.

1813 *Examiner* 10 May 300/2 The most convenient grave for the emerging of the deceased. **1831** HOWITT *Seasons* 262 Those sudden emergings from shadow and silence. **1837** CARLYLE *Fr. Rev.* (1872) III. II. vi. 79 We have got to another emerging of the Trial.

eˈmerging, *ppl. a.* [f. as prec. + -ING².] That emerges. *lit.* and *fig.*

1646 S. BOLTON *Arraignm. Err.* 265 The power of redressing emerging enormities in a church. **1703** POPE *Vertumnus* 115 Thro' clouds th' emerging sun appears. **1710** NORRIS *Chr. Prud.* ii. 101 They..lay down old Principles.. when..any emerging Juncture shall make it for their advantage. **1822** BYRON *Heav. & Earth* iii. 40 To hiss and sting through some emerging world. **1856** STANLEY *Sinai & Pal.* vi. 263 The waves..dash against the emerging rocks.

emerick, emeril(l, obs. forms of EMERY.

†**eˈmerit,** *a. Obs. rare.* [ad. L. *ēmerit-us*: see EMERITUS.] Superannuated. In quots. used contemptuously. Also as quasi-*sb.* Cf. EMERITUS.

1641 W. CARTWRIGHT *Ordinary* I. v. (1651) 17 That old Emerit thing..that rotten Antiquary. *a* **1643** —— *Birth P'cess Eliz.* (R.), The emerit ancient warbling priests. **1710** *Acc. Last Distemper of T. Whigg* II. 43 He scorn'd to..be thought an Emerite.

†**eˈmerit,** *v. Obs. rare*⁻¹. [f. L. *ēmerit-* ppl. stem of *ēmerē-re, -ri*, f. *ē* out + *merēre, -ri* to deserve, earn.] *trans.* To obtain by service, deserve.

1648 FAIRFAX, &c. *Remonstrance* 51 The persons that.. shall have emerited their pardons.

emerited (ɪˈmɛrɪtɪd), *ppl. a. arch.* [f. L. *ēmerit-us* (see next) + -ED.] Chiefly of soldiers and sailors: That has retired from active service, served out his time; *hence*, skilled through long practice or experience. See EMERITUS.

1664 EVELYN *Sylva* (1776) 579 Emerited and well deserving Seamen and Mariners. **1681** —— *Diary* (1827) III. 61 A Royal Hospital for emerited souldiers. **1859** SALA *Tw. round Clock* (1861) 294 The most emerited thieves. *Ibid.* 401 The abhorred 'Palmerstoni' whom papal gensd'arme imagine to be an emerited brigand.

‖**emeritus** (ɪˈmɛrɪtəs), *a.* and *sb.* [L. *ēmeritus* that has served his time (said of a soldier), pa. pple. of *ēmerēri* (see EMERIT *v.*) to earn (one's discharge) by service.]

A. *adj.* Honourably discharged from service; chiefly in mod.L. phrase ***emeritus professor***, the title given to a university professor who has retired from the office.

1794 *U.S. Register* (Philad.) 119 Emeritus professor of divinity. **1823** DE QUINCEY *Lett. on Educ.* v. (1860) 102 An emeritus Professor of Moral Philosophy. **1870** LOWELL *Study Wind.* (1886) 86 He would not claim to be emeritus. **1874** MORLEY *Compromise* (1886) 140 When Reason may possibly have no more to discover for us in the region of morals..and so will have become emeritus.

B. *sb.* One who has retired or been discharged from active service or occupation.

In mod. Dicts.

†**ˈemerods,** *sb. pl. Obs.* Forms: 5–7 emeraudes, -odes, (5 emerawntys, -owdys, emoroyades), 7 emrods, emeroids, emerods. [ad. L. *hæmorrhoïdes*, a. Gr. αἱμορροΐδες: see HÆMORRHOIDS.] = HÆMORRHOIDS. (Still sometimes used in allusions to *1 Sam.* v. 6, 7, in A.V.)

a **1400** in *Rel. Ant.* I. 190 A man schal blede ther [in the arm] also, The emeraudis for to undo. *c* **1440** *Promp. Parv.* 139 Emerawntys, or emerowdys. **1530** PALSGR. 182 A disease called the emerodes. **1610** BARROUGH *Meth. Physick* I. xxviii. (1639) 47 If the disease [melancholy] be caused through the stopping of Emerods. **1625** HART *Anat. Ur.* II. viii. 106 Such dust..is thought to signifie fluxe of the Emeraudes. **1631** GOUGE *God's Arrows* III. 362 He died of.. the Emeroids. **1770** ANDREW MITCHELL in Ellis *Orig. Lett.* Ser. II. IV. 527 He was seized..with a fit of the gout and the emerods at the same time. **1855** SMEDLEY *Occult Sc.* 335 The mice and emerods of gold..were essentially charms.

emersed (ɪˈmɜːst), *ppl. a.* [f. L. *ēmers-us*, pa. pple. of *ēmergĕre* to EMERGE + -ED.] Standing out from a medium in which a thing has been plunged. *lit.* and *fig.*

1686 GOAD *Celest. Bodies* I. xvi. 106 A perfect Trine emers'd above the Horizon. **1729** SAVAGE *Wanderer* I. 105 My winding steps up a steep mountain strain! Emers'd a-top, I mark the hills subside. **1870** HOOKER *Stud. Flora* 368 Leaves floating or emersed.

emersed, bad spelling of IMMERSED.

1794 SULLIVAN *View Nature* I. 91 Emersed under the waters of the ocean.

emersion (ɪˈmɜːʃən). [as if ad. L. **ēmersiōn-em*, n. of action f. *ēmergĕ-re* to EMERGE.]

1. The appearing (of what has been submerged) above the surface of the water. (Formerly sometimes in a narrower sense: see quot. 1731.)

1667 *Phil. Trans.* II. 440 The Immersion and Emersion of the Globe. **1693** KNATCHBULL *Annot.* 207 (T.) Their immersion into the water, and their emersion out of the same. **1731** BAILEY, vol. II. *Emersion*, the rising of any solid above the surface of a fluid specifically lighter than itself, into which it had been violently immersed. **1799** KIRWAN *Geol. Ess.* 26 The creation of fish was..subsequent to the emersion of the tracts just mentioned. **1875** *Wonders Phys. World* America, the emersion of which is comparatively recent.

fig. **1760** FOOTE *Minor* II. (1781) 58 Her emersion from the mercantile ruin. **1768–74** TUCKER *Lt. Nat.* (1852) II. 350 This emersion..of human nature from the floods of corruption.

2. The action of coming out or issuing (from concealment or confinement). Somewhat *rare.*

1763 C. JOHNSTONE *Reverie* II. 42 My emersion from.. solitude in which I had buried myself. **1835** KIRBY *Hab. Anim.* I. ii. 63 The animal's emersion from its hiding place.

b. *Astron.* The reappearance of the sun or moon from shadow after eclipse, or of a star or planet after occultation.

1633 H. GELLIBRAND in T. James *Voy.* Rb, The exact time of the Moones Emersion. **1759** JOHNSON *Rasselas* xl. (1787) 116 We were..watching the emersion of a satellite of Jupiter. **1833** SIR J. HERSCHEL *Astron.* ix. 294 An eclipse.. in which only the immersion, or only the emersion is seen.

†**3.** A coming into notice; an issuing into being. *Obs.*

1678 CUDWORTH *Intell. Syst.* 145 This Hylozoick Atheism hath been very obscure ever since its first Emersion. **1680** H. MORE *Apocal. Apoc.* 218 The emersion of the New Jerusalem into Being.

Emersonian (ɛməˈsəʊnɪən), *a.* and *sb.* [f. the name of the American author Ralph Waldo *Emerson* (1803–82) + -IAN.] **A.** *adj.* Of, pertaining to, or characteristic of Emerson or his writings. **B.** *sb.* An admirer or follower of Emerson. Hence **Emerˈsonianism.**

1848 A. H. CLOUGH *Let.* 16 July (1957) I. 216 He is much less Emersonian than his Essays. **1857** KINGSLEY *Two Y. Ago* III. i. 34, I almost think those Emersonians are right, when they crave the 'life of plants, and stones, and rain'. **1870** *Gentl. Mag.* July 160 He 'planted himself', in Emersonian language, 'upon his instincts'. **1884** J. HAWTHORNE in *N. Amer. Rev.* Aug. 166 To be Emersonian is to be American. **1888** *Athenæum* 24 Mar. 372/2 In later life he [*sc.* A. B. Alcott] went about the American cities as a peripatetic philosopher, displaying in 'conversations' the Emersonian jewels and Transcendental wares. **1902** W. JAMES *Var. Relig. Exper.* ii. 31 Modern transcendental idealism, Emersonianism, for instance, also seems to let God evaporate into abstract Ideality. **1918** *Hist. Amer. Lit.* I. 352 The volatile and heady liquid known as Emersonianism. **1936** *Times Lit. Suppl.* 12 Dec. 1022/3 Allowing to the individual an Emersonian freedom to himself. **1965** M. BRADBURY *Stepping Westward* vi. 291 There were extravagant Emersonians in white socks.

emery (ˈɛmərɪ), *sb.* Also 6 emerye, (ymree), 7–8 emeril(l, 7 emerick. [a. F. *émeri*, *émeril*, OF. *esmeril* = Sp. *esmeril*, It. *smeriglio*:—late L. *smericulum*, f. Gr. σμῆρις (σμίρις, σμύρις) a powder used for polishing.]

1. a. A coarse variety of corundum, used for polishing metals, stones, and glass.

1481–90 *Howard Househ. Bks.* (1844) 379 My Lord toke to ..the armore to by with emery xxd. **1505** *Ld. Treas. Acc. Scotl.* in Pitcairn *Crim. Trials* I. *123 Dichting of their steil sadilles with ymree. **1577** *Wills & Inv. N.C.* (1835) I. 415, Viij pounde emerye. **1610** HOLLAND *Camden's Brit.* II. 225 That most hard and sharpe stone Smyris (which we tearme Emerill). **1612** DRAYTON *Poly-olb.* i. 2 Jernsey..whose.. ground The hardned Emerill hath. **1646** SIR T. BROWNE *Pseud. Ep.* II. iii. 69 The Magnet attracteth..the Smyris or Emery in powder. **1677** MOXON *Mech. Exerc.* (1703) 15 Make it..smoother with Emerick. **1759** WILSON in *Phil. Trans.* LI. 336, I then, with a little emery, made that edge.. rough again. **1769** *De Foe's Tour Gt. Brit.* III. 349 The sharp and hard Stone Smyris or Emeril. **1816** J. SMITH *Panorama Sc. & Art* I. 33 Emery is..employed as the cutting powder. **1858** GREENER *Gunnery* 217 Polish the barrels with..a little washed emery.

b. = *emery bag. U.S.*

1864 *Hist. North-Western Soldiers' Fair* 71, 2 soldiers' reticules, 3 pin cushions, 5 emeries, 1 crochet tidy. **1900** M. E. WILKINS *Love of Parson Lord* 47 Her scissors, her emery, her thread, were on the ground. *Ibid.* 49 An emery of painted velvet in an ivory case.

2. (See quot.)

1789 MILLS *Strata Irel.* in *Phil. Trans.* LXXX. 97 An irregular bed of iron ore, called emery by the inhabitants.

3. *attrib.* and *Comb.*, as ***emery grinding, shaping, -stone***; also **emery bag**, a case containing emery, used for keeping needles bright; **emery board**, an emery-coated nail file (see also quot. 1889); **emery-cake** (see quot. 1853); **emery-cloth, -paper**, cloth or paper covered with emery-powder, to be used for polishing or cleaning metals, etc.; **emery cushion** = *emery bag*; **emery-file** (see quot.); **emery-grinder**, an emery-wheel mounted on a stand, to be used as a grind-stone; **emery planer**, a planer having an emery wheel as a cutter instead of a blade; **emery-powder**, ground emery, hence a *vb.*, to rub with emery-powder; **emery-roller**, a roller coated with emery; **emery-stick** (see quot.); **emery-wheel**, a wheel made of lead, or of wood covered with leather, coated with emery, and used for polishing.

1845 *Lowell* (Mass.) *Offering* V. 200 The strenuous application..soon taught me the value of an *emery-bag. **1893** 'MARK TWAIN' in *Century Mag.* Dec. 237/2 They [the slaves] would smouch provisions..or a brass thimble,..or an emery-bag. **1905** *Daily Chron.* 6 Apr. 4/7 A minority of Englishwomen who chafed against their educational inequalities, who loathed their emery-bag destiny. **1725** in *N. & Q.* (1942) CLXXXII. 76/2 (*London shop-sign*) Sieve & *emery board. Robert Bacon, wire sieve maker. **1889** *Cent. Dict.*, *Emery-board*, cardboard-pulp mixed with emery-dust and cast in cakes. **1907** *Yesterday's Shopping* (1969) 538/2 Emery Boards—pkt 0/6. **1938** D. DU MAURIER *Rebecca* vi. 63 He took an emery board out of his pocket and began filing his nails. **1968** P. GEDDES *High Game* i. 12 She had taken an emery board from her handbag. **1853** URE *Dict. Arts* (ed. 4) I. 644 *Emery-cake consists of emery mixed with a little beeswax. **1873** *Young Englishwoman* Feb. 94/1 This natty little *emery cushion is composed of grey leather..filled with emery. **1937** A. THIRKELL *Summer Half* ix. 241 Enchanting odds and ends, such as strawberry emery cushions and ivory stilettoes. **1884** F. BRITTEN *Watch & Clockm.* 101 *Emery File..a solid stick of Emery used as a file. *a* **1884** KNIGHT *Dict. Mech.* Suppl. 312/1 *Emery grinding machine. **1772** *Phil. Trans.* LXII. 360 The stem.. made very smooth with *Emery paper. **1812** *Examiner* 28 Dec. 824/2 Blacking and emery-paper manufacturers. **18..** *Oxford Bible Helps* 126 The corundum..which when ground is known to us as *emery powder. **1885** MRS. RIDDELL *Mitre Court* I. iv. 86 She had scrubbed, blackleaded..and *emery-powdered for that gentleman. **1879** *Cassell's Techn. Educ.* IV. 274/1 An *emery roller is geared upon the..main cylinder. **1883** *Encycl. Brit.* XV. 157/1 Emery wheels are now mounted for use in a great many different ways,—either on slide-rests as turning tools, in emery planers and *emery shaping machines [etc.]. **1884** F. BRITTEN *Watch & Clockm.* 101 *Emery stick..a stick of wood round which Emery paper is glued. **1610** W. FOLKINGHAM *Art of Survey* I. iii. 5 *Emeril-stones. **1765** BOWLES in *Phil. Trans.* LVI. 231 Great blocks of emery-stone. **1864** RAWLINSON *Anc. Mon.* II. vii. 187 The shamir, or emery-stone. **1873** J. RICHARDS *Wood-working Factories* 58 Grindstones, *emery wheels, buffing wheels.

emery (ˈɛmərɪ), *v.* [f. prec. sb.] *trans.* To rub or polish with emery; to coat with emery.

Hence **ˈemeried** *ppl. a.*

1844 *N. Brit. Rev.* II. 192 An emeried wheel. **1865** *Intell. Observ.* No. 38. 123 An emeried glass-plate.

emerylite (ˈɛmərɪlaɪt). *Min.* [f. EMERY *sb.* + -LITE.] A silicate of calcium and aluminium, occurring in trimetric hemihedral crystals, with a monoclinic aspect; = MARGARITE.

1849 J. L. SMITH in *Amer. Jrnl. Sc.* Ser. II. VII. 285, I have decided to call it Emerylite.

‖**emesis** (ˈɛmɪsɪs). *Path.* [Gr. ἔμεσις, f. ἐμέ-ειν to vomit.] The action of vomiting.

1875 H. WOOD *Therap.* (1879) 426 Emesis is the result of a very complicated series of actions.

†**emethen,** *adv. Obs. rare.* Also 4 **emethend.** [a. ON. *á meðan* (*á* = ON; *meðan* 'whilst', related to MID).] In the mean time.

a **1300** *Cursor M.* 5118 He..leues me beniamyn emeþen. *Ibid.* 26928 It es stikand eure emeþend.

emetia (ɪˈmiːtɪə). *Chem.* [f. Gr. ἐμετ-ος vomiting + -IA.] = EMETINE.

1830 LINDLEY *Nat. Syst. Bot.* 205 Emetia is found in Ipecacuanha. **1875** H. WOOD *Therap.* (1879) 432 There is no proof that emetia ever causes vaso-motor spasm.

emetic (ɪˈmɛtɪk), *a.* and *sb.* Also 7–8 **emetick,** (7 **hemettick**). [ad. Gr. ἐμετικ-ός provoking vomiting, f. ἐμέ-ειν to vomit.] **A.** *adj.*

1. Having power to produce vomiting. Also *fig.* sickening, mawkish.

1670 W. SIMPSON *Hydrol. Ess.* 47 Why these should not be Emetick. **1770** R. BAKER *Remarks Eng. Lang.* (1779) 8 Richardson..in his emetic history of Pamela. **1796** MORSE *Amer. Geog.* I. 460 The waters when drank, operate..as emetic. **1838** T. THOMSON *Chem. Org. Bodies* 74 It possesses emetic qualities.

2. In phraseological combinations: **emetic cup, goblet** (cf. ANTIMONIAL *a.* 1); **emetic root,** *Euphorbia corollata*; **emetic tartar,** (now usually) **tartar-emetic** [mod.L. *tartarus emeticus*], potassio-antimonious tartrate, $C_4H_4(NH_4)(SbO)O_6\cdot\frac{1}{2}H_2O$; **emetic weed,** *Lobelia inflata*; **emetic wine** = *antimonial wine.*

1679 tr. *Apol. Mdm. Manchini* 14 The Hemettick Wine.. quickly brought her to her Grave. **1789** A. CRAWFORD in *Med. Commun.* II. 305 A quarter of a grain of emetic tartar. **1720** *Lond. Gaz.* No. 5884/1 Emetick Wine. **1823** J. BADCOCK *Dom. Amusem.* 108 Emetic Tartar..ought to be employed pure. **1877** WATTS *Dict. Chem.* V. 685 A compound of tartar-emetic and cream of tartar.

B. *sb.* A medicine that excites vomiting.

1657 G. STARKEY *Helmont's Vind.* 194 Vomitories..they likewise call by a Greek name, Emeticks. **1788** LD. AUCKLAND *Diary* in *Corr.* (1861) II. 94 To take an emetic together. **1819** BYRON *Juan* II. xxi, The sea acted as a strong

emetic. **1875** H. Wood *Therap.* (1879) 426 Emetics are.. employed..for the purpose of producing..vomiting. *transf.* **1823** Byron *Juan* VIII. xii, Three hundred cannon threw up their emetic.

emetical (ɪˈmɛtɪkəl), *a.* [f. prec. + -AL^1.] = EMETIC *a. lit.* and *fig.*

1669 *Phil. Trans.* IV. 1131 A greater proportion of Salt.. would make it..Emetical. **1825** Ld. Cockburn *Mem.* i. 39 The emetical nature of the stuff that was swallowed. **1842** *Blackw. Mag.* LI. 22 It is nauseous and emetical to be told that our fellow-countrymen starve outside our gates.

emetically (ɪˈmɛtɪkəlɪ), *adv. rare.* [f. EMETICAL *a.* + -LY.] In the manner of an emetic.

1860 Dickens *Uncomm. Trav.* xvii, Sneaking Calais, prone behind its bar, invites emetically to despair.

emetine (ˈɛmɪtaɪn). *Chem.* Also (*obs.*) emetin, emetina. [f. Gr. ἔμετ-ος vomiting + -INE.] An alkaloid obtained from the root of *Cephaëlis ipecacuanha.*

1819 Children *Chem. Anal.* 292 Emetin is obtained from ipecacuanha. **1838** T. Thomson *Chem. Org. Bodies* 262 Emetina..was detected, in 1817..in ipecacuanha. **1876** Harley *Mat. Med.* 721 It resembles..emetine.

emeto-cathartic (ˌɛmɪtəʊkəˈθɑːtɪk), *sb.* and *a. Med.* [f. Gr. ἔμετο-ς vomiting + καθαρτικός purgative.]

A. *adj.* Having power to cause both purging and vomiting. **B.** *sb.* A substance having this power.

1879 *Syd. Soc. Lex.* s.v. *Ailanthus,* These preparations act as emetocathartics, as well as tæniafuges.

emetology (ɛmɪˈtɒlədʒɪ). *Med.* [f. Gr. ἔμετο-ς vomiting + -LOGY.] 'The doctrine of, or a treatise of, vomiting and emetics' (*Syd. Soc. Lex.*).

1847 in Craig; and in mod. Dicts.

emeu, obs. f. EMU.

émeute (emøt). [Fr.: f. *émouvoir* to agitate, set in motion.] A popular rising or disturbance.

1782 G. Selwyn *Let.* 1 Mar. in *15th Rep. Hist. MSS. Comm.* App. VI. 586 He was so candid to me as to own that from the beginning of this *émeute* he could not perceive in me the least expression of fear. **1862** H. W. Bellew *Mission Afghanistan* 430 These feuds and emeutes are of daily occurrence. **1886** *Manch. Exam.* 7 Jan. 5/1 That movement might be supported by an emeute in the town.

emfiteutic: see EMPHYTEUTIC.

†**em'forth,** *adv.* and *prep. Obs.* Also 4 evene forth. [f. *em,* EVEN *adv.* + FORTH.]

A. *adv.* Equally.

1377 Langl. *P. Pl.* B. XIII. 142 Louye..þine enemye.. euene forth with þi-selue. **1430** Lydg. *Chron. Troy* IV. xxxv, Who shall emforth and more be suer.

B. *prep.*

1. According to; in proportion to.

c **1314** *Guy Warw.* (A.) 6093 Amis emforþ his miȝt Confort him boþ day and niȝt. *c* **1385** Chaucer *L.G.W.* 2128 *Ariadne,* To save a gentyl man emforth hire myght. **1393** Langl. *P. Pl.* C. XVII. 222 Beatus, seith seynt bernard qui scripturas legit..emforth his power.

2. Equally with.

c **1400** *Solomon's Bk. Wisdom* 33 þi trewe frende emforþ thyself þou miȝth telle þi þouȝth.

-emia, var. -ÆMIA.

emic (ˈiːmɪk), *a.* [f. PHON)EMIC *a.*] (See quot. 1954.) Cf. ETIC *a.*

1954 K. L. Pike *Lang. in Rel. Human Behavior* I. ii. 8/1 In contrast to the etic approach an *emic* one is in essence valid for only one language (or one culture) at a time..; it is an attempt to discover and to describe the pattern of that particular language or culture in reference to the way in which the various elements of that culture are related to each other in the functioning of that particular pattern, rather than an attempt to describe them in reference to a general classification derived in advance of the study of that particular culture. **1969** [see ETIC *a.*]. **1970** *Language* XLVI. 78 An underbar is sometimes used to point up the correspondences between emic and etic transcriptions.

†**'emicant,** *a. Obs. rare*$^{-1}$. [ad. L. *ēmicānt-em,* pr. pple. of *ēmicā-re*: see next.] That darts or flashes forth.

1712 Blackmore *Creation* 354 Thou almighty vigour.. Which emicant did this and that way dart.

†**'emicate,** *v. Obs. rare.* [f. L. *ēmicāt-* ppl. stem of *ēmicā-re* to spring forth, flash out.] *intr.* To spring forth, appear. Also *fig.*

1657 Tomlinson *Renou's Disp.* 306 In whose summity little purpureous flowers emicate. **1708** Motteux *Rabelais* v. xxii, The studious Cupidity, that so demonstratively emicates at your external Organs.

†**emi'cation.** *Obs. rare.* [ad. L. *ēmicātiōn-em,* n. of action f. as prec.]

1. 'Sparkling: flying off in small particles, as sprightly liquors' (J.).

1646 Sir T. Browne *Pseud. Ep.* II. v. 90 Iron in Aqua fortis will fall into ebullition, with noise and emication. **1775** in Ash. **1847** in Craig; and in mod. Dicts.

2. The action of shining forth. In quot. *fig.*

1633 T. Adams *Exp. 2 Pet.* i. 19 Christ hath..divers names of light given him, according to the different degrees of his emication. **1656** in Blount *Glossogr.* **1721–1800** in Bailey.

emicatious (ɛmɪˈkeɪʃəs), *a. nonce-wd.* [f. EMICATI-ON + -OUS.] That shines or glitters.

1819 H. Busk *Vestriad* v. 473 Wood..Smooth, emicatious, free from knot or joint.

[†**'emich, 'emych.** A misspelling of EUNUCH (occurring several times in the work cited).

1491 Caxton *Vitas Patr.* (W. de Worde) I. clviii. (1495) 161 a/2 Emyches..men that lacke their membres of mankinde. *Ibid.* 163 a/1 Emiches.]

emiction (ɪˈmɪkʃən). *Phys.* [n. of action f. *ēmict-* ppl. stem of late L. *ēmingĕre,* f. *ē* out + *mingĕre* to make water.]

1. The action of voiding the urine.

1847 in Craig; and in mod. Dicts.

2. *concr.* Urine; that which is voided by the urinary passages.

1666 G. Harvey *Morb. Angl.* (J.), Gravel and stone.. effuse the blood apparent in a sanguine emiction. **1775** in Ash. **1847** in Craig; and in mod. Dicts.

emictory (ɪˈmɪktərɪ), *a.* and *sb. Med.* [f. as prec.: see -ORY.] **A.** *adj.* That has diuretic properties. **B.** *sb.* A diuretic; a medicine that promotes the discharge of urine.

In mod. Dicts.

emid, obs. var. of AMID. [The *e-* may perh. represent *in* rather than *on.*]

a **1300** *Cursor M.* 4252 (Cott.) In all..drightin was him emid. *Ibid.* 6612 þai fand bot wormes creuland emid.

emidward, var. form of AMIDWARD, *prep. Obs.*

a **1300** *Cursor M.* 16404 Vp he ras and wess his hend emidward þat folk bliue.

†**emigrane.** *Obs.* [ad. med.L. *ēmigrāneus,* L. *hēmicrānius* (*dolor*): see MIGRAINE.] = MIGRAINE.

1483 *Cath. Angl.* 114 þe Emygrane, *emigraneus.*

emigrant (ˈɛmɪɡrənt), *sb.* and *a.* [ad. L. *ēmigrānt-em,* pr. pple. of *ēmigrā-re*: see EMIGRATE.]

A. *sb.* **a.** One who removes from his own land to settle (permanently) in another. Freq. *attrib.* in sense 'of, pertaining to, or used by emigrants', as ***emigrant car, road, ship, trail.***

1754 (*title*), A Memorial of the Case of the German Emigrants settled in..Pensilvania. **1774** Warton *Hist. Eng. Poetry* I. Introd. 27 In these expeditions the northern emigrants were..attended by their poets. **1818** Cobbett *Resid. U.S.* (1822) 302, I greatly doubt of its being..of any benefit to the emigrants themselves. **1839** Thirlwall *Greece* II. xii. 82 The emigrants were headed by chiefs who claimed descent from Agamemnon. **1856** Emerson *Eng. Traits,* Wks. (Bohn) II. 100 The noise of embarking emigrants.

attrib. **1842** *Amer. Almanac* (Boston) 321 The emigrant ship called the Governor Fenner..comes in collision with the Nottingham Steamer. **1843** *Merchant's Mag.* XVIII. 540, 20 eight-wheeled emigrant,..and 4 eight-wheeled mail and baggage cars. **1845** J. C. Frémont *Exped.* 107 The usual emigrant road to the mountains. *Ibid.* 179, I had determined to leave the emigrant trail. **1850** Dickens *Dav. Copp.* lv. 556 The time drawing on rapidly for the sailing of the emigrant-ship, my good old nurse..came up to London. **1855** *Times* 9 July 10/5 Wreck of the Emigrant ship Lochmaben Castle. **1858** *Penn. Rail Road Annual Rep.* 14 The rolling stock.. consisted..of 31 Emigrant Cars. **1883** E. W. Nye *Baled Hay* 56 The tourists..got them onto the emigrant train. **1895** *Rat Portage* [Kenora] *News* (Ont.) 5 Apr. 2/2 A special train of six emigrant cars passed through here about five o'clock this morning from the east. **1942** M. Sandoz *Crazy Horse* 13 Many..left their bones for the wolves along the emigrant road.

b. *spec.* One of the French Royalists who fled at the time of the Revolution; = EMIGRÉ I.

1792 Gibbon *Misc. Wks.* (1814) I. 368 The deplorable state of the French emigrants. **1812** Amyot *Windham's Life* I. 39 An expedition, composed of Emigrants, proceeded against Quiberon. **1860** L. Harcourt *Diaries G. Rose* I. 162 The Emperor had insisted that the Emigrants should make no attempt to disturb the public tranquillity.

B. *adj.* That emigrates or leaves his own land for another. Also (of birds), migratory.

1794 Mathias *Purs. Lit.* (1798) 195 Emigrant Catholick priests. **1796** E. Darwin *Zoon.* I. 233 The same birds are emigrant from some countries and not so from others.

†**e'migrate,** *a.* [ad. L. *ēmigrātus,* pa. pple. of *ēmigrāre*: see next and -ATE.] That has migrated (from the body).

1654 Gayton *Pleas. Notes* 226 Let our souls emigrate meet.

emigrate (ˈɛmɪɡreɪt), *v.* [f. L. *ēmigrāt-* ppl. stem of *ēmigrā-re,* f. *ē* out + *migrā-re* to MIGRATE.]

1. *intr.* To remove out of a country for the purpose of settling in another.

1778 *Conversation* in Boswell *Johnson* lxii. (1848) 574 They don't emigrate, till they could earn their livelihood.. at home. **1782** Pownall *Stud. Antiq.* 60 (T.) The surplus parts of this plethorick [*printed* phletorick] body must emigrate. **1833** Wade *Middle & Working Classes* (1835) 342 It is only the..redundant portion of the community that ought to emigrate. **1881** W. Bence Jones in *Macm. Mag.* XLIV. 137 In 1880, 96,000 persons emigrated from Ireland.

b. In wider sense: To remove from one place of abode to another. *rare.*

1841 W. Spalding *Italy & It. Isl.* III. 352 The mountaineers..emigrate during the summer to the Tuscan coast.

2. *trans.* To cause or assist to emigrate; to send out to settle in a foreign country.

1870 C. B. Clarke in *Macm. Mag.* Nov. 51/2 Pauper children..I would emigrate. **1886** Miss Rye in *Pall Mall G.* 20 Apr. 2 It is now twenty-five years since I first began to emigrate women.

'emigrated, *ppl. a.* [f. prec. + -ED^1.] That has left his native land to settle in another.

1794 *Hist.* in *Ann. Reg.* 65 Their emigrated countrymen in the Spanish service. **1809** Pinkney *Trav. France* 57 The emigrated proprietor is not..without a chance of restitution. **1863** Blyth *Hist. Rec. Fincham* 168 Our emigrated countrymen in the colonies.

emigrating (ˈɛmɪɡreɪtɪŋ), *ppl. a.* [f. as prec. + -ING^2.] That emigrates.

1812 *Examiner* 9 Nov. 710/2 Many emigrating inhabitants. **1869** *Daily News* 12 June, What was best in your emigrating population.

†**b.** = MIGRATORY. *Obs. rare.*

1792 A. Young *Trav. France* 289 The mountains..are covered with good grass, that feeds a million of emigrating sheep.

emigration (ɛmɪˈɡreɪʃən). [ad. L. *ēmigrātiōn-em,* n. of action f. *ēmigrā-re* to EMIGRATE. (Of earlier occurrence than the vb.)]

1. *gen.* The action of migrating or departing out of a particular place or set of surroundings. In early examples often applied to the departure of the soul from the body, either *lit.* by death, or *fig.* with reference to ecstatic rapture.

1650 Bp. Hall *Balm Gil.* (R.), A scorching triall (upon the emigration) in flames little inferiour..to those of hell. **1656** More *Antid. Ath.* III. ix. (1712) 171 The Emigration of humane Souls from the bodies by Ecstasy. **1678** Jer. Taylor *Fun. Serm.* 250 Frequent Aspirations and Emigrations of his Soul after God. **1755** *Phil. Trans.* XLIX. 175 There is an emigration of a great number from hence to sea. **1794** G. Adams *Nat. & Exp. Philos.* IV. li. 414 Successive emigrations [of air-bubbles] towards the upper parts of the tube. **1796** H. Hunter tr. *St. Pierre's Stud. Nat.* (1799) II. Introd. 57 A new confirmation of the vegetable harmonies of Nature founded on the emigration of plants.

†**b.** *transf. Obs.*

1649 Jer. Taylor *Gt. Exemp.* Exhort. §12 Jesus had some ..acts of emigration beyond the lines of his even and ordinary conversation.

2. *esp.* The departure of persons from one country, usually their native land, to settle permanently in another. Also *attrib.,* as in ***emigration-agent.***

1677 Hale *Prim. Orig. Man.* 240 (R.) Plethory hath many times occasioned emigrations. **1768–71** A. Young *Farmer's Lett. to People* 198 It highly behoves us to stop immediately all further emigrations. **1791** Newte *Tour Eng. & Scot.* 125 Those melancholy emigrations..from the Islands..of Scotland. **1833** Wade *Middle & Working Classes* (1835) 106 The practicability of emigration as a means of relief. **1867** Buckle *Civilis.* (1873) III. i. 9 An overflow which in civilised times is an emigration, is in barbarous times an invasion.

3. The whole body of persons who emigrate.

1863 Bright *Sp. Amer.* 16 June, Of all the emigration from this country..a mere trifle went south.

emigrational (ɛmɪˈɡreɪʃənəl), *a. rare.* [f. prec. + -AL^1.] Of or pertaining to EMIGRATION.

1885 Ld. Rosebery in *Pall Mall G.* 26 Mar. 6/2 Twenty-five emigrational agencies in London.

emigrationist (ɛmɪˈɡreɪʃənɪst). [f. as prec. + -IST.] One who advocates emigration.

emigrator (ˈɛmɪɡreɪtə(r)). *rare.* [a. L. **ēmigrātor,* agent-n. f. *ēmigrā-re*: see EMIGRATE *v.*] = EMIGRANT.

1837 Lytton *Athens* I. 242 In the average equality of the emigrators were the seeds of a new constitution.

emigratory (ˈɛmɪɡreɪtərɪ), *a.* [f. L. *ēmigrāt-* ppl. stem of *ēmigrāre* + -ORY: see EMIGRATE *v.* Cf. *migratory.*]

1. Of animals: = MIGRATORY. *rare.*

1839 *Proc. Berw. Nat. Club* I. VII. 189 The great body of this emigratory species..moved southwards.

2. Occupied in emigrating; pertaining to emigration.

1854 H. Miller *Footpr. Creat.* xii. (1874) 222 Records of an emigratory process. **1865** W. G. Palgrave *Arabia* I. 288 A large emigratory detachment.

‖**emigré.** Also émigré. [Fr.: pa. pple. of *émigrer* to EMIGRATE.] **1.** A Frenchman who has left his country for another; *esp.* one of those Royalists who fled at the French Revolution.

1792 Gibbon *Misc. Wks.* (1814) I. 363 The Geneva emigrés..are hastening to their homes. **18..** T. Archer *Sword & Shuttle* i, Our emigrés..had settled in Spitalfields.

2. *transf.* An emigrant of any nationality, esp. a political exile.

1955 *Times* 3 May 5/5 Czechoslovakian *émigrés,* who were disaffected towards the then régime in Czechoslovakia. **1965** *New Statesman* 30 Apr. 686/2 Dusty attics in Munich and Berlin inhabited in and around 1920 by displaced Balts and seedy Russian émigrés.

3. *attrib.* and *Comb.,* as ***emigré artist, -club,*** etc.

1954 KOESTLER *Invisible Writing* xxii. 247 They read their emigré papers, frequented their emigré-clubs and cafés. **1956** *Ann Reg. 1955* 237 To persuade émigré Poles to return. **1962** *Times* 12 Oct. 15/7 When they [*sc.* Australian painters] have become *émigré* artists. **1964** V. NABOKOV *Defence* xiv. 222 Paying no attention to the speeches she heard at émigré political meetings.

†**e'mike**, *v. Obs. rare*⁻¹. [ad. L. *ēmic-āre*: see EMICATE *v.*] *intr.* To spring forth, appear.

1657 TOMLINSON *Renou's Disp.* 349 Two lesser nerves emike in its leafes.

Emilian (ɪ'mɪlɪən), *a.* and *sb.* Also 8–9 **Æmilian**. [f. *Emilia* (see below) + -AN.] **A.** *adj.* Of or pertaining to Emilia, a district of northern Italy (now part of the region of Emilia-Romagna), its inhabitants, or their dialect. **B.** *sb.* **1.** A native or inhabitant of Emilia. **2.** The dialect of Italian spoken in Emilia.

1660 E. WARCUPP tr. *Schottus' Italy* I. 82 At Piacenza begins the Emilian Way. **1776** GIBBON *Decl. & F.* I. xiv. 424 From Milan to Rome, the Æmilian and Flaminian highways opened an easy march of about four hundred miles. **1878** *Encycl. Brit.* VIII. 701/1 The dialects..of Upper Italy, including Genoese, Piedmontese, Venetian, Æmilian, and Lombard. **1880** *Ibid.* XIII. 435/1 The side of the Apennines, where the great Emilian Way..preserves an unbroken straight line from Rimini to Piacenza. *Ibid.* 493/1 Characteristic of the Piedmontese, the Lombard, and the Emilian is the continual elision of the unaccented final vowels. *Ibid.*, Gallo-Italian and more specially Emilian characteristics. **1893** G. A. GREENE *Ital. Lyrists* p. xxx, The Tuscans, Emilians, and Romans must be classed together. **1904** E. G. GARDNER *Dukes & Poets in Ferrara* i. 10 Transfigured in the glow of an Emilian sunset. **1936** A. W. CLAPHAM *Romanesque Archit.* iii. 41 It is..in the internal elevation that these Emilian churches differ most markedly from those of Lombardy. **1958** S. RUNCIMAN *Sicilian Vespers* vi. 88 He would have preferred to..bring the army over the Ligurian Alps, avoiding the lands of the Lombard and Emilian cities. *Ibid.* xiv. 233 On 1 May [1282] Guy of Montefeltro with a number of Tuscan and Emilian Ghibellines had ambushed the papal governor of Romagna.

‖**émincé** (emɛ̃se). Also **emincé**. [Fr.] (See quot. 1961.)

1907 G. A. ESCOFFIER *Guide to Mod. Cookery* xv. 446 An unalterable principle governs the preparation of emincés and hashes, which is that the meats constituting these dishes should never boil if it be desired that they be not hard. **1947** L. P. DE GOUY *Gold Cookery Bk.* viii. 515 (*heading*) Emincé of Chicken Belmont. **1961** *Larousse Gastronomique* 399/2 *Émincé*, a dish made with left-over roast or braised meat. The meat, thinly sliced, is put in an ovenware dish and covered with some sauce or other.

eminence ('ɛmɪnəns). [ad. L. *ēminentia*, f. *ēminēnt-em* EMINENT.]

I. In physical senses.

1. †**a.** Height, altitude, degree of elevation (*obs.*). **b.** A lofty or elevated position.

1658 EVELYN *Fr. Gard.* (1675) 278 Upon this water..pour sweet butter melted, to the eminence of two fingers. *c* **1800** K. WHITE *Poet. Wks.* (1837) 136 Draw the fix'd stars from their eminence. **1822** IMISON *Sc. & Art* I. 222 If a lighted candle be set..on an eminence.

†**2. a.** A prominence, protuberance. Chiefly in *Anat.* **b.** *Bot.* (See quot. 1688.) *Obs.*

1615 CROOKE *Body of Man* 438 Wherein the eminence.. shooting from the vpper part of the forehead is wanting. **1667** *Phil. Trans.* II. 493 The same Author hath discovered in it [the Tongue] many little Eminences. **1688** R. HOLME *Armoury* II. 115/1 Eminence, or Woolly Eminence, is the outward skin or husk that covers round roots, as in Onions, Tulipa's. **1743** tr. *Heister's Surg.* 168 There is a certain Eminence in this Edge of the Acetabulum.

3. An elevation on the earth's surface; a rising ground, hill. Also *fig.*

1670 COTTON *Espernon* III. XI. 567 He caus'd two good Forts to be trac'd out..upon two Eminences. **1748** ANSON *Voy.* III. v. (ed. 4) 452 There is a battery..on an eminence. **1797** BEWICK *Brit. Birds* (1847) I. 7 The other, perched on an eminence, watches the flight of the prey. **1814** WORDSW. *Excursion* IX. 53 We..speak..of Age As of a final Eminence. **1833** SIR J. HERSCHEL *Astron.* i. §19 (1858) 17 If we ascend a high eminence on a plain. **1844** LINGARD *Anglo-Sax. Ch.* (1858) I. i. 5 He was beheaded on a small eminence without the walls.

II. In non-material senses.

4. Distinguished superiority, elevated rank as compared with others. (Sometimes with *fig.* notion of 1.) **a.** in social or official position, wealth, or power.

1603 SHAKS. *Meas. for M.* I. ii. 168 Whether the Tirranny be in his Eminence that fills it vp. **1613** —— *Hen. VIII*, II. iii. 29 A Womans heart, which euer yet affected Eminence, Wealth, Soueraignty. *a* **1652** BROME *Queene's Exchange* I. i. (1657) 458 Your self A Queen of so great eminence. **1667** MILTON *P.L.* II. 6 Satan by merit rais'd to that bad eminence. **1767** *Lett. Junius* xxiii. 105 The eminence of your station gave you a commanding prospect of your duty. **1848** MACAULAY *Hist. Eng.* I. 165 No man could hope to rise to eminence and command but by their favour.

b. in reputation, intellectual or moral attainment, or the possession of any quality, good or (sometimes) bad.

1647 CLARENDON *Hist. Reb.* I. I. 36 His Son made a notable progress, by an early eminence in Practice and Learning. **1750** JOHNSON *Rambler* No. 157 ¶4 A young man that gave..hopes of future eminence. **1800** *Med. Jrnl.* IV. 406 Several surgeons of eminence. **1844** EMERSON *Nature, Young American* Wks. (Bohn) II. 307 No man of letters, be his eminence what it may, is received into the best society. **1868** M. PATTISON *Academ. Org.* 112 Eminence in science should be made the one statutable condition [for a headship]. **1870** HAWTHORNE *Eng. Note-bks.* (1879) II. 27 The poorer classes..excel..in the bad eminence of filth.

†**c.** Mastery, the 'upper hand'. Phrase ***to have the eminence of***: to have the advantage of. *Obs.*

1606 SHAKS. *Tr. & Cr.* II. iii. 266 You should not haue the eminence of him. **1613** HEYWOOD *Silver Age* III. i. Wks. (1874) 131 Long did we tugge For eminence.

†**d.** ***spirit of eminence***: pride, ambition. *Obs. rare.*

1597 DANIEL *Civ. Wares* VI. xxxiii, Devotion..abates the spirit of eminence.

5. a. As a title of honour, now borne only by Cardinals. (See quot. 1836.)

1653 CROMWELL *to Cdl. Mazarin* (Carlyle) V. App. No. 27 It's surprise to me that your Eminence should take notice of a person so inconsiderable as myself. **1717** BERKELEY *Tour in Italy* Wks. 1871 IV. 514 His eminence..put on his cardinal's square cap. **1836** *Penny Cycl.* VI. 291/1 Urban VIII, in 1630, gave to the cardinals the title of Eminence, which was shared with them by the grand master of the order of Malta, and the ecclesiastical electors of the German or Roman empire only. **1884** *Weekly Reg.* 11 Oct. 451/2 One word, his Eminence said he would add, concerning the Rosary.

b. Used occas. as a designation of an important person, an authority. Cf. next.

1935 A. HUXLEY *Let.* 5 June (1969) 396 Individual eminences are all right; but their importance, in this context, is greatly magnified if they represent professional organizations. **1966** M. R. D. FOOT *SOE in France* ii. 34 The eminences of various kinds consigned to SOE as a travel agent.

†**6.** Acknowledgement of superiority, homage.

1605 SHAKS. *Macb.* III. ii. 31 Present him Eminence, both with Eye and Tongue.

†**7.** An eminent quality, an excellence; a distinction, honour. *Obs.*

1609 *Man in Moone* (1849) 16 You assume it an eminence, to be rarely arrayed. **1655** FULLER *Ch. Hist.* II. 128 His Eminences were Painting and Graving. *Ibid.* IX. 101 So severall eminences met in this worthy man. **1659** PEARSON *Creed* (1839) 31 There must be therefore some great eminence in the object worshipped.

†**8. a.** Eminent degree or measure. *Obs.*

1651 HOBBES *Leviath.* I. x. 41 Naturall Power, is the eminence of the Faculties of Body, or Mind. **1710** STEELE *Tatler* No. 206 ¶2 Men of our Acquaintance, who had no one Quality in any Eminence.

b. *Gram.* (See quot.)

1824 L. MURRAY *Eng. Gram.* i. 91 [The superlative formed with *very*] is called..the superlative of eminence, to distinguish it from the other superlative.

c. Phrase, ***by (way of) eminence***: in an eminent or especial sense, *par excellence*. (In early examples sometimes in sense 7: by way of distinction.) *rare* in mod. use.

1621–31 LAUD *Sev. Serm.* (1847) 66 Now Jerusalem is by way of singular eminence called here 'a city compacted together'. **1765** BLACKSTONE *Comm.* I. 229 The principal council..is generally called, by way of eminence, the council. **1829** I. TAYLOR *Enthus.* ix. 253 This by eminence is the bright omen of the times. **1883** F. A. WALKER *Pol. Econ.* 399 One kind of money..may be called by eminence political money.

9. The highest development, the 'flower'.

1857 H. REED *Lect. Eng. Poets* i. 14 The portion of literature..which may be regarded as its eminence,—its Poetry.

‖**éminence grise** (eminɑ̃s griz). [F., = grey eminence: see EMINENCE 5.] A term originally applied to Père Joseph (1577–1638), the confidential agent of Cardinal Richelieu; now extended to describe one who wields real though not titular control.

1838 *Westm. Rev.* XXXI. 16 The attendants..left Richelieu alone with his celebrated secret agent, known by the soubriquet of *l'Eminence grise*—Father Joseph, the capuchin friar. **1937** *Times* 8 Apr. 18/2 (*headline*) Eminence grise. **1955** *Times* 2 May 11/1 Many Americans will no doubt find it strange that Mr. Menon,..whom they have come to regard as a sinister *éminence grise* standing between two countries, should choose to act as their ambassador. **1958** A. HOCKING *Epitaph for Nurse* i. 20 She was going to be the Eminence Grise, the power behind the throne.

'**eminency**. Also 7 **emminency**. [ad. L. *ēminentia*: see EMINENCE and -ENCY.]

I. In physical senses.

†**1.** Height; prominence, elevation above surrounding objects. *Obs. rare.*

1635 N. CARPENTER *Geog. Del.* II. vii. 105 The ordinary Eminency of the hight of the Earth aboue the Waters. **1657** AUSTEN *Fruit Trees* II. 137 Mighty hils and Mountaines in eminency. **1663** CHARLETON *Chorea Gigant.* 48 One..stone exceeding the rest in eminency.

†**2.** *concr.* A projection or prominence; a protuberance. *Obs.*

1668 CULPEPPER & COLE *Barthol. Anat.* III. ix. 148 Towards the Temples there grows a certain eminency. **1677** MOXON *Mech. Exerc.* (1703) 15 You do off the Eminencies or Risings. **1718** J. CHAMBERLAYNE *Relig. Philos.* (1730) I. x. §9 The Muscle..runs about the Eminency, like a Rope in a Pulley.

†**3.** An elevation on the earth's surface; a rising ground, hill. Also an elevated object. *Obs.*

1662 GERBIER *Princ.* 10 A Church or Steeple, or some other Eminency. **1703** MAUNDRELL *Journ. Jerus.* (1721) 68 Mount Calvary..is a small Eminency or Hill. **1737** WHISTON *Josephus Wars* VII. viii. §5 A certain eminency of the rock. **1748** ANSON *Voy.* II. xii. (ed. 4) 354 On the tops of some small eminencies there are several look-out towers.

II. In non-material senses.

†**4.** Distinguished superiority, elevation above the common standard in social position, wealth, power, reputation, or attainment, or in the possession of any special quality; = EMINENCE 4. *Obs.*

1628 EARLE *Microcosm.* lxi. 166 Men of parts and eminency. **1642** C. H. in Ellis *Orig. Lett.* II. 282 III. 302 We have lost..few of eminency. **1698** SIDNEY *Disc. Govt.* iii. §28 (1704) 351 Commoners, who in antiquity and eminency are no way inferior to the chief of the titular Nobility. **1727** DE FOE *Hist. Appar.* v. 48 This woman was a witch of some eminency.

†**b.** Of things, of places, towns, etc.: Importance. *Obs.*

1622 MISSELDEN *Free Trade* 6 To finde out a fit remedy is of high eminency. **1640** WILKINS *New Planet* vii. (1707) 217 There are but two places of any eminency, the Circumference and the Centre. **1651** tr. *Don Fenise* 296 We arrived at the doore of an house of eminency. **1673** *Vain Insolency Rome* 6 The first greatness of Rome was founded in the eminency of the City.

†**5.** As a title of honour, borne esp. by cardinals; = EMINENCE 5. *Obs.*

1655 MILTON *Lett. State* (1851) 331, I intreat your Eminency to give him entire Credit. **1670** G. H. *Hist. Cardinals* I. III. 72 Their Eminencies were all astonished at the Election.

†**6.** Acknowledgement of superiority, homage, deference; = EMINENCE 6. *Obs.*

1647 WARD *Simp. Cobler* (1843) 50 Equity is a due to People, as Eminency to Princes.

†**7.** That in which a person (or thing) excels or is remarkable; *esp.* in good sense, an excellence, special talent, honourable distinction. *Obs.*

1602 FULBECKE *Pandectes* 62 He hath beene accompted ignoble, who hath not beene..noted for some eminency. **1607** TOPSELL *Serpents* 595 Therefore it followeth unavoidably, that the eminency of their [serpents'] temperament is cold in the highest degree. *a* **1617** BAYNE *On Eph.* (1658) 51 This Adoption is called by the name of a dignity or eminency. *a* **1677** BARROW *Serm.* Wks. 1716 I. 298 Reason and discretion are the singular eminencies of men.

†**8.** Superiority in degree or measure; intensive magnitude. ***by (way of) eminency***: see EMINENCE 8 c. *Obs.*

1608 S. HIERON *Defence* III. 159 Some eminency of greatnes, power, or goodnes. **1622–62** HEYLIN *Cosmogr.* III. (1682) 51 Not only for distinctions sake, but in way of eminency. **1643** BURROUGHES *Exp. Hosea* ix. (1652) 307 The Sabbath is called an everlasting Covenant by way of eminency. **1651** *Abel Rediv. Luther* (1867) I. 38 The eminency of his good parts did more and more show themselves. **1703** MAUNDRELL *Journ. Jerus.* (1721) 24 The People of the Country call it..the Plain..by way of Eminency.

9. Prominence, or relative importance, in mental view.

1841–4 EMERSON *Ess. Art* Wks. (Bohn) I. 147 This rhetoric, or power to fix the momentary eminency of an object. **1873** M. ARNOLD *Lit. & Dogma* 367 Christian Churches do recommend the..secret of Jesus, though not.. in the right eminency.

¶**10.** Confused with IMMINENCY. Cf. EMINENT 6.

1680 *Life Edw. II* in *Select. fr. Harl. Misc.* (1793) 37 The Spencers..saw the eminency of their own dangers.

eminent ('ɛmɪnənt), *a.* [f. L. *ēminēnt-em*, pr. pple. of *ēminē-re* to project.]

I. In physical (and obvious metaphorical) senses.

1. High, towering above surrounding objects. Also *fig.* Now *poet.* or *arch.*

1588 ALLEN *Admon.* 22 Nero..deuised an eminent pillar. **1611** BIBLE *Ezek.* xvii. 22 Upon an high mountain and eminent. **1667** MILTON *P.L.* I. 587 He above the rest In shape and gesture proudly eminent Stood like a Towr. **1674** BREVINT *Saul at Endor* 363 Images..seated on the Eminentest Places of the Church. **1772–84** COOK *Voy.* (1790) IV. 1446 The eminent part..is the S.E. point. **1814** SOUTHEY *Roderick* XIV, Upon a stately war-horse eminent. *fig.* **1830** TENNYSON *Love & Death*, In the light of great eternity Life eminent creates the shade of death. **1851** MRS. BROWNING *Casa Guidi Windows* 87 The patriot's oath.. stands Among the oaths of perjurers, eminent.

b. In weaker sense: Projecting, prominent, protruding. Also *fig.*

1541 R. COPLAND *Guydon's Quest. Chirurg.*, A party of the orbytall, or emynent pomall. **1607** TOPSELL *Four-f. Beasts* (1673) 155 Females [elephants] carry..their Calves upon their snowts and long eminent teeth. **1644** BULWER *Chiron.* 67 The..Fingers..presented in an eminent posture. **1744** AKENSIDE *Pleas. Imag.* III. 407 The fairer [parts], eminent in light, advance. **1843** CARLYLE *Past & Pr.* (1858) 124 A very eminent nose. *fig.* **1870** LOWELL *Among my Bks.* Ser. II. (1873) 289 Some eminent verse lifts its long ridge above its tamer peers.

II. In non-material senses. (Formerly often with some notion of 1.)

2. Of persons: **a.** Exalted, dignified in rank or station.

1603 SHAKS. *Meas. for M.* IV. iv. 25 A deflowred maid, And by an eminent body. **1691** HARTCLIFFE *Virtues* 141 We may not lawfully be angry..with those in eminent Place. **1761** HUME *Hist. Eng.* III. liv. 175 The king was too eminent a magistrate to be trusted with discretionary power. **1786** BURKE *Art. W. Hastings* Wks. 1842 II. 140 A certain native person of distinction or eminent rajah.

b. Distinguished in character or attainments, or by success in any walk of life. (The use in bad sense is now *ironical*.)

1611 BIBLE *Job* xxii. 8 The honourable man [*marg.* eminent *or* accepted for countenance]. **1643** PRYNNE *Sov. Power Parl.* III. 66 These two eminentest Prophets..resist the Captaines, Souldiers, and unjust Executioners of their Princes. **1728** NEWTON *Chronol. Amended* i. 60 Eminent Musicians and Poets flourished in Greece. **1805** *Med. Jrnl.* XIV. 407 An eminent practitioner..entertains a different opinion. **1837** HT. MARTINEAU *Soc. Amer.* III. 5 Eminent cooks are paid 1200*l.* a-year. **1847** GROTE *Greece* II. xlvii. (1862) IV. 157 Thucydides..was eminent as a speaker.

c. ***Eminent Persons Group***, a group of Commonwealth politicians who visited South Africa in 1986 in order to investigate ways of ending the country's political unrest. Abbrev. *EPG* s.v. E. III.

1986 *Guardian* 5 Feb. 7/1 Sir Geoffrey won the support for the Commonwealth Eminent Persons Group of the EEC-Frontline States meeting. **1986** *Financial Times* 13 May 19/1 Pretoria sees the Eminent Persons Group as a useful channel of communication with the ANC and the international community. **1986** *Times* 20 May 1/7 The Commonwealth Eminent Persons Group (EPG), which is trying to mediate between Pretoria and the ANC, had left Lusaka..for Cape Town. **1987** *Financial Times* 10 June 10 The remark could equally have applied to..his contribution to the report of the Commonwealth Eminent Persons' Group on South Africa.

†**3.** Of things or places: Chief, principal, important; especially valuable. *Obs.*

1612 T. TAYLOR *Comm. Titus* i. 15 Their cheife and eminent inward parts are defiled. **1650** FULLER *Pisgah* II. v. 128 An eminent country in Idumea. **1676** ALLEN *Addr. Nonconf.* 176 Prayer..is an eminent part of Gods worship. **1677** MOXON *Mech. Exerc.* (1703) 130 If your Shop stands in an eminent Street. **1683** SALMON *Doron Med.* III. 644 It gives present ease, and is eminent against all..pains. **1748** HARTLEY *Observ. Man* I. ii. 218 These Muscles..drawing the Eye out on eminent Ocasions.

4. Of qualities: Remarkable in degree; †conspicuously displayed. Of actions, facts, phenomena: Signal, noteworthy (now chiefly in good sense).

c **1420** *Pallad. on Husb.* I. 90 The cok confesseth emynent cupide. **1454** in Ellis *Orig. Lett.* II. 38 I. 120 The emynent myscheve and ffynall destruccionne of the said Counte. **1594** HOOKER *Eccl. Pol.* I. xi. (1611) 34 After an eminent sort. **1655–60** STANLEY *Hist. Philos.* (1701) 5/2 There is an eminent place in Eusebius to prove this. **1657** G. STARKEY *Helmont's Vind.* 267 An eminent fright will take away.. Agues. **1677** FELTHAM *Resolves* I. xlv. Wks. (ed. 10) 72 His valor..is..eminent in his killing of the Bear and Lion. **1691** RAY *Creation* (1714) 159 A peculiar sort of voice..is.. eminent in Quails. *a* **1704** T. BROWN *Praise Drunkenn.* Poems (1730) I. 31 The god of wine..whose eminent perfection Drunkenness I intend to make the subject of.. discourse. **1709** STEELE *Tatler* No. 34 ⁋1 Mountebanks..do their most eminent Operations in Sight of the People. **1826** DISRAELI *Viv. Grey* III. i. 89 His success was eminent. **1862** LD. BROUGHAM *Brit. Const.* App. 453 The reputation justly acquired by his eminent services. **1869** GLADSTONE *Juv. Mundi* ii. 65 Their opponents..were..not Achaian in the same eminent sense.

b. *Crystallography.* (See quot.)

1831 BREWSTER *Optics* xxiii. 204 The plane of most eminent cleavage. **1860** TYNDALL *Glac.* I. §1. 3 One cleavage is much more perfect, or more eminent as it is sometimes called, than the rest.

5. Law. ***right of eminent domain***: see quots.

1738 *Hist. Crt. Excheq.* vi. 111 The King who had the eminent Dominion. **1853** WHARTON *Pa. Digest* 673 §3 The right of eminent domain, or inherent sovereign power gives the Legislature the control of private property for public use. **1880** BROWN *Law Dict.* s.v., Eminent domain is the ownership or *dominium* (domain) of an independent sovereign over the territories of his sovereignty, by virtue of which no other sovereign can exercise any jurisdiction therein. **1886** *Pall Mall G.* 14 July 5/1 The State exercising its right of eminent domain.

¶ **6.** Confused with IMMINENT (so freq. *eminens* in med.L. for *imminens*). *Obs.*

1600 HAKLUYT *Voy.* (1810) III. 377 The eminent dangers which euery houre we saw before our Eyes. **1612** WOODALL *Surg. Mate* Wks. (1653) 156 Let..your Patient be.. informed of the eminent danger of death. **1616** BRENT tr. *Sarpi's Hist. Council of Trent* (1676) 269 The actual and eminent departure of many Fathers. **1722** DE FOE *Plague* (1884) 94 The eminent Danger I had been in.

†**emi'nential**, *a. Math. Obs. rare.* [f. EMINENT *a.* + -IAL.] (See quot. 1796.)

1736 in BAILEY. **1751** in CHAMBERS. **1775** in ASH. **1796** HUTTON *Math. Dict.*, *Eminential equation*, a term used by some algebraists, in the investigation of the areas of curvilinear figures, for a kind of assumed equation that contains another equation eminently, the latter being a particular case of the former. **1847** in CRAIG; and in mod. Dicts.

Hence †**emi'nentially**, *Obs. rare*; = EMINENTLY 4.

1656 tr. *Th. White's Peripatetical Institutions* 328 This action, therefore, actuates the Creature with a certain indivisibility that eminentially contains divisibility.

eminently ('ɛmɪnəntlɪ), *adv.* [f. EMINENT *a.* + -LY².] In an eminent manner.

†**1.** On high; in a lofty or elevated position.

1620 VENNER *Via Recta* Introd. 5 Those houses..are somewhat eminently situated. **1675** OGILBY *Brit.* 10 A Bush ..eminently situate.

†**2.** Conspicuously, so as to attract the eye. *Obs.*

1610 GUILLIM *Heraldry* III. xii. (1660) 157 Their commander being so eminently clad. **1667** E. CHAMBERLAYNE *St. Gt. Brit.* I. III. viii. (1743) 191 In the middle of the Church is he or she eminently placed in the sight of all the people. **1677** HALE *Prim. Orig. Man.* I. iii. 89 The great Rocks in the Sea are..eminently visible to this day. **1774** JOHNSON in *Boswell* (1831) III. 147 The moon shone eminently bright.

3. In an eminent or especial degree; signally, notably.

1641 BP. J. HALL *Serm.* in *Rem. Wks.* (1660) II. 59 That all Nations should agree upon an universall cessation of armes ..it must needs be the Lords doing so much more eminently. **1746** M. TOMLINSON *Prot. Birthr.* 3 Nothing.. more Eminently distinguishes Man from the Brute Creation. **1817** W. BOSWELL in *Parl. Deb.* 805 Gentlemen who had eminently served their country. **1833** HT. MARTINEAU *Three Ages* iii. 105 Nowhere does virtue more eminently fail of its earthly recompense than in the church. **1851** CARLYLE *Sterling* II. iv. (1872) 118 A painter's eye..he ..eminently had.

4. *Philos.* and *Theol.* See quot. 1751.

In scholastic theology God is said to possess the excellences of human character not *formally* (i.e. according to their definition, which implies creature limitation) but *eminently* (L. *eminenter*), i.e. in a higher sense. In wider use, the word is nearly equivalent to *virtually*.

1640 FULLER *Joseph's Coat* (1867) 58 But, virtually and eminently..all his bones were broken, that is, contrited and grinded with grief and sorrow. *a* **1665** J. GOODWIN *Filled w. the Spirit* (1867) 211 The apostle..may be said eminently, though not formally, to have declared him [the Holy Ghost] to be God. **1691–8** NORRIS *Pract. Disc.* (1711) III. 15 Fire is Eminently and Potentially, though not Formally hot. **1751** CHAMBERS *Cycl.*, *Eminently*..in the schools, is used in contradistinction to *formally*..to denote that a thing possesses, or contains any other in a more perfect or higher manner than is required to a formal possesion thereof. **1845** J. H. NEWMAN *Ess. Develpm.* 323 A..university of sciences, containing all sciences either 'formally' or 'eminently'.

†**b.** *Math.* One equation is said to contain another eminently, when the latter is a particular case of the former. *Obs.*

1798 [see EMINENTIAL].

¶ †**5.** Of peril, danger: Imminently, urgently.

1646 H. LAWRENCE *Comm. Angells* Ep. Ded. 1 b, This warre..to which my leisure more eminently exposed me. **1670** G. H. *Hist. Cardinals* II. I. 114 Their ruine..I see most eminently..at hand.

†**'eminentness.** *Obs.*⁻⁰ [f. EMINENT *a.* + -NESS.] The state of being eminent.

1731–1800 in BAILEY.

†**'eminously,** *adv. Obs. rare*⁻¹. [f. L. *ēminus* at a distance + -OUS + -LY².] Remotely, distantly.

1657 TOMLINSON *Renou's Disp.* 303 Which [thistle down] eminously represents a running hare.

emir (ɛ'mɪə(r), 'iːmə(r)). Forms: 7 **emer, amir,** 7–9 **emeer,** 7– **emir.** [a. Arab. *amīr*, commander. See AMEER, ADMIRAL.]

1. A Saracen or Arab prince, or governor of a province; a military commander.

1632 LITHGOW *Trav.* (1682) pt. v. 195 An Emeer, or hereditary Prince. **1632** —— *Totall Discourse* 373 Having an Emeere of their owne, being subiect to none, but to his owne passions. **1686** *Lond. Gaz.* No. 2177/1 An Emir or Prince of the Arabs..has taken the Field with some Troops. **1781** GIBBON *Decl. & F.* III. lxiv. 616 The humble title of emir was no longer suitable to the Ottoman greatness. **1852** MISS YONGE *Cameos* (1877) I. xxiv. 185 Saladin..sent an emir to the camp with presents. **1848** LANE *Arab. Nts.* I. 87 The Emeers and Wezeers.

2. A title of honour borne by the descendants of Mohammed.

1625 PURCHAS *Pilgrimes* II. 1295 Mahomet's..kinsmen in greene Shashes, who are called Emers. **1688** *Lond. Gaz.* No. 2322/3, 56 Emirs..with green Shashes. **1708** KERSEY *Emir* (among the Turks) a Lord, especially any one descended from the false prophet Mahomet. **1721–1800** in BAILEY. **1813** BYRON *Giaour* xii, The foremost of the band is seen An Emir by his garb of green.

emirate (ɪ'mɪərət, 'ɛmɪrət). [f. EMIR + -ATE.] The jurisdiction or government of an emir.

1863 J. C. MORISON *St. Bernard* IV. i. 406 The Emirate of Mossul should be in the hands of a man of energy. **1883** *American* VI. 374 Whose adherence gave Abd-ur-Rahman-Khan the emirate.

†**e'miss,** *a. Obs. rare*⁻¹. In 7 **emisse.** [ad. L. *ēmiss-us*, pa. pple. of *ēmittĕ-re* to send forth, EMIT.] Emitted.

1647 H. MORE *Song of Soul* III. III. xxx, Rayes emisse From centrall Night.

emissary ('ɛmɪsərɪ), *sb.*¹ and *a.* [ad. L. *ēmissāri-us* adj., that is sent, also *absol.* an emissary, spy, f. *ēmiss-* ppl. stem of *ēmittĕre* to send out (see EMIT) + *-ārius*, -ARY¹.]

A. *sb.* **a.** A person sent on a mission to gain information, or to gain adherents to, or promote the interests of a cause. (Until recently used almost exclusively in bad sense, implying something odious in the object of the mission, or something underhand in its manner.) Also *fig.* Now freq. used without implication of odiousness or underhandedness.

In B. Jonson's *Staple of News* (see quot. 1625) the word is used app. as a novelty, and recurs constantly through the play as the official title of the agents employed by the imaginary 'office for the collection of news.'

1625 B. JONSON *Staple of N.* I. ii. (1631) 9 What are Emissaries? Men imploy'd outward, that are sent abroad To fetch in the commodity [news]. **1637–50** ROW *Hist. Kirk* (1842) 465 The Bishops purseivants, and others their emissaries. *c* **1650** DENHAM *Progr. Learn.* 126 Lucifer's.. faithful emissary, rose from hell To possess Peter's chair. **1665** GLANVILL *Sceps. Sci.* iv. §3 The *meatus*, or passages, through which those subtill emissaries [the 'Spirits'] are conveyed to the respective members. **1708** *Bickerstaff detected* in *Swift's Wks.* II. I. 168 Culprit aforesaid is a popish emissary. **1756** BURKE *Subl. & B.* I. §7 (1808) 134 Pain..is..an emissary of this king of terrours. **1810** WELLINGTON in Gurw. *Disp.* VII. 2, I am endeavouring to get this information by emissaries. **1841** D'ISRAELI *Amen. Lit.* (1867) 379 Burghley..had..emissaries to inform him of the ballads sung in the streets. **1876** GREEN *Short Hist.* vii. §6 (1882) 400 She viewed the Douay priests simply as political emissaries of the Papacy. **1968** J. A. W. BENNETT *Chaucer's Book of Fame* ii. 67 As Jove's emissary the bird speaks as though he has divined these limitations.

b. = SPY.

1676 in BULLOKAR. **1721–1800** in BAILEY.

†**c.** *attrib.* quasi-*adj. Obs.*

a **1637** B. JONSON *Lyrick Pieces* 8 (R.) Nor forth your window peepe, With your emissarie eye.

B. *adj.* That is sent forth.

†**1. a.** Emitted as an emanation. **b.** Sent forth on a mission (cf. A). **c.** In transl. L. *emissarius caper*, Levit. xvi. 8. = SCAPE-GOAT. *Obs. rare.*

1659 H. MORE *Immort. Soul* (1662) 121 Emissary atoms. **1688** —— *Para. Proph.* 399 Emissary Agents from the Roman See. **1688** —— *An Illustration* 311 The Rivers must be Emissary Powers of the said Kingdom. **1833** ROCK *Hierurg.* (1851) 55 The High-Priest..offered the emissary goat.

2. *Phys.* Of small vessels: Sent forth, branching out from a main trunk.

1831 R. KNOX *Cloquet's Anat.* 741 The veins.. communicate..by a multitude of emissary twigs.

emissary ('ɛmɪsərɪ), *sb.*² [ad. L. *ēmissārium* an outlet, f. *ēmiss-* (see prec.) + *-ārium*: see -ARY¹.] An outlet, channel, duct: chiefly of a lake or reservoir. Also *fig. Obs.* exc. in *Rom. Antiq.*

1601 HOLLAND *Pliny* II. 530 Without any emissaries, tunnels, or holes. **1727** SWIFT *To a very young Lady* Wks. 1755 II. II. 44 To be the common emissary of scandal. **1786** *Phil. Trans.* LXXVI. 368 The famous Emissary of the Emperor Claudius remains nearly entire. **1859** LD. BROUGHTON *Italy* II. xvii. 121 The great emissaries of the Alban lake.

†**b.** *Phys.* A canal by which any fluid passes out. *Obs.*

1657 TOMLINSON *Renou's Disp.* 166 *The emissaryes of the palate from the brain. **1732** ARBUTHNOT *Rules of Diet* 355 The Obstruction of the Emissaries of the Saliva.

'emissary,ship. *rare*⁻¹. [f. EMISSARY *sb.*¹ + -SHIP.] The position or office of an emissary.

1625 B. JONSON *Staple of N.* I. i, Give your worship joy, Of your new place, your emissaryship In the News-office!

emissile (ɪ'mɪsɪl), *a.* [f. L. *ēmiss-* ppl. stem of *ēmittĕre* to send forth: see -ILE, and cf. *missile.*] That is capable of being thrust out or protruded.

1732 in BAILEY. **1775** in ASH. **1848** J. WILKINSON *Swedenborg's Anim. Kingd.* I. i. 28 The emissile and retractile cornua..in snails. **1856–8** W. CLARK *Van der Hoeven's Zool.* I. 191 Tubule of mouth emissile.

emission (ɪ'mɪʃən). [ad. L. *ēmissiōn-em*, n. of action f. *ēmittĕre* to EMIT.] The action of the vb. EMIT.

†**1.** The action of sending forth. *Obs.* in gen. sense.

1607 TOPSELL *Four-f. Beasts* (1673) 181 Emission or sending away. **1646** SIR T. BROWNE *Pseud. Ep.* (L.), Populosity..requireth..emission of colonies. **1657** HOBBES *Absurd Geom.* Wks. 1845 VII. 398 The authority..of the Apostles in the emission of preachers to the infidels. **1827** G. S. FABER *Origin of Expiatory Sacrifice* 197, *note*, Noah seems to have twice selected that holyday for the emission of the dove.

†**2.** The issuing, publication (of a book, a notice).

1751 JOHNSON *Rambl.* No. 169 ⁋11 The tardy emission of Pope's compositions. **1779** JOHNSON *Life Pope* Wks. IV. 40 The emission..of the Proposals for the Iliad.

3. The issuing or setting in circulation (bills, notes, shares, etc.). Also *concr.*

1773 *Gentl. Mag.* XLIII. 295 All the emissions of their paper-currency..are forged. **1790** BURKE *Fr. Rev.* Wks. V. 415 Proposing the emission of assignats. **1865** H. PHILLIPS *Amer. Paper Curr.* II. 36 A subsequent emission of bills of credit.

4. a. The action of giving off or sending out (chiefly what is subtle or imponderable, light, heat, gases, odours, sounds, etc.). †Formerly also the sending forth (of the soul) in death; the allowing 'the animal spirits' to escape; and *fig.* the 'pouring out', 'breathing forth' (of affection, etc.).

a **1619** DONNE *Biathan.* (1644) 190 This actuall emission of his soule, which is death. *a* **1626** BACON (L.), Tickling causeth laughter: the cause may be the emission of the spirits. **1660** JER. TAYLOR *Duct. Dubit.* I. iv. Wks. IX. 161 The voice was..effective..in the direct emission. **1693** SOUTH *Serm.* (L.), Affection flamed up in collateral emissions of charity to its neighbour. **1751** JOHNSON *Rambl.* No. 146 ⁋9 Growing fainter..at a greater distance from the first emission. **1833** SIR J. HERSCHEL *Astron.* x. 311 The tail of the..comet..occupied only two days in its emission from the comet's body. **1853** —— *Pop. Lect. Sc.* i. §35. (1873) 26 Puffs of smoke, at every moment of their emission from the crater. **1859** G. WILSON *Gateways Knowl.* (ed. 3) 77 The emission of fragrance. **1871** BLACKIE *Four Phases* i. 71 The emission of sparks of light.

b. Optics. *theory of emission* = *emission theory*, sense 7 below.

1831 BREWSTER *Optics* xv. §94. 134 The Newtonian theory of light, or the theory of emission.

c. *Physics*. The action of giving off radiation or particles; a flow of electrons from a cathode-ray tube or other source.

1900 RUTHERFORD in *Phil. Mag.* XLIX. 12 The results seem to point to a uniform rate of emission of the emanation at all pressures. **1955** W. HEISENBERG in W. Pauli *Niels Bohr* 25 Let a measuring apparatus be placed in the neighbourhood, which registers the emission of an electron. **1955** *Sci. Amer.* June 40/3 It is from these bursts of emission that radio astronomers have obtained most of their new information about the Sun's activities.

5. *concr.* That which is emitted; an emanation, effluvium.

1664 POWER *Exp. Philos.* iii. 155 The Magnetical Emissions..are..Corporeal Atoms. **1664** EVELYN *Kal. Hort.* (1729) 218 Warm and benign Emissions of the Sun. **1871** TYNDALL *Fragm. Sc.* (ed. 6) I. ii. 43 We obtain the value of the purely luminous emission.

6. *Phys.* = L. *emissio seminis*.

1646 SIR T. BROWNE *Pseud. Ep.* 371 There is no generation without a joynt emission. **1665** GLANVILL *Sceps. Sci.* The other Instances of..Emissions. **1885** *Law Reports* Appeal Cases X. 176.

7. emission nebula *Astr.*, a nebula which shines with its own light, produced inside it; **emission spectrum**, a spectrum which shows the radiations from an emitting source; **emission theory**, any theory of light or other radiation according to which it consists of streams of particles rather than waves.

[**1954** *Physics Abstr.* LVII. 1018/2 Two fundamental types of nebulae follow from this discussion: (1) the emission-type nebulae, consisting of atomic and ionized H, without dust, and (2) dark nebulae, with dust, consisting mainly of H_2.] **1956** *Austral. Jrnl. Physics* IX. 227 Ordinary *emission nebulae emit radio waves as the result of their high electron temperature by the process of free-free transitions. **1974** *Sci. Amer.* Oct. 34/3 These reflection nebulas are useful for studying the properties of the interstellar dust grains, but they are distinguished from the true emission nebulas, which shine as a result of the atomic processes going on within them. **1978** PASACHOFF & KUTNER *University Astron.* xxiii. 573 The Great Nebula of Orion.. is an emission nebula. **1888** *Phil. Mag.* 5th Ser. XXVI. 289 Ångström thought it improbable that oxygen should have a spectrum of such a character, since he failed to obtain an *emission spectrum resembling it. **1930** G. THOMSON *Atom* ii. 22 It is from the position of these black lines (Fraunhofer lines) that the nature of the substances present in the sun has been found. Such a black line spectrum is called an 'absorption' spectrum, in contrast to the bright line 'emission' spectrum. **1962** *Listener* 31 May 949/2 Surrounding the Sun is a layer made up of tenuous gas, which, if seen on its own, would produce an emission spectrum made up of isolated bright lines. **1880** BASTIAN *Brain* 62 An *emission theory..will not hold for the diffusion of light. **1926** R. W. LAWSON tr. *Hevesy & Paneth's Man. Radioactivity* i. 5 Finally for cathode rays the emission theory, and for Röntgen rays the wave theory held the field.

†**emi'ssitious**, *a. Obs. rare*$^{-1}$. [f. L. *ēmissīci-us* sent out, f. *ēmiss-* ppl. stem of *ēmittĕre* + -OUS: see EMIT.]

1. *fig.* Prying, inquisitive, narrowly examining.

1620 BP. HALL *Hon. Mar. Clergy* II. viii, Cast backe those emissitious eyes. **1847** in CRAIG; and in mod. Dicts.

2. Cast out.

1731–36 in BAILEY. **1775** in ASH.

emissive (ɪˈmɪsɪv), *a.* [f. L. *ēmiss-* ppl. stem of *ēmittĕ-re* to send forth, EMIT + -IVE.]

1. Having power to emit; radiating.

1870 T. L. PHIPSON tr. *Guillemin's Sun* 236 A homogeneous gaseous mass..having a radiating or emissive power. **1881** PROF. STOKES in *Nature* No. 625. 596 The..body of the sun..is comparatively feebly emissive of light.

b. *emissive theory*: = *emission theory*.

1837 WHEWELL *Hist. Indust. Sc.* (1857) I. 63 The emissive, and the undulatory theory of light. **1842** W. GROVE *Corr. Phys. Forces* 64 The emissive or corpuscular theory.

†**2.** That is emitted; that is sent or flows forth. *Obs. rare.*

16.. R. LOVEDAY *Letters* (1663) 201 Thus their emissive venome..will fatally recoyl upon themselves. **1746–7** HERVEY *Medit.* (1818) 126 Freely..she distributes the bounty of her emissive sweets. **1737** H. BROOKE *Tasso* I. (R.), Soon a beam, emissive from above, Shed mental day.

emissivity (iːmɪˈsɪvɪtɪ). [f. EMISSIVE *a.* + -ITY.] Emissive or radiating power of heat or light; *spec.* in *Physics* (see quot. 1958).

1880 *Encycl. Brit.* XI. 577/2 We define thermal emissivity as the quantity of heat per unit of time. *Ibid.*, The first thoroughly trustworthy experiments giving emissivities in absolute measure. **1884** P. G. TAIT *Light* 248 We now define the emissivity of a body at a given temperature, for a particular radiation, as the ratio of its emission of that radiation to the emission of the same radiation by a black body at the same temperature. **1891** *Proc. R. Soc.* L. 166 (*heading*) The thermal emissivity of thin wires in air. **1902** *Encycl. Brit.* XXVII. 189/2 Fourier defined another constant expressing the rate of loss of heat at a bounding surface per degree of difference of temperature between the surface of the body and its surroundings. This he called External Conductivity, but the term Emissivity is more convenient. **1958** H. J. GRAY *Dict. Physics* 174/1 Emissivity of a surface is the ratio of its emissive power to that of a black body for a given wavelength and at the same temperature. The term is also used for the amount of heat emitted per second by unit area of the surface maintained at a temperature of one degree above its surroundings, but a better name..is heat transfer coefficient.

emissory (ɪˈmɪsərɪ). [f. as EMISSIVE *a.* + -ORY.] = EMISSARY *sb.*^{2}

1858 G. P. SCROPE *Geol. & Extinct Volcanoes of Central France* (ed. 2) 59 The emissory thus forcibly created.

emit (ɪˈmɪt), *v.* [ad. L. *ēmittĕ-re* to send forth, f. *ē* out + *mittĕ-re* to send.]

trans. To send forth: in certain special senses. (Not used with personal obj.)

1. To send forth as a stream or emanation.

a. To send forth, discharge (as a liquid or plastic substance); to exude (juices, etc.).

1646 SIR T. BROWNE *Pseud. Ep.* III. xiii. 137 [The liquid secreted by toads] is emitted aversely or backward. **1712** POPE *Spect.* No. 408 ¶3 So pure a Fountain emits no..troubled Waters. **1813** SIR H. DAVY *Agric. Chem.* (1814) 249 A tree which emits sap copiously from a wound. **1835–6** TODD *Cycl. Anat.* I. 209/1 The threads by which the spiders suspend themselves..are emitted from the extremity of the abdomen. **1879** SIR J. LUBBOCK *Sci. Lect.* iii. 71 The aphis emits a drop of sweet fluid.

b. To give off, throw out ('effluvia', light, heat, gases, flames, sparks, etc.).

1626 BACON *Sylva* §259 Both of them..do not appear to emit any Corporal substance. **1692** BENTLEY *Boyle Lect.* 227 By effluvia and spirits that are emitted. **1756–7** tr. *Keysler's Trav.* IV. 452 The water..emits an ill smell. **1794** J. HUTTON *Philos. Light, etc.* 206 Those bodies may be heated so as to emit light. **1848** MRS. JAMESON *Sacr. & Leg. Art* (1850) 64 The earth emits flames. **1869** E. A. PARKES *Pract. Hygiene* (ed. 3) 89 An adult man..emits..carbonic acid gas by the skin.

fig. **1805** FOSTER *Ess.* I. ii. 27 Emitting sentiment at every pore.

¶ *intr.*

1886 *Daily News* 16 Sept. 7/2 Summoned..for..permitting..smells to emit from his stable.

c. *transf.*

1754 HUME *Hist. Eng.* I. iii. 67 That multitude of nations which she had successively emitted.

†**2.** To throw out as an offshoot. *Obs.*

1660 SHARROCK *Vegetables* 117 More fresh sprouts..are emitted. **1676** WORLIDGE *Cyder* (1691) 57 Before its wound be healed, and new fibres emitted. **1756** P. BROWNE *Jamaica* 105 This plant..emits a few..stalks.

3. To give forth (sound).

1826 KIRBY & SP. *Entomol.* III. xxxii. 339 They emit a grating noise. **1860** TYNDALL *Glac.* II. §1. 224 A bell struck in a vacuum emits no sound. **1876** SMILES *Sc. Natur.* vii. (ed. 4) 107 It did not emit any cry, such as the hare does.

4. To utter, give expression to (a statement, opinions, etc.).

1753 *Stewart's Trial* App. 4 All these declarations were emitted by the..persons..mentioned. **1805** FOSTER *Ess.* III. i. 5 Emit plenty of antipathy in a few syllables. **1818** MILL *Brit. India* II. IV. vii. 261 Complaints were..emitted of the scarcity of money. **1831** CARLYLE *Sart. Res.* (1858) 179 How could a man..emit [thoughts] in a shape bordering so closely on the absurd?

†**5.** To issue, publish (books, documents, notices). *Obs.*

1637–50 ROW *Hist. Kirk* (1842) 361 Papers and books emitted for cleareing the wickednes of the Prelatt's apostasie. **1723** *Wodrow Corr.* (1843) III. 6 The public papers emitted that and next year. **1726** AYLIFFE *Parerg.* 180 A Citation..ought to be..emitted by the Judges Authority. **1779** JOHNSON *Life Pope* Wks. IV. 23 Pope having now emitted his proposals. **1847** SIR W. HAMILTON *Letter* 37 But this declaration, now emitted, is contradicted by that very declaration, emitted in February.

6. To issue formally and by authority (edicts, proclamations; also, and now chiefly, paper currency, bills, etc.).

1649 BP. GUTHRIE *Mem.* (1702) 103 A Declaration Emitted by the English Parliament. **1672** CLARENDON *Ess.* in *Tracts* (1727) 265 Lewis..condemned that excommunication and the pope that emitted it. **1761–2** HUME *Hist. Eng.* (1806) V. lxxi. 279 The edicts emitted..still wanted much of the authority of laws. **1791** T. JEFFERSON *Writ.* (1859) III. 268 A dollar of silver disappears for every dollar of paper emitted. **1863** DICEY *Federal St.* I. 124 No State shall..emit bills of credit.

†**7.** To send forth, let fly, discharge (a missile).

1704 SWIFT *Batt. Bks.* (1711) 263 Having emitted his Launce against so great a Leader. *c* **1720** PRIOR *2nd Hymn of Callimachus to Apollo* Poems 244 Lest..the far-shooting God emit His fatal arrows.

†**emi'trichie, e'mytrycke.** *Obs. rare.* [ad. Med.L. *(h)ēmitricius (morbus)*, *(h)emitricia (febris)*, corruptly ad. Gr. ἡμιτριταῖος semi-tertian (fever).] A kind of fever.

1398 TREVISA *Barth. De P.R.* IV. viii. (1495) 92 Feuers that hiȝt Emitrichie. [*Ibid.* VII. vii. 227 Some sykenes whyche is callyd Emitricius.] **1547** BOORDE *Brev. Health* cxliv. 53 In Englyshe it is named the Emytrycke fever.

emitted (ɪˈmɪtɪd), *ppl. a.* [f. EMIT *v.* + -ED^1.] That is given off, thrown off.

a **1711** KEN *Edmund* Poet. Wks. 1721 II. 258 Guilding each Motion by emitted Rays. **1837** WHEWELL *Hist. Induct. Sc.* (L.), An emitted fluid.

†**emittent**, *a. Obs.* [ad. L. *ēmittent-em*, pr. pple. of *ēmittĕ-re* to send forth.] That emits.

1665–6 *Phil. Trans.* I. 357 The bloud of the Emittent Animal, may mix..with that of the Recipient. **1692** RAY *Dissol. World* iv. (1732) 54 The emittent Body.

emitter (ɪˈmɪtə(r)). [f. EMIT *v.* + -ER.]

1. That which emits. Const. *of*.

1883 TYNDALL *Radiation* in *Contemp. Rev.*, Grasses were powerful emitters of heat. **1926** *Spectator* 17 Apr. 696/1 Tungsten a powerful emitter of ultra-violet rays, when it is incandescent. **1927** A. HUXLEY *Proper Studies* 72 No emitter of singular opinions is ever reasonable in the eyes of the..majority.

2. An electrode which emits current-carriers; an element in a transistor. Also *attrib.* and *Comb.*, as ***emitter-base***, ***-follower***, ***-junction***, ***-resistance***.

1948 *Physical Rev.* LXXIV. 230/1 Two [electrodes], called the emitter and collector, are of the point-contact rectifier type. **1957** *Electronic Engin.* XXIX. 3 The emitter resistance is inversely proportional to the emitter current. **1958** *Ibid.* XXX. 200 The linear emitter-follower is characterized by a low impedance emitter output terminal, whose voltage approximates that of its base. **1962** SIMPSON & RICHARDS *Junction Transistors* ii. 25 The material from which these injected carriers come..is called the emitter and the junction between it and the base is called the emitter junction. *Ibid.* ix. 202 Because the emitter-base junction is a high-efficiency hole injector, very few electrons are removed via the emitter.

emitting (ɪˈmɪtɪŋ), *vbl. sb.* [f. EMIT *v.* + -ING^1.] The action of the vb. EMIT.

1693 SIR T. BLOUNT *Nat. Hist.* 298 An alternate and successive retracting and emitting of the Sting.

e'mitting, *ppl. a.* [see -ING^2.] That emits.

1667 DR. E. KING in *Phil. Trans.* II. 450, I did often strike with my finger the upper part of the emitting Vein.

emma, used orig. in telephone communications and in the oral transliteration of code messages, hence *colloq.*, for *m*, as in ***ack emma***, for *a.m.* (see ACK); ***emma-emma-esses*** (see quot. 1919); ***emma-gee***, for *m.g.* = machine gun; ***pip emma***, for *p.m.* (see PIP *sb.*^{4}); ***toc emma***, for *t.m.* (see TOC EMMA).

1891 *Man. Instructions Signalling* 94 The reader may pronounce his letters in any distinctive method to distinguish those letters which resemble others in sound, e.g. B, V, D, E, or M, N, etc. may be called Beer, Vay, Do, E, and Emma and N, etc. **1898**, etc. [see ACK]. **1915** 'IAN HAY' *First Hundred Thousand* xix. 289 'Pip Emma'—as our friends the 'buzzers' call the afternoon. **1918** H. W. MCBRIDE *Emma Gees* i. 9 Emma Gee is signaler's lingo for M.G., meaning machine gunner. **1919** DOWNING *Digger Dialects* 22 *Emma-emma-esses*, smoke-oh. (From the signal alphabet, MMS, Men may smoke.) **1926** E. WALLACE *Door with Seven Locks* xiii. 125 Tell him I want to raid Gallows Cottage, Gallows Hill, at eleven-fifteen pip-emma. **1931** *Morning Post* 20 Aug. 8/5 He was the only infantry officer..who had a good word for the Trench Mortar crowd. 'Are you Toc Emmas? You're just the men I want.' **1969** WODEHOUSE *Pelican at Blandings* vi. 83 We shall meet at twelve pip emma.

emmantle, var. of IMMANTLE.

emmarble (ɛˈmɑːb(ə)l), *v.* Also **enmarble**. [f. EN- + MARBLE *sb.*] *trans.* To convert into marble, *fig.*; to sculpture in marble; to adorn or inlay with marble. Hence **emmarbled** *ppl. a.*

1596 SPENSER *Hymn to Love* 140 Wks. (1862) 487 Thou doest emmarble the proud hart of her. **1850** MRS. BROWNING *Crowned & Buried* Poems II. 223 Pictured or emmarbled dreams. **1864** *Blackfriars* I. 59 The richly enmarbled altar.

emmarvel (ɛˈmɑːvɪl). Also **enmarvel**, **em-**, **enmarvaile**. [f. EN- + MARVEL *sb.*^{1} or *v.*] *trans.* To fill with wonder. Hence **emmarvelled** *ppl. a.*

1740 GRAY *Let.* in Mason *Memoirs* (1807) I. 257 We are all enraptured and enmarvailed. **1829** A. H. HALLAM *Remains* 22 On that child's emmarvailed view. **1834** LD. HOUGHTON *Dream of Sappho*, They heard emmarvelled.

emme, obs. form of AM: see BE *v.*

emme, var. of EME, *Obs.*, uncle.

†**'emmele.** *Mus. Obs. rare*$^{-1}$. [ad. Gr. ἐμμελής, f. ἐν in + μέλος melody. (Boethius divides musical progressions into ἐμμελεῖς, those which can form part of a melody, and ἐκμελεῖς those which cannot.)] A term applied in the old Theory of Harmony to the imperfect concords.

1609 DOULAND *Ornith. Microl.* 79 Emmeles are..those which sound thirds, sixts, or other imperfect Concords.

emmenagogic (ɛˌmiːnəˈgɒdʒɪk), *a. Med.* Also 7 **emenagogic**. [f. EMMENAGOG-UE + -IC.] Having the property of, or related to, an emmenagogue.

1678 SALMON *Lond. Disp.* 45/2 Ground Pine..is..Diuretick, and Emenagogick. **1757** *Phil. Trans.* L. 79 Emmenagogic pills.

†**b.** *absol.* quasi-*sb.* = EMMENAGOGUE *sb. Obs.*

1742–1800 in BAILEY.

Hence **eˌmmenaˈgogical** *a.*

1805 *Edin. Rev.* VII. 109 Sage is..emmenagogical.

emmenagogology (ɛˌmiːnəgəʊˈgɒlədʒɪ). *Med.* [f. EMMENAGOG-UE + -(O)LOGY.] 'A treatise on emmenagogues' (*Syd. Soc. Lex.* 1884).

emmenagogue (ɛ'mi:nəgɒg), *a.* and *sb. Med.* Also 8 **emenagogue.** [f. Gr. ἔμμηνα the menses of women + ἀγωγός drawing forth.]

A. *adj.* Having power to excite the menstrual discharge; = EMMENAGOGIC.

1702 SIR J. FLOYER in *Phil. Trans.* XXIII. 1168 All..are ..Emmenagogue. **1830** LINDLEY *Nat. Syst. Bot.* 135 Common Rue, and another species, are..emmenagogue. **1860** in MAYNE *Exp. Lex.* **1861** R. BENTLEY *Man. Bot.* 625 *Petiveria alliacea* is reputed sudorific and emmenagogue. **1864** A. B. GARROD *Mat. Med.* (ed. 2) 182 Myrrh..is supposed to possess antispasmodic and emmenagogue properties. **1887** C. A. MOLONEY *Sk. Forestry W. Afr.* xx. 328 All parts of this plant are said to be emmenagogue.

B. *sb.* Agents which increase or renew the menstrual discharge.

1731–1800 in BAILEY. **1732** ARBUTHNOT *Rules of Diet* 273 Emenagogues are such things as produce a Plethora or Fulness of the vessels. **1875** H. WOOD *Therap.* (1879) 535 Emmenagogues are medicines..employed to promote the menstrual flux.

emmene: see EMONY, *dial.*, anemone.

emmenological (ɛ,mi:nəʊ'lɒdʒɪkəl), *a. Med.* [f. EMMENOLOGY + -IC + -AL[1].] 'Relating to menstruation' (*Syd. Soc. Lex.* 1881).

emmenology (ɛmɪ'nɒlədʒɪ). *Med.* [f. Gr. ἐμμηνο- stem of ἔμμηνα the menses + -LOGY.] A treatise on, or the doctrine of, menstruation.

1742 (*title*) Le Tellier's Critical Reflections upon the Emmenology of Dr. Friend. **1847** in CRAIG; and in mod. Dicts.

Emmental, Emmenthal ('ɛməntɑ:l). Also Emmentaler, -thaler (-tɑ:lə(r)). [G. *Emmentaler* (formerly, *-thaler*), f. *Emmental*, region in Switzerland.] In full ***Emmental*** (etc.) ***cheese.*** A Swiss cheese containing numerous holes.

1902 *Encycl. Brit.* XXVII. 355/2 Of the varieties of cheese made in Switzerland, the best known is the Emmenthaler. **1950** J. G. DAVIS *Dict. Dairying* 119 *Emmenthal cheese*, the classical Swiss hard-pressed cheese. **1953** *Sci. News* XXIX. 60 Cheese was made in prehistoric times, and the craft has developed great heights of skill in the creation of such cheeses as English Stilton, Swiss Emmentaler and French Roquefort. **1955** *Times* 10 May 12/4 Switzerland still offers the world its Emmenthal—commonly called Gruyere. **1958** *Catal. County Stores, Taunton* June 8 *Cheese*..Emmental (Gruyère)—8/-. **1959** *Times* 5 Oct. (Switzerland Suppl.) p. ix/2 Gruyère or Emmentaler cheese.

emmer ('ɛmə(r)). [Upper G. *emmer* (OHG., MHG. *amer*).] A species of wheat, *Triticum dicoccum.* Also *attrib.*

1908 P. T. DONDLINGER *Book of Wheat* iii. 56 The introduction of spelt and emmer must also be mentioned. **1921** G. A. F. KNIGHT *Nile & Jordan* iii. 32 One of the names of the primitive 'emmer-corn' in Babylonia was *bututtu*, which is akin to the Egyptian *bôti*. **1924**, **1965** [see EINKORN]. **1928** V. G. CHILDE *Most Anc. East* ii. 43 The wild ancestor of emmer wheat (*Triticum dicoccum* with fourteen chromosomes) is alleged to grow native in Western Persia and Mesopotamia, in Syria and Palestine. **1965** R. F. PETERSON *Wheat* v. 82 On the whole, wheats of the Einkorn group were more resistant than those of the Emmer group.

emmesh, variant of ENMESH *v.*

emmet ('ɛmɪt). Forms: 1 **æmete, -mette, -mytte, émete,** 3–4 **emete,** (5 **ematte**), 4–6 **emet,** (**emot(e,** 4 *Sc.* **a nemot,** *i.e.* an emot), 6 **emmette,** (**emmont**), 6–7 **emmot(t(e,** (9 *Sc.* **emmock**), 6– **emmet.** (For forms with initial *a*, see ANT.) [repr. OE. *ǽmete* wk. fem. (see ANT). The OE. *ǽ* in stressed initial syllables frequently underwent shortening in ME., and was in that case variously represented according to dialects by *ă* or *ĕ*. Hence the two forms *ămete* and *ĕmete*; the former of which became contracted into *amt*, ANT, while the latter retained its middle vowel and survives as *emmet*.]

1. a. A synonym of ANT. Chiefly *dial.*, but often used *poet.* or *arch.* **horse-emmet,** the Wood Ant (*Formica rufa*).

c **850** *Kentish Gloss.* in Wr.-Wülcker 85 *Formicæ*, emetan. *c* **1300** *Beket* 2141 Faste hi schove and crope ek as emeten. *c* **1375** *Sc. Leg. Saints, St. Jacobus* 137 Nocht a nemot. *c* **1450** *Metr. Voc.* in Wr.-Wülcker 625 *Formica*, ematte. **1509** BARCLAY *Shyp of Folys* (1570) 138 Learne man of the simple Emmet. **1609** BIBLE (Douay) *Prov.* vi. 6 Goe to the emmote ô sluggard. **1659** W. BROUGH *Sacr. Princ.* 215 All creatures, from the emmet to the angel. **1713** *Guardian* (1756) II. No. 153. 273 He is an emmet of quality. **1779** JOHNSON *Life Pope* Wks. IV. 99 Looking on mankind..as on emmets of a hillock. **1802** BINGLEY *Anim. Biog.* (1813) III. 293 The horse-emmet, or great hill-ant. **1855** SINGLETON *Virgil* I. 81 Emmet, apprehending helpless eld.

b. In Cornwall: a holiday-maker or tourist; a summer visitor. (Mildly disparaging.) Cf. GROCKLE.

1975 *Sunday Express* 15 June 6/3 A Devon lady mentioned in passing that emmets and grockles were about to come her way... 'Grockles' is favoured particularly in Devon's Torbay area, while 'Emmets' is the tag for tourists in Cornwall. **1984** *Listener* 20 Sept. 23/1 'Grockle' is the Devonian word for tourist, or tripper, or summer visitor. In Cornwall the word is 'emmet'—less difficult and more vivid because its true meaning is 'ant'.

2. *attrib.*, as ***emmet-swarm.*** Also **emmet-batch, -but, -cast** (*dial.*) = ANT-HILL; **emmet-hunter** (*dial.*), the Wryneck (*Yunx torquilla*).

1847–78 HALLIWELL *Emmet-batch, an ant-hill, *Somerset.* **1697** DAMPIER in *Phil. Trans.* XX. 49 *Emett Butts. *Mod. Kent Dial.* The field is so full of *emmet-casts. **1837** MACGILLIVRAY *Hist. Brit. Birds* III. 100 Wryneck, [Provincial name], *Emmet-hunter. **1885** *Academy* 10 Oct. 235 The *emmet-swarm of popular scribblers.

†**emmetris.** *Obs. rare*[−1]. A green-coloured gem, prob. a kind of emerald.

1621 BURTON *Anat. Mel.* II. iv. I. iv. (1651) 371 Which properties..Cardan gives to that green coloured Emmetris.

emmetrope ('ɛmətrəʊp). *Phys.* [f. Gr. ἔμμετρ-ος + ὤπ-: see next.] One whose sight is emmetropic.

1875 H. WALTON *Dis. Eye* 345 Emmetropes complain of fatigue only in using the eye for near objects.

‖**emmetropia** (ɛmə'trəʊpɪə). *Phys.* [mod.L. (invented by F. C. Donders of Utrecht), f. Gr. ἔμμετρ-ος in measure + ὠπ- stem of ὤψ the eye + -IA.] 'The normal or healthy condition of the refractive media of the eye, in which parallel rays are brought to a focus upon the retina when the eye is at rest and in a passive condition' (*Syd. Soc. Lex.*).

1864 MOORE tr. *Donders' Accomod. & Refr. Eye* 81. **1878** T. BRYANT *Pract. Surg.* I. 299 The former condition is known as emmetropia.

emmetropic (ɛmə'trɒpɪk), *a. Phys.* [f. as prec. + -IC.] Characterized by emmetropia.

1878 FOSTER *Phys.* III. ii. 402 The normal eye, the so-called emmetropic eye. **1879** PRIESTLEY SMITH *Glaucoma* 13 The refraction in each eye was..emmetropic.

emmetropy (ɛ'metrəpɪ). *Phys.* Anglicized form of EMMETROPIA.

1880 LE CONTE *Sight* 46 This normal condition is called emmetropy.

emmew, var. of IMMEW, to put in a MEW, to enclose.

†**e'mmoised,** *pple. Obs. rare.* In 5 **enmoysed.** [var. of *amesed*, from AMESE *v.*] Comforted.

c **1400** *Test. Love* I. (1560) 275/2 Desire..some speaking to have, or els at the least to be enmoysed with sight. **1692** in COLES. **1721–1800** in BAILEY. **1775** in ASH.

emmonite ('ɛmənaɪt). *Min.* Also **emmonsite.** [f. name of Ebenezer *Emmons* (1799–1863) an American geologist.] A variety of strontianite, so named by Thomson in 1836.

1837 DANA *Min.* 200 Another variety..he has named Emmonite.

emmonsite ('ɛmənzaɪt). *Min.* [f. the name of S. F. *Emmons* (1841–1911), American geologist: see -ITE[1].] A hydrated ferric tellurite that occurs in yellowish green crystals.

1886 W. F. HILLEBRAND in *Proc. Colorado Sci. Soc.* 25 Feb. 23, I..take great pleasure in naming it Emmonsite, in honor of S. F. Emmons. **1944** *Amer. Mineralogist* XXIX. 215 Emmonsite also occurs near Silver City, New Mexico, as green botryoidal crusts in crevices in quartz- and pyrite-rich vein material.

emmove, var. of ENMOVE *v.*, *Obs.*

emmunity, obs. var. of IMMUNITY.

Emmy ('ɛmɪ). *U.S.* [Said to be an alteration of *Immy*, f. *image orthicon* + -Y *suffix*[6].] A statuette awarded to an outstanding television programme or performer by the American Academy of Television Arts and Sciences.

1949 *Life* 28 Mar. 95/2 Grant-Realm Television Productions..won television's equivalent of an Oscar—the first Emmy. **1954** *Sun* (Baltimore) 25 Jan. B 9/2 Members of the Academy of Television Arts and Sciences..announced nominations for..the awards, called 'Emmies'. **1959** *Oxford Mail* 7 May 1/2 Fred Astaire, now 60, received nine U.S. television 'Emmy' awards..in a presentation in which the big awards went to old timers.

emne, obs. var. of EVEN *a.*

emni, obs. var. of EVEN *v.*

emodin ('ɛmədɪn). *Chem.* [f. mod.L. (*Rheum*) *Emodi*, an obs. name for Turkey rhubarb (from Gr. 'Ημωδός the Himalaya) + -IN.] A constituent of rhubarb root, obtained by treating chrysophanic acid with benzol. Its formula is $C_{40}H_{30}O_{13}$ (Watts *Dict. Chem.*).

1858 DE LA RUE & MÜLLER in *Q. Jrnl. Chem. Soc.* X. 305 This substance for which..we propose the name of Emodin, is of a bright deep orange colour.

†**emodu'lation.** *Mus. Obs.*[−0] [n. of action f. L. *ēmodulā-re* to sing, celebrate: see -ATION.] The action of singing in measure and proportion; 'phrasing'.

1731 in BAILEY. **1775** in ASH.

emollescence (ɪmɒ'lɛsəns). *Chem.* and *Min.* [f. L. *ēmollesc-ĕre* to grow soft + -ENCE.] 'A state of softening; the softened condition of a melting body before it fuses' (*Syd. Soc. Lex.*).

1794 KIRWAN *Min.* I. 43 The..lowest degree is emollescence. **1847** in CRAIG; and in mod. Dicts.

emolliate (ɪ'mɒlɪeɪt), *v.* [f. L. *ēmollī-re* to soften, f. *ē* intensive + *molli-s* soft + -ATE.] *trans.* To soften, render effeminate.

1802–17 PINKERTON *Geog.* (W.), Emolliated by four centuries of Roman domination. **1847** in CRAIG; and in mod. Dicts.

†**e'molliative,** *a. Obs. rare*[−1]. [f. as prec. + -ATIVE.] That tends to soften, assuage, relax.

1601 HOLLAND *Pliny* II. 138 The meale..of the three-moneth corn is more moist and emolliative.

†**e'mollid,** *a. Obs.*[−0] [ad. L. *ēmollid-us*, (? erroneous reading) Livy XXXIV. xlvii.] Soft, tender, nice, effeminate.

1656 in BLOUNT *Glossogr.* **1731** in BAILEY. **1775** in ASH.

emollient (ɪ'mɒlɪənt), *a.* and *sb. Med.* Also 7 **emolent,** 8–9 **emolient.** [f. L. *ēmollient-em*, pr. pple. of *ēmollī-re* to soften, f. *ē* intensive + *molli-s* soft.]

A. *adj.* That has the power of softening or relaxing the living animal textures. Also *fig.*

1643 J. STEER tr. *Exper. Chyrurg.* vii. 29, I use emolent Medicines. **1655** CULPEPPER, COLE & ROWLAND *Riverius* X. iii. 289 A Decoction of Emollient Herbs. **1796** BURKE *Regic. Peace* Wks. VIII. 135 All the emolient cataplasms of robbery and confiscation. **1833** MRS. BROWNING *Prometh. Bd.* Poet. Wks. (1850) I. 161 Mixtures of emollient remedies. **1876** GROSS *Dis. Bladder* 26 A large emollient poultice is applied to the vesicated surface.

B. *sb.* A softening application. Chiefly in *pl.* Also *fig.*

1656 RIDGLEY *Pract. Physick* 13 Lay not on the scarified place emollients. **1667** *Decay Chr. Piety* xix. §13 (1683) 368 This pacifick purpose, as a lenitive and emollient. **1727** POPE, etc. *Art Sinking* 92 The emollients and opiats of poesy. **1875** H. WOOD *Therap.* (1879) 582 True emollients are perfectly bland, fatty substances.

†**e'molliment.** *Obs.*[−0] [as if ad. L. **ēmollīment-um*, f. *ēmollīre*: see prec.] 'An asswaging' (Cockeram 1623).

emo'llition. ? *Obs.* Also 7 **emolition.** [as if ad. L. **ēmollītiōn-em*, n. of action f. *ēmollī-re* to soften.] The action of softening. Also *fig.*

a **1619** DANIEL *Coll. Hist. Eng.* (1626) 3 Which [land].. would have..not needed this emollition by learning. **1626** BACON *Sylva* §730 Bathing or Anointing give a Relaxion or Emollition. **1646** SIR T. BROWNE *Pseud. Ep.* 53 Powerful menstruums are made for its emolition. **1741** *Compl. Fam. Piece* I. i. 80 Let it lie on [the corn] till it have sufficiently done the designed Work of Emollition. **1775** in ASH. **1847** in CRAIG; and in mod. Dicts.

†**e'mollitive,** *a.* and *sb. Med. Obs.* [f. L. *ēmollīt-* ppl. stem of *ēmollī-re* to soften + -IVE.]

A. = EMOLLIENT *a.*

1601 HOLLAND *Pliny* II. 137 This is generally obserued, that all sorts of wax be emollitiue. **1657** TOMLINSON *Renou's Disp.* 499 The herbaceous part is emollitive.

B. = EMOLLIENT *sb.*

1601 HOLLAND *Pliny* II. 11 *Explan. of Wds. of Art*, Emollitiues, medicines that do soften any hard swelling.

†**'emologe,** *v. Obs. rare*[−1]. [ad. med.L. *emologāre* corrupt var. of *homologāre* to confirm; used techn. for 'to register a decree in the records of a (French) parliament'.] *trans.* To enter or register as in a diary or calendar.

1655 DIGGES *Compl. Ambass.* 186 These things..should be inrolled and emologed in their Parlaments.

emolument (ɪ'mɒljʊmənt). [ad. L. *ēmŏlŭ-*, *ēmŏlĭmentum* profit, advantage; in most Lat. Dicts. said to be f. *ēmŏlī-rī* to bring out by effort.

On this view, however, the quantity ought to be *ēmōlīmentum*; the quantity evidenced in L. poetry points to derivation from *ēmŏlĕre* to grind out. Possibly two distinct L. words of the same spelling may have been confused.]

1. Profit or gain arising from station, office, or employment; dues; reward, remuneration, salary.

1480 *Wardr. Acc. Edw. IV* (1830) 127 Certeyn offeringes ..and emoluments unto the said benefice due. **1637–50** Row *Hist. Kirk* (1842) 31 His former rents and emoluments. **1743** J. MORRIS *Serm.* viii. 216 Believers..deny themselves all the..emoluments..they might have injoyed here. **1803** F. JEFFREY in *Four C. Eng. Lett.* 423 The concern has now become to be of some emolument. **1881** P. BROOKS *Candle of Lord* 69 Men who want to be scholars for the emoluments ..scholarship will bring.

†**2.** Advantage, benefit, comfort. *Obs.*

1633 MASSINGER *New Way, etc.* IV. ii, Thou never hadst in thy house..A piece of..cheese..For their [men's] emolument. **1704** SWIFT *T. Tub* (1768) I. 119 That wind still continues of great emolument in certain mysteries. **1756** CHESTERFIELD *Lett.* IV. cccxvi. 80, I brought it [an emetic] all up again to my great satisfaction and emolument.

†**emolu'mental,** *a. Obs. rare.* [f. prec. + -AL[1].] = next.

1664 EVELYN *Sylva* Pref. Rdr., All that is laudable and truly emolumental. **1669** J. ROSE *Eng. Vineyard* Ep. Ded., All that is truely magnificent and emolumental in the culture of trees and fruits. **1721–1800** in BAILEY. **1847** in CRAIG; and in mod. Dicts.

emolumentary (ɪˌmɒljuːˈmɛntərɪ), *a.* [f. EMOLUMENT + -ARY.] That tends to emolument; profitable, beneficial, advantageous.

1775 WRAXALL in *Tour N. Europe* 87 Marriage is not encouraged by [any] emolumentary mark of favour. **1888** *Daily News* 22 May 6/5 My office is honorary rather than emolumentary.

†**e'mong**, *prep.* and *adv. Obs.* Forms: 4 **emang**, 5 **emaunge, -onge, -unge**, 5–7 **emong**. [variant of AMONG, IMONG.] = AMONG.

A. *prep.*

1375–1592 [see AMONG 1 β]. *a* **1400–50** *Alexander* 4817 And gods glorious gleme glent þam emaunge. *c* **1420** *Avow. Arthur* xlvi Emunge the grete and the smalle. **1470–85** MALORY *Arthur* Prol. (1817) 1 Moost to be remembred emonge vs englysshe men. **1571** DIGGES *Pantom.* I. Bij b, Emong Right lined figures, suche as haue onely three sides are Triangles.

B. *adv.*

1440–70 [see AMONG]. **1548** FORREST *Pleas. Poesye* 432 That wheareseoeure they shall come emonge, No fawte theare bee..fownde.

†**e'monges(t**, *prep.* Forms: 5 **emanges, -ez, emongis**, 6 **-es, -s, -est.** [f. prec. with advbl. genitive ending: see AMONGST.] = AMONGST.

1460–1569 [see AMONGST 6]. **1495** *Act 11 Hen. VII*, c. 53 That the seid Robert emongis other shuld stand and be convicted..of High Treason. **1571** ASCHAM *Scholem* I. (Arb.) 37 Witte is a singuler gifte of God, and so most rare emonges men.

emony (ˈɛmənɪ). Also 7 **emone, emmene.** [aphet. f. ANEMONE (? taken as *an emony*).]

1644 *Vind. Dr. Featley* Pref. 6 Robbing him of.. Emmenes or Tulips. **1657** COLES *Adam in Eden* (Britten and Holl.), The common people call them Emones. **1664** R. TURNER in Prior, Gardeners call them Emonies. **1731** BAILEY, *Anemone*, the emony or wind-flower. **1882** in *Devonshire Plant-n.*, Emony.

emoptoic, obs. form of HÆMOPTOIC.

emorodial, obs. form of HÆMORRHOIDAL.

emorogie, obs. form of HÆMORRHAGE.

emoroydes, obs. f. EMERODS, HÆMORRHOIDS.

emortise, obs. form of AMORTIZE.

1598 STOW *Surv.* xviii. (1603) 168 The emortising and propriation of the Priorie.

emote (ɪˈməʊt), *v.* orig. *U.S.* [Back-formation from EMOTION.] *intr.* To dramatize emotion; to act emotionally.

1917 MEGRUE & HACKETT *It pays to Advertise* III. 103 And you let me sit there and emote all over the place. **1927** A. W. L. FAWCETT *Films, Facts & Forecasts* xv. 142 In these surroundings the players must 'emote' all they know. **1931** *Observer* 26 July 15 'What were your emotions when you looked down..on to the Sea of Galilee?,' I asked Mr [G. B.] Shaw. 'I did not emote,' he replied a trifle reproachfully. **1949** *John o' London's* 16 Sept., In my experience, emoting is theatrical jargon for particularly ham emotional acting. **1960** *Times* 15 Mar. 6/1 [*Ballet*] Genuine inventiveness was betrayed by the closeness of the emoting hands. **1968** *Observer* 6 Oct. 28/7 After the first half-hour..she has little to do but emote in mostly painful situations. **1970** *Amateur Photographer* 11 Mar. 35/1 This was the reign of the *genre* picture when every male sitter had to be doing something... The female sitter had to emote in some way, either by dressing up or by gazing with drooping head into a bowl of flowers.

emotion (ɪˈməʊʃən). [ad. L. *ēmōtiōn-em*, n. of action f. *ē-movē-re*, f. *ē* out + *movē-re* to move.]

†**1.** A moving out, migration, transference from one place to another. *Obs.*

1603 KNOLLES *Hist. Turks* (1621) 3 The divers emotions of that people [the Turks]. **1695** WOODWARD *Nat. Hist. Earth* I. (1723) 45 Some accidental Emotion..of the Center of Gravity.

†**2.** A moving, stirring, agitation, perturbation (in physical sense). *Obs.*

1692 LOCKE *Educ.* 7 When exercise has left any Emotion in his Blood or Pulse. **1708** O. BRIDGMAN in *Phil. Trans.* XXVI. 138 Thunder..caused so great an Emotion in the Air. **1755** PORTER *ibid.* XLIX. 118 The horses rose from their litter with violent emotions. **1758** *Ibid.* L. 647 The waters continuing in the caverns..caused the emotion or earth-quake. **1772** MONRO *ibid.* LXII. 18 A diluted spirit of vitriol..occasioned no..emotion. *a* **1822** SHELLEY *Love's Philos.* 6 The winds of heaven mix forever With a sweet emotion.

†**3.** *transf.* A political or social agitation; a tumult, popular disturbance. *Obs.*

1579 FENTON *Guicciard.* II, There were..great stirres and emocions in Lombardye. **1709** ADDISON *Tatler* No. 24 ¶13 Accounts of Publick Emotions, occasion'd by the Want of Corn. **1757** BURKE *Abridgem. Eng. Hist.* Wks. X. 432 Even in England some emotions were excited in favour of the Duke [Robert of Normandy, in 1103].

4. a. *fig.* Any agitation or disturbance of mind, feeling, passion; any vehement or excited mental state.

1660 JER. TAYLOR *Duct. Dubit.* (R.), The emotions of humanity..the meltings of a worthy disposition. **1712** STEELE *Spect.* No. 432 ¶9 I hope to see the Pope..without violent Emotions. **1762** KAMES *Elem. Crit.* ii. §2. (1833) 37 The joy of gratification is properly called an emotion. **1785** REID *Int. Powers* 725 The emotion raised by grand objects is awful. **1828** SCOTT *F.M. Perth*, Desirous that his emotion should not be read upon his countenance.

b. *Psychology.* A mental 'feeling' or 'affection' (*e.g.* of pleasure or pain, desire or aversion, surprise, hope or fear, etc.), as distinguished from cognitive or volitional states of consciousness. Also *abstr.* 'feeling' as distinguished from the other classes of mental phenomena.

1808 *Med. Jrnl.* XIX. 422 Sea-sickness..is greatly under the dominion of emotion. **1841–4** EMERSON *Ess. Friendship* Wks. (Bohn) I. 81 In poetry..the emotions of benevolence and complacency..are likened to the material effects of fire. **1842** KINGSLEY *Lett.* (1878) I. 61 The intellect is stilled, and the Emotions alone perform their..involuntary functions. **1871** TYNDALL *Fragm. Sc.* (ed. 6) II. xi. 231 He..almost denounces me..for referring Religion to the region of Emotion. **1875** JOWETT *Plato* (ed. 2) I. 249 The..emotions of pity, wonder, sternness, stamped upon their countenances.

5. *attrib.* and *Comb.* **a.** attrib., as *emotion-marker, -reaction.* **b.** objective and obj. gen., as *emotion-arousing, -provoking* adjs. **c.** instrumental, as *emotion-charged, -shaken* adjs.

1884 W. JAMES *Coll. Ess. & Rev.* (1920) 258 What the action itself may be is quite insignificant, so long as I can perceive in it intent or *animus*. This is the emotion-arousing perception. **1937** *Burlington Mag.* June 262/1 He does not attempt to amend his emotion-charged statements. **1964** CRYSTAL & QUIRK *Prosodic & Paraling. Features in Eng.* iii. 41 The problem arises as to where arbitrary divisions in the cline of spasmodic emotion-markers should be made. **1951** J. M. FRASER *Psychol.* vi. 65 In ordinary life, however, emotion-provoking situations can seldom be solved by such actions. *a* **1930** D. H. LAWRENCE *Apocalypse* (1931) ix. 93 Nay, every image will be understood differently by every reader, according to his emotion-reaction. **1906** B. VON HUTTEN *What became of Pam* xiii. 316 The stern, nervous, emotion-shaken face.

emotionable (ɪˈməʊʃənəb(ə)l), *a.* [f. EMOTION + -ABLE.] = EMOTIONAL *a.* 2.

1889 *Universal Rev.* III. 46 The secret of his supremacy over an emotionable nation. **1893** *Daily News* 6 May 5/5 Mr. Asquith, not ordinarily an emotionable man.

emotional (ɪˈməʊʃənəl), *a.* [f. EMOTION + -AL¹.]

1. Connected with, based upon, or appealing to, the feelings or passions.

1834 J. S. MILL in *Monthly Repos.* VIII. 645 He [*sc.* Plato] adverts only to those genera which form the basis of our great moral and emotional (or as the Germans say, aesthetic) classifications. **1847** GROTE *Greece* II. xvi. III. 285 Every musical mode had its own peculiar emotional influences. **1860** FROUDE *Hist. Eng.* VI. 6 Uncoloured..with the emotional weaknesses of humanity. **1862** SHIRLEY in *Nugae Crit.* vi. 282 The use of emotional language. **1875** OUSELEY *Harmony* Pref. 7 Others..treat Music as..only an emotional art. **1875** W. JAMES *Coll. Ess. & Rev.* (1920) 24 One may deem that the lack of emotional bias which left him contented with the mere principle of parsimony as a criterion of universal truth was really due to a defect in the active or impulsive part of his mental nature. **1910** YEATS *Let.* 23 Feb. (1954) IV. 549 The stage, where we say a man is a 'character actor' meaning that he builds up a part out of observation, or we say that he is 'an emotional actor' meaning that he builds it up out of himself. **1936** *Discovery* July 201/1 If we say or do something to the subject which causes him to experience emotional stress..we find, after a pause of nearly two seconds, that the [electrical] resistance drops. **1956** A. H. COMPTON *Atomic Quest* 242 One of the young men..came to my office in a state of emotional stress.

2. Liable to emotion; easily affected by emotion. Also in philosophical sense, characterized by the capacity for emotion. Also *absol.* quasi *sb.*

1857 MRS. GASKELL *C. Brontë* (1860) 9 The natives of the West Riding..are not emotional. **1879** MCCARTHY *Own Times* II. 384 She [Mrs. Barrett Browning] speaks especially to the emotional in woman. **1884** A. HIND in *Athenæum* 19 Apr. 497/1 Soul..ceases to operate *qua* emotional and appetitive soul.

emotionalism (ɪˈməʊʃənəlɪz(ə)m). [f. prec. + -ISM.] Emotional character. Usually in disparaging sense: The habit of morbidly cultivating or of weakly yielding to emotion.

1865 *Pall Mall G.* 3 Nov. 112 Lively emotionalism is his special characteristic. **1869** *Spectator* 17 Apr. 475/1 Overstrained, and consciously indulged and petted bits of sentimentalism..passing the verge of maudlin emotionalism. **1883** L. ABBOTT in *Home Mission* Oct. 231 The religion of emotionalism [is] represented by the Negro.

emotionalist (ɪˈməʊʃənəlɪst). [f. as prec. + -IST.] **a.** One who bases his theories of conduct on the emotions. **b.** In contemptuous use: One who is unwisely emotional, or who appeals (unworthily) to the emotions instead of the reason.

a **1866** J. GROTE *Exam. Util. Philos.* iv. (1870) 62 Mill writes..as if he were a mere emotionalist. **1882** J. PARKER *Apost. Life* (1884) III. 66 Would he now be called fanatic, emotionalist, enthusiast? **1888** COSMO MONKHOUSE in *Academy* 23 June 425/1 He is no professional emotionalist, making capital out of pain.

emotionality (ɪˌməʊʃəˈnælɪtɪ). [f. as prec. + -ITY.] Emotional character or temperament.

1865 *Englishm. Mag.* Mar. 208 A high state of joyous emotionality. **1885** JEAFFRESON *Real Shelley* I. 392 Allowance must be made for Shelley's vehement emotionality.

e'motionaliˌzation. *nonce-wd.* [f. next + -ATION.] The process of cultivating the feelings, or heightening the sensibility.

1876 MAUDSLEY *Physiol. Mind.* vi. 366 To bring the low savage to the level of the cultivated European..a process of emotionalization [would be needed].

emotionalize (ɪˈməʊʃənəlaɪz), *v. rare.* [f. EMOTIONAL + -IZE.] *trans.* To render emotional; make a subject for emotional talk or display; to deal with emotionally.

1879 FROUDE *Cæsar* xxvi. 456 An oath with him was not a thing to be emotionalised away. **1882** —— *Carlyle* I. 66 A pious family, where religion was not..emotionalised.

emotionally (ɪˈməʊʃənəlɪ), *adv.* [f. as prec. + -LY².] In an emotional manner; with reference to the emotions.

1865 DICKENS *Mut. Fr.* I. ii, Nodding emotionally. **1866** *Ch. Times* 20 Feb., The Rinderpest is emotionally described ..as an affliction. **1874** SPURGEON *Treas. Dav.* Ps. xcii. 1 IV. 263 It is good emotionally for it is pleasant to the heart. **1876** GEO. ELIOT *Dan. Der.* IV. lii. 71 Passionate situations, which she never made emotionally her own.

†**e'motionate**, *a. nonce-wd.* [f. EMOTION + -ATE.] = EMOTIONAL 2.

1824 JAMES GILCHRIST *Etymologic Interpreter* 88 We are essentially sentimental and emotionate.

emotioned (ɪˈməʊʃənd) *ppl. a. rare.* [f. EMOTION + -ED.] Stirred by emotion.

a **1783** J. SCOTT (of Amwell) *Ess. Painting* Wks. (1822) 176 How all his form the emotion'd soul betrays.

emotionize (ɪˈməʊʃənaɪz), *v. rare.* [f. EMOTION + -IZE.] *trans.* To stir or affect with emotion.

1859 R. BURTON in *Jrnl. R. Geog. Soc.* XXIX. 341 Wild races seek..something..to emotionize them. **1883** *Wilfred's Widow* II. vi. 255 Moved—touched—emotionized.

emotionless (ɪˈməʊʃənlɪs), *a.* [f. as prec. + -LESS.] Without emotion, devoid of feeling or passion.

1862 F. HALL *Hindu Philos. Syst.* 177 Brahma is.. tranquil..emotionless. **1875** FLOR. MARRYAT *Open Sesame* I. x. 144 Her face..struck me as strangely emotionless.

emotionlessness (ɪˈməʊʃənlɪsnɪs). [f. EMOTIONLESS *a.* + -NESS.] The state or condition of being emotionless.

1921 T. R. GLOVER *Jesus in Exper. of Men* xiii. 219 One of their ideals was 'Emotionlessness'. **1926** *Chambers's Jrnl.* 357/1 The whole face had a suggestion of emotionlessness acquired by habit.

emotive (ɪˈməʊtɪv), *a.* [f. L. *ēmōt-* ppl. stem of *ēmovē-re* to move out + -IVE.]

1. †**a.** Causing movement (*obs.*). **b.** Tending to excite or capable of exciting emotion.

1735 BROOKE *Univ. Beauty* IV. 121 Eternal art, Emotive, pants within the alternate heart. **1883** H. M. KENNEDY tr. *Ten Brink's E.E. Lit.* 38 The emotive passionate quality of epic diction.

2. a. Pertaining to the emotions, or to emotion.

1830 MACINTOSH *Eth. Philos.* Wks. 1846 I. 160 Distinction between the percipient and what, perhaps, we may venture to call the emotive or the pathematic part of human nature. **1855** H. SPENCER *Princ. Psychol.* (1870) I. 484 Actions..at once, conscious, rational, and emotive. **1876** GEO. ELIOT *Dan. Der.* VII. lii. 492 It prepared her emotive nature for a deeper effect.

b. Eminently capable of emotion, emotional.

1881 MRS. PRAED *Policy & P.* II. 30 One must feel with the emotive, see with the spiritual.

c. *Philos.* and *Lit. Criticism.* Expressing or arousing feeling or emotion; not descriptive. *emotive theory*: the view that ethical and value judgements are not assertions or reports (even of the speaker's attitudes), but are expressions of feeling or attitude and prescriptions of action.

1923 OGDEN & RICHARDS *Meaning of Meaning* p. viii, A division of the functions of language into two groups, the symbolic and the emotive. **1936** A. J. AYER *Lang., Truth & Logic* vi. 160 The function of the relevant ethical word is purely 'emotive'. **1944** C. L. STEVENSON *Ethics & Lang.* iii. 59 Emotive meaning is a meaning in which the response (from the hearer's point of view) or the stimulus (from the speaker's point of view) is a range of emotions. **1951** *Mind* LX. 205 The so-called 'emotive theory' of value statements.

Hence **e'motively** *adv.*, emotionally. **e'motiveness**, the quality of being emotional. **e'motivism**, the emotive theory or adherence to it. **e'motivist**, one who maintains or accepts the emotive theory. **emo'tivity**, the capacity for emotion; also *spec.* in sense 2 c.

1884 *Athenæum* 5 Apr. 438/1 Thoughts must be emotively expressed before they can become poetry. **1876** GEO. ELIOT *Dan. Der.* xl, Sympathetic emotiveness..ran along with his speculative tendency. **1854** HICKOK *Ment. Philos.* 176 Emotivity [is a] term for the capacity of feeling. **1925** I. A. RICHARDS *Princ. Lit. Crit.* 131 Words..used symbolically or, scientifically, not figuratively and emotively. **1949** *Mind* LVIII. 39 It is..impossible to ascribe the logically undesirable character of emotivity to classes of sentences *en bloc.* **1951** *Ibid.* LX. 390 Showing where the Emotivist and the Existentialist go wrong. **1952** R. M. HARE *Lang. of Morals* ix. 144 The 'emotivity' of much moral utterance..is only a symptom..of an evaluative use of words. **1960** J. O. URMSON et al. *Conc. Encycl. West. Philos.* 142/1 Ayer..has since abandoned emotivism.

emove (ɪˈmuːv), *v. rare.* Also 5 emoyve. [In 15th c. *emoyue* (if this is not misread for *enioyne*), ad. OF. *emovoir*; in 18th c. directly ad. L. *ēmovēre*: see EMOTION.] *trans.* †**a.** To move, incite (to an action) (*obs.*). **b.** To affect with emotion.

a **1400** *Relig. Pieces fr. Thornton MS.* (1867) 2 He byddes .. þat all þat hase cure .. emoyue þaire parischenes, etc. **1748** THOMSON *Cast. Indol.* I. x, Kindly raptures them emove. **1835** *Fraser's Mag.* XI. 425 He for whose loss all gentle breasts are now emoved.

empacket (ɛmˈpækɪt), *v. rare.* [ad. Fr. *empaqueter*: cf. EN- and PACKET.] *trans.* To pack up.

1825 SCOTT *Betrothed* xii. (1832) 106 No other woman .. hath such skill in empacketing clothes.

empæstic (ɛmˈpiːstɪk), *a.* [ad. Gr. ἐμπαιστική (τέχνη) the art of embossing, f. ἐμπαίειν to beat in, emboss.] In phrase *empæstic art*: the art of embossing.

1850 LEITCH tr. *Müller's Anc. Art* §173. 152 Embossed silver plates with ornaments of gold riveted on them (therefore works of the empæstic art).

empair, -ment, etc., obs. ff. IMPAIR *v.*, etc.

†**emˈpale**, *v. Obs.* [f. EN- + PALE *a.*; OF. had *empalir* in same sense.] *trans.* To make pale.

1604 A. SCOLOKER *Daiphantus* in Arb. *Garner* VII. 400 The heart's still perfect; though empaled the face. **1610** G. FLETCHER *Christ's Vict.*, No bloudles maladie empales their face. **1664** POWER *Exp. Philos.* I. 75 This Artificial Claret .. you may empale as you please.

empale, empalement: see IMPALE, -MENT.

empall: see EM- *prefix.*

empalm, obs. form of IMPALM.

‖**empanada** (empaˈnaða). [Sp., f. *empanada* ppl. adj. (fem.), f. *empanar* to roll and bake or fry in pastry or dough.] A variety of esp. South American savoury pasty or turnover.

1939 C. L. B. BROWN *S. Amer. Cook Bk.* 58 Unlike the cold English pork and lark pies, *empanadas* are at their very best when eaten piping hot. The *empanadas* of Latin America are as varied as the *vol au vents* of France. **1969** R. & D. DE SOLA *Dict. Cooking* 93/1 *Empanada*, turnover filled with cheese, cooked fish, ground meat, or stewed vegetables. **1977** B. CHATWIN *In Patagonia* lxxviii. 180 She bought two empanadas for herself. **1985** *Washington Post* 27 June (Virginia Weekly) 14/3 The fourth offering was the best .. a deep-fried, flaky empanada filled with a choice of cheese, beef or chicken.

†**emˈpanel**, *sb. Obs.* Also 6 en-, inpanell, impanall, enpannell, 7 empannel. [f. next.] The list of jurors summoned by the sheriff. Also a jury so summoned.

1501 *Plumpton Corr.* 159 The Inpanell that .. shall passe agaynst you for your maner of Kenalton. *Ibid.* 161, I have sent you part the names of the enpannell. **1568** GRAFTON *Chron.* II. 630 The Maior .. began to call the empanels. **1667** *Decay Chr. Piety* v. §9. 228 May not Christ be permitted .. to make his challenge and exceptions against this so incompetent impanel? **1775** ASH, *Empannel*, the list of jurors summoned to appear in a Court of judicature.

empanel, impanel (ɛmˈpænəl), *v.* Forms: *α.* 5 empanelle, 6–8 enpanel, 6–9 empannell, 6– empanel. *β.* 6–8 impannell, 6–9 impannel, 6– impanel. [a. AF. *empanelle-r*, f. *en-* (see EN-) + *panel* (see PANEL).]

trans. To enter (the names of a jury) on a panel or official list; to enrol or constitute (a body of jurors). Hence **emˈpanelled** *ppl. a.*

[**1383** *Act 7 Rich. II* c. 7 Le meschief qavient as diverses gentz du roialme queux sont empanellez & retournez devant les Justices.]

α. **1487** in *Eng. Gilds* (1870) 404 The seid seriaunt empanelle no man to be in gret inquest. **1548** CRANMER *Catech.* 59 It is not nowe necessarie to empanel a quest. **1611** SPEED *Hist. Gt. Brit.* IX. xiii. §71 The King .. sent .. certaine Londoners .. to be there empanelled for Quests of Inquirie. **1630** J. TAYLOR (Water P.) *Vertue of Tayle* Wks. II. 128/1 A Jury here of Anagrams, you see .. empanneld. **17..** BURKE *Libel Bill* (R.), Jurors duly empannelled and sworn. **1876** GREEN *Short Hist.* ii. 82 A jury empanelled in each hundred.

β. **1514** FITZHERB. *Just. Peas* (1538) 89b, Persons impanellyd by the .. justices. **1586** in *10th Rep. Hist. MSS Comm.* App. v. 440 The Maior .. shall ympannell a jury of the best .. men. **1596** SPENSER *F.Q.* VI. vii. 34 A Jurie was impaneld streight. *c* **1600** SHAKS. *Sonn.* xlvi, To side this title is impannelled A quest of thoughts, all tennants to the heart. **1623** T. GOAD *Dolef. Euen-Song* 17 The Coroners Inquest was there impanelled vpon the dead corpses. **1710** *Tatler* No. 253 ¶1 Twelve Gentlemen of the Horse-Guards were impannelled. **1761** CHURCHILL *Rosciad* Poems (1763) I. 8 Twelve sage impannell'd Matrons. **1788** BURNS *Let. P. Hill* 1 Oct., Were I impannelled one of the author's jury. **1817** W. SELWYN *Law Nisi Prius* (ed. 4) II. 1127 The jurors that are impanelled to inquire of such issue. **1868** MILMAN *St. Paul's* vii. 137 A jury was .. impannelled to ascertain boundaries. **1872** *Wharton's Law Dict.* (ed. 5) 517/1 Women are impanneled as a jury .. where a female prisoner is condemned to be executed, and pleads pregnancy.

empanelling (ɛmˈpænəlɪŋ), *vbl. sb.* [f. prec. + -ING[1].] The action of the vb. EMPANEL.

1467 in *Eng. Gilds* (1870) 392 By crafte of enpanellynge. **1549** LATIMER *Serm. bef. Edw. VI* (Arb.) 143 The Iudge at the enpanelynge of the queste, hadde hys graue lookes. **1885** *Pall Mall G.* 11 May 8/1 They watched with great keenness the empanelling of the jury.

empanelment (ɛmˈpænəlmənt). [f. as prec. + -MENT.] = prec.

1883 *Sat. Rev.* LV. 519 With every fresh empanelment the risk of this is renewed. **1887** *Library Mag.* (New York) Apr. 531/1 After a definite period of empanelment.

†**emˈpannel**, *v. Obs. rare.* [f. EN- + PANEL, pack-saddle.] *trans.* To put a pack-saddle upon.

1620 SHELTON *Quix.* III. ii. I. 227 Good betide him that freed us from the pains of empannelling the grey Ass. **1881** DUFFIELD *Don Quix.* II. 326 Saddle Rozinante, and empannel thine ass.

empanoply, empaper: see EM- *prefix.*

emparadise, var. of IMPARADISE *v.*

emparchment: see EM- *prefix.*

†**emˈpare**, *v. Obs.* [ad. OF. *emparer* in same sense.] *trans.* To furnish, adorn.

1490 CAXTON *Eneydos* xvi. 63 My sone mercure .. take thy wynges empared with fedders.

†**emˈparel**, *sb. Obs. rare*⁻¹. In 5 enparel [altered form of APPAREL; see EN-.] = APPAREL.

c **1420** *Anters of Arthur* xxix, Hur enparel was a-praysut with princes of myȝte.

†**emˈparel**, *v. Obs.* Also 6 empareile [altered form of APPAREL *v.*; see EN-.] *trans.* To equip, array.

1480 CAXTON *Chron.* 243 Shippes that were ful wel arrayd and emparailled and enarmed. **1557** T. PAYNELL *Barcklaye's Bat. of Jugurth* 21 He assembled & empareiled an army.

empark, var. of IMPARK *v.*

emparl(e, emparlance: see IMPARL, -ANCE.

†**emˈparley**, *v. Obs. rare*⁻¹. [f. EN- + PARLEY; cf. OF. *emparler*, IMPARL.] *intr.* To parley.

1600 HOLLAND *Livy* XXVIII. xxxv. 695 They met for to emparley and commune together.

empart, obs. form of IMPART.

empash, -ment, obs. *Sc.* forms of IMPEACH to hinder, IMPEACHMENT hindrance.

†**emˈpasm.** *Med. Obs. rare.* [as if ad. Gr. *ἔμπασμα, regularly f. ἐμπάσσειν to sprinkle on.] **1.** 'A perfumed powder to be sprinkled on the body to restrain sweating or to destroy its smell' (*Syd. Soc. Lex.*).

1657 TOMLINSON *Renou's Disp.* 201 The less affinity falling in the denominations of Empasm and Diapasm. **1775** in ASH. **1847** in CRAIG; and in mod. Dicts.

2. (See quot.)

1657 *Phys. Dict.*, *Empasms*, medicinal pouders used to allay inflamations, and to scarifie the extremity of the skin. **1678** in PHILLIPS. **1721–1800** in BAILEY.

‖**emˈpasma.** *Med. Obs.*⁻⁰ [mod.L., f. as prec.] = EMPASM 1.

1708 in KERSEY. **1751** in CHAMBERS *Cycl.* **1860** in MAYNE *Exp. Lex.*; and in mod. Dicts.

empassion, -ate, -ment: see IMPASSION, etc.

empaste: see IMPASTE.

empathetic (ɛmpəˈθɛtɪk), *a. Psychol.* [f. EMPATH(Y + -IC, after such derivatives as *sympathetic* f. *sympathy*.] = EMPATHIC *a.* Hence **empaˈthetically** *adv.*

1932 *Nation* (N.Y.) 13 Apr. 432 The method .. condemns the biographer to immerse himself in his subject's mind, to take a view that is more than 'sympathetic', that is indeed empathetic. **1933** *Archit. Rev.* LXXIV. 222/1 What newly erected buildings have now any 'empathetic' influence on those they contain? **1949** KOESTLER *Insight & Outlook* xxvi. 359 The richer the personality .. the more empathetic understanding of others it will be capable of. **1961** *Listener* 31 Aug. 326/3 Backache on my part, empathetically produced by those ingenious and toiling rice-planters. **1963** H. READ *Contrary Experience* III. ix. 280 We both spring from the same yeoman stock .., and I think I have a certain 'empathetic' understanding of his personality.

empathic (ɛmˈpæθɪk), *a. Psychol.* [f. EMPATH(Y + -IC.] Of, relating to, or involving empathy; having empathy *to* or *with* (persons, etc.). Hence **emˈpathically** *adv.*

1909 E. B. TITCHENER *Lect. Exper. Psychol. Thought-Processes* v. 181 They shade off gradually into those empathic experiences which I mentioned in the first Lecture. *Ibid.* 185 The [mental] picture is combined with an empathic attitude. **1914** R. M. OGDEN *Introd. Gen. Psychol.* II. xiv. 195 A prominent feature of the aesthetic sentiment .. is its empathic character. **1929** C. J. DUCASSE *Philos. Art* x. 151 This way of reacting in the presence of the statue constitutes the empathic way. *Ibid.* 154 We can if we wish .. perceive empathically also lines, surfaces, motions. **1957** C. BROOKE-ROSE *Langs. of Love* iv. 32 She had sunk to crossword puzzles, and was becoming empathic with the mind of the man on the *Daily Chronicle*. **1957** W. H. WHYTE *Organization Man* 407 Be empathic to the values of the test maker.

empathist (ˈɛmpəθɪst). *Psychol.* [f. EMPATH(Y + -IST.] An adherent of a theory involving empathy.

1923 OGDEN & RICHARDS *Meaning of Meaning* ix. 312 It appeals to Empathists, Croceans and Solipsists. **1934** *Mind* XLIII. 235 It should be kept in mind that C.A.T. [C. A. Thomson] has been an 'Empathist'.

empathize (ˈɛmpəθaɪz), *v. Psychol.* [f. EMPATH(Y + -IZE.] *trans.* To treat something or someone with empathy. *intr.* To use empathy.

1924 R. M. OGDEN tr. *Koffka's Growth of Mind* iv. §7. 207 The chimpanzee is able to *empathize*, or feel itself towards, the end-situation of attaining its goal. **1929** C. J. DUCASSE *Philos. Art* x. 166 For the most part we empathize inanimate things only in so far as we are interested in them aesthetically. **1931** T. H. PEAR *Voice & Personality* v. 56 One may .. 'empathise' with the speaker. **1949** WELLEK & WARREN *Theory of Lit.* viii. 85 The realist .. chiefly observes behavior or 'empathizes'. **1957** G. M. CARSTAIRS *Twice-Born* 152 One has .. to empathise, to 'feel with' him before one can identify his elusive patterns of emotional response.

empathy (ˈɛmpəθɪ). *Psychol.* and *Æsthetics.* [tr. G. *Einfühlung* (see EINFÜHLUNG) (T. Lipps *Leitfaden d. Psychol.* (1903) 187), ad. Gr. ἐμπάθεια.] The power of projecting one's personality into (and so fully comprehending) the object of contemplation.

1904 'V. LEE' *Diary* 20 Feb. in 'Lee' & Anstruther-Thompson *Beauty & Ugliness* (1912) 337 Passing on to the æsthetic empathy (Einfühlung), or more properly the æsthetic sympathetic feeling of that act of erecting and spreading. **1909** E. B. TITCHENER *Lect. Exper. Psychol. Thought-Processes* i. 21 Not only do I see gravity and modesty and pride .. but I feel or act them in the mind's muscles. This is, I suppose, a simple case of empathy, if we may coin that term as a rendering of *Einfühlung*. *Ibid.* v. 185 All such 'feelings' .. normally take the form, in my experience, of motor empathy. **1912** *Academy* 17 Aug. 209/2 [Lipps] propounded the theory that the appreciation of a work of art depended upon the capacity of the spectator to project his personality into the object of contemplation. One had to 'feel oneself into it'... This mental process he called by the name of *Einfühlung*, or, as it has been translated, *Empathy*. **1913** J. M. BALDWIN *Hist. Psychol.* II. 126 'Æsthetic semblance' is the equivalent of 'empathy'. **1925**, **1929** [see EINFÜHLUNG]. **1928** 'R. WEST' *Strange Necessity* 102 The active power of empathy which makes the creative artist, or the passive power of empathy which makes the appreciator of art. **1955** D. DAVIE *Articulate Energy* iii. 30 This is a silent music, a matter of tensions and resolutions, of movements (but again not rhythmical movements) sustained or broken, of ease or effort, rapidity or languor. What we mean, in fact, is *empathy*. **1958** C. P. SNOW *Conscience of Rich* xxxiii. 240 It was not only consideration and empathy that held him back. **1963** R. L. KATZ *Empathy* i. 8 It is true that in both sympathy and empathy we permit our feelings for others to become involved.

†**emˈpatron**, *v. Obs. rare*⁻¹. In 6 enpatrone. [f. EN- + PATRON.] *trans.* To stand in the relation of patron to; to patronize.

1597 SHAKS. *Lover's Compl.* 224, For these of force must your oblations be, Since I their Aulter, you enpatrone me.

empawn, obs. var. of IMPAWN *v.*

empeach, obs. var. of IMPEACH *v.* to hinder, accuse, and *sb.* hindrance, accusation.

empearl, var. IMPEARL, to adorn as with pearls.

†**emˈpeiral**, *a. Obs. rare*⁻¹. [f. Gr. ἔμπειρος (see EMPIRIC) + -AL[1]] = EMPIRICAL.

1587 HARMAR tr. *Beza's Sermons* 421 (T.) Empeirall practicks, who use the medicines which they call narcoticall.

empenitent, obs. form of IMPENITENT *a.*

empennage (ɛmˈpɛnɪdʒ). [Fr., f. *empenner* to feather (an arrow).] An arrangement of stabilizing planes at the stern of an aeroplane or airship; also, the tail-surfaces or tail-plane. Also *transf.* and *fig.*

1909 A. BERGET *Conquest of Air* II. i. 132 The empennage will comprise a surface placed well to the rear of the sustaining surface .. to which it will be joined. **1911** *Aero* Nov. 232/1 The construction of the empennage or fixed 'non-lifting' tail plane. **1912** S. L. WALKDEN *Aeroplanes in Gusts* xii. 95 This .. only defines the path AH more obstinately than before, unless the empennage is made with considerable spread in the fore-and-aft direction. **1926** *Chambers's Jrnl.* 580/1 In every aeroplane the tail unit or 'empennage' comprises the rudder, .. the elevators, .. and the fin. **1927** E. W. SPRINGS *Nocturne Militaire* viii. 258 They vibrated like a hula dancer's empennage. **1959** *New Scientist* 7 May 1014/1 An empennage that could serve a satellite as a rudder.

†**emˈpeople**, *v. Obs.* Also en-, impeople. [f. EN- + PEOPLE.]

1. *trans.* To fill with people, populate.

1582 N. LICHEFIELD tr. *Lopes de Castanheda's Hist. Disc. E. Indies* 140b, He was desirous to encrease and enpeople his Citie. **1583** STUBBES *Anat. Abus.* II. 31 Before the world was impeopled. **1631** *Celestina* XVIII. 181 What does impeople Church-yards but it? **1646** SIR T. BROWNE *Pseud. Ep.* I. vi. 24 But we now know 'tis very well empeopled. **1648** J. BEAUMONT *Psyche* XVI. xix. (R.), Thou hast helpt to impeople hell. **1839** BAILEY *Festus* (1852) 173 With starry globes unnumberable .. Did He the void impeople.

2. *nonce-use.* To establish as the population.

1590 SPENSER *F.Q.* I. x. 56 And gan enquere .. what unknowen nation there empeopled were. **1775** in ASH. **1847** in CRAIG; and in mod. Dicts.

Hence **em'peopled** *ppl. a.*

1855 SINGLETON *Virgil* I. 164 Libya's shepherds.. And their empeopled kraals with scattered roofs.

†**'emperale.** *Obs. rare*⁻¹. [Corrupt form of *emperial*, IMPERIAL: see Du Cange s.v. *imperialis*.] A coin of an emperor.

a **1400** *Octouian* 1911 For emperales that were not smale I bought hym.

†**empe'rality.** *Obs. rare*⁻¹. In 5 **emperalyte.** [var. of IMPERIALITY: cf. prec.] = EMPIRE.

c **1470** HARDING *Chron.* lix. i, Able he was.. To haue ruled all the emperalyte.

†**em'peratrice.** *Obs. rare*⁻¹. [A 16th c. form of **imperatrice*, a. Fr. *impératrice*, ad. L. *imperātrīc-em*, fem. of *imperātor*: see EMPEROR.] = EMPRESS.

1542 HENRY VIII *Declar.* 201 Dauid Kyng of Scottis did homage to Matilde the Emperatrice.

emperess(e, obs. var. of EMPRESS.

emperial(l(e, obs. form of IMPERIAL *a.*

†**em'perial,** *v. Obs. rare*⁻¹. In 5 **emperialle.** [f. *emperial*, IMPERIAL *a.*] *trans.* To give a lordly or magnificent appearance to.

c **1460** J. RUSSELL *Bk. Nurture* in *Babees Bk.* (1868) 133 Emperialle þy Cuppeborde with Siluer & gild fulle gay.

emperic, -al, obs. ff. EMPIRIC, -AL.

emperice, obs. form of EMPRESS.

emperil, obs. form of IMPERIL.

†**em'periment.** *Obs. rare*⁻¹. [a. OF. *empirement* deterioration, f. *empirer* to make worse; cf. EMPYRE *v.* and -MENT.] The action of getting worse, of 'breaking up' physically.

1674 *Collect. Poems, To Flatman*, The minds incurable disease, That (till the last Emperiment) expects no ease.

emperious, obs. var. of IMPERIOUS *a.*

†**em'perish,** *v. Obs. rare.* Also 6 **emperysshe, emperyshe.** [app. f. F. *empirer*, on the erroneous analogy of words like *embellish*; afterwards perh. associated with PERISH.]

trans. To make worse, impair, enfeeble. Hence **em'perishing** *ppl. a.*

1530 PALSGR. 531 It is not utterly marred, but it is sore emperysshed. **1545** T. RAYNOLD *Womans Book* Y 5 The weedes.. wyll defourme and emperysshe the good grace of them. **1579** SPENSER *Sheph. Cal.* Feb., I deeme thy braine emperished bee Through rustie elde. **1593** NASHE *Christ's T.* (1613) 68, Rather.. then inward emperishing famine should too vntimely inage thee.

†**em'perishment.** *Obs.* [f. prec. + -MENT.] Impairment, injury.

1545 RAYNOLD *Womans Book* Y 6 Without any emperisshement of theyr helth.

†**'emperize,** *v. Obs. rare.* [f. EMPERY + -IZE.] **a.** *trans.* To rule as an emperor; to lord it over. **b.** *intr.* Const. *over.* Hence **'emperizing** *ppl. a.*

1598 BARCKLEY *Felic. Man* (1631) 167 He thought it greater.. 'ore Kings to emperize. **1609** HEYWOOD *Brit. Troy* Proem, The Apocalip Magog shall.. Emperise the world. **1601** CHESTER *Love's Mart.* cci, True loue is Troths sweete emperizing Queene.

†**'emperly,** *a. Obs. rare*⁻¹. [f. EMPER-OR + -LY.] = IMPERIAL.

1500–25 *Virgilius* in Thoms *Prose Rom.* (1858) II. 23 He saw his unkell.. in his emperly stole.

emperor ('ɛmpərə(r)). Forms: 3 emperere, 3–8 emperour(e, (3 amperur, aumperour, 4 emparour, -ur, empere, emperore, -ure, eemperour, 5 emperowre), 5–6 emproure, -ure, (6 emporour, empowr, empoure, -pre-, -prioure), (4 imparour, -ur, imperur, -owr, 4–6 imperour), 4, 6– emperor. [The ME. *emperere, emperoure*, are respectively ad. OF. *emperere(s* (nom. case) and *empereor* (oblique case):—L. *impe'rātor, imperā'tōrem*, agent-noun f. *imperāre* to command.

The L. *imperator*, orig. denoting in general the holder of a chief military command, became in the period of the Roman republic a title of honour, bestowed on a victorious general by the acclamation of the army on the field of battle. This title was afterwards conferred by the senate on Julius Cæsar and on Augustus, with reference to the military powers with which the chief of the state was invested; and in accordance with this precedent it was adopted by all the subsequent rulers of the empire except Tiberius and Claudius. In post-classical Latin it became the chief official designation of the sovereign, being interpreted in the sense of 'absolute ruler' (in Greek αὐτοκράτωρ). In this sense it continued to be applied to the rulers of the Western and Eastern Roman empires until they severally came to an end. In A.D. 800 when the Western empire was nominally revived, the Frankish king Charles the Great (Charlemagne) was crowned by the pope with the title of *imperator*, implying that he was invested with the same supremacy over European monarchs that the rulers of the earlier Roman empire had possessed. The title continued to be borne by his successors, the heads of the 'Holy Roman Empire' (popularly the 'Empire of Germany') down to its extinction in 1806. The Romanic (and hence the English) forms of the word were originally applied to the sovereigns of the Eastern empire, to those of the Romano-Germanic empire, and historically to those of the earlier Roman empire. For subsequent extensions of meaning (common to English with the Romanic langs.), see below in sense 3.]

I. 1. The sovereign of the undivided Roman Empire, or of the Western or Eastern Empire.

a **1225** *Ancr. R.* 244 þuruh Julianes heste þe Amperur. *a* **1300** *Cursor M.* 11277 (Cott.) In august time, þe Imparour, Was vs born vr sauueour. *c* **1300** *St. Margarete* 23 Liþer was þemperor Diocletian. **1340** HAMPOLE *Pr. Consc.* 4089 He sal be last emparour þat þare sal be. **1388** WYCLIF *Matt.* xxii. 21 ȝelde ȝe to the emperoure tho thingis that ben the emperouris. **1480** CAXTON *Chron. Eng.* IV. (1520) 27 b/2 He was commaunded by the letter of themperoure to come to Rome. **1549** *Compl. Scot.* 25 Marcus antonius vas venquest be the empriour agustus. **1603** KNOLLES *Hist. Turks* (1638) 36 Baldwin had before married Emanuel the Greek Emperors neece. **1790** BURKE *Fr. Rev.* Wks. V. 431 Rome, under her emperours, united the evils of both systems. **1833** CRUSE *Eusebius* IV. x. 137 This emperor [Adrian] having finished his mortal career.

2. The head of the Holy Roman Empire, also styled of Almaigne or Germany.

In German documents *Kaiser* (the Teutonic form of the imperial name CÆSAR) was used in this sense, and is therefore regarded as the German equivalent of 'emperor'.

1297 R. GLOUC. (1724) 486 The aumperour Frederic, & the king Philip of France Alle hii wende to Ierusalem. *c* **1450** *Guy Warw.* (C.) 4205 Therfore y sey yow, syr emperere. **1529** RASTELL *Pastyme* (1811) 81 Philyppe Auguste.. wanne a great battell agaynst Otton the emperour. *c* **1552** BALE *K. Johan* 1 My granfather was an empowr excelent. **1615** STOW *Annales* 661/1 His lordship.. taking leaue of the Emperour, departed from Vienna. **1735** OLDMIXON *Hist. Eng., Geo. I*, vi. 763 The Treaty of Vienna between the Emperor and King of Spain. **1804** [see 3]. **1873** BRYCE *Holy Rom. Empire* (ed. 4) xii. 186 No act of sovereignty is recorded to have been done by any of the Emperors in England.

3. a. In wider sense, as a title of sovereignty considered superior in dignity to that of 'king'.

In the Middle Ages, and subsequently, the title was often applied to extra-European monarchs ruling over wide territories. We still speak of the Emperors of China, Japan, Morocco, and historically of the Mogul Emperors of India and the Emperor of the Aztecs. Since the early part of the 16th c. the title has been used as the equivalent of the Russian TZAR (or *czar*). The Sultans of Turkey (who assumed the style of *Keisar-i-Rūm*, 'Cæsar of Rome', as successors of the Byzantine emperors) were occasionally spoken of as emperors. Until the present century 'the Emperor' always, unless otherwise interpreted by the context, denoted the 'emperor of Germany'. But in 1804 Napoleon I. assumed the title of 'Emperor of the French', and in the same year the emperor Francis II 'of Germany' added to his other titles that of 'Emperor of Austria', which he retained when in 1806 he put an end to the Holy Roman Empire by his abdication. Subsequently the style of emperor has been adopted in several other instances. 'At present (1889) the only sovereigns so called are (apart from Asiatic and African potentates) those of Russia, Austria, Germany (since 1870), and Brazil (since 1822); and in 1876 the title of Empress of India was assumed by Queen Victoria.' (*N.E.D.*)

c **1400** MAUNDEV. v. 42 The grete Cham.. is the gretteste Emperour.. of alle the parties beȝonde. **1533–4** *Act 25 Hen. VIII*, c. 22. §1 The laufull kinges and emperours of this realme. **1560** ROLLAND *Crt. Venus* Prol. 122 As I have red of Kingis and Empreouris. **1611** SHAKS. *Winter's T.* III. ii. 120 The Emperor of Russia was my Father. **1655** M. CARTER *Hon. Rediv.* (1660) 70 Yet our Kings have been styled Emperors, and this Realm of England called an Empire. **1772** SIR W. JONES *Ess.* i. (1777) 185 Being assisted by the emperours of India and China. **1804** tr. *Proclam. Francis II*, 11 Aug. in *Ann. Reg.* 695 Immediately after our title of elected emperor of the Romans shall be inserted that of hereditary emperor of Austria. **1836** *Penny Cycl.* V. 132 Napoleon, by the grace of God.. emperor of the French. *Ibid.* VII. 77 The government of China.. depends on the will.. of the reigning emperor. *a* **1859** DE QUINCEY *Autobiog. Sk.* Wks. 1858 I. 162 *note*, An emperor is a prince uniting in his own person the thrones of several distinct kingdoms. **1872** FREEMAN *Gen. Sketch* xvi. §3. (1874) 330 Since Buonaparte's time the title of Emperor, which once meant so much, has ceased to have any particular meaning.

b. *transf.* and *fig.*

a **1300** *Cursor M.* 18179 þou ert.. sa hei wit-all, Bath als king and emparur. **1393** LANGL. *P. Pl.* C. XXII. 429 Ich wolde þat.. peers.. [were] Emperour of alle the worlde. *c* **1400** *Rom. Rose* 7217 Of all this world is emperour Gyle my fadir. **1526** *Pilgr. Perf.* (W. de W. 1531) 7 b, In heuen, euery man.. shall be as an emperour. **1598** SHAKS. *Merry W.* I. iii. 9 Thou'rt an Emperor (Cesar, Keiser and Pheazar). **1602** —— *Ham.* IV. iii. 22 Your worm is your onely Emperor for diet. **1667** MILTON *P.L.* II. 510 Nor less Then Hells dread Emperour. **1697** POTTER *Antiq. Greece* III. xx. (1715) 149 Neptune the Great Emperor of the Sea.

4. a. In the popular names of certain butterflies: **purple emperor,** †**emperor of the woods,** *Apatura Iris*; †**emperor of Morocco,** a collector's name, perh. = *purple emperor.*

1773 WILKES *Eng. Moths & Butterfl.* pl. 120 The Purple Highflier, or Emperor of the Woods. **1775** HARRIS *Aurelian* pl. 3 Purple Emperor. **1788** P. PINDAR (J. Wolcott) *title*, Sir Joseph Banks and the Emperor of Morocco. **18..** LYTTON *Kenelm Chil.* v. v, A rare butterfly.. called the Emperor of Morocco.

b. *ellipt.* for *emperor fish, emperor penguin.*

1927 *Times* (weekly ed.) 3 Feb. 115/3 The King penguins .. are, next to the Emperors, the largest of the family. **1929** *Times* 2 Aug. 14/1 'Emperors', beautiful fish of about 30 lb., and of a rich red colour all over. **1967** M. E. GILLHAM *Sub-Antarctic Sanctuary* xx. 173 The almost impossibly rigorous conditions of the emperors' breeding colonies.

†**II. 5. a.** In the etymological sense = 'commander'. **b.** *Rom. Ant.* As the rendering of L. *imperator* in its republican sense (now replaced by the Lat. word). *Obs.*

c **1325** *K. Alis.* 1669 The messangers Buth y-come to heore emperis. **138.** WYCLIF *Sel. Wks.* III. 290 Oure emperoure Crist Comaundiþ. *c* **1400** *Destr. Troy* 3670 þai.. ordant hym [Agamynon] Emperour by opyn assent. **1533** BELLENDEN *Livy* v. (1822) 439 [The] grete justice of thare emprioure Camillus. **1598** W. PHILLIPS *Linschoten's Trav.* in Arb. *Garner* III. 23 The ships of an ancient custom, do use to choose an Emperor among themselves. **1598** GRENEWEY *Tacitus' Ann.* I. iii. (1622) 5 [Augustus] had beene honored with the name of Emperour one and twenty times. **1606** SHAKS. *Ant. & Cl.* IV. xiv. 90 My Captaine, and my Emperor. **1741** MIDDLETON *Cicero* II. vii. (1742) 193 Upon this success, Cicero was saluted Emperor.

III. 6. *attrib.* and *Comb.*, as ***emperor-king, -maker; emperor-less, -like*** adjs. (and adv.); also †**emperor-clerk,** contemptuously for a lord-spiritual; **emperor fish,** a brilliant-coloured food fish, *Holacanthus imperator*; **emperor goose,** a goose of Alaska, *Philacte canagica*, having handsomely variegated plumage; **emperor-moth** (*Saturnia pavonia minor*); **emperor penguin,** the largest of the penguin family, *Aptenodytes forsteri.*

138. WYCLIF *Sel. Wks.* III. 437 Alle degrees of *emperor clerkis. —— *Wks.* (1880) 447 Of popis, ne of oþere emperour clerkis. **1889** *Cent. Dict.*, Emperor of Japan... Also *emperor-fish. **1896** LYDEKKER *R. Nat. Hist.* V. 344 The splendidly-coloured emperor-fish (*H*[*olacanthus*] *imperator*) ..ranges from the east coast of Africa to the Indian and Malayan seas. **1949** *Oxf. Jun. Encycl.* II. 373/2 The best-known [Butterfly-fish] is the Emperor Fish of Indian seas, a very gaudy fish, with its yellow stripes crossing a blue or brown body, and blue and white markings on head and fins. **1872** COUES *Key N. Amer. Birds* 283 Painted Goose. *Emperor Goose. Wavy bluish-gray, with lavender or lilac tinting. **1940** GABRIELSON & JEWETT *Birds Oregon* 129 The Emperor Geese usually arrive here as single birds mingling with other species or in small bands. **1841** W. SPALDING *Italy & It. Isl.* III. 60 The *emperor-king passed through Piedmont in triumph. **1882** *Athenæum* 30 Dec. 879/2 The great-grand-nephew of the victor of Rossbach put an end.. to the *emperor-less period. **1579** TOMSON *Calvin's Serm. Tim.* 509/2 It is an *Emperour-like gouernance. **1601** *Imp. Consid. Sec. Priests* (1675) 54 Thus these great Emperour-like Jesuits do speak to her Majesty. *c* **1630** DRUMM. OF HAWTH. *Poems* Wks. (1711) 6 And emperourlike decore With diadem of pearl thy temples fair. **1581** SAVILE *Tacitus' Hist.* I. xxx. (1591) 18 Prouide that the raskallest sort be no *Emperour-makers. **1868** WOOD *Homes without H.* xiv. 279 The cocoon of the common *Emperor Moth. **1885** *Encycl. Brit.* XVIII. 492 '*Emperor' and 'King' Penguins. **1895** LYDEKKER *R. Nat. Hist.* IV. 546 The king-penguin.. and the still larger emperor-penguin. **1905** R. F. SCOTT *Voy. 'Discov.'* I. iv. 148 A small colony of Emperor penguins in process of moulting exhibited the most dishevelled appearance. **1959** *New Biology* XXIX. 107 The truly Antarctic birds are the Emperor and Adélie penguins and the southern forms of Antarctic skua.

'emperor, *v. nonce-wd.* [f. prec. sb.] *trans.* To rule over as emperor or supreme head.

1855 BAILEY *Mystic* 109 Seeking.. Their own names, to the tribes each emperor'd, To magnify.

'emperor,ship. [f. EMPEROR *sb.* + -SHIP.] The office or dignity of emperor; the reign of an emperor.

1575 T. ROGERS *Sec. Coming Christ* 23/1 Which ambiciously sought the Emperourship of al Italy. **1805** *Month. Mag.* XX. 147 Between the battle of Actium and the acceptance of the emperorship. **1882** *Athenæum* 25 Feb. 247 The last dozen years of his emperorship.

†**em'person,** *v. nonce-wd.* In 6 **enperson.** [f. EN- + PERSON.] *trans.* To unite with one's personality.

1548 GEST *Pr. Masse* 86 Christes body is not enpersoned in us, notwithstanding it is enbodied to us.

empery ('ɛmpərɪ), *sb.* Now only *poet.* or rhetorical. Forms: 3–7 emperie, -ye, (6 embery, empory), 7–9 empiry, -ie, (7 empyrie), 6– empery. Cf. IMPERY. [a. OF. *emperie* (Littré s.v. *empire*), ad. L. *imperium* EMPIRE.]

†**1.** The status, dignity, or dominion of an emperor. *Obs.*

1297 R. GLOUC. (1724) 85 He þer forþ com. And wende toward Rome to wynne þe emperie. **1563–87** FOXE *A. & M.* (1596) 8/2 The excellencie of the Romane emperie did advance the popedom of the Romane bishop aboue other churches. **1588** SHAKS. *Tit. A.* I. i. 201 Thou shalt obtaine and aske the Emperie.

b. In wider sense: Absolute dominion.

1548 UDALL, etc. *Erasm. Par. Matt.* i. 21 Ryches, honoure and emperye. **1591** DRAYTON in Farr *S.P. Eliz.* (1845) I. 132 The only God of emperie and of might. **1599** SHAKS. *Hen. V*, I. ii. 226 Ruling in large and ample Emperie, Ore France. *a* **1631** DONNE *Paradoxes* (1652) 11 All Victories and Emperies gained by War. **1655** JER. TAYLOR *Guide Devot.* (1719) 138 Sets us free From the ungodly Empirie Of Sin. **1812** SCOTT *Trierm.* III. xxv, Coin'd badge of empery it [the gold] bare. **1831** J. WILSON *Unimore* vi. 291 Every Passion in its empery Doth laugh Remorse to scorn. **1882** G. MACDONALD in *Good Words* 154 A wider love of empery.

†**c.** In the sense of L. *imperium*: The authority with which an officer or magistrate has been lawfully invested; legitimate government. *Obs.*

c **1374** CHAUCER *Boeth.* 51 þilke dignitee þat men clepiþ þe emperie of consulers. **1611** SPEED *Hist. Gt. Brit.* IX. vi. (1632) 504 To introduce that free Empery. **1642** BRIDGE *Wound. Consc. Cured* § 1. 10 If a Prince should.. change the form of the Common-weale from Empery to Tyranny.

2. a. The territory ruled by an emperor. **b.** In wider sense: The territory of an absolute or powerful ruler; also *fig.*

1550 COKE *Eng. & Fr. Herald* (1877) §50 Constantyne.. conquered the whole empery. **1601** R. JOHNSON *Kingd. & Commw.* 33 A larger Empery hath not be fallen any christian potentate. **1611** SPEED *Theat. Gt. Brit.* xxix. (1614) 57/1 Alfred or before him Offa shared the open circuit of their emperie into Principalities. **1820** KEATS *Lamia* II. 36 A want Of something more, more than her empery Of joys. **1833** H. COLERIDGE *Poems* I. 62 'Tis all thy own, 'tis all thy empery.

†**'empery,** *v. Obs. rare*⁻¹. [f. prec. sb.] *intr.* To exercise supreme power; to lord it. Const. *upon.*

1502 ARNOLDE *Chron.* (1811) 160 Alsoo emp'ryng vpon ful many cristen lordis.

empesche, -sshe, obs. ff. IMPEACH to hinder.

empest, impest (ɪm'pɛst), *v.* [ad. F. *empeste-r* (Montaigne, 16th c.), f. *em-* = IM-¹ + *peste* PEST, plague: with substitution of L. *im-*.] *trans.* To infect with a plague or pestilence. Also *fig.* Hence **impe'station,** the action of impesting.

a **1618** SYLVESTER *Honour's Fare-well* 50 A Soule devested Of worldly Pomp (which hath the World impested). **1655** H. LESTRANGE *K. Charles* 7 London being.. empested with a.. furious contagion. *a* **1748** CHR. PITT *Epistles, Imit. Spenser* (1810), Ne bitter dole impest the passing gale. **1808** J. BARLOW *Columb.* VI. 36 See the black Prison Ship's expanding womb Impested thousands, quick and dead, entomb. **1844** B. G. BABINGTON tr. *Hecker's Epidemics Mid. Ages* 233 The same attempt at impestation had been already often made in earlier times. **1884** *Med. Times* 19 July 99/2 Hospitalism spared the Calcutta Medical College Hospital during Dr. Mouat's incumbency and impested it in mine. **1923** A. HUXLEY *Antic Hay* v. 76 When two or three are gathered together.. they.. necessarily empest the air.

empester, *v. Obs.* var. of IMPESTER *v.*, to entangle.

empetrous ('ɛmpɪtrəs), *a. Zool.* [f. Gr. ἔμπετρ-ος growing on rocks + -OUS.] 'A term applied to animals like the seal, which have such short members or limbs that they lie directly upon the ground' (*Syd. Soc. Lex.*).

empeyre, obs. f. IMPAIR *v.*

†**'emphanist.** *Obs. rare*⁻¹. [ad. Gr. ἐμφανιστ-ής informer.] An informer, professional spy.

a **1631** DONNE *Aristeas* (1833) 105 You meane the Emphanists, where the Margin says.. false reporters or Spies.

‖**emphase** (ɑ̃faz), *sb. rare.* The Fr. form of EMPHASIS. (Defined by Littré 'exaggeration in expression, tone, voice, or gesture'.)

1882 SYMONDS in *Macm. Mag.* 323 We long.. for less *emphase*. *Ibid.* 327 The habitual *emphase* of his style.

†**em'phase,** *v. Obs.* (? *nonce-wd.*) [f. EMPHASIS.] *trans.* ? To lay emphasis upon.

1631 B. JONSON *New Inn* II. i. (1692) 728, I.. bid you most welcome. *Lady F.* And I believe your *most*, my pretty Boy, Being so emphased by you.

emphasis ('ɛmfəsɪs). *Pl.* emphases. [a. L. *emphasis*, a. Gr. ἔμφασις (in senses 1 and 7 below), f. ἐμφα(ν-, ἐμφαίνειν, mid. voice ἐμφαίνεσθαι, f. ἐν in + φαίν-ειν to show, φαίνεσθαι to appear.]

I. The rhetorical sense, and senses derived from it.

†**1.** (The Gr. and Lat. sense.) The use of language in such a way as to imply more than is actually said; a meaning not inherent in the words used, but conveyed by implication. *Obs.*

[Quintilian illustrates the meaning of 'emphasis' by the manner in which Virgil indicates the vast size of the Cyclops by saying that he 'lay along the cavern'.]

1589 PUTTENHAM *Eng. Poesie* (Arb.) 194 [*Side-note*, Emphasis, or the Renforcer] To inforce the sence of anything by a word of more than ordinary efficacie.. [the meaning of which] is not apparant, but, as it were, secretly conveyed. **1659** PEARSON *Creed* (1839) 215 The Lord of that Temple in the emphasis of an Hebrew article was Christ. **1764** HARMER *Observ.* iii. 8 There might be an emphasis in those words of Moses, which has not of late been at all understood.

b. Special or important significance in a word or phrase (cf. 4).

1612 BRINSLEY *Lud. Lit.* 213 Let them also be taught.. in what word the Emphasis lyeth.

2. Vigour or intensity of statement or expression. Now felt as *transf.* from 4.

1573 G. HARVEY *Lett.-Bk.* (1884) 32 The veri causis.. he knew fully as wel as mi self, with a good larg emphasis, I warrant you. *a* **1619** FOTHERBY *Atheom.* II. xii. (1622) 335 To expresse, with a greater Emphasis, the incredible power of Musick. **1685** STILLINGFL. *Orig. Brit.* ii. 51 Tertullian doth add the greater Emphasis to his Argument. **1839** DE QUINCEY *Recoll. Lakes* Wks. II. 9 She ceased to challenge notice by the emphasis of her solicitations. **1872** MORLEY *Voltaire* (1886) 122 He is the most trenchant writer in the world, yet there is not a sentence of strained emphasis or overwrought antithesis.

†**b.** *concr.* An emphatic expression. *Obs. rare*⁻¹.

1606 SHAKS. *Ant. & Cl.* I. v. 67 Be choak'd with such another Emphasis.

3. Intensity or force of feeling, action, etc.

1602 SHAKS. *Ham.* v. i. 278 What is he, whose griefes Beares such an Emphasis? *a* **1667** COWLEY *Oliver Cromwell* (1710) II. 655 It is only an Emphasis and Exaggeration of their Wickedness. **1670** D. LLOYD *State Worthies* 23 It's the emphasis of misery, to be too soon happy. **1784** COWPER *Task* v. 7 Are they not.. by an emphasis of int'rest his? **1876** GEO. ELIOT *Dan. Der.* I. x. 181 His.. figure.. was all the worse for its apparent emphasis of intention.

4. Stress of voice laid on a word or phrase to indicate that it implies something more than, or different from, what it normally expresses, or simply to mark its importance. (Cf. quot. 1612 in 1 b.)

1613 R. C. *Table Alph.* (ed. 3) *Emphasis*, a forcible expressing. **1748** J. MASON *Elocut.* 26 When we.. distinguish any particular Word in a Sentence, it is called Emphasis. **1775** T. SHERIDAN *Lect. Art Reading* i. §3 Mark the pauses and emphases by the new signs. **1849** DICKENS *Dav. Copp.* iii, Peggotty said, with greater emphasis than usual, that, etc. **1875** JOWETT *Plato* (ed. 2) V. 15 The emphasis is wrongly placed.

b. Manner of placing the 'emphasis' in speaking or reading.

1725 BP. DERRY in Ellis *Orig. Lett.* II. 450 IV. 338 Upon the Delivery of the enclosed speech from the Throne (which was done with as graceful an emphasis as I ever heard).

5. *transf.* 'Stress' laid upon, importance assigned to, a particular fact or idea.

1687 R. L'ESTRANGE *Answ. Diss.* 37 A Flower not to be pass'd over without an Emphasis. **1805** *Med. Jrnl.* XIV. 61 My laying emphasis on the previous effect of the vaccine inoculation. **1847** EMERSON *Repr. Men, Goethe* Wks. (Bohn) I. 384 The emphasis of conversation, and of public opinion, commends the practical man. **1870** —— *Soc. & Solit.* Wks. (Bohn) III. 49 Let not the emphasis of hospitality lie in these things. **1863** GEO. ELIOT *Romola* (1880) I. I. xvi. 222 A slight matter, not worth dwelling on with any emphasis.

6. Prominency, sharpness of contour.

1872 BLACKIE *Lays Highl.* Introd. 22 You never saw a Ben rising bolt upright with a more distinct emphasis. **1877** —— *Lang. & Lit. Scot. Highl.* The bones which mark the features.. lose their emphasis. **1885** *Harper's Mag.* Mar. 526/2 An.. oriel-window, the base of which is formed by a gradual emphasis of the brick wall.

†**II. 7.** An optical illusion, mere appearance. *Obs. rare*⁻¹.

1653 WHARTON *Disc. Comets* Wks. (1683) 156 Some think Comets.. a meer Emphasis or Apparency.

emphasize ('ɛmfəsaɪz), *v.* Also -ise. [f. EMPHASIS + -IZE.] *trans.* To impart emphasis to (anything); to lay stress upon (a word or phrase in speaking); to add force to (speech, arguments, actions, etc.); to lay stress upon, bring into special prominence (a fact, idea, feature in a representation, etc.).

1828 in WEBSTER. **1845** DICKENS *Cricket on Hearth* iii. (Househ. ed.) 106 This philanthropic wish Miss Slowboy emphasized with various new raps and kicks at the door. **1855** W. A. NICHOLLS *Nat. Draw. Master* 8 Accustoming the hand to emphasize strokes in every possible variety of manner. **186.** THACKERAY *Fitz-Boodle's Prof.* Misc. Works IV. 18 My conversion made some noise.. being emphasised as it were by this fact. **1865** TYLOR *Early Hist. Man.* iii. 44 Gesticulation goes along with speech to.. emphasize it. **1869** OUSELEY *Counterp.* xix. 156 When the change to the tonic, or dominant.. is emphasized.. by a longer note than the rest. **1871** BROWNING *Pr. Hohenst.* 432 The Present with .. Its indistinctness emphasized. **1882** HOWELLS in *Longm. Mag.* I. 45 The spruces and firs.. emphasise the nakedness of all the other trees. **1883** FROUDE *Short Stud.* IV. II. iv. 215 The emphasis of phrases may remain, but the point emphasised has been blunted.

Hence **'emphasized** *ppl. a.*

1855 W. A. NICHOLLS *Nat. Drawing Master* 8 The production of emphasized strokes. **1856** MRS. BROWNING *Aur. Leigh* II. 884 And talked with measured, emphasised reserve.

emphasizer ('ɛmfəsaɪzə(r)). [f. EMPHASIZE *v.* + -ER¹.] One who or that which emphasizes.

1887 *Outing* (U.S.) X. 111/1 By way of an emphasizer, striking the table a blow with his fist. **1922** *S.P.E. Tract* XI. 20 We have come to such a pass with this emphasizer [sc. *literally*] that [etc.].

'emphasizing, *vbl. sb.* [f. EMPHASIZE *v.* + -ING¹.] The action of EMPHASIZE *v.*

1888 MRS. H. WARD *R. Elsmere* I. vi, The emphasising rather than the surrender of self.

†**'emphasy.** Also 7 **emphasie** [as if. a. Gr. *ἐμφασία, f. ἐμφα-: see EMPHASIS.] = EMPHASIS.

1612 BRINSLEY *Pos. Parts* (1669) 55 Or else for more emphasie, that is, for speaking more significantly. **1656** in BLOUNT *Glossogr.* **1692** in COLES.

emphatic (ɛm'fætɪk), *a.* [ad. Gr. ἐμφατικ-ός (var. of ἐμφαντικός), f. ἐμφα(ν-: see EMPHASIS.] Characterized by, or imparting, emphasis. **A. 1. a.** Of language, modes of statement or representation; also of tones, gesture, etc.: Forcibly expressive.

1708 KERSEY, *Emphatick*, utter'd with a grace, significant, forcible. **1712** ADDISON *Spect.* No. 363 ¶4 The intercession of the Messiah is conceived in very Emphatic sentiments and Expressions. **1734** tr. *Rollin's Anc. Hist.* (1827) I. III. 249 An emphatic emblem. **1836** J. GILBERT *Chr. Atonem.* viii. (1852) 227 The emphatic representation of Scripture.

b. Of a word or syllable: That bears the stress in pronunciation. †Also (rarely) as quasi-*sb.* in *pl.* = 'emphatic syllables'.

1815 J. GRANT in *Month. Mag.* XXXIX. 118 The same care.. the moderns devote to that of their emphatics and unemphatics. **1837-9** HALLAM *Hist. Lit.* (1847) I. 29 The accented or.. emphatic syllables.

c. *Gram.* ***emphatic particle***: one used to impart emphasis to the portion of the sentence in which it occurs. ***emphatic state***: an inflexion of the sb. in Aramaic, having a function somewhat resembling that of the definite article.

2. Of persons: That expresses himself with emphasis of voice, gesture, or language.

1760 R. LLOYD *Actor* Wks. (1774) I. 16 None emphatic can that actor call, Who lays an equal emphasis on all. **1781** COWPER *Conversation* 269 The emphatic speaker dearly loves to oppose, In contact inconvenient, nose to nose. **1837** DICKENS *Pickw.* (1847) 272/1 The business.. was commenced by a little emphatic man. **1866** GEO. ELIOT *F. Holt* (1868) 29 Mr. Lingon was equally emphatic.

3. Of actions or their effects: Strongly marked, forcible, 'telling'.

1846 PRESCOTT *Ferd. & Is.* I. xi. 449 Still more emphatic honours were conferred on the Count de Cabra. **1872** MORLEY *Voltaire* (1886) 2 One of the emphatic manifestations of some portion of the minds of men. **1873** BURTON *Hist. Scot.* VI. lxx. 199 They threatened to show their opinion in emphatic shape.

B. *sb.* (esp. as pl.). A letter, linguistic form, part of speech, phrase, or syllable that is expressive or indicative of emphasis; *joc.*, an expletive.

1837 G. PHILLIPS *Elem. Syriac Gram.* 24 To the absolute and constructive state of nouns,.. the Syrians add a third, the Definite, or as it has been more generally called, the Emphatic. **1845** S. AUSTIN *Ranke's Hist. Ref.* III. 221 He declared in the most emphatic manner, that it was a.. duty to oppose the.. Turks. **1847** GROTE *Greece* (1862) III. xxxix. 405 An emphatic passage of.. Æschylus. **1873** GILBERT *More 'Bab' Ballads* 52, I have known him indulge in profane, ungentlemanly emphatics. **1905** *Daily Chron.* 23 Oct. 3/4 His emphatics, his luxuriant indulgence in the use of the 'and'. **1938** *Indogerman. Forsch.* Dec. 247 Adverbs include.. emphatics denoting emphasis or restriction, e.g. *indeed, also, only.* **1970** *Language* XLVI. 374 There remain still to be considered the instances of pronominalization in simplex sentences—reflexives, emphatics, and topicalized sentences.

emphatical (ɛm'fætɪkəl), *a. rare* in mod. use. Also 7 **emphaticall**. [f. as prec. + -AL¹.]

†**1.** That implies more than is directly expressed; allusive, suggestive. (Cf. EMPHASIS 1.) *Obs.*

a **1555** LATIMER *Serm. & Rem.* (1845) 274 Chrysostom hath many figurative speeches and emphatical locutions. *a* **1682** SIR T. BROWNE *Tracts* 24 The expression of Scripture is more emphatical than is commonly apprehended. **1702** *Eng. Theophrast.* 337 Great things must be delivered plainly, an emphatical tone would spoil all. **1775** ADAIR *Amer. Ind.* 56 It is an emphatical and emblematical term to express evil, by the negative of good.

2. Of speech or writing: Strongly expressive, forcible, pointed. Of a word: That has special importance in the sentence; hence, that receives the stress in pronunciation.

1577 HARRISON *England* II. xxv. I. 362 Hir owne image and emphaticall superscription. **1630** BRATHWAIT *Eng. Gentl.* (1641) 221 This.. forced from that.. Father this emphaticall discourse. **1713** *Guardian* No. 79 The emphatical expression of praise and blame. **1748** J. MASON *Elocut.* 26 And the emphatical Words.. in a Sentence are those which carry a Weight or Importance in themselves. **1818** JAS. MILL *Brit. India* II. IV. ix. 288 Used so many and such emphatical terms to impress a belief, that, etc. **1824** L. MURRAY *Eng. Gram.* I. 185 Other words.. may begin with capitals, when they are remarkably emphatical.

†**b.** That is designated emphatically or '*par excellence*'. *Obs.*

1644-52 J. SMITH *Sel. Disc.* VII. iv. (1821) 348 The time of that emphatical revelation of the great mystery of God. **1658** SIR T. BROWNE *Gard. Cyrus* II. 500 The Emphaticall decussation or fundamental figure. **1758** S. HAYWARD *Serm.* xvi. 484 The day of Christ's appearance is.. the emphatical day.

†**c.** Of or pertaining to emphasis. *Obs.*

1646 SIR T. BROWNE *Pseud. Ep.* VII. x. 357 They were mistaken in the Emphaticall apprehension.

3. Of actions, sentiments, etc.: Forcible, strongly marked.

1581 J. BELL *Haddon's Answ. Osor.* 436 We.. apply.. improper and borrowed speeches to make the matter seem more emphaticall. **1765** LAW tr. *Behmen's Myst. Magnum* xxxii. (1772) 168 Here we have a very excellent and emphatical example. *a* **1789** BURNEY *Hist. Mus.* (ed. 2) II. iv. 273 Musicians.. who.. ornament their persons in the most emphatical manner. **1805** FOSTER *Ess.* I. vii. 108 Some.. brand of emphatical reprobation.

4. Of a person: That uses emphasis in speech or action; that speaks or acts in a pointed and forcible manner.

1606 *Sir G. Goosecappe* I. i, in Bullen *Old Pl.* III. 10 My Captaine is the Emphaticall man. **1631** GOUGE *God's Arrows* v. i. 375 In setting downe this he is also very emphaticall. **1649** MILTON *Eikon.* 31 On this Theam the King was emphatical and elaborate. **1678** T. JORDAN *Tri. Lond.* in Heath *Grocers' Comp.* (1869) 528 Pleased with.. the promptitude of the emphatical speaker. **1831** CARLYLE *Misc.* (1857) II. 237 Dame Ute bids her not be too emphatical.

†**II. 5.** [cf. EMPHASIS 7.] Of colours: Merely apparent, illusory. *Obs.*

1646 SIR T. BROWNE *Pseud. Ep.* VI. ix. 322 That there is an emphaticall or apparent rednesse in one. **1663** BOYLE *Colours* (J.), Emphatical colours are light itself modified by refractions. **1708** KERSEY, Emphatical or apparent colours, those which are often seen in clouds; before the Rising, or after the setting of the Sun, etc. **1721-1800** in BAILEY.

em'phatically, *adv.* [f. prec. + -LY².]

1. In an emphatic or forcible manner or sense; with emphasis; decidedly, decisively.

1584 FENNER *Def. Ministers* (1587) 69 Saying emphetically, he determined. **1628** EARLE *Microcosm.* lvi. 152 And then they emphatically rail, and are emphatically beaten. **1663** COWLEY *Verses & Ess.* (1669) 128 The Rich poor Man's Emphatically Poor. **1711** STEELE *Spect.* No. 147 ⁋2, I heard the Service read..so emphatically, and so fervently. **1756** BURKE *Vind. Nat. Soc.* Wks. 1842 I. 9 It is always so; but was here emphatically so. **1824** W. IRVING *T. Trav.* I. 258 Striking his cane emphatically on the ground. **1830** FOSTER in *Life & Corr.* (1846) II. 184 The most emphatically evangelical piety. **1871** FREEMAN *Norm. Conq.* (1876) IV. xvii. 58 William the Tyrant, as the local historian emphatically calls him.

†**2.** In a pregnant manner, allusively, suggestively. *Obs.* Cf. EMPHASIS I.

1658–9 T. WALL *Char. Enemies Ch.* 18 Which Samuel does here emphatically insinuate. **1678** CUDWORTH *Intell. Syst.* 410 He often useth those words also emphatically, for 'One only supreme God'.

†**3.** In appearance, as opposed to 'in reality' or 'in fact'; cf. EMPHASIS 7. *Obs.*

1646 SIR T. BROWNE *Pseud. Ep.* v. ii. 235 What is delivered of their incurvitie, must..bee taken Emphatically, that is, not really but in appearance. **1679** PLOT *Staffordsh.* (1686) 127 Not emphatically, like the colours in a glass Prisme..but solidly and genuinly. **1775** in ASH.

†**em'phaticalness.** *Obs. rare.* [f. EMPHATICAL *a.* + -NESS.] The quality of being emphatical; = EMPHASIS 2.

a **1665** J. GOODWIN *Filled w. the Spirit* (1867) 166 Now this could not be expressed in more emphaticalness of words. **1668** JER. COLLIER *Several Discourses* (1725) 246 But then 'tis imply'd in the Emphaticalness of the Expression.

emphisode: see EMPHYSODE.

empholite ('ɛmfəlaɪt). *Min.* [f. (by Igelström 1883) Gr. ἐμφωλεύειν to lurk in + -ITE.] Hydrous silicate of alumina, found in Sweden in minute radiated crystals.

1883 *Amer. Jrnl. Sc.* Ser. III. XXVI. 156 Empholite.. occurs mixed with cyanite, and in cavities in schistose damornite.

emphractic (ɛm'fræktɪk), *a.* and *sb. Med.* [ad. Gr. ἐμφρακτικός, f. ἐμφράττειν to obstruct.]

A. *adj.* Having power to obstruct.

1727–51 in CHAMBERS *Cycl.* **1847** in CRAIG; and in mod. Dicts.

B. *sb.* A medicine which shuts up the pores of the skin.

1678 in PHILLIPS (Emphrastical in **1700**). **1775** in ASH. **1847** in CRAIG; and in mod. Dicts.

†**em'phractical,** *a. Med. Obs. rare.* [f. prec. + -AL¹.] = prec. adj.

1657 TOMLINSON *Renou's Disp.* 124 All are not emphractical or such as fill the pores with their lentor.

emphrensy, obs. var. ENFRENZY.

‖**emphysema** (ɛmfɪ'siːmə). *Med.* Also ? 9 emphysem. [mod.L., a. Gr. ἐμφύσημα inflation, f. ἐμφυσά-ειν to puff up.] 'The swelling of a part caused by the presence of air in the interstices of the connective tissue' (*Syd. Soc. Lex.*). Also (the usual sense of the unqualified word), an enlargement of the air vesicles of the lungs (***pulmonary*** or ***vesicular emphysema***).

1661 LOVELL *Hist. Anim. & Min.* 329 The emphysema or inflation thereof, which is a swelling, caused by external causes. **1764** WATSON in *Phil. Trans.* LIV. 242 The disorder ..was made infinitely worse by the emphysema. **1828** WEBSTER, *Emphysema, emphysem.* **1842** *Med.-Chir. Trans.* XXV. 103, I may mention emphysema of the lungs, which almost always affects both lungs in a symmetrical manner. **1883–4** *Med. Ann.* 40/2 Asthma..accompanied by emphysema. *a* **1883** C. H. FAGGE *Princ. & Pract. Med.* (1886) I. 875 Emphysema of the lungs—or 'emphysema', as it is often called without any addition, when there can be no doubt that a pulmonary affection is intended. **1920** *Nature* 26 Feb. 703/1 Reference is made to the question of the production of emphysema of the lungs (a condition of permanent distension with other changes) by the playing of wind-instruments. **1955** *Sci. News Let.* 4 June 354/1 Chronic bronchitis..may also be found in such other chest diseases as pulmonary emphysema, silicosis, [etc.]. **1966** WRIGHT & SYMMERS *Syst. Path.* I. x. 348 The term 'vesicular emphysema' is used by some authors for emphysema of air spaces to distinguish it from 'interstitial emphysema' in which air escapes from the air spaces into the interstitial structures of the lungs.

emphysematose (ɛmfɪ'siːməˌtəʊs), *a. Med.* [f. Gr. ἐμφυσηματ- stem of prec. + -OSE.] = next.

1776 *Phil. Trans.* LXVI. 432 When I struck it with my finger, it returned an emphysematose sound.

emphysematous (ɛmfɪ'siːmətəs), *a. Med.* [f. as prec. + -OUS.] Of the nature of or like emphysema; pertaining to emphysema.

1764 WATSON in *Phil. Trans.* LIV. 241 The whole substance of the lungs was in a state truly emphysematous. **1870** A. FLINT *Physiol. Man* viii. (1873) 235 Some observers have found the corresponding lung..emphysematous.

†**'emphysode,** *a. Med. Obs. rare*⁻¹. [ad. mod.L. *emphȳsōdes*, a. Gr. *ἐμφῡσώδης characterized by blisters, f. ἐμφυσά-ειν to puff up.]

In ***emphisode fever***: transl. of *Emphysodes febris* (see quot. 1731).

1547 BOORDE *Brev. Health* cxliii. 53 In Englyshe it is named the Emphisode fever. [**1731** BAILEY, *Emphysodes febris* (with Physicians) a vehement heat in fevers, which causes pustules and inflammation in the mouth.] **1775** in ASH.

†**emphy'teuciary.** *Obs. rare*⁻¹. [f. L. *emphyteusi-s* + -ARY.] = EMPHYTEUTICARY.

1676 R. DIXON *Two Testaments* 24 They have..right..to become..Emphyteuciaries, Vassals, or otherwise.

emphyteusis (ɛmfɪ'tjuːsɪs). *Law.* Also 8 empheuteusis. [a. L. *emphyteusis*, a. Gr. ἐμφύτευσις of same meaning; lit. 'implanting', f. ἐμφυτεύ-ειν to implant.] 'A perpetual right in a piece of land that is the property of another' (Stubbs).

a **1618** RALEGH in Gutch *Coll. Cur.* I. 71 Emphyteusis is.. a contract, whereby any moveable thing is granted, to be enjoyed under a certain rent, reserved to the grantor. **1818** HALLAM *Mid. Ages* (1841) I. i. 132 The usufruct or emphyteusis of the Roman code. **1875** BRYCE *Holy Rom. Emp.* viii. (ed. 5) 131 The divided ownership of feudal law found its analogies in the Roman tenure of emphyteusis. **1878** G. MARRIOTT tr. *Laveleye's Prim. Property* 51 An emphyteusis or hereditary lease.

‖**emphyteuta** (ɛmfɪ'tjuːtə). *Law.* [a. L. *emphyteuta*, ad. Gr. ἐμφυτευτής in same sense, f. ἐμφυτεύ-ειν: see prec.] 'A tenant of land which was subject to a fixed perpetual rent' (Maine).

1708 in KERSEY. **1721–1800** in BAILEY. **1775** in ASH. **1875** POSTE *Gaius* II. (ed. 2) 167 The proprietor had a reversion on failure of the heirs of the emphyteuta.

emphyteutic (ɛmfɪ'tjuːtɪk), *a. Law.* Also 7 emphyteutike, -tick, 8 emfiteutic. [ad. L. *emphyteutic-us* in same sense, f. Gr. ἐμφυτεύ-ειν: see EMPHYTEUSIS.] Of the nature of, or held by, EMPHYTEUSIS.

1651 HOWELL *Venice* 148 Goods Ecclesiastic holden as Emphyteutike. **1656** in BLOUNT *Glossogr.* **1768** BLACKSTONE *Comm.* III. 232 A tenant..might be ejected from such emphyteutic lands. **1787** J. TOWNSEND *Journ. Spain* (1792) III. 328 By the emfiteutic contract the great proprietor..has power to grant any given quantity [of land] for a term of years. **1880** MUIRHEAD *Instit. Gaius* 550 Emphyteutic grants of lands by a municipality.

†**emphy'teutical,** *a. Law. Obs. rare*⁻¹. [f. as prec. + -AL¹.] = prec.

a **1618** RALEGH in Gutch *Coll. Cur.* I. 71 It shall be an emphiteutical contract.

†**emphy'teuticary.** *Law. Obs. rare.* [ad. L. *emphyteuticāri-us* = *emphyteuta.*] = EMPHYTEUTA.

a **1656** HALES *Serm. at Eton* (1672) 11 We..may be some emphyteuticaries, or farmers, or usufructuaries. **1656** BLOUNT *Glossogr.*, *Emphyteuticary*, he that maketh a thing better than it was when he received it, that raiseth his rents or improves. **1677** in COLES; and in mod. Dicts.

empicture, var. of. IMPICTURE *v.*, to represent as in a picture, portray.

empiecement (ɛm'piːsmənt). [ad. F. *empiècement*, f. *em-* = *en* + *pièce* PIECE *sb.* + -MENT.] A piece of ornamental material inserted in a garment as a trimming.

1899 *Daily News* 26 Jan. 6/3 The cape matched the dress, and its empiecement and storm collar were covered with steel embroidery. **1902** *Westm. Gaz.* 17 Apr. 3/1 The skirt of this costume has the popular empiecement about the waist. **1927** *Observer* 13 Mar. 25 Empiecements in artistic and other geometrical designs are inserted on some, bars of a contrasting material on others.

†**'empiem.** *Med. Obs.* Anglicized f. EMPYEMA.

1598 SYLVESTER *Du Bartas* 209 The spawling Empiem.. With foule impostumes fills his hollow chest.

empierce, impierce (ɛm-, ɪm'pɪəs), *v.* Also 6 empierse, empeirce, enpearce, imperse. [f. EN-, IN- + PIERCE *v.*] *trans.* To pierce through keenly; to transfix. *lit.* and *fig.*

1578 T. PROCTOR *Gorg. Gallery, Pyramus & Th.*, Sweete pendant, now in wofull brest Impersid. **1592** SHAKS. *Rom. & Jul.* I. iv. 19 I am too sore enpearced with his shaft, To soare with his light feathers. **1593** NASHE *Christ's T.* (1613) 129 To arte-enamel your speech to empeirce..soules. **1621** QUARLES *Esther* §10 Like painted swords They near impierc'd Queen Esthers tender heart. **1642** H. MORE *Song of Soul* I. III. v, The vast thumps of massie hammers noise, Empierc'd mine ears. **1751** GILB. WEST *Educ.* xxxvii, [His] tender Breast Empierced deep with sympathizing Teen. **1855** *Fraser's Mag.* LI. 89 The horrible thorns empierced the bone.

b. *intr.*

1814 CARY *Dante* (Chandos ed.) 147 Through the orbs of all, A thread of wire, impiercing, knits them up.

Hence **em'pierced, em'piercing** *ppl. adjs.*

1604 DRAYTON *Moyses* (L.), He feels those secret and impiercing flames. **1612** —— *Poly-olb.* xxii. (1748) 341 The brinish tears drop'd down on mine impierced breast. **1652** BENLOWES *Theoph.* XIII. xlv. O, let our fleshly barks still ride At anchor in calm streams of His empierced side.

†**em'pight,** *v. Obs.* Also 4 enpight. [The pa. t. and pa. pple. of **empitch*, f. EN- + PITCH *v.*].

1. *trans.* Fixed in, implanted.

c **1400** *Test. Love* I. (1560) 273 b/2 In you is so mokel werking vertues enpight. **1596** SPENSER *F.Q.* III. v. 20 Exceeding griefe that wound in him empight. **1642** H. MORE *Song of Soul* II. iii. II. xlv, Nothing is empight In it. **1746** W. THOMPSON *Hymn to May* [an imitation of Spenser] xliii, Full suddenly the seeds of joy recure Elastic spring, and force within empight. **1721–1800** in BAILEY. **1847** in CRAIG; and in mod. Dicts.

2. *intr.* for *refl.*

1596 SPENSER *F.Q.* II. iv. 46 He..ere it empight In the meant marke, advaunst his shield atween.

empire ('ɛmpaɪə(r)), *sb.* Forms: 3 anpyre, empyere, 4 empir, (impire, imparre), 4–5 emper(e, 4–6 empyr(e, 4– empire. [a. F. *empire*:—L. *imperium* in same sense; related to *imperāre* to command, whence *imperātor* EMPEROR.

Owing partly to historical circumstances, and partly to the sense of the etymological connexion between the two words, *empire* has always had the specific sense 'rule or territory of an EMPEROR' as well as the wider meaning which it derives from its etymology.]

I. Imperial rule or dignity.

1. Supreme and extensive political dominion; *esp.* that exercised by an 'emperor' (in the earlier senses: see EMPEROR 1, 2), or by a sovereign state over its dependencies.

c **1325** *E.E. Allit. P.* B. 1332 For alle his empire so hiȝe in erþe is he grauen. *a* **1400** *Know Thyself* in *E.E.P.* (1862) 132 þauȝ þou haue kyngdam and empyre. *c* **1400** *Three Kings Cologne* 18 Octauianus..in þe ȝeer of his Empire XLII. **1535** COVERDALE *2 Chron.* xxxvi. 20 They became his seruauntes..tyll the Persians had the empyre. **1589** PUTTENHAM *Eng. Poesie* I. xxiii. (Arb.) 60 Your Maiestie haue shewed yourselfe..vertuous and worthy of Empire. **1681** NEVILE *Plato Rediv.* Pref., Many Treatises..alledged .. That Empire was founded in Property. **1711** POPE *Temp. Fame* 347 And swam to empire thro' the purple flood. **1821** BYRON *Sardan.* I. i. (1868) 350 Thirteen hundred years Of empire ending like a shepherd's tale. **1845** STOCQUELER *Handbk. Brit. India* (1854) 7 From this hour (1757) the establishment of the British empire in India may be dated.

2. *transf.* and *fig.* Paramount influence, absolute sway, supreme command or control.

c **1325** *E.E. Allit. P.* A. 454 My lady..haldez þe empyre ouer vus ful hyȝe. **1579** FULKE *Confut. Sanders* 628 What Empyre hath Master Sander in Grammer. **1601** SHAKS. *All's Well* I. i. 72 Thy blood and vertue Contend for Empire in thee. **1667** MILTON *P.L.* I. 114 To deifie his power Who from the terrour of this Arm so late Doubted his Empire. **1752** HUME *Ess. & Treat.* (1777) I. 182 The empire of philosophy extends over a few. **1838** LYTTON *Alice* 129 You know the strange empire you have obtained over me. **1886** STEVENSON *Treasure Isl.* III. xiv. 113 Silence had re-established its empire.

3. The dignity or position of an emperor; also, †the reign of an emperor (*obs.*); = EMPERORSHIP.

1606 G. WOODCOCKE tr. *Hist. Ivstine* Kk 3 b, He died..in the fiftene year of his empire. **1844** LINGARD *Anglo-Sax. Ch.* (1858) I. i. 6 Elevation of Constantine to the Empire.

4. A government in which the sovereign has the title of emperor.

1834 [see EMPLOYÉ]. **1850** MERIVALE (*title*) A History of the Romans under the Empire.

II. That which is subject to imperial rule.

5. a. An extensive territory (*esp.* an aggregate of many separate states) under the sway of an emperor or supreme ruler; also, an aggregate of subject territories ruled over by a sovereign state.

1297 R. GLOUC. (1724) 733 All thys were of hys anpyre. *c* **1330** R. BRUNNE *Chron.* (1810) 6 Adelard of Westsex was kyng of þe Empire. **1393** GOWER *Conf.* III. 282 God hath beraft him..his large empire. **1460** *Lybeaus Disc.* 843 A sercle..Of stones and of golde, The best yn that enpyre. **1606** SHAKS. *Ant. & Cl.* I. i. 34 Let the wide Arch of the raing'd Empire fall. **1735** BURKE *Sp. Conc. Amer.* Wks. III. 69 An empire is the aggregate of many states under one common head. **1848** MACAULAY *Hist. Eng.* I. 348 The position of London, relatively to the other towns of the empire. **1852** TENNYSON *Ode on Death Wellington* I. 2 Bury the Great Duke with an empire's lamentation. **1887** *Whitaker's Almanack* 297 The approximate population of the British Empire is now 321,000,000.

b. ***the Empire***: (*a*) before 1804 (and subsequently in *Hist.* use) often *spec.* the 'Holy Roman' or 'Romano-Germanic' empire.

1678 WANLEY *Wond. Lit. World* v. i. §100. 468/2 Rodolphus the second..was forced to..content himself with..the Empire. **1724** DE FOE *Mem. Cavalier* (1840) 35 The general diet of the empire.

(*b*) Great Britain with its dominions, colonies, and dependencies; the British Empire; freq. the overseas dominions, etc., as opposed to Great Britain. Since the Statute of Westminster (1931), *Commonwealth* has become the more usual term.

1772 R. CUMBERLAND Advt. to *Fashionable Lover* sig. A2ᵛ, Wherever..I have made any attempts at novelty, I have found myself obliged..to dive into the lower class of men, or betake myself to the outskirts of the empire. **1776** ADAM SMITH *W.N.* II. v. iii. 586 Countries which contribute neither revenue nor military force towards the support of the empire. **1847** in J. C. BYRNE *Twelve Years Wand. Brit. Colonies* (1848) II. iii. 86 This gentleman asked whether the colony was to remain the sink-hole of the empire. **1862** *Englishwoman's Dom. Mag.* Jan. 136 'The Hope of the Empire'—the Prince of Wales. **1900** *Daily News* 25 Oct. 4/4

Was it too much to say that in this last twelve months the Empire had been born anew? 1902 *Times* 18 July 8/2 Their fellow-subjects in other portions of the Empire. 1904 *Daily Chron.* 15 Nov. 6/7 Lord Rosebery, in his capacity of principal guest at a dinner of the Oxford Colonial Club last night, replied to the toast of the 'Empire'. 1917 R. MUIR *Char. Brit. Empire* 13 The British Navy has made the growth of the Empire possible. 1948 *Times Lit. Suppl.* 9 Oct., 'Empire', along with its adjective, has gone out of fashion, though it may still be used discreetly for the assemblage of the non-selfgoverning territories and the mother country.

(*c*) the rule of Napoleon Bonaparte as Emperor of the French, 1804–15, or the period of this.

1810 L. GOLDSMITH *Secret Hist. Cabinet Bonaparte* (1811) 112 (*heading*) The Government of France under the consulate and empire of Napoleon Bonaparte. 1830 HAZLITT *Life Nap. Buonaparte* III. xxxiv. 114 If the reign of terror excited their fears and horror, the establishment of the Empire under Buonaparte seemed an even greater affront. 1845 [see CONSULATE 2]. 1866 CROWE *Hist. France* xliii. (*title*) The Consulate and the Empire. 1902 J. H. ROSE *Life Napoleon I* I. xx. 470 At Metz, the troops and populace fretted against the Empire and its pretentious pomp. 1924 R. B. MOWAT *Diplom. Napoleon* xiii. 132 Bonaparte had ushered in the Empire by proclaiming his contempt for the law of nations. 1967 J. MARSHALL-CORNWALL *Napoleon* ii. 26 The French field-guns remained unchanged in range and calibre throughout the whole period of the Consulate and Empire.

(*d*) the rule of Napoleon III as Emperor of the French, 1852–70, or the period of this, usually as *Second Empire*.

1863 A. W. KINGLAKE *Invasion of Crimea* II. iii. 67 He [*sc.* Napoleon III] was very willing to try to earn for the restored Empire that kind of station and title which the newest of dynasties may acquire by signal achievements in war. 1873 *Young Englishwoman* Feb. 77/1 The multifarious skirts and retroussis of the Second Empire régime. 1876 C. M. YONGE *Womankind* xv. 114 Are we not still suffering from the expensive style begun in the Second Empire? 1904 M. BEERBOHM *Around Theatres* (1953) 332 My imagination roved back to lose itself in the golden haze of the Second Empire. 1961 M. HOWARD *Franco-Prussian War* i. 15 A régime so precarious as that of the Second Empire, bitterly opposed by an active and intelligent minority and resting on public apathy rather than popular consent.

6. *transf.* and *fig.* (Cf. *realm.*)

*c*1440 *York Myst.* xlvi. 200 Farewele, nowe I passe to þe pereles empire. 1526 *Pilgr. Perf.* (W. de W. 1531) 69 Called to be enherytours of the celestiall empyre. 1608 SHAKS. *Per.* II. i. 53 These fishers..from their watery empire recollect All that may men approve or men detect! 1656 W. MONTAGUE *Accompl. Wom.* 124 Love is an Empire only of two Persons. 1709 ADDISON *Tatler* No. 154 ¶2 Æneas is represented as descending into the Empire of Death. 1772 MACKENZIE *Man World* I. i. (1823) 241 Liberal minds will delight in extending the empire of virtue. 1821 SHELLEY *Prometh. Unb.* I. 15 Scorn and despair—these are mine empire.

7. A country of which the sovereign owes no allegiance to any foreign superior.

1532–3 *Act 24 Hen. VIII*, c. 12 This realme of England is an Impire. 1765 BLACKSTONE *Comm.* I. 242 The legislature ..uses..*empire*..to assert that our king is..sovereign and independent within these his dominions.

III. 8. a. *attrib.* and *Comb.*, as ***empire-plan***, ***-race***, etc.; ***empire-grown*** adj.; ***empire-maker***, ***-making*** ppl. a.; **empire-builder**, a man who acquires additional territory for his state; also formerly applied loosely to British administrators abroad; *transf.*, one who increases his authority or influence, or who expands unnecessarily the size of his offices, etc., or the number of his subordinates; so ***empire-building*** vbl. sb. and ppl. a.; **Empire City** *U.S.*, a name for the City of New York; **empire cloth**, a cloth or sheet used as an electrical insulator; **Empire Day**, May 24, the birthday of Queen Victoria, formerly observed as a (school) holiday in the British Empire and instituted as a memorial of the assistance given by the colonies to the mother country in the South African war of 1899–1902 (now *Commonwealth Day*); **Empire State** *U.S.*, a name for the State of New York; also applied to other American states.

1894 *Westm. Gaz.* 30 June 6/1 A reference to Mr. Cecil Rhodes's work as empire-builder. 1909 *Ibid.* 10 June 7/1 As if Shakespeare and Burns and Bunyan and Swift and all the rest of that superb gallery were not the greatest of British Empire-builders. 1927 V. WOOLF in *Forum* May 709 Her dreams of living in India, married to..some empire builder. 1959 *Camb. Rev.* 2 May 456/1 Running through the [Civil] service,..the approach of the empire builder. 1970 D. DEVINE *Illegal Tender* ii. 20 Wainwright was solely to blame for the inter-departmental tension. He was said to be an empire-builder. 1898 *Daily News* 12 Aug. 6/1 His exploits in the Empire-building line. 1962 J. BRAINE *Life at Top* ii. 31, I should have to continue as the despised administrator, the nasty unsympathetic accountant who kept his eye on office materials and methods and who..firmly checked any attempts at empire-building. 1962 *Times* 9 Nov. 13/4 One hesitates..to accuse the obstetricians of empire building. 1838 *Bentley's Misc.* IV. 48 The bustle and noise of the empire city. 1857 W. CHANDLESS *Visit Salt Lake* II. v. 222 The mint julep, that in the Crescent City you may enjoy for ten cents, costs you twelve and half in the Empire city. 1944 *Newsweek* 24 July 82/3 The Empire City meeting is typical of wartime racing. 1913 FLEMING & JOHNSON *Insulation & Design of Electrical Windings* iii. 107 Except in the case of Empire cloth no appreciable deterioration in the insulation was noted. 1945 *Electronic Engin.* XVII. 498 Among the insulating materials affected are..all cellulose products such as paper, varnished fabric, empire cloth and insulating tape. 1902 *Times* 18 July 8/1 Lord Meath..wrote suggesting that May 24..should be observed as an official holiday under the title of 'Empire Day'. 1922 CHESTERTON *Ballad St. Barbara* 74 For the spots are all red and the rest is all grey, And that is the meaning of Empire Day. 1901 *Empire Rev.* I. 370 A concession in support of Empire-grown wine. 1903 *Daily Chron.* 5 Dec. 4/4 Whether we had 'Empire-grown' cotton, or depended chiefly on American supplies. 1899 Empire-maker [see BEAN-FEAST b]. 1903 *Westm. Gaz.* 1 June 12/3 Gazing out across the silent waters at the granite hills that have seen the passage of how many empire-makers. 1894 *Daily News* 29 Jan. 5/2 Mr. Rhodes is an Empire-making man. 1864 PUSEY *Lect. Daniel* ii. 66 The great empire-plan of Alexander. 1878 MORLEY *Condorcet* 52 Its desire to be an empire-race. 1834 *Reg. Deb. Congress U.S.* 506 We are told, sir, of..the empire State of New York. 1835 *Knickerbocker* V. 51 Show him the public works of the Empire State, as well as those of Pennsylvania. 1841 J. Q. ADAMS in *Congress. Globe* Sept. App. 433 If there is an 'Empire State' in this Union, it is Delaware..[but] if my forty friends from New York choose to call it the Empire State, I will not quarrel with them. 1860 *Leisure Hour* 29 Nov. 765/2 Illinois, the 'Empire State' of the mighty West. 1889 FARMER *Americanisms* s.v., The term *Empire State of the South* has been applied to Georgia. 1903 *N. Y. Even. Post*, The saloon men of Tennessee have not, perhaps, the literary finish..of their brethren in the Empire State. 1948 *Arizona* (Phoenix) *Republican* 27 Feb. 6/1 The Empire State is 'in the bag' for the GOP. 1851 *Gentl. Mag.* CXXI. II. 54 God bless'd the empire-tree which thou didst plant.

b. Applied to styles of clothing (esp. a dress with a high waistline), furniture, etc., characteristic of the period of the French Empire (see 5 b (*c*) and (*d*)).

1869 LADY C. SCHREIBER *Jrnl.* (1911) I. 29 Green cup and saucer, imitating 'Empire' Sèvres. 1870 O. LOGAN *Before Footlights* 292 How do you manage to pay $60 for your new but ugly little Empire bonnet? 1879 *Encycl. Brit.* IX. 849/2 The 'empire' style, a stiff, affected classicalism, prevailed in France during the reign of Napoleon. 1887 *Academy* 18 June 440/1 She wore, of course, an Empire dress. 1888 *Weldon's Illust. Dressmaker* Dec., The Empire and Directoire styles are steadily increasing in popularity. 1889 R. BROOK *Elem. Style Furnit.* 29 As in all other French styles, 'Empire' was closely imitated in this country. *Ibid.*, It is impossible to have a better authority on 'Empire' Furniture, than the book of designs published in Paris, by the architects, Percier and Fontaine, in 1809. 1901 E. SINGLETON *Furnit. of our Forefathers* II. 573 Empire sofa owned by Mrs. William Young, Baltimore, Md. 1904 H. E. BINSTEAD *Furnit. Styles* x. 116 It is never difficult to determine what is Empire. 1905 A. HAYDEN *Chats on Old Furnit.* 208 The wood used for..Empire cabinets is rich mahogany. *a*1910 'O. HENRY' *Sixes & Sevens* (1916) xiii. 129 High-collared, baggy, empire-waisted, ample-skirted. 1958 *Vogue* Apr. 18 Choose this Empire-line charmer in swirling full length. 1967 E. SHORT *Embroidery & Fabric Collage* ii. 41 The same design would have been unthinkable on say an Empire dress of seventy years earlier. 1968 *Harrods Xmas Catal.* 15/2 An Empire line slip in nylon. 1970 *Oxford Times* 25 Sept. 11/5 She wore a full length white empire line dress with a guipure lace bodice and circular train trimmed with guipure lace.

c. Applied to wines and spirits grown in the British Empire (Commonwealth) and imported into Great Britain.

1937 AUDEN in Auden & MacNeice *Lett. f. Iceland* v. 57 Someone may think that Empire wines are nice. 1954 P. FRANKAU *Wreath for Enemy* III. v. 210 You would look like an advertisement for Empire Burgundy. 1965 R. JEFFRIES *Dead against Lawyers* ix. 94, I can offer you Empire sherry or a beer?

†'**empire**, *v. Obs.* Also impire, em-, impyre. [f. prec. sb.] *intr.* To rule absolutely as an emperor. Const. *above, of, on.*

1556 *Calvin's Com. Prayer Bk.* in *Phenix* (1708) II. 217 Strangers again empire above us. 1594 CAREW *Tasso* (1881) 75 At pleasure now on starres empyreth he. *a*1605 MONTGOMERIE *Sonn.* xxxi, Thy sprit..spurris thee..abone the planetis to impyre. 1599 JAS. I. Βασιλ. Δωρον (1682) 71 Your wrath empyring over your owne passion. 1637 HEYWOOD *Dial.* xiii. Wks. 1874 VI. 225, I empir'd o're All Caria.

empire, var. of EMPYRE *a.*, empyrean.

†'**empiredom.** *Obs. rare*⁻¹. [f. EMPIRE *sb.* + -DOM.] = EMPIRE II.

1591 HORSEY *Trav.* (1857) 158 He..assumed to himself two severall crowns and empirdoms.

empiric (ɛm'pɪrɪk), *a.* and *sb.* Forms: 6–7 emperic, -ike, -ique, -yke, empirike, -ique, -yke, empyrick, -yke, 7–8 emperick(e, empirick(e, empric(k(e, 6– empiric; also 6 impericke. [ad. L. *empiricus*, Gr. ἐμπειρικ-ός, f. ἐμπειρία experience, f. ἔμπειρος skilled, f. ἐν in + πεῖρα trial, experiment. In 17th c. usually ('ɛmpɪrɪk)]

A. *adj.* = EMPIRICAL in various senses. (The use as *sb.* occurs earlier in Eng., and the adjectival senses are chiefly derived from it.)

1605 BACON *Adv. Learn.* I. 8 It is accounted an errour, to commit a naturall bodie to Emperique Phisitions. *a*1649 DRUMM. OF HAWTH. *Jas. V.* Wks. (1711) 90 This empyrick balm could the French apply to cure the wounds of the Scottish common-wealth. 1667 MILTON *P.L.* V. 440 By fire Of sooty coal the Empiric Alchimist Can turn..Metals of drossiest Ore to perfet Gold. *a*1700 DRYDEN (L.), Bold counsels..Like empirick remedies..last are try'd. 1787 *Phil. Trans.* LXXVII. 43 They are only empiric, and not founded upon the theory and principles of gravitation. 1815 *Scribbleomania* 76 Empiric pigmies may prate about straws. 1877 E. CAIRD *Philos. Kant* II. v. 286 The combination of sensitive states by an empiric law of association.

B. *sb.*

1. A member of the sect among ancient physicians called *Empirici* ('Εμπειρικοί), who (in opposition to the *Dogmatici* and *Methodici*) drew their rules of practice entirely from experience, to the exclusion of philosophical theory.

1541 R. COPLAND *Galyen's Terap.* 2 Gij, The whiche thynge the Emperykes vnderstande by onely experyence. 1601 HOLLAND *Pliny* II. 344 Another faction and sect of Physitians, who..called themselues Empiriques. 1605 TIMME *Quersit.* Pref. 5 Among Physitians there are Empericks, Dogmaticks, Methodici, or Abbreuiators, and Paracelsians. 1738 J. KEILL *Anim. Œcon.* Pref. 30 The Doctrine of the Empiricks, which despises all Reasoning. 1805 *Med. Jrnl.* XIV. 446 The ancient empirics were peculiarly eminent for their talent of observation.

b. One who, either in medicine or in other branches of science, relies solely upon observation and experiment. Also *fig.*

1578 LYTE *Dodoens* VI. vi. 665 Broomrape is counted of some empiriques (or practisioners)..for an excellent medicine. 1613 R. C. *Table Alph.* (ed. 3), *Emperick*, he that hath all his skill in phisicke by practise. 1858 ROBERTSON *Lect.* i. 11 A mere empiric in political legislation. 1873 HALE *In His Name* viii. 65 The Florentine would be called only an empiric by the science of to-day. 1877 E. CAIRD *Philos. Kant* v. 100 The animals are pure empirics.

2. An untrained practitioner in physic or surgery; a quack.

[1527 ANDREW *Brunswyke's Distyll. Waters* Oj, Than came there an onlerned Empyricus.] 1562 BULLEYN *Bk. Simples* 68b, One called Edwardes, a doltish impericke. 1601 SHAKS. *All's Well* II. i. 125 We must not corrupt our hope, To prostitute our past-cure malladie To empericks. 1621 BURTON *Anat. Mel.* II. i. IV. i, There be many mountebanks, quack-salvers, Empericks, in every street. *a*1764 LLOYD *Ep. C. Churchill* Poet Wks. 1774 I. 85 Quack and Critic differ but in name. Empirics frontless both, they mean the same. 1806 *Med. Jrnl.* XV. 369 Bone setters are another set of empirics. 1835 BROWNING *Paracelsus* 164 They are hooting the empiric, The ignorant and incapable fool.

b. *transf.* A pretender, impostor, charlatan.

1640 QUARLES *Enchirid.* IV. lxxxix, Hee that beleeves with an implicite Faith, is a meere Empricke in Religion. 1670 EACHARD *Cont. Clergy* 22 A disesteemed pettifogger, or empyrick in divinity. 1777 W. DALRYMPLE *Trav. Sp. & Port.* cxii, The Bishop, supreme empiric, heals the minds and cures the consciences..by the same prescription. 1817 COLERIDGE *Lay Serm.* 386 Such are the political empirics, mischievous in proportion to their effrontery, and ignorant in proportion to their presumption.

3. Comb. ***empiric-like*** adj. and adv.

1620 MELTON *Astrolog.* 9 He delivered this Emperike like Oration. *a*1700 DRYDEN (J.), The illiterate writer, emp'rick like applies To each disease..chance remedies.

empirical (ɛm'pɪrɪkəl), *a.* Forms: 6–7 empericall, 7–8 empyrical, 7– empirical. [f. prec. + -AL¹.]

1. *Med.* **a.** Of a physician: That bases his methods of practice on the results of observation and experiment, not on scientific theory. **b.** Of a remedy, a rule of treatment, etc.: That is adopted because found (or believed) to have been successful in practice, the reason of its efficacy being unknown. †Also as quasi-*sb.* in *pl.* = 'empirical remedies'.

1569 J. SA[NFORD] *Agrippa's Van. Artes* 140b, Empericall, that is to saie, that consisteth in practise, of experimentes. 1612 WOODALL *Surg. Mate* Wks. (1653), Medicine composed by a Chymicall, Methodicall, or Empericall Surgeon. 1656 RIDGLEY *Pract. Physick* 26 Empiricalls are: Earth-worms provided divers wayes. 1685 EVELYN *Mem.* (1857) II. 216 He had a laboratory, and knew of many empirical medicines. 1830 MACKINTOSH *Eth. Philos.* Wks. 1846 I. 136 Sextus, a physician of the empirical, *i.e.* anti-theoretical school. 1869 E. A. PARKES *Pract. Hygiene* (ed. 3) p. i, Empirical rules..observations of what seemed good or bad for health.

2. That practises physic or surgery without scientific knowledge; that is guilty of quackery. Also of medicines: That is of the nature of a quack nostrum. Cf. EMPIRIC B. 2.

*a*1680 BUTLER *Rem.* (1759) II. 304 A Pedlar of Medicines ..and Tinker empirical to the Body of Man. 1839 JAMES *Louis XIV*, IV. 45 Empirical drugs for the cure of various diseases. 1840 H. AINSWORTH *Tower Lond.* (1864) 66 When all the physicians of the royal household were dismissed, and the duke sent messengers for empirical aid.

3. In matters of art or practice: That is guided by mere experience, without scientific knowledge; also of methods, expedients, etc. Often in opprobrious sense *transf.* from 2: Ignorantly presumptuous, resembling, or characteristic of, a charlatan.

1751 JOHNSON *Rambler* No. 183 ¶13, I have avoided.. that..empirical morality, which cures one vice by means of another. 1793 HOLCROFT *Lavater's Physiog.* xxix. 136 We are all more or less empirical physiognomists. 1825 MCCULLOCH *Pol. Econ.* I. 42 Their arguments..had somewhat of an empirical aspect. 1861 GOSCHEN *For. Exch.* 84 The application of hasty and empirical measures. 1872 YEATS *Techn. Hist. Comm.* 317 The great majority of accidents are..the results of empirical management.

4. Pertaining to, or derived from, experience. ***empirical ego*** = ***empirical self***; ***empirical formula***: in *Mathematics*, a formula arrived at inductively, and not verified by deductive proof; in *Chemistry*, a formula which merely enumerates the ultimate constituents of a

compound in any convenient order, without implying any theory of the mode in which they are grouped; *empirical law*: see quot. 1846; *empirical philosophy* = EMPIRICISM 2b (cf. also PRAGMATISM 4); *empirical psychologist*, an exponent or adherent of empirical psychology; *empirical psychology*, the science of the mind developed by observation and experiment, rather than by deduction from general principles (opp. *rational psychology*); *empirical self* (see quot. 1890).

1649 JER. TAYLOR *Gt. Exemp.* Pref. ¶46 The propositions of this philosophy being Empiricall and best found out by observation. **1798** *Month. Rev.* XXV. 585 His empirical acquaintance with the works of taste is not comprehensive. **1829** *Nat. Philos.* I. *Mechanics* III. v. 18 (Usef. Know. Ser.) By an empirical formula is meant one that is conceived or invented without any analysis or demonstration. **1830** SIR J. HERSCHEL *Stud. Nat. Phil.* 71 If the knowledge be merely accumulated experience, the art is empirical. **1834** MRS. SOMERVILLE *Connex. Phys. Sc.* viii. (1849) 70 An empirical law observed by Baron Bode, in the mean distances of the planets. **1836–7** SIR W. HAMILTON *Lect.* (1877) II. xxi. 26 Knowledge a posteriori is a synonym for knowledge empirical, or from experience. **1846** MILL *Logic* III. xvi. §i, An empirical law then, is an observed uniformity, presumed to be resolvable into simpler laws, but not yet resolved into them. **1850** DAUBENY *Atom. Th.* ix. (ed. 2) 297 $SO^3 + KO$ is the rational formula of the salt called sulphate of potass: S, O^4, K the empirical. **1851** H. L. MANSEL *Proleg. Logica* ix. 275 Among modern philosophers, empirical psychology..is frequently classified as metaphysical. **1869** BUCKLE *Civilis.* III. v. 385 The empirical corroboration of his doctrine by direct experiment. **1870** S. H. HODGSON *Theory of Practice* I. ii. 252 Every feeling and every object in the whole empirical ego stands in some relation to it [*sc.* the emotion of moral sense]. **1890** W. JAMES *Princ. Psychol.* I. x. 291 The Empirical Self of each of us is all that he is tempted to call by the name of *me*. **1892** —— *Coll. Ess. & Rev.* (1920) 321 We certainly need something more radical than the old division into 'rational' and 'empirical' psychology. **1901** —— in *Proc. Soc. Psychical Res.* XLII. 21, I can therefore speak..as a mere empirical psychologist, of Myers's general evolutionary conception. **1902** —— *Var. Relig. Exper.* xiv. 374 According to the empirical philosophy..all ideals are matters of relation. **1949** *Mind* LVIII. 124 The empirical psychologist is almost of necessity an epiphenomenalist in practice. **1963** R. P. WOLFF *Kant's Theory Mental Activ.* I. ii. 144 Only the empirical self is knowable. **1967** S. J. TODES in R. P. Wolff *Kant* 164 The distinguishing feature of the empirical ego is that all empirical knowledge must be in terms of it.

em'pirically, *adv.* [f. prec. + -LY².] In an empirical manner.

1. After the manner of an empiric or quack-doctor.

1631 BRATHWAIT *Whimzies, Almanack-maker*, He ha's some small scruple of physician..and can most empyrically discourse of the state of your body. **1643** SIR T. BROWNE *Relig. Med.* I. §31 His scholars: who..doe empirically practise without his advice. **1872** F. THOMAS *Dis. Women* (ed. 3) 64 The advice is too often given empirically.

2. By means of observaton and experiment.

1646 SIR T. BROWNE *Pseud. Ep.* VI. xii. 334 For wee shall emperically and sensibly discourse hereof. **1664** POWER *Exp. Philos.* III. 192 Philosophy..will Empirically and Sensibly canvass the Phænomena of Nature. **1809–10** COLERIDGE *Friend* (1865) 23 A schoolmaster is under the necessity of teaching a certain rule in simple arithmetic empirically. **1879** tr. *Du Moncel Telephone* 52, I sought..to discover empirically the exact effect of each element.

†**em'piricalness.** *Obs.* [f. as prec. + -NESS.] The quality of being empirical.

1654 W. DE RAND *Short Meth. of Surg.*, Not being offended at the appearance of Empiricalness in the discourse.

empiricism (ɛm'pɪrɪsɪz(ə)m). [f. EMPIRIC + -ISM.] The method or practice of an empiric.

1. *Med.* Practice founded upon experiment and observation; ignorant and unscientific practice; quackery. Also *transf.*

1657 G. STARKEY *Helmont's Vind.* 245 The Chymistry of the Galenical Tribe is a ridiculous..and..dangerous Empericism. **1756** C. LUCAS *Ess. Waters* II. 47 The art became debased with empiricism. **1791** MACKINTOSH *Vind. Gall.* Wks. 1846 III. 148 'The practical claim of impeachment'..is the most sorry juggle of political empiricism. **1880** SIR J. FAYRER in *Nature* XXI. 231 The empiricism of to-day is more scientific than it was in former days.

2. a. The use of empirical methods in any art or science. **b.** *Philos.* The doctrine which regards experience as the only source of knowledge.

1796 F. A. NITSCH *Kant's Princ. concerning Man* 218 The comfortless attacks of Fatalism, Scepticism, and Empiricism. **1798** A. F. M. WILLICH *Elem. Crit. Philos.* 7 A slavish dependence upon the Empiricism of Locke. **1803** *Edin. Rev.* I. 257 Made acquainted with the division of empiricism and rationalism. **1817** JAS. MILL *Brit. India* I. II. ix. 399 Mere observation and empiricism, not even the commencement of science. **1872** MINTO *Eng. Lit.* II. viii. 547 The empiricism popularly associated with the name of Locke. **1881** HUXLEY in *Nature* No. 615. 343 All true science begins with empiricism.

3. *concr.* A conclusion arrived at on empirical grounds.

1846 MILL *Logic* III. xiii. §5 The instances of new theories agreeing with..old empiricisms, are innumerable.

empiricist (ɛm'pɪrɪsɪst), *sb.* and *adj.* [f. as prec. + -IST.]

A. *sb.* **a.** An upholder of philosophical empiricism. **b.** One who follows empirical methods.

1698–1712 SHAFTESBURY *Phil. Regimen* (1900) 207 The prescriptions of the vulgar-wise, like those of the Empiricists. They know only the symptom; apply only to the symptom. **1857** T. E. WEBB *Intell. Locke* i. 17 Kant..regarded Aristotle as the head of the Empiricists. **1875** *N. Amer. Rev.* CXX. 469 Berkeley..a consistent empiricist. **1876** tr. *Wagner's Gen. Pathol.* 5 Medical men have been designated as Empiricists and Rationalists in matters of pathology. **1955** *Sci. Amer.* Aug. 86/1 Now, through Bertrand Russell, almost all British and American empiricists are to some degree disciples of Hume.

B. *adj.* Of, or relating to, or characterized by, philosophical empiricism.

1871 H. SIDGWICK in *Academy* 15 Nov. 521/1 It is impossible to state more boldly the empiricist view of geometry. **1890** W. JAMES *Princ. Psychol.* I. vii. 195 Empiricist writers are very fond of emphasizing one great set of delusions which language inflicts on the mind. **1907** —— *Pragmatism* ii. 51 Pragmatism represents a perfectly familiar attitude in philosophy, the empiricist attitude. **1953** H. H. PRICE *Thinking & Exper.* viii. 252 In any Empiricist theory of thinking..there has to be a doctrine of cashability. **1965** N. CHOMSKY *Aspects Theory Syntax* 206 There is no justification for the common assumption that there is an asymmetry between rationalist and empiricist views.

empirico- (ɛm'pɪrɪkəʊ), taken as comb. form of EMPIRICAL *a.*, EMPIRICISM, etc., usually in some such sense as 'partly empirical and partly...'. Also **em'pirio-**.

1895 A. C. ARMSTRONG tr *Falckenberg's Hist. Mod. Philos.* II. xvi. 622 The preponderance of natural science and the empirico-skeptical tendency of the philosophy of the day conditioned by it. **1897** C. H. JUDD tr. *Wundt's Outl. Psychol.* v. 318 This general principle is known as the *principle of psycho-physical parallelism.* It has an empirico-psychological significance and is thus totally different from certain metaphysical principles. **1937** C. B. WEINBERG (*title*) Mach's empirio-pragmatism in physical science. **1938** *Times Lit. Suppl.* 22 Jan. 52/3 A distinction of prime importance between the 'empirico-mathematical' and the 'empirico-schematic' sciences. *Ibid.* 52/4 The empiriometric and empirio-schematic analysis of observable reals. **1942** *Mind* LI. 306 Intuitionism..is particularly out of harmony with the more extreme types of empirico-formalism which are so influential at the moment.

empiri'cutic, *a.* *nonce-wd.* In 7 emperick-qutique. [f. EMPIRIC: on analogy of *pharmaceutic.*] Empirical.

1607 SHAKS. *Cor.* II. i. 128 The most soueraigne Prescription in Galen, is but Emperick qutique; and to this Preseruatiue, of no better report then a Horse-drench.

†**'empirie.** *Obs.* In 7 **empyrie.** [ad. Gr. ἐμπειρία. Cf. EMPIRIC.] = EMPIRICISM 1.

1651 WITTIE tr. *Primrose's Pop. Err.* I. vi. 23 Even Physicians do not disdain Empyrie.

empirio-criticism (ɛm,pɪrɪəʊ'krɪtɪsɪz(ə)m). *Philos.* [tr. G. *empiriokritizismus* (R. Avenarius 1894, in *Vierteljahrschr. f. Wiss. Philos.* XVIII. 138), f. *empirio-* EMPIRICO- + *kritizismus* criticism.] The philosophy of Richard Avenarius (1843–96), a form of positivism consisting primarily in the rejection of the dualism of body and mind, and the restriction of knowledge to a basis in experience treated critically and so deprived of all metaphysical elements.

1897 *Mind* VI. 449 (*title*) Richard Avenarius and his General Theory of Knowledge, Empiriocriticism. *Ibid.* 451 'Critical empiricism'..looks for the universal element in experience... Empiriocriticism, on the other hand, takes up the position that everything is experience when it has been stated as experienced by an individual—though it may be that..it is only experience for this one individual in question... This empiriocriticism also approaches experience critically, but it does not determine its concept of experience beforehand. **1933** *Mind* XLII. 379 All his [*sc.* Lenin's] philosophical work, the greater part of which appears in the volume *Materialism and Empirio-Criticism*, reveals his partisanship. **1955** H. B. ACTON *Illusion of Epoch* I. i. 19 Books by Ernst Mach and Richard Avenarius in which, under the name of 'empirio-criticism', a phenomenalist account of matter was advocated.

Hence **em,pirio-'critical** *a.*, of, or relating to, or characterized by, empirio-criticism.

1909 in *Cent. Dict.* Suppl. **1925** F. ZNANIECKI *Laws Soc. Psychol.* i. 1 The arguments against the possibility of psychological laws may be reduced to three. The first has been put forward by the so-called empirio-critical school of German philosophers (Avenarius, Petzoldt, and others), and..by the neo-criticists (Natorp, etc.). **1933** *Mind* XLII. 379 The Russian followers of the empirio-critical philosophy of Mach and Avenarius. **1949** I. DEUTSCHER *Stalin* iv. 106 Neo-Kantian or empirio-critical philosophy.

empirism ('ɛmpɪrɪz(ə)m). [f. Gr. ἔμπειρ-ος (see EMPIRIC) + -ISM.] = EMPIRICISM 2b.

1716 M. DAVIES *Dissert. Physick* 37 in *Ath. Brit.* III. **1852** SIR W. HAMILTON *Discuss.* 104 Empirism, Philosophy of Experience or of Observation. **1852** MORELL tr. *Tennemann's Hist. Phil.* 67 Empirism..would derive all our knowledge ultimately from experience.

empiristic (ɛmpɪ'rɪstɪk), *a.* [f. as prec. + -IST + -IC.] Of or pertaining to empirism.

1881 LE CONTE *Light* 103 The one is called the nativistic, the other the empiristic theory.

empiry, var. EMPYRE, obs., empyrean.

emplace (ɛm'pleɪs), *v.* [f. EN- + PLACE *sb.*; (really back-formation from EMPLACEMENT.)] *trans.* To put into a place or position. *spec.* To provide an emplacement for new guns.

1865 RAWLINSON *Anc. Mon.* III. v. 385 The shrine..was emplaced upon the topmost, or silver stage. **1900** *Daily News* 22 Jan. 3/2 This morning the Boers emplaced a five-pounder at the brick fields, and proceeded to drop shells into the market square. **1904** *Daily Chron.* 28 May 5/4 A series of batteries, strongly emplaced, crowded the crest of the hill. **1915** J. BUCHAN *Nelson's Hist. War* V. 26 They had an ordinary range of four to five miles, and this allowed them to be emplaced well to the rear out of any danger from the enemy. **1958** P. KEMP *No Colours or Crest* xii. 269 A detachment of our escort had emplaced itself behind a low bank.

emplacement (ɛm'pleɪsmənt). Rarely **im-**. [a. Fr. *emplacement*: see prec. and -MENT.]

1. The action of placing in a certain position; the condition of being so placed.

1869 RAWLINSON *Anc. Hist.* 64 The emplacement of each pyramid so as exactly to face the cardinal points.

2. a. Of a building, etc.: Situation, position. **b.** Site. *rare.*

1802 W. TAYLOR in Robberds *Mem.* I. 415 Buildings admired for their architecture, and well displayed by their emplacement. **1804** W. TAYLOR in *Ann. Rev.* II. 689 The station or implacement, would confer majesty even on an inferior edifice. **1837** *Blackw. Mag.* XLI. 362 The French might have found..a more appropriate emplacement for the obelisk. **1862** RAWLINSON *Anc. Mon.* I. v. 95 The exact emplacement of the second [story] on the first is also doubtful. **1880** *Blackw. Mag.* Jan. 115 The large amphitheatre, the emplacement of which can still be traced on the hill side.

3. *Mil.* A platform for guns, with epaulements for the defence of those serving them.

1811 WELLINGTON in Gurw. *Disp.* VII. 258 They ought to make an emplacement for their field pieces. **1862** ANSTED *Channel Isl.* I. iii. (ed. 2) 42 Two..square emplacements, covering rocks, have been constructed. **1881** *Daily News* 1 Sept. 2/4 A model emplacement, constructed of concrete. **1889** *Engineer* 5 Apr. 281 We understand that the heavy steel guns are to be mounted in Moncrieff implacements.

emplaistre, var. of EMPLASTER, *Obs.*

emplane (ɛm'pleɪn), *v.* Also **enplane.** [f. EM- 1 a + PLANE *sb.*⁵] *trans.* and *intr.* To take or go on board an aeroplane.

1923 *Westm. Gaz.* 2 July 3/2 Two Vickers-Victoria machines arrived, and emplaned the distressed garrison. **1930** *Air* July 292 The Prime Minister and Miss Ishbel MacDonald emplaning for a week-end in Edinburgh. **1941** F. H. JOSEPH in M. Wheeler *Britain at War* 95 Group was first enplaned, then those passengers taken on. **1944** *Cape Times* 25 May, Men of the Fifth Indian Division had no idea where they were going when they emplaned. **1966** *New Statesman* 14 Jan. 58/3 A popular radio actress.. is emplaned to Paris in the early Sixties. **1966** *Catholic Standard* 21 Oct. 4/6 He [*sc.* Krushchev] suddenly pulled up stakes and enplaned with all haste for Moscow. **1970** *Daily Tel.* 25 July 10 The usual Kennedy Airport congestion caused us to wait 2¼ hours, after emplaning, for takeoff.

emplant, obs. form of IMPLANT.

†**em'plaster**, *sb.* *Obs.* Forms: 4 **enplaster, -tre,** 5–7 **emplastre, -aister, -ayster, -aystre,** (6 *erron.* **emplasture**); also 6–7 **implaster, -aister.** [a. OF. *emplastre* (F. *emplâtre*), L. *emplastrum*, ad. Gr. ἔμπλαστρον plaster or salve, f. ἐμπλάσσειν, f. ἐν in + πλάσσειν to mould.]

1. *Med.* or *Surg.* = PLASTER.

1382 WYCLIF *Isa.* xxxviii. 21 Thei shulden taken an hep of fyges, and..make an enplastre vpon the wounde. **1430** LYDG. *Chron. Troy* I. vii, Lectuary, emplaystre, or pocyon. *a* **1500** *Med. Receipts* in *Rel. Ant.* I. 54 Tak everferne..and tak mynt, and mak ane emplaster. **1564** BECON *Gov. Virtue* (1566) 50b, Neither hearbe nor emplasture hathe healed them. **1578** LYTE *Dodoens* I. xcix. 141 Oyntments, oyles, or emplaisters. **1601** HOLLAND *Pliny* XX. ix, If the said implaister be made with bean-meale. *c* **1720** W. GIBSON *Farrier's Dispens.* xvi. (1734) 302 The whole is brought to the consistence of an Emplaster. **1751** CHAMBERS *Cycl.*, *Emplaster*, popularly called Plaster. **1809** PARKINS *Culpepper's Eng. Physic. Enlarged* 361 The Greek emplaisters consisted of these ingredients.

fig. **138.** WYCLIF *Sel. Wks.* III. 166 Enplaster of cursing for heele of monnis soule. **1563–87** FOXE *A. & M.* (1596) 256/2 Minister some spirituall implaster. *a* **1656** BP. HALL *Rem. Wks.* (1660) 79 Lay on the soveraign emplaisters of the ..mercy of our Blessed Redeemer.

2. Used to render L. *emplastrum*: see EMPLASTRATION 1.

1601 HOLLAND *Pliny* II. 518 The manner of graffing by way of emplaistre or scutcheon.

Hence †**em'plasterwise**, *adv.*, in the form of a plaster, as a plaster is applied.

1551 TURNER *Herbal* I. C iij b, It [amomum] helpeth them that are bytten of scorpiones laid to emplaisterwise with basill. **1562** *Ibid.* II. 13b, The sede [of sonne flower] layd to emplasterwise, dryeth away hanginge wartes.

†**em'plaster**, *v.* *Obs.* Forms: 4–6 **emplastre,** 6–7 **emplaster, -aistre, -ayster;** also 7 **implaistre.** [a. OF. *emplastre-r*, ad. L. *emplastrāre*, f. *emplastr-um*: see prec.]

1. a. To cover with a plaster; to plaster over; also *fig.* **b.** To spread on as a plaster.

c 1386 CHAUCER *Merch. T.* 1053 Als fair as ye his [Solomon's] name emplastre, He was a lecchour and an ydolastre. 1541 R. COPLAND *Guydon's Formul.* Y ij b, To emplayster the place with diaculum. 1585 H. LLOYD *Treas. Health.* D ij, Galbanum emplastered to the hed is of great efficacye. 1601 HOLLAND *Pliny* xx. ix, Colewort is soveraigne good to be implaistred upon those tumors. 1633 tr. *Bacon's Life & Death* (1651) 50 Let the body be Emplaistred with Mastick.

2. A rendering of L. *emplastrare* to bud trees (misinterpreted in quot. 1656); see EMPLASTRATION 1.

c 1420 *Pallad. on Husb.* VI. 86 The pechys in this moone Emplastred are. 1656 DUGARD *Gate Lat. Unl.* §324.91 He.. besmears them, being implanted (which is to emplaster).

Hence **em'plastering** *vbl. sb.*

c 1420 *Pallad. on Husb.* III. 350 Oon in the stok, on graffeth under rynde; Emplastering an other dothe in kynde. *Ibid.* VII. 92 Emplasturyng accordeth with the tree That hath a juce of fattenesse in the rynde. 1577 B. GOOGE *Heresbach's Husb.* (1586) 72 Emplastring or inoculation. 1633 tr. *Bacon's Life & Death* (1651) 50 Let this Bath with the Emplaistring .. be renewed every fifth day.

emplasteration, var. EMPLASTRATION, *Obs.*

1692 in COLES. 1775 in ASH.

†**em'plastic**, *a.* and *sb.* *Obs.* [ad. Gr. ἐμπλαστικός, f. ἐμπλάσσειν: see EMPLASTER *sb.*]

A. *adj.* Fit to be used as a plaster; *hence*, adhesive, glutinous, viscid. Also [after late Gr. use], that stops up the pores.

1618 LATHAM *2nd Bk. Falconry* (1633) 140 It is also of an emplasticke or clammy quality. 1634 T. JOHNSON tr. *Parey's Chirurg.* VII. xxvii. (1678) 189 Medicins.. acrid, oily, and emplastick. 1684 tr. *Bonet's Merc. Compit.* IV. 133 Wax.. through its.. emplastick faculty.. fastning it self like Glew. 1756 C. LUCAS *Ess. Waters* I. 53 Unctuous and emplastic bodies. 1832 in WEBSTER; and in mod. Dicts.

B. *sb.* An adhesive or glutinous substance.

1657 TOMLINSON *Renou's Disp.* 125 An Emplastick should be of a terrene substance. 1721–1800 BAILEY, *Emplasticks*, Medicines which constipate and shut up the Pores of the Body, that Sulphureous Vapours cannot pass. 1751 STACK in *Phil. Trans.* XLVII. 269 Burgundy-pitch, or any other powerful emplastic.

†**em'plastical**, *a.* *Obs. rare*$^{-1}$. [f. prec. + -AL[1].] = prec. *adj.*

1657 TOMLINSON *Renou's Disp.* 124 Their quality sounds not emplastrical but emplastical, or emphractical. *Ibid.* 125 An emplastical medicament should want all mordacity.

†**em'plasticate**, *v.* *Obs. rare*$^{-1}$. [f. EMPLASTIC + -ATE.] *trans.* To make into a plaster.

1657 TOMLINSON *Renou's Disp.* 335 Emplasticated with honey, it takes away dimness.. from the eyes.

†**empla'stration.** *Obs.* Also 5 **emplastracioun**, 6 **emplaistration**, 6 **implastration**. [ad. L. *emplastrātiōnem*, noun of action f. *emplastrāre*: see EMPLASTER *v.*]

1. A mode of budding trees mentioned by Latin writers; so called from the piece of bark surrounding the bud, which was attached like a 'plaster' (L. *emplastrum*) to the tree.

c 1420 *Pallad. on Husb.* VII. 91 In Juyl and nowe solempne insicion Hath treen, that men calle emplastracioun. 1601 HOLLAND *Pliny* II. Gloss., Emplastration in the Hortyard, is grafting by inocelation with a scutcheon. 1745 tr. *Columella's Husb.* v. xi, Emplastration, or.. Inoculation.

2. The application of a plaster.

1545 T. RAYNOLD *Womans Booke* 75 Ministred.. by fumes, or odours, or emplastration, etc. 1601 HOLLAND *Pliny* II. 394 To returne agaïne to the former emplastration. 1633 tr. *Bacon's Life & Death* (1650) 63 Closure up of the body by Emplastration.

‖**em'plastrum.** The Latin form of EMPLASTER *sb.*

1596 FITZ-GEFFRAY *Sir F. Drake* (1881) 19 Soules sweet Emplastrum, unguent of the eyes. 1878 T. BRYANT *Pract. Surg.* I. 171 If the carbuncle is small.. cover it with emplastrum plumbi spread on leather.

emplead, obs. form of IMPLEAD.

emplection, bad form of EMPLECTON.

emplectite (ɛm'plɛktaɪt). *Min.* [f. Gr. ἔμπλεκτος inwoven (f. ἐμπλέκειν, f. ἐν in + πλέκειν to weave) + -ITE; the name being given from its appearance.] A sulphide of bismuth and copper, occurring in bright tin-white needle-shaped crystals; found in Saxony and Chili.

1857 SHEPARD *Min.* 424. 1884 DANA *Min.* 86.

‖**em'plecton.** *Arch.* [mod.L., a Gr. ἔμπλεκτον: see prec.] 'A kind of masonry, in which the outsides of the wall are ashlar, and the interval filled up with rubbish' (Liddell and Scott).

1708–15 KERSEY, *Emplecton opus*, Masons-work well knit and couched together. 1731 in BAILEY, vol. II.

empledge, var. of IMPLEDGE.

empleomania (ˌɛmpliə'meɪnɪə). [Sp., f. *empleo* employment + MANIA.] A mania for holding public office.

1878 J. R. LOWELL in *Century Mag.* (1898) Nov. 144/1 The *empleomania*, which is the dry-rot of Spain. 1920 *Glasgow Herald* 23 Oct. 12 The evil which has sapped the vigour of so many nations—'empleomania'—has made its insidious way into British administrative departments. 1922 *Ibid.* 4 Jan. 4 This creed, adoption of which begets the insanity of empleomania.. has had a stranglehold upon the whole Ibero-American Continent.

†**em'plesance.** *Sc. Obs. rare*$^{-1}$. [as if OF. **emplaisance* f. **emplaisir*: see EMPLESS. Cf. PLEASANCE.] Pleasure.

1469 *Sc. Acts Jas. III* (1814) 94 It salbe leful to the kingis hienes to tak þe desisioun of ony actioune that cummis before him at his emplesance.

†**empleseur.** *Sc. Obs. rare*$^{-1}$. [f. OF. **emplaisir*: see next. Cf. PLEASURE.] = prec.

1560 *Letter* in McCrie *Knox.* I. 437 And this ye faill not to do, as ye will do us singular empleseur.

†**em'pless**, *v.* *Sc. Obs.* [ad. OF. **emplaisir*, orig. form of *emplaire* to please; cf. EN- and PLEASE.] *trans.* To please.

1478 *Act. Audit.* (1839) 61 Þe said Schir William to folou vpon personis for þe said some as it empless him.

emplie, obs. var. of IMPLY.

emplore, obs. form of IMPLORE.

employ (ɛm'plɔɪ), *sb.* Also 7–8 **imploy**. [ad. F. *emploi*, n. of action f. *employer* to EMPLOY; = Sp. *empleo*, It. *impiego*.]

†**1.** The action of employing a person or making use of a thing; = EMPLOYMENT 1. *Obs.*

1666 EVELYN *Mem.* (1807) III. 184 Employ of chirurgeons. a 1694 A. LITTLETON in Spurgeon *Treas. Dav.* Ps. xv. 5 The drone without a sting.. wanting a tool for employ. 1829 SOUTHEY *Sir T. More* ii. 76 The application of gunpowder.. was not brought into full employ, even after, etc.

2. The state or fact of being employed; *esp.* that of serving an employer for wages. In phrases, *in, out of, employ*; *in the employ of* (the person employing).

1709 STRYPE *Ann. Ref.* I. xliii. 473 The first mention.. of Thomas Sampson in publick employ. 1713 *Guardian* No. 158 We are obliged by duty to keep ourselves in constant employ. 1832 HT. MARTINEAU *Homes Abroad* ix. 114 New comers of their craft, or in their employ. 1841 MIALL *Nonconf.* I. 391 Operatives out of employ. 1885 *Act 48 & 49 Vict.* c. 56 Preamb., To permit electors in his regular employ to absent themselves.

3. Something on which a person or thing is employed; an employment, occupation. Now *poet.* or *arch.*

1680 SIR E. KING in *Academy* 15 May 502/2 A better employ to exercise his courage. 1704 SWIFT *T. Tub* iv. 64 Peter put these bulls on several employs. 1725 BRADLEY *Fam. Dict.* II. s.v. *Tree*, Drunken Fellows.. uncapable of so judicious Imploy. 1829 C. WELCH *Wesl. Polity* 89 An assiduity worthy of a better employ. 1877 M. ARNOLD *Poems* II. 89 The wind-borne, mirroring soul.. leaves its last employ.

†**b.** A regular business or occupation; a trade or profession. *Obs.*

1678 BUNYAN *Pilgr.* I. (1862) 114 To have but a poor imploy in the world. 1697 POTTER *Antiq. Greece* I. xxvi. (1715) 169 That Ferry-man shall be prohibited the exercise of his employ, who overturns his boat. 1771 WESLEY *Wks.* 1872 V. 297 Neglect of the worldly employ wherein.. God has placed us. 1795 J. AIKIN *Manchester* 238 From this variety of employ, population has more than doubled since 1772.

†**c.** An official position in the public service.

1691 LUTTRELL *Brief Rel.* (1857) II. 210 Being putt out of an employ.. at the custome house at Newcastle. 1691 RAY *Creation* II. (1704) 241 Great Commands & Employs in the Dutch Colonies. a 1734 NORTH *Lives* (1826) I. 76 Another employ fell to his Lordship's share. 1821 BYRON *Mar. Fal.* II. i. 113 The wariest of republics Has lavish'd all its chief employs upon him.

employ (ɛm'plɔɪ), *v.* Forms: 5 **en-**, 5– **employ**; also 6–8 **imploy**. [a. F. *employe-r* (var. of OF. *emplier*: see IMPLY, and cf. PLOY, PLY), a Com. Romanic word = Pr. *impleiar*, Cat. *implegar*, Sp. *emplear*, Pg. *empregar*, It. *impiegare*:—L. *implicāre*, f. *in* + *plicāre* to fold. Cf. IMPLY.

The senses of this word (exc. 5, 6) are derived from the late L. sense of *implicare* 'to bend or direct upon something'; the classical senses 'enfold, involve' are represented by IMPLY.]

1. *trans.* To apply (a thing) to some definite purpose; to use as a means or instrument, or as material. Const. *for, in, on*, †*to*.

α. 1483 CAXTON *Gold. Leg.* 433/4 Whan hir moder sawe the.. lynnen cloth thus employed she was moche wroth. 1553 BRENDE *Q. Curtius* 109 (R.) When he beheld the boorde.. employed to so base a use. 1624 LD. KENSINGTON in Ellis *Orig. Lett.* I. 301. III. 173 To employ her credit with the king her son. 1671 tr. *Frejus' Voy. Mauritania* 5 To employ eight hundred Piastres for his expence. a 1704 LOCKE (J.), The timber employed about the plough. 1718 *Free-thinker* No. 65. 68 Employ the Prerogative only for their [the people's] Good. 1759 B. MARTIN *Nat. Hist. Eng.* I. *Somerset* 53 The soil of this Country is.. employed in Grain and Pasturage. 1839 LANDOR *Andrea* Wks. 1846 II. 526 All have more knowledge than they will employ. 1856 RUSKIN *Mod. Paint.* III. IV. iv. §11 Art was employed for the display of religious facts.

β. c 1460 FORTESCUE *Abs. & Lim. Mon.* viii. (1885) 126 The kynges owne money, wich he mey than imploye to oþer vse. 153. STARKEY *Lett.* 73 Imploing such giftys God hathe gyuen me. 1601 R. JOHNSON *Kingd. & Commonw.* (1603) 85 The hils.. and river sides being onely imploied to vines. 1667 MILTON *P.L.* IV. 763 Heere Love his golden shafts imploies. 1689–92 LOCKE *Toleration* ii. Wks. 1727 II. 291 The best Design any one can imploy his Pen in. 1697 DRYDEN *Virg. Georg.* III. 244 This Curse.. Juno.. imploy'd for Iö's Punishment. 1772 PRIESTLEY *Inst. Relig.* (1782) I. 413 The rest of the inclosure imployed in tillage.

b. To apply, devote (effort, thought, etc.) to an object. (In later use merged in 4.)

1587 HARRISON *England* II. i. (1877) I. 37 To imploy their studies unto physike and the lawes. 1596 SHAKS. *Merch. V.* II. viii. 43 And imploy your chiefest thoughts To courtship. 1683 BURNET tr. *More's Utopia* 128 All other Animals imploy their bodily Force one against another. 1784 J. BARRY *Lect. Art* iii. (1848) 151 Any man.. who would generously employ his whole undivided attention to it.

c. To make use of (time, opportunities). Const. *in*, †*to*. In mod. use also (influenced by 4), 'to fill with business' (J.).

α. 1481 CAXTON *Myrr.* I. v. 20 He.. employed his tyme to studye. 1523 LD. BERNERS *Froiss.* I. cclxii. 387 What was best for them to do to employ forthe their season. 1664 EVELYN *Kal. Hort.* (1729) 185 How usefully you employ this glorious Recess. 1725 DE FOE *Voy. round W.* (1840) 319 Those intervals were employed to.. hunt for food. 1860 TYNDALL *Glac.* I. §27. 195 Having ten days at my disposal.. I was anxious to employ them.

β. 1621 G. SANDYS *Ovid's Met.* IV. (1626) 77 Some in life-practiz'd Arts imploy their times. 1732 LEDIARD *Sethos* II. ix. 277 He imploy'd the whole time in raising enormous machines.

†**2.** To bestow (something) *on* a person. *Obs.* [So *emploier* in OF.]

1548 GEST *Pr. Masse* 104 Melchisedech.. employing upon Abraham bred and wyne. 1598 GREENE *Jas. IV* (1861) 190 What reward.. May I employ on you for this your zeal?

3. To use the services of (a person) in a professional capacity, or in the transaction of some special business; to have or maintain (persons) in one's service.

α. 1584 POWEL *Lloyd's Cambria* 98 Emploied in affaires of the Commonwealth. 1771 *Junius Lett.* lix. 304 Let us employ these men in whatever departments their various abilities are best suited to. 1872 RAYMOND *Statist. Mines & Mining* 206 Scott & Co., employing nine men six months. 1872 MORLEY *Voltaire* (1886) 162 Lessing.. was employed by Voltaire.. in the Hirschel case.

β. 1590 SHAKS. *Mids. N.* I. i. 124, I must imploy you in some businesse Against our nuptiall. 1621 *Frailty of Life* in Farr *S.P. Jas. I* (1848) 201 To thinke, not one of those whome he imploy'd Should be aliue within one hundred yeares. 1662 STILLINGFL. *Orig. Sacr.* III. i. §2 Moses.. writ as a person imployed by God. 1728 NEWTON *Chronol. Amended* ii. 224 Cinyras.. imployed workmen in making armour.

†**b.** To send (a person) with a commission *to, towards* (a person), *to, into* (a place); also, *to employ out*. *Obs.*

α. 1611 SHAKS. *Cymb.* II. iii. 68 We shall haue neede T' employ you towards this Romane. 1618 BOLTON *Florus* III. vi. 190 Publius Servilius was employd out against them. 1654 R. CODRINGTON tr. *Hist. Ivstine* 289 The Lacedemonians, being unwilling to employ their forces into so remote a war. 1687 *Good Advice* 22 Bishop Usher was Employ'd to O. Cromwell by some of the Clergy.

β. 1606 SHAKS. *Ant. & Cl.* V. ii. 70 To Cæsar I will speake, what you shall please, If you'l imploy me to him. 1631 WEEVER *Anc. Fun. Mon.* 670 Iohn Wriothesley.. was imployed into Scotland, and with him Northumberland Herauld. 1650 J. HOWELL *Hist. Revol. Naples* 56 He imployed besides into the Castle three Gentlemen of speciall parts.

4. To find work or occupation for (a person, his bodily or mental powers); in *pass.* often merely to be occupied, to be at work. Const. *about, in, on*.

α. 1611 BIBLE *Ezra* x. 15 Were employed about this matter. 1655 FULLER *Ch. Hist.* I. iv. §19 He was principally employed farre off at Constantinople. 1713 STEELE *Englishm.* No. 11. 73 Whoever is well employed is then at Prayers. 1772 JOHNSON *Lett.* (1788) I. l. 60 By showing how much I am employed upon you. 1850 MCCOSH *Div. Govt.* II. ii. (1874) 215 How can the whole soul be so nobly.. employed? *Mod.* I cannot fully employ you. I found him employed in writing letters. Glad to see you so well employed.

β. 1651 HOBBES *Leviath.* III. xxxiv. 208 Men, that are otherwise imployed. 1691–8 NORRIS *Pract. Disc.* IV. 191 All .. imploy'd in the Contemplation of our Excellencies. 1704 SWIFT *Batt. Bks.* (1711) 262 He was imploy'd in drinking. 1705 STANHOPE *Paraphr.* II. 277 Imploying our Thoughts, upon the Occasions chosen by Our Lord.

b. *refl.* To apply (*obs.*), busy, or occupy oneself.

1579 LYLY *Euphues* (Arb.) 113 Employe thyselfe to marcial feates. 1764 REID *Inquiry* i. §2. (1785) 12 Castle-builders employ themselves.. in romance. 1856 R. VAUGHAN *Mystics* (1860) I. 4 More of genius than common was required to teach a man how to employ himself.

c. Said of the object to which attention is given.

1665 BOYLE *Occas. Refl.* (1675) 25 Occasional Reflections .. need not employ our hands. 1697 DRYDEN *Virg. Georg.* IV. 78 Their young Succession all their Cares employ. 1704 POPE *Summer* 47 Then might my voice thy list'ning ears employ. 1732 BERKELEY *Alciphr.* vii. §17. Wks. 1871 II. 317 Speculations to employ our curiosity. 1774 GOLDSMITH *Grecian Hist.* II. 170 Mithridates, who so long employed the Roman armies. 1833 HT. MARTINEAU *Manch. Strike* i. 13 A Pan's pipe employed his mouth. 1854 TENNYSON *Poems, To Rev. F. D. Maurice* i, Come, when no graver cares employ. *Mod.* He needs something to employ his mind.

†**5.** = IMPLY in various senses: **a.** To entwine, enclose, encircle. **b.** To involve, include, contain. **c.** To imply, signify. *Obs.*

1528 Fox in Pocock *Rec. Ref.* I. liii. 143 The causes.. imployed so manifest justness. 1529 MORE *Comf. agst. Trib.* I. Wks. (1557) 1146/2 We must expresse or imploy a condicion therin. 1579 *Poore Knight's Palace* B b, Crabbed Care, imployd with streeke of red. 1581 J. BELL *Haddon's*

answ. Osor. 31 Which wordes do employ nothyng els, but that, etc. **1605** CHAPMAN *All Fooles* Plays 1873 I. 134 Fortunio welcome, And in that welcome I imploy your wiues. **1606** HOLLAND *Sueton.* 129 Passed a decree, that the day on which hee beganne his Empire should be called Palilia, imploying thereby..a second foundation of the Cittie. *a* **1626** BACON *Max. & Uses Com. Law* 31 Which interest of marriage went still imployed..in every tenure called knight's service.

¶ **6.** To supply. *Obs. rare.*

1668 CHILD *Disc. Trade* (1694) 172 It employs the Nation for its Consumption, with Pepper, Indigo, Calicoes.

employability (ɛmplɔɪəˈbɪlɪtɪ). [f. EMPLOYAB(LE *a.* + -ILITY.] The character or quality of being employable.

1926 A. M. CARR-SAUNDERS *Eugenics* vii. 157 Categories (a) and (b) of employability account for 89·4 per cent. of the men and 88·2 per cent. of the women. **1927** *Daily Tel.* 28 June 7/2 The scheme..is for the purpose of so improving the general employability of young unskilled men. **1959** B. WOOTTON *Social Sci. & Social Path.* vii. 223 Even the test of employability or of working efficiency does not serve to distinguish the sick from the sound.

employable (ɛmˈplɔɪəb(ə)l), *a.* [f. EMPLOY *v.* + -ABLE] That can be employed.

a **1691** BOYLE (J.), The objections made..seem employable against this hypothesis. **1768–74** TUCKER *Lt. Nat.* (1852) II. 97 The materia medica of morality, that is, the conceptions..employable therein. **1808** BENTHAM *Sc. Reform* 69 Evidence alternately employable. **1840** MILL *Diss. & Disc.* I. 389 Means employable for important social ends.

‖**employé** (ɑ̃plwaje). [a. F. *employé*, pa. pple. of *employer* to employ.] One who is employed. (In Fr. use chiefly applied to clerks; in Eng. use *gen.* to the persons employed for wages or salary by a house of business, or by government.)

Hence also **employée**, a female employé.

1834 O. P. Q. in *Spectator* 22 Nov. 1112/2 An old bankrupt employé of the Empire. **1848** MILL *Pol. Econ.* I. ix. §2. (1876) 87 Connecting.. the interest of the employés with the..success of the concern. **1860** GEN. P. THOMPSON *Audi Alt.* III. cii. 4 No representations against a Government employé shall be entertained. **1862** *Macm. Mag.* July 257 All these employées should be women of character. **1879** HARLAN *Eyesight* v. 64 In Italy, all railroad employés are subjected to rigorous examination.

employed (ɛmˈplɔɪd), *ppl. a.* [f. EMPLOY *v.* + -ED.] That is in (another's) employ. Also *absol.* with pl. sense, the wage-earning class.

1625 BACON *Ess. Travel.* (Arb.) 523 The Secretaries, and Employd Men of Ambassadours. **1670** R. COKE *Disc. Trade* 55 You must do it as the imployed English please. **1818** CANNING in *Parl. Deb.* 964 An employed informer, and consequently a spy. **1860** GEN. P. THOMPSON *Audi Alt.* III. cxxiv. 76 Attachment to the class of the employed, rather than of the employers.

Hence †**emˈployedness**, the condition of being seriously busy. *Obs. rare*⁻¹.

a **1691** BOYLE *Wks.* VI. 48 (R.) Rhetoric and care of language [are not] consistent with..employedness.

employee (ɛmplɔɪˈiː, ɛmˈplɔiː). orig. *U.S.* [f. EMPLOY + -EE.]

a. A person employed for wages; = EMPLOYÉ, which it has now virtually superseded. **b.** (*nonce-use.*) Something that is employed.

1850 L. H. GARRARD *Wah-To-Yah* xii. 172 Horses and mules..were here herded, by their employees. **1854** THOREAU *Walden* iv. (1886) 113 They take me for an employee. **1879** TOURGEE *Fool's Err.* xxxv. 241 Their commands are..obeyed by the..employees. **1886** A. MORGAN in *Lit. World* (Boston, U.S.) 15 May 172/1 The supines of Shakespeare outnumber the employees of most authors. **1891** *Pall Mall Gaz.* 23 Oct. 2/1 To arrange a forty-eight hour week for the few binders, while retaining the fifty-four hours for the bulk of the employees. **1906** *Daily Chron.* 9 May 5/5 'I don't like this affectation of "employee",' observed Judge Addison, in the Southwark County Court. 'I prefer English words.' **1909** *Ibid.* 15 Dec. 1/3 The employee shares in the company are 50,000 of £1 each. **1928** *Britain's Industr. Future (Lib. Ind. Inq.)* III. 141 The stimulation of employee-ownership under schemes of profit-sharing and investment by employees. **1954** J. A. C. BROWN *Soc. Psychol. Industry* iii. 84 The supervisors of high production groups were those who were..more employee-centred.

In U.S. often written **employe**.

1904 *N.Y. Times* 26 Mar. 1 Receiver Taft called the employes of the failed firm into his office. **1923** CHILDS & CORNELL *Office Administr.* 258 The training of a new employe. **1930** *Chicago Daily News* 25 Aug., The first annual picnic of employes of The Daily News and their families.

employer (ɛmˈplɔɪə(r)). [f. EMPLOY *v.* + -ER.]

a. One who employs. Const. *of.* **b.** *spec.* One who employs servants, workmen, etc. for wages.

1599 SHAKS. *Much Ado* v. ii. 31 Troilous the first imploier of pandars. **1668** CHILD *Disc. Trade* (T.), Owner or employer of much shipping. **1742** RICHARDSON *Pamela* IV. 103 To present her Imployer with Bills for 500*l.* **1780** BURKE *Econ. Ref.* Wks. III. 286 Making it the interest of the contractor to exert..skill for..his employers. **1856** FROUDE *Hist. Eng.* (1858) I. i. 21 Agricultural labourers lived..in the houses of their employers. **1878** JEVONS *Prim. Pol. Econ.* 64 Employers are regarded as tyrants.

employing (ɛmˈplɔɪɪŋ), *vbl. sb.* [f. EMPLOY *v.* + -ING¹.] **a.** The action of the verb EMPLOY. †**b.** Employment, occupation (*obs.*).

1607 HIERON *Wks.* I. 245 For the lawfull imploying himselfe in the same. *a* **1665** J. GOODWIN *Filled w. the Spirit* (1867) 261 Such an employing of the Spirit as that we have described. **1707** J. STEVENS tr. *Quevedo's Com. Wks.* (1709) *Dog* 222 Whose whole Employing is like the Frogs, drinking and prating.

emˈploying, *ppl. a.* [f. as prec. + -ING².] That employs. *rare.*

1887 *Pall Mall G.* 8 Nov. 13/2 The main qualifications which the employing incumbents of England demand.

employment (ɛmˈplɔɪmənt). Also 7 em-, imploiement, -ploiment. [f. EMPLOY *v.* + -MENT.]

1. a. The action or process of employing; the state of being employed. Also in phrase, † (*man*, etc.) *of much, little*, etc. ***employment***.

1598 FLORIO *Dict.* Ep. Ded. 2 Your able emploiment of such servitours. **1602** SHAKS. *Ham.* v. i. 77 The hand of little Implyment hath the daintier sense. **1665** G. HAVERS *P. della Valle's Trav. E. India* 82 Bartolomeo Pontobuoni, a good Painter, and also a man of much Employment. **1665** BOYLE *Occas. Refl.* v. i. (1675) 299 So meritorious an Imploiment of her Greatness shew'd her to be worthy of it. **1689** HOWE *Ho. Com. Deb.* 29 Nov. in Cobbett *Parl. Hist. Eng.* (1809) V. 463 By the Employment of Mr. Shales. **1702** *Eng. Theophrast.* 136 It is good to compound employments of both [young and old]. **1871** B. STEWART *Heat* 26 The superior limit of its accurate employment.

†**b.** The service (of a person). Phrase, ***at your employment***. (*Obs.*)

1595 SHAKS. *John* I. i. 198 At your employment; at your seruice sir. **1603** BRETON *Poste w. Packet, Love L. & Answ.*, I have devoted myself to your Imploiment.

2. a. That on which (one) is employed; business; occupation; a special errand or commission.

1597 SHAKS. *2 Hen. IV*, I. ii. 85 Is there not wars? is there not imployment? **1598** —— *Merry W.* v. v. 135 How wit may be made a Iacke-a-Lent when 'tis vpon ill imployment. **1607** in Ellis *Orig. Lett.* I. 246. III. 87 His emploiments, he saith, have been five times to Venice, once into Persia. **1651** HOBBES *Leviath.* II. xxx. 181 The excuse of not finding employment. **1738–41** WARBURTON *Div. Legat.* IV. vi. (R.), Had Jesus..made use of the great and learned for this employment. **1742** RICHARDSON *Pamela* III. 345 Your Sunday Imployments charm us all. **1760** GOLDSM. *Cit. W.* cxix, I..went from town to town, working when I could get employment. **1837** SIR F. PALGRAVE *Merch. & Friar* (1844) Ded. 2 The character acquired for me by my employments.

†**b.** The use or purpose to which a thing is devoted. *Obs.*

1593 SHAKS. *Rich. II*, I. i. 90 Lendings he hath detain'd for lewd employments. **1658** *Whole Duty Man* viii. §11. (1687) 71 Making it less fit for any imployment.

c. A person's regular occupation or business; a trade or profession.

1648 GAGE *West Ind.* xv. (1655) 102 In their imployments they are..Grasiers. **1674** BREVINT *Saul at Endor* 72 They subdivide their Emploiements. **1839** ALISON *Hist. Europe* (1849–50) I. ii. §66. 185 They..proposed..to let every man exercise any profession..or carry on any employment.

†**3.** An official position in the public service; a 'place'. *Obs.*

1647 CLARENDON *Hist. Reb.* (1702) II. VI. 93 Restored to their Offices, and Employments. **1708** SWIFT *Sacram. Test* II. I. 128 The gentlemen of employments here make a very considerable number in the house of commons. **1734** tr. *Rollin's Anc. Hist.* (1827) II. II. 59 He was made prætor which seems to have been a very considerable employment.

¶**4.** = IMPLEMENT. *Obs. rare*⁻¹.

1612 CHAPMAN *Widdowes T.* Wks. 1873 III. 76 My stay hath been prolonged With hunting obscure nooks for these emploiments [a crowbar and a halter].

5. *attrib.* (in sense 2 c) ***employment agency, agent, bureau, exchange***, etc., professional intermediaries between applicants for work and employers.

1886 J. A. PORTER *New Stand. Guide Washington* 204 Dondore and Morse, Attorneys..also Employment Bureau. **1888** *12th Rep. Ohio Bur. Labour Statistics* 263 'Employment agencies'..have very appropriately been characterized as 'a class who trade on the needs of the inexperienced searcher for honest employment'. **1903** *Westm. Gaz.* 23 Dec. 5/2 All the corporations have resolved to support the bakers, with the object of obtaining the complete suppression of the employment agencies [in Paris]. **1909** *Lancet* 11 Sept. 830/1 (*heading*) An employment exchange for university undergraduates. **1921** *Dict. Occup. Terms* (1927) 771 Employment agent; employment bureau manager. **1945** *Archit. Rev.* XCVIII. 115/1 Mushroom employment-agencies and dubious correspondence courses play on the soldier's anxiety and issue him promissory notes which will never be honoured. **1961** *Technology* Feb. 45/2 Youth employment service. *Ibid.*, The company contact the youth employment officer. *Ibid.*, It is probably this kind of situation that evoked from Miss Avent the words 'employment exchange'.

emplume (ɛmpl(j)uːm), *v.* Also 7 implume. [a. Fr. *emplumer*, f. *en-* (see EN-) + *plume* PLUME, feather; cf. Sp. *emplumar*, It. *impiumare*.]

†**1.** *trans.* ? To 'tar and feather' (or the like). [So Sp. *emplumar*.] *Obs.*

1631 *Celestina* v. 33 That gadding to and fro Bawd, who for her villanies..hath been several times implumed.

2. To furnish with a plume, adorn as with plumes. Also in *ppl. a.* **emˈplumed**.

1623 MABBE tr. *Guzman d'Alfarache* II. 21 They might very well have put the implumed Hat vpon my head. **18..** MRS. BROWNING *Song Ragged Sch.*, Angelhoods, emplumed In such ringlets of pure glory.

emplunge, var. of IMPLUNGE, *Obs.*

emply, obs. var. of IMPLY *v.*

empocket, *v.* Var. IMPOCKET *v.*, to put into one's pocket.

empoison (ɛmˈpɔɪzən, z(ə)n), *v.* Forms: α. 4–6 enpoysen, -on, -oun, 5–6 enpoisen, -on, -oun, 4–8 empoyson, (7 empoysn), 6– empoison. β. 6–7 impoyson, 6– impoison. [a. F. *empoisonne-r*, f. *en-* (see EN-) + *poison* POISON.]

†**1.** *trans.* To administer poison to (a person); *esp.* to kill by poison. Also *absol.* *Obs.*

α. *c* **1350** *Will. Palerne* 4650 þei him bi-hiȝt..þat þei prieuli wold enpoysoun þe king. *c* **1386** CHAUCER *Monk's T.* 582 Empoysoned of thyn owene folk thou weere. **1480** CAXTON *Chron. Eng.* lviii. 42 King vortimer was enpoisened and dyed at london. **1523** LD. BERNERS *Froiss.* I. cccxvi. 486 In mynde to haue enpoysoned the frenche kynge. **1604** *Supplic. Masse Priests* ii, To murder and empoyson our late Queene. **1667** *Lond. Gaz.* No. 206/2 The Grand Visier was by..practises on his person empoisoned.

β. **1530** PALSGR. 590/1, I impoyson. **1580** *Apol. Pr. Orange* in *Phœnix* (1721) I. 464 The Cardinal of Grandvelle impoison'd the last Maximilian. **1599** *Warn. Faire Wom.* I. 44 Some..tyrant to obtain a crown Stabs, hangs, impoisons. **1649** *Alcoran* 406 He permitted one of his dearest friends to ..die impoysoned. **1670** BROOKS *Wks.* (1867) VI. 227 How many thousand children and servants are there impoisoned! **1795** BARRUEL *Hist. Clergy during French Rev.* 55 Impoisoned by these pestilent men.

†**b.** *transf.* and *fig.* To kill as if by poison; to affect as poison does. Also *absol.* *Obs.*

1607 SHAKS. *Cor.* v. vi. 11 A man by his owne Almes impoyson'd. **1626** BACON *Sylva* §546 The Surfeit of them [mushromes] may suffocate and empoyson. **1646** SIR T. BROWNE *Pseud. Ep.* III. vii. 119 This way a Basilisk may empoyson.

2. a. To put poison into (food or drink); to taint, render poisonous; to vitiate as with poison (the blood, animal tissues, etc.); to envenom. Also, to dip (an arrow) in poison. Now somewhat *rhetorical*.

α. **1634** T. JOHNSON tr. *Parey's Chirurg.* II. (1678) 274 Neither..could it [gunpowder] empoyson the bodies of such as are wounded. **1683** SALMON *Doron Med.* I. 155 When the Blood is empoysoned. **1725** SLOANE *Jamaica* II. 6 Bowmen with their arrows most villanously empoyson'd. **1825** SCOTT *Talism.* xxviii, The simoon empoisons the atmosphere.

β. **1602** WARNER *Alb. Eng.* x. lvi. (1612) 246. **1686** GOAD *Celest. Bodies* III. iii. 472 Our Two Superiours are more to be suspected in impoisoning the Fountains, and corrupting our Mass of Bloud. **1733** CHEYNE *Eng. Malady* I. vi. §2 (1734) 50 All which must necessarily..impoison..their natural Juices.

†**b.** *intr.* for *refl.*

1622 PEACHAM *Compl. Gentl.* xviii. (1634) 215 Yet much lyeth in our power to keepe that fount from empoysoning.

3. *fig.* **a.** To taint with sin or error; to corrupt, vitiate, spoil.

α. **1325** *E.E. Allit. P.* B. 242 þat en-poysened alle peplez þat parted fro hem boþe. **1401** *Pol. Poems* (1859) II. 73 Prechen what ȝou list, and with ȝour privy pestilence enpoisoun the peple. **1534** LD. BERNERS *Gold. Bk. M. Aurel.* (1546) S viij, Riches, youthe, solitarines, and libertee ben IIII. pestilences, that enpoison the prynce. **1599** SANDYS *Europæ Spec.* (1632) 18 Proceed on to empoyson their country. **1633** BP. HALL *Hard Texts* 144 Thou art.. empoysoned with the most deadly venome of wickednesse. **1738** WARBURTON *Div. Legat.* I. 292 The Deists..empoison everything they touch. **1882** T. A. POPE tr. *Capecelatro's Philip Neri* I. 48 An undisciplined will might..destroy or empoison all vigour of thought.

β. **1557** NORTH *Gueuara's Diall Pr.* A. Ded., Any newe thinge that mighte..impoison with erronious doctrine the consciences. *c* **1612** BEAUM. & FL. *Thierry* II. 454 She hath impoyson'd Your good opinion of me. **1656** TRAPP *Comm. Eph.* v. 3 Citizens' wives..were..impoisoned at stage-plays.

b. To render virulent, envenom (feelings); to 'poison', embitter (a person's mind) *against*. Also, to embitter, destroy all pleasure in (a means of enjoyment).

α. **1646** J. HALL *Horæ Vac.* 136 Jests empoysoned with bitternesse. **1806** *Ann. Rev.* IV. 774 Our social tables, which they conspire to empoison. **1832** *Blackw. Mag.* XXXII. 225 This distraction..will empoison all your joys. **1879** J. HAWTHORNE *Laugh. M.* 75 His soul had been empoisoned against them and all the world.

β. **1599** SHAKS. *Much Ado* III. i. 86 One does not know How much an ill word may impoison liking.

empoisoned (ɛmˈpɔɪzənd, -z(ə)nd), *ppl. a.* [f. prec. + -ED¹.]

†**1.** Killed by poison; poisoned. *Obs.*

1615 G. SANDYS *Trav.* IV. 307 The death of her impoisoned husband. **1616** *Overbury's Vis.* in *Harl. Misc.* (Malh.) III. 347 The pains of my impoison'd ghost.

2. Steeped in, impregnated or tainted with, poison; poisonous, envenomed. *lit.* and *fig.*

1598 CHAPMAN *Iliad* VIII. 365 Impoison'd strokes His wounding thunder shall imprint. **1601** HOLLAND *Pliny* I. 144 These Arabians..shooting their empoysoned arrowes, practise pyracie. **1678** WANLEY *Wond. Lit. World* v. i. §71. 465/2 A pair of empoysoned Gloves..procured his death. *a* **1711** KEN *Hymnotheo* Poet. Wks. 1721 III. 318 On Earth uncurs'd no Plants empoyson'd grew. **1799** CORRY *Sat. London* (1803) 162 Assassins, ready to lift their empoisoned

stillettos against your hearts. **1883** J. Parker *Tyne Ch.* 145 The serpent..shows its empoisoned fang.

empoisoner (ɛm'pɔɪzənə(r)). *Obs.* or *arch.* [f. as prec. + -ER.] One who empoisons.

c **1386** Chaucer *Pard. T.* 566 Thus ended..the false empoysonere. *a* **1577** Sir T. Smith *Commw. Eng.* (1609) 96 Impoysoners..shall bee boyled to the death. **1600** O. E. *Repl. Libel* I. v. 99 The father of all..murderers, empoisoners, and enemies to this state. **1622** Bacon *Hen. VII*, 2 The Impoisoner of his wife. **1650** Weldon *Crt. Jas. I* (1651) 65 They preferred Empoysoners to be servants to Sir Gervase Elwayes. **1829** Landor *Imag. Conv.* (1846) II. 234 We live among..empoisoners.
fig. **1579** Tomson *Calvin's Serm. Tim.* 810/2 A..wicked man that goeth about to sowe peruerse doctrine..what is hee els, but an impoisoner? **1653** Gauden *Hierasp.* 412 The divels Empericks and empoisoners.

†**em'poisoness.** *Obs. rare.* [f. EMPOISON-ER; cf. *murderess.*] A female empoisoner.

1628 tr. *Matthieu's Powerfvll Favorite*, Martina, that famous sorceresse and empoysonnesse.

em'poisoning, *vbl. sb.* [f. as prec. + -ING¹.] The action of the vb. EMPOISON.

c **1374** Chaucer *Boeth.* I. iii. 206 Þe empoysenyng of Socrates. **1494** Fabyan *Chron.* I. clvii, By the impoysonynge of his own wyfe. *ibid.* VII. 322 He dyed at Swynyshede..by the enpoysonynge of a munke of the same house. **1527** Andrew *Brunswyke's Distyll. Waters* A iij b, Columbyne water..is good for impoysyning. *a* **1569** Kingesmyll *Confl. Satan* (1578) 7 The deedes of the flesh are..impoisonings. **1678** Wanley *Wond. Lit. World* v. ii. §80. 472/2 He bribed the Bishop of Rome to the empoysoning of his brother Zemes. **1681** *Roxb. Bal.* (1883) IV. 655 From secret Impoysonings..*Libera nos, Domine.*

em'poisoning, *ppl. a.* [f. as prec. + -ING².] That empoisons, kills by poison, or renders poisonous.

1598 *Ord. for Prayer in Liturg. Serv. Q. Eliz.* (1847) 682 The sacred oil..is a sovereign Antidote..against..empoisoning confections. **1646** Sir T. Browne *Pseud. Ep.* (1650) III. xxviii. 151 Nor are all Snakes of such empoisoning qualities. **1653** Urquhart *Rabelais* II. xv. The smell..is so pestiferous and impoisoning. **1706** Watts *Horæ Lyr.* III. 258 The impoisoning taint O'erspreads the building.

empoisonment (ɛm'pɔɪzənmənt). Also 7–8 impoisonment. [f. as prec. + -MENT.]

1. The administration of poison to a person; the fact of being poisoned. *arch.* or *Obs.*

1569 R. Androse tr. *Alexis' Secr.* IV. III. 13 A more excellent remedie against empoysonments [*printed* empoysments]. **1600** O. E. *Repl. Libel* I. v. 104 The apostles .. neuer taught..empoisonment of princes. **1653** A. Wilson *Jas. I*, 84, I have found in the Book of God, examples of all other offences, but not any one of an Impoysonment. **1727** Swift *Further Acc. E. Curll* III. I. 154 The manner of Mr. Curll's impoisonment. **1815** *Month. Mag.* XXXIX. 309 Sudden death, so like an empoisonment. **1824** Landor *Imag. Conv.* Wks. 1846 I. xii. 49 You..rarely find an empoisonment..committed in England for policy.

2. The action of tainting or impregnating with poison. Also *fig.*

1626 Bacon *Sylva* §915 And these Empoisonments of air are the more dangerous in meetings of people. **1886** Farrar *Westm. Serm.* in *Libr. Mag.* (N.Y.) 16 Oct. 595 His bad example is a spiritual empoisonment.

empolder (ɛm'pəʊldə(r)), *v.* [f. EM- 1 b + POLDER¹.] *trans.* To make a polder of; to reclaim from the sea. Cf. IMPOLDER *v.* So **em'poldered** *ppl. a.*

1889 *Cent. Dict.*, *Empoldered*, reclaimed and brought into the condition of a polder; brought under cultivation. **1922** *Blackw. Mag.* July 14/2 A few acres have been cleared and empoldered with mud-dams. **1951** *New Biol.* XI. 77 By 1940 flood-fallowing experiments had been begun. An area of 100 acres..was empoldered (i.e. surrounded by earth walls).

emporetic (ɛmpɒ'rɛtɪk), *a. Antiq.* [ad. L. *emporēticus* (*emporetica charta* Pliny *H.N.* XIII. xii), a. Gr. *ἐμπορητικός, f. *ἐμπορέειν to trade, f. ἔμπορος merchant.] Pertaining to trade. *emporetic paper*: a coarse kind of papyrus used for wrapping up parcels. (Quincy *Lex. Phys.-Med.* 1719 wrongly explains this as 'paper made soft and porous, such as is used to filter with'.)

[**1662** Fuller *Worthies* I. 144 Imperial, Royal, Cardinal, and so downwards to that course Paper called Emporetica.] **1851** *Ancient Fishing* in *Fraser's Mag.* XLIII. 264 The Emporetic, or shop-paper..serving for wrapping up groceries, fruit, etc.

Hence †**empo'retical** *a. Obs.*$^{-0}$.

1656 Blount *Glossogr.*, *Emporetical*, pertaining to Merchants or Markets. **1678–1706** in Phillips. **1721–1800** in Bailey; and in mod. Dicts.

†**empo'reutic,** *a.* and *sb. Obs.* [ad. Gr. ἐμπορευτικ-ός, f. ἐμπορεύεσθαι to trade, f. ἔμπορος trader: see EMPORIUM.]

A. *adj.* Of or pertaining to trade.

B. *sb.* **a.** *sing.* (See quot.) **b.** *pl.* Articles manufactured for sale.

1612 Sturtevant *Metallica* (1854) 37 Emporeuticks which they [Joyners, Smiths, etc.] ordinarily make, as Presses..Bellowes, Tongs. *Ibid.* 50 The Emporeutick.. treateth of the worke of the art..wares for use and sale.

Hence †**empo'reutical,** *a. Obs.*; = prec. adj.

1612 Sturtevant *Metallica* (1854) 50 The first [part] is called Organic, and the other Emporeutical or Polecall.

†**em'porial,** *a. Obs.* [f. EMPORI-UM + -AL¹.] Of or pertaining to an emporium; having the character or function of an emporium.

1604 T. Wright *Passions* Pref., Great citties (specially emporiall) affoord..all sorts of politique prudence. **1802** *Month. Mag.* XIII. 12 Knives may have been brought..by the Phœnicians, and sold at their emporial sea-towns in the Isle of Wight and in Cornwall.

emporie, var. form of EMPORY, *Obs.*

emporium (ɛm'pɔərɪəm). *Pl.* 7–9 **emporiums**, 9 **emporia.** (See also EMPORY.) [a. L. *emporium*, a. Gr. ἐμπόριον, f. ἔμπορος merchant, f. ἐν in + vbl. stem πορ-, περ- to journey.]

1. A place in which merchandise is collected or traded in. Often as applied to towns or countries: A principal centre of commerce, 'a mart'.

1586 J. Hooker *Girald. Irel.* in *Holinsh.* II. 12/2 A Scotch Town is the cheefest emporium in a manner of all that land. **1621** Burton *Anat. Mel.* II. iii. III. (1651) 326 Paris, London, small Cottages in Cæsars time, now most nobel Emporiums. **1692** Ray *Dissol. World* II. v. (1732) 253 The best Emporium and Mart of this Part of the world. **1776** Adam Smith *W.N.* IV. ii. (1869) II. 27 The emporium, or general market, for the goods of all the different countries whose trade it carries on. **1805** Lucock *Nat. Wool* 44 Perhaps they [the Italian cities] would have remained much longer the emporia of the world. **1869** Buckle *Civilis.* III. v. 340 Emporiums of commerce. **1878** Bosw. Smith *Carthage* 8 Egypt..deigned to open an emporium at Naucratis for the ships and commerce of the Greeks.

†**b.** In the East Indies: A 'factory' of European merchants. *Obs.*

1727 A. Hamilton *New Acc. E. Ind.* II. xxxiv. 20 Half a League farther up..the Dutch Emporium stands.

c. Pompously applied to: A shop, warehouse.

1839 Dickens *Nich. Nick.* xxxii, Emporiums of splendid dresses. **1859** Sala *Tw. round Clock* (1861) 163 But I find the shop now expanded into a magnificent emporium.

2. *transf.* and *fig.*

1839 Murchison *Silur. Syst.* I. xxxv. 475 The rich emporium of the Scotch coal measures. **1852** Miss Mitford in L'Estrange *Life* (1870) III. xiii. 241 Her house in London was a perfect emporium of escaped state criminals. **1865** Merivale *Rom. Emp.* (1865) VIII. lxvi. 235 She [Alexandria] was an emporium for the interchange of ideas and speculations.

†**3.** (See quot.) *Obs.*

1721–1800 Bailey, *Emporium*, the common sensory of the brain. **1753** Chambers *Cycl. Supp.*

emport(e, obs. ff. IMPORT *v.*

†**em'portment.** *Obs. rare.* [a. F. *emportement* fit of passion, f. *emporter* to carry away, *s'emporter* to be carried away by anger.] A fit or 'transport' of passion, state of vehement anger.

a **1734** North *Examen* (1740) 653 (D.) Lay aside emportments so justly provoked. —— *Lives* II. 423 At which the Ambassador and his friend were in a furious emportment.

†**em'porture,** *v. Obs. rare*$^{-1}$. In other editions im-. (Meaning obscure; perh. misprint for *importuned.*)

c **1525** Skelton *Ph. Sparowe* (Dyce) 1154 She is playnly expresse, Egeria the goddesse, And like to her image Emportured with corage A louers pylgrimage.

†**'empory.** *Obs.* Anglicized f. of EMPORIUM.

1607 Bp. J. King *Sermon* (Nov.) 2 The renouned Emporie and Mart of the whole Kingdome. **1680** Morden *Geog. Rect.* Scot. (1685) 33 Dunfreis is a rich and well traded Emporie upon the River Nith. **1698** Farquhar *Love & Bottle* IV. (1728) 69 This is the great Empory of lewdness. **1774** T. West *Antiq. Furness* Introd. 15 Ulverston, the empory of Furness.

†**empo'ssess,** *v. Obs. rare.* Also 5 en-. [f. EN- + POSSESS *v.*] *trans.* To invest with possession, endow *with*.

c **1500** *Melusine* (E.E.T.S.) 99 He..charged them to edyfye..a Priorye of eyghte monkes, them to reueste and empossesse with landes. *Ibid.* 100 And enpossessed them wel for theire sustenaunce.

empostem, -ume, obs. ff. IMPOSTHUME.

empound, obs. form of IMPOUND.

†**em'pover,** *v. Obs. rare.* Also 5–6 enpouere, 6 enpover. [a. OF. *enpover-ir* to IMPOVERISH.] *trans.* To impoverish.

1474 Caxton *Chesse* III. iii. F iij, How enpouere they the comynte. **1523** Ld. Berners *Froiss.* I. cccvii. 462 The garysons..had greatly enpouered..the countre of Normandy. **1528** Roy *Sat.*, The charges to recover Lest they shulde theym selves enpover.

empoverish, obs. form of IMPOVERISH.

†**em'powder,** *v. Obs. rare.* [f. EN- + POWDER *sb.*] *trans.* To insert sparsely or in small patches like grains of powder.

1548 Udall, etc. *Erasm. Par. John* Pref., Clothe of golde empowdred emong patches of canuesse, or perles and diamondes emong peoblestones.

empower (ɛm'paʊə(r)), *v.* Also 7–9 impower, (6–7 impowre). [f. EN- + POWER.]

1. *trans.* To invest legally or formally with power or authority; to authorize, license.

α. **1654** H. L'Estrange *Chas. I* (1655) 75 Letters from the Pope..empowering them to erect this Colledge. **1786** T. Jefferson *Writ.* (1859) I. 567 A clause is inserted.. empowering the King to discontinue it at any time. **1827** Hallam *Const. Hist.* (1876) II. x. 266 The Petition and Advice had..empowered him to appoint a successor. **1860** Motley *Netherl.* (1868) I. i. 18 They were empowered..to levy troops by land and sea.
β. **1655** Fuller *Ch. Hist.* VIII. i. §8 These visitors, not as yet impowred by law. **1704** Swift *T. Tub* vii. 94, I do here impower him to remove it. **1801** Strutt *Sports & Past.* II. i. 51 The commissioners were..impowered to survey the lands adjoining to the city of London.

2. To impart or bestow power to an end or for a purpose; to enable, permit.

α. **1681–6** J. Scott *Chr. Life* (1747) III. 619 Much less can he empower others to do Miracles. **1727** De Foe *Syst. Magic* I. iv. (1840) 91 Some have doubted whether the Devil is empowered to take up any human shape. **1869** *Contemp. Rev.* XI. 260 Air and..exercise..empower the man for any intellectual or moral work.
β. **1667** Milton *P.L.* x. 369 Thou us impow'rd to fortifie thus farr. **1715–20** Pope *Iliad* XIV. 295 Impower'd the wrath of gods and men to tame.

†**b.** To bestow power upon, make powerful.

1690 Penn *Rise & Progr. Quakers* (1834) 17 Who empowered them as their work witnesseth.

†**3.** *refl.* To gain or assume power *over*. *Obs.*

1657 S.W. *Schism Dispach't* 167 When this strange Vsurpation impower'd itself over the whole Church. *Ibid.* 179 That William the Conquerour should have impower'd himself over England.

Hence **em'powering** *ppl. a.*

1674 N. Fairfax *Bulk & Selv.* 141 Some instance of Gods impowering ghost.

empowerment (ɛm'paʊəmənt). [f. prec. + -MENT.] The action of empowering; the state of being empowered.

1849 *Life Rev. J. Fisher* ii. 29 They followed up this remarkable empowerment..by removing the sentences, etc. **1882–3** Schaff *Encycl. Rel. Knowl.* II. 1369 An all-conquering conviction of divine vocation and empowerment.

†**emprent,** *v. Obs. rare*$^{-1}$. Used as transl. of L. *impetrare* to obtain by request.

c **1374** Chaucer *Boeth.* (1868) 159 Men byseken it and emprenten it.

emprent, obs. form of IMPRINT.

empress ('ɛmprɪs), *sb.*¹ Forms: 2–4 emperice, 3–8 emperess(e, 4 (amperesse), emperis(e, -isse, empiresse, 5 emprice, -ise, 5–7 empresse, 7– empress. Also 4–5 imperes, -ice. [ME. *emperesse*, a. OF. *emperesse*, fem. of *emperere* EMPEROR (late L. type **imperatorissa*). OF. had also *empereriz*, *-is*, = Pr. *emperairitz*, Sp. *emperatriz*:—L. *imperātricem*, and various mixed forms, as *emperice*, *amperice*, some of which occur in ME.]

1. The consort of an emperor. Also, a female sovereign having the rank equivalent to that of an emperor.

1154 *O.E. Chron.* an. 1140 Þe hæfde ben Emperice. **1297** R. Glouc. (1725) 440 He louede hyr, vor heo was eyr & hey emperesse. *Ibid.* 474 The nexte ȝer ther after the Amperesse Mold Wende out of this liue. *c* **1350** *Will. Palerne* 5343 And Melion..was crouned emperice. **1480** Caxton *Chron. Eng.* VII. (1520) 79 b/1 Wyllyam..helde warre agaynst Maude the empresse. **1559** Bp. Scot in Strype *Ann. Ref.* I. II. App. vii. 417 The emperesse Theodora that then was. **1704** Addison *Italy* (1733) 236 Among the Emperesses. *a* **1745** Swift *Wks.* (1768) IV. 301 The earl of Chester..commanded there for the empress. **1836** *Penny Cycl.* V. 132/2 Napoleon.. crowned his wife as empress. **1888** *Times* No. 32,573. 7/4 The Queen and the Empress Frederick were compelled to delay their departure from the Royal borough. *Mod.* In 1876 Queen Victoria was proclaimed Empress of India.

2. A female potentate exercising supreme or absolute power. Chiefly *transf.* and *fig.*

a **1300** *Cursor M.* 20801 Of heuen and erth..scho es quene, Bath imperice and heind leuedi. *c* **1374** Chaucer *Boeth.* (1868) 109 For felonie is emperisse and flowreþ ful of rycchesse. *c* **1460** *Towneley Myst.* 171 Thi moder is of helle emprise. **1588** Shaks. *Tit. A.* II. iii. 40 Harke Tamora, the Empresse of my Soule. **1634** Habington *Castara* 30 The pale-faced Empresse of the night Lent in her chaste increase her borrowed light. **1682** Dryden *Mac Fl.* 87 Now Empress Fame had publisht the renown Of Shadwells coronation. **1797** Mrs. Radcliffe *Italian* xii, Who..seemed the empress of the scene. **1832** *Blackw. Mag.* Feb. 353/1 The British capital has been called..the empress of all cities. **1844** Kinglake *Eöthen* v. (1878) 73 Yonder empress throned at the window of that humblest mud cottage.

3. *Comb.* **a.** *appositive.*

a **1661** Holyday *Juvenal* 93 Before his bed she chose a mat that stunk, And wore a night-hood too, an empress-punk! **1705** in *Lond. Gaz.* No. 4156/1 The Earl of Sunderland.. had Audience..of the Empress-Dowager. **1711** *Ibid.* 4875/2 His Excellency deliver'd her Majesty's Credentials to the Empress-Regent.

b. *empress-cloth*: a woollen fabric differing from merino chiefly in not being twilled. (App. not known as a trade term in England.)

1884 in Knight *Amer. Mech. Dict.*; and in later Dicts.

†**'empress,** *sb.*² *Obs.* Forms: 6 emprese, 7 empresse, empressa. See also IMPRESS *sb.*², IMPRESA. [A var. of IMPRESS *sb.*², ad. It. *impresa* of same meaning. The form with *em-* may be ad. the equivalent Sp. *empresa*, and is therefore treated separately.]

A motto or significant device; see IMPRESS *sb.*² Also *attrib.*

1593 NASHE *Christ's T.* 19 b, Let..this for an Empresse be engrauen. **1603** DRAYTON *Baron's Wars* vi. 43 Emblems, Empressas, Hirogliphiques. **1610** HOLLAND *Camden's Brit.* I. 287 A blew garter, carrying this Empresse..*Hony soit qui Mal y pense.* **1688** R. HOLME *Armoury* III. 146/2 Emblem or Empress work is drawing Faces from the Life.

†**em'press**, *v. Obs.* Forms: 4 enprece, -presse, 4–5 empresse. See also IMPRESS *v.* [a. OF. *empresse-r*, *emprecier*, f. *en-* (see EN-) + *presser* to PRESS.] *trans.* and *absol.* To subject to pressure, press, oppress. Also *intr.* to crowd, press eagerly *into.*

c **1325** *E.E. Allit. P.* C. 43 And pere as pouert enpresses, þaȝ mon pyne þynk. *Ibid.* 528 Pouerte me enprecez & paynez innoȝe. *c* **1386** CHAUCER *Chan. Yem. Prol. & T.* 518 Such feendly thoughtes in his hert empresse. *c* **1400** *Rom. Rose* 3691 No man..ne may..of the reisins have the wyne Til grapes..Be sore empressid. **1475** *Bk. Noblesse* 4 Every man in hym silf let the passions of dolours be..empressid into vyfnes.

‖**empressé** (ɑ̃prɛse), *a.* [Fr., pa. pple. of *empresser*, f. *em-* = *en-* + *presser* PRESS *v.*¹] Eager, zealous.

1837 J. F. COOPER *Recoll. Eur.* II. ii. 42 All the French women were exceedingly *empressées* in their manner towards the Great Unknown. **1878** L. W. M. LOCKHART *Mine is Thine* II. xvii. 23 Be low, be depressed, but, at the right moment, *empressé* and earnest. **1906** W. DE MORGAN *Joseph Vance* xxxiii. 325 'Was he very *empressé* in his manner?' I asked. 'Spooney, do you mean?'

‖**empressement** (ɑ̃prɛsmɑ̃). [Fr.; f. *empresser* to urge, *s'empresser* to be eager.] Animated display of cordiality.

1749 CHESTERF. *Lett.* No. 202 (1792) II. 262 You must do it..with alacrity and *empressement.* **1823** BYRON *Juan* XI. xlii, Juan was received with much 'empressement' [*rimed with* chessman]. **1866** HOWELLS *Venet. Life* v. 73 She acknowledges the compliment with life-like empressement.

empressite ('ɛmprɪsaɪt). *Min.* [f. the name of the *Empress*-Josephine mine, where it was first found: see -ITE¹.] A telluride of silver, of disputed composition (see quots.).

1914 W. M. BRADLEY in *Amer. Jrnl. Sci.* 4th Ser. XVIII. 163 Some years ago, what appeared to be a new mineral was found in the Empress-Josephine Mine in the Kerber Creek District of Colorado by Professor R. D. George of the University of Colorado... The mineral gives a ratio of practically Ag:Te::1:1... The name empressite has been given to it by Professor George. **1956** *Amer. Mineralogist* XLI. 722 Ag_5Te_3 is synthetic empressite. $Ag_{5-x}Te_3$ is the formula deduced, for the mineral, from cell dimensions and density of analyzed crystals. **1964** *Ibid.* XLIX. 326 Chemical analysis..and *x*-ray single crystal data on natural material from the type locality show that Bradley's original composition of AgTe was correct, and it is proposed that the name empressite be retained for this material. **1965** *Ibid.* L. 797 The mineralogy of the silver tellurides is still far from completely understood. Is it not then premature to redefine the term 'empressite' for which a composition near Ag_5Te_3 has long been accepted? **1968** *Ibid.* LIII. 1513 'Empressite' from the type locality consists of two optically distinct phases with the formulae AgTe and $Ag_{5-x}Te_3$.

†**em'pride**, *v. Obs. rare.* In 5 enpride, enpryde. [f. EN- + PRIDE.] *refl.* To pride oneself.

a **1440** *Relig. Pieces fr. Thornton MS.* (1867) 23 Thre thynges ere whare-of a man enprides hym. *c* **1440** *Gesta Rom.* (1879) 174 He Enpridid him not for the honours. **1502** *Ord. Crysten Men* III. iii. (1506) 158 By this meane fell & hym enpryded the pharysee.

†**em'prime**, *v. Obs.* In 6 empryme. *trans.* To separate a deer from the rest of the herd.

1575 TURBERVILE *Bk. Venerie* 242 When he is hunted and doth first leave the herde we say that he is syngled or emprymed. **1656** in BLOUNT. **1775** in ASH.

emprint, obs. form of IMPRINT *sb.* and *v.*

emprise, emprize (ɛm'praɪz), *sb. arch.* Forms: α. 4–5 empryse, (4 emperise), 5 emprys, enprise, ymprise, enpriss, 7 empries, 4– emprise, -ize. β. 4 enpress, em-, imprese, 4–6 impease. [a. OF. *emprise, emprinse*, com. Romanic = Pr. *empreza*, Sp. *empresa*, It. *impresa*:—late L. **imprensa*, f. ppl. stem of **imprendĕre* (in OF. *emprendre*) to take in hand, f. *in-* in + *prehendĕre* to take.

The 17th c. forms *em-, imprese* appear to be influenced by Sp. or It.; cf. EMPRESS *sb.*, IMPRESS *sb.*² which are ultimately the same word; the earlier *enpress* is difficult to explain. See also APRISE.]

1. An undertaking, enterprise; *esp.* one of an adventurous or chivalrous nature.

a **1300** *Cursor M.* 9802 Man to dei, godd for to rise, Moght nan tak elles þis emprise. **1375** BARBOUR *Bruce* III. 276 To bryng All thar enpress to gud ending. *c* **1386** CHAUCER *Knight's T.* 1682 The lord considered that it were destruccioun to gentil blood to fighten in this emprise. **1423** JAS. I. *Kingis Quair* II. i, Nature first begynneth her enprise. **1600** FAIRFAX *Tasso* II. lxxvii, If you atchieue renowne by this empries. **1600** HOLLAND *Livy* XXIII. xviii. 486 Annibal for very shame was faine to give over his imprease. **1725–6** POPE *Odyss.* IV. 602 Ambushed we lie, and wait the bold emprise. **1823** SCOTT *Romance* (1874) 86 The..most extravagant emprises of the heroes of romance. **1871** BROWNING *Pr. Hohenst.* 773 Dare first The great emprise.

†**b.** A purpose, intent. *Obs.*

c **1340** *Cursor M.* 6528 þei dud aȝeynes goddes emprise. **1393** GOWER *Conf.* III. 281 And eke I not for what emprise I shulde assote upon a nonne.

2. *abstr.* Chivalric enterprise, martial prowess.

a **1300** *Cursor M.* 8183 (Cott.) Knight he was o gret empris. *a* **1400** *Octouian* 1060 Ley on strokes with good empryse. *c* **1500** *Lancelot* 3455 The worschip of knychthed and empryss. **1667** MILTON *P.L.* XI. 642 Giants of mightie Bone, and bould emprise. **1782** HAN. MORE *David* I. 27 Let not thy youth be dazzled..With deeds of bold emprise. **1812** BYRON *Ch. Har.* II. xxxviii, He..whose..foes Shrunk from his deeds of chivalrous emprize. **1863** LONGF. *Wayside Inn* I. Interl. 37 The deeds of high emprise, I sing!

†**b.** Difficulty, greatness of undertaking. *Obs.*

c **1386** CHAUCER *Pers. T.* ¶617 Him thinkith it is so gret emprise for to undertake to doon werkes of goodnes. **1393** GOWER *Conf.* III. 252 It is..of none emprise To speke a word.

†**c.** Pre-occupation, absorption of thought. *Obs.*

c **1500** *Lancelot* 389 The vanyteis of slep..causith of sum maner influens, Empriss of thoght, ore superfleuytee.

†**3.** Renown, glory, distinction. *Obs.*

c **1430** *Syr Gener.* (Roxb.) 1937 This goode ladie of high emprise Did him kisse in herti wise. *c* **1500** *Lancelot* 269 He hath the worschip and emprise.

†**b.** Value, estimation. *Obs.* [? Influenced by PRICE.]

1375 BARBOUR *Bruce* X. 507 The Erll..hye Enpriss Set ay apon Souerane bounte. **1393** GOWER *Conf.* III. 147 But Manachaz saith other wise, That wine is of the more emprise.

†**4.** ? Spoil, prey. *Obs.*

a **1400** *Octouian* 769 Florent..tok of foweles greet empryse.

†**em'prise**, *v. Obs.* Also 5 en-, empryse. [f. prec. sb.] *trans.* To undertake, take on oneself.

c **1386** CHAUCER *Pers. T.* ¶329 Presumpcioun is whan a man undertakith and emprisith that him oughte not to do. **1485** CAXTON *Chas. Gt.* Pref. 3, I haue enprysed..to reduce this sayd book in to our englysshe. **1490** —— *Eneydos* 3, I knowleche my selfe ignorant of connynge to enpryse on me so hie and noble a werke. **1590** *Three Lords & Ladies Lond.* in Hazl. *Dodsley* VI. 376 Each in honour of his mistress, Hath here empris'd the challenge of his right. *a* **1608** SACKVILLE *Dk. Buckingham* lviii. (D.), Thereto trusting I emprised the same.

Hence **em'prising** *ppl. a.*, enterprising, adventurous.

a **1844** CAMPBELL *Lines Departure Emigrants*, Go forth and prosper then, emprising band.

emprison, obs. form of IMPRISON.

emproper, var. IMPROPER *v. Obs.* to appropriate.

empropriate, var. of IMPROPRIATE.

emprosthotonic (ɛm,prɒsθəʊ'tɒnɪk), *a. Path. rare.* [ad. Gr. ἐμπροσθοτονικ-ός suffering from tetanic procurvation.] Of or characterized by EMPROSTHOTONOS.

1883 LAUDER BRUNTON in *Nature* 15 Mar. 468 The convulsions change their character and become emprosthotonic.

‖**emprosthotonos** (ɛmprɒs'θɒtənɒs). *Path.* [mod.L., a. Gr. ἐμπροσθότονος drawn forward and stiffened, f. ἔμπροσθεν before + τόνος a stretching.] 'A condition in tetanus in which the body is drawn forwards by excessive action of the anterior muscles of the trunk' (*Syd. Soc. Lex.*).

1657 *Phys. Dict.*, *Emprostotonos*, a kind of cramp. **1685** T. COOKE *Marrow of Chirurg.* (ed. 4) 498 When the Body, Head, and Neck is drawn forwards, called Emprosthotonos. **1775** MACKENZIE, in *Phil. Trans.* LXVII. 7 A person in the emprosthotonos. **1781** SIR T. WATSON *Lect. Physic* (ed. 5) I. 559 The only example of emprosthotonos which I ever saw.

emprove, -ment, obs. f. IMPROVE, -MENT.

†**empse**, *a. Obs. rare*⁻¹. ? Desert, uninhabited.

1642 H. MORE *Song of Soul, Psychozoia*, xxxvi, The satyres..That in empse Ilands maken their abode.

empt (ɛmpt), *v. Obs.* exc. *dial.* Forms: 1 ǽmetȝian, ǽmtiȝan, ǽmtian, 2 æmtien, 4 emte(n, empte, 9 *dial.* emp, emt, 6– empt. [OE. *ǽmtian* (*ȝe-ǽmtian*), f. *ǽmt-a*, *ǽmetta* leisure; cf. EMPTY *a.* and *v.*]

†**1.** *intr.* and *refl.* To be at leisure. Only in OE.

c **825** *Vesp. Psalter* xlv[i]. 10 Ǽmetȝiað ant ȝesiað forðon ic eam dryhten. *c* **1000** ÆLFRIC *Gram.* xxxiii. 206 (Z.) Ǽmtiȝað eow to rædinge.

†**2.** *intr.* To become empty. *Obs.*

c **1205** LAY. 30408 Feollen ærm kempes; æmteden sadeles.

3. *trans.* To make empty; to drain, exhaust. *lit.* and *fig.* Const. *of.* Also *refl.* = EMPTY *v.* 2, 3.

1340 *Ayenb.* 58 Ase þo þet emteþ þe herte of hire guode. *c* **1386** CHAUCER *Chan. Yem. Prol. & T.* 188 Ther-by shal he nat wynne But empte his purs. **1398** TREVISA *Barth. De P.R.* XIII. xx. (1495) 450 Abyssus..maye neuer be stoppyd..ne emptyd. **1568** T. HOWELL *Arb. Amitie* (1879) 92 There I empt my laden hart. **1630** J. TAYLOR (Water P.) *Wks.* 27/1 Though a man in study take great paines, And empt his veines. **1640** BROME *Antipodes* III. vii, Unlesse I empt My brest of mercy to appease her for you. **1678** HOBBES *Nat. Philos.* iii. 27 That the Cylinder may empt itself. **1825** BRITTON *Beauties Wilts.* Gloss., *Empt*, to pour out, to empty. **1881** *I. of Wight Gloss.* (E.D.S.), *Empt*, to make empty.

4. To pour forth, discharge, clear out (the contents of a vessel, etc.).

1606 WARNER *Alb. Eng.* xiv. To Rdr., Muse, that..Emptedst poore wit poore winde to win. **1623** COCKERAM, *Extercorate*, to empt, or carry out dung.

†**'emptening**, *vbl. sb. Obs.* = EMPTYING *vbl. sb.*

1561 HOLLYBUSH *Hom. Apoth.* 20 b, Great voyding and emptening of the body is, etc.

'emptied, *ppl. a.* [f. EMPTY *v.* + -ED.] That has been exhausted of its contents.

1632 W. LITHGOW *Totall Discourse* 226 Water to..fill our emptied bottles. **1667** BOYLE in *Phil. Trans.* II. 425 The..emptied Receiver.

emptier ('ɛmptɪə(r)). [f. EMPTY *v.* + -ER¹.] He who or that which empties.

1605 TIMME *Quersit.* II. vi. 129 In the nature of balsamick salt thou hast..a purger, and an universal emptier. **1611** BIBLE *Nahum* ii. 2 The emptiers have emptied them out, and marred their vine branches. **1812** H. MACNEILL *Poet. Wks.* II. 77 Dear sober emptyers of the glass. **1879** BARING-GOULD *Germany* II. 269 The..cesspool-emptiers are town officials.

emptily ('ɛmptɪlɪ), *adv.* [f. EMPTY *a.* + -LY².] In an empty manner.

1591 PERCIVALL *Sp. Dict.*, *Vaziamente*, emptily. **1611–84** LEIGHTON in Spurgeon *Treas. Dav.* Ps. xxxix. 4 What we know emptily and barely, we may know spiritually and fruitfully. **1653** MANTON *Exp. James* i. 19 We do not vainly and emptily talk of the things of God. **1871** R. ELLIS *Catullus* lxiv. 142 A light wind emptily fleeting.

emptiness ('ɛmptɪnɪs). Also **emptyness(e.** [f. EMPTY *a.* + -NESS.] The condition of being empty.

1. *gen.* The condition of being void of contents, of not being filled, furnished, or inhabited.

1533 ELYOT *Cast. Helthe* II. (1541) 45 The moderation of slepe must be measured..by emptynesse or fulnesse of the body. **1535** COVERDALE *2 Esdras* vii. 25 Vnto the full, plenty: and to the emptye, emptynesse. **1597** SHAKS. *2 Hen. IV*, I. iii. 75 His Coffers sound With hollow Pouerty, and Emptinesse. **1626** BACON *Sylva* §300 Appetite consisteth in the Emptiness of the Mouth of the Stomack. **1680–1** PENN *Wks. Isaac Pennington* I. A iij b, In that emptiness they waited to be filled of him that filleth all things. **1719** WATTS *Hymns* I. cii, Blest are the humble souls that see Their emptiness and poverty. **1728** POPE *Dunc.* I. 33 Keen hollow winds howl thro' the bleak recess, Emblem of music caus'd by emptiness. **1747** WALPOLE *Lett. H. Mann* 178 (1834) II. 203 No idea of the emptiness of London. **1845–6** TRENCH *Huls. Lect.* II. vii. 261 This was the emptiness of which Christ's coming should be the answering fulness. **1885** *Manch. Exam.* 15 Apr. 3/1 Emptiness of subject and monotony of treatment.

b. *concr.* Void space; a vacuum.

1570 DEE *Math. Pref.* 35 Water..by descending to leaue Emptiness at his backe. **1625** DONNE *Serm.* iii. 22 a, A supplying of all Emptinesses in our Soules. **1691–8** NORRIS *Pract. Disc.* IV. 327 An Emptyness which they can never fill. **1713** WARDER *True Amazons* 35 The occasion of this vast Emptiness in the Hive. **1877** BRYANT *Lit. People Snow* 346 Where once they made their haunt, was emptiness.

2. The state of being void of certain specified contents, or of a specified quality. Const. *of.*

1593 HOOKER *Eccl. Pol.* III. i, Emptines of Christian loue and charity. **1642** FULLER *Holy & Prof. St.* III. iii. 157 Such boasting sounds proceed from emptinesse of desert. **1707** FLOYER *Physic. Pulse-Watch* 362 The Pulsus profundus..indicates..emptiness of Humours. **1875** MASKELL *Ivories* v. 45 To absence of composition..were added neglect and emptiness of form.

3. Want of solidity or substance; inability to satisfy desire; unsatisfactoriness; vacuity, hollowness.

a **1695** DRYDEN *Dufresnoy* Pref. xii, 'Tis this which causes the Graces..to subsist in the emptiness of Light and Shadows. **1710** STEELE *Tatler* No. 271. ¶4 To lay before my Readers the Emptiness of Ambition. **1781** COWPER *Hope* 156 Hope..has the wondrous virtue to educe From emptiness itself a real use. **1860** W. COLLINS *Wom. White* 125 Objections that rose to my lips..died away in their own emptiness. **1871** MISS BRADDON *Fenton's Quest* I. ii. 28 There was no more dulness or emptiness for Gilbert Fenton in his life at Lidford.

b. *pl.* Trifles, trivialities, 'vanities'.

1843 JAMES *Forest Days* (1847) 14 The little emptinesses which occupy free hearts in the early morning. **1884** A. MACLAREN in *Chr. Commw.* 11 Dec. 111/2 Unsubstantial emptinesses and moonshiny illusions.

4. Want of knowledge; lack of sense; inanity. Also, of an author or a composition: Lack of vigorous thought or expression; meagreness or poverty of matter.

1658 J. ROWLAND *Moufet's Theat. Ins.* 1013, I wonder at Pennius's brevity and emptiness in this argument. **1699** GARTH *Dispens.* IV. (1730) 12 Bur[ge]ss deafens all the list'ning Press With Peals of most Seraphick Emptiness. **1728** POPE *Dunc.* I. 185 Me emptiness and dulness could inspire, And were my elasticity, and fire. **1844** STANLEY *Arnold* (1858) I. iv. 168 The falsehood and emptiness of the Latin historians.

†**'empting**, *vbl. sb.* Also emptin. [f. EMPT *v.* + -ING.¹] = EMPTYING; in U.S. the *pl.* in the sense 'yeast' is pronounced ('ɛmptɪnz) but often written *emptyings*: see EMPTYING 2 b.

c **1440** *Promp. Parv.* 139 Emtyng or a voydynge. **1650** *Salem* (Mass.) *Q. Court Recs.* in *Essex Antiquarian* (1903) VII. 28 Elizabeth Pinion,..having come into the house to

borrow some emptings, Tobiah took her and threw her [etc.]. **1839** 'M. CLAVERS' *New Home* xviii. 120 Mrs. Doubleday..keeps her husband's house..in unexceptionable trim. Her *emptin's* are the envy of the neighbourhood. **1848** LOWELL *Bigelow Papers* IX. 131 'T will take more emptins..than this noo party's gut, To give such heavy cakes ez them a start. **1889** R. T. COOKE *Steadfast* vi. 74 Everybody wanted some of her 'empt'ins' to set their own. **1894** M. E. WILKINS *Pembroke* 46, I—wanted to see—if—Sylvy had any emptins. **1902** CLAPIN *Dict. Amer.* 173 *To run emptins*, to show signs of not holding out well, as for instance a speech or an enterprise of any kind.

emption ('ɛmpʃən). [ad. L. *emptiōn-em* buying, n. of action f. *emĕ-re* to buy.]

1. The action of buying: chiefly in phrases, ***right of (sole) emption***, etc., or with allusion to 2.

1461-83 *Ord. R. Househ.* 73 The chief Butler..taketh his resceytes of money..of the Thesaurer..for all the emptiones of his office. **1736** CARTE *Ormonde* I. 140 The proclamation for the sole emption..was offered to be revoked. **1783** BURKE *Rep. Aff. India* Wks. 1842 XI. 143 By a limitation of the right of emption of foreign opium.

2. *Roman Law.* Purchase, in the contract of sale (L. *emptio*, as correlated with *venditio*).

c **1555** HARPSFIELD *Divorce Hen. VIII*, (1878) 241 There is emption and vendition contracted as soon as the parties be condescended upon the price. **1727** ARBUTHNOT *Coins* (T.), There is a dispute among the lawyers, Whether Glaucus exchanging his golden armour with the brasen one of Tydides was emption or commutation.

emptional ('ɛmpʃənəl), *a.* [f. prec. + -AL[1].] That may be purchased.

†**emp'titious**, *a. Obs. rare*⁻¹. [f. L. *emptīci-us* f. *empt-* ppl. stem of *emĕre* to buy + -OUS: cf. *adventitious*.] Venal, capable of being bought.

1650 A. B. *Mutat. Polemo 11* Emptitious as he was..they ..knew well enough how to over value him.

‖**emptor** ('ɛmptɔː(r), -ə(r)). *Rom. Law.* [a. L. *emptor*, agent-n. f. *emĕre* to buy.] A purchaser.

1875 POSTE *Gaius* I. (ed. 2) 108 He had to utter the formula ..i.e. to invite the emptor to strike the scale with the ingot.

†'**emptory.** *Obs.* [ad. late L. *emptōrium* place of buying: see prec.] A mart, market-place.

1641 HEYLIN *Help to Hist.* (1680) 474 The common Mart or Emptory. **1665-76** RAY *Flora* 146 The flower-market, the common Emptory of trash and refuse.

empty ('ɛmptɪ), *a.* and *sb.* Forms: 1 **ǽmetiȝ, ǽmtiȝ, émtiȝ**, 3, 5 **amti, -tie**, 3-4 **emti, empti**, 4-7 **emty, emptie, -ye**, 4- **empty**. [OE. *ǽmetiȝ*, f. *ǽmetta* leisure + *-iȝ*, -Y.

The vowel of the middle syllable was dropped already in OE. The initial *ǽ*, being shortened, yielded as usual in ME. dialects the parallel forms *ă* and *ĕ*; hence the forms *amti* and *emti*; the former died out in 15th century; the latter (with the euphonic *p* normal between *m* and *t*) is represented by the mod. form.]

A. *adj.*

†**1.** Of persons: At leisure, not occupied or engaged. Also, unmarried. Only in OE.

c **897** K. ÆLFRED *Gregory's Past.* li. 401 Þæt hie ne wenen ðæt hie..ȝemengan mæȝen wið ða æmteȝan wifmen. *c* **1000** ÆLFRIC *Hom.* (Th.) II. 441 Martha swanc, and Maria sæt æmtiȝ.

2. a. Of a material receptacle: Containing nothing; opposed to *full*. Also *fig.* of anything that may be said to be 'filled'.

971 *Blickl. Hom.* 5 Heo [the Virgin Mary] wæs 'ful' cweden næs 'æmetuȝu'. *c* **1300** *Beket* 2178 The sculle al amti was: and no brayn therinne bilevede. *c* **1386** CHAUCER *Reeve's Prol.* 40 Almost al empty is þe tonne. **1514** BARCLAY *Cyt. & Uplondyshm.* (1847) 62 With empty belly and simple poore aray. **1599** SHAKS. *Hen. V*, IV. iv. 73 The empty vessel makes the greatest sound. *a* **1628** PRESTON *New Covt.* (1634) 62 Nothing is said to be empty, but when you look for a fullnesse in it. **1673** O. WALKER *Educ.* (1677) 103 They bring forth yellow and emty eares, before the harvest. **1732** POPE *Ep. Bathurst* 320 Which of these is worse, Want with a full or with an empty purse? **1732** ARBUTHNOT *Rules of Diet* 269 They might be taken in an empty Stomach. **1845** BUDD *Dis. Liver* 374 The gall-bladder and ducts are found empty. **1860** TYNDALL *Glac.* I. § 11. 80, I now filled our empty wine-bottle with snow.

b. Void of certain specified contents; *fig.* devoid of certain specified qualities, etc. Const. †*from*, †*in*, *of*.

1483 CAXTON *Cato* G j, Empty of alle goodes and fylled of alle euyll. **1588** SHAKS. *L.L.L.* v. ii. 878 And I shal find you emptie of that fault. **1596** —— *Merch. V.* IV. i. 5 Empty From any dram of mercie. **1600** —— *A.Y.L.* II. vii. 93 In ciuility thou seem'st so emptie. **1633** BP. HALL *Hard Texts* 97 We..are of ourselves emptie of all good. *a* **1727** NEWTON (J.), The heavens are much emptier of air than any vacuum we can make below. **1860** TRENCH *Mirac.* xxxi. (1862) 444 The Gentiles were empty of all fruits of righteousness. **1865** MILL *Exam. Hamilton's Philos.* 87 Metaphysical doctrines which..are empty of the smallest substance.

3. *transf.* †**a.** Having one's purse, etc. empty; destitute of money. (Only contextual.) *Obs.*

1581 J. BELL *Haddon's Answ. Osor.* 15 The Apostles.. should wander through the whole world emptie of all worldly furniture. **1722** DE FOE *Plague* (1756) 173 Those that had Money..were able to subsist themselves; but those who were empty suffered..great Hardships. **1724** —— *Mem. Cavalier* (1840) 151 The king [was] quite empty of money.

b. Having an empty stomach; hungry. Now only *colloq.*

1593 SHAKS. *2 Hen. VI*, III. i. 248 Wer't not all one, an emptie Eagle were set, To guard the Chicken from a hungry Kyte. **1620** SHELTON *Don Quix.* III. xxx. 209 And where there is plenty the Guests are not empty. **1719** DE FOE *Crusoe* (1840) II. viii. 182 I found myself empty.

†**c.** Of the body: Wanting fullness, shrunken, emaciated. Also of the pulse: Weak, 'slender'.

c **1374** CHAUCER *Boeth.* II. i. 4 Þe slak[e] skyn tremblеþ vpon myn emty body. **1486** *Bk. St. Albans* C j a, Sum put hawkys in mew..when they be Empty and lene. **1533** ELYOT *Castel Helthe* II. (1541) 45 b, Where the body is long empty by longe syknesse or abstinence, slepe comforteth nature. **1707** FLOYER *Physic. Pulse-Watch* 412 An empty Pulse shews small Strength.

d. Of a cow or other farm animal: not pregnant. Cf. FULL *a.* 1 e.

1900 in J. WRIGHT *Eng. Dial. Dict.* II. 252/1. **1950** *N.Z. Jrnl. Agric.* Feb. 100/1 Many cows thought to be empty have proved to be in calf when slaughtered at the works. **1960** *Farmer & Stockbreeder* 23 Feb. 80/3 Empty gilts shared in the general enthusiasm, averaging £41 15s 2d.

4. a. Of space, a person's place, etc.: Vacant, unoccupied. Of a house, etc: Devoid of furniture or inmates. Also *fig.* spec. ***Empty Quarter*** [rendering Arab. *Ruba el-Khali*], the great southern desert of Arabia (formerly identified with the Dahna); also *fig.*

971 *Blickl. Hom.* 37 Þæt on us ne sy ȝemeted næniȝu stow æmetiȝ gastlicra mæȝena. *c* **1000** ÆLFRIC *Gen.* i. 2 Seo eorþe ..wæs ydel ant æmtiȝ. *c* **1200** *Trin. Coll. Hom.* 87 He.. cumeð þerto and fint hit emti and mid beseme clene swopen. *a* **1225** *Ancr. R.* 156 Non empti stude iðe heorte to underuongen flesliche leihtren. **1297** R. GLOUC. 17 Amty place he made a boute, & folc fleu hym faste. *c* **1385** CHAUCER *L.G.W.*, 888 Tysbe..saw hire wympil & hise emty schede. **1514** BARCLAY *Cyt. & Uplondyshm.* (1847) 6 One maye clerely the emty nestes se. **1593** SHAKS. *2 Hen. VI*, v. ii. 4 And dead mens cries do fill the emptie aire. **1611** BIBLE *1 Sam.* xx. 25 Dauids place was emptie. **1627** MAY *Lucan* XI. 503 With empty Standards reft of Companies. **1697** DRYDEN *Virg. Georg.* IV. 516 Two rising Heaps of liquid Crystal stand, And leave a Space betwixt, of empty Sand. **1709** STEELE *Tatler* No. 182 ¶1 The Town grows so very empty. **1864** SKEAT *Uhland's Poems* 273 Every room seemed empty now.

[**1875** *Encycl. Brit.* II. 240/1 This greater desert, the 'Roba El Khaliyeh' or 'Empty Space' of geographers—the 'Dahna' or 'Crimson' of modern Arabs.] **1910** *Encycl. Brit.* II. 260/1 The great desert known as the Dahna or the Rub'a el Khali ('the empty quarter'). **1913** T. HOUTSMA et al. *Encycl. Islam* I. 370/2 Central Arabia... The desert has several names..generally it is called al-Dahnā', 'the red country', after the colour of the sand. On the maps it is indicated al-Rub' al-Ḵhālī, i.e. the empty quarter. **1929** T. E. LAWRENCE *Let.* 12 July (1938) 663 They can pass over the Ruba el Khali, the so-called 'Empty Quarter' of Arabia. **1932** B. THOMAS (*title*) Arabia felix, across the Empty Quarter of Arabia. **1959** *Listener* 19 Nov. 893/1 The Empty Quarter stretches for nine hundred miles across southern Arabia. **1963** *Guardian* 5 July 8/3 One hails him as the Hakluyt of that empty quarter where the parched intellect croaks for a swig of feeling.

b. quasi-*sb.* A void (space).

1535 COVERDALE *Job* xxvi. 7 He stretcheth out yᵉ north ouer the emptie.

5. Without anything to carry.

a. Of a carriage, ship, etc. (= sense 2). Hence *transf.* of a beast of burden: Without a load (*rare* in mod. use).

c **1330** *King of Tars* 201 And sadeles mony emptye. **1502** ARNOLDE *Chron.* (1811) 197 Item an emty horse only i. d'. **1586** MARLOWE *1st Pt. Tamburl.* I. ii, Return our mules and empty camels back. **1607** TOPSELL *Four-f. Beasts* (1673) 244 When you have used him [the horse] to leap empty, likewise accustome him loaded. **1697** DRYDEN *Virg. Georg.* III. 271 Persuade 'em first to lead an empty wheel. **1714** *Fr. Bk. of Rates* 412 Vessels..empty, or loaded with Masts, Planks, and other Timber. **1796** *Log* in Nicolas *Disp. Nelson* VII. p. lxv, A Ship and a Brig from Finale..proving..empty. **1884** SIR W. MᶜMURDO in *Pall Mall G.* 18 June 2/1 FitzGerald.. started with the empty camels in a bee-line across the desert.

b. Of the hand: Not bringing or carrying any thing away. Hence of persons: = EMPTY-HANDED; chiefly as predicative complement, e.g. ***to go, come away empty***.

c **1500** *New Notbr. Mayd* in *Anc. Poet. Tracts* 45 The poure may stande, With empty hande. **1535** COVERDALE *Ruth* iii. 17 Thou shalt not come emptye vnto thy mother in lawe. **1607** SHAKS. *Timon* III. vi. 40, I return'd you an empty Messenger. **1727** A. HAMILTON *New Acc. E. Ind.* I. xi. 119 The Custom, not to appear before great Men with an empty Hand.

fig. **1751** JORTIN *Serm.* (1771) VI. 198 The prayers of the Penitent return not empty. **1850** TENNYSON *In Mem.* III. iii, A hollow form with empty hands.

c. As a Biblical Hebraism, of a sword, ***to return empty***.

1611 BIBLE *2 Sam.* i. 22. **1677** HUBBARD *Narrative* 98 Whom [sixty of the enemy] they slew and took, so as their Sword returned not empty.

6. a. Of persons, their projects, etc.: Lacking knowledge and sense; frivolous, foolish.

1611 BIBLE *Pref.* 8 This was iudged to be but a very poore and emptie shift. **1664** POWER *Exp. Philos.* Pref. 18 Our best Philosophers will but prove empty Conjecturalists. *a* **1674** CLARENDON *Hist. Reb.* (1704) III. XIII. 307 A very empty and unprepared design. **1696** TATE & BRADY *Ps.* cxliv. 4 His Thoughts but empty are and vain. **1707-8** *Let.* in *Hearne's Coll.* II. 91 A silly, empty pretender to Greek. **1711** STEELE *Spect.* No. 75 ¶6 The empty Coxcomb has no Regard to any thing..Sacred. **1727** DE FOE *Syst. Magic* I. iv. (1840) 98 The meanest, emptiest, and most inconsistent project.

b. Of things: Wanting solidity and substance; unsatisfactory, vain, meaningless.

1340 *Ayenb.* 143 Zuo emti to þe ziȝþe of þo greate blisse. **1603** SHAKS. *Meas. for M.* II. iv. 2 Heauen hath my empty words. **1667** MILTON *P.L.* III. 454 Find Fit retribution, emptie as thir deeds. **1674** BREVINT *Saul at Endor* 230 It is but an emty Phantome. **1697** DRYDEN *Virg. Georg.* IV. 710 All his Hopes exhal'd in empty Smoke. **1711** STEELE *Spect.* No. 79 ¶9 All these Acts are but empty Shows. **1718** *Freethinker* No. 60. 34 It is not an empty Title..but a Right. **1728** POPE *Dunc.* I. 54 Weighs..solid pudding against empty praise. *a* **1764** LLOYD *Whim* Poet. Wks. 1774 II. 166 Wrangling wits..quarrel for an empty name. **1813** SHELLEY *Q. Mab* iv, Words..Empty and vain as his own coreless heart. **1837** THIRLWALL *Greece* IV. xxxii. 229 Nor were these mere empty professions. **1884** *Sat. Rev.* 14 June 766/1 Frightened by the emptiest of bugbears.

B. *sb. Comm.* An empty truck or wagon; an empty box, cask, etc. which has contained goods; an empty cab or taxi; an empty house or premises; an empty bottle, container, etc. *colloq.*

1865 *Morn. Star* 1 Feb., I was ordered..to..send the empties off first. **1879** F. H. GRUNDY *Pictures of Past* vi. 166 'Well,' says Leigh Hunt, 'I found him [*sc.* a cabman] returning from Hammersmith, and he said as an empty he would take me for half-fare.' **1881** *Daily News* 22. Aug. 3/2 George Whitehead, a dealer in empties at Mile-end New-town. **1884** *Harper's Mag.* May 874/2 They are..made into a long train in exchange for 'empties'. **1905** *Westm. Gaz.* 23 Aug. 8/2 Property owners throughout the various suburbs of London are making loud complaint of the steady increase in the proportion of 'empties'. **1914** *Evening Post* (Wellington, N.Z.) 24 Feb. 4 Get as many 'empties' [= bottles] as possible. **1924** *Ladies' Home Jrnl.* June 100 He delivers it by the case and calls for the empties. **1938** G. GREENE *Brighton Rock* VII. i. 277 A cupboard stood open full of empties. **1961** L. VAN DER POST *Heart of Hunter* I. v. 82 Some fuel-drums lay in a neat line..all empties.

C. *attrib.* and *Comb.* as (parasynthetic adjs.), ***empty-basketed, -bellied, -fisted, -headed, -hearted, -pannelled*** (in Falconry), ***-pated, -skulled, -stomached, -vaulted***; also EMPTY-HANDED. **empty-cell** used *attrib.* (see esp. quot. 1946); **empty nester** chiefly *U.S.*, either member of a couple whose children have grown up and left home (freq. in *pl.*); hence **empty nest**, a household in which only the parents now remain; also applied *attrib.*, as ***empty-nest syndrome***, to depression allegedly affecting women whose children have left home; **empty word** *Linguistics*, a word which has no meaning in itself but serves a grammatical function, e.g. *at*, *but*, *for*, etc.

1883 *Harper's Mag.* Apr. 702/2 Fisher people..coming back *empty-basketed. **1836-48** B. D. WALSH *Aristoph. Knights* I. iii, You've cut *Empty-bellied to the Town-hall. **1917** A. J. WALLIS-TAYLER *Preservation of Wood* vii. 199 This process [*sc.* the Rueping or Rüping Process] is on what is known as the *empty cell treatment. **1946** CARTWRIGHT & FINDLAY *Decay of Timber* xiii. 260 It is usual to treat poles and timber for building use by the empty cell process, by means of which the walls of cells of the wood are left coated with a layer of preservative, but the cavities are empty. **1968** W. E. WILLIS *Timber* iv. 86 The two empty cell methods are known as the Rueping and Lawry processes. **1664** H. MORE *Myst. Iniq.* xv. 52 Fear of the Saints displeasure, if they approach *empty-fisted. **1650** B. *Discollim.* 17 *Empty-headed, Fiddle-brain'd Men. **1873** SYMONDS *Grk. Poets* iii. 86 Trample on the empty-headed rabble. **1605** SHAKS. *Lear* I. i. 155 Nor are those *empty-hearted, whose low sounds Reuerbe no hollownesse. **1842** MANNING *Serm.* viii. (1848) I. 109 Empty-hearted followers of this vain-glorious world. **1962** *Economist* 15 Dec. 1131/2 Couples in the 45-65 age bracket—the so-called '*empty nesters', whose children have grown up and who have become bored with their large houses. **1972** *Ladies' Home Jrnl.* Feb. 124/4 Even the 'empty nest' syndrome hasn't seemed to hit her. She seems genuinely delighted by both of her daughters' marriages. **1973** *N.Y. Times* 21 Jan. x. 24/5 Not all empty-nest women have high-salaried husbands, but all feel less 'squoze' once their sons and daughters have addresses of their own. **1976** *Globe & Mail* (Toronto) 27 Aug. 12/4 Therapists who deal with parents during this stage of life have come to view the trivial-sounding 'empty nest' as a family crisis potentially as profound as divorce. **1980** *Sunday Times* 30 Mar. 50 Builders..have ignored an increasingly important category of housebuyer—the busy, well-off executive couple who either have no children or whose children have grown up and left. Americans call them 'empty nesters'. **1575** TURBERV. *Falconrie* 313 Let hir stande *emptiepanneld upon the same untill night. **1820** SCOTT *Abbot* xxxiii, There are *empty-pated coxcombs at each corner. **1863** MRS. C. CLARKE *Shaks. Char.* vi. 159 Quackery may, and does succeed for a season..with the *empty-skulled. **1527** ANDREW *Brunswyke's Distyll. Waters* A ij, Them that be *empty-stomaked thrughe overmoche hete of the stomake. **1861** DU CHAILLU *Equat. Afr.* vi. 58 The only empty-stomached individual of the company. **1634** MILTON *Comus* 249 They float..through the *empty-vaulted night. **1892** H. SWEET *New Eng. Gram.* I. 22. §58 When a form-word is entirely devoid of meaning, we may call it an **empty word*, as opposed to *full words* such as *earth* and *round*. **1953** W. J. ENTWISTLE *Aspects of Lang.* x. 298 Chinese..makes considerable use of 'empty words', that is of auxiliaries in the broad sense of the term, which includes prepositions as well as subordinate members of the verbal complex. **1968** P. KRATOCHVÍL *Chinese Lang. Today* iv. 117 Traditional Chinese linguists considered practically all minimal forms, beside what would be called nouns, as 'empty words'.

empty ('ɛmptɪ), *v.* Forms: [1 **ȝe-ǽmtiȝian**], 6-7 **emptie**, 6- **empty**. [f. EMPTY *a.*; the form with prefix *ȝe-* appears in OE.; subsequently the

word does not appear in our quots. before 16th c. Cf. EMPT.]

1. *trans.* To make empty; to pour out, draw off, or remove the contents of (anything); to clear (a house, etc.) of furniture or of inmates.

[*c* **1000** ÆLFRIC *Hom.* (Th.) I. 290 [Arius] wæs swa ȝeæmtoȝod on his innoðe swa swa he wæs ær on his ȝeleafan.] **1555** EDEN *Decades W. Ind.* II. i. (Arb.) 110 They had emptied theyr quyuers. **1602** CAREW *Cornwall* 20 b, An ill..saved Harvest soon emptieth their old store. **1623** CONWAY in Ellis *Orig. Lett.* I. 292 III. 157 Bleeding, [I will] emptie my vaynes. **1667** MILTON *P.L.* I. 633 These puissant Legions, whose exile Hath emptied Heav'n. **1697** DRYDEN *Virg. Georg.* IV. 493 Empty the woolly Rack, and fill the Reel. **1763** J. BROWN *Poetry & Mus.* iii. 31 The Kettle is in Part empty'd in the Morning. **1791** COWPER *Iliad* XVIII. 356 All our houses..Stand emptied of their hidden treasures. **1798** CANNING *New Morality* 40 in *Anti-Jacobin* 9 July (1852) 202 Empty all thy quiver on the foe.

b. To transfer the whole contents of (a vessel, etc.) to another receptacle. Const. †*in*, *into*, *upon*. Also *fig.*

1598 SHAKS. *Merry W.* III. iii. 15 Empty it in the muddie ditch. **1833** HT. MARTINEAU *Cinnamon & Pearls* v. 90 Markets into which we can empty our warehouses. **1865** DICKENS *Mut. Fr.* I. 122 Bob carried..one of those iron models of sugar-loaf hats..into which he emptied the jug.

c. To drain away, pour off, clear out (the contents of anything). Also *fig.*

1578 T. N. tr. *Conq. W. India* 31 That with two pumpes they might not emptie the water. **1823** LAMB *Elia*, Ser. II. xxiii. (1865) 396 To perceive all goodness emptied out of him.

2. To unburden, discharge, clear *of* (*with* obs.) certain specified contents. Chiefly *transf.* and *fig.*

1526 *Pilgr. Perf.* (W. de W. 1531) 103 Pryde..fylleth a man or woman full of..vaynglory..but mekenes emptyeth them. **1555** EDEN *Decades W. Ind.* Pref. (Arb.) 55 Whether the sandes of the ryuers..bee so emptied with golde. **1593** HOOKER *Eccl. Pol.* IV. x. (1611) 147 Emptying the Church of euery such rite and ceremony. *a* **1628** PRESTON *New Covt.* (1634) 397 The spirit of bondage..empties a man of all righteousness. **1667** MILTON *P.L.* III. 731 The neighbouring Moon With borrowd light her countenance triform Hence fills and empties. **1850** TENNYSON *In Mem.* VIII. ii, And all The chambers emptied of delight. **1874** MORLEY *Compromise* (1886) 140 Formularies, which he has first to empty of all definite..significance.

3. *refl.* Of persons: Chiefly said of Christ, after Gr. ἐκένωσε ἑαυτόν (A. V. 'made himself of no reputation') *Phil.* ii. 7. Formerly also, to exhaust all one's resources.

1579 FULKE *Heskins' Parl.* 114 He emptied himselfe..taking the shape of a seruant. **1651** N. BACON *Hist. Disc.* lvii. 170 But emptied themselves to the utmost for his delivery. **1658** *Whole Duty Man* xvii. § 11. 142 Christ emptied himself of all..glory and greatness. **1741** WATTS *Improv. Mind* (1801) 355 Jesus the mediator emptied himself for our sakes. **1882** FARRAR *Early Chr.* I. 380 He..emptied Himself of His glory..as the..co-equal Son.

4. *refl.* Of a river, etc.: To discharge itself *into* another river, the sea, etc; said also of a blood-vessel.

1555 EDEN *Decades W. Ind.* (Arb.) 284 A branche of Nilus which emptieth it selfe in owre sea. **1651** HOBBES *Leviath.* II. xxix. 173 The Veins..empty themselves into the Heart. **1725** DE FOE *Voy. round World* (1840) 306 A large river empties itself into this bay. **1860** TYNDALL *Glac.* I. 34 The river..empties itself into the lake.

b. *intr.* for *refl.* Now chiefly in *U.S.*

a **1682** SIR T. BROWNE *Tracts* 165 The Rivers Arnon, Cedron, Zaeth, which empty into this valley. **1692** tr. *Sallust* 50 All these together empty'd into Rome as into the common sewer of all disorder. **1796** MORSE *Amer. Geog.* I. 385 Sheepscot river..empties into the ocean. **1864** G. P. MARSH *Man & Nature* 402 Until the year 1714, the Kander ..emptied into the river Aar.

5. *intr.* for *refl.* To become empty.

1633 B. JONSON *Epithalamion* Wks. (1838) 718 The chapel empties; and thou may'st be gone Now, Sun. **1654** GAYTON *Festivous Notes* 100 As his purse failed, or pockets emptied. **1850** MRS. CARLYLE *Lett.* II. 109 Now that the town is emptying. **1885** *Manch. Exam.* 5 May 5/5 The benches had almost emptied for the dinner hour.

'empty-'handed, *a.* [see EMPTY *a.*] Having nothing in the hand: chiefly in phrases, *to go, come*, etc. *empty-handed.*

a. Bringing nothing, *esp.* no gift. Also *fig.*

1613 PURCHAS *Pilgr., Descr. India* (1864) 40 None..may come before the King with any Petition emptie-handed. **1775** SHERIDAN *Rivals* II. ii, I guessed you weren't come empty-handed. **1850** W. IRVING *Goldsmith* 31 His daughter ..entered her husband's family empty-handed. **1871** ROSSETTI *Poems, Last Confess.* 22, I passed a village-fair.. And thought, being empty-handed, I would take Some little present.

fig. **1855** SMEDLEY *Occult Sc.* 258 Proving..that the prescient spirit comes empty-handed.

b. Carrying nothing away.

1635 AUSTIN *Medit.* 137 Departing as he [Christ] did emptie-handed from the world. **1835** W. IRVING *Tour Prairies* 119 He [the hunter] returned empty-handed. **1868** FREEMAN *Norm. Conq.* (1876) II. vii. 102 At all events Swegen went away empty-handed.

'emptying, *vbl. sb.* [f. EMPTY *v.* + -ING[1].]

1. The action of making empty.

1605 SHAKS. *Macb.* IV. iii. 68 Intemperance..hath beene Th' vntimely emptying of the happy Throne. **1651** WITTIE tr. *Primrose's Pop. Err.* 297 Bloud-letting..is..called the emptying of the vessels.

2. *concr.* **a.** What is emptied out of any vessel; also *fig.* **b.** *pl.* Yeast (*obs.* exc. *U.S.* as an artificial spelling for *emptins*; see EMPTING).

1650 B. *Discollim.* 23 A few Brewers emptyings. **1813** SOUTHEY *Nelson* II. 36 Galley slaves, the emptying of the jails, and banditti. **1860** EMERSON *Cond. Life, Power* Wks. (Bohn) II. 333 If we will make bread, we must have..yeast, emptyings.

empurple (ɛm'pɜːp(ə)l), *v.* Also 7 **enpurple**, 6 **inpurple**, 7–8 **impurple**. [f. EN- + PURPLE.] *trans.* To make purple; to redden.

1590 SPENSER *F.Q.* III. vii. 17 Wildings.. whose sides empurpled were with smyling red. **1623** DRUMM. OF HAWTH. *Cypress Grove* Wks. (1711) 119 The violets.. impurple not the winter. *c* **1630** —— *Poems* Wks. (1711) 5 O sacred blush, enpurpling cheeks pure skies With crimson wings. **1667** MILTON *P.L.* III. 364 The bright Pavement impurpl'd with Celestial Roses smil'd. **1755** JOHNSON, *Empurple.* **1772** SIR W. JONES *Laura* 62 The rising flowers impurpled every dale. **1804** J. GRAHAME *Sabbath* 489 That setting sun Is now empurpling Scotland's mountain tops. **18..** MRS. BROWNING *Lam. for Adonis* v, The blood ran away And empurpled the thigh. **1884** HUNTER & WHYTE *My Ducats & Dau.* i. (1885) 2 A dye-work..daily empurpled the stream.

b. To robe or clothe in purple. *rare.*

1598 FLORIO, *Porporare*, to impurple or inroabe with scarlet. **1868** BEECHER *Serm. Crowned Suffering*, The ribald soldiery..empurple him [Christ].

empurpled (ɛm'pɜːp(ə)ld), *ppl. a.* [f. prec. + -ED[1].] That is made or turned purple; reddened.

1708 J. PHILIPS *Cyder* (1807) 60 Down rain th' impurpled balls, ambrosial fruit. **1790–1813** A. WILSON *Sheph. Dream* Poet. Wks. 11 Bleaters, nibbling o'er th' empurpled plain. **18..** MACAULAY *Ivry*, We thought of Seine's empurpled flood.

b. Clad in or covered with purple. Also *fig.*

1860 T. MARTIN *Horace* 55 Barbaric monarchs' mothers, and empurpled tyrants fear. **1878** *Masque Poets* 30 The empurpled ease Of her Greek couch.

empurpling (ɛm'pɜːplɪŋ), *ppl. a.* [f. as prec. + -ING[2].] **a.** That makes purple, reddens. **b.** That grows purple.

1793 COLERIDGE *Songs of Pixies* ix, The impurpling vale. **1797** MRS. RADCLIFFE *Italian* xxx. (1824) 696 An empurpling and reposing hue.

empusa (ɛm'pjuːzə). Also 7–9 **empuse**. [a. Gr. ἔμπουσα.]

1. In classical sense: A hobgoblin or spectre supposed to be sent by Hecate.

1603 HOLLAND *Plutarch's Mor.* 598 Little children, whom they use to scarre with the fantastical illusion *Empusa.* **1647** JER. TAYLOR *Dissuas. Popery* I. i. § 10 This was well tried of old against an Empuse that met Apollonius Tyaneus. **1855** SMEDLEY *Occult Sc.* 72 A near kinsman of the classical Empusa.

†**2.** A hobgoblin, spectre, phantom. *Obs.*

1621 MOLLE *Camerar. Liv. Libr.* IV. 264 This faire bride is an Empuse or Hag. **1678** CUDWORTH *Intell. Syst.* I. ii. 62 An Empusa, Phantom, or Spectre. **1708** in KERSEY. **1755** in ASH. **1847** in CRAIG; and in mod. Dicts.

†**3.** *Comb.*, as in ***empusa-land.*** *Obs.* (*nonce-wd.*)

1799 W. TAYLOR in Robberds *Mem.* I. 305 When I return from empusaland to reality.

4. A genus of the family *Entomophthoreæ.*

†**em'puzzle**, *v.* *Obs.* In 7 **empuzzel**. [f. EN- + PUZZLE *sb.* or *v.*] *trans.* To puzzle.

1646 SIR T. BROWNE *Pseud. Ep.* I. i. 1 It hath empuzzeled the enquiries of others..to make out how, etc.

empyema (ɛmpaɪ'iːmə, ɛmpɪ-). *Path.* [mod.L., a. Gr. ἐμπύημα a gathering, suppuration, f. ἐμπυέ-ειν to suppurate.]

1. 'A collection of pus in the cavity of the pleura, the result of pleurisy. The term has also been used to denote any chronic inflammatory effusion in the chest' (*Syd. Soc. Lex.*).

1615 CROOKE *Body of Man* 367 You shall open a mans side diseased of the Empyema. **1702** C. MATHER *Magn. Chr.* VII. (1852) App. 606 All his..skill in anatomy could not prevent its producing an empyema. **1878** T. BRYANT *Pract. Surg.* I. 569 Suppuration in the antrum, or Empyema.

2. In wider sense: Suppuration. *rare.*

1866 A. FLINT *Princ. Med.* (1880) 149 The term empyema only expresses the existence of pus, without indicating its situation. **1880** tr. *Ziemssen's Cycl. Med.* IX. 545 This so-called Empyema of the Gall bladder.

†**3.** 'An operation to discharge all sorts of matter with which the midriff is loaded by making a perforation in the Breast' (Kersey). *Obs.*[−0]

1721–1800 in BAILEY. **1775** in ASH.

†**empy'ematous**, *a.* *Med. Obs. rare*[−1]. [f. Gr. ἐμπυηματ- stem of ἐμπύημα + -OUS.] Belonging to or suffering from EMPYEMA. So †**empye'matic** [see -IC].

1661 LOVELL *Hist. Anim. & Min.* 45 Eaten by those that have the peripneumony, or are empyematous..and those that spit forth empyematous matter. **1684** tr. *Bonet's Merc. Compit.* [Nettle] is good for..empyematick persons.

†**em'pyic**, *a.* *Med. Obs. rare.* [ad. Gr. ἐμπυικός suppurating.] That suffers from EMPYEMA.

[**1657** *Phys. Dict.*, *Empyici*, are such as have an imposthume or bladder broken in the side of the lungs.] **1684** tr. *Bonet's Merc. Compit.* v. 141 This Sinus is especially considerable in tapping Empyick persons.

†**em'pyical**, *a.* *Path. Obs. rare*[−1]. [f. prec. + -AL[1].] = prec.

1758 J. S. *Le Dran's Observ. Surg.* 111 The weight of the Fluid in an empyecal [*sic*] Person.

†**empyre**, *v.* *Obs. rare*[−1]. [ad. F. *empirer*, variant of OF. *empeirer*: see IMPAIR.] *trans.* To impair, make worse.

1566 DRANT *Horace's Sat.* ii. F v b, Let furious fortune frowne..She cannot much empyre our cates.

†**empyre**, *a.* *Obs.* Also 4 **empiry**, 6 **empire**. [ad. med.L. (*cælum*) *empyreum*, *empyrium*: see EMPYREAL.] = EMPYREAL, EMPYREAN.

1340 HAMPOLE *Pr. Consc.* 7761 Þis heven is cald heven empiry. **1520** *Myrr. our Ladye* 302 Heuen empyre. **1549** *Compl. Scot.* 48 The hauyn empire. **1594** DICKENSON *Arisbas* (1878) 30 His heroique spirit..hath ascended to the Empyre heaven.

empyreal (ɛm'pɪrɪəl, ɛmpɪ'riːəl), *a.* Forms: 5 **imperyal**, 7 **empyreall**, **emperial**, **imperial(l**, 7–8 **empyrial(l**, 6– **empyreal**. [f. Med.L. *empyreus*, *empyræus*, f. Gr. ἐμπύρ-ος fiery) + -AL[1].]

1. Of or pertaining to the EMPYREAN or highest heaven. Also *fig.*

1481 CAXTON *Myrr.* III. xxxii. 184 And that is called the heuen Imperyal. *c* **1590** MARLOWE *Faust.* vi. 63 The seven planets, the firmament, and the empyreal heaven. **1652** CARYL *Job* xiv. 12. 604 The imperial heaven, which is called the Seat of the blessed. **1667** MILTON *P.L.* VII. 14 Into the Heav'n of Heav'ns I have presum'd..and drawn Empyreal aire. **1732** POPE *Ess. Man* II. 23 Go soar with Plato to th' empyreal sphere. **1850** W. IRVING *Mahomet* vii. (1853) 39 Seated securely in the empyreal heavens.

b. Of or pertaining to the sky or visible heaven; celestial.

1744 AKENSIDE *Pleas. Imag.* I. 202 Amaz'd she views The empyreal waste. **1882** WHINFIELD tr. *Omar Khayyam* 64 Yon palace whose roofs touch the empyreal blue.

c. quasi-*sb.*

1827 KEBLE *Chr. Y.*, *Quinquages. Sund.*, Happy souls.. Plunge in th' empyreal vast.

2. *fig.* Sublime, elevated, superior, rare.

1641 MILTON *Ch. Govt.* II. (1851) 143 A mortall thing among many readers of no Empyreall conceit. **1735–6** H. BROOKE *Univ. Beauty* I. 194 Empyreal natures with empyreal names. *a* **1797** W. MASON *Ode to Truth* iv. 39 Shall a form..of mould'ring clay, Vie with these charms empyrial?

3. In etymological sense: Fiery; composed of or resembling the pure element of fire. Also *fig.*

1601 DEACON & WALKER *Spirits & Divels* 93 They.. consist of empyriall or fierie bodies. *a* **1711** KEN *Hymns Evang.* Poet. Wks. 1721 I. 6 A chariot..Of brightest empyreal Substance built. **1809** W. IRVING *Knickerb.* I. i. (1849) 32 Certain empyreal, luminous or phosphoric clouds.

†**4.** *Chem.* Capable of supporting combustion. ***empyreal air***: Scheele's name for oxygen. *Obs.*

1780 tr. *Scheele's Experiments* 35 Since this air is absolutely necessary for the generation of fire..I shall henceforth..call it empyreal air. **1812** SIR H. DAVY *Chem. Philos.* 226 Only two undecompounded empyreal substances have been as yet discovered.

†**b.** (See quot.) *Obs.*

1801 HERSCHEL *Sun* in *Phil. Trans.* XCI. 303 An elastic gas, which may be called empyreal, is constantly formed [in the sun].

empyrean (ɛmpɪ'riːən, ɛm'pɪrɪən), *a.* and *sb.* Also 6 **empyrian**, 7–8 **empyræan**. [f. as prec. + -AN.]

A. *adj.* Of or pertaining to the sphere of fire or highest heaven. Also *fig.*

1614 RALEIGH *Hist. World* I. 3 It pleased God first of all to create the Empyrean Heaven. **1682** SIR T. BROWNE *Chr. Mor.* 93 The pearl we seek for is not to be found in the Indian, but in the empyrean ocean. **1796** MORSE *Amer. Geog.* I. 27 Above the starry sphere..finally the empyrean heaven, or heaven of heavens. **1805** WORDSW. *Prelude* IV. (1850) 98 Drenched in empyrean light. *a* **1839** PRAED *Poems* (1864) II. 306 From the Courts of the Empyrean dome Came forth what seemed a fiery car.

B. *sb.*

1. The highest heaven. In ancient cosmology the sphere of the pure element of fire: in Christian use, the abode of God and the angels. Also *fig.*

1667 MILTON *P.L.* VII. 73 Divine Interpreter sent Down from the Empyrean. **1755** in JOHNSON. **1847** LD. LINDSAY *Chr. Art* I. Introd. 32 The empyrean, the first work of creation and the residence and throne of God. **1878** NEWCOMB *Pop. Astron.* IV. 408 The empyrean, or kingdom of fire.

2. *transf.* **a.** The visible heavens or firmament. **b.** The whole extent of cosmic space.

1808 J. BARLOW *Columb.* IV. 456 O'er great, o'er small extends his physic laws, Empalms the empyrean. **1821** CRAIG *Lect. Drawing* v. 262 The vast empyrean of the sky. **1880** M. PATTISON *Milton* xiii. 179 The physical universe itself [becomes] a drop suspended in the infinite empyrean.

†**empy'reum.** *Obs.* Also **empyræum**. [a. L. *empyreum* (*cælum*) the fiery heaven or sphere of fire.] = EMPYREAN B. 1.

1647 CRASHAW *Music's Duel* 91 In th' empyræum of pure harmony. *a* **1680** BUTLER *Rem.* (1759) I. 11 Prove, if they are other Suns..Or Windows in the Empyreum. *a* **1711** KEN *Hymnotheo* Poet. Wks. 1721 III. 200 Through Empyreum ..Thousands of thousands their bright Beams display. **1777**

PRIESTLEY *Matt. & Spir.* (1782) I. vi. 67 When the Christian ..has ranged the regions of empyreum for some thousands of years.

†**empy'reum(e.** *Obs. rare.* Anglicized form of next.

1665 G. HARVEY *Advice agst. Plague* 24 They impress an Empyreume upon the intrails for want of subtil dissipative parts. **1727** BRADLEY *Fam. Dict.* s.v. *Angelica*, There may be Danger of an Empyreum from another Fire.

empyreuma (ɛmpɪ'ruːmə). Also 7 **empyruma**; *pl.* **empyreumata.** [a. Gr. ἐμπύρευμα a live coal covered with ashes, f. ἐμπυρεύειν to set on fire.]

†**1.** (See quots.) *Obs.*

1643 J. STEER tr. *Exp. Chyrurg.* vi. 20 That outward heat doth draw unto it Empyruma, that is, heat left by the fire in the burned part. **1656** RIDGLEY *Pract. Physick* 66 The Empyreuma, or Atoms of the fire must first be called forth.

2. The 'burnt' smell imparted by fire to organic substances.

1641 FRENCH *Distill.* i. (1651) 13 A certain Empyreuma, or smatch of the fire. **1736** BAILEY *Housh. Dict.* 188 If the cassia be drawn low it is very subject to an empyreuma. **1794-6** E. DARWIN *Zoon.* (1801) I. 195 Our victuals..are adulterated with salt, spice, oil, and empyreuma. **1858** HOGG *Life Shelley* II. 423 A disgusting taste..gravely pronounced to be only an empyreuma.

†**3.** In *pl.* 'Little feaverish remains, after a crisis. Also that thick viscous matter which settles at the bottom of distilled Water' (Phillips). *Obs.*—⁰

1721-1800 in BAILEY. **1775** in ASH.

empyreumatic (ɛm,pɪruː'mætɪk), *a.* [f. Gr. ἐμπυρευματ- stem of ἐμπύρευμα + -IC.] Pertaining to, or having the quality of, EMPYREUMA; tasting or smelling of burnt organic matter.

1669 W. SIMPSON *Hydrol. Chym.* 163 That fetid empyreumatic oyl which we see. **1746** R. JAMES *Introd. Moufet's Health's Improv.* 42 The Mass..is..of a disagreeable Smell, empyreumatic, bitter. **1791** HAMILTON *Berthollet's Dyeing* I. I. I. v. 78 A dark coloured and empyreumatic phlegm. **1862** *Cornh. Mag.* VI. 607 One pipe ..represents a dose of nicotine and empyreumatic oil.

empyreumatical (ɛm,pɪruː'mætɪkəl), *a.* [f. as prec. + -ICAL.] = prec.

1667 BOYLE *Orig. Formes & Qual.*, Other Empyreumaticall oyles. **1669** —— *Contn. New Exp.* II. (1682) 196 The Flesh had contracted a taste and a smell very empyreumatical. **1725** BRADLEY *Fam. Dict.* s.v. *Nutmeg*, To avoid the Empyreumatical Impression it would otherwise take. **1872** BAKER *Nile Tribut.* ii. 35 The Arabs..prepare their tanned skins with an empyreumatical oil.

†**empy'reumatism.** *Obs. rare*—¹. [f. as prec. + -ISM.] Infection with an EMPYREUMA.

1669 W. SIMPSON *Hydrol. Chym.* 191 Accusing its medical preparations of empyreumatism.

empyreumatize (ɛmpɪ'ruːmətaɪz), *v.* [f. as prec. + -IZE.] *trans.* To infect or taint with an EMPYREUMA. Hence **empy'reumatized** *ppl. a.*

1846 *Blackw. Mag.* LIX. 113 The smell of empyreumatised grease..wafted to the nostrils.

empyric, etc., obs. (erron.) f. of EMPIRIC, etc.

empyrical (ɛm'pɪrɪkəl), *a. rare*—⁰. [f. Gr. ἔμπυρος burnt + -IC + -AL¹.] **a.** Of or pertaining to burning or combustion. **b.** 'Containing the combustible principle of coal' (Smart 1847).

†**empy'rosis.** *Obs. rare*—¹. [a. Gr. ἐμπύρωσις n. of action f. ἐμπυρό-ειν = ἐμπυρεύειν to set on fire.] A general fire, conflagration.

1677 HALE *Prim. Orig. Man.* 217 The former Opinion that held these Cataclysms and Empyroses universal. **1755** in ASH. **1847** in CRAIG; and in mod. Dicts.

em quad, quadrat: see EM.

emrod(e, obs. var. of EMERALD, EMEROD.

†'**emrose.** *Obs.*—⁰ 'Probably a garden Anemone (*A. coronaria* L. ?)' (Britten and Holland).

1708 in KERSEY, *Emrose*, a flower. **1721-1800** in BAILEY. **1775** in ASH.

†'**em'selves,** *pron.* *Obs.* [See 'EM.] = THEMSELVES *sb.*.

1699 T. C. tr. *Tully's Offices* (1706) 31 They'd hardly ever trouble 'emselves so far.

emte, obs. variant of EMMET.

emtory, variant of EMPTORY, *Obs.*

emty, obs variant of EMPTY.

emu ('iːmjuː). Also 7 **emia, eme,** 7- **emeu,** 8-9 **emew.** [Alleged by early travellers (see quot. 1613) to be the name used by the natives of Banda and the neighbouring islands; now, however, believed to be a. Pg. *ema*, orig. denoting the crane, but afterwards applied to the ostrich and to various birds of ostrich-like appearance.

'The form *emu* is now more common in popular writing, and has latterly been adopted in the transactions of the Zoological Society. Prof. Newton, however, and some other eminent authorities prefer the older form *emeu*' (N.E.D., 1891).]

†**1.** = CASSOWARY I. *Obs.*

1613 PURCHAS *Pilgr.* I. v. xii. 430 The bird called Emia or Eme is admirable. **1656** H. MORE *Antid. Ath.* II. xi. (1712) 74 The Cassoware or Emeu.

†**2.** ? The American Ostrich, *Rhea americana.* [Perh. an error; the Pg. *ema* is applied to this bird.]

1774 GOLDSM. *Nat. Hist.* III. 37 The Emu which many call the American Ostrich. **1796** STEDMAN *Surinam* I. x. 245 The largest bird in Guiana is there called tuyew, and by others emu.

3. A genus (*Dromæus*) of birds, constituting the family *Dromæidæ* of the order *Megistanes*, subclass *Ratitæ*. It is peculiar to the Australian continent. The best known species (*D. novæ-hollandiæ*), discovered soon after the colonization of New South Wales in 1788, was originally regarded as a species of Cassowary; the Emu and Cassowary are closely allied, but the former is distinguished by the absence of the horny 'helmet' and of the caruncles on the neck, and by the presence of a singular opening in the front of the windpipe.

1842 *Penny Cycl.* XXIII. 145/2 The Emeu can produce a hollow drumming sort of note. **1871** DARWIN *Desc. Man* (1888) II. 224 The female of one of the emus (*Dromæus inoratus*) is..larger than the male. **1875** A. R. WALLACE *Geog. Distrib. Animals* II. 368 The Emeus are found only on the main-land of Australia. **1936** I. L. IDRIESS *Cattle King* v. 46 In a good season emus and kangaroos are fairly plentiful. **1944** *Living off Land* ii. 16 Grubs, snakes, emus, and kangaroos can be palatable. *Ibid.* 28 Emu meat, when cooked in the skin, is inclined to be oily. **1968** K. WEATHERLY *Roo Shooter* 76 Many people say that the emu is the fastest creature in the bush.

4. *Comb.* **emu-apple,** an Australian tree, *Owenia acidula*, which bears a red fruit; **emu-bush,** either of two Australian shrubs (see quot. 1889); **emu-tree,** a low tree or shrub, a native of Tasmania; **emu-wren,** an Australian bird, *Stipiturus* (or *Malurus*) *malacurus*, of the family *Sylviidæ*.

1898 MORRIS *Austral Eng.* 137/2 *Emu-apple. **1905** J. H. MAIDEN *Forest Flora N.S.W.* II. 90 It [sc. *Owenia acidula*] is called 'Sour Plum', 'Native Peach or Nectarine', and 'Emu Apple'. **1889** —— *Useful Nat. Plants Austral.* 132 Heterodendron oleæfolium..*Emu Bush..All the colonies except Tasmania. *Ibid.* 317 Eremophila longifolia..'Emu Bush', owing to emus feeding on the seeds of this and other species... In all the colonies except Tasmania. **1910** C. E. W. BEAN *On Wool Track* 86 The emu-bush, which droops like the bunch of an emu's tail and is very good to eat—as the rabbits have found. **1931** V. PALMER *Separate Lives* 211 Country that was a maze of emu-bush and mulga scrubs. **1936** F. CLUNE *Roaming round Darling* xvii. 165 The currant or emu bush: needle-leafed, with fruit like blackberries, each one the size of a pea—not caviare to emus. **1875** LASLETT *Timber Trees* 206 *Emu Tree. **1865** GOULD *Handbk. Birds Australia* I. 339 The *Emu Wren is..fond of low marshy districts.

†**e'mucid,** *a. Obs.*—⁰ [f. E- *pref.*³ + L. *mūcidus* mouldy.] Mouldy.

1656 in BLOUNT *Glossogr.* **1721** in BAILEY. **1847** in CRAIG.

†'**emulable,** *a. Obs. rare*—¹. [f. L. *æmul-āre* to EMULATE + -ABLE.] Worthy of emulation.

1693 LEIGHTON *Comm. 1st Pet.* iii. 13 (R.) None are so complete but they may espy some..emulable good..in meaner Christians. [In mod. Dicts.]

†'**emulate,** *a. Obs. rare*—¹. [ad. L. *æmulātus* pa. pple. of *æmulā-ri* to rival.] Ambitious, emulous.

1602 SHAKS. *Ham.* I. i. 82 Prick'd on by a most emulate Pride.

emulate ('ɛmjʊleɪt), *v.* Also 7 **æmulate.** [f. L. *æmulāt-* ppl. stem of *æmulā-ri* to rival.]

1. *trans.* Of persons: To strive to equal or rival (a person, his achievements or qualities); to copy or imitate with the object of equalling or excelling.

1589 WARNER *Alb. Eng.* Prose Addit. (1612) 347 So much doe I emulate, not enuie thy glorie. **1665** BOYLE *Occas. Refl.* v. ix. (1675) 330 The disparity of Circumstances betwixt their own Condition, and that of those they Æmulate. **1694** DRYDEN *To Sir G. Kneller* 80 Contemn the bad, and Emulate the best. **1752** HUME *Ess. & Treat.* (1777) I. 224 The whole world emulates Athens and Rome. **1883** F. M. PEARD *Contrad.* I. 12 When will you emulate Sir Archibald in the art of saying pretty things?

2. Implying some degree of success: To vie with, rival, attain or approach to equality with.

1807 G. CHALMERS *Caledonia* I. III. iii. 341 He emulated the Scottish kings in splendour. **1828** SCOTT *F.M. Perth* xiii, My royal nephew will soon emulate his father's wisdom. **1872** YEATS *Growth Comm.* 52 Many of the Greek states emulated Tyre in commerce and opulence.

b. Of things: To vie with, rival, equal or closely approach in any quality.

1598 SHAKS. *Merry W.* III. iii. 58, I see how thine eye would emulate the Diamond. **1660** BOYLE *New Exp. Phys. Mech.* xxxvii. 307 They were wont..to emulate..the apparition of Light. **1661** BOYLE *Examen* iii. (1682) 21 The Corpuscles..tend to..emulate a spring. **1725** BRADLEY *Fam. Dict.* s.v. *Sycomore*, The Liquor emulates that of the Birch. **1833** MISS MITFORD in L'Estrange *Life* III. i. 2 Lady Madalina Palmer is working one [a carpet] which emulates the paintings of Van Huysum.

c. *Computing.* To reproduce the action of or behave like (a different type of computer) with the aid of hardware or software designed to effect this; to run (a program, etc., written for another type of computer) by this means.

1965 *Communications Assoc. Computing Machinery* VIII. 755/2 The System/360 interrupt routine sets a flag which can be tested as part of the DIL instruction. It then returns to the routine which completes emulating the 7000 series instruction. **1971** *IEEE Trans. Computers* XX. 751/2 This effort has led to the development of microcomputers..with READ ONLY control memories containing microprograms that emulate a specific von Neumann-type computer. **1977** *Harvard Business Rev.* Nov.-Dec. 86/1 It is unlikely that competitors will be able to emulate the program. **1983** *Austral. Microcomputer Mag.* Aug. 72/2 Different processors are emulated by changing a personality card. Mice I has 8K of emulation memory. **1983** [see EMULATOR 3]. **1984** *Dr. Dobb's Jrnl.* Jan. 76 (*heading*) Emulate WordStar on TOPS-20. **1985** *Personal Computer World* Feb. 30/1 (Advt.), EP8000 can emulate and program all eproms up to 8K x 8 bytes.

†**3.** *intr.* To make it one's ambition, strive in a spirit of rivalry (to do or obtain something). Const. *inf.* *Obs.*

1597 J. PAYNE *Royal Exch.* 40 Emulate to be nerer there good begynnings. **1619** H. HUTTON *Follie's Anat.* 49 Vulcan ..did not strive, Or emulate to be superlative. **1649** G. DANIEL *Trinarch., Hen. V*, ccxvi, He..Emulated more to Dye.

†**4.** *trans.* To desire to rival (a person, his fortune, achievements, etc.); *hence*, to be jealous of, envy, feel a grudge against. *Obs.*

1611 TOURNEUR *Ath. Trag.* v. ii, I begin to emulate thy death. **1624** HEYWOOD *Gunaik.* 207 An opposite faction which emulated his goodnesse. **1654** TRAPP *Comm. Ps.* lxxiii. 3, I æmulated, and stomached their prosperity.

5. In occasional uses: †**a.** ? To woo, contend emulously for (*obs.*). ¶**b.** To excite the emulation of. *rare*—¹.

1603 DRAYTON *Bar. Wars* I. xlvii, We see the early rising Sunne, With his bright Beames to emulate our sight. **1804** MONSON in Owen *Wellesley Disp.* 529 Each emulated the other to deeds of glory.

emulating ('ɛmjʊleɪtɪŋ), *ppl. a.* [f. EMULATE *v.* + -ING².] That emulates. Also *fig.*

1610 HEALEY *St. Aug. Citie of God* XIV. iii. (1620) 474 Who is more enuious, contentious, emulating and wrathfull against them then he? *a* **1777** FAWKES tr. *Smart's Wks.* (1791) II. 159 If e'er a lyre at unison there be, It swells with emulating harmony.

emulation (ɛmjuː'leɪʃən). Also 7 **æm-.** [ad. L. *æmulātiōn-em*, n. of action f. *æmulā-ri.*]

1. The endeavour to equal or surpass others in any achievement or quality; also, the desire or ambition to equal or excel.

In early use the word is perh. more freq. applied to the mental emotion; in mod. use the notion of active effort is always in some degree present.

1552 HULOET, Emulation, *zelus.* **1555** EDEN *Decades W. Ind.* (Arb.) 59 To prouoke & encorage other forwarde natures to themulation of their vertues. **1612** BRINSLEY *Lud. Lit.* v. (1627) 48 Provoking emulation of the Schollers. **1622** B. JONSON *Pref. Verses* in Mabbe tr. *Aleman's Guzman D'Alf.*, This Faire æmulation, & no envy is. **1674** BOYLE *Theol. comp. w. Nat. Philos.* 197 Imitation or Emulation oftentimes makes many others addict themselves to it [a branch of study]. *c* **1790** BURKE *Sp. Short. Parl.* Wks. X. 85 The spirit of emulation has also been extremely increased. **1828** D'ISRAELI *Chas. I*, II. xi. 274 Their emulation.. terminated in personal antipathy. **1882** HINSDALE *Garfield & Educ.* I. 36 He was always generous in his emulations.

†**2.** Ambitious rivalry for power or honours; contention or ill-will between rivals. *Obs.*

1588 in *Harl. Misc.* (1809) II. 97 The dissension and emulation that I have seen..between private captains for vain-glory. **1594** SHAKS. *Rich. III*, II. iii. 25 Emulation, who shall now be neerest, Will touch vs all too neere. **1612** T. TAYLOR *Comm. Titus* i. 6 (1619) 105 What heart-greife was it to Iacob to see such daily emulation betweene Leah and Rahel? **1646** BUCK *Rich. III*, I. 13 Iulius Cæsar, was..a great Captaine, although his Emulation cost an infinite quantitie of..humane blood. **1651** *Reliq. Wotton* (1685) 608 A great emulation fallen between the Queens Agent, and the Polish Orator there.

†**3.** Grudge against the superiority of others; dislike, or tendency to disparagement, of those who are superior. *Obs.*

1561 EDEN *Arte Nauig.* Pref., This enuy of emulation proceadeth of some singuler vertue of them that are so maliced. **1596** DRAYTON *Leg.* iii. 323 For Emulation ever did attend Upon the Great. **1605** BACON *Adv. Learn.* I. vii. §6 Constantine the Great, in Emulation was woont to call him Parietaria, Wall Flower. **1606** SHAKS. *Tr. & Cr.* I. iii. 134 Pale and bloodlesse Emulation. **1695** BP. PATRICK *Comm. Gen.* 492 Zilpah's Sons..were thought to have less emulation to him, than the Sons of Leah. **1771** SMOLLETT *Humph. Cl.* (1815) 127, I am afraid we sometimes palliate this vice [envy], under the specious name of emulation.

¶**4.** As rendering of *æmulatio* (Vulg.), 'jealousy' (ascribed to God). *rare*—¹.

1609 BIBLE (Douay) *Ps.* lxxvii. 58 In their gravens they provoked him to emulation.

5. *Computing.* The technique by which a computer is enabled, by means of special hardware or software, to execute programs written for a different type of computer.

1965 *Communications Assoc. Computing Machinery* VIII. 753 (*heading*) Emulation of large systems. *Ibid.*, Emulation is the name given to the technique introduced in the IBM System/360 machine series for aiding in the conversion problem. **1970** A. CAMERON et al. *Computers & O.E.*

Concordances 25 You can also run programs that existed on a 1401 on a 360 through something called emulation..as opposed to paying a programmer..the cost of reprogramming. **1984** *Your Computer* Feb. 14/2 The VT200 terminals have full VT100 emulation capabilities, to enable customers to add VT200s to systems currently supporting VT100 terminals.

emulative (ˈɛmjʊlətɪv), *a.* [f. L. *æmulāt-* ppl. stem of *æmulā-ri* (see EMULATE *v.*) + -IVE.]

1. That results from or is characterized by emulation.

1593 R. HARVEY *Philad.* 23 Memprise slewe his manly brother..to be out of his emulative danger. *a* **1659** CLEVELAND *Poems, On Fly* 21 She..in an emulative Chafe..begg'd thy Shrine her Epitaph? **1763** HOOLE *Jer. Del.* v. (R.), All, with emulative zeal, demand To fill the number of th' elected band. **1828** D'ISRAELI *Chas. I*, I. iv. 65 The people were invited to ruin their families in emulative costliness.

2. That tends to emulation; disposed to rival, copy, or compete with. Const. *of* Also *fig.*

1748 RICHARDSON *Clarissa* (1811) I. xxxviii. 283 Noble minds, emulative of perfection. **1791** HUDDESFORD *Salmag.* 138 Dick's breast with emulative ardour glows. **1829** SCOTT *Anne of G.* ii, The sound was re-echoed..from precipice to precipice, with emulative thunders. **1871** RUSKIN *Fors Clav.* xi. 11 The peasant's wife..emulative of Queens Penelope, Bertha, and Maud.

ˈemulatively, *adv. rare.* [f. prec. + -LY².] In an emulative manner.

1754 RICHARDSON *Grandison* (1811) IV. vii. 56 Both hands were so emulatively passive.

emulator (ˈɛmjʊleɪtə(r)). Also 7 **æmulator, emulatour.** [a. L. *æmulātor* zealous imitator.]

1. One who emulates, in good or bad sense.

†**a.** A rival, competitor; also, one who enviously disparages. *Obs.*

1589 GREENE *Menaphon* (Arb.) 81 You are friendly emulators in honest fancie. **1600** SHAKS. *A.Y.L.* I. i. 150 An enuious emulator of every mans good parts. **1628** tr. *Camden's Hist. Eliz.* II. (1688) 198 George Buchanan, his Emulatour..set him forth..as one more mutable than the Chameleon. **1750** JOHNSON *Rambler* No. 54 The emotions which the death of an emulator or competitor produces.

b. A zealous imitator; one who strives to equal the qualities or achievements of another. Const. *of.*

1652 J. HALL *Height Eloquence* p. lxii, Hyperides is a great Emulatour of Demosthenes. **1738** WARBURTON *Div. Legat.* App. 30 A happy emulator of the eloquence of Cicero. **1837-9** HALLAM *Hist. Lit.* I. ciii. §128 A diligent emulator of Grocyn..was..Linacre. **1875** JOWETT *Plato* (ed. 2) I. 158 Emulators and disciples of the culture of the Lacedaemonians.

¶**2.** (In the Douay-Rheims Bible.) Used to render L. *æmulator*: **a.** One who is zealous for a cause, etc.; const. *of.* **b.** Applied to God: A 'jealous' being, one who brooks no competitor.

1582 *N.T.* (Rhem.) *Gal.* i. 14, I..being more aboundantly an emulator of the traditions of my fathers. **1609** BIBLE (Douay) *Ex.* xxxiv. 14 God is an emulatour. —— *2 Macc.* iv. 2 The..emulatour of the law of God.

3. *Computing.* A piece of hardware or software used with one device to enable it to emulate another, esp. to enable a computer to run programs written for a different type of computer.

1965 *Communications Assoc. Computing Machinery* VIII. 753/2 An emulator is a package that includes both special hardware and a complementary set of software. *Ibid.* 754/1 The speed of an emulator can be increased if more instructions are added to the emulating machine. **1983** *What's New in Computing* Jan. 18/2 The remote batch emulator lets the ACT Sirius 1 communicate with equipment that supports one or more members of the IBM family of remote batch entry stations. **1983** *Austral. Microcomputer Mag.* Sept. 65/1 The emulator divides the system's memory into two sections. One section holds the operating system and whatever applications program is running. The second section of memory is used to emulate a disk drive. **1985** *Byte* Mar. 404 (*heading*) An assembly-language emulator program.

†**ˈemulatory,** *a. Obs. rare*⁻¹. [f. prec.; see -ORY.] Of the nature of emulation.

1621 W. SCLATER *Tythes* (1623) 160 Too fond emulatory imitation of, etc. **1627** BP. HALL *Farew. Serm. Fam. Pr. Henry* Wks. 463 [At Court] you see..emulatory officiousnesse.

†**ˈemulatress.** *Obs. rare.* [f. EMULATOR + -ESS.] A female emulator. Also *fig.*

1620 SHELTON *Quix.* I. II. i. 65 History, the Emulatresse of Time. **1741** RICHARDSON *Pamela* (1824) I. lxxvii. 436, I was not willing my girl should give way to the noble emulatress. **1832** in WEBSTER; and in mod. Dicts.

†**emuˈlatrix.** *Obs. rare*⁻¹. [a. L. *æmulātrix*, fem. of *æmulātor* EMULATOR.] = EMULATRESS.

1651 HOWELL *Venice* 198 Genoa, her Sister Republic and old Emulatrix.

†**ˈemule,** *v. Obs. rare.* Also **æmule.** [ad. L. *æmul-āri* to EMULATE.] = EMULATE *v.*

1816 SOUTHEY *Poet's Pilgr.* iii. 20 The young Nassau, Emuling that day his ancestors' renown.

emulge (ɪˈmʌldʒ), *v. Phys.* [ad. L. *ēmulgē-re* to milk out.] *trans.* To drain (secretory organs) of their contents. Hence **eˈmulging** *vbl. sb.* and *ppl. a.*

1681 tr. *Willis's Rem. Med. Wks.* Voc., Emulging vessels or arteries, or veins. **1784** CULLEN *First Lines* clxxii. Wks. 1827 I. 625 Vomiting..emulges the biliary and pancreatic ducts. **1844** T. GRAHAM *Dom. Med.* 325 The pill No. 104..does not assist so much in emulging the biliary ducts, and giving tone to the bowels.

emulgence (ɪˈmʌldʒəns). *rare.* [f. as if ad. L. **ēmulgentia*, f. *ēmulgent-em*: see next and -ENCE.] The action of milking out.

1674 STAVELEY *Rom. Horseleach* (1769) 48 [Indulgences] for the purpose of drawing money from the people..have not improperly been called Emulgences. **1879** G. MEREDITH *Egoist* I. 254 As though it [a woman's worship] coud be bandied to and fro without emulgence of the poetry.

emulgent (ɪˈmʌldʒənt), *a.* and *sb. Phys.* [ad. L. *ēmulgent-em*, pr. pple. of *ēmulgē-re* to milk out: see EMULGE.]

A. *adj.* That 'milks out'; *esp.* 'applied to the vessels of the kidneys, which are supposed to strain or milk the serum through the kidneys' (*Syd. Soc. Lex.*).

1578 BANISTER *Hist. Man* v. 82 The Emulgent veynes. **1621** BURTON *Anat. Mel.* I. i. II. ii, The branches of the Caua are..inward seminall or emulgent. **1670** *Phil. Trans.* V. 2081 Passages, by which the Chyle may come into the Emulgent..Vessels. **1675** EVELYN *Terra* (1776) 23 The Fibres..are as it were the Emulgent veins. **1783** W. KEIR in *Med. Commun.* I. 130 The right emulgent vein was..large. **1835-6** TODD *Cycl. Anat.* I. 223/2 The case of the emulgent arteries.

B. *sb.* = *emulgent vessels.*

1612 S. H. *Ench. Med.* II. 128 An immoderate heate drawing ouermuch bloud by the emulgents. **1646** SIR T. BROWNE *Pseud. Ep.* IV. v. 188 The Azygos..in its descent doth furnish the left Emulgent with one veyne. **1788** BAILLIE in *Phil. Trans.* LXXVIII. 357 The right spermatic vein was found to open into the right emulgent.

†**emuˈlosity.** *Obs. rare* [f. EMULOUS (as if L. **æmulōs-us*) + -ITY.] Rivalry, dispute.

1716 M. DAVIES *Ath. Brit.* II. 147 Our Pamphlet decides the Emulosity with a short piece of Latin Prose and Verse. —— *Ibid.* 175 Historiological Emulosities.

emulous (ˈɛmjʊləs), *a.* Also 6 *Sc.* **ymulis,** 7-8 **æmulous.** [f. L. *æmul-us* of same meaning + -OUS.]

1. a. Desirous of rivalling, imitating, obtaining. Const. *of.* †**b.** Of things: Closely resembling, imitative *of* (*obs. rare*).

1398 TREVISA *Barth. De P.R.* VII. lxiv. (1495) 280 In theym that haue the Lepra that hyghte Elephancia the colour and hewe is emulous. **1667** MILTON *P.L.* VI. 822 By strength They measure all, of other excellence not emulous. *a* **1721** PRIOR *Ep. Mr. Howard* 59 Good Howard, emulous of the Grecian art. **1796** BURKE *Regic. Peace* Wks. VIII. 291 Emulous of the glory of the youthful hero. **1850** KINGSLEY *Alt. Locke* x. (1876) 110 Emulous of Messrs. Aaron Levi & Co. **1856** EMERSON *Eng. Traits, Result* Wks. (Bohn) II. 135 Kingdoms emulous of free institutions.

2. Filled with emulation; actuated by the spirit of rivalry. †Formerly also in weaker sense: = RIVAL *a.*

1617 BP. J. HALL *Contempl.* I. 147 The fire issuing from God upon their [Moses' and Aaron's] emulous opposites. **1625** K. LONG tr. *Barclay's Argenis* III. v. 164 The two æmulous suiters. **1649** BP. HALL *Cases Consc.* IV. ii. (1654) 300 The emulous Schools of Sammai and Hillel. **1725-6** POPE *Odyss.* VI. 105 Æmulous the royal robes they lave. **1851** LONGF. *Gold. Leg., School Salerno,* Where every emulous scholar hears..The rustling of another's laurels! **1876** GEO. ELIOT *Dan. Der.* VI. xlv. 421 The stream of emulous admirers.

†**3. a.** Greedy of praise or power. **b.** Envious.

1606 SHAKS. *Tr. & Cr.* II. iii. 243 He is not emulous, as Achilles is. **1633** BP. HALL *Hard Texts* 206, I am censured by some emulous accusers. **1655-60** STANLEY *Hist. Philos.* (1701) 111/1 What a Son thou hast, now may All my æmulous Neighbours say.

4. Of actions, feelings, etc.: Proceeding from, or of the nature of, emulation or rivalry. †Also, zealous, earnest (*obs.*).

1535 STEWART *Cron. Scot.* III. 431 Turne all your mad murning In ymulis prayer and [in] grit louing. **1693** SMALLRIDGE *Jul. Cæsar* in Dryden *Plutarch* IV. 466 This passion was a kind of æmulous struggle with himself. **1782** V. KNOX *Ess.* (1819) II. cxvi. 288 The profusion of emulous extravagance. **1848** MACAULAY *Hist. Eng.* I. 408 Poets sang with emulous fervour the approach of the golden age. **1871** ROSSETTI *Poems, Sonn.* iv. *Kiss,* Till love's emulous ardours ran, Fire within fire, desire in deity.

emulously (ˈɛmjʊləslɪ), *adv.* [f. EMULOUS *a.* + -LY.] In an emulous manner. Also *fig.*

1647-8 COTTERELL *Davila's Hist. Fr.* (1678) 2 Emulously getting possession of. **1677** *Life* in *Cleveland's Gen. Poems,* Many intermediate Stages..contended as emulously for his aboad, as the seven Cities for Homer's Birth. **1734** tr. *Rollin's Anc. Hist.* (1827) II. II. 108 Men emulously strove, who should show the greatest gratitude towards the gods. **1876** BANCROFT *Hist. U.S.* III. xxiii. 566 Women..emulously drive the spinning-wheel from sunrise until dark.

emulousness (ˈɛmjʊləsnɪs). *rare*⁻⁰. [f. EMULOUS *a.* + -NESS.] The state of being emulous.

1721-1800 in BAILEY. **1775** in ASH; and in mod. Dicts.

emulsic (ɪˈmʌlsɪk), *a. Chem.* [f. EMULS-IN + -IC.] Related to EMULSIN.

WATTS *Dict. Chem.* II. 486 *Emulsic acid.*

emulsification (ɪˌmʌlsɪfɪˈkeɪʃən). [f. EMULSIFY *v.* See -FICATION.]

a. The action of the vb. EMULSIFY. **b.** *spec.* in Pathology: 'The last stage of fatty degeneration in which the structures become softened and semi-liquid, consisting of an albuminous fluid containing oil-globules' (*Syd. Soc. Lex.*).

1876 HARLEY *Mat. Med.* 30 The process of emulsification.

emulsifier (ɪˈmʌlsɪfaɪə(r)). *Chem.* [f. EMULSIFY *v.* + -ER¹.] An agent or apparatus which effects the emulsification of an oil, etc.

1888 *Chemist & Druggist* XXXII. 28/2 An Emulsifier Wanted. **1902** C. J. S. THOMPSON *Pract. Dispensing* (ed. 3) iii. 28 When making an emulsion the oil to be emulsified should be added to the emulsifier. **1928** *Manch. Guardian Weekly* 26 Oct. 323/4 Milk..is being produced in increasing quantities from an 'emulsifier'. **1954** *Thorpe's Dict. Appl. Chem.* (ed. 4) XI. 345/2 The emulsifier, which promotes the dispersion of one liquid in another, acts as a bridge between the continuous phase and the dispersed phase.

emulsify (ɪˈmʌlsɪfaɪ), *v.* [f. L. *ēmuls-* ppl. stem of *ēmulgē-re* to milk out + -(I)FY.] *trans.* To convert into an emulsion. Also *absol.*

1859 TODD *Cycl. Anat.* V. 106/1 The fat had..been minutely subdivided and emulsified. **1881** *Times* 4 Jan. 3/5 Dr. Maddox obtained sensitive photographic plates by emulsifying bromide of silver in liquid gelatine.

Hence **eˈmulsifying** *vbl. sb.* and *ppl. a.*

1875 H. WOOD *Therap.* (1879) 442 No emulsifying substance was contained in the intestine. **1876** FOSTER *Phys.* II. i. (1879) 231 Bile..has by itself a slight..emulsifying power. **1883** TAYLOR *Hardwick's Photogr. Chem.* 378 He prefers emulsifying with a very small quantity of it.

emulsin (ɪˈmʌlsɪn). *Chem.* [f. EMULS-ION + -IN.] A neutral substance contained in almonds; = SYNAPTASE.

1838 T. THOMSON *Chem. Org. Bodies* 682 The investigation of emulsin was taken up by Mr. Richardson. **1872** THUDICHUM *Chem. Phys.* 4 Emulsine or synaptase of almonds. **1876** HARLEY *Mat. Med.* 627 The maceration allows of the solution and reaction of the..emulsin.

emulsion (ɪˈmʌlʃən). Also 7 **emulction.** [ad. mod.L. *ēmulsiōn-em*, n. of action f. L. *ēmulgēre* to milk out. In Fr. *émulsion.*]

†**1.** The action of 'milking out'. *fig.* Cf. EMULGE *v.*

1658 J. ROBINSON *Eudoxa* Pref. 4 My wished end is, by gentle concussion, the emulsion of truth.

†**2.** (See quot.) *Obs.*

1657 *Phys. Dict., Emulsions,* the steeping or dissolution by steeping of any seeds or kernels in liquor till it come to the thickness of a jelly.

3. a. A milky liquid obtained by bruising almonds, etc. in water. **b.** *Pharmacy.* 'A milky liquid, consisting of water holding in suspension minute particles of oil or resin by the aid of some albuminous or gummy material' (*Syd. Soc. Lex.*). Also *attrib.*

1612 *Ench. Med.* II. 138 Also an emulction prepared of Almonds. **1664** EVELYN *Kal. Hort.* (1729) 208 Emulsions of the cooler seeds bruised. **1712** tr. *Pomet's Hist. Drugs* I. 22 Gourd Melons..are chiefly us'd for Emulsions. **1875** DARWIN *Insectiv. Pl.* vi. 127 Leaves immersed in an emulsion of starch. **1880** *Nature* XXI. 436 A special arrangement upon a gelatine emulsion plate.

4. *Photogr.* A mixture consisting of a silver compound held in suspension in collodion or gelatin, used in coating plates, films, etc. Also *attrib.*

1840 J. F. W. HERSCHEL in *Phil. Trans.* CXXX. 8 My first attention was directed to the discovery of a liquid, or emulsion, which by a single application, whether by dipping or brushing over, should communicate the desired quality [of sensitiveness]. **1877** *English Mechanic* 23 Nov. 261/2 Emulsions..consisting of collodion and silver, ready for pouring upon plates. **1878** W. W. ABNEY *Treat. Photogr.* xvi. 115 All the different varieties of the emulsion processes. *Ibid.* xxii. 153 If a glass plate has to be coated with the emulsion, the same directions as those given for coating emulsion plates should be followed. **1880** [see Dict., 3]. **1908** *Westm. Gaz.* 18 Jan. 14/2 The emulsion side of the film or plate. *Ibid.* 25 July 14/2 This positive can be made on a silver emulsion plate. **1958** M. L. HALL *Newnes Complete Amat. Photogr.* 75 Individual semi-rigid sheets of thicker, transparent film, emulsion-coated, designed for darkroom loading into film-holders.

5. emulsion paint, a water-thinned paint containing a non-volatile substance, e.g. synthetic resin, as its binding medium.

1939-40 *Army & Navy Stores Catal.* 238/2 Hall's distemper. Oil-emulsion paint. **1944** G. M. SUTHEIM in J. J. Mattiello *Protect. & Decorat. Coatings* IV. xi. 331 Emulsion paint is a surface coating in which the vehicle is an emulsion. *Ibid.* 333 The main difference between emulsion paint and ordinary or improved water paints is the fact that emulsion paints form continuous hydrophobic films on drying. **1958** *Woman* 22 Feb. 2/1 Emulsion paint goes over old emulsion. **1960** *House & Garden* June 72/1 Emulsion paints..need no special undercoat, are speedy to apply, dry in a few hours.

emulsionize (ɪˈmʌlʃənaɪz), *v.* [f. EMULSION + -IZE.] *trans.* To make into an EMULSION.

Hence **eˈmulsionized** *ppl. a.*

1872 HUXLEY *Phys.* vi. 154 Fats are..emulsionized by the bile. **1881** G. L. CARRICK *Koumiss* 46 An emulsionised fluid, in which casein is suspended.

emulsive (ɪˈmʌlsɪv), *a.* [f. L. *ēmuls-* ppl. stem of *ēmulgē-re* (see prec.) + -IVE.] That has the nature of an EMULSION.

1861 HULME tr. *Moquin-Tandon* II. III. 189 Milk is an emulsive fluid.

emulsoid (ɪˈmʌlsɔɪd). *Chem.* [G. *emulsoid* (P. P. von Weimarn 1908, in *Zeitschr. f. Chem. & Ind. d. Kolloide* III. 27/2), f. EMULS(ION + -OID.] A liquid which appears to contain another liquid in colloidal suspension (see also quot. 1956).

1909 *Chem. Abstr.* III. 394 Classification of Colloids... The physical aggregations..are divided into two classes *suspensoids*..and *emulsoids*, in which the particles are minute drops of liquid. **1913** *Ibid.* VII. 2144 An experimental test for emulsoids lies in their coagulability to two liquid layers. **1925** J. ALEXANDER *Colloid Chem.* (ed. 2) 27 The reversible colloids are therefore called *emulsoids* and the irreversible colloids *suspensoids*. **1938** *Science* 4 Mar. 212/1 Originally 'emulsoids' included coagula, jellies and emulsions, the term being based on the assumption that jellies are fine emulsions. **1956** J. S. ANDERSON tr. *Remy's Treat. Inorg. Chem.* II. xvi. 686 Colloidal emulsions are called emulsoids. [*Note*] The terms 'emulsoid' and 'suspensoid' are often applied also to the sols of lyophilic and lyophobic colloids, respectively, without regard to the state of aggregation of the disperse phase.

†**e'munct**, *a. Obs. rare.* [ad. L. *ēmunct-us*, pa. pple. of *ēmungĕre* to wipe the nose. The L. phrase, *emunctæ naris homo* a man of 'keen scent' (*fig.*) gave rise to the use of the pple. in sense 'acute'.] Of the judgement: Keen, acute.

1679 PRANCE *Addit. Narr. Pop. Plot* 5 Your Highness, being of so deep and emunct a Judgment. **1697** EVELYN *Numism.* ix. 297 The Nose..as the Emunct Judicious.

†**e'munction.** *Obs. rare.* [ad. L. *ēmunctiōn-em* a wiping of the nose, n. of action f. *ēmungĕre* to wipe the nose.]

1. The action of wiping the nose; hence *transf.* of clearing any of the passages of the body.

1615 CROOKE *Body of Man* 538 We haue often seen that Medicines applied to the eyes haue through these holes past into the nose, and so haue beene cast out either by emunction or by the mouth. **1684** I. MATHER *Remark. Provid.* (1846) 212 After the use of unctions and emunctions.

†**2.** Excretion. *Obs.* Cf. EMUNCTORY.

1650 BULWER *Anthropomet.* ii. (1653) 71 The curious emunctions of the pores.

emunctory (ɪˈmʌŋktərɪ), *a.* and *sb. Phys.* [ad. mod.L. *ēmunctōri-us* excretory, *ēmunctōr-ium* a means of cleansing by excretion (in classical L. used for 'a pair of snuffers'), f. *ēmungĕre*: see prec.]

A. *adj.* **a.** Of or pertaining to the blowing of the nose. **b.** That has the function of conveying waste matters from the body.

1547 BOORDE *Brev. Health* ccxliv. 83 The nosethrylles be the emunctorye places of the brayne. **1725** BRADLEY *Fam. Dict.* s.v. *Musk*, It apparently filtrates thro' the emunctory Glands. **1858** POLSON *Law & L.* 160 He found a sufficient substitute in his emunctory powers. **1864** EASTWICKE *Resid. Persia* I. 11 There was nothing but coughing, sternutation and emunctory movements for the next half hour.

B. *sb.* 'A cleansing organ or canal; a term applied to the excretory ducts and organs of the body' (*Syd. Soc. Lex.*). Also *fig.*

[**1543** TRAHERON *Vigo's Chirurg.* Gloss., *Emunctoria* ben the clensyng places, as the flanckes, the armeholes, etc.] **1601** HOLLAND *Pliny* Gloss., *Emunctories* be those kernelly places in the body, by which the principall and noble parts doe void their superfluities. **1651** BIGGS *New Disp.* 172 ⁋234 God hath ordained sufficient Emunctories for any filth whatsoever. **1767** STERNE *Tr. Shandy* IX. xx, Blow your noses,—cleanse your emunctories,—sneeze, my good people. **1821** *New Monthly Mag.* I. 440 The nose is the emunctory of the brain. **1854** BUSHNAN in *Circ. Sc.* II. 21/2 A third great emunctory has to be added; namely, the kidney.

†**e'munctuary.** *Obs.*, bad form of prec.

1572 J. JONES *Bathes Buckstone* 15a, By the proper emunctuaries, as out of the head, by the nose, mouth, eares, eyes, palate, etc. **1649** BULWER *Pathomyot.* II. ii. 106 The extreme part of the Face..is the emunctuary of the senses.

†**e'muncture.** *Obs. rare.* [f. L. *ēmunct-* ppl. stem of *ēmungĕ-re* to wipe out + -URE.]

a. The action of wiping. *fig.* **b.** = EMUNCTORY.

1541 R. COPLAND *Guydon's Quest. Chirurg.*, The sayd parietalles..are the holes of the eares, and the instrumentes mamylares of yᵉ emunctures. **1674** TURNOR *Case of Bankers & Creditors* §7. 31 This neat Emuncture or wipe.

†**emun'dation.** *Obs.* [ad. L. *ēmundātiōn-em*, n. of action f. *ēmundā-re* to cleanse, f. *ē* out + *mund-us* clean.] The action of ceremonial cleansing or purification.

1609 BIBLE (Douay) *Ps.* lxxxviii. 45 Thou hast destroied him from emundation. **1652** GAULE *Magastrom.* 39 This they apply to the ceremoniall emundations or purifactions. **1731–1800** in BAILEY. **1775** in ASH.

†**e'munge**, *v. Obs.* [ad. L. *ēmungĕ-re* to wipe or blow the nose.] *trans.* To wipe out, cleanse; also *fig.* (as in Lat.), to cheat.

Hence **e'munging** *vbl. sb.*

1664 H. MORE *Myst. Iniq.* 127 The emunging of the people of their mony. **1846** LANDOR *Exam. Shaks.* Wks. 1846 II. 265, I did indeed spit it forth, and emunge my lips, as who should not?

emure, a var. of IMMURE *v.* and *sb.*, in the Shaks. folio 1623.

1588 SHAKS. *L.L.L.* III. i. 12 Thou wert emured, restrained. **1606** —— *Tr. & Cr.* Prol. 9 (1623) To ransacke Troy, within whose strong emures The rauish'd Helen..sleepes.

†**emu'scation.** *Obs.* [as if ad. *L. *ēmuscātiōn-em*, n. of action f. *ēmuscā-re* to cleanse from moss, f. *ē* out + *muscus* moss.] The action of cleansing (the trunk of a tree) from moss. Also *fig.*

1664 EVELYN *Sylva* (1679) Advt., Let them read for emuscation, cleansing it of the moss. **1679** PLOT *Staffordsh.* (1686) 385 They cure it..by emuscation. **1721–1800** in BAILEY. **1847** in CRAIG; and in mod. Dicts.

emydian (ɪˈmɪdɪən). *Zool.* [f. Gr. ἐμυδ- stem of ἐμύς the fresh-water tortoise + -IAN.] A tortoise of the genus EMYS.

1854 OWEN in *Circ. Sc.* (*c* 1865) II. 69/1 Side-walls..are added in the fresh-water species (*emydians*).

emydin (ˈɛmɪdɪn). *Chem.* [f. as prec. + -IN.] 'A substance obtained from the eggs of the tortoise, having probably a similar constitution to vitellin' (*Syd. Soc. Lex.*).

1882 WATTS *Dict. Chem.* II. 487 Emydin forms white, hard, transparent grains, very soluble in dilute potash.

emydosaurian (ˌɛmɪdəʊˈsɔːrɪən). *Zool.* [f. *emydo-*, combining form of EMYS, + SAURIAN.] A crocodile.

1837 *Penny Cycl.* VIII. 162/1 They [Crocodilidæ] form the Loricata of Merrem and Fitzinger, and the Emydosaurians of De Blainville.

emyr, obs. form of ADMIRE.

‖**emys** (ˈɛmɪs). *Zool.* In *pl.* **emydes.** [mod.L., a. Gr. ἐμύς the fresh-water tortoise.] The ordinary fresh-water tortoise.

1843 *Penny Cycl.* XXV. 57/2 Certain Emydes..tend to the Sea-tortoises or Turtles..and yet exhibit characters peculiar to themselves. **1873** GEIKIE *Gt. Ice Age* 492 App., Remains of the elephant..the beaver, the emys..and goats.

emyspery, obs. form of HEMISPHERE.

en (ɛn), *sb.* The name of the letter N. In *Printing*, the half square, formerly of the type n, used as a unit for measuring the amount of printed matter in a line, page, etc. Also *attrib.*, esp. in ***en quad***, ***quadrat***, a block of metal half the width of the *em quad* (see also quot. 1967); ***en rule***, a dash of the width of an en. Cf. N I 1 b.

1793, 1808 [see EM]. **1875** J. SOUTHWARD *Dict. Typogr.* (ed. 2) 32 *En dash.*—A dash..half the length of the em of the fount to which it belongs. **1888** *Pall Mall Gaz.* 10 Sept. 11/2 The 'justifier'..spaces out the lines with great regularity and in so short a time that 20,000 ens per hour is about the average output. **1891** *Printers' Register* 7 Dec., 49,000 American ems, equal to 98,000 English ens. **1893** HART *Rules for Compositors* 21 *En rules* are to be used in such cases as 1880–1, and not hyphens or em rules. **1904** GOODCHILD & TWENEY *Technol. & Sci. Dict.* 204/1 *En quads*, spaces exactly half of an em. **1921** *Glasgow Herald* 22 Feb. 10 The first scale paid to linotype operators was 3d. per thousand 'ens'. **1967** En quad [see EM].

‖**en** (ɑ̃), *prep.* [Fr., = in; as (a).] **en attendant**, in the meantime, while (one is) waiting; **en avant**, forward; **en axe** (see quot.); **en barbette** (see BARBETTE *sb.*); **en beau**, in a favourable manner; **en brosse**, of hair, cut short, giving a bristly effect; **en cabochon** (see CABOCHON and quot. 1940); **en casserole** (see CASSEROLE 2); **en clair**, in ordinary language (not in cipher); **en cœur**, in dressmaking, heart-shaped, V-shaped; **en coquille** (see quot. 1882); **en déshabillé**, in undress; also *fig.* (see DISHABILLE); **en évidence**, in evidence, in the forefront, conspicuous(ly); **en face**, from the front, facing forward, (*Bibliogr.*) opposite; **en famille**, in or with the family, as one of the family, at home; **en fête**, in festival array, keeping holiday; **en garçon**, as a boy, as a bachelor; **en grand seigneur**, like a lord; **en grande tenue**, in full dress; **en gros**, in general, in broad terms; **en l'air**, 'in the air'; (of troops) unsupported; **en noir**, on the black side; **en pantoufles**, lit. 'in slippers', hence, in a free and easy atmosphere; **en pension**, as a boarder in lodgings; **en permanence**, permanently; **en pointe(s)** *Ballet*, on the extremity of the toe(s); **en poste**, of a diplomat, in an official position (at a specified place); **en prince**, like a prince, in a princely manner; **en principe**, in principle; **en prise** *Chess* etc., in a position to be taken; **en rapport** (see RAPPORT *sb.* 3 and as separate entry); **en regard** *Bibliogr.* = *en face*; **en règle**, in due form; **en retraite**, in retirement, on half pay; **en revanche**, in return, as a quid pro quo; **en route** (see ROUTE *sb.* 5); **en secondes noces**, by a second marriage; **en suite** (see SUITE 5 and EN SUITE); **en train**, in progress; concerned, occupied (usu. const. *with*); **en ventre sa mère** [legal Fr.], in the womb, unborn; **en ville**, away from home. See also EN BLOC, EN MASSE, EN PASSANT, EN PLEIN, EN TOUT CAS.

1743 H. WALPOLE *Let.* 12 Oct. (1903) I. 389, I hope in time to have poems upon him... *En attendant*, I have sent you some pamphlets to amuse your solitude. **1793** GIBBON *Let.* 25 Nov. (1956) III. 365 Leave to go abroad to-morrow and to go out of town when I please en attendant the future measures of a radical cure. **1801** M. EDGEWORTH *Belinda* xii, *En attendant* here are your two hundred guineas. **1931** *N. & Q.* CLXI. 73/2 We are still waiting..for his work to be accessible in English. They [*sc.* our readers] may, *en attendant*, like to know of an article..in the current number of the *Dublin Review*. **1815** J. SIMPSON *Visit to Flanders* iii. 122 The man who, when the lives of *others* were concerned, could only cry, '*en avant, en avant*'. **1823** BYRON *Let.* 22 Apr. in Moore *Lett. & Jrnls.* (1830) II. 641 But never mind—*en avant!* live while you can. **1836** tr. *Bourrienne's Mem. N. Bonaparte* xiv. 176 'Very well,' said the chief consul, '*en avant*—let us proceed.' **1845** R. FORD *Handbk. Spain* I. II. 218/2 The easy victories of the French over the Spaniards were mainly owing to their dashing *en avant* charges. **1901** R. STURGIS *Dict. Archit.* 178/2 A monument is said to be *en axe* with a street when the centre line of the street passes through the centre of the monument. Two rooms are said to be *en axe*, or an opposite window or door, or two opposite doors, are said to be *en axe* when the axis of the room, pavilion, wing, or whole building passes through them, or even when they are centred upon one another with deliberate care to bring them exactly opposite. **1818** *Edin. Rev.* XXX. 315 We have every reason certainly to be satisfied with the account she gives of us... We are certainly painted *en beau*. **1832** MILL *Let.* 27 Dec. in *Wks.* (1963) XII. 132 A sketchy kind of book,..intended to throw light upon France, painting it & all it contains *en beau*. **1875** *Contemp. Rev.* XXVI. 553 Painted *en beau* by the Ins or *en noir* by the Outs. **1901** 'L. MALET' *Hist. Sir R. Calmady* VI. ii. 500 Zimmermann, the colossal Swiss-German courier, with his square, yellow beard and hair *en brosse*. **1909** H. G. WELLS *Tono-Bungay* II. iii. 192 Ewart had returned with his hair cut *en brosse*. **1924** M. KENNEDY *Constant Nymph* i. 15 He..wore his dark hair *en brosse*. **1957** R. MASON *World Suzie Wong* II. viii. 239 The familiar shape of the head under the *en brosse* hair. **1889** *N.E.D.* s.v. *cat's-eye*, A precious stone..which, when cut *en cabochon* [etc.]. **1910** J. BUCHAN *Prester John* (1922) xi. 150 There were fifty-five rubies in it... In shape they were oval, cut on both sides *en cabochon*. **1940** *Chambers's Techn. Dict.* 294/2 *En cabochon*, a style of cutting used in the case of certain gemstones, notably garnets... Such stones are not facetted, but a smooth-domed surface is produced, the plan of the stone being circular or oval. **1897** En clair [in use at the Foreign Office]. **1920** 'TAFFRAIL' *H.M.S. Anonymous* 189 The German commandant..made the following wireless signal 'en clair' to the British men-of-war. **1928** *Daily Tel.* 17 July 10/7 Making 'en clair' wireless signals. **1960** C. MACKENZIE *Greece in my Life* 53 He went back to the Chancery and sent off a rousing telegram to the Foreign Office *en clair*. **1873** *Young Englishwoman* Feb. 78/1 A dinner dress..with corsage open en cœur. **1874** *Echo* 30 Dec. 2/2 These bodies [*sc.* corsages] may be..opened *en cœur* or square. **1882** CAULFEILD & SAWARD *Dict. Needlework*, En cœur. **1878** *Cassell's Fam. Mag.* Apr. 295/1 The skirt is..bordered with a flounce en coquille. **1882** CAULFEILD & SAWARD *Dict. Needlework*, *En Coquille*, the French term to denote 'shell-shaped'. The ribbon or lace is laid like a succession of scallop-shells, one above or over the other, in groups of threes. **1699** M. LISTER *Journey to Paris* 35 A young Gentleman in a Fur Cap en dishabille. **1808** *Edin. Rev.* Oct. 133 A powerful mind *en deshabille*, and free from the fetters of study. **1877** C. READE *Woman Hater* I. vii. 172 Let me catch her *en déshabille*, with her porter on one side, and her lover on the other. **1818** LADY MORGAN *Fl. Macarthy* II. i. 6 Mr. Crawley now placed himself en evidence at his window. **1858** LYTTON *What will he do with It?* II. v. x. 226 George Morley and his fair cousin walked boldly, *en évidence*, before the prying ghostly windows. **1888** S. BUXTON *Handbk. Pol. Quest. Day* (ed. 7) 153 The anxiety of members to keep themselves *en évidence*. **1911** E. M. CLOWES *On Wallaby* vi. 162 The lack of courtesy, of patience, and consideration is all fully *en évidence*. **1768** STERNE *Sent. Journ.* I. 41, I..eyed him as he walk'd along in profile,—then *en face*. **1931** *Periodical* (Suppl.) Dec., The first edition text is printed with a transcript of the manuscript *en face*. **1936** *Burlington Mag.* Mar. 117/2 She has turned slightly to the right and is looking at the spectator, her head *en face*. **1726** A. POPE *Let.* June (1956) II. 380, I shall be much pleased to see you here *en famille*, but pray tell me the time..it being else a great uncertainty whether I may not..have strangers with me. **1787** P. BECKFORD *Italy* (1834) II. 55 We passed the day quite *en famille* at Belem with a whole legion of Marialvas. **1843** THACKERAY *Misc.* (1857) IV. 86 It was vary kaind of you to come upon us *en famille*, and accept a dinner *sans cérémonie*. **1915** P. JONES *War Lett.* (1918) 140 Flemish is almost always used by the people *en famille*. **1926** D. H. LAWRENCE *Plumed Serpent* i. 14 How could any man's coat-collar look so home-made, so *en famille*! **1965** C. D. EBY *Siege of Alcázar* (1966) iv. 82 A quiet luncheon *en famille*, and a nap in an olive grove. **1865** 'OUIDA' *Strathmore* I. xi. 120 The city was in its spring-tide gaiety, the dense crowds were sweeping down towards the barrières of the west, Paris was *en fête*. **1888** *Lancs. Even. Post* 3 Feb. 2/4 Haslingden Liberalism..is to be *en fête* this evening on the occasion of its annual soirée. **1942** G. MITCHELL *Laurels are Poison* xvii. 185 The whole of the College was prepared to be *en fête*. **1802** C. WILMOT *Let.* 13 Mar. in *Irish Peer* (1920) 51 The little girls, till they are eleven or twelve years old most frequently dress 'en garçon'. **1811** L. M. HAWKINS *C'tess & Gertr.* I. xv. 248 He soon settled himself again, *en garçon*, in chambers. **1866** MRS. H. WOOD *Elster's Folly* xvii, He was living quite *en garçon*, with only one man. **1929** S. MCKENNA *Happy Ending* II. i. 129 Mark Tollesbury will be in London *en garçon*. **1968** 'M. INNES' *Appleby at Allington* I. i. 9 He had invited Appleby to dinner—*en garçon*, since he was a bachelor and since Lady Appleby would not get back from London until next day. **1805** T. F. FREMANTLE *Let.* 24 July in *Wynne Diaries* (1940) III. 185 If I succeed in my band, I shall indeed be en grand Seignieur [*sic*]. **1831** DISRAELI *Young Duke* IV. i, [It] prevented him from receiving his friends *en grand seigneur* in

his hereditary castle. **1887** G. B. SHAW *Don Giovanni Explains* in *Wks.* (1932) VI. 109 Speaking to her..*en grand seigneur*, I bade her do instantly whatever she was told. **1834** H. GREVILLE *Diary* 27 Nov. (1883) I. 41 A farce at which all the Court *en grande tenue* was obliged to attend. **1872** W. CHAFFERS *Keramic Gallery* I. 59 A lady in the costume of Louis XIV., *en grande tenue.* **1927** *Blackw. Mag.* June 749/2 He found the Rissaldar-major *en grande tenue* just back from a wedding. **1953** C. DAY LEWIS *Italian Visit* iii. 42 Garish Campagna knocks at the back door, Rome calls *en grande tenue.* **1727** M. W. MONTAGU *Let.* 23 June (1966) II. 77, I was glad to hear Mr. Remond's History from you, thô the newspaper had given it me en gros and my Lady Stafford in detail some time before. **1831** LADY ELIZ. GROSVENOR *Let.* (1965) iv. 98 In some few things it might be advantageously altered, but en gros he is well pleased with it. **1904** W. JAMES *Coll. Ess. & Rev.* (1920) 446 Taking it [*sc.* a book] *en gros*, what strikes me most in it is the great sense of concrete reality with which it is filled. **1706** P. SIRIS tr. *Feuillet's Art of Dancing* vi. 9 A Bending and Springing Step, with a Foot *en l'Air. Ibid.* Pl. xv. 39 Forwards *en l'Air*, and afterwards falling on the same Leg. **1808** WELLINGTON *Disp.* (1838) IV. 130 Its retreat to the sea should be considered in some degree *en l'air.* **1853** C. BRONTË *Villette* II. xxvii. 280 What had a person devoted to a serious calling..to do with Counts and Countesses, hotels and châteaux? To him, I seemed altogether 'en l'air'. **1891** 'L. MALET' *Wages of Sin* v. i, I wait on circumstances. My plans are rather distractingly *en l'air* every way just at present. **1918** FARROW *Dict. Mil. Terms* 204 *En l'air*... Said of troops when too far from the main body, either to render assistance or to receive support. **1964** W. B. PEMBERTON *Battles of Boer War* vi. 164 The extreme right of the Boers was practically *en l'air* and deserted. **1860** E. EDEN *Semi-attached Couple* II. iii. 40 Perhaps I see things *en noir* today. **1875** En noir [see *en beau*]. **1905** MRS. H. WARD *Marr. W. Ashe* II. xi. 197 She must know that everything she does is seen there *en noir.* **1912** A. LANG *Shakes., Bacon & Gt. Unknown* xiii. 282 No wonder that he turned to tragedy..and saw life *en noir.* **1921** J. CONRAD *Wks.* XVIII. p. viii, The only thing that will not be found amongst those Figures and Things that have passed away will be Conrad *en pantoufles.* **1930** *Time & Tide* 2 May, His secretary..had a little work up his sleeve, all ready to be printed and published on the morrow of France's burial, in which he was to be exposed 'en pantoufles'. **1955** *Times* 12 May 13/4 The authority and erudition he can pack into eight pages on 'The North-East in the Eighteenth Century'..is yet one more proof that he is never *en pantoufles.* **1816** En pension [see PENSION *sb.* 6c]. **1889** *Athenæum* 14 Sept. 351/1 The persistence with which Mrs. Markenfeld..remains *en pension* in a gloomy house with such abominable company. **1848** THACKERAY *Van. Fair* liii. 474 There were dirty trays, and wine-coolers en permanence. **1872** E. BRADDON *Life in India* v. 178 His Lares and Penates are erected *en permanence.* **1934** A. J. TOYNBEE *Study Hist.* III. 12 To make themselves at home upon it *en permanence.* **1955** *Times* 29 Aug. 10/5 Juliet expresses her character, and especially her emotional agitation, en pointes. **1959** *Times* 1 Sept. 11/3 Miss Doris Lainë..did a wonderfully neat hop *en pointe.* **1932** N. MITFORD *Christmas Pudding* ix. 137 He..since being *en poste* at Cairo, had interested himself mainly in Egyptology. **1962** *John o' London's* 31 May 517/1 While he was *en poste* in Paris he gathered much of the material. *a* **1700** EVELYN *Diary* 16 Jan. an. 1679 (1955) IV. 162 A french Merchant, who had his house furnish'd *en Prince.* **1885** 'L. MALET' *Col. Enderby's Wife* I. II. iv. 143, I was assured that you would be treated *en prince.* **1954** E. JENKINS *Tortoise & Hare* vii. 69 When her father was alive they did a lot of racegoing... He used to do it *en prince.* **1928** T. S. ELIOT *For Lancelot Andrewes* v. 88 For Mr. Symons there is, at least *en principe*, a ritual..of 'vice' or 'sin'. **1959** *Encounter* XIII. 87, I agree *en principe* with most. [**1750** *Chess made Easy* p. ix, When one Piece can take another, that other is said to be *in Prise* of the first.] **1821** *Kaleidoscope* 13 Mar. 294/2 [He] had the privilege of taking such of the pieces.. as might be *en prise.* **1902** *Encycl. Brit.* XXVIII. 758/2 B moves anywhere not *en prise.* **1960** R. C. BELL *Board & Table Games* ii. 48 Alquerque... If another piece is then *en prise* it is taken in the same move by a second short leap. **1909** I. BYWATER *Aristotle on Art of Poetry* p. xxxiii, I give it as rendered into Latin by Dr. Margoliouth..with the Greek of A^c *en regard* for purposes of comparison. **1959** T. S. ELIOT tr. *St.-J. Perse's Anabasis* 13, I have always refused to publish the translation except in this way, *en regard* with the French text. **1816** T. L. PEACOCK *Headlong Hall* vi. 83 You are right, Miss Graziosa: your taste is correct—perfectly *en règle.* **1833** C. MACFARLANE *Lives of Banditti & Robbers* l. 63 Many of these Calabrians were banditti..and afterwards became robbers *en règle.* **1880** L. FAGAN *Panizzi* I. 42 Panizzi's passport being perfectly *en règle.* **1893** G. B. SHAW *Widowers' Houses* I. 4 On the steamboat a little négligé was quite en règle. **1936** C. S. LEWIS *Allegory of Love* i. 6 A treatise, with rules and examples *en règle* for the nice conduct of illicit loves. **1848** THACKERAY *Pendennis* i, Specimens of the costume of a military man *en retraite.* **1860** W. H. RUSSELL *Diary in India* I. 57, I receive as a reward for my services..a post, with which I am well satisfied. I live in it for years. I use all my energies in it, and for me there is no future except *en retraite.* **1827** E. BELGRAVE in G. Huxley *Lady Eliz. & Grosvenors* (1965) vii. 134 Dinner..is rather a long proceeding. But, 'en revanche' , they are a very short time at dessert. **1841** M. G. BLESSINGTON *Idler in France* I. 308 She offers him, *en revanche*, a cane, buttons, or a pin —in short, some present. **1883** L. OLIPHANT *Altiora Peto* vii. 125 She gave a comical look at that lady's waist and elbows, which was evidently *en revanche* for the well-bred stare to which she had been subjected. **1891** W. JAMES *Let.* 25 Aug. (1920) I. 316 My Cousin Elly Emmet..is about to marry *en secondes noces* a Scotchman. **1909** MRS. H. WARD *Daphne* vi. 142 The Duchess had been..married *en secondes noces*..by an epicurean duke. **1961** P. GREEN tr. *Oldenbourg's Massacre at Montségur* vi. 192 Petronilla, already married *en secondes noces* to Nuno Sanche. **1778** H. WALPOLE *Let.* 27 Nov. (1904) X. 349 You cannot justly expect him to be very punctual at first, till he is got *en train.* **1803** E. WYNNE *Diary* 9 Sept. (1940) III. 90 We found the Ball already *en train* by the time we arrived. **1855** MRS. GASKELL *Let.* ? July (1966) 360, I am en train for applying to Miss 'Temple'. **1891** E. SIMCOX in K. A. McKenzie *E. Simcox & G. Eliot* (1961) ii. 56 The Miners had another big Congress at Paris, when I was *en train* with Babylonian weights and measures. **1772** RUFFHEAD & MORGAN *Jacob's New Law Dict.* s.v. Infant, II. *Who are minors, and how far the law regards infants* in ventre sa mere... An infant *in ventre sa mere*, or in the mother's womb, is supposed in law, to be born for many purposes. **1848** WHARTON *Law Lex.* 9/2 A child *en ventre sa mère* is..a life in being. **1891** *Law Times* XC. 461/2 Beyond all question, for many purposes, a child *en ventre sa mère* is considered as being alive. **1860** *Once a Week* 11 Feb. 152/1 She was so huffy that I told Blot I would dine *en ville* for a short time. **1884** F. BOYLE *On Borderland* 336 The horrid cookshops which send dinners *en ville.*

en, early ME. variant of IN.

en-, *prefix*[1], the form assumed in Fr. (as also in Pr., Sp., Pg.) by the L. prepositional prefix *in-* (see IN-). The Eng. words in which it appears are partly adaptations of Fr. (occasionally Sp.) words, either of L. descent or formed in Romanic, and partly original formations upon Eng. words.

A. Forms.

1. In modern orthography and pronunciation *en-* becomes *em-* before *b* and *p*, and occasionally before *m*. This rule was not fully established in spelling before the 17th c.; in ME., as in OF. and OSp., *enb-*, *enp-* are more frequent than *emb-*, *emp-*, though the latter may perhaps represent what was the actual pronunciation.

2. In ME. (as in OF.) *en-*, *em-*, freq. became *an-*, *am-* (a form which survives in AMBUSH). This *an-*, *am-*, like the native prefix AN- 1, was often reduced to *a-*: see APPAIR, APRISE. Conversely, the prefix *a-* of various origin was often changed into *en-*, as in *embraid*.

3. From 14th c. onwards the prefix IN- (IM-) has been frequently substituted for *en-* (*em-*); and, conversely, *en-* (*em-*) has been substituted for the prefix IN- (IM-) of words of L. or It. origin, and for the native Eng. IN-. Nearly every word, of long standing in the language, which is formed with *en-* has at some period been written also with *in-*. Hence it is often impossible to determine whether in a particular word of Eng. formation the prefix *en-* or *in-* is due to the analogy of words of Fr., Lat., or purely Eng. origin; in many instances it must have been applied merely as a recognized Eng. formative, without reference to the analogy of any individual word. In 17th c. the form *in-* (*im-*) was generally preferred; the now prevailing tendency is to use *en-* (*em-*) in Eng. formations, and where the prefix represents Fr. *en-*; and in mod. reprints of 17th c. books, and in Dicts., the *in-* (*im-*) of the original texts is often replaced by *en-* (*em-*). In some words, however, as *em-*, *imbed*, *en-*, *inclose*, the form with *in-* still occurs, but in most cases less frequently than the *en-* forms; in a few instances *in-* has entirely superseded *en-*, even where the latter is etymologically more correct, as in *imbrue*, *impair*, *inquest*. In a few words (*e.g.* ENSURE, INSURE) the alternative forms have (in very modern times) been appropriated to express different senses. As a general rule the *en-* and *in-* forms are in this Dict. treated as belonging to one and the same word. A word still surviving in use is treated in the alphabetical place of its now more frequent form. In the case of obs. words, where there is no decided preponderance in usage, the choice of the typical form has been determined by etymological considerations: thus the adapted words from Fr. or Sp. with *en-*, and new formations app. on the analogy of these, are by preference placed under E; while words app. formed on Latin analogies, or prob. originating as compounds of the Eng. prep. IN, will appear under I.

The substitution of *in-* for *en-* has in part been due to notions of etymological fitness, the Romanic *en-* having been regarded as a corrupt and improper form of the L. *in-*, while the Eng. formations in *en-* were either referred to L. analogies or treated as compounds of the native preposition. The phenomenon seems, however, to be partly of phonetic origin. The sound of (ɛ) initial and unstressed has in careless speech a tendency to pass into (ɪ); cf. the colloq. pronunciation of *effect*, *ellipse*, *essential*. Hence such forms as *embed*, *imbed*, *enclose*, *inclose* are in familiar pronunciation really homophones; many persons use the *en-* forms in writing, and (unconsciously) the *in-* forms in speech. From the occurrence of spellings like *inbassed* for *embassade* in the fourteenth century, it may be surmised that the tendency to 'raise' the initial (ɛ) has existed from an early period.

B. Signification and uses.

The applications of the prefix in Fr. (Pr., Sp., Pg.), and hence in Eng., are substantially identical with those of the L. *in-*, which was used to form vbs. (1) from sbs., with sense 'to put (something) into or on what is denoted by the sb.', or 'to put' what is denoted by the sb. 'into or on (something)'; (2) from sbs. or adjs., with sense 'to bring or to come into a certain condition or state, to invest with a certain quality'; (3) from other vbs., with added notion of 'within', 'into', 'upon', or 'against', or with merely intensive force. Many L. or late L. words of this formation came down into Romanic, and have thence been adapted in Eng. In Romanic the prefix was extensively applied in the formation of new words, in strict accordance with L. analogies, exc. that in formations upon vbs. the notion of 'against' rarely or never occurs. In Eng. the analogy of the many words with *en-* adapted from Romanic gave rise to the extensive application of the prefix in the formation of Eng. words, its functions being the same as in Fr.

The compounds of EN- which have been in general use, or which require special comment, are given in their alphabetical place. The following are examples of those which are merely nonce-words, or of very rare occurrence. (See also EM-).

1. Verbs formed by prefixing *en-* to a sb.

a. With general sense 'to put (something) into or on what the latter member indicates':

†**enambush**, to place in ambush; † **enangle**, to put into an angle or corner; **encell**; **encentre**, to place in the centre of something; **enchair**; †**enchariot**; **encist**, to shut up in or as in a cist or chest; †**encoach**, to seat in a coach; **encoil**, to wrap in or as in a coil; †**encouch**, to lay upon a couch, *fig.*; **encraal**, *intr.* for *refl.*, to lodge in a kraal; **encrochet**, to enclose in brackets; **encup**, to place in or as in a cup; **encushion**, to seat on a cushion; **enfeature**, to exhibit on the features; †**engammon**, to put or (*intr.* for *refl.*) get into the haunch (of a pig); †**engaol** (in quots. *fig.*); **engarb**, to put into a garb, clothe; **engarment**, to case as in a garment; **englamour**, to surround with illusion; †**engown**, to dress in a gown; †**engyve**, to put in gyves or fetters; **enhusk**; †**enjourney**, (*refl.*) to start on a journey; †**enkennel**; **enkerchief**; †**enkernel**; †**enlabyrinth**, to entangle as in a labyrinth; †**enlead**; **enmagazine**, *fig.*; †**ennet**, to entangle; †**enniche**, to set up in a niche, as a statue, *fig.*; **enrib**, to put within the ribs; †**enseat**, to install; **enshadow**; **enshawl**, to wrap in or cover with a shawl; **enshell**; †**enshelter**; †**enslumber**, to lull to sleep, *lit.* and *fig.*; †**ensoap** (see quot.); †**enstage**, to put upon the stage (of a theatre); †**enstock**, to set in the stocks; †**entower**, to imprison in the Tower; †**envapour**, to shroud in vapour; **enwall**, to enclose within walls; **enzone**, to engirdle.

c **1611** CHAPMAN *Iliad* XVIII. 475 Within a vale..they ..*enambush'd them. *Ibid.* X. 257 Enambush'd enemies. **17..** CAWTHORN *Elegy Capt. Hughes* 28 Th' enambushed phalanx. ?*a* **1400** *Morte Arth.* 3782 His enmye ..*enangylles abowte oure excellente knyghttez. **1652** SPARKE *Prim. Devot.* (1673) 623 App., What a deal of sulphur..was *encelled against that day [Nov. 5]. **1856** R. VAUGHAN *Mystics* (1860) II. XIII. iii. 272 Here dwells chaste coolness, safe encelled. **1843** E. JONES *Sens. & Ev.* 111 If when the day was fine..*Encentred in this meadow, one revolved Inquiring gaze. **1859** TENNYSON *Last. Tourn.* 104 Sir Lancelot, sitting in my place *Enchair'd. **1652** BENLOWES *Theoph.*, Postill for Author, Speculations high, *Enchariot Thee Elijah-like to th' Skie! *Ibid.* X. lxxv. 188 Elijah-like..To be encharioted in fire. **1888** RHYS *Hibbert Lect.* 173 The dragons continued..*encisted in the subterranean lake. *a* **1618** J. DAVIES *Wittes' Pilgr.* Wks. (1876) 22 (D.) Tamburlaine..*encoacht in burnisht gold. **1839** BAILEY *Festus* (1848) 32/1 This world, within whose heartstrings I feel myself *encoiled. **1596** *Edward III*, II. i. 14 *Encouch the word..with such sweet laments. **1832** *Blackw. Mag.* May 729/1 The lane where gipsy gang had *encraal'd. **1806** SOUTHEY *Lett.* (1856) I. 397 He will ..*encrochet [ ] thus what Hyems has to copy. **1881** MRS. H. HUNT *Childr. Jerus.* 144 The convent..lay..*encupped in hills. **1819** H. BUSK *Vestriad* IV. 725 Or in gilt equipage *encushion'd sit. **1843** E. JONES *Poems, Sens. & Event* 43 The joy..in his face and eye..*enfeatured. **1673** R. LEIGH *Transpr. Reh.* 23 Ratts *engammon'd in the fat Hanches of the Arcadian Sow. **1593** SHAKS. *Rich. II*, I. iii. 166 Within my mouth you haue *engaol'd my tongue. **1844** LD. HOUGHTON *Mem. Many Sc., Valentia* 200 Engaoled in this unhealthy time. **1831** *Fraser's Mag.* IV. 139 The canting philanthropist, *engarbed as a quaker. **1859** MISS MULOCK *Romant. T.* 101 The form which *engarmented that pure.. soul. **1864** DICEY in *Daily Tel.* 15 July, The memory of a great past still *englamours them [the Danes]. **1613** G. FLETCHER *Christ's Bloody Sweat* in Farr *S.P. Jas. I* (1848) 336 Here saw he lawyers soberly *engoun'd. **1603** FLORIO *Montaigne* II. viii. (1632) 224 We..are *engived and shackled in them [arms]. **1788** BURNS *Ep. H. Parker* 12 A fiery kernel *Enhusked by a fog infernal. **1596** R. L[INCHE] *Diella* (1877) 82 The next day, They would *eniourney them. **1603** J. DAVIES *Microcosmos* 220 That alwaies in a Tub *enkenell'd lies. *c* **1800** KIRKE WHITE *Poems* (1837) 47 Sleep, baby mine, *enkerchieft on my bosom. **18..** M. ARNOLD *Switzerland* I. ii. 3 in Sel. Poems (1882) 123, I know that soft enkerchief'd hair. *a* **1843** SOUTHEY *Nondescr.* vi. (D.) A happy metamorphosis To be *enkernell'd thus. **1652** BENLOWES *Theoph.* I. liii, My soul, *enlabyrinth'd in grief. **1598** FLORIO, *Impiombare*, to *enlead or fasten or couer with lead. *Impiombatura*, an enleading or fastning with lead. **1887** *Harper's Mag.* July 268 The incendiary material *enmagazined in their pages. **1598** FLORIO, *Irretare*, to

ensnare or take in a net or ginne, to entramell, to *ennet. **1761** STERNE *Tr. Shandy* III. xxxviii, He..deserves to be *en-nich'd as a prototype for all writers. **1854** S. DOBELL *Balder* iii. 20 The strong *enribbed heart. **1602** FULBECKE *Pandectes* 65 Whether base artificers are to be *enseated..in places of worth. **1636** W. DENNY in *Ann. Dubrensia* (1877) 13 Pendant leaves his head *enshadow'd round. **1882** M. ARNOLD in *Macm. Mag.* XLVI. 143 The soft mantle of enshadowing hills. **1822** *Blackw. Mag.* XII. 69 With what an air of tenderness he *enshawls each ivory shoulder. **1877** BLACKIE *Wise Men* 302 None In mortal frame *enshelled. **1604** SHAKS. *Oth.* II. i. 18 If that the Turkish Fleete Be not *enshelter'd..they are drown'd. *c* **1611** CHAPMAN *Iliad* XXIV. 399 The guards..he *enslumber'd. *a* **1619** DONNE *Biathan.* (1644) 155 Content to enslumber themselves in an opinion. **1610** G. FLETCHER *Christ's Vict.* in Farr *S.P. Jas. I* (1848) When the senses half enslumbered lie. **1598** FLORIO, *Insaponare*, to *ensope, to sope clothes..to lay in suds. **1613** CHAPMAN *Rev. Bussy D'Ambois* Plays 1873 II. 114 The splenative Philosopher..were worthy the *enstaging. **16..** SYLVESTER *Du Bartas* (N.), I intend to tye th' Eternal's hands, and his free feet *enstock. *a* **1649** DRUMM. OF HAWTH. *Answ. Object.* Wks. (1711) 214 The *entowering of Henry the VI. **1605** SYLVESTER *Du Bartas* II. iii. *Vocation* 555 (D.) A black fume, that all *envapoureth. **1610** G. FLETCHER *Christ's Vict.* lvi, His Court with glitterant pearle was all *enwall'd. **1864** *Blackfriars* I. 32 The extent of ground thus enwalled. **1832** J. WILSON in *Blackw. Mag.* XXXI. 859 The groves that *enzone Greenbank. **1838** *Tait's Mag.* V. 218 Queens in luxury enzoned.

b. With general sense 'to put what the latter member indicates into or upon' (a person or thing).

enamber, to scent or flavour with ambergris (see AMBER 1); **encap**, to put a cap on; **encolumn**, to ornament (a wall) with columns; **encoronall**; **encoronet**; †**encowl**, to put on (a person) the cowl of a monk; **endiadem**, to crown, in quots. *fig.*; **enfigure**, to adorn with figures; †**enfrieze**, to ornament as with a frieze; †**enfringe**, to sew fringes upon; †**engall**; †**engold**; †**engrape**, to cover with grapes; †**enhoney**, *fig.*; †**enlaurel**, to crown with laurels; **enleaf**, to adorn with leaves, to wrap in leaves; †**enmitre**; **enmoss**; **enrut**; **ensaffron**, to tinge with yellow; **ensand**; **ensandal**, *fig.*; †**enscreen**; †**ensilver**; †**enscarf**; †**enspangle**; †**ensparkle**; **enspell**, to cast a spell upon; †**enspice**; †**enstomach**, to encourage; **ensulphur**; †**entackle**, to furnish (a ship) with tackle; †**entask**; **entincture**; †**entinsel**, to cause to glitter; †**enturf**; **enverdure**; **enwood**, to cover with trees.

1681 in *Phil. Collect.* XII. 105 Buying..Amber and other requisites, and *Enambering therewith..Sugar. **1847** *Illust. Lond. News* 16 Oct. 256/1 His brow *encapt With the gloomy crown of Care. **1808** R. PORTER *Trav. Sk. Russ. & Swed.* (1813) I. iv. 27 The regal pride of *encolumned walls. **1858** E. CASWALL *Poems* 170 With..golden pillars *encoronall'd. **1881** PALGRAVE *Vis. England* 47 If an alien King *Encoronet thy brow? **1612** DRAYTON *Poly-olb.* xxiv, King Alfred..Left his Northumbrian crown, and soon became *encoul'd. **1818** SHELLEY *Misery* 439 Lady whose imperial brow Is *endiademed with woe. **1819** *Blackw. Mag.* V. 322 Endiadem'd with..fleecy-silver'd cloud. **1774** *Poetry* in *Ann. Reg.* 211 Behold The tissued vestment of *enfigur'd gold. **1648** HERRICK *Hesper.* I. 233 The Roome is hung with the blew skin Of shifted snake; *enfreez'd throughout With eyes of peacocks trains. **1714** *Orig. Canto Spencer* xxxix. 2 White Robes, *enfring'd with Crimson Red. **1611** FLORIO, *Affielire*..to *engall or enbitter. **1382** WYCLIF *Bar.* vi. 7 Trees..*engoldid and ensiluered. —— *Rev.* xvii. 4 And the womman was..engoldid with gold, and with precious stoon. **1523** SKELTON *Garl. Laurel* (Dyce) 656 Vinis *engrapid. **1603** FLORIO *Montaigne* II. xii. (1632) 289 To *enhonny and allure us to these opinions. **1620** DAVIES *Past. to W. Browne*, Foe-men to faire skils *enlawreld Queene. **1789** P. SMYTH tr. *Aldrich's Archit.* (1818) 99 The bell of the capital..is *enleaved. **1837** L. HUNT *Bluestocking Revels* iii. 39 Fruit..Enleaf'd on the bough. **1598** FLORIO, *Inmetriare*, to *enmitre, to crowne with a mitre. **1818** KEATS *Endym.* I. 231 Meadows that outskirt the side Of thine *enmossed realms. **1882** H. MERIVALE *Faucit of B.* III. II. xix. 153 Over which distance these *enrutted tracks made their uneasy way. *c* **1630** DRUMM. OF HAWTH. *Poems* Wks. (1711) 6 Phœbus in his chair, *Ensaffroning sea and air. **1879** T. HARDY *Return Native* II. ii, A stratum of ensaffroned light. **1523** SKELTON *Garl. Laurel* (Dyce) 654 With alys *ensandid about in compas. **1853** B. TAYLOR in *Blackw. Mag.* LXXIII. 744 Belted with beech and *ensandal'd with palm. **1641** M. FRANK *Serm.* ii. (1672) 530 Heaven might now *enskarfe itself in a scarlet cloud. **1665** R. B. *Comment. 2 Tales* 42 Let night's sable Curtain *enskreen these dark actions. **1382** WYCLIF *Bar.* vi. 7 The trees of hem..also engoldid, and *ensiluered. **1648** HERRICK *Hesper., Mistress M. Willand*, Sent T' *enspangle this expansive firmament. **1593** NASHE *Christ's T.* (1613) 144 Why *ensparkle they their eyes with spiritualiz'd distillations? **1884** J. PAYNE *1001 Nights* VII. 285 Her glances *enspelled all who looked on her. **1598** FLORIO, *Inspeciare*, to *enspice. **1545** T. RAYNOLD *Womans booke* 59 The midwife..*enstomakyng her to pacience. *c* **1611** CHAPMAN *Iliad* x. 7 Or opes the gulfy mouth of war with his *ensulphur'd hand. **1819** *Blackw. Mag.* IV. 565 From the surge of hell's ensulphered sea. *a* **1529** SKELTON *Garl. Laurel* (Dyce) 545 Your storme driven shyppe I repared new So well *entakeled. **1606** SYLVESTER *Du Bartas* I. iv. (1641) 32/1 The Heav'ns have..*entaskt my layes. **1768** S. BENTLEY *River Dove* 6 Windows so Story-bedight: Entinctur'd, Devotion to aid. **1652** BENLOWES *Theoph.* XII. li, Spangles..*Entinseling like Stars the dew. **1523** SKELTON *Garl. Laurel* (Dyce) 655 The bankis *enturfid with singular solas. *Ibid.* 666 *Enverdured with laurel leves continually grene. **1850** MRS. BROWNING *Poems* I. 121 Enverduring the green Of every heavenly palm. **1816** L. HUNT *Rimini* iv. 81 The shade Of some *enwooded field.

2. Verbs formed by prefixing *en-* to a sb. or adj., with general sense 'to bring into a certain condition or state'.

†**enanger**, to make angry; **enapt**, to make fit, qualify; **enarbour**, to convert into an arbour; †**enazure**, to render azure; †**encalm** = BECALM; †**encanker**; **encannibal**; **encharnel** (see CHARNEL *sb.*[1]), to bury; †**encinder**, to burn to ashes; †**encluster**; **encommon**; †**endoubt** (*refl.*), to feel doubt, apprehend; **endragon** (in example as *endragoned* ppl. adj.); †**endrudge** (*refl.*), to enslave oneself; †**endry**; †**enearnest**; **enfamous**; †**enfavour**, to take into favour, to get (oneself) into favour, ingratiate; †**enfear**; †**enfertile**; †**enfierce**; †**enfort**, to convert into a fort, fortify; **enfree**; **enfoul**; **enfreedom**; **enfroward**; †**engallant**; †**engarboil**, to throw into commotion; **englad**; **engloom**, to render gloomy, change into gloom; **engod**; **engolden**, to make golden, also *intr.* to become golden; †**engrand**; **engreen**; †**enlength**; **enlife**; †**enlusty**, to delight; **enmass**; †**enripe**; †**enruby**; **enruin**; †**ensad**; †**ensafe**, whence **ensafer**; **ensaint**; **enscroll**; **enseraph**; **enserf**; †**ensober**; †**ensound**, to make sound; †**enstable**; **ensucket** (cf. SUCKET, sweetmeat), to sweeten; **entempest**; †**enthirst**; **entrough**, to hollow out like a trough; **envineyard**; **enwaiter**, to turn into a waiter; †**enwaste**; †**enwine**, to convert into wine; †**enwoman**; †**enworthy**, to make worthy; †**enwrack**, to bring to wrack, ruin.

1491 CAXTON *Vitas Patr.* I. xxxviii. (1495) 53 a/1 The lorde..strongly *enangred came to the sayd pytte. **1651** JACKSON *Creed* XI. xvii. in Wks. X. 346 A diligent servant to a..cruel master..is thereby well *enapted..to be diligent. **1883** *Harper's Mag.* Nov. 946/1 Stairs *enarboured by vines. **1630** BRATHWAIT *Eng. Gentlewom.* 301 That [woman] *enazures her seered veines. **1562** J. SHUTE *Cambine's Turk. Wars* 34 b, Seeinge the ship *encalmed. **1489** SKELTON *Elegy Earl Northumb.* (Dyce) 142 With my rude pen *enkankerd all with rust. **1854** *Blackw. Mag.* LXXV. 131 If Mr. Parkyns had not *encannibaled himself. **1875** MYERS *Poems, Renew. Youth*, The rulers came, *Encharnelled in their fatness. **1593** NASHE *Christ's T.* 31 b, Many goodly streets..they *encindred. *c* **1630** DRUMM. OF HAWTH. *Poems* 130 What Bands (*enclustred) neare to these abide. **1607** SYLVESTER *Du Bartas* II. IV. ii, Good becomes more Good, the more It is *en-common'd. **1661** FELTHAM *Resolves* II. lxxxii. 366 Their Mysteries might not..be..encommon'd. *c* **1400** *Rom. Rose* 1664 If I ne hadde *endoutet me To have ben hatid. **1876** G. M. HOPKINS *Wr. Deutschland* (1918) 20 In wind's burly and beat of *endragonèd seas. *a* **1656** BP. HALL *Rem. Wks.* (1660) 29 Such is every one that *endrudgeth himself to any known sin. *a* **1440** *Sir Degrev.* 418 My perkes ar stroyed And reveres *endreyde. **1603** FLORIO *Montaigne* (1634) 550 Vicissitude doth..*en-earnest my minde. **1613** BROWNE *Brit. Past.* II. i. (1772) II. 39 Padus silver stream..*Enfamoused by rebelles Phaëton. *a* **1650** SIR S. D'EWES *Autobiog.* (1845) I. 377 Some wit, to enfamous the rare confidence of Mr. Felton [made an anagram on his name.] **1639** SALTMARSHE *Policy* 275 How to *enfavour yourself with those you discourse with. **1650** FULLER *Pisgah* II. i. 62 For to *enfavour themselves with the Emperor. *Ibid.* vi. ii. 144 If any shall enfavor me so far. **1584** HUDSON *Du Bartas' Judith*, A woman's look his hart *enfeares. **1610** HOLLAND *Camden's Brit.* ii. 46 The rivers Dee..and Done..*enfertile the fields. **1680** MORDEN *Geog. Rect., Africa* (1685) 445 Enfertiles all the Countries through which it passes. **1596** SPENSER *F.Q.* IV. iv. 8 More *enfierced through his currish play. **1580** SIDNEY, etc. *Psalm* cxxv, With her hilly bullwarkes Roundly *enforted. **1885** D. C. MURRAY *Rainbow Gold* I. II. ii. 201 So is the stream of every human passion *enfouled or filtered by the heart it flows through. **1599** SANDYS *Europæ Spec.* (1632) 170 The Free Cityes..have..*enfreed themselves from the Pope. **1606** SHAKS. *Tr. & Cr.* IV. i. 38 To render him, For the enfreed Anthenor, the faire Cressid. **1874** PUSEY *Lent. Serm.* 181 Enfreed by God. **1588** SHAKS. *L.L.L.* III. i. 125 *Enfreedoming thy person. **1874** PUSEY *Lent. Serm.* 248 God's..enfreedoming, ennobling grace. **1599** SANDYS *Europæ Spec.* (1632) 195 The only prickles that so *enfroward mens affections. **1599** B. JONSON *Cynthia's Rev.* IV. i, If you could but endear yourself to her affection, you were eternally *engallanted. *a* **1641** BP. MOUNTAGU *Acts & Mon.* (1642) 67 To *engarboyle the Church upon high termes of Heresie. *Ibid.* 242 To engarboile disputes with needlesse assertions. **1523** SKELTON *Garl. Laurel* (Dyce) 530 The larke..Of the soneshyne *engladid with the lyght. **1604** *Supplic. Masse-priests* §1 [These things] doe..exceedingly possesse and englad our hearts. **1610** G. FLETCHER *Christ's Tri. over Death* ii. Th' engladded Spring. **1795–9** SOUTHEY & R. LOVELL *Poems* 89 Night's *englooming sway Steals on the fiercer glories of the day. **1874** PUSEY *Lent. Serm.* 108 We might have been as God, yea..*engodded. **1825** L. HUNT *Redi's Bacchus* in *Tuscany* Poet. Wks. (1860) 386 That Vaiano Which *engoldens and empurples in the grounds there of my Redi. **1849** *Tait's Mag.* XVI. 348 Yon wreath'd bower Engoldened with the westering sun. **1860** PUSEY *Min. Proph.* 521 The whole world was *engoldened with evangelical preachings. **1655** FULLER *Hist. Camb.* (1840) 186 This duke..by all means endeavoured to *engrand his posterity. **15..** F. DAVISON in Farr. *S.P., Eliz.* II. 327 *Engreening..those pleasant mountagnets. **1877** BLACKIE *Wise Men* 268 Engreen the hills. *c* **1530** MORE *Answ. Frith* Wks. 1037/1 He hath somewhat *enlengthed it of late. **1603** DANIEL *Panegyr. King* xvii, A new season..Begins to enlength the days. **1599** T. M[OUFET] *Silkwormes* Ded., A..little flame..to *enlife for aye the same. **18..** LOWELL *Poet. Wks.* (1879) 403 With wise lips enlife it. **1483** CAXTON *G. de la Tour* A j, This swete songe *enlustyed me. **1878** H. M. STANLEY *Dark Cont.* I. xv. 392 The heroes of the great raid are *enmassed in view. **1503** *Sheph. Kalender* ii, For I *enripe..Fruits of the earth. *a* **1520** SKELTON *Bowge of Courte* 2 The sonne..enryped hath our corne. **1611** FLORIO, *Arrobinare*, to *enruby, to make ruddy. **1876** J. ELLIS *Cæsar in Egypt* 344 That dread shock..Left here *enruin'd..A city. **1634** SIR S. D'EWES *Jrnl.* (1783) 55 A particular newes which much *ensadded my heart. **1652** SPARKE *Prim. Devot.* (1663) 564 To rescue and *ensafe us. *Ibid.* 111 *Ensafers of God's onely begotten Son. **1599** NASHE *Lent. Stuffe* 58 Saint Gildarde..the Pope so *ensainted. **1864** *Spectator* 538 Like Charlemagne a high ensainted king. **1880** *Argosy* XXIX. 469 The aspect of some ensainted phantom. **1842** *Gentl. Mag.* May XVII. 479 *note*, Three ostrich feathers *enscrolled. **1858** E. CASWALL *Poems* 144 The Seraphs..Amidst their songs *enseraph'd me. **1882** W. B. WEEDEN *Soc. Law Labor* 86 The *enserfed free-holders bought their freedom. **1651** JER. TAYLOR *Course Serm.* I. xiii. 170 God sent him sharpnesses..to *ensober his spirits. **1562** BULLEYN *Dial. Sorenes & Chir.* 23 a, This decoction..doeth *ensounde..the member. **1534** WHITTINTON *Tullyes Offices* II. (1540) 89 Whan..iustyce..*enstableth and encreaseth the ryches of theues. **1594** *Zepheria* xxiii, So did that sug'ry touch my lips *ensucket. **1800** COLERIDGE *Poet. Wks.* II. 155 Zeal unresisted *entempests your breast. **1640** BP. HALL *Chr. Moder.* (Repr.) 14/1 Wine; whereby he is inflamed and *enthirsted the more. **1876** R. BURTON *Gorilla L.* II. 129 The breadth of the *entroughed bed varies. **1848** CLOUGH *Amours de Voy.* III. 293 Farewell..ye *envineyarded ruins. **1865** *Athenæum* No. 1959. 650/1 The *enwaitered greengrocer. **1494** FABYAN VI. clxxvi. 172 But durynge this siege, the Danys eft *-enwasted yͤ lande of Fraunce. **1548** GESTE *Pr. Masse* 86 Christes..bloud [is] *enwyned. **1595** DANIEL *Sonn.* 42 That grace..doth more than *enwoman thee. **1626** T. H. *Caussin's Holy Crt.* 64 You desire..to *enworthy, and distinguish your nobility. **1686** W. DE BRITAINE *Hum. Prud.* xix. 84 You must study to enworthy your self. **1625** LISLE *Du Bartas, Noe* 4 O world *enwrackt and over flown.

b. Verbs formed (with sense as above) on adjs. or sbs. with the prefix *en-* and the suffix -EN[5], as ENLIVEN, ENLIGHTEN. Most of these verbs were formed by prefixing *en-* to an already existing verb in *-en*; but a considerable number seem to be directly f. the adj. or sb. on the analogy of those of the former class. For examples see 3.

3. Verbs, mostly transitive, formed by prefixing *en-* to a verb, with additional sense of *in*, or simply intensive (in poetry often merely to give an additional syllable); also vbs. f. *en-* + adj. or sb. + *-en* (see 2 b).

†**enaid**, to aid, assist; †**encarve**; †**encheck**, to represent in mingled hues; †**enchequer**, to arrange in a chequered pattern; †**enclaim**; †**encleanse**; †**enclog**; †**encolden**; †**encurb**; †**encurse**; †**endamnify**, to damnify, cause loss to; †**endart**; †**endazzle**; **endiaper**, to dapple, variegate; †**enditch**; **endizen**, to set forth; †**endrench**; †**endye**; †**eneich** (see ECHE *v.*), to improve; **enfasten**; †**enfester**; **enfoil**; †**enforge**, to invent; †**enfreeze**; **enfuddle**; **engarble**, to mutilate; **engaze**, to comprehend in one's gaze; **engerminate**; **engladden**; †**englaze**, to represent on glass; **enguard**; **enhamper**; †**enhang**; †**enhedge**; †**enjangle**, *intr.*; †**enjudge**; †**enlanguish**, to render languid; †**enlap**, to wrap in (something); †**enlengthen**; †**enlessen**; †**enmilden**; †**enmingle**; †**enmix**; †**enorder**; †**enquicken**; †**enrive**; †**enscale**, to climb; †**enscore**, to count; **enseem**, *intr.* = SEEM; †**ensoak**; †**enstuff**; **ensweep**; †**entame**; **enthunder**, *intr.*; †**entoast**, *intr.* to drink a health; †**entwist**, also *fig.*; †**enwallow**, *intr.*; †**enweaken**; †**enwed**; **enwiden**; **enwisen**, to make wise; **enwrite**; †**enwrong**, to deprive wrongfully *of*; †**enyoke**.

1502 *Ord. Crysten Men* (W. de W.) IV. vi. (1506) 178 Yf we haue poorenes of entencyon hym it shal *enayde. **1596** FITZ-GEFFRAY *Sir F. Drake* (1881) 22 *Encarving characters of memorie. **1611** SYLVESTER *Du Bartas* II. iv. *Schisme* (1641) 228/1 Th' artfull shuttle did *encheck the cangeant colour of a mallard's neck. **1648** HERRICK *Hesper., Oberon's Pal.* 56 Squirrels' and children's teeth late shed Are neatly here *enchequered. **1531–2** *Act 23 Hen. VIII*, c. 1 The ordinaries *enclaiminge such offenders by the liberties of the churche. **1493** *Festivall* (W. de W. 1515) 88 She was *enclensed with the clensynge of the holy ghoost. **1604** SHAKS. *Oth.* II. i. 70 Traitors ensteep'd, to *enclogge [*Qq.* clog] the guiltlesse Keele. **1627** FELTHAM *Resolves* I. xlvii. (1631) 174 The hands and feet..are by degrees *encoldned to a fashionable clay. **1555** *Fardle Facions* Pref. 10 The golden graueled springes, thei *encurbed with Marble. *a* **1450** *Knt. de la Tour* 12, Y durst never telle it..for drede of *encursinge. **1615** SANDYS *Travels* 276 Those who hired the fishing..were *endamnified much by the violent breaking in of the seas. **1592** SHAKS. *Rom. & Jul.* I. iii. 98 More deepe will I *endart mine eye. **1644** MILTON *Areop.*, An eagle..kindling her *endazzled eyes. **1607** *Tragedie Cl. Tiberius* G 2 (N.) The troubled bosome of the maine *Endiapred with cole-black porpesses. **1598** FLORIO, *Affossare*, to ditch..about, to *endich. **1589** WARNER *Alb. Eng.* v. xxviii, What so else Occurrants..may interrupt..Our Penne shall not *endizen. **1593** NASHE *Christ's T.* (1613) 44 My soule..will..*endrench mee in..dolour. *c* **1500** *Elegy Hen. V* in Percy *Reliq.* 117 Grounde..Whiche wert *endyed with rede blode. **1635** PAGITT *Christianogr.* App. 21 A thing..used to *eneich their health. **1848** CLOUGH *Amours de Voy.* v. 66 To *enfasten the roots of my floating existence In the rich earth. **1686** CHARDIN *Travels* 370 Rivulets, that..*enfertilized the neighbouring parts on every side. **1609** J. DAVIES *Holy Roode* (1876) 16 (D) Whiche His *enfestered sores exulcerates. **1773** J. ROSS *Fratricide* iv. 347 Resolved In this next cope to foil or be *enfoiled. *c* **1440** *Partonope* 2512 Such vntrouth wolde not he *Enforged..haue. **1596** SPENSER

Hymn to Love xxi, Thou hast *enfrosen her disdainefull brest. **1822** J. WILSON in *Blackw. Mag.* XII. 113 Punch our powers insidiously *enfuddles. **1609** BP. BARLOW *Answ. Nameless Cath.* 73 The *engarbled Anatomie of a damned wretch. **1877** BLACKIE *Wise Men* 212 If a man could.. soaring sun-ward..*Engaze the radiant round. **1874** PUSEY *Lent. Serm.* 305 Unless..grace *engerminate in what is spoken. *Ibid.* 246 Thee..Who didst..*engladden..me. **1610** G. FLETCHER *Christ's Vict.* in Farr *S.P. Jas. I* (1848) 75 In those windows doth his arms *englaze. **1605** SHAKS. *Lear* I. iv. 349 He may *enguard his dotage with their powres, And hold our lives in mercy. **1855–9** SINGLETON *Virgil* II. 163 Throughout many a year with awe Enguarded. **1881** PALGRAVE *Vis. England* 279 The swordhilt in the wound *enhamper'd caught. *c* **1386** CHAUCER *Monks T.* 677 Thow schalt *enhangid ben, fader, certayn. **1632** VICARS *Virgil* (N.), Matrons..In heaps *enhedg'd it. **1580** NORTH *Plutarch* (1676) 44 And touch the Harp without *enjangling jar. *c* **1380** *Sir Ferumb.* 1959 Wharfor to ȝow y make my mone; *eniugieþ ȝe my foos. **1603** FLORIO *Montaigne* III. xiii. (1632) 613 It is pitty a man should bee so..*enlanguished. **1654** COKAINE *Dianea* IV. 329 Her eyes, enlanguished by griefe. **1601** HOLLAND *Pliny* XXXVII. vii. 617 By reason of the clay wherein they [rubies] be *enlapped. **1646** SIR T. BROWNE *Pseud. Ep.* 80 A smaller thred and more *enlengthened filament. **1548** GESTE *Pr. Masse* 127 To *enlessen theyr paynes in [purgatory]. **1603** FLORIO *Montaigne* III. xii. (1632) 599 That *enmildens mee. **1781** BURGOYNE *Lord of Manor* I. i. (D.), Sweets bloom *enmingled around. **1526** SKELTON *Magnyf.* 2540 Fallyble flatery *enmyxed with bytternesse. **1669** EVELYN *Three late Impostors* 70 It seemeth right to these your just debts to *enorder you to make satisfaction. **1647** H. MORE *Song of Soul* Notes 145/2 He hath not yet *enquickened Men..with this Deiform life. *Ibid.* 162/2 The lower man is our enquicknedbody. **1596** SPENSER *Dolef. Lay Clorinda* i, That my *enriven heart may find relief. **1613** W. BROWNE *Brit. Past.* II. i, Then with soft steps *enscaled the meeknid vallies. *c* **1420** *Pallad. on Husb.* I. 640 Other iiii *enscore her place into. **1818** LAMB *Vis. Repent.* Poems 596 *Enseem'd it now, he stood on holy ground. **1523** SKELTON *Garl. Laurel* 23 *Ensokyt with sylt of the myry mose. *a* **1547** EARL SURREY *Aeneid* II. 27 Did *enstuff..The hollow womb with armed soldiers. **1730** THOMSON *Autumn* 1109 *Ensweeping first The lower skies. **1855** SINGLETON *Virgil* I. 157 The seas Ensweeping in its flight. **1600** SHAKS. *A.Y.L.* III. v. 48 'Tis not..your cheeke of creame That can *entame my spirits. **1855–9** SINGLETON *Virgil* II. 524 Æneas..terribly *enthunders in his arms. **1724** RAMSAY *Tea-t. Misc.* (1733) II. 138 Shall I not to her health *entoast. **1590** SHAKS. *Mids. N.* IV. i. 48 So doth the woodbine, the sweet Honisuckle Gently *entwist. **1800** T. JEFFERSON *Writ.* (1859) IV. 320 He will..entwist himself with the Envoys. **1596** SPENSER *F.Q.* V. xi. 14 One sencelesse lumpe..*Enwallow'd in his own blacke bloudy gore. **1672** W. DE BRITAINE *Dutch Usurp.* 23 They are sufficiently *enweakened. **1490** CAXTON *Eneydos* xvi. 62 Parys *enwedded the fayr heleyne. **1593** NASHE *Christ's T.* (1613) 18, I have..*enwidened Hell mouth to swallow thee. **1623** COCKERAM, *Expatiate*, to enwiden, to enlarge. **1646** S. BOLTON *Arraignm. Err.* 355 We had..need rather..seek to lessen than to enwiden our differences. **1965** D. J. MILLEN in *Earth & Sky* (Cath. Poetry Circle) 20 Man applauding man, enwidens And unfolds the praiser's joy. **1860** PUSEY *Min. Proph.* 427 *Enwisening, rejoicing, enlightening the soul. *a* **1849** POE *To Helen* Poems (1859) 64 Heart-histories seemed to lie *enwritten Upon those crystalline, celestial spheres. *c* **1485** *Plumpton Corr.* 65 Ye *enwrong her of certayne lands. **1879** FARRAR *St. Paul* II. 154 Be not again *enyoked with the yoke of slavery.

en-, *prefix*². The form taken by the Gr. ἐν, etymologically cogn. with the prec. Chiefly in combinations already formed in Greek, as *enallage*, *endemic*, *energy*, *enthusiasm*; occas. in mod. formations as *enderon*. (Before *b*, *m*, *p*, *ph*, it takes the form *em-*; and before *l*, *r* it becomes *el*, *er-* respectively.)

-en, *suffix*¹ :—OTeut. *-îno(m*, formally the neut. of *-îno-*, -EN⁴, is used to form diminutives from sbs. (esp. names of animals), as in CHICKEN *sb.*¹, KITTEN, MAIDEN, ME. *ticchen* kid; also in ME. *stucchen* small piece.

-en, *suffix*² :—WGer. *-innja*, repr. OTeut. *-inî*, occurs in several OE. fem. sbs., a few of which have survived into mod. Eng.

1. It is used to form feminines from sbs. denoting male persons or animals, as in OE. *gyden* goddess (f. *god*), *mynecen* nun (f. *munuc* monk), *wylfen* she-wolf (f. *wulf* wolf). The only surviving instance of this use is VIXEN female fox. 2. It is added in a few instances to the stem of a vb. or to that of a verbal-abstract sb., as in BURDEN *sb.*, BURIAN, OE. *ræden* condition.

-en, *suffix*³, the form assumed in ME. by the OE. *-an*, the termination of the nom., accus., and dat. plural of sbs. of the weak declension, as in *oxa* masc., ox, pl. *oxan*; *tunge* fem., tongue, pl. *tungan*; *éare* neut., ear, pl. *éaran*. In origin the suffix belonged to the stem; but as in OE. the nom. sing. of these sbs. ended in *-a*, *-e* (levelled in ME. to *-e*), while the OE. *-an* of the oblique cases sing. became *-e* in ME., the termination *-en* came to be regarded as a formative of the plural, and its use was extended in southern ME. to many other words of OE. and Fr. origin. It was also added to the remains of other old plurals, as *brether*, *childer* (OE. *cildru*), *ky* (OE. *cý*), whence the modern *brethren*, *children*, *kine*. Apart from these the sole surviving representative (in standard Eng.) of this inflexion is *ox-en*; but *hos-en* (OE. *hosan*) continued in use until 17th c. In southern and south midland dialects the plurals in *-en* are still of frequent occurrence.

-en, *suffix*⁴ (reduced to *-n* after *r* in unstressed syllables), corresponds to OS. *-in*, OHG. *-în* (Ger. *-en*), ON. *-in*, Goth. *-eina-*:—OTeut *-îno-*, = Gr. *-ῖνο-*, L. *-īno-* (see -INE), added to noun-stems to form adjs. with sense 'pertaining to, of the nature of'. In Teut. the adjs. so formed chiefly indicate the material of which a thing is composed. Of the many words of this formation which existed in OE. scarcely any survive in mod. use; but the suffix was extensively applied in ME. to form new derivatives. Some of these took the place of OE. words, from which they formally differ only by the absence of umlaut; compare OE. *gylden* with mod.Eng. *golden*, OE. *stǽnen* (early ME. *stenen*) with ME. and dial. *stonen*, made of stone. From 16th c. onwards there has been in literary English a growing tendency to discard these adjs. for the attrib. use of the sb., as in 'a gold watch'; hence many of them have become wholly obs., and others (as *golden*, *silvern*) are seldom used except metaphorically, or with rhetorical emphasis. It is only in a few cases (e.g. *wooden*, *woollen*, *earthen*, *wheaten*) that these words are still familiarly used in their lit. sense. In s.w. dialects, however, the suffix is of common occurrence, being added without restriction to all sbs. denoting the material of which anything is composed, as in *glassen*, *steelen*, *tinnen*, *papern*, etc.

-en, *suffix*⁵, forming verbs.

1. from adjs., as *darken*, *deepen*, *harden*, *madden*, *moisten*, *widen*. Most of the words of this type seem to have been formed in late ME. or early mod.Eng., on the analogy of a few verbs which came down from OE. or were adopted from ON.; e.g. *fasten*:—OE. *fæstnian*; ?*brighten*:—ONorthumb. *berhtnia*; *harden*:—ON. *harðna*. In Teut. there are two classes of vbs. formed upon the 'weak' or lengthened stems of adjs. (suffix *-on-*): (*a*) the intransitive (or in sense pass.) vbs. which in Goth. make the inf. in *-nan*, and the pa. t. in *-ôda*; e.g. *fullnan* to be filled, f. *fullan-* full; *gabignan* to be rich, f. *gabigan-* rich; *managnan* to abound, f. *managan-* many; (*b*) the originally trans. vbs. in OTeut. (*i*)*nôjan*, e.g. OHG. *festinôn* to fasten, f. *feston-* (:—*fastjon-*) fast. In Eng. these two classes of vbs. can scarcely be discriminated with precision, but in most cases the intr. sense (as in *deepen* = 'become deeper') appears to be derived from the trans. sense (as in *deepen* = 'make deeper').

2. from sbs. In OTeut. sbs. both of the weak and the strong declension gave rise to intr. verbs in -(*i*)*nôjan*, and this formation is represented by a few examples in OE., such as *hlystnian* to LISTEN. In 14th c. some additional vbs. occur, formed app. on the analogy of these, as *happen*, *threaten*. The majority of Eng. words f. sb. + *-en*, however, such as *heighten*, *lengthen*, *strengthen*, *hearten*, *barken*, appear first in mod.Eng., and seem to be due to the analogy of the verbs f. adjs.

3. In one or two cases (e.g. *waken*) the suffix *-en* represents OTeut. *-na-*, the formative of the present stem in certain strong verbs.

-en, *suffix*⁶, the ending of the past participle of many strong verbs, as *broken*, *spoken*, *sunken*. OE. *-en*, corresp. to OFris, *-en*, OS. *-an*, (M)Du. *-en*, OHG. *-an* (MHG., G. *-en*), ON. *-enn*, *-inn* (Sw. *-en*), Goth. *-ans*:—prim. Germ. *-inaz*, *-anaz* (Indo-Eur. *-énos*, *-ónos*), of which some languages generalized one and some the other, the first type being represented by mutated forms in OE., eg. *cymen* (:—**kuminaz*), pa. pple. of *cuman* to COME, beside *cumen* (:—**kumanaz-*).

enabit, obs. var INHABIT.

enable (ɛ'neɪb(ə)l), *v.* Forms: 5–6 **enhable**, **-bel**, 6 **enhabile**, **inhable**, **-bile**, 6–8 **inable**, 5– **enable**. [f. EN-¹ + ABLE *a.*: cf. ABLE *v.*]

†**1.** To invest with legal status; to habilitate. **1491** *Act 7 Hen. VII*, c. 20 Preamb., It was ordeyned.. that..Lord Roos and his heires shuld be restored, enhabled and have all suche name, dignite, estate, preeminence. **1558** in Strype *Ann. Ref.* I. II. App. v. 7 Your highness shall be from henceforth enabled in blood. **1570–87** HOLINSHED *Scot. Chron.* (1806) I. 199 Constantine..was..inabled as heire apparent to the crowne. **1615** WADSWORTH in Bedell *Lett.* (1624) 11 The passions which..moued King Henrie.. to disinherite Queene Mary, and enable Queene Elizabeth. **1622** CALLIS *Stat. Sewers* (1647) 193 Neither do the goods of the Church inable the Parson. **1721** STRYPE *Eccl. Mem.* II. I. xvi. 130 She was restored and enabled in blood.

2. To authorize, sanction, empower; to give legal power or license to. Const. *to* with *inf.* **1526** *Househ. Ord.* 217 If the purveyor shall enable the Beer or Ale to be sent to the Court. **1535** *Act 27 Hen. VIII*, c. 10. §6 She shall be..inhabeled to pursue haue and demaunde her dower. **1642** MILTON *Argt. Militia* 11 The Law will inable the two Houses of Parliament to put the Kingdome into a posture of warre. **1745** in *Col. Rec. Penn.* V. 32 An 'act to enable Jeremiah Langhorn..to build a Court House in the County of Bucks'. **1824** MARSHALL *Constit. Opin.* (1839) 303 Congress cannot enable a state to legislate. **1855** MACAULAY *Hist. Eng.* III. 224 An act was.. passed enabling beneficed clergymen..to hold preferment in England.

†**3. a.** To give power to (a person); to strengthen, make adequate or proficient. *Obs.* or *arch.* **1530** PALSGR. 532/1, I enable, I make good. **1534** LD. BERNERS *Gold. Bk. M. Aurel.* (1546) E vj, Now ye can enable his fleshe in good customes. **1581** MULCASTER *Positions* xli. (1887) 232 Exercise to enable the body. **1596** SPENSER *Irel.* Wks. (1862) 523 The English Lords..greatly encouraged and inabled the Irish. **1626** T. H. *Caussin's Holy Crt.* 496 Her Father..enabled her in Philosophy, Rhetorique, Poesy, and the other Artes. **1638** O. SEDGWICKE *Serm.* 97 By diligent practise so inable your selves, that, etc. **1652** GAULE *Magastrom.* 208 The devils..have a faculty and sagacity (both much enabled by long experience in things) above us men. **1888** *Pall Mall. G.* 20 Dec. 6 Irish stew, which is said to be very enabling as well as extremely 'filling'.

b. To impart to (a person or agent) power necessary or adequate for a given object; to make competent or capable. Const. *for*, *to*, *unto*. *rare* in mod. use. *c* **1460** *Stans Puer* in *Babees Bk.* (1868) 26 First thiself enable With all thin herte to vertuous disciplyne. **1594** T. B. *La Primaud. Fr. Acad.* II. 19 Euery thing..being inhabled thereunto through a quickening vertue infused into it. **1613** *Life Will. I* in *Select. Harl. Misc.* (1793) 10 The people.. were well enabled both with courage and skill, for all military atchievements. **1646** H. LAWRENCE *Comm. Angells* 154 It was all that Alexander had to inable him to the conquest of the world. **1705** STANHOPE *Paraph.* III. 2 The great things, our Blessed Saviour hath done..are not intended to excuse his Followers from Action, but to enable them for it. **1853** RUSKIN *Stones Ven.* III. ii. §26. 50 How much of it will enable us best for our work.

c. To supply with the requisite means or opportunities to an end or for an object. Const. *to* with *inf.* **1531** ELYOT *Gov.* I. iii, Vertue and lernynge do inhabile a man..to be thought worthy. **1597** I. T. *Serm. Paules C.* 33 God hath inhabled them to doe that great and weightie worke. **1611** BIBLE *Pref.* 1 We are enabled to informe others. **1650** BAXTER *Saints' R.* I. vii. (1662) 74 They..freely send the Spirit to inable us to perform these conditions. **1742** RICHARDSON *Pamela* III. 218 A new Recruit of Spirits.. inabled me to resume my Pen. **1770** WESLEY *Serm.* lvi. Wks. 1811 IX. 2 God enabled him to awaken several young persons. **1839** THIRLWALL *Greece* V. 281 A victory which he obtained over the Thebans enabled him to recover Coronea. **1872** MORLEY *Voltaire* (1886) 51 A solitude..which enabled him to work better there.

†**4.** To regard as qualified or competent; to ascribe qualifications to. *Obs.* (Cf. *disable* in Shaks. *A.Y.L.* V. iv. 80.) **1553** T. WILSON *Rhet.* 72 Euery one enhableth his owne goodes to deserve like dignitie with the beste. **1596** NASHE *Saffron Walden* I vj, That you may..be resolv'd what those good parts are you enable the Doctor for.

5. a. To make possible or easy; also to give effectiveness to (an action). **1620** O. SEDGWICKE *Christ's Counsell* 198 Things which will much availe to helpe and inable the remembrance of truths heard and received. **1647** CLARENDON *Hist. Reb.* (1703) II. VII. 332 Needful habiliments of War to enable our Defence. **1675** SIR M. HALE *Contempl.* I. (1969) 110 What are these divine truths which really and soundly believed doth inable the victory over the world. **1892** *Daily News* 2 Feb. 3/3 It will also enable the inclusion of others. **1902** A. NUTT *Leg. Holy Grail* 27 This has been held by some scholars to enable the dating of the romance. **1963** A. HERON *Towards Quaker View of Sex* iv. 42 What God asks he enables, provided only and always that we will to do his will.

b. Esp. in *Computing*. To make (a device) operational, to turn on. **1962** *Gloss. Terms Automatic Data Processing* (*B.S.I.*) 63 *Enabling signal*, a signal which allows an operation to take place. **1972** SCHMALZ & SIPPL *Computer Gloss. for Students & Teachers* 67/2 *Enabled*, the condition of an interrupt level wherein the level is not inhibited from advancing from the waiting state to the active state, except for priority considerations. **1981** *Event* 9 Oct. 28/2 *Enable*, *vb.* (*military/computers*), to arm a weapon or to make any electronic device operable. In short, to turn on. **1983** *Tandy TRS-80 Microcomputer News* July–Aug. 9/1 Both devices must be enabled in the system. **1986** *Byte* XI. 270/2 In the 2-MH_z mode, you can only enable the 80-column screen.

†**6.** *intr.* for *refl.* To become able, gain strength or power. *Obs. rare*⁻¹. *c* **1420** *Pallad. on Husb.* IV. 834 With stamped squylle embawme..And thai wol soone enable in that jointe.

enabled (ɛ'neɪb(ə)ld), *ppl. a.* [f. ENABLE *v.* + -ED¹.] **a.** Endowed with power, strong, mighty. **b.** Legally sanctioned or authorized. **1592** A. DAY *Engl. Secret* (1625) II. 114 The..matter wherein his inabled discretion may with greatest singularity be performed. **1608** R. JOHNSON *Seven Champions Chr.*

F iij b, This enabled and famoused Knight at armes. **1729** SAVAGE *Wanderer* III. 260 To justice soon th' enabled heir appeals.

enablement (ɛˈneɪb(ə)lmənt). [f. ENABLE *v.* + -MENT.] The action or means of enabling.

1. Habilitation, removal of legal disabilities.
1495 *Act 11 Hen. VII*, c. 40. §4 This acte of enhablement and restitucion of Thomas Erle of Surrey. **1503–4** *Act 19 Hen. VII*, c. 28 §1 The restitucions and enhablementes of the seid persones. **1964** GOULD & KOLB *Dict. Soc. Sci.* 460/2 A natural right may be defined as a liberty or immunity that ought to be protected or a service or enablement that ought to be provided for all men at all times and under all conditions.

2. a. The process of rendering able, competent, or powerful; the state of being so; *concr.* something by which one is enabled, a qualification.
1617 BACON *Adv. Learn.* I. 36 Learning..hath..efficacie in inablement towards..military virtue. **1646** S. BOLTON *Arraignm. Err.* 219 Some truths may be said to be..for strength and enablement. **1647** SPRIGGE *Anglia Rediv.* I. v. 35 Watson, whose continued diligence..redounded not a little to the enablement of the army. **1656** R. ROBINSON *Christ all* 351 We haue spiritual enablement from Christ. *a* **1703** BURKITT *On N.T.* Matt. xvii. 2 Those whom God singles out for the greatest trials, he will fit beforehand with the best enablements.

b. Support, sustenance, maintenance. *rare.*
1626 T. H. *Caussin's Holy Crt.* 368 Others distributed their reuenew in equall portions to Churches, needy persons, and their owne enablement. *Ibid.* 500 So much of my Fathers goods, which was meane inough, yet for my enablement sufficient.

3. An equipment, implement. Cf. ENABLE *v.* 3.
1495 *Act 11 Hen. VII*, c. 64 Armours Defensives, as.. Crosbowes and other enhabilmentis of Werres.

enabler (ɛˈneɪblə(r)). [f. ENABLE *v.* + -ER.] One who enables.
1615 HIERON *Wks.* I. 606 It was wholly by a certaine secret enabler. **1619** W. SCLATER *Expos. 1 Thess.* (1630) 108 God, the onely enabler to so great performances. **1825** *Ann. Reg.* 210 The word Habilitador might, if there were such a word, be translated Enabler.

enabling (ɛˈneɪblɪŋ), *vbl. sb.* [f. ENABLE *v.* + -ING[1].] The action of the vb. ENABLE.
1581 SIDNEY *Apol. Poetrie* (Arb.) 29 This..enabling of iudgment. **1617** HIERON *Wks.* II. 348 To depend vpon God's inabling. **1658** *Whole Duty Man* vii. §14 By doing those things, for the enabling of us whereunto it was given us. **1860** PUSEY *Min. Proph.* 413 The prophets..espying, by God's enabling, things beyond human ken. **1888** MYERS *Chr. Living* vii. 103 All God's commands are enablings.

enabling (ɛˈneɪblɪŋ), *ppl. a.* [f. ENABLE *v.* + -ING[2].] That enables: chiefly of legislative enactments. ***enabling statute***: sometimes applied *spec.* to the act 32 Hen. VIII. c. 28, by which tenants-in-fee and certain other persons were 'enabled' to make leases. ***enabling act***, a legislative enactment enabling or empowering a person or corporation to take certain action.
1677 FELTHAM *Resolves* I. viii. 11 (ed. 10) It..wounds him, to the loss of inabling Blood. **1851** HELPS *Comp. Solit.* xii. (1874) 221 Enabling powers. **1856** F. PIERCE in *Messages & Papers of Presidents* (1896–9) V. 358 The States of California, Michigan and others were self-organized, and as such were admitted into the Union without a previous enabling act of Congress. **1873** J. H. BEADLE *Undevel. West* xix. 364 Let Congress pass an enabling act for that Territory. **1881** *Times* 17 Jan. 13/4 Mr. Crump urged that the statute was 'enabling'. **1884** *Pall Mall. G.* 7 Nov. 1/1 The enabling bill..is only a draft measure. **1965** *Listener* 20 May 745/1 This final power of approving or rejecting Assembly measures was reserved to Parliament in the Enabling Act of 1919.

†**eˈnact**, *sb. Obs.* [f. next vb.] That which is enacted, an enactment; also *fig.* a purpose, resolution.
1467 in *Eng. Gilds* (1870) 390 By the enacte of this present yelde. *Ibid.* 404 This enacte so to endure by force of this present yelde. **1588** SHAKS. *Tit. A* IV. ii. 118 The close enacts and counsels of the hart.

enact (ɛˈnækt), *v.* Also 5–7 inact. [f. EN-[1] + ACT *sb.* and *v.* Cf. Anglo-Latin *inactitāre* (1432) = sense 1 (Du Cange).]

I. (from ACT *sb.*)

†**1.** *trans.* To enter among the *acta* or public records (see ACT *sb.* 6); also, to enter in a record or chronicle. *Obs.*
1467 in *Eng. Gilds* (1870) 379 The actes of the yelde.. shullen be enacted and engrossed on a quayer of parchemyn. **1475** *Bk. Noblesse* (1860) 24 It is..enacted in divers cronicles..that..William the duke of Guien died bethout heire masle. **1568** GRAFTON *Chron.* II. 647 When these agreements were done and enacted, the King dissolved his Parliament. **1640–1** *Kirkcudbr. War-Comm. Min. Bk.* (1855) 69 We have enacted this letter and will requyer and expect ane exact accompt thairof.

2. Of a legislative authority: To make into an act (see ACT *sb.* 5); hence, to ordain, decree. Also with obj.-clause introduced by *that.* (In early examples scarcely separable from 1.)
1464 EDW. IV. in *Paston Lett.* 493 II. 165 He shall..haue the said fundacon inacted and auctorised in the parlement next holden. **1566** PAINTER *Pal. Pleas.* I. 21 The tribunes were verie instant that at length lawes might be enacted. **1596** SHAKS. *Merch. V.* IV. i. 348 It is enacted in the Lawes of Venice. **1633** G. HERBERT *Temple, Size* iii, Wouldst thou His laws of fasting disanull? Enact good cheer? **1709** STRYPE *Ann. Ref.* I. xlix. 529 It was now declared and inacted, that the said act and statute..should stand. **1710** PRIDEAUX *Orig. Tithes* i. 22 The Law of the Sabbath was enacted from the beginning. **1776** ADAM SMITH *W.N.* I. xi. 190 In 1463 it was enacted that no wheat should be imported if, etc. **1844** H. H. WILSON *Brit. India* III. 557 To..amend the laws.. enacted by the Local Legislature.
absol. **1580** LADY PEMBROKE *Ps.* xcix. (1823) God did daigne to talk with men; He enacting, they observing, From his will there was no swerving. **1642** BRIDGE *Wound. Consc. Cured* §5. 38 There is an excellent temper of the three Estates in Parliament, there being..no power of enacting in one or two of them, without the third.

b. Said of the legislative measure. (See ENACTING *ppl. a.*; cf. *ordain, provide*, etc.)
1765–74 BLACKSTONE *Comm.* II. 82 Magna carta..enacts that, etc. *Mod.* The statute enacted no new provisions.

†**c.** *nonce-use.* To secure (rights) *to* a person by enactment.
1628 BP. J. HALL in *Rem. Wks.* (1660) II. 21 God's book is the true Magna Charta that enacts both king and people their own.

†**3.** To declare officially or with authority; to appoint. ***to enact into***: to constitute. *Obs.*
1611 SPEED *Hist. Gt. Brit.* IX. xix. (1632) 944 Enacting them enemies to their naturall Country. *c* **1677** *Act Securing Prot. Relig.* in Marvell *Growth Popery* 31 The person so consecrated, shall be, and is hereby Enacted to be complete Bishop of the said vacant See. **1715** BENTLEY *Serm.* x. 362 By slow degrees Transubstantiation was enacted into an Article of Faith.

II. (from ACT *v.*)

†**4.** To work in or upon; to actuate, influence. Also, to implant, inspire (a feeling, etc.) *into* a person. *Obs.* Cf. ACT *v.* 1.
1616 W. FORDE *Serm.* 43 Nature itselfe..seemeth to have ..inacted this desire into every one. **1645** RUTHERFORD *Tryal & Tri. Faith* (1845) 304 The wind of the Spirit doth not always enact the Soul to believe. **1647** H. MORE *Song of Soul* I. II. xlv, To enact his corps and impart might Unto his languide tongue. *Ibid.* II. iii. II. i, Her phantasie Strongly inacted guides her easie pen.

5. To represent (a dramatic work, a 'scene') on or as on the stage; to personate (a character) dramatically, play (a part); also *fig.* with reference to real life; = ACT *v.* 4–7.
1430 LYDG. *Chron. Troy* Prol., For they enacted and gilt with theyr sayes Theyr high renowne. **1602** SHAKS. *Ham.* III. ii. 108 I did enact Julius Cæsar. **1828** CARLYLE *Misc.* (1857) I. 199 Through life he enacted a tragedy, and one of the deepest. **1825** DE QUINCEY *Cæsars* Wks. 1859 X. 155 Marcus Antoninus is a scholar; he enacts the philosopher. **1860** MOTLEY *Netherl.* (1868) I. i. 9 Its main scenes were long enacted there.

b. To perform (a ceremony).
1846 KEBLE *Lyra Innoc.* (1873) 114 She sees him..Dimly enact some awful rite.

†**6.** To bring into act, accomplish, perform. *Obs.*
1594 SHAKS. *Rich. III*, v. iv. 2 The king enacts more wonders then a man. **1616** R. C[ROWLEY] *Times' Whis.* III. 1155 If ther be handes that dare enact a murder.

†**7.** *intr.* To act. Cf. ACT *v.* 9. *Obs.*
1593 NASHE *Christ's T.* (1613) 68, I may be the better able to enact with my hands. **1684** CHARNOCK *Attrib. God* (1834) II. 559 They punctually enact according to their commission.

†**eˈnact**, *pple.* = *enacted*, pa. pple. of ENACT *v.*
a. Enacted, decreed. **b.** Actuated, influenced.
1643 PRYNNE *Sov. Power Parl.* II. 61 That if anything should be enact done by Counsell. **1843** E. JONES *Sens. & Event* 189 Deception sometimes is by virtue enact.

enactable (ɛˈnæktəb(ə)l), *a.* [f. ENACT *v.* + -ABLE.] That may be enacted.
1882 *Advance* (Chicago), In the State of Illinois, constitutional prohibition is neither enactable nor enforcible.

enacted (ɛˈnæktɪd), *ppl. a.* [f. as prec. + -ED[1].]

1. Ordained by legislative authority.
1579 FULKE *Heskins' Parl.* 68 It cannot be an enacted trueth, without the consent of the higher house. **1863** FR. KEMBLE *Resid. Georgia* 253 Enacted statutes on which this detestable system is built. **1869** J. MARTINEAU *Ess.* II. 64 We judge by the datum of enacted law.

2. Performed (as on the stage); also, carried out in action, performed, perpetrated.
1647 H. MORE *Song of Soul* To Rdr. 7/1, I can seem no better to them then a piece of highly inacted folly. **1813** SCOTT *Rokeby* I. ii, Conscience, anticipating time, Already rues the enacted crime.

eˈnacting, *vbl. sb.* [f. as prec. + -ING[1].] The action of the verb ENACT in various senses.
1631 WEEVER *Anc. Fun. Mon.* 83 The murmuring of his Subiects, vpon the enacting of this Statute. **1782** BURKE *Penal L. agst. Irish Catholics* Wks. VI. 279 In the enacting of which [laws] they do not directly or indirectly vote.

eˈnacting, *ppl. a.* [f. as prec. + -ING[2].] That enacts. ***enacting clauses*** (of a statute): those in which new provisions are enacted, as distinguished from those which merely contain statements of fact or declarations of the existing law.
1644 HUNTON *Vind. Treat. Monarchy* v. 39 They have an enacting Authority. **1670–1** MARVELL *Corr.* Wks. 1872–5 II. 376 A long debate for bringing in an inacting clause. **1771** *Junius Lett.* lxiii. 323 It stands in no need of a bill either enacting or declaratory. **1867** *Times* 27 Nov. 11/6 The enacting part warranted a dismissal.

enaction (ɛˈnækʃən). [f. as prec.: cf. ACTION *sb.*]
a. The action of enacting (a law); = ENACTMENT 1. **b.** *concr.* = ENACTMENT 2.
1630 J. CRAVEN *Sermon* (1631) 14 Laudable enactions; but the misery is..lamentable executions. **1645** J. GOODWIN *Innocency Triumph.* 78 Without penall enactions against those that cannot obey. **1796** MORSE *Amer. Geog.* I. 316 *note*, His endeavours to prevent the enaction of the stamp act. **1825** WATERTON *Wand. S. Amer.* IV. ii. 328 Many a vexatious enaction might be put in force. **1888** A. GUSTAFSON in *Voice* (N.Y.) 15 Mar., For the enaction of good laws we must have good law-makers.

enactive (ɛˈnæktɪv), *a.* [f. as prec. + -IVE.] Relating to or concerned with the enactment of law; = ENACTING *ppl. a.*
1658 BRAMHALL *Schism Guarded* 271 (L.) An enactive statute regardeth only what shall be. **1881** *Daily News* 28 May 3/1 They had disposed of the enactive part of the Bill.

†**eˈnactize**, *v. Obs.*[−1] Used for ENACT *v.*
a **1618** SYLVESTER *Du Bartas* (1621) 1207 Lawes of vertue to enactize [*riming with* practize (*sb.*)].

enactment (ɛˈnæktmənt). [f. ENACT *v.* + -MENT.]

1. The action of enacting (a law).
1817 EARL LIVERPOOL *Sp.* in Evans Parl. Deb. I. 586 The enactment of the present bill. **1818** COBBETT *Pol. Reg.* XXXIII. 604 The enactment of them only confirmed men in their opinion. **1825** T. JEFFERSON *Autobiog.* Wks. 1859 I. App. 113 The laws of the State, as well of British as of Colonial enactment. **1868** MILMAN *St. Paul's* viii. 169 The enactment of the Six Articles.

b. The state or fact of being enacted.
1885 *Law Times* 137/1 The draft Criminal Code..appears to be no..nearer to enactment than it was three years ago.

2. That which is enacted; an ordinance of a legislative authority, a statute.
1821 SYD. SMITH *Edin. Rev.* Wks. 1859 I. 334/2 A prison is a place where men..should be made unhappy by public lawful enactments. **1827** HALLAM *Const. Hist.* (1876) I. i. 34 Many general enactments of this reign bear the same character of servility. **1862** *Fraser's Mag.* Nov. 635 Glass manufactories were crippled by harassing enactments. **1876** GREEN *Short Hist.* v. §2 (1882) 225 A crowd of enactments for the regulation of trade.

b. *pl.* The particular provisions of a law.
1839 THIRLWALL *Greece* III. 83 We know neither the occasion which gave rise to it, nor the precise nature and extent of its enactments. **1845** MCCULLOCH *Taxation* II. x. (1852) 353 The enactments were such as might be expected to follow a preamble of this sort.

3. The acting of a part or character in a play. *rare*[−0].
In mod. Dicts.

enactor (ɛˈnæktə(r)). Also 7 enacter, ennactor. [f. as prec. + -OR; cf. ACTOR.]

1. One who enacts (a law, etc.).
1609 *Man in Moone* (1849) 27 The lawes of the Highest Enacter of all decrees. **1695** BP. PATRICK *Comm. Gen.* i. 1 The enacter of their laws. **1861** WILSON & GEIKIE *Mem. E. Forbes* i. 13 The enactors of this law.

2. One who enacts (a part, scene, ceremony, incident, or transaction).
1829 LANDOR *Imag. Conv.* (1846) II. 45 The enactors and applauders..of the first and greatest crime. **1858** J. MARTINEAU *Stud. Chr.* 37 Skilful enactor of rites.

enactory (ɛˈnæktərɪ), *a.* [f. as prec. + -ORY.] Concerned with or relating to the enactment of law.
1844 *Blackw. Mag.* LV. 226 Whether Lord Aberdeen's bill were enactory..or declaratory. **1884** A. A. PUTNAM *10 Yrs. Police Judge* xii. 83 'Laws and Resolves', enactory and re-enactory.

†**eˈnacture.** *Obs.* [f. as prec. + -URE.] ? Carrying into act, fulfilment.
1604 SHAKS. *Ham.* III. ii. 207 (*Qq.*) The violence of either grief or joy Their own enactures [*Ff.* ennactors], with themselves destroy.

†**eˈnage**, *v. Obs.* Also 6–7 inage. [f. EN-[1] + AGE; cf. OF. *enaagier* to declare (one) to be of full age.] *trans.* To make old; to give the appearance of age to.
Hence **eˈnaged** *ppl. a.*, grown old, inveterate.
1593 NASHE *Christ's T.* (1613) 68 Famine should..inage thee. **1594** *Zepheria* xvi, Disdain should thus enage thy brow! **1598** SYLVESTER *Du Bartas* II. II. i. (1605–7) I. 276 Neuer frost, nor snow, nor slipp'rie ice The Fields enag'd. **1631** *Celestina* i. 20 O inaged vertue!

enaid: see EN- *pref.*[1] 3.

†**eˈnair**, *v. Obs. rare*[−1]. [f. EN-[1] + AIR *sb.* or *v.*] *trans.* To 'air'.
1602 DAVIES *Wittes Pilgr.* N ij, Who, when she lists (with Balme-breath's Ambrosie) Shee it [her tongue] enaires in Prose or Poesy.

enaliosaur (ɛˈnælɪəʊˌsɔː(r)). [f. Gr. ἐνάλιο-ς of the sea + σαῦρος lizard.] A 'marine lizard': a designation applied to the gigantic fossil reptiles (allied to the crocodiles) forming the orders *Sauropterygia* and *Ichthyopterygia.*
1863 LYELL *Antiq. Man* xx. 403 Remains of an enaliosaur ..in the coal of Nova Scotia.

enaliosaurian (ɛ,næliəʊ'sɔːrɪən), *a.* and *sb.* [f. as prec. + -IAN.]

A. *adj.* Pertaining to or resembling the enaliosaurs.

1860 GOSSE *Rom. Nat. Hist.* 361 The possibility of the present existence of the Enaliosaurian type. **1860** *Athenæum* 22 Dec. 875 The Enaliosaurian hypothesis. **1871** HARTWIG *Subterr. W.* ii. 20 Enaliosaurian reptiles.

B. *sb.* = ENALIOSAUR.

1837 *Penny Cycl., Enaliosaurians*..fossil marine animals. **1881** GRANT ALLEN *Vignettes fr. Nat.* viii. 72 The sea swarmed with gigantic enaliosaurians.

enallage (ɛ'nælədʒiː). Also 7-8 **enallagy, enalagy.** [a. L. *enallagē*, a. Gr. ἐναλλαγή change, related to ἐναλλάσσειν to change.]

1. *Gram.* The substitution of one grammatical form for another, *e.g.* of sing. for pl., of present for past tense, etc.

1583 FULKE *Defence* 126 In the participle..is a manifest enallage or change of the gender. **1614** SELDEN *Titles Hon.* 115 Their Grammarians make it [Elohim] an Enallage of Number..to express excellencie. **1656** OWEN *Wks.* 1851 VIII. 403 There may be an enallagy of number, the nation for the nations. **1737** WATERLAND *Eucharist* (ed. 2) 373 Enallage of tenses, which is frequent in Scripture. **1832** in WEBSTER; and in mod. Dicts.

†**2.** *Rhet.* (See quot.) *Obs.*$^{-0}$

1736 BAILEY, *Enallage*, a figure whereby we change or invert the order of the terms in a discourse.

†**e'naluron.** *Her. Obs.* Also 8 **enalyron.** [perh. a. AFr. phrase **en aileron* (*en* in, by way of; *aileron* pinion, also bordering, braiding of a doublet). If the traditional explanation be correct, cf. ALERION.] A bordure charged with birds. (According to Sir G. Mackenzie and Porny the word is an adv., = '*orlé*, or in manner of a bordure', the use by English heralds from Leigh onwards being erroneous.)

1562 LEIGH *Armorie* (1597) 111 The fifth [Bordure] is called Enaluron, when it is occupied with any foule or bird. **1610** GUILLIM *Heraldry* I. v. (1660) 29 A bordure, Azure charged with Enaluron of Martlets. **1766** PORNY *Heraldry* (1787), English armorists call a Bordure Enaluron if charged with eight birds. [And in mod. Dicts.]

‖**enam** (ɪ'nɑːm). *India.* Also **enaum, inām, inaám.** [Pers. (Arab.) *inʿām*, lit. 'favour', f. *naʿama* to be happy, in 4th conj. *anʿama* to favour, bless.] A grant of land free of the land-tax due to the State as supreme landlord; also, the land so held.

1803 DK. WELLINGTON in Gurwood *Desp.* V. 361 The Rajah gave him a village in enaum. **1850** W. H. MORLEY *Anal. Digest* I. 302/1 An Inaámdár is not competent to alienate any part of his Inaám. **1858** J. B. NORTON *Topics* 240 Short-sighted sovereigns..granted away an enormous quantity of land in enam.

enamber: see EN- *prefix*[1] 1 b.

enambush: see EN- *prefix*[1] 1.

‖**e,nam'dar.** *India.* [a. Pers. *inʿāmdār*, f. *inʿām* ENAM + *dār*, stem of *dāshtan* to hold.] One who holds an ENAM; an assignee of land free of land-tax.

1850 [see ENAM]. **1858** J. B. NORTON *Topics* 52 The dispossessed enamdar..nurse[s] a sullen..vengeance against us. **1866** *Daily Tel.* 8 Feb. 4/4 What can his views be upon..ryotwarree, Enamdars, Indian taxation?

enamel (ɛ'næməl), *sb.* Forms: 5 **innamyl,** 6 **inamel(l, enamell,** 7 **enammel,** 7- **enamel.** [f. ENAMEL *v.*; the etymological senses are 'means of enamelling', 'process or result of enamelling'; the former includes the sense of AMEL *sb.*, which became obs. in 18th c.]

1. a. A semi-transparent or opaque composition of the nature of glass, applied by fusion to metallic surfaces, either to ornament them in various colours, or to form a surface for encaustic painting; also (in 19th c.) used as a lining for culinary vessels, etc.

1463 in *Bury Wills* (1850) 35 A ruby with iiij labellys of white innamyl. **1586** T. B. *La Primaud. Fr. Acad.* I. (1594) 208 All works of gold, silver, and inammell. **1662** EVELYN *Chalcogr.* (1769) 44 Silver, to fill with a certain encaustic or black enamel. **1712** tr. *Pomet's Hist. Drugs* I. 193 Being finely ground, it is used by the Goldsmiths for Enamel. **1837** DISRAELI *Venetia* I. ii. (1871) 5 Wild hyacinths..spread like patches of blue enamel. **1875** URE *Dict. Arts* I. 277 The enamel of these saucepans is quite free from lead.

b. *fig.*; formerly with notion of an additional or perfecting adornment; now chiefly with reference to the hardness and polish of enamel.

a **1680** S. CHARNOCK in Spurgeon *Treas. Dav.*, Ps. cxxxv. 13 Unchangeableness is the thread that runs through the whole web; it is the enamel of all the rest. **1678** JER. TAYLOR *Serm.* Ded., Those Truths..are the enamel and beauty of our Churches. **1825** MACAULAY *Milton, Ess.* (1851) I. 14 None of the hard and brilliant enamel of Petrarch in the style. **1858** HAWTHORNE *Fr. & It. Jrnls.* II. 35 A genuine love of painting and sculpture..formed a fine and hard enamel over their character.

c. A glassy 'bead' formed by the blowpipe.

d. In recent use applied to any composition employed to form a smooth hard coating on any surface (*e.g.* on pottery, wood, leather, paper, etc.). Cf. ENAMEL *v.* 2. Also used *attrib.*, as ***enamel paint.***

1865 M. W. BROWN *U.S. Patent 49,708* 2/2 In the use of my enamel-paint for the purposes of covering iron, steel, or other solid metallic substances..I apply a heat to the articles so covered or coated..not to exceed 300° Fahrenheit. **1895** *Montgomery Ward Catal.* 623/2 Enamel paint..for general decorative purposes. **1911** *Encycl. Brit.* XX. 458/1 The term 'enamel paint' was first given to a compound of zinc white, petrol and resin, which possessed on drying a hard glossy surface. The name is now applied to any coloured paint of this nature. **1946** M. DICKENS *Happy Prisoner* viii. 153 She had managed to buy a whole range of enamel paints.

2. *Phys.* [after Fr. *émail.*] The substance which forms the hard glossy coating of teeth; the similar substance forming the coating of the bony scales of ganoid fishes.

1718 J. CHAMBERLAYNE *Relig. Philos.* (1730) I. iii. §2 The Teeth are surrounded with a hard Substance..the Enamel. **1782** A. MONRO *Anatomy* 114 Each tooth is composed of its *cortex*, or *enamel*, and an internal bony substance. **1847** CARPENTER *Zool.* §586 Fishes of this order [Ganoidians] are covered by angular scales, composed internally of bone, and coated with enamel. **1863** *Lond. Rev.* 10 Jan. 35/2 To nations good manners are what modesty is to chastity, or enamel to the teeth. **1873** MIVART *Elem. Anat.* vii. 250 The enamel is the hardest structure in the human body and almost entirely a mineral, containing but two per cent. of animal substance.

3. An artistic work executed in enamel; an enamel-painting.

1762 H. WALPOLE *Let.* 6 June (1903) III. 95, I have not lost one enamel, nor bronze. **1861** *Sat. Rev.* 7 Sept. 253 The leather drinking-cup, helmet, and enamels, bespeak a thegn of high rank. **1863** SIR G. SCOTT *Glean. Westm. Ab.* 61 The execution of these enamels is truly exquisite. **1865** *Reader* Mar. 278/2 Henry Bone..for a single enamel..is said to have received 2,200 guineas.

4. *transf.* (*poet.* and *rhetorical*) Applied to any smooth and lustrous surface-colouring (sometimes with added notion of varied colours); *esp.* to verdure or flowers on the ground.

1600 FAIRFAX *Tasso* (J.), Down from her eyes welled the pearles round Upon the bright enamel of her face. **1665** BOYLE *Occas. Reflec.* IV. i. (1675) 169 The various and curious Enammel of the Meadows. **1814** CARY *Dante's Inf.* IV. 113 On the green enamel of the plain Were shown me the great spirits. **1847** EMERSON *Poems, Each & All* Wks. (Bohn) I. 399 The bubbles of the latest wave Fresh pearls to their enamel gave. **1864** SKEAT *Uhland's Poems* 51 Leaf's enamel, blossom's beauty.

5. *attrib.* and *Comb.*, as ***enamel-colour, -lining, -manufactory, -painting, -plate, -powder, -work***; also **enamel-kiln**, a kiln for firing porcelain that has been printed on the glaze; **enamel-painting**, the production of a picture by fusing vitrifiable colours laid on a metal surface; **enamel-paper**, paper covered with a glazed metallic coating. Also (in dental anatomy), **enamel-cell**, one of the cells of the *enamel-organ*, sometimes called collectively 'enamel-membrane'; **enamel-cuticle**, that which covers the outer surface of the enamel; **enamel-germ**, a portion of thickened epithelium, which afterwards develops into the **enamel-organ**.

1784 S. JONES *Let.* 8 Mar. in *Sel. Lett. J. Wedgwood* (1965) 288 A man that can make as good..*Enamel coulers as any man in the country. **1799** G. SMITH *Laboratory* I. 114 To prepare the flux for enamel-colours. **1774** J. WEDGWOOD *Let.* 18 Dec. (1965) 170 Mr. Rhodes must fix them with a little Borax &c in his *enamel Kiln. **1881** *Porcelain Wks. Worcester* 30 Its true character is revealed after it has passed through the enamel kiln. **1884** *Daily News* 24 July 6/3 The *enamel linings of cooking utensils used in the Royal Navy. **1754** BP. POCOCKE *Travels* (1889) II. 69 The china and *enamel manufactory at Battersea. **1878** T. BRYANT *Pract. Surg.* I. 558 Enamel developed from the *enamel organ. **1847** LD. LINDSAY *Chr. Art* I. Introd. 209 Miniature and *enamel painting. **1875** URE *Dict. Arts* II. 272 All enamel paintings are in fact, done on either copper or gold. **1855** OWEN *Skel. & Teeth* 267 The *enamel plates in the elephant's grinder. **1875** URE *Dict. Arts* II. 273 The *enamel powder is spread with a spatula. **1756-7** tr. *Keysler's Trav.* (1760) II. 6 An *enamel-work of the ancient arms of Florence. **1879** SIR G. SCOTT *Lect. Archit.* I. 312 Of enamel-work you have splendid relics in the monument of William de Valence.

enamel (ɛ'næməl), *v.* Forms: 4 **enaumayl,** (4-5 **anamal, -el, -yl,** 5 **annamal**), 4-6 **enamyl,** (5 **ennamel**), 6-8 **enamell,** 7 **en-, inammel(l,** (**enamol, inamil,** 8 **enamle**), 4- **enamel.** [ad. AFr. *enamayller, enameler* (1313 in Godef.), f. *en-* (see EN-[1]) + *amayl*, AMEL *sb.*]

1. a. *trans.* To inlay or encrust (metal) with a vitreous composition (see ENAMEL *sb.*) applied to the surface by fusion. Also *absol.*

In early use chiefly denoting the inlaying or partial covering of a metallic surface in order to ornament it by the contrast between the colour of the enamel and that of the metal; afterwards applied to the process of entirely covering metals with enamel, to form a ground for painting in vitrifiable colours, or for any ornamental or economic purpose.

c **1325** *E.E. Allit. P.* B. 1457 Brende golde..enaumaylde with azer. *c* **1400** MAUNDEV. xix. 219 Foules, alle of gold, & richely wrought & enameled. **1420** in *E.E. Wills* 41 & þe cnap of þe couercle ys an-amylyd with blewe. *a* **1440** *Sir Degrev.* 634 Anamelede with azoure. **1458** *Test. Ebor.* (1855) II. 226 Silver that is anameled. ? *c* **1475** *Sqr. lowe Degre* 746 Your chaynes enameled many a folde. **1503** *Privy Purse Eliz. of York* (1830) 96 A payre of smalle knyves inamyled for the Quenes owne use. **1634** SIR T. HERBERT *Trav.* 38 Jewels of gold inammeld and set with stones of worth. *a* **1691** BOYLE (J.), It were foolish to colour or enamel upon the glasses of telescopes. **1716-8** LADY M. W. MONTAGUE *Lett.* I. xxxii. 112 A large bouquet of jewels made like natural flowers..well set and enamelled. **1799** G. SMITH *Laboratory* I. 122 It will become fit to enamel with on gold or other metals. **1837** GORING & PRITCHARD *Microgr.* 40 A piece of dial plate enamelled black. **1872** YEATS *Tech. Hist. Comm.* 211 Kitchen utensils of tin and iron are enamelled.

b. To inlay or cover metal surfaces with (figures or ornaments of enamel); to portray with enamel.

1494 FABYAN VII. 538 And therin imagery grauen & enamelyd moste curyouslye. **1558** *Lanc. Wills* I. 88 A ring of gold wᵗʰ letters one yᵉ outside enamyled. **1756-7** tr. *Keysler's Trav.* (1760) IV. 260 A golden triangle..on which is enamelled the image of the virgin Mary.

c. *transf.* To variegate like enamelled work; to adorn or beautify (any surface) with rich and varied colours.

1650 FULLER *Pisgah* II. vi. 143 The countrey thereof was enamelled with pleasant rivers. **1653** H. COGAN tr. *Pinto's Trav.* xxxix. (1663) 156 The Lord..enamels the Firmament with stars. *c* **1750** SHENSTONE *Elegies* xxvi. 4 Spring ne'er enamell'd fairer meads than thine. **1834** PRINGLE *Afr. Sk.* ix. 298 Millions of flowers of the most brilliant hues enamel the earth. **1875** J. BENNET *Winter Medit.* II. xi. 387 In Corsica the roadside in the valleys..is enamelled with the purple Cyclamen.

†**d.** *fig.* To adorn magnificently; to impart an additional splendour to what is already beautiful; to embellish superficially.

1593 NASHE *Christ's Teares* 63 You [preachers] count it prophane to arte-enamel your speech. **1597** INGMETHORPE *Serm. 2 John* Ep. Ded., You have enameld, as it were, and embroiderd that graund benefite with infinite other kindnesses. **1599** NASHE *Lent. Stuffe* (1871) 35, I might enamel and hatch ouer this device more artificially. *a* **1631** DONNE *Serm.* x. 97 And being enameled with that beautiful Doctrine of good Workes too. **1670** EVELYN in *Phil. Trans.* V. 1057 How do such Persons enamel their Characters, and adorne their Titles with lasting and permanent honors!

2. In various extended uses (see ENAMELLED).

a. To apply a vitreous glaze by fusion to (surfaces of any kind, *e.g.* pottery).

b. To cover (any material, *e.g.* wood, paper, cardboard, leather) with a smooth polished coating resembling enamel.

1889 *Pall Mall Gaz.* 17 Oct. 1/3 The craze for enamelled furniture and enamelled nick-nacks gets worse and worse. Everybody enamels. Bachelors enamel their own furniture and rooms. **1937** *Discovery* Feb. 57/2 Enamelled kitchen stoves.

†**c.** Used by Holland as transl. of L. *inurere*: To 'burn in' the colours (applied with wax crayons) in encaustic painting. *Obs.*

1601 HOLLAND *Pliny* II. 546 As touching the feat of setting colours with wax, and enamelling with fire. *Ibid.*, And to inamel by the means of fire.

d. As a cosmetic process: To apply certain preparations to (the face) in order to impart an appearance of smoothness to the skin.

1804 M. WILMOT *Let.* 9 Apr. in *Russ. Jrnls.* (1934) 92 The fashion of their country ordains that every woman shou'd enamel their face. **1868** *N. & Q.* 68 Enamelling the face. This practice..is partly described in a fragment of Ovid.

enamellar, enamelar (ɛ'næmələ(r)), *a.* [f. ENAMEL *sb.* + -AR.] Consisting of enamel, resembling enamel; smooth, glossy.

1828 in WEBSTER. **1847** in CRAIG; and in mod. Dicts.

enamelled, enameled (ɛ'næməld), *ppl. a.* [f. ENAMEL *v.* + -ED[1].]

1. Ornamented or covered with enamel, or with a glossy coating resembling enamel. ***enamelled board***: cardboard with a glazed surface. ***enamelled leather***: a glazed leather used for boots, for parts of carriages, etc. ***enamelled photograph***: a photograph on metal or pottery, covered with a thin layer of enamel; also (in 19th c. use) a photograph on paper, overlaid with a film of gelatine.

1621 BURTON *Anat. Mel.* III. ii. III. iii. (1651) 474 Inamelled jewels on their necks. **1740** SWIFT *Will* Wks. 1745 VIII. 384 The enamelled silver plates to distinguish bottles of wine by. **1864** S. BEETON *Dict. Univ. Inform.* 712 Enamelled culinary utensils are now both cheap and common. **1879** J. J. YOUNG *Ceram. Art* 39 Walls entirely cased with enamelled tiles of deep blue.

b. *Phys.* Of teeth, etc.: Having a coating of enamel. See ENAMEL *sb.* 3.

1870 ROLLESTON *Anim. Life* Introd. 68 The enamelled scales of Ganoidei. **1872** NICHOLSON *Palæont.* 423 There are always two sets of enamelled teeth.

2. Having naturally a hard polished surface, resembling enamel.

1590 SHAKS. *Mid. N.* II. i. 255 And there the snake throwes her enammel'd skinne. **1591** —— *Two Gent.* II. vii. 28 He makes sweet musicke with th' enameld stones. **1854** WOODWARD *Mollusca* (1856) 101 Those [shells] acquire a glazed or enamelled surface, like the couries.

3. Beautified with various colours.

1613 PURCHAS *Pilgr.* I. I. v. 20 Delighting themselves in the enamelled walkes. **1633** MILTON *Arcades* 84 O'er the smooth enamelled green..Follow me. **1760** J. SCOTT *Elegy* Poet. Wks. (1786) 29 Blows not a flow'ret in th' enamel'd vale. **1860** WHYTE-MELVILLE *Holmby House* 337 The enamelled meadows..of that fairyland.

†**b.** *fig.* Ornate. *Obs.*

1604 T. WRIGHT *Passions* IV. i. 112 Inameld speakers.. condemned others as barbarous and ignorant. 1656 S. WINTER *Serm.* Ep. Ded., I have not affected enamel'd phrases.

enameller, enameler (ɛ'næmələ(r)). [f. ENAMEL *v.* + -ER.] One who enamels, or executes enamelled work.

1623 COCKERAM, An Enammeller, *Encasticke.* 1761 (*title*) The Life of Theodore Gardelle, Limner and Enameller. 1800 tr. *Lagrange's Chem.* I. 64 You may employ funnels formed at an enameller's lamp. 1861 A. B. HOPE *Eng. Cathedr. 19th C.* vii. 251 Enamellers of tiles are rising in general estimation.

enamelling, enameling (ɛ'næməlɪŋ), *vbl. sb.* Also 6 Sc. enamelyne. [f. ENAMEL *v.* + -ING[1].]

1. a. The action or process of covering or adorning with enamel. **b.** *concr.* A covering or ornamentation of enamel. Also *attrib.*

enamelling-furnace, a furnace for fusing the coating of enamel on earthenware, glass, etc. ***enamelling-lamp***, a lamp with blowpipe attached for ornamenting glass with enamel.

*c*1449 PECOCK *Repr.* 127 Thei schulden leie rather blew enameling than reed or whijt. 1550 LYNDESAY *Sqr. Meldram* 123 Wks. 1879 I. 163 Of gold [was] ane garland of her heid Decorit with enamelyne. 1652 EVELYN *Mem.* (1857) I. 286, I went to one Mark Antonio, an incomparable artist in enamelling. 1688 R. HOLME *Armoury* III. 382/1 An Enamelling point.. is for the ordering and setling Ammell.. in its place. 1729 SIR J. CLERK in *Bibl. Topogr. Brit.* III. 258 A sort of enamelling on the gold socket. *c*1760 IBBOTS in *Times* (1884) 18 Apr. 4/3 Many curiosities of bronzes, enamellings, miniatures, etc. 1822 BEWICK *Mem.* 56 The latter taught his brother.. enamelling and painting. 1868 *Times* 22 Sep. 9/4 Cosmetics, bath preparations and enamelling.

2. *fig.*

15.. LD. BURLEIGH *Advice to Q. Eliz.* in *Harl. Misc.* (1809) II. 277 A fair enamelling of a terrible danger.

attrib. 1823 MOORE *Rhymes on Road* Ext. vii. 49 The small, enamelling touch Of smooth Carlino.

enamellist (ɛ'næməlɪst). [f. ENAMEL *sb.* + -IST.] An artist in enamel.

1885 *Mag. Art* Sept. 479/2 The pale fawn-colour employed by the great enamellists of the age.

†**e'namelure.** *Obs. rare*[−1]. [f. ENAMEL *v.* + -URE.] An enamelling, covering of enamel.

*c*1430 *Pilg. Lyf Manhode* I. xcv. (1869) 51 Eche of them was enameled, and in each enamelure ther was propre scripture.

‖**enamo'rado.** *Obs.* [Sp., f. *enamorar* to ENAMOUR] = INAMORATO.

1677 SIR T. HERBERT *Trav.* 74 (T.) An enamorado neglects all other things to accomplish his delight.

†**e'namorate,** *v. Obs. rare.* [f. It. *innamorat-* ppl. stem of *innamorare* 'to enamour, to fall in loue' (Florio).] *trans.* To inspire with love.

Hence **e'namorating** *ppl. a.* Also **e,namo'ration**, ecstasy of love.

1591 PERCIVALL *Sp. Dict.*, *Enamorar*, to enamorate. 1624 HEYWOOD *Gunaik.* VI. 297 The place and object which made him first grow enamorated. *a*1711 KEN *Hymnotheo* Poet. Wks. 1721 III. 112 Still upon my Spirit stream, In sweet enamourating Beam. *Ibid. Damoret* Wks. 1721 IV. 529, I felt enamourations sweet.

†**e'namorate,** *a.* and *sb. Obs.* Also 7 enamoret, -ourite. [ad. It. *innamorato*: see prec.] **A.** *adj.* Enamoured. **B.** *sb.* A lover.

Hence **e'namorately,** *adv.*

1607 HEYWOOD *Fair Maid Exch.* i. Wks. 1874 I. 21, I am a poor enamorate. 1614 COOKE *City Gallant* in Hazl. *Dodsley* II. 289 A kind enamoret I did strive to prove. 1621 BURTON *Anat. Mel.* III. ii. III, Is this no small servitude for an enamourite to be every hour combing his head? 1599 NASHE *Lent. Stuffe* (1871) 38 A third writes passing enamorately, of the nature of white-meats.

enamorato, enamorata, obs. forms of INAMORATO, INAMORATA.

enamour (ɛ'næmə(r)), *v.* Forms: 4-5 anamo(u)r, -er, 4-9 enamor (6 ennamor), 5 enamur, 7 enamore, inamor, -our, 4- enamour. [a. OF. *enamour-er*, f. *en-* (see EN-[1]) + *amour* love (see AMOUR); equivalent formations are Pr., Sp., Pg. *enamorar*, It. *innamorare.*]

1. *trans.* To inspire or inflame with love. Chiefly pass. ***to be enamoured***: to be in love. Const. *of*, †*on*, †*upon*, *with*. Also *fig.*

1303 R. BRUNNE *Handl. Synne* 8170 A grete mayster and a syre Was anamourde so on hyre. *c*1385 CHAUCER *L.G.W.* 1606 She wex enamoured vpon this man. 1494 FABYAN VI. clxxvii. 174 Of this Lowys, it is testifyed.. that he shulde enamoure hymselfe vpon a menchon [*i.e.* nun]. 1530 PALSGR. 532/1 She hath as many craftes to enamour a foole upon her as any queene in this towne. 1549 COVERDALE *Erasm. Par. 2 Cor.* iii. 8 So is oure soule euerye daye more and more secreatelye enamoured. 1590 SHAKS. *Mids. N.* IV. i. 82 Me-thought I was enamoured of an Asse. *a*1626 W. SCLATER *Sermons Experimentall* (1638) 210 Methinks, therefore, that I might enamore you of love towards this mercy of God in Christ Jesus. 1629 DONNE *Whitsund. Serm., Gen.* i. 2 Wks. 1839 I. 58 Lord, thou hast enamoured me, made me in love. 1671 MILTON *P.R.* II. 211 Should she ..Descend with all her winning charms begirt To enamour. *c*1750 SHENSTONE *Solicitude* 5 With her mien she enamours the brave. 1801 WELLINGTON in Gurw. *Disp.* I. 336 It appears that he was much enamored of one of the Koorg Rajah's sisters. 1858 LONGF. *Epimeth.* x, Him whom thou dost once enamour. 1878 BROWNING *La Saisiaz* 32 Where that lady lives of whom enamoured was my soul.

2. In weaker sense: To charm, delight, fascinate. Chiefly *pass.* Const. *of*, †*on*, †*with.*

1590 SHAKS. *Mids. N.* III. i. 141 Mine eare is much enamored of thy note. 1647 SALTMARSH *Sparkl. Glory* (1847) 107 Those only graces that the world can..be enamoured on in God's people. 1692 SOUTH *Serm.* (1697) I. 11 Whether..Anger..Revenge..Wantonness..could have at all affected or enamour'd the mind of the same Socrates. 1742 RICHARDSON *Pamela* III. 55 Lord Davers himself is become inamour'd of your Letters. 1790 BURKE *Fr. Rev.* 83 They are so much enamoured of your fair and equal representation. 1866 DICKENS *Lett.* (1880) II. 262, I am not so much enamoured of the first and third subjects.

¶**3.** To desire passionately, fall in love with.

1854 BAILEY *Festus* (ed. 5) 445 The pining spirit Which doth enamour immortality.

enamoured (ɛ'næməd), *ppl. a.* [f. prec. vb. + -ED[1].] Full of the passion of love; in love. Also, in weaker sense, charmed, fascinated.

*a*1631 DONNE *Poems* (1650) 38 Th' inamour'd fish will stay. 1665 GLANVILL *Sceps. Sci.* xiv. 83 The enamour'd Intellect. 1669 WOODHEAD *St. Teresa* I. xxxvi. 268 This Glass was..set in our Lord himself, with such an enamoured communication of himself. 1709 STEELE *Tatler* No. 27 ¶6 Love..had that Effect on this enamour'd Man. 1814 WORDSW. *White Doe* I. 85 Where the enamoured sunny light Brightens her that was so bright. 1855 MILMAN *Lat. Chr.* (1864) V. VIII. viii. 23 The enamoured princess could not endure life without him. 1877 DOWDEN *Shaks. Prim.* vi. 82 The enamoured Venus.

Hence **e'namouredness.** *rare.*

*a*1678 WOODHEAD *Holy Living* (1688) 56 Sensual loves, or enamour'dness of any earthly person or thing. 18.. MRS. C. CLARKE *On Coriolanus* II. i. 164 Among the most intense utterances of spousal enamouredness.

enamouring (ɛ'næmərɪŋ), *ppl. a.* [f. ENAMOUR *v.* + -ING[2].] That enamours; lovely.

1667 *Decay Chr. Piety* viii. §3. 265 The..enamouring invitations he makes to us. *c*1680 BEVERIDGE *Serm.* (1729) II. 460 They enjoy..infinite and enamouring perfections. *a*1716 SOUTH *Serm.* (1717) III. 392 He..grasped at the most enamouring Proposals of Sin. 1939 *Times* 2 June 21/2 The large sinking fund..is not an enamouring feature for many trustees.

enamourite: see ENAMORATE *sb.*

enamourment (ɛ'næməmənt). [f. ENAMOUR *v.* + -MENT; cf. OF. *enamourement.*] The state of being enamoured.

*a*1711 KEN *Hymns Evang.* Poet. Wks. 1721 I. 25 Pure like the Saints Enamouraments above. 1886 J. PAYNE tr. *Boccaccio's Decameron* II. 23 The countess, beginning with her first enamourment.

[**enanation:** given in some mod. Dicts. with a reference to R. Brown *Botany* (1874) where it is a misprint for ENATION.]

enanger, enangle: see EN- *pref.*[1] 2, 1.

enanthem (ɛ'nænθəm). *Path.* [Anglicized form of next or a. G. *enanthem.*] = next.

1885 C. H. FAGGE *Princ. & Pract. Med.* I. 170 He seems to have thought that an important argument..could be based upon an analogy which he drew between the specific cutaneous eruption of a contagious fever and the lesions in this disease [*sc.* enteric fever] which affect Peyer's patches and the solitary follicles. To express this very relation, the word *enanthem* had been already coined by German writers as a correlative to the term *exanthem.* 1962 *Lancet* 12 May 997/1 This is an atypical history [of smallpox]—the rash developing on the first day of fever and illness. There was a well-marked enanthem, and between 5000 and 10,000 lesions on the skin. *Ibid.* 999/1 The enanthem varied from one or two lesions on the palate to a severe eruption all over the palate and fauces.

enanthema (ɛnæn'θiːmə). *Path.* [mod.L., ad. Gr. ἐνάνθημα eruption.] A mucosal, as opposed to a cutaneous, eruption.

1842 DUNGLISON *Dict. Med. Sci.* (ed. 3) 263/1 *Enanthema*, a name recently given to certain eruptions of the mucous membrane. 1964 *Brit. Med. Jrnl.* 25 Apr. 1121/3 How then would he describe the difference between exanthema and enanthema?

enantioblastic (ɛn,æntɪəʊ'blæstɪk), *a. Bot.* [f. Gr. ἐναντίος opposite + βλαστός (-BLAST) + -IC.] Having the radicle turned away from the micropyle. Also **e,nantio'blastous** *a.*

1858 A. GRAY *Introd. Struct. & Syst. Bot.* 531/2 *Enantioblastous*, with the embryo at the end of the (orthotropous) seed diametrically opposite the hilum, as in Tradescantia. 1878 M. T. MASTERS *Henfrey's Elem. Bot.* (ed. 3) I. ii. 157 The radicle generally points to the hilum (homoblastic), rarely away from it (enantioblastic). 1887 BENTLEY *Man. Bot.* (ed. 5) 347 We have already observed, that the radicle as a general character is turned towards the micropyle... Some apparent exceptions to these relative positions occur..when the radicle is described as enantioblastic.

enantiodromia (ɛn,æntɪəʊ'drəʊmɪə). [a. Gr. ἐναντιοδρομία running in contrary ways, f. ἐναντίος opposite + δρόμος running.] The process by which something becomes its opposite, and the subsequent interaction of the two: applied esp. to the adoption by an individual or by a community, etc., of a set of beliefs, etc., opposite to those held at an earlier stage. Hence **enantio'dromiacal, enantio'dromic** *adjs.*, resulting from enantiodromia.

1917 D. HECHT in C. E. Long tr. *Jung's Coll. Papers Anal. Psychol.* (ed. 2) xiv. 415 Heraclitus..discovered the most wonderful of all psychological laws, namely, the regulating function of antithesis. He termed this 'enantiodromia' (clashing together), by which he meant that at some time everything meets with its opposite. *Ibid.* 417 Enantiodromia is the being torn asunder into the pairs of opposites. 1923 H. G. BAYNES tr. *Jung's Psychol. Types* xi. 542, I use the term enantiodromia to describe the emergence of the unconscious opposite... A good example of enantiodromia is seen in the psychology of Saul of Tarsus and his conversion to Christianity. 1943 E. L. MASCALL *He who Is* x. 128 Islam is submission... And by that *enantiodromia*, which is so marked a feature of human activity, Mohammedanism becomes the most militant religion in history, for once the believer has made his submission he..sees himself as an instrument of the divine ruthlessness. 1946 *Brit. Jrnl. Med. Psychol.* XX. 214/1 Just as the repressions that went with the increasing dogmatism and formalism of the Middle Ages had produced the enantiodromiacal reaction of the Renaissance, so the repressions of the age of materialism and respectability produced its deadly challenge out of itself. 1953 *Times Lit. Suppl.* 25 Sept. 612/5 We are reminded also of that other—excruciatingly enantiodromic—answer..: 'Nes. Yo.' 1959 R. F. C. HALL tr. *Neumann's Archetypal World of Henry Moore* 4 The dialectal law of Heraclitus, the law of enantiodromia, according to which any given position is always superseded by its negation.

enantiomorph (ɛn'æntɪəʊmɔːf). [a. G. *enantiomorph* (C. F. Naumann *Elemente d. theoretischen Krystallogr.* (1856) II. ii. 104), f. Gr. ἐναντίος opposite + μορφή form.] A form which is related to another as an object is related to its image in a mirror; a mirror image. Also *adj.* = **enantio'morphic, -'morphous** *adjs.*; whence **-'morphously** *adv.* So **enantio'morphism, enantio'morphy**, the condition or property of being enantiomorphous, esp. in *Cryst.*

1885 A. C. BROWN in *Encycl. Brit.* XIX. 312/1 Two figures or two portions of matter are said to be enantiomorph to each other when these forms are not superposable, i.e., the one will not fit into a mould which fits the other, but the one is identical in form with the mirror image of the other. *Ibid.*, As an example of enantiomorphism we may take our two hands, which will not fit the same mould or glove, but the one of which resembles in figure the mirror image of the other. *Ibid.* 313/2 The crystallographic theory of enantiomorph crystals. *Ibid.* 314/1 We now know a considerable number of cases where..both enantiomorphs have been discovered, and many where only one has as yet been found. 1892 *Science* XX. 89/1 Optical isomers..may.. be taken as the analogues of enantiomorphous crystals, as of quartz, right-handed and left-handed; the pairs in each case being perfectly equivalent, but not superposable. 1895 STORY-MASKELYNE *Crystallogr.* vi. §150. 169 The configuration of the one tetartohedron will then correspond to that of the other as seen in a mirror. In a word, the two tetarto-symmetrical forms are enantiomorphous. 1895 *Bloxam's Chem.* (ed. 8) 600 The crystals..of the racemate differ from each other in the position of a certain unsymmetrical face; this is on the right hand in the one kind and on the left hand in the other (enantiomorphous). 1898 *Nature* 8 Sept. 454/1 Enantiomorphism is possible only in the case of asymmetric solid figures. *Ibid.* 454/2 The special one-sided asymmetry of the base will modify its mode of combination with the two enantiomorphous acids. *Ibid.* 455/1 Asymmetric agents can only display selective action in dealing with enantiomorphs. 1898 *Jrnl. Chem. Soc.* LXXIII. 608 The question of the proportion in which enantiomorphously related crystals are deposited. 1900 A. HILL *Introd. Sci.* ii. 86 The lævo-rotary crystals look like the dextro-rotary when they are seen in a looking-glass. They are reversed or enantiomorphic in the language of crystallography. 1900 J. LARMOR *Æther & Matter* 209 Enantiomorphy [of a molecule] reverses the signs of all its electrons and perverts their relative position. 1902 H. A. MIERS *Min.* 50 Two supplementary forms which are similar but not identical are said to be 'enantiomorphous'; all forms which have neither a centre nor a plane of symmetry are enantiomorphous to another form. 1929 *Times* 2 Feb. 8/3 The whole is a perfect enantiomorph (mirror image) of the coast of Holland and the Zuyder Zee. 1951 N. F. M. HENRY et al. *Interpr. X-Ray Diffraction Photogr.* I. 6/1 Enantiomorphous crystals lack all elements of symmetry which would produce a right-handed arrangement from a left-handed one, and vice versa. *Ibid.*, Enantiomorphism is an important property because of its connection with optical activity, and because of its occurrence in substances of great biological and technical importance. 1956 *Daily Tel.* 6 Feb. 6/2 Guessing the time from enantiomorphic clock faces. 1964 N. G. CLARK *Mod. Org. Chem.* iii. 30 Optical isomerism occurs whenever a molecule is not identical with its image as seen in a plane mirror; the two spatial arrangements ('object' and 'image') thereby give rise to two isomeric forms of the compound. These are known as *enantiomorphic forms, enantiomorphs* or *antimers.* 1965 *New Scientist* 5 Aug. 352/3 The melting point attributed by your correspondent to the D form [of thalidomide] referred to a compound used in the synthesis of this enantiomorph.

enantiopathic (ɛn,æntɪəʊ'pæθɪk), *a. Med.* [f. as next + -IC.] Of or pertaining to ENANTIOPATHY; that acts by causing effects contrary to those of the disease.

1830 *Edin. Rev.* L. 513 The..enantiopathic..opposes contrary to contrary. 1884 in *Syd. Soc. Lex.*

enantiopathy (ɛ,næntɪ'ɒpəθɪ). *Med.* [as if ad. Gr. *ἐναντιοπάθεια, f. ἐναντιοπαθής of contrary properties, f. ἐναντίος opposite + πάθος feeling.]

An occasional synonym of ALLOPATHY; the treatment of disease by contraries.

1852 SIR W. HAMILTON *Discussions* App. iii. C. 682 Enantiopathy, and not homœopathy, is the true medicine of minds. **1884** in *Syd. Soc. Lex.*

enantiosis (ɛ,næntɪˈəʊsɪs). *Rhet.* [mod.L., a. Gr. ἐναντίωσις, f. ἐναντιό-εσθαι to oppose, f. ἐναντίος contrary.] A figure of speech in which the opposite is meant to what is said; irony.

1657 J. SMITH *Myst. Rhet.* 118 *Enantiosis*, a figure when we speak..by a contrary. **1721–1800** BAILEY, *Enantiosis*, contrariety; a Rhetorical Figure. In mod. Dicts.

enantiotropy (ɛ,næntɪˈɒtrəpɪ). *Physical Chem.* [ad. G. *enantiotropie* (O. Lehmann *Molekularphysik* (1888) I. 119), f. Gr. ἐναντίο-ς opposite + τροπή turning.] The existence of two stable polymorphs of a substance which at a certain transition temperature are interconvertible. Hence **enantioˈtropic** *a.*

1900 *Jrnl. Chem. Soc.* LXXVIII. II. 83 Enantiotropy of Tin. **1903** H. C. JONES *Princ. Inorg. Chem.* 172 Substances which like sulphur exist in two phases of the same state of aggregation, and the two phases can be reciprocally transformed into one another by changing the temperature, are known as enantiotropic. **1904** A. FINDLAY *Phase Rule* 42. **1937** *Nature* 31 July 202/2 Barium carbonate shows an enantiotropic change at 800° from the rhombic to the hexagonal form. **1948** GLASSTONE *Physical Chem.* (ed. 2) vi. 469 Two crystalline forms of a substance are said to be enantiotropic, or to exhibit enantiotrophy, when each has a definite range of stability, and the change from one form to the other takes place at a definite temperature in *either* direction.

enantyr: see ENAUNTER.

enapt, enarbour: see EN- *prefix*[1] 2.

†**enarch** (ɛˈnɑːtʃ). *v. Obs.* Cf. INARCH. [f. EN-[1] + ARCH *sb.*; cf. OF. *enarchier.*] **a.** *trans.* To build or set in the form of an arch. **b.** To arch in or over, draw an arch over. **c.** *Her.* In *pass.* of a chevron: To have an arch within its inner angle. Hence **eˈnarched** *ppl. a.*

c **1430** LYDG. *Stor. Thebes* (E.E.T.S.) 1253 A porche bilt of square stonys ful myghtely enarched. **1562** LEIGH *Armorie* (1597) 105 b, The fielde Argent, a Cheueron enarched Sable. **1611** SPEED *Hist. Gt. Brit.* IX. xii. (1632) 705 Enarching the ayre with a spatious Rainebow. **1610** GUILLIM *Heraldry* II. vi. (1611) 57 Sometimes enarched sometimes reuersed. **1631** WEEVER *Anc. Fun. Mon.* 842 This enarched Monument.

eˈnarching *vbl. sb.*, variant of INARCHING.

1727 BRADLEY *Fam. Dict.* s.v. *Grafting*, Grafting by.. Enarching. **1872** H. MACMILLAN *True Vine* iii. 117 Grafting by enarching.

enargite (ɛˈnɑːdʒaɪt). [f. Gr. ἐναργ-ής clear (from its cleavage being apparent) + -ITE.] A black sulph-arsenide of copper, of metallic lustre.

1852 SHEPARD *Min.* 350 Enargite..massive, granular or columnar.

†**eˈnarm**, *v. Obs.* [a. OF. *enarme-r* to arm, f. *en-* in + *armer* to arm; cf. ANARMED.] = ARM *v.*

1. *trans.* To put into arms; to fit or equip with armour or weapons. Also *refl.*

c **1320** *Cast. Love* 1351 He was en-armed ful stronge. **1430** LYDG. *Chron. Troy* I. vii, The nauye..Well enarmed and rychely vitayled. **1500–20** DUNBAR *Lament Makaris* vi. Anarmit vnder [Maitland MS. enarmit baith with] helme and scheild. *c* **1565** LINDESAY (Pitscottie) *Chron. Scot.* (1728) 60 We exhort your Majesty to enarm yourself. **1584** HUDSON tr. *Du Bartas' Judith* I. 371 (1613) (D.) While shepherds they enarme vnus'd to danger. **1830** J. MAYNE *Siller Gun* 128 Dumfries, in mony a chosen band, Enarm'd appears.

b. *fig.*

c **1420** *Pallad. on Husb.* I. 623 Thei wol..his courage enarme. **1541** BECON *News out of Heaven* Wks. (1843) 46 And the better enarm himself with courageous valiance to fight against the crafty and subtile assaults of his enemy [the Devil]. **1581** ANDRESON *Serm. Paules Crosse* 61 Our wicked nature..enarmeth hautie contempt against them.

2. *transf.*

?*a* **1400** *Morte Arth.* 910 The vesare, þe aventaile, enarmede so faire. *c* **1420** *Pallad. on Husb.* I. 502 And hete eke wol thi hous enarme. **1496** *Bk. St. Albans, Fishing* 27 The carpe..is..stronge enarmyd in the mouthe.

3. *Cookery.* To lard, garnish with bacon.

c **1420** *Liber Cocorum* (1862) 29 The crane is enarmed ful wele..With larde of porke. **1494** FABYAN VII. 599 Bore hedes in castellys of golde and enarmed.

4. *Her.* To depict in various colours the arms (beak, hoofs, tusks, etc.) of a bird or beast. Also *transf.* (*nonce-use*), to describe as if heraldically the 'arms' of (a hawk).

14.. *Praise of Vere* 74 in Todd *Illust. Gower & Chauc.* 306 [His auncestry] Beryth hym [the boar] azure enarmyd with gold. **1486** *Bk. St. Albans* A vij b, To begynne at hir fete and goo vpwarde as knyghttis been harnesside and armeed, & so we shall enarme her [the hawk]. **1818** in TODD.

Hence **eˈnarmed** *ppl. a.*, furnished with armour, equipped for battle.

c **1400** *Destr. Troy* xxx. 12262 In company with knightes enarmit. **1572** KNOX *Hist. Ref.* Wks. 1846 I. 222 With the hole bandis of French men enarmed. **1582–8** *Hist. Jas. VI* (1804) 93 Requyring support of enarmit men for defence of the King's caus.

enarm, var. of INARM, to embrace.

enarme (ɛˈnɑːm). [a. OF. *enarme* buckler-strap.] The strap by which a shield or buckler was held on the arm.

1885 H. DILLON ed. *Fairholt's Costume* Gloss. s.v.

†**eˈnarme(e.** *Obs.* [f. OF. *enarmer* to arm (see ENARM *v.*); Godef. cites *masse enarmee* armed body.] = ARMY.

c **1430** LYDGATE *Bochas* (1558) I. viii. 112 She bad Barach ..that he shoulde a great enarme take. But he for drede thys iourney gan forsake. *Ibid.* III. x. 36 Thenarme of Xerxses to sustene, This woman faught lyke a fell woluesse. *Ibid.* III. xxi. 3 With him he had a full great enarmee, Chose out of Cartage in stele armed bryght.

†**eˈnarmoure.** *Sc. Obs. rare*[−1]. [f. ENARM *v.*, after *armour.*] Armour; a suit of armour.

1513 DOUGLAS *Æneis* VIII. ix. 57 Of als mony enarmouris spulȝeit clene.

†**eˈnarrable**, *a. Obs. rare.* Also 5 enarrabulle. [ad. L. *ēnārrābilis*, f. *ēnārrāre*: see next.] That may be related or told.

1623 COCKERAM II, Which may bee Declared, *Narrable, Enarrable.*

¶ Used by mistake for *innarrable* [ad. L. *innārrābilis*], that cannot be described.

1482 *Monk of Evesham* (Arb.) 47 This gold smyth..wyth an enarrabulle gestur..joyde to my leder. **1491** CAXTON *Vitas Patr.* (W. de W. 1495) I. xliv. 76 a/2 This day haue I seen thynges enarrable.

†**enarrate**, *v. Obs.* [f. L. *ēnārrāt-* ppl. stem of *ēnārrā-re*, f. *ē-* out + *nārrāre* to relate.] *trans.* To tell out clearly.

1750 tr. *Leonardus' Mirr. Stones* 41 The causes..it would be useless here to enarrate.

†**enarration.** *Obs.* Also 6 ennaration. [ad. L. *ēnārrātiōn-em*, n. of action f. *ē-nārrā-re*: see prec.]

1. An exposition, a commentary.

1563–87 FOXE *A. & M.* (1596) 48/2 Heraclitus..first began to write..ennarations upon the new testament. **1570** BILLINGSLEY *Euclid* I. xxvi. 37 As witnesseth Eudemus in his booke of Geometricall enarrations. **1609** BIBLE (Douay) *Ps.* cl. *comm.*, S. Augustin in the conclusion of his Enarrations or Sermons upon the Psalmes, explicateth a mysterie. **1647** TORSHEL *A Designe* 8 The Ancients framed their Commentaries, Enarrations, Scholies, etc.

2. A description, detailed story or narrative.

1592 tr. *Junius on Rev.* xvii. 7 There is [in the Apocalypse] ..an enarration of the beast. **1666** J. SMITH *Old Age* (1676) 68 An Anatomical Enarration of the..compounding parts of these limbs. **1678** CUDWORTH *Intell. Syst.* I. v. 802 In that enarration which is written, concerning the Rich man and Lazarus. **1717** DAVID WILKINS in Monk *Life of Bentley* (1833) II. 21 The whole discourse contained..nothing but an enarration of his performances. **1826** G. S. FABER *Difficulties of Romanism* (1853) 301 Augustine's Enarrations on the Psalms.

†**eˈnarrative.** *Obs. rare.* [f. L. *ēnārrāt-* ppl. stem of *ēnārrāre*: see ENARRATE and -IVE; cf. *narrative.*] **a.** A story, tale. **b.** An argument, reasoning.

1560 ROLLAND *Crt. Venus* I. 256 Me to perswade with wrang enarratiue Lufe to abstene. *Ibid.* 757 Thay all hard Venus enarratiue.

†**enaˈrrator.** *Obs.* [a. L. *ēnārrātor*, agent-n. f. *ēnārrā-re*: see ENARRATE.] He who proclaims or tells forth clearly.

1610 GUILLIM *Heraldry* III. xxiv. (1660) 241 Not..only a Spectator, but also a..Zealous Enarrator of his Wisdome.

enarthrodial (ɛnɑːˈθrəʊdɪəl), *a. Anat.* [f. mod.L. *enarthrōdia* (f. Gr. ἐν in + ἀρθρωδία ARTHRODIA) = ENARTHROSIS + -AL[1].] Of the nature of, or belonging to, the ball-and-socket joint.

1836–9 TODD *Cycl. Anat.* II. 884/1 A true enarthrodial or cotyloid articulation is developed. **1845** TODD & BOWMAN *Phys. Anat.* I. 71 An enarthrodial or ball-and-socket joint.

enarthrosis (ɛnɑːˈθrəʊsɪs). *Anat.* [a. Gr. ἐνάρθρωσις jointing in, f. ἔναρθρος jointed. Cf. *arthrosis.*] The jointing of the ball-like head of a bone into a socket; the ball-and-socket joint.

1634 T. JOHNSON tr. *Parey's Chirurg.* VI. xlii. (1678) 166 Enarthrosis, when the head of a bone is wholly received in the cavity of another. **1741** MONRO *Anat.* (ed. 3) 249 The superior round Head of this Bone of the Arm is articulated by Enarthrosis, with the Glenoid Cavity of the Scapula. **1816** KIRBY & SP. *Entomol.* (1828) III. xxxiv. 412 M. Latreille calls the articulation of the head in this genus Apoderus Enarthrosis. **1870** ROLLESTON *Anim. Life* 33 The ..needs of these limbless animals [Ophidia] are met by the 'ball and socket' articulation or enarthrosis of the procoelian bodies of their vertebrae.

enascent (ɪˈnæsənt), *a. rare.* [ad. L. *ēnāscent-em*, pr. pple. of *ēnāsci*, f. *ē-* out + *nāsci* to be born.] That is just coming into being. Also *fig.*

1745 WARBURTON *Occas. Refl.* II. Wks. (1811) 385 An enascent equivocation. **1791** E. DARWIN *Bot. Gard.* I. 61 The new annals of enascent time. *Ibid.* I. iv. 489 Enascent leaves expand.

†**enatant**, *a. Obs. rare*[−1]. [ad. L. *ēnatantem*, pr. pple. of *ēnatā-re* to float up, f. *ē-* out + *natāre* to swim.] Floating up, coming to the surface.

1657 TOMLINSON *Renou's Disp.* 552 Then should..the enatant bran [be] received into a sieve.

†**enaˈtation.** *Obs. rare*[−0]. [ad. L. *ēnatātiōn-em*, n. of action f. *ēnatāre* to swim out.] A swimming out, an escape by swimming.

1731–1800 in BAILEY. **1775** in ASH; and in mod. Dicts.

enate (ˈiːneɪt), *a. Phys.* [ad. L. *ēnāt-us*, pa. pple. of *ēnāsci*, f. *ē-* out + *nāsci* to be born.] That has grown out: said of the apophysis of a bone.

1666 J. SMITH *Old Age* (1676) 176 The Enate parts..or the Apophyses of the bones. **1884** in *Syd. Soc. Lex.*

enation (ɪˈneɪʃən). *Bot.* [ad. L. *ēnātiōn-em* outgrowth, f. *ēnāsci*: see prec.] (See quot.)

1842 GRAY *Struct. Bot.* vi. §3 (1880) 179 Outgrowths, mostly from the anterior or sometimes posterior face of organs = Enation.

en attendant: see EN *prep.*

†**eˈnaunter**, *conj. Obs. rare.* Also 4 enantyr. [A variant of *an, in, on aunter*, Fr. *en aventure*: see ADVENTURE *sb.* I c.] In case that; lest by chance.

c **1307** *Coer de Lion* 484 Enantyr hym tydde swylk a chaunce. **1579** SPENSER *Sheph. Cal.* Feb. 200 Anger nould let him speake to the tree, Enaunter his rage mought cooled bee. **1589** *Mar Martine* 5 For men of litrature t'endite so fast, them doth not sitte, Enaunter in them, as in thee, thair pen outrun thair witt.

en avant: see EN *prep.*

†**eˈnavigate**, *v. Obs.*[−0] [ad. L. *ēnāvigāt-* ppl. stem of *ēnāvigā-re* to sail over, f. *ē-* out + *nāvigāre* to sail.] *trans.* To sail out or over.

1623 in COCKERAM. **1847** in CRAIG; and in mod. Dicts.

Hence **enaviˈgation.**

1731–6 in BAILEY. **1775** in ASH.

en axe: see EN *prep.*

enazure: see EN- *pref.*[1] 2.

enb-, obs. spelling of EMB-.

†**enˈbaissing**, *vbl. sb. Obs.* In 4 enbaissynge, enbasshinge. [corrupt var. of *abaissing*, ABASHING.] Abashment, dismay.

c **1374** CHAUCER *Boeth.* IV. i. 109 A grete meruayle and an enbaissynge [*v.r.* enbasshinge] wiþouten ende [L. *infiniti stuporis*].

†**enˈbaned**, *pple. Obs.* [Etymology and meaning obscure: Mätzner compares Pr. *embanamen* a kind of defensive work, f. *en-* (see EN-) + *bana* horn.] ? Fortified.

c **1325** *E.E. Allit. P.* B. 1458 Couered cowpes..as casteles arayed, Enbaned vnder batelment. *c* **1340** *Gaw. & Gr. Knt.* 790 Enbaned vnder þe abataylment.

†**enˈbasted**, *pple. Obs. rare*[−1]. Of uncertain formation and meaning; the Parker Soc. editor explains '*basted*' or steeped.

a **1555** PHILPOT tr. *Curio's Def.* in *Wks.* (1842) 375 The Holy Ghost, which may not..permit the same [Scriptures] notwithstanding to be oppressed with superstition, and to be enbasted [L. *imbui*] with vain opinions.

en beau: see EN *prep.*

†**enˈbene**, *v. Cookery. Obs.* Also enbane. [? var. of EMBAIN to bathe, steep.] *trans.* ? To baste; to steep.

c **1420** *Lib. Cure Coc.* 26 Enbene hit [a capon on the spit] wele withe þy ryȝt honde. *Ibid.* 27 With ȝolkes of eyren enbene hit [þo ox tonge] ay whille þat hit rostes. *c* **1450** *Noble Bk. Cookry* (Napier) 107 Take whit bred and lay it in a disshe, and enbane it with wine. *Ibid.* 118 Enbane it with yolks of eggs.

enbewte: see EMBEAUTY.

enbibe, enbibing, obs. ff. IMBIBE, -ING.

‖**en bloc** (ɑ̃ blɒk), *adv. phr.* [Fr.] In a block, as a whole. Also *attrib.*

1861 J. S. MILL *Repr. Govt.* xvii. 312 The amount assigned to each being levied by the local assembly..and paid *en bloc* into the national treasury. **1878** L. W. M. LOCKHART *Mine is Thine* I. xii. 241 You judge all your old friends, *en bloc*, simply from your own point of view. **1888** *Contemp. Rev.* Jan. 81 We are bound to take Nature *en bloc*, with all her laws and all her cruelties, as well as her beneficences. **1900** *Westm. Gaz.* 11 July 2/2 We agree, *prima facie*, that there is every kind of objection to *en bloc* disfranchisements. **1905** *Spectator* 28 Jan. 111/1 He was all but ready to..accept the tenets of the elder Church *en bloc.* **1908** *Westm. Gaz.* 17 Nov. 5/3 This machine is the new 1909 model, the en bloc engine, four-speed gear-box, and thermo-syphon cooling denoting the only departure from standard practice. **1930** G. R. DE BEER *Embryol. & Evol.* i. 10 It is not the 'stage' which is shifted *en bloc*, but certain characters which may be peculiar to that stage. **1934** *Discovery* June 174/1 Nearby..are villages whose inhabitants in summer migrate *en bloc*,..to the islands off the coast where they spend their time fishing. **1966** *English Studies* XLVII. 65 A mere *en bloc* rendering of the phrase obscures an image.

†**enˈblow**, *v. Obs. rare.* In 4 *pa. pple.* enblowid, enblawen. [var. of INBLOW *v.*]

a. To inflate, puff up. **b.** To inspire.

1382 WYCLIF *Pref. Ep. Jerome* ix, But perauenture Tullyus is to be wenyd enblowid with the spirit of retorik. *c* **1400** *Apol. Loll.* 30 Bischopis, enblawen wiþ enuy of þe fendis temptacoun.

†**en'bord**, *v. Her. Obs.* [? f. Fr. phrase *en bord.*] = BORDURE *v.*

Hence **en'bording** *vbl. sb.* = BORDURE *sb.*

1486 *Bk. St. Albans, Her.* Bjb, A differens calde enbordyng. **1586** FERNE *Blaz. Gentrie* 154 The thirde brother had his coate Enborded. *Ibid.* 155 The fifth brother had his enbordinge chequie of two tracts.

enbrade, -braid(e, var. ff. EMBRAID. *Obs.*

[**enbreame**, a misprint for *extreame*, EXTREME; in some Dicts with definition 'sharp, powerful'.

1577 NORTHBROOKE *Dicing* (1843) 4 To..indure the operation of enbreame purges.]

†**enbreston.** *Obs. rare*⁻¹.

c **1450** *Noble Bk. Cookry* (Napier) 87 Sethe it till it be on enbreston.

en brosse, en cabochon: see EN *prep.*

enbusche, -busshe, obs. ff. of AMBUSH.

‖**en'cadré.** *Crystallog.* [a. F. *encadré*, pa. pple. of *encadrer* to frame, f. *en-* in + *cadre* a frame.] (See quot.)

1817 R. JAMESON *Char. Min.* 212 A crystal is named encadré, when it has facets which form kinds of squares around the planes of a more simple form already existing in the same species.

encænia (ɛn'siːnɪə). Also 4 **encenia, encennia**, 5 **encenye.** [a. L. *encænia*, a. Gr. (τὰ) ἐγκαίνια dedication festival, f. ἐν in + καινός new.]

†**1.** A renewal; a dedicatory festival.

138. WYCLIF *Serm.* Sel. Wks. II. 105 Encennia is as myche as newinge in our speche. **1387** TREVISA *Higden* (Rolls) IV. 119 þat halowynge [of the temple] is i-clepede Encenia.

2. The anniversary festival of the dedication of a temple or church: *esp.* (among the Jews) of the Temple at Jerusalem.

1398 TREVISA *Barth. De P.R.* IX. xxxiv. (1495) 370 Encennia is the dedicacion and halowynge of a newe temple. **1483** CAXTON *Gold. Leg.* 285/1 The fest of Encenye..was the dedycacion of the Temple. **1673** CAVE *Prim. Chr.* I. vi. 124 The Encænia of the ancient Church are annual festivals in memory of the dedication of their particular Churches. **1721–1800** BAILEY, *Encænia*, among Christians signifies the Consecration or Wake-days of Churches.

3. The annual Commemoration of founders and benefactors at Oxford University, held in June.

1691 WOOD *Ath. Oxon.* II. 474 Jeremias Wells..spoke in verse in the first Encænia at the dedication of Sheldons Theater. **1870** W. COLLINS *Man & Wife* (1871) 466 App., The Vice-Chancellor announced that if the proceedings were interrupted any more the Encænia would be abruptly closed.

encage, incage, (ɛn-, ɪn'keɪdʒ), *v.* [f. EN-¹, IN- + CAGE *sb.*; cf. Fr. *encager.*] *trans.* To confine in, or as in, a cage. Hence **en'caged**, *ppl. a.*

1593 SHAKS. *3 Hen. VI*, IV. vi. 12 Such a pleasure as incaged Birds Conceiue, When, etc. **1595** SPENSER *Sonn.* lxxiii, Doe you him..in your bosome bright..encage. *a* **1631** DONNE *Poems* (1635) 152 Bajazet encag'd, the shepheards scoffe. **1633** P. FLETCHER *Purple Isl.* II. xlii, A cave the winds encaging. **1633** EARL MANCH. *Al Mondo* (1636) 191 Like as a Bird that hath beene long encaged. **1791** BENTHAM *Panopt.* 37 Noise, the only offence by which a man thus encaged could render himself troublesome. **1812** BYRON *Ch. Har.* I. lxxxi, The generous soul..Which the stern dotard deemed he could encage. **1843** *Blackw. Mag.* LIII. 675 The Æolus [is there] to recall and encage the tempestuous elements of strife. **1854** THACKERAY *Newcomes* I. 114 The two little canary birds encaged in her window.

†**en'cagement.** *Obs. rare*⁻¹. In 7 in-. [f. prec. + -MENT.] The state of being encaged.

1620 SHELTON *Quix.* IV. xxi. 540 Your incagement, and as you imagine, inchantment, in that coop.

encalendar: modernized spelling of INCALENDAR *v.*, *Obs.*

†**en'calf**, *a. Obs. rare*⁻¹. [f. phrase *in calf*: see EN- *pref.*¹.] Of a cow: That is in calf.

1556 *Richmond. Wills* (1853) 90 To everye of the sonnes of Evan Haddocke my sonne in lawe one encalf qwye.

encallow (ɛn'kæləʊ), *sb. local.* = CALLOW *sb.* 3. Hence **encallow** *v.*

1836 *Penny Cycl.* V. 408/1 The encallow, as it is technically called, or the top-soil. **1850** E. DOBSON *Bricks & Tiles* 21 The first operation [in digging clay] is to remove the mould and top soil... In London the vegetable mould is called the encallow, and the operation of removing it, encallowing. **1884** C. T. DAVIS *Manuf. Bricks* 103.

encalm: see EN- *pref.*¹ 2.

encamp (ɛn'kæmp), *v.* Also 6–8 **incamp.** [f. EN-¹ + CAMP *sb.*²]

1. *trans.* In military sense: To form into a camp; to settle or lodge in a camp.

1568 GRAFTON *Chron.* II. 618 He encamped his armye very stronglye, both with trenches and artillery. **1588** SHAKS. *Tit. A.* V. ii. 126 Bid him encampe his Souldiers where they are. **1640** E. DACRES tr. *Machiavelli's Prince etc.* 83 It is almost impossible that an army can lye incampt before a towne for the space of a whole yeere. **1727** POPE, etc. *Art Sinking* 110 The almighty encamping his regiments. **1748** ANSON *Voy.* II. xiii. (ed. 4) 369 There were large parties of them incamped in the woods. **1863** GEO. ELIOT *Romola* (1880) I. II. xxvi. 325 The terrible soldiery were encamped in the Prato.

†**b.** *refl. Obs.*

1549 CHEKE *Hurt Sedit.* (1641) 15 Yee have..encamped your selfe in field. **1592** SHAKS. *Rom. & Jul.* II. iii. 27 Two such opposed Kings encampe them still.

c. *intr.* for *refl.*

1579 FENTON *Guicciard.* (1618) 111 The French men went to incampe in the wood of Incoronato. **1596** SHAKS. *1 Hen. IV*, IV. iv. 82 What, is the King encamp'd? **1603** KNOLLES *Hist. Turks* (1638) 171 The yong Emperor..incamped in the same place where he before lay. **1759** ROBERTSON *Hist. Scot.* I. VII. 500 The nobles encamped at St. Ninian's. **1858** KNIGHT *Pop. Hist. Eng.* IV. 394 The Earl of Feversham..encamped on this morass [Sedgmoor].

2. *transf.* (*intr.* and *pass.*) To lodge in the open in tents or other portable or improvised habitations.

1725 DE FOE *Voy. round World* (1840) 261 We followed up the stream..encamping each night. **1794** SULLIVAN *View Nat.* II. 191 De la Condamine..was encamped months on the volcanos of Peru. **1815** MOORE *Lalla R.* (1824) 170 The place where they encamped..was the first delightful spot they had come to. **1855** EMERSON *Misc.*, *Tantalus* Wks. (Bohn) III. 321 We are encamped in nature, not domesticated.

†**en'camper.** *Obs. rare.* [f. ENCAMP *v.* + -ER.] One who encamps (soldiers); a tactician.

1598 BARRET *Theor. Warres* V. iii. 152 The best Italian and Spanish encampers.

encamping (ɛn'kæmpɪŋ), *vbl. sb.* Also **incamping.** [f. ENCAMP *v.* + -ING¹.]

1. The action of the vb. ENCAMP; an encampment. Also *attrib.*

1590 SIR J. SMYTH *Disc. conc. Weapons* 48 Many encampings of armies..dislodgings, marchings. **1604** EDMONDS *Observ. Cæsar's Comm.* 85 The Romaines reckned their iourneys with their army by their incampings. **1622** BACON *Hen. VII*, 99 (R.) The French knew well enough how to make warre with the English by strong encampings. **1706** HEARNE *Collect.* (Oxf. Hist. Soc.) I. 214 A..Camp, or place of Encamping. **1859** LANG *Wand. India* 310 Our incamping ground.

†**2.** Transl. of Gr. σταθμός: The distance between one encampment and another. *Obs. rare.*

1623 BINGHAM *Xenophon* 7 The Riuer Euphrates..was about 12 encampings from thence. **1655–60** STANLEY *Hist. Philos.* (1701) 116/2 The distance of the place..being one hundred twenty two Encampings.

encampment (ɛn'kæmpmənt). Also 8 **incampment.** [f. ENCAMP *v.* + -MENT.]

1. The action of encamping; the state of being encamped.

1686 LUTTRELL *Brief Rel.* (1857) I. 381 The encampment of his majesties forces on Hounslow Heath. **1709** STEELE *Tatler* No. 60 ¶9 The whole Art of Encampment. **1750** *Phil. Trans.* XLVII. iii. 5 During our incampment in Dutch Brabant. **1774** GOLDSMITH *Grecian Hist.* I. 222 They were once more obliged to forsake culture for encampment. **1776** GIBBON *Decl. & F.* I. (R.), A square of about seven hundred yards was sufficient for the encampment of twenty thousand Romans. **1836** W. IRVING *Astoria* II. 245 Two or three days after the encampment in the valley.

2. The place where a body of troops is lodged in tents or other temporary means of shelter, with or without intrenchments; = CAMP *sb.*² 1. Also *attrib.* and *fig.*

1598 BARRET *Theor. Warres* V. ii. 150 Strong encampements, if commodities be cut off, not much available. **1713** POPE in *Guardian* No. 173 ¶8 A green encampment yonder meets the eye, And loaded citrons bearing shields and speares. **1732** LEDIARD *Sethos* II. VIII. 169 An incampment which was forming in haste. **1838** LYTTON *Leila* I. i, The immense and murmuring encampment of the Spanish foe.

b. *transf.* The temporary quarters, formed by tents, vehicles, etc., occupied by a body of nomads or men on the march, travellers, etc.; = CAMP *sb.*² 4. Also *fig.*

1725 DE FOE *Voy. round World* (1840) 64 The creek..where they had formed their encampment. **1825** *Bro. Jonathan* III. 418 Signs of a small Indian encampment. **1864** LOWELL *Fireside Trav.* 127 A lobster..So old that barnacles had spread Their white encampments o'er its head. **1884** *Harper's Mag.* Feb. 339/1 Encampments are common..along the Thames.

†**3.** A Masonic meeting. *Obs.*

1787 in *Burns' Wks.* (1856) II. 83 *note*, At a general encampment held this day, the following brethren were made Royal Arch Masons, viz.—Robert Burns, etc. **1878** WOODFORD *Kenning's Masonic Cyclop.*, *Encampment*, the name formerly given to the assemblies of Masonic Knights Templar.

encanker, encannibal: see EN- *pref.*¹ 2.

encanthis (ɛn'kænθɪs). *Med.* Also 7 **enchanthis, encanthe.** [a. Gr. ἐγκανθίς tumour in the inner corner of the eye, f. ἐν in + κανθός the corner of the eye.] 'A small red excrescence in the inner canthus of the eye, growing from the caruncula lacrymalis and semilunar fold of the conjuctiva' (*Syd. Soc. Lex.*).

1586 WALTER BAILEY *Preserv. Eye-sight* (1633) 16 Encanthis is an excrescence of the same flesh which is in the greater Cantho. **1657** *Phys. Dict.*, *Enchanthis.* **1685** COOKE *Marrow Chirurg.* (ed. 4) IV. §2 i. 193 Encanthe is an increase of the Glandule in the great corner of the Eye. **1708** in KERSEY. **1721–1800** in BAILEY. **1840** LISTON *Surgery* (ed. 2) II. 312 Encanthis is a tumour situated in the corner of the eye. **1847** in CRAIG; and in mod. Dicts.

encap: see EN- *pref.*¹ 2b.

encapsulate (ɛn'kæpsjʊleɪt), *v.* Also **in-.** [f. EN-¹, IN-² + L. *capsula* small chest or box, capsule + -ATE³.]

trans. To enclose (as) in a capsule. Also *fig.*, to summarize or isolate as if in a capsule.

1874 JONES & SIEV. *Pathol. Anat.* (ed. 2) 150 The tumours are sometimes clearly defined and incapsulated. **1876** DUHRING *Dis. Skin* 26 A membrane encapsulating the corpuscle. **1939** R. G. COLLINGWOOD *Autobiogr.* x. 113 But this secondary life is prevented from overflowing into my primary life by being what I call incapsulated, that is, existing in a context of primary or surface knowledge which keeps it in its place and prevents it from thus overflowing. *Ibid.* 114 Historical knowledge is the re-enactment of a past thought incapsulated in a context of present thoughts. **1954** D. RIESMAN in *Amer. Jrnl. Sociol.* Jan. 382/2 Institutions incapsulate them or awaken them or destroy them. **1955** M. BELOFF *Foreign Policy & Democratic Process* 50 It may simply be that the older nations of Europe have retained, incapsulated within them, sufficient relics of their predemocratic leadership to provide the necessary ballast for the democratic sails. **1958** N. R. HANSON *Patterns of Discovery* i. 27 Language can encapsulate scenes and sounds, teeth and growls, smiles and laughs. **1958** *Oxford Mag.* 20 Nov. 109/1 They are forced to work for two terms for an exam... which encapsulates that dreary anachronism, compulsory Latin. **1961** *Guardian* 22 May 5/1 May one, if need arise, be encapsulated and shot into space, but not, I beg, with members of one's family. **1962** W. NOWOTTNY *Lang. Poets Use* vii. 146 To offer such a definition is to attempt to incapsulate a number of critical trends. **1967** *Listener* 29 June 863/3 This charming little creation..encapsulates an aspect of history for all time. **1972** *Country Life* 6 Jan. 56/3 For his ministers the problem was often to incapsulate him [*sc.* William IV] or walk round him.

So **en'capsulated** *ppl. a.*, **en'capsulating** *vbl. sb.* and *ppl. a.*: applied *fig.* to certain languages in which modifying elements are inserted in the body of a word.

1868 MAX MÜLLER *Stratific. Lang.* 22 The infixing or incapsulating languages are but a variety of the affixing class. **1913** *Chambers's Jrnl.* Aug. 553/2 The cell becomes encapsulated and pointed. **1958** *Times Rev. Industry* May 70/1 The bulk of encapsulating production is pharmaceutical. **1959** *Oxford Mail* 2 Feb. 5/4 Another interesting, though less successful, experiment involves a small nude encapsulated in a large abstract design. **1959** *New Scientist* 13 Aug. 192/2 One way of encapsulating is akin to blowing bubbles.

encapsulation (ɛnkæpsjuː'leɪʃən). Also **in-.** [n. of action from prec.] The action or process of incapsulating; enclosure in a capsule. Also *fig.* (*spec.* in relation to languages).

1860 FARRAR *Orig. Lang.* viii. 172 Every subordinate clause being inserted in the main one by a species of incapsulation. **1861** T. R. JONES *Anim. Kingd.* (ed. 3) 49 The encapsulation of *Plæsconia Charon*..presented analogous phenomena. **1888** *Lancet* 30 June 1288/1 [In cancer] Encapsulation means not only the surrounding of the growth by a capsule which consists of the cellular tissue which formerly occupied the site now occupied by the tumour, but also of the blood vessels. **1934** PRIEBSCH & COLLINSON *German Lang.* viii. 344 Though German has recently turned away from such *Einschachtelung* or 'incapsulation', it still retains as a regular feature the relegation of the finite verb to the end-position of the subordinate clause. **1959** *Times Lit. Suppl.* 27 Feb. 110/3 This comes perilously near to incapsulation. **1960** *Aeroplane* XCVIII. 254/2 Encapsulation of electronic equipment is undesirable. **1960** *New Left Rev.* Nov.–Dec. 4/2 The polite encapsulation of the Liberal Press.

encapsule (ɛn'kæpsjuːl), *v. Phys.* [f. EN-¹ + CAPSULE.] *trans.* To enclose in a capsule; cf. CAPSULE 2. Hence **en'capsuled** *ppl. a.*

1877 F. ROBERTS *Handbk. Med.* (ed. 3) I. 64 It may become encapsuled by some dense tissue. **1885** W. K. PARKER *Mam. Descent* (Hunt. Lect.) ii. 52 *note*, The bones and cartilages that encapsule it.

encaptivate: see INCAPTIVATE, *Obs.*

†**encaptive** (ɛn'kæptɪv). *Obs.* Also 6–7 **incaptive.** [f. EN-¹ + CAPTIVE *a.*] To make into a captive; to captivate, enthral.

1592 NASHE *P. Penilesse* Bijb, These two Earth wormes [Greediness and Niggardize] encaptiued this beautifull substaunce [gold]. **1599** —— *Lenten Stuffe* 59 To..encaptiue him to her trenchour. **1605** DANIEL *Trag. Philotas* I. ii, More Than my incaptiv'd Fortune doth allow.

†**en'cardion.** *Bot. Obs.*⁻⁰ [a. Gr. ἐγκάρδιον the heart or core of wood.] 'Old name for the pith of vegetables' (*Syd. Soc. Lex.*).

1727–51 in CHAMBERS *Cycl.*; and in mod. Dicts.

encarn, var. of INCARN, *Obs.*

encarnadine, var. of INCARNADINE.

encarnalize (ɛn'kɑːnəlaɪz) *v.* Also 9 **incarnalize.** [f. EN- + CARNALIZE.] *trans.* To clothe in flesh and blood; *fig.* to make (an idea) palpable, to embody. Also to make carnal, fleshly, gross, or sensual. Hence **en'carnalized**, *ppl. a.*

1847 TENNYSON *Princ.* III. 298 Those monstrous males..Encarnalize their spirits. **1850** H. COLERIDGE *Poems* II. 157 So incarnalise The strong idea. **1860** ELLICOTT *Life Our Lord* ii. 42 The pagan of the East may have fabled of his

encarnalized divinities. **1876** FARRAR *Marlb. Serm.* 225 The poor, vain..intellect..is encarnalised and depraved.

encarnate, obs. form of INCARNATE.

‖**en'carpa**, *sb. pl. Arch. Obs. rare*⁻¹. [L. *encarpa*, a. Gr. ἔγκαρπα, neut. pl. of ἔγκαρπος; cf. ENCARPUS.] Festoons of fruit (as an architectural ornament).

1662 EVELYN *Sylva* (1776) 387 The Berry adorning the Intercolumniations with scarlet festoons and Encarpa. **1709** in KERSEY. **1721–1800** in BAILEY. **1775** in ASH.

†**en'carpous**, *a. Phys. Obs.*⁻⁰ [f. Gr. ἔγκαρπ-ος (see next) + -OUS.] 'Pregnant' (*Syd. Soc. Lex.*).

encarpus (ɛn'kɑːpəs). *Arch.* [ad. Gr. ἔγκαρπος containing fruit, taken as = ἔγκαρπα; see ENCARPA.] 'The festoons on a frieze; consisting of fruit, flowers, leaves, etc.' (Gwilt).

encarve: see EN- *pref.*[1] 3.

encase, incase (ɛŋ-, ɪŋ'keɪs), *v.* [f. EN-[1], IN- + CASE *sb.*[2] Cf. Fr. *encaisser.*]

1. *trans.* To put into or enclose within a case or receptacle. Also *fig.*

1727 DE FOE *Hist. Appar.* v. (1840) 45 Souls which have been encased in flesh. **1792** A. YOUNG *Trav. France* 243 Are not individuals to..incase the dead bodies, in whatever manner they please? **1823** SCOTT *Peveril* xlviii, The creature was incased [in a violoncello] and mounted on a man's shoulders! **1856** KANE *Arct. Expl.* I. xix. 240 The body was encased in a decent pine coffin. **1875** JOWETT *Plato* (ed. 2) III. 671 A little soul is encased in a large body.

2. To overlay, surround, hem in as with a case.

1633 P. FLETCHER *Purple Isl.* v. xxxiv, The glassie wall (that round encasing The moat of glasse is named from that enlacing). **1791** COWPER *Iliad* x. 348 Whose horns I will encase with gold. **1795–7** SOUTHEY *Poet. Wks.* II. 149 Green moss shines there with ice incased. **1827** M'MURTRIE *Cuvier's Anim. Kingd.* 170 The sternum..is divided by a moveable articulation into two lids, which..completely encase the animal in its shell. **1862** STANLEY *Jew. Ch.* (1877) 321 The sanctuary was..encased with buildings.

b. To clothe, cover, invest. Chiefly *humorous.*

1725 POPE *Odyss.* I. 333 In radiant Panoply his limbs incas'd. **1833** MARRYAT *P. Simple* xxxi, His legs were encased in silk stockings. **1871** BLACKIE *Four Phases* i. 13 Well encased in warm sheepskin jackets and felt shoes.

encased (ɛn'keɪst), *ppl. a.* [f. ENCASE *v.*] In phr. *encased knot*, a knot of dead wood that has not been connected by living matter with the adjacent wood but is often partly or wholly enclosed in bark.

1917 C. H. SNOW *Wood & Org. Struct. Materials* iv. 42 An encased knot is one which is surrounded wholly or in part by bark or pitch. **1931** G. A. GARRATT *Mech. Prop. Wood* ii. 55 Dead branches result in what are known as encased knots, which are, in effect, nothing more than pegs in a hole. **1968** G. TSOUMIS *Wood as Raw Material* x. 176 The knots resulting from such branches [*sc.* dead branches enclosed in living stems] and called *encased* or *loose.*

encasement (ɛn'keɪsmənt). Also **incasement.** [f. ENCASE *v.* + -MENT.] **1. a.** That which encases; receptacle, covering, sheath.

1741 MONRO *Anatomy* (ed. 3) 152, I have..described the incasement of the teeth. **1849** *Fraser's Mag.* XXXIX. 664 Gorgons and dragons..look grim from out of their stony encasement. **1856** KANE *Arct. Expl.* I. vi. 56 His..horn, from the tip to its bony encasement, four feet. **1863** SALA *Capt. Dang.* III. v. 176 Wedge after wedge [was] driven in between his Legs..and the Iron Incasement.

b. *Biol.* = EMBOÎTEMENT. (See quot.)

1879 tr. *Haeckel's Evol. Man.* I. ii. 36 Encasement..the false idea that the germs of innumerable generations previously formed and encased one in another, existed in every organism.

2. The act of encasing; the condition of being encased; *spec.* in *Bee-keeping.* Also *concr.* (see quot. 1884).

1825 *New Monthly Mag.* XVI. 598 This incasement of our feet in icy boxes was very annoying. **1884** J. HUNTER *Man. Bee-keeping* (ed. 3) 15 In the case of a strange Queen's appearance in the hive..the stranger is seized by the Workers, who gather round her and form a closely packed ball..technically called 'an encasement'. **1888** F. R. CHESHIRE *Bees* II. 431 During examination..an encasement of the queen in her own hive is commenced.

encash (ɛn'kæʃ), *v.* [f. EN-[1] + CASH *sb.*[1]: cf. Fr. *encaisser.*]

1. *trans.* To convert (drafts, bills, notes, etc.) into cash; to CASH.

1861 GOSCHEN *For. Exch.* 103 The seller of such a bill..would send his bill to be encashed. **1880** *Daily News* 17 Dec. 7/4 Messrs. Morton, Rose and Co. are prepared to Encash the Coupon, falling due 1st January next.

2. To receive or obtain in the form of cash payments; to realize.

1861 GOSCHEN *For. Exch.* 77 The silver thus encashed is to be actually shipped to England. **1879** R. H. LANG in *Macm. Mag.* Sept., The communication of the revenue encashed. **1888** *Pall Mall G.* 5 Apr. 12/1 A sum which it will take many nights to encash.

encashable (ɛn'kæʃəb(ə)l), *a.* [f. ENCASH *v.* + -ABLE.] Capable of being cashed.

1913 J. M. KEYNES *Indian Currency & Finance* iii. 42 If the Government had made its notes encashable at a great variety of centres, it would have been taking on itself the expense and responsibility [etc.]. **1927** *Daily Tel.* 7 Mar. 2 This loan bears ½ per cent. more interest than the Savings Bonds, but whereas the latter are encashable at any time without loss of capital, the price receivable for the Conversion Loan would depend on the market value when sold.

encashment (ɛn'kæʃmənt). [f. ENCASH *v.* + -MENT.] The action of encashing; *concr.* the amount of cash receipts.

1861 GOSCHEN *For. Exch.* 26 Encashment of dividends or other sources of revenue. **1882** *Standard* 23 Aug. 5/4 The *Moniteur*..publishes the encashment to the 31st of July.

encastellate, var. of INCASTELLATE, *Obs.*, to make into a fortress.

[**en'castic.** *Obs.*⁻⁰ ? Misprint for ENCAUSTIC.

1623 COCKERAM, *Encasticke*, one that can enamell.]

†**en'cauma.** *Obs.*⁻⁰ [a. Gr. ἔγκαυμα result of burning in.]

1. 'The scoria of silver' (*Syd. Soc. Lex.*).

2. A deep, foul ulceration of the cornea, followed by destruction of the eye.

1708 in KERSEY. **1847** in CRAIG; and in mod. Dicts.

3. Formerly used for the mark left by a burn, or the vesicle produced by it' (*Syd. Soc. Lex.*).

1708 in KERSEY. **1775** in ASH. **1847** in CRAIG.

†**en'cause**, *v. Obs.* Also 6 incawse. [f. EN-[1] + CAUSE *v.*] *trans.* To cause.

14.. CAXTON *Chron.* 226 The which disguysynges..encaused many myshappes. **1527** ANDREW tr. *Brunswykes Distyllacions* F. iv, Thre or foure droppes of the same water put in defe eares..incawseth heryng againe.

‖**encaustes** (ɛn'kɔːstiːz). [a. Gr. ἐγκαυστής in same sense, f. ἐγκαίειν to paint in encaustic.] A painter in encaustic.

1775 in ASH. **1850** LEITCH *Müller's Anc. Art* §310. 354 Nicias the great encaustes.

encaustic (ɛn'kɔːstɪk), *a.* and *sb.* Also 7–8 in Gr. or L. form **encausticе**, 8 **encaustica.** [ad. Gr. ἐγκαυστικός, f. ἐγκαίειν to burn in.]

A. *adj.*

1. Pertaining to, or produced by, the process of 'burning in': **a.** with reference to the ancient method of painting with wax colours, and fixing them by means of fire; also to modern processes of similar nature.

1756 *Phil. Trans.* XLIX. 654 The new encaustic painting, or painting in burnt wax. **1762–71** H. WALPOLE *Vertue's Anecd. Paint.* (1786) V. 2 The revival of encaustic painting. **1841** W. SPALDING *Italy & It. Isl.* I. 193 The processes of the ancient art, now lost..particularly the Encaustic method. **1867** A. BARRY *Sir C. Barry* vi. 184 The great fresco and encaustic pictures.

b. in wider sense, with reference to any process by which pigments are 'burnt in', *e.g.* enamelling, painting on pottery, etc. ***encaustic brick, tile***: one decorated with patterns formed with different coloured clays, inlaid in the brick or tile, and burnt with it.

1656 BLOUNT *Glossogr.*, *Encaustick* (encausticus), enameled, wrought with fire, varnished. **1781** HAYLEY *Tri. Temper* VI. 174 The..artist, whose nice toils aspire To fame eternal by encaustic fire. **1860** SMILES *Self-Help* ii. 45 The manufacture of encaustic tiles. **1879** SIR G. SCOTT *Lect. Archit.* I. 177 The splendid encaustic floor is still perfect.

2. *transf.* and *fig.*

1822 DE QUINCEY *Confess.* Wks. V. 232 Those encaustic records which in the mighty furnaces of London life had been burned into the undying memory. **1872** H. MACMILLAN *True Vine* vi. 260 The encaustic lichen on the rock.

B. *sb.*

1. [ad. Gr. ἐγκαυστικὴ τέχνη.] The art or process of encaustic painting. Chiefly applied to the ancient method of painting so called, or its mod. imitations (see A. 1 a); occasionally to enamelling, painting on pottery, etc.

1601 HOLLAND *Pliny* II. 546 The art of painting with fire (called Encaustice). **1708** KERSEY, *Encaustice* or *Encaustica*, the Art of Enamelling..with fire. **1838** B'NESS BUNSEN in Hare *Life* (1879) I. xi. 481 The method of painting in encaustic, practised by the ancients. **1844** DISRAELI *Coningsby* III. iv. 106 The walls..entirely painted in encaustic by the first artists of Germany. **1848** WORNUM *Lect. Paint. by R.A's* 221 *note*, Encaustic..practised by the later Greeks..appears to have been nothing more than burning-in with a heater (cauterium) the ordinary wax colours.

†**2.** A pigment or glaze applied by 'burning in'.

1662 EVELYN *Chalcogr.* iv. *Misc. Writ.* (1805) 277 A certain encaustic or black enamel.

encaustically (ɛn'kɔːstɪkəlɪ), *adv.* [f. ENCAUSTIC + -AL[1] + -LY[2].] In encaustic.

1857 DE QUINCEY in Page *Life* (1877) II. xviii. 139 Burnt in, encaustically painted.

†**encave**, *v. Obs. rare*⁻¹. [a. OF. *encave-r* f. *en* in + *cave* cellar.] To put into a cellar; to hide.

1604 SHAKS. *Oth.* IV. i. 82 Do but encaue your selfe.

-ence, *suffix.* [a. Fr. *-ence*, ad. L. *-entia*, forming abstr. sbs., usually of quality, rarely of action, on ppl. stems in *-ent-*, e.g. *sapient-em* knowing, *sapient-ia* knowingness, sapience; *audient-em* hearing, *audient-ia* the process of hearing, audience. As the ppl. stem had *-ent-*, *-ant-*, the derivative sbs. had *-entia* (*prūdentia*), *-antia* (*īnfantia*); but all these were levelled in OFr. to *-ance*, in words that survived in popular use, or were formed analogically on the pr. pple. in *-ant*; as *aidance*, *assistance*, *complaisance*, *contenance*, *nuisance*, *parlance*, *séance.* These were sbs. of action or process, the value with which the suffix was retained in Fr. as a living formative. But subsequently other L. words in *-ntia*, which had not survived in the living language, were readopted on the analogy of these, but with *-ence* or *-ance* according to the L. vowel, e.g. *absence*, *clémence*, *diligence*, *élégance*, *présence*, *providence*, *prudence*, *tempérance*, *violence.* These were sbs. of quality or state; all Fr. words in *-ence* are of this class. Both classes were adodpted in ME. in their actual Fr. forms and senses, which they generally still retain; but since 1500, some of those in *-ance* have been altered back to *-ence* after L. All words since adopted from or formed on L., follow L. precedent as to *-ence* or *-ance.* The result is that the modern spelling of individual words, and still more of groups of cogn. words, is uncertain and discordant; cf. assist*ance*, consist*ence*, exist*ence*, resist*ance*, subsist*ence*; attend*ance*, superintend*ence*; ascend*ant*, *-ent*, *-ancy*, *-ency*, condescend*ence*; depend*ant*, *-ent*, *-ance*, *-ence*, independ*ence*; appear*ance*, appar*ent*; pertin*ence*, appurten*ance.* In sense, words in *-nce* are partly nouns of action, as in OFr., partly of state or quality, as in L. The latter idea is more distinctly expressed by the variant *-ncy* (see -Y = *-ie*:—*-ia*) which has been formed in Eng. as a direct adaptation of L. *-ntia*; see -ENCY, -ANCY.]

‖**enceinte** (ɑ̃sɛ̃t), *sb.* [Fr.; f. on late L. type **incincta*, f. ppl. stem of *incingĕre* to gird, surround closely.] An enclosure; chiefly in *Fortification* (see quots.).

1708 KERSEY, *Enceinte*, Compass, Inclosure. **1753** CHAMBERS *Cycl. Supp.*, *Enceinte*, in fortification, the wall, or rampart, which surrounds a place, sometimes composed of bastions and curtains, either faced or lined with brick, or stone, or only made of earth. **1866** KINGSLEY *Herew.* I. i, It did not seemingly form part of the enceinte of the mediaeval castle of the Wake. **1879** *Cassell's Techn. Educ.* IV. 136/2 The 'enceinte' or 'body of the place' is the main enclosure of the fortress.

‖**enceinte** (ɑ̃sɛ̃t), *a.* Forms: 6 [insented] 6–8 enseint, 7 einsent, inseint, 8- enceinte. [Fr.; = Pr. *encinta*, Sp. (written as two words) *en cinta*, It. *incinta*:—late L. *in-cincta*, explained by Isidore (6th c.) as 'ungirt', f. *in-* negative prefix + *cincta*, pa. pple. of *cingĕre* to gird.

Others explain the word as the pa. pple. of *incingĕre* to put a girdle on, gird (the It. and Pr. forms of this verb being used for 'to render pregnant'), or as phrase (late L. **in cinctā* = *in cinctū*) in a girdle. See Diez and Scheler.]

Of women: Pregnant. †***privement enseint*** (legal AF.): see quot. 1613.

[**1599** *Will of G. Taylard* (Somerset Ho.), Yf my wife be pryvyment insented wt a manchilde.] **1602** in J. P. Rylands *Chesh. & Lanc. Fun. Certif.* (Record Soc. 1882), Agnes was priviement enseint wth a sonne. **1613** SIR H. FINCH *Law* (1636) 117 His wife priuement inseint (that is, so with childe as it is not discerned). **1723** SHEFFIELD (Dk. Buckhm.) *Wks.* (1753) II. 114 During a possibility of being left enceinte. **1766** BLACKSTONE *Comm.* II. xi. 61 Leaving his wife enseint or big with child. **1860** TANNER *Pregnancy* i. 26 Those Parisian ladies who were fortunately enceinte.

enceinteship (ɑ̃'sætʃɪp). *nonce-wd.* [f. ENCEINTE *a.* + -SHIP.] The state of being ENCEINTE.

1841 *Fraser's Mag.* XXV. 14 Another anecdote of her in her enceinteship, if such a word may be allowed.

enceladite (ɛn'sɛlədaɪt). *Min.* [f. L. *Encelad-us*, the name of one of the giants + -ITE.] 'A borotitanate of magnesia and iron, with 15 to 20 p.c. of boric acid' (Dana); = WARWICKITE.

1846 HUNT in *Amer. Jrnl. Sc.* Ser. II. II. 30, I..would propose for it the name Enceladite.

encell: see EN- *pref.*[1] 1.

encendiary, obs. form of INCENDIARY.

encennia: see ENCÆNIA.

encens(e, obs. forms of INCENSE.

encense, variant of ENSENSE *v. Obs.*

†**en'censer.** *Obs.* Also 4 enscenser, 5 encensor. [a. OF. *encensier*:—late L. Type **incensārium*, f. *incens-um* INCENSE. Hence aphetically CENSER.] A censer.

1382 WYCLIF *Ex.* xxxvii. 16 And enscensers of most clene gold. **1480** CAXTON *Ovid's Met.* XIII. xiii, Eneas..gaf to the Kynge of his jewels..a moche ryche encensor.

†**en'cent**, *v. Obs.*⁻⁰ [? Back-formation from INCENTIVE.] ? *trans.* ? To excite. Only in **en'centing** *vbl. sb.* (*rare*⁻¹).

c **1400** *Lay Folks' Mass-bk.* App. iii. 125 Deuoute sterynge þorou3 goostely encentynge of herte.

encent(i, var. ENSENT, *obs.*, to consent.

encentive, obs. var. of INCENTIVE.

encentre: see EN- *pref.*¹ 1.

‖**Encephala** (ɛn'sɛfələ), *sb. pl. Zool.* [mod.L., f. Gr. ἐν in + κεφαλή head.] A division of Mollusca, including those which have a distinct head.

1854 WOODWARD *Mollusca* (1856) 24 In the Encephala, the tongue is armed with spines.

‖**en'cephali**, *sb. pl. Obs.*—⁰ [mod.L., f. as prec.] Worms generated in the head.

1736 in BAILEY. **1775** in ASH.

encephalic (ɛnsɪ'fælɪk), *a.* [f. Gr. ἐγκέφαλ-ος the brain + -IC.] Pertaining to the brain or ENCEPHALON.

1831 R. KNOX *Cloquet's Anat.* 447 Every encephalic nerve is enveloped by an external membrane. **1865** GROTE *Plato* II. xxiii. 159 The..(encephalic) soul, located in the head. **1870** *Daily News* 1 Nov., Typhoid fever of the encephalic type.

encephalitic (ɛnsɛfə'lɪtɪk), *a. Path.* [f. next; see -IC.] Pertaining to encephalitis.

1866 A. FLINT *Princ. Med.* (1880) 717 This encephalitic softening is generally red in color.

encephalitis (ɛnsɛfə'laɪtɪs). *Path.* [f. Gr. ἐγκέφαλ-ος the brain + -ITIS.] Inflammation of the brain and its membranes. Now chiefly in sense: 'Inflammation of the substance of the brain as distinct from its membranes' (*Syd. Soc. Lex.*).

1843 SIR T. WATSON *Lect. Physic* (1871) I. 348 The disorder I am about to consider has been called encephalitis. **1866** A. FLINT *Princ. Med.* (1880) 717 The terms encephalitis and cerebritis denote inflammation of the substance of the brain. **1880** H. M. JONES in *Med. Temp. Jrnl.* July 185 One was complicated with encephalitis.

encephalitogenic (ɛn,sɛfəlaɪtəʊ'dʒɛnɪk, ɛn,kɛf-), *a.* Also occas. **encephalogenic.** [f. ENCEPHALIT(IS + -O + -GENIC *suffix.*] Producing or able to produce encephalitis.

1923 *Jrnl. Amer. Med. Assoc.* 24 Nov. 1788/2 Levaditi distinguishes the two kinds of active materials or viruses contained in the naso-pharyngeal secretions as 'salivary keratogenic' and 'salivary encephalogenic', according as they resemble..the herpes virus or..the encephalitis virus. **1925** *Jrnl. Exp. Med.* XLI. 215 (*heading*) An exotic strain of encephalitogenic virus. **1940** VAN ROOYEN & RHODES *Virus Dis. Man* lx. 841 Beans, corn, and other substances were alleged to be acted on by bacteria and in this way an encephalitogenic agent produced. **1958** *Immunology* I. 111 Encephalitogenic bacillary fractions produce histological reactions at the injection site.

encephalization (ɛn,sɛfəlaɪ'zeɪʃən). [f. Gr. ἐγκέφαλ-ος brain + -IZATION.] **1.** An evolutionary increase in the complexity or relative size of the brain; a shift of function from non-cortical parts of the brain to the cortex.

1938 J. F. FULTON *Physiol. Nerv. Syst.* p. viii, Owing to greater encephalization, experimental evidence drawn from the primates is more immediately applicable to the human being than that drawn from studies of other mammals. **1940** C. S. SHERRINGTON *Man on his Nature* 310 What is called 'encephalization' is an evolutionary change which is strikingly exemplified in ourselves. It is a shifting of the function in the brain from older and more primitive to newer and more complex parts. **1972** *Science* 19 May 804/1 A major trend in Cenozoic primate evolution has been the progressive neocortical encephalization. **1976** *Sci. Amer.* Jan. 95/2 The step from reptiles to mammals required a certain amount of encephalization (approximately a fourfold increase in relative brain size to transform a reptilian polygon into an archaic mammalian polygon).

2. Special Comb.: **encephalization quotient**, the ratio of the actual size of the brain of an animal to the size that would be expected from the size in other animals, allowing for differences in body weight.

1970 H. J. JERISON in *Science* 11 Dec. 1224/2 We may now define our measure of relative brain size as the *encephalization quotient EQ$_i$ for species *i*, the ratio of its brain size E_i to the expected brain E_e in a living mammal of the same body size P_i. **1975** *Nature* 24 Apr. 687/2 Using Holloway's estimates of endocranial volumes (442 cm³ for *A. africanus* and 530 cm³ for *A. robustus*), the encephalisation quotient is 4.0 for *A. africanus* and 4.0 for *A. robustus*. **1981** *Sci. Amer.* Feb. 95/2 Overall, the encephalization quotient of the pterosaur—the ratio of the volume or weight of its brain to that of the brain of an earthbound reptile of the same size—was relatively large.

encephalo- (ɛn'sɛfələʊ, ɛn'kɛfələʊ), comb. form of Gr. ἐγκέφαλος brain, as in **encephalogram** (ɛn'sɛfələʊgræm, ɛn'kɛf-), an X-ray photograph of the brain; **encephalograph** (ɛn'sɛfələʊgrɑːf, -æf, ɛn'kɛf-), (*a*) = *encephalogram*; (*b*) an instrument for recording the electrical activity of the brain, *electro-encephalograph*; **encepha'lography** [ad. G. *encephalographie* (A. Bingel 1921, in *Fortschr. auf d. Gebiete d. Röntgenstrahlen* XXVIII. 205)], the radiological examination of the brain (see quot. 1955); hence **encephalo'graphic** *a.*; **en'cephalolith**, a concretion in the brain (Billings); **encepha'lology**, a description of the brain; the science of the brain; **en,cephaloma'lacia**, softening of the brain; **en,cephalome'ningocele**, protrusion through a fissure in the skull of brain-substance with the attached membranes; **en,cephalomye'litis**, inflammation of both the brain and the spinal cord; any of various virus diseases characterized by fever and lack of co-ordination and damage to the central nervous system.

1928 *Bull. N.Y. Acad. Med.* IV. 828 (*title*) Case report illustrating the early diagnostic significance of the encephalogram. **1959** B. WOOTTON *Social Sci. & Social Path.* x. 306 The possibility that the encephalograms are themselves affected by experience deserves at least to be considered. **1934** WEBSTER, Encephalograph. **1955** *Oxf. Jun. Encycl.* XI. 307/1 The 'encephalograph', a device which records electrical effects of the activity of the brain. **1922** *Jrnl. Amer. Med. Assoc.* LXXVIII. 622/2 Bingel discusses his..technic for encephalography or the roentgenographic representation of the brain. *Ibid.*, He reported 100 cases in which encephalographic data had been secured. **1955** *Gloss. Terms Radiology* (*B.S.I.*) 21 *Encephalography*, the radiological examination of the ventricles and subarachnoid space following the injection of air by cisternal or lumbar puncture. **1962** *Lancet* 8 Dec. 1205/1 The electroencephalogram shows that the cerebral cortex has been extensively destroyed, and this can readily be confirmed by air encephalography. **1824** (*title*) Encephalology, or a very brief Sketch of Dr. Hirnschadel's Ologies of the Cranion and Phren perfected by the Rationals. **1842** DUNGLISON *Med. Lex.* (ed. 3) 263/2 *Encephalomalacia*, mollities cerebri. **1863** D. MACLACHLAN *Pract. Treat. Dis. Advanced Life* viii. 172 (*heading*) Encephalomalacia, necrencephalus, ramollissement cérébral, or softening of the brain. **1912** ADAMI & MCCRAE *Path.* 487 The result of such embolism is encephalomalacia. **1900** *Index Catal. Libr. Surgeon-General's Off., U.S. Army* 2nd Ser. V. 1/2 Encephalomeningocele, *See* Brain (*Hernia of*). **1905** *T. H. Green's Path.* (ed. 10) 11 They [*sc.* pouches in the cranium] may contain brain-substance (*encephalocele*), or brain-substance and fluid (*encephalomeningocele*). **1908** *Jrnl. Nerv. & Ment. Dis.* XXXV. 388 (*title*) A case of probable encephalomyelitis. **1939** *Ann. Reg. 1938* 376 Man is susceptible to equine encephalomyelitis. **1963** GREENFIELD & NORMAN in W. Blackwood *Greenfield's Neuropath.* (ed. 2) viii. 475 Encephalomyelitis as a sequel to acute infectious disease, especially smallpox..and measles.., has been known for two centuries. **1966** WRIGHT & SYMMERS *Systemic Path.* II. xxxiv. 1197 Rabies is essentially an acute encephalomyelitis.

encephalocele (ɛn'sɛfələʊ,siːl). *Med.* [f. Gr. ἐγκέφαλο-ς the brain + κήλη tumour.] 'Protrusion of a portion of the brain through a preternatural opening in the skull' (*Syd. Soc. Lex.*).

1835–6 TODD *Cycl. Anat.* I. 744/1 That malformation termed encephalocele. **1878** T. BRYANT *Pract. Surg.* I. 239 In the true encephalocele, the brain itself is pressed out of the skull into the external tumour.

encephaloid (ɛn'sɛfəlɔɪd), *a. Path.* [a. Fr. *encéphaloïde* (Laennec) f. Gr. ἐγκέφαλ-ος the brain + -OID.] That resembles the brain or brain-structure; the distinctive epithet of soft cancer (sarcoma).

1846 W. H. WALSHE *Cancer* 8. **1872** PEASLEE *Ovar. Tumours* 20 The encephaloid variety is more common than the scirrhous.

encephalon (ɛn'sɛfələn). *Anat.* [a. Gr. (τὸ) ἐγκέφαλον what is within the head.] What is within the skull; the brain.

1741 MONRO *Anat. Nerves* (ed. 3) 14 The Cortex of the *Encephalon*. **1802** *Med. Jrnl.* VIII. 98 The meninges of the encephalon, as well as the brain itself, were in a state of high inflammation. **1881** MIVART *Cat* 259 The..Encephalon, is that enlarged part of the nervous centres which is contained within the cranium.

encephalopathy (ɛnsɛfə'lɒpəθɪ). *Path.* [f. Gr. ἐγκέφαλο-ς brain + -πάθεια, f. πάθος suffering.] Disease of the brain in general. Hence **encephalo'pathic** *a.*, pertaining to encephalopathy.

1866 A. FLINT *Princ. Med.* (1880) 767 Saturnine Encephalopathy. **1876** tr. *Wagner's Gen. Pathol.* 585 Polyuria had occurred in consequence of violent encephalopathies. **1866** A. FLINT *Princ. Med.* (1880) 767 Other manifestations of lead-poisoning..may..precede the encephalopathic attack.

‖**encephalos** (ɛn'sɛfələs). *rare.* [a. Gr. ἐγκέφαλος the brain.] = ENCEPHALON.

1708 KERSEY, *Encephalos*, whatever is contained within the Scull. **1836–7** SIR W. HAMILTON *Metaph.* I. App. 411 The female encephalos is considerably smaller than that of the male.

encephalous (ɛn'sɛfələs). *a. Zool.* [f. ENCEPHAL-A + -OUS.] Of molluscs: Possessing a distinct head; belonging to the ENCEPHALA.

1851 RICHARDSON *Geol.* viii. 229 The encephalous orders possess organs of sense. **1875** BLAKE *Zool.* 243 Encephalous molluscs, with locomotive and prehensile organs.

encerche, var. of ENSEARCH, *v. Obs.*

†**en'certain**, *v. Obs. rare.* [f. EN-¹ + CERTAIN *a.*] *trans.* To certify, inform.

c **1530** LD. BERNERS *Arthur* (1814) 515 At laste she was encertayned that, etc.

encertin, *Sc.* var. of INCERTAIN *a.* (*adv.*) *Obs.* uncertain, without purpose.

†**en'ceur.** *Obs.* [a. obs. Fr. *encueur*, *encœur* (? f. phrase *en cœur* in the heart).] A disease of the chest affecting horses and oxen.

1616 SURFL. & MARKH. *Countr. Farme* 139 The Enceur doth bring present death to horses.

ench, obs. var. of INCH.

enchace, obs. form of ENCHASE.

enchafe (ɛn'tʃeɪf), *v. Obs.* or *arch.* Forms: 4 **enchaufye**, 4–7 **enchauf(e**, 4– **enchafe**; also 7 **inchafe.** [ME. *enchaufe*, an alteration of *eschaufe*, ACHAFE.]

1. *trans.* To make hot or warm. Also *fig.* to excite, irritate.

c **1374** CHAUCER *Boeth.* III. iv. 73 As fire..ne stinteþ nat to enchaufen [*Camb. MS.* eschaufen] and to ben hote. **1375** BARBOUR *Bruce* II. 395 The gude, at enchaufyt war Off Ire. **1470–85** MALORY *Arthur* XVIII. xv, Syr Lauayne was ryden to playe hym to enchauffe his hors. *c* **1534** tr. *Pol. Verg. Eng. Hist.* (1846) I. 43 The legates of Rome being enchafed with such woords. **1601** HOLLAND *Pliny* I. 225 Hee alone after this maner inchafeth himselfe, and giues an edge vnto his anger. *Ibid.* XVIII. xxx, The Frument..soone catcheth a heat, and is quickly enchaufed. **1611** SHAKS. *Cymb.* IV. ii. 174 They are as rough (Their Royall blood enchaf'd) as the rud'st winde. **1812** H. & J. SMITH *Rej. Addr.* 86 Thy embryo form..The dark enlightens, and enchafes the cold.

2. *intr.* To grow hot. Also *fig.*

c **1380** *Sir Ferumb.* 2256 He louaþ þat fyr; let hym enchaufe ynne. **1382** WYCLIF *Job* vi. 17 As thei enchaufe, thei shul be losid fro ther place.

en'chafed, *ppl. a.* [f. ENCHAFE *v.* + -ED¹.] Furious, excited, irritated. Also *fig.*

1604 SHAKS. *Oth.* II. i. 16, I neuer did like mollestation view On the enchafed flood. **1801** JOANNA BAILLIE *Met. Leg. W. Wallace.* lxxx, Like th' enchafed lion bound.

enchain (ɛn'tʃeɪn), *v.* Forms: 4 **encheinen**, 5–7 **enchayn**, 7 **encheine**, 6–8 **inchain**, 7 **inchayn**, 6– **enchain.** [a. OF. *enchaine-r*, f. *en-* (see EN-¹) + *chaine* CHAIN *sb.*]

1. *trans.* To put in or bind with chains; to chain up, fetter.

1491 CAXTON *Vitas Patr.* (W. de W. 1495) I. xxx. 26 b/2 Some men broughte to hym a chylde enchayned. **1603** KNOLLES *Hist. Turks* (1621) 1331 Putting into their [Christian slaves] places the Turkes which had inchained them. **1756** NUGENT *Gr. Tour* France IV. 73 The statue of Lewis XIV..with four slaves enchained, denotes his victories.

†**b.** To surround or hem in as with a chain.

1581 STYWARD *Mart. Discip.* II. 129 The Turke..doth inchaine and fortifie the Campe.

2. *fig.* **a.** To 'fetter', restrain; to impede the free or natural action of.

1751 JOHNSON *Rambl.* No. 159 ¶5 Bashfulness..may flush the cheek..and enchain the tongue. **1838–9** HALLAM *Hist. Lit.* IV. IV. vii. §57 He was never enchained by rules. **1880** MAZZINI *Royalty & Repub.* 187 Do not enchain one of its [the intellect's] faculties.

b. To hold fast, rivet (the attention); to bind, attach (the emotions) closely to an object. Hence with personal obj. See ENCHAINING *ppl. a.*

1658 T. WALL *God's Rev. Enemies Ch.* 17 Great affection ..believes a possibility of that to the liking of which it is enchained. **1844** A. WELBY *Poems* (1867) 46 Thy song enchained a thousand hearts. **1851** C. BRONTË in Mrs. Gaskell *Life* (1857) II. 236 Rachel's acting..enchained me with interest, and thrilled me with horror. **1863** BURTON *Bk. Hunter* 48 In a noble library the visitor is enchained to reverence and courtesy by the genius of the place.

†**c.** *intr.* for *refl.* To become closely united. *Obs.*

c **1400** *Test. Love* II. (1560) 285/2 Dignitie with honour, and reverence, causen harts to encheinen.

†**3.** To link together as in a chain. *Obs.*

1642 HOWELL *For. Trav.* (1869) 33 One contracts and enchaines his words. **1768** BP. WARBURTON *Lett. Eminent Divine* (1809) 422 The parts of the argument are so enchained with one another that, etc.

Hence **en'chained** *ppl. a.*

1654 R. CODRINGTON tr. *Hist. Ivstine* 297 He..filled not, as his Father, the prisons with enchained Citizens.

‖**enchaînement** (ɑ̃ʃɛːnmɑ̃). *Ballet.* Also **enchainement.** [Fr.] A connected series or sequence of steps.

1830 R. BARTON tr. *C. Blasis' Code of Terpsichore* II. vii. 85 Previous to the commencement of a pirouette, either from the inside or outside, the dancer may pause in any sort of attitude or arabesque in which he pleases to end his enchaînement. **1934** A. HASKELL *Balletomania* iii. 67 Dancing is so subtle that six *ballerinas* will perform the same *enchainement* in an almost identical manner, and yet create an entirely different impression. *Ibid.* xi. 229 Some Maryinsky teacher, who has a rich repertoire of *enchaînements.* **1936** —— *Prelude to Ballet* iii. 19 Any competent dancer can arrange a small dance..by drawing upon various *enchainements* (combinations of steps) with which she is familiar. **1948** *Ballet Ann.* II. 69 The student's ..ability to assimilate new steps and new *enchaînements.*

enchaining (ɛn'tʃeɪnɪŋ), *ppl. a.* [f. ENCHAIN *v.* + -ING².] That enchains.

†**1.** Forming a chain or linked series. *fig. Obs.*

1658 R. WHITE tr. *Digby's Powd. Symp.* (1660) 143 These ..causes are so enchaining one within the other.

2. That holds or rivets the attention.
1823 *Sismondi's Lit. Europe* (1846) I. ii. 55 Scarcely a volume..contains passages breathing a more enchaining eloquence. **1866** J. MARTINEAU *Ess.* I. 64 The most enchaining and irresistible is James Mill.

enchainment (ɛnˈtʃeɪnmənt). [f. ENCHAIN *v.* + -MENT.] The action of enchaining; the state of being enchained.
1750 WARBURTON *Julian* II. iii. Wks. (1811) VIII. 132 A connection and enchainment of one fact to another. **1849** MISS MULOCK *Ogilvies* xxxix. (1875) 298 Passing enchainments of sense or fancy. **1855** *Ess. Intuit. Morals* 101 The doctrine of the necessary enchainment of action with action.

†**enˈchaip,** *v. Sc. Obs. rare.*⁻¹ [= **encheap*, f. EN-¹ + CHEAP *sb.* or *vb.*] *intr.* or *absol.* To 'do a trade'.
c **1475** *Rauf Coilȝear* 318 Quhair ony Coilȝear may enchaip I trow till encheif.

enchair: see EN- *pref.*¹ 1.

†**enˈchance,** *sb. Obs. rare*⁻¹. In 5 **enchaunce.** [as if OF. **encheance* f. *encheoir* to happen: see EN-¹ and CHANCE.] = CHANCE.
1432-50 tr. *Higden* (Rolls) I. 151 Enchaunce movenge [L. *agitante sorte*].

†**enˈchance,** *v. Obs. rare.* In 5 **enchaunse.** [? f. EN-¹ + CHANCE *sb.*] *trans.* ? To adventure. (But prob. a mere mistake for *enhaunsest*: see ENHANCE.)
1483 CAXTON *Cato* C v, Thou takest on the and enchaunsest thyself for to doo hygh and excellent promesses.

†**enˈchant,** *sb. Obs. rare*⁻¹. [f. next vb.] Magic, enchantment.
1634 *Malory's Arthur* (1816) I. 120 By the damsel's enchant [1470–85 enchauntement], the sword Excalibur fell out of sir Accolon's hand.

enchant (ɛnˈtʃɑːnt, -æ-), *v.* Forms: 4 **enchaunten,** 4–6 **enchaunt,** 6–8 **incha(u)nt,** 4– **enchant.** [a. F. *enchante-r*:—L. *incantāre*, f. *in-* upon, against + *cantāre* to sing; cf. CHANT *v.*, INCANTATION.]
1. *trans.* To exert magical influence upon; to bewitch, lay under a spell. Also, to endow with magical powers or properties. Also *fig.*
1377 LANGL. *P. Pl.* B. xx. 376 The frere with his phisik this folke hath enchaunted. **1393** GOWER *Conf.* III. 137 With word the serpent is enchaunted. *c* **1440** *York Myst.* xxxiii. 288 He enchaunted & charmed oure knyghtis. **1578** T. N. tr. *Conq. W. India* 122 The Indians thought that the Spaniardes were inchaunted. *a* **1619** DANIEL in Farr *S.P. Eliz.* (1845) II. 399 T' inchant your fame to last so long a while. **1635** PAGITT *Christianography* (1646) I. 235 Thus had the Popes by this time learnt to inchant these words of holy scripture, to make them serve for a cloake of disobedience. **1642** FULLER *Holy & Prof. St.* v. xiv. 411 Cockering mothers inchant their sonnes to make them rod-free. **1741** RICHARDSON *Pamela* I. 55 This little Slut has the Power of Witchcraft..she inchants all that come near her. **1772** PENNANT *Tours Scotl.* (1774) 232 Both these amulets have been enchanted. **1818** JAS. MILL *Brit. India* I. II. vii. 321 The murdered individual had enchanted them.
absol. **1610** SHAKS. *Temp.* Epil. 13 Now I want Spirits to enforce: Art to inchant.
†**2.** *fig.* To influence irresistibly or powerfully, as if by a charm; to hold spellbound; in bad sense, to delude, befool. *Obs.*
c **1374** CHAUCER *Troylus* IV. 1395, I shal hym so enchaunten with my sawes. *c* **1380** *Sir Ferumb.* 4187 Þan was Char[lis] enchanted so With Þees traytour, and othre mo. **1523** LD. BERNERS *Froiss.* I. xlvi. 63 To forsake the kyng of Englande, who had enchaunted them. **1591** SHAKS. *1 Hen. VI*, III. iii. 40 Speake Pucell, and enchaunt him with thy words. **1678** CUDWORTH *Intell. Syst.* I. ii. 69 Philosophers, and Theologers enchanting mens Understandings.
†**b.** To attract, win over, compel or induce, as if by magic (to do something). *Obs.* (cf. INCENTIVE).
1393 LANGL. *P. Pl.* C. XVIII. 288 Eueriche busshope.. sholde fere hem [his people] fro synne..And enchaunte hem to charite. **1577** HOLINSHED *Chron.* III. 1106/1 Vnlearned men may be inchanted to thinke and iudge those that be things indifferent..to be great treasons. **1597** SHAKS. *Lover's Compl.* 128 He..sexes both enchanted To dwell with him in thought.
3. To charm, delight, enrapture.
Originally with conscious metaphor as in 2; now employed more freely, after the mod.Fr. use of *enchanter*.
1592 SHAKS. *Ven. & Ad.* 145 Bid me discourse, I will enchant thine ear. **1672** DRYDEN *Assignation* II. iii, This time I will absolutely inchant 'em. **1713** STEELE *Guardian* No. 22 ¶1 Our eyes inchanted with flowery meadows. **1831** LYTTON *Godolph.* 13 Godolphin was enchanted at this proposal. **1872** MORLEY *Voltaire* (1886) 68 Voltaire is enchanted to hear that his niece reads..Locke.

enˈchanted, *ppl. a.* [f. ENCHANT *v.* + -ED.¹]
1. Invested with magical powers or properties. Also *fig.*
1596 SPENSER *F.Q.* IV. vi. 26 The same which..in that enchaunted glasse she saw. **1610** SHAKS. *Temp.* V. i. 112 Where thou bee'st he or no, Or some inchanted triffle to abuse me. **1671** MILTON *Samson* 932, I know..thy fair enchanted cup. **1815** MOORE *Lalla R.* (1824) 330 So powerfully on every soul That new, enchanted measure stole. **1877** W. JONES *Finger-ring L.* 113 The enchanted rings of the Greeks.
2. Bewitched, laid under a spell.
1710 STEELE & ADDISON *Tatler* No. 254 ¶1 All is Enchanted Ground, and Fairy Land. **1769** *Junius Lett.* xx. 96 The enchanted castles of ministerial magic. **1810** SCOTT *Lady of L.* I. xxvi, On Heaven and on thy lady call, And enter the enchanted hall!
†**b.** Deluded, captivated as by magic. *Obs.*
1617 HIERON *Wks.* (1619–20) II. 220 His owne inchaunted and beguiled heart.
3. Delighted, charmed, enraptured.
1593 SHAKS. *Lucr.* 83 Therefore that praise which Collatine doth owe Enchanted Tarquin answers with surmise In silent wonder of still-gazing eyes. **1846** KEBLE *Lyra Innoc.* (1873) 208 Drink the loved cadence with enchanted ear.

enchanter (ɛnˈtʃɑːntə(r), -æ-). Forms: 4 **enchantour, -eor, enchauntur, -or,** (**enchauntonour**), 4–5 **enchauntour,** 4–6 **-ter,** 5 **-eure,** 6 **inchaunter,** 6–7 **inchanter,** 3– **enchanter.** [f. ENCHANT *v.* + -ER; but the ME. forms in *-ur, -or, -our*, etc., are formally a. OF. *enchanteor* :—L. *incantātōrem.*]
1. One who enchants, uses magic (see ENCHANT *v.* 1); formerly also, a 'conjuror', one who practises sleight of hand.
1297 R. GLOUC. (1724) 28 Þe kyng Baþulf..gret enchanter was. *c* **1305** *St. Lucy* in *E.E.P.* (1862) 104 Myne enchantours bynyme schulle þi wicchinge. *c* **1386** CHAUCER *Pers. T.* ¶615 Fflatereres been the deueles Enchauntours. **1398** TREVISA *Barth. De P.R.* XVI. xl. (1495) 566 This stone Eliotrop dyscerneth the foly of enchauntours. *c* **1430** *Pilg. Life Manhode* II. cxxii. (1869) 121 If evere thou seye an enchantour pleye with an hat, how he maketh the folk to wene there be somewhat under. *c* **1450** *Merlin* vii. 113 Now hath the enchauntor well spoken. **1541** ELYOT *Image Gov.* 7 Using the counsayle of witches and inchaunters, he made his sacrifice with young children. **1598** HAKLUYT *Voy.* I. 56 He must pay a great summe of money to the inchanter to be purified. **1634** MILTON *Comus* 645 By this means I knew the foul enchanter. **1727** DE FOE *Syst. Magic* I. ii. (1840) 58 Whether..we consider the Magicians to be philosophers, or ..enchanters and conjurers. **1875** JOWETT *Plato* (ed. 2) I. 215 The art of the enchanter is a mode of charming snakes and spiders.
b. *transf.* A 'charmer', bewitching woman.
a **1704** T. BROWN *Beauties* (1730) I. 42 With sure success each fair enchanter set Toyles for my heart.
2. enchanter's nightshade, *Circæa lutetiana.*
1597 GERARD *Herbal* II. lix. 280 Inchaunters Nightshade hath leaues like vnto Petimorell. **1775** ASH, *Enchanters-nightshade.* The name of a plant, the circæa. **1861** MISS PRATT *Flower. Pl.* II. 290 Order *Onagrariæ. Circæa Lutetiana* (common Enchanter's Night-shade).

†**enˈchantery.** *Obs. rare.* Also 3 **enchaunterye,** 6 **inchauntry.** [a. OF. *enchanterie*, f. *enchanteor* : see prec.] Magic, enchantment.
1297 R. GLOUC. (1724) 148 Ac þer was som enchantery þer to, ich vnderstonde. **1591** SPARRY tr. *Cattam's Geomancie* 37 The Arte of diuination and inchauntry.

†**enˈchanting,** *vbl. sb. Obs.* [f. ENCHANT *v.* + -ING¹.] The action of the vb. ENCHANT.
1553 T. WILSON *Rhet.* (1567) 95 a, I maie call it rather an enchaunting then a murther. **1571** CAMPION *Hist. Irel.* II. v. (1633) 85 Whom the Bishop ascited to purge the same of inchaunting and Witch-craft.

enchanting (ɛnˈtʃɑːntɪŋ, -æ-), *ppl. a.* [f. ENCHANT *v.* + -ING².]
1. That enchants or lays under a spell.
1555 EDEN *Decades W. Ind.* (Arb.) 53 Stoppe thyne eares from..the inchauntynge mermaydes. **1590** GREENE *Fr. Bacon* (1861) 172 The enchanting forces of the devil. **1626** G. SANDYS *Ovid's Met.* VII. 135 On Pelias..she hung a deathlike sleepe with her inchanting tongue.
2. Charming, delightful, enrapturing.
1606 SHAKS. *Ant. & Cl.* I. ii. 132, I must from this enchanting Queene breake off. **1667** MILTON *P.L.* x. 355 Sin, his faire inchanting Daughter, thus the silence broke. **1718** LADY M. W. MONTAGUE *Lett.* II. xlviii. 50 It has an enchanting effect. **1872** MORLEY *Voltaire* (1886) 120 No spectrum analysis can decompose for us that enchanting ray.

enchantingly (ɛnˈtʃɑːntɪŋlɪ, -æ-), *adv.* [f. prec. + -LY².] In an enchanting manner.
1600 SHAKS. *A.Y.L.* I. i. 174 Hee's..of all sorts enchantingly beloued. **1748** SMOLLETT *Rod. Rand.* lvi. (1804) 403 Why are you so enchantingly good? **1766** C. ANSTEY *Bath Guide* xiii. 110 This Place is enchantingly pretty. **1804** MOORE *Poet. Wks.* I. 369 Blessed and bright are thy rays O'er the brow of creation enchantingly thrown.

enchantingness (ɛnˈtʃɑːntɪŋnɪs, -æ-). *nonce-wd.* [f. ENCHANTING + -NESS.] The quality of being enchanting.
1879 G. MEREDITH *Egoist* II. iv. 82 Clara's enchantingness ..assured him she was worth winning.

enchantment (ɛnˈtʃɑːntmənt, -æ-). Forms: 4–7 **enchaunt(e)ment,** 5–8 **inchaunt(e)ment,** 3– **enchantment.** [a. OF. *enchantement*, f. *enchanter* to ENCHANT: see -MENT.]
1. The action or process of enchanting, or of employing magic or sorcery.
1297 R. GLOUC. (1724) 10 A clerk þoru enchantement hym bi gan to telle. *c* **1386** CHAUCER *Knts. T.* 1943 Thenchauntementz of Medea and Circes. *c* **1400** MAUNDEV. iv. (1839) 25 It is made be Enchauntement. **1470–85** MALORY *Arthur* IV. x, By the damoysels enchauntement the swerd..felle oute of Accolons hande. **1526** TINDALE *Rev.* xviii. 23 With thyne inchantment were deceaved all nacions. **1651** HOBBES *Leviath.* III. xxxvii. 236 There is no place of Scripture, that telleth us what an Enchantment is. **1710** STEELE *Tatler* No. 9 ¶2, I saw his great Coach..by a strange Inchantment turned into many different Vehicles. **1828** SCOTT *F.M. Perth* xxxiv, That he was under the influence of enchantment, was a solution which superstition had suggested. **1841** W. SPALDING *Italy & It. Isl.* II. 79 Poetical fables have placed Charlemagne in a world of heroism and enchantment.
2. *fig.* Alluring or overpowering charm; enraptured condition; (delusive) appearance of beauty.
1678 BUTLER *Hud.* III. I. 1179 Th' inchantment of her Riches. *a* **1704** T. BROWN *Praise Drunk.* Poet. Wks. 1730 I. 32 The soft enchantment of the vine. **1799** CAMPBELL *Pleas. Hope* I. 7 'Tis distance lends enchantment to the view. **1823** LAMB *Elia* I. xviii. (1865) 137 Is there not..some of the child's heart left, to respond to its earliest enchantments. **1870** EMERSON *Soc. & Solit., Farming* Wks. (Bohn) III. 60 There is a great deal of enchantment in a chestnut rail. **1872** MORLEY *Voltaire* (1886) 3 The delight of enchantment among ideas of grace and beauty.

enchantress (ɛnˈtʃɑːntrɪs, -æ-). Forms: 4–6 **enchaunteresse,** 6 **enchanteresse,** 6–8 **inchantresse,** 8– **enchantress.** [a. OF. *enchanteresse*, fem. of *enchantere*, *-eor* ENCHANTER.] A female enchanter.
1. A female who employs magic; a witch, sorceress. Also *fig.*
c **1374** CHAUCER *Boeth.* IV. iv. 123 O feble and lyȝt is þe hand of Circes þe enchaunteresse. **1480** CAXTON *Ovid's Met.* XII. xii, Broteon and..Orion wer sones of Mycale the enchaunteresse. **1598** GRAFTON *Chron.* II. 538 A develish Witch, and a fanaticall Enchaunteresse. **1614** RALEIGH *Hist. World* II. 299 Endor, famous by reason of the Inchantresse. **1641** MILTON *Ch. Govt.* II. iii. (1851) 157 The fucus which these inchantresses..have laid upon the features..of Truth. **1725** POPE *Odyss.* x. 162 The soft Enchantress dame..to whom the powers belong Of dreadful magic. **1794** G. ADAMS *Nat. & Exp. Philos.* II. xxi. 389 Philosophy becomes a vain babbler, and Religion a superstitious enchantress. **1815** MOORE *Lalla R.* (1824) 414 The Enchantress now begins her spell.
2. *fig.* A charming or bewitching woman.
1713 C'TESS WINCHELSEA *Misc. Poems* 194 There shalt thou meet Of soft Enchantresses th' Enchantments sweet. **1866–8** MISS BRADDON *Lady's Mile* i. 3 The girl he loved was the most capricious little enchantress.

†**enˈcharge,** *sb. Obs.* [a. OF. *encharge*, f. *encharger*: see next.] An injunction.
1595 COPLEY *Wits* (Nares), His trumpetter..refus'd this encharge and push'd the nobleman himselfe forward.

encharge (ɛnˈtʃɑːdʒ), *v.* Also in-. [a. OF. *encharger*, f. *en-* (see EN-¹) + *charge* CHARGE *sb.*]
†**1.** *trans.* To impose as a charge or duty; to command, enjoin (an action); to give (a thing) in charge. Const. *to*, or dat. of the person. *Obs.*
c **1374** CHAUCER *Boeth.* V. vi. 178 Grete necessite of prowesse and vertue is encharged and comaunded to ȝow yif ȝe nil nat dissimulen. **1598** BARRET *Theor. Warres* II. i. 17 So shall he accomplish what is encharged and commanded him. *Ibid.* 20 The Ensigne..the Captaine..deliuereth..vnto his Ensigne-bearer, encharging him the custodie and defence thereof. **1656** FINETT *For. Ambass.* 54 It was beforehand incharged to me to put them from that hope. **1828** LAMB *Lett.* in C. & Mrs. C. Clarke *Recoll. Writers* (1878) 160 Mrs. Hazlitt to whom I encharged it.
†**2.** To enjoin or commission (a person) *to* do something. *Obs.*
c **1535** DEWES *Introd. Fr.* in *Palsgr.* 897 The whiche hath me commanded and encharged to reduce and to put by writtyng the maner. **1598** GRENEWEY *Tacitus' Ann.* I. xiv. (1622) 26 He encharged the Germanes to breake in. **1670** G. H. *Hist. Cardinals* II. I. 130, I have encharged Monsignor Burlemont..to wait upon you. **1681** P. RYCAUT *Critick* 199 It had [been] better he had encharged us not to suffer, etc.
3. To burden, entrust, commission *with*.
1640 BP. HALL *Episc.* III. i. 220 Encharging them with the flocke over which Christ hath made them Bishops. **1671** *True Non-conf.* 161 It is a..necessary thing, that the more.. gifted, be peculiarly incharged with the inspection of the Clergie. **1750** BEAWES *Lex Mercat.* (1752) 6 The magistracy it encharged with their execution. **1868** R. QUICK *Ess. Educ. Ref.* iv. 68 A man..who found himself encharged with the bringing up of a young nobleman.

enchariot: see EN- *pref.*¹ 1.

enˈcharm, *v.* Also 7 **incharm.** [a. OF. *encharme-r*, f. *en* in + *charme* CHARM *sb.*¹] *trans.* To throw a charm or spell over; to enchant.
1480 CAXTON *Ovid's Met.* XIV. i, She..encharmed them [the herbes] with sorrowful and hevy charmes. **1497** BP. ALCOCK *Mons Perfect.* B iij, This wylde beste must be encharmed wᵗ yᵉ scripture of god. **1611** SPEED *Hist. Gt. Brit.* VII. iv. 206 Rowena..saluted the King with a cup of gold full of sweet Wine, incharming it with these words. **1890** M. W. HUNGERFORD *Life's Remorse* I. xv. 200 Such a knowledge of horseflesh as should encharm the soul of any Irishman. **1905** W. HOLMAN HUNT *Pre-Raphaelitism* I. xiii. 358 [Christ].. encharming the simple by His love and lovableness.

encharnel: see EN- *pref.*¹ 2.

†**enˈcharter,** *v. Obs. rare*⁻¹. [ad. OF. *enchartrer*, f. *en* in + *chartre*:—L. *carcer-em* prison.] *trans.* To incarcerate.
1483 CAXTON *G. de la Tour* H ij b, Whiche comforted and vysyted the poure enchartered and emprysoned.

†**enˈchase,** *sb. Obs. rare*⁻¹. In 5 **enchace.** [f. ENCHASE *v.*¹] Chase; hunting.
1486 *Bk. St. Albans* e. j I shall yow tell which be beestys of enchace.

†**en'chase**, *v.*[1] *Obs.* Also 4–5 **enchace**, 5 **enchasse**. [a. OF. *enchacier*, f. *en-* (see EN-[1]) + *chacier* (see CHASE, CATCH): cf. It. *incacciare* to drive.]

trans. To drive away, banish; to hunt, pursue. *c* **1380** *Sir Ferumb.* 2906 To the Galwis-warde..þay enchacede þan baroun. **14..** *Tundale's Vis., Purific. Marie* 128 And then all fylth from hur to enchase. **1430** LYDG. *Chron. Troy* I. vi, Aurora..Is wonte t' enchase the blacke skyes doune. **1480** CAXTON *Chron. Eng.* v. (1520) 43/2 The folke of Saxon..you have dryven and enchased. **1491** Act 7 *Hen. VII.* c. 20 §6 The distres so take to lead dryve enchace and bere awey, etc. **1583** STANYHURST *Æneis* I. (Arb.) 30, Swans twelue in coompany flushing..enchast with a murtherus eagle. **1741** T. ROBINSON *Gavelkind* II. viii. 263 He may lawfully enchase and drive them out.

enchase (ɛn'tʃeɪs), *v.*[2] Forms: 6–8 **enchace**, 6–9 **inchase**, 7 **inchace**, 5– **enchase**. [In senses 1–3, 6 clearly a. F. *enchâsser* to enshrine (sacred relics), enclose, set (gems), encase; f. *en* in + *châsse* shrine, casket, case, setting:—L. *capsa* CASE *sb.*[2] Whether senses 4–5 belong to the same word appears doubtful; they may naturally have been developed from 3, but in our quotations 4 appears as the earliest recorded sense, both of this word and of CHASE *v.*[2] which is supposed to be an aphetic form of it.]

I. With the idea of ornamentation.

1. To 'set' as a jewel *in* (gold or other setting); also, of the enchasing material (quots. *fig.* only), to serve as a setting for.

1534 LD. BERNERS *Gold. Bk. M. Aurel.* (1546) Q, A man being a diamond enchaced among men, yet..quicke and mery amonge women. **1660** JER. TAYLOR *Worthy Commun.* I. v. 98 Because the Sacrament is not without the word, they are a jewel enchas'd in gold when they are together. **1831** BREWSTER *Nat. Magic* vii. 159 A speaking head..of the sage Minos, which he had enchased in gold. **1877** W. JONES *Finger-ring L.* 246 A gold ring with a ruby enchased. *fig.* **1590** SPENSER *F.Q.* I. xii. 23 My ragged rimes are all too rude and bace Her heavenly lineaments for to enchace. **1607** CHAPMAN *Bussy D'Ambois* Plays 1873 II. 9 Thou hast ..Glosse enough T'enchase in all shew, thy long smothered spirit. **1761** H. WALPOLE in *Four C. Eng. Lett.* 268 Gray has translated two noble incantations..They are to be enchased in a history of English bards. **1765** GRAY *Lett.* in *Poems* (1775) 314 Four small lakes..whose deep blue waters.. contrasted with the black desert in which they were inchased. **1867** SWINBURNE in *Fortn. Rev.* Oct. 420 Interludes..known..to many ignorant of their original setting, in which they are now again enchased.

2. To set (gold, etc.) *with* gems.

1615 G. SANDYS *Rel. Journ.* I. 75 The ornament of her head..of beaten gold, and inchaced with gems. **1690** *Songs Costume* (1849) 196 In box of beaten gold..Inchas'd with diamonds. *a* **1882** LONGF. *Morit. Salutamus* 199 Golden cups enchased with rubies.

b. *transf.* and *fig.*

1589 GREENE *Menaphon* (Arb.) 77 Like to the purest molde, Enchac'de with daintie daysies soft and white. **1593** DRAYTON *Eclog.* I. 38 Whose floore with Stars is gloriously inchased. *c* **1611** CHAPMAN *Iliad* (1857) Pref. 71 Plato..with his [Homer's] verses, as with precious gems, everywhere enchaceth his writings.

c. Said of the gems.

1697 DRYDEN *Virg. Georg.* II. 725 To drink in Bowls which glitt'ring Gems enchase.

3. To inlay or variegate (metal, etc.) *with* gold or silver.

1640 G. SANDYS *Christ's Passion* 18 See those Roofs..the Beams With burnisht gold inchac'd, and blazing Gems. **1716–8** LADY M. W. MONTAGUE *Lett.* I. x. 36 There was.. a set of fine china for the tea-table enchased in gold. **1725** POPE *Odyss.* XV. 129 This silver bowl, whose costly margins shine Enchas'd with gold. **1781** GIBBON *Decl. & F.* II. xliii. 603 His armour was enchased with gold.

4. To adorn with figures in relief, *esp.* of repoussé-work. Hence in wider sense, to engrave, ornament with engraved figures or patters.

1463 *Bury Wills* (1850) 23, I wille she haue..my flat pece enchased to make with a saltsaler of sylver [*in this document freq.* chased *in same sense*]. **1682** WHELER *Journ. Greece* II. 181 Figures of Inchased Work. **1717** BERKELEY in Fraser *Life* (1871) 515 The house..being enchased with beautiful relievos of antiquity. **1828** MACAULAY *Misc. Writ.* (1860) I. 259 They are not enchased and relieved with the same skill.

b. To engrave (figures) *on*, *in* a surface; to portray by engraved figures.

1579 SPENSER *Sheph. Cal.* Aug. 27 Wherein is enchased many a fayre sight. **1601** HOLLAND *Pliny* II. 566 Within the hollow part and concauitie he inchased the conflict between the gods and the gyants. **1766** *Chron.* in *Ann. Reg.* 112/2 He [a type-founder] has found means to enchase the points or vowels, without which that character would be unintelligible. **1868** SILL *Poet's Apol.* I. v, Truth enchased upon a jewel rare, A man would keep.

5. *transf.* and *fig.* To adorn or variegate with figures resembling engraving.

1590 SPENSER *F.Q.* II. ix. 24 A wandring vine, Enchaced with a wanton yvie twine. **1610** G. FLETCHER *Christ's Vict.* in Farr *S.P. Jas. I* (1848) 47 A thousand colours did the bow enchace. **1612** DRAYTON *Poly-olb.* viii. 117 His manly breast inchaste With sundry shapes of Beasts. **1816** COLERIDGE *Lay Serm.* 346 The vegetable creation..inchases the.. volume of the earth with the hieroglyphics of her history.

II. With the idea of inclusion.

6. To enshrine (as a relic) *in*. [The original sense in Fr.]

1643 EVELYN *Mem.* (1857) I. 46 Enchased in a crystal covered with gold. **1688** H. WHARTON *Enthus. Ch. Rome* 24 [He] might..have his Bones enchased in Gold. **1823** SCOTT *Romance* (1874) 68 The highly ornamented Church with which superstition has surrounded and enchased it [the famous hut of Loretto].

b. *fig.* (often passing into 7.)

1615 CHAPMAN *Odyss.* II. 415 And if, like him, there be in thee enchac'd Virtue to give words works. **1626** T. H. *Caussin's Holy Crt.* 37 God seemeth to haue enchased all Christian perfection, in Charity. **1649** JER. TAYLOR *Gt. Exemp.* I. vii. 31 Thy holy Humanity inchased in the adorable Divinity. *a* **1711** KEN *Hymns Evang.* Poet. Wks. 1721 I. 100 Thy bright Idea in my Heart Enchase.

†**7.** To close in, shut in, enclose. *Obs.*

1591 SPENSER *M. Hubberd* 626 The Lyon..Enchaste with chaine and circulet of golde. **1601** HOLLAND *Pliny* II. 626 They [magicians] giue direction..to inchase or inclose it [Chlorites] with a piece of yron. *c* **1611** CHAPMAN *Iliad* XII. 56 They charge him close, and stand (as in a tow'r They had inchas'd him) pouring on of darts an iron show'r. *Ibid.* XIX. 346 Herself the skies again enchased. **1715** tr. *Pancirollus' Hist. Mem. Th.* I. IV. xvi. 219 Samothrace..where was first invented the Art of encircling, or enchasing Iron with Gold [*cf.* 3].

8. To 'let in' to a 'chase' or mortice. Also *transf.* and *fig.*

1611 COTGR., *Iabler*, to make the Croes of a Caske: viz. a furrow or hollow..whereinto the head-peeces may be enchased. **1616** J. B. *Sermon* 18 The Soule and the Body are olde friends, so enchased, one into another, that, etc. *a* **1774** GOLDSMITH tr. *Scarron's Comic Romance* (1775) i. 81 His whole head was enchased into his hat.

enchased (ɛn'tʃeɪst; *poet.* ɛn'tʃeɪsɪd), *ppl. a.* [f. prec. + -ED[1].] In senses of the verb.

1616 LANE *Squire's T.* VI. 53 Bold Camballo..came armd in bright enchaced steele. **1818** KEATS *Endym.* Vain as swords Against the enchased crocodile.

†**en'chasement.** *Obs.* [f. as prec. + -MENT; cf. OF. *enchacement* of same meaning.] That in which anything is enchased; a setting, frame.

1651 tr. *Coveras' Hist. Don Fenise* 27 He..prepared the jewell of his soule for a more pretious inchasement. **1686** tr. *Chardin's Trav.* 100 The Mingrelians have a greater Esteem for the Enchasements, then for the Reliques themselves. **1772** J. R. FORSTER *Kalm's Trav.* II. 222 The enchasement of the doors and windows.

enchaser (ɛn'tʃeɪsə(r)). [f. ENCHASE *v.*[2] + -ER.] One who enchases or engraves metal.

1859 C. BARKER *Assoc. Princ.* ii. 49 The piety and liberality..of our early..enchasers. **1873** *Echo* 18 Aug. 4/4 A very skilful enchaser. **1887** *Pall Mall G.* 20 Aug. 5/1 Mr. Stevenson is not a patient enchaser of far-fetched, costly jewel-words.

enchasing (ɛn'tʃeɪsɪŋ), *vbl. sb.* [f. ENCHASE *v.*[2] + -ING.] The action of the verb ENCHASE; the putting of a jewel into its setting; in quot. *fig.*

1831 E. IRVING *Expos. Rev.* I. 49 Without such a setting and enchasing in the conditions of time and place.

‖**enchâssure.** *rare*[−1]. [Fr.; f. *enchâsser*: see ENCHASE *v.*[2]] The casing of a relic.

1716 LADY M. W. MONTAGUE *Lett.* I. 14 The rich images of the saints, and the enchassures of the relics.

enchasten (ɛn'tʃeɪsən), *v. rare*[−1]. [f. EN-[1] + CHASTEN.] *trans.* To make chaste, purify.

c **1800** K. WHITE *Time* 357 Castaly enchasten'd with its dews.

enchauf(e, -ffe, -fye, obs. ff. ENCHAFE.

enchaunt, obs. form of ENCHANT.

enche, obs. form of INCH.

†**en'cheason.** *Obs.* Forms: 3–5 **enchesun, -oun(e -own(e**, 4–7 **encheson(e**, (4 **encheison, -eyson**, 5 **enchesen**, ? **encihoson, inchessoun**, 6 **enchesson**,) 6–7 **encheason.** Also ANCHESOUN. [a. OF. *encheson, encheison*, f. *encheoir*, lit. to fall in, hence to be in fault (whence *encheement* 'instigation, cause', Godef.). The OF. word was influenced in meaning, if indeed its formation was not actually suggested, by the earlier *acheson* (see ACHESOUN):—L. *occāsiōn-em* occasion; the two words seem to have been entirely synonymous, *acheson* being more usual in continental OF., and *encheson* in AF. and in Eng.]

1. Occasion, cause, reason, motive.

1297 R. GLOUC. (1724) 111 He ascode hem..for wat encheson heo come. *c* **1315** SHOREHAM *Poems* 120 More encheyson hadde oure levedy..blythe for to be. *c* **1340** *Cursor M.* 2237 (Fairf.) Quen we se enchesoun..we may clymbe vp and doun. **1393** LANGL. *P. Pl.* C. VII. 40 Couetyse contreuede how ich myghte Be holde for holy..by þat encheison. *c* **1430** HENRYSON *Mor. Fab.* 83 For what enchesson this Dogs skin haue ye borne? *a* **1450** *Le Morte Arth.* 56 He made inchessoun for to abyde. *c* **1450** LONELICH *Grail* xxxix. 466 Thanne knew he wel be his owne enchesown that he was a synnere ful grette. **1579** SPENSER *Sheph. Cal.* May 147 Thou..blamest hem much, for small encheason. **1597** *Guistard & Sismond* B ij, Ease, rest, and delicates, what great encheason, They give to starre a man to corage. *a* **1618** J. DAVIES *Eglog.* (1772) 110 Who whilom no encheson could fore-haile. **1641** *Termes de la Ley* 135 b, *Encheson*..signifies..the occasion, cause, or reason for which any thing is done. **1642** BIRD *Magazine of Honour* 86 Upon divers encheasons and occasions.

2. *by, for encheason of*: by reason of, because of.

c **1386** CHAUCER *Melibeus* ¶627 The ydel man excuseth him..in somer by enchesoun of the grete heat. **1488** CAXTON *Chast. Goddes Chyld.* 86 They trowen that by encheson of suche manere temptacyon they ben forgoten of her god. **1494** FABYAN VI. clxxxvi. 187 For encheson that yᵉ sayd William ayded a noble man of Pycardy. **1609** SKENE *Reg. Maj.* 112 The King be encheson [*margin*, Be reason, or because], that the overlord is within his wairid, afterward giues that land to any man as escheit.

†**en'cheat**, *sb. Obs.* [a. OF. *encheoite*, f. *encheoir* to fall in; cf. ESCHEAT.] Revenue derived from escheats or confiscations.

1387 TREVISA *Higden* (Rolls) VII. 259 He ȝaf hym eche day a litel what of enchetes [*parum de fisco*] to lyve by. *Ibid.* 323 Odo wastede and destroyede the kynges rentes and enchetes [*fiscos regios*]. **1494** FABYAN VII. 306 By theyr meanys, yᵉ Kyng loste many forfaytes and encheatis.

†**en'cheat**, *v. Obs. rare*[−1]. In 5 **enchete.** [f. prec.; cf. ESCHEAT *v.*] *trans.* To confiscate for the royal treasury.

1460 CAPGRAVE *Chron.* 288 Ye have stered the Kyng to enchete alle the temporaltes that longyng to the Frensch munkis. **1483** *Cath. Angl.* 114 To Enchete, *fiscare.*

†**en'cheater.** *Obs.* In 4 **enchetour**, 5 **encheter.** [f. prec. + -ER.] = ESCHEATOR.

1387 TREVISA *Higden* (Rolls) V. 43 Enchetour [*fisci advocatus*]. **1483** *Cath. Angl.* 114 An Encheter, *fiscator.*

encheck: see EN- *pref.*[1] 3.

encheer (ɛn'tʃɪə(r)), *v.* Also 7 **enchear, inchear.** [f. EN-[1] + CHEER *v.*] *trans.* To cheer, render cheerful. Hence **en'cheering** *ppl. a.*

1605 DANIEL *Philotas* (1717) 311 Ded., That in better place And better comfort they may be inchear'd Who shall deserve, etc. *c* **1630** DRUMM. OF HAWTH. *Poems* Wks. (1711) 38 The flower of princes ..Enchearing all our dales..Is come. **1652** BENLOWES *Theoph.* VIII. lxxv, I' th' Orient Sols enchearing rays. *c* **1800** K. WHITE *Christiad* ix, No sweet remain of life encheers the sight.

enchein, obs. form of ENCHAIN.

‖**en'cheiria.** *Obs. rare.* [Gr. ἐγχειρία.] Method of manipulation.

1672 NEWTON in Rigaud *Corr. Sci. Men* (1841) II. 346 The want of a good encheiria.

enchequer: see EN- *pref.*[1] 3.

†**en'cherish**, *v.* [a. OF. *encheriss-*, lengthened stem of *encherir*: see EN-[1] and CHERISH.] *trans.* ? = CHERISH. Implied in †**en'cherishing**, *vbl. sb.*, in quot. app. used in sense 'benefit, advantage'.

c **1480** in *Pol. Poems* (1859) II. 286 Yt were..expedyent for oure Kyngs And a gret enscherychyng to all the Comynalte.

†**en'chest**, *v. Obs.* Also 7 **in-**. [f. EN-[1] + CHEST *sb.*] *trans.* To shut up in, or as in, a chest.

1632 VICARS *Æneid* (N.), Can thy breast enchest such anger still? **1632** SHERWOOD, To inchest, *encaisser.*

†**en'chested**, *ppl. a. Obs.* [f. EN-[1] + CHEST *sb.* + -ED.] Furnished with coffers or sunken panels.

1730 A. GORDON *Maffei's Amphith.* 285 The Roof is enchested and waved.

†**en'cheve**, *v. Obs. rare.* Also 5 *Sc.* **encheif.** [altered form of *acheve*, ACHIEVE.] *trans.* To win, gain possession of. Also *intr.* To succeed. Hence **en'cheving** *vbl. sb.*

c **1475** [see ENCHAIP]. **1470–85** MALORY *Arthur* I. iii, He is not here..that shall encheue the swerd. *Ibid.* II. iv, The encheuynge of the swerd.

‖**enchilada** (ɛntʃɪ'lɑːdə). [Amer. Sp., fem. of *enchilado*, pa. pple. of *enchilar* to season with chili, f. Sp. *en* in + *chile* chili.] A tortilla served with a sauce seasoned with chili.

1887 F. C. GOOCH *Face to Face with Mexicans* xii. 410 They go to some stand..and eat *enchiladas* and *tamales* and drink *pulque.* **1895** *Jrnl. Amer. Folk-Lore* Jan.–Apr. 62 *Enchiladas* are practically corn fritters allowed to simmer for a moment in chile sauce, and then served hot with a sprinkling of grated cheese and onion. **1934** J. M. CAIN *Postman always rings Twice* i. 5 Fried eggs and bacon, enchilada, flapjacks, and coffee. **1968** N. BENCHLEY *Welcome to Xanadu* viii. 180 He..ordered a bowl of chili and enchiladas.

enchiridion (ɛnkaɪ'rɪdɪən). [a. Gr. ἐγχειρίδιον, f. ἐν in + χείρ hand + dim. suff. -ιδιον.] A handbook or manual; a concise treatise serving as a guide or for reference.

1541 COVERDALE *Old Faith* Wks. 1844 I. 49 He [Moses] made..an enchiridion and sum of all the acts of his time. **1658** BP. REYNOLDS *Medit. Lord's Supper* Ded., I have been emboldened to present this small enchiridion..unto the hands and patronage of so..judicious a person. *a* **1789** BURNEY *Hist. Mus.* (ed. 2) II. ii. 122 The Enchiridion of Hubald..appears first in the volume. **1829** I. TAYLOR *Enthus.* (1850) 224 The Bible..is the heavenly enchiridion of those who are beset with the cares, etc. of the world. **1885** *Blackw. Mag.* June 775/1 This enchiridion or little handbook was published in 1575.

enchisel: see EN- *pref.*[1] 2.

‖**enchondroma** (ɛnkɒn'drəʊmə). *Path. Pl.* **enchondromata.** Also (formerly) in adapted form **enchondrom.** [mod.L., as if a. Gr. *ἐγχόνδρωμα, f. ἐν in + χόνδρος cartilage.] Orig., a

tumour having a structure resembling cartilage. In later use usu. restricted to mean: a chondroma arising within a bone.

1847 SOUTH tr. *Chelius's Surgery* II. 674 John Müller has described it most minutely as Enchondrom..such conglomeration is peculiar to the Enchondrom. **1847–9** TODD *Cycl. Anat.* IV. 133/1 Enchondroma exhibits itself as a tumour of moderate size. **1878** T. BRYANT *Pract. Surg.* I. 112 Enchondromata..are most commonly met with in connection with bone. **1958** H. L. JAFFE *Tumors of Bones* xi. 170 An enchondroma beginning within a metaphysis may eventually involve a large portion of the shaft.

enchondromatous (ɛnkɒn'drəʊmətəs), *a. Path.* [f. mod.L. *enchondrōmat-* stem of prec. + -OUS.] Of or pertaining to ENCHONDROMA.

1847 TODD *Cycl. Anat.* IV. 121/2 Growths of all kinds.. enchondromatous, erectile, etc. **1872** COHEN *Dis. Throat* 140 A case of large enchondromatous tumor on the under surface of the hard palate.

enchondrosis (ɛnkɒn'drəʊsɪs). [f. ENCHONDR(OMA + -OSIS.] A chondroma arising from cartilage.

1871 T. H. GREEN *Introd. Path.* xvii. 132 The enchondromata must for the most part be regarded as innocent growths. Those homologous forms which originate from cartilage, and have been called 'Enchondroses', differ in all respects from the heterologous. **1908** *Practitioner* Dec. 763 On the inner aspect of the second toe there is an enchondrosis. **1967** R. A. WILLIS *Path. Tumours* (ed. 4) xliii. 686 A once prevalent idea that multiple enchondroses and multiple exostoses are only different varieties of one disease has been discarded.

enchorial (ɛn'kɔːrɪəl), *a.* [f. Gr. ἐγχώρι-ος in or of the country (f. ἐν in + χωρά country) + -AL¹.] That belongs to, or is used in, a particular country: **a.** Used (after Gr. ἐγχώρια γράμματα, occurring on the Rosetta stone) as the distinctive epithet of the popular (as distinguished from the hieroglyphic and the hieratic) form of the ancient Egyptian written character; in technical use now commonly superseded by DEMOTIC. **b.** In general sense (somewhat *rare.*)

1822 *Q. Rev.* XXVIII. 189 A close comparison of the enchorial or demotic character with the corresponding Greek on the Rosetta stone. **1864** SIR F. PALGRAVE *Norm. & Eng.* III. 98 The name..transmitted by the enchorial tradition..is clearly Teutonic. **1882** *Pall Mall G.* 8 June 4/2 That indescribable enchorial something which is British and not Netherlandish.

†**en'chronicle,** *v. Obs.* Also 6 encronicle, incronicle. [f. EN-¹ + CHRONICLE.] *trans.* To enter in a chronicle; to register, put on record.

1513 BRADSHAW *St. Werburgh* (1848) 137 Encronicled foloweth..A briefe compilacion of Kynge Edward seniour. **1587** R. LONG (MS. Brit. Mus.), Yt hath bene th' order of all antiant orators..to..incronicle all such worthye persons. **1593** G. HARVEY *Pierce's Super.* 115 Let it be enchronicled for one of the..miracles of this age, that, etc.

†**en'church,** *v. Obs. rare.* Also 8 inchurch. [f. EN-¹ + CHURCH.] *trans.* To form into, or organize as, a church. Hence **en'churched** *ppl. a.*

a **1658** J. DURHAM *Exp. Revel.* II. iii. (1680) 85 The governing of Churches, and inchurched members. **1677** I. MATHER *Preval. Prayer* (1864) 257 Never baptized, nor of the inchurched Indians. **1681** *Whole Duty Nations* 64 If Two or three agree, and are..enchurch'd in my Name, I will be in the midst of them. **1702** C. MATHER *Magn. Chr.* V. II. (1852) 283 Its communication to the inchurched Gentiles..is clearly held forth.

enchylema (ɛnkɪ'liːmə). *Biol.* [G. (J. von Hanstein *Das Protoplasma als Träger d. pflanzlichen & thierischen Lebensverrichtungen* (1880) iv. 39): see EN-² and CHYLE.] In some old theories of the structure of cytoplasm: **a.** A clear liquid supposed to constitute the ground-substance of a cell nucleus and to contain a fibrillar network. **b.** A liquid supposed to exist in the form of 'alveolar spheres' in a continuous, usu. more viscous liquid.

1886 *Science* VIII. 125/1 This basal substance, enchylema, is probably more or less nearly fluid during life. **1888** ROLLESTON & JACKSON *Forms Anim. Life* p. xxi, Protoplasm..appears sometimes to be structureless, but as a rule it is more or less vesicular, consisting of a denser substance (mitome) enclosing droplets of a more fluid character (enchylema, paramitome). **1896** E. B. WILSON *Cell* i. 17 According to the view most widely held, one of its [*sc.* protoplasm's] essential features is the presence of two constituents, one of which, the ground-substance, cytolymph, or enchylema, is more liquid, while the other, the spongioplasm or reticulum, is of a firmer consistency, and forms a sponge-like network. **1940** L. H. HYMAN *Invertebrates* I. i. 2 The spumoid or alveolar theory [of protoplasm], developed by Bütschli, and widely accepted, even today, states that protoplasm is composed of spheres, the alveoli, filled with a clear fluid, the hyaloplasm or enchylema, and suspended in a continuous interalveolar substance.

enciclopaidion, bad form of ENCYCLOPÆDIA.

1693 W. FREKE *Sel. Ess.* i. 7 Let us..state any one of the Arts and Sciences in the whole Enciclopaidion.

‖**encierro** (en'θjerro). [Sp., lit. act of enclosing or locking up.] The driving of bulls through the streets of a Spanish town from a corral to the bull-ring, freq. for the specific purpose of giving amateurs an opportunity to 'play' the bulls.

1845 R. FORD *Handbk. Trav. Spain* I. ii. 179 The *encierro*, the driving them to the arena, is a service of danger. **1901** *Encycl. Sport* I. 153/2 Soon the whole herd of bulls..is rattled along the lanes..in the direction of the bull-ring. The horsemen are assisted in this operation, called the *encierro* ('enclosing') by numerous amateurs. **1959** *Times* 10 July 8/6 A quaking fear seizes every English stomach before the *Encierro* begins. **1966** G. SIMS *Sleep no More* xii. 84 He's taken part in the *encierro* at Pamplona—that's a run of about half a mile down zigzagging boarded-up streets to the bull ring. They let loose six young bulls to chase you.

encincture (ɛn'sɪŋktjʊə(r)), *v.* [f. EN-¹ + CINCTURE *sb.*] *trans.* To surround with, or as with, a belt or girdle; to girdle.

1821 SHELLEY *Prometh. Unb.* II. iii, [The lake] Encinctured by the dark and blooming forests. **1839** *Fraser's Mag.* XX. 44 Clusters of fire-flies..encinctured the green foliage.

en'cincture, *sb. rare.* [f. EN-¹ + CINCTURE *sb.*] The process of surrounding as with a girdle; the fact of being so surrounded: *concr.* an enclosure.

1814 WORDSW. *Excursion* v. (1850) 143 The chancel only showed..marks of earthly state..with the Encincture's special sanctity But ill according. **1881** H. G. HEWLETT in *19th Cent.* Aug. 296 The encincture of Kent on two or even three sides with water.

encinder: see EN- *pref.*¹ 2.

encipher (ɛn'saɪfə(r)), *v.* Also 6 incipher. [f. EN-¹ + CIPHER *sb.*] *trans.* **a.** To write (a letter) in cipher: to record in cipher. **b.** To combine in a cipher or monogram *with.*

1577 HOLINSHED *Chron.* III. 1229/2, I saw two letters, the one inciphered and the other disciphered. **1651** *Life Father Sarpi* 141 That under the Quadragesimale, there were three persons enciphred. **1826** E. IRVING *Babylon* II. v. 22 [Napoleon] Permitting his name to be enciphered with the ..name of Jehovah.

encircle (ɛn'sɜːk(ə)l), *v.* Also 4 ? enserde, 7–8 incircle, (7 incircule). [f. EN- + CIRCLE.]

1. *trans.* To enclose in a circle.

a. Of things, bodies of people, etc.: To form a circle round, surround. **b.** To surround, gird, encompass *with.*

? *a* **1400** *Morte Arth.* 3943 The..kynge..Ses theme alle in a soppe in sowte by theme one, With þe Sarazenes unsownde enserchede [*corrected* (? *conjecturally*) *in Gloss. to* enserclede] abowte. **1597** SHAKS. *2 Hen. IV*, IV. ii. 6 Your Flocke.. Encircled you, to hear with reverence Your exposition. **1611** SPEED *Hist. Gt. Brit.* VI. xxiv. 116 Incircuiling their heads with this word, *æternitas imperi.* **1642** HOWELL *For. Trav.* (1869) 46 Great Britaine being encircled by the Sea..need not feare any one Earthly power. **1741** RICHARDSON *Pamela* II. 106, I found myself incircled in the Arms of my..Father. **1775** R. CHANDLER *Trav. Asia M.* I. 106 The people..were encircling the trunks with tar. **1775** JOHNSON *Tax. no Tyr.* 42 Encircle with a diadem the brows of Mr. Cushing. **1844** *Mem. Babylonian P'cess* II. 20 Some of the nuns encircle their naked waists with a girdle of thorns. **1848** MACAULAY *Hist. Eng.* II. 295 The close which encircles the venerable cathedral.

c. *transf.* and *fig.*

1774 GOLDSM. *Retal.* 83 Satire and censure encircled his throne. **1791** COWPER *Iliad* I. 46 God of the silver bow, who with thy power Encirclest Chrysa. **1833** BROWNING *Pauline* 24 Sense supplies a love Encircling me. *a* **1876** J. H. NEWMAN *Hist. Sk.* I. I. iv. 171 The divinity which.. encircled the hideous form of Attila.

2. To make a circling movement about (a person or thing).

1598 SHAKS. *Merry W.* IV. iv. 57 Then let them all encircle him about. **1624** CAPT. SMITH *Virginia* III. ii. 48 Till they had twice incirculed the fire. **1638** WILKINS *New World* I. (1684) 137 Jupiter hath four [Moons] that Incircle him with their Motion. *a* **1717** PARNELL *Hesiod, Rise of Woman* (R.), Hermes..Her brows encircled with his serpent-rod.

en'circled, *ppl. a. rare.* Also 7 incircled. [f. prec. + -ED¹.] In senses of the verb.

1632 LITHGOW *Totall Discourse* 416 On the incircled plaine there groweth nothing but Wheate, Rye, Barley, Pease, and Beanes. **1695** BLACKMORE *Pr. Arth.* VI. 566 Incircled Wrestlers now their Manhood try. **1789** T. WHATELY in *Med. Commun.* II. 388, I..attempted to separate the encircled piece.

encirclement (ɛn'sɜːk(ə)lmənt). [f. ENCIRCLE *v.* + -MENT.] The act or fact of encircling or of being encircled: used esp. with reference to countries that believe themselves to be surrounded by hostile nations.

1919 G. B. SHAW *Peace Conference Hints* ii. 20 The famous encirclement (*Einkreisung*) which was the masterstroke of the Allied strategy. **1920** H. G. WELLS *Outl. Hist.* 456/2 Their [*sc.* the French] government set about the encirclement of the colonies and their subjugation in a terrifyingly systematic manner. **1927** *Observer* 24 July 14/2 A ring of Verey lights..that exaggerated..the encirclement and nearly completed it. **1940** *Ann. Reg. 1939* 63 The Reich Government in official declarations raised the cry of 'encirclement', and accused Great Britain of planning the destruction of German trade. **1957** *Times* 11 May 6/2 The threat of attack by Israel to prevent her encirclement by an Arab federation bent on her destruction. **1966** *Listener* 10 Mar. 339/2 The Chinese now see their encirclement by what they like to call 'imperialist' intrigues. **1967** S. BECKETT *Eh Joe* 38 E [camera] now begins a much wider encirclement.

encircler (ɛn'sɜːklə(r)). *rare.* Also 7 incircler. [f. ENCIRCLE *v.* + -ER.] He who or that which encircles, girds, or surrounds.

1631 *Celestina* VI. 75 O girdle, incircler of so incomparable a creature. **1831** E. IRVING *Expos. Rev.* I. 58 The supporters and encirclers of the throne of God.

encircling (ɛn'sɜːklɪŋ), *vbl. sb.* [f. ENCIRCLE *v.* + -ING¹.] The action of the vb. ENCIRCLE.

1632 LITHGOW *Totall Discourse* 265 About it [this chapel], I meane without the vtter sides of it, and the inward incirclings of the compassing Quiere, there are alwayes burning about fifty Lampes. **1836** ARNOLD *Lett.* (1844) II. viii. 48 An image..of the encircling of the everlasting arms.

encircling (ɛn'sɜːklɪŋ), *ppl. a.* Also incircling. [f. as prec. + -ING².] That encircles.

1632 LITHGOW *Totall Disc.* 265 Within incircling bandes of pure Gold. **1633** P. FLETCHER *Purple Isl.* V. (R.), The third..is like a grape Which all entwines with his encircling side. **1725** POPE *Odyss.* I. 526 A realm defended with incircling seas. **1832** J. H. NEWMAN *Hymn*, '*Lead, kindly Light*,' Amidst the encircling gloom Lead thou me on. **1871** FREEMAN *Norm. Conq.* (1876) IV. xviii. 236 The minster looks down on the encircling stream of the Wear. **1873** W. BLACK *Pr. Thule* ix. 138 The blinding white of the incircling hills.

encircular (ɛn'sɜːkjʊlə(r)), *a. rare*⁻¹. [f. EN-¹ + CIRCULAR.] Circular.

1804 J. GRAHAME *Sabbath* (1839) 20/2 The host of heaven ..adored..nor changed their form Encircular.

†**en'circulize,** *v. Obs. rare*⁻¹. [see -IZE.] *trans.* To surround as with a circle; to hem in.

1624 [SCOTT] *Vox Coeli* Ded. 4 To make his territories and Dominions encirculize great Brittaine and France.

encist: see EN- *pref.*¹ 1.

†**encla.** *Obs.* [obscure: prob. some error.] The throat or gullet.

1541 R. COPLAND *Quest. Chirurg.* F ij a, Wherof serueth the encla & the amygdales, and faulses..they serue to prepare the breth. *Ibid.* F ij b, The throte called gulle or encla.

enclad (ɛn'klæd). *pple. rare.* [f. EN-¹ + CLAD.] Equivalent to *enclothed*, pa. pple. of ENCLOTHE.

1863 *Sat. Rev.* 386 Enclad in the spoils of wolf and of wild cat.

enclaim: see EN- *pref.*¹ 3.

en clair: see EN *prep.*

†**en'claret,** *v. Obs. rare*⁻¹. [f. EN-¹ + CLARET.] *trans.* To tinge with claret; to overlay with a claret-like hue.

1648 HERRICK *Hesper.* I. 192 Cheeks like creame enclarited.

enclasp (ɛn'klɑːsp, -'klæsp), *v.* Also 7 inclasp (inclaps). [f. EN-¹ + CLASP *sb.* and *v.*] *trans.* To hold in or as in a clasp or embrace; to clasp tightly; also *fig.* Hence **en'clasping** *ppl. a.*

1596 FITZ-GEFFRAY *Sir F. Drake* (1881) 14 Enclaspeth with her winged eminence The worlds orbicular circumference. **1607** TOPSELL *Four-f. Beasts* 106 You are inclasped in..inextricable nets. *a* **1618** J. DAVIES *Bien Venu* Wks. (1876) 5 (D.) O Union, that enclaspest in thyne armes All that in Heau'n and Earth is great or good. **1647** CUDWORTH *Serm. 1 John* ii. 3–4 (1676) 65 He..inclaspeth the whole world within his outstretched arms. **1783** LEMON *Eng. Lang.* Pref. 1 (Jod.) Why do the ivy and eglantine enclasp so eagerly their oak? **1834** DISRAELI *Rev. Epick* I. xlix. 5 Thy fond hand still I enclasp. **1848** H. MILLER *First Impr.* v. (1857) 81 Grey lichened rocks, enclasped by sprigs of ivy. **1877** M. ARNOLD *Poems* II. 17 The islands feel the enclasping flow.

‖**enclave** ('ɛnkleɪv, ɛn'kleɪv, ɑ̃klav) *sb.* [Fr. *enclave*, f. *enclaver* to enclose, shut in, ad. late L. *inclāvāre*, f. *in* in + *clāv-is* key (Scheler), or *clāv-us* nail (Littré).] A portion of territory entirely surrounded by foreign dominions. Also *fig.*

1868 G. DUFF *Pol. Surv.* 38 Russia looks upon them [the Roumans] as destined to be a mere enclave in a Slavonic empire. **1870** *Contemp. Rev.* XV. 89 Enclaves in the territory of the greatest-happiness idea. **1884** *Spectator* 2 Feb. 150 Purely human enclaves in an inspired book. **1885** *Pall Mall G.* 16 Feb. 9/1 Portugal..possesses an enclave extending from Massabe to Red Point.

en'clave, *a. Her.* Also inclave. [a. Fr. *enclavé*, pa. pple. of *enclaver* to dovetail: see prec.] Of the border of an ordinary: Having a contour like that of a dovetail joint. So **en'claved** *ppl. a.*

1661 S. MORGAN *Sph. Gentry* I. i. 8 This chiefe issuing into the sable field of darkness may properly called Inclave, breaking forth into a label of one point. **1731** in BAILEY vol. II. Enclave. **1828** BERRY *Encycl. Heraldica, Inclave*, the same as pattée, or dovetailed.

‖**enclavure.** *rare*⁻¹. [Fr.] = ENCLAVE *sb.*

1851 SIR F. PALGRAVE *Norm. & Eng.* I. 637 In such enclavures as we have named Vermandois did not possess direct authority.

†**en'clawed,** *pa. pple. Obs. rare*⁻¹. Of uncertain origin and meaning: Robson suggests the sense 'riveted', in which case the word might be for *enclowet*, f. OF. *encloué* nailed.

c **1420** *Anturs of Arth.* xxx, His mayles were mylke quyte, enclawet ful clene.

encleanse: see EN- *pref.*[1] 3.

†**en'clear**, *v. Obs.* Also 6 inclear, inclere. [f. EN-[1] + CLEAR *a.*]

1. *trans.* To make bright or clear; to give clearness to (sight).

1526 SKELTON *Magnyf.* 2548 A myrrour incleryd is this interlude. **1556** ABP. PARKER *Psalter* cxix, Encleare my sight: and me reuiue.

2. To light up, illumine. *lit.* and *fig.*

1509 BARCLAY *Shyp of Folys* (1874) I. 290 Blynde man inclere thy wylfull ignoraunce. *c* **1510** —— *Mirr. Good Mann.* (1570) Dij, Christ hath inclered his minde with inwarde light. **1580** SIDNEY *Ps.* lxxvii, Light of lightnings flash Did pitchy cloudes encleare.

‖**en'clere**, *adv. Obs.* [? OF. phrase *en cler*; cf. CLEAR *a.*] Brightly.

a **1440** *Sir Degrev.* 1061 The sonne schonne en clere.

†**enclin**, *a. Obs.* [a. F. *enclin*:—late L. *inclīnis* of same meaning, related to *inclīnāre* to INCLINE.] Bowed down.

c **1430** *Pilgr. Lyf. Manh.* II. xxiv. (1869) 85 If it ne were, alle rude wittes woldin ben enclyn and humble hem.

†**enclinant**, *a. Obs.* In 4 enclinaunt, enclynaunt. [a. OF. *enclinant*, pr. pple. of *encliner* to INCLINE.] **a.** ? Doing homage, submissive. **b.** Inclined, prone (*to*).

1330 R. BRUNNE *Chron. Wace* (Rolls) 5320 Of pritty reomes euery kynge Were enclinaunt til his coronyng. **1388** WYCLIF *Exod.* xxxii. 22 This puple..is enclynaunt to yuel. —— *Prov.* xxii. 9 Enclinaunt [*v.r.* redi] to merci.

encline, obs. var. INCLINE *sb.* and *v.*

enclipse, incorrect form of ECLIPSE *v.*

1606 G. W[ODCOCKE] tr. *Hist. Ivstine* 110 b, The Moone was Enclipsed.

enclisis ('ɛnklɪsɪs). *Gram.* [mod.L., f. Gr. ἔγκλισις f. ἐν on + κλίνειν to lean.] Pronunciation as an enclitic; the transference of accentuation to a previous word.

1885 *Amer. Jrnl. Philol.* VI. 218 Retaining the convenient terms orthotonesis and enclisis to designate this alternating accent. **1949** *Archivum Linguisticum* I. 169 The expanded or composite form, which results from enclisis with members of the paradigm of the third personal pronoun. **1963** in Brown & Foote *Early Eng. & Norse Studies* 134 An unusual postpositive use of the article, though with no suggestion of enclisis as in Scandinavian.

enclitic (ɛn'klɪtɪk). *a.* and *sb. Gram.* Also 8 enclytick. [ad. L. *enclitic-us*, a. Gr. ἐγκλιτικ-ός, f. ἐν on + κλίνειν to lean.]

A. *adj.* That 'leans its accent on the preceding word' (Liddell and Scott): in Greek grammar the distinctive epithet of those words which have no accent, and which (when phonetic laws permit) cause a secondary accent to be laid on the last syllable of the word which they follow. Hence applied to the analogous Latin particles *-que*, *-ve*, *-ne*, etc., and in mod. use (with extension of sense) to those unemphatic words in other langs. that are treated in pronunciation as if forming part of the preceding word.

1656 BLOUNT *Glossogr.*, *Enclitick*, that inclines or gives back. **1750** HARRIS *Hermes* I. v. (1786) 85 *note*, The Diversity between the Contradistinctive Pronouns, and the Enclitic, is not unknown even to the English Tongue. **1855** BROWNING *Grammarian's Fun.*, Gave us the doctrine of the enclitic De. **1867** RAWLINSON *Anc. Mon.* IV. iv. 227 The pronouns had in certain cases an enclitic form.

B. *sb.* An enclitic word.

1663 in BULLOKAR. **1709** STEELE *Tatler* No. 18 ⁋1 They are busy in making Emendations upon some Enclitics in a Greek Author. **1750** HARRIS *Hermes* I. v. (T.), When we say, 'Give me content', the *me* in this case is a perfect enclitick. **1878** PARRY *Grk. Gram.* 175 If several Enclitics come together, each throws its accent on the preceding.

†**enclitical** (ɛn'klɪtɪkəl), *a. Obs.* Also 7 (*erron.*) enclytical. [f. as prec. + -AL[1].]

1. = ENCLITIC *a.*

1612 BRINSLEY *Lud. Lit.* 110 The Enclyticall Coniunction *que.* **1656** BLOUNT *Glossogr.*, *Enclitical* conjunctions..cast back the accent to the syllable going before.

2. *nonce-use.* That leans against something.

1773 GRAVES *Spir. Quix.* II. vii. (D.), A little shed or enclitical penthouse.

Hence **en'clitically** *adv.*, in an enclitic manner, as an enclitic.

1845 STODDART in *Encycl. Metrop.* (1847) I. 84/1 The Latin *que*, used only enclitically indeed in modern Latin. **1871** EARLE *Philol. Eng. Tong.* §598 (1880), The second and third words lean enclitically upon the first.

encliticism (ɛn'klɪtɪsɪz(ə)m). [f. as prec. + -ISM.] (See quot.)

1887 EARLE *Philol. Eng. Tong.* §254 Accentual leaning on some other word..is Encliticism [*printed* Enclyt-].

enclog: see EN- *pref.*[1] 2.

†**en'cloister**, *v.* Also 7 encloystre, -ter, incloyster, incloister. [f. EN-[1] + CLOISTER: cf. F. *encloîtrer*, and OF. *encloistre* sb., cloister.]

1. *trans.* To shut up in a cloister or monastery.

1612 DRAYTON *Poly-olb.* xxiv, Maids, and widow'd queens Incloister'd that became. *a* **1670** HACKET *Cent. Serm.* (1675) 221 Is..to be incloystered in an unmarried estate for ever.

2. *transf.* and *fig.* To shut in; to immure or imprison; to confine.

1596 R. L. *Diella*, 1596 When day incloistred is In dustie pryson of infernall night. **1627** DRAYTON *Agincourt* 208 Poems..In priuate chambers, that incloistered are. *a* **1638** MEDE *Ch. for Chr. Worship* Wks. II. 336 This notion of encloistering a Deity by an Idol. **1654** SIR R. BAKER tr. *Balzac's Lett. to Card. Richelieu* God hath not conferred such extraordinary endowments upon you, to be for ever encloistered within your self. **1670** PENN *Truth Rescued* 49 They were not there encloyster'd for not agreeing in their Verdict. **1710** *Brit. Apollo* III No. 91. 2/1 Such Damps could be..Encloistered and Pent in.

3. To furnish with cloisters. See ENCLOISTERED 2.

en'cloistered, *ppl. a.* Also 6 incloistered. [f. prec. + -ED[1].]

1. Shut up in cloisters or monasteries. Also *fig.*

1550 LEVER *Serm.* (Arb.) 73 Settyng abrode incloystred papistes. **1908** BELLOC *On Nothing* 72 The smoke also of the train as it skirts the Downs is part and parcel of what has become (thanks to the trains) our encloistered country life.

2. Surrounded by or furnished with cloisters.

1622–62 HEYLIN *Cosmogr.* I. (1682) 232 Several Quadrangles, every one encloystered. **1632** LITHGOW *Totall Disc.* 268 Having incloystered lodgings ioyned to the walls thereof. *Ibid.* 444 The eleven incloystered petty Courts.

†**en'close**, *sb. Obs. rare.* [f. next; in Caxton perh. a. OF. *enclos* or *enclose*.] = ENCLOSURE.

1. The space enclosed by a boundary; the precincts.

1484 CAXTON *Curial* (1888) 16 Wythin thenclose of thy pryue hous.

2. A letter or document enclosed within another.

1648 EVELYN *Mem.* (1857) III. 32 Since my last, I received..an enclose from Mr. Warcupp.

enclose, inclose (ɛn-, ɪn'kləʊz), *v.* Forms: α. (? 4 encless), 6 encloyse, 4– enclose. β. 5– inclose, 6 incloise, -cloiss. [f. EN-[1] + CLOSE *v.*, after OF. *enclore* (pa. pple. *enclos*) of same meaning. (Cf. INCLUSE.) The majority of recent Dicts. give *inclose* as the typical form; but the preponderance of usage (in England at least), as well as etymological propriety, is in favour of *enclose*. The statutes providing for the enclosure of land use the spelling *inclose*.]

1. a. *trans.* To surround (with walls, fences, or other barriers) so as to prevent free ingress or egress.

α. ? *a* **1400** *Morte Arth.* 2396 Here es a knyghte in theis klevys, enclesside [? *read* enclosside] with hilles. *c* **1430** LYDG. *Compl. Bl. Knt.* vi, A parke, enclosed with a wal. **1481** CAXTON *Myrr.* II. iii 67 The paradies terrestre..is enclosed with fyre brennyng.

β. *c* **1400** *Destr. Troy* 848 In an yle..This clene flese was inclosede all with clere water. **1523** FITZHERB. *Surv.* 2 And the felde be inclosed about. **1601** HOLLAND *Pliny* I. 91 There is a gulfe of 516 miles, inclosed within the promontory or cape of the mountain Barce. **1611** BIBLE *2 Macc.* i. 34 Then the king inclosing the place, made it holy. **1716–8** LADY M. W. MONTAGUE *Lett.* I. xxxvi. 137 The gardens..are inclosed with very high walls. **1743** J. DAVIDSON *Æneid* VII. 185 And incloses it with a Parapet.

b. To fence in (waste or common land) with the intention of taking it into cultivation, or of appropriating it to individual owners. Also *fig.*

α. **1503–4** *Act 19 Hen. VII*, c. 29 §2 Landes..whiche..be encloysed of newe with a Pale. **1523** FITZHERB. *Surv.* 2 It is at the lordes pleasure to enclose them and kepe them in tyllage or pasture. **1593** SHAKS. *2 Hen. VI*, I. iii. 24 Against the Duke of Suffolke, for enclosing the Commons of Melforde. **1725** DE FOE *Voy. round W.* (1840) 305 It was not ..enclosed after the English manner. **1833** HT. MARTINEAU *Brooke Farm* i. 12 An Act of Parliament is to be obtained for enclosing Brook common.

β. [**1538** STARKEY *England* 97, I thynke hyt veray necessary to haue thys inclosyng of pasturys for our catayl and bestys. **1633** G. HERBERT *Temple*, *Ch. Porch* iv, If God had laid all common, certainly Man would have been th' incloser.] **1712** *Act 12 Anne* c. 14 §1 It shall..be lawful..to inclose any Part of the Wastes or Common Grounds..not exceeding Sixty Acres. **1744** JACOB *Law Dict.* s.v. *Inclosure*, If the Lord of a Manor inclose Part of the Waste or Common, and doth not leave sufficient Room for the Commoners; they may break down such Inclosure, or have Writ of Assize. **1756** *Act 29 Geo. II.* c. 36 (*title*) An Act for inclosing by the mutual Consent of Lords and Tenants, Part of any Common. **1777** W. DALRYMPLE *Trav. Sp. & Port.* xvi, The late bishop improved this spot of ground..by planting and inclosing it. **1812–16** J. SMITH *Panorama Sc. & Art* II. 594 The general advantages of inclosing land can admit of no question.

fig. **1562** *Apol. Private Masse* (1850) 8 To enclose that to some one sort of private profit, that ought to remain in common. *a* **1618** RALEIGH *Maxims St.* (1651) 43 Charles the fifth..purposed to enclose their [the Netherlanders] priviledges. **1667** MILTON *P.L.* III. 420 This round World, whose first convex divides The luminous inferior Orbs, enclos'd From Chaos. **1668** HOWE in H. Rogers *Life* iv. (1863) 126 It is an enclosed pleasure; a joy which the stranger cannot intermeddle with.

2. a. To shut up in a room or building; to seclude, imprison. *Obs.* exc. with reference to monastic seclusion.

α. *c* **1325** *E.E. Allit. P.* B. 334 Of vche clene comly kynde enclose seuen makez. **1375** BARBOUR *Bruce* IV. 219 The quhethir, men said, enclosit he had Ane spirit. **1393** GOWER *Conf.* III. 200 Many a day..he lay..Withinne walles fast enclosed. **1577** HANMER *Anc. Eccl. Hist.* (1619) 147 Infinite multitudes were everywhere enclosed. *c* **1590** MARLOWE *Faust* (2nd version) 120 In the strongest tower Enclose him fast. **1872** O. SHIPLEY *Gloss. Eccl. Terms* 169 The nuns live in community, but are not enclosed.

β. **1585** ABP. SANDYS *Serm.* (1841) 74 Manasses was never reclaimed until he was inclosed in prison. **1632** LITHGOW *Totall Disc.* 451 He caused inclose mee in a little Cabinet within the Parlour.

†**b.** To put (a jury) in the 'box'. *Sc. Obs.*

1759 HUME *Hist. Eng.* (1806) III. xxxix. 271 The jury was enclosed, of which the earl of Caithness was chancellor. **1795** *Scots. Mag.* LVII. 610/2 Eleven o'clock..at which time the jury was inclosed.

3. a. To insert in a frame or setting, or in a surrounding mass of material; to shut up in a case, envelope, or receptacle. Also *fig.*

α. *c* **1386** CHAUCER *Pers. T.* ⁋965 In the orisoun of the Paternoster hath oure Lord Jhesu Crist enclosed most thinges. ? *a* **1400** *Morte Arth.* 506 And lettres hym bedes Of credence enclosyde. **1611** BIBLE *Ex.* xxxix. 6 They wrought Onix stones enclosed in ouches of gold. **1611** SHAKS. *Wint. T.* I. ii. 435 That lyes enclosed in this Trunke, which you Shall beare along impawnd. **1626** BACON *Sylva* §318 The Apple, Enclosed in Wax was..Green and Fresh. **1664** EVELYN *Kal. Hort.* (1729) 218 About the middle of this Month quite enclose your tender Plants.

β. **1596** DALRYMPLE tr. *Leslie's Hist. Scot.* VI. 340 The Reliques of Malcolme..war Jncloset and keipet in the selfe buist. **1611** BIBLE *Song Sol.* viii. 9 If she bee a dore, we will inclose her with boords of Cedar. **1713** *Guardian* No. 1 ⁋1 A robe or mantle inclosed in a circle of foliages. **1750** tr. *Leonardus' Mirr. Stones* 147 Whatever extraneous matter it finds is inclosed in the gum.

b. In mod. use *esp.*: To place (a letter, document, etc.) for transmission within the cover of another. Also said of the containing letter.

1707 ADDISON *Lett.* (1941) 68 My Lord Hartford desiring me to enclose this Letter to the Electoress. **1708** *Ibid.* 109, I this morning receiv'd..your Lordship's letter..with several others enclosed in the same packet. **1768** BP. WARBURTON *Lett. Eminent Divine* (1809) 422, I looked over my papers to see if I could explain the matter in another sheet, which I would have inclosed. **1835** DICKENS *Let.* 8 Aug. (1965) I. 72 My dear Tom.—I inclose you the proof we spoke of, agreeably to your request. **1838** —— *Let.* 28 Dec. 478, I inclose to Mrs. Blanchard an Invitation from my worser half. **1840** MRS. F. TROLLOPE *Widow Married* iii, I inclose you a lock of his dear little hair. *a* **1891** *Mod.* (*Comm.*) I beg to enclose my price list. I have received his letter enclosing a cheque. **1903** J. JOYCE *Let.* 9 Mar. (1966) II. 35, I enclose you self-explaining documents.

4. In various occasional uses:

†**a.** To blindfold (the eyes). *Obs.*

1475 CAXTON *Jason* 102 b, [Jason] made them to ere foure mesures of lond, enclosing their eyen.

†**b.** To harness, put in the shafts. *Obs. rare*[−1].

1615 CHAPMAN *Odyss.* III. 658 They went to coach, and did their horse inclose [Gr. ζεύγνυντο].

†**c.** To fasten (a door). *Obs. rare.*

1563 BECON *Articles Chr. Relig.* xix, We celebrate the mysteryes, the dores beyng shut and enclosed.

5. a. Of things: To surround, bound on all sides; to envelop, contain.

α. **1340** HAMPOLE *Pr. Consc.* 6610 þe sese..encloses alle þe erthe oboute. **1382** WYCLIF *Jonah* ii. 6 Depnesse encloside me. **1734** tr. *Rollin's Anc. Hist.* IV. IX. 294 A province enclosed between Cilicia and Cappadocia. **1834** McMURTRIE *Cuvier's Anim. Kingd.* 409 The semi-nymph only differs from the larva in the presence of the cases which enclose the wings. **1884** BOWER & SCOTT *De Bary's Phaner. & Ferns* 585 A normal cambium..encloses a large pith. **1887** STEVENSON *Underwoods* I. i. 1 A house with lawns enclosing it.

β. **1503** DUNBAR *Thistle & Rose* 156 A coistly croun..This cumly quene did on hir heid incloiss. **1645** BOATE *Irel. Nat. Hist.* (1652) 40 The Sea..upon the East-side, where the same is inclosed betwixt Ireland and Great-Britain. **1796** KIRWAN *Elem. Min.* (ed. 2) I. 18 Many of them [crystals] inclose organized substances which they could not have admitted but when in a soft or liquid state. **1839** G. BIRD *Nat. Philos.* 106 The air inclosed between E and A will escape through the valve E.

b. *Math.* Of lines or surfaces: To bound on all sides (a portion of space); also (loosely) to intercept (an angle).

1762 SIMSON *Euclid's Elem.* Axiom, Two straight lines cannot enclose a space. **1860** TYNDALL *Glac.* I. §2. 15 The number of degrees in the angle enclosed by the two mirrors. **1885** WATSON & BURBURY *Math. The. Electr. & Magn.* I. 63 The space within any closed surface *S'* enclosing *S*.

6. Of an army, a number of persons, etc.: To surround, hem in on all sides.

1601 SHAKS. *Jul. C.* v. iii. 27 Titinius is enclosed round about With Horsemen. **1611** BIBLE *Judg.* xx. 43 They inclosed the Beniamites round about. **1667** MILTON *P.L.* I. 617 They..half enclose him round With all his Peers. **1770** LANGHORNE *Plutarch* I. (1879) I. 125/1 The rest of the forces ..enclosed the enemy's rear. **1865–6** H. PHILLIPS *Amer. Paper Curr.* II. 91 Endeavor to enclose the British army and navy in the Delaware bay.

†**en'close**, *pple. Obs.* In 5 inclose. [a. Fr. *enclos*, pa. pple. of *enclore*: see prec. Cf. ENCLUSE.] Used as pa. pple. of ENCLOSE *v.*

? *c* **1475** *Sqr. lowe Degre* 986 It was my stewarde, Syr Maradose, That ye so longe have kept inclose.

enclosed, inclosed (ɛn-, ɪn'kləʊzd), *ppl. a.* [f. ENCLOSE *v.* + -ED[1].] **a.** In the senses of the verb. *spec.* of religious communities who are secluded from relations with the outside world.

1552 HULOET, Inclosed, *inclusus.* **1573–80** BARET *Alv.* I. 94 Inclosed: shut in. **1607** TOPSELL *Four-f. Beasts* (1673) 361 To shew the food of tame and enclosed Lions. **1648**

GAGE *West Ind.* xviii. (1655) 122 Which I shall observe with inclosed Parentheses as I goe along. **1797** BEWICK *Brit. Birds* (1847) I. 355 They prefer woody and heathy wastes to inclosed ground. **1848** MACAULAY *Hist. Eng.* I. 312 A region ..which contained only three houses and scarcely any enclosed fields. **1884** ADDIS & ARNOLD *Cath. Dict.* (1897) 911/2 The nuns were to be strictly enclosed. **1905** *Athenæum* 30 Sept. 431/1 Catherine de' Ricci belonged to an enclosed community of Dominican Tertiaries. **1957** *Oxf. Dict. Chr. Ch.* 296/2 The enclosure is more strict in women's orders than men's, and most strict of all in the enclosed orders.

b. quasi-*sb.* A letter or other enclosure within a letter.

1618 J. CHAMBERLAIN *Let.* 5 May (1939) II. 162 The inclosed stands me in two shillings. *c* **1645** HOWELL *Lett.* (1650) II. 23 Yours of the third of August came to safe hand in an inclos'd from my brother. **1707** ADDISON *Lett.* (1941) 72, I was to wait on you..with the enclosed from the Ambassadour Cornara. **1839** DICKENS *Let.* 25 Jan. (1965) I. 494 The best way of answering the inclosed which I found lying at home last night.

†**en'closement.** *Obs. rare*$^{-1}$. [f. ENCLOSE *v.* + -MENT.] = ENCLOSURE.

1580 HOLLYBAND *Treas. Fr. Tong, Toute closture,* an enclosement. **1694** CHILD *Disc. Trade* (ed. 4) 76 Regular and just inclosements of our forests.

encloser (ɛn'kləʊzə(r)). [f. ENCLOSE *v.* + -ER.]

1. One who encloses; *esp.* one who appropriates common land (see ENCLOSE *v.* 1 b). Also *fig.*

1597 J. KNEWSTUB *Confutation* 596 The number of his perfect ones are become inclosers, and haue taken in this heauen. *a* **1616** BEAUM. & FL. *Scornful Lady* II. iii, Thanks to my dear incloser, Master Morecraft. **1633** G. HERBERT *Temple, Ch. Porch* iv, If God had laid all common, certainly Man would have been th' incloser. **1633** MASSINGER *New Way, &c.* IV. i, They call me..grand encloser Of what was common. **1857** TOULM. SMITH *Parish* 468 The encloser would appropriate a permanent personal advantage. **1885** *Spectator* 18 July 950/2 The rescue of Epping Forest from the enclosers.

†**2.** transl. L. *clusor* (Vulg.), a literal rendering of Heb. *masgēr* 'one who closes', a smith. *Obs. rare*$^{-1}$.

1382 WYCLIF *2 Kings* xxiv. 16 He ladde in to caytifte fro Jerusalem..craftise men, and enclosers, a thousand.

en'closing, *vbl. sb.* [f. ENCLOSE *v.* + -ING[1].]

1. The action of the vb. ENCLOSE in various senses.

1538 [see ENCLOSE *v.* 1 b]. **1543–4** *Act 35 Hen. VIII,* c. 9 The recoueringe, inclosinge and inninge of..Wappinge marshe. **1719** DE FOE *Crusoe* (1840) I. x. 173, I began my enclosing of this piece of ground. **1832** in Picton *L'pool. Munic. Rec.* (1886) II. 355 The necessity of the gradual inclosing of the strand.

†**b.** The state of being enclosed. *Obs. rare*$^{-1}$.

c **1440** HYLTON *Scala Perf.* (W. de W. 1494) I. xvi, þou sholdest..be mispaid with thy enclosyng.

†**2.** *concr.* The setting of a gem. *Obs.*

1611 BIBLE *Ex.* xxviii. 20 They shalbe set in gold in their inclosings.

enclosing (ɛn'kləʊzɪŋ), *ppl. a.* [f. ENCLOSE *v.* + -ING[2].] That encloses.

1856 STANLEY *Sinai & Pal.* vii. (1858) 282 Within these two enclosing walls. **1873** TRISTRAM *Moab* xvi. 311 Within the enclosing colonnade we could find no traces of building.

enclosure (ɛn'kləʊʒ(j)ʊə(r), -ə(r)). Also in-. [a. OF. *enclosure* in same sense: see ENCLOSE *v.* and -URE.

The statutes providing for the enclosure of land use the spelling *inclosure.*]

1. The action of enclosing. **a.** *spec.* The action of surrounding or marking off (land) with a fence or boundary; the action of thus converting pieces of common land into private property. Also *attrib.* in ***Enclosure Act, Commissioner.*** Also *fig.*

An Enclosure Act is a private Act of Parliament authorizing the 'enclosure' of common land in some particular locality. In many cases, however, the land dealt with by these Acts was not 'common' land in an absolute sense, but was private property encumbered with the right of commoning during a few weeks in autumn; and the usual procedure was to give each of the commoners a piece of land in absolute ownership as compensation for his surrender of this right.

α. **1574** tr. *Littleton's Tenures* 49a, Three causes of disseisin of rente service..rescous, replevine, and enclosure. **1577** B. GOOGE *Heresbach's Husb.* II. (1586) 50 The first needefull thing for a Garden is water. The nexte to that is enclosure. **1611** SCLATER *Key* (1629) 303 There is, then, no enclosure of this blessing of righteousnesse to any nation, person, sexe, or condition of men. **1642** FULLER *Holy & Prof. St.* II. ix. 86 The gifts and graces of Christians lay in common, till base envy made the first enclosure. **1776** ADAM SMITH *W.N.* I. I. xi. 160 The advantage of enclosure is greater for pasture than for corn. **1801** STRUTT *Sports & Past.* II. i. 50 [Stow] attributes the decay of archery among the Londoners to the enclosures made near the metropolis. **1863** FAWCETT *Pol. Econ.* II. viii. (1876) 238 In the case of almost all these enclosures the interests of the poor have been systematically neglected. **1872** E. PEACOCK *Mabel Heron* vi. 89 The enclosure commissioner..had set out a wide road. **1883** SEEBOHM *Eng. Village Community* 13 Nearly 4000 Enclosure Acts were passed between 1760 and 1844.

β. **1538** STARKEY *England* 98 Hyt ys no thyng necessary for the nuryschyng of our bestys to haue so grete inclosurys of pasturys, wych ys a grete dekey of the tyllage of thys reame. **1614** BP. HALL *Recoll. Treat.* 1035 Whence are our depopulations, and inclosures? **1631–2** *Star Chamb. Cases* (1886) 180 Suffer noe inclosures tending to depopulation. **1712** *Act 12 Anne* c. 4 (*title*) An Act for making Inclosures of some Part of the Common-Grounds in the West-Riding. **1780** BURKE *Sp. Econ. Ref.* Wks. III. 272, I propose to have those rights of the Crown valued as manorial rights are valued on an inclosure. **1801** *Act 41 Geo. III,* c. 109 (*title*) An Act for consolidating in one Act certain Provisions usually inserted in Acts of Inclosure. **1818** CRUISE *Digest* (ed. 2) II. 542 It shall be lawful for the commissioners in inclosure acts. **1845** *Act 8 & 9 Vict.* c. 118 §2 The Commissioners..shall be styled 'The Inclosure Commissioners for England and Wales'. **1873** *Act 36 & 37 Vict.* c. 19 Preamb., Lands allotted under Local Acts of inclosure for the benefit of the poor.

b. *gen.* The action of closing in, surrounding, etc. Somewhat *rare.*

1605 TIMME *Quersitanus* III. C c, Another most excellent lute for the like incloser is made of glasse and vermilion. **1658** SIR T. BROWNE *Hydriot.* i. 35 The Ægyptians..by..handsome Inclosure in glasses, contrived the notablest wayes of integral conservation. **1878** FOSTER *Phys.* III. vii. §1. 531 The complete enclosure of the glottis..is..a part of the act of coughing.

2. The state of being enclosed (in a monastery).

1816 MARY SCHIMMELPENNINCK *Biogr. Jansenius* II. 52 She resolved, therefore, to re-establish that enclosure which the rule of St. Bennet so strictly enjoins. **1872** O. SHIPLEY *Gloss. Eccl. Terms* 179 The nuns keep strict enclosure, and lead the contemplative life.

3. That wherewith something is enclosed:

a. An encompassing fence or barrier; buildings round a court. Also *fig.*

1517 *Domesday Inclos.* (1897) I. 248 Landes enclosid by hedgys, dikes, or other Inclousours. **1543–4** *Act 17 Hen. VIII,* c. 17 §17 If thinclosure or inclosures of any of the saide Coppies..happen to be broken or pulled downe. **1556** *Chron. Gr. Friars* (1852) 59 There was a boke made and send up to the commyns of Cornwalle and Devynshere..be cause of their rysynge and pullynge downe of incloseres. **1594** PLAT *Jewell-ho.* III. *Chem. Concl.* 33 Pales and other enclosures. *c* **1710** CELIA FIENNES *Diary* (1888) 8 Fruitfull Country's for Corn, graseing, much for inclosures that make the wayes very narrow. **1725** POPE *Odyss.* VII. 145 Th' allotted space of ground, Fenc'd with a green enclosure all around. **1742** YOUNG *Nt. Th.* IV. 93, I see the circling hunt, of noisy men, Burst law's inclosure. **1754** POCOCKE *Trav.* (1889) II. 72 A court of large buildings..the enclosure of the court seems..very old. **1823** SCOTT *Quentin D.* iii, The second enclosure rising higher than the first.

b. An outer covering or case; an envelope.

1551 BIBLE *Exod.* xxxix. 13 (R.) A turcas, an onix, & a jaspis closed in ouches of gold in their inclosers. **1594** PLAT *Jewell-ho* III. *Chem. Concl.* 2 All the outwarde couers and enclosures whatsoeuer. **1595** MARKHAM *Sir R. Grinvile* cxxii, O why should such..enuie dwell, In the inclosures of eternall mould? **1601** CORNWALLYES *Disc. Seneca* (1631) 39 He that aspireth to this flight to the starres, must..make apt his grosse inclosure of earth. **1633** P. FLETCHER *Pisc. Ecl.* I. v, The raw blossome of my youth was yet In my first childhood's green enclosure bound.

4. That which is enclosed: **a.** A space included within or marked off by boundaries. *spec.* on a racecourse (see quot. 1963).

1552 HULOET, Inclusure called a barton to feade fowles in, *chors.* **1580** HOLLYBAND *Treas. Fr. Tong* s.v. *Pourprendre,* The roote of that tree did occupy in compasse a great inclosure. **1636** HEALEY *Epictetus' Man.* 106 In the greatest enclosure of all, there was a gate. **1772** PRIESTLEY *Inst. Relig.* (1782) I. 413 The whole inclosure was..converted into a chace. **1836–9** DICKENS *Sk. Boz* (1850) 131/1 We were seated in the enclosure of St. James's Park. **1864** SKEAT *Uhland's Poems* 361, I..Sell fortress, town, and hill, With servants, rents, inclosures, woods. **1867** 'OUIDA' *Under Two Flags* I. iii. 46 The horses were being led into the enclosure for saddling. **1910** *Encycl. Brit.* XIII. 737/2 [France] There are none of the clubs and special enclosures such as at Sandown, Kempton, Hurst, Lingfield, Gatwick, etc., though portions of the stand are set apart for privileged persons. **1963** BLOODGOOD & SANTINI *Horseman's Dict.* 72 *Enclosure,* space set apart on the grounds of a racecourse for some specific purpose; the Royal Enclosure, the Jockey Club Enclosure, the Members' Enclosure, etc. **1968** J. FLEMING *Kill or Cure* ix. 115 She wasn't allowed into the Royal Enclosure at Ascot.

b. A document or letter enclosed within the cover of another.

1776 *Jrnls. Cont. Congress* IV. 107 Two letters from General Schuyler..with an account of his expedition to Tryon county, with 9 enclosures. **1776** J. HANCOCK in Sparks *Corr. Amer. Rev.* (1853) I. 235 Your letter of the 21st instant..with the inclosure, was duly received. *Mod.* I have received your letter with its enclosures.

enclothe (ɛn'kləʊð), *v.* [f. EN-[1] + CLOTHE *v.*] *trans.* To clothe, cover, invest.

1832 *Fraser's Mag.* VI. 602 It enclothes the banks with a show of light and glory. **1833** MRS. BROWNING *Prometh. Bound* Poems 1850 I. 176 Enclothed with wings. **1885** W. K. PARKER *Mammal. Desc.* iii. 60 The three membranes that enclothe the embryo.

encloud (ɛn'klaʊd), *v.* Also 6–7 enclowd, 7 incloude, -owd. [f. EN-[1] + CLOUD *sb.*] *trans.* To surround with or envelop in a cloud; to overshadow, darken. Also *fig.* Hence **en'clouded** *ppl. a.*

1591 SPENSER *Virg. Gnat* 571 The heauens on euerie side enclowded bee. **1602** DAVISON *Rhapsody* (1611) 25 Darknesse oft that light incloudes. **1606** SHAKS. *Ant. & Cl.* v. ii. 212 In their thicke breathes shall we be enclowded. **1610** HEALEY *St. Aug. Citie of God* I. xxi. (1620) 31 Mortall men..are most commonly inclowded in a mist of ignorance and errour. *a* **1641** BP. MOUNTAGU *Acts & Mon.* (1642) 117 Stars are enclowded oftentimes. *Ibid.* 126 Now for the secret and enclouded sense. **1844** A. WELBY *Poems* (1867) 11 When death's shadows my bosom encloud. **1856** R. VAUGHAN *Mystics* (1860) II. IX. iii. 141 Mark the advantage of this enclouded state.

†**en'clow,** *v. Obs. rare*$^{-1}$. (See ENCLAWED). [ad. OF. *enclo-er,* f. *en* in + *clou* nail.] *trans.* To nail up.

c **1430** *Pilgr. Lyf. Manhode* I. cxvii. (1869) 61 With the nailes with which was nayled the sone of the smith..the mailes weren enclowed.

†**en'cloy,** *v. Obs.* [a. OF. *encloye-r, encloër* (mod. *enclouer*), to drive in a nail. Cf. prec. and ACCLOY.] *trans.* To lame or maim by driving in a nail. Also *fig.*

1393 GOWER *Conf.* II. 47 And halted, as he were encloied. *c* **1430** LYDG. *Bochas* (1558) VIII. xxi. 18 False ambicion and froward duplicite Hath many a realme & many a land encloid.

enclude, obs. form of INCLUDE.

†**en'cluse,** *pple.* and *ppl. a. Obs.* Also incluse. [a. OF. *enclus,* ad. L. *inclūs-us,* pa. pple. of *inclūdĕre*: see INCLUDE.] Enclosed: chiefly said of monks or nuns.

c **1340** HAMPOLE *Prose Tr.* (1866) 42 ȝa and þou sall be safe as ane ankir incluse. *c* **1420** *Pallad. on Husb.* IV. 261 The caules that of seede encluse uppe wynde Wol bygger be. *c* **1440** HYLTON *Scala Perf.* (W. de W. 1494) I. lx, As done pryncypally ancres encluse and true religyous.

encluster: see EN- *pref.*[1] 2.

encoach: see EN- *pref.*[1] 1 a.

encode (ɛn'kəʊd), *v.* [EN-[1] + CODE *sb.*[1] 3 b.] *trans.* To translate into cipher or code; also *techn.* of computers (see quot. 1955). Also *transf.*

1919 in L. TISSOT-DUPONT *Dict. Termes de Telegraphie-Telephonie.* **1931** H. O. YARDLEY *Amer. Black Chamber* xiv. 187 If his cable, even after translation into Japanese and encoded in his code, still retains the proper name, I'm sure I can find it. **1932** D. L. SAYERS *Have his Carcase* xxvi. 341 It's the kind of thing that young Alexis could easily learn to encode and decode. **1955** *Gloss. Terms Autom. Digital Computers (B.S.I.)* 10 *Encode,* to express information by means of a *code.* Colloquially, 'to code'. **1959** B. C. BROOKES in Quirk & Smith *Teaching of English* v. 155 The lecturer..encodes [his] information in appropriate speech signals. **1959** E. PULGRAM *Introd. Spectrogr. Speech* i. 12 The membranes of telephones and microphones are obstacles of this type receptive to air waves. The energy that strikes them is translated, or encoded, into electric currents, which are in the receiver electronically decoded again into sound waves.

Hence **en'coding** *vbl. sb.* (also *attrib.*).

1953 *Encounter* Oct. 21/1 Communism itself [is] only a secondary encoding of the completely unmentioned Soviet Union. **1954** *Electronic Engin.* XXVI. 84 The technique of encoding and programming, the 'training of the robot'. **1956** J. WHATMOUGH *Language* i. 13 A striking utterance is found, on inspection, to disturb commonplace encoding and decoding processes.

encoder (ɛn'kəʊdə(r)). [f. the vb.] Someone or something that encodes; *spec.* a part of a computer that converts data under specific conditions.

1944 *Harper's Mag.* Oct. 468/1 The Italian radio operator ..did not have the mechanical encoder and had to encode the messages by hand. **1956** *Electronic Engin.* XXVIII. 37 At the rear of the machine is the perforator or 'encoder' which produces the punched tape. **1958** *Ibid.* XXX. 685 The comparator described..compares two voltages at constant intervals of time, a process required for example in voltage encoders. **1959** *Times Rev. Industry* Feb. 86/1 Separation of the directional information from two normal left and right stereo signals in an encoder. **1964** J. Z. YOUNG *Model of Brain* ix. 159 Cells with long spreading dendrites provide the encoders. **1966** *Electronics* 17 Oct. 38 Low-drift gyros are still desirable, but the encoder function and analog-to-digital requirements tied to gimbaling are bypassed.

en cœur: see EN *prep.*

en'coffin, *v.* Now *rare.* Also 7 encoffen. [f. EN-[1] + COFFIN.] *trans.* To put into a coffin; hence, to shut up, hide away. Also *fig.* Hence **en'coffining** *vbl. sb.*

1598 E. GILPIN *Skial.* (1878) 54, I had rather be encoffin'd in this chest. **1631** WEEVER *Anc. Fun. Mon.* 868 His bones were..solemnly encoffined in the Chancell. **1670** PENN *Case Liberty Consc.* 15 They condemn the Papists for encoffening the Scriptures..in an unknown tongue. **1856** *Chamb. Jrnl.* V. 214 The encoffining..of the dead was regarded as of greater consequence.

encoffined (ɛn'kɒfɪnd), *ppl. a.* [f. ENCOFFIN *v.* + -ED[1].] Enclosed in a coffin.

1904 M. CORELLI *God's Good Man* 59 The encoffined saint whose sarcophagus had been unearthed. **1907** E. WILDER tr. *Werder's Hamlet's Myst.* i. 49 The secret of the encoffined and unprovable crime. **1908** *Daily Chron.* 17 Aug. 5/6 An encoffined body.

encoffinment (ɛn'kɒfɪnmənt). [f. ENCOFFIN *v.* + -MENT.] The action of encoffining.

1882 R. K. DOUGLAS *China* xvi. 294 The encoffinment takes place on the third day after death.

‖**encoignure** (ɑ̃kɔɲyr). [Fr., f. *en-* in + *coin* corner.] A piece of furniture, esp. of ornamental design, made with an angle to fit into a corner.

1848 H. R. FORSTER *Stowe Catal.* 22 A pair of very handsome encoigneures, of rich buhl on tortoiseshell. **1936**

Burlington Mag. Oct. 187/1 Among the masterpieces of French furniture in Windsor Castle are a commode and a pair of *encoignures*. **1962** *Internat. Art Treasures Exhib.* (*Vict. & Albert Mus.*) 21/2 A Louis XVI suite of lacquer furniture attributed to P. Garnier comprising a Commode and a pair of Encoignures.

encoil, encolden: see EN- *pref.*[1] 1, 3.

encollar, encolumn: see EN- *pref.*[1] 2.

encolour (ɛn'kʌlə(r)), *v.* [f. EN-[1] + COLOUR *sb.*[1] Cf. OF. *encolour-er.*] *trans.* To put colour upon, tinge. Hence **en'colouring** *vbl. sb., concr.* a tinge or colouring overlaid.

1648 HERRICK *Hesper.* I. 181 Wings, With thousand rare encolourings. **1850** MRS. BROWNING *Poems* II. 309 Oval cheeks, encoloured faintly.

encolure (ɛnkəʊ'l(j)ʊə(r)). *nonce-wd.* [a. Fr. *encolure* the neck of an animal.] Used by Browning for: The mane (of a horse).

1855 BROWNING *Statue & Bust* in *Men & Wom.* I. 157 Hair.. Crisped like a warsteed's encolure.

encomber, -ment, obs. ff. ENCUMBER, etc.

encomiac (ɛn'kəʊmɪæk), *a. nonce-wd.* [f. Gr. ἐγκώμι-ον (ἔπος) ENCOMIUM + -AC.] Of or pertaining to eulogy; panegyrical.

1869 *Contemp. Rev.* XII. 230 The study of the Greek of Theocritus, especially in his encomiac and more heroic idylls.

†**en'comiasm.** *Obs. rare*⁻¹. [as if. ad. Gr. *ἐγκωμίασμ-α, f. ἐγκωμιάζειν: see next.] A laudatory discourse, panegyric.

1634 JACKSON *Creed* VII. xxvii, This author's encomiasm of wisdom.

encomiast (ɛn'kəʊmɪæst). [ad. Gr. ἐγκωμιαστ-ής, f. ἐγκωμιάζειν to praise, laud, f. ἐγκώμιον ENCOMIUM.] One who composes or pronounces an encomium; a praiser, eulogizer, flatterer.

1610 G. FLETCHER *Christ's Vict.* xlix, Of faire Eclecta.. the.. smooth Encomiast. *a* **1626** BACON *Q. Eliz.* Mor. & Hist. Wks. (Bohn) 492 The only proper encomiast of this lady is time. **1772** *Let.* in Pettigrew *Lettsom* (1817) III. 394 Having undertaken the office of the biographer, not that of the encomiast. **1875** JOWETT *Plato* (ed. 2) III. 132 We hear the encomiasts of Homer affirming that he is the educator of Hellas.

†**encomi'aster.** *Obs. rare*⁻¹. [as if ad. Gr. *ἐγκωμιαστήρ = ἐγκωμιαστής: see prec.] = prec.

1676 GROVE *Vind. Conform. Clergy* (1680) 21 You may see by this how far you may trust this eloquent Encomiaster.

encomiastic (ɛn,kəʊmɪ'æstɪk), *a.* and *sb.* [ad. Gr. ἐγκωμιαστικ-ός, f. ἐγκωμιάζειν: see ENCOMIAST.]

A. *adj.* That conveys or confers an encomium; laudatory, commendatory, eulogistic.

1599 B. JONSON *Cynthia's Rev.* I. iv. 75 To frame some encomiasticke speech upon this our Metropolis. **1630** BRATHWAIT *Eng. Gentl.* (1641) 306 Doting on nothing more than these encomiasticke bladders of their desertlesse praises. **1795** R. ANDERSON *Brit. Poets* 448 An Ode, which, though less elevated, has some fine encomiastic strains. **1841** HOR. SMITH *Moneyed Man* I. v. 154, I made a slight encomiastic allusion to Fanny Hartopp.

†**B.** *sb.* A eulogistic discourse or composition; a formal encomium. *Obs.*

1632 B. JONSON *Magn. Lady* I. i, I thank you, master Compass, for your short Encomiastic. **1644** JOHN CARTER *Nail hit on the head* (1647) 39 A sumptuous and magnificent Sepulchre.. and upon it written Encomiastiques, the high praises of his vertue. **1707** HEARNE *Coll.* (Oxf. Hist. Soc.) II. 25 Sends an 'Encomiastic' to be prefixed to Hudson's edition of Dionysius. **18..** MOORE *Devil among Schol.* 584 Wise Encomiastics Upon the Doctors and Scholastics.

encomiastical (ɛn,kəʊmɪ'æstɪkəl), *a.* [f. prec. + -AL[1].] = ENCOMIASTIC *a.*

1592 G. HARVEY *Pierce's Super.* 59 This deserveth a more famous encomiasticall oration. **1691** WOOD *Ath. Oxon.* II. 112 A white marble table, and thereon an Epitaph.. with encomiastical Verses. **1721–1800** in BAILEY. **1815** *Scribbleomania* 25 Plaudits encomiastical, That stride on stilts, bombastical.

en,comi'astically, *adv. rare.* [f. prec. + -LY[2].] In an encomiastical manner.

a **1631** DONNE *Lett.* (1651) 32 If I have not spoken of your Majesty encomiastically. **1871** *Athenæum* 9 Sept. 339 A short notice.. written in good taste, if a little too encomiastically.

†**en'comiate,** *v. Obs. rare*⁻¹. [f. ENCOMI-UM + -ATE.] *trans.* To pronounce an encomium upon; to extol, commend.

1651 BIGGS *New Disp.* 146 They encomiate Phlebotomy chiefly for that end.

encomienda (ɛnkəʊmɪ'ɛndə). *Hist.* [Sp., = commission, charge, sb. corresp. to the vb. *encomendar* to commit, charge; cf. med.L. phr. *in commendam* (see COMMENDAM).] An estate granted to a Spaniard in America, with powers to exact taxation and corvée from the Indian inhabitants; such authority; a system derived from such authority. Also **encomen'dero,** the holder of an encomienda.

1810 *Eclectic Rev.* VI. II. 1065 The systematic slavery of the *encomiendas* having been annulled by Charles III. **1818** *Docs. Congr. U.S. For. Rel.* (1834) IV. 325 (Stanford), All these regulations were found ineffectual to secure the Indians against the rapacity of the encomenderos, and encomiendas were abolished. **1877** *Encycl. Brit.* VI. 174/1 That system of *repartimientos* or *encomiendas* which was afterwards to work such cruel mischief among the conquered. **1885** *Ibid.* XVIII. 677/2 'Encomiendas', or grants of estates on which the inhabitants were bound to pay tribute and give personal service to the grantee. **1952** BERTRAND & PETRIE *Hist. Spain* (ed. 2) xxiii. 198 The *encomenderos*, to whom territories and whole populations of Indians were granted on the condition of feeding them and instructing them in the Christian faith—these colonists declared that there was nothing to be done with the Indians. **1964** M. HARRIS *Patterns of Race in Americas* ii. 18 In the highlands.. the dominant form of labour appropriation.. was known as the *encomienda*... A man who had performed service.. in the conquest of the new territories was rewarded with the privilege of collecting tribute and drafting labor among a stated group of Indians... Cortes.. received an *encomienda* consisting of twenty-two townships.

†**en'comion.** *Obs.* The Gr. form of ENCOMIUM; occas. used in 16th and 17th c.

1598 B. JONSON *Ev. Man in Hum.* IV. ii. 69 You have a simple servant here, that crownes your beauty with such encomions. *a* **1640** JACKSON *Creed* XI. xlvi, Mellifluous encomions of divine love. **1646** G. DANIEL *Poems* Wks. 1878 I. 88 How deckt In her Encomions ffollie doth appeare.

†**en'comionize,** *v. Obs. rare.* [f. prec. + -IZE.] *trans.* To pronounce an encomium upon; to eulogize.

1599 NASHE *Lent. Stuffe* 23 Tart and galingale.. Chaucer preheminentest encomionizeth aboue all.. confectionaries. **1647** R. BARON *Cyprian Acad.* 70 Hark.. how I anatomize My Julietta, and her encomionize.

encomium (ɛn'kəʊmɪəm). *Pl.* **encomiums;** also (now *rarely*) **encomia.** Also ENCOMION. [a. L. *encōmium*, ad. Gr. ἐγκώμιον (ἔπος) eulogy.] A formal or high-flown expression of praise; a eulogy, panegyric.

1589 PUTTENHAM *Eng. Poesie* I. xx. (Arb.) 58 The immortall gods were praised by hymnes, the great Princes and heroicke personages by ballades of praise called Encomia. **1613** BEAUM. & FL. *Honest Man's Fort.* III. i, You .. Should sing encomiums on't [marriage]. **1711** STEELE *Spect.* No. 139. ¶3 If we consider this wonderful Person, it is Perplexity to know where to begin his Encomium. **1846** DICKENS *Old C. Shop* xxx, He brought in the bread, cheese and beer, with many high encomiums upon their excellence. **1875** JOWETT *Plato* (ed. 2) I. 139 Many tales, and praises, and encomia of ancient famous men.

†**b.** *abstr. Obs. rare*⁻¹.

1784 COWPER *Task* VI. 715 Encomium in old times was poets' work.

†**enco'mmend,** *v. Obs. rare*⁻¹. [a. Sp. *encomendar* in same sense, f. *en-* (see EN-[1]) + *comendar* to COMMEND.] *trans.* To entrust (a military function).

1598 BARRET *Theor. Warres* V. i. 121 Encommended and bestowed vpon personages of great grauitie.

encommon: see EN- *pref.*[1] 2.

†**en'company,** *v. Obs.* [ad. OF. *encompaignier*, f. *en-* (see EN-[1]) + *compaignie* COMPANY.]

1. *trans.* To accompany.

1494 FABYAN VII. 515 The sayd prouost beynge encompanyed with .viii. score or .cc. men. **1533** MORE *Answ. Poisoned Bk.* Wks. 1088/1 Theyr glose was of faythe not alone, but encompained with two good felowes perdye.

2. To bring into company, associate. Const. *to.*

c **1530** LD. BERNERS *Arth. Lyt. Bryt.* (1814) 345 Encompanyed by maryage to ony persone.. ayenst her herte.

encompass (ɛn'kʌmpəs), *v.* Also 6–8 **incompass.** [f. EN-[1] + COMPASS *sb.*; cf. obs. Sp. *encompasar* of equivalent formation.]

1. To encircle as a ring or girdle; to surround, bound on all sides.

α. **1555** EDEN *Decades W. Ind.* III. VI. (Arb.) 161 The northe landes which the frosen sea encompaseth vnder the northe pole. **1697** DRYDEN *Virg. Georg.* IV. 688 Baleful Styx encompasses around.. th' unhappy Ground. **1725** DE FOE *Voy. round W.* (1840) 130 A kind of a city, encompassed all round, the river making a kind of double horse-shoe. **1776** WITHERING *Bot. Arrangem.* (1796) II. 423 Some encompassed with a membranaceous border, deeper than half the breadth of the seed. **1872** JENKINSON *Guide Eng. Lakes* 251 Behind are the mountains encompassing Borrowdale.

β. **1596** SPENSER *State Irel.* Wks. (1862) 527/2 You have very well declared the originall of their mounts and great stones incompassed. **1652** NEEDHAM tr. *Selden's Mare Cl.* 79 This Dominion.. incompassed their Empire round like a girdle. **1659** HAMMOND *On Ps.* lx. 304 Part of Syria which is incompast with Tigris and Euphrates. **1723** SHEFFIELD (Dk. Buckhm.) *Wks.* (1753) II. 221 My iron pallisade that incompasses a square court.

2. a. Of persons: To surround, form a circle about, whether for protection, in attendance, or with hostile intent. Also *fig.* Also *absol.*

α. **1555** EDEN *Decades W. Ind.* II. I. (Arb.) 107 Encoompasinge the vyllage where they laye. **1667** MILTON *P. L.* III. 149 Th' innumerable sound of Hymns.. wherewith thy Throne Encompass'd shall resound thee ever blest. **1704** SWIFT *T. Tub* Wks. 1760 I. 36 Encompassed with a ring of disciples. **1781** GIBBON *Decl. & F.* II. xxx. 258 His throne was encompassed with domestic enemies. **1850** TENNYSON *In Mem.* CXXVI. ii, I.. sleep Encompass'd by his faithful guard.

β. **1590** WEBBE *Trav.* (Arb.) 24 The Turkes power did incompasse Prester Iohns sonne. **1591** SHAKS. *1 Hen. VI,* III. ii. 53 Hag of all despight, Incompass'd with thy lustfull Paramours. *a* **1699** LADY HALKETT *Autobiog.* (1875) 72, I was now Incompased with misfortunes.

†**b.** Of right lines: To contain, include (an angle). *Obs. rare*⁻¹.

1660 BARROW *Euclid.* I. xlvii. Probl. 3 The sides *A B, A C,* encompassing the right angle.

†**3.** To make a circuit about, go all round (anything). *Obs.*

1640 WILKINS *New Planet* vii. (1707) 216 The Planets.. do by their Motion encompass the Body of the Sun. **1654** GAYTON *Pleas. Notes* IV. iv. 192 Drake encompass'd the world with a ship. **1727** SWIFT *Gulliver* III. i. 179, I encompassed it almost round before I could find a convenient place to land in. **1772–84** COOK *Voy.* (1790) IV. 1275 Mr. Gore encompassed the hill, and joined them.

4. To surround entirely, overlay as with an envelope or shell; to contain.

1553 EDEN *Treat. New Ind.* (Arb.) 35 A thinne skinne.. encompassing the shell of the nutte. **1571** DIGGES *Pantom.* IV. xxv, This figure.. may be incompassed of a sphere. **1626** BACON *Sylva* §587 A Stalk of Wheat.. encompassed with a case of Wood. **1650** BAXTER *Saints' R.* I. vii. (1662) 102 Had onely Faith to live upon, and were incompassed with flesh. **1678** HOBBES *Nat. Philos.* ix. 115, I thought nothing had encompassed the Earth but Air. **1794** G. ADAMS *Nat. & Exp. Phil.* I. 56 They are kept together by the air that incompasses them in the receiver. **1875** H. E. MANNING *Mission H. Ghost* vii. 192 Walk in the light with which He encompasses you.

†**5.** *nonce-use.* To outwit, take advantage of, 'get round' (a person). *Obs.*

1598 SHAKS. *Merry W.* II. ii. 158 Ah ha, Mistresse Ford and Mistresse Page, haue I encompass'd you?

6. Used for COMPASS *v.*[1] 2.

1882 P. ROBINSON *Under Sun* III. v. 201 Whatever the method employed for encompassing his death. **1889** MRS. H. L. CAMERON *Lost Wife* I. iv. 69 What earthly reason could Captain Thistleby have for encompassing my destruction?

en'compasser. *rare.* [f. ENCOMPASS *v.* + -ER.] One who or that which encompasses.

1666 J. SMITH *Old Age* (ed. 2) 241 Vessels.. which bring home the noble Travellour, the encompassour of the little World.

en'compassing, *vbl. sb.* [f. ENCOMPASS *v.* + -ING[1].] The action of the vb. ENCOMPASS.

1628 EARLE *Microcosm.* lxi 166 They meet in some foreign region, where the encompassing of strangers unites them closer.

encompassing (ɛn'kʌmpəsɪŋ), *ppl. a.* [f. ENCOMPASS *v.* + -ING[2].] That encompasses.

1571 DIGGES *Pantom.* IV. xxiii, His encompassing Icosaedrons side is an Apotome. **1724** WATTS *Logic* (1736) 121 The encompassing Parts are the Walls and Gates. **1888** *Pall Mall G.* 13 Sept. 4/2 The Emperor of Morocco has fought his way out of his encompassing enemies.

encompassment (ɛn'kʌmpəsmənt). *rare.* [f. ENCOMPASS *v.* + -MENT.]

1. The action of encompassing; †'talking round' a subject (*obs. rare*⁻¹).

1602 SHAKS. *Ham.* II. i. 10 Finding By this encompassement and drift of question, That they doe know my sonne.

2. The state of being encompassed.

1882 *Century Mag.* Oct. 945 A sense of absolute encompassment by perfect good.

†**en'compassure.** *Obs. rare*⁻¹. [f. ENCOMPASS *v.* + -URE.] That which encompasses; environment.

1600 TOURNEUR *Transf. Met.* lxxvii. 536 Fogs, damps, trees, stones, their sole encompassure.

†**en'comy.** *Obs. rare.* Anglicized form of ENCOMIUM.

1533 CRANMER in Ellis *Orig. Lett.* I. 114 II. 38 Diverse other encomyes spoken of chyldren. **1542** BECON *David's Harp* Wks. (1843) 285 He will.. lift it up with perpetual encomies, lauds, and praises. **1544** BALE in *Sel. Wks.* (1849) 7 Many popish parasites.. have written large commendations and encomies of those.

encoop (ɛn'kuːp), *v. poet.* [f. EN-[1] + COOP *sb.*[1]] *trans.* To coop up.

1867 J. B. ROSE tr. *Virgil's Æneid* 267 Again besieged, again encooped in hold. **1906** HARDY *Dynasts* II. I. viii. 172 Her fleet at any minute can encoop Yours in the Baltic.

en'coppicement. [f. EN-[1] 2 + COPPICE *sb.* + -MENT.] The promotion and preservation of coppices.

1935 *Forestry* IX. 11 The object of the encoppicements.. was coppice in which hazel and ash figured largely. **1958** *Wilts. Arch. Mag.* LVII. 65 Although encoppicement was legally sanctioned, the hedges of a coppice are [etc.].

en coquille: see EN *prep.*

encorbellment (ɛn'kɔːbəlmənt). [f. EN- + CORBEL + -MENT; after Fr. *encorbellement.*]

1886 BALDW. BROWN *Schola to Cathedral* iv. 136 *note,* A pseudo arch or vault formed by encorbellment (i.e. the continuous projection of each horizontal course over the one immediately below it).

encore (ɑ̃'kɔr, often ɒŋ'kɔə(r)), *int.* and *sb.* Also 8 **encora.** [a. Fr. *encore* still, yet (in some contexts translated by 'again'); cf. the synonymous Pr. *encara, enquera,* OSp. *encara,* It. *ancora.* (Usually these words have been

regarded as:—L. (*in*) *hanc hōram* until this hour; but the phonology is not wholly clear, and other explanations have been proposed, e.g. by Havet in *Romania*, VIII. 94.) The use of It. ANCORA occurs in Eng. equally early; the form *encora* in 18th c. is due to confusion between the Fr. and the It. word.

There appears to be no evidence that either the Fr. or the It. word was ever similarly used in its native country. The corresponding word both in Fr. and It. is *bis*; in It. *da capo* was formerly used.]

A. *int.* Again, once more: used by spectators or auditors to demand the repetition of a song, piece of music, or other performance, that has pleased them.

1712 STEELE *Spect.* No. 314 ¶9 Whenever any Gentlemen are particularly pleased with a Song, at their crying out Encore.. the Performer is so obliging as to sing it over again. **1766** ANSTEY *Bath Guide* (1767) 114 Pray speak to Sir Toby to cry out encore. **1781** J. MOORE *View Soc. It.* (1795) I. 189 A Duo.. drew an universal encora from the spectators. **1825** HONE *Every-day Bk.* I. 1464 Loud shouts of 'encore' roused him.

B. *sb.* A call for the repetition of a song, etc.; the repetition itself. Also *attrib.*

1763 J. BROWN *Poetry & Mus.* xii. 206 If the Audience were warmed by the Subject of an Opera.. the Encore, instead of being desireable, would generally disgust. **1811** BYRON *Hints from Hor.* 310 His anguish doubling by his own 'encore'. **1839** DICKENS *Nich. Nick* xxii. That'll be a double encore if you take care, boys. **1883** *Athenæum* 2 June 697/3 There is nothing in the twenty pages.. to warrant an encore. **1884** G. MOORE *Mummer's Wife* (1887) 192, I know all the words except the encore verse. *Mod.* No encores allowed.

en'core, *v.* [f. prec.] *trans.* To call applaudingly for the repetition of (a song, etc.); to demand a repetition from (a performer).

1748 RICHARDSON *Clarissa* (1811) III. 341 They encored it. **1754** —— *Grandison* (1781) VI. xxxi. 204 The wretches.. encored him [Sir Charles] without mercy. **1826** MISS MITFORD *Village* Ser. II. (1863) 268, I got a part of the audience.. to encore my swoon. **1863** MRS. C. CLARKE *Shaks. Char.* iv. 98 The idea of a man pluming himself on the possibility of being encored in a roar. **1879** FROUDE *Cæsar* xiii. 182 Lines.. reflecting on Pompey.. were encored a thousand times.

b. *transf.* To go over again (*nonce-use*).

1806 BERESFORD *Miseries* (ed. 5) I. 24 Till you are.. necessitated to turn back, and encore all your sufferings.

encoronall, encoronet: see EN- *pref.*[1] 1 b.

encorownment, var. of ENCROWNMENT, *Obs.*

encorporate, obs. form of INCORPORATE.

†**en'corpore**, *v. Obs.* Also 5 encorpere. [a. OF. *encorpore-r*, ad. L. *incorporāre* to INCORPORATE.]

1. *intr.* in *Alchemy*: To form one body with; to amalgamate.

c **1386** CHAUCER *Chan. Yem., Prol. & T.* 262 Oure matires enbibyng And eek of oure matires encorporyng. *c* **1460–70** *Bk. Quintessence* 13 Putte þe element of watir.. vpon j ib of mater and putte by vij daies to encorpere wel.

2. *trans.* To insert in a body of documents; to enrol or enter in the records of a court.

1523 LD. BERNERS *Froiss.* I. ccxii. 260 We woll.. that the sayd letters before encorpored, be of none effecte.

†**en'corsive**, *a. Obs. rare.* [f. OF. *encorser* to make flesh, grow fat, f. *en* in + OF. *cors* (F. *corps* body + *-if*, -IVE.] Fat, fleshy.

a **1340** HAMPOLE *Cant., Psalter* 516 Encorsyfe is þe lufyd & he kest vp.

[**encortif**, erroneous f. of *encorsif*, ENCORSIVE.

Wyclif's Sel. Wks. (1869) III. 36 (from Hampole: see ENCORSIVE.)]

encortin, obs. f. ENCURTAIN.

encouch: see EN- *pref.*[1] 1 a.

encounter (ɛn'kaʊntə(r)), *sb.* Forms: 3 encontre, 5 encountre, 6- encounter. Also 6–8 incounter. [a. OF. *encontre* masc. and fem. (cf. Pr. *encontre*, Sp. *encuentro*, It. *incontro*), f. late L. *incontrāre*: see next.] A meeting face to face.

1. A meeting face to face; a meeting (of adversaries or opposing forces) in conflict; *hence*, a battle, skirmish, duel, etc.

1297 R. GLOUC. (Rolls) 8051 He vond hard encontre in norþhumberlande. *c* **1430** *Syr Gener.* (Roxb.) 5083 But than cam encountre strong Folk of higher Inde among. **1575** *Chr. Prayers* in *Priv. Prayers* (1851) 542 How unseemly an encounter is this, wherein the flesh being matched against the spirit.. striveth with him for victory. **1586** T. B. *La Primaud. Fr. Acad.* I. (1589) 104 An incounter of their armies, wherein Cæsar, being at that time the weaker, had the woorst. **1594** SHAKS. *Rich. III*, I. ii. 115 To leaue this keene encounter of our wittes. **1667** MILTON *P. L.* II. 718 Winds the signal blow To joyn thir dark Encounter in mid air. **1672** MARVELL *Reh. Transp.* I. 229, I.. have no heart to this encounter. **1828** SCOTT *F.M. Perth* i, In these vales.. the Saxons.. and the Gael.. had many a desperate and bloody encounter. **1853** ROBERTSON *Serm.* Ser. III. xvii. 221 We *must* shrink from the encounter with death.

†**b.** *attrib. Obs. rare.*

1598 STOW *Surv.* xxxix. (1603) 386 [A champion in the lists says] Though my horse fayle me I will not fayle an incounter companion.

2. The fact of meeting with (a person or thing), *esp.* undesignedly or casually. Const. *of*, *with*.

1656 FINETT *For. Ambass.* 22 In case he should be put to it upon any incounter of negotiation or otherwise. **1665** EVELYN *Mem.* (1857) III. 161 We are infinitely defective as to.. excuses.. upon sudden and unpremeditated encounters. *a* **1699** LADY HALKETT *Autobiog.* (1875) 9, I must here relate a little odd Incounter. **1794** GODWIN *Cal. Williams* 230 The state of calamity to which my.. persecutor had reduced me, had made the encounter even of a den of robbers, a fortunate adventure. *a* **1859** MACAULAY *Hist. Eng.* V. 93 There was constant risk of an encounter which might have produced several duels. **1870** EMERSON *Soc. & Solit.* Wks. (Bohn) III. 5 The encounter with superior persons on terms allowing the happiest intercourse.

†**b.** An amatory interview. *Obs. rare.*

1599 SHAKS. *Much Ado* III. iii. 161 The Prince.. saw a far off in the Orchard this amiable incounter. *Ibid.* IV. i. 94 Who hath indeed most like a liberall villaine, Confest the vile encounters they haue had A thousand times in secret.

†**c.** An accosting, address. *Obs.* Cf. ENCOUNTER *v.* 7.

1591 SHAKS. *Two Gent.* II. vii. 41 For I would preuent The loose encounters of lasciuious men.

d. (A session of) encounter therapy; the experience of participating in an encounter group. Also *spec.*, the name of an organization (also called the Human Potentials Movement) which originally promoted encounter groups. See *encounter group*, etc., sense 7 below.

1967 C. R. ROGERS in J. F. Bugental *Challenges Humanistic Psychol.* 263/1 The interaction is best thought of.. as a varied tapestry.. with certain kinds of trends evidenced in most of these intensive encounters. **1968** J. HOWARD in *Life* 12 July 57/2 The movement is.. known in some quarters as the 'encounter' and in others as the 'T-group'. **1970** —— *Please Touch* 4 Encounters, one leader of the movement says, 'teach intimacy, which gives life a whole new dimension'. *Ibid.* 16 After the Advanced Encounter I was persuaded easily to remain for the weekend. **1972** *Times* 5 June 13/3 Encounter, or the Human Potential Movement, or the Growth Movement, as its devotees call it, is rapidly catching on in this country from America. **1973** *Nation Rev.* (Melbourne) 31 Aug. 1462/1 The irrational core of the encounter movement.. is that the complexity of human growth can be reduced to programmed emotional experience... The encounter experience, a feature of the middle class American search for utopia, has now become an entity in our own country. **1976** *New Yorker* 5 Jan. 30/1 It is true that encounter—which has been described as a way of achieving personal growth through the exploration of feelings among people gathered together for that purpose—owed a great deal of its vogue to the development it underwent at Esalen. **1986** G. SLOVO *Death by Analysis* iii. 23 He started a series of bio-energetic groups with a bit of gestalt and encounter thrown in on the side.

†**3.** Manner of meeting another; style of address, behaviour. *Obs.*

1596 SHAKS. *Tam. Shr.* IV. v. 54 That with your strange encounter much amazed me. **1602** —— *Ham.* V. ii. 197 The tune of the time, and outward habite of encounter. **1611** —— *Wint. T.* III. ii. 50 With what encounter so uncurrent I have strained to appear thus.

†**4.** An idea that suddenly presents itself, as it were by accident; a happy thought. *Obs. rare.*

1651 HOBBES *Leviath.* I. viii. 34 Many times with encounters of extraordinary Fancy. **1678** —— *Nat. Philos.* i. 11 Wonder.. I never thought upon't before, for it is a very happy encounter.

5. The fact of being met with; occurrence. *rare.*

1870 LOWELL *Among my Bks.* Ser. I. (1873) 203 Things of daily encounter.

†**6.** Proposed as a name for the rhetorical figure ANTITHESIS. *Obs. rare*[−1].

1589 PUTTENHAM *Eng. Poesie* III. xix. (Arb.) 219 Ye haue another figure very pleasant and fit for amplification, which to answer the Greeke terme, we may call the encounter.

7. Special Comb. **encounter group** orig. *U.S.*: in group therapy, a group which meets in order to improve the emotional adjustments of its members through body contact, emotional expression, and confrontation; also ***encounter therapy***.

1967 C. R. ROGERS in J. F. Bugental *Challenges Humanistic Psychol.* 262/2 Since then I have been involved in more than forty ventures of what I would like to term—using the label most congenial to me—*basic *encounter groups*. **1968** J. HOWARD in *Life* 12 July 65/3 Will all that remains be a few yellowing Christmas cards from friends we met in encounter groups? **1978** G. A. SHEEHAN *Running & Being* viii. 105 Sport.. reminds me of an encounter group I once attended. In the first exercise, the person next to me asked me again and again, 'Who are you?' **1985** *Verbatim* Spring 17/2 Many articles and books, radio and television programs, and self-help and encounter groups are designed to help us curb our tempers. **1970** J. HOWARD *Please Touch* 24 A weekend of 'Nude *Encounter Therapy' run in some swimming pool near Los Angeles by a therapist. **1986** *New Yorker* 22 Sept. 68/2 People.. practised growth-movement therapies: rolfing.. and encounter therapies.

encounter (ɛn'kaʊntə(r)), *v.* Also 4 encountre, 6–8 incounter. [a. OFr. *encontre-r*, a Com. Romanic word, = Pr., Sp., Pg. *encontrar*, It. *incontrare*:—late L. *incontrāre*, f. *in* in + *contra* against.]

1. *trans.* To meet as an adversary; to confront in battle, assail. Sometimes *absol.* with reciprocal sense. Also *fig.*

c **1300** *St. Brandan* 411 And encountrede this lithere fisch and smot to him faste. **1475** CAXTON *Jason* 6 They that encountrid hercules. *c* **1500** *Lancelot* 3261 And ywons king.. Encounterit hyme in myddis of the gren. **1577** VAUTROUILLIER *Luther on Ep. Gal.* 146 But let us suffer the law and the promise to encounter together. **1601** HOLLAND *Pliny* II. 544 Astonied at the sight of a monstrous bull let loose and ready to incounter him. **1624** CAPT. SMITH *Virginia* I. 2 He was provided with a Navy able to incounter a Kings power. **1626** MEAD in Ellis *Orig. Lett.* I. 336 III. 250 The Duke was hotly encountered by the Sailors about this day sennight. **1697** DRYDEN *Virg. Georg.* IV. 125 They challenge, and encounter Breast to Breast. **1781** GIBBON *Decl. & F.* II. xxxviii. 394 The two kings encountered each other in single combat. **1792** BURKE *Pres. St. Affairs* Wks. VII. 90 Enemies very different from those she has hitherto had to encounter. **1851** CREASY *Decis. Battles* (1864) 187 To encounter Varus's army in a pitched battle.

†**b.** *intr.* Const. *against*, usually *with*. *Obs.*

1530 WOLSEY in Cavendish *Life* (1825) I. 324 Against whom the King was constrained to encounter in his royal person. **1555** EDEN *Decades W. Ind.* II. I. (Arb.) 107 Encounteryng with them, he was repulsed with shame and damage. **1684** *Contempl. State of Man* I. (1699) 109 That dreadful day wherein the Army of Vengeance.. are to encounter with the Army of Sin. **1728** R. MORRIS *Ess. Anc. Archit.* 18 The single Enemies I have to encounter with.

†**2.** *trans.* To go counter to, oppose, thwart; to contest, dispute. Also *absol.* *Obs.*

1549 COVERDALE *Erasm. Par. Rom.* 17 But some will againe encounter and saye. **1583** GOLDING *Calvin on Deut.* vi. 32 When they withstand God and incounter his Word. **1589** PUTTENHAM *Eng. Poesie* III. xxiii. (Arb.) 276 Nothing is so vnpleasant to a man, as to be encountred in his chiefe affection. **1638** *Penit. Conf.* vi. (1657) 99 Saint Augustine incountring that opinion.. reasoneth thus. **1677** HALE *Prim. Orig. Man.* 79 From the intrinsecal nature of the things that encounter the possibility of an eternal successive duration in them. **1786** BURKE *Art. agst. W. Hastings* Wks. XII. 144 The evidence of this man, not having been encountered at the time.

†**b.** *intr.* Const. *with*. *Obs.*

1677–8 MARVELL *Corr.* No. 340 Wks. 1872–5 II. 604 Lest I should happen to encounter with our proceedings.

†**3.** *trans.* To be placed opposite, or in opposite directions, to (each other). *Obs.*

1610 GUILLIM *Heraldry* VI. v. (1660) 405 She beareth.. three Swords barwayes proper, the middlemost encountring the other two.

†**b.** *intr.* Const. *with*. *Obs.*

1659 LEAK *Water-wks.* 34 There are Pins AE, incountring with Pins which are in PH.

4. To meet, fall in with (a person or thing), *esp.* casually. Sometimes *absol.* Also *fig.*

1520 *Caxton's Chron. Eng.* III. 26/1 Pompei and he encountred togyder. **1528** FOXE *Let. to Gardiner* 12 May in N. Pocock *Rec. Reform.* (1870) I. 141 Encountering Mr. Silvester Darius in the same place, who then was sent from the king's highness.. into Spayne. **1614** RALEIGH *Hist. World* II. 395 Two men should incounter him by Rahel's Sepulchre. **1662** EVELYN *Chalcogr.* (1769) 56 Some rare things in stampi to be encountred amongst the collections of the curious. **1776** JOHNSON in Boswell (1816) III. §49 The most extraordinary young man that has encountered my knowledge. **1822** BYRON *Werner* I. i. 322 We never met before, and never.. may again encounter. **1860** TYNDALL *Glac.* I. §8. 57, I encountered a considerable stream rushing across it [the glacier]. **1875** HAMERTON *Intell. Life* III. iii. 91 He knew the dictionary meaning of every word he encountered.

†**b.** *intr.* Const. *with*. *Obs.*

1632 LITHGOW *Trav.* V. 190 A Christian Amaronite, who accidently encountred with vs. **1672** MARVELL *Reh. Transp.* I. 142 It would be difficult to quote twenty lines in Mr. Bayes but we should encounter with the Roman Empire. **1767** *Babler* I. 67 xv. Some how or other my eye encountered with Miss Maria's at the end of this speech.

5. To meet with, experience (difficulties, opposition, etc.). Also with notion of 1: To face resolutely.

1814 D'ISRAELI *Quarrels Auth.* (1867) 336 The Royal Society.. encountered fierce hostilities. **1844** H. H. WILSON *Brit. India* III. 68 Disease was not, however, the only enemy which the British had to encounter. **1876** GREEN *Short Hist.* iii. §5 (1882) 141 From the Church he [Henry III] encountered as resolute an opposition.

†**b.** *intr.* Const. *with*. *Obs.*

1581 *Apol. Pr. Orange* in *Phenix* (1721) I. 450 If.. I had not incounter'd with the Hatred of the Spanish Nation. **1776** G. SEMPLE *Building in Water* 14 They had not any Difficulties of Water to encounter with.

†**6.** To go to meet. Also *fig.* *Obs.*

1603 SHAKS. *Meas. for M.* III. i. 84, I will encounter darknesse as a bride And hugge it in mine armes. **1611** —— *Cymb.* I. iii. 32 At the sixt houre of Morne, at Noone, at Midnight, T' encounter me with Orisons.

¶ Bombastically used for: To go to, approach (*nonce-use*).

1610 SHAKS. *Twel. N.* III. i. 82 Will you incounter the house.

†**7.** To accost, address. *Obs.*

1579 LYLY *Euphues* (Arb.) 36 With.. smiling face.. encountered him on this manner. **1590** GREENE *Never too late* (1600) 25 Isabel.. incountred him thus. Gentle sir, etc.

†**en'counter**, *adv. Obs. rare*[−1]. [ad. OF. *encontre* against.] Opposite, contrary; = COUNTER *adv.*

1660 *Hist. Indep.* 82 The rogue of all the Kingdom ran directly encounter to their designs.

†**en'counterable**, *a. Obs. rare*[−1]. [f. ENCOUNTER *sb.* + -ABLE: cf. *profitable*.] ? Ready for encounters.

1576 FLEMING *Panoplie Ep.* 346 Whiche time, I woulde I had spent,.. in the extolling of your.. encounterable valiauntnesse.

†**en'counterer.** *Obs.* Also 6 encounterer. [f. ENCOUNTER *v.* + -ER.] One who or that which encounters; an adversary, opponent.

1523 LD. BERNERS *Froiss.* I. clxix. 206 They..rode close togyder in good aray..but they founde no encounterers. **1589** PUTTENHAM *Eng. Poesie* III. xxv. (Arb.) 310 In another respect arte is as it were an encountrer and contrary to nature. *c* **1611** CHAPMAN *Iliad* XX. 151 The earth did groan With feet of proud encounterers. **1656** H. MORE *Antid. Ath.* II. x. (1712) 70 The Lion..will strike such a stroke with his tail, that he will break the back of his Encounterer with it.

b. One who meets (another) half-way; a 'forward' person, coquette. *rare*$^{-1}$.

1606 SHAKS. *Tr. & Cr.* IV. v. 58 Oh these encounterers so glib of tongue.

en'countering, *vbl. sb.* [f. ENCOUNTER *v.* + -ING^1.] The action of the vb. ENCOUNTER.

1482 CAXTON *Trevisa's Higden* III. vi. 121 In the encountrynge and fyghtyng Brutus..and Arnus..slough eyther other. **1523** LD. BERNERS *Froiss.* I. xlviii. 69 And dyuers encountrynges was bytwene them. **1581** *Apol. Pr. Orange* in *Phenix* (1721) I. 450 That the Race of [a man's] life be..prosperous without..any wicked incountring. **1610** GUILLIM *Heraldry* II. v. 50 By reason of the opposition and encountering of some other current. **1623** DRUMM. OF HAWTH. *Cypress Grove* Wks. (1711) 126 So many shadows cast out and caused by the encountring of these superiour celestial bodies. **1704** SWIFT *T. Tub* Author's Apol., The accidental encountering of a single thought.

encountering (ɛnˈkaʊntərɪŋ), *ppl. a.* [f. ENCOUNTER *v.* + -ING^2.] That encounters.

In the use of G. M. Hopkins (see quot.).

1586 MARLOWE *1st Pt. Tamburl.* II. vi. 19 Let us put on our meet encountering minds. **1626** G. SANDYS *Ovid's Met.* XI. 219 Keepe the bankes that lead Along th' incountring Current to his head. **1667** MILTON *P.L.* VI. 220 Millions of fierce encountring Angels fought. **1738** GLOVER *Leonidas* V. 350 Betwixt th' encountring chiefs. **1856** BRYANT *Poems, Winter Piece* 119 The encountering winds shall oft Muster their wrath again. **1878** G. M. HOPKINS *Let. to Bridges* 30 May (1935) 53 The rhythm is anacrustic or, as I should call it, 'encountering'.

†**en'countery.** *Obs. rare*$^{-1}$. In 6 incountrie. [ad. OF. *encontree* a meeting, f. *encontrer* ENCOUNTER *v.*] The shock of attack or encounter.

1566 PAINTER *Pal. Pleas.* Ded., To him whose frequent vse of mightye incountrie and terrible shocke of shield and launce, is familier in court.

†**en'countrance.** *Obs. rare*$^{-1}$. In 6 incountraunce. [f. ENCOUNTER *v.* + -ANCE.] = ENCOUNTERING *vbl. sb.*

1592 WYRLEY *Armorie* 94 Great semblaunce And shew of loue made at incountraunce.

†**en'courage,** *sb. Obs. rare*$^{-1}$. [f. next.] = ENCOURAGEMENT.

1535 *Act 27 Hen. VIII*, c. 23 §2 To the great animacion and encourage of thoffendours.

encourage (ɛnˈkʌrɪdʒ), *v.* Forms: α. 5 encorage, 6– encourage. β. 7 incorage (incurrage), 7–8 incourage. [ad. OF. *encoragier*, Fr. *encourager*, f. *en* (see EN-^{1}) + *corage*: see COURAGE.]

1. *trans.* To inspire with courage, animate, inspirit.

α. **1490** CAXTON *Eneydos* (1889) 31 They were..gretly encoraged wyth goode hope. *a* **1593** H. SMITH *Serm.* (1637) 404 God would have Joshua encouraged with all the encouragement that may be. *a* **1649** DRUMM. OF HAWTH. *Skiamachia* Wks. (1711) 203 By encouraging those, who for ..their own interest pretend religion. **1722** DE FOE *Plague* (1754) 6 That which encourag'd them was, that the city was healthy. **1847** EMERSON *Repr. Men, Napoleon* Wks. (Bohn) I. 376 Whatever appeals to the imagination..wonderfully encourages and liberates us.

β. **1551** ROBINSON tr. *More's Utop.* (Arb.) 16 This verely is yᵉ chieffe cause, yᵃᵗ hath incouraged me. **1647** WARD *Simp. Cobler* 71 Prayers..that the God of power and goodness, would incourage your hearts. **1713** STEELE *Guardian* No. 24 ¶2 Jack was incouraged at this success.

2. Const. *to* with sb. as obj. or with *inf.*

a. To inspire with courage sufficient for any undertaking; to embolden, make confident.

α. **1553** EDEN *Treat. Newe Ind.* (Arb.) 5 Yat they mighte.. bee encouraged to do the like. **1651** HOBBES *Leviath.* II. xxvii. 158 Presumeth on his force..which encourages him to commit the same again. **1785** COWPER *Lett.* 9 Nov., John Gilpin..first encouraged you to write. **1824** MISS FERRIER *Inher.* xxxv, I feel encouraged to the liberty I am going to take, by the kindness you showed me. **1880** MRS. FORRESTER *Roy & V.* I. 31 Encourage yourself to say these things now you are in Paris.

β. **1538** STARKEY *England* 153 The wych thyng undowtydly wold incorage basse stomakys to endevur themselfys dylygently. **1641** PRYNNE *Antip.* 3 Ded., To the which I have beene the more incouraged by a Divine Providence. **1743** TINDAL *Rapin's Hist. Eng.* II. XVII. 53 Incouraged the Protestants to stand upon their defence.

b. To incite, induce, instigate; in weaker sense, to recommend, advise.

1483 CAXTON *Cato* G j b, They encorage somme persone to do euyl. **1612** SIR R. DUDLEY in *Fortesc. Papers* 7 *note*, To incurrage his Highnes to undertake a matter of that consequence. **1697** DRYDEN *Virg. Georg.* III. 201 Water him, and..Encourage him to thirst again, with Bran. **1875** JOWETT *Plato* (ed. 2) IV. 44 We are not encouraging individuals to make right or wrong for themselves.

†**c.** *ellipt.* To encourage to come, to invite. *Obs. rare.*

1728 T. SHERIDAN *Persius* vi. (1739) 86 Ennius..[was] encouraged to Rome by Cato the Quæstor.

3. To stimulate (persons or personal efforts) by assistance, reward, or expressions of favour or approval; to countenance, patronize; also, in bad sense, to abet.

1668 HALE *Pref. Rolle's Abridgment* 9 A Book published.. not to abate their [Students'] Industry, but to incourage it. **1716** LADY M. W. MONTAGUE *Lett.* xi. I. 38 No woman dares..encourage two lovers at a time. **1777** SHERIDAN *Sch. Scand.* IV. i, Paying them [tradesmen] is only encouraging them. **1857** BUCKLE *Civiliz.* I. xi. 629 Why should we call upon government to encourage those who write our books? **1866** ROGERS *Agric. & Pr.* I. xxvi. 642 The bailiffs were allowed to encourage venturous boys in bringing young birds for purposes of training. **1876** GREEN *Short. Hist.* vi §3 (1882) 293 Among the group who encouraged the press of Caxton [was]..Richard, Duke of Gloucester.

b. To allow or promote the continuance or development of (a natural growth, an industry, a sentiment, etc.); to cherish, foster.

1677 YARRANTON *Engl. Improv.* 63 If the Iron Manufacture be not incouraged. **1694** CONGREVE *Double Dealer* I. v, Hum! I have encouraged a pimple here too. **1788** V. KNOX *Winter Even.* I. iii. 31 Books of controversy..are less encouraged. **1856** KANE *Arct. Expl.* II. xviii. 184 Sunshine..encouraged a perceptible growth of flowering plants. **1863** GEO. ELIOT *Romola* II. xxiii, [He] grasped at a thought more actively cruel than any he had ever encouraged before.

4. *nonce-use.* **a.** Humorously: To put spirit into (liquor). **b.** To make up for, compensate for.

1628 HOBBES *Thucyd.* (1822) 71 Encouraging their want of knowledge with store of men. **1655** FULLER *Hist. Camb.* v. §48, 87 Erasmus..sometimes incouraged his faint Ale with the mixture.

encouragement (ɛnˈkʌrɪdʒmənt). Also 6–8 incouragement. [a. F. *encouragement*: see prec. and -MENT.] The action or process of encouraging, the fact of being encouraged (see senses of the vb.); *concr.* a fact or circumstance which serves to encourage.

1568 GRAFTON *Chron.* II. 257 King Edward purposyng a lyke encouragement of noble and worthie knightes. **1598** J. DICKENSON *Greene in Conc.* (1878) 143 For his more incouragement viewing in his mistris countenance, no cloudes of discontent. **1638** LD. GORING in *Hamilton Papers* (1880) 65 What encouragement whatever those ill affected with you may gather. **1677** YARRANTON *Engl. Improv.* 62 To the Incouragement of the Iron, and Iron Manufactures. **1700** WALLIS in *Collect.* (Oxf. Hist. Soc.) I. 319 This riding-master went hence, finding little or no encouragement, of any desirous to learn. **1711** SHAFTESB. *Charac.* (1737) II. 124 Inward deformity growing greater, by the incouragement of unnatural affection. **1748** ANSON *Voy.* (ed. 4) Introd., Such employments could not long be wanting, if due incouragement were given to them. **1828** SCOTT *F.M. Perth* vi, The wooer had begun to hold the refusal of the damsel as somewhat capricious..after the degree of encouragement which, in his opinion, she had afforded. **1875** JOWETT *Plato* (ed. 2) V. 186 [Plato] gives no encouragement to individual enthusiasm. **1883** *Law Rep. Queen's B.* XI. 569 The object of the society being the encouragement of saving.

encourager (ɛnˈkʌrɪdʒə(r)). [f. ENCOURAGE *v.* + -ER.] He who or that which encourages.

1562 BP. HOOPER (*title*), An Apologye againste the Report that he should be a Maintainer and Encorager of suche as cursed the Quenes Highnes. **1563** FOXE *A. & M.* (1596) 72/2 To which notable thing and great force of faith, Mauritius himselfe was a great incourager. **1607** TOPSELL *Serpents* (1658) 592 My worshipful good friend, and dayly encourager unto all good labours. **1738** *Daily Post* 17 Aug. *Mary-le-Bonne Gardens*, Mr. Gough begs leave..to return the encouragers of his Musical Entertainment thanks. **1777** WATSON *Philip II* (1839) 125 They were considered as fomenters of the tumults, and encouragers of heresy. **1844** H. H. WILSON *Brit. India* III. 209 He was an encourager of letters and the arts.

en'couraging, *vbl. sb.* [f. ENCOURAGE *v.* + -ING^1.] The action of the vb. ENCOURAGE.

1578 *Chr. Prayers* in *Priv. Prayers* (1851) 539 That I may have a longing to [the true good things] through thine encouraging. **1637** *Decree Star Chamb.* §11 in Milton *Areop.*, For the..incouraging of Printers in their honest.. endeauours. **1658** *Whole Duty Man* i. §22 (1687) 4 To the incouraging of us in sins.

encouraging (ɛnˈkʌrɪdʒɪŋ), *ppl. a.* [f. ENCOURAGE *v.* + -ING^2.] That encourages or tends to encourage.

1663 EARL LAUDERD. in *L. Papers* (1884) I. 176 The Bishop..hath written a brave incouraging Epistle to our Chancellor. **1783** BURKE *Rep. Affairs India* Wks. XI. 29 The choice of Mr. John Stables..was by no means..an encouraging example to either Service. **1855** MACAULAY *Hist. Eng.* III. 661 He sate down..to write a kind and encouraging letter to the unfortunate general.

Hence **en'couragingly** *adv.*, in an encouraging manner.

1646 P. BULKELEY *Gospel Covt.* IV. 332 Those about him speak encouragingly to him. **1741** RICHARDSON *Pamela* II. 170 How encouragingly kind was all this! **1856** KANE *Arct. Expl.* I. xiv. 164 We talked encouragingly of spring hopes.

encover, incover (ɛn-, ɪnˈkʌvə(r)), *v. rare.* [f. EN-^{1}, IN- + COVER *v.*^{1}] *trans.* To cover completely; to enclose and cover. Hence **en'covered, en'covering** *ppl. adjs.*

1520–30 SKELTON *Garl. Laur.* 1164 Slimy snails Encoverde over with gold of tissew fine. **1596** R. L. *Diella*, The gold encoverd booke. **1851** D. WILSON *Prehist. Ann. Scotl.* (1863) I. 117 The incovering mound is about..forty-four feet in diameter.

encowl, encraal: see EN- *pref.*^{1}

encradle (ɛnˈkreɪd(ə)l), *v.* Also 7 incradle. [f. EN-^{1} + CRADLE *sb.*] *trans.* To lay in a cradle.

1596 SPENSER *Hymne Heavenly Love* 225 Where he encradled was In simple cratch, wrapt in a wad of hay. **1655** FULLER *Church Hist.* I. iv. 213 Three Child-Constantines encradled. **1662** —— *Worthies, Linc.* II. 165 Though there incradled.

†**encrain.** *Obs.*$^{-0}$

1731–36 BAILEY vol. II, *Encrain* [with Horsemen], a horse that is wither wrung or one that is spoilt in the withers.

†**en'crampish, -ise,** *v. Obs. rare.* [f. EN-^{1} + CRAMP *a.* + *-ish*, after words like *impoverish*.] *trans.* To cramp, hamper. Hence **en'crampised** *ppl. a.*, cramped, distorted.

c **1430** *Pilgr. Lyf Manhode* II. (1869) 108 I hatte Peresce, þe goutous, þe encrampised, þe boistous, þe maymed. **1523** SKELTON *Garl. Laurel* 15 Encraumpysshed so sore was my conceyte.

†**en'crass,** *v. Obs. rare*$^{-1}$. [ad. F. *encrasse-r*, f. *en-* (see EN-^{1}) + *crasse* thick, CRASS; cf. late L. *incrassāre*.] *intr.* To thicken; to become thick.

1575 TURBERV. *Falconrie* 241 The..moysture of the head distilling from aboue, vpon those breathing partes, and there encrassed..breede difficultie of breathing.

Encratism (ˈɛnkrətɪz(ə)m). [f. Gr. ἐγκρατ-ής + -ISM.] The doctrinal system and practice of the Encratites.

1885 G. SALMON *Hist. Introd. N.T.* xi. 240 Several of the Gnostic sects had in common this feature of Encratism..the rejection..of marriage, of flesh meat, and of wine.

Encratite (ˈɛnkrətaɪt). Chiefly in *pl.* [ad. late L. *encratīta*, late Gr. ἐγκρατῖτης (Hippolytus), f. ἐγκρατ-ής continent + -ῑτης: see -ITE.] One of those early Christian heretics (chiefly Gnostic) that abstained from flesh, from wine, and from marriage. Also *attrib.*

1587 T. ROGERS *39 Art.* (1621) 295 The Encratites..use no wine at all. **1702** ECHARD *Eccl. Hist.* (1710) 500 Justin's scholar, Tatian..formed a new sect called by the name of Encratites, or Continents. **1883** *Ch. Q. Rev.* XV. 394 By Encratites and Marcionites intoxicating liquors would have been denounced with as much fervour as by Dr. Kerr. **1885** G. SALMON *Hist. Introd. N.T.* 241 The principal apocryphal Acts of the Apostles proceeded from men of Encratite views.

†**en'cre,** *v. Obs. rare*$^{-1}$. [app. a corrupt form of *encrese*, INCREASE.] ? To grow, thrive.

c **1420** *Pallad. on Husb.* XII. 66 Wel wot this tree Encre in litel moiste and places hie.

encrease, -crece, -crees(e, -cresce, -cres(e, -cress(e, obs. forms of INCREASE.

†**en'credit,** *v. Obs. rare*$^{-1}$. [f. EN- + CREDIT.] To gain credit for (a person). In quot. *refl.*

1642 ROGERS *Naaman* 436 Thinking to encredit and ingratiate themselves into their affections.

encrely, var. of ENKERLY *a.*, *Obs. Sc.*

encrimson (ɛnˈkrɪmzən), *v.* Also 9 in-. [f. EN- + CRIMSON.] *trans.* To make or dye crimson.

1773 J. ROSS *Fratricide* I. 528 Lips encrimson'd o'er With vestal modesty! **1882** FARRAR *Early Chr.* II. 215 Steps encrimsoned by the uncleansed pools of gore.

encrimsoned (ɛnˈkrɪmzənd), *ppl. a.* [f. prec. + -ED^1.] Dyed crimson; red like crimson. Also *fig.*

1597 SHAKS. *Lover's Compl.* xxix, In bloodlesse white, and the encrimson'd mood. **1824** *Month. Mag.* LVIII. 144 Grasping this incrimsoned steel. **1839** POE *House of Usher* Wks. 1864 I. 294 Feeble gleams of encrimsoned light made their way through the trellissed panes. **1882** FARRAR *Early Chr.* I. 10 Bands of gladiators..hacked each other to pieces on the encrimsoned sand.

encrinal (ˈɛnkrɪnəl), *a. Geol.* [f. ENCRIN-US + -AL^1.] = ENCRINITAL.

1845 in *Proc. Berw. Nat. Club* II. xii. 159 The blue encrinal limestone so abundant at Holy Island. **1858** GEIKIE *Hist. Boulder* xi. 205 The rock with its included encrinal stems and shells.

encrinic (ɛnˈkrɪnɪk), *a. Geol.* [f. ENCRIN-US + -IC.] = ENCRINITAL.

1847 in CRAIG; and in mod. Dicts.

encrinital (ɛnkrɪˈnaɪtəl), *a. Geol.* [f. ENCRINITE + -AL^1.]

1. Of or pertaining to, or having the character of, Encrinites.

1847 ANSTED *Anc. World* viii. 177 Living chiefly on the crabs, lobsters, and shell-fish, or on the encrinital animals. **1875** CROLL *Climate & T.* xviii. 298 Encrinital fragments in the greatest abundance.

2. Containing Encrinites.

1876 PAGE *Adv. Text-Bk. Geol.* xiv. 245 The frequent synonym of 'encrinal' or 'encrinital limestone'.

encrinite (ˈɛnkrɪnaɪt). *Zool.* and *Geol.* [f. ENCRIN-US + -ITE.] A fossil crinoid; formerly sometimes extended to crinoids generally.

1808 PARKINSON *Organ. Rem.* II. 153 (in Rees). **1819** REES *Cycl.*, *Encrinites*, a kind of columnar extraneous or organized fossil. **1835** KIRBY *Hab. & Inst. Anim.* II. xiii. 10 A tribe of lily-like animals..which, from a supposed resemblance..to the blossom of a liliaceous plant have been denominated Encrinites. **1854** F. BAKEWELL *Geol.* 30 The prevailing characteristic fossils being encrinites and

madrepores. **1880** GEIKIE *Phys. Geog.* iv. §21. 191 A piece of limestone is..made up of the crowded joints of the encrinite or stone-lily—a marine animal.

attrib. **1822** G. YOUNG *Geol. Surv. Yorksh. Coast* (1828) 21 Masses of the encrinite limestone. **1847** E. FORBES in Wilson & Geikie *Mem.* xii. (1861) 413, I went to seek out the localities for the encrinite heads.

encrinitic (ɛnkrɪˈnɪtɪk), *a. Geol.* [f. ENCRINITE + -IC.] Containing fossil Encrinites.

1863 *Cambrian Jrnl.* Sept. 154 The carbonate shell marble of South Wales, and the encrinitic of North Wales. **1864** in *Proc. Amer. Phil. Soc.* IX. 482 The metamorphosis of encrinitic limestone.

encrinoid (ˈɛnkrɪnɔɪd), *a. Geol.* [f. ENCRIN-US + -OID.] Resembling an Encrinite.

1841–71 T. R. JONES *Anim. Kingd.* (ed. 4) 179 An Encrinoid Echinoderm in its perfect condition.

‖**Encrinus** (ˈɛnkrɪnəs). *Zool.* Also 8 encrinos. [mod.L., f. Gr. ἐν in + κρίνον lily. The word was invented by Harenberg (1729) as a name for a fossil which two years before he had proposed to call a 'stone lily'.]

1. †A name formerly applied generally to fossil crinoids; = ENCRINITE (*obs.*). **b.** Now the name of a particular (extinct) genus of crinoids, the type of the family *Encrinidæ*.

1762 [see 2]. **1841–71** T. R. JONES *Anim. Kingd.* (ed. 4) 181 To convert an Encrinus into an animal capable of locomotion. **1851** RICHARDSON *Geol.* viii. 228 In encrinus, it is composed of different-sized circular plates.

†**2.** Applied to certain extant animals which were supposed to resemble the fossil encrinus: **a.** The *Pennatula Encrinus* of Linnæus = the mod. genus *Umbellula* (class *Anthozoa*, sub-kingdom *Cœlenterata*). **b.** A crinoid described by Ellis as found on the coast of Barbadoes. *Obs.*

1762 ELLIS in *Phil. Trans.* LII. 358 As it comes nearest to the fossils called encrini..I shall keep to that name, and call it encrinus. **1788** *Chambers' Cycl.* (Rees), *Encrinos.* **1819** REES *Cycl.*, *Encrinus.*

†**en'crisp**, *v. Obs. rare.* [f. EN- + CRISP; cf. late L. *incrispāre.*] *trans.* To curl (hair or wool) tightly or crisply. Hence **en'crisped** *ppl. a.*

c **1420** *Pallad. on Husb.* III. 139 Thai shall have softe encrisped wolle. **1523** SKELTON *Garl. Laurel* 289 With heris encrisped, yalowe as the golde.

en'croach, *sb.* Also 7 incroch. [f. ENCROACH *v.*] Encroachment; gradual approach.

1611 SPEED *Hist. Gt. Brit.* IX. xxi. (1632) 1000 The further incroch of the French. **1666** J. SMITH *Old Age* (1676) 99 The insensible encroach of age is no where so soon discovered. *a* **1716** SOUTH *12 Serm.* (1717) IV. 393 Grew into it by insensible Encroaches. **1920** *Conquest* Nov. 39/3 Rocks are affected by micro-fungi, and may crumble as a result of their encroach into crevices and their subsequent action. **1924** *Chambers's Jrnl.* Nov. 714/1 From a line square of posts, bordering on the marshes, and on the mud-flats' farthest encroach, the one safe track leads shorewards.

encroach (ɛnˈkrəʊtʃ), *v.* Forms: α. 4–7 encroch(e, (6 engroche), 6– encroach. β. 5–7 incroch(e, 6 incroatch, (ingroche), 6–8 incroach. [a. OF. *encrochier* to seize, also *refl.* and *intr.* to perch, fasten upon, f. *en-* (see EN-) + *croc* hook.]

†**1.** *trans.* To seize, acquire wrongfully (property or privilege). Also *absol. Obs.*

α. ? *a* **1400** *Morte Arth.* 2036 The renkez..Encrochede alle Cristyndome be craftes of armes. **1494** FABYAN, VII. ccxxx. 262 He wolde haue encroched thynges appertaynynge to yᵉ Crowne of Fraunce.. **1523** FITZHERB. *Surv.* Prol., I make this boke..to thentent that the lordes..shuld nat..haue their landes lost nor imbeselde nor encroched by one from another. *a* **1593** H. SMITH *Wks.* (1866–7) I. 364 Base-born honours which they have encroached from men. **1605** VERSTEGAN *Dec. Intell.* (1634) 115 The Scottish men..did lastly encroach unto themselves a Kingdome. **1606** G. W[OODCOCKE] tr. *Hist. Ivstine* H h 6 a The tribute which Iustinius had couetously enchroched.

β. *a* **1528** SKELTON *Death Edw. IV*, 51 And more euer to incroche redy was I bent. *c* **1534** tr. *Pol. Verg. Eng. Hist.* I. 65 Ingroching bootie echewhere plentifullie. **1587** *Myrr. for Mag.*, *Brennus* iv, Hee warned me I should not seeke t' incroatch That was not mine.

†**b.** *Law.* (See quot.) *Obs.*

1641 *Termes de la Ley* 135 b, A Rent is said to be encroched, when the Lord by distresse or otherwise compells the tenant to pay more rent than he ought.

†**c.** In good or neutral sense: To obtain, gain. *Obs. rare.*

c **1325** *E.E. Allit. P.* A. 1116 Delyt þat his come encroched. *Ibid.* C. 18 For þay schal comfort encroche in kyþes ful mony.

2. *intr.* To trench or intrude usurpingly (*esp.* by insidious or gradual advances) on the territory, rights, or accustomed sphere of action of others. Also *transf.* and *fig.* of things: To make gradual inroads on, extend (its) boundaries at the expense of, something else. Const. *on*, *upon* (the territory, rights, etc. invaded, or the person whose rights are infringed); also *simply*.

α. *c* **1534** tr. *Pol. Verg. Eng. Hist.* (1846) I. 137 Bie littell and littell engroched on the sowthe partes of the Ile. **1600** HAKLUYT *Voy.* (1810) III. 423 See you that you suffer him not to encroch vpon you. **1713** STEELE *Englishm.* No. 29. 185, I shall not encroach upon your Time. **1791** SMEATON *Edystone L.* §357 The sea encroached upon these cliffs. **1855** MACAULAY *Hist. Eng.* III. 260 Restraining both churches..from encroaching on the functions of the civil magistrate. **1875** JOWETT *Plato* (ed. 2) V. 116 He who encroaches shall pay twofold the price of the injury.

β. **1541** ELYOT *Image Gov.* 155 b, He woulde not suffer his libertines to incroche vpon his possessions. **1660** R. COKE *Power & Subj.* 136 Laws made by the Kings of this realm did never incroach upon the ghostly power which our Saviour by divine positive institution left only to his Church. **1794** G. ADAMS *Nat. & Exp. Philos.* IV. xliv. 201 The nucleus of a spot..often changes its figure, by umbra incroaching irregularly upon it.

†**b.** *trans.* To impose (an unfair burden or condition) *upon. Obs. rare*⁻¹. (Doubtful: perh. *what* is used adverbially.)

1548 LD. SOMERSET *Epist. Scots* 244 What wil they not encroche vpon you?

3. *intr.* To advance, intrude beyond natural or conventional limits. †**b.** *refl.* in same sense (*obs. rare*).

1555 *Fardle Facions* App. 323 When the coueitous manne will encroche beyonde his boundes. **1599** T. M[OUFET] *Silkwormes* 48 Lest heate by stealth encroch it selfe too soone. **1618** BOLTON *Florus* III. v. 181 Lucius Sulla..shoved the Enemie backe..from encroaching any farther. **1680** BUTLER *Rem.* (1759) I. 214 Those that falsly venture to encroach, Where Nature has deny'd them all Approach. **1830** M. DONOVAN *Dom. Econ.* I. 3 A state which encroaches beyond the boundaries of sleep. [See also ENCROACHING *ppl. a.*]

c. *trans.* To encroach upon.

1578 LYTE *Dodoens* 660 This [Bramble] taketh roote easily ..incroching grounde with the toppes of his branches. *Ibid.* 648 It incrocheth and winneth more ground.

†**4.** *intr.* To get oneself connected *with. Obs. rare.*

1579 GOSSON *Apol. Sch. Abuse* (Arb.) 73 Penelopes suters ..were glad to encroche with some of her maides.

encroacher (ɛnˈkrəʊtʃə(r)). [f. ENCROACH *v.* + -ER.] One who encroaches (*on*).

1581 J. BELL *Haddon's Answ. Osor.* 491 Why is Haddon accused..as an encrocher upon other mens possessions? **1689** R. WRIGHT *Benefice* 16, I am a bold Incroacher on the Gods, And steal their Free-hold. **1720** SWIFT *Run upon Bankers* Wks. 1755 IV. I. 22 The bold encroachers on the deep. **1742** RICHARDSON *Pamela* III. 11, I would not for the World be thought an Incroacher. **1861** *Sat. Rev.* 22 June, Those irregular encroachers who border and trespass on the domain of history.

†**en'croaching**, *vbl. sb. Obs.* [f. ENCROACH *v.* + -ING¹.] The action of the vb. ENCROACH.

1539 TAVERNER *Gard. Wysed.* I. 40 a, By thy incrochyng of other mens realms. *a* **1639** W. WHATELEY *Prototypes* II. xxix. (1640) 144 Murder is a sinne..wronging God extreamely in presumptuous incroching upon his prerogative. **1643** PRYNNE *Sov. Power Parl.* III. 36 The encroaching of the said royall power to them.

encroaching (ɛnˈkrəʊtʃɪŋ), *ppl. a.* [f. ENCROACH *v.* + -ING².] That encroaches.

1593 SHAKS. *2 Hen. VI*, IV. i. 96 The House of Yorke thrust from the Crowne, By lofty proud incroaching tyranny. **1649** MILTON *Eikon.* xi. (1851) 426 It concern'd them first to sue out their Livery from the unjust wardship of his encroaching Prerogative. **1742** RICHARDSON *Pamela* IV. 50 Ladies in your Way, are often like incroaching Subjects. **1853** KANE *Grinnell Exp.* xxix. (1856) 250 Our nobly-strengthened little craft rose up upon the encroaching floes bodily. **1873** SYMONDS *Grk. Poets* i. 26 The cold encroaching policy of Sparta.

encroachingly (ɛnˈkrəʊtʃɪŋlɪ), *adv.* [f. prec. + -LY².] In an encroaching manner.

1822 *Month. Mag.* LIV. 592 Whether Bodmer availed himself of Wieland's pen too encroachingly.

encroachment (ɛnˈkrəʊtʃmənt). Also 7–8 in-. [f. ENCROACH *v.* + -MENT: in AF. (1437) *encrochement.*] The action of encroaching, in various senses; *spec.* in *Law* (see quot. 1613).

1523 FITZHERB. *Surv.* 15 But and there shalbe made any new incrochementes or intackis inclosed or taken in out of the commens. **1556** J. HEYWOOD *Spider & F.* xxi. 49 Ye thus.. Usurpe on vs by meane of encrochement. **1613** R. C. *Table Alph.* (ed. 3), *Encrochment*, when the Lord hath gotten and seised of more rent or seruices of his tenant then of right is due. **1646** SIR T. BROWNE *Pseud. Ep.* I. iii. 8 The people.. being ready with open armes to receive the encroachments of Error. **1667** MILTON *P.L.* XII. 72 But this Usurper his encroachment proud Stayes not on Man. **1768** BLACKSTONE *Comm.* III. 111 Encroachment of jurisdiction, or calling one *coram non judice*, to answer in a court that has no legal cognizance of the cause. **1794** G. ADAMS *Nat. & Exp. Philos.* IV. xliv. 201 By these incroachments the nucleus of a spot is divided into two or more nuclei. **1830** H. ROGERS *Ess.* (1850) II. iv. 199 We..find the Latin element making undue encroachments. **1878** BOSW. SMITH *Carthage* 433 The intervening strip of land, narrower now than then owing to the encroachment of the waves.

encrochet: see EN- *pref.*¹ 1 a.

encrown (ɛnˈkraʊn), *v.* Also 6 encroun. [f. EN-¹ + CROWN *sb.*]

1. *trans.* To put a crown on (any one); to crown.

1486 *Bk. St. Albans, Her.* A j a, Aungelis encrowned full hye with precious stones. **1841** T. J. OUSELEY *Eng. Melodies* 49 Whilst Flowers en-crown thy Fairy head. **1854** BAILEY *Festus* (ed. 5) 530 Encrowned with peaks of quivering fire. **1884** *Sword & Trowel* Feb. 63 Our fathers were wont to encrown themselves with a tasselled triangle.

†**2.** ? To mark or stamp with the figure of a crown. *Obs.*

1538 LELAND *Itin.* V. 110 And one Quene Elenor was buried..under a flat Stone of Marble with an Image of plaine Plate of Brasse encrounid.

†**en'crownment.** *Obs. rare*⁻¹. In 4 encorownment. [f. ENCROWN *v.* + -MENT.] The action or ceremony of encrowning; coronation.

? *a* **1400** *Morte Arth.* 4198 Encorownmentes of kynges enoynttede.

†**en'cruelize**, *v. Obs. rare*⁻¹. [f. EN-¹ + CRUEL + -IZE.] *trans.* To make cruel or savage.

1654 COKAINE *Dianea* IV. 344 Those minds, which, encruelized, had not distinction to know their madnesse.

encrust, incrust (ɛn-, ɪnˈkrʌst), *v.* [Prob. of twofold formation: (1) ad. Fr. *incrust-er* or It. *incrustare* (used in sense 1), ad. L. *incrustāre*, f. *in* upon + *crusta* CRUST. (2) f. EN-¹, IN- + CRUST, or ad. Fr. *encroûter* (in 16th c. *encrouster*) of equivalent formation. The *en-* and *in-* forms are both in common use, without any differentiation of sense; the Dictionaries mostly favour *incrust*, but *encrust* appears to be the more frequent in actual use.]

1. *trans.* To ornament (a surface) by overlaying it with a crust of precious material. Also ***to encrust into.***

α. **1776** GIBBON *Decl. & F.* I. xii. 262 The outside of the edifice was encrusted with marble. **1825** *Bro. Jonathan* I. 142 As if the whole tree were encrusted with molten jewellery. *a* **1859** MACAULAY *Hist. Eng.* V. 196 A staircase encrusted with jasper. **1875** FORTNUM *Maiolica* xi. 101 The painted and incised bacini, which are encrusted into her church towers.

β. **1641** EVELYN *Mem.* (1857) I. 35 The church of the Jesuits is..a glorious fabric without and within, wholly incrusted with marble. **1781** GIBBON *Decl. & F.* III. liii. 295 The walls were incrusted with marbles of various colours. **1885** STONE *Chr. bef. Christ* 44 Vases incrusted with diamonds and *lapis lazuli.*

2. To cover with a crust or thin coating (*e.g.* of rust, sedimentary deposits, etc.). Also of scales, shellfish, etc.: To form a crust or hard coating on (a surface).

α. **1774** GOLDSM. *Nat. Hist.* (1776) I. 313 In those dreary countries, the instruments..that are kept in the pocket..are quickly encrusted. **1806** *Med. Jrnl.* XV. 535 He now was encrusted with one scab over every part of his face and body. **1828** STARK *Elem. Nat. Hist.* I. 482 Scales encrusting the soft part of the dorsal and anal fins. **1854** F. BAKEWELL *Geol.* 87 Sulphur is found..encrusting the sides in considerable quantities. **1878** BOSW. SMITH *Carthage* 433 The blocks of masonry..are now encrusted by shell fish and sea weeds.

β. *a* **1691** [see ENCRUSTING *ppl. a.*]. **1695** WOODWARD *Nat. Hist. Earth* IV. (1723) 219 Some Rivers do thus bring forth ..mineral Matter in great Quantity so as to cover and incrust the Stones, Sticks and other Bodyes lying therein. **1733** POPE *Hor. Sat.* II. i. 73 Let Jove incrust Swords, pikes, and guns, with everlasting rust. **1756** C. LUCAS *Ess. Waters* II. 23 Such..waters..incrust vessels in which they are contained. **1863** FR. KEMBLE *Resid. Georgia* 23 Their bare feet being literally incrusted with dirt.

b. *fig.*

α. **1806** SOUTHEY *Lett.* (1856) I. 359 Some rejected Christ as unfit nucleus to encrust with their fables. **1861** MILL *Utilit.* iii. 42 The simple fact is..encrusted over with collateral associations.

β. **1742** YOUNG *Nt. Th.* I. 157 How was my heart incrusted by the world! **1837** J. H. NEWMAN *Par. Serm.* III. xvii. 265 Satan..may incrust it with his own evil creations. **1858** HOLLAND *Titcomb's Lett.* viii. 80 You get habits of thought and life that incrust you. **1873** H. ROGERS *Orig. Bible* viii. (1875) 326 Many languages..were still so incrusted with barbarism.

3. To form into a crust, deposit as a crust.

1726 THOMSON *Winter* 756 The winter snow Incrusted hard. **1837** W. IRVING *Capt. Bonneville* (1849) 151 It was sufficiently incrusted to bear a pedestrian.

4. a. *intr.* for *refl.* To form itself into a crust. **b.** *intr.* To form or deposit a crust *upon.*

1725 HUXHAM in *Phil. Trans.* XXXIII. 381 The Pustules ..did not incrust yellow. **1754** *Ibid.* XLIX. 26 This chanel of fire..is covered by the..lava, which cools and incrusts on its surface. **1865** PUSEY *Truth Eng. Ch.* 30 A mass of unauthorized traditional glosses..had encrusted over the Thirty-nine Articles.

5. To shut up, imprison as within a crust. *rare.*

a **1711** KEN *Poet. Wks.* (1721) IV. 528 Tho' I should..In Alps of Ice encrusted, freeze. **1830** SIR J. HERSCHEL *Stud. Nat. Phil.* 79 The statue might be conceived encrusted in its marble envelope.

encrustation, var. INCRUSTATION.

encrusted, incrusted (ɛn-, ɪnˈkrʌstɪd), *ppl. a.* [f. ENCRUST *v.* + -ED¹.] In senses of the vb.

1663 J. BEALE *Let.* 21 Jan. in *Boyle's Wks.* 1772 VI. 387 A black incrusted substance, which he found in Mendipp-hills, bedecked very delightfully with artificial branches of the exact form of ferns, which they say is an infallible discoverer of a coal-mine. **1816** J. SCOTT *Vis. Paris* (ed. 5) 59 The olive branch in one hand, and the encrusted pike in the other. **1853** KANE *Grinnell Exp.* xxxviii. (1856) 351 Trailing his hind quarters over the incrusted snow. **1859** GULLICK & TIMBS *Paint.* 121 The first kind, or 'incrusted enamels' is subdivided into two classes. **1866** TATE *Brit. Mollusks* iv. 292 Solid concretions..of an organized skeleton and incrusted salts.

encrusting, incrusting (ɛn-, ɪnˈkrʌstɪŋ), *ppl. a.* [f. ENCRUST *v.* + -ING².] That encrusts.

a **1691** BOYLE *Hist. Air* (1692) 140, I visited the incrusting spring..and could not find anything incrusted within 26 yards of the rise of it. **1766** PENNANT *Zool.* (1768) I. Pref. 3

The excellence and number of our springs, whether medicinal or incrusting. **1856-8** W. CLARK *Van der Hoeven's Zool.* I. 79 Polypary incrusting, formed of stolons. **1861** DICKENS in *All Y. Round* IV. 461, I was content to take a foggy view of the Inn through the window's encrusting dirt. **1878** G. MACDONALD *Phantastes* v. 81 A kiss cannot reach her through the incrusting alabaster.

encrustment (ɛnˈkrʌstmənt). [f. ENCRUST *v.* + -MENT.] *concr.* That which is deposited by the action of encrusting; an outer encrusted layer or shell. Also *fig.*

1861 CRAIK *Hist. Eng. Lit.* I. 561 That rich..spirit of drollery..penetrating through all enfoldings and rigorous encrustments into the kernel of the ludicrous. **1876** BLACKMORE *Cripps* II. xiv. 211 The trees..glistened rather with soft moisture than with stiff encrustment.

encrystal: see INCRYSTAL.

†**enculȝe.** *Sc. Obs. rare*⁻¹. [Cf. ACCOIL, which in Sc. form would be *aculȝie.] ? Coaxing.

1375 *Sc. Leg. Saints, St. Tecla* 34 Quhene he saw he sped nathinge For his enculȝe or entysing.

enculturation (ɛnˌkʌltjʊəˈreɪʃən). *Social Sciences.* [f. as CULTURATION: see EN-¹.] (See quot. 1948.)

1948 M. J. HERSKOVITS *Man & Works* iii. 39 The aspects of the learning experience which mark off man from other creatures, and by means of which..he achieves competence in his culture, may be called enculturation. This is in essence a process of conscious or unconscious conditioning, exercised within the limits sanctioned by a given body of custom. **1955** *Yearbk. Anthropol.* I. 315/1 The training of students involves the usual problems of enculturation. **1968** *Indian Mus. Jrnl.* V. 24 Normally, education is part of the process called by some anthropologists 'enculturation' (the culture inculcating its own values). **1968** N. O. LURIE in J. A. Clifton *Introd. Cultural Anthropol.* 297/1 Our biological evolutionary heritage means that we must learn our cultural adaptations for survival, and for this vital technique to work, a culture must be firmly implanted in the members of the society which shares it. The term 'enculturation' is sometimes used to describe this process.

†**enˈcumber**, *sb. Obs.* Forms: 4 encumbre, encumbir, 6 encombre, 7 encomber, encumber. Also 6 incomber, incumber. [a. OF. *encombre* = Pr. *encombre*, It. *ingombro*:—late L. *incumbrum*, f. *incumbrāre*: see ENCUMBER *v.*] The state of being encumbered; *concr.* an encumbrance, embarrassment, trouble, annoyance.

c **1330** R. BRUNNE *Chron.* (1810) 327 With many grete encumbre of in hard stoure. **1546** GARDINER *Decl. Artic. Joye* 43 Saynt Austen..auoydinge thencombre of these subtyll heretiques. **1557** NORTH tr. *Guevara's Diall of Princes* (1582) 422 b Why they should suffer so many incombers, broiles, and troubles as they do. *a* **1618** RALEIGH *To P. Henry* in *Rem.* (1661) 252 The greater [ship] is slow; unmaniable, and ever full of encumber. *c* **1630** DRUMM. OF HAWTH. *Poems* 10 Sleep..follow'd with a troope of golden Slumbers Thrust from my quiet Braine all base encumbers. **1642** HOWELL *For. Trav.* v. (Arb.) 28 Too great a number of such Friends, is an encomber and may betray him.

encumber (ɛnˈkʌmbə(r)), *v.* Forms: α. 4-7 encomber, -bre, (5 encounbre, emcombre), 5-8 encumbre, 6- encumber. β. 6-8 incomber, incumbre, 7 incombre, incumber. See also ACCUMBER. [a. OF. *encombre-r* to block up, obstruct, a Com. Rom. word (Pr. *encombrar*, It. *ingombrare*):—late L. *incombrāre*, f. *in* in, upon + *combrus* barricade, obstacle, prob. repr. L. *cumulus* heap. (In Eng. the fig. uses appear much earlier than the literal.)]

1. *trans.* To hamper, embarrass (persons, their movements, actions, etc.) *with* a clog or burden. Also of things: To act as a clog or restraint upon. Also *fig.*

α. *c* **1386** CHAUCER *Pers. T.* ¶613 Of accidie cometh first, that a man is annoyed and encombrid for to do eny goodnes. **1600** HOLLAND *Livy* XLIII. xxiii. 1169 They marched heavily armed and encombred. **1660** BLOUNT *Boscobel* II. (1680) 31 He travers'd..near three hundred (miles)..encombered with a portmanteau. **1781** GIBBON *Decl. & F.* III. lii. 261 The royal camp was encumbered by the luxury of the palace. **1842** BISCHOFF *Woollen Manuf.* II. 44 There were various branches of our trade which it had been thought necessary to encumber with high duties. **1855** MACAULAY *Hist. Eng.* IV. 408 He could not be persuaded to encumber his feeble frame with a cuirass. **1875** JOWETT *Plato* (ed. 2) IV. 407 The study of philosophy..may encumber him.

β. ? **1612** BRINSLEY *Lud. Lit.* iii. (1627) 13 Schoolemasters who are incumbred with this inconvenience. **1610** HEALEY *Epictetus' Man.* (1636) xiii. 17 Lamenesse incombers the legges, but not the resolution. **1688** in Somers *Tracts* I. 306 Such Statutes..seem to incumber what Papists think his Majesty's Prerogative. **1726** ADDISON *Dial. Medals* ii, She draws back her garment..that it may not incumber her in her march. **1738** [G. SMITH] *Cur. Relat.* II. 314 They sold their Commodities..in order to be less incombert when they should go about to conquer.

†**2.** To engage, involve, entangle *in. Obs.*

138. WYCLIF *Wks.* (1880) 70 Procuratours of þe fend to encombre [mennus soulis] in synne. *c* **1386** CHAUCER *Prol.* 508 And lefte his scheep encombred in the myre. *a* **1662** HEYLIN *Laud* I. 128 To deliver him out of that War in which they had incumbred..him. *c* **1720** PRIOR *Poems* (J.) Encumbered in the silken string.

†**3.** To cause suffering or inconvenience to. *Obs.*

c **1330** R. BRUNNE *Chron.* (1810) 254 Ȝit salle Edward be encombred þorgh dame Blanche schene. **1481** CAXTON *Myrr.* I. xii. 37 In mannes body whan ony maladye or sekenes encombreth hit. **1514** BARCLAY *Cyt. & Uplondyshm.* (1847) 51 Sometime these Courtiers them more to incumber Slepe all in one chamber. **1563-87** FOXE *A. & M.* (1596) 191/2 Greefes wherwith your mind is dailie incombred. **1605** BACON *Adv. Learn.* I. vii. §7 (1873) 56 His mind..being no ways charged or incumbered, either with fears, remorses, or scruples.

†**b.** Of enemies, etc.: To press hardly upon, harass, give trouble to. *Obs.*

1413 LYDG. *Pilgr. Sowle* I. i. (1859) 2 To what purpoos had god formed me for to ben encombred with soo moche meschyef. *c* **1440** *Gesta Rom.* I. xxxi. 104 The fleshe, the worlde, and the Devil..encomberithe a man. **1485** CAXTON *Chas. Gt.* 120 Ye shal be here encombred and assaylled. **1633** P. FLETCHER in Farr *S.P. Jas. I* (1848) 197 Much were the knights encumbred with these foes.

†**c.** To overcome, master; said *esp.* of temptations, passions, etc. *Obs.*

1377 LANGL. *P. Pl.* B. XIX. 223 That ydelnesse encombre hym nouȝt. **1393** GOWER *Conf.* III. 267 The King.. Incombred of his lustes blinde The lawe tornith out of kinde. *c* **1430** LYDG. *Bochas* II. v. (1554) 46 b, The auoutour ..Thee encumbred of very force.

4. To burden with duties, obligations, or responsibilities.

a **1593** H. SMITH *Wks.* (1867) II. 355 Martha is sore encumbered with much serving. **1607** HIERON *Wks.* I. 336 It is a burthen to them to bee so employed; they cannot abide to be so encombred. **1781** BURKE *Sp. Repeal. Marriage Act* X. 137 A man that breeds a family without competent means of maintenance, encumbers other men with his children. **1879** FROUDE *Cæsar* xi. 119 Aurelia had objected to be encumbered with a stepson.

5. To burden (a person or an estate) with debts; *esp.* to charge (an estate) with a mortgage. [Cf. OF. *encombrer* to mortgage.]

α. **1632** MASSINGER *City Madam* I. ii, Such lands..As are not encumbered. **1729** BERKELEY *Serm.* Wks. 1871 IV. 639 If you were..encumbered with debt. **1843** LEVER *J. Hinton* vii. (1878) 46 His large estates, loaded with debt and encumbered by mortgage. **1858** LD. ST. LEONARDS *Handy Bk. Prop. Law* xiv. 95 If he make a mortgage after having otherwise encumbered the estate.

β. **1677** YARRANTON *Engl. Improv.* 8 There being so many ways to incumber the Land privately. **1767** BLACKSTONE *Comm.* II. 313 The new occasions and necessities..required means to be devised of charging and incumbering estates.

6. To load or fill (places, things) *with* what is obstructive or useless; to block up; *fig.* to complicate, render difficult.

c **1400** *Rom. Rose* 3007 Thorough the breres anoon wente I, Wherof encombred was the hay. **1555** EDEN *Decades W. Ind.* (Arb.) 310 All iorneys incumbered with continuall waters. **1561** T. NORTON *Calvin's Inst.* I. 38 Seruetto and other like..haue encombred al things with new deceites. **1777** PRIESTLEY *Matt. & Spir.* (1782) I. 34, I have not.. encumbered my doctrine with..difficulties. **1796** MORSE *Amer. Geog.* I. 129 Copper Mine River..is encumbered with shoals and falls. **1816** SCOTT *Bl. Dwarf* ii, The ground about the pillar was strewed, or rather encumbered, with many large fragments of stone. **1868** MILMAN *St. Paul's* 472 Newton's monument..adorns or incumbers the Church of St. Mary-le-Bow. **1876** GREEN *Short Hist.* vi. §2 (1882) 276 The Statutes of Apparel..begin at this time to encumber the Statute-Book.

†**7.** In pa. pple.: Constipated. *Obs. rare*⁻¹.

1486 *Bk. St. Albans* C iij b, When yowre hawke is encombred in the bowillis.

†**8.** ? To fold (the arms). *Obs. rare*⁻¹.

1602 SHAKS. *Ham.* I. v. 174 With Armes encombred thus, or thus, head shake.

encumbered (ɛnˈkʌmbəd), *ppl. a.* [f. ENCUMBER *v.* + -ED¹.] In the senses of the verb: Hampered, burdened, etc. Of an estate: Charged with a mortgage.

1784 COWPER *Task* IV. 498 Society grown weary of the load, Shakes her incumber'd lap, and casts them out. **1847** BRIGHT *Sp. Irel.* 13 Dec., The encumbered condition of landed property in Ireland. **1859** JEPHSON *Brittany* ii. 9 Those who travelled in more dignified and encumbered style. **1884** MACKESON & SMITH ed. *Coote's Law of Mortg.* 473 The Incumbered Estates Court [West Indies].

enˈcumberer. [f. as prec. + -ER.] One who encumbers.

encumbering (ɛnˈkʌmbərɪŋ), *ppl. a.* [f. ENCUMBER *v.* + -ING².] That encumbers.

1641 MILTON *Animadv.* (1851) 188 Whosoever..labours to keep such an incumbring surcharge of earthly things. **1795** SOUTHEY *Joan of Arc* I. 404 From his belt he took The encumbering sword. **1838-9** HALLAM *Hist. Lit.* IV. IV. vii. 319 *note*, The feeble encumbering pronoun 'which'. **1872** H. MACMILLAN *True Vine* vii. 300 These barren, encumbering branches.

Hence **enˈcumberingly** *adv.*

encumberment (ɛnˈkʌmbəmənt). *Now rare.* Also incumberment. [a. OF. *encombrement*: see ENCUMBER *v.* and -MENT.]

1. The action of encumbering; the state or fact of being encumbered.

c **1330** R. BRUNNE *Chron.* (1810) 148 God..Saued þam alle þo tymes fro þer encumberment. *a* **1619** DANIEL *Coll. Hist. Eng.* (1626) 98 Their numbers growing so great, as bred many incomberments. **1678** CUDWORTH *Intell. Syst.* 151 Subjecting him [the Deity] to Sollicitous Encumberment. **1854** *Tait's Mag.* XXI. 454 Escaping from the rich encumberment of the metropolitan port. **1877** *Daily News* 3 Dec. 6 Droves of cattle..add to the incumberment of the way.

†**b.** Contextually used for: Satanic temptation. *Obs.* Cf. ENCUMBER *v.* 3 c.

c **1330** *Arth. & Merl.* 706 It was..The deuels foule encumberement. **15..** *Merlin* 645 in Furniv. *Percy Folio* I. 442 Thorrow the ffeendes incomberment.

†**c.** Molestation, disturbance. *Obs.*

1509 HAWES *Past. Pleas.* 14 Without Saturnus blacke encombrement. **1596** SPENSER *F.Q.* VI. viii. 38 To let her Sleepe out her fill without encomberment.

†**d.** Misfortune, mishap. *Obs.*

c **1440** *Gesta Rom.* 129, I have thorowe Encomberment slayne a man, and he is here with me.

†**2.** *concr.* Something that encumbers; = ENCUMBRANCE. *Obs.*

1600 ABP. ABBOT *Exp. Jonah* 634 Let us shake off all incumberments. **1660** H. MORE *Myst. Godl.* To Rdr. 29 Devested of those many encumberments of humane inventions both false and useless. **1664** —— *Myst. Iniq.* iii. 8 A troublesome and useless incumberment upon Christianity.

encumbrance (ɛnˈkʌmbrəns). Forms: α. 4-5 encombraunce, (-beraunce), 4-6 encumbraunce, 4-7 encombrance, 7- encumbrance; β. 6 incomb(e)raunce, 6-7 incombrance, (7 incumberance), 7-9 incumbrance. [a. OF. *encombrance*, f. *encombrer* to ENCUMBER; see -ANCE.]

†**1.** Encumbered state or condition; trouble, molestation, perplexity. *Obs.*

c **1314** *Guy Warw.* (A.) 5509 The douke Otous..His gret encumbraunce him telde. **1377** LANGL. *P. Pl.* B. XVIII. 265 (Wright's text) Care & encombraunce is comen to vs alle. *c* **1430** *Syr Gener.* (Roxb.) 2657 So I me drede..To haue som grete encomberaunce. **1509** FISHER *Fun. Serm. C'tess Richm.* (1708) 28 A lyfe voyde of all sorrow and encombrance. **1559** *Homilies* I. *Fear of Death* III. (1859) 103 The great encombrance which our spirit hath by this sinful flesh.

†**b.** Satanic temptation: = ENCUMBERMENT 1 b.

c **1450** *Merlin*, Wyte ye well that this is the encombraunce of the deuell.

2. *concr.* That which encumbers; a burden, impediment, 'dead weight'; a useless addition; in stronger sense, an annoyance, trouble.

1535 *Stat. 27 Hen. VIII*, c. 3 Which..shall be a great incumberance to all such the Kinges subiectes. **1583** GOLDING *Calvin on Deut.* ii. 8 The incomberaunces are..so great as it would bee vnpossible for vs to ouercome them if God assisted vs not. **1653** MILTON *Hirelings* (1659) 95 To hire incumbents or rather incumbrances for life-time. **1748** ANSON *Voy.* I. i. (ed. 4) 16 This incumbrance of a convoy gave us some uneasiness. **1764** BURN *Poor Laws* 172 Housekeepers will be freed from the intolerable incumbrance of beggars at their doors. **1833** I. TAYLOR *Fanat.* ii. 35 Malign dispositions and vindictive habits are.. miserable encumbrances of the mind. **1851** MARIOTTI *Italy in 1848* iv. 234 The great mass of volunteers, especially Lombards, were looked upon as a mere encumbrance. **1860** TYNDALL *Glac.* I. §27. 196 Divesting my limbs of every encumbrance.

3. A person dependent on another for support; *esp.* in phrase ***without encumbrance*** = 'having no children'.

1742 FIELDING *Jos. Andrews* IV. ii, I will have no more incumbrances brought on us. **1751** JOHNSON *Rambler* No. 165 §4. 148 Left the younger sons encumbrances on the eldest. **1833** HT. MARTINEAU *Three Ages* iii. 109 The widow ..may advertise herself as 'without incumbrance', to undertake any situation. **1865** *Pall Mall G.* 28 Nov. 10 Coachmen..rarely have children, or, as they say.. incumbrances.

4. *Law.* A burden on property: 'A claim, lien, liability attached to property; as a mortgage, a registered judgment, etc.' (Wharton).

a **1626** BACON *Max. & Uses Com. Law* 27 These acts are collaterall encombrances. **1642** PERKINS *Prof. Bk.* iv. §269. 120 He hath this Land without encombrance of Action. **1658** SLINGSBY *Diary* (1836) 200 That my ancient and lineally descended estate, might without incumbrance fall upon you my elder son. **1770** *Junius Lett.* xl. 204 You accepted the succession with all its encumbrances. **1836** KENT *Comm. Amer. Law* (1873) II. xxxix. 483 If a vendor, knowing of an encumbrance upon an estate, etc.

encumbrancer (ɛnˈkʌmbrənsə(r)). *Law.* Also in-. [f. ENCUMBRANCE + -ER.] One who has an encumbrance or legal claim on an estate.

1858 LD. ST. LEONARDS *Handy Bk. Prop. Law* viii. 50 A preferable title to any former purchaser or encumbrancer. **1863** GLADSTONE *Financ. Statem.* 22 A large body of mortgageors, incumbrancers, and life-renters.

†**enˈcumbrancy.** *Obs. rare*⁻¹. In 6 in- [f. as prec.: see -ANCY.] = ENCUMBRANCE 4.

1554 in *Archæol.* XXXIX. 188 The Quenes Matie to dischardge the purchaser of all incumbrauncy.

†**enˈcumbrous,** *a. Obs.* Forms: α. 4 encumberous, 4-5 encomb(e)rous(e, 6- encumbrous. Also β. 4 incombrous. [a. OF. *encombros*, f. *encombre*: see ENCUMBER *sb.* and -OUS.] Cumbersome, distressing, troublesome.

c **1384** CHAUCER *H. Fame* 862 Harde langage..ys encombrouse for to here. *c* **1392** —— *Compl. Venus* 42 But ful encomberous [*v.r.* encombrous] is þe vsing. **1413** LYDG. *Pilgr. Sowle* II. xliv. (1859) 50 The mooste encomberous melodye that euer I herde byfore. **1694** STRYPE *Cranmer* II. iii. *note* (D.), To avoid many encumbrous arguments.

†**en'cumbry.** *Obs. rare*⁻¹. In 6 incombrye. [f. ENCUMBER *v.* + -Y.] = ENCUMBRANCE.

1546 GARDINER *Decl. Artic. Joye* 82b, To make the husband amendes for that encombrye, ye teach men..that they may haue as lawfully two wyues at ones, as one.

encup: see EN- *pref.*¹ 1 a.

encur, obs. form of INCUR.

encurb, encurse: see EN- *pref.*¹ 3.

encurl (ɛn'kɜːl), *v.* Also incurl. [f. EN-¹ + CURL.] *trans.* To twist, twine, interlace.

1647–8 HERRICK *Poems* (1869) *App. Epithal.* viii, Like streames which flow Encurlld together. —— *Hesper* Wks. (1876) II. 253 Be she bald or do's she weare Locks incurl'd of other haire.

encursion, obs. var. INCURSION.

encurtain (ɛn'kɜːtɪn, -t(ə)n), *v.* Forms: 4 encortin, 6 encurtine, incorteyn, incurtain, -teyn, 7 en-, incourtaine, 7– encurtain. [a. OF. *encortine-r, encourtine-r*, f. *en-* in + *cortine, courtine* CURTAIN.]

1. *trans.* To surround, or envelop with curtains.

1393 GOWER *Conf.* I. 71 A softe bedde of large space They hadde made and encortined. *c* **1530** LD. BERNERS *Arth. Lyt. Bryt.* (1814) 6 To lye in the bed incorteyned wyth sylke. **1601** HOLLAND *Pliny* XIX. i, They began at Rome to encourtaine their Theatre with such vailes dyed in colours.

2. *trans.* and *fig.* To surround as with a curtain; to shroud, veil.

1596 FITZ-GEFFRAY *Sir F. Drake* (1881) 97 Since first these clouds his [the sunne's] face incurtained. *c* **1800** K. WHITE *Poet. Wks.* (1837) 71 Encurtain'd in the main. **1869** SPURGEON *Treas. Dav.* Ps. xviii. 11 Blessed is the darkness which encurtains my God.

†**3.** *Fortification.* (See quot.) *Obs. rare*⁻¹. [So *encortiner* in OF.; cf. CURTAIN *sb.*]

1598 FLORIO, *Cortinare*, to encurtine, to flank or fortifie about with a wall.

Hence **en'curtained** *ppl. a.*

1595 MARKHAM *Sir R. Grinvile* lxxxviii, Bright day is darkned by incurtaind light. **1606** CHAPMAN *M. D'Olive* Plays 1873 I. 190 Through the encourtaind windowes..I see light Tapers. **1631** BRATHWAIT *Whimzies, Gamester* 40 At the end of every act, the encurtain'd musique sounds.

encushion: see EN- *pref.*¹ 1 a.

-ency, ad. L. *-entia*, the termination of abstract sbs. formed upon pr. pples. (ppl. adjs. or sbs.) in *-ent-* by means of the suffix *-ia* (whence Eng. *-y* in *modesty, fallacy*, etc.: see -Y, -CY). The L. sbs. in *-entia* (like those in *-ia* generally) denoted primarily qualities or states; but some of them came by development of sense to be nouns of action or process, and in late L. and in Romanic the formation of nouns of action became the normal function of the suffix. Consequently the Eng. sbs. in -ENCE (which are adaptations of L. types in *-entia* either through Fr. or according to Fr. analogies) have very frequently the sense of action or process, either in addition to, or to the exclusion of, that of quality or state. The sbs. in *-ency*, on the other hand, being purely English adaptations of the Latin types, have properly only the sense of quality or state, and concrete senses thence developed. As exemplifying this difference of use between the two suffixes, cf. *recurrence* and *currency*, *confluence* and *fluency*, *residence* and *presidency*. When the same word exists in both the *-ence* and the *-ency* forms, the tendency is (where the sense of the verbal etymon permits) to restrict the former to action or process (*i.e.* to connect its meaning rather with that of the vb. than with that of the adj.), while the latter is used to express quality; cf. *coherence* and *coherency*, *persistence* and *persistency*. In a few instances both forms of a word have equally the sense of quality or condition; in most of these cases the one or the other of the forms has become obsolete or archaic; where they are both in current use, the distinction usually is that *-ency* has a more distinct reference to the sense of the related adj. or sb. in *-ent*, considered as the predicate of some particular subject; cf. for example, 'sentience is an attribute of animals' with 'some maintain the sentiency of plants'. See -ANCY.

encyclic (ɛn'saɪklɪk), *a.* and *sb.* [ad. late L. *encyclicus*, an altered form (with substitution of suffix) of *encyclius*, a. Gr. ἐγκύκλιος of same meaning, f. ἐν in + κύκλ-ος circle.]

A. *adj.*

1. = ENCYCLICAL A. 1, 2.

1824 *Hist. Europe* in *Ann. Reg.* 195/2 His recovery was followed by the promulgation of an Encyclic letter. **1866** FELTON *Anc. & Mod. Gr.* I. ix. 438 The encyclic, or liberal education at this period, embraced seven departments.

2. *nonce-use.* Encircling.

1850 MRS. BROWNING *Vis. Poets* I. 202 Dropping from Heaven's encyclic rim.

B. *sb.* = ENCYCLICAL B.

1851 MARIOTTI *Italy in 1848* iv. 251 The Papal encyclic of the 19th April, entered into no man's views. **1864** *Q. Rev.* July 127 The terms of the Encyclic imply a separation between liberty and Roman Catholicism.

‖**en'cyclica.** *rare.* [mod.Lat. fem. of *encyclicus*: see prec.] = ENCYCLICAL B.

1888 *Catholic Househ.* 18 Aug. 5/3 To the Encyclica of September 1883, the Catholics fully responded..To the Pontifical Encyclicas follow, etc.

encyclical (ɛn'saɪklɪkəl), *a.* and *sb.* [f. late L. *encyclicus* (see ENCYCLIC) + -AL¹.]

A. *adj.*

1. *Antiq.* Used as transl. of Gr. ἐγκύκλιος (παιδεία), *i.e.* general (education); cf. ENCYCLOPÆDIA 1.

1616–61 HOLYDAY *Persius* 301 The learning, which they call encyclical.

2. Of an ecclesiastical epistle: Circular, intended for extensive circulation. Now chiefly of letters issued by the pope.

1647 JER. TAYLOR *Dissuas. Popery* II. II. §2 Wks. (1822) XI. 85 Their [the Greeks'] prime and most learned prelate ..did..publish an encyclical epistle against the definition of the council. **1805** BP. HORSLEY *Sp. Petit. Rom. Cath. Speeches* (1813) II. 242, The apostolical vicars put forth an encyclical letter forbidding the people..to take the oath. **1882** FARRAR *Early Chr.* II. 35 The encyclical letter from the Church of Jerusalem, of which St. James was the main author.

B. *sb.* An encyclical letter; see A. 2.

1837 J. H. NEWMAN in *British Critic* XXII. 282 When a new Encyclical issues from Rome, etc. **1864** *Sat. Rev.* 3 Dec. 791 No one can read the Pope's new Encyclical without feeling, etc. **1871** MACDUFF *Mem. Patmos* v. 56 This most deeply spiritual encyclical. **1875** MANNING *Mission H. Ghost* xiii. 376 Pius IX..in the Encyclical..condemned.. the separation of Philosophy and Science from revelation.

encyclopædia, encyclopedia (ɛn,saɪkləʊ'piːdɪə). Also 7 in adapted forms encyclopædie-y, -pedie, -pedy, -ped(e. [a. late L. *encyclopædia*, a. pseudo-Gr. ἐγκυκλοπαιδεία, an erroneous form (said to be a false reading) occurring in MSS. of Quintilian, Pliny, and Galen, for ἐγκύκλιος παιδεία 'encyclical education', the circle of arts and sciences considered by the Greeks as essential to a liberal education (cf. ENCYCLICAL A. 1).

The spelling with *æ* has been preserved from becoming obs. by the fact that many of the works so called have Latin titles, as *Encyclopædia Britannica, Londinensis*, etc.]

1. The circle of learning; a general course of instruction.

1531 ELYOT *Gov.* I. xiii, The circle of doctrine..is in one worde of greke Encyclopedia. **1646** SIR T. BROWNE *Pseud. Ep.* a3a, To Rdr., In this Encyclopædie and round of knowledge. **1654** WHITLOCK *Zootomia* 187 Borrowed from the Bank of the Encyclopædia, or generall Learning. **1662** PHILLIPS *Dict.* Advt., A Dictionary for the English Tongue, would require an Encyclopedy of knowledge. **1681** T. MANNYNGHAM *Disc.* 54 They make..the whole Encyclopede of Arts and Sciences but a brisker Circulation of the blood. **1686** GOAD *Celest. Bodies* III. iii. 459 The Student..who shall think fit to take so useful a Theory in his Encyclopaedy. **1708** MOTTEUX *Rabelais* v. xx, In you are lodg'd a Cornucopia, an Encyclopedia, an unmeasurable Profundity of Knowledge. **1868** M. PATTISON *Academ. Org.* 277 An education which aimed at a little encyclopædia of elementary knowledge.

2. A literary work containing extensive information on all branches of knowledge, usually arranged in alphabetical order.

The word in this sense appears first as the title of certain works published in the 17th cent. *esp.* that of Alstedius (see quot. 1819).

1644 T. DICONSON in Bulwer *Chirologia* a2 Thy Enchiridion..became th' Encycloped. **1662** EVELYN *Chalcogr.* (1769) 123 A kind of encyclopedia of all..and memorable things. **1716** M. DAVIES *Ath. Brit.* II. 342 Mr. Record had scarce any Precedents or Patterns in his *Encyclopædy of Learning* to copy after. **1768** (*title*) Encyclopædia Britannica. **1819** *Pantologia* s.v. *Encyclopædia*, The first work we have seen under the title of Encyclopædia, is J. H. Alstedii Encyclopædia, which was published in 1632, in two vols. folio. **1841** MYERS *Cath. Th.* III. ii. 4 The Bible is..by no means indeed an Encyclopædia. **1859** DARWIN *Orig. Spec.* i. (1873) 24 An ancient Chinese encyclopædia.

humorously. **1837** DICKENS *Pickw.* xxiv, Mr. Pickwick.. looked encyclopædias at Mr. Peter Magnus. **1885** *Illust. Lond. News* 19 Dec. 648 Maida [a girl] was an encyclopædia of knowledge.

b. Sometimes applied *spec.* to the French work 'Encyclopédie ou Dictionnaire raisonné des Sciences, des Arts, et des Métiers' (1751–1765), by Diderot, D'Alembert, and other eminent scholars and men of science.

1773 (*title*) Select Essays from the Encyclopedy. **1790** BURKE *Fr. Rev.* Wks. V. 207 The vast undertaking of the Encyclopædia. **1872** MORLEY *Voltaire* (1886) 161 Diderot was busy (1750) with the first volume of the Encyclopædia.

3. An elaborate and exhaustive repertory of information on all the branches of some particular art or department of knowledge; *esp.* one arranged in alphabetical order.

1801 (*title*) The Encyclopædia of Wit. **1807** (*title*) The Vocal Encyclopædia: comprising a variety of popular songs, etc. **1859** SMILES *Self-help* 61 Introduced in the historical part of his [Loudon's] laborious Encyclopædia of Gardening..The result of which appeared in his Encyclopædias. **1881** (*title*), Hamersly's Naval Encyclopædia.

Hence **en,cyclo'pædiac** *a.* [see -AC], = ENCYCLOPÆDIC; **en,cyclopæ'diacal** *a.* [see -ACAL], = prec.; **en,cyclo'pædial** *a.* [see -AL], of or pertaining to an encyclopædia (see ENCYCLOPÆDIA 2).

1886 *Athenæum* 27 Feb. 298/3 His encyclopædiac knowledge renders it probable he will make an excellent librarian. **1836** *Blackw. Mag.* XL. 589 It is the object of many..to render instruction encyclopædiacal. **1848** *Fraser's Mag.* XXXVII. 216 The tendency of the Alexandrian school was encyclopædiacal throughout. **1818** *Blackw. Mag.* III. 658 Our Encyclopaedial lion is fangless and toothless.

encyclopædian (ɛn,saɪkləʊ'piːdɪən), *a.* and *sb.* [f. prec. + -AN.]

A. *adj.* **a.** Embracing the whole circle of learning; comprising a wide range of subjects. **b.** Of the nature of or resembling an encyclopædia.

1837 *New Monthly Mag.* XLIX. 439 A work of this order ..is in its nature encyclopædian.

B. *sb.*

†**1.** = ENCYCLOPÆDIST 1 b. *Obs. rare*⁻¹.

1834 BECKFORD *Italy* II. 249 Voltaireists and encyclopedians have poisoned all sound doctrine.

¶**2.** app. = ENCYCLOPÆDIA 1. [? Meant for a Gr. accusative.]

1621 BURTON *Anat. Mel.* I. ii. III. xv. (1651) 132 Let them have that Encyclopædian, all the learning in the world.

en,cyclo'pædiast. *rare*⁻¹. [f. ENCYCLOPÆDIA, on the analogy of *Ecclesiast.*] = ENCYCLOPÆDIST 1 b.

1818 *Blackw. Mag.* III. 26 Had he been less munificent in his patronage of French encyclopædiasts.

encyclopædic, encyclopedic (ɛn,saɪkləʊ'piːdɪk), *a.* [f. as prec. + -IC.] Of, pertaining to, or resembling an encyclopædia (see ENCYCLOPÆDIA 1); that aims at embracing all branches of learning; universal in knowledge, very full of information, comprehensive.

1824 *Blackw. Mag.* XVI. 26 Attempts at bringing knowledge into encyclopedic forms. **1838–9** HALLAM *Hist. Lit.* II. II. viii. 335 So comprehensive a notion of zoology displays a mind accustomed to encyclopedic systems. **1862** MERIVALE *Rom. Emp.* (1865) VI. liv. 470 Another feature of Lucan's Pharsalia is its affectation of encyclopædic knowledge. **1872** MINTO *Eng. Lit.* I. ii. 92 That encyclopædic statistician [Macaulay's father]. **1876** GREEN *Short Hist.* i. §4 (1882) 37 The encyclopædic character of his researches left him in heart a simple Englishman.

encyclopædical, encyclopedical (ɛn,saɪkləʊ'piːdɪkəl), *a.* [f. as prec. + -AL¹.] = prec.

1651 FULLER *Abel. Rediv.* 104 Encuclopedicall wisdome.. he esteemed rather a learned sort of madnesse, then etc. **1837** WHEWELL *Hist. Induct. Sc.* (1857) I. 192 An encyclopedical view of human knowledge. **1858** CARLYLE *Fredk. Gt.* (1865) X. XXI. viii. 156 The King's encyclopedical conversation enchanted me completely.

encyclopædically (ɛnsaɪkləʊ'piːdɪkəlɪ), *adv.* [f. ENCYCLOPÆDIC: see -ICALLY.] In an encyclopædic manner; comprehensively.

1855 ROSSETTI *Let.* 25 Nov. (1965) I. 280, I found his [*sc.* Browning's] knowledge of early Italian art beyond that of anyone I ever met—*encyclopaedically* beyond that of Ruskin himself.

encyclopædism, encyclopedism (ɛn,saɪkləʊ'piːdɪz(ə)m). [f. ENCYCLOPÆDIA + -ISM.]

1. Encyclopædic learning; the possession of the whole range of knowledge.

1833 CARLYLE, *Diderot*, Misc. V. 45 This exaggerated laudation of Encyclopedism. **1856** R. VAUGHAN *Mystics* (1860) I. I. i. 6 Not that he [Gower] sets up for Encyclopædism; on the contrary, he laments..the scantiness of his knowledge.

2. The doctrines of the Encyclopædists (see ENCYCLOPÆDIST 1 b).

1835 *Fraser's Mag.* XI. 102 A time of Tithe Controversy, Encyclopedism, Catholic Rent, Philanthropism, and the Revolution of Three Days! **1840** MILL *Diss. & Disc.* (1859) II, French philosophy, with us, is still synonymous with Encyclopedism.

encyclopædist, encyclopedist (ɛn,saɪkləʊ'piːdɪst). [f. as prec. + -IST.]

1. A compiler of or writer in an encyclopædia.

1651 EVELYN *Mem.* (1857) I. 278 Curtius had been scholar to Alstedius, the Encyclopedist. **1845** FORD *Handbk. Spain* §1. 31 *note*, St. Isidore..was the Pliny, the Bede, the Encyclopedist of his age.

b. *esp.* one of the writers of the French *Encyclopédie* (see ENCYCLOPÆDIA 2 b); often with a disparaging allusion to the tenets they promulgated.

1796 HUTTON *Math. & Philos. Dict.* Pref. 5 To have recourse to..the still more stupendous performance of the French Encyclopædists. **1800** *Month. Mag.* VIII. 597 The encyclopedists undertook to new model..the old-fashioned religious..opinions of that country [France]. **1829** CARLYLE *Misc.* (1857) II. 53 What Steam-engine..did these Encyclopedists invent for mankind?

2. One who attempts to deal with every branch of knowledge, or whose studies have a very extensive range.

1871 BLACKIE *Four Phases* i. 132 Aristotle..like a true encyclopædist, was content to register the gods whom he had not the heart to worship.

encyclopædize, encyclopedize (ɛnsaɪˈklɒpiːdaɪz), *v.* [f. as prec. + -IZE.] *trans.* **a.** To arrange as an encyclopædia (see ENCYCLOPÆDIA 1); to exhibit (knowledge) in a systematic form. **b.** To describe in an encyclopædia (see ENCYCLOPÆDIA 2).

1824 BYRON *Juan* XV. lxviii, Dictionaries Which encyclopedise both flesh and fish. **1824** *Blackw. Mag.* XVI. 32 The attempt to exhibit all Science in one body, the attempt to exhibit all Science to one mind, which are the two forms of the attempt to encyclopedize knowledge.

‖**encyliglotte.** *Obs.* [Fr. *encyliglotte* (Rabelais), app. a corruption of Gr. ἀγκυλόγλωσσον (*-γλωττον), the condition of being tongue-tied; cf. mod.Fr. *ancyloglosse*.] The string of the tongue.

a **1693** URQUHART *Rabelais* III. xxxiv, The Encyliglotte, which she had under her tongue being cut, she spoke.

encyse, obs. form of INCISE *v.*

encyst (ɛnˈsɪst), *v.* [f. EN-[1] + CYST.] *trans.* To enclose in a cyst, capsule, or bag; only in *pa. pple.* and *refl.* Also *absol.* or *intr.*

1845 BUDD *Dis. Liver* 272 Gall-stones in the substance of the liver..are often encysted. **1854** WOODWARD *Mollusca* (1856) 67 Shell represented by two short styles, encysted in the substance of the mantle. **1882** *Nature* XXVI, The cercaria..soon came to rest, showing a tendency to encyst itself on surrounding objects. **1896** tr. *Boas' Zool.* 86 A great many forms..have the power of encysting. **1966** *McGraw-Hill Encycl. Sci. & Technol.* VI. 439/2 The ability of protozoans to encyst is at least one of the reasons for their world-wide distribution.

fig. **1873** SYMONDS *Gk. Poets* xii. 418 Even in Pindar, moral mysticism is, as it were, encysted, like an alien deposit, in the more vital substance of aesthetic conceptions.

encystation (ɛnsɪˈsteɪʃən). *Biol.* [f. prec. + -ATION.] The process (observed in some Protozoa) of becoming surrounded with a cyst, bag, or capsule; = ENCYSTMENT.

1869 NICHOLSON *Zool.* 61 Reproduction in Vorticella..by a process of encystation and endogenous division. **1877** HUXLEY *Anat. Inv. An.* xii. 660 The Heliozoa propagate by simple division with or without previous encystation.

encysted (ɛnˈsɪstɪd), *ppl. a.* [f. as prec. + -ED[1].] That is contained in a cyst or sac. ***encysted tumour***: a tumour consisting of a fluid or other substance enclosed in a cyst. Also *fig.*

1705 T. GREENHILL in *Phil. Trans.* XXV. 2010, I..found it to be of that sort of Wens or encisted Tumors called Atheroma. **1782** S. F. SIMMONS in *Med. Commun.* I. 102 The dropsy was supposed to be of the encysted kind. **1824** COLERIDGE *Aids Refl.* (1848) I. 256 The encysted venom, or poison-bag, beneath the adder's fang. **1861** O. W. HOLMES *Elsie V.* 222 Encysted griefs, if we may borrow the chirurgeon's term.

encysting (ɛnˈsɪstɪŋ), *vbl. sb.* [f. ENCYST *v.* + -ING[1].] The action of the verb ENCYST.

1875 H. WALTON *Dis. Eye* 501 An eye may be destroyed while the encysting is going on.

encystment (ɛnˈsɪstmənt). [f. as prec. + -MENT.] **a.** 'The condition of an encysted tumour' (*Syd. Soc. Lex.*). **b.** *Biol.* The process of becoming surrounded by a cyst.

1865 *Pall Mall G.* No. 354. 1016/2 The encystment of the parasites. **1877** HUXLEY *Anat. Inv. An.* ii. 96 These Flagellata..present various modes of agamic multiplication by fission, preceded or not by encystment.

encyte, obs. form of INCITE.

end (ɛnd), *sb.* Forms: 1–7 ende, (2 aend, -e, 4 eende, hende, 4, 6 eande, 4 aend, eond, 5 heynd, 7 *dial.* eend), 3– end. Also 3–5 ȝende, 4 ȝend, 5 ȝynde, 6 yende. [Common. Teut.: OE. *ęnde* str. masc., corresponds to OS. *endi* (Du. *einde*), OHG. *enti* masc. (also neut.; MHG. *ende* masc., neut., mod.G. *ende* neut.), ON. *ender* (also *ende* wk. masc.; Sw. *ände* masc., *ända* fem., Da. *ende*), Goth. *andeis*:—OTeut. **andjo-z*:—pre-Teutonic **an'tjo-s*, cogn. with Skr. *ánta* masc., neut., end, boundary, with AND *conj.*[1] formerly *prep.*, and with OHG. *andi, endi*, ON. *enne* neut. (:—OTeut. **anþjo(m*:—**'antjo(m*) forehead.

In some dialects of ME. the *e* became long. The forms *ȝend(e, ȝynd(e, yende* may be merely phonetic developments of *ēnd*, or they may possibly be due to the influence of the vb. Y-END (OE. *ȝeendian*).]

I. With reference to space.

1. a. The extremity or outermost part (in any direction) of a portion of space, or of anything extended in space; utmost limit. *Obs.* in general sense; retained in phrase, ***the end(s of the earth.***

c **825** *Vesp. Psalter* Ps. xviii. [xix.] 4 In alle eorðan uteo de swoeᵹ heara and in endas ymbhwyrftes eorðan word heara. *c* **1000** *Ags. Ps.* xviii. [xix]. 4 Ofer ealle eorðan endas [færð] heora word. *c* **1305** *St. Kenelm* 150 in *E.E.P.* (1862) 51 Forto pleyen him bi þe wodes ende. **1389** in *Eng. Gilds* (1870) 7 Wt oute þe cite townes ende. *a* **1400–50** *Alexander* 173 All þe erth of Egipt fra end vnto othere Bees conquirid. **1599** ? GREENE *George a Greene* (1861) 265 But darest thou walk to the towns end with me? **1657** J. SMITH *Myst. Rhet.* 66 Christ shall..reign from the River to the end of the land. **1713** POPE *Windsor For.* 399 Earth's distant ends our glory shall behold. *Mod.* I would go with him to the world's end.

b. A limit of magnitude or multitude.

c **825** *Vesp. Psalter* Ps. cxliv. [cxlv.] 3 Micel dryhten and herᵹendlic swiðe and micelnisse his nis ende. **1600** SHAKS. *A.Y.L.* III. iii. 53 Many a man knowes no end of his goods. **1865** MILL in *Evening Star* 10 July, There was no end to the advantages.

†**c.** A boundary. In *pl.* territorial boundaries [? after L. *fines*]. *Obs.*

1388 WYCLIF. *Isa.* x. 13 Y haue take awei the endis of peplis. **1483** CAXTON *Gold. Leg.* 72/2 The Ryuer of the endes of the phylisteis. **1526** TINDALE *Acts* xvii. 26 And the endes of their in habitacion. **1570** BILLINGSLEY *Euclid* I. def. 5. 2 A line is the ende and terme of a superficies.

d. ***the end.*** *fig.* and *colloq.* (*a*) Of persons and things, a term to express the extreme in disparagement; the 'limit' (cf. LIMIT *sb.*): the 'last straw'.

[**1929** WODEHOUSE *Mr. Mulliner Speaking* ii. 55 'This,' he said in a shaking voice, 'is the end. From this moment I go off the stuff.'] **1938** N. MARSH *Death in White Tie* iii. 43 The sort of people who go there are just simply The End..the most unspeakable curiosities. **1944** 'BRAHMS' & 'SIMON' *Titania has Mother* v. 41 But the damage had been done... It was The End. **1953** E. TAYLOR *Sleeping Beauty* x. 175 You simply *are* the end. **1959** G. FREEMAN *Jack would be Gentleman* v. 85 Donald, you really are the absolute end.

(*b*) In U.S. slang use (esp. jazz), a term of extreme approbation: the best, the ultimate (ULTIMATE *sb.* 1). Also *attrib.*

1950 *Neurotica* Autumn 45 Senor this shit [*sc.* narcotic] is the end! **1954** *Time* 8 Nov. 70 A term of high approbation in the swing era was 'out of this world', in the bop era it was 'gone', and today it is 'the greatest' or 'the end'. **1957** J. KEROUAC *On Road* II. iv. 127 That Rollo Greb is the greatest... Man, he's the end! **1960** W. MORRIS in D. Cerulli et al. *Jazz Word* 123 One of my paintings is named requiem for bird, a tribute for the end alto. **1963** *Nugget* Feb. 46, I was blowing some jazz in the student lounge on this end Steinway.

†**2. a.** A 'quarter', division, region (of the world, of a country or town). *Obs.* (but cf. EAST-END, WEST-END, where this sense blends with 3).

c **893** K. ÆLFRED *Oros.* II. i, þas feower heafodricu sindon on feower endum þyses middangeardes. *a* **1225** *St. Marher.* (1862) 16 Ant al þe ende þæt tu ant heo habbeð in ierðet. **1297** R. GLOUC. (1724) 377 Al þat aȝt was in Engelond he let somony in ech ende To Salesbury. *c* **1330** R. BRUNNE *Chron.* (1810) 32 Alle þe north ende was in his kepyng. *c* **1450** LONELICH *Grail* lii. 540 ȝoure fadir sendeth Into every ende aftyr his knyhtes.

b. An outlying part of a village or small country town, the end of an estate, or an outlying property, usually preceded by a descriptive name. (For place-names and field-names in *-end* see A. H. Smith *Eng. Place-Name Elements* (1956) s.v. *ende*[1].)

1866 GEO. ELIOT *F. Holt* I. viii. 196 Mr Goffe, of Rabbit's End, had never had it explained to him that..land must inevitably be given up when it would not yield a profit. **1906** *Bungalow* Dec. 8/2 It is the typical 'end' so beloved of the novelist, the disreputable quarter which the parsimonious squire neglects. **1910** E. M. FORSTER (*title*) Howards End. **1925** *Victoria Hist. County Bucks.* III. 465/1 The soil [at Winslow] is of Oxford clay, which has been worked in a pit at Tinker's End. **1954** M. BERESFORD *Lost Villages* x. 339 Bedfordshire... The form of settlement..gives us the characteristic 'Ends'. Here, farms are scattered.

3. a. One of the two extremities of a line, or of the 'length' or greatest dimension of any object; that part of anything that includes the extremity of its length. ***from end to end***: from one extremity to the other; throughout the length.

a **1225** *Ancr. R.* 430 He þe well bloweð went þe neruwe ende of þe horne to his owune muðe. *c* **1340** *Cursor M.* 23201 (Edinb.) þe pitte of helle pin, it es sa dep..þat end ne bes þar neuir apon. *c* **1394** J. MALVERNE *Contn. Higden* (Rolls) IX. App. 3 Perrexitque ad locum qui Anglice vocatur 'Mile ende.' *c* **1400** *Destr. Troy* 8795 Euer folowand the fell to þe fyngur endys. *a* **1533** LD. BERNERS *Huon* xxv. 75 Oberon satte at the tables ende. **1551** RECORDE *Pathw. Knowl.* I. xiv, In the eande of the other line. **1602** *Return fr. Parnass.* II. vi. (Arb.) 32 Your Hobby will meete you at the lanes end. **1632** LITHGOW *Totall Discourse* 22, I haue trod foure seuerall times from end to end of it [Italy]. **1664** EVELYN *Kal. Hort.* (1729) The Air Ground-pipe, laid the whole length of the Green-house..and reaching from end to end. **1688** R. HOLME *Armoury* II. 79/1 The Billberry, or Windberry, is round at the end. **1721–1800** BAILEY, *Cann-Hook*, an iron hook made fast to the end of a rope. **1758** JOHNSON *Idler* No. 33 ¶25 Mutton-chops off the worst end. **1760** WESLEY *Jrnl.* 30 June (1827) III. 9, I was quickly wet to my toe's end. **1863** KINGSLEY *Water Bab.* 39 The end of his own nose. **1867** W. W. SMYTH *Coal & Coal-mining* 166 On the floor of the cage or at the ends of a rod passing through its upper bar.

†**b.** The point of a spear. *Obs.*

c **1400** *Destr. Troy* 9432 He bare hym þurgh the brest with a bright end.

c. (see LAND'S END.)

d. ? *transf.* In the game of Bowls: The portion of a game which is played from one 'end' of the green to the other (see quot. 1876). Formerly also a definite portion of a game in Billiards and some other sports.

1688 R. HOLME *Armoury* III. 263/1 Five Ends make a Game by Day light, and three by Candle light. **1747** *Scheme Equip. Men of War* 37 Playing an End or two at that innocent ..Game, called Push Pin. **1876** H. F. WILKINSON *Bowls* in *Encycl. Brit.* IV. 181 The bowling generally takes place alternately from the two 'ends' of the green. A 'void end' is when neither side can score a cast.

e. *Archery.* (*a*) The place at which a mark is set up. (*b*) The number of arrows shot from one end of a range.

1801 T. ROBERTS *Eng. Bowman* 288 *End*, the place where a mark is fixed. **1836** in A. E. Hargrove *Archery* (1845) 89 Any member who shall draw an arrow before the *end* has been determined by the Judges, shall forfeit his right to count for such arrow. **1879** M. & W. THOMPSON *Archery* x. 52 By the rules of the York Round three arrows to each archer constitute an end. **1887** W. BUTT *H. Ford's Archery* 289 On July 5, 1877, he made 3 golds in one end at 100 yards.

f. Of a sports pitch or court; also, the half occupied by a team or individual player. Phr. ***to change ends***: to play in the opposite direction to that in which the team or individual had previously played; so ***change of ends***; ***to choose ends***: to indicate the direction in which one prefers to play; so ***choice of ends***.

1851 W. BOLLAND *Cricket Notes* v. 87 The safest plan is to stipulate..that the disputed man shall not be put on at either end—as a doubtful bowler should never be permitted. **1865** J. PYCROFT *Cricketana* xiii. 235 He used at Lord's to bowl from the Pavilion end in order that he might have the slope against him. **1867** G. H. SELKIRK *Guide to Cricket-Ground* iv. 59 The finest bowler might change ends every over, and bowl continuously. **1881** *Two Codes Football* (ed. 3) 28 Ends shall only be changed at half-time. **1890** C. G. HEATHCOTE in J. M. Heathcote *Tennis*, etc. 253 The winner of the toss should choose the best end, taking note in doing so not only of the position of the sun at the moment, but of what it will be in the course of the match. **1933** D. L. SAYERS *Murder must Advertise* xviii. 313 The slogger smote a vigorous ball from the factory end. **1960** J. R. WITTY in Fabian & Green *Assoc. Football* I. II. iii. 167 Choice of ends has always been decided by a toss of the coin. **1963** R. B. STRATFORD *Netball* ix. 70 Unless the weather conditions make the choice of ends desirable, it is better [for the captain who wins the toss] to choose the centre pass. **1970** *Times* 22 Oct. 13/4 (*Soccer*) Five minutes after the change of ends came the body blow.

g. In American and Canadian football, one stationed at the end of a line or team of players; a wing; the position occupied by such a player.

1892 *Outing* (U.S.) Dec. 50/1 Long gains at the tackles, ends, and around the ends, were common. **1899** A. H. QUINN *Pennsylv. Stories* 22 The ends and the backs came together as though drawn by a magnet and the pyramid toppled and fell. **1944** *Greeley* (Colo.) *Daily Tribune* 24 Sept. 2/1 The Wizards team is well spiked with verterans this year having a veteran backfield, two ends and a letterman tackle. **1968** *Globe & Mail* (Toronto) 13 Feb. 29/1 Of their 10 selections, seven were offensive ends or flankers.

h. Phr. ***the end of the road*** (*transf.* and *fig.*).

1924 DILLON & LAUDER *End of Road* 4 Keep right on to the end of the road. Keep right on to the end. **1954** M. PROCTER *Hell is City* III. vi. 108 It'll be the end of the road for him. He won't care what he does. **1959** 'A. FRASER' *High Tension* x. 99 It isn't any good pretending. We've come to the end of the road. **1968** *Guardian* 8 Oct. 1/2 The end of the road for Mr. Dubcek's Czechoslovakia may not have been reached after all.

4. The surface which bounds an object at either of its two extremities; the 'head' of a cask.

1526 *Pilgr. Perf.* (W. de W. 1531) 274 b, The hopes kepeth fast the bordes of the vessell..& holdeth in yᵉ endes that they start not. **1816** J. SMITH *Panorama Sc. & Art* I. 224 Draw lines across each end of the stone. *Mod.* The ends of the cask were stove in. The ends of the box are of hard wood.

5. a. A piece broken, cut off, or left; a fragment, remnant. Cf. CANDLE-END. Of cloth: A half-length, or half-piece. Also in *odds and ends* (see ODDS).

1481–90 *Howard Househ. Bks.* (1841) 141 My lord sent to Stoke be the carter ij.c. xxiiij. lb. yren, conteyning xj. endes. **1583** STUBBES *Anat. Abus.* II. 39 Scraps or shreds or short ends of lace. **1605** BACON *Adv. Learn.* II. 66 A brokers shop that hath ends of everything. **1647** WARD *Simp. Cobler* 13 Give him leave to sell all his rags, and odde-ends. **1704** in *Lond. Gaz.* No. 3986/4 Lost..5 yards and a half of superfine ..Black, 12 yards and a half of refine Black..being both Last Ends. **1712** E. HATTON *Merch. Mag.* 22 An End or Half Cloth, or a Long or Whole Cloth. **1713** SWIFT *Frenzy of J. Dennis* Wks. 1755 III. I. 140 On his table were some ends of verse and of candles. **1887** RIDER HAGGARD *Jess* xxxii, The bit of candle..was..burnt out, so..he produced a box full of 'ends.'

b. *fig. Obs.* exc. in *odds and ends* (q.v.).

1599 SHAKS. *Much Ado* I. i. 290 Ere you flout old ends any further, examine your conscience. **1605** B. JONSON *Volpone* Prol. Nor hales he in a gull, old ends reciting, To stop gaps in his loose writing. **1607** R. WILKINSON *Merch. Royall* 26 Euerie Ladie..if her husband haue bribed out but an end of an office, yet she reuels and playes Rex. **1634** BP. HALL *Occas. Medit.* Wks. (1808) 104 To improve these short ends of time, which are stolen from his more important avocations. **1654** WHITLOCK *Zootomia* 251 They call.. language of a finer Dresse, Ends of Playes.

c. A part, proportion; only with adjs. of quantity, as in † ***micel ende*** (OE.) a great part; † ***most end***, also ***most an end*** [? corruption of **mosten ende*, OE. *mæstan ende*], used adverbially = 'for the most part', 'almost entirely', 'especially'; † ***none end***, no portion; ***a good (great) end*** (*dial.*), a large proportion (*of*).

O.E. Chron. an. 1052, Harold..ofsloh mycelne ende þes folces. *c* **1340** *Cursor M.* (Trin.) 14478 [The Jews] souȝten him to slone And moost ende for þat resoun þat he vp reised lazaroun. ? *c* **1400–40** *How a Merchande, etc.* 106 in *E.P.P.* (Hazl.) I. 201 To speke wyth none ende of my kynne. **1623** LISLE *Ælfric on O. & N.T.* Jeremias..was oft in bands and cast into prison..and bore most an end the peoples sinnes. **1676** HALE *Contempl.* I. 58 The credit of the Relator, which most an end depends upon another's credit. **1739** *Grobianus* 122 Tipplers most an end are roaring Boys. **1869** R. B.

PEACOCK *Lonsdale Gloss.* s.v., It cost me a girt end of a pound. *Ibid., Most on End*..used adverbially; continually, unremittingly. *Mod. Derbysh.*, It cost me a good end of ten pounds. I have been waiting a good end of an hour.

d. A share or portion; a part or side. orig. *U.S.*

1903 A. H. LEWIS *Boss* xiv. 181 That's always th' Tammany end; forty per cent. **1907** in ASHER & HEAL *Send No Money* (1942) 115 After the genial and affable derelicts in the money changing end received the money..no stove has arrived. **1926** J. BLACK *You can't Win* ix. 105 Didn't him and Smiler bring it [*sc.* $200] up here for my end of that chippy gambling house's bankroll? **1928** *Publishers' Weekly* 30 June 2598 To talk to such a person about the editorial end of a publishing business means little or nothing. **1948** 'N. SHUTE' *No Highway* v. 126 Honey would have to come back to this country to tell us his end of it. **1962** B. KNOX *Little Drops of Blood* ii. 39 How about your end of it?

6. In various technical uses. **a.** *Coal-mining.* The furthest part of a gallery or working. ***end of coal*** (see quot. 1881). Also phr. ***on the end*** (see quots.).

1865 *Morning Star* 7 Jan. The men are of course usually at work in the 'ends'. **1867** W. W. SMYTH *Treat. Coal* xii. 140 A far better proportion of round coal will be obtained by working on the end, *i.e.*, in the direction of such cleat. **1878** HUXLEY *Physiogr.* 238 This direction is sometimes called the end of the coal. **1881** RAYMOND *Mining Gloss.*, *End of coal*, the direction or section at right-angles to the face; sometimes called the butt. **1892** H. W. HUGHES *Text-bk. Coal-min.* vii. 158 If the face is parallel to the cleat, the coal is said to be 'on the end'.

b. *Naut.* ***cable's end***, or simply ***end***: the last length of a cable. ***rope's end***: a short length of rope bound at the ends with thread, used as an instrument of punishment. ***bitter end*** (see BITTER).

1663 PEPYS *Diary* 23 June, I beat him, and then went up in to fetch my rope's end. **1801** SIR H. PARKER *Let.* 6 Apr. in Duncan *Nelson* (1806) 140 They [ships] were riding with two cables end. **1867** SMYTH *Sailor's Word-bk.*, *Rope's end*, the termination of a fall, and should be pointed or whipped. Formerly much used for illegal punishment. **1882** NARES *Seamanship* (ed. 6) 145 Have plenty of end in the bows ready to make fast.

c. ***a shoemaker's end***: a length of thread armed or pointed with a bristle; = WAX-END. ***to pack up one's ends and awls*** (*Sc.*): i.e. all one's effects.

1598 FLORIO, *Lesina*, a shooe-makers ende or awle. **1656** MORE *Antid. Ath.* II. xi. (1712) 74 Two strings like two shoemakers ends come from the hinder parts of the male. **1713** SWIFT *Elegy on Partridge* Wks. 1755 III. II. 82 Ariadne kindly lends Her braided hair to make thee ends. *a* **1745** MESTON *Poems* (1767) 98 Laden with tackle of his stall, Last, ends, and hammer, strap, and awl. **1798** WOLCOTT (P. Pindar) *Tales Hoy* Wks. 1812 IV. 389 Crispin too forgets his End and Awl. **1823** GALT *R. Gilhaize* I. 271 They arrived at Edinburgh, and constrained the Queen Regent..to pack up her ends and awls.

d. *Spinning* and *Weaving.* (*a*) ***card-end***: a sliver or carding. (*b*) A worsted yarn in a Brussels carpet.

1875 URE *Dict. Arts* I. 978 For spinning coarse numbers ..six card-ends are usually converted into one riband.

e. ***end of steel*** (also formerly ***end of the steel***): the limit to which tracks have been laid during the construction of a railway; a railway terminus; so ***end-of-steel town***, a town at a railway terminus. *Canad.*

[**1884** *Prince Albert Times* (Sask.) 4 July 3/1 A number of leading citizens of Calgary waited on Inspector Steele..on the eve of his departure to End of Track.] **1909** A. D. CAMERON *New North* ii. 21 Edmonton is the end of steel. Three lines converge here. **1912** H. FOOTNER *New Rivers of North* 276 We came to the end of the steel, but there was no construction work going on. **1912** J. B. BICKERSTETH *Let.* 3 Nov. in *Land of Open Doors* (1914) x. 199 An end-of-steel town is a wicked place. **1933** *Meccano Mag.* Mar. 195/1 Greatly reduced the time required for the journey from the 'end of steel', as the railway terminus is called in Canada. **1933** THOMPSON & EDGAR *Canadian Railway Devel.* 247 An engine drawing a train of ballast trucks..steamed to the end of steel. **1962** R. SLOBODIN *Band Organiz. Kutchin* 12 The railroad terminus—the 'end of steel'—is at Waterways, Alberta.

f. ***big end***: see BIG *a.* B. 2.

II. With reference to time or serial order.

7. a. The limit of duration, or close, of a period of time; the termination, conclusion, of an action, process, continuous state, or course of events; the terminal point of a series; the conclusion of a discourse, book, chapter, etc.

c **1000** *Ags. Gosp.* Matt. x. 22 Soðlice se þurhwunað oð ende, se byð hal. *c* **1200** ORMIN 4356 Forr seffne daȝhess brinngenn aȝȝ þe wuke till hiss ende. *c* **1230** *Hali Meid.* 17 Blisse þat cumeð..withuten ani ende. *a* **1300** *Cursor M.* 4236 Es noght his murning mai amend I wen bifor his liues ende. *Ibid.* 26595 If þou þis bok will se till end. **1340** *Ayenb.* 262 þis boc is ycome to þe ende. *a* **1400-50** *Alexander* 880 Philip..lofes hire [Olympias] lely to his lyfes ende. **1535** COVERDALE *1 Cor.* xv. 24 Then the ende, whan he shal delyuer vp the kyngdome vnto God the father. **1568** GRAFTON *Chron.* II. 22 Robert had heard this message unto the ende. **1709** ADDISON *Tatler*, No. 24 ¶3 This Felicity attending him to his Life's End. **1803** R. ANDERSON *Cumbld. Ball., Calep Crosby*, Frae week en to week en. **1862** STANLEY *Jew. Ch.* (1877) I. x. 198 The passage of the Jordan was not the end, but the beginning of a long conflict. **1876** TREVELYAN *Macaulay* I. i. 13 He worked unceasingly.. from year's end to year's end.

b. The latter or concluding part (of a period, action, etc.).

1398 TREVISA *Barth. De P.R.* II. xx. (1495) 47 In the ende of the worlde the deuyll shall be..moche the more feruent to woodnesse. *a* **1200** *Moral Ode* in *E.E.P.* 26 Ac ȝif þe ende is euel, al it is uuel. **1596** SHAKS. *Merch. V.* I. iii. 82 The Ewes In end of Autumne turned to the Rammes. *a* **1744** BROOME *Epic Poetry* (J.), The..designs of an action are the beginning;..the difficulties that are met with..are the middle; and the unravelling and resolution of these difficulties are the end. **1847** MRS. A. KERR *Hist. Servia* 170 Kara George..towards the end of the summer of 1806, approached the eastern frontier.

c. in attrib. uses of phrases, as ***end-account, end-August, -year*** (also followed by a specified year-date); ***end-of-December, end-of-season, end-of-term*** (also ***end-of-termy*** adj.), ***end-of-the-century, end-of-the-year.*** **end-of-(the)-day**, designating glassware made by combining different-coloured glass (allegedly oddments left over at the end of the day); cf. WHIMSY *sb.* 7 b.

1891 *Literary World* 20 Nov. 422/3 Our end-of-the-century civilisation. **1902** *Westm. Gaz.* 12 June 7/2 The end-of-December account. **1903** *Ibid.* 21 Aug. 9/1 The final details of the end-August settlement. **1909** *Ibid.* 9 Dec. 10/1 The end-of-the-year requirements are likely to be satisfied. **1911** H. WALPOLE *Mr. Perrin* iii. 42 The end-of-termy feelings. **1923** *Manch. Guardian Weekly* 10 Aug. 106/1 Smith Minor has been cruelly flogged by an avaricious head master who had discovered that his end-of-term rose-bowl was only electro plate instead of the solid silver which he had stipulated in his letter to the lad's parents. **1928** *Daily Chron.* 9 Aug. 8/6 The falling off in the average shown in latest developments, accentuated by end-account sales. **1937** *Antiques* Feb. 80/1 For years past, many collectors have found much to admire in what they called *End of the Day* glass. **1938** *New Statesman* 8 Jan. 39/1 The end-year issue of *The Bookseller*. **1947** WYNDHAM LEWIS *Let.* 21 Dec. (1963) 423, I was sorry to hear of your end-of-the-year feeling of nervous exhaustion. **1948** *Glass Club Bull.* Mar. 5/1 'End of the day' is a fanciful term given in support of the story that at the end of the working day the odds and ends ..were..remelted..and..appeared as beautiful pieces of purple and white glass. **1954** *Economist* 11 Sept. 1/2 The show [*sc.* Farnborough]..is both a shop-window and an end-of-term report. **1955** *Times* 6 July 16/1 The effects of end-account selling. **1959** *Ibid.* 12 June 15/1 An end-of-season concert. **1960** *Ibid.* 13 Jan. 17/2 There has recently been some movement of funds from London—quite apart from the Swiss end-year transactions. **1966** *Rep. Comm. Inquiry Univ. Oxf.* I. 182 At end-1965 prices. **1966** *Listener* 23 June 914/3 But it was the end-of-term exam that really made him anxious. **1969** *Canad. Antiques Collector* June 24/1 'End of day' novelties, blown for fun from remaining glass, are..the most interesting from a collector's point of view. **1981** P. PHILLIPS *Encycl. Glass* 163/3 These multi-coloured bottles were often made from the glass left in various pots at the close of work—hence the common name 'end-of-day' glass in England (also 'splashed glass' in America).

d. In hackneyed phr. ***at the end of the day***, eventually; when all's said and done.

1974 H. MCKEATING *God & Future* vi. 96 Eschatological language is useful because it is a convenient way of indicating..what *at the end of the day* we set most store by. **1976** *South Notts. Echo* 16 Dec. 1/4 'At the end of the day,' he stated, 'this verifies what I have been saying against the cuts in public expenditure.' **1978** *Jrnl. R. Soc. Arts* CXXVI. 213/2, I want to make a number of points to you, which we believe invalidate..the recommendations they make at the end of the day. **1982** B. BEAUMONT *Thanks to Rugby* iii. 39 But, at the end of the day, it is an amateur sport and everyone is free to put as much or as little into the game as he chooses. **1986** *Independent* 17 Nov. 4 At the end of the day businessmen can talk to the city in a way chief executives cannot.

8. a. Termination of existence; destruction, abolition. (The early examples of *end of the world* should perhaps be referred to 7, as *world* may have been taken in its older temporal sense; cf. however Fr. *fin du monde.*) ***It isn't*** (or ***wouldn't be***, etc.) ***the end of the world***, it is not a calamity, it is not a matter of great importance. Also ***end-of-the-world*** used attrib. or as adj.

832 *Charter* in Sweet *O.E.T.* 447 ðet he ðas god forðleste oð wiaralde ende. *c* **1340** *Cursor M.* 22390 (Edinb.) His dome þat him sale driue til ende. **1662** STILLINGFL. *Orig. Sacr.* III. i. §8 The world may have an end before he proves his Atoms could give it a beginning. *a* **1704** LOCKE (J.), There would be an end of all civil government, if the assignment of civil power were by such institution. **1907** G. B. SHAW *Major Barbara* III, Nothing's going to happen to you;..it wouldnt be the end of the world if anything did. **1964** J. CREASEY *Guilt of Innocence* xvi. 136, I know exactly what a shock you had... But it isn't the end of the world, you know. **1964** A. WILSON *Late Call* ii. 78 'I don't see the numbers very clearly...' 'Well, it isn't the end of the world if you don't.'

1916 D. H. LAWRENCE *Let.* 7 Nov. (1932) 375 The book frightens me: it is so end-of-the-world. *a* **1963** L. MACNEICE *Astrol.* (1964) ix. 286 A recent 'end-of-the-world' forecast.

b. The death (of a person); a mode or manner of death.

c **1305** *Edmund Conf.* 590 in *South-Eng. Leg.* (1887) 448 þe more is bodi ipined was: þe ner he was þen ende. *c* **1340** *Cursor M.* 3905 (Trin.) Rachel bare..beniamyn þat was þe cause of hir ende. *c* **1325** *E.E. Allit. P.* C. 426 Bed me bilyue my bale stour, & bryng me on ende. *c* **1400** *Destr. Troy* 1438 Ffele folke forfaren with a ffeble ende. *a* **1440** *Sir Eglam.* 756 The dragon hath tan hys ȝynde. **1568** GRAFTON *Chron.* II. 650 This ende had the valiant Lorde, Richard Plantagenet Duke of Yorke. **1596** SHAKS. *Merch. V.* III. ii. 44 Then if he loose he makes a Swan-like end, Fading in musique. **1667** PEPYS *Diary* (1879) IV. 338 Great talk of the good end that my Lord Treasurer made. **1732** POPE *Epit. Gay*, Unblam'd through life; lamented in thy end. **1807** CRABBE *Par. Reg.* III. 38 Call then a priest and fit him for his end. **1879** FROUDE *Cæsar* vi. 52 To be murdered was the usual end of exceptionally distinguished Romans.

†**c.** In phrase ***to be the end of*** (cf. ***to be the death of***). Now used, somewhat trivially, in the sense 'to be the downfall of, to put an end to (ambition, promotion, etc.)'.

1594 SHAKS. *Rich. III*, II. i. 15 Lest..the..King of Kings award Either of you to be the others end. **1597** —— *2 Hen. IV*, IV. iv. 130 This Apoplexie will (certaine) be his end. **1934** G. B. SHAW *On Rocks* I. 200 He was just ripe for the Cabinet when his wife..made money by journalism. That was the end of him. **1936** J. B. PRIESTLEY *They walk in City* iv. 76 She and the bow-legged chap would be pushing a pram up the road..and that..would be the end of them.

9. Ultimate state or condition. Chiefly in Bible phrases, in which, however, *end* is often misinterpreted in sense 8 b.

c **825** *Vesp. Psalter* xxxviii. [xxxix.] 5 Cuð me doa dryhten ende minne. **1611** BIBLE *Ps.* xxxvii. 37 Marke the perfect man, and behold the vpright: for the end of that man is peace.

10. ***latter*** (†***last***) ***end***: variously used in senses 7 b, 8 b, 9. Also Sc. ***hinder end.***

1382 WYCLIF *Ecclus.* i. 13 Wel shal be in the laste endys. **1568** GRAFTON *Chron.* II. 158 The latter ende of this moneth of July..the Legate..tooke his leave of the king. **1601** SHAKS. *All's Well* II. v. 30 A good Trauailer is something at the latter end of a dinner. **1664** EVELYN *Kal. Hort.* (1729) 193 The middle or latter end of this month. **1670** COTTON *Espernon* I. II. 57 Towards the Dukes latter end, I read this History to him.

†**11.** A termination of doubt or debate; a resolution, device, expedient; an agreement, settlement. *Obs.*

1297 R. GLOUC. (1724) 169 To London vorte wende, To nyme þer ys conseyl, wuch were best ȝende. *c* **1386** CHAUCER *Man of Law's T.* 168 Wel sche saugh ther nas non other ende. *c* **1460** FORTESCUE *Abs. & Lim. Mon.* (1714) 66 Unto the time his said Kyng had made such End, with him, his Adherents, and Fautours, as he desired. **1489** *Plumpton Corr.* 82 The dayes men cannot agre us, so Mr. Mydleton to make the end. **1542-3** *Act 34 & 35 Hen. VIII*, c. 27 §100 Parties, to whome any such offence shall hap to be committed, shall in nowise take any ende or agreement with the offenders.

†**12.** The completion of an action; the accomplishment of a purpose: chiefly in phrases, ***to have, make, take, bring to, be at (an) end.*** Also, the acme, utmost reach. *Obs.*

a **1300** *Cursor M.* 10127 Prophecies com al to end. *Ibid.* 25862 þat þou mai noght do to end. *Ibid.* 27783 For drede þat he may noght mak end. *c* **1340** *Ibid.* 8580 Al þat his fader be-gynne muȝt salamon til hende hit broȝt. **1375** BARBOUR *Bruce* IV. 660 Feill anoyis thoill ȝhe sall, Or that ȝour purposs ende haf tane. *c* **1440** *Boetus, Laud MS.* 559. 10 Withouten hym may hit nought To an eende our purpose be brought. *c* **1590** MARLOWE *Massac. Paris* I. ii. 142 To bring the will of our desires to end. **1632** MASSINGER. *Maid of Hon.* I. i, To eat and sleep supinely is the end Of human blessings. **1679** BURNET *Hist. Ref.* Ep. Ded. 3 To have been at the end of their designs.

13. a. Event, issue, result.

c **1385** CHAUCER *L.G.W.* 1774 *Lucrece*, What ende that I make, it shal be so! *c* **1400** *Apol. Loll.* 28 Onli in name, & as to ȝend & effect is nowȝt. **1483** *Cath. Angl.* 114 An Ende, *exitus.* **1559** *Myrr. Mag., Dk. Suffolk* xix, But note the ende. **1581** SAVILE *Tacitus' Hist.* III. xix. (1591) 125 The ende went on his side. **1633** HEYWOOD *Eng. Trav.* IV. Wks. 1874 IV. 73 The end still crownes the deede. **1641** J. JACKSON *True Evang. T.* ii. 160 It is the end that crownes the worke. **1878** B. TAYLOR *Deukalion* I. vi. 50 The end shall crown us: The Gods are just.

†**b.** ***to have its end(s) upon***: to have influence upon. *Obs.*

1638 CHILLINGW. *Relig. Prot.* I. ii. §49. 71 The Authority of one holy man, which has apparently no ends upon me. **1736** BUTLER *Anal.* viii. 396 Religion considered as a probation has had its end upon all persons, to whom, etc.

14. a. An intended result of an action; an aim, purpose. (Cf. L. *finis.*) ***to accomplish, answer, fulfil, gain,*** † ***make, serve one's end(s***: see those verbs.

c **1305** *Edmund Conf.* in *E.E.P.* (1862) 72 Hit schal ȝut likie wel bi þan 3 e wite þan ende. **1581** SIDNEY *Apol. Poetrie* (Arb.) 30 The Sadlers next end is to make a good saddle. *a* **1628** PRESTON *New Covt.* (1634) 232 A right end never hath a crooked rule leading to it. **1654** WHITLOCK *Zootomia* 184 They study..not to make their ends on any mans weaknesse. **1719** DE FOE *Crusoe* (1840) I. x. 174 This answered my end. **1735** BERKELEY *Free-think. in Math.* §6 Wks. 1871 III. 304, I have no end to serve but truth. **1759** ROBERTSON *Hist. Scot.* I. III. 260 She had fully gained her end. **1832** HT. MARTINEAU *Life in Wilds* vii. 88 I am rather afraid of our people mistaking the means for the end. **1857** D. JERROLD *St. Giles* x. 102[He] was delighted..that the ends of justice would be satisfied. **1875** JOWETT *Plato* (ed. 2) V. 323 They may fairly use a little violence in order to accomplish their end.

b. In phrases, ***for*** or ***to this (that, what, which) end, to no end.*** Also in conjunctional phrase, ***to the end (that)***; formerly also, † ***to the end to*** (with *inf.*).

Now somewhat archaic or rhetorical; the ordinary phrase is *in order* (*that* or *to*).

138. WYCLIF. *Sel. Wks.* III. 354 Han power of him to þise ende. *c* **1400** MAUNDEV. v. 51 ȝee schulle knowe and preve, to the ende that ȝee schulle not ben disceyved. **1474** CAXTON *Chesse* IV. ii. (1860) K iij b, The faders had dyuerse wyues.. to thende whan one was [with] childe, they myght take another. **1558** WARDE tr. *Alexis Secr.* (1568) 64 a, To thende they may al equally receive of the honnye. **1605** BACON *Adv. Learn.* I. ii. §9 (1873) 17 To the end to peruse the Greek authors. **1634** SIR T. HERBERT *Trav.* 28 To which end, King Abbas, sends his Ambassadour to Constantinople. **1684** BUNYAN *Pilgr.* II. 70, I am come forth to withstand them,

and to that end will back the Lions. **1692** Bp. Ely *Answ. Touchstone* 187 It is to no end to look what St. Austin saith. **1712** Addison *Spect.* No. 305 ⁋12 To the End that they may be perfect also in this Practice. **1728** Sheridan *Persius* iii. (1739) 47 Study..for what end ye were created. **1769** Robertson *Chas. V*, V. ii. 244 For this end he summoned Luther to appear at Rome. **1848** Macaulay *Hist. Eng.* I. 170 For these ends, and for these ends alone, he wished to obtain arbitrary power.

c. *Sc.* ***end's errand***: the special design.

1821 Galt *Sir A. Wylie* II. 158 Did they say nothing of the end's errand they had come upon?

15. A final cause; the object for which a thing exists; the purpose for which it is designed or instituted.

1534 Whittinton *Tullyes Offices* i. (1540) 4 Suche offyces ..pertayne to the ende of felycitie. **1587** Golding *De Mornay* xvi. 261 And as man is the end of the World, so is God the end of Man. **1648** *Shorter Catech.*, Man's chief end is to glorify God and to enjoy him for ever. **1722** Wollaston *Relig. Nat.* vii. 147 The end of Society is the common welfare and good of the people associated. **1776** Gibbon *Decl. & F.* I. xxiv. 702 I have considered the happiness of the people as the end of government. **1869** Ruskin *Q. of Air* §60 The flower is the end or proper object of the seed. *a* **1876** J. H. Newman *Hist. Sk.* I. iv. ii 375 The highest end of Church union..is quiet and unanimity.

III. Idiomatic phrases.

16. With various prepositions forming advb. phrases.

a. ***at the end*** (ME. ***at þen, atten ende***), †***at end***: at last. †**b.** ***for (an) end***: in conclusion, finally, 'to cut the matter short'. **c.** ***in the end***, †***in end***: ultimately, in the long run. †**d.** ***to an end***: consecutively, through the whole period specified.

a. *c* **1300** *Beket* 81 Attan ende bi cas; Tho heo com aȝe thulke hous ther this Gilbert was. *a* **1300** *Cursor M.* 14879 (Gött.) þai at end him did on rod. **1340** *Ayenb.* 128 Atenende þe zeneȝere..is ase þe ilke þet slepþ amide þe ze. *c* **1320** *Sir Tristr.* 407 Of þyng þat is him dere Ich man preise at ende. *Ibid.* 3287 þai hadde woundes ille At þe nende. **1632** Lithgow *Totall Disc.* 127 In end..the slaves..runne the Galley a shoare. **1872** Browning *Hervé Riel*, My friend, I must speak out at the end, Though I find the speaking hard.

b. **1570–6** Lambarde *Peramb. Kent* (1826) 221 For an end therefore I tel you, etc. **1576** Flemming *Panoplie Ep.* 10 For ende, he counselleth Curio to take charge of the common wealth. **1607** Shaks. *Cor.* ii. i. 260 For an end, we must etc.

c. *c* **825** *Vesp. Psalter* ix. 19 Nales in ende oferȝeotulnis bið ðearfena. **1568** Grafton *Chron.* II. 165 But in the end the losse fell to the Englishmen. **1828–40** Tytler *Hist. Scot.* (1864) I. 25 His [Edward I's] power and influence would in the end induce the different parties to appeal to him. **1885** *Manch. Exam.* 13 July 5/5 The match in the end was very narrowly won by Harrow.

d. **1583** Stubbes *Anat. Abuses* (1877) 50 Never content with one colour or fashion two dayes to an ende. **1657** Serjeant *Schism Dispach't* 478 Would any government.. remain on foot three years to an end, if, etc. **1717** J. Fox *Wanderer* 160 Octavius..told him he should not live another Hour to an End.

17. ***on end*** (see also an-end): †**a.** at last; **b.** consecutively, without intermission; also ***right*** or ***straight on end***: (*a*) consecutively, uninterruptedly; (*b*) immediately; †**c.** on (one's) way, forward, along; (whence ***to come on end***, to come forward; (ME.) ***to set spell*** or ***tale on end***, to begin a discourse); **d.** in an upright position, resting on (its) end.

a. *c* **1175** *Lamb. Hom.* 25 Al swa he doð swa þe swica þe biswikeð hine seolfe on-ende. *c* **1320** *Cast. Love* 1064 þat foreward on ende wel was i-holde. *c* **1325** *E.E. Allit. P.* A. 186, I drede on ende quat schulde byfalle.

b. **1634** Rutherford *Lett.* No. 32 (1862) I. 111 And was brought, thrice on end, in remembrance of you in my prayer to God. [**1778** Strait an end: see straight *adv.* 2 c.] **1836** in *Byron's Wks.* (1846) 552/1 The ministerial prints raved for two months on end. **1837** T. Hook *Jack Brag* i. 16 The fox going away right on-end across a heavy country. **1867** Smyth *Sailor's Word-bk.* 574 *Right on end*, in a continuous line; as the masts should be. **1882** Besant *All Sorts* vii, Working sixteen hours on end at two-pence an hour. **1883** S. Baring-Gould *John Herring* I. xi. 154, I be going to die right on end, I be.

c. *c* **1340** *Cursor M.* (Trin.) 1295 Seeth set tale on ende [*Cott* . spell o-nend] And tolde whi he was sende. **1621** Sanderson *Serm.* I. 188 These would be soundly spurred up, and whipped on end. **1630** *Ibid.* II. 266 Others will not come on end chearfully.

d. *a* **1300** *Cursor M.* 25049 þe cros..quen it es sett on end vp euen, It takens pes tuix erth and heuen. **1598** Grenewey *Tacitus' Descr. Germany* vi. (1622) 269 The Sueuians..haue their hair standing on end. **1784** Cowper *Task* iv. 86 Katerfelto, with his hair on end At his own wonders. **1836** *Random Recoll. Ho. Lords* xvi. 383 His dark hair..stands on end on the fore part of his head. **1839** W. Irving *Wolfert's R.* (1855) 143 A great hotel in Paris is a street set on end.

18. ***without end*** (ME. ***buten ende***): endlessly, for ever; also in adjectival sense, endless. ***world without end***: used as transl. late L. ***in secula seculorum***, 'for ever and ever'; also *attrib.*

a **1000** *Boeth. Metr.* xxi. 44 þæt micle leoht..is..Ece butan ende. *c* **1200** Ormin 409 Rihhtwise menn..shulenn habbenn..A butenn ende blisse inoh. *c* **1320** *Sir Tristr.* 2417 He ȝaf to blaunchefiour Wales wiþ outen end Bidene. **138.** Wyclif *Wks.* (1880) 24 Helle wiþ-outen hende. **1450–1530** *Myrr. our Ladye* 326 The vyrgyn mary..rayneth with cryste without enden. **1549** *Bk. Com. Prayer, Gloria Patri*, As it was in the beginning, is now and ever shall be: world without end. **1577** *St. Aug. Manual* 23 Pleasaunt tunes..are song to thy glory..without all end. **1588** Shaks. *L.L.L.* v. ii. 799 A time me thinkes too short, To make a world-without-end bargaine in. **1667** Milton *P.L.* i. 67 Torture without end Still urges.

19. †**a.** ***end for end***: (*Naut.*, of a cable) paid out to the full length (*obs.*). **b.** ***to shift, turn end for end***: to put each end of (a thing) where the other was; chiefly *Naut.*, to reverse (a rope), to upset (a boat). ***to go end for end***: (of a boat) to be upset. Also in same sense, ***end over end***. **c.** ***end to end***: with the ends in contact, lengthwise.

a. **1627** Capt. Smith *Seaman's Gram.* vii. 30 End for end is when the Cable runneth cleere out of the Hawse, or any Rope out of his shiuer. **1769** Falconer *Dict. Marine* (1789) *Filer le cable bout par bout*, to veer away the cable to the end, to veer out the cable end-for-end.

b. *a* **1734** North *Exam.* ii. v. §2 (1740) 316 We must turn our Style End for End. **1758** in *Phil. Trans.* LVIII. 284 The axis of the telescope was turned end for end; that is, the telescope..was turned upside down. **1804** A. Duncan *Mariner's Chron.* I. 224 A heavy sea striking the afterpart, it [the boat] went end for end over. **1805** W. Hunter in *Naval Chron.* XIII. 23 It would turn the Cutter end-over-end. **1867** Smyth *Sailor's Word-bk.*, To shift a rope end for end, as in a tackle, the fall is made the standing part, and the standing part becomes the fall. **1870** Lowell *Study Wind.* 201 He turns commonplaces end for end. **1875** Bedford *Sailor's Pocket-bk.* §6 (ed. 2) 219 The boat will be thrown.. end over end.

c. **1860** Tyndall *Glac.* ii. §1. 228, 39000 waves of red light placed end to end would make up an inch.

20. **a.** ***end on***: (*a*) placed so as to present the end directly towards the eye, or towards any object; opposed to *broadside on*. Also *attrib.* Chiefly *Naut.* Also *transf.*, applied to an educational course in which students spend six months at college and six months in industrial work alternately.

1832 Marryat *N. Forster* xlvii, She..being then nearly end on. **1834** Mrs. Somerville *Connex. Phys. Sc.* xxxiv. (1849) 373 A single pole end-on is sufficient. **1836** E. Howard *R. Reefer* xli, From the end-on view we had of her, we could not count her ports. **1866** Ballantyne *Shifting Winds* iv. (1881) 31 The lifeboat met the next breaker end-on. **1880** Mac Cormac *Antisept. Surg.* 229 The accident was caused by a scaffold plank of wood..falling end-on upon the man's head. **1888** *Encycl. Brit.* XXIV. 366/1 Several ships have been built for the 'end-on attack'. **1894** *Pall Mall Gaz.* 23 Oct. 2/1 Ships built mainly for end-on fire. **1898** Kipling in *Morn. Post* 10 Nov. 5/1, I meant my shot for an end-on shot. **1908** *Chambers's Jrnl.* Mar. 256/1 The greatest care should be taken on this road, else an end-on collision is possible. **1910** *Installation News* IV. 59/1 In a Tungsten lamp only 50% of the light is directed below the horizontal and the end-on candle power. **1959** P. F. R. Venables *Sandwich Courses* vi. 101 If half [the students] are away, and half at the firm..training and production [are] facilitated by this Cox and Box arrangement of end-on courses, i.e. two equivalent groups within the year.

(*b*) 'Working a seam of coal, &c., at right angles to the cleat, or natural planes of cleavage' (Gresley, 1883).

b. ***end up***: with the end uppermost. Esp. in phr. ***all ends up***: completely, utterly.

1921 A. W. Myers *Twenty Yrs. Lawn Tennis* 19 Barrett beat him 'all ends up' in an early round. **1932** *Times Educ. Suppl.* 10 Dec. 1/3 Larwood bowled him all ends up. **1954** P. Frankau *Wreath for Enemy* iii. iv. 203 In two months' time you'll be cursing me all ends up.

21. ***no end***: (*colloq.*) a vast quantity or number (*of*). Also (*mod. slang*) as adv., = 'immensely', 'to any extent'; and (with *of*) qualifying a predicate. Cf. 1 b.

1623 Bingham *Xenophon* 143 You..made no end of promises. **1856** Reade *Never too late* x, Box at the opera costs no end. **1859** Farrar *Eric* 55 You are no end cleverer and stronger. **1865** Trollope *Belton Est.* xxvii. 321 What comfort have I in a big house, and no end of gardens? **1871** F. C. Burnand *More Happy Thoughts* (ed. 2) xix. 143 He 'makes no end of stuff', or 'loses no end of stuff'..on the Derby. **1872** E. Peacock *Mabel Heron* I. i. 9 You will have no end of trouble. **1883** Besant *All in Garden Fair* viii, Keats was no end of a fellow. **1909** R. E. Knowles *Attic Guest* 54 You'll have no end of fun with him. **1912** *Chambers's Jrnl.* Dec. 769/1 'I really must show this to Champneys,' thought Michael; 'it will please him no end.' **1955** *Essays & Studies* VIII. 5 A few clean strokes of Occam's razor would have helped Mr. Jackson no end. **1958** H. Babcock *I don't want to shoot an Elephant* 8, I often walk fifteen miles a day while hunting... This puzzles my wife no end. **1970** *New Yorker* 3 Oct. 90/2 Thomas had been impressed no end by the sight of Klüver..fixing an art-and-technology malfunction with a pair of pliers.

22. With verbs. (See also 12–14.) **a.** ***to be at an end***: (of resources, etc.) to be exhausted; (of periods of time) to be completed; (of an action or state) to terminate. In corresponding senses, ***to bring, come to an end***. **b.** ***to be at the end of*** (one's resources, etc.): to have no more to spend; ***to be at one's wits' end***: to be utterly at a loss, to be quite perplexed. **c.** ***to put an end to***, †***to set end of***: to terminate, put a stop to, abolish. **d.** ***to have, take an end***: to be terminated, concluded. **e.** ***to make an end***: to conclude, finish (*absol.*); also const. *of*, *with*. **f.** ***to keep one's end up*** (also ***to keep*** or ***hold up one's end***): to sustain one's part or bear one's share fully in an undertaking or performance.

a. *c* **1340** *Cursor M.* 22263 (Edinb.) His rigning es brote til ende. **14..** in *Tundale's Vis.* (1843) 155 Then schulde oure trobul be at a nende. *c* **1590** Marlowe *Dido* v. i. 1409 Our travels are at end. **1588** Shaks. *L.L.L.* v. ii. 430 Speake for your selues, my wit is at an end. **1664** Evelyn *Kal. Hort.* (1729) 186 A Gard'ner's work is never at an end. **1711** Steele *Spect.* No. 284 ⁋2 Their affairs will be at an end. **1850** Mrs. Stowe *Uncle Tom's C.* xxxvii. 325 Will these years and years of misery come to an end?—shall we be free? **1875** Jowett *Plato* (ed. 2) I. 49 This part of the festival was nearly at an end. **1877** Morley *Carlyle, Crit. Misc.* Ser. i. (1878) 198 Imposture must come to an end.

b. **1555** Eden *Decades W. Ind.* iii. i. (Arb.) 140 They were at theyr wyttes endes whither to turne them. **1655** W. F. *Meteors* iii. 68 It would make men..to be at their Wits End if they were not accustomed to such Tumultuous Tempests. **1712** Arbuthnot *John Bull* (1755) 33 He is at an end of all his cash. **1875** Jowett *Plato* (ed. 2) I. 280, I am..at my wits' end.

c. *a* **1300** *Cursor M.* 25870 þar has þi schrift sett end o pyne. **1647** Clarendon *Hist. Reb.* i. §22 Put a quick end to this treaty. **1681–6** J. Scott *Chr. Life* (1747) III. 471 The Day of Judgment..shall..put an End to all their Mischiefs for ever. **1792** *Anecd. W. Pitt.* III. xlii. 150 If an end is not put to this war there is an end to this country.

d. *c* **1590** Marlowe *Edw. II*, ii. iv. 1137 My sorrows will have end. **1605** Verstegan *Dec. Intell.* i. (1628) 5 This so great a worke now ceased and tooke an end.

e. *c* **893** K. Ælfred *Oros.* ii. ii. §1 Biddende þæt hie..þæs ȝewinnes sumne ende ȝedyden. **1570–6** Lambarde *Peramb. Kent* (1826) 241 To make an end, heere was sometime a religious College. **1611** Bible *Ezra* x. 17 And they made an ende, with all the men that had taken strange wiues. *Mod.* The government has resolved to make an end of the insurgents.

f. **1867** *Baily's Monthly Mag.* Aug. 291 Mr. Appleby kept up his end very seasonably. **1878** Mrs. Stowe *Poganuc People* vi. 63 Nobody can say she hain't been a good yoke-fellow; she's kept up her end. **1887** Tourgée *Button's Inn* 131 She'd be worn out..trying to keep up her end [of the work]. **1892** Stevenson & Osbourne *Wrecker* i. 21 Do you think..that a man who can paint a thousand-dollar picture has not grit enough to keep his end up in the stock market? **1899** *Westm. Gaz.* 24 Nov. 5/1 Colonel Baden-Powell and his gallant garrison will have to keep their end up unassisted. *a* **1910** 'O. Henry' *Rolling Stones* (1916) 90 The Diamond-Cross'll hold its end up with a man who'll look after its interests. **1926** P. C. Standing *Anglo-Australian Cricket* xxiii. 103 Ranjitsinhji, who scored 42 and not out 93 and was still 'keeping up his end' when time was called. **1928** *Observer* 18 Mar. 15/3 Not a single woman who appears..in this play is able to keep her end up after the cosmic announcer informs the inhabitants of the world that the world is about to end. **1970** E. McGirr *Death pays Wages* v. 99 Piron had a certain enthusiasm for the Great Apes and was able to hold his end up, thanks to his good memory.

23. Elliptically. ***and there*** (*so*) ***an end***: = 'this is, shall be, an end.' *Obs.* or *arch.*

[**1382** Wyclif *1 Cor.* xv. 24 Aftirward an ende, whanne, etc.] **1591** Shaks. *Two Gent.* i. iii. 65 What I will, I will, and there an end. **1608** S. Collins *Serm.* 51 Which I will speak a word or twain unto, and so an end. **1615** Jn. Day *Festivals* 340 As for his Carkasse, a Coffin shall cover it, and there an ende of our great Purchaser.

24. Proverbial phrases: ***to begin at the wrong end***. †***not to care which end goes forward***: to be negligent. †***to get by the end***: to get command of, so as to have ready for use. ***to get the better end of***: to get the advantage of. ***to have the better, or worse, end of the staff***, 'to get the best, or worst, of it'. ***to have at one's fingers'*** or ***tongue's end***: to know by heart, be able to quote with readiness. †***at the hinder end of the bargain***: when accounts are settled, *fig.* ***to be at an idle end***, to be unoccupied; (to live) ***at a loose end***, with no fixed occupation. †***to live at stave's end***, ? to be unsociable, keep every one at a distance. ***to make both, two ends, the two ends of the year, meet***: to live within one's income [cf. Fr. *joindre les deux bouts, les deux bouts de l'an*]. ***to come to the end of one's tether***: see tether *sb.* 4; ***to go (in) off the deep end***, etc.: see deep *a.* 1 d.

1387 Trevisa *Higden* (Rolls) II. 29 Men of þat side schal haue the worse ende. **1562** J. Heywood *Prov. & Epigr.* (1867) 34, I liue here at staues end. **1573** G. Harvey *Letter-bk.* (1884) 3 Thai that have the wors end of the staf shal be sure to be wrung to the wors. **1588** Shaks. *L.L.L.* v. i. 81 Thou hast it..at the fingers ends, as they say. **1608** Withals *Dict.* 86 Negligently, as caring not what ende goes forward. **1638** Sanderson *Serm.* II. 97 We have rather cheated the devil, than he us; and have gotten the better end of him. **1662** Fuller *Worthies, Cumberl.* (D.), Worldly wealth he cared not for, desiring onely to make both ends meet. *c* **1680** Beveridge *Serm.* (1729) I. 55 Getting a scripture-word by the end. **1690** B. E. *Dict. Cant. Crew* s.v. *Ends*..Tis good to make both ends meet. **1722** De Foe *Col. Jack* (1840) 124 The devil will have you at the hinder end of the bargain. **1736** Bailey, To have the better end of the Staff. **1742** Richardson *Pamela* III. 178 Your Lordship has got a Word by the End, that you seem mighty fond of. **1748** Smollett *Rod. Rand.* x, He made shift to make the two ends of the year meet. **1865** *Pall Mall G.* 22 Apr. 1/1 And living completely at a loose end. **1876** Miss Broughton *Joan* ii. iv, By five-and-thirty the best of us has pretty well come to the end of her tether. *Ibid.*, Anthony struggling to make two ends meet! **1878** Huxley *Physiogr.* Pref. 6 Most of the elementary works I have seen begin at the wrong end. **1882** T. Mozley *Remin. Oriel College* (ed. 2) 183 He might sometimes seem to be at an idle end. **1884** *Illust. Lond. News* 11 Oct. 338/3 She ..had Shakespeare and Milton at her tongue's end. **1884** *Graphic* 23 Aug. 198/2 Her mother has to contrive to make both ends meet.

IV. 25. *Comb.*, chiefly *attrib.* with sense 'placed at the end', 'coming at the end', or 'last used'; as ***end-body, -brush, -bud, -handkerchief, -loop, -man, -parlour, -process, -result, -rhyme, -shoot, -situation, -spurt, -wall, -wheel***; also **end-around**, (*a*) *N. Amer. Football*, an offensive running play in which an end (sense 3 g) carries the ball behind his own team's line and round the opposite end; freq. *attrib.*; (*b*) *Computing*,

used *attrib.* to designate an operation of a cyclic nature in which a digit is transferred from one end of a register to the other; **end-artery** *Anat.* [ad. G. *endarterie* (J. Cohnheim *Untersuchungen ueber d. embolischen Processe* (1872) i. 18), f. END *sb.* + ARTERY], an artery which supplies almost all the blood to a part of the body and does not anastomose with itself or with other arteries; **end-board,** (*a*) (see quot.); (*b*) a BOARD (sense 4) of a book; **end-bulb** (see quot.); **end-fast** *a.*, fixed on end, standing upright; **end-fire array,** a radio antenna array in which the direction of reception of electromagnetic waves is in line with the elements of the array; so *end-fire radiation*, etc.; **end game** *Chess* (see quot.); also *attrib.* and *Bridge*; **end-gate** *U.S.* = TAIL-BOARD 1; also *attrib.* and *fig.*; **end-gatherer,** a collector of refuse wool; **end-grain** (*attrib.*), (of wood) placed with the end of the grain turned outwards; †**end-hand,** the hand nearest to the end of anything; **end-hole** (see quot. 1796); **end-hooping,** the hoop that binds the end of a vessel; **end-iron,** a movable plate in a kitchen range which serves to enlarge or contract the grate; †**end-land,** ? a frontier region; **end-leaf,** a (usually blank) leaf inserted at one or other end of a bound book; **end-making,** conclusion, settlement; **end moraine** = *terminal moraine* (TERMINAL *a.* 3); **end-organ** (see quot.); **end-paper** usu. in *pl.*, the blank leaves placed at the beginning and end of a book; **end-piece** (see quot.); a piece forming the end of a box, etc.; in watchmaking, the support for the end of a pivot; **end-plate,** the extreme fibres of a muscle or nerve; **end-play** *Bridge*, any of various methods of play which (usually at about the eleventh trick) force an opponent into making a lead which will cost him a trick; hence as *v. trans.*; **end-position** *Philol.*, the position at the end of a clause or phrase; **end-rib** (see quot.); **end run** *N. Amer.*, (*a*) in American football, an attempt by the ball-carrier to run round his own end (sense 3 g) and towards the goal; (*b*) *fig.*, an evasive tactic, esp. in war or politics; a ploy which allows one to advance by bypassing the opposition; **end-scraper** *Archæol.* = GRATTOIR; **end-shake,** a freedom of motion in a spindle at its end; †**end-sith** [OE. *síð* fate], death-fate; **end-speech,** a speech tacked on at the end, an epilogue; **end standard** *Metrology*, a standard of length in the form of a metal bar or block whose end faces are the standard distance apart under specified conditions; cf. LINE STANDARD a.; **end-stone,** one of the plates of a watch-jewel supporting a pivot; **end-stopping,** (of blank verse) a division of the lines, such that they end with a pause or stop; so **end-stopped** *ppl. a.*; **end table** *U.S.*, a table suitable for placing at the end of a couch or beside another piece of furniture; **end-time,** the end of a period of time; *spec.* the end of the world; **end-use,** the final specific use to which a product is put; so *end-user*; **end-wool,** refuse wool; **end zone** *N. Amer.*, (*a*) in football (see quots. 1916 and 1935); (*b*) in ice hockey, either of two sections of the rink which extend to the goal line from the neutral zone.

1934 *Birmingham* (Ala.) *News* 4 Nov. 15/1 The famous *end-around play accounted for Alabama's initial touchdown. **1946** *Annals Computation Lab. Harvard Univ.* I. 15 All storage counters are equipped with..end around carry. **1954** G. H. ALLEN *Encycl. Football Drills* v. 35 (*heading*) How to drill for end around. **1958** J. OLIVER *Offensive Football* v. 48 A very fine counter play in all series is the end-around play. **1975** *IEEE Trans. Computers* XXIV. 953/1 A set of shift registers..connected for end-around shifting. **1983** *N.Y. Times* 31 Jan. A1/2 The Redskins gained 44 yards on an end-around play and scored the winning touchdown on a 43-yard run. **1880** *Glasgow Med. Jrnl.* Dec. 490 Although not anatomically, the superior mesenteric is *functionally* an '*end artery'. **1883** J. COATS *Man. Path.* 35 There are parts of the body in which the arteries are distributed to a perfectly definite piece of tissue, and have no anastomotic connections. In the case of such arteries, to which Cohnheim gives the name of End Arteries, the results of obstruction are very serious. **1964** S. DUKE-ELDER *Parsons' Dis. Eye* (ed. 14) i. 11 The retinal arteries are end-arteries and have no anastomoses at the ora serrata. *c* **1860** H. STUART *Seaman's Catech.* 70 What are the '*end boards'? They are boards which cover and form the ends of the meetings. **1936** *Burlington Mag.* May 213/1 Adhering to the inside of the end-boards of a great ninth-century book of the Gospels. **1875** *Encycl. Brit.* I. 861/2 Nerve fibres at their peripheral extremities terminate in connection with peculiar structures, named *end-bodies, terminal bodies. *Ibid.*, The peripheral end-bodies in the skin. **1903** DORLAND *Med. Dict.* (ed. 3), *End-body*, that one of the two elements of the serum of an immunized animal which serves actually to kill the bacteria. The other element, the Between-body or Immune-body, simply fastens the end-body to the bacteria. The end-body is also called the complement and addiment. **1710** LONDON & WISE *Compl. Gardener* (1719) 152 The same course of pinching off *End-Buds is very profitable in Summer also. **1900** J. S. KINGSLEY *Text Bk. Vert. Zool.* 68 Allied to the sense organs of the lateral line are structures known as end buds. **1879** CALDERWOOD *Mind & Br.* iii. 42 This terminal expansion [of a nerve] is known as an *end-bulb, or touch organ. **1535** STEWART *Cron. Scot.* (1858) I. 282 Neir by the boundis of Brigantia thair stude Ane *end fast stane. **1936** R. S. GLASGOW *Princ. Radio Engin.* xiv. 458 If..there is a progressive phase difference between the currents of the adjacent antennas, the radiation will be concentrated along the axis of the array instead of at right angles to it. This type of structure is known as an *end-fire array. **1939** *Amat. Radio Handbk.* (*Radio Soc. Gt. Brit.*) x. 147 Aerials do not usually radiate uniformly in all directions. .. The effect of the ground is generally disadvantageous.. but it does help in allowing end-on or 'end-fire' radiation from a horizontal wire. **1943** *Gloss. Terms Telecomm.* (*B.S.I.*) 66 *End-fire array*, a type of directive aerial-array the principal direction of radiation of which is in the direction of the array line. **1949** *Electronic Engin.* XXI. 346 A wealth of information on broadside and end fire arrays. **1884** HORWITZ in *Academy* 12 Apr. 256/1 The real *end game consists of a position where the method can be analytically demonstrated by which the slightly superior force can win. **1897** *Westm. Gaz.* 15 Feb. 4/1 A fine end-game player. **1899** *Ibid.* 1 June 6/3 Skill in end-game play. **1947** T. REESE *Reese on Play* IV. 143 (*heading*) End game. **1952** I. MACLEOD *Bridge* xv. 190 Bridge writing tends to concentrate on the end game. **1964** V. NABOKOV *Defence* viii. 121 We'll simply take the endgame position at the point it was interrupted today. **1873** *Newton Kansan* 15 May 2/2 An iron *end gate rod was thrust easily into the excavation. **1905** *Emporia* (Kan.) *Gaz.* 3 Mar., Henry kept right on lamming the end-gate of the band wagon of reform with a poker. **1911** H. QUICK *Yellowstone Nights* vi. 165 Two boys..tied to the feed-rack by Allens's hired man and spanked with the end-gate of his wagon. **1764** BURN *Poor Laws* 53 All *end-gatherers offending against an act of the 13 Geo. c. 23..shall be deemed incorrigible rogues. **1882** *Worc. Exhib. Cat.* iii. 41 The flooring is laid in *end-grain sections of pine. **1884** *Health Exhib. Catal.* 88/2 End-grain wood pavements, etc. **1677** MOXON *Mech. Exerc.* (1703) 17 You must dip your Handle-hand, and mount your *end-hand a little. **1753** *Scots Mag.* Feb. 100/2 The *end-handkerchiefs would sell as well as the other ten. **1796** C. JONES *Hoyle's Games Improved* 296 (*Cribbage*) It is of Advantage to the last Player to keep as close Cards as possible, in Hopes of coming in for Fifteen, a Sequence, or Pair, besides the *End Hole, or Thirty-one. **1877** *Encycl. Brit.* VI. 576/1 (*Cribbage*) The go, end hole, or last card is scored by the player who approaches most nearly to thirty-one. **1905** F. H. COLLINS *Author & Printer* 108/1 **Endleaves*, the blank fly-leaves at the beginning and end of a book. *Ibid.*, *End papers*, see end leaves. **1954** N. R. KER *Pastedowns in Oxf. Bindings* p. vii, This method of strengthening the binding has been used since the Middle Ages, the only difference being that the endleaves then consisted of parchment instead of paper. **1712** J. JAMES *Gardening* 90 Fixing the two *End Loops upon the Stakes A and C. *a* **1796** BURNS (Jam.), She sprung an *end-hooping. *c* **1200** ORMIN 17916 Nohht ferr þær inn an *endeland þatt wass Ennon ȝehatenn. *c* **1490** *Plumpton Corr.* 82 Beseching your sayd mastership..to be at the *end-making. **1903** A. GEIKIE *Text-bk. Geol.* (ed. 4) II. Index 1446/2 Terminal moraines (*end-moraines). **1954** W. D. THORNBURY *Princ. Geomorphol.* xv. 374 Three types of glacial deposits—end moraine, lateral moraine, and ground moraine—may be distinguished, depending upon whether deposition took place at the end of, at the side of, or beneath an ice stream. **1960** B. W. SPARKS *Geomorphol.* xiii. 291 The edges of former ice sheets are often marked by terminal or end moraines, which are ridges of glacial material not usually exceeding 150–200 feet in height in lowlands. **1878** BELL *Gegenbauer's Comp. Anat.* 42 Sensory organs are the *end-organs of the sensitive nerves. **1818** H. PARRY *Art Bk.-binding* 31 Common marble paper pasted between the first and second leaf of the *end-papers. **1846** DODD *Brit. Manuf.* VI. 94 The end-papers are..glued to the boards. **1885** W. J. E. CRANE *Bookbinding* vii. 59 The 'end papers' are those blank leaves which are found at the beginning and end of every bound book. **1901** *Athenæum* 4 May, The end-papers were a little spotted, but the general condition was splendid. **1960** *Times* 6 Oct. 17/4 There are endpaper maps. **1824** MISS MITFORD *Village* Ser. I. (1863) 228 There is one little *end-parlour, an after-thought of the original builder. **1839** *Penny Cycl.* XIII. 118/1 The *end-pieces, when real diamonds are used, are what are called rose-diamonds, and are procured from Holland, where they are cut. **1878** W. W. ABNEY *Treat. Photogr.* xxx. 216 A movable end-piece through which the plate passes into the holder. **1881** RAYMOND *Mining Gloss.*, *Wall-plates*, the two-side pieces of a timber frame in a shaft... The other two pieces are the end-pieces. **1878** FOSTER *Phys.* III. i. 393 Between the lingual fibres and the *end-plates of the glossal muscular fibres. **1884** *Syd. Soc. Lex.*, *End-plate, motorial*, the branched, expanded, termination of a nerve fibre or one of its branches on a muscular fibre. **1931** *Bridge Mag.* VI. 213/1 All *end plays are divided into three large groups; negative, positive and neutral. **1936** E. H. DOWNES (*title*) Squeezes coups and end plays. *Ibid.* 51 The Declarer.. knows that the opponent being End-Played will be forced to make a return lead in a suit in which the Declarer holds a tenace position. **1950** G. S. COFFIN (*title*) Endplays. *Ibid.* p. ix, Although an endplay situation usually occurs when all four hands are played down to a few cards, endplays sometimes embrace so many cards that a player is 'endplayed' even on the opening lead! **1928** H. POUTSMA *Gram. Late Mod. Eng.* (ed. 2) viii. 442 When they [*sc.* adverbial adjuncts] have to be thrown into prominence, they not infrequently have front-position or *end-position. **1962** S. STUBELIUS in F. Behre *Contrib. Eng. Syntax* 198 End-position adverbials. *a* **1942** B. MALINOWSKI *Sci. Theory Culture* (1944) x. 92 The supply of physical material, the conditions in which the digestive processes can be carried out and the sanitary arrangements of the *end-processes. **1963** *Times Lit. Suppl.* 1 Mar. 156/5 The end-process of a long evolution. **1912** J. S. HUXLEY *Individual in Animal Kingdom* ii. 52 These substances—its food—may be varied ..and the *end-result, its protoplasm, yet be the same. **1958** *Spectator* 1 Aug. 157/1 Mr. Gaitskell can claim to have been surprisingly successful; but the end-result is unappetising. **1966** *Lancet* 31 Dec. 1458/1 The same end-result can be achieved by the subsequent use of a promoting agent. **1855** H. CLARKE *New Dict. Eng. Lang.* 332/1 **End-rhyme*, chiming at the end of each verse. **1907** *Cambr. Hist. Eng. Lit.* I. 62 The consistent use of end-rime and alliteration in one and the same poem. **1927** E. V. GORDON *Introd. Old Norse* 296 End-rhyme was called *runhending*. **1953** G. TURVILLE-PETRE *Orig. Icelandic Lit.* i. 41 Egill was before his time in using end-rime regularly. **1852** SEIDEL *Organ* 37 Between the upper and under-board there are six boards, viz. two.. called *end-ribs. **1902** *Record-Herald* (Chicago) 28 Sept. III. 1/4 Perkins made a fifteen-yard *end run. **1920** *Montgomery* (Ala.) *Advertiser* 7 Mar. 6/3 Stubbs follows with an end run for 25 yards. **1952** W. S. CHURCHILL *Second World War* V. xxiv. 378, I had..always been a partisan of the 'end run', as the Americans call it, or 'cat-claw', which was my term. **1961** W. VAUGHAN-THOMAS *Anzio* ii. 16 An end run occurs when the forward lines clash together into immobility and the backs race round the supine mass towards the goal. **1968** *Economist* 17 Aug. 29/2 An 'end run' around to Congress, bypassing the Secretary of Defence, is the time-honoured way for the military to put pressure on the Secretary to yield on weapons and budgetary matters. **1973** *Times* 17 Apr. 9/1 Denouncing proposed draft legislation, Mr Humphrey said in the Senate that it was a 'bold-faced grab' and 'outrageous end-run' by the Pentagon designed to evade congressional control. **1915** W. J. SOLLAS *Anc. Hunters* (ed. 2) 298 The grattoirs or *end scrapers are generally short and rough. **1937** GARROD & BATE *Stone Age Mt. Carmel* I. I. iii. 32 End-scrapers. **1881** HASLUCK *Lathe Work* 169 The face of the pulley forms the bearing to prevent the *endshake. **1858** GLENNY *Gard. Every-day Bk.* 89/1 Nearly all the *end-shoots may be safely taken away, for they take up the strength of the plant. *c* **1250** *Gen. & Ex.* 3777 Alle he [Korah, etc.] sunken ðe erðe wiðin..Swilc *endesið vn-biwen hauen. **1924** R. M. OGDEN tr. *Koffka's Growth of Mind* iii. §8. 103 When the animal has attained his goal, he has arrived at a situation which to him is an *end-situation. **1918** C. S. MYERS *Present-Day Applic. Psychol.* 13 Thus when the fatigue involved is slight, and the influence of practice or of *end-spurt is sufficiently great, a larger instead of a smaller output of work will occur towards the end of the day's work. **1963** J. M. FRASER *Psychol.* (ed. 2) xvii. 222 A very dramatic effect in speeding up the tempo..by.. extending the influence shown in the 'end-spurt'. **1888, 1906** *End standard [see LINE STANDARD a]. **1975** BRAM & DOWNS *Manuf. Technol.* i. 7 With few exceptions to the rule, most engineering devices depend upon end standards. **1884** F. BRITTEN *Watch & Clockm.* 101 In most English watches all the escapement pivots run on *end stones. **1881** *Athenæum* 23 Apr. 557/2 Mr. Rhoades's blank verse..is distinguished..by a frequent tendency to *end-stopping. **1877** DOWDEN *Shaks. Prim.* iv. 39 At first..the verse is *end-stopt. **1851** C. CIST *Cincinnati* 206 Circular, center, card, and *end tables. **1917** J. H. MCCONKEY *End of Age* 28 Similar to this will be the conditions in the *end-time. **1953** *Scottish Jrnl. Theol.* VI. 162 We believe that..although the full pattern and purpose belongs to the End-Time, reflections of it can be mirrored in the corporate meetings of the Church. **1953** BERG *Dict. New Words* 74/2 *End-use. **1958** *Times Rev. Industry* Feb. 11/1 Forecasts..are not made simpler by the ease with which one kind of fuel can be substituted for another in many of the end-uses. **1963** *Economist* 16 Feb. 627/2 Esso policy of not selling chemicals to the *end-user. **1664** EVELYN *Kal. Hort.* (1729) 229 The Flue, Shaft, Fire, and Ash-hole to be without, though joining close to the *End-wall. **1848** *App. to Report Dep. Keeper Public Records* IX. 111 The cleft wool to be kept by itself and the *endwool by itself. **1916** J. H. BANCROFT *Handbk. Athletic Games* 129 *End-zone, ten-yard territory between the end line and the goal line. **1935** *Encycl. Sports* 528/1 American rugby... The playing field is..divided into the field of play and end zones. These are, respectively, 100 yds. and 10 yds. each in length. **1961** F. C. AVIS *Sportsman's Gloss.* 245/1 *Face-off spot*...in the end zone, they are 15 ft. from goal line. **1963** *Dict. Canadian English* (*Intermediate*) 292/2 *End zone.* 1. in rugby football, the part of the field between each goal line and the corresponding end of the field. 2. in hockey, the ice between each blue line and the corresponding end of the rink. **1968** *Globe & Mail* (Toronto) 11 July 32/5 Then Gabler..threw a perfect one [*sc.* pass] into the end zone to Profit.

†**end**, var. of ANDE, *Obs.*, breath.

1597–1605 POLWART *Flyting* 568 His stinking end corrupted as men knawes. *a* **1600** *Poems 16th Cent.* 29 (Jam.) The sillie saul is quyte foryet, Quhill haistelie gais out his end. **1609** SKENE *Reg. Maj. Act K. William* 7 Gif blude be drawen (in anie part of the bodie) vnder the end (or mouth) [*L. subtus anhelitum*].

end (ɛnd), *v.*[1] Forms: 1 endian, 2–4 endien, enden, endenn (*Orm.*), 3–5 e(ende, (4 endy, hende, eondi, *pa. pple.* 4 ent), 4– end. See also Y-END. [OE. *ęndian*, corresp. to OFris. *endia*, OS. *endôn, endiôn*, (Du. *einden*), OHG. *entôn, entiôn*, (MHG., mod.G. *enden*), ON. *enda* (Sw. *ända*, Da. *ende*):—OTeut. **andjôjan*, f. **andjo-* END *sb.*]

I. Transitive and absolute senses.

†**1. a.** *trans.* To carry through to the end; to finish, complete. Also (in ME.), to perform (religious duties). *Obs.*

c **975** *Rushw. Gosp.* John iv. 34 þætte ic endigo werc his. *c* **1175** *Lamb. Hom.* 43 Men þe on þisse liue her hare scrift. enden nalden. *a* **1225** *Ancr. R.* 44 Goð biuoren ower weouede & endeð ðer þe graces. *a* **1300** *Cursor M.* 8310 þis wark..mai noght thoru þi-self be don, þin sun sal end it, salamon. *c* **1400** *Destr. Troy* 4 Graunt me þi helpe..þis werke for to ende. **1483** *Cath. Angl.* 114 to Ende, *conficere*. **1593** SHAKS. *Lucr.* 1843 He..kiss'd the fatal knife, to end his vow. **1597** MORLEY *Introd. Mus.* Annot., When I had ended my booke..I was requested to explaine some thing. **1601** SHAKS. *Jul. C.* v. i. 114 This same day Must end that worke, the Ides of March began. **1738** POPE *Epit. Sat.* ii. 254 Pray end what you began.

b. To be the end or result of.

a **1300** *Cursor M.* 9699 Pes endes al þat wel es wroght.

2. a. To bring to an end, conclude, come to a termination of (an action, a speech, a period of time, one's life, etc.; formerly sometimes with inf. as obj.). Often with adv. of manner or advb. phrase, or with *off*, *up*; also const. *with*.

c **1305** *Pilate* 259 in *E.E.P.* (1862), þus pilatus endede his lyf. *c* **1330** R. BRUNNE *Chron.* (1810) 47 Eilred at London endid his life. **1340** *Ayenb.* 110 Huet may þe zone betere acsy to his uader: þanne bread wyþoute more uor þane day to endy? *c* **1340** *Cursor M.* (Trin.) 10487 Whenne she had endede hir preyere She pleyned efte on þis manere. **1483** *Cath. Angl.* 115 It is Endit, *explicit*. **1557** NORTH *Diall of Princes* 229 b/2 We neuer cease to behold them, nor yet end to bewayle them. **1609** BIBLE (Douay) 2 *Esdras* vii. 1 When I had ended to speake these wordes. **1697** DRYDEN *Virg. Georg.* II. 560 Not then the drudging Hind his Labour ends. **1713** BERKELEY *Guardian* viii. Wks. III. 170 He has ended his discourse with a Prayer. **1717** —— *Tour Italy* Wks. IV. 530 We ended the day with music at St. Agnes. **1830** TENNYSON *Amphion* 50 Ere his song was ended. **1860** RUSKIN *Mod. Paint.* V. IX. xii. §1, I find that I have only now the power of ending this work, not of concluding it. **1862** GRANT *Capt. of Guard* xxxix. He ended his life in misery. **1884** G. ALLEN *Philistia* III. 250 Capital sentence to end off one's speech with. **1926** *Ladies' Home Jrnl.* Aug. 109 Those things you use to divide off words and end up sentences with.

b. *absol.*; esp. with reference to speech: To finish, conclude.

a **1340** HAMPOLE *Psalter* xxvi[i]. 15 End as þou has bygunen. *c* **1340** *Cursor M.* (Trin.) 5459 Whenne he endide of his sawe His sones he blessed on a rawe. **1585** ABP. SANDYS *Serm.* (1841) 329, I will therefore add somewhat concerning the disgrace which cometh unto marriage..and so end. **1591** SHAKS. *Two Gent.* II. iv. 31, I know it wel, sir, you alwaies end ere you begin. **1667** MILTON *P.L.* II. 106 He ended frowning, and his look denounc'd Desperate revenge. *a* **1704** T. BROWN *Sat. agst. Woman* Wks. 1730 I. 57 Quite tired of the nauseous theme, I end. **1879** FURNIVALL *Rep. E. Eng. T.S.* 24 To end, the Society wants more money. *Mod.* I shall end with a motion.

c. Colloq. phr. ***to end it*** (*all*), to commit suicide.

1911 *Maclean's Mag.* Sept. 172/1 Sometimes I wonder if it's all worth while; sometimes I'm half inclined to end it. **1925** F. HARRIS *My life & Loves* IV. iv. 90 This is the end; the sooner I put a bullet through my head the better... I took up the rifle to end it all when suddenly my eye caught sight of the..tins of sardines.

†**3.** To rid (a person) *of*. *Obs.*

1598 GREENE *Jas IV* (1861) 211 What may I do to end me of these doubts?

4. a. To put an end to, cause to cease, abrogate, destroy; formerly also to dissolve (a parliament).

c **1000** *Ags. Ps.* ix. 6 Ða hi hit endian sceoldan. *c* **1200** ORMIN 19797 Þe33 unnderstodenn wel, þatt..te33re la3he all endedd ben þurrh Cristess newe lare. *c* **1330** R. BRUNNE *Chron.* (1810) 214 At þis parlement..was it ent, aliens to auance. **1490** CAXTON *Eneydos* viii. 36 The swerde..ended in that hour hir lyf. **1568** GRAFTON *Chron.* II. 647 The king dissolved his Parliament, which was the laste parliament that ever he ended. **1598** SHAKS. *Merry W.* I. i. 41 If I were yong againe, the sword should end it. **1737** POPE *Hor. Epist.* II. i. 53 End all dispute: and fix the year precise. **1801** SOUTHEY *Thalaba* IV. xxvi, That merciful deed For ever ends thy suffering. **1808** J. BARLOW *Columb.* I. 79 The desperate crew..Resolve at once to end the audacious strife. **1877** MORLEY *Crit. Misc.* Ser. I. (1878) 200 To talk of France seeing good to end Protestantism in a night.

†**b.** To make an end of (a person); to kill. *Obs.*

a **1340** HAMPOLE *Cant. Psalter* 497 Ffra morne til eueyn þou sall end me. **1340–70** *Alex. & Dind.* 1064 Hit is riht þat þe rink be reufully ended. *a* **1400–50** *Alexander* 453 All his enmys in þat erd he endid in a stounde. **1596** SHAKS. *1 Hen. IV*, v. iii. 9 This Sword hath ended him. **1609** BP. BARLOW *Answ. Nameless Cath.* 300 The Pope mingled powder with Gemens Sugar, which should not End him presently, but Waste him by little and little. **1623** FLETCHER *Bloody Brother* IV. iii, Power enough..To end the murtherer.

II. Intransitive senses.

5. a. Of a period of time, action, continuous state, series, book, chapter, etc.: To come to an end. Also colloq. ***to end up***.

a **1000** *Guthlac* 21 (Gr.) Ær þou endien ealle ȝesceafte. *c* **1200** ORMIN 6514 Her endeþþ nu þiss Goddspell þuss. *c* **1250** *Gen. & Ex.* 166 Forð endede ðat fifte ni3t. *a* **1300** *Cursor M.* 7840 Þat eild bigan at abraham. It endes her in godds nam. **1340** HAMPOLE *Pr. Consc.* 1770 When his lif sal here ende, He what never whider he sal wende. *c* **1350** *Will Palerne* 540 Þis bitter bale botlesse wol hende! **1398** TREVISA *Barth. De P.R.* IX. ii. (1495) 346 Whan meuynge fayllyth thenne tyme endyth. **1486** *Bk. St. Albans* D iij a, Here endyth the proceis of hawkyng. **1526** *Pilgr. Perf.* (W. de W. 1531) 2 Here endeth the prologue, and here after foloweth the fyrst boke. **1601** SHAKS. *All's Well* v. i. 25 All's well that ends well, yet. **1605** DANIEL *Queen's Arcadia* IV. iv, All extremities must mend or end. **1676** HOBBES *Iliad* I. 289 Thus in disorder the Assembly ends. **1697** DRYDEN *Virg. Past.* IV. 9 The base degenerate Iron off-spring ends. **1728** POPE *Dunc.* II. 245 But that this well-disputed game may end, Sound forth, my brayers. **1812** J. WILSON *Isle of Palms* IV. 654 To-day our woes can never end. **1870** MORRIS *Earthly Par.* I. i. 305 For thinking how all stories end with this. **1874** SPURGEON *Treas. Dav.* Ps. cii. Introd., It ends up right gloriously with calm confidence for the future. **1875** BRYCE *Holy Rom. Emp.* viii. (ed. 5) 124 The line of Charles the Great ended in A.D. 911. *Mod.* The quarter ending June 24.

b. To issue or result *in*.

a **1225** *Ancr. R.* 102 Þe worldes urakele urouren..schulen enden ine sor & ine seoruwe. *c* **1400** *Destr. Troy* 194 Couetous þere come knightes full ofte, And endit in auerys to ay lastand sorowe. **1651** HOBBES *Leviath.* I. vii. 30 No Discourse whatsoever, can End in absolute Knowledge of Fact. **1664** EVELYN *Kal. Hort.* (1706) 24 Sobbing the Leaves of the Plant..ends in scorching. **1709** STEELE *Tatler* No. 10 ⁋1 There is a contagious Sickness, which, it is feared, will end in a Pestilence. **1808** *Med. Jrnl.* XIX. 380 The controversy..ended in both parties admitting, etc. **1870** H. MACMILLAN *Bible Teach.* x. 204 A life of godliness ends in a saintly death. **1885** *Manch. Exam.* 6 July 4/7 The cricket match..ended in a draw.

c. Of persons, Const. *in*, or *by*, with gerund: To come ultimately to (do something).

1825 COLERIDGE *Aids to Refl.* 101 He, who begins by loving Christianity better than Truth, will..end in loving himself better than all.

6. To die. *rare* in mod. use. Also *to end up* (*slang*).

c **1200** ORMIN 8347 Affterr þatt tatt Herode king Wass ended inn hiss sinne. **1297** R. GLOUC. (1724) 370 Steuene.. suþþe was kyng of Engelond, & endede myd ssame. *c* **1340** *Cursor M.* 6724 Þe beest shal wiþ stonyng ende. *c* **1435** *Torr. Portugal* 1389, I yeve..To thy doughter alle my lond, Yf that I end there. **1590** SHAKS. *Mids. N.* v. i. 353 Farwell friends, thus Thisbie ends. **1858** CARLYLE *Fredk. Gt.* (1865) VI. xv. x. 63 A cannon-ball smites the life out of him, and he ended here. **1886** RIDER HAGGARD *K. Solomon's Mines* ii. 32 We should only end up like my poor friend Silvestre.

7. Of a portion of space, material object, treatise, etc.: To terminate, have its end or extremity.

1611 COTGR., *Aboutir en pointe*, to end sharpe, or pointed. **1882** GEIKIE *Text-bk. Geol.* VI. v. (1885) 890 It [the glacier] ended off upon the land. **1877** *Encycl. Brit.* VI. 424 The promontory which ends in the Lizard. *Mod.* His property ends at the fifth milestone. An iron rod ending in a sharp point. The plateau ends abruptly in a precipice.

III. 8. *trans.* To furnish with an end of a particular kind, for protection or ornament.

1889 *Cent. Dict.* s.v., To end a cane with an iron ferrule.

9. To put *up* on end; to up-end.

1889 *Cent. Dict.*, *End*..to set on end; set upright. **1890** *Century Mag.* Aug. 617/1 We ended-up an old plank.. against the twelve-foot brick wall. **1890** J. SERVICE *Thir Notandums* x. 72 There's aye a wheen toom barrels endit up and waiting to be filled.

¶ ***to end or mend***: see *to mend or end* (MEND *v.* 12 c).

a **1670** S. COLLINS *Pres. State Russia* (1671) ii. 9 It is a strange chastisement to kill, seeing the design hereof was never intended to end people, but to mend them. **1820** SCOTT *Monast.* II. v. 177 My fate calls me elsewhere, to scenes where I shall end it or mend it.

end, *v.*² *Obs.* exc. *dial.* [perh. a dial. variant or corruption of INN *v.*, influenced by END *v.*¹

It has been suggested that the word is a corruption of **in-do*, corresponding to Ger. *einthun* used in the same sense; but this seems impossible.]

trans. To put (corn, hay, etc.) into (a barn, stack, etc.); to 'get in'. Also *fig.* Hence **'ended** *ppl. a.*

1607 SHAKS. *Cor.* v. vi. 37, I..holpe to reape the Fame Which he did end all his. **1632** MILTON *L'Allegro* 109 His shadowy flail hath threshed the corn That ten day-labourers could not end. **1858** *Hereford Times* 23 Jan. in Dyce *Shaks. Cor.* v. vi. 37 Three well-ended hay-ricks..a rick of well-ended hay.

†**end**, *v.*, var. ANDE *v. Obs.*, to breathe, blow.

a **1300** *Cursor M.* 21075 Als a slepand aends oft. **1596** DALRYMPLE tr. *Leslie's Hist. Scot.* (1885) 29 Thair mouthis had blawne vpon or endet as we speik.

-end, a formative element representing the termination *-endus, -a, -um* of the gerundive of Latin verbs in *-ēre* and *-ĕre*. Examples are *agend, dividend, minuend, repetend, reverend, subtrahend*. The meaning of these words is passive, thus *agend* 'that which is to be done'. Like -AND² this element has never been a living suffix, having no separate existence apart from the Latin gerundive form from which it is derived. The gerundial endings are sometimes retained in their Latin (neut.) form (with pl. *-a*), as in *addendum, agendum, corrigendum, reddendum, referendum*.

†**'endable**, *a. Obs.* [f. END *v.*¹ + -ABLE.] That admits of being ended; terminable.

1693 W. ROBERTSON *Phraseol. Gen.* 530 Endable, *terminabilis*. **1775** in ASH. **1864** in WEBSTER; and in mod. Dicts.

end-all ('ɛnd-ɔːl). [f. END *v.*¹ + ALL.] That which 'ends all' (see quot. 1876). Now only *dial.* exc. in Shaksperian phrase, ***the be-all and the end-all***. (See BE-ALL.)

1605 SHAKS. *Macb.* I. vii. 5 That but this blow Might be the be all, and the end all. **1876** *Mid-Yorksh. Gloss.* (E.D.S.), *End-all*, more freely used than customarily, and with a wider interpretation in the sense of an act of completion. Also a finishing stroke. **1883** G. HOWELL in *Contemp. Rev.* Sept. 345 The latter aim was the be-all and end-all almost of those industrial combinations.

endamage (ɛn'dæmɪdʒ), *v.* Forms: *α.* 6–7 endammage, (-dge), 5–7 -dommage, -domage, (7 -damnage), 4–5 endamage(n, 4– endamage. *β.* 5–7 indamage, 6 -domage, 6–7 -dammage. [In 14th c. f. EN-¹ + DAMAGE *sb.*, or a. OF. **endamagier* (cf. the parallel formation *adamagier* in 13th c.). In 15th c. refashioned as *endommage, -domage*, after the contemporary Fr. *endommagier* of equivalent formation; but this form died out early in 17th c.]

trans. To inflict damage or injury upon.

1. To affect (persons, a community, etc.) detrimentally with regard to property, health, reputation, or general well-being. Also *absol.*

α. *c* **1374** CHAUCER *Boeth.* I. iv. 15 It [coempcioun] schulde greetly tourmentyn and endamagen al þe prouince of compaigne. **1477** EARL RIVERS (Caxton) *Dictes* 107 The kyng shal contynuelly be endommaged, seke of body and of the soule. *a* **1521** *Helyas* in Thoms *Prose Rom.* (1828) III. 12 If I thought to haue endomaged you of one seile [? *read* selie] ferdynge. **1546** LANGLEY *Pol. Verg. De Invent.* I. i. 1 a, To euery man..wer allotted two angels: wherof thone went about to endamage vs. **1596** SPENSER *F.Q.* VI. xii. 38 That never more he mote endammadge wight With his vile tongue, which many had defamed. **1635** QUARLES *Embl.* I. xi. (1718) 47 The Devil smileth that he may endamage. **1642** FULLER *Holy & Prof. St.* II. xiii. 101 Inclosure with depopulation endamnageth the parties themselves. **1655** H. VAUGHAN *Silex Scint.* I. (1858) Pref. 8 No loss is so doleful as that gain, that will endamage the soul. **1694** CHILD *Disc. Trade* (ed. 4) 211 The Dutch..will in all probability never endamage this Kingdom by the growth of their Plantations. **1768** TUCKER *Lt. Nat.* I. 346 That justice is better than iniquity, springs from the powers of men to benefit or endamage one another. **1828–40** TYTLER *Hist. Scot.* (1864) II. 161 That..neither the proprietor nor the cultivator [be] endamaged by the sudden desertion of the ground.

β. **1495** *Act 11 Hen. VII*, c. 22 Pream., Many..subgettis ben..lette and indamaged in their bilding and husbondry. **1641** MILTON *Ch. Govt.* II. (1851) 37 The man could not.. much indammage the Roman Empire. **1667** *Decay Chr. Piety* v. §16, I am indammag'd in my goods.

b. To damage, injure (reputation, health, welfare); to injure, prejudice, discredit (a cause, etc.).

α. **1579** FENTON *Guicciard.* (1618) 98 They might in many sorts endomage the common safetie of Italy. **1581** J. BELL *Haddon's Answ. Osor.* 187 b, That the majestie of Freewill may not by any meanes bee endamaged. **1610** GUILLIM *Heraldry* I. viii. (1660) 46 A guilt of endamaging the lives of millions. **1620** VENNER *Via Recta* (1650) 13 The South winde..endamageth our healths. **1674** BURNET *Royal Martyr* (1710) 43 Nor was Christianity endamaged by all that fury. **1691** LOCKE *Money* Wks. 1727 II. 14 There is so much want of Money, and Trade is still endamag'd by it. **1828** *Blackw. Mag.* XXIV. 624 These proceedings..were endamaging their reputation. **1882** FARRAR *Early Chr.* I. 177 Theologians..seriously endamage a sacred cause.

β. **1698** *Christ Exalted* §10. 9 These Sermons could not indamage the good Correspondence between the Brethren.

†**2.** To damage physically, inflict material injury upon (a person or thing); to spoil (a thing) so as to make it less fit for its purpose. *Obs.*

α. **1475** CAXTON *Jason* 30 Tronchonyng their speris upon his shelde, withoute endomagyng his shelde. **1576** BAKER *Jewell of Health* 62 Those partes endammaged or grieved with the Goute. **1578** BANISTER *Hist. Man* II. 39 Their substance was light, and Cartilaginous, to be lesse endammaged by outward force. **1583** MASCALL *Plant. & Graff.* (1592) 47 Take heede of those graffes, the which many wormes and Flyes doe endomage. **1667** H. STUBBE in *Phil. Trans.* II. 495 The Guns..were not much endammaged by Rust. **1690** LUTTRELL *Brief. Rel.* (1857) II. 28 A great storm..had endamaged several of the ships. **1708** J. CHAMBERLAYNE *St. Gt. Brit.* I. III. x. (1743) 205 The Thames swells..over its banks, and Westminster is a little endamaged in its Cellars. **1816** SCOTT *Antiq.* iii. [Calthrops] to endamage the sitting part of a learned professor of Utrecht.

β. **1583** MASCALL *Plant. & Graff.* (1592) Exhort., Cattell, indomaging your plants or Trees. **1686** *Voy. Emp. China to E. Tartary* in *Misc. Cur.* (1708) III. 190 The Bark..was.. indammaged by the agitation of the Waves.

†**3.** In military sense: To do harm to (the enemy, a hostile country). *Obs.*

1555 *Fardle Facions* II. ix. 191 There neuer medled any power with theim, that was able to conquer theim: or muche to endamage theim. **1611** SPEED *Hist. Gt. Brit.* VIII. vii. 404 Then coasting the shore, shrewdly endammaged Kent. **1633** T. STAFFORD *Pac. Hib.* xxvi. (1821) 471 To endammage the Enemy that hee may not hinder you. **1697** POTTER *Antiq. Greece* I xxvi. (1715) 151 The Cause of weakening or endamaging my Country.

¶**4.** Used for ENDANGER *v.* 4.

a **1648** LD. HERBERT *Hen. VIII* (1783) 341 He will endamage the loss of one half of his Realm.

†**en'damageable**, *a. Obs.*—⁰ [f. prec. + -ABLE.] Capable of receiving damage, susceptible to injury; perishable.

1864 in WEBSTER; and in mod. Dicts.

†**en'damageance.** *Obs. rare*—¹. In 6 endammageance. [f. as prec. + -ANCE.] Harm, injury.

1594 CAREW *Huarte's Exam. Wits* v. (1596) 55 If the other two [ventricles] remained not sound, and without endammageance, a man should thereby become witles, and void of reason.

endamagement (ɛn'dæmɪdʒmənt). [f. ENDAMAGE *v.* + -MENT.] The action of endamaging; the state of being endamaged; injury, harm, loss.

1593 NASHE *Four Lett. Confut.* 60 That vnaduised indammagement I haue done you. **1657** W. COLES *Adam in Eden* 167 The inhabitants of Middleborough..eat thereof [flax-seed] to the great endammagement of their healths. *a* **1674** CLARENDON *Hist. Reb.* (1704) III. XVI. 583 To the least indamagement of them. **1675** COCKER *Morals* 60 Who in their Youth refused to be taught, To numerous Endammagements are brought. **1789** BENTHAM *Princ. Legisl.* xviii. 35 The offence may be termed wrongful endamagement. **1836** *Fraser's Mag.* XIII. 301 The endamagement of their credit.

en'damaging, *vbl. sb.* [f. as prec. + -ING¹.] The action of the vb. ENDAMAGE.

1567 MAPLET *Gr. Forest* 7 Efestides..keepeth a man safe from all perill and endamaging. **1586** FERNE *Blaz. Gentrie, Lacye's Nobil.* 31 From the endomaging of his country. **1643**

MILTON *Divorce* II. iii. (1851) 64 That which was the endammaging onely of their estates was narrowly forbid.

†**en'damask,** *v. Obs.* [f. EN-[1] + DAMASK.] *trans.* **a.** To tinge with an interspersed shade of paler colour. **b.** To paint in various colours. Cf. DAMASK *sb.* and *v.*

1580 SIDNEY *Arcadia* (1622) 298 A prety feare came vp, to endamaske her rosie cheekes. **1611** SPEED *Hist. Gt. Brit.* v. vii. 42 Carrying these rasures on their pictured limbes, as badges of their Noblenesse, thus endamasked.

endamnify: see EN-[1] 3.

endanger (ɛn'deɪndʒə(r)), *v.* Forms: 6 en-, indaunger, 7–8 indanger, 6– endanger. [f. EN-[1] + DANGER *sb.*]

†**1.** *trans.* To subject (a person) to the absolute control of another; to render (an official) liable to dismissal or punishment at the will of a superior. Const. *to. Obs. rare.*

1551 ROBINSON tr. *More's Utop.* (Arb.) 60 Another giueth the kynge counsel to endaunger unto his grace the iudges of the Realme. **1579** TOMSON *Calvin's Serm. Tim.* 489/1 A slaue of Satan, one indangered to the wicked.

†**2.** *pass.* To incur the liability to punishment by another person; to be liable to arrest or seizure of goods on the part of a creditor. Const. *to* (a judge, creditor, etc.). *Obs.*

1477 J. PASTON in *Paston Lett.* No. 790 III. 179 He..is fere endangeryd to dyvers in thys contrey. **1548** COVERDALE *Erasm. Par. Rom.* xiii. 3 Nowe yf thou be lothe to be endaungered to magistrates or lawes. **1579** TOMSON *Calvin's Serm. Tim.* 172/2 For while we are indaungered to God, we can in no wise stand before him. **1596** SPENSER *State Irel.* Wks. 1805 VIII. 367 Being close hooded..from knowledge of any to whom he is indangered.

†**b.** To be liable *to* (punishment, evil of any kind.) Also const. *to* with *inf. Obs.*

1549 COVERDALE *Erasm. Par. Jude* II. 23 That he should be endaungered to diseases. *a* **1569** KINGESMYLL *Man's Est.* xiii. (1580) 98 We were fashioned of earth, but not endaungered to turne againe into yearth. **1577** tr. *Bullinger's Decades* (1592) 571 God accuseth vs and pleadeth vs guiltie of sinne, and indangered to punishment.

†**3.** To put (a person) in peril (of something untoward). Const. *of*, oftener *to* with *inf. Obs.*

1548 UDALL, etc., *Erasm. Paraph. John* 15 The confessing what he was himself endaungered him to lose his owne estimacion. **1603** W. WATSON in Dodd *Ch. Hist. Eng.* (1841) IV. xlix, To live in this miserable estate..would indanger me of losing quite my senses. **1626** BACON *Sylva* §977 It indangereth the Child to become Lunaticke. **1658** *Whole Duty Man* vi. §13 Where-ever this sin hath possession, it endangers men to fall into any other. **1737** WHISTON *Josephus' Antiq.* IX. iv. §5 That they might not endanger one another to perish, by treading on one another.

†**4.** To cause the danger of (something untoward happening); to render imminent or probable. Sometimes with gerund or inf. (with *to*) as obj.

1612 BRINSLEY *Lud. Lit.* 117 Grammaticall translations.. can neuer indanger any waie to make truants. **1644** BULWER *Chirol. & Chiron.* 102 To fling the Hand up and downe to endanger the offending of those that are nigh. **1663** BP. PATRICK *Parab. Pilgr.* xxxvii. (1668) 493 The very puff of a confident mans breath doth indanger to make me reel. *a* **1716** BLACKALL *Wks.* (1723) I. 227 Such ill Courses as will endanger his Ruin. **1791** SMEATON *Edystone L.* (1793) §313 They would have endangered the breaking the glass. **1796** SOUTHEY *Lett. Spain & Port.* (1808) I. 15 So as to endanger setting it on fire.

†**5.** To incur the danger of; to chance, risk. *Obs.*

15.. *Quest. Prof. & Pleas. Conc.* 30 a I alwaies..endanger your displeasure with my troublesome speeches. *c* **1611** CHAPMAN *Iliad* VIII. 16 Endanger it the whiles and see. **1691** RAY *Creation* (1714) 370 But would endanger to be quite destroyed. **1726** ADDISON *Dial. Medals* i. 34 Unless they turned back quickly they would endanger being benighted. **1771** *Muse in Min.* 31 Who dares blaspheme my name, endangers death.

6. To expose to danger, cause danger to. (The only modern sense.)

α. **1509** FISHER *Fun. Serm. C'tess Richmond* (1708) 31 Wrapped and endaungered with the myseres of this wretched Worlde. **1591** SHAKS. *Two Gent.* v. iv. 133, I hold him but a foole that will endanger His Body, for a Girle that loues him not. **1647** in *Nicholas Papers* (1886) I. 81 The City is..ridden by every party and wilbe so rather then endanger Trade. **1671** MILTON *Samson* 1009 Wedlock-treachery endangering life. **1725** DE FOE *Voy. round World* (1840) 212 Not so great a wind as to endanger us. **1770** *Junius Lett.* xxxvii. 181 It is not an act..that can ever endanger the liberties of this country. **1866** CRUMP *Banking* ix. 211 The convertibility of the note would be endangered.

β. **1601** HOLLAND *Pliny* I. 136 Lest one day or other the riuer with his violent streame should indanger the city of Babylon. **1691–8** NORRIS *Pract. Disc.* (1707) IV. 322 They would avoid a World that indangers their Innocency.

en'dangered, *ppl. a.* [f. prec. + -ED[1].]

a. That is or has been exposed to danger.

1597 DANIEL *Civ. Wares* IV. xlix. (1609) 99, Had he not speedy succour lent To his indangered father. **1692** SOUTH *Serm.* (1697) I. 85 Ded., The drift [of these discourses] is to carry the most Endangered, and Endangering Truth, above the Safest, when sinfull, Interest. **1846** GROTE *Greece* I. I. viii. 235 Protectors of the endangered mariner.

b. *spec.* (of an animal or plant) in danger of extinction; esp. in ***endangered species*** (also *transf.* and *fig.*).

1964 *Congress. Rec.* 8 July 16099/1 A partial list of extinct and endangered species of the United States and Puerto Rico is attached. **1976** *New Yorker* 12 Jan. 58/2 Seven hundred and sixty-one plants were designated as 'endangered', meaning their survival was in serious doubt. **1980** *Alabama Hist. Q.* Spring–Summer 102 The buildings illustrated were selected on the basis of their presence on the endangered species list. **1984** *Sunday Times* 22 Apr. 3/3 Dangerfield is being forced to close his collection of endangered birds. **1985** *Times* 11 Jan. 13/4 Freestanding art schools are becoming a rare and endangered species in this country.

endangerer (ɛn'deɪndʒərə(r)), *vbl. sb.* [f. ENDANGER *v.* + -ER.] One who endangers.

1672 BAXTER *Bagshaw's Scand.* iii. 32 Rash..spirits..will be continual endangerers of your liberties. **1824** COLERIDGE *Aids Refl.* (1848) I. 89 Scolds and endangerers of the public peace.

endangering (ɛn'deɪndʒərɪŋ), *vbl. sb.* [f. as prec. + -ING[1].] The action of the vb. ENDANGER.

1585 *Act 27 Eliz.* c. 2 §1 (Ruffhead), The great Endangering of the Safety of her most Royal Person. **1605** *Narr. Murthers Sir J. Fitz* (1860) 13 Also an indangering to Sir John his own life. *a* **1649** DRUMM. OF HAWTH. *Skiamachia* Wks. (1711) 203 Your petition is for the endangering of our peace and liberties. **1858** BRIGHT *Sp.* 27 Oct. *Reform*, The endangering of the Constitution.

en'dangering, *ppl. a.* [f. as prec. + -ING[2].] That endangers; dangerous.

1597 DANIEL *Civ. Wares* VII. xv, Peace with more indangering wounds offends Then Warre can doe. **1656** S. H. *Gold. Law* 44 Endangering..to the Publike. **1692** [see ENDANGERED *ppl. a.*]

endangerment (ɛn'deɪndʒəmənt). [f. as prec. + -MENT.] The action of putting in danger; the condition of being in danger.

1645 MILTON *Tetrach.* (1851) 160 The endangerment of our souls. **1809–10** COLERIDGE *Friend* (1865) 171 An unmitigated war of insult, alarm, and endangerment. **1871** NICHOLS *Fireside Sc.* 98 Serious endangerment to health.

endarch ('ɛndɑːk), *a. Bot.* [f. Gr. ἔνδον END(O- + ἀρχή beginning, origin.] Having a primary xylem developing outwards and a central protoxylem.

1900 B. D. JACKSON *Gloss. Bot. Terms.* **1902** *Encycl. Brit.* XXV. 413/1 When..there are several protoxylem strands situated at the internal limit of the xylem..the stele is endarch. **1910** J. M. LOWSON *Textbk. Bot.* (ed. 5) xiv. 361 The lower part of the stem has a single central protoxylem, i.e. it is endarch and monarch. **1957** H. C. BOLD *Morphol. Plants* xix. 370 Development of the xylem is endarch, for the first-formed annular and spiral protoxylem cells arise near the inner limit of each procambium strand.

†**en'dark,** *v. Obs. rare.* Also 4 endirke-n. [f. EN-[1] + DARK *a.*] *trans.* To render dark, cast into the shade; to dim (the sight). Hence **en'darked** *ppl. a.*, made dark, obscure (*fig.*).

c **1374** CHAUCER *Boeth.* IV. iii. 120 Ne no wickednesse shal endirken it. **1523** SKELTON *Garl. Laurel*, xvi. Of such an endarked chapter. **1556** ABP. PARKER *Psalter* cxxxix., For sure the dark so dark: cannot endarke thy louely sight. **1631** *Celestina* in Hazl. *Dodsley* I. 62 Her skin of whiteness endarketh the snow.

†**en'darken,** *v. Obs.* [f. EN-[1] + DARKEN *v.*] *trans.* To obscure, make dark. *lit.* and *fig.*

1595 DANIEL *Sonn.* xxi, My lifes light wholly endarkened is. **1651** BP. HALL *Soliloquies* (ed. 2) xii. 38 Light endarkened causeth the greatest darkness. **1755** T. H. CROKER tr. *Ariosto's Orl. Fur.* XXXI. l, But soon as Sol from th' earth endarken'd went.

endart: see EN- *pref.*[1] 3.

endarteritis: see ENDO-.

endaspidean (ɛndæ'spɪdɪən), *a.* [f. mod.L. *Endaspideæ* (C. J. Sundevall *Methodi Naturalis Avium Disponendarum Tentamen* (1872) I. 55), f. Gr. ἔνδον within + ἀσπίς shield.] Pertaining to passerine birds that have an anterior series of scutella on the inner side of the tarsus.

1889 in *Cent. Dict.* **1902** R. RIDGWAY *Birds North & Middle Amer.* IV. 328 The several modifications of the tarsal envelope in the present group may be described as follows. .. II. *Endaspidean.*—The above arrangement (exaspidean) reversed, the acrotarsium extending to and around the tarsus from the *inner* side, the narrow plantar space being thus external instead of internal. **1959** VAN TYNE & BERGER *Fund. Ornith.* ii. 48 Several types of passerine tarsal scutellation have been described... Endaspidean... Anterior, scutellated segment of tarsal sheath extends across the inner side of the tarsus.

†**en'daunt,** *v.*[1] *Obs.* [f. EN-[1] + DAUNT *v.* to tame.] *trans.* To tame.

1393 LANGL. *P. Pl.* C. XVIII. 171 He endauntede a douue.

†**en'daunt,** *v.*[2] *Obs.* [f. EN-[1] + DAUNT *v.* to fondle.] *trans.* To caress; to make much of, hold in high esteem.

1399 LANGL. *Rich. Redeles* III. 127 Ffor her dignesse endauntid of dullisshe nollis. *Ibid.* 351 þe while þe Degonys domes weren so endauntid.

†**en'daunture.** *Obs. rare*[−1]. [f. EN-[1] + OF. *danture* taming; suggested by the phrase *en sa danture* in the original text.] ? Taming, breaking in. (But the passage is nonsense, the translator not having understood his original.)

1340 *Ayenb.* 220 Huo þet tekþ colte endaunture, hyalde hit wyle þerhuyle hit ilest. [Fr. *quaprent poulain en sa danture, il le tendra tant comme il dure.*]

end-away, *adv. dial.* One after another, successively.

1888 *Sheffield Gloss.* (E.D.S.) He won six games end-away.

endazzle: see EN- *pref.*[3] 3.

†**end-day.** *Obs.* See END *sb.* and DAY. Also 5 enday. [OE. *ęnde-dæȝ*, f. *ęnde* END *sb.* + *dæȝ* DAY. Cf. OHG. *endi-dago* (MHG. *ende-tac*).] The last day; the day of one's death.

Beowulf (Gr.) 638 Ic..sceal..ოþðe ende-dæȝ..minne ȝebidan. *c* **1175** *Lamb. Hom.* 17 þet he icherre from þan uuelnesse ear his ende dei. *c* **1200** ORMIN 5674 He shall att his endedaȝȝ þurrh Drihhtin wurrþenn frofredd. *c* **1305** *Edmund Conf.* 580 in *South-Eng. Leg.* (1887) 448 And þou treweliche at min ende-day: art i-come me to. *c* **1340** *Cursor M.* 21063 (Fairf.), Quen þat [John] seye his ende-day comande neye..he did his graue to delue. *c* **1425** WYNTOUN *Cron.* VI. iv. 80 And led hys lyf till hys enday.

†**'ende.** *Obs.* Forms: 1 ænid, ænit, enid, ened, 3 hende, 4–5 enede, 5 heynde, ende. [OE. *ęned* str. fem. = MDu. *aned, anet*, Du. *eend*, OHG. *anat, -et, -it, -ot* (Ger. *ente*), ON. *önd* (Sw., Da. *and*). Cf. Lat. *anat-em.*] A duck.

a **700** *Epinal Gloss.* 17 *Aneta*, ænid [*a* **800** *Erfurt Gloss.* ænit, *Corpus Gloss.* enid]. *c* **1300** *Havelok* 1241 Ne was ther spared gos ne henne, Ne the hende, ne the drake. *c* **1325** *Gloss. W. de Biblesw.* in Wr.-Wülcker 143 En marreis ane iaroille [enede queketh]. *c* **1430** *Bk. Hawkyng* in *Rel. Ant.* I. 302 For to make hawke high of astate..take the weng of an enede. *c* **1440** *Promp. Parv.* 139 Ende, dooke byrde, *anas.* *c* **1475** *Voc.* in Wr.-Wülcker 760 *Hec anata*, a heynd.

ende, erron. var. HENDE *a. Obs.* gracious.

endear (ɛn'dɪə(r)), *v.* Also α. 7 endeere, -deare; β. 7 indear, indeere. [f. EN-[1] + DEAR *a.*]

†**1.** *trans.* To render costly or more costly; to enhance the price of. *Obs.*

α. **1603** FLORIO *Montaigne* 523 Enhancing the price of the place we raise the price and endeare the desire. **1618** *K. James's Procl. conc. Buildings* in Rymer (1717) XVII. 107 All Victualls and other Provision endeared. **1803** *Ann. Rev.* I. 390 Bread..would be cheapened by the competition, not endeared by the combination of bakers.

β. **1729** *Seasonable Remarks Trade* 11 There are several Accidents which indear a Commodity to the Merchant.

†**2.** To enhance the value of; to render precious or attractive. *Obs.*

α. **1580** SIDNEY *Arcadia* II. 125 He would endeare his own service. **1594** SOUTHWELL *M. Magd. Fun. Teares* 92 Love.. endeareth the meanest things, and doubleth the estimate of things that are precious. **1657** J. SMITH *Myst. Rhet.* 185 Her wit endeared by youth, her affection by birth, and her sadnesse by her beauty. *a* **1662** HEYLIN *Laud* I. 209 All those several motives which might not only serve to justifie, but endear the work.

β. **1622** BACON *Hen. VII*, 103 Making a body of forces of themselves, the more to indear their merit. **1672** DRYDEN *Marr. a-la-Mode* I. IV. i. Dram. Wks. 1725 III. 267 'Tis as Physicians show the desperate Ill T' indear their Art, by mitigating Pains They cannot wholly cure.

†**b.** To represent as valuable or important, to lay stress upon; also, to exaggerate. *Obs.*

1620 SHELTON *Quix.* III. xvii. 113, I must leave them here abruptly, since I want words to endear them. **1622** MABBE tr. *Aleman's Guzman d' Alf.* II. 97 May without indearing be truly said to be a princely and royall seat. **1656** COWLEY *Davideis* IV. (1710) II. 443 Not that I'd clear Their Guilt, or mine own Innocence indear. **1661** HOWELL *Twelve Sev. Treat.* 215 In all his declarations ther was nothing that he endear'd and inculcated more often.

3. To render (a person) dear *to* another; to inspire or create affection for (a person or thing). (The modern sense.) Also const. †*with.*

α. **1647** CLARENDON *Hist. Reb.* (1702) I. II. 121 His Majesty exceedingly desired to endear her to the People. **1748** RICHARDSON *Clarissa* (1811) II. xxxiii. 218 She endeared herself to me ten times more by her soothing concern for me. **1781** GIBBON *Decl. & F.* II. xxvii. 56 His gentle and amiable disposition endeared him to his private friends. **1821** BYRON *Juan* IV. xvi, That which destroys Most love, possession, unto them appear'd A thing which each endearment more endear'd. **1856** EMERSON *Eng. Traits, Relig.* Wks. (Bohn) II. 98 It [the Church] endears itself thus to men of more taste than activity. **1879** C. GEIKIE *Christ* lxiv. 809 One endeared by long companionship.

β. **1611** BARREY *Ram Alley* in Dodsley *Old Pl.* (1780) V. 444 Stand thou propitious, indear me to my love. **1647** CLARENDON *Hist. Reb.* (1702) I. II. 113 To indear himself with that Nation.

†**4.** To hold dear; to love. *Obs.*

1622 WITHER *Lines* in Farr's *S.P. Jas. I* (1848) 221 But to my heart they sit this day as neare As when I most endear'd them. **1639** SALTMARSHE *Policy* 20 Something he endears. *a* **1711** KEN *Sion* Wks. 1721 IV. 375 God..most amiable appear'd, Endearing most, and most to be endear'd.

†**5.** To treat affectionately or fondly; to caress. *Obs.* Cf. ENDEARING *ppl. a.*

1683 LORRAIN *Muret's Rites Fun.* 161 Embraced, hug'd, caressed, endeared and applauded by all the spectators.

†**6.** To win the affection of; to conciliate, attract. Also, to deepen (affection). *Obs.*

1580 SIDNEY *Arcadia* (1622) 247 Leauing no office vnperformed, which might either witnesse, or endeare her sonnes affection. **1628** EARLE *Microcosm., Weak Man* (Arb.) 58 You cannot endeare him more then by coozening him. *a* **1631** DONNE *Poems, etc.* (1633) 354 Not that God is endeared by that, or wearied by this. **1671** MILTON *Samson* 793, I sought by all means, therefore, How to endear..thee to me firmest. *a* **1704** T. BROWN *Sat. agst. Woman* Wks. 1730 I. 57 No law can bind them, and no love endear. **1704** HEARNE *Duct. Hist.* (1714) I. 390 This generous Act endeared the People..to him.

†**b.** To bind by obligations of gratitude. Sometimes const. *to* with inf. *Obs.*

α. **1607** SHAKS. *Timon* III. ii. 35, I am so much endeered to that Lord; hee's euer sending. **1626** T. H[AWKINS] *Caussin's Holy Crt.* 81 He must..frugally endeare Auditors..dissemble with his enemyes. **1652** J. WADSWORTH tr. *Sandoval's Civil Wars of Spain* 21 To endeer the Elector of Brandenburg the more to vote in his behalf. *Ibid.* 280 They gave them ten daies paie more to endear them to go before Tordesillas. **1654** tr. Scudery's *Curia Politiae* 107 Whereby the House of Lancaster..hath for ever indeared and obliged the House of York.

β. **1613** R. C. *Table Alph.* (ed. 3), *Indeere*, make bound to one. **1633** G. HERBERT *Temple, Ch. Militant* 12 Early didst thou arise to plant this vine, Which might the more indeare it to be thine.

endearance (ɛnˈdɪərəns). *rare.* [f. ENDEAR *v.* + -ANCE.] The action of endearing, or the state of being endeared.

1766 ANSTEY *New Bath Guide* (ed. 2) 77, Show it young Lady Betty, by way of Endearance. **1871** BREWER *Eng. Studies* (1881) Introd. 45 His language is so much governed by this feeling of Divine endearance.

endeared (ɛnˈdɪəd), *ppl. a.* [f. ENDEAR *v.* + -ED[1].]

1. Of friendship, etc.: Affectionate, cordial. *arch.*

1649 ROBERTS *Clavis Bibl.* 140 Jonathan's endeared love to David. **1692** BEVERLEY *Disc. Dr. Crisp* 14 The Warmest and Indearedst Love. *a* **1714** ELLWOOD *Autobiog.* (1765) 376 Unto you is the Salutation of my endeared Love. **1812** GEN. BROCK *Proclam. 22 July* in *Exam.* 5 Oct. 629/1 The endeared relations of its first settlers. **1842** H. ROGERS *Introd. Burke's Wks.* I. 3 With the son of the master..Edmund formed a most endeared friendship.

2. Regarded with affection, beloved.

1841 D'ISRAELI *Amen. Lit.* (1867) 698 All solicitations of the author to retrieve his endeared volume proved fruitless.

†**enˈdearedly**, *adv. Obs. rare.* [f. ENDEARED *ppl. a.* + -LY[2].] In an endeared manner.

1624 HEYWOOD *Gunaik.* III. 119 Both endeeredly affected their husbands. **1663** BAXTER *Divine Life* 306 A Jonathan..will endearedly love that man..who is appointed to deprive him of a Kingdome.

†**enˈdearedness.** *Obs.* [f. ENDEARED *ppl. a.* + -NESS.] The state of being endeared; feeling of affection, fondness.

1654 GAYTON *Pleasant Notes* III. v. 98 The other..to shew his Indeeredness, prest often to know the Murderer of his friend. **1679** *Prot. Conformist* 3 That vertue or rather grace of Moderation has graven the most deep and indelible characters of endearedness upon me. *a* **1703** BURKITT *On N.T.* Matt. iii. 17 The endearedness of his person: This is my beloved Son. *a* **1714** M. HENRY *Wks.* (1835) I. 278 Embrace each other with a cordial endearedness.

enˈdearing, *vbl. sb.* [f. ENDEAR *v.* + -ING[1].] The action of the vb. ENDEAR; †*concr.* a caress, mode of showing affection.

1622 E. MISSELDEN *Free Trade* 106 The..losse that thereby will fall..vpon all men in the endearing of all things. **1654** WHITLOCK *Zootomia* 324 Endearings, minted current, according to the lawfullnesse or unlawfullnesse of the Love they would procure. **1678** *Yng. Man's Cali.* Introd. 3 Intended for the endearing of God.

enˈdearing, *ppl. a.* [f. ENDEAR *v.* + -ING[2].] That endears: **a.** That wins or inspires affection. **b.** Manifesting affection, caressing.

1667 MILTON *P.L.* IV. 337 Nor gentle purpose, nor endearing smiles Wanted. **1680** H. MORE *Apocal. Apoc.* 50 This is but a just reward of Thy endearing sufferings upon the Cross. **1742** RICHARDSON *Pamela* IV. 266, I have a better and more indearing Husband than ever. **1878** Q. VICTORIA *Let.* in *Lond. Gaz.* 27 Dec., The noble and endearing qualities of her whom all now mourn.

endearingly (ɛnˈdɪərɪŋlɪ), *adv.* [f. ENDEARING *ppl. a.* + -LY[2].] In an endearing manner.

a **1711** KEN *Edmund* Poet. Wks. 1721 II. 202 Each he endearingly salutes. **1836** E. HOWARD *R. Reefer* lxi, We patted them endearingly with our hands. **1876** BANCROFT *Hist. U.S.* I. ix. 286 Who called him endearingly his son.

enˈdearingness. *rare*[−1]. [f. as prec. + -NESS.] The state of being ENDEARING, exhibition of affection.

1701 COLLIER *M. Aurel.* (1726) 316 They make up to them with great endearingness.

endearment (ɛnˈdɪəmənt). Also 7–8 indearment. [f. ENDEAR *v.* + -MENT.]

1. The action of endearing or the fact of being endeared; *concr.* something that endears, that excites or increases affection.

1663 *Aron-bimn.* 3 The Object of all this Care, this Indeerment and joy, is the Ark of God. **1673** *Lady's Call.* II. 82 One of the greatest endearments of Abraham to God. **1688** H. WHARTON *Enthus. Ch. Rome* 78 The belief of his endearment to God, made him often presume upon the Favour of Heaven. **1690** NORRIS *Beatitudes* (1694) I. 202 The Heathen, to whom the Unity and Agreement of the First Christians was a great indearment. **1881** P. BROOKS *Candle of Lord* 164 The enlargement of the faith brings the endearment of the faith.

†**b.** An obligation of gratitude, a bond of attachment. Cf. ENDEAR *v.* 6 b. *Obs.*

1628 EARLE *Microcosm., World's wise man* (Arb.) 61 His deepest indearment is a communication of mischiefe. **1677** HALE *Contempl.* II. 72 That Lust..which the..Saviour, upon the Indearment of his own Blood, begs us to Crucifie.

2. An action or utterance expressive of love or fondness; a caress. Also *abstr.*

1702 ROWE *Tamerl.* I. i. 341 Are War and Slavery the soft Endearments With which they court the Beauties they admire? **1742** RICHARDSON *Pamela* IV. 141 His Indearments and Tenderness to his Lady..was alone worthy of all her Risque. **1853** C. BRONTË *Villette* xxxvi. (1876) 401 M. Paul petted and patted her; the endearments she received were not to be wondered at. **1867** FREEMAN *Norm. Conq.* I. iv. 180 A mere name of endearment.

†**3.** Affection, fondness. *Obs.*

1709 STRYPE *Ann. Ref.* I. xliii. 477 Between these two there was a long and great endearment. **1746–7** HERVEY *Medit.* (1818) 19 If you really love the offspring of your own bodies; if your bowels yearn over those amiable pledges of conjugal endearment. **1821** CLARE *Vill. Minstr.* I. 60 Travellers returned from foreign ground Feel more endearments for their native earth.

4. The making (a commodity) dearer. *rare.*

1864 *Guardian* 21 Dec. 1218 People bought in provisions against the endearments of Sella's new tariffs.

†**5.** The action of enhancing the value of anything; also, praise, exaggeration. *Obs.*

1612 SHELTON *Quix.* I. III. xiii. 249 It is rather a poetical Endearment, than an approv'd Truth. **1647** CLARENDON *Hist. Reb.* (1702) I. II. 113 If his condition..were so good that it needed no indearment.

endeavour (ɛnˈdɛvə(r)), *sb.* Forms: see the verb. [app. f. next verb, which however appears later in our quots.]

1. The action of endeavouring; effort, or pains, directed to attain an object; a strenuous attempt or enterprise.

α. **1417** LD. FURNYVAL in Ellis *Orig. Lett.* Ser. II. I. 56 The great laboures, travels, and endevoures made by your said Lifetenaunte. **1440** [See ENDEAVOUR *v.*]. **1549** CROWLEY *Last Trump.* 496 Se thou apply the to learnynge Wyth all thy busy endevoure. **1605** BACON *Adv. Learn.* I. v. §10 (1873) 42 The scope that men propound to themselves, whereunto they bend their endeavours. **1618** SIR R. BOYLE *Diary* (1886) I. 204, I gave Mr. Richard Archdeacon a young gelding for his endevors about my purchaze of dongarvan. **1655–60** STANLEY *Hist. Philos.* (1701) 79/2 We should employ therein our utmost study and endeavour. **1745** in *Col. Rec. Penn.* V. 19 We will use our Endeavours to that End. **1750** JOHNSON *Rambler* No. 25 ¶5 To walk with circumspection..ought to be the constant endeavour of every reasonable being. **1814** WORDSW. *White Doe* v. 52 On him and on his high endeavour The light of praise shall shine for ever. **1856** RUSKIN *Mod. Paint.* III. IV. vi. §4 The life of Angelico was almost entirely spent in the endeavour to imagine the beings belonging to another world.

β. **1563** SHUTE *Archit.* A iij b, The firste frutes of my poor attemptes and indeuors. **1611** BIBLE *Pref.* 10 That hath bene our indeauour, that our marke. **1663** MARVELL *Corr.* xli. Wks. 1872–5 II. 89 You have that fruit of our former indevors. **1663** *Flagellum or O. Cromwell* (1672) 12 Both which he studied with the same indifference and infide and falicious indeavour. **1743** J. MORRIS *Serm.* ii. 45 Kind indeavours to promote their happiness.

b. *to do one's endeavour(s*: to exert oneself to the uttermost; to do all one can (in a cause or to an end). *arch.*

α. **1480** *Robt. Devyll* 42 The Emperoure charged every man to do his endever. **1551** ROBINSON tr. *More's Utop.* I. (Arb.) 56 Doynge my endeuoure to plucke out of hys mynde the..causes of vice. **1596** SHAKS. *Merch. V.* II. ii. 182 My best endeuors shall be done herein. **1688** EVELYN *Mem.* (1857) II. 281, I did my endeavour with the Lords of the Treasury to be favourable to him. **1716–8** LADY M. W. MONTAGUE *Lett.* I. xiv. 48, I have done my best endeavour to find out something worth writing to you. **1745** BUTLER *Serm.* Wks. 1874 II. 287 We are to do our endeavours to promote virtue and religion amongst men. **1827** F. COOPER *Prairie* II. xvi. 255 Yes, lad, yes; you would do your endeavours. **1873** BROWNING *Red Cott. Night-c.* 271 Do your endeavour like a man.

β. *c* **1530** H. RHODES *Bk. Nurture* in *Babees Bk.* (1868) 74 There doe your true indeuour. **1612** BRINSLEY *Lud. Lit.* iii. (1627) 13 Every one is to doe his best indeavour to know how to make it most easie.

†**2.** *Philos.* Used by Hobbes: (see quot.; in Latin *conatus*). *Obs.*

1651 HOBBES *Leviath.* I. vi. 23 These small beginnings of Motion, within the body of Man..are commonly called Endeavour. **1656** —— *Elem. Philos.* (1839) 206, I define endeavour to be motion made in less space and time than can be given. **1667** BOYLE *Orig. Formes & Qual.* 3 Local Motion, or an Endeavour at it, is not included in the nature of Matter.

endeavour (ɛnˈdɛvə(r)), *v.* Forms: α. 5 endevoyre, endover, (endower, -re), 5–6 endevoir, endever, 5–7 endevor(e, 6 endevyr, endevur, endevre, 6–7 endevour(e, 6– endeavour. β. 5–7 indevor, 6 indevur, 6–7 indever, indevour, 7–9 indeavour. [f. EN-[1] + DEVOIR *sb.*; cf. the Fr. phrase *se mettre en devoir de faire quelquechose* to make it one's duty to do something; hence, to set about, to endeavour. Cf. also the following quot.:

1504 *Nottingham Borough Rec.* III. 325 And þat euery Mair for þe tyme beyng put in devoire to calle..his said Chaumberleyns..to performe the same.]

†**1.** *refl.* To exert oneself, use effort. Const. *to* with *inf.*; (rarely) *for, to,* with *sb.*; also *simply.*

α. *c* **1400** *York Myst.* iv. 30 So that ye may endower To susteyn beast and man..Dwell here if that ye canne, This shall be your endowre. **1483** CAXTON *Gold. Leg.* 422/3 He..moche endeuoyred hym to make hym to lerne the deuyne Scripture. **1485** *Procl. agst. Henry Tudor* in *Paston Lett.* No. 883. III. 319 Like gode and true Englishmen to endover themselfs..for the defence of them. **1491** *Act 7 Hen. VII*, c. 22 Preamb., Endevoir youre self and put to your hand and spare no cost. **1521–2** *Compl. North* in Furniv. *Ballads fr. MSS.* I. 338 Wherfor I moste, & wyll do evyr, to pray for hys grace my selfe endevyr. **1540–1** ELYOT *Image Gov.* (1549) Pref. 2, I endeuoured my selfe whiles I had leysour, to translate it into Englishe. **1642** J. JACKSON *Bk. of Conscience* 86, I endeavour my selfe constantly both to refuse the evill and choose the good.

β. **1495–6** *Plumpton Corr.* 115, I shall indevor me for you as farre as I can. **1535** FISHER *Wks.* I. 412 If thou wilt indeuer thee vpon thy parte. **1589** PUTTENHAM *Eng. Poesie* I. viii. (Arb.) 36 They are as it were inforced to indeuour them selues to armes. **1614** LODGE *Seneca* Ep. 166 Indevour thyselfe as much as in thee lieth to the end, etc. **1655** *Francion* VII. 25 In the morning he did indeavour himself to make us friends.

†**b.** *trans.* To exert (one's power), thoughts, etc. *Obs. rare.*

1574 HELLOWES *Gueuara's Fam. Ep.* (1577) 397 Marcus Aurelius..endeuoured his power to persecute the Christians. **1606** G. W[OODCOCKE] tr. *Hist. Ivstine* 124 b, Euery man endeuored his thoughts how to make his duty, love, [etc.] encrese to him. *Ibid.* Ll. 5 b, Maximilian endeuored al his power against the Turke. **1642** *Lanc. Tracts Civil War* (1844) 18 Our high Sheriff..will readily..endeavour the power of the County against our proceedings.

†**2.** *intr.* for *refl.* To strive, try, exert oneself; to direct one's efforts. *Obs.* exc. as in 3.

1551 TURNER *Herbal* I. (1568) 142 A gourde hath long runnyng branches, whiche naturally indevour upwarde. **1588** ALLEN *Admon.* 55 The pardon of his Holines, giuen to all..that..indeuor in this quarrell. **1606** G. W[OODCOCKE] tr. *Hist. Ivstine* 100 b, All the realme endeuored after his steps. **1624** BARGRAVE *Serm. agst. Self-Policy* 24 Let us indeuour with words and workes.

3. *intr.* (The only mod. use.) To try, make an effort for a specified object; to attempt strenuously.

a. Const. *to* with *inf.* Also (rarely) used impersonally in *passive.*

α. **1594** SHAKS. *Rich. III*, I. iv, Every man that means to live well, endeavours to trust to himself. **1607** TOPSELL *Serpents* (1658) 591 He endevoureth to disperse and distribute the knowledge of his Majesty. **1649** EARL MONMOUTH tr. *Senault's Use of Passions* (1671) 306 'Tis endeavoured to part them from themselves. **1651** in *Nicholas Papers* (1886) 269, I will endeavour..to save something of my estate. **1759** HUME *Hist. Eng.* III. liii. 133 It was even endeavoured to revive the first institution of the college of justice. **1883** FROUDE *Short Stud.* IV. I. iv. 44 He [the pope] sent the Archbishop of Rouen to England to endeavour to compromise matters.

β. **1597** HOOKER *Eccl. Pol.* v. xv. (1611) 207 The teares of their grieued eyes the Prophets indeuoured..to wipe away. *c* **1620** in *Hatton Corr.* (1878) 3 To know God's will and to indever to doe it. **1743** J. MORRIS *Serm.* ii. 47 He indeavours to preserve peace.

b. With clause introduced by *that.*

16.. FATHER WALSH in *Scotsman* (1883) 17 Sept. 2/6 It were more charitable to endeavour that the errors might be taken away.

c. Const. *after,* †*at,* †*for.*

1641 FRENCH *Distill.* vi. (1651) 194 All the Chymicall discoveries are..found out by..endeavouring after this. **1649** JER. TAYLOR *Gt. Exemp.* I. viii. 113 A bloody king endeavoured for his destruction. **1704** SWIFT *T. Tub* Author's Apol., Which the world never..gave them any thanks for endeavouring at. **1711** ADDISON *Spect.* No. 106 ¶8, I could heartily wish that more of our Country-Clergy would..endeavour after a handsome Elocution. **1750** JOHNSON *Rambler* No. 9 ¶9 Every man ought to endeavour at eminence. **1851** HT. MARTINEAU *Hist. Peace* (1877) III. v. ix. 386 He was endeavouring after that enjoyment of domestic life. **1860** MILL *Repr. Govt.* ii. (1865) 10 If we are endeavouring after more riches.

†**4.** *trans.* To use effort or pains for; to attempt. *Obs.* exc. *arch.*

α. **1581** J. BELL *Haddon's Answ. Osor.* 468 The Lutherans ..have never endevoured anything more carefully. **1620** *Horæ Subsecivæ* 109 Hate Couetousnesse, but endeuour thrift. **1647** CLARENDON *Hist. Reb.* (1703) II. VII. 288 We shall..endeavour the extirpation of Popery. **1656** MORE *Antid. Ath.* (1712) Pref. Gen., He is to endeavour the adorning of himself with such accomplishments. **1751** JOHNSON *Rambler* No. 87 ¶6 He who endeavours the cure of our intellectual maladies, mistakes their cause. **1818** JAS. MILL *Brit. India* I. III. iii. 530 He was stimulated to endeavour the restoration. **1871** RUSKIN *Fors Clav.* viii. 17 Had it never been endeavoured until now.

β. **1586** T. B. *La Primaud. Fr. Acad.* (1589) 405 To indevor the spoile of all that is therein. **1601** R. JOHNSON *Kingd. & Commw.* (1603) A b, I could..indevor a draught of your most Honourable praises. **1672** MARVELL *Reh. Transp.* I. 146, I have here indeavoured the utmost ingenuity toward Mr. Bayes.

†**b.** To try to fulfil (a law). *Obs.*

1643 MILTON *Divorce* II. xx. (1851) 116 Every act of true faith..as that whereby we endeavour the law.

†**5.** To make a (hostile) attempt upon; to attack. *Obs. rare.*

1589 NASHE *Almond for P.* 17 a, It is nought but a learned ministry which their champion Martin endeuors. **1606** R. TURNBULL in Spurgeon *Treas. Dav.* Ps. xv. 5 It [teredo] hath such teeth as endeavoureth and consumeth the hard timber. [But perh. a nonce-wd. f. EN-[1] + DEVOUR.]

enˈdeavoured, *ppl. a. rare.* [f. ENDEAVOUR *v.* + -ED[1].] That has been tried or attempted.

1595 H. OLNEY in *Sidney's Apol. Poetrie* (Arb.) 16 Mine endeuored hardiment.

enˈdeavourer. [f. ENDEAVOUR *v.* + -ER.]

†**a.** One who endeavours; an aspirant. *Obs.*

1586 W. WEBBE *Disc. Eng. Poetrie* (Arb.) 15 Your worshyppe cannot chuse, but continue your wonted fauourable benignitie towardes all the indeuourers to learning. **1645** J. LILBURNE in Prynne *Fresh Disc. Blazing Stars* 34 An endeavourer to set the Princes of the earth

together by the ears. **1663** COWLEY *Verses & Ess.* (1669) 83 'Tis crowded..with the most burdensome sort of Guests, the Endeavourers to be witty. **1709** STEELE *Tatler* No. 167 ¶1 Labour and Industry will but push the unhappy Endeavourer..the further off his Wishes.

b. In full, ***Christian Endeavourer***: a member of the Young People's Society of Christian Endeavour, a religious association which originated in the United States in 1881.

1893 *Rep. Third Nat. Christian Endeavour Convention* 41 Wherever she went she met as many of the Endeavourers as she could, and all gave her one promise..'We mean to try and do all we can for Jesus'. **1896** *Harper's Weekly* 22 Aug. 822/2, I found restless Endeavourers still going into and coming out of their state-rooms. **1897** *Helping Words* Nov. 247 'There are some directions in the Bible that you can't follow.'.. 'That is a remarkable admission for an Endeavourer to make.' **1900** H. LAWSON *On Track* 136 At one end of the table a Christian Endeavourer endeavouring.

endeavouring (ɛn'dɛvərɪŋ), *vbl. sb.* [f. as prec. + -ING[1].] The action of the vb. ENDEAVOUR.

1548 R. HUTTEN *Sum of Diuinitie* L 2 a, Good intencions or endeuoringes of reason. **1583** GOLDING *Calvin on Deut.* vi. 35 An indeuoring to renounce the worlde and all his owne affections. **1665** MANLEY *Grotius' Low-C. Warres* 2 The unhappy endeavouring of Forraign Aid. **1840** CARLYLE *Heroes* (1858) 261 No dining at Freemason's Tavern..and infinite other jangling and true or false endeavouring. **1877** *Mem. Bp. of Argyll* iii. 32 In addition to his other endeavourings.

en'deavouring *ppl. a.* [f. ENDEAVOUR *v.* + -ING[2].] That endeavours. Also *transf.* and *fig.*

1628 MILTON *Poems, Vacat. Exerc.* 2 Hail, native language! that..Didst move my first endeavouring tongue to speak. **1656** tr. *Hobbes Elem. Philos.* (1839) 334 The parts, which are pressed by both the endeavouring bodies. **1850** LYNCH *Theop. Trin.* ii. 20 His net of endeavouring thought. **1876** GEO. ELIOT *Dan. Der.* II. xxiii. 107 The hard, climbing path of an endeavouring artist.

†**en'deavourment.** *Obs. rare.* [f. ENDEAVOUR *v.* + -MENT.] The action of endeavouring; = ENDEAVOUR *sb.*

1523 SKELTON *Garl. Laurel* 400 Your endeuorment So have ye done. **1591** SPENSER *M. Hubberd* 298 The goodman was meanly well content, Triall to make of his endeuourment.

†**en'deavourous,** *a. Obs. rare*[−1]. [f. ENDEAVOUR *sb.* + -OUS.] Full of endeavour, zealous, forward. Hence †**en'deavourously** *adv.*

1597 BEARD *Theatre Gods Iudgements* 48 Whilst hee thus strongly and endeauourously emploied himself about these affaires. *a* **1631** DONNE *Ess. Divinity* (1651) 28 For no man was euer more endeavourous than he.

endebt, -ed: see IND-.

endeca, an incorrect form of HENDECA-, a. Gr. ἕνδεκα eleven; occurring in **en'decagon**, a plane figure of eleven sides; **ende'cagynous** *a. Bot.*, having eleven pistils; **ˌendeca'phyllous** *a.*, having eleven leaflets; **ˌendecasy'llabic** *a.*, having eleven syllables; **ˌendeca'syllable**, a verse of eleven syllables. See HENDECAGON, -GYNOUS, -PHYLLOUS, -SYLLABIC, -SYLLABLE.

ended ('ɛndɪd), *ppl. a.* [f. END *v.* and *sb.* + -ED.]

1. That has come to an end.

1598 CHAPMAN *Iliad* II. 479 Every ended year..th' Athenian youths please him with offerings. **1599** SHAKS. *Much Ado* I. i. 299 When you went onward in this ended action. **1677** SEDLEY *Ant. & Cl.* v. i. (1766) 191 Let not his blood now stain the ended war. **1882** ELLEN M. TAYLOR *Madeira* 59 In bidding the ended day farewell.

2. [From the *sb.*] With prefixed adj. or numeral: Having its end (of a certain kind); having (a certain number of) ends.

endeictic (ɛn'daɪktɪk), *a.* [ad. Gr. ἐνδεικτικός f. ἐνδεικνυναι, f. ἐν in + δεικνύναι to show.] Serving to show or exhibit; probative.

(A name of one of the classes into which the Platonic Dialogues were divided by ancient grammarians or commentators. Cf. Diog. Laert. III. 49.)

1655-60 STANLEY *Hist. Philos.* (1701) 175/1 Agonistick [discourse is] Endeictick [or] Anatreptick. **1791** ENFIELD *Hist. Philos.* I. 215 The Agonistic dialogues, supposed to resemble the combat, were either Endeictic, as exhibiting a specimen of skill, or Anatreptic presenting the spectacle of a perfect defeat. **1855** BUTLER *Lect. Anc. Philos.* (1874) 323 Another classification [of Platonic Dialogues] of great antiquity is based vpon the style and purpose of the dialogue,—as maieutick, anatreptick, endeictick, and so forth. **1876** tr. *Zeller's Plato* 97 *note.*

†**en'deign,** *v.*[1] *Obs. rare.* In 4 endeyne, endyne. [ad. OF. *(s')endaignier*:—L. *indignāri*: see INDIGNANT.] *intr.* To be indignant. Const. *in, upon.*

1382 WYCLIF *1 Kings* xxi. 4 Thanne Achab cam into his hows, endeynynge, and grutchynge upon the word that Naboth Jezraelite hadde spoken to hym. —— *Wisd.* xii. 27 In the whiche suffring thei endeyneden. —— *Isa.* lvii. 6 Whether vp on these thingus I shal not endyne.

†**en'deign,** *v.*[2] *Obs. rare.* [f. EN-[1] + DEIGN *v.*] *refl.* = DEIGN.

a **1400** *Relig. Pieces fr. Thornton MS.* (1867) 87 [He] þat for dule endeynede hym to dye.

†**en'deignous,** *a. Obs. rare*[−1]. [f. ENDEIGN *v.*[1] + -OUS.] Disdainful. Cf. DEIGNOUS.

c **1400** *Test. Love* I. (1560) 274/2 If any would [be] endeynous, or prowd, or be envious.

endellionite (ɛn'dɛlɪənaɪt). *Min. Obs.* exc. *Hist.* [orig. called *endellion*, f. the place-name St. *Endellion*, Cornwall: see -ITE[1].] = BOURNONITE.

1809 J. L. DE BOURBON in *Jrnl. Nat. Philos., Chem. & Arts* XXIV. 229, I have given this the name of *endellion*; which avoids the termination in *ite*, so frequent in the nomenclature of mineral substances. **1837** DANA *Syst. Min.* 413 Other localities are..Endellion near Redruth, in Cornwall, where it was first found, and whence it was called Endellionite, by Count Bourbon. **1954** G. W. HIMUS *Dict. Geol.* 17 *Bournonite*... Also called Wheel-Ore and Endellionite.

†**endement.** *Obs. rare*[−1].

a **1490** CAXTON *Eneydos* (1889) 16 Entendynge to gyue comforte..and counseyl, to thendementes [? *read* thentendementes] and engynes of the werkmen.

†**endemete.** *Obs.* Also 4 enedmete, 5 edmette, enmotte. [f. ENDE + *-mete* MEAT.] Duckweed, *Lemna minor*.

a **1387** *Sinon. Bartl.* 27 *Lentigo* super aquam crescit, an[ce] enedmete. *c* **1440** *Promp. Parv.* 140 Ende mete [*v.r.* endmete, endmette, enmotte], *lenticula.*

endemial (ɛn'diːmɪəl), *a.* [f. Gr. ἐνδήμι-ος of or belonging to a state or people + -AL[1].] = ENDEMIC *a.*

1672 SIR T. BROWNE *Let. Friend* § 14. (1881) 137 Endemial and local infirmities proper unto certain regions. **1683** W. HARRIS *Pharmacologia* xiv. 255 The Dutch have a Natural, and Endemial aversion to all Emeticks. **1756** C. LUCAS *Ess. Waters* III. 245 We find them subject to no particular endemial disorder. **1808** BENTHAM *Sc. Reform* 8 Another vice endemial among lawyers. **1830** GODWIN *Cloudesley* III. xii. 237 Not one company of these endemial brigands was any longer to be heard of.

endemic (ɛn'dɛmɪk), *a.* and *sb.* [f. Gr. ἐν in + δῆμ-ος people + -IC.]

A. *adj.* Constantly or regularly found among a (specified) people, or in a (specified) country: *esp.* **a.** [ad. Fr. *endémique* (A. P. de Candolle 1820, in *Dictionnaire des Sciences Naturelles* XVIII. 412).] Of plants or animals: Having their ordinary habitat in a certain country; opposed to *exotic*. Now used *spec.* of plants and animals that are indigenous only in a specified area. **b.** Of diseases: Habitually prevalent in a certain country, and due to permanent local causes.

1759 GOLDSM. *Bee* No. 1 A deformity which, as it was endemic..it had been the custom..to look upon as the greatest beauty. **1776** ADAM SMITH *W.N.* I. I. viii. 77 *note*, Famines are periodical or endemic in Hindostan. **1802** *Med. Jrnl.* VIII. 450 The author..proceeds..to show in what sense the plague may be termed endemic. **1830-2** LYELL *Princ. Geol.* (1875) II. III. xli. 413 The endemic, and other species of animals and plants in the Atlantic Islands. **1876** DARWIN *Cross-Fertil.* xi. 415 Bees..visit many exotic flowers as readily as the endemic kinds. **1905** F. E. CLEMENTS *Res. Methods Ecol.* iv. 227 (*heading*) Endemism. .. Since its first use by De Candolle, the term endemic has been employed..by phytogeographers with the meaning of 'peculiar to a certain region'. *Ibid.* 228 In its proper sense, endemic refers to distribution, and not to origin. **1937** *Discovery* July 204/1 Of the *Carabidae*, 169 genera are represented, of which 63 are endemic. **1951** *Jrnl. Ecol.* XXXIX. 215 The term 'endemic' is relative in that it means, as now generally used in biology, a taxon or an ecological group limited in range to the geographical area under consideration.

c. *fig.*

1852 BLACKIE *Stud. Lang.* 1 An unreflecting habit of routine that seems endemic among official men in our country. **1905** *Westm. Gaz.* 15 Nov. 2/1 The same endemic series of murders of a more or less political character as in Macedonia. **1969** *Times* 15 Jan. 7/2 Until a few years ago warfare was endemic. **1970** *Daily Tel.* 14 Apr. 16 That bane of British economic policy-makers—an endemic tendency for imports to rise more rapidly than exports.

B. *sb.* **1.** An endemic disease. Also *fig.*

1662 J. CHANDLER *Van Helmont's Oriat.* 191 It is not manifest, that Endemicks or things proper to people in the Countrey where they live, are drawn by the Arteries. **1809** W. IRVING *Knickerb.* VII. viii. (1849) 417 That talking endemic, so prevalent in this country. **1857** BUCKLE *Civilis.* I. 118 European diseases, some of which, such as smallpox, have passed from epidemics into endemics. **1859** *Sat. Rev.* VIII. 261/2 Snobbishness is an insidious endemic.

2. A plant native to a certain limited area.

1932 FULLER & CONARD tr. *Braun-Blanquet's Plant Sociol.* xi. 282 The original dry sod, untouched by fire, is composed exclusively of the old Mascarene Tertiary endemics. **1947** R. GOOD *Geogr. Flowering Plants* iii. 48 While one part of a large region possesses a high proportion of endemics another and adjacent region may have considerably fewer. **1960** N. POLUNIN *Introd. Plant Geogr.* vii. 206 Some endemics are confined to very limited areas.

endemical (ɛn'dɛmɪkəl), *a.* [f. prec. + -AL[1].] = ENDEMIC *a.*

1657 G. STARKEY *Helmont's Vind.* 92 Those endemical malignant vapours, which infect the air. **1684** tr. *Bonet's Merc. Compit.* VI. 208 With the Ægyptians..the Plague is commonly endemical. **1788** BURKE *Sp. agst. W. Hastings* Wks. XIII. 424 Bribery was the ancient, radical, endemical, and ruinous distemper of the Company's affairs. **1831** CARLYLE *Sart. Res.* (1858) 94, I mean the epidemic, now endemical, of View-hunting. **1870** J. CAMERON *Phases Thought* 149 The endemical disorder passing rapidly into epidemical.

en'demically, *adv.* [f. ENDEMICAL *a.* + -LY[2].] In an endemical manner; as an endemic.

1661 HICKERINGILL *Jamaica* 100 There is no Countrey Disease..endemically raging throughout the Isle. **1824-9** LANDOR *Imag. Conv.* (1846) I. 21 It..prevents the expansion of principles endemically noxious through incalculable ages. **1855** *Househ. Wds.* XII. 71 Goître prevails endemically.

endemicity (ɛndə'mɪsɪtɪ). [f. ENDEMIC *a.* + -ITY.] The quality or fact of being endemic.

1886 MYERS *Phant. Living* 298 The sporadic endemicity of certain traditions of folk lore. **1887** *Q. Rev.* Jan. 206 The limits of the area of endemicity.

†**en'demious,** *a. Obs. rare*[−1]. [f. Gr. ἐνδήμι-ος (see ENDEMIAL) + -OUS.] = ENDEMIC.

1684 tr. *Bonet's Merc. Compit.* I. 37 The Iapanois..in their endemious Cod-rupture.

endemism ('ɛndɪmɪz(ə)m). [f. ENDEM(IC + -ISM.] The character or quality of being endemic; *spec.* of a plant or animal species, the state or condition of being indigenous only in a specified area.

1886 *Encycl. Brit.* XX. 126/1 In their fauna also the Pyrenees present some striking instances of endemism. **1905** F. E. CLEMENTS *Res. Methods Ecol.* iv. 228 The primary causes of endemism are two, lack of migration and presence of barrier... Endemism is readily recognized by methods of distributional statistics, applied to areas limited by natural barriers to migration. **1931** *Nature* 7 Mar. 338 The endemism is tremendous, and the fauna has the aspect of great antiquity. **1951** *Jrnl. Ecol.* XXXIX. 88 One of the most striking features of chasmophyte communities is the restricted distribution of their constituents; endemism is the rule.

endemnify, -ity: see IND-.

†**ende'moniasm.** *Obs. rare*[−1]. [f. Gr. ἐν in + δαίμων, δαίμον-ος DEMON[1], on analogy of *enthusiasm*.] Inspiration by a demon.

1751 BYROM *Enthus.* Poet. Wks. 1773 II. 24 The variety of delusion with which a different spirit may then possess its votaries will centre..in endemoniasm.

enden, var. HENDEN, *Obs.*, hence.

endeni'zation. *Obs. rare.* Also indenization. [f. ENDENIZE *v.* + -ATION.] The process of making (a person) a denizen or citizen.

1579 J. STUBBES *Gaping Gulf* C j, They..are accompted members with us of thys body by endenization or enfraunchisement. **1643** PRYNNE *Open. Gt. Seale* 17 Secondly, of Indenization or Enfranchisment. **1685** EVELYN *Mem.* (1857) II. 258 There were also another pardon, and two indenizations. **1709** L. MILBOURNE *Melius Inq.* 8 Our law-books give us an account of endenization.

†**en'denize,** *v. Obs.* Also indenize. [altered form of ENDENIZEN, assimilated to verbs in *-ize*.]

1. *trans.* To make a denizen or citizen of; to naturalize, enfranchise. Also *transf.* and *fig.*

1598 FLORIO, *Patriare*, to endenize, or enfranchise into a countrie. **1603** DANIEL *Def. Rhime* (1717) 7 Every language hath her proper Number or Measure..which Custom..doth indenize and make natural. **1614** BARGRAVE (1615) *Serm.* B iij b, Dauid made hast to be indenized, and possessed of the Kingdome of Heauen. **1687** LUTTRELL *Brief Rel.* (1857) I. 404 Several French..are lately gott out of France..and the King hath indenized several of them.

2. To remove into another order of being; to change into a superhuman or supersensuous form, and so to 'spirit away,' to 'translate'. Hence, to metamorphose.

1610 HEALEY *St. Aug. Citie of God* 498 Æneas was not to be found; some said he was indenized. **1633** J. FISHER *True Trojans* II. iii, in Hazl. *Dodsley* XII. 172 The perverse and peevish Are next indeniz'd into wrinkled apes.

Hence **en'denized** *ppl. a.*, **en'denizing** *vbl. sb.*

1610 W. FOLKINGHAM *Art of Survey* I. vii. 14 What choice, selected, and endenized Hearbes, Plants, Fruits and Physicall Simples be implanted and bestowed. **1643** W. BURTON tr. *Alstedius' Beloved City* To Rdr. 2 The generall welcome and long entertainment, which the other learned workes of this same Authour have had in our Schooles..seemed to me not to deny this piece an endenizing, or freedome.

endenizen (ɛn'dɛnɪzən), *v.* Forms: 6 endenison, 7 en-, indenizon, indenizen, 6- endenizen. [f. EN-[1] + DENIZEN.]

1. *trans.* To make a denizen or citizen of; to naturalize, enfranchise. Also *transf.* and *fig.*

1592 G. HARVEY *New Letter* 6 Oh that the worthy Du Bartas were so endenisoned. *a* **1637** B. JONSON *Eng. Gram.* Words indenizened, i.e. derived from the Greek, and commonly used as English: as azure, zeal, zephyre, etc. **1652** URQUHART *Jewel* Wks. (1834) 195 Liberty to endenizon new citizens in the commonwealth of languages. **1708** PENN in *Pa. Hist. Soc. Mem.* X. 292, I shall get them either naturalized or endenizened by the Queen. **1823** LAMB *Elia, Detached Th. Bks.* 420 The books..have not endenizened themselves..in the national heart. **1830** GODWIN *Cloudesley* III. ii. 33, I would have endenisened myself in a country where I could make myself respected.

†**2.** *intr.* To become a denizen or citizen. *Obs.*

1598 FLORIO, *Inurbare*, to endenizen, to become..a citizen or a ciuill man.

endent, endenture: see INDENT, INDENTURE.

†**en'dently**, *a.* or *adv. Her. Obs. rare.* Also in 6 endentallye. [f. F. *endenté* indented + -LY.] = INDENTED.

1486 *Bk. St. Albans, Her.* B iij b, The fifthe quadrate is calde endently of iij diuerse weis. **1586** FERNE *Blaz. Gentrie* 207 The last of the quadrates finall was called endentallye.

endentus.

1567 *Trial Treasure* in Hazl. *Dodsley* III. 263 For of mans living here there is no point endentus, Therefore a little mirth is worth much sorrow, some say.

ender ('ɛndə(r)), *sb.* [f. END *v.* + -ER.] He who or that which ends.

a. He who or that which puts an end or termination to anything. Formerly also, He who brings a person to his end.

c **1386** CHAUCER *Knight's T.* 1918 Myn hertes lady, ender of my lyf! **1587** TURBERV. *Trag. T.* (1837) 193 The day thou sawste me last, Was ender of my life. **1612** ROWLANDS *More Knaues Yet* 27 When the ender of all mortals comes, Pale death. **1675** BAXTER *Cath. Theol.* II. 131 The maker but not the ender of Controversies. **1879** R. K. DOUGLAS *Confucianism* iii. 76 Destiny is called the giver and ender of life.

b. He that brings anything to completion.

1382 WYCLIF *Hebr.* xii. 2 Biholdinge into the maker of feith and ender [Vulg. *consummator*], Ihesu. **1413** LYDG. *Pilgr. Sowle* v. xiv. (1483) 108 The hooly ghoost that is the ender and the fulfiller.

†**'ender**, *a. Obs.* Forms: 3-4 endir, -ur, 5 endyr, 3-5 ender. Also 5 endurs, endris, enderes, endyrs, *Sc.* andyrs. [app. a. or f. ON. *endr* adv., 'formerly, else, again', corresp. to Goth. *andiz-(uh)* 'either' (conj.), and perh. to dial. Ger. *ender, ehnder* 'before, sooner'; the OTeut. type **andiz* is an adv. in the compar. deg. related to AND. It seems probable that *ender-day, ender-night*, were originally compounds of the adv., though a trace of adjectival flexion occurs in the ON. compound *endra-nær* 'at some other time'. The forms with final *s* are of obscure origin.]

Only in phrase, ***this ender day, night, year***, indicating a day, etc. recently past.

a **1300** *Cursor M.* 4561 Me thoght in drem, þis ender night, þat i com in a medu slight. *Ibid.* 5672 Wil þou sla me als þou has slain þis endir dai þe egypcian? *c* **1330** *Arth. & Merl.* 917 So Y slepe this ender-night Bi me lay a selcouthe wight. **1393** GOWER *Conf.* II. 381 This ender day as I gan fare. *c* **1400** *Thomas of Erceldoune* 25 (*Cambr. MS. c* **1450**) As I me went þis Andyrs day [*Thornton* Endres daye, *Lansd.* this thender day], ffast on my way makyng my mone. *c* **1440** *Ipomydon* 830 I am..the strange squyère, That servyd my lady this endris yere. *c* **1450** *Guy Warw.* (C.) 2828 He slewe my lordys sone þe emperowre This endurs day in a stowre. *a* **1450** *Le Morte Arth.* 1017 Thinke ye not on this endris day.

Hence **andersith** *adv.* [OE. *síð* time, occasion], previously, beforetime.

a **1300** *Cursor M.* 2110 Affrik..That andesith [*Fairf.* sum tide] was cald Libi. *Ibid.* 24268 (Gött.) Mi schepe er funden ..þat tint war andersith [*Edinb.* andersiþe].

†**'ender**, *v. Obs. rare*$^{-1}$. [? var. of ENTER; but cf. **ender* implied in next.] *intr.* To enter.

c **1325** *Sir Tristr.* 323 Ysett he haþ þe long asise And endred beþ þer inne.

†**'enderest**, *a. Obs. rare*$^{-1}$. [superlative of **ender*, INDER, inner.] Inmost.

1450-1530 *Myrr. our Ladye* 80 Prayse hym..in the enderest of youre harte for the benefytes.

endermatic (ɛndə'mætɪk), *a.* [f. Gr. ἐν + δερματ- stem of δέρμα skin + -IC.] = next.

In mod. Dicts.

endermic (ɛn'dɜːmɪk), *a.* [f. Gr. ἐν + δέρμ-α skin + -IC.] That acts on the skin, or by penetrating beneath the skin. ***endermic method*** (see quot. 1831).

1831 J. DAVIES *Man. Mat. Med.* 263 He administers it by the endermic method; that is, applied in the form of a salve on a part deprived of the epidermis. **1875** H. WOOD *Therap.* (1879) 21 The endermic method is very rarely employed.

endermical (ɛn'dɜːmɪkəl), *a.* [f. ENDERMIC *a.* + -AL[1].] = prec. Hence **en'dermically** *adv.*, by the endermic method.

1849-52 TODD *Cycl. Anat.* IV. 1260/1 Certain medicines ..applied endermically, may induce a similar condition. **1875** H. WOOD *Therap.* (1879) 164 Veratria is exceedingly irritating..producing when given hypodermically or endermically severe pain.

†**'endermost**, *a. Obs. rare*$^{-1}$. [Irregularly f. END *sb.*, after the analogy of HINDERMOST, etc.] Nearest to the end; furthest.

1803 S. PEGGE *Anecd. Eng. Lang.* 102 Our Cockney has analogy to warrant him in his compounds when he talks of the endermost house in a street.

enderon ('ɛndərən). *Phys.* [Irregularly f. Gr. ἐν in + δέρ-ος, δέρ-μα skin.] A term introduced by Prof. Huxley to denote the inner derm or true skin, or any homologous structure. Opposed to ECDERON. Hence **ende'ronic** *a.*

1859 HUXLEY in Todd *Cycl. Anat.* V. 476/1 The entire internal (deep) area of metamorphosis [I call] the Enderon. **1872** MIVART *Elem. Anat.* 237 The name Enderon is applied to the deeper or dermal layer wherever situate.

en déshabillé: see EN *prep.*

endesith: see END *sb.* 25.

endetted, obs. form of INDEBTED.

c **1386** CHAUCER *Chan. Yem. Prol. & T.* 181 And yet I am endetted so therby Of gold. **1561** tr. *Calvin's Foure Godlye Serm.* ii. sig. Dv, If we be so endetted and bounde to god.

endeure, obs. form of ENDURE.

†**en'dew**, *v. Obs.* In 6 endue. [f. EN-[1] + DEW *sb.*] *trans.* To moisten as with dew; to bedew.

c **1510** BARCLAY *Mirr. Good Mann.* (1570) A iij, Swete showres descending with droppes Christaline Endueth the dry ground.

endew, endeyne, obs. f. ENDUE, ENDEIGN.

†**'endfull**, *a. Obs. rare*$^{-1}$. [f. END *sb.* + FULL.] Full of ends or aims; ambitions, busy.

Hence ?**'endfully** *adv. rare*$^{-1}$. (But perhaps should be read as two words, *end fully.*)

1645 QUARLES *Sol. Recant.* v. 58 Bend Thy endfull heart to make heav'ns glory th' end. *c* **1400** *Apol. Loll.* 61 He is þe midyl, end, ordeyning, & gouerning, He is endfully consuming & keping.

†**endiablee**, *v. Obs. rare*$^{-1}$. [ad. F. *endiabler*, f. *en* in + *diable* devil.] *trans.* To put a devil into, possess as with a devil.

a **1734** NORTH *Exam.* (1740) 571 Such an one as might best endiablee the Rabble, and set them a bawling against Popery.

†**endi'ablement.** *Obs. rare*$^{-1}$. [as if a. Fr. **endiablement*, f. *endiabler*: see prec.] Diabolical possession.

a **1734** NORTH *Exam.* III. viii. ¶ 35 (1740) 608 There was a terrible Rage of Faces made at him [Sir John Moor], as if an Endiablement had possessed them all.

endiadem, endiaper: see EN- *prefix*[1].

endict, endight, etc., obs. ff. INDICT, INDITE.

ending ('ɛndɪŋ), *vbl. sb.* [f. END *v.*[1] + -ING[1].]

1. The action of the verb END[1]: termination, conclusion, completion; †death, etc.

c **1000** *Ags. Gosp.* Matt. xiii. 39 Soðlice þæt rip is woruldе endung. *c* **1175** *Lamb. Hom.* 71 God..ȝefe us..riht scrift et ure endunge. *c* **1330** R. BRUNNE *Chron.* (1810) 10 Whan þe Kyng Kynwolf had don his endyng. **1340** HAMPOLE *Pr. Consc.* 34 Swa sal he [God] mak endyng Of alle thing. **1375** BARBOUR *Bruce* III. 276 To bryng All thair empress to gud endying. *c* **1420** *Chron. Vilod.* 1 And ȝeve me grace to breng to godde heyndynge. *c* **1485** *Digby Myst.* (1882) I. 324, I pray god bryng hym to an ille endyng. **1562** *Act 5 Eliz.* c. 15 §1 (Ruffhead), The Expiration and Ending of the Statute. **1594** HOOKER *Eccl. Pol.* I. x. (1611) 33 For the ending of strifes touching matters of Christian beleefe. **1629** MILTON *Nativity* 239 Time is our tedious song should here have ending. **1655** FULLER *Hist. Camb.* (1840) 139 Her death.. did not finally obstruct the ending of St. John's College. **1766** ENTICK *London* IV. 34 The terms, or times for pleading and ending of causes in the civil courts. **1818** CRUISE *Digest* (ed. 2) IV. 72 Every lease must contain a sufficient degree of certainty, as to its beginning, continuance, and ending. **1848** CLOUGH *Bothie* I The sports were now at the ending. **1868** MORRIS *Earthly Par.* (1870) II. III. 400 A fair ending crowned a troublous day.

2. The concluding part of a piece of work, a book, etc.; formerly also, of a space of time.

c **1400** *Rom. Rose* 2163 The book is good at the eendyng. **1635** PAGITT *Christianogr.* III. (1636) 88 Although we live in the latter ending of the world. **1875** JOWETT *Plato* (ed. 2) I. 114 The Dialogue fails in unity, and has not a proper beginning, middle, and ending.

3. The last part or termination of an organic structure: an extremity.

1884 BOWER & SCOTT *De Bary's Phaner. & Ferns* 232 With blind endings only in the growing-points and at the ends of peripheral branches.

4. The concluding part of a word, of a metrical line, piece of music, etc.; also, an inflexional or formative suffix.

1599 SHAKS. *Much Ado* v. ii. 40, I can find out no rhyme to lady but baby..for scorn, horn..for school, fool..verie ominous endings. **1814** L. HUNT *Feast Poets* (1815) 7 But volumes of endings, lugg'd in as you need 'em, Of *hearts* and *imparts*. **1857** HELMORE *Psalter Noted* Pref. viii, Each of the Tones..has a variety of endings. **1864** *Reader*, 24 Sept. 375 Replacing all the endings of its oblique cases by their prepositional value. **1875** JOWETT *Plato* (ed. 2) I. Introd. 13 The want of case endings.

5. *attrib.*; *esp.* †**ending-day**, the day of death; †**ending-post**, the winning-post; **ending-stone** (*U.S.*), a particular kind of millstone (see quots.).

.. *Chart. Thurkytel* in *Cod. Dipl.* IV. 294 Bute he it ðe deppere bete er his ending day. *c* **1320** *Sir Tristr.* 1672 Her loue miȝt no man tvin Til her endingday. **1523** LD. BERNERS *Froiss.* I. cccxxxii. 520 At last came his endyng day. **1760** R. HEBER *Horse Matches* ix. 29 As she or they come in by the ending-post each heat. **1791** 'G. GAMBADO' *Acad. Horsem.* xv. (1809) 126 One was seen to arrive at the ending Post without his bridle. **1883** E. INGERSOLL in *Harper's Mag.* June 76/1 Now the ending-stones are encountered, which break the germinal point off each grain.

ending ('ɛndɪŋ), *ppl. a.* [f. END *v.*[1] + -ING[2].]

1. That ends, finishes, or puts an end to; final.

a **1300** *Cursor M.* 25863 (Cott.) To ending fir sal þou be send. **1581** SIDNEY *Apol. Poetrie* (Arb.) 30 The ending end of all earthly learning, being vertuous action. **1826** E. IRVING, *Babylon* II. vii. 228 This ending act of judgment and desolation may begin.

†**2.** In *intr.* sense: Dying, near one's end. *Obs.*

1597 SHAKS. *2 Hen. IV*, IV. v. 80 This bitter taste Yeeld his engrossements To the ending Father.

Hence †**'endingly**, *adv. Obs.*

1611 COTGR., *Periodiquement*, endingly, concludingly, or towards the conclusion.

'endingless, *a.* [f. ENDING *vbl. sb.* + -LESS.] Without ending.

1946 *Language* XXII. II. 160 Here one may question the analysis of endingless forms in attributive positions as uninflected variants of overtly marked forms. **1957** R. W. ZANDVOORT *Handbk. Eng. Gram.* IV. 188 Adjectives and adverbs of *one syllable* usually take *-er* and *-est*... This also applies to the endingless adverbs discussed in 953: *He could not speak any plainer.*

endip, obs. var. INDIP.

endirke(n, obs. form of ENDARK.

en'distance, *v. Theatr.* and *Cinematogr.* [f. EN-[1] + DISTANCE *sb.* 3.] *trans.* To produce an effect of 'alienation' (sense 1 d) in an audience; to 'distance' (cf. sense 1 a). So **en'distancement**; **en'distancing** *vbl. sb.* (*attrib.*).

1961 *Times* 23 May 15/1 The experiment in 'endistancement' involved in putting most of the characters in..masks. **1961** *Times Lit. Suppl.* 30 June 400/2 There are few if any exponents of 'the new drama' who have not at some stage leavened realism with..the exploitation of 'endistancing' techniques..according to the dictates of Brecht's heroic theatre. *Ibid.* 400/3 Here we are 'endistanced' from the action with a vengeance. **1963** *Times* 20 Apr. 9/3 But the idea of screens so big that they filled the audience's wide field of vision, or as much as possible, and left no possibility of 'endistancement', has continued to haunt the cinema industry.

enditch: see EN- *pref.*[1] 3.

endite ('ɛndaɪt), *sb. Zool.* [f. Gr. ἔνδ-ον within + -ITE[1].] An appendage on the inner side of a limb of a crustacean.

1881 E. R. LANKESTER in *Q. Jrnl. Microsc. Sci.* XXI. 348 The median portion may be spoken of as the axis or corm, whilst the processes may be called 'phyllites' or 'apophyses', those ranged along the ventral or neural border of the corm being called 'endites', and those given off from the dorsal border being called 'exites'. **1888** ROLLESTON & JACKSON *Forms Anim. Life* 532 The Phyllopod type of appendage,.. with its branchia and external respiratory plate, and its series of internal lobes or endites. **1902** *Encycl. Brit.* XXV. 695/2 It is by the specialization of two 'endites' that the endopodite and exopodite of higher Crustacea are formed. *Ibid.* 696/1 The conversion of the Arthropod's limb into a jaw..is effected by the development of an endite near its base into a hard..gnathobase. **1965** PARKER & HASWELL *Text-bk. Zool.* (ed. 6) I. VIII. 390 The proximal endite..is small, and bears strong spines.

endite, etc., obs. f. of INDICT, INDITE, etc.

endive ('ɛndɪv). Forms: 5-6 endyve, (5 endywe), 6-7 endiue, 6- endive. [a. Fr. *endive* = Pr., Sp. and It. *endivia*:—late L. **intybea* adj. fem. f. *intibus* (*intubus, intybus, -um*). A late Gr. ἔντυβον (10th c.) is prob. ad. L.] The name of two species of Chicory (*Cichorium*, N.O. *Compositæ*).

a. *C. Intybus*, now called Wild Endive, Succory, or Chicory, indigenous in Europe, and common in a wild state in many parts of England. **b.** In mod. use chiefly applied to *C. Endivia*, alleged by some writers to have been imported into Europe from China in the 16th c. Of this there are two varieties, the Batavian or broad-leaved, formerly called also Scariole, and that with a curled or frizzled leaf, which is commonly blanched for use as salad, etc.

Both species have pale blue flowers; the 'blue endive' of the poets is *C. Intybus*.

c **1440** *Promp. Parv.* 140 Endyve, herbe, *endivia*. **1533** ELYOT *Cast. Helthe* (1541) 28 b, Endyve and Scariole be moche like in their operation to Cykorie. **1597** GERARD *Herbal* II. xxvii. §4 Curled Endive hath leaues not vnlike to those of the curled or Cabbage Lettuce. **1655** CULPEPPER *Riverius* I. I. 21 But in Summer we can allow a moderate use of Herbs..as Endive, Succory, Sorrel. **1710** PHILIPS *Pastorals* iv. 8 Daisies white and Endive blue. **1720** GAY *Poems* (1745) I. 113 Upon her grave the rosemary they threw The daisy, butter-flower and endive blue. **1832** *Veg. Subst. Food* 302 Endive..cultivated, if not found wild, in China and Japan. **1882** *Garden* 28 Jan. 62/3 Endive, both curled and Batavian, must be got into cold frames and blanched as required for use.

endizen: see EN- *pref.*[1] 3.

endleofan, -leofeða, -lyfta, -leofte, -left, obs. forms of ELEVEN, ELEVENTH.

c **1175** *Lamb. Hom.* 117 Endleofte unþeau is folc beo butan steore. *c* **1300** *K. Alis.* 57 Genner was the endleft [*misprinted* endlest] Feverel the tweolthe.

endless ('ɛndlɪs), *a.* and *adv.* [OE. *ęndeléas*, f. *ęnde*, END *sb.*: see -LESS.] Having no end.

1. Having no end or limit of duration; unending, eternal.

c **888** K. ÆLFRED *Boeth.* xxxviii. §3 þa earmþa beoþ endelease þe ece bioþ. *c* **1175** *Lamb. Hom.* 77 Hit scal king bon on þet endelese kineriche. *a* **1225** *Ancr. R.* 146 þi mede

þet were endeleas ȝif þi god dede were iholen. **1297** R. GLOUC. (1724) 152 'Alas!' he seyde, 'þe deolful harm, þat ys endeless!' *a* **1340** HAMPOLE *Psalter* lxxv. 4 Lightyn-and þou wondirfully fra hilles endles [Vulg. *a montibus æternis*]. **1393** GOWER *Conf.* II. 70 Whos name shall be endeles For the merveiles which he wrought. **1450–1530** *Myrr. our Ladye* 321 And I byleue endelesse lyfe. **1593** SHAKS. *Rich. II*, I. iii. 222 My.. time-bewasted light Shall be extinct with age, and endlesse night. **1651** HOBBES *Leviath.* IV. xlvi. 374 Eternity .. an Endlesse Succession of Time. **1711** STEELE *Spect.* No. 75 ¶8 Death.. is a short Night followed by an endless Day. **1827** POLLOK *Course T.* v, Heard the burning of the endless flames. **1850** TENNYSON *In Mem.* XLVII. iii, And we shall sit at endless feast.

b. *hyperbolically* for: Interminable; perpetual, incessant, constant.

c **888** K. ÆLFRED *Boeth.* xxxvi. §1 þat.. is endeleas wundor. **1577** B. GOOGE *Heresbach's Husb.* II. (1586) 52 b, To speake of all sortes of hearbes and flowers, were an endlesse labor. **1594** HOOKER *Eccl. Pol.* I. x. (1611) 26 Strife and troubles would be endlesse. **1633** P. FLETCHER *Psalm* 63 There we laid, asteeping Our eyes in endless weeping. **1655–60** STANLEY *Hist. Philos.* (1701) 103/1 How long a night is this, how endless! **1751** JOHNSON *Rambler* No. 141 ¶10 It were endless to recount the shifts to which I have been reduced. **1796** BURKE *Regic. Peace* Wks. 1842 II. 325 All the multiplied, endless, nameless iniquities. **1820** KEATS *St. Agnes* xxi, The lover's endless minutes slowly pass'd. **1847** LEWES *Hist. Philos.* (1867) I. 213 Hence the endless repetitions, divisions, and illustrations of positions almost self-evident. **1872** E. PEACOCK *Mabel Heron* I. i. 4 Pouring out endless platitudes.

2. Of things extended in space: Boundless, infinite; now chiefly with reference to length. Formerly also of depth: Bottomless. Often *hyperbolical*.

1413 LYDG. *Pilgr. Sowle* v. i. (1859) 72 The grete heuen.. is nought endeles, ne infynyte. **1432–50** tr. *Higden* (Rolls) I. 331 In þe west side he haþ þe endeles occean. **1594** R. SOUTHWELL in *Shaks. C. Praise* 14 How endlesse is your labyrinth of blisse. **1633** P. FLETCHER *Elisa* I. xxiv, Els had the endlesse pit too quickly caught me. **1647** COWLEY *Mistress* iv. (1669) 42 By Thee the one does changing Nature through Her endless Labyrinths pursue. **1856** KANE *Arct. Expl.* II. xx. 199 Weary of the endless waste of ice to seaward. **1864** MRS. CARLYLE *Lett.* III. 238 An old manor house, with endless passages. **1873** BLACK *Pr. Thule* viii. 129 The endless miles of moor.

3. Of immaterial things, quality, number, etc.: Unbounded, limitless, infinite.

138. WYCLIF *Sel. Wks.* III. 509 þe reule ȝoven of Crist of his endeles wisdom and his endeles charitee to mankinde. **1450–1530** *Myrr. our Ladye* 4 Of the blessyd endeles Trinite. **1595** SHAKS. *John* v. vi. 12 Thou, and endles night, Haue done me shame. *a* **1658** R. HARRIS in Spurgeon *Treas. Dav.* Ps. cxxxvi. 1 Mercy.. is negatively endless.. because unboundable for being. **1776** ADAM SMITH *W.N.* I. I. xi. 175 For the amusement of those desires which cannot be gratified, but which seem altogether endless. **1863** E. NEALE *Anal. Th. & Nat.* 53 A phase in itself endless, as Kant calls it, since no limit can be put to the possible modifications of quality. **1875** JOWETT *Plato* (ed. 2) III. 161 The individual man has an endless value in the sight of God.

†**b.** quasi-*sb.* (Arithmetical) infinity. *Obs.*

1398 TREVISA *Barth. De P.R.* XIX. cxxvi. (1495) 926 The nombre lineall begynnyth fro one and is wryte arowe and lyne vnto endlesse.

4. Having no definite extremity or terminal point of length. †**a.** ***endless gut***: the colon (perhaps including the rectum). *Obs.*

c **1450** *Voc.* in Wr.-Wülcker 574 *Colon*, the endelez gutte. *Ibid.* 603 *Podex*, the endeles gut.

b. *Mech.* ***endless band, -cable, -chain, -strap***: one whose ends are joined for the purpose of continuous action over wheels, etc. ***endless knife, saw***: a continuous band of steel with either a sharp, or a toothed edge for a similar purpose. ***endless screw***: a short length of screw revolving on an axis, by which continuous motion is imparted to a toothed wheel.

1816 J. SMITH *Panorama Sc. & Art* I 98 A rapid motion is communicated.. by means of an endless strap from a large fly wheel. **1822** IMISON *Sc. & Art* (ed. Webster) I. 58 Screws with sharp threads, have more friction than those with square threads; and endless screws have more than either. **1833** HOLLAND *Manuf. Metal* II. 144 (Cabinet Cycl.) Projecting points.. acting in the links of an endless chain. **1854** J. HOGG *Microsc.* I. ii. (1867) 142 By a slight variation in their positions produced by an endless-screw motion. **1884** *Health Exhib. Catal.* 113/1 One Brazing Machine for endless knives. **1885** *Law Times* LXXX. 101/1 The cloth.. being caught in an endless leathern band running over a pulley on the shaft. **1887** *Daily News* 8 Feb. 6/3 The cars will be worked on the successful endless-cable principle.

†**5.** ? Fruitless, profitless. *Obs.* $rare^{-1}$.

a **1625** FLETCHER *Lover's Pilgr.* II. iii, All loves are endlesse.

†**B.** *adv.* **a.** Infinitely, in an infinite degree. **b.** For an infinite period, for ever. *Obs.*

c **1325** *E.E. Allit. P.* A. 737 Hit [the pearl] is endelez rounde & blyþe of mode. *c* **1340** *Cursor M.* 23326 (Trin.) þei haue lost hit endeles. **138.** WYCLIF *Eng. Wks.* (1880) 71 Endeles mercyful & goode lord, helpe þi pore wrecchide prestis. **1398** TREVISA *Barth. De P.R.* VIII. i. (1495) 294 Men saye that a geaunt is endlesse moche. *c* **1400** *Destr. Troy* 8502 Exiled for euermore endles to sorow.

Hence †'**endlesshede** [see -HEAD], the quality or condition of being endless; eternal existence.

a **1340** HAMPOLE *Cant. Psalter* 509 Fra þe wayes of his endleshede.

endlessly ('ɛndlɪslɪ), *adv.* [f. prec. + -LY^{2}.] In an endless manner; everlastingly, for ever; perpetually, unceasingly.

c **1400** *Apol. Loll.* 55 To be quicknid ȝendlesly. *c* **1450** LONELICH *Grail* xlix. 64 For they ben Goddis endelesly. **1450–1530** *Myrr. Our Ladye* 4 Endelesly.. presente in the syghte of hys Godly forknowynge. **1509** FISHER *Fun. Serm. C'tess Richmond* (1708) 36 To whome be laude and honoure endlessly. **1616** LANE *Sqr. Tale* xi. 208 Curious galleries.. endlesselie roundinge. **1865** PUSEY *Truth Eng. Ch.* 41 Lest they should endlessly lose Him. **1878** HUXLEY *Physiogr.* Pref., The multiform and endlessly shifting phenomena of nature.

endlessness ('ɛndlɪsnɪs). [f. as prec. + -NESS.]

1. The quality of being endless.

1340 HAMPOLE *Pr. Consc.* 8129 Ffor if endlesnes any end moght hald, þan war it endlesnes unproperly cald. **1580** HOLLYBAND *Treas. Fr. Tong, Infinité*, endlesnesse. **1601** DEACON & WALKER *Spirits & Divels* 47 There would be a progresse in endlesnesse. *a* **1656** HALES *Gold. Rem.* (1688) 382 This dispute for its endlessness was like the mathematical line. **1858** ROBERTSON *Lect.* ii. 181 Bewildering the eye with the feeling of endlessness.

2. *concr.* Something that has no end.

a. An infinite or everlasting existence. **b.** Something indefinitely extended or lengthened; an infinite space, an interminable length.

a **1631** DONNE *Serm.* clvii. VI. 258 God hath provided us an Endlessness in the world to come. **1820** L. HUNT *Indicator* No. 26 (1822) I. 205 Any thing in the starry endlessness of existence. **1864** LOWELL *Fireside Trav.* 6 Fancy decorates him with an endlessness of airy pigtail.

endlichite ('ɛndlɪxaɪt, 'ɛndlɪkaɪt). *Min.* [f. the name of F. M. *Endlich*, Amer. mining engineer + -ITE^{1}.] An arsenio-vanadate of lead.

1885 GENTH & VOM RATH in *Proc. Amer. Phil. Soc.* XXII. 367 Endlichite, or Vanadium-Mimetite, a new species... The name has been suggested by Mr. N. H. Muhlenberg in honor of Dr. F. M. Endlich, Superintendent of the Sierra Mines at Lake Valley [New Mexico]. **1944** C. PALACHE et al. *Dana's Syst. Min.* II. 897 Endlichite... Contains As in substitution for V, with As:V = 1:1 in the material from Hillsboro, New Mexico.

endlong ('ɛndlɒŋ), *prep.*, *adv.*, and *a.* Forms: 3 **andelong**, 3–4 **endelong**, (4 **endelyng**), 4– **endlong**, 4– *north. dial.* **endlang**. [The early southern ME. *endelong*, f. *ende* END *sb.* + LONG, seems to have been substituted by popular etymology for the preposition *andlang* (see ALONG *prep.*), the first element of this having ceased to be intelligible, while the new compound yielded an identical sense (cf. *on end*, *end on*, ENDAWAY). In purely southern English *endelong* did not long survive, its place being taken by ALONG, the reduced form of the earlier *andlang*. But from 14th c. onwards *endlang*, *endlong* appear (as *prep.* and *adv.*) in northern and midland dialects, where they may be f. ON. *endelangr*, *endlangr* adj. (f. *ende-r* END + *langr* LONG), synonymous with OE. *andlang* adj. 'the whole length of'. In our quots. the adjectival use of *endlong* first occurs in a passage of Caxton's ed. of Trevisa's Higden, where it is substituted for *evelong* (= AVELONGE, oblong), used by Trevisa himself. Subsequently (in 17th c.) the adv. assumed the sense 'on end', 'end foremost or downwards', in accordance with the analogy of words like *headlong*, *sidelong*, where *-long* is a perversion of the OE. suffix *-lunga*. This use still occasionally appears in standard Eng.; the other uses are now peculiar to *Sc.* and northern dialects, except as deliberate archaisms.

Prof. Sievers (*Festgaben für Böhtlingk* 1888) considers that the second element in OE. *andlang* is not identical with LONG *a.*, but is directly from the OTeut. vb. **ling-an, lang, lung-ano-* to reach, extend. The ON. *endlanger*, Eng. *endlong*, he regards as altered from *andlangr*, OE. *andlang* by popular etymology.]

A. *prep.* From end to end of; through or over the length of (as opposed to across), following the line of, onwards by the side of; along. Chiefly of *place*, rarely of *time*.

a **1225** *Juliana* 30 Ant healden on hire heauet þat hit urne endelong hire leofliche bodi. *a* **1225** *St. Marher.* 10 Ant droh þa endelong hire ant þwertouer þrefter þe derewurðe taken. **1375** BARBOUR *Bruce* III. 414 Endlang the louchhis syd.. besyly thai socht. *c* **1386** CHAUCER *Sqr's T.* 408 The rede blood Ran endelong [*v.r.* endelyng] the tree. *c* **1450** *Cookery Bk.* 97 Bynde the threde with the frute A-bought a rownde spete, endelonge þe spete. **1470–85** MALORY *Arthur* X. lxiv, Sir Helyus.. drofe sir Palomydes ouerthwart and endlonge alle the feld. **1508–** DUNBAR *Gold. Targe* xv, Ladyes to dance full sobirly assayit.. Endlang the lusty rywir. *a* **1547** EARL SURREY *Aeneid* IV. 328 Like to the foule, that endlong costes and strondes.. flies sweping by the sea. **1600** HOLLAND *Livy* 921 (R.) The singular discipline and order of that nation in old time, was going downward and endlong many yeeres and ages alredie. *a* **1758** RAMSAY *Poet. Wks.* (1844) 86 Lay them [thir tangs] en'lang his pow or shin.

B. *adv.*

†**1.** Extended at full length; at one's whole length; horizontally. *Obs.* exc. *north. dial.*

1393 GOWER *Conf.* II. 233 And everything in his degre endelong upon a bourde he laide. *c* **1430** LYDG. *Bochas* VII. ix. (1554) 175 a, Beaten he was.. Whipped, scourged, endlong, and vpright. **1864** ATKINSON *Whitby Gloss.*, I tummell'd end lang.

2. From end to end, lengthwise, longitudinally, as distinguished from *crosswise* or *athwart*. *arch.* exc. *north. dial.*

c **1300** *Havelok* 2822 Him to binden faste Vpon an asse.. Andelong, nouht ouerthwert. *c* **1386** CHAUCER *Knt's T.* 1133 Dores.. I-clenched overthward and endelong With iren tough. **1470–85** MALORY *Arthur* X. lxxxvi. (1816) 153 Thurghoute alle this reame, endlonge and ouerthwart. **1574** HYLL *Planting* 78 Of eyther [vine] pare away halfe endlong upon the pith. **1594** BLUNDEVIL *Exerc.* III. II. vi. (ed. 7) 382 Foure barley kernels couched close together side by side, and not endlong, are said to make a finger breadth. **1825** SCOTT *Talism.* vii, Galloping in full career.. about and around, crossways and endlong. **1886** BURTON *Arab. Nts.* (abr. ed.) I. 162 The street had been pulled down endlong.

†**3.** Of motion in a longitudinal direction: Right along, straight on, straight through. *Obs.* exc. *north. dial.*

1375 BARBOUR *Bruce* XVI. 548 Endlang furth held thai thar vay. **1470–85** MALORY *Arthur* X. lxviii. These four knyghtes came into the feld endlonge and thurgh. **1517** TORKINGTON *Pilgr.* (1884) 47 An howge.. Serpent.. ranne endlong vpon the ryght Syde of the Chirche wall. **1700** DRYDEN *Pal. & Arc.* III. 691 Spurring at full speed, ran endlong on. **1854** H. MILLER *Sch. & Schm.* ix. (1857) 186 He was driven endlong against the wall of the kiln.

b. Of speech: Continuously.

1815 SCOTT *Guy M.* xi, He never could preach five words of a sermon endlang.

4. On end, perpendicularly, vertically.

1600 HOLLAND *Livy* III. xxviii. 107 They.. set two of them [speares] pitched in the ground endlong, and the third overthwart. **1656** HEYLIN *Surv. France* 148 They stood not up endlong but lay one upon the other. **1725** POPE *Odyss.* x. 667 Full endlong from the roof the sleeper fell, And snap'd the spinal joint.

C. *adj.*

†**1.** Extended lengthwise, oblong. *Obs.*

1480 CAXTON *Trevisa's Higden* (Rolls) II. 55 Britayne is endlong [**1387** TREVISA eve longe] and larger in the myddel than in thendes. **1541** R. COPLAND *Guydon's Quest. Chirurg.*, Of what shape is the stomacke?.. It is rounde endlong.

2. (Adjectival use of B. 4; cf. *headlong* adj.) Set on end, perpendicular. *rare.*

1716 M. DAVIES *Ath. Brit.* II. 203 His Grace's Wife being in that end-long Posture [viz., head downwards in a chest] was in jeopardy to break her neck. **1840** BROWNING *Sordello* III. 347 Giant rushes.. grew Like demons' endlong tresses.

†'**endlonges, -gs**, *adv.* and *prep.* *Obs.* or *dial.* [f. ENDLONG with adverbial genitive ending, as in *alway*(*s*, *betime*(*s*, etc.] = ENDLONG, q.v.

A. *adv.*

1473 WARKW. *Chron.* 22 It flammed Endlonges fro the Est to the Weste. **1593** NASHE *Christ's T.* (1613) 63 Many goodly streets end-longs to the very earth they encindred.

B. *prep.*

c **1380** *Sir Ferumb.* 498 Endelonges is side þat blod him ran. **1515** in Pitcairn *Crim. Trials* I. 262* To pass endlangis the Cost.

†'**endly**, *a.* and *adv.* *Obs.* Also 5 **eendli**, **endely(e**, **endlyche**. [f. END *sb.* + -LY$^{1, 2}$.]

A. *adj.* **a.** Conclusive, final. **b.** Extreme, excessive.

1436 *Pol. Poems* (1859) II. 201 Ane endely processe of pease by auctorite. *c* **1475** *Partenay* 4011 It goth vnto decline, Rather or later to an endly fine. **1494** FABYAN VII. 558 Toke therwith such an endelye fere, that he fell therwith dystraught.

B. *adv.* **a.** At last, finally. **b.** Extremely, very.

c **1410** LOVE *Bonavent. Mirr.* iii. (Gibbs MS.) Sche was endlyche þorgh plente of charyte knytte to hire blessed sone. *c* **1440** *Generydes* 4844 The whiche was endly fayre. *c* **1449** PECOCK *Repr.* IV. vii. 462 And so fynali and eendli y mai conclude.

'**end-man.** Also **end man.** [f. END *sb.* + MAN *sb.*^{1}] A man at an end of a line or row; *U.S.* the man at either extremity of the semi-circle of performers in a nigger-minstrel entertainment, a corner-man.

1865 SALA *Diary* II. 395 He propounded conundrums to his brother 'end man' who played the banjo. **1884** *Sat. Rev.* 7 June 740/1 At the ends are Bones and Tambo, the 'end-men'. **1886** *Harper's Mag.* Nov. 837/1 Binns.. sang.. appearing to Roxy as he sang as delightful a personage as an end man. **1889** *Cent. Dict.* s.v., In the early days of negro minstrelsy each troupe had two end-men... The larger troupes have since had two, and sometimes four, of each class of end-men. **1909** T. C. DE LEON *Beaux, Belles & Brains of 60's* xxxi. 356 Emmett was the star of Birch and Backus, as endman. **1956** M. STEARNS *Story of Jazz* (1957) xi. 116 The usual half circle of players with the end-men and interlocutor cracking jokes and doing their various specialties.

endmete, var. of ENDEMETE. *Obs.*

'**endmost**, *a.* *rare.* [f. END *sb.* on analogy of *hindmost*; Bosw.-Toller cites OE. *endemǽst* from Dicts.] Nearest to the end, furthest, most distant.

1775 in ASH. **1819** in *Pantologia*. **1879** BROWNING *Ivan Ivanov.* 196 And see, a rose-light dyes The endmost snow.

endo- ('ɛndəʊ; before two unstressed syllables ɛn'dɒ), *prefix* (before a vowel sometimes reduced to *end-*), employed as comb. form of Gr. ἔνδον within, in many compounds of mod. formation, as ˌ**endarte'rectomy** (also (now *rare*) **-arte'riec-**) *Surg.*, an operation to remove part of

the diseased inner lining of an artery, as when it is atheromatous; cf. *thromboendarter(i)ectomy* s.v. THROMBO-. ˌ**endarteˈritis, ˈendo-arteˈritis** [see ARTERITIS], *Pathol.*, inflammation of the inner coat of an artery; hence ˌ**endarteˈritic** *a.*, relating to or affected with endarteritis (*Cent. Dict.* Suppl., 1909). ˌ**endobiˈotic** *a. Bot.* (see quot.). ˈ**endoblast** *Biol.* = HYPOBLAST 2; = *entoblast* (b). **endoˈbronchial** *a.*, situated or occurring within a bronchus. ˌ**endoˈcannibalism** [ad. G. *endokannibalismus* (R. S. Steinmetz 1896, in *Wein. Anthrop. Ges. Mitth.* XXVI. 1)], the practice of eating parents and relatives. ˌ**endocerviˈcitis** *Path.*, inflammation of the lining of the canal of the cervix uteri. **endoˈchondral** *a. Anat.*, situated or occurring within the substance of a cartilage. ˈ**endochone** *Zool.*, the innermost structure of a chone. ˌ**endoˈchorion,** *Anat.* [see CHORION], the inner layer of the chorion or membrane that encloses the fœtus. ˈ**endochrome** (see quot.). **endoˈclinal** *a. Geol.*, of the nature of an ˈ**endocline**, a fan-fold of anticlinal type. ˌ**endocorˈpuscular** *a. Path.*, within a corpuscle. ˈ**endocrane** [Gr. κράνιον skull; also in Lat. form *endoˈcranium*], the inner surface of the skull. **endoˈcranial** *a.*, of or pertaining to the endocranium (Cent. Dict., 1889). **endoˈcyclic** *a.*, *Chem.* situated within the ring. ˈ**endocyst** (see quots., also CYST and ECTOCYST). **endocyˈtosis** *Biol.*, the taking in of matter by a living cell. ˌ**endodynamoˈmorphic** *a.* (see quot. 1930). **endoˈgastric** *a. Zool.*, situated within the abdomen. ˈ**endognath** *Zool.*, the inner branch of the oral appendages of a crustacean. **endoˈgnathal** *a.*, *Zool.* [Gr. γνάθ-ος jaw + -AL[1]], that is placed within the jaw; ***endognathal palp***, a palpiform appendage in certain Crustacea. ˌ**endolaˈryngeal** *a.* [cf. LARYNGEAL], pertaining to the interior of the larynx; hence ˌ**endolaˈryngeally** *adv.* ˈ**endolith** [Gr. λίθος stone], one of a number of coloured designs on slabs of marble or ivory, sawn from a block on the surface of which chemically prepared colour has been laid, that permeates the material; hence **endoˈlithic** *a.* ˈ**endolymph,** *Anat.* [see LYMPH], the fluid contained in the membranous labyrinth of the ear. **endoˈmetrial** *a.*, pertaining to the endometrium. ˌ**endometriˈoma** [*endometri(um* + -OMA], a tumour containing endometrial tissue; a localized swelling due to an area of endometriosis. ˌ**endometriˈosis** *Path.*, a condition resulting from the development of endometrial tissue in an abnormal, esp. extra-uterine, situation; so ˌ**endometriˈotic** *a.* ˌ**endomeˈtritis,** *Pathol.* [Gr. μήτρα womb + -ITIS (= Gr. -ῖτις)], inflammation of the lining membrane of the womb. **endoˈmetrium** *Anat.*, the mucous membrane lining the uterus. **enˈdometry,** *Med.* [Gr. -μετρια; see -METRY], the measurement of an internal part. ˌ**endomiˈtosis** *Biol.* [ad. G. *endomitose* (L. Geitler 1939, in *Chromosoma* I. 7)], division of chromosomes in a nucleus without subsequent division of the nucleus; hence ˌ**endomiˈtotic** *a.*, pertaining to or involving endomitosis. **endoˈnormative** *a. Linguistics*, of language standardization: drawing on native models of usage rather than on the standards for the language that are already established in other countries; contr. with *exonormative* adj. s.v. EXO-. **endoˈnuclease** *Biochem.*, any enzyme that cleaves a polynucleotide chain by separating nucleotides other than the two end ones; cf. *exonuclease* s.v. EXO-. **endoˈparasite,** *Zool.*, an animal that lives and finds nourishment in the internal organs of another; hence ˌ**endoparaˈsitic** *a.* **endoˈpeptidase** *Biochem.*, any of a group of proteolytic enzymes which split peptide bonds other than the terminal ones. ˌ**endophleˈbitis,** *Pathol.* [Gr. φλέψ, φλεβός vein + -ITIS (a. Gr. -ῖτις)], inflammation of the lining membrane of a vein. ˈ**endophragm** [Gr. φράγμα partition], (*a*) *Bot.* a transverse diaphragm or septum; (*b*) *Zool.* the chitinous covering of the neural canal in the thorax of some Crustacea; hence **endoˈphragmal** *a.* **endoˈphyllous** *a. Bot.* [Gr. φύλλον leaf + -OUS] (see quot.). ˈ**endophyte,** *Bot.* [Gr. φυτόν plant], †(*a*) (see quot. 1835); (*b*) a plant growing inside another, an internal fungus. **endoˈphytic** *a. Bot.*, of, pertaining to, or of the nature of an endophyte (also **enˈdophytous** *a.*). ˈ**endoplasm** *Biol.* [Gr. πλάσμα something moulded or formed], the inner soft layer of the cytoplasm; hence **endoˈplasmic** *a.*, of, pertaining to, or consisting of endoplasm (Cent. Dict., 1889). ˈ**endoplast** [Gr. πλαστός formed], 'a large protoplasmic corpuscle in the external parenchyma of the body of the Infusoria' (*Syd. Soc. Lex.*); hence **endoˈplastic** *a.* **endoˈplastule** [see -ULE], 'a bright rod-like mass lying in the interior or on the outside of the endoplast of Protozoa; supposed to be a male sexual organ' (*Syd. Soc. Lex.*). **endoˈpleura,** *Bot.* [Gr. πλευρά side], the internal covering of a seed; hence **endoˈpleurite,** *Zool.* [see prec.], the portion of the apodeme of the thorax in Crustacea, which arises from the interepimeral membrane connecting each pair of somites. ˈ**endopod** = ENDOPODITE. **enˈdopodite** [Gr. πούς ποδ-ός foot + -ITE], 'the innermost of the two processes appended to the basal process of the hinder limbs of some of the Crustacea' (*Syd. Soc. Lex.*). ˌ**endopoˈditic** *a.*, of or pertaining to the endopodite. **endoˈpsychic** *a.*, that is within the mind. **enˈdoptile** *a. Bot.* [Gr. πτίλον feather], 'said of an embryo, whose plumule is rolled up by the cotyledon, as in endogens' (*Treas. Bot.*). ˌ**endoˈradiosonde**, an encapsulated electronic device which when placed within the body transmits radio signals giving information about conditions inside the body. **endoˈreism, endoˈrheism** *Geogr.* [ad. F. *endorrhéisme*, 'ou, si l'on admet une orthographe simplifiée', *endoréisme* (E. de Martonne 1926, in *Compt. Rend.* CLXXXII. 1396)], land drainage not reaching the sea; interior drainage; so **endoˈreic, endoˈrheic** *adjs.* ˈ**endo(r)rhiz,** *Bot.* [Gr. ῥίζα root], 'the sheath-enclosed radicle of an endorrhizous plant, which does not lengthen, but gives origin from its termination or from its sides to short rootlets' (*Syd. Soc. Lex.*); hence **endoˈr(r)hizal, -ous,** *adjs.* ˈ**endosarc,** *Zool.* [Gr. σάρξ, σαρκ-ός flesh], the inner sarcode-layer of certain rhizopods, such as the Amœba. ˈ**endoscope,** *Med.* [Gr. -σκοπος watching], 'an instrument so arranged as to give a view of some internal part of the body through a natural canal' (*Syd. Soc. Lex.*); hence **endoˈscopic** *a.* **enˈdoscopy,** the examination of internal parts by means of the endoscope. **endoˈsiphon,** the internal tube of certain cephalopods; SIPHUNCLE 1; hence **endoˈsiphonal, -nate** *adjs.* ˌ**endoˈskeletal,** of or pertaining to the ˌ**endoˈskeleton,** *Anat.* [see SKELETON], the internal framework of the *Vertebrata*, consisting of bone and cartilage, as distinguished from the bony and leathery integuments of some animals. ˌ**endosoˈmatic** *a. Biol.*, designating or pertaining to a device that an animal uses which is part of its own body; hence ˌ**endosoˈmatically** *adv.*, in the manner of an endosomatic organ. ˈ**endosome,** (*a*) the innermost part of a sponge; (*b*) *Cytol.*, a deeply staining mass of chromatin in the middle of a vesicular nucleus in certain protozoans. ˈ**endosperm,** *Bot.* [Gr. σπέρμα seed], the nutritive element, also called albumen, enclosed with the embryo in many seeds; hence **endoˈspermic** *a.* ˈ**endospore,** *Bot.* [Gr. σπορά sowing], (*a*) the inner coat of a spore in lichens; (*b*) a spore formed in the interior of a theca; hence ˌ**endoˈsporous** *a.*, a term applied to fungi whose spores are contained in a case. **enˈdosteal** *a.*, *Anat.* [see -AL[1]], pertaining to the *endosteum* (q.v. below); hence **enˈdosteally** *adv.* **endoˈsternite,** Zool. [Gr. στέρνον breast + -ITE], the portion of the apodeme of the thorax in Crustacea which arises from the intesternal membrane. **enˈdosteum,** *Anat.* [mod.L., f. Gr. ὀστέον bone], the internal periosteum. **enˈdostoma,** *Zool.* [Gr. στόμα mouth] (see quot.). ˈ**endostome,** *Bot.* [see prec.], the aperture in the inner integument of an ovule. **endoˈstosis** [Gr. ὀστέον bone, on the analogy of ἐξόστωσις], an internal growth of bone. **enˈdostracum,** the inner layer of the shell of a crustacean. ˈ**endostyle,** *Zool.* [Gr. στῦλος column], 'a rigid, hollow, whitish, rod-like structure on the floor of the ventral groove of *Tunicata*' (*Syd. Soc. Lex.*); hence **endoˈstylic** *a.* **endoˈtheca** [Gr. θήκη case], (*a*) *Zool.*, the inner layer of the wall of the sac of the gonosome of the *Hydrozoa*; (*b*) *Bot.*, the inner membrane of the wall of the cells of the anther; hence **endoˈthecal** *a.*, (dissepiments) horizontal plates growing inwards from the septa of a corallite (*Syd. Soc. Lex.*). **endoˈthecium** *Bot.* [mod.L. (J. E. Purkinje *De cellulis antherarum Fibrosis* (1830) i. 1], a layer in the wall of the anther. **endoˈthelial** *a.*, relating to endothelium. **endoˈthelioid** *a.*, resembling endothelium. **endoˈthelium,** *Phys.* [Gr. θηλή nipple], the layer of cells lining a blood-vessel or serous cavity, in structure similar to EPITHELIUM; also pl. **endoˈthelia,** vessel-cells. **endoˈthorax** *Anat.*, the system of internal processes of the thorax or cephalothorax of arthropods. **endoˈtoxin,** a toxin contained within a bacterial cell, *spec.* one that is not released until disintegration of the cell. ˌ**endoˈtracheal** *a.*, within the trachea (Billings, 1890).

1950 *Proc. R. Soc. Med.* XLIII. 548 At the present time the indications for recanalizing *endarteriectomy should be restricted to cases of arteritis of non-acute form. **1974** R. M. KIRK et al. *Surgery* vi. 118/1 In selected patients the condition [*sc.* intestinal angina] can be ameliorated by arterial bypass or endarterectomy. **1978** *Sci. Amer.* Apr. 64/1 Endarterectomy is now a standard method of reestablishing blood flow through the extracranial arteries of the neck. **1866** A. FLINT *Princ. Med.* (1880) 196 **Endarteritis*. **1876** tr *Wagner's Gen. Pathol.* 161 An habitual use of alcohol..causes chronic endarteritis. **1883** *Jrnl. Anat. & Physiol.* XVII. II. 180 (*title*) Obliterative endarteritis, and the inflammatory changes in the coats of the small vessels. *Ibid.* 182 It is now known that the so-called organisation of thrombus is in reality an obliterative endarteritis, in which the thrombus plays merely a passive part. **1900** B. D. JACKSON *Gloss. Bot. Terms*, **Endobiotic*, living within as a parasite. **1930** H. M. FITZPATRICK *Lower Fungi: Phycomycetes* iii. 44 When, in parasitic species, the summer sporangia or resting spores are formed within the host cell they are termed endobiotic (endophytic when the host is a plant, endozoic when it is an animal). **1895** *Endoblast [see CŒLOBLAST]. **1928** G. H. CARPENTER *Biol. Insects* vii. 152 The insinking of a mass of cells ('middle plate') along the axis of the germ-band to form a lower layer (endoblast). **1932** *Jrnl. Thoracic Surg.* I. 435 By means of closed *endobronchial anesthesia..it is possible to maintain complete control of anesthetic concentration in a single lung. **1966** *Lancet* 31 Dec. 1449/2 Fundamental principles of physics as applied to anæsthesia..are described in some detail, and so also is endotracheal and endobronchial intubation. **1900** tr. *Deniker's Races of Man* v. 148 *Endocannibalism is but the remains of a natural state of primitive man. **1960** R. & C. NEEDHAM tr. *Hertz's Death & Right Hand* 44 Endocannibalism..secures for the flesh the most honourable of sepultures. **1879** *St. George's Hosp. Rep.* IX. 443 One case [of retroversion of uterus] was accompanied by severe *endocervicitis. **1882** *Quain's Anat.* (ed. 9) II. 113 Since the cartilage grows in every dimension by interstitial expansion, the bone which is invading it (*endochondral bone) becomes gradually wider as the ossification advances. **1913** [see *ectochondral* adj.]. **1887, 1888** *Endochone [see *ectochone*]. **1857** BULLOCK *Cazeaux Midwif.* 195 The internal or allantoid is essentially vascular, and has been denominated the *endochorion. **1835** LINDLEY *Introd. Bot.* (1848) II. 121 *Endochrome, the granular contents of spores and sporidia. **1884** *Syd. Soc. Lex.*, *Endochrome*..specially applied to the colouring matter of vegetable cells when any other colour than green. **1901** *Nature* 19 Sept. 514/1 The Silurian tableland,..its *endoclinal and exoclinal structures. **1889** *Geol. Mag.* Feb. 62 We must naturally expect to find the deepest strata in the 'fan structure' (**endocline*) or pseudo-synclinal form and the highest in the folds of the inverted fan structure (*exocline*) or pseudo-anticlinal. **1901** *Practitioner* Mar. 276 The new generation of *endocorpuscular parasites. **1878** BARTLEY tr *Topinard's Anthrop.* II. iii. 294 How much more [importance] should we [attach] to its interior or *endocrane? **1924** *Glasgow Herald* 10 May 7 Sir Arthur Keith..delivered..the annual lecture..his subject being 'Phrenological Studies of the Skull and *Endocranial Cast of Sir Thomas Browne'. **1946** *Nature* 6 July 5/1 The study of endocranial casts assumes some importance in palæontology, and particularly in the palæontology of man and the other primates. **1877** HUXLEY *Anat. Inv. An.* vii. 403 In addition to these externally visible sclerites, there is a sort of internal skeleton (*endocranium or tentorium). **1913** *Endocyclic [see *exocyclic* adj. s.v. EXO-]. **1872** NICHOLSON *Palæont.* 191 The *endocyst is invariably flexible and membranous. **1880** *Athenæum* 23 Oct. 536/1 Within the cell [in Polyzoa] comes the body-wall known as the endocyst. **1963** C. DE DUVE in De Rueck & Cameron *Lysosomes* 412 The new term..simply indicates that materials are coming into the cell (*endocytosis) rather than going out (exocytosis). **1969** N. S. COHN *Elem. Cytol.* (ed. 2) v. 124 Foreign protein or other material could undergo digestion within the cell as a result of such endocytosis (pinocytosis and phagocytosis). **1927** *Endodynamomorphic [see *ectodynamomorphic* adj. s.v. ECTO-]. **1930** *Nature* 19 July 89 Endodynamomorphic soils are those in which external factors have not yet exerted their full influence and which are therefore immature. **1932** FULLER & CONARD tr. *Braun-Blanquet's Plant Sociol.* ix. 256 The endodynamomorphic soils are either limited to desert and mountain regions with sparse vegetation or they are to be considered merely as early stages of development of the ectodynamomorphic climax soils. **1888** ROLLESTON & JACKSON *Forms Anim. Life* 795 The *endogastric septa of Haeckel. **1902** *Encycl. Brit.* XXX. 795/2 Ultimately the coil becomes ventral or endogastric. **1899** *Proc. Zool. Soc.* 705 The middle lobe of the *endognath (the proximal division of the *lacinia externa* in Boas's nomenclature). **1877** HUXLEY *Anat. Inv. An.* vi. 345 The *endognathal palp. **1888** SIR M. MACKENZIE *Frederick the Noble* 191, I had twice done an *endolaryngeal operation on this patient. *Ibid.* 230 By previously removing a portion *endolaryngeally. **1884** *Globe* 29 Apr., Dr. Hand-Smith's *Endoliths at Piccadilly Hall. **1886** *Pall Mall G.* 12 Dec. 8/2 Dr. Hand-Smith lent a splendid endolith of Lord Beaconsfield and various *endolithic marbles. **1836–9** TODD *Cycl. Anat.* II. 539/1 The *endolymph is in birds as limpid as in the Mammifera. **1878** FOSTER *Phys.* III. iii. §1. 449 Waves of sound can and do reach the endolymph of the labryinth by direct conduction through the skull. **1859** TODD *Cycl. Anat.* V. 702/2 *Endometrial inflammations have been distinguished..as croupy..catarrhal, and the like. **1932** S. ZUCKERMAN *Soc. Life Monkeys & Apes* v. 71 Endometrial growth during the ovarian phase of follicular growth. **1922** W. B. BELL in *Jrnl. Obstet. & Gynæcol.*

XXIX. 443 These extra-uterine growths have been described as 'adenomyomata' and 'adenofibromyomata'.. I have referred to such tumours as '*endometriomata' or as 'endometriomyomata' and 'endometriofibromyomata'. I hope that gynæcologists will adopt this in the place of the older nomenclature. **1962** J. W. HUFFMAN *Gynecol. & Obstetrics* xlv. 1035 The ovaries are buried in the adherent mass or are converted into endometriotic cysts or endometriomas. **1925** J. A. SAMPSON in *Amer. Jrnl. Obst. & Gyn.* X. 462 (*title*) Inguinal *endometriosis (often reported as endometrial tissue in the groin, adenomyoma in the groin, and adenomyoma of the round ligament). *Ibid.*, Ectopic endometrial tissue in the wall of the uterus.. has arisen from the direct invasion of the myometrium by the mucosa lining the uterine cavity. We might call such a condition a direct or primary endometriosis of the uterus. **1940** *Amer. Jrnl. Obstet.* XL. 554 Peritoneal endometriosis associated with endometrial cysts of the ovary. **1961** *Lancet* 23 Sept. 696/2 It is still debatable whether endometriosis can be permanently cured by hormone therapy. **1942** A. H. CURTIS *Textbk. Gynecol.* (ed. 4) xxxiii. 511 *Endometriotic tissue lodged in a vein. **1966** WRIGHT & SYMMERS *Syst. Path.* I. xxvii. 894 Endometriotic lesions of the uterus. **1872** F. THOMAS *Dis. Wom.* 117 Senile *endometritis. **1876** tr. *Wagner's Gen. Pathol.* 592 Puerperal endometritis. **1882** *Syd. Soc. Lex.*, *Endometrium. **1907** *Practitioner* Dec. 792 The endometrium was normal. **1912** ADAMI & MCCRAE *Text-bk. Pathol.* 647 The histological appearances of the endometrium in certain stages of the menstrual cycle. **1956** *Nature* 14 Jan. 59/1 Mechanical irritation of the endometrium during the luteal phase of the œstrous cycle will provoke the formation of decidual cells. **1878** BARTLEY tr. *Topinard's Anthrop.* II. iii. 244 We shall only mention two of them..*endometry and endoscopy. **1942** *Biol. Abstr.* XVI. 1930/2 Chromocenter formation depends on failure of the daughter chromatids to move apart in the *endomitoses by which polyploidy occurs. **1943** *Ibid.* XVII. 1344/2 Inner multiplication of chromosomes, i.e., polyploidy arisen through 'endomitosis'. **1959** SOUTHWOOD & LESTON *Land & Water Bugs* xii. 351 The phenomenon of endomitosis has been studied in this bug. **1951** M. J. D. WHITE in G. H. Bourne *Cytol. & Cell Physiol.* (ed. 2) v. 209 Geitler has also described what he calls '*endomitotic' cycles of condensation and decondensation during the formation of endopolyploid nuclei. **1960** L. PICKEN *Organiz. Cells* iv. 128 This cycle of changes in the chromosomes only becomes linked with the formation of the gigantic quasi-spindle.. after the genome population has been built up to a high level by repeated endomitotic divisions. And..the 'anaphase' movement does not separate daughter chromosomes. **1968** W. A. STEWART in J. A. Fishman *Readings Sociol. of Lang.* 534 The form of standardization prevalent in any one country may be either *endonormative*, when it is based upon models of usage native to that country, or *exonormative*, when it is based upon foreign models of usage. **1980** *Word 1979* XXX. 43 The Yugoslav-Albanian change involved planned shift from an endonormative to an exonormative mode of standardization. **1984** *English World-Wide* V. I. 145 The authors come down in favour of endonormative standards for SgE, which would guarantee the satisfaction of internal communicational needs as well as international intelligibility. **1962** *Jrnl. Biol. Chem.* CCXXXVII. 819/1 This enzyme produces scissions at many points along the deoxyribonucleic acid chain and hence can be classed as an *endonuclease. **1982** T. M. DEVLIN *Textbk. Biochem.* xvii. 802 Some endonucleases have been particularly useful in the development of early methodologies for sequencing of RNA polynucleotides. **1884** P. GEDDES in *Ency. Brit.* XVIII. 261 *Endoparasites he [Leuckart] divides according to, etc. **1883** *Athenæum* 24 Mar. 381/3 Simondsia is a genus of *endoparasitic nematodes. **1936** BERGMANN & ROSS in *Jrnl. Biol. Chem.* CXIV. 723 It is therefore possible to classify the two types of peptidases as *exopeptidases*, which are restricted to terminal peptide linkages, and **endopeptidases*, which are not thus restricted. **1962** A. SPECTOR in A. Pirie *Lens Metabolism Rel. Cataract* 330 An endopeptidase called β-protease..will attack lens protein in acid pH. **1874** JONES & SIEV. *Pathol. Anat.* 400 *Endophlebitis is hardly seen in an acute form. **1877** HUXLEY *Anat. Inv. An.* vi. 333 A complex mass of fibres, which is attached in part to the *endophragms of the thorax in front. *Ibid.* 361 A strong apodeme..passing inwards and forwards meets with its fellow, to form an *endophragmal arch, which supports the œsophagus and stomach. **1835** LINDLEY *Introd. Bot.* (1848) II 65 Dumortier adds to these names *endophyllous.. because the young leaves of monocotyledons are evolved from within a sheath. *Ibid.* I. 21 A division..separates, in trees, the bark from the internal part, or *endophyte as he [Count de Tristan] terms it. **1854** J. HOGG *Microscope* II. i. (1867) 293 Endophytes..originate from germs which penetrate healthy plants and develop a mycelium. **1887** H. M. WARD tr. *Sachs' Lect. Physiol. Plants* xxiii. 371 (*heading*) *Endophytic parasites. **1898** H. C. PORTER tr. *Strasburger's Text-bk. Bot.* 308 Some species also are endophytic and inhabit cavities in other plants. **1902** Endophytic [see *ectophytic* adj. s.v. ECTO-]. **1935** F. E. FRITSCH *Struct. & Reprod. Algae* I. 155 An endophytic green alga..has been reported in the skin of the carp. **1964** V. J. CHAPMAN in *Oceanogr. & Marine Biol.* II. 210 The asexual generation is represented by a unicellular endophytic plant. *a* **1889** C. V. RILEY (Cent. Dict.), The larvæ of the castnians are ..*endophytous, boring the stems and roots of orchids and other plants. **1883** J. E. ADY in *Knowledge* 15 June 355/2 Its [Amœba's] jelly-like body becomes faintly parcelled out into an outer firm (ectoplasm) and an inner soft (*endoplasm) layer. **1934** *Nature* 19 May 761/2 The *endoplasmic streaming which is the most striking feature in the pseudopodium of an amœba is not..present in most other rhizopods. **1955** *Sci. News Let.* 28 May 338/2 The endoplasmic reticulum. **1853** *Endoplast [see PERIPLAST]. **1859** TODD *Cycl. Anat.* V. 475/1 On the outer side of the line lie the close-set endoplasts of the deepest layer of the epidermis. **1877** HUXLEY *Anat. Inv. An.* i. 47 The endoplast may take on more and more definitely the characters of a reproductive organ. *Ibid.* ii. 95 Magosphæra is thus very nearly an *endoplastic repetition of the moneran Protomonas. *Ibid.* 96 Nor do any of them exhibit a structure analogous to the *endoplastule of the Ciliata. **1842** GRAY *Struct. Bot.* viii. (1880) 306 The inner coat, called ..*Endopleura..is always conformed to the nucleus. **1870** BENTLEY *Bot.* 331 The endopleura is generally of a soft and delicate nature. **1877** HUXLEY *Anat. Inv. An.* vi. 310 The *endopleurite, likewise, divides into three apophyses. **1893** T. R. R. STEBBING *Hist. Crustacea* iv. 36 In describing a crustacean appendage he [*sc.* T. H. Huxley] names the first two joints the protopodite, which bears on its extremity on the inner side the endopodite, and on the outer side the exopodite. For these terms the shortened forms exopod and *endopod will here be preferred—exopod for exopodite, and endopod for endopodite and protopodite combined. **1959** *Chambers's Encycl.* IV. 278/2 In the walking legs of crabs and lobsters only the endopod remains, but in the corresponding thoracic limbs of some more primitive Malacostra the exopod is presented as a many-pointed flagellum and is used for swimming. **1870** ROLLESTON *Anim. Life* 94 Two multiarticulate filaments representing an 'exopodite' and an '*endopodite'. **1877** HUXLEY *Anat. Inv. An.* vi. 281 To this end the joints of the endopodite are greatly expanded, and converted into a hemispherical bowl. **1880** T. H. HUXLEY *Crayfish* 218 The inner or *endopoditic division of the antenna. **1913** *Lancet* 19 Apr. 1116/1 The repressing factor in the waking consciousness is named by Freud the **endopsychic censor*. **1922** J. RIVIERE tr. *Freud's Introd. Lect. Psycho-anal.* 240 The *why* of the symptom, its tendency, is..always an endo-psychic process. **1927** C. MACKENZIE *Vestal Fire* I. i, A *frisson* that no endo-psychic censor is capable of providing. **1932** *Brit. Jrnl. Psychol.* Oct. 160, I shall include in the term anxiety that special form which by reason of its endopsychic conditioning is thought of as guilt. **1957** *Lancet* 15 June 1224/1 The *endoradiosonde described here embodies a mechano-chemical transducer that changes its dimensions with pH. **1927** E. DE MARTONNE in *Geogr. Rev.* XVII. 397 In this paper we shall attempt to define the extent of the *endoreic, or interior-basin, domain and explain its causes. **1957** G. E. HUTCHINSON *Treat. Limnol.* I. iv. 226 The Caspian basin, into which the Volga drains, adds greatly to the area of the endorheic regions of the north temperate zone. **1927** E. DE MARTONNE in *Geogr. Rev.* XVII. 397 It is convenient to describe each of these two great regions by a single word: we may term through-flowing, or ocean, drainage 'exoreism' (ex-o-rē-ism, from the Greek ἐξ, out, and ῥεῖν, to flow), interior basin drainage '*endoreism' (en-do-rē-ism, from ἐν, in, and ῥεῖν). **1963** D. W. & E. E. HUMPHRIES tr. *Termier's Erosion & Sedimentation* 404 *Endorheism*, inland drainage, drainage toward the center of a land mass. **1869** NICHOLSON *Zoology* 43 The *endosarc contains the only organs possessed by the animal. **1877** HUXLEY *Anat. Inv. An.* xii. 659 The line of separation between the endosarc and the ectosarc. **1861** BUMSTEAD *Ven. Dis.* (1879) 87 In learning the use of the *Endoscope..commence with the simplest instruments. **1872** THOMAS *Dis. Wom.* 93 If the cervix be dilated, the endoscope may be at once introduced. **1861** BUMSTEAD *Ven. Dis.* (1879) 90 An *endoscopic examination is attempted. *Ibid.* 87 Writers on *endoscopy. **1883** HOLMES *Surgery* (ed. 3) III. 214 Endoscopy is of very little value in stricture. **1883** HYATT in *Proc. Boston Soc. Nat. Hist.* 261 The '*endosiphon', here spoken of for the first time by that name, is the internal tube long known in Actinoceras, and lately demonstrated in Piloceras. *Ibid.* 273 The *endosiphonal tube is narrow and regular. **1883** —— *Proc. Amer. Assoc. Adv. Sci.* XXXII. 328 The *endosiphonate.. types [of cephalopods]. **1883** *Athenæum* 30 June 833/1 The muscular and *endoskeletal systems of *Limulus* and *Scorpio*. **1839–47** TODD *Cycl. Anat.* III. 846/2 The..skeleton and *endoskeleton..become appendages one of the other. **1872** NICHOLSON *Palæont.* 30 Some of the fishes..possess no 'endoskeleton'. **1877** HUXLEY *Anat. Inv. An.* i. 53 Old Echinoderms have a calcareous endoskeleton. **1951** *New Biol.* XI. 21 Nearly all the effector and receptor organs of nearly all animals are of the type..called *endosomatic. Roughly, this means that they are material parts of the organism and are made of the organism's own stuff. **1957** P. B. MEDAWAR *Uniqueness Individual* vii. 140 Cameras have eye-like and clothes have skin-like functions, and motor-cars the functions *endosomatically performed by legs. **1887** *Encycl. Brit.* XXII. 415 A reticulation of ectosome on the one side and of endoderm and mesoderm, i.e., *endosome, on the other. **1912** E. A. MINCHIN *Introd. Study Protozoa* vi. 73 In the condition with a single, or one greatly preponderating, mass of chromatin, the nuclear space.. presents the appearance of a vesicle containing the chromatin-mass at or near its centre;..the chromatinic mass may be termed..an endosome. *Ibid.* 76 The endosome..in most cases..is composed of a matrix or ground-substance of plastin in which the chromatin is lodged. An endosome of this kind is termed a karyosome. **1926** G. N. CALKINS *Biol. Protozoa* ii. 59 Endosomes may consist entirely of chromatin ..or they may be composed of chromatin and plastin in various combinations. **1961** MACKINNON & HAWES *Introd. Study Protozoa* I. 12 The term karyosome (the endosome of some authors) is here used descriptively as the name of any conspicuous, deeply staining body lying in the nuclear sap. *c* **1850** *Nat. Encycl.* I. 388 It is also named *endosperm. **1875** DARWIN *Insectiv. Pl.* xv. 302 The endosperm is not actually united with..the embryo. **1882** VINES *Sachs' Bot.* 227 A special mass of tissue, the so-called Endosperm. **1875** COOKE *Fungi* 23 The covering of the spore is double consisting of an exospore and an *endospore. **1882** VINES *Sachs' Bot.* 277 An external rough dark-brown exospore and an inner endospore. **1868** *Endosteal [see *ectosteal* adj. s.v. ECTO-]. **1878** T. BRYANT *Pract. Surg.* I. 537 The endosteal membrane..lines the bone. **1870** ROLLESTON *Anim. Life* 39 This merely *endosteally ossified bone. **1877** HUXLEY *Anat. Inv. An.* vi. 309 Each *endosternite is distinguishable into three apophyses. **18..** CARPENTER *Physiol.* (1881) 48 [The shaft of a bone] is lined by a..delicate layer of the same tissue, to which the term '*endosteum' is applied. **1877** HUXLEY *Anat. Inv. An.* vi. 341 And the plate [in Astacus] which stretches backwards and supports the labrum, within its posterior forked boundary, is the *endostoma. **1835** LINDLEY *Introd. Bot.* (1848) I. 21 In the language of Mirbel, exostome in the outer integument, and *endostome in the inner integument. **1842** GRAY *Struct. Bot.* vi. §8 (1880) 277 When the ovule has two coats, the foramen of the outer one is called Exostome, of the inner Endostome; literally the outer and the inner orifice. **1870** ROLLESTON *Anim. Life* 38 Ossified both by ectostosis and *Endostosis. **1880** T. H. HUXLEY *Crayfish* iv. 194 This zone [*sc.* the ectostracum] may be distinguished from the *endostracum which makes up the rest of the exoskeleton. **1960** I. F. & W. D. HENDERSON *Dict. Sci. Terms* (ed. 7) 160/2 Endostracum... The inner layer of mollusc shell. **1854** WOODWARD *Mollusca* (1856) 345 In Salpa..the dorsal sinus contains the long tubular filament called the *endostyle. **1877** HUXLEY *Anat. Inv. An.* x. 597 On each side of the endostyle the posterior part of the hæmal wall of the pharynx presents two oval apertures. *Ibid* 612 The *endostylic cone elongates. **1833** *Athenæum* 10 Feb. 188/3 Edwards and Haime described..the absence of *endothecal dissepiments. **1832** LINDLEY *Introd. Bot.* I. ii. 128 The lining of the anther has received particular illustration from M. Purkinje, who calls it **endothecium*. **1959** FOSTER & GIFFORD *Compar. Morphol. Vascular Plants* xix. 495 This well-marked outer layer of the microsporangium wall is usually designated as endothecium. **1876** tr. *Wagner's Gen. Pathol.* 150 The lymphatic capillaries have an *endothelial covering. **1866** A. FLINT *Princ. Med.* (1880) 225 The tubercles present the typical *endothelioid and giant-celled structure. **1872** PEASLEE *Ovar. Tumours* 5 The *endothelium of blood-vessels. **1876** tr. *Wagner's Gen. Pathol.* 227 Their endothelia are more easily separated. **1881** MIVART *Cat* 189 The layer of epithelium thus lining a serous cavity is called endothelium. **1878** J. BELL tr. *Gegenbauer's Comp. Anat.* v. 249 These processes..are found chiefly in the head and thorax in many orders of the Insecta..where they form a complicated structure known as the '*endothorax'. **1957** RICHARDS & DAVIES *Imms's Gen. Textbk. Ent.* (ed. 9) I. 60 Under the term endothorax is included the endoskeleton of the thorax. **1905** A. C. ABBOTT *Princ. Bacteriol.* (ed. 7) xxv. 568 We now regard the toxic action of these bacteria to be due to the formation of *endotoxins or intracellular toxins. **1907** *Jrnl. Amer. Med. Assoc.* 923 The serum injected into the patient has brought about a local disintegration of the gonococci and a liberation of endotoxins. **1964** M. HYNES *Med. Bacteriol.* (ed. 8) vi. 67 The toxins of bacteria which do not produce exotoxins are termed endotoxins and are thought to be firmly bound to the bacterial proteins in a non-diffusible form. **1910** *Practitioner* June 861 *Endotracheal stenosis, due to syphilis. **1962** *Lancet* 28 Apr. 879/2 To protect the patient against obstruction of the airway, endotracheal intubation with a cuffed tube is highly desirable during abdominal surgery.

endocardial (ɛndəʊ'kɑːdɪəl), *a. Phys.* [f. Gr. ἔνδο-ν (see ENDO-) + καρδία heart + -AL[1].]
a. That is within the heart. **b.** Relating to the endocardium.

1847–9 TODD *Cycl. Anat.* IV. 139/1 Induration-matter.. appears on the endocardial and valvular surfaces. **1861** T. GRAHAM *Pract. Med.* 329 Endocardial inflammation. **1877** ROBERTS *Handbk. Med.* (ed. 3) II. 7 Abnormal sounds originating within the heart, named endocardial murmurs.

endocarditis (ˌɛndəʊkɑː'daɪtɪs). *Med.* [f. ENDOCARDI-UM + -ITIS.] Inflammation of the lining membrane of the heart. Hence **endocarditic** (-'dɪtɪk) *a.*, of or pertaining to endocarditis.

1836–9 TODD *Cycl. Anat.* II. 646/2 Chronic endocarditis affects the valves of the heart. **1866** A. FLINT *Princ. Med.* (1880) 335 Simultaneous involvement of the mitral valve in the endocarditic process. **1882** *Pop. Sc. Monthly* XX. 712 Trivial injuries to the mitral-valve curtains by endocarditis.

‖**endocardium** (ɛndəʊ'kɑːdɪəm). *Phys.* [mod.L., f. Gr. ἔνδο-ν (see ENDO-) + καρδί-α heart.] The smooth membrane lining the cavities of the heart.

1872 HUXLEY *Phys.* ii. 36 There is an internal..lining called the endocardium. **1877** ROBERTS *Handbk. Med.* (ed. 3) II. 36 It rarely happens that the endocardium is seen in the early period of inflammation.

endocarp ('ɛndəʊkɑːp). *Bot.* [f. as prec. + Gr. καρπ-ός fruit.] The inner layer of a pericarp, which lines the cavity containing the seeds. It is fleshy, as in the orange; membranous, as in the apple; or hard, as in the peach.

1830 LINDLEY *Nat. Syst. Bot.* 132 Fruit consisting of several capsules..the endocarp separating entirely from the sarcocarp. **1835** —— *Introd. Bot.* (1848) II. 3 In the peach ..the stone [is] the endocarp or putamen. **1883** *Evang. Mag.* Oct. 460 The stone in the centre is..not the seed..but the 'endocarp' become stony by thickening and hardening of its cells.

endoce, variant of ENDOSS *v.*, *Obs.*

endocentric (ɛndəʊ'sɛntrɪk), *a. Linguistics.* [f. ENDO- + CENTRIC *a.*] Applied to a construction or compound having the same grammatical function as one of its constituent parts. Opp. to EXOCENTRIC *a.* Hence **endo'centrically** *adv.*

1933 BLOOMFIELD *Lang.* xii. 194 The forms *John* and *poor John* have, on the whole, the same functions. Accordingly, we say that the English character-substance construction (as in *poor John, fresh milk*, and the like) is an *endocentric* construction. *Ibid.* xiv. 235 Since a *blackbird* is a kind of a *bird*, and a *door-knob* a kind of a *knob*, we may say that these compounds have the same function as their head members; they are endocentric. **1942** BLOCH & TRAGER *Outline Ling. Analysis* v. 76 If a phrase has the same function as one or more of its immediate constituents, it is an endocentric phrase and has an endocentric construction. **1957** S. POTTER *Mod. Ling.* v. 114 Inasmuch as *good men* is a phrase without predication, it is said to be an *endocentric construction*. As a unit *good men* has the same function as one or more of its constituents. **1964** R. H. ROBINS *Gen. Ling.* vi. 238 Only *all* and *both* can be endocentrically preposed to constructions closed in this way (*both my big black dogs*, etc.). **1968** B. M. H. STRANG *Mod. Eng. Structure* (ed. 2) v. 77 Nominal groups (*every conceivable kind of flower, the finest recording I've ever heard*) have heads (*flower, recording*) and these heads are, like the groups they belong to, nominal. Structures of this..kind are *endocentric*.

endochorion, -chrome, -crane: see ENDO-.

endocrine ('ɛndəʊkraɪn, -ɪn), *a.* and *sb. Physiol.* Also -crin. [f. Gr. ἔνδον ENDO- + κρίνειν to separate. Cf. It. *glandole endocrine* (N. Pende, 1909), *endocrinico* (ibid.), F. *glandes endocrines*

(Gottignies, 1912), Sp. *glándulas endocrinas* (R. Mollá, 1912).] Denoting a gland having an internal secretion which is poured into blood or lymph; a ductless gland, as the thyroid, pituitary, and adrenal glands. As *adj.* also = endocrinal.

Stedman's *Med. Dict.*, 1911, has *endocrin* with the erroneous def. 'The internal secretion of a gland'.

1914 E. A. SCHÄFER *Introd. Study Endocrine Glands* 5 Organs..passing such material into the blood or lymph are termed internally secreting or endocrine organs. **1914** *Lancet* 12 Sept. 714/1 The organs of internal secretion, or endocrine glands. **1921** *Amer. Jrnl. Med. Sci.* CLIX. 800 Thyroid and other endocrin disturbances. **1922** *N.Y. Med. Jrnl.* CXV. 393 The diagnostic and therapeutic rôle of the endocrines. **1924** R. MUIR *Text-bk. Pathol.* 721 Several of the endocrine glands exert..a co-ordinated action on the metabolism of carbohydrates. **1925** J. LAIRD *Our Minds & Their Bodies* 52 Secretions from the endocrines. **1925** W. J. H. SPROTT tr. *Kretschmer's Physique & Char.* 84 Whether the thyroid plays here a rôle as primary cause of an endocrine nature..one cannot say for certain. **1927** HALDANE & HUXLEY *Anim. Biol.* ix. 190 The endocrine system or sum total of the ductless glands. **1954** *Sci. News* XXXIII. 17 In spring, the lengthening hours of light or rising temperature cause endocrine changes in many birds and fishes. **1957** *Encycl. Brit.* X. 392/1 The mode of secretion may be toward the outside of the body (exocrine) or toward the blood and lymph vessels (endocrine).

Hence **'endocrinal, endocrinic** (-'krınık), **'endocrinous** *adjs.*, pertaining to, of the nature of, or relating to endocrine organs; **,endocri'nology**, the physiology or study of the endocrines; whence **,endocri'nologist**; **,endocrino'logical** *a.*

1913 DORLAND *Med. Dict.* (ed. 3), Endocrinology. **1914** *Brit. Med. Jrnl.* 14 Feb. 369/1 Deficiency of endocrinic glandular secretion. **1914** *Lancet* 4 Apr. 952/2 Influence of the Endocrinous Glands upon Uterine Hæmorrhage. **1919** *Nature* CIV. 208/1 'Endocrinology', or physiology of the internally secreting glands. **1923** *Glasgow Herald* 10 Nov. 4 Variations in the endocrinal or regulatory system. **1930** *Times Lit. Suppl.* 25 Dec. 1103/1 For the endocrinologist there are three papers dealing respectively with the chemical properties of the oxytocic principle of the pituitary gland, with oestrin and with a comb-growth-promoting substance obtained from testes and urine. **1949** M. MEAD *Male & Female* ii. 29 Nor do we..find what..endocrinological clues set them on these paths. **1956** E. L. MASCALL *Christian Theol. & Nat. Sci.* vi. 212 Some new discovery of the endocrinologists about the influence of our glandular secretions upon our behaviour.

†**en'doctrine**, *v. Obs. rare.* [ad. OF. *endoctriner*: see EN-¹ and DOCTRINE *sb.*] *trans.* To train, instruct; = INDOCTRINATE.

*c*1500 MELUSINE (1889) 258 This lady had..a sone..whiche was fayre and wel endoctryned. *Ibid.* 186 To endoctrine them, & shew to tham the way of good governance. **1633** DONNE *Hist. Sept. 2* (T.) Ptolomeus Philadelphus was endoctrined, in the science of good letters, by Strabo.

endocuticle ('ɛndəʊ,kjuːtık(ə)l). Also **endocu'ticula**. [f. ENDO- + CUTICLE.] The inner part of a cuticle. **a.** The flexible, laminated, innermost part of the cuticle of an insect or other arthropod.

1929 F. L. CAMPBELL in *Ann. Entomol. Soc. Amer.* XXII. 415 Following the suggestion of Mr. R. E. Snodgrass, of the Bureau of Entomology, the writer calls the extremely thin outermost layer (Grenzlamelle) the epicuticula, the brittle, pigmented outer layer (epidermis, Pigmentschichte) the exocuticula, and the flexible, colorless inner layer (dermis, Hauptlage) the endocuticula. **1935** BORRADAILE & POTTS *Invertebrata* (ed. 2) x. 309 The arthropod cuticle has a thin, impermeable, non-chitinous external layer (epicuticle) and a thick, elastic, permeable, lamellar inner layer (endocuticle), largely composed of chitin. **1967** P. A. MEGLITSCH *Invert. Zool.* xvi. 676 The endocuticle is a continuous layer..and particularly important in the flexible membranes between the skeletal plates.

b. The innermost part of the cuticle that surrounds animal fibres or hairs, etc.

1949 [see EPICUTICLE b]. **1956** *Nature* 18 Feb. 319/1 [They] described sections of hair in their study of the cuticle layer. They now believe..that the endocuticle is non-keratinous in character. **1962** W. J. ONIONS *Wool* ii. 16 Electron microscopy of silver stained, reduced fibres suggests that the exocuticle contains more sulphur than the endocuticle, which is a layer resistant to alkaline extraction but not to trypsin.

endocyst: see ENDO-.

endoderm ('ɛndəʊdɜːm). [f. Gr. ἔνδο-ν (see ENDO-) + δέρμ-α skin.]

1. *Bot.* **a.** A layer of large cambium cells lying beneath the liber. **b.** The inner layer of the wall of a vegetable cell.

1835 LINDLEY *Introd. Bot.* (1848) I. 193 The cellular face of the liber..A. Richard distinguishes by the name of subliberian layer, or Endoderm.

2. *Biol.* **a.** The inner layer of the blastoderm. **b.** The lining of the internal cavity of the *Cœlenterata*. **c.** *attrib.*

1861 J. R. GREENE *Man. Anim. Kingd.*, *Cœlent.* 21 The endoderm, whose free surface forms the lining of the large internal cavity. **1862** H. SPENCER *First Princ.* II. xix. §152 (1875) 417 The..blastoderm..divides into two layers..the ectoderm and the endoderm. **1877** HUXLEY *Anat. Inv. An.* iii. 113 The endoderm..is composed of a layer of very distinct cells. **1885** *Encycl. Brit.* XIX. 14/2 The endoderm cells..are almost wholly taken up in the chemical work of digesting and assimilating the food received into the cavity, the lining of which they form. **1914** E. W. MACBRIDE *Text-bk. Embryol.* I. viii. 171 The formation of a cap of small ectoderm cells resting on larger endoderm cells and gradually investing the latter by the process called epibole. **1940** *Chambers's Techn. Dict.* 297/1 *Endoderm disc*, in certain *Malacostraca*, a posterior unpaired thickening on the ventral surface of the blastoderm during early development.

Hence **endo'dermal, endo'dermic,** *adjs.*, pertaining to or of the nature of an endoderm; **endo'dermis** [on the analogy of *epidermis*], *Bot.*

1877 HUXLEY *Anat. Inv. An.* i. 57 The endodermal lining of the enterocœle. *Ibid.* iii. 114 The flagellæ of the endodermic cells. **1884** BOWER & SCOTT *De Bary's Phaner. & Ferns* 121 The endodermis is a sheath consisting in all cases of one single layer of cells.

endodontia (ɛndəʊ'dɒntıə). [See next.] = next.

1946 (*title*) Journal of endodontia. **1949** M. COHEN in V. R. Trapozzano *Rev. Dentistry* xiii. 374 (*heading*) Endodontia. What is the objective of root canal therapy? **1969** *Gloss. Terms Dentistry* (*B.S.I.*) 21 *Endodontia*, the part of dentistry concerned with the pulp cavity and periapical tissues.

endodontics (ɛndəʊ'dɒntıks). [f. Gr. ἔνδον END(O- + ὀδούς, ὀδόντ- tooth + -ICS.] The branch of dentistry that deals with the prevention, diagnosis, and treatment of diseases of the pulp and periapical tissues.

1946 *Dentistry* VI. 771/1 (*index*) Endodontics, penicillin in. **1960** H. J. HEALEY *Endodontics* iii. 85 Endodontics requires..ability in the digital manipulation and use of specially designed instruments.

Hence **endo'dontal, endo'dontic** *adjs.*, pertaining to endodontics; **endo'dontically** *adv.*, according to the methods of endodontics; **endo'dontist**, one who practises or specializes in endodontics.

1946 *Jrnl. Endodontia* I. 1 The 'endodontist' is not any more a rebel against the ruling of 'science' but a recognized specialist of dentistry. *Ibid.* 25 Only exact endodontic technique can save a tooth without in the least endangering the patient. **1960** H. J. HEALEY *Endodontics* i. 15 Odontalgia of this nature is of particular importance to the endodontist. *Ibid.* iii. 71 The selection of cases for endodontic therapy is of utmost importance in the ultimate success or failure in endodontically treated teeth. **1960** A. B. WADE *Basic Periodontology* vi. 274 Endodontal therapy. **1965** L. I. GROSSMAN *Endodontic Practice* (ed. 6) xx. 450 Endodontal treatment..concerns itself with the health of the supporting structures of the teeth.

endogamous (ɛn'dɒgəməs), *a.* [f. Gr. ἔνδο-ν (see ENDO-) + γάμ-ος marriage + -OUS.]

Characterized by, of the nature of, or pertaining to, endogamy.

1865 MC LENNAN *Prim. Marriage* iii. 48 Tribes which we shall call endogamous tribes. **1875** LUBBOCK *Orig. Civiliz.* iii. 115 Tribes which have marriage by capture and yet are endogamous. **1880** *Academy* 10 July 26 The opinion of the ancient Arabs—that the children of endogamous marriages are weakly and lean.

endogamy (ɛn'dɒgəmı). [f. as prec. on the analogy of *polygamy*.] **1.** The custom of marrying only within the limits of a clan or tribe. Hence **endo'gamic** *a.* [see -IC], pertaining to endogamy.

1865 MCLENNAN *Prim. Marriage* 48 *note*, The words endogamy and exogamy are new. **1875** LUBBOCK *Orig. Civiliz.* iii. 95 Some tribes branched off into endogamy, others into exogamy. **1873** *Contemp. Rev.* XXII. 423 The transition..from the exogamic to the endogamic system.

2. *Bot.* The fusion or coalescence of two or more female gametes.

1937 GWYNNE-VAUGHAN & BARNES *Struct. & Devel. Fungi* (ed. 2) 5 The power of movement of attached gametangia is very limited, so that, when endogamy is possible, it is likely to occur.

endogen ('ɛndəʊdʒın). *Bot.* [Fr. *endogène* (De Candolle 1813) f. Gr. ἔνδο-ν (see ENDO-) + -γενής born, produced. (A Gr. ἐνδογενής is found with sense 'born in the house').] A plant in which new wood is developed in the interior of the stem, which is not differentiated into wood and bark; opposed to EXOGEN. Also *fig.*

Hence **endoge'neity** [badly formed after *homogeneity*], the fact of being ENDOGENOUS.

1842 GRAY *Struct. Bot.* iii. §3 (1880) 70 Endogenous, or inside growing, and for such plants the name of Endogenous Plants, or Endogens. **1867** J. MARTINEAU *Ess.* II. 167 Man is still definable as a mere intellectual endogen. **1872** H. MACMILLAN *True Vine* iii. 76 The peculiarity of the endogen is to be simple and unbranched in all its parts. **1835** LINDLEY *Introd. Bot.* (1848) I. 234 What is called Endogeneity.

endogenesis (ɛndəʊ'dʒɛnısıs). *Biol.* [mod.L., f. Gr. ἔνδον ENDO- + γένεσις origin, production.] The production of structures or bodies within the organism.

1882 *Syd. Soc. Lex.*, *Endogenesis*, the development of one or more cells in the interior of a parent cell.

endogenetic (,ɛndəʊdʒı'nɛtık), *a.* [f. as prec.: see -GENETIC.] **a.** *Path.* Developed internally. **b.** *Biol.* Produced from within. **c.** *Geol.* (i) (See quot. 1904); (ii) formed by processes originating within the earth.

1874 DUNGLISON *Dict. Med. Sci.* 358/2 *Endogenetic*,..having an origin from internal causes, as *endogenetic diseases.* **1902** *Encycl. Brit.* XXV. 439/2 The inflorescence may be endogenetic, the ovule may consist of nucellus alone, and frequently there is no ovule. **1904** A. W. GRABAU in *Amer. Geologist* Apr. 229 A group which owes its origin chiefly to chemical agents or agents acting from within, or so intimately associated with the forming rock mass that the process of formation may be called *endogenetic*. Endogenetic rocks may also be called non-clastic. **1914** T. CROOK in *Min. Mag.* XVII. 73 *Endogenetic rocks*, formed by processes of internal origin, which processes operate deep-seatedly or from within outwards. **1937** WOOLDRIDGE & MORGAN *Physical Basis Geogr.* v. 54 Internal uplifting, distorting or disrupting forces, which may be grouped as 'endogenetic'. **1953** CZECH & BOSWELL tr. *Penck's Morphol. Analysis of Land Forms* i. 2 The activity of those *endogenetic* forces, originating within the planet, which are responsible for raising individual portions of the crust above sea level.

endogenic (ɛndəʊ'dʒɛnık), *a. Geol.* [f. ENDO- + -GENIC.] = ENDOGENETIC *a.* c (ii).

1942 O. D. VON ENGELN *Geomorphology* iv. 56 The relief features..are created..by internal, that is, *endogenic* forces. **1961** L. D. STAMP *Gloss. Geogr. Terms* 176/1 Endogenetic is the usual English form, endogenic the American. **1963** D. W. & E. E. HUMPHRIES tr. *Termier's Erosion & Sedimentation* x. 202 Deformation will occur simultaneously with diagenesis, giving rise to domes or folds. It has been called 'endogenic folding' by Grabau.

endogenous (ɛn'dɒdʒınəs), *a.* [f. ENDOGEN + -OUS.] **a.** Growing from within. **b.** *Path.* (see quot. 1883). **c.** Of or pertaining to an ENDOGEN.

1830 LINDLEY *Nat. Syst. Bot*, Introd. 20 Palms, which are endogenous in the strictest sense of the word. **1856** EMERSON *Eng. Traits, Relig.* Wks. (Bohn) II. 100 No chemist has prospered in the attempt to crystallize a religion. It is endogenous, like the skin. **1874** LUBBOCK *Wild Flowers* iii. 48 Endogenous plants..are those in which the bud is developed from a sheath-like cavity on one side of the cotyledon. **1876** tr. *Wagner's Gen. Pathol.* 250 Oser also holds to the endogenous formation of cells.

d. *Geol.* Formed within a mass of rock, or within the earth's surface; *spec.* applied to intrusive rock changed by contact with surrounding rocks.

1845 A. PRICHARD tr. *von Humboldt's Κοσμος* I. 452, I entitled (1832) the plutonic and volcanic eruptive rocks *endogenous* (that which is engendered in the interior,) the sedimentary and flœtz rocks *exogenous*, (externally engendered). **1859** D. PAGE *Handbk. Geol. Terms*, *Endogenites*, fossil stems and fragments exhibiting the endogenous structure are so termed. **1878** T. S. HUNT *Chem. & Geol. Ess.* (ed. 2) xi. 196 The endogenous character of this granite is well shown by its banded structure. **1890** *Bull. Geol. Soc. Amer.* I. 48 The growth of the continent, so far as through marine waters, may be said to have been endogenous. It began to be exogenous on the Atlantic side in the Cretaceous era. **1954** W. D. THORNBURY *Princ. Geomorphology* xix. 488 Volcanism arises from forces which are endogenous in nature and are produced by physical and chemical changes taking place in the earth's interior.

e. *Psychiatry.* Applied to disorders originating within the individual.

1925 G. V. T. HAMILTON *Introd. Obj. Psychopath.* ix. 283 Conjointly acting exogenous and endogenous stimuli..may..lead to seriously morbid habits of indirect reaction. **1962** *Lancet* 29 Dec. 1341/1 Genetic factors are known to be important in the ætiology of so-called endogenous depressions, the predisposition being inherited, and the depressive illness often being precipitated by other factors which may be physical or exogenous.

Hence **en'dogenously** *adv.*, in an endogenous manner.

1876 tr. *Wagner's Gen. Pathol.* 250 The endogenously formed pus-corpuscle is born in the conjunctiva of the rabbit like a young trout. **1883** *Fortn. Rev.* 1 Aug. 177 An endogenous contagion is one that passes direct from the sick body to the sound.

endogeny (ɛn'dɒdʒını). [f. ENDO- + -GENY.] = ENDOGENESIS.

1882 *Syd. Soc. Lex.*, *Endogeny*, the condition of growing or developing from within, as when young or daughter cells are developed in the interior of a mother cell.

endognathal, -lith: see ENDO-.

endolour (ɛn'dɒlə(r)), *v. rare* [a. Fr. *endolorir*: see EN-¹ and DOLOUR.] *trans.* To plunge in grief.

1884 J. PAYNE *Tales fr. Arabic* II. 101 A heart endolored.

endolymph, endometrial, etc.: see ENDO-.

endomixis (ɛndəʊ'mıksıs). *Biol.* [f. ENDO- + Gr. μῖξις mixing, (sexual) intercourse.] A process that occurs in some lower ciliates, in which the old macronucleus disintegrates and a new one is formed from micronuclear material without conjugation taking place.

1914 WOODRUFF & ERDMANN in *Jrnl. Exper. Zool.* XVII. 491 This [rearrangement] involves a more profound intermingling of nuclear and cytoplasmic substances than is possible during the typical vegetative life of the cell. Since this intermingling occurs within a cell we term this reorganization process endomixis. **1936** *Jrnl. Morphology* LIX. 13 The term 'endomixis' has been applied to a variety of nuclear reorganization processes which may not have very much in common. **1961** MACKINNON & HAWES *Introd. Study Protozoa* 292 Many of the books continue to give detailed accounts of endomixis, which almost certainly does not occur in *Paramecium*... Endomixis does occur in some of the lower ciliates. **1965** V. A. DOGIEL *Gen. Protozool.* (ed. 2) vii. 383 In its simplest form endomixis is accomplished in *Epistylus articulata*.

endomorph ('ɛndəʊmɔːf). [f. ENDO- + Gr. μορφ-ή form.] **1.** *Min.* (See quot.)

1882 Geikie *Text-bk. Geol.* ii. ii. §2. 61 A mineral which encloses another has been called a Perimorph; one enclosed within another an Endomorph.

2. *Anthropometry.* A person with a soft round body-build in which the physical structures developed from the endodermal layer of the embryo predominate: one of W. H. Sheldon's three constitutional types (cf. ECTOMORPH, MESOMORPH).

1940 W. H. Sheldon *Varieties Human Physique* iii. 34 Those whose physiques show a predominant endomorphy we call *endomorphs. Ibid.* vii. 251 The endomorph likes soft, overstuffed furniture,..luxurious general furnishing, and ceremonial eating equipment. **1951** Auden *Nones* (1952) 56 An endomorph with gentle hands. **1954** R. Fuller *Fantasy & Fugue* 75 I've a soft body, big chest, bigger stomach. A typical viscerotonic endomorph—easy going, fond of people and fonder still of jugged hare. **1963** [see ECTOMORPH].

Hence **'endomorphic** *a.*, (*a*) *Min.* [ad. F. *endomorphique* (J. Fournet 1858, in *Ann. Sci. Physiques Soc. d'Agric., Lyon* II. Procès-verbaux, p. iii)], of or pertaining to an endomorph; (*b*) *Anthropometry*, characterized by endomorphy. Also **'endomorphy** (see quots.).

1888 F. H. Hatch in J. J. H. Teall *Brit. Petrography* 430 *Endomorphic*, applied, first by Fournet, to contact-metamorphism when produced in the erupted rock. It is used in contradistinction to *exomorphic. Syn.* Endogenous. **1940** W. H. Sheldon *Varieties Human Physique* i. 5 *Endomorphy* means relative predominance of soft roundness throughout the various regions of the body. *Ibid.* iii. 38 The whole endomorphic head is constructed on a spherical plan. **1944** A. Huxley *Let.* 19 July (1969) 508 The massive mixtures of endomorphy and mesomorphy who sing at the opera. **1955** *Lancet* 5 Feb. 291/1 Endomorphy, characterised by ready accumulation of fat, deep chest, round skull and thick upper arm and thigh but relatively thin wrists and ankles.

endopterygote (ˌɛndəʊp'tɛrɪgəʊt), *a.* and *sb. Ent.* Also -ic, -ous *adjs.* [f. mod.L. *Endopterygota* (D. Sharp 1899, in *Proc. IV Int. Congr. Zool. 1898* 246), f. Gr. ἔνδον within + πτερυγωτός winged.] Belonging to the division Endopterygota of insects, which develop their wings internally until the pupa stage. Also as *sb.* Hence **ˌendoptery'gotism**.

1899 *Proc. Intern. Congress Zool. 1898* 248 The great majority of existing insects are endopterygotic. **1902** *Encycl. Brit.* XXIX. 502/2 Some of the Palæozoic insects, though we infer them to have been exopterygotous, were really endopterygotous. *Ibid.* 503/1 The change from exopterygotism to endopterygotism..by an intermediate period of anapterygotism. **1928** G. H. Carpenter *Biol. Insects* xii. 329 The orders of winged insects—whether exopterygote or endopterygote—are distinguished mainly, as regards the adults, by the characters of their jaws and their wings. **1957** Richards & Davies *Imms's Gen. Textbk. Ent.* (ed. 9) iii. 255 There is no doubt that the Megaloptera ..include some of the most primitive recent Endopterygotes. **1964** V. B. Wigglesworth *Life of Insects* 320 This [*sc.* Neuroptera] is the first of the 'endopterygote' orders or Holometabola.

†**en'dore**, *v. Obs.* Also 4 endorre, 5–6 endour. [a. OF. *endore-r* to gild.] To cover with a yellow glaze of yolk of egg, saffron, etc.

Hence **en'dored** *ppl. a.*, **en'doring** *vbl. sb.*, *concr.* a glaze of yolk of egg, etc.

?*c* **1390** *Form of Cury* (1780) 106 Put yt on a broche and rost yt and endorre yt wyth ȝolkys of eyryn. ?*a* **1400** *Morte Arth.* 199 Ffesauntez enflureschit in flammande silver With darielles endordide, and daynteez ynewe. *c* **1420** *Anturs of Arth.* xxxvi, Ryche daintes en-doret, in dysshes bi-dene. *c* **1420** *Liber Cocorum* (1862) 37 Endore hit wit ȝolkes of egges then. *c* **1450** *15th C. Cookery Bks.* 98 Endore the coffyn withoute with saffron & almond mylke. *c* **1450** *Noble Bk. Cookry* (Napier 1882) 66 When the endoringe is stiff let them rost no more. *c* **1460** *Towneley Myst.* 90 Here is to recorde the leg of a goys, With chekyns endorde, pork, partryk, toroys. **1513** *Bk. Keruynge* in *Babees Bk.* 278 Chekyns or endowred pygyons.

endored, obs. var. of ADORED, *ppl. a.*

endorphin (ɛn'dɔːfɪn). *Biochem.* [ad. F. *endorphine* (E. Simon: see *Compt. Rend.* (1976) Ser. D. CCLXXXII. 785), f. *endogène* ENDOGENOUS *a.* + *morphine* MORPHINE.] Any of a group of peptides that occur naturally in the brain and bind to the same receptors as does morphine.

1976 *Proc. Nat. Acad. Sci.* LXXIII. 3942/1 We have reported isolating from a crude extract of (porcine) hypothalamus-neurohypophysis three peptides named endorphins. **1978** *Nature* 22 June 675/1 Recent research has led to the hypothesis that acupuncture produces analgesia through the release of endorphins. **1983** *Oxf. Textbk. Med.* II. xxi. 21/1 Electrical stimulation of nerve trunks or of cutaneous nerves can result in endorphins appearing in the cerebrospinal fluid, presumably indicating activation of pain inhibitory mechanisms.

endor(r)hiz, -al, -ous: see ENDO-.

endorsable (ɛn'dɔːsəb(ə)l), *a.* Also 8–9 indorsable, en-, indorsible. [f. ENDORSE *v.* + -ABLE.] That may or can be endorsed.

1704 *Act 3 & 4 Anne* c. 8 §1 Every such note..shall be assignable or indorsible. **1767** Blackstone *Comm.* II. 467 These also..are made assignable and indorsable in like manner. **1809** R. Langford *Introd. Trade* 12 A Promissory Note..is endorsible from one person to another. *Ibid.* 20 The latter act..renders them indorsable.

endorsation, var. INDORSATION, endorsement.

endorse (ɛn'dɔːs), *sb.* Also 6 endorce, 7 endors. [app. f. ENDORSE *v.*; but the reason for the name in sense 1 is obscure.]

1. *Her.* A vertical division of a shield, one-eighth (others say one fourth) of the breadth of a PALE. According to some of the early writers, so called only when a pale is between two of them; but others deny this.

1572 Bossewell *Armorie* 12 An Endorce..is the fourth parte of the Pallet. **1661** Morgan *Sph. Gentry* ii. iii. 33 The Pale..is divided again into the pallet, which is half the pale, and the Endors which is half the pallet. **1725** Bradley *Fam. Dict., Endorse*..the eighth Part of a Pale. **1864** Boutell *Heraldry, Hist. & Pop.* v. 23 A Pale between two Endorses is said to be endorsed.

†**2.** ? The reverse of a coin. *Obs. rare*$^{-1}$.

1688 R. Holme *Armoury* iii. 32/1 A Doller of Saxony ..[had] on the Endorse two Mens Heads.

endorse, indorse (ɛn-, ɪn'dɔːs), *v.* Forms: α. 6 endorce, 7– endorse. β. 7 indorce, 6– indorse. [Altered form of ME. *endosse* (see ENDOSS), assimilated to the equivalent med.L. *indorsāre* f. *in* upon + *dorsum* back, which was used in law-books in sense 1; cf. the OF. gloss 'indorso, *endorseir*' cited by Godef.

Indorse is the form found in legal and statutory use, and in most political economists; it is also that approved in all American dictionaries; in English use, according to Bithell (*Counting-house Dictionary*, ed. 1893), 'as to the forms *Indorse* and *Endorse*, practice appears to be entirely controlled by the taste of the writer'; but *endorse* is now almost universal in English commercial use. So with the derivatives except *indorsation* (which is now almost exclusively in Scotch use).]

I. To write on the back of something.

1. *trans.* To write on the back of (a document); to inscribe (words) *on* (the back of) a document.

a. In general sense: *e.g.* to inscribe (a document) on the back *with* words indicating the nature of its contents, one's opinion of its value, some extension or limitation of its provisions, etc. **b.** *Comm.* To sign one's name on the back of (a bill, promissory note, or cheque). **c.** *to endorse* (a sum of money) ***off***: to write on the back of a bill, etc. a receipt for a portion of its amount.

A bill, cheque, etc. payable 'to order' must be 'endorsed' by the payee before it can be paid. If ***endorsed in blank*** (i.e. without the addition of words making it payable to a particular person), it becomes payable 'to bearer'. Such documents may also be 'endorsed' by a subsequent holder, who thereby becomes responsible for their being paid (hence the *fig.* sense 2). Similarly, a bank note is often 'endorsed' to show that it has passed through the endorser's hands.

α. [**1381–1613** see ENDOSS.] **1581** Lambarde *Eiren.* iv. vii. (1588) 518 He..should endorce his name upon the backside of it. **1601–2** Fulbecke *2nd Pt. Parall.* 60 An obligation endorsed with this condition. **1686** *Lond. Gaz.* No. 2144/4 A Note..for 400*l.*..with 250*l.* Endorsed off. **1706** *Ibid.* No. 4207/4 A Bill drawn by Mr. Henry Jones..endorsed by John Spurstow and Robert Sparke. **1788** H. Walpole *Remin.* ix. 72 Sir Robert always carried them to George II, who endorsed and returned them. **1838** *Murray's Handbk N. Germ.* Introd. 17 The traveller will naturally..not endorse them till he receives the money. **1865** *Morning Star* 28 Jan., He would not now give the defendant the option of paying a fine, but would commit him for a month, and endorse that upon his licence. **1868** Rogers *Pol. Econ.* ii. (1876) 21 The bill may be subsequently endorsed by a firm of high character.

β. **1547** *Act 1 Edw. VI*, c. 5 §5 The said Wardens shall cause the Number of the said Horses..to be indorsed..on the Back-side of the said Licence. **1592** West *Symbol.* A iij, With & vpon condition thereupon indorsed for the true performance of the couenants. **1685** *Lond. Gaz.* No. 2051/4 Those Gentlemen..are desired to Indorse their Names and Places of abode, on the backside of their Tickets. **1709** *Tatler* No. 113 ¶18 A bundle of letters..indorsed..'Letters from the Old Gentleman.' **1777** Sheridan *Sch. Scand.* iii. ii, My friend Brush has indorsed it, and I thought..'twas the same as cash. **1822** Scott *Nigel* x, Pointing out.. the royal warrant indorsed thereon. **1849** Gilbart *Banking* (ed. 5) 20 All legal writers write *indorse.* **1866** Crump *Banking* 122 On indorsing a bill or note to another person, care should be taken to spell the indorsee's name correctly. **1891** *Law Times* XC. 409/1 The writ was indorsed with a claim for the removal of two of the trustees. **1893** *Law Times Rep.* LXVIII. 441/1 A memorandum of that date was indorsed upon the indenture of the 6th Oct. 1887.

d. To make (a bill, note, cheque) payable *to* another person by endorsement. Also, *to **endorse over***: to make over one's rights in (a bill, etc.) *to* another person; also *fig.*

1866 Crump *Banking* 122 On endorsing a bill or note to another person, care should be taken, etc. **1873** Burton *Hist. Scot.* VI. lxix. 162 They would not have the king indorse over to his bishops or anybody else the reverence which they submitted to be due to himself.

e. To make an entry of an offence on (a licence, e.g. of a publican or motorist).

1902 *Hansard Commons* 30 Jan. 1436 The justices will not exercise the power given them of endorsing licenses, the effect of which, on the third endorsement, would be to deprive a man of the value of his license. **1970** *Oxford Times* 18 Sept. 2/1 For driving without insurance, he was jailed for three months..and his licence was endorsed.

f. *S. Afr.* In pass. phr. ***to be endorsed out***, of Blacks: to be moved away from an urban area by the authorities because one lacks certain endorsements in an identity pass (see quot. 1963).

1963 Wilson & Mafeje *Langa* 2 A man is 'endorsed out' if he is without employment, and has not lived in Cape Town for at least fifteen years, or been with one employer for at least ten years; a woman if she is neither employed nor the wife of a man 'exempted'. **1965** *Economist* 7 Aug. p. viii/2 When they [*sc.* people of Transkai] lose jobs in the white towns..they are 'endorsed out' by officials. **1970** *Observer* 19 Apr. 25/6 The rich African, too, can be sent to jail without a pass, or 'endorsed out' from the townships into the reserves. **1980** J. Cock *Maids & Madams* 245 A woman living in an urban township may..be endorsed out if she is widowed or divorced.

2. *fig.* **a.** To confirm, sanction, countenance, or vouch for (statements, opinions, acts, etc.; occasionally, persons), as by an endorsement. Chiefly mod.; but perhaps implied in the punning quot. *a* 1637, and in quot. 1633 in ENDORSEMENT 2.

α. [*a* **1637** B. Jonson *To Earl Newcastle*, Nay, so your seate his beauties did endorse As I began to wish myself a horse.] **1847** Emerson *Repr. Men, Montaigne* Wks. (Bohn) I. 344 This book of Montaigne the world has endorsed, by translating it into all tongues. **1861** Stanhope *Pitt* II. xxii. 404 Such were the statements of Mr. Fox, but is there at the present day even one man willing to endorse them? **1874** Morley *Compromise* (1886) 67 Superstition does a little good by accidentally endorsing rational conclusions in one or two matters.

β. **1862** Bright *Sp. America* 18 Dec., The majority were supposed to indorse the policy. **1880** Carpenter in *19th Cent.* No. 38. 599 This conclusion I unhesitatingly indorsed.

†**b.** To characterize, describe, entitle. (Cf. *ticket, label.*) *Obs. rare.*

1596 Nashe *Saffron Walden* 161 He endorseth him the puling Preacher of *Pax vobis* & humilitie. *c* **1645** Howell *Lett.* iv. i. (R.) This perchance may be your policy, to endorse me your brothir.

c. To declare one's approval of, 'crack up' (a person or thing).

1914 *Concise Oxf. Dict., Endorse* (vulgar in advertisements), declare one's belief in. **1914** H. G. Wells *Englishman looks at World* vi. 61 Larkinism comes to endorse me since this was written. **1925** *Publishers' Weekly* 26 Dec. 2013/1, I am told..that even the endorsing of articles by prominent stage-folk is now not so eagerly sought after by astute manufacturers. **1926** *Ibid.* 20 Feb. 563 The New York Times, The New York Post,..and many others endorsed the book so highly that we are now setting it up ourselves. *Ibid.* 18 Sept. 960 From the standpoint of the man or woman who endorses college and college education. **1968** *Down Beat* 7 Mar. 38/1 He didn't endorse any breakfast cereals.

II. To put something on the back. (Merely literary, and chiefly humorous or pedantic.)

3. a. To load the back of (an animal) *with.* **b.** To take (something) upon one's back. **c.** To pile (something) *upon.*

1671 Milton *P.R.* iii. 329 Elephants indorsed with towers. **1808** J. Barlow *Columb.* vi. 304 The freemen.. Endorse their knapsacks. **1837** *Blackw. Mag.* XLII. 111 The heads of camels 'endorsed' with human beings. **1839** De Quincey *Recoll. Lakes* Wks. 1862 II. 98 Nightcaps, surmounted by handkerchiefs indorsed upon handkerchiefs.

4. a. To sit or ride on the back of (a horse). *nonce-use* (with pun on 2).

a **1637** [see 2]. *a* **1845** Hood *To Bad Rider* i, Why, Mr. Rider, why Your nag so ill indorse, man? —— *Desert-Born*, I cannot ride—there's something in a horse That I can always honour, but I never could endorse.

†**b.** To mount upon. *Obs. rare*$^{-1}$.

1594 Carew *Tasso* (1881) 63 The Painim troupe this while seekes to endorce, Defeated, flying, chac'd, the Citie wall.

III. 5. *Her.* In pa. pple. *endorsed.*

a. = ADDORSED; 'borne or set back to back' (Porny). **b.** Of a pale: Placed between two endorses. **c.** Of wings: Thrown backwards

α. *c* **1500** *Sc. Poem Heraldry* 131 *ibid.* 98 The ix regardand is; The x endorsit. **1572** Bossewell *Armorie* ii. 42 Dors an Dors i.e. Backe to Backe or Endorsed. **1611** Speed *Hist. Gt. Brit.* v. iii. 14 His armes to be Gules, charged with two lyons rampant endorsed Ore. **1727** Bradley *Fam. Dict.* s.v. *Endorsed*, When two Lions are born rampant, and turning their Backs to each other, the Heralds say they are endorsed. **1850** W. D. Cooper *Winchelsea* 161 A griffin passant, wings endorsed. **1864** [see ENDORSE *sb.*].

β. **1611** Cotgr., Addorsé, indorced; or, set backe to backe; a tearme of Blason. **1761** *Brit. Mag.* II. 581 Crest. On a wreath, a gryphon's head couped..wings indorsed.

endorsee, indorsee (ˌɛn-, ˌɪndɔː'siː). [f. ENDORSE *v.* + -EE.

The spelling *indorsee* was usual until recently.]

One in whose favour a note or bill is endorsed, or to whom it is assigned by endorsement.

1754 *Dict. Arts & Sc.* I. 300 The indorsee is to receive the money of the first drawer, if he can. **1766** W. Gordon *Gen. Counting-ho.* 340 The holder or last indorsee. **1767** [see ENDORSER]. **1785** Arnot *Trials* (1812) 318 The point in dispute was, whether this forgery was contrived by..the drawer and indorser, or..the indorsee. **1809** R. Langford *Introd. Trade* 22 They become answerable to their indorsee. **1817** W. Selwyn *Law Nisi Prius* (ed. 4) II. 1186 The legal title..of the indorsee of a bill of lading, may be impeached on the ground of fraud. **1849** Gilbart *Banking* (ed. 5) 55 The person who indorses a bill is called the indorser; the person to whom it is indorsed is called the indorsee [*ed.* 2, 1828, *has* endorses, endorser, endorsed, endorsee]. **1866**

CRUMP *Banking* 122 A payee indorsing a bill not negotiable is liable to his indorsee; for each indorser as it were takes the place of a new drawer. **1888** *Times* 3 Nov. 9/4 The indorsee of the bill was a fictitious person.

endorsement, indorsement (ɛn-, ɪn'dɔːsmənt). [f. ENDORSE *v.* + -MENT.] The action of endorsing.

1. The action of endorsing (a document): *concr.* a signature, memorandum, or remark endorsed upon a document. See ENDORSE *v.* 1. *spec.* the entering of an offence on a licence.

1547 *Act 1 Edward. VI*, c. 5 §5 The same Endorsement to be signed with the Hand of the said Warden. **1586** SIR A. PAULET in Ellis *Orig. Lett.* I. 220 III. 7 By reason as did appeare by an indorsement, that they had bene mistaken and were sent to Wyndsor. **1682** SCARLETT *Exchanges* 34 By his Endorsement he made it his own Bill. **1767** BLACKSTONE *Comm.* II. 468 The payee..may by indorsement, or writing his name *in dorso* or on the back of it, assign over his whole property to the bearer. **1783** BURKE *Rep. Committee on India* Wks. XI. 289 When he made the endorsement, or whether in fact he has made it at all, are matters known only to himself. **1848** MILL *Pol. Econ.* II. 46 Many bills..are at last presented for payment quite covered with indorsements. **1866** CRUMP *Banking* 121 An indorsement is a conditional contract on the part of the indorser to pay the immediate or any succeeding indorsee, in case of the acceptor's or maker's default. **1902** [see ENDORSE *v.* 1 e]. **1903** 'IAN HAY' & WODEHOUSE *Baa, Baa, Black Sheep* II. 47 May I see your licence, my dear B. B.?.. I hope it has no endorsements on it! **1960** *Act 8 & 9 Eliz. II.* c. 16. 86 (*heading*) Endorsement of licences.

2. *fig.* Confirmation, ratification, approving testimony.

1633 G. HERBERT *Temple, Sunday* i, Th' indorsement of supreme delight Writ by a friend. **1863** DRAPER *Intell. Devel. Europe* (1865) 552 It received a most emphatic endorsement from the organic world. **1879** H. GEORGE *Progr. & Pov.* I. i. (1881) 18 This doctrine..bears the indorsement of the very highest names.

endorser, indorser (ɛn-, ɪn'dɔːsə(r)). [f. ENDORSE *v.* + -ER. (In law-books sometimes *indorsor*: see -OR.)] One who endorses. *lit.* and *fig.*

1682 SCARLETT *Exchanges* 57 If an Endorser commit any Error in the endorsing..then the said Endorser is obliged to make good the Loss. **1743** FIELDING *J. Wild* II. vii, The drawer was not to be found..and consequently the money was now demanded of the indorser. **1767** BLACKSTONE *Comm.* II. 469 The indorsee..may call upon either the drawer or the indorsor. **1777** SHERIDAN *Sch. Scand.* II. ii, In all cases of slander currency, whenever the drawer of the lie was not to be found, the injured parties should have a right to come on any of the indorsers. **1849** FREESE *Comm. Class-bk.* 35 An indorser of a bill is liable in all respects. **1883** J. G. BUTLER *Bible Work, Comm. Acts* xi. 22 We remember him..first as Joses, and next as the endorser of Saul to Peter and James.

endosarc, -scope, etc.: see ENDO-.

†**en'dose.** *Obs. rare*$^{-1}$.

c **1400** *Ywaine & Gaw.* 1461 When that he [a knight newly married] has grete endose, Than war tyme to win his lose.

endosmic (ɛn'dɒzmɪk), *a.* [f. Gr. ἔνδο-ν + ὠσμό-ς (see ENDOSMOSIS) + -IC.] Of or pertaining to endosmosis.

c **1865** J. WYLDE in *Circ. Sc.* I. 62/2 Gases have an astonishing tendency to mix together, by what is called endosmic action.

endosmodic (ɛndɔz'mɒdɪk), *a. rare.* [f. as prec., after *spasmodic*.] = ENDOSMIC.

1839–47 TODD *Cycl. Anat.* III. 484/1 The original appearance was speedily reinduced, owing to the endosmodic action of the sirop.

endosmometer (ɛndɔz'mɒmɪtə(r)). [f. Gr. ἔνδο-ν + ὠσμό-ς (see ENDOSMOSIS) + -METER.] An instrument for exhibiting and measuring the phenomena of endosmosis.

1836–9 TODD *Cycl. Anat.* II. 98/2 An apparatus to which I gave the name of endosmometer. **1858** LARDNER *Hand-bk. Nat. Phil., Hydrost.* 77 Endosmometer.—Dutrochet contrived an instrument to which he gave this name.

endosmose ('ɛndɒzməʊs). *Phys.* [a. Fr. *endosmose*, formed by Dutrochet as if ad. mod.L. *endōsmōsis*: see next. Cf. EXOSMOSE, OSMOSE.] = next. Hence **endos'mosic** *a.*, of or pertaining to endosmose.

1829 *Edin. Rev.* L. 159 Endosmose, or impulsion inward. **1855** H. SPENCER *Princ. Psychol.* (1872) II. VI. xi. 139 Solubility in the saliva, without which its particles cannot be carried by endosmose through the mucous membrane of the tongue. **1882** VINES *Sachs' Bot.* 423 The vesicle..swells up strongly in water by endosmose, as is shown in Fig. 293. **1835** TODD *Cycl. Anat.* I. 41/2 These filamentary organs.. were endowed with an endosmosic power.

endosmosis (ɛndɔz'məʊsɪs). *Physics* and *Phys.* [mod.L. (quasi-Gr.), f. Gr. ἔνδο-ν (see ENDO-) + ὠσμός pushing, thrusting. = ENDOSMOSE. (The two forms appear to be equally frequent in use; *endosmosis* is more in accordance with Eng. analogies.)] The passage of a fluid 'inwards' through a porous septum, to mix with another fluid on the inside of it.

1836–9 TODD *Cycl. Anat.* II. 99 All alkalies and soluble salts produce endosmosis. **1844–57** G. BIRD *Urin. Deposits* (ed. 5) 428 The well-known phenomena described by Dutrochet, under the terms of endosmosis and exosmosis. **1880** J. W. LEGG *Bile* 55 The appearance of sugar in the bile is due to endosmosis from the liver itself.

endosmotic (ɛndɔz'mɒtɪk). [f. as prec. on Gr. analogies; cf. *anastomosis, anastomotic*.] Of or pertaining to endosmosis.

1836–9 TODD *Cycl. Anat.* II. 108/1 Two opposite endosmotic currents. **1876** tr. *Wagner's Gen. Pathol.* 537 Albumen possesses endosmotic properties. **1882** VINES *Sachs' Bot.* 673 The endosmotic force of grape-sugar.

endos'motically, *adv.* [f. ENDOSMOTIC *a.*: see -ICALLY.] In an endosmotic manner.

1881 K. SEMPER *Nat. Conditions* vi. 184 They [*sc.* desert-snails] may..be capable of absorbing a larger amount of water endosmotically through the skin than the snails in our damp climates. **1884** SEDGWICK & HEATHCOTE tr. *Claus's Zool.* 307 The nutritive fluid passes endosmotically into the body parenchyma.

endosperm, -spore, etc.: see ENDO-.

†**en'doss,** *v. Obs.* Forms: 4–7 endosse (*pa. pple.* 4 endost, 5 endoost, indoost, indost), 5 endos, 6 endoce, 9 (*rare*) endoss. [ME. *endosse*, a. OF. *endosse-r* corresp. to med.L. *indorsāre* ENDORSE, f. *in* upon + *dorsum* (Fr. *dos*) back].

1. *trans.* To write on the back of (a document); to inscribe (words) *on* (the back of) a document; = ENDORSE, *v.* 1.

1381 *Pol. Poems* (1859) I. 225 Charters were endost. **1460–70** LYDG. *Ord. Fools* 8 in *Q. Eliz. Academy* 79 Endosyd theyre patente that they shall neuer the. **1502** ARNOLDE *Chron.* (1811) 119 Wee award yt ether of theym by his obligacion be bounde to other x. li. stg. wyth condycion, endoced. **1613** R. C. *Table Alph.* (ed. 3) *Endosse*, put on the back, or write on ye back.

2. In extended sense: To inscribe or portray (something) upon any surface. *Obs.*

1447 BOKENHAM *Seyntys* 145 Mynerve..Wyth al hir wyt ne coude provide More goodly aray Thow she dede endos Wyth ynne oo web al methamophosyos. **1595** SPENSER *Col. Clout* 634 Her name in euery tree I will endosse. **1596** — *F.Q.* v. xi. 53 A shield in which he did endosse His deare Redeemers badge vpon the bosse.

3. a. To put (clothing) on one's back. **b.** ? To clothe with armour.

c **1460** *Towneley Myst.* 166 Both ye and I Agains the fynde are welle endoost. **1805** W. TAYLOR *Monthly Mag.* XIX. 574 He endosses the black robe.

4. To load the back; in quot. *transf.*

c **1460** *Towneley Myst.* 201 For his great boost With knoks he is indoost. *Ibid.* 254 With tormentes keyn bese he indost For ever more.

endosteal, etc.: see ENDO-.

†**en'dote,** *v. Obs. rare*$^{-1}$. [f. EN-[1] + F. *doter*, ad. L. *dōtāre*, f. *dōt-em* dowry.] = ENDOW *v.* 2.

1528 TINDALE *Obed. Chr. Man* Wks. I. 249 Their own heirs do men disinherit, to endote them [the friars].

endothecal, -thelial, etc.: see ENDO-.

endothelioma (,ɛndɒθiːlɪ'əʊmə). *Path.* Pl. -ata. [ad. G. *endotheliom* (C. O. Block 1875, in *Arch. d. Heilkunde* XVI. 412), f. ENDOTHELI(UM + -OMA.] A tumour of endothelium. Hence **endotheli'omatous** *a.*

1880 H. OSGOOD tr. *von Ziemssen's Cycl. Pract. Med.* IX. 344 Under the name of primary melanotic endothelioma of the liver, Block recently described a case of diffuse or infiltrated pigment cancer. **1886** *Buck's Handbk. Med. Sci.* II. 812/1 *Endothelioma* (psammoma) of the optic nerve consists of alveolar connective tissue, in which cells lie embedded in more or less concentric layers. **1888** J. F. PAYNE *Gen. Path.* 302 Endothelioma is a name sometimes given to this [*sc.* psammoma] and other growths originating in, and composed of, endothelium. **1894** D. J. HAMILTON *Text-bk. Path.* II. II. lxxxv. 738 Cylindromatous endotheliomata are found in various parts of the brain or projecting into the brain from the membranes. **1906** *Practitioner* Nov. 666 The endotheliomatous areas consisted of tubules, columns or sheets of cells. **1964** S. DUKE-ELDER *Parsons' Dis. Eye* (ed. 14) xxv. 369 Some of these may be endotheliomatous growths. *Ibid.* xxxiii. 530 Primary tumours of the optic nerve... A few are endotheliomata or fibromata.

endothermic (ɛndəʊ'θɜːmɪk), *a. Chem.* [ad. F. *endothermique* (M. Berthelot *Essai de mécanique chimique* (1879) II. IV. ii. 18), f. ENDO- + THERMIC *a.*] Characterized by, or attended with, the absorption of heat.

1884 M. M. P. MUIR *Princ. Chem.* I. iv. 254 To found a system of classification on the difference between exothermic and endothermic changes. **1890** *Bloxam's Chem.* (ed. 7) 141 When C is burnt into CO_2 by 2 N_2O, it evolves 40,400 more units of heat than when burnt in O_2, showing that, contrary to the usual law, heat is evolved in the decomposition of the N_2O, amounting to 20,200 units per molecule. Such a compound is said to be endothermic. **1898** *Nature* 18 Aug. 375 The true chemical equivalent of light energy can only be measured by means of an endothermic irreversible reaction. **1902** *Encycl. Brit.* XXV. 37/1 Such endothermic bodies are nearly always found to show considerable violence in their decomposition. **1927** *Jrnl. Iron & Steel Inst.* CXVI. 479 Practically all clays undergo an endothermic reaction between 100° and 650°C. **1945** *Electronic Engin.* XVII. 670 The individual process of induced transformation is just as likely to be endothermic as exothermic. **1960** *New Biol.* XXXI. 62 The formation is analogous to an endothermic compound or to any molecule in which energy is stored. **1963** HIGHAM *Handbk. Papermaking* v. 109 In the case of the sulphate process the reaction given above is endothermic and, as such, requires considerable heat to achieve completion. **1965** *New Scientist* 4 Nov. 345/1 Beyond Mach 5 the heat to be absorbed will be so great that it will be necessary to use 'endothermic fuels' which undergo chemical reactions which absorb heat.

endothermy ('ɛndəʊθɜːmɪ). [f. ENDO- + Gr. θερμός heat + -Y[3].] (See quot. 1922).

1922 *Lancet* 3 June 1109/1 Endothermy is the production of heat in the tissues from within, the active electrode being cold when applied, the process differing therefore from other methods of cauterisation by heat. **1933** *Times* (Electricity Supply No.) 5 Dec. p. xxiii/6 Endothermy, a modification of diathermy..which enables him to carry out certain operations that were previously impossible.

endotrophic ('ɛndəʊtrɒfɪk), *a. Bot.* Also (erron.) endotropic. [ad. G. *endotropisch* (B. Frank 1887, in *Ber. d. Deut. Bot. Ges.* V. 398).]

Chiefly of Mycorrhiza: nourished from within; growing within the cells of plant roots. Opp. ECTOTROPHIC *a.*

1899 *Ann. Bot.* XIII. 7 The presence of an endotropic mycorhiza in the roots of the *Aplectrum* would lessen the tendency to the formation of an ectotropic layer with a second fungus. **1903** [see ECTOTROPHIC *a.*]. **1926** TANSLEY & CHIPP *Study of Vegetation* ix. 158 Endotrophic [fungi] are found mainly within the cells of the roots of herbaceous plants. **1959** [see ECTOTROPHIC *a.*].

endoubt: see EN- *pref.*[1] 2.

endow (ɛn'daʊ), *v.* Also 7–8 indow. [f. EN- *pref.*[1] + F. *douer*:—L. *dōtāre*, f. *dōt-em* dowry. In legal AF. (15th c.) *endouer*.]

1. *trans.* †**a.** To give a dowry to (a woman) (*obs.*). **b.** To provide dower for (a widow). Formerly const. *of*.

1535 *Act 27 Hen. VIII*, c. 10 §7 Suche woman shalbe endowed of as muche of the residue of her husbandes tenementes. **1574** tr. *Littleton's Tenures* 8 b, The wife..shall bee endowed of the thirde parte of such landes. **1607** *Shaks. Timon* I. i. 139 How shall she be endowed, If she be mated with an equall Husband? **1635** AUSTIN *Medit.* 106 Lest hee should be thought unable to endowe his Spouse. **1767** BLACKSTONE *Comm.* II. 131 An alien also cannot be endowed, unless she be queen consort. **1818** CRUISE *Digest* (ed. 2) I. 180 If the wife be past the age of nine years, at the time of her husband's death, she shall be endowed.

†**c.** To give as a dowry. *fig. Obs. rare*$^{-1}$.

1475 CAXTON *Jason* 4 [Death] the dowaire that nature hath endowed to me.

2. To enrich with property; to provide (by bequest or gift) a permanent income for (a person, society, or institution).

c **1460** FORTESCUE *Abs. & Lim. Mon.* (1714) 69 How that the Crown may be best endowed. **1480** CAXTON *Chron. Eng.* VII. (1520) 150 b/2 Whiche preest is sufficyently endowed for hym and a servaunt. **1569** *Bk. Com. Prayer*, Matrimony, With al my worldly Goodes I thee endowe. **1570** *Act 13 Eliz.* c. 10 §1 Ecclesiastical Persons.. being endowed and possessed of ancient Palaces..and other Edifices. **1580** STOW *Annales* 559 He indowed them with rents and reuenues taken from the priories..which hee suppressed. **1638** *Penit. Conf.* vii. (1657) 136 Let an Hospital be once erected, and endowed. **1772** BURKE *Sp. Ch. Claims Bill* 17 Feb. Wks. X. 146 Not that the Church of England is incompetently endowed. **1856** EMERSON *Eng. Traits, Cockayne* Wks. (Bohn) II. 64 A testator endows a dog or a rookery, and Europe cannot interfere with his absurdity. **1857** TOULM. SMITH *Parish* 19 The piety of the wealthy led them to build and endow these [churches].

3. *fig.* **a.** To invest *with* (privileges, etc.).

1601 HOLLAND *Pliny* I. 75 All Achæa generally throughout, Domitius Nero endowed with freedom. **1661** BRAMHALL *Just Vind.* vi. 126 Justinian did new-found the Patriarchate..and indow it with ample priviledges.

b. To enrich or furnish *with* (†*in*, †*of*) any 'gift', quality, or power of mind or body.

a **1420** OCCLEVE *De Reg. Princ.* 143 Hym ought endowed be in sapience. **1425** *Paston Lett.* 5. I. 21 Ye are..of worshepe and cunnyng worthyly endowed. **1475** CAXTON *Jason* 34 b, Thinking on the vertues wher in he was endowed they complayned him moche. **1526** *Pilgr. Perf.* (W. de W. 1531) 169 b, He hath endowed vs christians..with the spiryte of adopcyon. **1661** BRAMHALL *Just Vind.* v, Our Saviour endowed them with all the fulness of power that mortal men were capable of. **1743** J. MORRIS *Serm.* ii. 34 They..who were indowed with any extraordinary gifts. **1856** EMERSON *Eng. Traits, Lit.* Wks. (Bohn) II. 114 Tennyson is endowed precisely in points where Wordsworth wanted. **1872** YEATS *Techn. Hist. Comm.* 212 Inorganic matter becomes first endowed with life and organisation during the growth of plants. **1872** MORLEY *Voltaire* (1886) 142 Considered as statuesque figures endowed with speech, Brutus, Cæsar, and the rest are noble and impressive.

c. To invest (imaginatively) *with* a quality.

1888 MISS YONGE *Hannah More* 62 The ladies not only believed in her wonderful genius, but endowed her with all imaginable virtues.

†**d.** Said of the qualities with which one is 'endowed'. Cf. ENDUE *v.* 9 b. *Obs.*

1611 SHAKS. *Cymb.* I. i. 24 I do not thinke So faire an Outward, and such stuffe within Endowes a man, but hee.

†**4.** ? Confused with ENDUE. To put on (garments).

1483 CAXTON *G. de la Tour* C ij, The deuylle..dyde her endowe her gownes.

†**en'dowage.** *Obs. rare*$^{-1}$. In 6 endowege. [f. ENDOW *v.* + -AGE.] = ENDOWMENT.

1530 *Proper Dialogue* (1863) 34 Ye people to swere for to maynteyne this endowege of ye clerkes and religious folke.

endowed (ɛn'daʊd), *ppl. a.* [f. ENDOW *v.*] In senses of the vb. Chiefly of societies or

institutions: Possessing a secured income from property bequeathed or given.

1700 DR. WALLIS in *Collect.* (Oxf. Hist. Soc.) I. 324 They are schools endowed; with exhibitions.. for the education of youth. **1846** McCULLOCH *Acc. Brit. Empire* (1854) II. 315 The names, free school, endowed school, grammar school, etc., are often used with some degree of confusion. **1870** *Echo* 9 Nov., There are the endowed charities which derive a steady annual income from invested property.

¶ **b.** Used *transf.* of the secured income. *rare.*

1845 R. HAMILTON *Pop. Educ.* viii. 191 The endowed stipend would not yield the master the most meagre support.

endower (ɛnˈdaʊə(r)), *sb.* [f. ENDOW *v.* + -ER.] One who endows.

1624 DARCIE *Birth of Heresies* xviii. 75 Authors, Restorers, Endowers, and augmenters of the Missall Sacrifice. **1765-9** BLACKSTONE *Comm.* (1793) 604 The right of visitation of the former results.. to the king; and of the latter to the patron or endower. **1885** *Ch. Q. Rev.* XXI. 139 If the State regarded itself as the endower of the Church.

†**enˈdower**, *v. Obs.* [ad. OF. *endouairer*, f. *en-* (see EN-[1]) + *douaire* DOWER.] *trans.* To dower (a woman); also *fig.*

1606 G. W[OODCOCKE] *Hist. Ivstine* Ff 4 a, He maried to a most honorable man the daughter of his enemy Vitellius, being most largely endowred. **1653** WATERHOUSE *Apol. Learning* 142 (T.) This once renowned church was gloriously deckt with the jewels of her espousals.. and frankly endowered. **1654** R. CODRINGTON *Hist. Iustine* 15 The wife being endowred with the blood of her husband, delivered.. herself to her adulterer.

endowing (ɛnˈdaʊɪŋ) *vbl. sb.* [f. ENDOW *v.* + -ING[1].] The action of the vb. ENDOW.

c **1460** FORTESCUE *Abs. & Lim. Mon.* xix. (1714) 139 How grete Goode wyll growe of the forme endowyng of the Crowne. **1631** WEEVER *Anc. Fun. Mon.* 199 In building and endowing of an Hospitall. **1740** J. CLARKE *Educ. Youth* (ed. 3) 189 The Building and endowing of Colleges. **1867** PEARSON *Early & Mid. Ages Eng.* I. 167 This endowing of the first adventurers.

endowment (ɛnˈdaʊmənt). Also 6-8 indow(e)ment. [f. ENDOW *v.* + -MENT.]

1. The action of endowing, in various senses.

c **1460** FORTESCUE *Abs. & Lim. Mon.* (1714) 78 We have found undoubtydly what maner of Revenuz, is beste for the Endowment of the Crowne. **1494** FABYAN, IV. lxix. 47 Of this firste Indowement of the Churche. **1641** *Termes de la Ley* 135 Indowment.. signifies properly the giving or assuring of dower to a woman. **1642** PERKINS *Prof. Bk.* v. §315. 139 Possession of the freehold by the endowment is vested in, etc. **1852** LEVER *Daltons* II. 259 You are anxious about the endowment of the Ursulines, and so am I.

2. *concr.* The property or fund with which a society, institution, etc. is endowed.

1597 HOOKER *Eccl. Pol.* v. lxxix. (1611) 429 The goods of the Church are the sacred indowments of God. **1649** BP. REYNOLDS *Hosea* i. 39 O therefore that every Parish had an endowment fit for a learned, laborious, and worthy Pastor. **1757** BURKE *Abridgm. Eng. Hist.* Wks. X. 411 Alms, and endowments, the usual fruits of a late penitence. **1845** S. AUSTIN *Ranke's Hist. Ref.* II. 501 The estates of benefices.. were applied to increasing the endowments of parish churches and schools. **1870** *Daily News* 16 Feb., The sacrifice of the endowments of the Irish Church.

†**3. a.** Commercial advantage, profit. **b.** Property, possessions. *Obs. rare.*

1615 G. SANDYS *Trav.* 12 The Lentiske tree, which is welnigh onely proper to Sio doth giue it the greatest renowne and endowment. **1816** SCOTT *Old Mort.* xxxiii, Basil Olifant, who had agreed to take the field if he were ensured possession of these women's worldly endowments.

4. A 'gift', power, capacity, or other advantage with which a person is endowed by nature or fortune.

c **1610** SIR J. MELVIL *Mem.* (1735) 12 The King's rare natural Endowments. **1611** SHAKS. *Cymb.* I. iv. 6 Though the Catalogue of his endowments had bin tabled by his side. **1672** DRYDEN *Assignation* I. i. Dram. Wks. 1725 III. 296 A man of my extraordinary Indowments. **1710** PRIDEAUX *Orig. Tithes* ii. 69 No Endowments of the Mind.. were at all necessary. **1847** EMERSON *Repr. Men, Shaks.* Wks. (Bohn) I. 362 With this wisdom of life is the equal endowment of imagination and of lyric power. **1859** DARWIN *Orig. Spec.* xv. (1873) 428 All corporeal and mental endowments will tend to progress towards perfection.

5. *attrib.* and *Comb.*: (sense 2) **endowment assurance, insurance**, a form of life insurance providing for the payment of an endowment or fixed sum to the insured person at a specified date, or (usually) to his representatives on his death, should that take place before the specified date of payment; **endowment (insurance) policy**, a policy which provides for payment according to the above method; so **endowment plan; endowment mortgage**, a mortgage that is linked to an endowment policy such that the capital is repaid only when the policy matures or on the death of the borrower.

1865 *Nation* (N.Y.) I. 157 Endowment Assurance Policies.. are issued to persons desirous of making provisions for advanced life. **1871** *Harper's Mag.* Aug. 477 Benjamin P. Gunn.. explaining the endowment plan to his guide. **1880** *Encycl. Brit.* XIII. 168/2 Endowment-Assurances. **1889** *Cent. Dict.*, Endowment policy, or, in full, Endowment insurance policy. **1895** E. CARROLL *Princ. Finance* 298 Insurance is divided into Accident and Casualty Insurance, Endowment Insurance, Fire Insurance, Life Insurance, Marine Insurance, etc. **1898** *Westm. Gaz.* 5 Feb. 6/3 The Equity and Law seems to be the only office to which the public should take their endowment assurance business. **1898** *Daily News* 26 Feb. 8/1 The favourite system of insurance is the endowment plan, is it not? **1962** *Which?* June 183/1 In this report, we compare non-profit and with-profits endowment assurance policies. **1965** *Building Societies Inst. Q.* Apr. 101 The paragraphs on endowment mortgages are rather confused and incomplete. **1986** *What Mortgage* June 14/3 An endowment mortgage is automatically linked to an endowment assurance policy provided by an insurance company.

†**enˈdowry.** *Obs. rare.* [f. ENDOW *v.*, after DOWRY.] = DOWRY.

1523 LD. BERNERS *Froiss.* I. cxvi. 139 Johane, eldest daughter to the duke of Brabant.. went to the lande of Buyche, the which was her endowrie. *c* **1530** —— *Arth. Lyt. Bryt.* (1814) 26 Ye shall gyue to Perron your wyf this nyght yͤ charter of her endowry.

ˈend-point. [f. END *sb.* + POINT *sb.*[1]] The end or latter part of a period, process, etc.

1. *spec.* in *Chem.*, etc. The point in a titration, or the stage of a process of dilution, at which a definite effect is observable.

1899 HENDERSON & PARKER *Introd. Anal. Chem.* 114 The exact point at which neutralization takes place ('the end point') is determined by means of an indicator. **1919** *Chemist & Druggist* XCI. 243 The solution is very slowly decolorised at first... The end point was taken as the faintest visibly pink tint, permanent for one minute. **1946** *Nature* 19 Oct. 556/2 The concentration of chloride in the blood of agouti and black mice has been investigated.. but with only 0.22 c.c. of serum the end-point is not certain. **1956** *Ibid.* 18 Feb. 303/2 Tobacco seedlings show systemic symptoms sooner when inoculated with tobacco sap diluted almost to the infection end-point than when they are inoculated with undiluted sap from infected Prince beans. **1961** *Lancet* 29 July 228/1 In the tube dilution methods the end-point was taken as the last tube showing visible growth after 48 hours incubation at 35-37°C. **1963** *Ibid.* 5 Jan. 52/2 'Total acid' meant titratable acidity to an end-point about pH 8-10 (phenolphthalein).

2. *transf.* and *fig.*

1921 E. SAPIR *Language* (1922) v. 115 The starting-point and end-point of the flow of activity. **1927** L. CLENDENING *Human Body* iv. 109 (*caption*) An air sac. The end point of a lung branch. **1959** J. C. CATFORD in Quirk & Smith *Teaching of English* vi. 183 The variations in the vertical dimension.. represent.. different types of end-point, or 'second term', for the relations represented. **1965** W. S. ALLEN *Vox Latina* ii. 60 Scaurus.. who comments on the current end-point of the dipthong as *e* rather than *i*.

end-ˈproduct. [f. END *sb.* + PRODUCT *sb.*[1] 3.]

1. *Chem.* A stable, non-radioactive nuclide that is the final product of a radioactive series.

1905 RUTHERFORD in *Phil. Mag.* X. 306 The view that lead is the final or end product of the transformation of radium is supported by the fact that lead is always found in the radioactive minerals in about the amount to be theoretically expected from the content of uranium, when the quantity of helium, present in the mineral, is used to compute its probable age. **1907** B. C. A. WINDLE *Sci. Facts* 10 The element thorium appears to be constantly engaged in generating from itself another solid element which again decays, its end-product being so far unknown. **1922** *Encycl. Brit.* XXXII. 221/2 The atomic weight of the end-product of uranium is close to that of lead. **1958** F. E. ZEUNER *Dating the Past* (ed. 4) 320 Actinium.. decays until finally, after the emission of 7 atoms of helium, the inactive end-product is reached, which.. is actinium-lead with the atomic weight of 207.

2. A finished article in a manufacturing process.

1939 *Fortune* Apr. 1 An automobile.. is the end-product of a long line of manufacturing, mining and farming activities. **1950** *Engineering* 24 Feb. 222/2 The.. engineering product.. may be an end-product or a component. **1958** *Listener* 5 June 931/2 We speak of the end-product in a factory. **1959** *Times Lit. Suppl.* 13 Mar. 140/4 Miró.. can rely on the interpretative sensibility of craftsmen.. whose end-products he describes as.. 'authentic in their plastic statement'.

3. *transf.* and *fig.*

1923 J. S. HUXLEY *Ess. Biologist* ii. 79 His adult self, the end-product of that development. **1924** J. GLOVER in E. Jones *Social Aspects Psycho-Analysis* 44 The earliest nascent manifestations of these instincts and their most complicated and remote end products. **1931** *Nature* 7 Feb. 214/2 The end-products of soil formation are closely similar from the two contrasted types of parent rock. **1942** M. McCARTHY *Company she Keeps* (1943) v. 131 The prodigality was merely an end-product of asceticism. **1961** J. WILSON *Reason & Morals* ii. 112 Of course 'I must not fight' *might* be the end product of a calculation: perhaps for some pacifists it is.

endragoned, *ppl. a.*: see EN- *prefix*[1] 3.

†**enˈdraper**, *v. Obs. rare*[−1]. [app. irregularly a. OF. *endraper*, f. *en-* (see EN-[1]) + *drap* cloth.] *trans.* To weave into cloth.

Hence **enˈdrapering** *vbl. sb.*

1461-83 *Pol. Poems* (1859) II. 287 By the endraperyng theroff [of wool] they haue theyre sustynaunce.

endrench: see EN- *pref.*[1] 3.

endrin (ˈɛndrɪn). [Prob. f. EN-[2] + *-drin* as in ALDRIN, DIELDRIN.] An insecticide that is a stereo-isomer of dieldrin.

1953 *Jrnl. Econ. Ent.* XLVI. 164/1 (*title*) Control of Mosquitoes with DDT, Aldrin, Dieldrin, Endrin and Isodrin. *Ibid.* 199/1 Report of the Committee on Insecticide Terminology.. The Committee has approved endrin as a coined name for the insecticidal chemical [etc.]. **1956** *Nature* 25 Feb. 356/1 DDT and some of its analogues, rotenone and endrin. **1964** *New Statesman* 3 Apr. 538/2 Almost coincident with the recommendation to withdraw endrin and dieldrin came a report on the damage done by these two pesticides.. in the Mississippi basin.

†**enˈdroit.** *Obs. rare.* Also endrayghte, -eyte. [a. OF. *endroit, -ait*, in same sense.] Quality, species.

c **1400** *Beryn* 404 The statis that were above had of the feyrest endreyte. **1480** CAXTON *Ovid's Met.* XII. xii, A yonge Centaure, the moste fayre creatur of his endroit. *c* **1488** *Liber Niger* in *Househ. Ord.* (1790) 36 The clerk of kychyn.. shall go see the kings servyse and deyntes of flesshe and fish, that it be alwey chosen of the best endrayght.

endrudge, endry: see EN- *pref.*[1] 2.

†**ˈendship.** *Obs.* [f. END *sb.* + -SHIP. Cf. *township*.] A small suburb, a hamlet.

1589 R. HARVEY *Pl. Perc.* 8 All the picked yoouths straind out of an whole Endship. *a* **1688** BUNYAN *Barren Fig-tree*, They shake the whole family, the endship, the whole town. **1701** DE FOE *Freeh. Plea agst. Stockj. Elect.* 18 They are not to be Nam'd among the List of the most despicable Endships, or Village[s] in the County.

ˈendsville, *sb. U.S. slang.* Also Endville, Endsville. [f. END *sb.* 1 d (b): see -VILLE.] **a.** The greatest, the best; the imaginary home of good things or people.

1957 *N.Y. Times Mag.* 18 Aug. 26/1 Endville (obs.) means the best. **1959** *Esquire* Nov. 70/1 *Endsville*, the greatest. **1960** *Amer. Speech* XXXV. 313 *Endsville*.. refers to the home of a person, in this case that of a brilliant one ('He's the end from Endsville').

b. = *the end of the road* s.v. END *sb.* 3 h; also, 'the limit', 'the end' (sense 1 d).

1962 *Radio Times* 17 May 43 Endsville man, I got no bread. **1969** *Time* 21 Nov. 48/3 At the windup of his two-week tour, Soviet Cosmonaut Georgy Beregovoy announced that New York was strictly Endsville: 'Saturated. Tense. Not fun at all.' **1977** *Times Lit. Suppl.* 17 June 722/1 In a more depressing sense, however, a Last Frontier can be the last place left to go, a last chance, a forlorn hope, endsville. **1984** F. SINATRA in J. Rockwell *Sinatra* 231 You can be the most artistically perfect performer in the world, but the audience is like a broad—if you're indifferent, endsville.

enduce, obs. variant of INDUCE.

endue, indue (ɛn-, ɪnˈdjuː), *v.* Forms: α. 5-7 endew, 5- endue; β. 5-7, indew, (6 yndue), 5- indue. [ad. OF. *enduire* (also in semi-learned form *induire*), corresp. to Pr. *endurre*, Cat. *induir*, It. *indurre* (cf. the 'learned' forms Sp. *inducir*, Pg. *induzir*, It. *inducere*):—L. *indūcĕre* (see INDUCE), f. *in* into, on + *dūcĕre* to lead, draw. The etymological senses 'lead into', 'draw into', 'lead on', 'draw on', account for the Eng. senses 1-6, which approximately follow the senses of OF. *enduire, induire*. In senses 5-6, however, the word was associated with the nearly synonymous L. *induĕre* to put on (a garment), which it often renders in early translations from Latin. (Perhaps it would not be incorrect to say that the L. *induĕre* was adapted in a form coinciding with that of the verb ad. OF. *enduire*.) Senses 7-9 are of mixed origin: they are partly derived from the fig. use of sense 6 'to clothe' (cf. *invest*); but the forms *endew, indew* in 15th c. (sense 8) are etymologically equivalent to ENDOW (cf. OF. *deu* 1 pers. pres. indic. of *doër* to endow). Hence in 16th and 17th c. the verb *endue* had all the senses of ENDOW in addition to those which it derived from OF. *enduire* and L. *induĕre*. In sense 9 the meanings proceeding from the three sources have so completely coalesced that it is often impossible to say which of them is the most prominent in a particular use of the word.

The form *endue* is now the more common in all the living senses, though some writers employ it and *indue* indiscriminately, while others appropriate the latter to those uses (*esp.* senses 5, 6) which suggest an etymological connexion with L. *induere*. The obs. sense 2, when referred to by mod. writers, has commonly the spelling *endew*.]

I. To bring in, introduce.

†**1.** To induct (a spiritual person) into a living, or (a secular person) into a lordship. In ME. const. *in* (= into). *Obs.*

c **1400** *Apol. Loll.* 50 For bischoppis, abbots, or oþer personis, to be putt in þer segis, or prestis to be induyd, or inled in Kirks. **1460** CAPGRAVE *Chron.* 256 Othir dukes he schal endewe in the lordchippis of Itaile.

II. [after Fr. *enduire*.]

†**2.** Of a hawk: In early use, app. = 'to put over', *i.e.* to pass (the food contained in the 'gorge') into the stomach; in later use, to digest. (In 15th c. only *absol.*; from 16th c. also, *to endue her gorge, her meat.*) Hence *transf.* of other animals or of persons: To digest. *Obs.*

α. *c* **1430** *Bk. Hawkyng* in *Rel. Ant.* I. 296 And ye shall say this hawke is ful y-gorged, and hath endewedd, or i-put over. **1486** *Bk. St. Albans* A vij a, An hawke enduth neuer as long as hir bowellis bene full at her fedyng. *a* **1528** SKELTON *Col. Cloute* 216 Your gorge not endewed Without a capon stewed. **1530** PALSGR. 643/1, I mute, as a hauke dothe whan she hath endued her gorge. **1577** B. GOOGE *Heresbach's Husb.* IV. (1586) 161 b, Give them [fowls] no newe, till you

perceive..that the olde bee endewed. **1615-33** LATHAM *Falconry* Gloss., *Endew*, is when a Hawke digesteth her meat, not onely putting it ouer from her gorge, but also cleansing her pannell. **1622** FLETCHER *Sp. Curate* v. ii, A good stomach will endue it easilie. **1626** DONNE *Serm.* lxviii. 684 Meat..such as they are able to digest and endue. **1708** MOTTEUX *Rabelais* v. ii, They eat and drank like men.. endued or digested like men. **1721** in BAILEY.

β. **1575** TURBERV. *Bk. Falconrie* 327 Shee will have indewed it out of hande. **1615** LATHAM *Falconry* (1633) 85 If the stomacke..do not digest and indue well. **1618** —— *2nd Bk. Falconry* (1633) 114 Small birds..are meetest for that purpose, and easiest to be indued.

†**b.** *fig.* To take in, 'inwardly digest'. *Obs.*

1596 SPENSER *F.Q.* III. x. 9 None but she it vewd, Who well perceived all, and all indewd.

†**3.** *intr.* To be digested. *Obs. rare.*

c **1575** *Perfect Bk. for kepinge Sparhawkes* (1886) 7 Meates wch endew sonest and maketh the hardest panell.

†**III. 4.** To lead on; to bring up, educate, instruct. *Obs.* [See examples of *enduire* in Godef.]

1526 *Pilgr. Perf.* (W. de W. 1531) 16 The purpose of God was so to endewe man that he sholde neuer thynke this worlde his fynall habitacyon. **1541** PAYNEL *Catiline* iii. 4 He was indued and brought up in conditions like Catiline. **1580** BARET *Alv.* I. 135 To indue, instruct, or teach, *imbuo.* **1581** J. BELL *Haddon's Answ. Osor.* 323 Paule..endued you at the first with a farre other manner of doctrine.

†**b.** To bring *to* a certain state or condition. *Obs. rare*$^{-1}$.

1604 SHAKS. *Oth.* III. iv. 146 For let our finger ake, and it endues Our other healthfull members, euen to a sense Of paine.

IV. To put on as a garment; to clothe or cover. [Influenced by L. *induere.*]

5. To assume, take upon oneself (a different form) [cf. L. *induere personam*, etc.]; in later use, to put on (garments, etc.). Also *fig.*

1432-50 tr. *Higden* (Rolls) I. 369 A man and a woman be constreynede to indue an other forme. **1596** SPENSER *F.Q.* III. vi. 35 Infinite shapes of creatures there are bred..Some fitt for reasonable sowles t' indew. **1626** G. SANDYS *Ovid's Met.* XI. 232 Next, Phantasus..indues a tree, Earth, water, stone. **1814** SCOTT *Wav.* xii, The Baron..had indued a pair of jack-boots of large dimensions. **1830** TENNYSON *Poems* 122 Could I..indue i' the spring Hues of fresh youth. **1848** LYTTON *Harold* XII. vii, Who had not yet endued his heavy mail. **1859** J. H. STIRLING *Crit. Ess. Tennyson* (1868) 71 How perfectly Tennyson can endue what state of mind he pleases. **1880** MISS BROUGHTON *Sec. Th.* II. III. v. 209 Regarding..the perfectly new Tweed suit which..he has endued.

6. To clothe (a person) *with.*

1432-50 tr. *Higden* (Rolls) I. 239 The victor was induede with the coote of Iupiter. *a* **1700** DRYDEN tr. *Ovid's Met.* Wks. 1821 XII. 147 Endu'd with robes of various hue. **1850** HAWTHORNE *Scarlet L.* viii. (1879) 123 A loose gown..such as elderly gentlemen loved to endue themselves with. **1866** R. CHAMBERS *Ess.* Ser. I. 182 His feet are raised upon the fender..he is endued with slippers and gown.

b. *transf.*

a **1649** DRUMM. OF HAWTH. *Fam. Ep.* Wks. (1711) 136 The spring the woods with new [leaves] indews. **1857-8** SEARS *Athan.* iv. 27 Every particle of the poor dust that has ever indued us. **1869** BLACKMORE *Lorna D.* ii. (ed. 12) 7 John Fry's..hat was indued with a plume of marsh-weed. **1875** *Wonders Phys. World* II. iv. 305 This species indued in a thick shaggy fur.

†**c.** To overlay, cover. [The current sense of Fr. *enduire.*] *Obs. rare.*

1644 EVELYN *Mem.* (1857) I. 128 The miraculous Sudarium indued with the picture of our Saviour's face. **1794** BLUMENBACH *Mummies* in *Phil. Trans.* LXXXIV. 187 The hard compact ones, wholly indued with rosin.

V. To 'invest' or endow with dignities, possessions, qualities, etc.

†**7.** To invest with honours, dignity, etc. *Obs.*

1565 T. RANDOLPH in Ellis *Orig. Lett.* I 184. II. 201 All dignities that she cane indue hym with, are all reddie given and graunted. **1513-75** *Diurn. Occurr.* (1833) 70 The quenis grace..maid thir personis following knychtis, and indewit thame with the honour thairof.

†**8.** To invest (a person or body of persons) *with* property; = ENDOW *v.* 2. Const. *of.* *Obs.*

c **1440** *Promp. Parv.*, Induyn, *doto.* *c* **1449** PECOCK *Repr.* 347 Founders and Endewers of eny persounes or comountees, if thei endewiden so richeli..weren not..to be blamed. **1494** FABYAN VII. 370 He sette therin monkes of Cisteaux ordre, whyte monkes, and endewed them with ryche possessyons. **1496-7** *Plumpton Corr.* 124 That it wyll please your sayd mastership to indue this woman in some lordship of yours of xx marke duryng hir lyfe. **1529** *Act 21 Hen. VIII*, c. 13 Noo..Parsonage that hath a Vicar indued, nor any Benefice perpetually appropriate. **1568** GRAFTON *Chron.* II. 258 The same Jaques had promised the king..to endue his sonne the Prince of Wales therewith [Flaundyrs]. **1579** FENTON *Guicciard.* (1618) 231 To indue his brother with Ecclesiastical reuenues. **1590** GREENE *Never too Late* C iij, What substance hath Francesco to endue thee with? **1611** BIBLE *Gen.* xxx. 20 And Leah said, God hath endued me with a good dowry. **1647** LILLY *Chr. Astrol.* xviii. 102 A man modestly indued with the Goods and Fortune of this world.

†**b.** To endow (an institution). *Obs.*

a. **1539** *Act 31 Hen. VIII*, c. 5 The king hath of late erected..a goodly sumptuous house..and the same endewed with parkes, orchardes, gardein. **1565** CALFHILL *Answ. Treat. Crosse* (1846) 207 Constantinus..liberally did endue the church. **1601** F. GODWIN *Bps. of Eng.* 232 [He] very largely endued..the Abbey of Eynsham. **1603** KNOLLES *Hist. Turks* (1621) 838 How to endue the same with lands and revenues sufficient.

β. **1462** J. PASTON in *Lett.* 461 II. 113 Sir John Fastolf.. mad his will in especiall that a college of vij monks shuld be stabilisshed, founded, and indewed. **1538** LELAND *Itin.* I. 10 St. Thomas Hospitale is..induid with sum Landes, al by the Citisens of Northampton.

†**c.** To supply *with* anything. *Obs.*

1595 SHAKS. *John* IV. ii. 43 More strong [reasons] I shall indue you with. **1607** —— *Cor.* II. iii. 147 The Tribunes endue you with the Peoples Voyce.

†**d.** To bestow, grant. Const. *dat.* of pron.; cf. ENDOW *v.* 1 c. *Obs. rare.*

1587 M. GROVE *Pelops & Hipp.* (1878) 55 Let Clio muse to paint the gifts, which Ioue doth her endue.

9. To invest *with* a power or quality, a spiritual gift, etc. Often in pass. *to be endued with* = to be possessed of (a certain quality).

Nearly synonymous with ENDOW; the two verbs may often be used interchangeably, but in mod. use *endow* suggests that the power or quality is of the nature of a permanent advantage.

a. **1447** BOKENHAM *Seyntys* (1835) 13 With vertuhs ful excellently In hyr soule inward endewyd was she. **1509** FISHER *Fun. Serm. C'tess Richmond* (1708) 8 She being endued with so grete towardness of Nature. **1605** BACON *Adv. Learn.* I. iii. §6 Learning endueth mens mindes with a true sence of the frailtie of their persons. **1616** HIERON *Wks.* II. 37 Was it with what religion is the woman endewed, or with what portion is shee endowed? **1669** BOYLE *Contn. New Exp.* II. (1682) 27 The Apples seemed..endued with a most pleasant Taste. **1709** BERKELEY *Ess. Vision* §86 Our sight would be endued with a far greater sharpness. **1736** BUTLER *Anal.* I. i. Wks. 1874 I. 14 We know we are endued with capacities of action, of happiness and misery. **1791** COWPER *Iliad* XVII. 898 Two mules with strength for toil endued. **1874** HOLLAND *Mistr. Manse* xxi. 92 Contented with the hue which endues its wings with beauty.

β. **1536** R. BEERLEY in *Four C. Eng. Lett.* 34 Most reuerent lord yn God..ynduyd with all grace and goodnes. **1655** FULLER *Ch. Hist.* I. i. §17 An oake in New Forest..is indued with the same quality, putting forth leaves about the same time. **1692** WASHINGTON tr. *Milton's Def. Pop.* ii. (1851) 63 Kings, tho indued with the Supream Power are not..Lords over the People. **1727** POPE, etc. *Art Sinking* 118 The less a man is indued with any virtue, the more need he has to have it plentifully bestowed. **1754** EDWARDS *Freed. Will* III. iii. 156 Let us suppose a Scale of a Balance..indued with a self-moving Power. **1860** HOLLAND *Miss Gilbert* xvii. 305 A heart indued and informed with love for God and man.

†**b.** Of a quality, etc.: To be inherent in. *Obs.*

1631 MILTON *Sonn.* ii. 8 And inward ripeness doth much less appear, That some more timely-happy spirits endu'th. **1655-60** STANLEY *Hist. Philos.* (1701) 27/2 Whose Souls deceit and vanity endue.

Hence †**en'duable** *a.*, capable of being invested with, or put in possession of. Const. *of.* †**en'duer**, one who invests a person or body of persons (with lands, etc.).

1558 *Richmond. Wills* (1853) 124 Of the whyc my sayd wyffe schal be endewebl accordyng to comone lawys. *c* **1449** [See ENDUE *v.* 8].

†**en'duement.** *Obs.* Also 7 **induement.** [f. ENDUE *v.* + -MENT.] The action of enduing; *concr.* that with which one is endued.

a. That which is put on or worn; a covering (*rare*). **b.** *fig.* A qualification, accomplishment, adornment.

1609 HOLLAND *Amm. Marcel* XV. viii. 45 They had.. perused the old bookes, the reading whereof declareth by bodily signes the physiognomie or inward induements of the mind. **1641** MILTON *Ch. Discip.* I. (1851) 23 They prostitute every induement of grace, every holy thing to sale. **1650** BULWER *Anthropomet.* xxi. 229 Shoes or any other enduements of the Feet are besides Nature. *c* **1674** *Scotl. Grievances under Lauderdale* I Our great perswasions of his singular enduements..were the only measures of our concessions.

†**endugine.** *Obs. rare*$^{-1}$. ? = DUDGEON.

1638 *Gratiæ Ludentes* 118 (N.) Which shee often perceiving, and taking in great endugine, roundly told him, etc.

enduing (ɛn'dju:ɪŋ), *vbl. sb.* [f. ENDUE *v.* + -ING^1.] The action of the verb ENDUE (sense 2).

1575 TURBERV. *Bk. Falconrie* 327 The heate [in the liver] ..is the cause of all kindly digestion and indewing.

en'duing, *ppl. a.* [f. as prec. + -ING^2.] That endues.

1644 BULWER *Chirol.* 143 The enduing ensigne..by evidence ensures the priviledges of investiture.

†**en'dulce,** *v. Obs.* [ad. OF. *endoulcir*, f. *en-* (see EN-^{1}) + *doulx, doulce*:—L. *dulcem* sweet.] *trans.* To sweeten, perfume.

1611 SPEED *Hist. Gt. Brit.* VII. xlii. 352 Her body shee endulced with the sweetest balmes.

endulge, obs. form of INDULGE *v.*

†**en'dull,** *v. Obs.* [f. EN-^{1} + DULL *a.*] *trans.* To render dull; to blunt, weaken; to deprive of sanity.

1395 PURVEY *Remonstr.* (1851) 28 Endullynge the regalie and power of seculer lordis. **1490** CAXTON *Eneydos* xxvi. 96 She [Dido] is..endulled and fallen in dysperacyon. **1520** BARCLAY *Jugurth.* 51 b His mynde was a lytell endulled and priuate of reason and memorie.

endungeon (ɛn'dʌndʒən), *v.* Also 9 **indungeon.** [f. EN-^{1} + DUNGEON.] *trans.* To put into or shut up in a dungeon. Hence, to enclose in any receptacle. Hence **en'dungeoned** *ppl. a.*

a. **1599** NASHE *Lent. Stuffe* 56 Endungeond in his pocket a tweluemonth. **1623** DRUMM OF HAWTH. *Flowers Sion* (1630) 31 That Prince of Sin..shall endungeoned dwell. *a* **1711** KEN *Hymnotheo* Poet. Wks. 1721 III. 153 By Faith they mock'd, scourg'd, chain'd, endungeon'd lay. **1820** COLERIDGE in *Lit. Rem.* (1836) IV. 114 To endungeon through the magistrate the honest and peaceable Quaker. **1827** MONTGOMERY *Pelican Isl.* IX. 163 'Twas a spectacle for angels..To see a dark endungeon'd spirit roused.

β. **1808** J. BARLOW *Columb.* I. 41 Who now beneath his tower indungeon'd lies. **1884** TENNYSON *Becket* IV. ii. 156 Could you keep her Indungeon'd from one whisper of the wind.

Endura (ɛn'djʊrə). [mod.L., f. O. Prov. *endurar* to fast, endure.] A practice among the Cathari, in which those who have received the consolamentum undergo physical privations, freq. resulting in death, in order to prevent recontamination of the soul.

1888 H. C. LEA *Hist. Inquisition* I. iii. 95 When this heretication occurred on the death-bed, it was commonly followed by the 'Endura' or 'privation'. **1922** H. J. WARNER *Albigensian Heresy* iv. 85 Every inducement was now made to the sick man to end his life by any means other than by direct violence. He was urged to undergo the *Endura*, which took various forms. **1961** P. GREEN tr. *Oldenbourg's Massacre at Montségur* ii. 51 Certain *perfecti* were so passionately addicted to extreme fasting that they incurred the charge of wanting to put an end to their own lives. This is the explanation behind the legend of the *endura*, or voluntary death by starvation. **1970** R. HAUGHTON *Love* iii. 94 The Cathars, whose extreme doctrine could culminate in the ecstatic suicide of fasting of the 'Endura'.

endurability (ɛn,djʊərə'bɪlɪtɪ). *rare.* [f. ENDURABLE *a.* + -ITY.] The quality of being endurable.

1837 CARLYLE *Fr. Rev.* I. III. vi, It begins questioning Lettres-de-Cachet generally, their legality, endurability.

endurable (ɛn'djʊərəb(ə)l), *a.* Also 7 **indurable.** [f. ENDURE *v.* + -ABLE.]

1. That can be endured, suffered, put up with.

1800 WORDSW. *Michael* 454 There is a comfort in the strength of love; 'Twill make a thing endurable, which else, etc. **1823** LAMB *Elia* (1860) 208 His Iago was the only endurable one which I remember to have seen. **1856** FROUDE *Hist. Eng.* (1858) II. xi. 458 Life had become at least endurable to her.

2. Able or likely to endure, durable. *rare.*

1607 TOPSELL *Four-f. Beasts* (1673) 434 The mule.. ought to be brought up in..hard places, that so the hoofs may grow hard and indurable. **1616** *Withals' Dict.* 549 Good manners are endurable, but beauty is lost by age. **1826** *Blackw. Mag.* XX. 328 Rock-rooted castles, that seem endurable till the solid globe shall dissolve. **1885** *Manch. Wkly. Times* Supp. 20 June 4/3 This sheepskin is not nearly so strong and endurable as the material it is made to simulate. **1886** *Northern N. & Q.* I. 51 The author has done a solid and endurable piece of work.

Hence **en'durableness.** *rare.* The state or character of being endurable.

1795 COLERIDGE *Plot Discov.* 18 If its only excellence, if its whole endurableness consist in motion.

endurably (ɛn'djʊərəblɪ), *adv.* [f. ENDURABLE *a.* + -LY^2.] In an endurable manner; so as to be endured.

In recent Dicts.

endurance (ɛn'djʊərəns). Also 6-8 **indurance.** [f. ENDURE *v.* + -ANCE; in OF. *endurance.*]

1. a. The fact of enduring (pain, hardship, annoyance); the habit or the power of enduring; often *absol.* as denoting a quality, longsuffering, patience.

a. **1667** MILTON *P.L.* II. 262 We can create, and work ease out of pain Through labour and endurance. **1839** JAMES *Louis XIV*, IV. 449 He was forgiving, and of long endurance. **1856** KANE *Arct. Expl.* II. xxvi. 267 The disciplined endurance of the men. **1861** GEO. ELIOT *Silas M.* 59 Their aged wisdom was constantly in a state of endurance mitigated by sarcasm. **1879** FROUDE *Cæsar* viii. 76 The endurance of the inequalities of life by the poor is the marvel of human society. **1888** *Amer. Humorist* 5 May 3/2 Prolonging his visit beyond all endurance.

β. **1599** SHAKS. *Much Ado* II. i. 246 O she misusde me past the indurance of a block. **1744** HARRIS *Three Treat.* III. I. (1765) 137 Not a grain more of Magnanimity, of Candour and Calm Indurance.

†**b.** Durance, captivity, imprisonment. *Obs.*

1603 KNOLLES *Hist. Turks* (1621) 1256 Which.. composition..made in the absence and indurance of their Generall, was by the Turkes faithfully kept.

c. Of inanimate things: the power of holding out; the capacity (e.g. of steel) of withstanding strain.

1890 *Daily News* 13 Nov. 5/7 Her speed was 18 knots an hour. Her coal endurance is given as 475 tons stowage, and with that stowed she could have steamed 7,000 miles. **1911** *Proc. Inst. Mech. Engin.* IV. 878 Annealed cast-steel showed rather less endurance than annealed mild-steel, in spite of the much greater tenacity of the cast-steel. **1930** *Jrnl. Iron & Steel Inst.* CXXII. 597 The heat-treatment of the rails was found to have markedly increased the endurance of the steel. **1932** *Discovery* May 143/2 The endurance of spiral and laminated springs..is much less than that of the steel of which they are composed.

2. a. Duration or continued existence in time. Also, power of lasting, capacity of continued existence.

1494 FABYAN V. cxxix. 111 Some accompt ye enduraunce therof to the laste yere of Burdredus. **1692** LADY RUSSELL *Lett.* II. cxxxvii. 112 The joys of eternal endurance. **1799** J. ROBERTSON *Agric Perth* 74 The leases now commonly granted are of endurance nineteen years. **1811** L. HAWKINS *C'tess & Gertr.* I. 27 Sermons of four hours' endurance. **1855** BAIN *Senses & Int.* I. ii. §23 (1864) 63 The undying endurance of an electric wire. **1865** M. ARNOLD *Ess. Crit.* i.

(1875) 7 This is why Byron's poetry had so little endurance in it, and Goethe's so much.

β. **1596** SPENSER *State Irel.* 2 Others more late and of lesse indurance. **1614** RALEIGH *Hist. World* II. 381 The long indurance of the Siege [of Troy].

†**b.** ? Protraction of an existing condition. *Obs. rare*⁻¹.

1613 SHAKS. *Hen. VIII*, v. i. 122, I should haue tane some paines..to haue heard you Without indurance further.

3. *concr.* That which is endured; a hardship.

a. **1608** SHAKS. *Per.* v. i. 13 If thine consider'd prove the thousandth part Of my endurance, thou art a man. **1622** BACON *Hen. VII*, 158 Wee shall also unyoke our People from all heauie Burthens and Endurances. **1812** J. HENRY *Camp. agst. Quebec* 134 The endurances we underwent in conjunction. **1865** DICKENS *Mut. Fr.* I. 286 Is my present endurance none?

β. *a* **1555** RIDLEY *Wks.* 428 I never had of him which suffered indurance at my entrance to the see of London, one penny of his moveable goods. **1622** J. RAWLINS *Recor. Ship Bristol* in Arb. *Garner* IV. 591 Which he must procure, or incure sorer indurances.

4. *attrib.* (esp. in spec. sense of the durability of metals), as ***endurance limit, range, test*** (= *fatigue limit, range, test*).

1925 *Jrnl. Iron & Steel Inst.* CXI. 563 Increase in the elastic ratio increase, the ratio of endurance limit to tensile and torsional strength. *Ibid.*, With low elastic ratio the full endurance range can be utilised only when the range is between nearly equal and opposite stresses. **1902** *Phil. Trans.* A. CXCIX. 289 The breaking stress for annealed specimens of the type used in the endurance tests was 23·1 tons for Lowmoor iron, and 48 tons for cast-steel. **1930** [see ATTRITION 2 b *fig.*]. **1930** *Engineering* 3 Jan. 27/3 Endurance tests on the complete springs. **1932** AUDEN *Orators* III. 109 Are you sure of passing the endurance test?

endurant (ɛnˈdjʊərənt), *a.* [f. ENDURE *v.* + -ANT; in F. *endurant.*] Ready to endure; that endures or is capable of enduring. Const. *of.*

1866 NEALE *Sequences & Hymns* 137 Doing good, and endurant of evil. **1874** PUSEY *Lent. Serm.* 314 We should be endurant of evil and subservient to all. **1881** PALGRAVE *Visions Eng.* 240 Calm adamantine endurant chief.

endurate, obs. form of INDURATE.

endure (ɛnˈdjʊə(r)), *v.* Forms: *α.* 4 endeure, 5 enduer, 4– endure; *β.* (5 induyr), 5–8 indure. [a. OF. *endure-r* to make hard, to endure, = Pr. *endurar*, It. *indurare*:—L. *indūrāre*, f. *in* (see IN-) + *dūrāre* to harden, to endure, f. *dūr-us* hard.]

†**I. 1.** To indurate, harden. Hence *fig.* to make callous or indifferent. Also, in good sense, to make sturdy or robust, to strengthen. *Obs.*

a. **1382** WYCLIF *Acts* xix. 9 Summe weren endurid, or maad hard. **1407** *Exam. W. Thorpe* in Arb. *Garner* VI. 58 O thine heart is full hard, endured as was the heart of Pharoah. **1483** CAXTON *Gold. Leg.* 128/3 And she endured and enformed all the other in prayer. **15..** *New Not-broune Mayd, Passion Cryste* 388 in Hazl. *E.P.P.* III. 16 So endured With synne and vyce is he. **1596** SPENSER *F.Q.* IV. viii. 27 And manly limbs endur'd with litle care Against all hard mishaps and fortunelesse misfare.

β. **1578–1600** *Sc. Poems 16th C.* II. 183 Priests, curse no more, And not your heartes indure. **1588** A. KING tr. *Canisius' Catech.* 146 That suithlie, quhilk maks the mynde of man stubbornlie indured agains gud admonition.

II. To last; to suffer continuously.

2. *intr.* To last, continue in existence. Also, to persist, 'hold out' in any action, etc. †Formerly also, to continue in a certain state or condition, remain in a certain place (with complement expressing the state or place).

a. c **1386** CHAUCER *Man Law's T.* 655 In the castel noon so hardy was That eny while dorste therin endure. *c* **1400** MAUNDEV. v. (1839) 47 Who so stopped that watre from hem, thei myghte not endure there. *c* **1400** *Sowdone Bab.* 1220 Thou maiste not longe endure. *c* **1430** LYDG. *Chorle & Byrde* (1818) 14 A wrecche never lyke to thryve But for tendure in poverte all my live. **1477** EARL RIVERS (Caxton) *Dictes* 10 b, His lordship and power in this worlde may not long endure. *a* **1555** LATIMER *Serm. & Rem.* (1845) 33 So this great king endured a leper all the days of his life. **1607** TOPSELL *Serpents* (1653) 613 Snakes and Adders..will not endure neer those places where they hear their voice. **1664** EVELYN *Kal. Hort.* (1729) 218 Myrtles will endure abroad near a month longer. **1711** *Col. Rec. Penn.* II. 558 A free and open trade with us whilst the Sun endures. **1814** SOUTHEY in *Q. Rev.* XII. 65 Such corruptions endure only for a season. **1845** S. AUSTIN *Ranke's Hist. Ref.* II. 407 Such a relation was too wide a departure from the ordinary nature and course of human affairs to endure long. **1878** BROWNING *La Saisiaz* 35 Take the hope therein away, All we have to do is surely not endure another day.

β. c **1450** *Merlin* ii. 24 Thus it indured longe tyme. *c* **1460** *Towneley Myst., Processus Noe* 24 It shalle begyn fulle sone to rayn uncessantle..and induyr dayes fourty. **1542** BOORDE *Dyetary* xxviii. (1870) 291 As long as the Agew doth indure. **1596** BELL *Surv. Popery* I. I. ii. 5 The floud indured one whole yeare. **1616** SURFL. & MARKH. *Countr. Farme* 407 If you wash them in salt brine, you shall make them white, and to indure long. **1676–7** MARVELL *Corr.* Wks. 1872–5 II. 524 The debate upon the Nine-pences..indured the whole day. **1743** *Lond. & Country Brew.* II. (ed. 2) 147 Neither Fermentation, nor Age, can ever disunite or separate such its ill Properties, while the Drink indures.

†**b.** To keep up *with*. *Obs. rare.*

1588 R. PARKE tr. *Mendoza's Hist. China* 180 Men..did trauaile with the same [burdens] with so great ease and swiftnes, that the horse could not indure with them.

†**c.** To be continued through space; to extend from one point to another. *Obs. rare.*

1523 LD. BERNERS *Froiss.* I. cccxxxvii. (1812) 527 Highe wodes and forestes, that endured to the cyte of Constances. *c* **1530** —— *Arth. Lyt. Bryt.* (1814) 303 Thei [woundes] began at his shouldres and endured downe to his thyghes. **1588** R. PARKE tr. *Mendoza's Hist. China* 229 These Ilands endured vntill they came vnto a little gulfe. *Ibid.* 328 Many townes of Indians of this nation, the which indured twelue dayes iourney.

†**d.** quasi-*trans.* with *out*: To last out, persist during the continuance of (an event or action).

1636 E. DACRES tr. *Machiavel's Disc. Livy* I. 133 They would sooner accept of the Kings, than endure out the warre.

3. *trans.* To undergo, bear, sustain (continuous pain, opposition, hardship, or annoyance); *properly*, to undergo without succumbing or giving way. Also *absol.*

a. c **1325** *E.E. Allit. P.* A. 475 What more-hond moȝte he a-cheue þat hade endured in worlde stronge. **1340** HAMPOLE *Pr. Consc.* 6865 For-why na whitt of man may endure To se a devel in his propre figure. **1570–6** LAMBARDE *Peramb. Kent* (1826) 145 One sort founde him more than a Pope, the other felt him more than a King, and they both endured him an intollerable tyrant. **1667** MILTON *P.L.* II. 206 To endure Exile, or ignominy, or bonds, or pain. **1795** SOUTHEY *Joan of Arc* v. 380 He can brave his cruelty, And triumph by enduring. **1876** GREEN *Short Hist.* ii. §8 (1882) 101 Such anarchy as England had endured under Stephen.

β. **1594** H. WILLOBIE in *Shaks. C. Praise* 7 To indure the burning heate. **1671** *True Nonconf.* 169 Your N.C. must indeed be very simple, that he could indure such imposing. **1711** SHAFTESB. *Charac.* (1737) II. 383 See how you can indure the prospect. **1782** PRIESTLEY *Corrupt. Chr.* I. II. 238 These writers had..to indure..the punishment.

b. Of things: To support (a strain, pressure, wear and tear, etc.) without receiving injury; formerly also *absol.* Also in weaker sense, to undergo, suffer, be subjected to.

1413 LYDG. *Pylg. Sowle* IV. xxx, Gold wylle well enduren under the hamoure enlargyng hymself withouten crasure. **1611** BIBLE *Pref.* 1 The same endured many a storm of gaine-saying. **1658** EVELYN *Fr. Gard.* (1675) 70 Old trees, whose rind being very tough, can endure the wedge without splitting. **1860** TYNDALL *Glac.* II. §3. 247 The loss [of heat] endured..through radiation into space.

†**c.** To withstand as an adversary, support, sustain. *Obs.*

1375 BARBOUR *Bruce* II. 429 His men..war sa few that thai na mycht Endur the forss mar off the fycht. *c* **1450** *Merlin* ix. 134 That noon myght his strokes endure. **1470–85** MALORY *Arthur* x. i, Yet shalle I ryght wel endure you. **1724** DE FOE *Mem. Cavalier* (1840) 64 We were obliged to endure the whole weight of the imperial army.

4. To suffer without resistance, submit to, tolerate; to contemplate with toleration.

a. **1475** CAXTON *Jason* 78 Notwithstanding he endured the malice of Zethephius..a certayn space. **1601** SHAKS. *Jul. C.* IV. iii. 29 Brutus, baite not me, Ile not indure it. **1609** B. JONSON *Sil. Wom.* I. i. (1616) 533 He cannot endure a Costard-monger. **1651** HOBBES *Leviath.* II. xxiv. 129 Commonwealths can endure no Diet. **1716–8** LADY M. W. MONTAGUE *Lett.* I. xvi. 54 Men endure everything while they are in love. **1732** BERKELEY *Alciphr.* ii. §24 The tendency of your opinions is so bad that no good man can endure them. **1845** E. HOLMES *Mozart* 136 The French gentlemen have only so far improved their taste as to be able to endure good things.

β. **1617** MARKHAM *Caval.* II. 86 Your horse..will not indure their companie. **1617** HIERON *Wks.* (1619–20) II. 342 God..can indure none but cheerefull Seruitors. **1678** BUNYAN *Pilgr.* I. 135, I could never indure him.

¶ Used for: To entertain the possibility of.

1677 FELTHAM *Resolves* I. xxvii. (ed. 10) 47 St. Augustine would by no means indure the Antipodes: we are now of nothing more certain.

b. With object inf. (with *to*), subord. cl., or accus. and inf.

a. **15..** *New Not-broune Mayd* (1842) 51 When your pleasure Was to endure To lye my sydes betwene. **1607** TOPSELL *Serpents* (1653) 815 The people of Europe in no place..can endure them to be set on their Tables. **1611** BIBLE *Esther* viii. 6 For how can I endure to see the evil that shall come unto my people? *a* **1627** HAYWARD *Four Y. Eliz.* (1840) 44 He had openlie reproched the French soldiers, for enduringe their master's enimies to lyve. *a* **1718** PENN *Maxims* Wks. 1726 I. 836 Those that have employments should not be endured to leave them humourously. **1732** BERKELEY *Alciphr.* i. §5 We..cannot endure that truth should suffer through complaisance. **1792** G. WAKEFIELD *Answer to Priestley* 14 But my friends..must, and will, endure me both to speak and write of them and their opinions, etc. **1798** —— *Reply to the Bp. of Landaff's Address* 5 The public ear must endure to vibrate with an incessant application of wholesome doctrine. **1871** BROWNING *Pr. Hohenstiel* 1314 The man endured to help, not save outright the multitude.

β. **1597** HOOKER *Eccl. Pol.* v. vii. (1611) 195 The world will not indure to heare that we are, etc. **1601** R. JOHNSON *Kingd. & Commw.* (1603) 205 They will not indure any of the common people to come neare them. **1654** TRAPP *Comm. Ps.* iv. 3 Wee cannot indure to hear sweet words from a stinking breath. **1660** *Trial Regic.* 106 They ought not to indure to have their Jurisdiction so much as questioned.

†**5.** Of things: To permit of, be compatible with. *arch.*

1593 BILSON *Govt. Christ's Ch.* 166 The wordes doe well endure it. **1823** SCOTT *Peveril* xiii, I have that to say to this youth which will not endure your presence.

†**enˈdured**, *ppl. a. Obs. rare.* In 6 indured. [f. ENDURE *v.* + -ED¹.] Hardened, callous; = INDURATED.

1540 SURREY *Poems* 103 In blind indured hearts light of thy lively name Cannot appear. **1578–1600** *Sc. Poems 16th C.* II. 171 Their false indured heart.

†**enˈdurement.** *Obs.* [f. ENDURE *v.* + -MENT.] The action of enduring; *concr.* that which is endured; hardship, suffering.

1608 SYLVESTER *Du Bartas* (1621) 626 Or too-much idle feare of sufferings and endurements. *a* **1716** SOUTH *Serm.* (1744) VIII. ix. 254 These examples..should make us couragious in the endurement of all worldly misery.

endurer (ɛnˈdjʊərə(r)). *rare.* [f. ENDURE *v.* + -ER.] One who endures.

1596 SPENSER *State Irel.* (J.), They are..great endurers of cold, labour, hunger, and all hardiness. *a* **1625** BEAUM. & FL. *Nice Valour* IV. i, I'll fit you with my scholars, new practitioners, Endurers of the time. **1832** tr. *Tour Germ. Prince* II. ix. 155 What a man was this sublime endurer!

enˈduring, *vbl. sb.* Also 7 induring. [f. ENDURE *v.* + -ING¹.] The action of the vb. ENDURE.

c **1374** CHAUCER *Boeth.* III. xi. 98 Acordynge to hyr nature in conservacioun of hyr beynge and enduryng. **1413** LYDG. *Pilgr. Sowle* V. i. (1859) 73 Seculum is taken for the enduryng of the world. **1603** KNOLLES *Hist. Turks* (1638) 103 The induring of a long siege. **1659** PEARSON *Creed* (1839) 329 The descent into hell is not the enduring the torments of hell. **1684** BUNYAN *Pilgr.* II. 114 His Faith, his Courage, his Enduring, and his Sincerity under all, has made his Name Famous.

enduring (ɛnˈdjʊərɪŋ), *ppl. a.* Also 7 in-. [f. ENDURE *v.* + -ING².] That endures, lasting.

1532–3 *Act 24 Hen. VIII*, c. 1 Fewe of them..haue any good or strong horse-harneis of lether, ne any endewringe saddelles. **1816–7** BYRON *Manfred* I. i. 4 My slumbers—if I slumber—are not sleep, But a continuance of enduring thought. **1883** FROUDE *Short Stud.* IV. I. x. 125 The most enduring incidents of English history.

†**enˈduring**, *prep. Obs.* Also 6–8 induring. [Orig. the pr. pple. of ENDURE *v.*, in concord with the sb. (e.g. *enduring his life* = 'while his life endures'), afterwards taken as prep.] = DURING.

a. **1494** FABYAN VI. clxxv. 172 Enduryng whiche trowbles, the Danys entred the lande. **1513** BRADSHAW *St. Werburge* I. 987, I wyll obserue, enduryng this lyfe mortall. **1548** UDALL *Erasm. Par.* Pref. 12 a All my lyfe enduryng..to employe, etc. *a* **1615** *Brieue Cron. Erlis Ross* (1850) 16 Iohne Ila was Erll of Ross..enduring his lyftyme.

β. **1524** *Diurn. Occurr. Scot.* (1833) 9 All the kirkis of thar dyocies wer interdyted induring their wairding. **1588** A. KING tr. *Canisius' Catech. Confess.* 9 Gif being pairted for adulterie lauchfullie prouen, any marie induring the vyers [other's] lyf quhilk is adulterie. **1637–50** ROW *Hist. Kirk* (1842) 179 And I promise, indureing the conference, not to countenance any enemies to that religion.

enduringly (ɛnˈdjʊərɪŋlɪ), *adv.* [f. ENDURING *ppl. a.* + -LY².] In an enduring manner.

1831 *New Monthly Mag.* LIII. 545 How assiduously and enduringly they toiled. **1862** R. PATTERSON *Ess. Hist. & Art* 378 The great empires which have enduringly impressed themselves upon the world's memory. **1888** *Harper's Mag.* July 215 The work was done cheaply and flimsily, not massively and enduringly.

enduringness (ɛnˈdjʊərɪŋnɪs). [f. ENDURING *ppl. a.* + -NESS.] The quality of being enduring.

a **1867** JAS. HAMILTON in Spurgeon *Treas. Dav.* Ps. xc. 16 In so far as it was to have any success or enduringness, it must be God's work. **1878** DOWDEN *Stud. Lit.* 155 The enduringness of nerve needed for sane and continuous action.

enduro (ɛnˈdjʊərəʊ). Chiefly *U.S.* [f. ENDUR(ANCE + -O².] A long-distance race for motor vehicles (orig. for motorcycles) or boats, designed to test endurance rather than speed.

1935 *Motorcyclist* Mar. 6/1 My mount, by virtue of my showing in the enduro, was a Twin-cylinder Thor. **1967** *Boston Sunday Herald* 26 Mar. I. 49/6 There's a smattering of local interest again on this 16th year of the Florida enduro. **1967** *Boston Sunday Globe* 23 Apr. 5/1 A motorcycle owner..can..compete in a cross-country race (enduro), or chase another rider around a bumpy, circular track (scrambles). **1976–77** *Sea Spray* (N.Z.) Dec./Jan. 13/1 (Advt.), Prototype versions of our V-6 [outboard motor] have stepped into the winner's circuits around the world, including the Paris,..and the Milan, Italy, enduros. **1986** *Kart & Superkart* Aug. 19/1 Nothing logical ever happens in Endurance racing, so..all the Enduro professionals..had put in lot of time and effort to get the equipment, pits and back-up crew all working well.

enduyce, obs. form of INDUCE.

†**ˈendware.** *Obs. rare*⁻¹. [? perh. some error; OE. **ęnde-waru* (collect. sing.) would mean 'the inhabitants of an end' (cf. END *sb.* and -WARE). Halliwell gives '*Endware*, a hamlet, *Linc.*'; but it is not in the Linc. glossaries.] ? = ENDSHIP.

1577 HARRISON *England* II. xiii. (1877) I. 261 The moonkes were authors of manie goodlie borowes and endwares neere unto their dwellings..But alas..they wrought oft great wickedness and made those endwares little better than brodelhouses.

end-way(s, -wise (ɛndweɪ, -weɪz, -waɪz), *adv.* [f. END *sb.* + -WAY(S, -WISE.]

1. Of position: With the end (as distinguished from the side) uppermost, foremost, or turned towards the spectator. Also ***endways on***.

1657 R. LIGON *Barbadoes* (1673) 87 To dig small holes..and put in the Plants endwise. **1679** PLOT *Staffordsh.* (1686) 193 Set obliquely like a pack of Cards, endways or edgways. **1709** BERKELEY *Ess. Vision* §2 Distance being a line directed endwise to the eye. **1722** DE FOE *Col. Jack* (1840) 47 The book lay end-way. **1855** LONGF. *Hiaw.* VIII. 68 The birch canoe stood endwise. **1857** MRS. GASKELL *C. Brontë* (1860) 3 The flag-stones with which it is paved are placed endways. **1869** BLACKMORE *Lorna D.* xiii. (ed. 12) 78 A stone was set up endwise. **1879** MISS JACKSON *Shropsh. Word-bk.* s.v.,

The house standing endways-on to the street. **1884** *Times* (weekly ed.) 3 Oct. 13/1 A little town looking end-ways on to the river from a terraced slope.

b. In the direction of the ends; also, end to end. *a* **1608** SIR F. VERE *Comm.* 125 The Poulder..broad-wayes lay due West, and end-ways North and South. **1862** *Jrnl. Soc. Arts* X. 327/1 Strips of vulcanised india-rubber cemented endways.

2. Of motion: †**a.** End on, in a direct line, continuously. (*Obs.* exc. *dial.*) **b.** End foremost. **c.** In the direction of the ends, lengthwise; also quasi-*adj.*

a. **1575** TURBERV. *Venerie* 86 Hartes which have bene hunted, do most commonly runne endwayes as farre as they have force. **1641** HOBBES *Lett.* Wks. 1845 VII. 456 As if a footman should run with double swiftnesse endwayes. **1855** *Whitby Gloss.*, *Endways*, forward.

b. **1765** GRIFFITH *Storm* in *Phil. Trans.* LV. 277 More than one [splinter] flew end-ways like an arrow. **1796** MORSE *Amer. Geog.* I. 480 A large pine has been seen..to pitch over endwise. **1870** BARNUM in R. Anderson *Missions Amer. Bd.* IV. xlii. 421 Taking the gun in both hands and striking with it endwise. **1871** 'MARK TWAIN' *Screamers* 31 He was all ready for the dog too, and knocked him endways with a rock when he came to tear him.

c. *c* **1790** IMISON *Sch. Arts* I. 138 Take the tube..and shaking it endways, the mercury will run into the tube. **1791** SMEATON *Edystone L.* (1793) 196 The stress upon the legs is always endways. **1819** PLAYFAIR *Nat. Phil.* (ed. 3) I. 165 The strength of the beam to resist a force applied to it endwise. **1850** *Chubb's Locks & Keys* 13 A compound of both endway pushing and revolving motion. **1882** *Nature* XXVI. 599 The endwise action of so large a force.

†**en'dwell**, *v. Obs. rare.* [f. EN-¹ + DWELL. Cf. IN-DWELL.] *trans.* To dwell in, stay in.

Hence **en'dweller**, an inhabitant.

c **1420** *Pallad. on Husb.* I. 437 Herdde it [the cistern] weel Tyl water wol endwelle it and abyde. *c* **1630** DRUMM. OF HAWTH. *Poems* 136 Rich Pallace, and Endweller ever blest.

endye: see EN- *pref.*¹ 3.

En'dymiony. *nonce-wd.* [f. *Endymion* proper name + -Y.] Sleepiness like that of Endymion.

1600 TOURNEUR *Transf. Met.* vi, Long Endimionie Hath pierc'd the clearenes of thy sight.

†**ene**, *a. Obs. rare.* Also 4 **eene, ȝene, ȝeeene, yeene, yn.** [related to OE. *éanian*, EAN *v.*] Of sheep: With young, in lamb.

1388 WYCLIF *Ps.* cxliii. 13 The scheep of hem ben with lambre [*v.r.* eene, yn, ene, ȝeeene, ȝene; **1382** ful of frut; Vulg. *fœtosæ*.] —— *Isa.* xl. 11 He schal bere scheep with lomb [*v.r.* ene, *ether* with lomb, yeene, *ether* with lomb; **1382** ful of frut; Vulg. *fœtas*.]

†**'ene**, *adv.* Forms: 1 *ǽne*, 2-4 ene, (3 æne). [OE. *ǽne*, instr. case of *án* one. Cf. MHG. *eine*.]

1. Once, on one occasion; opposed to *often*.

Beowulf (Gr.) 3020 Ac sceal..Oft nalles æne elland tredan. *c* **1000** ÆLFRIC *Gen.* xviii. 31 Nu ic æne begann to sprecanne to minum Drihtne. *c* **1175** *Lamb. Hom.* 15 Ne beo þu nefre ene wrað þer fore. *a* **1250** *Owl & Night.* 1105 Vor hit bitidde ene swo, Ich am the blithur ever mo. *c* **1325** *Chron. Eng.* in Ritson *Met. Rom.* II. 304 Ene heo [the Danes] him [Edmund] overcome.

2. In phrases. ***for ene***: once for all. ***at ene***: (*a*) at one stroke, = AT ONCE 1; (*b*) in one group or set, = AT ONCE 2. ***to make at ene***: to arrange, settle; cf. AT ONE 2. See also BEDENE.

c **1275** LAY. 20462 For ene and for euere. **1297** R. GLOUC. 47 Thou nart one y payed oure tresour to nyme at ene. *c* **1325** *E.E. Allit. P.* A. 291 Þre wordez hatz þou spoken at ene. *Ibid.* 952 In þat on oure pes watz mad at ene.

ene, obs. form of EVEN *sb.*; also obs. pl. of EYE.

-ene, *suffix*, in *Organic Chemistry* the termination of many names of hydrocarbons, e.g. *benzene, camphene, napthalene, toluene*, etc. In systematic nomenclature, proper to compounds of the olefine group, with formula C_nH_{2n}, but also more widely used.

†**en'eager**, *v. Obs.* Also 6 **eneigre.** [f. EN-¹ + EAGER.] *trans.* To make eager or fierce; to irritate; to whet (an appetite).

1594 R. CAREW *Tasso* (1881) 26 The thought of this his natiue sauage mood..Angring eneigres. **1649** AMBROSE *Media* xiii. (1652) 350 If it be..eneagred with a longing desire.

enearnest: see EN- *pref.*¹ 2.

†**en'ebrie**, *v. Obs. rare*⁻¹. [ad. L. *inebriāre* INEBRIATE.] *trans.* = INEBRIATE.

c **1430** *Speculum* (1888) 35 This wyne, the king of heven enebried fulle swetely.

†**'enecate**, *v. Obs.* [f. L. *ēnecāt-* ppl. stem of *ēnecāre*, f. *ē* out + *necāre* to kill.] *trans.* To kill outright. In quot. *absol.*

1657 *Phys. Dict.*, *Enecated*, killed. **1665** G. HARVEY *Advice agst. Plague* 10 Some..enecate in two or three hours, suddenly corrupting or extinguishing the vital spirits. **1721-1800** BAILEY, *Enecated*, killed.

Hence **ene'cation**, *Obs.* [see -ATION], the action of killing outright, destruction.

1657 TOMLINSON *Renou's Disp.* 182 The enecation of small wormes. **1661** LOVELL *Hist. Anim. & Min.* 430 Vlcers ..are cured if verminose, by extraction, and enecation.

en échelon: see ECHELON.

ened, enedmete, var. of ENDE, etc., *Obs.*

eneich: see EN- *pref.*¹ 3.

Eneid, variant of ÆNEID.

eneigre, variant of ENEAGER *v. Obs.*

enelpi, variant of ONELEPY *a. Obs.* only.

c **1175** *Lamb. Hom.* 29 On enelpi luttele hwile mon mei underfon ane wunde on his licome.

enema ('ɛnɪmə, ɛ'niːmə). *Med.* Pl. **enemas**; in techn. use often **enemata.** [a. Gr. ἔνεμα, f. ἐνιέναι, f. ἐν in + ἑ- stem of ἱέναι to send.

The normal pronunciation is ('ɛnɪmə), but the incorrect form has been in very general use.]

1. A liquid or gaseous substance (either medicinal or alimentary) introduced mechanically into the rectum; a clyster, an injection. Also *attrib.*, as in ***enema-apparatus, -instrument, -pump, -syringe.***

1681 tr. *Willis' Rem. Med. Wks.* Voc., *Enema*, a clister. **1751** CHAMBERS *Cycl.*, *Enema* in medicine denotes a clyster. **1794-6** E. DARWIN *Zoon.* (1801) I. 32 A dram of it [laudanum] was used as an enema. **1800** *Med. Jrnl.* III. 230, I then exhibited a laxative and antispasmodic Enema. **1847** E. SEYMOUR *Severe Dis.* I. 9, I recommended him..the use of enemata. **1872** COHEN *Dis. Throat* 87 We can resort to nutritive enemas. **1879** T. BRYANT *Pract. Surg.* II. 3 The.. india-rubber enema apparatus..may be employed. **1886** C. H. FAGGE *Princ. & Pract. Med.* II. 208 Enemata may be continued somewhat longer still.

2. Short for 'enema-apparatus'.

Mod. One of——'s patent enemas.

†**enemiable**, *a. Obs. rare*⁻¹. [ad. OFr. *anemiable, ennemiable*: see ENEMY and -ABLE, and cf. *amiable*.] Having the disposition of an enemy; hostile.

1382 WYCLIF *Ecclus.* xlvi. 7 A bure he made aȝen the enemyable [*v.r.* enmyable] folc.

enemicitious, var. of INIMICITIOUS, assimilated to ENEMY.

1691 ED. TAYLOR *Behmen's Theos. Philos.* xviii. 27 Mortal, and the Properties of it became Enemicitious.

†**'enemious**, *a. Obs.* In 6 **enmious.** [a. OF. *enemieux*, f. *enemi*: see ENEMY and -OUS.] Hostile, unfriendly.

1529 S. FISH *Suppl.* 9 An enmious and an enuious laughing. **1547** RECORD *Judic. Uryne* 42 b These [colors] ar the most enemious to nature.

Hence **'enemiously** *adv.*, in a hostile manner; spitefully.

1529 MORE *Heresyes* IV. ix. 107 b 1 Neuer eny secte.. wolde..so enemyously blaspheme & oppugne yᵉ church of Cryste.

enemity, obs. form of ENMITY.

enemony, obs. form of ANEMONE.

enemy ('ɛnəmɪ), *sb.* and *a.* Forms: 4-7 **enemi(e, -mye, enmie, -y(e,** 4-6 **enne-, ennymy(e,** 5-7 **enimie, -ye,** (4 **ennymei, en(e)me,** 5 **annemy, elmy, enmei,** 6 **ennimie**), 4- **enemy.** [a. OF. *enemi* (Fr. *ennemi*), *anemi, -y*, corresp. to Pr. *enemie*, Cat. *enemig*, Sp. *enemigo*, It. *nemico*:—L. *inimīcus*, f. *in-* negative prefix + *amīcus* friendly, friend.]

A. *sb.*

I. An unfriendly or hostile person.

1. a. One that cherishes hatred, that wishes or seeks to do ill to another; also in weaker sense, an adversary, antagonist, opponent. Const. *of* (or *genitive case*), *to*.

a **1300** *Cursor M.* 14827 Quar es he þat godds enemy? *c* **1340** *Ibid.* 25350 (Fairf.) Forgiue þine eneme. **1362** LANGL. *P. Pl.* A. XI. 148 He..biddeþ [vs]..Blessen vr enemys. **1398** in *Eng. Gilds* (1870) 5 Enpresoned falslich by enme. *c* **1440** *York Myst.* xvii. 329 Herowde is oure enmye. **1538** STARKEY *England* ii. 49 The handys..defend the rest of the body from the iniury of ennymys vtward. **1592** SHAKS. *Rom. & Jul.* I. v. 143 Prodigious birth of Loue it is to me, That I must loue a loathed Enemie. **1600** —— *A.Y.L.* II. iii. 18 Within this roofe the enemie of all your graces liues. **1653** *Trial Major Faulconer* in Howell *St. Trials* (1816) V. 359 He was an enemy to himself in spending his estate. **1664** MARVELL *Corr.* Wks. 1872-5 II. 98 A worke of their enimyes and not of their neighbours and friends. **1792** *Aneed. W. Pitt* I. ii. 44 An enemy to his fellow-subjects. **1845** S. AUSTIN *Ranke's Hist. Ref.* II. 215 A stake was driven into the ground before his door, as a token that he was a public enemy. **1859** TENNYSON *Geraint & Enid* 282 Where can I get me..arms to fight my enemy? **1872** MORLEY *Voltaire* (1886) 12 The man of the world, that worst enemy of the world.

b. spec. ***the Enemy***: the Devil (cf. *fiend*). Also ***(our) ghostly*** or ***great enemy***; ***the old enemy***, †***the enemy of hell***; ***the enemy of mankind***, ***of souls***, etc. (*b*) ***enemy of the people***, a common form of indictment used by popular leaders, esp. Communists, against their political opponents.

1382 WYCLIF *Luke* x. 19, I haue ȝouun to ȝou power of defoulinge, other tredinge..on al the vertu of the enemy. **1387** TREVISA *Higden* (Rolls) V. 131 The olde enemy cryde openliche in þe ayer. **1447** BOKENHAM *Seyntys* (1835) 9 That tentacyoun Betoknyth..Of oure goostly enmye. *a* **1450** *Knt. de la Tour* (1868) 125 She had vij husbondes, the whiche were mischeued and slayne bi the Annemy of helle. **1526** *Pilgr. Perf.* (W. de W. 1531) 4 The prynce of derknes..our goostly ennemy the deuyll. **1535** STEWART *Cron. Scot.* II. 221 Be illusion of the ennimie. **1549** *Bk. Com. Prayer, Visit. Sick*, Defend him from the danger of the enemy. **1712** ADDISON *Spect.* No. 273 ¶8 Another Principal Actor in this Poem is the great Enemy of Mankind. **1820** SCOTT *Abbot* xvi, I defy the Old Enemy to unmask me when I choose to keep my vizard on.

(*b*) **1888** E. M. AVELING tr. *An Enemy of Society* IV. in H. Ellis *Plays by Ibsen* 288 He's an enemy of the people! **1904** CONRAD *Nostromo* III. xiii. 477 Comrade Fidanza,..you have refused all aid from that doctor. Is he really a dangerous enemy of the people? **1938** *Encycl. Brit. Bk. of Yr. 1938* 680/1 The purge against Trotskyists and the hunt for 'enemies of the people and socialism'. **1955** *Treatment Brit. P.O.W.'s in Korea* (*H.M.S.O.*) 13 The battered condition of those who had just returned to the compound as an example of what could happen to anyone who showed himself to be 'an enemy of the people'. **1958** *Economist* 15 Nov. 589/2 The deputy minister of the interior recently admitted that about 700,000 enemies of the people..still exist in Hungary.

c. ***the great*** or ***last enemy***: death (cf. *1 Cor.* xv. 26).

1885 *Border Lances* 166 Looking to see the great Enemy arise from the waters, and come up to enter within the house where the knight lay.

d. *transf.* and *fig.* (*a*) One who hates or opposes (a cause, custom, state of things). (*b*) Something that operates prejudicially upon, counteracts the action of.

1398 TREVISA *Barth. De P.R.* VII. xx. (1495) 237 Eyen ben enmyes and theues. **1595** SHAKS. *John* III. i. 263 So mak'st thou faith an enemy to faith. **1658** EVELYN *Fr. Gard.* II. §3 (1675) 173 To destroy these Enemies [Palmer worms], you should, etc. **1679** PENN *Addr. Prot.* I. viii. (1692) 31 Vice, the Enemy of Religion, is at the same time, the Enemy of Humane Society. **1782** *Let.* in Amyot *Windham* (1812) I. 18 One was an enemy to thinking;—the other to drinking. **1875** JOWETT *Plato* (ed. 2) V. 229 The true judge..ought to be the enemy of all pandering to the pleasure of the spectators.

e. Phr. ***(to be) nobody's enemy but one's own***: (to be) responsible only for one's own misfortunes.

[**1592** GREENE *Upst. Courtier* sig. H2r, I thinke him an honest man if he would but liue within his compasse, and generally no mannes foe but his owne.] **1639** J. CLARKE *Paræmiologia* 21/1 He is no mans enemy but his owne. **1719** DE FOE *Crusoe* (1840) II. xi. 242, I had been nobody's enemy but my own. **1849** LYTTON *Caxtons* II. XIII. iv. 325 Guy Bolding, with all his faults, was one of those excellent creatures who are nobody's enemies but their own. **1850** DICKENS *Dav. Copp.* xxv. 263 He is quite a good fellow—nobody's enemy but his own.

2. One belonging to a hostile army or nation; an armed foe.

a **1300** *Cursor M.* 6592, I ledd ȝou thoru þe strand, Vte of all ȝour enmys hand. *c* **1325** *E.E. Allit. P.* B. 1204 And harde hurles þurȝ þe oste, er enmies hit wyste. **1393** GOWER *Conf.* III. 15 The higher hond he [Bacchus] hadde And victoire of his enemies. *c* **1460** FORTESCUE *Abs. & Lim. Mon.* (1714) 121 His Highness schal be..of Power to subdue his Ennymyes. **1461** J. PASTON *Let.* 23 Aug. in *Paston Lett.* No. 410 II. 42 God..send yowe vyttorye of yowr elmyes. **1601** SHAKS. *Jul. C.* v. iv. 22 No Enemy Shall euer take aliue the Noble Brutus. *a* **1674** CLARENDON *Hist. Reb.* IX. (1843) 581/2 To take charge of those horse whom only their friends feared, and their enemies laughed at. **1712** STEELE *Spect.* No. 350 ¶1 The Relief which a Man of Honour would bestow upon an Enemy barbarously treated. **1769** BLACKSTONE *Comm.* IV. 83 A rebel is not an enemy. **1874** BANCROFT *Footpr. Time* i. 46 All outside the family, tribe, or nation were usually held as enemies.

3. a. The hostile force. Originally only as quasi-personified, with concord in *sing.*; now also as *collect.* with concord in *pl.* Also, a hostile ship.

1601 SHAKS. *Jul. C.* IV. iii. 199 'Tis better that the Enemie seeke vs. **1793** BURKE *Corr.* (1844) IV. 159 They strike at the enemy in his weakest and most vulnerable part. **1813** WELLINGTON in Gurw. *Disp.* XI. 35 To draw the attention of the enemy to this quarter. **1855** MOTLEY *Dutch Rep.* VI. i. (1866) 771 He sprang on board the enemy alone. **1867** PEARSON *Early & Mid. Ages Eng.* I. 471 A storm of arrows completed the rout of the first line of the enemy; and their men-at-arms were, etc.

b. *fig.*

1879 PROCTOR *Pleas. Ways Sc.* viii. 174 Cold is the real enemy which bars the way towards the Pole.

c. *colloq.* or *slang.* ***how goes the enemy***: = 'what is the time?'

1839 DICKENS *Nich. Nick.* xix. **1839** BAILEY *Festus* xiv. (1848) 154.

†**II. 4.** [app. a subst. use of B. 1.] = ENMITY. *Obs. rare.*

1398 TREVISA *Barth. de P.R.* VIII. xiii. (1495) 320 Vnder the planete Mars is conteyned werre and batayle, prison and enmye. *c* **1400** *Apol. Loll.* 15 Þat cursing be riȝtwyse longen [pre condicious]..vnriȝtwisnes in þe kirk..vnriȝtwisnes in þe man cursid, & enmey of þe obstinat. *Ibid.* 87 On sleþ an oþer bi enemy. *c* **1420** *Chron. Vilod.* 212 For to him he hadde a prevyȝe enmyȝe.

III. *Comb.*: instrumental, as ***enemy-controlled, -held, occupied*** adjs.

1918 *Act 8 & 9 Geo. V* c 31 §8 Any property belonging to a company which is an enemy-controlled corporation. **1937** *Daily Tel.* 19 Oct. 15/2 Enemy-held Channel ports would no more have deprived England of the command of the sea than enemy-held Ostend and Zeebrugge did. **1946** W. S. CHURCHILL *Secret Session Speeches* 45 The enemy-held Atlantic ports and airfields. **1919** J. M. KEYNES *Econ. Conseq. Peace* (1920) 108 To maintain the civilian French population in the enemy-occupied districts. **1944** J. S. HUXLEY *On Living in Rev.* iii. 38 The enemy-occupied countries.

B. *adj.* (In many examples the word admits of being regarded as the *sb.* used *attrib.*)

† **1.** Adverse, hostile, ill-disposed, unfriendly. Const. *to*, *with*. *Obs.*

c **1340** *Cursor M.* 12930 (Trin.) Þe enemy fend þo him [Jesus] souȝt. **1382** Wyclif *1 Cor.* xv. 26 Forsoth at the laste, the enemy deeth schal be distroyed. **1514** Barclay *Cyt. & Uplondyshm.* (1847) 63 Enemie to muses is wretched povertie. **1553** N. Grimald tr. *Cicero's Duties* (*c* **1600**) 131 b To mans nature..cruelty is most enimy. **1596** Shaks. *Merch. V.* iv. i. 447 Your wife..would not hold out enemy for euer. **1607** Topsell *Four-f. Beasts* (1673) 100 The enemy beasts to harts:—Harts are opposed by wolves. **1643** Sir T. Browne *Relig. Med.* 137, I have beene shipwrackt, yet am not enemy with the sea or winds. **1654** Earl of Orrery *Parthenissa* (1676) 125 He has nothing that's enemy to us but his name. **1726** Swift *Gulliver* ii. vii. Some evil genius, enemy to mankind, must have been the first contriver.

2. Of or pertaining to a hostile army or nation; standing in the relation of an enemy, hostile.

1388 Wyclif *Ecclus.* xlvi. 7 He made assauȝt aȝens the folk enemy [**1382** enmyable folc]. **1598** Grenewey *Tacitus' Ann.* xi. viii. (1622) 149 Being captaines of the enemy nations. **1623** Bingham *Xenophon* 82 The Countrey is enemy, and we in danger to lose many Souldiers. **1653** Holcroft *Procopius* iv. 149 Narses medled not with Ariminum..nor with any other Enemy-towne. **1655–60** Stanley *Hist. Philos.* (1701) 116/2 The Carduchi, a People Enemy to the Persians. **1768–74** Tucker *Lt. Nat.* II. 429 There is a party of enemy Indians coming that way. **1793** T. Jefferson *Writ.* IV. 25 (1859) Enemy goods are lawful prize. **1881** J. Westlake in *Academy* 15 Jan. 14/3 Distinguishing.. between the enemy character of individuals and of their State. **1891** Meredith *One of our Conq.* III. vi. 108 The young..have either emotion or imagination to fold them defensively from an enemy world. **1902** *Westm. Gaz.* 5 Aug. 6/3 Stock requisitioned during the late war from private enemy owners. **1909** *Ibid.* 5 Apr. 1/3 The destination..is presumed to exist if the goods are consigned to enemy authorities, or to a contractor established in the enemy country who..supplies articles of this kind to the enemy. *Ibid.* 2/1 If goods consigned to any trader supplying an enemy population could be seized. **1915** J. H. Morgan tr. *German War Bk.* 113 Usages of war in regard to enemy territory and its inhabitants. **1915** *N.Y. Tribune* 30 Mar. 8/3 British naval officers in their reports have also referred to 'enemy' ships and fleets. **1942** E. Waugh *Put out more Flags* iii. v. 233 'No, not an enemy agent.' 'Certainly not, sir, but a frivolous, talkative girl.' **1946** 'G. Orwell' *Crit. Ess.* 137 Koestler..was once again thrown into prison as an enemy alien.

† **'enemy**, *v. Obs. rare*$^{-1}$. [f. prec.] *intr.* To be hostile *to*. Hence † **'enemying** *vbl. sb.*

1382 Wyclif *Ps.* xxxiv. 19 Ouer ioȝe not to me that enemyen [**1388** ben aduersaries] to me wickeli. **1529** S. Fish *Suppl.* 9 So then here was enmying, enuying, laughing, etc.

enemy, dial. corruption of anemone.

18.. Tennyson *N. Farmer* ix, They fun 'um theer a-laäid of 'is faäce Doon i' the woild 'enemies.

† **'enemyful**, *a. Obs. rare*$^{-1}$. [f. enemy + -ful.] Resulting from the action of an enemy; hostile. Hence **'enemyfully** *adv.*, after the manner of an enemy.

1382 Wyclif *Isa.* i. 7 Ȝoure regioun..shal be desolat as in enemyful wastete. **1450–1530** *Myrr. our Ladye* 260 That had enmefully enuye to the glory of them that were made.

† **'enemylike**, *a.* and *adv. Obs.* Also 4 enemylich. [f. enemy + like *a.* and *adv.*]

A. *adj.* Resembling an enemy; having the bearing or disposition of an enemy.

1561 T. Norton *Calvin's Inst.* iv. 166 To be caried with an enemylike mynd against his aduersarie. **1623** Bingham *Xenophon* 7 As for Cyrus, where he is..an enemie, no man more sowre, nor more enemie-like.

B. *adv.* After the manner of an enemy; as an enemy does.

1382 Wyclif *Num.* xxv. 18 The Madianytees..enemylich han doo aȝeyns ȝow. **1561** T. Norton *Calvin's Inst.* iv. xx. (1634) 739 To defend with warre the dominions committed to their charge, if at any time they be enemy-like assailed. **1631** Gouge *God's Arrows* iii. ii. 183 They were the first that enemie-like set upon Israel. **1651** Howell *Venice* 178 But whether he is to be acknowledg'd as a Father, who enemy-like robs his children, judge you.

† **'enemyly**, *a.* and *adv. Obs. rare.* Also 4 enmyly. [f. enemy *a.* + -ly^{1} and ^{2}.]

A. *adj.* Hostile. **B.** *adv.* In a hostile manner.

1382 Wyclif *2 Macc.* xiv. 11 Other frendis hauynge hem enmyly, enflawmiden Demetrie aȝeinus Judee. **1561** Daus tr. *Bullinger on Apoc.* (1573) 139 b, The Lord is..describyng the enemylie warre agaynst Antichrist.

'enemyship, *nonce-wd.* [f. enemy + -ship.] The position or relation of an enemy.

1776 Paine *Com. Sense* (1791) 30 Is the nearest and only true way of proving enemyship, if I may so call it.

† **e'nent**, and with advb. gen. suffix *-es* **enentes**, *prep. Obs.* Forms: *α.* 4 enent. *β.* 4 enentes, -is, 6 enens. [var. ff. anent.] In various senses of anent: *e.g.* in the eyes or opinion of = anent 6; opposite = anent 7; towards; in favour of = anent 9; as regards = anent 10.

a **1300** *Cursor M.* 6880 (Gött.) Als enent þis moyses. *Ibid.* 10858 (Cott.) Þou has enent vr lauerd spedd. *Ibid.* 14459 Enentis þe Iuus al was for noght. *Ibid.* 14878 All for noght enent him stode. *Ibid.* 25312 Þou hald wreth enents þi broiþer. *a* **1400–50** *Alexander* 3245 Suld neuir na gome be to glade..Of his neȝbour noy enentis him-selfe. **1516** *Will Rd. Peke of Whd.* 4 June, Even enens my stall.

† **e'nentise, -ish**, *v. Obs.* In 4 ene(y)ntis, -ysch. [var. ff. of anientise.] *trans.* To bring to nothing, exhaust (the contents of a vessel).

Hence **e'nentising** *vbl. sb.*, exhaustion, fainting.

a **1340** Hampole *Psalter* lxxiv. 8 The groundis that is the pyne of hell is noght enentist [*ibid* enentyscht] that it ne last withouten ende. **1388** Wyclif *Judith* xiii. 29 Achior..felde doun on his face..and his soule suffride eneyntisyng.

eneolithic, var. aeneolithic *a.*

1911 J. L. Myres *Dawn Hist.* x. 224 The result was a long chalcolithic (or as the Italians say, eneolithic) phase, in which good cheap stone and bad expensive bronze were in use concurrently. **1932** *Antiquity* VI. 480 Rock-engravings near Lake Gokcha (Sevang) [Armenia]..rather akin to paintings on eneolithic pottery. **1934** A. J. Toynbee *Study Hist.* I. i. C. iii. 168 Local conditions of life in the 'Eneolithic Age'. **1956** *Antiquity* XXX. 99 Two round eneolithic pits also penetrated the palaeolithic level.

enepidermic (ɛnɛpɪ'dɜːmɪk), *a.* [f. en-^{2} *pref.* + epiderm-is skin + -ic.] Of or pertaining to (medical) applications to the skin.

† **e'nerd**, *v. Obs.* In *pr. pple.* **enerdand, -ond.** [Prob. f. en-^{1} + erd to dwell; but cf. enherd.] *intr.* To dwell in.

c **1400** *Destr. Troy* 4117 A londe þere ledis in dwelt..byg men with all, Enerdond by hor one. *Ibid.* 12587 Enmys enerdand in ylis aboute.

† **'energate**, *v. Obs. rare.* [f. energ-y + -ate.] *trans.* To energize; to give energy to.

1647 M. Hudson *Div. Right Govt.* ii. x. 152 Religion must be the foundation of all Policy..cementing all societies, and energating all lawes.

energetic (ɛnə'dʒɛtɪk), *a.* [ad. Gr. ἐνεργητικός active, f. ἐνεργέ-ειν to operate, effect. Now treated as if derived from energy.]

† **1.** Operative, engaged in action. *Obs. rare.*

1701 Grew *Cosm. Sacr.* i. i. (R.) If then we will conceive of God truly..we must look upon him..as a being eternally energetick.

2. Powerfully operative.

1651 Biggs *New Disp.* 204 An energetick remedy. **1839** G. Bird *Nat. Philos.* Introd. 33 A most energetic force presiding over the internal constitution of bodies. **1860** Tyndall *Glac.* i. §20. 141, I..found an energetic polarity in a mass at some distance below the summit. **1876** Tait *Rec. Adv. Phys. Sc.* vi. 152 The most energetic chemicals.

3. Characterized by energy. Of persons: Strenuously active. Of movements, actions, expressions: Forcible, vigorous, emphatic.

1796 Burke *Regic. Peace* Wks. VIII. 240 The active and energetick part of the French nation, itself the most active and energetick of all nations. **1845** Whately *Rhet.* (1850) 213 Many others, who are allowed to be elegant, are yet by no means vigorous and energetic. **1842** A. Combe *Physiol. Digestion* 126 The active and energetic respiration attendant on cheerfulness and buoyance of spirits. **1876** Emerson *Lett. & Soc. Aims, Resources* Wks. (Bohn) III. 203 The world belongs to the energetic, belongs to the wise. **1881** Jowett *Thucyd.* I. 99 All men are energetic when they are making a beginning.

Hence **ener'getics** *sb. pl.* [on the analogy of *mathematics*, etc.], the doctrine or science of energy.

1855 W. Rankine in *Edin. Philos. Jrnl.*, The basis of the science of energetics. **1881** Armstrong in *Nature* No. 619. 452 That branch of science which..I may provisionally term 'Animal Energetics'.

ener'getical, *a.* [f. as energetic *a.* + -al^{1}.]

1. *Philos.* Operative, that produces effects; active as opposed to passive. *arch.*

1603 Sir C. Heydon *Jud. Astrol.* xxiii. 506 Their inward formes, and energeticall faculties. **1644–52** J. Smith *Sel. Disc.* iv. 119 Resembling the passive powers of the intellect to colours, the active or energetical to light. **1678** Cudworth *Intell. Syst.* 161 Fate..ought..to be looked upon..as an energetical and effectual principle. **1850** Maurice *Mor. & Met. Philos.* (ed. 2) 88 All things are efficient and energetical only in their harmony.

† **2.** Powerfully operative. *Obs.*

1631 R. H. *Arraignm. Whole Creature* i. 8 When it worketh it is energeticall indeed, and powerfull in operation. **1644–52** J. Smith *Sel. Disc.* v. 160 As this is more strong and active, so is happiness itself more energetical within us. **1661** *Origen's Opin.* in *Phœnix* (1721) I. 73 That most excellent and most energetical part in us which The Scripture calls Spirit.

3. Full of energy; strenuously active; forcible, emphatic. *rare* in mod. use.

1631 *Star Chamb. Cases* (1886) 46 A very energeticall phrase, grynding the faces of the poore. **1773** J. Allen *Serm. St. Mary's Oxf.* 23 The energetical fervent prayers of this church's champions. **1839** James *Louis XIV*, III. 409 This rapid, and energetical method of continuing the war.

energetically (ɛnə'dʒɛtɪkəlɪ), *adv.* [f. energetical *a.* + -ly^{2}.] In an energetical manner.

1775 De Lolme *Eng. Const.* (1784) Pref. 1 Which he so energetically applauds. **1836** *Random Recoll. Ho. Lords* xiv. 339 His longest and most energetically delivered speeches. **1855** Macaulay *Hist. Eng.* IV. 86 He did not approve of the plan: but he executed it..zealously and energetically. **1883** H. Spencer in *Contemp. Rev.* XLIII. 8 The primitive man ..can exert himself energetically for a time.

‖ **ener'gia**. *rare.* The Lat. form of energy; used in the sense of energy 6.

1861 Graham in *Phil. Trans.* 184 The colloid possesses Energia.

† **e'nergial**, *a. Obs. rare.* [f. energy + -al^{1}.] Of or pertaining to energy; operative, efficacious.

c **1525** Skelton *Replyc.* 368 A mysticall, Effecte energiall As Greekes do it call.

energiatype (ɛ'nɜːdʒɪətaɪp). *Obs.* [f. *energia* (see energy) + type.] An earlier name for the photographic process called ferrotype.

1845 *Athenæum* 22 Feb. 203 The Energiatype, or, as the discoverer now names the process, the Ferrotype. **1859** *Encycl. Brit.* XVII. 550/2 Under the name of the energiatype, Mr. Hunt published an account of a process in which the salts of iron were used.

energic (ɛ'nɜːdʒɪk), *a.* [f. energ-y + -ic; cf. F. *énergique*, It. *energico*.]

† **1.** Powerfully operative; = energetic 2. *Obs.*

1665 G. Harvey *Advice agst. Plague* 7 Not so Energick as to venenate the intire mass of blood in an instant. **1689** —— *Curing Dis. by Expect.* xvi. 124 The most Energick Simples. **1753** Smollett *Ct. Fathom* (1784) 13/2 A juice much more energick than the milk of goat, wolf, or woman.

2. Characterized by energy; strenuous, forcible, vigorous; = energetic 3. Now *rare*.

1702 tr. *Le Clerc's Prim. Fathers* 45 Expressions..not.. energick enough to express such Thoughts. **1792** A. Young *Trav. France* 65 The energic exertions of ardent minds. **1818** J. H. Frere *Whistlecraft's Nat. Poem* iii. xli, The strong Fryingpan's energic jangle. **1876** J. Ellis *Caesar in Egypt* 32 Caesar, astute, energic, press'd the war.

3. *nonce-uses.* (See quots.)

1796–7 Coleridge *Poems, Lines on Friend*, To me hath Heaven with bounteous hand assigned Energic reason. **1834** —— *Let.* 1 Mar., My mind is always energic—I don't mean energetic: I require in everything what, for lack of another word, I may call propriety,—that is, a reason, why the thing *is* at all, and why it is *there* or *then* rather than elsewhere or at another time. **1859** *Blackw. Mag.* LXXXVI. 242/2 The energic faculty that we call Will.

† **e'nergical**, *a. Obs. rare.* [f. as energic *a.* + -al^{1}.] = prec.

1565 Jewel *Def. Apol.* (1611) 241 Your Figuratiue, Tropicall, & Energicall Doctrine touching this blessed Sacrament. **1653** Waterhouse *Apol. Learn.* 85 (T.) The learned and moderate..confess our polity to be productive of more energical..preachers than any church in Europe. **1720** Welton *Suffer. Son of God* I. xii. 300 Whose Works of Penitence..become Powerful and Energical to procure those Great and Extraordinary Graces.

‖ **energico** (e'nerdʒiko), *adv. Music.* [It.] With energy. In mod. Dicts.

energid (ɛ'nɜːdʒɪd). *Biol.* [ad. G. *energide* (J. Sachs 1892, in *Flora* LXXV. 57), f. *energie* energy: see -id^{2}.] The nucleus of a cell together with its active cytoplasm regarded as a vital unit.

1897 *Nat. Sci.* Dec. 393 We may introduce that change from the word cell to that of energid (Sachs). *Ibid.*, The distinguishing characteristic of an energid is the living element (protoplasm and nucleus), whilst that of a cell is the membrane. **1900** I. B. Balfour tr. *von Goebel's Organ. Plants* i. 24 A polyergic plant is either an *energid-colony* or *cœnobium* (cellular or non-cellular) in which..each energid is capable of living for itself; or the energids exhibit a division of labour and..form an *energid-dominion*. **1960** L. Picken *Organization of Cells* x. 444 It is by no means the case, that mitosis and cytoplasmic cleavage are inseparable phenomena, or the formation of a polynuclear energid an exceptional event. **1965** Bell & Coombe tr. *Strasburger's Textbk. Bot.* 14 It can be envisaged that each nucleus has its own volume of protoplasm. The term 'energid' has been suggested for these physiological units lacking morphological delimitation.

† **e'nerging**, *ppl. a. Obs. rare*$^{-1}$. [? f. *energe vb. (back-formation from energy) + -ing^{2}.] ? Powerfully acting. (But perh. misprint for emerging.)

1749 Smollett *Regicide* i. vi. (1777) 15 To stifle and repress Th' energing dictates of my native right.

energism ('ɛnədʒɪz(ə)m). *Metaphysics.* [ad. G. *energismus* (F. Paulsen *Einleitung in d. Philos.* (1892) 432), f. late L. *energia* energy: see -ism.] The theory that the supreme good does not lie in pleasure but in a contented activity of mind (see also quot. 1931). Hence **ener'gistic** *a.*

1895 F. Thilly tr. *Paulsen's Introd. Philos.* (1898) 421 This view is opposed by another theory, which does not seek the highest good in subjective feelings, but in an objective content of life, or, since life is activity, in a *specific mode* of life. Permit me to call this view *energism*. **1913** *Hastings's Encycl. Relig.* VI. 511/1 'Energism' is Paulsen's title for his revived Greek position. In this third use of the term it [*sc.* happiness] includes, rather than excludes, perfection as an end. **1931** A. Wolf in W. Rose *Outl. Mod. Knowl.* 544 The view which identifies it [*sc.* the sole attribute of ultimate reality] with energy is called *energism*. *Ibid.* 548 Philosophy which was more or less materialistic, or energistic, or at least positivist.

energist ('ɛnədʒɪst). ? *nonce-wd.* [f. energy + -ist.] A writer who aims at 'energy' of style.

1804 *Edin. Rev.* III. 349 Want of dignity in the mode of chastising the absurdities of the Energists.

energize ('ɛnədʒaɪz), *v.* [f. ENERG-Y + -IZE: cf. Fr. †*énergiser* (Boiste).]

1. *trans.* **a.** To rouse into energy or activity, call into active operation. **b.** To infuse energy into, supply with energy. (Now esp. in technical use.)

1753 MISS COLLIER *Art Torment.* 136 From a desire of energizing this his [Jonathan's] favourite affection. **1812** G. CHALMERS *Dom. Econ. Gt. Brit.* Pref. 9 The office of Inspector-General was greatly improved, and energized, during the first administration of Mr. Pitt. **1875** MCLAREN *Serm.* Ser. II. viii. 147 Faith will energize us for any sort of work. **1886** P. BENJAMIN *Age of Electricity* vi. 80 An electro-magnet is energized or de-energized..by simply establishing or stopping the current in the coil. **1909** *Westm. Gaz.* 12 Jan. 4/3 The Blaisdell energised solid tyre. **1958** *Times* 26 July 4/7 When the fence was energized it was highly dangerous.

2. *intr.* To be in active operation; to put forth energy, exercise one's powers.

1752 FIELDING *Amelia* XI. v. Wks. 1784 IX. 278 The same passion cannot much energize on two different objects at one and the same time. **1818–60** WHATELY *Comm-pl. Bk.* (1864) 23 In attending to an interesting play..we can energise without much fatigue. **1852** SIR W. HAMILTON *Discuss.* 39 We exist only as we energise. **1871** FROUDE in *Devon. Assoc. Trans.* IV. 20 We have no reason to believe that in the past condition of the earth..there were functions energizing of which we have no modern counterparts. **1895** *Contemp. Rev.* Jan. 16 That Law would revive and energise the monster our backs were turned. **1908** *Westm. Gaz.* 11 Dec. 2/1 The stray Tories who chanced to go with the Liberal tide in 1906, and who now energise on the Liberal benches. **1920** *Pilgrim* Oct. 105 The act of speaking makes words..the actual vehicle and expression of a concrete personality here and now locally energising in them. **1922** J. Y. SIMPSON *Man & Attainm. Immort.* i. 8 Theology..must in some degree be a knowledge of the world as an expression of God, and of Him as energising in and through it.

Hence **'energized** *ppl. a.*

1885 MRS. LINTON *Chris. Kirkland* II. 54 A huge cosmic joke and energized satire.

energizer ('ɛnədʒaɪzə(r)). [f. prec. + -ER.]

a. He who or that which energizes.

(Used by Harris for: The agent of an action.)

1750 HARRIS *Hermes* I. ix. (1786) 174 Every Energy is necessarily situate between two Substantives, an Energizer which is active, and a Subject which is passive. *Ibid.* 175 Brutus loved Portia. Here Brutus is the energizer; loved, the energy; and Portia, the subject. **1882** W. B. WEEDEN *Social Law Labor* 28 He may be his..own energizer. **1959** *Daily Tel.* 4 June 10/2 We do not want a sponsor of South Sea bubbles, but we do want an energiser of practical plans. **1961** *New Scientist* 6 July 13/2 Of the 120 patients selected, half were given the 'tranquillizer' and half the 'energizer'.

b. *spec.* A carbonate mixed with charcoal to increase carburizing speed.

1938 D. K. BULLENS *Steel & its Heat Treatment* (ed. 4) I. II. x. 264 Energizers. The richness of the CO may be further enhanced by mixing barium or sodium carbonate with the C... These compounds are called 'energizers' because they produce a more energetic carburization. **1948** J. E. GARSIDE in H. W. Baker *Mod. Workshop Technol.* I. vii. 154 The materials consist essentially of a mixture of wood, bone, or leather charcoal, with compounds such as carbonates of barium, calcium, or sodium, which are termed 'energizers'.

energizing ('ɛnədʒaɪzɪŋ), *vbl. sb.* [f. as prec. + -ING¹.] The action of the verb ENERGIZE.

a. The action or process of awakening to energy or activity. **b.** The action of displaying energy; energetic action.

1851 *Fraser's Mag.* XLIII. 323 The curbing of our mischievous propensities, and the energizing of our good ones. **1854** HICKOK *Sc. Mind* 241 A *nisus*, or energizing towards a presented object. **1862** GOULBURN *Pers. Relig.* iii. (1873) 22 The fruits of the spirit..are not the result of the energizing of our own will.

'energizing, *ppl. a.* [f. as prec. + -ING².]

a. That supplies energy, or rouses into energy; exciting, stimulating. **b.** That is in active operation; that puts forth energy.

1750 HARRIS *Hermes* I. ix. (T.), As all energies are attributes, they have reference of course to certain energizing substances. **1786** BP. HORSLEY *Serm. Sons of the Clergy* (T.), To taste these nobler exercises of energising love. **1811** BUSBY in *Byron's Waltz* ii. *note*, When energising objects men pursue. **1849** STOVEL *Introd. Canne's Necess.* 21 A practical and energizing spirit breathes through them all. **1862** DANA *Man. Geol.* 743 The energizing light of the sun shining on the earth.

energumen (ɛnə'gjuːmən). Also 9 (? Fr.) **energumene.** [ad. late L. *energūmenus*, a. Gr. ἐνεργούμεν-ος, pass. pple. of ἐνεργέειν to work in or upon, f. ἐν in + ἔργ-ον work: cf. Fr. *energumène*. The Lat. pl. *energumeni* sometimes occurs.]

1. One that is wrought upon or possessed by a devil; a demoniac.

[**1685** tr. *Bergerac's Satyr. Char.* xiii. 59 If then this Energumenus, hath a thousand lengths and breadthes that are so many Crosses about her.] **1706** tr. *Dupin's Eccl. Hist. 17th C.* I. v. 98 From Catechumens he passes to the Energumens. **1820** SCOTT *Abbot* xxxii, If there was ever an *Energumene*, or possessed demoniac..there is a devil speaking with that woman's tongue! **1855** SMEDLEY *Occult Sc.* 173 Such catechumens as were not at the same time energumens. **1863** GEO. ELIOT *Romola* (1880) I. I. v. 69 Of an energumen whose dwelling is among tombs.

2. A 'possessed' person, an enthusiast, a fanatical devotee. Also *attrib.*

1702 C. MATHER *Magn. Chr.* I. iii. (1852) 63 Quakers and Seekers, and other such Energumens. *Ibid.* III. II. xxvi. 493 The man..of an energumen countenance. **1818** T. JEFFERSON *Writ.* IV. 451 When General Washington was withdrawn, the energumeni of royalism..mounted on the car of State. **1860** GEN. P. THOMPSON *Audi Alt.* III. civ. 12 Suppose some 'energumene' were to make the declaration, etc. **1885** MORLEY in *Macm. Mag.* Feb. 255/2 The seeming peril to which priceless moral elements of human character were exposed by the energumens of progress.

Hence †**e,nergu'menical** *a. Obs.*, having the characteristics of a demoniac or 'possessed' person. **ener'gumenist** = ENERGUMEN I.

1684 I. MATHER *Remark. Provid.* (1856) 121 Certain arguments of an energumenical person. **1646** GAULE *Cases Consc.* 37 The meerly Passive be simply deemoniacks, but not Energumenists.

energy ('ɛnədʒɪ). [ad. late L. *energīa*, Gr. ἐνέργεια, f. ἐνεργής, f. ἐν + ἔργον work. Cf. Fr. *énergie*. Senses 1 and 2 belong to ἐνέργεια as used by Aristotle, whereas sense 5 answers to that of Gr. δύναμις.]

1. a. With reference to speech or writing: Force or vigour of expression.

[This sense (found in late L. and in Romanic) is originally derived from an imperfect understanding of Aristotle's use of ἐνέργεια (*Rhet.* III. xi. §2) for the species of metaphor which calls up a mental picture of something 'acting' or moving. In mod. use it blends with 3.]

[**1581** SIDNEY *Def. Poesie* (Arb.) 67 That same forciblenes, or Energia, (as the Greekes cal it) of the writer.] **1599** THYNNE *Animadv.* 42 The frenche Hollybande, not vnderstandinge the true energye of our tongue. *a* **1696** HOLDER (J.), When animated by elocution [Speech] acquires a greater life and energy. **1729** STACKHOUSE *Body Divin.* IV. i. §2 These are all of them terms of a peculiar energy. **1845** WHATELY *Rhet.* (1850) 203 The transposition of words which the ancient languages admit of, conduces, not merely to variety, but to Energy. **1847** EMERSON *Repr. Men, Shaks.* Wks. (Bohn) I. 357 The Liturgy, admired for its energy and pathos.

†**b.** *transf.* Impressiveness (of an event). *Obs.*

1764 HARMER *Observ.* II. 7 This thunder..added considerably to the energy of this event [Saul's inauguration].

2. a. Exercise of power, actual working, operation, activity; freq. in philosophical language. †Formerly also *concr*: The product of activity, an effect.

a **1626** BACON (J.), They are not effective of any thing, nor leave no work behind them, but are energies merely. **1642** H. MORE *Song of Soul* Gloss., *Energie*..is the operation, efflux or activity of any being: as the light of the Sunne is the energie of the Sunne, and every phantasm of the soul is the energie of the soul. **1644–52** J. SMITH *Sel. Disc.* VIII. v. (1821) 399 Their life is nothing else but a strong energy of fancy and opinion. **1646** SIR T. BROWNE *Pseud. Ep.* II. v. 87 The conceited remedy..carryeth often the honour of the capitall energie, which had no finger in it. **1744** HARRIS *Three Treat.* (1841) 18 Call every production, the parts of which exist successively..a motion or an energy: thus a tune and a dance are energies. **1798** BAY *Amer. Law Rep.* (1809) I. 23 Naturalization had a retrospective energy. **1833** I. TAYLOR *Fanat.* ii. 42 The transition of the passions from momentary energies to settled dispositions. **1859** SIR W. HAMILTON *Lect.* (1877) II. xxi. 25 The faculty of which this act of revocation is the energy, I call the Reproductive.

†**b.** Effectual operation; efficacy. *Obs.*

a **1719** SMALRIDGE (J.), Beg the blessed Jesus to give an energy to your imperfect prayers. **1725** POPE *Odyss.* xx. 226 Blows have more energy than airy words.

3. Vigour or intensity of action, utterance, etc. Hence as a personal quality: The capacity and habit of strenuous exertion.

1809–10 COLERIDGE *Friend* (1865) 37 To lose the general and lasting consequences of rare and virtuous energy. **1839** THIRLWALL *Greece* V. 110 The prudence and energy displayed at this critical juncture by Agesilaus. **1841–4** EMERSON *Ess. Prudence* Wks. (Bohn) I. 93 The poet admires the man of energy and tactics. **1855** MACAULAY *Hist. Eng.* III. 726 He took his measures with his usual energy and dexterity. **1856** KANE *Arct. Expl.* I. xi. 121 When the hatches were opened, the flame burst out with energy. **1856** FROUDE *Hist. Eng.* I. i. 71 Henry, with the full energy of his fiery nature, was flinging himself into a quarrel.

4. a. Power actively and efficiently displayed or exerted. Sometimes in *pl.* in same sense.

1665 GLANVILL *Sceps. Sci.* xii. 66 If this motive Energie..must be called Heat..I contend not. **1813** SIR H. DAVY *Agric. Chem.* (1814) 185 Soils..which act with the greatest chemical energy in preserving Manures. **1849** MRS. SOMERVILLE *Connex. Phys. Sc.* Introd. 2 Impress the mind with some notion of the energy that maintains them [the heavenly bodies] in their motions. *Ibid.* iii. 15 The disturbing energy of the planets. **1860** TYNDALL *Glac.* I. §7. 51 Struggle with the slow energy of a behemoth. **1865** DICKENS *Mut. Fr.* II. 24 The united energies of two horses, two men, four wheels, and a plum-pudding carriage dog. **1870** E. PEACOCK *Ralf Skirl.* II. 1 Throwing all their energies into worldly concerns.

b. *pl.* Individual powers in exercise; activities.

a **1742** BENTLEY (J.), How can concussion of atoms beget ..powers and energies that we feel in our minds? **1783** in *Phil. Trans.* LXXIII. 160 Nature unquestionably abounds with numberless unthought-of energies, and modes of working. **1801** SOUTHEY *Thalaba* III. xvi, There might his soul develope best Its strengthening energies. **1849** RUSKIN *Sev. Lamps* vii. 184 A measure of license is necessary to exhibit the individual energies of things. **1861** MAY *Const. Hist.* (1863) I. i. 6 The troublesome energies of Parliament.

5. Power not necessarily manifested in action; ability or capacity to produce an effect.

1677 HALE *Prim. Orig. Man.* I. i. 26 We find in so small a particle of a created Being this admirable energy. **1691** T. H[ALE] *Acc. New Invent.* p. xxiii, Some vain Authors have essayed in print to give reasons for such energy of that Fish. *a* **1732** ATTERBURY *Serm.* IV. ix. (T.), Discoursing of the energy and power of church music. *a* **1862** BUCKLE *Civiliz.* (1869) III. v. 420 An occult principle, which he termed the Animal Power or Energy of the brain. **1887** LOWELL *Democr.* 36 Institutions which could bear and breed such men as Lincoln and Emerson had surely some energy for good.

6. a. *Physics.* The power of 'doing work' possessed at any instant by a body or system of bodies. First used by Young (with reference to sense 4) to denote what is now called ***actual, kinetic,*** or ***motive energy***, i.e. the power of doing work possessed by a moving body by virtue of its motion. (Young expressed the quantity of 'energy' in a particle as the product of the mass into the square of the velocity; it is now found more convenient to express it as the *half* of this product.) Now extended (first by Rankine) to include ***potential, static,*** or ***latent energy***, or ***energy of position***, i.e. the power of doing work possessed by a body in virtue of the stresses which result from its position relatively to other bodies. Also with adjs., ***mechanical, molecular, chemical, electrical energy***, etc.; ***atomic energy***, see ATOMIC *a.* 2 d; ***radiant energy*** (see quots. 1901, 1942).

conservation of energy: the doctrine that the quantity of energy in any system of bodies cannot be increased or diminished by any mutual action of those bodies, and that the total energy in the universe is a constant quantity.

1807 T. YOUNG *Nat. Philos.* viii. (1845) I. 59 The term energy may be applied, with great propriety, to the product of the mass or weight of a body, into the square of the number expressing its velocity. **1852** THOMSON in *Philos. Mag.* 304 (*title*), Dissipation of Mechanical Energy. **1853** W. RANKINE *Transform. Energy* in *Scient. Papers* (1881) 203 [Defines 'actual or sensible energy', 'potential or latent energy', 'conservation of energy']. **1863** TYNDALL *Heat* i. §9 Asserting that mechanical energy may be converted into heat. **1876** M. FOSTER *Physiol.* II. v. (1879) 420 The animal body is a machine for converting potential into actual energy. **1878** HUXLEY *Physiogr.* 199 But whether this is the sole source of volcanic energy or not is uncertain. **1879** THOMSON & TAIT *Nat. Phil.* I. I. §278 In every case in which energy is lost by resistance, heat is generated. **1901** S. NEWCOMB in J. M. Baldwin *Dict. Philos.* I. 326/1 *Radiant energy or radiance.* Every hot body radiates its heat through the space around it, thus imparting energy to the ether. The energy..is now believed to take a form of waves of electric energy..and its amount is exactly equal to that which the hot body loses. **1936** *Nature* 25 Jan. 135/1 Mass and energy are equivalent, and mass is to be regarded in a sense as a concentrated source of energy. **1942** J. D. STRANATHAN *Particles* ix. 374 Although sufficient quantitative evidence has already been presented..to convince one of the interchangeability of mass and energy..when an electron and a positron combine the two masses disappear and there appears simultaneously a definite amount of radiant energy. **1956** G. THOMSON *Atom* (ed. 5) xvi. 156 It is one of the consequences of the theory of relativity that mass and energy are closely connected, so closely that when one appears the other must disappear. *Ibid.* 161 Uranium.. splits into two nuclei..with a diminution of mass and consequent release of energy.

†**b.** Suggested as a name for MOMENTUM.

1808 *Edin. Rev.* XII. 130 This modification of power [that of a moving body, 'proportional to the quantity of matter multiplied into the velocity'] might be called Energy.

c. Veget. Phys. ***energy of growth***: see quot.

1882 VINES *Sachs' Bot.* 821 If the power of any particular zone to attain a definite length is called its Energy of Growth.

d. **(*mental*) *energy*** (see quots.).

1901 S. NEWCOMB in J. M. Baldwin *Dict. Philos.* I. 326/2 It is sometimes supposed that thought or mental action.. may be a distinct form of energy... But the energy itself can be only that of the matter comprising the brain and nervous system. **1944** J. S. HUXLEY *On Living in Rev.* xv. 192, I shall use the term mental energy in the broad popular sense, as denoting the driving forces of the psyche, emotional as well as intellectual.

7. *attrib.* and *Comb.*, as ***energy-change, consumption, -density, -exchange, -level, -producer, -production, -state, unit, value***; ***energy-carrying, -giving, -producing, -rich*** adjs.

1905 *Westm. Gaz.* 28 Apr. 2/1 The energy-carrying power of a beam of light. **1884** M. M. P. MUIR *Princ. Chem.* II. iii. 453 The energy-changes attending the formation of various compounds. **1909** *Installation News* III. 109/1 The energy consumption should not be below 500 watts. **1958** H. J. GRAY *Dict. Physics* 175/2 *Energy density*, amount of (e.g. radiant) energy in unit volume. **1910** W. JAMES *Let.* 17 June (1920) II. 345 Physically a dinosaur's brain may show as much intensity of energy-exchange as a man's. **1941** J. S. HUXLEY *Uniqueness of Man* III. iv. 96 The fertilizing, energy-giving belt of cyclonic weather. **1951** *Good Housek. Home Encycl.* 374/2 Energy-giving food. **1910** W. JAMES *Let.* 17 June (1920) II. 345 Certain arrangements of matter *on the same energy-level* are, from the point of view of man's appreciation, superior, while others are inferior. **1922** A. D. UDDEN tr. *Bohr's Theory of Spectra* III. iv. 116 The values of the atomic energy corresponding to these states are frequently referred to as the 'energy levels' of the X-ray spectra. **1930** G. THOMSON *Atom* xi. 164 The first outstanding fact in the theory of these extra nuclear electrons is the existence of what are called Energy Levels. The idea is that each electron in the atom requires an amount of energy to remove it completely from the atom, which is characteristic of the particular atom, and the particular electron, though more than one electron may be at the same energy level. **1912** J. S. HUXLEY *Individual in Animal Kingdom* vi. 146 Some of the existing materials must be sacrificed as energy-producers. **1909** *Daily Chron.* 8 July 6/4 An energy-producing food. **1927** HALDANE & HUXLEY *Animal Biol.* iii. 92 Children need a great deal more food per pound of their own weight for energy-production alone,

besides their requirements for growth. **1952** *New Biol.* XIII. 125 The limited stock of abiotically formed energy-rich molecules. **1955** W. HEISENBERG in W. Pauli *Niels Bohr* 14 Schrödinger had recognized that the wave functions were the elements of the transformation matrices for the transition from energy states to position states. **1948** *Mind* LVII. 299 We pay for our electric current in kilowatt-hours, which are energy units. **1938** R. W. LAWSON tr. *Hevesy & Paneth's Man. Radioactivity* (ed. 2) xi. 109 For the disruption of aluminium nuclei it is found that there are certain energy values (resonance levels) of the incident α-particles.

b. Special Comb.: **energy crisis, crunch,** a serious shortage of energy-producing fuels; **energy-efficient** *a.* orig. *U.S.*, that makes economical use of available energy, esp. fuel; conducive to fuel economy; also **energy efficiency; energy gap,** (*a*) *Physics*, a gap between adjacent energy bands, such that a particle cannot pass from the lower to the higher without some minimum increase in its energy; *esp.* that between the valence band and the conduction band in an insulator or semi-conductor; (*b*) = *energy crisis* above.

1970 *Sci. News* 28 Nov. 415/1 The current short-term *energy crisis. **1971** *Washington Post* 10 Jan. F8/1 Although some progress has been made in dealing with the U.S. 'energy crisis', the likelihood of..blackouts in the coming year is not being ruled out. **1985** G. T. NURSE et al. *Peoples of S. Afr.* x. 250 Recurrent energy crises are endemic in African agricultural societies. **1974** *News & Press* (Darlington, S. Carolina) 25 Apr. 8/7 There is..a distinct change of pattern in the automotive industry that was brought about by the *energy crunch. **1978** *N.Y. Times Mag.* 4 June 110 (*heading*) The real meaning of the energy crunch. **1972** H. PERRY *Conservation of Energy* 2 The principal theme of this report is that energy conservation and *energy efficiency are important issues. **1977** *Sci. Amer.* Dec. 47/3 The specification, which is called the energy efficiency ratio..is the quantity of heat energy (in British thermal units) removed from the air per hour divided by the electric power (in watts) supplied to the machine. **1986** *Options* Aug. 33/1 Energy efficiency is not..a subject on which the British can talk with much authority. **1972** H. PERRY *Conservation of Energy* II. 50 As energy prices rise.. a shift toward more *energy-efficient methods of moving people and freight can be expected to occur. **1975** *Economist* 27 Sept. 71/2 The car..must be made less polluting and more energy efficient. **1984** *Today in Gainesville* (Florida) Mar. 3A These homes are equipped with..energy-efficient insulation. **1937** SEITZ & JOHNSON in *Jrnl. Applied Physics* VIII. 190/1 The conductivity σ..depends on *E*, the *energy gap between the filled and unfilled bands. **1954** F. LONDON *Superfluids* II. 53 Various attempts have been made to modify the energy spectrum of the ideal Bose-Einstein gas in such a way as to fit the thermal data of liquid helium. The conclusion..is that something as drastic as an energy gap is required. **1959** R. A. SMITH *Semiconductors* i. 16 If the forbidden energy gap *ΔE* between the highest filled band and the next empty band is large, no electronic conduction can take place as no 'neighbouring' empty levels exist into which electrons may be accelerated. **1969** *East Europe* Apr. 19/1 Recent economic difficulties in some communist countries can be linked to a developing energy gap, that is, the difference between their domestic energy resources at competitive prices and total energy requirements. **1977** *Undercurrents* June–July 8/1 Although North Sea oil and gas will make energy growth in Britain feasible during the 1980s, by the 1990s these reserves will be running out and we'll be faced with an 'energy gap'. **1978** H. M. ROSENBERG *Solid State* (ed. 2) viii. 131 If the energy gap is not too large, say 1 eV or less, a few electrons can be excited across the gap at room temperature and so a small current can flow... This is the behaviour typical of a semiconductor. **1985** *Electronics* 8 July 20/1 The energy gap for pyrite is 0.9 eV, which compares with 1.1 eV for silicon.

enerthand, *pr. pple.* of ENHERD, *Obs.*

enervate (ɪ'nɜːvət), *a.* Also 8 **ennervate**. [ad. L. *ēnervāt-us*, pa. pple. of *ēnervāre*: see next.]

1. Wanting in strength of character; spiritless, unmanly, effeminate.

1603 HOLLAND *Plutarch's Mor.* 11 They waxe carelesse, dissolute, and enervate. **1675** DRYDEN *Aurungz.* II. i, The Dregs and Droppings of enervate Love. **1749** J. WARTON *Ode West's Pindar* (T.), Away enervate bards, away. **1774** GOLDSMITH *Grec. History* I. 176 We are to behold an ennervate and factious populace. **1822** WORDSW. *Eccl. Sonn.* I. ix, Poet. Wks. IV. 201 The Pictish cloud darkens the enervate land By Rome abandoned. **1830** *Fraser's Mag.* I. 515 The enervate candidates for place and patronage.

b. of artistic style, etc.

a **1704** T. BROWN *Prol. to 1st Sat. Persius* (1730) I. 51 Nor Virgil's great majestick lines Melted into enervate Rhimes. **1762** J. BROWN *Poetry & Mus.* xii. (1763) 209 Certain Greeks..brought a refined and enervate Species of Music to Rome. **1884** *Blackw. Mag.* Apr. 432/2 Let it not be supposed that this art..was enervate, monotonous, or slow.

2. Wanting in bodily strength or physical power.

1703 ROWE *Ulyss.* I. i. 335 My cold enervate hand. **1737** POPE *Hor. Epist.* II. i. 153 On each enervate string they taught the note, To pant. **1741** BETTERTON in Oldys *Eng. Stage* vi. 110 Such a languid and enervate Hoarsness. **1762** FALCONER *Shipwr.* I. 672 When eastern breezes, yet enervate, rise. **1849** LYTTON *Caxtons* II. lvi, The enervate slightness of his frail form.

3. *Bot.* Having no rib or nerve; ribless.

enervate ('ɛnəveɪt), *v.* [f. L. *ēnervāt-* ppl. stem of *ēnervāre* to extract the sinews of, weaken, f. *ē* out + *nervus* sinew (see NERVE *sb.*). The later use is influenced by the mod. sense of *nerve*. Cf. ENERVE *v.*

(In 17–18th c. the accentuation was usually *e'nervate.*)]

†**1.** *trans.* To cut the tendons of; chiefly *spec.* to hamstring, hough (a horse). Also (see quot. 1751.). *Obs.*

1638 FEATLY *Transubst. Exploded* 183 You cut your selfe in the hammes, and enervate your maine argument. **1656** BLOUNT *Glossogr.*, *Enervate*..to cut off sinews. **1702** BP. PATRICK *Comm. Josh.* xi. 9 They were wont thus to enervate all the horses they found in the king's stables after his death. **1751** CHAMBERS *Cycl.* s.v., Cutting two tendons on the side of a horse's head..they thus enervate horses, to make their heads small and lean.

†**2.** To emasculate. *Obs. rare*$^{-1}$.

1610 J. H[EALEY] tr. *Augustine's City of God* VII. xxiv. 285 If earth were held no goddesse, men would..not [lay their hands] upon themselves, to enervate themselues for her.

3. To weaken physically (a person or animal); now only of agencies that impair nervous 'tone', as luxury, indolence, hot or malarious climates.

a **1668** DENHAM *Of Old Age* ii. (R.), I feel no weakness, nor hath length Of winters quite enervated my strength. **1757** DYER *Fleece* I. (R.), No..myrtle bowers, The vigorous frame..of man Enervate. **1781** GIBBON *Decl. & F.* (1869) II. xlii. 559 The conquerors were enervated by luxury. **1796** MORSE *Amer. Geog.* II. 303, I, therefore, the King of Poland, enervated by age. **1805** NELSON *Let.* 1 Oct. in A. Duncan *Life* (1806) 243, I have had..one of my..spasms, which has almost enervated me. **1855–60** MAURY *Phys. Geog. Sea* iii. §184 Their crews enervated in tropical climates.

†**b.** To impair the strength of (inanimate things). *Obs.*

1667 WATERHOUSE *Fire Lond.* 69 Chapels, Churches, Monuments..it..flaked and enervated.

4. To weaken mentally or morally; to destroy the capacity of (a person, a community, etc.) for vigorous effort of intellect or will. Said *esp.* of the effects of luxury or sloth. Also, to destroy or impair the vigour of (sentiments, expressions, etc.).

1614 RALEIGH *Hist. World* III. 64 Luxury, wherewith most Empires that ever were, have beene enervated. **1625** DONNE *Serm.* lxvi. 665 God shall..enfeeble and enervate.. that Constancy. **1652** BP. PATRICK *Fun. Serm.* in *J. Smith's Sel. Disc.* 555 Do not..enervate your souls by idleness. **1697** DRYDEN *Virg. Georg.* IV. 290 No Lust enervates their Heroick Mind. **1753** HANWAY *Trav.* (1762) I. III. xxviii. 118 By imputing vice to nature..we enervate that detestation which arises..upon the mention of those things which we denominate unnatural. **1868** M. PATTISON *Academ. Org.* §5. 149 The tendency of abstract thought..to enervate the will is one of the real dangers of the highest education.

†**5.** To destroy the force of (arguments, testimony, etc.); to destroy the grounds of (a doctrine, an opinion); to render ineffectual (a law, an authority, an opponent's efforts, etc.). *Obs.* Sometimes expanded into ***to enervate the force of***.

1610 DONNE *Pseudo-Martyr* 271 Because the Glosse is now by some thought to be of equal Authoritie with the Text it is not an inconvenient way to enervate both. **1634** *Acts Durham High Com. Crt.* (1857) 99 To enervate the testimony of the wittnesses. **1653** ASHWELL *Fides Apost.* 271, I..have enervated most of those Arguments, which I have found brought against either. **1672** NEWTON in Rigaud *Corr. Sci. Men* (1841) II. 318 So acute an objector hath said nothing that can enervate any part of it [my discourse]. *a* **1674** CLARENDON *Surv. Leviath.* (1676) 108 A..Prince, who hath not enervated those Machinations. **1702** ECHARD *Eccl. Hist.* (1710) 538 He might..enervate the force and vigour of all divine injunctions. *a* **1718** PENN *Wks.* (1726) I. 452 Something that can resolve its Doubts, answer its Objections, enervate its Propositions. **1765** BLACKSTONE *Comm.* I. 417 In the next year..this wise provision was enervated, by only, etc. **1836** J. GILBERT *Chr. Atonem.* iii. (1852) 82 Enervate the force of legislative sanctions.

†**b.** To disparage the power or value of (something). *Obs.*

a **1619** DONNE *Biathanatos* (1644) 207 To enervate and maime..that repentance which is admitted for sufficient in the Romane Church. **1655–60** STANLEY *Hist. Philos.* (1701) 216/1 Not that..he [Zeno] did enervate Vertue.

enervated ('ɛnəveɪtɪd), *ppl. a.* [f. ENERVATE *v.* + -ED^1.] That is deprived of nerve and strength, *lit.* and *fig.*; effeminate, weakly.

1660 JER. TAYLOR *Duct. Dubit.* I. iv. Wks. IX. 162 The gods which they worshipped, those poor enervated demons. *a* **1735** ARBUTHNOT & POPE (J.), Their enervated lords are softly lolling in their chariots. **1841** EMERSON *Addr., Man the Ref.* Wks. (Bohn) II. 241 The enervated and sickly habits of the literary class.

'enervating, *vbl. sb.* [f. as prec. + -ING^1.] The action of the verb ENERVATE. *lit.* and *fig.*

a **1674** CLARENDON *Surv. Leviath.* (1676) 277 The method that must be taken towards the enervating those high pretences. **1751** CHAMBERS *Cycl.*, *Enervating*, the act of destroying the force, use, or office, of the nerves.

enervating ('ɛnəveɪtɪŋ), *ppl. a.* [f. ENERVATE *v.* + -ING^2.] That enervates, in the various senses of the verb.

1821 BYRON *Cain* II. i. 57 A most enervating and filthy cheat. **1850** PRESCOTT *Peru* II. 12 The enervating influence of a tropical climate. **1870** LOWELL *Among my Bks.* Ser. I. (1873) 362 The enervating incense that women are only too ready to burn.

enervation (ɛnə'veɪʃən). [ad. late L. *ēnervātiōn-em*, f. *ēnervāre* (see ENERVATE *v.*).]

†**1.** = L. *enervatio*, used as transl. of Gr. ἀπονεύρωσις in transl. Galen *De Loc. Aff.* i. 6 (see quot. 1751). *Obs.*

1578 BANISTER *Hist. Man* IV. 47 A broad Membraneous eneruation. **1751** CHAMBERS *Cycl.* s.v., The fibres of the recti of the abdomen..are intersected by several nervous places, called by the antients, enervations; though they be real tendons.

2. The action of enervating; the state of being enervated: see ENERVATE *v.*

c **1555** HARPSFIELD *Divorce Hen. VIII* (1878) 219 The enervation and evasion of her adversaries intention. **1597** BACON *Coulers Good & Evill* i. (Arb.) 140 This couler of melioritie and preheminence is oft a signe of enervation and weakenesse. **1639** CADE *Serm. Necess. for these Times* App. 36 An enervation or dissolution of good laws. **1660** R. COKE *Power & Subj.* 207 To the final destruction and enervation of the Estates of the same Incumbents. *a* **1718** PENN *Tracts* Wks. 1726 I. 485 An Enervation of the Romanist's Faith. **1849** GROTE *Greece* VI. II. xlvii. 25 A love for knowledge without enervation of character. **1850** KINGSLEY *Alt. Locke* xiv. (1879) 177 The luscious softness of the Italian airs overcame me with a delicious enervation.

'enervative, *a. rare*$^{-0}$. [f. ENERVATE *v.* + -IVE.] Tending to enervate.

1864 in WEBSTER; and in mod. Dicts.

enervator ('ɛnəveɪtə(r)). [as if a. L. **ēnervātor*, agent-n. f. *ēnervāre* to ENERVATE.] He who or that which enervates.

1840 THACKERAY *Paris Sk. Bk.* Wks. 1879 XVI. 84 Calling our darling romances foolish..enervators of intellect.

†**enerve,** *a. Obs. rare*$^{-1}$. [? ad. L. *ēnerv-is* nerveless; but the sense is obscure.]

a **1521** *Prol. to Helyas* in Thoms *E.E. Prose Romances* III. 16 Wythout hygh style and enerve industry, I have al onely folowed mine auctour as nyghe as I coulde.

†**e'nerve,** *v. Obs.* [ad. Fr. *énerver*, ad. L. *ēnervāre*: see ENERVATE *v.*] = ENERVATE *v.* in various senses. Hence **e'nerved, e'nerving** *ppl. adjs.*

1613 ZOUCH *Dove* 28 Like feeble Miloes armes eneru'd, and dead. **1644** HAMMOND *Loyal Convert* 19 [Their] effeminacies have enerv'd the strength of their declining Kingdoms. *a* **1648** DIGBY *Lett. conc. Relig.* ii. (1651) 18 A fore-laid designe to enerve their authority. **1649** G. DANIEL *Trinarch., Hen. IV*, ccvi, Unsteddy doctrines, which attend Enerved minds. *c* **1680** EARL DORSET *Antiq. Coquet* (R.), Age has enerv'd her charms. **1727** ARBUTHNOT *Coins* Ded., Riot..Enerv'd those Arms, that snatch'd the Spoil before. **1795–9** R. LOVELL & SOUTHEY *Poems* 109 Beware Luxury's enerving snare. **1828** in WEBSTER. **1847** in CRAIG; and in mod. Dicts.

†**e'nervity.** *Obs. rare*$^{-0}$. [ad. if ad. L. **ēnervitas*, f. *ēnervis* nerveless, f. *ē* out + *nervus* nerve.] The condition of being nerveless.

1656 in BLOUNT *Glossogr.*

†**e'nervous,** *a. Obs. rare.* [f. L. *ēnerv-is* (see prec.) + -OUS.] Bereft of nerve and strength; powerless, futile, spiritless. (Used several times by R. North.)

1677 I. L. & S. D. *Ded. to Cleveland's Poems* A iiij b, We have only an enervous effeminate froth offered. *a* **1734** NORTH *Exam.* I. iii. ¶93 (1740) 188 After the Plot became enervous, and all farther Use of it was despaired of.

†**'enes,** *adv. Obs.* Forms: 2–3 **ænes, enes,** *Orm.* **æness,** (3–5 **ens,** 3 **eanes,**) 4–5 **enis, -us, -ys).** [Early ME. *ænes*, *enes*, var. of OE. *ánes* once, assimilated to *æne*, ENE.]

1. Once, on one occasion.

1154 *O.E. Chron.* an. 1120 Ðises ȝeares com þet leoht to Sepulchrum Domini innan Jerusalem twiȝes, ænes to Eastron and oðre siðe to Assumptio sancte Marie. *c* **1175** *Lamb. Hom.* 37 Uwilc mon scal beon twiȝen awesscen of his sunne, enes et þam fulhtbeda..oðer siðe..et soð scrifte. *a* **1200** *Moral Ode* 93 in *E.E.P.* 28 Enes drihte helle brac. *c* **1200** ORMIN 1078 Þatt wass aȝȝ æness o þe ȝer. **1426** AUDELAY *Poems* (1844) 43 At the lest enus a ȝere. *c* **1460** *Towneley Myst.* 187, I pray the that thou wold kys me enys.

2. At any one time, either past, present, or future; *esp.* to mark the completion of an action; at some time or other, formerly; once upon a time.

c **1205** LAY. 29325 Ænes an ane tide an cniht þer com ride. *c* **1230** *Hali Meid.* 11 Meidenhad is tresor þat beo hit eanes forloren ne beð hit neauer ifunden. *a* **1300** *Cursor M.* (Cott.) 10699 Vou þat es ens mad rightwis to brek aght naman þat es wis. *c* **1308** *Pol. Songs* (Camden Soc.) 203 Be the soule enis ute, A vilir caraing nis ther non. *c* **1340** *Cursor M.* (Fairf.) 3631 For ware he þar-of enys fedde..his benysoun walde he him gife. *c* **1400** *Destr. Troy* 873 Þat I may see thee come sounde to þis sale enys. **1483** CAXTON *G. de la Tour* Prol. 2 The woman that enis he hathe truli loued. **1542** BOORDE *Introd. Knowl.* xxxiii. 2, I was borne in Bion; ens English I was.

3. *at enes*, at one and the same time; = AT ONCE 3.

a **1225** *Ancr. R.* 420 Ne ne nime, et enes, to ueole disceplines.

[**enest,** misreading in Cursor Mundi for EVEST, malice, q.v.]

enetide, obs. form of EVENTIDE.

eneuch, eneugh, Sc. form of ENOUGH.

en évidence, en face, en famille: see EN *prep.*

†**e'new**, *v. Obs.* Forms: 5 ennewe, 7 ineaw, 6–7 enew. [ad. OF. *enewer*, *eneauer*, f. *en* in (see EN-¹) + *eau* water.]

trans. Of a hawk: To drive (a fowl) into the water. *refl.* Of a fowl: To plunge in the water. (In Shaks. spelt *emmew*, either by confusion with *emmew* ENMEW, or merely by a misprint.)

1486 *Bk. St. Albans* D ij a, Yowre hawke hath ennewed the fowle in to the ryuer. **1575** TURBERV. *Bk. Falconrie* 150 If your falcon do stoupe them and enewe them once or twice. **1603** SHAKS. *Meas. for M.* III. i. 91 This outward-sainted Deputie Whose.. deliberate word.. follies doth emmew, As Falcon doth the Fowle. **1611** MARKHAM *Countr. Content.* I. v. (1668) 32 Let her enew the fowl so long till she bring it to the plunge. **1612** DRAYTON *Poly-olb.* xx, Themselves for very fear they instantly ineaw.

enew, obs. and dial. form of ENOW.

enew, var. of ENNEW *v.*¹ and ², *Obs.*

enewre, obs. var. of INURE.

enexorable, obs. form of INEXORABLE.

eneye, var. of INEYE *v. Obs.* to inoculate.

enface (ɛn'feɪs), *v.* [f. EN-¹ + FACE *sb.*, on the analogy of ENDORSE.] *trans.* To write, print, or stamp a form of words upon the face of (a bill, etc.). Also *to enface* (words) *upon*. Hence **en'faced** *ppl. a.* Also **en'facement**, what is written or printed upon the face of a bill or note.

1861 *Times* 20 Mar. 6/4 With a memorandum enfaced, as the term was, upon them to the following effect 'Interest payable in London by draught on Calcutta'. **1869** *Daily News* 14 Dec., 'Enfaced' rupee paper, 92¼. **1886** *Blackw. Mag.* Sept. 342/1 Identified by a parcel area and reference number both enfaced on the map itself. **1861** *Times* 20 Mar. 6/4, 6,000,000*l.* [of these notes] bore the simple enfacement 'Interest payable in London by draught in Calcutta'.

†**en'faimle**, *v. Obs. rare*⁻¹. [obscurely f. EN-¹ + OF. *faim* hunger, or some derivative of that word.] ? *intr.* To suffer from famine (or possibly *trans.*, to starve).

c **1475** *Partenay* 1300 A myghty towne.. Which, enfaimling [Fr. *affamee*], Almoste gan purchace The soudan bigly the town beseging.

enfain: see EN- *pref.*¹ 2.

†**en'fame**. *Obs. rare.* [a. OF. *infame*, *enfame*, ad. L. *īnfāmia* INFAMY.] = INFAMY.

c **1400** *Test. Love* I. in *Chaucer's Wks.* (1561) 291 The people wol lye & bringe aboute soche enfame. *Ibid.* 292 Some men there been that their owne enfame can none otherwise voide, or els excuse, but be hindoring of other mennes fame.

enfame, obs. form of INFAME.

†**en'famine**, *sb. Obs.* [f. next vb.] Famine, starvation.

c **1450** LONELICH *Grail* xii. 352 [The castle] myhte neuere i-wonnē be But only thorwgh enfamyne.

†**en'famine**, *v. Obs.* Also 4–5 enfamyne. [f. EN-¹ + FAMINE *sb.*]

1. *intr.* To perish by famine.

c **1325** *E.E. Allit. P.* B. 1194 Faste fayled hem þe fode, enfaminied monie.

2. *trans.* To cause to suffer famine; to starve. Also *fig.*

138. WYCLIF *Wks.* (1880) 150 þes ben euele fadris þat þus cruelly enfamynen here sugetis soulis. *c* **1430** LYDG. *Bochas* II. xxiv. (1554) 60 b, When men enfamined haue nether grein ne bred. **1480** CAXTON *Chron. Eng.* clxxi, Within the first yere he had enfamyned the londe.

†**en'famish**, *v. Obs.* Forms: 5 enfamych, -yssh. [Altered form of AFFAMISH: see EN- *pref.*¹] *trans.* To famish, starve.

c **1400** *Sowdone Bab.* 2141 Thay shalle enfamyched be. *a* **1400–50** *Alexander* 2153 (Dubl. MS.) Thare negh was fey for defaute enfamyshyd [*Ashmole*, enfamyschist] hys oste. **1491** CAXTON *Vitas Patr.* (W. de W. 1495) III. xxxv. 327 b/1, They sawe that they were enfamysshed. **1766–1800** in BAILEY. **1828** in WEBSTER; and in mod. Dicts.

†**en'famishment**. *Obs. rare.* [f. ENFAMISH *v.* + -MENT.] The action of starving to death.

1611 SPEED *Hist. Gt. Brit.* IX. xiv. §19 So exquisite a barbarisme, as Richards enfamishment.

enfamous: see EN- *prefix*¹ 2.

†**en'fantement**. *Obs. rare*⁻¹. [a. Fr. *enfantement* child-bearing, f. *enfanter* to bear a child.] Offspring.

1483 CAXTON *Gold. Leg.* 260/3 Where thou arte thenfantemente or fruyte of my wombe.

‖**enfant gâté** (ɑ̃fɑ̃ gɑte). [Fr., = spoilt child.] A person who is accorded excessive adulation or indulgence.

1802 GIFFORD tr. *Juvenal's Satires* p. xlvi, In a word, Horace seems to have been the *enfant gaté* of the palace. **1833** SCOTT *Introd. Novels* I. 479 The Author of the Waverley Novels.. might.. have been termed *L'Enfant Gâté* of success. **1892** E. DOWSON *Lett.* (1967) 275, I.. think that there is.. beneath her double perversity of enfant gâtée and jeune fille coquette a solid foundation of affection. **1937** A. J. CRONIN *Citadel* III. vi. 298 Frances.. had an amused affection for the *enfant gâté*. **1960** *Times* 2 June 12/3 As a person he has survived the period of being the *enfant gâté* of post-war Germany.

enfantillage (ɑ̃fɑ̃tijaʒ). [Fr., f. *s'enfantiller* (f. *enfant* child): see -AGE.] A childish action or prank.

1827 [see BÊTISE]. **1914** E. SIDGWICK *Duke Jones* 384 The talk distracted itself again owing to Charles' enfantillages.

‖**enfant terrible** (ɑ̃fɑ̃ tɛribl). [Fr., = terrible child.] A child who embarrasses his elders by untimely remarks; *transf.* a person who compromises his associates or his party by unorthodox or ill-considered speech or behaviour; loosely, one who acts unconventionally.

1851 *Fraser's Mag.* Mar. 322/1 He.. seemed to tell all these stories just as an *enfant terrible* might, without fully understanding them. **1854** THACKERAY *Newcomes* I. xxi. 194 The *enfant terrible*, young Alfred,.. announcing to all the company at dessert, that Ethel was in love with Clive. **1885** 'L. MALET' *Col. Enderby's Wife* II. III. v. 27 That *enfant terrible* of Mrs. Farrell's is not coming back, I trust? **1930** T. KARSAVINA *Theatre Street* III. xxiv. 293 A permanent figure of the theatre was Jean Cocteau, the *enfant terrible* of rehearsals. **1939** D. CECIL *Young Melbourne* iii. 87 She.. spoke her mind with *enfant terrible* candour. **1940** *Ann. Reg. 1939* 10 The *enfant terrible* of the party, who once more did not see eye to eye with his colleagues.

†**en'farce**, *v. Obs.* Also 5 **enfarse**, 6–7 **infarce**, -se. [a. F. *enfarc-ir*, ad. L. *infarcīre*.]

1. To stuff **a.** (a sucking pig, etc.) with forcemeat; **b.** (the belly, oneself) with food.

c **1420** *Liber Cocorum* (1862) 36 Put alle in body of þo pygge, Rost hit on broche of irne bygge Enfarsed. **1543** BECON *New Year's Gift* Wks. (1843) 322 How doth the glutton.. enfarce it [his belly] with all kind of dainties! **1574** NEWTON *Health Mag.* 12 If the partie.. have not longe afore enfarced himselfe with plentie of meate.

2. *transf.* and *fig.*

1531 ELYOT *Gov.* I. iii. (1883) I. 27 Redynge this warke, infarced througly with suche histories and sentences. *Ibid.* II. vi. II. 55 A man.. by furie chaunged in to an horrible figure, his face infarced with rancour. **1533** —— *Cast. Helthe* III. i. (1541) 53 b, The body is infarced eyther with choler, yelowe or blacke, or with fleume. **1542** BECON *Potat. Lent* Wks. 1564 I. 35 b, Souls, replenished and enfarsed with celestiall meate. **1543** GRAFTON *Contn. Harding* 528 Letters enfarced and replenysshed with all humanytee.

3. To stuff (something) *into*. Also *fig.* (contemptuously) to interpolate.

1564 *Brief Exam.* *iiij b, Ye woulde not be so busie to infarce in your bookes the reproche of these men. **1566** DRANT *Horace* a iv. b, Thauthors must be full Of fostred arte, infarst in ballasde breste. **1578** BANISTER *Hist. Man* I. 13 This neither iawe.. hath on eche side propper cauities with marey infarced. **1601** HOLLAND *Pliny* XXXV. xiv, The earth thus infarced [between planks] continueth a world of yeres. **1623** LISLE *Ælfric on O. & N.T.* Pref. 5 The Latin Copy-clarke.. hath enfarced these words, Quamvis ipse, etc. **1624** F. WHITE *Repl. Fisher* Pref. 8 He.. infarceth here a rapsodie.

Hence **en'farcing** *vbl. sb.*

1623 LISLE *Ælfric on O. & N.T.* Pref., By the infarcing afterward of these Epistles.. into their bookes of Canons.

enfasten: see EN- *pref.*¹ 3.

†**en'fat**, *v. Obs.* Also 4 **infat**. [f. EN-¹, IN- + FAT *a.*] *trans.* To fatten; *fig.* to make gross.

1382 WYCLIF *Matt.* xiii. 15 The herte of this peple is enfattid. —— *Acts* xxviii. 27 The herte of this puple is infattid [*Vulg. incrassatus*].

enfatuate, obs. form of INFATUATE *a.* and *v.*

†**en'faunce**. *Obs. rare*⁻¹. [a. OF. *enfaunce*, Fr. *enfance*.] Childhood.

c **1400** *Rom. Rose* 4288 The which devel in hir enfaunce Hadde lerned of Loves arte.

†**en'faunt**, *sb. Obs. rare*⁻¹. [a. OF. *enfaunt* (Fr. *enfant*). Cf. INFANT.] A child, a young person.

c **1450** *Bk. Curtasye* 644 in *Babees Bk.* 141 Yf that þou be a ȝong enfaunt, And thenke þo scoles for to haunt.

†**en'faunt**, *v. Obs. rare*⁻¹. [ad. OF. *enfaunter* (Fr. *enfant-er*), in same sense. Cf. INFANT *v.*] *trans.* To bear (a child).

1483 CAXTON *Gold. Leg.* 128/2 The place in whych the vyrgyne marye enfaunted and childed Jhesu cryst.

enfavour: see EN- *pref.*¹ 2.

enfear, enfeature: see EN- *pref.*¹ 2 and 1 a.

enfect, obs. form of INFECT *a.* and *v.*

enfeeble (ɛn'fiːb(ə)l), *v.* Forms: α. 4 **enfebil**, 4–5 **enfeble**, 6 **enfeable**, -**febel**, 7– **enfeeble**. β. 6–7 **infeeble**. [a. OF. *enfebl-ir*, f. *en-* (see EN-¹) + *feble* FEEBLE. Cf. AFFEEBLE.] *trans.* To make feeble, weaken.

α. *a* **1340** HAMPOLE *Psalter* xxvi. 4 þei þat angirs me vnskylwysly are sekyd that is enfebild. **1485** CAXTON *St. Wenefr.* 12 She was enfeblyd with ouermoche payne. **1533** MORE *Apology* xxvii. Wks. 892/1 They both enfeable and also dishonour the realme. **1600** HAKLUYT *Voy.* (1810) III. 203 He was enfeebled of abilitie. **1764** GOLDSM. *Trav.* 270 Praise.. Enfeebles all internal strength of thought. **1860** TYNDALL *Glac.* I. §20. 142 The [magnetic] action was greatly enfeebled. **1872** YEATS *Growth Comm.* 293 England was enfeebled.. by the Wars of the Roses.

β. **1576** FLEMING *Panoplie Ep.* 79 Your owne health.. is much infeebled. **1614** RALEIGH *Hist. World* II. 441 With intent to infeeble them for want of water. **1667** MILTON *P.L.* IX. 488 So much hath.. paine Infeebled me.

enfeebled (ɛn'fiːb(ə)ld), *ppl. a.* [f. ENFEEBLE *v.* + -ED¹.] Made feeble, weakened.

1649 G. DANIEL *Trinarch., Hen. V*, clxxiv, Let his enfeebled Temples, for one Night Beat orderlie. **1746–7** HERVEY *Medit.* (1818) 150 To invigorate the enfeebled knees. *a* **1859** MACAULAY *Hist. Eng.* V. 287 Emotions too violent to be borne by an enfeebled body and mind.

enfeeblement (ɛn'fiːb(ə)lmənt). [f. ENFEEBLE *v.* + -MENT.] The action or process of enfeebling; the state of being enfeebled.

1667 H. MORE *Div. Dial.* II. xxiii. (1713) 163 The great.. Enfeeblements of Mind and Body. **1805** *Month. Mag.* XIX. 327 The enfeeblement, or smothering of his argument. **1861** MILL *Utilit.* ii. 33 The enfeeblement of the feeling of veracity is one of the most hurtful things to which our conduct can be instrumental. **1869** SEELEY *Lect. & Ess.* ii. 54 The enfeeblement produced by the.. introduction of civilisation.

en'feebler. *rare.* [f. as prec. + -ER.] One who or something which enfeebles.

1609 *Man in Moone* (1849) 12 He is his own strengths enfeebler. **1612** W. PARKES *Curtaine Dr.* (1876) 16 Lust.. the azure infeebler of the braine. **1724** A. PHILIPS *Ode Signora Cuzzino* 6 Sweet enfeebler of the heart! **1846** *Edin. Rev.* LXXXIV. 362 It is well said by Plato in the *Phaedrus*, that the invention of letters was the great enfeebler of memory.

en'feebling, *vbl. sb.* [f. as prec. + -ING¹.] The action of the vb. ENFEEBLE.

1503–4 *Act 19 Hen. VII*, c. 4 Preamb., The great hurte and enfebelyng of this Realme. **1531–2** *Act 23 Hen. VIII*, c. 16 A great enfeblyng of the kinges saide subiectes. **1705** STANHOPE *Paraphr.* III. 567 Those Parts.. which Nature hath left liable.. to great enfeeblings.

enfeebling (ɛn'fiːblɪŋ), *ppl. a.* [f. ENFEEBLE *v.* + -ING².] That enfeebles.

1599 MARSTON *Sco. Villanie* II. vii. 206 Infeebling ryot. *a* **1661** HOLYDAY *Juvenal* 216 Passion.. does in a trice By th' ear and eie admit infeebling vice. **1838–9** HALLAM *Hist. Lit.* II. II. v. §85. 236 The enfeebling expletives 'do' and 'did'. **1887** *Spectator* 1 Oct. 1300 England survives all things, even.. her own enfeebling tolerances.

†**en'feeblish**, *v. Obs.* Forms: 4 **enfeblesch**, -**ish**, 5 -**yssh**, 6–7 **enfeeblish**. [a. OF. *enfebliss-*, lengthened stem of *enfeblir*: see ENFEEBLE.]

a. *intr.* To become or grow feeble. **b.** *trans.* To make feeble, enfeeble.

1382 WYCLIF *Ex.* xxii. 14 Who of his neiȝbore eny thing of thes askith to borwe, and it were enfeblished or deed.. he shal be compellid to ȝeeld. ? *a* **1400** *Morte Arth.* 2484 The Fraunche-mene enfeblesches, ne farly me thynkkys! **1491** CAXTON *Vitas Patr.* (W. de W. 1495) III. xliii. 329 b/1, He was thus enfeblysshed in his membres. **1576** NEWTON *Lemnie's Complex.* (1633) 131 Manly strength, by immoderate heat, is resolved and enfeeblished.

Hence †**en'feeblishing** *vbl. sb.*

1626 W. SCLATER *Expos. 2 Thess.* (1629) 91 Vndergoing so many, so continuall mutations, and.. enfeeblishings.

†**en'fellowship**, *v. Obs.* [f. EN-¹ + FELLOWSHIP.] **a.** *trans.* To join in fellowship. **b.** *intr.* To enter into fellowship.

1470–85 MALORY *Arthur* VIII. xxvii. 315, I wille see sir launcelot and enfelaushippe me with hym. *Ibid.* IX. xix. 367 And they enfelaushypped to gyder. **1553** GRIMALDE *Cicero's Offices* I. (1558) 25 When good men alike in condicions be enfelowshipt in familiaritie together.

†**en'felon**, *v. Obs.* or *arch.* [ad. OF. *enfelonner*, f. *en-* (see EN-¹) + *felon* furious.] *trans.* To make furious, infuriate. Hence **en'feloned** *ppl. a.*

1475 CAXTON *Jason* 101 b, Anon as the monstre had apperceyued Jason he enfelonned him self. **1596** SPENSER *F.Q.* V. viii. 48 Like one enfelon'd or distraught. **1864** SIR K. JAMES *Tasso* X. lii, With a less wicked and enfeloned brow.

enfence, obs. form of INFENCE.

enfeoff (ɛn'fɛf), *v.* Forms: α. 5 **enfeffe**, **enfefe**, 6 **enfeoffe**, 5– **enfeoff**. Also 5 **enfeffee**. β. 5–7 **infeof(f**, 6 **infeffe**, 7 **infeft**. Also 6 **infeoffe**. See also ENFIEF. [a. OF. *enfeffer*, *enfieffer* (AF. *enfeoffer*), f. *en-* (see EN-¹) + *fief* FIEF. In Anglo-Lat. *infeoffāre*.]

1. *trans.* To invest with a fief; to put (a person) in possession of the fee-simple or fee-tail of lands, tenements, etc. Also *absol.* Const. *in*, *of*, †*on*, later *with*; also *simply*.

α. *a* **1400–50** *Alexander* 2793 [Alexander] enfeffid þaim belyue, In palais, in prouince, in principall regnes. **1411** SIR T. LANGEFORD in *E.E. Wills* (1882) 18 Y pray alle ȝow þat bene enfeffeed in my londes.. þat ȝe fulfylle my forseyd wylle. **1426** *E.E. Wills* (1882) 71 þay wolde enfeffe Philippe Dene on vj marces of rente. **1467** *Mann. & Househ. Exp.* 172 Karowe and I withe oder waren enfefed in a howese and land. **1531** *Dial. Laws Eng.* II. xvi. (1638) 86 The grantor enfeoffeth the grantee of one of the said acres. **1590** GREENE *Fr. Bacon* x. 14, I will enfeoff fair Margaret in all. **1611** SPEED *Hist. Gt. Brit.* IX. ix. (1632) 614 The Scottish King claimed that Country from King John, who by his deed enfeoffed him thereof. **1655** FULLER *Ch. Hist.* III. vi. §13 We.. shall take such tenements into our hand, and shall enfeoffe others therein. **1785** BURKE *Sp. Nabob Arcot's Debts* Wks. IV. 308 A criminal.. is.. enfeoffed with an estate. **1818** CRUISE *Digest* I. 43 If the lord enfeoffs another of the tenancy, this makes the land frank fee. *a* **1845** BARHAM *Ingol.*

Leg. (1877) 337 The veteran was enfeoffed in the lands and Manor. **1876** BANCROFT *Hist. U.S.* I. xiii. 433 Charles II.. enfeoffed his brother, the Duke of York, with the counties between Pemaquid and the St. Croix.

β. **1491** *Act 7 Hen. VII*, c. 12. §5 Tenementes whereof they by this Acte be infeoffed. **1590** H. SWINBURNE *Treat. Test.* 93 If a man seased of lande in fee doe infeoffee a straunger. **1592** NASHE *P. Penilesse* (ed. 2) 33 b, The sonne seeks the death of the father, that he may be infeoffed in his wealth. **1628** COKE *On Litt.* 42 b, Whosoeuer is disabled by the Common Law to take, is disabled to infeoffe. **1640** *Canterburians Self-Conviction* 99 They set up a rubricke, feafing and infefling the officiating Priest in the halfe of all the oblations. **1662** FULLER *Worthies Westmorl.* III. 141 Richard Gilpin..was infeoffed..in the Lordship of Kentmire-hall by the Baron of Kendal. **1752** CARTE *Hist. Eng.* III. 566 He should infeofe her in a jointure of 40,000 crowns a year out of the dutchy of Berry.

b. *transf.* and *fig.*

α. **1407** *Will. Thorpe's Exam.* in Arb. *Garner* VI. 57 This office that ye would now enfeoff me with. **1460** *Pol. Rel. & L. Poems* (1866) 64 For strengthe, ner force, may nat atteyne certayne a wille þat stant enfeffyd in Fraunchise. **1593** NASHE *Christ's T.* (1613) 179 The Fathers of our earthly bodies..cannot..enfeofe vs in glory perpetuall. **1638** *Penit. Conf.* viii. (1657) 247 The commodity is yours, for whose good we are enfeoffed with this power. **1834** H. MILLER *Scenes & Leg.* xvii. (1857) 251 The fish in which they had enfeoffed themselves at the expense of Nannie Fizzle.

β. *a* **1626** BP. ANDREWES *Serm.* (1886) I. 43 To set before us this flesh; and..to infeoffe us in it. **1684** CHARNOCK *Attrib. God* (1834) II. 431 Infeoffing them in a land flowing with milk and honey.

2. To hand over as a fief; to surrender, give up entirely. *fig.*

1596 SHAKS. *1 Hen. IV*, III. ii. 69 The skipping King.. Enfeoff'd himselfe to Popularitie. **1610** *Histrio-m.* v. 251 Hee that is most infeoft to Tyrannie. **1833** H. COLERIDGE *Poems* I. 46 The choicest terms are now enfeoff'd to folly. **1880** BLACKMORE *Mary Anerley* I. ii. 12 The weak lot which is enfeoffed to popularity.

†**enfeo'ffee.** *Obs.* In 5 enfeffe. [a. pa. pple. of AF. *enfeoffer*: see -EE.] One who is enfeoffed.

1424 R. FLORE in *E.E. Wills* (1882) 61, I wul þat my said enfeffez make astate þerof to my said son Thomas.

enfeoffment (ɛn'fɛfmənt). Also 5 enfeft-, 6 infeoff-, 8 enfeofment. [f. ENFEOFF + -MENT.]

a. The action of enfeoffing. **b.** The deed or instrument by which a person is enfeoffed. **c.** The fief or estate, in quot. *fig.* **d.** The possession of a fief.

1460 *Pol. Rel. & L. Poems* (1866) 112 For the in paradyse I ordeynnyd A plase: fulle Ryche was thyn enfeftment. **1597** DANIEL *Civ. Wares* VII. lxxxii, The King, as husband to the crown, doth by The wifes infeoffment hold. **1614** SELDEN *Titles Hon.* 190 By their Charters, Enfeoffments, and Testaments recorded in old storie. **1762** tr. *Busching's Syst. Geog.* VI. 166 Otho..invested the houses of Stolberg and Schwarzburg with the joint enfeoffment of it. **1769** ROBERTSON *Chas. V*, III. VII. 54 The Spanish ambassador would not be present at the solemnity of his enfeofment. **1839** KEIGHTLEY *Hist. Eng.* I. 238 That an enfeoffment to that effect might be executed.

enfer, enferre, obs. forms of INFER.

†**en'ferme,** *v. Obs. rare*⁻¹. [ad. F. *enferme-r* to shut up.] *trans.* To shut up, enclose.

1481 CAXTON *Myrr.* II. xviii. 104 That whiche is enfermed and closed in the erthe is helle.

†**en'fermer.** *Obs.* [a. OF. *enfermier*:—late L. *infirmārius*.] The superintendent of a (monastic) infirmary: see INFIRMARER.

c **1325** *Metr. Hom.* 29 A blak munk of an abbaye was enfermer of all.

enfermerere, var. of INFIRMARER, *Obs.*

enfermi: see ENFIRM.

enfertile, enfertilize: see EN- *pref.*¹ 2, 3.

†**en'fested,** *ppl. a. Obs. rare*⁻¹. [? for **infested*, f. INFEST *a.* bitterly hostile + -ED¹; or error for *enfestered*.] Embittered.

1591 SPENSER *Muiopotmos* 354 That olde Enfested grudge.

enfester: see EN- *pref.*¹ 3.

en fête: see EN *prep.*

enfetter (ɛn'fɛtə(r)), *v.* Also 7 infetter. [f. EN-¹ + FETTER *sb.*] *trans.* To put into fetters, *lit.* and *fig.*; also, to enslave *to*.

1604 SHAKS. *Oth.* II. iii. 351 His Soule is so enfetter'd to her Loue. **1611** SPEED *Hist. Gt. Brit.* IX. viii. (1632) 581 Those seruitudes wherewith..they were supposed to be enfettered. **1626** G. SANDY'S *Ovid's Met.* IV. 75 Like a Serpent by an Eagle truss't; Which to his head and feet, infettered, clings. **1637** BASTWICK *Litany* I. 4 They haue the keys..of all the prisons..to infetter any at their beck. **1860** C. LANGSTER *Hesperus*, etc. 186 Love should be enfettered, hand and foot, For the long æon of a human year.

enfeud, obs. form of INFEUD.

enfever (ɛn'fiːvə(r)), *v.* [f. EN-¹ + FEVER *sb.*] *trans.* To throw into a fever; *fig.* to exasperate, incense. Hence **en'fevering** *ppl. a.*

1799 SEWARD *Horace's Odes* I. i., To blend the enfevering draught with its pellucid waves. **1647** EVELYN *Mem.* (1857) III. 6 To enfever the people against him [the King].

en'fevered, *ppl. a.* [f. ENFEVER *v.* + -ED¹.] Fever-stricken.

1893 *Pall Mall Mag.* I. 887 His enfevered brain. **1901** *Daily Chron.* 2 July 3/1 Whilst the last chill comes To that enfevered clay and makes it pure.

enfief (ɛn'fiːf), *v. rare.* [f. EN-¹ + FIEF.] = ENFEOFF.

1861 A. B. HOPE *Eng. Cathedr. 19th C.* 153 Enfiefed with spacious places of worship..by Constantine. **1882** W. B. WEEDEN *Soc. Law L.* 169 The privileges were all enfiefed.

Enfield ('ɛnfiːld). The name of a town in Middlesex (now in Greater London), near which the Government has a manufactory of small arms. Used *attrib.* with various military terms, as in ***Enfield rifle***, etc.

1854 C. A. WINDHAM *Crimean Diary* (1897) 91 The Enfield rifle..should be the arm for the infantry. **1858** GREENER *Gunnery* 377 The length of the Enfield bullet is ⅞ inch. **1858** BEVERIDGE *Hist. India* III. IX. iv. 633 One hundred Enfield riflemen of the 64th. *Ibid.* Covered at discretion by Enfield skirmishers. *Ibid.* 634 The power of the Enfield rifle in British hands. **1860** [see BROWN BESS]. **1876** [see MINIÉ]. **1959** *Chambers's Encycl.* V. 674/2 The Enfield system of rifling..was adopted. In 1895 the Lee-Enfield rifle was introduced.

enfierce, enfigure: see EN- *pref.*¹ 2 and 1 b.

enfilade (ɛnfɪ'leɪd), *sb.* [a. Fr. *enfilade*, f. *enfiler* to thread on a string, hence to pierce or traverse from end to end, f. *en-* (see EN- *pref.*¹) + *fil* thread.]

†**1.** A suite of apartments, whose doorways are placed opposite to each other. Hence in phrase, ***in enfilade***. Also applied to a long 'vista', as between rows of trees, etc. *Obs.*

1705-30 S. GALE in Nichols *Bibl. Topogr. Brit.* III. 41 Rooms which..are placed in enfilade. **1727** BRADLEY *Fam. Dict.* s.v. *Garden*, Groves form'd of Rows of Fruit-trees and Forest-trees..make..very agreeable Enfilades. **1762-71** H. WALPOLE *Vertue's Anecd. Paint.* (1786) IV. 265 An enfilade of correspondent gates. **1779** SWINBURNE *Trav. Spain* xxxviii, The trees have swelled out beyond the line traced for them, and destroyed the enfilade, by advancing into the walks, or retiring from them. **1805** REPTON *Landsc. Garden.* (ed. 2) 105 A magnificent enfilade through a long line of principal apartments.

2. *Mil.* †**a.** (See quot.) *Obs.*

1706 PHILLIPS, *Enfilade* [in Military Affairs] is the Situation of a Post, so that it can discover and scour all the length of a straight line. **1715** in KERSEY. **1721-1800** in BAILEY.

b. A 'fire' from artillery or musketry which sweeps a line of works or men from one end to the other. Also *attrib.* in ***enfilade fire***.

1796-7 *Instr. & Reg. Cavalry* (1813) 175 Its [the echelon's] prolongation shall not be exposed to an enfilade. **1803** WELLINGTON in Gurw. *Disp.* II. 286 You would have iron guns instead of brass for your enfilade. **1863** KINGLAKE *Crimea* (1877) IV. xii. 255 Threatening..his batteries with an enfilade fire. **1876** BANCROFT *Hist. U.S.* VI. liv. 425 The space within the works..was exposed to enfilade.

enfilade (ɛnfɪ'leɪd), *v.* [f. prec. sb.]

†**1.** *trans.* To set (trees) so as to form an enfilade. *Obs.* (*nonce-use.*)

1725 BRADLEY *Fam. Dict.* s.v. *Quincunx*, Take care that the trees be well squar'd or laid out by a line, and, as it were, enfiladed one with another.

2. *Mil.* To subject to an enfilade; to 'rake' or to be in a position to 'rake' (a line of fortification, a line of troops, a road, etc.) from end to end with a fire in the direction of its length.

1706 PHILLIPS, *Enfilade*, or *Enfile* the Courtin, Rampart, etc., is to scour or sweep the whole length of such a Work with the Shot. *a* **1755** *Expedition to Carthagena* (J.), The avenues, being cut through the wood in right lines, were enfiladed by the Spanish cannon. **1772** SIMES *Mil. Guide*, A work is said to be enfiladed when a gun can be fired into it, so that the shot may go all along the inside of the parapet. **1828** *Blackw. Mag.* XXIV. 357 This success made it an operation of no difficulty to enfilade the enemy's position on the left bank. **1846** PRESCOTT *Ferd. & Is.* I. v. 237 The bridge..was enfiladed by the enemy's cannon. **1879** Low *Jrnl. Gen. Abbott* iv. 333 Our course..was completely enfiladed by a stone breastwork.

b. *transf.*

a **1845** BARHAM *Ingol. Leg.* (1877) 413 The level beams of the rising or setting sun as they happened to enfilade the gorge. **1848** THACKERAY *Bk. Snobs* (1872) 119 The bow-window of the Club..enfilades Pall Mall.

Hence **enfi'laded** *ppl. a.*, **enfi'lading** *ppl. a.*

1812 *Examiner* 14 Sept. 581/1 Two enfiladed batteries. **1828** SPEARMAN *Brit. Gunner* 33 The continued fire of the first or enfilading batteries. **1866** *Harvard Mem. Biog. N. L. Abbott* II. 101 The Twentieth..advanced..under an enfilading fire of artillery.

†**en'file,** *v. Obs.* Also 7 infile. [a. Fr. *enfile-r*: see ENFILADE.]

1. *trans.* To put on a string or thread. Also, ***to enfile up***: to hang up on a string, etc.

1393 GOWER *Conf.* III. 237 They taughten him [Sardanapallus] to lace a braide..and to enfile A perle. **1601** HOLLAND *Pliny* II. 124 To cut the root..into thin roundles, and to keep them enfiled vp. *Ibid.* II. 133 The swine mushromes..are hanged vp to dry infiled vpon a rush running through them. **1675** HOBBES *Odyssey* (1677) 116 When they had slain my men, they them enfil'd..like fishes hung in ranks.

2. *Her.* In pa. pple. (See quot.)

1830 ROBSON *Brit. Herald.* Gloss. s.v., When the head of a man or beast, or any other charge, is placed on the blade of a sword, the sword is said to be enfiled with whatever is borne upon it.

†**en'fire,** *v. Obs.* Also 6 enfyre. [f. EN-¹ + FIRE *sb.*]

1. *trans.* To set on fire.

1513 DOUGLAS *Æneis* XIII. Prol. 13 The son enfyrit haill, as to my sycht. **1605** SYLVESTER *Du Bartas* I. vii. (1605-7) I. 234 Th' Orbe of Flame..doth not enfire the frame.

b. To inflame.

1545 T. RAYNOLD *Womans booke* 79 By the which the bloude is enfyred and chawfed.

2. *fig.* **a.** To kindle (a passion, zeal, etc.). **b.** To fire, inflame (a person) with anger, passion.

1596 SPENSER *Hymn to Love* xxv, So hard those heavenly beauties he enfyred. **1603** FLORIO *Montaigne* I. xxxviii. (1632) 119 Great cares of sharpe desire Doe carefull man distract, torment, enfire. **1620** BP. HALL *Hon. Mar. Clergy* I. §12 (Wks. 1628) 752 The touch of whom hath so much enfired his ghostly zeale. **1652** BENLOWES *Theoph.* VI. xiv, Fruition Love enfires. **1855** SINGLETON *Virgil* I. 260 Cupid ..with the presents should the raging queen Enfire.

†**en'firm,** *v. Obs. rare.* Also 3 enfermi. [ME. *enfermi*, a. OF. *enferme-r*, f. *en-* (see EN-¹) + *ferme*:—L. *firm-us* FIRM; the later *enfirm* prob. a new formation on EN-¹ + FIRM *a.*]

trans. To strengthen, fortify.

1297 R. GLOUC. (1724) 552 To Gloucetre hii wende, to enfermi þen toun. **1649** G. DANIEL *Trinarch., Hen. IV*, liii, The Gascoynes thus enfirm'd, and noe great feare Of French Invasion.

enfix, rare var. of INFIX.

enflame, -flaumbe, obs. ff. INFLAME.

enflesh (ɛn'flɛʃ), *v.* Also 6-7 inflesh. [f. EN-¹, IN- + FLESH *sb.*]

trans. **a.** To make into flesh. **b.** To cause a growth of flesh upon (the limbs). **c.** To plant or establish in the flesh, to ingrain. **d.** To give a fleshly form to. Hence **en'fleshing** *vbl. sb.*

1548 GESTE *Pr. Masse* 86 No more then the deytie is recompted enfleshed for that it is substancially in us. *Ibid.*, The incarnation or enfleshing of Christes Godhead. **1598** FLORIO, *Incarnare*, to incarnate, to inflesh. *Ibid.*, *Incarnamento*, an enfleshing, an incarnating, incarnation. **1603** —— *Montaigne* I. lvi. (1632) 173 Those vices, which are habituated, inbred, setled, and enfleshed in him. **1633** P. FLETCHER *Purple Isl.* VI. (R.), Who th' Deity infleshṭ, and man's flesh deified. **1648** HERRICK *Hesper., To his Mistresses*, Bring your magicks, spels, and charmes, To enflesh my thighs and armes. **1883** J. PARKER *Apost. Life* II. 212 Our love must incarnate, enflesh, and embody itself.

enfleurage (ɑ̃flœrɑːʒ). [Fr.] The process of extracting perfumes from flowers by means of fats such as lard and olive oil; INFLOWERING.

1855 G. W. S. PIESSE *Art of Perfumery* i. 15 Absorption, or Enfleurage. **1880** *Encycl. Brit.* XIII. 595/2 The aroma is extracted by the process known as 'enfleurage', *i.e.*, absorption by a fatty body, such as purified lard or olive oil. **1885** [see INFLOWERING]. **1966** *New Scientist* 15 Sept. 624/1 Enfleurage, a very old process in which essential oils from blooms are extracted by absorption into thin films of olive oil or lard.

†**en'flourish,** *v. Obs. rare*⁻¹. [f. EN-¹ + ME. **flureschen*, *flurisen*, FLOURISH.] *trans.* To display flourishingly; to trick out with ornaments.

?*a* **1400** *Morte Arth.* 198 Ffesauntez enflureschit in flammande silver.

enflower (ɛn'flaʊə(r)), *v.* Also 6 enflore. [f. EN-¹ + FLOWER *sb.*] *trans.* To adorn or deck with flowers. Hence **en'flowered** *ppl. a.*

1523 SKELTON *Garl. Laurel* 1164 The margent Enflorid with flowris. *c* **1598** B. JONSON *Case Altered* v. i, Milan, these odorous and enflower'd fields Are none of thine. *c* **1602** DAVISON in Farr *S.P. Eliz.* (1845) II. 327 All engreening and enflowering Those pleasant mountagnets. *c* **1611** CHAPMAN *Iliad* VIII. 2 The cheerful Lady of the light.. Dispersed her beams through every part of this enflow'red globe. **1888** A. J. BUTLER *Dante, Paradise* x. 132 Thou wouldst know from what plants this garland is enflowered.

enfluence, obs. form of INFLUENCE.

enfoil: see EN- *prefix*¹ 3.

†**en'fold,** *sb. Obs.* [f. next.] A convolution (of the brain or intestines).

1578 BANISTER *Hist. Man.* v. 72 The intrels..are circunduced into diuers, and many enfoldes,and turnynges. *Ibid.* VIII. 100 The brayne..seemeth to shew many infoldes and turnynges.

enfold, infold (ɛn-, ɪn'fəʊld), *v.*¹ Also 7 infould. *Pa. pple.* occas. 7 infold, 9 enfolden. [f. EN-¹, IN- + FOLD *sb.* and *v.*] To put into a fold, or within folds.

1. *trans.* To wrap up, envelope *in* or *with* a garment, or a surrounding medium of any kind. Also with the garment, etc. as subject.

a. **1776** WITHERING *Bot. Arrangem.* (1796) I. 192 Seed single..enfolded in the cup. **1860** TRENCH *Mirac.* xvi. (1862) 272 The oak is enfolded in the acorn. **1869** FREEMAN *Norm. Conq.* III. 34 The royal robes in which the body had been enfolded were borne away.

β. *c* **1425** *Found. St. Bartholomew's* (E.E.T.S.) 8 Many to ynfoldeyn and many with hym to adde. **1596** SHAKS. *Merch. V.* II. vii. 69 Guilded timber [*mod. edd.* tombes] doe wormes infold. **1613** PURCHAS *Pilgrimage* (1614) 175 Even as..the white of the Egge comprehendeth the yolke, so that first intelligible world infoldeth the second. **1617** MORYSON *Itin.* III. 111 The Silke-wormes..infold themselves in a piece of silk thei weave of an ovall forme and yellow color. **1647** H. MORE *Song of Soul* IV. xxxvi, She in the body was infold, Of this low life. **1668** CULPEPPER & COLE *Barthol. Anat.* I. xx. 52 Two Membranes..infolding the whole bladder. **1713** POPE *Windsor For.* 393 The pearly shell [shall] its lucid globe infold. **1725** —— *Odyss.* III. 540 Artist divine, whose skilful hands infold The victim's horn with circumfusile gold. **1728** YOUNG *Love Fame* v. (1757) 137 Gay rainbow silks her mellow charms infold. **1875** B. TAYLOR *Faust* II. ii. II. 101 Cast o'er The knight your magic mantle and infold him.

b. *fig.*

a. **1674** FAIRFAX *Bulk & Selv.* Ep. Ded., The kindness..is wont to be enfolded mainly within the rank or stock..of the same. *a* **1711** KEN *Hymnotheo* Poet. Wks. 1721 III. 319 All Plants..A confluential Loveliness enfold. *a* **1822** SHELLEY *Witch Atl.* ii, She lay enfolden In the warm shadow of her loveliness. **1850** MRS. STOWE *Uncle Tom's C.* xxiv. 233 His love enfolded her childish heart with more than mortal tenderness.

β. **1592** SHAKS. *Rom. & Jul.* III. iii. 73 Vnlesse the breath of Hartsicke groanes Mist-like infold me from the search of eyes. **1641** MILTON *Ch. Govt.* (1851) Pref. 95 That book within whose sacred context all wisdome is infolded. **1867** G. MACDONALD *Poems* 58 Night infolds the day.

2. To encompass, encircle; to clasp, embrace. Also *fig.*

1596 SPENSER *F.Q.* (T.), For all the crest a dragon did infold With greedy paws. **1618** CHAPMAN *Hesiod* II. 236 She never knew how to enfold The force of Venus swimming all in gold. **1633** P. FLETCHER *Elisa* II. v. *Poet. Misc.* 119 Her snow-white arms..their now dead lord infold. **1725** POPE *Odyss.* XIX. 555 His neck with fond embrace infolding fast. **1850** MRS. BROWNING *Poems* II. 414 While the Muses hang enfolding Knee and foot with faint wild hands. **1855** SINGLETON *Virgil* I. 132 [Vines] with lusty stems Their elms infolding. *Ibid.* I. 277 Each snake, inclipping them, infolds. **1876** BANCROFT *Hist. U.S.* III. xx. 302 Its people, infolding at one extreme the offspring of colonists from Greece, and at the other the hardy children of the Northmen.

†**3.** = INVOLVE. **a.** To imply or necessarily include. **b.** To involve or plunge *in* (disaster). Also *refl.* **c.** To involve in obligation, to oblige.

1579 TOMSON *Calvin's Serm. Tim.* 250/1 God should infolde vs in one selfe same destruction. **1586** T. B. *La Primaud. Fr. Acad.* I. (1589) 145 We infold our selves in that fault, which we reproove in others. *Ibid.* 430 All covetous men..infold themselves in many griefs. **1625** GILL *Sacr. Philos.* I. 24 That any thing be, infolds necessarily the will and power of God thereto. **1646** N. LOCKYER *Sermon* 11 There be many difficulties about the creature, but may be all infolded in one, to wit, sinne.

4. To put into the shape of a fold or succession of folds; formerly often *fig.* to render involved or intricate. Also *refl.* and *intr.* for *refl.*

1605 BACON *Adv. Learn.* I. vii. §4 Fitter for a Declamation than agreeable to a Treatise infolded as this is. **1611** BIBLE *Ezek.* I. 4 A great cloude, and a fire infoulding itselfe. **1612** *Drayton's Poly-olb.* Introd. A ij, The verse oft..so infolds that suddaine conceipt cannot abstract a forme of the clothed truth. **1875** DARWIN *Insectiv. Pl.* xiv. 324 As the rim is enfolded. **1882** VINES *Sachs' Bot.* 950 The cambium layer ..becomes deeply infolded where it extends inwards.

Hence **enˈfolded** *ppl. a.*, **enˈfoldedly** *adv.*

1617 MORYSON *Itin.* III. 111 That the infolded wormes may die. *c* **1633** MILTON *Arcades* 64 The celestial Sirens..That sit upon the nine infolded spheres. **1879** FARRAR *St. Paul* I. 92 A semblance as of infolded flame. **1624** F. WHITE *Repl. Fisher* 280 [It] is neither expresly nor infoldedly taught in holy Scripture.

enfold (ɛnˈfəʊld), *v.*[2] *rare.* Also 7 infold. [f. EN- *pref.*[1] + FOLD *sb.*[1]] To shut up (sheep, etc.) in a fold.

c **1611** CHAPMAN *Iliad* VIII. K vj, Then Troians in their wals Had beene infolded like meeke Lambs, had Ioue winkt at their fals. **1683** CHALKHILL *Thealma & Cl.* 94 She left the Lovers to enfold her Sheep. **1882** J. PARKER *Apost. Life* I. 13 Until the last little lamb had been safely enfolded.

enfolder, infolder (ɛn-, ɪnˈfəʊldə(r)). [f. ENFOLD *v.*[1] + -ER.] One who or something which enfolds; †in quot. *spec.* an enveloping membrane.

1545 RAYNALD *Womans booke* (1564) 45 Bryngyng from thence the veine of the chylde, betweene his seconde and the innermost infolder. *Ibid.* I. (1634) 79 The third or the inmost infolder of the child..is so thinne that one may easily see through it. **18..** MRS. BROWNING *Wine of Cyprus* Poet. Wks. (1883) 30 That shadow, the enfolder of your quiet eyelids.

enfolding, infolding (ɛn-, ɪnˈfəʊldɪŋ), *vbl. sb.* [f. as prec. + -ING[1].] The action of the verb ENFOLD. Also *concr.* in various applications: (*a*) a wrappage, envelope, † in *pl.* garments; (*b*) a fold, convolution.

1586 W. WEBBE *Disc. Eng. Poetrie* (Arb.) 65 The turning of verses; the infolding of wordes. **1611** SHAKS. *Wint. T.* IV. iv. 755 Seest thou not the ayre of the Court, in these enfoldings? **1873** MIVART *Elem. Anat.* ix. 372 Infoldings of the surface of the organ. **1880** A. WILSON in *Gentl. Mag.* CCXLVI. 45 The infolding of this blastoderm. **1882** VINES *Sachs' Bot.* 533 The cells which contain chlorophyll exhibit the infoldings of the cell-wall. **1885** W. K. PARKER *Mammal. Descent* iii. 88 The embryo and its inner enfoldings.

enfolding, infolding (ɛn-, ɪnˈfəʊldɪŋ), *ppl. a.* [f. as prec. + -ING[2].] That enfolds.

1669 BUNYAN *Holy Citie* 169 An infolding Mystery wrapped up, and inclosed. **1735** H. BROOKE *Univ. Beauty* I. (R.), In balm imbosom'd every region lies, Of ambient ether and infolding skies. **1827** KEBLE *Chr. Y., St. Michael* ix, Waft us heaven-ward with enfolding wing. **1879** FARRAR *St. Paul* (1883) 144 An infolding fire and a supernatural sound arrested their progress.

enfoldment (ɛnˈfəʊldmənt). *arch.* [f. as prec. + -MENT.] The action of enfolding; †*concr.* that which enfolds.

1593 NASHE *Christ's T.* (1613) 45 That in mine amorous enfoldment, I might whyrle her [Ierusalem] to Heauen with me. **1624** GATAKER *Transubst.* 94 O most divine and holy Mysterie, symbolically discovering those enigmaticall Enfoldments. **1825** SCOTT *Talism.* ix, His long slender dark fingers were..almost buried in the large enfoldment of King Richard's hand.

†**enˈfollow,** *v. Obs. rare.* In 4-5 infolewe, en-, infolowe. [f. EN- *pref.*[1] + FOLLOW *v.*] **a.** *trans.* To follow after; *fig.* to imitate. **b.** *intr.* To follow on; to ensue, result.

Hence **enˈfollowing** *vbl. sb.*

1382 WYCLIF *Ecclus.* xxxii. 23 In his infolewingis he shal ben vndernome [Vulg. *insectationibus arguetur*]. *c* **1449** PECOCK *Repr.* III. vi. 313 In-folewing Crist in the seid pouerte. **1485** CAXTON *St. Wenefr.* 4 Moche good shold therof enfolowe.

enfonce (ɛnˈfɒns), *v. rare.* [ad. Fr. *enfoncer*, f. *en-* (see EN-[1]) + *foncer* to sink.] *trans.* To sink in; to place in a low or retired position.

1834 R. MUDIE *Brit. Birds* (1841) I. 147 The eyes of this one [the screech owl] not being so deeply enfonced as those of most of the others.

enfondre, var. of ENFOUNDER *v.*, *Obs.*

†**enˈforce,** *sb. Obs.* [f. next vb.: cf. AFFORCE.] Effort, exertion.

1375 BARBOUR *Bruce* XVII. 448 Thai that var With gret enforss assalȝeand thar. **1491** CAXTON *Vitas Patrum* (W. de W. 1495) I. xlii. 68 b/2, All her enforce auaylled her not. **1526** *Pilgr. Perf.* (1531) 13 b, We desyre..with all the enforce and myght of our hertes to be with hym. **1671** MILTON *Samson* 1220 A petty enterprise of small enforce.

enforce (ɛnˈfɔəs), *v.* Forms: *α.* 4-7 enforse, (4 ? enforth, 6 enfoarce), 4- enforce. *β.* 4-7 inforse, (6 infors), 5- inforce. [ad. OF. *enforcier, enforcir*:—late L. *infortiāre, infortīre*, f. *in-* (see IN-) + *fortis* strong; see also EN- *prefix*[1] and FORCE *sb.*]

I. To put force or strength into.

†**1.** *trans.* To strengthen (a fortress) by extra works, (an army, navy, town, etc.) by extra ships, troops, etc.; to occupy in force; to reinforce. *Obs.*

a. **1340-70** *Alisaunder* 908 Enforced were þe entres with egre men fele. *c* **1425** WYNTOUN *Cron.* VIII. xxxvii. 177 Morys of Murrawe..Ðat syne enforsyt it [þat Castelle] grettumly. **1523** LD. BERNERS *Froiss.* I. xlvi. 63 The frenche kynge enforced his great nauy that he had on the see. **1557** PAYNEL *Barclay's Jugurth* 52 He ordeyned as it were a forward enforced with a threfold subsidie, or socour. **1668** TEMPLE *Lett. Ld. Arlington* Wks. 1731 II. 61 To enforce the Towns of Flanders by..our Troops. **1755** EDWARDS *Wks.* (1834) I. Introd. 209/2 The French were in constant expectation of being greatly enforced by a large body.

β. **1375** BARBOUR *Bruce* IV. 65 [Thai] inforsit the castell sua. **1652** NEEDHAM tr. *Selden's Mare Cl.* 376 Provided and inforced with men of war in divers forein Parts. **1697** DRYDEN *Virg.* (1806) IV. 153 The brave Messapus shall thy troops inforce With those of Tibur.

†**2.** To strengthen in a moral sense; to impart resolution or fortitude to (a person); to encourage (const. *to* with *inf.*); to strengthen (a resolve, a purpose). *Obs.*

c **1386** CHAUCER *Pers. T.* ¶656 This vertu..enhaunsith and enforceth the soule. **1483** CAXTON *Gold. Leg.* 178/3 Yet was saynt barnabe a man enforced to suffre paynes. **1534** LD. BERNERS *Gold. Bk. M. Aurel* (1546) O vj, By suche examuples..the good people shoulde enforce them selues. **1626** BACON *Sylva* (1677) §314 To enforce the Spirits by some Mixture, that may excite and quicken them. **1685** R. BERKELEY in *Mem.* (1857) III. 275 Sir, if the entreaties of a friend can enforce the resolves of so great a philosopher.

†**3.** To add force to, intensify, strengthen (a feeling, desire, influence); to impart fresh vigour or energy to (an action, movement, attack, etc.). *Obs.*

a. **1375** BARBOUR *Bruce* v. 355 Douglass..enforsit on thame the cry. *c* **1400** *Rom. Rose* 4499 Now mote my sorwe enforced be. *c* **1450** *Merlin* ix. 136 And so began the turnement newe to enforse for the rescewe of theire felowes. **1523** LD. BERNERS *Froiss.* I. lxxvi. 97 The next day to enforce the assaut. **1563** MAN *Musculus' Commonpl.* 34 a, Enforcing up his noyse littel and littel. **1727** POPE, etc., *Art Sinking* 76 Hang on lead to..enforce our descent. **1741** MIDDLETON *Cicero* (1742) III. xii. 287 He [Cicero]..used to enforce the severity of his abstinence. **1750** JOHNSON *Rambler* No. 63 ¶12 The temptations to do ill are multiplied and enforced. **1775** T. SHERIDAN *Art Reading* 102 Their [the consonants'] sound should be enforced.

β. **1513** DOUGLAS *Æneis* I. ii. 31 Infors thi wyndis. **1534** LD. BERNERS *Gold. Bk. M. Aurel.* (1546) N iv, He..inforceth his appetite, to know more. **1691-8** NORRIS *Pract. Disc.* IV. 374 Conviction of the Worlds Vanity..as an inner spring actuates and inforces all our outward motions. *a* **1716** SOUTH *Serm.* I. vi. (R.), The same authority, and evidence, that inforced the former.

†**b.** To give legal force to; to ratify. *Obs. rare*[—1].

1756 P. BROWNE *Jamaica* 5 His majesty..always inforces or makes void all the acts passed by them.

4. To press home (an argument, etc.); to urge (a demand, etc.); formerly, also, to lay stress upon, emphasize (a fact, circumstance).

a. *c* **1449** [see ENFORCING *vbl. sb.*]. **1593** SHAKS. *Rich. II*, IV. i. 90 Against Aumerle we will enforce his Tryall. **1600** HOLLAND *Livy* v. iv. 181 Much against my stomacke, O Quirites, enforce I this point. **1635** NAUNTON *Fragm. Reg.* (Arb.) 43 The Warrant for his execution [being] tendered, and somewhat enforced, she [the Queen] refused to sign it. *a* **1674** CLARENDON *Hist. Reb.* (J.), Enforcing the ill consequence of his refusal to take the office. **1711** SHAFTESB. *Charac.* II. 68 Where infinite rewards are thus inforc'd..natural motives to goodness are apt to be neglected. **1751** JOHNSON *Rambler* No. 87 ¶14 The preacher..enforcing a precept of religion. **1832** HT. MARTINEAU *Ireland* ii. 33 In order to enforce what he had said. **1870** ANDERSON *Missions Amer. Bd.* II. ix. 74 Hoapile enforced his claim by an argument from a reciprocity of rights and duties. **1878** BROWNING *La Saisiaz* 76 Failed ye to enforce the maxim.

β. **1586** A. DAY *Eng. Secretary* II. (1625) 92 How much every degree is still inforced one above another. **1605** B. JONSON *Volpone* I. iv, To inforce..Your cares, your watchings, and your many prayers. **1628** T. SPENCER *Logick* 308 The presence of that doth inforce the absence of the rest. **1750** JOHNSON *Rambler* No. 24 ¶5 This monition might very properly be inforced. **1775** ADAIR *Amer. Ind.* 61 To inforce their musical speech.

†**b.** With obj. clause, or accus. and inf.: To assert, argue forcibly. *Obs.*

1579 J. KNEWSTUB *Confut.* 5 Upon order taken for procuring things to be done, H.N. will necessarily enforce that the same are done. **1613** *Life Will. Conq.* in *Select. fr. Harl. Misc.* (1793) 8 He inforced it to be a good title.

†**5.** To exert (one's strength). *Obs.*

1490 CAXTON *Eneydos* (1889) 18 By grete myghte and bodyli strengthe enforced his puyssaunce for to arache and plucke vp the same tree.

†**b.** *refl.* To exert oneself, strive. Const. *to* with *inf.* Also *to* with *sb.*: To strive after, rush into. *Obs.*

a. *c* **1340** *Cursor M.* 18089 Enforseþ ȝou wiþ myȝte & meyn Stalworþely to stonde aȝeyn. *c* **1386** CHAUCER *Melibeus* ¶209 Suche as enforcen hem rathere to prayse youre persone by flaterie. *a* **1450** *Knt. de la Tour* (1868) 61 Eve..enforced her to excuse her of her misdede and synne. **1526** TINDALE *Rom.* xv. 20 So have I enforsed my selfe to preache the gospell. **1533** BELLENDEN *Livy* III. (1822) 213 He enforcit himself to batall. **1535** FISHER *Wks.* 381 Such soules also as..enforce them selues to a great loue. **1557** NORTH *Gueuara's Diall Pr.* Prol. A i *a*, We may enforce our selfes to worke amendes. **1693** W. ROBERTSON *Phraseol. Gen.* 535 To enforce, or strain himself earnestly, *conari*.

β. *c* **1460** FORTESCUE *Abs. & Lim. Mon.* (1714) 60 [Man] inforsith hymself to be alway gretter and gretter. **1513** DOUGLAS *Æneis* X. vii. 177 Pallas..Inforcis hym to greif hys fays that tyde. **1541** ELYOT *Image Gov.* 43 He..inforceth him selfe to brenne the houses. **1633** BP. HALL *Hard Texts, N.T.* 85 Inforce yourselves to use all diligent..indeavours.

†**6.** *intr.* for *refl.* To strive, attempt, physically or mentally. Of a ship: To make way. *Obs.*

a. *c* **1340** HAMPOLE *Prose Tr.* 2 It enforthis for to halde besyly in it the swetteste name of Ihesu. *c* **1374** CHAUCER *Boeth.* II. i. 30 She vseþ ful flatryng familarite wiþ hem þat she enforceþ to bygyle. **1382** WYCLIF *1 Kings* xix. 10 Saul enforside to fitche to gidre with a spere Dauid in the wal. —— *Acts* xxv. 15 The schipp was rauyschid, and myȝte not enforse into the wynd. **1490** CAXTON *How to Die* 4 The deuylle enforseth to brynge to him sorowe vpon sorow. **1557** *N.T.* (Genev.) *1 Thess.* ii. 17 We enforsed the more to se your face. **1595** SPENSER *Col. Clout* 482 Thrise happie Mayd, Whom thou doest so enforce to deifie.

β. **1513** DOUGLAS *Æneis* v. i. 37 Nor we may nocht strife, nor enforce [*ed.* 1557 inforce] sa fast Agane the storme. **1581** MARBECK *Bk. of Notes* 377 False Prophets..inforce to quench the true vnderstanding of the lawe.

II. To bring force to bear upon.

†**7.** *trans.* To drive by force: **a.** by physical force, as a stone *from* a sling, a person *from* a place. Also, *to enforce open*, and *simply*.

c **1325** *E.E. Allit. P.* B. 938 And enforsed alle fawre forth at þe ȝatez. **1555** *Fardle Facions* I. vi. 94 There come into that coaste, infinite swarmes of Gnattes, without any drifte of winde to enforce them. **1596** HARINGTON *Metam. Ajax* (1814) 109 The very nature of fire helpeth to enforce [air] upward. **1599** SHAKS. *Hen. V*, IV. vii. 65 As swift as stones Enforced from the old Assyrian slings. **1600** HAKLUYT *Voy.* (1810) III. 189 If we be inforced by contrary windes. **1627** SPEED *England* xxi. §8 Yet hath she [Lincoln] not escaped the calamitie of sword, as in the time of the Saxons; whence Arthur enforced their Host. **1644** QUARLES *Barnabas & B.* (1851) 194 Nor can my stronger groans enforce the portals open. **1649** SELDEN *Laws Eng.* II. xii. (1739) 67 Those that would reduce him, he enforces into foreign Countries.

b. by mental or moral force: To drive a person *to* or *from* a belief, sentiment, or course of action.

1542 HENRY VIII *Declar. Scots* 192 Beying novve enforced to the warre. **1591** DRAYTON *Noah* in Farr *S.P. Jas. I* (1848) 119 From remorce In his own nature you doe him inforce. **1635** AUSTIN *Medit.* 101 To this observance [fasting]..Nature should inforce us. **1646** SIR T. BROWNE *Pseud. Ep.* I. i. 1 It..hath enforced them unto strange conceptions. **1664** DRYDEN *Rival Ladies* II. i. (1725) 209, I am inforc'd to trust you with my most near Concerns.

†**8.** To use force upon; to press hard upon. Also *fig.* to press hard upon, urge, with arguments, taunts, entreaties, etc. *Obs.*

138. WYCLIF *Wks.* (1880) 378 [Naaman] enforsid hym þat he schuld haue take þo giftis. *c* **1400** *Rom. Rose* 6409 Thou shalt not streyne me a dele, Ne enforce me. **1494** FABYAN VII. ccxlv. 288 Eyther prynce enforsed so straytly that other, that eyther of theym were vnhorsed. **1568** GRAFTON *Chron.*

II. 176 If you thinke not this..truth, I will not enforce you. **1601** SHAKS. *Jul. C.* IV. iii. 112 The Flint..much inforced, shewes a hastie Sparke. **1605** CAMDEN *Rem.* 212 He besieged Orleans, and had so enforced it, that the Inhabitants were willing..to yeelde themselves. *a* **1618** RALEIGH *Rem.* (1644) 36 It is not the part of a just Civil Prince..to enforce such a Countrey. **1662** FULLER *Worthies* (1840) III. 279 He enforced him no further.

b. *intr.* in same sense: ***to enforce upon.*** *Obs.*

1561 T. NORTON *Calvin's Inst.* I. To Rdr., How much more the sickenesse enforced vpon me, so much lesse I spared myselfe. **1568** GRAFTON *Chron.* II. 98 The French men..so enforced upon them, that they..tooke the sayde Arthur prisoner. **1586** J. HOOKER *Girald. Irel.* in *Holinshed* II. 16/1 They still pressing & inforcing vpon him.

†**9.** To overcome by violence; to take (a town) by storm; to force, ravish (a woman); also *fig.*

a. *c* **1386** CHAUCER *Pers. T.* ¶900 If the womman maugré hir heed hath ben enforced or noon. **1483** CAXTON *G. de la Tour* E vj b, He..enforced their wyues. **1579** FENTON *Guicciard.* 165 They enforced it in two dayes, and likewise the Castle, making slaughter of all the footmen that were withdrawne thither. **1594** T. B. *La Primaud. Fr. Acad.* II. 423 Howsoeuer they labour to enforce (as it were) their conscience. **1631** CHAPMAN *Cæsar & Pompey* Plays 1873 III. 172 The great authority of Rome Would faine enforce me by their mere suspitions.

β. **1560** DAUS tr. *Sleidane's Comm.* 250 A, Inforce theyr wyues and their children. **1577** *Test. 12 Patriarchs* 52 Ye shall..inforce maidens in Jerusalem.

10. To compel, constrain, oblige. Said of both persons and circumstances. Const. *to* with *inf.* *arch.*

a. **1523** LD. BERNERS *Froiss.* I. xii. 12 They were xi days in the shyppe, and enforced it to saile as moche as they myghte. **1553** EDEN *Treat. Newe Ind.* (Arb.) 13 [They] were at the length, enforsed to departe. **1573** TUSSER *Husb.* (1878) 5 My seruing you..Enforced this to come to pas. **1632** LITHGOW *Trav.* III. (1682) 107 Accompanied with two Goddesses; the one was (Eloquence) to perswade them, and the other was (Violence) to enforce them. **1649** SELDEN *Laws Eng.* II. ii. (1739) 15 The Parliament was sometimes enforced to adjourn it self for want of number sufficient. **1733** NEAL *Hist. Purit.* II. 387 [He] had been..enforced to enter into a bond of a thousand pounds. **1801** SOUTHEY *Thalaba* V. xxxv, Only by strong and torturing spells enforced. **1837** SIR F. PALGRAVE *Merch. & Friar* i. (1844) 17 You would have been enforced to compress your missive within..scanty bounds.

β. **1509–10** *Act 1 Hen. VIII*, c. 12 Pream., The Parties..were inforced and constrayned to sue ther Lyverey..oute of the Handes of the seid late Kyng. **1581** W. STAFFORD *Exam. Compl.* III. (1876) 82 The husbandman was necessarily inforced..to sel his Victayles dearer. **1691** LOCKE *Money* Wks. 1727 II. 33 The Bargain being made, the Law will inforce the Borrower to pay it.

III. To produce, impose, effect, by force.

†**11.** To produce by force, material or immaterial; to extort (tears, concessions, etc.) *from* a person; to force (a passage); to bring on (a quarrel, etc.) by force; to force on. *Obs.*

a. **1586** MARLOWE *1st Pt. Tamburl.* III. ii, With shivering spears enforcing thunder-claps. **1586** A. DAY *Eng. Secretary* I. (1625) 42 My paper burthened with this long discourse..enforceth an end. **1594** GREENE & LODGE *Looking Glasse* (1861) 131 Dare you enforce the furrows of revenge Within the brows of royal Radagon? **1598** B. JONSON *Ev. Man in Hum.* IV. iii. (1616) 48 Why, how now, brother, who enforst this brawle? **1633** T. STAFFORD *Pac. Hib.* xi. (1821) 134 The White Knight..condemned both his Sonne and people for their folly, to enforce a fight. **1812** J. HENRY *Camp. agst. Quebec* 134 The endurances we underwent..enforced many a tear.

β. **1531–46** ELYOT *Governour* (1883) II. 215 Iniurie apparaunt and with power inforced..may be with lyke powar resisted. **1583** GOLDING *Calvin on Deut.* Pref. Ep. 1 The long interceassing of so great a benefite, inforced through the tyrannie of Antichrist. **1611** LANYER *Salve Deus* in Farr *S.P. Jas. I* (1848) 230 Your cries inforced mercie, grace, and loue, From Him whom greatest princes would not moue. **1621** BURTON *Anat. Mel.* I. iii. III. (1651) 212 By the striking of a flint fire is inforced. **1636** G. SANDYS *Paraphr. Div. Poems* Ex. xv. (1648) 2 Pharaohs Chariots..Twixt walls of Seas their way inforce. **1674** PLAYFORD *Skill Mus.* I. 54 To feign them, or at the least to inforce Notes.

†**12.** To force, obtrude (something) *on* a person.

1601 SHAKS. *All's Well* II. i. 129, I will no more enforce mine office on you.

13. To compel by physical or moral force (the performance of an action, conformity to a rule, etc.); to impose (a course of conduct) *on* a person.

1649 SELDEN *Laws Eng.* I. xiii. (1739) 23 This course was..inforced upon them by a Roman Constitution. **1712** BERKELEY *Pass. Obed.* §3 A supreme power of making laws, and enforcing the observation of them. **1828** SCOTT *F.M. Perth* xiv, To enforce upon his fiery temper compliance with the rules of civil life. **1844** H. H. WILSON *Brit. India* I. I. ii. 143 He declared his determination to enforce obedience to the order. **1859** KINGSLEY *Misc.* (1860) II. 63 The bloated tyrant..enforced payment by scourge and thumbscrew. **1875** JOWETT *Plato* (ed. 2) V. 123 They are to enforce the education of their children upon unwilling parents.

14. To compel the observance of (a law); to support by force (a claim, demand, obligation).

a. **1603** SHAKS. *Meas. for M.* IV. iv. 25 A deflowred maid, And by an eminent body, that enforc'd The Law against it! **1732** BERKELEY *Alciphr.* III. §13 There was neither jail nor executioner in his kingdom to enforce the laws. **1774** GOLDSM. *Nat. Hist.* (1776) II. 131 It should be the business of the legislature..to enforce this Divine precept. **1839** THIRLWALL *Greece* V. 265 Sparta..paid no regard to the sentence, which, after the battle of Mantinea, there was none to enforce. **1841** ELPHINSTONE *Hist. Ind.* I. 503 They sent a body of 1000 infantry and 300 horse to enforce their demand.

β. **1848** MACAULAY *Hist. Eng.* I. 652 This law was inforced ..with a rigour at once cruel and ludicrous.

b. *absol. rare.*

1876 GROTE *Eth. Fragm.* ii. 39 If as an individual he is obliged to obey, as one of the public he is entitled to enforce upon other individuals.

enforceability (ɛn-, ɪnfɔəsə'bɪlɪtɪ). [f. ENFORCEAB(LE + -ILITY.] The character or quality of being enforceable.

1921 B. M. SQUIRES in J. R. Commons *Trade Unionism & Labor Problems* xliv. 786 An admission of illegality must necessarily reflect upon the enforceability of the provisions of the act. **1925** *Glasgow Herald* 9 Sept. 10 The danger of 'a Legislature which has grown accustomed to pass any number of laws without concern for their consequences or their enforceability'. **1928** *Britain's Industr. Future* (*Lib. Ind. Inq.*) III. xvii. 212 The possibility of obtaining legal enforceability for their decisions.

enforceable (ɛn'fɔəsəb(ə)l), *a.* Also 6 inforcible, 9 enforcible. [f. ENFORCE *v.* + -ABLE.] Capable of being enforced. †Also = FORCIBLE.

1589 *Marprel. Epit.* C ij b, See..what may be brought to reproche the credit of such inforcible proofes. *a* **1677** BARROW Sermon VI. *Wks.* I. 71 (L.) Grounded upon plain testimonies of Scripture, and enforcible by good reason. **1863** H. COX *Instit.* II. viii. 495 An obligation enforceable in equity. **1870** *Contemp. Rev.* XV. 555 Either party..may..get damages, enforceable by distress. **1875** BRYCE *Holy Rom. Emp.* xv. (ed. 5) 245 Feudal rights no longer enforcible.

en'forced (ɛn'fɔəst), *ppl. a.* [f. as prec. + -ED[1].]

1. That is subjected to force or constraint. *rare.*

1654 R. CODRINGTON tr. *Hist. Ivstine* 74 This concurse..of the water doth take down with it into the bottom of the deeps the enforced spirit, and there suffocates and keeps it down, etc. **1861** GEN. P. THOMPSON *Audi Alt.* III. cxlvi. 134 They pleaded themselves enforced agents.

2. That is forced upon or exacted from a person; that is produced by force; forced, constrained.

1576 FLEMING *Panoplie Ep.* 203 He hath constrayned such to yeelde to inforced obedience and servitude. **1594** SHAKS. *Rich. III*, III. v. 9 Gastly Lookes Are at my seruice, like enforced Smiles. **1625** K. LONG tr. *Barclay's Argenis* V. x. 364 The slavery of an inforced marriage. **1837** HT. MARTINEAU *Soc. Amer.* II. 128 A country where a degraded class is held to enforced labour. **1868** HELPS *Realmah* v. 68 How Sir John could have endured the enforced silence.

enforcedly (ɛn'fɔəsɪdlɪ), *adv.* Also 6–7 inforcedly. [f. prec. + -LY[2].] In an enforced manner. †**a.** By force, forcibly (*obs.*). **b.** Under compulsion. **c.** With constrained utterance.

1579 TWYNE *Phisick agst. Fortune* II. lxvii. 244 a, I am enforcedly dryuen into banishment. **1594** SOUTHWELL *M. Magd. Fun. Teares* 18 She for whom he died [was] inforcedly left alive. **1635** R. H. *Arraignm. Whole Creature* xiv. §1. 226 They should doe it of necessity, inforcedly, and compulsorily. **1656** S. H. *Gold. Law* 15 Suppose that Perkin Warbeck..had inforcedly and so usurpingly gained the Government. **1864** LOWELL *Fireside Trav.* 180 Whose Geography we studied enforcedly at school. **1882** H. MERIVALE *Faucit of B.* III. II. x. 7 The oracle spoke—enforcedly—slowly—cruelly.

†**en'forcely**, *adv. Obs.* In 4 inforcely, enforsaly. [irregularly f. ENFORCE *v.* + -LY[2].] In a forcible manner; violently, furiously.

1375 BARBOUR *Bruce* II. 314 Saw thaim cum swa inforcely. *Ibid.* v. 324 Than suld thai, full enforsaly..assale The ynglis men.

enforcement (ɛn'fɔəsmənt). Also 6–8 in-. [a. OF. *enforcement*: see ENFORCE *v.* and -MENT.] The action or process of enforcing.

†**1.** The action or process of increasing the strength of anything (*esp.* an armed force, etc.); *concr.* a reinforcement. *Obs.*

1643 PRYNNE *Sov. Power Parl.* IV. 35 Such a force of Irish Rebels now ready to be shipped..for their assistance and enforcement. **1682** TEMPLE *Mem.* Wks. 1731 I. 406 The Prince of Conde was sent in haste out of Flanders, with a great Enforcement. **1762** *Acc. of Bks.* in *Ann. Reg.* 250/1 Something equivalent to those enforcements and lowering of sounds which gives such a pleasant variety.

†**2.** Energetic activity; an effort. *Obs. rare.*

1547–64 BAULDWIN *Mor. Philos.* (Palfr.) To Rdr., Their busie inforcement hath kindled in others the like hatred and contempt. **1551** RECORDE *Pathw. Know.* To Rdr., To accomplishe so haulte an enforcement.

3. The urging a demand, pressing home an argument, representation, or statement.

1586 A. DAY *Eng. Secretary* I. (1625) 33 Forcible reasons, enforcements, rebukes, and perswasions. **1587** GOLDING *De Mornay* xxxiii. 537 What inforcements..to perswade men? **1635** AUSTIN *Medit.* 165 These preach (as St. John, after, did;) using the same manner of Enforcement. **1751** JOHNSON *Rambler* No. 162 §10 Persuaded the tenants..to entreat his enforcement of their representations. **1861** SMILES *Engineers* II. 160 It cost him many years of arguing, illustration, and enforcement. **1880** E. WHITE *Cert. Relig.* 54 How large a space is occupied with the enforcement of this claim.

†**4.** The action of bringing force to bear upon, doing violence to, or overcoming by force (a person or thing). Also *fig.* a strained interpretation (of words). *Obs.*

1577–87 HOLINSHED *Chron.* III. 1061/1 Where he did so much by batterie & other kinds of inforcement. **1583** FULKE *Defence* Answ. Pref. §10. 28, I marvel at your bold assertions, and abhor your impudent enforcements. **1597** SHAKS. *Rich. III*, III. vii. 8 And his enforcement of the Citie Wiues. **1597** —— *2 Hen. IV*, I. i. 120 As the Thing, that's heauy in it selfe, Vpon enforcement, flyes with greatest speede.

5. Constraint, compulsion; a constraining or compelling influence. *rare* in mod. use.

1475 CAXTON *Jason* 19 b, He dremed of his lady for thenforcement of loue. **1548** UDALL, etc. *Erasm. Par. Mark* 41 The soule..throughe thenforcement of disease had forsaken the bodye. **1553** T. WILSON *Rhet.* 57 b, Often tymes the soldiour saieth, his capitaines biddyng was his enforcement. **1670** MILTON *Hist. Eng.* III. Wks. (1851) 125 For any enforcement that Artur with all his Chivalry could make. **1820** KEATS *Ode to Psyche* 2 O Goddess! hear these tuneless numbers, wrung By sweet enforcement. *a* **1845** HOOD *Lamia* vii. 60 By thy own enforcement [I] come to force thee, Being passion-mad.

6. The forcible exaction of a payment, an action, etc.; the enforcing or compelling the fulfilment of (a law, demand, obligation); †*concr.* a means of enforcing, a 'sanction'.

1597 DANIEL *Civ. Wares* IV. lxiv, Though hee had then inforcements of expence Both for offence, retaynements, and defence. **1642** MILTON *Apol. Smect.* (1851) 266 To see the ruine of our Protestation, and the inforcement of a Slavish life. **1690** LOCKE *Hum. Und.* II. xxi. (1695) 150 The Rewards and Punishments..which the Almighty has established as the Enforcements of his Law. **1756** BURKE *Vind. Nat. Soc.* Wks. I. 78 Is it consistent with the divine wisdom to prescribe rules to us, and leave the enforcement of them to the folly of human institutions? **1828** SCOTT *F.M. Perth* xxv, The occasion seemed to require an enforcement of domestic discipline. **1876** GREEN *Short Hist.* iii. §7 (1882) 150 [The] weakness [of the Charter] in providing no means for the enforcement of its own stipulations.

7. *attrib.* and *Comb.* (sense 6) ***enforcement officer, staff, work.***

1946 *How Britain was fed in War Time* (Ministry of Food) iv. 40 At the end of 1944 there were 415 Ministry of Food Statutory Orders in force... The wide new field of offences resulting from the Ministry's Orders made it necessary to appoint a special enforcement staff. **1947** *Evening News* 17 Dec. 1/1 After weeks of secret inquiry by his enforcement staff, Mr. Strachey [Minister of Food] has..been presented with a report. *Ibid.*, All Ministry enforcement officers are now empowered to search premises and confiscate any meat suspected of having been illegally killed. **1948** *Hansard Commons* 11 Mar. 1405 Eighty-four inspectors are employed on all forms of enforcement work. **1959** *Times* 17 July 8/3 Devon County Council agreed to spend £500 on the appointment of four plain clothes litter wardens... The wardens, officially called enforcement officers, will be in action for eight weeks.

b. Special Comb. **enforcement notice**, the official notification from a local planning authority that a particular development is considered to be in breach of planning legislation, and requiring that the breach be remedied within a specified time.

1947 *Town & Country Planning Act* 10 & 11 Geo 6 c. 51 § 23(2) Any notice served under this section (hereinafter called an '*enforcement notice') shall specify the development which is alleged to have been carried out without the grant of..permission. **1976** *Southern Even. Echo* (Southampton) 2 Nov. 18/4 A Cadnam man, who failed to obey enforcement notices served on him by New Forest District Council, was summoned at Totton court.

enforcer (ɛn'fɔəsə(r)). [f. ENFORCE *v.* + -ER.]

1. One who enforces.

1580 HOLLYBAND *Treas. Fr. Tong, Forceur*, a conqueror, an enforcer. **1649** SELDEN *Laws Eng.* II. i. (1739) 6 The Contrivers, Advisers and Enforcers. **1884** H. H. WILSON *Brit. India* I. 234 A rigorous advocate and unrelenting enforcer of measures of public economy and retrenchment. **1855** GROTE *Greece* II. xci. XII. 20 A paramount obligation of which he was the enforcer. **1885** J. RAE in *Contemp. Rev.* June 902 Besides its function as enforcer of morality..the State has another office.

2. *slang* (orig. *U.S.*). One who enforces his will by violence and intimidation; a strong-arm man, esp. in an underworld gang.

1934 *Survey Graphic* Oct. 480/2 December 19, 1932, Frank ('The Enforcer') Nitto, Capone's cousin and business manager of the Capone gang, was shot three times in the neck. **1951** E. KEFAUVER *Crime in Amer.* x. 143 Dead beside him was his lieutenant and 'enforcer', Charlie Gargotta. **1972** *N.Y. Times* 1 June 47/4 His subordinates include 'enforcers' or strong-arm men, and freelance 'cutters'. **1976** *Reader's Digest* Mar. 34 Every team employs swashbuckling ..'enforcers'... Dave 'Hammer' Schultz..excels at..ferocious attacks on opposing teams' stars. **1983** *Times* 28 Apr. 3/6 An east London wholesaler was cleared at the Central Criminal Court yesterday of the gangland execution of an underworld 'enforcer'.

enforcible: see ENFORCEABLE.

enforcing (ɛn'fɔəsɪŋ), *vbl. sb.* [f. ENFORCE *v.* + -ING[1].] The action of the vb. ENFORCE in its various senses. †*concr.* that which enforces.

138. WYCLIF *Sel. Wks.* I. 245 Of sich enforsinge mote nedis come mede. **1398** TREVISA *Barth. De P.R.* II. iv. (1495) 31 Aungels dystroye the reeses and the enforcynges of fendes. *c* **1440** *Gesta Rom.* xxxi. 116 (Harl. MS.) When the lion had sight of hem, he Ran to him with a cruell enforsynge. *c* **1449** PECOCK *Repr.* IV. iv. 446 This hool argument with alle hise enforcingis. **1531** ELYOT *Gov.* I. v. (1883) I. 35 Without any violence or inforsinge. *c* **1610–5** *Female Saints* (1866) 80 After long enforcing she must needes yield nature her due. **1641** H. AINSWORTH *Orth. Foundat. Relig.* 12 Love is the inforcing, or motive of the Will, to the thing loved.

en'forcing, *ppl. a.* [f. as prec. + -ING[2].] That enforces or presses upon.

1649 G. Daniel *Trinarch., Hen. V*, clxiv, The thin-film'd Bladder breakes Prest with the burthen of enforceing Ayre. **1662** H. Stubbe *Ind. Nectar* ii. 12 A drink invented by an enforcing necessity.

Hence **en'forcingly** *adv.*, in a forcible manner; earnestly, impressively.

1571 Golding *Calvin on Ps.* xliv. 5 Onlesse it bee put enforcingly for assurance sake. **1754** Richardson *Grandison* (1781) VI. 9, I am wished to write more enforcingly to you.

† **en'forcive,** *a. Obs.* [f. enforce *v.* + -ive.]

1. a. Tending to enforce. **b.** Urgent, forcible.

1606 G. W[oodcocke] tr. *Hist. Ivstine* 83 b With these and such like inforciue arguments the harts of his souldiors were greatly incouraged. *c* **1611** Chapman *Iliad* viii. 212 [An eagle] who seasde in her repayre A sucking hind calfe, which she trust in her enforciue seeres. *Ibid.* x. 128 Why stir ye thus so late? Sustain we such enforcive cause? **1693** Beverley *True St. Gospel Truth* 6 Those Attributes of God, that are most enforcive of a gracious Answer.

2. As quasi-*sb.* (nonce-use), after the analogy of *motive*: A means of compelling.

1686 A. Horneck *Crucified Jesus* (1695) 373 If these Motives cannot prevail, God hath Enforcives which shall.

Hence † **en'forcively** *adv.*, by compulsion.

1880 Webster cites Marston.

† **enforest** (ɛn'fɒrɛst), *v. Obs.* Also 7 en-, inforrest. [f. en-[1] + forest. Cf. afforest.]

trans. To convert (arable or pasture land) into forest or hunting-ground. Cf. afforest.

a **1619** Daniel *Coll. Hist. Eng.* (1626) 128 All such as were found to haue beene inforrested since the first Coronation of Henry the Second to bee disafforested. **1627** Speed *England* vi. §7 Thirtie miles of circuit inforrested for his game of Hunting. **1662** Fuller *Worthies* ii. 174 Henry the Eight enforrested the grounds hereabouts [Hampton Court].

enforge: see en- *pref.*[1] 3.

enform, etc.: see inform, etc.

† **enforsothe,** *v. Obs. rare*$^{-1}$.

1460 in *Pol. Rel. & Love Poems* (1866) 153 Whanne y enforsoþe me oþer whilis, and þinke y wolde lyue o trewe lijf.

enfort: see en- *pref.*[1] 2.

en'forth, variant of emforth, *Obs.*

c **1385** Chaucer *L.G.W.* 2128 *Ariadne*, To save a gentilmanne enforthe [*v.r.* emforth] hir might.

enforth, obs., ? var. of enforce *v.*

† **enfor'tune,** *v. Obs.* [f. en-[1] + fortune.]

trans. To invest with a property or quality.

c **1374** Chaucer *Compl. Mars* 105 But he that wroght hit enfortuned hit so, That every wight that had hit shulde have wo.

† **en'fouble,** *v. Obs. rare*$^{-1}$. [a. OF. *enfuble-r*:—L. *īnfibulā-re* to buckle in, f. *in* in + *fibula* buckle; cf. F. *affubler*, repr. med.L. *affibulāre* of same meaning.] *trans.* To wrap up, veil closely.

c **1340** *Gaw. & Gr. Knt.* 959 Hir frounte folden in sylk, enfoubled ay quere.

enfoul: see en- *pref.*[1] 2.

† **en'foulder,** *v. Obs. rare*$^{-1}$. [app. f. en-[1] + OF. *fouldre* (mod.Fr. *foudre*) thunderbolt.]

Implied in **en'fouldred** *ppl. a.*, ? charged with thunder-bolts, black as a thunder-cloud.

1590 Spenser *F.Q.* i. xi. 40 With fowle enfouldred smoake and flashing fire.

† **en'founder,** *v. Obs. rare.* Also 5 enfonder. [ad. F. *enfondrer*, f. *en-* in + *fondrer* in same senses.]

a. *trans.* To drive in, batter in. **b.** *intr.* Of a horse: To stumble, drop down.

1475 Caxton *Jason* 25 b, At the thirde stroke he enfondrid .. his helme. *c* **1530** Ld. Berners *Arth. Lyt. Bryt.* (1814) 87 His hors enfoundred vnder hym.

enfourm, obs. form of inform.

† **en'frain,** *v. Obs. rare. Pa. pple.* enfraint. [ad. OF. *enfraindre* (F. *enfreindre*):—L. *īnfringĕre*, f. *in* (see in-) + *frangĕre* to break.] *trans.* To violate (a promise, an obligation).

1475 Caxton *Jason* 63 b, Ofte times they [promises] ben enfrainte and broken. **1483** —— *G. de la Tour* xcviii. 129 She hadde .. enfraynt her mariage, for the whiche she shulde be bete with stones. *Ibid.* cxliii. 203 This commaundement I have enfrayned and broken.

enframe (ɛn'freɪm), *v.* Also 9 inframe. [f. en-[1] + frame *sb.*] *trans.* **a.** To set (a picture, etc.) in or as in a frame. **b.** Of surrounding objects: To serve as a frame to. Also *fig.*

Hence **en'framed** *ppl. a.*

1848 *Fraser's Mag.* XXXVIII. 514 The boats and rafts; the floating bodies .. all enframed by the gaping ruin of the fallen dwellings. **1877** Tennyson *Harold* i. i, But all the powers of the house of Godwin Are not enframed in thee. **1878** *Tinsley's Mag.* XXIII. 40 Masses of golden-brown hair inframing the exquisite face. **1886** G. B. Brown *Schola to Cathedr.* iv. 171 Mosaics, and gold-enframed enamels.

† **en'franch,** *v. Obs.* Also 6 enfraunch, 7 infranch. [a. AF. *enfraunch-er*, f. *en-* in + *franc* free.] = enfranchise.

Hence **en'franched** *ppl. a.*

1581 Marbeck *Bk. of Notes* 193 By him we be enfraunched from the captivitie and thraldome of the Divell. **1606** Shaks. *Ant. & Cl.* iii. xiii. 149 He has Hiparchus, my enfranched Bondman, whom He may at pleasure whip. **1621** Quarles *Argalus & P.* (1678) 55 The sovereigntie of thy worth infranches Thy captive beautie. **1633** P. Fletcher *Purple Isl.* ix. xlii, Little caps and shaved head .. infranched bondmens guise.

enfranchisable (ɛn'frɑːntʃɪzəb(ə)l, -'fræn-, -tʃaɪzəb(ə)l), *a.* [f. next + -able.] That admits of being enfranchised; capable of being enfranchised.

1880 Muirhead *Ulpian* i. §25 It being .. competent to enfranchise the twenty-five enfranchisable within the lower numbers.

enfranchise (ɛn'frɑːntʃɪz, -'fræn-, -tʃaɪz), *v.* Forms: 6 **enfraunches(e, -ize, 7 -ise, enfranchiz,** 6- **enfranchize;** also 6–7 **infranchese, -ise, infraunchise.** [ad. OF. *enfranchiss-*, lengthened stem of *enfranchir*, f. *en* (see en- *pref.*[1]) + *franc* free: see frank *a.* Cf. affranchise.

By Johnson regarded as f. en-[1] + franchise, a view of the derivation which has influenced the later use. The pronunciation of *enfranchise, affranchise*, has from 18th c. followed the same course as that of *franchise*: Buchanan (1766), an orthoepist of no great authority, has (-tʃaɪz) in all three words: Perry (1793) has (-tʃiːz); Sheridan, Walker (1790) and the majority of later orthoepists, have (-tʃɪz), but (-tʃaɪz) reappears in Knowles (1835) and in Ogilvie (1850), and is given as an alternative in many recent Dicts.]

I. To admit to personal freedom.

1. To admit to freedom, set free (a slave or serf).

1531 Elyot *Gov.* ii. vii. (1883) II. 77 Thou in a priuate jugement were ouercommen of a poore man but late infraunchised. **1577–87** Holinshed *Chron.* I. 123/1 He did not onelie baptise them, but also infranchised them of all bodilie seruitude and bondage. **1636** G. Sandys *Paraph. Div. Poems* 1 Sam. ii. 1, Those who served, infranchised. **1776** Adam Smith *W.N.* I. iii. ii. 393 A villain enfranchised .. could cultivate it only by means of what the landlord advanced to him. **1876** Ouida *Moths* (1880) III. 119 The Tsar has not enfranchised me.

fig. **1548** Gest *Pr. Masse* 127 He is both blessed and enfranchised from al travayl. **1695** Tryon *Dreams & Vis.* iii. 37 [The] beginning of each Christians Regeneration .. whereby he Infrancheses himself from the world. *a* **1754** W. Hamilton *Youngest Grace* (R.), Psyche, infranchis'd from all mortal pain. **1888** *British Weekly* 24 Aug. 273/1 The soul .. should become mellow and enfranchised.

† **b.** To set free from political subjection. *Obs.*

c **1600** Norden *Spec. Brit., Cornw.* (1728) 7 Vntill the Britons enfraunchized themselves by a generall reuolte. **1606** Shaks. *Ant. & Cl.* i. i. 23 Take in that Kingdome, and Infranchise that. **1648** Milton *Observ. Art. Peace* (1851) 556 To be infranchiz'd with full liberty equall to thir Conquerours.

2. To release from confinement; chiefly *transf.* or *fig.* (Freq. in Shaks.)

1568 Grafton *Chron.* 93 If you finally refuse to deliuer him, I thinke verily the counsayle will enfraunches hym. **1588** Shaks. *Tit. A.* iv. ii. 125 From that wombe where you imprisoned were He is infranchised and come to light. **1598** [see enfranchised.] **1626** T. H. tr. *Caussin's Holy Crt.* 160 Break your fetters, enfranchiz your selfe. **1878** S. Cox *Salv. Mundi* ix. (ed. 3) 201 Liberate and enfranchise that which is good.

† **b.** *humorously.* To get (a thing) free.

1682 D'Urfey *Butler's Ghost* 16 This .. Fierce Blade from peaceful sheath he lugs; For, putting chape betwixt his Feet, He, with much ease, Enfranchis'd it.

3. To release from obligatory payments, legal liabilities, etc. ***to enfranchise a copyhold*** or ***leasehold estate***: to convert it into freehold.

1594 Carew *Huarte's Exam. Wits* xiii. (1596) 220 His house shalbe enfranchised in Israel from all maner tribute. **1818** Cruise *Digest* III. 107 The lord of a manor enfranchised a copyhold .. and then disputed the right of common with the copyholder he had enfranchised.

II. To admit to municipal or political privileges.

† **4.** To make 'free' of a municipality or corporation. Const. *into.* Also *fig. Obs.*

1514 *Act 5 Hen. VIII*, c. 6 The crafte and misterye of Surgeons enfraunchesid in the Citie of London. **1602** Fulbecke *Pandects* 56 If they were enfraunchised of a hundred cities. *a* **1628** F. Greville *Sidney* (1652) 53 This was the first prize which did enfranchise this Master Spirit into the mysteries and affairs of State. *a* **1655** Vines *Lord's Supp.* (1677) 170 He .. must submit to the laws and rules of that Corporation he is free of, whether to be enfranchized or disfranchized.

5. To make (a city or town) 'free' by charter; to invest (it) with municipal rights. Now *chiefly*, to invest with the right of being represented in parliament.

1564 Haward *Eutropius* vi. 53 When he cam into Siria he enfraunchised Seleucia. **1655** Fuller *Ch. Hist.* i. iv. §2 Verolam-cestre was at this time enfranchised with many Immunities. **1844** Ld. Brougham *Brit. Const.* xiv. (1862) 212 She added no less than sixty-two burgh members, chiefly by enfranchising petty burghs.

6. To admit to membership in a body politic or state; to admit to political privileges; †to naturalize (an alien). Now *chiefly*, to admit to the electoral 'franchise' or right of voting for members of parliament.

1683 *Brit. Spec.* 196 He hath by his Prerogative Power to enfranchise an Alien. **1711** Strype *Parker* an. 1595 (R.), He [Dr. Baro] being an alien, ought to have carried himself quietly and peaceably in a country where he was so humanely harboured and infranchised. **1839** Thirlwall *Greece* II. 74 He is said to have enfranchised not only aliens .. but slaves. **1884** *Times* (weekly ed.) 26 Sept. 2/1 We want .. to enfranchise those great masses of the people.

b. *fig.* To naturalize (foreign words; rarely, foreign plants). ? *Obs.*

1601 Holland *Pliny* I. 359 Cherry-trees, Peach-trees, .. are held for aliens in Italy. Howbeit, some of them now are infranchised and taken for free denizens among vs. **1668** Wilkins *Real Char.* i. ii. §2. 8 By enfranchising strange forein words. *a* **1748** Watts (J.), These words have been enfranchised amongst us.

enfranchised (ɛn'frɑːntʃɪzd, -'fræn-, -tʃaɪzd), *ppl. a.* [f. enfranchise *v.* + -ed[1].] In senses of the verb.

1579–80 North *Plutarch* 531 (R.) Fabius Rullus .. put from the senate certain bondmen infranchised. **1598** Chapman *Iliad* i. 94 Till her enfranchis'd feet Tread Chrysa under. **1643** Milton *Divorce* xiii. (1851) 54 The enfranchiz'd life and soul of man. *a* **1720** Sheffield (Dk. Buckhm.) *Wks.* (1753) I. 49 Where the enfranchis'd soul at ease can play. *a* **1845** Barham *Ingol. Leg.* (1877) 15 Many a mischievous enfranchised Sprite Had long since burst his bonds of stone or lead. **1884** Gladstone in *Standard* 29 Feb. 2/5 Enfranchised occupiers of buildings of 10*l.* clear annual value.

enfranchisement (ɛn'frɑːntʃɪzmənt, -'fræn-). Also 6–7 in-. [f. as prec. + -ment.] The action of enfranchising; the state or fact of being enfranchised.

1. Liberation from imprisonment, servitude, or political subjection. Also *fig.*

1595 Shaks. *John* iv. ii. 52 My selfe and them .. heartily request Th'infranchisement of Arthur. **1601** —— *Jul. C.* iii. i. 81 Cry out Liberty, Freedome, and Enfranchisement. *a* **1626** Bacon *Max. & Uses Com. Law* vi. 30 An instrument of manumission, which is an evidence of my enfranchisement. **1630** Prynne *Anti-Armin.* 147 He hath procured an absolute enfranchisement from hell. **1693** Dryden *Persius* Sat. iii. (R.), False enfranchisement with ease is found. **1848** tr. *Mariotti's Italy* II. i. 7 The enfranchisement of Italy formed the text of all their proclamations. **1850** Mrs. Stowe *Uncle Tom's C.* xxviii, He had commenced the legal formalities for his enfranchisement. **1872** Morley *Voltaire* (1886) 4 The enfranchisement of the individual from bondage to a collective religious tradition that had lost its virtue.

2. a. Admission to the 'freedom' of a city, borough, or corporation, or to the citizenship of a state; admission to political rights, now *esp.* to the electoral franchise. **b.** The conferring of privileges (now chiefly the right of parliamentary representation) upon a town.

1628 Coke *On Litt.* i. 137 b, Enfranchisement .. the incorporating of a man to bee free of a Company or Body Politique. **1630** Wadsworth *Sp. Pilgr.* viii. 83 His .. Maiestie .. would confirme vnto me my Patent of Infranchisement. **1654** W. Mountague *Devout Ess.* ii. i. §3 (R.), The amplitude and infranchisement of humane reason cannot be said properly to be impair'd by these limits. **1685** Baxter *Paraphr. N.T.* Acts xvi. 37 Paul was a Roman by enfranchisment. **1753** Melmoth *Cicero* iii. xxiv. (R.), Certain cities .. of which he is desirous to procure the enfranchisement. **1794** S. Williams *Vermont* 232 The same privileges, immunities, and enfranchisements. **1869** Seeley *Lect. & Ess.* i. 13 It was not enfranchisement that they wanted, it was simply military protection.

3. The action of making lands freehold.

1876 Digby *Real Prop.* x. 396 Enfranchisement .. consists in the conveyance of the freehold by the lord to his copyhold tenant.

en'franchiser. [f. as prec. + -er.] One who or that which enfranchises; in senses of the vb.

1632 Sherwood, Enfranchiser, *affranchisseur.* **1650** R. Stapylton *Strada's Low C. Warres* vii. 80 Boasting himselfe to be the sole Infranchiser of Holland. **1673** *Lady's Call.* i. v. 36 He will tell us that the disbelief of God and another life, is the great enfranchiser of mankind. **1796** *Month. Mag.* II. 778 Timoleon, the enfranchizer of Sicily. **1880** Muirhead *Gaius* ii. §56 The estates of [deceased] latins belong to their enfranchisers.

en'franchising, *vbl. sb.* [f. enfranchise *v.* + -ing[1].] The action of the verb enfranchise, in its various senses.

1574 tr. *Littleton's Tenures* 42 b, The Lorde maye make manumission and infraunchissinge to his villaine. **1600** Holland *Livy* 870 (R.) The multitude, so augmented by the enfranchising of slaves. **1688** *Addr. fr. Totness* in *Lond. Gaz.* No. 2347/1 Your most Gracious Declaration of Indulgence, for the enfranchizing of Conscience. **1787** T. Jefferson *Writ.* (1859) II. 92 The enfranchising the port of Honfleur at the mouth of the Seine.

enfraught (ɛn'frɔːt), *a. rare*$^{-1}$. [f. en-[1] + fraught.] Laden, charged, filled. Const. *with.*

1866 J. Rose tr. *Ovid's Fasti* ii. 818 The regal youth, Enfraught with envy .. Burnt with a lover's fires.

enfray, obs. form of affray.

enfree, -freedom, -freeze: see en- *pref.*[1]

enfrenzy (ɛn'frɛnzɪ), *v.* Also 7 (after Gr. analogies) **emphrensy.** [f. en-[1] + frenzy.] *trans.* To throw into a frenzy. In quot. *absol.*

Hence **en'frenzied** *ppl. a.*

a **1656** Bp. Hall *St. Paul's Combat* (R.), His tooth like a mad dog's envenomes and emphrensies. **1823** *Blackw. Mag.* XIII. 327 Blanch .. enfrenzied shrieks. *a* **1845** Barham *Ingol. Leg., Jarvis's Wig.*, With an enfrenzied grasp.

enfrieze, enfringe, enfroward, enfuddle: see EN- *pref.*[1] 1 b, 2, 3.

†en'fume, *v. Obs.* Also 7 infume. [ad. F. *enfume-r*:—L. *infūmāre* (see INFUMATE *v.*) f. *in* + *fūm-us* smoke.]

trans. To expose to the action of smoke. **a.** To give a smoky taste to (wine). **b.** To dry in smoke; = INFUMATE *v.* **c.** To make dingy, obscure with smoke. **d.** To blind as with smoke. Hence **en'fumed** *ppl. a.*, **en'fuming** *vbl. sb.*

1601 HOLLAND *Pliny* I. 406 Other [grapes] they suffer to be dried in the smoke of smiths forges, wherby they get the very tast of infumed wine. **1603** DAVIES *Microcosmos* (1876) 38 (D.) Perturbations.. so enfume them that they cannot see. **1607** TOPSELL *Four-f. Beasts* (1673) 21 The brain of an Asse steeped in sweet water and infumed in leaves.. easeth the falling evill. **1611** FLORIO, *Infumatione*, an infuming, a bloting. **1623** COCKERAM, *Infume*, to dry in the smoake. **1658** HEWYT *Serm.* 177 (T.), Let them no more produce their enfumed titles.

†en'fundying, *vbl. sb. Sc. Obs.* In 4 enfundeyng. [app. f. **enfundy*, a. OF. *enfondre* to be benumbed with cold + -ING[1].] Benumbed with cold.

c **1375** BARBOUR *Bruce* xx. 75 (Edin. MS.) This malice of enfundeyng [*other texts* ane fundyng] Begouth, for throw hys cald lying.. Him fell that hard perplexity.

engage (ɛn'geɪdʒ), *sb.* [f. next vb.; cf. It. *ingaggio*.]

†**1. a.** Engagement, bargain. **b.** The state of being engaged or entangled; embarrassment, peril (cf. ENGAGE *v.* 13). *Obs.*

1589 PUTTENHAM *Eng. Poesie* III. xix. (Arb.) 241 Nor that it came by purchase or engage. **1626** G. SANDYS *Ovid's Met.*, XIII. 76 Nestor.. implor'd to his ingage Vlysses helpe.

2. In Sword-exercise: (the vb. in the imperative used *subst.*: see ENGAGE *v.* 17).

1833 *Regul. Instr. Cavalry* I. 142 Come to the 'Engage'. **1871** *Daily News* 14 Jan., Men.. sat down cheerfully in their saddles, and brought their swords to the 'engage'.

engage (ɛn'geɪdʒ), *v.* Forms: *α.* (6 **enguage,** 7 **engadge**), 6- **engage.** *β.* 6-8 **ingage.** [a. F. *engage-r*, f. *en* (see EN-[1]) + *gage* pledge (see GAGE, WAGE): cf. the equivalents Pr. *engatgar*, *enguatjar*, *engatjar*, It. *ingaggiare*.

The *trans* and *refl.* senses (exc. 19) approximately follow the senses of Fr. *engager*; the *intr.* senses and the *trans.* sense 19 are of English development.]

I. To deposit or make over as a pledge.

†**1.** *trans.* To pledge or pawn (movable property); to mortgage (lands, houses, etc.). *Obs.*

1525 LD. BERNERS *Froiss.* II. cxiii. [cix.] 322 His brother had before that engauged the thre forsaid castels for florens. **1577** HOLINSHED *Chron.* II. 28 Duke Robert.. engaged a portion of his duchie of Normandie to his youngest brother Henrie for a great sum of gold. **1581** LAMBARDE *Eiren.* II. vii. (1588) 280 The Ciuilians doe adiudge it theft, if one (that laieth his goods to pledge) do embesell them from the partie to whom they were engaged. **1624** CAPT. SMITH *Virginia* I. 3 For an armour he would haue ingaged vs a bagge of pearle. **1669** PENN *No Cross* xviii. §9 Persons, who by their Excess.. have deeply engaged their Estates.

2. *fig.* To pledge, offer as a guarantee (one's life, honour, etc.); also, to expose to risk, compromise. *rare* in mod. use.

1568 NORTH tr. *Gueuara's Diall of Princes* (1619) 709, I.. admonish the.. Officers of Princes not to sell, chaunge, nor engage their liberties as they doe, etc. **1599** DANIEL *Civ. Wares* v. The Queene perceiuing in what case she stoode, To lose her Minion, or ingage her State. **1600** SHAKS. *A. Y. L.* v. iv. 172 This to be true, I do engage my life. **1631** HEYWOOD *Maid West* II. III. Wks. 1874 II. 378 My honour, faith and country are ingag'd. **1655-60** STANLEY *Hist. Philos.* (1701) 477/1 All this we say without engaging our Opinion. **1677** *Govt. Venice* 63 By a ridiculous Custom this Admiral.. engages his Life there shall be no Tempest that day. **1776** GIBBON *Decl. & F.* I. xviii. 493 Others had engaged their doubtful fidelity to the emperor. **1855** CDL. WISEMAN *Fabiola* 238 But my honour is engaged.

II. To bind or secure by a pledge.

†**3.** To make (a person) security for a payment, the fulfilment of an undertaking, etc.; 'to render liable for a debt *to* a creditor' (J.). *Obs.*

1596 SHAKS. *Merch. V.* III. ii. 264, I haue ingag'd my selfe to a deere friend, Ingag'd my friend to his meere enemie To feede my meanes. **1639** MASSINGER *Unnat. Combat* III. iii, Yet detain from us The debt.. We have made you stand engaged for. **1651** HOBBES *Leviath.* II. xxii. 117 He that lendeth it.. understandeth those onely for his debtors, that are engaged.

4. a. To bind by a contract or formal promise.

1603 FLORIO *Montaigne* (1634) 493 Hazarding rather to consume, then engage themselves to feminine embracements. **1617** HIERON *Wks.* II. 332 These vowes were the solemne promises, by which he.. ingaged himselfe to God. **1702** ROWE *Amb. Step-Moth.* IV. i. 1644 My Father's Fate dissolves that Truce to which I stood ingag'd. **1855** MOTLEY *Dutch Rep.* v. i. (1866) 659 He declined engaging himself not to recall his foreign soldiery.

b. *spec.* To bind by a promise of marriage; to betroth. Chiefly *pass.* and *refl.* (See also 6 c.)

1727 FIELDING *Love in Sev. Masq.* Wks. 1775 I. 31 Since nothing else will do, I am engaged by all the strength of vows and honour. **1848** MACAULAY *Hist. Eng.* I. 648 He was engaged to a young lady of gentle blood. **1867** TROLLOPE *Chron. Barset* I. xxx. 257 What would you think of a girl who could engage herself to any man under such circumstances?

c. In mod. use often in *pass.* with weaker sense: To have promised one's presence, made an appointment, etc., for any purpose of business or pleasure.

1885 L. B. WALFORD *Nan*, &c. I. 79 He has asked Nan [to dance] before, but she was engaged. *Mod.* I am engaged for to-morrow, but could dine with you on Monday.

5. [With etymological sense of securing by payment of earnest-money: see GAGE, WAGE.]

a. To hire, secure the services of (a servant, workman, agent, etc.). Also *refl.* of a servant, etc.: To enter into an agreement for service.

1753 HANWAY *Travels* (1762) I. Introd. 13 A british subject who engaged himself as a factor to the russia company. **1860** TYNDALL *Glac.* I. §24. 169 Balmat was engaged at this time as the guide of Mr., etc. **1862** TROLLOPE *Orley F.* xiii. 100 We have engaged the services of Mr. Aram. **1876** GREEN *Short Hist.* vi. §6. (1882) 325 Thomas Cromwell.. was certainly engaged as the commercial agent to one of the Venetian merchants. *Mod.* He has engaged himself to an engineer.

b. To bespeak or secure (something) for one's own or another's use or possession.

1760 WASHINGTON *Diary* 7 Jan. (1925) I. 109 Accompanied Mrs. Bassett to Alexandria and engaged a Keg of Butter of Mr. Kirkpatrick, being quite out of that article. **1795** SOUTHEY *Lett. fr. Spain* (1799) 10 The boxes [in the theatre] are engaged by the season. **1820** MOORCROFT *Trav.* (1841) I. 199, I laid in a considerable quantity of wheat flour at Tandi, and engaged carriers and ponies for its transport. *Mod.* I have engaged rooms at the hotel. This seat is engaged. Engage places for us in the coach.

6. *intr.* for *refl.* (in senses 4, 5). **a.** *gen.* To pledge oneself; to enter into a covenant or undertaking. Const. *to* with *inf.*, or subordinate clause; †rarely *into*, *unto* with sb. as obj. Also, to 'warrant', pledge one's credit, assert on one's own responsibility *that*.

1613 R. C. *Table Alph.* (ed. 3), *Ingage*, lay to pledge, binde himselfe. **1647** FULLER *Good Th. in Worse T.* (1841) 127 How proper the remedy for the malady I engage not. **1649** BP. REYNOLDS *Hosea* iv. 57 A manifestation of that love in some promise or other, ingageing unto assistance. **1650** *Nicholas Papers* (1886) I. 184 His Lordship.. was to engadge it should be repaid in that time [3 yeares]. **1661** *Papers on Alter. Prayer Bk.* 100 Renouncing the flesh, etc. And ingageing into the Christian belief. **1672** CAVE *Prim. Chr.* III. iv. (1673) 335 When Christ promises so much to them who engage with him. **1720** *Col. Rec. Penns.* III. 100 Our Indians have repeatedly engaged to me that they would go no more out to War. **1751** JOHNSON *Rambler* No. 118 ¶9 The man.. has no other care than to collect interest, to estimate securities, and to engage for mortgages. **1787** T. JEFFERSON *Writ.* (1859) II. 303 The court of London engaged not to abandon Prussia. **1869** FREEMAN *Norm. Conq.* III. xii. 242 Harold further engaged to give his sister in marriage to an unnamed Norman noble. **1878** BROWNING *Poets Croisic* xviii, Croisic, I'll engage, With Rome yields sort for sort, in age for age.

b. *to engage for*: to be answerable for, guarantee; *later*, to undertake to perform, to promise. Rarely in *indirect passive.*

1680 BUTLER *Rem.* (1759) II. 70 Some near Friend.. engaged for his Honesty and good Behaviour. **1708** SWIFT *Sacram. Test*, How chearfully they engaged for the safety of the nation. **1727** A. HAMILTON *New Acc. E. Ind.* II. xxxviii. 68 He could not engage for their [Fakires'] Safety among his Countrymen. **1748** RICHARDSON *Clarissa* (1811) IV. 348 Her wishes.. were gently intimated, and as readily engaged for. **1813** JANE AUSTEN *Pride & Prej.* i. 2 It is more than I engage for, I assure you. **1866** CARLYLE *Inaug. Addr.* 171 That is pretty much all I can engage for.

†**c.** To betroth oneself (see 4 b.). *Obs. rare.*

1722 DE FOE *Relig. Courtsh.* I. i. (1840) 9 She will know how it is as to that, before she engages.

d. To agree *with* a servant, workman, or employé for hired service. Occas. with *indirect pass.* (Mostly superseded by 5 a.)

1791 SMEATON *Edystone L.* (1793) §309 Till proper persons could be engaged with and sent off. **1825** T. COSNETT *Footman's Directory* 217 Many ladies and gentlemen will not engage with any one who does not know town well.

e. Of a servant, etc.: To take service (*with* a master or employer). Cf. 5 a.

1766 J. WEDGWOOD *Let.* 15 Sept. (1965) 42, I should expect him to engage for three years at least. *Mod.* Before I engage with another master, I will, etc.

7. a. *trans.* In wider sense: To bind by moral or legal obligation. Const. *to* with *sb.* or *inf.*

164. CHAS. I *Answ. Earles of Bristol & Dorset* 5 The municipall and fundamentall Lawes of that Nation ingage the Subject to.. strictnesse of obedience. **1659** HAMMOND *On Ps.* xviii. 1 Paraphr. 94, I stand ingaged, most passionately to love, and bless, and magnifie thee. **1672** GREW *Anat. Plants, Idea Philos. Hist. Pl.* §8 The present Design will ingage us, to an accurate and multifarious Observation of Plants.

†**b.** To lay under obligations of gratitude; to oblige. Const. *to* (a person), or *simply. Obs.*

1626 D'EWES in Ellis *Orig. Lett.* I. 322 III. 214 By which I assure my selfe further ingaged, then by your most kind acknowledgement anye way discharged. **1631** HEYWOOD *Maid West* II. III. Wks. 1874 II. 376 Good gentlemen Ingage me so far to you. **1648** CROMWELL *Lett.* 8 Mar. (Carlyle), I am engaged to you for all your civilities. **1655-60** STANLEY *Hist. Philos.* (1701) 101/1 If thou protect him, thou wilt preserve our friend and infinitely engage us.

†**c.** In *pass.*: To be 'committed' *to* (certain opinions). *Obs.*

1677 HALE *Prim. Orig. Man.* IV. vi. 339 They are destitute of any satisfactory Evidence, to any person that is not strangely and impotently engaged to them.

8. a. To urge, exhort, persuade, induce; said both of persons and of motives, etc. In 18th c. often approaching the sense of Fr. *engager* 'to invite'. Now *rare.*

1647 SPRIGGE *Anglia Rediv.* IV. vii. (1854) 280 That all may be rather convinced and engaged by argument and truth. **1667** MILTON *P.L.* IX. 963 O.. example high! Ingaging me to emulate. **1716-8** LADY M. W. MONTAGUE *Lett.* I. xxii. 66 Her highness.. when I left her, engaged me to write to her. **1761** HUME *Hist. Eng.* I. viii. 166 He engaged the grand-master of the templars by large presents.. to put him in possession of Gisors. **1791** SMEATON *Edystone L.* (1793) §313 The high wages.. did not engage them to secure themselves with a sufficient stock of provisions. **1839** KEIGHTLEY *Hist. Eng.* I. 105 He engaged them to declare in his favour. **1862** KINGTON *Fredk. II*, II. xiii. 171 Enzio had engaged the Castle.. to surrender.

†**b.** with sb. of action as obj. *Obs.*

1742 JOHNSON *L.P.*, *Sydenham*, The author which gave him most pleasure, and most engaged his imitation.

9. a. To gain, win over, as an adherent or helper. Cf. 5 a. *arch.*

1697 POTTER *Antiq. Greece* III. vii. (1715) 65 Whom Paris had engagd to his Party by a large sum of Money. **1741** WATTS *Improv. Mind* xv. (1801) 14 Engage the God of truth on our side. **1751** JOHNSON *Rambler* No. 95 ¶19 Such is the hazard of.. engaging reason against its own determinations. **1779** —— *L.P.*, *Blackmore* Wks. III. 174 To engage poetry in the cause of virtue. **1818** JAS. MILL *Brit. India* II. v. ii. 372 For the sake of the bribes with which the Duan took care to engage him.

†**b.** To secure for oneself (help, sympathy, approval). *Obs.*

1725 POPE *Odyss.* XIII. 345 Alcinous to persuade, To raise his wonder, and engage his aid. **1748** RICHARDSON *Clarissa* (1811) I. ii. 8 Those whose approbation we wish to engage.

10. To attach by pleasing qualities; to attract, charm, fascinate. Cf. 14. Also *absol.* Now *rare*; cf. ENGAGING *ppl. a.*

1711 ADDISON *Spect.* No. 106 ¶3 This Humanity and Good-nature engages every Body to him. *a* **1721** PRIOR (J.), When beauty ceases to engage. **1751** CHESTERF. *Lett.* III. ccxlv. 126 If you engage his heart, you have a fair chance for imposing upon his understanding. **1773** JOHNSON *Lett.* 6 Sept. (1788) I. 126 She engaged me so much that I made her a present of Cocker's arithmetick. **1784** COWPER *Tiroc.* 147 If books that could engage Their childhood, pleased them at a riper age. **1814** CHALMERS *Evid. Chr. Revel.* i. 22 Their heart is engaged by the amiable morality [of the gospel]. *a* **1876** J. H. NEWMAN *Hist. Sk.* I. II. iv. 257 Cicero engages our affections by the integrity of his public conduct.

III. To cause to be held fast; to involve, entangle.

[The physical sense 11 (adopted from Fr.) appears to be a development from the sense 'to put in pledge' = 1. Senses 12–16 are chiefly fig. applications of 11, but often influenced by the notion of branch II.]

11. In physical senses.

a. To entangle, *e.g.* in a snare or net, in a bog. *Obs.* or *arch.*

1602 SHAKS. *Ham.* III. iii. 69 Oh limed soule, that strugling to be free, Art more ingag'd. **1603** FLORIO *Montaigne* (1634) 266 The Barble fishes, if one of them chance to be engaged. **1652** J. WORDSWORTH tr. *Sandoval's Civil Wars of Spain* 362 The Foot stuck fast, engaged in the mire to the very knees. **1697** DRYDEN *Virg. Georg.* III. 625 Thou mayst.. beamy Stags in Toils engage.

fig. **1631** HEYWOOD *London's Jus Hon.* Wks. 1874 IV. 271 Upon them stand Two dangerous rocks, your safety to ingage. **1638** FORD *Fancies* v. i, Those ties of nature.. How much they do engage. **1671** MILTON *P.R.* III. 347 That thou may'st know I seek not to engage Thy virtue.

b. *Arch.* To fasten, attach. In *pass.* of a pillar: To be let into (a wall), so as to be partly enclosed. See ENGAGED 2.

1766 SMOLLETT *Trav.* 94 Twelve columns engaged in the wall. **1776** G. SEMPLE *Building in Water* 4, I did not engage them to the Brace Beams. **1849** RUSKIN *Sev. Lamps* iii. §10. 73 The lowest with its pillars engaged. **1865** *Athenæum* No. 1947. 230/3 The columns are 'engaged' to the square outer piers. **1877** A. B. EDWARDS *Nile* xviii. 495 Engaged in the brickwork on either side of the principal entrance to this hall are two stone door-jambs.

c. *Mech.* (*intr.* for *refl.*) of a portion of machinery, as a cog-wheel, etc.: To interlock *with*, fit into a corresponding part.

1884 *Pall Mall G.* 28 Aug. 5/2 Engages with the cylinder and locks it for firing.

12. †**a.** *trans.* To cause (esp. an armed force) to penetrate *into* the interior of a country, into a defile, mountain pass, etc. (so as render withdrawal difficult); also *refl.* (*obs.*). **b.** *intr.* †To enter *into* a country, etc. (*obs.*); to involve oneself *in* (an intricate path, etc.).

1645 CROMWELL *Lett.* 9 Apr. (Carlyle), Lest we should engage our Body of Horse too far into that enclosed country. **1686-7** BURNET *Trav.* iii. (1750) 166 We engage into that Range of Hills that carry the Name of Apennines. **1693** *Mem. Ct. Teckley* IV. 55 The hardness of the Season, hindered him from engaging himself further into Transylvania. **1854** THACKERAY *Newcomes* I. 127 Mr. Bayham made an abrupt tack larboard, engaging in a labyrinth of stables.

†**13. a.** To entangle, involve, commit, mix up (in an undertaking, quarrel, etc.). Const. *in*, less often *into*, *to*, *with*. *Obs.*

a **1586** SIDNEY (J.), So far had we engaged ourselves.. that we listed not to complain. **1625** BACON *Ess. Travel* (Arb.) 523 They will engage him into their owne Quarels. **1635** EVELYN *Mem.* (1857) I. 8 When she perceived the peril whereto its excess had engaged her. **1662-3** SIR C. LYTTELTON in *Hatton Corr.* (1878) 29 For I was deeply engaged wth him upon a planting interest. **1680** BUTLER

Rem. (1759) I. 217 These Follies had such Influence on the Rabble, As to engage them in perpetual Squabble. *a* **1714** BURNET *Own Time* (1823) I. 440 Into this the King of Sweden, then a child, was engaged: so it was called the triple alliance. **1727** SWIFT *To Very Young Lady*, To engage you, by his insinuations, in misunderstanding with your best friends. **1734** tr. *Rollin's Anc. Hist.* (1827) VII. XVII. 272 He had engaged his city in the Achæan league.

†**b.** *intr.* for *refl.* To entangle, involve, or mix oneself up. Const. *in*, less often *among*, *into*. *Obs.*

1657 S. W. *Schism Dispach't* 567 Yet hee will needs have mee engage into such questions. *a* **1667** COWLEY *Obscurity*, If we engage into a large Acquaintance..we set open our gates to the Invaders of most of our time. **1750** JOHNSON *Rambler* No. 36. ¶3 Much earlier than we engage among the actions and passions of mankind. **1796** MORSE *Amer. Geog.* II. 208 The nation again engaged in debt.

14. *trans.* To attract and hold fast (attention, interest); formerly also with personal obj., 'to hold by the attention' (J.). Cf. 10.

1642 FULLER *Holy & Prof. St.* IV. x. 286 Their Auditours, generally as engaged as the Disputants, will succour their Champion with partiall relations. **1691–8** NORRIS *Pract. Disc.* IV. 221 Nothing..fit to stay or ingage a Soul that is Capable of Enjoying God. **1711** SHAFTESB. *Charac.* i. (1737) III. 351 He admires, he contemplates; but is not yet ingag'd or interested. **1712** STEELE *Spect.* No. 503 ¶2 Her form..engaged the eyes of the whole congregation in an instant. **1773** MRS. CHAPONE *Improv. Mind* (1774) I. 2, I will hope that your attention may be engaged, by Truths of the highest importance. **1832** HT. MARTINEAU *Life Wilds* Pref. 12 Will impress the memory and engage the interest.

15. *trans.* To provide occupation for, employ (a person, his powers, thoughts, efforts, etc.). Now nearly always *passive*. Formerly also, †to make use of (an instrument).

1648 GAGE *West Ind.* xx. (1655) 157 Beginning now to repent me of what I was now ingaged in. **1651** *Life Father Sarpi* (1676) 89 It would be necessary to engage a volume of praises. **1677** MOXON *Mech. Exerc.* (1703) 219 The Iron Pin in the Hole of the Beam kept it to its due distance from the Center; so that neither hand was ingaged to guide it. **1678** BUNYAN *Pilgr.* I. Author's Apol., Behold how he ingageth all his Wits. **1680** BUTLER *Rem.* (1759) X. 5 Both Armies..Are in a bloody Fight engag'd. **1756** C. LUCAS *Ess. Waters* II. 31 It [is] a question which has engaged better heads and pens than mine. **1815** *Scribbleomania* 242 Mr. Dibdin is engaged in writing a list of the classical library of the Earl of Spencer. *a* **1847** MRS. SHERWOOD *Lady of Manor* IV. xxvi. 246, I contrived to seem engaged with my guitar. **1864** J. H. NEWMAN *Apol.* App. 11 Many of them are engaged on one subject. **1872** RAYMOND *Statist. Mines & Mining* 306 Producing excellent milling ore at a handsome profit to the men engaged in it.

16. *intr.* for *refl.* 'To embark in any business' (J.); to enter upon or employ oneself in an action. Const. *in*, formerly *on*, *upon*, and *simply*. Cf. 13 b.

1646 CHAS. I *Church Govt.* (1849) 43, I will not engage upon new questions not necessary for my purpose. **1671** GUMBLE *Life Monck*, In whatsoever condition he had engaged, he had found or made a great Fortune. **1672** PETTY *Pol. Anat.* (1691) 47 The restored Irish.. will be careful how they engage any more upon a frivolous, impious Undertaking. **1732** BERKELEY *Serm.* Wks. III. 241 Those who at this day engage in the propagation of the gospel. **1749** CHESTERF. *Lett.* II. ccvii. 292 He engaged young and distinguished himself in business. **1825** SOUTHEY *Paraguay* IV. vi, Not desiring to engage Upon the busy world's contentious stage. **1830** R. KNOX *Béclard's Anat.* Introd. 18 He had..engaged deeply in the study of languages. **1848** MACAULAY *Hist. Eng.* I. 191 The government engaged in war with the United Provinces. **1875** JOWETT *Plato* (ed. 2) I. 364 If I had engaged in politics, I should have perished long ago.

IV. With reference to combat. [Specialized uses of III.]

17. *trans.* Of combatants: To interlock (weapons). Cf. Fr. *engager le fer*, to cross swords. Also *absol.*, as ***to engage in tierce, in quart***.

1697 DRYDEN *Virg. Georg.* III. 341 The stooping Warriors ..Engage their clashing Horns. **1833** [See ENGAGING *vbl. sb.*] **1881** WAITE *Sabre, Singlestick*, etc. 101 A man thus armed engages in quarte or tierce.

18. a. *trans.* To bring (troops) into conflict *with* the enemy. **b.** ***to engage a combat*** (*rare*; after Fr. *engager le combat*). **c.** *intr.* for *refl.*: To enter into combat (*with*); also *fig.*

a. 1868 E. EDWARDS *Ralegh* I. ii. 30 [They] could scarcely have reached the camp before they found themselves engaged with the enemy. *Mod.* He had taken care not to engage the whole of his troops.

b. 1855 MOTLEY *Dutch Rep.* V. v. (1866) 748 The mortal combat between the Inquisition and the Reformation was already fully engaged. *Ibid.* VI. i. 770 The fierce combat had already been engaged in the darkness.

c. 1647 CLARENDON *Hist. Reb.* II. 48 The earl of Holland was sent with a body of three thousand horse..to meet it [a party of the Scots army] and engage with it. **1697** DRYDEN *Virg. Georg.* I. 509 East and West ingage, And at their Frontiers meet. *Ibid.* III. 418 Ev'n the fearful Stag dares for his Hind engage. **1762–71** H. WALPOLE *Vertue's Anecd. Paint.* (1786) II. 239 On the outside is Fairfax himself on his chestnut horse, men engaging at a distance. **1783** CRABBE *Village* I. Wks. 1834 II. 81 That hoary swain, whose age Can with no cares except its own engage. **1823** SOUTHEY *Hist. Penins. War* I. 102 The mob..did not venture to engage against musketry and cannon with their knives. **1837** HT. MARTINEAU *Soc. Amer.* III. 59 One day he met a man muffled in a cloak, who engaged with him..and stabbed him.

19. *trans.* (= 'to engage with': see 18.) To attack, enter into a combat with (an army, a ship); also (now *rarely*) *fig.*

1698–9 LUDLOW *Mem.* I. 47 We lost..a favourable opportunity of engaging the enemy. **1704** HEARNE *Duct. Hist.* (1714) I. 365 Tarquin..engaged the Romans, and was defeated. **1709** POPE *Ess. Crit.* 556 These monsters, Critics! with your darts engage. **1709** *Lond. Gaz.* No. 4547/2 He..was obliged to engage her to Leeward. **1748** ANSON *Voy.* II. xi. 252 We had not been inattentive to the means of engaging her to advantage. **1786** T. JEFFERSON *Writ.* (1859) I. 549, I have engaged the abuses of the tobacco trade on a more general scale. **1839** KEIGHTLEY *Hist. Eng.* I. 68 On the right bank of the river they were engaged by the Earls Edwin and Morcar.

‖**engagé** (ɑ̃gaʒe), *ppl. a.* [F.] Of (the work of) writers, artists, etc. = COMMITTED *ppl. a.* b. (See also ENGAGED *ppl. a.* 4.)

[**1948** H. READ *Art Now* (ed. 3) 139 'L'art engagé', art in the service of the revolution.] **1955** G. GREENE *Quiet American* 121, I don't know what I'm talking politics for. They don't interest me and I'm a reporter. I'm not *engagé*. **1956** *Essays in Crit.* VI. 388 His [*sc.* Hazlitt's] temper was active, sympathetic and *engagé*, rather than philosophical. **1959** *Encounter* Oct. 54/1 Surrealism built a functional, utilitarian literature—the first *engagé* art of our time. **1966** *Listener* 17 Mar. 378/1 We hear a lot of talk about the duty of the artist to be 'committed' or '*engagé*'.

‖**enga'geants**, *sb. pl. Obs.* Also 7 en-, ængageant(e)s. [Fr.] (See quot. 1694.)

1690 *Songs Costume* (1849) 188 About her sleeves are engageants. **1694** *Lady's Dict.*, *Ængageants* are double ruffles that fall over the wrists. **1695** MOTTEUX *St. Olon's Morocco* 94 Sleeves of these Vests..would be much like our Womens Engageantes. **1748** *Earthq. Peru* iii. 257 They are sometimes open like long engageants, worn also in the days of King Henry V. **1872** *Young Englishwoman* Nov. 594/1 The sleeves, open to the elbow over print lace engageantes, are edged..with..velvet.

engaged (ɛn'geɪdʒd), *ppl. a.* [f. ENGAGE *v.* + -ED[1].]

1. In various senses of the verb. **a.** †Entangled. **b.** †Obliged, attached by gratitude. **c.** Locked in fight. **d.** That is under a promise to marry; betrothed. Hence ***engaged ring*** (? Obs.) = *engagement ring*.

1615 G. SANDYS *Trav.* 137 The sands..with a lingring cruelty swallowed the ingaged. **1665** WALTON *Life Hooker* I. 99 Not as an engaged person, but indifferently. **1673** *Vain Insol. Rome* 12 Your engaged well wishing Friend and Servant. **1692** LOCKE *Toleration* III. iii, This.. is..like an engaged Enemy, to vent one's Spleen upon a Party. **1719** DE FOE *Crusoe* (1858) 219 Never man had a more faithful, loving, sincere servant than Friday was to me..perfectly obliged and engaged. **1869** *London Society* XVI. 513 (*title*) The Engaged Ring. *a* **1870** DICKENS *Edwin Drood* iii, It is so absurd to be an engaged orphan. **1873** C. M. YONGE *Pillars of House* II. xxii. 252 It is not a proper engaged-ring. You can't wear it. *a* **1891** *Mod.* At a certain party last week, there were six engaged couples.

2. a. *Arch.* ***engaged column***, one partly let into a wall in the rear. ***engaged tower*** (see quot.). **b.** *Mech.* ***engaged wheels***, wheels in gear with each other. The driver is the engaging wheel, and the follower is the wheel engaged.

1847 *Engl. Ecclesiology* 154 Of the quadrangular tower there are two varieties: the one where it is engaged, i.e. has the aisles flush with its western face. **1867** A. BARRY *Sir C. Barry* ii. 51 Engaged columns—colonnades walled up. **1880** C. T. NEWTON *Ess. Archæol.* iii. 83 A Doric peristyle with engaged columns. **1882** *Athenæum* No. 2859. 212 The later pillars of the nave..are accompanied by eight engaged shafts. **1886** *Ibid.* 21 Aug. 248/1 The church at Acton possesses what is called an engaged tower.

3. *Teleph.* Of a number or line: in use and therefore unavailable to a second caller; of a person: telephoning. Hence ***engaged signal***, ***-test***, ***-tone***.

1891 J. POOLE *Pract. Telephone Handbk.* viii. 151 (*heading*) Engaged test. *Ibid.* 153 If she then hears a click in her receiver, she knows that the number is engaged. *Ibid.* 154 If a subscriber's line is engaged. **1893** PREECE & STUBBS *Man. Telephony* xvi. 271 (*heading*) Switch with distinct 'engaged signal' circuit. **1921** G. B. SHAW *Back to Methuselah* III. 137 Engaged! Who is she calling up now? **1927** *Electr. Communication* VI. I. 14/2 If the busy signal is heard in the receiver..then the called subscriber is engaged. **1935** G. GREENE *England made Me* I. 17, I hoped it was the engaged tone, but I knew it was the ringing tone.

4. A term of literary and artistic criticism: = COMMITTED *ppl. a.* b. (Cf. ENGAGÉ *ppl. a.*)

1947 J. HAYWARD *Prose Lit. since 1939* 47 This is not to say that literature must become 'engaged', as one school of continental writers now insists; that it must..'take sides' in the social revolution. **1957** *Observer* 27 Oct. 14/3 He [*sc.* François Mauriac] had written a rather wry little note in *L'Express*, suggesting that I had treated him, in his capacity as an 'engaged' writer, like some sole-surviving specimen of an extinct race. **1958** *Sunday Times* 20 July 6/5 The faults usual in 'engaged' literature.

Hence †**en'gagedly** *adv. Obs.*, in an engaged or interested manner; with the feeling of a partisan.

1654 WHITLOCK *Zootomia* 233 (T.) Engagedly biassed to one side or the other.

†**en'gagedness.** *Obs.* [f. prec. + -NESS.] The quality or state of being engaged, occupied, or interested; devotion to a purpose.

1668–83 OWEN *Expos. Hebrews* III. 36 Intenseness and engagedness of heart and soul. **1742** MRS. EDWARDS in *Jon. Edwards' Wks.* (1834) I. Introd. 105/2, I felt a great earnestness of soul and engagedness in seeking God for the town. **1763** WHEELOCK *Serm.* 30 June (1767) 5 The engagedness of their hearts for the good of others.

†**engagee** (ɛn,geɪ'dʒiː), *sb. Obs.* [ad. Fr. *engagé*: see ENGAGE *v.* and -EE.] One who is engaged or hired for service.

1808 PIKE *Sources Mississ.* II. 123 A Canoe manned with three engagees of Mr. ——. **1817** *Ann. Reg., Chron.* 551 One of our engagees informed us that he had seen them.

engagement (ɛn'geɪdʒmənt). Also 7–8 in-. [f. as prec. + -MENT.]

I. The action of engaging; the state, condition, or fact of being engaged.

†**1.** The pledging or mortgaging (of property); a mortgage, 'encumbrance'. *Obs.*

1630 BRATHWAIT *Eng. Gentlew.* (1641) 351 And preserved his patrimony from ingagement. **1656** H. PHILIPPS *Purch. Patt.* (1676) 58 An House or Land..free from all ingagements.

2. a. A formal promise, agreement, undertaking, covenant.

In 17th c. applied *spec.* to various political compacts, *esp.* to the secret treaty negotiated at Carisbrooke in 1647 between Charles I and commissioners representing the Scottish government. See ENGAGER 2.

1624–47 BP. HALL *Rem. Wks.* (1660) 24 He had my engagement to preach the Sunday following. **1646** E. F[ISHER] *Mod. Divinity* 22 The parties that were bound, are freed and released from their ingagements. **1651** *N. Riding Rec.* V. 96 The engagement was in theis words:—'I doe declare,' etc. **1662** D. DICKSON in Spurgeon *Treas. Dav.* Ps. cxvi, This Psalm is a threefold engagement of the Psalmist unto thanksgiving unto God. **1742** RICHARDSON *Pamela* IV. 209 Such is your Will, and such seem to be your Ingagements. **1790** BURKE *Fr. Rev.* Wks. V. 57 The engagement and pact of society, which generally goes by the name of the constitution. **1856** KANE *Arct. Expl.* II. xvii. 178 An engagement was drawn up..and brought to me with the signatures of all the company.

b. An 'appointment' made with another person for any purpose of business, festivity, etc. Also *attrib.*, as ***engagement book***.

1806–7 J. BERESFORD *Miseries Hum. Life* (1826) VI. iii, Starting for a long ride on a dinner engagement. **1831** DISRAELI *Yng. Duke* II. iii. (L.), We damsels shall soon be obliged to carry a book to enrol our engagements..if this system of reversionary dancing be any longer encouraged. **1850** THACKERAY *Pendennis* II. ii. 15 Anatole, his man..got a sight of her ladyship's engagement-book. **1860** TYNDALL *Glac.* I. §24. 170, I..would have spent the night there were it not for my engagement with the Guide Chef. **1875** JOWETT *Plato* (ed. 2) I. 122 If you have no engagement, suppose that you sit down and tell me what passed. **1886** *Sat. Rev.* 6 Mar. 328/1 On the following morning he [a racehorse] was found to be..incapable of fulfilling an engagement. **1959** T. S. ELIOT *Elder Statesman* I. 19 But what a time for your engagement book! You know what the doctors said: complete relaxation.

c. *Comm.* in *pl.* Promises to pay; pecuniary liabilities. In phrase, ***to meet one's engagements***.

1848 MACAULAY *Hist. Eng.* I. 215 They were consequently unable to meet their own engagements. *Mod.* We regret to inform you that Mr. A. B. is unable to meet his engagements.

d. The fact of being engaged to be married; betrothal. Also *attrib.*, esp. as ***engagement ring***.

[**1742** FIELDING *Jos. Andrews* (L.), She knew her engagements to Horatio.] **1811** JANE AUSTEN *Sense & Sens.* II. vii. 114 'If your engagement had been carried on for months and months..before he chose to put an end to it.' ..'Engagement!' cried Marianne, 'there has been no engagement.' **1859** DICKENS *Lett.* (1880) II. 86 Much excited and pleased by your account of your daughter's engagement. **1861** GEO. ELIOT *Silas M.* 10 She [Sarah] held her engagement to him at an end. **1861** *Cassell's Illustr. Family Paper* 2 Feb. 160/2 The gentleman wears the engagement ring on the third finger of the left hand; the lady on the third finger of the right hand. **1875** MRS. STOWE *We & Neighbors* xxxix. 372 Angie wore on her finger an engagement-ring. **1884** Q. VICTORIA *More Leaves* 103 Our blessed Engagement Day! A dear and sacred day. **1909** *Daily Chron.* 5 Aug. 7/1 Though they had not yet reached the engagement-ring stage, all of her friends were wondering how soon they could begin to plan for the wedding. **1970** C. KERSH *Aggravations of Minnie Ashe* xiv. 202 He bought an engagement ring (later to be pawned by his widow and never redeemed).

3. The fact of being engaged by an employer; an 'appointment', salaried post.

1884 MRS. KENDAL in *Daily News* 24 Sept. 6/1 He had decided to go on the stage, and all that he wanted was an engagement. *Mod.* Immediately after his engagement as secretary. He has obtained a lucrative engagement.

†**4. a.** Moral or legal obligation; a tie of duty or gratitude. *Obs.*

1627 MASSINGER *Gt. Dk. Florence* V. ii, Since my engagements are so great that all My best endeavours to appear your creature Can but proclaim my wants. **1675** BROOKS *Gold. Key* Wks. 1867 V. 416 There is no engagement from God upon any of his people, to run themselves into sufferings wilfully. **1726** *Col. Rec. Pennsylv.* III. 257 He is known to lie under deep Engagements to that Party. **1794** GODWIN *Cal. Williams* 294 Engagement and inclination equally led me to pass a considerable part of every day in this agreeable society.

†**b.** Attachment, prepossession, bias. Cf. ENGAGE *v.* 7 c, 10. *Obs. rare.*

1689 BURNET *Tracts* I. 77 The ingagement that People have to their native Homes appears signally here. **1708** SWIFT *Sentiment Ch. Eng. Man*, Impartially and without engagement..to examine their actions.

c. In *Literary Criticism*, etc.: = COMMITMENT 6 c. Sometimes with Fr. pronunc. (ɑ̃gaʒmɑ̃).

1948 P. MAIRET tr. *Sartre's Existentialism & Humanism* 16 ..[An] important Sartrean concept—*engagement*—is here translated as 'commitment'. .. The French word..conveys a shade of meaning different from that of our word 'engagement'; the existentialism *engagement* is essentially unilateral. **1950** *Theology* LIII. 477 This kind of Christian engagement has been continued. **1952** H. READ *Philos. Mod. Art* iv. 79 Modern protagonists of 'engagement' in art, of socialist realism, of nationalism, etc. **1956** C. WILSON *Outsider* ii. 38 Sartre, whose theory of commitment or 'engagement'..led him to embrace a modified communism. **1960** *Times* 16 Mar. (Canberra Suppl.) p. xv/1 In this age of *engagement*, escapism is deplored.

†**5.** The fact of being entangled; involved or entangled condition. *Obs.*

1642 MILTON *Apol. Smect.* (1851) 325 From which mortall ingagement wee shall never be free. **1648** GAGE *West. Ind.* xx. (1655) 158 Who had been the cause of their ingagement in that great danger. **1648** SYMMONS *Vind. Chas. I* 335, I thought it to be a matter of so great ingagement.

6. The fact of being engaged *in* any occupation; a piece of business requiring attention.

1665 GLANVILL *Sceps. Sci.* xiv. 80 By the most close meditation and engagement of your minds. *a* **1700** ROGERS (J.), Play, either by our too constant or too long engagement in it becomes like an employment or profession. **1781** COWPER *Retirement* 513 From all his wearisome engagements freed.

7. *Swordsmanship.* The action of crossing swords. See ENGAGE 17.

1881 WAITE *Sabre, Singlestick*, etc. 19 On crossing swords, which should be about nine inches apart, when it is called an equal engagement, press your blade, etc.

8. The state of being engaged in fight; a battle, conflict, encounter; also formerly, a single combat.

1665 BOYLE *Occas. Refl.* II. xv. (1675) 144 He will never despair of victory in an ingagement, where he may justly hope to have God for his Second. **1700** DRYDEN *Fables* Ded., Your supposed death in that engagement was so generally lamented through the nation. **1710** *Lond. Gaz.* No. 4685/2 We daily expect to hear of an Engagement between the Swedish and Danish Fleets in the Baltick. **1862** STANLEY *Jew. Ch.* (1877) I. ix. 180 It was the first engagement in which they were confronted with the future enemies of their nation.

†**II. 9.** *concr.* in active sense: That which engages or induces to a course of action; an inducement, motive. Cf. ENGAGE *v.* 8. *Obs.*

1642 MILTON *Arg. conc. Militia* 12 What stronger ingagement can there be..to encourage men in any desperate designe? **1680** BURNET *Rochester* (1692) 95 The great expressions of his Love in Dying for us are mighty Engagements to Obey and imitate him. **1691-8** NORRIS *Pract. Disc.* IV. 173 The great Motives and Ingagements to Obedience.

engager (ɛnˈgeɪdʒə(r)). [f. ENGAGE *v.* + -ER.]

1. a. One who enters into an engagement or agreement; †a surety, guarantor. **b.** One who engages in an enterprise or occupation. **c.** One who engages the service of another; an employer.

1653 WATERHOUSE *Apol. Learn.* 125 (L.) Rash motions have lost noble enterprises and their engagers. **1691** WOOD *Ath. Oxon.*, II. 293 That [the Italian Opera] might be performed with all decency..several sufficient Citizens were engagers. **1865** *Reader* No. 143. 342/2 Such pastimes ..the engager in them.

†**2.** *spec.* One of those who signed or approved of the 'Engagement' of 1647: see ENGAGEMENT 2. *Obs.* exc. *Hist.*

1650 DONNE JUNR. in *Donne's Lett.* (1651) Ded., What of them that were both Covenanters and Engagers too. **1650** LD. CASSILIS in *Nicholas Papers* (1886) 188 The confluence of Malignants and Engagers about him [Chas. II] in the Army. **1761-2** HUME *Hist. Eng.* (1806) IV. lx. 521 An army which admitted any engagers or malignants among them.

engaging (ɛnˈgeɪdʒɪŋ), *vbl. sb.* [f. as prec. + -ING¹.] The action of the vb. ENGAGE, in various senses. Also *attrib.*, as in ***engaging guard*** (*Mil.*).

1647 CLARENDON *Hist. Reb.* I. (1843) 10/1 The engaging the Parliament in the war. **1680** BURNET *Rochester* 111 The ingaging into much Passion. **1803** CAPT. BISSELL in *Naval Chron.* XI. 241 This kind of engaging lasted more than an hour. **1833** *Regul. Instr. Cavalry* I. 138 Forming quickly his 'Engaging Guard' to any point required. *Ibid.* I. 147 Engaging..the action of joining the sword of an opponent, either previous to his, or your own attack.

engaging (ɛnˈgeɪdʒɪŋ), *ppl. a.* [f. ENGAGE *v.* + -ING².] That engages, in various senses.

1. †**a.** Obliging (*obs.*). †**b.** Absorbing, interesting (*obs.*). **c.** Winning, attractive.

1673 *Vain Insol. Rome* 11, I have not forgot your engaging Charity. **1692** E. WALKER *Epictetus' Mor.* lxi, These ingaging Virtues are the Tyes, That more oblige, than Arts, or Amorous Eyes. **1713** BERKELEY *Ess. in Guardian* vi. Wks. III. 163 Virtue has in herself the most engaging charms. **1817** J. SCOTT *Paris Revisit.* 104 The walk on the old ramparts presents several most engaging views. **1833** B'NESS BUNSEN in Hare *Life* (1879) I. ix. 405 She..has always the same engaging manner. **1848** MACAULAY *Hist. Eng.* I. 250 His countenance was eminently handsome and engaging.

2. That makes an engagement or gives a pledge.

1883 *Glasgow Week. Her.* 8 Sept. 3/2 The father of the infant baptised used to be addressed [in the Scotch baptismal service] as 'the engaging parent'.

3. *Mech.* ***engaging and disengaging machinery***: that in which one part is alternately united to, or separated from, another part, as occasion may require. (Nicholson.)

engagingly (ɛnˈgeɪdʒɪŋlɪ), *adv.* [f. prec. + -LY.] In an engaging manner.

1. So as to involve a pledge; cf. prec. 2.

1651 BAXTER *Inf. Bapt.* 124 Were it [baptism] performed more solemnly, particularly, and engagingly.

2. Attractively, charmingly, winningly.

1694 *Pindaric Ode to Sancroft*, How his Rays Engagingly Surprize! **1742** RICHARDSON *Pamela* III. 104 One more learned..could not write as you do..so very ingagingly. **1805** S. & HT. LEE *Canterb. T.* V. 345 Too engagingly peremptory, to admit of any denial from him. **1812** L. HUNT in *Exam.* 4 May 275/1 [He] is..engagingly tolerant.

enˈgagingness. [f. as prec. + -NESS.] The quality of being engaging or fascinating; attractiveness, seductiveness.

1727 BAILEY vol. II, *Insinuatingness*,..insinuating Nature, Engagingness. **1768-74** TUCKER *Lt. Nat.* (1852) II. 313 The engagingness of mischief. **1906** G. SAINTSBURY *Minor Poets of Caroline Period* II. 371 A certain quality of engagingness which it has.

†**enˈgaigne.** *Obs.* [a. OF. *engaigne* deception (cf. It. *ingannare* to deceive), also indignation, resentment.] Resentment.

1375 BARBOUR *Bruce* XVIII. 508 (Edinb. MS.) He had at hym rycht gret engaigne [ed. *Skeat* disdeyne].

†**enˈgalared,** *pple.* *Obs.* *rare*⁻¹. Also ?engolerid. [perh. f. EN-¹ + *galari* GALLERY.] ? Furnished with galleries.

1523 SKELTON *Garl. Laurel* (Dyce) 460 A palace.. Engolerid [ed. 1568 Engalared] goodly with hallis and bowris.

engall, -gallant, -gammon, -gaol, -garb, -garble, -garboil: see EN- *pref.*¹ 1 a, 1 b, 3.

en garçon: see EN *prep.*

engarland (ɛnˈgɑːlənd), *v.* Also 7 engyrland, ingarland. [f. EN- *pref.*¹ + GARLAND; cf. Fr. *enguirlander*.]

1. *trans.* To put a garland upon; to wreathe *with*. Also with flowers, etc. as subj. Also *fig.*

1581 SIDNEY *Apol. Poetrie* (Arb.) 60 Laurels..to engarland our Poets heads. **1613-6** W. BROWNE *Brit. Past.* II. i, Powers..Whose milde aspect engyrland Poesie. *a* **1631** DRAYTON *Leg. Piers Gaveston* (1748) 205 With funeral wreaths ingarlanding his brows. **1830** TENNYSON *Arab. Nts.* xiv, [A cloth of gold] Engarlanded and diaper'd With inwrought flowers. **1853** F. W. NEWMAN tr. *Odes Horace* 110 To tempt the little gods, whom myrtle Frail and rosemary engarlands.

2. To surround, as with a garland.

1598 E. GILPIN *Skial.* v, You rotten-throated slaves Engarlanded with coney-catching Knaves. **1814** CARY *Dante* (Chandos) 147 That part of the cornice, where no rim Engarlands its steep fall. **1879** CHR. ROSSETTI *Seek & F.* 91 Snowy heights form a water-shed for the low-lying fertility which engarlands their base.

Hence **enˈgarlanded** *ppl. a.*

1858 W. JOHNSON *Ionica* 82 A sister's engarlanded brows.

engarment: see EN- *pref.* 1 a.

†**enˈgarrison,** *v.* *Obs.* Also 7 ingarrison. [f. EN-¹ + GARRISON.] **a.** *trans.* To serve as a garrison in. **b.** To protect by a garrison. **c.** To station as a garrison; *pass.* only. **d.** *refl.* To establish (oneself) *in*, as in a garrison or fortification; to entrench (oneself).

1612-15 BP. HALL *Contempl. N.T.* IV. xxxii, They that would hold fair correspondence with the citizens, where they were engarrisoned. **1640** HOWELL *Dodona's Gr.* 9 Neptune..with a flying gard of brave winged Coursers doth engarrison her. **1641** HEYLIN *Help to Hist.* (1671) 270 There lay engarrison'd the Captain of the Crispinian Horsemen. **1668** W. CHARLTON *Ephes. & Cimm. Matrons* 46 Think it below their Courage to engarrison that Fort. **1682** BUNYAN *Holy War* 27 The giant had..ingarrisoned himself in the town of Mansoul. **1683** CAVE *Ecclesiastici* 397, I will not.. engarrison myself within crowds of People. *a* **1716** SOUTH *Serm.* IX. v. (R.), He has engarrison'd himself in a strong hold. **1775** ADAIR *Amer. Indians* 314 In the various nations where they ingarrisoned themselves. **1853** STOCQUELER *Mil. Encycl.*, *Engarrison*, to protect any place by a garrison.

engastration (ɛŋgæˈstreɪʃən). *rare.* [f. Gr. ἐν in + γαστ(ε)ρ- stem of γαστήρ belly + -ATION.] The action of stuffing one fowl inside another.

1814 *Sch. Gd. Living* 87 Engastration of stuffed pies, one bird within another..The passion for engastration seems to have had its admirers in all ages.

†**enˈgastriloque.** *Obs.* *rare*⁻¹. [f. as next + L. *-loquus* speaking.] = next.

1720 HUTCHINSON *Witchcr.* i. 11 Such People are call'd Engastriloques, or Ventriloquists.

†**enˈgastrimyth.** *Obs.* Also 6 engastromith, 7 (*erron.* in *Dicts.* -mich, -imuch). [ad. Fr. *engastrimythe*, ad. Gr. ἐγγαστρίμυθος, f. ἐν in + γαστρί, dat. of γαστήρ belly + μῦθος speech.] One who appears to speak in the belly, a ventriloquist.

1598 SYLVESTER *Du Bartas* I. ii. *Deceipt* (1605-7) I. 309 All incenst, the pale Engastromith..Speakes in his wombe. **1623** COCKERAM, *Engastromich*, one possessed, which seemes to speak in his belly. **1656** BLOUNT *Glossogr.*, *Engastrimuches* (engastrimuchi), were those, that being possessed, seemed to speak out of their belly. **1708** MOTTEUX *Rabelais* IV. lviii. (1737) 238 The first, were call'd *Engastrimythes*.

Hence †**engastriˈmythian** *a.*, that practises ventriloquism; **engastriˈmythic** *a.*, pertaining to, of the nature of ventriloquism.

a **1693** URQUHART *Rabelais* III. xxv, The Engastrimythian Prophetess. **1849** S. R. MAITLAND *Illustr. & Enquiries Relating to Mesmerism* I. 58, I cannot help saying that there seems to me to be something engastrimythic in this case. **1851** G. S. FABER *Many Mansions* (1862) 125 Upon this, she abandoned her engastrimythic whisperings, and uttered a loud cry of alarm and distress.

engaze: see EN- *pref.*¹ 3.

enge, obs. f. ING(E meadow.

†**enˈgeal,** *v.* *Obs.* *rare*⁻¹. In 5 engeyle. [ad. OF. *engiel-er*, *engel-er*, f. *en-* (see EN-¹) + *geler* to freeze: cf. CONGEAL.] *trans.* To freeze.

14.. *MS. Cantab.* Ff. i. 6, f. 11 (Halliw.) Stones engeyled falleth doune arow, Whenne that hit hayleth.

engel, obs. form of ANGEL *sb.*

Engelmann (ˈɛŋgəlmən). The name of Dr. George *Engelmann* (1809-84) of St. Louis, a botanist, used *attrib.* or in the genitive to designate a spruce (*Picea engelmannii*) native to western North America.

1866 'J. SENILIS' *Pinaceæ* 48 Abies Engelmani [*sic*]: Engleman's [*sic*] Spruce Fir. **1868** J. HOOPES *Bk. Evergreens* 177 A[bies] Engelmanni, *Parry*.—Engelmann's Spruce. **1908** *Bot. Gaz.* May 333 The two trees that dominate the society are the Engelmann spruce (*Picea Engelmanni*) and the subalpine fir (*Abies lasiocarpa*). **1948** A. L. RAND *Mammals E. Rockies* 8 The forests of the east slopes of the mountains are characterized by Engleman spruce, lodgepole pine, alpine fir (near timberline), white-barked pine. **1964** GLEASON & CRONQUIST *Nat. Geogr. Plants* xx. 366 (*caption*) The trees here [*sc.* in Idaho] are alpine fir, Engelmann spruce, and white-bark pine.

engem (ɛnˈdʒɛm), *v.* *rare.* Also 9 ingem. [f. EN-¹ + GEM.] *trans.* To set with, or as with, gems; to bejewel.

c **1630** DRUMM. OF HAWTH. *Poems* Wks. (1711) 6/2 When clouds engemm'd shew azure, green, and red. **1803-49** J. C. MANGAN *Poems* (1859) 98 A ring, ingemmed with a chrysolite. **1814** CARY *Dante* (Chandos) 262, I pray thee, living topaz! that ingemm'st This precious jewel, let me hear thy name.

engender (ɛnˈdʒɛndə(r)). *v.* Also 4-5 engendre, 5-7 ingender. [a. F. *engendrer*, corresp. to Pr. *engenrar*, It. *ingenerare*:—L. *ingenerāre*, f. *in* + *generāre* to beget, GENERATE, f. *genus*, *gener-is*, breed, race.]

1. *trans.* Of the male parent: To beget. Const. *on*, *of*. Now only *rhetorical* or *fig.*

c **1325** *E.E. Allit. P.* B. 272 En-gendered on hem Ieauntez with her Iapez ille. *c* **1386** CHAUCER *Merch. T.* 28 Than schuld he take a yong wif and a fair, On which he might engendre him an hair. *c* **1400** MAUNDEV. xxi. 223 Of his Sone Chuse, was engendred Nembrother the Geaunt. **1475** CAXTON *Jason* 77 The one espoused that other and engendryd on her a daughter. **1513** DOUGLAS *Æneis* x. Prol. 42 The Fader..His only Son engendris evirmoir. **1568** GRAFTON *Chron.* II. 625 The sayde Richarde was espoused to Lady Alice..of which woman he engendered Richard, John and George. **1651** HOBBES *Leviath.* III. xxxvii. 233 When a man..engenders his like..it is no Miracle. **1796** JEFFREY in Ld. Cockburn *Life J.* (1853) II. xiii, I haue to seek out some angelic partner, and engender a dozen or two of children. **1836-7** SIR W. HAMILTON *Metaph.* xxxix. (1870) II. 394 The offspring of experience engendered upon custom.

†**2.** Of the female parent: To conceive, bear.

1340-70 *Alex. & Dind.* 587 3e were alle..bred of þat modur þat..storms engendreþ. ? *a* **1400** *Morte Arth.* 612 Sexty geauntes be-fore engenderide with fendez. **1509** HAWES *Past. Pleas.* IV. xx, Seven doughters..she had well engendred. **1601** SHAKS. *Jul. C.* v. iii. 71 O Error soone conceyu'd, Thou..kil'st the Mother that engendred thee. **1683** *Brit. Spec.* 57 The Father and Mother, and simply those that beget and ingender do..rule over all their Children.

3. Of both parents, also vaguely of ancestors, and *transf.* of countries, situations, conditions, etc.: To produce, give existence to (living beings). In *passive*, to be produced, begotten (const. *between*, *of*); to be descended.

1393 LANGL. *P. Pl.* C. XI. 215 A rybaud þei engendrede and a gome vnryghtful. **1480** CAXTON *Descr. Irel.* (1520) 2/2 Men of relygyon eet barnacles upon fastynge dayes bycause they ben not engendred with flesshe. **1549** *Compl. Scot.* Ep. Q. Mary 2 Illustir princes, engendrit of magnanime genoligie. **1577** B. GOOGE *Heresbach's Husb.* III. (1586) 125 b, Of the shee Asse and the Horse, is engendred the shee moile. **1651** C. CARTWRIGHT *Cert. Relig.* I. 232 For what hath man deserved, why his parents should ingender him such, or such? **1777** ROBERTSON *Hist. Amer.* (1778) I. III. 202 Elevated at some distance from the odious reptiles ingendered in the putrid waters. **1814** CARY *Dante's Inf.* III. 97 The human kind, the place, the time, and seed, That did engender them and give them birth. **1830** LYELL *Princ. Geol.* (1875) I. I. ii. 16 [Anaximander has been alleged to

have taught that] the first imperfect and short-lived creatures had been engendered in slime.

†**4.** *absol.* To copulate, have sexual intercourse. Said of both sexes. Const. *with.* Also *fig.* *Obs.*

c **1400** *Destr. Troy* 7959 Luff ingendreth with ioye, as in a iust sawle. **1547** J. HARRISON *Exhort. Scottes* 213 Thei ingendered with spirites, & brought furth l. Giauntes. **1577** B. GOOGE *Heresbach's Husb.* III. (1586) 127 Camel.. engendreth..backward, as the Elephantes. **1599** MASSINGER, etc. *Old Law* III. ii, His goodness has gone backward, and engendered With his old sins again. **1667** MILTON *P.L.* II. 794 And in embraces forcible and foule Ingendring with me. **1774** GOLDSM. *Nat. Hist.* (1776) III. 174 With the wild boar..they are never known to engender. **1826** KIRBY & SP. *Entomol.* (1828) III. xxxviii. 25 That Insecta engender only once in the course of their lives.

¶ *trans.* Misused for: To couple.

1791 PAINE *Rights M.* (ed. 4) 80 By engendering the church with the state.

5. *trans.* †**a.** To produce by natural processes, develop, generate (plants, minerals, material substances) (*obs.*). **b.** To give rise to, produce (a state of things, a disease, force, quality, feeling, etc.). †**c.** To contract (a disorder). *Obs.*

a. c **1386** CHAUCER *Prol.* 4 Of which vertue engendred is the flour. c **1430** LYDG. *Chorle & Byrde* (1818) 12 Ther is a stone, which is callid is a Jagounce Of olde engendrid within myn entraylle. **1553** EDEN *Treat. Newe Ind.* (Arb.) 6 Golde ..is engendred almost in al regions neare vnto the *Æquinoctial* line. **1563** T. GALE *Antid.* II. 51 It doeth ingender fleshe on the bones that are bare. **1570–6** LAMBARDE *Peramb. Kent* (1826) 261 Those brookes..doe ingendre the river Stowre. **1653** CULPEPPER *Eng. Physic.* 144 To..clense the Kidnies from Gravel or Stones ingendered in them. **1671** J. WEBSTER *Metallogr.* xiii. 202 The ground and soil of this Mountain..neither ingenders, nor brings forth any fruit, grass, nor grain. **1775** ADAIR *Amer. Ind.* 237 Others resemble the onyx, being engendered of black and thick humours.

b. **1340** HAMPOLE *Pr. Consc.* 1141 Lust and lykyng, that es flesshely Engendres the syn of lychery. **1477** NORTON *Ord. Alch.* in Ashm. (1652) 64 Darknes with hardnes ingendred shall be. **1526** *Pilgr. Perf.* (W. de W. 1531) 47 To plucke out all the olde euyll customes that by synne be engendred in vs. **1628** T. SPENCER *Logick* 124 These similitudes..ingender truth. **1646** RECORDE, etc. *Gr. Artes* 167 The quotient will shew you the number that engendreth the Progression. **1692** DRYDEN *St. Euremont's Ess.* 296 Immoderate Study engenders a grossness in the Mind. **1752** HUME *Pol. Disc.* vii. 118 Taxes..when carried too far, destroy industry, by engendring despair. **1841** CATLIN *N. Amer. Ind.* (1844) II. xlviii. 111 This stupid and useless fashion..has most unfortunately been engendered on these ignorant people. **1863** TYNDALL *Heat* i. §10 The heat engendered by the friction.

c. **1525** LD. BERNERS *Froiss.* II. clxxxviii. 575 They answered howe the kyng of longe tyme had engendred the same malady. **1632** LITHGOW *Trav.* v. 192 When Italians.. eate any quantity thereof, they presently fall into the bloudy fluse, or else ingender some other pestilentious fever.

†**6.** *intr.* **a.** Of living things: To breed, multiply. **b.** Of inorganic substances: To form, originate, be produced. **c.** Of maladies, etc.: To originate, develop. Also *fig.* *Obs.*

c **1386** CHAUCER *Prol.* 421 He knew the cause of every maladye..And where thei engendrid. c **1420** *Pallad. on Husb.* I. 308 For causes pestilent Engendring there, and wormes violent. **1523** LD. BERNERS *Froiss.* I. ccccviii. 710 Thus ther engendred hatred dayly bytwene Fraunce and Flaunders. **1567** MAPLET *Gr. Forest* 5 b, The Cristall.. engendreth not so much of the waters coldenesse. **1578** LYTE *Dodoens* I. lxx. 104 Fleas will not come nor ingender where it [Fleabane] is layed. a **1618** RALEIGH *Instruct. Sonne* ix. (1651) 24 As the worm that engendereth in the Kernel of the Nut. **1651** HOWELL *Venice* 195 An illfavourd black cloud began to engender against her in the Levant. **1653** CULPEPPER *Eng. Physic.* 62 To cause the stone not to ingender. a **1700** DRYDEN (J.), Thick clouds are spread, and storms engender there. **1726** LEONI *Alberti's Archit.* I. 44 a, Damp that may happen to engender or gather under ground. **1786** tr. *Beckford's Vathek* (1868) 53 Bats will engender in thy belly. **1865** DRAPER *Intell. Devel. Europe* xx. 471 In Italy..a dismal disbelief was silently engendering.

†**en'gender,** *sb.* *Obs.* Also 6 ingender. [a. OF. *engendre,* n. of action f. *engendrer*: see prec.] The action of engendering or begetting; *concr.* that which is engendered; offspring, produce.

a **1528** SKELTON *Vox Populi* 365 Withe comons and comon ingenders. **1556** J. HEYWOOD *Spider & F.* xxix. 17 To know his grandam butterflise estate, With all vncles and auntes, of their engender. **1647** CRASHAW *Poems* 129 From th' rising son, obtaining by just suit, A spring's ingender, and an autumn's fruit.

engendered (ɛn'dʒɛndəd), *ppl. a.* [f. ENGENDER *v.* + -ED.] Begotten or produced; (of a disease) arising within the body, non-contagious.

1633 G. HERBERT *Temple, Providence* xiv, Nothing ingendred doth prevent his meat. **1841** LANE *Arab. Nts.* I. 60 Diseases engendered are..leprosy, hectic, epilepsy, etc.

engenderer (ɛn'dʒɛndərə(r)). Also 6–7 engendrer, ingenderer. [f. ENGENDER *v.* + -ER.] One who or that which engenders.

1561 T. NORTON *Calvin's Inst.* II. 152 The mothers are called *genitrices,* that is engenderers. **1587** GOLDING *De Mornay* v. 59 One is an ingenderer and another is ingendred, among men, a father and a sonne. **1596** BP. ANDREWES *Serm.* II. 94 These [the prophets] also he strove to forget, and as ingenderers of melancholy to remove them far away. **1625** HART *Anat. Ur.* I. v. 45 Ease and idlenesse, the engendrers of all manner of crudities. **1636** DAVENANT *Witts* in *Dodsley* (1780) VIII. 481 Thou dull ingenderer; Male rather in the back than in the brain. **1852** *Tait's Mag.* XIX. 53 Still more disgusting engenderers of filth.

en'gendering, *vbl. sb.* [f. as prec. + -ING[1].] The action of the vb. ENGENDER, in various senses.

c **1450** *Merlin* v. 81 The recorde of the engenderinge of the childe. **1580** TWYNE (*title*) Shorte and pithie Discourse concerning the engendering..of all Earthquakes. **1711** SHAFTESB. *Charac.* (1737) III. 412 Not only the mere engendring of the young, but the..methods of providing for them, are all foreknown.

engendering (ɛn'dʒɛndərɪŋ), *ppl. a.* [f. as prec. + -ING[2].] That engenders.

1607 TOPSELL *Four-f. Beasts* (1673) 267 The excesse, or lack of engendring seed. a **1631** DONNE *Poems* (1650) 175 Though ingendring force from whence they came Be strong enough. **1646** J. BENBRIGGE *Vsura Acc.* Introd. 3 Anatomizing the engendring wombe of his sinfulnesse against God. **1826** SCOTT *Woodst.* ii, A bunch of engendering adders.

en'genderment. [f. as prec. + -MENT.] The action of engendering; procreation.

1835–6 TODD *Cycl. Anat.* I. 129/1 The engenderment of new individuals.

engendrure (ɛn'dʒɛndr(j)ʊə(r)). *arch.* Also 5 engenderure. [a. OF. *engendreure* (= Pr. *engenradura*), f. *engendrer*: see ENGENDER *v.*]

†**1.** The action of engendering. **a.** Generation, procreation. **b.** Copulation. *Obs.*

c **1315** SHOREHAM 139 Folye hyt hys to meche to thynche Of the engendrure..Of Fader and Sone. c **1386** CHAUCER *Pers. T.* ¶301 Whan he useth his wyf withoute soverayn desir of engendrure. **1447** BOKENHAM *Seyntys* (1835) 51 Be kyndly engenderure To joyen in the lykenesse of ther nature. **1555** *Fardle Facions* I. ii. 31 Those [beastes].. encreased by mutuall engendrure, the varietie, and nombre.

2. Parentage, descent, origin.

1362 LANGL. *P. Pl.* A. VII. 219 Go to Genesis þe Ieaunt engendrure [**1377** engendroure] of vs alle. c **1475** *Partenay* 5750 Off Tristram-is line was hys engendrure. **1483** CAXTON *Gold. Leg.* 380/4 Fortune onely of engendrure and happe doth al. **1884** SALA in *Illust. Lond. News* 16 Feb. 147 It is singular that so many prominent members of the *Times* staff should have been of West Indian engendrure.

engendure (ɛn'dʒɛndjʊə(r)). *arch.* Also 5 inngendure. [Bad form of prec.] = prec. *lit.* and *fig.*

? a **1400** *Morte Arth.* 3744 Of siche a engendure fulle littylle joye happyns. c **1450** *Merlin* i. 18 My moder..natht knoweth of that thow puttest on hir in thy Inngendure. a **1454** OCCLEVE *MS. Soc. Antiq.* 134. f. 259 (Halliwell) Leefulle luste is necessarie, Withouten that may be non engendure. **1823** LAMB *Elia* (1860) 135 Crown-office Row (place of my kindly engendure). **1864** LOWELL *Biglow P.* Poet. Wks. (1879) 247 Knowledge of the..engendure and affinities of our noble language.

engeny, var. of INGENY, *Obs.*

engerminate: see EN- *pref.*[1] 3.

enghle: see INGLE *sb.* and *v.*

engild (ɛn'gɪld), *v.* [f. EN-[1] + GILD *v.*] *trans.* To gild; also *fig.* to brighten with golden light.

c **1400** *Apol. Loll.* 85 Trees polist of forgars, & engilt, & siluerid. **1590** SHAKS. *Mids. N.* III. ii. 187 Faire Helena; who more engilds the night. **1855** SINGLETON *Virgil* I. 206 His [Eridanus'] twain horns Engilt on bull-like face.

engine ('ɛndʒɪn), *sb.* Forms: α. 4–7 engin, 4–8 engyn(e, 4–6 engynne, (5 *pl.* engenys, 7 enging), 4– engine. β. 5–8 ingin(e, 6–7 ingyn(n)e, (5–6 yngyne, 6 injyne, ingen, 7 ingene). See also INGENY. [a. OF. *engin,* corresp. to Pr. *engen, engein, engienh,* Sp. *ingenio,* Pg. *engenho,* It. *ingegno*:—L. *ingenium* (whence INGENIOUS), f. *in* in + *gen-* root of *gignĕre* to beget.

The β forms, some of which are directly influenced by the Lat. *ingenium,* appear to occur after 16th c. only in senses 1–3.]

†**1. a.** Native talent, mother wit; genius. *Obs.*

From the middle of 17th c. app. only Sc. in β forms, retaining the older accentuation *in'gine,* and prob. regarded as a distinct word from *engine.*

α. c **1386** CHAUCER *Second Nun's T.* 339 A man hath sapiences thre, Memorie, engin, and intellect also. c **1391** —— *Astrol.* Prol. 2, I ne usurpe nat to haue fownde this werk of my labour or of myn engin. **1483** CAXTON *Gold. Leg.* 276/1 Saynt Augustyn concluded all the other by engyn and by scyence. **1589** PUTTENHAM *Eng. Poesie* II. viii. [ix.] (Arb.) 95 Such..made most of their workes by translation..few or none of their owne engine. **1632** LITHGOW *Trav.* IX. (1682) 379 High Press thy [Etna's] Flames..But higher moves the scope of my Engine.

β. **1477** NORTON *Ord. Alch.* Proem, in Ashm. (1652) 7 It is no small ingine To know all secreats pertaining to the Myne. **1535** STEWART *Cron. Scot.* II. 100 It will transcend the strenth of my ingyne, To tell ȝow all thair godlines diuyne. a **1572** KNOX *Hist. Ref.* Wks. (1846) I. 64 Kennedy ..one of excellent injyne in Scotish poesye. **1598** B. JONSON *Ev. Man in Hum.* v. iii, If thy master..be angrie with thee, I shall suspect his ingine, while I know him for't. **1599** JAMES I *Βασιλικον Δωρον* To Rdr., Which I wrote for exercise of my own ingene. **1651** FULLER *Abel Rediv., Colet* (1867) I. 117 Great respect had wont to be had both to the ingine and ingenuity of the intrants. **1785** BURNS *1st Ep. Lapraik* v, A' that ken't him round declar'd He had ingine. **18..** SCOTT *Monastery* 531/2 A man of quick ingine and deep wisdom.

†**b.** Natural disposition, temper. Chiefly *Sc.*

c **1565** LINDESAY (Pitscottie) *Chron. Scot.* 55 (Jam.), Wikkitness, to which he was given allenarly, through the impiety of his own ingyne. **1572** *Lament. Lady Scot.* in *Scot. Poems 16th C.* II. 239 To quhom can I this throuch propyne Bot unto one of excellent ingyne. **1600** FAIRFAX *Tasso* I. lxxxiii, His fell ingine His grauer age did somewhat mitigate.

†**2. a.** Skill in contriving, ingenuity; also, in bad sense, artfulness, cunning, trickery. *Obs.*

c **1320** *Sir Beues* 2003 Ac now icham from him ifare þrouȝ godes grace & min engyn. c **1320** *Seuyn Sag.* (W.) viii. 1959 Gold and siluer to wille he wan Bi losengerie an bi engin. **1393** GOWER *Conf.* II. 83 The women were of great engine. c **1450** *Merlin* i. 20, I am the sone of the enmy that begiled my moder with engyn. **15..** tr. *Sir T. More's Edw. V* (1641) 2 By what crafty engin he first attempted his ungracious purpose. **1549** *Compl. Scot.* Ep. Q. Mary 4 Be ane diuyne miracle, rather nor be the ingyne of men. a **1628** B. JONSON in Sir J. Beaumont *Bosworth F.* 13 All Monuments of Praise, That Art, or Engine, or the Strength can raise.

†**b.** In OF. phrase *mal engin* evil machination: see MALENGIN. Also in similar sense, *false, malicious engin.* *Obs.*

c **1440** *Partonope* 1440 Thought his counsell was fals engyne. **1545** T. RAYNOLD *Womans booke* B. 4 This knowledge also ministreth yet a farther ingyn and polycye to inuent infynitely the better how, etc. **1557** *K. Arthur* (Copland) IV. xii, Brought to the purpose by fals engyn and treason and by false enchauntement. **1637–50** ROW *Hist. Kirk* (1842) 156 Their malicious ingyns in conspyreing aganis Kirk, King, and countrey.

†**3.** An instance or a product of ingenuity; an artifice, contrivance, device, plot; and in bad sense, a snare, wile (cf. 5 c. and GIN *sb.*[1]); also, in weaker sense, an appliance, means.

The later instances are partly *fig.* from 4, 5 c, or 7.

a **1300** *Floriz & Bl.* 759 He het him telle his engin Hu he to blauncheflur com in. c **1400** *Rom. Rose* 4549 The develles engynnes wolde me take. c **1430** LYDG. *MS. Cott. Aug.* iv. 28 b, By what engyne the fylthes fer nor nere Were borne awaye. **1477** NORTON *Ord. Alch.* i. in Ashm. (1652) 20 To make trew..Gold is noe ingin, Except..the Philosophers medicine. **1523** LD. BERNERS *Froiss.* I. ccccxiv. 724 To fynde way and engin howe to passe the bridge. **1583** STANYHURST *Æneis* I. (Arb.) 18 Shee [Juno] soght al possibil engins In surging billows too touze thee coompanie Troian. **1625** BACON *Ess. Superst.* (Arb.) 345 Astronomers..did faigne Eccentricks, and Epicycles, and such Engines of Orbs. **1635** QUARLES *Embl.* iii. 9 (D.) The hidden engines, and the snares that lie So undiscovered. **1667** MILTON *P.L.* I. 750 Nor did he scape By all his engins. **1683** TEMPLE *Mem.* Wks. 1731 I. 376 The Dutch and the Spaniards set on Foot all the Engines they could. **1719** *Cordial Low Spirits* I. 129 Falshood is the only Engine they have left to defend the Reputation of the Crape. **1781** GIBBON *Decl. & F.* II. xxxiii. 252 The warrior could dexterously employ the dark engines of policy.

4. A mechanical contrivance, machine, implement, tool; in 15th c. also *collect.* apparatus, machinery. *arch.* in gen. sense. (For *fig.* uses see 10.)

c **1330** R. BRUNNE *Chron. Wace* (Rolls) 8816 Geauntz.. sette þem [the stones at Stonehenge] on an hil ful hey With engyns fulle queyntely. a **1400–50** *Alexander* 5292 Þis selere was be sorsry selcuthely foundid, Made for a mervall to meeue with engine. c **1440** *Promp. Parv.* 140 Engynne, or ingyne, *machina.* c **1550** SIR J. BALFOUR *Practicks* (1754) 38 He or sche sall be put and haldin in the stokkis or sic uther ingine. **1571** *Mem. Ripon* (1882) I. 309 Ropes and other yngynes. **1635** PAGITT *Christianogr.* III. (1636) 48 The Image with all his engines was openly showed at Pauls crosse. **1662** FULLER *Worthies* (1840) III. 58 Some thieves (with what engines unknown)..forced it [a chest] open. **1664** POWER *Exp. Philos.* Pref. 7 Our modern Engine the Microscope. **1712–4** POPE *Rape Lock* III. 132 He..extends The little engine [a pair of scissors] on his fingers' ends. **1727** SWIFT *Gulliver* I. viii. 87 With ropes and engines, I made a shift to turn it. **1747** CARTE *Hist. Eng.* I. 535 Being drawn from his horse by an engine with an iron hook at the end. **1866** BRYANT *Death Slavery* vii, At thy feet Scourges and engines of restraint and ease.

5. *spec.* **a.** A machine or instrument used in warfare. Formerly sometimes applied to all offensive weapons, but chiefly and now exclusively to those of large size and having mechanism, *e.g.* a battering-ram, catapult, piece of ordnance, etc.

a **1300** *Cursor M.* 9889 (Cott.), Na maner engine o were Mai cast þar-til it for to dere. **1387** TREVISA *Higden* (Rolls) IV. 429 Vespacianus destourbed þe wal wiþ þe stroke of an engine [Higden *arietis*]. c **1440** *Bone Flor.* 859 And they wythowte, yngynes bende, And stones to the walles they sende. **1549** COVERDALE, etc. *Erasm. Par. Hebr.* xi. 30 Sodaynely to fall without any violence of Engynes. **1598** HAKLUYT *Voy.* I. 21 They haue expelled Lions, Beares, & such like vntamed beasts, with their bowes, and other engines. **1667** MILTON *P.L.* VI. 518 Whereof to found their Engins and their Balls. **1676** D'URFEY *Mad. Fickle* v. ii, And I shall make a private Room in your guts for this Engine here [a rapier]. **1719** DE FOE *Crusoe* (1858) 409 Bows and arrows, great clubs..and such like engines of war. **1737** FRANKLIN *Ess.* Wks. 1840 II. 292 The stage and the press..became battering engines against religion. **1777** WATSON *Philip II,* (1839) 405 Farnese..got possession of more than thirty of the enemy's ships, with all the artillery and engines that were on board. **1843** PRESCOTT *Mexico* (1850) I. 365 They had no weapons to cope with these terrible engines.

†**b.** An 'engine of torture'; *esp.* the rack. *Obs.*

c **1430** *Life St. Kath.* (1884) 55 Graunt þat þis peynfull engyn be destruyed by þe strook of heuenly thonder & leuen. **1477** EARL RIVERS (Caxton) *Dictes* 15 a, [He] was commanded to be put in engyne and tormented. **1579** FULKE *Heskins' Parl.* 286 The words..by no engin can be wrested. **1605** SHAKS. *Lear* I. iv. 290 Which like an Engine, wrencht my frame of Nature From the fixt place. **1689** SHADWELL *Bury F.* I. i, What an engine is this fop.

c. A contrivance for catching game; a snare, net, trap, decoy, or the like. Cf. GIN. Still used for appliances used in the illicit catching of salmon, etc.

1481 CAXTON *Myrr.* II. vi. 77 The hunters..by their engyns that they haue propire for the same take hym. **1523** *Act 14 & 15 Hen. VIII*, c. 13 Diuers weres & ingins for fisshynge. **1686** N. COX *Gentl. Recr.* III. 141 Partridges are ..most easily to be deceived or beguiled with any Train, Bait, Engine, or other Device. *Ibid.* III. 145 Make an Engine in the form and fashion of a Horse, cut out of Canvas, and stuff it with Straw, or such light matter. **1861** *Act 24 & 25 Vict.* c. 109 §11 No fixed Engine of any Description shall be placed or used for catching Salmon in any inland or tidal Waters. **1873** J. W. W. BUND *Law rel. Salmon Fisheries* x. 270 The nets were illegal fixed engines. **1923** *Act 13 & 14 Geo. V* c. 16 §11 No fixed engine of any description shall be ..used for taking..salmon or migratory trout. **1968** *Times* 23 May 17/5 The appellant was convicted for unlawfully using..a fixed engine—a net which he had left unattended, secured by anchors.

¶**d.** App. confused with *henge*, HINGE, or with the synonymous HENGLE. *Obs.*⁻⁰

1552 HULOET, Engin of a dore, *vertebra.* **1580** in BARET *Alv.* E 237.

†**6.** Taken as the equivalent of L. *machina* (see MACHINE) in certain specific uses. **a.** *engine of the world*, after L. *machina mundi* (Lucretius): the 'universal frame'. **b.** The mechanism by which in a Greek theatre gods, etc. were made to appear in the air: cf. L. *deus ex machina. Obs.*

a. 1450–1530 *Myrr. our Ladye* 220 The cloyster of mary beryth hym that gouernyth the thre engynes..heuen, erthe, and helle. **1529** MORE *Heresyes* I. Wks. 129/1 There was a god, eyther maker or gouernour or both, of al this hole engine of the world. **1539** BP. HILSEY *Primer* in *Myrr. our Ladye* 349 The governor of the triple engine, The Son of God of mightes most. **1561** T. NORTON *Calvin's Inst.* I. xiv. (1634) 73 In governing of the so swift whirling about of the engine of heaven.

b. 1633 T. JAMES *Voy.* 107 As if they had beene brought home in a dreame or engine. **1654** TRAPP *Comm. Ps.* lxviii. 20 He appeareth as out of an Engin, and pulleth us out of Death's jaws.

7. a. A machine, more or less complicated, consisting of several parts, working together to produce a given physical effect.

As in recent use the word has come to be applied *esp.* to the STEAM-ENGINE (q.v.) and analogous machines (see 8, 9), the wider sense expressed in the above definition has become almost obsolete, surviving chiefly in the compounds *beer-engine, calculating-engine, fire-engine, garden-engine, water-engine* (q.v. under their initial elements).

1635 N. CARPENTER *Geog. Del.* I. i. 12 An artificiall Clock, Mill, or such like great Engine. **1651** HOBBES *Govt. & Soc.* Author's Pref., As in a watch, or some such small engine. **1667** in *Phil. Trans.* II. 425 A Glass-Receiver of the above mentioned Engine [an air-pump]. **1708** J. C. *Compl. Collier* (1845) 28 If the Pit be sunk more than thirty Fathom, then we use the Horse Engin. **1712** ARBUTHNOT *John Bull* (1755) 15 I'll rather wheel about the street an engine to grind knives and scissars. *c* **1730** E. BURT *Lett. N. Scotl.* (1818) I. 106 An engine to chop straw withal. **1776** ADAM SMITH *W.N.* (1869) II. IV. viii. 243 The exportation of frames or engines for knitting gloves or stockings is prohibited. **1816** WORDSW. *Thanksg. Ode* (1850) II. 215 The tubed engine feels the inspiring blast.

b. *transf.* and *fig.*

1633 *Costlie Whore* II. i. in Bullen *O. Pl.* IV, I feele within my breast a searching fire Which doth ascend the engine of my braine. **1667** BOYLE *Orig. Formes & Qual.* 4 Those curious and elaborate Engines, the bodies of living Creatures. **1697–8** WATTS *Reliq. Juv.* (1789) 180 Our Sovereign Creator formed our souls, and sent them to inhabit these two engines of flesh. **1842** TENNYSON *Two Voices* 347 No life is found..only to one engine bound.

c. *spec.* (*a*) Short for *beer-engine, fire-engine, garden-engine*, etc. †(*b*) = *engine-loom*: see 11. †(*c*) See quot. 1696.

In 18th c. and still later the word *engine*, when used *spec.* without defining word or contextual indication, usually meant 'fire-engine'.

1645 PAGITT *Heresiogr.* (1647) B iij b, Your Engines to cast water upon the houses. **1670** TRIGG in Bedloe *Popish Plot* (1679) 23 This Fire was most mischievously designed, as being in a place where no Engine could come. **1696** *Phil. Trans.* XIX. 345 Some [Mills] go with Sails, and serve also to Dreyn the Fens, and are called Engines. **1725** *Lond. Gaz.* No. 6364/3 By Trade a Silk-Weaver on the Engine. **1779** JOHNSON in *Boswell* III. 234 The engines will soon extinguish the fire. **1796** C. MARSHALL *Garden.* iv. (1813) 54 An engine to water the leaves of vines and all other wall trees. **1798** CAPT. MILLER in Nicolas *Disp. Nelson* (1846) VII. Introd. 156 A boat that was taking in a hawser..I filled with fire-buckets..and was putting the engine in another. **1844** W. H. MAXWELL *Sports & Adv. Scotl.* viii. (1855) 87 'Him wot was drawin' at the engine, as you passed the bar.'

8. = STEAM-ENGINE. (This was for long the prevailing sense, and often influenced the later use of the word in other senses.) Often with defining word, as ***locomotive-***, ***marine***, ***pumping***, ***railway engine***.

1816 *Encycl. Perthensis* XXI. 384 In consequence of the great superiority of Mr. Watt's engines..they have become of most extensive use. **1838** F. W. SIMMS *Public Wks. Gt. Brit.* 69 The adhesion of the wheels of an engine upon the rails was sufficient to effect its progression. **1852** CLOUGH *Songs in Absence* I. 2 His iron might the potent engine plies. **1856** EMERSON *Eng. Traits, Manners* Wks. (Bohn) II. 46 Little is left for the men but to mind the engines, and feed the furnaces. **1869** *Eng. Mech.* 26 Mar. 5/2 The goods engines were moderate in weight. **1878** F. WILLIAMS *Midl. Railw.* 654 A good engine-man takes a pride now in his engine.

9. Applied to various other machines analogous to the steam-engine; *i.e.* to machines including in themselves the means of generating power. Now esp., an internal-combustion engine, such as the motor of a road vehicle.

10. *fig.* (Chiefly after sense 4.) †**a.** Of a person: An agent, instrument, tool. *Obs.*

1568 GRAFTON *Chron.* II. 610 He was..the very organ, engine, and deviser of the destruction of Humfrey the good Duke of Gloucester. **1672** MARVELL *Reh. Transp.* I. 92 That Politick Engine who..was employed..as a Missionary amongst the Nonconformists. **1713** STEELE *Englishm.* No. 54. 344 Sir Francis Walsingham..was one of the great Engines of State. **1767** BLACKSTONE *Comm.* II. 69 Empson and Dudley, the wicked engines of Henry VII.

b. Of a thing: An instrument, means, organ.

1590 GREENE *Fr. Bacon* (1630) 56 Now farewell world, the engin of all woe. **1650** MAJOR-GEN. HARRISON in Ellis *Orig. Lett.* II. 297 III. 354, I thinke Faith and Praier must bee the cheife engines. **1664** POWER *Exp. Philos.* I. 68 The Animal Spirits..are the chief Engine of Sight. **1762** J. BROWN *Poetry & Mus.* vii. (1763) 147 The Exhibition of Plays and Shews was one of the very Engines of Corruption. **1789** BENTHAM *Princ. Legisl.* xviii. §18 The State has two great engines, punishment and reward. **1855** PRESCOTT *Philip II*, I. II. ix. 244 Never..had the press been turned into an engine of such political importance. **1871** BLACKIE *Four Phases* i. 73 Logical analysis, the characteristic engine of Socrates.

11. *attrib.* and *Comb.*: **a.** attrib. (chiefly in sense 8), as ***engine-box***, ***-funnel***, ***-furnace***, ***-hose***, ***-house***, ***-pump***, ***-room***, ***-shaft***, ***-wheel***, ***-work***; **b.** objective with vbl. sb. or agent-noun, as ***engine-†artificer***, ***-construction***, ***-driver***, ***-maker***, ***-tender***, ***-tenter***, ***-wright***; ***engine-less***, ***-like*** adjs.; also **engine-bearer** (see quot.); **engine-bell**, (*a*) a device for internal communication on a ship; (*b*) a bell rung as a warning on a railway train; **engine-lathe**, a lathe worked by machinery; †**engine-loom**, one in which the shuttle was driven by a mechanical contrivance, instead of being thrown by hand; **engine-pit**, (*a*) a pit for an engine; (*b*) a trough in the ground or floor constructed to allow a mechanic to work on the underside of a machine (esp. a vehicle); (*c*) (see quot. 1940); **engine-sized (paper)**, sized by a machine, not by hand in separate sheets; hence **engine-sizing**, the process of coating paper fibres in a beating machine with size or resin-mixture; the size itself; **engine-turned**, ornamented with engine-turning; also *fig.*; **engine-turner**, one who performs engine-turning; **engine-turning**, the engraving of symmetrical patterns upon metals by machinery.

1647 HAWARD *Crown Rev.* 21 *Engine Artificer: Fee *per diem* 4*d.* **1867** SMYTH *Sailor's Word-bk.*, *Engine-bearers, sleepers, or pieces of timber placed between the keelson, in a steamer, and the boilers of the steam-engine, to form a proper seat for the boilers and machinery. **1845** *Knickerbocker* XXV. 59 The short, sharp ring of our *engine-bell was heard. **1846–7** THOREAU *Walden* (1957) 145 When the engine bell rings. **1880** *Contemp. Rev.* Feb. 250 As if tired pedestrians should mount the *engine-box of headlong trains. **1887** *Athenæum* 8 Oct. 463/3 The gradual improvement in *engine construction. **1828** F. A. KEMBLE *Let.* Nov. in *Rec. Later Life* (1882) I. 180 *Engine drivers, and persons connected with the railroads and coaches. **1878** JEVONS *Prim. Pol. Econ.* 66 Enginedrivers and guards in America sometimes strike when a train is halfway on its journey. **1849** F. B. HEAD *Stokers & Pokers* iii. (1851) 43 The reeking *engine-funnel of an up-train is seen darting out of the tunnel. **1838** *Knickerbocker* XII. 373 A small *engine-hose..coiled up like a huge snake on the deck. **1825** HONE *Every-Day Bk.* I. 1217 An *engine-house, belonging to the Hope Fire Assurance Company. **1840** F. WHISHAW *Railways of Gt. Brit. & Irel.* 4 The carriage-house and engine-house. **1832** G. PORTER *Porcelain & Gl.* 49 A milled edge is given to earthenware in what is called an *engine lathe. **1885** *Pall Mall G.* 13 May 11/2 By me swept the trim, *engineless, and almost silent railway carriage, driven by an invisible electro motor. **1674** FAIRFAX *Bulk & Selv.* 136 A sort of mechanical or *engine-like twitchings. **1676** SHADWELL *Virtuoso* v. i, He that invented the *Engine-Loom. **1591** PERCIVALL *Sp. Dict.*, *Enginero*, an *engine maker, *machinarius.* **1839** R. S. ROBINSON *Naut. Steam Eng.* 150 The power of an engine..is estimated differently by different engine makers. **1839** URE *Dict. Arts* II. 970 In every winning of coal, the shape of the *engine-pit deserves much consideration. **1853** J. A. BEIL *Technol. Wörterbuch* 365/2 The engine pit (the pit in which the engine works), *der Maschinenschaft*, puits pour la machine. [**1883** *Encycl. Brit.* XX. 237/2 Between the rails of each radiating line a pit is constructed to afford access below the engines for inspection.] **1886** *Proc. Inst. Civil Engineers* LXXXVII. 392 The engine-pits are 2 feet 7 inches deep, 3 feet 10 inches wide, and extend the full length of the roads. **1904** GOODCHILD & TWENEY *Technol. & Sci. Dict.* 201/1 *Engine pit*, a depression or pit into which a man can get to examine the lower parts of a locomotive, motor car, etc. **1940** *Chambers's Techn. Dict.* 298/2 *Engine pit*..an engine sump or crank pit; the box-like lower part of the crank-case. **1838** DICKENS *O. Twist* xlviii, The clanking of the *engine-pumps. **1839** R. S. ROBINSON *Naut. Steam Eng.* Introd. 8 We go into *engine rooms. **1807** CARNE *Realistian Tin Mine* in *Phil. Trans.* XCVII. 293 The *engine shaft..is situated 8 fathoms north of the widest part of the lode. **1880** J. DUNBAR *Pract. Papermaker* 29 *Engine-sized papers. **1911** *Encycl. Brit.* XX. 732/1 Some form of animal or vegetable size or glue ..mixed with the pulp in the beating engine... Known as '*engine-sizing'..filling up the interstices of the fibres with a chemical precipitate. **1954** J. SOUTHWARD *Mod. Printing* (ed. 7) II. xlii. 443 Engine sizing—a soap consisting of resin and alum, colouring matter, [etc.]. **1825** J. NICHOLSON *Operat. Mechanic* 671 Valves, placed out of the reach of the operative engineer, or *engine tender. **1870** *Daily News* 22 Apr., Intimation was given to the *engine-tenter that they wished to be lowered down. **1765** J. WEDGWOOD *Let.* 6 July (1965) 35, I intend sending two setts of Vases, Creamcolour, *engine-turned. **1844** DICKENS *Mart. Chuz.* xiii, A gold hunting-watch..engine-turned. **1858** O. W. HOLMES *Aut. Breakf. T., Self-made Men*, Your self-made man..deserves more credit..than the..engine-turned article. **1879** *Print. Trades Jrnl.* XXVIII. 12 Pencil-cases elaborately engine-turned. **1769** J. WEDGWOOD *Let.* 19 Nov. 84 We have not one *Engine Turner left Here now. **1909** *Westm. Gaz.* 7 Jan. 5/2 The engine-turner who used the wonderful 'rose engine' to engrave the background. **1764** J. WEDGWOOD *Let.* 28 May (1965) 27, I..have sent you a semple of one hobby horse (*Engine turning). **1884** F. BRITTEN *Watch & Clockm.* 102 Engine turning..the wavy circular curves cut into the outside of watch cases for decoration. **1873** *St. Paul's Mag.* Mar. 266 The *engine-wheels could not bite. **1609** HOLLAND *Amm. Marcel.* 127 (R.) They would not lend their helping hand to any man in *engine-worke. **1862** SMILES *Engineers* III. 55 George Stephenson was, in 1812, appointed *engine-wright of the colliery.

engine ('ɛndʒɪn), *v.* [orig. a. OF. *engin-ier*, *engyner*, corresp. to Pr. *engenhar*, OSp. *engeñar*, Pg. *engenhar*, It. *ingegnare*:—med.L. *ingeniāre*, f. *ingenium*: see prec.; in later use f. ENGINE *sb.*]

†**1.** *trans.* To contrive, plan, either in a material or an immaterial sense. Also *absol.* with inf. of purpose. ***to engine together***: to frame or fit together by art. *Obs.*

1377 LANGL. *P. Pl.* B. XVIII. 250 For gygas þe geaunt · with a gynne engyned To breke & to bete doune · þat ben aȝeines ihesus. **1393** GOWER *Conf.* I. 79 With fair beheste and yeftes grete Of gold, that they hem have engined Togider. **1413** LYDG. *Pilgr. Sowle* II. li. (1859) 54 The synne that thou hast done was..not by very malyce engyned of withynne. *c* **1570** THYNNE *Pride & Lowl.* (1841) 10 With golden lace ful craftely engined. **1609** BP. BARLOW *Answ. Nameless Catholic* 198 The most horrible designe..that euer was engined. **1611** FLORIO, *Aggegnare*, to frame..to engine together.

†**2.** To take by craft; to ensnare, deceive. *Obs.*

c **1325** *Body & Soul* in *Map's Poems* 249 (M.) Ho may more trayson do, or is loverd betere engine Than he that al is trist is to. **1340** *Ayenb.* 122 Alle þo..þet habbeþ..þe herten engined ine þe dyevles nette. **1393** GOWER *Conf.* I. 71 A softe bedde..Where she was afterward engined. *c* **1400** *Beryn* 1501 His tung he gan to whet Sotilly to engyne hym.

3. †**a.** To put on the rack; to torture. †**b.** To assault with engines. **c.** *nonce-use.* To find engines or instruments for.

c **1386** CHAUCER *Nun's Priest's T.* 240 The mynistres of that toun..the hostiller sore engyned. **1613** T. ADAMS *Pract. Wks.* (1861) I. 29 (D.) We fear not..professed enemies to engine and batter our walls. **1820** KEATS *Hyperion* II. 161 Tell me..How we can war, how engine our great wrath!

4. To fit up (a vessel) with steam engines.

1868 *Express* 20 May, The Victoria, iron-clad frigate.. engined by Messrs. John Penn and Son. **1872** *Daily News* 5 Sept., Build the largest ironclad ships, engine them. **1882** *W. Hedley* 36 On December 3rd [1881] the first vessel built, engined, and masted above Newcastle, passed down the river.

engineer (ɛndʒɪ'nɪə(r)), *sb.* Forms: α. 4 engyn(e)our, 6 yngynore, ingenor. β. 6–7 en-, inginer, -are, engyner, ingener. γ. 7 en-, ingenier(e, -ir, ingeneer(e, en-, inginier, ingineer, 7– engineer. [ME. *engyneour*, a. OF. *engigneor* (for which mod.F. has the semi-learned form *ingénieur*, perh. influenced by It.), corresp. to Pr. *enginhador*:—late L. *ingeniātōrem*, f. *ingeniāre*: see prec. In 16th c. the word assumed the form *en-*, *inginer*, as if f. ENGINE *v.* + -ER (a derivation which yields the same sense as the Romanic word). Early in 17th c. appear the forms in *-ier(e, -eer.* The precise origin of these is uncertain; they may be ad. Fr. *ingénieur*, or perh. ad. It. *ingegniere*, which is a distinct word = Sp. *engeñero* (Minsheu), Pg. *engenheiro*, OF. *engignier* (Cotgr. *enginier*):—L. type **ingeniārius*, f. *ingenium* (see ENGINE *sb.*); on the other hand they may be f. ENGINE *sb.* + *-ier*, *-eer*, this suffix having in 16th c. already become familiar in military words of Romanic origin.]

†**1.** One who contrives, designs, or invents; an author, designer (const. *of*); also *absol.* an inventor, a plotter, a layer of snares. *Obs.* In the later quots. perh. a *fig.* use of 2.

α. *c* **1420** *Metr. Life St. Kath.* (Halliw.) 14 In hys court was a false traytoure, That was a grete Yngynore.

β. **1592** G. HARVEY *Pierce's Super.* 8 The dreadfull enginer of phrases insteede of thunderboltes. **1602** CAREW *Cornwall* 99 a, The Inginer of this practise..was a Portugall. **1605** B. JONSON *Sejanus* I. i, No, Silius, we are no good inginers. **1611** RICH *Honest. Age* (1844) 36 Yet you cannot deny them to be the deuil's enginers.

γ. *a* **1635** R. SIBBES in Spurgeon *Treas. Dav.* Ps. ix. 15 That great engineer, Satan. *a* **1680** BUTLER *Rem.* (1759) I. 300 Certainly these are the most prime Engineers of Oaths, that ever the World knew. **1702** SWIFT *Wks.* (1841) II. 478 The engineers of this bill [a bill before the House of Commons] thought they had obtained a great advantage against me.

2. †**a.** A constructor of military engines (*obs.*) [So L. *ingeniator* in Pipe Rolls 12th c.] **b.** One who designs and constructs military works for attack or defence; also *fig.* Also in *comb.*, as †***engineer-general***.

α. *c* **1325** *Coer de L.* 1387 A tour ful strong, That queyntyly engynours made. *c* **1380** *Sir Ferumb.* 3223 Þe Amyral made

his engyneour; þe engyns to sette & bende. **1607** Norden *Surv. Dial.* 189 M. William Englebert, an excellent Ingenor.

β. **1579** Digges *Stratiot.* 144 Expert Enginers and menne of excellente knouledge in the art of Fortification. **1583** T. Stocker *Hist. Civile Warres Low Countries* I. 50b, The buylder and Engyner whereof [of the Castle of Antwerpe] was one Pachiotto. **1600** Holland *Livy* xxiv. xxxiv. 532 But a more wonderful enginer for devising and framing of artillerie, ordinance, fabrickes, and instruments of warre. **1602** Shaks. *Ham.* iii. iv. 206 (Globe), For 'tis the sport to have the enginer Hoist with his own petar. **1631** Weever *Anc. Fun. Mon.* 591 Sir William Heydon..a valiant Souldier, and an expert Enginer.

γ. **1551** Edw. VI *Jrnl.* (1858) II. 369 Baron de la Garde had seene it [Portesmouth castell] having an ingenir with him, and, as it was thought, had the platte of it. **1627** Drayton *Agincourt* 8 The Engineer prouiding the Petar To breake the strong Percullice. **1637** Blount *Voy. into Levant* 31 The Gran Master and a chiefe Engeniere. **1638** Suckling *'Tis now, since, etc.* (R.), My tongue was engineer; I thought to undermine the heart By wispering in the ear. **1653** Holcroft *Procopius* II. 49 By the advise of Theodorus, a famous Ingineer. **1686** *Lond. Gaz.* No. 2023/4 Major Martin Beckman, His Majesties chief Ingenier. **1707** Farquhar *Beaux' Strat.* v. ii, Rise thou prostrate Ingineer, not all thy undermining Skill shall reach my Heart. **1710** *Lond. Gaz.* No. 4706/2 Mr. Secretary Addison and the Engineer-General informed the Committee. **1759** in Picton *L'pool Munic. Rec.* (1886) II. 150 Captain More one of His Majesty's Engineers. **1813** Wellington in Gurw. *Disp.* XI. 29, I hope that he will be able to send an engineer to undertake [the works]. **1866** Kingsley *Herew.* xviii. 231 She began praising his skill as an engineer.

c. A soldier belonging to the division of the army called *Engineers*, composed of men trained to engineering work. Also *attrib.*, as in *engineer-officer, -regiment, -warrant.*

1787 *Lond. Gaz.* 24–28 Apr. No. 12850 p. 197 The Corps of Engineers shall in future take the name of the Corps of Royal Engineers. **1794** Burke *Sp. agst. W. Hastings* Wks. XV. 63 Colonels of artillery and engineers. **1810** Wellington in Gurw. *Disp.* VI. 81 An army composed of divisions..artillery, engineers, etc., complete. **1889** Gen. Porter *Hist. Royal Engineers* 143 This day [26 May 1716] may therefore be taken as that on which the Engineer branch of the British army blossomed into a distinct Corps.

3. One whose profession is the designing and constructing of works of public utility, such as bridges, roads, canals, railways, harbours, drainage works, gas and water works, etc. From 18th c. also *civil engineer*, for distinction from 2b.

Not in Johnson 1755 or Todd 1818; the former has only the military senses, to which the latter adds 'a maker of engines', citing Bullokar. In the early quots. the persons referred to were probably by profession military engineers, though the works mentioned were of a 'civil' character. Since 2b has ceased to be a prominent sense of *engineer*, the term 'civil engineer' has lost its original antithetic force; but it continues to be the ordinary designation of the profession to which it was first applied, distinguishing it from that of 'mechanical engineer' (sense 4). Other phraseological combinations, as *electric* (now usu. *electrical*), *gas, mining, railway, telegraph engineer*, are used to designate those who devote themselves to special departments of engineering.

1606 Holland *Sueton.* 249 An Enginer also..promised to bring into the Capitoll huge Columnes with small charges. **1680** *Lond. Gaz.* No. 1547/1 A new Port at Nizza..A famous French Ingenier..has been consulted about it. *a* **1792** Smeaton *Reports* (1797) I. Pref. 7 The first meeting of this new institution, the Society of civil engineers, was held on the 15th of April 1793. **1793** —— *Edystone L.* Introd. 8 My profession of a civil Engineer. *Ibid.* §101 The engineer and his deputy. **1836** *Hull & Selby Railw. Act* 102 A civil engineer of eminence. **1861** *Sat. Rev.* 14 Dec. 615 Sir Hugh Myddleton, the enterprising goldsmith, has been called the first English engineer. **1880** Haughton *Phys. Geog.* v. 228 Without much assistance from engineers, they will make a network of natural navigable channels.

4. A contriver or maker of 'engines'. The precise sense has varied from time to time in accordance with the development of meaning in engine *sb.*; in present use the *engineer* in this sense (specifically *mechanical engineer*) is a maker of steam engines or of heavy machinery generally.

In this sense (but not in 3) the term is applied to the working artisan as well as to the employer of labour.

β. **1575** Laneham *Lett.* (1871) 45 Painterz, Karuerz, Players, Engyners. **1589** Puttenham *Eng. Poesie* I. viii. (Arb.) 34 There could be no politique Captaine, nor any witty enginer or cunning artificer. **1598** Florio, *Macanopoietico*, an inginer, an engine-maker.

γ. *a* **1628** F. Greville *Sidney* (1652) 40 A skilful Engenier, an excellent Musician, or any other Artificer of extraordinary fame. **1654** Bate *Myst. Nat. & Art* 72 According to the fancy and invencion of the artist or Engineer. **1691** T. H[ale] *Acc. New Invent.* p. liv., This Engine was invented by..an excellent Engineer. **1734** Desaguliers *Course Nat. Philos.* I. 69 The skill of a good engineer may be advantageously applied in changing the form or altering the parts and motions of a machine. **1747** R. Campbell *Lond. Tradesman* 248 By engineer I..mean..the tradesman who is employed in making engines for raising of water, etc. **1831** Sir J. Sinclair *Corr.* II. 62 This celebrated engineer [Robert Fulton] does great credit to the talents of America. **1887** *Pall Mall G.* 29 Nov. 11/1 The payment of 'tips' ranging from ten to twenty shillings to working engineers and others.

5. One who manages an 'engine' or engines.

†**a.** One who manages engines of war; an artilleryman. *Obs.*

1600 Heywood *Edw. IV*, II. Wks. 1874 I. 101 It was not you, At whom the fatall enginer did aime. **1633** G. Herbert *Temple, Ch.-Porch* xli, Wit's an unruly engine, wildly striking Sometimes a friend, sometimes the engineer. *a* **1659** Cleveland *Lond. Lady* 46 Like the Death-darting Cockatrice (that slye Close Engineer) that murders through the Eye. *a* **1719** Addison (J.), An author, who points his satire at a great man, is like the engineer who signalized himself by this ungenerous practice. **1800** *Naval Chron.* III. 287 In which are included sailors, marines, and the engineers.

b. *Mod.* One who has charge of a steam-engine; in England only with reference to marine engines; in U.S. often applied to the driver of a locomotive engine.

1832 *Amer. Railroad Jrnl.* I. 356/2 Engineers and attendants on the Engine. **1839** R. S. Robinson *Naut. Steam Eng.* 174, I am not able to speak of the engineers in Her Majesty's ships. **1856** Emerson *Eng. Traits, Wealth* Wks. (Bohn) II. 75 Steam, from the first..was dreadful with its explosion..engineers and firemen..have been sacrificed in learning to tame and guide the monster. **1860** Bartlett *Dict. Amer., Engineer*, the engine-driver on our railroads is thus magniloquently designated. **1946** *Chicago Daily News* 10 July 11/2 The engineer was killed and several passengers shaken up.

6. (With defining word, as ***human engineer, spiritual engineer***), one who is claimed to possess specialized knowledge, esp. as regards the treating of human problems by scientific or technical means.

1931 J. C. Richey (*title*) The social engineer. **1936** Mencken *Amer. Lang.* (ed. 4) vi. vi. 290 *The Engineering News-Record* also discovered..a socio-religious e[ngineer] (an uplifter), a social-e[ngineer] (the same),..a human-e[ngineer] (another variety of psycho-analyst).

engineer (ɛndʒɪˈnɪə(r)), *v.* [f. prec. sb.]

1. *intr.* To act as an engineer.

1681 [see engineering *ppl. a.*]. **1769** J. Watt *Lett. Dr. Small*, Our present magistracy..have employed me in engineering for them. **1870** Emerson *Soc. & Solit.* vii. 131 What of the grand tools with which we engineer, like kobolds and enchanters.

2. a. *trans.* To employ the art of the engineer upon; to construct or manage as an engineer.

1843 Vignoles *Life C. B. Vignoles* (1889) 294 The..road magnificently engineered through the pass. **1848** *Tait's Mag.* XV. 428 The drainage..had been engineered to admiration. **1856** Olmstead *Slave States* ix. 546 The roads are admirably engineered and constructed. **1888** *Pall Mall G.* 19 Sept. 5/1 Mr. Baker..with Sir John Fowler, engineers the undertaking [the Forth Bridge].

b. *fig.* To arrange, contrive, plan, superintend. Also (*U.S.*), to guide or carry through a measure or enterprise; to manœuvre, (occas.) to 'shepherd'.

1864 *Daily Tel.* 7 July, The lobbying or engineering a bill through the Legislature. **1865** S. S. Cox *Eight Yrs. Congress* 99 When he..undertakes to engineer a resolution through this House for the expulsion of a brother member, [etc.]. **1873** W. S. Mayo *Never Again* vii. 99 With good looks, a good voice,..and Mr. Boggs to engineer matters for her. **1882** Jay Gould in *Standard* 28 Dec. 6/5 The corner in grain engineered by parties in Chicago. **1883** *American* VII. 24 An exhibition engineered by a native prince. **1889** *Sat. Rev.* 16 Mar. 299/2 The jealousies and interests of workmen against employers are engineered remorselessly by professional wirepullers. **1890** *Fortn. Rev.* May 716 To 'engineer' a party..throughout a holiday expedition in a foreign country is an arduous..undertaking. **1959** *Daily Tel.* 28 July 1/1 The late debate had been engineered by the Opposition.

3. *fig. nonce-use.* To assail laboriously (*humorous*).

1781 Cowper *Let.* in Wks. (1837) XV. 64 Unless we engineered him with question after question we could get nothing out of him.

Hence **engiˈneered** *ppl. a.*; **engiˈneering** *ppl. a.*, that engineers, contriving, scheming.

1872 *Daily News* 3 Sept., From the safe ledge of a cleverly engineered road. **1681** N. N. *Rome's Follies* 26 Since I have begun to set my engineering brains to work.

engineering (ɛndʒɪˈnɪərɪŋ), *vbl. sb.* [f. prec. + -ing¹.]

1. a. The action of the verb engineer; the work done by, or the profession of, an engineer. **b.** The art and science of the engineer's profession.

Often used with defining words, as in *civil, mechanical, military engineering; agricultural, electric, gas, hydraulic, railway, sanitary, telegraph engineering*; see engineer *sb.* 2–4. *chemical, electrical, human, social engineering*: see the first elements.

1720 De Foe *Capt. Singleton* xv. (1840) 262 This [a contrivance in defensive warfare] is..the cunningest piece of Indian engineering. **1829** C. Welch *Wesl. Polity* 172 A Sunday School Teacher's labour is not much unlike civil engineering. **1840** *Civil. Eng. & Archit. Journ.* 59 There is room for..a school of Engineering on sound principles. **1858** Greener *Gunnery* 267 That portion of engineering which would define what power of engine would work a thousand cotton spindles. **1866** *Engineering* 5 Jan. 1 The title of this journal has been chosen..as typifying the business, art, and profession of the Engineer. **1873** Tristram *Moab* xiv. 270 An ancient roadway of which the engineering..could be easily traced. **1879** *Cassell's Techn. Educ.* I. 29 Civil Engineering is the term applied to that science which treats of the construction of canals, railroads, roads, bridges..aqueducts and such like. **1887** *Daily News* 24 Oct. 2/5. Shipbuilding and marine engineering have lately been doing better.

c. *fig.* Contriving, manœuvring.

1780 Cowper *Progr. Err.* 321 With some cold moral think to quench the fire; Though all your engineering proves in vain. **1884** *St. James's Gaz.* 21 Mar. 3/2 Party engineering and the trickery of elections.

2. *attrib.* ***engineering geology, shop, yard.*** Also **engineering science**, engineering regarded as a field of study, esp. that part of it which can be treated according to the laws of mathematics and the physical sciences; used esp. as the name of a department in places of higher education.

1792 Burke *Consid. Pres. St. Affairs* Wks. VII. 93 One arm is extremely good, the engineering and artillery branch. **1865** Brande *Dict. Sci.* (ed. 2) I. 779/2 Engineering geology. **1961** J. Challinor *Dict. Geol.* 68/1 *Engineering geology*, geology applied to engineering, including building construction. **1884** *Athenæum* 27 Sept. 397/3 The military and engineering policy of the rulers of the kingdom. **1901** *Engineering* 6 Sept. 331/2 The policy of the University [of Glasgow]..is to offer to students a course of study in engineering science, and to leave them to acquire their experience and practice in the office or in the workshop. **1907** *Oxf. Univ. Gaz.* 15 Oct. 68/1 The above Statute proposes to establish a Professorship of Engineering Science... The Professor will give Laboratory—but not Workshop—Instruction. **1911** *Engineering* 7 July 40/3 The classification and analysis of the phenomena presented to the engineer in the practice of his art conveniently called 'Engineering Science', occupies a position intermediate between biology..and physics... It is founded on the laws of motion, of heat, and of electricity, whose action is investigated in the physical laboratory; but it is concerned with the working of these laws under conditions comparable in their complexity with those under which the same laws work in living things. **1930** *Ibid.* 24 Jan. 98/3 His laboratory ..was used to enlarge the boundaries of engineering science. **1919** *Brit. Manufacturer* Nov. 24/1 Engineering shops. **1822** Byron *Juan* vii. xi, Excuse this engineering slang. **1739** Labelye *Westm. Br.* v, Very great masters in the Building or Engineering Way. **1758** Warburton *Div. Legat.* Pref. (R.), The Roman Conclave succeeded to the Roman Senate in this engineering work. **1919** *Brit. Manufacturer* Nov. 24/2 Engineering yards.

engineership (ɛndʒɪˈnɪəʃɪp). [f. engineer *sb.* + -ship.] **a.** The business, or occupation, of an engineer. **b.** The office, or position, of an engineer.

1649 Blithe *Eng. Improv. Impr.* (1653) To Rdr., Their pretences of great abilities in Engineership. **1661** Earl Orrery *State Letters* (1743) I. 62, I..pretend something to engineership. **1883** Nasmyth *Autobiog.* xvi. 288 The railway had been constructed under the engineership of Major Whistler. **1889** *Illust. Lond. News* 23 Feb. 242/3 Mr. Hawksley retired from the joint engineership.

†**engiˈneery.** *Obs. rare.* [f. engineer *sb.* + -y.] Used by Smeaton for 'the science of engineering'. Cf. enginery.

1793 Smeaton *Edystone L.* §39 Mr. Rudyerd's method.. of keying and securing, must be considered as a material accession to the practical part of Engineery. *Ibid.* §40 The great principle of Engineery, that weight is the most naturally and effectually resisted by weight.

†**ˈengineful,** *a. Obs. rare*⁻¹. [f. engine *sb.* + -ful.] Full of ingenuity, ingenious.

c **1300** *K. Alis.* 4869 Hy ben..gode, and engyneful to fighth.

engineman (ˈɛndʒɪnmən). [f. engine *sb.* + man.] **a.** One who works, or helps to work, a fire-engine. **b.** One who attends to a stationary steam-engine. **c.** The driver of a locomotive.

1835 Parsons *Tourist's Comp.* 243 No gratuity is allowed to be taken by any guard, engineman, porter, etc. **1852** Hawthorne *Blithedale Rom.* xxii. (1885) 171 A fire.. brought out the engine-men. **1859** Smiles *Self-Help* iv. 81 Stephenson taught himself arithmetic and mensuration while working as an engineman. **1871** M. Collins *Mrq. & Merch.* viii. 261 He saw..only the guards and enginemen.

enginery (ˈɛndʒɪnərɪ, -nrɪ). Forms: 7 en-, inginarie, 7–8 enginry, 7– **enginery.** [f. engine *sb.* + -(e)ry; cf. It. *ingegneria* (which may be the source), OF. *engignerie.*]

†**1.** The art of constructing 'engines' (cf. senses of engine *sb.*); also, the art of the (military) engineer. Also *attrib. Obs.*

1605 Bacon *Adv. Learn.* II. viii. §2 Astronomie, Cosmographie, Architecture, Inginarie and diuers others. [The corresponding passage *De Augm.* III. vi. has *machinaria.*] **1610** W. Folkingham *Art of Survey* I. ix. 20 Some Enginarie aide must bee assistant to mount the water by Screwes, Pullies, Poizes. **1644** Howell *Engl. Teares* in *Harl. Misc.* (Malh) V. 444 Nor can all thy elaborate circumvallations, and trenches, or any art of enginery, keep him [famine] out of thy line of communication. **1672** Petty *Pol. Anat.* (1691) 25 The Irish..had [no] Architecture, Enginery, Painting, Carving, nor any kind of Manufacture.

2. Engines collectively; apparatus, machinery. Frequent in *fig.* use.

1742 Young *Nt. Th.* vi. 261 A feeble Aid! Dedalian Engin'ry. **1774** Johnson *Diary* 20 Sept. in *Boswell* xlvi, Boulton..led us through his shops—I could not distinctly see his enginery. *c* **1840** Thirlwall in *Rem.* (1878) III. 1 The enginery of war is often brought out. **1851** Tennyson *Ode Internat. Exhib.* iii. 6 Harvest-tool and husbandry, Loom and wheel and enginery. **1862** Dana *Man. Geol.* 747 An animal is a self-propagating piece of enginery.

fig. *a* **1763** Shenstone *Economy* Wks. (1764) I. 320 The fraudful engin'ry of Rome. **1844** R. Chambers *Vest. Creat., Early Hist. Man*, A complete social enginery for the securing of life and property.

b. *esp.* Engines of war, artillery. Chiefly *poet.* or *rhetorical.* Also *fig.*

1641 Milton *Ch. Discip.* II. (1851) 54 The impregnable situation of our Liberty and Safety, that laught such weake enginry to scorn. **1667** —— *P.L.* vi. 553 In hollow Cube Training his devilish Enginrie. **1708** J. Philips *Cyder* (1807) 57 The loud disploded roar Of brazen enginry. **1764** Grainger *Sugar Cane* II. 322 Not all the brazen engineries of man, At once exploded, the wild burst surpass. **1839**

THIRLWALL *Greece* VI. xlix. 162 His enginery soon made a breach in the wall.

3. The work of an engine, the application of engine-power. Also *fig.*

1804 *Ann. Rev.* II. 370 The article..incurs a smaller charge for the wages of enginery.

fig. **1838** STERLING in Carlyle *Life* II. vii. (1872) 146 A few drawings,—all with the stamp of his [Michael Angelo's] enginery upon them.

†**'enginist.** *Obs.* [f. ENGINE + -IST.] = ENGINEER *sb.*

1579 FENTON *Guicciard.* (1618) 35 The great fame of Archimedes and other notable enginists. *Ibid.* 185 The Pisans..had..certain enginists to dresse their fortifications.

†**'enginous,** *a. Obs.* Also 4 engynous. [a. OF. *engineus, engigneus, engignos,* corresp. to Pr. *enginhos,* OSp. *engeñoso,* It. *ingegnoso*:—L. *ingeniōsus,* f. *ingenium*: see ENGINE *sb.*]

1. Clever, crafty, cunning; deceitful.

c **1325** *Coer de L.* 3945 Thomas, a knyghte engynous, Wente with hys host to Orlyons. **1393** GOWER *Conf.* III. 99 It [coler] maketh a man ben enginous. **1599** B. JONSON *Cynthia's Rev.* III. ii, For that's the mark of all their enginous drifts, To wound my patience. **1615** CHAPMAN *Odyss.* I. 452 Open force, or projects enginous.

2. Of or belonging to an engine; partaking of the nature of an engine. *lit.* and *fig.*

1606 DEKKER *Sev. Sinnes* IV. (Arb.) 30 For all the Enginous Wheeles of the Soule are continually going. **1630** B. JONSON *New Inn* II. ii, *Lady F.* Sure, petards To blow us up. *Lord L.* Some enginous strong words.

engird (ɛn'gɜːd), *v.* Also 7 ingird. Pa. pple. engirt. [f. EN-[1] + GIRD *v.*] *trans.* To surround with, or as with, a girdle; to encircle, as a girdle does. Also, *to engird in.*

1566 GASCOIGNE *Iocasta* ii, in Child *Four Old P.* (1848) 190 Let cruell discorde beare thee companie, Engirt with snakes. **1623** FAVINE *Theat. Hon.* I. i. 7 Round about engirt with a frindge of Gold. **1628** HOBBES *Thucyd.* (1822) 139 Paches..arrived at Mitylene and ingirt it with a single wall. **1745** W. THOMPSON *Sickness* II. (R.), She saw him smile along the tissu'd clouds..Engirt with cherub wings. *a* **1785** GLOVER *Athenaid* xxvii. (R.), A sash of tincture bright..Engirds his loins. **1813** WORDSW. *View fr. Top of Black Comb,* Main ocean..visibly engirding Mona's Isle. **1820** MOIR in *Blackw. Mag.* VI. 385 The hoary mountain tops..that engird the horizon in. **1851** NICHOL *Archit. Heav.* 22 He would manifestly be engirt by heavens having the general aspect of ours.

b. *fig.*

1586 MARLOWE *1st Pt. Tamburl.* v. ii, Ugly Darkness..Engirt with tempests, wrapt in pitchy clouds. **1593** SHAKS. *2 Hen. VI,* III. i. 200 My Body round engyrt with miserie. **1798** W. TAYLOR in Robberds' *Mem.* I. 219 Engird their brows With glittering crowns of praise.

Hence **en'girding** *ppl. a.*

1852 D. MOIR *Defeat Winter* viii, Love, with an engirding belt, Hath beautified the solitude.

engirdle (ɛn'gɜːd(ə)l), *v.* Also 7 ingirdle. [f. EN-[1] + GIRDLE.] *trans.* To surround with, or as with, a girdle; to serve as a girdle or enclosure to; to encompass. Also *fig.*

1602 DAVISON in Farr *S.P. Eliz.* (1845) II. 325 As mountaines great on euery side Engirdle faire Jerusalem. **1621** LADY M. WROTH *Urania* 225 He was ingirdled with his enemies. **1785** GLOVER *On Sir Isaac Newton,* Comets..with hideous grasp the skies engirdle round. **1830** J. WILSON in *Blackw. Mag.* XXVII. 665 A metropolitan city..engirdled with groves. **1852** MISS YONGE *Cameos* (1877) II. ix. 111 To die engirdled by the cord of St. Francis was the sure means of safety.

en'girdling, *vbl. sb.* [f. prec. + -ING[1].] The action of prec. vb.; *concr.* that which engirdles.

1598 FLORIO, *Cingolo,* a girdle or a garter, an engirdling.

engirdling (ɛn'gɜːdlɪŋ), *ppl. a.* [f. as prec. + -ING[2].] That engirdles, surrounds, encloses.

1855 MAURY *Phys. Geog. Sea* xi. §512 Vapour rising up from the engirdling ocean. **1859** DE QUINCEY *Ceylon* Wks. XII. 14 The people of the engirdling zone are called the Cinghalese. **1883** *Knowledge* 15 June 357/1 The protecting embrace of his [Saturn's] engirdling rings.

†**en'girt,** *v. Obs.* Also 7–8 ingirt. [f. EN-[1] + GIRT *v.*]

1. *trans.* To gird, encircle *with.* Also *simply.*

1590 MARLOWE *Edw. II,* v. i, Engirt the temples of his hateful head! **1613** PURCHAS *Pilgr.* VI. xiv. §1 (R.) The insulting waters..engirting meane while all the townes with a strait siege. **1634** SIR T. HERBERT *Trav.* 146 The coat..ingirted with a towell of silke and gold.

2. To surround as a girdle does; to encircle. Also *fig.*

15.. in Farr *S.P. Eliz.* (1845) II. 423 So feruent griefe engirts the King of Glory. **1599** NASHE *Lenten Stuffe* (1871) 33 This flinty ring that ingirts it. **1613–6** W. BROWNE *Brit. Past.* II. i. (R.), She prepar'd to cut the wat'ry zone Ingirting Albion. **1742** COLLINS *Ode* iv. 28 And [God] pour'd the main engirting all.

b. To enclose partially or wholly; to hem in; to envelope.

1627 MAY *Lucan* III. 591 They make their hornes t'engirt the adverse fleet. **1634** T. JOHNSON tr. *Parey's Chirurg.* III. iv. (1678) 57 The skin is double..ingirting the whole body.

Hence **en'girting** *vbl. sb.,* the action of the vb. ENGIRT; *concr.* that which engirts, the rim.

1599 NASHE *Lenten Stuffe* (1871) 17 In the ninth year of the ingirting his anointed brows with the refulgent Ophir circle. **1623** FAVINE *Theat. Hon.* VI. ix. 159 Another Circle, which made the engirting of the Seale.

engiscope: see ENGYSCOPE.

†**'engislet.** *Her. Obs.* [Obscure: possibly a mistake in *Bk. St. Alban's,* which the rest follow.]

1486 *Bk. St. Alban's, Her.* B iij a, Fesy target is whan a scogion or an engislet is made in the myddull of the cootarmure. **1586** FERNE *Blaz. Gentrie* 178 A scutcheon of pretence or Engislet borne ouer the foure coates. **1610** GUILLIM *Heraldry* II. vi. (1611) 61.

†**en'gist,** *v. Obs.* In 4 engyste. [f. EN-[1] + GIST *sb.*[1] a resting-place.] *trans.* To appoint the resting-places or lodgings in (a journey).

? *a* **1400** *Morte Arth.* 445, I salle thi journaye engyste, enjoyne theme my selvene.

englacial (ɛn'gleɪʃ(ɪ)əl), *a.* [f. EN-[1] + GLACIAL *a.*] Embedded in or being within a glacier. So **en'glacially** *adv.*

1891 *Amer. Geologist* Dec. 376 The purpose of this paper is to call attention of glacialists to the means of discrimination of the portion of the drift which, at the time of final melting of the ice-sheet, was enclosed within the ice and therefore is called englacial drift by Pres. Chamberlin, and the portion which was subglacial, lying under the ice. **1896** *Jrnl. Geol.* IV. 961 Superglacial and englacial streams might be supposed to make deposits in their channels. **1904** CHAMBERLIN & SALISBURY *Geol.* (1905) I. 268 A surface load ..buried by snow and ice..is englacial. **1925** ODELL in E. F. Norton *Fight for Everest: 1924* 315 The medial moraine from the north-east shoulder of Everest, carried englacially. **1933** *Geogr. Jrnl.* LXXXI. 304 The greatest part of the englacial debris. **1935** *Nature* 20 Apr. 605/2 The blanketing effect of the silt brought down by en-glacial and sub-glacial streams.

englad, -gladden, -glamour: see EN- *pref.*[1]

England ('ɪŋglənd). Forms: 1 Engla land, 2 Engle land, 3 Englene, Engle lond, 3–4 Engelond(e, 3 Enkelonde, 4 Engelande, Ingland, Yng(e)lond, 5 En-, Inglonde, 4– England. [OE. *Engla land,* lit. 'the land of the Angles': see ENGLISH, ANGLE[3].

This word and its cognates, *English,* etc. are the only instances in which in mod. standard English the letter *e* stands in an accented syllable for (ɪ). The change of an earlier (ɛŋ) into (ɪŋ) is strictly normal, and in all other examples the spelling has followed the pronunciation. Cf. *wing,* ME. *wenge*; *string,* OE. *strenge*; *link,* OE. *hlence.*]

†**1.** The territory of the Angles, as distinguished from that of the Saxons. Only in OE. (*rare.*)

c **890** K. ÆLFRED *Bæda* IV. xxvi. § Ðæt mynster Æbbercurniʒ ðæt is ʒeseted on Engla lande [L. *in regione Anglorum.*]

2. The southern part of the island of Great Britain; usually, with the exception of Wales. Sometimes loosely used for: Great Britain. Often: The English (or British) nation or state. ***Old England***: the 'old country' (as distinguished from *New England*).

In the writings of Ælfred and the earlier parts of the O.E. Chronicle, the name *Angel-cynn* race of the Angles (= Bæda's *gens Anglorum*) is used to denote collectively the Teutonic peoples in Britain, and also the territories which they occupied. This seems to have been the only general name for the country until the Danish conquest, when it was superseded by *Engla land.*

[*c* **897** K. ÆLFRED *Gregory's Past.* 5 Hu ða ciricean ʒiond eall Angelcynn stodon maðma..ʒefyldæ. *a* **1050** *O.E. Chron.* an. 1014 And æfre ælcne Deniscne cyng utlah of Engla lande ʒecwædon. *a* **1122** *O.E. Chron.* an. 1002 Se cyng het ofslean ealle ða Deniscan men þe on Angel cynne wæron.] **1154** *O.E. Chron.* an 1131 Swa hit næfre ær ne wæs on manne ʒemynd ofer eall Engle land. *c* **1205** LAY. 17 Wonene heo comen þa Englene londe ærest ahten. *Ibid.* 6317 Engelondes deorling. *a* **1225** *Ancr. R.* 82 Eresie, God beo iðoncked, ne rixleð nout in Engelond. *a* **1250** *Prov. Ælfred* in *O.E. Misc.* 12 On Englene londe [*a* **1275** in Enkelonde] he wes kyng. ? *a* **1300** *O.E. Misc.* xviii. 1 Engle lond is eyhte hundred Myle long. *a* **1300** *Cursor M.* 8 þe first conquerour of Ingland. *Ibid.* 24893 Quen þou cums in-til england. *c* **1340** *Ibid.* 24774 (Fairf.), þen bare William þe seigniorie of Ingelonde & of normandie. **1538** STARKEY *England* I. ii. 67 Hyt be almost impossybul to..set such a commyn wele among vs here in Englond. **1605** SHAKS. *Macb.* III. i. 31 Our bloody Cozens are bestow'd In England, and in Ireland. **1631** T. DUDLEY *Let.* Mar. in *Coll. New-Hampshire Hist. Soc.* (1834) IV. 243 Wee were free enough in Old England, to turne our in sides outwards. **1638** *Essex Inst. Hist. Coll.* (1862) IV. 184/1 George Ropes is to have 20 acres of Land to be Laid out for him at his retorne from old England. *a* **1700** EVELYN *Diary* 26 May an. 1671 (1955) III. 579 To know in what condition *New-England was*; which appearing to be very independent as to their reguard to old England, [etc.]. **1702** *Addr. fr. Lancaster* in *Lond. Gaz.* No. 3804/5 A Princess born in Old England. **1775** in *Mass. Hist. Soc. Coll.* (1836) 3rd Ser. V. 87 Thus stands the matters betwixt Old England and America. **1884** *Boston* (Mass.) *Jrnl.* 30 Dec. 2/4 Our goods are crossing the water to keep alive old England.

b. ***England, home, and beauty***: a phr. from a poem of *c* 1812 (see quot.) expressing idealistic patriotism, used allusively or ironically.

c **1812** J. BRAHAM *Death of Nelson* 4 In honor's cause I fall at last. For England home and beauty, For England, home and beauty. **1850** DICKENS *Dav. Copp.* lii. 536 Let it be.. said of me, as of a gallant and eminent naval Hero..that what I have done, I did..'For England, home, and Beauty'. **1874** M. CLARKE *His Natural Life* I. vii. 54 'England, home, and beauty!' said Vetch, with a mock-heroic air.

3. *transf.* A country or district peopled by men of English origin, or of a kindred race. *rare.*

1834 GEN. P. THOMPSON *Exerc.* (1842) III. 40 [Belgium], an older England than our own. **1883** W. SIKES in *Harper's Mag.* Feb. 342/2 The part of Pembrokeshire which for centuries has been dubbed 'Little England beyond Wales.' **1886** *Pall Mall G.* 7 Dec. 1/1 A Conference of all the Englands over sea.

4. Short for *the King of England,* also for the inhabitants of England, or a portion of them, as in 'Young England', for which see YOUNG.

1595 SHAKS. *John* II. i. 482 Speake England first, that hath bin forward first To speake vnto this Cittie.

Englander ('ɪŋgləndə(r)). *rare.* [f. prec. + -ER (in quots. 1836, 1855, after Ger. *Engländer*).]

1. A native of England, an Englishman.

1820 SCOTT *Abbot* iv, I marvel what blood thou art—neither Englander nor Scot. **1836** CARLYON *Early Years* 67 Coleridge, being a noticeable Englander, and a poet withal. **1855** THACKERAY in Lewes *Life Goethe* VII. vii, The admission of these young Englanders.

2. *Little Englander*: see LITTLE A. *adj.* 13.

‖**englanté,** *a. Her.* [Fr. *englanté,* f. *en-* (see EN-[1]) + *gland*: —L. *gland-em* acorn.] Bearing acorns.

1731 in BAILEY, vol. II.

†**en'glass,** *v. Obs.* [f. EN-[1] + GLASS.] *trans.* **a.** To fit (a window) with glass; to glaze. **b.** To figure in coloured glass.

1530 PALSGR. 535/1, I englasse a window with glasse. **1572** BOSSEWELL *Armorie* II. 25 b, The cote Armors..to bee paynted..graued, englassed.

englaze: see EN- *pref.*[1] 3.

engle, obs. f. ANGEL *sb.*; also of INGLE, *Obs.*

Englechery, -schire, obs. ff. ENGLISHRY.

†**en'gleim,** *v. Obs.* Also 4–5 englayme, (4 glym), 5 yngleym. [f. EN-[1] + GLEIM slime.]

1. *trans.* To make slimy, clammy, or sticky; to set fast with slime. Also, to clog, choke, surfeit (the stomach).

1377 LANGL. *P. Pl.* B. xv. 56 The man that moche hony eteth · his mawe it engleymeth. **1387** TREVISA *Higden* (Rolls) V. 253 Wiþ aer infecte and engleymed [Lat. *aere corrupto*]. **1398** —— *Barth de P.R.* VII. xlix. (1495) 261 Ache and tourment that comyth of humours engleymed in the guttes. ? *a* **1400** *Morte Arth.* 1131 þe guttez and the gorre..þat alle englaymez þe gresse, one grounde þer he standez! *c* **1440** *Promp. Parv.* 198 Gleymyn, or yngleymyn, *visco, invisco.*

2. *fig.* To set fast, as in slime, or as a bird with birdlime; to entangle, ensnare. Const. *in, with.*

a **1340** HAMPOLE *Psalter* xliii. 27 Clemyd [*S.* englymede] is in erthe oure wambe. **1340–70** *Alex. & Dind.* 676 Englaymed was in glotenye · & glad to be drounke. *c* **1380** WYCLIF *Sel. Wks.* III. 150 þese prestis and þese clerkis.. ben most engleymed [wiþ coveteise]. *c* **1440** HYLTON *Scala Perf.* (W. de W. 1494) I. xliii, Yf thy herte be taken & engleymed with a veyne luste. *c* **1470** HARDING *Chron.* liv. ii, The Barons were so with gold englaymed.

3. *intr.* To settle, to stick.

c **1420** *Pallad. on Husb.* I. 692 That noon offes white Englayme uppon the rootes of her tonnge.

Hence **en'gleimed** *ppl. a.*: of the tongue: furred.

1493 *Festivall* (W. de W. 1515) 16 b, His tongue engleymed and his nose blacke, etc.

†**en'gleimous,** *a. Obs.* In 4 englaymous. [f. prec. + -OUS.] Slimy, venomous.

? *a* **1400** *Morte Arth.* 3685 Som gomes thourgh gyrde with gaddys of yryn Comys gayliche clede englaymous wapene!

Englifier ('ɪŋglɪfaɪə(r)). *Sc.* [f. next + -ER.] One who renders (a work) into English; a translator.

1824 *Blackw. Mag.* XV. 565, I only wonder how either Foscolo or his Englifier had the wit to pick them out.

Englify ('ɪŋglɪfaɪ), *v. Sc.* [f. ENGL-ISH + -(I)FY.]

trans. To make English; to cause to resemble English persons or manners.

1829 WILSON in *Blackw. Mag.* XXVI. 394 Our magnates have been Englified in all their notions.

English ('ɪŋglɪʃ), *a.* and *sb.* Forms: 1 Ænglisc, Englisc, 2–4 Englisch(e, 3–6 Englis(s, -ys, (3 Ænglis, Engleis, -is(s)ce, 4–6 Englissh(e, -issch, -yss(h(e, -yssche, Inglis(s, -ish(e, -isshe, (4 Englisch, -ijs, Engelis(sh, -ysch, Ingelis, Ynglisse, 6 Englush, Ynglyche), 4– English. [OE. *englisc, ænglisc*:—OTeut. **anglisko-,* f. **Angli-* (OE. *Engle*) pl., the Angles, one of the Teutonic peoples who settled in Britain in 5th c.; see ANGLE[3].]

A. *adj.*

1. In early uses now only *Hist.* Often with ellipsis of pl. sb. as in 2 d.

When the adj. first occurs in OE., it had already lost its etymological sense 'of or belonging to the Angles' (as distinguished from Saxons). The earliest recorded sense is: Of or belonging to the group of Teutonic peoples collectively known as the *Angelcynn* ('Angle-kin' = Bæda's *gens Anglorum*), comprising the Angles, Saxons, and Jutes, who settled in Britain during the 5th c. With the incorporation of the Celtic and Scandinavian elements of the population into the 'English' people, the adj. came in the 11th c. to be applied to all natives of 'England', whatever their ancestry. But for a generation or two after the Norman Conquest, the descendants of the invaders, though born in

England, continued to be regarded as 'French', so that the word *English*, as applied to persons, was for a time restricted to those whose ancestors were settled in England before the Conquest. In formal state documents the distinction between the 'French' and 'English' inhabitants of England survived after it had ceased practically to exist; cf. ENGLISHRY.

c **880** *Ælfred & Guthrum's Treaty* (Thorpe) ii, Gif man ofslaʒen weorðe, ealle we læteð efen dyrne, Engliscne & Deniscne. *a* **1000** *Ordinance respecting Dúnsæte* (Thorpe) vi, Nah naðer to farenne ne Wylisc man on Ænglisc lond ne Ænglisc on Wylisc, butan, etc. *a* **1016** *Laws of Æthelred* (Thorpe), Gif Ænglisc man Deniscne ofslea. *a* **1087** *Charter Will. I* in Stubbs *Sel. Chart.* 83 Will'm kyng gret.. ealle þa burhwaru binnan Londone Frencisce and Englisce. *c* **1205** LAY. 29404 Þat folc þæt was Ænglis. *Ibid.* 29457 Of Englisce leoden. *Ibid.* 31673 Penda king is Englisc. **1809** BAWDWEN *Domesday Bk.* 345 The English have four ploughs in the demesne. **1860** HOOK *Lives Abps.* (1869) I. iv. 174 Since the English came into Britain. **1872** E. ROBERTSON *Hist. Ess.* 215 The gradual extension of the English name in the course of the 10th century is very perceptible.

2. a. Of or belonging to England or its inhabitants.

c **1290** *Lives Saints* (1887) 73 Þe englische barones. **1375** BARBOUR *Bruce* I. 193 Schyrreffys and bailȝheys maid he [Edward I].. of Inglis nation. **15..** EARL SURREY *Death Sir T. Wyat* Poems (Aldine ed.) 60 A worthy guide to bring Our English youth by travail into fame. **1613** SHAKS. *Hen. VIII*, III. i. 143 Would I had neuer trod this English Earth. **1645** FULLER *Gd. Th. in Bad T.* (1841) 37 The English ambassador. **1796** H. HUNTER tr. *St. Pierre's Stud. Nat.* (1799) III. 707, I embarked on board an English ship which had sailed round the world. **1805** SCOTT *Last Minstr.* IV. xvii, Now every English eye, intent, On Branksome's armed towers was bent. **1842** BISCHOFF *Woollen Manuf.* (1862) II. 125 English wools rose in price. **1852** EARP *Gold Col. Australia* 102 To give the English reader an idea of its present condition.

b. In the names of various trees and plants; as **English elm**, *Ulmus campestris* (see ELM); **E. galingale**, *Cyperus longus*; **E. maidenhair**, *Asplenium Trichomanes*; **E. myrtle**, *Ligustrum vulgare*; **E. treacle**, *Teucrium Scordium*.

1578 LYTE *Dodoens* III. xxiii. 346 The roote of Cy[p]erus or *English Galangal, is hoate and dry in the third degree. **1861** MISS PRATT *Flower. Pl.* VI. 12 Order. *Cyperaceæ*.. Sweet or English Galingale. **1562** TURNER *Herbal* II. 157 b, Trichomanes (that is our *English Maydens heare) is supposed, etc. **1578** LYTE *Dodoens* III. lxix (Heading), Of English or Common Maydenheare. **1879** in PRIOR *Plant-n.* **1846** SOWERBY *Brit. Bot.*, *English Myrtle, the Common privet, *Ligustrum vulgare*. **1551** TURNER *Herbal* I. I iiij a, Germander, whyche is also called in Cambrige shyre *Englyshe triacle, is called in Greke Chamedrys. **1670** RAY *Catal. Plant. Angliæ* 67 (Britten & Holl.) In agro Cantabrigiensi English Treacle dicitur. **1886** In BRITTEN & HOLLAND.

c. In the names of certain diseases: ***English cholera***, †***English sweat***: see the sbs. †***English disease*** (***malady***), ***English melancholy***: the 'spleen'.

[**1733** CHEYNE *Eng. Malady* (1734) Pref. 1 By Foreigners.. Nervous Distempers, Spleen, Vapours, and Lowness of Spirits, are, in Derision, call'd the English Malady. **1834** M. GOOD *Study of Med.* (ed. 4) III. 113 English Melancholy.

d. *ellipt.* = 'English people, soldiers', etc.

(A 17th c. Sc. writer has the pl. *Englishes.*)

1599 SHAKS. *Hen. V*, I. ii. 111 O Noble English, that could entertaine With halfe their Forces, the full pride of France. **1671** *True Nonconf.* 221 The violences, wherewith the Englishes, during their Domination among us, can be charged. **1711** SWIFT *Lett.* (1767) III. 181 Pray observe the inhabitants about Wexford; they are old English. **1765** T. HUTCHINSON *Hist. Col. Mass.* i. 146 Freedom might be.. granted to all truly English. **1859** KNIGHT *Pop. Hist. Eng.* V. 165 That terrible battle-field, which the French call Neerwinden and the English call Landen.

e. Misc. special Combs.: **English bond**: see BOND *sb.*[1] 13 a; **English breakfast**, a large breakfast including cooked food, opp. *Continental breakfast*; **English Canadian**, an English-speaking Canadian, as opp. to a FRENCH CANADIAN; so **English-Canadian** *a.*, of, or pertaining to, English Canadians or the predominantly English-speaking parts of Canada; **English disease**, (*a*) (see 2 c); (*b*) rickets; (*c*) loosely applied to various disorders in the English economy or foreign policy; also **English sickness**; **English finish**, a relatively smooth machine-finish given to paper, or paper so treated; **English horn**: see HORN *sb.* 13 d; **English Miss** [MISS *sb.*[2] 4] a somewhat derisive term for an unmarried woman implying primness, or prudishness, etc.; **English pink** [PINK *sb.*[5]] (*a*) = *Dutch pink*, a yellow lake pigment, or shade of yellow; (*b*) [PINK *sb.*[4]] a pink colour (see quot. 1963); **English rose**, a typically attractive light-complexioned English girl; **English setter** [SETTER *sb.*[1] 11 a], a breed of long-haired sporting dog, usu. white or white with patches of colour; a dog of this breed; **English sickness** (see *English disease* above); **English-speaker**, a speaker of English; **English springer** [SPRINGER[1] 8 b], a small variety of spaniel; **English Sunday**, Sunday kept as a day of rest and worship, as traditionally in England; opp. *Continental Sunday*; **English toy terrier**, a variety of miniature terrier; cf. TOY *sb.* 12 c.

1807 C. WILMOT *Let.* 5 Aug. in Londonderry & Hyde *Russ. Jrnls.* (1934) II. 256 Cavanaugh.. routed up all his House & prepared an English Breakfast. **1857** C. M. YONGE *Dynevor Terrace* II. v. 71 The English breakfast, which had been established.. had quite vanished; each of the family had a cup of chocolate in private. **1964** P. JONES *Month of Pearl* v. 46 Continentals have a name for the kind of breakfast we habitually eat.. the 'English Breakfast'. It means an impossible mess of fried eggs, ham, and toast, and the biggest pot in the house full of tea. **1968** P. LORAINE *Dead Men of Sestos* x. 134, I used to like what I believe is called an English breakfast—a great deal of bacon and egg and sausage, and then a great deal of toast and butter and that delicious bitter marmalade. *a* **1820** G. HEAD *Forest Scenes* (1838) 307 There was an old man among them, an English Canadian, called Mr. Weller. **1886** J. G. BOURINOT *Intell. Devel. Canadian People* iii. 80 The most widely circulated English and French Canadian papers. **1897** —— *Canada* xxix. 448 The spirit of conciliation and justice.. has happily influenced the action of leading English and French Canadian statesmen. **1964** M. GALLANT in R. Weaver *Canad. Short Stories* (1968) 2nd Ser. 79 The English Canadians in the room agreed, glancing nervously at the French. **1967** *Times* 28 Feb. (Canada Suppl.) 24 Similarly, English-Canadians would be adversely affected. **1871** C. E. HACKLEY tr. *T. Billroth's Gen. Surg. Path. & Therapeutics* xvi. 451 It [*sc.* rachitis] was often called 'English disease'. **1939** DRUMMOND & WILBRAHAM *Englishman's Food* viii. 182 Rickets.. came to be generally known on the Continent as 'The English Disease' (*Die englische Krankheit*). **1969** *Physics Bull.* Apr. 132/1 British industry suffered grievously from the re-establishment of the university-industry barrier in the years that followed the war. It would be very interesting to discover why this happened, for it is, perhaps, one of the symptoms of the socalled 'English disease' in economics. **1970** *Daily Tel.* 9 Feb. 12 There can be no doubt that to a very large degree the improvement of Britain's trade figures during recent months has been due to the spreading of the 'English disease' over other industrial countries. **1970** B. LEVIN *Pendulum Years* ix. 149 The 'English disease' can be defined in a dozen different ways, and has been, but they have in common that irreducible minimum of amateurism that seems to cling to matters British. **1934** WEBSTER, English finish. **1960** G. A. GLAISTER *Gloss. Bk.* 124/1 *English finish*, a calendered paper with a smooth, matt surface. **1817** H. C. B. CAMPBELL *Jrnl.* 3 Sept. in *Journey to Florence* (1951) 59 Two ugly English Misses very stiff and prim. **1866** TROLLOPE *Claverings* xviii. 80 [Frenchman loq.] Your English meess is so much and so grand. **1879** C. M. YONGE *Magnum Bonum* II. xxvi. 520 Just the insipid English Mees... You should hear what the French think of the ordinary English girl. **1928** R. H. MOTTRAM (*title*) The English Miss. **1960** *Housewife* Oct. 34/2 You are not used to strong drink... The typical little English Miss. **1703** English pink [see PINK *sb.*[5]]. **1835** G. FIELD *Chromatogr.* ix. 84 *Dutch Pink, English* and *Italian Pinks*, are sufficiently absurd names of yellow colours prepared by dyeing, whitening, &c. with vegetal yellow tinctures, in the manner of rose pink, from which they borrow their name. **1901** G. H. HURST *Dict. Chemicals used in Paints* 147 *English pink*, a name given to yellow pigments prepared from Persian berries; they are similar to Dutch pinks. **1963** *Times* 25 May 11/6 Chrome-tin pink.. became known on the Continent as 'English pink'. **1902** B. HOOD *Merrie Eng.* II. 211 Dan Cupid hath a garden Where women are the flow'rs... And Oh! the sweetest blossom That in the garden grows,—The fairest Queen, it is, I ween, The perfect English rose. **1918** 'D. LYALL' *Eng. Rose* xx. 275 The two girls kissed one another, and the English rose was received in that happy corner of Ireland's garden and found it good. **1967** D. CILENTO *Manipulator* i. 13 Rose had.. won a seven-year contract with a film company on the strength of her English rose good looks. **1968** H. R. F. KEATING *Inspector Ghote hunts Peacock* v. 67 She was the ideal English Rose.. her hair was crisply golden... Her complexion was a vigorous pink and white. **1859** 'STONEHENGE' *Dog, in Health & Disease* I. iv. 95 The English setter imitated the pointer; but whether it was effected by crossing with that dog is difficult to say. **1910** *Encycl. Brit.* VIII. 378/1 The English setter should have a silky coat with the hair waved but not curly; the legs and toes should be hairy, and the tail should have a bushy fringe. **1950** A. C. SMITH *Dogs since 1900* 120 At the beginning of last century English Setters were often described as spaniels by old-fashioned sportsmen. **1963** *Economist* 14 Sept. 886/2 An article [German].. called 'The English Sickness' [= isolationism]. **1969** *Daily Tel.* 18 Apr. 18 The only obvious result of so much effort.. has been an abysmal economic growth rate scarcely known elsewhere to post-Keynesian economics. Humiliatingly, the English Sickness has become almost a by-word for economic inefficiency and economic failure. **1970** *Sci. Jrnl.* Apr. 26/1 'The English sickness' is a term widely used in Europe to describe high levels of absenteeism, restrictive practices and wildcat strikes. **1853** THACKERAY *Let.* 4 Mar. in *Lett. A. T. Ritchie* (1924) iv. 48 A great hearty nation [*sc.* the U.S.] of 26 millions of English-speakers. **1894** J. J. ASTOR *Journey in other Worlds* 38 This has given the English-speakers, especially the United States, a free hand. **1961** *Guardian* 30 June 12/2 English-speakers [of South Africa] opposed to the excesses of nationalism. **1808** English springer [see SPRINGER[1] 8 b]. **1922** R. LEIGHTON *Compl. Bk. Dog* 186 It is only recently that the Kennel Club has officially recognized the variety known as the English Springer. **1879** C. M. YONGE *Magnum Bonum* II. xvii. 333 The afternoon was spent in an easy-going, loitering way, more like a foreign than an English Sunday. **1903** A. BENNETT *Leonora* iii. 79 The smooth calm of the English Sunday. **1966** *Guardian* 22 Nov. 1/1 The grim visage of the traditional English Sunday looks like disappearing quite soon. **1907** F. T. BARTON *Terriers* xi. facing p. 98 (*caption*) Typical hind-quarters and stern of a white English Toy Terrier. **1962** *Times* 10 Feb. 6/3 English Toy Terriers (Black and Tan).

3. *transf.* Marked by the characteristics of an Englishman. Often in laudatory sense: Possessed of the virtues claimed as peculiarly 'English'.

1539 TONSTALL *Serm. Palm Sund.* (1823) 71 Only take an englyshe hart vnto the. **1695** *Eng. Anc. Const. Eng.* Pref. 6 He will find the design to be truly English, that is, sincere and honest. **1883** PHELPS *Eng. Style* 40 A mind compact with sturdy and solid English elements.

quasi-*adv.* **1784** COWPER *Tiroc.* 671 His address.. Not English stiff, but frank and formed to please.

4. a. As the designation of a language (see B. 1). Hence of words, idioms, grammar, etc.: Belonging to the English language. Of literary compositions, speeches, etc.: Written or spoken in the English language.

c **1000** ÆLFRIC *Hom.* (Thorpe) II. 358 (Bosw.) Ic [Ælfric Abbod] ʒesett hæbbe wel feowertiʒ larspella on Engliscum ʒereorde. *c* **1000** —— in Sweet *Ags. Reader* 57 Ðu bæde me for oft Engliscra ʒewrita. *c* **1230** *Hali Meid.* 5 And seið syon ase muchel on englische leodene ase heh sihðe. *a* **1240** *Ureisun* in *Cott. Hom.* 199 Ich habbe i-sungen þe ðesne englissce lai. *c* **1250** *Gen. & Ex.* 14 Ut of latin ðis song is draȝen On Engleis speche. *a* **1300** *Cursor M.* 24 (Cott.) Sanges.. Inglis, frankys, and latine. *Ibid.* 233 (Gött.) Þis ilke boke es translate vnto engliss tung to rede. *c* **1440** *Promp. Parv.* 140 Englysshe speche, *Anglicum.* **1526** *Pilgr. Perf.* (W. de W. 1531) 1 b, It was put into my mynde to drawe it in the englysshe tonge. **1580** BULLOKAR *Orthogr.*, There be eight vowels of differing sounds in Inglish speech. **1611** BIBLE Dedic., There should be one more exact translation of the Holy Scripture into the English Tongue. **1840** MACAULAY *Ranke* (1854) II. 541/2 We now see this book take its place among the English Classics. **1847** EMERSON *Repr. Men, Shaks.* Wks. (Bohn) I. 357 Our English Bible is a wonderful specimen of the strength and music of the English language.

b. with limiting words as in B. 1 b.

1579 FULKE *Refut. Rastel* 763 Prayers remaine still in the Saxon or old English tongue. *a* **1891** *Mod.* An Old-English grammar. Middle-English literature. It is not a modern English word.

B. *sb.*

1. a. The English language. First in the adverbial phrase, †*on* (now *in*) *English*. Also in phrase ***the King's, the Queen's English***, app. suggested by phrases like 'to deface the king's coin'. Also *attrib.* as ***English scholar***.

In 9th c., and prob. much earlier, *Englisc* was the name applied to all the Angle and Saxon dialects spoken in Britain. The name *English* for the language is thus older than the name *England* for the country. In its most comprehensive use, it includes all the dialects descended from the language of the early Teutonic conquerors of Britain; but it is sometimes popularly restricted to the language since the close of the 'Anglo-Saxon' or fully inflected stage; sometimes to the language and dialects of England proper, as distinguished from those of Scotland, Ireland, U.S., etc.; and sometimes to the literary or standard form of the language as distinct from illiterate or ungrammatical speech, etc.

[The use as sb. seems to have originated, not in the ellipsis of any particular word (e.g. *ʒereord*) meaning 'language', but in a vague absol. use of the neuter adj. A similar use is found in the other Teut. langs. and in Romanic; cf. Ger. *auf deutsch*, Fr. *en français*, Sp. *en castellano*.]

c **890** K. ÆLFRED *Bæda* III. xix, On sumre ceastre þe is nemned on Englisc Cneoferisburh. *c* **1000** *Ags. Gosp.* Matt. xxvii. 46 Heli, Heli, lema zabdani? þæt ys on Englisc, Min God, min God, to hwi forlete þu me? *c* **1175** *Lamb. Hom.* 103 On [sin] is icweden, *Gula*, þet is ȝifernesse on englisc. *c* **1205** LAY. 6317 Wrat þa laȝen on Englis. *a* **1300** *Cursor M.* p. 988 *Resurrection* 240 (Cott.) Raboni (þat is on englis maister). *c* **1340** *Ibid.* 26545 (Fairf.) Þat now in Ingelis [v.r. *Cott.* englis] wil I rede. *c* **1380** WYCLIF *Wks.* (1880) 429 Þe same sentense in engliȝsch. **1447** BOKENHAM *Seyntys* Introd. 4 Wych I purpose now to declare On ynglysh. **1526** *Pilgr. Perf.* (W. de W. 1531) 1 b, The mater is spirytuall, and requyreth moche declaracion in englysshe. *c* **1530** LD. BERNERS (*title*) The hystory of the moost noble and valyaunt knyght Arthur of lytell brytayne, translated out of frensshe in to englushe. **1598** SHAKS. *Merry W.* I. iv. 6 Abusing of Gods patience, and the Kings English. **1704** *Lond. Gaz.* No. 4046/4 Maurice Roberts.. a Shropshire Man, speaking very bad English. **1782** WESLEY *Wks.* (1830) IV. 267 Why has he then bad English on every page? **1836** E. HOWARD *R. Reefer* xxxv, They.. put the king's English to death so charmingly. **1869** ALFORD (*title*), Plea for the Queen's English.

b. The 'English' of a special period or district, or that which appears in the writings of an individual author. ***Old English***: in popular use applied vaguely to all obsolete forms of the language. According to the nomenclature now generally adopted in this country, the ***Old English*** period ends about 1100–1150, the ***Middle English*** period about 1500, when the period of ***Modern English*** begins. The name ***Early English*** is often used vaguely for Early Middle English, or for Middle and Early Modern English.

a **1225** *St. Marher* 23, I þe moneþ þat on ure ledene is old englisch efterlið inempnet, iulius o latin. **1303** R. BRUNNE *Handl. Synne* 7672 Yn a prouerbe of olde englys. **1340** *Ayenb.*, Engliss of Kent. **1691** WOOD *Ath. Oxon.* I. 257 To these books of Euphues, tis said, that our Nation is indebted for a new English in them. [**1822** J. GRIMM *Deutsche Grammatik* I. I. 506 Mittel-englische buchstaben.] **1836** M. DE LARENAUDIÈRE tr. *T. Wright's Lit. Anglo-saxonne en Angleterre* 38 Que l'on peut appeler l'anglais intermédiaire (middle english). **1839** T. WRIGHT *Lit. & Learning under Anglo-Saxons* 107 The form of our language during the twelfth and the first half of the thirteenth century is generally termed *Semi-Saxon*; from that period to the time of the Reformation it has received from modern philologists the name of *Middle-English*. **1871** H. SWEET *Alfred's transl. Gregory's Pastoral Care* pref. p. v, I use 'Old English' throughout this work to denote the unmixed, inflectional stage of the English language, commonly known by the barbarous and unmeaning title of 'Anglo-Saxon'. **1879** —— in *Trans. Philol. Soc. 1878* 377 It is a relief to turn to Germany, where Old and Middle English are not regarded as 'fringes'. **1887** RUSKIN *Præterita* II. x, Hooker's English was the perfectest existing model. **1927** *Englische Studien* Nov. 75 This tendency grows stronger in later Middle English. **1933** BLOOMFIELD *Lang.* i. 17 By comparing our

records of Old English (say, in the writings of King Alfred) with modern English, we can see how English has changed in the last thousand years.

c. English English, English as spoken in England as differentiated from that spoken, e.g., in the United States of America.

1804 M. WILMOT *Let.* 30 May in Londonderry & Hyde *Russ. Jrnls.* (1934) I. 102 If the other side is not *English* English, it is just the sort of language that might make one blush for what it is. **1943** *Spectator* 5 Feb. 120/1 Of the two hundred million people speaking English nearly seventenths live in the United States, and another tenth in the British Dominions are as much influenced by American as by English English. **1958** *Listener* 18 Dec. 1050/1 To get round the difficulty of putting Lorca across full-bloodedly, producers have had recourse to Irish, Cockney, and West Country speech... Lorca's plays suffer in English English because we do not like to grasp his nettles. **1961** H. R. F. KEATING *Rush on Ultimate* i. 13 'I never know what's Australian and what's English... Can you call it the gen over here?'.. 'From what I gather from the boys it's a bit dated now, but it's English English all right.' **1966** S. HARVESTER *Treacherous Road* i. 9 Most educated Egyptians spoke English English.

2. The 'English' at an author's command; means of expression in English. Also, the English word or equivalent (*for*).

c **1385** CHAUCER *L.G.W. 66 Prol.*, Allas, that I ne had Englyssh, ryme, or prose, Suffisant this flour to preyse aryght! *c* **1386** —— *Sqr's. T.* 29 Myn Englissh eek is insufficient. **1631** WEEVER *Anc. Fun. Mon.* 553, I will set downe in such English as I haue in the said Legend, or Agon. **1824** *Oriental Herald* I. 90 Whose patience is equal to the reading of the 'Bahar Damash' in Dr. Scott's English? **1890** T. HARDY *Melancholy Hussar* in *Three Notable Stories* 170 Phyllis used to say that his English, though not good, was quite intelligible to her. **1926** R. KEARTON *Naturalist's Pilgr.* vii. 74 'What are they mining for..., Herr Sonbergh?' 'Ah,' he exclaimed, 'I know quite well, but I cannot remember the English for it.' **1930** *N. & Q.* 11 Oct. 270/1 Throughout the English is apt, for spaces, to be careless and dull.

3. †**a.** An English sentence to be rendered into a foreign language. †**b.** An English equivalent for a foreign word. **c.** (*School slang*) An English translation; a 'crib'.

c **1000** ÆLFRIC *Gram.* (*Z.*) 259 Ealle ðas habbað an Englisc, þeah hi for faegernysse fela synd on Ledenspræce. **1552** HULOET, *Englyshe* or vulgare geuen by a maister to scholers to be made in latine. **1612** BRINSLEY *Pos. Parts* (1669) 49 The Englishes of our [Latin] Prepositions. *Ibid.* 53 When an English is given to be made Latine, what must you do first? **1679** W. WALKER *Dict. Eng. Particles* Pref., The first column contains some Englishes. **1862** H. C. ADAMS *First June* 66, I sometimes have half suspected him of learning his lessons with Englishes.

d. English language or literature as a school or university subject or examination.

1889 F. LEVANDER in A. Herbert *Sacrifice of Education to Examination* 42 The school in question was a small one... The subjects were English, Geography,..German, and Drawing. **1911** W. OWEN *Let.* 11 Sept. (1967) 79 Have just got home from the 'English'. Am fairly confident of a pass in this. **1926** KIPLING *Debits & Credits* 276 Howell, a favourite in 'English' as well as Latin. **1950** A. WILSON *Such Darling Dodos* 107 Mr. Rogers said we should read *Barnaby Rudge* for English, it will be the last book I shall read in class at St. Bertram's. **1968** *Listener* 29 Feb. 275/3 The journalistic addiction of our academic intellectuals..is now the menacing disease of university 'English'. **1970** *Guardian* 29 May 9/1 The UCCA clearing scheme..doesn't hold much hope if he wants to read English.

4. *ellipt.* for 'The sense expressed in plain English', the plain sense; also, ***plain, true English***; †***English out***; and in phrase, ***in plain English***: to speak plainly.

1645 *Liberty of Consc.* Pref. A iij, The plain english of the question is this: whether the Christian Magistrate be keeper of both Tables. **1647** WARD *Simp. Cobler* 12 The true English of all..their false Latine, is nothing but a generall Toleration of all Opinions. **1659** SCOTT in Burton *Diary* (1828) IV. 377 That is English out. **1679** PENN *Addr. Prot.* II. §5 (1692) 184 This is the English of their Doctrine. **1705** STANHOPE *Paraph.* III. 376 The plain English of what he thanks God for is in effect but Thus much. **1749** FIELDING *Tom Jones* VII. v. (1840) 86 The English of all which is..that I am in the wrong. **1856** EMERSON *Engl. Traits* VII. 121 When they unmask cant, they say, 'The English of this is ', etc.

†**5.** A Flemish coin (see quot.). *Obs.*

? *a* **1500** in *Athenæum* (1867) 7 Dec. 767 Viij mytis ys an englishe, that is the iij^de^ parte of *jd.* **1540** *Act 32 Hen. VIII*, c. 14 A piece of flemmishe mony called an Englyshe.

6. *Printing.* **a.** The name of a size of type smaller than Great Primer and larger than Pica.

1598 *Ord. Stationer's Co.* in *Hist. O.E. Lett. Foundries* (1887) 129 Those in pica Roman and Italic and in English. **1676** MOXON *Print Lett.* 8 The Stem of English Capitals is 6 parts. **1824** J. JOHNSON *Typogr.* II. 78 English is called Mittel by the Germans.

b. *Old English*: a form of 'Black Letter' resembling that used by early English printers; now occasionally employed for ornamental purposes; see OLD ENGLISH A. 2.

7. *Billiards.* = SIDE *sb.*[1] 14 d. Also *transf. U.S.*

1869 'MARK TWAIN' *Innoc. Abr.* 116 You would infallibly put the 'English' on the wrong side of the ball. **1898** R. HUGHES *Lakerim Athletic Club* xv. 242 Eaton would slash the ball with a stiffened wrist, an elbow swing, and a quick, hard jump into the air at the same time, to put the 'English' on. **1959** *Sunday Times* 5 Apr. 4/5 The billiard term 'putting on the english', which Atticus states is current parlance in American bowling circles. The story goes that an enterprising gentleman from these shores travelled to the United States during the latter part of the last century and impressed the Americans with a demonstration of the effect of 'side' on pool or billiard balls. His name was English. **1966** H. NIELSEN *After Midnight* (1967) iii. 53 When Simon tried to close the door..he encountered difficulties. The officer lent a hand. 'You have to put a little English on it,' he explained. 'There's a defect in the catch.'

C. *Comb.* **a.** Prefixed to ppl. adjs., as ***English-born, -bred, -built, -managed, -manned, -reading, -rigged, -speaking.*** **b.** Forming parasynthetic derivatives, as ***English-hearted, -minded.*** **c.** Prefixed to other adjs., as †***English-Indian***, †***-Irish***, †***-Popish***; †**English-Saxon**, = ANGLO-SAXON; also ***English-French, -German, -Latin***, etc., said of dictionaries in which English words are followed by their renderings into other languages.

18.. LYTTON *E. Maltrav.* (1851) 6 But I am *English-born. **1880** EARLE *Philol. Eng. Tong.* §155 A large body of French words in our language..pronounced as English-born words. **1808** BENTHAM *Sc. Reform* 80 Such ingenuity is not wanting to *English-bred technicalism. *c* **1677** *List Ships* in Marvell *Growth Popery* 61 The John and Sarah, of 120 Tun, *English Built. **1848** LYTTON *Harold* II. i, Many of Godwin's noblest foes sighed for the *English-hearted Earl. **1613** PURCHAS *Pilgr., Descr. India* (1864) 127 Our *English-Indian Societie. **1700** TYRELL *Hist. Eng.* II. 888 All the *English-Irish Knights..ran away. **1815** SCOTT *Guy M.* xlii, Three English-Irish peers. **1740** J. CLARKE *Educ. Youth* (ed. 3) 37 Such sort of *English-Latin Dictionaries. **1888** *Daily News* 26 Nov. 2/5 This estate has always been what has been called an *English-managed estate. **1799** NELSON in Nicolas *Disp.* (1845) IV. 97 An *English-manned Frigate. **1882** J. H. BLUNT *Ref. Ch. Eng.* II. 162 Thoroughly *English-minded men such as Gardiner. **1641** SANDERSON *Serm.* II. 8 This clamouring against *English-Popish ceremonies. **1907** W. JAMES *Pragmatism* i. 17 Religious philosophy in our day and generation is, among us *English-reading people, of two main types. **1959** *Listener* 24 Dec. 1120/3 The great insufflators of artistic interest in the English-reading world. **1832** MARRYAT *N. Forster* xxxvi, She is English built and *English rigged. **1610** HOLLAND *Camden's Brit.* I. Pref., The most ancient British and *English-Saxon tongues. **1695** *Enq. Anc. Const. Eng.* 33 As all his English-Saxon predecessors. **1777** NICOLSON & BURN *Westmoreland* I. 309 Our English-Saxon word *evil* seems to spring from the same source. **1829** BENTHAM *Justice & Cod. Petit.* IV. 6 Thence was created the necessity of employing these so little trustworthy trustees..as interpreters between the *English-speaking parties and the French-speaking judges. **1873** F. HALL *Mod. English* 146 The English-speaking people. **1883** LOWELL in *Daily News* 5 July 6/2 We continually hear nowadays of the 'English-speaking race,' of the 'English-speaking population'. **1887** *Spectator* 26 Feb. 300/1 Of this happy gift..Mr. Lowell has among English-speaking men almost a monopoly. **1937** *Discovery* June 185/1 The English-speaking nations. **1940** 'G. ORWELL' *Inside Whale* 79 Dickens is scarcely intelligible outside the English-speaking culture. **1970** C. L. CLINE *Lett. George Meredith* p. xxix, Meredith stood almost without rival at the head of letters in the English-speaking world.

Hence **English-hood** (*rare*).

1883 MRS. LYNN LINTON *Ione* II. xxiii. 260 The Englishhood of long walks in the lanes and fields.

English ('ɪŋglɪʃ), *v.* Forms: 4 Englysch, 4-6 -isshe, -ys(s)he, 4- English. [f. prec. adj.]

1. a. *trans.* To translate into English (a book, passage, etc.); to give the English equivalent for (a word or phrase).

1388 WYCLIF *Bible* Prol. xv, To Englisshe it aftir the word wolde be derk and douteful. *Ibid.*, I Englishe it thus. *c* **1430** LYDG. *Chorle & Byrde* (1818) 18 Out of frenssh how that hit englisshid be. **1490** CAXTON *Eneydos* (1889) 4 For hym, I knowe for suffycyent to expowne and englysshe euery dyffyculte that is therin. **1533** MORE *Apol.* v. Wks. 854/2 Howe be it the preacher englisheth it thus. **1660** BOYLE *Seraph. Love* xvii (1700) 106 Purchas'd for a Ransom, the Original Word English'd Redemption. **1728** MORGAN *Algiers* I. Pref. 19 It fully excuses my not Englishing them from the Greek my own self. **1807** *Ann. Rev.* V. 510 All German verses can be Englished in fewer syllables. **1872** SPURGEON *Treas. Dav.* Ps. lxii. 1 If we Englished the word, by our word 'verily'.

b. To render in English orthography. *rare.*

1807 G. CHALMERS *Caledonia* I. II. vi. 284 The common word..is *ruadh*, or as it is englished *roy*.

†**2.** To render into plain English; to describe in plain terms. *Obs.*

1598 SHAKS. *Merry W.* I. iii. 51 The hardest voice of her behauiour (to be english'd rightly) is, I am Sir John Falstafs. **1649** MILTON *Eikon.* v. 44 Those gracious Acts..may be english'd more properly Acts of feare. **1671** FLAVEI *Fount. Life* viii. 22, I am ashamed that my pen should English what mine eyes have seen.

3. To make English, to anglicize. **a.** To adopt (a word) into the English language; to give it an English character or form. **b.** To subject to English influence.

1824-9 LANDOR *Imag. Conv.* (1846) I. 157 *Liqueur* is not yet Englished. **1879** WALFORD *Londoniana* II. 99 The word 'Comfort' originally Norman and afterwards englished. **1880** GRANT WHITE *Every-Day Eng.* 21 When a foreign word has been transplanted into our speech and has taken firm root there, it should be thoroughly Englished. **1880** BROWNING *Dram. Idylls* II. *Clive* 9 The man Clive—he fought Plassy..Conquered and annexed and Englished! **1934** H. G. WELLS *Exper. Autobiogr.* II. viii. §5. 622, I think Conrad owed a very great deal to their early association; Hueffer helped greatly to 'English' him and his idiom. **1965** *Evening Standard* 10 Dec. 6/6 A New York tailor is advertising:..Let us take your Stateside suit and English it up.

'**Englishable**, *a. Obs.*[−0] [f. prec. + -ABLE.] Capable of being translated into, or expressed in, English.

1864 in WEBSTER; and in mod. Dicts.

Englished ('ɪŋglɪʃt), *ppl. a.* [f. ENGLISH *v.* + -ED[1].] That is translated into English.

1659 BAXTER *Key Cath.* II. i. 389 Is not his Doctrine here given you in his Englished words? **1879** FURNIVALL *E.E.T.S. Rep.* 20 Trevisa's englisht Higden's Polychronicon. **1881** *Academy* 16 Apr. 277 Which the testator got in exchange for a copy of an englished version.

Englisher ('ɪŋglɪʃə(r)). [f. ENGLISH *a.* and *v.* + -ER.]

1. [f. the adj.] An English subject; a native or inhabitant of England. Chiefly *Sc.*

1683 G. MARTINE *Reliq. Divæ Andreæ* ii. §1. (1797) 10 Within twentie two years as some Englishers grant. **1814** SCOTT *Wav.* xxix, That..the young Englisher should pay dearly for the contempt with which he seemed to regard him. **1835** LYTTON *Rienzi* I. xii, William the Bastard could scarce have found the hardy Englishers so easy a conquest as, etc. **1861** RAMSAY *Scot. Life & Char.* vi. (ed. 18) 187 Not in very good humour with the Englishers.

2. [f. the vb.] One who translates into English.

1800 *Month. Mag.* X. 319 The most fortunate englisher of Klopstock. **1879** FURNIVALL *E.E.T.S. Rep.* 8 The englisher of the French Romance, probably a clergyman of..Exeter. **1881** *Academy* 12 Mar. 187 Few Englishers have been so successful in giving the flavour of French verse.

Englishing ('ɪŋglɪʃɪŋ), *vbl. sb.* [f. ENGLISH *v.* + -ING[1].] **a.** The action of the vb. ENGLISH. **b.** *concr.* An English rendering or version.

a **1340** HAMPOLE *Psalter* Metr. Pref. 42 This holy man..in all his englysching ryʒt aftur the latyn taketh cours. **1586** W. WEBBE *Eng. Poetrie* (Arb.) 34 The englishing of Æneidos of Virgill. **1607** TOPSELL *Serpents* (1658) To Rdr., The second exception taken against the former Treatise, was the not Englishing or translating of the Latine Verses. **1674** N. FAIRFAX *Bulk & Selv.* 199 Which [word] they have stuck so closely to in their Englishings of Latine. **1886** *Athenæum* 9 Jan. 65/1 Some of Mr. Sieveking's 'Englishings' seem to have stopped rather short of English.

Englishism ('ɪŋglɪʃɪz(ə)m). *rare.* [f. ENGLISH + -ISM.] **1.** In various occasional senses: The characteristics peculiar to the English; English modes of procedure; a manifestation or product of English character; attachment to what is English.

1855 *Tait's Mag.* XXII. 177 He..certificated his patriotism when only an excess of English-ism was imputed. **1865** J. W. KAYE *Sepoy War* (heading of chapter) The Progress of Englishism [i.e. the remodelling of land tenure in India according to English notions]. **1868** MAYNE REID *Child Wife* xix. (1888) 101 In his own features..there was an unmistakable expression of 'Englishism'. **1879** *Indian Daily N.* 2 Oct., An Englishism..which foreigners note.

2. An English idiom or form of speech.

1893 in *Funk's Stand. Dict.* **1923** *Blackw. Mag.* Aug. 203/2 We..do the best we might with blunt Englishisms.

englishite ('ɪŋglɪʃaɪt). *Min.* [f. the name of George L. *English* (1864–1944), American mineral dealer + -ITE[1].] A hydrated phosphate of potassium, calcium, and aluminium found at Fairfield, Utah County, Utah.

1930 LARSEN & SHANNON in *Amer. Mineralogist* XV. 328 Layers of a clear, glassy, cleavable mineral that resembles crusts of gordonite..were found on microscopic examination to be a different species... The name englishite is proposed for this mineral. **1951** C. PALACHE et al. *Dana's Syst. Min.* (ed. 7) II. 957 *Englishite*... Probably monoclinic. Occurs as layers and aggregates of subparallel plates.

Englishize ('ɪŋglɪʃaɪz), *v.* [f. ENGLISH *a.* + -IZE.] *trans.* To make English.

1858 *Brownson's Q. Rev.* Apr. 190, I want the Church Americanized no more than I want her..Englishized or Gallicized. **1922** *Blackw. Mag.* Sept. 281/1 F...had been accustomed to meet the Englishised Indian in the privacy of his board-room in London. **1928** *Sunday Dispatch* 22 July 22/3 The Englishised sport from the other side of the Atlantic. **1949** *Hansard Commons* 16 May 50/2 The conditions that exist in the North of Ireland, in those Six Counties which have been cut away and 'Englishised'.

Englishly ('ɪŋglɪʃlɪ), *adv.* [f. ENGLISH *a.* + -LY[2].] In an English manner. †**a.** By means of an English word; in English (*obs.*). **b.** After the manner of the English people, like an Englishman or Englishmen. (*rare* in mod. use.)

1529 MORE *Dial. Heresyes* I. Wks. 221/1 If he wold call the priestes englishly. **1565** J. HALLE *Hist. Expost.* 113 Scarificatio, uel cutis Sculptura, englishly Scarification. **1602** WARNER *Alb. Eng.* XII. lxxii. (1612) 300 Arm'd be euery hand and heart hence, Englishly, to beat Spaine. **1641** SIR B. RUDYARD in Rushw. *Hist. Coll.* III. (1692) I. 315 It behoves us..to be Englishly sensible of the Injustice. **1765** H. WALPOLE *Let. H. Mann* (F. Hall). **1818** JAS. MILL *Let.* 30 Apr. in *Macvey Napier's Corr.* (1879) 19 Englishly-educated people are all hostile to him. **1859** SALA *Gas-light & D.* xv. 168 Voices anything but (Englishly) human.

Englishman ('ɪŋglɪʃmən). [f. ENGLISH + MAN.]

1. a. A man who is English by descent, birth, or naturalization. The historical senses of course follow those of ENGLISH *a.*; in mod. use, unless otherwise determined by context (as in ***Englishman by descent, naturalized Englishman***), the word means one born in England or of English parents.

c **950** *Laws of Æthelstan* i. prm. (Thorpe), Ic wille ðæt ʒe fedaþ ealle wæʒa an earm Engliscmon. *c* **1205** LAY. 1973 Ah Engliscemen [*c* **1275** Englissemen] hit habbed awend. *a* **1300** *Cursor M.* 242 (Gött.) Of ingland þe nacione Er englijs men in comune. **1387** TREVISA *Higden* 33 To calle the

men of the londe englisshmen. **1480** CAXTON *Chron. Eng.* ccxli. 267 Thurugh helpe and comfort of our englysshmen. **1523** LD. BERNERS *Froiss.* I. cvii. 129 Ther was no Englysshman of armes, but that had ii. or iii. prisoners. **1593** SHAKS. *Rich. II*, I. iii. 309 Though banish'd, yet a true-borne Englishman. **1624** BEDELL *Lett.* iv. 80 Many Englishmen, conuertentur ad Dominum Deum. **1701** DE FOE *True-born Eng.* I. 310 Englishman's the common Name for all. **1791** MRS. RADCLIFFE *Rom. Forest* ii, That Englishman that used to come with his master to our house. **1863** *Lond. Rev.* 10 Jan. 35/2 A thoroughly vulgar Englishman is as offensive an animal as the human mind can well imagine.

b. *Englishman's foot* (American): see quot.

1687 CLAYTON *Virginia* in *Phil. Trans.* XLI. 145 Our Plantain..they call the Englishman's-foot. **1861** MRS. LANKESTER *Wild Flowers* 109 Plantain..has been named, by the natives in some of our settlements, 'the Englishman's Foot'.

2. An English ship.

1823 J. F. COOPER *Pilot* xxxiii, Griffith saw his own ship borne away from the Englishman. **1885** W. C. RUSSELL *Strange Voyage* I. iv. 36 She was not an Englishman, though I really forget the nationality of the colour she flew at the peak.

'Englishness. [f. as prec. + -NESS.] The quality or state of being English, or of displaying English characteristics.

1804 W. TAYLOR in Robberds *Mem.* I. 512 The Englishness of several fairy-tales supposed to be French. **1838** *New Monthly Mag.* LIII. 118 The Englishness of everything about man, woman, and child born in the island. **1884** *Athenæum* 19 Jan. 93/3 The attraction of the face of the Hon. G. Seymour Conway..lies in its Englishness.

Englishry ('ɪŋglɪʃrɪ). Forms: 5 Englisherie, 7 englechery, -esherie, Englichiré, -ishiré, -ishrye, 8 Englecerie, -eschiré, -escyre, -icherie, 7– Englishry. [ad. AFr. *englecherie*, f. *englesche*, ad. ME. *englisch*, ENGLISH; see -RY.]

1. a. The fact of being an Englishman. Chiefly in legal phrase ***Presentment of Englishry***: the offering of proof that a slain person was an Englishman, in order to escape the fine levied (under the Norman kings) upon the hundred or township for the murder of a 'Frenchman' or Norman.

Bracton, followed by the legal antiquaries of the 17th c., represents this as the continuation of a similar practice under the Danish kings; but no evidence to that effect seems to be known.

[*c* **1292** BRITTON I. vii. (1865) 38 Et volums qe nul murdre soit ajugie par la ou acun parent al mort peuse estre trové, qi peuse monstrer qe il fust Engleys, et issi presenter de ly Englescherie]. **1620** J. WILKINSON *Treat. Coroners & Sherifes* 8 By a statute made 14 E. 3. c. 4 the presentment of Englechery was wholly abrogated and annulled. **1649** SELDEN *Laws Eng.* I. xl. (1739) 62 This custom lasted long after the Normans time, the Dane being only changed into the Norman, and was called Englishire. **1741** T. ROBINSON *Gavelkind* II. ix. 275 Before the Presentment of Engleschire was taken. **1861** PEARSON *Early & Mid. Ages Eng.* 280 Unless proof of 'Englishry' were made by the four nearest relatives of the deceased. **1883** FREEMAN *Impress. U.S.* iv. 16 All accepted the statement of what I may call their Englishry.

b. = ENGLISHNESS, ENGLISHISM.

1894 *Westm. Gaz.* 21 Sept. 2/1 Our Englishry is often a shallow veneer. Scratch the Teuton, and you find an O'Shaughnessy. **1924** *Year's Work in Eng. Stud. 1923* 37 Related..is the fable of the decline and fall of English philology since the mid-nineteenth century, and its loss of Englishry and of appeal to the English. **1940** E. C. BENTLEY *Those Days* i. 3 Palmerston's death brought out in Brooks the essential Englishry of that time. **1958** *Times Lit. Suppl.* 26 Sept. 543/3 The high romance, the doggedness, the talent for nonsense that are still, to the connoisseur of Englishry, staples of life in this drab, unhygienic island.

2. a. That part of the population, esp. in Ireland, that is of English descent. *Obs.* exc. *Hist.*

c **1470** HARDING *Chron.* ccxxxi. iv, Loue of all the land He [the duke of York] had amonge the Englisherie alwaye. **1600** DYMMOK *Ireland* (1843) 6 Such good lawes as tende to the preservation of the Englishrye. **1792** BURKE *Let. Sir H. Langrishe* Wks. 1842 I. 552 The popery laws..as applied between Englishry and Irishry. **1876** GREEN *Short Hist.* vii. §8 (1882) 434 The..English law..made treasonable any marriage of the Englishry with persons of Irish blood.

b. An English population; English people generally. In a town: An English quarter. *rare.*

1867 HOWELLS *Ital. Journ.* 165 There was, beside numerous Englishry in detached bodies, a troop of Germans. **1867** FREEMAN *Norm. Conq.* (ed. 3) I. v. 310 There was an English and a Welsh town, an Englishry and a Welshry. *a* **1910** 'MARK TWAIN' *Autobiogr.* (1924) I. 120 The Norman Conqueror came over to divert the Englishry.

'Englishwoman. [f. ENGLISH + WOMAN.] A woman who is English by descent, birth, or naturalization: see ENGLISHMAN.

1530 PALSGR. 217/1 Englysshewoman, *anglesche.* **1647** WARD *Simp. Cobler* 23 Never was any people under the Sun so sick..of new fashions as English-women. **1817** BYRON *Beppo* lxxxix, Where an Englishwoman sometimes faints, Italian females don't do so outright. **1860** FROUDE *Hist. Eng.* VI. 42 Above all things let her remember to be a good English-woman.

'Englishy, *a.* [f. as prec- + -Y.] Characteristic of what is English (as opposed to American, etc.).

1873 W. D. HOWELLS *Chance Acquaintance* vi. 133 The people, too, had such Englishy faces. **1880** *Scribn. Mag.* Feb. 633 'A fogger going to fodder his cattle'..'before the summer ricks are all carted'..how Englishy such sentences sound! **1903** *Westm. Gaz.* 4 Feb. 10/1 He spoke in a high Englishy way, which rather jarred on the ears of a Scotch boy. **1912** D. H. LAWRENCE *Let.* 13 May in F. Lawrence *Not I, but the Wind* (1934) 39 It's a quiet, dead little village [in Germany]..a bit Englishy. **1930** *Times Educ. Suppl.* 26 Apr. 183/3 The English teacher [in Canada] needs much tact, for if she is suspected of being 'Englishy', there will not be much reward of gratitude from the parents. **1967** *Guardian* 1 Feb. 9/6 Englishy pubs..have sprung up in New York.

Eng. Lit. Short for *English Literature*, considered as an academic subject of study.

1850 MRS. GASKELL *Let.* 25 Jan. (1966) 103 Mr Tom Taylor (the late Professor of Eng. Lit. in University College). **1869** LADY AMBERLEY *Diary* 24 Feb. in B. & P. Russell *Amberley Papers* (1937) II. 260, I went to the two Introductory Lectures given by Prof. Morley on Eng. Lit. and by Prof. Forster on Experimental Physics. **1937** S. POTTER *Muse in Chains* 17 Eng. Lit. is an example of the interpretation of the greater by the lesser: of great English writers by anecdotalists, antiquarians, hero-worshippers, pedants, and collectors. **1948** *N. & Q.* 6 Mar. 89/2 Joan Curl's pleasant story has a distinct flavour of Eng. Lit. **1957** *Listener* 19 Dec. 1025/1 The donnish or Eng. Lit. attitude toward the drama. **1958** *Observer* 30 Nov. 19/7 Earnest students of Eng. Lit. in the U.S.S.R. **1967** G. STEINER *Lang. & Silence* 82 It seems to me that the wide gap between the orthodox academic formulation of 'Eng. Lit.'..and the realities of our intellectual and psychological situation may account for the general *malaise* in the field.

englobe (ɛn'gləʊb), *v.* Also 7 in-. [f. EN-[1] + GLOBE. Cf. Fr. *englober.*] **1.** *trans.* **a.** To form into a globe, make globular; to round; in quot. *refl.* and *fig.* **b.** To enclose in, or as in, a globe; in quots. *fig.*

1611 FLORIO, *Agglobare*, to en-globe or make round. **1641** MILTON *Ch. Govt.* Wks. 1738 I. 53 Prelaty..must be forc'd to dissolve and unmake her own pyramidal figure..inglobe or incube her self among the Presbyters. *a* **1843** FOSTER in *Life & Corr.* (1846) I. 184 If..it [youthful energy] could be englobed..within the bosom of the young adventurer. **1858** SEARS *Athan.* II. x. 235 The degree in which the heavens are englobed within us.

2. *Biol.* To absorb (bacteria, etc.) within a phagocyte or the like. So **en'globed** *ppl. a.*; **en'globement**, the process or state of being englobed; **en'globing** *vbl. sb.*

1900 GOULD *Pocket Med. Dict.* (ed. 4) 233 *Englobing*, the taking in of an object by a phagocyte. **1902** *Encycl. Brit.* XXXI. 536/2 Red blood corpuscles are often englobed by this amœba. **1902** *Jrnl. Exper. Med.* VI. 155 The bodies of englobed parasites. *Ibid.*, The englobement of parasites in the liver is more active at certain periods of the cycle.

engloom: see EN- *pref.*[1] 2.

†en'glose, *v. Obs. trans.* ? To paint, polish.

1430 LYDG. *Chron. Troy* I. v, In his chambre englosed bryht and cleare That shone full shene with gold & with asure.

†en'glue, *v. Obs.* Also 4 engleue. [a. Fr. *englue-r*, f. *en-* (see EN-[1]) + *glu* birdlime.]

1. *trans.* To fasten down or close with, or as with, glue. *lit.* and *fig.*

1393 GOWER *Conf.* III. 312 He sighe and redy fonde This coffre made and well englued. *c* **1430** LYDG. *Bochas* II. xxviii. (1554) 65 a, And that theyr iyen by none yllusions Be not englued. **1475** CAXTON *Jason* 81 But whan their mosels ben englued.

b. To attach, connect closely. *fig.*

c **1430** LYDG. *Bochas* VI. xii. (1554) 159 a, Euery surfet englued es to other And one misrule bringeth in an other.

2. To fix to the spot, as (a bird) with birdlime; hence, to ensnare, fascinate.

1393 GOWER *Conf.* I. 331 He hath my lady so engleued She woll nought that he be remeued. *c* **1430** LYDG. *Bochas* II. xxx. (1554) 66 b, Deceit, that..Folkes englueth.

englut (ɛn'glʌt), *v. arch.* Forms: α. 5 englot, 6 englouette, 6– englut. β. 6 inglutte, 7, 9 inglut. [Really two words: (1) ad. OF. *englotir* (Fr. *engloutir*):—L. *ingluttīre*, f. *in-* (see IN-) + *gluttīre* to gulp, swallow; (2) f. EN-[1] + GLUT *v.*]

1. *trans.* To swallow, swallow up; to gulp down.

1491 CAXTON *Vitas Patr.* (W. de W. 1495) I. li. 108 a/1, Bounden with the boundes of the deuyll, and englotted in his bely. **1534** LD. BERNERS *Gold. Bk. M. Aurel.* (1546) R viij, Wyll ye..entre agayne into the swalowe of the see, for to engloutte you? **1581** J. BELL *Haddon's Answ. Osor.* 320 b Themselves engluttyng Partriches, Peacockes, Woodcockes. **1607** SHAKS. *Timon* II. ii. 175 How many prodigall bits haue Slaues and Pezants This night englutted. **1814** CARY *Dante* (Chandos) 169 Inveterate wolf! whose gorge ingluts more prey, Than any beast beside. **1832** L. HUNT *Transl.* Wks. 262 Night..hath got thee; To clutch and to englut thee.

2. To glut, satiate. *lit.* and *fig.* Also *refl.*

1571 ASCHAM *Scholem.* I. (Arb.) 50 Being once inglutted with vanitie, he will streight way loth all learning. **1593** NASHE *Christ's T.* (1613) 157 Whosoeuer englutteth himselfe, is guilty of his owne death. **1610** *Histrio-mastix* v. 183 To englut Their bestiall and more brutish appetites. **1619** *North's Gueuara's Diall Pr.* 701/2 Hee hadde inglutted himselfe with the variety of meates hee did eat at the feast. *c* **1800** DOWNEMAN *Ragnar Lodbrach*, There the wild beast inglutted stood. **1872** BLACKIE *Lays Highl.* 53 Hungry war Engluts his tiger-maw.

Hence **en'glutted,** *ppl. a.*

1814 CARY *Dante* (Chandos) 86 Wretched ventricle, That turns th' englutted aliment to dross.

†en'glute, *v. Alch. Obs.* [app. ad. med.L. **inglūtāre*, corresp. to F. *engluer*: see ENGLUE. Cf. Pr. *englutir.*] *trans.* To close with slime or glue; to seal up (a vessel), make air-tight; implied in **en'gluting,** *vbl. sb.* (See ENLUTE.)

c **1386** CHAUCER *Chan. Yem. Prol. & T.* 213 What sholde I tellen..Of the pot and glasses englutyng [*v.r.* enlutyng] That of the Eyr myghte passe out no thyng. **1584** R. SCOT *Disc. Witchcr.* XIV. i. 294 Mysticall termes of art, as..their subliming, amalgaming, engluting [*marginal note*, enluting]. **1692** COLES, *Engluting*, gluing or glued, stopped.

‖'englyn. Sometimes in Welsh pl. **englynion.** [Welsh.] In Welsh poetry, a stanza (now always a quatrain) of a certain metrical structure.

1612 DRAYTON *Polyolbion* iv. 59 In Englins some there were that on their subiect straine. *Ibid. note* p. 67 Englins are couplets interchanged of 16 and 14 feet called Paladiries and Pensels. **1866** *Cornh. Mag.* Mar. 28 About 2000 englynion or epigrammatic stanzas. **1875** *Anderida* I. XII. 236 Bards, your choicest englyns sing.

‖engobe (ɛn'gəʊb). [Fr.] (See quot.)

1857 BIRCH *Anc. Pottery* (1858) II. 326 An engobe or white coating of pipe-clay, with which the potter has covered the vase. **1875** FORTNUM *Maiolica* i. 9 The translucent coat through which the white 'slip' or 'engobe' became apparent.

engod, -gold, -golden: see EN- *pref.*[1] 1 b, 2.

engore (ɛn'gɔə(r)), *v.*[1] Also 6 engoar, ingore, 7 ingoar. [f. EN-[1] + GORE *sb.*] *trans.* To steep in gore; to make gory, stain with blood.

1593 NASHE *Christ's T.* (1613) 39 He shall..Oxen, Sheepe, Cammels, idely engore. **1597** DANIEL *Civ. Wares* VIII. ii. This new chosen Lord..with the sword..Ingor'd his new-worne crowne. *c* **1611** CHAPMAN *Iliad* XII. 212 A high-flowne eagle..sustain'd a dragon all engor'd In her strong seres. *Ibid.* XXI. 22 (D.) The flood blush'd to be so much engor'd With such base souls. **1615** W. HULL *Mirr. of Maiestie* 86 This bloud, wherewith I am ingoared. *c* **1800** DOWNMAN *Ragnar Lodbrach* in Evans *O. Ball.* III. iv. 113 With hunger keen the trenchant sword Wide the Scarfian rocks engor'd.

Hence **en'gored,** *ppl. a. Obs.*

1602 *Return fr. Parnass.* II. v. iv. (Arb.) 69 There shall engoared venom be my inke.

†en'gore, *v.*[2] *Obs. rare.* [f. EN-[1] + GORE *v.*] *trans.* To gore, wound deeply; *fig.* to 'goad', infuriate. Hence **en'gored,** *ppl. a.*

1590 SPENSER *F.Q.* II. viii. 42 As salvage Bull..When rancour doth with rage him once engore. *Ibid.* III. v. 28 By the great persue which she there perceav'd; Well hoped shee the beast engor'd had beene. **1596** *Ibid.* IV. ix. 31 As when an eager mastiffe once doth prove The tast of bloud of some engored beast.

engorge (ɛn'gɔːdʒ), *v.* Also 6 ingurge, 6–8 ingorge. [a. F. *engorge-r*, f. *en* in + *gorge* GORGE, throat.]

1. *trans.* To fill the gorge of; to gorge, feed or fill to excess; chiefly *refl.* Also (rarely) *intr.* for *refl.*

Prob. first used (in Eng.) with ref. to hawks; see GORGE.

1515 BARCLAY *Egloges* II. (1570) A vj/1 A birde well ingorged kepes well her nest. **1549** COVERDALE *Erasm. Par. 1 Cor.* viii. 4 Engorge and pamper vppe themselues with flesh offered to idolles. **1557** NORTH *Diall of Princes* 62 a, To ingurge themselves with wyne. **1603** HOLLAND *Plutarch's Mor.* 1213 You sit downe to meat..but touch not one dish, leaving them afterwards for your servants to engorge themselves therewith. **1667** MILTON *P.L.* IX. 791 Greedily she ingorg'd without restraint.

fig. *a* **1559** DOLMAN in *Mirrour for Magistr.* (1568) N 8 b, With pleasures cloyed, engorged with the fyll. **1689** T. PLUNKET *Char. Gd. Commander* 16 A Cur engorged with asperity.

b. *transf.* in *passive*: To be filled to excess, crammed. Chiefly *Path.* of animal tissues or organs: To be congested with blood.

1599 *Broughton's Lett.* i. 6 Virulent letters..ingorged with impudent lies. **1632** LITHGOW *Trav.* x. 499 The Riuers are ingorged with Salmond. **1834** J. FORBES *Laennec's Dis. Chest* (ed. 4) 213 The surrounding pulmonary substance..was red and engorged. **1869** H. USSHER in *Eng. Mech.* 3 Dec. 272/2 These vessels are congested, or engorged with blood.

2. To put (food) into the gorge; to devour greedily. Also *transf.* and *fig.* to swallow up (as a vortex).

1541 ELYOT *Image Gov.* (1556) 72 b, Also ingorgeyng meate upon meate. **1609** HOLLAND *Amm. Marcel.* XXIII. vi. 237 Neither doth any man, after he hath once satisfied his hunger, engorge superfluous meats. **1798** *Month. Mag.* VI. 366 Prepare not to ingorge The eternal pyramids. **1850** NEALE *Med. Hymns* 48 Engorg'd in former years, their prey Must Death and Hell restore today.

absol. **1739** *Grobianus* 142 Ingorge once more. *Ibid.* 179 Largely ingorge, and labour thro' the Treat.

Hence **en'gorged** *ppl. a.*, **en'gorger** *sb.*, **en'gorging** *vbl. sb.*

1562 BULLEYN *Def. agst. Sickness, Sicke men, &c.* 65 a, This will not helpe to digest your ingorged full stomack. **1598** FLORIO, *Diuoratore*, a deuourer, a glutton, an engorger. **1611** COTGR., *Ingorger*, A rauener, glutton, gulch, ingorger. *Ibid.*, *Engorgement*, a glutting, rauening, deuouring, ingorging.

engorgement (ɛn'gɔːdʒmənt). [f. ENGORGE *v.* + -MENT.] **a.** The action of engorging. **b.** The state of being engorged, in various senses, esp. *Path.*

the congestion (of a tissue or organ) with blood, secretions, etc.

1611 SPEED *Hist. Gt. Brit.* IX. xvi. (1632) 844 The warre eates on still in the body of France, but not with so sharpe teeth, nor so full engorgement as before. **1866** A. FLINT *Princ. Med.* (1880) 163 The period during which the affected lobe is in the state of active congestion or engorgement. **1872** DARWIN *Emotions* xiii. 325 The engorgement of the face, ears, and eyes with blood. **1873** HOLLAND *A. Bonnic.* vii. 118 His aim was..never to press to engorgement the receptive faculties. **1878** NAPHEYS *Phys. Life Woman* II. 233 Averting the violent rush of the milk.. and the consequent engorgement of the breast. **1881** RAYMOND *Mining Gloss., Engorgement*, the clogging of a furnace.

†**en'gotish**, *v. nonce-wd.* [f. EN-¹ + GOT(H + -ISH.] *trans.* To class or designate as 'Gothic'.

1664 EVELYN tr. *Freart's Archit.* Pref. 5 To Engotish.. after their own capricious humour an infinite many which do all pass under this appellation.

‖**engouement** (ãguːmã). Also 9 **engoument**. [Fr.: lit. obstruction in the throat.]

Unreasoning fondness.

1848 THACKERAY *Van. Fair* xxxiv. (1866) 280 She repaid Miss Crawley's *engoument* by artless sweetness and friendship. **1851** SIR F. PALGRAVE *Norm. & Eng.* I. Introd. 44 Swayed by the *engouement* for classical literature.

engouled (ɛn'guːld), *a. Her.* [ad. Fr. *engoulée*, fem. pa. pple. of *engouler*, f. *en* in + OF. *goule* (F. *gueule*) mouth (of a beast). The mod. Dicts. give the Fr. form *engoulée*.]

An epithet applied to bends, crosses, saltiers, etc., the extremities of which enter the mouths of animals.

1830 ROBSON *Brit. Her.* Gloss.

†**en'gouted**, *ppl. a. Obs.* Also 5 **engowted**. [? f. EN-¹ + GOUT drop.] ? Marked with spots like drops of blood.

c **1450** *Bk. Hawkyng* in *Rel. Ant.* I. 296 This hawke is engowted into braell ende. **1677** N. COX *Gentl. Recreation* II. (1706) 58 Her Brail feathers are engouted betwixt red and black.

engown: see EN- *pref.*¹ 1 a.

†**en'gowschede**, *ppl. a. Obs. rare*⁻¹. [Etymology and meaning uncertain: cf. OF. *engoussé* stout, fleshy.]

?*a* **1400** *Morte Arth.* 2053 A dragone engowschede.

engrace (ɛn'greɪs), *v.* Also 7 **in-**. [f. EN-¹ + GRACE *sb.*] †**a.** To introduce into favour (cf. *ingratiate*) *obs.* **b.** To put grace into.

Hence **en'graced**, *ppl. a.* **en'gracer**, one who or that which engraces.

1610 G. FLETCHER *Christ's Vict.* in Farr *S.P. Jas. I* (1848) 74 Ingrac't into so high a favour. *a* **1641** BP. R. MOUNTAGU *Acts & Monum.* (1642) 235 His intent was..to ingrace his service with King Herod. **1874** PUSEY *Lent. Serm.* 109 He.. made it a violence to their engraced nature, not to choose Him. **1866** —— *Mirac. Prayer* 5 God is its Engracer, its Indweller.

†**en'graded**, *ppl. a. Her. Obs. rare*⁻¹. Also **in-**. [f. EN-¹ + GRADE + -ED.] (See quot.)

1486 *Bk. St. Alban's, Her.* D ij b, Off a cros engraylid or engradid. *Ibid.* Thei ar calde armys engradit for they ar made of ij colouris the wich graditly ar broght to gedir oon coloure into another coloure. *Ibid.* D iij b, Ther is also a partyng of armys of ij colours ingradyt.

†**en'graff, in'graff**, *v. Obs.* or *arch.* [f. EN-¹, IN- + GRAFF *v.*]

1. = ENGRAFT *v.* 1.

c **1420** *Pallad. on Husb.* IV. 33 He..nygh the roote ingraffeth his sarment. **1590** MARLOWE *2nd Pt. Tamburl.* II. iii, That Zoacum, that fruit of bitterness, That in the midst of fire is ingraff'd. *a* **1617** BAYNE *On Eph.* (1658) 140 Before wee engraffe a Science, wee cut it, and set it for incision. *a* **1667** COWLEY *Shortness Life* Wks. (1688) 138 Who does a slight and annual Plant engraff Upon a lasting stock. **1765** A. DICKSON *Treat. Agric.* iii. (ed. 3) 35 There is scarcely a kind of tree, but may be ingraffed into any other kind. *a* **1803** BEATTIE tr. *Virgil's Past.* I. (R.), Mow Melibœus, now ingraff the pear, Now teach the vine its tender sprays to rear!

2. *fig.* = ENGRAFT *v.* 2.

a **1400** WYCLIF *1 Tim.* vi. 10 The which sum men coueitynge, erreden fro the feith, and bisettiden [*v.r.* ingraffiden; L. *inserebant*] hem with many sorwis. *c* **1449** PECOCK *Repr.* 563 He is ouer greet to be ingraffid here. **1542** BECON *Christm. Banq.* Wks. (1843) 74 He is 'the vine,' in whom we being ingraffed must needs bring forth much fruit. **1561** T. NORTON *Calvin's Inst.* II. 145 He did after a certain maner engraffe them into yᵉ household of Abraham. **1596** DALRYMPLE tr. *Leslie's Hist. Scot.* II. 142 To ingrafe and poure in the hartis of the ignorant people, diuine rites. **1605** *Answ. Supposed Discov. Rom. Doctr.* &c. 46 They be matriculated and ingraffed to the University. **1641** MILTON *Ch. Discip.* I. (1851) 20 How many surreptitious works are ingraff'd into the legitimate writings of the Fathers. **1660** R. COKE *Power & Subj.* 83 That there is a God..is..naturally ingraffed into the minds of all men. **1695** E. WELCHMAN *Husbandm. Manual* (1707) 43 There are too many, who, tho' engraffed into the Church, live no better..than many Heathens. **1739** *Grobianus* 224 The better to ingraff In Mem'ry ev'ry useful Paragraph.

b. To beget. *rare.*

1864 SWINBURNE *Atalanta* 963 [Children] All holy born, engraffed of Tantalus.

†**c.** In *passive*: To be closely attached *to*. *Obs.*

1597 SHAKS. *2 Hen. IV*, II. ii. 67 You haue beene so lewde, and so much ingraffed to Falstaffe.

Hence **en'graffed**, *ppl. a.* **en'graffer**, **en'graffing**, *vbl. sb.* **en'graffment** = ENGRAFTMENT.

1586 T. ROGERS 39 *Art.* (1621) 125 Before men be regenerate, they are..not engraffed, but wild olives. **1604** SHAKS. *Oth.* II. iii. 145 With one of an ingraft Infirmitie. *a* **1619** DONNE *Βιαθανατος* (1644) 81 This first ingraffed and inborne desire. **1643** T. GOODWIN *Trial Chr. Growth* 8 He is the ingraffer, and implanter of all the branches into this Vine. *a* **1655** VINES *Lord's Supp.* (1677) 285 The one seals our engraffing and implanting into Christ. **1705** STANHOPE *Paraphr.* III. 52 Engraffing..incorporates one sort of Plant with a Tree of another. *a* **1638** MEDE *Wks.* I. xlii. 236 By their spiritual engraffment into him.

engraft, ingraft (ɛn-, ɪn'grɑːft, -græft), *v.* In 7 *pa. pple.* **engraften**. [f. EN-¹, IN- + GRAFT.]

1. *trans.* To graft in; to insert (a scion of one tree) as a graft *into* or *upon* (another). Also *absol.*

a **1677** BARROW *Serm.* III. xxiii. (R.), Upon the wildest stock divine husbandry can engraft most excellent fruit. **1701** CUNNINGHAM in *Phil. Trans.* XXIII. 1206 When they ingraft, they do not slit the Stock as we do, but cut a small slice off the outside of the Stock. **1732** BERKELEY *Alciphr.* I. § 14 If upon a plum-tree peaches and apricots are engrafted. **1797** HOLCROFT tr. *Stolberg's Trav.* (ed. 2) II. lx. 367 Trees ..which, by engrafting, bear two kinds of fruit. **1816** J. SMITH *Panorama Sc. & Art* II. 640 Pear-trees are propagated by engrafting..upon free stocks.

b. *transf.* To set firmly *in*.

1793 SMEATON *Edystone L.* § 83 The foundation stones of every course were engrafted into, or rather rooted in the rock. *Ibid.* § 245 A socket, whereby the courses would have been mutually engrafted.

2. *fig.* (Often with express reference to a metaphorical 'tree', 'stock', etc.) **a.** To implant (virtues, dispositions, sentiments) *in* the mind; to incorporate (a thing) *into* a previously existing system or unity, (an alien) *into* a race or community; and the like. **b.** Const. *on*, *upon*: To super-add (something adventitious) to something already existing which serves as a basis. †**c.** *Comm.* To add to the stock of a trading company (cf. ENGRAFTMENT 3).

a. 1585 ABP. SANDYS *Serm.* (1841) 114 This word..would root out vice and ingraft virtue. **1633** EARL MANCH. *Al Mondo* (1636) 203 This ardent Love engrafting me into God by her uniting vertue. **1634** T. JOHNSON tr. *Parey's Chirurg.* XXIV. ii. (1678) 538 Lest that their sad..and pensive cogitations, should be..engraften in the issue. **1635** SWAN *Spec. M.* v. § 2. (1643) 161 Finding that some false tenets were engrafted amongst the ignorant. **1642** ROGERS *Naaman* Ep. Ded. 3 Yet God hath ingrafted your Honour into another stocke. **1643** MILTON *Divorce* II. iii. (1851) 70 This cannot be lesse then to ingraft sin into the substance of the law. **1737** WHISTON *Josephus' Antiq.* XVII. xii. § 1 A certain young man..ingrafted himself into the kindred of Herod by the resemblance of his countenance. *a* **1754** FIELDING *Remedy Afflict.* Wks. 1775 IX. 247 Acquiring solid lasting habits of virtue, and ingrafting them into our character.

b. 1667 MILTON *P.L.* XI. 35 All his works on mee Good or not good ingraft, my Merit those Shall perfet, and for these my Death shall pay. **1736** BERKELEY *App. Querist* II. § 106 It may..be fatal to engraft trade on a national bank. **1790** BURKE *Fr. Rev.* Wks. V. 232 You can..ingraft any description of republick on a monarchy. **1800** DUNDAS in J. Owen *Wellesley's Disp.* 563 The addition made to your European infantry..being engrafted on old disciplined well seasoned regiments. **1827** J. POWELL *Devises* (ed. 3) II. 245 An executory limitation [is] engrafted on an alternate contingent remainder in fee on another. **1839** ALISON *Hist. Europe* (1849–50) I. Introd. § 18 On the decayed stock of urban liberty they ingrafted the vigorous shoots of pastoral freedom. **1855** MACAULAY *Hist. Eng.* III. 524 A bill of pains and penalties..should be..engrafted on the Bill of Indemnity. **1881** GRANT *Cameronians* I. i. 14 It had been added to, or engrafted on, the tall, old, square baronial tower.

c. 1697 LUTTRELL *Brief Rel.* (1857) IV. 164 Whether they would admit talleys and their own notes to be engrafted upon their stock.

3. To graft (a tree), to furnish with a graft.

1794 MARTYN *Rousseau's Bot.* vii. 73 Fruit-trees are somewhat in the same case, by being ingrafted.

†**b.** To introduce small-pox virus into (a person's system); = INOCULATE. *Obs.*

1717 LADY M. W. MONTAGUE *Lett.* (1887) I. 228 The boy was engrafted last Tuesday..I cannot engraft the girl.

engraftation (ɛngrɑː'fteɪʃən, -græf-). *rare.* [f. prec. + -ATION.] The action of engrafting.

1816 G. S. FABER *Origin Pag. Idol.* II. 432 Engraftation. **1817** —— *Eight Dissert.* (1845) III. 372 Ingraftation. *a* **1853** ROBERTSON *Serm.* Ser. IV. xxviii. 213 The result of that engraftation was, that the fruit..savored partly of the new graft, and partly of the old stock.

engrafted (ɛn'grɑːftɪd, -græf-), *ppl. a.* [f. ENGRAFT *v.* + -ED¹.] In the senses of the vb. *lit.* and *fig.* †*engrafted holding*: = EMPHYTEUSIS.

c **1600** SHAKS. *Sonn.* xxxvii, I make my love engrafted to this store. **1611** BIBLE *Jas.* i. 21 Receiue with meeknesse the engrafted word. **1657** AUSTEN *Fruit Trees* II. 21 The Tree is certainly good, an ingrafted Tree. **1721** *Lond. Gaz.* No. 5934/2 The Proprietors of the ingrafted stock are required to make the Payment of 3*l.* per cent. **1762** J. BROWN *Poetry & Mus.* xi. (1763) 186 On their first Entrance into Rome, these dramatic Shews were no longer in their natural, but in an ingrafted State. *c* **1766** BURKE *Tracts Popery Laws* Wks. IX. 391 The Romans..therefore invented this species of engrafted holding. **1807** J. E. SMITH *Phys. Bot.* 35 He found a layer of new wood under the engrafted bark.

†**en'grafter**. *Obs.* [f. as prec. + -ER.] One who engrafts.

1721 R. KEITH tr. *T. à Kempis' Soliloq. Soul* xvi. 235 He is the Lover and the Ingrafter of Cleanness.

engrafting (ɛn'grɑːftɪŋ, -græf-), *vbl. sb.* [f. ENGRAFT *v.* + -ING¹.] The action of the verb ENGRAFT in various senses.

1667 *Phil. Trans.* II. 553 The curious engrafting of oranges. **1717** LADY M. W. MONTAGUE *Lett.* I. xxxv. 130 The small-pox..is here entirely harmless by the invention of ingrafting, which is the term they give it.

engraftment (ɛn'grɑːftmənt, -græf-). Also **in-**. [f. as prec. + -MENT.]

1. The action of engrafting. *lit.* and *fig.* Also *concr.* the shoot engrafted, a graft.

1647 M. HUDSON *Div. Right Govt.* II. x. 165 The engraftment and plantation of Christian principles in the heart of an Infidel. *a* **1743** SAVAGE *Ep. Dyer* 46 Those trees ..Which from our own engraftment fruitful rise. **1745** tr. *Columella's Husb.* IV. xxix, I engaged to give directions about ingrafting of vines, and preserving the ingraftments. **1774** BP. HALIFAX *Anal. Rom. Law* (1795) Pref. 21 The laws of England have received great improvements by ingraftments from the Roman. **1837** WHITTOCK *Bk. Trades* (1842) 370 The consequent ingraftment of Norman French upon the previous Saxonish dialects. **1858** *Sat. Rev.* 14 Aug. 166/1 On that fatal day [Bosworth Field] the White Rose withered for ever, and he cannot stomach its engraftment on the rival stalk.

†**2.** = INOCULATION. *Obs.* Cf. ENGRAFT *v.* 3 b.

1722 NETTLETON *Inoculation* in *Phil. Trans.* XXXII. 210 This Distemper is raised by an Ingraftment from the Small Pox.

†**3.** The issuing of additional stock in a trading company. *Obs.* Cf. ENGRAFT *v.* 2 c.

1721 *Lond. Gaz.* No. 5934/3 The 7*l.* per cent. which was due..pursuant to the Terms of the Ingraftment. **1776** ADAM SMITH *W.N.* I. II. ii. 319 The Bank was allowed to enlarge its capital by an engraftment of 1,001,171*l.* 10*s.*

†**en'grafture**. *Obs.* In 7 **ingrafture**. [f. as prec. + -URE.] The action of engrafting; the state of being engrafted.

1654 WARREN *Unbelievers* 104 It is compared to an ingrafture of a branch in a tree. **1658** BP. REYNOLDS *Lord's Supp.* xi, We often read..of his more peculiar presence with and in his people, and of our spiritual ingrafture into him by faith.

engrail (ɛn'greɪl), *v.* Forms: α. 4–5 **engrele**, 5 **engreyl, -grale**, 6–7 **engraile, -ayl**, 6– **engrail**. β. 5 **ingrayl**, 6–7 **ingrail, -ale, -eyl**, (6 **ingrele**). [ME. *engrele*, a. OF. *engresle-r* (mod.F. *engrêler*), commonly believed to be f. *en-* (see EN-¹) + *gresle*, *grêle* hail.

The original sense would thus be 'to pit or indent as by a shower of hail.' The writer of the Book of St. Albans (see quot. 1486 s.v. ENGRAILED) supposed that the word was derived from *gree* (L. *gradus*) step, and hence he gives *ingradatus* as the Lat. equivalent of 'engrailed.' Cf. ENGRADED.]

1. a. *Her.* To indent the edge of (an ordinary) with a series of contiguous curvilinear notches. **b.** Hence *gen.* to ornament the edge of (anything) with an indented pattern of this kind.

Almost exclusively in pa. pple.: see ENGRAILED *ppl. a.*

c **1420** *Anturs of Arth.* xl, With his griffuns of gold engrelet fulle gay. *a* **1440** *Sir Degrev.* 1030 He beres in cheef of azour Engrelyd with a satur [*i.e.* saltire]. *c* **1500** *Sc. Poem Her.* 136 in *Q. Eliz. Acad.* 99 The first, hole croce; the tother, engrelit be. **1572** BOSSEWELL *Armorie* II. 27 The quarters in the division of the Escocheon be engrayled. **1605** CAMDEN *Rem.* (1637) 214 They bare for their Armes Argent a Bend ingreyled Gules. **1695** *Lond. Gaz.* No. 3081/4 A Lyon Rampant with Ermine in a border ingral'd. **1766** PORNY *Heraldry* Gloss., *Engrailed*, This word signifies a thing the hail has fallen upon, and broken off the edges, like the leaves of a tree notched by hail-stones. **1840** BARHAM *Ingol. Leg.* Pref. 4 The Ingoldsby escutcheon, a saltire engrailed Gules. **1864** BOUTELL *Heraldry Hist. & Pop.* xv. (ed. 3) 186 They also engrail the bend itself. **1877** W. JONES *Finger-ring L.* 248 A curious ring was exhibited..It is engrailed.

2. *transf.* To give a serrated appearance to; formerly sometimes, to roughen, render prickly.

1576 NEWTON tr. *Lemnie's Complex.* 286 Their bodyes.. engrayled with lothsome blisters. **1594** NASHE *Unfort. Trav.* 53 The eighth had all his armour throughout engrayled like a crabbed brierie hawthorne bush. **1612** DRAYTON *Poly-olb.* xxix. (1748) 380, I [the river Wear] indent the earth, and then I it engraile With many a turn and trace. **1661** MORGAN *Sph. Gentry* I. ii. 23 Ingraling the earth by the waved lines of water. **1832** TENNYSON *Palace Art* xxix, Or over hills with peaky tops engrail'd.

†**3.** To indent, sculpture in intaglio. *Obs.*

1548 HALL *Chron. Hen. VIII*, 73 A fountayne of enbowed woorke, gylte with fine gold, and bice, ingrayled with anticke woorkes. **1566** DRANT *Horace Sat.* III. F viij b, The executours of Staberie engraylde on his grave, What were his ample legaces. **1567** *Ibid., Arte Poet.* B v, Lawes to ingrale in during brasse. **1577** STANYHURST *Descr. Irel.* in Holinshed *Chron.* VI. 26 The famous conquest of so woorthie a potentate should be ingrailed in perpetuall memorie. **1602** FULBECKE *Pandects* 63 Their countenances were resembled and engrailed in their Armorie.

†**4.** ? To variegate, adorn with mixture of colours.

In the first two quots. possibly: To surround with an indented border.

1483 in *Antiq. Repert.* (1807) I. 50 Rede cloth engreyled with vj yerdes of white woolen cloth. **1548** HALL *Chron.* (1809) 516 Cloth of golde set with redde roses ingreyled with gold of brouderye. *c* **1611** CHAPMAN *Iliad* XXIII. 761 Æacides then shows..a caldron new, engrail'd with twenty hues.

5. In mod. poetry sometimes used for: To ornament *with* (metal).

It is not clear whether any more definite sense is intended in the examples here quoted.

1814 SOUTHEY *Roderick* I, White turbans, glittering armour, shields engrail'd With gold. **1823** BOWLES *Grave Last Sax.* IV. 552 The lion ramps Upon his mailed breast, engrailed with gold. **1870** BRYANT *Iliad* I. x. 318 The car Engrailed with brass.

engrailed (ɛn'greɪld), *ppl. a.* [f. ENGRAIL *v.*]

1. (See ENGRAIL *v.* I.) **a.** *Her.* Of an ordinary: Having a series of curvilinear indentations in the edge. **b.** *gen.* Of the edge of any object, of a line, a circle, etc.: Ornamented with a series of curvilinear indentations. **c.** Of a coin: Having a margin formed by an engrailed circle, or with a ring of dots. **d.** *Entom.* ***engrailed moth***, *Tephrosia biundularia*; ***small engrailed moth***, *T. crepuscularis* (Newman *Brit. Moths* 66).

?*a* **1400** *Morte Arth.* 4183 He had sothely for-sakene þe sawturoure engrelede. **1486** *Bk. St. Albans, Her.* E ij b, Sych a bordure is calde a bordure ingraylit for the colowre of hym is put *gre* by *gre* into the felde of tharmys. **1830** E. HAWKINS *Anglo-Fr. Coin.* 128 Legend..within two concentric engrailed circles. **1848** RICKMAN *Goth. Archit.* xx, The nail-head, and engrailed ornaments. **1856** SMYTH *Rom. Fam. Coins* 97 A well struck engrailed coin of excellent workmanship. **1871** W. H. TURNER *Publ. Harl. Soc.* V. 86 A cross engrailed between four water bougets.

†**2.** (See ENGRAIL *v.* 3.) Incised, carved in intaglio. *Obs.*

1784 J. BARRY *Lect. Art* i. (1848) 69 The intaglio or engrailed figures on our Gothic tombs.

†**en'grailing,** *vbl. sb. Obs.* [f. as prec. + -ING[1].] The action of the verb ENGRAIL. Also *concr.* an engrailed edge.

1486 *Bk. St. Albans, Her.* C vj a, This engraylyng is no propur langage aftir the sight of thys cros, bot rather an endentyng. **1611** COTGR., *Engreslure*, an ingrayling, or inuecking; a kind of small indenting..in a coat of Armes. **1753** HOGARTH *Anal. Beauty* x. 61 Those regular engralings (as the heralds express it) which displeased the eye before. **1784** J. BARRY *Lect. Art* iii. (1848) 150 This ridiculous carved work and engrailing.

en'grailment. [f. as prec. + -MENT.] **a.** *Her.* The state of being engrailed or indented in curved lines. **b.** The engrailed circle round the margin of a coin, etc.

1856 SMYTH *Rom. Fam. Coins* 31 The laureated and ringletted profile of Apollo within an engrailment.

engrain, ingrain (ɛn-, ɪn'greɪn), *v.* Also 4 engreyne, 6 engrene. [f. EN-[1], IN- + GRAIN.

Palsgr. 1530 gives a Fr. *engrainer* to dye. The word, whether first formed in Fr. or Eng., was suggested by the Fr. phrase *en graine* (adapted in Eng. as *in grain*) where *graine* means the cochineal dye. Hence *to engrain* and *to dye in grain* meant originally to dye with cochineal, and subsequently to dye in any fast colour. But afterwards they came to be associated with the word *grain*, a. Fr. *grain*, the 'fibre' or minute structure of a thing; so that in mod. use 'to dye in (the) grain' means to impregnate the very substance of the material with the dye, to dye the wool before it is woven; and the present senses of the vb. *engrain* have distinct reference to *grain* 'minute structure.' On the whole the form *engrain* is now preferred to *ingrain*; see however the note on ENGRAINED *ppl. a.*]

†**1.** *trans.* To dye scarlet or crimson with cochineal; hence, to dye in fast colours, dye in grain. Also *transf.* and *fig. Obs.* or *arch.*

Already regarded as an archaism in Spenser's time, as the glossary to *Shep. Cal.* explains *engrained* by 'dyed in grain.'

α. *c* **1377** LANGL. *P. Pl.* B. II. 15 Hire robe was ful riche of red scarlet engreyned. **1465** *Mann. & Househ. Exp.* 162 Fyne crymysyne engreyned. **1502** ARNOLDE *Chron.* (1811) 264, I delyuered my clothes engrened to Mayster Foster. **1532-3** *Act 24 Hen. VIII*, c. 13 Clothe of the colours of scarlet, crimosen, or violet engrayned. **1579** SPENSER *Sheph. Cal.* Feb. 131 With Leaues engrained in lusty greene. **1591** —— *Virgils Gnat* 666 The Rose engrained in pure scarlet die. **1596** FITZ-GEFFRAY *Sir F. Drake* (1881) 35 His worth in honours purest dye engraine.

β. **1561** DAUS tr. *Bullinger on Apoc.* (1573) 144 b They shall not be clothed in soft or precious apparell, as veluet, sattin, or damaske, or crimosine ingrayned but in sacke-cloth. **1597** DANIEL *Civ. Wares* II. cxvii, Our fields ingrayn'd with blood. **1607** TOPSELL *Serpents* (1653) 695 A colour ingrained with the dung of a Crocodile. **1674** N. FAIRFAX *Bulk & Selv.* 171 It being true blew Gotham or Hobbes ingrain'd. **1855** SINGLETON *Virgil* I. 163 Milesian wools.. ingrained With Tyrian crimsons.

2. To cause (a dye) to sink into the texture of a fabric; to work (a foreign substance) into the 'fibre', the intimate structure of anything. Chiefly *fig.* to implant ineradicably (habits, convictions, prejudices, tastes) *in* a person.

α. *a* **1641** BP. R. MOUNTAGU *Acts & Monum.* (1642) 129 When the spots are engrained, and will not out by scouring, etc. **1820** SCOTT *Ivanhoe* xxxv, The stain hath become engrained by time and consuetude. *a* **1862** BUCKLE *Civiliz.* (1873) III. i. 43 With such force had the circumstance just narrated engrained superstition in the Scotch character. **1862** MAX MÜLLER *Chips* (1880) I. ix. 184 The feeling..is so deeply engrained in human nature.

β. **1746-7** HERVEY *Medit.* (1818) 42 Evil habits.. thoroughly ingrained in the disposition. **1878** *N. Amer. Rev.* CXXVII. 20 This republicanism the Talmudists have ingrained in him.

3. In *passive*: To be indelibly marked *with*.

1863 BARING-GOULD *Iceland* 160 A post very old, and ingrained with filth.

4. †**a.** To give a certain kind of texture to (*obs. rare*[−1]). **b.** *nonce-use.* To form a granular surface on (the skin).

1593 NASHE *Christ's T.* (1613) 147 She was wont in Asses milke to bathe her, to engraine her skin more gentle, plyant, delicate and supple. **1862** BURTON *Bk.-Hunter* 32 The countless little wrinkles which engrained his skin.

†**en'grain,** *v.*[2] *Obs. rare*[−1]. [ad. F. *engrener*, f. *en-* (see EN- *pref.*[1]) + *grain* lit. 'grain'.]

intr. Of a toothed wheel, etc.: To fit into a corresponding toothed piece of machinery.

a **1774** GOLDSMITH *Exper. Philos.* (1776) II. 52 By means of the toothed wheel F engraining in the toothed rack Dd.

engrained, ingrained (ɛn-, ɪn'greɪnd), *ppl. a.* [f. ENGRAIN *v.*[1] + -ED[1]. In the ppl. adj. used attrib., though not in the vb., the form with *in-* is more common than that with *en-*. In sense 2 the word is often heard with secondary (sometimes even with primary) stress on the prefix *in-*.]

†**1.** Dyed in grain: see ENGRAIN *v.*[1]

1599 MARSTON *Sco. Villanie* I. iv. 189 Ingrain'd Habits, died with often dips, Are not so soone discoloured.

b. *fig.* with sbs. characterizing persons: Thoroughly permeated with the characteristic qualities; thoroughgoing, incorrigible. Cf. 'a rogue in grain'.

1630 RUTHERFORD *Lett.* xii. (1862) I. 62 The bloody tongues, crafty foxes, double ingrained hypocrites shall appear as they are. **1715** *Wodrow Corr.* (1843) II. 53 Multitudes of engrained enemies of the succession, under the cloak of the Abjuration, served the interests of the Pretender. **1857** MAYHEW *Lond. Labour* I. 329 Many ingrained beggars certainly use the street trade as a cloak for alms-seeking. **1870** LOWELL *Among my Bks.* Ser. I. (1873) 277 He is an ingrained sceptic.

2. Of a dye, or foreign matter of any sort: Wrought into the inmost texture of something. Chiefly *fig.* of habits, sentiments, prejudices: Deeply rooted, inveterate.

1843 GLADSTONE in *For. & Col. Q. Rev.* II. 567 Deeply engrained mischiefs and corruptions. **1855** BAIN *Senses & Int.* II. i. §22 (1864) 109 A receiver of posted letters acquires an engrained sensibility to half an ounce. **1867** SMILES *Huguenots Eng.* viii (1880) 140 The engrained absolutism and egotism of Louis XIV..were at their acme from his earliest years. **1855** SINGLETON *Virgil* II. 142 From others, underneath the wasteful gulf, Their ingrained wickedness is washed away, Or is burnt out by fire. **1866** KINGSLEY *Herew.* vii. 129 It had its usual ingrained element of cant. **1869** *Echo* 20 Mar., His sinewy hands have got an odd, grimy appearance, as of ingrained coal-dust.

Hence **en'grainedly** *adv.*

1869 *Athenæum* 16 Oct. 495 She is a liar by instinct and by principle—designedly and undesignedly a liar; an utterly, ingrainedly untrue creature.

†**en'grainer, in'grainer.** [f. as prec. + -ER.] One who engrains.

1805 *Ann. Rev.* III. 17 Chemistry may hope one day to publish the scarlet dyer's vade-mecum, or every man his own ingrainer.

†**en'gralee,** *a. Her. Obs.* [a. OF. *engrallé* (mod. *engrêlé*): see ENGRAIL *v.*] = ENGRAILED.

1572 BOSSEWELL *Wks. Armorie* II. 27 b, To beare the same [colours] plaine, and neither engralee, rasie, enueckie or dentellie.

engram ('ɛngræm). [ad. G. *engramm* (R. Semon *Die Mneme* (1904) ii. 20), f. Gr. ἐν EN- + γράμμα letter.] A memory-trace; a permanent and heritable physical change in the nerve tissue of the brain, posited to account for the existence of memory. So **engraphy** ('ɛngrəfɪ), the action of exciting an organism in such a way that a permanent change or engram results. So **en'graphic** *a.*, of or pertaining to engraphy; **en'graphically** *adv.* Cf. ECPHORE.

1908 *Mind* XVII. 275 Forel..uses the 'engram' theory of Semon. **1921** L. SIMON tr. *R. Semon's Mneme* ii. 24 When an organism has been temporarily stimulated and has passed, after the cessation of the stimulus, into the condition of 'secondary indifference', it can be shown that such organism ..has been permanently affected. This I call the engraphic action of a stimulus, because a permanent record has been written or engraved on the irritable substance. I use the word engram to denote this permanent change wrought by a stimulus; the sum of such engrams in an organism may be called its 'engram-store'. *Ibid.* 32 Neither can such influences act engraphically. *Ibid.* 274 The engram-association is a result of engraphy and becomes manifest on ecphory. **1923** OGDEN & RICHARDS *Meaning of Meaning* iii. 138 Past strikings [of a match] have left, in our organisation, engrams, residual traces which help to determine what the mental process will be. **1925** C. FOX *Educat. Psychol.* 10 When a child simultaneously sees his nurse and receives food, both the optical stimulus and the taste stimuli produce their engraphic effects and the engrams are permanently associated. **1927** JOAD *Mind & its Workings* 40 What I am aware of when I appear to remember something is not the past occurrence which, as I say, I remember, but a present state or modification of my body. This present state or modification is called an engram. **1951** G. HUMPHREY *Thinking* viii. 226 The tendency to substantialize the end product of a part of the activity, and to speak..of engrams, neural imprints, sensation, [etc.]. **1967** *New Scientist* 27 July 206/1 The two most popular chemical contenders for this elusive 'memory trace' or 'engram' have been ribonucleic acid (RNA) and protein.

engrammatic (ɛngrə'mætɪk), *a.* [f. prec. + -ATIC.] Of, or pertaining to, an engram.

1925 *Brit. Jrnl. Med. Psychol.* V. 119 The author considers that the 'engrammatic sediment' of primitive symbolism is part of the reflex pattern of human cerebration. **1944** J. LAIRD in P. A. Schilpp *Philos. B. Russell* 310 If..mnemic connection is not physiologically engrammatic, there is room for the logical construction of minds which are not material. **1964** *New Scientist* 10 Sept. 643/2 The 'engrammatic' molecules that..store information in the central nervous system.

engrand: see EN- *pref.*[1] 2.

†**en'grandize, -ise,** *v. Obs.* Also 7 ingrandize. [a. Fr. *engrandiss-* extended stem of *engrandi-r*, ad. It. *ingrandire*:—late L. *ingrandīre*, f. *in-* (see IN-) + *grandi-s* great (see GRAND). Cf. AGGRANDIZE.] *trans.* To make great, increase in estimation, importance, power, rank, or wealth.

1625 in Rushw. *Hist. Coll.* (1659) I. 159 Curing the Kings Evil..a device to ingrandize the vertue of Kings when Miracles were in fashion. **1653** A. WILSON *Jas. I*, 55 To ingrandize all, the King created him..Viscount Rochester. **1670** G. H. *Hist. Cardinals* I. III. 95 He engrandiz'd his own Nephews amongst them. *Ibid.* III. I. 225 Alexander.. endeavoured what he could to ingrandize the Title of Cardinal. **1883** tr. *Allocution Pope Leo XIII* in *Daily News* 1 Sept. 2/2 Many..who are led away by the idea of constituting and engrandising the nation.

Hence **en'grandizing.** *vbl. sb.* and *ppl. a.*

1670 G. H. *Hist. Cardinals* II. III. 192 He began..to bend his mind to the ingrandizing this Kinsman. **1653** A. WILSON *Jas. I*, 52 With this Ingrandizing Title the King added a great Revenue. **1657** REEVE *God's Plea* 83 Elate.. imaginating, engrandising, preheminencies.

en grand seigneur, en grande tenue: see EN *prep.*

†**en'grange,** *v. Obs. rare*[−1]. [a. F. *engrange-r*, f. *en* in + *grange* barn.] *trans.* To put (crops) into a barn; to store, fill (a treasure-house).

1480 CAXTON *Ovid's Met.* XI. xii, Them..I shall enrych, and shall engrange theire tresoure with fruyt delytable.

engrape: see EN- *pref.*[1] I b.

engrapple, variant of INGRAPPLE *v. Obs.*

engrasp (ɛn'grɑːsp, -'græsp), *v.* [f. EN-[1] + GRASP.]

trans. To take, or try to take, in one's grasp; to embrace, grasp, seize. Also *fig.*

1593 NASHE *Christ's T.* (1613) 123 Who shall engraspe and bound the heauens body? **1667** H. MORE *Div. Dial.* v. xviii. (1713) 469 Without any design of engrasping great Mysteries. **1855** SINGLETON *Virgil* I. 274 Ulysses, too.. engrasped The holy image.

engrate, var. of INGRATE *v. Obs.* to regrate.

engratiate, obs. form of INGRATIATE.

engrave (ɛn'greɪv), *v. Pa. pple.* engraved, engraven. Also 6-8 ingrave; *pa. pple.* 6-8 ingraved, 6-9 ingraven. [f. EN-[1] + GRAVE *v.*; after the equivalent Fr. *engraver* (13-17th c.). (The strong pa. pple. *engraven* is now somewhat archaic or formal.)]

†**1.** *trans.* To sculpture; to portray or represent by sculpture. *Obs.*

1542 UDALL *Apophth.* 305 b, For his surname, Cicero, he engraved the figure and proporcion of a cicer. **1545** JOYE *Exp. Dan.* iii. (R.), For he shall make ye no image (saithe the Lorde) nor engrave non (nor set vp non). **1583** LYLY *Ep. T. Watson* in *Poems* (Arb.) 30 Lysippus engraued Vulcan with a streight legge. **1577-87** HOLINSHED *Chron.* III. 904/2 The kings my predecessors and ancestors, whose pictures are ingrauen and set heere in order within this hall. **1591** SHAKS. *1 Hen. VI*, II. ii. 15 Vpon the which Shall be engrau'd the Sacke of Orleance. **1614** RALEIGH *Hist. World* II. 312 His Sepulchre remained in S. Hierome's time, and over it the Sunne engraven.

†**2. a.** To cut into (a hard material) (*obs. rare*). **b.** To mark by incisions; to inscribe with incised characters; to ornament with incised marks.

1590 SPENSER *F.Q.* III. viii. 37 That seemes rough masons hand with engines keene Had long while laboured it to engrave. **1661** LOVELL *Hist. Anim. & Min.* Introd., Others that yeeld to iron may be Ingraven. **1859** SMILES *Self-help* v. 104 To engrave spoons and forks with crests and ciphers. **1832** TENNYSON *Œnone* 72 Behold this fruit, whose gleaming rind ingrav'n 'For the most fair'.

3. a. To carve (an inscription, figures, etc.) upon a surface; hence, to record by engraved or incised letters; also *fig.* †**b.** To make (wounds, cavities) by incision.

α. **1542** UDALL *Apophth.* 42 A golden aple with this poysee written or engraved about it. *Ibid.* We have perfecte knowelage of no more then is engraven in our memorie. **1578** BANISTER *Hist. Man* I. 24 The first & extremest ribbes ..haue likewise lesser cauities or gutters, to their substaunce engraued. **1594** GREENE *Selimus* Wks. 1881-3 XIV. 285 But we shall soone with our fine tempered swords, Engrave our prowesse on their burganets. **1600** HOLLAND *Livy* 127 (R.) The decemvirall lawes, they set up openly to be seene, engraven in brasse. **1766** GOLDSM. *Vic. W.* ii. (1857) 6 As he had engraven upon his wife's tomb. **1802** MAR. EDGWORTH *Moral T.* (1816) I. xii. 94 His coat of arms engraven upon the seal. **1870** HAWTHORNE *Eng. Note-bks.* (1879) II. 43 A cross engraven along its whole length.

β. **1557** *N.T.* (Genev.) *Epist.* *iij, In all partes of the worlde, he..as it were ingraued the glorie of his might. **1626** G. SANDYS *Ovid's Met.* XII. 251 The fatall steele..he waues Deepe in his guts, and wounds on wounds ingraues. **1663** GERBIER *Counsel* 41 The old Carver..had ingraven his own Name and Portraiture..in the Shield of Pallas. **1684** BUNYAN *Pilgr.* II. 63 If their Crimes had been ingraven in some Plate of Iron or Brass. **1738** WESLEY *Short Hymns* (1762) I. 355 Ingraven with an iron pen My name upon Thy hands is seen.

c. *fig.* To impress deeply; to fix indelibly.

α. **1509** HAWES *Past. Pleas.* XXX. xii, In my mynde..I had engraved Her goodly countenaunce. **1633** G. HERBERT *Temple, Nature* iii, O smooth my rugged heart, and there Engrave thy rev'rend law. **1790** BURKE *Fr. Rev.* Wks. V. 56 Whose penetrating style has engraved..in our hearts the words and spirit of that immortal law. **1875** OUSELEY *Mus. Form* iii. 30 To engrave them on his memory.

β. **1513** MORE *Rich. III* (1641) 240 By love or by grudge ingraved and imprinted in your heart. **1612** DRAYTON *Polyolb.* i. 2 And in your dreadfull verse ingrau'd the prophecies. *a* **1619** FOTHERBY *Atheom.* I. vii. §2 (1622) 52 It is naturally ingrauen into the mindes of all men, to beleeue There is a God. *a* **1649** DRUMM. OF HAWTH. *Jas. V*, Wks. (1711) 115 A prince's name is surer preserved, and more ingraven in paper than in..rusting medals.

4. To represent (a figure, landscape, etc.) by lines incised upon metal plates (in mod. use, also by lines carved in relief on wood blocks) with the view of reproducing it by printing. Also *absol.*

1667 EVELYN *Mem.* (1857) III. 199 Cause the best of your statues..to be..engraven in copper. **1672** PETTY *Pol. Anat.* (1691) 59 He hath caused distinct Maps to be made of every Barony..engraven in Copper. **1683** RAY *Corr.* (1848) 132 Whether he designs to engrave and publish any of those icons. **1710** HEARNE *Collect.* (Oxf. Hist. Soc.) 20 Dr. Sacheverell's Picture has been ingrav'd several Times. **1728** R. MORRIS *Ess. Anc. Archit.* Advt., Prospects of the Church and Monuments curiously engraven. **1821** R. TURNER *Arts & Sc.* (ed. 18) 73 How do people engrave on wood? **1827–32** J. M. W. TURNER (*title*) Picturesque Views in England and Wales, engraved by the best artists.

engrave, var. INGRAVE *obs.*, to entomb.

en'graved, *ppl. a.* [f. ENGRAVE *v.* + -ED¹.] In the senses of the verb.

1557 N. T. (Genev.) *Heb.* i. 3 Which Sonne beyng the bryghtnes of the glorie, and the ingraued forme of his personne. **1561** T. NORTON *Calvin's Inst.* I. 29b, Should very vnproprely yea fondly be called the engraued form of him. **1837** *Penny Cycl.* IX. 439/1 One of the first books illustrated with designs on engraved plates was the production of Italian artists.

†**en'gravement.** *Obs.* Also 7 ingravement. [f. ENGRAVE *v.* + -MENT.] The action of engraving; that which is engraved, an incised figure or inscription; also *fig.* an imprint, record, trace.

1604 BROUGHTON *Corrupt. Handl. Relig.* 99 The Patriarks engrauement in the twelv stones. **1617** *Janua Ling.* 118 Ingrauements in cleere plates endure long. **1637** J. RUTTER tr. *Corneille's Cid* I. i, The furrowes in his forehead seem to be Th' ingravements of his noble actions. **1727** DE FOE *Syst. Magic* I. vi. 141 If such writing or engravement were made by Cham.

†**en'graven**, *ppl. a. Obs.* Also 6–7 in-. [str. pa. pple. of ENGRAVE *v.*] = ENGRAVED.

1583 HARSNET *Serm. Ezek.* (1658) 130 God..had his Son, the Ingraven Image of his Father. **1588** FRAUNCE *Lawiers Log.* I. i. 2 That ingraven gift and facultie of wit and reason. **1593** *Tell-trothes N.Y. Gift* (1876) 34 But engrauen thoughtes will not be rubbed forth. **1642** ROGERS *Naaman* 535 Was not the Temple full of Lyons and Cherubims, and ingraven forms? **1688** R. HOLME *Armoury* III. 325/2 I have procured..some..since my former engraven ones.

†**en'graven**, *v. Obs.* Also 7 in-. [perh. f. prec.; perh. an alteration of ENGRAVE, due to analogy of vbs. with prefix EN-¹ and suffix -EN⁵.] = ENGRAVE. *lit.* and *fig.*

1605 CAMDEN *Rem.* 27 A name which was ingravened in the revestiarie of the Temple. **1650** T. BAYLY *Herba Parietis* 59 To engraven a similitude. **1704** *Gentleman Instructed* 250 (D.) Our Maker..has also engraven'd the knowledge of Himself in our souls. **1713** *Lond. Gaz.* 5165/4 Lost..Two silver Trencher Plates of Her Majesty's Engraven'd A.R.

†**en'gravening**, *vbl. sb. Obs.* [f. ENGRAVEN *v.* + -ING¹.] The action of the verb ENGRAVEN; the characters in which anything is engraved.

1645 RUTHERFORD *Tryal & Tri. Faith* (1845) 12 The engravening of free grace. **1655** GURNALL *Chr. in Arm.* I. 129 These places whose engravening is too curious to be long pored on by a weak eye.

engraver (ɛn'greɪvə(r)). Also 6–8 ingraver. [f. ENGRAVE *v.* + -ER.]

1. One who engraves; one whose business it is to cut devices, figures, or letters in wood, metal, stone, etc. Now often *spec.* one who engraves pictures on metal or wood from which prints are to be taken.

1586 T. B. *La Primaud. Fr. Acad.* II. (1594) 47 From what paterns doe Painters and Ingrauers take the fashion and forme of those Images and pictures. **1611** BIBLE *Exod.* xxxviii. 23 Aholiab, son of Ahisamach, of the tribe of Dan, an engraver. **1666** PEPYS *Diary* 26 Mar. To see the famous engraver, to get him to grave a seal for the office. **1690** TEMPLE *Ess. Heroic Virtue* Wks. 1731 I. 215 This Odin was ..the first Engraver of the Runick Letters or Characters. **1705** HEARNE *Collect.* 18 Aug. (Oxf. Hist. Soc.) I. 30 Cole the Ingraver. *a* **1779** WARBURTON *Lett. Literary Property* (R.), Could we easily think that a printseller or engraver should be able to obtain that for his baubles? **1815** *Scribbleomania* 192 (*note*), His engraver..undertook to procure a similar stone. **1865** DICKENS *Mut. Fr.* I. vii, His eyes are like the over-tried eyes of an engraver.

2. An engraving tool, a graver. *rare.*

1821 CRAIG *Lect. Drawing* vii. 371 The implements for this species of art are five or six engravers of various lengths and thicknesses.

3. *attrib.* and *Comb.*, as ***engraver student***; **engraver beetle**, any beetle of the family Scolytidæ; a bark-beetle.

1896 *Daily News* 11 Dec. 8/6 In the first year..the number of students [at the Royal Academy] was 77..and four were engraver students. **1897** J. H. COMSTOCK *Insect Life* v. 216 These smoothly cut figures are the mines of the engraver-beetle. Many kinds of these engravings can be found, each characteristic of a particular kind of engraver-beetle.

†**en'gravery.** *Obs.* Also 6–7 ingravery, -ie. [f. as prec.: see -ERY.] The art or work of the engraver; *concr.* the productions of the engraver's art; also (*rarely*) an individual work of the kind, a piece of engraving.

1566 PAINTER *Pal. Pleas.* (18..) II. 533. **1611** COTGR., *Manequinage*, anticke ingrauerie, or caruing, in Wainscot, or Stone-worke. **1638** BAKER tr. *Balzac's Lett.* (1654) IV. 44 He hath in charge to present you with my..small Ingravery. **1676** *Phil. Trans.* XI. 554 The Cabinets, copper Cuts and Engravery of Monsieur de Marolles. *a* **1682** SIR T. BROWNE *Tracts* 4 They wonder to find the art of ingravery so ancient upon pretious stones and signets. *Ibid.* (1684) 210 Some handsome Engraveries and Medals.

engraving (ɛn'greɪvɪŋ), *vbl. sb.* [f. ENGRAVE *v.* + -ING¹.]

1. The action of the verb ENGRAVE; the art of the engraver.

1601 HOLLAND *Pliny* II. 569 There is in marble of his portraying and ingrauing, an old woman drunken. **1696** BP. PATRICK *Comm. Ex.* xxxii. (1697) 632 Interpreters take it [a Heb. word] here for an Instrument of Engraving. **1776** GIBBON *Decl. & F.* I. 397 The elegance of his designs and engraving. **1837** *Penny Cycl.* IX. 439/2 In Germany engraving made more rapid strides towards excellence.

2. *concr.* That which is engraved; an engraved figure or inscription. *rare.* †Also *fig.* a deep impression (*e.g.* on the mind).

1611 BIBLE *Ex.* xxviii. 11 The worke of an engrauer in stone; like the engrauings of a signet. **1677** HALE *Prim. Orig. Man.* IV. vii. 355 The Fall of Man did [not] wholly raze out the Engravings of those common Notions. **1738–41** WARBURTON *Div. Legat.* IV. v. (R.), It appears..from the engravings on Aaron's breast-plate, that letters were in common use. **1884** *Cyclist* 13 Feb. 243/1 Beautiful specimens of Doulton's ware, salad bowls and servers, with silver mounts and a suitable engraving.

3. An impression from an engraved plate.

1803 *Med. Jrnl.* X. 187 Two painted Engravings of Cow-Pock and other Eruptions. **1816** SINGER *Hist. Cards* 224 It was not until the latter part of the sixteenth century that engravings on copper were used as embellishments for books in England. **1860** SALA *Hogarth* 117 A handsome cabinet of paintings, drawings, and engravings.

†**en'gravure.** *Obs. rare*⁻¹. [f. ENGRAVE *v.* + -URE.] An engraving.

1716 MYLES DAVIES *Athen. Brit.* III. 90.

†**en'grease**, *v. Obs. rare*⁻¹. [f. EN-¹ + GREASE, after Fr. *engraisser.*] *trans.* To fill with grease; to fatten.

1563–87 FOXE *A. & M.* (1843) V. 615 They are fatted and engreased like swine.

†**en'greaten**, *v. Obs.* [f. EN-¹ + GREAT *a.* + -EN⁵.] *trans.* To make great; to increase, aggrandize; also *fig.* to aggravate (an offence). Hence **en'greatening** *vbl. sb.*

c **1614** CORNWALLYES in Gutch *Coll. Cur.* I. 156 The late working of these conjunctions between them, to the engreatning of them, and peril of us. **1641** *Relation Answ. Earl Strafford* 4 He had engreatned and advanced the Kings Revenues. **1681** NEVILE *Plato Rediv.* 186 To engreaten the King against the Interest and Liberty of their own Country. **1684** *Contempl. State Man.* II. x. (1699) 238 Sin is..much engreatned by the circumstances which attend it.

†**en-gree**, *adv. Obs.* Also en gre. [F. *en gré.*] In good part.

14.. *Pol. Rel. & L. Poems* (1866) 38 Beseching you, Dere heret, as Enterly as y cane, to take en gre this poure gifte. *c* **1475** *Partenay* 3819 Off aduersite en-gree take the porte.

engreen: see EN- *pref.*¹ 2.

†**en'grege**, *v. Obs.* Also 4 engredge, -gge. [ad. OF. *engregier*, f. late L. **ingraviāre* (cf. L. *ingravāre* ENGRIEVE), f. *in-* + *gravi-s* heavy. See AGGREGE.] *trans.* **a.** To make heavy or dull; hence, to harden (the conscience, heart). **b.** To increase the importance of; to aggravate.

1382 WYCLIF *Ex.* vii. 14 Engregid is the herte of Pharao. *Ibid.* viii. 15 Pharao forsothe seynge that there was ȝeue rest, his herte engredgide. *c* **1386** CHAUCER *Pers. T.* ¶905 Alle thise thynges after þat they been grete or smale engreggen [v.r. engregen] the conscience of man. —— *Melibeus* ¶321 Everych of hem encreseth and engreggith other. ? *a* **1600** *Dial. betw. Clerk & Courtier* 4 (Jam.) Ye wald lufe it, And not engrege the case sa hie.

engreif(f, Sc. var. of ENGRIEVE *v. Obs.*

engrele, -greyl, var. of ENGRAIL *v. Obs.*

‖**engrenage** (ɑ̃grənaːʒ). [Fr.] *fig.* Gearing, putting into gear, meshing.

1918 G. B. SHAW *What I wrote about War* (1930) 237 The prison machine would not release the two men caught in its *engrenage.* **1931** *Times Lit. Suppl.* 10 Sept. 675/2 The new political romanticism of Communism believes that the reality can be dissipated by a new ordering of society; but probably it will succeed only in loosening one *engrenage* by imposing another. **1963** *Economist* 19 Jan. 203/1 'Good Europeans'..sought consolation in the..theory of *engrenage* (getting into gear).

engrene, -greyn, obs. forms of ENGRAIN *v.*

†**en'grieve**, *v. Obs.* Forms: α. 4 engreve, (*Sc.* engrief(f), 4–5 engreive (*Sc.* engrew), 6 engreue, -eeue, 6–7 engreve, 6– engrieve. β. 4 ingreve, 6 ingreeue, -ieue. [ad. OF. *engrever*:—L. *ingravāre*, f. *in-* (see IN-) + *grav-is* heavy; cf. EN-¹ and GRIEVE.]

1. *trans.* To cause grief or pain to; to annoy, hurt, vex. Also *absol.* To do harm, be troublesome.

1375 BARBOUR *Bruce* XI. 504 Myscheif..that suld swa engreiff, That na hys vorschip suld thame releif. *Ibid.* XIII. 210 The scottis archeris..Ingrevand [*v.r.* engrewand] thame so gretumly..That thai vayndist a litell we. *Ibid.* XX. 200 For it, he said, mycht nocht releif, And mycht [thaimself] gretly engreif. *c* **1400** *Rom. Rose* 3444 Yit no thyng engreveth mee. *c* **1425** WYNTOUN *Cron.* VIII. XXXV. 190 He þat mast engrewyt þere..Suld have þe grettast Prys, wyth þi Ðat he engrewyt honestly. **1513** DOUGLAS *Æneis* X. xiii. 19 Bot pryncipally Mezentyus all engrevit. **1626** BACON *Sylva* (1651) §828 Aches, and Hurts, and Cornes, do Engrieve, either towards Raine, or towards Frost.

2. To make grievous; to represent as grievous; to aggravate.

1535 CROMWELL *Let. Gardiner* in Burnet *Collect.* 460 In which part ye shall somewhat engrieve the matter. *a* **1555** BP. GARDINER in Foxe *A. & M.* (1563) 734b, To engreue it to be an importable burden. **1592** *Conspir. Pretended Ref.* 40 Seeking also to engreeue their faultes.

3. To make a grievance of; to take as a ground of accusation or reproach.

1577–87 HOLINSHED *Chron.* III. 1111/2 Mine owne confession is ingreeued against me. *Ibid.* III. 1114/1, I am sorie to ingreeue anie other mans doings.

Hence **en'grieved** *ppl. a.*

1591 SPENSER *Vis. World's Van.* 159, I gan in my engrieued brest To scorne all difference of great and small.

†**en'grin**, *v. Obs. rare*⁻¹. [f. EN-¹ + GRIN snare.] *trans.* To ensnare.

1340 *Ayenb.* 154 Alle þo..þet habbeþ zuo þe herten engrined ine þe dyeules nette.

engroce, obs. form of ENGROSS.

engroche, obs. form of ENCROACH.

engroove, ingroove (ɛn-, ɪn'gruːv), *v.* [f. EN-¹, IN- + GROOVE *sb.* or *v.*] *trans.* **a.** To work (something) into a groove. **b.** To form a groove in.

a **1842** TENNYSON *Love thou thy land* xii, Let the change which comes be free To ingroove itself with that which flies. **1880** BLACKMORE *Mary Anerley* II. iii. 39 A narrow glen, engrooved with sliding water.

en gros: see EN *prep.*

engross (ɛn'grəʊs), *v.* Forms: α. 4 engrosy, 5–7 engrose, 6–7 engrosse, 5 engroce, 5– engross. β. 5–8 ingrosse, 5–7 ingrose, (5 ingroos), 5–6 ingroce. [Three distinct formations, from elements ultimately identical. (1) In senses 1–2 a. AF. *engrosse-r* (med.L. *ingrossāre*) to write in large letters, f. *grosse* = med.L. *grossa* large writing, a transcript in large letters (fem. of *grossus* large, thick: see GROSS *a.*). (2) In senses 3–7 f. phrase *in gross*, Fr. *en gros* = 'in the lump, by wholesale'. AF. *engrosser* and Anglo-Lat. *ingrossare* in sense 3 are found in the Statutes. (3) In senses 8–11 a. Fr. *engrosser* to make big, thick, or gross, corresp. to Pr. *engrossar*, Sp. *engrosar*, It. *ingrossare*:—late L. *ingrossāre*, f. *in-* (see IN-) + *gross-us* stout, thick, GROSS.]

I. To write in large.

1. *trans.* To write in large letters; chiefly, and now almost exclusively, to write in a peculiar character appropriate to legal documents; *hence*, to write out or express in legal form. Also *absol.*

α. [**1304** *Year-bks. 32–33 Edw. I*, 315 Quant une fin est engrossé em ne resortira james a bref ne a note chalanger.] *c* **1430** LYDG. *Story Thebes* 2098 Engrosed vp..And enrolled only for witnesse In ȝoure regestres. **1467** in *Eng. Gilds* (1870) 379 The actes of the yelde..shullen be enacted and engrossed in a quayer of parchemyn. **1557** *Ord. Hospitalls* Fvij, The whole accompt..yow shall engrosse and write faire into a Booke. **1591** *Wills & Inv. N.C.* (1860) II. 199 For engrossing his will, twice unto paipar, after unto parchment. **1595** SPENSER *Col. Clout* 636 Her name..I will ..in the ground..engrosse, And fill with stones. **1632** *Star Chamb. Cases* (1886) 164 Bampton and his wife brought their answere readie drawen to him and desired him to engrosse it. **1664–5** PEPYS *Diary* II. 337 The story of the several Archbishops of Canterbury, engrossed in vellum. **1735** POPE *Prol. Sat.* 18 A clerc..Who pens a Stanza when he should engross. **1818** CRUISE *Digest* v. 79 The fine being

engrossed and completed as a fine of Michaelmas term. **1818** SCOTT *Hrt. Midl.* xxiv, The Clerk of Court, proceeded to engross in the record the yet unknown verdict. **1860** FORSTER *Gr. Remonstr.* 213 That the Declaration should be duly engrossed, and again brought in..the next day.

β. **1564** BULLEYN *Dial. agst. Feuer Pest* (1888) 21 Wee haue drawen and ingrossed his bookes. **1587** HARRISON *England* II. viii. (1877) I. 176 They will haue the bille ingrossed, that is to saie, put in parchment. **1600** HOLLAND *Livy* IV. 147 This was openly ingrossed in publicke Tables. **1640-4** in Rushw. *Hist. Coll.* III. (1692) I. 350 The Charge ingrossed against Inigo Jones upon the Complaint of the Parishioners of St. Gregories. **1660** MARVELL *Corr.* Wks. 1872-5 II. vi. 25 The Bill, upon reading the amendments, was ordered to be ingrossed. **1793** SMEATON *Edystone L.* §314 Instructions.. fairly ingrossed.

†**b.** Hence, to put into regular shape; to arrange (a matter). *Obs.*

1430 LYDG. *Chron. Troy* IV. xxxiv, To call his lordes.. And his lyeges to assemble yfere Fynally to engroce this mattere. **1526** SKELTON *Magnyf.* 2467 Yet, let us se thys matter thorowly ingrosed.

†**c.** To name in a formal document, to write the name of; hence, to include in a list. *Obs.*

1589 NASHE in Greene *Menaphon* (Arb.) Introd. 6 Mongst this kinde of men..I can but ingrosse some deepe read Grammarians. **1605** *Answ. Supposed Discov. Romish Doctr.* 2 Engrossing him in the Catalogue of censured, excommunicate and denounced Hereticks. **1621** QUARLES *Argalus & P.* (1678) 36 T'ingross their names within his Register. **1660** SHARROCK *Vegetables* 2 They stand aloof from the knowledge of most of the particulars therein to be ingrost.

†**2.** *transf.* To portray in large. *Obs. rare*$^{-1}$.

1538 LELAND *Itin.* VI. 3 An High Tumbe of Marble, but no Image engrossid on it.

II. To deal with 'in the gross'.

†**3.** To buy up wholesale; *esp.* to buy up the whole stock, or as much as possible, of (a commodity) for the purpose of 'regrating' or retailing it at a monopoly price. *Obs.* exc. *Hist.*

a **1400** in *Eng. Gilds* (1870) 353 No regratour ne go owt of town for to engrosy þe chaffare. **1591** G. FLETCHER *Russe Commw.* (1857) 9 Their nobilitie..use to engrosse it. **1622** MISSELDEN *Free Trade* 71 Some one or few..doe ioine together to engrosse and buy in a Commodity. *a* **1640** DAY *Parl. Bees* (1881) 73 Fucus, you That engrost our Hony deaw, Bought wax and honey up by th' great. **1647** MAY *Hist. Parl.* I. ii. 17 Disarming the people by engrossing of Gunpowder..and setting so high a rate upon it. **1827** HALLAM *Const. Hist.* (1876) II. viii. 35 One man was fined and set in the pillory for engrossing corn. **1872** YEATS *Growth Comm.* 379 Edicts..against engrossing the market.

β. **1548** CRANMER *Catech.* 77 Forstallyng, regratyng.. ingrossing of marchaundise. **1622** MALYNES *Anc. Law-Merch.* 123 Salt..they by authoritie did ingrosse for the king. **1672** MARVELL *Reh. Transp.* I. 262 You have so ingrossed and bought up all the ammunition of Railing.

†**b.** with reference to land. *Obs.*

1719 W. WOOD *Surv. Trade* 172 The false..notion.. induces them to Engross great Tracts of Land. **1728** SWIFT *Answ. Memorial*, Grasiers..were ready to ingross great quantities of land. **1767** A. YOUNG *Farm. Lett. to People* 53 Complaints are every where made of engrossing farms.

4. *transf.* and *fig.* †**a.** To get together, collect from all quarters; also ***to engross up*** (*obs.*). **b.** To gain or keep exclusive possession of; to concentrate (property, trade, privileges, functions) in one's own possession (often with the notion of unfairness or injury to others); to 'monopolize'.

a. **1596** SHAKS. *1 Hen. IV*, III. ii. 148 Percy is but my Factor..To engrosse vp glorious Deedes on my behalfe. **1599** B. JONSON *Cynthia's Rev.* IV. ii. 16 An' you engrosse 'hem all for your owne use. **1628** FORD *Lover's Mel.* II. i, You, Aretus, and I engross..The affairs of government. **1643** SIR T. BROWNE *Relig. Med.* II. §5 (1656) With my friend I desire not to share or participate, but to engrosse his sorrowes. **1694** DR. SLARE in *Phil. Trans.* XVIII. 218 He.. engrossed all the Pyrites or Copperas-stone to himself. *a* **1740** TICKELL *To Addison on Cato* (R.), Too long hath love engross'd Britannia's stage. **1781** J. MOORE *View Soc. It.* (1790) I. iii. 34 The men being allowed to engross as many women as they can maintain. **1832** AUSTIN *Jurispr.* (1879) I. vi. 243 In most actual societies the sovereign powers are engrossed by a single member of the whole. *a* **1862** BUCKLE *Civiliz.* (1869) III. iv. 212 Seeing a single person engross the conversation.

β. **1598** SHAKS. *Merry W.* II. ii. 203, I haue..ingross'd opportunities to meete her. **1606** —— *Ant. & Cl.* III. vii. 37 Your Marriners are Militers, Reapers, people Ingrost by swift Impresse. **1641** WILKINS *Math. Magick* I. xi. (1648) 75 Abundance of wealth..was then ingrossed in the possession of some few particular persons. **1645** MILTON *Tetrach.* (1851) 153 Som..would ingrosse to themselves the whole trade of interpreting. **1691-8** NORRIS *Pract. Disc.* IV. 310 Alms-giving..is so eminent a part of Charity that it has in a Manner ingross'd the Name of it. **1775** ADAIR *Amer. Ind.* 457 Our rulers ought not to allow..the Mushohge to ingross this vast forest. **1790** BEATSON *Nav. & Mil. Mem.* 309 Grasping at an opportunity to ingross this trade to themselves.

†**c.** *nonce-use.* To attribute exclusively *to*.

1641 *Vind. Smectymnuus* §7. 95 A power of remitting sinnes, which we hope he will not ingrosse to Bishops excluding Presbyters.

5. Of things: To require the entire use of, take altogether to itself; to occupy entirely, absorb.

1602 WARNER *Alb. Eng.* XII. lxxiii. (1612) 304 Skarlet Hats, Stoles, and Coules too much ingrost the sport. **1655** FULLER *Ch. Hist.* VII. i. §21 Norfolke Rebellion, as nearer London, engrossed all warlike provisions. **1768** BEATTIE *Minstr.* II. (R.) Pondering on former days by guilt engross'd. **1804** COLEBROOKE *Husb. & Comm. Bengal* (1806) 154 From this country [India]..Europe was antiently supplied with it [indigo] until the produce of America engrossed the market. **1846** MCCULLOCH *Acc. Brit. Empire* (1854) I. 527 Potatoes engross the whole manure of the little farmers. **1874** SPURGEON *Treas. Dav.* Ps. lxxx. 8 The old trees, which long had engrossed the soil.

b. Of an object of thought or feeling: To draw entirely to itself, occupy exclusively, absorb (the affections, attention, mind, time, etc.).

a. **1665** GLANVILL *Sceps. Sci.* viii. 46 Philosophy would not have engrossed our pen. **1732** POPE *Ess. Man* I. 119 If man alone engross not Heaven's high care. **1746-7** COLLINS *Poems* (1796) 112 They, whose sight such dreary dreams engross. **1769** *Junius Lett.* xi. 44 A measure so singularly daring that it..engrosses all our resentment. **1781** COWPER *Let.* 2 Apr., My morning is engrossed by the garden. **1820** HAZLITT *Lect. Dram. Lit.* 4 Letting the generation we live in engross nearly all our admiration. **1868** E. EDWARDS *Raleigh* I. iii. 45 The captain obtained his audience, and engrossed the watchfulness of the retainers.

β. **1665** BOYLE *Occas. Refl.* III. i. (1675) 147 Without leaving behind them any thing that can..entertain our Sight in the very place, where before they Ingross'd it. **1742** RICHARDSON *Pamela* IV. 148 This will so ingross the dear Lady's Pen. **1777** WATSON *Philip II* (1793) I. IX. II. 368 The attention of the French king was ingrossed.

6. To absorb or engage the whole attention or all the faculties of.

1709 STEELE *Tatler* No. 50. ¶1 Orlando believed himself ..not to be engross'd by any particular Affection. **1729** BUTLER *Serm.* Wks. (1874) II. 135 The degree in which self-love engrosses us. **1814** JANE AUSTEN *Lady Susan* xx. (1879) 247 The folly of the young man and the confusion of Frederica entirely engrossed him. **1856** KANE *Arct. Expl.* II. xxii. 219 Marsumah and Meteh had been engrossed with their bird-catching. **1872** BLACK *Adv. Phaeton* viii. 118 He was entirely engrossed in attending to her wants.

¶**7.** In certain strained fig. uses, app. derived from 3: †**a.** To include altogether (*obs. rare*$^{-1}$; suggested by the rime). †**b.** In 17th c.: To get hold of (an idea); to conceive (a sentiment) (*obs.*).

c **1460** *Towneley Myst.* 170 Almyghty God in persons thre, Alle in oone substance ay ingroost. **1632** HEYWOOD *Iron Age* II. v. Wks. 1874 III. 429 Proiects..for which I haue ingrost a mortall enuy here. **1633** FORD *Broken H.* III. iii, Thou hast there engross'd Some rarity of wit to grace the nuptials Of thy fair sister. *a* **1643** W. CARTWRIGHT *To King on Return fr. Scotl.* (R.), Your prolong'd delay..made our jealousy engross New feares.

III. To render gross, dense, or bulky.

†**8.** To render (fluids) gross or dense; to condense (vapours). Also *intr.* for *refl. Obs.*

1561 EDEN *Art. Nauig.* II. xix. 51 Rayne is made or engendred of moyste vapours which..are ingroced. **1582** HESTER *Secr. Phiorav.* I. xl. 49 The liuer..not beyng able to digest them [crude humours]..they ingrose and become maligne. **1586** COGAN *Haven Health* cxli. (1636) 271 Vapours and fumes..being ingrossed by coldnesse of the braine, distil to the lower parts. **1590** SPENSER *F.Q.* II. vi. 46 The waves thereof..were Engrost with mud.

9. †**a.** To make (the body) gross or fat; to fatten (*obs.*). **b.** To make (the mind) gross or dull (*arch.*); formerly also *intr.* for *refl.*

1587 HARRISON *England* II. vi. (1877) I. 142 They [the Scotch]..so ingrosse their bodies. **1594** SHAKS. *Rich. III*, III. vii. 76. **1626** T. H. *Caussin's Holy Crt.* 120 It happeneth to soules, which are great louers of sensuall pleasures, to engrosse, thicken themselues. *a* **1628** F. GREVILLE *Humane Learn.* liii, Poems (1633) 33 Engrosse the minde. **1826** E. IRVING *Babylon* II. VI. 89 They were in the last stage of the heart's ossification, their faculties engrossed and imbruted.

†**10.** *trans.* To make thick or bulky; to increase in size. *Obs.*

c **1611** CHAPMAN *Iliad* XVIII. 640 Fire, invading city roofs, is suddenly engrost And made a wondrous mighty flame. **1624** WOTTON *Archit.* (1672) 27 Though Pillars by channelling, be seemingly ingrossed to our Sight. **1663** GERBIER *Counsel* 47 Materials of weight, as Sauder, wherewith an unconscionable Plummer can ingrosse his Bill.

†**11.** *Mil.* [Cf. It. *ingrossare* in same senses.] To increase the numerical strength of (an army); also, to draw up (a battalion) in a compact body.

1526 *St. Papers, Hen. VIII*, VI. 376 Our armye was ingrocyd by the newe comyng of thies lanceknightes. **1581** STYWARD *Mart. Discip.* I. 26 The companies being thus doubled & the battailes ingrosed..euerie ensigne maie seeke out his owne band. *Ibid.* I. 27 Then doubling ye ranks of these hargubuseirs..they must bee ingrossed. **1650** HOWELL *Giraffi's Rev. Naples* 53 They went on in ingrossing the militia. **1654** EARL MONM. tr. *Bentivoglio's Warrs Flanders* 202 His Camp was not then very great, but he hoped to have it speedily ingrost by some Germans.

engrossed (ɛnˈgrəʊst), *ppl. a.* [f. ENGROSS *v.* + -ED^{1}.] In various senses of the vb.: *e.g.* **a.** Written out large, written in a legal hand; expressed or incorporated in a legal document. †**b.** Collected from various quarters, amassed in large quantity (*obs.*). †**c.** Thickened, swollen (*obs.*).

a. **1640-4** in Rushw. *Hist. Coll.* III. (1692) I. 59 The Ingrossed Articles were again presently read in the House. **1748** J. MASON *Elocut.* 14 Such a Monotony as Attorney's Clerks read in when they examine an engrossed Deed.

b. **1599** MARSTON *Sco. Villanie* III. 227 Nere his tongue shall lie Till his ingrossed iests are all drawne dry.

c. **1578** BANISTER *Hist. Man* I. 20 Where the body of the Vertebre should be, that is to say, the engrossed part. *c* **1611** CHAPMAN *Iliad* XIII. 613 When the engrossed waves Boil into foam.

Hence **enˈgrossedly** *adv.*, in an engrossed manner; with absorbed attention.

1865 DICKENS *Mut. Fr.* III. v, Bella's eyes dropped more engrossedly over her book.

engrosser (ɛnˈgrəʊsə(r)). [f. ENGROSS *v.* + -ER.] One who engrosses.

†**1.** One who buys in large quantities, esp. with the view of being able to secure a monopoly. Also, one who buys up large quantities of land, or obtains possession of many tenements, to the detriment of his neighbours. *Obs.* exc. *Hist.*

c **1460** FORTESCUE *Abs. & Lim. Mon.* (1875) 135 The said brogers and engrossers of offices. **1549** LATIMER *1st Serm. bef. Edw. VI* (Arb.) 33 Ingrossers of tenamentes and landes, throughe whose couetousnes, villages decaye and fall downe. **1636** HEALEY *Life Epictetus'*, That is, to the unlearned engrosser of books. **1692** TRYON *Good Housew.* xix. 171 The first Ingrossers and Buyers thereof [Canary] were Apothecaries. **1778** R. H. LEE in Sparks *Corr. Amer. Rev.* (1853) II. 216 An artificial scarcity, created in the midst of plenty, by an infamous set of engrossers. **1783** BURKE *Report Affairs India* Wks. XI. 144 The engrossers of opium.

b. One who 'monopolizes' or obtains exclusive possession of (anything).

1630 NAUNTON *Fragm. Reg.* (Arb.) 52 My Lord of Essex ..was noted for too bold an ingrosser both of fame and favour. **1729** GAY *Polly* III. Wks. (1772) 198, I am too no engrosser of power. **1782** V. KNOX *Ess.* 119 (R.) The engrossers of that part of the creation which God and nature have constituted free. **1816** SCOTT *Bl. Dwarf* v, You should, in compassion, cease to be such an engrosser.

2. One who copies (a document) in large fair character, or in legal style; †an engrossing clerk.

1607 DEKKER *Knts. Conjur.* (1842) 20 Euery market day you may take him in Cheap-side, poorely attyrde like an ingrosser.

engrossing (ɛnˈgrəʊsɪŋ), *vbl. sb.* [f. ENGROSS *v.* + -ING^{1}.] The action of the verb ENGROSS.

1. The action of buying (any article) in large quantities with the view of obtaining a monopoly; the action of buying up (land).

1542 BRINKLOW *Compl.* ii. 10 The latyng and engrossing of..leassys. **1647** CLARENDON *Hist. Reb.* (1702) I. IV. 250 The ingrossing Gunpowder, and suffering none to buy it without Licence. **1683** BURNET tr. *More's Utopia* 25 Restrain those engrossings of the Rich, that are as bad almost as Monopolies. **1776** ADAM SMITH *W.N.* I. III. ii. 386 This original engrossing of uncultivated lands.

b. *fig.* (See ENGROSS *v.* 4, 5.)

1597 DANIEL *Civ. Wares* v. lxxii, Griev'd at such ingrossing of Command. **1625** BACON *Ess. Envy* (Arb.) 514 An vnnecessary, and Ambitious Ingrossing of Businesse. **1694** CHILD *Disc. Trade* 39 The abatement of interest tends to the engrossing of trade into a few rich mens hands.

2. The action of writing out a document in a fair or legal character. Also *attrib.*

1483 *Act 1 Rich. III*, c. 7, §1 After the engrossing of every Fine..the same Fine shall be openly and solemnly read. **1583** GOLDING *Calvin on Deut.* Pref. 5 The gathering of these sermons and the ingrosing of them faire again afterwarde. **1765** BLACKSTONE *Comm.* I. 183 It..passes through the same forms as in the other house (except engrossing, which is already done). **1837** LOCKHART *Scott* (1839) 196 A sort of flourish..adopted in engrossing as a safeguard against the intrusion of a forged line. **1875** STUBBS *Const. Hist.* III. xviii. 262 The enrolment and engrossing of the acts of parliament.

attrib. **1709** STEELE *Tatler* No. 26. ¶4 All Ingrossing Work ..is risen 3s. in the Pound for want of Hands. *Mod.* It was written in a sort of engrossing hand.

engrossing (ɛnˈgrəʊsɪŋ), *ppl. a.* [f. as prec. + -ING^{2}.] That engrosses.

1. †**a.** That claims a large share; presumptuous, pretentious (*obs. rare*).

a **1797** H. WALPOLE *Mem. Geo. III* (1845) I. vi. 84 A term so engrossing gave offence and handle to ridicule.

b. That fully occupies or absorbs the attention, faculties, etc.

1820 SCOTT *Abbot* i, The engrossing nature of his occupation. **1825** LYTTON *Falkland* 20, I had one deep, engrossing, yearning desire. **1875** HELPS *Ess.*, *Aids Contentm.* 12 An alternation of the engrossing pursuit.

†**2.** That makes gross or brutish. *Obs. rare.*

a **1626** BP. ANDREWES *Serm.* vi. *Repentance & Fast.* 147 The Devil's only way, to rid Hypocrisie, by engrossing Epicurisme.

Hence **enˈgrossingly** *adv.*, in an engrossing manner. **enˈgrossingness**, the quality of being engrossing.

1835 *New Monthly Mag.* XLIV. 6, I intend to surprise the world whenever politics..draw less engrossingly on its attention. **1857** *Fraser's Mag.* LVI. 672 India has of late.. engrossingly occupied the English mind. **1848** *Tait's Mag.* XV. 682 They temper in his mind the engrossingness of present things.

engrossment (ɛnˈgrəʊsmənt). [f. ENGROSS *v.* + -MENT.] The action of engrossing; the state of being engrossed.

1. The action of buying up in large quantities, of collecting greedily from all quarters: *concr.* that which is so bought up or collected.

1597 SHAKS. *2 Hen. IV*. IV. v. 80 This bitter taste yeelds his engrossements, To the ending Father. **1598** FLORIO, *Monopolo*, an engrossement of any merchandize into one mans handes. **1648** *Regall Apol.* 31 Ingrossement of all Places and Offices of profit into Members hands. **1818** JAS. MILL *Brit. India* II. v. v. 530 *note*, He kept the grain on board the ships, to make his profit out of its engrossment. **1885** *L'pool Daily Post* 4 Feb. 4/7 The gradual engrossment of the ancient common lands.

2. The state or fact of being engrossed or absorbed in occupations, thoughts, etc.

1837 HOWITT *Rur. Life* IV. ii. (1862) 332 Graceful and happy in the engrossment of her simple duties. **1851** CAIRNS *Mem. J. Clark* 29 Amidst the engrossment of other studies. **1874** CARPENTER *Ment. Phys.* II. xv. (1879) 608 The entire engrossment of the mind with whatever may be for a time the object of its attention.

3. The action of writing out in a fair or legal character. Also *concr.* what is thus written; a record; *fig.* in quot.

1526 *Ord. R. Househ. Hen. VIII*, 140 The Clerkes of the Green cloath or one of them, be dayly attendant in the compting-house for the engrossement of daily bookes of the expences of the day before. **1638** JACKSON *Creed* IX. xii. Wks. VIII. 259 The true belief or persuasion of our interest in this promise is but the ingrossment of our former apprehension in our hearts. *a* **1674** CLARENDON *Life* II. 495 (T.) Which clause being afterwards added to the engrossment it [the bill] was again thus reformed. **1710** H. BEDFORD *Vind. Ch. Eng.* 123 Was not this Ingrossment subsequent to that Paper? **1837** SIR F. PALGRAVE *Merch. & Fr.* i. (1844) 17 The shred or remnant.. of the membrane previously used for the engrossment of some charter.

enguard: see EN- *pref.*[1] 3.

engulf, ingulf (ɛnˈgʌlf), *v.* Also 6-9 **en-**, ingulph. [f. EN-[1] + GULF; cf. Fr. *engouffrer*, earlier *engoulfer* (which may be the source).]

1. *trans.* To swallow up in a gulf, abyss, or whirlpool; to plunge into a gulf; to plunge deeply and inextricably into a surrounding medium. Also *refl.* and *intr.* for *refl.*

α. **1555** EDEN *Decades W. Ind.* (Arb.) 261 They were engulfed by chance in the great sea. **1580** SIDNEY *Ps.* clxii. (R.) In destruction's river Engulph and swallow those Whose hate, etc. **1600** FAIRFAX *Tasso* XV. xxiv. 271 Now deepe engulphed in the mightie flood They saw not Gades. **1796** MORSE *Amer. Geog.* II. 425 A city..having formerly been engulphed by an earthquake. **1831** CARLYLE in Froude *Life* i. (1882) II. 151 Not upon the quicksand, where resting will but engulph you deeper. **1869** FREEMAN *Norm. Conq.* (1876) III. xii. 235 In that dangerous passage the careless traveller might easily be engulfed.

β. *c* **1630** DRUMM. OF HAWTH. *Poems* Wks. 34/1 Her [Earth's] surface shakes..Towns them ingulf..Now nought remaineth but a Waste of Sand. *a* **1711** KEN *Poet. Wks.* (1721) IV. 29 They expire, Ingulfing in infernal Fire. **1735** SOMERVILLE *Chase* III. 135 Another in the treach'rous Bog Lies flound'ring, half ingulph'd. **1816** SHELLEY *Alastor* 365 A cavern there..Ingulphed the rushing sea. **1855** H. REED *Lect. Eng. Lit.* x. 323 Shelley was overtaken by a Mediterranean thunder-storm, and ingulfed in the deep waters.

b. *refl.* and *pass.* Of a river: To discharge itself into, be lost in, the sea; also, to disappear underground.

1634 SIR T. HERBERT *Trav.* 43 Made by the River Indus which their ingulfes herselfe into the Indian Seas. **1667** MILTON *P.L.* IV. 225 A River..through the shaggie hill Pass'd underneath ingulft. **1772** MASON *Eng. Garden* II. (R.), That hallow'd spring; thence, in the porous earth Long while ingulph'd. **1821** BRYDGES *Lett. Continent* 12 [The Rhone] makes itself a passage among the rocks at the extremity of Mount Jura, ingulphs itself for some time, etc.

2. *transf.* (chiefly *humorous*). To swallow up like an abyss; to bury completely.

1829 GEN. P. THOMPSON *Exerc.* (1842) I. 124 The autumnal glutton who engulphs their [oysters'] gentle substances within his own. **1863** FR. KEMBLE *Resid. Georgia* 58 Shirt gills which absolutely ingulfed his black visage. **1879** *Cassell's Techn. Educ.* I. 182/2 To procure these insignificant morsels, he engulfs a whole shoal of them at once in his capacious jaws.

3. *fig.*

α. **1603** HAYWARD *Answ. Doleman* viii. (T.) Upon every giddy and brainless warrant to engulph ourselves. **1669** WOODHEAD *St. Teresa* II. 264 That holy Soul went wholly immersed and engulfed in God. **1877** MOZLEY *Univ. Serm.* iii. 62 The power which mere sensual pleasure has of engulphing us in the vulgar sensation of life.

β. **1597** MORLEY *Introd. Mus.* Pref., To leaue that unbrought to an end, in the which I was so farre ingulfed. **1647** WARD *Simp. Cobler* 57 Into what importable head-tearings and heart-searchings you will be ingulfed. **1784** COWPER *Task* III. 816 London ingulphs them all. The shark is there And the shark's prey. **1864** LOWELL *Fireside Trav.* 126 O Death, thou ever roaming shark, Ingulf me in eternal dark!

†**II. 4.** To cut into gulfs or bays. *Obs. rare.*

1632 LITHGOW *Trav.* x. 496 Because of the Sea ingulfing the Land, and cutting it in so many Angles.

engulfed (ɛnˈgʌlft), *ppl. a.* [f. ENGULF *v.* + -ED[1].] In senses of the verb.

1590 SPENSER *F.Q.* III. ii. 32 Like an huge Aetn' of deepe engulfed gryefe, Sorrow is heaped in thy hollow chest. **1636** HEALEY *Cebes* 135 Her owne receipt..purgeth out all their ingulphed evils, as by vomit. **1728** THOMSON *Spring* 22 The bittern knows his time, with bill ingulpht To shake the sounding marsh. **1860** TYNDALL *Glac.* II. §8 267 We should find the engulfed rocks in the body of the glacier.

engulfing (ɛnˈgʌlfɪŋ). *vbl. sb.* [f. ENGULF *v.* + -ING[1].] The action of the verb ENGULF.

1658 *Whole Duty Man* ii. §4 (1684) 87 It is..the ingulfing him..in that most tormenting passion of jealousie. *a* **1711** KEN *Hymnarium* Poet. Wks. 1721 II. 27 Love..Strove her ingulfing to prolong. **1875** WHITNEY *Life Lang.* x. 195 The engulfing or burying of extant species.

enˈgulfing, *ppl. a.* [f. as prec. + -ING[2].] That engulfs.

a **1777** FAWKES *Eulogy I. Newton* (R.), Waves..bare the dangers of th' engulphing sand. **1852** D. MOIR *Thomson's Birth-pl.* iv. Wks. I. 213 The rapturous lark..less and less visible..'mid heaven's engulfing blue. **1871** TYLOR *Prim. Cult.* I. 304 The list of myths of engulphing monsters.

engulfment (ɛnˈgʌlfmənt). [f. as prec. + -MENT.] The action of engulfing; the process of being engulfed. Also *fig.*

1822 DE QUINCEY *Confess.* Wks. V. 69 And the most frightful abysses, up to the very last menace of engulfment. **1833** LYELL *Princ. Geol.* (1875) II. II. xxvi. 3 The cone [of Etna]..has more than once been destroyed either by explosion or engulphment. **1832** CARLYLE in *Fraser's Mag.* V. 399 What shape soever, bloody or bloodless, the descent and engulfment assume. **1860** TYNDALL *Glac.* II. §26. 367 The successive engulfments and disgorgings of the blocks.. have broken up the moraines.

engyre: see INGYRE.

engyscope (ˈɛndʒɪskəʊp). Also 9 (incorrectly) engiscope. [f. Gr. ἐγγύ-ς near at hand + -σκοπος looker: see -SCOPE.]

†**a.** In 17th and 18th c.: = MICROSCOPE (*obs.*).

b. Subsequently variously employed in narrower sense. Goring (1830) applied it to denote a compound microscope of any kind; but as the term was most frequently used by him in his description of the Amician and similar reflecting microscopes, it is now commonly understood as a distinctive name of that class of instruments.

1684-5 BOYLE *Min. Waters* 73 With differing Engyscopes, and in differing Lights. **1692** COLES, *Engyscope*, an Instrument to discern the proportion of the smallest things. **1697** EVELYN *Numism.* iv. 167 Engyscops, Microscops, and other Optick Glasses. **1731** BAILEY vol. II, *Engyscope*..the same as a microscope. **1832** *Optic Instr.* (Usef. Knowl. Soc.) xiv. §92. 48 The section of this Engiscope. **1837** GORING & PRITCHARD *Microgr.* 70 The ocular end of the engiscope.

engyve: see EN- *pref.*[1] 1 a.

enhabil, -bile, -ble, etc., obs. ff. ENABLE, etc.

enhabill, obs. form of INHABILE, unqualified.

†**enˈhabit**, *v.*[1] *Obs. rare*[−1]. [f. EN-[1] + HABIT dress.] *trans.* To clothe; in quot. *refl.*

c **1485** *Digby Myst.* III. 683, I wol en-abyte me with humelyte.

†**enˈhabit**, *v.*[2] *Obs. rare*[−1]. In 6 *pa. ppl.* **enhabyte.** [bad form of INHIBIT.] To forbid.

1502 *Ord. Crysten Men.* II. xv. 122 All rauayne & couetousness is enhabyte.

enhabit, -ant, obs. forms of INHABIT, -ANT.

†**enˈhach**, *v. Obs. rare*[−1]. [a. Fr. *enhacher* to fit into, be attached.] *trans.* To fit, inlay, adorn.

1523 SKELTON *Garl. Laurel* 40, I saw a pavylyon.. Enhachyde with perle and stones preciously.

enhale, obs. form of INHALE.

enhalo (ɛnˈheɪləʊ), *v.* [f. EN-[1] + HALO.] *trans.* To surround with, or as with, a halo; to throw a halo round. Also *fig.*

1842 LOWELL *Forlorn* Poet. Wks. (1879) 16/1 Enhaloed by a mild, warm glow. **1860** LD. LYTTON *Lucile* II. IV. §10 That dim circlet of light Which enhaloes the moon. **1864** LOWELL *Fireside Trav.* 41 Such admiring interest as that with which we enhaloed some larger boy.

†**enˈhalse**, *v. Obs.* [f. EN-[1] + HALSE *v.* in same sense.] *trans.* To salute, greet.

1559 BALDWIN in *Myrr. Mag.* (1563) M iij a, The other me enhalse With welcum coosyn.

enhamper: see EN- *pref.*[1] 3.

enhance (ɛnˈhɑːns, -ˈhæns), *v.* Forms: α. 4-7 **enhaunce**, 4-8 **enhaunse, enhanse**, (4 **enhawse, enhawnse,** 5 **henhawnes,** 7 **enhaunch**), 5- **enhance.** β. 5-6 **inhaunse,** 6-8 **inhaunce, inhanse, inhance.** [a. AF. *enhaunce-r*, prob. a mere corruption of OF. *enhaucer* = It. *innalzare*:—late L. **inaltiāre*, f. *in-* (see IN-) + *alt-us* high. Cf. ENHAULSE.

Formally, the AF. *enhauncer* might correspond to Pr. *enansar* to advance, enhance, repr. late L. type **inantiāre*, f. phrase *in ante* before (cf. ADVANCE *v.*); but this word is not known to have existed in OF.]

†**1. a.** *trans.* To lift, raise, set up; also, to raise the level of (ground). *Obs.*

By lawyers of 17th c. used *spec.* in the sense 'to raise (a weir in a river) to an (excessive) height', after AF. *enhancer* in certain statutes. See ENHANCER, ENHANCING *vbl. sb.*

1388 WYCLIF *Ps.* lxxiv. 5 Nyle ȝe enhaunce the horn. *c* **1391** CHAUCER *Astrol.* II. §26 Wher as the pol is enhawsed vp on the orisonte. *c* **1400** MAUNDEV. viii. (1839) 95 Thei [the Walles] han ben so filled agen, & the ground enhaunced. *a* **1400-50** *Alexander* 5068, I, Alexander þe athill..þine pilars en-haunsid. *c* **1430** LYDG. *Bochas* I. xv. 31 Cruelly he gan enhaunce his honde With his sweorde to yeue her a wounde. **1485** CAXTON *Chas. Gt.* 206 It was a stone..the whyche was enhaunced vpryght. **1548** UDALL, etc. *Erasm. Par. John* xvi. 100 b, The cause why..was to enhaunce you to heauen. **1583** STANYHURST *Æneis* III. (Arb.) 78 But father Anchises his palms from strond plat inhauncing. **1590** SPENSER *F.Q.* I. i. 17 Who, nought agast, his mightie hand enhaunst. **16..** tr. *Act 1 Hen. IV*, xii, Them [Weares] that they finde too much enhanced or straited [orig. *trop enhancez ou estretiez*] to correct, pull downe, and amend.

b. *Her.* To put (a bend, etc.) in a higher position in the field.

1864 BOUTELL *Heraldry Hist. & Pop.* xxi. 359 Three bendlets enhanced arg.

†**c.** *transf.* To 'lift up' (the voice, a prayer).

1483 CAXTON *Gold. Leg.* 33/2 Thirdly it [the church] is halowed by cause that the orysons be enhaunsed there. *Ibid.* 441/2 The preest enhauncyng hys voys sayth, etc.

¶**d.** ? Misused for: To surpass in height.

1632 LITHGOW *Trav.* v. 191 Their circle-spred tops, do kisse or enhance the lower clouds.

†**2.** In various *fig.* or immaterial senses, with personal obj.: **a.** To exalt in dignity, rank, estimation, or wealth. **b.** To elevate spiritually or morally. **c.** To lift up with pride; *refl.* to exalt oneself, assume superiority. **d.** To praise, extol.

a. *c* **1374** CHAUCER *Boeth.* IV. iii, Oonly bounte and prowesse may enhawnse euery man ouer oþer men. **1393** LANGL. *P. Pl.* C. xii. 58 So is pruyde en-hansed In religion and al þe reame, among ryche and poure. **1447** BOKENHAM *Seyntys* (1835) 112 To wurshyp I wyl enhaunsen the. **1489** CAXTON *Faytes of A.* IV. xv. 276 Fortune enhaunceth men att her owne plaisire. **1595** SPENSER *Col. Clout.* 359 The Shepheard of the Ocean Unto that Goddesse grace me first enhanced. **1643** PRYNNE *Sov. Power Parl.* 29 He enhaunsed men of low birth to great honours. *a* **1649** DRUMM. OF HAWTH. *Wks.* 40 To inhaunce with favours this thy reign.

b. *c* **1380** WYCLIF *Wks.* (1880) 42 þis haþ maad ȝou pore in þingis & enhaunsed ȝou in vertues. *a* **1450** *Knt. de la Tour* (1868) 7 Praiers to God makithe the man and woman to be enhaunsed. **1526** *Pilgr. Perf.* 12 This gyfte..enhaunceth or lyfteth vp the mynde of man to goostlynes and heuenly meditacyons.

c. *c* **1380** WYCLIF *Sel. Wks.* III. 396 Freris falsely enhansen homself abofe Crist and his apostils. *c* **1386** CHAUCER *Pers. T.* ⁋ 540 Flaterie makith a man to enhaunsen his hert and his countenaunce. *c* **1449** PECOCK *Repr.* I. xii. 63 That noon of ȝou..enhaunce ȝou silf aboue alle othere Cristen. **1590** SPENSER *F.Q.* I. v. 47 There also was king Crœsus, that enhaunst His hart too high. **1642** ROGERS *Naaman* 170 So content to enlarge Grace, that therewith she will enhaunse her selfe.

d. *a* **1400-50** *Alexander* 2498 þe mare I spek him dispite ..þe hiȝere I here him enhansed. **1485** CAXTON *Paris & V.* 71 That the name of our lord Ihesu cryst were more sayntefyed and enhaunced. **1450-1530** *Myrr. Our Ladye* 289 Erthe mote blesse the lorde..and enhaunce hym on wythouten ende. **1627** DRAYTON *Nymphidia*, Those [poets] more ancient do inhance Alcides in his fury.

3. a. To raise in degree, heighten, intensify (qualities, states, powers, etc.).

1559 *Mirr. Mag., Dk. Suffolk* v. 7 My lucky spede mine honor did enhaunce. **1583** GOLDING *Calvin on Deut.* xxxv. 209 Such a shameful thanklesnesse as inhaunceth their rebelliousnesse a hundredfold. **1691** RAY *Creation* ii. 450 That which enhanses this Injury, is that it is irreparable. **1781** GIBBON *Decl. & F.* II. xxxi. 201 These delights were enhanced by the memory of past hardships. **1853** C. BRONTË *Villette* xxi. (1876) 223 This dusky wrapper..enhancing by contrast the fairness of her skin. **1872** YEATS *Hist. Comm.* 94 Strawberries, bilberries, and currants, enhance their flavour in this zone to an excellence unknown in England. **1873** BURTON *Hist. Scot.* VI. lxxi. 245 They had what greatly enhanced their effective force—four brass field pieces.

b. To magnify subjectively, make to appear greater; to heighten, exaggerate.

c **1400** *Rom. Rose* 7248 And where is more wode folye Than to enhaunce chyvalrie. **1529** MORE *Suppl. Soulys* 315/1 Enhauncyng the merite and goodnes of Christs passion. **1669** GALE *Crt. Gentiles* I. Introd. 5 How much wil their Divine Majestie..be enhansed thereby? **1738** GLOVER *Leonidas* II. 275 Beyond the reach of fiction to inhance. **1788** BURKE *Sp. agst. W. Hastings* Wks. 1842 II. 211 He did, in the libel aforesaid, enhance his services. **1832** G. DOWNES *Lett. Cont. Countries* I. 438 The satirist wished to enhance the infirmity of Philip.

4. a. To raise (prices, value); to increase (charges, etc.).

1542-3 *Act 34 & 35 Hen. VIII*, c. 7 To mittigate, and enhaunce the price of wynes..as..occasion shall require. **1587** HARRISON *England* II. v. (1877) I. 135 Their freends are brought unto pouertie by their rents inhanced. **1616** R. C. *Times' Whis.* I. 694 Enhaunce The faire revennewes of the English crowne. **1632** QUARLES *Div. Fancies* I. lviii. 25 Why could not hungery Esau strive t' enhaunce His price a little? *a* **1649** DRUMM. OF HAWTH. *Irene* Wks. 173 Taxes and customs daily enhansed. **1697** EVELYN *Numism.* i. 6 The Value of the Denarius was inhaunced from..ten Asses to that of Sixteen. **1712** HEARNE *Coll.* III. 430 The Price should be rather inhanc'd than lessen'd. **1866** ROGERS *Agric. & Pr.* I. xx. 511 The price was considerably enhanced by the charge of conveyance.

b. *intr.* †Of prices: To rise. *Obs.* In more recent use, (of property, etc.) to increase in value or price.

1494 FABYAN *Chron.* VII. 463 Corne the yere folowynge was scant, whereof the pryce this yere began to enhaunce. **1671** F. PHILIPPS *Reg. Necess.* 235 Upon complaint of enhancing. **1889** *Cent. Dict.* s.v., A debt enhances rapidly by compound interest. [Rare.] **1892** *Pall Mall Gaz.* 15 Nov. 3/2 Until the property enhanced sufficiently to sell. **1904** *N.Y. Even. Post* 31 Mar. 2 With stationary or diminishing incomes, their living expenses are constantly enhancing.

5. a. To raise or increase *in* price, value, importance, attractiveness, etc. †**b.** Formerly used *simply*, = 'to increase in price or value'; *esp.* to raise the intrinsic value of (coin). Also (*rarely*) = 'to increase in attractiveness,' to beautify, improve.

1526 WRIOTHESLEY *Chron.* (ed. 1875) I. 15 This yeare, in November, the Kinge enhaunsed his coyne. **1542** BRINKLOW *Compl.* ii. A vij, They neuer inhaunsed theyr landes, nor toke so cruell fynes. **1598** STOW *Surv.* vii. (1603) 57 The Angell was enhanced to vii.*s.* vi.*d.* **1647** WARD *Simp. Cobler* 76, I honour them..more, that study wisely and soberly to enhance their native language. **1651** HOBBES *Leviath.* II. xxiv. 130 Base Mony, may easily be enhansed, or abased. **1699** WAFER *Voyage* (1729) 263 Thereby..to

enhance a part of the mines. **1718** POPE *Iliad* XII. 376 Our feasts enhanced with music's sprightly sound. **1836** HOR. SMITH *Tin Trump.* (1876) 250 The Poet enhances By beautiful fancies The strain. **1862** BURTON *Bk. Hunter* 44 The book has been..greatly enhanced in value by the profuse edging of manuscript notes.

enhanced (ɛn'hɑːnst, -'hænst), *ppl. a.* [f. ENHANCE *v.* + -ED[1].] **1. a.** In various senses of the verb.

1536 BELLENDEN *Chron. Scot.* (1821) II. 10 Nothir the feir of deith, nor present calamite, micht draw thaim fra thair inhansit sinne. **1594** GREENE *Selimus* Wks. 1881–3 XIV. 232 To..save himselfe from his enhanced hand. **1796** BURKE *Wks.* VIII. 566 Giving the enhanced price to that war. **1872** YEATS *Growth Comm.* 379 Buying up the stock of any commodity to sell it again at an enhanced price.

b. *Spectroscopy.* Applied to the lines of a metallic spectrum which are strengthened, or which only appear, under the action of the spark.

1897 J. N. LOCKYER in *Proc. R. Soc.* LX. 476 In these stars iron is practically represented by the enhanced lines alone. **1903** *Phil. Trans.* Ser. A. CCI. 211 The majority of the lines are due to metallic vapours, the enhanced lines and the arc lines being of about equal prominence. **1907** N. LOCKYER *Spectroscopic Comp. Metals* 24 The enhanced lines of titanium are..considerably weaker in the stellar spectrum than in the sun. **1922** *Encycl. Brit.* XXX. 298/2 The 'enhanced lines' of strontium 4077 and 4215 are relatively strong in stars of high luminosity and weak in those of low luminosity. **1951** L. H. ALLER in J. A. Hynek *Astrophysics* ii. 31 The chromosphere lines are enhanced lines.

2. *enhanced radiation*: ionizing radiation of increased intensity; *spec.* (freq. *attrib.*) that from certain low-yield thermonuclear weapons which produce less blast and heat, so as to be harmful to life but less destructive of property (cf. *neutron bomb* s.v. NEUTRON 2).

1976 *Manch. Guardian Weekly* 14 Nov. 6/3 The new type, low-yield weapons..release up to 80 per cent of their energy in prompt radiation... This characteristic is known as 'enhanced radiation' (ER). **1977** *Congress Q. Almanac* 381/1 President Carter..had asked Congress to give him the option of going ahead with production and deployment of the enhanced radiation weapons. **1978** *Sci. Amer.* May 44/1 The enhanced-radiation warhead..is the latest development in the U.S. military's search for a 'cleaner'..nuclear weapon. **1979** *Summary World Broadcasts: Soviet Union* (B.B.C.) 29 June A26 Another cause of disruption of the natural radio background is seismic processes. Crack formation in the Earth's crust is accompanied by enhanced radiation. **1982** *Daily Tel.* 29 July 4/8 The shell would be the third enhanced-radiation warhead to be built for a deployed American weapon system. **1985** *Military Sapce* 5 Aug. 8/1 Storage rings operating at or near 1 GeV..will extract and use synchrotron and undulator-enhanced radiation from the storage ring.

enhancement (ɛn'hɑːnsmənt, -'hæns-). [f. ENHANCE *v.* + -MENT.] The action or process of enhancing; the fact of being enhanced. (See senses of the vb.)

1577 in W. H. Turner *Select. Rec. Oxford* 388 Wthowt any further inhansemt or raysing of rents. **1610** HEALEY *St. Aug. Citie of God* 261 If Venus deserved her enhansement..why then is Minerva famous? **1622** MALYNES *Anc. Law-Merch.* 323 The said Lyon Doller (albeit decreed after the former enhancement) is still valued at fortie stiuers. **1674** *Govt. Tongue* (T.), Jocular slanders have, from the slightness of the temptation, an enhancement of guilt. **1710** *Lond. Gaz.* No. 4686/3 To..enquire of the Reason of the Dearness and Inhancement of the Price of such Book. **1787** BENTHAM *Def. Usury*, A few per cent. enhancement upon the price of goods is a matter that may easily enough pass unheeded. **1875** GLADSTONE *Glean.* VI. xxxvi. 128 Augmentation of ritual..without any corresponding enhancement of devotion.

attrib. **1883** *19th Cent.* Sept. 430 After having obtained an enhancement decree.

enhancer (ɛn'hɑːnsə(r), -'hæns-). [f. ENHANCE *v.* + -ER.[1]]

1. *gen.* One who, or that which, enhances.

1388 WYCLIF *Exod.* xxii. 15 And Moises bildide an auter and clepide the name thereof The Lord myn enhaunsere. **1568** *Like Will to Like* in Hazl. *Dodsley* III. 316 Thou art the enhancer of my renown. **1611** RICH *Honest. Age* (1844) 65 Pride is the inhaunser of all our miseries. **1832** LYTTON *Eugene A.* iv. 96 Errors of life as well as foibles of characters are often the real enhancers of celebrity.

2. *spec.* **a.** One who sets up or raises a weir to an excessive height. (Cf. quot. 1622 s.v. ENHANCING *vbl. sb.*)

1622 CALLIS *Stat. Sewers* (1647) 205 It gives the like penalty against him which shall relevy the annoyance, as against the inhauncer.

b. One who raises or seeks to raise prices. †Formerly also *absol.* (cf. *engrosser, forestaller*).

1549 LATIMER *Serm. bef. Edw. VI* (Arb.) 111 Money makers, inhauncers, and promoters of them selues. **1577** B. GOOGE *Heresbach's Husb.* (1586) 47 In no wise to be a raiser or enhaunser of rentes. **1631** *Star Chamb. Cases* (1886) 46 Yet he was adjudged an inhauncer for but advising the same. *a* **1680** BUTLER *Rem.* (1759) I. 151 The Jew, Forestaller and Enhancer To him for all their Crimes did answer.

enhancing (ɛn'hɑːnsɪŋ, -'hæns-), *vbl. sb.* [f. ENHANCE *v.* + -ING[1].] The action of the verb ENHANCE.

1490 CAXTON *Eneydos* xxviii. 109 Dydo hath defyled vylaynsly the good name and the enhaunsynge of the cytee. **1495** *Will Spilman* (Somerset Ho.), The bylding & the henhawnesyng of the Rooffe. **1534** MORE *On the Passion* Wks. 1292/2 Reseruynge theyr actuall enhaunsynge into heauen vntyll the great mistery of Christes passyon shoulde bee perfourmed. **1577–87** HOLINSHED *Chron.* III. 963/2 For the inhancing of gold to eight & fortie shillings, & siluer foure shillings the ounce. **1622** CALLIS *Stat. Sewers* (1824) 304 For the enhancing of such weres, mills, stanks, stakes, and kiddels. **1637** SANDERSON *Serm.* II. 71 Enhaunsing of fees, trucking for expedition.

†**en'hancing,** *ppl. a. Obs.* [f. as prec. + -ING[2].] That enhances.

1382 WYCLIF *Prov.* xxi. 24 The proud man and the enhaunsende hymself [Vulg. *arrogans*] is cleped vntaȝt. **1590** GREENE *Orl. Fur.* (1861) 90 Saba, whose enhancing streams Cut 'twixt the Tartars and the Russians. **1606** HIERON *Wks.* I. 44 The engrossing merchant, the enhaunsing husbandman. **1715** M. DAVIES *Ath. Brit.* I. 10 A gradual and more enhauncing Augmentation of the Expression.

enhancive (ɛn'hɑːnsɪv, -'hæns-), *a.* Also *U.S.* **enhansive.** [f. ENHANCE *v.* + -IVE.] That tends to enhance or intensify; *spec.* designating a sentence or word of which the second part is more forcible than the first, or the second part itself.

1853 [see ANNEXIVE *a.*]. **1889** *Blackw. Mag.* Nov. 708 What so..enhancive of the glow of the bright firelight..as that delightful ball of warm dark-grey fur coiled up upon the hearth? **1904** A. B. DAVIDSON *Theol. O.T.* iii. 99 *Elohim*—a plural not numerical, but simply enhancive of the idea of *might*.

enhang: see EN- *pref.*[1] 3.

†**en'happy,** *v. Obs.* [f. EN-[1] + HAPPY.] *trans.* To make (a person) happy; to make (an enterprise) prosperous.

1626 SIR S. D'EWES *Journal* (1783) 34 Do but enhappie him that sent it [a carcanet] in the ordinarie vse of it. **1641** SYMONDS *Serm. bef. Ho. Comm.* ¶3 What better then..to see our Kingdom enhappied? **1645** *City Alarum* 12 The pretious Elixar, which we must seeke out to enhappie this war. **1742** OWEN *Nat. Hist. Serpents* 83 That Tree, so enhappy'd flourishes all Winter.

en'harbour, *v.* Also 6 **inharbour.** [f. EN-[1] + HARBOUR *sb.* or *v.*] *trans.* **a.** To harbour within itself. **b.** To dwell in, as in a harbour.

1596 FITZ-GEFFRAY *Sir. F. Drake* (1881) 21 Spenser, whose hart inharbours Homers soule. **1613–6** W. BROWNE *Brit. Past.* I. iii, O true delight, enharbouring the breasts Of those sweet creatures with the plumy crests. *a* **1907** F. THOMPSON *Coll. Poetry* (1913) 322 As lovers..do their hearts Enharbour in its continent heart.

†**en'hard,** *v. Obs.* [f. EN-[1] + HARD; in early use possibly ad. Fr. *enhardir*, f. *en-* + *hardi* bold, HARDY.] *trans.* **a.** To make bold or hardy; = ENHARDY. **b.** To make hard, harden.

Hence **en'harded** *ppl. a.*, hardened.

a **1450** *Knt. de la Tour* (1868) 56 That worde..enharded hym [the develle] to speke to her. **1475** *Bk. Noblesse* 27 Accustumyng hem ayene to werre, were by experience lerned and enhardid. **1491** CAXTON *Vitas Patr.* IV. 333 b/2, I haue an herte so enharded that, etc. **1523** SKELTON *Garl. Laurel* 305 Enharded adyment the cement of your wall.

enharden (ɛn'hɑːd(ə)n), *v. Obs.* or *arch.* Also 6 **inharden.** [f. EN-[1] + HARDEN *v.*] *trans.* To make hard, harden. *fig.*

1502 *Ord. Crysten Men* V. i. (1506) 355 The dampned may by length of eternyte be enhardened. **1583** GOLDING *Calvin's Serm. Deut.* lxvii. 407 Wee may well inharden our selues in our wicked customes. **1643** SIR T. BROWNE *Relig. Med.* I. §40 Nor hath conversation, age or travell, been able to effront, or enharden me. **1875** MYERS *Poems* 26 She..Whom very stripes enharden.

¶ Used in sense of ENHARDY.

1779 T. A. MANN in *Ellis Orig. Lett.* (1843) 417 Your friendship for me enhardens me to try your advice on this head.

†**en'hardy,** *v. Obs.* [f. EN-[1] + HARDY *a.*; cf. F. *enhardir.*] *trans.* To make hardy, embolden.

1483 CAXTON *Gold. Leg.* 233/4 Alle the other bysshoppes that Eusebe had enhardyed. **1502** *Ord. Crysten Men* III. iii. (1506) 156 To comforte and to enhardy those to do well the whiche ben weyke in speryte. **1525** LD. BERNERS *Froiss.* II. cciv. [cc.] 630 Than this kynge..enhardyed himselfe to the warre with these barones.

†**enhar'moniac,** *a. Obs.*$^{-0}$ [f. as next + -AC.] = ENHARMONIC.

1681 BLOUNT *Glossogr.*, *Enharmoniack.*

†**enhar'monian,** *a. Obs. rare*$^{-1}$. [f. Gr. ἐναρμόνι-ος + -AN.] = next.

1603 HOLLAND *Plutarch's Mor.* 1252 Olympus..is reputed..the inventor of the Musicke called Enharmonian.

enharmonic (ɛnhɑː'mɒnɪk), *a.* and *sb. Music.* Also 7 **enarmonic, enharmonique,** 8 **-ick.** [ad. L. *enharmonic-us*, Gr ἐναρμονικός, f. ἐν in + ἁρμονια: see HARMONY. Cf. Fr. *enharmonique.*]

A. *adj.*

1. Pertaining to that genus, style, or scale of music current among the Greeks, in which an interval of two and a half tones was divided into two quarter tones and a major third.

[**1597** MORLEY *Introd. Mus.* Annot., *Enharmonicum* is that which riseth by *diesis, diesis*..and *ditonus.*] **1603** HOLLAND *Plutarch's Mor.* 1252 These were the beginnings of the enharmonique Musicke. **1726** SWIFT *London strewed with Rarities* Wks. 1841 I. 827 He sings..with equal facility in the chromatic, enharmonic, and diatonic style. **1774** STEELE in *Phil. Trans.* LXV. 71 The enharmonic genus requires intervals of the *diesis*, or quartertone. **1852** *Fraser's Mag.* XLVI. 656 Greek music..in its most approved form, the enharmonic, proceeded by quartertones.

2. Pertaining to, or concerned with, intervals smaller than a semitone; *esp.* with reference to the interval between those notes (belonging to different keys), which in instruments of equal temperament are rendered by the same tone: e.g. between G♯ and A♭. ***enharmonic change*** or ***modulation***: see quots. 1879.

a **1794** SIR W. JONES *Mus. Modes Hindus* in *Asiat. Res.* III. (1799) 75 Those, it seems, were the first enharmonick melodies. **1865** DE MORGAN in *Athenæum* No. 1975. 312/2 An enharmonic organ. **1879** PARRY in Grove *Dict. Mus.* s.v. *Change*, Changes are of three kinds..1. The Diatonic..2. The Chromatic..3. The Enharmonic, where advantage is taken of the fact that the same notes can be called by different names, which lead different ways, and..into unexpected keys.

fig. **1876** J. C. MORISON in *Macm. Mag.* XXXIV. 93 The modulation and enharmonic change with which writers of a totally different cast of genius..surprise the ear.

3. quasi-*sb.*

1883 DAVENPORT *Elem. Music* (1887) 30 Each of the three sounds [C, ♯B, ♭♭D] is called the Enharmonic of the one next above or below it alphabetically.

B. *sb. pl.* Enharmonic music.

1603 HOLLAND *Plutarch's Mor.* 1252 Thus you see what were the first rudiments and beginnings of Enharmoniques. **1865** *Pall Mall G.* 24 Nov. 10 Others seem sanguine that congregations can be got to sing anything—close enharmonics, perhaps.

Hence **enhar'monical** *a.* = prec. **enhar'monically** *adv.*

1751 CHAMBERS *Cycl.* s.v. *Diesis*, Enharmonical Diesis is the difference between a greater and lesser semi-tone. **1879** *Sat. Mus. Rev.* 6 Sept. 506 It roves through seven keys in fifteen bars, and such keys as G major, F minor, E flat, A flat minor, G flat major, F sharp major (enharmonically).

†**en'harness,** *v. Obs. rare.* In 5 **enharnash, -ysh.** [ad. F. *enharnacher*, F. *en-* (see EN-[1]) + *harnaschier, harneschier* to harness: see HARNESS.] *trans.* To harness (a horse).

1490 CAXTON *Eneydos* xxxviii. 128 A honderd fayre horses welle rychely enharnyshed. *c* **1500** *Melusine* 9 Oon of her seruaunts..ledd a palfroy richely enharnashed.

†**en'harped,** *ppl. a. Obs. rare*$^{-1}$. [? f. EN-[1] + med.L. *harpa*, Gr. ἅρπη sickle + -ED.[1]] ? Shaped like a sickle or scimitar; hooked.

a **1529** SKELTON *Dethe Erle Northumberland* 125 With thy sword, enharpit of mortall drede.

enhart(e, variant of ENHEART *v. Obs.*

†**en'haste,** *v. Obs.* [ad. OF. *enhaster*, f. *en-* (see EN-[1]) + *haster* (mod. *hâter*) to hasten.] *trans.* To hasten, hurry; also *refl.*

1430 LYDG. *Chron. Troy* I. ii. Many worthy in knighthode..Enhasted were unto their deth. *c* **1430** —— *Stor. Thebes* III. (R.), They enhasted hem, making none abode.

enhat (ɛn'hæt), *v.* [f. EN- 1 b + HAT *sb.*] *trans.* To invest with a cardinal's hat.

1925 *Times Lit. Suppl.* 26 Nov. 795/1 The rings ceremonially presented to Cardinals when enhatted. **1925** *Times* 18 Dec. 13/2 Five Cardinals Enhatted.

†**en'haulse,** *v. Obs. rare*$^{-1}$. [ad. OF. *enhalcer, enhauser.*] *trans.* = ENHANCE, q.v.

1600 HOLLAND *Livy* XXII. lviii. 468 The horsemens raunsome was somewhat enhaulsed..above that summe.

enhaunce, -ch, -se, obs. ff. ENHANCE.

†**en'haunt,** *v. Obs.* Also 6–7 **inhaunt.** [ad. Fr. *enhanter*, f. *en-* (see EN-[1]) + *hanter* to haunt.]

1. *trans.* To practise, exercise.

1382 WYCLIF *2 Chron.* xix. 6 3e [jugis] enhaunten [Vulg. *exercetis*] not dome of man, bot of the Lord. —— *Esther* ix. 12 Hou myche slaȝter wenest thou them to enhaunten in alle prouyncis?

2. a. *trans.* To frequent, haunt. **b.** *refl.* To betake oneself to a haunt, accustom oneself. **c.** *intr.* To keep company *with.*

1530 PALSGR. 535/2, *I enhaunte*, I haunt ones companye. **1547–64** BAULDWIN *Mor. Philos.* (Palfr.) XII. 185/2 Better it is to liue solitary, Then to enhaunt much company. **1549–62** STERNHOLD & H. *Ps.* xciv. 20 Wilt thou inhaunt thy selfe and draw, With wicked men to sit. **1562** TURNER *Baths* 4 b, I neuer sawe in anye place..more inhaunted then they [the baths near Baden] be. **1658** MANTON *Exp. Jude* 16 It argueth they do inhaunt with traitors.

Hence †**en'haunting** *vbl. sb.*

1382 WYCLIF *Ps.* liv. 3, I am maad al sory in myn enhaunting [**1388** exercising, Vulg. *exercitatio*].

†**en'havoc,** *v. Obs. rare*$^{-1}$. In 6 **enhavac.** [f. EN-[1] + HAVOC *v.*] To make havoc, devastate.

Hence **en'havocking** *vbl. sb.*, devastation.

1613 T. ADAMS *Pract. Wks.* I. 87 Our concealings have been close, our enhavacings ravenous, our transportations lavish.

enhawnse, -hawse, obs. ff. ENHANCE.

†**en'hazard,** *v. Obs.* [f. EN-[1] + HAZARD *sb.*] *trans.* To expose to hazard, to risk.

Hence **en'hazarding,** *vbl. sb.*

1562 SHUTE *Cambine's Turk. Wars* 8 They were willing to avoide the danger of anye more enhazarding their force. **1599** SANDYS *Europæ Spec.* (1632) 154 How often his State

hath beene afflicted by him [the Turke], and sometimes enhazarded. *Ibid.* 201 With the utter enhazarding of both Christendome and Christianity. **1611** SPEED *Hist. Gt. Brit.* IX. ii. §17 The Citizens, and souldiers..to secure their liues from the fire, did enhazard them on the fury of the sword.

enhearse, inhearse (ɛn-, ɪnˈhɜːs), *v.* Also 7 inhearce. [f. EN-¹ + HEARSE.] *trans.* To put into a hearse. Also *transf.* and *fig.*

1600 SHAKS. *Sonn.* lxxxvi, You..did my ripe thoughts in my braine inhearce. **1633** FORD *Love's Sacrifice* V. iv. 444 The shrine Of fairest purity which hovers yet About these blessed bones inhearsed within. **1635** BRATHWAIT *Arcad. Pr.* II. 20 Enhearse thy sable soule in lasting feares. **1855** SINGLETON *Virgil* II. 6 We My godlike sire's remains and bones inhearsed In earth.

†**enˈheart,** *v. Obs.* Also 6 enhart(e, 7 inhart. [f. EN-¹ + HEART.] *trans.* **a.** *fig.* To put heart into, make hearty; to encourage, inspirit. **b.** To enclose within the substance of the heart.

1545 RAYNOLD *Womans Booke* 71 She must be..strenthened with good comfortable meates & drinkes, which may enhearte her. **1548** GEST *Pr. Masse* 86 No more then the sayd holy ghost is adjudged embodied or enharted, for yᵗ he is wholly in us and in our hartes. **1603** H. CROSSE *Vertues Commw.* (1878) 113 Others may be inharted to rush carelesly forward into vnbrideled libertie.

enhearten (ɛnˈhɑːt(ə)n), *v.* Now *rare.* Also 7 inhearten. [f. EN-¹ + HEARTEN *v.*] *trans.* To make hearty or courageous; to strengthen, cheer.

1611 SPEED *Hist. Gt. Brit.* IX. viii. §33 Their Commaunder's inuinceable constancy against yeelding, which enheartened the better sort, dismayed the baser. **1656** EARL MONM. *Advt. fr. Parnass.* 120 The Venetian poet incouraged and inheartned Juvinal. **1859** I. TAYLOR *Logic in Theol.* 131, I seek to enhearten myself for a labour so arduous. **1881** PALGRAVE *Vis. Eng.* 241 O names that enhearten the soul, Blenheim and Waterloo.

transf. **1610** W. FOLKINGHAM *Art of Survey* I. x. 25 Sommer-eating doth greatly enhearten weake Medowes.

Hence **enˈheartening** *ppl. a.*

1836 J. GILBERT *Chr. Atonem.* ix. (1852) 270 This enheartening visitant. **1861** I. TAYLOR *Spirit Hebr. Poetry* (1873) 248 That modesty, that calm philosophic balance of the mind..enheartening especially to those who bear testimony for wisdom and goodness.

enheaven, inheaven (ɛn-, ɪnˈhɛv(ə)n), *v.* [f. EN-¹ + HEAVEN.] *trans.* To place in or raise to heaven, *lit.* and *fig.*; to entrance.

1652 BENLOWES *Theoph.* I. lxxii, Their perfume Enheav'ns the sense. **1839–48** BAILEY *Festus* 60/1 He Himself Conceiving, bearing, suffering, ending all, Affiliating and inheavening. **1851** S. JUDD *Margaret* III. (1871) 358 The one circumflows and inheavens us.

enhedge: see EN- *pref.*¹ 3.

[**enhendee,** *a. Her.* A spurious word found in some heraldic and other Dicts. in the phrase *cross enhendee* (given as synonym of *cross potenee*) where the adj. appears to be a corruption of OF. *enheudée* having a handle. The misreading occurs in Fr. writers, e.g. Palliot, 1664.]

†**enˈherd,** *v. Sc. Obs.* Forms: 4 aneherd, (*pr. pple.* enerthand), 4–5 anerd, (6 annerd), 5–6 enherde. [a. OF. *enherdre*:—late L. *inhærēre*, altered form of L. *inhærēre* (see INHERE), f. *in-* in. upon + *hærēre* to stick. The OF., and hence the Eng., word correspond in sense with L. *adhærēre* (late L. *-ĕre*) to ADHERE, whence the synon. OF. *aherdre*; prob, as in other instances, the OF. words with prefixes *en-* and *a-* have been confounded in use.]

intr. To adhere, assent. Const. *to*; also *simply.*

c **1375** *Sc. Leg. Saints, Paulus* 1090 Vthir womene..aneherdit to Petir and Paule. *Ibid., Andreas* 207 Myne barne, þat þis has me done, To þis aldmane enerthand is [L. *adhæsit*]. *c* **1375** BARBOUR *Troy-bk.* II. 1404 Kynges sere That to hys will anerdande were. *c* **1425** WYNTOUN *Cron.* VIII. xxix. 164 Hys wil wes til enherde To þe Scottis mennys Party. *c* **1440** *Gaw. & Gol.* in Pinkerton *Scot. Poems Repr.* II. 8 (Jam.), Thare anerdis to our nobill to note..Tuelf crounit kingis in feir. **1513** DOUGLAS *Æneis* II. xi. 164 Plat he refusis, enherding to his entent. *Ibid.* XII. xiii. 118 Juno anerdit [*v.r.* annerdit], and gaif consent thareto.

Hence **anˈherdand** [the pr. pple. used subst.], an adherent.

1478 *Acta Dom. Audit.* 71 (Jam.), That James of Lawthress..salbe harmless & scathless of thaime, thair freindis, partij and anherdandis. **1480** *Acta Dom. Concilii* 54 (Jam.) That Johne M'Gille sall be harmeles of the said Williame and his anherdens bot as law will.

†**enˈhere,** *v. Obs. rare*⁻¹. [Of uncertain formation: perh. f. EN-¹ + HEIR.] *trans.* ? To possess as an inheritance.

a **1400–50** *Alexander* 1132 Sir, anec..That þe erth of egipt enhered some tyme.

enherit, etc.: see INHERIT, etc.

†**enˈhigh,** *v. Obs.* In 5 enhie. [f. EN-¹ + HIGH.] *trans.* To make high, exalt.

c **1440** *Gesta Rom.* xxii. 123 That I and al my kin myght be enhied & honovrid.

enhoney: see EN- *pref.*¹ 1 b.

†**enˈhonour,** *v. Obs.* Also 6 in-. [f. EN-¹ + HONOUR.] *trans.* To put honour upon; to honour.

1571 GOLDING *Calvin on Ps.* xviii. 2 Tytles to enhonour God withall. **1583** —— *Calvin's Serm. Deut.* iv. 22 Euerie of them ought to considir..howe greatly God hath inhonored him. **1578** *Priv. Prayers* 547 Thou hast inhonoured me with the co-partnership of the everlasting inheritance.

enhoril: see ENOURLE.

†**enˈhort,** *v. Obs.* Also 4 enhurte, 4–5 enort. [a. OF. *enhort-er, enort-er*:—L. *inhortāri*, f. *in-* (see IN-) + *hortāri* to exhort.] *trans.* To exhort, encourage, incite. Const. *to* with *inf.*, and *simply.* Also with sb. as obj.: To recommend, suggest, insist upon.

1382 WYCLIF *2 Sam.* xi. 25 Coumfort thi fiȝters aȝens the cytee..and enhurte hem. **1388** —— *Ep. Jerome* iii, To Tymothe..he [Paul] wryteth, and enorteth the studie of lessoun. **1483** CAXTON *G. de la Tour* G iij, Euery good woman ought to enhorte her husbond to serue God.

Hence **enˈhorting,** *vbl. sb.*; **enˈhortment,** the action of exhorting, an exhortation.

1483 CAXTON *Gold. Leg.* 150/2 Eue by thenhortyng of the deuyl gaf ther consente to doo the synne of Inobedyence. **1475** —— *Jason* 124 Peleus sente you into colchos by his enhortement.

†**enˈhouse,** *v. Obs.* Also 6 in-. [f. EN-¹ + HOUSE.] *trans.* To settle or establish in a house.

1596 FITZ-GEFFRAY *Sir F. Drake* (1881) 99 O Death inhous'd in hells profundities. **1597** MIDDLETON in Farr *S.P. Eliz.* II. 535 These raigne enhoused with their mother night.

†**enˈhuile,** *v. Obs. rare.* [ad. OF. *enhuilier*, f. *en-* (see EN-¹) = *huile* oil: see ENOIL.] *trans.* To put oil upon, anoint with oil; to oil.

1601 HOLLAND *Pliny* II. 409 With a barbars brasen bason well enhuiled. **1603** —— *Plutarch's Mor.* 1138 He approched nere unto her house all enhuiled and anointed as he was.

enhunger (ɛnˈhʌŋgə(r)), *v.* Also 5 enhongre, inhungre. [f. EN-¹ + HUNGER.] *trans.* To put into a state of hunger, make hungry. Only in *pa. pple.*

1480 *Robt. Devyll* (1828) 34 He gate the bone alone, and laye and gnewe it; for he was sore enhongred. **1632** LITHGOW *Trav.* 38 We, being inhungred and also ouerioyed. **1845** J. MARTINEAU *Relig. Enq.* 7 Those animal passions which vice had..enhungered to feed on innocence and life. **1871** *Daily News* 13 Feb., What a terribly big maw Paris has, especially when she is enhungered.

enhusk: see EN- *pref.*¹ 1 a.

enhydrite (ɛnˈhaɪdraɪt). [f. as next + -ITE.] A mineral containing water occluded in its cavities.

Hence **enhyˈdritic** *a.* [+ -IC], of the nature of an enhydrite.

1812 PINKERTON *Petralogy* I. 60 Enhydritic agates found near Vicenza.

enhydrous (ɛnˈhaɪdrəs), *a.* [f. Gr. ἔνυδρ-ος (f. ἐν in + ὕδωρ water) + -OUS.] Having water within: containing water or some other fluid.

1812 PINKERTON *Petralogy* I. 90 Chalcedonies..are sometimes enhydrous, or contain a drop of water.

enhypostasia (ɛnhaɪpəʊˈsteɪzɪə). *Theol.* [mod.L., f. Gr. ἐνυπόστατος really existent.]

a. Substantial or personal existence. **b.** Personality existing not independently but in union with another personality; often describing the human nature of Christ as related to His divine nature as God the Son. So **enhypoˈstatic** *a.*

1877 [see ANHYPOSTASIA]. **1889** *Cent. Dict.*, Enhypostatic. **1917** H. M. RELTON *Study Christology* 78 Hypostasis distinguishes an individual by its characteristic properties, enhypostatic shows that it is not an attribute, which has existence in something else and is not seen in itself. *Ibid.* 226 The doctrine of the Enhypostasia..secures that the self-consciousness of the God-man is a single-consciousness which is not purely human, not merely human, but truly human. **1946** [see ANHYPOSTASIA]. **1954** *Scottish Jrnl. Theol.* VII. 249 By *enhypostasia*..it [*sc.* classical Christology] asserted that in the *assumptio carnis* the human nature of Christ was given a real and concrete subsistence within the hypostatic union—it was enhypostatic in the Word.

enhyˈpostatize, *v. rare*⁻¹. [f. EN-² + HYPOSTATIZE.] *trans.* To unite in one 'hypostasis' or 'person'.

1882–3 SCHAFF in *Herzog's Encycl. Rel. Knowl.* I. 458 His humanity was enhypostatized through union with the Logos, or incorporated into his personality.

enigma (ɪˈnɪgmə). Forms: 6–9 ænigma, 7 æ-, enigm(e, (anigma, inigma), 6- enigma. *Pl.* enigmas; also 6–7 æ-, enigmata. [a. L. *ænigma*, Gr. αἴνιγμα (pl. αἰνίγματα), f. αἰνίσσεσθαι to speak allusively or obscurely, f. αἶνος apologue, fable. The adapted forms *æ-, enigm(e* in 17th c. may be due to the Fr. *énigme.*]

1. a. A short composition in prose or verse, in which something is described by intentionally obscure metaphors, in order to afford an exercise for the ingenuity of the reader or hearer in guessing what is meant; a riddle. †**b.** In wider sense: An obscure or allusive speech; a parable (*obs.* exc. as *transf.* from 1 a).

1539 TAVERNER *Erasm. Prov.* 69 He pronounced also many Enigmata or Symboles. **1588** SHAKS. *L.L.L.* III. i. 128 Some enigma, some riddle, come, thy Lenuoy begin. **1603** HOLLAND *Plutarch's Mor.* 1354 Hidden under darke ænigmes and covert speeches. **1644–52** J. SMITH *Sel. Disc.* VI. iii. (1821) 201 Those ænigmata of Joseph's sun, moon, stars, and sheaves. **1681** H. MORE *Exp. Dan.* vi. 159 Delivering the matter without any Prophetick Ænigm or Parable. **1684** —— *An Answer* 249 Symbols, Parables, or Enigmes. **1715** POPE *Let. Sir W. Trumbull* 16 Dec., It was one of the Enigma's of Pythagoras, 'When the winds rise, worship the Eccho'..when popular tumults begin, retire to solitudes. **1781** HARRIS *Philol. Enq.* (1841) 441 Nor ought a metaphor to be farfetched, for then it becomes an enigma. **1797** MRS. RADCLIFFE *Italian* xxiv, You speak in enigmas, father. **1809–10** COLERIDGE *Friend* (1865) 158 In a complex enigma the greatest ingenuity is not always shown by him who first gives the complete solution. **1849** W. FITZGERALD tr. *Whitaker's Disput.* 186 Ænigmas which Œdipus himself could never solve.

2. *fig.* Something as puzzling as an enigma; an unsolved problem.

c **1605** ROWLEY *Birth Merl.* V. i. 349, I will erect a monument..A dark enigma to the memory. **1609** *Ev. Woman in Hum.* II. i. in Bullen *O. Pl.* IV, All which to me are problematique mines, Obsurde inigmaes. *a* **1667** JER. TAYLOR *Serm.* (1678) 340 A person both God and Man, an ænigma to all Nations, and to all Sciences. **1795** BURKE *Let. Dr. Hussey* (1844) IV. 325 As to Spain, it certainly has been, and long will be, an enigma. **1836** THIRLWALL *Greece* II. xiv. 200 If the fleet..could be supposed to solve this enigma. **1875** FARRAR *Silence & V.* ii. 33 Separated from the thought of God, the conscience becomes an idle enigma.

enigmatic (iːnɪgˈmætɪk, now usu. ɛn-), *a.* [ad. late L. *ænigmatic-us*, f. *ænigmat-* stem of *ænigma* (see ENIGMA). Cf. Fr. *énigmatique.*] Pertaining to, or of the nature of, an enigma, containing or resembling an enigma: ambiguous, obscure, perplexing. Of persons: Mysterious; baffling conjecture as to character, sentiments, identity, or history.

1628–1677 FELTHAM *Resolves* I. xxvii. (1677) 47 These fruitless and ænigmatic questions, are bones the Devil hath cast among us. **1648** JOS. BEAUMONT *Psyche* ix. 59 (R.) That ænigmatick foe, whose ammunition Is nothing else but want of all provision. **1669** GALE *Crt. Gentiles* I. I. ii. 11 Plato's usual way [was]..to wrap up those Jewish Traditions in..enigmatic Parables. **1828** CARLYLE *Misc.* I. (1857) 137 Being excessively reserved withal, he becomes not a little enigmatic. **1876** G. ELIOT *Dan. Der.* IV. xxxiv. 297 He saw the figure of the enigmatic Jew.

enigˈmatical, *a.* [f. prec. + -AL¹.] = prec.

1576 FLEMING *Panoplie Ep.* 399 Sydonius is so enigmaticall..that a man can scarse tell where to finde out his meaning. *c* **1645** HOWELL *Lett.* (1650) II. 44 The mud of Nile..that enigmaticall vast river. **1723** S. MATHER *Vind. Bible* 218 They did use ænigmatical discourses. **1823** LINGARD *Hist. Eng.* VI. 75 The meaning of this enigmatical remark was not disclosed till eighteen months afterwards. **1850** W. IRVING *Mahomet* vi. (1853) 34 The enigmatical career of this extraordinary man.

enigmatically (iːnɪgˈmætɪkəlɪ, now usu. ɛn-), *adv.* [f. prec. + -LY².] In an enigmatical manner; after the manner of, or by means of, an enigma; ambiguously, obscurely.

1590 GREENE *Never too late* (1600) 106 For young men 'tis too soone, for olde men too late to marry; concluding so enigmatically, it were not good to marry at all. **1641** FRENCH *Distill.* i. (1651) 15 Philosophers when they wrote any thing too excellent for the vulgar to know, expressed it enigmatically. **1744** BERKELEY *Siris* §365 He writes..enigmatically and briefly in the following terms. **1831** CARLYLE *Sart. Res.* II. iii. (1871) 82 So ends abruptly as is usual and enigmatically this little incipient romance.

†**enigˈmaticalness.** *Obs. rare.* [f. as prec. + -NESS.] The quality of being enigmatical.

1684 H. MORE *An Answer* 257 Plainness, in opposition to ænigmaticalness.

†**eˈnigmatist.** *Obs.* [ad. L. *ænigmatista*, ad. Gr. αἰνιγματιστ-ής, f. αἴνιγμα ENIGMA.] **a.** A writer of enigmas. **b.** One who speaks enigmatically.

1621 AINSWORTH *Annot. Pentat. Num.* xxi. 27 In Greeke, Ænigmatists, they that speake riddles. **1710** ADDISON *Whig-Exam.* i. ¶3, I shall deal more ingenuously with my Readers than the above-mentioned Enigmatist has done.

enigmatize (ɪˈnɪgmətaɪz), *v.* [ad. Gr. *αἰνιγματίζ-ειν (implied in αἰνιγματιστής, see prec.), f. αἰνιγματ- ENIGMA.]

1. *trans.* †**a.** To symbolize. **b.** To render enigmatical or puzzling.

a **1631** DONNE *Polydoron* 71 Acteon pursued by his houndes..may ænigmatize a lover chased and Devoured by his Thoughts. **1800** *Monthly Mag.* X. 437 Manuscripts..so ænigmatised with insertions and repetitions and alterations. *a* **1834** COLERIDGE *Lit. Rem.* (1836) I. 213 A poetic tissue of visual symbols..by which the Apocalypt enigmatized the Neronian persecutions. **1841** *Blackw. Mag.* XLIX. 151 It is precisely the disregard of details that enigmatizes humanity to Michelet.

2. *intr.* To utter or talk in enigmas; to deal in riddles.

In mod. Dicts.

enigmato-, combining form of ENIGMA, as in **enigmaˈtographer** [Gr. -γράφ-ος writer + -ER], a maker or explainer of enigmas.

enigma'tography [Gr. -γραφία writing], the making or collecting of enigmas. **enigma'tology** [see -LOGY], the study of enigmas.
1753 in CHAMBERS *Cycl. Supp.*

enimicitious, etc., var. of INIMICITIOUS, etc.

enimity, obs. form of ENMITY.

enisle, inisle (ɛn-, ɪ'naɪl), *v.* [f. EN-¹, IN- + ISLE.] **a.** To make into an isle. **b.** To place or settle on an isle. Also *fig.* To isolate, sever, cut off.
a. *c* **1630** DRUMM. OF HAWTH. *Sextain*, Mine eyes en-isle themselves with floods. **1848** M. ARNOLD *Poems* (1877) II. 17 In the sea of life enisled.. We mortal millions live alone. **1887** BROWNING *Parleyings, F. Furini* x, My self-consciousness 'Twixt ignorance and ignorance enisled.
β. **1612** DRAYTON *Poly-olb.* viii. 357 Into what sundry gyres her wondered self she [a river] throws, And oft inisles the shore. **1614** SELDEN *Titles Hon.* 91 This Chazaria or Gazaria.. almost inisled by the Seas Delle Zabache and Maggiore. **1812** COLERIDGE *Lit. Rem.* (1836) I. 366 Knots of curds inisled by interjacent whey at irregular distances. **1878** SEELEY *Stein* II. 156 Let the wild sea inisle thee.
Hence **i'nisled**, *ppl. a.*
1809–10 COLERIDGE *Friend* (1865) 38 The base of the inisled Ararat. **1880** BETHAM-EDWARDS *Forestalled* I. I. ii. 19 Far away lay many an inisled kingdom of fisherfolk.

†**e'nixed**, *pple. Obs. rare*⁻¹. [f. late L. *ēnixus* brought forth, born, pass. pple. of *ēnītī* to bring forth (orig. to strive: see ENIXLY).] Brought forth, born.
1607 TOPSELL *Four-f. Beasts* (1658) 69 A Calf, is a young or late enixed Bull or Cow.

†**e'nixibility.** *nonce-wd.* (bombastic.) [f. *ēnix-* ppl. stem of *ēnītī*: see prec.; after *visibility*, etc.] ? Possibility of being brought forth.
1652 URQUHART *Jewel* Wks. (1834) 210 With parturiencie for greater births, if a malevolent time disobstetricate not their enixibility.

†**e'nixly**, *adv. Obs. rare*⁻¹. [f. L. *ēnixē* with strong effort (f. *ēnixus*, pass. pple. of *ēnītī* to exert one's strength) + -LY².] Forcibly, stringently.
1671 *True Nonconf.* 92 They are.. enixely commanded the lowliest humility.

enjail, injail (ɛn-, ɪn'dʒeɪl), *v.* See also **engaol** (EN- *pref.*¹ 1). [f. EN-, IN- + JAIL. Cf. OFr. *enjaioler.*] *trans.* To shut up in, or as in, a jail; to imprison.
a **1631** DONNE *Progr. Soul* 18 (R.) Her firm destiny.. enjail'd her.. Into a small blew shell. **1855–9** SINGLETON *Virgil* II. 245 One of the kine returned The sound.. And, [though] injailed, the hope of Cacus balked.

†**en'jamb**, *v. Obs. rare*⁻¹. In 7 iniamb. [ad. Fr. *enjamber* to stride, encroach, f. *en-* in (see EN- *pref.*¹) + *jambe* leg.] *intr.* To encroach.
1600 O. E. *Repl. Libel* I. i. 33 In Juliers and Italy the Spaniard hath iniambed vpon others right.

enjambment (ɛn'dʒæmbmənt, ɑ̃ʒɑ̃bmɑ̃). *Pros.* Also **enjambement.** [ad. Fr. *enjambement*, f. *enjamber*: see ENJAMB *v.*] The continuation of a sentence beyond the second line of a couplet. Now also applied less restrictedly to the carrying over of a sentence from one line to the next.
1837–9 HALLAM *Hist. Lit.* II. v. II. §54. 216 Du Bartas almost affects the enjambement or continuation of the sense beyond the couplet. **1880** E. GOSSE *Eng. Poets* II. 271 Waller was the first English poet to adopt the French fashion of writing in couplets, instead of enjambments. **1881** SAINTSBURY *Dryden* 17 It [the couplet] was turned by enjambements into something very like rhythmic prose. **1929** *Trans. Amer. Philol. Assoc.* LX. 202, I use the term *enjambement* by itself in its largest sense, that of the running over of the sentence from one line to another. The word is often used by writers on prosody with the narrower force which it originally had, that of the running over of a group of closely joined words.

enjangle: see EN- *pref.*¹ 3.

†**en'jealous**, *v. Obs.* Also 7 **injealous.** [f. EN-¹ + JEALOUS *a.*] *trans.* To make jealous.
1619 SIR H. WOTTON in *Eng. & Germ.* (1865) 49 The King will thereby.. be soe injealoused, as maie.. keepe him from molesting thease nearer seas. **1689** *Irreg. Actions Papists* in *7th Collect. Papers Pres. Affairs* 13 Two or three gentlemen of Estate may.. enjealous a whole County.

†**en'jealousy**, *v. Obs.* [f. EN-¹ + JEALOUSY.] *trans.* To plunge into or provoke to jealousy.
1665 *Surv. Aff. Netherl.* 140 They.. enjealousied them one against the other.

†**en'jeopard**, *v. Obs.* In 6 **enjubarde**, 7 **enieopard.** [f. EN-¹ + JEOPARD *v.*] *trans.* To put in jeopardy, jeopardize, endanger.
1523 *St. Papers Hen. VIII*, I. 130 Ere His Grace wold enjubarde his people in thenfection thereof. **1638–48** G. DANIEL *Eclog.* v. 317 May it not Be his too much Affection to the Scott Enieopards him?

enjewel (ɛn'dʒ(j)uːəl), *v.* Also 7 **injewel.** [f. EN-¹ + JEWEL.] *trans.* **a.** To set jewels upon, adorn with jewels. **b.** To rest upon or adorn as a jewel does. In quots. *transf.*
Hence **en'jewelled**, *ppl. a.*
1648 HERRICK *Hesper. Nupt. Song Clipseby Crew*, Faire injewel'd May Blowne out of April. *a* **1849** POE *Al Aaraf* Wks. (1859) 198 The many star-isles That enjewel its breast.

enjoin (ɛn'dʒɔɪn), *v.* Forms: *α.* 3 enjunȝe, (anjoyni, ? angeonni), 3–4 enyoyn, 4–8 enjoyn(e, 4 (enjon), enjoign, (6 enjun), 7 enjoine, 7– enjoin. *β.* 6–7 inioyn(e, injoyn(e, (7 inoyne), 6–9 injoin. (See also ADJOIN ¶.) [a. Fr. *enjoign-* (stem of *enjoindre*, corresp. to Pr. *enjunher*, It. *ingiugnere*:—L. *injungĕre* to join on, to impose (a penalty or duty), f. *in-* + *jungĕre* to join.]
†**1.** *trans.* To join together. *Obs.*
1382 WYCLIF *Matt.* xix. 6 Therfore a man departe nat that thing that God enioynyde, or knytte to gidre. **1393** LANGLAND *P. Pl.* C. XI. 130 With wynd and water wittyliche en-ioyned. **1502** *Ord. Crysten Men* v. ii. (1506) 366 To enioyne hete and colde in one selfe torment. **1559** *Homilies* I. *Adultery* II, Through whoredome to be enjoyned [**1547** joined] and made all one with a whore. *c* **1600** NORDEN *Cornwall* in Johns *Week Lizard* (1848) 224 The forces of manie strong men enjoyned can doe no more in moving it. **1684** CHARNOCK *Wks.* (1864) I. 115 A reflection upon what God hath done should be enjoined with our desires of what we would have God to do for us.
†**b.** To take part in; also, to attach oneself to, join (a company). *Obs.*
1546 GARDINER *Decl. Articles Joye* 59 His ministers.. enioyning his glory and his honour. **1571** DIGGES *Pantom.* Pref., Enjoyning the company of Euclide, Archimedes, etc.
†**c.** *intr.* for *refl.* To join, make common cause *with*. *Obs. rare*⁻¹.
1734 tr. *Rollin's Anc. Hist.* II. VII. 382 Theron enjoined [**1739** (ed. 2) joined] with his father-in-law.
2. In early use: To impose (a penalty, task, duty, or obligation); said *esp.* of a spiritual director (*to enjoin penance*, etc.). Hence in mod. use: To prescribe authoritatively and with emphasis (an action, a course of conduct, state of feeling, etc.). Const. *on*, *upon* (a person); formerly *to*, or *dative* (or *acc.*: see 2b); also *simply*.
'It is more authoritative than *direct*, and less imperious than *command*' (J.).
a **1225** *Ancr. R.* 346 Al þet vuel þet tu euer þolest uor þe luue of Iesu Crist, wiðinnen þine ancre wowes,— al ich on iunne [*better readings* enjunȝe, angeonni] þe. **1340** *Ayenb.* 172 þet he habbe power.. him penonce to anioynj be þe zenne. *c* **1380** WYCLIF *Wks.* (1880) 43 þo mynystris.. schullen wiþ mercy enyonye hen penaunce. **1377** LANGL. *P. Pl.* B. XIII. 412 Penaunce þat þe prest enioigneth. *c* **1400** *Apol. Loll.* 32 It semiþ þat God enioniþ to doctors & dekunis þe minstri of presthed & of dekunhed. *a* **1533** LD. BERNERS *Huon* lxv. 223 That was eniunyd hym on payne of deth. **1577** HANMER *Anc. Eccl. Hist.* (1619) 503 And enioyned him no other punishment. **1616** HIERON *Wks.* II. 31, I perswade not a neglect of reading; nay, I intend and inioyne these. **1669–70** MARVELL *Corr.* cxxxvi. Wks. 1872–5 II. 302 The Lords.. have enjoyned their clerks secrecy. **1667** POOLE *Dial. betw. Protest. & Papist* (1735) 30 [The Romish Church] enjoyns these Practices to all her Members. *a* **1778** CHATHAM *Lett. Nephew* iv. 22 Pythagoras enjoined his scholars an absolute silence for a long noviciate. **1841** MYERS *Cath. Th.* III. §5. 17 A law enjoining all that ought to be done by man. **1863** BRIGHT *Sp. America* 26 Mar., In spite of all that morality may enjoin upon them.
b. The construction with dat. of person and acc. of thing is formally identical in mod. Eng. with the construction with double acc. Hence sometimes in *passive* with acc. of the thing.
1644 MILTON *Areop.* 54 But to be enjoyn'd the reading of that at all times.
†**c.** *to enjoin* (a person) *to* a penalty, observance, etc. *Obs.*
c **1380** WYCLIF *Antecrist* in Todd 3 *Treat. Wyclif* 149 þei enioynen hem to brede & watur & to go barefote. **1586** COGAN *Haven Health* (1636) 291 Not much greater punishment than the Nunne was enjoyned to. **1678** C. HATTON in *Hatton Corr.* (1878) 163 He wispers it about as a great secret, injoyning all persons to privacy. **1693** *Col. Rec. Penn.* I. 372 He wold Enjoine the Senecas to peace and friendship with them.
†**d.** To impose rules on (oneself). *Obs. rare*⁻¹.
1626 BACON *Sylva* §292 Monkes and Philosophers, and such as do continually enjoyne themselves.
e. with personal obj. (orig. indirect, in dative or preceded by *on, to*; afterwards direct) and inf. or subord. clause.
1297 R. GLOUC. 234 He hem enyoynede bocsomnesse do To þe herchebyssop of Kanterbury. **1480** CAXTON *Chron. Eng.* cxlvii. 126 Atte last the pope.. enioyned to the bisshops of englond that they sholde done general enterdyting thurgh oute al Englond. **1526** TINDALE *Acts* xv. 5 To inioyne them to keepe the lawe of Moses. **1611** SHAKS. *Wint. T.* II. iii. 173 We enioyne thee.. that thou carry This female Bastard hence. *c* **1680** BEVERIDGE *Serm.* (1729) I. 8 There are several canons enjoyning bishops to visit. **1712** STEELE *Spect.* No. 268 ⁋7 They injoined me to bring them something from London. **1825** T. JEFFERSON *Autobiog.* Wks. 1859 I. 18 They were enjoined.. to do nothing which should impede that object. **1883** FROUDE *Short Stud.* IV. I. iii. 42 The pope.. advised and even enjoined him to return to his duties.
f. without personal obj. and with inf. or subord. clause. Hence impersonally in passive.
1547 *Homilies* I. Pref. 5 A Sermon according as it is injoined in the book of her Highness Injunctions. *a* **1694** TILLOTSON (T.), Enjoining that truth and fidelity be inviolably preserved. **1868** STANLEY *Westm. Ab.* ii. 74 In his will he enjoined that his image on his tomb, etc. *Mod.* Christianity enjoins that we love our enemies.
3. To prohibit, forbid (a thing); to prohibit (a person) *from* (a person or thing). Now only in *Law*: To prohibit or restrain by an INJUNCTION.
1589 PUTTENHAM *Eng. Poesie* (1869) 30 Sore agreeued.. for that he had enioyned them from their wiues. **1814** LD. ELDON in Vesey & Beame *Reports* II. 412 The Court.. would.. injoin that action for ever. **1884** SIR C. BOWEN in *Law Rep.* Chanc. Div. XXVI. 709 We are now asked to.. enjoin him for ever from infringing a right which does not exist.
Hence †**en'joinance**, an injunction, command. **en'joined**, *ppl. a.* **en'joiner**, one who enjoins. **en'joining**, *vbl. sb.* **en'joinment**, the action of enjoining, injunction.
1782 ELPHINSTON *Martial* III. ii. 132 That is thy father's own enjoinance. **1594** HOOKER *Eccl. Pol.* II. viii. (1611) 78 That which the bond of.. enioyned duty tied him vnto. **1601** SHAKS. *All's Well* III. v. 97 Of inioyn'd penitents There's foure or fiue, to great S. Iaques bound. **1587** GOLDING *De Mornay* xxxiii. 532 The founder or Inioyner thereof by Lawe. **1662** FULLER *Worthies Sussex* III. 101 He was a great punisher of Pluralists, and injoyner of Residence. *a* **1570** BECON *New Catech.* Wks. (1844) 217 The enjoining of this outward baptism doth not save. **1646** SIR T. BROWNE *Pseud. Ep.* (J.), Critical trial should be made by publick enjoinment. **1816** SCOTT *Antiq.* xxxix, Letters of more strict enjoinment and more hard compulsion. **1868** BROWNING *Ring & Bk.* II. IV. 777 Her putative parents had impressed On their departure, their enjoinment.

enjoinder (ɛn'dʒɔɪndə(r)). [f. ENJOIN *v.* after *rejoinder.*] Something imposed upon one, a duty, an obligation.
1894 *Westm. Gaz.* 1 Sept. 3/1 No distinction is made in the analysis of conscience between its objectively rational evolution and its subjectively ultra-rational enjoinders. **1951** I. COMPTON-BURNETT *Darkness & Day* ii. 64 Then act on Alice's unspoken enjoinder.

†**en'joint.** *Obs.* [a. OF. *enjoincte*, f. *enjoindre*: see ENJOIN *v.*] That which is enjoined; a charge, duty.
1413 LYDG. *Pilgr. Sowle* I. xxv. (1859) 30 He has done his enioynte withouten ony peyn.

†**en'journ**, corruption of ADJOURN: see EN- *pref.*¹ A. 2; = ADJOURN 3.
1494 FABYAN *Chron.* VII. 593 And yᵉ foresayd parlyament was eniourned vnto yᵉ xx. day of Cristemas.

enjourney: see EN- *pref.*¹ 1 a.

†**en'joy**, *sb. Obs.* [f. next vb.] = ENJOYMENT.
1589 PUTTENHAM *Eng. Poesie* (1869) 249 As true loue is content with his enioy.

enjoy (ɛn'dʒɔɪ), *v.* Forms: *α.* 4–7 enjoye, (4 enyoie, 5–6 enyoy), 5 enjoye, 7 enjoie, 6– enjoy. *β.* 5–8 injoy, 6–7 injoye, injoie. [a. either OF. *enjoie-r* (cf. It. *ingiojare*) to give joy to, *refl.* to enjoy, f. *en-* in + *joie* JOY; or OF. *enjoir* to *enjoy*, *rejoice*, f. *en-* + *joir* (Fr. *jouir*):—L. *gaudēre*; cf. *rejoice.*]
1. a. *intr.* To be in joy, or in a joyous state; to manifest joy, exult, rejoice.
c **1380** WYCLIF *Tracts* Wks. (1880) 243 Enyoie ȝe to him wiþ quakynge. **1382** —— *Luke* i. 14 And manye schulen enioye in his natyuite. *c* **1440** *Gesta Rom.* (1878) 122 (Harl. MS.) He enioyed and was glad in al his herte. **1483** CAXTON *Gold. Leg.* 250/3 He sechyng the kyngdome of heuen enioyeth as a vaynqueur. **1549** LANEHAM *Let.* Pref. 41 Yet he neuer enioied after, but in conclusyon pitifully wasted his painful lyfe.
†**b.** *to enjoy of*: = sense 3 or 4 [Fr. *jouir de*].
1515 BARCLAY *Egloges* (1570) Civ/3 Likewise mayst thou inioy of our science. **1557** NORTH *Diall of Princes* 238 a/1 Of all that I haue had, possessed, attained, and whereof I haue enioyed, I haue onely two thinges, etc.
†**2. a.** *trans.* To put into a joyous condition; to make happy, give pleasure to. *Obs.*
1484 CAXTON *Ryall Bk.* Cj, For to gladde and enjoye the people. *c* **1500** *Melusine* 150 Whos taryeng enjoyed her moche. **1502** *Ord. Crysten Men* IV. xxvii. (1506) 324 That it hym may enioye & recomforte in his spyryte. **1610** MARKHAM *Masterp.* II. li. 107 No meat will enioy or do good vnto him.
b. *refl.* To experience pleasure, be happy; now chiefly, to find pleasure in an occasion of festivity or social intercourse, in a period of recreation, etc.
1656 H. MORE *Antid. Ath.* (J.), Creatures are made to enjoy themselves, as well as to serve us. **1711** SHAFTESB. *Charac.* III. §2 (1737) I. 310 When I employ my Affection in friendly and social Actions.. I can sincerely enjoy myself. **1712** STEELE *Spect.* No. 422 ⁋2 The agreeable Man makes his Friends enjoy themselves. *Mod.* Did you enjoy yourself at the party? He is enjoying himself at the seaside. They have nothing to do but enjoy themselves.
3. a. *trans.* To possess, use, or experience with delight. Also with reference to the feeling only: To take delight in, relish. Also *absol.*
1462 *Paston Lett.* No. 457 II. 109 Iche off us all schuld injoy the wylleffar off odyr. **1538** STARKEY *England* ii. 67 No one can long Enyoy plesure. **1597** SHAKS. *2 Hen. IV*, IV. iv. 108 Such are the Rich, That haue aboundance, and enioy it not. *a* **1639** *Reliq. Wotton.* 12 Both well enough injoying the present. **1667** MILTON *P.L.* IX. 829 Adam wedded to another Eve, Shall live with her enjoying, I extinct. **1713** ADDISON *Cato* (T.), I could enjoy the pangs of death And smile in agony. **1742** RICHARDSON *Pamela* III. 137 How he .. injoys.. the Relations of his own rakish Actions. **1870** E. PEACOCK *Ralf Skirl* II. ii. 10 William enjoyed the novelty

very much. **1872** Ruskin *Eagle's N.* §85 It is appointed for all men to enjoy, but for few to achieve.

b. with inf. as obj. *colloq.* or *vulgar.*

1864 *Realm* 22 June 3 She would greatly enjoy to dance at a ball once more.

4. a. In weaker sense: To have the use or benefit of, have for one's lot (something which affords pleasure, or is of the nature of an advantage).

c **1460** Fortescue *Abs. & Lim. Mon.* (1714) 144 We schal now enjoye our own Goods [in peace under Edward IV]. **1535** Coverdale *Job* xxxiii. 28 Latteth him enioye the light of yͤ lyuinge. **1577–87** Holinshed *Chron.* III. 811/2 He had of so long continuance inioied the name of iust and vpright. **1651** Hobbes *Leviath.* I. xiv. 67 Mony is thrown amongst many, to be enjoyed by them that catch it. **1676** Hobbes *Iliad* I. 88 As long as I enjoy my life. **1749** Fielding *Tom Jones* I. iv. (1840) 3/2 It [Allworthy's house] stood..high enough to enjoy a most charming prospect. **1818** Cruise *Digest* VI. 300 Anne..shall hold and enjoy the same as a place of inheritance. **1830** Disraeli *Chas. I,* III. iv. 52 Wentworth had not enjoyed the royal favour. **1874** Carpenter *Ment. Phys.* (1879) I. vii. 324 Animals enjoying a much lower degree of intelligence.

¶ Sometimes used *catachr.* with obj. denoting something *not* pleasurable or advantageous.

Chiefly in expressions like 'to enjoy poor health,' 'to enjoy an indifferent reputation', where the sb. has properly a favourable sense, qualified adversely by the adj. (Cf. the similar use of *jouir de,* censured by Fr. grammarians.) Uses like those in quots. 1577, *a* 1633, to which this explanation does not apply, could not now occur.

1577 Hanmer *Anc. Eccl. Hist.* 469 What shall I speake of Pertinax and what of Iulian? Enjoyed not both they one kinde of death? *a* **1633** Munday *Palmerin* (1639) I. liv. His Father, Mother and all his friends..were not a little sorrowfull to enjoy his absence. **1834** Venn *Life & Lett.* (1835) 407 At best she enjoys poor health. **1871** Macduff *Mem. Patmos* ii. 148 The reigns of Alexander Severus and Caracalla..enjoyed an unhappy distinction for their grinding taxation.

b. To have one's will of (a woman).

1598 Shaks. *Merry W.* II. ii. 265 You shall, if you will, enioy Fords wife. **1667** Milton *P.L.* IX. 1032 Never did thy Beautie..so enflame my sense With ardor to enjoy thee. **1950** A. Clarke *Coll. Plays* (1963) 284 *Brother.* Her present marriage has been consummated. *Abbot.* But lacking true consent, is null and void. *Brother.* Although her husband frequently enjoyed her?

enjoyable (ɛn'dʒɔɪəb(ə)l), *a.* [f. enjoy *v.* + -able.]

1. Capable of being enjoyed.

1645 Milton *Colast.* (R.), Unfitness and contrariety.. leaves nothing between them enjoyable. **1746–7** Hervey *Medit.* (1818) 269 A portion enjoyable only through such a fortuitous term. **1825** Ld. Cockburn *Mem.* 309 Enjoyable only by the young and active. **1839** Dickens *Lett.* (1880) I. 24 The last gratification is enjoyable all our lives.

2. Affording pleasure, delightful.

a **1744** Pope *Lett.* (T.), The evening of our days is generally the calmest and the most enjoyable of them. **1867** Dickens *Lett.* (1880) II. 304 This passage in winter time cannot be said to be an enjoyable excursion. **1882** Braddon *Mt. Royal* III. vi. 95 Plymouth seemed a very enjoyable place.

en'joyableness. [f. prec. + -ness.] The quality of being enjoyable.

1868 *Lessons Mid. Age* 10 Would that things would keep their first fresh feeling and racy enjoyableness! **1885** *Advance* (Chicago) 9 July 445 A cold rain detracted somewhat from the enjoyableness of the occasion.

enjoyably (ɛn'dʒɔɪəblɪ), *adv.* [f. as prec. + -ly²: see -ably.] In an enjoyable manner.

1877 Bigg-Wither *Pion. S. Brazil* I. II. iv. 288, I passed my first night..uneventfully, but yet supremely enjoyably. **1887** *Charity Org. Rev.* III. Aug. 324 The meeting, which was throughout enjoyably informal, dissolved.

†**en'joyance.** *Obs.* [f. enjoy *v.* + -ance.] = enjoyment.

1627 Sanderson *Serm.* I. 267 They had but a very small enjoyance of the light of God's word.

enjoyer (ɛn'dʒɔɪə(r)). [f. enjoy *v.* + -er.¹] One who enjoys. Const. *of.*

c **1600** Shaks. *Sonnets* lxxv, A miser..proud as an inioyer. **1607** Hieron *Wks.* I. 101 Many enioyers of Gods blessing. **17..** De la Pryme *Diary* (1869) 315 Enjoyers of yͤ drained lands in their parishes. **1856** Emerson *Eng. Traits* v. 79 We ..use the names [Saxon and Norman]..one to represent the worker, and the other the enjoyer. **1884** *Sat. Rev.* 7 June 734/2 A nation cannot be a mere..placid enjoyer of the dividends on the savings and gains of its forefathers.

en'joying, *vbl. sb.* [f. enjoy *v.* + -ing¹.] The action of the verb enjoy; enjoyment.

1536 Anne Boleyn *Let. Hen. VIII* in *Select. Harl. Misc.* (1793) 149 Must bring you the enjoying of your desired happiness. **1603** Florio *Montaigne* (1634) 495 All enjoyings are not alike. **1651** Hobbes, *Leviath.* III. xli. 264 The enjoying of Immortality, in the Kingdome of the Son of Man.

pl. **1621** Lady M. Wroath *Urania* 148 Those loose and wicked enjoyings which we coveted. *Ibid.* 229, 297, 371.

enjoying (ɛn'dʒɔɪɪŋ), *ppl. a.* [f. enjoy *v.* + -ing².] That enjoys; cheerful, happy.

1655 Earl Orrery *Parthen.* (1676) 5 An enjoying Lover. **1857** De Quincey *Bentley* Wks. VII. 97 In the same cheerful and enjoying frame of mind did Bentley sit by his happy fireside in Trinity Lodge. **1866** Geo. Eliot *F. Holt* xxxiv. He was..less bright and enjoying than usual.

enjoyingly (ɛn'dʒɔɪɪŋlɪ), *adv.* [f. prec. + -ly².] In an enjoying manner; with enjoyment.

1835 *Fraser's Mag.* XI. 568 To recognise most enjoyingly 'original' reflections and 'novel' remarks. **1877** Furnivall *Leopold Shaks.* Introd. 114 Shakspere..took enjoyingly the pleasures..that the fates provided.

enjoyment (ɛn'dʒɔɪmənt). Also 7–8 **injoyment.** [f. enjoy *v.* + -ment.]

1. The action or state of deriving gratification from an object. Also, in weaker sense, the possession and use of something which affords pleasure or advantage. Const. *of.*

1553 Brende *Q. Curtius* 119 (R.) Why do you doubt for the enioyment of those thinges to breake out of this imprisonment? **1665** Manley *Grotius' Low-C. Warres* 378 Injoyment of many Lands. **1718** Lady M. W. Montague *Lett.* II. lvi. 86 The honest English squire..believes..that ..there is no perfect enjoyment of this life out of Old England. **1848** Macaulay *Hist. Eng.* II. 212 He would protect the Established Church in the enjoyment of her legal rights. **1877** Sparrow *Serm.* xxiii. 312 The depth of the peace which flows from the enjoyment of his love.

2. Gratification, pleasure; *concr.* something which gives pleasure.

1665 Boyle *Occas. Refl.* v. iii. (1675) 305 He cuts them off, in the height of their Injoyments. **1732** Berkeley *Alciphr.* I. §9 Food, drink, sleep, and the like animal enjoyments being what all men like and love. **1842** Miss Mitford in L'Estrange *Life* III. ix. 154 Such a life might have had its enjoyments even in London. **1874** Lady Barker *Stat. Life in N.Z.* iv. 25 We..were only fit for the lowest phase of human enjoyment—warmth, food, and sleep.

†**en'joyse,** *v. Obs.* [ad. OF. *enjoiss-* extended stem of *enjoir,* f. *en-* (see en-¹) + *joir* (mod.F. *jouir*) to enjoy.] *refl.* and *intr.* To make oneself joyful; to be delighted, rejoice. Const. *of.*

c **1470** Harding *Chron.* XVI. vi, Of euill gotten good the third should not enioyse. **1483** Caxton *Gold. Leg.* 430 Of whiche good lyf and chyldehode his debonayr moder enioysyng hirself sayd ofte tymes, etc.

enjubard, var. of enjeopard *v. Obs.*

enjudge: see en- *pref.*¹ 3.

†**'enjury,** obs. form of injure *v.*

1491 Caxton *Vitas Patr.* (W. de W. 1495) I. lxvi. 115 a/1 He was euyll content wyth hym, estemyng to be eniuryed bi the wordes aforesayd.

enk, obs. form of ink.

†**en'kennel,** *v. Obs.* Also 6 **inkennel.** [f. en-¹ + kennel.] *trans.* To lodge as in a kennel.

1577–87 Holinshed *Chron.* III. 1029/2 Comming to S. Leonards hill..they [Ket's followers] inkennelled themselues there on the same hill. **1603** Davies *Microcosmos* 84 (D.) [Diogenes] that alwaies in a tub enkennell'd lies.

enkephalin (ɛn'kɛfəlɪn). *Biochem.* Also (*rare*) enceph-. [f. Gr. ἐγκέφαλ-ος brain + -in¹.] Either or both of two pentapeptide endorphins.

1975 J. Hughes et al. in *Life Sci.* XVI. 1753 There is mounting evidence that the brain contains an endogenous constituent which acts as an agonist at morphine receptor sites... This substance..we have termed enkephalin. **1977** *Sci. Amer.* Mar. 51/1 A variety of evidence now indicates that the enkephalins are neurotransmitters of specific neuronal systems in the brain that mediate the integration of sensory information having to do with pain and emotional behaviour. **1978** *Lancet* 5 Aug. 293/1 Encephalins and opiate receptors are particularly concentrated in pain-related areas of the C.N.S. **1983** *Oxf. Textbk. Med.* I. xii. 50/2 The smallest of the endorphins are the two 5-amino-acid enkephalins which differ by one amino-acid—methionine enkephalin and leucine enkephalin.

†**'enker,** *adv. Obs. rare.* [a. OF. *encré* lit. 'inked,' in phrase *vert encré* dark green.] In ME. phrase *enkergrene,* dark green.

c **1340** *Gaw. & Gr. Knt.* 150 Ouer-al enker grene. *Ibid.* 2477 Þe knyȝt in Þe enker grene.

enkerchief: see en- *pref.*¹ 1 a.

†**'enkerly,** *adv. Obs.* In 4 encrely, enkerly, enkrely, ynkirly, -urly, 5–6 inkirly. [Origin uncertain; possibly a. ON. **einkarliga* (cf. mid.Da. *enkorlig* adj. especial) f. *einkar-* prefix; specially, very (= *einkan-* whence *einkanliga* especially). But this is not quite satisfactory with regard to the sense. Cf. Sc. *inkirt* 'anxious' (Jam.).] Earnestly, heartily, fervently.

1375 Barbour *Bruce* I. 301 For he thocht ay encrely To do his deid awysily. *Ibid.* VII. 183 The kyng..slepit nocht full ynkurly. *Ibid.* x. 534 He has seyn The Erll sa ynkirly hym set Sum sutelte or [wile] to get. *c* **1375** *Sc. Leg. Saints, Andreas* 678 For þat I has luffit þe lange enkrely. ? *a* **1400** *Morte Arth.* 507 Thene the emperour was egere, and enkerly fraynes þe answere of Arthure. **1513** Douglas *Æneis* VI. i. 8 The kyng ..inkirly from his hart Maid this orisone.

enkernel: see en- *pref.*¹ 1 a.

enkindle (ɛn'kɪnd(ə)l), *v.* Also 6 enkendle, 6–8 inkindle. [f. en-¹ + kindle *v.*]

1. *trans.* To cause (a flame, etc.) to blaze up. Chiefly *fig.* to excite (passions, war, etc.).

1583 Stanyhurst *Aeneis* II. (Arb.) 63 Whose sight thy passion angrye Enkendleth. **1593** Nashe *Christ's T.* (1613) 38 A short blazd straw-fire, to tinde or inkindle Hell-fire. **1652** Bp. Patrick *Fun. Serm.* in *J. Smith's Sel. Disc.* 533 He who inflames our souls with love to God, will certainly enkindle a subordinate love within us to himself. *a* **1691** Boyle *Wks.* VI. 531 (R.) The apprehension..ran..of its [the Fire of London] being inkindled with design by the French and Dutch. **1751** Johnson *Rambler* No. 185 ⁋7 Fresh remembrance of vexation must still enkindle rage. **1794** S. Williams *Vermont* 307 All parties had cautiously avoided enkindling a civil war. **1819** *Month. Mag.* XLVIII. 307 This poetic fury appears to have been first enkindled in Bodmer by the appearance of the five first books of Klopstock's Messiah. **1858** Kingsley *Andromeda* 329 In her heart new life was enkindled.

2. To set (a combustible) on fire. In lit. sense *Obs.* or *arch.*

1548 Udall etc. *Erasm. Par. Rom.* xiii. (R.) Nor let us extinguish the smoldering flaxe, but enkendle it. **1638** Wilkins *New World* iii. (1707) 29 Such solid Orbs, that by their swift Motion might heat and enkindle the adjoining Air. **1747** Hales in *Phil. Trans.* XLIV. 582 (2) Some Means ..to inkindle the sulphureous Vapours. **1794** T. Taylor *Pausanias' Descr. Greece* I. 43 But then the pieces of wood.. were enkindled without fire.

b. *fig.* To inflame with passion, desire, etc. †Former const. *to* (an action, object of pursuit).

1561 T. Norton *Calvin's Inst.* IV. xvi. (1634) 662 They shall hereby be the more inkindled to the endevor of renuing. **1605** Shaks. *Macb.* I. iii. 120 That trusted home, Might yet enkindle you unto the Crowne. *a* **1619** Daniel *Coll. Hist. Eng.* (1626) 25 The King..inkindled with this affront, spared not his Person, to auenge his wrath. **1628** Bp. Hall *Old Relig.* 34 He is inwardly inkindled to an indeauour of good. **1834** Disraeli *Rev. Epick* III. xiii. 10 That voice that like a trump Their blood enkindled.

c. *transf.* To light up, illuminate.

1870 Lowell *Study Wind.* 114 That literary heaven.. artificially enkindled from behind. **1876** Swinburne *Erechth.* 1372 And the light of their eyeballs enkindled so bright with the lightnings of death.

†**3.** *intr.* To take fire; to burst forth in flame.

1553 Grimald tr. *Cicero's Duties* (*c* 1600) 87 a, Those things wherunto most men inkindled with greedinesse bee haled. **1671** Salmon *Syn. Med.* I. xxxvii. 84 Wet Hay laid together..soon inkindles. **1747** Hales in *Phil. Trans.* XLIV. 584 Those who have been on high Hills have observed Lightening to inkindle among the Clouds.

enkindled (ɛn'kɪnd(ə)ld), *ppl. a.* [f. prec. + -ed¹.] In the senses of the verb.

1549–62 Sternhold & H. *Ps.* cvi. 29 And in his so inkindled wrath the plague upon them broke. **1595** Shaks. *John* IV. ii. 163 Eyes as red as new enkindled fire. **1713** Derham *Phys.-Theol.* I. iii. 21 Lightening, and other enkindled Vapours. **1877** Morley *Crit. Misc.* Ser. II. 257 The enkindled summits of the soul.

enkindler (ɛn'kɪndlə(r)). [f. enkindle *v.* + -er.] One who or that which enkindles.

1853 Bowring in *Fraser's Mag.* XLVIII. 350 A lamp.. when enkindled, is Th' enkindler of a thousand. **1868** *Contemp. Rev.* IX. 563 The Irish Government..has been.. not the enkindler, not the leader, not the abetter of aggressive Protestantism in Ireland.

enkindling (ɛn'kɪndlɪŋ), *ppl. a.* [f. as prec. + -ing.] That enkindles.

1626 T. H. tr. *Caussin's Holy Crt.* 93 The enkindling tinder of his lust. **1674** N. Fairfax *Bulk & Selv.* 121 Until this loses its enkindling leavening strength. **1817** Coleridge *Biog. Lit.* 297 For this is really a species of animal magnetism, in which the enkindling reciter..lends his own will and apprehensive faculty to his auditors.

enlabyrinth: see en- *pref.*¹ 1 a.

enlace (ɛn'leɪs), *v.* Also 4–6 enlase, 6,9 inlace. [a. F. *enlace-r* = Pr. *enlassar,* Sp. *enlazar,* Pg. *enlaçar,* It. *inlacciare*:—late L. **inlaciāre,* f. *in-* (see in-) + **laci-us* (OF. *las* lace, snare = It. *laccio,* Sp. *lazo*):—L. *laqueus* noose. Cf. L. *illaqueāre.* In later use taken as f. en-¹ + lace.]

1. *trans.* To lace about, encircle tightly with many folds or coils. Also *fig.*

c **1374** Chaucer *Boeth.* I. iv. 13 Þat man..enlaceþ hym in þe cheyne wiþ whiche he may be drawen. **1430** Lydg. *Chron. Troy* IV. xxx, To perce nerfe and vayne And them enlace in his [Cupid's] fyry chayne. **1502** *Ord. Crysten Men* (W. de W. 1506) I. iii. 17 To breke the bondes of the deuyll, of yͤ whiche he hym helde enlasyd. **1587** Turberv. *Trag. T.* (1837) 163 And felt himselfe enlaste in love. **1859** Tennent *Ceylon* II. IX. vi. 520 The figs, and particularly the banyan ..speedily seize upon the palmyra, enlacing it with their nimble shoots. **1877** *Daily News* 26 Dec. 3/1 They will enlace him in the coils of their red tape.

b. *transf.* To surround closely, enfold, embrace.

1633 P. Fletcher *Purple Isl.* v. xi, The second all the city round enlaces. —— *Elisa* ii. 49 While he again her in his arms enlac'd. **1865** Carlyle *Fredk. Gt.* IX. xx. v. 78 The old Town..is enlaced..by a set of lakes and quagmires.

2. To interlace, entwine, entangle. Also *fig.*

c **1374** Chaucer *Boeth.* v. i. 149 Þe questioun of þe deuyne purueance is enlaced wiþ many oþer questiouns. **1509** Barclay *Shyp of Folys* (1570) 241 The violet..in bosome by me alway I beare, The same oft time inlased with my heare. **1868** Hawthorne *Amer. Note-bks.* (1879) I. 65 The leafy boughs and twigs of the underbrush enlace themselves. **1870** Morris *Earthly Par.* III. IV. 200 His fingers lovingly enlaced By other fingers.

3. To cover as with a network.

1850 Kingsley *Alt. Locke* xxxvi. (1879) 375 The vast plains of Hindostan, enlaced with myriad silver rivers and canals.

†**4.** [See unlace, lace *vbs.*] To take off (the wings of a bird) in carving. *Obs.*

c **1460** J. Russell *Bk. Nurture* in *Babees Bk.* (1868) 142 Take capoun or hen so enlased, & devide.

Hence **en'laced** *ppl. a.*

1851 MRS. BROWNING *Casa Guidi W.* 56 Doth he.. Keep house.. with inlaced Bare brawny arms about his favourite child.

enlacement (ɛnˈleɪsmənt). [f. ENLACE *v.* + -MENT.] The action of enlacing; the condition of being enlaced.

1830 SOUTHEY *Yng. Dragon* I. 87 His tail about the imp he roll'd, In fond and close enlacement. **1888** *Blackw. Mag.* Feb. 174 Joyce detached herself suddenly from that close enlacement.

enˈlacing, *vbl. sb.* [f. as prec. + -ING.] = prec.

1633 P. FLETCHER *Purple Isl.* 55 The moat of glasse is named from that enlacing.

enlaik: see INLAKE.

en l'air: see EN *prep.*

†**enˈlangoured,** *ppl. a. Obs.* [ad. OF. *enlangouré*, f. *en-* (see EN- *pref.*¹) + *langour* (mod.F. *langueur*):—L. *languōr-em* languor.] Languid, pale.

c **1400** *Rom. Rose* 7401 Of such a colour enlangoured, Was Abstinence.

enlanguish, enlap: see EN- *pref.*¹ 3.

†**enˈlard,** *v. Obs.* Also 6–7 inlard. [f. EN-¹ + LARD.] *trans.* **a.** To lard, fill with lard or fat; in quots. *fig.* **b.** = INTERLARD.

1556 ABP. PARKER *Psalter* cxix. 351 Inlarded is their hart with pride. **1606** SHAKS. *Tr. & Cr.* II. iii. 205 That were to enlard his fat already pride. **1621** BURTON *Anat. Mel.* III. iv. I. i, A fifth part of the world.. so inlarded and interlaced with several superstitions.

enlarge (ɛnˈlɑːdʒ), *v.* Also 4 enlargen, 7 enlardge, 6–8 inlarge. [a. OF. *enlarge-r*, *enlargir*, f. *en-* (see EN-¹) + *large* (see LARGE). Some of the mod.Eng. uses are influenced by those of Fr. *élargir*, OF. *eslargir*, *alarger* (see ALARGE).]

I. To make larger.

1. *trans.* To render more spacious or extensive; to extend the limits of (a territory, enclosure, etc.); to widen (boundaries).

In later use this merges in the more generalized sense 2; the fig. applications in 3 however remain distinct.

c **1400** MAUNDEV. v. 45 Thei may not enlargen it [Egypt] toward the desert, for defaute of watre. *c* **1420** *Pallad. on Husb.* I. 316 The fundament enlarge it half a foote Outwith the wough. **1535** COVERDALE *Jer.* xxxi. 38 The cite of yᵉ Lorde shalbe enlarged from the towre of Hananeel, vnto yᵉ gate of the corner wall. *a* **1687** PETTY *Pol. Arith.* 72 Any Prince willing to inlarge his Territories, will give, etc. **1748** HARTLEY *Observ. Man* I. ii. §1. 123 Grinding inlarges the sphere of their attractions. **1856** KANE *Arct. Expl.* II. xv. 164 He will rear himself upon his hind-legs to enlarge his circle of vision.

2. a. To increase the size of (a material object); to add to, augment (a literary work, a person's wealth, the number or amount of anything). Formerly also (cf. uses of *large*) with reference to intensive magnitude: to increase (a person's renown, the force of anything, etc.). †Sometimes with *out* (*obs. rare*). Also, to increase in apparent size, magnify. Also *absol.*

c **1380** *Antecrist* in Todd *3 Treat. Wyclif* 120 þe deuyl shal enlarge his taile more wickudly in þe eende of þe worlde. **1576** FLEMING *Panoplie Ep.* 117 That the dignitie of Plancus might be augmented, & his honour inlarged. **1591** SPENSER *M. Hubberd* 745 T'enlarge his breath, (large breath in armes most needfull). **1594** CAREW tr. Huarte *Exam. Wits* (1616) 280 By means whereof it extendeth and enlargeth out the naturall heat. **1614** RALEIGH *Hist. World* II. IV. vii. §1. 246 He.. enlarged the Centurions of Horsemen. **1628** HOBBES *Thucyd.* (1822) 57 The Athenians much enlarged their own particular wealth. **1683** SALMON *Doron Med.* I. 155 It inlarges its Narcotick Force. *a* **1687** PETTY *Pol. Arith.* x. 116 Selling of Lands to Foreigners for Gold and Silver, would inlarge the Stock of the Kingdom. **1703** ROWE *Fair Penit.* I. i. 202 Enthusiastick Passion.. Enlarg'd her Voice. **1732** POPE *Ep. Cobham* I. 35 Fancy's beam enlarges, multiplies, Contracts. **1742** YOUNG *Nt. Th.* IV. 462 O how is man inlarg'd, Seen thro' this medium. **1774** MONBODDO *Language* (ed. 2) I. Pref. 10 In this second edition, so much inlarged. **1810** SCOTT *Lady of L.* I. xxxiv, Slowly enlarged to giant size. **1845** BUDD *Dis. Liver* 126 The spleen is found enormously enlarged. **1866** WALCOTT *Cathedr. Reform.* in *Ch. & World* 15 At the very time when the numbers and learning of parish clergy were rapidly being enlarged. **1883** *Manch. Exam.* 24 Oct. 5/1 Their salaries will be enlarged out of the episcopal and capitular incomes.

†**b.** To magnify, exaggerate in statement. Also, to set forth at length. *Obs.*

1586 A. DAY *Eng. Secretary* (1625) A ij b, To.. enlarge my paines taken in publishing the other. **1646** H. LAWRENCE *Comm. Angells* 23, I shall not enlarge this now particularly. **1703** MAUNDRELL *Journ. Jerus.* (1732) 15 The Asiatick way of enlarging. **1728** MORGAN *Algiers* I. iii. 52 Report generally inlarges matters.

†**c.** *intr. to enlarge on*: to make an addition to (a plan); to amplify (a hint). *Obs.* (Cf. 5 b.)

1711 ADDISON *Spect.* No. 58 ⁋13 It is so very easy to enlarge upon a good Hint. **1790** PALEY *Horæ Paul.* i. 8, I have so far enlarged upon this plan, as to take into it, etc. **1800** *Med. Jrnl.* IV. 233 Those gentlemen.. will.. enlarge on the plan I have hinted thus lightly.

d. *Photogr.* To make a picture larger than (the original negative). Also *absol.*

1866 J. TOWLER *Negative & Print* xiv. 132 The screen will have to be shoved further off from the lens on the opposite side, and the picture becomes thereby enlarged. **1871** *English Mechanic* 24 Feb. 549/3 Cheap Enlarging Camera. *Ibid.* 5 May 166/2 [A] condenser.. for enlarging with a ¼ plate lens. **1878** ABNEY *Treat. Photogr.* Index, Enlarged photographs. **1903** A. WATKINS *Photogr.* (ed. 2) 43 Daylight Enlarging. *Ibid.* 44 In commencing.. to calculate enlarging exposures. *Ibid.*, The indicated exposure will be right for a decidedly dense negative without taking into account the increase for the enlarging factor. *Ibid.* 47 Most photographers want to enlarge from a negative of settled size to one size of paper. **1959** *Chamber's Encycl.* X. 688/2 The position of the enlarging lens is adjustable with respect to the negative.

3. Figurative applications of 1.

a. To extend the range or scope of. †Also, to spread, promote the diffusion of (a belief) (*obs.*).

1553 EDEN *Treat. Newe Ind.* Title (Arb.) 3 God is glorified and the Christian fayth enlarged. **1594** HOOKER *Eccl. Pol.* I. iii, We somewhat more enlarging the sence thereof. **1656** H. PHILIPPS *Purch. Patt.* (1676) 139 To enlarge this Table, that so it may shew not only.. half inches, but the quarters, or tenth parts of Inches. **1668** in *Phil. Trans.* II. 3 The endeavours of the Authour for the improving and enlarging his Philosophical Commerce. **1742** RICHARDSON *Pamela* IV. 102 Till I have catch'd her a little inlarging her innocent Freedoms, as she calls them. **1782** PRIESTLEY *Corr. of Christianity* II. x. 244 Justinian greatly enlarged this kind of authority. **1884** EARL SELBORNE in *Law Times Rep.* New Ser. L. 3 He cannot.. enlarge in his own favour the legal.. operation of the instrument.

b. To widen, render more comprehensive (a person's thoughts, sympathies, affections); to expand, increase the capacity of (the mind).

1665 GLANVILL *Sceps. Sci.* 74 Science indeed inlargeth: But there's a knowledge that only puffeth up. *a* **1704** T. BROWN *Dk. Ormond's Recov.* Wks. 1730 I. 51 His mind enlarg'd, and boundless as the sky. **1736** BUTLER *Anal.* I. i, Persons' notions of what is natural, will be enlarged. **1850** MᶜCOSH *Div. Govt.* II. i. (1874) 152 Geologists would enlarge our conceptions of Time. **1868** FREEMAN *Norm. Conq.* (1876) II. vii. 41 His own mind was enlarged and enriched by foreign travel.

c. *to enlarge the heart*: to 'expand', 'swell' the heart with gratitude or affection (in this sense sometimes with personal obj., after 2 *Cor.* vi. 13); now usually, to increase the capacity of the heart for affection, widen the range of the affections.

1611 BIBLE *2 Cor.* vi. 11 O yee Corinthians, our mouth is open vnto you, our heart is enlarged. *Ibid.* 13 Be ye also inlarged. **1638** ROUSE *Heav. Univ.* v. x. (1702) 151 Be thou enlarged in thy return of Thanks and Glory to Him. **1667** MILTON *P.L.* VIII. 590 Love refines The thoughts, and heart enlarges. **1741** RICHARDSON *Pamela* II. 156 My Heart is.. more inlarg'd with his Goodness and Condescension. **1848** MACAULAY *Hist. Eng.* I. 162 All hearts.. were enlarged and softened. **1852** ROBERTSON *Lect.* 177 Enlarge your tastes, that you may enlarge your hearts as well as your pleasures.

d. *to enlarge the hand*: to open the hand wide, be liberal. *Obs.* or *arch.* Cf. *large-handed*.

1651 *Life Father Sarpi* (1676) 63 It was thought necessary for him to enlarge his hand to those that managed Bread and wine.

†**e.** To extend (the time allowed for an action); to grant or obtain an extension of time for (a lease, bankruptcy, etc.). *Obs.*

1656 H. PHILIPPS *Purch. Patt.* (1676) B vij b, Leases.. lately inlarged to 60 years. **1677** MARVELL *Corr.* cccv. Wks. 1872–5 II. 548 We shall perceive whether his Majesty thinke fit to.. inlarge the adjournment. **1725** *Lond. Gaz.* No. 6435/3 The.. Time was.. enlarged for Joseph Lacy.. for surrendring himself. **1812** *Exam.* 24 Aug. 537/1 *Bankruptcy Enlarged*, J. Chatterton.. flour-merchant, from June 27 to September 9. **1863** H. COX *Instit.* I. vi. 36 An Act.. for enlarging the time of continuance of Parliaments.

f. *Law. to enlarge an estate*: said of the effect of a release which, e.g. converts a life-interest, or a tenancy for a term of years, into a fee-simple or fee-tail. (The sense may perh. belong to branch II.)

1574 tr. *Littleton's Tenures* 97 b, Releases.. sometime have theire effecte by force to enlarge the estate [AF. *enlarger lestate*] of them, to whome the release is made. **1597** DANIEL *Civ. Wares* VIII. lix, To confer First, how he might have her estate inlarg'd. **1818** CRUISE *Digest* VI. 321 If Popham.. should not enlarge his estate to an estate tail.

4. a. *refl.* (in senses 1–3.) To increase or widen in extent, bulk, or scope.

1413 LYDG. *Pilgr. Sowle* IV. xxx. (1483) 77 Gold wylle well enduren under the hamoure enlargyng hymself withouten crasure. **1591** SHAKS. *1 Hen. VI*, I. ii. 134 Glory is like a Circle in the Water, Which neuer ceaseth to enlarge it selfe. **1823** LAMB *Elia* Ser. II. (1865), Enlarging themselves, if I may say so, upon familiarity. **1875** JOWETT *Plato* (ed. 2) III. 28 Our ideas will have to enlarge themselves.

b. *intr.* for *refl.*

1481 CAXTON *Myrr.* III. i. 132 Yf therthe were gretter than the sone, thenne the shadowe of þᵉ sone shold goo enlargyng. **1541** R. COPLAND *Guydon's Quest. Chirurg.*, Fro whiche cometh a corde that thre fyngre brede fro the elbowe enlargeth and compriseth all the elbowe. **1756–82** J. WARTON *Ess. Pope* (1782) I. vii. 406 The figure of Fame enlarging and growing every moment. **1776** WITHERING *Bot. Arrangem.* (1796) IV. 265 The hollow very fine, but soon enlarging by the shrinking of the spongy flesh. **1845** BUDD *Dis. Liver* 352 His belly began to enlarge. **1875** JOWETT *Plato* (ed. 2) IV. 281 As our knowledge increases, our perception of the mind enlarges also. **1879** CARPENTER *Ment. Phys.* I. ii. §61. 62 A sort of core.. which enlarges in the parts of the Cord that give off the nerve-trunks.

†**c.** Of the wind, thunder: To increase in force. *Obs.*

1628 DIGBY *Voy. Medit.* (1868) 15 If the wind had not suddainely enlarged. **1762–9** FALCONER *Shipwr.* III. 436 Loud, and more loud, the rolling peals enlarge.

5. †**a.** *refl.* To expand (oneself) in words, give free vent to one's thoughts in speech. Also, in similar sense, *to enlarge one's heart*. *Obs.*

1614 RALEIGH *Hist. World* II. v. iii. §15. 441 It will appeare more commendable in wise men, to enlarge themselues, and to publish, etc. **1651** FULLER *Abel Rediv.*, *Bradford* (1867) I. 221 He enlarged himself in a most sweet meditation, of the wedding garment. **1660** *Trial Regic.* 154, I found he began to inlarge his heart to me. **1678** CUDWORTH *Intell. Syst.* I. i. §39. 48 The Platonists frequently take occasion from hence to enlarge themselves much in the disparagement of Corporeal things.

b. *intr.* for *refl.* To speak at large, expatiate. Const. *on*, *upon*; formerly also *simply*.

1659 HAMMOND *On Ps.* 3, I shall not here inlarge to insert. **1664** BUTLER *Hud.* II. II. 68, I shall enlarge upon the Point. **1771** *Junius Lett.* liv. 283 [He] enlarges with rapture upon the importance of his services. **1818** JAS. MILL *Brit. India* II. v. v. 500 He was somewhat disposed to enlarge in praise of himself. **1830** LYELL *Princ. Geol.* I. 323 Respecting Southern Italy, Sicily, and the Lipari Isles, we need not enlarge here. **1833** HT. MARTINEAU *Vanderput & S.* vi. 99 He enlarged once more on the avarice and cowardice of the banks.

II. 6. a. To set at large; to release from confinement or bondage. Somewhat *arch.* Cf. Fr. *élargir*.

1494 FABYAN VI. cxlix. 136 In this passe tyme, Gryffon, the yonger brother, was enlargyd frome pryson. **1560** DAUS tr. *Sleidane's Comm.* 453 b, The captiue Cardinalles at the length putting in suerties are inlarged. **1580** SIDNEY *Arcadia* (1622) 329 Like a Lionesse lately enlarged. **1605** CAMDEN *Rem.* 22 Edward the third enlarged them first from that bondage. **1616** J. LANE *Sqr.'s Tale* IX. 277 Algarsifes soldiers.. demaundes theire General enlardgd. **1761–2** HUME *Hist. Eng.* (1806) V. lxvii. 108 No man, after being enlarged by order of court, can be recommitted for the same offence. **1878** SIMPSON *Sch. Shaks.* I. 39 He was enlarged upon sureties.

b. *spec.* in *Hunting*.

1880 *Daily Tel.* 20 Oct., We are close to the spot where the stag is to be enlarged.

c. *transf.* and *fig.*

1593 B. BARNES in Farr *S.P. Eliz.* (1845) I. 43 Deare Davids Sonne [who should from hell].. poore sinners both inlarge and save. **1597** SIR W. SLINGSBY in Slingsby *Diary* (1836) 252 If we [wind-bound sailors] be not inlarged within these 20 dayes. **1639** FULLER *Holy War* III. viii. (1840) 130 King Richard would not enlarge him from the strictness of what was concluded. **1725** POPE *Odyss.* IV. 796 The friendly Gods a springing gale inlarg'd. **1796** MORSE *Amer. Geog.* I. 683 A round ball.. in the heat of summer, opens and enlarges a number of male insects.

†**III. 7.** To bestow liberally; to endow with bountiful gifts. [So OF. *enlargir*; cf. L. *largīrī*.]

1491 CAXTON *Vitas Patr.* (W. de W. 1495) I. xliv. 73 b/1, He enlarged to the poore grete quantite of his goodes temporall. **1513** BRADSHAW *St. Werburge* I. 1669 Clothes of Dyaper, Rychely enlarged with syluer and with golde. **1607** H. ARTHINGTON *Goodl. God* in Farr *S.P. Jas. I* (1848) 263 How much are we, Lord, bound to thee, For all thy favours every way, Inlarged so aboundantly. **1657** S. PURCHAS *Pol. Flying Ins.* I. i. 2 The great Artifex of Nature hath enlarged the smaller creatures with wisdome, and invention.

IV. 8. *to enlarge a horse* (see quot.) [after OF. *élargir*].

1753 CHAMBERS *Cycl. Supp.*, *Enlarge*, in the manege, is used for making a horse go large, that is, making him embrace more ground than he before covered.

Hence **enˈlarge** *sb.*, the action of setting free. **enˈlargeable** *a.*, capable of being enlarged. **enˈlargeableness**, the quality of being enlargeable.

1608 T. MIDDLETON *Fam. of Love* (1885) I. ii. 127 My absence may procure thy more enlarge. **1653** SHIRLEY *Crt. Secret* II. iii, I may entreat her grace's mediation To the King for his enlarge. **1881** PALGRAVE *Visions Eng.* Pref. 11 The more large or enlargeable are their technical powers. **1878** LOCKYER *Stargazing* 457 If the negative is well defined—that is, if it possesses the quality of enlargeableness.

enlarged (ɛnˈlɑːdʒd), *ppl. a.* [f. ENLARGE *v.* + -ED¹.]

1. Increased, widened, dilated, extended; also *fig.* free from narrowness, liberal.

1599 THYNNE *Animadv.* Ded. 3 The enlarged contynuance of Youre honorable fauour. **1674** N. MATHER in Owen *Holy Spirit* (1693) Pref. 2 Abundant Cause of Enlarged Thankfulness. **1754** RICHARDSON *Grandison* (1781) V. xxxi. 206 His enlarged heart can rejoice in the happiness of his friends. **1790** BURKE *Fr. Rev.* Wks. V. 95 More sober minds and more enlarged understandings. **1868** FREEMAN *Norm. Conq.* (1876) II. vii. 109 A sinner for whom the most enlarged charity could hardly plead.

2. Liberated, set free.

1645 MILTON *Tetrach.* (1851) 155 Som delightfull intermissions, wherein the enlarg'd soul may leav off a while her severe schooling. **1886** BESANT *Childr. Gibeon* II. xxxii, The enlarged captive.

Hence †**enˈlargedly** *adv.*, in an enlarged manner; (*a*) with extended meaning; (*b*) with free utterance. †**enˈlargedness**, the state or condition of being enlarged in heart, speech, etc.

1625 BP. MOUNTAGU *App. Cæsar.* 172 Iustification is taken.. enlargedly for that Act of God, etc. **1655** GURNALL *Chr. in Arm.* ix. §2 (1669) 105/1 Thou hearest how enlargedly they pray. **1642** G. HUGHES *Serm.* To Rdr., If, of truth and enlargednesse of heart to Christ, etc. **1646** LILBURNE & OVERTON *Out-cryes Oppr. Commons* (ed. 2) 9 So say we in the inlargednesse of our soules. *a* **1688** BUNYAN *Solomon's Temple* xviii, God's true Gospel Church should have its enlargedness of heart still upward.

enlargement (ɛnˈlɑːdʒmənt). Also 6–8 inlargement. [f. ENLARGE *v.* + -MENT.] The action of enlarging; the state of being enlarged.

1. a. Increase in extent, capacity, magnitude, or amount: an instance of such increase.

1564 HAWARD *Eutropius* VI. 53 He gave the Daphnenses a percell of lande for the enlargemente of theyr groves or copyes. **1594** HOOKER *Eccl. Pol.* III. xi, The enlargment or abridgement of functions ministeriall. **1664** EVELYN *Sylva* (1679) 4 The repetition of graffing, for the inlargement and melioration of fruit. **1736** BUTLER *Anal.* i. 18 The vast enlargement of their locomotive powers. **1866** GEO. ELIOT *F. Holt* (1868) 46 An enlargement of the chapel..absorbed all extra funds and left none for the enlargement of the minister's income. **1875** H. WOOD *Therap.* (1879) 330 Malarial enlargements of the spleen.

b. *concr.* Something added so as to enlarge.

a **1691** BOYLE *Wks.* I. 587 (R.) Divers notes..to be inserted here and there, as inlargements in the next edition.

c. *Photogr.* The process of enlarging a picture; a negative or print made of a larger size than the original.

1866 J. TOWLER *Negative & Print* xiv. 129 *(heading)* The solar camera and solar enlargements. **1871** *English Mechanic* 17 Mar. 621/2 The inner body of large camera for enlargement. **1878** ABNEY *Treat. Photogr.* xxix. 209 It can also be shown that an enlargement from a small negative is better than a picture of the same size taken direct as regards sharpness of detail. **1884** —— *Instr. Photogr.* (ed. 6) 188 Enlarged negatives can be produced either by making an enlarged transparency, or by enlarging the negative from it in the camera. In all cases of enlargement the camera must be employed. **1903** A. WATKINS *Photogr.* (ed. 2) 47 The five separate influences which decide an enlargement exposure. **1919** C. C. TURNER *Struggle in Air* xv. 203 Often enlargements of these photographs revealed important changes undetected by the naked eye.

†**2.** Diffusion, propagation. *Obs.* Cf. ENLARGE 3 a.

1607 HIERON *Wks.* I. 247 We haue not laboured the inlargement of Gods truth. **1644** MILTON *Educ.* (1738) 135 A great furtherance to the enlargement of a truth.

3. The widening or expanding of the mind, of a person's thoughts, sympathies, or affections; the quality of being 'enlarged' in mind, thought, etc.

1806 A. KNOX *Rem.* (1844) I. 96 His own enlargement of mind may raise him above..Judaism. **1847** EMERSON *Repr. Men, Swedenborg* Wks. (Bohn) I. 331 His judgments are those of a Swedish polemic, and his vast enlargements purchased by adamantine limitations. *a* **1862** BUCKLE *Civiliz.* (1873) III. iii. 182 It prepared them for a certain enlargement of mind, which is the natural consequence of seeing affairs under various aspects.

4. Copious discourse or expatiation on a subject; also, verbal amplification. *arch.*

1659 O. WALKER *Instr. Art Oratory* 95 Doubled Sentences and enlargements by Synonymal Words..are but necessary. **1669** BUNYAN *Holy Citie* 5 You must not from me look for much inlargement. **1683** BURNET tr. *More's Utopia* (1684) 97 The old Men take occasion to entertain those about them, with some useful and pleasant Enlargements. **1741** WARBURTON *Div. Legat.* II. 162 The Subject little needs Enlargement. **1747** GOULD *Eng. Ants* Ded., I shall therefore forbear those usual Enlargements. *a* **1765** MALLET *To Dk. Marlb.* (R.), I restrain my pen from all enlargement.

5. a. Release from confinement or bondage.

1540 *Act 32 Hen. VIII*, c. 2 §9 After his enlargement and commyng out of pryson. **1611** BIBLE *Esther* iv. 14 Then shall there enlargement and deliuerance arise to the Jewes from another place. **1709** STANHOPE *Paraphr.* IV. 250 That Enlargement from the Slavery of Lusts and vicious Habits. **1774** GOLDSM. *Nat. Hist.* (1862) I. ii. 157 The enclosed animal..by repeated efforts, at last procures its enlargement. **1875** 'STONEHENGE' *Brit. Sports* I. II. ii. §1. 153 The enlargement of the deer. **1883** TREVELYAN in *Daily News* 24 Feb. 2/7 The enlargement from prison of Mr. Parnell.

†**b.** Freedom of action; *concr.* a right of free action, a privilege. *Obs.*

1611 SHAKS. *Cymb.* II. iii. 125 Yet you are curb'd from that enlargement, by The consequence o' th' Crown. **1646** J. WHITAKER *Uzziah* 3 The enlargements bestowed upon this person. **1648** MILTON *Observ. Art. Peace* (1851) 556 Such freedoms and enlargements, as none of their Ancestors could ever merit.

c. In religious use: Conscious 'liberty', absence of constraint, in prayer, etc. *arch.*

1648 TH. HILL *The Strength of the Saints* 19 Ministers find they have preached such a Sermon in such a place with very much enlargement. *a* **1733** D. WILCOX in Spurgeon *Treas. Dav.* Ps. xxvii. 4 What entertainments I have had! what enlargements in prayer, and answers thereto! **1739** J. TRAPP *Serm. Righteousn. over-m.* (1758) 61 They talk much of..their enlargements in devotion. **1766** WESLEY *Jrnl.* 31 July, I preached with great enlargement of heart. **1870** ANDERSON *Missions Amer. Bd.* II. xviii. 147 Church members had wonderful enlargement and assistance in prayer.

enlarger (ɛnˈlɑːdʒə(r)). Also 7 inlarger. [f. ENLARGE *v.* + -ER.] He who or that which enlarges.

1. a. In senses of ENLARGE 1–5.

1545 UDALL, etc. *Erasm. Par.* (1548) *Luke* 191 a, See ye what maner ministers and enlargers of his dominion..he chose out for the nons. **1612** BREREWOOD *Lang. & Relig.* xxi. 185 Jacobus..was in his time a mighty inlarger of Eutyches sect, and maintainer of his opinion. **1660** JER. TAYLOR *Duct. Dubit.* III. iii. §4 If religion be the..enlarger of kingdoms. **1774** T. WEST *Antiq. Furness.* (1805) 424 The right reverend and very learned enlarger of Camden's Britannia. **1846** GROTE *Greece* I. xxi. II. 269 The author of the Odyssey is not identical either with the author of the Achilleis or his enlargers.

b. *spec.* in *Photogr.* One who, or an apparatus which, enlarges photographs.

1886 in W. D. Welford *Photographer's Indispensable Handbk.* (1887) 334 Bromised paper affords wonderful facilities to the enlarger, whether he be a professional or only a casual. **1894** *Brit. Jrnl. Photogr. Almanac 1895* 1034 (Advt.), The snap shot enlarger. **1911** B. E. JONES *Cassell's Cycl. Photogr.* 221/2 The fixed-focus enlarger, a piece of apparatus in the form of a double box, which allows one degree of enlargement only. **1940** F. J. MORTIMER *Wall's Dict. Photogr.* (ed. 15) 245 *(heading)* The vertical enlarger. **1959** *Chambers's Encycl.* X. 688/2 In some types of enlarger focusing is automatically adjusted to match the distance from enlarger lens to baseboard.

†**2.** One who sets (a person) at large. *Obs.*

1611 SPEED *Hist. Gt. Brit.* IX. xvi. §8 Whereby the maine drift of his enlargers was not much aduanced.

enˈlarging, *vbl. sb.* [f. ENLARGE *v.* + -ING[1].]

1. The action of ENLARGE *v.* in its various senses.

1494 FABYAN V. cxv. 89 He releuyd greatly the poore people, by enlargyng of his liberall almes. *Ibid.* VI. clxxxvii. 189 For the enlargynge of the Kyng. **1553** EDEN *Treat. Newe Ind.* (Arb.) 37 They fyght not for the enlargeing of theyr dominion. **1656** MORE *Antid. Ath.* II. ii. (1712) 41 The inlarging of our Understanding by so ample Experience. *a* **1717** PARNELL *To Ld. Bolingbroke* Wks. (1810) 413 Where mean acrostics..control The great enlargings of the boundless soul. **1843** BROWNING *Blot 'Scutcheon* I. iii, Thorold's enlargings, Austin's brevities.

attrib. **1875** URE *Dict. Arts* II. 729 The hammer used for beating the first packet [of gold-leaf] is called the flat, or the enlarging hammer.

2. *concr.* An expansion, swelling.

1562 TURNER *Herbal* II. 111 b, The herbe..healeth the enlarginges of wind or puls veynes.

enlarging (ɛnˈlɑːdʒɪŋ), *ppl. a.* [f. ENLARGE *v.* + -ING[2].] That enlarges, in various senses.

Hence **enˈlargingly,** *adv.*

1694 VAN LEUWENHOEK in *Phil. Trans.* XVIII. 196 A much more enlarging Microscope. **1746–7** HERVEY *Medit.* (1818) 177 Your deep, prolonged, enlarging, aggravated roar. **1762–9** FALCONER *Shipwr.* III. 65 While round before the enlarging wind it falls. **1765** BLACKSTONE *Comm.* I. 87 So that this was an enlarging statute. **1856** EMERSON *Eng. Traits, Lit.* Wks. (Bohn) II. 109 With patriotic and still enlarging generosity. **1882** J. PARKER *Apost. Life* I. 19 The power was to be used enlargingly.

†**enˈlargisse,** *v. Obs.* Also 5 enlargise. [ad. OFr. *enlargiss-* lengthened stem of *enlargir*: see ENLARGE *v.*] *trans.* **a.** To make larger, enlarge. **b.** To bestow bountifully; to vouchsafe.

c **1430** *Pilgr. Lyf Manhode* I. li. (1869) 31 He wolde..yiue almesse and enlargise it to poore erraunt pilgrimes. **1440** J. SHIRLEY *Dethe K. James* (1818) Advt., The Kyng of Scottes hadde leve enla[r]gissid, and had saufecondit of his maister the kyng of England, (for so the Kyng of Scottes clepid hym,) to return safe and sownde ayene ynto his region of Scotteland. *c* **1448** in *R. Glouc.* (1724) II. 483 His fader in his tymes enlargissed his marches.

enlaurel: see EN- *pref.*[1] 1 b.

enlay: see INLAY.

enlead, enleaf: see EN- *pref.*[1] 1 a, b.

enleague (ɛnˈliːg), *v.* Also 7 inleague. [f. EN-[1] + LEAGUE *sb.* or *v.*] *trans.* To unite in or as in a league.

1602 WARNER *Alb. Eng.* X. lv. (1612) 244 Not for Maries Title, or her any virtuous Gifts, Think that they her inleagued. **1628–1677** FELTHAM *Resolves* I. xxxi. (1677) 54 To inleague ourselves with an undividable love. **1633** FORD *Broken Hrt.* III. iv, I..Could..with a willingness inleague our blood With his. **1759** W. WILKIE *Epigon.* I. (1769) 14 Greece enleagued a full assembly held. **1821** JOANNA BAILLIE *Poems*, Now it doth appear That he, enleagued with robbers, was the spoiler.

enlegeance, corruption of ALLEGEANCE[1], *Obs.*

enlength, -en: see EN- *pref.*[1] 2, 3.

enlepi, variant of ONELEPY *a. Obs.* only.

c **1175** *Lamb. Hom.* 75 Ich ileue on þe helende crist · filium eius unicum · his enlepi sune.

enlessen: see EN- *pref.*[1] 3.

†**enˈleve,** *v. Obs rare*[−1]. [a. OF. *enleve-r*, f. *en-* (see EN-[1]) + *lever* to raise.] *trans.* To raise (a figure) in relief; to represent in relief.

c **1400** MAUNDEV. xvii. 188 In the Plates ben Stories & Batayles of Knyghtes enleved [orig. *enleuez*].

‖**enlevé** (ɑ̃ləve), *a. Her.* [Fr. *enlevé*, pa. pple. of *enlever* (see prec.).] Raised or elevated, = *enhanced*: see ENHANCE 1 b.

In mod. Dicts.

enlevement (ɛnˈliːvmənt, ɑ̃lɛvmɑ̃). *Sc. Law.* [Fr. *enlèvement*, f. *enlever* to carry off, f. *en-*:—L. *inde* away + *lever* to lift.] A carrying off (of a woman or child); an abduction.

Sometimes employed by mod.Eng. writers merely as Fr., without reference to its earlier adoption.

1769 LD. PRESIDENT in *Scots Mag.* Sept. 687/1 As to the enlevement of Mignon's child..such enlevement happened in July 1748. **1818** SCOTT *Hrt. Midl.* i, The development, *enlèvement*, the desperate wound etc...become a mere matter of course. **1852** THACKERAY *B. Lyndon* xvi, All the town being up about the *enlèvement*.

enle(v)en, -enth, obs. ff. ELEVEN, -TH.

†**enˈliberty,** *v. Obs. rare*[−1]. In 6 enlyberte. [f. EN-[1] + LIBERTY.] *trans.* To put within the 'liberty' or absolute control of; to give up entirely.

c **1500** *Melusine* (1889) 99, I enlyberte & habaundonne it to them [the monkes] for theire vse.

enlife: see EN- *pref.*[1] 2.

†**enlight** (ɛnˈlaɪt), *v. Obs.* or *arch.* Forms: 1 inlíhtan, -léhtan, -lýhtan, 4 ynliȝte-n, 7 inlight, 6– enlight. [OE. *inlíhtan*, f. *in-* + *líhtan* (see LIGHT *v.*) to shine. But the word in 17–18th c. is prob. independently f. EN-[1] + LIGHT *v.* Cf. ALIGHT *v.*[3]]

1. *trans.* To shed light upon, illuminate. Also *fig.* and *absol.*

c **975** *Rushw. Gosp.* Luke xi. 36 Swa leht leȝedes in-lihteð ðec. *a* **1000** *Guthlac* 70 (Gr.), Siððan hine inlyhte, se þe lifes weȝ gæstum ȝearwað. **1382** WYCLIF *2 Cor.* iv. 6 God..hath ynliȝtid in oure hertis. **1605** SYLVESTER *Du Bartas* I. iv. (1605–7) I. 143 Seeing the Lampe which doth enlight the Whole. **1634** HABINGTON *Castara* (Arb.) 137 The Cymmerians, whom no ray Doth ere enlight. **1665** WITHER *Lord's Prayer* 84 Some who have been in a good measure inlighted. **1675** COCKER *Morals* 24 How dark's the Lesser Worlds sad Winters Night, When Reasons radiant Rays do not enlight. **1709** POPE *Ess. Crit.* II. 403 That sun..Enlights the present, and shall warm the last.

2. *trans. to enlight up*: to light up, kindle, cause to shine.

1818 LAMB *Sonn.* iii. Wks. 603 What rare witchery.. Enlighted up the semblance of a smile In those fine eyes.

enlighten (ɛnˈlaɪtən), *v.* Forms: α. 6– enlighten. β. 4 inliȝten, 6–8 inlighten, (7 illighten). [f. EN-[1] + LIGHT *sb.* + -EN[5]: see EN- *pref.*[1] 2 b.

(As in many vbs. with the same prefix and suffix, the precise mode of formation is doubtful. Possibly *inlighten* (14th c.: see sense 4) was a secondary form of *inlight* (see prec.); formation on IN-, EN-[1] + LIGHTEN *v.* is also possible. Cf. ALIGHTEN.)]

†**1.** *trans.* To put light into, make luminous.

1587 GOLDING *De Mornay* i. 1 Which should take vpon them to enlighten the Sunne wᵗ a Candle. **1602** WARNER *Alb. Eng.* XIII. lxxviii. (1612) 323 One Sunne inlighteneth euery Light. **1678** CUDWORTH *Intell. Syst.* 350 Thou rollest round the Heavens, enlightnest the Sun. *a* **1763** BYROM *Thanksg. Hymn* Wks. (1810) 254 And the Moon is enlighten'd to govern the night.

†**b.** To light, set light to (a lamp, a combustible). *Obs.*

1613–16 W. BROWNE *Brit. Past.* I. iii, Now had..all the lamps of heav'n inlightned bin. *a* **1634** CHAPMAN *Revenge Hon.* Wks. 1873 III. 322, I ere long enlightened by my anger Shall be my own pile and consume to ashes.

2. To shed light upon, illuminate (an object, scene, etc.); to give light to (persons). Also *absol.* Now chiefly *poet.* or *rhetorical.*

1611 BIBLE *Ps.* xcvii. 4 His lightnings inlightned the world. **1635** SWAN *Spec. M.* iii. §2 (1643) 48 The element of fire..whose act and qualitie is to enlighten. **1711** SHAFTESB. *Charac.* (1737) II. 372 Vital treasures which inlighten and invigorate the surrounding worlds. **1761** SMOLLETT *Humph. Cl.* (1815) 109 Ranelagh..enlightened with a thousand golden lamps. **1784** COWPER *Task* I. 348 Shadow and sunshine..darkning and enlightning..ev'ry spot. **1831** BREWSTER *Newton* (1855) I. iv. 80 The sun..enlightened some such clouds near him. **1842** LONGF. *Sp. Stud.* II. x, Thou moon..all night long enlighten my sweet lady-love! **1871** B. TAYLOR *Faust* (1875) II. II. iii. 162 What fiery marvel the billows enlightens.

†**b.** *fig.* To throw light upon, elucidate (a subject). *Obs.*

1587 GOLDING *De Mornay* xxxi. 505 Which end of the Law..is greatly inlightened vnto vs by the comming of our Lord. **1607** TOPSELL *Four-f. Beasts* (1673) 464 The difference of Regions do very much enlighten the discription or history of Sheep. **1694** R. BURTHOGGE *Reason* 150 This Discourse..will seem a little Mysterious; and, therefore, to Inlighten it, etc. **1738** J. KEILL *Anim. Œcon.* 54 By whose bright Genius..we see the Theory of Medicine enlightened and illustrated.

†**3. a.** To light, give light to (a room or building) by lamps, etc., or by windows. **b.** To light (a district, town, etc.); to furnish with lighting apparatus. *Obs.*

1645 EVELYN *Mem.* (1857) I. 179 Enlightened with 44 apertures or windows, artificially disposed. **1706** *Lond. Gaz.* No. 4292/3 Letters Patents for Enlightening the Suburbs of London..by new invented Lights. **1737** in Picton *L'pool. Munic. Rec.* (1886) II. 142 An Act..for enlightening round the Dock. **1768** *Chron.* in *Ann. Reg.* 73/1 The bill for enlightening..the parish of St. Mary le bone in the county of Middlesex. **1773** NOORTHOUCK *Hist. Lond.* 599 The body is enlightened by a single series of large gothic windows. **1817** HUGHAM *Walks through London* 292 A plain brick building, well enlightened.

†**4.** In Biblical phrase: To remove dimness or blindness from (the eyes, and *fig.* the heart). *Obs.*

1382 WYCLIF *Ephes.* i. 18 The yȝen of ȝoure herte inliȝtened. *c* **1535** FISHER *Wks.* (1883) 439 He must beseche our sauiour Christ to enlighten his harte by clere faith. **1611** BIBLE *1 Sam.* xiv. 29 See..how mine eyes haue beene enlightened, because I tasted a little of this honie. *a* **1703** BURKITT *On N.T.* Mark x. 52 He stood still, he called him, and enlightened his eyes.

5. *fig.* To supply with intellectual light; to impart knowledge or wisdom to; to instruct. In

mod. use often humorously in trivial sense: To inform, remove (one's) ignorance of something.
1667 MILTON *P.L.* XI. 115 Reveale To Adam what shall come.. As I shall thee enlighten. **1712** ADDISON *Spect.* No. 419 ⁋5 Before the World was enlightened by Learning and Philosophy. **1763** JOHNSON *Ascham* Wks. IV. 621 To inlighten their minds, and to form their manners. **1832** HT. MARTINEAU *Demerara* ii. 28 As much as you please in enlightening those who are unaware of them. **1863** FR. KEMBLE *Resid. Georgia* 9 The moment they [slaves] are in any degree enlightened, they become unhappy. **1884** *Manch. Exam.* 2 May 4/7 The letter which follows his own ..will enlighten him on this point.

b. In religious use: To supply with spiritual light.
1577 tr. *Bullinger's Decades* (1592) 517 Blasphemie against the Sonne of man is committed of the ignorant, which are not yet inlightned. **1611** BIBLE *Pref.* 5 (The Seuentie) were ..enlightened with propheticall grace. **1644** *Jus. Pop.* 4 When Civilitie began to be illightned by Christianitie. **1650** BAXTER *Saints' R.* IV. iv. (1662) 677 That heavenly Light, wherewith your own souls were never illightened. **1877** MOZLEY *Univ. Serm.* vi. 141 Outward nature cannot of itself enlighten man's conscience.

†**6.** Contextually: To revive, exhilarate. (Cf. *lighten, brighten*, in similar connexion.) *Obs.*
1667 MILTON *P.L.* VI. 497 He [Satan] ended, and his words thir drooping chere Enlightn'd.

enlightened (ɛn'laɪt(ə)nd), *ppl. a.* [f. ENLIGHTEN *v.* + -ED[1].]
†**1.** That has been made luminous; blazing, light-giving. *Obs.*
1611 COTGR., *Fouldroyer*, to blast with lightning, or (inlightened) thunderbolts. **1803** PIGOTT in *Phil. Trans.* XCV. 152 The enlightened stars are those that have already attained the highest degree of perfection.

2. That receives light from a luminous object; illuminated.
1638 WILKINS *New World* v. (1707) 39 The nearer any enlightened Body comes to the Light. **1789** HERSCHEL *Saturn* in *Phil. Trans.* LXXX. 8 We must..see the rounding part of the enlightened edge. **1821** CRAIG *Lect. Drawing* iv. 236 Part of the enlightened surface of the flesh.

3. Possessed of mental light; instructed, well-informed; free from prejudices or superstition.
1663 BUTLER *Hud.* I. i. 498 Prolongers to enlightned stuff [1689 snuff]. **1732** BERKELEY *Alciphr.* I. §9 The select spirits of this enlightened age. **1814** D'ISRAELI *Quarrels Auth.* (1867) 448 Many enlightened bishops sided with the philosopher [Hobbes]. **1868** PEARD *Water-farm.* vii. 80 The most enlightened culture was bestowed on the bed of the Galway rivers.

Hence **en'lightenedness.**
1847 SOUTHEY *Doctor* VI. 373 Where your enlightenedness (if there be such a word) consists..it would puzzle the Devil to tell.

enlightener (ɛn'laɪt(ə)nə(r)). Also 8 **inlightener.** [f. ENLIGHTEN *v.* + -ER[1].] One who, or that which, enlightens; one who imparts intellectual light, informs or instructs. Rare in physical sense.
1582 BENTLEY *Mon. Matrones* III. 225 O mine Inlightener, it is thou that hast taught and instructed me. **1667** MILTON *P.L.* XII. 271 O sent from Heav'n, Enlightner of my darkness. **1750** WARBURTON *Doctr. Grace*, Is it possible, then, to suppose them [the Apostles] to be deserted by their divine Inlightener? **1840** MILL *Diss. & Disc.*, *Civiliz.* (1859) I. 187 Literature..has almost entirely abandoned its mission as an enlightener and improver of them [the current sentiments]. **1851** G. S. FABER *Many Mansions* (1862) The great Enlightener of Life and Immortality.

†**b.** In pl.: The party of enlightenment, the 'illuminatists'. *Obs.* (? *nonce-use.*)
1800 *Month. Mag.* VIII. 597 The first practical victory won by the Enlighteners over their antagonists, was the suppression of the Order of Jesuits by Clement XIV.

enlightening (ɛn'laɪt(ə)nɪŋ), *vbl. sb.* [f. ENLIGHTEN *v.* + -ING[1].] The action of the verb ENLIGHTEN, in various senses.
1561 T. NORTON *Calvin's Inst.* II. 82 To whome the Holy ghost by his enlightening shall make a new minde. **1613–16** W. BROWNE *Brit. Past.* II. v, Whose new inlightning will be quench'd with teares. **1665** WITHER *Lord's Prayer* 67 My Rush-candle may perhaps occasion the enlightning of many Torches hereafter. **1727** DE FOE *Syst. Magic* I. i. (1840) 16 To shine..for the further enlightening the world.

en'lightening, *ppl. a.* [f. as prec. + -ING[2].] That enlightens, in various senses of the verb.
1641 MILTON *Ch. Govt.* Pref. (1851) 96 The supreme inlightning assistance. **1678** NORRIS *Coll. Misc.* (1699) 101 'Twas a Crime to taste th' inlightning Tree. **1791** COWPER *Odyss.* x. 236 Where sets The all enlight'ning sun. **1824** COLERIDGE *Aids Refl.* (1848) I. 5 This seeing light, this enlightening eye, is reflection.

enlightenment (ɛn'laɪt(ə)nmənt). [f. as prec. + -MENT.]
1. The action of enlightening; the state of being enlightened. Only in fig. sense (see ENLIGHTEN *v.* 5). The imparting or receiving mental or spiritual light.
1669 LE BLANC in Spurgeon *Treas. Dav.* Ps. lxxxiv. 13 His lightnings, that is his divine enlightenments, are best seen. **1798** *Month. Mag.* VI. 554 A truth..the power of comprehending which implies a high degree of enlightenment. **1846** W. H. MILL *Five Sermons* (1848) 5 The highest spiritual enlightenment. **1855** DICKENS *Lett.* (1880) I. 398, I should be ready to receive enlightenment from any source. **1860** FROUDE *Hist. Eng.* V. 3 He imagined .. that an age of enlightenment was at hand. **1881** W. COLLINS *Bl. Robe* I. ii. 16, I needed no further enlightenment.

2. Sometimes used [after Ger. *Aufklärung, Aufklärerei*] to designate the spirit and aims of the French philosophers of the 18th c., or of others whom it is intended to associate with them in the implied charge of shallow and pretentious intellectualism, unreasonable contempt for tradition and authority, etc.
1865 J. H. STIRLING *Secret of Hegel* p. xxvii, Deism, Atheism, Pantheism, and all manner of *isms* due to Enlightenment. *Ibid.* p. xxviii, Shallow Enlightenment, supported on such semi-information, on such weak personal vanity, etc. **1889** CAIRD *Philos. Kant* I. 69 The individualistic tendencies of the age of Enlightenment.

†**en'limn,** *v. Obs.* In 5–6 en-, inlymn. [f. EN-[1] + LIMN: see ENLUMINE.] *trans.* **a.** To illuminate (a book); = ENLUMINE 4. **b.** To paint in bright colours.
1453 *Test. Ebor.* (1855) II. 190, j par of tables enlymned with Seyntes. **1530** PALSGR. 536/1 I enlymnye, as one enlymneth a boke, *Ie enlumine.* This boke is well written and richely enlymned, *Ce liure est bien escript et richement enluminé.* **1603** SIR C. HEYDON *Jud. Astrol.* ii. 71 Origen called heauen a booke, in which God hath as it were inlymned all that his pleasure is should come to passe in this world.

enlink (ɛn'lɪŋk), *v.* Also 6 enlincke, -lynck, inlin(c)k. [f. EN-[1] + LINK.] *trans.* To fasten as with links; link together as in a chain; to join in company *with*; to connect closely; *lit.* and *fig.* Const. *in, to, with.*
1560 DAUS tr. *Sleidane's Comm.* 193 a, Cities of the Empire inlincked with the Protestantes. **1567** DRANT *Horace' Epist.* To Rdr. *iiij, Maruaile that I wil now any longer enlincke my selfe in things so small. **1596** SPENSER *F.Q.* v. iv. 3 That lovely payre, Enlincked fast in wedlockes loyall bond. **1599** SHAKS. *Hen. V,* III. iii. 18 Fell feats, Enlynckt to wast and desolation. **1606** G. W[OODCOCKE] tr. *Hist. Ivstine* 24 b, He fled vnto Tissaphernes..with whom.. he in-linked himself in such great friendship [etc.]. **1620** T. GRANGER *Div. Logike* 159 The observation of these conditions. Concludeth, and inlinketh, true, and genuine Conjugates together. *Ibid.* 292. **1813** SCOTT *Trierm.* III. xxx, Maids enlinked in sister-fold. **1846** DE QUINCEY *Christianity* Wks. XII. 264 The one idea is enlinked with the other. **1883** T. WATTS in *19th Cent.* Mar. 415 Coleridge was enlinked to modern life and thought.

Hence **en'linked** *ppl. a.*; **en'linkment** (*rare*), a linking on.
1599 NASHE *Lenten Stuffe* (1871) 50 The inlinked consanguinity betwixt him and Lady Lucar. **1881** *Athenæum* 17 Sept. 370/2 The enlinkment of Condate with the camp at Kinderton near Middlewich.

enlist (ɛn'lɪst), *v.* Also 8 **inlist.** [f. EN-[1] + LIST *sb.* or *v.*
If from the sb., possibly suggested by Du. *inlijsten* to inscribe on a list or register. So far as our quots. show, the vb. *list* (now usually written *'list* as if aphetic) occurs considerably earlier than *enlist*, and may possibly be its source. The form *inlist*, now wholly disused, was in 18th c. much the more frequent.]

1. *trans.* To enrol on the 'list' of a military body; to engage as a soldier.
1698–9 E. LUDLOW *Mem.* III. 99 That the like number was enlisted [ed. 1751 inlisted] under my command in the western parts of England. **1755** JOHNSON, *List*, to enlist [the word is not under *En-* or *In-*]. **1762** *Gentl. Mag.* I The Dutch..were very busy inlisting men. **1776** GIBBON *Decl. & F.* I. xiii. 272 The bravest of their youth he enlisted among his land or sea forces. **1858** FONBLANQUE *How We are Governed* 99 The number of soldiers to be employed, and the terms upon which they shall be enlisted.

2. *transf.* and *fig.* To engage (a person) for domestic service (*humorous*); to secure (a person or his services) as an aid in any enterprise; to range (persons) in a particular class, or (feelings, etc.) in support of a cause; to make (natural forces, science, etc.) available for a special purpose.
1753 SMOLLETT *Ct. Fathom* (1784) 90/1 He likewise inlisted another footman and valet de chambre into his service. **1781** COWPER *Conversation* 205 A graver fact, enlisted on your side, May furnish illustration well applied. **1791** BOSWELL *Johnson* an. 1738 He was..inlisted by Mr. Cave as a regular coadjutor in his magazine. **1826** *Q. Rev.* XXXIV. 117 It was clever to inlist on his side those venerable prejudices. **1837** DISRAELI *Venetia* IV. ix. (1871) 259 So he resolved to enlist the aunt as his friend. **1842** W. MORGAN in Abdy *Water-cure* (1843) 218 The continued use of such liquors..enlists the moderate man into the ranks of the drunkard. **1867** SMILES *Huguenots Eng.* ii. (1880) 31 The Reformers early enlisted music in their service. **1884** *Manch. Exam.* 4 June 5/1 To enlist public interest in the wretched lot of the Dorsetshire labourer.

3. *refl.* Chiefly in sense 1. Now *rare*: superseded by 4.
1750 JOHNSON *Rambl.* No. 19 ⁋4 That class in which he should inlist himself. **1774** CHESTERF. *Lett.* I. 72 The people ..refused to enlist themselves in military service. **1783** WATSON *Philip III* (1839) 57 [He] persuaded many of his countrymen to enlist themselves under his banners.

4. *intr.* for *refl.* To have one's name inscribed in a list of recruits; to engage for military service. Also *transf.* and *fig.*
1776 GIBBON *Decl. & F.* I. vii. 137 His victory was rewarded by..a permission to inlist in the troops. **1790** BEATSON *Nav. & Mil. Mem.* I. 274 Part of them inlisted with the Corsicans. **1793** BURKE *Conduct of Minority* Wks. VII. 265 The former class..would be ready to enlist in the faction of the enemy. **1840** DICKENS *Barn. Rudge* xxxi, A carter in a smock-frock seemed wavering and disposed to enlist. **1865** H. PHILLIPS *Amer. Paper Curr.* II. 100 Specie was also proposed as a bounty to induce men to enlist.

Hence **en'listed** *ppl. a.*, enrolled for military service. **en'lister,** one who enlists men for military service; a recruiting officer. **en'listing** *vbl. sb.*, the action of the vb. ENLIST; also *attrib.*
1724 *Briton* 118 The enlisted Men were, for the most part, Irish Papists. **1882** HINSDALE *Garfield & Educ.* 431 The majority of the twenty-five thousand enlisted men in the army are native-born citizens. **1865** CARLYLE *Fredk. Gt.* VIII. XIX. ix. 272 The whole German Reich was deluged with secret Prussian Enlisters. **1807** J. MARSHALL *Const. Opin.* iv. (1839) 50 The mere enlisting of men without assembling them is not levying war. **1846** MCCULLOCH *Acc. Brit. Empire* (1854) II. 443 The enlisting money and other expenses.

enlistment (ɛn'lɪstmənt). [f. ENLIST *v.* + -MENT.]
1. The action or process of enlisting men for military service; the action of engaging oneself for military service. Also *fig.* and *attrib.*
1765 T. HUTCHINSON *Hist. Col. Mass.* i. 139 Lest there should not be a voluntary inlistment. **1810** WELLINGTON in Gurw. *Disp.* VI. 78 The enlistment of persons of this description in the corps of this army. **1864** SALA in *Daily Tel.* 27 July, By enlistment huts and rendezvous tents for the army and navy. **1871** MACDUFF *Mem. Patmos* viii. 108 Different subjects for the enlistment of their immortal energies. **1879** *Soldiering* in *Cassell's Techn. Educ.* III. 139 The smooth-sounding title of 'lowering the standard of enlistment'.

2. 'The document by which a soldier is bound' (Webster). ? *U.S.* only.

†**en'live,** *v. Obs.* Also 7 inlyve, -live. See *enlife* (EN- *prefix*[1] 2). [f. EN-[1] + LIFE; cf. the pl. *lives.*]
1. *trans.* To impart natural or spiritual life to, animate (a body, an individual). Also *fig.*
1593 NASHE *Christs' T.* (1613) 158 The diuel, who..goes and enliueth such licentious shapes. **1616** R. CARPENTER *Past. Charge* 45 Seruants of the Lord, quickned and enlived with the spirit of grace and power of godlinesse. **1633** BP. HALL *Hard Texts, N.T.* 233 The body of the first man..was informed and enlived by a living and reasonable soule. **1642** J. BALL *Answ. Can* ii. 71 The true church of God, all whose members were not..spiritually enlived.
transf. **1642** SIR E. DERING *Sp. on Relig.* 110 There wanteth..the formall power that should actuate and enlive the worke. *a* **1659** OSBORN *Queries* Wks. (1673) 606 The Spring by which a small Watch is Inlived.

2. To impart freshness and vivacity to; to make lively; to cheer. Also to revive (beauty).
1617 [see ENLIVING]. **1628** C. POTTER *Consecr. Serm.* (1629) 71 His speech should be..quickned and enlived with action. **1647** J. COTTON *Sing. Ps.* i. 5 The sound of the Harpe ..quickned and enlived as it were by a spirituall song. **1649** LOVELACE *Poems* 19 Loÿsa's pencills..With which she now enliveth more Beauties, then they destroy'd before.

Hence **en'living,** *vbl. sb.*
1602 HIERON *Answ. Popish Rime* To Rdr., The well neere breathlesse body of poperie beginneth to entertaine some hope of a new enliuing. **1617** —— II. 60 The singing of a psalme..is a notable meanes for the enliuing and stirring vp of our dull spirits. **1631** R. H. *Arraignm. Whole Creature* xx. 334 Wanting that vivification, inlightning and inliving, which is from that Sonne of Righteousnesse.

enliven (ɛn'laɪv(ə)n), *v.* [f. EN-[1] + LIFE + -EN[5]; see ENLIVE.]
†**1.** *trans.* To give life to; to bring or restore to life; to animate (as the soul the body). *Obs.*
1633 EARL MANCH. *Al Mondo* (1636) 14 Death..is but a departed breath from dead earth, inlivened at first by breath cast upon it. **1674** N. FAIRFAX *Bulk & Selv.* 28 That ghostly being which enlivens the body of man. **1681** CHETHAM *Angler's Vade-m.* xxxviii. §12. (1689) 248 Leaving it [i.e. spawn] to be enlivened by the sun's heat. **1732** WESLEY *Wks.* (1872) VII. 478 When God hath raised this body, he can enliven it with the same soul that inhabited it before.

2. To give fuller life to; to animate, inspirit, invigorate physically or spiritually; to quicken (feelings), stimulate (trade, etc.).
1644–52 J. SMITH *Sel. Disc.* VII. iv. (1821) 333 The Divinity derives itself into the souls of men, enlivening and transforming them into its own likeness. **1659** HAMMOND *On Ps.* cxix. 29 Paraphr. 598 To inliven me to a pious virtuous life. **1677** YARRANTON *Eng. Improv.* 127 There is no way..to inliven Trade..but this way. **1679** PLOT *Staffordsh.* (1686) 384 For enlivening old trees. **1684** BUNYAN *Pilgr.* II. 51 They came out of that Bath..much enlivened and strengthened in their Joynts. *a* **1745** SWIFT (J.), A small quantity of fresh coals..very much enlivens it [the fire]. **1799** DUNDAS in J. Owen *Wellesley's Disp.* 640 The bullion which has been sent from this country..has tended to enliven your circulation. **1827** C. BRIDGES *Expos. Ps.* cxix. (1830) 15 What is the motive that enlivens the believer in the pursuit of more extended spiritual knowledge?

3. To make 'lively' or cheerful, cheer, exhilarate; to impart liveliness to, relieve the monotony of, diversify agreeably (circumstances, conditions); to brighten, render cheerful in appearance.
1691 RAY *Creation* (1714) 179 Their eminent Ends and Uses in illuminating and enlivening the Planets. **1711** ADDISON *Spect.* No. 10 ⁋ 1, I shall endeavour to enliven Morality with Wit. **1730** THOMSON *Autumn* 27 A serener blue With golden light enlivened. **1760** J. SCOTT *Elegy* i. Poet. Wks. (1786) 25 The Voice of Song [shall] enliven ev'ry Shade. **1778** MISS BURNEY *Evelina* (1784) II. i. 3 Our house has been enlivened to-day by the arrival of a London visitor. **1824** DIBDIN *Libr. Comp.* 516 He is a sage to consult, rather

than a companion to enliven. **1858** DORAN *Crt. Fools* 61 The Jews themselves employed jesters to enliven their own wedding feasts. **1875** JOWETT *Plato* (ed. 2) IV. 504 A picture, which is well drawn in outline, but is not yet enlivened by colour.

Hence **en'livened**, *ppl. a.*; **en'livener**, he who or that which enlivens.

1640 W. BRIDGE *True Souldiers Convoy* 9 Enmity being nothing els but enlivened contrariety. **1665** COWLEY *Pindar. Odes, Destiny* i, Lo, of themselves th'enlivened chesmen move. **1678** CUDWORTH *Intell. Syst.* 793 This Enlivened Terrestrial Body, or Mortal man. **1663** BOYLE *Consid. Exper. & Nat. Philos.* I. ii. 43 He calls Him the Preserver, or . . the enlivener of them all. **1774** MRS. DELANY *Corr.* Ser. II. II. 34 The deer . . are beautiful enliveners of every scene. **1821** *Blackw. Mag.* X. 332 He was the enlivener and inspiriter of conversation. **1874** HARTWIG *Aerial W.* iv. 38 Echo, the charming enlivener of the silent glen.

enlivening (ɛnˈlaɪv(ə)nɪŋ), *vbl. sb.* [f. prec. + -ING^1.] **a.** The action of the vb. ENLIVEN. **b.** *concr.* Something that enlivens.

1628–1677 FELTHAM *Resolves* I. lxxxiv (R.), The good man is full of joyful enlivenings. **1674** N. FAIRFAX *Bulk & Selv.* 141 Without insouling or inlivening of it [the body]. **1772** *Ann. Reg.* 48/1 One of the greatest objects of his [Sully's] policy . . was the enlivening the provinces by agriculture, the true source of riches. **1859** R. BURTON *Centr. Afr.* in *Jrnl. Geog. Soc.* XXIX. 21 Central Africa . . appeared upon the maps a blank of white paper, with enlivenings of ostriches and elephants.

en'livening, *ppl. a.* [f. ENLIVEN *v.* + -ING^2.] That enlivens; in the senses of the verb.

1664 H. MORE *Myst. Iniq.* iv. 9 The sincere doctrine and enlivening spirit of the Gospel of Christ. **1746–7** HERVEY *Medit.* (1818) 107 Does the grape refresh you with its enlivening juices? *c* **1790** IMISON *Sch. Art* I. 105 This enlivening quality in air is also destroyed by the air's passing through fire. **1862** BURTON *Bk. Hunter* I. 34 The enlivening talk has made a guest forget 'The lang Scots miles'.

Hence **en'liveningly**, *adv.*

1867 *Morning Star* 19 July, The people . . became more numerous, and at times enliveningly demonstrative.

enlivenment (ɛnˈlaɪv(ə)nmənt). [f. ENLIVEN *v.* + -MENT.] The action of enlivening; the state or fact of being enlivened; *concr.* something that enlivens.

1883 *Harper's Mag.* Apr. 688/1 Not to mention an occasional kermesse and other enlivenments.

enlock (ɛnˈlɒk), *v.* Also 7–9 inlock. [f. EN-^{1} + LOCK *v.*] *trans.* To lock up, shut in, enclose, hold fast. Also *fig.*

1596 SPENSER *F.Q.* IV. Prol. 4 My soveraigne Queene, In whose chast brest all bountie naturall And treasures of true love enlocked beene. **1812** CRABBE *Tales* xxi. Wks. 1834 V. 248 He observed . . His friend enlock'd within a lady's arm. **1831** CARLYLE *Sart. Res.* (1858) 123 Inlock both Editor and Hofrath, in the labyrinthic tortuosities and covered-ways of said citadel. **1870** MYERS *Poems* (1875) 75 Lamps enlock the tomb in golden glamour.

†**b.** (See quot.)

1632 SHERWOOD, To Inlocke (mortaise in), *enclaver.*

en'lodge, *v. rare.* In 7 inlodge. [f. EN-^{1}, IN- + LODGE *v.*] *trans.* To locate or lodge in a place or within a given space. Hence **en'lodged** *ppl. a.*; **en'lodgement**, the action of locating in a place.

1678 NORRIS *Coll. Misc.* (1699) 69 Some more inlodg'd excellence. **1884** *Punch* 16 Feb. 75 The history of a writ from the original lawyer's letter to enlodgement in Holloway.

†**en'long**, *v. Obs. rare.* [f. EN-^{1} + LONG *a.*] Implied in **en'longing**, *vbl. sb.*, app. meaning 'prolongation, extension'.

1509 HAWES *Past. Pleas.* (1554) Ccj b, God graunt the mercy, but no tyme enlongyng. —— *Conv. Swearers* 27, I do graunte mercy but no tyme enlongynge.

†**en'longate**, *v. Obs. rare*$^{-1}$. ? Mistake for ELONGATE *v.* 2 b.

1686 GOAD *Celest. Bodies* I. xvii. 113 The Quadrates of ♀ are consider'd under another Name, viz. when she is elongated from the Sun.

†**en'lumine**, *v. Obs.* Also 4–5 enlumyne, enlomyne. [a. OF. *enlumine-r*, ad. late L. *inlūmināre* (in classical Lat. *illūmināre*), f. *in-* (see IN-) + *lūmen, lūmin-is* light. Cf. ILLUMINE, ILLUMINATE, ALLUMINE. In sense 4 the word assumed the aphetic forms LUMINE, LIMN, the latter of which survives with modified sense.]

1. *trans.* To light up, illuminate; also *transf.*

1375 BARBOUR *Bruce* VIII. 228 Thair speris, thair pennownys, & thar scheldis Of licht Illumynit [*v.r.* enlumymyt] all the feldis. **1481** CAXTON *Myrr.* III. xix. 176 The Sonne . . enlumineth alle the other by his beaulte. **1581** J. BELL *Haddon's Answ. Osor.* 488 So were ye powers of her soule enlumined with the orient beames of his divine inspiration. **1596** SPENSER *F.Q.* v. Prol. 7 That same great glorious lampe of light, That doth enlumine all these lesser fyres.

b. To give sight to.

1495 CAXTON *Vitas Patr.* (W. de W.) III. viii. 320 a, How fyue lytyll lyons beyng blynde were enlumyned by an holyman.

2. *fig.* To enlighten (ignorance, etc.); to throw light upon (a subject).

1393 GOWER *Conf.* III. 86 Theorike principalle . . is enlumined Of wisdome. *c* **1400** *Test. Love* I. (1560) 272 b/2 Worldes and cloud atweene us twey woll not suffer my thoughts of hem to be enlumined. *c* **1430** LYDG. *Lyfe & Pass. St. Albon* (1534) A. ij, In hope his influence shall shyne My tremblyng penne by grace to enlumyne. **1509** BARCLAY *Shyp of Folys* (1874) I. 121 Strengthynge the body, the herte enlumynynge. **1581** J. BELL *Haddon's Answ. Osor.* 56 This kinde of people, enlumined by the Prince of darknes . . did rayse out of hell, this newfangled monster of Transubstantiation.

3. To light, kindle (a fire).

1475 CAXTON *Jason* 19 Whiche enlumyned in him so terryble a fyre.

4. [Cf. med.L. *lumina* (lit. 'lights') the paintings in a MS.] To illuminate, adorn (MSS.) with coloured designs or miniatures. Also *fig.*

c **1366** CHAUCER *A.B.C.* 73 Kalendeeres enlumyned ben þei. *c* **1400** *Rom. Rose* 1695 For it so welle was enlomyned. **1430** LYDG. *Chron. Troy* Prol., For he enlumineth by craft and cadence, This noble storye with many freshe coloure Of Rethorik. **1525** LD. BERNERS *Froiss.* II. cc. (cxciv.) 609, I had engrosed in a fayre boke well enlumyned.

5. *fig.* To shed lustre upon, render illustrious or brilliant.

c **1386** CHAUCER *Clerke's T.* Prol. 33 Fraunces Petrark . . Enlumyned al Ytaille of poetrie. *c* **1450** *Merlin* xx. 326, Xij sones, where-of the londe of Bretaigne was after enlumyned. **1579** E. K. in *Spenser's Sheph. Cal.* Ep. Ded., Those rough and harsh tearmes enlumine . . the brightnesse of brave and glorious wordes.

†**en'lure**, *v. Obs.* Also 7 inlure. [f. EN-^{1} + LURE *sb.*: cf. ALLURE.] *trans.* To entice (a hawk) by a lure; hence *fig.* to draw on, entice; also *absol.*

1486 *Bk. St. Albans* D iij b, And thyse ben not enlured ne reclaymed bycause y^t they ben so ponderous to the perche portatyf. **1581** J. BELL *Haddon's Answ. Osor.* 297 b The other . . enlured Henry the 5 . . unto lyke outrage agaynst his own Father. **1607** *Barley-Breake* (1877) 20 Whereby he might the better her inlure. **1607** *Schol. Disc. agst. Antichr.* I. i. 13 Euery pleasant fountaine . . that may enlure to returne.

Hence **en'luring** *vbl. sb.*

1613 T. ADAMS *Pract. Wks.* (1861–2) I. 311 (D.) Provocations, heats, enlurings of lusts.

enlusty: see EN- *pref.*^{1} 2.

†**en'lute**, *v. Alch. Obs.* [f. EN-^{1} + L. *lūt-āre* to plaster with clay, f. *lūt-um* clay.] *trans.* To stop or cement with clay. (See ENGLUTE.)

c **1386** CHAUCER *Chan. Yem. Prol. & T.* 213 The pot and glas enlutyng, That of the aier mighte passe no thing. **1584** R. SCOT *Discov. Witchr.* XIV. i. 294 Enluting [*marginal note to* engluting].

enlyance, by-form of ALLIANCE.

†**en'lyme**, *v. Obs.* [? f. EN-^{1} + **lyme*, LEME; cf. ME. *alime*, ALEME. But perh. var. of ENLIMN.] *trans.* To illuminate, brighten.

c **1440** *Partonope* 1920 Alle the feelde Was enlymed wyth the bryghtnesse.

enmagazine: see EN- *pref.*^{1} 1 a.

†**en'manché, e'mmanché.** *Her. Obs.* Also 6 emaunche. [a. Fr. *emmanché*, f. *en-* (see EN-^{1}) + *manche*, masc., handle.

In Fr. heraldry the word is used (1) of an axe or other weapon, having the handle of a certain tincture different from that of the blade; (2) of the field, denoting what Eng. heralds call *barry-pily*. Neither of these senses is recognised in England, though the former appears in some recent Eng. Dicts. The Eng. senses given below are of doubtful authenticity; sense 2 is perh. founded on the erroneous derivation from *manche*, fem., sleeve.]

1. Of the field: (Sir J. Ferne's engraving represents 'per fesse dancetté of two points').

1586 FERNE *Blaz. Gentrie* I. 199 He beareth Emaunche [*printed* Emanuche] Arg. and Gewles.

2. Of a chief: (see quot.).

1736 BAILEY, *Enmanché* [in Heraldry] is derived from *manche*, F. a sleeve, and is when the chief has lines drawn from the upper edge of the chief on the sides, to about half the breadth of the chief, signifying as if it had sleeves on it. **1847** in CRAIG; and in mod. Dicts.

enmantle, var. of IMMANTLE.

enmarble, enmarvel, -vail: see EMM-.

enmass: see EN- *pref.*^{1} 2.

‖**en masse** (ɑ̃ mas). Also 9 en mass. [Fr.] In a mass or body; bodily, all at once.

1802 PLAYFAIR *Illustr. Hutton. The.* 334 The transition from gneiss to granite *en mass*, is not uncommon. **1815** *Scribbleomania* 53 The public *en masse*, Hath affirmed that these Lays other efforts surpass. **1848** MRS. GASKELL *M. Barton* v, The things were . . lifted *en masse* to the drawer.

enmesh, emmesh, immesh (ɛnˈmɛʃ, ɛˈmɛʃ, ɪˈmɛʃ), *v.* Also 7 enmash. [f. EN-^{1} + MESH.]

1. *trans.* To surround with meshes; to catch or entangle in, or as in, a net. Also of the net, and *fig.*

α. **1604** SHAKS. *Oth.* II. iii. 367 The Net that shall en-mash them all. *a* **1669** LE BLANC in Spurgeon *Treas. Dav.* Ps. cxix. 61 A gladiator with net and sword . . endeavouring to enmesh any one who comes near him. **1831** CAPT. TRELAWNY *Adv. Younger Son* I. 202 They have here a ring-fence of posts, in which the King of Candy is enmeshed. **1847** GROTE *Greece* II. xi. III. 132 Declining to haul up the net when the fish were already enmeshed. **1884** *Harper's Mag.* Sept. 499/1 Vines . . enmeshing every stone in their tenacious threads.

β. **1870** MORRIS *Earthly Par.* I. II. 606 A past song . . Emmeshed for ever in the memory's net.

γ. **1774** GOLDSM. *Nat. Hist.* VII. 236 Spider . . careful to observe when the fly is completely immeshed. **1853** C. BRONTË *Villette* xvi. (1855) 160, I got immeshed in a network of turns unknown.

2. *fig.* To entrap, entangle; to make (thought) complicated.

α. **1822** SHELLEY *Let. Hunt*, Debts, responsibilities, and expenses will enmesh you round about. **1863** MRS. C. CLARKE *Shaks. Char.* xviii. 469 Buckingham's career with Richard contains an impressive lesson on weakness enmeshed by unscrupulous strength.

β. **1870** MORRIS *Earthly Par.* II. III. 242 Such things emmeshed his dying troubled thought.

γ. **1865** DICKENS *Mut. Fr.* I. xv, The undesigning Boffin had become so far immeshed.

Hence **en'meshment**, the state or condition of being enmeshed; entanglement.

1885 'C. E. CRADDOCK' (Miss Murfree) in *Atlantic Monthly* Apr. 434/2 In that enchanted enmeshment were tangled all the fancies of the night. **1885** *Punch* 30 May 258 As concerns Egyptian darkness, and the Muscovite enmeshment.

enmew: see IMMEW.

enmie, -y(e, obs. forms of ENEMY.

enmilden, enmingle: see EN- *pref.*^{1} 3.

†**en'mind**, *v. Obs. rare*$^{-1}$. [f. EN-^{1} + MIND *sb.*] *trans.* To put in mind, remind.

1644 J. FARY *Gods Severity on Mans Sterility* (1645) 1 Upon the hearing of this newes, our Saviour en-mindes them of what hapned even in their owne City.

†**en'mine**, *v. Obs. rare*$^{-1}$. [App. f. EN-^{1} + MINE *sb.* or *v.*] *trans.* To fix in a hole in the ground.

c **1420** *Pallad. on Husb.* I. 768 Yf the lacke a welle, a winche enmyne.

enmious: see ENEMIOUS.

enmitre: see EN- *pref.*^{1} 1 b.

enmity (ˈɛnmɪtɪ). Forms: 4–6 enem-, enmyte(e, enemite, -yte, 4 enmit(y)e, 5 enymyte, 6 enem-, enimitie, ennimitie, enim-, inimity, 6– enmity. [ad. OF. *enemistié, ennemistié* (Fr. *inimitié*), = Pr. *enemistat*, Sp. *enemistad*:—late L. **inimīcitāt-em*, f. *inimīcus*: see ENEMY.]

1. The disposition or the feelings characteristic of an enemy; ill-will, hatred.

a **1300** *Cursor M.* 4078 (Gött.) Ne wald þai neuer apon him se, Fra þat day bot wid enmite [*Trin.* enemyte]. *c* **1380** WYCLIF *Sel. Wks.* III. 301 For enemyte þat þei han to a man. **1483** CAXTON *Cato* I viii b, For enymyte and hate are contrary to frendship and concorde. **1535** COVERDALE *Isa.* xi. 13 The hatred of Ephraim, and ye enmyte of Iuda shalbe clene rooted out. **1596** DALRYMPLE tr. *Leslie's Hist. Scot.* (1885) 92 The . . inimity borne toward thair parents to instil in the hartes of thair barnes. **1667** MILTON *P.L.* I. 431 Can . . works of love or enmity fulfill. **1768** STERNE *Sent. Journ., Riddle* (1778) II. 115 A man who values a good night's rest will not lie down with enmity in his heart, if he can help it. **1875** JOWETT *Plato* (ed. 2) I. 353 He hated me, and his enmity was shared by several who were present.

2. The condition of being an enemy; a state of mutual hostility; *esp.* in phrase *at* or *in enmity*.

? *a* **1400** *Chester Pl.* (1843–7) 31 And enmitye betwene you towe . . I shall make. **1483** CAXTON *Gold. Leg.* 379/3 By cause there shold noo debate ne enemyte falle betwene the brethren. **1579** NORTH *Plutarch* 541 So civill and temperate were mens enmities at that time. **1593** SHAKS. *Rich. II*, II. ii. 68, I will dispaire, and be at enmitie With couzening hope. **1602** SEGAR *Hon. Mil. & Civ.* I. iii. 4 When the Romanes were divided, one faction labouring to oppresse another . . such enimitie was called Sedition. **1611** BIBLE *Jam.* iv. 4 Know yee not that the friendship of the world is enmity with God? **1667** PEPYS *Diary* (1879) IV. 479 It will prevent much trouble by having of him out of their enmity. *a* **1704** LOCKE (J.), In an age at enmity with all restraint. **1837** HT. MARTINEAU *Soc. Amer.* III. 188 The growing enmity of opinion to the punishment of death. **1845** STEPHEN *Laws Eng.* II. 407 Provided their parents were not at the time in enmity with our sovereign. **1855** MACAULAY *Hist. Eng.* IV. 581 The adventures, the attachments, the enmities of the lords and ladies who, etc.

b. *transf.*

1818 JAS. MILL *Brit. India* II. IV. ix. 300 That system of patronage . . is at irreconcilable enmity with the very principle of good government.

†**c.** *to be of (a person's) enmity*: to be at enmity with (him). *Obs.*

1641 W. HAKEWIL *Lib. of Subject* 123 All Merchants Denizens and Forreins (except those which be of our enmitie) may, etc.

†**3.** Something that is prejudicial; a baneful influence. *Obs.*

1387 TREVISA *Higden* (Rolls) IV. 99 It is grete enemyte [*inimicissimum*] to werriours forto norsche sleuþe and leccherie. *c* **1391** CHAUCER *Astrol.* II. §4 A fortunat assendent clepen they whan . . no wikkid planete haue non aspecte of enemyte up-on the assendent. *c* **1470** HARDING *Chron.* liii. i, The water myght not the enemytee Kepe of [warre] from his trewe Britayn lande. **1605** SHAKS. *Lear* II. iv. 212, I abiure all roofes, and chuse To wage against the enmity oth' ayre.

enmix: see EN- *pref.*^{1} 3.

enmoised: see EMMOISED, *Obs.*

†**en'montery.** *Obs. rare*$^{-1}$. [ad. F. *émonctoire*, f. mod.L. *ēmunctōrius*: see EMUNCTORY.] = EMUNCTORY *sb.*; in quot. *spec.* the armpit.
1655 FULLER *Ch. Hist.* x. v. §12 He was shot through the Emnontery of the left Arm.

†**en'mortise,** *v. Obs. rare*$^{-1}$. In 5 enmortese. [ad. OFr. *enmortiss-* lengthened stem of *enmortir*, var. of *amortir*: see EN- *pref.*^{1} A. 2 and AMORTIZE.] *trans.* To convey (property) to a corporation; = AMORTIZE 3.
1439 in *E.E. Wills* (1882) 119, I woll that myn executours enmortese vnto the howse of Tewkesbery C mark.

enmoss: see EN- *pref.*^{1} 1 b.

enmove, var. of INMOVE *v. Obs.*

†**en'muffle,** *v. Obs.* [f. EN-^{1} + MUFFLE *v.*] *trans.* To muffle up. Hence **en'muffling** *vbl. sb.*
1611 FLORIO, *Imbauagliamento*, an enmuffling.

†**en'muse,** *v. Obs. rare*$^{-1}$. [var. of AMUSE: see EN- *pref.*^{1} A. 2.] *trans.* To bewilder, confound; = AMUSE 2.
1502 *Ord. Crysten Men* III. iii. (W. de W. 1506) 159 The deuyll dysceyueth, enmuseth, and entyseth the pore creature humayne.

enmyable, var. of ENEMIABLE *a. Obs.*

enmye, -myȝe, obs. forms of ENEMY.

enmyly, var. of ENEMYLY *a. Obs.*

ennated, var. of INNATED, innate.

[**ennation, enneation**, 'the ninth segment in insects', for which mod. Dicts. cite 'Maunder', is a blunder for *ennaton* (a. ἔννατον late spelling of Gr. ἔνατον ninth) which appears in Maunder's *Treas. Nat. Hist.* 1848–54, but not in later editions. We have no evidence that the word was ever in Eng. use.]

ˌ**enneaconta'hedral,** *a. rare.* [f. Gr. ἐννεάκοντα (erron. for ἐνενήκοντα; see Dindorf in *Stephani Thes.*) ninety + ἕδρα base + -AL^1.] Of a crystal: Having ninety faces.
1817 R. JAMESON *Char. Min.* 202.

ennead ('ɛniːæd). [ad. Gr. ἐννεάς, ἐννεάδ-ος, f. ἐννέα nine.]
†**1.** The number nine. *Obs.*
1655–60 STANLEY *Hist. Philos.* (1701) 384/1 The Ennead is the first square of an odd number.
2. A set of nine persons or things (discourses, points, etc.); *spec.* one of the six divisions in Porphyry's collection of Plotinus' works, each of which contains nine books.
1653 H. MORE *Conject. Cabbal.* (1713) 186 In his fifth Ennead..he makes the Universe a necessary Emanation of God. **1678** CUDWORTH *Intell. Syst.* 213 Though Tertullian be yet more Liberal, and encrease the Number to an Ennead. **1854** MAURICE *Mor. & Met. Philos.* (ed. 2) 58, I disposed them, he [Porphyry] says, into 6 Enneads, gladly availing myself of the perfect numbers (6 and 9). **1870** PROF. CAYLEY in *Nature* 29 Dec. 178/1 The name 'ennead' is given to any nine points in plano which are the intersections of 2 cubic curves: or to any nine lines through a point which are the intersections of two cubic curves. **1881** *Ch. Q. Rev.* 172 The exquisite language of the prophecy of Isaiah, especially in its last three enneads. **1884** E. W. BUDGE *Babylon. Life & Hist.* ix. 128 The most important ennead [of Gods] among the Babylonians was as follows.
Hence **enne'adic** *a.* pertaining to an ennead.

enneaeteric (ˌɛnɪəɪ'tɛrɪk), *a. rare.* [f. as if on Gr. *ἐννεαετηρίς a cycle of nine years (f. ἐννέα nine + ἔτος year, after the analogy of τριετηρίς, etc.) + -IC.] Consisting of nine years.
1846 GROTE *Greece* II. ii. II. 353 *note*, The fact..does not establish a knowledge of the properties of the octaeteric or enneaeteric period.

enneagon ('ɛniːəgɒn). Also 7 -one. [f. Gr. ἐννέα nine + γωνία angle.] A plane figure with nine angles. Hence **enne'agonal,** *a.*, having nine angles.
1660 BARROW *Euclid* IV. xi, Then is *AB* the side of Enneagone. **1721–1800** in BAILEY. **1817** H. T. COLEBROOKE *Algebra* 92 The regular pentagon, heptagon, and enneagon.

enneagynous (ɛnɪ'ædʒɪnəs), *a. Bot.* [f. Gr. ἐννέα nine + γυν-ή woman + -OUS.] Having nine pistils.
In mod. Dicts.

enneahedral (ˌɛnɪə'hiːdrəl), *a.* Also 9 enneaedral. [f. Gr. ἐννέα nine + ἕδρα base + -AL^1.] Having nine faces.
1802 BOURNON in *Phil. Trans.* XCII. 253 Which..render the pyramids enneaedral.

†'**ennealogue.** *nonce-wd.* [f. Gr. ἐννέα + λόγ-ος word, after the analogy of DECALOGUE.]
1655 FULLER *Ch. Hist.* II. iv. §42 When this [commandment] was wanting, the Decalogue was but an ennealogue.

†'**ennean,** *a. Obs.*$^{-0}$ [f. Gr. ἐννέα + -AN.]
1623 COCKERAM, *Ennean number*, the number of nine.

enne'andrian, *a. Bot.* [f. mod.L. *enneandria* one of the Linnean classes (f. as next) + -AN.] = next.

enneandrous (ɛnɪ'ændrəs), *a. Bot.* [f. Gr. ἐννέα nine + ἀνδρ- male + -OUS.] Having nine stamens.
1870 BENTLEY *Bot.* 246 A flower having 9 stamens is Enneandrous.

enneapetalous (ˌɛnɪə'pɛtələs), *a. Bot.* [f. Gr. ἐννέα nine + πέταλ-ον leaf + -OUS.] Having nine petals. So **ennea'phyllous** *a.* [Gr. φύλλον leaf], having nine leaves or leaflets. **ennea'sepalous** [SEPAL], having nine sepals. **ennea'spermous** [Gr. σπέρμα seed], having nine seeds.
1847 in CRAIG; and in mod. Dicts.

enneastyle ('ɛnɪəstaɪl), *a. Arch.* [f. Gr. ἐννέα nine + στῦλος column.] Having nine columns or pillars.
1875 *Encycl. Brit.* II. 410/2 An enneastyle arrangement.

enneatic (ɛnɪ'ætɪk), *a. rare.* [f. Gr. ἐννέ-α + -ATIC.] Occurring once in nine times, days, or years, etc.; ninth.

enne'atical, *a.* [f. as prec. + -AL^1.] = prec. †*enneatical day*: every ninth day of a disease. †*enneatical year*: every ninth year of life.
1751 CHAMBERS *Cycl.* **1847** in CRAIG; and in mod. Dicts.

ennet: see EN- *pref.*^{1} 1 a.

†**e'nnew,** *v.*^{1} *Obs.* Also 7 ennue. [f. EN-^{1} + NEW.] *trans.* **a.** To make new; to restore. **b.** To make anew; to repeat.
1382 WYCLIF *Ecclus.* xxxvi. 6 Ennewe thou signes, and chaunge merueiles. **1523** SKELTON *Garl. Laurel* 389 Maister Chaucer..nobly enterprised How that Englishe myght freshely be ennewed. **1623** COCKERAM, Made New, *Ennued.*

†**e'nnew,** *v.*^{2} *Painting. Obs.* Also 5–6 ennue, enewe. [perh. f. EN-^{1} F. *nuer* to shade, tint see quots. s.v. *nuer* in Godef.).] *trans.* To tint, shade; to graduate (colours). Also *fig.*
1430 LYDG. *Chron. Troy* I. v, The medlynge in conclusion So was ennewed by proportion That fynally excesse was there none. *Ibid.* II. x, I must procede with sable and with blacke And in ennuyng where ye fynde a lacke. **1470–85** MALORY *Arthur* III. ix. (1889) 110 The one shylde was enewed with whyte and the other shelde was reed. **1507** in Hazl. *E.P.P.* II. 123 Roses ennued moost swetely By dame nature. **1530** PALSGR. 536/2 I ennewe, I set the laste and freshest coloure upon a thing, as paynters do whan their worke shall remayne to declare their connynge. *Je renouuelle.* **1573** *Art of Limning* 5 This colour shalbe enewed (that is to say) darked or sadded with blacke ynke.

enniche: see EN- *pref.*^{1} 1 a.

ennoble (ɛ'nəʊb(ə)l), *v.* Also 7–8 enoble, 6–8 innoble, 7 inoble. [ad. F. *ennoblir*, f. *en-* (see EN- *pref.*^{1}) + *noble*, NOBLE *a.*] *trans.*
1. To give the rank of nobleman to (a person).
1594 SHAKS. *Rich. III*, I. iii. 81 To ennoble those That scarse, some two dayes since were worth a Noble. *a* **1638** MEDE *On Deut.* xxxiii. 8 Wks. I. 179 Levi was enobled.. specially as being of kin to Moses the Prince of the Congregation. **1791** *Gent. Mag.* LXI. 1105 His [Columbus'] family was ennobled. **1812** H. & J. SMITH *Horace in Lond.* 122 Virtue builds herself a throne, Ennobling whom she touches. **1845** LD. CAMPBELL *Chancellors* (1857) II. xxxviii. 146 Most of the Executors ennobled themselves, or took a step in the Peerage.
2. To impart nobility to (a person or thing). Formerly also, to attribute nobility to.
1502 *Ord. Crysten Men* I. iv. (W. de W. 1506) 43 Enryched and ennobled with holy mysteryes. **1583** STUBBES *Anat. Abus.* II. 103 The more to innoble and set foorth the excellencie of this honorable calling of a bishop. **1601** SHAKS. *All's Well* II. iii. 179 She..so ennobled, Is as 'twere borne so. **1647** R. STAPYLTON *Juvenal* 149 Cicero innobled the meannesse of his birth. **1838** EMERSON *Addr. Cambr. Mass.* Wks. (Bohn) II. 191 He who does a good deed, is instantly ennobled. **1876** GREEN *Short Hist.* viii. §i. (1882) 451 The meanest peasant felt himself ennobled as a child of God.
3. To impart a higher character to (a person or thing); to dignify, elevate, refine.
1636 E. DACRES tr. *Machiavel's Disc. Livy* II. 511 Mens hands and tongues two of their worthiest instruments to ennoble them. **1667** MILTON *P.L.* IX. 992 Much won that he his Love Had so enobl'd. **1713** BERKELEY *Ess.* ix. in *Guardian* No. 70 Wks. III. 174 The Christian Religion ennobleth and enlargeth the mind. **1784** COWPER *Task* v. 603 The loss of all That can enoble man. **1825** in Hone *Every-day Bk.* I. 441 These palaces [are] now ennobled into a refuge. **1846** TRENCH *Mirac.* i. (1862) 118 The Son of God ..ennobling all that He touches.
†**4.** To render famous or illustrious. *Obs.*
1565 GOLDING *Caesar* 266 b Surus, a Heduan, a man both for manhood and birth greatlye ennobled. *a* **1626** BACON (J.), The Spaniards..ennobled some of the coasts thereof with shipwrecks. **1679** PLOT *Staffordsh.* (1686) 407 Tho' the place..were enobled with the martyrdoms of a 1000 Christians. **1725** POPE *Odyss.* XXII. 313 Bear Thy death, ennobl'd by Ulysses' spear. **1775** ADAIR *Amer. Ind.* 378 They have..enobled themselves by war actions.
5. Of light: To render conspicuous. *Obs. rare.*
1665 BOYLE *Occas. Refl.* v. iv. (1675) 310 The light that ennobles him, tempts Inquisitive men to keep him..from sleeping. **1667** —— *Orig. Formes & Qual.*, Striæ, that enoble the darker Body.

ennobled (ɛ'nəʊb(ə)ld), *ppl. a.* [f. prec. + -ED^1.]
1. Made noble in rank, nature, or character.
1586 A. DAY *Eng. Secretary* (1625) Aij, Your L. may please of your owne ennobled condition to wel-doing..to vouchsafe your liking to this latter. **1607** ROWLANDS *Hist. Guy Warw.* 3 Right worthily Enobled and truly Honourable Lord. **1793** SOUTHEY *Tri. Wom.* 393 Raised supreme the ennobled race among. **1858** ROBERTSON *Lect.* i. 25 The newly ennobled looks down upon the newly rich.
†**2.** Celebrated, famous, noted. *Obs.*
1571 GOLDING *Calvin on Ps.* xxii. 14 The hill of Basan was ennobled for battling and rank pastures. **1601** HOLLAND *Pliny* I. 136 Other cities there are..in Mesopotamia.. innobled for their learning.

ennoblement (ɛ'nəʊb(ə)lmənt). [f. as prec. + -MENT.] The action of ennobling; the state or fact of being ennobled. †*concr.* Something that ennobles.
1622 BACON *Hen. VII*, 15 He added to his former creations, the Innoblement or aduancement in Nobilitie of a few others. **1665** GLANVILL *Scep. Sci.* i. 2 Æternal Wisdome..inrich't us with all those enoblements. **1840** MARRYAT *Olla Podr.* xxx, They look to ennoblement in the Academy. **1852** *Fraser's Mag.* XLVI. 243 They never heard of the man's name..before they heard of his ennoblement. **1871** H. B. FORMAN *Living Poets* 266 The..faculties.. necessary for the flawless ennoblement of so serious a subject.

ennobler (ɛ'nəʊblə(r)). [f. as prec. + -ER.] One who or that which ennobles.
1782 *Poetry* in *Ann. Reg.* 188 The prime ennobler of th' aspiring mind. **1814** CARY *Dante* (Chandos) 318 Ennobler of thy nature. **1875** LOWELL in *N. Amer. Rev.* CXX. 357 But the sweetener and ennobler of the street and the fireside.

e'nnobling, *vbl. sb.* [f. ENNOBLE *v.* + -ING^1.] The action of the verb ENNOBLE.
1596 HARINGTON *Metam. Ajax* (1814) For the enobling of this rare invention. **1614** SELDEN *Titles Hon.* Pref., Particular ennobling, by the Princes autoritie, came in vse.

ennobling (ɛ'nəʊb(ə)lɪŋ), *ppl. a.* [f. as prec. + -ING^2.] That ennobles; elevating, refining.
1790 BURKE *Fr. Rev.* Wks. V. 255 He feels no ennobling principle in his own heart. **1818** BYRON *Ch. Har.* IV. clxxvii, Ye Elements!—in whose ennobling stir I feel myself exalted. **1868** M. PATTISON *Academ. Org.* §5. 167 The ennobling influences of the pursuit of knowledge.
Hence **e'nnoblingly** *adv.*
1823 MOORE *Rhymes Road* v. 14 All that in man most ennoblingly towers.

†**e'nnoblish,** *v. Obs.* Also 5 ennoblessh, 7 enoblish. [ad. F. *ennobliss-* lengthened stem of *ennoblir*: see ENNOBLE.] *trans.* = ENNOBLE in various senses; also, to distinguish by favours or gifts.
1483 CAXTON *Gold. Leg.* 219/2 He ennoblesshed seynt John to fore al other with the swetnes of his famyliarite. **1572** BOSSEWELL *Armorie* 16 b, Because they..ennoblish their owne Houses, whereof they descended. **1582** BENTLEY *Mon. Matrones* II. 16 That I so vile a creature, am so ennoblished by thee to so honourable an husband. **1599** HAKLUYT *Voy.* II. II. 75 These streames and barges do ennoblish very much the City, and make it..seeme another Venice. **1600** DYMMOK *Ireland* (1843) 37 His other acts haue enoblished him for a most worthy soldier. **1610** GUILLIM *Heraldry* I. ii. (1660) 14 To persons ennoblished by the Soveraign, by precious Stones. **1610** HOLLAND *Camden's Brit.* Irel. II. 94 To augment his honour by more enoblishing him with honourable Armes. **1630** R. JOHNSON *Kingd. & Commw.* 402 Ennoblished it [Saros Patak] is besides with the greatest College belonging to the reformed religion in all these parts.
Hence †**e'nnoblishment,** *Obs.* = ENNOBLEMENT.
1591 (*title*), A Reuocation of all such Letters for Ennoblishment, as haue not been verified in the Chamber of accountes of Normandy. **1610** HOLLAND *Camden's Brit.* (1637) 175 He that hath obtained such letters of ennoblishment is enabled to be dubbed knight.

†**e'nnoblize,** *v. Obs.* Also 7 enoblize. [ad. Fr. *ennobliss-* lengthened stem of *ennoblir*, assimilated to vbs. in -IZE. See ENNOBLISH.]
trans. To confer nobility upon, make noble; *lit.* and *fig.*
1598 BARCKLEY *Felic. Man* III. (1603) 263 Let him endevour to ennoblize himselfe by his owne vertue. **1601** W. PARRY *Trav. Sir A. Sherley* (1863) 32 If the king purpose to make any man great by enoblizing him. **1635** BARRIFFE *Mil. Discip.* (1643) Ep. Ded. 2 Many Heroicall Ancestours.. have ennobliz'd your potent Family. **1654** COKAINE *Dianea* II. 111 He was the most celebrated King..that enoblized the Glories of his bloud, by the wonders of his Vertue.

en noir: see EN *prep.*

[**ennoisies,** misreading for ENVOISIES.]

†**e'nnoy,** *sb. Obs.* Also 5–6 ennoye. [Variant of ANNOY *sb.* (q.v.)] A troubled state of mind, grief, vexation; also *concr.* a cause of trouble.
1491 CAXTON *Vitas Patr.* (W. de W. 1495) II. 272 a/1 That other heuynesse that corrupteth the soule..tholde faders called it ennoye or greuaunce. **1513** DOUGLAS *Æneis* Contents Bk. 3 The secund buik schawis the finale ennoy The great mischeif, and subversioun of Troye. *Ibid.* XI. iv. 54, I mycht haue ȝald this saule full of ennoy.

†e'nnoy, *v. Obs.* Also 5 enoye, ennuye. [Variant of ANNOY *v.*, after OF. *ennoyer*.]

1. *trans.* in *pass.* To be ruffled in mind, troubled, vexed; = ANNOY 3. Const. *of*; also const. *to* with *inf.* To find (a thing) irksome.

1485 CAXTON *Paris & V.* 36 Whereof he was sore ennoyed in hymself. **1491** —— *Vitas Patr.* (W. de W. 1495) I. i. 6 a/2 He was ennoyed to contynue his prayers. *c* **1500** *Melusine* 192 Many one were wery and ennuyed [*misprinted* enimyed] of theire harneys.

2. *absol.* **a.** To do harm; = ANNOY 4 b. **b.** To be irksome, produce tedium.

c **1420** *Pallad. on Husb.* II. 163 Yf Est or Southeryn wyndes nought enoye. *c* **1430** *Pilgr. Lyf Manhode* I. cliii. (1869) 76 With oute jntervalle alle thing enoyeth; both the faire weder, and thicke of reyn.

Hence **e'nnoying**, *vbl. sb.*

c **1430** *Pilgr. Lyf Manhode* II. lxvi. (1869) 101, I am þilke þat shortliche maketh the time passe with oute enoyinge.

†ennoynt, obs. variant of ANOINT.

†e'nnoyous, *a. Obs. rare.* Also 5 ennoyes. [ad. OF. *ennoyeus*, *ennieus* (mod.F. *ennuyeux*): see ANNOYOUS.] Annoying, troublesome; harmful.

c **1420** *Pallad. on Husb.* IV. 612 Yf amites unto thayme ennoyes be. **1481** CAXTON *Myrr.* II. xxvii. 120 The tempeste . . is greuous & ennoyous to many thynges.

†e'nnoysance. *Obs. rare*$^{-1}$. [Var. of ANNUISANCE.] A state of ennui; weariness.

1502 *Ord. Crysten Men* IV. xxx. (W. de W. 1506) 350 By heuynes in all thynges falleth in languour & in ennoysaunce of his lyfe.

‖**ennui** (ɑ̃nɥi), *sb.* [a. Fr. *ennui*, OF. *enui*:—L. *in odio*: see ANNOY, ENNOY, which are older adoptions of the same Fr. word.

So far as frequency of use is concerned, the word might be regarded as fully naturalized; but the pronunciation has not been anglicized, there being in fact no Eng. analogy which could serve as a guide.]

The feeling of mental weariness and dissatisfaction produced by want of occupation, or by lack of interest in present surroundings or employments.

[**1667** EVELYN *Mem.* (1857) III. 161 We have hardly any words that do . . fully express the French naivete, ennui, bizarre, etc. **1732** BERKELEY *Alciphr.* II. §17 They should prefer doing anthing to the *ennui* of their own conversation.] **1758** CHESTERF. *Lett.* IV. 117 In less than a month the man, used to business, found that living like a gentleman was dying of ennui. **1789** MRS. PIOZZI *Journ. France* II. 388 Muse! prepare some sprightly sallies To divert ennui at Calais. **1801** MAR. EDGWORTH *Angelina* i. 10 She felt insupportable ennui from the want of books and conversation suited to her taste. **1871** DARWIN *Desc. Man* I. ii. 42 Animals manifestly enjoy excitement and suffer from ennui.

b. Personified. **c.** *concr.* A cause of ennui.

1790 CATH. GRAHAM *Lett. Educ.* 290 It would entirely subdue the dæmon Ennui. **1812** H. & J. SMITH *Rej. Addr., Cui Bono* i, The fiend Ennui awhile consents to pine. **1847** W. E. FORSTER in T. W. Reid *Life* (1888) I. vii. 208 We drove to a first-class hotel . . a stylish, comfortless temple of ennui. **1849** C. BRONTË *Shirley* vii. 87 Every stitch she put in was an ennui.

ennui, *v.* [f. prec. sb.; only in pa. pple., which is occas. spelt with *y*, after Fr. *ennuyer*.] *trans.* To affect with ennui; to bore, weary.

1805 SYD. SMITH *Moral Philos.* xviii. (1850) 266 They [animals] rejoice, play, are ennuied as we are. **1808** *Edin. Rev.* XI. 360 If the common people are ennui'd with the fine acting of Mrs. Siddons. **1865** *Cornh. Mag.* July 58 The Shoddy lady . . ennuied with the superb house and uncongenial surroundings. **1888** *Pall Mall G.* 20 Aug. 1/1 The Roman public, jaded and ennuyed, found life not worth living without the stimulus of the sight of death.

Hence **ennuying**, *ppl. a.* (*rare.*)

1858 MRS. CARLYLE *Lett.* II. 388 Evenings . . sacred to reading on his part, and mortally ennuying to myself.

†en'number, *v. Obs. rare.* [f. EN-^{1} + NUMBER; cf. ANNUMBER.] *trans.* To number.

1535 *Goodly Primer* Expos. Ps. li, That I may be ennumbered among them.

‖**ennuyé** (ɑ̃nɥije), *a.* [Fr.: pa. pple. of *ennuyer* to bore.] Affected with ennui.

1757 GRAY *Let. Hurd*, 25 Aug., I am alone, and *ennuyé* to the last degree yet do nothing. **1822** T. MITCHELL *Aristoph.* II. 18 A sort of ennuyé, triste, pitiable busy-idler. **1847** DISRAELI *Tancred* v. vii. (1871) 394 He must be terribly ennuyé here.

b. quasi-*sb.* (also *fem.* **ennuyée**), one who is troubled with ennui.

1826 MRS. JAMESON (*title*), Diary of an Ennuyée.

Eno ('iːnəʊ). *Pharm.* [The name of J. C. *Eno* (*c* 1828–1915), English pharmacist, who first sold it.] A proprietary name for a laxative and antacid containing sodium bicarbonate, tartaric acid, and citric acid. Also *Eno's* (*Fruit Salt*) (also proprietary).

1889 F. D. LUGARD *Diary* 8 Dec. (1959) I. 48/2 Eno's Fruit Salts. **1894** E. A. EVEREST *Let.* 14 Feb. in R. S. Churchill *Winston S. Churchill* (1967) I. Compan. I. vii. 443 Take some Eno it will purify the Blood. **1908** *Trade Marks Jrnl.* 30 Sept. 1598 *Eno's Fruit Salt*... A medicinal preparation, for human use. J. C. Eno, Limited, London. *a* **1914** J. JOYCE *Stephen Hero* (1944) xvii. 43 You have connected Ibsen and Eno's fruit salt forever in my mind. **1920** *Trade Marks Jrnl.* 12 May 902 *Eno*... A saline, being a medicinal preparation included in Class 3. J. C. Eno, Limited. **1924** J. BUCHAN *Three Hostages* ix. 127 'I can take it that there's nothing wrong with me?' 'Nothing that a game of squash and a little Eno won't cure'. **1942** E. WAUGH *Put out more Flags* 27 There was an unfamiliar buoyancy in his bearing as though he had been at somebody's Eno's. **1976** *Southern Even. Echo* (Southampton) 18 Nov. 10/2 They've got a better chance than most thanks to the wave of bonhomie that washes over us like a dose of Boxing Day Eno's.

Enochian (iː'nɒkɪən), *a.* [f. *Enoch* + -IAN.] Of, belonging to, or characteristic of Enoch (see Gen. v. 24), or the apocryphal Book of Enoch. Also **E'nochic** *a.*

1893 R. H. CHARLES *Bk. Enoch* 313 The term 'the Son of Man' . . may have been derived from a current Enochic usage. **1902** *Encycl. Brit.* XXV. 496/1 Slavonic Book of Enoch... This new fragment of the Enochic literature has only recently come to light. **1919** S. C. CARPENTER *Christianity acc. Luke* iv. 41 [Our Lord's] actual use of the Enochian conception [of the Messiah]. **1920** V. BURCH in Harris & Burch *Testimonies* II. x. 85 Peter's use of the Enochic writings makes in the direction of a close relation between his citations from them and his citations from Isaiah.

enoculate, obs. f. INOCULATE.

†e'nodable, *a. Obs.*$^{-0}$ [ad. L. *ēnōdabilis*, f. *ēnōdāre*: see next.] Capable of being made clear, or of being freed from knots.

1623 COCKERAM II, To be Loosed, *Enodable.*

†e'nodate, *v. Obs.* [f. L. *ēnōdāt-* ppl. stem of *ēnōdā-re*, f. *ē* out + *nōd-us* knot.] *trans.* To free from knots; also *fig.* to unravel, clear of difficulties.

1656 BLOUNT *Glossogr.*, *Enodate*, to unknit, to cut away the knot, to declare or make manifest, to untie. **1681** *Relig. Clerici* 51 When they cannot enodate your argument, they serve you . . the same trick that Alexander did with the Gordian knot.

Hence **†eno'dation**, the action of loosing or unravelling.

1603 HOLLAND *Plutarch's Mor.* 1024 Thus much for the enodation of this knot. **1623** COCKERAM, *Enodation*, a declaration. **1653** W. SCLATER *2nd Fun. Serm.* (1654) 28 Scarcely any thing, that way, proved too hard for him, for his enodation or descision. **1736** in BAILEY.

enode (iː'nəʊd) *a. Bot.* [ad. L. *ēnōdis* free from knots (f. *ē* out + *nōd-us* knot).] Free from knots.

In mod. Dicts.

†e'node, *v. Obs. rare.* [ad. L. *ēnōdāre*: see ENODATE.] *trans.* To loose, untie (a knot); also *fig.* to solve (a riddle).

1623 COCKERAM, *Enode*, to declare. **1657** TOMLINSON *Renou's Disp.* Pref., Enode the knot, and throw open the gates. **1684** WILLARD *Mercy magn.* 4 Riddles which require great study to enode them.

†e'nodous, *a. Obs.* [f. L. *ēnōd-is* (see ENODE *a.*) + -OUS.] Free from knots.

1657 TOMLINSON *Renou's Disp.* 373 Others [orenges] are enodous and sterile.

†e'noil, *v. Obs.* Also 5–7 enoyle. [f. EN-^{1} + OIL *sb.* Cf. ANOIL, ENHUILE.]

1. *trans.* To put oil upon. **a.** To anoint, *esp.* a king, etc. **b.** To mix with oil. Cf. ENHUILE.

c **1420** *Pallad. on Husb.* I. 687 Half a strike Of barly mele enoyled. **1546** LANGLEY *Pol. Verg. De Invent.* v. iii. 100 b, Priestes and also Kynges . . oughte to be enoyled. **1575** TURBERV. *Falconrie* 279 She may . . enoyle hir feathers with hir beake. **1643** PRYNNE *Sov. Power Parl.* II. 93 Other kings persons . . who are not annointed, are as sacred . . as those who are enoyled.

2. *transf.* and *fig.*

1526 *Pilgr. Perf.* (W. de W. 1531) 115 Thou shalt enoyle & mollifye his herte that enuyeth the. **1647** SANDERSON *Serm.* (1681) II. 216 To enoil a rotten post with a glistering varnish.

†e'noiling, *vbl. sb.* [f. ENOIL *v.* + -ING.] The action of the vb. ENOIL. **a.** The action of anointing, *esp.* a king. **b.** The sacrament of extreme unction. Also *concr.* The oil used for anointing.

1526 *Pilgr. Perf.* (W. de W. 1531) 222 He ordeyned also the sacrament of extreme vnccyon or enoylynge. **1555** *Fardle Facions* II. xii. 279 The godfathers, to the ende the enoilyng [in confirmacion] should not droppe awaie . . clappe on a faire filette on the foreheade. **1643** PRYNNE *Sov. Power Parl.* III. 93 This enoyling . . derives no personall Prerogatives or Immunities at all to kings.

†e'noine, *v. Obs. rare.* [a. OF. *enoign-* present stem of *enoindre*, *enuindre*:—L. *inung(u)-ĕre*, f. *in* on + *ung(u)-ĕre* to anoint. Displaced by the form *enoint*, ANOINT, from the pa. pple.] *trans.* = ANOINT.

1340–70 *Alex. & Dind.* 410 Fonde wiþ fals craft hure face to enoine.

enoint, obs. form of ANOINT.

†e'noisel, *v. Obs.*$^{-0}$ [a. OF. *enoisel-er*, f. *en-* (see EN-^{1}) + *oiseler* 'to flye out at birds, like a giddie Hawke' (Cotgr.), f. *oisel* (mod. *oiseau*) bird.]

intr. Of a hawk: To fly at a bird.

c **1535** DEWES *Introd. Fr.* in Palsgr. 952 To enoisel as a hauke.

enol ('iːnɒl). *Chem.* [f. -EN(E + -OL.] Any organic compound that contains the unsaturated alcoholic group ·CH:C(OH)· and is a tautomeric form of a corresponding keto compound. Hence **e'nolic** *a.*, of or pertaining to an enol; **'enolase**, a crystalline enzyme that acts as a catalyst; **'enolate**, a metallic derivative of an enol; **enoli'zation**, conversion into enols or enolic groups.

1894 *Jrnl. Chem. Soc.* LXVI. II. 433 Compounds containing the group :C:C(OH) are said to be 'enolic'. *Ibid.* 434 No evidence supporting the existence of the tautomeric enolic form sometimes attributed to malonic acid was obtained. **1937** *Nature* 31 July 198/1 An *in vitro* intramolecular shifting of the enol linkage along the carbon chain in hexoses... Such a shifting of enol linkages would make it possible to understand how *l*-lactic acid can derive from *d*-glucose *in vivo*. *Ibid.*, The enolase and dismutase of hexosediphosphate breakdown. *Ibid.*, The occurrence of enolization and dismutation would explain the inhibition of glucolysis proper by fluoride and iodoacetate. **1946** *Ibid.* 21 Dec. 910/1 Furthermore, N-phenylsydnone exhibits its relationship to enols in that it undergoes instantaneous bromination in glacial acetic acid solution. **1962** S. G. WALEY in A. Pirie *Lens Metabolism Rel. Cataract* 354 The product (the enolate) has the negative charge on the oxygen atom. **1964** N. G. CLARK *Mod. Org. Chem.* xv. 297 It is possible to prepare one or other of the pure tautomers from ordinary ethyl acetoacetate by reason of the greater volatility of the 'enol' form. **1965** PHILLIPS & WILLIAMS *Inorg. Chem.* I. xvii. 646 Other interesting carbon carriers are enolates which pick up CO_2 via a carbanion mechanism.

enology: see ŒNOLOGY.

enomotarch (ɛ'nɒmətɑːk). *Gr. Antiq.* [ad. Gr. ἐνωμοτάρχ-ης, f. ἐνωμοτ-ια + ἄρχειν to command.] The commander of an ENOMOTY.

1623 BINGHAM *Xenophon* 54 The Coronels . . appointed Captaines ouer them . . Penteconters, and Enomotarches. **1850** GROTE *Greece* II. lvi. VII. 109 The [Spartan] soldier thus received no immediate orders except from the enomotarch.

enomoty (ɛ'nɒməti). *Gr. Antiq.* [ad. Gr. ἐνωμοτία a band of sworn soldiers, f. ἐν in + ὀμνύναι to swear.] A division in the Spartan army.

1623 BINGHAM *Xenophon* 54 They filled the middest . . if very wide by Enomoties. **1838** THIRLWALL *Greece* V. xxxviii. 75 The *enomoty*, of thirty-six men, stood in three files.

enophthalmus, -mos (ɛnɒf'θælməs, -ɒs). *Ophthal.* [mod.L., f. Gr. ἐν in + ὀφθαλμός eye.] Abnormal retraction of the eyeball into the orbit.

1883 *Index-Catal. Libr. Surg.-General's Office, U.S. Army* IV. 253 (*heading*) Enophthalmus. **1892** GRADLE in *Hare's Syst. Pract. Therap.* 1075 The . . receding of the eyeball into the orbit, enophthalmos, is apparently produced by any condition of emaciation or extreme anæmia. **1907** *Practitioner* Nov. 734 The intermittent exophthalmos occurs when the head is depressed, such as occurs in stooping, whereas enophthalmos follows when the head is in the erect position. **1964** S. DUKE-ELDER *Parsons' Dis. Eye* (ed. 14) x. 109 When all the sympathetic function on one side is lost, resulting in miosis, a narrowed palpebral fissure and slight enophthalmos (due to loss of tone of Müller's muscle) [etc.].

enoptromancy (ɛ'nɒptrəʊmænsɪ). In Dicts. erron. enopto-. [ad. F. *énoptromancie*, f. Gr. ἔνοπτρο-ν mirror + μαντεία: see -MANCY.] Divination by means of a mirror.

1855 SMEDLEY *Occult Sc.* 321 Enoptromancy, is a species of divination by the mirror.

enorder: see EN- *pref.*^{1} 3.

enorganic (ɛnɔː'gænɪk), *a. rare.* [f. EN-^{2} + ORGANIC.] Inherent in the organism.

1846 SIR W. HAMILTON *Dissert.* in Reid *Wks.* 864 The mental effort to move . . I would call the Enorganic volition.

enorm (ɪ'nɔːm). Forms: 5–7 enorme, 6– enorm. [a. Fr. *énorme*:—L. *ēnormis*, f. *ē* out + *norma* mason's square, pattern.]

†1. Deviating from the ordinary rule or type; unusual, extraordinary, extravagant. *Obs.*

c **1510** BARCLAY *Mirr. Good Mann.* (1570) D iiij, A pure minde and simple . . With none enorme maners, nor grieuous spot of crime. **1535** STEWART *Cron. Scot.* III. 53 Seand the se so furius and enorme. **1638** READ *Chirurg.* xxiv. 180 If any enorme wound fall out whereby there is a solution of unity in the jaw bones. **1647** H. MORE *Song of Soul* II. i. II. xxii, Nought scorching, nought glowing, nothing enorm. *a* **1734** NORTH *Exam.* II. v. ¶163 (1740) 420 The Author . . should have . . said not a Word of the Matter, much less given in the enorm Depositions in the very Words.

†2. Of sins and crimes (rarely of persons): Abnormally wicked, monstrous, outrageous. *Obs.*

1481 CAXTON *Myrr.* II. viii. 82 The grete and enorme synnes that they [Sodom and Gomorrha] commysed. **1563–87** FOXE *A. & M.* (1596) 17/2 Heere commeth the enorme and horrible abuse of excommunication. **1570–87** HOLINSHED *Scot. Chron.* (1806) II. 447 The said desperate & enorme persons. **1600** FAIRFAX *Tasso* VIII. lxxi, The neast of treason false and guile enorme. *a* **1639** SPOTTISWOOD *Hist. Ch. Scot.* VI. (1677) 318 The enorm crimes . . whereof he was guilty.

3. Abnormally large, vast, monstrous; = ENORMOUS 3. *arch.*

1581 SAVILE *Tacitus' Agric.* (1622) 188 But there is beside a huge and enorme tract of ground. **1609** HOLLAND *Amm. Marcel* XXXI. ii. 402 The Alani..wander..in..enorme and huge cantons [*pagos immensos*]. *a* **1734** NORTH *Lives* (1826) III. 286 Expecting to see an enorm spectre. **1817** COLERIDGE *Sibyl. Leaves* II. 281 Condensed blackness and abysmal storm..Arms the Grasp enorm. **1871** G. MACDONALD *Wks. Fancy & Imag.* II. 169 Mocking the enorm Strength on its forehead.

b. *Sc. Law.* ***enorm*** *†**hurt**, **lesion*** (in Roman Civil Law *læsio ultra dimidium vel enormis*). An injury (sustained by one of the parties to a contract) which amounts to more than one-half the value of the subject-matter.

c **1550** SIR. J. BALFOUR *Practicks* (1754) 179 (Jam.) All contracts,—made by minoris in thair les age, to thair enorm hurt and skaith, ar of nane avail. **1888** LD. HALSBURY in *Law Times Rep.* (N.S.) LIX. 2/2 Validity, subject to reduction on the ground of enorm lesion, of the contract in question.

4. quasi-*sb.*

1535 STEWART *Cron. Scot.* II. 356 It sould proceid..As neidfull war withoutin ony enorme.

†e'norm, *v. Obs.* In 7 also inorm. [f. prec.] *trans.* To make monstrous. Frequent in Davies.

1602 J. DAVIES *Mirum in Mod.* C iii. Then lets hee Fiends the fantacie enorme With strong delusions and with passions dire. **1612** —— *Muse's Sacrifice* (Grosart) 15 To help my hatefull hands that sinne inorm'd.

†e'normance, *Obs. rare*⁻¹. ? = ENORMITY.

1682 D'URFEY *Butler's Ghost* 142 Tho he each Sabbath bangs his Desk, In laying the Enormance home, And preaching Torments are to come.

†e'normand, *Obs. rare*⁻¹. ? = ENORMITY.

1719 D'URFEY *Pills* (1872) I. 200 When Lawn Sleeves, and Plays Were cry'd down, an equal enormand.

†enor'mantic, *a. Obs.* Also 7 enormontick. [app. f. as if Gr. *ἐνορμαντικ-ός f. ἐν (see EN-*pref.*[2]) + ὁρμαίνειν to set in violent motion.] That sets in motion; impulsive.

1651 BIGGS *New Disp.* 114 Awakened by enormantick power of an exotick motor. **1693** J. BEAUMONT *On Burnet's The. Earth* I. 29 Typhoeus being that Enormontick Spirit..or that protrusive Impetus, still reigning in the Chaos.

†e'norment. *Obs. rare.* = ENORNMENT.

1513 BRADSHAW *St. Werburge* II. 549 The people..Gaue diuers enormentes vnto this place. *Ibid.* II. 1226 Endowed it with riches and enormentes many on.

enormification (ɪˌnɔːmɪfɪ'keɪʃən). *rare*⁻¹. [f. L. *ēnormi-s* ENORM + -FICATION.] The action or process of making enormous.

1881 GRANT WHITE *Eng. Without & Within* vii. 205, I mused wondering..upon that sad gradual enormification by which she passed from a tall blooming beauty into her present tremendous proportions.

†e'normious, *a. Obs.* Also 6 -iouse, -eous, inormious. [f. L. *ēnormi-s* (see ENORM) + -OUS.]

1. Deviating from ordinary rule or type, irregular, extraordinary; = ENORMOUS 1 and 3.

1613 R. C. *Table Alph.* (ed. 3) *Enormious*, out of square, vnorderly. **1622** CALLIS *Stat. Sewers* (1647) 151 And I have ..beheld much enormious proceedings..both in the Commissioners and in their Officers. **1656** *Artif. Handsom.* 60 (T.) The enormious additions of their artificial heights.

2. Of persons or their actions: Extraordinarily wicked, outrageous, monstrous; = ENORMOUS 2.

1545 UDALL tr. *Erasm. Par.* Luke 67 a, Enormeous..sins. **1552** BALE *Apol.* 99 That detestable professyon of a lyfe so enormiouse. **1583** STUBBES *Anat. Abus.* (1877) 47 To give the King to vnderstand the inormious abuse thereof. **1609** BIBLE (Douay) *Jer.* l. comm., God..is severe when he punisheth enormious sinners. **1649** BP. HALL *Cases Consc.* (1650) 420 To prevent some enormious act. **1656** EARL OF MONMOUTH *Advert. from Parnassus* 24 Those inormious and hatefull loathsomenesses. **1665** J. SERGEANT *Sure-footing* 91 If the motions he had to keep him good were very strong and efficacious, he is still more enormious.

Hence **†e'normiously**, *adv.*

a **1641** BP. R. MOUNTAGU *Acts & Mon.* (1642) 59 Those many errors and mistakings, whereinto they so often and enormiously fell. *Ibid.* 68 Thousands of bad Christians, who have..profaned enormiously that sacred name of Unction.

†e'normitan. *Obs. rare*⁻¹. [f. ENORMIT-Y + -AN.] One who exceeds ordinary bounds; one who behaves extravagantly.

1654 H. L'ESTRANGE *Chas. I* (1655) A ij, What St. Augustine said of some enormitans of his time.

enormity (ɪ'nɔːmɪtɪ). Forms: *α.* 5–6 enormyte(e, -ie, -ye, 6–7 -itie, 6– enormity. *β.* 7 inormitie, -y, innormity. [ad. Fr. *énormité*, ad. L. *ēnormitātem*, f. *ēnormis* (see ENORM).]

†1. Divergence from a normal standard or type; abnormality, irregularity. *Obs.* or *arch.*

1538 STARKEY *England* I. iii. 84 The partys in proportyon not agreyng..leue much enormyte..in thys polytyke body. **1647** H. MORE *Song of Soul* II. iii. III. lxx, The strange absurd enormity Of staggering motions in the azure skie. **1865** MOZLEY *Mirac.* v. 95 Pure, boundless enormity, then is itself incredible.

†b. *concr.* Something that is abnormal; an irregularity, extravagance, eccentricity. *Obs.*

1494 FABYAN VI. cxlix. 135 For his dulnesse and his other enormytes in hym exercysyd. *Ibid.* VII. ccxxiv. 251 That tyme clerkes..rode with gylte spurres, with vsynge of dyuerse other enormytees. **1577** VAUTROUILLIER *Luther on Ep. Gal.* 26 And yet we can not remedie this enormitie. **1687** *Death's Vis.* ix. (1713) 41 *note* 4 The Irregularities and Enormities that appear in the Mundane System. **1710** ADDISON *Tatler* No. 250 ¶1 Enormities in Dress and Behaviour. **1781** J. MOORE *View Soc. It.* (1790) I. xxxix. 432 Keep the citizens from reflecting on..the enormities of the new form of government.

2. Deviation from moral or legal rectitude. In later use influenced by ENORMOUS 3: Extreme or monstrous wickedness.

1563 *Homilies* II. *Repentance* II. (1859) 537 Our natural uncleanliness and the enormity of our sinful life. **1777** ROBERTSON *Hist. Amer.* (1778) II. v. 138 Stained an illustrious name by deeds of peculiar enormity and rigour. **1863** BRIGHT *Sp. Amer.* 30 June, The protest..against the enormity of the odious system. **1872** BLACK *Adv. Phaeton* xxvi. 358 Lecture her two boys on the enormity of telling a fib.

b. *concr.* A breach of law or morality; a transgression, crime; in later use, a gross and monstrous offence.

1475 CAXTON *Jason* 134 b, Certes Madame sayd yet Jason for these enormytes know that I have left and repudied her. **1549** COVERDALE *Erasm. Par. Hebr.* 16 Beware that we fal not agayne into our olde enormyties. **1664** H. MORE *Myst. Iniq.* 10 Provided there be but found a colour for these gross enormities. **1713** ADDISON *Guardian* No. 116 ¶1 There are many little enormities in the world which our preachers would fain see removed. **1766** FORDYCE *Serm. Yng. Wom.* (1767) II. xiv. 267 A single look is construed into I know not what enormity. **1842** H. ROGERS *Introd. Burke's Wks.* (1842) I. 28 The enormities of Debi Sing, one of the worst agents of Indian tyranny. **1879** FROUDE *Cæsar* xi. 119 Other enormities Catiline had been guilty of.

†3. Excess in magnitude; hugeness, vastness. *Obs.*; recent examples might perh. be found, but the use is now regarded as incorrect.

1792 *Munchhausen's Trav.* xxii. 93 A worm of proportionable enormity had bored a hole in the shell. **1802** HOWARD in *Phil. Trans.* XCII. 204 Notwithstanding the enormity of its bulk. **1830** *Fraser's Mag.* I. 752 Of the properties of the Peak of Teneriffe accounts are extant which describe its enormity. **1846** DE QUINCEY *Syst. Heavens* Wks. III. 183 The whitish gleam was the mask conferred by the enormity of their remotion. [*Mod.* '"You have no idea of the enormity of my business transactions", said an eminent Stock Exchange speculator to a friend. He was perhaps nearer the truth than he intended'.]

b. *concr.* Something enormous. (*humorous.*)

1825 HONE *Every-day Bk.* I. 436 This waxen enormity [an enormous taper] was lighted.

†enormly (ɪ'nɔːmlɪ), *adv. Obs. rare.* [f. ENORM *a.* + -LY[2].] Enormously, monstrously. Also in *Sc. Law* (cf. *enorm lesion*).

1538 *Prymer Salisb.* in Maskell *Mon. Rit.* II. 273 How enormely thou hast synned. **1540** *Acts Jas. V* (1597) §70 And therethrow we ar greatumlie and enormelie hurte.

enormous (ɪ'nɔːməs), *a.* Also 6 innormous. [f. L. *ēnorm-is* (see ENORM) + -OUS.]

†1. Deviating from ordinary rule or type; abnormal, unusual, extraordinary, unfettered by rules; hence, mostly in bad sense, strikingly irregular, monstrous, shocking. *Obs.*

1531 FRITH *Judgm. on Tracy* (1829) Pref. 246 So shall this enormous fact be looked upon with worthy correction. **1590** BARROW & GREENWOOD in *Confer.* 43 Innumberable enormous Canons & Constitucions of Antichrist. **1620** VENNER *Via Recta* viii. 168 Whether the appetite be enormous, or too irregular. **1667** MILTON *P.L.* v. 297 Nature here plaid at will Her Virgin Fancies, pouring forth more sweet, Wilde above rule or Art; enormous bliss. **1733** POPE *Ess. Man* III. 242 The enormous faith of many made for one. **1774** T. WARTON *Hist. Eng. Poetry* xvi. II. 370 Entered the choir in a military habit, and other enormous disguises. **1818** HALLAM *Mid. Ages* (1872) II. 149 The absurd and enormous provisions of the spurious constitution.

b. Extending beyond definite limits; redundant. *Obs.*

1704 NEWTON *Opticks* (1721) 88 The enormous part of the Light in the circumference of every lucid Point ought to be less discernible in shorter Telescopes than in longer.

†2. Of persons and their actions: Departing from the rule of right, disorderly. Of a state of things: Disordered, irregular. Hence, excessively wicked, flagitious, outrageous. *Obs.*

Expressions like 'enormous wickedness' are now felt as belonging to sense 3, perh. with some slight mixture of the older sense.

1593 BILSON *Govt. Christ's Ch.* 146 Avoyd the companie of such enormous persons. **1612** SHAKS. & FL. *Two Noble K.* v. i, Oh great corrector of enormous times. **1631** WEEVER *Anc. Fun. Mon.* 363 The Popes rapines and enormous proceedings in those dayes. *a* **1677** BARROW *Serm.* (1810) I. 168 Constantine..chose Christianity as the only religion, that promised impunity and pardon for his enormous practices. **1737** HERVEY *Mem.* II. 241 Speaking of the enormous behaviour of the City of Edinburgh in this transaction. **1744** JOHNSON *L.P.*, *Savage* Wks. III. 321 The enormous wickedness of making war upon barbarous nations because they cannot resist. **1827** POLLOK *Course T.* VI, Some last, enormous, monstrous deed of guilt. **1827** SOUTHEY *Hist. Penins. War* II. 65 The enormous wickedness with which they abused their victory. *Ibid.* II. 112 The enormous guilt of destroying the city and its inhabitants.

3. Excessive or extraordinary in size, magnitude, or intensity; huge, vast, immense.

This is the only current sense, and appears to have influenced the later use of senses 1 and 2.

1544 PHAËR *Regim. Lyfe* (1560) I iij, Paine of the stone is one of yᵉ moste enormous paynes that the body of man is vexed with. **1667** MILTON *P.L.* I. 511 Titan Heav'ns first born With his enormous brood. **1774** GOLDSM. *Nat. Hist.* (1776) III. 31 The urus..of the large enormous kind of Lithuania. **1827** POLLOK *Course T.* I, Worn and wasted with enormous woe. **1836** MACGILLIVRAY tr. *Humboldt's Trav.* xxvii. 421 The line of enormous cracks and fissures. **1848** MACAULAY *Hist. Eng.* I. 190 The fortress of Tangier..was repaired and kept up at an enormous charge. **1860** TYNDALL *Glac.* I. §2. 11 These avalanches..consist of enormous blocks of ice.

†b. Overgrown in power or importance. *Obs.*

1641 MILTON *Ch. Discip.* I. (1851) 11 Doe wee suffer misshapen and enormous Prelatisme..thus to blanch and varnish her deformities. **1759** ROBERTSON *Hist. Scot.* II. 97 This great princess and her enormous subject.

4. quasi-*adv.*

1566 DRANT *Wail. Hierim.* K viij, My peoples crymes.. were more innormous vyle Then Sodom sinne.

enormously (ɪ'nɔːrməslɪ), *adv.* [f. ENORMOUS + -LY[2].] In an enormous manner.

†1. a. Abnormally, eccentrically, irregularly. **b.** Lawlessly, criminally, immorally. *Obs.*

1617 HIERON *Wks.* II. 289 He, that preacheth most enormously, professeth the cleane contrarie. *a* **1619** DONNE *Βιαθανατος* (1644) 94 There Bull-baytings, to which they are so enormously addicted. **1686** BOYLE *Enq. Notion Nat.* 260 From which the monster does enormously deviate. **1689** *Myst. Iniq.* 20 Popery..provides for their living as enormously as they please. **1713** DERHAM *Phys. Theol.* (1786) I. 408 Had man's body been made..too enormously gigantic, it would, etc.

2. To a vast extent; vastly, hugely, prodigiously.

a **1728** WOODWARD (J.), A notion so enormously absurd and senseless. **1741–2** WALPOLE *Lett. H. Mann* (1834) I. xviii. 66 It will be enormously long, but I have prepared you for it. **1797** BURKE *Regic. Peace* iii. Wks. VIII. 381 The rise in the last year..is enormously out of all proportion. **1860** TYNDALL *Glac.* II. §20. 338 The alleged temperature was so enormously below the freezing point. **1867** DICKENS *Lett.* (1880) II. 306 The city has increased enormously.

e'normousness. [f. as prec. + -NESS.]

†1. Divergence from a right moral standard; also in stronger sense, gross wickedness, heinousness; = ENORMITY 2. *Obs.*

a **1631** DONNE *Serm.* xvi. 159 Such is the infinitenesse and Enormousnesse of our rebellious Sin. **1667** *Decay Chr. Piety* ii. §5. 210 Those who have not opportunity to examine our faith, see the enormousness of our works.

2. The quality of being excessive in size; vastness, hugeness.

1802 C. WILMOT *Let.* 15 Nov. in *Irish Peer* (1920) 114 The Gothic Cathedral [at Milan]..is not yet finish'd from the enormousness of the expense. **1885** W. C. RUSSELL *Strange Voy.* II. vii. 110 The enormousness of the ocean.

†e'norn, *v. Obs.* Also 4–6 enn-, enourne(n, (4 enhorne, en(n)urn(e, ennowrn), enorn(e, 5 enoorne, 6 -ourne. [Altered form of ANORN, q.v.]

1. *trans.* To adorn, deck, trim; to set out (a table); = ANORN; also *fig.*

c **1325** *E.E. Allit. P.* A. 1026 Þe wonez with-inne enurned ware Wyth alle kynnez perre þat moȝt repayre. *c* **1340** *Gaw. & Gr. Knt.* 2027 His cote..Ennurned vpon veluet vertuuus stonez. *c* **1375** *Sc. Leg. Saints, Margarete* 15 Til enhorne vchis & cronis. **1382** WYCLIF *Ecclus.* xxix. 33 Go, gest, and enourne the bord. *c* **1400** *Destr. Troy* 1675 An auter enournet in nome of a god. *a* **1430** *Pilgr. Lyf. Manhode* III. li. (1869) 162, I was oones arayed and enoorned with you riht queyntliche. **1513** BRADSHAW. *St. Werberge* I. 3431 This sacrat relique..Enowrned with riches sumptuous.

2. To adore, worship. (See ANORN ¶.)

c **1375** *Sc. Leg. Saints, Theodora* 666 Al þai knychtis a-pone kne Ennornyt hyme.

Hence **†e'norning** *vbl. sb. Obs.*, the action of the vb. ENORN; in quot. *concr.* ornamentation. **†e'nornment**, *Obs.*, adornment, ornamentation.

1382 WYCLIF *Ecclus.* xxii. 23 As grauely enournynge [*v.r.* Enuyrownynge] in a briȝt wal. —— *Jer.* ii. 32 Whether forȝete shal the maiden of hir enournement? *c* **1400** MAUNDEV. (Roxb.) xxxii. 145 We hald swilk enournement grete foly. *c* **1483–4** *Will Taylour* (Somerset Ho.), Item, I bequeth to my Cosyn Robert Sturmyn..all the enournamente belonging vnto my Chapell. [**1513** see ENORMENT.]

e'northotrope (ɛ'nɔːθətrəʊp). [f. Gr. ἐν in + ὀρθό-ς upright + -τροπ-ος turning.] A toy consisting of a card on which confused objects are transformed into various figures or pictures, by causing it to revolve rapidly.

In mod. Dicts.

†e'nose, *v. Obs. rare.* Also 5 enoyse. [? a. OF. *enosse-r*, *enoisse-r*, lit. to choke with a bone, f. *en-* (see EN- *pref.*[1]) + *os* bone.] *trans.* ? To choke. Only in Lydgate, in somewhat obscure fig. senses; ? to baffle, perplex, hamper.

1430 LYDG. *Chron. Troy* Prol., Falshed with trouthe that makethe the men enosed To which parte that they shall theym holde. *c* **1430** —— *Bochas* II. xxviii. (1554) 65 With suche false craft neuer to be enoysed. *Ibid.* III. xxi. 93 b, His indigent hert so streitly is enosed To Erebus. *a* **1460** —— *MS. Soc. Antiq.* 134, f. 4 (Halliw.), For ayther muste y playnely hire accuse Or my gilte with this gilt ennose. **1530** PALSGR. 536/1. I ennose, I abuse (the monk of Berye Lydgate). *Ie abuse.*

‖**enosis** (ɛ'nəʊsɪs, 'ɛnəsɪs). [f. mod.Gr. ἕνωσις, f. ἕν-, εἷς one.] The proposed union of Cyprus and

Greece. Also *transf.* Hence **e'notic** *a.*, of enosis; **'enotist**, one who advocates enosis.

1928 [see NONCURANTIST *a.*]. **1948** *Times* 13 Aug. 4/4 The constitutional issue has been to some extent obscured by manifestations in favour of Enosis or self-government. **1954** L. DURRELL *Let.* (1969) 126, I am grappling with the moribund Information Services of the island, trying to make our case against the united howls of Enotists, British pressmen and fact-finding M.P.s. **1955** *Times* 2 July 6/7 The Archbishop and his *enosis* followers remain uncompromising in their demand for immediate self-determination. **1956** *Ann. Reg. 1955* 125 The Turks.. asked for assurances that *enosis* with Greece would not be permitted. **1958** *Punch* 29 Jan. 172/3 He himself [*sc.* Gladstone] was not ablaze with the enotic flame. **1958** *Economist* 18 Oct. 219/1 Next year Somalia is likely to become independent, whereupon the cry of enosis may go up in British Somaliland.

enostosis (ɛnɒ'stəʊsɪs). [f. Gr. ἐν in + ὀστέον bone, on the analogy of ἐξόστωσις.] (See quot.)

1874 JONES & SIEV. *Anat.* 145 If, as occasionally happens, a bony tumour grows inward into the medullary canal of a bone, it is termed an Enostosis.

enough (ɪ'nʌf), *a.*, *sb.*, and *adv.* Forms: 1 **ȝenóȝ**, **ȝenóh**, 2–3 **ȝenoh**, (2 **onoh**), 2–5 **inoch**, 3 **anoȝ**, **inouh**, **inooȝ**, 3–5 **in-**, **ynogh**, **-oȝ(h**, **-oh(g**, **-ouȝ**, **-owȝ**, **-ug(h**, 4 **enogh(t**, **-oȝ**, **-oh**, **enohw**, **ynowh**, 5 **inowhe**, 6 **in-**, **ynowghe**, **enohut**, (4 **anough**, **-ouȝ**, **inoht**, **inogh**, 5 **enoghe**, **ynought**), 4–7 **an-**, **in-**, **ynough(e**, (4 **ynowþȝ**, 5 **inowge**, **ynoughf**, 6–8 **enoff**, **inoffe**, 6 **yenough**, 7 **eno'**, **-ouch**, **-out**, 8 **enought**,) 7–8 **enufe**, **-uff**, 6– **enough**. Also *north.* 4–6 **in-**, **yneuch**, **-ewch(t**, (6 **aneuch(e**, **-gh**, **en(n)ewche**, 7 **æneuche**), 8–9 *Sc.* **eneuch**, **-gh**. See also ENOW¹. [OE. *ȝenóȝ*, later *ȝenóh* adj. (used in acc. neut. as adv.), corresp. to OFris. *enôch*, OS. *ginôg* (Du. *genoeg*), OHG. *ginuog* (MHG. *genuog*, *genuoc*, mod.G. *genug*), ON. *gnógr* (Sw. *nog*, Da. *nok*), Goth. *ganôh-s*:—OTeut. **ganôgo-z*, related to the impers. vb. (pret. -pres.) OE. *ȝeneah*, OHG. *ginah*, Goth. *ganah* 'it suffices', f. OTeut. **ga-* (see Y-) + **nah*, occurring also with different prefix in OE. *beneah* he enjoys, requires, Goth. *binah* it is right or needful. The OTeut. root **nah*:—Aryan **nak* appears also in L. *nancisci* (pa. pple. *nac-tus*) to obtain, Skr. *naç* to reach.

The earlier OE. form *ȝenóȝ*, and the forms with inflexional termination, have their normal phonetic representative in ENOW. In later OE. the ȝ when final after a long vowel became in most dialects *h* (= x), but when medial remained unchanged; thus in this adj. the nom. sing. and the acc. sing. masc. and neut. became *ȝenóh*, whence the mod. *enough*, while the nom. and acc. pl. were *ȝenóȝe*, yielding ENOW as their regular mod. form. Hence in many dialects, though not in all, the word *enough* (or its local equivalent), is employed in the sing. and in the advb. uses, while ENOW serves for the plural. In 18th c. this distinction was recognized (e.g. by Johnson) as standard English; now, however, *enow* is in literary use entirely superseded, exc. as an intentional archaism, by *enough*.

The frequent ME. forms with final *t* may possibly be due to influence of the ON. neut. *gnógt*; cf. however forms like *boght* for BOUGH, *borcht* for *borch*, BOROUGH, etc., where the *t* is merely excrescent.]

A. *adj.* Sufficient in quantity or number.

1. in concord with sb. expressed or implied: **a.** with sb. in sing., which it usually follows. Also with ellipsis of sb. in sing. Also, with intensive force, † ***enough and enough***, and *U.S. dial.* in phr. ***enough sight better***, etc.: cf. SIGHT *sb.*¹ 2 b. (For advbl. phrase † ***time enough***, see TIME.)

a **1000** *Andreas* 1536 (Gr.) Þær wæs ælcum ȝenoȝ fram dæȝes orde drync sona ȝearu! *a* **1200** *Moral Ode* 235 Hi hem deð wa inoch. *c* **1250** *Gen. & Ex.* 3365 Anoȝ adden he ðanne drinc. *a* **1300** *Cursor M.* 4799 (Gött.) Tresur enohut wid ȝu ȝe take. *c* **1330** *Roland & V.* 162 Thow byrd to haue nurtour aneuch. *c* **1400** *Destr. Troy* 13119 Past of his pouer to pouert ynugh. **1475** SIR J. PASTON in *Paston Lett.* No. 754 III. 130, I have pytte yow to cost, charge, and losse i nowge. **1518** *Dispatch* in Ld. Berners *Froiss.* Pref. I. 12 With payne and trauayle anough, we made toward the Cowrte. **1535** STEWART *Cron. Scotl.* (1858) I. 40 It stude rycht stark quhair it had strenth aneuche. **1610** SHAKS. *Temp.* I. ii. 314 There's wood enough within. **1766** GOLDSM. *Vic. W.* iii, He had not resolution enough to give any man pain by a denial. **1780** MAD. D'ARBLAY *Diary* 23 Feb. The play has wit enough and enough, but..incidents don't appear to me interesting. **1816** J. WILSON *City of Plague* II. ii. 36 That thought is happiness Enough for me. **1845** S. JUDD *Margaret* I. xiv. 110 Their music is enough sight better than ours. **1856** A. CARY *Married, not Mated* 63 Granmam likes Hal, in fact, enough sight the best. **1860** TYNDALL *Glac.* I. §11. 74, I..thought that we had light enough, and ought to make use of it. **1887** M. E. WILKINS *Humble Romance* 160 If it's got to be done by anybody I'd enough sight rather 'twoud be done by the town. **1891** —— *New Eng. Nun* 407 They'd keep dusted 'nough sight cleaner. **1911** J. C. LINCOLN *Cap'n Warren's Wards* xvi. 251 It was enough sight damper amongst the seats than in those cloth waves.

b. with sb. in plural. Also with ellipsis of pl. sb. (The OE. and ME. forms with pl. inflexion will be found under ENOW; the early examples below should perh. be regarded as belonging to the absol. use with gen. pl.)

c **1200** *Trin. Coll. Hom.* 35 Mið oðre wowe inohg. *a* **1330** *Rom. Alexander* in *Roland & V.* (1836) Introd. 23 About him com barouns anough. *c* **1500** *God Speed Plough* 78 Then commeth the tipped-staves for the Marshalse, And saye they haue prisoners mo than Inough. **1665** BOYLE *Occas. Refl.* II. viii. (1675) 124 'Tis not many, or few, that are requir'd, but enough. **1818** COBBETT *Pol. Reg.* XXXIII. 108 Now, there are candidates enough, who will pretend that they are for Reform. **1878** BROWNING *La Saisiaz* 12 Two, enough and none to spare.

2. predicatively.

c **1040** *Rule St. Benet* (Logeman) 92 Genoh bið munece twa tunican. *a* **1200** *Moral Ode* 389 in *Trin. Coll. Hom.* 232 Crist sal one ben inoȝh alle his derlinges. *c* **1386** CHAUCER *Clerk's T.* 995 This is y-nough, Grisilde myn. **1535** COVERDALE *2 Sam.* xxiv. 16. It is ynough, holde now thy hande. **1579** SPENSER *Sheph. Cal.* June 79 Enough is me to paint out my vnrest. **1600** SHAKS. *Sonn.* cxxxiii, Is't not ynough to torture me alone. **1649** MILTON *Eikon.* Pref. B., It is anough to remember them the truth of what they know. **1664** BUTLER *Hud.* II. ii. 93 Is't not enough w'are bruised and kicked With sinfull members of the wicked? **1855** MACAULAY *Hist. Eng.* III. 213 It was enough for him that those bills seemed, etc.

3. *absol.* in *sing.* **a.** That which is sufficient; as much as is requisite or desired. Often const. *of* (in OE. partitive genitive). Also const. *to* (†*at*) with inf., or *for* with sb., indicating the purpose. ***to have had enough*** (*of* anything): to have become tired of (it), desire no more.

c **888** K. ÆLFRED *Boeth.* xxiv. §4 He hæfþ on his aȝenum ȝenoh. *a* **1000** *Genesis* 619 (Gr.) Þonne gife ic him þæs leohtes ȝenoȝ. *a* **1200** *Moral Ode* 387 Inoh he haued þe hine haueð. *a* **1300** *Cursor M.* 13501 (Gött.) All þai had enoght at ett. **1340** HAMPOLE *Pr. Consc.* 1466 Now haf we ynogh, now haf we noght. **1377** LANGL. *P. Pl.* B. VII. 86 He hath ynough þat hath bred ynough. **1398** TREVISA *Barth. De P.R.* XII. vii. (1495) 417 They arere not vp theyr heedes whanne they drynke or they haue dronke inough. *c* **1470** HENRY *Wallace* I. 446 Quhen thou wantts gud, cum fech ynewch fra me. **1526** TINDALE *Matt.* xxv. 9 Not so, lest there be not ynought for vs and you. **1562** J. HEYWOOD *Prov. & Epigr.* (1867) 159 As good ynough as a feast. **1568** GRAFTON *Chron.* II. 300, I have and shall have inough to mainteine my poore estate, as long as I live. *c* **1645** *Roxb. Ballads* (1886) VI. 321 And Captain Puff will have enuff To make him brag and vapor. **1697** SOUTH *Serm.* (1737) VI. 126 Carrying enough and enough about him to assure his final doom. **1704** *London. Gaz.* No. 3989/3 The French Man having enough of it, sheared off. **1705** TATE *Warrior's Welcome* ii, Enoff is Dar'd; Secure the Lawrels won. **1722** DE FOE *Col. Jack* (1840) 241, ..I had had enough of fighting. **1767** A. YOUNG *Farmer's Lett. People* 294 The plea of growing enough for family use of wheat, oats, &c. is a mistaken one. **1814** JANE AUSTEN *Mansf. Park* (1851) 65, I have had enough of the family for one morning. **1850** MRS. STOWE *Uncle Tom's C.* xix. 189 Augustine! Augustine!.. I'm sure you've said enough. **1875** JOWETT *Plato* (ed. 2) I. 369, I am in want, and he has enough.

b. ***to have enough to do*** (†*ado*) *to* (accomplish something): to have great difficulty, have to exert all one's powers. (In ME. the explanatory *to do* was not expressed.)

a **1154** *O.E. Chron.* an. 1137 Thre men hadden onoh to bæron onne. *a* **1340** *Cursor M.* 16906 (Cott.) A mikel stan to turn i-nogh had tuent. **1568** GRAFTON *Chron.* II. 265 They thought they should have ynough to do to defende the towne. **1622** BACON *Henry VII.* 246 He had enough to do to saue and helpe. **1746** SIR J. COPE *Rep. Cond.* 126 She would have enough ado to get home.

c. *ellipt.* = 'Enough has been done, said, etc.'; quasi-*interj.*; also followed by *of* in interjectional phrases.

c **1340** *Sir Gaw. & Gr. Knt.* 1948 Inoȝ.. I þonk yow, bi þe rode. **1605** SHAKS. *Macb.* V. viii. 34 And damn'd be him that first cries hold, enough. **1645** CHAS. I *Let. Wife* in *Rep. Comm. Hist. MSS.* App. 6 But anuf of this, I know thy affection. **1712** E. COOKE *Voy. S. Sea* 354 But enought of this, since it was not our Fortune to take her. **1728** POPE *Dunc.* III. 357 Enough! enough! the raptur'd monarch cries. **1808** SCOTT *Marm.* I. xvi, Enough of him.

d. Idiomatically, † ***his enough***: = 'enough for him' (*obs.*). Also (nonce-uses) as sb. with article.

1651 N. BACON *Hist. Disc.* lix. 176 It's his enough. **1655** FULLER *Ch. Hist.* IV. iii. §3 If some Courtiers were to stint the enough of Clergy-men. **1858** HAWTHORNE *Fr. & It. Jrnls.* II. 149 There is no enough short of a little too much.

e. Phr. ***enough is enough***, one must be satisfied with what has been achieved, etc.

1546 J. HEYWOOD *Prov.* II. xi, Here is enough, I am satisfied (saide he) Sens enough is enough (saide I)..For folke saie, enough is as good as a feast. **1721** J. KELLY *Scot. Prov.* 93 Enough is enough of Bread and Cheese. **1834** SOUTHEY *Doctor* I. xx. 199 As for money, enough is enough. **1941** G. B. SHAW *How to become Musical Critic* (1960) 319, I could multiply instances; but enough is enough. **1947** N. STREATFEILD *Grass in Piccadilly* 225 It's been very nice, but enough is enough.

B. *adv.* (In mod.Eng. *enough* nomally follows an adj. or adv. which it qualifies; in OE. and ME. it often preceded it, and occasional instances of this order occur in writings of the present century.)

1. a. Sufficiently; in a quantity or degree that satisfies a desire, meets a want, or fulfils a purpose.

c **888** K. ÆLFRED *Boeth.* xxxvi. §3 Genoȝ sweotole me is þæt ȝesæd. *c* **1200** *Trin. Coll. Hom.* 217 Þis chirche is riche inoh. *c* **1250** *Gen. & Ex.* 600 It adde lested long a-noȝ. *a* **1300** *Cursor M.* 8103 Bi-halden vs inogh has þou. **1513–75** *Diurn. Occurr.* (1833) 59 To assy gif thair ladderis wer convenient and lang aneuch. **1535** COVERDALE *1 Chron.* xxiii. 1 He [Dauid] himselfe was olde, and had lyued ynough. **1597** J. PAYNE *Royal Exch.* 3 Soone ynoughe yf well ynoughe. **1664** EVELYN *Kal. Hort.* (1729), Your choice Tulips..will be more secure, and forward enough. **1667** MILTON *P.L.* IV. 124 Yet not anough had practised to deceive Uriel once warnd. **1716–8** LADY M. W. MONTAGUE *Lett.* I. xix. 59, I hope you know me enough to take my word. **1742** RICHARDSON *Pamela* III. 231 They have vex'd me more than enough. **1804** W. MILFORD *Harmony* 238 Enough aware that, etc. **1809** ROLAND *Fencing* 61 You are not always quick enough to parry as has been recommended. **18..** COLERIDGE *Ch. & State* (1839) 206 Enough thankful. **1875** JOWETT *Plato* (ed. 2) I. 161 He who is moderately good, and does no evil, is good enough for me.

b. quasi-*adj.* qualifying a sb. used as predicate.

1711 ADDISON *Spect.* No. 130 ¶1 The Butler has been Fool enough to be seduced by them. *Mod.* He was not man enough to confess the truth. **1878** HARDY *Return of Native* I. II. ii. 247 Looking at a spot into which she was not climber enough to venture.

c. *ellipt.*, with omission of *done*, i.e. *boiled*, *cooked*, *roasted*, etc. *Obs.* exc. *dial.*

c **1440** *Anc. Cookery* in *Househ. Ord.* (1790) 432 When thai arne ynoughf, take hem up, and let hem kele. **1658** EVELYN *Fr. Gard.* III. iv. (1675) 294 You shall discover, if it be enough boyled, by putting into it a Hens egg; if it sink, it is not yet enough. **1725** BRADLEY *Fam. Dict.* s.v. *Tart*, Bake it in the oven, and when enough, strew Sugar again over it. **1796** MRS. GLASSE *Cookery* iii. 29 As soon as you find the greens are shrunk and fallen to the bottom..they are enough. **1863** ATKINSON *Provinc. Danby*, *Eneugh*, adv., sufficiently cooked, enough done (of any article of food).

2. In vaguer sense (qualifying an adj. or adv.).

a. With intensive force: Fully, quite, abundantly, as much as well could be. Now only in certain customary (chiefly *colloq.*) phrases, as ***sure enough***, ***you know well enough***, etc. Also in weaker sense, implying 'a slight augmentation of the sense of the positive' (J.), as in ***aptly enough***, ***oddly enough***.

c **888** K. ÆLFRED *Boeth.* xxxvi. §3 Ða cwæþ ic; Genoȝ open hit is. *a* **1175** *Cott. Hom.* 223 God wot ȝenoh ȝeare ȝif ȝe of þan treowe aeteð. *a* **1225** *Ancr. R.* 420 Sum wummon inouh reaðe wereð þe brech of heare ful wel i-knotted. *a* **1300** *Fall & Passion* 101 in *E.E.P.* (1862) 15 Ihsu was sikir inoȝ. **1375** BARBOUR *Bruce* I. 286 Hys landis that war fayr Inewch Thai to the lord off clyffurd gave. *c* **1450** *Merlin* iv. 68 And these othir tymes I parceyved it wele I-nough. **1529** MORE *Comf. agst. Trib.* II. Wks. 1204/1 This poynte is..metely playn inough. *a* **1568** *Sempill Ballates* 237 The Quhyt is twiche and fresche ennewche. **1594** *Battell Balrinness* in *Scot. Poems 16th C.* II. 351 For weill aneugh they understood. **1630** LANE *Sqr's T.* p. 151 *note*, This heard, Leyfurco with his mates thus prate, theare wheare weare safe enuff topp of the gate. *a* **1774** GOLDSM. *Double Transf.* 28 Though she felt his usage rough, Yet in a man 'twas well enough. **1783** HAILES *Antiq. Chr. Ch.* ii. 15 Which, aptly enough, might be denominated the journals of the senate. **1871** BROWNING *Hervé Riel*, You shall look long enough ere you come to Hervé Riel.

b. Implying disparagement of the importance or relevance of a conceded proposition.

1606 SHAKS. *Tr. & Cr.* V. i. 57 An honest fellow enough ..but he has not so much Braine as eare-wax. **1719** DE FOE *Crusoe* (1840) II. xvi. 327 Good bread enough, but baked as biscuits. **1822** *Blackw. Mag.* XII. 69 Calashes are good things enough, when the weather's wet and muggy. **1831** MACAULAY *Essays, Johnson*, Wks. (1866) V. 509 The conceit is wretched enough, but, etc. **1856** MRS. CARLYLE *Lett.* II. 286 A good enough man in his way—sober and laborious, and all that.

3. With comparatives: amply, sufficiently. *U.S. dial.*

a **1852** F. M. WHITCHER *Widow Bedott P.* (1883) xvi. 59 It's enough ginteeler 'n them flambergasted blue and yaller things. **1897** R. M. STUART *In Simpkinsville* 18 You'd see one thet was enough pinker an sweeter 'n the rest to make you climb for it.

† **e'noughbote.** *Obs.* [f. ENOUGH + BOTE, BOOT *sb.*¹] Satisfaction for an injury.

1340 *Ayenb.* 180 After þe ssrifte comþ ynoȝbote, þet is þe amendinge þet me ssel do..bi þe rede of þe ssrivere.

† **e'noughly**, *adv.* *Obs. rare*⁻¹. In 4 **ynoȝliche**. [f. as prec. + -LY².] Sufficiently.

1340 *Ayenb.* 55 An hondred poure miȝten libbe and ynoȝliche by ueld.

enoumbre: see ENUMBER.

enounce (ɪ'naʊns), *v.* [ad. F. *énoncer*, ad. L. *ēnuntiā-re* (see ENUNCIATE), after the analogy of ANNOUNCE.]

1. *trans.* To state (a proposition, principle, opinion) in definite terms; = ENUNCIATE.

1805 FOSTER *Ess.* IV. iii. 152 Whatever sentences will justly enounce them. **1837–8** SIR W. HAMILTON *Logic* xv. (1866) I. 281 The Antecedent comprises the two propositions, the one of which enounces the general rule. **1851** SIR F. PALGRAVE *Norm. & Eng.* I. 199 The proposition is incontestable yet incompletely enounced. **1878** DOWDEN *Stud. Lit.* 144 Wordsworth's theory..was perhaps not enounced with perfect clearness.

2. To state publicly; to proclaim.

1807 T. THOMSON *Chem.* II. 222 Landriani..enounced the alteration of lime-water by it [carbonic acid gas] as a proof of his opinion. **1829** SOUTHEY *Sir T. More* II. 233 [To] enounce without disguise the most revolutionary sentiments. **1834** *Fraser's Mag.* X. 722 Plunkett enounced.. the following to be his deliberate sentiments.

3. To utter, pronounce (words, etc.); cf. ENUNCIATION.

1829 SOUTHEY *All for Love* IX, At his command the Chorister Enounced the Prophet's song. **1852** A. M. BELL *Elocut. Man.* (1859) 58 The student should be able to enounce these [sounds] independently. **1857** C. BRONTË *Professor* I. xiv. 235 Language enounced with such steam-engine haste.

enouncement (ɪ'naʊnsmənt). [f. prec. + -MENT.] The action of enouncing; a definite statement, proclamation, utterance.

1836–7 SIR W. HAMILTON *Metaph.* xxxviii. (1870) II. 353 The enouncement of this criterion was..a great discovery in the science of mind. **1856** DOVE *Logic Chr. Faith* III. ii. 139 An enouncement of the laws of thought.

†**e'nourle**, *v. Obs. rare.* Also 5 enhoril. [as if a. Fr. **enourler*, f. *en* (see EN- *pref.*[1]) + *ourler* to edge.] *trans.* To border; ? to surround.

c **1325** *E.E. Allit. P.* B. 19 Þe kyng þat al weldez..With angelez enourled in alle þat is clene. ? *a* **1400** *Morte Arth.* 3244 Enhorilde with arborye and alkyns trees.

enourn: see ENORN.

enow (ɪ'naʊ), *a.* and *adv.*[1] Now only *arch.* and *dial.* Forms: α. (with apparent traces of pl. inflexion) 1 ȝenóȝe, 2 inóȝe, 3–5 in-, ynoghe, -oghȝe, -oȝe, -oȝhe, -ohe, -ouȝe, in-, ynowe, -owȝe, 4–5 anowe, (5 enoghe, enughe, inowhe), 3–6 ynowe, 6 enowe. β. (without traces of inflexion) 3–5 in-, ynou, 3–7 in-, ynow, (4–6 inew, ynew, 4 aney, 6–9 *Sc.* anew, 8–9 *dial.* enew, enoo), 4– enow. [See ENOUGH. The forms of ENOUGH and *enow* cannot always be discriminated with certainty, as the phonetic value of the ME. and early mod. 3, *gh*, was not uniform. The same graphic form, indeed, may sometimes represent two different pronunciations, one belonging to each series.]

A. *adj.*

1. 'The plural of ENOUGH' (J.). (The recent literary use is almost peculiar to Sc. writers.)

Beowulf 3103 (Gr.), þæt ȝe ȝenoȝe ne on sceawiað beagas and brad gold. *c* **1033** *Charter Cnut* in *Cod. Dipl.* VI. 183 Leofric eorl, and Osgod Clape, and Đored, and oðre ȝenoȝe. *c* **1175** *Lamb. Hom.* 13 Ic eou wille ȝeuen wela and westme inoȝe. *c* **1200** ORMIN 7932 Þatt witenn menn inoȝhe. *a* **1225** *Leg. Kath.* 514 Ah wordes þu hauest inohe. *a* **1300** *Cursor M.* 4563 (Götting.) In a medow sliht, floures and gress i-now i fand. *c* **1320** *Seuyn Sag.* (W.) 921 He kest the bor doun hawes anowe. **1375** BARBOUR *Bruce* I. 558 His Systir Son him slew, And gud men als, ma then Inew. *a* **1400–50** *Alexander* 3931 Bernes was diȝt þe deth with dintis enoghe. *c* **1430** *Hymns Virg.* (1867) 76 God haþ mercies y-now in stoore For a þousand worldis. **1486** *Bk. St. Albans* C j b, Yeue hir birdis Inow both morow and euyn. **1513** DOUGLAS *Æneis* II. vii. (vi.) 23, I than, by cleir takynnis anew, Manifestlie all the Greikis falsheid knew. **1535** COVERDALE *Ezek.* xxxix. 10 They shall haue weapens ynew to burne. **1581** SIDNEY *Apol. Poetrie* (Arb.) 67 He would be sure to name windes enovve. *c* **1611** CHAPMAN *Iliad* xx. 24 His mere looks threw darts enow t'impress Their pow'rs with trembling. **1656** SANDERSON *Serm.* (1689) 266 The Devil will be sure to suggest enow of these pretensions. **1702** ADDISON *Dial. Medals* i. 24, I think there are at Rome enow modern works of Architecture to employ any reasonable man. **1752** HUME *Ess. & Treat.* (1777) I. 23 There are enow of zealots on both sides. **1820** SCOTT *Ivanhoe* xxxii, Take with you enow of men. **1824** L. MURRAY *Eng. Gram.* I. 254 Enow was formerly used as the plural of enough; but it is now obsolete. **1828** STEUART *Planter's G.* 253 Accidents enow will happen, without aggravating them by carelessness. **1868** G. MACDONALD *Eng. Antiphon* 210 Without yet having generated thoughts enow concerning the subject itself.

b. predicatively.

1647 MAY *Hist. Parl.* Pref. 5 Any English man, whose yeares have been enow to make him know the Actions that were done. **1760** STERNE *Serm. Yorick* (1773) IV. 31 As if the causes of anguish in the heart were not enow. **1796** C. MARSHALL *Garden.* xii. (1813) 154 Three or four [fruits] on a long and strong branch are quite enow. **1825** SCOTT *Talism.* xix, Those charges, which there are enow to bring against him in his absence.

c. *absol.* = 'persons enough'.

1583 STUBBES *Anat. Abus.* II. 25 There are inow, and more than a good meanie. **1646** CRASHAW *Steps Temple* 74 There are enow, whose draughts, as deep as hell, Drink up all Spain in sack. **1669** SHADWELL *Royal Shepherdess* I. i, Thou wilt surely have Enow to court thee. **1805** WORDSW. *Prelude* v. (1851) 91 Enow there are on earth to take in charge Their wives, their children, and their virgin loves.

2. As *adj. sing.* = ENOUGH *a.* 1 a.

1297 R. GLOUC. (1724) 388 Þe kyng and Roberd..wyþ gret ost and strengþe ynou to Engelond come. *a* **1300** *Cursor M.* 2190 (Götting.) Of þat nacion sprang foli enou. **1393** LANGL. *P. Pl.* C. xv. 139 Ich haue mete more þan ynowe. *c* **1420** *Chron. Vilod.* 130 Plenteythe of fysshe þey hadden ynowe. **1471** SIR J. PASTON in *Lett.* 670 III. 7, I have hey i new of myn owne. **1672–5** COMBER *Comp. Temple* (1702) 90 And hence we see we have Reason enow to confess our Sins.

b. predicatively; = ENOUGH *a.* 2.

a **1200** *Moral Ode* 385 in *Lamb. Hom.* 183 Crist scal one beon inou . alle his durlinges. **1607** TOURNEUR *Rev. Trag.* v. i, That's enow a' conscience! **1814** BYRON *Lara* I. xxviii, It was enow To seal his lip, but agonise his brow.

c. *absol.* = ENOUGH *a.* 3.

a **1300** *Cursor M.* 27601 (Cott.) Inow no mai man find o þaa. **1413** LYDG. *Pilgr. Sowle* II. lvii. (1859) 56 Ynowe to doo for many a day herafter. *a* **1440** *Sir Degrev.* 1024 Whedur he wol tornay or fyȝthe, He shal have i-now! **1597** DANIEL *Trag. Philotas* in Farr *S.P. Jas. I* (1848) 275, I know t'have said too much, but not ynow.

B. *adv.* = ENOUGH *adv.* in various senses.

1297 R. GLOUC. (1724) 83 Þat folk was þo of þis lond y payed wel ynow. *c* **1300** *Beket* 2213 Honurede that holi bodi: and custe hit ynoȝe. *c* **1340** *Cursor M.* 1404 (Fairf.) Lorde I-noghe [*Trin.* Inouȝe] now liued haue I. *c* **1385** CHAUCER *L.G.W.* 893 *Tisbe*, To make myn wounde large I-now I gesse. *a* **1449** PECOCK *Repr.* 295 It may weel ynowȝ accorde with resoun. *a* **1553** UDALL *Royster D.* I. ii. (Arb.) 14 Bee of good cheere; anon ye shall doe well ynow. **1676** HOBBES *Iliad* XIII. 271 Or if you had been hurt 'tis sure enow, Nor in your back nor neck had been the wound. **1814** SOUTHEY *Paraguay* I. 19 A few firm stakes..Circling a narrow space, yet large enow. **1850** MRS. BROWNING *Rom. Ganges* xxiii, None are frail enow For mortal joys to borrow! **1870** MORRIS *Earthly Par.* III. IV. 235 Bright enow With gold and gems.

b. *ellipt.* = ENOUGH *adv.* 1 c.

c **1440** *Anc. Cookery* in *Househ. Ord.* (1790) 451 When hit is innowe take hit up.

enow (ɪ'naʊ), *adv.*[2] *dial.* [? Short for *e'en* (= *even*) *now*. (But cf. Ger. *im nu*, Sw. *i detta nu*.)] Just now (*Sc.*); by and by; presently.

1816 SCOTT *Antiq.* xxiv, 'We canna howk for't enow.' **1855** ROBINSON *Whitby Gloss.*, I will come enow.

enoy, -ing, var. of ENNOY, -ING, *Obs.*

enoynt, obs. var. ANOINT *ppl. a.* (*obs.*) and *v.*

enoyse, var. of ENOSE *v. Obs.*

enp-: see EMP-.

enpair, obs. form of IMPAIR.

en pantoufles: see EN *prep.*

†**en'parelling**, *vbl. sb. Obs.*, var. of APPARELLING *vbl. sb.*

1496 *Will Snaw* (Somerset Ho.), Towards the garnesshing & enparellyng of the Image of saynte Mary Magdalene in the chapell of Yelde Hall of London.

‖**en passant** (ɑ̃ pasɑ̃), *adv.* [Fr.]

1. In passing; by the way; in the course of a narrative, etc.

1665 BOYLE *Occas. Refl., Disc. Medit.* (1675) 57 Having given you this Advertisement, *en passant*, we may now proceed. **1720** WELTON *Suffer. Son of God* I. viii. 162 We ought not to receive them but *en Passant*, and by the way. **1838** S. LOVER *Handy Andy* iii, His pursuer..gave a back-handed slap at the window-bottles, *en passant.* **1860** ADLER *Fauriel's Prov. Poetry* viii. 161 It is sufficient..to indicate ..*en passant* the existence of the histories in question.

2. *Chess.* *to take* (a pawn) ***en passant***: to take with one of your own pawns an adversary's pawn that has been moved forward two squares, passing over the square on which it would by the general rule have been liable to capture by your pawn.

1818 W. S. KENNY *Pract. Chess Exerc.* 106 You prevent him by pushing immediately your queen's knight's pawn upon his knight, which..obliges the adversary to take your pawn *en passant.*

†**en'payn**, *v. Obs. rare*[−1]. [ad. OF. *enpain-er*, f. *en* (see EN- *pref.*[1]) + OF. *paine* (mod. *peine*) trouble.] *refl.* To put oneself to pains; to exert oneself.

c **1380** *Sir Ferumb.* 633 Eyþer enpaynede him other to slo.

en pension, en permanence: see EN *prep.*

†**en'per**, *v. Obs. rare*[−1]. [? corruptly ad. OF. *aperir*, ad. L. *aperīre* to open.] *trans.* ? To open, make plain.

c **1420** *Anturs of Arth.* xix, Prophetes haue told, And enperit to the pepulle in hor preching.

†**en'pite**, *v. Obs.* [? f. EN-[1] + *pite*, PITY.] *trans.* ? To affect with compassion, touch the heart of.

c **1400** *Test. Love* II. (1560) 284/2 Yet I am glad and greatly enpited, how continually thou haddest me in mind.

enplane, var. EMPLANE *v.*

enplant, enpowder, etc.: see IMP-.

‖**en plein** (ɑ̃ plɛ̃). [Fr., = in full.] **1.** Of a bet in roulette and other banking games: placed entirely upon one number or side; of a number or side, backed with the whole bet.

1881 HARDY *Laodicean* II. IV. iv. 258 Leaving off backing numbers *en plein*, he laid his venture..*à cheval.* **1933** MRS. C. S. PEEL *Life's Enchanted Cup* xiii. 161 Suddenly I knew that I must risk my last five francs *en plein* on number thirteen. **1966** G. GREENE *Comedians* I. ii. 88, I had already won once *en plein.* **1966** C. ROBERTSON *Judas Spies* i. 9 He had been sitting at a roulette table..playing the even chances mostly, occasionally trying his luck *en plein.*

2. ***en plein air***, in the open air.

1888 *Practitioner* Oct. 258 Typhus..is..very uncommon amongst the class of people..who..live largely a life *en plein air.* **1962** *Observer* 1 July 19/8 The Greek tradition of performing the classics *en plein air* is not..continuous since antiquity.

3. In other phrases.

1865 'OUIDA' *Strathmore* I. vi. 103 We are so proud of our stolen nuts that we crack them *en plein jour* instead of keeping them to enjoy in the darkness of night. **1896** E. DOWSON *Let.* 5 July (1967) 371 Have I not been peacefully rusticating these five months en pleine campagne? **1940** J. JOYCE *Let.* 11 Feb. (1966) III. 465 He had practically to kidnap the child *en pleine rue.* **1944** A. L. ROWSE *Eng. Spirit* viii. 62 The Portuguese Empire was *en pleine déchéance.*

en pointe(s), en poste, en prince, en principe, en prise, en regard: see EN *prep.*

†**en'praynt.** *Obs. rare.* [a. OF. *empreinte* (see IMPRINT), f. *empreindre*:—Lat. *imprimĕre*, f. *in-* upon + *primĕre* to press.] A shock, encounter.

c **1489** CAXTON *Sonnes Aymon* xx. 453 Eche of them overthrew vii knightes at that enpraynt.

enprent, obs. var. IMPRINT.

†**enpresoné.** *Sc. Obs. rare.* Also enpresowné; pl. -eis, -eys. [a. F. *emprisonné* put in prison.] A prisoner.

c **1425** WYNTOUN *Cron.* VIII. xxvii. 14 Na man..durst say ..þat he Wes yholden before Enpresowné. *Ibid.* VIII. xxvii. 141 Þe Kyng gert cry All þe enpresowneys slayne to be.

†**en'press**, *v. Obs. rare.* Also 4 enprece. [a. OF. *enpresse-r*, f. *en-* (see EN-[1]) + *presser* to PRESS. See IMPRESS.] *trans.* To press hard upon; to oppress. Also *absol.*

c **1325** *E.E. Allit. P.* C. 43 As pouert enpresses. *Ibid.* 528 When pouerte me enprecez.

enpress, obs. var. of EMPRISE.

c **1325** *E.E. Allit. P.* A. 1096 Þis noble cite of ryche enpresse Watz sodanly ful with-outen sommoun Of such vergynez.

enprint, enprison, enproper: see IMPR-.

enprowe, obs. form of IMPROVE.

enpugne, obs. var. IMPUGN.

†**en'quarter**, *v. Obs.* Also 7 inquarter. [f. EN-[1] + QUARTER *sb.* Cf. Ger. *einquartieren*, = sense 1.]

1. *trans.* To put (troops) into quarters; to billet. Also *absol.*

1642 CHARLES I *Declar. about Brentford* 10 Part of it [the army] was inquartered at Brainford. **1673** H. STUBBE *Further Vind. Dutch War* To Rdr. 9 Neither could the Captain General..enquarter in any City, without the Consent of the Province.

2. *Her.* To place (armorial bearings) in a quarter of the shield; to quarter.

1622–62 HEYLIN *Cosmogr.* I. (1682) 204 Varying the Coat of France, which they enquartered with their own. **1635** BRERETON *Trav.* (1844) 135 The arms of this see..and Bishop Hampton's own coat arms enquartered together.

Hence **en'quartering** *vbl. sb.*, the action of placing (troops) in quarters, or of going into quarters.

1639 *Lawes & Ord. Warre* 14 Their marching, retreating, or enquartering in or thorow any townes or countryes.

enquere, obs. var. ENQUIRE, INQUIRE.

†**enquerouresse.** *nonce-wd.* [f. OF. *enquereour* one who holds a judicial inquiry + -ESS.] A female inquisitor.

c **1430** *Pilgr. Lyf Manhode* II. viii. (1869) 78 Art thou meyresse? or a newe enquerouresse? Shewe thi commission.

enquest, obs. form of INQUEST.

†**en'question.** *Obs. rare*[−1]. [a. OF. *enquestion.*] Question, inquiry.

a **1641** BP. R. MOUNTAGU *Acts & Mon.* (1642) 55 Three Divines of Spaine..haue of purpose defended and explained that Doctrine without taxe, enquestion, or imputation.

†**en'queyntance.** *Obs.* = ACQUAINTANCE 1.

1297 R. GLOUC. (1724) 330 Þat ne wylnede enqueyntance of hym.

enquicken: see EN- *pref.*[1] 3.

enquiet, -ation, etc.: see INQUIET, etc.

†**en'quile**, *v. Obs. rare*[−1]. [a. OF. *encueillir* (written also *anqillir*) to take. See AQUILE.] *trans.* To obtain.

c **1325** *E.E. Allit. P.* C. 39 Any by quest of her quoyntyse enquylen on mede.

enquire (ɛn'kwaɪə(r)), *v.* An alternative form of INQUIRE. The mod. Dicts. give *inquire* as the standard form, but *enquire* is still very frequently used, esp. in the sense 'to ask a question'. For the relation in history and use between the two forms, see INQUIRE. Hence **enquirer, enquiry**, etc., for which see the forms with IN-.

†**en'race**, *v. Obs. rare.* [f. EN-[1] + RACE *sb.*] *trans.* To introduce into a race of living beings; to implant. Hence **en'raced** *ppl. a.*, that is implanted in the race, inborn, inbred.

a **1577** SIR T. SMITH *Commw. Eng.* (1633) 56 The enraced love of tenants..to such Noblemen. **1590** SPENSER *F.Q.* III. v. 52 He it fetcht out of her native place, And did in stocke of earthly flesh enrace. **1596** —— *Hymn Beauty* 114 When she in fleshly seede is eft enraced.

†**en'rach.** *v. Obs. rare*[−1]. [ad. OF. *enrach-ier*, corrupt var. of *esrachier*: see ARACHE.] *trans.* To tear out, ravish.

1509 HAWES *Past. Pleas.* 137 Myne only lady and maystres also, Whose goodly beaute hath my harte enrached.

†**en'racined**, *ppl. a. Obs. rare*$^{-1}$. [ad. Fr. *enraciné*, f. *en-* (see EN- *pref.*^{1}) + *racine* root.] That has taken root, rooted.

1656 SIR R. GORDON *Hist. Earls Sutherl.* 295 (Jam.), A quarrell..deiplie grounded, and enracined for many other preceiding debates.

†**en'rage**, *sb. Obs.* [f. next.] Rage, fury.

1502 *Ord. Crysten Men* (W. de W. 1506) v. iii. 377 Is multyplyed the enrage of enuy of those the whiche ben dampned.

enrage (ɛn'reɪdʒ), *v.* Also 6–8 **in-**. [ad. OF. *enrage-r*, f. *en-* (see EN- *pref.*^{1}) + *rage* rabies, RAGE.

The Fr. word is used only intr.; the trans. use in Eng. appears to have arisen (*c* 1600) from the pa. pple. *enraged* (= Fr. *enragé*) taken as passive.]

†**1.** *intr.* To be distracted, 'driven wild' (by hunger, thirst). Const. *for* [after Fr. *enrager de faim, soif*]. *Obs.*

1502 *Ord. Crysten Men* (W. de W. 1506) v. ii. 364 Nor never shall cease to..enrage for thyrste. **1523** LD. BERNERS *Froiss.* I. cxlvi. 174 So sore strayned that we haue nat to lyue withall, but..muste all dye, or els enrage for famyn. **1557** PAYNEL *Barclay's Jugurth* 95 Serpentes whiche were so muche more violent and fiers for lacke of meat..as al other wilde beastes be wont to inrage for honger.

†**2.** To get into a rage, become very angry. *Obs.*

a **1533** LD. BERNERS *Huon* civ. 345 He enraged & was nere out of his wyt. **1632** LITHGOW *Trav.* x. 466 Whereat the Alcalde, inraging, set my teeth asunder with a payre of iron cadges. **1782** MISS BURNEY *Cecilia* IX. x. V. 192 My father.. will only enrage at the temerity of offering to confute him.

†**3.** Of famine, persecution, etc.: To rage. *Obs.*

1560 BIBLE (Genev.) *Ex.* Arg., The more that the tyranny of the wicked enraged against his Church. **1606** WARNER *Alb. Eng.* XIV. xcii. (1612) 372 Such famine had inrag'd within the walles so sore.

†**4.** *Pa. pple.* Maddened (with anger, love, pain, etc.); inspired with poetic frenzy. Also, affected with rabies.

1513 DOUGLAS *Æneis* XIII. v. 20 And sine, half deill enragit ..in ruschis he Amyd the rowt. **1592** SHAKS. *Ven. & Ad.* 317 His love, perceiving how he is enraged, Grew kinder. *a* **1619** FOTHERBY *Atheom.* I. xiv. §3 (1622) 151 Yea one that is enraged, not with frenzie, but with furie. **1635** SWAN *Spec. M.* vi. §4 (1643) 252 Such as are enraged by the biting of a mad dog. **1650** EARL MONMOUTH tr. *Senault's Man become Guilty* 65 Poets droop, when not inraged. **1697** DRYDEN *Virg. Georg.* III. 388 To battel Tygers move; Enrag'd with Hunger, more enrag'd with Love. **1719** DE FOE *Crusoe* (1840) II. xiv. 293 The poor beast, enraged with the wounds, was no more to be governed.

5. *trans.* To throw into a rage; to make furious, exasperate; also with *on*, and *absol.*

1589 WARNER *Alb. Eng.* VI. xxx. (1612) 149 Successlesse therefore, and inrag'd. **1590** SPENSER *F.Q.* I. i. 17 Therewith enrag'd she loudly gan to bray. **1597** SHAKS. *2 Hen. IV*, IV. i. 211 Like an offensive wife, That hath enrag'd him on, to offer strokes. **1605** —— *Macb.* III. iv. 118 Question enrages him. **1624** BEDELL *Lett.* iv. 77 The Protestants making the Pope Antichrist..is a point that inrageth much at Rome. **1667** MILTON *P.L.* II. 698, I reing King, and to enrage thee more, Thy King and Lord. **1709** STANHOPE *Paraphr.* IV. 531 Shall we be inraged and impatient for Affronts and Disgrace. **1774** GOLDSM. *Nat. Hist.* (1776) IV. 103 He [the dog] stands enraged and barking. **1864** *Blackfriars* II. 224 Little the worse for..his fall, but madly enraged at the galling mischance. **1872** DARWIN *Emotions* x. 240 A man may intensely hate another, but until his bodily frame is affected, he cannot be said to be enraged.

†**6.** *transf.* **a.** To add fury or violence to; to make violent or virulent; to exacerbate. **b.** To cause heat or fever in (the blood, a wound). *Obs.*

a. *c* **1500** *Melusine* 164 The see was enraged thrugh the stormes and horryble tempeste. **1614** RALEIGH *Hist. World* IV. i. §1. 457 Great rivers are at once swollen, fast running inraged. **1639** FULLER *Holy War* v. xv. (1840) 269 Unwholesome diet enraging the climate against us. **1656** RIDGLEY *Pract. Physick* 49 A double poyson, one putrifying which is enraged by suppurating remedies. **1692** E. WALKER *Epictetus' Mor.* xxi, To tell him he's mistaken will inrage His grief. **1713** YOUNG *Last Day* II. 248 Angels drive on the wind's impetuous course, T'enrage the flame. **1759** B. MARTIN *Nat. Hist. Eng.*, *Somerset* I. 84 Enrages the Gout or strikes it in.

b. **1597** SHAKS. *2 Hen. IV*, I. i. 144 My Limbes (Weak'ned with greefe) being now inrag'd with greefe, Are thrice themselues. **1626** G. SANDYS *Ovid's Met.* VI. 119 In-bred lust Inrag'd his blood. **1635** R. BOLTON *Comf. Affl. Consc.* v. 215 They will..rather enrage the wound, then weaken the rage. **1693** R. LYDE *Recov. Friend's Adventure* in Arb. *Garner* VII. 449 My left thumb..was very much swelled and enraged.

enraged (ɛn'reɪdʒd), *ppl. a.* [f. prec. + -ED^1.]

†**1.** In various senses. Of matter: Enfevered, vitiated. Of creatures: Made furious, maddened. Of men: Savage. *Obs.*

1398 TREVISA *Barth. De P.R.* v. lvii. (1495) 173 Bones often tymes ben greuyd of fretynge and gnawynge of wode and enragyd matere. **1533** BELLENDEN *Livy* v. (1822) 449 Bot the place and hichtis quhare thay dwell has maid thame sa enragit and wilde. **1601** HOLLAND *Pliny* II. 226 All the horses..become inraged. **1652** HOWELL *Masaniello, 2nd Part* 47 Like so many enraged lions.

†**2.** Of desires, passions, etc.: Inflamed, ardent, furious. *Obs.* or *arch.*

1580 SIDNEY *Arcadia* (1622) 166 With the sword of reuerent dutie gaine-stand the force of so many enraged desires. **1599** SHAKS. *Much Ado* II. iii. 103 But..she loues him with an inraged affection, it is past the infinite of thought. **1651** *Life Father Sarpi* (1676) 50 Such an inraged hatred.

3. Of persons: Thrown into a rage, infuriate.

1732 BERKELEY *Alciphr.* III. §16 Would you help an enraged man to his sword? **1757** BURKE *Abridgm. Eng. Hist.* Wks. X. 466 He was unwilling to keep pace with the violence of that enraged bishop. **1855** MACAULAY *Hist. Eng.* IV. 526 The prosecutors had with difficulty escaped from the hands of an enraged multitude.

Hence **en'ragedly** *adv.*, in an enraged manner, furiously. **en'ragedness**, the state or condition of being enraged.

a **1572** KNOX *Hist. Ref.* Wks. (1846) I. 178 Then more enraigedlye, thei cry, 'We shall never departe till that we see him'. **1639** CHARLES I *Declar. Tumults Scot.* 37 The barbarous multitude run most inragedly upon them. **1611** COTGR., *Furie*, enragednesse, frenzie, madnesse.

enragement (ɛn'reɪdʒmənt). [f. ENRAGE *v.* + -MENT.] The action of enraging; the state or condition of being enraged. †Also in good sense: Rapture.

1596 SPENSER *Hymn Heav. Love* 286 With sweete enragement of celestiall love. **1648** J. GOODWIN *Right & Might* 8 They..were now under a great additionall enragement. **1669** W. SIMPSON *Hydrol. Chym.* 78 By symptomatical enragements of that furibund animal. **1881** D. C. MURRAY *Joseph's Coat* I. viii. 169 Examining the drawing there to John's satisfaction and George's enragement.

enraging (ɛn'reɪdʒɪŋ), *ppl. a. rare.* [f. ENRAGE *v.* + -ING^2.] That enrages; provoking, exasperating. (So Fr. *enrageant*.)

1880 DISRAELI *Endym.* xii. 47 Myra was always unmoved and enraging from her total want of sensibility.

†**en'rail**, *v. Obs.* var. of INRAIL *v.*

†**en'range**, *v. Obs.* Also 6 **enraunge**. ? In Spenser only. [f. EN-^{1} + RANGE *sb.* and *v.*]

1. *trans.* To place in a range or rank; to arrange.

1590 SPENSER *F.Q.* III. xii. 5 After whom marcht a jolly company, In manner of a maske, enraged orderly. **1596** —— *Hymn Heav. Beauty* 83 More faire is that, where those Idees on hie Enraunged be, which Plato so admyred.

2. To range or ramble in (a forest).

1596 SPENSER *F.Q.* VI. ii. 9 In all this forrest and wyld wooddie raine Where, as this day I was enraunging it.

enrank (ɛn'ræŋk), *v.* Also 7 **enranck**. [f. EN-^{1} + RANK *sb.*] *trans.* To set in a rank or row; *esp.* to draw up (soldiers) in order of battle.

1591 SHAKS. *1 Hen. VI*, I. i. 115 No leysure had he to enranke his men. **1610** HEALEY *St. Aug. Citie of God* 585 Hee begat the sonne who is enranked in this genealogicall rolle. **1613–6** W. BROWNE *Brit. Past.* II. i, His rusty teeth.. Did through his pallid cheekes..Bewray what number were enranckt within. **1834** *Fraser's Mag.* IX. 119 Her sons, thus side to side Enranked.

‖**en rapport** (ɑ̃ rapɔr). In relation (*with*); in mesmeric 'rapport': see RAPPORT.

enrapt (ɛn'ræpt), *pple.* [f. EN-^{1} + RAPT.]

'Carried away' by prophetic ecstasy; hence, absorbed in contemplation, enraptured.

1606 SHAKS. *Tr. & Cr.* v. iii. 65, I myself Am like a Prophet suddenly enrapt. **1790** A. WILSON *Invocation* Poet. Wks. (1846) 53 Enrapt with the prospect, the bard gazed around. **1805** WORDSW. *Prelude* x. (1850) 289 On the fulgent spectacle..I gazed Enrapt.

¶This sense is in some applications undistinguishable from the fig. sense of *enwrapt* (see ENWRAP *v.*, and cf. Shaks. *Twel. N.* IV. iii. 3). Hence a frequent confusion between the two words. In the following passage Johnson regards *enrapt* as erroneously written for *enwrapt*:

c **1730** POPE, etc. *Mart. Scriblerus* (1742) 130 Nor hath he been so enrapt in these Studies as to neglect, etc.

enrapture (ɛn'ræptjʊə(r)), *v.* Also 8 **inrapture**. [f. EN-^{1} + RAPTURE.]

1. *trans.* To throw into a rapture, inspire with overmastering poetic fervour. Only in *passive*.

1742 P. FRANCIS tr. *Horace' Odes* IV. ii. (1807) New words he rolls enraptur'd down Impetuous through the dithyrambic strains. **1827** [see ENRAPTURED 1].

2. To delight intensely.

1740 DYER *Ruins Rome* 134 The brow We gain enraptur'd. **1821** MOORE *Irish Mel.* Poet. Wks. (1850) 200 Such eyes, As before me..enraptured I see. **1866** GEO. ELIOT *F. Holt* (1868) 12 She had not been enraptured when her son had written..that, etc. *Mod.* He quite enraptured his audience.

enraptured (ɛn'ræptjʊəd), *ppl. a.* [f. prec. vb. + -ED^1.]

1. Full of poetic rapture.

1751 J. BROWN *Shaftesb. Charac.* 389 The inraptured strains of Philocles. **1827** KEBLE *Chr. Y.*, *Circumcision* xii. 4 One high enraptured strain.

2. Rapturously delighted; entranced, ravished.

1757 HURD *Poet. Imitation* Wks. (1811) II. 146 Hardly considered by the inraptured thought as fiction. *a* **1763** SHENSTONE *Poems* Chalm. XIII. 308 Oft gazing on her shade, th'enraptured fair Decreed the substance well deserv'd her care. **1836** J. GILBERT *Chr. Atonem.* iv. (1852) 62 They broke forth in strains of enraptured admiration. **1853** ROBERTSON *Serm.* Ser. III. ii. (1872) 26 Its glories.. pour in melody upon the enraptured ear.

enrapturer (ɛn'ræptjʊərə(r)). [f. ENRAPTURE + -ER.] One who or that which enraptures.

1850 L. HUNT *Autobiog.* I. viii. 300 Evil..is..the crown of patience, the enrapturer of the embraces of joy.

enrapturing (ɛn'ræptjʊərɪŋ), *ppl. a.* [f. ENRAPTURE + -ING^2.] That enraptures, or transports with delight; entrancing, ravishing.

1801 MOORE *Catalogue* ii. 13 This lesson of dear and enrapturing lore I have never forgot. **1883** J. PARKER *Apost. Life* II. 299 An unutterable and enrapturing expectation.

†**en'rase**, *v. Obs. rare*$^{-1}$. [var. of ARASE: see EN-^{1} A. 2.] *trans.* To erase, obliterate.

1491 CAXTON *Vitas Patr.* (W. de W. 1495) 159 b/1 For the loue of Johan my seruaunte thy synne is enrased oute.

†**en'ravel**, *v. Obs. rare.* Also 7 **inravel**. [f. EN-^{1} + RAVEL, *Sc.*, rail.] *trans.* To enclose within railings. Hence **en'ravelled** *ppl. a.*

1632 LITHGOW *Trav.* IX. 410 A gaudy beede inraueled betweene fiue small fast made irons. *Ibid.* x. 441 Two milk white Hennes, enraueled in an Iron Cage. *Ibid.* i. 32 The inravled images with sparrets of iron.

enravish (ɛn'rævɪʃ). *rare* in mod. use. Also 6–7 **inravish**. [f. EN-^{1} + RAVISH.] *trans.* To transport with intense delight; to enrapture.

1596 SPENSER *Hymn Love* 119 What wonder then if with such rage extreme, Fraile men..so much enrauisht bee? **1596** FITZ-GEFFRAY *Sir F. Drake* (1881) 25 Whose Muse is so inravish'd with the lookes Which from your Mistresse ivorie browes do fall. **1677** HALLYWELL *Saving Souls* 88 (T.) Which cannot but enravish every generous breast. *a* **1714** ABP. SHARP *Serm.* (1829) II. 458 We shall..spend the whole eternity..in loving God..in being enravished with all his wise contrivances.

Hence **en'ravished** *ppl. a.*

1662 H. MORE *Enthus. Tri.* (1712) 45 The divine Love and Beauty descending into their enravished Souls. [Not in ed. 1656.]

†**en'ravishing**, *ppl. a.* [f. prec. + -ING^2.] That enravishes; enrapturing, delightful.

1681–6 J. SCOTT *Chr. Life* V. 30 The most sublime and enravishing objects. **1685** H. MORE *Illustration* 376 Such enravishing news. *a* **1714** ABP. SHARP *Serm.* Wks. (1829) I. 55 These [the pleasures of religion] are of so excellent a kind, so delicious, so enravishing that, etc.

Hence **en'ravishingly** *adv.*

1687 H. MORE *App. Antid.* (1712) 221 The subtilty of the Matter [spiritual matter] will more..enravishingly move the Nerves, than any terrestrial Body can possibly.

enravishment (ɛn'rævɪʃmənt). *rare.* [f. ENRAVISH *v.* + -MENT.]

1. The state of being enravished.

1656 H. MORE *Antid. Ath.* (1712) Ep. Ded. 2 Plato, if he were alive again..to the enravishment of his amazed Soul might behold Vertue become visible.

2. An emotion that forms part of such a state; an ecstatic or rapturous feeling.

1665 GLANVILL *Sceps. Sci.* xxiv. (R.), The enravishments of her [Nature's] transported admirers.

†**en'reason**, *v. Obs. rare*$^{-1}$. In 3 **enreson**. [a. OF. *enresoner*, *enraisonner* to address, talk to, f. *en-* (see EN- *pref.*^{1}) + *raison* REASON.] *trans.* To address in words.

1297 R. GLOUC. (1724) 34 [Canute] enresonede hys men, as hii byuore hym stode.

enregiment (ɛn'rɛdʒ(ə)mənt), *v.* [ad. Fr. *enrégimenter*, f. *en-* (see EN- *pref.*^{1}) + *régiment* REGIMENT.] *trans.* To form into a regiment or organized body; hence, to bring under rule and discipline.

1831 CARLYLE in Froude *Life* (1882) II. 206 Enregiment and organise them [knaves] as cunningly as you will. **1835** *Fraser's Mag.* XI. 560 The writers..enregimented in the service of diffusion. **1874** T. G. BOWLES *Flotsam & Jetsam* 118 An atom in a mass of other men to be..enregimented.

enregister (ɛn'rɛdʒɪstə(r)), *v.* Also 6 **enregester**, 6–7 **inregister**, 8 **enrigister**. [ad. Fr. *enregistrer*, f. *en-* (see EN- *pref.*^{1}) + *registre* REGISTER *sb.*]

1. a. *trans.* To enter in a register or official record. (In mod. use as a gallicism.)

1579 TOMSON *Calvin's Serm. Tim.* 525/2 Our sinnes..he [God] hath not forgotten..they are all inregistred before him. **1591** HORSEY *Trav.* (1857) App. 350 Enregistred by the agent in writing. **1612** W. PARKES *Curtaine-Dr.* (1876) 9 Fixed a copious Scedule ore his head, Where all his mischiefes are inregistred. **1795** tr. *Barruel's Hist. Clergy Fr. Rev.* 240 Enregister their names. **1850** W. IRVING *Mahomet* xiii. (1853) 60 The Syrian Greeks came in..to have their names enregistered in the book of tributaries. **1918** *Times Lit. Suppl.* 21 Mar. 137/2 The three hundred thousand enregistered by the barrister Chenaux.

b. *transf.* and *fig.*

1523 LD. BERNERS *Froiss.* I. i. 1 That the honorable and noble aventures of feates of armes..shulde notably be inregistered. **1596** SPENSER *Hymn Heav. Love* 130 As in a brasen booke, To read enregistred in every nooke His goodnesse. *a* **1631** DONNE *Hist. Septuagint* (1633) 217 He hath himself written and inregistred his own proper faults. **1831** *Fraser's Mag.* III. 323 We now have the wild follies of those Alchemists enregistered as a warning. **1896** *McClure's Mag.* VI. 479/2 The works of men too numerous to be enregistered here. **1928** *New Statesman* 27 Oct. 81 The young spiders..are obeying what is nowadays a racially enregistered tropism to climb.

2. To put on record as law; to ratify and put on record. Now *rare*.

1651 *Life Father Sarpi* (1676) 88 The Court..do their uttermost endeavour to enregister and authenticate the exclusion of Princes. **1702** *Anguis in Herba* 31 He obliged himself to enrigister the Renunciation in the Council of State. **1819** SHELLEY *Cenci* II. i. 147 Executioners Of his decree enregistered in heaven. **1838–9** HALLAM *Hist. Lit.* III. III. vii. 364 Letters patent..which the Parliament of Paris enregistered with great reluctance.

Hence **en'registering** *vbl. sb.*

1604 E. G. *D'Acosta's Hist. Indies* IV. vi. 222 The first discovery and inregistring of the Mines of Potozi. **1791** PAINE *Rights M.* (ed. 4) 100 The Parliament..ordered the enregistering to be struck out.

en'registrate, *a. nonce-wd.* [f. prec. + -ATE.] Placed on permanent record.

1599 JAMES I *Βασιλ. Δωρον* (1603) 117 Your writing which is nothing else but a forme of en-registrate speech.

enregistration (ˌɛnrɛdʒɪ'streɪʃən). [f. ENREGISTER *v.*: see -ATION.] The registering, on the brain, of previous actions, so that performance becomes automatic or instinctive.

1922 J. Y. SIMPSON *Man & Attainm. Immortality* xi. 241 Increased cerebral development involves in some way a wider and more complex range of enregistration and combination of action and reaction, and so, through the presence of alternatives, of choice. **1927** *Glasgow Herald* 24 Mar. 4 Experiments with rats that quickly master a labyrinth of the Hampton Court maze type point to an enregistration of tactile and muscular sensations. **1930** *John o'London's* 8 Mar. 878/3 Enregistration of the past is characteristic of life.

†**en'registry.** *Obs. rare.* [f. ENREGISTER *v.*; cf. *registry*.] The action of enregistering (a law).

1825 T. JEFFERSON *Autobiog.* Wks. 1859 I. 70 The determined opposition of the Parliament to their ['the taxes'] enregistry.

en règle, en retraite, en revanche: see EN *prep.*

†**en'rheum,** *v. Obs.* [ad. OF. *enrheum-er* (mod. *enrhumer*), f. *en-* (see EN- *pref.*[1]) + *rheume*, ad. Gr. ῥεῦμ-α RHEUM.] *trans.* To affect with rheum or catarrh; to give a cold to.

1666 G. HARVEY *Morb. Angl.* xiv. 170 The party..hath taken could, and is enrheumed.

enrib: see EN- *pref.*[1] 1 a.

enrich (ɛn'rɪtʃ), *v.* Forms: α. 4–6 **enrych,** 6 **enriche,** (**enritch,** *Sc.* **enreache**), 5– **enrich.** β. 6 **inrych,** 6–8 **inrich(e.** [a. Fr. *enrich-ir*, f. *en-* (see EN- *pref.*[1]) + *riche* rich.]

1. a. *trans.* To make rich, wealthy, or opulent. Also *absol.*

1382 WYCLIF *Gen.* xxx. 20 The Lord hath enrychide me with a good dower. *c* **1460** FORTESCUE *Abs. & Lim. Mon.* (1714) 142 He hath than enryched his Corowne with such Riches and Possessions, as never Kyng schal may take from yt. **1530** *Act 22 Hen. VIII*, c. 8 §1 Denizens..after they be so inriched..convey themselves, with their said Goods, to their own Country. *a* **1572** KNOX *Hist. Ref.* Wks. 1846 I. 398 Nor yitt to enreache the Crowne..with your substance. **1677** YARRANTON *Engl. Improv.* 61 Set all the poor in England at work, and much inrich the Country. **1732** BERKELEY *Alciphr.* II. §2 Many men are enriched by all the forementioned ways of trade. **1838** EMERSON *Addr. Camb. Mass.* Wks. (Bohn) II. 191 Thefts never enrich; alms never impoverish. **1856** KANE *Arct. Expl.* I. xvii. 209 Enriching them in return with needles and beads.

b. *refl.* and (rarely) *intr.* for *refl.*

1525 LD. BERNERS *Froiss.* II. xcii. [lxxxviii.] 273 Their desyre is euer to enryche and to haue all themselfe. **1549** CHEKE *Hurt Sedit* B i b, But and we beyng wery of pouertye woulde seke to enryche ourselues we shold go, etc. **1848** MACAULAY *Hist. Eng.* I. 654 That they were able to enrich themselves by so odious a trade. **1880** B. PRICE in *Fraser's Mag.* May 677 Enabling industry to expand and enrich.

2. *fig.* To make rich, endow, with mental or spiritual wealth.

1502 *Ord. Crysten Men* (W. de W. 1506) I. iv. 43 Sacerdotales the whiche is as moche for to saye as enryched and ennobled with holy mysteryes. **1597** HOOKER *Eccl. Pol.* v. lxxviii, Men specially enritcht with the gifts of the Holy Ghost. **1604** *Bk. Com. Prayer, For R. Family*, Enrich them with thy heauenly grace. **1730** THOMSON *Autumn* 1353 Enrich me with the knowledge of thy works. **1838** WORDSW. *Sonn. to Planet Venus*, Are we aught enriched in love and meekness?

3. a. To fill or store with wealth; to add to the valuable contents of.

1579 LYLY *Euphues* (Arb.) 112 Enrich thy cofers. **1593** SHAKS. *Rich. II*, I. iii. 141 Till twice fiue Summers haue enrich'd our fields. **1601** HOLLAND *Pliny* II. 632 Italy..inriched with captaines, souldiers, and slaues. **1634** MILTON *Comus* 505 All the fleecy wealth That doth enrich these downs. **1794** MRS. RADCLIFFE *Myst. Udolpho* i, Was enriched by a collection of the best books. **1831** SIR J. SINCLAIR *Corr.* II. 347 Who is travelling to enrich the Zoological Museum.

b. *fig.* To increase the wealth or copiousness of (a language); to add to, improve (a science, etc.).

1598 F. MERES in *Shaks. C. Praise* 21 The English tongue is mightily enriched. **1601** HOLLAND *Pliny* II. 537 Hee alone did illustrate and inrich it [sculpture] as much, if not more, than all his predecessors. **1664** POWER *Exp. Philos.* Pref. 18 Without inriching his discourse with any real Experiment or Observation. **1841** D'ISRAELI *Amen. Lit.* (1867) 136 Chaucer has been accused of having enriched the language with the spoils of France. **1848** MACAULAY *Hist. Eng.* I. 256 In that year [1679] our tongue was enriched with two words, Mob and Sham. **1856** EMERSON *Eng. Traits, Lit.* Wks. (Bohn) II. 113 Richard Owen has..enriched science with contributions of his own.

4. To make (the soil, etc.) rich in productive power; to fertilize.

1601 HOLLAND *Pliny* XVII. vi. I. 505 They have a great opinion of the same [Marle] that it mightily enricheth it [the ground] and maketh it more plentifull. **1622** WITHER *Sonn.* in Farr *S.P. Jas. I* (1848) 216 The hony, milky plaine, That is inricht by Jordan's watering. **1813** SIR H. DAVY *Agric. Chem.* (1814) 359 Substances, which in their use and decomposition must enrich the land.

5. To make 'rich' or splendid with decoration; often with added notion of costliness. Also *fig.*

1601 HOLLAND *Pliny* II. 456 The Gaules..were wont to goe to the wars brauely set out and inriched with gold. **1727** SWIFT *Gulliver* I. ii. 34 The hilt and scabbard were gold enriched with diamonds. **1742** COLLINS *Eclog.* III. 3 While ev'ning dews enrich the glitt'ring glade. *a* **1876** J. H. NEWMAN *Hist. Sk.* I. I. ii. 67 A lofty dome, the sides of which are enriched with agate.

6. a. To make 'richer' in quality, flavour, colour, etc.; to heighten, enhance (excellences).

1620 QUARLES *Div. Poems, Jonah*, When heaven's bright favours shone upon my face, And prosper'd my affairs, inrich'd my joyes. **1756** P. BROWNE *Jamaica* 11 The sugar cane..requires abundance of vegetable mould to inrich its sap. **1849** KINGSLEY *Lett.* (1878) I. 207 The green fern and purple heather have enriched the colouring since the spring. **1884** W. C. SMITH *Kildrostan* 46 You take a wild-flower And plant it in a garden to enrich Its life and beauty.

b. To raise (gas) to a required calorific value by the admixture of another gas.

1921 *Chem. Abstr.* XV. 1070 The gas to be enriched enters through a pipe and..passes through an outlet provided with a metal grid. **1958** *Times* 2 June p. iii/2 This gas is then enriched to the declared calorific value by the automatic addition of neat refinery gas.

c. To increase the abundance of a specific isotope in (a material); occas., to increase the abundance of (a specific isotope).

1945 H. D. SMYTH *Devel. Methods of using Atomic Energy* 130 Uranium which had already been partially enriched. **1949** *Atomics* Oct. 66 The O^{18} isotope of oxygen is being enriched by a factor of 100 at Harwell by a thermal diffusion plant. **1970** *Daily Tel.* 13 Nov. 5/1 Russia has offered to enrich uranium for Sweden's boiling water reactors.

Hence **en'riched** *ppl. a.*

1664 EVELYN *Kal. Hort.* (1729) 204 Temperately enrich'd Water, such as is impregnated with Neat and Sheeps-dung. **1816** J. SMITH *Panorama Sc. & Art* I. 158 The Tudor flower..forms a most beautiful enriched battlement. **1936** *Physical Rev.* XLIX. 404 The enriched sample [of carbon] may be removed for analysis. **1940** *Chambers's Techn. Dict.* 136/2 Carburetted (or enriched) water-gas. **1945** H. D. SMYTH *Devel. Methods of using Atomic Energy* 22 Such proposed arrangements are usually called 'enriched piles'. *Ibid.* 23 A chain reaction bomb in pure, or at least enriched, U-235 or plutonium. **1955** *Ann. Reg. 1954* 393 A full scale reactor to generate electricity..was to use slightly enriched uranium as fuel. **1957** *Times* 22 Aug. 4/4 Enriched uranium... Enriched nuclear fuel... Enriched fuel. **1970** *Daily Tel.* 4 Nov. 5 Enriched uranium with a uranium-235 share of more than 20 per cent. is the material used in atomic bombs.

enricher (ɛn'rɪtʃə(r)). [f. ENRICH *v.* + -ER[1].] One who or that which enriches.

c **1610** *Women Saints* 30 [Helena] the builder and enricher of churches throughe the worlde. **1616** SURFL. & MARKH. *Country Farme* 493 Because Turneps, Nauets, and Fetches are enrichers, and (as it were) manurings of the ground. **1738** WESLEY *Hymns, Come Holy Spirit, send down those Beams* i, Come, Thou enricher of the Poor. **1776** T. BOWDEN *Farm. Direc.* 20 Juicy plants, that much shade and cover the ground, are found to be enrichers of land.

†**enrichesse,** *v. Obs. rare*$^{-1}$. [f. EN-[1] + *richesse* RICHES.] *trans.* = ENRICH 1.

c **1430** *Pilgr. Lyf Manhode* I. (1869) 47 But i haue riht priuely hid it, for to enrichesse with the poore folk.

enriching (ɛn'rɪtʃɪŋ), *vbl. sb.* [f. ENRICH *v.* + -ING[1].] The action of the verb ENRICH.

1494 FABYAN VI. cxci. 194 Lothayr spoyled the kynges paleys and other places, to the great enrychynge of hym and his hoost. **1581** SIDNEY *Apol. Poetrie* (Arb.) 29 This enritching of memory..which..we call learning. **1677** YARRANTON *Engl. Improv.* 144 Made here of our own growth, to the Nations great enriching. **1812** COBBETT in *Exam.* 19 Oct. 671/2 The enriching and pampering of those who render no public service. **1856** EMERSON *Eng. Traits, Relig.* Wks. (Bohn) II. 101 The wise legislator..will shun the enriching of priests.

enriching (ɛn'rɪtʃɪŋ), *ppl. a.* [f. as prec. + -ING[2].] That enriches; in the senses of the vb.

1674 J. B[RIAN] *Harv. Home* iv. 25 Rain down from heav'n enriching floods. **1674** COLLINS in Rigaud *Corr. Sci. Men* (1841) II. 587 Your advice and assistance will be obliging and enriching to the commonwealth of learning. **1799** J. ROBERTSON *Agric. Perth* 268 Or lay enriching manure on the most barren ground. **1864** PUSEY *Lect. Daniel* v. 250 The enriching neighbourhood of the sea of Galilee to Naphtali. **1958** *Times* 2 June p. iii/1 Gas released as a by-product from a neighbouring petrochemical industry has been used for some years on a small scale as an enriching gas at Partington gas works.

Hence **en'richingly** *adv.*

1817 J. GILCHRIST *Intellect. Patrimony* 111 The operation is at first toilsome; but it is enrichingly profitable. **1865** R. PAUL *Let.* in *Mem.* xix. (1872) 322 Let the word of Christ dwell in you enrichingly.

enrichment (ɛn'rɪtʃmənt). [f. as prec. + -MENT.]

1. a. The action or process of enriching, in various senses; the condition of being enriched. Now *spec.* of a mixture of isotopes, esp. nuclear fuel: cf. ENRICH *v.* 6 c.

a **1626** BACON *Holy War* Wks. VII. (1859) 14 Not without great and ample additions, and enrichment thereof. **1631** MARKHAM (*title*), The Inrichment of the Weald of Kent. **1665** MANLEY *Grotius' Low C. Warres* 247 To behave themselves valiantly..would not onely be for their everlasting Honour, but Enrichment. **1724** WATTS *Logic* I. vi. §1 A vast hindrance to the enrichment of our understandings. **1748** ANSON *Voy.* I. i. 8 It was not principally intended for the enrichment of the Agents. **1875** WHITNEY *Life Lang.* vii. 120 Material..which furnishes notable enrichment to speech. **1876** GREEN *Short Hist.* vii. §1. 342 The smaller gentry shared in the general enrichment of the landed proprietors. **1936** *Physical Rev.* XLIX. 404 (*heading*) Evidence for the enrichment of carbon in the heavier isotope by diffusion. **1945** H. D. SMYTH *Devel. Methods of using Atomic Energy* 40 The amount of enrichment to be expected in a single production unit..was very small. **1958** *Engineering* 4 Apr. 423/3 Though it is stated that the new reactor uses enriched fuel, enrichment is normally unnecessary when the moderator is heavy water.

b. *concr.* A means of enriching; an addition of wealth.

1649 BLITHE *Eng. Improv. Impr.* (1653) 45 He [the merchant] fetches it from farre, and tis a gallant Inrichment to this Nation.

2. *spec.* The imparting of 'richness' of effect by decorative additions. Also *concr.* in sing. and in pl., the ornament used for enriching a building, etc.

1664 EVELYN tr. *Freart's Archit.* (R.), Neither did they often fill the pedestals with relieuo..and rarely euer allow the corona any enrichment. **1708** *New View Lond.* I. 101/2 A large Column..having Enrichments of Fruit, Leaves. **1837** WHITTOCK *Bk. Trades* (1842) 231 Filigree working is a kind of enrichment on gold or silver. **1864** BOUTELL *Heraldry Hist. & Pop.* xix. 316 The Effigy of Edward II..still retains..its sculptured enrichments.

†**enridged,** *ppl. a. rare*$^{-1}$. Thrown into ridges, ridged: see quot.

1605 SHAKS. *Lear* IV. vi. 71 *Qo.* 1 & 2 He had a thousand Noses, Hornes wealk'd, and waued like the enridged [1 *Fol.* enraged] sea.

†**en'right,** *v. Obs.* Also 7 **inright.** [f. EN-[1] + RIGHT *sb.*] *trans.* To put (a person) into (his) right; to invest *with* a right or title.

1587 TURBERV. *Trag. T.* (1837) 58, I my selfe enright thee with the conquest of the fielde. **1654** J. SPITTLEHOUSE *Vind. Fifth Monarchy Men* 7 Our principle doth not lead us forth to entitle our selves to such Offices; it being the Word of God that inrights us thereunto. **1656** S. H. *Gold. Law* 2 All the people must perish, to inright one unrighteous man.

enring (ɛn'rɪŋ), *v. poet.* Also 7 **inring.** [f. EN-[1] + RING *sb.*] *trans.* To put within a ring.

1. To form a ring round; to surround, encircle. *lit.* and *fig.* Also, to form into a ring.

1589 WARNER *Alb. Eng.* VI. xxxiii. (1612) 162 Inringed by his complices, their chearefull Leader said. **1594** CAREW *Tasso* (1881) 63 For Tancred and Reynold brake through the traine, That thicke of men and armes enringde tofore. **1613–6** W. BROWNE *Brit. Past.* I. iii, She rais'd the youth, then with her armes inrings him. *Ibid.* II. i, Sweet rest inrings The tyred body of the swarty clowne. **1833** MRS. BROWNING *Prometh. Bd.* Poems 1850 I. 188 The deep glooms enringing Tartarus! **1839–48** BAILEY *Festus* xxi. 267 Like the pure pearl-wreath which enrings thy brow.

2. To put a ring or rings on; to adorn with a ring. In quots. *transf.*

1590 SHAKS. *Mids. N.* IV. i. 49 The female Iuy so Enrings the barky fingers of the Elme. **1825** *Blackw. Mag.* XVIII. 434, I will leave..the enringing with eternal shackles One's right-hand fingers,—to whoever likes.

enripe: see EN- *pref.*[1] 2.

enripen (ɛn'raɪp(ə)n), *v. rare.* Also 7 **inripen.** [f. EN-[1] + RIPEN.] *trans.* To make ripe; to mature. *lit.* and *fig.* Hence **en'ripened** *ppl. a.*

a **1631** DONNE *Poems* (1650) 92 The summer how it inripened the yeare. **1855** SINGLETON *Virgil* I. 66 Vintager of your enripened bough.

enrive: see EN- *pref.*[1] 3.

enrobe (ɛn'rəʊb), *v.* Also 7 **inrobe.** [f. EN-[1] + ROBE *sb.*[1] Cf. OF. *enrober*.] *trans.* To put a robe upon, dress in a robe. Also *transf.* and *fig.*

1593 NASHE *Christ's T.* (1613) 41 The Sun..shall enrobe himselfe in scarlet. **1598** SHAKS. *Merry W.* IV. vi. 41 Quaint in greene, she shall be loose en-roab'd. **1614** SIR W. LEIGHTON in Farr *S.P. Jas. I* (1848) 265 This leprous corps of sinne with rags enrobe. **1738** WESLEY *Ps.* civ. 2 With Light Thou dost Thyself enrobe. **1850** *Chamb. Jrnl.* XIV. 30 The Nepaulese envoy, all sumptuously enrobed and glittering with jewels. **1862** NEALE *Hymns East. Ch.* 138 Enrob'd in earthly frame.

Hence **en'rober,** one who enrobes.

1598 FLORIO, *Inuestitore*, an inuestor, an installer, an enrober, an endower, a presentor.

en'rockment. [f. EN-[1] + ROCK + -MENT.] A mass of large stones thrown into water at random to form the bases of piers, breakwaters, etc.

1846 WORCESTER cites FRANCIS. **1864** in WEBSTER.

enrol, enroll (ɛn'rəʊl), *v.* Forms: 4 **enrolly,** 6–7 **enroule,** (7 **enrowle**), 5– **enrol(l;** also 5–8 **inrol(l,** (7 **inrowle**). [ME. *enrolly*, ad. OF. *enroll-er*,

(mod.F. *enrôler*), f. *en* (see EN-[1]) + OF. *rolle*, *roolle* (mod. *rôle*) ROLL.]

I. To write upon a roll.

1. *trans.* To write (a name), inscribe the name of (a person) on a roll, list, or register; to make a list of. Also † *to enrol up.*

c **1350** *Usages Winchester* in *Eng. Gilds* 359 Euerych soutere..shal..þe clerke a peny for to enrolly hys name. **1523** SKELTON *Garl. Laurel* 938, I, iwus, Endeuoure me Yowr name to se It be enrolde Writtin with golde. **1572** T. CARTWRIGHT in Whitgift *Answ. Cartwright* 91 Their Names written and enrouled vp. **1691** T. HALE *Acc. New Invent.* p. xc, Our Sea-men and their numbers were carefully enroll'd. *a* **1763** SHENSTONE *Elegies* XIII. 19 Myriads, in time's perennial list inroll'd. **1777** WATSON *Philip III* (1839) 93 The soldiers..were emulous to have their names enrolled for that dangerous service. **1846** MCCULLOCH *Acc. Brit. Empire* (1854) I. 595 Many also of the menial servants..are enrolled in the official returns in other classes.

2. To place upon a list; to incorporate as a registered or acknowledged member (*in* a society, corporate body, etc.). Also *fig.*

1613 SHAKS. *Hen. VIII*, I. ii. 119 This man..was enrold 'mongst wonders. *a* **1677** BARROW *Serm.* Wks. 1830 I. 351 To be deemed considerable in this faculty, and enrolled among the wittes. **1770** LANGHORNE *Plutarch* (1879) I. 27/1 When more were enroled in their body, [they were called] Conscript Fathers. **1824** W. IRVING *T. Trav.* I. 233, I now determined..to enrol myself in the fraternity of authorship. **1877** MRS. OLIPHANT *Makers Flor.* ii. (1877) 33 They were permitted to enrol themselves in any guild or art.

3. *esp.* To place on the list of an army; to enlist, incorporate in the ranks of an army; to levy (an army). Also *refl.* to enlist, take service.

1576 FLEMING *Panoplie Ep.* 77 If he..had not..enrolled, and mustered an armie of tried souldiours. **1611** BIBLE *1 Macc.* x. 36 There be enrolled amongst the kings forces about thirtie thousand men of the Iewes. **1651** HOBBES *Leviath.* II. xxi. 112 He that inrowleth himselfe a Souldier. **1716-8** LADY M. W. MONTAGUE *Lett.* I. xxxi. 109 In Asia any man that is rich is forced to enrol himself a janisary. **1798** MALTHUS *Popul.* (1878) 173 Those who are..tempted to enrol themselves as soldiers. **1876** J. H. NEWMAN *Hist. Sk.* I. I. ii. 77 They were enrolled as guards to the Caliph.

†4. To write (an agreement, deed, obligation, etc.) upon a roll or parchment; to engross, give legal form to. *Obs.*

Most of the instances may possibly belong to sense 5.

c **1430** LYDG. *Story Thebes* 1141 Thaccord enrolled in the toune. **1458** *Lease* in Ld. Campbell *Chancellors* (1857) I. xxii. 322, My dede enrolled and subscribed with myne owne hande. **1531-2** *Act 23 Hen. VIII*, c. 6 §5 The saide person so to be assigned..to write make and enroll suche obligacions. **1588** SHAKS. *L.L.L.* I. i. 38 Which I hope well is not enrolled there. **1628** COKE *On Litt.* 309 b, By Deed indented and inrolled according to the Statute.

5. To enter among the rolls, *i.e.* upon the records of a court of justice.

1495 *Act 11 Hen. VII*, c. 38 Pream., Indentures..inrolled in your Courte of the Chauncery of recorde. **1592** in *Vicary's Anat.* (1888) App. xv. 278 Euerie Maister shall enrolle the Indentures of his aprentice in the comon chartres office. **1660** MRQ. WORC. in Dircks *Life* xiv. (1865) 229 Having this Commission inrolled or assented unto by his Council. **1818** CRUISE *Digest* IV. 230 Where the deed was directed to be enrolled in a particular court, it must be enrolled in that court. **1875** STUBBS *Const. Hist.* III. xviii. 263 By which time..the really important petitions..were enrolled.

6. To record, *lit.* and *fig.*; also, to record with honour, celebrate.

1530 PALSGR. 357/1, I enrolle, I fyxe a thynge in my mynde. **1597** DANIEL *Civ. Wares* III. xxi, Be it enrold..how firm thy courage stood. **1633** G. HERBERT *Temple, Praise* vii, Small it is, in this poore sort To enroll thee. **1641** MILTON *Ch. Govt.* II. iii. (1851) 157 It had bin long agoe enroul'd to be nothing els but a pure tyrannical forgery. **1737** POPE *Hor. Epist.* II. i. 373 Dubb'd historians by express command To enrol your triumphs o'er the seas and land. **1742** YOUNG *Nt. Th.* VIII. 48 He..in heav'n's register inrolls The rise, and progress, of each option there. **1850** TENNYSON *In Mem.* xliii, So that still garden of the souls In many a figured leaf enrolls The total world.

II. To form into a roll.

7. a. To form into rolls or coils. b. To wrap up or enfold *in* or *with*; also *transf.* and *fig.*

1530 PALSGR. 537/1, I enrolle, I rolle up a writyng, or any other thing rounde. **1586** MARLOWE *1st Pt. Tamburl.* II. iii, Bullets..Enroll'd in flames and fiery smouldering mists. **1591** SPENSER *Virgil's Gnat* 257 [A snake] Now more and more hauing himselfe enrolde. **1596** —— *F.Q.* IV. iii. 41 Great heapes of them, like sheepe in narrow fold For hast did over-runne, in dust enrould. *c* **1630** DRUMM. OF HAWTH. *Poems* Wks. 5/2 Nor snow of cheeks with Tyrian grain enrol'd. **1659** C. NOBLE *Moderate Answ. Immod. Queries* 2 Wherein their own welfares and concerns were inrolled and bound up. **1694** ADDISON *Ovid's Met.* Wks. 1726 I. 196 Now in a maze of rings he lies enrowl'd. **1762** FALCONER *Shipwr.* II. 158 The folding reefs in plaits inroll'd they lay. **1836** G. S. FABER *Answ. Husenbeth* 17 Folds in which the small limbs of the Refutation itself have been..enrolled.

Hence **en'rolled** *ppl. a.* (sense 2).

1840 G. S. FABER *Regeneration* 234 Her acknowledged, and enrolled, and accredited members. **1853** STOCQUELER *Mil. Encycl., Enrolled Pensioners*, the out-pensioners of Chelsea Hospital, who are formed into companies for garrison and colonial duty. *Mod.* The society has a thousand enrolled members.

†**en'roll** *sb. Obs. rare*$^{-1}$. [f. prec. vb.] That in which anything is enrolled, a register.

1533-4 *Act 25 Hen. VIII*, c. 21 §9 One sufficient clerke..shall intitle in his bokes and enroll of recorde such other writinges.

en'roller. [f. ENROL *v.* + -ER.] One who enrols or registers.

1631 MAY tr. *Barclay's Mirr. Mindes* II. 30 Enrollers of the ancient vertue. **1755** in JOHNSON. **1828** in WEBSTER.

enrolling (ɛn'rəʊlɪŋ), *vbl. sb.* [f. ENROL *v.* + -ING[1].] The action of the verb ENROL.

1467 *Mann. & Househ. Exp.* (1841) 402 Item, for inrollynge of the forseid wrytt uppon the patent of lyvelode, ijs. iiijd. **1712** ARBUTHNOT *John Bull* 15 Fees for enrollings, exemplifications, bails, vouchers, returns, caveats, etc.

attrib. **1840** DICKENS *Barn. Rudge* xxxvi, How do our numbers stand since last enrolling-night?

enrolment (ɛn'rəʊlmənt). [f. ENROL *v.* + -MENT.] The action of enrolling.

1. The action of enrolling soldiers, citizens, etc.; the process of being enrolled.

1552 HULOET, Enrolemente or engrosement, *conscriptio*, *Perscriptio.* **1581** SAVILE *Tacitus' Hist.* Annot. (1591) 51 The number of souldiers in a Legion..at the first enrolment. **1619** SCLATER *Exp. 1 Thess.* (1630) 442 Enrolement in the number of the predestinate. **1640-4** *Parl. Orders* in Rushw. *Hist. Coll.* III. (1692) I. 744 Their first Inrollment of any such Horse and Horse-men. **1810** WELLINGTON in Gurw. *Disp.* V. 480 The enrolment, organization and equipment of this large force. **1845** R. HAMILTON *Pop. Educ.* iv. (ed. 2) 83 Many may need that education who are not of that religious enrolment. **1885** *Act 48 Vict.* c. 15 Sched. iii. Precept. §8 Premises..which would qualify him for enrolment as a burgess.

2. The action of recording in official archives; *esp.* the registering a deed, judgement, recognizance, acknowledgement, etc. in a court of record.

1535 *Act 27 Hen. VIII*, c. 27 Which regester of enrollementes, shall remaine and be safelie kepte in the said courte. *a* **1626** BACON *Max. & Uses Com. Law* 55 This needeth no inrollment as a bargaine and sale doth. **1641** *Termes de la Ley* 190 Inrolment is the registring, recording, or entring of any act or deed in the Chancery or else-where. **1818** CRUISE *Digest* IV. 131 All conveyances or incumbrances..prior to the enrolment, are..void. **1875** STUBBS *Const. Hist.* III. xviii. 262 To view the enrolment and engrossing of the acts of parliament.

b. *concr.* The entry or official record of a deed, etc.; a record in general.

1603 *Eng. Mourn. Garment* in *Harl. Misc.* (Malh.) II. 506 In no inrollment such a king is found. **1607-13** DAVIES *Hist. Tracts Irel.* (J.), The king..delivered the enrolments, with his own hands, to the bishop of Salisbury. **16..** *Dryden's Patent* in *Prose Wks.* I. App. (R.), These presents, or the inrolment thereof, shall be..a sufficient warrant.

3. Honourable celebration.

1602 *Metamorphosis Tabacco* (Collier) viii, [It] merits enroulement with Mæonian quill.

enrood, var. of INROAD *v. Obs.*

enroot (ɛn'ruːt), *v.* Only in pa. pple. Also 5 enrot, 9 inroot. [f. EN-[1] + ROOT.] *trans.*

1. To fix by the root.

1490 CAXTON *Eneydos* (1889) 17 Smalle busshes or lytyll trees, by humydite and hete, depely enroted in the erthe. **1590** SPENSER *F.Q.* III. iii. 22 And eke enrooted deepe must be that Tree, Whose big embodied braunches shall not lin Till they to hevens hight forth stretched bee. **1836-9** TODD *Cycl. Anat.* II. 553/1 In old persons close to the entrance [of the ear] hairs..are enrooted.

b. *fig.* To implant deeply in the mind; to fix firmly in custom or habit.

1596 SPENSER *Hymn Heav. Love* 24 The guilt of that infected cryme Which was enrooted in all fleshly slyme. **1688** JAS. II *Let. Feversham* in *4th Coll. Papers Pres. Juncture Affairs* 28 Your former Principles are so enrooted in you. **1805** *Ann. Rev.* III. 255 It has not the courage of the antient parliaments, because it is less inrooted.

2. To entangle root with root.

1597 SHAKS. *2 Hen. IV*, IV. i. 207 His foes are so en-rooted with his friends, That plucking to vnfixe an Enemie, Hee doth vnfasten so, and shake a friend.

enrough (ɛn'rʌf), *v.* Also 7 inrough. [f. EN-[1] + ROUGH *a.*] *trans.* or *refl.* To make (the sea) rough. Also *fig.*

1601 DONNE *Poems* (1650) 295 In vaine this sea shall..enrough It selfe. **1635** VALENTINE *Foure Sea-Serm.* 39 Our life inroughed with some tempests. **1840** BROWNING *Sordello* 257 He snuffs The aroused hurrican, ere it enroughs The sea.

†**en'round**, *v. Obs.* [f. EN-[1] + ROUND *sb.*]

1. *trans.* To surround, encircle.

c **1420** *Pallad. on Husb.* I. 590 And other while an hen wol have the pippe, A white pellet that wol the tonge enrounde. **1580** SIDNEY *etc. Ps.* xlvi. Kings with siege her walls enround. **1599** SHAKS. *Hen. V*, IV. Prol. 36 How dread an Army hath enrounded him. **1600** TOURNEUR *Transf. Met.* lxii, And spies the multitude that him enround.

2. To 'compass,' try to bring about. *Obs. rare*$^{-1}$.

1606 EARL NORTHAMPTON in *True & Perfect Relation* Bbb j a, A crafty pate, enrounding violently the ruine of our Soueraigne.

‖**en route** (ɑ̃ rut). [Fr.] On the way, in the course of the journey: see ROUTE.

enruby, enruin: see EN- *pref.*[1] 2.

enrut: see EN- *pref.*[1] 1 b.

‖**ens** (ɛnz), *sb. Pl.* entia ('ɛnʃɪə). [Late L. *ēns*; a neuter pr. pple. formed from L. *esse* to be, on the supposed analogy of the compds. *absēns, potēns*, etc.]

1. *Philos.* a. Something which has existence; a 'being', entity, as opposed to an attribute, quality, etc.

1614 T. ADAMS in Spurgeon *Treas. Dav.* Ps. ciii. 19 Eternity is properly the duration of an uncreated Ens. **1650** BULWER *Anthropomet.* 71 An ens is such naturally, that it should act or suffer something. **1677** HALE *Prim. Orig. Mankind* 323 Men have needlessly multiplied *Entia.* **1678** GALE *Crt. Gentiles* III. 113 For it's necessary that every ens or being be derived from the first Being.

b. An entity regarded apart from any predicate but that of mere existence. Also, the predicable 'ens' regarded as an abstract notion.

1581 SIDNEY *Apol. Poet.* (Arb.) 55 The quiddity of Ens. [**1628** MILTON *Vacation Exerc.*, Ens is represented as father of the Predicaments.] **1791** E. DARWIN *Bot. Gard.* I. 41 Ens without weight, and substance without shade. **1870** BOWEN *Logic* iv. 90, I cannot see why ens is not thinkable.

†2. = ESSENCE. *Obs.*

1649 J. E. tr. *Behmen's Ep.* 9 The dark fiery soule conceiveth the Ens and Essence of the Divine light in her selfe. **1730** *Phil. Trans.* XXXVI. 288 It is the very Ens, or Being most pure of Flame.

†b. *Alch.* (See quots.) *Obs.*

1662 R. MATHEW *Unl. Alch.* §109. 178 Weigh its weight of fresh Ens well ground together. **1683** SALMON *Doron Med.* I. 327 Reduce the Mercury of the Vulgar into its first liquid Ens. **1715** KERSEY, *Ens Primum*, the most efficacious Part of any natural Mixt Body. *Ens Veneris*, sublimation of equal Parts of the calcin'd Powder or Cyprus Vitriol, and of Sal Armoniack. **1721-1800** in BAILEY; and in mod. Dicts.

ens, var. of ENES *adv. Obs.* once.

Ensa ('ɛnsə). Also E.N.S.A., ENSA. [f. the initials of *Entertainments National Service Association.*] An organization established in 1939 to arrange entertainments for the services during the war of 1939–45.

1939 *War Illustr.* 11 Nov. 275 During the first two weeks of the war ENSA—Entertainments National Service Association—came into being with its headquarters at Drury Lane Theatre, London, to organize concert parties. **1940** *Times Weekly* 10 Jan. 19 Miss Gracie Fields..gave her third concert (organized by E.N.S.A. on behalf of N.A.A.F.I.) to the men of the Forces. **1941** G. GREENE *Nineteen Stories* (1947) 181 Not even an Ensa show? **1943** J. B. PRIESTLEY *Daylight on Saturday* xi. 68 General Office rang up to say that there had been a message from ENSA reminding him that they were giving a show in the canteen to-day. *Ibid.*, Proscot had cheered up a little when first he had been reminded that an ENSA show was coming to-day.

†**en'sacre**, *v. Obs.* [f. EN-[1] + SACRE.] *trans.* To consecrate to an ecclesiastical office.

1491 CAXTON *Vitas Patr.* (W. de W. 1495) I. cliii. 158 a/2, I was promoted to the dignytee of Archebysshopp ensacred & receyued in the holy chyrche of Alexandrye.

ensad, ensafe, -er, ensaffron: see EN- *pref.*[1] 2 and 1 b.

ensaigne, obs. variant of ENSIGN *sb.*

ensaim, var. of ENSEAM *v.*[1] *Obs.*

en'sained, *ppl. a.* [ad. OF. *enseignié, ensagnié*, marked, blazoned, instructed, skilled, adept.] Skilled, trained, learned.

1484 CAXTON *Curiall* (1888) 10 And alleway emong us courtyours ensayned [*printed* enfayned] we folowe more the names of thoffyces than the droytes and ryghtes.

ensaint: see EN- *pref.*[1] 2.

†**en'salve**, *v. Obs. rare*$^{-1}$. [f. EN-[1] + SALVE *sb.* or *v.*] *trans.* To put salve upon; to anoint.

c **1485** *Digby Myst.* (1882) IV. 916, I haue bought here oyntmentes..To ensalue his body.

†**en'sampial, en'saumplal**, *a. Obs. rare.* [f. ENSAMPLE + -AL[1]: it is uncertain which of the two forms was written by Pecock.] Only in phrase ***historial ensampial*** (*ensaumplal*): of the nature of a historical example.

c **1449** PECOCK *Repr.* 293 Or it is historial ensampial of the now bifore seid Moral Conversacioun. *Ibid.* III. vi. 309 No parti..being historial ensaumplal, lettith the seid endewing.

ensample (ɛn'sɑːmp(ə)l, -'sæm-), *sb. arch.* Forms: 4 ensamp-, ensaumpel, -ul(le, -il(l)e, (insampil, -saumpill, 5 emsampelle), 4–5 ensaumple, -nple, ensawmp(i)l(e, -yl, 3– ensample. [Altered form of ASAUMPLE, a. OF. *essample*: see EXAMPLE *sb.* (An AF. *ensample* occurs in some editions of Britton, but Nichols reads *essaumplarie.*)] = EXAMPLE in various senses.

The mod. archaistic use is almost wholly due to reminiscence of the passages in which the word occurs in the New Testament. In four of these passages it is used in sense 2, and is retained unaltered in the R.V.; in the remaining two it has the sense 3, and has in the R.V. been replaced by *example.*

1. An illustrative instance.

a **1300** *Cursor M.* 10595 (Gött.), Be þis ensampil may men sy, Godd wald scho grew and clamb on hij. **1393** GOWER *Conf.* III. 138 Wherof ensample if thou wilt seche, Take hede. **14..** *Pol. Rel. & L. Poems* 98 A gode Ensampille y wille telle. **1436** *Pol. Poems* (1859) II. 174 An emsampelle of deseytte. **1485** CAXTON *Pref. Malory's Arthur*, Also certeyn

bookes of ensaumples and doctryne. **1548** W. PATTEN *Exp. Scot.* in Arb. *Garner* III. 80 That if, for ensample like to this, I should rehearse to you out of the Old Testament, how the seven plentiful years, etc. **1597** MORLEY *Introd. Mus.* 20 Here is an ensample, peruse it. *a* **1850** ROSSETTI tr. *Dante's Vita Nuova* I. (1874) 81 By which ensamples this thing shall be made manifest.

†**b.** quasi-*adv.* = 'for example'. *Obs.*

c **1391** CHAUCER *Astrol.* II. §45 Ensampulle as thus: the ȝere of ovre lord 1400, etc.

2. A precedent which may be followed or imitated; a pattern or model of conduct.

1297 R. GLOUC. (1724) 446 And, vor ensample of hem, oþere ensentede þerto. *a* **1340** HAMPOLE *Psalter* cxliv. 22 Bi myn ensaumpill all fleyss..loue him wiþouten end. *c* **1386** CHAUCER *Prol.* 520 To drawen folk to heuen..By good ensample. *c* **1440** *York Myst.* xxvii. 86 Here schall I sette ȝou for to see þis ȝonge childe for insaumpills seere. *c* **1489** CAXTON *Sonnes of Aymon* xii. 295 A worthy capytayn is the myrrour & ensaunple to thother for to doo well. **1531** *Dial. on Laws Eng.* I. xxvi. (1638) 42 It seemeth that he doth against the ensample of God. **1556** *Chron. Gr. Friars* (1852) 90 He..askyd them mercy and foryefnes for his evylle insampulle. **1611** BIBLE *Phil.* iii. 17 Marke them which walke so, as ye haue vs for an ensample. —— *1 Thess.* i. 7. **1641** J. JACKSON *True Evang. T.* I. 85, I have Esay for an ensample. **1847** EMERSON *Poems, To Rhea* Wks. (Bohn) I. 403, I make this maiden an ensample To Nature.

b. Phrases: †*in* (†*to*) *ensample*; *to give, set* (*an*) *ensample*; *to take ensample* (†*at, by, of*).

c **1250** *Old Kent. Serm.* in *O.E. Misc.* 27 þer-of us yeft ensample þo þrie kinges of heþenesse. *c* **1305** *Edmund Conf.* 498 in *E.E.P.* (1862) 84 þis holi man euere nam his ensample bi seint Thomas. *Ibid.* 522 Nym ensample of me. *a* **1300** *Cursor M.* 17288. 175 (Cott.) Ensample at him he toke. *a* **1340** HAMPOLE *Psalter* xxvii. 1 Crist..settand him ensaumpile til rightwismen. **1393** LANGL. *P. Pl.* C. XVII. 324 What sorwes he suffrede in ensample of ous alle. *c* **1400** MAUNDEV. (Roxb.) xxiv. 111 To giffe his men ensaumple and will to feight. *c* **1410** LOVE *Bonavent. Mirr.* xxvii. (1510) H iij, He prayeth to ensample of us that we shulde oftsyth pray. *c* **1440** *Lay Folks Mass-bk.* (MS. C.), Grete ensaumple he settes þereto. **1483** CAXTON *G. de la Tour* C iij b, I pray yow that ye take ensample here at me. **1568** GRAFTON *Chron. Edw. III*, III. 284 Ye shall geve by this an evill ensample. **1865** PUSEY *Truth Eng. Ch.* 160 The ensample which He gave us in His Holy Childhood.

†**c.** *in ensample*: after the model (*of*); in imitation of the fact (*that*). *Obs.*

c **1391** CHAUCER *Astrol.* I. §21 In ensample that the zodiak in hevene is ymagened to ben a superfice contienyng a latitude of 12 degrees. *c* **1400** *Destr. Troy* 1610 In Ensample of this Cite [*sc.* Troy]..Rome on a Riuer rially was set.

3. A deterrent instance of punishment, or of the evil consequences of any course of conduct; a practical warning. Const. *to*, *of* (the person to be warned), also with possessive pronoun. Phrases, *for*, †*in ensample*.

c **1340** *Cursor M.* 47 (Trin.) Ensaumpel herby to hem I sey, þat rage in her riot al wey. **1375** BARBOUR *Bruce* I. 119 Walys ensample micht have bene To ȝow, had ȝe It forow sene. **1480** CAXTON *Chron. Eng.* cclvii. 336 They..were sore punysshed in ensample of other. **1523** LD. BERNERS *Froiss.* I. cccl. 561 They shulde neuer haue peace with him, in ensample to all other townes. **1547** J. HARRISON *Exhort. Scottes* 232 May not the ruine of yᵉ Grekes..suffyce for your ensample? **1611** BIBLE *2 Peter* ii. 6 Making them [Sodom and Gomorrha] an ensample vnto those that after should liue vngodly. **1858** GEN. P. THOMPSON *Audi Alt.* I. xlviii. 189 Now these things happened for our ensamples.

†**en'sample**, *v.* *Obs.* [f. prec. sb.]

1. *trans.* **a.** To authorize by example; also, to set forth as an example.

c **1380** WYCLIF *Serm.* Sel. Wks. I. 10 Dedis ben nouȝtis þat ben not ensaumplid and wrouȝt by þis fadir. **1393** GOWER *Conf.* I. 1 Some matere Ensampled of the old wise.

b. To give an example or instance of.

c **1380** WYCLIF *Sel. Wks.* III. 512 ȝif þes newe reules weren [etc.]..[he] shulde have taught hem boþe and ensaumpled, boþe in his lif and spekinge. **1393** GOWER *Conf.* II. 148 In what maner it is grevous, Right fain I wolde ensample here. *c* **1449** PECOCK *Repr.* III. vi. 311 Crist ensamplid thilk greet pouerte. **1589** SPENSER *F.Q.* Pref., Homere..hath ensampled a good governour and a vertuous man. *a* **1599** —— in Farr *S.P. Eliz.* (1845) I. 16 He..Ensampled it by this most righteous deede.

2. To give an example to; to instruct by example. Also, to model (something, oneself) *by*, *upon*.

c **1380** WYCLIF *Sel. Wks.* III. 360 For Cristis lyf was þe beste, þat shulde ensaumple alle oþir. **1393** GOWER *Conf.* III. 241 Wherof all other..Ensampled hem upon the dede. **1654** GAYTON *Pleas. Notes* II. iv. 47 Of him that had the view of the Temple (for I cannot ensample you in all) take this small account. *Ibid.* III. iv. 86 But if ever he had a true one [*sc.* sword], it must be made and ensampled by that of Chinons of England.

b. *intr.* To give an example (*to*).

c **1449** PECOCK *Repr.* II. v. 168 Forto ensaumple to othere men. *Ibid.* 314 For strengthe of her ensampling..tho circumstauncis for which thei so ensampliden.

ensampler (ɛn'sɑːmplə(r), -'sæm-). Forms: 4 **ensamplaire**, 4–5 **ensaumpler**. [ad. OFr. *essamplaire*:—L. *exemplārium*, f. *exemplum* EXAMPLE. Cf. EXEMPLAR *sb.*]

a. A copy, pattern. **b.** A 'copy' of a book.

c **1374** CHAUCER *Boeth.* III. ix. 87 þou drawest alle þinges of þi souereyne ensampler. **1388** WYCLIF *Joshua* Prol., Men of my language, the whiche oure ensaumpleris deliten. *c* **1449** PECOCK *Repr.* III. xix. 412 Thei ouȝten be ensaumplers of moral vertues.

†**en'sampling**, *vbl. sb.* *Obs.* [f. ENSAMPLE *v.* + -ING[1].] The action of the vb. ENSAMPLE.

c **1449** PECOCK *Repr.* III. vi. 309 If eny ensaumpling schulde lette the seid endewing, it schulde be the ensaumpling of Crist. **1598** FLORIO, *Rasempiatura*, an ensampling.

ensand, ensandal: see EN- *pref.*[1] 1 b.

ensanguine (ɛn'sæŋgwɪn), *v.* [f. EN-[1] + L. *sanguin-em* blood. Cf. It. *insanguinare*.] *trans.* To stain with blood.

1667 [see next]. **1797** *Monthly Rev.* XXIII. 509 In tyrannizing over, desolating, ensanguining, and dishonouring France. **1878** SPURGEON *Treas. Dav.* Ps. cv. 29 The beloved Nile and other streams were all equally tainted and ensanguined.

ensanguined (ɛn'sæŋgwɪnd), *ppl. a.* [f. ENSANGUINE *v.* + -ED[1].]

1. Blood-stained, bloody.

1667 MILTON *P.L.* XI. 654 Now scatterd lies With Carcasses and Arms th' ensanguind Field. **1726** THOMSON *Winter* 828 He lays them [the deer] quivering on the ensanguined snows. **1803** *Ann. Reg.* 706 The ferocity of an ensanguined rabble. **1816** BYRON *Parisina* xvii, The dust, which each deep vein Slaked with its ensanguined rain. **1851** MAYNE REID *Scalp Hunt.* xxix. 216 His eye was caught by the ensanguined object upon the rock.

b. *fig.*

1806 *Naval Mag.* XV. 243 The ensanguined fury with which it was fought. **1829** K. DIGBY *Broadst. Hon.* I. *Godefridus* 128 The most ensanguined pages of profane history. **1886** *Pall Mall G.* 18 June 10/2 The turbulent and ensanguined history of Ireland.

2. *transf.* Dyed or stained blood-colour; crimson.

1784 COWPER *Task* IV. 217 Ensanguin'd hearts, clubs typical of strife. **1812** H. & J. SMITH *Rej. Addr., Drury's Dirge* ix, Jealousy's ensanguin'd chalice, Mantling pours the orient wave. *a* **1845** BARHAM *Ingol. Leg., Metempsychosis* 132 Liquid of the same ensanguined hue.

ensate ('ɛnseɪt), *a. Bot.* [ad. mod.L. *ensātus*, f. L. *ēnsis* sword: see -ATE.] Sword-shaped.

1830 LINDLEY *Nat. Syst. Bot.* 277 The ensate or grassy ones [leaves] of Asphodeleæ.

ensaumpel, -ul(le, etc., var. of ENSAMPLE.

†**en'say**, *v.* *Obs. rare*[−1]. [prob. ad. Sp. *ensayar*; cf. OF. *ensayer*.] = ASSAY *v.* 4.

1740 tr. *Barbas' Metals, Mines, & Min.* 103 The people..brought me some of the Oar to ensay it.

ensayme, var. of ENSEAM *v.*[1] *Obs.*

†**en'scale**, *v.* *Obs. rare*[−1]. [? f. EN- *pref.*[1] + SCALE (in music).] *trans.* ? To attune.

1638–48 G. DANIEL *Eclog.* v. 115 When the flood Of devine fury, might enscale our Ears T' astonishment.

enscance, obs. var. ENSCONCE.

enscarf: see EN- *pref.*[1] 1 b.

†**en'schedule**, *v.* *Obs. rare*[−1]. [f. EN-[1] + SCHEDULE *sb.*] *trans.* To insert in a schedule; to write down on a list; to schedule.

1599 SHAKS. *Hen. V*, v. ii. 73 Whose Tenures and particular effects You haue enschedul'd briefely in your hands.

enscheryching: see ENCHERISH.

†**en'sclaundre**, *v.* *Obs. rare*[−1]. [Corrupt var. of ESCLANDRE.] *trans.* To bring scandal upon.

1389 in *Eng. Gilds* (1870) 4 Eny riotour, oþer contekour, oþer such by whom þe fraternite myght be ensclaundred.

ensconce (ɛn'skɒns), *v.* Forms: 6 **enscance**, 7 **ensconse**, 6–7 **inskonce, -se**, 6–8 **insconce, -se**, 6– **ensconce**. [f. EN-[1] + SCONCE *sb.*, small fortification, earthwork, prob. ad. OF. *esconse* hiding-place, place of shelter, whence *esconser* to hide, shelter, which may be the source of some of the uses of this verb. Cf. SCONCE *v.*

The form *enscance* in Barret suggests derivation from Du. *skans* = SCONCE.]

†**1.** *trans.* To furnish with 'sconces' or earthworks; to fortify. Also *absol.* *Obs.*

1590 SIR J. SMYTHE *Disc. Weapons* 12 b, A vaine opinion of insconsing of Sconces in the drie grounds of England. **1611** FLORIO, *Bastionare*, to ensconce, to blocke. **1752** CARTE *Hist. Eng.* III. 674 To insconce the bridges, to stop the fords. **1867** SMYTH *Sailor's Word-bk.*, *Ensconce*, to intrench; to protect by a slight fortification.

absol. **1598** BARRET *Theor. Warres* II. i. 16 He is to enscance and fortifie as commodity and the place will permit.

†**2.** To shelter within or behind a fortification; also *transf.* and *fig.* *Obs.*

1590 SHAKS. *Com. Err.* II. ii. 38, I must get a sconce for my head, and Insconce it to. **1593** —— *Lucr.* 1515 He entertain'd a show, so seeming iust, And therein so ensconc't his secret euill, that, etc. *a* **1628** DENISON *Heav. Banq.* (1631) 80 The Israelites were insconsed with strong bulwarkes. **1663** BUTLER *Hud.* I. iii. 1349 A Fort of Error, to ensconce Absurdity and Ignorance. **1686** W. DE BRITAINE *Hum. Prud. Convers.* 21 'Tis my Complacency that Vest to have, T' insconce my Person from Frigidity. *a* **1734** NORTH *Exam.* III. viii. ¶79 (1740) 644 His Person..is insconsed.

†**b.** *refl.* Also *fig.* *Obs.*

1590 SIR J. SMYTH *Disc. Weapons* 13 Wet grounds where they may ensconce themselves with small cost within little Ilands. **1624** CAPT. SMITH *Virginia* I. 6 Inskonsing my selfe euery two dayes, where I would leaue Garrisons for my retreat. **1678** BUTLER *Hud.* III. i. 1115 He..Insconc'd himself as formidable As could be underneath a Table.

fig. *c* **1600** SHAKS. *Sonn.* xlix, Against that time do I insconce me here Within the knowledge of mine owne desart. **1627** SPEED *England, etc., Wales* xiv. §3 The Country hath not naturall prouision to ensconce her selfe against the extremitie of winds and weather.

†**c.** *intr.* for *refl.*

1600 CAPT. SMITH in Hakluyt *Voy.* III. 257, I would haue holden this course of insconsing euery two dayes march. **1663** BUTLER *Hud.* I. iii. 416 The Fort where he ensconc'd. **1721** D'URFEY *New Operas* 250 E'er I could Ensconce, comes up this Devil agen.

3. *trans.* To establish in a place or position for the purpose **a.** of concealment; **b.** of security, comfort, 'snugness', etc. Chiefly *refl.*

a. **1598** SHAKS. *Merry W.* III. iii. 97, I will ensconce mee behinde the Arras. **1826** SCOTT *Woodst.* viii, He must discover where this Stewart hath ensconced himself. **1841** CATLIN *N. Amer. Ind.* (1844) I. xxi. 155, I have been closely ensconced in an earth-covered wig-wam. **1849** MISS MULOCK *J. Halifax* (ed. 17) 329, [I] ensconced myself behind the sheltering bank blinds. **1877** CLERY *Min. Tact.* xii. 147 Bodies of French skirmishers ensconced themselves in the undulations of the ground.

b. **1820** W. IRVING *Sketch Bk.* II. 126 The parson, who was deeply ensconced in a high-backed oaken chair. **1840** DICKENS *Old C. Shop* xviii, Ensconcing themselves, in the warm chimney-corner. **1847** LD. LINDSAY *Chr. Art.* I. 121 A vine, emblematical of the church..the four doctors of the Latin church ensconced among its branches. **1862** LYTTON *Str. Story* II. 73 His guest had ensconced himself in Forman's old study.

Hence **en'sconcing** *vbl. sb.*

1590 SIR J. SMYTH *Disc. Weapons* 13 Their ensconcings in the drie grounds upon the Havens of England, are to small purpose. *a* **1652** BROME *Mad Couple* II. i. Wks. 1873 I. 31, I need no more insconsing now in Ram-alley.

enscore, enscreen, enscroll: see EN- *pref.*[1] 3, 1 b, 2.

ensculpture: see INSCULPTURE.

enseal (ɛn'siːl), *v.* *arch.* Forms: 4–5 **ensele**, (5 **enceyl**), 6–7 **enseal(l)e**, 5– **enseal**. Also 5–7 **inseal**. [a. OFr. *enseel-er*, *enceel-er*, *enseal-er*, f. *en-* (see EN-[1]) + *seel* (mod. *sceau*) SEAL.]

1. *trans.* To affix a seal to (a document); to attest or confirm by sealing.

c **1330** R. BRUNNE *Chron.* (1810) 258 Boþe to hold couenanz with scrite enselid þe dede. **1377** LANGL. *P. Pl.* B. II. 112 In þe date of þe deuel þis dede I assele [*v.r.* ensele]. **1443** *Test. Ebor.* (1855) II. 134 A speciall wille enceylyd with the seale of myn armes. **1466** in *Paston Lett.* No. 554. II. 284 Divers old deeds, some without date, insealed under autenticke seales. **1574** tr. *Littleton's Tenures* 107 b, The heire of the disseysour that ensealeth the deede. *a* **1709** ATKYNS *Parl. & Pol. Tracts* (1734) 175 The Statutes..require Indentures ensealed by the Electors to be tack'd to the Writ.

fig. *a* **1500** *Chaucer's Dreme* 1016 For every thing he said there, Seemed as it insealed were. **1581** J. BELL *Haddon's Answ. Osor.* 444 That one onely Sacrifice, which Christ..did enseale, and Ratify with his owne precious body.

b. To put a seal or stamp upon (a measure or weight) in token of its being up to the standard.

1467 in *Eng. Gilds* (1870) 383 That it be made after the wyght ensealed accordynge to the kynges standard. *c* **1610** in Gutch *Coll. Cur.* II. 15 That every Vintner have their pots and their measures sized and insealed after the standard of the University.

2. To close with a seal, seal up.

a **1340** HAMPOLE *Psalter* Prol., þis boke is cald garthen closed wel enseled. **1465** *Paston Lett.* No. 502. II. 187 A box enselyd with hys owyn seall. **1613** SIR H. FINCH *Law* (1636) 22 A boxe insealed with charters. **1714** SCROGGS *Courts-leet* (ed. 3) 110 A Box ensealed with writings. **1886** BURTON *Arab. Nts.* (abridged) I. 78 A well-shut house With keyless locks and doors ensealed.

fig. *c* **1374** CHAUCER *Troylus* v. 151 But this enseled [*v.r.* ensealed] til an other day.

en'sealing, *vbl. sb.* [f. ENSEAL *v.* + -ING[1].] The action of the verb ENSEAL. *lit.* and *fig.*

1531–2 *Act 23 Hen. VIII*, c. 6 §8 At the tyme of ensealynge of the proces for execucion. **1561** DAUS tr. *Bullinger on Apoc.* (1573) 100 He himselfe geeveth them faith and his spirite, which is the insealyng of their mynds. **1755** MAGENS *Insurances* II. 386 At the Ensealing and Delivery hereof.

†**en'sealing**, *ppl. a.* *Obs.* [f. ENSEAL *v.* + -ING[2].] That enseals or confirms.

1563 MAN *Musculus' Commonpl.* 278 b, They [Sacraments] doe confirme us, not as the very ensealing spirite himselfe doth, but as ensealing signes.

†**en'sealment.** *Obs.* [f. ENSEAL *v.* + -MENT.] The action of ensealing; that which enseals or confirms; a confirmation.

1581 MARBECK *Bk. of Notes* 92 Our Baptime is a certaine..ensealement and Sacrament of our attonement with God.

†**en'seam**, *sb.* *Obs.* In 5 **ensayme**. [? f. next vb.] That which is enseamed or cleansed away; superfluous fat; scourings.

1486 *Bk. St. Albans* B j a, Ensayme of an hawke is the grece.

†**en'seam**, *v.*[1] *Obs.* Forms: 5 **enceym**, 5–7 **ensayme, -seame**, (7 **ensaim, -sayn**), 6– **enseam**; also 7–8 **inseame**. [ad. OF. **ensaime-r* (cf. *ensemer* in Cotgr.), altered form of *essaimer*

(mod. *esseimer*, *essimer*), f. *es-*, L. *ex-* + OF. (**saim*), *saïn* grease (mod. *sain-doux* lard) :—med.L. *sagīmen* stuffing. Cf. SEAM *sb.* grease, lard.]

1. *trans.* To cleanse (a hawk, later also a horse) of superfluous fat.

c **1450** *Bk. Hawkyng* in *Rel. Ant.* I. 308 Withdrawe his mete in the mewe sevennyghe and wasch it eche tyme, and sumtyme with vinegre til he be enceymyd. **1486** *Bk. St. Albans* B j a, It is tyme for to fede hir with wash mete and to begynne to ensayme hire. *a* **1528** SKELTON *Ware Hawke* 78 She was not clene ensaymed. **1575** TURBERV. *Falconrie* in *Edin. Rev.* (1872) Oct. 356 How you shall enseame a hawke, or give her castings and scourings. **1598** FLORIO, *Alenare*, to enseame a horse. **1611** COTGR., *Ensemer*, to inseam; unfatten. **1614** MARKHAM *Cheap Husb.* (1623) 55 Till you have enseamed him [your hunting horse], hardned his flesh, taken away his inward grease. **1639** T. DE GREY *Compl. Horsem.* 340 If you bee in the way of ensaying your horse. **1774** GOLDSM. *Nat. Hist.* III. 69 Twenty days before we enseam a falcon.

¶ **b.** (See quot.: perh. only a misapprehension.)

1611 COTGR., *Affener*, to feed or inseame with hay; to stall-feed.

2. *intr.* for *refl.* of the hawk: To become clear of superfluous fat, etc.

1486 *Bk. St. Albans* B iij a, As she ensaymeth hir fete will wax yolow and smothe. **1615** LATHAM *Falconry* (1633) 62 Reasonable time..that she may enseame inwardly, and outwardly together.

Hence **en'seaming** *vbl. sb.*

c **1575** *Perfect Bk. Sparhawkes* (1886) 15 Ensayming is to take her gresynes and foulnes awaye. **1615** LATHAM *Falconry* (1633) 45 No one of the other sort of hawks is in a quarter of that danger in their inseaming that she is in.

†**en'seam,** *v.*² *Obs.* [ad. Fr. *enseimer* (now *ensimer*); OFr. *ensaimer*, f. *en-* (see EN-¹) + OF. **saim*, *saïn*: see ENSEAM *v.*¹] *trans.* To load with grease. Hence **en'seamed** *ppl. a. fig.*

The Fr. word is now used only in sense 'to grease (cloth)', whence perh. the fig. use in Shaks.

1562 LEIGH *Armorie* (1597) 57 Hee is not enseamed with much fatnesse, but is all of muscles and senues. **1602** SHAKS. *Ham.* III. iv. 92 In the ranke sweat of an enseamed bed.

enseam (ɛn'siːm), *v.*³ Also 7–8 **inseam.** [f. EN-¹ + SEAM *sb.* and *v.*]

†**1.** *trans.* To sew or stitch up in. *Obs.*

1605 CAMDEN *Rem.* (1636) 35 A jewel..which one stale away and enseamed it in his thigh. *Ibid.* (1657) 66 Jupiter halted when Bacchus was enseamed in his thigh.

2. To mark as with a seam. Cf. SEAM *v.*

1611 BEAUM. & FL. *4 Plays in One, Triumph of Death* vi, Take him dead-drunk now, without repentance, His lechery inseam'd upon him. **1725** POPE *Odyss.* XIX. 544 Deep o'er his knee inseam'd, remain'd the scar. **1856** T. AIRD *Poet. Wks.* 79 Gray men enseamed with many a scar.

†**en'seam.** *v.*⁴ *Obs. rare.* [Of obscure etymology: cf. ME. *in same*, *inseme* together; also ON. *semja* to put together.] *trans.* ? To bring together. **a.** To include or contain together. **b.** To introduce to company.

1596 SPENSER *F.Q.* IV. xi. 35 And bounteous Trent, that in him selfe enseames Both thirty sorts of fish, and thirty sundry streames. **1607** CHAPMAN *Bussy D'Ambois* Plays 1873 II. 16 Beaupres, come I'le enseame thee: Ladies..I haue heere a friend that I would gladlie enter in your graces.

†**en'sear,** *v. Obs.* [f. EN-¹ + *sear*, SERE *a.*] *trans.* To dry up.

1607 SHAKS. *Timon* IV. iii. 187 Enseare thy Fertile and Conceptious wombe.

†**en'search,** *sb. Obs.* [ad. OF. *encerche*, f. *encerchier*: see next vb.] The action of the vb. ENSEARCH; search.

a **1509** *Instr. Hen. VII to Ambass.* in *Brit. Mag.* II. 403 The kings..servants..shall make inquisician, and enserche. **1529** MORE *Heresyes* II. Wks. 191/2 The church by dylygent enserche, fyndeth the life of a man holy. **1530** PALSGR. Introd. 3 After enquery and enserche made for them, dyvers came unto my handes. **1605** VERSTEGAN *Dec. Intell.* i. (1628) 11 Such insearch and enquirie as he most diligently made.

ensearch (ɛn'sɜːtʃ). *v. Obs.* exc. *arch.* Forms: 4–5 **encerche**, 4–6 **enserch(e**, **-searche**, (6 **ensertche**), 6– **ensearch.** Also 6 **inserch(e**, **-search(e.** [ME. *encerche(n*, *enserche(n*, ad. OF. *encerchier*, *enserchier*, f. *en* (see EN-¹) + *cerchier* (Fr. *chercher*) to SEARCH.]

1. *trans.* To look carefully through (a country, place, book or document); to examine, pry into, scrutinize, search. Also *fig.*

1382 WYCLIF *Gen.* xxxi. 37 Thou..hast enserchid alle my necessaryes of hows. *c* **1400** MAUNDEV. xxxi. (1839) 314 For to encerche tho Contrees. *c* **1449** PECOCK *Repr.* I. xiii. 71 It is no nede me forto..encerche the writingis of Doctouris. **1531** ELYOT *Gov.* II. ix. (1883) II. 110 He folowing with his swerde redy drawen wolde therwith enserche the bedde, cofers, and all other places of his chambre. **1563–87** FOXE *A. & M.* (1596) 965/2 Studiously to ensearch and peruse the places of holy Scripture. **1577** STANYHURST *Descr. Irel.* in *Holinshed* VI. Ep. Ded., If it shall stand with your honor his pleasure..at vacant houres to insearch it, you shall find therein etc. **1855** SINGLETON *Virgil* I. 124 But to ensearch the cursed cold [soil] is hard.

fig. *c* **1430** *Hymns Virg.* (1867) 117 Graunte þat we may oure silf to enserche & se. **1537** *Inst. Chr. Man* M vj b, But if he diligently enserche his own harte. **1549** CHALONER tr. *Erasm. Moriæ Enc.* F iij b, An ungodly curiositee to ensearche the secrets of Nature. **1566** DRANT *Wail. Hierim.* K vj b, Let us insearche and trye our selves, and turne to God againe. **1627–77** FELTHAM *Resolves* I. xvii. 29 If we giue repulses, we are presently..insearched for the cause.

2. To seek for (a person or thing); to inquire after. Also with *out.*

1382 WYCLIF *Zeph.* i. 6 Whiche souȝten..not the Lord nether enserchiden hym. **1436** *Pol. Poems* (1859) II. 203 Pease men shulde enserche with besinesse. **1530** PALSGR. Introd. 3, I dyd my effectuall devoire to ensertche out suche bokes. **1538** STARKEY *England* I. ii. 39 We must now seke out and enserch the veray true commyn wele.

3. To search into (facts, errors, etc.); to inquire into, investigate. Also with obj. sentence: To inquire.

c **1400** *Prymer in Eng.* in Maskell *Mon. Rit.* II. 130 That thou enquere my wickidnesse and enserche my synne. **1530** TINDALE *Answ. More* IV. iii. Wks. III. 171 Then we will ensearch whether it may be a sacrament or no. **1541** ELYOT *Image Gou.* 61 Than wolde he diligently ensearche, of what perfection their woorkes were. **1577** STANYHURST *Descr. Irel.* in *Holinshed* VI. 35 Cambrensis insearcheth diverse philosophicall reasons in finding out the cause. **1581** W. STAFFORD *Exam. Compl.* i. (1876) 30 Would ensearch the default, and then certifie the good man of the house thereof.

4. *intr.* To make search; to inquire.

1382 WYCLIF *Deut.* xix. 18 Whanne moost bisily enseerchynge thei fynden, etc. *c* **1450** *Bk. Curtasye* 232 in *Babees Bk.* (1868) 306 Enserche no fyr pen falles to the. **1481** CAXTON *Myrr.* III. x. 152 Tholomeus..was he..that most enserched of the sterres. **1494** FABYAN VI. clxxxv. 184 Enserchynge thorugh his landes for suche a knyght. **1533–4** *Act 25 Hen. VIII*, c. 9 §6 To enserch or make any inquerie thereof. **1587** M. GROVE *Pelops & Hipp.* (1878) 15, I wil that ye ensearch foorthwith, and it reueale to me.

†**en'searcher.** *Obs.* Forms: 4 **enserchere**, 5–6 **enserchour**, 6 **enserchеr**, **insearcher.** [f. ENSEARCH *v.* + -ER: in ME. a. OF. *encerchere*, *-eor.*] One who searches, pries, or inquires into.

1382 WYCLIF *Ecclus.* xiv. 22 Who thenketh out the weies of hym in his herte..goende aftir it as enserchere. *c* **1440** *Gesta Rom.* xvi. 55 (Add. MS.) The first of you is a stronge werriour, The second best counseilloure, and the thirde the sotelest enserchour. *a* **1535** MORE *Wks.* 3 A desirous enserchour of the secretes of nature. **1577–87** HOLINSHED *Chron.* I. 9/1 Cambrensis..was a curious insearcher therof.

†**en'searching,** *vbl. sb. Obs.* [f. ENSEARCH *v.* + -ING¹.] The action of the verb ENSEARCH; the action of looking for, or inquiring into.

c **1430** tr. *T. à Kempis' Imit.* I. iii, What auailiþ grete enserching of hidde & derke þinges? **1531–2** *Act 23 Hen. VIII*, c. 8 §1 The inserchinge, finding and wasshinge of the saide tinne. **1605** VERSTEGAN *Dec. Intell.* i. (1628) 11 Tacitus a man curious in the insearching..for the originall of the Germans.

enseat: see EN- *pref.*¹ 1 a.

en secondes noces: see EN *prep.*

†**enseel** (ɛn'siːl), *v. Obs. rare*⁻¹. In 5 **ensile.** [f. EN-¹ + SEEL *v.*] *trans.* To stitch up the eyelids of (a hawk).

1486 *Bk. St. Albans* A ij b, He most take with hym needell and threde to ensile the hawkes that ben takien. **1678–1706** in PHILLIPS. **1721–80** in BAILEY; and in mod. Dicts.

enseem: see EN- *pref.*¹ 3.

†**en'seer,** *sb. Obs.* Also 5 **inseer.** [f. EN-¹ + SEER.] One who sees or looks into (anything).

c **1400** *Test. Love* III. (1560) 293/1 This leude book..by a good inseer may be understande. **1535** JOYE *Apol. Tindale* 20 God..is onely the enseer and sercher of herte and mynde.

ensege, -segge, var. of ENSIEGE.

enseigne, -eyne, -eygne, obs. ff. ENSIGN *sb.*

enseignment, var. of ENSIGNMENT.

†**en'seise,** *v. Obs. rare*⁻¹. [ad. OF. *enseisir*, *ensaisir*, f. *en-* (see EN-¹) + *saisir* to SEISE.] *trans.* To put (a person) in possession.

c **1420** *Anturs of Arth.* xxiii, That segge schalle ensese him atte a session.

ensemble (ɑ̃sɑ̃bl), *adv.* and *sb.* Also 5 **insamble.** [a. Fr. *ensemble*:—late L. *insimul*, f. *in* in + *simul* at the same time.]

A. *adv.* Together, at the same time.

c **1440** *Anc. Cookery* in *Househ. Ord.* (1790) 457 And when hit is boylet ensemble in the settynge doune, put therto a lytel vynegur. **1494** FABYAN VII. 482 The .ii. cardynallys ensemble sped theim vnto Parys. *Ibid.* VII. 574 Vpon the .vii. daye in lyke wyse played insamble an Henauder, and one Iohn Standysshe, esquyer. *a* **1528** SKELTON *Sp. Parrot* 417 For ffrantiknes and wylfulnes and braynles ensembyll, The nebbis of a lyon they make to trete and trembyll. **1861** G. MEREDITH *Let.* 19 Nov. (1970) I. 115 Before dinner we all bathed in Como, ladies and gentlemen ensemble. **1966** AUDEN *About House* 44 He, she, or both ensemble Emerge from a private cavity to be reborn.

‖**B.** *sb.* (Only as Fr.)

1. a. All the parts of anything taken together so that each part is considered only in relation to the whole; the general effect (of a person's appearance, a whole work of art, etc.). Also **tout ensemble** (tut ɑ̃sɑ̃bl) [Fr. *tout* all] in same sense.

1703 TATE *Portrait-Roy. H.M. Picture* Notes 22 There must be, what Painters call, an agreement of the Tout Ensemble. **1750** CHESTERF. *Lett.* (1792) III. 70 All these trifling things..collectively form that pleasing *je ne sçais quoi*, that *ensemble* which they are utter strangers to. **1782** POWNALL *Antiq.* 81 The *ensemble* of the piece will be hid from us and unintelligible. **1802** M. BERRY *Jrnl.* 16 Mar. (1866) II. 137 A long *pas de deux* was performed with such a perfect *ensemble* and precision, that [etc.]. **1823** BYRON *Juan* XIV. xl, The 'tout ensemble' of his movements wore a Grace. **1833** HT. MARTINEAU *Briery Cr.* v. 108 One might almost call his ensemble slovenly to-day. **1855** H. SPENCER *Princ. Psychol.* (1872) II. VI. ix. 126 The proportions of its body and limbs in their ensemble and details, are nearly the same. **1879** BEERBOHM *Patagonia* iii. 37 A shaggy beard and moustache completed the toutensemble of his really striking face. **1915** M. E. PERUGINI *Art of Ballet* III. xxxiii. 293 There had hardly been, perhaps, quite that unity and perfection of *ensemble* which the coming of a dancer of superb technique made possible.

b. A woman's dress, hat, etc., as a complete whole.

1927 *Weekly Dispatch* 6 Nov. 16 A simple ensemble..in shades of brown. *Ibid.*, The afternoon ensemble is by no means dead. **1930** *Daily Express* 8 Sept. 5/5 White rabbit, brocade, velvet..add considerable chic to the evening ensemble. **1969** *J. C. Penney Catal.* Fall & Winter 105 A coat and dress *ensemble* made of Orlon acrylic knit.

2. *Mil.* (See quot.)

1853 STOCQUELER *Mil. Encycl.*, *Ensemble*, together; the exact execution of the same movements, performed in the same manner, and by the same motions.

3. a. *Mus.* The united performance of all voices or all instruments in a piece of concerted music, or of a chorus and orchestra; also, the manner in which this is done; the musicians comprising such a concert group or orchestra.

In quot. 1951 applied to the united performance of voices in an operatic chorus.

1844 *Musical Examiner* 28 Sept. 809 It was really possible for five principal vocalists to achieve a perfect *ensemble*. **1880** GROVE *Dict. Mus.* II. 659/2 A feeling of carelessness..which the conductor must be quick to detect lest the *ensemble* be marred thereby. **1915** *Musical Q.* I. 83 We must put up with *ensemble* when we want to talk of that part of music, which is produced by the co-operation of several performers. *Ibid.*, Much care is required to secure a good ensemble in a vocal piece. **1927** *Observer* 27 Nov. 14/4 The ensemble between pianoforte and violoncello was good. **1929** *Encycl. Brit.* VIII. 616/2 The 'ensemble numbers' of an opera (trio, quartet and so forth). By extension the term is applied to the process of combining in this manner and to the skill with which it is accomplished. Thus in this sense it may be said that the ensemble of a choir or of a quartet was poor. **1934** S. R. NELSON *All about Jazz* iv. 71 His band can rank with the world's finest symphony orchestras in precision..and all those other attributes which go to make the finest musical ensembles. **1946** *Penguin Music Mag.* I. 20 The present management of Covent Garden..will cordially welcome occasional visits from complete foreign ensembles. **1947** A. EINSTEIN *Mus. in Romantic Era* xvi. 242 Here again are ensembles like the quintet at the end of the first half of the last act, even though it is no dramatic Mozartian ensemble. **1951** AUDEN & KALLMAN *Rake's Progress* III. 45 At the end of the ensemble, the voices of Rakewell and Shadow are again heard from the street. **1970** *N.Y. Times* 8 Nov. 84/5 The New York Rock Ensemble.

b. In ballet, musical comedy, or variety, a 'chorus' of dancers; a dance performed by such a group.

1915 M. E. PERUGINI *Art of Ballet* III. xxxiv. 303 'Ship Ahoy!' a nautical one-scene *divertissement*... The final *ensemble*, when the lady passengers..danced beneath the soft glow of the swinging lanterns was a particularly novel, pretty and inspiriting picture. **1921** WODEHOUSE *Jill the Reckless* xi. 161 The ladies of the ensemble were changing their practice-clothes after a particularly strenuous rehearsal. **1922** BEAUCLERK & EVRENOV tr. *Svetlov's Thamar Karsavina* 61 Karsavina's *rôle* is..devoid of incident and overwhelmed by the too brilliant and confusing *ensemble* that surrounds her. **1930** T. KARSAVINA *Theatre Street* II. xvi. 213 The ensemble lagged; Fokine..suddenly..flew at me. 'How can I blame the *corps de ballet* if the star herself gives a bad example.' **1933** A. G. MACDONELL *England, their England* vii. 102 Complete with..hand-made smocks for ye gaffers..and aluminium Eezi-Milk stools for the dairymaids (or Ladies of the Dancing Ensemble). **1936** A. HASKELL *Prel. Ballet* x. 50 Instead of one brilliant individual and a mechanical group in the background there must now be an *ensemble* of dance artists, whose function it is to interpret instead of merely being occupied in keeping time and keeping line. **1958** *Times* 11 Sept. 4/5 Lifar's opening *Noir et Blanc* made an impressive stage spectacle as it put the company through its paces in a series of testing solos and ensembles.

4. *Math.* A collection or combination of systems of identical constitution but in possibly differing states.

1902 J. W. GIBBS *Statist. Mech.*, p. xi, We consider especially ensembles of systems in which the index..of probability of phase is a linear function of the energy. *Ibid.* 116 A microcanonical ensemble of systems. *Ibid.* 169 The time-ensemble, or ensemble of phases through which a single system passes in the course of time. *Ibid.* 190 A grand ensemble is therefore composed of a multitude of petit ensembles. **1938** R. C. TOLMAN *Princ. Statist. Mech.* xiii. 524 The properties of a thermodynamic system..may be studied with the help of the average properties of an appropriately chosen representative ensemble of systems. **1965** D. MIDDLETON *Topics Communication Theory* i. 1 We are concerned not with the transmission and reception of just one particular 'message', but rather with the set, or ensemble, of all possible messages for the purpose at hand.

5. *attrib.*

1929 [see sense 3 a]. **1938** G. FFRANGCON-DAVIES in R. D. Charques *Footn. Theatre* IV. 241 One gathers from contemporary records that 'ensemble' playing as we know it to-day was non-existent. **1939** W. HOBSON *Amer. Jazz Music* 204 *Do Your Duty* has an ensemble introduction after which Bessie sings thirty-two bars with a loose ensemble background. **1958** A. MILLER *Coll. Plays* 16, I saw the

productions of the Group Theatre..the brilliance of ensemble acting. **1958** *Spectator* 27 June 831/3 The Youth Theatre concerns itself with ensemble playing, not with turning out miniature stars.

en'semble, *v.* [a. OF. *ensemble-r* in same sense. Cf. ASSEMBLE.] *trans.* To bring together, assemble; also *refl.* and *intr.* for *refl.*

a **1300** *Leg. St. Gregory* 982 þe cardinals al togider come, Ensembled þai were alle þo. *c* **1380** *Sir Ferumb.* 5467 þay ensemblede þanne to-gadre anon. **1491** CAXTON *Vitas Patr.* (1495) II By very charite were they [the hermits] ensembled, alied and unyed. **1533** MORE *Apol.* xlvii. Wks. 920/2 Openly by day they ensembled themselfe together to the noumber of an hundred. **1966** *Observer* 20 Mar. 11/1 Our driver carefully changed his bowler for the modish Cossack tea-cosy, ensembled with string gloves.

†**en'sembly.** *Obs. rare*⁻¹. In 5 ensemble. [a. OF. *ensemblee*, f. *ensembler*: see prec.] = ASSEMBLY.

c **1480** *Kyng & Hermit* 21 in Hazl. *E.P.P.* (1864) 13 With ryall fests and feyr ensemblè, With all yᵉ lordys of that contrè: With hym ther gan thei dwell.

†**en'semplary.** *Obs.* Also 4 ensamplarie. [app. a doublet of ENSAMPLER; Gower's use suggests that he regarded it as f. ENSAMPLE + -ERY.] Examples collectively; example in the abstract.

1393 GOWER *Conf.* II. 292 A tale..Which is of olde ensamplarie. *Ibid.* III. 48 [History] is of great ensemplary Agein the vice of sorcery.

ensence, -ense, obs. forms of INCENSE.

ensenȝe, -ȝhe, -ye, -yhe, obs. ff. ENSIGN *sb.*

ensense, obs. form of INSENSE *v.*, to instruct.

†**ensent,** *sb. Obs. rare*⁻¹. [f. next.] Assent.

1297 R. GLOUC. (1724) 317 þoru ensent of hyr tueye sones.

†**en'sent,** *v. Obs.* In 3-4 encent, -senti. [var. of ASSENT.] *intr.* To assent or consent *to*.

c **1290** *Lives Saints* (1887) 280 þe pope makede him dauncherous: and nolde ensenti þer-to. **1297** R. GLOUC. (1724) 171 þe kyng þoru ys conseyl encented wel her to. *c* **1305** *Edmund Conf.* 81 in *E.E.P.* (1862) 73 He ne dude neuere lecherie: ne neuere ensentede þerto.

ensepulchre (ɛn'sɛpəlkə(r)), *v.* [f. EN-¹ + SEPULCHRE.] *trans.* To put into a sepulchre; to entomb. Also *transf.*

1820 MILMAN *Fall Jerusalem* (1821) 160 The vast common doom ensepulchres the world. **1827** POLLOK *Course T.* VII, Cities..ensepulchred beneath the flood. **1841** MOIR in *Blackw. Mag.* L. 390 The oblivious gulf, whose mazy gloom Ensepulchres so many things. **1885** TENNYSON *Balin Poems* 146 Let the wolves' black maws ensepulchre Their brother beast.

enseraph: see EN- *pref.*¹ 2.

enserch, obs. form of ENSEARCH.

†**en'serchise.** *Obs.* [as if a. OF. *encerchise, f. *encerchier* to ENSEARCH.] A search, inquiry.

1436 *Pol. Poems* (1859) II. 195 Thus was he wonte..One suche enserchise busily to abyde.

†**en'sered,** *ppl. a. Obs. rare*⁻¹. [f. EN-¹ + SERE + -ED¹.] Furnished with 'seres' (defined in *Bk. St. Albans* as 'the skin on the legs').

1486 *Bk. St. Albans* A vij a, This hawke has..a faire enseryd legge.

enserf: see EN- *pref.*¹ 2.

ensete (ɛn'siːtiː). [Native name.] An African relative of the banana, *Ensete ventricosum* (*Musa ensete*).

1790 J. BRUCE *Trav. to Nile* V. 36 The Ensete is a herbacious [*sic*] plant. It is said to be a native of Narea. **1864** J. A. GRANT *Walk across Africa* p. xv, Ensete; a species of wild plantain..called m'seegwah and m'tembah by natives, who make necklaces of its seeds. **1961** H. P. HUFFNAGEL *Agric. Ethiopia* xxviii. 292 The main product of the ensete is a fermented starch of high nutritive value.

ensew(e, obs. forms of ENSUE.

enshade (ɛn'ʃeɪd), *v.* [f. EN-¹ + SHADE *sb.*] *trans.* To envelop in shade.

18.. HALL CAINE *After Sunset* in Sharp *Sonnets this Cent.* (1886) 38 While we lie Enshaded, lulled, beneath heaven's breezeless sky.

enshadow, enshawl: see EN- *pref.*¹ 1 a.

ensheath(e (ɛn'ʃiːθ, -ð), *v.* Also 7 insheath. [f. EN-¹ + SHEATH *sb.*, SHEATHE *v.*] *trans.* To enclose in, or as in, a sheath.

1593 NASHE *Christ's T.* (1613) 50 My throat..hath quite swallow'd vp and ensheath'd my tongue. **1737** OZELL *Rabelais* III. xxxiii. III. 39 The velvet scabbard that insheatheth it. **1835-6** TODD *Cycl. Anat.* I. 8/2 By the triple partition of its tendon, it ensheaths the lumbar muscles. **1860** LD. LYTTON *Lucile* II. vi. §9 In the young heart..A love large as life, deep and changeless as death, Lay ensheathed.

Hence **en'sheathing** *ppl. a.*

1877 KINGLAKE *Crimea* VI. vi. 317 The ensheathing columns were roughly handled.

enshell, enshelter: see EN- *pref.*¹ 1 a.

†**'enshield,** *a. Obs. rare*⁻¹. [Usually taken as = *enshielded*, pa. pple. of next, which suits the apparent sense; but the accent is peculiar. Perh. f. EN-¹ + SHIELD *sb.*] ? Shielded, concealed.

1603 SHAKS. *Meas. for M.* II. iv. 80 These blacke Masques Proclaime an en-shield beauty.

enshield (ɛn'ʃiːld), *v. rare.* [f. EN-¹ + SHIELD *v.*] *trans.* To guard or screen as with a shield.

1855 SINGLETON *Virgil* I. 293 This altar will Enshield us all. **1859** MISS MULOCK *Romant. T.* 301 The frail, trembling child stood still enshielded by Olof's arms.

enshore, obs. form of INSHORE.

enshrine (ɛn'ʃraɪn), *v.* Also 6-8 inshrine, (6 enshryne, 7 inscrine). [f. EN-¹ + SHRINE.]

1. *trans.* To enclose (a sacred relic, the image of a deity or saint) in a shrine; to place (a revered or precious object) in an appropriate receptacle.

1586 WARNER *Alb. Eng.* II. xiii. (1612) 60 Philoctes..His ashes did conuay To Italy, inshrined in his Temple there to stay. **1623** MASSINGER *Dk. Milan* II. i, Though but a ducat, We will enshrine it as a holy relic. **1667** MILTON *P.L.* I. 719 To inshrine Belus or Serapis thir Gods. *a* **1744** POPE *Wife of Bath* 249 [The tomb] where enshrin'd the great Darius lay. **1820** W. IRVING *Sketch-bk.* I. 267 The remains of those saints and monarchs which lie enshrined in the adjoining chapels. **1826** KIRBY & SP. *Entomol.* xlvii. (1828) IV. 413 The snake-devouring ibis these inshrine.

fig. **1591** SHAKS. *1 Hen. VI*, III. ii. 119 Burgonie Inshrines thee in his heart. **1661** MORGAN *Sph. Gentry* I. vii. 98 Next to his bosom in whom she [Eve] was inscrined. **1671** MILTON *P.R.* IV. 598 True image of the Father..enshrined In fleshly tabernacle. *a* **1743** SAVAGE *Verses to Knight* (R.) In whose transcendent mind Are wisdom, purity, and truth enshrined. **1841** W. SPALDING *Italy & It. Isl.* II. 264 Papal orthodoxy sat enshrined in the Escurial.

humorously. **1851** D. JERROLD *St. Giles* ix. 89 He was, ere the church-bell ceased, enshrined in the family pew.

†**b.** To conceal as within a shrine. *Obs.*

1583 STANYHURST *Æneis* III. (Arb.) 89 Thee stars imparted no light..And the moon enshryned with closet clowdye remayned. **1596** SPENSER *Hymn Beauty* 188 What booteth that celestiall ray, If it in darkness be enshrined ever.

2. To contain as a shrine does; to serve as a shrine for (something sacred or precious). Also *fig.*

1621 G. SANDYS *Ovid's Met.* VII. 128 The greatest God of all My brest inshrines. **1849** ROBERTSON *Serm.* Ser. I. iii. (1866) 41 A poetical shape..enshrining an inner and a deeper truth. **1856** KANE *Arct. Expl.* I. xxi. 266 The first warm snows..enshrine the flowery growths.

Hence **en'shrined** *ppl. a.* **en'shrinement,** the action of enshrining, in quot. *fig.*; also *concr.* that which enshrines or envelopes; in *pl.* the surroundings. **en'shrining** *vbl. sb.*

1795 SOUTHEY *Joan of Arc* IV. 135 The slant sunbeam Falls on the arms inshrined. **1849** *Fraser's Mag.* XXXIX. 717 This mystery, in all its enshrinements, has the ædes of Egypt striven to express. **1872** HOLLAND *Marb. Proph.* 8 The enshrinement of the Christian faith In sign and symbol. **1868** BUSHNELL *Serm. Living Subj.* 271 The enshrining of his glorious divinity in them.

enshroud (ɛn'ʃraʊd), *v.* Also 7 inshrowd. [f. EN-¹ + SHROUD.] *trans.* To cover as with a shroud; to envelope completely; to hide from view. Also *fig.*

1583 STANYHURST *Æneis* I. (Arb.) 31 Venus enshrowds theym with a thick fog. **1613-6** W. BROWNE *Brit. Past.* I. iv, In gloomy vaile of night, Inshrowd the pale beams of thy borrowed light. **1761** CHURCHILL *Apol.* 4 They lurk enshrouded in the vale of night. **1876** BLACKIE *Songs Relig. & Life* 200 Trails of thick blue mist enshroud The green far-gleaming glens. **1879** DIXON *Windsor* II. xxiii. 243 The crimes..were enshrouded in the deepest mystery.

Hence **en'shrouded** *ppl. a.*

1830 TENNYSON *Dirge* ii, Nothing but the small, cold worm Fretteth thine enshrouded form.

ensialic (ɛnsaɪ'ælɪk), *a. Geol.* [f. EN-² + SIALIC *a.*¹] Originating or occurring in or on sialic material; of or pertaining to such structures or phenomena.

1949 F. G. WELLS in *Bull. Geol. Soc. Amer.* LX. 1927 (*heading*) Ensimatic and ensialic geosynclines. *Ibid.*, The terms ensialic and ensimatic are proposed to designate these distinctly different types [of deposit in geosynclines]. **1960** *Gloss. Geol.* (Amer. Geol. Inst.) (ed. 2) 96/2 *Ensialic geosyncline*, a geosyncline that forms on a floor composed of sial..and is composed largely of sediments derived from the weathering of the crust. **1972** *Sci. Amer.* Mar. 34/3 The plate-tectonic version of the geosynclinal cycle predicts that miogeoclines are ensialic, or laid down on continental crust (sial). **1976** *Tectonophysics* XL. 101 (*heading*) Precambrian mobile belts of southern and eastern Africa: ancient sutures or sites of ensialic mobility? **1979** *Nature* 15 Mar. 223/1 A controversial subject in orogenesis is whether plate tectonics had an important role in the Proterozoic or whether *in situ* ensialic models fit the facts in the best way.

†**en'siege,** *sb. Obs. rare*⁻¹. In 5 ensegge. [f. next vb.] Siege; in phrase *to lay ensiege*.

? *a* **1500** *MS. Lincoln* A i. 17 f. 4 (Halliw.) He went unto the citee of Tyre, and layde ensegge abowte it.

†**en'siege,** *v. Obs.* In 4 ensege, -segge. [a. OF. *enseger, -segger* (mod.F. *assiéger*). Cf. ASSIEGE.] *trans.* To besiege. Also *fig.*

c **1380** WYCLIF *Serm.* Sel. Wks. I. 25 Titus and Waspasian ..ensegiden Jerusalem. *Ibid.* II. 155 þei ensegen þe soulis of men. ? *a* **1400** *Morte Arth.* 1337 Ensegge all þa cetese be the salte strandez. *c* **1400** MAUNDEV. (Roxb.) XIII. 58 When twa rewmes er at were and owþer party ensegez citee, toune or castell.

ensient (ɛnsɪ'ɛnt), *a. Law.* Later spelling of *enseint* = ENCEINTE.

1827 J. POWELL *Devises* (ed. 3) II. 359 A natural child of which a particular woman is ensient. **1818** CRUISE *Digest* VI. 181 If..his said wife should be ensient with one or more children.

Hence **ensi'enture,** the state of being with child, pregnancy.

1775 in ASH.

ensiew, obs. form of ENSUE.

†**en'siferous,** *a. Obs.*⁻⁰ [f. L. *ēnsi-s* sword + *-fer* bearing + -OUS.] That bears a sword.

1656 in BLOUNT *Glossogr.* **1721-1800** in BAILEY. **1847** in CRAIG; and in mod. Dicts.

ensiform ('ɛnsɪfɔːm), *a.* and *sb. Biol.* [f. L. *ensi-s* sword: see -FORM.] **A.** *adj.* Sword-shaped. (Often said of leaves.) ***ensiform cartilage***, a cartilage appended to the sternum or breast-bone.

1541 R. COPLAND *Guydon's Quest. Chirurg.*, Belowe in the furcule is an addycyon cartylagynous called Ency forme. **1794** MARTYN *Rousseau's Bot.* xiv. 155 Linnaeus calls them Ensiform or sword-shaped. **1816** KIRBY & SP. *Entomol.* (1828) II. xxiii. 324 Ensiform antennæ. **1845** LINDLEY *Sch. Bot.* viii. (1858) 151 Leaves ensiform, with parallel veins. **1872** MIVART *Elem. Anat.* 300 The diaphragm is attached to the ensiform cartilage and several ribs.

B. *sb.* = *ensiform cartilage*.

1907 *Practitioner* Oct. 467 Even when it travels directly downwards, in the same line as the pulmonary murmur, it [*sc.* an aortic murmur] travels much further, and is usually clearly audible at the ensiform.

ensight, obs. form of INSIGHT.

ensign ('ɛnsaɪn), *sb.* Forms: 4, 6 an-, as-, ensenȝe, -ȝhe, -ye, -yhe, 4 ensaigne, 5-7 ensigne, 5 ensygne, 6 enseigne, essenȝe, (6 insigne, 8 insign), 6- ensign. See also ANCIENT *sb.*², INSIGNE. [a. OF. *enseigne, enseine, ensaigne, ansigne*, corresp. to Pr. *enseigna, ensegna, essenha*, Cat. *insignia*, It. *insegna*:—L. *īnsignia*, pl. of *īnsigne*, neut. of *īnsignis* adj., f. *in* + *signum* sign.

The INSIGNE used in sense 4 by some writers late in 18th c. and in 19th is prob. intended as Lat., and is therefore treated as a distinct word.]

†**1.** A signal; a rallying or battle-cry, watchword. Chiefly *Sc. Obs.*

1375 BARBOUR *Bruce* II. 378 Hys assenȝhe gan he cry. *Ibid.* V. 323 His ensenȝhe mycht heir him cry. *c* **1450** *Merlin* X. 161 The Duke..cride his ensigne. *c* **1500** *Lancelot* 3347 Thar essenȝeis lowd thai gon to cry. **1513** DOUGLAS *Æneis* VII. ix. 86 The hyrdis ensenȝe loud wp trumpis sche.

2. A sign, token, characteristic mark. *arch.*

1474 CAXTON *Chesse* 85 Entyse them to lawghe and jape by ony dysordynate ensignes or tokenes. **1491** —— *Vitas Patr.* (W. de W. 1495) I. i. 3 a/1 In exposynge to hym very ensygnes of his vysage and clothynge. **1609** B. JONSON *Sil. Wom.* III. vi, We see no Ensigns of a Wedding here. **1632** MASSINGER & FIELD *Fatal Dowry* I. i, Are these the ensigns of so coarse a fellow? **1644** *Jus Pop.* 48 The prime ensignes of Majestie, which consists in making Laws. **1650** BULWER *Anthropomet.* xii. 132 The Beard is the ensigne of manhood. **1765** BLACKSTONE *Comm.* I. 84 From these three strong marks and ensigns of superiority. **1830** GEN. P. THOMPSON *Exerc.* (1842) I. 206 A well-dressed man, with all the ensigns of respectability and good-fellowship about him.

¶ *humorously.* Cf. 5 and Fr. *enseigne* signboard.

1854 THACKERAY *Newcomes* I. 90 There was never a card in her window, whilst those ensigns in her neighbours' houses would remain exposed..for months together.

3. A conventional sign; an emblem, badge.

1579 E. K. *Gloss. Spenser's Sheph. Cal.* Apr. 123 The Oliue was wont to be the ensigne of peace. **1665** G. HAVERS *P. della Valle's Trav. E. India* 46 Whether this fillet..was a badge of Religion, or only an Ensign of piety. **1750** JOHNSON *Rambler* No. 55 ¶4 My mother appeared again without the ensigns of sorrow. **1825** MISS MITFORD in L'Estrange *Life* II. x. 209 She left those ensigns of authority, the keys, in his possession. **1860** ABP. THOMSON *Laws Th.* §22. 33 The Sculptor raises a tomb, and covers it with the ensigns of piety and death.

4. *esp.* A badge or symbol of dignity or office; chiefly *pl.* = L. *insignia*; also, heraldic arms or bearings.

1513 DOUGLAS *Æneis* VII. iv. 53 Sceptour and croun, And of justice wthir ensenȝeis seyr. **1536** *Act 28 Hen. VIII*, c. 16 §3 Thoffice..of an archebyshop..with all tokens, insignes and ceremonies thereunto lawfully belongyng. **1676** HOBBES *Iliad* I. 15 Having in his hands the Ensigne meet.. A Golden Scepter and a Crown of Bays. **1691** *Lond. Gaz.* No. 2653/3 Then the King put on the Blue Ribon with the George, Garter King at Arms reading the usual Admonitions upon the putting on each of the said Ensigns. **1710** PALMER *Proverbs* 359 The ornaments and insigns of a family. **1750** C. LUCAS *Ess. Waters* II. 125 There is nothing ..but a black marble table, ornamented with ensigns armorial. **1772** *Ann. Reg.* 77/2 A new order was instituted by her Danish Majesty..the ensign of which is a cypher of her Majesty's name. **1776** GIBBON *Decl. & F.* I. xvi. 428 A white robe was the ensign of their dignity. **1873** TRISTRAM *Moab* xii. 226 Two fine Saker falcons..his pets, the ensign and crest of his tribe.

5. a. A military or naval standard; a banner, flag. In the Royal Navy pronounced ('ɛns(ə)n).

In British nautical use applied *spec.* to a flag with a white, blue or red field, and the union in the corner. Since 1864 the ensign of the Royal Navy and the Royal Yacht Squadron has

been white, that of the naval reserve, of ships in the service of public offices, and of certain yacht clubs, blue, and the 'merchant ensign' red. (See *Encycl. Brit.* ed. 9 s.v. *Flag.*)
c **1400** *Rom. Rose* 1200 And that was he that bare the ensaigne Of worship. **1513** DOUGLAS *Æneis* XI. ix. 45 Charge thame thar ensenȝeis for to rais on hycht. **1591** GARRARD *Art Warre* 65 The valiant Alfierus with his ensigne in one hand and his sword in another. *a* **1656** BP. HALL *Occas. Medit.* 79 We are wont to fight cheerfully under this ensign abroad. **1707** *Royal Proclam.* 28 July in *Lond. Gaz.* No. 4356/1 We have..thought fit..to Order and Appoint the Ensign Described on the..Margent hereof, to be Worn on Board all Ships. **1838** *Hist. Record 3rd Regt. Foot* 27 And each Company had a colour which was designated an ensign. **1848** M. ARNOLD *Poems* (1877) I. 85, I still bear on The conquering Tartar ensigns through the world.

b. *transf.*

1598 CHAPMAN *Iliad* VI. 175 Lycia, where Xanthus doth display The silver ensigns of his waves. *a* **1678** MARVELL *Poems* 26 Then flowers their drowsy eyelids raise, Their silken ensigns each displays.

†**6.** A body of men serving under one banner; a company, troop. Sometimes used to render the L. *cohors* or *ordo*. *Obs.*

The number of men in an 'ensign' seems to have varied from 100 to 500.

1552 in Strype *Eccl. Mem.* II. II. x. 328 The Bishops of Colen and Treves..did send unto the Emperor 1500 horse, and six ensigns of foot. **1581** SAVILE *Tacitus' Hist.* (1591) Annot. 51 The Hastati were diuided againe into ten Enseignes, or *ordines*. **1584** BALNUIS *Lett.* in Keith *Hist. Ch. & State Scotl.* (1734) App. 44 (Jam.) The payment of our futemen extendis monethlie everie Ansenye (whiche are now sex in number) to 29*ol.* sterl. **1590** J. SMYTH *Disc. Weapons* 8 b, Our English Milicia of footmen monie yeares past, did consist of bands but of 100 to an Ensigne. *Ibid.* 9 b, At which time their bands did consist of five hundred to everie Ensigne. **1600** HOLLAND *Livy* II. xi. 51 Valerius..set forth from mount Cœlius certaine ensignes [*cohortes*] of his best and choice souldiors. **1650** R. STAPYLTON *Strada's Low C. Warres* VI. 17 She commanded Count Mansfeldt to goe before with 16 ensignes, of her best Foote.

7. The soldier who carries the ensign; a standard-bearer. See ANCIENT *sb.*[2] Formerly commissioned officers of the lowest grade in the infantry bore this title, which has been replaced by that of sub-lieutenant.

1513–75 *Diurn. Occurr.* (1833) 225 Alexander Bog ansenyie to capitane Daniel Meluile with the said ensenyie, and lxx suddartis. **1579** DIGGES *Stratiot.* 89 Let the Ensigne be a man of good accompte. **1677** W. HUBBARD *Narrative* 19 Ensign Savage, that young Martial Spark. **1682** BUNYAN *Holy War* 51 His Ensign was Mr. Thunder. **1756–7** tr. *Keysler's Trav.* (1760) I. 309 The sons of many of the noblest and wealthiest families are ensigns and lieutenants. **1846** MCCULLOCH *Acc. Brit. Empire* (1854) II. 559 The mortality of captains from battle is double that of ensigns.

8. †**a.** transl. Fr. *enseigne de vaisseau*, midshipman (*obs.*). **b.** In the U.S. navy, the designation of the lowest rank of commissioned officers.

1708 *Lond. Gaz.* No. 4420/7 Mr. de Villeville, Ensign of the Ship. **1886** *Encycl. Amer.* III. 819 Officers of the Navy ..Ensign, ranking with Second Lieutenant in the Army.

9. *Comb.*, as ***ensign-staff*** (in sense 5); **ensign-fly**, a parasitic hymenopterous insect of the family Evaniidæ.

1707 *Lond. Gaz.* No. 4380/2 His Boltsprit carried away our Ensign-Staff. **1799** *Naval Chron.* I. 269 Nailed the Flag to the ensign staff. **1894** COMSTOCK *Man. Insects* 628 We have named these insects Ensign-flies, because they carry the abdomen aloft like a flag. **1897** —— *Insect Life* 86.

ensign (ɛn'saɪn), *v. Obs.* exc. *Her.* Forms: 5–6 ensigne, -sygne, 5 enseigne, -seygne, enseyne, (6 ensine, -syne, 7– ensign). Also 5 inseygne, 6 insygne, 6–8 insigne. [a. OF. *ensignier*, *enseigner*, corresp. to Pr. *enseignar*, Cat. *ensenyar*, Sp. *enseñar*, Pg. *ensinar*, It. *insegnare*:—med.L. *insignāre*, f. *in* (see IN-) + *signum* sign.]

†**1.** *trans.* To indicate, point out, show. Also *absol.* to give indications. *Obs.*

1475 CAXTON *Jason* 37 b, As to the waye that he had holden he ensigned to the lady. **1483** —— *Gold. Leg.* 288/3 Why callest thou them traitours whiche ben Doctours and enseygne the lyf perdurable. **1541** R. COPLAND *Galyen's Terapeutyke* 2 C iij, But I can nat coniect what may shewe and ensygne the tyme. **1548** UDALL, etc. *Erasm. Par. John* 67 a, He did ensigne theim in time to come a terrible iudgemente. **1576** BAKER *Jewell of Health* 29 a, The matter ought afore to be put into the vessels, as this letter X insigneth to us.

†**2.** To direct (a person) *to* an object; to instruct, inform. Also with double acc.: To teach (a person, a thing). *Obs.*

1474 CAXTON *Chesse* 16 He is taught, enseygned and norisshed in his yougth. **1477** EARL RIVERS (Caxton) *Dictes* 74 b, Wylle ye that I enseygne and teche you howe ye shal mowe escape from alle euyll. **1508** BARCLAY *Shyp of Folys* (1874) I. 236 A folysshe Father full hardly shall ensyne His sone to good lyfe. **1598** BARRET *Theor. Warres* II. i. 16 [The Caporall] himselfe ensigning and teaching the Bisognios. *Ibid.* III. i. 33 Ensigning them the vse of their weapon.

3. †**a.** To mark with a distinctive sign or badge; also, to serve as a badge of (*obs.*). **b.** *Her.* To distinguish (a charge) by a significant mark or ornament placed upon it, as a crown, coronet, or mitre.

1572 BOSSEWELL *Armorie* II. 71 The Cocke aboue other birdes is ensigned with a peculiare Creste. **1586** FERNE *Blaz. Gentrie* 138 Princes..which do insigne their chapeau and helme with a crowne of flowers and crosses. **1610** GUILLIM *Heraldry* I. i. (1660) 5 Osyris bare a Scepter royall, insigned on the top with an Eye. **1610** JONSON *Prince Henry's Barriers*, Henry but join'd the roses, that ensign'd Particular families. **1766** PORNY *Heraldry* (1787) 150 The sixteenth is Argent, a man's Heart Gules, ensigned with a Crown Or. **1808** J. BARLOW *Columb.* VI. 272 A warrior ensign'd with a various crown. **1842** M. LOWER *Eng. Surnames* (1875) II. App. 148 A cross ensigned by XP. **1864** BOUTELL *Heraldry Hist. & Pop.* xiii. 96 Archbishops and Bishops..ensign their Shields with their Mitres.

†'**ensign-ˌbearer.** *Obs.* One who carried a company's ensign; = ENSIGN *sb.* 7.

1579 DIGGES *Stratiot.* 89 The ensigne bearer ought, when the warre is ended, to deliver up to hys captayne agayne hys Ensigne. **1582–8** *Hist. James VI* (1804) 134 Alexander Bog ansenȝie bearer to Capitane Meluill. **1604** E. GRIMSTONE *Hist. Siege Ostend* 72 An Ensigne-bearer..was slaine. **1672** VENNE *Mil. Observations, Exercise Foot* 177.

ensigncy ('ɛnsaɪnsɪ). [f. ENSIGN *sb.* + -CY (cf. *captaincy*).] The rank or position of an ensign in the army.

1767 HUGH KELLY, etc. *Babler* II. 166 A paltry little ensigncy. **1771** SMOLLETT *Humph. Cl.* (1815) 227, I purchased an ensigncy. **1800** WELLINGTON in Gurw. *Disp.* I. 239 Recommended for the first vacant ensigncy in the 33rd regiment. **1860** J. KENNEDY *Quodlibet* xvii. 227 Accepting an ensigncy from the hands of Washington.

ensignhood ('ɛnsaɪnhʊd). *nonce-wd.* [f. ENSIGN *sb.* + -HOOD.] The state of being an ensign.

1842 MRS. GORE in *Tait's Mag.* IX. 569 The first fortnight of escape from cubhood to ensignhood.

†**en'signment.** *Obs.* [a. OF. *enseignement*, f. *enseigner* to teach; cf. ENSIGN *v.* and -MENT.]

1. a. The action or process of showing or teaching, instruction; **b.** *concr.* that which is taught, a lesson; also, a means of instruction.

1398 TREVISA *Barth. De P.R.* v. iii. (1495) 107 He that hath the brayne nesshe, thynne and clere is swifte and good of enseynement and techynge. **1483** CAXTON *G. de la Tour* L iij, I shalle telle yow what Salamon therof seyth in the book of thenseygnement. **1493** *Festivall* (W. de W. 1515) 154 And whan all yᵉ people come soo togyder at this ensygnement. **1502** *Ord. Crysten Men* (W. de W. 1506) IV. vi. 177 A ryght profytable insygnement of the practyse that the confessour ought to holde. **1575** in *Laneham's Let.* (1871) 93 He ensued not the ensygnementes nor the doctryne of the dyuyne sapyence. **1600** HOLLAND *Livy* v. li. 212 We are made an example and ensignement [*documento*] to the whole world.

2. A badge or symbol of office; = ENSIGN *sb.* 4.

1567 R. MULCASTER *Fortescue's De Laud. Leg.* 121 A white quoife of silke: whiche is the principal and chief insignement of habite wherewith serjeantes at lawe in their creation are decked. **1611** SPEED *Hist. Gt. Brit.* IX. xii. (1632) 703 King Edward also deuised..distinctive habites and ensignements, whereof the principall was the azure Garter.

†'**ensignship.** *Obs. rare*⁻¹. [f. ENSIGN *sb.* + -SHIP.] = ENSIGNCY.

1745 *Observ. Conc. Navy* 44 Sales of Ensignships, Adjutancies, Quarter-Master-ships, etc.

ensilage ('ɛnsɪlɪdʒ), *sb.* [a. F. *ensilage*, f. *ensiler*: see ENSILE *v.*]

1. The process of preserving green fodder in a silo or pit, without having previously dried it.

1881 *Salem* (Mass.) *Gaz.* 10 June 1/2 On ensilage of Green Forage Crops in Silos. **1882** *Macm. Mag.* No. 278. 114 Ensilage is the packing of green forage in air- and water-tight structures. **1882** *Times* 30 Nov. 11 The object of ensilage is to maintain the sap as nearly as possible in its original state. **1884** *Boston* (Mass.) *Jrnl.* 20 Nov. 2/4 Norfolk is the county where the ensilage of fodder is most practised.

2. The material resulting from the process.

1881 *Echo* 11 June 1/6 Ensilage..is produced by cutting green fodder of different kinds when well matured..and pressing it down in water-tight pits, subsequently also made air-tight. **1882** *Times* 30 Nov. 11 About 3 in. of the ensilage was found to be mouldy.

3. *attrib.*

1883 *Edin. Rev.* Jan. 150 Five separate manufacturers advertised ensilage cutters. **1888** *Times* 24 July 13/1 Those who were prepared to make ensilage stacks.

ensilage ('ɛnsɪlɪdʒ), *v.* [f. prec. sb.] *trans.* To subject to the ensilage process; to convert into ensilage. Hence '**ensilaged** *ppl. a.*

1883 *West Chester Pa. Republican* VI. No. 37. 4 An ensilaged crop. **1883** *Chamb. Jrnl.* 274 Pease, oats, maize, and vetches might be ensilaged together. **1883** *Edin. Rev.* Jan. 149 Preserving green fodder by ensilaging it.

ensilate ('ɛnsɪleɪt), *v.* [f. Fr. *ensil-er* + -ATE.] = ENSILAGE *v.*

1883 *Chamb. Jrnl.* 5 May, Green forage should be ensilated without mixture of any dry substances.

ensile (ɛn'saɪl), *v.* [ad. F. *ensile-r*, ad. Sp. *ensilar*, f. *en-* (see EN-¹) + *silo* (see SILO) pit for preserving green fodder, repr. L. *sīrus* a. Gr. *σῖρός*, *σειρός* underground granary.] *trans.* To put (forage) into a silo for preservation; to convert into ensilage. Hence **en'siled** *ppl. a.*, **en'siling** *vbl. sb.*

1883 *Manch. Exam.* 29 Nov. 5/3 Of the 24 tons of grass ensiled in June it was calculated that there was at least 21 tons available for winter use. **1885** *Spectator* 21 Feb. 249 Lucern, red clover, and spurrey have all been successfully ensiled. **1885** *Pall Mall G.* 29 Apr. 5/1 Alcoholic silage is produced by the action of the cells of the ensiled plants. *Ibid.*, The ensiling of immature fodder.

ensile: see ENSEEL.

'**ensilist.** [f. ENSILE + -IST.] One who preserves his crops by ensilage.

1883 *Hibernia* July 103/2 Concrete has been adopted by many ensilists.

ensilver: see EN- *pref.*¹ 1 b.

†**en'sindon,** *v. Obs. rare*⁻¹. [f. EN-¹ + SINDON.] *trans.* To wrap in a sindon or linen cloth.

1609 DAVIES *Holy Rood* I. vi, Now doth this..Synaxie..Ensindon Him with choicest Draperie.

ensine, obs. form of ENSIGN *sb.*

†**en'sise.** *Obs.*⁻⁰ [var. of ASSIZE *sb.*]

1721–1800 BAILEY, *Ensise*, quality, stem *O*[*ld word*].

ensisternal (ɛnsɪ'stɜːnəl), *a.* [f. L. *ensi-s* sword + mod.L. *stern-um*, Gr. *στέρν-ον* breast-bone + -AL¹.] 'Relating to the ensiform cartilage' (*Syd. Soc. Lex.*).

ensky (ɛn'skaɪ), *v.* [f. EN-¹ + SKY.] *trans.* To place in the sky or in heaven: *pass.* only.

1603 SHAKS. *Meas. for M.* I. iv. 34, I hold you as a thing en-skied, and sainted. *a* **1763** SHENSTONE *Odes* Wks. 1765 I. 255 Thou seem'st chang'd; all sainted, all ensky'd. **1814** CARY *Dante* (Chandos) 226 Of seraphim he who is most ensky'd. **1858** PATMORE *Angel in Ho.* 136 This truth 's a star, Too deep-enskied for all to see.

Hence **en'skied** *ppl. a.*

1852 MRS. JAMESON *Leg. Madonna* (1857) 109 The most majestic of the enthroned and enskied Madonnas.

enslave (ɛn'sleɪv), *v.* Also 7–8 **inslave.** [f. EN-¹ + SLAVE.]

1. *trans.* To reduce to slavery; to make a slave of. Also *absol.*

1656 COWLEY *Davideis* II. (1710) I. 348 Enslav'd, and sold to Ashur by his Sins. **1793** BLACKSTONE *Comm.* (ed. 12) 539 Much less can it give a right to kill, torture, abuse, plunder, or even to enslave, an enemy, when the war is over. **1796** MORSE *Amer. Geog.* I. 277 Prevent them from..enslaving their brethren, of whatever complexion. **1867** PEARSON *Hist. Eng.* I. 50 The ungrateful freedman might be enslaved again. **1878** BOSW. SMITH *Carthage* 348 Scipio..had moved forward from his head quarters at Tunis, plundering and enslaving as he went.

2. *transf.* and *fig.* **a.** To reduce to political 'slavery', deprive of political freedom.

α. **1643** PRYNNE *Treachery & Disloy. Papists* II. 43 (R.) Corrupt publicke officers and judges of late times..have..endeavoured to enslave both us and our posterities. **1660** R. COKE *Just. Vind.* 18 A nation may enslave it self by its too much wit. **1775** JOHNSON *Tax. no Tyr.* 64 May with the same army enslave us. **1848** MACAULAY *Hist. Eng.* I. 297 Such an army..was not very likely to enslave five millions of Englishmen. **1877** MRS. OLIPHANT *Makers Flor.* x. 241 She [Florence] was enslaved, she, once the freest of the free.

β. **1700** DRYDEN *Fables, Cock & Fox* 384 Joseph..Who by a dream inslav'd th' Egyptian land. **1767** T. HUTCHINSON *Hist. Prov. Mass.* iv. 425 Confederating..to inslave the Dutch.

b. In moral or intellectual sense: To render (a person) a 'slave' to passion, habit, superstition, etc.

α. *c* **1645** HOWELL *Lett.* III. xxi, Who doth enslave himself too strictly to words. **1651** BAXTER *Inf. Bapt.* 28 Those whose consciences are not wholly enslaved to their fancies. **1738** WESLEY *Hymn, From whence these dire Portents around* vi, Let Sin no more my Soul enslave! **1821** SHELLEY *Prometh. Unb.* II. iv. 110 All spirits are enslaved which serve things evil. **1825** LYTTON *Zicci* 24, I am enslaved by her beauty. **1876** GREEN *Short Hist.* vi. §5 (1882) 315 Luther declared man to be utterly enslaved by original sin. **1884** CHURCH *Bacon* ix. 223 His Latin, without enslaving itself to Ciceronian types..is singularly forcible and expressive.

β. **1665** BOYLE *Occas. Refl.* IV. viii. (1675) 218 To which unbridl'd Passions hurry the criminally unhappy Persons they have Inslav'd. **1705** STANHOPE *Paraphr.* II. 301 Pleasure inslaves us by often indulging. **1746** HURD *Remarks Weston's Enquiry* (R.), Inslaved to the tenets of a conceited philosophy.

enslaved (ɛn'sleɪvd), *ppl. a.* [f. ENSLAVE *v.* + -ED¹.] Reduced to slavery. Also *fig.*

1667 MILTON *P.L.* XI. 797 The conquerd also, and enslav'd by Warr. **1756** C. LUCAS *Ess. Waters* II. 34 France and other inslaved countries. **1790** BURKE *Fr. Rev.* Wks. V. 139 The enslaved minister of that captive king. **1817** COLERIDGE *Sibyl. Leaves*, Not yet enslaved, not wholly vile, O Albion! **1859** LD. BROUGHTON *Italy* II. 224 The enslaved subjects of the Cæsars.

Hence **en'slavedness.**

1847 in CRAIG; and in mod. Dicts.

enslavement (ɛn'sleɪvmənt). [f. ENSLAVE *v.* + -MENT.] The action of enslaving; the state of being enslaved.

1692 SOUTH *Serm.* (1697) I. 474 Returning to a fresh Enslavement to their Enemies. **1821** *New Monthly Mag.* II. 136 The unjust enslavement of Italy. **1839** J. BRENAN (*title*), Old and New Logic, shewing how Lord Bacon delivered the Mind from its 2000 years' Enslavement under Aristotle. **1844** LORD BROUGHAM *Brit. Const.* (1862) Introd. 21 No alternations of enslavement and emancipation. **1849** GROTE *Greece* II. lxvii. (1862) VI. 67 How lamentably they [Greek philosophers] were hampered by enslavement to the popular phraseology.

enslaver (ɛn'sleɪvə(r)). [f. ENSLAVE *v.* + -ER.] One who enslaves; *esp.* the woman by whose charms a man is 'enslaved'.

1727 SWIFT *To Stella*, Enslavers of mankind! Base kings, and ministers of state. **1748** SMOLLETT *Rod. Rand.* lxv. (1804) 474 The delicate nerves of my fair Enslaver. **1816**

BYRON *Ch. Har.* III. lxvii, The earth Forgets..The enslavers and the enslaved. **1818** PRAED *Poems* (1865) II. 243 Hail, fair Enslaver! at thy changing glance Boldness recedes. **1849** LYTTON *Caxtons* 15 A name..borne by the enslaver of Athens. **1856** WHYTE-MELVILLE *Kate Cov.* iii, Young fledglings pining madly for their enslavers.

enslumber: see EN- *pref.*[1] 1 a.

ensmall (ɛn'smɔːl), *v. rare.* [f. EN-[1] + SMALL.] *trans.* To make smaller. Hence **en'smalled** *ppl. a.*

1857 THOMSON *Land & Book* IV. xl. 612 To reconcile my previous anticipations with the vastly ensmalled reality.

ensnare (ɛn'snɛə(r)), *v.* Also 6–9 insnare. [f. EN-[1] + SNARE.] *trans.* To catch (animals, etc.) in a snare; to SNARE. Chiefly *transf.* and *fig.* to entangle (persons) in difficulties; to entrap, beguile, lure. Also *absol.*

1576 FLEMING *Panopl. Epist.* 213 Many have beene so insnared and intangled..in nettes of doubtfull reasons. **1594** SHAKS. *Rich. III*, I. iii. 243 That Bottel'd Spider, Whose deadly Web ensnareth thee about. **1768** BEATTIE *Minstr.* II. xxviii, Spiders ensnare, snakes poison, tigers prowl. **1782** V. KNOX *Ess.* (1819) I. liv. 288 Would rather shoot a pheasant or insnare a trout. **1836** W. IRVING *Astoria* I. 133 These people..ensnare the waterfowl of the ponds and rivers.

transf. and *fig.* **1593** SHAKS. *Lucr.* 485 Thy beauty hath ensnar'd thee to this night. **1597** HOOKER *Eccl. Pol.* v. ix. (1611) 199 That which hath..insnared the iudgements of sundry good..men. **1667** MILTON *P.L.* IV. 717 She ensnar'd Mankind with her faire looks. **1685** BAXTER *Paraphr. N.T.* Matt. xxii. 16 They sought to insnare Christ. **1730** THOMSON *Autumn* 1292 Let these Ensnare the wretched in the toils of law. **1749** SMOLLETT *Regicide* IV. iii, Curse on these faithless drops Which fall but to ensnare! **1866** FREER *Regency Anne Austria* II. 18 Ensnared by her beauty and so egregiously duped. **1876** BANCROFT *Hist. U.S.* II. xxxix. 466 A troop of horse, insnared by a false guide in an ambush among large trees.

Hence **en'snared** *ppl. a.*

1643 MILTON *Divorce* I. xiv. (1851) 56 Committing two ensnared souls..to kindle one another..with a hatred inconcileable. **1658** J. ROWLAND *Moufet's Theat. Ins.* 1068 The ensnared little creatures..do lie still.

ensnarement (ɛn'snɛəmənt). [f. as prec. + -MENT.] The action of ensnaring; the state or fact of being ensnared; *concr.* that which ensnares: an allurement, enticement, bait.

1617 HIERON *Wks* (1619–20) II. 259 And to beware of insnarement with the desire and loue of earthly things. **1649** ROBERTS *Clavis Bibl.* 367 The only Antidotes against worldly ensnarements. **1678** GALE *Crt. Gentiles* III. 97 God leaves men to the Blandishments, Allurements, and Ensnarements of an heart-bewitching world.

ensnarer (ɛn'snɛərə(r)). [f. as prec. + -ER.] One who ensnares.

1631 T. MAY tr. *Barclay's Mirrour Mindes* I. 63 They account all strangers..as enemyes & ensnarers of their liberty. **1651** J. F[REAKE] *Agrippa's Occ. Philos.* 399 The Tempters and Ensnarers have the last place. **1751** JOHNSON *Rambler* No. 155 ¶13 These ensnarers of the mind.

ensnaring (ɛn'snɛərɪŋ), *vbl. sb.* [f. as prec. + -ING[1].] The action of the vb. ENSNARE.

1660 R. COKE *Power & Subj.* 97 All the Acts made before ..for the ensnaring of the Subjects.

en'snaring, *ppl. a.* [f. as prec. + -ING[2].] That ensnares, entraps.

1630 R. JOHNSON *Kingd. & Commw.* 174 Th' ensnaring Lawes let Crowes goe free, While simple Doves entangled bee. **1643** MILTON *Divorce* II. xiv. (1851) 98 The debtor.. flattered with insufficient and insnaring discharges. *a* **1704** T. BROWNE *Satire Woman* Wks. 1730 I. 56 Gay laughter now, then sighs, with an ensnaring tear. **1826** MISS MITFORD *Village* Ser. II. (1863) 328 The insnaring seductions of the tap-room at the King's Head.

Hence **en'snaringly** *adv.*, in an ensnaring manner.

1853 LYNCH *Self-Improv.* vi. 151 Till wisdom free us, we are insnaringly and slavishly dependent.

en'snarl, *v.*[1] Forms: 6–7 ensnarle, 5 insnarl. [f. EN-[1] + SNARL *sb.*[1]] *trans.* To catch or entangle in, or as in, a 'snarl' or ravelled knot. Also *fig.*

c **1440** *Promp. Parv.* 262/2 Intrykyd or insnarlyd, *intricatus.* **1593** NASHE *Christ's T.* (1613) 148 As an Angler ensnarleth his hooke amongst weedes. **1596** SPENSER *F.Q.* v. ix. 9 They would closely him ensnarle, Ere to his den he backward could recoyle. **1608** TOPSELL *Serpents* 782 Untill they [Spiders] have throughly insnarled him within their clammy and viscous gins. **1655** GURNALL *Chr. in Arm.* II. 657 The ensnarling our own thoughts, by thinking to fathom the bottomlesse depths of God's justice, with the short cordage of our reason. **1675** J. SMITH *Chr. Relig. Appeal* I. 66 The Roman Empire is ensnarl'd in some or other War. **1894** W. R. THAYER *Poems New & Old* 19 The soul of Halid is ensnarled in a secret and pardonless crime. **1896** P. BROOKS *New Starts in Life* xiv. 239 Shall life be one great deep stream of joy, ever and anon darkening and ensnarling itself in suffering? **1924** *Public Opinion* 1 Aug. 104/2 Exhibiting an amazing capacity to get at the ensnarled kinks of the mind and soul.

†**en'snarl**, *v.*[2] *Obs.*[−0] [f. EN-[1] + SNARL *v.*] *intr.* 'To gnash the teeth' (Cockeram 1623).

‖**ens necessarium** (ɛnz nɛkɛ'sɑːrjʊm, nɛsɪ'sɛərɪəm). *Philos.* [L., necessary being.] A necessarily existent being; God.

1900 J. H. STIRLING *What is Thought?* ii. 32 We draw into consideration what concerns..the *constitution* of the ens necessarium. *a* **1910** W. JAMES *Some Probl. Philos.* (1911) iii. 43 God..cannot lack being therefore: He is *Ens necessarium, Ens realissimum*, as well as *Ens perfectissimum.* **1937** A. HUXLEY *Ends & Means* xiv. 278 The argument..that if there is an *ens necessarium* it must be at the same time an *ens realissimum.* **1949** *Mind* LVIII. 75 If by God we mean an *ens necessarium* or a Being that exists with 'necessity'.

ensoak: see EN- *pref.*[1] 3.

ensoap, ensober: see EN- *pref.*[1] 1 a, 2.

†**en'soigne**, *sb. Obs.* Forms: 4 ensoyne, -soygne, -soyngne, 5 ensoigne. [a. OF. *ensoigne*, var. of *essoigne*: see ESSOIN.]

1. Excuse, delay: only in phr. ***without ensoigne.***

c **1325** *Coer de L.* 1467 Forth they wente, withouten ensoyne. *c* **1380** *Sir Ferumb.* 945 So þat euerech with-oute ensoygne haþ a-slawe his. *Ibid.* 2827 And Gy Answerede wiþ-oute ensoyngne as he him stod afforn.

2. Embarrassment, inconvenience.

1475 CAXTON *Jason* 42 Certes the sekeness is of grete ensoigne and payne.

†**en'soigne**, *v. Obs. rare.* In 4 ensoyne. [ad. OF. *ensoignier*, f. *ensoigne*: see ESSOIN.] *trans.* To excuse.

a **1400** *Leg. Rood* (1871) 132 Mi sone from þe schulde beon ensoynet. *a* **1400** *Sir Degrev.* 275 There myght no sege be ensoynd That faught in the ffeld.

ensong, obs. variant of EVENSONG.

En-Soph (eɪn səʊf). Also -Sof. [See ENSOPHIC *a.*] In Cabbalistic doctrine, the absolute infinite and incomprehensible God.

1791 BRUCKER & ENFIELD *Hist. Philos.* II. IV. iii. 217 The chief heads of the Cabbalistic Doctrine are these... The Being from whom all things proceed is a Spirit, uncreated, eternal,..existing by the necessity of its nature, and filling the immensity of space. This spirit is *En-Soph*, the Infinite Deity. *Ibid.* 221 The En-soph, or Deity, contains all things within himself. **1865** C. D. GINSBURG *Kabbalah* ii. 64 No one has seen the *En Soph* at any time. **1902** *Jewish Encycl.* III. 468/1 An expression of the will of the En-Sof is not necessary in the act of emanation.

en'sophic, *a. Cabbala.* [f. late Heb. *ēin sōph* 'no end, infinity' + -IC.] (See quot. 1693.)

1693 *Phil. Trans.* XVII. 801 The Ensophick, or Infinite World, from which all the other do spring. **1873** C. G. LELAND *Egypt. Sketch-Bk.* xvi. 202 The supermundane and ensophic universe.

ensorcell (ɛn'sɔːsəl), *v.* [a. OF. *ensorceler*, f. *en-* (see EN-[1]) + *sorceler*, f. *sorcier* SORCERER.] *trans.* To enchant, bewitch, fascinate.

a **1541** WYATT in Puttenham *Eng. Poesie* III. xix. (Arb.) 232 Your Princely happes..ensorcell all the hearts Of Christen kings. **1855** G. MEREDITH *Shav. Shagpat* (1872) 93 A sorceress ensorcelled. **1886** BURTON *Arab. Nts.* (Abridged) I. 24 The damsel..whom this gazelle had ensorcelled.

Hence **en'sorcelling** *ppl. a.*; **en'sorcellment**, magic, enchantment.

1883 PAYNE *1001 Nts.* III. 104 His eyes were more ensorcelling than Haront and Maront. **1931** M. SUMMERS *Supernatural Omnibus* 10 Egypt the ancient..is the very womb of wizardry, of ghost lore, of ensorcellment, of scarabed spells and runes.

†**en'sorde**, *v. Obs. rare*[−1].

a **1528** SKELTON *Col. Cloute* 2585 Ensordyd with the wavys savage wode, Without our shyppe be rare, it is lykely brast.

†**en'sordid**, *a. Obs. rare*[−1]. = SORDID.

1627–77 FELTHAM *Resolves* I. iv. 5 Vice..in her bared skin, or her own ensordid rags!

†**en'sorrow**, *v. Obs.* Also 4 insorwe-n. [ME. *insorwen*, f. IN- + *sorwen* SORROW *v.*; in 16th c. independently f. EN-[1] + SORROW *sb.*] **a.** *intr.* To be in pain or sorrow; to sorrow. **b.** *trans.* To render sorrowful; to annoy, distress.

1382 WYCLIF *Rom.* viii. 22 Ech creature insorwith, and childith, or worchith with angwis, til ȝit. **1593** NASHE *Christ's T.* (1613) 78 To the ensorrowing the frontiers of sinne. **1603** FLORIO *Montaigne* III. iii. (1632) 46 The body.. is wasted, and ensorrowed.

†**en'sorte**, *v. Obs.* [f. EN-[1] + Fr. *sort* spell:—L. *sort-em* lot.] *trans.* To enchant, bewitch.

1475 CAXTON *Jason* 135 Ymagined lyghtly that Medea hadde ensorted or bewicched him [Jason].

ensoul, insoul (ɛn-, ɪn'səʊl), *v.* [f. EN-[1] + SOUL.]

1. *trans.* To put or take into the soul; to unite with the soul: †*refl.* to be absorbed into, become part of, the (Divine soul).

1633 EARL MANCH. *Al Mondo* (1636) 201 They laboured ..to insoule themselves in God. **1652** BP. PATRICK *Fun. Serm.* in *J. Smith's Sel. Disc.* 544 He had incorporated, shall I say, or insouled all principles of justice and righteousness. **1799** SOUTHEY *Eng. Eclog., etc.* Poet. Wks. III. 175 Only in some few faithful memories Insoul'd. **1881** PALGRAVE *Visions Eng.* 333 Insoul us to the nobler part, The chivalrous loyalty of thy life and word!

2. To infuse a soul into; to fill with 'soul'. Also, to dwell in, animate, as a soul.

1652 W. DENNIE *Glance at Theoph.* in Benlowes *Theoph.*, The hallowed air Seems all ensould with sweet Perfume. **1832** *Blackw. Mag.* XXXI. 653 He ensouls all dead insensate things. **1841–4** EMERSON *Ess. Love* Wks. (Bohn) I. 78 The soul is wholly embodied, and the body is wholly ensouled. **1879** G. MACDONALD *Sir Gibbie* I. xii. 177 The one visible symbol informed and insouled of the eternal. **1888** C. GORE *Ministry Chr. Ch.* 24 *note*, An organism ensouled by the indwelling word.

Hence **en'souled** *ppl. a.*; **en'souling** *ppl. a.*

18.. *Nat. Encycl.* I. 901 Christ was ἔνσαρκος, 'incarnate', but not ἔμψυχος 'insouled'. **1865** DRAPER *Intell. Devel. Europe* iv. 71 He [Thales] taught that the world is an insouled thing. **1826** *Blackw. Mag.* XX. 490 Infinitely penetrating—ensouling. **1868** BUSHNELL *Serm. Living Subj.* 459 The Word itself became the ensouling principle.

ensound: see EN- *pref.*[1] 2.

ensourge: variant of INSURGE. *Obs.*

ensoyne, obs. form of ENSIGN *sb.*

ensoyne, -soygne, variants of ENSOIGNE.

enspangle, ensparkle: see EN- *pref.*[1] 1 b.

†**en'special**, *adv.* and *a. Obs.* [Phrase *in special*, OFr. *en especial.*]

A. *adv.* Especially. **B.** *adj.* Especial.

c **1530** LD. BERNERS *Arth. Lyt. Bryt.* (1814) 24 She that fro hensforth wyl be your enspecyall louer and frende. **1534** WHITTINTON *Tullyes Offices* I. (1540) 26 Ayde of this lyfe is due to them enspecyall.

†**en'speer**, *v. Obs. rare*[−1]. In 5 enspere. [f. EN-[1] + SPEER.] *intr.* To enquire. Const. *of.*

c **1440** *Gesta Rom.* lxix. 317 (Harl. MS.) The Emperour enspered of the prioress.

enspell: see EN- *pref.*[1] 1 b.

ensphere (ɛn'sfɪə(r)), *v.* Also 7 en-, insphear(e, 7–9 insphere. [f. EN-[1] + SPHERE.]

†**1.** *trans.* To place in a (celestial) 'sphere'.

1615 *Val. Welshm.* (1663) B iij a, Eternal peace Insphear thy soul, and mount it to the stars. **1634** MILTON *Comus* 3 Where those immortal shapes Of bright aereal spirits live inspheard.

2. To enclose in, or as in, a sphere; to encircle, enclose. Also *fig.*

1616 CHAPMAN *Homer's Hymns, To Hermes* 394 His ample shoulders in a cloud enspher'd Of fierie chrimsine. *c* **1630** DRUMM. OF HAWTH. *Poems* Wks. 13 As that high circle, which the rest enspheres. *a* **1634** CHAPMAN *Sonn.* iii, None like Homer hath the world enspher'd, Earth, seas and heaven fix'd in his verse. **1648** HERRICK *Hesper., To King on Taking Leicester*, Victory do's rest, Enspher'd with palm on your triumphant crest. **1850** MRS. BROWNING *Poems* I. 345 The clear strong stars..insphere Our habitation. **1876** T. HARDY *Hand Ethelberta* II. 98 Being completely ensphered by the fog.

b. To contain as a sphere does.

1612 DONNE *Elegy Mrs. Drury, 2nd Anniv.* 78 Wks. 1872 I. 133 Shee whose eyes enspheard Star light inough, t' have made the south controll..the star-full northern pole.

3. To make into a sphere, give spherical form to. Also *fig.*

1640 T. CAREW *Poems, Obseq. Lady A. Hay*, Virgins.. Shall draw thy picture..One shall ensphere thine eyes. **1852** H. ROGERS *Ecl. Faith* (1853) 24 His true emblem is the hedgehog ensphered in his prickles. **1856** MRS. BROWNING *Aur. Leigh* I. 1007 Who..turning grandly on his central self Ensphered himself in twenty perfect years.

Hence **en'spherement, en'sphering** *vbl. sb.* and *ppl. a.*

1841 *Blackw. Mag.* L. 153 Man's belief..received by historic tradition and customary enspherement. **1868** BUSHNELL *Serm. Living Subj.* 13 A visible insphering in flesh. **1652** BENLOWES *Theoph.* IV. xxii, Twining Embraces with 's ensphearing arm of love. **1856** MASSON *Ess. 3 Devils* 73 The ensphering atmosphere and the storms that rage in it.

enspice: see EN- *pref.*[1] 1 b.

enspire, enspirit, obs. ff. INSPIRE, INSPIRIT.

enspiritualize (ɛn'spɪrɪtjuːəlaɪz), *v. rare.* [f. EN-[1] + SPIRITUALIZE *v.*] *trans.* To give a spiritual character to.

1886 SHORTHOUSE *Sir Percival* iii. 85 [A building] Enspiritualised, it seemed to me, by the fleeting clouds that swept over the sky.

enspisse: see INSPISSE.

‖**ens rationis** (ɛnz ræti'əʊnɪs, ræʃ-). *Philos.* Pl. entia rationis ('ɛntɪə, 'ɛnʃɪə). [L., being of the mind: see ENS.] An entity of reason, a being that has no existence outside the mind (opp. *ens reale*). Cf. ENTITY 3.

1565 T. HARDING *Confutation Apol. C. of E.* III. v. fol. 144[v], Disputations..about *genus* and *species*, and the rest of the universals.., whether they were *entia relia* [sic], or *rationis.* **1652** N. CULVERWEL *Lt. Nature* 201 The soul..will set up Beings of its own, *Entia Rationis*; Reason's creatures. **1707–8** BERKELEY *Philos. Commentaries* (1944) No. 535 The distinction betwixt entia Realia & entia rationis may be made as properly now as ever. **1883** F. H. BRADLEY *Princ. Logic* I. vi. 175 It is a metaphysical *ens rationis*, an abstract universal which can not be real. **1948** *Mind* LVII. 364 Later the view that its [*sc.* the supersensible world's] existence is not even problematic, that it is a mere *ens rationis*, 'a concept not an existent', is considered.

‖**ens reale** (ˌɛnz reɪ'ɑːlɪ, riː'eɪlɪ). *Philos.* Pl. entia realia ('ɛntɪə reɪ'ɑːlɪə, 'ɛnʃɪə riː'eɪlɪə). [L., real being.] A being that exists independently of any finite mind (opp. *ens rationis*). Hence *superl.* **ens**

realissimum (ɛnz reɪəˈlɪsɪmʊm, riːəˈlɪsɪməm), the most real being; God.

1565, **1707-8** [see ENS RATIONIS]. **1847** J. D. MORELL *Hist. Philos.* (ed. 2) I. ii. 257 Kant..allows that we inevitably trace all conditions of existence up to the supreme condition, the 'ens realissimum', and thus attain to the idea of a God. **1877** [see HYPOSTATIZE *v.*]. *a* **1910**, **1937** [see ENS NECESSARIUM]. **1958** W. STARK *Sociol. Knowl.* iv. 187 Movement is the *ens realissimum*, and not fact as commonly understood.

enstable: see EN- *pref.*¹ 2.

†**en'staff**, *v. Obs.*⁻⁰ [f. EN-¹ + STAFF.] *trans.* To put (a flag) on a staff; to hoist.

1611 FLORIO, *Alberáre*..also to enstaffe as a..banner.

enstage: see EN- *pref.*¹ 1 a.

enstall, enstalment: see INSTALL, -MENT.

enstamp (ɛnˈstæmp), *v.* Also 7-8 **instamp.** [f. EN-¹ + STAMP *v.*] To stamp, imprint (marks, figures, etc.) *on* anything. Also *fig.*

1611 SPEED *Hist. Gt. Brit.* v. vi. 31 Cunobeline (for so upon his coines his name is instamped). *Ibid.* v. vi. (1632) 32 Many coynes instamped of him. *c* **1630** JACKSON *Creed* IV. viii. Wks. III. 135 There must be such a correspondence as is between the character and the letter enstamped. **1653** GATAKER *Vind. Annot. Jer.* 106 A natural power enstamped on them by God their Creator. **1702** C. MATHER *Magn. Chr.* II. (1852) App. 221 On the other side were enstamped the towers of Zion. **1753** *Ess. Celibacy* 79 Nature is a system.. instamped with the goodness of the Deity. **1827** *Gentl. Mag.* XCVII. II. 33 Our Gray had likewise enstamped upon his imagination the forms and shadows of things which are presented to us in this visible creation. **1855** SINGLETON *Virgil* I. 86 The ploughman..on his cattle hath enstamped the brand.

Hence **en'stamped** *ppl. a.*

1597 DANIEL *Civ. Wars* VI. xxxvii, Make, that instamped Characters may send Abroad to Thousands, Thousand Men's Intent.

enstar, enstate: see INSTAR, INSTATE.

enstatite (ˈɛnstətaɪt). *Min.* [f. Gr. ἐνστάτ-ης adversary (from its refractory nature) + -ITE.] A variety of diallage, tinted variously from greyish- or greenish-white to olive-green and brown.

1857 C. SHEPARD *Min.* 425 Enstatite..in prisms, resembling pyroxene or scapolite. **1879** RUTLEY *Stud. Rocks* x. 120 Enstatite also affords two other directions of less perfect cleavage.

Hence **ensta'titic** *a.* [+ -IC].

1885 *Geol. Mag.* Feb. (*Title of Article*), The Enstatitic Lavas of Eycott Hill.

†**en'steep**, *v. Obs. rare*⁻¹. [f. EN-¹ + STEEP *v.*] *trans.* To immerse, station under water.

1604 SHAKS. *Oth.* II. i. 70 Congregated Sands, Traitors ensteep'd, to enclogge the guiltless Keele.

enstock, enstomach: see EN- *pref.*¹ a and b.

enstool (ɛnˈstuːl), *v.* [f. EN-¹ + STOOL *sb.* 1 e.] *trans.* To place (a west African chief) on his 'stool'. Hence **en'stoolment.**

1895 *Times* 16 Nov. 5/4 The King of Kokofu..is one of the three chiefs who, by ancient custom, perform the ceremony of 'enstooling' the King of Kumassi as King paramount [of the Ashanti Confederation]. **1895** *Daily News* 25 Nov. 3/5 The enstooling of Prempeh on March 26, 1886. **1925** *Public Opinion* 11 Oct. 396/1 Should a Chief be enstooled. **1959** A. ABBS *Ashanti Boy* v. 191 We had many people in Dwamanoa..because of the white Queen's enstoolment.

†**en'store**, *v. Obs.* Also 4 **enstoore**, 4-7 **instore.** [Probably two formations: (1) var. of ASTORE *v.*, influenced by L. *instaurāre* to fit up, repair, restore; (2) f. EN-¹ + STORE *sb.* or *v.*; but the two cannot be accurately distinguished in the examples.]

1. *trans.* To renew, repair (transl. L. *instaurare*).

1382 WYCLIF *2 Kings* xii. 5 And enstoore thei the coveryngis of the hows. —— *Ezek.* xxxvi. 10 Ruynouse thingis shaln be instorid, or maad aȝein. —— *Ephes.* i. 10 For to instore [**1388** enstore] alle thingis in Crist. —— *Rom.* xiii. 9 If there be ony othir maundement, it is instorid or enclosid [Vulg. *instauratur*] in this word.

2. To fit up, provide, store *with*. Also const. *of*.

c **1450** LONELICH *Grail* xxxv. 585 And for his Maner.. Enstored ful wel it was. **1494** in Blyth *Hist. Notices & Rec. Fincham* (1863) 155 Enstored with all my catail of shepe. **1502** ARNOLDE *Chron.* (1811) 215 He [the Keper] shal yelde to the eyer whan so he come to ful age all his lande instored of husbondry. **1557** PAYNEL *Barclay's Jugurth* 98 Thys castle was..instored with men, wepyn, vitayles, and with all other ordinaunce. **1597** DANIEL *Civ. Wares* III. xxxii, He that is with Life and will instor'd, Hath for revenge inough. *a* **1633** MUNDAY *View Sundry Examples* 79 Of money and riches sufficiently instored.

†**en'strait**, *v. Obs.* Forms: 5 **enstreit**, 6 **enstreighte.** [f. EN-¹ + STRAIT *a.*] *trans.* = STRAITEN. **a.** To make narrow. **b.** To bring into straits or difficulties.

c **1475** tr *T. à Kempis' Imit.* I. xxiv, Coueitouse men shul be enstreited wiþ most wrecchid nede. **1581** in W. H. Turner *Select Rec. Oxf.* 413 To enstreighte or make narrowe the way.

†**en'straiten**, *v. Obs. rare.* [f. EN-¹ + STRAITEN.] *trans.* **a.** To make strait or narrow; to curtail (property). **b.** To bring into straits; to put under constraint.

1590 R. PAYNE *Descr. Irel.* (1841) 11 He hath already to plesure his countrie instraightned his demeanes. **1618** BOLTON *Florus* II. xvii. (1636) 142 But the Romans had enstraitned her before she was aware thereof.

†**en'strange**, *v. Obs.* Also 5 **enstraunge.** [f. EN-¹ + STRANGE.] *trans.* **a.** To remove far *from*. **b.** To make strange or a stranger *to*.

1483 CAXTON *Gold. Leg.* 253/2 She was as fer enstraunged fro the payne of the flesshe as she was fro corrupcion of her body. *a* **1763** SHENSTONE *Elegies* XIX. 55, I smile, but from a soul enstrang'd to peace.

†**en'strangle**, *v. Obs. rare*⁻¹. [var. of ESTRANGLE, *Obs.*] *trans.* To strangle.

c **1400** MAUNDEV. xviii. (1839) 194 Whan thei ben thus enstrangled, thei eten here Flesche.

†**en'strength**, *v. Obs.* [f. EN-¹ + STRENGTH.] *trans.* To endow with strength, strengthen.

1483 CAXTON *Gold. Leg.* 122/2 Thys vyncent was tormented for to dwelle wyth God..he was beten to be enstrengthed.

†**en'strengthen**, *v. Obs.* [f. EN-¹ + STRENGTHEN.] *trans.* To strengthen, make strong.

1538 LELAND *Itin.* II. 75 A famose Toun or Castelle apon a very Torre or Hille, wunderfully enstrengthenid of nature. **1539** *Proclam. Hen. VIII* in Froude *Hist. Eng.* III. 366 Until such time as they, enstrengthened, may be able to go in like pace with them. **1654** COKAINE *Dianea* II. 162 Enstrengthening himselfe to receive that soule which by the right of Love he supposed belonged to him.

enstruct, obs. form of INSTRUCT.

enstuff: see EN- *pref.*¹ 3.

†**en'style**, *v. Obs.* Also 7 **enstile.** [f. EN-¹ + STYLE *sb.* or *v.*] *trans.* To style, denominate.

1599 B. JONSON *Cynthia's Rev.* v. viii. 30 Our eye doth reade thee (now enstil'd) our Crites. **1623** *Vox Graculi* in Brand *Pop. Antiq.* (1870) I. 38 Vulgarly enstiled Shrove Tuesday. **1638** SANDERSON *Serm.* (1681) II. 112 Why the Apostle should chuse to enstile Almighty God from these two [attributes] of Patience and of Consolation. **1648** HERRICK *Hesper.*, *Oberon's Pal.* 92 By some enstyl'd The luckie omen of the child.

†**en'suable**, *v. Obs.* [f. ENSUE *v.* + -ABLE; for the sense cf. *conformable*, *suitable*.] That logically ensues; likely to result.

1548 GEST *Pr. Masse* 93 An issue..resonable an[d] ensuable. It is nothing ensuable, because the apostles sacrificed, they sacrificed Christes bodye and bloud. **1635** J. HAYWARD *Banish'd Virg.* 183 Which they would not have done, if they had but considered or foreseene their ensueable inconveniences.

†**en'suance.** *Obs.* [f. as prec. + -ANCE.] The fact of ensuing.

1652 EARL MONM. tr. *Bentivoglio's Hist. Relat.* 114 Upon the insuance of peace, and due observation of all things on this side the line.

ensuant (ɛnˈsjuːənt), *a.* [f. ENSUE *v.* + -ANT. Cf. OFr. *ensiwant.*] †**1.** Appropriately following, sequent *to*. *Obs. rare*⁻¹.

1589 PUTTENHAM *Eng. Poesie* II. x. [xi.] (Arb.) 104 If..the maker do..make his dittie sensible and ensuant to the first verse in good reason.

2. Following or consequent *on*.

1897 *Daily News* 21 Oct. 7/7 His condition, ensuant on a paralytic stroke, left little room for hope. **1900** *Ibid.* 2 July 5/6 The stoppage of trade ensuant on the war.

ensucket: see EN- *pref.*¹ 2.

ensue (ɛnˈsjuː), *v.* Forms: 5-7 **ensew(e**, 5 **ensiewe**, **-yew**, 5-6 **insue**, 6 **insew(e**, 6-7 **inshow**, 5- **ensue.** [ad. OF. *ensiw-*, *ensu-*, stem of *ensivre*, *ensuivre* (mod.F. *ensuivre*), corresp. to Pr. *enseguir*, It. *inseguire*:—late L. *insequĕre*, L. *insequi* to pursue, follow close upon, f. *in* (see IN-) + *sequi* to follow.]

†**1.** *trans.* To follow in (a person's steps); to follow (a leader, etc.). *Obs.*

?*a* **1500** *Flower Womanhede* in *Pol. Rel. & L. Poems* 43 Whos stepes glade to ensue Ys eueri woman in their degre. **1509** HAWES *Examp. Virt.* xiii. 255 And xv. ladyes her dyd ensue. **1596** SPENSER *F.Q.* IV. ix. 5 Whom straight the Prince ensuing in together far'd. *a* **1626** BP. ANDREWES *Serm.* 147 All that have ensued the steppes of their faith.

b. *absol.* and *intr.*

c **1500** *New Not-br. Mayd* 235, I must ensue Where fortune doth me lede. **1513** DOUGLAS *Æneis* II. xii. [xi.] 77 Neir at our bak Crewse, my spous ensewis. *a* **1577** SIR T. SMITH *Commw. Eng.* (1633) 56 Which pricketh forward to ensue in their fathers steps.

†**2.** *fig.* To follow the guidance of (a person, etc.); to imitate (an example); to follow (inclination, passion, etc.), conform to (advice, orders).

1430 LYDG. *Chron. Troy* II. x, I am so dull certayne that I ne can Guido ensewe. **1481** CAXTON *Myrr.* I. xiv. 47 Tho philosophres ensieweth better Plato than Aristotle. *c* **1500** *Doctr. Gd. Servaunts* in *Poet. Tracts* (1842) 7 Seruauntes ought not to ensue Theyr owne wyll. **1530** *Proper Dyaloge* (1863) 23 In this they ensued Christes lawyng and his doctrine. **1541** ELYOT *Image Gov.* 13 All honourable women ensued the Empresses exaumple. **1599** DAVIES *Immort. Soul* (1876) I. 99 While these receiv'd opinions I ensue.

†**b.** Of things: To take after, correspond to.

1398 TREVISA *Barth De P.R.* I. Prol. (1495) 3 The proprietees of thynges folowe and ensewe their substaunces. **1533-4** *Act 25 Hen. VIII*, c. 21 §19 An ordenance.. insewing muche the olde auncient customes of this realme in that behalfe. **1628** COKE *On Litt.* 13 a, The recompense shall ensue the loss.

†**3.** To follow with the intention of overtaking; to pursue. *Obs.*

1513 BRADSHAW *St. Werburge* I. 1079 This venerable prynce ensuynge this great harte approched to his cell. **1569** J. SANFORD *tr. Agrippa's Van. Artes* 125 b, To ensue them that flee.

b. *fig.* To follow or seek after, strive to obtain, aim at. *arch.* Also †*intr.* with *after*.

1483 CAXTON *Cato* 2 b, Eschewe alle vyces and ensiewe vertue. **1535** COVERDALE *Ps.* xxxiii. 14 Let him seke peace and ensue it. **1642** ROGERS *Naaman* To Rdr. §2 To affect and ensue the meanes of it owne safety. **1759** ROBERTSON *Hist. Scot.* II. 119 For him I desire to ensue courage. **1874** MORLEY *Compromise* (1886) 113 They have sought truth and ensued it.

†**4.** To follow out (a plan, course of life, profession, etc.); to follow up (a train of thought), 'pursue' (a subject). Also *catachr.* to spend (a period of life). *Obs.*

1509 HAWES *Past. Pleas.* XXXI. xii, But that in joye you may your youth ensue. **1531** ELYOT *Gov.* I. iv. (1883) I. 28 Semblable ordre will I ensue in the fourmynge the gentill wittes of noble mennes children. **1581** LAMBARDE *Eiren.* II. iv. (1602) 136, I will ensue that also. **1590** SPENSER *Ep. Sir John Norris*, And Precedent of all that armes ensue. *a* **1613** OVERBURY *A Wife* (1638) 172 They are not pauled with insuing idle cogitations.

5. †**a.** *trans.* Of an event, state of things, portion of time, portion of a book or discourse: To follow, succeed, be subsequent to. Also of persons: To succeed (some one) in an office, or in the performance of an action. Chiefly implying *immediate* sequence: To come next to. *Obs.*

1491 *Act 7 Hen. VII*, c. 20 §5 By the space of ij monethes next ensuyng any of the seid festis. **1542** in W. H. Turner *Sel. Rec. Oxford* 168 The feast..next insuying the date herof. **1578** TIMME *Caluine on Gen.* 159 How long it was ere that the flood insued the creation of the world. **1591** SPENSER *Teares Muses* 54 And let the rest in order thee ensew. **1609** BP. BARLOW *Answ. Nameless Catholic* 16 What are these Aggreeuances..that..ensued that desperate Plot? **1612** DRAYTON *Poly-olb.* xxiv. (1748) 360 Him Erkenwald ensues th' East-English Offa's son. **1649** SELDEN *Laws Eng.* (1739) Pref. 8 For three hundred years next ensuing the Normans.

b. *intr.* Of a portion of time, part of a book or discourse: To be subsequent. Of an event, a state of things: To occur or arise subsequently. Chiefly implying immediate succession. Cf. ENSUING *ppl. a.*

The phrase ***next ensuing***, now somewhat pleonastic, is still in formal use with reference to dates.

1485 CAXTON *Chas. Gt.* 5 Thre partyes by chapytres ensyewyng declared. **1494** FABYAN 5 The Cronycle shall ensewe, In his dewe ordre. **1528** *Test. Ebor.* (Surtees) V. 265 To be disposed in maner and forme that ensuyeth. **1559** in *Vicary's Anat.* (1888) App. iii. 139 Gouernors of the sayd hospytalles for the yere now next insuynge. **1584** POWEL *Lloyd's Cambria* 91 The yeare insuing. **1591** in Picton *L'pool Munic. Rec.* (1883) I. 96 The copie of wᶜʰ said Letter ensueth. **1667** MILTON *P.L.* IV. 991 Now dreadful deeds Might have ensu'd. **1669** BUNYAN *Holy Citie* 195 These and the words ensuing. **1709** STEELE & SWIFT *Tatler* No. 74 ¶ 11 On Saturday the 15th of October next ensuing. **1729** T. COOKE *Tales, Proposals, etc.* 36 Bleak Winds and Storms ensue, they [the Flowers] droop, they dy. **1770** LANGHORNE *Plutarch* (1879) I. 204/1 Several skirmishes ensued in the difficult passes. **1866** KINGSLEY *Herew.* xvii. 216 Conversations ensued thereon between Baldwin and his courtiers.

†**c.** In *pr. pple.*: In succession, 'running'. *Obs. rare.*

1583 STOCKER *Hist. Civ. Warres Lowe C.* I. 107 b, Then they should giue two nights ensuing at midnight a signe with fire, etc.

6. †**a.** *trans.* To follow as a result or consequence; to result from. *Obs.*

1514 BARCLAY *Cyt. & Uplondyshm.* (1847) p. xlvi, Surfet ensuing gluttony. **1566** DRANT *Horace' Sat.* II. A viij, Such lyke blame That doth ensue outragiouse spence. **1607** TOPSELL *Serpents* (1653) 701 The accidents that follow, are like to those which ensue the bitings of Vipers. *a* **1677** BARROW *Serm.* (Wks. 1716) I. 1 By peace [may be meant] the content..ensuing such a course of actions. *a* **1754** FIELDING *Conversation* Wks. 1784 IX. 364 Nor would any inconvenience ensue the admittance of such exceptions.

b. *intr.* To follow as a result; to result. Const. †*by*, *from*, †*of*, *on*, *upon*.

1483 CAXTON *Cato* B iij, The grete multitude of synnes whyche ensueth and cometh thereof. **1525** E. LEE in Ellis *Orig. Lett.* Ser. III. II. 71, I need not advertise your Grace what infection & danger may ensue hereby. **1598** BARKCLEY *Felic. Man* (1631), The service of God, whereof ensueth the enjoying of his heavenly kingdome. *a* **1700** DRYDEN *Ovid's Met.* XII. Wks. 1821 XII. 167 From the wound ensued no purple flood. **1774** GOLDSM. *Nat. Hist.* (1776) II. 318 What devastation might not ensue were the elephant..as fierce.. as the tiger. **1837** G. BIRD *Nat. Philos.* 238 Decomposition of water will, of course, ensue, and hydrogen will be evolved. **1850** TENNYSON *In Mem.* cxvii, That out of distance might ensue Desire of nearness doubly sweet.

¶ To proceed, issue *from*.

1599 MARSTON *Sco. Villanie* II. vii. 208 Soules of men, from that great soule ensue.

7. *intr.* To follow as a logical conclusion. Usually *impers.* with virtual subject-clause. *rare* in mod. use.

1581 LAMBARDE *Eiren.* IV. iv. 399 It doeth of necessitie ensue, that he, etc. **1600** SHAKS. *A.Y.L.* I. iii. 31 Doth it therefore ensue that you should loue his Sonne deerelie?

ensuer (ɛn'sjuːə(r)). *rare.* [f. ENSUE *v.* + -ER.] One who ensues, a follower.

1550 PAYNEL *Notable Sayings Script.* Ded. Ep., Diligent ensuers of his will and steps. **1885** *Blackw. Mag.* 736/2 The poor ensuer of the peace.

en'suing, *vbl. sb.* [f. as prec. + -ING[1].] The action of the vb. ENSUE, in various senses.

1561 NORTON & SACKV. *Gorboduc* I. i, In right ensuynge of your life. **1581** J. BELL *Haddon's Answ. Osor.* 103 b, The ensuyng of whose studious industry we do not neglect. **1605** VERSTEGAN *Dec. Intell.* viii. (1628) 242 A iust insuing of the vse of reason.

ensuing (ɛn'sjuːɪŋ). *ppl. a.* etc. [f. ENSUE *v.* + -ING[2].] **A.** *ppl. adj.*

1. In various applications of the sense of ENSUE *v.* 5. **a.** Coming afterwards, subsequent, posterior in time or order (? *obs.*). **b.** Immediately subsequent, coming next; also ***next ensuing***. **c.** That is shortly to happen, approaching, imminent.

a. 1604 DEKKER *King's Entertainm.* 270 To a more royall and serious ensuing entertainment. **1610** BEAUM. & FL. *Maid's Trag.* IV. i, A great example of their justice To all ensuing eyes. **1627–77** FELTHAM *Resolves* I. xxiv. 43 Men, rather than they will want insuing memory, will be spoken by the branded Statue. **1680** *Life Edw. II* in *Select. Harl. Misc.* (1793) 49 A perfect mirror, wherein ensuing kings may see, etc.

b. 1611 RICH *Honest. Age* (1844) 20 What conceipt I have ..I will partly make manifest by this insuing circumstance. **1697** DRYDEN *Virg. Georg.* I. 112 Th' ensuing Season, in return, may bear The bearded product of the Golden Year. **1747** WESLEY *Prim. Physic* (1762) Introd. 27, I have had many Opportunities of trying the Virtues of the ensuing Remedies. **1766** GOLDSM. *Vic. W.* xxviii, For the three ensuing days I was in a state of anxiety. **1875** SCRIVENER *Lect. Grk. Test.* 11 In the two next ensuing Lectures.

c. 1603 KNOLLES *Hist. Turks* (1638) 306 By the small number of their army divining their ensuing overthrow. **1678** *Trans. Crt. Spain* II. 158 There is appearance of an ensuing rupture. **1734** *Grub St. Jrnl.* 2 May 4/3 The ensuing Elections of Members to serve in parliament. **1828** SCOTT *F.M. Perth* xxxiii, To make some arrangements for the ensuing combat.

2. In sense of ENSUE *v.* 6: Resulting.

1604 DEKKER *Honest Wh.* Wks. 1873 III. 75 To guard you safe from all ensuing danger. **1642** MILTON *Apol. Smect.* (1851) 290 Their manifest crimes serve to bring forth an ensuing good. **1665** EARL ROTHES in *Lauderd. Papers* (1884) I. 216 To prevent ffurdier inshowieng danger.

†**B.** *pple.* (quasi-*prep.*). With respect to. *Obs.*

1645–62 PAGITT *Heresiogr.* (ed. 6) 201 Ensuing this voice, we see that St. Peter calls it, etc.

†**en'suingly,** *adv. Obs.* [f. ENSUING *ppl. a.* + -LY[2].] In an ensuing manner. **a.** Congruously, fittingly. **b.** In due order or sequence.

c **1510** BARCLAY *Mirr. Good Mann.* (1570) A ij, After mine estate My stile and my writing ensuingly to sounde. *a* **1535** MORE *On the Passion* Wks. 1321/1 Linked and cheined ensewinglye together. **1556** J. HEYWOOD *Spider & F.* xxxi. 112 What waie was had? ensueth ensuingly.

‖**en suite**: see SUITE.

ensulphur: see EN-[1] *pref.* 1 b.

†**en'surance.** *Obs.* exc. in form INSURANCE. [a. OF. *enseurance*: see ENSURE *v.* and -ANCE.]

1. The action of ensuring or making certain; *concr.* a means of ensuring.

1654 WHITLOCK *Zootomia* 143 Were some mens Petitions to men, as non-sensicall as their Prayers to God, they would need no other ensurance of their deniall. **1688** *Objection agst. Repeal Penal Laws & Tests* 16, I will never seek or value an Ensurance by Oaths and Tests.

2. Betrothal. Cf. ENSURE *v.* 4.

1469 MARG. PASTON in *Paston Lett.* No. 601 II. 340, I have non very knowleche of your ensuraunce.

3. *Comm.* The securing against loss in return for a fixed payment; = INSURANCE.

1661 T. MUN *Eng. Treas.* (1664) 6 To be well acquainted with the laws..of the Ensurance office. *a* **1695** MRQ. HALIFAX (T.), There will be no ensurance here to make you amends, as there is in the case of fire. **1755** in JOHNSON.

†**en'surancer.** *Obs.* Also 7–8 insurancer. [f. ENSURANCE + -ER.] He who or that which gives assurance or confidence.

1665 STILLINGFL. *Grounds Prot. Relig.* 162 Our Ensurancer in the main Principle of Faith concerning the Scriptures being the Word of God, is Apostolical Tradition.

†**en'sure,** *a. Obs. rare*$^{-1}$. [a. AF. *ensur*, f. *en-* (see EN-[1]) + *sur* SURE; but perh. to be taken as phrase *en sur* in a state of security.] Sure, confident.

c **1430** *Hymns Virg.* (1867) 18 In þis world is hard auenture: Who-so þerof is moost ensure, Sunnest schal he be schamed and schent.

ensure (ɛn'ʃʊə(r)), *v.* Forms: 5 ensuer, -sewer, 4– ensure. See also INSURE. [ad. AF. *enseurer*, f. *en-* (see EN-[1]) + OF. *seur* (mod.F. *sûr*) sure: the AF. vb. may be regarded as an alteration of OF. *asseurer* to ASSURE.

The word freq. occurs in individual MSS. of Chaucer, but the better attested reading in these passages is app. *assure*.

The form INSURE is properly a mere variant of *ensure*, and still occasionally appears in all the surviving senses. In general usage, however, it is now limited to the financial sense (with reference to 'insurance' of life or property), in which the form *ensure* is wholly obsolete.]

†**1.** *trans.* To make (a person) mentally sure; to convince, render confident. Followed by *subord. clause.* Chiefly *pass.* and *refl. Obs.*

c **1500** *Melusine* 68 They were ensured that they wold & sought but good. **1568** GRAFTON *Chron. Hen. V*, II. 495 The French enemies..ensured themselves to gaine..whatsoever before they had lost. **1674** N. FAIRFAX *Bulk & Selv.* 147 That the body do not lock up [souls] there for the sake of its hardfastness or closeness, we are ensured.

†**2.** To give security to, pledge one's faith to (a person) for the execution of a promise. *Obs.*

1413 LYDG. *Pilgr. Sowle* IV. xxxviii. (1859) 63, I ensure you feythfully, I shall brynge you to a place where ye shalle sene hym. **1557** *K. Arthur* (Copland) II. xiii, Here I ensure you by the faithe of my body neuer to departe.

†**3.** To pledge one's credit to (a person); to tell (a person) confidently *that* (something is true).

c **1385** CHAUCER *L.G.W.* 2115 *Ariadne*, I swere & yow ensure This sevene yer I have your servaunt be. *c* **1450** *Why I can't be a Nun* 364 in *E.E.P.* (1862) 147 So God me spede, I yow ensewer, Ellys yowre habyte ys no trew token. **1483** CAXTON *Cato* C iiij, I ensure you that it is trouthe. **1534** LD. BERNERS *Gold. Bk. M. Aurel.* (1546) Z viij, I ensure the, the worme in the tymbre..doth not so muche domage. **1642** FULLER *Holy & Prof. St.* IV. xv. 314 She advised him rather to marry, ensuring him that no Lady in the land..would refuse him.

†**4.** To guarantee (a thing) to a person; to warrant (a fact). Const. *to* or *dat. Obs.*

1460 in *Pol. Rel. & L. Poems* (1866) 62 Nay, that I you ensure. **1483** CAXTON *Gold. Leg.* 424/1 Testefyeng and ensuryng that the holy man fiacre was ful of wicked & euyl arte. **1528** ROY *Sat.*, I durst ensure the one thynge. **1733** NEAL *Hist. Purit.* II. 574 All which he ensured upon his royal word.

†**b.** To guarantee (an expense). *Obs.*

1738 JOHNSON *Let. Cave* in *Boswell* (1887) I. 122 And since the expense will be no more, I shall contentedly insure it.

†**5.** To engage (a person) by a pledge or contract.

c **1400** *Rowland & O.* 160 He es ensurede to myn eme & mee. **1440** J. SHIRLEY *Dethe K. James* (1818) 9 Yn the same wise bene ye sworne and ensurid to kepe youre peple.

†**b.** *esp.* To engage by a promise of marriage, or (rarely) by marriage itself; to betroth, espouse. Cf. ASSURE 4. *Obs.*

c **1450** LONELICH *Grail* lii. 1019 So that ensured thanne bothe they were, And for the Mariages they ordeyned there. **1523** LD. BERNERS *Froiss.* I. cxl. *heading*, Howe the yonge erle of Flaunders ensured the kynges doughter of Englande. *c* **1530** —— *Arth. Lyt. Bryt.* (1814) 237 Let vs..sende for the archbysshop, to thentent to ensure you togyther. *c* **1550** CHEKE *Matt.* i. 18 After his mother Mari was ensured to Joseph. **1558** BP. WATSON *Sev. Sacram.* xxviii. 177 When the two parties..haue sayde these woordes, then bee they ensured and iustly married together. **1606** G. W[OODCOCKE] tr. *Hist. Ivstine* 79 b, No other maide should be contracted and ensured to any husband, etc.

6. To secure, make safe (*against*, *from* risks).

a **1704** L'ESTRANGE (J.), A mendicant contracted with a country fellow..to ensure his sheep for that year. **1776** SIR J. REYNOLDS *Disc.* vii. (1876) 424 Sufficient to ensure us from all error and mistake. **1847** MRS. A. KERR *Hist. Servia* 426 To ensure her friends against any sort of reaction. **1883** *Manch. Exam.* 26 Nov. 5/3 The Swiss lake steamers are..too toylike to ensure their passengers against reasonably probable risks.

†**7.** *Comm.* To INSURE (a person's life, property, etc.). *Obs.*

1693 E. HALLEY in *Phil. Trans.* XVII. 602 The price of ensuring the Life of a Man of 20. **1747** *Scheme Equip. Men of War* 40 'Tis natural for us to ensure our Effects.

8. To make certain the occurrence or arrival of (an event), or the attainment of (a result); = ASSURE 5.

1742 YOUNG *Nt. Th.* VII. 633 All promise, some ensure, a second scene. **1796** BURKE *Regic. Peace* Wks. 1842 II. 380 Whether the authority..can ensure their execution. **1839** THIRLWALL *Greece* II. 339 Having taken no precautions to ensure regular supplies. **1879** W. H. WHITE in *Cassell's Techn. Educ.* IV. 80/1 By this arrangement it is ensured that there shall be no leak.

9. To make (a thing) sure *to* or *for* a person; to secure.

1770 LANGHORNE *Plutarch* (1879) I. 518/2 Ensuring them the victory. **1799** WELLINGTON in Gurw. *Disp.* I. 48 The only rule, which..can ensure for the officers..the conveniences which they have a right to expect. **1847** L. HUNT *Jar Honey* x. (1848) 138 It ensures us an intercourse with a nation we esteem. **1861** MAY *Const. Hist.* (1863) I. i. 12 A constitutional government ensures to the King a wide authority.

en'surer. *rare.* [f. prec. + -ER.] He who or that which ensures. †**a.** One who vouches for, guarantees. †**b.** One who guarantees another against loss; an underwriter; = INSURER. **c.** One who or that which renders (anything) certain.

1654 WHITLOCK *Zootomia* 35 Wouldest thou have a Policy on Heaven?..make the Poore thy Ensurers. *a* **1660** HAMMOND *Wks.* (1684) IV. 481, I will once set up the Ensurer's Office, that whatever goes out on that Voyage, shall never miss to come home with gain. **1693** LUTTRELL *Brief Rel.* (1857) III. 29, 9 merchants on the Exchange, great ensurers, are all withdrawn for considerable summs. **1694** S. JOHNSON *Notes Past. Let. Bp. Burnet* I. 5 The Pulpits were the Ensurers of the King's Word. *a* **1734** NORTH *Exam.* III. vi. §91 (1740) 490 Just as if the Ensurers brought in a Catalogue of Ships lost, taking no Notice of Ships arrived.

ensurge, var. of INSURGE *v. Obs.*

†**en'suring,** *vbl. sb. Obs.* [f. ENSURE *v.* + -ING[1].] The action of the verb ENSURE; *attrib.* in ***ensuring-office*** = *insurance-office*.

1709 E. W. *Life Donna Rosina* 12 The Ensuring Office in the Spanish West Indies.

†**en'swamp,** *v. Obs. rare*$^{-1}$. [f. EN-[1] + SWAMP *sb.*] *trans.* To plunge into or entangle in a swamp. Implied in **en'swamped** *ppl. a.*

1702 C. MATHER *Magn. Chr.* II. (1852) App. 183 They were like to make no weapons reach their enswamped adversaries. **1821** T. NUTTALL *Trav. Arkansa* vi. 108, I was now obliged more deeply to wade through the enswamped forests..which surround the habitable prairie lands.

enswathe, inswathe (ɛn'sweɪð), *v.* [f. EN-[1] + SWATHE *sb.* or *v.*] *trans.* To bind or wrap in a swathe or bandage. Also *refl.*

1597 SHAKS. *Lover's Compl.* 49 Letters sadly pend in blood,..Enswath'd and seald to curious secrecy. **1827** DE QUINCEY *Last Days Kant* Wks. III. 116 Nesting and enswathing himself in the bedclothes. **1830** H. N. COLERIDGE *Grk. Poets* (1834) 340 Then did they bathe thee in a fresh pure stream..and enswathed thy limbs In a white robe.

b. *transf.* and *fig.*

1830 AIRD in *Blackw. Mag.* XXVIII. 821 A lucid air enswathed her head. **1842** TENNYSON *St. Simeon Stylites* 74 Inswathed sometimes in wandering mist. **1857** J. PULSFORD *Quiet Hours* 174 Dense vapours were enswathing the soul. **1873** BROWNING *Red Cott. Night-c.* 235 Your smile enswathes me in beatitude.

enswathement (ɛn'sweɪðmənt). [f. prec. + -MENT.] The action of enswathing, or the condition of being enswathed: *concr.* that in which anything is enswathed or enfolded. Also *fig.*

1877 BLACKIE *Wise Men* 65 All vital power..in moist enswathement grows. **1883** H. DRUMMOND *Nat. Law in Spir. W.* vii. (1884) 225 We..define the soul as an invisible enswathement of the body. **1887** E. C. DAWSON *Life Bp. Hannington* 27 The cramping enswathements of the Roman system.

ensweep: see EN- *pref.*[1] 3.

†**en'sweeten,** *v. Obs.* Also 7 insweeten. [f. EN-[1] + SWEETEN *v.*] *trans.* To infuse sweetness into; to sweeten. Also *fig.*

1607 WALKINGTON *Opt. Glass* 58 Which more ensweeteneth the breath. **1627–77** FELTHAM *Resolves* I. viii. 11 The bitterness of Reprehension is insweetned. *a* **1640** JACKSON *Creed* XI. xxv. Wks. X. 477 The very name of peace would ensweeten our thoughts.

ensynopticity (ˌɛnsɪnɒp'tɪsɪtɪ). *rare*$^{-1}$. [f. EN-[2] + SYNOPTIC + -(I)TY.] A capacity for taking a general view of a subject.

1855 WHATELY *Select. Writings* 38 There is, perhaps, no faculty so much the gift of nature as Totality (or ensynopticity).

ent[1]. *Obs.*$^{-0}$ [a. Fr. *ente*:—late L. **impota*: cf. IMP.] A scion or graft.

1648 HEXHAM *Dutch Dict.*, Eester, an Ent, a Scion, a Sprig, or a Graft.

ent[2] (ɛnt), *a.* (quasi-*sb.*) *Metaph. rare.* [ad. late L. *ens*, *ent-is*: see ENS.] See quot. (rendering of Gr. τὸ ὄν).

188. H. JACKSON in *Encycl. Brit.* XVIII. 315 Starting from the formula 'the Ent (or existent) is, the Nonent is not', Parmenides attempted, etc. *Ibid.*, The Ent, *i.e.* the existent unity..which reason discovers beneath the variety and mutability of things.

ent (ɛnt). Also 'ent, e'nt, etc. Dial. and colloq. var. *isn't*: see BE *v.* A I. 1. Cf. AIN'T[1].

1685 C. COOPER *Grammatica Linguæ Anglicanæ* xix. 79 *De Barbara dialecto*... Facilitatis causa dicitur. *Bellis Bellows* follis *'ent is not* nonne est. **1710** [see BE *v.* A I. 1]. **1711** SWIFT *Jrnl. to Stella* (1948) I. 188 En't that right now? **1888** in *Eng. Dial. Dict.* **1961** [see PERSONAL *sb.* 5]. **1977** J. JOHNSTON *Shadows on our Skin* 86 Bit young, ent he, for a girl like you?

-ent, *suffix*, a. Fr. *-ent*, ad. L. *-ent-em*, the ending of pr. pples. of vbs. of the 2nd, 3rd, and 4th conjugation, as *rident-em*, *currentem*, *audientem*. (In the pples. of the 3rd and 4th conjugation this ending represents OAryan *-nt-*, or perh. *-ent-*, of the ablaut-series *-ent-*, *-ont-*, *-nt-*; cf. Skr. *-ant-*, *-at-*, Gr. *-οντ-*, Goth. *-and-*, OE. *-end-*; in those of the 2nd conjugation it represents this suffix combined with the thematic *-e-* of the vb.; similarly the *-ant-* of the 1st conjugation includes a thematic *-a-*.) In OFr. this suffix and the corresponding *-ant-em* of the 1st conjugation were levelled under *-ant*, the sole ending of the Fr. pr. pple., as *riant*, *courant*, *mourant*, *levant* (:—L. *levantem*). At a later time many L. forms in *-ent-*, which had acquired an adj. sense, were adopted in Fr. as adjs. with the *-ent-* unchanged, as *diligent*,

évident; some of these were duplicates of living ppl. forms in *-ant*, as *convénient* = *convenant*, *provident* = *pourvoyant*, *confident* = *confiant*. The Fr. words in *-ant*, *-ent*, which were adopted into Eng., have generally retained the form of the suffix which they had in Fr.; but since 1500 there has been a tendency to refashion them after Lat., and hence several words in *-ant* have changed that ending for *-ent*, either entirely or in certain senses. In mod.Eng. also many Lat. words in *-entem* have been directly adopted, always in the form *-ent*. The conflict between Eng. and Fr. analogies occasions frequent inconsistency and uncertainty in the present spelling of words with this suffix; cf. e.g. *assistant*, *persistent*; *attendant*, *superintendent*; *dependant*, *-ent*, *independent*.

2. In sense the words in *-ent*, *-ant* are primarily adjs., sometimes distinctly ppl., as *convergent*, *obsolescent*, *errant*, *peccant*; some, however, are, like many words of the same type in Lat. and Fr., used as sbs. (either in addition to the adj. use or exclusively), meaning (*a*) a personal agent, as *agent*, *claimant*, *president*, *regent*; (*b*) a material agent, as *coefficient*, *current*, *ingredient*, *secant*, *tangent*, *torrent*; *esp.* in *Medicine*, as *aperient*, *astringent*, *emollient*, *expectorant*.

entablature (ɛnˈtæblətjʊə(r)). Also 7–8 in-. [ad. (? through Fr.; see quot. 1611) It. *intavolatura*, f. *intavolare*, f. *in* in + *tavola* table.]

1. *Arch.* That part of an order which is above the column; including the architrave, the frieze, and the cornice.

1611 COTGR. *Entablature*, an intablature. **1664** EVELYN tr. *Freart's Archit.* xiv. 38 The Entablature [orig. Fr. *entablement*] (that is to say, Architrave, Freeze, and Cornice). **1726** LEONI *Alberti's Archit.* I. 13b, Columns, Architraves, Intablatures, and Coverings. **1760** GRAY *Corr.* (1843) 203 Large Corinthian columns of fine alabaster.. bear up an entablature, and form a sort of canopy over it. **1841** W. SPALDING *Italy & It. Isl.* II. 223 In the classical orders, the entablature overpowered the columns. **1875** MERIVALE *Gen. Hist. Rome* lxxviii. (1877) 665 He was allowed to engrave his own name upon the entablature of the temple.

2. *Mech.* **a.** In the marine steam-engine: A strong iron frame supporting the paddle-shaft. **b.** The platform which supports the capstan.

1867 *Times* 23 Jan. 10 Among other repairs..has been that of the engine entablature, which was split across. **1886** J. M. CAULFIELD *Seamanship Notes* 3 Parts of the Capstan.. Throw off, spindle, entablature.

entablatured (ɛnˈtæblətjʊəd), *ppl. a.* [f. prec. + -ED².] Furnished with an entablature.

1849 FREEMAN *Archit.* 22 An entablatured mask cloking an arched body. **1859** SALA *Tw. round Clock* (1861) 199 No entablatured colonnade, with nothing to support.

entable (ɛnˈteɪb(ə)l), *v.* *rare*⁻¹. [f. EN-¹ + TABLE.] *trans.* To set up or inscribe on a table.

1865 E. BURRITT *Walk Land's End* 277 A letter of thanks which he requested should..be entabled and hung up.

entablement (ɛnˈteɪb(ə)lmənt). [a. F. *entablement*, f. *entabler*, f. *en-* (see EN-¹) + *table* TABLE.] **a.** = ENTABLATURE. **b.** The horizontal platform or graduated series of platforms supporting a statue and placed above the dado and the base.

1664 EVELYN tr. *Freart's Archit.* (R.), They differ nothing either in height, substance, or entablement from the feminine Ionic, and masculine Doric. **1708** *New View Lond.* II. 402/1 Columns and Entablement of the Corinthian Order. **1800** *Month. Mag.* XIII. 18 Dado..means (1) the cubic part of the pedestal of a column, or of a statue, included between the base and the entablement. **1865** *Reader* 9 Dec. 662 The figure..standing upon a series of entablements.

†**en'tach**, *sb.* *Obs.* *rare*⁻¹. In 4 entecche. [f. next vb.] A symptom of an illness.

c **1350** *Will. Palerne* 558, I..told him al treuly þe entecches of myn evele.

†**en'tach, en'tech**, *v.* *Obs.* Forms: 4–5 entech, -tecch, -tetch, 5 entatch, (entachch), 5–6 **entach.** [a. OF. *entachier*, *entechier*, to imbue with any quality, infect (cf. mod.F. *enticher* to infect), f. *en-* (see EN-¹) + *tache*, *teche*, spot, mark, contagion, 'trait' of character, etc.; perh. ultimately identical with *tache*, **tac* TACK: see ATTACH.]

1. *trans.* To stain, defile; to infect.

c **1374** CHAUCER *Boeth.* IV. iii. 120 Who so þat euer is entecched and defouled wiþ yuel. *c* **1450** LONELICH *Grail* l. 259 Non Of hem Entachched was with non Maner Synne. **1481** CAXTON *Myrr.* III. x. 156 Alle we abyde entetched and soylled therby [by Adam's sin]. **1483** —— *G. de la Tour* D iij, And of this manere the moost parte of the world is entatched and ouercome. **1509** HAWES *Past. Pleas.* (1845) 137 With fervent love and fyry lemes entached.

2. To imbue with any quality, good or evil. See ENTECHED *ppl. a.*

3. ? To link together. [? var. ATTACH.] *rare*⁻¹.

c **1450** *Merlin* xviii. 288 Thei were so thikke and so entacched ech amonge other, that mo than a thousand fill in to the river.

Hence **en'teched** *ppl. a.*, imbued with certain qualities or dispositions; only with qualifying advbs. [So OFr. *bien*, *mal entechié*.]

c **1374** CHAUCER *Troylus* v. 832 On of the best enteched creature, That is or shal, while that the world may dure. *a* **1420** HOCCLEVE *De Reg. Princ.* 150 A croked hors never the better is entecchede, Althoughe his bridelle glistre of golde and shyne.

entachch, entatch: see ENTACH.

entackle: see EN- *pref.*¹ 1 b.

entad (ˈɛntæd), *adv.* *Anat.* and *Zool.* *rare.* [f. Gr. ἐντός within + -AD.] On or towards the inner side or interior *of*; in or into a position nearer to the centre *of*.

1882 [see ECTAD *adv.*].

†**en'tail**, *sb.*¹ *Obs.* Forms: 4 entaille, 4–7 entaile, -yle, (4 *Sc.* eyntayill, 5 entaylle, -eyle). [a. OF. *entaille* fem., n. of action f. *entailler* ENTAIL *v.*¹; cf. Pr. *entalh*, OSp. *entalle*, Pg. *entalho*, It. *intaglio* masc., of similar meaning.]

I. Cutting, carving; pattern or shape.

1. Ornamental carving; sculpture. Also *concr.*

c **1300** *K. Alis.* 4671 A schryne, Of entaile riche and fyne. *c* **1400** *Rowland & O.* 412 Ane helme of riche entayle, Of precyouse stanes the appayrayle. *c* **1400** *Destr. Troy* 1650 Caruen in Cristall by crafte of Entaile. **1430** LYDG. *Chron. Troy* I. vi, A ryche ymage of sylver..of meruaylous entayle. *c* **1530** LD. BERNERS *Arth. Lyt. Bryt.* (1814) 139 Foure condytes meruaylously wrought by subtyll entayle.

concr. *c* **1430** LYDG. *Bochas* II. xv. (1554) 54b, Nothing seyn of all the whole entaile.

2. *transf.* 'Cut', fashion of a garment; shape, pattern, outline; figure, stature. Also, guise, semblance.

c **1320** *Seuyn Sag.* (W.) 2671 Honge we him in his entaile. *c* **1325** *Poems temp. Edw. II* (Percy) lvi, A new entaile have thei i-fend..The raye is turned overthwart. *c* **1400** *Rom. Rose* 1081 Aboute hir nekke of gentyl entayle Was shete the riche chevesaile. *c* **1430** LYDG. *Bochas* II. xxvii. (1554) 63a, Among which hilles..Been craggy roches most hidous of entaile. *c* **1570** THYNNE *Pride & Lowl.*, Another was there, much of his entaile.

3. The phrase *of good* (*rich*) *entail* (sense 1, 2) was app. taken as = 'of good quality'. Hence (persons) *of entaile*: of 'quality' or rank.

c **1330** R. BRUNNE *Chron. Wace.* *c* **1380** *Sir Ferumb.* 730 A smot him on þe helm an heȝ þat was of god entaille. *c* **1430** *Syr Gener.* (Roxb.) 3608 With ix hundreth knightes of good entaile. *c* **1430** LYDG. *Min. Poems* (1840) 188 Cytryne of colour, lyke garnettes of entayle. *a* **1450** *Le Morte Arth.* 3273 And yiffe we may wyth spechys spede Wyth trew trowthes of entayle.

II. The keeping accounts by tallies.

c **1488** *Liber Niger* in *Househ. Ord.* 70 He [Chief Pantrer] receivythe the brede of the Sergeaunt of the bake-house by entayle. *Ibid.* 77 Ale or beer..pourveyede by entayle.

entail (ɛnˈteɪl), *sb.*² *Law.* Forms: see ENTAIL *v.*² [f. ENTAIL *v.*²] The action of entailing; the state of being entailed.

1. The settlement of the succession of a landed estate, so that it cannot be bequeathed at pleasure by any one possessor; the rule of descent settled for any estate; the fixed or prescribed line of devolution. Also in phrases: ***to break, cut (off) the entail, statute of entails, entail male.***

c **1380** [see transferred use 2 a.]. **1467** *Bury Wills* (1850) 47, I wylle that myn executoʳˢ and myn feffeis see the best mene that they can in restoryng ageyn to the olde intaile of the seid place. *Ibid.* 50 Not conteynyd in myne dede of entayle. **1580** POWEL *Lloyd's Cambria* 138 To his heires male by an especial Entaile aforesaid. **1601** SHAKS. *All's Well* IV. iii. 313 For a Cardceue he will..cut th' intaile from all remainders. **1660** BURNEY *Κέρδ. Δῶ ρον* (1661) 54 In passing of Fines and cutting of the Entails. **1712** ARBUTHNOT *John Bull* (1755) 49 His sister Peg's name being in the entail, he could not make a thorough settlement without her consent. **1742** RICHARDSON *Pamela* III. 405 My father too..might have cut off the Intail. **1759** ROBERTSON *Hist. Scot.* (1802) I. I. 223 By introducing entails..to render their possessions unalienable and everlasting. **1796** JANE AUSTEN *Pride & Prej.* (1833) 268 This son was to join in cutting off the entail. **1839** KEIGHTLEY *Hist. Eng.* I. 252 The statute of entails..is also to be referred to this reign. **1876** BANCROFT *Hist. U.S.* III. iii. 341 Entails were not perpetual; land was always in the market.

2. *transf.* and *fig.* in various senses: **a.** The securing (an office, dignity, privilege) to a predetermined line of successors; a predetermined order of succession. **b.** The transmission, as an inalienable inheritance, of qualities, conditions, obligations, etc. **c.** Necessary sequence. **d.** *concr.* That which is entailed; a secured inheritance.

a. *c* **1380** WYCLIF *Wks.* (1880) 391 Men supposen þis entaile [of tithes] was not expresly confermyd bi criste. **1555** BRADFORD in Strype *Eccl. Mem.* III. App. xlv. 131 Thoughe the Quene..disheryt the right heyres apparent, or breake her fathers intayle. **1622** BACON *Hen. VII* Wks. (Bohn) 315 So as the entail might seem rather a personal favour to him and his children, than a total disinherison to the house of York. *a* **1699** STILLINGFL. *Serm.* II. i. (R.), How comes the entail to be made to all his [St. Peter's] successors? **1827** HALLAM *Const. Hist.* (1876) III. xv. 182 Harley..zealously supported the entail of the crown on the princess Sophia.

b. **1706** DE FOE *Jure Div.* VIII. 188 They're Traytors else to the Entails of Sense. **1780** BURKE *Econ. Ref.* Wks. 1842 I. 246 An intail of dependence is a bad reward of merit. **1866** J. MARTINEAU *Ess.* I. 218 The natural entail of disease and character. **1879** GEO. ELIOT *Theo. Such* ii. 36 That entail of social ignorance.

c. **1662** STILLINGFL. *Orig. Sacr.* II. vi. §10 If God by his immediate hand of providence did not cut off the entail of effects upon their natural causes. *a* **1847** R. HAMILTON *Rew. & Punishm.* ii. (1853) 82 The entail of vice upon the circumstances of the present life.

d. **1822** BYRON *Werner* II. ii. 305 Ignorance And dull suspicion are a part of his Entail will last him longer than his lands.

†3. *pl.* (See quot.; app. humorous use of phrase belonging to 1.)

1790 W. MARSHALL *Midl. Counties* (E.D.S.) s.v., When the reapers come near to the finish, they cut off each other's entails, or ends of the lands: the whole finish together.

†**en'tail**, *v.*¹ *Obs.* Forms: 4–5 **entaille, entaylle,** *Sc.* **entailze,** (6 **entally**), 4–7 **entaile.** Also 6 intaile, -yle. [a. OF. *entaille-r*, corresp. to Pr. *entalhar*, *entaillar*, Sp. *entallar*, It. *intagliare*:—late L. *intaleāre*, f. *in* into + *taleāre* (Fr. *tailler*) to cut.]

1. *trans.* To carve, sculpture; to make carvings upon, ornament with carvings; to portray or represent by carving.

c **1394** *P. Pl. Crede* 167 A curious cros craftly entayled. *c* **1400** *Rom. Rose* 140 Wel entailled With many riche portraitures. **1481** CAXTON *Myrr.* III. xi. 158 In thyse grete colompnes or pylers..were entaylled & grauen the vii scyences. **1483** —— *Gold. Leg.* 355/3 They wold not entaylle ne kerue hit [an ydolle]. **1555** *Fardle Facions* II. i. 117 Plate ..curiously wrought and entallied. **1590** SPENSER *F.Q.* II. iii. 27 Golden bendes, which were entayld With curious antickes. **1637** J. ANCHORAN *Porta Linguarum* 183 A Carver or an image maker, graves, carves, and entailes a statue.

absol. *a* **1500** *Chaucer's Dreme* 11 Couth well entayle in imagery.

b. *transf.* with reference to embroidery.

c **1340** *Gaw. & Gr. Knt.* 612 Tortors and trulofez entayled so þyk.

c. In *passive* (cf. *mould*, *carve*, etc.) of a living body.

1501 DOUGLAS *Pal. Hon.* I. xxxix, His bodie weill entailȝeit euerie steid.

2. To engrave in intaglio. *rare* as distinct sense.

1538 LELAND *Itin.* VII. 57 [Cornelines] and other Stonys wel entaylid for Seales. **1577–87** HARRISON *England* in *Holinshed* xxiii. 128 Costlie stones alreadie intailed for seales.

3. To cut into, make an incision in.

1601 HOLLAND *Pliny* (1634) II. 259 Leafed after the maner of passe-floures..but that they be intailed or indented deeper.

b. *absol.*

1590 SPENSER *F.Q.* II. vi. 29 The mortall steele despiteously entayld Deepe in their flesh.

4. To cut notches in a 'tally'; to keep an account by tally.

c **1488** *Liber Niger* in *Househ. Ord.* 78 The yomen of the pycher house..intayle with both buttlers of wyne & ale.

entail (ɛnˈteɪl), *v.*² Forms: *α.* 4–6 **entaile,** 5 **entayle,** 7– **entail.** *β.* 5–6 **intaile, -yle,** 7–8 **intail.** [f. EN-¹ + AF. *tailé* TAIL *a.* or *taile* sb., entail. In legal Anglo-Lat. (16th c.) *intalliāre*. See further under TAIL *a.*]

1. Law. *trans.* To convert (an estate) into a 'fee tail' (*feudum talliatum*); to settle (land, an estate, etc.) on a number of persons in succession, so that it cannot be bequeathed at pleasure by any one possessor. Const. *on*, *to*, *upon*.

1380 WYCLIF *Wks.* (1880) 390 Lande entaylid by mannys lawe. **1466** *Mann. & Househ. Exp.* (1841) 341 The said Herry schalle bye and entayle v. markes worthe of londe to hym and his eyres. **1495** *Act 11 Hen. VII*, c. 60 Pream., Londes and tenementis whiche were intailed to him and to his Auncestres. **1590** GREENE *Never too late* (1600) 55 What Lands to sel, how they were either tied by Statute, or Intaild? **1642** FULLER *Holy & Prof. St.* I. xiv. 45 The old man being onely Tenant for life, and the lands entaild on one young Gentleman. **1670** MILTON *Hist. Eng.* VI. Wks. (1851) 241 An old craft of the Clergy to secure thir Church Lands, by entailing them on some Saint. **1765** *Act 5 Geo. III*, c. 26 Pream., [They] should convey, settle, and intail the lands so to be purchased. **1824** MISS MITFORD *Village* Ser. I. (1863) 87 The house and park..were entailed on a distant cousin. **1856** EMERSON *Eng. Traits, Aristocr.* Wks. (Bohn) II. 86 They cannot sell them [houses], because they are entailed.

2. *transf.* and *fig.* To bestow or confer as if by entail; to cause to descend to a designated series of possessors; to bestow as an inalienable possession.

1509 HAWES *Examp. Virt.* xii. 240 The other gardyn is celestyall..And is entayled to vs in generall. **1513** MORE *Edw. V*, 3 The Crowne of the Realme [was] entayled to the Duke of Yorke and his Heires. **1589** *Pappe w. Hatchet* B, Neuer entaile thy wit to the eldest. **1593** SHAKS. *3 Hen. VI*, I. i. 194, I here entayle The Crowne to thee and to thine Heires for euer. **1630** PRYNNE *God no Impostor* 2 The benefits of the Gospell are intayled vpon them alone. **1649** SELDEN *Laws Eng.* I. xii. (1739) 22 Nor then had the Pope the whole power herein intailed to his Triple Crown. **1682** BURNET *Rights Princes* ii. 57 Bishops might have entailed their Sees to their Kinred or Friends. **1703** POPE *Thebais* 111 Thou Fury, then, some lasting curse entail. **1752** FIELDING

Amelia II. iii, Can I bear to think of entailing beggary on the posterity of my Amelia? **1800** COLQUHOUN *Comm. Thames* Pref. 7 Intails distress and obloquy on an innocent offspring. **1870** LOWELL *Study Wind.* 214 Luther..entailed upon us the responsibility of private judgement.

†**b.** In occasional uses: To make (a person) 'heir' *to* a possession, condition, etc.; to cause a person to become permanently (something). *Obs.*

1627–77 FELTHAM *Resolves* I. xxxvi. 61 Either of these intail a mans mind to misery. *a* **1659** OSBORN *Characters, &c.* (1673) 639 For he did undo By writing them, what Wit entayl'd thee to. **1683** *Penn. Archives* I. 79 Amount to soe vast a sume as will entail me yᵒʳ Perpetuall Debtor.

†**3.** To attach as an inseparable appendage *to, upon*, an estate or inheritance; hence *gen.* to 'tack on', attach. *Obs.*

1593 NASHE 4 *Lett. Confut.* 63 It hath pleased M. Printer ..to intaile a vaine title to my name. **1607** HEYWOOD *Woman Kilde* Wks. 1874 II. 94 All his mad tricke were to his land intailed, And you are heyre to all. *c* **1645** HOWELL *Lett.* (1650) II. 17 Upon the latter of which the Musulman empire is entayld. **1669** BUNYAN *Holy Citie* 89 His Name was always so entailed to that Doctrine. **1713** DERHAM *Phys. Theol.* IV. 188 The allotment of Food is..entailed to the very Constitution and Nature of Animals.

4. To impose (inconvenience, expense, labour) *upon* a person. Chiefly said of cirumstances or actions; hence occas. of personal agents.

1665 BOYLE *Occas. Refl.* IV. xix. (1675) 281 Yet Custom has so Entail'd some ways of Expence upon some Stations in the World. **1771** *Junius Lett.* xlii. 223 What an enormous expense is entailed..upon this unhappy country. **1826** SCOTT *Provinc. Antiq.* Which shall, so long as the building stands, entail disgrace on all who have had to do with it. **1846** PRESCOTT *Ferd. & Is.* I. i. 95 The long wars..which a disputed succession entailed on the country. **1851** GLADSTONE *Glean.* IV. lxi. 42, I..shall not entail upon your Lordship the charge of handing to and fro replications and rejoinders. **1860** TYNDALL *Glac.* I. §16. 104 The great amount of labour which this [assistance] might entail upon him.

5. *Simply.* To bring on by way of necessary consequence. Of premises: To involve logically, necessitate (a particular conclusion).

1829 SOUTHEY *Sir T. More* I. 267 A conquest which brought with it no evil and entailed no regret. **1839** E. D. CLARKE *Trav.* 134/1 The scheme..was found to entail greater evils than those he was labouring to put down. **1854** THACKERAY *Newcomes* I. 32 The weight of business which this present affliction entails. **1856** DOVE *Logic Chr. Faith* Introd. 4 That failure would not entail the conclusion that, etc.

entailable (ɛn'teɪləb(ə)l), *a.* [f. ENTAIL *v.*² + -ABLE.] Capable of being bequeathed or transmitted by entail.

1689 *Consid. Succession & Alleg.* 16 The Crown has.. been declared entailable. **1796** MORSE *Amer. Geog.* I. 627 [In Virginia] Slaves as well as lands were entailable during the monarchy. **1807** *Ann. Rev.* V. 176 The entailable amount might be proportioned to the rank of peerage.

entailed (ɛn'teɪld), *ppl. a.* [f. as prec. + -ED¹.] Of land, an inheritance, etc.: Transmitted by entail. Also *fig.*

1531 *Dial. on Laws Eng.* I. xxix. (1638) 52 The..recovery must be taken in this case..as recoveries of other lands intailed bee. **1767** MRS. S. PENNINGTON *Lett.* IV. 38 To restore to his destitute family an entailed estate. **1790** BURKE *Fr. Rev.* Wks. V. 78 To claim and assert our liberties, as an entailed inheritance derived to us from our forefathers. **1818** CRUISE *Digest* VI. 21 If B. claimed a share of the entailed lands. **1845** MᶜCULLOCH *Taxation* I. iv. (1852) 125 Owners of entailed estates. **1860** PUSEY *Min. Proph.* 14 Until the entailed curse be cut off by repentance.

†**en'tailer¹**. *Obs.* [f. ENTAIL *v.*¹ + -ER.] A carver, engraver.

1570 DEE *Math. Pref.*, More then the common Sculptor, Entayler, Kerver. **1611** COTGR., *Burineur*, intayler.

entailer² (ɛn'teɪlə(r)). [f. ENTAIL *v.*² + -ER.] One who entails an estate; one who executes an entail.

1779 ARNOT *Hist. Edin.* iv. (1816) 128 The will of the entailer. **1815** SCOTT *Guy M.* l, We must..serve him heir to his grandfather Lewis, the entailer. *a* **1868** BROUGHAM, The entailer cannot disappoint those children who have rights to a portion of his property.

entailing (ɛn'teɪlɪŋ), *vbl. sb.* [f. as prec. + -ING¹.] The action of ENTAIL *v.*²

1538 STARKEY *England* I. iv. 113 For thys intaylyng.. makyth many richles heyrys. *a* **1674** CLARENDON *Hist. Reb.* XII. 707/2 The entailing upon Them and their Posterities, a lasting War. **1818** CRUISE *Digest* I. 305 A custom of entailing.

en'tailment¹. *rare*⁻¹. [f. ENTAIL *v.*¹ + -MENT.] The action of 'cutting' or excising.

1822 *Monthly Mag.* LIII. 127 He seems to approve of Mr. Bowdler's entailments.

entailment² (ɛn'teɪlmənt). [f. ENTAIL *v.*² + -MENT.] **1.** The action of entailing (property).

a **1641** BP. MOUNTAGU *Acts & Mon.* (1642) 19 By which new way of entaylement..God..was..made his by peculiar Appropriation. **1832** MARRYAT *N. Forster* xxv, Entailment of property..upon the male heir. **1875** T. HILL *True Order Stud.* 128 Laws of primogeniture, entailment of estates.

2. *Philos.* [cf. ENTAIL *v.*² 5.] The strict or logically necessary implication of one proposition by another.

1933 L. S. STEBBING *Mod. Introd. Logic* xv. 286 Professor Moore's analysis of the distinction between material implication and entailment makes it possible. **1957** G. H. VON WRIGHT *Logical Stud.* 166 (*title*) The Concept of Entailment. **1965** P. CAWS *Philos. Sci.* xiv. 106 The weak kind..is called material implication, as distinct from strong implication or entailment.

†**entain**, *v. Obs.* In 4 enteyn. [alteration of ATTAIN, q.v.] *trans.* To overtake, affect = ATTAIN 5.

c **1380** *Sir Ferumbr.* 2590 Sche is so mat sche may noȝt go: so hunger hur haueþ enteynte.

ental ('ɛntəl), *a. Anat.* and *Zool.* [f. Gr. ἐντός within + -AL.] Inner; internal.

1881 [see ECTAL *a.*]. **1889** *Buck's Handbk. Med. Sci.* VIII. 111 The ental surface of the pia.

†**en'talent**, *v. Obs. rare*⁻¹. [a. OF. *entalenter*, f. *en-* (see EN-¹) + *talent* (ad. L. *talent-um* a weight, that which makes the balance incline, hence) inclination, desire.] *trans.* To inspire with desire or passion; to excite. Hence **en'talented** *ppl. a.*

c **1374** CHAUCER *Boeth.* V. v. 168 Al be it so þat þe qualites of bodies..entalenten þe instrumentes of þe wittes. **1402** HOCCLEVE *Let. Cupide* in *Chaucer's Wks.* (1532) 373 Feruent wyl, and entalented corage. **1616** BULLOKAR, *Entalented.*

entally, obs. form of ENTAIL *v.*¹

†**'entally**, *adv. Obs.* [f. med.L. *ent-* stem of *ens* (see ENS) + -AL¹ + -LY²; after *really*, etc.]

1691 ED. TAYLOR *Behmen's Theos. Philos.* 337 Yet are truely, and entally or really, but not essentially.

†**en'tame**, *v.*¹ *Obs.* Also 4 entamy, 5 enteme. [a. Fr. *entame-r* = *atamer*: see ATTAME.]

1. *trans.* To make a cut into, wound. Also *fig.*

c **1330** R. BRUNNE *Chron. Wace* (Rolls) 12387 He.. entamed boþe his bryn. *c* **1380** *Sir Ferumb.* 3699 Þe helm was so hard y-wroȝt, þat he miȝt entamy him noȝt, Wyþ no dynt of swerde. **1393** GOWER *Conf.* I. 66 If thou thy conscience Entamed hast in such a wise. ? *a* **1400** *Morte Arth.* 1160 They fande no flesche entamede. **1480** CAXTON *Ovid's Met.* XII. xii, Loves of bred hole & entamed. **1490** —— *Eneydos* iv. 18 The whiche trees soo cutte and entamed.

2. To make the first cut in. Hence *fig.* To open (a discussion, conversation, etc.). Cf. F. *entamer.*

1475 CAXTON *Jason* 90 She entemed and began to opene her mater in this wyse. **1483** —— *Gold. Leg.* 110/3 Whyche of them bothe shold entame or bygynne to take of the breed. *c* **1500** *Melusine* 299 He had not entamed nor shewed the matere to no man.

entame (ɛn'teɪm), *v.*² [f. EN-¹ + TAME.] **a.** *trans.* To tame; to subdue. †**b.** *intr.* To grow or become tame. *Obs.*

1600 SHAKS. *A.Y.L.* III. v. 48 'Tis not..your cheek of cream, That can entame my spirits to your worship. **1768** J. ROSS *Ode on Loss of Friend*, MS. Wks. 223 My trembling frame With some felt impulse shrinks, and all my pow'rs entame. **1855** SINGLETON *Virgil* I. 111 All are..at much cost entamed.

entamœba (,ɛntə'miːbə). Also *U.S.* **entameba**. [mod.L. *entamoeba* (Casagrandi and Barbagallo 1897, in *Ann. d'Igiene Sperimentale* VII. 163), f. ENT(O- + AMŒBA.] A member of a genus of amœbas so called, including several species parasitic on vertebrates.

1914 FANTHAM & PORTER *Some Minute Animal Parasites* vii. 147 Entamœbae are extremely important, as they occur commonly in the intestine of man in tropical countries. *Ibid.* 151 The multiplication of Entamœba occurs usually by simple division into two daughter forms. **1926** C. M. WENYON *Protozool.* I. ii. 227 Entamœbae are of common occurrence in the intestine of animals. **1962** *Lancet* 8 Dec. 1209/1 The presence of the entamœbae was held to be proven only if the trophozoites could be found in permanent fixed preparations. **1964** M. HYNES *Med. Bacteriol.* (ed. 8) xxviii. 426 Two entamœbæ are found in the fæces of man: *Entamœba coli* a harmless commensal, and *Entamœba histolytica*, the cause of amœbic dysentery and liver abscess.

entamœbiasis (,ɛntæmiː'baɪəsɪs). *Path.* Also *U.S.* **entamebiasis**. [f. ENT(O- + AMŒB(A + -(I)ASIS.] A disease caused by entamœbæ, esp. *Entamœba histolytica.*

1929 THOMSON & ROBERTSON *Protozool.* xiii. 151 Relapses in entamœbiasis are of common occurrence.

entangle (ɛn'tæŋg(ə)l), *v.* Also 6 entangel, 6–8 intangle. [f. EN-¹ + TANGLE *sb.* and *v.*

(The primary reference may have been to boats or oars caught in 'tangle' or sea-weed (this being the original sense of the sb.), but the wider sense appears in our earliest quots.)]

I. To catch or impede with a tangle.

1. *trans.* To involve, impede, cause to stick fast in coils, network, or anything 'tangled' or interlaced. Hence in wider sense: To involve in surroundings that impede movement, or from which extrication is difficult.

α. **1555** EDEN *Decades W. Ind.* I. III. (Arb.) 77 Attemptinge to goo throwgh the grasse & herbes they were soo entangled & bewrapte therin. *Ibid.* (Arb.) 193 In them [the sandes] many shyppes are entangled. **1665** MANLEY *Grotius' Low-C. Warres* 213 One of the greatest Ships..entangled with another Ships Cables. **1710** J. CLARKE *Rohault's Nat. Phil.* (1729) I. 115 All these Particles of Matter must be broken where-ever they are..intangled with those that join to them. **1711** ADDISON *Spect.* No. 42 ¶1 Lest she should entangle her Feet in her Petticoat. **1722** SEWEL *Hist. Quakers* (1759) I. III. 205 Being entangled in the ropes in leaping down. **1726** THOMSON *Winter* 926 Entangled in the gathering ice. **1777** WATSON *Philip II* (1839) 203 If any of them should.. be entangled in the mud. **1824** W. IRVING *T. Trav.* II. 236 A vessell entangled in the whirlpools. **1835–6** TODD *Cycl. Anat.* I. 229/1 Agaric and sponge entangled the blood and retained a coagulum on the spot.

β. **1533** FRITH *Answ. More* Wks. (1573) 148/2 For anone ye shall see hym so intangled in briers, that he shall not witte where to become. **1570** LEVINS *Manip.* 128 Intangil, *illaqueare.* **1616** SURFL. & MARKH. *Countr. Farme* 317 Sheepe..loosing some of their lockes of Wooll vpon the hedges..poore Bees now and then become intangled therein.

b. *esp.* To catch or hold fast in a snare or net; to ensnare. Also *fig.*

α. **1568** GRAFTON *Chron.* II. 741 The Devill is wont with such witchcrafts, to wrap and entangle the myndes of men. **1651** HOBBES *Leviath.* I. 23 He will find himself entangled in words, as a bird in lime twigs. **1711** STEELE *Spect.* No. 139 ¶1 The Snares in which France has entangled all her Neighbours. **1773** BURKE *Sp. Relief Prot. Dissenters* Wks. X. 33 Nets that entangle the poor fluttering silken wings of a tender conscience. **1841** D'ISRAELI *Amen. Lit.* (1867) 592 Entangled in the meshes of political parties. **1870** BRYANT *Iliad* I. II. 40 Saturnian Jove hath in an evil net Entangled me most cruelly.

β. **1526** *Pilgr. Perf.* (W. de W. 1531) 41 b, Intryked or intangled in the affeccyon or loue of worldly goodes and honours. **1576** FLEMING *Panoplie Ep.* 287 They intangle themselves in the same webbes of woe. **1611** BIBLE *Matt.* xxii. 15. **1692** E. WALKER tr. *Epictetus' Mor.* xxv, Be not here intangled by The too great Lustre that beguiles your eye.

c. *transf.* To involve in intricate paths or among obstacles; also *fig.* with reference to a metaphorical 'maze' or 'labyrinth'.

1611 BIBLE *Ex.* xiv. 3 They are intangled in the land, the wilderness hath shut them in. *a* **1649** DRUMM. OF HAWTH. *Irene* Wks. 173 That labyrinth wherein they are like to intangle and lose themselves. **1725** DE FOE *Voy. round World* (1840) 90 Our Madagascar ship was..entangled among rocks and currents. **1790** BURKE *Fr. Rev.* Wks. V. 58 Entangled in the mazes of metaphysic sophistry. **1823** LAMB *Elia* Ser. I. x. (1865) 83 You get entangled in another man's mind, even as you lose yourself in another man's grounds. **1850** PRESCOTT *Peru* II. 245 The Spanish commander became entangled in the defiles of the mountains.

†**d.** *intr.* To become entangled. *Obs. rare.*

1628 COWLEY *Piramus & Thisbe* iv, A Bird..By struggling more entangles in the Gin. *a* **1673** HORTON in Spurgeon *Treas. Dav.* Ps. xciv. 19 Boughs usually catch, and intangle one in another.

2. *fig.* To involve in difficulties; to engage (a person) in undertakings, quarrels, etc., from which it is difficult to withdraw; to embarrass, hamper; to involve in mental difficulties, perplex, bewilder. Formerly also *absol.* †to cause entanglements.

α. **1540** *Act 32 Hen. VIII*, c. 38 §1 The vsurped power of the Byshoppe of Rome hath always entangled and troubled to the mere iurisdiction and regall power of this realme. **1555** EDEN *Decades W. Ind.* II. IX. (Arb.) 132, I fynde my wytte more entangeled in the description hereof. **1606** SHAKS. *Ant. & Cl.* IV. xiv. 48 Yea, very force entangles It selfe with strength. **1683** TEMPLE *Mem.* Wks. 1731 I. 410 The others were entangled still in some Difficulty or other. **1798** NELSON 25 Oct. in Nicclas *Disp.* (1845) III. 159 You will..not entangle yourself by undertaking to embark the troops for France. **1833** HT. MARTINEAU *Manch. Strike* viii. 87 Getting entangled in a complimentary speech. **1858** FROUDE *Hist. Eng.* IV. xviii. 52 The Pope..had endeavoured to entangle his nephew in the conspiracy. **1871** TYNDALL *Fragm. Sc.* I. xviii. 462 He was long entangled in Electrochemistry.

β. **1563–87** FOXE *A. & M.* III. 357 He might intangle himself, but should do his Brother no good. **1597** DANIEL *Civ. Wares* I. lxxi, Intestine strife, of force, The apt-divided State intangle would. **1699** BURNET *39 Art.* i. (1700) 20 This is rather a flight of Metaphisicks that intangles one, than a plain and full conviction. **1750** JOHNSON *Rambler* No. 22 ¶5 Intangled in consequences which she could not foresee.

†**b.** To bind by embarrassing engagements *to* another person. *Obs.*

1620 *Horæ Subsec.* 106 A Prodigall..is so entangled to other men, that hee is neuer master of himselfe. **1632** LITHGOW *Trav.* vii. 331 Not being intangled to wife and children, etc.

c. To involve (a person) in compromising relations *with* another. Cf. 3.

1888 F. HUME *Mad. Midas* I. i, He became entangled with a lady whose looks were much better than her morals. **1888** A. K. GREEN *Behind Closed Doors* iii, She could never have become entangled with him.

†**d.** To encumber (land, an estate). *Obs.*

1601–2 FULBECKE *2nd Pt. Parall.* 63 The partie morgaging, incumbring, entangling, or aliening the land. **1616** SIR R. DUDLEY in *Fortesc. Papers* 16 My Estate in England is entangled, partly by a suite in the Chauncery.

II. 3. To make tangled; to twist, interlace, or mix up in such a manner that a separation cannot easily be made.

1555 EDEN *Decades W. Ind.* I. III. (Arb.) 77 The sea was euery where entangeled with Ilandes. *Ibid.* 196 The formes of their letters are muche more crooked and entangeled. **1601** HOLLAND *Pliny* I. 199 They have not so soone clasped and intangled it [the trunke] with their taile, but they set their venomous teeth in the Elephants eare. **1671** MILTON *Samson* 763 Entangl'd with a poisonous bosom snake. **1713** *Lond. & Country Brew.* I. (1742) 50 The spirituous Parts are more entangled, and kept from making their Escape. **1860** TYNDALL *Glac.* I. §27. 212 The flakes were composed of these exquisite [snow] blossoms entangled together.

b. *fig.* To render (a subject, etc.) complicated or intricate; to complicate *with*.

1672 A. MARVELL *Reh. Transp.* I. 104 He had intangled the matter of Conscience with the Magistrates Power. **1677** *Govt. Venice* 269 Your Scholars..rather intangle and perplex Councils than clear them. **1695** LD. PRESTON *Boeth.* v. 212 The Question..was intangled with many others. **1768** STERNE *Sent. Journ. Mystery*, Two other circumstances which entangled this mystery. **1879** FROUDE *Cæsar* xxviii. 481 The story is entangled with legends.

entangled (ɛnˈtæŋg(ə)ld), *ppl. a.* [f. prec. + -ED¹.] In the senses of the vb.: **a.** Caught or held fast in anything tangled; ensnared. **b.** Involved in difficulties; embarrassed, perplexed. †**c.** Of an estate: Encumbered (*obs.*). **d.** Interlaced; complicated, intricate.

1561 T. NORTON *Calvin's Inst.* I. 30 Such as in Scripture are to our capacitie doubtfull and entangled. **1598** J. DICKENSON *Greene in Conc.* (1878) 134 Now wrought she on his intangled wits as on an anuill. **1653** MILTON *Hirelings* Wks. (1851) 384 The obscure and intangl'd Wood of Antiquity. **1662** STILLINGFL. *Orig. Sacr.* III. i. §7 Nothing can bee a greater evidence of an intangled mind. **1670** MARVELL *Let. Mayor of Hull* Wks. I. 160 The discourses growing long and intangled, one of the members..rose up. **1680** BURNET *Rochester* 167 To recover an intangled Estate. **1735** SOMERVILLE *Chase* I. 160 Seek'st thou for Hounds to..brush th' Entangled Covert? **1762** FALCONER *Shipwr.* II. (1819) 47 All the entangled cords in order placed. **1768** BLACKSTONE *Comm.* III. 329 Heaps of entangled conveyances or wills of a various obscurity. **1856** STANLEY *Sinai & Pal.* ii. 121 A somewhat entangled and delicate question. **1862** H. SPENCER *First Princ.* II. xx. (1875) 440 Each deposit must be differently distributed by the entangled currents.

Hence †**en'tangledly** *adv.*, in an entangled manner. †**en'tangledness**, the state of being entangled.

1611 COTGR., *Perplexement*, perplexedly, intricately, intangledly, troublesomely. **1687** H. MORE *Contn. Remark. Stor.* 428 It was usual with these Goblins..to wind all this Yarn on these old pieces of Lumber, so perplexedly and entangledly. **1611** COTGR., *Perplexité*, intangledness. **1684** T. BURNET *Th. Earth* I. 241 Much of that intangledness which we find now in astronomy, would be taken away.

entanglement (ɛnˈtæŋg(ə)lmənt). Also 7-8 **in-**. [f. ENTANGLE *v.* + -MENT.]

1. a. The action of entangling; the fact or condition of being entangled, confused medley; *spec.* a compromising relationship, an unsuitable liaison.

1687 H. MORE *App. Antid.* (1712) 194 The intanglement of multifarious Contradictions in the Conception. **1748** RICHARDSON *Clarissa* (1811) III. 80 The different webs that offer to him for the entanglement of a haughty charmer. **1835-6** TODD *Cycl. Anat.* I. 229/1 The entanglement of blood in the cellular coat of the vessel. **1845** DARWIN *Voy. Nat.* viii. (1879) 160 Produced by the entanglement of the single threads. **1856** KANE *Arct. Expl.* I. iv. 42 Serious risks of entanglement among the broken ice-fields. **1860** TYNDALL *Glac.* I. §2. 21 Great was the entanglement of fissures. **1861** TULLOCH *Eng. Purit.* i. 109 In all that concerns Cromwell the entanglement is extreme. **1863** MRS. GASKELL *Dark Night's Work* v. 60 This foolish entanglement of Ralph's; they would not call it an engagement. **1871** BLACKIE *Four Phases* i. 122 He kept himself out of all political entanglement. **1875** STUBBS *Const. Hist.* I. xiii. 638 Without entanglement of machinery or waste of power. **1957** 'D. RUTHERFORD' *Long Echo* i. 24 Maria..dead could not involve him in any entanglement.

b. An instance of entanglement.

a **1690** E. HOPKINS in Spurgeon *Treas. Dav.* Ps. xi. 6 All the involucra and entanglements of Providence shall be fully unfolded. **1836** J. GILBERT *Chr. Atonem.* viii. (1852) 239 Thus entanglements arise not easy to be unravelled. **1868** FREEMAN *Norm. Conq.* (1876) II. viii. 278 The first entanglements between Normandy and Anjou.

2. a. A means of entangling; that by which a person or thing is entangled; an embarrassment, a snare; a circumstance which complicates or confuses a matter.

1637-50 ROW *Hist. Kirk* (1842) 475 These civile honors and employments are verie great entanglements to Christ's ministers. **1644** MILTON *Judgm. Bucer* Wks. 1738 I. 281 The Roman Antichrists have knit many a pernicious entanglement to distressed Consciences. **1691-8** NORRIS *Pract. Disc.* (1711) III. 17 A very great let and intanglement to him in his enquiry after Truth. **1727** BRADLEY *Fam. Dict.* s.v. *Corn*, Those salts..cut and remove the entanglements of the different buds which are contained in each seed. **1768-74** TUCKER *Lt. Nat.* (1852) II. 552 Pleasure is a sly enchantress..we have need of all our eyes to keep clear of her entanglements. **1875** JOWETT *Plato* (ed. 2) IV. 267 These are a few of the entanglements which impede the natural course of human thought. **1878** SEELEY *Stein* III. 357 Here was a new entanglement, the plot of a quite new historical drama.

b. *Naut.* 'A cable stretched athwart the mouth of a river or harbour, with stout spars of wood lashed to it, to prevent the entrance of an enemy' (Adm. Smyth).

1888 *Daily News* 20 July 6/1 The booms, or rather entanglements, which are to protect each of the entrances to our anchorage.

3. *Mil.* An extensive barrier arranged so as to impede an enemy's movements; an abatis formed of trees and branches, or an obstruction formed of stakes and barbed wire.

1834 J. S. MACAULAY *Field Fortif.* iv. 83 The boughs of the brushwood..interlacing with one another, will thus form a very good obstacle, called an entanglement. **1876**, **1879** [see *wire entanglement*]. **1899** *Westm. Gaz.* 17 Nov. 2/1 Where a wood enters into the scheme of defence, an abattis—in this case called an 'entanglement'—forms naturally one of the best resources of the defenders. **1916** 'BOYD CABLE' *Action Front* 47 Slowly and cautiously, with the officer leading, they began to wend their way out under their own entanglements. **1917** [see WIRE *sb.* 1 e]. **1922** BLUNDEN *Shepherd* 69 They've all died on the entanglements.

entangler (ɛnˈtæŋglə(r)). [f. as prec. + -ER¹.] He who, or that which, entangles or ensnares.

1591 PERCIVALL *Sp. Dict.*, *Marañador*, an intangler. **1719** D'URFEY *Pills* III. 126 Upon the Exchange 'twixt Twelve and One, Meets many a neat entangler. *a* **1821** KEATS *Sleep & Poetry* Poems 256 Silent entangler of a beauty's tresses.

en'tangling, *vbl. sb.* [f. ENTANGLE *v.* + -ING¹.] The action of the verb ENTANGLE.

1573-80 BARET *Alv.* I 199 An intangling, a wrapping, or folding in. **1591** PERCIVALL *Sp. Dict.*, *Embaraço*, let, stop, entangling. *a* **1649** DRUMM. OF HAWTH. *Irene* Wks. 170 Anxious entangling and perplexing of consciences. **1649** JER. TAYLOR *Gt. Exemp.* II. Disc. viii. §41. 83 The implication and intanglings of ten thousand thoughts. **1754** RICHARDSON *Grandison*, This entangling with all its painful consequences.

entangling (ɛnˈtæŋglɪŋ), *ppl. a.* [f. as prec. + -ING².] That entangles.

a **1628** SIR J. BEAUMONT *Poems, Dial. betw. World, Pilgr., & Vertue*, My paces with intangling briers are bound. **1636** *Destr. Troy* 210 Then him..They seiz'd, and with intangling folds imbrac'd His neck. **1735** SOMERVILLE *Chase* III. 42 Thick with entangling Grass, or prickly Furze. **1746-7** HERVEY *Medit.* (1818) 47 Escaped from an entangling wilderness. **1884** *Chr. World* 12 June 433/1 Entangling alliances with foreign nations are to be avoided.

Hence **en'tanglingly**, *adv.*, in an entangling manner.

1878 *Scribn. Mag.* XVI. 38/1 The rest of the road presented..deeper bogs, and more entanglingly strewn rocks.

†**en'tapisse**, *v. Obs. rare*⁻¹. [a. OF. *entapisser*, f. *en-* (see EN- *pref.*¹) + *tapisser*, f. *tapis* carpet.] *trans.* To carpet.

1595 LODGE *Fig for Momus* Sat. v, An humble cote entapissed with mosse.

†**en'tappesse**. *Obs. rare*⁻¹. [f. OF. *entapiss-* lengthened stem of *entapir*, f. *en-* (see EN-¹) + *tapir* to hide.] The action of seeking covert: said of a fox.

(If the reading of the original ed. be correct the word must app. have been confused with UNTAPIS to break covert.)

1719 D'URFEY *Pills* II. 269 The Fox has broke Covert, let none lag behind, We've had an [*ed.* **1872** no] Entappesse, she runs up the Wind.

‖**entasis** (ˈɛntəsɪs). [mod.L., a. Gr. ἔντασις, f. ἐντα-, ἐντείνειν to strain.]

1. *Arch.* 'A delicate and almost imperceptible swelling of the shaft of a column' (Gwilt).

1827 *Gentl. Mag.* XCVII. II. 605 The very idea of an entasis in the columns. **18..** *Nat. Encycl.* I. 202 They diminish, with an imperceptible entasis. **1866** FELTON *Anc. & Mod. Gr.* II. viii. 144 The external lines of the columns are carved also, forming a hyperbolic entasis.

†**2.** *Pathol.* 'Old term for tonic spasm' (*Syd. Soc. Lex.*).

1753 in CHAMBERS *Cycl. Supp.*

entask: see EN- *pref.*¹ 1 b.

entassment (ɛnˈtæsmənt). [ad. F. *entassement*, f. *en-* (see EN-¹) + *tas* heap.] A heap, accumulation.

1864 in WEBSTER; and in mod. Dicts.

†**entatic** (ɛnˈtætɪk), *a. Med. Obs.* Also erron. **entastic**. [a. Gr. ἐντατικ-ός, f. ἐντα-, ἐντείνειν: see ENTASIS 2.] Of or pertaining to entasis. Of medicines: Aphrodisiac.

1822 J. M. GOOD *Study of Med.* I. 265 The spasms were sometimes clonic or agitatory, instead of being entastic or rigid. **1847** CRAIG, *Entastic*. So **1864** in WEBSTER; and in later Dicts. **1882** *Syd. Soc. Lex.*, *Entatic*.

†**'enté**, *a. Her. Obs.*⁻⁰ [a. Fr. *enté* pa. pple. of *enter* to graft.] Said of an emblazonment in which one coat of arms is engrafted or impaled in another.

1736 in BAILEY: and in mod. Dicts.

†**entech, -tecch**, variants of ENTACH, *Obs.*

†**en'techment**. *Obs. rare*⁻¹. [? f. *enteche*, ENTACH *v.* + -MENT; in Douglas perh. f. EN-¹ + TEACH + -MENT.] The action of teaching; a lesson.

1513 DOUGLAS *Æneis* XI. iv. 41 And rycht hard bene the first entechment [L. *rudimenta*] Of haisty batall to thame bene nocht acquent.

enteer(e, obs. form of ENTIRE.

entelechy (ɛnˈtɛləkɪ). *Philos.* Also 7 **entelechie**, **entelech**; 6 in Gr. form **entelecheia**; 7-9 in Lat. **entelechia**. [ad. Gr. ἐντελέχεια, f. ἐν + τέλει, dat. of τέλ-ος perfection + ἔχ-ειν to have.]

1. In Aristotle's use: The realization or complete expression of some function; the condition in which a potentiality has become an actuality.

1603 FLORIO *Montaigne* II. xii. (1632) 304 Aristotle..cal'eth [the soul] Entelechy, or perfection moving of itselfe. **1652** J. SMITH *Sel. Disc.* x. 500 Wickedness is the form and entelech of all the wicked spirits. **1655-60** STANLEY *Hist. Philos.* (1701) 256/1 The Soul is the first Entelechy of a natural organical body, having life potentially. **1837** WHEWELL *Hist. Induct. Sc.* (1857) I. 43 The Entelechy, or Act, of a moveable body. **1842** SIR W. HAMILTON in *Reid's Wks.* I. 202/2 *note*, Aristotle defines the soul, the Form or Entelechy of an organized body. **1850** MAURICE *Mor. & Met. Philos.* (ed. 2) 194 Motion is the entelechy (the perfecting power or principle) of the potential as potential.

2. In various applied senses (apparently due to misconceptions of Aristotle's meaning): **a.** That which gives perfection to anything; the informing spirit. **b.** The soul itself, as opposed to the body.

1603 HARSNET *Pop. Impost.* 5 When his Holiness the King of Spaine and Parsons theyr Entelechie were plotting beyond the seas. *a* **1652** J. SMITH *Sel. Disc.* iv. 114 He seems to make it [the soul] nothing else..but an entelechia or informative thing. **1652** URQUHART *Jewel* Wks. (1834) 231 The purest parts of the separated entelechises [*sic*] of blessed saints. **1659** SHIRLEY *Honoria & Mam.* I. i, Soul..that bright entelecheia Which separates them from beasts.

3. The name given by Leibnitz to the monads of his system.

1877 E. CAIRD *Philos. Kant* v. 92 It is better to give the general name of monads or entelechies to those simple substances that have only perception.

‖**entellus** (ɛnˈtɛləs). [mod.L. app. from the proper name Entellus: see Virg. *Æn.* v. 437-472.

The name was first proposed by Dufresne, *Bulletin Soc. Philomath.*, 1797; but he does not explain the reason for his choice of it. Cf. other (past or present) specific names of Indian monkeys, *anchises*, *priamus*, *rhesus*, *irus*.]

An East Indian species of monkey of the genus Semnopithecus (*S. entellus*).

1843 *Jrnl. Asiat. Soc. Bengal* XII. 169 It [the Semnopithecus Johnii] is more suspicious and wary than the Entellus. **1847** CARPENTER *Zool.* §151 The Entellus abounds over almost every part of India.

enteme, var. of ENTAME *v.*² *Obs.*

†**en'temper**, *v. Obs.* Also 4 **entempre**, **-i**. [var. of ATTEMPER; in AF. *entemprer* (Bozon).]

1. *trans.* **a.** To temper, qualify by admixture; to modify or moderate by blending with something of different or opposite quality. **b.** To modify the temperature of (*e.g.* water).

c **1290** *Lives Saints* (1887) 319 Euerech of þeos foure elemenz entempriez oþur. *Ibid.* Ake ȝif þov nimst riȝt puyr hot watur and dost cold þar-to þov miȝt it makien euene wlach and entempri it so. *c* **1400** tr. *Lanfranc's Cirurgie* 29 The neschenesse is entempered & ystrengthyde.

2. To moderate, to restrain; = ATTEMPER 4.

c **1380** *Sir Ferumb.* 164 Entempre þou beter þy tonge.

entempest: see EN- *pref.*¹ 2.

entemple (ɛnˈtɛmp(ə)l), *v.* [f. EN-¹ + TEMPLE.] *trans.* To enclose as in a temple; to enshrine. Also *fig.* Hence **en'templing** *vbl. sb.*

1603 DEKKER *Grissil* (1841) 14 What virtues were entempled in her breast. **1685** H. MORE *Para. Prophet.* 246 There to be entempled in more illustrious Temples. *Ibid.* 247 Theodosius..allows the entempling of them with all Magnificence. **1830** W. PHILLIPS *Mt. Sinai* I. 282 Natural effluence of spirit within Mystic entempled. **1858** BUSHNELL *Serm. New Life* 13 In that manner to receive and entemple the Infinite Spirit.

entempre, var. ATTEMPRE *a. Obs.*, temperate.

1297 R. GLOUC. (1724) 429 Entempre he was of mete, and drynke, and of slep also.

entencion, -sion, -tion, -tional: see INT-.

entend, -ance, -ible, -ment: see INTEND.

†**en'tendant**, *a. Obs.* Also 4-5 **entendaunt**. [a. Fr. *entendant*, pr. pple. of *entendre* to hear, attend to.] **a.** Attentive (*to*). **b.** In attendance. = ATTENDANT *a.* 1 and 2.

α. [**1292** BRITTON I. ii. §18 Et voloms qe nos viscountes et nos baillifs soint entendauntz a eux et a lour maundementz.] *c* **1340** *Cursor M.* 2542 Bad alle til him entendaunt be. **1387** TREVISA *Higden* (Rolls) III. 425 And but þou be entendaunt ..to myn commaundements..I schal sende men þat schal scourge þe. **1389** *Eng. Gilds* 93 And if yᵉ deen be comaundeed for to be entendaunt hem for to helpen. **1393** GOWER *Conf.* III. 365 Jewes eke and Sarazines, To him I sigh all entendaunt. **1480** CAXTON *Chron. Eng.* II. (1520) 15 b/1 The Kynge of Fraunce..commaunded that al men sholde be as entendant to Kynge Leyr..as it were unto hymselfe.

†**en'tender**, *v. Obs.* Also 7-8 **intender**. [f. EN-¹ + TENDER *a.*] *trans.* To make tender; to melt (the heart); to enervate; to weaken.

1594 SOUTHWELL *M. Magd. Fun. Teares* 126 And my innocent blood [would] entender his adamant heart. **1618** BOLTON *Florus* III. iii. 171 The daintinesse of the ayre and soyle entendred their spirits. **1669** WOODHEAD *St. Teresa* I. Pref. 14 All which do much serve for intendring the same. **1742** YOUNG *Nt. Th.* II. 525 Virtue alone entenders us for Life: I wrong her much—entenders us for ever. **1753** SMOLLETT *Ct. Fathom* (1813) I. 34 Her heart was too much intendered to hold out..against all the forms of assault. **1765** GOLDSM. *Ess.* 13 A social heart entender'd by the practice of virtue.

entent, etc.: see INTENT, etc.

‖**entente** (ɑ̃tɑ̃t). [Fr.] **a.** An understanding; most freq. used as a shortening of ENTENTE CORDIALE. **b.** A group of states or powers connected by an *entente cordiale*.

1854 LD. BLOOMFIELD *Let.* 9 Dec. in G. Bloomfield *Remin.* (1883) II. 47 Just at the moment that the King [of Prussia] was proclaiming the happy *entente* with Austria. **1878** L. W. M. LOCKHART *Mine is Thine* II. xxxv. 325 Esmé held out her hand, which he took; and thus the friendly *entente* was sealed! **1907** *Times* 20 Apr. 8/2 But was there not an *entente* which must be the great ideal of every Briton—the *entente cordiale*, the *entente commerciale* between Great and Greater Britain? **1907** *Westm. Gaz.* 16 Aug. 2/2 The reforms introduced in the Macedonian vilayets by the *entente* Powers. **1908** *Daily Chron.* 14 Aug. 1/5 Why, asked Mr. Lloyd George, cannot we have an agreement with Germany, seeing that Great Britain has already concluded ententes with France, Russia, and the United States? **1920** *Glasgow Herald* 5 Aug. 7 The young Austrian republic, whose existence would be endangered unless the Entente intervened. **1923** *Westm. Gaz.* 23 Jan., The Little Entente (Roumania, Czecho-Slovakia, and Jugo-Slavia).

Hence **en'tentist**, one who favours an entente.

1915 *Times* 30 Aug. 5/7 Oh! you stupid Quadruple Ententists! **1924** *Glasgow Herald* 24 Jan. 7 Carlotti, the Italian Ambassador at Petersburg and an Ententist.

‖**entente cordiale** (ɑ̃tɑ̃t kɔrdjal). [Fr.] A friendly understanding, esp. one between two or more political powers or states; *spec.* with reference to the understanding arrived at between England and France in 1904, and between these two countries and Russia in 1908.

1844 T. RAIKES *Jrnl.* 3 June (1857) IV. 400 Still less had he [*sc.* the Tsar] the slightest wish or intention to derange or counteract this *entente cordiale* between England and France. **1845** FORD *Hand-bk. Spain* I. 227 But all this breeds bad blood and mars, on the Spaniards' part, the *entente cordiale*. **1847** H. GREVILLE *Diary* (1883) I. 189 If Guizot remains in office Normanby must be recalled, as the only chance of a renewal of the *entente cordiale*. **1860** F. NIGHTINGALE *Notes on Nursing* vi. 36 The *entente cordiale*.. between the doctor and his head nurse. **1870** J. R. LOWELL *Among my Bks.* 320 Something that would break the *entente cordiale* of placid mutual assurance. **1904** *Spectator* 31 Dec. 1070/1 The Cologne Gazette last week discounted M. Jaurès's reply to Count von Bülow, and warned its readers that the *entente cordiale* with England was aimed against Germany. **1908** *Times* 11 Mar. 11/6 The agreements which constitute the *entente cordiale* with France. **1965** A. J. P. TAYLOR *Eng. Hist. 1914–45* xii. 417 There had always been something strained and artificial in the *entente cordiale* with France. **1970** *New Yorker* 25 July 8/2 The dining is an *entente cordiale* between East and West. Dancing. Closed Mondays.

ententophil, -phile (ɑ̃'tɑ̃:təʊfɪl, -faɪl), *a.* and *sb.* [f. ENTENTE + -(O)PHIL, -PHILE.] (One who is) friendly to a particular *entente*.

1920 *Glasgow Herald* 9 May 9 (Greece) A Government formed with the least possible delay should declare itself ententophile. *Ibid.* 15 June 7 Signor Meda is the most Ententophile, or the least Germanophile, personality of the 'Popular Party'. *Ibid.* 14 Oct. 6 M. Take Jonescu,.. the staunchest Ententophile in Eastern Europe. **1932** R. H. B. LOCKHART *Mem. Brit. Agent* IV. iii. 231 Trotsky was not to be placated... 'While your fools of spies are trying to prove that I am a German agent, my friends down there.. are calling me an Ententophile.'

entepicondylar (ɛntɛpɪ'kɒndɪlə(r)), *a. Anat.* [f. Gr. ἐντός within + EPICONDYLE, after *condylar*.] ***entepicondylar foramen***: a foramen in the humerus of many vertebrates just above the medial epicondyle.

1893 *Athenæum* 18 Nov. 701/2 An entepicondylar (ulnar) foramen in the humerus. **1949** *Buchanan's Man. Anat.* (ed. 8) vi. 282 The supracondylar process represents a portion of bone that forms an entepicondylar foramen in many vertebrates. **1964** PARKER & HASWELL *Text-bk. Zool.* (ed. 7) II. 771 In the armadillos.. the humerus is short and powerful, with well-developed processes and ridges, and with a foramen (entepicondylar foramen) above the inner condyle.

†'**enter**, *sb. Obs.* [f. the verb.

(The form *entre* may in some instances belong to this word; but the examples cannot be distinguished from those in which it belongs to ENTRY.)]

1. The action of entering; the power or right of entering; a legal entry; *concr.* a means or way of entrance; a passage.

c **1430** LYDG. *Bochas* VIII. xiii. (1554) 185a, Gaue hym enter and possession. **1563** BP. GARDINER in Foxe *A. & M.* 732b, My brother of S. Dauids, maie like a champion with his sword in his hand make enter for the rest. **1588** SHAKS. *L.L.L.* v. i. 141 His enter and exit shall bee strangling a Snake.

2. [Confused with Fr. *enter* to graft.]

1693 EVELYN *De la Quint. Compl. Gard.* II. 105 Graffing and Enter, or Ingraffing, are Sinonimous Terms.

enter ('ɛntə(r)), *v.* Forms: 3–8 entre, (3 entri, 4 entere, entur), 4–5 entree, entyr(e, 4– enter. [a. Fr. *entrer* = Pr. *entrar, intrar*, Sp., Pg. *entrar*, It. *entrare, intrare*:—L. *intrāre*, related to *inter* between, *intrō* inwards, *intrā* within.

The L. vb. was used both as trans., and as intr. with *in* = into; in Fr. the intr. use was alone adopted, and passed into Eng. The trans. senses 9–15 are derived from the similar senses of *enter into* (1–8), perh. with some influence from Lat.]

I. To go or come in.

* *intr.* (Often conjugated with *be.*)

1. To go or come into a place, building, room, etc.; to pass within the boundaries of a country, region, portion of space, medium, etc. Also *fig.*

a. Const. *into*, †*in* (= 'into'), rarely †*unto*. Now largely superseded by the trans. use 10, but retained where the notion of penetration into the interior of a place is sought to be emphasized.

c **1300** *K. Alis.* 4488 In a castel he entred thare. *c* **1325** *E.E. Allit. P.* A. 38, I entred in þat erber grene. *c* **1386** CHAUCER *Miller's T.* 399 That ilke nyght, That we ben entred into schippes boord. *c* **1400** *Destr. Troy* 3007 Honerable Elan was entrid in þe tempull. *c* **1400** MAUNDEV. v. (1839) 37 In his tyme, entred the gode Kyng Edward of Englond in Syrye. *Ibid.* 56 At that Cytee entrethe the Ryvere of Nyle into the See. **1568** GRAFTON *Chron.* II. 263 Syr for Gods sake enter againe into your Ship. **1703** MAUNDRELL *Journ. Jerus.* (1732) 5 We entred into a Woody Mountain. **1796** H. HUNTER tr. *St. Pierre's Stud. Nat.* (1799) III. 339 Enter into it [harbour] then at this time.. while day-light remains. **1843** MARRYAT *M. Violet* xxxv. 290 We.. entered into a noble forest.

fig. *c* **1384** CHAUCER *H. Fame* III. 19 Now [O Apollo] entreth in my brest anoon. **1547** *Homilies* I. *Good Works* (1859) 58 What man.. doth not see and lament to have entered into Christs religion such false doctrine. **1712** STEELE *Spect.* No. 284 ¶1 When this Humour enters into the Head of a Female. **1875** JOWETT *Plato* (ed. 2) III. 450 A spirit of reverence enters into the young man's soul.

b. *simply.* To come into the place indicated by the context. Of an actor: To come upon the stage; in the stage-directions of plays used constantly in 3rd pers. imper. sing. and pl. Also *fig.*

As to the grammatical character of 'enter' as a stage direction, cf. the Lat. directions in *Calisto & Melibœa* 1520, which has frequently *intret, exeat*, and those in Udall's *Roister Doister* 1553, where *exeat, exeant, cantent*, etc. appear throughout; also Bales' *Kynge Johan*: 'Here the Kyng delevyr the crowne to the Cardynall', 'Her go owt Sedwsion', 'Here the Pope go out', 'Here cum Dyssimulacyon syngyng of the letany', etc.

a **1300** *Cursor M.* 8341 (Cott.) For-þi hir enterd bersabe. *c* **1391** CHAUCER *Astrol.* II. §12 The howr of Mercurie entryng vnder my west orisonte at eue. **1398** TREVISA *Barth. De P.R.* XVII. xx. (1495) The stocke of boxe.. hath noo poores where ayre myghte entree. *c* **1400** *Destr. Troy* 9107 Þan vnarmyt he entrid, euyn to þe citie. *c* **1425** WYNTOUN *Cron.* VIII. xxxv. 75 Ramsay til hym coym in hy And gert hym entre. **1557** tr. *More's Edw. V.* (1641) 16 When he is once entred, he creepeth forth so farre. **1590** SHAKS. *Mids. N.* v. i. 186 She [Thisbie] is to enter, and I am to spy Her through the vvall. **1594** HOOKER *Eccl. Pol.* IV. ix. §3 A way made for Paganism or for extreme barbarity to enter. **1635** AUSTIN *Medit.* 194 John.. did.. before Christ entred, play the Mediator. **1664** EVELYN *Kal. Hort.* (1729) 231 The Air .. entring by the Furnace-pipes. **1767** T. HUTCHINSON *Hist. Prov. Mass.* ii. 138 The minister.. discovered near 20 entring. **1839** THIRLWALL *Greece* VII. liv. 41 The king and his troops entered first through a postern.

c. with pleonastic *in* (adv.). Somewhat *arch.* or *rhetorical*.

1297 R. GLOUC. (1724) 47 Þei entrede in at Temse mouþ. *c* **1325** *Coer de L.* 75 And there we may, withouten dent, Enter in now, verament. *c* **1425** WYNTOUN *Cron.* II. viii. 114 And entryde in wytht hys menyhe. *a* **1535** MORE *De quat. Noviss.* Wks. 81/2 While he wer entring in at yᵉ gate. **1847** TENNYSON *Princ.* v. 472 Empanoplied and plumed We entered in.

2. *Law.* To make entry (into lands) as a formal assertion of ownership; to take possession. Const. †*in, into*, and *simply*. (For *to enter upon* see 9a.)

1523 FITZHERB. *Surv.* 12b, For and he do, the lorde may entre as in landes forfayte to hym. *a* **1619** DALTON *Country Just.* lxxxiii. (1630) 213 If after the death of the father a stranger.. entereth into his land by force. **1721** *St. German's Doctor & Stud.* 32 Though his successor have right to the lands, yet he may not enter. **1809** TOMLINS *Law Dict.* s.v. *Entry*, This entry into lands is where a man enters into or takes possession of any lands, etc., in his proper person. **1818** CRUISE *Digest* II. 375 Upon the death of the testator his sister entered and married.

3. To penetrate into the substance of anything; to be plunged deeply. Const. *into*; also *simply*.

1491 CAXTON *Vitas Patr.* (W. de W. 1495) I. xxxiii. 28a/1 The grounde was soo softe and moryssh that they entred up to the raynes. **1539** BIBLE (Great) *Ps.* cv. 18 The iron entered into his soul. **1667** MILTON *P.L.* VI. 326 The sword of Michael.. deep entring, shar'd All his right side.

†**b.** *fig.* (*a*) To be absorbed (*in* thought). (*b*) In phrase, ***to enter far within*** (a person), i.e. to have great influence over (him). *Obs.*

c **1400** *Destr. Troy* 3844 Euermore ymaginand & entrond in thoghtes. **1601** HOLLAND *Pliny* XX. xiv, Vindex so far entred within him, as he obtained whatsoever he would at his hands.

4. To become a member in a society, etc. Cf. 23c.

1389 *Eng. Gilds* (1870) 3 Who þᵗ entryth in þe same ffraternite. **1674** BREVINT *Saul at Endor* 266 By entring into a Confraternity. **1791** BOSWELL *Johnson* an. 1730 He fairly told Taylor that he could not.. suffer him to enter where he knew he could not have an able tutor. **1854** *Prospective Rev.* X. XL. 525 He.. entered at Oriel College. *a* **1891** *Mod.* He entered at St. John's College.

†**5.** To come or be brought into any state or condition (sometimes with additional notion of place); to fall into a disorder, etc. Const. *into*, occas. *to, unto*. *Obs.*

c **1340** *Cursor M.* 23368 (Fairf.) Þa iois sere þat ihesus crist has diȝt til his qua-sim mai entre in-to þat blis. **1382** WYCLIF *Matt.* xxv. 21 Entre thou into the ioye of thi lord. **1483** CAXTON *Gold. Leg.* 238/1 Alle they that so consented entred in to frenesye and myght not be hool. **1535** COVERDALE *Matt.* xviii. 9 To entre in vnto life. **1568** GRAFTON *Chron.* II. 675 Determined to take part with king Edwarde, with whome.. he in small space entred into great grace and high favour. **1657** W. COLES *Adam in Eden* 155 Those that be entred into a Ptisick. **1710** STEELE *Tatler* No. 251 ¶6 He that has entred into Guilt has bid Adieu to Rest.

6. To make a beginning, engage (in any action, course of conduct, discourse, etc.). **a.** Const. *in* (arch.), *into*, occas. †*to*.

a **1450** *Knt. de la Tour* (1868) 8 To the entent that thei might praie and entre in orisones. **1552** ABP. HAMILTON *Catech.* (1884) 28 Afoir we enter to the special declaratioun of the x commandis. **1597** MORLEY *Introd. Mus.* Pref., There be many who will enter into the reading of my booke for their instruction. **1611** BIBLE *Ps.* cxliii. 2 Enter not into iudgement with thy seruant. **1647** CLARENDON *Hist. Reb.* I. (1843) 11/1 Though the War was entred in, all hope of obtaining money to carry it on was even desperate. **1712** STEELE *Spect.* No. 426 ¶1 He entered into the following Relation. **1841** BREWSTER *Mart. Sc.* vi. (1856) 89 The commissioners entered into an active correspondence with Galileo. **1855** MRS. CARLYLE *Lett.* II. 264 We entered into conversation without having been introduced. **1863** H. COX *Instit.* I. viii. 113 The returning officer has not.. any power of entering into a scrutiny of votes. **1879** MᶜCARTHY *Own Times* II. 24 Ireland would be entered in rebellion.

†**b.** *simply.* Also of a period of time or state of things: To begin. *Obs.*

1548 UDALL, etc. *Erasm. Par. Matt.* iii. 13 Began and entred with the matter that he came for. **1563** SHUTE *Archit.* D iij a, To beginne with the Pedestal of Corinthia, ye shal enter thus. **1586** J. HOOKER *Girald. Irel.* in *Holinshed* II. 149 There entred a verie fervent affection and good will between them. **1669** EVELYN *Mem.* (1857) II. 41 Imploring His blessing for the year entering. **1688** *Penn. Archives* I. 107 The winter.. is now entred with some severity.

7. *intr.* for *refl.* of branch II. (See 20c, 23c.)

8. to enter into (†**in**): in various senses, in which the intrans. vb. does not occur simply.

†**a.** To look at a particular place in (a mathematical table). *Obs.* So Fr. *entrer dans*. Cf. 16.

c **1391** CHAUCER *Astrol.* II. §44 With so many entere into thy tabelis in þe furst lyne.

b. To take on oneself (an engagement, a relation, the duties of an office, etc.). Sometimes in *indirect passive*. †***to enter into religion***: to embrace a monastic life. Cf. 14.

c **1250** *Kent. Serm.* in *O.E. Misc.* 35 We.. bieþ i-entred into cristes seruise. *c* **1290** *Lives Saints* (1887) 125 For-to entri into Answere: þare he ne ouȝte nouȝt to do. *c* **1380** WYCLIF *Sel. Wks.* III. 349 Who is beterid by entryng into þes ordris. *c* **1386** CHAUCER *Merch. T.* 312 Auyseth yow.. How that ye entren in to mariage. **1597** HOOKER *Eccl. Pol.* v. lxi. §2 Such kind of baptism barred men afterwards from entering into holy orders. *a* **1631** DONNE *Paradoxes* (1652) 28 The Allegoricall death of entring into Religion. **1647** MAY *Hist. Parl.* II. v. 92 That they all entered into Pay. **1711** STEELE *Spect.* No. 79 ¶3, I have a mind to put off entering into Matrimony till another Winter is over my Head. **1796** PEGGE *Anonym.* (1809) 388 Our great man was entered in Religion, as they called it. **1876** J. H. NEWMAN *Hist. Sk.* I. I. iii. 140 Trade.. does not care for the religious tenets of those who offer to enter into relations with it.

c. To become a party to; to bind oneself by (a league, treaty, etc.); to append one's name to (a bond). See also RECOGNIZANCE, SECURITY.

1535 COVERDALE *2 Kings* xxiii. 3 And all the people entred in to [WYCLIF: assentyde to] the couenaunt. **1590** SHAKS. *Com. Err.* IV. iv. 128 Master, I am heere entred in bond for you. **1593** —— *Rich. II*, v. ii. 65 'Tis nothing but some bond, that he is enter'd into. **1637** *Decree Star Chamb.* §16 in Milton *Areop.* (Arb.) 16 The like Bond shall be entred into by all. **1711** ADDISON *Spect.* No. 69 ¶1 A Subject of the Great Mogul entering into a League with one of the Czar of Moscovy. **1767** T. HUTCHINSON *Hist. Prov. Mass.* ii. 201 They entred anew into articles of submission. **1802** MAR. EDGEWORTH *Mor. T.* (1816) I. 220 The agreement, into which he had entered. **1886** *Manch. Exam.* 2 Jan. 5/3 He refused to enter into a treaty with the Indian Government.

d. To engage in the consideration of (a subject).

1553 EDEN *Treat. Newe Ind.* (Arb.) 9 To entre into another matter. **1586** A. DAY *Eng. Secretary* I. (1625) 112 The second of these must by insinuation be entred into. **1662** STILLINGFL. *Orig. Sacr.* I. vi §9 If we should enter into their Theology, and the History of that. **1711** STEELE *Spect.* No. 95 ¶3. I.. should be obliged to you if you would enter into the Matter more deeply. **1839** G. BIRD *Nat. Philos.* Introd. 34 To enter into these speculations would however be useless and unprofitable. **1869** J. MARTINEAU *Ess.* II. 45 Into its physiology we do not propose to enter.

†**e.** To take part in, intermeddle with. *Obs.*

1710 STEELE *Tatler* No. 176 ¶2 Our Affections must never enter into our Business. *a* **1714** BURNET *Own Time* II. 207 Other princes would not.. enter into the laws and establishment settled among us.

f. To take an interest in; to take an intelligent interest in, understand, sympathize with.

1797 GODWIN *Enquirer* I. vi. 43 It is by comparison only that we can enter into the philosophy of language. **1833** B'NESS BUNSEN in Hare *Life* I. ix. 404 Entering into everything and enjoying everything like a child. **1851** HELPS *Friends in C.* II. 11, I should enter into his feelings rather than into those of the ordinary spectator. **1885** SIR J. HANNEN in *Law Rep.* Prob. Div. X. 89 She entered into all the arrangements.. in a methodical and rational manner.

g. To form part of; to be a constituent element in. So also with adv., ***to enter in***.

1715 DESAGULIERS *Fires Impr.* 152 Lapis Calaminaris, which enters into the Composition of the Brass. **1793** SMEATON *Edystone L.* §193 The quantity and species of sabulous matter that entered into the texture of the limestone. **1796** H. HUNTER tr. *St. Pierre's Stud. Nat.* (1799)

I. 567 These universal correspondencies.. enter into all the plans of Nature. **1811** PINKERTON *Petral.* I. 231 Where no secondary stone enters in its composition, I do not see why, etc. **1879** HUXLEY *Hume* 74 Those compound states of consciousness, which so largely enter into our ordinary trains of thought. **1888** *Spectator* 30 June 884/1 Other considerations, some of them trifling enough, enter in.

h. In Bible phrase, ***to enter into*** (another's) ***labours*** (lit. from the Gr. and the Vulg.): to reap the benefits of what has been done by another.

1382 WYCLIF *John* iv. 38 Othere men traueliden, and ȝe entriden in to her trauelis. **1526** *Pilgr. Perf.* (W. de W. 1531) 11 They laboured.. the vynyarde.. & we haue entred into theyr labours, takynge the fruyte of the same.

9. to enter on, upon:

a. *Law.* (Cf. 2.) To make an entry into (land) as an assertion of ownership; to assume possession of (property); †to dispossess (a holder of property).

1467 *Bury Wills* (1850) 47, I will that myn feffeis and myn executo^rs entre vppon hym and put hym owth. **1655–60** STANLEY *Hist. Philos.* (1701) 23/2 It shall not be lawful for any Woman to enter upon the goods of the dead. **1712** STEELE *Spect.* No. 263 ¶6, I shall immediately enter upon your Estate for the Arrear due to me. **1809** BAWDWEN *Domesday Bk.* 599 Ausfrid, the Priest, entered forcibly upon this land of Ralph's. **1818** CRUISE *Digest* III. 319 He will not distrain or enter on the premises conveyed for the recovery of his rent charge.

b. To make an entrance on; to take the first steps upon (a path, a tract travelled over).

c **1380** *Sir Ferumb.* 59 And forþward faste on hure way þey wente, and entrede on þe brigge. **1659** HAMMOND *On Ps.* ci. 8 The season wherein David, as a Judge, entring on the Tribunal, etc. **1826** FOSTER in *Life & Corr.* (1846) II. 96 He is saved from entering on a scene of infinite corruptions. **1860** TYNDALL *Glac.* I. §12. 88 My guide and myself entered upon this portion of the glacier.

c. *fig.* To take the first steps in; to do the first part of; to begin, take in hand, engage in (a process, enterprise). Cf. Fr. †*entrer sur* (Littré). Also, to begin (a period of time).

1618 BOLTON *Florus* I. i. 3 Which of them should first enter upon the government and Rule. **1655** FULLER *Ch. Hist.* Ded., I after was entred on a Resolution to dedicate it to his Memory. **1672–5** COMBER, *Comp. Temple* (1702) 89 By his offering and entring on a treaty. **1704** ADDISON *Italy* Pref., For before I enter'd on my Voyage I took care, etc. **1719** DE FOE *Crusoe* (1840) I. xvi. 274, I was now entered on the seven-and-twentieth year of my captivity. **1844** STANLEY *Arnold* II. x. 288 He entered on his Professorial duties. **1883** GILMOUR *Mongols* xvii. 206 To enter upon a contest with evil.

†**d.** To begin an attack upon. *Obs.*

1490 CAXTON *Eneydos* xliii (*heading*), How Nysus and Eryalus made theym redy to entre vpon the hoost of Turnus. **1607** TOPSELL *Four-f. Beasts* (1673) 540 The Beare dareth not to enter upon the wilde Boar, except behinde him.

e. To begin to deal with (a subject).

1632 *Star Chamb. Cases* (1886) 124 Then the Kinges Councell entred upon their proofes. **1649** SELDEN *Laws Eng.* I. vi. (1739) 14 Thus entred the Prelates upon affairs of Kings and Kingdoms. **1712** ADDISON *Spect.* No. 339 ¶5 The Day is not too far spent for him to enter upon such a Subject. **1727** *Wodrow Corr.* (1843) III. 295 This day the Committee.. entered on the Church's grievances. **1796** JANE AUSTEN *Pride & Prej.* v. 191 Her fear, if she once entered on the subject.

**** *trans.*** (formerly sometimes conjugated with *be.*)

10. To go or come into (a closed space, *e.g.* a house); to go within the bounds of (a country, etc.); to go within (a gate); to step upon (a path, a bridge); to go on board (a ship). Cf. 1 a.

1340 HAMPOLE *Pr. Consc.* 402 Yhe sal noght entre, be na way Hevenryke that sal last ay. *c* **1400** *Destr. Troy* 13880 No buerne was so bold þe brigge for to entre. *c* **1400** MAUNDEV. xiii (1839) 144 He most entre the See, at Gene. **1509** FISHER *Fun. Serm. C'tess Richmond* Wks. 302 He hathe entred the heuen, to appere before the vysage of his fader for vs. **1576** FLEMING *Panoplie Ep.* 171 Who being discomfited with the storms and tempestes thereof, never enter shippe. **1568** GRAFTON *Chron.* II. 165 The which with great courage entered Wales. **1592** SHAKS. *Rom. & Jul.* III. i. 7 One.. that when he enters the confines of a Tauerne, claps me his Sword vpon the Table. **1711** STEELE *Spect.* No. 178 ¶2 He ..returns as if he were entring a Gaol. **1737** WHISTON *Josephus' Hist.* IV. iv. §7 They soon came to know who they were.. that were entered the city. **1756–7** tr. *Keysler's Trav.* (1760) III. 165 The gate which thou enterest. **1801** SOUTHEY *Thalaba* III. i, Some traveller, who shall enter Our tent, may read it. **1840** DICKENS *Barn. Rudge* i, Who was the young lady that I saw entering a carriage? **1876** GREEN *Short Hist.* i. 18 The band of monks entered Canterbury bearing before them a silver cross.

fig. c **1380** WYCLIF *Last Age Church* (1840) p. xxv, þis was þe firste tribulacioun þat ontrede þe Chirche of God. **1644** MILTON *Areop.* (Arb.) 71 Entring the glorious waies of Truth. **1843** MRS. CARLYLE *Lett.* I. 201 It never enters his head to lie under the walnut-tree here. **1862** TROLLOPE *Orley F.* xv. 121 The idea that Lady Mason was guilty had never entered her head.

†**b.** To take possession of (the throne, the crown). Cf. 9 a. *Obs.*

1563 FOXE *Life* in *Latimer's Serm. & Rem.* (1845) Introd. 20 Till the time that blessed King Edward entered his crown. **1649** SELDEN *Laws Eng.* II. xxii. (1739) 102 Henry the Fourth entred the Throne by his Sword.

c. To take up one's abode in. Chiefly with mixed notion of 12, as ***to enter a monastery, the cloister*** (= to become a monk or nun), ***to enter a college***, etc.

1603 SHAKS. *Meas. for M.* I. ii. 182 This day my sister should the Cloyster enter.

d. To force an entrance into; to break into (a house, etc.); †to board (a ship).

1586 J. HOOKER *Girald. Irel.* in *Holinshed* II. 49/1 His lodging.. was entred with fire. **1627** CAPT. SMITH *Seaman's Gram.* xii. 57 There is more men lost in entering, if the chase stand to her defence. **1726** SHELVOCKE *Voy. round World* vi. (1757) 202 And seeing their forecastle full of men,.. I concluded they had come to a resolution of entering us. **1817** W. SELWYN *Law Nisi Prius* II. 777 Judgment was arrested in trespass for breaking and entering a free fishery.

11. To make a way into or pass between the parts of anything; to pierce; to penetrate. Cf. 3.

1613 SHAKS. *Hen. VIII*, II. iv. 182 This respite.. enter'd me; Yea, with a spitting power.

†**b.** Of the agent: To pierce, make a hole into. Also *fig.* to 'get an idea into' (a person). *Obs.*

1703 MOXON *Mech. Exerc.* 154 Entring the Post first with an Augure. *a* **1718** PENN *Tracts* Wks. 1726 I. 526, I almost despair of entering some of our Adversaries.

†**c.** Of male animals: To copulate with. *Obs.*

1607 TOPSELL *Four-f. Beasts* (1673) 18 A Mare which a Horse hath formerly entred. *Ibid.*, A female asse which hath been entered by a male asse.

12. To become a member of (a society or organized body). So ***to enter the army, the church, a university***, etc. Cf. 4.

a **1891** *Mod.* He entered the army at nineteen. A lad of seventeen is too young to enter a university.

†**13.** To take the first steps in (an action or work); to begin. Often with *obj. inf. Obs.* Cf. 6.

c **1515** *Cocke Lorell's B.* (1843) 12 Some to howse the tope sayle dyde entre. **1548** UDALL, etc. *Erasm. Par. Matt.* iv. 17 To begynne and enter his prechyng. **1563–87** FOXE *A. & M.* (1596) 77/1 Constantinus.. entred his journie, comming towards Italie. **1576** FLEMING *Panoplie Ep.* 49 The souldiers ..having no stomache to enter conflict and skyrmishe, betooke them to flight. **1594** NASHE *Terrors Night* G b, Which before I enter to describe, thus much I will informe ye. **1642** ROGERS *Naaman* 256 A worke well entred, is truly said to be halfe done. **1703** MOXON *Mech. Exerc.* 29 Made, or, at least, entred at the Forge.. yet sometimes Smiths do it on cold Iron.

b. To begin (a period of time).

a **1617** BAYNE *On Eph.* (1658) 75 Kings.. in entring their reigns. **1801** STRUTT *Sports & Past.* I. i. 13 *note*, Her majesty had just entered the seventy-seventh year of her age.

†**14.** To come, or be brought, into a certain state; to take upon oneself (a condition, office, or relation of any kind); to embrace (a profession). *Obs.* exc. in phrase ***to enter religion*** (cf. 8 b).

1563 *Homilies* II. *Resurr. Christ* (1859) 430 Then are they in very evill case.. that be entred their sleepe in Christ. **1576** FLEMING *Panoplie Ep.* 282 Over hastie bee they to enter wedlocke. *Ibid.* 342 If you doe enter acquaintance and familiaritie with him. **1590** GREENE *Orl. Fur.* (1861) 91 Would these princes.. enter arms as did the Greeks against Troy. **1596** *Edw. III*, I. ii, We with England will not enter parley. **1611** SPEED *Theat. Gt. Brit.* xvii. (1614) 33/2 Sigebert.. entered the profession of a monke. *Ibid.* xxviii. 55/1 P. O. Scapula entred his Lieutenantship in Britaine. **1651** W. G. tr. *Cowel's Inst.* 23 Make Oath not to enter marriage again without the Kings consent. **1888** BERNARD *World to Cloister* 9 If he enter religion.

†**15. *to enter bond***: = 'to enter into a bond' (see 8 c). *Obs.*

1650 *Bury Wills* (1850) 224 Soe that within a moneth after my death she enter bond to my trustees of my estate. *Ibid.*, If she shall refuse to enter such bond.

16. To turn to a particular place in (a mathematical table). Still in nautical use. Cf. 8 a.

1593 FALE *Dialling* 11/2 With this quocient Sine I enter the Table. **1644** NYE *Gunnery* (1670) 60, I enter the Table under the Title inches. **1840** RAPER *Navigation* 80 Enter Table 5 with the first number of points at the top, and the second number of points at the side.

II. To cause to enter.

17. *trans.* To put or bring (a person) into something: *esp.* to take or put (men) on board a vessel. *arch.*

1523 LD. BERNERS *Froiss.* I. cxx. 143 They decked thre shyppes, and entred into theym a certayne. **1588** R. PARKE tr. *Mendoza's Hist. China* 387 Whereby to enter the lawe of the Gospel into the mightie kingdome of China. **1607** DEKKER *Northw. Hoe* III. i. Wks. 1873 III. 36 But come enter him [*i.e.* 'show in' a visitor]. **1611** CHAPMAN *Iliad* III. Comm. (1857) 81 And thus to the last twelve books.. with those free feet that entered me, I haste. **1674** *Lond. Gaz.* No. 870/4 Laying him on board on the Bow.. [he] entered his Men, and made him surrender. **1720** DE FOE *Capt. Singleton* xi. (1840) 193 The boat.. was to enter her men in the waste. **1845** HAMILTON *Pop. Educ.* vii. (ed. 2) 146 Each citizen has a legal right to enter his children [in the primary schools]. **1847–8** H. MILLER *First Impr.* viii. (1857) 124 He would, he said, fairly enter me on the grounds, and introduce me.

†**b.** *fig.* To admit into a society, etc.; to introduce into a condition or state. Const. *into*, rarely *in. Obs.*

1594 HOOKER *Eccl. Pol.* III. i. (1611) 83 Entered wee are not into the visible Church, before our admittance by the doore of baptisme. **1606** SHAKS. *Ant. & Cl.* IV. xiv. 113 This sword but shewne to Cæsar with this tydings, Shall enter me with him. *a* **1617** BAYNE *On Eph.* (1658) 8 This blessing entreth them into assured possession. **1658** *Whole Duty Man* i. §31 (1684) 23 Baptism.. enters us into covenant with God. **1719** DE FOE *Crusoe* (1840) I. i. 4 He would.. endeavour to enter me fairly into the station of life which, etc. **1723** BLACKALL *Wks.* I. 184 By which [Baptism] we are entred and initiated into the Christian Church.

†**c.** with complement. *Obs.*

1607 SHAKS. *Cor.* II. ii. 103 His Pupill age Man-entred thus, he waxed like a Sea. **1631** MASSINGER *Believe as You List* I. i, With this charitie I enter thee a begger.

†**18.** To introduce (to the knowledge of anything) by instruction; to give (a person) initiatory information or instruction *in*; to instruct initially; to initiate. *Obs.* or *arch.*

1540 HYRDE tr. *Vives' Instr. Chr. Wom.* (1592) C iij, The precepts of wise men, which she had been entred in. **1548** UDALL, etc. *Erasm. Par.* Pref. 13 b, Sounde meate for such as are wel entred. **1607** SHAKS. *Cor.* I. ii. 2 They of Rome are entred in our Counsailes. **1674** PLAYFORD *Skill Mus.* I. ii. 41 So that he be already entred upon the Theorie of Musick. *a* **1714** ELLWOOD *Autobiog.* 202 He asked me.. If I would enter his Children in the Rudiments of the Latin Tongue. **1732** BERKELEY *Alciphr.* II. §4 Cleophon.. entered him [his son] betimes in the principles of his sect. **1864** BURTON *Scot Abr.* I. iv. 229 You are entered in all the secrets of his workshop.

b. To exercise initially; to train; to fly (a hawk) for the first time; to break in (a horse). Also, ***to enter a dog at*** or ***to***: to put him (while yet untrained) on the scent of.

1481–90 *Howard Househ. Bks.* (1844) 508 A kest of hakys, when he went to enter them to the rever. *c* **1575** *Perfect Bk. Sparhawkes* (ed. Hasting 1886) 17 Enter her in this order folowinge. **1598** FLORIO, *Accarnare*, to flesh, to enter a dog. **1668** PEPYS *Diary*, 21 Dec., Not daring yet to use the others [horses] too much, but only to enter them. *a* **1670** HACKET *Abp. Williams* II. 143 (D.) Like hounds ready to be entred. **1727** BRADLEY *Fam. Dict.* s.v. *Entering of Hounds*, The Hare is esteemed the best Game to enter your Hounds at. **1875** 'STONEHENGE' *Brit. Sports* 124 The young hounds should be entered to fox. **1881** MICHELL *Hawking* in *Macm. Mag.* XLV. 39 It remains only to break him to the lure, and to 'enter' him, each of which processes is soon completed.

19. To put (something) *into* (another thing); to put in, insert, introduce. Now chiefly *techn.* [So Fr. *entrer* (Littré), though the use is not recognized by the Academy.]

1375 BARBOUR *Bruce* I. 623 This lettir sall I entyr heyr. **1647** H. MORE *Song of Soul* II. II. III. i, He much perplexed is.. Where to make choice to enter his rugg'd saw. **1691** RAY *N.C. Words* 31 *Gavelock*.. an Iron Bar to enter stakes into the ground. **1703** MOXON *Mech. Exerc.* 122 Enter the edge of the Draw-knife into the Work. **1787** BEST *Angling* (ed. 2) 29 You must enter the hook at the tail of the worm. **1806–7** J. BERESFORD *Miseries Hum. Life* (1826) x. xcv, Entering your watch at the wrong opening, when it instantly dives to your knee. **1830** GEN. P. THOMPSON *Exerc.* (1842) I. 244 It is therefore politic to enter the wedge by this end. **1859** F. GRIFFITHS *Artil. Man.* (1862) 208, 5.. enters shot or shell, and rams home. *c* **1860** H. STUART *Seamen's Catech.* 11 The ball will be entered the largest end downward. **1865** BUSHNELL *Vicar. Sacr.* i. (1866) 4 A special care is needed lest we enter something into the meaning from ourselves.

†**b. *to enter foot***: to begin. Also *refl.* in same sense. *Obs.*

1618 CHAPMAN *Hesiod* I. 141 When first thou enter'st foot to plow thy land. **1742** FIELDING *J. Andrews* I. x, He.. entered himself into an ejaculation on the numberless calamities which attended beauty.

c. In backgammon. To place a man again on the board after it has been taken up, and unable to come in again because the point indicated by the throw is already full.

1870 HARDY & WARE *Mod. Hoyle, Backgammon* 143.

20. To put (a name) into a list in writing, (a fact or particular) into a description or record; to write down (on paper, a tablet, etc.). Const. *in*, *into*, *on*, and simply. ***to enter*** (money, goods, etc.) ***to***, ***against***: to put down to a person's account.

1362 LANGL. *P. Pl.* A. XI. 253, I was markid, withoute mercy and myn name entrid In þe legende of lif longe er I were. *c* **1391** CHAUCER *Astrol.* II. §44 Consider thy rote furst ..& entre hit in-to thy slate for the laste merydye of December. *c* **1400** MAUNDEV. xxii. (1839) 238 Thei [alle the Mynstrelle] ben.. entred in his Bokes, as for his owne men. **1523** FITZHERB. *Surv.* 20 To entre their copyes truely in the lordes courte roll. **1576** FLEMING *Panoplie Ep.* 196 Such discourses, as you have already with painefull pen entered into paper. **1668** HALE in *Rolle's Abridgm.* Pref. 8 Let him enter the Abstract.. into his Common-place Book. **1727** A. HAMILTON *New Acc. E. Ind.* I. C viij, The Publisher.. has duly entred this Book in the Register of Stationers-hall, London. **1783** BURKE *Report Affairs India* Wks. XI. 136 He did not.. think it proper to enter his answer on the records. **1802** MAR. EDGEWORTH *Moral T.* (1816) I. xix. 154 If you received the note from us.. it must be entered in our books. **1812** *Examiner* 28 Sept. 624/1 They.. determined to enter goods to people who never had any dealings. **1828** SCOTT *F. M. Perth* ix, And not entered against him at the long and dire day of accounting. **1844** LINGARD *Anglo-Sax. Ch.* (1858) I. App. 361 Parish Churches are entered in the ancient record of Domesday.

b. To hand in at the Custom House a statement of the amount and value of (goods exported or imported). Also, to register (a vessel) as arriving in or leaving a port.

1634 SIR T. HERBERT *Trav.* A ij b, Such as.. like Merchants with their goods, enter them, before they ship them. **1840** R. DANA *Bef. Mast* xiii. 28 The cargo having been entered in due form, we began trading. **1845** MCCULLOCH *Taxation* II. x. (1852) 342 The teas entered for consumption. *Mod. Newspaper* (Heading of paragraphs), Vessels entered inwards. Vessels entered outwards.

c. To insert by name on the list of competitors (in a race, athletic contest, etc.). Also *intr.* for *refl.*

1684 *Lond. Gaz.* No. 1938/4 The first Horses to be shown and entred there a week before for this year. **1702** *Ibid.* No. 3832/4 The Horses to be enter'd.. 14 days before. *a* **1891** *Mod.* Please enter me for the Sack Race and Hurdles. Have you entered for the Quarter-mile?

d. To get (land) recorded in a land-office in one's name as the intending occupier. *U.S.*

1799 *Columbian Centinel* (Boston, Mass.) 1 July 3/1 Real Estates, entered at the Register of Deed's Office. **1835** in H. Howe *Hist. Coll. Ohio* (1847) 387 Much land was entered in the county, and many settlements made. **1843** 'R. Carlton' *New Purchase* xiv. 100 Out there, a settlement usually takes its name from the person that first 'enters the land', i.e. buys a tract at the land office. **1871** Schele de Vere *Americanisms* (1872) 173 All other lands can be obtained by entering them. **1884** H. Butterworth *Zigzag Journ. Western States* 217 'What does it usually cost to make a farm on government land?'..'It costs fourteen dollars to enter one hundred and sixty acres of land.'

21. ***to enter up*****: a.** To enter in regular form (a series of items); to complete the series of entries in (a book) to a certain date.

Mod. (*Comm.*) Have you entered up your payments? The cash-book had not been properly entered up.

b. *Law.* To cause (a verdict, judgement, etc.) to be written down in the records of a court.

a **1734** North *Exam.* i. ii. §48 (1740) 54 Corruptions by the Way, use not to be entered up upon Record. **1875** Poste *Gaius* iii. (ed. 2) 414 A judge's order authorizing the plaintiff to enter up judgment and issue execution.

22. a. *Law.* ***to enter an action, caveat, writ,*** etc.; to bring it before the court in due form, usually in writing. **b.** ***to enter a protest*****:** primarily of the minority in a deliberative body, *esp.* the House of Lords, to record a protest on the journals or minutes; hence *gen.* to protest. So also, ***to enter a caution, protestation,*** etc.

a. 1579 Fulke *Heskins' Parl.* 129 Chrysostome may enter action against him of slaunder and defamation. **1597** Shaks. *2 Hen. IV*, ii. i. 2 Mr. Fang, haue you entred the Action? **1884** *Law Rep.* Prob. Div. IX. 23 The defendant..entered a caveat.

b. 1679 Dryden *Tr. & Cress.* Ep. Ded., Whatever Protestation you might enter to the contrary. **1699** Bentley *Phal.* 139, I enter'd no caution about it to the Reader. **1728** in Picton *L'pool Munic. Rec.* (1886) II. 86 A motion..made for entring a protest against the above order. **1821** Q. Caroline *Remonstr. Geo. IV*, 17 July, The Queen feels it to be her bounden duty to enter her most deliberate and solemn protest against the said determination. **1884** Pennington *Wiclif* ix. 290 He entered his decided protest against the system of the Schoolmen.

c. To put down or cause to be put down upon the record.

1692, 1809 [see docket *v.* 2]. **1860** *Act 23 & 24 Vict.* c. 38. §3 No Judgment which has not already been or shall not hereafter be entered or docketed under the several Acts.. shall have any Preference against Heirs. **1896** A. Pulling *Law Rep., Five Years' Digest* 679/1 The defendant failed to appear, and judgment was entered. **1930** *Daily Express* 6 Nov. 7/2 No judgment was entered.

23. From sense 20, with mixed notion of 17 b: **a.** To admit as a pupil, or member of a society; to engage (a servant, workman, etc.). **b.** To procure admission for (a person) as such. **c.** *refl.* and *intr.* for *refl.* Const. *among, in, into, of.*

a. 1651 Baxter *Inf. Bapt.* 23 They that are entered under him as their Master. **1662** Stillingfl. *Orig. Sacr.* ii. ii. §5 And if the King were chosen out of the Souldiers, he was presently entred among the Priests. **1691** Wood *Ath. Oxon.* III. 358 In the year 1655 making a return to the University, he was entred into Ch. Ch. **1748** Anson *Voy.* iii. viii. 370 He had entered twenty-three men during his stay at Macao. **1793** Smeaton *Edystone L.* §129, I immediately entered another able seaman, which..made the number six. *Ibid.* §130, I likewise entered three masons and nine tinners..to take the first turn or week.

b. 1670 Walton *Lives* iv. 266 Having entred Edward into Queens Colledge. **1675** *Art Contentm.* ix. §11. 227 He was never enter'd in those academies of luxury. **1712** Budgell *Spect.* No. 307 ¶12 He was entered in a College of Jesuits. **1722** De Foe *Col. Jack* (1840) 224 Some..officers..entered me into the army. **1791** Boswell *Johnson* an. 1730 Taylor was entered of that college.

c. 1689–92 Locke *Toleration* Wks. 1727 II. iii. 324 They are free from it who enter themselves of the Company. **1702** *Lond. Gaz.* No. 3839/4 All others that enter to pay Five Guineas. **1725** De Foe *Voy. round World* (1840) 77 The people who were willing to take service with us, and enter themselves on board. **1870** E. Peacock *Ralf Skirl.* I. 6 He therefore entered himself as a clerk to a solicitor.

† **'enter,** *prep. Obs. rare*⁻¹. [ad. Fr. *entre*:—L. *inter.*] Between.

c **1420** *Pallad. on Husb.* iii. 455 Northwarde of fervent grounde, southwarde of colde, And enter both of hilly lande thai wolde.

enter, obs. var. entire, and inter, to bury.

enter-, entre-, *prefix*, a. Fr. *entre-*:—L. *inter* (see inter-), with senses 'between', 'among', 'mutually'. Occurring first in words a. Fr., as enterfeat, entermise, enterprise, entertain; also as an early variant of *inter-* in words ad. Lat. In 14–17th c. it was often prefixed to Eng. words, many of the compounds so formed being imitations of synonymous compounds in Fr. Since the middle of 17th c. this prefix has ceased to be employed in the formation of new words; the compounds (of Eng. origin) in which it occurs are either obs. or have been refashioned with *inter-*. The more important compounds of *enter-* will be found in their alphabetical place; the following are nonce-words or of rare occurrence:

enter-'advertise *v.* (Fr. *s'entre-avertir*), *refl.*, to inform each other; **enter'bathe** *v.* [cf. Fr. *s'entrebaigner*], *refl.*, to bathe each other; **enter'bear** *v.* [tr. Fr. *s'entreporter*], ? to carry mutually; **enter'brace** *v.*, to embrace mutually; **enter'braid** *v.*, to intertwine; **enter'break** *v.* [cf. OF. *entrerompre*], *trans.*, to break between, make a break in; **enter'breath,** breathing between; time for taking breath; **enter'call** *v. trans.*, to call mutually; **enter'capering** *vbl. sb.*, intermingled capering, intricate movement; **enter'carriage,** carriage to and fro between two places; **enteren'gender** *v. trans.*, to produce (each other) reciprocally; **enter'glancing** *vbl. sb.*, interchange of glances; **enter'grave** *v. trans.*, to engrave between; hence **enter'graving** *vbl. sb.*; **enter'hinder** *v. trans.*, to hinder mutually; **enter'hold** *v. trans.*, to observe (a treaty) reciprocally; **enter'kissing** *ppl. a.*, mutually kissing; **enter'lend** *v.* [cf. Fr. *s'entreprêter*] *trans.*, to lend to one another; **enter'love** *v.* [cf. Fr. *s'entr'aimer*] *trans.*, to love mutually; **enter'march** *v. intr.*, to tread on each other's toes; **enter'mine** *sb.*, an intervening mine; **enter'mine** *v. intr.*, to drive mines between or in an interval; hence **entermining** *vbl. sb.*; **ente'rowe** *v.* [cf. Fr. *s'entredevoir*] *trans.*, to owe one another; **enter'pillar** [tr. L. *intercolumnium*], the space between two pillars; **enter'seek** *v.* [cf. Fr. *s'entrechercher*], *trans.*, to seek mutually; **enter'shew** *v.* [cf. OF. *s'entremostrer*], *trans.*, to show one to another; **enter'shine** *v.* [cf. Fr. *entreluire*], *intr.*, to shine or show up between; to appear partially; to glance, glimmer; **enter'shoulder** *v. trans.*, to shoulder mutually, to jostle; hence **enter'shouldering** *vbl. sb.*; **enter'split** *v.* [cf. Fr. *entrefendre*], *refl.*, to split one another; **enter'spoil** *v.* [tr. Fr. *s'entrepiller*], *trans.*, to pillage mutually; **enter'suck** *v. trans.*, to suck mutually; **enter'take** *v.* [cf. Fr. *entreprendre* and enterprise *v.* 3], *trans.*, to receive, entertain; **enter'tear** *v.* [cf. Fr. *s'entredéchirer*], *trans.*, to tear mutually; **enter'warn** *v.* [cf. Fr. *s'entr'avertir*], *trans.*, to warn mutually.

1603 Florio *Montaigne* iii. viii. (1632) 528 We profitably *enter-advertize our selves of our defects. **1598** Sylvester *Du Bartas* ii. i. *Handie-crafts* 21 [They] cast away their spears, And rapt with joy, them *enterbathe with tears. **1603** Florio *Montaigne* i. xxvii. (1632) 90 Children killed their parents..to avoid the hindrance of *enterbearing one another. **1483** Caxton *Gold. Leg.* 110/3 Atte last he opened hys dore and sith *enterbraced eche other. **1598** Sylvester *Du Bartas* ii. i. *Handie-crafts* 209 Their shady boughs first bow they tenderly, Then *enterbraid. **1541** R. Copland *Guydon's Quest. Chirurg.*, The syxth vtylyte that Galyen putteth is to *entrebreake [1579 enterbrake], and intercyde the matter. **1631** Brathwait *Whimzies, Gamester* 40 At the end of every act..the encurtain'd musique sounds, to give *enterbreath to the actors. **1603** Florio *Montaigne* i. xxx. (1632) 104 Those that are much about one age, doe generally *entercall one another brethren. *Ibid.* i. xxii. 47 By the changes and *entercaprings of which, the revolutions..of the..planets are caused. **1598** Norden *Spec. Brit., M'sex* ii. 6 For the more easie *entercarriage of thinges between London and it [Hartford]. **1603** Florio *Montaigne* iii. xiii. (1632) 617 Paine and pleasure..*enter-engender and succeed one another. **1575** Gascoigne *Flowers* (R.), Their chiefe repast was by *enterglancing of lookes. **1609** Bible (Douay) *I Kings* vii. 28 The verie worke it selfe of the feete, was *entergraven: and *entergravinges betwen the joyntures. **1603** Florio *Montaigne* ii. ii. (1632) 190 They are two occupations that *enterhinder one another, in their vigor. **1491** Caxton *Vitas Patr.* (W. de W. 1495) i. lxiii. 114 a/1 The whyche paccyon they made and *entrehelden; For after ofte times they vysited eche other. **1591** Sylvester *Du Bartas* i. ii. 1050 Water, 'noynting with cold-moist the brims Of th' *enterkissing turning Globes extreams Tempers the heat. **1603** Florio *Montaigne* iii. iii. (1632) 463 They are things which *enterlend and *enterowe one another their essence. *Ibid.* i. xxvii. 94 They *enterlove one another, and love me as much. **1475** Caxton *Jason* 105 They [Medea and Jason] *entremarched with their feet under the tables. *c* **1611** Sylvester *Du Bartas* ii. iv. *Decay* 949 Just in the mouth of th' *entermine he [fir'd]. **1541** Elyot *Image Gov.* (1556) 135 b, Craftie *enterminynge. **1609** Bible (Douay) *I Kings* vii. 31 The middle *enterpillers [were] square not round. **1603** Florio *Montaigne* i. xxxiv. (1632) 111 There are ever conditions that *enterseeke one another. *Ibid.* ii. xii. 265 It was..a singular pleasure to observe the love..each endevored to *entershew one another. **1562** Phaër *Æneid* ix. B b iiij b, Soldiours round ryng not so thicke, Where wal most *entershines. **1603** Florio *Montaigne* ii. xii. (1632) 301 An overshadowed and darke picture, *entershining with an infinit varietie of false lights. *a* **1649** Drumm of Hawth. *Jas. V* Wks. 113 At his very sight ..a tumult, confused clamour, and *enter-shouldering of male-contents arose. **1605** Sylvester *Du Bartas* ii. iii. *Vocation* 301 If that any [stones] fail their foes to hit In full, in flight themselves they *entersplit. **1603** Florio *Montaigne* iii. vii. (1632) 517 Superiority and inferiority.. must perpetually *enterspoile one another. *Ibid.* ii. xxvi. 387 They.. mutually *entersuck't each one the others [thumb]. **1596** Spenser *F.Q.* v. ix. 35 So did this mightie Ladie..with more myld aspect those two to *entertake. **1603** Florio *Montaigne* ii. xi. (1632) 240 All are pleased to see them [beasts]..*enterteare one another. *Ibid.* i. xxxiv. 111 This means of *enterwarning one another would bring no small commoditie into common commerce and societie.

enterable ('ɛntərəb(ə)l), *a.* [f. enter *v.* + -able.]

That may be entered, in various senses of the vb.; †*spec.* of an article of commerce, that is allowed to be imported.

1714 *Fr. Bk. of Rates* 57 Merchandizes, which are Enterable in the former Account of Goods. **1787** Nelson 12 Aug. in Nicolas *Disp.* (1845) I. 252 Tamarinds and noyeau I must get smuggled..The latter is not enterable. **1793** A. Bell in Southey *Life* (1844) I. 461 Walked all round Pondicherry. Enterable by the sea face from the south. **1858** Hawthorne *Fr. & It. Jrnls.* I. 245 The hotel is..enterable through an arch. **1879** G. Macdonald *Sir Gibbie* I. ix. 123 On neither could he be required to live and act—as now in this waste of enterable and pervious extent.

enteradenography, -ology: see entero-.

enterance: see entrance.

enterate ('ɛntərət), *a. Zool.* [ad. mod.L. *enterāt-us*, f. Gr. ἔντερα bowels: see -ate.]

Having an intestine distinctly separated from the outer body-wall.

1877 Huxley *Anat. Inv. An.* xi. 652 The possibility that anenterous parasites are not necessarily modifications of free, enterate ancestors.

enterbathe, -bear, -break, -breath, -call, -caper, -carriage: see enter- *pref.*

entercept, enterchaine, etc.: see inter-.

† **'enterclose, 'interclose.** *Obs.* [a. OF. *entreclos*, f. *entre* between + *clos*: see close *sb.*]

1. A partition, 'septum'.

1398 Trevisa *Barth. De P.R.* xvii. lxxxi. (1495) 653 In the fruyte of Mirtus ben thre celles and in euery celle thre greynes or foure joyned wythout interclose [*sine pariete.*] *Ibid.*, Some greyne is dowble wythoute interclose [Lat. *absque pariete*] as in Celidoyne, and some is double wyth interclose as the greyne of Narstucium.

2. *Arch.* ? A screen, partition. Also *attrib.*

c **1450** *Voc.* in Wr.-Wülcker 590 Interclausum, an enterclos. **1479** *Will Wulwurth* (Somerset Ho.), Lego ad facturam le enterclose beate Marie ecclesie. **1485** in *Finchale Priory Acc.* (1837) 370 Lez enterclose walles tenementorum in Ballio. **1601** F. Godwin *Bps. of Eng.* 308 Ouer against which place, vpon the enterclose of the Quier I find written, etc. **1851–3** Turner *Dom. Archit.* II. v. 216 [tr. *Liberate Roll* of 1248] An interclose with door and locks at the entrance of the queen's new chamber.

b. ? A space partitioned off.

The architectural dicts. give the definition 'a passage between two rooms', referring to the following example:

1478 Wyrcestre *Itin.* (1778) 288 Le enterclose per quam vadit a porta ad aulam [in Wookey cavern] est longitudinis dimidium furlong, et archuata, etc.

entercommon, -commune, etc.: see in-.

enterdeal, obs. form of interdeal.

enterdese, variant of interdice, *Obs.*

‖**'enter-deux.** *Obs. rare*⁻¹. [a. Fr. *entre-deux* 'between two'.] A 'go-between'; in quot. a proxy bridegroom.

1602 Fulbecke *Pandectes* 25 James King of Scots..was married to Anne..by a substitute or *enter-deux*.

enterdice, var. of interdice, *Obs.*

enterdict: obs. form of interdict.

enterdit(e: var. of interdite, *Obs.*

enterduce: var. of interdice, *Obs.*

entere, obs. form of entire.

entered ('ɛntəd), *ppl. a.* [f. enter *v.* + -ed¹.] In various senses of the verb, *e.g.*: That has gone or advanced within; that a person, etc. has gone into; that has been placed on a register.

1534 Ld. Berners *Gold. Bk. M. Aurel.* (1546) M iij, A lorde of noble bloude, and somewhat entred in age. **1796** Coleridge *Ode Departing Year* i, Ere yet the entered cloud foreclosed my sight. **1887** *Pall Mall G.* 4 Aug. 2/1 The entered vassal..supposed by a legal fiction still to be the holder of the estate.

enterengender: see enter- *pref.*

enterer ('ɛntərə(r)). [f. enter *v.* + -er.]

1. One who goes or comes into.

1590 Spenser *F.Q.* iii. xii. 42 Those dreadfull flames.. That erst all entrers wont [*v.r.* won] so cruelly to scorch. *a* **1617** Hieron *Wks.* (1619) I. 11 The entrers into this gate of life. **1760** J. Scott *Elegy* iv. (1786) 45 The hope-flushed ent'rer on the stage of life. **1858** R. S. Surtees *Ask Mamma* v. 16 On went the vehicle, leaving the enterer to settle into a seat by its shaking.

†**2.** One who is being initiated. *Obs.*

1565 Jewel *Def. Apol.* (1611) 147 Beginners, or Enterers of the Faith, called Catechumeni. **1612** Brinsley *Lud. Lit.* iii. 18 If any require any other little booke meet to enter children; the Schoole of Vertue is one of the principall, and easiest for the first enterers.

3. One who 'enters' for a race, etc.

1746 *Brit. Mag.* 48 A constant Enterer at New-market Races.

enteres, var. of entresse, entrance.

enterfa(i)re, -feir, -fire, obs. ff. INTERFERE *v.*

†**enter'feat.** *Obs.* Also 7 interfeat. [ad. Fr. *entrefaite*, f. *entrefaire* to do (something) between or mutually, f. *entre* (see ENTER- *pref.*) + *faire* to do.] *pl.* Deeds (of arms) on both sides.

1614 RALEIGH *Hist. World* III. 139 The varietie of which enter-feates was such that the Thebans themselves were drawne by the losse of the haven of Corinth to sue for peace. *a* **1662** HEYLIN *Laud* II. 465 During which Interfeats of Arms, and Exchange of Pens.

enterflow, obs. form of INTERFLOW.

enterglance, -grave, etc.: see ENTER- *pref.*

enteric (ɛn'tɛrɪk), *a.* and *sb. Anat.* and *Path.* [ad. Gr. ἐντερικ-ός, f. ἔντερον an intestine.] **A.** *adj.* Of or pertaining to the intestines. ***enteric fever***: typhoid fever.

1869 E. A. PARKES *Pract. Hygiene* (ed. 3) 541 The fatal cases of 'continued fever' are from enteric (typhoid) fever. **1878** BELL *Gegenbauer's Comp. Anat.* 112 The enteric cavity. *Ibid.* 523 These plexuses are distributed on the enteric tube.

B. *sb.* Enteric fever.

1900 *Westm. Gaz.* 31 Jan. 5/2 The preventive inoculation for enteric. **1926** W. R. INGE *Lay Thoughts* 99 Two of the worst scourges, enteric and tetanus.

entering ('ɛntərɪŋ), *vbl. sb.* [f. ENTER *v.* + -ING[1].]

1. a. The action of the vb. ENTER in various senses.

c **1385** CHAUCER *L.G.W.* 2139 *Ariadne*, His dwellynge Right faste bi the dore at his entrynge. **1388** WYCLIF *1 Kings* xvi. 4 The eldere men of the citee..camen to hym..and seiden, Whether thin entryng is pesible? **1526** *Pilgr. Perf.* (W. de W. 1531) 274 In the entrynge of the vij dayes iourney of this pilgrimage of perfeccyon. **1553** LATIMER *Serm. Lord's Pr.* II. 3 'Our Father'. These words pertain not to the petitions, they be but an entering. **1653** URQUHART *Rabelais* I. iv, In the entering of the spring. **1702** *Lond. Gaz.* No. 3839/4 The Horses to be kept in that Parish from the Entring to the Running. **1714** STRINGER (*title*), The Experienc'd Huntsman..with directions concerning the Breeding and Entring of Hounds. **1842** H. E. MANNING *Serm.* (1848) I. i. 3 The entering in of sin proves the presence of an Evil Being. **1880** MCCARTHY *Own Times* III. 334 From the entering of Moscow to the arrival at St. Helena.

†**b.** ***to give entering to***: to admit. *Obs.*

1491 CAXTON *Vitas Patr.* (W. de W. 1495) II. 192 a/2, In the mornyng gyuyng to hym entrynge he sayd to hym.

†**2.** The place where one enters; an entrance; a door, etc. Of a bodily organ: An opening. *Obs.*

1382 WYCLIF *Ezek.* viii. 5 The ydol of envye in that entrynge. *c* **1540** BOORDE *The boke for to Lerne* B iij a, The gate howse in the mydse of the fronte entrynge into the place. **1541** R. COPLAND *Guydon's Quest. Chirurg.*, It [testis fellis] hath two entrynges or neckes betwene whiche is a dystaunce.

3. *Attrib.*, as ***entering-breach, -clerk, -door, -landmark, -room, -stone***; also *Naut.* with reference to the means of entrance into a vessel, as ***entering-hatchway, -ladder, -port, -rope***; and *Mech.* in the names of certain tools, as ***entering-chisel, -file***; **entering edge** *Aeronaut.*, that edge of a surface which is the front edge in flight; now called *leading edge*.

1562 PHAËR *Æneid* IX. B b iiij b, Some seeke their *entryng breach on skalyng ladders clambring quicke. **1701** *Lond. Gaz.* No. 3723/4 Whereby *Entring-clerks and others may be furnished with proper Words. **1723** *Ibid.* No. 6191/2 Each Horse..paying..Half a Crown to the entring Clerk. **1886** *Pall Mall G.* 29 Apr. 2/1 Chained to the desk of an entering clerk. **1632** LITHGOW *Trav.* VIII. (1682) 353 The chiefest Mosque in it..having thirty four *entring Doors. **1908** H. MAXIM *Artif. & Nat. Flight* vii. 100 Our planes must have a certain length of *entering edge—that is, the length of the front edge must bear a certain relation to the load lifted. **1626** CAPT. SMITH *Accid. Yng. Seamen* 13 An *entring ladder. **1853** KANE *Grinnell Exp.* xxxi. (1856) 272 This cape is the great *entering landmark of the northern shores of Lancaster Sound. **1758** J. BLAKE *Plan Mar. Syst.* 2 The *entring ports. **1830** MARRYAT *King's Own* vii, Out of the larboard entering-port. **1886** *Daily News* 20 Oct. 6/2 The huge press that stood in the *entering room..went for a beggarly six shillings. **1627** CAPT. SMITH *Seaman's Gram.* vi. 27 The *Entering rope is tied by the ships side, to hold by as you goe vp the Entering ladder, cleats, or wailes. **1596-7** S. FINCHE in Ducarel *Hist. Croydon* (1783) 153 b, There is space..for a *enteringe stone of eache side.

'entering, *ppl. a.* [f. ENTER *v.* + -ING[2].] That enters; coming or going in; †beginning.

1483 CAXTON *Gold. Leg.* 99/2 The next moneth of august the thirde day entryng. **1594** SOUTHWELL *M. Magd. Fun. Teares* 198 To her now entring and never-ending pleasures. **1633** P. FLETCHER *Purple Isl.* v. xlvi, Receives the ent'ring sounds. **1666** DRYDEN *Ann. Mirab.* cxxix, Grim death.. urges entering billows as they flow. **1795** SOUTHEY *Joan of Arc* IX. 260 Nor heard the coming courser's sounding hoof, Nor entering footstep. **1855** MACAULAY *Hist. Eng.* III. 57 Streams of entering and departing courtiers.

enteritis (ɛntə'raɪtɪs). *Path.* [f. Gr. ἔντερον + -ITIS.] Inflammation of the bowels; *esp.* of the small intestines; usually understood of the acute rather than the chronic form.

1808 *Med. Jrnl.* XIX. 276 Those patients..were very liable to them [febrile affections] in the form of Enteritis. **1878** HABERSHON *Dis. Abdomen* 4 Pain..of a very intense form..in enteritis.

enterkiss: see ENTER- *pref.*

†**enter'know, inter'know,** *v. Obs.* [f. ENTER-, INTER- + KNOW *v.*; after Fr. *s'entreconnaître.*] *trans.* To know (one another) mutually; to know and be known by (a person). Hence **enter'knowing** *vbl. sb.*

1603 FLORIO *Montaigne* II. xviii. (1632) 376 If that [our word] faile us..we enterknow one another no longer. **1652** BP. HALL *Invis. World* Pref., I have desired..to enterknow my good God, and his blessed Angels and Saints. *Ibid.* II. iv, Why should we abridge our souls more than them of the comfort of our interknowing?

†**enter'knowledge.** *Obs.* In mod. editions and Dicts. inter-. [f. ENTER- + KNOWLEDGE; cf. prec.] Mutual knowledge.

a **1626** BACON *New Atl.* (1650) 11 All Nations have Enterknowledge one of another, either by Voyage into Forraine Parts, or by Strangers that come to them.

enterlace, obs. form of INTERLACE.

†**enter'lade,** *v. Obs. rare*$^{-1}$. [? misprint for *enterlace*, as in later editions; or var. of *enterlard.*]

1545 RAYNOLD *Womans Booke* 18 They [the vessels] begin to intermingle, enbrade, and enterlade each other.

enterlard, -league: see INTER-.

enterlend, -love: see ENTER- *pref.*

†**enter'lesse,** *v. Obs. rare*$^{-1}$. [a. OF. *entrelesse-r, -laisser* to omit, f. *entre-* (see ENTER-*pref.*) + *laisser* to leave.] *trans.* To omit.

1548 HALL *Chron.* (1809) 184 Abstinence of War was concluded betwene the Kyng of Englande & the Duchesse of Burgoyne (Enterlessyng the Duke and his name).

enterline, obs. form of INTERLINE.

enterlude, obs. form of INTERLUDE.

enterly, var. of ENTIRELY.

†**en'term,** *v. Obs. rare*$^{-1}$. In 7 entearm. [f. EN-[1] + TERM *v.*] To apply a term to; to name.

1607 WALKINGTON *Opt. Glass* 108 The receptacle of choler entearmed the gall.

entermarriage, -meddle, etc.: see IN-.

†**enter'meene,** *v. Obs. rare.* [Of uncertain formation; perh. f. ENTER- + MEAN *sb.* community, participation; but cf. OF. *entremener* to lead between.] *intr.* ? To meddle, interfere.

c **1449** PECOCK *Repr.* 50 Sporiorie and Cutellerie entermeeneden and enterfereden with goldsmyth craft.

entermell, var. of INTERMELL, *Obs.*

entermes: see ENTREMESS. *Obs.*

†**enter'mete,** *v. Obs.* Forms: 3-5 enter-, entreme(t)te(n, 3 entermitti, 4-5 entremet, 5 entre-, entromytte. Also 5 intremet, 6 intermete; and see INTERMIT, INTROMIT. [a. OF. *entremetre* (mod. *entremettre*), repr. two distinct Lat. formations, *intermittĕre* (cf. Sp. *entremeter*, It. *intermettere*) to interrupt, discontinue, in late L. also to put (something) between, and *intrōmittĕre* (cf. Sp. *entrometer*, It. *intromettere*) to send or admit within, introduce; f. *inter* between, *intrō* within + *mittĕre* to send. In ME. the word was adopted as refl. and intr. with sense 'to introduce oneself, meddle'; in early mod. Eng. the sense 'interpose (something, or oneself)' was taken up from Fr., but rarely occurs. The verbs INTERMIT, INTROMIT, adapted from the original Lat. forms, were formerly often used in the senses of *entremete*, of which they may therefore to some extent be regarded as refashioned forms; now, however, they are used only in senses directly due to their Latin etymology.]

1. *refl.* To concern or occupy oneself, intermeddle, take part; to have dealings or intercourse. Const. *in, of, with.* Also, to set oneself, undertake *to* (do something).

a **1225** *Ancr. R.* 172 Heo entermeteð hire of þinges wiðuten. *a* **1300** *Cursor M.* 7403 (Cott.) O þe kingrike al gouerning He [Dauid] entir-mett him in na dede [*Trin. MS.* he entermeted him of no þing in dede]. *Ibid.* 8759 He [Salomon] can him entermet þe temple mak. *c* **1400** *Rom. Rose* 5949 She is neither so fool ne nyce, To entremete hir of sich vice. **1406** HOCCLEVE *Misrule* 440 Right wole eek, that I me entremete. *c* **1430** *Pilgr. Lyf Manhode* III. xxix. (1869) 151 The hand..entermeteth hire to taste and to visite so ofte the tunge. *c* **1440** HYLTON *Scala Perf.* (W. de W. 1494) III. ix, To..intermette the with worldly besynes. **1485** MALORY *Arthur* XVI. xv, Yf ye entermete [**1634** intermit] yow in this I shall slee you. **1490** CAXTON *Eneydos* xxiii. 87 All thartes and scyences magicque wherof this lady and prestresse entromytteteth [*read* entromytteth] herself. *c* **1500** *Melusine* 69 That none of us shall entremete hym to doo that ye spek of. **1517** in Turner *Sel. Rec. Oxf.* 17 All those that entremetyde them of merchantyse should be taxed.

b. *intr.* for *refl.*

a **1300** *Floriz & Bl.* 204 Ne þer nis non so riche king þat dorste entermeten of eni such þing. *c* **1300** *Beket* 1253 Lete him iworthe so Than entermitti of holi churche. *a* **1420** HOCCLEVE *De Reg. Princ.* 1089 Our Lorde God wolde entermete Of no richesse. *c* **1449** PECOCK *Repr.* I. 145 To be forbode from entermeting with the Bible. **1467** in *Eng. Gilds* (1870) 404 That non seriaunt name nor entremet of the seid eleccion. *c* **1475** *Partenay* 215 He..loue of al shal haue wher he entermet. **1485** MALORY *Arthur* X. xxvi, The kyng.. badde hym entermete [**1634** intermeet] with hym self and with his wyf and of his knyghtes. **1490** CAXTON *Eneydos* 3 Yf ony man wyll enter-mete in redyng of hit. **1491** —— *Vitas Patr.* (W. de W. 1495) I To entremete to recyte..suche hystoryes. **1494** FABYAN VI. clxiv. 158 That nother ye one nor the other shulde intremet with the foresayd londes. **1548** HALL *Chron.* (1809) 88 It longeth not to clerkes to intermete of them.

c. *trans.* To meddle with, be occupied upon. *rare.*

1393 GOWER *Conf.* I. 161 My thought will entermete him sone. **1502** ARNOLDE *Chron.* (1811) 38 Of him that entyrmeten the thyngis aboue sayd.

2. To mix, alternate.

c **1530** in *Pol. Rel. & Love Poems* (1866) 43 Entirmet this with woo And gladnes.

3. To put (oneself) *between.*

a **1541** WYATT *Poems* in *Tottell's Misc.* (Arb.) 74 The hylles that doth them entermete Twene me, and those shene lightes.

Hence **enter'meting** *vbl. sb.* and *ppl. a.*

c **1375** *Sc. Lives Saints, Petrus* 311 Four concubynes he.. gerte refuse þe entremetynge Forthir till have with Agrippine. **1377** LANGL. *P. Pl.* B. XI. 406 Ac for thine entermetyng here artow forsake. *c* **1400** *Test. Love* III. (1560) 296 b/2 Thyne entremeting maners into stedfastnesse shullen be chaunged. *c* **1449** PECOCK *Repr.* II. xii. 220 We muste haue manye othere entermetingis with him than the entermeting of remembring oonli. **1583** T. STOCKER *Trag. Hist. Civ. warres* II. 15 By the entermeetyng and intercession..of the Lordes here vnder named, etc.

†**enter'meter.** *Obs.* [ad. Fr. *entremetteur*, f. *entremettre*: see prec.] A broker, mercantile intermediary.

1491 CAXTON *Vitas Patr.* (W. de W. 1495) II. 260 a/1, He was a grete marchaunt and entermeter.

entermine: see ENTER- *pref.*

entermingle, obs. form of INTERMINGLE.

†**enter'mise.** *Obs.* [a. Fr. *entremise*, f. *entremettre* to place in the midst, interfere, f. *entre* (see ENTER-) + *mettre* to put.]

a. Occupation, business. **b.** Interposition, intervention, mediation.

1490 CAXTON *Eneydos* 55 Withstandynge the grete entermyse and besy occupacion that they had In hande. **1624** *Brief Inform. Affairs Palatinate* 36 Hee was offered a Treatie of Peace, by the entermise of the Elector. **1638** tr. *Balzac's Lett.* III. (1654) 112 By the entermise of words.

entermix, obs. form of INTERMIX.

entero- ('ɛntərəʊ; before two unstressed syllables ɛntə'rɒ), (before a vowel sometimes reduced to *enter-*), combining form of Gr. ἔντερο-ν intestine, in many compounds of mod. formation, occurring in Biology, Pathology, etc. The most important only are here given; as **enterade'nography** *Anat.* [see ADENOGRAPHY], 'a description of the intestinal glands' (*Syd. Soc. Lex.*); **enterade'nology** *Anat.* and *Phys.* [see ADENOLOGY], 'an account of the intestinal glands' (*Syd. Soc. Lex.*); **ente'ralgia** *Med.* [Gr. ἄλγος pain], pain in the intestines, colic; **,ente'rectomy** *Surg.* [-ECTOMY], removal of a portion of the intestine; **,entero-anasto'mosis** *Surg.*, the joining of two portions of an intestine so as to make a continuous tube; **entero'biasis** *Path.* [-IASIS], infection of the intestines by pinworms of the genus *Enterobius*; **'entero,cele** *Surg.* [Gr. κήλη tumour], a hernial tumour whose contents are intestine; hence **entero'celic** *a.*; **,entero'chlorophyll** *Chem.*, a form of chlorophyll present in some animals; **entero'coccus** *Bacteriol.* [ad. F. *enterocoque* (Thiercelin 1899, in *Compt. rend. Soc. Biol.* V. 55)], one of several species of streptococcus found in the intestine; **'enterocœle, -cœl** *Zool.*, (part of) a cœlom or body-cavity that is or has been in communication with the archenteron; hence **entero'cœlic, -ous** *adjs.*; **,enteroco'litis** *Path.*, inflammation of the small intestine and colon; **entero'crinin, en'terocrinin** *Biochem.* [Gr. κρίνειν to separate: cf. ENDOCRINE], an intestinal hormone that stimulates digestion; **,entero'dynia** *Med.* [Gr. ὀδύνη pain] = *enteralgia*; **,entero-ente'rostomy** *Surg.*, an operation for forming a permanent opening between two non-continuous portions of the intestine; **,enteroe'piplocele** *Surg.* [see EPIPLOCELE], a hernia in which portions of intestine and omentum are both protruded; **,entero'gastrocele** *Surg.*, a term for an abdominal hernia containing intestine; **entero'gastrone** *Biochem.*, a humoral agent

from the intestinal mucosa that retards gastric secretion and motor activity; **ente'rography**, 'a description of the intestines' (*Syd. Soc. Lex.*); **ˌentero-he'patic** *a. Med.*, relating to the intestines and liver; **ˌentero-hepa'titis** *Med.* and *Vet.*, inflammation of the intestines and liver, *spec.* in gallinaceous birds; = BLACK-HEAD 5; **ˌentero'hydrocele** *Surg.* [see HYDROCELE], 'intestinal hernia conjoined with hydrocele' (*Syd. Soc. Lex.*); **ˌentero'kinase** *Biochem.*, an enzyme found in the intestinal mucous membrane that brings about the conversion of trypsinogen to trypsin; **'enteroˌlite**, altered form of **'enteroˌlith** *Path.* [Gr. λίθος a stone], a stony concretion in the stomach or intestinal canal of animals, and occasionally of man; **ente'rology** *Anat.* [+ -LOGY], 'a treatise on, or the consideration of the history of, the intestines' (*Syd. Soc. Lex.*); **entero'nephric** *a. Zool.*, designating a nephridial system in which the septal nephridia open into the intestine; **ente'ropathy** *Path.* [Gr. -παθεια, f. πάθος suffering], 'intestinal disorder or disease' (*Syd. Soc. Lex.*); **'enteroˌplasty** *Surg.* [+ Gr. πλαστ-ής fashioner + -Y], the restoration by plastic operation of a solution of continuity of the intestine; **ˌentero'ptosis** *Path.* [Gr. πτῶσις falling], abnormally low position of the small intestines; **ˌente'rorrhaphy** *Surg.* [Gr. ραφή suture], the sewing up of a wound in the intestines; **'enterospasm** *Path.*, spasmodic contraction of the intestine; **ente'rostomy** *Surg.* [Gr. στόμα mouth], the operation for making a permanent opening into the intestine; **'enterotome** [Gr. τομίς knife], an instrument for opening the intestinal canal; **ente'rotomy** *Surg.* [Gr. -τομια cutting], the opening of the intestine to release its contents, as sometimes in hernia, or to remove a foreign body; **ˌenteroto'xæmia** *Vet.*, toxæmia caused by disease of the small intestine; **entero'toxin** *Med.*, a toxin originating in the intestine, causing food poisoning; *spec.* a cytotoxin; **Entero-Vioform** *Pharm.*, a proprietary name for a preparation of Clioquinol formerly used for the prevention and treatment of (travellers') diarrhoea.

1830 J. P. KAY in *N. of England Med. & Surg. Jrnl.* 1 Nov. 220 (*title*) Gastralgia and *enteralgia, or morbid sensibility of the stomach and bowels. **1840** A. TWEEDIE *Syst. Pract. Med.* IV. 152 The treatment of enteralgia may be commenced by insuring the removal of any cause of irritation within the canal. **1897** *Trans. Amer. Pediatric Soc.* IX. 119 These cases are common in the practice of every physician and are commonly diagnosed as 'gastralgia' or 'enteralgia'. **1877** L. A. STIMSON tr. *Ziemssen's Cycl. Pract. Med.* VII. 662 In case..the volvulus cannot be withdrawn, ..it has been recommended to excise it completely (*enterectomy), and then..to insert the upper end through an opening into the cæcum (Hacken), and to ligate the other: entero-anastomosis. **1908** *Practitioner* Mar. 368 To..wait for an improvement in the patient's condition to perform an enterectomy. **1877** *Entero-anastomosis [see *enterectomy* above]. **1908** *Practitioner* Sept. 459 Entero-anastomosis without resection. **1930** *Q. Cumul. Index Medicus* VII. 894/2 (*title*) Diagnosis and epidemiology of *enterobiasis. **1970** PASSMORE & ROBSON *Compan. Med. Stud.* II. xix. 30 Communal living, infrequent bathing and contaminated clothing combine to produce epidemics of enterobiasis. **1661** LOVELL *Hist. Anim. & Min.* 62 Pounded with honey it [the ashes of a Hare] helps the *enterocele. **1878** T. BRYANT *Pract. Surg.* I. 646. **1736** BAILEY, *Enterocelick. **1883** C. A. MACMUNN in *Proc. R. Soc.* XXXV. 133 It..can be detected in the bile of specimens of *Helix* after a six months' fast; for this colouring-matter, since it is found in the appendages of the enteron, the name *enterochlorophyll is proposed. **1888** ROLLESTON & JACKSON *Forms Anim. Life* (ed. 2) 117 The secretion of the liver is acid, and has been found to have a diastatic and a peptic action in *H. pomatia*. It contains entero-chlorophyl in *Helix pomatia*. **1908** PARK & WILLIAMS *Pathogenic Micro-Organisms* (ed. 3) xx. 252 **Enterococcus.* —Thiercelin in 1903 described the enterococcus proteiformis (Fig. 93) as occurring as a coccus. *Ibid.* (*caption*), Fig. 93 Represents the gradation of the Enterococcus (Thiercelin) from the apparent bacillary forms to the coccus without a capsule. **1925** R. E. BUCHANAN *Gen. Syst. Bacteriol.* III. 301 *Enterococcus*, a casual name given by various writers to cocci found in the intestinal tract. **1955** *Sci. News Let.* 19 Feb. 118/1 A member of a streptococcus germ family is now blamed for causing tooth decay. Studies showing that this strep., called an enterococcus, caused tooth decay in rats [etc.]. **1877** *Enterocœle [see ENDODERMAL *a.*]. **1951** G. DE BEER *Vertebrate Zool.* (ed. 2) xix. 238 In *Amphioxus*, the cœlomic cavities of the somites, when they arise, are in open communication with the gut, and are hence known as enterocœls. **1950** J. Z. YOUNG *Life of Vertebrates* iii. 48 In earlier chordates..the cœlom is continuous with the archenteron and is said to be an enterocoele. **1888** *Nature* 2 Feb. 334/2 The 'Schlauchförmiger Kanal'..being *enterocœlic in origin. **1888** ROLLESTON & JACKSON *Forms Anim. Life* (ed. 2) 592 The anterior enterocoelic pouch. **1964** PARKER & HASWELL *Text-bk. Zool.* (ed. 7) II. 61 The cavities in these [folds], continuous with the archenteron, are the beginnings of the enterocœlic system. **1875** E. R. LANKESTER in *Q. Jrnl. Microsc. Sci.* XV. 165 You have..in the former an '*entero-cœlous' condition, to use Professor Huxley's terminology. **1857** DUNGLISON *Med. Lex.* (ed. 15), *Enterocolitis. **1886** *Buck's Handbk. Med. Sci.* II. 435/1 In entero-colitis the inflammation is mostly confined to the lower end of the ileum. **1964** M. HYNES *Med. Bacteriol.* (ed. 8) xi. 145 It [*sc. Staph. aureus*]..can cause a very dangerous enterocolitis when it invades an intestine sterilized by antibiotic therapy. **1938** E. S. NASSET in *Amer. Jrnl. Physiol.* CXXVIII. 481 The name **enterocrinin* (intestinal secretagogue) is proposed for this hormone. **1957** *Encycl. Brit.* VII. 380/2 The existence of a hormone, enterocrinin, has been demonstrated and a highly active, crystalline product has been obtained. Injection of this hormone produces an outpouring of intestinal juice. **1848** DUNGLISON *Med. Lex.* (ed. 7), *Enterodynia. **1870** GARROD & BAXTER *Mat. Med.* (ed. 3) 406 Painful affections of the stomach and duodenum, as in gastrodynia, enterodynia. **1896** A. E. MAYLARD *Treat. Surg. Alim. Canal* lxvi. 543 *Entero-enterostomy (short-circuiting).—This operation is performed when it is impossible to remove the diseased portion of the bowel. **1955** R. MAINGOT *Abdominal Operations* (ed. 3) xxix. 655 Entero-enterostomy is then carried out proximal to these anastomoses in order to deflect the gastric contents into the distal jejunum. **1736** BAILEY, *Enteroepiplocele. **1878** T. BRYANT *Pract. Surg.* I. 646 When both intestine and omentum occupy the sac [they form an] entero-epiplocele. **1930** KOSAKA & LIM in *Proc. Soc. Exper. Biol. & Med.* XXVII. 891 An inhibitory agent may be formed in the mucosa of both the small and large intestine as the result of contact with fat... The name *Entero-gastrone (derived from *entero/n*, *gastr/on* and *chal/one*) is suggested for the gastric inhibitory agent. **1937** *Amer. Jrnl. Physiol.* CXVIII. 475 A method is described for the preparation of an extract (entero-gastrone) from the duodenal mucosa of hogs, which exhibits an inhibitory action on gastric mobility and secretion. **1961** *Lancet* 19 Aug. 395/2 The absorption of large amounts of urobilinogen from the gut into the *entero-hepatic circulation which were then re-excreted by the liver. **1895** *U.S. Dept. Agric. Bull.* VIII. 7 (*heading*) An infectious disease among turkeys caused by protozoa (infectious *entero-hepatitis). **1900** DORLAND *Med. Dict.* 233/2 *Enterohepatitis*, inflammation of the bowel and liver. **1906** [see BLACK-HEAD 5]. **1959** *Times* 7 Dec. (Agric. Suppl.) p. vii/4 Blackhead disease (enterohepatitis). **1902** W. H. THOMPSON tr. *Pawlow's Work of Digestive Glands* ix. 160 We had, therefore, discovered a ferment, not for this or that constituent of the food, but a ferment of other ferments. I propose to give it the name of **Enterokinase.* **1907** Enterokinase [see TRYPSIN]. **1923** T. R. PARSONS *Fund. Bio-Chem.* iii. 32 This enterokinase is an example of the group of substances termed 'kinases', which have the power of activating the mother substances or precursors of enzymes. **1961** W. J. E. JESSOP *Fearon's Introd. Biochem.* (ed. 4) xiv. 223 In acid solution, pH5 to 6, the conversion of trypsinogen to trypsin is catalysed by the intestinal enzyme, enterokinase. **1884** *Syd. Soc. Lex.*, *Enterolith. **1721** BAILEY, *Enterology. **1919** K. N. BAHL in *Q. Jrnl. Microsc. Sci.* LXIV. I. 101 The elaborate '*entero-nephric' type of the nephridial system in Pheretima. **1963** R. P. DALES *Annelids* i. 33 The enteronephric system is apparently related to water conservation. **1897** *Enteroptosis [see VISCERO-]. **1907** *Practitioner* Dec. 771 Patients with very lax abdominal walls and marked enteroptosis. **1949** H. W. FLOREY *Antibiotics* I. i. 55 One of the most ingenious uses to which yeast has been put was due to Günzburg (1896), who proposed to treat enteroptosis with it. **1807** MORRIS & KENDRICK *Edin. Med. Dict.*, **Entero-raphia*, the suture of a gut when wounded. **1889** *Buck's Handbk. Med. Sci.* VIII. 299/1 The immediate restoration of the continuity of the gut by circular enterorrhaphy. **1897** H. ILLOWAY *Constipation* viii. 88 *Enterospasm occurs most frequently in gastric and intestinal indigestions. **1908** *Practitioner* Aug. 219 A localised enterospasm. **1923** P. L. MUMMERY *Dis. Rectum & Colon* xvii. 408 In view of..the presence of blood in the stools, it seemed probable that the enterospasm was set up by an ulcer in the colon. **1878** J. ASHHURST *Princ. & Pract. Surg.* (ed. 2) xxxviii. 747 *Enterostomy..to provide an opening for the introduction of food into the small intestine, has been suggested by Surmay. **1948** H. & J. DEVINE *Surg. Colon & Rectum* xi. 143 An enterostomy is a great affliction: the liquid faeces of the small intestine pour on to the abdominal wall, irritate and excoriate it,..and thus make the patient almost a complete invalid. **1842** DUNGLISON *Med. Lex.* (ed. 3) 267/1 *Enterotome. **1882** WILDER & GAGE *Anat. Technol.* i. 70 The enterotome supplied in post-mortem cases is a pair of long scissors, one blade of which is enlarged and rounded, and projects beyond the other so as to precede it in opening an intestine. **1948** H. & J. DEVINE *Surg. Colon & Rectum* xxi. 233 Should the small bowel be included in the enterotome the patient will complain of severe pain. **1878** T. BRYANT *Pract. Surg.* I. 627 Of these [means] '*enterotomy' is most applicable. **1932** H. W. BENNETTS in *Coun. Sci. & Ind. Res. Bull.* LVII. 10 In order to remove confusion, the name infectious *entero-toxaemia is herewith adopted for the Western Australian disease. **1957** *Times* 3 Sept. 15/5 Enterotoxaemia often occurs when the flock is suddenly moved to better pasture. **1936** *Jrnl. Infectious Dis.* LVIII. 321 The ability to produce an *enterotoxin may be restored to certain food poisoning organisms which have lost this power by serial transfers on starch agar. **1964** M. HYNES *Med. Bacteriol.* (ed. 8) xi. 145 Enterotoxin-producing strains are a common cause of food poisoning. [**1900** *Trade Marks Jrnl.* 15 Aug. 856 *Vioform...* Basle Chemical Works,..Bâle, Switzerland.] **1957** *Official Gaz.* (U.S. Patent Office) 7 May TM12/1 Ciba Pharmaceutical Products, Inc...**Entero-Vioform...* For antidiarrheal agent. First use Apr. 1, 1955. **1958** *Trade Marks Jrnl.* 25 June 644/2 *Entero-Vioform*..for use in the treatment of intestinal complaints. CIBA Limited..Basle, Switzerland. **1959** L. DURRELL in *Sunday Times* 27 Dec. 13/1 A single tube of magic Enterovioform..will enable one to throw off all grim forebodings about melons and grapes. **1965** 'M. BRETT' *Plague of Dragons* iii. 31 'I expect my men to look after themselves.' 'In that case I'll pack enterovioform.' **1977** B. PYM *Quartet in Autumn* v. 41 'Enterovioform,' said Letty. He smiled pityingly, 'All those English on package tours on the Costa Brava may find it helpful, but my case is rather different.' **1983** *Fortune* 11 July 94/1 Japanese courts in 1978 ruled that clioquinol, a drug Ciba-Geigy introduced and sold under the name Entero-Vioform as a cure for diarrhea, caused a disease of the spinal and optic nerves called subacute myelo-optico-neuropathy (SMON).

enterodelous (ˌɛntɛrəʊ'diːləs), *a. Biol.* [f. mod.L. *enterodēla* sb. pl., f. ENTERO- + Gr. δῆλ-ος manifest + -OUS.] Having an intestine plainly visible; applied to those Polygastria that have a perfect intestinal tube, terminated by a mouth and anus.

1847-9 TODD *Cycl. Anat.* IV. 3/2 The Enterodelous Polygastria.

enteroid (ɛntə'rɔɪd), *a. Biol.* [f. Gr. ἔντερ-ον + -OID.] Resembling a bowel.

1835-6 TODD *Cycl. Anat.* I. 171/1 An enteroid vessel.

enteron ('ɛntərɒn). *Anat.* Pl. **entera**. [mod.L., a. Gr. ἔντερον an intestine.] The alimentary canal; the intestine or gut.

1842 DUNGLISON *Med. Lex.* (ed. 3) 267/1 Enteron. **1878** F. J. BELL tr. *Gegenbaur's Comp. Anat.* iii. 165 Separate glands are almost always absent from the mid-gut of the Vermes, but the epithelium is generally found to be different from the epithelia of the other divisions of the enteron. **1880** *Encycl. Brit.* XII. 548/1 By the formation of a mouth to the sac, the enteron acquires the functions of a digestive retort. **1927** HALDANE & HUXLEY *Anim. Biol.* xii. 268 The mouth leads into a cavity called the coelenteron, because it fulfils the functions both of the coelom and of the enteron or gut of higher forms. **1963** BORRADAILE & POTTS *Invertebrata* (ed. 4) v. 155 The enteron or cavity of the colony [of polyps] is continuous and common to all its members.

enteropneustal (ˌɛntərəʊp'njuːstəl), *a.* [f. Gr. ἔντερο-ν intestine + πνευστ-, f. πνέειν to breathe + -AL[1].] Of or pertaining to the *Enteropneusta*, worm-like animals having the breathing apparatus borne on the intestinal canal.

1877 HUXLEY *Anat. Inv. An.* xii. 674 *note*, Either Vertebrate, Enteropneustal or Tunicate branchiæ.

enterovirus (ˌɛntərəʊ'vaɪərəs, 'ɛntərəʊˌvaɪərəs). *Path.* [f. ENTERO- + VIRUS 2.] Any of a group of RNA viruses which primarily infect the lymphoid tissue of the alimentary tract but which may also involve the nervous system or other tissues, causing poliomyelitis or other diseases. Hence **entero'viral** *a.*

1957 *Amer. Jrnl. Publ. Health* XLVII. 1556/1 The National Foundation for Infantile Paralysis, recognizing that the poliomyelitis, Coxsackie, and ECHO viruses all inhabit the alimentary tract as well as share other properties, has changed the name of its Committee on the ECHO Viruses to the Committee on the Enteroviruses. **1961** *Lancet* 29 July 248/2 The enteroviruses such as poliomyelitis and Coxsackie. *Ibid.* 23 Sept. 684/2 Our methods of stool extraction were suitable for enteroviral isolations.

enterowe: see ENTER- *pref.*

†**enter'parlance.** Also 7 in-. [ad. AF. *entreparlaunce*, f. *entreparler*: see next.] A conference.

1603 KNOLLES *Hist. Turks* (1621) 954 The first enterparlance of peace betwixt the Persians and the Turks. **1625** *Modell Wit* 61 b, In which time of so serious interparlance. **1643** *Three Letters* 41 They would apply themselves unto him for an enterparlance.

†**enter'parle,** *v. Obs.* Also 7 **interparle**. [ad. F. *entreparler*, f. *entre* between + *parler* to speak.] *intr.* To talk mutually, confer.

1536 *St. Papers Hen. VIII*, II. 343 Enterparlling togithers by a mediatour. **1567** TURBERV. in Chalmers *Eng. Poets* II. 642/1 And hope..To enterparle with thee my Friend.

Hence **'enterparle** *sb.*, the action of the verb; a conference, parley. **enter'parling** *vbl. sb.*, (*a*) taking part in a conversation; (*b*) intercession.

1597 DANIEL *Civ. Wares* II. xxiii, From Lancaster.. Arrived Northumberland, as to confer..And therefore doth an enterparle exhort. **1529** MORE *Comf. agst. Trib.* II. Wks. 1170/1 With ofter enterparlyng vpon your parte. **1656** TRAPP *Comm. 1 Tim.* ii. 1 Interparlings with God, either for ourselves..or for others.

†**enter'parley.** *Obs.* Also 6 **inter-**. [f. ENTER- + PARLEY.] A mutual talk; a conference, conversation; also *Mil.* a parley.

1590 LODGE *Euphues Gold. Leg.* in Halliw. *Shaks.* VI. 38 Leaving off these interparleys, you shall hear my last sonnetto. **1594** —— *Wounds Civ. War* v. in Hazl. *Dodsley* VII. 186 The younger Marius..Vouchsaf'd an inter-parley at the last. **1603** FLORIO *Montaigne* I. vi. (1632) 12 During their enter-parlie and businesse about taking hostages. **1620** SHELTON *Quix.* IV. xxx. 237 With that they gave over their Enterparly.

†**enter'part,** *v. Obs. rare*$^{-1}$. In 4 **entrepart-yn**. [a. OF. *entrepartir*: see ENTER- and PART *v.*] *trans.* To share, participate in.

c **1374** CHAUCER *Troylus* I. 592 To entrepartyn wo, as gladly as disport.

†**enter'parten,** *v. Obs.* [? Secondary form of prec.; perh. influenced by *partner*.] *trans.* To share or divide with a partner, or between partners.

Hence **enter'partening** *vbl. sb.*

1561 T. NORTON *Calvin's Inst.* I. 34 He..enterparteneth the gouernment of the world with his Father. *Ibid.* II. 163 By enterpartening of himself with vs. **1553** GRIMALDE *Cicero's Offices* (1556) 8 The enterpartening of mannes life.

†**enter'pen,** *v. Hawking. Obs.* [a. OF. *entrepener*, f. *entre* between + *penne* wing feather.] (See quots.)

1486 *Bk. St. Albans* A vij a, This hawke is entirpenned, that is to say when the federis of the wyngis bene bitwen the

body and the thighis. **1736** BAILEY s.v., A Hawk enterpenneth, that is, she hath her Feathers wrapt up, snarled or intangled.

enterpendant: see INTERPENDENT.

enterpillar: see ENTER- *pref.*

enterpleader, -polish: see INTER-.

enterpone, var. of INTERPONE, *Obs.*

enterpose, -produce: see INTER-.

† **enter'prenant**, *a. Obs.* In 6 enterprenaunt. [a. OF. *entreprenant*, pr. pple. of *entreprendre* to take in hand ENTERPRISE.] Enterprising.

c **1500** *Melusine* 122 The sawdan is hardy and enterprenaunt.

enterpret, form of INTERPRET.

enterprise ('ɛntəpraɪz), *sb.* Forms: 5–6 enter-, entreprys(e, (5 enterprinse), entrepris(e, 6 enterprice, -yce, 6–9 enterprize, 5– enterprise. Also 6–7 interprise, -yse, *Sc.* -yiss, 7 -yze. [a. OFr. *entreprise, -prinse*, f. *entreprendre* to take in hand, undertake, f. *entre* between + *prendre* to take.]

1. A design of which the execution is attempted; a piece of work taken in hand, an undertaking; *chiefly*, and now exclusively, a bold, arduous, or momentous undertaking.

c **1430** *Syr Gener.* (Roxb.) 4310 Whan the Soudon wist of this That thei lost such an entrepris. **1475** *Bk. Noblesse* (1860) 6 Entreprinses and werris taken and founded vppon a just cause. **1530** PALSGR. 868 The great diffyculte of myne entrepryse. **1535** STEWART *Cron. Scot.* II. 185 Met in the middis with mony interpryiss. **1557** PAYNEL *Barclay's Jugurth* 95 b, He proceded in his interprise and purpose. **1603** KNOLLES *Hist. Turks* (1621) 1308 They resolved..to make an enterprise upon some townes of Albania. **1618** E. ELTON *Expos. Romans vii.* (1622) 398 We must not be ignorant of Satan's Enterprizes. **1704** SWIFT *Batt. Bks.* (1711) 261 He..had wander'd long in search of some Enterprize. **1748** *Anson's Voy.* Introd., A Voyage round the World is still considered as an enterprize of a very singular nature. **1814** CHALMERS *Evid. Chr. Revel.* viii. 215 We must restrain the enterprizes of fancy. **1875** HELPS *Ess. Organiz. Daily Life* 132 In those enterprises which we call joint-stock undertakings.

b. *abstr.* Engagement in such undertakings.

1769 *Junius Lett.* iii. 17 You ought to have pointed out some instances of..well-concerted enterprise. **1783** WATSON *Philip III*, II. vi. 151 Times of national enterprize. **1806** BERESFORD in *Lond. Gaz.* 13 Sept. 1213/2 Some of the existing Duties bear too hard on the Enterprize of Commerce. **1829** I. TAYLOR *Enthus.* iv. (1867) 71 Theology offers no field to men fond of intellectual enterprise.

2. Disposition or readiness to engage in undertakings of difficulty, risk, or danger; daring spirit.

1475 *Bk. Noblesse* 20 Was never so worshipfulle an act of entreprise done in suche a case. **1540–54** CROKE *Ps.* (1844) 22 Thyne entrepryse dyd neuer quayle. **1792** BURKE *Heads Consid. Pr. Aff.* Wks. VII. 93 In such [piratical] expeditions enterprise supplies the want of discipline. **1869** FREEMAN *Norm. Conq.* (1876) III. xiv. 332 With an expression of contempt for his lack of enterprise.

†**3.** The action of taking in hand; management, superintendence. *Obs.*

1534 LD. BERNERS *Gold. Bk. M. Aurel.* (1546) D vij b, Some abode there charged with the enterpryse of the sonne. **1803** in Nicolas *Disp. Nelson* (1845) V. 370 The enterprise and conduct of the Fleet devolved on Lord Nelson.

4. Special Comb. **enterprise zone** *Econ.*, a designated zone within an area of high unemployment and low investment, usu. in an inner city, where the government encourages new enterprise by granting financial concessions such as tax and rate relief to businesses.

1978 *Times* 27 June 2/1 A suggestion that '*enterprise zones' should be created in Britain's derelict inner cities.. was made last night by Sir Geoffrey Howe..in a speech to the Bow Group. **1981** *Record* (Columbia, S. Carolina) 31 Aug. D9 Cities would design projects under the 'enterprise zone program' using tax breaks, deregulation or other investment incentives such as job training. **1984** *Daily Tel.* 24 Sept. 17/7 Enterprise zones and the like..have had an imperceptible effect on jobs.

enterprise ('ɛntəpraɪz), *v. arch.* Forms as in sb. [partly f. prec.; partly f. Fr. *entrepris*, pa. pple. of *entreprendre* (see prec.), from which vb. the senses are chiefly taken.]

1. *trans.* To take in hand (a work), take upon oneself (a condition), attempt or undertake (a war, an expedition, etc.), run the risk of or venture upon (danger). *arch.*

1485 MALORY *Arthur* Contents VII. v, How Trystram enterprysed the Batayll to fyght for the trewage of Cornwayl. **1526** *Pilgr. Perf.* (W. de W. 1531) 51 It boldeth hym to..enterpryse without feare suche ieoperdy. **1548–9** (Mar.) *Bk. Com. Prayer, Offices* 13 Matrimonie..is not to bee enterprised.. vnaduisedlye. **1602** PATERICKE tr. *Gentillet agst. Machiavel* 314 Appius could not obtaine the tyrannie which hee had enterprised. **1691** LOCKE *Money* Wks. 1727 II. 89 This was enterprized by a Prince, who could stretch his Prerogative very far upon his People. **1728** WOOLSTON *Disc. Miracles* iv. 55 That the Bearers of the poor man should enterprise a trouble and a difficulty. **1788** COWPER *Corr.* (1824) II. 174 Impossible for Mrs. Unwin to enterprize a cake. **1807** G. CHALMERS *Caledonia* I. I. ii. 57 Roman ambition first enterprized the conquest of the common parent of the British nations. **1871** RUSKIN *Fors Clav.* v. 12 What the *Times* calls 'Railway Enterprise'. You Enterprised a Railroad through the valley.

†**b.** with *inf.* (rarely with *clause*) as obj. *Obs.*

1481 CAXTON *Myrr.* III. xxiv. 193 Them that haue late enterprysed agayn right and reson to make warre. **1523** SKELTON *Garl. Laurel* 388 Maister Chaucer..nobly enterprysed How that our Englysshe myght freshly be ennewed. **1581** MARBECK *Bk. of Notes* 497 Ananias, thou hast enterprised to lye vnto the Holie ghost. **1605** BACON *Adv. Learn.* II. ii. §13 To circle the Earth..was not done nor enterprised till these later times. **1617** HALES *Gold. Rem.* (1688) 7 He therefore enterpris'd to handle this Argument.

†**2.** With personal obj.: **a.** To take in hand, attack. **b.** In *pa. pple.* [after Fr. *entrepris*]: Embarrassed, non-plussed, rendered helpless.

c **1450** *Merlin* xx. 315 Whan the kynge Arthur saugh hem so enterprised. **1480** CAXTON *Ovid's Met.* XII. xviii, I am so moche enterprised of dystresse and anger. *c* **1510** MORE *Picus* Wks. 26 He lieth at hande, and shall vs enterprise. **1513** BRADSHAW *St. Werburge* II. 135 Danes and Norwaies enterprised this lande.

†**3.** *intr.* To make an attempt, undertake an operation, form a design. Of military commanders: To direct operations, make an attack (*upon*). Cf. Fr. *entreprendre sur*. *Obs.*

a **1527** tr. *Machiavelli's Prince* iii. (1883) 25 France..with its own forces alone, had been able to have enterprised upon Naples. **1588** J. UDALL *Diotrephes* (Arb.) 28 Be sure of the court, before you enterprise any other where. **1640** YORKE *Union Hon.* 37 One Robert Huldern..with 15,000 strong enterprized for Yorke. **1651** tr. DE LAS COVERAS *Hist. Don Fenise* 207 He had a design to enterprise upon the honour of his owne Sister. **1701** COLLIER *M. Aurel.* (1726) 296 We should enterprise with a reserve for disappointment. **1732** NEAL *Hist. Purit.* I. 111 It behoved the learned, grave, and godly ministers of Christ to enterprize farther. **1813** SIR R. WILSON *Diary* II. 248 Buonaparte..might, perhaps, enterprize towards Prague.

Hence †'**enterprised** *ppl. a.*, that has been undertaken, ventured upon.

1560 DAUS tr. *Sleidane's Comm.* 193 b, The Duke and the Lantzgraue made aunswere..recyting the causes of this enterprised defence. **1572** R. H. tr. *Lauaterus' Ghostes* (1596) 33 He woulde persist in his enterprised purpose.

enterpriser (ɛntə'praɪzə(r)). [f. ENTERPRISE *v.* + -ER[1].] One who attempts an undertaking. Const. *of, in.* †Also in bad sense, an adventurer.

1523 LD. BERNERS *Froiss.* I. cclxxxiv. 424 A great enterpriser of dedes of armes. **1545** RAYNOLD *Womans Booke* D 2 The gud courages of al honest enterpreyers [*sic*] in those matters & al other. **1577–87** HOLINSHED *Chron.* III. 802/2 The enterprisers of these iusts, was Thomas lord Howard, etc. **1594–5** in Chambers *Dom. Ann. Scot.* I. 259 He was ane simple gentleman, and not ane enterpriser. **1681** *Ess. Peace & Truth Ch.* 17 The Enterprizers of that new Babel. **1711** SHAFTESB. *Charac.* II. §2 (1737) I. 233 The Boast of almost every Enterprizer in the Muses Art. **1748** RICHARDSON *Clarissa* I. xix. 138 The attempts of enterprisers and fortune-seekers. **1830** R. CHAMBERS *Life Jas. I*, I. iii. 93 An enterpriser in the great and hazardous schemes. **1882** W. B. WEEDEN *Social Law Labor* 32 These are not simply undertakers, inter-takers, or enterprisers.

'**enterprising**, *vbl. sb. rare.* [f. ENTERPRISE *v.* + -ING[1].] The action of the vb. ENTERPRISE; the action of undertaking or attempting.

1572 H. MIDDELMORE in Ellis *Orig. Lett.* II. 190 III. 5 In the entirprisinge of which matter I doe wishe, etc. **1652** GAULE *Magastrom.* 24 As to the enterprizing or atchieving of naturall, politicall, and religious actions, etc. **1675** MARVELL *Corr.* Wks. 1872–5 II. 442 His late entirprising to subvert in all manners the libertyes of this city, etc.

enterprising ('ɛntəpraɪzɪŋ), *ppl. a.* Also 7 in-. [f. as prec. + -ING[2].] **a.** That undertakes. **b.** Forward and prompt to undertake. In early use chiefly in bad sense, foolhardy, also ambitious, scheming: now chiefly in favourable sense, full of the spirit of enterprise.

1611 COTGR. s.v. *Fol.*, An enterprizing foole needs little wit. **1672** MARVELL *Reh. Transp.* I. 139 Mr. Bayes is so interprising you know. **1720** DR. WILCOCKS in Ellis *Orig. Lett.* II. 440 IV. 321 The King of Prussia..has a brisk enterprising look. **1776** GIBBON *Decl. & F.* I. 364 Diocletian ..justly dreaded the enterprising spirit of Carausius. **1855** MACAULAY *Hist. Eng.* III. 605 The sagacious Caermarthen and the enterprising Monmouth agreed in blaming these cautious tactics. **1876** J. H. NEWMAN *Hist. Sk.* I. I. i. 36 Marco Polo..was one of a company of enterprising Venetian merchants.

Hence **enter'prisingly** *adv.*

1822 *New Monthly Mag.* V. 298 The claims which he had so enterprisingly advanced. **1887** *Times* 19 Oct. 7/4 Some couple of thousand of the roughest enterprisingly made their way to Trafalgar-square yesterday.

enterre, enterrupt, obs. var. INTER, INTERRUPT.

enterseek, -shew, -shine: see ENTER- *pref.*

entershock: see INTERSHOCK.

entershoulder, -split, -spoil, -suck: see ENTER- *pref.*

entersole: var. of ENTRESOL.

enterspace, -sperse, obs. var. of INTERSPACE, -SPERSE.

† **enter'tain**, *sb. Obs.* Also 6–7 entertaine, 6 -ayne, 7 intertaine. [f. next: cf. Fr. *entretien.*] = ENTERTAINMENT.

1. a. Pleasure; delight. **b.** An amusement, a merry-making.

1601 WEEVER *Mirr. Mart.* E iiij b, On whose [a river's] prowde banke such entertaine I had. **1638–48** G. DANIEL *Eclog.* III. 30 Rurall entertains Had noe ill-meanings. **1669** *Addr. Hopeful Yng. Gentry Eng.* Ep. Ded. A viij, Our masquerades and longer festivous entertains. **1678** SIR T. BROWNE *Let.* Wks. 1852 III. 448 Intending to live in Surrey House, and there to make his entertaines; so that he contrives what pictures to lend, etc.

2. Conversation; social behaviour.

1602 MARSTON *Ant. & Mel.* I. Wks. 1856 I. 11 With most obsequious sleek-browed intertain They all embrace it as most gratious. **1639** G. DANIEL *Ecclus.* xlii. 12 To restraine A wife Immodest in her entertaine.

3. The reception of a guest; also, the treatment of a person as a guest.

1591 SPENSER *M. Hubberd* 1085 Who..Receyued them with chearefull entertayne. **1605** HEYWOOD *If you know not me* Wks. 1874 I. 202 Those plausive shouts, which giue you entertaine. **1608** SHAKS. *Per.* I. i. 119 Your entertain shall be As doth befit our honour and your worth. **1640** T. CAREW *Poems, My Mistr. Commanding me to Return Lett.* 15 Tell your Soveraigne..I gave you courteous entertaine. **1651** tr. DE LAS COVERAS *Hist. Don Fenise* 50, I thought to enjoy the deare entertaine of Hipolite.

b. A meal; *esp.* a formal or elegant meal; a feast, banquet. Cf. ENTERTAINMENT II c.

1632 HEYWOOD *1st Pt. Iron Age* III. i. Wks. 1874 III. 302 All welcome to this peacefull intertaine. **1639** G. DANIEL *Ecclus.* xlii. 40 Abstaine To meet with Woemen at an Entertaine. *a* **1682** SIR T. BROWNE *Misc. Tracts* (1684) 203 The dismal Supper and strange Entertain of the Senatours. **1686** OLDHAM *Art Poetry* 30 Ill Music..is what the entertain might spare.

4. Reception into the mind; acceptance.

1616 R. NICCOLS *Overbury's Vis.* in *Harl. Misc.* (Malh.) III. 357 My counsel might find entertain With those, whose souls, etc. **1646** SIR T. BROWNE *Pseud. Ep.* v. iv. 237 Sathan appeared..with a Virgins head, that thereby..his temptation might finde the easier entertaine.

entertain (ɛntə'teɪn), *v.* Forms: 5–7 enterteyn(e, 5 entreteyne, (entertien, entretene, -iene), 6–7 entertaine, -ein(e, 6 -ayne, (-ene, 7 -ean, -eign), 6–8 intertain(e, 6–7 -ayn(e, -ein, -eyn(e, (6 interteny, intertynie), 6– entertain. [late ME. *entertene*, ad. F. *entretenir* = Pr. *entretenir*, Sp. *entretener*, It. *intrattenere*:—late L. *intertenēre*, f. L. *inter* among + *tenēre* to hold.]

†**I. 1.** *trans.* To hold mutually; to hold intertwined. Also *absol.* with reciprocal sense. *Obs.*

1481 CAXTON *Myrr.* II. x. 88 They [bananas] entretiene and cleue to gydre wel an hondred in a clustre. **1578** BANISTER *Hist. Man.* VIII. 111 An other lesser [nerve] trunke is intertained among the fore partes of the legge.

II. To maintain, keep up.

†**2.** *trans.* To keep (a person, country, etc.) in a certain state or condition; to keep (a person) in a certain frame of mind. *Obs.*

1490 CAXTON *Eneydos* xiii. 49 His swete wordes and drawynge atysen and enterteyne her in a contynualle thoughte towarde hym. **1538** STARKEY *England* II. ii. 191 Hys owne clyent..was interteynyd in long sute. **1581** SAVILE *Tacitus' Agric.* (1622) 191 By a kind of courteous and mild regiment intertained the countrey in quiet. **1664** MARVELL *Corr.* Wks. 1872–5 II. 170 The Fidelity and prudence of their Ministers seems rather to entertain them in mutual cautele and suspicion. *a* **1714** BURNET *Own Time* (1823) I. 425 Cromwell was certainly fond of her, and she took care to entertain him in it.

3. To keep up, maintain (a state of things, a process); to retain in use (a custom, law, etc.); to maintain, persist in (a course of action, 'attitude', state of feeling). *Obs.* in gen. sense; retained (but somewhat *arch.*) in a few special uses, as ***to entertain a correspondence, discourse***.

1490 CAXTON *Eneydos* vii. 31 To enterteyn hir pudyque chastyte in perpetuall wydowhed. **1587** FLEMING *Contn. Holinshed* III. 1375/1, I intertained intelligence with the Scottish queane. **1593** DRAYTON *Idea* Introd. Sonn., My Muse..cannot long one Fashion intertaine. *c* **1630** DRUMM. OF HAWTH. *Irene* Wks. 164 b, So careful hath he been to intertain peace amongst his subjects. *a* **1639** SPOTTISWOOD *Hist. Ch. Scot.* v. (1677) 253 Morton..entertained a long fight with them. **1672** CAVE *Prim. Chr.* I. ii. (1673) 21 To entertain the discipline of our Forefathers. **1794** J. HUTTON *Philos. Light, &c.* 182 This heat, in the burning body, is entertained by the extrication of light. **1825** SOUTHEY *Paraguay* III. 18 The Empress Queen..did not disdain..to entertain Discourse with him. **1855** MILMAN *Lat. Chr.* (1864) II. III. vii. 137 Entertaining a friendly correspondence with the orthodox Queen Theodelinda. **1860** MOTLEY *Netherl.* (1868) I. iv. 111 Philip..might direct all his energies towards entertaining civil war in France.

†**4.** To maintain (something) in existence; to keep in repair or efficiency. *Obs.*

1475 CAXTON *Jason* 72 b, And for to entretiene his astate were ordeyned certayn nombre of peple. **1586** BRIGHT *Melanch.* ii. 5 These varieties of humours are entertained by nourishments. **1670–98** LASSELS *Voy. Italy* I. 42 It's [a bridge] entertain'd at the cost of the king of Spain.

†**5.** To keep, retain (a person) in one's service; to be at the charges of (a person) in return for services rendered by him. *Obs.*

1559 *Mirr. Mag., Dk. Gloucester* vii, With princely wagies dyd me enterteyne. *a* **1593** H. SMITH *Wks.* (1866–7) I. 15, I

was..entertained with a stipend raised by voluntary contribution. **1625** in *Vicary's Anat.* (1888) App. iii. 167 Two..Phisitions to bee interteyned and ymployed by this Cittie. **1636** tr. *Florus' Hist.* 130 They were entertained in pay by King Perses. **1650** FULLER *Pisgah* III. ii. 361 Notwithstanding so many labourers entertained in the work, seven years was this Temple in building. **1762–71** H. WALPOLE *Vertue's Anecd. Paint.* (1786) I. 195 No wonder when so many Italians were entertained in the king's service.

†**b.** To take (a person) *into* one's service; to hire (a servant, etc.); to retain as an advocate.

1579 FENTON *Guicciard.* (1618) 147 They entertained into their pay Charles Vrsin and Bartlemew Aluiano with two hundred men at armes. **1591** SHAKS. *Two Gent.* II. iv. 110 Sweet Lady, entertaine him for your Seruant. **1613** PURCHAS *Pilgr.* I. v. iii. 392 Gave order..to entertaine halfe of them for the warres. **1676** MARVELL *Corr.* Wks. 1872–5 III. 498, I have enterteind Mr. Hall likewise, an able Exchequer atturny. **1721** PERRY *Daggenh. Breach* 71, I.. directly entertain'd all the Hands I could get.

†**6.** To maintain; to support; to provide sustenance for (a person). *Obs.*

1640 *Bk. War Committee Covenanters* 67 Sex musqueteires and ane sergand to be enterteanit upon the publict. **1655–60** STANLEY *Hist. Philos.* (1701) 99/1 Hermogenes, falling into Poverty, Socrates perswaded Diodorus his Friend to entertain. *a* **1657** BALFOUR *Ann. Scotl.* (1824–5) II. 145 That also they take order for intertaining the poore in ilk parochin. **1703** DK. QUEENSBERRY in Ellis *Orig. Lett.* II. 396 IV. 240, I thought it necessary to entertain him with some money. **1771** *Antiq. Sarisb., Lives Bps.* 169 Ten widows of Clergymen are here entertained, with a very comfortable provision.

III. To maintain relations with.

†**7.** To deal with, have communication with (a person). *Obs.*

1568 GRAFTON *Chron.* II. 720 He is a deepe dissimuler.. entertayning all men for his owne profite. **1655–60** STANLEY *Hist. Philos.* (1701) 141/2 A Friend is not be entertained out of useful or necessary Ends, nor when such fail, is to be cast off.

†**8.** To treat in a (specified) manner. *Obs.*

c **1489** CAXTON *Sonnes of Aymon* xxvi. 549 He entreteyneth vs above all other honourabli for the love of you. **1591** SHAKS. *1 Hen. VI*, II. iii. 72, I am sorry, that with reuerence I did not entertaine thee as thou art. **1608–11** BP. HALL *Medit.* (1851) 76 And entertained with all variety of persecution. **1630** M. GODWYN tr. *Bp. Hereford's Ann. Eng.* 28 He was very disgracefully entertained by Sir Amias Powlet, who clapt him in the stocks. **1662** GUNNING *Lent Fast* 44 Art thou rich? do not contumeliously entertain the [Lent] fast.

IV. To hold engaged, provide occupation for.

9. To engage, keep occupied the attention, thoughts, or time of (a person): also with *attention*, etc. as obj. Hence, to discourse to (a person) *of* something. *Obs.* exc. *arch.*

1598 SHAKS. *Merry W.* II. i. 68, I thinke the best way were, to entertaine him with hope. **1605** DANIEL *Philotas* in Farr *S. P. Jas. I* (1848) 274 With what strange formes and shadowes ominous Did my last sleepe my griev'd soul intertaine! **1614** RALEIGH *Hist. World* IV. i. §4 The Phocians hoped so to entertain the Thessalians at home, as, etc. **1665** BOYLE *Occas. Refl.* (1675) 60 Noble enough, and worthy to entertain the Eyes of God. **1684** *Contempl. State Man* II. viii. (1699) 218 Entertaining thy self in Pleasures, thou hast for Toys and Fooleries lost Heaven! **1686** W. DE BRITAINE *Hum. Prud.* §2. 5 Nor is the World any longer to be entertained with Dark Lanthorns. **1692** BP. ELY *Answ. Touchstone* A v, I hope I shall neither tire the Reader, nor entertain him unprofitably. **1748** CHESTERF. *Lett.* II. clxxiii. 142, I have so often entertained you upon these important subjects. *a* **1850** ROSSETTI *Dante & Circ.* I. (1874) 186 Of thee she entertains the blessed throngs.

†**b.** To occupy, fill up, wile away (time). *Obs.*

1589 PUTTENHAM *Eng. Poesie* III. xxv. (Arb.) 306 To entertaine time and ease at home. **1593** SHAKS. *Lucr.* 1361 The weary time she cannot entertain. **1667** MILTON *P.L.* II. 526 Where he may likeliest find Truce to his restless thoughts, and entertain The irksome hours, till his great Chief return. **1673** RAY *Journ. Low C.* 287 We entertained our time pleasantly enough in searching out and describing of plants.

†**c.** To give occupation to (an enemy's forces); to engage. *Obs.*

1590 SIR J. SMYTH *Disc. Weapons* 12 They presentlie sending certen troupes..to skirmish and entertaine the Mosquettiers. **1599** SHAKS. *Hen. V*, I. ii. 111 O Noble English, that could entertaine With half their Forces, the full pride of France. **1647** SPRIGGE *Anglia Rediv.* II. i. (1854) 70 They [colonel Butler's regiment] entertained sir Charles Lucas. **1654** R. CODRINGTON tr. *Ivstine's History* 192 Porus ..had prepared an Army to entertain him [Alexander].

10. To engage agreeably the attention of (a person); to amuse. In recent use often also *ironical*: = 'to try to entertain' (with something stupid or uninteresting). Also *refl.* and *absol.*

1626 BACON *Sylva* §953 All this to entertain the Imagination that it waver less. **1655–60** STANLEY *Hist. Philos.* (1701) 92/2 We entertained our selves with discourse till the Prison was opened. **1662** STILLINGFL. *Orig. Sacr.* I. iv. §10 Such relations, which though not true, might yet please and entertain his readers. **1716–8** LADY M. W. MONTAGUE *Lett.* I. xxvii. 89, I am very much entertained with him. **1738** *Common Sense* (1739) II. 127 Thus was poor Lucinda entertain'd out of her Innocence, and diverted into Infamy and Contempt. **1775** JOHNSON *Let. Mrs. Thrale* 11 June, You never told me..how you were entertained by Boswell's Journal. **1806–7** J. BERESFORD *Miseries Hum. Life* (1826) v. xv, A lady whom you consider it as your duty to entertain. **1823** LAMB *Elia* Ser. II. xxiii. (1865) 399 My favourite occupations..now cease to entertain. **1863** FR. KEMBLE *Resid. Georgia* 55 He entertained me with an account of the Darien Society.

V. To find room for; to give reception to.

†**11.** To admit and contain; to 'accommodate'.

1622–62 HEYLIN *Cosmogr.* I. (1682) 277 The most safe and capacious Haven..capable of entertaining the greatest Navy. **1664** EVELYN *Kal. Hort.* (1729) 200 Hot-beds to entertain..exoctick Plants. **1703** MOXON *Mech. Exerc.* 42 Cut out so much Iron in the Fore and Backsides, as would entertain the main Spindle. **1721** PERRY *Daggenh. Breach* Title-p., Rendering the Ports of Dover and Dublin Commodious for Entertaining large Ships.

†**12.** To give reception to; to receive (a person). Also *fig.* Sometimes const. *into*. *Obs.*

1568 GRAFTON *Chron.* II. 659 Divers other..came humbly and submitted themselves, whome he gently enterteined & lovingly receyved. **1590** SHAKS. *Com. Err.* III. i. 120 Since mine owne doores refuse to entertaine me. **1624** HEYWOOD *Gunaik.* I. 37 Ino..with her sonne Melicerta, were entertained into the number of the Sea-gods. **1650** BAXTER *Saints' R.* I. v. (1654) 51 If the King of Israel riding on an Ass, be entertained into Jerusalem with Hosanna's. **1667** MILTON *P.L.* IV. 382 Hell shall unfould, To entertain you two, her widest Gates.

13. To receive as a guest; to show hospitality to. Also *absol.*

1490 CAXTON *Eneydos* xx. 74, I haue them not onely receyued but entreteyned, furnyshed and susteyned, etc. **1513–75** *Diurn Occurr.* (1833) 102 Directit be our souerane lady to intertynie the said ambassatour vntill hir cummyng. **1542** UDALL *Erasm. Apoph.* 2 In receiuyng and interteinyng of geastes and straungers. **1641** J. JACKSON *True Evang. T.* II. 93 Thou never gavest me a Kid, to entertaine my friends. **1677** HALE *Contempl.* II. 131 This World is little other than our Inn to entertain us in our Journey to another Life. **1781** GIBBON *Decl. & F.* III. 16 Gregory was entertained in the house of a pious and charitable kinsman. **1859** JEPHSON *Brittany* xvi. 267 The Emperor was entertained at dinner. **1880** MRS. E. EDWARDS *Pezazi* in *Macm. Mag.* No. 253. 74 We were in such confusion..that we could not entertain.

†**14.** To give reception (to something); to allow (something) to enter; to accept (pay, etc.); to receive (news, events, etc.) in a certain manner.

1586 A. DAY *Eng. Secretary* I. (1625) 119 And being also informed with what great extreamitie you have entertained the newes of his losse. **1590** SPENSER *F.Q.* II. ix. 6 But were your will her sold to entertaine. **1595** MARKHAM *Sir. R. Grinvile* (Arb.) 77 Abr'ams faire bosome lyes to entertaine it [thy soule]. **1614** RALEIGH *Hist. World* IV. iii. §15 The Athenians with immoderate joy entertained this happy seeming proclamation. **1620** QUARLES *Pentelogia* in Farr *S. P. Jas. I* (1848) 138 Did thy cheekes entertaine a traytor's lips? **1696** STANHOPE *Chr. Pattern* (1711) 74 We are to.. entertain the most calamitous accidents without murmuring or discontent. *c* **1710** C. MATHER in Blaikie *Ministr. Word* (1883) 295 To have the truths well entertained with the auditory.

b. To admit to consideration (an opinion, argument, request, proposal, etc.); to receive (an idea) into the mind.

1614 BP. HALL *Recoll. Treat.* 45 But I will suspect a novell opinion, of untruth; and not entertaine it, unlesse, etc. **1665** BOYLE *Occas. Refl.* II. xi. (1675) 130 Who thinks it not time to entertain thoughts of Death. **1709** STEELE *Tatler* No. 128 ¶7, I..have..entertained the Addresses of a Man who I thought lov'd me more than Life. **1875** JOWETT *Plato* (ed. 2) I. 409 That is a question which he refuses to entertain. **1885** *Act 48 Vict.* c. 17 §8 The case shall be stated and the appeal entertained and heard.

c. To keep, hold, or maintain in the mind with favour; to harbour; to cherish; in weaker sense, to experience (a sentiment).

1576 FLEMING *Panoplie Ep.* 4 Nothing (blame and offence excepted) Can chaunce in the life of any man wherein horror is harboured, or feare intertained. **1647** COWLEY *Mistr., Despair* ii, When thoughts of Love I entertain. **1711** ADDISON *Spect.* No. 123 ¶5 Leonilla..entertained..a secret Passion for Florio. **1730** BERKELEY *Let.* 7 May, I entertained some thoughts of applying to his Majesty. **1770** LANGHORNE *Plutarch* (1879) I. 144/1 The King entertained a deep resentment against him. **1827** SCOTT *Highl. Widow* v, [She] perhaps for the moment actually entertained the purpose which she expressed. **1876** J. H. NEWMAN *Hist. Sk.* I. i. iv. 200 To learn from others, you must entertain a respect for them.

†**15.** To encounter, meet with. *Obs. rare.*

1591 SPENSER *Virgil's Gnat* 563 Th' Argolicke Power returning home againe..Did happie winde and weather entertaine. **1634** SIR T. HERBERT *Trav.* 29 That he chose rather to be his owne Executioner, then to entertaine the cruell aspect of his Master.

†**16.** To take upon oneself (an obligation, a relation); to engage in, enter upon (a task). *Obs.*

1579–80 NORTH *Plutarch* (1676) 75 Knowing themselves unmeet to entertain wedlock. **1603** KNOLLES *Hist. Turks* (1621) 277 That the King should..entertaine that honourable warre. **1624** CAPT. SMITH *Virginia* VI. 221, I was imploied by many my friends of London to entertaine this plantation. **1667–8** MARVELL *Corr.* Wks. 1872–5 II. 232 We onely made one order, that the House would entertein no new businesse till it be calld over. **1719** W. WOOD *Surv. Trade* 10 Trade was first entertain'd..by little States.

entertainable (ɛntəˈteɪnəb(ə)l), *a.* [f. ENTERTAIN *v.* + -ABLE.] Capable of being entertained, of being received into the mind.

1684 CHARNOCK *Attrib. God* (1834) I. 113 Whatsoever favours the ambition..of men, is easily entertainable.

entertained (ɛntəˈteɪnd), *ppl. a.* [f. ENTERTAIN *v.* + -ED[1].] In senses of the verb.

†**1.** Taken into service; enlisted. *Obs.*

1589 GREENE *Menaphon* (Arb.) 34 Love that smiled at his newe interteined champion.

2. a. That is receiving hospitality; **b.** that is the object of efforts to amuse or gratify. Chiefly *absol.*

1856 MISS YONGE *Daisy Chain* I. xx. (1879) 206 It was perfect delight to entertainers and entertained. **1860** O. W. HOLMES *Prof. Breakf.-t.* 32 We are the entertainer and the entertained.

entertainer (ɛntəˈteɪnə(r)). Also 6–7 **interteiner**, (6 **enterteiner, interteinour**). [f. ENTERTAIN *v.* + -ER[1].]

1. One who receives a guest; one who shows hospitality; a host. Also *fig.*

1576 FLEMING *Panoplie Ep.* 116 Democritus Sicyonius is ..my friendly interteiner. **1670** WALTON *Life Wotton* 21 He was a great lover of his neighbours, and a bountiful entertainer of them. **1772–84** COOK *Voy.* (1790) VI. 2220 Their entertainer was very corpulent. **1829** LYTTON *Disowned* 11 Having thanked his entertainers for their hospitality. **1856** MRS. BROWNING *Aur. Leigh* IV. 728 A graceful diner-out And entertainer more than hospitable. *fig.* *a* **1656** BP. HALL *Rem.* 89 (T.) We become the receptacles and entertainers of his [God's] good Spirit.

b. One who admits to consideration (requests or proposals); one who harbours or cherishes (sentiment, etc.).

1610 SHAKS. *Temp.* II. i. 17 When euery greefe is entertaind, That's offer'd comes to th'entertainer. **1612–15** BP. HALL *Contempl. N.T.* IV. xxx, Good purposes, when they are not held,..turn enemies to the entertainer of them.

2. One who or that which furnishes amusement; one who gives a public 'entertainment'.

a **1535** MORE *On the Passion* Wks. 1273/2 She was content to be talkatiue with a straunger, & wax a proper enterteiner. **1793** (*title*), Wonderful Magazine and Marvellous Chronicle, or new weekly entertainer. **1870** H. SMART *Race for Wife* i, Conjurors, lecturers, monologue entertainers.

†**3.** That which keeps up or promotes. *Obs.*

1635 PAGITT *Christianogr.* (1646) 187 Equality in government is the entertainer of confusion.

†**enterˈtainess.** *Obs. rare*[−1]. [f. as prec.: see -ESS.] A female entertainer; a hostess.

1709 E. W. *Life Donna Rosina* 41 She told her Entertainess that she was extreamly troubled.

entertaining (ɛntəˈteɪnɪŋ), *vbl. sb.* [f. ENTERTAIN *v.* + -ING[1].] The action of the vb. ENTERTAIN, in various senses.

1568 GRAFTON *Chron.* II. 663 What profite this gentle entertaynyng of his people brought him to..all men may easely conjecture. **1642** ROGERS *Naaman* 27 Both the message of Elisha and Naaman's entertaining thereof. *a* **1687** PETTY *Pol. Arith.* i. (1691) 30 By this entertaining of Strangers for Soldiers, their Country becomes more and more peopled. **1883** *Athenæum* 27 Oct. 534/2 The club expect also to have the entertaining of..distinguished guests.

attrib. **1791** in Picton *L'pool Munic. Rec.* (1886) II. 268 The present Assembly room was to be appropriated for an entertaining room.

entertaining (ɛntəˈteɪnɪŋ), *ppl. a.* [f. as prec. + -ING[2].] That entertains.

†**1.** Affording sustenance, supporting life. *rare.*

1691–8 NORRIS *Pract. Disc.* 202 The Air Temperate and Healthy, the Earth Fruitful and Entertaining.

2. Agreeable; interesting; now chiefly, amusing.

1697 COLLIER *Ess. Mor. Subj.* I. (1709) 12 For the Presence of any desirable Object, we know is more Acceptable and Entertaining, than either the Notion or Prospect of it. **1713** BERKELEY *Hylas & Phil.* III. Wks. 1871 I. 339 A part of knowledge both useful and entertaining. **1729** BUTLER *Serm.* Wks. 1874 II. 44 The secondary use of speech is to please and be entertaining to each other in conversation. **1796** C. MARSHALL *Garden.* i. (1813) 6 Of all the employments in life, none is more..entertaining, than the cultivation of plants. **1860** RAMSAY *Remin.* Ser. I. (ed. 7) 105 Enterteening has in olden Scottish usage the sense not of amusing but of interesting.

†**3.** That exercises hospitality; hospitable. *rare.*

1659 PEARSON *Creed* (1839) 498 This is the heavenly fellowship represented unto entertaining Abraham.

Hence **enterˈtainingly** *adv.*, in an entertaining manner; †in the manner of one who receives guests (*obs.*); in an interesting or amusing way. **enterˈtainingness**, the quality of being entertaining.

1621 LADY M. WROTH *Urania* 455 He bark't not..but look'd soberly and entertainingly, like a steward, on the strangers. **1754** SHERLOCK *Disc.* 36 (R.) He can talk entertainingly upon common subjects. **1809–10** COLERIDGE *Friend* (1865) 3 The entertainingness of moral writings. **1882** DR. J. BROWN *John Leech, etc.* 320 The question is ably and entertainingly handled. **1884** HALE *Christm. in Narragansett* v. 117 No method known by which you can inspissate entertainingness into a dull article.

entertainment (ɛntəˈteɪnmənt). Forms: see ENTERTAIN *v.* [f. ENTERTAIN *v.* + -MENT.]

†**1.** The action of upholding or maintaining. *Obs.*

1610 *Death Rauil.* in *Harl. Misc.* (Malh.) III. 114 Letters patent..for the intertainement of the edict made in Nantes.

†**2. a.** The action of maintaining persons in one's service, or of taking persons into service. Also, the state or fact of being maintained in or taken into service; service, employment. *Obs.*

1577–87 HOLINSHED *Chron.* I. 78/1 The Saxons.. desirous of intertainment to serue in warres. **1601** SHAKS. *All's Well* IV. i. 17 He must thinke vs some band of strangers, i'th aduersaries entertainment. **1604** —— *Oth.* III. iii. 250

Note if your Lady straine his [Cassio's] Entertainment With any strong, or vehement importunitie. **1647** SPRIGGE *Anglia Rediv.* IV. vii. (1854) 269 All officers and soldiers that shall desire to take entertainment from any foreign kingdom. *a* **1662** HEYLIN *Laud* II. 259 To undertake some Stipendary Lecture, wheresoever they could find entertainment.

b. Provision for the support of persons in service (*esp.* soldiers); *concr.* pay, wages. *Obs.*

1535 *Act 27 Hen. VIII*, c. 11 §1 The kings clerks..haue for their enterteinements and their clerkes, no fees nor wages certaine for those offices. **1596** SPENSER *State Irel.* 89 The which eighteene thousand pounds will defray the entertainment of 1500 Souldiers. **1612** DAVIES *Why Ireland, etc.* (1787) 24 The Earl of Stafford's entertainment was, for himself six shillings and eight pence per diem. **1682** EVELYN *Mem.* (1857) II. 172 And other officers, with their several salaries and entertainments. **1709** STRYPE *Ann. Ref.* Introd. ii. 16 Granting him 20*s.* a day..towards the entertainment of an hundred horsemen serving there under him.

†**3.** Maintenance; support; sustenance. *Obs.*

1603 KNOLLES *Hist. Turks* (1621) 1391 Lands for the intertainement of them and their horses. **1692** RAY *Dissol. World* iii. (1732) 36 Most convenient for the Entertainment of the various Sorts of Animals. **1705** STANHOPE *Paraphr.* III. 468 Creatures..designed for the Service and Entertainment of Mankind. **1754** ERSKINE *Princ. Sc. Law* (1809) 89 The expence laid out upon the minor's entertainment. **1761** HUME *Hist. Eng.* III. 71 James..erected a college at Chelsea for the entertainment of twenty persons.

†**4.** Manner of social behaviour. *Obs.*

1531 ELYOT *Gov.* II. xii, With hir good maners and swete enterteinements. **1572** J. JONES *Bathes Buckstone* Pref. 3 The maners that to Phisicions belonged, are that thei be of gentle entertaynment. **1598** BARRET *Theor. Warres* IV. i. 118 Gouerne them with convenient speeches, and good entertainment and curtesie.

†**5.** Treatment (of persons). *Obs.*

1568 GRAFTON *Chron.* II. 669 He was of the Nobilitie receyved, and with all honorable entertainement conveyed to the Kinges presence. **1645** PAGITT *Heresiogr.* (1662) 45 This [viz. burning] was the entertainment that these sectaries had in times past. **1660** BOYLE *Seraphic Love* 74 The savage entertainment He met with in it [the World].

†**6.** Discussion of a subject. *Obs.*

1675 R. BURTHOGGE *Causa Dei* 329 To conclude this tedious Entertainment of the Gentile Divinity, I will add, etc.

7. Occupation; spending (of time). Now *rare.*

1551 ROBINSON tr. *More's Utop.* I. iiij b, What familiar occupieng and enterteynement there is amonge yᵉ people. **1588** SHAKS. *L.L.L.* v. i. 126 Sir Holofernes, as concerning some entertainment of time. **1860** MOTLEY *Netherl.* (1868) I. iii. 91 A dallying entertainment of the time.

8. a. The action of occupying (a person's) attention agreeably; interesting employment; amusement.

1612 BRINSLEY *Lud. Lit.* xxviii. (1627) 282 An Oration by the highest, to giue the visitours intertainment. **1756–7** tr. *Keysler's Trav.* (1760) III. 123 A person who is fond of seeing natural curiosities cannot but meet here with the highest entertainment. **1824** COLERIDGE *Aids Refl.* (1850) Introd. 47 He who seeks to find instruction in the following pages, will not fail to find entertainment likewise. **1857** WILLMOTT *Pleas. Lit.* xxi. 123 Biography..furnishes entertainments to the reader.

b. That which affords interest or amusement.

1659 *Gentl. Call.* (1696) 83 Other Mens [Affairs]..are the usual entertainment of those that neglect their own. **1683** DRYDEN *Life Plutarch* 80 It [history] has alwayes been the most delightful entertainment of my life. **1713** STEELE *Spect.* No. 423 ¶1 Gloriana shall be the name of the Heroine in to Day's Entertainment. **1756** BURKE *Subl. & B.* III. iv, These fine descriptive pieces..have been the entertainment of ages. **1788** REID *Aristotle's Logic* iv. §3. 81 His appetite for this kind of entertainment.

c. *esp.* A public performance or exhibition intended to interest or amuse.

Johnson (1755) assigns to the word a specific application to 'the lower comedy'; in recent use it often denotes an assemblage of performances of varied character, as when music is intermixed with recitations, feats of skill, etc.

1727 J. THURMOND (*title*), The Miser; or Wagner and Abericock. A Grotesque Entertainment. **1806–7** J. BERESFORD *Miseries Hum. Life* (1826) v. xiii, The entertainments at Astley's or the Circus. **1847** EMERSON *Repr. Men, Shaks.* Wks. (Bohn) I. 353 Importunate for dramatic entertainments. **1881** SAINTSBURY *Dryden* 18 Davenant succeeded in procuring permission from the Protector..to give what would now be called entertainments.

9. The accommodation of anything in a receptacle. *Obs.*

1697 POTTER *Antiq. Greece* III. xx. (1715) 152 Harbours were Places render'd..commodious for the Entertainment of Ships. **1721** PERRY *Daggenh. Breach* 122 Sufficient room for the Entertainment of Ships in this Harbour.

†**10.** Reception (of persons); manner of reception.

1589 GREENE *Menaphon* (Arb.) 66 Hath your hot intertainment cooled your courage? **1606** SHAKS. *Ant. & Cl.* III. xiii. 140 Get thee backe to Cæsar, Tell him thy entertainment. **1690** LOCKE *Hum. Und.* II. ix. (1695) 67 According to the divers circumstances of Childrens first entertainment in the World. **1692** BP. ELY *Answ. Touchstone* A iv, In the very Prisons, where the Romish-Priests could meet with any entertainment.

11. a. The action of receiving a guest. Also, the action of treating as a guest, of providing for the wants of a guest.

1594 HOOKER *Eccl. Pol.* I. x. (1611) 32 The courteous entertainment of forreiners and strangers. **1649** ROBERTS *Clavis Bibl.* 421 Hezekiah's entertainment of them with gladnesse. **1698–9** LUDLOW *Mem.* I. 19 (R.) Where [at Whitehall] a constant table was provided for their entertainment. **1702** J. LOGAN in *Pa. Hist. Soc. Mem.* IX. 110 The entertainment has been some charge, his retinue and company being great. **1725** DE FOE *Voy. round World* (1840) 245 Not the custom of the Spaniards to let their wives appear in any public entertainment of friends. **1848** MACAULAY *Hist. Eng.* I. 385 The improvement of our houses of public entertainment. **1883** E. T. PAYNE in *Law Times* 27 Oct. 432/2 The proprietor of [an inn]..undertakes to provide for the entertainment of all comers.

b. *concr.* Hospitable provision for the wants of a guest; *esp.* provision for the table. Somewhat *arch.*

1540 in Ellis *Orig. Lett.* I. 146. II. 126 The most bountiful gifts, the chere and most gratiouse enterteignment. **1590** SPENSER *F.Q.* I. x. 37 His office was to giue entertainement And lodging unto all that came. **1661** PEPYS *Diary* 22 Aug., To my uncle Fenner's, where there was..great deal of company, but poor entertainment. **1728** MORGAN *Algiers* II. iv. 260 Provided of all requisite Entertainment for at least a Twelvemonth. **1849** JAMES *Woodman* xii, Take order that lodging and entertainment be prepared at York.

c. A meal; *esp.* a formal or elegant meal; a banquet. Somewhat rare in recent use.

1607 SHAKS. *Timon* I. ii. 153 You have done our pleasures Much grace (faire Ladies) Set a faire fashion on our entertainment. **1669** MARVELL *Corr.* Wks. 1872–5 II 285 A Bill..against giving of interteinments of meat or drink. **1681** R. KNOX *Hist. Ceylon* 89 The Entertainment is, green Leaves..which they eat raw, with Lime and Betel-nut. **1766** GOLDSM. *Vic. W.* xxxii, A very genteel entertainment..dressed by Mr. Thornhill's cook. *c* **1775** BURKE *Sp. Durat. Parl.* Wks. X. 81 Entertainments, drinkings, open houses. **1841** LANE *Arab. Nts.* I. 90 When the man returned from an entertainment.

12. †**a.** The action of accepting (a present or proposal); the receiving in a certain manner (news, events, etc.); the 'reception' (*esp.* favourable reception, welcome), *e.g.* of a newly published book, of a new idea or doctrine, etc. *Obs.*

1586 A. DAY *Eng. Secretary* I. (1625) 124 By patient sufferance, and entertainment of our harmes. **1612** ROWLANDS *More Knaues Yet* 31 If a bribe doe entertainement finde. **1612** BRINSLEY *Pos. Parts* (1669) Introd. 4 By the welcome and kind entertainment of my first labours, etc. **1648** BP. HALL *Select Th.* xxiv, Evils, which we look for, fall so much the less heavily, by how much we are foreprepared for their entertainment. **1672** TILLOTSON in Wilkins *Nat. Relig.* Pref., The ensuing treatise..needs nothing else to make way for its entertainment. **1699** BENTLEY *Phal.* 343 His Forgery met with good Entertainment. **1727** S. SWITZER *Pract. Gardiner* xxxvii. 196 The Scorzonera has of late met with great entertainment at the tables of the curious.

b. The taking into consideration; entering upon the discussion (of a question).

1841 MYERS *Cath. Th.* IV. §13. 253 Men will grow more and more averse to the entertainment of questions which, etc.

c. The cherishing (an idea) in the mind.

1841 MIALL *Nonconf.* I. 17 The deliberate entertainment of this selfish design.

13. *attrib.* and *Comb.*

1904 *Westm. Gaz.* 29 Aug. 3/1 A prince among provincial entertainment-mongers of the humbler order. **1922** *Punch* 25 Oct. 385 No entertainment tax. **1937** *Burlington Mag.* Feb. 96/2 Gives the book a high entertainment-value. **1946** G. B. SHAW *Shaw on Theatre* (1958) 268 The critics reported that my plays were not plays, whatever other entertainment value they might possess. **1951** MCLUHAN *Mech. Bride* 75/1 The reciprocal connections between *chic* and the entertainment industries. **1958** *Listener* 6 Nov. 742/2 She was wonderful entertainment value and a rare spirit. **1959** HALAS & MANVELL *Technique Film Animation* 10 Potentialities [of animation] which..extend much more widely than the entertainment film.

entertake, -tangle, -tear: see ENTER- *pref.* and INTER-.

entertise, var. of INTERDICE, *Obs.*

entertissue: see INTER-.

enterval, -view, obs. forms of INTERVAL, INTERVIEW.

enterwarn: see ENTER- *pref.*

enterwoven, enterwrought: see INTER-.

†**en'test**, *a. Obs. rare*⁻¹. ? Variant of INTEXT, interwoven.

1607 TOPSELL *Serpents* 627 His shield an hundred Snakes, his Fathers crest, An Hydra in their compass is entest.

enthalpy ('ɛnθəlpɪ, ɛn'θælpɪ). *Physics.* [ad. Gr. ἐνθάλπειν to warm in, f. ἐν in + θάλπειν to heat.] A thermodynamic property of a system: the sum of its internal energy and the product of its volume and the pressure exerted on it; usu. measured relative to an arbitrarily defined zero.

1927 H. MOSS tr. *Mollier's Steam Tables* 3 The quantity *E* is known as the internal or intrinsic energy while the quantity *H* is termed the total heat, enthalpy or (sometimes) heat content. **1930** *Engineering* 8 Aug. 162/1 The calculation of the enthalpy, or heat contained in saturated air will show that most of the heat present..is the latent heat in the associated steam. **1950** *Jrnl. R. Aeronaut. Soc.* LIV. 73/2 This is the usual enthalpy-entropy diagram, drawn on the assumption of no internal losses or increase in entropy. *Ibid.* 76/1 Since there can be no loss in energy, the enthalpy levels of each of the points of the cycle diagram prior to the final expansion remain the same as for the ideal cycle. **1962** *Engineering* 23 Feb. 276/2 The total heat content (enthalpies) of the coolant gas at inlet. **1967** CONDON & ODISHAW *Handbk. Physics* (ed. 2) v. i. 5 In a change occurring at constant pressure..all the heat added to the system goes to increase the enthalpy.

†**'entheal**, *a. Obs.* [f. as next + -AL¹.] = next.

1736 in BAILEY; **1847** in CRAIG; and in mod. Dicts.

†**'enthean**, *a. Obs.* [f. Gr. ἔνθε-ος (see ENTHEOS) + -AN.] Inspired by an indwelling god.

1635 HEYWOOD *Hierarch.* I. 25 Some of their prophets in an Enthean fury, Predicted that a King should come from Iury, To Monarchise the World. **1652** BENLOWES *Theoph.* XII. ciii, Canzons, tin'd with Enthean fire.

†**'entheasm.** *Obs. rare*⁻¹. [as if ad. Gr. *ἐνθεασμός, f. ἐνθεάζειν (see next).] = ENTHUSIASM.

1751 BYROM *Enthus.* Poet. Wks. (1810) 251 Altho' in one absurdity they chime To make religious entheasm a crime.

†**enthe'astic**, *a. Obs. rare*⁻¹. [ad. Gr. ἐνθεαστικ-ός, f. ἐνθεάζειν to be the subject of 'possession' by a god, f. ἔνθεος ENTHEOS.] (See quot.)

Hence **enthe'astical** *a.*, **enthe'astically** *adv.*

1794 T. TAYLOR tr. *Plotinus* Introd. 23 The entheastic (or such as are agitated by a divine fury). —— tr. *Pausanias' Greece* III. 266 Wisdom..delivered..entheastically, or according to a deific energy.

†**'entheate**, *a. Obs.* Also 7 **entheat.** [ad. L. *entheāt-us*, pa. pple. of **entheāre*, f. *entheus*: see next.] Possessed or inspired by a god.

c **1630** DRUMM. OF HAWTH. *Poems* Wks. 29/2 Stars..entheate from above, Their sovereign Prince laud, glorify, adore. **1640** W. HODGSON *Commend. Verses* in *B. Jonson's Wks.*, His Genius justly in an Entheat Rage, Oft lash't the dull—sworn Factors for the Stage.

‖**'entheos, -us.** *Obs. rare.* [a. L. *entheos, -us*, Gr. ἔνθεος divinely inspired, f. ἐν in + θεός god.

The use by Eng. authors appears to be suggested by some such L. phrase as *entheus ardor*.]

An indwelling divine power; inspiration.

1594 J. DICKENSON *Arisbas* (1878) 78 The diuine Entheos..should be affoorded to other nations. *c* **1595** —— *Sheph. Compl.* (1878) 23 Matchlesse perfections, wrought in them by vertue of a diuine Entheos. **1782** J. SCOTT *Painting* Wks. (Anderson) 770 Without the Entheus Nature's self bestows, The world no painter nor no poet knows.

Hence †**'entheous** *a.* [+ -OUS.] divinely inspired.

1682 H. MORE *Annot. Glanvill's Lux O.* 33 Men of a more Æthereal and Entheous temper.

enthetic (ɛn'θɛtɪk), *a. Med.* [ad. Gr. ἐνθετικ-ός, f. ἐνθε- aor. stem of ἐντιθέναι, f. ἐν in + τιθέναι to place.] Put in; introduced from without. Said of 'diseases produced by inoculation or implantation, and especially syphilitic diseases' (*Syd. Soc. Lex.*).

1867 *Abyss. Exped.* in *Standard* 23 Nov., Most danger is to be apprehended from the outbreak of epidemics—of smallpox, cholera, and enthetic disease. **1888** SIR M. MACKENZIE *Frederick the Noble* 226 The man..urged that the disease might be of an enthetic character.

enthirst: see EN- *pref.*¹ 2.

enthral(l (ɛn'θrɔ:l), *v.* Also in-. [f. EN-¹ + THRALL *sb.*

The sb. *thrall* may here be taken in either of its two senses, 'slave' and 'slavery.']

1. *trans.* To reduce to the condition of a thrall; to hold in thrall; to enslave, bring into bondage. Now *rare* in lit. sense.

α. **1656** COWLEY *Pindar. Odes, Brutus* iii, Ingrateful Cæsar who could Rome enthrall. **1659** PEARSON *Creed* (1839) 512 A ransom is..that which is detained, or given for the releasing of that which is enthralled. **1777** WATSON *Philip II* (1839) 321 The danger..of being again enthralled by the Spaniards. **1871** B. TAYLOR *Faust* (1875) I. xxv, I am free! No one shall enthrall me.

β. **1614** RALEIGH *Hist. World* I. 39 Those people, which he [the Turk] hath subjected and inthralled. **1636** E. DACRES tr. *Machiavel's Disc. Livy* II. 495 It is as hard and dangerous..to inthrall a people, that would live free.

2. *fig.* To 'enslave' mentally or morally. Now *chiefly*, to captivate, hold spellbound, by pleasing qualities.

α. **1576** NEWTON tr. *Lemnie's Complex.* (1633) 170 A man should not give over or enthrall his credit and honour to Harlots. **1590** SHAKS. *Mids. N.* III. i. 142 So is mine eye enthralled to thy shape. **1695** LD. PRESTON *Boeth.* IV. 177 Vice doth enthral Men's strongest Powers. **1797** MRS. RADCLIFFE *Italian* xvii, He was inclined to believe that a stratagem had enthralled him. *a* **1839** PRAED *Poems* (1864) II. 123 And M—, in that simple dress, Enthralls us more by studying less. **1878** E. JENKINS *Haverholme* 136 He was enthralled by the wizard spell of the orator.

β. **1603** DANIEL *Def. Rhime* (1717) 12 Seeking to please our Ear, we inthral our Judgment. **1636** HEALEY *Theophrast., Impert. Diligence* 53 This fellow perswades him not so much to inthrall himselfe to his Physicians directions. *c* **1720** PRIOR *Poems* (1866) 12 She soothes, but never can inthral my mind. *a* **1803** BEATTIE *Hermit* (R.), Spring shall return, and a lover bestow And sorrow no longer thy bosom enthrall. **1859** KINGSLEY *Raleigh* Misc. I. 30 The sense of beauty inthralls him at every step. **1876** BANCROFT *Hist. U.S.* I. xviii. 516 To inthrall his mind by the influences of religion.

Hence **en'thralled** *ppl. a.* **en'thraller**, one who enthralls. **en'thralling** *vbl. sb.* and *ppl. a.*

1591 SHAKS. *Two Gent.* II. iv. 134 Loue hath chas'd sleepe from my enthralled eyes. **1600** HOLLAND *Livy* II. xxiv. 59 The enthralled debtors..were immediatlie by name enrolled. **1644** MILTON *Areop.* (Arb.) 75 Through our..backwardnes to recover any enthrall'd peece of truth out of

the gripe of custom. **1640–4** in Rushw. *Hist. Coll.* III (1692) I. 93 The subjecting and inthralling all Ministers under them. **1669** COKAINE *Poems* 149 Her sweetest mouth..[is] All hearts enthraller. **1797** BURKE *Regic. Peace* iii. Wks. VIII. 311 With an enthralled world to labour for them. **1820** SCOTT *Monast.* xiii, Those of the *Sucken*, or enthralled ground, were liable in penalties. **1871** MACDUFF *Mem. Patmos* xiv. 195 To break loose from the enthralling chains of earth.

enthraldom (ɛn'θrɔːldəm). *rare.* [f. ENTHRAL *v.* + -DOM.] The state or condition of being enthralled. *lit.* and *fig.*

1641 JER. BURROUGHS *Serm.* 19 Tending..to the enthraldome of the estates, liberties, consciences of their posteritie. **1715** M. DAVIES *Ath. Brit.* I. 223 Full of marks of their Popish Enthraldom. **1843** *Tait's Mag.* X. 559 It is not yours to weep The land's enthraldom. **1884** *Public Opinion* 5 Sept. 289/1 The emancipation of multitudes of men and women from their enthraldom to a vitiated appetite.

enthralment (ɛn'θrɔːlmənt). [f. ENTHRAL *v.* + -MENT.] The action of enthralling; the state of being enthralled; slavery; sometimes in *pl.* Chiefly *fig.*

1611 SPEED *Hist. Gt. Brit.* IX. xvi. §21 The King of France might seeme to haue sustained a grieuous losse by the enthralment of this Duke. **1636** tr. *Florus* 258 Cataline..was thrust into a treason for inthralment of his native Countrey. **1645** MILTON *Tetrach.* (1851) 187 Ther can be neither peace, nor joy, nor love, but an enthrallment. **1794** G. WAKEFIELD *Dk. of York* 33 To weep over the enthralment of our species. **1805** WORDSW. *Prel.* (1850) 87 Life, In its late course of even days with all Their smooth enthralment. **1818** KEATS *Endym.* I. 798 There are..enthralments far More self-destroying. **1828** D'ISRAELI *Chas. I*, I. iv. 77 This tenderness in all probability was but the temporary enthralment of the eyes. **1876** BANCROFT *Hist. U.S.* V. Index 545 [Religious freedom] rises from inthralments of the hand of violence.

†en'thrill, *v. Obs.* [f. EN-[1] + THRILL *v.*] *trans.* To pierce.

1559 SACKVILLE *Mirr. Mag., Induct.* R i. liii, Pale Death Enthrylling it [her brest] to reue her of her breath. **1593** NASHE *Christ's T.* (1613) 182 The yron fist, that holds out nought but a knife to enthrill vs.

enthrone (ɛn'θrəʊn), *v.* Also 7–8 **inthrone**. [f. EN-[1] + THRONE: cf. F. *enthroner* (Cotgr.).]

1. *trans.* To seat on a throne; *esp.* to set (a king, bishop, etc.) on a throne as a formal induction to office; to invest with regal or episcopal authority.

1606 SHAKS. *Ant. & Cl.* III. vi. 5 Cleopatra and himselfe in Chaires of Gold Were publikely enthron'd. **1651** BAXTER *Inf. Bapt.*, A King is..King..incompleatly till he be solemnly Crowned and Inthroned. **1726** AYLIFFE *Parerg.* 63 This Pope..was no sooner elected and enthron'd in France ..but that he, etc. **1848** MACAULAY *Hist. Eng.* I. 135 He was not crowned and anointed in Westminster Abbey, but was solemnly enthroned. **1876** GREEN *Short Hist.* iii. 119 [The] Bishop of Norwich was elected by the monks of Canterbury at his bidding and enthroned as Primate.

fig. *a* **1628** SIR J. BEAUMONT *Epiph.* in Farr *S.P. Jas. I* (1848) 143 There pride, enthroned in misty errours, dwels. **1727** THOMSON *Summer* 400 One [maid], chief, in gracious dignity inthron'd Shines o'er the rest. *a* **1790** WARTON *Enthusiast* (R.), Where happiness and quiet sit enthron'd. **1844** STANLEY *Arnold* (1858) II. 148 To enthrone the very mystery of falsehood and iniquity. **1868** MISS BRADDON *Dead-Sea F.* II. ix. 211 If she seem an angel to you, enthrone her in your heart of hearts.

2. To set as on a throne; to place in a high position, exalt.

1699 ADDISON *Imit. Milton* 42 By every God that sits enthroned on high. **1856** STANLEY *Sinai & Pal.* iii. (1858) 171 Enthroned..on a mountain fastness. *a* **1859** MACAULAY *Hist. Eng.* V. 300 In every parish from Mile End to Saint James's was to be seen enthroned on the shoulders of stout Protestant porters a pope.

Hence **†enthro'nation**, *Obs.*, in 7 **inthronation**, the action of enthroning. **en'throned** *ppl. a.*, in 8 **inthroned**.

1611 SPEED *Hist. Gt. Brit.* x. i. §10 The antique Regall Chaire of Inthronation. *a* **1711** KEN *Div. Love* Wks. (1838) 247 Glory be to thee, O Love inthroned!

enthronement (ɛn'θrəʊnmənt). Also 7 **in-**. [f. as prec. + -MENT.] **a.** The action of enthroning; *esp.* the ceremony of enthroning a king or bishop. **b.** The fact of being enthroned.

1685 *Addr. Virginia* in *Lond. Gaz.* No. 2051/2 Your Majesties peaceable and safe Inthronement in your Rightful and Lawful Imperial Seat. **1878** SPURGEON *Treas. Dav.* Ps. cxviii. 24 The day of David's enthronement was the beginning of better times. **1885** *Manch. Exam.* 9 Apr. 5/3 It was at Bishop Temple's own request that his enthronement ..took place so early in the morning.

†en'throng, in'throng, *v. Obs. rare.* [f. EN-[1], IN- + THRONG *sb.* and *v.*] **a.** *intr.* To crowd in. **b.** *trans.* To encircle in a throng, beset.

1600 FAIRFAX *Tasso* XV. xli, The seas betwixt those Isles inthrong. *Ibid.* XIX. xxxvii, His people like a flowing streame inthrong. **1603** FLORIO *Montaigne* III. xiii. (1632) 627 Alcibiades..enthronged by his enemies.

enthroning (ɛn'θrəʊnɪŋ), *vbl. sb.* [f. ENTHRONE *v.* + -ING[1].] The action of the verb ENTHRONE; the action of formally inducting a king or bishop to office; = ENTHRONEMENT. Also *fig.*

1668 WILKINS *Real Char.* 295 Coronation, inthroning, is solemnity of King-making, or King-declaring. **1697** tr. *Dupin's Eccl. Hist.* II. 32 These two letters were written a little while after the Enthroning of George. **1705** STANHOPE *Paraphr.* III. 94 Of that Enthroning the Holy Ghost shed abroad..was a convincing Demonstration. **1848** MACAULAY *Hist. Eng.* II. 651 The enthroning of Henry the Fourth.

enthronization (ɛn,θrəʊnaɪ'zeɪʃən). Forms: 6 intronyzacion, -izacion, 6–8 inthronization, 7– enthronisation, -ization. [f. ENTHRONIZE + -ATION.] = ENTHRONEMENT. Also *fig.* and *attrib.*

1517 TORKINGTON *Pilgr.* (1884) 11 A Riche Cappe which every Duk ys Crowned with at hys ffirst Intrononyzacions. **1552** BALE *Apol.* 96 The feast of Sathans intronizacion. **1574** *Life 70th Abp. Canterb.* A viij, The installinge off Archbisshopps his predecessors (which they commonly call inthronization). **1614** SELDEN *Titles Hon.* 147 The Great Sophi hath at his inauguration a kind of miter horn'd put on by his Chaliph, at his inthronization. **1656** TRAPP *Comm. Acts* xiii. 9 Popes..change their names at their enthronization. **1663** *Aron-bimn.* 3 All Israel shall be invited to wait upon the Solemnity of its [the sacred Ark's] Inthronization. **1750** HODGES *Elihu* (1755) Prel. Disc. 77 In this vision we have a representation of the..inthronization of the Lamb. **1838** *Fraser's Mag.* XVII. 628 Unanimous enthronisation of his genius above surrounding and inferior men. **1860** FREER *Henry IV*, II. III. iii. 318 Opposite, was a chair..for the occupation of the king before his enthronization. **1879** W. BENHAM *Mem. Tait* 454 Immediately after the enthronisation the Archbishop and his family went to Lambeth.

attrib. **1751** MILLES in *Phil. Trans.* XLVII. 116 *note*, The enthronization-feast of archbishop Neville.

†en'thronize, *v. Obs.* exc. *arch.* Forms: α. 4 entronize, 6–7 enthronise, (-oanize, -onishe), 6–8 enthronize. β. 4–6 intronise, -ze, 6–7 inthronise, -yse. [ad. OF. *introniser* (13th c. in Littré) ad. late L. *int(h)ronizāre*, ad. Gr. ἐνθρονίζειν, f. ἐν in + θρόνος THRONE.

In the poetical examples the accent is variously '*enthronize, en'thronize*; the former accords best with mod. analogies.]

1. *trans.* = ENTHRONE *v.* 1. Also *fig.* and *refl.*

α. **1393** GOWER *Conf.* III. 167 What emperour was entronized The firste day of his corone. **1563–87** FOXE *A. & M.* (1684) II. 437 He in his whole pomp mitred sat there enthronized. **1594** J. DICKENSON *Arisbas* (1878) 41 Chastitie sate enthronizde as gardian of her lookes. **1609** BP. BARLOW *Answ. Nameless Catholic* 304 Kings are enthroanized by Diuine ordinance. **1646** J. HALL *Poems* 78 With what grace Doth mercy sit enthroniz'd on thy face! **1651** GATAKER *Parker* in Fuller *Abel Rediv.* (1867) II. 16 The first [archbishop] that..was enthronized in that seat.

β. **1393** GOWER *Conf.* I. 254 Thus was he pope canonised with great honour and intronised. **1460** CAPGRAVE *Chron.* 252 And aftir him [Urban] was intronized Bonifacius the IX. **1579** FULKE *Heskins' Parl.* 296 The reuerend M. Doctor Heskins..inthronized in his Doctours chayer. **1637** POCKLINGTON *Altare Chr.* 28 Ambition to step up into the highest roomes and seats, and there to inclose and inthronize themselves. **1685** *Acc. Coron.* in *Lond. Gaz.* No. 2028/2 Te Deum being Sung, He Ascended the Throne, and being Inthronized, the Arch-Bishops, etc. **1838** *Rubric Coron. Q. Vict.* in Maskell *Mon. Rit.* III. 123 The Queen will ascend the Theatre, and be lifted up into her Throne..being Inthronized, or placed therein.

2. To set as on a throne; to place in a high position, exalt; to raise in dignity.

α. **1583** GOLDING *Calvin on Deut.* clxxi. 1063 Enthronished with the Angels of Paradise. **1614** R. TAILOR *Hog hath lost Pearl* v. in Hazl. *Dodsley* XI. 485 Here sits enthronis'd The sparkling diamond. **1623** DRUMM. OF HAWTH. *Cypress Grove* Wks. 125 The sun enthronized in the midst of the planets. *a* **1711** KEN *Hymns Festiv.* Poet. Wks. 1721 I. 259 An heav'nly Mind can never miss, To sit like Jesus enthroniz'd in Bliss.

β. **1557** *Primer, Laudes* B ij, O Glorious floure of womanhed Above the sterres inthronised. **1614** RALEIGH *Hist. World* II. 378 Now inthronized he sits on high, In golden Palace of the starry Skie.

Hence **en'thronized** *ppl. a.*, **en'thronizing** *vbl. sb.*

1572 N. ROSCARROCK in Bossewell *Armorie* Prel. Verses, Thenthronizing of Ioue. **1581** J. BELL *Haddon's Answ. Osor.* 305 b, After the enthronizyng of Hildebrand..Kynges were called Kynges onely in name. **1601** BP. BARLOW *Serm. Paules Crosse* 25 The inthronising and deposing of Princes, is Gods onely prerogative royall. **1640** HOWELL *Dodona's Grove* 58 The newly enthroniz'd Oke. *a* **1734** NORTH *Exam.* II. v. §27 (1740) 332 The heroic Carriage..of some of the enthronised Clergy. **1871** R. ELLIS *Catullus* xxxiv. 6 Latonia, thou that art Throned daughter of enthronis'd Jove.

enthunder: see EN- *pref.*[1] 3.

enthuse (ɛn'θjuːz), *v.*, orig. *U.S.* (*colloq.* or *humorous.*) [An ignorant back-formation from ENTHUSIASM.] **a.** *trans.* To kindle with enthusiasm. **b.** *intr.* To grow enthusiastic; to go into ecstasies.

1827 in *Amer. Speech* (1947) XXII. 286/2 My humble exertions will I trust convey and enthuse, and draw attention to the beautifully varied verdure of N.W. America. **1852** *N.Y. Weekly Tribune* 24 Jan. 3/2 We were probably not so much 'enthused' as they were. **1859** *Congress. Globe* 16 Feb. 1058/3 They are what they call in the country 'enthused'—run mad on the subject [of Cuba]. **1869** *Ohio newspaper* in *N. & Q.* Ser. IV. IV. 512 The only democrat whose nomination could enthuse the democracy of Ohio. **1872** LYTTON *Parisians* II. viii, The American..whispered ..'I am not without a kinkle that you will be enthused'. **1880** GRANT *Confess. Frivolous Girl* iv. 180, I admit he began to enthuse a little. **1887** H. P. KIMBALL in *Pall Mall G.* 22 June 5/1, I don't get enthused at all, sir, over all this Greek business. **1909** *Daily Chron.* 27 Oct. 3/3 A little too much of the enthusing forest lover. **1912** W. OWEN *Let.* 22 Sept. (1967) 162, I cannot enthuse over the things as Leslie does. **1918** E. WALLACE *Down under Donovan* v. 44 A million francs, think of it! Isn't it sufficient to enthuse a man without a profession? **1938** 'D. HUME' *Good-Bye to Life* v. 61 The prospect of a stay at Three Gables was nothing to enthuse about. **1957** *Times* 11 Nov. 13/3 She enthused rapturously on the advantages of being on the telephone. **1964** C. CHAPLIN *Autobiogr.* xxv. 432 *The Great Dictator* opened..to a glamorous audience who were elated and enthused. **1968** *Guardian* 13 July 8/6 Edmund Blunden's sudden resignation, in mid-term, has enthused nobody.

†en'thusiac, *a. Obs.* In 7 **-aque**. [f. Gr. ἐνθουσία (correctly inferred from its derivatives: see ENTHUSIASM) + -AC.] Causing prophetic ecstasy.

1603 HOLLAND *Plutarch's Mor.* 1321 These Enthusiaque and divining spirits.

†en'thusian. *Obs.* [f. as prec. + -AN.] = ENTHUSIAST 1.

1621 BURTON *Anat. Mel.* III. iv. I. iii. (1676) 406/1 Of Prophets, Enthusians and Impostors, our Ecclesiastical stories afford many examples. **1692** in COLES. **1707** E. WARD *Hudibras Rediv.* (1715) II. viii, Those..confusions, Occasioned by such vile Enthusions [*sic*] Who had already robb'd the Throne.

enthusiasm (ɛn'θjuːzɪæz(ə)m). Also 7 **enthusiasme**, (**entousiasm**, 8 **enthysiasm**). [ad. late L. *enthūsiasm-us*, Gr. ἐνθουσιασμός, f. ἐνθουσιάζειν, f. ἐνθουσία (Zonaras *Lex.*) the fact of being ἔνθεος possessed by a god. Cf. Fr. *enthousiasme*.

The word ἐνθουσία has been explained by Leo Meyer as for *ἐνθεουσία, abstr. sb. f. *ἐνθεοῦντ- stem of pr. pple. of *ἐνθεεῖν to be ἔνθεος.]

†1. a. Possession by a god, supernatural inspiration, prophetic or poetic frenzy; an occasion or manifestation of these. *Obs.*

[**1579** E. K. *Gloss. Spenser's Sheph. Cal.* Oct. *Argt.*, A certaine ἐνθουσιασμός and celestiall inspiration. **1608** SYLVESTER *Du Bartas* 210, I feel the vertue of my spirit decayed, The Enthousiasmos of my Muse allaid.] **1603** HOLLAND *Plutarch's Mor.* 1342 The Dæmons use to make their prophets and prophetesses to be ravished with an Enthusiasme or divine fury. **1620** J. PYPER tr. *Hist. Astrea* I. v. 146 The Bacchanals runne thorow the streets raging and storming, full of the Enthusiasme of their god. **1651** BAXTER *Inf. Bapt.* 87 Doth he think they knew it by Enthusiasm or Revelation from Heaven? **1674** HICKMAN *Hist. Quinquart.* (ed. 2) 8 Nothing made the Anabaptists so infamous as their pretended enthusiasms or revelations. **1693** URQUHART *Rabelais* III. Prol., It is my sole Entousiasm. **1807** ROBINSON *Archæol. Græca* III. xii. 253 The second sort of θεομάντεις.. were such as pretended to enthusiasm.

b. (cf. 3.) Poetical fervour, impassioned mood or tone. *Obs.*

1693 DRYDEN *Juvenal* Pref. (J.), Poetry, by a kind of enthusiasm, or extraordinary emotion of soul, makes it seem to us that we behold, etc. **1779–81** JOHNSON *L.P., Cowley* Wks. II. 70 He [Cowley] was the first who imparted to English numbers the enthusiasm of the greater ode, and the gaiety of the less.

2. Fancied inspiration; 'a vain confidence of divine favour or communication' (J.). In 18th c. often in vaguer sense: Ill-regulated or misdirected religious emotion, extravagance of religious speculation. *arch.*

1660 H. MORE *Myst. Godl.* To Rdr., If ever Christianity be exterminated, it will be by Enthusiasme. **1711** SHAFTESB. *Charac.* §7 (1737) I. 53 Inspiration is a real feeling of the Divine Presence, and Enthusiasm a false one. **1747** DODDRIDGE *Life Col. Gardiner* §137. 163 There is really such a Thing as Enthusiasm, against which it becomes the true Friends of the Revelation to be diligently on their Guard. **1766** WALPOLE *Let.* 10 Oct., Towards the end he [Wesley] exalted his voice and acted very ugly enthusiasm. **1772** PRIESTLEY *Inst. Relig.* (1782) I. 121 Enthusiasm [makes us] imagine that we are the peculiar favorites of the divine being. **1829** I. TAYLOR *Enthus.* ii. (1867) 20 The most formal and lifeless devotions..are mere enthusiasm unless, etc. **1841–4** EMERSON *Ess. Over-Soul* Wks. (Bohn) I. 118 Everywhere the history of religion betrays a tendency to enthusiasm.

3. a. The principal current sense: Rapturous intensity of feeling in favour of a person, principle, cause, etc.; passionate eagerness in any pursuit, proceeding from an intense conviction of the worthiness of the object.

1716 KENNETT in Ellis *Orig. Lett.* II. 429 IV. 306 The King of Sweden..must have much more enthusiasm in him to put it in execution. **1766–7** MRS. S. PENNINGTON *Lett.* III. 167 Different religions have introduced prejudices, Enthusiasms, and Scepticisms. **1792** *Anecd. W. Pitt* I. xviii. 282 A passion for glory which was nothing short of enthusiasm. **1808** SIR JOHN MOORE in Jas. Moore *Camp. Spain* 76 The armies you see are also without enthusiasm, or even common obstinacy. **1817** MISS MITFORD in L'Estrange *Life* II. i. 11 Enthusiasm is very catching, especially when it is very eloquent. **1863** MARY HOWITT tr. *F. Bremer's Greece* I. ii. 56 Enthusiasm for the ideals of his country and of humanity.

b. An object of (freq. temporary) enthusiasm; an action or idea about which one feels enthusiastic, a 'craze'.

1916 JOYCE *Portrait of Artist* ii. 102 The letters cut in the stained wood..stared upon him, mocking his bodily weakness and futile enthusiasms. **1931** M. SADLEIR *Bulwer* IV. v. 224 Godwin, whose enlightened political philosophy and actual achievements in fiction were among Bulwer's youthful enthusiasms. **1937** H. G. WELLS *Brynhild* v. 58 Cummington's enthusiasms always annoyed him and this last enthusiasm just now he felt might annoy him very much.

enthusiast (ɛnˈθjuːzɪæst). [ad. Gr. ἐνθουσιαστής, f. ἐνθουσιάζειν (see prec.). Cf. Fr. *enthousiaste*.]

†**1.** One who is (really or seemingly) possessed by a god; one who is under the influence of prophetic frenzy. Also *fig. Obs.*

a **1641** Bp. Mountagu *Acts & Mon.* (1642) 162 So did those Enthusiasts amongst the Pagans deliver that..wherof they had no..apprehension. **1660** Stillingfl. *Iren.* I. v. (1662) 96 Their proper Enthusiasts as the Sybils, and the Pythian Prophetess. **1677** W. Hubbard *Narrative* II. 48 The Indians..will not as yet return any of our Captive Friends, till God speak to the foresaid Enthusiasts [two sagamores claiming divine inspiration].

fig. **1647** Crashaw *Music's Duel* Poems 90 She is placed Above herself—Music's enthusiast! **1700** Dryden *Alexander's Feast* 163 The sweet enthusiast from her sacred store Enlarg'd the former narrow bounds.

2. †**a.** transl. Lat. *Enthusiasta*: In *Eccl. Hist.* the designation of a sect of heretics of the fourth century, who pretended to special revelations. *Obs.* (The Lat. form is now used *Hist.*)

1637 Hieron *Wks.* I. 82 There were in the elder times certaine heretiques called Enthusiasts, which..contemned the written word. **1639** F. Robarts *God's Holy H.* x. 75 The haeresie of the Messalini otherwise called Euchites and Enthusiastes.

b. *gen.* One who erroneously believes himself to be the recipient of special divine communications; in wider sense, one who holds extravagant and visionary religious opinions, or is characterized by ill-regulated fervour of religious emotion.

(Pagitt and other 17th c. writers give *enthusiasts* as the actual name of a contemporary sect of Anabaptists; but this is probably a misapprehension.)

1609 Downam *Chr. Liberty* 27 If there be no freedom in our wills before we be called, then belike..we must looke with the Enthusiasts for violent raptures. **1614** T. Adams *Devil's Banquet* 328 Sottish Enthusiastes condemne all learning, all premeditation. **1665** Glanvill *Sceps. Sci.* xiii. 73 Hence we may derive the Visions, Voyces, Revelations of the Enthusiast. **1746** Wesley *Princ. Methodist* 54 It is the believing those to be Miracles which are not, that constitutes an Enthusiast. **1806** Earl Westmorld. in Cobbett *Parl. Deb.* VII. 230 Atheists, enthusiasts, jacobins, and such descriptions of persons. **1856** R. Vaughan *Mystics* (1860) II. 164 This very Church of Rome incarcerated Molinos and Madame Guyon as dangerous enthusiasts.

3. One who is full of 'enthusiasm' (see enthusiasm 3) for a cause or principle, or who enters with enthusiasm into a pursuit. Const. *for*, *in*, *of*, †*to*. Sometimes with unfavourable notion (*transf.* from 2 b.): A visionary, self-deluded person.

In present use the disparaging sense is more frequent than in the case of the related words enthusiasm and enthusiastic.

1764 Goldsmith *Hist. Eng.* in *Lett.* (1772) II. 224 An enthusiast to the discipline of the field. **1769** *Junius Lett.* xxxv. 158 Hardly serious at first, he is now an enthusiast. **1790** Burke *Fr. Rev.* Wks. V. 197 We shall believe those reformers to be then honest enthusiasts. **1791** —— *Th. Fr. Affairs* VII. 74 At present the king..can send none but the enthusiasts of the system. **1793** Holcroft tr. *Lavater's Physiogn.* viii. 52 Paracelsus..an astrological enthusiast. **1856** Sir B. Brodie *Psychol. Inq.* I. i. 26 The energy and sincerity of enthusiasts is powerful in all ages. **1878** Morley *Carlyle* in *Crit. Misc.* 196 The arbitrary enthusiast for external order.

¶ Sometimes defined by the context in its etymological sense, in order to give a different complexion to its use in sense 2 or 3.

c **1771** Fletcher *4th Check* Wks. 1795 III. 59 The true Enthusiasts, those who are really inspired by the grace and love of God. **1879** R. H. Smith in *Sunday Mag.* 507 He was an enthusiast in the best and truest sense of the word, for he was filled with the fulness of God.

4. *attrib.* or *adj.* That is an enthusiast; pertaining to an enthusiast, enthusiastic.

1681 Luttrell *Brief Rel.* (1857) I. 88 The enthusiast maid of Hatfeild predicted the royall blood should be poysoned. **1742** Collins *Ode Pity* 29 Shall raise a wild enthusiast heat. **1862** Thornbury *Turner* II. 325 In a room that resembled the miserable Barry's, he lived his enthusiast life.

enthusiastic (ɛnˌθjuːzɪˈæstɪk), *a.* and *sb.* [ad. Gr. ἐνθουσιαστικ-ός, f. ἐνθουσιάζειν: see prec.]

A. *adj.* Of or pertaining to enthusiasm, full of or characterized by enthusiasm.

†**1.** Pertaining to, or of the nature of, possession by a deity. Also *fig. Obs.*

1603 Holland *Plutarch's Mor.* 1348 For an instrument..to set it [divination] aworke, we allow a spirit or winde, and an exhalation enthusiasticke. **1647** Crashaw *Poems* 112 Enthusiastic flames, such as can give Marrow to my plump genius. **1669** Gale *Crt. Gentiles* I. III. i. 12 The Forme..wherein the first Divine Poesie was delivered, was Enthusiastic. **1849** Fitzgerald tr. *Whitaker's Disp.* 295 We do not speak of any enthusiastic influence of the Spirit.

†**2.** Pertaining to, characterized by, or of the nature of mystical delusions in religion. *Obs.*

1690 Temple *Ess. Heroic Virtue* Wks. 1731 I. 220 Being built upon Foundations wholly Enthusiastick, and thereby very unaccountable to common Reason. **1727** Swift *Let. Eng. Tongue*, During the usurpation..an infusion of enthusiastic jargon prevailed. **1748** Hartley *Observ. Man* II. ii. 194 The several Enthusiastic Sects that arise from time to time among Christians.

†**b.** *transf.* Irrational, 'quixotic'. *Obs.*

1692 Dryden *St. Euremont's Ess.* 34 The Decii who sacrificed themselves for the good of a Society whom they went to forsake, seem to me truly enthusiastick. **1775** Johnson *Tax. no Tyr.* 10 An absurd and enthusiastick contempt of interest.

3. Of feelings, convictions, etc.: That is of the nature of, that amounts to, enthusiasm 3; intensely ardent, rapturous. Of persons, their temperaments, actions, language, etc.: Characterized by or manifesting enthusiasm 3.

1786 Burke *W. Hastings* Wks. 1813 XII. 401 Their military and enthusiastick spirit. **1791** —— *Lett. Member Nat. Assemb.* Wks. VI. 39 A style, glowing, animated, enthusiastick. **1793** Gouv. Morris in Sparks *Life & Writ.* (1832) II. 276 The English will be wound up to a pitch of enthusiastic horror against France. **1808** Sir John Moore in Jas. Moore *Camp. Spain* (1809) 294 In aid of an enthusiastic brave people. **1841** Lane *Arab. Nts.* I. 72 Enthusiastic admirers of literature. **1876** Green *Short Hist.* vii. 361 A burst of enthusiastic joy hailed the accession of Elizabeth.

†**B.** *sb.* = enthusiast 1, 2 b. *Obs.*

1610 Healey *St. Aug. Citie of God* 56 There we saw Enthusiastikes, persons rapt with fury. **1634** Sir T. Herbert *Trav.* (1677) 326 (T.), The dervis and other santoons, or enthusiasticks. **1692** Luttrell *Brief Rel.* (1857) II. 547 Some troopes were ordered to suppresse and seize upon the ring-leaders of these enthusiasticks. **1707** E. Ward *Hud. Rediv.* (1715) II. IX, Enthusiasticks flock'd in Shoales, To fight, not for their Lives, but Souls.

enthusiˈastical, *a.* [f. prec. + -al[1].]

†**1.** Of the nature of possession by a deity; = enthusiastic 1. *Obs. rare.*

a **1652** J. Smith *Sel. Disc.* vi. 183 This way of communicating truth to the souls of men is originally nothing else but prophetical or enthusiastical.

†**2.** = enthusiastic 2. *Obs.*

1656 H. More *Enthus. Tri.* (1712) 25 We are speaking now of Enthusiastical Sanguine. **1677** W. Hubbard *Narrative* II. 61 Squando..that Enthusiastical, or rather Diabolical Miscreant. **1679** Puller *Moder. Ch. Eng.* (1843) 299 This one enthusiastical conceit of the 'Light within'. **1696** C. Leslie *Snake in Grass* (1697) 92 The..Enthusiastical Murthers, Rapines, and Outrage of the Zealots. **1729** Butler *Serm.* Wks. 1874 II. 174 The subject is a real one: there is nothing in it enthusiastical or unreasonable. **1752** Carte *Hist. Eng.* III. 82 The enthusiastical and seditious opinions of Muncer and the Anabaptists. *a* **1847** Mrs. Sherwood *Lady of Manor* I. ix. 401 A set of enthusiastical Methodists.

†**b.** *transf.* Moved by irrational impulses; visionary; fanatically devoted to an idea or belief.

1614 T. Adams *Devil's Banquet* 331 Some will minister nothing, but what comes next into their heads and hands: these are Enthusiasticall Phisitians. **1680** Burnet *Rochester* 82 They are neither hot nor enthusiastical but under the power of calm and clear Principles. **1711** Shaftesb. *Charac.* (1737) III. 64 There have been in reality Enthusiastical Atheists. **1750** Johnson *Rambler* No. 63 ¶4 That all are equally happy..none is sufficiently enthusiastical to maintain.

3. = enthusiastic 3. *arch.*

1782 V. Knox *Ess.* (1819) III. cxviii. 1 The enthusiastical admirers of a favourite author. **1802** Mar. Edgeworth *Mor. T.* (1816) I. x. 82 The old man, whose temper was not quite so enthusiastical. **1837** W. Ware *Zenobia* (1844) I. 4 A birth transcending human expectation could not create a more enthusiastical sensation.

enˌthusiˈastically, *adv.* [f. prec. + -ly[2].]

†**a.** In the manner of one under mystical religious delusion. *Obs.* **b.** In the manner of one full of enthusiasm; with a display of ardent or rapturous feeling.

a. 1691 Wood *Ath. Oxon.* (R.), He [John Oxenbridge] preached very enthusiastically in several places. **1696** C. Leslie *Snake in Grass* (1697) 90 If they shou'd Enthusiastically Believe, or Hypocritically Pretend. **1722** De Foe *Plague* (1754) 26 Some were so Enthusiastically bold as to run about the Streets, with their Oral Predictions.

b. 1786 W. Gilpin in *Mrs. Delany's Corr.* Ser. II. III. 346 Plants, of which she is enthusiastically fond. **1848** Macaulay *Hist. Eng.* I. 362 His scheme was enthusiastically applauded. **1876** Grant *Burgh Sch. Scotl.* Pref. 5 Mr. Innes ..always entered enthusiastically into any proposal calculated to elucidate the past history of his native country.

enˈthusiastly, *adv. rare.* [f. enthusiast + -ly[2].] In the manner of an enthusiast.

1884 W. J. Linton *Poor Woman* in *Transl. Eng. Verse*, 155 The young..Of her great beauty raved enthusiastly.

enthwite, var. of entwite *v.*, *Obs.*

enthymematic (ˌɛnθɪmɪˈmætɪk), *a.* [ad. Gr. ἐνθυμηματικός, f. ἐνθύμημα (see next).] Of, or pertaining to, or of the nature of an enthymeme; containing an enthymeme; consisting of enthymemes. Also ˌ**enthymeˈmatical** *a.* in same sense.

1588 Fraunce *Lawiers Log.* II. ix. 98 b, An argument called Sorites by this enthymematicall progression. **1681** Hobbes *Rhet.* II. xxii. 84 Enthymematical; that is, have in themselves the force of an Enthymeme. **1827–53** Whately *Logic* II. iv. §7 Here the Minor Premiss is what is called an Enthymematic sentence. **1860** Abp. Thomson *Laws Th.* §110. 206.

enthymeme (ˈɛnθɪmiːm). Also 7–9 **enthymem**; in Lat. form **enthymema**. [ad. L. *enthȳmēma*, a. Gr. ἐνθύμημα, f. ἐνθυμέεσθαι to think, consider, infer, f. ἐν in + θυμός mind.]

†**1.** *Rhet.* After Aristotle's use: An argument based on merely probable grounds; a rhetorical argument as distinguished from a demonstrative one. *Obs.*

1600 Holland *Livy* XXIII. xii. 481 These strange Enthymemes and conclusions. **1642** Milton *Apol. Smect.* (1851) 256 To wreath an Enthymema with maistrous dexterity. *a* **1677** Barrow *Serm.* (1686) III. ii. 18 Oratours back their Enthymemes (or rational Argumentations) with Inductions (or singular Examples). **1841** De Quincey *Rhetoric* Wks. X. (1862) 27 [Explains Aristotle's use, as distinguished from that of later logicians].

†**2.** Cicero (*Top.* xiii.) uses *enthymema* for a striking antithesis closing a rhetorical period. Hence the following definitions:

1657 J. Smith *Myst. Rhet.*, An Enthymem..is, as Cicero saith, when the sentence concluded consisteth of contraries. **1731** Bailey, *Enthymem* (with Rhetoricians) is when the concluding sentence consists of contraries.

3. *Logic.* A syllogism in which one premiss is suppressed.

[This sense is due to a misapprehension (already in Boethius *a* 524), the description of the enthymeme (sense 1) as 'an imperfect syllogism' (ἀτελὴς συλλογισμός) having been interpreted as referring to its form instead of its matter.]

1588 Fraunce *Lawiers Log.* II. ix. 98 b, An Enthymeme is nothing but a contracted syllogisme. **1656** Cowley *Pindar. Odes* 50 *note*, In Enthymemes..half is left out to be supplyed by the Hearer. **1712** Arbuthnot *John Bull* (1755) 95, I desire to know whether you will have it by way of Syllogism, Enthymem, Dilemma, or Sorites. **1764** Reid *Inquiry*, Perhaps Des Cartes meant not to assume his own existence in this enthymeme, but the existence of thought. **1795** Wythes *Decis. Virginia* 15 The argument included in this opinion is an enthymema. **1827–36** Whately *Logic* 265 In an Enthymeme the suppressed Premiss should be always the one of whose truth least doubt can exist. **1870** Bowen *Logic* iii. 57 The Common form of argumentation is Enthymeme, which consists of but two propositions.

entice (ɛnˈtaɪs), *v.* Forms: α. 3–6 **entyce**, **-tyse**, 4–7 **entise**, (4 **entythe**, 7 **entize**,) 4– **entice**. β. 4 **intisce**, 5–6 **intyce**, 6–7 **intise**, 5–8 **intice**. [a. OF. *enticier* (in ONF. *enticher*) = sense 1; the etymological sense was prob. 'to set on fire, add fuel to (a fire)'; app. repr. Lat. type **intitiāre*, f. *in-* (see in-) + **titi-us* (class. L. *titio*) firebrand. Cf. attice (of which this is a parallel form) and tice; for the development of sense cf. embrace *v.*[3]]

†**1.** *trans.* To stir up, incite, instigate (*to* a course of action); also to provoke (*to* anger). *Obs.*

1297 R. Glouc. (1724) 235 Edelfred..He entyced and oþer kynges..þat hii wende to Walys. *c* **1315** Shoreham 114 Glotonye entythyth [? *read* entychyth, entyssyth; *rime* norysseth] To lecherye her. *c* **1325** *E.E. Allit. P.* B. 1136 þou dryȝtyn dyspleses with dedes ful sore, & entyses hym to tene more traybly þen euer. ? *a* **1400** *Chester Pl.* (1843–7) 207 When he intisced hym through his read. ? *a* **1400** *Morte Arth.* 307 To entyce the Emperour to take overe the mounttes. **1538** Bale *Thre Lawes* 1998 Therein to do as ye shall me entyce. **1568** Grafton *Chron.* II. 720 Your maister, is..entised and provoked by the Duke of Burgoyn. **1628** Hobbes *Thucyd.* (1822) 62 Not suffering the Athenians to give them the least way but enticing them to the war.

2. To allure, attract by the offer of pleasure or advantage; *esp.* to allure insidiously or adroitly. Often const. *from*, *to* (a course of conduct, a place). Also with *away*, *in*.

1303 R. Brunne *Handl. Synne* 1503 ȝyf þou..entycedest any fro relygyoun, Gostly þou mayst hym slo. **1401** *Pol. Poems* (1859) II. 33 What charity is this..to intice him to be buried among you from his parish church. **1550** *Act 3 & 4 Edw. VI*, c. 16 §13 If..the father..steale, or intise away any such child. **1577** B. Googe *Heresbach's Husb.* IV. (1586) 187 [Bees]..entised with these newe flowres..feed..greedilie. **1607** Dekker *Westw. Hoe* Wks. 1873 II. 306 Intist from mine owne Paradice, To steale fruit in a barren wildernes. **1648** Gage *West. Ind.* xix. (1655) 144 Those that keep the Bodegones..will commonly intice in the Indians, and make them drunk. **1664** Evelyn *Kal. Hort.* (1729) 209 Beer mingled with Honey, to entice the Wasps. **1706** Addison *Rosamond* III. iii, That no foul minister of vice Again my sinking soul intice. **1748** *Anson's Voy.* III. vi. 348 We could not entice them on board. **1786** H. Tooke *Purley* Introd. 6, I shall not be at all inticed by them to take upon my shoulders a burthen. **1807** Crabbe *Par. Reg.* III. (1810) 31 No curious shell, rare plant..Inticed our traveller, from his home, so far. **1872** Black *Adv. Phaeton* xxv. 343 My Lady strove to entice him into the general talk. **1880** T. Spalding *Eliz. Demonol.* 22 The most successful method of enticing stragglers into its folds.

†**b.** *transf.* To attract physically. *nonce-use.*

1646 Sir T. Browne *Pseud. Ep.* II. iii. 76 It would not intice it [the Needle] from A to B, but repell it from A to Z.

†**3.** [? A distinct word, a. OF. *entechier*: see entach.] ? To catch (an infection or stain). *Obs.*

c **1340** *Gaw. & Gr. Knt.* 3436 How tender hit is to entyse teches of fylþe.

Hence †**enˈticeable** *a.*, *Obs.*, in 7 **intiseable**, fitted to entice, seductive. †**enˈticeful** *a.*, *Obs. rare*, enticing, full of enticement.

1607 *Exam. Geo. Blakwel* 156 Intiseable perswasions of mens alluring reasons. **1556** T. Hoby tr. *Castiglione's Courtyer* II. (1561) L b, Women enticefull past shame.

enticement (ɛnˈtaɪsmənt). Also 4–8 **inticement**. [a. OF. *enticement*: see prec. and -ment.]

†**1.** Incitement, instigation. Also *concr.* something that incites. *Obs.*

1303 R. Brunne *Handl. Synne* 2146 Al ys entycement of þe deuyl. *c* **1380** Wyclif *Apocalypse* xiii. in *Bible* Pref. 8 *note*, Fals prelates that don by the conseil and the enticement of hem that sechen erthelich things. *c* **1425** Wyntoun

Cron. VIII. xxiv. 199 Ðis wes þe fyrst entycement Ðat amovyd on þis were. **1494** FABYAN V. cxv. 89 Chylperiche hadde by intycement of Fredegunde wrongfullye turmentyd tharchebyshop of Roan. **1555** EDEN *Decades W. Ind.* (Arb.) 331 They lacke breade, salte, and other intysements of glutteny. **1587** FLEMING *Contn. Holinshed* III. 1367/2 By intisements of certeine seditious and traitorous persons.

2. The action of alluring or attracting; attractive quality, fascination; *concr.* a means or method of enticing; something which entices, an allurement.

1549 L. COXE *Erasm. Par. Titus* ii. 14 A newe peculyar people, which..should contemne yᵉ euyls of this world, & treade downe yᵉ entysementes & giftes of it vnder their fete. **1607** FLETCHER *Woman Hater* I. iii, Banquets, Masques, Shews, all inticements That Wit and Lust together can devise. **1634** MILTON *Comus* 524 Here to every thirsty wanderer, [Comus] By sly enticement gives his baneful cup. **1692** BENTLEY *Boyle Lect.* i. 31 What inticement is there in common profane Swearing? **1727** BRADLEY *Fam. Dict.* s.v. *Horse-Feeder*, The Horse-Feeder..must..win him [the Horse] by gentle Enticements. **1738** BIRCH *Life Milton* Wks. I. 75 No Enticements of any kind were wanting. Great sums of Money were proffer'd. **1844** EMERSON *Tantalus* Wks. (Bohn) III. 322 There is in woods and waters a certain enticement and flattery.

enticer (ɛn'taɪsə(r)). [f. as prec. + -ER¹.] One who, or that which, entices; †an instigator (*obs.*); a seducer, tempter.

c **1386** CHAUCER *Pers. T.* ¶943 If that another man be occasioun or ellis enticer of his synne. *c* **1500** *Hye Way to Spytal H.* 833 in Hazl. *E.P.P.* IV. 60 Applesquyers, entycers, and ravysshers. **1583** BABINGTON *Commandm.* vii. Wks. (1637) 58 The eye is a vehement inticer unto lust. **1640** BP. REYNOLDS *Passions* xvi. 173 Rarity is a marveilous Lenocinium, and inticer of Desire. *a* **1703** BURKITT *On N.T.* Matt. xxvi. 75 Either the first enticers, or the accidental occasions were women. **1858** *Plain Serm. Var. Subj.* 227 How many a wretched being..might but for some lustful enticer, have followed the Lamb of God in eternal glory!

enticing (ɛn'taɪsɪŋ), *vbl. sb.* [f. as prec. + -ING¹.] The action of the vb. ENTICE.

a **1340** HAMPOLE *Psalter* xviii. 13 Synnes þat comes of ill eggyngis [*S.* euel entysynge]. **1450–1530** *Myrr. our Ladye* 194 They felle through the entysynge of the wycked spyryte. **1535** COVERDALE *Ecclus.* ix. 4 Heare hir not, lest thou perish thorow hir entysinge. **1823** SCOTT *Peveril* viii, Pardon my enticing away from your service the young woman.

enticing (ɛn'taɪsɪŋ), *ppl. a.* [f. as prec. + -ING².] That entices or instigates; insidiously attractive; alluring, beguiling, seductive.

1553 T. WILSON *Rhet.* 40 A brothell house where entisinge harlottes lived. **1593** SHAKS. *2 Hen VI*, I. iii. 92 My selfe haue..plac't a Quier of such enticing Birds. **1611** BIBLE *Col.* ii. 4 Lest any man should beguile you with entising words. **1697** DRYDEN *Virg. Georg.* III. 337 The soft Seducer, with enticing Looks, The bellowing Rivals to the Fight provokes. **1788** BURKE *Sp. agst. W. Hastings* Wks. XIII. 305 Ladies recommended..by sweet and enticing names. *Mod.* I do not find the prospect enticing.

enticingly (ɛn'taɪsɪŋlɪ), *adv.* [f. prec. + -LY².] In an enticing manner.

1720 WELTON *Suffer. Son of God* I. iv. 71 An Enemy, so much the more formidable, as it, the more Enticingly, sooths our Natural Inclinations. **1831** LYTTON *Godolph.* 9 The idea..more enticingly put than it was at first. **1877** LADY BRASSEY *Voy. Sunbeam* xiv. (1878) 240 We found the table most enticingly laid out.

entier, entierty, obs. ff. ENTIRE, etc.

entifical (ɛn'tɪfɪkəl), *a. rare.* [f. assumed L. **entific-us* (f. *ent-* stem of ENS + *-ficus*: see -FIC) + -AL¹.] That bestows essential existence.

1743 J. ELLIS *Knowledge Div. Things* IV. 367 Nothing being contingent but God foreknew it, and he..could not know it without an eternal entifical Idea of it.

entify ('ɛntɪfaɪ), *v. rare.* [ad. assumed L. **entificāre*, f. as prec.: see -FY.] *trans.* To make into an entity, attribute objective existence to. Hence **entifi'cation**.

1882 tr. *T. Vignoli's Myth & Sc.* (Internat. Sci. Series) 154 The primitive and constant act of all animals..is that of entifying the object of sensation..Such entification is the result of spontaneous necessity.

†en'tiltment. *Obs. rare*⁻¹. [f. EN-¹ + TILT *sb.* + -MENT.] A temporary covering; an awning.

1599 NASHE *Lenten Stuffe* 80 The best houses and walls there were of mud, or canvas or poldavies entiltments.

entincture, entinsel: see EN- *pref.*¹ 1 b.

†en'tine, *v. Obs.* [f. EN-¹ + TINE (Spenser), TIND to kindle.] *trans.* To kindle, light up.

1612 LANE *Sqrs. Tale* E.E.T.S. 318 This aunswer.. taught Videria this new brond t'entine. *Ibid.* 326 Whose dauncinge plumes..seemd at the sonns beames many sonns t'entyne.

entir, var. of INTER.

entirchawnge, entirdite: see INTERCHANGE, INTERDICT.

entire (ɛn'taɪə(r)), *a.*, *adv.* and *sb.* Forms: α. 4–6 enter(e, 5–6 entier(e, -tyer(e, (4 entre, 4–7 enteer(e), 7 entyre, 6– entire. β. 4 intier, 5–6 intere, 5–7 intyre, 6 *Sc.* inteir, 6–9 intire. [a. OF. *entier, entir* = Pr. *entier, entieyr*, Cat. *enter*, Sp. *entero*, It. *intero*, Pg. *inteiro*:—L. *in'tegr-um*, f. *in* not + **tag-* root of *tangĕre* to touch.

The L. *integer* was used in the lit. senses 'whole, unbroken, sound', and in the fig. of 'untainted, upright'; these senses remained in early French and consequently in Middle English, but with very few exceptions only the lit. senses have survived to the present time.]

A. *adj.* **I.**

1. Whole; with no part excepted.

a **1400** *Symbols Passion* 229 in *Leg. Rood* 196 To sen it a twelf-moneth ich day enter. *a* **1400–50** *Alexander* 1261 To tell þair torfer in tere it wald tary me to lang. **1494** FABYAN 5 Of bothe landes the Cronycles entyere. *a* **1535** MORE *On the Passion* Wks. 1337. 2 The very real things that is conteyned vnder both those fourmes, is one entiere bodye. **1618** SIR H. CAREY in *Fortesc. Papers* 56, I have yourself to be my noble wittness for my intyre proceedeing. **1667** MILTON *P.L.* XII. 264 The Sun shall in mid Heav'n stand still A day entire. **1747** WESLEY *Prim. Physic* (1762) 111 The entire Creation was at Peace with Man. **1816** KIRBY & SP. *Entomol.* (1828) II. xviii. 107 Destroys an intire colony, of which she would be the founder. **1860** TYNDALL *Glac.* I. §7. 48 Sufficiently strong to bear the entire weight of the body.

2. a. Complete; constituting a whole; including all the essential parts. †In early use also, perfect, containing all that is desirable.

c **1430** LYDG. *Bochas* I. i. (1544) 1 b, Paradyse, a place most entiere. **1571** DIGGES *Pantom.* I. xxxv. L j b, You shall make one entier table of all, conteyning the number of myles, furlongs, etc. **1688** R. HOLME *Armoury* III. 322/1 The Drill, the Drill Bow, and the Drill Plate, go all together as one entire Instrument. **1697** DRYDEN *Virg. Past.* Pref. (1721) I. 93, I do not design an intire Treatise in this Preface. **1804** *Ann. Rev.* II. 77/1 The occupier of what is called an entire farm. **1873** SYMONDS *Grk. Poets* iii. 81 Phocylides says: In justice the whole of virtue exists entire.

†b. Applied about 1722 to a kind of malt liquor (similar to what is now called 'porter'). (See quot. 1802.) *Obs.*; but see C. 4.

1742 *Lond. & Country Brew.* I. (ed. 4) 25 For intire small Beer, five or six Barrels off a Quarter. **1754** *Connoisseur* xv, A publican..ventured an hogshead of entire butt on the candidate who serves him with beer. **1771** SMOLLETT *Humph. Cl.* (1815) 148 Calvert's entire butt beer. **1802** [J. FELTHAM] *Picture of London* 249 Porter obtained its name about the year 1730..[it had previously been] the practice to call for a pint of *three threads*, meaning a third of ale, beer, and twopenny... A brewer of the name of Harwood conceived the idea of making a liquor which should partake of the united flavours of [all three]..calling it *entire* or *entire* butt. **1839** BAILEY *Festus* xviii. (1848) 181 And porter and stout, entire and brown.

3. a. Of a quality, state of feeling, condition, fact, or action: Realized in its full extent, thorough, complete, total. (*entire affection, friendship*, etc., may sometimes occur in this sense, but chiefly belong to the obs. sense 10.)

c **1400** *Pol. Rel. & L. Poems* 256 Than schalt þou sacrifice accepte Of riȝtwisnesse & treuþe entere. **1413** LYDG. *Pilgr. Sowle* IV. xx. (1483) 64, I had ioye entier and eke gladnesse. **1642** ROGERS *Naaman* 587 Gods cures are like himselfe, perfect, intire, and absolute. **1647** CLARENDON *Hist. Reb.* I. (1843) 5/2 That he..might..present to his majesty the entire peace and restitution of his family. **1692** SOUTH *Serm.* (1697) I. 475 The Intire overthrow of this mighty..Host of the Midianites. **1712** W. ROGERS *Voy.* p. vi, I wish you intire Health and Happiness. **1755** YOUNG *Centaur* ii. Wks. 1757 IV. 141 Hell is nothing but an intire absence from Him. **1793** BURKE *Corr.* (1844) IV. 186 If you did not give entire credit to my declarations. **1836** J. GILBERT *Chr. Atonem.* vi. (1852) 161 The statements of Scripture are in entire harmony with this representation. **1855** MACAULAY *Hist. Eng.* III. 220 Granting entire liberty of conscience. **1879** R. K. DOUGLAS *Confucianism* iii. 80 Entire sincerity is required of them who approach the altar.

b. With agent-noun or sb. descriptive of a person: That is thoroughly of the character described. †Also formerly as predicate: Thoroughly established in (an opinion, a resolve, knowledge, etc.); cf. Fr. *entier* 'qui maintient entières ses idées, ses volontés' (Littré).

1534 LD. BERNERS *Gold. Bk. M. Aurel.* (1546) G g, All these mortall men ar so entier in their owne wylles. **1641** HINDE *J. Bruen* lvii. 190 All such..as were most sound and entire in the Knowledge of the Truth. **1655** *Francion* xi. 23 They did not know her to be entire in her resolutions, and that she would not forsake them for any Remonstrances. **1657** EARL MONMOUTH tr. *Parata's Pol. Disc.* 85 The Romans never laid down Arms but when they were entire Victors. *Mod.* He is an entire believer in Christianity.

†c. Of persons: Wholly devoted to another, perfectly beloved. In later use, of friends and friendly intercourse: Unreserved, familiar, intimate. *Obs.* [cf. Fr. *ami entier*, and equivalent in It. and Sp.]

c **1420** *Pallad. on Husb.* I. 279 Hym nil I undertake That is thi dere entere. **1430** LYDG. *Chron. Troy* I. v, Thy doughter deare That was to the so passingly entere. **1608–11** BP. HALL *Medit. & Vows* II. §38 It is best to be courteous to all; entire with few. **1611** CORYAT *Crudities* Ep. Ded., My most sincere and entire friend M. Lionel Cranfield. **1641** BP. HALL *Rem. Wks.* II. (1660) 89 It troubled him an hundred times more to be cast out from this (more entire) presence. **1643** HORN & ROBOTHAM *Gate Lang. Unl.* xciii. §909 Waiwardnesse estrangeth the entirest friends. *a* **1718** PENN *Life* Wks. 1726 I. 232 An entire and constant Friend.

4. a. Whole, unbroken, intact; not mutilated or decayed; undiminished in quantity or extent.

a **1631** DONNE *Paradoxes* (1652) 86 [A miser's treasure profits no one;] Yet it remains intire. **1656** MORE *Antid. Ath.* III. viii. (1712) 113 His body was found entire. **1666** EVELYN *Diary* 7 Sept., Nothing remaining intire but the inscription in the architrave. **1697** POTTER *Antiq. Greece* I. xxv. (1715) 132 Their Estates, which were all that time preserv'd entire to them. **1727** A. HAMILTON *New Acc. E. Ind.* I. x. 102 The Portugueze capitulated to leave Ormuze, with all the Fortifications intire. **1805** WORDSW. *Prel.* IV. (1850) 101 In military garb, Though faded yet entire. **1826** KIRBY & SP. *Entomol.* (1828) IV. xxxvii. 19 The headless animal made the same movements as when intire.

b. *spec.* Of male animals: Not castrated. [So in all Romanic langs.]

1799 MALTHUS *Jrnl.* 13 July (1966) 146 Entire horses are in general use here. **1834–43** SOUTHEY *Doctor* (1849) 339 What the Spaniards..call a Caballo Padre, or what some of our own writers..appellate an entire horse. **1876** WHYTE MELVILLE *Katerfelto* vii. 78 The animal, though an entire horse..responded lovingly and gently to his caress.

c. Of immaterial things: Unimpaired, undiminished.

1601 HOLLAND *Pliny* I. 136 But there continue still in their entire and as flourishing state as euer the city Hebata and Oruros. **1635** A. STAFFORD *Fem. Glory* (1869) 107 The first Principles of my Religion..I will preserve entyre. **1667** MILTON *P.L.* I. 146 If he our Conquerour..Have left us this our spirit and strength intire. **1736** BUTLER *Anal.* I. i. 25 Apprehension, Memory, Reason, all entire. **1853** ROBERTSON *Serm.* Ser. III. xvi. 219 When Christian principles were left entire.

†d. Of a question: Intact; that has not been entered upon. Of an offence: In no degree atoned for or 'purged'. *Obs.*

1598 GRENEWEY *Tacitus' Ann.* III. xvi. (1622) 71 Yet that the offence committed against his father, was entire. **1698** SIDNEY *Disc. Govt.* i. §3 (1704) 8 So that the Question remains intire, as if he had never mention'd it.

e. Of persons: With unimpaired strength, not fatigued or worn, fresh. [So L. *integer*.] *arch.*

1590 SPENSER *F.Q.* I. vi. 44 Backe to fight againe, new breathed and entire. **1628** HOBBES *Thucyd.* (1822) 104 Won to the war when you were entire but repenting it upon the damage. **1665** MANLEY *Grotius' Low-C. Warres* 291 Six hundred intire, beside two hundred sick and wounded. **1853** ROBERTSON *Serm.* Ser. III. i. (1872) 8 He is entire, powerful because he has not spent his strength.

5. a. Wholly of one piece; continuous throughout; one and undivided. Now only in scientific use.

1590 SPENSER *F.Q.* I. vii. 33 But all of Diamond perfect pure and cleene It framed was, One massie entire mould. **1604** SHAKS. *Oth.* V. ii. 144 Of one entyre and perfect Chrysolite. **1679** PENN *Addr. Prot.* I. ix. (1692) 46 Being but one Entire Interest throughout the World. **1699** DAMPIER *Voy.* II. I. i. 14 A turn on the Last side of the River, which is here entire: for a little before..we met the main stream where it parts into the 2 channels. **1703** MAUNDRELL *Journ. Jerus., Euphrates, &c.* (1732) 4 Intire blocks of wood. **1726** LEONI *Alberti's Archit.* I. 42 a, All Stone should be entire.. you may know whether it is entire or crack'd. **1786** tr. *Beckford's Vathek* (1868) 28 The chasm closed, and the ground became as entire as the rest of the plain. **1817** W. SELWYN *Law Nisi Prius* II. 860 If a man be imprisoned..on the 1st day of January, and kept in prison till the 1st day of February..the whole is one entire trespass. **1834** MᶜMURTRIE *Cuvier's Anim. Kingd.* 200 The first dorsal entire; while on the contrary the last rays of the second, as well as those of the anal which correspond to them, are detached. **1880** GRAY *Struct. Bot.* vi. §5. 245 The calyx or corolla when gamophyllous..is said to be..entire, when the union is complete to the summit or border.

b. Of troops: Forming an unbroken body. Now only in techn. phrase ***rank entire***.

1568 GRAFTON *Chron.* II. 505 The Duke of Bedford.. made likewise an entier battayle. **1691** *Proc. agst. French* in *Select. Harl. Misc.* (1793) 476 They marched intire through the body of the country. **1833** *Regul. Instr. Cavalry* I. 126 The Squads should..be formed rank entire. **1879** A. FORBES in *Daily News* 13 June 5/6 That the true tactic is to work in rank entire.

c. In scientific use: Having an unbroken outline, without notches or indentations. Said, *e.g.* of leaves, shells, certain parts of animal bodies.

1757 MILLER in *Phil. Trans.* L. 435 The leaves are intire, and come to a point at their base. **1817** COLERIDGE *Biog. Lit.* (1847) II. 209 The gable ends..towards the street, some in the ordinary triangular form and entire as the botanists say. **1828** STARK *Elem. Nat. Hist.* II. 180 Last segment of the abdomen entire or notched. **1835** LINDLEY *Introd. Bot.* (1848) I. 261 The entire blade of the Box tree. **1866** TATE *Brit. Mollusks* iii. 45 The aperture is entire that is not notched or produced into a canal.

d. *Her.* Of a bearing, e.g. a cross: attached to the sides of the shield.

1688 [see FIXED *ppl. a.* 1 b]. **1825** W. BERRY *Encycl. Her.* I. Bb 2/1 *Entire*, or *Through out*, sometimes called *fixed* and *firm*, being attached to the sides of the shield, as a *cross pattée entire*. **1889** [see FIRME *a.*]. **1969** FRANKLYN & TANNER *Encycl. Dict. Heraldry* 96/1 Cross-crosslet..when extended to the limits of the field..is not..'anchored'..but is cross-crosslet 'entire'.

6. †a. Wholly of one kind, homogeneous; free from alien admixture. *Obs.*

1622–62 HEYLIN *Cosmogr.* III. (1673) 41/2 And yet those Maronites though intire without intermixture are held, etc. **1640** QUARLES *Enchirid.* IV. xcvii, It is..a plaine suit of one entyre cloth. **1648** *Petit. Eastern Assoc.* 14 Were both the Houses..so intire from Opinionists..as we could wish. **1683** *Brit. Spec.* 39 The old Language of the Britains who have been..curious to preserve it entire without any mixture. **1683** SALMON *Doron Med.* III. 671 It preserves it safe and intire from filth. **1699** DAMPIER *Voy.* II. viii. 157 It was brackish: for though the fresh water is born up by the Salt, and it might be intire without mixture, yet, etc.

b. Of qualities, feelings, etc.: Pure, unmixed. Cf. 3.

1597 SHAKS. *2 Hen. IV*, II. iv. 352 See now whether pure Feare, and entire Cowardise, doth not make thee wrong this vertuous Gentlewoman, to close with vs? **1667** MILTON *P.L.*

III. 265 Wrauth shall be no more Thenceforth, but in thy presence Joy entire.

7. a. Wholly reserved; unshared. ***entire tenancy*** (Law): see quot.

1641 *Termes de la Ley* 137 Entire Tenancie is that which is contrary to severall Tenancie, and signifieth a sole possession in one man. **1707** HEARNE *Collect.* (Oxf. Hist. Soc.) I. 339 Mr. Foulkes keeping it intire to himself. *Mod.* He has the entire control of that department. I will take the entire responsibility of this step.

b. ***entire to itself***: secluded, kept apart, private.

a **1618** RALEIGH *Rem.* (1644) 10 That Aristocracy be not too magnificent nor intire to it self, but communicate with the people some commodities of State or Government. **1649** MILTON *Eikon.* xxviii, Those few mortifying hours that should have been entirest to themselves.

II. In ethical sense.

†8. Of reputations or persons: Free from reproach, unblemished, blameless. *Obs.*

1577 HOLINSHED *Chron.* II. 193 Richard Grafton was a right reverend man whiles he lived and of entier name also being dead. **1667** MILTON *P.L.* IX. 292 Daughter of God and Man, immortal Eve, For such thou art, from sin and blame entire. **1678** R. BARCLAY *Apol. Quakers* x. §16. 304 The Bishops and Apostles..should be men of most intire manners and Life. **1779** J. MOORE *View Soc. Fr.* (1789) I. i. 5 He who has the vigour to disentangle himself from the snares of deep play..with his character entire may be esteemed a fortunate man.

†9. Of persons and their actions: Characterized by integrity; incorruptible, honest, upright. *Obs.*

c **1430** LYDG. *Bochas* III. v. (1554) 77 b There was a prince, full notable and entere Called Otanes. *c* **1500** *Doctr. Gd. Servaunts* in *Poet. Tracts* (Percy) 3 Be of thy mynde peasyble and entere. **1647** CLARENDON *Hist. Reb.* (1702) I. v. 516 Some very honest and intire Men stayed still there. *Ibid.* II. VI. 54 From whom he could expect no entire, and upright dealing. **1707** HEARNE *Collect.* 30 May (Oxf. Hist. Soc.) II. 17 John Urry of Xt Church, an intire Man.

†10. Of feelings, the heart, etc.: Unfeigned, sincere, genuine, earnest. *Obs.*

The examples of this sense are often not easily to be distinguished from those of the still current sense 3, to which expressions like *entire affection*, etc., if used at all, would now belong.

c **1380** WYCLIF *Wks.* (1880) 106 Treuly assoiled of god for his entre sorwe of synne. *c* **1430** *Syr. Gener.* (Roxb.) 7365 He hem met with hert entier. **1509** FISHER *Fun. Serm. C'tess. Richmond* Wks. 302 But we shall with moost entyer mindes beseche hym. **1535** —— *Wks.* 382 Draw nygh vnto hym with entiere deuotion. **1556** LAUDER *Tractate* 528 With hert Inteir I wald beseik your Maiesteis. **1596** SHAKS. *Tam. Shr.* IV. ii. 23 Your entire affection to Bianca. **1650** HUBBERT *Pill Formality* 193 That love, and intire affection that you bear to their poor souls. *a* **1716** BLACKALL *Wks.* (1723) I. 112 The strictest Friendships, the most intire Love, and the firmest Peace.

†11. The notion 'intimate' developed in sense 3 b seems to have suggested an association of *entire* with *interior*. Hence perh. Spenser's ***parts entire*** = 'inward parts'.

[**1483** *Cath. Angl.*, Entyrly, intime. **15..** COOPER *Lat. Dict.*, *Intime*, entirely.] **1590** SPENSER *F.Q.* IV. viii. st. 48 Casting flakes of lustful fire..into their hearts and parts entire.

†B. *adv.* **a.** Wholly, completely. **b.** Heartily, sincerely, unfeignedly. *Obs.*

a. ? *a* **1400** *Chester Pl.* (1843) I. 193 Seith fourtie daies are gone intier. [Cf. 1707 in A. 7.]

b. *c* **1430** *Syr. Gener.* (Roxb.) 7609 He that me loued most entier. *c* **1430** LYDG. *Smyth & his Dame* 467 in Hazl. *E.P.P.* III. 218 She..thanked God intere.

C. *sb.*

1. The whole; the assemblage of all the parts; the full extent (of anything). In recent use somewhat *rare*.

1597 BACON *Coulers Good & Evill* v. (Arb.) 145 It is not safe to deuide, but to extoll the entire still in generall. **1609** TOURNEUR *Fun. Poem* 375 The parts: the entire; and every circumstance That was contingent. **1804** CASTLEREAGH in S. J. Owen *Wellesley's Disp.* 250 We have by two wars..bound up the entire of Mysore in our dominions. **1832** G. DOWNES *Lett. Cont. Countries* I. 234 A range of seven graves, enclosed each by lofty railings—so that the entire resembles, etc. **1842** S. LOVER *Handy Andy* viii, The death of her husband, who left her the entire of his property. **1876** GLADSTONE *Synchr. Homer* 193 In the entire of the Poems we never hear of a merchant ship of the Greeks.

2. Entirety; completeness.

1622 BACON *Hen. VII*, 158 Maintaining the Liberties of Holy Church in their Entire. **1859** THACKERAY *Virgin.* lxiii. (D.). Too long to print in entire.

3. An entire horse; a stallion.

1881 J. F. KEANE *Journ. Medinah* 160 He bought two young bay entires for one hundred dollars each. **1886** *Daily News* 14 Dec. 3/1 Four heavy-looking grey entires.

4. Short for *entire beer*: see A 2 b.

Not now in current use exc. on tavern sign-boards and the like, where 'A.B.C. & Co's entire' is still advertised.

1825 HONE *Every-day Bk.* I. 691 Hagger's entire [humorously for 'ginger-beer'], two-pence a bottle. **1854** WYNTER *Curiosities Civiliz.* 239 On countless sign-boards of the metropolis this [porter]..is advertised by the title of entire.

5. *Philately.* (See quot. 1967.)

1897 O. FIRTH *Postage Stamps* vii. 148 The advisability of collecting 'entires', or 'Ganz Sachen', as the Germans more expressively have it, is a problem that sooner or later presents itself to the ardent collector. **1937** *Daily Tel.* 16 Oct. (Stamp Suppl.) p. ix/1 The air mail has stimulated the collecting of entires. **1967** *Scott's New Handbk. Philatelists* 13 *Entire*, a whole stamped envelope, letter sheet or wrapper, used or unused.

†enˈtire, *v. Obs.* [f. prec. adj.]

1. *trans.* To make a whole of; to unite.

1678 SIR J. SPELMAN *Alfred Gt.* (1709) 28 The West Saxon Kingdom and the Kingdom of Kent became again entired in one in his hand.

2. To attach exclusively; also in weaker sense, to attach closely or intimately.

1624 HEYWOOD *Gunaik.* 305 Lamia was..entyred to Demetrius. *Ibid.* VII. 323 Shee had a bedfellow, unto whom above all others shee was entired. **1655** —— *Fortune by Land & S.* v. Wks. 1874 VI. 432, I take my Sisters husband, unto me Therefore one most intir'd.

Hence **enˈtired** *ppl. a.* = ENTIRE 3 c.

1635 HEYWOOD *Hierarch.* I. 37 Theseus in Search of his deare and Entired friend Perithous.

entirely (ɛnˈtaɪəlɪ), *a.* and *adv.* Forms: see ENTIRE and -LY[1] and [2]. [f. ENTIRE *a.* + -LY.]

†A. *adj.* (ME. only). **a.** Full, complete. **b.** Sincere, having integrity. *Obs.*

14.. *Pol. Rel. & L. Poems* 41 Besechinge you euer with myn enterly hert. **1488** CAXTON *Chast. Goddes Chyld.* 10 Yeuing up thankynges with enterly deuocyon. **1497** BP. ALCOK *Mons Perfect.* B iij, Y^e very enteerly folowers of Cryste Ihesu.

B. *adv.*

†1. In an entire state; without diminution or division, as a whole. *Obs.*

(As in the case of the synonyms *whole* etc., the adj. would now be used instead of the adv.)

1491 *Act 7 Hen. VII*, c. 12 Pream., To preserve the possessions of the Crown hoolly and entierly without any severaunce or decreasing therof. **1512** *Act 4 Hen. VIII*, c. 19 §10 The hole summes..delyverd fully & enterely. **1659** ANNESLEY in *Burton's Diary* (1828) IV. 464 The which was read first intirely, and afterwards, in parts.

2. Wholly, completely, perfectly; without exception or reservation.

c **1400** MAUNDEV. xii. (1839) 139 Thei kepen entierly the Comaundement. *c* **1430** *Freemasonry* 241 ȝef that the mayster a prentes have, Enterlyche thenne that he hym teche. **1481** CAXTON *Myrr.* III. x. 155 Adam knewe all the seuen scyences lyberall entyerly without fayllyng of a worde. **1667** MILTON *P.L.* VII. 549 And behold all was entirely good. **1706** HEARNE *Collect.* (Oxf. Hist. Soc.) I. 171 He was intirely an Enemy to the Gross Errors of Popery. **1761** HUME *Hist. Eng.* II. xxxi. 201 His resolution of breaking intirely with the court of Rome. **1769** GOLDSMITH *Rom. Hist.* (1786) I. 121 He was the son of a man entirely respected by both parties. **1797** BEWICK *Brit. Birds* (1847) I. 66 Another circle of dark rusty brown entirely surrounds the face. **1875** JOWETT *Plato* (ed. 2) I. 20, I entirely agree..and accept the definition.

¶ In humorous representations of the speech of Irishmen, often placed at the end of a sentence.

Mod. 'He's a fine gentleman entirely'.

3. Wholly and exclusively, solely.

1647 CLARENDON *Hist. Reb.* I. (1843) 4/2 He [Villiers] entirely disposed of all the graces of the king. **1672** CAVE *Prim. Chr.* III. iv. (1673) 331, I shall set down the story intirely out of the Author himself. **1732** ARBUTHNOT *Rules of Diet* 400 If a Gouty Person can bring himself intirely to a Milk Diet. **1833** H. COLERIDGE *North. Worthies* (1852) I. 16 Middleton composed his life of Cicero, Jortin his life of Erasmus, almost entirely from the epistles of their respective subjects. **1850** MISS MITFORD in L'Estrange *Life* III. xii. 223 He [Charles Kingsley] did win his own sweet wife entirely by this charm of character.

†4. a. Heartily, sincerely. **b.** Earnestly. *Obs.*

In the later instances these uses seem to approach or coincide with the still current sense 2.

a. *a* **1340** HAMPOLE *Psalter* vi. 4 Fulhard it is to be turnyd enterly til þe bryghthed and þe pees of godis lyght. **1393** LANGL. *P. Pl.* C. XVIII. 142 Loue þyn enemy entyerly · godes heste to ful-fille. **1467** *Mann. & Househ. Exp.* (1841) 172 Ryte worschepeful and my enterly welbeloved frend. **1586** A. DAY *Eng. Secretary* I. (1625) 27 The griefe that by my selfe among many others, for his losse, is entirely conceived. **1596** SHAKS. *Merch. V.* III. ii. 228 They are intirely welcome. **1647** WARD *Simp. Cobler* 22, I intirely wish..more wisdom to that Plantation. **1711** ADDISON *Spect.* No. 170 ⁋2 The Apprehension that he is not equally beloved by the Person whom he entirely loves. **1722** *Journ. through Eng.* (ed. 2) I. 131, I that love the Country entirely..have fixt my Residence here [Epsom].

b. *a* **1400** *Isumbras* 434 To Ihesu Criste than prayes he, And enterely hym bysoghte. *c* **1420** *Chron. Vilod.* 1183 þat þey wolden preyȝe for Alfynes soule enterly. *Ibid.* 311 He loked þo more entierlocure towarde þat tombe. **1455** *Paston Lett.* No. 230 I. 319 Praying you interlych to bie with me at dyner on Seynt Benett day. **1548–9** (Mar.) *Bk. Com. Prayer* 128 Entierly desiryng thy fatherly goodnes. **1590** SPENSER *F.Q.* I. xi. 32 Gan to highest God entirely pray. **1606** G. W[OODCOCKE] tr. *Hist. Ivstine* 91 a, They intirely besought them..they would now be bould in the ouerthrow.

entireness (ɛnˈtaɪənɪs). [f. as prec. + -NESS.] The quality, state, or condition of being entire.

1. Wholeness, completeness; undiminished, unbroken, or undivided condition. ***in its entireness***: as a whole. Of qualities, states, actions, etc.: Thoroughness, fullness, perfectness.

1599 SANDYS *Europæ Spec.* (1637) 132 To reprint them in their first entirenesse. **1605** BACON *Adv. Learn.* II. v. §2 A steme [of a tree] hath a dimension and quantitie of entyrenes and continuance before it come to discontinue and break itself into Armes. **1614** BP. HALL *Heaven upon Earth* §18 One is sicke of his neighbour's field, whose misshapen angles..hinder his Lordship of entirenesse. **1680** S. MATHER *Iren.* 11 A Church in an Island..must not be denyed intireness of Jurisdiction within itself. **1703** MOXON *Mech. Exerc.* 75 The evenness and entireness of the Edge. **1796** BURKE *Regic. Peace* Wks. 1842 II. 325 They come to attack your king..together with the entireness of the empire. **1817** COLERIDGE *Biog. Lit.* 159 That satisfying entireness, that complete adequateness of the manner to the matter which so charms us in Anacreon. **1861** MILL *Utilit.* iii. 49 That entireness of sympathy with all others. **1870** BOWEN *Logic* 7 We can more easily grasp it in thought, and contemplate it at once in its entireness.

†2. Wholeness or oneness of feeling with another; close friendship, familiarity, intimacy.

1599 SANDYS *Europæ Spec.* (1632) 171 Their alliance or rather meere entirenesse with Spaine. **1612–5** BP. HALL *Contempl. O.T.* VI. i, Whither shall wee impute it, but to his more intyrenesse with God. **1620** *Horæ Sub.* 43 Their entirenesse and inwardnesse with the men of the greatest name. **1673** *Lady's Call.* II. §2. 69 That entireness and affection which is the soul of marriage.

†3. Wholeness of feeling or thought; integrity, honesty, sincerity. *Obs.*

1549 COVERDALE *Erasm. Par. Coloss.* ii. 5 If I espye your entiernes and godly condicions either to be in ieoperdie or to be inconstant & wauer. —— *2 Cor.* viii. 18 Whose faythe and entyrenesse in preachynge the gospell..is well tryed. **1631** GOUGE *God's Arrows* I. §56. 98 An especiall point of sincerity consisteth in the fore-said intirenesse.

entirety (ɛnˈtaɪətɪ, ɛnˈtaɪərɪtɪ). Forms: 6 entiertee, 7, 9 entierty, 8 entierity, 9– entirety. Also 7 intierty. [ad. AF. *entiertie*, OF. *entiereté*:—L. *integritāt-em*, f. *integer*: see ENTIRE.]

Johnson 1755 has only the form *entierty*, which continued in legal use into the nineteenth century.

1. The state or condition of being entire; completeness, fullness, integrity, perfection; *esp.* in phrase ***in its entirety***: in its complete form, as a whole.

1548 GEST *Pr. Masse* 89 Deragotorye to the entiertee and fulnes of Christes ones sacrifice. **1630** PRYNNE *Anti-Armin.* 163 They haue an intirety, a fulnesse in themselues. **1765–9** BLACKSTONE *Comm.* (R.), This is the natural and regular consequence of the union and entirety of their interest. **1847** J. WILSON *Chr. North* (1857) I. 259 Its entirety—its unity, which is so perfect. **1853** ROBERTSON *Serm.* Ser. III. xv. 181 The Christian Church taken in its entirety. **1878** BOSW. SMITH *Carthage* 183 All chance of fulfilling it [his religious mission] in its entirety had passed away for ever.

b. *Law.* The entire or undivided possession of an estate; *esp.* in phrase ***by entireties***, when two parties are jointly seised of a whole estate, and neither is exclusive possessor of a part. Cf. MOIETY.

1613 SIR H. FINCH *Law* (1636) 10 They shall not haue the land by entierties, but by moities ioyntly. *a* **1626** BACON *Office of Alienations* (R.), Sometimes the attorney..setteth down an entierty, where but a moiety, a third, or fourth part only was to be passed. **1809** BAWDWEN *Domesday Bk.* 615 Rayner claims the Entierty of the Church. **1818** CRUISE *Digest* V. 356 A husband seised jointly with his wife, whether by moieties or entireties. **1858** LD. ST. LEONARDS *Handy Bk. Property Law* II. 7 A purchaser cannot be compelled, even in equity, to take an undivided part of an estate..if he contracted for the entirety.

2. The whole; the sum total.

1856 KANE *Arct. Expl.* II. i. 21 You have the entirety of our outfit. **1870** ROLLESTON *Anim. Life* Introd. 24 Those other characters must relate..to the entirety of the organism as such. **1885** *Times* (weekly ed.) 10 July 20/3 The entirety containing about 26 acres.

entitative (ˈɛntɪtətɪv), *a. Metaph.* [ad. med.L. *entitātivus*, f. *entitāt-em*: see ENTITY.]

1. Pertaining to the mere existence of anything. ***entitative act***: transl. L. *actus entitātivus*, a term used by the Scotists to denote 'material' as opposed to 'formal' or 'quiditative' actuality.

The word *act* in this phrase has its scholastic sense, 'that which differentiates an "actual" from a "potential" existence'. Duns Scotus, differing from Aquinas, recognized two kinds of 'act', i.e. two senses or degrees in which a thing might be said to have 'actual' existence: in one sense it is 'actual' if it simply possesses the 'matter' by virtue of which it has *any* existence other than merely potential; in the other sense, it is actual only when it possesses the 'form' which gives it *specific* existence. Hence in the language of his disciples the *entitative act* is the 'matter' of an actually existing thing, while the *formal act* is its 'form'; or, more accurately, they denote the possession of 'matter' and 'form' respectively.

[*a* **1308** DUNS SCOTUS *Sent.* XI. iii. §11 Uno modo *actus* est differentia entis opposita potentiæ..Alio modo *actus* dicit habitudinem illam quam dicit forma ad informabile et ad totum cujus est. **1520** LYCHETUS *Comm. on Duns Scotus' Sent.* II. xii. §19 Sicut forma est actus formalis quia potest informare per receptionem ipsius, ita etiam materia est actus entitativus.] *c* **1600** *Timon* IV. iii. (1842) 66 Whether there be a man in the moone..which may have there really and intrinsecally an entitative acte and essence, besides a formall existence. **1628** BP. HALL *Old Relig.* 49 The bold Schooles dare say that the naturall and entitatiue value of the Workes of Christ was finite, though the morall value was infinite. *c* **1630** JACKSON *Creed* VI. xi. Wks. VI. 116 There is more entitative goodness in being a man than in being a lion. **1743** J. ELLIS *Knowl. Div. Th.* iv. 289 Whether..the entitative material act of sin be physically or morally good? **1890** *Tablet* 29 Nov. 860 The vexed question as to the entitative simplicity or not of the living principles of mere plants and brute animals. **1907** *Dublin Rev.* July 188 St. Thomas, with all the Scholastics, maintained the absolute entitative distinction of God from creatures. **1909** M. H. DZIEWICKI *Wyclif's De Ente* 243 The commission of sin as an entitative act.

2. Of the nature of an entity; having real existence.

1862 F. HALL *Hindu Philos. Syst.* 272 When a man mistakes a rope for a snake..the man's misconception, which is entitative, is the cause of his fear.

Hence **'entitatively** *adv.*, in an entitative manner; as a mere existence.

1677 GALE *Crt. Gentiles* III. 55 The whole act considered entitatively and naturally. **1696** LORIMER *Goodwin's Disc.* vii. 135 There cannot be a Conditional Will in God, that is ..subjectively, or entitatively Conditional. **1751** CHAMBERS *Cycl.* s.v., Peter, entitatively taken, is Peter, as a thing, a substance, a man, etc. without any regard to his being a lord, a husband, learned, etc. **1818** in TODD; and in mod. Dicts.

entitle (ɛn'taɪt(ə)l), *v.* Forms: 5-7 **entytle,** (**entytel, -titele**), 5- **entitle.** Also 5-7 **intytle,** (**intitele**), 5-9 **intitle.** See also INTITULE. [a. AF. *entitle-r*, OF. *entiteler*, *entituler*, mod.Fr. *intituler*, corresp. to Pr. *entitolar*, *intitular*, It. *intitolare*, late L. *intitulāre*, f. *in* in + *titulus* TITLE.]

I. From TITLE = 'superscription, designation'.

1. *trans.* To furnish (a literary work, a chapter, etc.) with a heading or superscription; in early use *gen.* (cf. TITLE *sb.*). Subsequently only in narrower sense: To give to (a book, etc.) a designation by which it is to be cited, or which indicates the nature of its contents. Chiefly with complementary obj.; also const. †*by*, †*with*.

α. *c* **1381** CHAUCER *Parl. Foules* 30 This booke..Entitled was right thus..Tullius of the dreame of Scipion. **1388** WYCLIF *Jerome's Prol. Rom.*, The epistil..that to Ebrues ys writen..is not entitlid with his [Paul's] name. **1483** CAXTON *Cato* A ij b, This booke..ought to be entytled the reule and gouernement of the body and of the sowle. **1581** MULCASTER *Positions* Ep. Ded. (1887) 5, I haue entitled the booke Positions. **1605** BACON *Adv. Learn.* I. iii. §9 To dedicate them [books]..to private and equal friends, or to entitle the books with their names. **1792** *London Rev.* Nov. 363 This section Mr. S. entitles, 'Of the Use and Abuse of general Principles in Politics'. **1888** H. MORLEY *Eng. Writers* III. 179 A book entitled 'De Nugis Curialium'.

β. **1432-50** tr. *Higden* (Rolls) I. 25 In his Policraticon, whom he intitlede de Nugis Curialium. **1534** LD. BERNERS *Gold. Bk. M. Aurel.* (1546) B iij b, I will intitle this boke the Golden boke. **1542-3** *Act 34 & 35 Hen. VIII*, c. 1 Bookes ..intiteled..the psalter, primers, praiers, statutes and lawes of this realme. **1738** BIRCH *Life Milton* Wks. 1738 I. 76 The Icon was at first intitled by the King Suspiria Regalia. **1793** SMEATON *Edystone L.* Contents 7 Extracts from a Book intitled the Storm.

†**b.** To inscribe, dedicate (a book) *to* a person.

1460 CAPGRAVE *Chron.* 152 Doctour Gylis..entitelid it [the bok of Governauns of Princes] to Philip, dauphin of Frauns. **1607** HIERON *Wks.* Ded. before p. 429 I. Pp iiij, I haue thought good to commend some of my poore labours vnto you, by a more particular entitling them to your name.

†**c.** To ascribe (a literary work) *to* an author. With mixed notion of 5 c.

1550 CRANMER *Defence* 50 b, In an other booke, entitled to saint Augustine, is written thus, etc. **1575** FULKE *Confut. Doctr. Purg.* (1577) 216 Ecclesiasticus and the booke of Wisdome, falsely intitled to Salomon. **1671** STUBBE *Reply* 17 My Adversaries will here allow no other Book to be Entitled unto the R.S. but what is licensed by their President. **1699** BENTLEY *Phal.* Introd. 14 Dionysius made a Tragedy called Parthenopæus, and intitled it to Sophocles. **1724** SWIFT *Let.* 28 Apr. The other [tract] is entitled to a Weaver..but thought to be the work of a better hand.

†**d.** ? To prefix the name of (an alleged author) *to*. *Obs.* (Perh. belongs to 5.)

a **1745** SWIFT (T.), We have been entitled, and have had our names prefixed at length to whole volumes of mean productions.

2. To bestow on (a person) a certain title or designation expressing his rank, office, or character; to speak of (a person) by a certain title. Formerly also, to give a certain designation to (a thing). Const. as in 1.

α. **1447** BOKENHAM *Seyntys* (1835) Introd. 3 Galfryd of Ynglond in his newe werk Entytlyd thus as I can aspye Galfridus Anglicus. **1589** R. HARVEY *Pl. Perc.* 7 It were enough to entitle those Browne Sectaries of the Blacke Prince, with the name of traytors. **1602** FULBECKE *Pandectes* 21 The kings and Queenes of England entitling themselues kings and Queenes of Fraunce. **1667** MILTON *P.L.* XI. 171 Next favourable thou, Who highly thus to entitle me voutsaf'st. **1683** RAY *Corr.* (1848) 135 He entitles it *Conyza acris annua alba.* **1711** HEARNE *Collect.* (Oxf. Hist. Soc.) III. 147 Please entitle S. only Bart. **1860** PUSEY *Min. Proph.* Joel iii. 16 Here entitled by the incommunicable name of God.

β. **1593** SHAKS. *Rich. II*, I. ii. 33 That which in meane men we intitle patience, Is pale cold cowardice. **1596** —— *Tam. Shr.* IV. v. 61 And now by Law, as well as reuerent age, I may intitle thee my louing Father. **1605** CAMDEN *Rem.* 35 Mawd ..who intitled herselfe Empresse. **1728** MORGAN *Algiers* II. ii. 232 They intitled him Sultan.

†**3.** To write down under proper titles or headings. *Obs.*

α. *c* **1430** LYDG. in *Lay Folks Mass Bk.* (1879) 394 Somme entytlenn hem in smale bookes of Report. **1463** *Paston Lett.* No. 477 II. 138 And more thinges..which I entytelyd in a scrowe. **1533** FRITH *Answ. More's Lett.* Pref. A ij b, He desired me to entitle the somme of my wordes & wryte them for hym.

β. **1533-4** *Act 25 Hen. VIII*, c. 21 §9 One sufficient clerke ..shall intitle in his bokes and enroll of recorde such other writinges. **1582** BENTLEY *Mon. Matrones*, After the good example of the learned fathers of our time, to intitle, reduce, & applie those other godlie meditations & praiers.

II. From TITLE = 'right to possession'.

4. To furnish (a person) with a 'title' *to* an estate. Hence *gen.* to give (a person or thing) a rightful claim *to* a possession, privilege, designation, mode of treatment, etc. Const. *to* with *sb.* or *inf.*; also *simply*. Now said almost exclusively of circumstances, qualities, or actions; formerly often of personal agents.

α. **1468** W. WORCESTER in *Paston Lett.* No. 582 II. 314, I ..entitled no crettur to na place. **1530** PALSGR. 538/1 By what meanes is he entyteled unto these landes. **1649** SELDEN *Laws Eng.* I. xlvii. (1739) 77 The Emperor could entitle the Pope to no power here, because none he had. **1652** T. WHITFIELD *Doctr. Armin.* 8 His dying for the elect is a sufficient ground to entitle him. **1711** ADDISON *Spect.* No. 257 ¶8 [God] will hereafter entitle many to the Reward of Actions which they had never the Opportunity of Performing. **1725** DE FOE *Voy. round World* (1840) 289 Such a quantity as might entitle that water to the name of the Golden Lake. **1798** FERRIAR *Certain Varieties Man* 223 Every man thinks himself entitled to observe and to publish. **1818** CRUISE *Digest* I. 138 The first tenant in tail who is born becomes entitled to any timber felled by the tenant for life. **1826** HENRY *Elem. Chem.* I. 635 The remaining salts of alumina have no properties sufficiently important to entitle them to a separate description. **1832** HT. MARTINEAU *Demerara* ii. 15 Better entitled than most of his brethren to complain of neglect. **1838** DE MORGAN *Ess. Probab.* 188 If each had been entitled to his fraction of the sum which would have become due had he lived to the end of the year. **1875** POSTE *Gaius* III. comm. (ed. 2) 396 The obligation by which the co-creditors are entitled.

β. **1495** *Act 11 Hen. VII*, c. 2 §4 It shalbe laufull to every man intitled to have the seid penaltie to distreyne for it. **1571** CAMPION *Hist. Irel.* (1633) 70 Intytled to thirty thousand marks yearely. **1695** tr. *Colbatch's New Light Chirurg. Put out* p. iii, With how much Justice it's intitled to such a Name. **1741** RICHARDSON *Pamela* I. 46 Who..thinks himself intitled to call me Bold-face. **1769** ROBERTSON *Chas. V*, III. IX. 133 A higher rank in the temple of fame than either his talents or performances intitle him to hold.

b. *spec.* To furnish with a TITLE to orders.

1720 BP. KENNETT *Monit. Clergy Peterbor.* I. 16, I must expect and insist upon it, that you Intitle no Curate, without, etc.

†**c.** To invest *with* an office, etc. *Obs.*

1584 FENNER *Def. Ministers* (1587) 38 Seeing you must.. intitle the Magistrate with the Pastors office. **1662** FULLER *Worthies* (1840), Bring the last who was entitled..with that dignity.

†**d.** To qualify, render apt. Const. *to*. *Obs.*

1627-77 FELTHAM *Resolves* I. xix. 33 There is a nobleness in the mind of man, which of it self, intitles it to the hatred of what is ill. **1650** FULLER *Pisgah* 402 The Temple..visibly intitled itself to fortification.

†**e.** To assign the possession of (something) *to*; to settle (an estate) *on* a person. *Obs.*

1608 HIERON *Defence* II. 25 The attribute 'your Prince', giuen to Michael, entitleth the name Michael to Christ only. **1674** R. GODFREY *Inj. & Ab. Physic* 145 He intitled his Inheritance on his Sister.

†**f.** Phrase, ***to entitle and engage***.

1641 MILTON *Ch. Discip.* I. 4 To entitle and engage a glorious name to gross corruption. **1649** *Nicholas Papers* (1886) 149 To intitle and engage the Queen to espouse as her owne quarrell whatever reflects upon Lord Jermyn.

†**5.** To regard or treat (a person) as having a title *to* something. Hence, to represent (a person or thing) as the agent, cause, or subject of a particular action, effect, condition, or quality. Const. *in*, *to*, with *sb.*, rarely with *inf.* *Obs.*

α. **1646** JASPER MAINE *Serm. agst. False Proph.* 2 Never plot was hatcht to disturb the Commonwealth, but the writings of some Sybill or other were entitled to that plot. **1662** STILLINGFL. *Orig. Sacr.* III. iii. §7 Supposing Gods giving man this freedom of will, doth not entitle him to be the author of evill. **1672** SIR T. BROWNE *Lett. Friend* vii. (1881) 131, I was not so curious to entitle the stars unto any concern of his death. **1690** LOCKE *Govt.* I. xi. §154 How ready Zeal for Interest and Party is to entitle Christianity to their Designs.

β. **1607-12** BACON *Ess. Praise* (Arb.) 352 Wherein a man is ..most defective..that will the flatterer intitle him to perforce. **1649** JER. TAYLOR *Gt. Exemp.* II. 100 Nor intitle God in our impotent..fansyes. **1663** J. SPENCER *Prodigies* (1665) 359 An event to which I incline to intitle the especial agency of the Devil.

†**b.** *refl.* To lay claim *to*. *Obs.*

1655 FULLER *Ch. Hist.* I. i. §4 Churches are generally ambitious to entitle themselves to Apostles, for their Founders. **1672** BP. LLOYD *Fun. Serm. Bp. Wilkins*, To entitle themselves to dying men, even those, whose whole life was a testimony against them. *a* **1718** PENN *Life* Wks. 1726 I. 155 Such as intitle themselves to Christianity, whilst Strangers to the Terrors of the Lord for Sin.

†**c.** To impute (something) *to*. *Obs.* Cf. 1 c.

1630 PRYNNE *Anti-Armin.* 267 What Testimonies their opposite Arminian Errors..can rake vp together, to intitle them vnto our Church. **1647** H. MORE *Poems* Pref., If we can but once entitle our opinions..to Religion. *a* **1662** [see ENTITLING *vbl. sb.*] **1665** GLANVILL *Sceps. Sci.* 37 Intitling the Opinion of Intentional Species to Aristotle.

Hence **en'titled** *ppl. a.*, that has a title or qualification; qualified. **en'titling** *vbl. sb.* **en'titlement**, a means of entitling; a designation, name. **en'titler**, one who entitles, or gives a title or name to.

1869 *Daily News* 9 Dec., The objections of entitled opposers. *a* **1662** HEYLYN *Life Abp. Laud* (1668) 127 The entitling of these Doctrines to the name of Arminius. **1835** *Tait's Mag.* II. 670 Objections were raised..against so unlucky an entitlement. **1653** ASHWELL *Fides Apost.* 225 And this may be therefore judged the..most likely to be intended by the first entitlers.

entitule, obs. var. INTITULE *v. arch.* = ENTITLE.

entity ('ɛntɪtɪ). Forms: 7 **entitie, -ye,** (**entite**), 7- **entity.** [ad. late L. *entitāt-em*, f. *ēns*, *enti-s*: see ENS. Cf. Fr. *entité*, It. *entità*, Sp. *entitad*.

The orig. sense was *abstr.*, but, in accordance with the usual tendency of such words, it early acquired a *concr.* sense (= ENS), which predominates in mod. use.]

1. Being, existence, as opposed to non-existence; the existence, as distinguished from the qualities or relations, of anything.

1596 BELL *Surv. Popery* III. ix. 372 God..is the principall agent of the real and positive entities thereof. **1647** H. MORE *Song of Soul, Antipsychopannychia* III. xxix, Both Night and Coldnesse..have reall entitie. **1656** HOBBES *Liberty, Necess. & C.* (1841) 135 Entity is better than nonentity. **1710** BERKELEY *Princ. Hum. Knowl.* §81 The positive abstract idea of quiddity, entity, or existence. **1830** HERSCHELL *Stud. Nat. Phil.* 108 In the τὸ ὂν and the τὸ μὴ ὄν, that is to say, in entity and nonentity. **1837-9** HALLAM *Hist. Lit.* (1847) III. iii. §9. 305 Entity or real being.

2. That which constitutes the being of a thing; essence, essential nature.

1643 R. O. *Man's Mort.* vii. 54 He, that is, his Entite, person, even all that went to make him man. **1648** CRASHAW *Steps to Temple* 81 Dear hope!.. The entity of things that are not yet. *a* **1688** CUDWORTH *Immut. Morality* (1731) 16 It is impossible any Thing should Be..without a Nature or Entity. **1785** REID *Int. Powers* 399 For the entity of all theoretical truth is nothing else but clear intelligibility.

3. *concr.* Something that has a real existence; an ENS, as distinguished from a mere function, attribute, relation, etc. †***rational entity***: = L. *ens rationis*, a thing which has an existence only as an object of reason.

1628 T. SPENCER *Logick* 209 The specificall difference is a rationall entitie and no more. **1685** BOYLE *Enq. Notion Nat.* 22 This Death..is neither a Substance, nor a Positive Entity, but a meer Privation. **1735-8** BOLINGBROKE *On Parties* 139 'Till it becomes an ideal Entity, like the Utopia. **1855** H. SPENCER *Princ. Psychol.* (1872) I. v. x. 626 No effort of imagination enables us to think of a shock, however minute, except as undergone by an entity. **1871** DARWIN *Desc. Man* I. vii. 228 Those..must look at species either as separate creations or..distinct entities.

†**b.** An actual quantity (however small). *Obs.*

1626 BACON *Sylva* §123 Eruptions of Aire, though small and slight, give an Entitie of Sound.

c. (See quot.)

1881 SPOTTISWOODE in *Nature* No. 624. 572 In some tubes, the exhaustion of which is very moderate..the blocks of light termed entities by Mr. De La Rue are formed.

4. *indefinitely.* What exists; 'being' generally.

1604 EDMONDS *Observ. Cæsar's Comm.* 39 Our knowledge were equal to vniuersall entitie. **1670** EACHARD *Cont. Clergy* 56 We be but mites of entity, and crumbs of something. **1699** GARTH *Dispens.* 3 How the dim Speck of Entity began T'extend its recent Form, and stretch to Man. **1829** I. TAYLOR *Enthus.* ii. (1867) 31 He has become..infinitely less than an atom..an incalculable fraction of positive entity!

ento- ('ɛntəʊ), *prefix* (before a vowel commonly reduced to *ent-*), repr. Gr. ἐντός within, inside, in many compounds of mod. formation relating to anatomy and biology, as **'entoblast** [Gr. βλαστός sprout], (*a*) the nucleolus of a cell; (*b*) an inner germ-layer of an embryo; = *endoblast*, HYPOBLAST 2; **,entocal'caneal** *a.* (see quot. and CALCANEAL); **ento'chondral** *a. Anat.*, situated or occurring within cartilage; **'entocœle** *Zool.*, that portion of the gut-cavity of certain polyps which lies between a pair of mesenteries (see quot. 1885); so **ento'cœlic** *a.*; **ento'condyloid** *a.* [Gr. κόνδυλ-ος knuckle + -OID] (see quot.); **ento'cuneiform** *a.* (see quot. and CUNEIFORM); **'entocyst** (see quot. and CYST); **'entoderm** [Gr. δέρμα skin], the outer layer of the blastoderm, also called *hypoblast*; **ento'dermal, -mic** *adjs.* = ENDODERMAL, -IC *adjs.*; **ento'gastric** *a.* [see GASTRIC], pertaining to the interior of the stomach or of the gastric cavity; **ento'glossal** *a.* [Gr. γλῶσσ-α the tongue + -AL[1]], a term applied to one of the bones of the hyoidean arch in some fishes, which supports the tongue; **entomere** *Embryol.*, each of the more granular cells produced by segmentation of the primitive ovum; **ento'metarse** [mod.L. *metatarsus*], the bones between the tarsus and the toes; **ento'parasite** (see quot. 1861); hence **,entopara'sitic** *a.*; **,entope'ripheral** *a.* (see quot. and PERIPHERAL); **'entophyte** [Gr. φυτόν plant], a plant growing within the substance of other plants or animals; hence **ento'phytic** *a.*; **ento'plastral** *a.*, pertaining to the entoplastron; **ento'plastron** in turtles (see quot.); **ento'proctous** *a.* [Gr. πρωκτός anus, rump], belonging to the *Entoprocta*, a class of Polyzoa, in which the anus lies within the circle of tentacles; **ento'pterygoid** *a.* [see PTERYGOID] (see quot.); **en'toptic** *a.* [see OPTIC], relating to the appearance of the different internal structures of the eye; hence **en'toptics** *sb.* (see quot.); **ento'sclerite** *Ent.*, an internal sclerite; **ento'septum**, in corals, a septum developed interiorly; **ento'sternal** *a.* [see STERNAL], pertaining to the *entosternum* or median piece of the sternum or breastbone, very largely

developed in birds; **ento'sternite** *Anat.*, an internal fibro-cartilaginous plate giving support to a series of muscles in various arthropods; **ento'sternum** *Ent.*, an internal process or system of processes of the sternum of an arthropod; **en'totic** *a.* [see OTIC], pertaining to or occurring in the inner ear; **,entotym'panic** *a.* [see TYMPANIC], situated within the *tympanum* or drum of the ear.

1864 WEBSTER, *Entoblast, the nucleolus of a cell. **1892** E. L. MARK tr. *Hertwig's Textbk. Embryol.* v. 86 The inner germ-layer (entoblast or entoderm) lines the cœlenteron and provides for nutrition. **1926** JORDAN & KINDRED *Textbk. Embryol.* ix. 67 We are compelled to postulate an earlier solid stage of the blastula in which ectoblast (epiblast) and entoblast (hypoblast) are prelocalized. **1945** W. J. HAMILTON et al. *Human Embryol.* viii. 105 An *entoblast* which gives origin to the epithelial linings of the digestive and respiratory tracts. **1854** OWEN in *Circ. Sc.* (c. 1865) II. 74/1 One [process], called the '*entocalcaneal', projects from below the entocondyloid cavity, and from the back part of the upper end of the entometatarse. **1889** *Entochondral [see *ectochondral* (ECTO-)]. **1885** G. H. FOWLER in *Q. Jrnl. Microsc. Sci.* XXV. 578 For the chambers (Radialtaschen, Loges,) into which the cœlenteron is periaxially divided by the mesenteries, I am compelled to coin new names; to those chambers which lie between a 'pair' of mesenteries the term *entocœle is applied..; to those chambers of which one lies between every two pairs of mesenteries the term exocœle. **1902** *Trans. Linnean Soc.* Oct. 304 The appearance of a new mesenterial pair is followed very closely by the outgrowth of a tentacle from its entocœle. **1963** BORRADAILE & POTTS *Invertebrata* (ed. 4) v. 182 In the typical sea-anemone..and in coral polyps..the secondary mesenteries..are situated in the spaces between two adjacent pairs (exocoeles), never between two members of a pair (entocoeles). **1888** *Q. Jrnl. Microsc. Sci.* XXVIII. 5 The tentacles are probably *entocœlic only. **1902** *Trans. Linnean Soc.* Oct. 304 The tentacles are outgrowths of both the entocœlic and exocœlic mesenterial chambers. **1854** OWEN in *Circ. Sc.* (c. 1865) II. 74/1 The inner of the two cavities for the condyles..is the '*entocondyloid' cavity. **1855** —— *Skel. & Teeth* 254 The brachial artery pierces the entocondyloid ridge. **1854** —— in *Circ. Sc.* (c. 1865) II. 81/2 The *entocuneiform bone. **1872** MIVART *Elem. Anat.* 186 Of the three cuneiform bones, the innermost, the ento-cuneiform is the largest. **1884** *Syd. Soc. Lex*, *Entocyst, the inner layer of the cuticular envelope of the Polyzoa. **1879** tr. *Haeckel's Evol. Man* I. iii. 67 The lower, which forms the organs of digestion and reproduction, Huxley called the *Entoderm, or Inner-layer. **1892** Entoderm [see *entoblast* above]. **1884** SEDGWICK & HEATHCOTE tr. *Claus' Zool.* iii. 100 The *entodermal lining of the gastro-vascular canals. **1886** *Buck's Handbk. Med. Sci.* III. 172/1 The division of the margin of the ectodermal disk into two parts, one resting directly on the *entodermic yoke. **1877** HUXLEY *Anat. Inv. An.* iii. 150 The details of this process of *entogastric gemmation have been traced by Haeckel in *Carmarina hastata.* **1878** BELL *Gegenbauer's Comp. Anat.* 472 The rudimentary first arch fuses to form the so-called *entoglossal bone. **1890** BILLINGS *Med. Dict.* I. 455/1 *Entomere. **1854** *Entometatarse [see *entocalcaneal*]. **1861** HULME tr. *Moquin-Tandon* II. VII. 324 Some writers have proposed to call them [Entozoa] *Ento-parasites. **1876** DAVIS *Polaris Exp.* App. 653 All the animals should be examined for ecto- and ento-parasites. **1861** H. MACMILLAN *Footn. Page Nat.* 167 Animals of feeble vitality .. are rarely, if ever, free from these *ento-parasitic plants. **1855** H. SPENCER *Princ. Psychol.* (1870) I. 250 Those [feelings] internally initiated, which we may conveniently call *ento-peripheral. **1861** H. MACMILLAN *Footn. Page Nat.* 167 Upwards of ten species of *entophytes have already been discovered parasitic upon man. **1847–9** TODD *Cycl. Anat.* IV. 118/1 This substance [White Thrush] is in part *ento-phytic. **1861** H. MACMILLAN *Footn. Page Nat.* 227 Entophytic fungi spring from beneath the cuticle of living plants. **1896** R. LYDEKKER *R. Nat. Hist.* V. 77 Owing to the absence of the unpaired *entoplastral bone. **1871** T. H. HUXLEY *Man. Anat. Vert.* v. 202 The *entoplastron and the two epiplastra correspond with the median and lateral thoracic plates of the Labyrinthodont *Amphibia.* **1877** HUXLEY *Anat. Inv. An.* xii. 680 The lowest known term..of the Malacozoic Series is an *entoproctous Polyzoon. **1854** OWEN in *Circ. Sc.* (c. 1865) II. 79/1 The *entopterygoids. **1880** GUNTHER *Fishes* 55 The entopterygoid, an oblong and thin bone attached to the inner border of the palatine and pterygoid. **1876** BERNSTEIN *Five Senses* 80 All such phenomena are called *entoptic, because they deal with the perceptions of the internal portions of the eye. **1876** *Catal. Sci. App. S. Kens.* 551 Apparatus to determine the position of entoptic objects—in the humours of the eye. **1864** *Reader* 2 July 11 The light that enters the eye may, under certain conditions, cause one to see objects that exist within the eye-ball; and an investigation of these conditions is called *Entoptics. **1902** *Proc. Zool. Soc.* 17 June 174 From the middle of its area arises a stout, hooked *entosclerite, which projects backwards into the cavity of the prosoma. **1885** G. H. FOWLER in *Q. Jrnl. Microsc. Sci.* XXV. 578 The septa lying in these two classes of chambers are similarly called exosepta and *entosepta. **1903** *Ann. & Mag. Nat. Hist.* Feb. 147 The union of the entoseptum within each pair of the second cycle mesenteries with the adjoining exosepta. **1835–6** TODD *Cycl. Anat.* I. 284/1 A middle one [*i.e.* centre] which supports the keel, termed..the *entosternal. **1854** OWEN in *Circ. Sc.* (c. 1865) II. 69/2 The median piece of the plastron, called 'entosternal', answers to the sternum of the crocodile. **1884** E. R. LANKESTER in *Q. Jrnl. Microsc. Sci.* XXI. 547 In order to make a close comparison of these *Entosternites, it will be necessary to determine exactly the insertions of the muscles to which they give origin. **1888** ROLLESTON & JACKSON *Forms Anim. Life* 526 An entosternite or chitinoid fibro-cellular plate. **1902** *Nature* 25 Sept. 529 The entosternite of Mygale. **1902** *Encycl. Brit.* XXV. 527/2 The affinity between Limulus and the Arachnids, indicated by the presence of a free suspended *entosternum or plastron or entosternite in both. **1878** FOSTER *Phys.* III. iii. 457 Corresponding to entoptic phenomena there are various *entotic phenomena. **1881** MIVART *Cat* 65 An internal, much wider part, the *ento-tympanic.

entoast: see EN- *pref.*[1] 3.

entoil (ɛn'tɔɪl), *v. arch.* Also 6–7 **entoyle**, 7 **intoyl**. [f. EN-[1] + TOIL *sb.*[2]] *trans.* To bring into toils or snares; to entrap, ensnare. Chiefly *fig.*

1621 G. SANDYS *Ovid's Met.* v. 104 None more The chace affected, or t'intoyle the Bore. **1875** BROWNING *Inn Album* 11 You entoil my legs, And welcome, for I like it.

fig. **1581** W. CLARKE in *Confer.* IV. (1584) Ffiij b, Thus you are entoyled. **1590** BARROW & GREENWOOD in *Confer.* 46 The furder and more you striue against the truth, the furder and faster you entoyle your self. *a* **1626** BACON *New Atl.* (1650) 13 Entoyled both their Navy, and their Campe, with a greater Power than theirs, both by Sea and Land. **1652** BENLOWES *Theoph.* XI. lxxix, Nere in the net of Slothfulnesse entoyl'd. **1820** KEATS *St. Agnes* xxxii, So mused awhile, entoyled in woofed fantasies. **1879** BROWNING *Ned Bratts* 43 Mounting until its mesh Entoiled all heads in a fluster.

Hence **en'toilment** *rare*, the action of entoiling; the state of being entoiled.

1855 BROWNING *Men & Wom.* II. *Before*, In torture and entoilment.

†**en'toire**, *a.* (quasi-*sb.* and quasi-*adv.*) *Her. Obs.* Also 6–8 **entoyre**. [perh. a misspelling of Fr. *entouré* pa. pple. of *entourer* to surround. See ENTOUR *v.*] (See quots.)

1562 LEIGH *Armorie* (1597) iij, The third [sort of bordure] is called Entoyre, the which is, when dead things do occupy the same bordure, as mollets, Roundels, and such like. **1661** MORGAN *Sph. Gentry* II. vi. 61 Or, a Bordure Sable charged with Entoyre of 8 Besants. **1721–1800** BAILEY, *Entoyre*..is when a Border is charged with any sort of Things which have not Life, except Leaves, Flowers, and Fruits. [And in mod. Dicts.]

entomb (ɛn'tuːm), *v.* Also 6 **entoumbe**, 6–8 **intomb(e**, (6 **intumb**). [a. OF. *entoumbe-r*, *entumbe-r*, Fr. *entombe-r*, f. *en* in (see EN-) + *tombe* TOMB.]

1. *trans.* To place in a tomb; to bury, inter.

α. **1578** HUNNIS *Hyvefull Honye* 130 Entoumbe thou me in Canaan. **1634** SIR T. HERBERT *Trav.* 133 Therein is richly entombed Fatima, daughter and heire of their greatest Prophet Mahomet. **1756–7** tr. *Keysler's Trav.* (1760) I. 202 Here is entombed the heart of an unconquered hero. **1842** PRICHARD *Nat. Hist. Man* 189 The remains of the dead found entombed in various parts of Europe.

β. **1576** FLEMING *Panoplie Ep.* 115 The exhibiting of deserved honor unto him after he was intumbed. **1611** SPEED *Theat. Gt. Brit.* vi. (1614) 11/1 K. Henry VI...was intombed at Windsor. **1775** ADAIR *Amer. Ind.* 187 [The dead husband] is intombed in the house under her bed.

2. *transf.* and *fig.* To enclose as in a tomb; to overwhelm; to bury. Also *absol.*

1593 SHAKS. *Lucr.* 679 Entombs her outcry in her lips sweet fold. **1593** NASHE *Christ's T.* 5 b, Thou art.. entombed in Ashes like Gomorra. **1599** —— *Lenten Stuffe* (1871) They intomb and balist with sudden destruction. **1665** J. MALL *Offer of F. Help* 118 Seas of wrath are.. threatning to entomb you. **1742** YOUNG *Nt. Th.* IX. 2429 When Time..In Nature's ample ruins lies intomb'd. **1830** LYELL *Princ. Geol.* (1875) II. III. xlv. 526 During the great Earthquake of 1693 in Sicily, several thousand people were at once entombed in the ruins of caverns in limestone. **1874** MORLEY *Compromise* (1886) 37 The spirit of the Church is eternally entombed within the four corners of acts of parliament.

3. To serve as a tomb for; to receive as in a tomb. *lit.* and *fig.*

a **1631** DONNE *Lett.* (1651) 113 To seem to entomb those affections of mine to your service. **1633** G. HERBERT *Temple, Ch. Porch* viii, Let not a common ruine thee intombe. **1638** COWLEY *Love's Riddle* v. Wks. (1684) 117 Some steepy mountain bury me alive, Or Rock intomb me in its stony entrails! **1812** H. & J. SMITH *Rej. Addr., Hampsh. Farmer*, None of your Ægyptian pyramids, to entomb subscribers' capitals. **1821** SHELLEY *Hellas* 8 If Hell should entomb thee.

entombed (ɛn'tuːmd), *ppl. a.* [f. ENTOMB *v.* + -ED[1].] Laid in a tomb; buried. *lit.* and *fig.*

1626 G. SANDYS *Ovid's Met.* xv. 305 Alemons sonne erects his citie walls: Which of th'intombed he Crotona calls. **1647** WARD *Simp. Cobler* 58 The vast heritage of sinne your Intombed father left upon your score. **1746–7** HERVEY *Medit.* (1818) 51, I bid adieu to this entombed warrior. **1866** G. MACDONALD *Ann. Q. Neighb.* xiii. (1878) 248 From a living Now to an entombed and consecrated Past.

entombing (ɛn'tuːmɪŋ), *vbl. sb.* [f. as prec. + -ING[1].] The action of the vb. ENTOMB; the state of being entombed.

1564–78 BULLEYN *Dial agst. Pest.* (1888) 17 The worthy entombing of his bones. **1644** BP. HALL *Rem. Wks.* II. (1660) 130 Lazarus was called (after three dayes entombing) out of his grave. **1668** WILKINS *Real. Char.* 287 Entombing, Tomb, Sepulchre, Monument, Epitaph.

†**en'tombless**, *a. Obs. rare*⁻¹. [f. as prec. + -LESS.] Exempt from entombing; undying.

1601 WEEVER *Mirr. Mart.* F ij, Set forth Immortall verse for my entomblesse worth.

entombment (ɛn'tuːmmənt). [f. as prec. + -MENT.] The action of entombing; *lit.* and *fig.*

1666 ALSOP *Maryland* (1869) 78 They give him no other intombment than, etc. *a* **1677** BARROW *Wks.* (1686) III. 218 It [idleness] is the very entombment of a man. **1842** *Blackw. Mag.* LII. 420 The double entombment of Napoleon. **1877** MOZLEY *Univ. Serm.* iii. 61 What an entombment of mind should we have!

entometatarse: see ENTO- *pref.*

entomic (ɛn'tɒmɪk), *a.* [f. Gr. ἔντομ-α insects (see ENTOMO-) + -IC.] Of or pertaining to insects.

1862 MRS. SPEIR *Last Years Ind.* 28 Farewell to Egypt,.. its dust and its entomic activities. **1880** M. COLLINS *Th. in Garden* II. 102 A society which should take accurate record of all ornithic, entomic, and botanic facts.

entomical (ɛn'tɒmɪkəl), *a.* [f. as prec. + -AL[1].] = prec.

In mod. Dicts.

entomo- (before two unaccented syllables (ɛntə'mɒ-); before one unacc. syll. (ɛn'tɒmə-); before an acc. syll. (,ɛntəməʊ-), combining form of Gr. ἔντομος adj. 'cut up', in neut. pl. used in sense 'insects', with reference to the division of their bodies into segments: cf. L. *insecta*: see INSECT. Occurring with sense 'insect' in many scientific compounds of modern formation, as **ento'mogenous** *a. Bot.* [Gr. -γενής born, produced + -OUS], having its growth in the body of insects. **en'tomolite**, *Geol.* [Gr. λίθος stone], a fossil insect. **ento'mometer** [Gr. μέτρον measure], an instrument for measuring the parts of insects. **ento'mophagan**, *Zool.* [Gr. φαγ-εῖν to eat + -AN], one of the *Entomophaga* or insect-eaters—in mammals, a division of the *Marsupialia*, in insects of the *Hymenoptera*. **ento'mophagous** *a.* [Gr. φαγ-εῖν to eat + -OUS], insect-eating. **ento'mophilous** *a. Bot.* [Gr. φίλ-ος friend + -OUS], applied to plants in which fertilization is effected through the agency of insects. **ento'mostracan** *a. Zool.* and *Geol.* [Gr. ὄστρακ-ον shell + -AN], of or belonging to the *Entomostraca*, one of the orders of the *Crustacea* (see quot.); also as *sb.* **ento'mostracous** *a.* [Gr. ὄστρακ-ον + -OUS] = prec. **ento'motomist**, *Zool.* [f. next + -IST], one who dissects insects. **ento'motomy**, *Zool.* [Gr. -τομία cutting], the science of the dissection of insects to ascertain their structure, insect anatomy.

1865 *Reader* No. 119. 406/1 Curious *entomogenous fungi. **1840–3** HUMBLE *Dict. Geol. & Min.*, *Entomolite, a fossil insect; a petrified insect. **1840** W. WHEWELL *Philos. Induct. Sci.* I. p. cx, The words *Carnivores* and *Insectivores* are better..than Greek terms; otherwise we might..speak of *Zoophagans* and *Entomophagans. **1839–47** TODD *Cycl. Anat.* III. 259/2 But in most of the *Entomophagous genera ..the canines present a marked inferiority of development. **1880** GRAY *Struct. Bot.* vi. §4. 217 Delpino has classified flowers into Anemophilous and *Entomophilous. **1882** G. ALLEN in *Nature* 17 Aug. 373 Plantago must be descended from an entomophilous ancestor. **1835** KIRBY *Hab. & Inst. Anim.* II. xiii. 7 To place the Cirripedes immediately before the *Entomostracan Crustaceans. **1835** Entomostracan [see MALACOSTRACAN *a.* and *sb.*]. **1847** *Proc. Berw. Nat. Club* II. 199 He had added two Entomostracans. **1835–6** TODD *Cycl. Anat.* I. 43 Small animals, such as *entomostracous crustacea.

entomoid ('ɛntəmɔɪd), *a.* [f. as prec. + -OID.] Having the form or appearance of an insect; inset-like. Also quasi-*sb.*

1835–6 TODD *Cycl. Anat.* I. 112/1 These entomoid aquatic animals are generally carnivorous.

entomological (,ɛntəməʊ'lɒdʒɪkəl), *a.* [f. ENTOMOLOG-Y + -IC + -AL[1].] Of, or pertaining to, entomology or insects.

1816 KIRBY & SP. *Entomol.* (1843) I. 202 The utility of Entomological knowledge. **1826** SYD. SMITH *Wks.* (1859) II. 81 All nature is alive, and seems to be gathering all her entomological hosts to eat you up. **1846** MᶜCULLOCH *Acc. Brit. Empire* (1854) I. 117 Three years of entomological research in Brazil. **1870** YEATS *Nat. Hist. Comm.* 222 Sandal-wood is much used for entomological cabinets.

entomologist (ɛntə'mɒlədʒɪst). [f. as prec. + -IST.] One who studies entomology.

1771 *Phil. Trans.* LXI. 240 The entomologists have ranked the bivalve insects under the genus of the monoculi. **1816** KIRBY & SP. *Entomol.* (1843) I. 30 The remark of an author who himself is no entomologist. **1875** HAMERTON *Intell. Life* I. vii. 39 We have heard..even of a blind entomologist.

entomologize (ɛntə'mɒlədʒaɪz), *v.* [f. as prec. + -IZE.] *intr.* To study entomology; to collect specimens, or observe the habits, of insects.

1815 TAYLOR in Robberds *Mem.* II. 455 The engineer.. is not to lose his time in zoologizing, entomologizing, etc. **1828** J. M. HERBERT in *Darwin's Life & Lett.* (1887) I. 168 On these occasions Darwin entomologised most industriously. **1849** KINGSLEY in *Life* (1877) I. 211 It is too ..wet for entomologising.

entomology (ɛntə'mɒlədʒɪ). [ad. Fr. *entomologie* (1764 in Littré), mod.L. *entomologia* f. ENTOMO- + λογία (see -LOGY).] That branch of natural history which deals with the physiology, distribution, and classification of insects.

1766 tr. *Bonnet's Contemp. Nat.* IX. ix. I have given the name *insectology* to that part of natural history which has insects for its object: that of *entomology*..would undoubtedly have been more suitable..but its barbarous sound terryfy'd me. **1771** G. WHITE *Selborne* xxxiv. 91 Nothing would recommend entomology more than, etc. **1828** STARK *Elem. Nat. Hist.* II. 213 The branch of science

named Entomology. **1856** EMERSON *Eng. Traits, 1st Visit Eng.* Wks. (Bohn) II. 3 Landor despised entomology.

entone (ɛn'təʊn), *v.* [a. Fr. *entonne-r*: see INTONE.] *trans.* = INTONE; occas. used *arch.* and *techn.* with reference to church music.

c **1485** *Digby Myst.* (1882) IV. 1498 Now may thou entone a mery songe. *Ibid.* 1620 Entone sum ermonye! **1833** MRS. BROWNING *Prometh. Bd.* Poet. Wks. 1850 I. 158 All the mortal nations.. Are a dirge entoning.

Hence **en'tonement**, the action of intoning.

1849–53 ROCK *Ch. of Fathers* IV. xii. 137 Each took his own side of the choir for the entonement of the antiphons.

entonic (ɛn'tɒnɪk), *a.* *Med.* [f. Gr. ἔντον-ος strained (f. ἐν in + τόνος a straining) + -IC.]

'Intense, having exaggerated action, or great tension or tone' (*Syd. Soc. Lex.*).

In mod. Dicts.

entoparasite, -parasitic, -peripheral, -phyte, -phytic, -proctous, -pterygoid, -optic(s: see ENTO- *pref.*

†**en'tortill**, *v.* *Obs.* Also 7 entortle, intortle, -tell. [ad. F. *entortiller*, f. *en* (see EN-) + *tortiller* to twist, ad. late L. *tortillāre*, f. *tort-us*, pa. pple. of *torquēre* to twist.] *trans.* To entwine, coil.

1641 J. JACKSON *True Evang. T.* II. 143 The red scarlet lace of Christs blood, must be entortled and interwoven into a bracelet. **1652** SCLATER *2nd Cir. Auth.*, Ep. Ded., All which, so intortelled as they are within each other, etc. **1653** H. COGAN tr. *Pinto's Trav.* xxviii. (1663) 110 His tail might be some twenty fathoms long, and was entortilled about such another Monster.

Hence †**en'tortilled**, *ppl. a.*, †**entorti'llation**, *Obs.*, the action of twisting or entwining.

1629 J. MAXWELL tr. *Herodian* (1635) 236 By which darke and intortled Speeches he meant they should rather ghesse at what was done, than directly understand him. *a* **1631** DONNE tr. *Aristeas' Septuagint* (1633) 47 Borders, Raysings, Flowries, Wrappings, Entortilations and such like.

entosternal: see ENTO- *pref.*

entosthoblast (ɛn'tɒsθəʊblɑːst, -blæst). [f. *entostho-* taken as combining form of Gr. ἔντοσθε from within + -BLAST.] (See quot.)

1884 *Syd. Soc. Lex.*, *Entosthoblast*, a term for a granule within the nucleolus of a nucleated cell.

entotic, entotympanic: see ENTO- *pref.*

†**en'touch**, *v.* *Obs.* *rare*$^{-1}$. [f. EN-^{1} + TOUCH *v.*] *trans.* To touch upon, touch.

1426 *Pol. Poems* (1859) II. 136 After hem.. The boke also entouchid with his hond, Was Herry sworne.

entoumbe, obs. form of ENTOMB.

†**en'tour**, *v.* *Obs.* Also 7 entower. [ad. F. *entourer*: see prec.]

1. To surround (with a halo or the like).

1623 FAVINE *Theat. Hon.* II. xiii. 235 Entoured with beames. **1653** A. ROSS *View all Relig.* (1658) 349 The Image of the Virgin Mary entowered with a Golden Sun.

2. *Her.* In *pa. pple.* (See quot.)

1847 PARKER *Gloss. Brit. Her.* s.v., A shield decorated with branches, an ornament not strictly heraldic, is said by some to be *entoured* with them. In mod. Dicts.

‖**entourage** (ɑ̃turɑʒ). [Fr.; f. *entourer* to surround, f. *entour* that which surrounds, f. *en* in + *tour* circuit.] Surroundings, environment; *esp.* the assemblage of persons who surround, or are in attendance on, a superior.

1832–4 DE QUINCEY *Cæsars* Wks. X. 231 The simplicity of its republican origin had.. affected the.. *entourage* of the imperial office. **1850** THACKERAY *Pendennis* lix. (1885) 578 The house and its entourage. **1860** FROUDE *Hist. Eng.* VI. 52 Renard.. had been nervously struck by the entourage which surrounded Elizabeth. **1886** *Magd. College & Jas. II* (Oxf. Hist. Soc.) VI. Introd. 32 The appearance and *entourage* of the original paper.

‖**en tout cas** (ɑ̃ tu kɑ). [Fr., = in any case or emergency.] **1.** A parasol which also serves the purpose of an umbrella.

1874 *Cassell's Fam. Mag.* Dec. 20/1 'En-tout-cas' are larger than parasols and smaller than the usual umbrellas, and are suspended by a chain. **1889** *Chambers's Jrnl.* 28 Dec. 827/1 The parasol and the popular *en tous cas.* **1915** GALSWORTHY *Little Man* 39 Maud comes running,.. dragging a bull-dog.. by the crutch end of her en-tout-cas. **1928** *Daily Express* 17 July 5/2 The useful en-tout-cas that will withstand a summer shower. **1951** E. PAUL *Springtime in Paris* vi. 124 A torn *en-tout-cas* (combination umbrella and sunshade) turned inside out.

2. (Properly *En-Tout-Cas.*) A trade name for an all-weather hard lawn-tennis court.

1928 *Trade Marks Jrnl.* 17 Oct. 1644 *En-Tout-Cas*, marking tapes, and pins used.. for marking out hard lawn tennis courts... The En-Tout-Cas Company (Syston) Limited.. London E.C.2. **1931** *U.S. Lawn Tennis Assoc. Official Program* 23 Mar. 4 'En-Tout-Cas' courts are ready for play thirty minutes after heavy rain. **1953** *Landfall* 7 Feb. 121 But mostly we played.. in doubles.. shouting and sweating on the mossy en-tout-cas court. **1955** *Newsweek* 29 Aug. 46/3 Italians.. prefer the slow, high bounces of European entout-cas to the speedy skids of a tennis ball on grass.

entower: see EN- *pref.*^{1} 1 a.

entoyre, variant of ENTOIRE.

entozoon (ɛntəʊ'zəʊən). *Zool.* [mod. f. ENTO- + ζῷον animal.] A parasitic animal that lives within another. Also *attrib.* In *pl.* **Ento'zoa**, a class of animals taking their name from their mode of existence, though, as regards structure, they belong to various classes.

1836–9 TODD *Cycl. Anat.* II. 114 This singular Entozoon [*i.e.* Trichina] I discovered in a portion of the muscles of a male subject. **1875** H. WALTON *Dis. Eye* 25 The entozoon was about the size of a garden-pea. **1856** *Lancet* 12 Jan., Entozoon worms inhabiting the living body. **1882** O'DONOVAN *Merv* II. 105 The stagnant rain-pools almost invariably contain the eggs of entozoon animals.

pl. **1834** MCMURTRIE *Cuvier's Anim. Kingd.* 475 The second order of the Entozoa comprises, etc. **1851–9** OWEN in *Adm. Man. Sci. Enq.* 383 They should be examined for the presence of entozoa. **1876** tr. *Wagner's Gen. Pathol.* 109 The fate of entozoa depends more upon chance than that of any other animals.

Also **ento'zoal** *a.*, (*a*) of or pertaining to the *Entozoa*; (*b*) of disease: caused by the presence of *Entozoa*. **ento'zoic** *a.* [+ -IC.] = prec. **ˌentozoo'logically** *adv.*, with reference to entozoology; from the point of view of an entozoologist. **ˌentozo'ologist**, one who studies entozoology; one who makes the *Entozoa* an especial study. **ˌentozo'ology**, that branch of zoology which treats of the *Entozoa*.

1864 *Reader* IV. 669/2 For preventing the ravages of this, as of all other forms of *entozoal disease. **1866** *Ibid.* No. 159 36/3 The entozoal portions. **1861** HULME tr. *Moquin-Tandon* II. VII. 324 Crustaceous Entozoa.. *Entozoic Worms. **1869** E. A. PARKES *Pract. Hygiene* (ed. 3) 490 Some entozoic influence may be at work. **1879** G. ALLEN *Col. Sense* iii. 24 The lower vermiform Articulata are mostly entozoic, and these of course are quite blind. **1865** *Reader* 4 Feb. 143/2 Still, *entozoologically speaking, no harm follows.

entrable, obs. var. of ENTERABLE.

†**en'tract**, *v.* *Obs.* [var. of ENTREAT, after L. *tractāre*.] *trans.* To treat.

a **1572** KNOX *Hist. Ref.* Wks. 1846 I. 107 Some.. had better deserved then so to have bene entracted.

‖**entr'acte** (ɑ̃trakt). [Fr. *entr'acte*, f. *entre* between + *acte* act.] **a.** The interval between two acts of a play in a theatrical performance. **b.** A performance of music, dancing, etc., taking place between the acts.

[**1750** CHESTERF. *Lett.* (1774) I. clxxxvii. 563 Play.. is only the 'inter-acts' of other amusements.] **1842** J. F. WARNER *Univ. Dict. Mus. Terms* p. xxxvi, *Entr' Acte*, the music played between the acts of a French play. **1849** (*title*) The theatrical programme, and entr'acte. 23 July. **1863** OUIDA *Held in Bondage* (1870) 52 That old man there, who droops his head, takes snuff during the entr'actes. **1884** STEVENSON *New Arab. Nts.* 310 It was more like an entr'acte in a farce of Molière's.

‖**en'trada, en'trado**. *Obs.* [Sp. *entrada* entry, revenue. For the form *entrado* cf. -ADO^{2}.]

1. A ceremonial entry into a place.

1671 CROWNE *Juliana* IV. 40 As souls make their Entradoes in the skies.

2. Income, revenue.

1618–29 in Rushw. *Hist. Coll.* (1659) I. 15 It would be a profitable course to increase your Entrada. **1632** MASSINGER *Maid of Honour* I. i, And talked of nothing But your rents and your entradas. **1654** H. L'ESTRANGE *Chas. I* (1655) 111 Upon this account was brought into the Exchequer, an entrado of at least One hundred thousand pounds.

†**en'trade.** *Obs.* *rare*$^{-1}$. [Anglicized form of prec.: see -ADE.] = ENTRADA 1.

1670 G. H. *Hist. Cardinals* II. II. 150 All was pacify'd and set right.. before the Entrade.

entrail ('ɛntreɪl), *sb.*^{1} Chiefly in pl. Forms: *α.* 4–7 **entraile**, 4–5 **entraille**, 5–7 **entrayle**, 5 **-traylle**, (5 **entrell(e, -treyll)**, 6–7 **entral(l(e**; *β.* 6–8 **intrail(e**, 6–7 **intral(l(e**, (6 **intrayle**, 7 **interal**). [a. OF. *entraille* (now only in pl. *entrailles*) = Pr. *intralia*:—late L. *intrālia* inward parts, intestines, neut. pl. of **intrālis* adj. 'inward', f. *inter* between, among: see INTERIOR. Cf. L. *interānea* entrails, whence OF. *entraigne*, Sp. *entrañas*. As the word, like others with same termination, represents a Lat. neut. pl. taken as a fem. sing., it had primarily a collective sense, the sing. and pl. being in early use equivalent.]

I. In *sing.*

†**1. a.** *collect.* The intestines or internal parts generally; the 'inside'. *Obs.*

a **1300** *Cursor M.* 26756 Þis entrail in fire þat brennes bi-takens þin vn-scriuen sinnes. *c* **1300** *K. Alis.* 3628 He smot that duk, on the breost; Thorugh livre, and his entraile. *c* **1400** *Destr. Troy* 11800 The bestis were britnet & broght to þe auter, With the entrell euermore euyn vppo lofte. **1652** ASHMOLE *Theat. Chem. Brit.* liii, 224 Yet have y mor poyse closyd in mine entrayle.

b. *Cookery.* A stuffed paunch. *Obs.*

c **1430** *Cookery Bk.* 38 *An Entrayle*—Take a chepis wombe; take Polettys y-rostyd.. and do in the wombe.

2. a. [With sense inferred from the pl.: see 3 a.] An internal organ of the body; = L. *viscus*. Now *rare*.

1677 BARROW *Serm.* (1686) III. 135 The heart, that material part and principal entrail of our Body, is the chief seat of the soul. **1807** G. GREGORY *Dict. Arts & Sc.* II. 444/1 s.v. *Plants*, Linnæus defines them [stamina] to be an entrail of the plant. **1856** KANE *Arct. Expl.* II. iii. 41 To taste an occasional entrail of our last half dozen rabbits.

b. *esp.* A bowel, intestine.

1483 *Cath. Angl.* 116 An Entrelle, *vbi* A tharme.

II. In *pl.*

3. a. *gen.* The organs and parts enclosed in the trunk of man or (formerly) other animals.

α. *a* **1300** *Cursor M.* 26752 Alle your entrailles ilkon in well-and pottes sal be don. **1481** CAXTON *Myrr.* II. xv. 100 The spyther.. spynneth and weueth of his entraylles the thredes of whiche he maketh his nettes. **1555** EDEN *Decades W. Ind.* III. II. (Arb.) 42 Whether perles bee the byrthe or spaune of there entrals. **1610** HEALEY *St. Aug. Citie of God* 526 The lungs, the softest of all the entrailes but for the marrow. **1734** tr. *Rollin's Anc. Hist.* (1827) I. 56 The divine vapour.. had diffused itself through the entrails of the priestess. **1772** PRIESTLEY *Inst. Relig.* (1782) I. 200 The priests used to.. devour the entrails of goats. **1838–43** ARNOLD *Hist. Rome* II. xxix. 143 The signs given by the entrails of the sacrifice. **1889** 'MARK TWAIN' *Conn. Yankee* 46 They would have dug his entrails out.. to get at that tale and squelch it. **1915** W. S. MAUGHAM *Of Human Bondage* c. 527 Hunger was gnawing at his entrails. **1916** JOYCE *Portrait of Artist* iii. 159 He sprang from the bed, the reeking odour pouring down his throat, clogging and revolting his entrails.

β. **1557** NORTH tr. *Gueuara's Diall Princes* 43 b/1 The wormes shall eate hys intrayle sin the graue. **1588** SHAKS. *Tit. A.* I. ii. 144 And intrals feede the sacrifising fire. **1629** DAVENANT *Albovine* (1673) 431 All m'interals are shrunk up. **1728** T. SHERIDAN *Persius* Sat. II. (1739) 31 Is it by the fat Intrails of Beasts?

b. *spec.* The contents of the abdominal cavity; the bowels; the intestines.

α. **1382** WYCLIF *Acts* i. 18 Alle his [Judas'] entrailis ben sched abrood. **1486** *Bk. St. Albans* C v b, For sekenes that haukis haue i their entrellis. *c* **1489** CAXTON *Sonnes of Aymon* ix. 251 The wounde of Rycharde was soo greefull to see.. For all the entraylles appyered oute of his body. **1594** T. B. *La Primaud. Fr. Acad.* II. Ep. Rdr., The lower story of this frame, where the guttes and entrailes of the body.. haue their abiding. **1667** MILTON *P.L.* II. 783 Thine own begotten, breaking violent way Tore through my entrails. **1768–74** TUCKER *Lt. Nat.* (1852) II. 142 The flattering bait of pride to get her swallowed down into the entrails.

β. **1467** in *Eng. Gilds* (1870) 372 That intrailles of bestes and blode putts be clansed.. by night. **1594** SHAKS. *Rich. III*, IV. iv. 23 Wilt thou, O God, flye from such gentle Lambs, And throw them in the intrailes of the Wolfe? **1617** MARKHAM *Caval.* III. 41 It also purgeth the stomacke and intrals of all molten grease. **1704** SWIFT *Batt. Bks.* (1711) 240 If the Materials be nothing but Dirt, spun out of your own Intrails (the Guts of Modern Brains). **1726** SLOANE *Jamaica* II. 304 The intrails were the same as those of other pigeons.

†**4.** The inward parts regarded as the seat of the emotions, thoughts, etc.; = 'heart', 'soul'; also in phrase †***entrails of mercy***. Cf. BOWEL 3.

c **1374** CHAUCER *Boeth.* III. xii. 107 Þe most[e] ardaunt loue of hys wijf brende þe entrailes of his brest. *c* **1380** WYCLIF *Serm.* Sel. Wks. II. 255 Ofte holy writt clepiþ mercy þe entrailis of mercy. **1382** —— *Ecclus.* xix. 23 The entrailes of hym ben ful of treccherie. *c* **1430** LYDG. *Bochas* IV. xiv. (1554) 114 a, In her entrayles all malice was enclosed. **1574** HELLOWES *Gueuara's Fam. Ep.* (1584) 264 That I shoulde bee of malicious entrailes, either double in wordes. **1593** SHAKS. *3 Hen. VI*, I. iv. 87. **1611** HEYWOOD *Gold. Age* I. i. Wks. 1874 III. 11 Her Intrails were all in a mutiny. **1790** BURKE *Fr. Rev.* 128 In England we have not yet been completely embowelled of our natural entrails.

5. *transf.* **a.** The inner parts of anything; the interior, internal contents (of the earth, etc., often with personification). Now somewhat *rare*.

1490 CAXTON *Eneydos* xix. 73 The rotes haue hidde hemself wythin the entraylles of therthe their moder. **1576** FLEMING *Panoplie Ep.* 282 Such a one searcheth the very heart and entrayles of the ground, for gold and silver. **1602** FULBECKE *Pandectes Law Nations* 73 The other entralles of the earth: as Pitch, Chalke, lyme. **1610** SHAKS. *Temp.* I. ii. 295, I will rend an Oake And peg thee in his knotty entrailes. **1624** CAPT. SMITH *Virginia* VI. 215 The Riuer doth pierce many daies iourney the entrailes of that Country. *a* **1661** FULLER *Worthies* (1840) II. 263 The entrails of such utensils [pillow, or bolster] amongst the Romans were made but of dust. *a* **1682** SIR T. BROWNE *Chr. Mor.* 92 Even the sun.. May have dark and smoaky entrails. **1683** PETTUS *Fleta Min.* II. 12 The Monochord whose Entrals are curiously composed of Metals. **1772–82** MASON *Eng. Garden* II. (R.), Nor thou, fell tube! Whose iron entrails hide the sulphurous blast. **1866** HARTWIG *Harmonies Nat.* in Spurgeon *Treas. Dav.* Ps. xcv. 4 Filtering through the entrails of the earth.. the thermal springs gush forth.

†**b.** of immaterial things. *Obs.*

1584 FENNER *Def. Ministers* (1587) 74 He must rippe vp the verie intrayles of our wordes, ere hee can fetche out this meaning. **1642** ROGERS *Naaman* 867 Sinne.. hath seated it selfe deeply in the entrals of thy soule. *a* **1655** VINES *Lord's Supp.* (1677) 324 To look into the entrals of this Sacrament.

†**en'trail**, *sb.*^{2} *Obs.* *rare*. [f. next vb.; cf. AF. *entrail* 'reticulum'.] The action of the verb ENTRAIL; a coil.

1590 SPENSER *F.Q.* I. i. 16 Folds.. stretcht now forth at length without entraile.

†**en'trail**, *v.* *Obs.* Also 6 **entrayl, intrail**. [ad. OF. *entreillier*, f. *en-* (see EN-^{1}) + *treille* trellis-work.] *trans.* To entwine; interlace.

1577–87 HOLINSHED *Chron.* III. 856/2 A wreath of gold curiouslie wrought and intrailed. **1579** SPENSER *Sheph. Cal.* Aug. 30 And over them spred a goodly wilde vine Entrailed with a wanton yvy twine. **1595** —— *Prothalamion* 25 A little wicker basket, Made of fine twigs, entrayled curiously. **1736** W. THOMPSON *Epithalamium* [Imitation of Spenser], Myrtle-girland green, Entrail'd with flowrets.

†**en'trailed**, *ppl. a. Obs.* [f. prec. + -ED¹.]
1. Entwined, interwoven.
1599 MIDDLETON *Micro-cynicon* Wks. V. 492 Her high-pric'd necklace of entrailed pearls.
2. *Her.* ***entrailed cross***: one drawn in outline, with looped flourishes at the corners (see figures in Leigh *loc. cit.* and Elvin *Dict. Her.*). Sir J. Ferne refers disapprovingly to a use of the word as = UMBRATED.
1562 LEIGH *Armorie* (1597) 36 He beareth argent a crosse entrailed..it is alwaies sable, and is no bigger then touched with a pensell, or tricked with a pen. **1586** FERNE *Blaz. Gentrie* 175 You haue been taught to call this crosse entrailled.

entrain (ɛn'treɪn), *v.*¹ [ad. Fr. *entraîn-er*, f. *en-* (L. *inde*) away + *traîner* to drag.] **1.** *trans.* To draw away with or after oneself; in early use *fig.* to bring on as a consequence; in mod. use *lit.* but *rare.*
1568 T. HOWELL *Arb. Amitie* (1879) 40 Faith true obtaine ..Friend deere entraine. **1603** FLORIO *Montaigne* III. v. (1632) 471 Yeares entraine me if they please, but backward. **1657** TOMLINSON *Renou's Disp.* Ded., You entrain Humility and Integrity for your Retainers. **1698** VANBRUGH *Æsop* II. i, The Stomach..with its destiny entrain'd their fate. **1835** LYTTON *Rienzi* IV. ii. 198 Thou wert entrained to the slaughter. **1858** MAYNE REID in *Chamb. Jrnl.* IX. 172 Entrained in the crowd. **1881** J. HILL in *Metal World* 8 Oct. 342 Independent of the water entrained.
2. *spec.* Of a fluid: to carry (particles) along by its flow; *spec.* of steam which carries along particles of water through a pipe or particles of sugar from an evaporating pan during the manufacture of sugar; also, to incorporate (air-bubbles) in concrete. Hence **en'trainer**, 'a device for saturating a current of gas or steam with liquid, usually a hollow or pocket for collecting a liquid in such a way that it will be picked up by a passing current of gas or steam' (*Cent. Dict.* Suppl.); **en'training** *vbl. sb.* and *ppl. a.*; **en'trainment**¹, the action of the verb in these senses.
1892 *Mod. Lang. Notes* Nov. 393 *Entrain, entrainement* —evidently from Fr. *entrainer*. The action of carrying over particles of syrup or sugar by the steam exhausted from vacuum-pans in boiling sugar. **1930** *Engineering* 14 Feb. 213/1 Resulting in further steam being entrained in the jet. **1955** BROWN & DEY *India's Mineral Wealth* (ed. 3) ix. 350, 0.63 ton of cement would be used for 100 cubic feet of concrete, without the help of pozzolanas or air entrainment. **1955** *Bull. Atomic Sci.* Jan. 2/1 He wrote down the mathematical equations for the entrainment of air in the balance wheel of the watch. **1956** Entraining [see AIR *sb.*¹ B. I. 1]. **1958** *New Scientist* 7 Aug. 573/1 There are actual droplets of liquid boiler water which have been carried out of the boiler, or entrained, by the steam. **1959** *Oceanogr. & Marine Biol.* I. 157 This figure shows the existence of an entrainment current (that is, water dragged along). **1962** *Engineering* 30 Mar. 430 Manufacturers of air-entraining Portland cement.

entrain (ɛn'treɪn), *v.*² [f. EN-¹ + TRAIN *sb.*]
1. *trans.* To put into a railway-train.
1881 *Standard* 11 July 6 The Volunteers were en-trained and despatched to their destinations without either undue hurry or delay. **1882** ALISON in *Standard* 7 Aug. 5/7 The guns and troops were quietly entrained at the..Junction.
2. *intr.* To go on board a train.
1890 *Daily News* 8 Apr. 3/3 The troops should be back.. in sufficient time to..entrain for London. **1899** *Ibid.* 21 Nov. 5/4 The debarkation and entraining of the troops as they arrive here is being carried out rapidly... The troops entrain at the docks. **1914** R. BROOKE *Coll. Poems* (1918) Mem. p. cxxx, We..entrained in the last train left. **1938** AUDEN & ISHERWOOD *On Frontier* II. i. 68 The clerk entraining for the office. **1968** G. JONES *Hist. Vikings* II. i. 65 If he entrains at Malmö..for Stockholm and Uppsala.
Hence **en'training** *vbl. sb.*
1881 *Volunteer Rev.* in *Scotsman* 29 Nov., The entraining and detraining of the men was carried on satisfactorily.

‖**entrain** (ɑ̃trɛ̃), *sb.* [Fr.] Enthusiasm, animation.
1859 *Once a Week* 8 Oct. 304/2 The result of all this is to be seen in a greater degree of *entrain* than can perhaps be found in any other congregation of holiday-seeking Britons. **1888** MRS. H. WARD *R. Elsmere* III. v. xxxi. 12 The instruments dashed into the opening allegro with..an *entrain* that took the room by storm. **1919** J. C. SNAITH *Love Lane* xxiii. 117 Corporal Hollis could not be expected to display the entrain of a sergeant of the Black Watch. **1954** E. JENKINS *Tortoise & Hare* ix. 93 She wanted to put her head out of the window, but that would have shown too much *entrain*.

en train: see EN *prep.*

entrainment¹: see ENTRAIN *v.*¹

entrainment² (ɛn'treɪnmənt). [f. ENTRAIN *v.*² + -MENT.] The act or fact of entering a train.
1891 *Pall Mall Gaz.* 8 July 2/2 The early hour of entrainment is..still maintained.

†'**entral.** *Obs. rare*⁻¹. In 7 entrall. [f. ENTER *v.* + -AL¹. (OFr. had *entraille* in same sense.)] Entrance; entry.
1647 H. MORE *Song of Soul* II. iii. II. vi, None would vouchsafe the entrall [*rime* tricentrall] Into this life.

entrammel (ɛn'træməl), *v.* Also 7 entramel. [f. EN-¹ + TRAMMEL.] *trans.* **a.** To put into trammels or nets. Only *fig.* To entangle, fetter, hamper. †**b.** ? To bind, plait (the hair) (*obs.*).
Hence †**en'trammelled** *ppl. a.*; also †**en'trammelling** *vbl. sb.*
1598 FLORIO, *Lucignoli*..entramelings or curlings of haires wrought and enterlaced togither with ribands. **1603** —— *Montaigne* III. v. (1632) 492 They ensnared, glewed, entrameled, haltred and shackled themselves. **1611** COTGR., *Passe-fillons*..any frizled lockes, or entrammelled tufts of haire. *a* **1670** HACKET *Abp. Williams* I. (1692) 104 Entramell'd with fictions and ignorance. **1841** *Fraser's Mag.* XXIII. 278 To thee alone can I entrust the duty of entrammelling and fettering this bold spirit. **1880** F. HUEFFER in *Macm. Mag.* Nov. 45 Twanging his guitar with no..rule to entrammel his passionate effusion.

entrance ('ɛntrəns), *sb.* Forms: 6-8 **enterance**, 6-7 **enter-**, **entraunce**, 6- **entrance**; also 6 **intraunce.** [a. OF. *entrance*, f. *entrer* to ENTER: see -ANCE.]
1. a. The action of coming or going in.
1601 SHAKS. *Twel. N.* III. i. 93, I will answer you with gate and entrance, but we are preuented. **1612** *Enchir. Med.* 154 The dose is..to bee taken at the entrance into bed. **1628** PRYNNE *Cens. Cozens* 38 He hath prescribed vs a short Eiaculation..at our entrance into the Church. **1720** DE FOE *Capt. Singleton* vi. (1840) 100 In the..first entrance of the waste, we were..discouraged. **1791** MRS. RADCLIFFE *Rom. Forest* i, La Motte was interrupted by the entrance of the ruffian. **1839** JAMES *Louis XIV*, II. 286 To witness the entrance of the Royal party.
b. *spec.* The coming of an actor upon the stage.
1600 *A.Y.L.* II. vii. 141 They haue their Exits and their Entrances. **1679** DRYDEN *Tr. & Cr.* Pref. A iiij b, After an Entrance or two he lets 'em [Pandarus and Thersites] fall. **1681-6** J. SCOTT *Chr. Life* (1747) III. vii. 193 Appearing and acting upon the Stage without either Entrance or Exit. **1874** MORLEY *Compromise* (1886) 126 Progress would mean something more than mere entrances and exits on the theatre of office.
c. *Eccl.* [transl. Gr. εἴσοδος] ***Great*** and ***Little Entrance***: in the Eastern Church, the bringing in respectively of the elements and of the gospels, in the eucharistic service.
1855 P. FREEMAN *Princ. Divine Service* I. 147. **1859** NEALE *Liturg.* Introd. xv. **1876** *Dict. Christ. Antiq.* s.v.
†**d.** Words spoken, or ceremonies observed, on entering. *Obs.*
1693 TEMPLE *Mem.* Wks. 1731 I. 396, I wou'd leave him there after the first Entrances were past.
2. *fig.* **a.** Generally.
1526 *Pilgr. Perf.* (W. de W. 1531) 1 b, After my entraunce to religyon, consyderynge to what I had bounde myselfe. **1535** COVERDALE *Wisdom* vii. 6 All men then haue one intraunce vnto life, & one goinge out in like maner. **1614** RALEIGH *Hist. World* II. 399 This gave occasion to young David..to make a famous entrance into publique notice of the people. **1750** JOHNSON *Rambler* No. 1 ⁋2 Wishing that ceremonial modes of entrance [before the publick] had been anciently established. **1888** *Spectator* 28 Apr. 562/2 A measure for facilitating the entrance of Life-Peers into the House of Lords.
b. *esp.* The entering *into* or *upon* (office, duties, etc.). †Formerly also *absol.* accession (of a sovereign, etc.).
1559 HETHE in Strype *Ann. Ref.* I. App. vi. 8 Paul the IVth of that name..ever since his first entraunce into Peters chayre. **1612** WOODALL *Surg. Mate* Ep. Salut. 3 In the year of the great Plague at the first entrance of King James of blessed memorie. **1647** CLARENDON *Hist. Reb.* I. (1843) 8/2 Before they made an entrance upon more solemn debates. **1649** SELDEN *Laws Eng.* I. xvi. (1739) 30 Kings furthermore bound themselves (at their entrance into the Throne) hereunto by an Oath. **1709** STRYPE *Ann. Ref.* I. xiii. 175 Not long from the beginning of the Queen's entrance upon her government. *a* **1891** *Mod.* The oath required to be taken by magistrates at entrance into office.
†**c.** 'Intellectual ingress' (J.); initiation. *Obs.*
1612 BRINSLEY *Lud. Lit.* viii. 107 To attaine to make a more easie entrance, to that purity of the Latine tongue. **1625** BACON *Ess. Trav.* (Arb.) 521 He that trauaileth into a Country, before he hath some Entrance into the Language, goeth to Schoole, and not to Trauaile.
d. Short for *entrance fee, money.*
1681 W. ROBERTSON *Phraseol. Gen.* (1693) 539 An entrance into a school or entrance money. **1702** *Lond. Gaz.* No. 3807/4 To pay a Guinea and a half Entrance 4 Days before they Run. **1713** *Ibid.* No. 5131/4 Subscribers to pay One Guinea Entrance. **1887** C. D. WARNER *Their Pilgr.* (1888) xi. 253 Paying their entrance, and passing through the turnstile..they stood in the Congress Spring Park.
3. Power, right, or opportunity of entering; admission. *lit.* and *fig.*
1576 FLEMING *Panoplie Ep.* ⁋3 It was my happie chance to have entrance into a goodly Gardene plotte. **1590** SPENSER *F.Q.* I. iv. 6 A Porter..Cald Malvenu, who entrance none denide. **1695** WOODWARD *Nat. Hist. Earth* III. §1 (1723) 132 The Fissures whereinto it can get Admission or Enterance. **1703** MOXON *Mech. Exerc.* 124 The Nail (unless it have good entrance) will start aside. *Ibid.* 224 To find how great a Dy should have Entrance at a small Hole. **1798** SOUTHEY *St. Patrick's Purgatory* 29 The gates of Paradise unclose, Free entrance there is given. **1838** LYTTON *Leila* II. i. 17, I have your royal word, sire, for free entrance and safe egress. **1849** JAMES *Woodman* vii, He retired a step or two to give him entrance.
fig. **1576** FLEMING *Panoplie Ep.* 281 Upon these premisses, I see entraunce to this plaine conclusion. **1602** DAVISON in Farr *S.P. Eliz.* (1845) II. 323 That my cries may entraunce gayne. **1647** H. MORE *Song of Soul* II. iii. IV. xviii, Gods lovely life hath there no enterance. **1722** SEWEL *Hist. Quakers* (1795) I. 35 All these reasons found little entrance with priests, magistrates and others.

†**4. a.** The beginning or commencement (of a course or period of time). **b.** The first part, the opening words (of a chapter or book). *Obs.*
a. **1549** COVERDALE *Erasm. Par. Philip.* i. 5 Euer synce the fyrst entraunce of your profession, euen vnto this daye. **1621** LADY M. WROTH *Urania* 545 This is scarce the enterance: what will be the successe? **1639** SALTMARSHE *Policy* 70, I know no better Policy in the Preface or entrance upon a designe than, etc. **1658** USSHER *Ann.* I. 1 Upon the entrance of the night. **1693** EVELYN *De la Quint. Compl. Gard.* I. 32 At the Entrance of the Spring.
b. **1552** LATIMER *Serm. Lord's Prayer* II. 2 The entrance is this; Cum oratis, dicite, Paternoster, qui es in coelis. **1638** CHILLINGW. *Relig. Prot.* I. iv. §43. 212 Adde to this place, the entrance to his History. **1697** POTTER *Antiq. Greece* III. xi. (1715) 100 As we learn from the very Entrance of the first Iliad, where he speaks of Achilles' Anger. **1765** BLACKSTONE *Comm.* I. 219 This was observed in the entrance of the last chapter.
5. *concr.* That by which anything is entered, whether open or closed; a door, gate, avenue, passage; the mouth (of a river). Also, the point at which anything enters or is entered.
1535 COVERDALE *Ezek.* xl. 38 A chambre also, whose intraunce was at the dore pilers. **1553** EDEN *Treat. New Ind.* (Arb.) 26 At the entraunce at the great desert. **1606** SHAKS. *Tr. & Cr.* III. iii. 38 Achilles stands i' th' entrance of his Tent. **1652** NEEDHAM tr. *Selden's Mare Cl.* 33 The more Northerly enterance of Nilus..served instead of Bounds to the South part of the Land of Israel. **1719** DE FOE *Crusoe* 69, I made up the Entrance, which till now I had left open. *a* **1849** SIR R. WILSON *Life* (1869) I. iii. 140 We were beating off the harbour's entrance. **1860** TYNDALL *Glac.* I. §8. 60 The glacier is forced through the entrance of the trunk valley. **1879** HARLAN *Eyesight* iii. 38 This blind spot is at the entrance of the optic nerve.
fig. **1535** COVERDALE *Ecclus.* i. 5 The euerlastinge commaundementes, are the intraunce of her [wyszdome]. **1592** MARLOWE *Jew Malta* v. ii, And now, as entrance to our safety, To prison with the Governor. **1605** CAMDEN *Rem.* 17 That these were the fowre entraunces into the church. **1725** DE FOE *Voy. round World* (1840) 270 The very entrance into eternal horror.
6. *Naut.* The part of a ship that comes first (in the water); 'the bow of a vessel, or form of the fore-body under the load-water line' (Adm. Smyth).
1781 NELSON 24 Aug. in Nicolas *Disp.* (1845) I. 43 She [the Albemarle] has a bold entrance, and clean run. **1869** SIR E. REID *Shipbuild.* v. 85 In ships which have a very fine entrance the breasthook plates are not run right forward to the stem.
†**7.** The action of entering (something) in a record; *concr.* an entry. *Obs.* (cf. ENTRY).
1588 MELLIS *Briefe Instr.* D iiij, The enterance of these parcels. **1620** J. WILKINSON *Of Courts Baron* 190 The bailife ..delivers to the Sherife a copie of the entrance of the court when the cause was removed thus. ?**1857** MRS. GASKELL *Let.* ?Aug. (1966) 462 The contradiction..involved in the 3£ entrance..on the one page, and the 1£ entrance for clothes on the next.
8. *attrib.*, as ***entrance-channel***, ***-cue*** (Theatr.), ***-door***, ***-fee***, ***-hall***, ***-lodge***, ***-money***, ***-road***, ***-way***.
1839 DE LA BECHE *Rep. Geol. Cornwall* xv. 520 The *entrance-channel would be much better than at present. **1955** FRIEDMAN & WEISSKOPF in W. Pauli *Niels Bohr* 148 In the optical model, compound nucleus formation and absorption..represent the removal of the particle from the entrance channel. **1901** C. MORRIS *Life on Stage* (1902) ix. 59 The canary breeches were always there, ready to..break a buckle just at the moment of my *entrance-cue. **1961** BOWMAN & BALL *Theatre Lang.* 124 *Entrance cue*, a cue for an actor to come onstage. *a* **1817** JANE AUSTEN *Persuasion* (1818) IV. viii. 149 As she ceased, the *entrance door opened again. **1880** 'MARK TWAIN' *Tramp Abroad* 168 At the entrance-door up-stairs. **1844** *Mem. Babylonian P'cess* II. 4, I paid her *entrance fee. **1856** FROUDE *Hist. Eng.* (1858) I. i. 52 The children of those who could afford the small entrance fees were apprenticed to trades. **1677** in M. M. Verney *Verney Lett.* (1930) I. iv. 55 Is there an *Entrance Hall?—No, but a wide passage that serves the purpose. **1841** ORDERSON *Creol.* xi. 111 He found his master seated in the entrance-hall. **1864** PUSEY *Lect. Daniel* viii. 501 Thereon follows eternal life, to which death is the entrance-hall. **1970** *N.Y. Times Mag.* 25 Oct. 87 The neo-Gothic entrance hall is furnished with Victorian chairs and bench. **1881** MISS BRADDON *Asph.* I. 290 Nobody ever saw a man at an *entrance lodge. **1681** W. ROBERTSON *Phraseol. Gen.* (1693) 539 *Entrance money, which Schollars paid to the Master at their first coming to school. **1833** MARRYAT *P. Simple* v, And, as for entrance money, why I think I must not charge you more than a couple of guineas. **1833** BREWSTER *Nat. Magic* iii. 45 Driving up the *entrance-road to the house. **1883** H. H. KANE in *Harper's Mag.* Nov. 945/1 The *entranceway looked dirty.

entrance (ɛn'trɑːns, -'træns), *v.* Also 7 **entraunch**, **intranse**, 6-8 **intrance.** [f. EN-¹ + TRANCE.]
1. *trans.* To throw into a trance.
α. **1608** SHAKS. *Per.* III. ii. 94 She hath not been entranced Above five hours. **1712** ADDISON *Spect.* No. 303 ⁋4 The Nine Days' Astonishment, in which the Angels lay entranced..is a noble circumstance.
β. **1667** MILTON *P.L.* I. 301 He stood and call'd His Legions, Angel Forms, who lay intrans't. *Ibid.* XI. 420 Adam..Sunk down, and all his Spirits became intranst.
†**b.** *transf. Obs.*
1686 N. COX *Gentl. Recreat.* III. 133 If you would restore any of these entranced [with drugged bait] Fowl to their former health.
2. To throw into a state of mind resembling a trance; to put 'out of oneself'; to overpower with strong feeling, as delight, fear, etc.
α. *a* **1599** SPENSER (J.), With delight I was entranced and carried so far from myself. **1621** QUARLES *Div. Poems, Esther*

(1717) 16 So stand the Sea-men..Entraunch'd with what this man of God recited. **1634** Milton *Comus* 1005 Celestial Cupid..Holds his dear Psyche, sweet entranced. *a* **1765** Mallet *To Dk. Marlborough* (R.), Entranc'd in wonder at th' unfolding scene. **1820** Keats *St. Agnes* xxviii, So entranced, Porphyro gazed upon her empty dress. **1868** Helps *Realmah* vii. (1876) 158 Throughout that night, Realmah sat entranced in thought.

β. **1598** Marston *Pygmal.* Sat. iv. 154 Fond Bryart.. Intrance thy selfe in thy sweet extasie. **1743** J. Davidson *Æneid* 25 Intranced in fear and wonder. **1771** Mackenzie *Man Feel.* xxxv. (1803) 69 He was too much intranced in thought, to observe her at all.

b. To carry away in or as in a trance (*from, to*).

1593 Nashe *Christ's T.* (1613) 118 When a man is so.. entranced from himselfe, with Wealth, Ambition, and Vaine-glory, that, etc. *Ibid.* 176 That reuerend Pastor, (entranced to hell in his thoughts for the distresse of his people). **1877** Mrs. Oliphant *Makers Flor.* i. 17 The Vita Nuova that entrances the young poet into its charmed circle.

Hence **en'tranced** *ppl. a.* **en'trancedly** *adv.*, in the manner of one entranced.

1686 [see 1 b]. **1768** Beattie *Minstr.* i. xxxiii, Sleep A vision brought to his entranced sight. **1837** Lytton *E. Maltravers* 25 Her entranced and silent lover. **1871** Macduff *Mem. Patmos* i. 12 The Evangelist..awaking from his entranced dream. **1873** Browning *Red Cott. Nt.-Cap* 1610 So wrote entrancedly to confidant Monsieur L. M.

entrancement (ɛn'trɑːnsmənt, -'træns-). [f. ENTRANCE *v.* + -MENT.] The action of entrancing; the condition of being entranced.

1652 Cokaine tr. *Cassandra* 84 His spirits a little recovered from that entrancement. **1680** Otway *Poet's Compl. Muse* v, As we did in our Entrancements lie. **1772** Mackenzie *Man World* i. xxii. (1823) 448 She received it with an intrancement of sorrow. **1817** Coleridge *Sibyl. Leaves, Keepsake,* The entrancement of that maiden kiss. **1837** Howitt *Rur. Life* vi. xviii. (1862) 610 The feelings of delicious entrancement with which I approached the outskirts of Dartmoor.

entrancing (ɛn'trɑːnsɪŋ, -'træns-), *ppl. a.* [f. ENTRANCE *v.* + -ING^{2}.] That entrances; transporting.

1842 Lytton *Zanoni* 26 The Siren's voice poured forth its entrancing music. **1846** Keble *Lyra Innoc.* (1873) 5 In that entrancing dream. **1881** *Athenæum* No. 2825. 807 The entrancing tale of the Tegethoff.

Hence **en'trancingly** *adv.*, in an entrancing manner or degree.

1854 *Tait's Mag.* XXI. 273 It steals entrancingly over the ear. **1856** Ruskin *Mod. Paint.* III. iv. vi. §6 Never sublime, never perfectly nor entrancingly beautiful.

entrant ('ɛntrənt), *sb.* and *a.* See also INTRANT. [a. Fr. *entrant*, pr. pple. of *entrer* to ENTER.]

A. *sb.* One who or that which enters. Also *fig.*

1. One who comes or goes into (a room, etc.); a person entering; an incomer; a visitor.

a **1856** H. Miller *Rambles Geol.* (1858) 252 Remarking that the entrant was 'only the green lady'. **1866** R. Chambers *Ess.* Ser. ii. 23 Mr. Sydenham was there..to welcome the entrants, manage introductions. **1884** *Times* 15 Oct. 9/1 The abuse of public meeting involved in a selection of the entrants.

fig. **1857** G. Wilson *Gateways Knowl.* (1859) 15 As the privileged entrant counsels, the great arms and limbs of the body are set in motion. **1889** *County Govt. Rev.* 2 Jan. 417 The latest entrant to the controversy is our contemporary the Law Times.

b. One who makes legal entry; one who enters into the possession of land, etc.

1635 Pagitt *Christianogr.* iii. (1636) 36 Because one entred upon the Priory of Barnewell by the Popes Bull, the said Entrant was committed to the Tower.

2. One who enters into or becomes a member of an institution or profession. Const. *into*.

1800 A. Carlyle *Ant.* 249 The sudden call for young men to fill up vacancies..obliged the Church to take their entrants from the lower ranks. **1839–57** Alison *Hist. Europe* IX. xxii. 8 The influences of these new entrants appeared in the secrecy and ability with which the measures were taken. **1845** McCulloch *Taxation* i. iv. (1852) 122 There would be a greater influx of entrants into professional businesses. **1875** *Modern Circular,* Mutual Entrants in 1876 participate in the Eighth Division of Profits. **1880** *Fraser's Mag.* No. 701 The entrant to the Scotch National Church..is only legally required to subscribe the Confession of Faith.

b. One who 'enters' as a competitor. Also *fig.*

1838 *Fraser's Mag.* XVIII. 725 We have in the victors.. the names and material of the successful entrants. **1883** H. Drummond *Nat. Law in Spir. W.* xii. (1884) 411 Of the millions of possible entrants for advancement..the number ultimately selected for preferment is small. *Mod.* The prizes will depend on the number of entrants.

B. *adj.* That enters, in senses of the verb.

1640–1 *Kirkcudbr. War-Comm. Min. Bk.* (1855) 12 The entrant tenants, at Whitsounday last..shall be lyable for mantainance of the foote sogers. **1651** *Life Father Sarpi* (1676) 18 The Father..could not be satisfied how the humour of Gold could be made entrant.

entrap (ɛn'træp), *v.*^{1} Forms: 6–7 entrappe, 6–8 intrap(pe, 6– entrap. [ad. OF. *entraper, entrapper*, f. *en-* (see EN-^{1}) + *trappe* TRAP.]

1. *trans.* To catch in or as in a trap. Also *transf.* and *fig.* to bring unawares into a position of difficulty or danger; to bring (a person) into one's power by artifice.

α. **1590–6** Spenser *F.Q.* (J.), That guileful net In which.. eyes entrapped are. **1598** Barret *Theor. Warres* i. ii. 9 Being first entrapped and foundred with the like vice of drunkennesse. **1713** Warder *True Amazons* 55 Many [Wasps in Pots] will be entrap'd. **1774** Goldsm. *Nat. Hist.* (1776) IV. 272 The wild elephant, upon seeing himself entrapped in this manner, instantly attempts to use violence. **1835** Kirby *Hab. & Inst. Anim.* xix, Spiders were divided.. according to the mode in which they entrap or seize their prey. **1835** Lytton *Rienzi* x. v. 419 He had entrapped the confidence of another. **1860** Tyndall *Glac.* ii. §27. 376 The residue of the air originally entrapped in the interstices of the snow. **1868** J. H. Blunt *Ref. Ch. Eng.* I. 137 The king was trying to entrap the Pope.

β. **1534** Barnes *Supplic. Hen. VIII* (R.), Neither to intrappe them, nor betray them. **1561** Daus tr. *Bullinger on Apoc.* (1573) Pref. 7 The seconde [persecution]..which intrapped also the Authour of this worke. *a* **1649** Drumm. of Hawth. *Jas. V*, Wks. 109 This interview was to intrap his person. **1678** Wanley *Wond. Lit. World* v. ii. §59. 471/1 Manuel..was..intrapped in the straights of Cilicia, and his Army miserably cut off.

b. To beguile, bring by artifice *to* or *into*.

1851 Hussey *Papal Power* i. 38 Having been at first persuaded or entrapped, into an approval of Pelagius' doctrines. **1868** Freeman *Norm. Conq.* (1876) II. viii. 261 Entrapping men to destruction by the literal fulfilment of an oath. **1884** *Manch. Exam.* 14 June 4/8 Entrapping the Legislature into conclusions which are not openly declared.

2. With reference to speech: To involve in contradiction, draw into an erroneous statement or compromising admission.

a **1611** Bible *Ecclus.* viii. 11 Rise not vp (in anger) at the presence of an iniurious person, least he lie in waite to entrap thee in thy words. *a* **1714** Sharp *Serm.* (1754) IV. viii. 139 The Pharisees and Herodians..had taken counsel together how they might entrap our Saviour in his talk. **1870** Bowen *Logic* ix. 291 Then the respondent is entrapped whether he answer in the Affirmative or the Negative.

†**en'trap**, *v.*^{2} *Obs. rare.* [f. EN-^{1} + TRAP *v.*] *trans.* To furnish with trappings.

1654 R. Codrington tr. *Hist. Ivstine* 534 He did ride..in a Chariot drawn with two horses richly entrapped.

entrapment (ɛn'træpmənt). [f. as prec. + -MENT.] **1.** The action of entrapping; the condition of being entrapped or caught by artifice.

1597 Daniel *Civ. Wares* iv. lxxx, Northumberland.. given to understand Of some entrapment by conspiracy, Gets into Wales. **1613** Sherley *Trav. Persia* 38 His first victory would rather haue proued a snare to his intrapment. **1812** *Examiner* 28 Sept. 618/2 For whose entrapment are you thus affecting no intention of entrapping? **1865** Dickens *Mut. Fr.* iv. xv, Appealing from the irregular entrapment of this mode of examination. **1875** Darwin *Insectiv. Pl.* xvii. 408 The entrapment of various minute crustaceans.

2. *Law.* A method of criminal investigation in which the police instigate, initiate, or encourage the commission of a crime by a suspected offender in order to secure his or her arrest; the result of such action. (Used as grounds for defence outside the U.K.)

1899 *Amer. Digest* (Century ed.) VIII. 1567/1 Entrapment by detectives. **1930** *Publishers' Weekly* 11 Jan. 213/1 The use of entrapment methods by Chicago reformers to bring about the arrest of booksellers on charges of handling immoral literature has aroused city-wide indignation among the trade. **1931** *Federal Reporter* (U. S.) LI. 676/1 It might be urged, perhaps, that the object of the conspiracy was to entrap certain suspected offenders. Nevertheless, such entrapment was to be accomplished through the violation of the Prohibition Act. **1957** *Encycl. Brit.* VI. 717/2 The defense of entrapment is available to persons who have committed a crime at the instigation of public officers... The central issue to be determined is whether the police took the initiative in urging the commission of the crime or whether they merely secured evidence of on-going criminality. **1973** *N.Y. Law Jrnl.* 19 July 5/3 The court reaffirmed the 'subjective' view of the entrapment defense taken by the majority in Sorrells v. United States. **1985** *Sunday Times* (Johannesburg) 5 May 22/2 Those who dislike entrapment know that informers in illicit gold and diamond dealing cases can claim one-third of the money confiscated after conviction.

entrapper (ɛn'træpə(r)). [f. as prec. + -ER.] One who entraps.

1593 Nashe *Christ's T.* (1613) 182 The Pyt-fal..that sathan (our old entrapper) layes for vs. **1798** Edgeworth *Pract. Educ.* (1822) I. 176 'Oh, ho!' exclaims the entrapper, 'I have you now!' **1863** Maguire *Father Mathew* 219 The practised entrapper of unsuspecting youth.

en'trapping, *vbl. sb.* [f. as prec. + -ING^{1}.] The action of the vb. ENTRAP; †also the means of entrapping, a device, stratagem, wile.

1561 T. Norton *Calvin's Inst.* Pref., When he nothyng preuailed, he turned to suttle entrappynges. **1584** Powel *Lloyd's Cambria* 19 They durst not persue the Welsh to the Mountaines for feare of Intrapping. **1594** Carew *Tasso* (1881) 45 Sweete things to heare, entrappings very sweet. **1603** Knolles *Hist. Turks* (1638) 316 *marg.*, A notable stratagem of Scanderbeg for the intrapping of his enemies.

en'trapping, *ppl. a.* [f. as prec. + -ING^{2}.] That entraps. Of questions, etc.: Adapted to entrap. Hence **en'trappingly** *adv.*, so as to entrap.

1625 B. Jonson *Staple of N.* v. ii, I have an entrapping question or two more, To put unto them. **1642** Milton *Apol. Smect.* Wks. 1738 I. 103 The hurt that might be done among the weaker by the intrapping Authority of great Names titled to false opinions. **1856** R. Vaughan *Mystics* (1860) II. 282 *note*, Wrong terms and entrapping questions. **1857** W. Collins *Dead Secret* (1861) 31 Innovating young recruits in the Church army might entrappingly open the Thirty-nine Articles under his very nose.

‖**entrata** (ɛn'trɑːtə). *Obs. rare.* [It.] = ENTRY.

1656 Earl Monm. *Advt. fr. Parnass.* 378 Never was there seen a more signal pleasing spectacle in Pernassus..then the entrata made by these Gentlemen.

†**entrate.** *Obs. rare*$^{-1}$. [ad. It. *entrata*, f. *entrare* to enter.] That which comes in, a revenue.

a **1670** Hacket *Abp. Williams* i. (1692) 83 The Lord Treasurer Cranfeild, a good husband for the Entrates of the Exchequer.

entraunce, -che, obs. forms of ENTRANCE.

†**entraverse**, *adv. Her. Obs. rare.* [ad. OF. *entravers*, f. *en-* (see EN-^{1}) + *travers* across.] Athwart, crosswise.

c **1450** *Merlin* x. 163 Crownes of goolde and asure bendes entrauerse lysted as grene as a mede.

entrayle, -ylle, obs. forms of ENTRAIL.

entre, etc., obs. form of ENTIRE, etc.

entreague: obs. form of INTRIGUE.

entreasure (ɛn'trɛʒjʊə(r)), *v.* [f. EN-^{1} + TREASURE *v.*]

1. *trans.* To store up in or as in a treasury.

1597 Shaks. *2 Hen. IV*, iii. i. 85 Which in their Seedes, And weake beginnings lye entreasured. **1610** G. Fletcher *Christ's Vict.* i. iv, The memories of heav'n entreasur'd lie. **1613** Alexander *Sidney's Arcadia* iii. Supp. (1629) 338 They would securely entreasure it in a more precious Place. **1828** Lamb in *Blackw. Mag.* XXIV. 772 She should entreasure up a secret In the peculiar closet of her breast.

†**2.** To stock with treasure. *Obs.*

a **1634** Chapman *On B. Jonson's Sejanus*, He [the jeweller] entreasures princes' cabinets.

†**en'treat**, *sb. Obs.* Also 5 entrete, 6 entreate, 6–7 intreat(e. [f. next vb.; OF. had *entraite*, f. *entraitier* vb.] The action of the vb. ENTREAT. †**a.** Negotiation, intervention (*obs.*). **b.** Entreaty, supplication.

1485 Malory *Arthur* i. ii, By the entrete at the last the kyng & she met to gyder. **1568** T. Howell *Arb. Amitie* (1879) 68 By great entreate and humble sute. *a* **1592** Greene *Poems* 99 Use no entreats, I will relentless rest. **1621** Lady M. Wroth *Urania* 14, I..with all the intreates that I could frame, perswaded him to entertaine that seruant of mine. **1639** G. Daniel *Ecclus.* xlv. 4 At his entreat The wonders ceas'd. **1650** *Don Bellianis* 142 Which..you will not do at my intreats.

entreat (ɛn'triːt), *v.* Forms: α. 4–6 entrete, 5–6 -ede, 6–7 -eate, (6 -ait(e), 4– entreat; β. 6–7 intreate, 6 intrait, -ete, (-eit), 6–9 intreat. [ad. OF. *entraiter, entraitier*, f. *en-* (see EN-^{1}) + *traiter* to TREAT. In the archaistic use 1 the spelling *intreat* still sometimes occurs.]

†**I.** To treat; to handle. *Obs.* or *arch.*

1. *trans.* To treat, deal with, act towards (a person, etc.) in a (specified) manner. *Obs.* exc. *arch.*

α. *c* **1430** *Hymns Virg.* 22 So betyn, so woundyd, Entretyd so fuly. **1480** Caxton *Chron. Eng.* ccxlviii. 317 The other Capytayns were..entreated as men of warre ben acustomed. **1551** Wotton in Froude *Hist. Eng.* (1881) V. 6 My aunt, her mother, was evil entreated by the king that dead is. **1577** B. Googe *Heresbach's Husb.* iii. (1586) 139 The olde Ewes..be easlyer to be entreated. **1639** Fuller *Holy War* iii. xxxi. (1840) 173 The pope ill entreated and imprisoned his [Frederick's] messengers. *c* **1720** Prior *Poems* (J.), Well I entreated her, who well deserv'd. **1864** Burton *Scot Abr.* II. i. 62 Their authors..spitefully entreated as monomaniacs.

β. **1509** Fisher *Fun. Serm. C'tess Richmond* Wks. 296 To ..intrete euery persone..accordynge to theyr degre and hauour. **1604** E. Grimstone *Hist. Siege Ostend* 153 Intreating whole troopes of Prince Maurices as friendes. **1622** R. Hawkins *Voy. S. Sea* 271 Shee [the ship] fell over upon that side suddenly, intreating many of them which were in her, very badly. **1657** S. Purchas *Pol. Flying-Ins.* 147 How hee might best order, and intreat them [Bees] according to their kind. **1718** *Col. Rec. Penn.* III. 52 They ought to be well used and Civilly Intreated. **1800** Addison *Amer. Law Rep.* 277 To wound, beat, and evilly intreat. **1875** Jowett *Plato* (ed. 2) I. 135 They evil intreated one another.

†**2.** To take (a thing) in hand; *esp.* to treat, handle (a subject or question). *Obs.*

α. **1509** Fisher *Fun. Serm. C'tess Richmond* Wks. 290 As say the doctours entreatynge this gospell, & her lyfe. **1526** *Pilgr. Perf.* (W. de W. 1531) 1 The seconde boke.. entreateth what is the iourney of religion. **1545** Raynold *Byrth Mankynde* (1564) 98 In this third booke shalbe entreated what is to be done to the Infant borne. **1581** Marbeck *Bk. of Notes* 555 That yeares actes..were sufficientlye entreated of all three. **1681** W. Robertson *Phraseol. Gen.* (1693) 540 To entreat or handle, *tractare*.

β. **1536** Latimer *2nd Serm. Convoc.* i. 43 It should be too long to intreat, how the children of light are ingendered. **1538** Starkey *England* i. iii. 86 Yf they juge be hys frend whose cause ys intretyd. **1563** *Homilies* ii. *Repairing Churches* (1859) 276 That house of God..wherein be intreated the Sacraments and mysteries of our redemption. **1597** Morley *Introd. Mus.* 184 Musick cannot be intreated or taught without the knowledge of all other sciences.

†**b.** To occupy oneself in. *Obs.*

1590 Spenser *F.Q.* ii. vii. 53 A thick Arber..In which she often usd from open heat Her selfe to shroud, and pleasures to entreat.

†**c.** To beguile, pass (time). *Obs.*

1592 SHAKS. *Rom. & Jul.* IV. i. 40 My Lord you must intreat the time alone.

†**3.** *intr.* Of a speaker or writer, a book, etc.: To treat *of* or *upon* a subject. *Obs.*

1513 MORE *Rich. III*, Wks. 37/1 Richarde the third sonne, of whom we nowe entreate. **1534** LD. BERNERS *Gold. Bk. M. Aurel.* (1546) B iiij b, Marc Aurele the emperour, of whome this present boke entreateth. *c* **1540** *Life Fisher* Wks. II. Introd. 58 This excellent man of whom we intreate, John Fysher, Bishopp of Rochester. **1594** PLAT *Jewell-ho.* I. *Divers New Exper.* 4 Wherevpon Valetius entreateth in this maner. **1610** MARKHAM *Masterp.* II. lxxxiii. 364 Of which wee shall speake.. when wee intreate of paring and shooing. **1611** *Coryat's Crudities, Panegyr. Verses,* Of steeples, townes and towers entreats his goose's quill. **1632** SANDERSON *12 Serm.* 4 To intreate at this time of Saint Paul's advice. **1681** W. ROBERTSON *Phraseol. Gen.* (1693) 540 Atticus in one book did entreat of.. the Records of things done in 700 years.

b. in *indirect passive.*

1561 T. NORTON *Calvin's Inst.* vi. (1634) 19 This matter indeed is worthy.. to bee largely entreated of. **1589** PUTTENHAM *Eng. Poesie* I. xv. (Arb.) 50 Except Eglogue whereof shalbe entreated hereafter. **1638** CHILLINGW. *Relig. Prot.* I. iii. §74. 175 The subject here entreated of.

c. *simply* (with ellipsis of prep. and obj.).

c **1386** CHAUCER *Pard. T.* 302 A word or tuo, as other bookes entrete. *c* **1534** tr. *Pol. Verg. Eng. Hist.* (1846) I. 5 As towchinge the situation thereof hereafter.. I meane to entreate in places convenient. **1571** DIGGES *Pantom.* III. x. R iij, Although it would seeme I had entreated sufficiently.

†**4.** *intr.* To enter into negotiations; to treat *with* a person; *of* (occasionally *about, for*) a thing; also *simply*. *Obs.*

c **1340** *Cursor M.* 24795 (Fairf.) To entrete of þe pais betwix him & þa danais. **14..** *Epiph.* in *Tundale's Vis.* (1843) 106 Herode.. of thys mater entredes pryvylly. **1482** WARKW. *Chron.* 27 That will speke and entrete with ther enemyes. **1523** LD. BERNERS *Froiss.* I. clxxxv. 219 Bytwene these parties entreated for a peace, the archbysshoppe of Senns.. the lorde of Saynt Venant. **1560** DAUS tr. *Sleidane's Comm.* 44 b, In the assemblie at Norinberge.. the Princes entreated of peace. **1598** GRENEWEY *Tacitus' Ann.* I. vi. (1622) 10 Being sent vnto you from the Germane campe, to entreat of the common profit and good.

β. **1534** LD. BERNERS *Gold. Bk. M. Aurel.* (1546) Dd iiij, She was intreatynge to mary an nother husbande. **1568** GRAFTON *Chron.* II. 664 And this mariage agreed upon (which semeth more likely to be intreated of then concluded). **1586** T. B. *La Primaud. Fr. Acad.* I. (1594) 395 Attilius Regulus.. being.. sent to Rome upon his faith to intreat about a peace. **1593** SHAKS. *2 Hen. VI*, IV. iv. 9 Ile send some holy Bishop to intreat. **1603** KNOLLES *Hist. Turks* (1621) 119 To intreat with him of peace.

†**5.** *trans.* To parley with (a person). *Obs.*

1523 LD. BERNERS *Froiss.* I. ccxxix. 307 So they entreated the sayd Companyons, and offred them golde.

II. With additional sense of asking, asking *of* somebody or *for* something.

†**6.** *intr.* To intercede, plead *for* (a person). *Obs.*

a. *c* **1430** *Compl. Criste* 127 in *Pol. Rel. & L. Poems* 169 Lete merci for us entrete. **1526** *Pilgr. Perf.* (W. de W. 1531) 84 He wyll make other persones to.. perswade & entreate for hym. **1605** SHAKS. *Lear* III. iii. 4 They.. charg'd me.. neither to speake of him, entreat for him, or any way sustaine him. **1611** BIBLE *Ex.* viii. 9 When shall I entreat for thee?

β. **1600** SHAKS. *A.Y.L.* IV. iii. 73, I will neuer haue her, vnlesse thou intreat for her.

†**7.** *intr.* To sue, plead *for* (a concession or favour). *Obs.*

1573 TWYNE *Æneid* XI. (R.), Then lets intreat for peace. **1818** JAS. MILL *Brit. India* II. v. viii. 645 The prisoners entreated for their release.

8. *trans.* To ask earnestly for (a thing); chiefly with *clause* as obj. Occas. const. *of* (a person).

a. **1610** SHAKS. *Temp.* v. i. 118, I.. doe entreat Thou pardon me my wrongs. **1771** GOLDSM. *Hist. Eng.* IV. 200 He entreated that they would elect such, in particular, as had, etc. **1780** BURKE *Execution Rioters* Wks. IX. 266 For God's sake entreat of Lord North to take a view of the sum total. **1797** MRS. RADCLIFFE *Italian* x, I entreat you will speak explicitly. **1878** JOAQUIN MILLER *Songs Italy* 94 To entreat of the gods what they will not give.

β. *a* **1600** *Creation* in *Evergreen* (1761) I. 166 The serpent.. persuadit me.. Intreiting, be eiting, That we suld be perfyte. **1602** MARSTON *Ant. & Mel.* II. Wks. 1856 I. 28 Our tyred limbes.. intreat soft rest. **1611** BIBLE *Ps.* xlv. 12 The rich among the people shall intreate thy fauour. **1653** WALTON *Angler* Ep. Ded., To intreat that they [former favours] may be enlarged to the patronage.. of this Book. **1712** HEARNE *Collect.* (Oxf. Hist. Soc.) III. 496, I intreat therefore y^t^ you would insert it in ye Post-Boy.

9. To make an earnest prayer or request to; to beseech, implore. Chiefly with *subord. clause* or const. *to* with *inf.* Formerly also const. *of*, or with sb. as second obj.

a. **1502** ARNOLDE *Chron.* (1811) 134 Wherfore he entredyd the sayde brydge-maysters of respyte in the mater. **1509** HAWES *Past. Pleas.* xxxii. (1845) 158 Dame Correccion.. Did me entreat a while to abyde. **1534** WHITTINTON *Tullyes Offices* III. (1540) 132 To entreat the iudge.. what thynges he may do sauying his conscience. **1584** POWEL *Lloyd's Cambria* 94 They promised to Intreate the King for him. **1611** BIBLE *Gen.* xxv. 21 Isaac intreated the Lord for his wife, because she was barren. **1735** BERKELEY *Free-thinking in Math.* §48 Wks. 1871 III. 330, I entreat my reader to think. **1840** DICKENS *Barn. Rudge* vi, Ask me no questions, I entreat you. **1859** TENNYSON *Geraint & Enid* 760 Entreat her by my love.. That she ride with me in her faded silk. **1875** JOWETT *Plato* (ed. 2) I. 384 Let me entreat you once more to take my advice and escape.

β. **1611** BIBLE *Ex.* viii. 8 Intreat the Lord, that hee may take away the frogges from me. **1676** HOBBES *Iliad* I. (1686) 170 I'le not intreat you for my sake to stay. **1751** JOHNSON *Rambler* No. 153 ⁋ 19 All whom I intreat to sing are troubled with colds. **1792** *Munchhausen's Trav.* xxiii. 97 Intreating me to assist in the war against Russia.

†**10.** To prevail on by supplication or solicitation; to persuade by pleading. Also, of circumstances, considerations, etc.: To induce. *Obs.*

a. **1551** BIBLE *2 Chron.* xxxiii. 13 And he was entreated of hym & herd his praier. **1563** *Homilies* II. *Idolatry* III. (1859) 264 A dog that would be entreated and hired with part of the prey to suffer the wolves to worry the sheep. **1586** MARLOWE *1st Pt. Tamburl.* I. i, This should entreat your highness to rejoice. **1593** *Prodigal Son* I. 91 Ah my beloved son, be entreated, and go not hence.

β. **1568** GRAFTON *Chron.* II. 768 Howbeit she could in no wise be intreated with her good wyll to delyver him. **1576** FLEMING *Panoplie Ep.* 241 For he is a man full of affabilitie.. and easie to be intreated. **1638** *Penit. Conf.* i. (1657) 4 God was intreated and Moses prevailed.

†**en'treatable, in'treatable,** *a.* *Obs.* [f. ENTREAT *v.* + -ABLE.]

1. a. Of a thing: That admits of being taken in hand, treated of, or discussed. **b.** Of a person: That admits of being dealt with, manageable.

1548 GEST *Pr. Masse* D viij, The next entretable matter is y^t^ ye sayd sacrifice is, etc. **1581** J. BELL *Haddon's Answ. Osor.* 499 That you should not have hadd a more entreatable aunswerer.

2. That can be prevailed on by entreaty; compliant, placable.

1556 ABP. PARKER *Psalter* xc, Most pityfull: intreatable in hart. **1576** NEWTON tr. *Lemnie's Complex.* (1633) 210 Quicke, testy, not entreatable. **1611** SPEED *Hist. Gt. Brit.* VI. vii. 70 A man of a softer, and more intreatable condition. *a* **1718** PENN *Tracts* Wks. 1726 I. 900 Be Intreatable.

Hence **en'treatableness**, the quality of being 'easy to be entreated'.

1534 WHITTINTON *Tullyes Offices* I. (1540) 39 There is nothynge more laudable nor comly in a great and noble man, than.. facylite and easynesse, and entretablenesse.

†**en'treatance, in'treatance.** *Obs.* [f. ENTREAT *v.* + -ANCE.]

1. Treatment; dealing with, or behaviour towards, a person.

1577 A. M. *Captiv. J. Fox* in Arb. *Garner* I. 205 Having been thirteen or fourteen years under their gentle entreatance. **1616** SURFL. & MARKH. *Country Farme* 21 Gentle and courteous intreatance of their Master towards them.

2. Intercession; entreaty.

1548 HALL *Chron.* (1809) 837 There was no feare but that a little Intreataunce should purchase favour enough for hym. **1569** GOLDING *Heminges Post.* Ded. 21 The entreatance of certain godly shepheards, compelled me to publishe. **1578** *Chr. Pr.* in *Priv. Prayers* (1851) 488 Save them at our entreatance for them. **1600** FAIRFAX *Tasso* I. xix, Entreatance faire with counsell he vnites. **1606** G. W[OODCOCKE] tr. *Hist. Ivstine* 102 a, At length by much intreatance they grannted him a truce for two monthes.

en'treated, *ppl. a. rare.* [f. ENTREAT *v.* + -ED[1].]

In senses of the verb. **a.** That is the object of entreaty; besought. **b.** (*nonce-use.*) 'Begged' or assumed without proof.

1631 *Celestina* II. 33 There is a great distance betweene the intreater and the intreated. **1634** SIR T. HERBERT *Trav.* 224, I will lead you through no more extravagancies, lest your entreated patience turne into exoticke passion. **1646** SIR T. BROWNE *Pseud. Ep.* 296 Which we shall labour to induce not from postulates and entreated Maximes.

†**en'treater.** *Obs.* [f. ENTREAT *v.* + -ER.]

1. A negotiator; an agent; a mediator.

1523 LD. BERNERS *Froiss.* I. ccxxiv. 483 Then these Entreatours went and made report to their lordes. **1568** GRAFTON *Chron.* II. 477 This mocion succeded worse than the entreators desired.

2. One who makes a petition; a suitor.

1588 J. UDALL *Demonstr. Discip.* (Arb.) 9 [They] haue reiected a request so holy.. yea, and handled the intreaters.. so cruelly. **1624** F. WHITE *Repl. Fisher* 564 It seemed.. to be vnlawfull.. that the Martyrs should be Intreatours. **1673** O. WALKER *Education* 270 (F. Hall).

†**en'treatful,** *a. Obs. rare.* In 6 in- [f. ENTREAT + -FUL.] Full of entreaty; supplicating.

1596 SPENSER *F.Q.* v. x. 6 To seeke for succour.. With humble prayers and intreatfull teares.

en'treating (ɛn'triːtɪŋ), *vbl. sb.* [f. ENTREAT *v.* + -ING[1].] The action of the verb ENTREAT in various senses.

1. a. Treatment (of); dealing (with a person).

1529 MORE *Heresyes* II. Wks. 190/2 Thanke me for ye good intreting of them both. **1594** CAREW *Huarte's Exam. Wits* (1616) 193 Subiections, bondages and ill intreatings. **1614** J. DAY *Festivals* (1615), What St. Austin tels us.. to put us in minde of the good intreating of our Servants.

b. Discussion (of); dealing (with a subject).

1526 *Pilgr. Perf.* (W. de W. 1531) 234 In the entreatynge of these matters. **1551** TURNER *Herbal* I. K j a, One of them is spoken of in the intreatyng of Camomyll. **1580** HOLLYBAND *Treas. Fr. Tong, Maniement*, a handling, a vsing, an intreating.

c. Negotiation.

1599 HAKLUYT *Voy.* II. 89 A towne that will heare intreatings is halfe lost.

2. Beseeching.

1603 KNOLLES *Hist. Turks* (1638) 52 Yet had he with great intreating so preuailed.

entreating (ɛn'triːtɪŋ), *ppl. a.* [f. ENTREAT *v.* + -ING[2].] That entreats, in senses of the verb.

1718 ROWE tr. *Lucan* I. 629 When for Redress intreating Armies call. **1863** GEO. ELIOT *Romola* I. vi, Her eyes.. made a timid entreating appeal.

Hence **en'treatingly** *adv.*

1850 J. A. ST. JOHN in *Tait's Mag.* XVII. 25 Looking entreatingly into the face of the baker. **1866** GEO. ELIOT *F. Holt* II. xxvii. 179 'No', said Felix, entreatingly. 'Don't move yet'.

†**en'treatise.** *Obs.* In 5 **entreatyse, -ze.** [f. ENTREAT *v.*, after the analogy of *treatise.*] = ENTREATY. **a.** Treatment. **b.** Negotiation.

1494 FABYAN V. cxxvii. 108 They.. by fayre entreatyze contentyd.. the fader. *Ibid.* VI. clvi. 144 Alcinnus was not sent for any entreatyse of peace.

†**en'treative,** *a. Obs.* Also in-. [f. ENTREAT + -IVE.] Of the nature of an entreaty; characterized by entreaty.

1607 A. BREWER *Lingua* I. i. in Hazl. *Dodsley* IX. 341 And oft embellish'd my entreative phrase. **1650** *Don Bellianis* 139 The Soldan would not free the Knight of the golden Image, and the Duke, by intreative means. **1748** RICHARDSON *Clarissa* (1811) V. viii. 100 All gentle, all intreative, my accent.

entreatment (ɛn'triːtmənt). *Obs.* exc. *arch.* Also in-. [f. ENTREAT *v.* + -MENT.]

1. The action of entreating: †**a.** Discussion, investigation. †**b.** Negotiation, settlement. **c.** Treatment (of persons).

1557 PAYNELL *Barclay's Jugurth* 118 b, The night before that day, which was assigned to intreatment of the peace. **1560** ROLLAND *Crt. Venus* II. 89 Quhair all science hes daylie Entreitment. **1850** BLACKIE *Æschylus* II. 215 Evil entreatment he repaid with evil. **1862** *Luck Ladysmede* II. 161, I will only thank you for his gentle entreatment in the cloister of St. Mary.

†**2.** Conversation, interview. *Obs.*

1602 SHAKS. *Ham.* I. iii. 122 Set your entreatments at a higher rate Then a command to parley.

†**en'treature.** *Obs.* In 7 in-. [f. ENTREAT *v.* + -URE: cf. OF. *entraiture.*] ? = ENTREATY 4.

1577 *Test. 12 Patriarchs* 64 [He] made us a feast, & with much intreature gave me his daughter Bethoue to wife.

entreaty (ɛn'triːtɪ), *sb.* Forms: *α.* 6–7 **entreatie,** 7– **entreaty.** *β.* 6 **intreati(e, (-tye, -die, intrety),** 7–9 **intreaty.** [f. ENTREAT *v.* + -Y.]

†**1.** Treatment (of persons); handling. Also management (of cattle). *Obs.*

1567 FENTON *Trag. Disc.* 16 You have founde worse entreatie att my handes. **1579** J. STUBBES *Gaping Gulf* C vj, For if the Spaniard.. did.. beare away harde intreadie for hys vnwonted pryde towards vs. **1607** TOPSELL *Four-f. Beasts* (1673) 561, I have also recited before in another place of the intreaty of Oxen. **1622** R. HAWKINS *Voy. S. Sea* 224 He would give us our lives with good entreatie. *a* **1670** HACKET *Abp. Williams* I. (1692) 22 The Lord Privy Seal.. gave civil entreaty when the Esquire Beadles.. came to him.

†**b.** Reception (of guests), entertainment. *Obs.*

1609 B. JONSON *Sil. Wom.* Prol., They shall find guests entreaty, and good roome. **1615** CHAPMAN *Odyss.* xv. 679 None that could bestow Your fit entreaty.

†**2.** Treatment, discussion, investigation (of a question, subject, etc.). *Obs.*

c **1534** tr. *Pol. Verg. Eng. Hist.* (1846) I. 26 Before I entered into the entreatie of battailes. **1538** STARKEY *England* I. i. 24 The intrety of materys of the commyn wele. **1570** BILLINGSLEY *Euclid* IV. Introd. 110 The maner of entreatie in this booke is diuers from the entreaty of the former bookes. *a* **1626** BP. ANDREWES *Serm.* (1661) 172 Whereout ariseth naturally the entreaty of these four points.

†**3.** Negotiation (of a peace). *Obs.*

1523 LD. BERNERS *Froiss.* I. ccxxix. 305 Then it was ordayned.. to treat with the erle Mountfort.. on ye state of peace.. And at the first entreaty therle Mountfort answered, etc. **1607** TOPSELL *Serpents* (1653) 627 By truce and entreaties of Peace.

4. Earnest request, solicitation, supplication.

1573 G. HARVEY *Letter-bk.* (1884) 9, I wil not do ani thing for intreati. **1611** BIBLE *Prov.* xviii. 23 The poore vseth intreaties, but the rich answereth roughly. **1647** CLARENDON *Hist. Reb.* I. (1843) 7/1 The Prince.. by his humble and importunate entreaty.. in the end prevailed. **1726** ADDISON *Dial. Medals* (1727) 40 To move his haughty soul they try Intreaties, and perswasion soft apply. **1821** BYRON *Two Foscari* I. i, Alas! my life Has been one long entreaty. **1875** JOWETT *Plato* (ed. 2) V. 339 The judges.. shall be inaccessible to entreaties.

†**en'treaty,** *v. Obs.* [a. OFr. *entraiti-er*: see ENTREAT *v.*] *intr.* = ENTREAT 4.

1523 LD. BERNERS *Froiss.* I. ccccxxvi. 746 They of Gaunt had a saue conduct.. to entreatie for a peace.

‖**entrechat** (ɑ̃trʃa). [Fr. *entrechat*, ad. It. (*capriola*) *intrecciata* a complicated caper, f. *intrecciare*, f. *in* in + *treccia* tress, plait.] A figure or feat in dancing, in which the performer, during a leap from the ground, strikes the heels together a number of times.

1775 JEANS in *Lett. 1st Earl Malmesbury* (1870) I. 309 He found that he was incapable of himself to rival his brother performer in his entrechats. **1821** EDGEWORTH *Mem.* II. 120 He could actually complete an entrechat of ten distinct beats. **1826** MISS MITFORD *Village* Ser. II. (1863) 282 Such pirouettes and entrechats as none but French heels could achieve. *a* **1845** BARHAM *Ingol. Leg., House Warming,* Gracious me what an entrechat! Oh, what a bound!

entrecomune, obs. form of INTERCOMMUNE.

‖**entrecôte** (ɑ̃trəkoːt). [Fr., lit. = between rib.] In full *entrecôte steak*. A boned steak cut off the sirloin.

1841 THACKERAY in *Fraser's Mag.* June 715/1, I dined.. with a friend. We had.. two entrecotes aux épinards. *Ibid.* 715/2 Whenever.. you go to Paris, call at once for the *entrecote*; the filet in comparison.. is a poor *fade* lady's meat. **1877** E. S. DALLAS *Kettner's Bk. of Table* 63 The rib-steak or entrecôte, cut from the ribs of beef. **1928** A. CHRISTIE *Myst. Blue Train* xix. 150 The Comte de la Roche had just finished.. an *entrecôte Béarnaise*. **1962** *Punch* 28 Nov. 774/1 Tartan Plate, consisting of fried egg, entrecôte steak, grilled tomato, roll and butter.

†**entre'counte**, *v. Obs.* In 5 entercounte. [Bad form of next.] *intr.* To run one against another; to meet in opposition.

1413 LYDG. *Pilgr. Sowle* v. i. (1859) 70 The spyeres tornynge so swetely.. entercounted to geders in their circute about the erth. **1481** CAXTON *Myrr.* II. xxix. 122 The wyndes.. entrecounte and mete in som place.

†**entre'counter**, *v. Obs. rare.* [a. OF. *entrecontrer*: cf. ENTER- *pref.* and COUNTER *v.*] *intr.* To set oneself in opposition, cavil.

1553 T. BROKIS *Serm.* in *Foxe's A. & M.* (1849) VIII. 782 Sir Cooke (saith he) it is your office to see to pottage making.. and not to controule Goddes doctrine, neither to entrecounter against holy writte.

entrecourse, obs. form of INTERCOURSE.

entrede, obs. form of ENTREAT.

‖**entredeux** (ɑ̃trədø). *Sewing.* [Fr., lit. = between two.] An insertion of lace, linen, or other material; = BEADING *vbl. sb.* 2.

1850 *Harper's Mag.* I. 432 Morning cap trimmed with Valenciennes and gauze ribbons.. muslin *guimpe bouillonné*, with embroidered *entre-deux*. **1902** *Daily Chron.* 1 Feb. 8/3 A milk-white gown, most delightfully arranged about the waist in corselet form by means of lace entre-deux. **1904** *Ibid.* 3 May 8/5 A way of using medallions and entredeux of stitched linen on gowns of fine cloth. **1928** *Observer* 12 Feb. 23 Such felts are.. simple compared to many another which is complicated by endredeux of straw. **1964** *McCall's Sewing* ii. 28/2 *Entre-deux*, another term for beading or veining.

‖**entrée** (ɑ̃tre). Also † **entré, entree**. [Fr.: for the earlier adoption of the word see ENTRY.]

1. a. The action or manner of entering. **b.** The privilege or right of entrance; admission; *spec.* the privilege of admission to a Royal Court.

a. **1782** COWPER *Let.* 5 Jan., My public entrée therefore is not far distant. **1803** MAR. EDGEWORTH *Tales & Nov.* IV. (1832) 326 Nothing could be more awkward.. than our entrée. **1888** W. R. CARLES *Life Corea* iii. 28 Women have the right of entrée everywhere.

b. **1762** EARL OF MARCH *Let.* 20 Oct. in J. H. Jesse *Selwyn & Contemp.* (1843) I. 212 It is a charming house, and as I have.. a partiality for the French, I am very glad to have the *entré*. **1786** *Lounger* (1787) II. 243, I was the only person to whom she gave the constant entrée into her boudoir. **1822** SCOTT *Peveril* IV. ix. 210 The.. nobility who had from birth.. the privilege of the *entrée*. **1827** LYTTON *Pelham* xxiii, My Mother's introductions had procured me the entrée of the best French houses. **1898** *Westm. Gaz.* 25 Feb. 1/1 Several papers have announced that the Queen has granted the privilege of the *entrée* for this afternoon's Drawing Room to.. the two daughters of Lord Rosebery. As a matter of fact the wife and unmarried daughters of an ex-Cabinet Minister have the *entrée* for life as a matter of right. One of the *entrée* presentations this afternoon will be Lady Marjorie Carrington. **1966** *Listener* 10 Mar. 354/2 He was portraying a luxurious social life to which he had no *entrée*. **1969** H. PERKIN *Key Profession* v. 161 This.. gave the A.U.T. the entrée to Government offices.

c. The entrance of performers in any large spectacle or show; the ceremonial procession of circus performers round the arena; the coming of an actor upon the stage; = ENTRANCE *sb.* 1 b.

1824 in M. W. Disher *Greatest Show on Earth* (1937) 101 It [*sc.* the programme] began with a Grand Amazonian Entrée. **1824** K. DECASTRO *Mem.* 121 Their 'Grand Entree', as it is now called. **1830** N. AMES *Mariner's Sks.* 278 An actor no more comes on the stage, he makes his 'entree'. **1870** O. LOGAN *Before Footlights* xxviii. 367 In the circus dressing-room they are preparing for the 'grand *entree*'.

2. *Cookery.* A 'made dish', served between the fish and the joint. Also *attrib.*, as *entrée dish.* (Littré explains *entrées* as 'mets qui se servent au commencement du repas'.)

1759 W. VERRAL *Cookery* 46 Roasted ham. For this *entrée* is generally provided a new Westphalia or Bayonne ham. **1773** J. WEDGWOOD *Let.* 21 Nov. (1965) 156 Poach'd Egg Cups; Entre Dishes; Cover'd Dishes. **1846** SOYER *Gastron. Regenerator* 713 (*heading*) New pagodatique entrée dish. **1850** THACKERAY *Pendennis* xxiii, Two little entrées of sweetbread and chicken. **1880** SIR H. THOMPSON *Food & Feeding* 84 A family dinner may.. consist of soup, fish, entrée, roast and sweet. **1901** *Connoisseur* Dec. 275/2 A nice pair of Sheffield plate entrée dishes.

3. *Music.* †**a.** 'A small piece of music in slow 4-4 time, with the rhythm of a march, and usually containing two bars, each repeated' (*obs.*). **b.** 'The opening piece (after the overture) of an opera or ballet' (Grove *Dict. Mus.* s.v.). Also, a number or divertissement in a ballet or ballet-opera.

1724 *Short Explic. For. Wds. in Musick Bks.* 29 *Entree*, or *Entre*, is a particular Kind of Air so called. **1776** J. HAWKINS *Hist. Sci. & Pract. Mus.* IV. ix. 239 The operas of Lully consist of recitatives, short airs,.. choruses in counterpoint, with entrées, and splendid dances. **1949** *Ballet Ann.* III. 92 The choreographers.. retain the extremely rigid forms of *entrée* and build-up of *enchaînement*, which are found in the old French ballets.

4. Phr. **entrée en matière** [Fr., lit. = entry into the matter], the beginning (of discourse, etc.), the broaching of a subject.

1930 E. F. THOMAS *Nevertheless the Duke* xii. 203 'I have known you before!'.. As an *entrée en matière* it was, to say the least, time-worn. **1938** *N. & Q.* CLXXIV. 272/1 Mr. Peter Quennell, who makes his *entrée en matière* with the pleasantly disputable assertion that [etc.]. **1960** *20th Cent.* Sept. 279 A most delightful *entrée en matière* for the very full and substantial biography.

†**entregent**. *Obs. rare.* [a. Fr. *entregent*, f. *entre* among + *gent* people.] Social intercourse.

1651 J. DONNE JR. in *Mathewes' Eng. Lett.* To Rdr., [Letter-writing] is the Entregent of absent Persons. **1750** CHESTERF. *Lett.* (1774) I. 549 Your chit-chat or *entregent* with them.

entremedle, obs. form of INTERMEDDLE.

†**entre'medly**, *a. Obs. rare*$^{-1}$. [ad. OFr. *entremeslé* intermixed: cf. *meddle*.] Intermixed.

c **1430** LYDG. *MS. Soc. Antiq.* 134. 14 (Halliw.) So entremedly by successioun Of bothe was the generacioun.

†'**entremess**. *Obs.* Forms: 4 entremass, -mees, -mes(se, entermews, entyrmes, 5 entermes, -mis, 7–8 entremess. [a. OFr. *entremès* (mod.F. *entremets*: see ENTREMETS), f. *entre* between + *mès* (mod.F. *mets*) course of viands:—L. *missum* something sent or placed.] Something served between the courses at a banquet; also *fig.*

1340 *Ayenb.* 56 And huanne þe mes byeþ y-come on efter þe oþer: þanne byeþ þe burdes and þe trufles uor entremes. **1375** BARBOUR *Bruce* XVI. 457 Thai had ane felloune entremass. *c* **1400** MAUNDEV. xxxi. (1839) 309 In stede of entre messe, or a sukkarke. *c* **1430** LYDG. *Bochas* v. xxv. (1554) 138a, Thus can this lady.. Her entermis forth serue. *c* **1450** *Bp. Grosseteșt's Househ. Stat.* in *Babees Bk.* 329 Commauned ȝe þat youre dysshe be welle fyllyd and hepid, and namely of entermes. *c* **1460** Ros *La Belle Dame* 156 in *Pol. Rel. & L. Poems* 57 For to juge his ruful semblance, god wote it was a piteous entemes [? *read* entermes]. **1672** MARVELL *Reh. Transp.* I. 130 The Entremesses shall be of a Fanaticks Giblets. **1708** MORTIMER *Husb.* (ed. 2) I. 444 The true Chard used in pottages and Entre-messes.

entremet, var. of ENTERMETE, *Obs.*

‖**entremets** (ɑ̃trmɛ) *sb. pl.* Also 5 **entremetes**. [mod.Fr.: see ENTREMESS.]

1. a. Side dishes.

1475 CAXTON *Jason* 119 Of the metes and entremetes.. I will make no mencion. **1756** *Connoisseur* No. 137 (1774) IV. 246 The duly adjusting the entremets. **1820** T. MITCHELL *Aristoph.* I. 207 Soup piquant and entremets. **1833** MARRYAT *P. Simple* xxxii, First and second course entremets.

†**b.** Used as *sing. Obs. rare.*

1739 *Common Sense* II. 13 It is.. easy to distinguish.. the puny Son of a compound Entremets from the lusty Offspring of Beef and Pudding.

c. Freq. in *sing.* A sweet dish.

1846 E. ACTON *Mod. Cookery* (ed. 5) Index b. §592 All sweet puddings are served as *entremets*, except when they replace the roasts of the second course. **1846** 'A LADY' *Jewish Man.* vi. 110 Fill *vol-au-vents* with fruits richly stewed with sugar..; it forms a very pretty entremêt. **1877** E. S. DALLAS *Kettner's Book of Table* 380 There is no sweet entremet more simple.. than.. plain boiled rice with preserved or stewed fruit and cream. **1935** M. MORPHY *Recipes of all Nations* 86 Pancakes have been one of the most popular of French entremets. **1969** R. & D. DESOLA *Dict. Cooking* 94/2 *Entremets*, dessert course served in France after the cheese course.

2. *Antiq.* A spectacular entertainment between the courses of a banquet.

1863 KIRK *Chas. Bold* I. 88 To these exhibitions—entremets as they were called.

entrench, intrench (ɛn-, ɪnˈtrɛnʃ), *v.* Also 7 **entrensh**. [f. EN-^{1}, IN- + TRENCH *sb.* and *v.*

The form *intrench* is that favoured by mod. Dicts., but in recent use *entrench* seems to be more frequent.]

1. *trans.* (*Mil.*) To place within a trench; to surround or fortify (a post, army, town, etc.) with trenches. Also *refl.*

a. **1563** GOLDING *Cæsar* 205 They shoulde be as good as entrenched. **1629** *S'hertogenbosh* 47 The Gouernour.. propounding that the Vuchteren wall should be entrenched. **1643** CROMWELL *Lett.* 11 Sept., The Enemy hath entrenched himself over against Hull. **1693** *Mem. Cnt. Teckeley* IV. 34 One side covered by a Hill, which was not entrenched. **1783** WATSON *Philip III* (1839) 23 Giving them instructions to entrench themselves at the village of Hervorden. **1813** WELLINGTON in Gurw. *Disp.* XI. 177 A camp which they had strongly entrenched. **1845** S. AUSTIN *Ranke's Hist. Ref.* II. 353 They might entrench themselves opposite to the enemy. **1873** DIXON *Two Queens* I. i. 3 They lay entrenched along the Ebro.

β. **1555** EDEN *Decades W. Ind.* I. III. (Arb.) 78 Open gardens, not intrenched with dykes. **1603** KNOLLES *Hist. Turks* (1638) 303 Mustapha intrenched his army vpon the rising of a hill. **1757** BURKE *Abridgm. Eng. Hist.* Wks. 1808 X. 409 Here he found the enemy strongly intrenched. **1810** WELLINGTON in Gurw. *Disp.* VI. 39 It might be advantageous to intrench one or more positions. **1864** SALA in *Daily Tel.* 21 Sept., They retire, and intrench themselves somewhere else.

b. *absol.*

1583 T. STOCKER *Civ. Warres Lowe Countr.* II. 59 This night, likewise, the Enemie beganne to entrenche in Isseene waie. **1590** MARLOWE *2nd Pt. Tamburl.* III. iii, Raise mounts, batter, intrench, and undermine. **1623** BINGHAM *Xenophon* 31 Hee is intrenching or raising a wall somewhere to blocke vp our way. **1769** GOLDSM. *Rom. Hist.* (1786) I. 461 Cæsar.. began to entrench also behind him.

2. *transf.* and *fig.*; *spec.* in *Politics*, to safeguard the position of (an individual, a group, etc.) by constitutional provisions.

a. *a* **1594** MARLOWE & NASHE *Dido* I. i, Finding Æolus entrench'd with storms. **1609** HOLLAND *Amm. Marcel.* xxiv. ii. 242 The same [stronghold] entrenched, as it were about with the course of the river. **1649** SELDEN *Laws Eng.* II. i. (1739) 7 Against this danger he entrenches himself in an Act of Parliament. **1732** BERKELEY *Alciphr.* IV. §3 Entrenched within tradition, custom, authority, and law. **1866** G. MACDONALD *Ann. Q. Neighb.* xxxii. (1878) 553 Still keeping himself entrenched in the affectation of a supercilious indifference. **1962** *Listener* 12 Apr. 627/1 The most weighty criticism which can be made of all schemes to draw up a list of human rights and to entrench them in a constitution relates to the practical problem of selecting the rights to be protected and of formulating them in legal language.

β. **1607** *Schol. Disc. agst. Antichr.* I. ii. 78 Within which [bound] God hath intrencht all humane power. **1759** JOHNSON *Idler* No. 61 ¶7 He intrenches himself in general terms. **1796** BURKE *Regic. Peace* Wks. 1842 II. 332 One of the parties to a treaty intrenches himself up to the chin in these ceremonies.

†**3.** To make (a wound) by cutting. *Obs. rare.*

1590 SPENSER *F.Q.* III. xii. 20 A wide wound therein.. Entrenched deep with knyfe accursed keene. **1601** SHAKS. *All's Well* II. i. 45 One Captaine Spurio his sicatrice, with an Embleme of warre.. this very sword entrench'd it.

4. *intr.* = TRENCH. *to entrench upon*: to take, use, or occupy a portion of (something) reserved; to encroach or trespass upon; to infringe (rights, †laws); to come within the definition of. Now *rare.*

a. **1640** *Canterb. Self-convic.* Postscr. 4 Exceeding the Sphere of man, and entrenshing upon Gods proper glorie. **1710** PRIDEAUX *Orig. Tithes* ii. 119 This would be to entrench upon his own Grant. **1769** WESLEY *Wks.* (1872) XIII. 18 Let not the gentleman entrench upon the Christian. **1831** *Q. Rev.* XLIV. 269 Far.. from entrenching upon the privileges of parliament. **1837** J. H. NEWMAN *Proph. Office Church* 15 Without seeming to entrench upon political principles.

β. **1633** FORD *Broken H.* III. i, Intrenching on just laws Whose sovereignty is best preserved by justice. **1642** FULLER *Holy & Prof. St.* III. xiii. 183 Intrench not on the Lord's day to use unlawfull sports. **1649** JER. TAYLOR *Gt. Exempl.* I. §1 (R.) It intrenches very much upon impiety. **1722** WOLLASTON *Relig. Nat.* i. 17, I might intrench upon truth by doing this. **1761** HUME *Hist. Eng.* I. viii. 180 Concessions which intrenched so deeply on the honour and dignity of the crown.

†**b.** *simply.* To make encroachments. *Obs. rare.*

1634 SIR T. HERBERT *Trav.* 86 The kings prime House is within the Mydan, yet no way entrenching further than the other Houses. *a* **1635** NAUNTON *Fragm. Regalia* (Arb.) 46 Where it did not intrench, neither invade her interest.

entrenched, intrenched (ɛn-, ɪnˈtrɛnʃt), *ppl. a.* [f. ENTRENCH *v.* + -ED^1.] In senses of the verb. **a.** Surrounded with a trench; fortified. Also *fig.* **b.** Dug out like a trench, excavated.

1570–6 LAMBARDE *Peramb. Kent* (1826) 247 An entrenched ground with three ditches. *c* **1590** MARLOWE *Faust.* 44 Environ'd round with airy mountain-tops, With walls of flint, and deep-entrenched lakes. *a* **1667** COWLEY *To his Majesty*, Wk. II. 571 No deeply entrench'd Islands. **1785** BURKE *Sp. Fox's E. Ind. Bill* Wks. X. 229 Their Stativa, or stations.. were strong intrenched camps. **1811** WELLINGTON in Gurw. *Disp.* VII. 164 An intrenched camp should be marked out. **1861** *Times* 23 July, Attacking the entrenched position of the rebels.

c. *Politics.* Esp. in *entrenched clauses, provisions*, constitutional legislation that may not be repealed except under more than usually stringent conditions.

1950 *Newsweek* 23 Jan. 45/3 It was pretty well agreed that the right to two official languages, freedom of religion, and provincial control over education would be 'entrenched' clauses of the constitution [of Canada], not to be changed without approval of every province. **1952** *Ann. Reg. 1951* 103 The Government were still bound by the 'entrenched clauses' of the South Africa Act. **1957** ELLIOTT & SUMMERSKILL *Dict. Politics* 106 *Entrenched Provisions*, those sections of the South Africa Act, 1909, which can be altered or repealed only by a Bill passed by both Houses of Parliament sitting together, and agreed to at the third reading by not less than two thirds of the total number of members of both Houses. **1962** *Listener* 12 Apr. 626/2 A constitutionally entrenched Bill of Rights.

entrenching, intrenching (ɛn-, ɪnˈtrɛnʃɪŋ), *vbl. sb.* [f. as prec. + -ING^1.] The action of the vb. ENTRENCH, in various senses. Also *attrib.*; also *entrenching clause* = *entrenched clause.*

1598 BARRET *Theor. Warres* I. ii. 13 The ground where the Campe shall then be, with the manner of the intrenching, etc. *c* **1629** LAYTON *Syon's Plea* (ed. 2) 24 An intrenching upon the King's Prerogative. **1633** G. HERBERT *Temple, Search* x, Thy will such an intrenching is As passeth thought! **1775** *Let.* 26 June in N. Bouton *Provincial Papers* (1873) VII. 531 We now send what entrenching Tools we have prepared. **1809** WELLINGTON in Gurw. *Disp.* IV. 474 Intrenching tools and other baggage belonging to the 31st regiment. **1877** *Field Exerc. Inf.* 312 Axes and intrenching tools, to enable it [rear guard] to block up bridges. **1956** *Times* 10 Nov. 7/2 The supposition that the 'entrenching' clause 152 was so fundamental to the constitution that any

legislation to make its evasion even indirectly possible was bad law.

entrenchment, intrenchment (ɛn-, ɪnˈtrɛnʃmənt). [f. ENTRENCH *v.* + -MENT.]

1. a. The action of enclosing within trenches.

In mod. Dicts.

b. *concr.* That which is formed by entrenching; a line of trenches, a post fortified by trenches; *loosely*, a fortification. Also *fig.*, *spec.* the establishment of constitutional safeguards by entrenched clauses.

a. **1590** SPENSER *F.Q.* II. xi. 6 Seven of the same against the Castle gate In strong entrenchments he did closely place. **1649** CROMWELL *Lett.* 17 Sept., They got ground of the enemy, and by the Goodness of God, forced him to quit his entrenchments. **1670** COTTON *Espernon* I. IV. 166 A great Ditch, which the torrent of Land floods had worn, and hollow'd into the form of a regular entrenchment. **1772** PENNANT *Tours Scotl.* (1774) 74 A strong entrenchment on a steep and lofty clay cliff. **1813** WELLINGTON in Gurw. *Disp.* XI. 177 The 52nd regiment..carried the entrenchment with the bayonet. **1847** EMERSON *Repr. Men, Napoleon* Wks. (Bohn) I. 372 A thunderbolt in the attack, he was found invulnerable in his entrenchments.

β. **1622** F. MARKHAM *Bk. War* v. iv. 175 Intrenchments, fortifications, places of approach. **1647** CLARENDON *Hist. Reb.* (1702) II. VII. 357 He Besieged them in their own Intrenchment. **1732** LEDIARD *Sethos* II. x. 371 To surprize him in the middle of his intrenchments. **1796** BURKE *Corr.* IV. 353 Had your miserable slanderers been there, to make an intrenchment of their worthless carcasses.

fig. *c* **1630** B. JONSON *To Inigo Marquis Would-be*, When thou..canst of truth the least entrenchment pitch. **1741** MIDDLETON *Cicero* I. II. 147 Had forced the entrenchments of the Nobility. **1865** DICKENS *Mut. Fr.* II. 27 This sally on a weak point of Mrs. Wilfer's entrenchments. **1876** E. MELLOR *Priesth.* viii. 385 The sacerdotalists have here an intrenchment from which they can never be dislodged. **1961** *Ann. Reg.* *1960* 92 The only entrenchment in the Constitution was that guaranteeing the equal status of the two official languages, English and Afrikaans.

†**2.** The action of trenching *upon* something; encroachment, intrusion. *Obs.*

1649 SELDEN *Laws Eng.* I. (1739) 202 Kings looking upon this as an intrenchment upon their Prerogative. **1684** CHARNOCK *Attrib. God* (1834) I. 760 All the speeches of men ..are intrenchments upon God's wise disposal of affairs. **1691-8** NORRIS *Pract. Disc.* IV. 182 An intrenchment upon Publick Decency. *a* **1694** TILLOTSON *Serm.* xl. (1742) III. 159 A high entrenchment upon the office of, etc.

‖**entre nous** (ɑ̃trə nu), *phr.* [Fr.] Between ourselves; in private.

1689 SHADWELL *Bury F.* I. ii. 10 I'll tell the more *entre nous*: But, in the mean time [etc.]. **1705** CIBBER *Careless Husband* II. ii. 17 Why then, *Entre Nous*, there is a certain *Fille de Joye* About the Court here. **1766** GOLDSMITH *Vicar* I. xii. 112 Entre nous, I protest I like my Lady Blarney vastly. **1819** KEATS *Cap & Bells* xxxiv, And master is too partial, *entre nous*. **1833** DICKENS *Let.* ? Jan. (1965) I. 14, I suppose the story is to be *entre nous*. **1889** E. DOWSON *Let.* 29 June (1967) 87 It's sublimely fatuous that I should mind —but entre nous it has quite spoofed me quite. **1922** JOYCE *Ulysses* 613 A religious silence of the strictly *entre nous* variety.

entrepone, var. of INTERPONE *v. Obs.*

‖**entrepôt** (ɑ̃trpo). Also 8 erron. **entre-port.** [Fr.:—Lat. type *interpositum*, neut. pa. pple. of *interpōnĕre*, f. *inter* between + *pōnĕre* to place.]

1. Temporary deposit of goods, provisions, etc.; chiefly *concr.* a storehouse or assemblage of storehouses for temporary deposit. Also *fig.*

1721 C. KING *Brit. Merch.* I. Pref. 25 A place of Entre-Port for the Depository of their Goods. **1782** POWNALL *Antiq.* 68 The people..settled..many entrepôts, and out-distant factories. **1802** PLAYFAIR *Illustr. Hutton. Th.* 363 It may have..served for an entrepot, as it were, where those debris were deposited. **1811** WELLINGTON in Gurw. *Disp.* VIII. 410 Their [the troops'] surplus means of transport might be applied..to form an entrepôt at a convenient distance. **1871** MAINE *Vill. Commun.* vi. 197 The merchant ..carries his goods from the place of production, stores them in local entrepôts.

2. A commercial centre; a place to which goods are brought for distribution to various parts of the world. Also *attrib.*, as in ***entrepôt-trade***.

1758 CHESTERF. *Lett.* (1792) IV. 118 The place where you are now is the great entrepôt of business. **1812** *Examiner* 19 Oct. 658/2 Moscow is the *entrepot* of Asia and Europe. **1866** ROGERS *Agric. & Prices* I. xxiv. 607 The most important entrepot of the herring fishery was Yarmouth in Norfolk. **1883** *Pall Mall G.* 5 Apr. 2/1 A diversion from our entrepôt trade.

3. A mart or place where goods are received and deposited, free of duty, for exportation to another port or country.

†**entreˈpreignant**, *a. Obs. rare.* [a. F. *entrepreignant*, obs. form of pr. pple. of *entreprendre* to undertake.] Enterprising.

c **1475** *Partenay* 2504 A ful good knight..wurthy, Entrepreignant, coragious, and hardy. *Ibid.* 5073, 5355.

entrepreneur (ˌɒntrəprəˈnɜː(r), ‖ɑ̃tr(ə)prənœr). [Fr.: see ENTREPRENOUR.] **a.** The director or manager of a public musical institution. **b.** One who 'gets up' entertainments, *esp.* musical performances.

1828 J. EBERS *Seven Years King's Theatre* iv. 115 The payment of the benefit expenses by the unfortunate *entrepreneur*. A manager is..an animal whom it is supposed lawful and commendable to bleed at every vein. **1838** *Actors by Daylight* I. 230 On the first landing of the Bayaderes at Bordeaux this active *entrepreneur* despatched a messenger *instanter* to that city. **1878** GROVE *Dict. Mus.* I. 104 Concerts were started by..a well-known entrepreneur of the day. **1882** *Musical Times* 1 Feb. 108/1 Mr... begs to inform Projectors of Concerts, Secretaries of Institutions, and Entrepreneurs generally.

c. *Pol. Econ.* One who undertakes an enterprise; one who owns and manages a business; a person who takes the risk of profit or loss.

1852 CARLYLE *Let.* 15 Sept. in J. A. Froude *Life of Carlyle* II. xx. 107 A public set of rooms—*Kursaal* they call such things, finer than some palaces, all supported by gambling, all built by one French gambling *entrepreneur*. **1883** F. A. WALKER *Pol. Econ.* I. i. 203 The employer, or entrepreneur, receiving profits. *Ibid.* VI. xi. 432 The state as capitalist is at no small disadvantage; as entrepreneur, that disadvantage is vastly aggravated. **1889** R. T. ELY *Introd. Pol. Econ.* (1891) 170 We have..been obliged to resort to the French language for a word to designate the person who organizes and directs the productive factors, and we call such a one an *entrepreneur*. **1922** F. LAVINGTON *Trade Cycle* iii. 19 In modern times the entrepreneur assumes many forms. He may be a private business man, a partnership, a joint stock company, a co-operative society, a municipality or similar body. **1930** J. M. KEYNES *Treat. Money* I. ix. 124 The individuals who perform entrepreneur functions. *Ibid.* xi. 159 Entrepreneurs will sometimes begin to act before the price-changes which are the justification of their action have actually occurred. **1959** J. BRAINE *Vodi* viii. 123 Tom's father looked every inch the successful *entrepreneur*. **1959** *Listener* 26 Nov. 915/2 Where their predecessors were flanked by engineers and scientists, the new-style entrepreneurs will be buttressed by sales managers and advertising experts.

Hence **entrepreˈneurship**.

1934 in WEBSTER. **1959** *Economist* 14 Feb. 588/1 Entrepreneurship..might be common to all developing economies. **1968** *Sci. Jrnl.* Dec. 79/1 MIT-based entrepreneurship.

entrepreneurial (ˌɒntrəprəˈnɜːrɪəl, -prəˈnjʊərɪəl), *a.* [f. ENTREPRENEUR + -IAL.] Of or pertaining to an entrepreneur or entrepreneurs.

1922 H. L. REED *Devel. Federal Reserve Policy* i. 6 Occasionally entrepreneurial activity is injured by the rising scale of prices, as..in the public utility and railroad fields. **1940** *Economist* 24 Feb. 333/1 The mature economy theory is confined to academic..circles; it is rarely encountered in business or financial, and never in entrepreneurial, groups. **1951** C. W. MILLS *White Collar* I. ii. 26 The small businessman has been deprived of his old entrepreneurial function. **1964** *Economica* Aug. 332 He was a solid Kent landowner and farmer of the businesslike kind with his risks well spread in land, trade and government contracting... Dr. Coleman's biography is a model of what real entrepreneurial history can do for economic history. **1966** *New Scientist* 17 Nov. 366/2 It is an entreprenurial business venture, designed to take advantage of the rapid development of data processing.

So **entrepreˈneurially** *adv.*

1960 *New Left. Rev.* Sept.-Oct. 28/2 The entrepreneurially-minded who could not move so rapidly in the managerial world of the big corporations.

†**entreprenour.** *Obs.* In 5 enterprenour, entreprennoure. [ad. F. *entrepreneur*, agent-n. f. *entreprendre* to undertake.] One who undertakes; a manager, controller; champion.

1475 *Bk. Noblesse* (1860) 64 That most noble centoure Publius Decius, so hardie an entreprennoure in the bataile. **1485** CAXTON *Chas. Gt.* 166 Rychard went to fore as chyef enterprenour.

†**entre-pressed**, *ppl. a. Obs. rare*$^{-1}$. (The original has *fraposta*, interposed, placed between.)

1641 EARL MONMOUTH tr. *Biondi's Hist. Civ. Warres Engl.* IV. v. 134 Those of Rhoan, having made themselves masters of two towres [*misprinted* townes] by whose entre-pressed curtain they might give him entry.

†**entreˈproche**, *v. Obs. rare*$^{-1}$. [as if a. F. **entreproche-r*, f. *entre* between + *proche* near. Cf. Fr. *approcher* APPROACH.] *intr.* To approach one another.

c **1475** *Partenay* 2225 When entreproched thys huge hostes to.

†**entresalle** (ɑ̃tr(ə)sal). [Fr. *entresalle*, f. *entre* between + *salle* room.] An anteroom.

1884 *Health Exhib. Catal.* 48/2 The above [furniture] arranged to show a salon and entresalle, completely furnished.

†**entresaˈlue**, *v. Obs.* Also 5 entresalew(e. [a. OF. *entresalue-r*, f. *entre* (see ENTER-) + *saluer* to salute.] *trans.* To greet or salute mutually.

1481 CAXTON *Myrr.* II. vi. 76 Olyfauntes..bowe their heedes that one to that other lyke as they entresalewed eche other. **1491** —— *Vitas Patr.* (W. de W. 1495) II. 269 a/2 After that they were entresalued.

†**ˈentresign.** *Obs. rare.* Also 5 entresygn(e. [a. OF. *entreseigne* sign, mark, f. *entre* (see ENTER-) + *seigne* (mod.F. *signe*):—L. *signum*.] A sign or token; *esp.* a badge on a knight's armour.

1480 CAXTON *Ovid's Met.* XI. xxi, To gyue her [Alcyone] entresignes, by whyche she may see apertly the nawfrage and peryll of her husbonde. **1489** —— *Faytes of A.* IV. xv. 274 The lordes in a bataylle myght be knowen by his armes and entresygnes.

‖**entresol** (ˈɛntəsɒl, Fr. ɑ̃tr(ə)sɔl). Also 8 **entresole, entersole,** 9 **intersole.** [Fr.; f. *entre* between + *sol* the ground.] A low story placed between the 'ground floor' and the 'first floor' of a building; sometimes so contrived as to appear externally part of the former; a mezzanine story. Also *attrib.*

1711 R. NEVE *Builder's Dict.* (ed. 2) *Entresole*, sometimes call'd Mezanine, is a kind of little Story, contrived occasionally at the top of the first Story, for the conveniency of a Ward-robe, etc. **1789** P. SMYTH tr. *Aldrich's Archit.* (1818) 140 The lesser rooms have entersoles with winding stair-cases leading to them. **1823** NICHOLSON *Pract. Builder* 438 In this case, the upper story is termed a mezzanine or inter-sole. **1848** THACKERAY *Van. Fair* xxxvi. (1853) 305 They could take the premier now, instead of the little entresol of the Hotel which they occupied. **1864** *Leeds Mercury* 15 Nov., The inhabitants..on the borders of the Arno hastened to remove their valuables from the ground floors and even entresols. **1887** *Times* (weekly ed.) 17 June 4/1 A small back room on the entresol floor of Palace-chambers.

†**ˈentress(e.** Chiefly *Sc. Obs.* Also 6–7 **entres,** 6 **enteres, intres.** [app. irregularly f. ENTER *v.* + -ESS, after *duress, largess*.] = ENTRANCE, ENTRY, in certain senses. **a.** The opportunity, right, or permission to enter. **b.** A means or place of entering. **c.** Entrance, initiation into a subject.

c **1430** HENRYSON *Mor. Fab.* 9 Of which the entresse was not hie nor brade. **1509** HAWES *Past. Pleas.* (1845) 16 Into the toure for to have an intres. *Ibid.* xxiv. 109 The eres are but an intres To commyn wytte. —— *Joyful Medit.* 4 As in this arte having small intres, But for to lerne is all myn appetite. **1519** HORMAN *Vulg.* 255 Yf ye stande to thynne: ye geue entresse to your ennemies. **1560-78** *Bk. Discip. Ch. Scot.* (1621) 41 And to have some entres in the first rudiments of Grammer. *c* **1565** LINDESAY (Pitscottie) *Chron. Scot.* (1728) 3 The Chancellor..gave her Entress to visit her young Son. *a* **1572** KNOX *Hist. Ref.* Wks. 1846 I. 17 Yet is it the entress unto eternall lyif. **1600** *Gowrie's Conspir.* in *Harl. Misc.* (Malh.) II. 345 The double dore..did byde them..halfe an houre..before they coulde get it broken and have entresse. *a* **1657** SIR J. BALFOUR *Ann. Scotl.* (1824-5) II. 187 Nobilitey and caualleros striuing to gett entresse to see the ceremoney.

entresse, var. of INTERESS, *Obs.*, interest.

†**enˈtrete.** *Obs. rare*$^{-1}$. [a. OF. *entrait* adhesive plaster.] A plaster.

c **1440** *MS. Linc. Med.* f. 302 (Halliw.) It sal..hele it withowttene any entrete, bot new it evene and morne.

†**enˈtrike**, *v. Obs.* Also 5–6 **entryke,** (6 **entriek**), 5 **intrike.** [a. OF. *entriqu-er, intriquer* = Pr. *entricar, intricar*, ad. It. *intricare*, var. of *intrigare* (see INTRIGUE):—L. *intrīcāre*, f. *in* in + *trīcæ* quirks, tricks. Cf. INTRICATE, INTRIGUE.

In Ital. *intrigare* (see INTRIGUE) is the form of the inf. required by phonetic law; but in other parts of the vb. the forms *intrico, intrica*, etc. are normal, and the *c* was introduced into the inf. by analogy.]

1. *trans.* To entangle (a person), ensnare, beguile.

c **1380** WYCLIF *Sel. Wks.* II. 421 To dispence and assoile men of synnes, þat ben entrikid wiþ sich ritis. *c* **1381** CHAUCER *Parl. Foules* 403 But which of ȝow, that loue most entrikyth. **1430** LYDG. *Chron. Troy* Prol., His misty speche ..intriketh readers that it see. **1496** *Dives & Paup.* (W. de W.) li. 91/1 Moche of my nacyon is entryked and blente with such fantasyes. **1530** PALSGR. 538/2 He that his entryked with wordly busynesse is nat mete to be a studyent. **1545** UDALL *Erasm. Par.* (1548) *Luke* xi. 34 In case the iye of thy bodye be corrupted..then shall all the whole bodye be entrieked.

2. To make (a sentence) entangled; to complicate, involve.

1393 GOWER *Conf.* I. 358 That he the worde entriketh, That many a man of him compleigneth. *c* **1430** LYDG. *Stor. Thebes* 2892 His Cleer conceyte..Nat entryked with no doublenesse. **1545** UDALL *Erasm. Par.* (1548) *Luke* viii. 9, Entrieked or wrapped in derke parables. **1549** COVERDALE *ibid. Rom.* Argt., The same [sentences] are oftetymes, as a man maye saye, entriked or entangled.

entrism, var. ENTRYISM.

entrochal (ˈɛntrəkəl), *a.* [f. ENTROCH-US + -AL^{1}.] Pertaining to, or largely composed of, entrochi.

1872 NICHOLSON *Palæont.* 126 Crinoidal limestone or entrochal marble.

entrochite (ˈɛntrəkaɪt). [f. as prec. + -ITE.] = ENTROCHUS.

In mod. Dicts.

‖**entrochus** (ˈɛntrəkəs). *Palæont.* Pl. entrochi. [mod.L., f. Gr. ἐν in + τροχός wheel.] A name sometimes given to the wheel-like plates of which certain crinoids are composed.

1676 BEAUMONT in *Phil. Trans.* XI. 727 Most of the oval Entrochi grow crooked and twisting. **1755** AMORY *Mem.* (1769), The vault and walls are decorated with entrochi and shells. **1794** SULLIVAN *View Nat.* I. 488 The entrochi and the relics of other fishes.

†**enˈtroop**, *v. Obs. rare.* In 7 entroup. [ad. Fr. *entrouper* (Cotgr.), f. *en* (see EN-^{1}) + *troupe* troop.] *trans.* To form into a troop, assemble.

1609 HOLLAND *Amm. Marcel.* XVI. xi. 73 The horsemen strongly entrouped themselves.

entropic (ɛnˈtrɒpɪk), *a.* [f. ENTROP(Y + -IC.] Of or pertaining to entropy; characterized by or resulting from entropy. Freq. *fig.*, with allusion to the randomness, uniformity, and unavailability of energy for work that entropy measures.

1930 W. H. AUDEN *Poems* 58 But taking the first steps falters, is vexed By opposite strivings for entropic peace. **1946** KOESTLER *Thieves in Night* 274 A solar spot has burst and expanded its heat into the great pool of entropic indifference. **1971** *Nature* 4 June 313/1 The free energies of these interactions are entropic in origin. **1977** J. L. HARPER *Population Biol. Plants* xxiii. 748 There is nothing in the process of evolution..to suggest that the collective evolution of the populations in a community is towards some ideal—community structure, stability,..information content, entropic level. **1980** S. NAIPAUL *Black & White* II. iv. 182 After the initial frenzy, entropic exhaustion was bound to set in. **1983** *Nature* 3 Feb. 399/1 Invoking the expansion of the Universe provokes us to contemplate the entropic qualities of the cosmological gravitational field.

Hence **enˈtropically** *adv.*, as regards entropy; in an entropic manner.

1974 *Physics Bull.* Dec. 580/3 The number of possible arrangements of water molecules is greater, and entropically favoured, if the contact between nonpolar groups and water is minimized, and that between polar groups and water maximized. **1983** *Nature* 3 Feb. 399/1 Nucleosynthesis became entropically favoured. **1983** *Observer* 22 May 31/1 Jack Kerouac..for a few unconsecutive months in the mid-1950s consented to be billeted, fed and adored by her, before drifting back entropically to the road.

‖**entropion, entropium** (ɛnˈtrəʊpɪɒn, -əm). *Path.* [mod.L., f. Gr. ἐντροπή, related to ἐντρέπειν to turn inwards, f. ἐν in + τρέπειν to turn.]

Inversion of the eyelids.

1875 H. WALTON *Dis. Eye* 685 Idiopathic entropium is met with in three states. **1878** T. BRYANT *Pract. Surg.* I. 344 Entropion signifies a rolling inwards of the whole lid, the whole row of lashes being completely turned towards the eyeball.

entropy (ˈɛntrəpɪ). *Physics.* [f. Gr. τροπή transformation (lit. 'turning'), after the analogy of ENERGY. First proposed by Clausius (1865) in Ger. form *entropie*.

Clausius (*Pogg. Ann.* CXXV. 390), assuming (unhistorically) the etymological sense of *energy* to be 'work-contents' (*werk-inhalt*), devised the term *entropy* as a corresponding designation for the 'transformation-contents' (*verwandlungsinhalt*) of a system.]

1. The name given to one of the quantitative elements which determine the thermodynamic condition of a portion of matter. Also *transf.* and *fig.*

In Clausius' sense, the entropy of a system is the measure of the unavailability of its thermal energy for conversion into mechanical work. A portion of matter at uniform temperature retains its entropy unchanged so long as no heat passes to or from it, but if it receives a quantity of heat without change of temperature, the entropy is increased by an amount equal to the ratio of the mechanical equivalent of the quantity of heat to the absolute measure of the temperature on the thermodynamic scale. The entropy of a system = the sum of the entropies of its parts, and is always increased by any transport of heat within the system: hence 'the entropy of the universe tends to a maximum' (Clausius). The term was first used in Eng. by Prof. Tait (see quot. 1868), who however proposed to use it in a sense exactly opposite to that of Clausius. In this he was followed (with an additional misunderstanding: see quot. 1875) by Maxwell and others; but subsequently Tait and Maxwell reverted to the original definition, which is now generally accepted.

1868 TAIT *Sketch Thermodynamics* 29 We shall..use the excellent term Entropy in the opposite sense to that in which Clausius has employed it—viz., so that the Entropy of the Universe tends to zero. **1875** MAXWELL *Th. Heat* (ed. 4) 189 *note*, In former editions of this book the meaning of the term Entropy as introduced by Clausius was erroneously stated to be that part of the energy which cannot be converted into work. The book then proceeded to use the term as equivalent to the available energy... In this edition I have endeavoured to use Entropy according to its original definition by Clausius. **1885** WATSON & BURBURY *Math. Th. Electr. & Magn.* I. 245 As in the working of a heat engine, the entropy of the system must be diminished by the process, that is, there must be equalisation of temperature. **1925** A. & J. STRACHEY tr. *Freud's Coll. Papers* III. v. 599 In considering the conversion of psychical energy no less than of physical, we must make use of the concept of an entropy, which opposes the undoing of what has already occurred. **1933** W. E. ORCHARD *From Faith to Faith* xi. 280 The deduction which one of our greatest physicist astronomers draws from the second law of thermodynamics: namely, that since there must be a maximum entropy, there must have been once its maximum opposite. **1955** *Sci. Amer.* May 124/2 Certain combinations of balls yield a greater change in entropy than others. Those combinations in which entropy change reaches maximum value lead to solutions. **1955** *Ibid.* June 64/1 This equilibrium state..is the thermodynamic condition of maximum entropy—the most disordered state, in which the least amount of energy is available for useful work. **1965** *Financial Times* 11 Aug., Moralising by those whose industrial entropy is an accepted fact of life is neither likely to persuade the workers nor assist the trade unions in the task of trying to meet the nation's difficulties.

2. a. *Communication Theory.* A measure of the average information rate of a message or language; *esp.* the quantity $-\Sigma p_i \log p_i$ (where the p_i are the probabilities of occurrence of the symbols of which the message is composed), which represents the average information rate per symbol.

1948 *Bell Syst. Techn. Jrnl.* XXVII. 396 Consider a discrete source of the finite state type... There is an entropy H_i for each state. The entropy of the source will be defined as the average of these H_i weighted in accordance with the probability of occurrence of the states in question... This is the entropy of the source per symbol of text. **1953** S. GOLDMAN *Information Theory* 329 The amount of language information (*i.e.*, entropy) in the sequence is..a measure of the choice that was available when the sequence was selected. **1953** D. A. BELL *Stat. Methods Electr. Engin.* x. 145 Since entropy increases as the arrangement of a system becomes less distinguishable from other possible arrangements, while the value of a pattern for conveying information depends on its uniqueness, the information capacity of a signal is the negative of its entropy. **1960** D. MIDDLETON *Introd. Stat. Communication Theory* vi. 301 H(X) is called the (communication) entropy of the X ensemble, since..it is the direct mathematical analogue of the more familiar entropy measure of statistical mechanics. **1964** *Language* XL. 210 The basic probability concept, 'entropy', and its quantum, the 'bit', are now part of the metalanguage of linguistics.

b. *Math.* In wider use: any quantity having properties analogous to those of the physical quantity; *esp.* the quantity $-\Sigma x_i \log x_i$ of a distribution $\{x_1, x_2, \ldots\}$.

1951 *Jrnl. R. Statistical Soc.* B. XIII. 60 The idea of selective entropy provides us with a new and important concept in the analytical theory of probability. **1961** *Proc. Cambr. Philos. Soc.* (*Math. & Physical Sci.*) LVII. 839 The analogue of Boltzmann's H-theorem is not a statement about the monotonicity of the entropy of the chains..but a statement about the 'entropy' of the frequency distribution $(s_1, .. s_n)$. **1968** P. A. P. MORAN *Introd. Probability Theory* i. 50 Since $-x \log x$ is a convex function the entropy of a finite set of events is a maximum when their probabilities are equal.

entror (ˈɛntrə(r), -ɔː(r)). *Law. rare.* [ad. AF. *entrour*, f. *entrer* to enter: see -OR.] One who makes legal entry.

1865 NICHOLS *Britton* II. 303 The voucher shall be from person to person..of the persons named..in order up to the first disseisor, or other entror.

†**enˈtrouble,** *v. Obs. rare.* In 5 entrowble. [a. OF. *entrouble-r*, f. *en-* (see EN-[1]) + *trouble* trouble.] *trans.* To render troubled.

1475 CAXTON *Jason* 86 b, Medea entrowbled at that time her mayntene.

entrusion, obs. form of INTRUSION.

entrust, intrust (ɛn-, ɪnˈtrʌst), *v.* [f. EN-[1] + TRUST *sb.*

The form *intrust*, though preferred in many recent Dicts., is now rare in actual use.]

1. *trans.* To invest with a trust; to confide a task, an object of care to (a person, etc.); to commission or employ in a manner implying confidence.

a. Const. *to* with *inf.*, †*for* (a purpose), *in* (a business); also *simply. Obs.* or *arch.* exc. in *Law.*

α. **1602** CAREW *Cornwall* 82 b, They.. were wont to be entrusted, for the Subsidiary Cohort, or band of supply. **1646** SIR T. BROWNE *Pseud. Ep.* III. xi. 130 The Griffin.. doth..well make out the properties of a Guardian, or any person entrusted. **1665** G. HAVERS *P. della Valle's Trav. E. India* 31 The last Advertisements..argue that the King still entrusts him. **1666** PEPYS *Diary* (1879) IV. 108 The report we received from those entrusted in the fleete to inform us. **1691** in W. Perry *Hist. Coll. Amer. Col. Ch.* (1860) I. v a. 4 The Archbishop of Canterbury..was wholly entrusted by the King and Court for all Ecclesiastical affairs. **1759** ROBERTSON *Hist. Scot.* I. II. 112 The clergy were entrusted because they alone were properly qualified for the trust. **1836** J. GRANT *Random Recoll. Ho. Lords* xiii. 290 Earl Grey ..entrusted his son-in-law in the execution of so important a task. **1885** *Law Rep. Q. Bench Div.* XIV. 202 The Attorney General only..was entrusted by the constitution to sue for the King.

β. **1649** MILTON *Eikon.* Wks. 1738 I. 387 The Governor besought humbly to be excus'd, till he could send notice to the Parlament who had intrusted him. *a* **1674** CLARENDON *Hist. Reb.* (1704) III. XII. 254 Sr Benjamin Wright; who was intrusted by them to sollicite at Madrid for their Pass.

b. Const. *with* (the charge or duty confided).

α. **1651** HOBBES *Leviath.* II. xx. 105 Monarchs, or Assemblies, entrusted with power. **1688** SHADWELL *Sqr. Alsatia* v. Wks. (1720) 103 Who are the ladies you have entrusted me with, Ned? **1748** *Anson's Voy.* I. iii. 26 A carpenter, whom he entrusted with a large sum of money. **1848** MACAULAY *Hist. Eng.* II. 203 The other was entrusted with all the mysteries of Tory diplomacy. **1879** M. ARNOLD *Porro unum, &c.* in *Mixed Ess.* 160 New..universities.. ought not to be entrusted with power to confer degrees.

β. **1672** WILKINS *Nat. Relig.* II. viii. (R.), They..are careful to improve the talents they are intrusted withall. **1741** RICHARDSON *Pamela* II. 165 Mrs. Jewkes, I am going to intrust you with a Secret. **1848** MACAULAY *Hist. Eng.* I. 541 He..was so little disposed to intrust them with political power that he thought them unfit even to enjoy personal freedom.

2. To confide the care or disposal of (a thing or person), the execution of (a task) *to*, †*with* a person. Also, to trust, commit the safety of (oneself, one's property, etc.) *to* a thing.

α. **1618** BOLTON *Florus* II. vi. 106 Entrusting a part of their Army to Appius Consull. **1655–60** STANLEY *Hist. Philos.* (1701) 75/2 His Father dying, left him..fourscore Minæ, which being entrusted with a Friend for Improvement, they miscarried. **1722** DE FOE *Col. Jack* (1840) 31 An errand of too much consequence to be entrusted to a boy. **1792** *Anecd. W. Pitt* I. xvii. 281 The Defence of the island was entrusted to a constitutional and well-disciplined militia. **1818** BYRON *Ch. Har.* IV. clxx, How we did entrust Futurity to her! **1868** MILMAN *St. Paul's* iii. 72 The temporalities of the see were entrusted to the Dean and Chapter. *Mod.* I should not like to entrust my safety to such a boat as that.

β. **1601** R. JOHNSON *Kingd. & Commw.* (1603) 155 To intrust so great a power to noblemen. **1715** *Addr.* in *Lond. Gaz.* No. 5332/1 The Business of the Commission intrusted with us. **1805** WORDSW. *Prelude* v. 427 When I was first intrusted to the care Of that sweet Valley. **1855** PRESCOTT *Philip II*, I. II. ii. 160 A suitable person to whom the reins of government might be intrusted. **1875** STUBBS *Const. Hist.* II. xiv. 6 The Tower was intrusted to the archbishop.

Hence **enˈtrusted** *ppl. a.* **enˈtrusting** *vbl. sb.*

1642 *Declar. Lords & Com., Ordinance Lond.* 13 Apr. 3 Such entrusted persons as they shall appoint. **1660** MILTON *Free Commw.* 451 Having..many Commonwealths under one united and entrusted Sov'ranty. *a* **1700** DRYDEN *Charac. Good Parson* Wks. 1821 XI. 397 Intrusted riches to relieve the poor. **1818** KEATS *Endym.* I. 758 Then wherefore sully the entrusted gem Of high and noble life with thoughts so sick? **1851** G. S. FABER *Many Mansions* 309 The seat of the Fallen Hierarch's Entrusted Dominion. **1884** RUSKIN in *Pall Mall G.* 20 Sept. 4/2 After twelve hundred years' entrusting of the Gospel to them [the clergy].

entrustment (ɛnˈtrʌstmənt). [f. ENTRUST *v.* + -MENT.] The action of entrusting; the fact of being entrusted. Formerly also, a position of trust; a duty with which one is entrusted.

1643 HERLE *Answ. Ferne* 29 'Tis but a power of ordinary entrustment. **1657** J. GOODWIN *Triers Tried* 18 God hath called or advanced them to their respective entrustments. **1657** PETTUS in *Loveday's Lett.* (1663) A 3 b, I wish I had leisure to peruse the whole Packet..but..I cannot spare so much time from my Intrustment. **1877** *Act 40 & 41 Vict.* c. 39 §2 Where any person has been entrusted with, etc...any revocation of his entrustment..shall not affect the title, etc.

entry (ˈɛntrɪ). Forms: 4–7 entre, 4–6 -ee, 6–7 entrey, -ie, -ye, 6 entery (-ie), 5– entry. [ME. *entre(e*, a. Fr. *entrée*, corresp. to Pr. *intrada*, Sp., Pg. *entrada*, It. *intrata*:—late L. *intrāta*, f. *intrāre* (Fr. *entrer*) to ENTER.]

1. a. The action of coming or going in; the coming (of an actor) upon a stage; the entering into or invading (a country), etc. In phrases, *to make* (†*have*) *entry*. Also *fig.*

c **1330** R. BRUNNE *Chron.* (1810) 179 Now has R. entre, and Acres taken es. *c* **1400** *Ywaine & Gaw.* 2961 Als Sir Ywaine made entre. **1475** CAXTON *Jason* 96 [He] thought.. of what purpoos he mighte make to her his entree. **1568** GRAFTON *Chron.* II. 723 The king of Englandes entrie and invasions. **1594** T. B. *La Primaud. Fr. Acad.* II. 507 Their opinion touching the birth of soules, their entrie into the bodie. **1746–7** HERVEY *Medit.* (1818) 129 No actor on a stage ..can make a more regular entry, or a more punctual exit! **1833** HERSCHEL *Astron.* viii. 258 The entry and egress of the planet's center [across the sun's disc]. **1853** KANE *Grinnell Exp.* xiii. (1856) 99 Since our entry into the ice. **1866** CRUMP *Banking* x. 226 The first entry of gold into the mint for coinage purposes.

fig. **1587** FLEMING *Cont. Holinshed* III. 1550/2 Then began such an entrie of acquaintance, knowledge, love.. betwixt them. **1604** JAMES I *Counterbl.* (Arb.) 99 The first entry thereof [*i.e.* of Tobacco taking] among vs. **1690** TEMPLE *Ess. Learn.* Wks. 1731 I. 167 Very soon after the Entry of Learning upon the Scene of Christendom. **1833** CHALMERS *Const. Man* (1835) I. iii. 155 Finds entry into the mind.

b. The ceremonial entrance (of a king, etc.).

1534 LD. BERNERS *Gold. Bk. M. Aurel.* (1546) O vj, Thus this emperour adressed his entre with his capitaynes. *a* **1714** BURNET *Own Time* (1766) I. 27 His entry and coronation were managed with such magnificence that the country suffered much for it. **1845** S. AUSTIN *Ranke's Hist. Ref.* III. 261 Their solemn entry into the imperial city.

†**c.** The action of boarding (a ship). *Obs.*

1591 RALEIGH *Last Fight Rev.* (Arb.) 21 To make any more assaults or entries.

†**d.** ? The paying of formal visits, 'making calls'. *Obs. rare.*

1755 T. AMORY *Mem.* (1769) I. 219 She can even pass the Sunday evenings away at cards and in visiting, and waste at play and entry the hours of the sacred day. *Ibid.* II. 81 They renounced custom and false notions, the propensities and entries, the noise and splendor of the world.

e. The beginning of the part of a performer or instrument in a canon or other musical composition; also *attrib.* in *entry sign*.

1879 GROVE *Dict. Mus.* I. 390/2 Those who can stand the enormous strain which is implied in the recollection of every *nuance* and the exact entry of every instrument in a long and complicated work. **1893** J. S. SHEDLOCK tr. *Riemann's Dict. Mus.* 220/1 Entry Signs are the marks in a canon (of which only one part is written out) for the entry of the imitating parts... The sign which a conductor gives to a player or singer to come in after a long pause is also called an Entry Sign. **1965** *New Statesman* 9 Apr. 586/2 The Mahler performance..had all the marks of under-rehearsal..and every now and again a fluffed entry.

f. In Bridge, (a card providing) an opportunity to transfer the lead to one's partner or to one's dummy. Also *Comb.*, as ***entry-creating***, ***entry-killing*** ppl. adjs.

1884 'CAVENDISH' *Whist* (ed. 14) 135 In case his only card of entry in that suit should be an honour, not an ace. **1906** W. DALTON *'Saturday' Bridge* ii. 53 When you hold six or more cards of a black suit, thoroughly established, and one other card of entry, No Trumps should always be declared at the score of love. **1934** E. CULBERTSON in *Amer. Speech* IX. 10/1 Contract Bridge terms that are almost an indispensable part of every player's vocabulary..such as ..*entry*. **1939** N. DE V. HART *Bridge Players' Bedside Bk.* 149 An entry-killing play which consists in refusing to take a trick in an opponent's suit until the other opponent is exhausted of the suit. **1959** *Listener* 19 Mar. 530/2 The ace of spades still provided an entry to the dummy. *Ibid.* 17

Sept. 462/1 There are countless entry-killing and entry-creating plays.

2. *Law.* **a.** The actual taking possession of lands or tenements, by entering or setting foot on the same.

1491 *Act 7 Hen. VII*, c. 16 §1 Thentre, season and possession of your seid Subgiet..into all the premisses. **1540** —— *32 Hen. VIII*, c. 2 §2 No..person..shall..maintein any..writ o[f] entry vpon disseason done to any of his auncestors. *a* **1626** BACON *Max. & Uses Com. Law* 23 Where a man findeth a piece of land that no other possesseth ..and he that so findeth it doth enter, this entry gaineth a property. **1742** FIELDING *Jos. Andrews* I. xii, He'd warrant he soon suffered a recovery by writ of entry. **1817–8** COBBETT *Resid. U.S.* (1822) 271 Mr. Birkbeck informs me he has made entry of a large tract of land. **1866** KINGSLEY *Herew.* I. xvi. 298, I advise you as a friend not to make entry on those lands.

b. One of the acts essential to complete the offence of burglary.

1769 BLACKSTONE *Comm.* IV. 227 As for the [burglarious] entry, any the least degree of it, with any part of the body, or with an instrument held in the hand, is sufficient; as, to step over the threshold.

†**3. a.** A dance introduced between the parts of an entertainment; an interlude. Cf. Fr. *entrée* or *entrée de ballet* (Littré). **b.** *Music.* = ENTRÉE 3.

1651 EVELYN *Mem.* (1857) I. 276 A masque at Court, where the French King in person danced five entries. **1675** SHADWELL *Psyche* I. Wks. 1720 II. 16 Then an Entry danc'd by four Sylvans. **1728** R. NORTH *Memoirs Musick* (1846) 102 The Entrys of Baptist ever were and will be valued as most stately and compleat harmony.

4. *transf.* †**a.** The entering upon an office; the accession of a sovereign. *Obs.* †**b.** The becoming a member of an institution. *Obs.*

c **1380** WYCLIF *Sel. Wks.* III. 310 For symonye don in here entre. **1389** in *Eng. Gilds* (1870) 107 To make ye paiement of his couenauns for his entre. *c* **1500** *Blowbol's Test.* 45 in Hazl. *E.P.P.* I. 94 Of so grete reverens werre the universities, That men toke entrie knelyng on their knees. **1576** *Thanksgiv.* in *Liturg. Serv. Q. Eliz.* (1847) 548 The day of the Queens Majestys entry to her reign.

c. The initial training of young hounds (cf. ENTER *v.* 18 b); now, more commonly *collect.*, young hounds who are being entered. Also *transf.*, the younger generation (see also quot. 1946).

1845 W. YOUATT *Dog* iii. 83 There must always be a little flesh in hand for the sick, for bitches with their whelps, and for the entry of young hounds. **1856** 'STONEHENGE' *Man. Brit. Sports* II. iv. 124/2 Your chance of good sport through this season and the next depends more upon your young entry than upon the old draft-hounds. *Ibid.* 125/1 In order to have an opportunity of rating the young ones for speaking to 'riot', while under the fresh recollections of the encouragement which they have received in their entry to their own particular game. **1881** *Encycl. Brit.* XII. 315/2 The young entry are sure to run riot. **1897** *Encycl. Sport* I. 543/2 It is better to keep steadily on, confining hounds as much as possible to covert, or the entry will forget what they have learned. **1899** SOMERVILLE & 'ROSS' *Irish R.M.* vi. 130 Dr. Jerome Hickey was having a stirring time with the young entry and the rabbit-holes. **1924** J. BUCHAN *Three Hostages* vii. 101 Thank God that we have a man like him among the young entry. **1946** M. C. SELF *Horseman's Encycl.* 453 Hounds are 'entered' when they are first put into the pack during the cubbing season. Young riders are 'entered' by being brought by their fond parents to the covert side. Both are known as 'Young Entry'.

†**5.** The right or opportunity of entering; admission, ENTRANCE. *Obs.*

a **1300** *Cursor M.* 13079 Þe king þam lete haf fre entre. *c* **1325** *Coer de L.* 1884 The galyes..had nigh won entrie. *c* **1330** R. BRUNNE *Chron.* (1810) 272 Now has þe Baliol a stounde lorn issu & entre. **1377** LANGL. *P. Pl.* B. XI. 118 Þanne may alle Cristene come..and cleyme þere entre. **1491** CAXTON *Vitas Patr.* (W. de W. 1495) II. 195 b/2, The entre of the cyte of Athenes forsayd was graunted unto hym. **1574** tr. *Littleton's Tenures* 15 a, Yet shall hee have free entree, egresse, and regresse in the same house. **1615** CHAPMAN *Odyss.* I. 191 In this discourse, he first saw Pallas standing, Unbidden entry.

6. a. The coming in (of a period of time); the entrance upon (a journey, work, etc.). *Obs.* exc. *U.S.*

a **1300** *Cursor M.* 13259 To nazareth he went again..Tua dais in aueril entre. *c* **1400** *Destr. Troy* 2248 What proffet any prowes with a prowde entre, To begyn, any goode, on a ground febill. *c* **1450** *Merlin* xiii. 191 A-boute the entre of may. **1535** GARDINER in Strype *Eccl. Mem.* I. xxx. 212, I required your advice in mine entry and beginning thereof. **1568** GRAFTON *Chron.* II. 618 When the Duke of Yorke had thus framed the entry into hys long entended jorney. **1587** HARRISON *England* II. vi. (1877) I. 166 Some making their entrie [at supper] with egs. **1655–60** STANLEY *Hist. Philos.* (1701) 555/2 Not to stay longer in the entry. **1907** *Springfield Weekly Republ.* 24 Oct. 1 An act of the Legislature which became operative with the entry of the month.

†**b.** The preface or opening words (of a book, etc.). *Obs.*

1340 HAMPOLE *Pr. Consc.* 369 Alle þat byfor es wryten.. Es bot als an entre of þis buk. **1581** SIDNEY *Apol. Poetrie* (Arb.) 52 The Poet..for hys entry, calleth the..Muses to inspire into him a good inuention. **1659** PEARSON *Creed* (1839) 225 And thus even in the entry of the Article we meet with the incarnation.

7. *concr.* **a.** That by which any place open or closed is entered; a door; a gate; an approach or passage to a country, etc.; the mouth of a river. In a dwelling, an entrance-hall; lobby. Also *fig.*

1297 R. GLOUC. (1724) 158 Bute entre on þer nys, And þat ys vp on harde roches. **1340–70** *Alisaunder* 908 Enforced were þe entres with egre men fele. *c* **1420** *Pallad. on Husb.* I. 1059 Her [the hive's] entre tourne it faire upon the southe. **1535** COVERDALE *Acts* xii. 14 She opened not the entrye for gladnes. **1580** NORTH *Plutarch* (1676) 669 It was a passage and entrey into the Countrey of Laconia. **1598–1600** HAKLUYT *Voy.*, At the entrie of which riuer he stayed his course. **1605** SHAKS. *Macb.* II. ii. 66, I heare a knocking at the South entry. *a* **1652** BROME *Eng. Moor* II. ii, Her's a letter thrown into the entry. **1727** SWIFT *Descr. Morning*, Prepar'd to scrub the entry and the stairs. **1826** T. J. WHARTON in *Pa. Hist. Soc. Mem.* I. 156 He tells truly who signed that paper in the entry or porch.

fig. **1340** HAMPOLE *Pr. Consc.* 1763 Þat es entre and way.. Til lyf or ded. *c* **1386** CHAUCER *Melibeus* ¶73 Werre at his bygynnyng hath so greet an entre and so large, that every wight may entre. *a* **1450** *Knt. de la Tour* 14 Humilite is the furst entre and wey of frenship. **1570** BILLINGSLEY *Euclid* XI. Introd. 312 The first booke was a ground, and a necessarye entrye to all the rest following. **1855** O. W. HOLMES *Poems* 191 Gone, like tenants that quit without warning, Down the back entry of time.

¶ A sense 'innermost part, sanctuary' has been erroneously inferred from the following passage, in which Chaucer confuses L. *adytum* with *aditus*.

c **1374** CHAUCER *Boeth.* II. i. 30 Sentences..drawen oute of myne entre, þat is to seyne out of myn informacioun.

b. *transf.* A passage between houses, whether or not leading to an open space beyond; an alley. Now only *dial.* †Also, an avenue, approach to a house (*obs.*).

c **1400** *Destr. Troy* 1600 All maister men þat on molde dwellis, Onestly enabit in entris aboute. **1632** HEYWOOD *2nd Pt. Iron Age* III. Wks. 1874 III. 391 Through many a corner and blind entries mouth. *a* **1639** W. WHATELY *Prototypes* I. xxi. (1640) 260 A dark entrie leading to the glorious palace of glory. **1694** PHILLIPS *Life Milton* xx, A pretty Garden House..at the end of an Entry. **1792** WOLCOTT (P. Pindar) *Odes Kien Long* Wks. 1812 III. 155 The souls of many Kings are vulgar Entries..A long, dark, dangerous, dreary Way, past finding. **1866** R. CHAMBERS *Ess.* Ser. I. 129 A chimney-sweep..has been established for years in one of the murky entries. *Mod.* The entrance to these houses [in Birmingham] is not in the front which faces the street, but in the 'entry' [*i.e.* passage common to two adjoining houses].

c. *Hunting.* (See quots.)

1630 J. TAYLOR (Water P.) *Wks.* I. 93/1 For what Necromanticke spells are, Rut, Vault, Slot, Pores, and Entryes. **1727** BRADLEY *Fam. Dict.* s.v. *Hart*, Let him draw into Covert as he passes observing the size of entries. **1774** GOLDSM. *Nat. Hist.* (1862) I. II. v. 325 When a deer has passed into a thicket, leaving marks whereby his bulk may be guessed, it is called an entry.

d. *Mining.* (See quot.)

1881 RAYMOND *Mining Gloss.*, *Entry*, an adit. Applied to the main gangway in some coal mines.

†**8.** A room or house into which one enters to lodge; a lodging, hostel. *Obs.* exc. *Hist.*

1544 *Late Exp. Scotl.* in Arb. *Garner* I. 125 Upon the approachment of the men to their entries. **1852** SIR W. HAMILTON *Discuss.* 412 All scholars should be members of some College, Hall or Entry. **1864** BURTON *Scot Abr.* I. v. 258 Officers of the collegiate institutions—colleges, halls, inns, and entries.

9. a. The action of entering or registering something in a list, record, account-book, etc. Also *concr.* a statement, etc. entered upon a record; an 'item' in a list or an account-book.

1553 GRIMALDE *Cicero's Offices* III. (1558) 163 The enteries and ponnishments of the censors declare as much. **1562** *Act 5 Eliz.* c. 12 §6 The said Clerk..shall register..a brief Declaration or Entry of the said Licence. *a* **1626** BACON *New Atl.* (J.), A notary made an entry of this act. **1712** ARBUTHNOT *John Bull* 15 Fees for..examinations, filings of writs, entries, etc. **1802** MAR. EDGEWORTH *Moral T.* (1816) I. xix. 154 The sailor..appealed..to the entry in the books. **1849** STOVEL *Canne's Necess.* Introd. 11 The following entries, copied from the Lords' Journal..determine the date. **1863** MARY HOWITT tr. *F. Bremer's Greece* I. viii. 259 Making an entry in my diary, of the daily occurrences.

b. *double entry*: the method of bookkeeping in which every item entered to the credit of one account in the ledger is entered to the debit of another, and *vice versa*. *single entry*: the method in which each transaction (as a general rule) is entered only in *one* account. Also *fig.*

1721 W. WEBSTER *Ess. Bk.-keeping* (ed. 2) 1 Book-keeping is the Art of stating our Accompts,..to which end, the Italian manner of Debtor and Creditor, by double entry, is by experience, found most conducive. **1741** MAIR *Book-keeping Methodiz'd* (ed. 2) 14 Italian Book-keeping is said to be a Method of Keeping Accompts by double Entry because, etc. **1883** CARISS *Book-keeping* 3 Book-keeping by Double Entry..was devised centuries ago, and has since become..generally adopted. **1961** S. CHAPLIN *Day of Sardine* i. 22 But if my writing's bad my double entry memory is good. It all goes down and sooner or later comes shooting out.

c. The list of names of the competitors (for a race, etc.).

1885 *Truth* 28 May 854/1 The entry for the Royal Hunt Cup is smaller than usual.

d. The entering at the custom-house of the nature and quantity of goods in a ship's cargo. ***bill of entry***: see quot. 1809. ***port of entry***: the port at which imported goods are entered.

1692 in Picton *L'pool Munic. Rec.* (1883) I. 300 If ye entrey be right. **1715** *Lond. Gaz.* No. 5311/3 Keeper of the Books of Entry of all Ships coming into the Port of London. **1796** BURKE *Regic. Peace* Wks. VIII. 385 The increase on the face of our entries is immense during the four years of war. **1809** R. LANGFORD *Introd. Trade* 130 Bill of entry, a note specifying goods entered at the custom house.

10. *attrib.* and *Comb.*, as ***entry-book***, ***-card***, ***-clerk***, ***-door***, ***-end***, ***-list***, ***-mat***, ***-money***, ***-mouth***, ***-pegs***, ***-point***, ***-way***, ***-winning***; **entry form**, (*a*) an application form setting out a person's entry in a competition; (*b*) in *Lexicography*, the canonical form in which a word is entered in a dictionary; the head-form; **entryman** *U.S.*, one who enters upon public land with the intention of settling; **Entryphone**, a proprietary name for a type of intercom device by which persons identify themselves in order to gain admittance to a building, etc.; also (with lower-case initial) used generically; cf. *speak-box* s.v. SPEAK *v.* 36.

1678 *Trial Ireland, etc.* 47 As appears by their *Entry-Books. **1880** *Quart. Rev.*, No. 297. 12 *Lord Bolingbroke*, There is no trace of his residence to be found in the entry-books of the Dean. **1907** *Strand* Nov. 507/1, B might easily have an *entry card in spades or clubs. **1751** *Phil. Trans.* XLVII. xliii. 280 An *entry-clerk in the court of Chancery. **1526** TINDALE *Acts* xii. 13 Peter knocked at the *entry dore. *a* **1804** J. MATHER *Songs* (Sheffield 1862) 88 Who tell their fond tales at an *entry end. **1924** *Competitions* I. 147/1 An official *entry form must be used. **1961** 'J. WYNDHAM' *Consider her Ways* 218 Where is that Pools entry-form? **1962** K. MALONE in Householder & Saporta *Probl. in Lexicogr.* 115 The entry-form should be *self/selv-* (not simply *self*). **1976** *Daily Tel.* (Colour Suppl.) 16 July 29/4 Keep this copy of the *Daily Telegraph Magazine* safely meanwhile. You will need it for your entry form. **1980** *Amer. Speech 1976* LI. 235 Choice of the entry-form spelling is made on the basis of frequency, historical importance, and phonetic regularity. **1908** *Westm. Gaz.* 13 Aug. 4/1 It was only with the greatest difficulty that the R.A.C. managed to get anything like a representative *entry list. **1886** *N. Amer. Rev.* Jan. 59 The *entryman, under the timber culture act, is not compelled to plant any trees until the third year from date of entry, when if he likes he may file a relinquishment of his claim, and the land is again open for entry. **1912** *Out West* June 418 His report was heard read with great satisfaction by upwards of a hundred of the entrymen of Los Angeles and vicinity. **1855** *Whitby Gloss.*, 'The *entry mat', the street door mat. *c* **1490** *Cely Papers* in *English Studies* (1961) XLII. 143 Coket siluer othirwyse callid *entree money. **1864** A. M^c^KAY *Hist. Kilmarnock* 210 Each member to pay the usual entry-money. **1880** *Antrim & Down Gloss.*, **Entry mouth*, sb., the end of an entry or lane, where it opens upon a street. **1865** *Gayworthys* II. 169 The two women lifted thin gingham bonnets from the *entry-pegs. **1958** *Certificate of Incorporation* (Companies' House) No. 614411 The *Entryphone Company Limited is this day incorporated. **1969** D. GRAY *Murder on Honeymoon* xviii. 111 The front door had an entry-phone with the names of the six lots of tenants beside six buzzers. **1972** *Observer* (Colour Suppl.) 6 Feb. 39/1 An Entryphone breathes 'Come in, I'll be down in a second'. **1976** *Trade Marks Jrnl.* 28 July 1573/2 Entryphone... Goods..for use in the control of entry of persons to buildings... Entryphone Company Limited,.. London. **1982** *Financial Times* 17 Dec. 15/3 The well secured home probably includes an entryphone, grilles,.. and an alarm. **1926** J. S. HUXLEY *Ess. Pop. Sci.* 234 The sperm *entry-point. **1964** A. EDEL in I. L. Horowitz *New Sociology* 218, I should like to..make a start on analyzing the entry-points, if we may so call them, where value issues enter into social science. **1746** *Probate Rec. N.H.* III. 391 It is also agreed by us that the said Cellar great Doors and the yard the *Entryway Stairs..all be in Common. **1854** M. J. HOLMES *Tempest & Sunshine* iii. 44 There was no entry way to the building. **1889** R. T. COOKE *Steadfast* xxii. 236 His study door opened from the left hand of the little entry-way into which they stepped from without. **1893** S. MERRILL in M. Philips *Making of Newspaper* 96 Patrolman Blucher had finished his nap in the entry-way leading to Eckstein's cigar factory. **1471** *Hist. Arriv. Edw. IV.* (Camd. Soc.) 6 At the first *Entrie-winning of his right to the Royme and Crowne of England.

'entryism. *Pol.* Also entrism. [f. ENTRY + -ISM; cf. F. *entrisme*.

The term is thought to have arisen from advice given by Leon Trotsky to his followers in *La Vérité*, Sept. 1934: En disant ce qui est, il faut entrer dans le parti Socialiste. Cf. also J. P. CANNON *Hist. Amer. Trotskyism* (1944) xi. 224 We began negotiations with the leaders of the 'Militants' over the terms and conditions of our entry into the Socialist Party.]

The policy or practice of joining an organization with the intention of subverting its aims and activities (see quots.); organized infiltration.

1963 I. DEUTSCHER *Prophet Outcast* 272 'Entrism' is the term by which the Trotskyists described and discussed this move even thirty years later [than 1934–5]. **1975** J. CARMICHAEL *Trotsky* xii. 409 In the 1930s Trotsky advised his little coteries to join the Socialists..to 'carry the revolutionary programme to The Masses'... This recommendation..has been calcified in the jargon as 'entrism'. **1976** *Daily Tel.* 8 July 16 Those who would..gag at the mere mention of 'entryism'. **1976** *Guardian Weekly* 19 Dec. 3/4 There was also much huffing and puffing in Labour's parliamentary ranks about the infiltration—or, euphemistically, entryism—into the party by Trotskyists and Marxists. **1980** *Times* 15 Jan. 1/5 The two documents in the hands of *The Times*, *Entrism*, published in 1973, and *British Perspectives and Tasks*, 1976, were among 10 such publications..submitted to the Labour Party national executive in 1977. **1981** *Daily Tel.* 23 Nov. 16/4 It is virtually impossible to establish hard details of far Left penetration and entryism in charities. **1983** *Times Lit. Suppl.* 9 Dec. 1382/3 ILP entrism encountered quite different problems in different unions.

Hence **'entryist**, a practitioner or supporter of entryism; also *attrib.* or as *adj.*

1964 in *Times* (1985) 17 Dec. 10/4 By 'Tendency Paper' was meant an entrist propaganda paper, applying the programme of Trotskyism within the Labour Party. **1976** *Times* 6 Dec. 1 The report..referred to 'entryist activities' adopted by an organization which, because it was ineligible for affiliation to the party decided that its members should enter as individuals to carry out activities within it as

directed by the outside organization. **1977** *Listener* 24 Mar. 388/1 The 'entrists' who are persuading constituency parties that their MP is a representative and not a delegate. **1980** *Times* 15 Jan. 1/6 The perspective for the next period opens up the prospect for entrist work to be really fruitful. **1982** *Encounter* Mar. 31/2 McCormick and Lewis soldiered on, meeting the military entryists.

‖**Entscheidungsproblem** (ɛn'tʃaɪdʊŋsprɒ ˌblɛm). *Math.* and *Logic.* [G., f. *entscheidung* decision + *problem* PROBLEM.] = *decision problem* (DECISION 5).

[**1922** *Mathematische Annalen* LXXXVI. 163 (*title*) Beiträge zur Algebra der Logik, insbesondere zum Entscheidungsproblem.] **1930** *Proc. London Math. Soc.* XXX. 271 The *Entscheidungsproblem* is to find a procedure for determining whether any given formula is valid, or, alternatively, whether any given formula is consistent. **1938** *Mind* XLVII. 445 Gödel's example belongs to the field of investigations of the *Entscheidungsproblem.* This problem is to discover whether the accepted primitive propositions and rules of inference of mathematical logic allow us to conclude either the truth or the falsehood of every propositional formula, and if so to give a general method by which this can be done. **1958** M. DAVIS *Computability & Unsolvability* viii. 134 Hilbert declared that the decision problem..(often referred to simply as the *Entscheidungsproblem*) was the central problem of mathematical logic.

entuite, var. of ENTWIT(E.

†**en'tune,** *sb. Obs. rare*⁻¹. [f. next verb.] Tune; song; melody, music.

c **1369** CHAUCER *Dethe Blaunche* 309 So mery a sowne, so swete entunes.

†**en'tune,** *v. Obs.* Also 5 **en-, intewne.** [var. of ENTONE, INTONE, a. OF. *entone-r*, *-onne-r* = Pr. and Sp. *entonar*:—late L. *intonāre*, f. *in-* (see IN-) + *ton-us* TONE: see TUNE.]

1. *trans.* To sing, chant, intone. Also *absol.*

c **1374** CHAUCER *Troylus* IV. Proem 4 And can to folis so her song entune. **1450–1530** *Myrr. our Ladye* 300 Cristen peple intewne praysynges to the vyrgyn marye. **1483** CAXTON *Gold. Leg.* 253/2 Alle they that were comen with Jhesu Cryste entewned swetely. **1627** HAKEWILL *Apol.* IV. x. §2 (1630) 429 Hymness and sonnets..entuned in a solemne and mournfull note.

2. To bring (a voice or instrument) into tune.

a **1500** *Flower & Leaf* xxvi, The company answered all, With voices sweet entuned, & so small. **1523** SKELTON *Garl. Laurel* 276 Whose hevenly armony was so passing sure, So duly entunyd with every measure. **1530** PALSGR. 538/2, I entune, I set an instrument in tune or a companye of syngars... Have you entuned these organes?

enturf: see EN- *pref.*¹ 1 b.

enturret (ɛn'tʌrɪt), *v. rare.* [f. EN-¹ + TURRET.] *trans.* To surround with towers.

1866 J. ROSE tr. *Ovid's Fasti* IV. 246 Did she [the goddess] enturret first a Phrygian town?

entwine, intwine (ɛn-, ɪn'twaɪn), *v.* [f. EN-¹, IN- + TWINE *v.*]

1. *trans.* To twine or twist together; to plait, interlace, interweave.

1616 W. BROWNE *Brit. Past.* II. iii. Intwine..the flesh-like Columbine With Pinckes. **1667** MILTON *P.L.* IV. 174 But further way found none, so thick entwin'd, As one continu'd brake. **1712** BUDGELL *Spect.* No. 425 ⁋3 The Graces with their Arms intwined within one another. **1772** SIR W. JONES *Poems, Solima*, Where bloom intwin'd the lily, pink, and rose. **1801** SOUTHEY *Thalaba* III. xviii, Patiently the Old Man Entwines the strong palm-fibres. **1807** CRABBE *Par. Reg.* II. 281 Entwine their withered arms 'gainst wind and weather.

b. *intr.* for *refl.*

1663 BP. PATRICK *Parab. Pilgr.* xiii. (1668) 92 There they entwine in the dearest embraces. *a* **1771** *Stanzas* in *P. Fletcher's Pisc. Ecl.* (1771) iii. st. 15 *note*, Fly and entwine amid those locks of gold. **1849** S. R. MAITLAND *Illustr. and Enquiries* I. 76 Two serpents, who rear up and entwine in the light of a candle stick.

c. To form by twining; to weave.

a **1700** DRYDEN (J.), The vest and veil divine, Which wand'ring foliage and rich flow'rs intwine. *a* **1743** SAVAGE *Valentine's Day* Wks. 1777 II. 218 For him may Love the myrtle wreath entwine.

d. *fig.*

1597 HOOKER *Eccl. Pol.* V. i, This opinion, though false, yet entwined with a true. **1613** DONNE *Epith. Ct. Palatine & Lady Eliz.*, You two have one way left yourselves t'entwine Besides this bishop's knot. **1684** CHARNOCK *Attrib. God* (1834) I. 10 It [the belief of a God] is so entwined with reason. **1829** I. TAYLOR *Enthus.* x. (1867) 287 The [Christian] doctrine is entwined with the [English] language. **1868** STANLEY *Westm. Ab.* Pref. 11 The murder of Becket..was inseparably entwined with the whole structure of the building.

2. To wreathe or encircle (an object) *with* (another); to wreathe (the one) *about*, *round* (the other). Also *intr.* for *refl.*

1796 MORSE *Amer. Geog.* II. 625 They entwine their bodies with the entrails of cattle. **1809** W. IRVING *Knickerb.* (1861) 182 No more entwines with flowers his shining sword. **1845** DARWIN *Voy. Nat.* vii. (1879) 137 Trees intwined with creepers. *Ibid.* xx. (1873) 454 The pepper-vine intwining round its trunk. **1874** BOUTELL *Arms & Arm.* iv. 61 A vine-branch entwined about a rod or staff.

b. *fig.*

1835 BROWNING *Paracelsus* 132 Tangle and entwine mankind with error. **1843** NEALE *Hymns for Sick* 31 In earthly joys entwined, I had forgot The things above. **1848** tr. *Mariotti's Italy* II. iii. 75 Schiller entwined himself round the heart. **1874** SAYCE *Compar. Philol.* viii. 317 Similarity of name or local celebrity may cause a myth to entwine itself about some personage or event of actual history.

3. To clasp as a twining plant; to enfold, embrace. Also *fig.*

1633 P. FLETCHER *Purple Isl.* II. xxxv, Divided flames, the iron sides entwining. **1633** G. HERBERT *Temple, Affliction* ii, Thy glorious houshold-stuffe did me entwine. **1667** MILTON *P.L.* X. 512 His Armes clung to his Ribs, his Leggs entwining Each other. *a* **1803** BEATTIE *Poems, Hares* 94 The flowering thorn..The hazle's stubborn stem entwin'd. **1832** TENNYSON *Miller's Dau.* xxix, True wife, Round my true heart thine arms entwine. **1878** *Masque Poets* 36 Let my arm your waist entwine.

Hence **en'twinement**, the action of entwining; the state of being entwined; also *concr.* **en'twining** *vbl. sb.*, the action of the verb ENTWINE. **en'twining** *ppl. a.*, that entwines.

a **1670** HACKETT *Abp. Williams* I. (1692) 81 That it might be like a mixture of roses and wood-binds in a sweet entwinement. **1834** SIR F. B. HEAD *Bubbles Brunnen* 307 No foot tore asunder the entwinement. **1674** N. FAIRFAX *Bulk & Selv.* 193 The unthinkable care and forecast in all its [the world's] evennesses and entwinings. **1738** GLOVER *Leonidas* III. 222 Among the intwining branches of the groves. **1821** SHELLEY *Prometh. Unb.* I. 148, I feel Faint like one mingled in entwining love.

entwist, intwist (ɛn-, ɪn'twɪst), *v.* [f. EN-¹ + TWIST *v.*] *trans.* **a.** To clasp with a twist. **b.** To form into a twist. **c.** To twist in *with*.

α. **1590** SHAKS. *Mids. N.* IV. i. 48 So doth the woodbine, the sweet Honisuckle, Gently entwist. **1683** A. SNAPE *Anat. Horse* I. x. (1686) 20 They [the guts] are gathered up and entwisted in the folds of the Mesentery. **1705** PHILIPS *Blenheim* 249 (Jod.) Th' unweeting prey Entwisted roars. **1750** JOHNSON *Rambler* No. 68 ⁋5 Very few..have their thread of life entwisted with the chain of causes on which armies or nations are suspended. **1769** MRS. MONTAGU *Lett.* II. 114 Though the single thread will not bear handling, yet twisted, and entwisted..it is hard to be broken. **1837** *New Monthly Mag.* XLIX. 399 Some had a maze of horsehair.. entwisted round their polls.

β. **1649** ROBERTS *Clavis Bibl.* iii. 63 Intwisted or woven together like a curious silken web. **1711** J. GREENWOOD *Eng. Gram.* 282 When a twister a-twisting, will twist him a twist For the twisting of his twist, he three twines doth intwist. **1805** SOUTHEY *Madoc* II. xii, His untrimm'd hair, a long and loathsome mass, With cotton cords intwisted. **1864** NEALE *Seaton. Poems* 111 The endless lines Intwisted, and enlinked.

Hence **en'twisted** *ppl. a.*

a **1800** COWPER & HAYLEY tr. *Andreini's Adam* IV. i. The fatal sound of these entwisted pipes. *a* **1813** A. WILSON *Ep. C. Orr* Poet. Wks. (1846) 170 His noontide walks, his vine entwisted bowers. **1855** SINGLETON *Virgil* II. 38 A pliant collar of entwisted gold.

†**en'twit(e,** *v. Obs.* Also 6 **entwyte,** (**entuite, intwight**) 7 **enthwite.** [Altered form of ATWITE; cf. TWIT.] *trans.* **a.** To twit, rebuke, reproach (a person). Const. *of*, *with*. **b.** To make (a thing) a subject of reproach.

1542 UDALL *Erasm. Apoph.* 146 Thou doest naught to entwite me thus. *a* **1553** —— *Royster D.* II. iii. (Arb.) 36 No good turnes entwite, Nor olde sores recite. **1560** *School House for Women* 828 in Hazl. *E.P.P.* IV. 137 In case they doo you but one benefit They wil you ever with that one entwit. **1582** N. T. (Rhem.) *Matt.* xxiii. 29 *note*, Christ.. entwyteth them of their malice. **1583** STANYHURST *Æneis* Ded. (Arb.) 8, I may bee perhaps entwighted of more haste then good speede. **1588** BP. ANDREWES *Serm.* 10 April (1629) 8 By that word he meanes to enthwite them. *a* **1603** T. CARTWRIGHT *Confut. Rhem. N.T.* (1618) 68 He doth somewhat bitingly taxe and entuite the Corinthians. **1608** [HIERON] *Defence* II. 42 He entwitteth the suspended and deprived ministers with want of learninge.

entyer, -e, obs. ff. of ENTIRE.

entyr, obs. form of INTER *v.*

entyr-: see INTER-.

entyre, obs. form of ENTIRE.

entyrement, obs. form of INTERMENT.

entyrmes, obs. form of ENTREMESS.

e'nubilate (ɪ'njuːbɪleɪt), *v.* [f. L. *enūbilāt-* ppl. stem of *ēnūbilāre*, f. *ē* out + *nūbil-us* cloudy, f. *nūbes* a cloud.] *trans.* To make clear.

1736 in BAILEY. **1847** in CRAIG. **1903** *Sat. Rev.* 10 Jan., Maeterlinck is gradually enubilating himself from those enchanted mists in which first he strayed. **1928** 'BRENT OF BIN BIN' *Up Country* xv. 252 The M'Eacherns..asked Bert to help the mounted troopers in clearing out the Eagle Hawk Gullies crowd, and thus enubilate the atmosphere.

†**e'nubilous,** *a. Obs.*⁻⁰ [f. L. *ē* + *nūbil-us* + -OUS.] Fair, without clouds.

1736 in BAILEY. **1847** in CRAIG; and in mod. Dicts.

enucleate (ɪ'njuːklɪeɪt), *v.* Also 6 **enucleat.** [f. L. *ēnucleāt-* ppl. stem of *ēnucleāre* to remove the kernel of, f. *ē* out + *nucleus* kernel. The fig. sense, till modern times the exclusive one in Eng., was fully developed in Lat.]

1. *fig.* To extract the 'kernel' from; to bring out from disguise; to lay open, clear, explain.

1548 HALL *Chron.* (1809) 407 Thinkyng that he would enucleate and open to her all these thinges. **1560** ROLLAND *Crt. Venus* III. 896 All obscure probleme..ȝe can.. Enucleat. **1622** AILESBURY *Serm.* (1623) 19 We sweat to enucleate the mystery. **1774** T. WEST *Antiq. Furness* (1805) 37 No inscription..that can serve to enucleate its original name. **1787** SCHWARTZ in *Phil. Trans.* LXXVII. 359 To enucleate the family relation of this hitherto unknown vegetable. **1846** LANDOR *Exam. Shaks.* Wks. II. 272 To enucleate and bring into light their abstruse wisdom. **1859** *Sat. Rev.* 3 Sept. 284/1 Enucleating the sense which underlies a difficult construction.

2. *Surg.* **a.** To extract (a tumour, etc.) from its shell or capsule. Also *absol.*

1878 A. HAMILTON *Nerv. Dis.* 196 They are easily enucleated. **1878** T. BRYANT *Pract. Surg.* I. 115 To remove them it is only necessary to divide their capsule and the soft parts covering them in and to enucleate. **1887** *Brit. Med. Jrnl.* 17 Dec. 1359/1 Dr. Keith's success in enucleating uterine tumours.

b. To extract (an eye) from the socket.

1867 G. LAWSON *Injuries Eye, Orbit, & Eyelids* vii. 277 The opening in the conjunctiva, through which the eye has been enucleated, may be closed by drawing it together by a fine thread. **1906** A. BENNETT *Whom God hath Joined* vii. 260, I had to have an oculist at last. I couldn't sleep, and he enucleated the eye, as the term is. **1968** *May & Worth's Man. Dis. Eye* (ed. 13) iv. 137 When an eyeball containing a malignant growth is enucleated, as much of the optic nerve as possible should be removed.

3. *Biol.* To deprive (a cell) of its nucleus.

1909 in *Cent. Dict.* Suppl. **1968** *Science* 7 June 1115/3 Kinetics of protein synthesis were measured in oocytes of *Rana pipiens* enucleated at various times during and following pituitary-induced maturation.

Hence **e'nucleating** *ppl. a.*

1862 LOWELL *Biglow P.* 92 Runick inscriptions..offer peculiar temptations to enucleating sagacity.

enucleate (ɪ'njuːklɪeɪt), *a. Biol.*, etc. [ad. L. *enucleatus*, pa. pple. of *enucleare* to ENUCLEATE.] Without a nucleus.

1889 in *Cent. Dict.* **1910** F. KEEBLE *Plant-Anim.* iv. 113 The enucleate green cell may be connected by fine processes with another green cell still possessed of nuclear substance. **1921** L. W. SHARP *Introd. Cytology* iv. 69 The mammalian erythrocyte..loses its nucleus at an early stage and may continue to exist in the enucleate state for..30 days. **1968** H. HARRIS *Nucleus & Cytoplasm* i. 2 (*heading*) Lessons from an enucleate cell.

e'nucleated, *ppl. a.* [f. ENUCLEATE *v.* + -ED¹.] Having the kernel or nucleus extracted. Also *fig.*

1885 R. F. BURTON *Arab. Nts.* VII. 14 Arab ''Ajwah', enucleated dates pressed together into a solid mass. **1896** E. B. WILSON *Cell* vii. 248 The nucleated fragments quickly heal the wound... On the other hand, enucleated fragments, consisting of cytoplasm only, quickly perish. **1900** *Daily News* 17 May 6/3 The most enucleated invalid might stand the intellectual strain of the 'Southern Cross' and the 'Northern Lights'. **1960** L. PICKEN *Organization of Cells* IV. vi. 139 The possibility of dividing cells into nucleated and enucleated halves.

enucleation (ɪˌnjuːklɪ'eɪʃən). [as if ad. L. **ēnucleātiōn-em*, f. *ēnucleāre*: see ENUCLEATE *v.* Cf. Fr. *énucleation.*]

1. The action of enucleating, or getting out the 'kernel' of a matter; unfolding, explanation.

1650 S. CLARKE *Eccl. Hist.* I. (1654) 326 To which they added an enucleation of hard texts. **1686** GOAD *Celest. Bodies* I. ix. 27, I say therefore, toward the Enucleation of the Question, etc. **1796** PEGGE *Anonym.* VIII. lxxxiii. (1809) 382 Another enucleation of this difficult ecclesiastical term. **1840** *Blackw. Mag.* XLVIII. 274 The enucleation of separate parts of that which his ambitious intellect yearned towards the production of as a whole. **1862** F. HALL *Hindu Canons of Dramaturgy* (1865) 9 Its writer rarely propounds for scholastic enucleation such an enigma as, etc.

2. *Surg.* **a.** 'The shelling out of a tumour, or a structure, or a part, from its capsule or enclosing substance' (*Syd. Soc. Lex.*).

1874 ROOSA *Dis. Ear* 107 Sebaceous tumours should be removed by enucleation. **1876** J. S. BRISTOWE *Theory & Pract. Med.* (ed. 2) 53 They..are..capable of pretty easy enucleation from the tissues in which they are imbedded.

b. The removal of an eye from the socket.

1867 H. POWER *Dis. Eye* x. 582 Enucleation of the eye. **1949** A. D. RUEDEMANN in C. Berens *Eye & its Diseases* (ed. 2) lxix. 983 The nerve may be grasped with enucleation forceps to facilitate the excision of a long piece of the optic nerve.

3. *Biol.* The extraction of a nucleus from its cell.

1909 in WEBSTER. **1960** L. PICKEN *Organization of Cells* IV. vi. 139 The amoeba is unable to spread after enucleation and remains rounded up.

enuff, enuȝhe, obs. ff. ENOUGH.

enula campana: see ELECAMPANE.

1542 BORDE *Dyetary* xix. (1870) 278 The rootes of Enulacampana, soden tender. **1634** H. R. *Salerne's Regim.* 141 **1712** tr. *Pomet's Hist. Drugs* I. 52.

†**e'number,** *v. Obs. rare.* Also 5 **enoumbre.** [a. OF. *enombre-r*, *enumbrer* = Pr. *enombrar*, It. *inombrare*:—L. *inumbrāre*, f. *in* in + *umbra* shadow. Cf. INUMBRATE.] *trans.* To put in the shade; to overshadow, shroud. Also *refl.*

c **1400** MAUNDEV. (1839) Prol., He wolde of his blessednesse enoumbre him in the seyd blessed & gloriouse Virgin Marie. *Ibid.* xii. 136 God sente his Wysdom in to Erthe and enumbred him in the Virgyne Marie.

enumer (ɪ'njuːmə(r)), *v. trans.* = ENUMERATE *v.* 1.

1936 AUDEN *Look, Stranger!* 36 Among the foes which we enumer You are included. **1936** —— & ISHERWOOD *Ascent of F6* (1937) II. iii. 103 Ignore the Law, it's a bore, Don't enumer all the rumours of a war.

enumerability (ɪˌnjuːmərəˈbɪlɪtɪ). [f. ENUMERABLE *a.* + -ILITY.] The fact or quality of being enumerable.

1939 *Yale Rev.* Spring 497 Arithmetic abstracts objects of all qualities save their enumerability; the symbol π abstracts in a single Greek letter a complicated relation between the parts of all circles. **1941** *Mind* L. 286 Mr. Ayer might have used the same argument in the case of enumerability. **1941** J. S. HUXLEY *Uniqueness of Man* i. 28 Arithmetic abstracts objects of all their qualities save their enumerability.

enumerable (ɪˈnjuːmərəb(ə)l), *a.* [f. ENUMER(ATE *v.* + -ABLE.] That can be enumerated; having a definite number; numerable; *spec.* in *Math.* = DENUMERABLE *a.*

1889 in *Cent. Dict.* **1907** E. W. HOBSON *Theory of Functions* ii. 66 An aggregate which contains an indefinitely great number of elements is said to be enumerable, or countable (*abzählbar, dénombrable*), when the aggregate is such that a (1, 1) correspondence can be established between the elements and the set of integral numbers 1, 2, 3, [etc.]. *a* **1910** W. JAMES *Some Probl. Philos.* (1911) xi. 171 The terms are not 'enumerable' in that order. **1940** A. J. AYER *Found. Emp. Knowl.* ii. 124 If the sense-data do not appear to be enumerable, they really are not enumerable. **1968** P. A. P. MORAN *Introd. Probability Theory* i. 1 We suppose that the number of ways in which the event can occur is either finite.., or 'enumerable', i.e. that the events can be numbered off, or put into one-to-one correspondence with the integers.

Hence **eˈnumerably** *adv.*

1968 P. A. P. MORAN *Introd. Probability Theory* i. 4 If the number of E_i is enumerably infinite, the number of A_i is non-enumerably infinite.

enumerable, enumerate, erroneous forms (freq. in 17th c.) of INNUMERABLE, INNUMERATE.

†**eˈnumerate,** *pa. pple. Obs.* [ad. L. *ēnumerāt-us*, pa. pple. of *ēnumerāre*: see next.] Equivalent to the later ENUMERATED.

1646 G. GILLESPIE *Male Audis* 3 So many scandals as are enumerate in the Ordinance. **1671** *True Nonconf.* 226 All these vain Popish Inventions, and Superstitions, enumerate in this Covenant. **1711** C. M. *Lett. to Curat* 35, I proceed now Particularly to consider our Reformers enumerate by your author.

enumerate (ɪˈnjuːməreɪt), *v.* [f. L. *ēnumerāt-* ppl. stem of *ēnumerāre*, f. *ē* out + *numerāre* to count, f. *numerus* NUMBER.]

1. *trans.* To count, ascertain the number of; more usually, to mention (a number of things or persons) separately, as if for the purpose of counting; to specify as in a list or catalogue.

For the primary sense 'ascertain the number of', see esp. ENUMERATED *ppl. a.*, and cf. ENUMERATION, ENUMERATOR.

1647 JER. TAYLOR *Dissuas. Popery* II. i. §11 (R.) If the priest pardons no sins but those which are enumerated. **1671** J. WEBSTER *Metallogr.* vii. 113 Again, he enumerateth eight sorts of Cachimies that were known unto him. **1744** BERKELEY *Siris* §244 There would be no end of enumerating the like cases. **1803** G. S. FABER *Cabiri* II. 34 Atalanta is enumerated, by Apollodorus, among the Argonauts. **1816** J. SMITH *Panorama Sc. & Art* I. 561 The satellites of Jupiter ..are enumerated and distinguished in a regular manner. **1836** J. H. NEWMAN *Par. Serm.* (1837) III. xvii. 261 St. Paul ..enumerates many of the Ancient Saints. *a* **1856** H. MILLER *Test. Rocks* xi. (1857) 469 Adolphe Brogniart had enumerated only seventy species of plants.

†**b.** with clause as obj. *Obs. rare.*

1653 CROMWELL *Lett. & Sp.* 4 July, Enumerating how businesses have been transacted from that time.

2. *Gram.* To 'qualify' numerically. *rare.*

1876 A. DAVIDSON *Hebr. Gram.* §48 The other numerals are nouns and disagree in gender with the words which they enumerate.

†**3.** [? Cf. L. *enumerare* to pay in full.] ? To bestow abundantly. *Obs. rare.*

1717 L. HOWEL *Desiderius* (ed. 3) 76 Prayers that he would ennumerate his spiritual Gifts to this holy Society.

Hence **eˈnumerated** *ppl. a.*, **eˈnumerating** *vbl. sb.* (in quot. *attrib.*).

1721 *Roy. Proclam.* 5 Feb. in *Lond. Gaz.* No. 5928/4 Such enumerated Goods. **1767** T. HUTCHINSON *Hist. Prov. Mass.* i. 4 Contraband and enumerated commodities. **1871** *Census Eng. & Wales, Prelim. Report* 6 The enumerated population of London..was 3,251,804. **1864** BURTON *Scot. Abr.* I. v. 253 That enumerating function of the Roman officer.

enumeration (ɪˌnjuːməˈreɪʃən). [a. F. *énumeration*, ad. L. *ēnumerātiōn-em*, n. of action f. *ēnumerāre*: see prec.]

1. The action of ascertaining the number of something; *esp.* the taking a census of population; a census.

1577 tr. *Bullinger's Decades* (1592) 629 That holy man did rightly know the enumeration of the sacred Trinitie. **1810** in *Risdon's Surv. Devon* 394 According to the enumeration in 1801, the population amounted to 1600 persons. **1819** *Gentl. Mag.* 529 He produced an enumeration of the inhabitants of the island. **1848** MACAULAY *Hist. Eng.* I. 340 *note*, In 1740, the population of Nottingham was found, by enumeration, to be just 10,000.

2. The action of specifying seriatim, as in a list or catalogue.

1551 GARDINER *Of The Presence in Sacrament* 21 To multiply language by enumeraciOun of partes. **1581** LAMBARDE *Eiren.* IV. xvi. (1588) 576, I shall not need to make long enumeration of the sortes of executions, which, etc. **1646** SIR T. BROWNE *Pseud. Ep.* VI. i. 279 The enumeration of Genealogies, and particular accounts of time. **1793** T. BEDDOES *Math. Evid.* 34 The definition of a complex term consists merely in the enumeration of the simple ideas, for which it stands. **1858** LD. ST. LEONARDS *Handy Bk. Property Law* XVIII. 136 The enumeration of these circumstances is not to restrict the generality of the enactment.

b. *concr.* A catalogue, list.

1724 WATTS *Logic* I. ii. §2 Though they are not all agreed in this enumeration of elements. **1772** *Junius Lett.* lxviii. 351 The enumeration includes the several acts cited in this paper. **1830** HERSCHEL *Stud. Nat. Phil.* 135 We should possess an enumeration..of her materials and combinations. **1875** JOWETT *Plato* (ed. 2) I. 184 In this enumeration the greatest good of all is omitted.

3. *Rhet.* transl. L. *enumeratio*: A recapitulation, in the peroration, of the heads of an argument.

1862 in MAUNDER *Sci. & Lit. Treas.*; and in mod. Dicts.

enumerative (ɪˈnjuːmərətɪv), *a.* [f. ENUMERATE *v.* + -IVE.] That has the function of enumerating; concerned with enumeration. Const. *of.*

1651 JER. TAYLOR *Holy Dying* v. §3 Being particular and enumerative of the variety of evils which have disordered his life. **1848** H. MILLER *First Impr.* vi. (1857) 102 He [Thomson] rather enumerates than describes..Now the prospect from the hill at Hagley furnished me with the true explanation of this enumerative style. **1880** MUIRHEAD tr. *Gaius Instit.* Comm. IV. §47 *note*, Whether his *uelut* is to be taken as enumerative..or as merely indicative.

enumerator (ɪˈnjuːməreɪtə(r)). [as if a. L. *ēnumerātor, agent-n. f. *ēnumerāre* to ENUMERATE.] One who enumerates; *spec.* one of the subordinate officers employed in taking a census.

1856 GROTE *Greece* II. xcvi. XII. 492 *note*, The enumerators take account of the slave women and children. **1881** *Daily News* 5 Apr. 6/1 The enumerator has to leave from a hundred to two hundred schedules and after a few days to call for them again.

enunciable (ɪˈnʌnsɪəb(ə)l, -ʃɪ-), *a.* [as if ad. L. *ēnuntiābilis, f. *ēnuntiāre*; see next.] That admits of being enunciated.

1652 URQUHART *Jewel* Wks. (1834) 198 All the words enunciable are in it contained. **1824** COLERIDGE *Aids Refl.* (1848) I. 261 John..enunciates the fact itself, to the full extent in which it is enunciable for the human mind.

enunciate (ɪˈnʌnsɪeɪt, -ʃɪ-), *v.* [f. L. *ēnuntiāt-* ppl. stem of *ēnuntiāre* (incorrectly *enunciare*), f. *ē* out + *nuntiāre* to announce, f. *nuntius* messenger.]

1. *trans.* To give definite expression to (a proposition, principle, theory, etc.); = ENOUNCE 1.

1623 COCKERAM, *Enunciate*, to declare. **1656** tr. *Hobbes' Elem. Philos.* (1839) 204 Which also may more briefly be enunciated thus, velocity is the quantity of motion determined by time and line. *a* **1691** T. BARLOW *Rem.* 553 The truths that may be enuntiated concerning him [Plato]. **1842** GROVE *Corr. Phys. Forces* 2 The theory consequent upon new facts..is generally enunciated by the discoverers themselves. **1853** MARSDEN *Early Purit.* 220 The dogmas enunciated in the Lambeth articles. **1878** HUXLEY *Physiogr.* 95 The same principle may be enunciated in another form.

b. Of words: To form, or serve as a statement of.

1859 MILL *Liberty* (1865) 20/2 The words which enunciate a truth.

2. To state publicly; to proclaim.

1864 PUSEY *Lect. Daniel* Pref. 24 Moses enunciated as simple, undemonstrated truth, 'In the beginning God created the heaven and the earth'. **1875** MANNING *Mission H. Ghost* i. 3 It can therefore never err in enunciating or declaring the revealed knowledge which it possesses.

3. To utter, pronounce (articulate sounds). Also *absol.* = ENOUNCE 3.

1759 HART *Vision of Death* (R.), Each enunciates with a human tone. **1791** BOSWELL *Johnson* an. 1744 *note*, Not.. marked by any peculiar emphasis, but only..distinctly enunciated. **1873** BROWNING *Red Cott. Nt.-Cap* 223 How distinct enunciating, how Plain dealing!

Hence **eˈnunciated** *ppl. a.*

1664 H. MORE *Myst. Iniq.* 534 That Incongruity betwixt enunciated Falsity and the Minde and Things has no moral evil in it. **1817** H. T. COLEBROOKE *Algebra* 266 Putting the enunciated divisor sixteen. **1835** WHEWELL in Todhunter *Acc. of Whewell's Writings* (1876) II. 213 A distinction or resemblance in enunciated principle.

enunciation (ɪnʌnsɪˈeɪʃən, -ʃɪ-). [ad. L. *ēnuntiātiōn-em*, n. of action f. *ēnuntiāre*: see prec. Cf. Fr. *énonciation.*] The action of enuntiating.

1. The action of giving definite expression to (a law, principle, etc.).

1808 *Med. Jrnl.* XIX. 482 Enunciation of the Principle, and Observations respecting it. **1830** HERSCHEL *Stud. Nat. Phil.* 95 The most extensive and general enunciation of the laws of nature. **1873** J. COOKE *New Chem.* 13 This word.. selected by Avogadro in the enunciation of his law.

†**b.** *concr.* A proposition, statement. *Obs.*

1628 T. SPENCER *Logick* 222 A compound axiome, is but one proposition, or enuntiation, as Aristotle calls it. **1637** GILLESPIE *Eng. Pop. Cerem.* IV. vii. 32 Christ..used no prayer in the distribution, but that demonstrative enunciation, *This is my body.* **1717** S. CLARKE *Mr. Leibnitz's 5th Paper* (R.), Every intelligible enunciation must be either true or false. **1765** WARBURTON *Div. Legat.* (ed. 4) VI. §4 V. 194 *note* And verifies the enunciation of the gospel.

c. *Math.* The form of words in which a proposition is stated.

1793 T. BEDDOES *Math. Evid.* 50 The enunciation of proposition the 29th. **1885** LEUDESDORF *Cremona's Proj. Geom.* 99 These are precisely the two directly equal pencils mentioned in the enunciation.

2. †**a.** ? Verbal expression (quot. 1551). **b.** The action of declaring or asserting (a fact, doctrine, etc.); formal declaration or assertion.

1551 GARDINER *Of The Presence in Sacrament* 41 a, The callyng of bread by enunciation, for a name is not material. **1651** JER. TAYLOR *Clerus Dom.* (R.), By way of interpretation and enunciation, as an ambassador. **1827** BENTHAM *Ration. Evid.* Wks. 1843 VII. 81 The proposition in question..is not, properly speaking, the enunciation of a matter of fact. **1844** LEVER *T. Burke* xviii, He never missed an opportunity for the enunciation of such doctrines.

3. The uttering or pronouncing of articulate sounds; manner of utterance.

1750 CHESTERF. *Lett.* 9 July (1870) 179 Remember of what importance Demosthenes and one of the Gracchi, thought Enunciation. **1812** *Examiner* 9 Nov. 716/1 His enunciation is perfectly articulate. **1879** FROUDE *Cæsar* xi. 129 He mocked at his bad enunciation and bad grammar.

enunciative (ɪˈnʌnʃɪətɪv). [ad. L. *ēnuntiātīv-us*, f. *ēnuntiāre*: see ENUNCIATE.]

1. That serves to enunciate; predicative; declaratory. Const. *of.*

1531 ELYOT *Gov.* III. xxv, Yet be their warkes compacte in fourme of narrations whiche by oratours be called enunciatiue. *c* **1555** HARPSFIELD *Divorce Hen. VIII* (1878) 219 These enunciative words do not prove them man and wife. **1628** T. SPENCER *Logick* 160 An enuntiatiue speech is either simple, or compounded of those that be simple. **1654** JER. TAYLOR *Real Pres.* 74 And if these words..be exegetical, and enunciative of the change that is made by prayers and other mystical words. **1726** AYLIFFE *Parerg.* 306 In respect of the dispositive Words of an Instrument, and not in regard of the Enunciative Terms thereof. **1816** BENTHAM *Chrestom.* 41 The simply enuntiative parts of the propositions will serve by themselves. **1862** F. HALL *Hindu Philos. Syst.* 284 The words are..more directly enunciative of the doctrine.

†**b.** *Gram.* (See quot.) *Obs.*

c **1620** A. HUME *Brit. Tongue* (1865) 33 The conjunction enunciative coples the partes of a period..The ratiocinative couples the parts of a ratiocination.

†**c.** Of a command: Explicit, express. *Obs.*

1664 H. MORE *Synopsis Proph.* 534 His absolute and enunciative command.

†**2.** Of the nature of outward expression. *Obs.*

1655–60 STANLEY *Hist. Philos.* (1701) 480/1 As to Enunciative discourse..there are some Dogmatists who condemn it..whence they kept silence. **1656** JEANES *Mixt. Schol. Div.* 63 Here by the word is understood, not the word enunciative [L. *prolativum*], the word written or preach't, But the Word substantiall: And the word was God.

3. Pertaining to vocal utterance or elocution.

1831 *Fraser's Mag.* III. 485 Time had palsied your strength and weakened your enunciative powers. **1850** *Ibid.* XLI. 449 He gave scope to the extraordinary enunciative powers of Bannister.

Hence **eˈnunciatively** *adv.*, in an enunciative manner; declaratively.

1637 GILLESPIE *Eng. Pop. Cerem.* IV. vii. 32 It is not a thing indifferent, to omit the repetition of those words, *This is my body*, enunciatively and demonstratively.

enunciator (ɪˈnʌnsɪˌeɪtə(r), -ʃɪ-). [a. L. *ēnuntiātor*, f. *ēnuntiāre*: see ENUNCIATE.] **a.** One who or that which enunciates.

1809–12 MAR. EDGEWORTH *Ennui* xv, The news, of which she was the first, and not very intelligible enunciator. **1863** HUXLEY *Man's Place Nat.* II. 85 As for the second [proposition], one can only admire the surpassing courage of its enunciator. **1870** *Psalms Chronologically Arranged* 113 The Prophets..were acknowledged as the enunciators of God's present purpose.

b. A self-acting telegraphic signal.

1847 *Rep. Comm. Pat. 1847* (U.S.) 101 Letters patent have also been granted for an improved enunciator, for use in hotels, &c. **1889** *Pall Mall G.* 21 Jan. 6/3 An electric enunciator in the box-office which will register the numbers, etc.

†**eˈnunciatory,** *a. Obs. rare.* [f. L. *ēnuntiāt-* (see ENUNCIATE) + -ORY.] = ENUNCIATIVE.

a **1693** URQUHART *Rabelais* III. xxxviii. 317 Predicable and enunciatory fool.

enunction, var. of INUNCTION, *Obs.*

enundation, obs. form of INUNDATION.

†**eˈnuny,** *v. Obs.* [ad. late L. *inūnī-re*, f. *in* in + *ūnī-re* to unite, f. *ūnus* one.] *trans.* To unite.

1542 BECON *Christmas Banquet* Works 1560 I. xxvii. b. Repentance without faith auaileth nothing, but enunied and ioined with faith is a singuler and high treasure. *Ibid.* Except by fayth they be enunied and joined together.

enure (ɛˈnjʊə(r)), *v.* Also 5 **enewre.** [f. EN-[1] + URE, a. OF. *oeuvre* operation; cf. *poure*, POOR, a. OF. *povre*.

An earlier form of INURE, by which it is now superseded exc. in the legal sense 3 below.]

†**1.** *trans.* To put into operation or exercise; to carry into act; to commit (a crime). *Obs.*

1549 CHALONER *Erasm. on Folly* E j a, Who neither is skilled in thyngs daiely enured. **1580** SPENSER *Let. G. Harvey* Wks. (Globe) App. ii. 709/1 I also enure my penne sometime in that kinde. **1581** J. BELL *Haddon's Answ. Osor.* 39 b, Whereby the..dueties of Christian lyfe may be dayly enured and preserved. **1596** SPENSER *F.Q.* IV. ii. 29 Ne certes can that friendship long endure..That doth ill cause or evill end enure. *Ibid.* v. ix. 39 Many haynous crymes by her enured. *a* **1599** —— *Epigr.* Wks. (Globe) 587/2 But he,

soone after, fresh againe enured His former cruelty. *a* **1612** HARRINGTON *Epigr.* II. (1633) 101 T' enure on vertuous wives such wrong suspitions. **1667** MILTON *P.L.* VIII. 239 But us he sends .. as Sovran King, and to enure Our prompt obedience.

2. Of persons: To bring by use, habit, or continual exercise to a certain condition or state of mind, to the endurance of a certain condition, to the following of a certain kind of life, etc. Const. *to* with *sb.* or *inf.* Now only in form INURE, q.v.

c **1489** CAXTON *Sonnes of Aymon* viii. 187 A fayre company, and well enewred to the warre. **1489** CAXTON *Faytes of A.* I. xiv. 38 To enure hem self so to peyne and trauayll. **1553** T. WILSON *Rhet.* 8 Enuryng our selves to do that in dede whiche we know in woorde. **1577** tr. *Bullinger's Decades* (1592) 106 Wee must .. enure our selues to chastise them [children], if they delight to lie. **1638** SUCKLING *Aglaura* I. i, The slave whom tedious custom has enur'd And taught to think of miserie as of food. **1645** USSHER *Body Div.* (1647) 334 Yet, as a Master of defence, enureth us to the conflict, by contending with us. **1675** HOBBES *Odyssey* (1677) 55 Henceforth his people let no king enure To gentle government. **1713** ADDISON *Cato* II. i, Troops enured to toil. **1791** NEWTE *Tour Eng. & Scot.* 237 The nature of their country enures them to exercise and temperance. **1818** JAS. MILL *Brit. India* I. II. vi. 202 He .. enured these sentient creatures to pleasure and pain, cold and heat. **1827** HARE *Guesses* (1859) 197 He must enure himself to bear sudden and violent changes. **1837** WHITTOCK *Bk. Trades* (1842) 350 To enure youths to habits of industry.

†**b.** In early use const. *with.*

1509 FISHER 7 *Penit. Ps.* Wks. 16 They shall be enured with contynuall hatred. **1555** W. WATREMAN *Fardle Facions* I. i. 26 Before they had .. enured them selues with their [progenitors'] facions and maners. **1561** T. NORTON *Calvin's Inst.* I. 31 That by litle and litle they may be enured with that profitable maner of speach.

3. *intr.* Chiefly *Law.* To come into operation; to take place, have effect; to be available; to be applied (to the use or benefit of a person). Const. *to* or *simply*.

1607 COWEL *Interpr., Enure* signifieth to take place or effect, to be avaylable. **1628** COKE *On Litt.* 307 a, This shall enure by force and way of grant. **1642** PERKINS *Prof. Bk.* i. §69. 32 This grant shall not enure to such intent to determine the seignorie but shall enure by way of convenant. **1677** YARRANTON *Eng. Improv.* 183 That all the Benefit of the said River Sharwell .. shall be and enure to the several Companies named in this Act. **1726** AYLIFFE *Parergon* 469 In a Donative a Resignation to one of the Founders or Patrons of the Church .. is sufficient, .. for it enures to them all. **1765** BLACKSTONE *Comm.* I. 401 Else the dignity enures only to the grantee for life. **1849** J. P. KENNEDY *W. Wirt* (1860) II. xv. 242 The cessions of land .. have generally enured to the special benefit of Georgia. **1875** POSTE *Gaius* II. §88 It enures exclusively to the bonitary proprietor. **1888** BRYCE *Amer. Commw.* I. 84 The suspension enures to the benefit of the President, who becomes a sort of dictator.

b. *trans.* To make available; to hand over.

1736 CARTE *Ormonde* II. 205 To enure to any person or persons .. any estate sold or disposed of.

Hence †**e'nurement**, *Obs.*, use; practice. †**e'nurer**, *Obs.*, one who practises or puts into operation. **e'nuring** *vbl. sb.*

1611 COTGR., *Exercice*, exercise; enurement, use, practise; action, execution. **1556** J. HEYWOOD *Spider & Fl.* xxvii. 243 As lawles enurers, Of verdites false or foolish. **1606** G. W[OODCOCKE] tr. *Hist. Justine* 55 a, So .. did .. the customary envring to the discipline of warre giue him bouldnes to put them to death.

enuresis (ɛnjʊ'riːsɪs). [mod.L., f. Gr. ἐνουρεῖν to urinate in.] Incontinence of urine, esp. minor incontinence not associated with any organic disease. Hence **enu'retic** *a.* and *sb.*

1800 tr. *W. Cullen's Nosology* 173 (*heading*) Enuresis. Involuntary but not painful flux of urine. **1822** J. M. GOOD *Study Med.* IV. 492 Paruria incontinens .. is the enuresis of most of the nosologists. **1907** *Practitioner* Apr. 542 For a year past he had terrors practically every night, and often .. enuresis. **1909** *Lancet* 1 May 1245/2 He had frequently known nocturnal enuresis to persist after very thorough removal of adenoids and tonsils. **1937** C. L. C. BURNS in E. Miller *Growing Child* vi. 180 It might be said that the neurotic attitude of an enuretic child is an effect of the enuresis rather than a cause. **1943** *Our Towns* iii. 85 The mother of the enuretic .. does not teach her child .. control of its natural functions. **1968** *Encycl. Brit.* VIII. 619/2 Enuresis .. usually means bed-wetting.

enurn, obs. variant of INURN.

enurny (ɛ'nɜːnɪ), *a. Her.* Also enurney. [a. AF. *enorné, enourné*, altered form of OF. *aourné* adorned: see ANORN, ENORN.] Of a bordure: Charged with beasts. By some writers improperly used as sb. for a charge of this kind upon a bordure.

1562 LEIGH *Armorie* (1597) 111 The fourth [bordure] is called Enurney, that is, when it is occupied with any beast. **1610** GUILLIM *Heraldry* I. v. (1660) 29 This term Enurny is proper to all bordures charged with any beasts. **1727** BRADLEY *Fam. Dict.*, *Enurny*, the Heralds Term for a Bordure of a Coat of Arms, being charged with any kind of Beasts. **1847** *Gloss. Brit. Her.* s.v. *Bordure of England* 63 Some would say enurney of lions, or charged with an enurney of lions.

enus, -ys, var. forms of ENES *adv. Obs.* once.

envade: see INVADE.

†**en'vahisshe**, *v. Obs.* Also 5 envaysshe, envahysshe. [ad. Fr. *envahiss-* lengthened stem of *envahir*: see ENVAYE *v.*] *trans.* To attack. Also *absol.* Hence **en'vahisshing** *ppl. a.*

1489 CAXTON *Faytes of A.* I. ii. 30 To enuahisshe leping vpon his enemyes. *Ibid.* II. xxxv. 148 Thus is the fortresse enuaysshed. *c* **1500** *Melusine* 147 We dide yssue yesterday, and enuahysshed our enmyes.

envapour: see EN- *pref.*[1] 1 a.

†**en'vassal**, *v. Obs.* Also 7 envassaile, -all, invassal, -el. [f. EN-[1] + VASSAL.] *trans.* To reduce to the condition of a vassal; to reduce to servitude or subjection; to make subservient *to.* Also *fig.*

1605 DANIEL *Queen's Arcadia* Wks. (1717) 165 That intolerable Misery, Whereto Affection now invassels me. **1609** BP. BARLOW *Answ. Nameless Cath.* 60 Awing our Princes, enuassaling our Prelates. **1647** CUDWORTH *Serm.* 1 *John* ii. 3–4 (1676) 57 Many of us .. have our minds .. envassalled to Riches, Gain, Profit. **1660** FULLER *Mixt Contempl.* (1841) 194 They would have seized on our persons too, and have envassalled us for ever unto them.

Hence **en'vassalled** *ppl. a.*, **en'vassaling** *vbl. sb.*

1609 BP. BARLOW *Answ. Nameless Cath.* 25 Yeelded vnto by timorous Princes, ambitious and tumultuous Prelates, enuassalled Parasites. **1642** *Vind. Parl.* in *Harl. Misc.* (Malh.) V. 275 For the strength and safety, and not inflaming or invassaling of his subjects and people.

†**en'vassalage.** *Obs. rare.* Also 8 in-. [f. prec. + -AGE.] **a.** The state of being reduced to vassalage. **b.** The action of reducing to vassalage.

1646 SIR J. TEMPLE *Irish Rebell.* Pref. 6 They speak as if their oppressions might be paralelled with the Israelitish envassalage in the Land of Egypt. **1652** PEYTON *Catastr. Ho. Stuarts* 90 By that derivation they .. augmented the power of invassalage.

†**en'vault**, *v. Obs.* Also 6 envawte. [f. EN-[1] + VAULT *sb.*]

1. *trans.* To arch over, cover the arched roof of.

1523 SKELTON *Garl. Laurel* (Dyce) 477 Enuawtyd with rubies the vawte was of this place.

2. To entomb.

a **1745** SWIFT *A Conclusion*, I wonder, good man, that you are not envaulted; Prithee, go and be dead, and be doubly exalted.

†**en'vay(e**, *sb. Obs.* Also 5 envahye. [a. OF. *envahie, envaye*, f. *envahir*: see next.] An attack.

c **1450** *Merlin* xx. 318 We shull .. chastice hem at this enuay. *c* **1500** *Melusine* 201 His peuple .. made a fyers enuahye vpon the poyteuyns.

†**en'vaye**, *v. Obs.* Also 5 envahye, envayhe. [ad. Fr. *envahi-r* = Pr. *envair*, Sp. *envadir*:—late L. **invadīre*, L. *invādĕre*: see INVADE, ENVAHISSHE.] *trans.* To attack.

1475 CAXTON *Jason* 28 For to go with him for to enuahye and fighte with their enemyes. **1483** —— *Gold. Leg.* 74/4 The chaldeys .. haue enuayhed thy camels and taken them.

envaysshe: see ENVAHISSHE.

envecked, -ee, obs. ff. INVECKED, -EE. *Her.*

enveigh, etc., **enveigle**: see IN-.

enveil (ɛn'veɪl), *v.* Also 6 enveile, envele. [f. EN-[1] + VEIL *sb.* Cf. OF. *envoiler.*] *trans.* To cover with a veil, place a veil upon (*e.g.* a woman when received into a religious order). Also *transf.* and *fig.* to shroud as with a veil.

1555 *Fardle Facions* Pref. 16 Hauyng thus with his subtilties enueiled our mindes. *Ibid.* II. xii. 268 The Bisshoppe was giuen authoritie to enueile virgines, and to hallow them. **1837** *Foreign Q. Rev.* XIX. 305 Kerner again has taken up the whole black mantle of Novalis, and enveiled himself with it. **1850** BLACKIE *Æschylus* II. 170 When dark night enveils the welkin.

†**en'veleny**, *v. Obs. rare*[—1]. [ad. It. *invelenire*, f. *in* in + *veleno*:—L. *venēnum* poison.] *trans.* To envenom, to poison.

c **1534** tr. *Pol. Verg. Eng. Hist.* (1844) I. 249 A man .. enveleyed [? envelenyed] with the delicius poyson of ease.

envelop (ɛn'vɛləp), *v.* Forms: α. 4–5 envolupe(n, -ipe(n, 7–8 envellop, 6– envelop(e. β. 6 involup, 7–8 invellop(e, 6–8 invelop(e. [a. OF. *envolupe-r, enveloper* (mod. *envelopper*) = Pr. *envolupar, envelopar*, f. *en-* (see EN-[1]) + **volup-*, **velop-*, cogn. with It. *viluppo* bundle, whence *inviluppare* to envelope. Cf. DEVELOP, VOLUPER.

The Romanic base *volup-, vilup-* is of obscure origin; some regard it as Teut., comparing ME. *wlappen* to LAP, wrap, which, however, is not known outside Eng., and is by Prof. Skeat regarded as an altered form of *wrap.* Diez suggested that a late L. **volutuāre* (f. *volvĕre* to roll) became **voluppāre*, but the analogies offered for this phonetic process are unsatisfactory.]

1. *trans.* To wrap up in, or as in, a garment or outer covering. Also *fig.*

1386 CHAUCER *Pard. T.* 614 For he is most envoliped in synne. **1406** HOCCLEVE *Misrule* 245 If that yee been envolupid in cryme. **1513** DOUGLAS *Æneis* VII. iii. 67 With ane grene branche of tre He did involup and aray his heid. **1650** BULWER *Anthropomet.* 93 Eares so large, that they invelope their whole bodies with them. **1809** PINKNEY *Trav. France* 216 In digging a vault a body was discovered enveloped in a long robe. **1875** LYELL *Princ. Geol.* (ed. 12) II. III. xl. 377 They had been packed up in a box, and enveloped in cotton.

b. To serve as a wrapping or case for. Also *fig.*

1595 SHAKS. *Hen. V*, I. i. 31 Leauing his body as a Paradise T'inuelop and containe Celestiall Spirits. **1738** GLOVER *Leonidas* x. (R.), The silken plumes Of sleep envelop his extended limbs. **1797** M. BAILLIE *Morb. Anat.* (1807) 357 The cellular membrane, which envelopes the vessels of the spermatic chord. **1830** R. KNOX tr. *Béclard's Anat.* 116 These membranes .. were long confounded .. with the organs which they envelope. **1834** MCMURTRIE *Cuvier's Anim. Kingd.* 235 Their mantle unites under the body, forming a muscular sac which envelopes all the viscera. **1870** H. MACMILLAN *Bible Teach.* viii. 152 His body must be enveloped by the earth, as his soul is enveloped by the body.

2. To wrap, cover closely on all sides with a surrounding medium (*e.g.* clouds, darkness, flames, an atmosphere, etc.). Const. *in, with.* Also with the surrounding medium as subject.

1590 SPENSER *F.Q.* II. xii. 34 Suddenly a grosse fog overspred .. And heavens chearefull face enveloped. **1603** SHAKS. *Meas. for M.* IV. ii. 77 The best, and wholsomst spirits of the night, Inuellop you, good Prouost. **1664** H. MORE *Myst. Iniq.* 503 Raies of light and glory envelop His Body. **1675** COCKER *Morals* 41 Our chearin Sun, our Glory and Delight, Are soon inveloped in shades of Night. **1700** DRYDEN *Fables, Pal. & Arc.* 1863 A cloud of smoke envelops either host. **1762** DUNN in *Phil. Trans.* LII. 471 They are so invelloped in vapours, as to be undiscernible. **1791** COWPER *Iliad* XVII. 716 Jove with storms Enveloped Ida. **1800** tr. *Lagrange's Chem.* I. 58 The azote which is disengaged, envelops the carbon. **1847** *Illust. Lond. News* 10 July 19/3 Mr. Huntley's property was enveloped in one broad sheet of flame. **1847** L. HUNT *Jar Honey* ii. (1848) 15 One of these cliffs towers to such a height, that its summit is for ever enveloped in clouds.

fig. **1474** CAXTON *Cheese* 109 The thought is enuoluped in obscurete. **1670** COTTON *Espernon* I. II. 64 The extreme danger they saw themselves envellop'd in. **1670** *Moral State Eng.* 137 When we cloud our Reason, and envelope it in mists. **1837** DISRAELI *Venetia* II. i. (1871) 105 What mystery was this that enveloped that great tie? **1846** SIR W. HAMILTON *Dissert.* in *Reid's Wks.* 752 The peasant employs all the principles of abstract philosophy, only inveloped, latent, engaged.

†**3.** *catachr.* **a.** 'To line; to cover on the inside' (J.). **b.** Of a body of men: To surround.

1590 SPENSER *F.Q.* II. vii. 4 His yron cote, all overgrowne with rust, Was underneath enveloped with gold. **1683** TEMPLE *Mem.* Wks. 1731 I. 388 The Prince of Orange .. was at first envelop'd by his own flying Men.

Hence **en'veloped** *ppl. a.* (in senses of the vb.; in quot. *fig.*), enshrouded, darkened. **en'veloper**, one who envelops or wraps up. **en'veloping** *vbl. sb.*, the action of the vb. ENVELOP; also *concr.* a wrapping; an enclosing membrane.

1607 WALKINGTON *Opt. Glasse* 11 The inveloped and deformed night of ignorance. **1883** CLODD in *Knowl.* 15 June 353/1 The rain-clouds are imprisoned in dungeons or caverns by Vritra the 'Enveloper'. **1693** J. BEAUMONT *on Burnet's Th. Earth* I. 52 The envelopings also with which the Infant is encompast, being very thin. **1831** R. KNOX tr. *Cloquet's Anat.* 239 The Enveloping Aponeuroses vary much in their thickness. **1879** G. PRESCOTT *Sp. Telephone* 133 Magnetization .. impressed upon a soft iron rod by the action of an enveloping helix. **1882** VINES *Sach's Bot.* 702 Salts .. present in solution in the enveloping strata of water.

envelope ('ɛnvələʊp, 'ɒnv(ə)ləʊp), *sb.* Also 8–9 envelop. [ad. Fr. *enveloppe*, f. *envelopper*: see ENVELOP *v.*

Walker 1791 records the custom then prevailing of pronouncing this word like the Fr. *enveloppe* (ɑ̃vlɔp). In sense 2 this pronunciation, or rather some awkward attempt at it (ɑ̃vələʊp, 'ɒnvələʊp) is still very frequently heard, though there is no good reason for giving a foreign sound to a word which no one regards as alien, and which has been anglicized in spelling for nearly 200 years.]

1. a. That in which anything is enveloped; 'a wrapper, integument, covering' (J.).

1715 KERSEY, *Envelope*, a cover for anything. **1796** C. BURNEY *Mem. of Metastasio* III. 142 He has consigned to my messenger .. six volumes .. not only without a box, but without any kind of envelope, or direction. **1811** *Edin. Rev.* XVIII. 226 The earth which serves as the envelope of the bones [in certain caverns]. **1830** HERSCHEL *Stud. Nat. Phil.* 79 The statue might be conceived encrusted in its marble envelope. **1845** STOCQUELER *Handbk. Brit. India* (1854) 346 The better class of females .. are covered with an immense piece of cloth .. these envelopes are of white cloth. **1854** BREWSTER *More Worlds* ii. 21 The Earth is surrounded with an aerial envelope or atmosphere. **1865** *Sat. Rev.* 28 Oct. 555 The spirits have behind them the crass and heavy envelope of their earthly tenement. **1873** H. ROGERS *Orig. Bible* ii. (ed. 3) 90 The envelope which protects the chrysalis.

b. *fig.*

1741 WARBURTON *Div. Legat.* II. 629 Their obvious sense that serves only for the envelope. **1797** GODWIN *Enquirer* II. xii. 370 Style should be the transparent envelop of our thoughts. **1829** I. TAYLOR *Enthus.* iv. (1867) 78 The leading intention of both [Antinomianism and Stoicism] is to enclose the human mind in a perfect envelop of abstractions. **1865** LECKY *Ration.* (1878) I. 300 Every dogmatic system .. should be regarded as the vehicle or envelope of pure religion. **1952** *Brit. Jrnl. Psychol.* July 239 The 'envelope' is the late Dr. Plant's name for the processes by which the individual selects from the environment those features with which he can deal and shuts out the rest. **1957** N. FRYE *Sound & Poetry* 136 Traditional literary scholarship, chiefly .. concerned with the sender and receiver in reaction with the cultural envelope. **1963** *Listener* 28 Feb. 370/2 The Liverpool building .. is a palpable *volume*, held in place by a semi-translucent envelope of concrete and glass, to which the ribs are clearly accessory.

2. *spec.* The cover of a letter; now a small sheet of paper folded and gummed to serve as a cover for a letter.

a **1714** BURNET *Own Time* I. (1724) 302 A letter from the King of Spain was given to his daughter by the Spanish Ambassador, and she tore the envelope, and let it fall. **1726** SWIFT *To Grub St. Poets*, Wks. 1735 II. 368 Lend these to Paper-sparing Pope..No letter with an Envelope Could give him more Delight. **1826** J. NEAL *Bro. Jonathan* III. 351 Our hero was tearing off the envelope. **1839** SIR R. HILL in G. B. Hill *Life* (1880) I. 346 The little bags called envelopes. **1874** BURNAND *My Time* xxvii. 250 He quickly opened the envelope to see if the enclosed fee was in notes or a cheque.

3. In physical science often used in general sense; also *spec.* in *Bot.* the calyx or the corolla, or both taken together; in *Astron.* the nebulous covering of the head of a comet, the coma.

1830 R. KNOX *Béclard's Anat.* 234 The envelopes of the muscles, or the enveloping aponeuroses..furnish.. insertions to muscular fibres. **1830** LINDLEY *Nat. Syst. Bot.* 99 Stamens single, without any floral envelope. **1834** MRS. SOMERVILLE *Connex. Phys. Sc.* xxxvi. (1849) 404 The luminous envelope was of a decided yellow. **1851** CARPENTER *Man. Phys.* 519 A general contraction of the mantle or muscular envelope. **1870** HOOKER *Stud. Flora* 14 Papaveraceæ..envelopes and stamens very caducous.

4. *Fortification.* (See quot.)

1707 in *Glossogr. Angl. Nova.* **1715** KERSEY, *Envelope*, In Fortification, a Work of Earth rais'd either in the Ditch of a Place, or beyond it. **1853** STOCQUELER *Mil. Encycl.*, *Envelope*, in fortification, a work of earth, sometimes in form of a single parapet, and at others like a small rampart.

5. a. *Math.* The locus of the ultimate intersections of consecutive curves (or surfaces) in a 'family' or system of curves (or surfaces).

1871 TODHUNTER *Diff. Calc.* xxv. (1875) 359 The locus of the ultimate intersections of a series of curves is called the envelop of the series of curves. **1873** WILLIAMSON *Diff. Calc.* xv. 250 The envelope of the system..is touched by every curve of the system.

b. *Electr. Engineering.* A curve formed by joining the successive peaks of a graph of an oscillation, esp. a modulated wave.

1928 *Exper. Wireless & Wireless Engin.* V. 302/1 When the voltages..are applied to the grid of an anode bend detector whose A.C. characteristic is a straight line, the envelopes indicated by curves 1 and 2 (Fig. 8) are rectified. **1929** *Ibid.* VI. 620/1 R, when plotted against time, will give the outline of the envelope representing the succession of carrier wave peaks. **1970** D. F. SHAW *Introd. Electronics* (ed. 2) xi. 256 The audio-frequency signal is represented by the envelope of the radio-frequency wave and..a device is employed which will give an output voltage proportional to the positive (or negative) envelope of the waveform.

6. *Aeronaut.* The gas or air container of a balloon or airship.

1901 *Sci. Amer.* 10 Aug. 89/3 The balloon is inflated with hydrogen, and in order to maintain at all times a tension on the envelope—that is to say, perfect inflation—a compensating balloon filled with air is placed in the interior. **1909** *Rep. Advisory Committee Aeronautics* 15 July 121 There will be some risk of [electrical] discharges between the airship and a charged cloud..while with a non-conducting envelope, if wet, there would be the same risk. **1950** *Gloss. Aeronaut. Terms (B.S.I.)* I. 49 Envelope. *a.* The gas-containing unit of a balloon or non-rigid or semi-rigid airship. *b.* The outer cover of an airship in which the gas-containing units are surrounded by a layer of air or inert gas. **1961** R. HIGHAM *Brit. Rigid Airship* vii. 118 This was despite the fact that the engineer had to climb on to the top of the envelope each time it was necessary to switch to a new tank of petrol.

7. The outer containing-vessel of a vacuum tube.

1932 F. E. TERMAN *Radio Engineering* xi. 395 The 280 tube has two cathodes and two anodes and so is essentially two half-wave rectifiers enclosed in one envelope. **1959** *Listener* 12 Mar. 454/1 Extra high pressure mercury vapour lamps in quartz envelopes.

8. *attrib.* and *Comb.*, as ***envelope cementer***, ***cutter***, ***flap***, ***folder***; **envelope conditions** *Aeronaut.* (see quot.); **envelope delay** *Electr. Engineering* (see quot. 1940).

1904 *Daily Chron.* 12 Jan. 10/6 Envelope Cementer wanted... Envelope Folder wanted. **1944** *Jrnl. R. Aeronaut. Soc.* XLVIII. 117 Tests at other heights can then be confined to what are termed 'envelope' conditions; that is, the engine conditions which will give the maximum economy at any given speed. **1901** *Daily Chron.* 16 Apr. 8/6 Envelope Cutter. **1940** *Chambers's Techn. Dict.* 301/1 *Envelope delay*, the time taken for the envelope of a signal to travel through a transmission system, without reference to the time taken by the individual components. **1943** F. E. TERMAN *Radio Engineers' Handbk.* v. 443 Envelope delay is of particular importance in tuned amplifiers handling television signals, because any variation in the envelope delay with modulating frequency adds to the total delay error of the system. **1956** AMOS & BIRKINSHAW *Television Engin.* II. i. 20 A more sensitive indication of the seriousness of any phase distortion is given by the slope of the curve itself, usually measured by the slope of the tangent to the curve... The slope of the tangent is the *envelope delay* or *group delay*. **1891** KIPLING *Light that Failed* xi. 191 A letter with a black M. on the envelope flap. **1904** Envelope folder [see *envelope cementer*].

Hence **'envelope**, *v. colloq.* to put (a letter) in an envelope.

1857 DE MORGAN in Graves *Life Sir W. R. Hamilton* III. (1889) 519 You write letters..Lady Hamilton finds them, envelopes them, puts them before you, etc.

envelopment (ɛn'vɛləpmənt). [f. ENVELOP *v.* + -MENT; cf. Fr. *enveloppement.*] The action of enveloping; the state of being enveloped. *concr.* That which envelops; a wrapping, covering. Also *fig.*

1763 TUCKER *Free Will* Pref. (R.), It is become difficult to see any sense at all, through their envelopements. **1831** CARLYLE *Sart. Res.* II. ii, Reverence..springs forth undying from its mean envelopment of Fear. **1842** J. H. NEWMAN *Ch. of Fathers* 34 Various diseases were cured..by the touch of the holy bodies or their envelopments. **1879** RUTLEY *Stud. Rocks* x. 160 Microscopic envelopments of quartz have been met with in chabasite.

†**en'venom**, *sb. Obs.* In 4 envenyme. [f. next vb.] That which envenoms; a poison.

1377 LANGLAND *P. Pl.* B. II. 14 Orientales and ewages enuenymes to destroye.

envenom (ɛn'vɛnəm), *v.* Forms: α. 4–6 envenim, -ym(e, 4–5 envenem(e, -om, 4 envinim, 5 envemyn, (envemon), 7 envenome, 6– envenom. β. 6 inveneme, (invennom), 7 invenim, -ome, 7–8 invenom. See also ANVENOM. [ME. *envenime-n*, ad. OFr. *envenimer*, f. *en* (see EN-[1]) + OFr. *venim* (mod. *venin*) VENOM:—L. *venēn-um* poison.]

†**1.** *trans.* To venom (a person, an animal); to poison by contact, bite, inoculation, etc. Also *absol.*

c **1300** *K. Alis.* 5611 Addres, guiures [*printed* quinres], and dragouns Wolden this folk mychel and lyte, Envenymen and abite. **1340** *Ayenb.* 26 Þe eddre þet al enuenymeþ. *c* **1400** MAUNDEV. v. (1839) 54 The serpentes byten hem & envenyme hem. *c* **1450** LONELICH *Grail* lii. 240 Thanne sawh he wel that envemyned he was. **1535** MORE *On the Passion* Wks. 1274/1 Being..so sore envenomed with so mani poison spottes. **1665–6** *Phil. Trans.* I. 391 A Toad may envenome outwardly. **1665** *Flagellum; or O. Cromwell* (1672) Pref., That poyson of Asps under his lips which.. will envenome even those of the Species that come near it. **1725** BRADLEY *Fam. Dict.* s.v. *Vives*, Do not touch them with your Fingers, for it will invenom them.

fig. *c* **1380** WYCLIF *Sel. Wks.* III. 272 Weiward disciplis, þat envenymyn and distroien holy Chirche. *c* **1386** CHAUCER *Wife's Prol.* 474 But age, allas! that al wol envenyme. **1612** W. PARKES *Curtaine Dr.* (1876) 6 He in-venomes all the eares that heare him.

2. To put venom or poison on (a weapon, etc.); to taint (the air, ground, etc.) with poison; to render noxious or poisonous. Cf. ENVENOMED *ppl. a.*

c **1325** *Coer de L.* 4349 Envenymyd ther takyl was. **1393** GOWER *Conf.* I. 234 An arwe..Whiche he to-fore had envenimed. *c* **1450** LONELICH *Grail* l. 603 A knyf..the wheche envemyned was. *c* **1500** *Melusine* 161 The king was wounded with a dart enuenymed by the sawdans hand. **1555** EDEN *Decades W. Ind.* III. IX. (Arb.) 177 The women..vse to inueneme their arrowes. **1602** SHAKS. *Ham.* v. ii. 332 The point envenom'd too, Then venome to thy worke. **1616** SURFL. & MARKH. *Country Farm* 291 The Caper-tree inueniming the whole ground, and making of it barren. **1675** TRAHERNE *Chr. Ethics* xxvi. 405 Because the colours are envenomed wherewith he painteth his face. **1871** NAPHEYS *Prev. & Cure Dis.* I. ii. 73 Plants which thus envenom the sweet.

b. To infuse venom or bitterness into (actions, relations, etc.); to impart bitterness to (the feelings or words of a person); to embitter, make virulent.

1533 BELLENDEN *Livy* v. (1822) 395 Knaw ye nocht how thir wageis war invennomit be poisoun of inemyis. **1568** GRAFTON *Chron.* II. 634 Their wordes were swete as sugar, and their thoughtes were all envenomed. **1658** *Lady's Call.* II. §3. 87 It rather envenoms the crime and adds unnaturalness to deceit. **1859** MILL *Liberty* iv. 152 Nothing in the..practice of Christians does more to envenom the hatred of Mahommedans. **1866** FELTON *Anc. & Mod. Gr.* II. viii. 424 The complicated passions that envenomed the strife.

3. *fig.* To impregnate with moral 'venom'; to corrupt, vitiate.

c **1374** CHAUCER *Boeth.* IV. iii. 120 Þe vtteriste wikkednesse ..infectiþ and enuenemyþ hem gretely. *c* **1400** *Rom. Rose* 7474 For men may finde alway sopheme The consequence to enveneme. *c* **1440** *Gesta Rom.* ii. 7 Þe devill had envenemyd all mankynd. **1641** MILTON *Church Discip.* I. (1851) 19 A universall tetter of impurity had invenom'd every part. **1705** STANHOPE *Paraphr.* III. 433 We will hope ..that no Minds so invenom'd can be found. **1883** I. TAYLOR *Fanat.* iv. 71 The imagination..envenomed by hatred.

en'venomed, *ppl. a.* [f. prec. + -ED[1].]

1. †**a.** Of a reptile, insect, etc.: Charged with venom (*obs.*). **b.** Of a weapon, etc.: Smeared with venom. Of air, food, etc.: Poisoned, tainted. **c.** Of a wound: Infected with venom, poisoned.

c **1300** *K. Alis.* 5436 Her bytt envenymed was. *c* **1330** R. BRUNNE *Chron.* (1810) 228 Envenomed knyfe he bare also priuely. **1393** GOWER *Conf.* III. 281 As a morcel envenimed. **1577** tr. *Bullinger's Decades* (1592) 48 The enuenomed bytinges of the Serpents. *c* **1590** MARLOWE *Faust.* vi. 22 Halters and envenom'd steel Are laid before me. **1621** G. SANDYS *Ovid's Met.* III. 47 Th' inuenom'd gore, which from his palate bled. **1667** MILTON *P.L.* II. 543 As when Alcides ..felt th'envenom'd robe. **1695** BLACKMORE *Pr. Arth.* VI. 832 Some only breath th' envenom'd Air, and die. **1708** J. PHILIPS *Cyder* II. 63 Happy Iërne, whose most wholsome Air Poisons envenom'd spiders. **1810** SCOTT *Lady of L.* II. xxxiii, Thy dart Plunged deepest its envenomed smart.

2. *fig.* Chiefly of temper, feelings, etc.: Virulent, malignant, embittered.

c **1375** WYCLIF *Antecrist* in Todd *Three Treat.* (1851) 141 Takyng of temporaltees envenymed. **1647** CLARENDON *Hist. Reb.* (1702) I. v. 425 The reiterated complaints, and invenom'd repetitions. **1649** SELDEN *Laws Eng.* I. lxix. (1739) 180 The invenomed spirits of the Judges of those days. **1781** COWPER *Truth* 159 Of temper as envenomed as an asp. **1821** SHELLEY *Prometh. Unb.* I. i. 289 Till thine Infinity shall be A robe of envenomed agony. **1879** FROUDE *Cæsar* xix. 331 They at least had no sympathy with such envenomed animosities.

†**en'venomer.** *Obs. rare.* In 6 invenomer. One who envenoms.

1598 FLORIO, *Intossicatore*, a poisoner, an inuenomer.

en'venoming, *vbl. sb.* [f. ENVENOM *v.*] The action of the verb ENVENOM. Also *concr.*

c **1386** CHAUCER *Merch. T.* 816 Thy tayl is deth, thurgh thin envenymynge. *c* **1450** LONELICH *Grail* l. 607 The ton was for the envemynenge, þe toþer for scharpnesse. **1627–77** FELTHAM *Resolves* I. xxi. 38 The ways he strews with serpents and invenomings.

†**en'venomize**, *v. Obs. rare*[−1]. [f. EN-[1] + VENOM *sb.* + -IZE.] *trans.* To infect with poison. In quot. *absol.*

1598 TOFTE *Alba* (1880) 85 Fierce Serpents (not milde Doues) enuenomise.

†**en'venomous**, *a. Obs.* In 5 envenymous, 7 invenomous. [ad. OF. *envenimeus*, f. *envenimer* to ENVENOM.] Full of venom; poisonous. *lit.* and *fig.*

a **1420** HOCCLEVE *De Reg. Princ.* (1860) 4918 Her rede and counceile is envenymous. **1475** CAXTON *Jason* 137 Alway machining a right envenymous will. **1597** R. JOHNSON *Seven Champions* II. (N.), [The dragon] stroake with her invenomous wings. **1624** HEYWOOD *Gunaik.* I. 41 She cast an invenomous confection into the fountaine.

en ventre sa mère: see EN *prep.*

enverdure: see EN- *pref.*[1] 1 b.

†**en'vermeil**, *v. Obs.* Also 4 envermail. [ad. OF. *envermeiller*, f. *en* (see EN-[1]) + *vermeil*, *vermeille* vermilion-coloured: see VERMEIL.]

trans. To tinge as with vermilion; to give a ruddy colour to. Hence **envermeiled** *ppl. a.*, roseate, ruddy.

14.. [? LYDG.] *Ball. our Ladie* in *Chaucer's Wks.* (1561) cccxxix b, Uinarie enuermailed, refresher of our blood. **1625–6** MILTON *Death Fair Infant* 1 That lovely dye That did thy cheek envermeil. **1822** BEDDOES *Bride's Tragedy* IV. iii, How blushes open their envermeiled leaves On her fair features.

enveron, enverroun, obs. ff. ENVIRON.

†**en'versed**, *ppl. a. Obs. rare*[−1]. [ad. OF. *enversé*, pa. pple. of *enverser* to overturn.]

Inverted.

a **1648** LD. HERBERT *Poems* (1881) 5 Her Waist's an envers'd Pyramis.

envest, obs. form of INVEST.

†**'envesure.** *Obs. rare*[−1]. [a. OF. *enveisure*, f. *enveisier* to divert. Cf. ENVOISIES.] Game, play.

c **1300** *K. Alis.* 5543 Hy lowghen and maden enuesure [*printed* ennesure].

envey, obs. form of INVEIGH.

envia'bility. [f. ENVIABLE *a.*: see -ITY.] The character or quality of being enviable.

a **1916** H. JAMES *Middle Years* (1917) 74 The enviability of certain complacencies of faith and taste. **1930** *Times Lit. Suppl.* 16 Oct. 839/3 The enviability or ultimate fatuity of his pleasant life.

enviable ('ɛnvɪəb(ə)l), *a.* [f. ENVY *v.* + -ABLE.] That is to be envied.

1602 CAREW *Cornwall* (J.), An enviable mediocrity of fortune. **1779** BURKE *Corr.* (1844) II. 278 My situation is anything rather than enviable. **1812** G. CHALMERS *Dom. Econ. Gt. Brit.* 293 The foe never sets his foot on this enviable island. **1855** MACAULAY *Hist. Eng.* III. 3 William was, at this time one of the most enviable of human beings. **1860** TYNDALL *Glac.* I. §27. 196 Unlike the enviable ostrich, I cannot shut my eyes to danger when it is near.

Hence **'enviableness**, *rare*, the quality or condition of being enviable. **'enviably** *adv.*, in an enviable manner or degree.

1833 HT. MARTINEAU *Charmed Sea* iii. 36 The enviableness of her calm state of feeling. **1823** J. BADCOCK *Dom. Amusem.* 140 That enviably brilliant covering. **1855** MACAULAY *Hist. Eng.* IV. 380 There was scarcely in all Europe a residence more enviably situated.

envidious, obs. form of INVIDIOUS.

envied ('ɛnvɪd), *ppl. a.* [f. ENVY *v.* + -ED[1].] That is the object of envy.

1631 T. MAY tr. Barclay *Mirrour of Mindes* I. 187 Hee himselfe was glad to haue himselfe saluted..by noe high or envied names, but sometimes plaine William. **1667** MILTON *P.L.* II. 244 Our envied Sovran. **1750** GRAY *Elegy* 24 No children..climb his knees the envied kiss to share. **1815** *Scribbleomania* 59 The envied honours of Parnassus. *a* **1859** MACAULAY *Hist. Eng.* V. 199 Grandees who had the envied privilege of going in coaches and four through the streets.

absol. **1685** *Gracian's Courtier's Orac.* 151 Enviers die as often as they hear the praises of the Envied revive. *c* **1800** K. WHITE *Lett.* (1837) 263 Yet it often happens that the condition of the envier is happier than that of the envied. **1886** BURTON *Arab. Nts.* I. 107 It would besit thee to pardon me even as the Envied pardoned the Envier.

envier ('ɛnvɪə(r)). Also 6 enviour, 6–7 envyer. [f. ENVY *v.* + -ER¹ (earlier -OUR.).] One who envies.

1509 BARCLAY *Shyp of Folys* (1874) I. 8 Gluttons, wasters, enuiours, enchantours. **1555** EDEN *Decades W. Ind.* III. IX. (Arb.) 175 These malycious enuyers of other mens trauayles. **1606** BACON in *Four C. Eng. Lett.* 40 You are great, and therefore have the more enviers. **1630–88** tr. *Camden's Hist. Eliz.* IV. 603 He was presently censured as an envier of the Earl's honour. *a* **1762** LADY M. W. MONTAGUE *Let. Mrs. Hewet* xcii. 152 Never bride had fewer enviers, the ..man is so..detestable. **1841** D'ISRAELI *Amen. Lit.* (1867) 316 Its opulence was an object it could not conceal from its enviers. **1874** MOTLEY *Barneveld* II. xv. 180 The enviers of our peace and tranquillity.

envigor, var. INVIGOUR *v. Obs.* to invigorate.

en ville: see EN *prep.*

†**en'vined**, *ppl. a. Obs. rare*⁻¹. In 4 envyned. [ad. Fr. *enviné*, f. *en* (see EN-¹) + *vin* wine.] Stored with wine.

c **1386** CHAUCER *Prol.* 342 A bettre envyned man was nowher noon.

envineyard: see EN- *pref.*¹ 2.

enviour, obs. form of ENVIER.

envious ('ɛnvɪəs), *a.* Forms: 4–6 envyous(e, 5 -ose, (4 enviose, -vios, -vius, -vyus, -wius, 5 enviyus, -vyows, *pl.* envyeusis), 4– envious. Also 5 invyowse. [a. AF. *envious*, OF. *envieus, -vius* (mod.F. *envieux*) = Pr. *envejos, envios*, Cat. *envejos*, Pg. *invejoso*, Sp. *envidioso*, It. *invidioso*:—L. *invidiōsus*, f. *invidia* ENVY.]

1. Full of envy, affected or actuated by envy; vexed or discontented at the good fortune or qualities of another. Const. †*against*, †*at*, *of*, †*to* with *sb.* or *inf.*

a **1300** *Cursor M.* 27658 (Cott.) Þe enuius man ai lufes he leste þam þat he wate er moste honeste. *c* **1386** CHAUCER *Man of Lawes T.* 267 O Sathan envyous. *a* **1450** *Knt. de la Tour* (1868) 53 There be other that be envious to see other in gretter degre thanne they. **1526** *Pilgr. Pref.* (W. de W. 1531) 78 And..the enuyous man, for to do a displeasure to his ennemy, wyll suffre rebuke and blame. **1611** BIBLE *Prov.* xxiv. 19 Neither be thou enuious at the wicked. **1636** *Ariana* 328 They thought it envious against their repose, to have shed so much as a teare for them. **1697** DRYDEN *Virg. Past.* vii. 37 If he blast my Muse with envious Praise. **1842** LYTTON *Zanoni* 28 Our good Loredano is envious of my diamond. **1872** MORLEY *Voltaire* (1886) 108 Envious scribes in his life-time taunted him with avarice.

absol. *a* **1300** *Cursor M.* 27706 (Cott.) Forþi sais Senec on þe envius, Quine, etc. **1340** *Ayenb.* 28 Vor þe more þet þe guodes byeþ greate, þe more zorȝeþ þe enuious. **1816** BYRON *Monody Death Sheridan*, The envious who but breathe in others' pain. **1846** RUSKIN *Mod. Paint.* I. Pref. (ed. 2) 14 The envious, because they like not the sound of a living man's praise.

†**2.** Full of ill-will; malicious, spiteful. *Obs.* 'Still current *dial.* in Suffolk' (F. Hall).

c **1330** R. BRUNNE (1810) 180 Grete scathe..Com tille Kyng R. for þat envios sawe. *c* **1430** LYDG. *Chorle & Byrde* (1818) 12 Hit maketh accorde betwene folk envyous. **1579** LYLY *Euphues* (Arb.) 40 Who more envious than Tymon denouncing all humaine societie. **1673** PENN *Chr. Quaker* iv. 531 Envious Displeasure against an Harmless Suffering People. *a* **1713** ELLWOOD *Autobiog.* (1765) 384 Printed by one of his Party with very envious Reflections upon it.

†**3.** Full of emulation; emulous. Const. *of.*

a **1300** *Floriz & Bl.* 356 For he is suþe couetus And at þescheker enuius. *a* **1450** *Knt. de la Tour* (1868) 150 Thei be envyeusis whiche shalle goo furst up on the offerande. **1594** T. B. *La Primaud. Fr. Acad.* II. 318 Be enuious of the best gifts. **1821** KEATS *Lamia* 217 Lycius Charioting foremost in the envious race.

†**4.** Grudging, parsimonious, sparing, excessively careful. *Obs.*

1580 LYLY *Euphues* (Arb.) 368 Beautie was no niggard of hir slippes in this gardein, and very enuious to other grounds. *a* **1667** JER. TAYLOR (W.), No men are so envious of their health.

†**5.** Calculated to excite ill-will; invidious; odious. *Obs.*

1635 R. N. tr. *Camden's Hist. Eliz.* (ed. 3) I. 90 Which sect began presently to be knowne by the envious name of Puritans. **1640** BP. HALL *Episc.* Ep. Ded. 5 Hath put my pen upon this envious, but necessarie taske.

†**6.** That is or may be an object of envy; enviable.

1590 SPENSER *F.Q.* I. iv. 39 He to him lept, and that same envious gage Of victors glory from him snatcht away. **1651** *Reliq. Wotton.* 69 A glorious harvest..which could not but have made an envious addition. **1665** PEPYS *Diary* 8 Dec. (ed. Bright) III. 327 So envious a place.

7. *Comb.*, as ***envious-hearted.***

1873 L. WALLACE *Fair God* II. vii. 128 Time was when no envious-hearted knave could have made him believe, etc.

enviously ('ɛnvɪəslɪ), *adv.* [f. prec. + -LY².] In an envious manner.

†**a.** In a spirit of emulation or rivalry. *Obs.* **b.** Maliciously, spitefully, grudgingly.

c **1350** *Will. Palerne* 1129 Burnes he sent Enuiously to þemperour & egged him swiþe Bi a certayne day bataile to a-bide. *c* **1430** LYDG. *Story Thebes* in *Chaucer's Wks.* (1561) ccclxxv b, They on Greekes enuiously gan to shout. **1509** FISHER 7 *Penit. Ps.* xxxviii. II. Wks. 86 All they..enuyously haue conspyred the deth of a symple persone. **1602** SHAKS. *Ham.* IV. v. 6 She..beats her heart, Spurnes enuiously at Strawes. **1639** FULLER *Holy War* III. viii. (1840) 130 The cross enviously concealed by the Turks. **1664** H. MORE *Myst. Iniq.* iii. 7 Those Doctrines of Devils, which they enviously and insultingly entangled poor mankind withall.

enviousness ('ɛnvɪəsnɪs). [f. as prec. + -NESS.] The quality of being envious.

1561 T. NORTON *Calvin's Inst.* III. 227 Nor will with enuiousnesse against god complayne of his Fortune. **1562** TURNER *Baths* I b, For enuiusnes [the Physicians] wold not send the sik folk..unto these bathes. **1628** WITHER *Brit. Rememb.* III. 941 A spightfull enviousnesse. **1652** SIR A. COCKAYNE tr. *Cassandra* I. 62 Courtiers, who, forcing the enviousnesse of their nature, lookt upon his fortune with joy and applause.

†'**enviousty.** *Obs. rare*⁻¹. [f. as prec. + -TY.] = ENVIOUSNESS.

1382 WYCLIF *Ecclus.* xxvi. 6 The dyuyseoun [*v.r.* envyouste] of the cite, and the gederyng togidere of the puple.

†**en'vire**, *v. Obs.* Also ? 4 envere, 6 envoyre. [a. OF. *envire-r* (occuring in sense 'to turn round') f. *en* (see EN-¹) + *virer* to VEER.] = ENVIRON *v.* (It is doubtful whether the first quot. belongs here.)

[? *a* **1400** *Morte Arth.* 1694 Myne armez are of ancestrye enueryde with lordez]. **14..** LYDG. *MS. Soc. Antiq.* 134 (Halliw.) Of the Holy Gost rounde aboute envirid. **1513** BRADSHAW *St. Werburge* (1848) 137 The sayd abbay Enuired with walles myghty to assay. *c* **1530** LD. BERNERS *Arth. Lyt. Bryt.* (1814) 252 Enuoyred with greate and depe dyches ful of water.

environ, *sb. Obs.* in *sing.* In 4 envyroun, -own. [a. OF. sing. *environ* (subsequently a mod.F. pl. *environs*), f. the adv.: see ENVIRON *adv.*]

†**1.** In ME. *sing.* Compass, circuit. Only in phrases *by, in environ, by environ of*; = F. *à l'environ* (*de*).

1382 WYCLIF *Gen.* xxiii. 17 The feeld..as wel it as the spelunk and alle the trees of it, in alle the termes of it bi enuyroun. —— *Ex.* vii. 24 Alle the Egipciens deluyden bi enuyroun of the floode. —— *Mark* vi. 6 And he wente aboute castelis in enuyrown, techinge.

2. In mod. Eng. *pl.* **environs** (ɛn'vaɪrənz, 'ɛnvɪrənz). The outskirts, surrounding districts, of a town.

1665 EVELYN *Mem.* (1857) I. 419 The pestilence still increasing in London and its Environs. **1750** CHESTERF. *Lett.* III. ccxxix. 43 When you go to Genoa, pray observe carefully all the *environs* of it. **1772–84** COOK *Voy.* (1790) V. 1808 The environs of Hudson's Bay. **1831** SIR J. SINCLAIR *Corr.* II. 184 The neighbourhood of Brock is quite enchanting..with its painted houses..and delightful environs. **1847–8** H. MILLER *First Impr.* xix. (1857) 331 Without having once seen the sun shine on the city or its environs.

b. *transf.* in *sing. rare*⁻¹. Surrounding.

1823 BYRON *Let. Ld. Blessington* 14 Apr., The peccant part and its immediate environ are..black.

environ (ɛn'vaɪrən), *v.* Forms: *α.* 4–5 enviroun, -vyroun, (4–5 enverom, -on), 4–7 envyron, (4 envyrown, -weron, 5 enverroun, -wyroun, 5–6 environne), 4– environ. *β.* 6 invyroun, -veron, (6–7 invi(e)orn), 6–8 inviron. [a. F. *environ-ner* (in AF. *c* 1300), f. *environ* round about: see ENVIRON *adv.*]

1. *trans.* Of things: To form a ring round, surround, encircle. Also *fig.* of circumstances or conditions, *esp.* (with notion of 2 b) of dangers, troubles, etc.

c **1400** MAUNDEV. v. (1839) 45 This Ryvere.. envyronnethe all Ethiop. *c* **1430** LYDG. *Compl. Bl. Knt.* xii, The bankys rounde, the welle environyng. **15..** in *Athenæum* (1870) 6 Aug. 181 All invieorned on the South parte with a freshe water ryver. **1631** GOUGE *God's Arrows* III. xii. 208 Ilands environed by the sea, with good shippings. **1670–98** LASSELS *Voy. Italy* II. 21 The circle of white marble pavement which environeth the altar of St. Peter. **1681** COLVIL *Whigs Supplic.* (1751) 24 A cowl lin'd with iron, Which did his temples so inviron. **1720** WELTON *Suff. Son of God* I. vi. 117 Quickening Flames..Environ and surround me. **1816** W. HOLLAR *Holbein's Dance of Death* 69 A great cloister, environning a plot of ground. **1872** JENKINSON *Guide Eng. Lakes* (1879) 24 A quiet and fertile spot, environed by green meadows.

fig. **1382** WYCLIF *Ecclus.* li. 5 Manye tribulaciouns that enuyrouneden me. *a* **1400–50** *Alexander* 4632 Mekill variaunce of vertus enveronis oure saules. **1563** FOXE *A. & M.* III. 297 Hypocrisie, arrogancy, and obstinate security environ me. **1604** T. WRIGHT *Pass.* v. §4. 191 A number of sound and substantiall reasons..environ the question proposed on every side. **1663** BUTLER *Hud.* I. iii. 1 What Perils do inviron The Man that meddles with cold Iron! **1686** *Voy. Emp. China into W. Tartary* in *Misc. Cur.* (1708) III. 199 All the Marks of Grandure, with which he was invirorned at the Court at Pekin. **1851** D. MITCHELL *Fresh Gleanings* 106 Whatever pleasant or painful circumstances may environ me.

†**b.** To include, take in (a certain space). *Obs.*

1570–6 LAMBARDE *Peramb. Kent* (1826) 166 The ruines of which building..do environne almost ten acres of grounde. **1613** PURCHAS *Pilgr.* (1864) 18 The whole Monarchie en-uironeth nine hundred leagues.

c. To surround, encircle, encompass *with* anything. Also *fig.* Chiefly *pass.*

1382 WYCLIF *Luke* xix. 43 Thin enemyes schulen enuyroune thee with pale. *c* **1400** MAUNDEV. xxvii. (1839) 278 And alle envyround with ston of Jaspre. **1536** *Act 26 Henry VIII*, c. 12 A Parke, walled and envyronned with brycke and stone. **1590** SIR J. SMYTH *Disc. Weapons* 13 Where..they may environ themselves with water on everie side. **1632** LITHGOW *Trav.* II. 67 Peloponnesus..is all inuironed with the sea, saue onely at a narrow strait. **1658** EVELYN *Fr. Gard.* II. §2. (1675) 161 Inviron them with dung to blanch them. **1701** LAW *Counc. Trade* (1789) 105 Our coasts were..invironed and surrounded with fish. **1748** ANSON *Voy.* II. xii. 261 The harbour is invironed on all sides ..with high mountains. **1864** BOUTELL *Heraldry Hist. & Pop.* xxiv. (ed. 3) 407 The Royal Shield of England environed with the fleurs de lys of France.

fig. **1675** TRAHERNE *Chr. Ethics* 384 The holy soul of a quiet man is..invironed with its own repose. **1794** MRS. RADCLIFFE *Myst. Udolpho* xvi, Were environed with delights both from nature and art. **1847** J. WILSON *Chr. North* (1857) I. 422 Our boyhood was environed with the beautiful. **1855** MILMAN *Lat. Chr.* (1864) II. iii. 81 That enthusiasm in himself which would environ him with wonder.

2. Of persons: To form a ring round, stand round, throng; to be in attendance upon; to be stationed round, as guards. Also, To surround †*of*, *with* (persons).

1382 WYCLIF *Zech.* ix. 8 Any y shal enuyroune myn hous of these that holden knyȝthode to me. **1393** GOWER *Conf.* III. 253 There founden they..Lucrece..all environed With women. **1490** CAXTON *Eneydos* lix. 158 We enuyronne hym rounde aboute wyth goode men of armes. **1552** LYNDESAY *Monarche* 5569 The Angellis of the Ordoris Nyne Inueron sall that throne Diuyne. **1598** YONG *Diana* 94 Enuironed rounde about with a troupe of Nymphes. **1670** COTTON *Espernon* II. VIII. 350 He dy'd environ'd by three of his Children, several Divines, and all his Domestick Servants. **1855** MILMAN *Lat. Chr.* (1864) II. III. vii. 151 Every Christian was environed with a world of invisible beings.

b. To surround with hostile intention; to beset; to beleaguer (a city, fortress, etc.). Also, To beset *with.*

1375 BARBOUR *Bruce* XI. 640 All enveronyt vith fayis is he. *a* **1400–50** *Alexander* 3617 To enverom alle þe vaward of all þe vile yndes. **1475** CAXTON *Jason* (1477) 17 Jason was enuironned and assayled on alle sides. **1568** GRAFTON *Chron.* II. 748 The Capitaynes..planted a strong siege, and environed it [the Castell] round about. **1603** KNOLLES *Hist. Turks* (1638) 92 They hauing long before so streitly inuironed the city. **1761–2** HUME *Hist. Eng.* (1806) IV. lix. 459 Colonel Pride..had environed the house with two regiments.

3. To surround on all sides, envelop, enclose. Now chiefly of the atmosphere, light, etc. †Formerly also, to wrap up, clothe; to screen or conceal *from.*

1413 LYDG. *Pilgr. Sowle* I. iii. (1483) 4 The Centre of the erthe was wonder derck in itself and was aboute enuyronned by less derke mater and lesse. **1474** CAXTON *Chesse* 65 Al the thynges that the ayer goth about and enuyronneth. **1483** —— *Gold. Leg.* 237/1 He sawe an auncient man.. enuyronned in a whyte mantel. **1571** DIGGES *Pantom.* IV. xxv. Hhj, One comprehending sphere inuironeth all his angles. **1607** DEKKER *Hist. Sir T. Wyatt* Wks. (1873) III. 88 Thus like a Nun..Liue I inuirond in a house of stone. **1659** LEAK *Waterwks.* 3 The Pestle..well invironed with leather. **1699** POMFRET *Reason* 155 'Tis now environ'd from our eyes. **1846** LANDOR *Hellenics* Wks. (1868) II. 482 Gravely-gladsome light environed them. **1860** TYNDALL *Glac.* I. §11. 73 We were environed by an atmosphere of perfect purity.

†**4.** To describe a circle or make a circuit round; to go round in a circle. *Obs.*

1340 HAMPOLE *Pr. Consc.* 7608 And þe heven þat þe erth envirouns. *c* **1400** MAUNDEV. (1839) xvii. 182 Men may envirowne all the Erthe of alle the World, as well undre as aboven and turnen aȝen to his Contree. **1483** CAXTON *Gold. Leg.* 34/2 By envyronyng or goyng aboute the aultre. **1570–6** LAMBARDE *Peramb. Kent* (1862) 311, I will begin at the North east corner..and from thence environ the whole Bishopricke. **1647** LILLY *Chr. Astrol.* cxliiii. 617 The Luminaries [being] in angles not environed of the Planets.

†**b.** To travel about (a country, etc.). *Obs.*

1382 WYCLIF *1 Tim.* v. 13 Thei ydel lernen for to enuyrowne housis. *c* **1400** MAUNDEV. (Roxb.) Pref. 1 It lyked him..to enuirun þat land with his blissed fete. *c* **1400** *Rom. Rose* 7019 We envyroune bothe londe and se.

†**en'viron**, *adv.* and *prep. Obs.* Forms: *α.* 4–6 enviroun(e, 4–5 envyron, 6 enveron, 5– environ. *β.* 4 in viroun, 6 invirone, 7 inviron. [a. Fr. *environ*, f. *en* in + OF. **viron* circuit, related to *virer* to VEER. Cf. Pr. *en viro* of same meaning.]

A. *adv.* Round about; in the neighbourhood.

c **1375** WYCLIF *Serm.* Sel. Wks. II. 311 In viroun and wiþinne þei weren ful of iȝen. *c* **1385** CHAUCER *L.G.W.* Prol. 300 And with that word, a compas enviroun They sitten hem ful softely adoun. **1436** *Pol. Poems* II. (1859) 157 Exhortynge alle Englande to kepe the see enviroun. **1513** DOUGLAS *Æneis* XIII. v. 4 And with large clamour fillis inveroun Thair myndis all. **1519** *Four Elements* Interlude in Hazl. *Dodsley* I. 6 Which doth illumine the world environ. **1600** FAIRFAX *Tasso* II. lxxx. 35 Lord Godfreyes eie three times enuiron goes.

B. *prep.* Round, about.

1393 GOWER *Conf.* III. 76 The Serpent..Went environ the shelle aboute. *c* **1400** *Rom. Rose* 3618 He ladde me..Alle environ the vergere. *c* **1450** *Merlin* vii. 113 Somme seide that thei wolde ley siege environ the baile.

environage (ɛn'vaɪrənɪdʒ). *rare.* [f. ENVIRON + -AGE.] The assemblage of surrounding objects or circumstances; surroundings.

1836 *New Monthly Mag.* XLVIII. 320 The slightest changes in the environage of the party. **1838** *Ibid.* LIII. 122 That which is rendered indecent by the circumstances of its environage.

environal (ɛn'vaɪrənəl), *a. rare.* [f. ENVIRON + -AL¹.] (See quot.)

1888 GULLICK in *Linn. Soc. Jrnl.* XX. 222 Environal Segregation is Segregation arising from the relations in which the organism stands to the environment.

en'vironed, *ppl. a. Her.* [f. ENVIRON *v.* + -ED[1].] Of a charge: Set round with other objects, as a head with a wreath, a lion with bezants, etc.

Perh. never in actual Eng. use. In Chambers only as transl. Fr. *environné* as a term of French heraldry.

1727-51 in CHAMBERS *Cycl.* **1847** in CRAIG. [**1864**: see ENVIRON *v.* 1 c.] In mod. Dicts.

† **enviro'nee,** *adv.* and *prep. Obs. rare.* [app. the writer's blunder for ENVIRON, after Fr. *environné* pa. pple.; see ENVIRON *v.*] Round about.

c **1475** *Partenay* 5480 Figured knightis were enuironee. *Ibid.* 3874 Thre tymes the castell enuironee [she] went. *Ibid.* 2717.

† **en'vironer.** *Obs.* [f. ENVIRON *v.* + -ER[1].] One who, or that which, environs or surrounds.

1562 BULLEYN *Bk. Simples* 12 a, The Ocian..seperature of landes, environer of Ilandes.

environing (ɛn'vaɪrənɪŋ), *vbl. sb.* [f. ENVIRON *v.* + -ING[1].] The action of the verb ENVIRON. Also *concr.* That which environs or surrounds; the circumference.

c **1374** CHAUCER *Boeth.* II. vii. 56 Al þe envyronynge of þe erþe aboute ne halt but þe resoun of a prykke at regard of þe gretnesse of heuene. *Ibid.* V. iv. 165 But þe eye of intelligence is heyȝer for it sourmounteþ þe environynge of þe vniuersite, etc. **1656** HEYLIN *Surv. France* 34 The principal environings are made by the Seine and the Marne. **1879** *Athenæum* 11 Oct. 476/2 In the midst of his customary environings the Duc de Richelieu receives a visit from a young lady.

environing (ɛn'vaɪrənɪŋ), *ppl. a.* [f. ENVIRON *v.* + -ING[2].] That environs, surrounds, envelops.

1641-1706 EVELYN *Mem.* (1819) I. 136 Full of sweet shrubbs in the invironing hedges. **1832** DOWNES *Lett. Cont. Countries* I. 72 Blocks of granite, detached from the environing heights. **1860** RUSKIN *Mod. Paint.* V. VII. ii. § 4. 113 London..loses at least two out of three sunrises, owing to the environing smoke. **1951** D. RIESMAN in A. W. Loos *Relig. Faith & World Culture* 62 We can distinguish conceptually between the needs of society (as a system of social organization) and those of the environing group (as a system of psychological ties and expectations). **1957** G. CLARK *Archæol. & Society* (ed. 3) i. 36 Their environing habitats and biomes.

environment (ɛn'vaɪrənmənt). [f. ENVIRON *v.* + -MENT. Cf. OF. *environnement.*]

1. The action of environing; the state of being environed. (With quot. cf. ENVIRON *v.* 4.)

1603 HOLLAND *Plutarch's Mor.* 1009, I wot not what circumplexions and environments [*orig.* περιελεύσεις].

2. *concr.* **a.** That which environs; the objects or the region surrounding anything.

1830 CARLYLE in *For. Rev. & Cont. Miscell.* v. 34 Baireuth, with its kind picturesque environment. **1831** CARLYLE *Sart. Res.* II. i. (1871) 56 The whole habitation and environment looked ever trim and gay. **1867** FROUDE *Short Stud.* (1883) IV. §2. i. 166 The flame..burnt hot in my own immediate environment. **1872** BLACKIE *Lays Highl.* Introd. 37 The environment of this loch put me in mind of Grasmere. **1956** P. S. SEARS in W. L. Thomas *Man's Role in changing Face of Earth* II. 473/1 The situation is clouded by a widespread confidence that this impact of man upon environment can continue indefinitely. **1967** K. MELLANBY *Pesticides & Pollution* ii. 31 Perhaps the most obvious way in which man has contaminated his environment is by polluting the air with smoke. **1968** *Biol. Conservation* I. 70/1 EDF is attempting to establish..a body of common law under which the general public can assert its constitutional right to a viable, minimally-degraded, environment.

fig. **1862** SHIRLEY *Nugæ Crit.* 278 What is poetic in the story is disengaged from its casual environment. **1870** M. CONWAY *Earthw. Pilgr.* xxv. 300 Every belief has an environment of related beliefs.

b. *esp.* The conditions under which any person or thing lives or is developed; the sum-total of influences which modify and determine the development of life or character.

1827 CARLYLE *Misc., Goethe* (1869) 192 In such an element with such an environment of circumstances. **1855** H. SPENCER *Princ. Psychol.* (1872) I. III. iii. 301 The division of the environment into two halves, soil and air. **1874** SIDGWICK *Meth. Ethics.* v. 167 The organism is continually adapted to its environment. **1881** ROMANES in *Fortn. Rev.* Dec. 740 Environment—or the sum total of the external conditions of life.

c. *spec.* in *Phonetics.* (See also quot. 1951.)

1951 Z. S. HARRIS *Methods Struct. Ling.* ii. 15 The environment or position of an element consists of the neighbourhood, within an utterance, of elements which have been set up on the basis of the same fundamental procedures which were used in setting up the element in question. **1960** *Medium Ævum* XXIX. 27 There was evidently a phonemic distinction between forms which ultimately had the assibilated consonant and those which did not, even in the environment of front vowels. **1963** *Amer. Speech* XXXVIII. 50 Consonant and pause probably made up just about this percentage of environments for all finals. **1966** *Ibid.* XLI. 258 In all other phonetic environments.

d. *Art.* A large structure designed to be experienced and enjoyed as a work of art with all (or most) of one's senses while surrounded by it, rather than from outside.

1962 *Listener* 5 Apr. 603/3 Last summer, at the Martha Jackson gallery in New York, there was an exhibition of 'environments, situations, places'. **1970** *New Yorker* 3 Oct. 93/1 About the only idea that everyone present did agree on was Whitman's suggestion that the Pepsi pavilion be an 'environment' in which visitors could create their own experience. **1977** *Times* 19 Aug. 12/5 In the jargon of modern art, an environment is a work of environmental art: a form of art that encompasses the spectator instead of confronting him with a fixed image or object. **1979** *United States 1980/81* (Penguin Travel Guides) 427 Along Haight Street the trees are decorated with Japanese parasols to create 'environments'.

3. *attrib.*, as ***environment area, control, minister***.

1963 *Daily Tel.* 28 Nov. 16/2 The future pattern of cities should be conceived as a patchwork of 'environment areas' of residence, commerce or industry from which traffic other than that concerned with the area would be excluded. **1968** *Listener* 26 Sept. 393/2 A house to Bucky is an environment control. **1970** *Times* 27 Oct. 2/7 (*heading*) Mr. Walker defines role of environment minister.

environmental (ɛn,vaɪrən'mɛntəl), *a.* [f. prec. + -AL[1].]

1. Of or pertaining to environments or the environment.

1887 *Athenæum* 7 May 611/3 The external or environmental explanation of evolution. **1891** *Blackw. Mag.* CL. 853/1 Some general environmental cause appears to be necessary for the explanation of the facts. **1902** W. JAMES *Var. Relig. Exper.* xiv. 360 Utopian dreams of social justice ..are, in spite of their impracticability and non-adaptation to present environmental conditions, analogous to the saint's belief in an existent kingdom of heaven. **1917** A. S. PRINGLE-PATTISON *Idea of God* 75 Terms like stimulus, response, behaviour, all imply the notion of selection, the power of adaptation to environmental change. **1928** R. N. CHAPMAN in *Ecology* IX. 114 It seems evident that we have in nature a system in which the potential rate of reproduction of the animal is pitted against the resistance of the environment, and that the quantity of organisms which may be found is a result of the balance between the biotic potential or the potential rate of reproduction, and the environmental resistance. **1945** KOESTLER *Yogi & Commissar* III. ii. 171 The socialist attitude to criminology, based on environmental psychology. **1950** *New Biol.* VIII. 18 Any peculiar character induced in a parent by special environmental conditions does not appear in the offspring, unless the same environmental conditions are reproduced. Non-hereditary variation due to external conditions is known as environmental variation. **1957** *Financial Times Ann. Rev. Brit. Industry* 85/5 This raises a question wider than occupational safety—namely environmental safety. **1962** *Listener* 24 May 903/1 There must be a proper relationship between the traffic capacity of the main distributory system and the capacity of the intervening areas (which for convenience I call the 'environmental areas'). *Ibid.* 30 Aug. 304/1 Allied to the earth sciences are the environmental sciences. Meteorological forecasts will be greatly improved in the future. **1967** K. MELLANBY *Pesticides & Pollution* i. 15 The rather special case of pesticides, which have recently been shown to constitute such an important contribution to environmental pollution. **1970** P. R. & A. H. EHRLICH *Population, Resources, Environment* xi. 275 Environmental consulting firms have begun to appear. **1970** *New Yorker* 15 Aug. 42/1 Under its control is an environmental-health commission.

2. Special collocations: **environmental engineer**, one who specializes in controlling damage to the environment caused by pollution and other hazards (see also quot. 1972); also **environmental engineering**.

c **1962** D. R. SCOTT in *Proc. Internat. HEVAC Conf. Heating, Ventilating & Air Conditioning* 19/1 Emergence of new technologist: the Environmental Engineer, who will take his specialist place with the civil, mechanical, electrical and chemical engineers. **1972** *Accountant* 21 Sept. 361/1 On the front cover of the report Young, Austen and Young describe themselves as 'Environmental Engineers', which seems to be an increasingly popular form of description for what used to be called heating and ventilating engineers. *c* **1971** *Loughborough Univ. of Technol. Cal. 1971-72* 90 The undergraduate courses offered by each School of Studies are: *School of Engineering* Aeronautical Engineering and Design..Civil Engineering..Environmental Engineering ..[etc.]. **1980** *Engin. News-Rec.* 23 Oct. 20/1 Forces of the marketplace cannot fill the need for environmental engineers..because 53% of the environmental work force is employed by government or educational institutions.

Hence **environ'mentally** *adv.*, with reference to or by means of (one's or the) environment.

1884 *Mind* July 338 Environmentally-initiated Sensations are classified according to the nature of the agent by which they are aroused. **1918** *Times Lit. Suppl.* 2 May 205/1 A cell may environmentally acquire a new property and keep it. **1928** *Daily Tel.* 21 Aug. 13/1 If you cannot indict a nation, neither can you fully describe a nation, environmentally or spiritually. **1958** *Punch* 12 Feb. 238/2 Both..knew that the most important thing in life—it is something we first heard of from the Americans—is to get 'environmentally well-adjusted'. **1965** *Language* XLI. 277 An environmentally conditioned allophone of terminal fade.

en,viron'mentalism. [f. ENVIRONMENTAL *a.* + -ISM.] A theory of the primary influence of environment on the development of a person or group.

1923 A. A. GOLDENWEISER *Early Civilization* xiv. 292 Attempts to interpret forms of civilization..by environmental conditions... The staunch environmentalism of Buckle still has its charms for many of his readers. **1931** *Encycl. Social Sci.* V. 561/1 Environmentalism is the tendency to stress the importance of physical, biological, psychological or cultural environment as a factor influencing the structure or behavior of animals, including man. **1957** K. A. WITTFOGEL *Oriental Despotism* i. 11 Static theories of environmentalism.

en,viron'mentalist, *sb.* (and *a.*) [f. as prec. + -IST.] **A.** *sb.* One who believes in or promotes the principles or precepts of environmentalism; also, one who is concerned with the preservation of the environment (from pollution, etc.).

1916 *Amer. Jrnl. Sociol.* XXI. 628 The environmentalist will often agree with the anti-environmentalist that certain changes in a culture may be due..to certain cultural features ..but, objects the environmentalist, these cultural features were, in their turn, produced by the physical environment. **1925** F. THOMAS *Environmental Basis of Society* xi. 288 The environmentalist holds, for example, that the snow house of the Eskimo is determined by the surrounding Arctic environment. **1936** *Nature* 26 Sept. 530/1 Whether our outlook be mainly that of the eugenist or that of the environmentalist, we must not 'cease from mental fight' until we have..'built Jerusalem in England's green and pleasant land'. **1940** R. S. WOODWORTH *Psychol.* (ed. 12) vii. 225 The age-long dispute between the hereditarians and the environmentalists. **1941** J. S. HUXLEY *Uniqueness of Man* ii. 39 Sentimental environmentalists, who adhered to the crudest form of Lamarckism. **1959** *Archit. Rev.* CXXV. 304/2 The people are the Environmentalists... Their means of expression are the relationships between buildings and between spaces, and the element in which they work is time. **1970** *New Yorker* 9 May 33/2 Dr. Robert N. Rickles, a thirty-four-year-old chemist and an environmentalist,.. took the helm of the city's Department of Air Resources last month. **1970** *Nature* 15 Aug. 655/2 The project to build a supersonic transport has run into renewed complaints from the environmentalists.

B. *adj.* Of, pertaining to, or relating to environmentalism.

1934 in WEBSTER. **1952** W. SPROTT *Social Psychol.* II. viii. 147 Blackburn who champions the environmentalist position shows that..it is only among the poorer classes that the negative correlation is significant.

Also **en,viron,menta'listic** *a.*

1941 *Natural Hist.* Feb. 112 The truths of environmentalism...serve Doctor Peattie well in this revival of the environmentalistic philosophy. **1962** H. J. EYSENCK *Know your own I.Q.* 36 This method of investigation..favours the hereditary rather than the environmentalistic point of view.

† **en'vironry.** *Obs.* [f. ENVIRON + -RY.] = ENVIRONMENT.

1600 TOURNEUR *Transf. Met.* (1878) Prol. 28 The azure-colour'd skie, Is now transform'd to hel's environrie. *Ibid.* xxi. 142 Did make her temples' rich environrie.

environs: see ENVIRON *sb.*

† **en'virtue,** *v. Obs.* Also 6 envertue. [a. OF. *(s')envertue-r, s'envirtue-r,* f. *en* (see EN-[1]) + *vertu* virtue; cf. *s'esvertuer,* mod. *s'évertuer.*]

1. *refl.* To exert one's strength; to strive.

1475 CAXTON *Jason* 31 He envertued hym selfe defending. **1480** —— *Ovid's Met.* x. viii, Ypomenes envirtued & enforced hym So moche in th' end that he passed her. *c* **1500** *Melusine* 200 The kyng of Anssay..envertued hym self strong, and made with his handes grete vasselage.

2. *trans.* To endue with virtue.

1692 O. WALKER *Hist. Illustr.* 67 A little cake..which they put into the Serpents mouth, to sanctifie and envirtue it for the recovery of the sick.

envisage (ɛn'vɪzɪdʒ), *v.* [a. Fr. *envisage-r,* f. *en-* (see EN-[1]) + *visage* VISAGE, face.]

1. *trans.* To look in the face of; *fig.* to face (danger, etc.); to look straight at.

1820 KEATS *Hyperion* II. 204 To envisage circumstance, all calm, That is the top of sovereignty. **1823** *New Monthly Mag.* VII. 328 Envisaging his fate With regal valour. **1879** G. MEREDITH *Egoist* II. v. 98 Must I recognize the bitter truth?..I have envisaged it.

2. To obtain a mental view of, set before the mind's eye; to contemplate; *chiefly,* to view or regard under a particular aspect.

1837 HERSCHEL in Babbage *Bridgew. Treat.* App. i. 246 Envisaging the case algebraically. **1837** JERROLD in *New Monthly Mag.* LI. 317 We could not perfectly envisage the atrocity. **1845-6** TRENCH *Huls. Lect.* Ser. II. vi. 238 Men continually envisaged the highest benefits which their souls could attain. **1853** DE MORGAN in Graves *Life Sir W. R. Hamilton* III. (1889) 443 If he [Argand] really envisaged the logarithmic property of the angles, he made a most decisive step. **1855** *Ess. Intuit. Morals* 16 In whatever way we envisaged the moral attributes of God.

b. *Philos.* To perceive by intuition.

1860 MANSEL *Prolegom. Log.* iv. 116 *note,* I have availed myself of the term *envisage,* as the best English equivalent that has yet been proposed to the German *anschauen.* **18..** MCCOSH (Ogilv.), From the very dawn of existence the infant must envisage self, and body acting on self.

3. Of an object: To present itself under a particular aspect. *rare.*

1884 *Pall Mall G.* 10 Oct. 5/1 The New England summer as it envisaged itself to the eyes of Thoreau.

Hence **en'visagement,** the action of presenting (an object) to one's own consciousness. **en'visaging** *vbl. sb.*, the action of the vb. ENVISAGE.

1877 E. CAIRD *Philos. Kant* II. viii. 365 This imaginative envisagement of the categories. **1883** W. SMART *Disciple Plato* 37 It is the envisaging of the one idea.

envision (ɛn'vɪʒən), *v.* [f. EN-[1] + VISION *sb.*] *trans.* To see or foresee as in a vision; to envisage; to visualize. So **en'visioning** *vbl. sb.*

1921 L. STRACHEY *Q. Vict.* vii. 221 His blackest hypochondria had never envisioned quite so miserable a Catastrophe. **1925** *Chambers's Jrnl.* Dec. 800/1 Namitie.. resigned himself apparently to envisioning her in the arms of the perfidious cousin. **1927** *Observer* 15 May 6 Karel Capek has..envisioned a world in which atomic energy, having been harnessed, first provides mankind with a new religion and then sets all the world at war. **1933** J. BAILLIE *And Life*

Everlasting (1934) ii. 24 The indictment is .. that the glories of heaven have always blinded the eyes of those that envisioned them to the more intimate glories of earth. **1938** *Observer* 18 Dec. 11/2 Mr. Houghton .. is addicted to words like 'envisioning' which are not to be found in Webster or in the New English Dictionary. **1952** M. McCarthy *Groves of Academe* (1953) iii. 40 And the more he envisioned this prospect, the more he was of two minds about it. **1953** S. Spender *Creative Element* iii. 67 The development of modern literature today away from such highly individualistic envisionings. **1963** *Economist* 31 Aug. 744/2 The Negro firebrands, who .. envisioned the march as an excuse for swarming into the very offices of Congressmen.

†**en'vive**, *v. Obs.* [f. EN-[1] + Fr. *vif*, *viv-e*:—L. *vīv-us* alive.] *trans.* To enliven, quicken.

1523 Skelton *Garl. Laurel* 872 To envyve Pandarus' appetyte. *a* **1528** —— *Magnyf.* 1569 A fayre maystresse that quyckly is envyved with rudyes of the rose.

enviyus, obs. form of ENVIOUS.

†**envoisies**, *a. Obs. rare*[−1]. [a. OF. *envoisié* (nom. sing. and pl. *-ez*, *-es*), f. *envoisier*, *enveisier* to divert: see ENVESURE.] Gay, lively.

c **1450** *Merlin* vi. 106 To hem that we[re] Ioly and enuoisies [*printed* ennoisies] he yaf the Iuwellis.

envoke, obs. form of INVOKE.

†**en'volde**, *v. Obs. rare.* [a. OF. *envoldre*:—L. *involvĕre* to INVOLVE.] = INVOLVE.

1451 *Paston Lett.* No. 140 I. 185, I dar not envolde me in the same.

†**envolume** (ɛn'vɒljuːm), *v. Obs.* In 7 involum. [f. EN-[1] + VOLUME.] **a.** To form into a volume; to write at length. **b.** To incorporate with a volume.

1632 Lithgow *Trav.* I. 8, I could inuolume, as large a discourse, vpon this heart-grieuing proiect, as, etc. **1864** in Webster; and in mod. Dicts.

envolupe(n, obs. form of ENVELOPE *v.*

envolve: see INVOLVE.

†**en'vomish**, *v. Obs.* In 5 envomyssh. [Corruptly a. Fr. *esvomiss-* lengthened stem of *esvomir*, f. *es-* (:—L. *ex*) out + *vomir* to vomit.] *intr.* To vomit.

1480 Caxton *Ovid's Met.* XI. viii, Cylenus .. so moche dranke of the wyn, that he went casting & envomysshynge.

envoy ('ɛnvɔɪ), *sb.*[1] In sense 1 also 4–7 envoye, 9 envoi, and (with prefixed Fr. article) 6–7 l'envoy(e, 9 *arch.* l'envoi, -voy. [a. OF. *envoy(e* (mod. *envoi*), n. of action f. OF. *envoiier* (mod. *envoyer*) to send, f. phrase *en voie* on the way; cf. Sp. *enviar*, It. *inviare*.] Sending forth.

1. The action of sending forth a poem; hence, the concluding part of a poetical or prose composition; the author's parting words; a dedication, postscript. Now chiefly the short stanza which concludes a poem written in certain archaic metrical forms. *arch.*

c **1398** Chaucer (*title*), Th' enuoye of Fortune. **1485** Caxton *Chas. Gt.* 250 Thenuoye of thauctour. **1508** Barclay *Shyp of Folys* (1874) II. 230 Thenuoy. **1576** Turberv. (*title*), Tragical Tales .. with the Argument and L'Envoye to ech Tale. **1611** Cotgr., *Envoy* .. th' Enuoy, or conclusion of a Ballet, or Sonnet. **1640** B. Jonson *Underwoods, Misc. Poems* lx, Another answers, 'las! those silks are none, In smiling l'envoy. **1823** *Sismondi's Lit. Eur.* (1846) I. vi. 173 The songs are usually in seven stanzas, followed by an envoy, which he calls a tornada. **1823** *New Monthly Mag.* VII. 194 The last chapter .. the moral and envoy of the whole. **1880** Hueffer *Macm. Mag.* No. 253. 49 There are .. six lines to a stanza and six stanzas to a poem, not counting the tornada or envoi of three lines.

†**b.** *transf.* The conclusion of a play; also, a catastrophe, dénouement. *Obs.*

1609 B. Jonson *Sil. Wom.* v. i, I have given the bride her instructions to breake in upon him in the l'envoy. **1636** Massinger *Bashful Lover* v. i, Long since I look'd for this l'envoy.

2. The action of dispatching a messenger or parcel; hence, a mission, errand (*arch.*). ***letter of envoy*** (rare), transl. Fr. *lettre d'envoi*, a letter advising dispatch of goods.

1795 Southey *Joan of Arc* v. 496 Nor did I feel so pressing the hard hand Of want in Orleans, ere he parted thence On perilous envoy. **1872** in *Proc. Amer. Phil. Soc.* XII. 322 A letter of envoi was received.

envoy ('ɛnvɔɪ), *sb.*[2] Forms: (7 envoyé, -ée), envoy(e, 7– envoy. [app. an alteration (in the latter part of 17th c.) of Fr. *envoyé* (pa. pple. of *envoyer* to send), which had previously been adopted unchanged.]

1. A public minister sent by one sovereign or government to another for the transaction of diplomatic business. Now applied *esp.* to diplomatic ministers of the second rank ('ministers plenipotentiary') as distinguished from those of the highest rank ('ambassadors'), and those of the third rank ('chargés d'affaires').

The term ***envoy extraordinary***, formerly denoting a minister charged with a special or temporary mission, is now merely the fuller designation of the 'envoy' in the narrower sense = minister plenipotentiary.

[**1660** Evelyn *Mem.* (1857) I. 359 The Envoyée of the king of Poland. **1664** Marvell *Corr.* Wks. 1872–5 II. 172 He hathe taken care to supply it in the meantime by his Extraordinary Envoyè. **1691** Rycaut in *Gentl. Mag.* May (1786) 396/1 To treat the Turkish envoyées so ill, as, etc.] **1666** Pepys *Diary* 11 July, A galliott .. that is going to carry the Savoy Envoye [? *meant for* envoyé] over. **1667** Evelyn *Mem.* (1857) II. 31 To the audience of a Russian Envoy in the Queen's presence-chamber. **1710** in *Lond. Gaz.* No. 4688/1 The Earl of Stair, her Britannick Majesty's Envoy-Extraordinary to King Augustus. **1716** Lady M. W. Montague *Lett.* I. vi. 18 Madame .. the wife of our king's envoy from Hanover. **1779** J. Moore *View Soc. Fr.* II. 175, I have been introduced to all of them by Mr. Harris, his Majesty's envoy extraordinary. **1803** *Med. Jrnl.* IX. 453 A correspondence which I have begun, by means of the British Envoy. **1860** Motley *Netherl.* (1868) I. i. 3 Sir Edward Stafford, English envoy in Paris. **1875** H. Reeve in *Encycl. Brit.* (ed. 9) I. 657 Diplomatic envoys are of three ranks .. 1. Ambassadors .. 2. Envoys extraordinary or ministers plenipotentiary, accredited to sovereigns .. 3. Chargés d'affaires.

2. In wider sense: An agent, commissioner, deputy, messenger, representative.

[**1643** Denham *Dido* Poems (1668) 134 Jove's Envoyé through the Air Brings dismal tydings.] **1696** Tate & Brady *Ps.* cvi. 16 God's Envoy Moses they oppose. **1712** Blackmore *Creation* vi. 678 Where [*sc.* in the brain] their Report the Vital Envoys make. **1820** Irving *Sketch Bk.* I. 99 Men .. have been envoys from England to ransack the poles. **1859** Thackeray *Virgin.* vi. 48 The intrepid young envoy made his way from Williamsburg almost to the shores of Lake Erie.

3. *attrib.*

a **1711** Ken *Christophil* Poet. Wks. 1721 I. 487 An Envoy-Star, whose Ray Shou'd shew the world where Jesus lay.

†'**envoy**, *v. Obs.* [ad. Fr. *envoy-er* to send.]

a. To send. **b.** To write as an 'envoy' or concluding stanza.

1481 Caxton *Myrr.* I. v. 24 A new lignage was enioyed [? *read* enuoyed] from heuen on hygh. **1508** Barclay *Shyp Folys* (1874) II. 230 Alas what may I vnto you nowe enuoy.

envoyship ('ɛnvɔɪʃɪp). [f. ENVOY *sb.* + -SHIP.] The office, position, or function of an envoy.

1736 H. Coventry *Philemon to Hydaspes* iii. (T.), Cain paid all due reverence to this lunar envoyship. **1817–8** Cobbett *Resid. U.S.* (1822) 217 The Boroughmongers may easily add a legation of mendicity to their Envoyships and Consulships. **1843** *Blackw. Mag.* LIV. 812 You remember Marston .. at Brunswick, in his envoyship.

envy ('ɛnvɪ), *sb.* Forms: 3–7 envie, envye, (4 envi, enevi, envyȝe, enwie, 5 inwy(e, 4–6 invy), 3– envy. [a. F. *envie*, corresp. to Pr. *enveia*, Cat. *enveja*, Pg. *inveja*, Sp. *envidia*, It. *invidia*:—L. *invidia*, f. *invid-us* envious, related to *invidēre* to look maliciously upon, to envy, f. *in* upon + *vidēre* to see.]

†**1.** Malignant or hostile feeling; ill-will, malice, enmity. *Obs.*

a **1300** *Cursor M.* 15389 Of all venime and eneui ful kindeld vp he ras. *c* **1300** *Seyn Julian* 88 Ich [Belial] made þoru a lutel enuye þat on sle þat oðer. *c* **1400** *Ywaine & Gaw.* 3522 So grete envy .. bitwix tham twa was than. *c* **1430** *Syr Gener.* 5266 To him he had so grete envie. **1526** Skelton *Magnyf.* 1989 Full fewe but they have envy at me. **1596** Shaks. *Merch. V.* IV. i. 10 No lawful meanes can carrie me Out of enuies reach. **1611** Bible *Mark* xv. 10 For hee knew that the chiefe Priests had deliuered him for enuie. **1640** *Queen of Arragon* II. i. in Hazl. *Dodsley* XIII. 355 Misfortune brings Sorrow enough; 'tis envy to ourselves T'augment it by prediction. **1707** E. Ward *Hud. Rediv.* (1715) II. ix, In Naseby-Fields both Armies met, Their Envy, like their Numbers, great.

†**b.** Unwillingness, reluctance. *Obs. rare.*

1557 North tr. *Gueuara's Diall of Princes* 185 b/1 For speaking the truth: the man which hath enuy to seme olde doth delite to liue in the lightnes of youth.

†**c.** Odium, unpopularity, opprobrium; used to translate L. *invidia*. *Obs.*

1598 Grenewey *Tacitus' Ann.* I. x. (1622) 19 As well the fact, as the enuie of it, should light vpon their owne necks. **1622** Bacon *Henry VII*, 100 This Taxe (called Benevolence) was deuised by Edward the Fourth, for which hee sustained much Enuie. **1651** *Fuller's Abel Rediv., Calvin* (1867) I. 327 This accident procured great envy unto Calvin from all places. **1679** Burnet *Hist. Ref.* I. II. 62 He had the Legates between him and the Envy or Odium of it.

†**2.** Active evil, harm, mischief. *Obs.*

ME. *enuy(e* may perh. sometimes represent ENNOY, ANNOY.

a **1400** *Chester Pl.* (Shaks. Soc.) 199 Envye doe by no woman, To doe her shame by nighte nor daie. *c* **1400** *Apol. Loll.* 26 Discese & oþer enuyes. *c* **1460** *Battle Otterbourne* in Percy *Reliq.* 46 Yf thou hast haryed all Bamborowe shyre, Thou hast done me grete envye.

3. The feeling of mortification and ill-will occasioned by the contemplation of superior advantages possessed by another. Const. †*at*, *of*, †*to*, †*upon* (persons), *at*, *of* (things). Phrases, ***to feel*** (†***have***) ***envy***.

c **1280** *Fall & Passion* in *E.E.P.* (1862) 13 To him þe deuil had envie, þat he in his stid schold be broȝte. *a* **1300** *Cursor M.* 27694 (Cott.) He þat by caus of enuy werrayes anoþer wrangwisly. *a* **1340** Hampole *Psalter* ii. 10 Enuye couaitis, iolifte & oþer vices. *c* **1386** Chaucer *Knt's. T.* 49 Haue ye so gret envye Of myn honour? **1393** Langl. *P. Pl.* C. XXIII. 246 Haueþ non enuye To lerede ne to lewide. *a* **1440** *Relig. Pieces fr. Thornton MS.* 23 Envy .. es joye of oþer mens harme and sorowe of oþer mens welefare. **1475** Caxton *Jason* 77 Zethephius began to haue enuy vpon the king appollo. **1540** Hyrde tr. *Vives' Instr. Chr. Wom.* (1592) X j, It is much more shame to have envy at other for money, clothings, or possessions. **1588** A. King tr. *Canisius' Catech.* 143 Invy at our brothers charitie. **1601** Shaks. *Jul. C.* v. v. 70 All the Conspirators saue only hee, Did that they did, in enuy of great Cæsar. **1611** Bible *Transl. Pref.* 2 Enuie striketh most spitefully at the fairest. **1684** Winstanley in *Shaks. C. Praise* 400 Honour is always attended on by Envy. **1737** Whiston *Josephus' Antiq.* I. xviii. §2 He was hindered .. by his envy at him. **1836** H. Smith *Tin Trumpet* (1876) 145 Envy—punishing ourselves for being inferior to our neighbours. **1875** Jowett *Plato* (ed. 2) V. 75 Let every man contend in the race without envy.

†**b.** In the phrase ***to envy***, i.e. to such a point as to excite envy; to the heart's content; to admiration; to perfection. *Obs.* Cf. 5.

Perh. suggested by Fr. *à l'envi*, emulously, which is of different etymology. Cf. ENVY *v.*[2], to which the first quot. may belong.

c **1369** Chaucer *Dethe Blaunche* 173 They had good leyser for to route To envye, who might slepe beste. **1650–3** tr. *Hales' Dissert. de Pace* in *Phenix* (1708) II. 370 That Contemplation, happy even to Envy, awaits us in the Heavens. **1668** Pepys *Diary* 10 Mar., Captain Cocke .. told me .. that the Solicitor General do commend me, even to envy.

c. *pl.* Instances of envy; envious feelings, jealousies; rivalries.

1622 Bacon *Hen. VII*, 239 Little Enuies or Emulations upon Forraine Princes. **1668** Dryden *Ess. Dram. Poesy* (J.), The little envies of them [women] to one another. **1888** *Poor Nellie* 26 Whilst .. our statesmen inflame the mean envies of classes.

d. *concr.* The object of envy.

1836 Ld. Lytton *Duchess* III. ii, Duchess la Vallière .. The envy of the beauty and the birth Of Europe's court.

4. Without notion of malevolence: †**a.** Desire to equal another in achievement or excellence; emulation. *Obs. rare.*

1541 Elyot *Image Gov.* (1549) 129 His aduancement shall ingender in noble men an honest enuie. **1606–35** Ford (Webster), Such as cleanliness and decency Prompt to a virtuous envy.

b. A longing for the advantages enjoyed by another person.

1723 Pope *Lett.* (1737) VI. 99 My innocent envies and wishes of your state. *Mod.* Your success excites my envy.

†**5.** Wish, desire, longing; enthusiasm. *Obs.* Cf. Fr. *envie*.

a **1300** *Cursor M.* 2240 (Trin.) þese foles .. wiþ greet envye þis werk bigon. *c* **1430** *Syr Tryam.* 341 They rode forthe with grete envy To seke aftur the quene. **1481** Caxton *Myrr.* I. v. 19 And had enuye at none other thinge, but only for to lerne suche science. **1607** Topsell *Four-f. Beasts* (1673) 261 Uncivilized men do participate, in their conditions, the labours and envie of brute beasts.

6. *Comb.*

1817 Coleridge *Biog. Lit.* 26 He must be envy-mad. **1871** Palgrave *Lyr. Poems* 135 Judges with envy-dim eye.

¶ In the following quots. *enuy* is prob. a mere misprint for *enemy*. Cf. ENVYTE.

c **1430** Lydg. *Bochas* I. ix. (1544) 16 b, Yᵉ great sodein fall Of mighty Jabin for his iniquitie Which unto Jewes was enuy [*ed.* **1494** enmy] full mortall. **1483** Caxton *G. de la Tour* E ij, The enuy or deuylle. **1579** Lyly *Euphues* (Arb.) 189 Greater is thy credit in susteining wrong, then thy enuyes in committing injury.

envy ('ɛnvɪ), *v.* Forms: 4–7 envie(n, envye, (5 invye), 4– envy. [ad. Fr. *envier*, corresp. to Pr. *enveiar*, Cat. *envejar*, Pg. *invejar*, Sp. *envidiar*, It. *invidiare*:—med.L. *invidiāre*, f. L. *invidia* ENVY *sb.* The older accentuation (ɛn'vaɪ) survived into the 17th c. and is still common dialectally, esp. in Sc.]

1. *trans.* To feel displeasure and ill-will at the superiority of (another person) in happiness, success, reputation, or the possession of anything desirable; to regard with discontent another's possession of (some superior advantage which one would like to have for oneself). Also in less unfavourable sense: To wish oneself on a level with (another) in happiness or in the possession of something desirable; to wish oneself possessed of (something which another has).

a. with obj. a thing; †(rarely) with obj. clause.

c **1386** Chaucer *Wife's Prol.* 142, I nyl nat enuye no virginitee. **1393** Gower *Conf.* I. 254 Every worship is envied. **1595** W. C[larke] in *Shaks. C. Praise* 15 Let other countries (sweet Cambridge) envie .. thy petrarch, divine Spenser. **1600** Shaks. *A.Y.L.* III. ii. 78, I .. owe no man hate, enuie no mans happinesse. *c* **1632** *Poem* in *Athenæum* No. 2883. 121/3 Eolus such monstrous wracks envyes. **1696** Whiston *Th. Earth* IV. (1722) 368 We have but too much reason to envy the Ancient Happiness of our Forefathers. **1728** T. Sheridan *Persius* iii. (1739) 49 Do not envy that the wealthy Lawyer increases his Stores beyond you by Knavery and Oppression. **1857** Ruskin *Pol. Econ. Art* 4 A power not indeed to be envied, because it seldom makes us happy.

b. with obj. a person.

1526 *Pilgr. Perf.* (W. de W. 1531) 115 Thou shalt .. mollifye his herte that enuyeth the. **1562** J. Heywood *Prov. & Epigr.* (1867) 26 Better be enuied than pitied, folke sey. **1613** Shaks. *Hen. VIII*, II. ii. 125 They will not sticke to say, you enuide him. **1741** Middleton *Cicero* II. x. 458, I envy him for walking, and joking with you. **1841–4** Emerson *Ess.* viii. *Heroism* Wks. (Bohn) I. 110 Who does not envy those who have seen safely to an end their manful endeavour? **1872** Ruskin *Eagle's N.* §34 We may be envied, but shall not be praised, for having been allowed, etc.

c. with double obj., person and thing.

1797 MRS. RADCLIFFE *Italian* xii, I envy your friend those tears. **1807** CRABBE *Par. Reg.* I. 554 Ah! much I envy thee thy boys.

†**2.** To feel a grudge against (a person); to regard (a person or an action) with dislike or disapproval. *Obs.*

1557 NORTH tr. *Gueuara's Diall Pr.* 105 b/2, I knowe well, Faustine, that for that I haue sayed.. thou and others suche lyke, shall greatlye enuye me. **1577** NORTHBROOKE *Dicing* (1843) 163 Bicause you are aged, and nowe are not able to doe as other yong men and women do, and this maketh you to enuy it so much. **1602** WARNER *Alb. Eng.*, Epit. 389 Much was this distraction of Regalitie from Richard the second, enuied by those of his Line and Affinitie. **1630** R. JOHNSON *Kingd. & Commw.* 553 The Grand Seignior doth much envie him [Emir of Sidon] for suffering the Florentines to harbour and water within his Port of Tyrus.

†**b.** ? To injure; cf. ENVY *sb.* 2. *Obs. rare.*

1621 FLETCHER *Pilgrim* II. i, If I make a lie To gain your love, and envy my best mistress, Pin me against a wall.

†**3.** *trans.* To grudge, give reluctantly, refuse to give (a thing) *to* (a person); to begrudge (a thing); to treat (a person) grudgingly. Also *absol.*

1575–85 ABP. SANDYS *Serm.* (1841) 217 God hath not envied us: he oweth us nothing, but he giveth us much. **1590** SPENSER *F.Q.* III. v. 50 But that sweet Cordiall.. She did to him envy. **1616** SURFL. & MARKH. *Country Farm* 83 The dung of Peacockes is verie soueraigne against the diseases of the eyes.. but the Peacock so much enuieth the good of man, that he eateth his owne dung. **1667** MILTON *P.L.* VIII. 494 Thou has fulfill'd Thy words, Creator bounteous.. nor enviest. *Ibid.* IV. 517 Why should thir Lord envie them that? **1693** DRYDEN *Ess. Satire* Wks. 1821 XIII. 5 Jonson, who by studying Horace, had been acquainted with the rules, yet seemed to envy to posterity that knowledge. **1707** *Curios. in Husb. & Gard.* 25 We ought.. to make our own Advantage of that Knowledge, and not to envy it to others. **1770** LANGHORNE *Plutarch* (1879) II. 785/2 Thou enviedst me the glory of giving thee thy life.

†**b.** With clause as obj.: To grudge *that* (something should take place). *Obs.*

c **1430** LYDG. *Story Thebes* III, For euery man of high and lowe degree Enuieth now, that other should thrive. **1548** UDALL, etc. *Erasm. Par. John* 40 b, Enuying that God shoulde haue his owne prayse and glory. **1605** BACON *Adv. Learn.* I. 23 Antiquity enuieth there should be new additions. **1663** BUTLER *Hud.* I. ii. 835 Magnano.. did envy That two should with so many men vye. **1682** D'URFEY *Butler's Ghost* 176 Envying that he should ground his fame on Deeds so Essential to his Honour.

†**4.** *intr.* To have envious, grudging, or malevolent feelings. Sometimes with the occasion of the feeling expressed by inf. *to envy at* = senses 1–3. *Obs.*

1477 EARL RIVERS *Dictes* 52 To be envied at of mightier men then he is. **1549** COVERDALE *Erasm. Par. Gal.* iv. 30 Whose libertie they enuye at. **1595** SHAKS. *John* III. iv. 73 But now I enuie at their libertie. **1649** MILTON *Eikon.* 30 The king envying to see the Peoples love devolv'd on another object. **1656** COWLEY *Pindaric Odes, Life & Fame* (1687) ii, Oh Life! that epicures envy to hear! **1658** J. COLES *Cleopatra* VII. 271 Those to whom this fortune is denied have so much cause to envie at it, etc. *a* **1677** BARROW *Serm.* (1810) II. 227 Envying at those who have more worldly advantages. *a* **1700** DRYDEN *Pal. & Arc.* iii, Envy'd to behold The Names of others, not their own inroll'd.

†**b.** To be jealous *for* another. *Obs. rare*$^{-1}$.

1382 WYCLIF *Numb.* xi. 29 What, he seith, enuyest thow for me [Vulg. *æmularis pro me*].

†**en'vy**, *v.*^{2} [a. OF. *envier*:—L. *invītāre* to challenge, INVITE. Cf. the aphetic form VIE.

The identity in form and close resemblance in sense between this and prec. render it prob. that the two words were confused even in the earliest use; the examples in 16–17th c. may perh. belong to ENVY *v.*^{1}]

a. *intr.* To vie, contend for mastery. **b.** *trans.* To vie with, seek to rival.

c **1369** CHAUCER *Dethe Blaunche* 406 As thogh the erthe enuye wolde To be gayer than the heuen. **1384** —— *H. Fame* III. 141 For that she wolde envien, lo, To pypen bet than Appollo. **1509** HAWES *Past. Pleas.* xiv. xvi. (1845) 56 My mayster Lydgate I wyll not envy. **1590** SPENSER *F.Q.* I. ii. 17 Each others equall puissance enuies. **1621** FLETCHER *Island Princ.* I. ii, Each tree As if it envied the old Paradise.

envy, obs. var. of INVEIGH *v.*

1611 SCLATER *Key* 367 With what earnestness of affection envies hee [St. Paul] against those that, etc.

†**'envyful**, *a.* Chiefly *Sc. Obs.* [f. ENVY *sb.* + -FUL.] Full of envy, malice, or spite. Const. *of.*

1450–1530 *Myrr. our Ladye* 183 The enuyful sturrer and suggestoure. **1549** *Compl. Scot.* vii. (1872) 71 Aduerse fortoune hes bene inuyful contrar my veil fayr. **1594** J. MELVILL *Diary* 194 Close the mouthes of invyfull sclanderers. *a* **1651** CALDERWOOD *Hist. Kirk* (1843) II. 353 Their latent adversareis, invyfull of their place and vocatioun.

envying ('ɛnvɪɪŋ), *vbl. sb.* [f. ENVY *v.*^{1} + -ING^{1}.] The action of the verb ENVY; *concr.* in *pl.* jealousies, etc.

1586 J. HOOKER *Ireland* Ep. Ded. in Holinshed *Chron.*, You.. haue through so much enuienges.. perseuered in your attempts. **1611** BIBLE *2 Cor.* xii. 20 Debates, enuyings, wraths, strifes. —— *Rom.* xiii. 13 Let us walke.. not in strife and enuying. **1658** *Whole Duty Man* xiii. §25. 103 This envying at God's goodness to others, is in effect a murmuring against God. **1864** MRS. GATTY *Parab. Nature* Ser. iv. 23 What could put comparisons, and envyings into their heads?

envying ('ɛnvɪɪŋ), *ppl. a.* [f. ENVY *v.* + -ING^{2}.] That envies.

1382 WYCLIF *Isa.* xxvi. 11 The enuyende puples.

Hence **'envyingly** *adv.*

1861 *Romance Dull Life* xli. 300 She noticed envyingly the force of mild and intelligent silence.

†**'envyless**, *a. Obs. rare*$^{-1}$. [f. ENVY *sb.* + -LESS.] Without envy, not exposed or liable to envy. In quot. quasi-*adv.*

a **1628** R. BROOKE *Fame & Honour* lxiv, In Honour they should envilesse excell.

envyous, -ows, -us, obs. ff. ENVIOUS.

envyron, var. of ENVIRON *adv. Obs.*

[**envyte**, app. a misprint for *enmyte*, ENMITY. Cf. ENVY *sb.* ¶.

c **1430** LYDG. *Story Thebes* III. Kiiij, They on Grekes, enuyously gan shoute And of despyte, and grete enuyte Bad hem foles, gone home to her contre. **1480** CAXTON *Chron. Eng.* III. (1520) 25/2 Antigonus broder unto the kynge was slayne thrugh the envyte of the quene. *a* **1569** *Sqr. Low Degree* 392 in Hazl. *E.P.P.* II. 38 For yf it may be founde in thee, that thou them (de)fame for envyte.]

enwall, inwall (ɛn-, ɪn'wɔːl), *v.* [f. EN-, IN- + WALL.] *trans.* **a.** To enclose within a wall; also *transf.* and *fig.* **b.** To serve as a wall to.

1523 SKELTON *Garl. Laurel* (Dyce) 569 A felde.. Enwallyd aboute with the stony flint. **1580** C'TESS PEMBROKE *Ps.* lxxviii, Heaped waves an uncouth way enwall. **1596** SPENSER *State Irel.* Wks. (1862) 543/2 They would bee able with little to in-wall themselves strongly. **1601** DANIEL *Epistles* Wks. (1717) 356 In-wall'd within a living Tomb. **1610** G. FLETCHER *Christ's Vict.* lvi, His Court with glitterant pearle was all enwall'd. **1627** SPEED *England* xxxiv. §8 The close [was] inwalled by Bishop Langton. **1864** *Blackfriars* I. 32 The extent of ground thus enwalled. **1879** *Cornh. Mag.* Jan. 43 London was inwalled in the year 306 A.D.

Hence **en'walling** *ppl. a.*

1647 H. MORE *Song of Soul* I. III. xxxi, And strong Pantheotheus inwalling might.

enwallow: see EN- *pref.*^{1} 3.

enwarp: see INWARP.

enwaste: see EN- *pref.*^{1} 2.

†**en'wave**, *v. Obs.* Also 7 in-. [f. EN-^{1} + WAVE *v.*] *trans.* **a.** To form into waves. **b.** To plunge into the waves.

1610 G. FLETCHER *Christ's Vict.* in Farr *S.P. Jas. I.* (1848) 46 Those [waters (depicted in embroidery)] that neare the margin pearl did play, Hoarcely enwaved were with hastie sway. **1627–77** FELTHAM *Resolves* I. xxvii. 91 Learning is like a river.. it inwaves itself in the unfathom'd Ocean.

enweaken: see EN- *pref.*^{1} 3.

†**en'wealthy**, *v. Obs.* Also in-. [f. EN-^{1} + WEALTHY.] *trans.* To make wealthy; = ENRICH.

1593 DRAYTON *Eclog.* v, Where of herself she 'xacts such usury, That she's else needy by inwealthying this. **1594** *Zepheria* vi. in Arb. *Garner* V. 68, I then enwealthy thy exchequer.

enweave, enwoven: see IN-.

enwed: see EN- *pref.*^{1} 3.

en'wheel, *v. Obs.* exc. in echoes of Shakespeare's use. Also 7 in-. [f. EN-^{1} + WHEEL *sb.*] *trans.* To encircle, surround.

1604 SHAKS. *Oth.* II. i. 87 The grace of Heauen.. Enwheele thee round. **1621** FLETCHER *Pilgrim* I. ii, Heaven's grace in-wheele ye. **1766–1800** in BAILEY. **1897** F. THOMPSON *New Poems* 42 The Presence-hall where Angels Do enwheel their placèd King. **1912** L. A. HARKER *Mr. Wycherly's Wards* ix. 129 Enwheel'd around with love on every hand.

enwiden: see EN- *pref.*^{1} 3.

enwind, inwind (ɛn-, ɪn'waɪnd), *v.* [f. EN-^{1} + WIND *v.*] *trans.* To wind itself around (something); to surround as with windings or coils. Also, to make into a coil. *lit.* and *fig.*

1850 MRS. BROWNING *Poems* II. 245 A sound, a sense of music.. Softly, finely, it inwound me. **1850** TENNYSON *In Mem.* xcviii, Let her great Danube rolling fair Enwind her isles, unmark'd of me. **1859** —— *Guinevere* 598 The moony vapour rolling round the king.. Enwound him fold by fold. **1876** SWINBURNE *Erechth.* 806 With what blossomless flowerage of sea-foam and blood-coloured foliage inwound. **1877** M. ARNOLD *Fragm. Antigone* Poems II. 40 The bond Original, deep-inwound, Of blood.

Hence **en'winding** *vbl. sb.*

1598 FLORIO, *Falde*.. a folding, an inwinding or a plaiting of a garment. **1697** *View Penal Laws* 257 Neither he or any other shall make any Inwinding within the Fleece.

enwine: see EN- *pref.*^{1} 2.

enwisen, enwoman: see EN- *pref.*^{1} 3 and 2.

enwomb (ɛn'wuːm), *v.* Also 7–8 inwomb(e. [f. EN-^{1} + WOMB.]

1. *trans.* To cause to bear in the womb; to make pregnant. Also *fig.*

1590 SPENSER *F.Q.* II. i. 50 Me then he left enwombed of this childe. **1633** P. FLETCHER *Purple Isl.* x. xxxvii, Her daintie breasts.. may seem to sight To be enwombed both of pleasure and delight.

2. To hold or to place in the womb. ? *Obs.*

1601 SHAKS. *All's Well* I. iii. 150, I am your mother, And put you in the Catalogue of those That were enwombed mine. *a* **1625** BOYS *Wks.* (1630) 144 Mary did inwombe the Father of Mercies. **1647** H. MORE *Song of Soul* III. App. li, Him whose chaste soul enwombd in Virgin chast, etc. *a* **1711** KEN *Hymns Evang.* Wks. 1721 I. 205 God inwomb'd.

3. *transf.* **a.** To contain as in the womb; in quots. *fig.* **b.** To plunge *into*, bury *in*, the womb or bowels of (something); to enclose, shut up as in the womb.

a **1591** SPENSER *Ruins of Rome* 67 Her great spirite rejoyned to the spirite Of thir great masse, is in the same enwombed. *a* **1625** BOYS *Wks.* (1630) 10 The heaven of heavens cannot contain him [God], much lesse any barren braine inwombe him. *a* **1631** DONNE *Funeral Elegies* (R.), The Affrique Niger streame enwombs Itselfe into the earth. **1633** P. FLETCHER *Elisa* xxx, Why is he living, then, in earth enwombed? **1840** BROWNING *Sordello* v. 418, I enwomb Some wretched Friedrich with his red-hot tomb. **1855** SINGLETON *Virgil* II. 442 If thou Enwombest such high courage in thy breast. **1859** MISS MULOCK *Romant. T.* 40 The dull dead metals that lie enwombed there.

Hence **en'wombed** *ppl. a.*, pregnant.

1820 SHELLEY *Witch Atl.* x, Wondering how the enwombed rocks Could have brought forth so beautiful a birth.

enwood, -worthy, -wrack: see EN-^{1} 1 b, 2.

enwrap, inwrap (ɛn-, ɪn'ræp), *v.* [f. EN-^{1}, IN- + WRAP *v.*]

1. *trans.* To wrap, envelop, enfold *in* or *with* (a garment, case, or covering, coils or folds of anything); also, with the thing enveloping as subject. *lit.* and *fig.* †In early use also: To fold up (a garment).

α. **1382** WYCLIF *Jer.* x. 8 A tree.. with siluer enwrappid. **1548** GEST *Pr. Masse* 71 To enwrap. **1572** BOSSEWELL *Armorie* II. 95 b, Twoo Cypres trees.. enwrapped with Ivy proper. **1578** BANISTER *Hist. Man* IV. 51 Membranes enwrappyng round the ioyntes. *Ibid.* VIII. 105 They are enwrapped both with the thinne, and also the hard Membrans. **1601** HOLLAND *Pliny* II. 280 It ought to be applied enwrapped well in wooll. **1683** A. SNAPE *Anat. Horse* IV. xxi. (1686) 188 For it enwrappeth almost all the Muscles of the Thigh. **1725–6** POPE *Odyss.* VIII. 339 Down rushed the toils, enwrapping as they lay The careless lovers. **1775** R. CHANDLER *Trav. Asia M.* (1825) I. 82 The women of the Turks.. when they go out, are enwrapped in white linen. **1830** LINDLEY *Nat. Syst. Bot.* 144 Petals.. enwrapping the stamens. **1845** *P. Parley's Ann.* VI. 80 The body of a man.. enwrapped in a shroud.

β. **1382** WYCLIF *2 Kings* ii. 8 Helyas tooke his mantyll, and inwrappyde it. —— *Prov.* xxix. 6 The sinnende wicke man a grene shal inwrappe. **1555** EDEN *Decades W. Ind.* II. IX. (Arb.) 132 When shee seeth her younge chekyn inwrapped in towe or flaxe. **1605** BACON *Adv. Learn.* II. xxii. §6 How they [the affections] are enwrapped one within another. *a* **1661** FULLER *Worthies, Wiltshire* III. 165 His Armes.. three Children-heads.. Inwrapped about their necks, with as many Snakes Proper. **1750** G. HUGHES *Barbados* 253 Inwrapped in sometimes ten or eleven green husky leaves.

b. *transf.* To wrap, enfold closely in a surrounding medium, *e.g.* clouds, darkness, vapour. Of the medium: To envelop. Also *fig.*

α. **1545** UDALL *Erasm. Par. Luke* (1548) xxiii. 806 Enwrapping his minde and sentence in the mistical darknesse of parables. **1563** SACKVILLE *Mirr. Mag.* Induct. 5 The mantels rent, wherein enwrapped been The gladsome groves. **1640** BP. HALL *Rem. Wks.* II. (1660) 38 Neither can it ever see more than half the World at once; darkness the while enwraps the other. **1768–74** TUCKER *Lt. Nat.* (1852) II. 415 The fiery meteor, enwrapt in clouds and darkness. **1848** MILLER *First Impr.* xi. (1857) 172 It stands half enwrapped in tall wood. *a* **1849** POE *E. B. Browning* Wks. 1864 III. 403 A mystical something or nothing enwrapped in a fog of rhapsody.

β. **1590–6** SPENSER *F.Q.* (J.), Arachne.. Spread her subtil net, Inwrapped in foul smoak. **1668** HOWE *Bless. Righteous* (1825) 53 And inwraps it in the blackness of darkness for ever. **1878** G. MACDONALD *Phantastes* III. xxii. 161 Inwrapt me like an odorous vapour.

c. Const. *from.*

a **1849** POE *Valentine* Poems (1859) 57 Her own sweet name that nestling lies upon the page, enwrapped from every reader. **1883** T. HARDY in *Longm. Mag.* July 254 The inevitable glooms of a straitened hard-working life occasionally enwrap him from such pleasures as he has.

2. *fig.* **a.** To contain implicitly, involve.

1642 *Observ. on his Majesty's Answ. to Decl. Parl.* 13 Whether this or that Doctrine enwraps the greatest Danger. **1649** ROBERTS *Clavis Bibl.* 619 The benefits enwrapped in this salvation for the Church. **1882** *Pop. Science Monthly* XXII. 148 An act which inwraps so much of irreparable loss.

b. To 'wrap' in slumber, trance, etc.; to absorb or engross in contemplation, thought, etc.

In some applications of this sense the pa. pple. is liable to be confused with ENRAPT, q.v.

α. *a* **1600** FAIRFAX *Tasso* XIV. xvii, Enwrapt in fond desire. **1601** SHAKS. *Twel. N.* IV. iii. 3 Though 'tis wonder that enwraps me thus, Yet 'tis not madnesse. **1629** MILTON *Nativity* 134 If such holy song Enwrap our fancy long.

β. **1589** GREENE *Arcadia* (1616) 41 His trance, wherein the present wonder had inwrapt him. **1641** MILTON *Ch. Discip.* II. (1851) 68, I doe now feele my selfe inwrapt on the sodaine into those mazes and Labyrinths of dreadfull and hideous thoughts. **1836–9** DICKENS *Sk. Boz* 176/2 Too much inwrapped in the contemplation of his happiness.

†**c.** To involve, implicate, entangle (in danger, guilt, suffering); to involve in a common fate *with* another. *Obs.*

α. **1382** WYCLIF *1 Sam.* xv. 6 Departith fro Amalech, lest perauenture I enwrappe thee with hem. **1617** COLLINS *Def. Bp. Ely* I. i. 74 We should feare to be enwrapped in his danger. **1636** SANDERSON *Serm.* II. 47 And from

enwrapping himself within the guilt of their transgressions. **1826** E. IRVING *Babylon* II. VI. 133 That day of wrath.. fearfully enwrappeth them all in the horrors of its last hour. *β.* **1563-87** FOXE *A. & M.* (1596) 97/1 They inwrapped themselues in..miserie and desolation. **1635** N. R. tr. *Camden's Hist. Eliz.* IV. 178 His confession..inwrapped many. **1675** BROOKS *Gold. Key* Wks. 1867 V. 147 The first Adam..plunged himself into all unrighteousness, and so inwrapped himself in the curse.

Hence **en'wrapped, -'wrapt** *ppl. a.*

1598 CHAPMAN *Iliad* I. 313 To heaven the thick fumes bore Enwrapped savours. **1605** BACON *Adv. Learn.* II. xxiii. §33 Somewhat viscous and inwrapped, and not easy to turn. *a* **1638** MEDE *Wks.* I. xliv. 250 When the inwrapped Promises were unfolded and revealed. **1868** *Selden's Table-t.* (Arb.) Introd. 9 Their inwrapped principles may be understood in their nature.

†**en'wrapment, in'wrapment.** *Obs. rare.* [f. ENWRAP *v.* + -MENT.] The action of enwrapping; the state of being enwrapped. Also *concr.* a wrapping, covering.

1753 SHUCKFORD *Creation* 203 They wreathed together a foliature of the fig-tree, and made themselves enwrapments. **1798** *Month. Mag.* VI. 552 The inwrapment in surplices of linen.

enwrapping, inwrapping (ɛn-, ɪn'ræpɪŋ), *vbl. sb.* [f. ENWRAP, *v.* + -ING[1].] The action of the verb ENWRAP. Also *concr.* a fold. *lit.* and *fig.*

1543 TRAHERON *Vigo's Chirurg.* I. x. 10 The third and laste of the smal guttes..hathe many involutions and inwrappynges. **1561** T. NORTON *Calvin's Inst.* IV. 62 Darke by reason of many douteful enwrappyngs. **1567** MAPLET *Gr. Forest* 34 It [Bindweede]..troubleth them with the inwrapping and circumplication about yᵉ other their stem or stalk. **1619** W. SCLATER *Expos. 1 Thess.* (1630) 22 In respect of their promiscuous enwrapping in common calamities. **1840** ARNOLD in Stanley *Life & Corr.* (1844) II. App. 420 Their [the Apennines'] infinite beauty of outline, and the endless enwrappings of their combes.

enwrapping, inwrapping (ɛn-, ɪn'ræpɪŋ), *ppl. a.* [f. ENWRAP *v.* + -ING[2].] That enwraps; enclosing; enveloping.

1850 BROWNING *Christm. Eve & Easter Day* 243 See the enwrapping rocky niche. **1862** H. SPENCER *First Princ.* II. x. §84 (1875) 258 Radiation from the enwrapping cloud.

enwreathe, inwreathe (ɛn-, ɪn'riːð). Also 7 inwreath. [f. EN-[1] + WREATHE *v.*] *trans.* †**a.** To wrap or envelop *in* (*obs.*). **b.** To wreathe, intertwine *with.* **c.** To surround as with a wreath; to encircle as a wreath does. *lit.* and *fig.*

1620 SHELTON *Quix.* II. xiv. (R.), Enwreathed in a sail and thrown into the sea. **1630** BRATHWAIT *Eng. Gentl.* 87 Such plants as they [the endive or misselto] inwreath. **1667** MILTON *P.L.* III. 361 With these that never fade the Spirits Elect Bind thir resplendent locks inwreath'd with beams. **1730** THOMSON *Autumn* 937 Nor less the palm of peace enwreathes thy brow. **1791** MRS. RADCLIFFE *Rom. Forest* ii, The lofty battlements, thickly enwreathed with ivy. **1850** MRS. BROWNING *Poems* II. 47, I gaze upon her beauty Through the tresses that enwreathe it. **1853** G. JOHNSTON *Nat. Hist. E. Bord.* I. 75 Groups of thorn, hazel and sloe, enwreathed with honeysuckle. **1859** GEO. ELIOT *A. Bede* 70 It was not at all a distressed blush, for it was inwreathed with smiles and dimples. **1879** BROWNING *Pheidippides* 49 Oak and olive and bay,—I bid you cease to enwreathe Brows made bold by your leaf!

Hence **en'wreathed** *ppl. a.*

1631 BRATHWAIT *Whimzies, Gamester* 42 Walking..with ..an enwreathed arm like a dissassionate lover. **1820** KEATS *Hyperion* I. 219 Bowers of fragrant and enwreathed light.

enwrite, enwrong: see EN- *pref.*[1] 3.

enwrought: see INWROUGHT.

eny, obs. variant of ANY.

enykynnes, variant of ANYKYNS, *Obs.*

1377 LANGL. *P. Pl.* B. II. 200 Fettereth fast falsenesse for enykynnes ȝiftes.

enymy, obs. form of ENEMY.

1375 BARBOUR *Bruce* VIII. 80 Magre all his enymyss, etc.

enyoke: see EN- *pref.*[1] 3.

enys, variant of ENES *adv. Obs.* once.

enyyn-, enyntysch, var. ff. ANIENTISHE *v. Obs.*

Enzed (ɛn'zɛd). *Austral.* and *N.Z.* [repr. pronunc. of initial letters of *New Zealand.*] A popular written form of 'New Zealand'; also, a New Zealander. Hence **En'zedder,** a New Zealander.

1918 *Chrons. N.Z.E.F.* 24 May 179/1 Another interesting struggle was the tug-of-war between the 'En-Zeds' and the 'Ossies'. *Ibid.* 21 June 225/1 We christened the Adjutant 'Kiwi'—the symbol of En-Zed. **1934** *Bulletin* (Sydney) 1 Aug. 11/4 During the war years it was an honored title for all Enzeds serving overseas. **1941** BAKER *N.Z. Slang* v. 43 *Enzed* and *Enzedder* were also coming into colloquial use by the end of last century. **1944** J. H. FULLARTON *Troop Target* iii. 25 Pack my..body back to Enzed in a wheel-chair. **1946** T. E. HAUGHEY *Railway Reminisc.* 6 He was back in En-Zed on a holiday. **1948** R. FINLAYSON *Tidal Creek* ix. 214 Uncle Ted, like a real Enzedder with no use for this snobby business, has renounced the title. **1956** S. HOPE *Diggers' Paradise* 99 Two ace shearers, an Aussie and an Enzedder.

enzone: see EN- *pref.*[1] 1 a.

enzootic (ɛnzəʊ'ɒtɪk), *a.* and *sb.* [f. Gr. ἐν in + ζῷον animal + -IC, on the analogy of *chaotic, hypnotic,* etc. Cf. Fr. *enzootique.*]

A. *adj.* 'Applied to diseases of cattle peculiar to a district, climate, or season, in the same manner as *Endemic* is employed to indicate those of human beings' (*Syd. Soc. Lex.*).

B. *sb.* An enzootic disease.

1880 *Times* 15 Sept. 7/6 Fortified by a knowledge of endemics and enzootics in other regions. **1882** G. FLEMING *Vivisection* in *19th Cent.* No. 61. 472 The disease [anthrax] is enzöotic in the half-submerged valleys..of Catalonia.

enzyme ('ɛnzaɪm). [f. Gr. ἐν in + ζύμη leaven.]

1. The leavened bread with which the Eucharist is administered in the Greek Church.

1850 J. M. NEALE *Eastern Ch.* 1074 'If,' says he [Theorianus, A.D. 1170], 'the Divine virtue changes the oblations into the Body and Blood of Christ, it is superfluous to dispute whether they were of Azymes or Enzymes, or of red or white wine.'

2. *Biochem.* [ad. G. *enzym* (W. Kühne 1877, in *Verhandl. Naturhist.-Medic. Ver. Heidelberg* I. 194), f. mod. Gr. ἔνζυμος leavened.] Any of the proteins produced by cells which catalyse specific biochemical reactions; formerly called (*unorganized*) *ferment.* Also *attrib.* and *Comb.* Hence **enzy'matic, en'zymic** *adjs.*; **enzy'matically, en'zymically** *advbs.*

1881 W. ROBERTS in *Proc. R. Soc.* XXXII. 146, I would suggest the desirability of adopting this term [G. *enzym*] into English, with a slight change of orthography, as 'enzymes', and also of coining from this root the cognate words which are requisite for clear and concise description. The action of an enzyme may be designated *enzymosis,* and the nature of the action may be spoken of as *enzymic.* **1890** [see ZYMOLYSIS]. **1898** *Ann. Bot.* XII. 491 The alcoholic fermentation of sugar is effected by the activity of an enzyme or soluble ferment. **1899** [see ZYMASE]. **1900** A. J. EWART tr. *Pfeffer's Physiol. Plants* I. viii. 503 Even in an actively growing plant an abundant supply of the products of enzymatic action may partly or wholly inhibit the formation of the enzyme in question. **1902** *Jrnl. Chem. Soc.* LXXXI. 373 The phenomenon of fermentation is caused by enzyme action. **1903** *Westm. Gaz.* 20 Oct. 8/2 An enzyme-secreting organism..has been conveyed to the farm. **1908** *Chambers's Jrnl.* July 541/2 The hydrogen peroxide is decomposed by the enzyme catalase present in the milk into water. **1927** HALDANE & HUXLEY *Anim. Biol.* iv. 106 Each digestive enzyme is a definite substance with the property of bringing about, or enormously speeding up, a particular chemical reaction. **1930** *Chem. Abstr.* 1654 The polypeptidase group includes enzymes which require the presence of a free NH_2 and others which require a free COOH in the substrate. Probably these groups are the point of attachment in the formation of enzyme-substrate compd. **1942** *Ann. Reg. 1941* 344 [Enzyme research] suggested strongly that enzymatic activity is vested in the protein molecule itself. **1944** *Ann. Rev. Physiol.* VI. 277 Renin which was released by the ischemic kidney acted enzymatically upon a serum globulin. **1948** *Sci. News* VII. 125 They are the parts of digestive juices which break up and dissolve the fat, starch and meat of food; they are also responsible for fermentation: the word 'enzyme' in fact means merely 'in yeast'. **1949** MILES & PIRIE *Nature Bacterial Surface* i. 5 There is a group of mucopolysaccharides whose presence in certain organisms is essential for the stability of the cell membrane, and..these can be destroyed enzymically. **1953** *New Biol.* XV. 112 The enzyme-catalyzed reactions which make up this machinery [of a living organism] are nearly always reversible. **1956** *Nature* 14 Jan. 80/1 Since..cresolase activity is an enzymic ..process, molecular oxygen must combine at some stage with enzyme or enzyme-substrate complex. *Ibid.* 24 Mar. 575/1 Even in the presence of enzymatically generated peroxide, catalase did not catalyse the oxidation of *p*-hydroxyphenylpyruvic acid to homogentisic acid. **1962** A. PIRIE *Lens Metabolism Rel. Cataract* 429 Lactic acid was estimated colorimetrically..and enzymically. **1968** *Listener* 11 July 49/1 The biochemical enzymic machinery in the muscles. **1968** *Times* 19 Nov. 6/7 Sulphur compounds are known to be important inhibitors of enzymatic processes. **1968** *Physics Bull.* Dec. 433 Several different species of spherical cells were treated enzymatically to remove their outer coats. **1969** *New Scientist* 16 Oct. 122/1 Its great breakthrough with the enzyme wash powders brought troubles at both ends of the product.

enzy'mology. [f. ENZYM(E + -OLOGY.] The division of biochemistry which deals with enzymes. Hence **enzy'mologist**; **enzymo'logical** *a.*

1900 B. D. JACKSON *Gloss. Bot. Terms.* Add., Enzymology. **1939** *Industr. & Engin. Chem.* (*News Ed.*) 10 Oct. 652 Biochemist-Enzymologist, experienced in Bromelin and Papain production and research publications. **1941** *Manch. Guardian Weekly* 17 Jan. 52 Just after I had read about the triumphs of Swedish enzymology, I met the village milkman. *Ibid.,* Meanwhile we may remain careless of 'what the Swede intend' and let the enzymologists go their way. **1956** *Nature* 24 Mar. 559/1 Enzymological studies on polysaccharide syntheses in plants. **1961** *Times* 17 July 3/1 Biochemistry with emphasis on enzymology. **1970** *Nature* 9 May 500/1 The creeping computerization that is spreading through biochemistry is now beginning to permeate the activities of enzymologists.

E O. A game of chance, in which the appropriation of the stakes is determined by the falling of a ball into one of several niches marked E or O respectively. Also *attrib.*

1750 COVENTRY *Pompey Lit.* I. xv. (1785) 36/2 For the sake of playing at E O. **1801** M. EDGEWORTH *Belinda* III. xxv. 53 He likes the lady's EO table better than the lady. **1827** HONE *Every-Day Bk.* II. 112 The profits gained by E O Tables, Rouge et Noir, etc.

eo-, *prefix,* employed as combining form of Gr. ἠώς dawn, in scientific terms of recent origin, chiefly *Geol.* and *Palæont.* First used in EOCENE, with the sense 'characterized by the "dawn" or faintly recognizable beginnings of' (the recent fauna and flora); subsequently, with similar notion, in **eophytic** (iːəʊ'fɪtɪk), *a.* [+ Gr. φυτόν plant + -IC], characterized by the earliest appearance of plant-life. **eozoic** (iːəʊ'zəʊɪk), *a.* [+ Gr. ζῷον animal], characterized by the earliest appearance of animal life; said of the Laurentian strata and the period represented by them. Also in mod.L. names of fossil genera, believed to be the earliest representatives of types still existing, as **Eohippus** (iːəʊ'hɪpəs) [+ Gr. ἵππος horse], the oldest known genus of the horse family. **Eopteris** (iː'ɒptərɪs) [+ Gr. πτερίς fern], a genus including the oldest known fern. **Eosaurus** (iːəʊ'sɔːrəs), the oldest known genus of saurians. **Eozoon** (iːəʊ'zəʊən) [+ Gr. ζῷον animal], a supposed genus of foraminifers or rhizopods, at one time regarded as the earliest known animal; its alleged remains are now believed to be of inorganic origin; hence **Eo'zoonal** *a.,* pertaining to the eozoon.

1879 LE CONTE *Elem. Geol.* 504 *Eohippus..a small animal no bigger than a fox, having three toes on the hind foot and four perfect ones on the fore foot. **1880** HUXLEY in *Times* 25 Dec. 4/1, I do not see..any reason to doubt that the eocene equidæ were preceded by mesozoic forms, which differed from eohippus in the same way as eohippus differs from equus. **1880** DAWSON *Earth & Man* ii. 32 An *Eophytic period preceding the Eozoic. **1879** LE CONTE *Elem. Geol.* 404 Unless we except the *Eosaurus, these are the first true reptiles found. **1873** DAWSON *Earth & Man* ii. 18 *Eozoic or those [rocks] that afford the traces of the earliest known living beings. **1871** HUNT in *Proc. Amer. Assoc. Sci.* 53 Subsequently to the eozoic times, silicated rocks..are comparatively rare. **1872** DARWIN *Orig. Spec.* x. 287 The existence of the *Eozoon in the Laurentian formation of Canada is generally admitted. **1879** LE CONTE *Elem. Geol.* 275 A section of an *Eozoönal mass. **1881** R. ETHERIDGE in *Jrnl. Geol. Soc.* XXXVIII. 54 The prevalent limestones, Eozoonal or otherwise.

Eoan (iː'əʊən), *a.* [f. L. *ēō-us,* a. Gr. ἠῷος, f. ἠώ-ς dawn + -AN.] Of or pertaining to the dawn; eastern.

a **1822** SHELLEY *Liberty* xv, The morning-star Beckons the Sun from the Eoan wave. **1827** SIR H. TAYLOR *Com. nenus* iii. 5 (D.) The Mithra of the middle world, That sheds Eoan radiance on the West.

Eoanthropus (iːəʊ'ænθrəpəs). [f. EO- + mod.L. *anthropus*: see ANTHROPO-.] The name given to a genus or a member of a genus represented by what was formerly believed to be the skull of a prehistoric man. See PILTDOWN.

1913 A. S. WOODWARD in *Q. Jrnl. Geol. Soc.* LXIX. 135 The facial parts of the skull..differed..from those of any typically human skull. I therefore propose that the Piltdown specimen be regarded as the type of a new genus of the family Hominidæ, to be named *Eoanthropus* [*Ibid.* 137 The species of which the skull and mandible have now been described in detail may be named *Eoanthropus dawsoni,* in honour of its discoverer.] **1935** HUXLEY & HADDON *We Europeans* ii. 59 It is perhaps a million years since Eoanthropus and Sinanthropus roamed the earth.

eobiont (iːəʊ'baɪɒnt). [f. EO- + Gr. βιουντ- pr. pple. stem of βιοῦν to live, f. βίος life.] A hypothetical chemical structure, supposed to arise during biopoesis, that has certain characteristics of living matter but is not alive in the fullest sense.

1953 N. W. PIRIE in *Discovery* Aug. 242/2 In early systems, which may be called eobionts, functions may have been performed by other materials, inefficiently no doubt but well enough to get things started. [*Note*] Eobiont = 'dawn organism'. **1967** J. D. BERNAL *Orig. Life* iii. 27 He [*sc.* Oparin] showed that such colloidal bodies could carry on complex chemical reactions and could gradually form what were afterwards referred to as eobionts or pre-vital masses which could carry on a chemical evolution of their own.

Eocene ('iːəsiːn), *a. Geol.* [f. Gr. ἠώ-ς dawn (see EO-) + καινός new, recent.]

1. The epithet applied to the lowest division of the Tertiary strata, and to the geological period which they represent.

1831 W. WHEWELL *Let.* (1876) II. 111, I propose for your four terms 1 acene, 2 eocene, 3 miocene, 4 pliocene. **1833** LYELL *Princ. Geol.* (ed. 2) III. 54 The period next antecedent we shall call Eocene. **1851** RICHARDSON *Geol.* vii. 174 The eocene group is characterised by a total absence of cycadeæ. **1878** HUXLEY *Physiogr.* 214 The Eocene rocks once spread over the whole surface of this chalk.

fig. **1856** DARWIN *Let.* 17 June (1887) II. 73 His Geology also is rather eocene as I told him. **1864** LOWELL *Fireside Trav.* 103 These eocene periods of the day are not fitted for sustaining the human forms of life. **1870** *Daily Tel.* 22 Sept., Its deep roots shot back into the eocene strata of civilisation.

2. quasi-*sb.*

1851 RICHARDSON *Geol.* xi. 370, 1. Upper Eocene. 2. Middle Eocene. 3. Lower Eocene.

fig. **1877** BLACKMORE *Erema* II. xxxvi. 221 The calm deep eocene of British rural mind.

eode, ME. and OE. pa. t. of GO.

eofen, obs. form of HEAVEN.

eoile, obs. form of OIL.

‖**eo ipso** (ˌeɪəʊ ˈɪpsəʊ), *advb. phr.* [L., ablative of *id ipsum*, that (thing) itself.] By that very act (or quality); through that alone; thereby. Cf. IPSO FACTO.

1696 J. SERGEANT *Method to Science* I. v. 50 Nothing can be said to be *Divisible*, or capable to be made *more*, but it must be said *eo ipso* to be Actually and truly *One*. **1846** W. HAMILTON *Suppl. Diss.* in *Reid's Wks.* (ed. 2) Note A. §4. 754/2 For when a belief is necessary it is, *eo ipso*, universal. **1890** W. JAMES *Princ. Psychol.* II. xxi. 300 What is lively and interesting stimulates *eo ipso* the will. **1901** A. E. TAYLOR *Probl. Conduct.* v. 295 A piece of benevolent legislation which compelled the consumer to pay more for the necessaries of life would *eo ipso* diminish the funds he can afford to devote to the pursuits of the higher culture. **1955** J. L. AUSTIN *How to do Things with Words* (1962) viii. 98 To perform a locutionary act is in general..also and *eo ipso* to perform an illocutionary act, as I propose to call it.

E.O.K.A., EOKA, Eoka (eɪˈəʊkə). [f. initials of mod. Gr. Ἐθνικὴ Ὀργάνωσις Κυπριακοῦ Ἀγῶνος National Organization of Cypriot Struggle (for the furthering of the Greek cause in Cyprus).] The name of a Greek-Cypriot liberation movement.

1955 *Times* 11 July 10/1 These were the first terrorist outrages for a week, and may have been caused by a 'lone wolf' terrorist, as Eoka, the underground movement, has refrained from all activity. **1956** *Ann. Reg. 1955* 124 The extremist societies, the Communists on the one hand and E.O.K.A. (National Organization for the Cyprus Struggle) on the other. **1957** *Observer* 28 July 3/3 Leaflets..spoke of an organization calling itself EOKA..which had decided to begin the 'struggle for liberty'. **1957** *Times* 11 Nov. 10/4 In a public declaration this weekend the [Greek] Government strongly rebuked the Eoka Cypriot underground organization for interfering in Greek foreign affairs.

eoli, variant of ELE, oil, *Obs.*

Eolian, Eolic, Eolipyle, var. ff. ÆOLIAN, etc.

éolienne, eolienne (iːəʊlɪˈɛn). Also æ-. [ad. F. *éolienne*, fem. of *éolien*, f. Gr. αἰόλος quick-moving, glittering, sheeny + *-ien* = -IAN.] A fine dress fabric of silk and wool. Also *attrib.*

1902 *Westm. Gaz.* 27 Feb. 3/2 Crêpes de Chine and éoliennes and taffetas. **1909** *Ibid.* 28 June 5/3 Éolienne skirts trimmed with lace. **1918** *Home Chat* 4 May 106 A tunic..of ..fine coating serge, or wool Eolienne. **1920** *Glasgow Herald* 17 Apr. 4 A navy blue aeolienne frock. **1957** M. B. PICKEN *Fashion Dict.* 117/2 Eolienne..or aeolian.

eolith (ˈiːəʊlɪθ). *Archæol.* [f. EO- + LITH, after *neolith*. Cf. F. *éolithe*.] The name given to certain flints which have been found in Tertiary deposits in England, France, and elsewhere, which have been claimed to be the earliest traces of human handiwork, but whose origin is much disputed.

1895 A. H. KEANE *Ethnol.* 74 Other modern savages, who are quite incapable of fashioning any of these British *eoliths*, as they are called. **1907** T. R. HOLMES *Anc. Brit.* 26 Flints of divers shapes..which have been termed 'eoliths', or stone implements of a dawning age. **1921** R. A. S. MACALISTER *Text-bk. European Archæol.* I. 148 Certain flint flakes to which the name 'Eoliths' has been given. **1950** G. E. DANIEL *Hundred Years Archæol.* vii. 230 Benjamin Harrison, a village shop-keeper of Ightham in Kent..began to collect stone tools in Kent, especially in the plateau gravels. Here he found what are now referred to as Harrisonian eoliths.

eolithic (iːəʊˈlɪθɪk), *a.* (and *sb.*) *Archæol.* [ad. F. *éolithique* (G. de Mortillet *Le Préhistorique* (1883) I. iv. 18), f. EO- + LITHIC *a.*¹, after *neolithic, palæolithic*.] Pertaining to the earliest age of man that is represented by the use of worked flint implements. Also *fig.* and as *sb.*

1890 T. WILSON in *Rep. Smithsonian Inst. 1888* 604 The first or Eolithic period belongs entirely to the tertiary geologic epoch. **1893** J. A. BROWN in *Jrnl. Anthropol. Inst.* XXII. 94, I venture to suggest the following four divisions of the Stone age..1. Eolithic; Roughly hewn pebbles and nodules and naturally broken stones, showing work with thick ochreous patina, found on the plateaux of the chalk. *Ibid.* 97 Flint implements of the Eolithic period (Plateau). **1920** QUIGGIN & HADDON *Keane's Man Past & Pr.* 10 The tools exhibit deliberate flaking, and mark the transition between eolithic and palaeolithic work. **1926** T. E. LAWRENCE *Seven Pillars* (1935) li. 294 We.., after killing the sheep in relay, had recourse to stray flints to cut them up... We used them in the eolithic spirit. *a* **1936** KIPLING *Something of Myself* (1937) vii. 177 *The Times* leaders on 'motor-cars' were eolithic in outlook. **1948** A. L. KROEBER *Anthropol.* (ed. 2) xvi. 631 Rutot's Mesvinian stage of the Eolithic is recognized as probably a Belgian facies of the oldest Levalloisian or Pre-Mousterian. But his still earlier Eolithic stages..find little acceptance by the prehistorians as containing real artifacts.

eom, obs. form of *am*: see BE *v.*

eom, variant of EME, *Obs.* uncle.

eon, variant form of ÆON.

Eonism (ˈiːəʊnɪz(ə)m). Also **eonism**. [f. the name of the Chevalier Charles d'*Éon* (1728–1810), a French adventurer who wore women's clothes: see -ISM.] Transvestism, esp. by a man. So **ˈEonist**, one who wears the clothes of the opposite sex.

1928 H. ELLIS *Studies Psychol. Sex* VII. i. 10 It was clearly a typical case of what Hirschfeld later termed 'transvestism' and what I would call 'sexo-aesthetic inversion', or more simply, 'Eonism'. *Ibid.* 12 The Eonist (though sometimes emphatically of the apparent sex) sometimes shows real physical approximations towards the opposite sex. **1970** *Times* 5 Sept. 8/4 Today we can see that the Chevalier was an a-sexual transvestite. From his name Havelock Ellis coined the term *eonism* to describe this minor deviation.

‖**eo nomine** (ˌeɪəʊ ˈnəʊmɪniː), *advb. phr.* [L., ablative of *id nōmen*, that name.] Under that name; that is so called; explicitly.

1627 *Let.* 23 Nov. in Birch *Court & Times Chas. I* (1848) I. 292 The Earl of Bridgewater hath, *eo nomine*, disbursed £10,000. **1822** [see ARMINIANISM]. **1870** S. H. HODGSON *Theory of Practice* II. ii. 69 He who seeks happiness, eo nomine, misses it. **1938** R. G. COLLINGWOOD *Princ. Art* iv. 72 The case of religious art *eo nomine*..hardly needs analysis.

†**ˈeont.** [OE. *ęnt*.] A giant.

a **1000** *Ruin* (Gr.) 2 Brosnað enta ȝeweorc. *c* **1175** *Lamb. Hom.* 93 Eontas wolden areran..anne stepel.

eorl, obs. and Hist. form of EARL.

eorne, var. of EARN *adv. Obs.* earnestly.

eornen, variant of *rinnen*: see RUN.

eornest, obs. form of EARNEST.

eorre, var. f. IRRE *sb.* and *a. Obs.*, anger, angry.

eosin (ˈiːəsɪn). *Chem.* [f. Gr. ἠώς the morning red, the dawn + -IN.] A red dye-stuff produced by the addition of bromine to a solution of fluorescin in glacial acetic acid. Its potassium salt, known in commerce as 'soluble eosin' or 'eosin', is used as a rose-coloured dye. Also *attrib.*

1866 A. FLINT *Princ. Med.* (1880) 866 The addition of some coloring agent, such as iodine or eosine, is of assistance in searching for them. **1879** WATTS *Dict. Chem.*, Eosin. **1885** *Athenæum* 27 June 827/3 Coal-tar colours, especially eosine reds, have been employed in the artificial flower manufacture.

eosinophil (iːəʊˈsɪnəfɪl), *a.* and *sb. Med.* Also **-phile**. [G. *eosinophil* (P. Ehrlich 1878–9, in *Farbenanalyt. Untersuch. z. Histol. d. Blutes* (1891) 7), f. EOSIN + -O + -PHIL, -PHILE.]

A. *adj.* Having an affinity for eosin; staining readily with eosin. **B.** *sb.* A cell readily stained by eosin. Hence **eosinoˈphilic**, **eosiˈnophilous** *adjs.* = A above; also, pertaining to **eosinoˈphilia**, a condition of the blood marked by the formation and accumulation of an excess of eosinophil cells.

1886 H. M. BIGGS tr. *Hueppe's Meth. Bacteriol. Invest.* ii. 68 The elements of the blood..are divided, according to Ehrlich, into—1. Lymphoid elements... 2. Myeloid cells (eosinophile). 3. Undetermined (spleen and..marrow). *Ibid.* 69 The *a* or eosinophile granule..can be stained in all the acid aniline-dyes. **1892** GOULD *Pocket Med. Dict.* 105 Eosinophilous. **1899** J. R. GREEN *Soluble Ferments* xxii. 382 An eosinophilous substance diffused out of the nucleus into the cytoplasmic zone. **1900** DORLAND *Med. Dict.* 234/2 Eosinophil, eosinophilic, eosinophilous. **1900** W. MYERS tr. *Ehrlich & Lazarus' Histol. Blood* 149 By eosinophilia we understand an increase only of the polynuclear eosinophil cells in the blood. Confusion of this form of leucocytosis with leukæmia is quite impossible. **1905** *Medical Annual* 140 Of 158 non-infected persons 91.1 per cent had under 5 per cent of eosinophiles. *Ibid.*, The eosinophilia may persist some time after the disappearance of ova. **1907** J. G. ADAMI *Inflammation* II. xi. 82 During the height of the infection the eosinophils were found collected in the blood-vessels, actively migrating into the peritoneal cavity. **1907** *Practitioner* Sept. 455 The Eosinophil Cells. **1910** H. W. ARMIT tr. *Ehrlich & Lazarus' Anæmia* iii. 167 The Post-infective Form of Eosinophilia... There may even be a distinct eosinophilic leucocytosis. **1912** ADAMI & MCCRAE *Text-bk. Path.* 99 All verminous parasites set up eosinophilia, an increase in the number of eosinophile leukocytes in the circulating blood. *Ibid.* 128 The leukocytes that take part [in inflammation] are the polynuclear..cells, the lymphocytes, and the eosinophiles. **1949** H. W. FLOREY et al. *Antibiotics* II. xlv. 409 Eosinophilia developed in 14 out of 16 patients at some time during 120 days of treatment with 3 g. daily of highly purified streptomycin. In 7 patients the eosinophil cells amounted to 10 per cent. or more of the white blood cells. **1958** *Immunology* I. II. 116 A homogeneous eosinophilic cytoplasm interspersed with areas of necrosis.

eotand, -end, var. of ETEN, *Obs.* giant.

eotechnic (iːəʊˈtɛknɪk), *a.* [f. EO- + Gr. τεχνικ-ός (see TECHNIC *a.* and *sb.*).] Denoting or belonging to the first stage of industrial development, when technical advances are first applied to the making of machines.

1934 L. MUMFORD *Technics & Civilization* iii. 109 The demonstration that industrial civilization was not a single whole..was first made by Professor Patrick Geddes... In defining the paleotechnic and neotechnic phases, he however neglected the important period of preparation, when all the key inventions were either invented or foreshadowed. So, following the archeological parallel he called attention to, I shall call the first period the eotechnic phase: the dawn age of modern technics. *Ibid.* 112 At the bottom of the eotechnic economy stands one important fact: the diminished use of human beings as prime movers, and the separation of the production of energy from its application and immediate control. **1954** J. A. C. BROWN *Social Psychol. Industry* i. 22 The eotechnic or medieval phase of industry stretches roughly from about A.D. 1000 to 1750.

Eötvös (ˈøtvøʃ). The name of R. *Eötvös* (1848–1919), Hungarian physicist, used *attrib.* or in the possessive to designate certain apparatus invented and principles enunciated by him.

1913 *Jrnl. Chem. Soc.* A. CIV. II. 300 The surface-tension formulæ of Young and Eötvös... Eötvös' formula. **1920** A. S. EDDINGTON *Space Time & Gravit.* vii. 112 But it was shown by experiments with the Eötvös torsion-balance that the ratio of weight to mass for uranium is the same as for all other substances. **1922** *Encycl. Brit.* XXXI. 207/1 The quantities which the Eötvös balance is capable of measuring are almost incredibly small. **1930** N. K. ADAM *Physics & Chem. of Surfaces* v. 153 Eötvös' 'law'...[154] Eötvös deduced his equation theoretically from considerations of 'corresponding states' of liquids of similar molecular constitution... The central point of the theory is, however, that surfaces should be compared on the basis of the number of molecules per unit area. *Ibid.* 159 The orientation and shape of the surface molecules.., their mutual attractions and details of their shape, size, and packing..may all affect the value of the Eötvös 'constant'. **1957** *Encycl. Brit.* VII. 846/1 The Eötvös or *Polflucht* force. **1963** JERRARD & MCNEILL *Dict. Sci. Units* 46 *Eotvos unit* (E), a unit used in geophysical prospecting to indicate the change in the intensity of gravity with change in horizontal distance. It has the dimensions of 10^{-9} gal per horizontal centimetre.

-eous, *suffix*, occurring in adjs., is chiefly f. L. *-e-us* + -OUS. The Eng. words with this suffix are for the most part practically mere adaptations of L. adjs. in *-eus*, the senses of which they generally retain. While, however, the L. adjs. in *-eus* f. sbs. denoting material substances have usually the sense 'composed of', as well as the sense 'of the nature of, resembling', their Eng. derivatives in *-eous* express the latter meaning only: compare, e.g. *argenteous, ligneous, vitreous*, with the corresponding words in Latin. In a very few cases (e.g. *aqueous*) Eng. adjs. in *-eous* have been formed directly on L. sbs. The L. ending *-eus* also occurs as part of a complex suffix, as in the words in *-āceus* (see -ACEOUS) and *-āneus* (cf. *consentaneous, instantaneous*).

2. In *beauteous, bounteous, duteous, plenteous*, the ending *-eous* arises from the addition of the suffix *-ous* to *-te*, earlier form of -TY; but in the older words of this formation *-teous* replaces an earlier *-tivous*, f. Fr. *-tif* + -OUS; e.g. *bounteous* was originally *bountivous*, f. Fr. *bontif*, f. *bonté*: see BOUNTY.

3. In a few instances *-eous* is an analogical deformation of other suffixes, as in *righteous* (for *rightwise*), *courteous*, for ME. *curteis* a. OFr. *curteis* (*-eis*:—L. *-ēnsem*).

eovese, obs. form of EAVES.

eow, obs. form of YEW.

eow, -er, etc., obs. forms of YOU, YOUR, etc.

eowberge, obs. form of YEWBERRY.

†**eowde.** *Obs.* [OE. *éowde*:—OTeut. type **awidjo(m*, f. **awi-s*, OE. *éowu* EWE. Cf. OHG. *ewit*, Goth. *awêþi* of same meaning, but different formation.] A flock of sheep.

a **1000** *Andreas* 1669 Ne scealt þu þæt eowde anforlætan. *c* **1000** *Ags. Ps.* lxxviii. 14 We þin folc wærun and fæle sceap eowdes þines. *a* **1175** *Cott. Hom.* 245 ȝif he hit þan ȝemet, he hit berð an his eaxlun to þara eowde oder falde.

eozoic, Eozoon, etc.: see EO- *pref.*

ep-, *prefix*, in words a. or ad. Gr., or f. Gr. elements, represents ἐπ-, shortened form of ἐπί before a vowel: see EPI-.

epacrid (ɛˈpækrɪd). *Bot.* [ad. mod.L. *epacrid-em*, f. Gr. ἐπί + ἄκρις summit; so called by Forster (1776) because 'the plants of this genus are generally found on mountain tops' (Forster, *Characteres Generum Plant.* 10). In sense b. f. mod.L. *Epacrid-eæ*.]

a. A plant of the genus *Epacris*. **b.** A plant of the N.O. *Epacrideæ*, of which this is the typical genus; the order consists of corolliflоral dicotyledons, growing in Australia and the Indian Archipelago, which resemble the heaths of other countries.

1881 BLACKMORE *Christowell* i, Choice geraniums lived here, and roses, heaths and epacrids.

epacris (ɛˈpækrɪs). [mod.L. (J. R. & J. G. A. Forster *Characteres Generum Plantarum* (1776) 19), f. Gr. ἐπί + ἄκρις summit; see EPACRID.] A

plant of the genus of Australian evergreen heath-like shrubs so called.

1805 *Curtis's Bot. Mag.* XXII. 844 (*heading*) Rigid Epacris. **1807** *Ibid.* XXV. 982 This beautiful Epacris was sent us in blossom. **1841** *Florist's Jrnl.* (1846) II. 137 A 'New Subscriber'..wishes to know the reason his Epacrises are losing their foliage. **1884** 'R. BOLDREWOOD' *Old Melbourne Mem.* xi. 77 Special species of Epacris grew there. **1885** H. H. HAYTER *Carboona* 7 Of our tribe she is the flower, Lily, epacris and orchid. *a* **1963** B. JAMES in *Austral. Short Stories* (1963) 48 And an Australian garden for..epacris, for mint bush, Geraldton wax and indigofera.

epact ('i:pækt, 'ɛpækt). [ad. Fr. *epacte*, L. *epacta*, Gr. ἐπακτή, f. ἐπακτός, vbl. adj. of ἐπάγειν to intercalate, f. ἐπί on + ἄγειν to bring.]

1. a. (Also pl. *epacts*.) The number of days that constitutes the excess of the solar over the lunar year of 12 months. **b.** The number of days in the age of the moon on the first day of the year (now Jan. 1st, but formerly March 1st or 22nd).

a. 1588 A. KING *Canisius' Catech.* N vj b, Y^e Epact, quhilk is ye nombre of ye dayes quhairby y^e ȝere of ye sone do exceid y^e ȝere of ye moone. **1603** SIR C. HEYDON *Jud. Astrol.* xviii. 383 The Epact, or 11. daies ouerplus. **1725** BRADLEY *Fam. Dict.* s.v. *Year*, These eleven Days are call'd Epacts. **1750** *Phil. Trans.* XLVI. 421. **1787** BONNYCASTLE *Astron.* xiv. 237.

b. 1552 *Bk. Com. Prayer*, Almanack, *heading* of col. 3 The Epacte. **1561** EDEN *Art Nauig.* II. vi. 31 This nomber of Epact or concurrent is founde. **1594** BLUNDEVIL *Exerc.* VII. i. (ed. 7) 654 The Epact [beginneth] the first of March. **1594** J. DAVIS *Seaman's Secr.* (1607) 6 There are two numbers especially required, named the Prime and the Epact. **1696** WHISTON *Th. Earth* II. (1722) 214 The Eccentricity of the Sun is..exactly coincident with the Epact of the Moon. **1704** HEARNE *Duct. Hist.* (1714) I. 5 The Epact is the number of Days of the Moon's age on the last day of December. **1704** J. HARRIS *Lex. Techn.* s.v., Divide by 3; for each one left add Ten; 30 reject; the Prime makes Epact then. **1816** PLAYFAIR *Nat. Phil.* II. 137 The Epacts..the ages of the moon..at the beginning of every year. **1867** DENISON *Astron. without Math.* 95 The moon's age at that time is called the epact of the year.

2. Any intercalated day or days. *rare.*

1603 HOLLAND *Plutarch's Mor.* Gloss., *Epact*, the day put to, or set in, to make the leape yeere. **1880** *Contemp. Rev.* Apr. 585 The five days which the Egyptians added by way of epact to the twelve months of thirty days each.

3. *attrib.*

1876 *Prayer-bk. Interleaved* 55 By means of the Epact Almanack, Easter-day for any year may be readily found.

epactal (ɪ'pæktəl, ɛ'pæktəl), *a. Anat.* [f. Gr. ἐπακτός (see prec.) + -AL¹.] 'Imported; foreign' (*Syd. Soc. Lex.*). *epactal bone*: the Wormian bone at the superior angle of the occipital bone.

1878 BARTLEY tr. *Topinard's Anthrop.* II. i. 207 The exceptionally large ossa Wormiana..an epactal, for example.

†**epæ'netic**, *a. Obs.* Also 7 epænitic, 8 epainetic. [ad. Gr. ἐπαινετικός, f. ἐπαινέειν to praise.] Laudatory, panegyrical.

1675 PHILLIPS *Theatr. Poet.* Pref. **5 b, In whatever kind of Poetry, whether the Epic, the Dramatic..the Epænetic, the Bucolic, or the Epigram. **1687** WINSTANLEY *Lives Eng. Poets* Pref., Some addicting themselves most to the Epick.. other to the Elegiack, the Epænitick, the Bucolick, or the Epigram. **1736** BAILEY, *Epainetick Poem* comprehends the Hymn, the Epithalamium, the Genethliacon, or what else tends to the praise or congratulation of the Divine persons and persons eminent upon earth.

‖**epagoge** (ɛpə'gəʊgi:). [Gr. ἐπαγωγή, f. ἐπάγειν to bring in, f. ἐπί to + ἄγειν to bring.] The method of bringing forward a number of particular instances to lead to a general conclusion; argument by induction. **epa'gogic** *a.* [ad. Gr. ἐπαγωγικ-ός], of an inductive nature.

In mod. Dicts.

epagomenal, epagomenous (ɛpæ'gɒmənəl, -əs), *adjs.* = EPAGOMENIC *a.*

1906 *Expositor* Apr. 342 The five epagomenous days of the year. **1924** W. M. F. PETRIE *Relig. Life Anc. Egypt* v. 165 On the first of the epagomenal days at the end of the year. **1928** C. DAWSON *Age of Gods* vii. 151 The Egyptian solar calendar with its 12 months of 30 days and 5 epagomenal days, which is so marked an improvement on the Babylonian lunar year.

epagomenic (ˌɛpəgəʊ'mɛnɪk), *a.* [f. Gr. ἐπαγομέν-η (ἡμέρα) intercalated (day), pass. pple. of ἐπάγειν (see EPAGOGE) + -IC.] Intercalary (days); (gods) worshipped on intercalary days.

1839 *Fraser's Mag.* XX. 211 The epagomenaic [*sic*], *i.e.* as the gods of the five days which formed no part of the month, or of the old solar year. **1880** *Athenæum* 23 Oct. 535/3 Rites to be performed or omitted on the epagomenic days.

epale'aceous, *a. Bot.* [f. E- *pref.*³ + L. *palea* chaff + -ACEOUS.] Having no chaffy scales.

In mod. Dicts.

epalpate (i:'pælpət), *a. Ent.* [f. E- *pref.*³ + L. *palpus* the soft palm of the hand, in mod.L. a feeler.] Having no palpi or feelers.

1884 in *Syd. Soc. Lex.*

epalpebrate (i:'pælpɪbrət), *a.* [f. E- *pref.*³ + L. *palpebra* eyelid + -ATE².] Having no eyebrows.

1884 in *Syd. Soc. Lex.*

epana-, before stems beginning with a vowel *epan-*, a combination of two Greek prepositions ἐπ(ί) upon, in addition + ἀνά up, again, occurring in some rhetorical terms, adopted from Greek. **eˌpanadi'plosis** [Gr. δίπλωσις a doubling; cf. ANADIPLOSIS], (see quots.). **ˌepana'lepsis** [Gr. λῆψις a taking, f. ληβ-; cf. ANALEPSY], a figure by which the same word or clause is repeated after intervening matter; so **epanaleptic** (-'lɛptɪk) *a.* [Gr. ἐπαναληπτικός], characterized by epanalepsis or repetition of a word or phrase; also as *sb.*, such repetition. **epa'naphora** [Gr. φορά a carrying] = ANAPHORA. **epa'naphoral** *a.*, characterized by epanaphora. **epa'nastrophe** [Gr. στροφή turning; cf. ANASTROPHE], a figure by which the end-word of one sentence becomes the first word of the next. **e'panodos**, also *erron.* 6 epanodis, 7, 9 epanados [Gr. ὁδός way; cf. ANODE], (*a*) the repetition of a sentence in an inverse order; (*b*) a return to the regular thread of discourse after a digression. **ˌepanor'thosis** [Gr. ὄρθωσις a setting straight, f. ὀρθόειν, f. ὀρθός straight], a figure in which a word is recalled, in order to substitute a more correct or stronger term. Hence **ˌepanor'thotic** *a.*

1678 PHILLIPS, **Epanadiplosis*..a Rhetorical figure wherein a sentence begins and ends with the same word; as Severe to his servants, to his children severe. **1736** BAILEY, *Epanadiplosis*..In Latin this figure is called *Inclusio*. **1847** CRAIG, *Epanadiplosis*. **1584** D. FENNER *Artes Logike & Rethorike* sig. D3^v, *Epanalepsis, which signifieth to take backe. **1589** PUTTENHAM *Eng. Poesie* III. xix. (Arb.) 210 *Epanalepsis*, or the Eccho sound..Much must be be beloued, that loueth much. *a* **1619** FOTHERBY *Atheom.* (1622) Pref. 10 A Poeticall Epanalepsis or reduplication. **1736** BAILEY, *Epanalepsis*, a repetition. **1847** CRAIG, *Epanalepsis*. **1927** F. J. E. RABY *Hist. Chr. Latin Poetry* iii. 96 Luxorius..shows a vicious taste for the cento and for *epanaleptic verses. **1956** AUDEN *Old Man's Road*, The language they loved was coming to grief, Expiring in preposterous mechanical tricks, epanaleptics, rhopalics, anacyclic acrostics. **1678** PHILLIPS, **Epanaphora*, a figure in which the same word begins several sentences. **1864** WEBSTER, *Epanaphora*. **1906** *Athenæum* 10 Mar. 303/2 Under cover of all this *epanaphoral fury..Mr. Campbell has in more than one instance shifted his ground. **1864** WEBSTER, **Epanastrophe*. **1589** PUTTENHAM *Eng. Poesie* III. xix. (Arb.) 229 *Epanodis, or the figure of Retire. *a* **1679** HOBBES *Rhet.* (1840) 523 Epanados..signifies the turning to the same tune. **1812** KNOX & JEBB *Corr.* II. 79 The epanodos, or..speaking first, to the latter of two propositions; afterwards, to the former. **1847** CRAIG, *Epanodos*..a rhetorical figure, when a sentence or member is inverted, or repeated backward. **1579** E. K. *Gloss. Spenser's Sheph. Cal.* Jan. 61 A prety *Epanorthosis in these two verses. **1672** H. MORE *Brief Reply* 172 By a seasonable Epanorthosis he straightway adds, etc. **1736** BAILEY, *Epanorthosis*. **1847** CRAIG, *Epanorthosis*.

epanthous (ɛ'pænθəs), *a. Bot.* [f. Gr. ἐπ(ί) + ἄνθ-ος flower + -OUS.] Growing upon flowers, as certain fungi.

In mod. Dicts.

eparch ('ɛpɑ:k). Also 7 eparck. [a. Gr. ἔπαρχ-ος, f. ἐπ(ί) over + ἀρχός ruler.]

1. a. *Hist.* Used as equivalent to the L. *præfectus* perfect. **b.** In mod. usage: The governor of an eparchy or administrative division in the kingdom of Greece.

1656 BLOUNT *Glossogr.*, *Eparch*, the President of a Province. **1788** GIBBON *Decl. & F.* (1846) V. liii. 245 The eparch or præfect of the city. **1827** SIR H. TAYLOR *Comnenus* II. iii, The eparchs will resort To the Bucoleon. **1884** J. T. BENT in *Macm. Mag.* Oct. 431/2 These eparchs again look after the demarchs or mayors of the various towns.

2. *Eccl.* **a.** *Hist.* The metropolitan (bishop) of a province. **b.** In the Greek (Russian) Church: The metropolitan (bishop) of an eparchy.

1691 GRASCOME *Reply to Vind. Disc. Unreasonableness New Separ.* 21 The African Fathers were such Enemies to the Titles of Eparck or Patriarck. **1882–3** SCHAFF *Encycl. Relig. Knowl.* III. 1927 Under him [the patriarch] the eparchs in the provinces.

Hence **'eparchate** [see -ATE¹], = next.

1882–3 SCHAFF *Encycl. Relig. Knowl.* III. 1763 The three eparchates of Palestine.

e'parchial, *a.* [f. next + -AL¹.] Pertaining to an eparchy.

1882–3 SCHAFF *Encycl. Relig. Knowl.* 2082 Under these chief academies are the eparchial seminaries, with many circuit and parish schools.

eparchy ('ɛpɑkɪ). [ad. Gr. ἐπαρχία, f. ἔπαρχος: see prec.] A district or province under the government of an eparch.

1. One of the subdivisions of the modern kingdom of Greece; a division of a nomarchy.

1838 *Penny Cycl.* XI. 433/2 Deputies from the communes assemble at the chief town of the eparchy. *c* **1850** *Nat. Encycl.* I. 839 It forms part of the eparchy of Naxos. **1880** *Encycl. Brit.* XI. 85 (art. *Greece*) The [13] nomarchies are sub-divided into 59 eparchies.

2. In the Russian (Greek) Church: A diocese.

1796 MORSE *Amer. Geog.* II. 87 Bishops..preside over dioceses called Eparchies. **1798** MALTHUS *Popul.* (1878) 153 It [a statistical work on Russia] contains all the eparchies except Bruzlaw. **1862** NEALE *Ess. Liturg.* (1867) 302 All the sees are divided into eparchies.

eparterial (ɛpɑ:'tɪərɪəl), *a. Anat.* [See EP-.] Situated above the pulmonary artery (see quots.).

1882 E. A. SCHÄFER *Quain's Elem. Anat.* (ed. 9) II. 511 The right bronchus..soon gives off a branch..which comes off *above* the place where the right pulmonary artery crosses the bronchus (eparterial branch). **1921** A. KEITH *Hum. Embryol.* (ed. 4) xxii. 349 The bronchus of the upper right lobe..commonly lies above its artery—that is to say, it is eparterial. The other bronchi are hyparterial. **1962** *Gray's Anat.* (ed. 33) 1340 After giving off a branch to the upper lobe of the right lung—termed the superior lobe (eparterial) bronchus because it arises above the right pulmonary artery —the right (hyparterial) bronchus passes below the artery.

†**epaˌssyte'rotically**, *adv. nonce-wd.* [f. Gr. ἐπασσύτερον one upon another; cf. *chaotically*.]

1652 URQUHART *Jewel* Wks. (1834) 249 He killed seven of them epassyterotically, that is, one after another.

‖**épatant** (epatɑ̃), *a.* [Fr., pres. pple. of *épater* (see next).] Shocking (to the conventionally-minded). (Usually with implied reference to the next.) Also *absol.*

1925 G. B. SHAW *Shaw on Theatre* (1958) 171 The old anti-bourgeois weeklies..always Frondeur and *épatant* no matter who was in power, have disappeared. **1945** W. STEVENS *Let.* 16 May (1967) 500 No one seems to be more addicted to the *epatant* (but it is not in any meretricious sense). **1961** *Listener* 16 Nov. 825/3 It has to be striking, astonishing, titillating, in a particular way—it has to be *épatant*. **1963** AUDEN *Dyer's Hand* 502 When Benedick says, 'Well, a horn for my money when all's done,' he is being deliberately *épatant*.

‖**épater** (epate). [Fr., to flabbergast.] Phr. ***épater le(s) bourgeois***: to startle or shock the 'man in the street' or the uncritical adherent of traditional (artistic or ethical) theories.

The Fr. phrase 'Je les ai épatés, les bourgeois' is attributed to Alexandre Privat d'Anglemont (d. 1859).

1903 G. B. SHAW *Man & Superman* Epist. Dedic. p. v, You once asked me why I did not write a Don Juan play... You meant me to épater le bourgeois. **1920** O. W. HOLMES *Let.* 30 Aug. (1953) I. 277 One is that you refer to things not generally known by your readers without explanation—a thing which inferior people do to '*épater les bourgeois*'. **1938** W. S. MAUGHAM *Summing Up* 233 Sometimes he [*sc.* an author]..to *épater le bourgeois* has paraded the red waistcoat of Théophile Gautier. **1941** L. MACNEICE *Poetry of Yeats* v. 95 Moore..is writing like a naughty boy *pour épater les bourgeois*. **1958** B. NICHOLS *Sweet & Twenties* i. 21 Tallulah's wickedness is really a pose—a mask to *épater les bourgeois*.

epatic, -ke, obs. ff. HEPATIC, etc.

‖**epaule** (ɛ'pɔ:l). *Fortif.* Also 8 espaule. [a. Fr. *épaule* (earlier *espaule*) shoulder.] The 'shoulder' of a bastion, *i.e.* the place where the face and flank meet.

1702 *Mil. Dict.*, *Epaule*. **1704** J. HARRIS *Lex. Techn.*, *Epaul, espaul*. **1727** CHAMBERS, *Epaule*, or *Espaule*. **1748** *Earthquake of Peru* i. 48 Which makes the Angle of the Epaule 130 Degrees. **1853** STOCQUELER *Mil. Encycl.* s.v.

epaulement (ɛ'pɔ:lmənt). Also 7 espaulment, 9 epaulment. In sense 2 ‖**épaulement** (epolmɑ̃). [a. Fr. *épaulement* (earlier *esp-*), f. *épauler* to protect (troops) by an epaulement, f. *épaule* shoulder.]

1. *Fortif.* 'A covering mass raised to protect from the fire of the enemy, but differing from a parapet in having no arrangement made for the convenient firing over it by defenders' (Adm. Smyth).

1687 J. RICHARDS *Jrnl. Siege Buda* 8 To beat the Enemy from an Espaulment they had made to flank the Breach. **1748** SMOLLETT *Rod. Rand.* xlv. (1804) 306, I never saw an epaulement but once—and that was at the siege of Namur. **1811** PINKERTON *Petral.* I. 43 Fasces of prisms, projecting from the wall, like epaulements. **1859** F. GRIFFITHS *Artil. Man.* (1862) 251 On the balls striking the epaulment, they ricoched.

‖**2.** *Ballet.* The placing of the shoulders, one forward and the other drawn back, with the head turned to look over the forward shoulder.

1830 R. BARTON tr. *Blasis's Code of Terpsichore* 67 *Epaulement*, opposition of the body. *Ibid.*, Opposition, *épaulement du corps*; half-arm in opposition and legs in the third position. **1952** *Ballet Ann.* VI. 121/1 The shortcomings of the French school—poor *port de bras* and *épaulement*, bent knees and weakness in *pirouettes*. **1961** *Guardian* 8 June 8/4 Sticklike arms and an almost complete lack of *épaulement*.

epaulet, epaulette ('ɛpəlɛt). [a. Fr. *épaulette*, f. *épaule* shoulder.

The anglicized spelling *epaulet* is preferable, on the ground that the word is fully naturalized in use; but the form in *-ette* is at present more common.]

1. A shoulder-piece; an ornament worn on the shoulder as part of a military, naval, or sometimes of a civil uniform. ***to win one's epaulets***: (of a private soldier) to earn promotion to the rank of officer.

1783 NELSON 26 Nov. in Nicolas *Disp.* (1845) I. 89 Here are two Navy Captains..with epaulettes. **1800** *Naval Chron.* III. 495 The Post Captain under three years standing..wears one epaulet upon the right shoulder. **1816** 'QUIZ' *Grand Master* VIII. 220 Gorget, epaulets, and sash, Lion and crown—a perfect dash. **1838** *Hist. Rec. 4th Dragoon Guards* 63 The Officers were ordered to wear two Silver Epaulettes and an Aiguillette. **1848** W. H. KELLY tr. *L. Blanc's Hist. Ten Y.* I. 220 Obliged to borrow from

Rothschild, the banker, the epaulettes he wore as Austrian consul. **1875** HAMERTON *Intell. Life* III. vi. 101 A soldier wins his epaulettes before the enemy.

b. As equivalent for 'officer', 'commission'.

1829 MARRYAT *F. Mildmay* xvi, My captain elect.. herded not with his brother epaulettes. **1848** THACKERAY *Bk. Snobs* ix, When epaulets are not sold.

2. *Entom.* The plate that covers the base of the anterior wings in hymenopterous insects.

1834 MCMURTRIE *Cuvier's Anim. Kingd.* 435 At the base of each of the superior wings is a kind of epaulette, prolonged posteriorly, that corresponds to the piece called *tegula* in the Hymenoptera. **1874** LUBBOCK *Orig. & Met. Ins.* iii. 56 The ciliated lobes or epaulets.

3. Used by antiquarian writers as a name for the smaller forms of the shoulder-piece or 'pauldron' in a suit of armour.

1824 MEYRICK *Anc. Arm.* III. 87 A suit of armour.. resembling the halecrets of Henry the Eighth's time in having epaulettes for the shoulder.

4. A piece of trimming forming an ornament for the shoulder of a lady's dress.

1865 DICKENS *Mut. Fr.* I. ii, A shoulder—with a powdered epaulette on it—of the mature young lady.

5. *Comb.*, as *epaulet-like* adj.

1841–71 T. R. JONES *Anim. Kingd.* (ed. 4) 221 Four epaulet-like wreaths of long cilia. **1889** *Daily News* 12 Nov. 3/1 Oversleeves of the velvet are heaped up in epaulet-like folds upon the shoulders.

Hence **'epauˌletted** *ppl. a.*, furnished or ornamented with epaulets; wearing epaulets.

1810 *Naval Chron.* XXIII. 351 His epauletted coat. **1836** E. HOWARD *R. Reefer* xxviii, Heavily-epauletted shoulders. **1849** *Blackw. Mag.* LXV. 30 How were the Kabyles to distinguish between the acts of the private soldier and of the epauleted chief. **1860** GEN. P. THOMPSON *Audi Alt.* III. cxxiv. 77 To don the dress of epauletted hangmen.

epaxial (ɛ'pæksɪəl), *a.* *Anat.* [f. EP- + L. *axi-s* + -AL[1].] Situated on or above the axis (of the body): said of muscles, cartilages, etc. that lie upon or above the vertebral column looked at in a horizontal position.

1872 MIVART *Elem. Anat.* 219 Such arches, as they extend above the axis, have been called epaxial arches.

Hence **e'paxially** *adv.*, in an epaxial position or direction.

†**epe**, *v.* *Obs. rare.* [a. ON. *œpa*:—OTeut. *wôpjan*: see WEEP.] *intr.* To cry aloud.

c **1200** ORMIN 9198 Þe rowwste iss herrd off ænne mann þatt epeþþ þuss i wesste.

epe, var. of YEPE *a.*, *Obs.*, active, bold.

epecedean, obs. form of EPICEDIAN.

‖**épée** (epe). [Fr., = sword.] The sharp-pointed sword used in duelling and (blunted) in fencing. Hence **épé(e)ist** [cf. F. *épéiste*, also used], an épée fencer.

1889 W. H. POLLOCK et al. *Fencing* vii. 112 The fencer who has never handled the practice *épée* may at first find some difficulty when he exchanges the foil for it. **1910** *Encycl. Brit.* IX. 668/1 English épéists have also been coming to the front. *Ibid.* 668/2 Épée fencing can be, and often is, conducted indoors. **1910** *Westm. Gaz.* 11 Apr. 14/1 Mr. Seligman is a very fine épéeist. **1922** G. F. LAKING *Rec. Eur. Armour* V. 59 The Court or 'small' sword, the use and rules of which are practically identical with those of the modern *épée*. **1955** *Times* 4 July 4/1 In the men's bouts, fought with the *épée*, London had 13 wins to three. **1958** *Times* 28 Nov. 16/6 There are 14 of the current top 16 amateur épéeistes entered.

epeiric (ɛ'paɪərɪk), *a.* *Geol.* [f. Gr. ἤπειρος mainland, continent + -IC.] *epeiric sea*: see quot. 1930.

1917 *Bull. Geol. Soc. Amer.* XXVIII. 780 Stormy epeiric seas are represented by Lake Erie and the North Sea. **1925** J. JOLY *Surface-Hist. Earth* iii. App. 65 We are justified in ascribing the epeiric seas, attending the coming of a revolution, to the density-changes arising from the change of state of a basaltic substratum. **1930** *Ibid.* (ed. 2) 208 *Epeiric seas*, shallow marine waters connected with the oceans but wholly within the continental platform. **1964** A. B. SHAW *Time in Stratigr.* ii. 7 Great currents of the type characteristic of today's open oceans probably did not occur in epeiric seas of the past.

Epeirid (ɛ'paɪərɪd). *Zool.* [ad. mod.L. *Epeiridæ* (see below), ? f. Gr. ἐπί on + εἴρειν to string together.] A member of the family of web-spinning spiders, formerly called Epeiridæ, now known as Argiopidæ. Also *attrib.* or as *adj.*

1881 O. PICKARD-CAMBRIDGE *Spiders of Dorset* II. 587 The studding of the lines of their snares, by some Epeirids, with viscid globules intended to entrap their prey. *Ibid.*, The cross-lines of Epeirid snares. **1902** *Trans. S. Afr. Philos. Soc.* XI. p. xlvi, The garden.. was tenanted by numerous Epeirid spiders (*Argyope australis*). **1909** A. E. SHIPLEY in Sedgwick *Text-bk. Zool.* III. xv. 408 Perhaps our commonest Epeirid, *Meta segmentata*.

epeirogeny (ɛpaɪə'rɒdʒɛnɪ). [f. as EPEIRIC *a.* + -GENY.] The formation of continents; the deformation of the earth's crust by which continents and ocean basins are produced. So **epeiro'genesis** [-GENESIS] = EPEIROGENY; **epeiroge'netic** [-GENETIC], **epeiroge'netical**, **epeiro'genic** [-GENIC] *adjs.*

1890 G. K. GILBERT *Lake Bonneville* viii. 340, I shall take the liberty to apply to the broader movements the adjective *epeirogenic*... The process of mountain formation is *orogeny*, the process of continent formation is *epeirogeny*, and the two collectively are diastrophism. **1894** *Geol. Mag.* 449 The gentle but varying amount of epeirogenic deformation. **1898** J. E. MARR *Princ. Stratigr. Geol.* 32 Those wide-spread, fairly uniform movements which are spoken of as epeirogenic or continent-forming. **1903** A. GEIKIE *Text-bk. Geol.* (ed. 4) II. 1428/1 Epeirogeny or continent-making. **1909** WEBSTER, Epeirogenetic. **1925** J. JOLY *Surface-Hist. Earth* x. 162 The relations which exist between epeirogenic movements and glacial phenomena. *Ibid.* 189 Orogenesis and epeirogenesis.. are forms of diastrophism. **1937** WOOLDRIDGE & MORGAN *Physical Basis Geogr.* v. 62 Radial movements, due to forces acting vertically, which have been styled epeirogenetic (continent building or plateau building). **1937** *Geogr. Jrnl.* XC. 91 Epeirogenetical changes. **1939** *Nature* 4 Feb. 184/1 So far as the post-Franciscan history of Southern California is concerned, tectonically comparable areas seem to have been affected at all times by orogenic and epeirogenic forces. **1963** D. W. & E. E. HUMPHRIES tr. *Termier's Erosion & Sedimentation* i. 13 In fact, a universal epeirogeny occurred during the late Precambrian and the Carboniferous.

epencephalic (ɛ,pɛnsɪ'fælɪk), *a.* *Anat.* [f. EPENCEPHAL-ON + -IC.] Of or pertaining to the epencephalon; covering the epencephalon.

1851 [see RHINENCEPHALON]. **1854** OWEN in *Circ. Sc.* (*c* 1865) II. 53/2 Epencephalic arch. **1880** GÜNTHER *Fishes* 85 Epencephalic arch, composed of the occipitals.

epencephalon (ɛpɛn'sɛfələn). *Anat.* [f. EP- + ENCEPHALON.] The anterior of the two enlargements into which the posterior primary vesicle of the brain divides. Also called *hind-brain.*

1854 OWEN in *Circ. Sc.* (*c* 1865) II. 59/2 The epencephalon.. derives a further.. bony covering from the basisphenoid and the parietals. **1881** MIVART *Cat* 358 The anterior part of this third vesicle is sometimes called the Epencephalon.

ependyma (ɛ'pɛndɪmə). [a. Gr. ἐπένδυμα, f. ἐπενδύειν, f. ἐπί over + ἐν on + δύειν to put. Cf. Fr. *épendyme.*] 'Virchow's name for the lining membrane of the cerebral ventricles and of the central spinal canal' (*Syd. Soc. Lex.*). So **e'pendymal** *a.*, pertaining to the ependyma; **ependy'mitis**, inflammation of the ependyma.

1872 MIVART *Elem. Anat.* 366 Another very delicate epithelial layer called the ependyma. **1874** A. E. J. BARKER tr. *H. Frey's Histology & Histochem. Man* 575 To this [*sc.* the neuroglia of the spinal cord] several names have been given, such as 'central ependymal thread', 'grey central nucleus'. **1887** ELLIS *Anat.* (ed. 10) 213 Four of them [ventricles].. are lined throughout by a thin membrane named ependyma. **1889** *Cent. Dict.*, Ependymitis. **1898** Ependymal [see ASTROCYTE]. **1902** CUNNINGHAM *Text-bk. Anat.* 419 The ependymal cells. *Ibid.* 436 The ependymal layer. **1910** *Practitioner* July 65 Definite signs of post-basic meningitis or ependymitis about the fourth ventricle were found. **1962** E. C. CROSBY et al. *Correl. Anat. Nerv. Syst.* ix. 577 The ependymal cells of the choroid plexus are usually regarded as secreting the cerebrospinal fluid. **1965** R. P. MOREHEAD *Human Path.* xxxv. 1411 This condition, known as granular ependymitis, may cause obstruction of the ventricular system.

epenthesis (ɛ'pɛnθɪsɪs). *Gram.* [late L. *epenthesis*, a. Gr. ἐπένθεσις, f. ἐπί in addition + ἐν in + θέσις placing, f. τι-θέ-ναι to place. Cf. Fr. *epenthèse.*] (See quot. 1657) Subsequently used in a wider sense to account for the presence of an unetymological vowel (cf. ANAPTYXIS) or consonant.

In mod. philology applied *spec.* to the phonetic change which consists in the transference of a semi-vowel to the syllable preceding that in which it originally occurred, as in Gr. χαίρω from an earlier *χαρjω.

1657 J. SMITH *Myst. Rhet.* 171 *Epenthesis* is the interposition of a letter or syllable in the midst of a word. **1888** KING & COOKSON *Sound & Inflex. Gr. & Lat.* 197 In such presents as φθείρω, the ει is not to be regarded as the result of Epenthesis. **1954** PEI & GAYNOR *Dict. Linguistics* 66 *Epenthesis*, the interpolation in a word or sound-group of a sound or letter which has no etymological justification for appearing there. **1955** *Sci. Amer.* Aug. 79/2 Sometimes you hear a consonant inserted where the spelling of the word suggests no such sound: fambly for family, chimbley for chimney. The name of this phenomenon, from the Greek, is 'epenthesis'. **1968** *Language* XLIV. 281 A number of phonetic treatments which are shared by Gathic and Younger Avestan but not by either Sogdian or Ossetic: (1) There is no trace of *i-* or *u-*epenthesis.

e'penthesized, *ppl. a.* [See -IZE.] Of a letter or sound: inserted by or resulting from epenthesis.

1880 WILKINS & ENGLAND tr. *Curtius' Gr. Vb.* xi. 216 The epenthesised ι.

† **e'penthesy**, obs. var. of EPENTHESIS.

In mod. Dicts.

epenthetic (ɛpɛn'θɛtɪk), *a.* [ad. Gr. ἐπενθετικός: see prec. and -IC.] Pertaining to, or of the nature of, epenthesis. Of a letter or sound: Inserted in the middle of a word.

1831 M. STUART *Heb. Gr.* (ed. 4) §308 Future with epenthetic Nun. **1859** *Lit. Churchm.* V. 87/2 The א is considered epenthetic, as the true word would be [*krw*]. **1883** *Edin. Rev.* Oct. 442 An epenthetic *t* to fill up the sound.

epeolatry (ɛpɪ'ɒlətrɪ). [f. Gr. ἔπος, ἔπεος word: see -LATRY.] The worship of words.

1860 O. W. HOLMES *Professor* v. 104 Time, time only, can gradually wean us from our *Epeolatry*, or word-worship, by spiritualizing our ideas of the thing signified. **1928** *Daily Express* 28 Jan. 8/7 Many writers suffer from this disease of epeolatry, or word-worship. **1968** *Observer* 21 Jan. 27/7 A long farewell to Marshall McLuhan, most treacherous of clerks and a threat to all who cherish epeolatry.

epergne (ɪ'pɜːn). Also 8 **epergn**, **epargne**. [perh. a corruption of Fr. *épargne* saving, economy; cf. quot. 1779; but there is no evidence to show how the word acquired its present meaning.] A centre-dish, or centre ornament for the dinner-table, now often in a branched form, each branch supporting a small dish for dessert or the like, or a vase for flowers. (From our quots. it appears that the earlier use was chiefly to hold pickles.)

1761 *Bill of Fare* in Pennant *London* (1813) 562, 2 Grand Epergnes filled with fine Pickles. **1775** in Picton *L'pool Munic. Rec.* 199 That Mr. Mayor be desir'd to order a handsome silver Epergn. **1779** MACKENZIE in *Mirror* No. 34 §6 In the centre.. stood a sumptuous *epargne*, filled [with sweetmeats]. **1804** *Verses to Dr. Warton* in *Ann. Reg.* 928 [His pupils present him with an epergne on his resigning the head-mastership of Winchester, hoping that it may remind him 'of "Pickles" left behind']. **1819** *Banquet* 60 Waiter, epergne, and tankard, beaker, vase. **1861** DICKENS *Gt. Expect.* xi, An epergne or centre-piece of some kind was in the middle of the cloth.

epetite, obs. var. of HEPATITE.

epexegesis (ɛ,pɛksɪ'dʒiːsɪs). [a. Gr. ἐπεξήγησις, f. ἐπεξηγεῖσθαι, f. ἐπί in addition + ἐξηγεῖσθαι to explain: see EXEGESIS.] The addition of a word or words to convey more clearly the meaning implied, or the specific sense intended, in a preceding word or sentence; a word or words added for this purpose.

1621 BP. MOUNTAGU *Diatribæ* 163 The latter part of the Apostles assertion is an epexegesis, or explication, of the former. *a* **1641** —— *Acts & Mon.* 130 Primarily and literally, not Princes, but Prophets, which is an epexegesis of Anointed. **1888** *Pall Mall G.* 4 Oct. 3/1 The above may be very sound epexegesis. **1889** M. B. EDWARDS *A. Young* Introd. 33 These jottings of old age, interesting as they are, err on the side of redundancy and epexegesis.

epexegetic (ɛ,pɛksɪ'dʒɛtɪk). [ad. Gr. ἐπεξηγητικός, f. ἐπεξηγεῖσθαι: see prec.] Pertaining to, or of the nature of, an epexegesis; given as an additional explanation. Const. *of.*

1888 *Athenæum* 3 Nov. 590/1 Ep. I., vv. 18–20.. are epexegetic of the preceding verse.

epexegetical (ɛ,pɛksɪ'dʒɛtɪkəl), *a.* [f. prec. + -AL[1].] = prec. Hence **e,pexe'getically** *adv.*, in an epexegetical manner, by way of epexegesis.

1864 F. HALL in Wilson tr. *Vishnú-puráńa* I. 104 According to the commentator, 'fierce' and 'mild' are epexegetical of 'agreeable' and 'hideous'. **1865** *Athenæum* No. 1986. 692/1 This superfœtation of epexegetical help. **1871** tr. *Lange's Comm. Jeremiah* 160 'Hunters' is therefore epexegetical. **1882** J. ROBERTSON tr. *Müller's Heb. Synt.* 52 To attach.. epexegetically some additional specification: 'The great river, the river Euphrates'.

ephah ('iːfə). *Heb. Antiq.* Forms: 4 (ephi), 7–8 **epha**, 7– **ephah**. [a. Heb. *ēphāh*, believed to be of Egyptian origin.

Cf. Egyptian *âpit*, a dry measure containing 40 *hin*, or according to Hultsch 18·18 litres = 4 gallons. The form *ephi* is a. L. *ephi* (Vulg.) = Gr. οἰφί (LXX.). The Gr. and Lat. forms cannot be adoptions of the Heb. word, but appear to be taken directly from Egyptian; the Gr. is stated by Hesychius to be the name of an Egyptian measure.]

A Hebrew dry measure, identical in capacity with the bath; see BATH *sb.*[3]; it is variously said to have contained from $4\frac{1}{2}$ to 9 gallons. Also *fig.*

1398 TREVISA *Barth. De P.R.* XIX. cxxviii. (1495) 932 Batus is in fletynge thynges.. Ephi in drye thynges. **1611** BIBLE *Ezek.* xlv. 10 Ye shall haue iust ballances, and a iust Ephah, and a iust Bath. **1622** A. COOKE *Pope Joan* in *Harl. Misc.* (Malh.) IV. 10 By your Grace's means, the epha, wherein popish wickedness sitteth, may be lifted up between the earth and the heaven. **1660** FULLER *Mixt Contempl.* (1841) 177 Some have had a hin.. others an ephah of afflictions. **1721** BAILEY, *Epha.*

ephebe (ɛ'fiːb). *Gr. Antiq.* [ad. L. *ephēb-us*, a. Gr. ἔφηβος, f. ἐπί upon + ἥβη early manhood.] Among the Greeks, a young citizen from eighteen to twenty years of age, during which he was occupied chiefly with garrison duty. Also in L. form **ephebus** (ɛ'fiːbəs). Hence **e'phebic** *a.*, of or pertaining to an ephebus, or to early manhood.

[**1697** POTTER *Antiq. Greece* I. ix. (1715) 48 They who were enroll'd amongst the Ephebi. **1807** ROBINSON *Archæol. Græca* II. xviii. 175 The ephebi.. were youths that had arrived at the age of eighteen years.] **1880** WALDSTEIN *Pythag. Rhegion* 5 So soon as they became ephebes.. their hair was cut off to the length, etc. **1865** GROTE *Plato* I. iii. 116 *note*, His [Æschines'] two ephebic years. **1884** L. MORRIS *Songs Unsung* in *Times* 9 June 5, I.. marked.. my youngest born.. doffing his ephebic robe.

ephebeum (ɛfiː'biːəm). *Antiq.* [L., a. Gr. ἐφηβεῖον, f. ἔφηβος EPHEBE.] A court in the palæstra for the young men to exercise themselves.

1697 POTTER *Archæol. Græcæ* I. viii. 40 (*caption*) The Ephebeum. **1851–2** *Archit. Publ. Soc., Detached Ess.* (1853)

Baths 3/1 The ephebæum (or young men's hexedra). **1901** R. STURGIS *Dict. Archit.*, *Ephebeion*; *-eum*. In Greek archæology, a place for the youths (*epheboi*) to exercise; hence, in Greco-Roman archæology, any place for gymnastic exercises, as in connection with Roman thermæ.

ephectic (ɛˈfɛktɪk), *a.* [ad. Gr. ἐφεκτικός, f. ἐπέχειν to check, hold back, hence to suspend (one's judgement), f. ἐπί upon + ἔχειν to hold.]
Characterized by suspense of judgement. In ancient use, a distinctive epithet of the Sceptic school of philosophers.
a **1693** URQUHART *Rabelais* III. xxxvi. 303 The Schools of the Pyrronian..Sceptick, and Ephectick Sects. **1883** SAINTSBURY in *Daily News* 20 Dec. 6/2 Montaigne's attitude was ephectic.

ephedra (ɛˈfɛdrə). [mod.L. (Tournefort in Linnæus *Genera Plantarum* (1737) 312), f. Gr. ἐφέδρα sitting upon.] A member of the genus of low evergreen trailing shrubs so called, belonging to the family Gnetaceæ and sometimes called shrubby horsetails. Hence **ˈephedroid** *a.*, resembling ephedra.
1914 W. J. BEAN *Trees & Shrubs Hardy in Brit. Isles* I. 515 The Ephedras..usually inhabit dry, inhospitable regions. **1933** *Tropical Woods* XXXVI. 7 Ephedroid Perforation Plate.—A plate having a small group of bordered, circular openings (as in *Ephedra*). **1951** *Dict. Gardening* (R. Hort. Soc.) II. 748/2 The hardy Ephedras are best accommodated in well-drained places in the rock-garden. **1953** K. ESAU *Plant Anat.* xi. 225 (*caption*) End walls of vessel members showing..different types of perforation plates..foraminate (ephedroid). **1963** V. NABOKOV *Gift* ii. 118 Those plants that to the last remain faithful to travellers: stunted ammodendrons, lasiagrostis, and ephedras.

ephedrine (ˈɛfədrɪn). *Med.* Also **-in.** [S. Nagai 1887, in *Pharmazeut. Zeit.* XXXII. 700, f. *Ephedra* (see prec.) + -INE[5].] An alkaloid, $C_{10}H_{15}NO$, that occurs in certain species of *Ephedra* in four optically active forms and is made synthetically; 2-methylamino-1-phenylpropanol; *spec.* one of the lævorotatory isomers, used in the form of its salts as a sympathomimetic drug.
1889 *Jrnl. Chem. Soc.* LVI. 1020 Nagai, some years ago, isolated an alkaloïd, ephedrine, from the *Ephedra vulgaris*, but through lack of material was unable to do more than determine its physiological action. **1900** DORLAND *Med. Dict.*, Ephedrin. **1929** *Irish Jrnl. Med. Sci.* Apr. 184 In cases where the blood-pressure falls very low, ephedrin will control the fall. **1940** *Thorpe's Dict. Appl. Chem.* (ed. 4) IV. 317/1 The difference between ephedrine and *ψ*-ephedrine is limited to the carbon atom bearing the hydroxyl group. **1949** T. A. HENRY *Plant Alkaloids* (ed. 4) 642 Being more stable to metabolic conditions, ephedrine can be given by mouth, whereas adrenaline has to be used by injection. **1967** G. A. SWAN *Introd. Alkaloids* ii. 9 As ephedrine has been used successfully in the treatment of bronchial asthma, hay fever and other allergic conditions, many syntheses of it have been devised.

ephelis (ɛˈfiːlɪs). *Med.* Pl. **ephelides** (ɛˈfiːlɪdiːz). [a. L. *ephēlis*, f. Gr. ἔφηλις (or ἐφηλίς), in pl. rough spots on the face, or perh. freckles.] A freckle; also *collect.* for various kinds of skin discoloration.
1756 J. GREIVE tr. *Celsus' Of Medicine* VI. v. 327 It is almost a folly to cure vari, lenticulæ and ephelides; but 'tis impossible to prevent women from being nice in what regards their beauty. *Ibid.*, An ephelis is cured by resin. **1813** T. BATEMAN *Pract. Synopsis Cutaneous Dis.* viii. 317 The term Ephelis denotes not only the freckles..which appear on persons of fair skin, and the larger brown patches, which likewise arise from exposure to the direct rays of the sun, as the name imports; but also those large dusky patches, which are very similar in appearance, but occur on other parts of the surface, which are constantly covered. *Ibid.* 318 Sauvages has improperly classed with Ephelis, the mottled, and dusky red hue of the shins of those, who expose their legs constantly to strong fires in the winter; and also the livid patches of scurvy. **1833** J. FORBES et al. *Cycl. Pract. Med.* II. 70 Ephelis diffusa, an eruption of distinct or confluent large, irregular, round patches, of a tawny, yellow, or brown colour. **1908** *Practitioner* Aug. 348 Some dermatologists include freckles, lentigo, or ephelides under the heading of sexual pigmentation. **1954** ORMSBY & MONTGOMERY *Dis. Skin* (ed. 8) v. 703 Ephelides do not occur on the palms or soles. **1961** P. BORRIE *Roxburgh's Common Skin Dis.* (ed. 12) xx. 370 When heat is applied frequently to the skin..a dark brown network is formed, the so-called Ephelis ab igne.

†**eˈphemera**, *a.* and *sb.*[1] *Path. Obs.* Forms: 4–7 **effimera**, 6 **ephimera**, 7–9 **ephemera**; *pl.* 7 **ephemeraes**, 8–9 **-æ**, **-as**. Also in adapted forms 6–7 **effimere**, 6 **ephimer**. [a. med.L. *ephēmera* (sc. *febris*), fem. of *ephēmerus*, a. Gr. ἐφήμερος lasting only for a day, f. ἐπί (see EPI-) + ἡμέρα day. The adapted forms are perh. through OF. *effimere.*]
A. *adj.* Of a fever: Lasting only for a day; 'ephemeral'. **B.** *sb.* An ephemeral fever.
1398 TREVISA *Barth De P.R.* VII. xxxiv. (1495) 248 Effimera, one dayes feuer is as it were the heete of one daye. **1528** PAYNEL *Salerne Regim.* C, A feuer effimere is engendred of vapours and smudge fumes. **1547** BOORDE *Brev. Health* cxxxvi. 50 In Englyshe it is named the Ephimer fever..The fever doth dye that daye in the which he doth infest any man. **1585** LLOYD *Treas. Health* R iij, Of the Agew callyd ephimera which endureth but one daye. **1625** HART *Anat. Ur.* II. ix. 112 That Feauer which we call Ephemera, not exceeding foure and twentie houres. **1707** FLOYER *Physic. Pulse-Watch* 115 Ephemeras oft end in Hectics, or Intermittents, because the Pulse is a-like frequent in all of them. **1813** J. THOMSON *Lect. Inflam.* 105 The ephemera from cold may be regarded as an idiopathic fever.

ephemera (ɪˈfɛmərə), *sb.*[2] Pl. **ephemeræ, -as.** [a. mod.L. *ephēmera* (? sc. *musca*): see prec.
In med.L. *ephemera* was neut. pl., a. Gr. ἐφήμερα used in this sense by Aristotle (see EPHEMERON). The earlier Eng. instances are possibly due to the common practice of treating plurals in *-a* as sing. Linnæus however used the word as fem., making it the name of a genus (of much wider extent than the genus now so called.)]
1. An insect that (in its imago or winged form) lives only for a day. In mod. entomology the name of a genus of pseudo-neuropterous insects belonging to the group *Ephemeridæ* (Day-flies, May-flies).
1677 HALE *Prim. Orig. Man.* II. vi. 170 But Ephemeraes in duration, and little other than Insects in extent. **1750** JOHNSON *Rambler* No. 82 ¶7, I..have discovered a new ephemera. **1813** BINGLEY *Anim. Biog.* (ed. 4) III. 235 The Common Ephemera, or Day-fly. **1873** DAWSON *Earth & Man* vi. 136 Shad-flies or ephemeras, which spend their earlier days under water.
2. *transf.* and *fig.* One who or something which has a transitory existence.
1751 JOHNSON *Rambler* No. 145 ¶11 These papers of a day, the Ephemeræ of learning. **1785** CRABBE *Newspaper* Wks. 1834 II. 119 These base ephemeras, so born To die before the next revolving morn. **1815** *Scribbleomania* 58 When the new-fangled ephemeræ of fashion shall be no more. **1886** H. F. LESTER *Under 2 Fig Trees* 33 [A charwoman is] a kind of domestic ephemera which flutters briefly in the scullery and then is seen no more.

ephemeral (ɪˈfɛmərəl), *a.* (*sb.*) [f. Gr. ἐφήμερ-ος (see prec.) + -AL[1].]
A. *adj.*
1. a. Of diseases: Beginning and ending in a day. **b.** Of insects, flowers, etc.: Existing for one day only, or for a very few days.
a. 1576 NEWTON tr. *Lemnie's Complex.* (1633) 164 The corruption of the Ayre is the cause of this grievous maladie or Ephemerall Ague. **1866** A. FLINT *Princ. Med.* (1880) 945 If very short, lasting only a single day, it is..an ephemeral fever.
b. 1826 KIRBY & SP. *Entomol.* (1828) IV. xlix. 523 Some insects are so ephemeral that they are to be found only for a few days. **1864** *Intell. Observ.* No. 33. 149 The perfect Ephemeral imago. **1875** HELPS *Ess., Exerc. Benevolence* 36 The insects..poor ephemeral things. **1880** GRAY *Struct. Bot.* vi. §5. 243 Ephemeral or Fugacious, lasting for only a day; as the petals of Poppy.
2. a. In more extended application: That is in existence, power, favour, popularity, etc. for a short time only; short-lived; transitory.
a **1639** SIR H. WOTTON *Reliq. Wotton.* (1685) 220 An ephemeral fit of applause. *a* **1659** BP. MORTON *Episc. Justified* (1670) 142 A Deambulatory, Hebdomatical (or peradventure Ephemeral) Office. **1810** T. JEFFERSON *Writ.* (1830) IV. 137 His ministers, however weak and profligate in morals, are ephemeral. **1821** KNOX *On Grammar Schools* 157 The gale of ephemeral popularity. **1825** SYD. SMITH *Sp.* Wks. 1859 II. 204/2 Their ephemeral liberty. **1867** FREEMAN *Norm. Conq.* (1876) I. vi. 481 Empires like those of Alexander, Charles, and Cnut are in their own nature ephemeral.
b. *absol.*
1875 BROWNING *Aristoph. Apol.* 127 May I, the ephemeral, ne'er scrutinize Who made the heaven and earth. **1878** BOSW. SMITH *Carthage* 381 When the due distinction had been drawn between the ephemeral and the lasting.
B. *sb.* in *pl.* Insects which live only for a day. Also *transf.* of books, persons, etc.
1817 COLERIDGE *Biog. Lit.* II. xx. 121 Gnats, beetles, etc. ..the whole tribe of ephemerals..may flit in and out. **1831** *Blackw. Mag.* XXX. 965 Let the breezy sunshine but bring out the winged ephemerals. **1870** SWINBURNE *Ess. & Stud.* (1875) 106 Assemblies of important ephemerals who met to dispute the respective claims, etc. **1878** W. E. A. AXON *Bk. Rarities Warrington Museum* 11 Some of these books are pure ephemerals.
Hence **eˈphemerally** *adv.*; **eˈphemeralness.**
1848 MILL *Pol. Econ.* II. xiv. §4. 1. 467 The most ephemerally celebrated, and the really greatest poets (Byron and Shelley). **1911** G. H. MAIR *Eng. Lit.: Mod.* ii. 48 Pamphlets or text books that have been preserved by accident from the ephemeralness which was the common lot of hundreds of their fellows. **1922** W. J. LOCKE *Tale of Triona* ix. 101 Let him make good, not ephemerally..but definitely. **1941** WYNDHAM LEWIS *Let.* 10 Aug. (1963) 295 The book-business, in America has been..reduced to a level of ephemeralness, news-value, and mere fact-finding past belief. **1969** *Daily Tel.* 21 Apr. 16/3 Some of the enjoyment of a good performance lies in its very ephemeralness.

ephemerality (ɪˌfɛməˈrælɪtɪ). [f. prec. + -(I)TY.] The quality of being ephemeral; *concr.* in *pl.* ephemeral matters.
1822 CARLYLE *Early Lett.* (1886) II. 67 Speculation on ephemeralities. **1861** READE *Cloister & H.* III. 222 This lively companion..often looked in on him, and chattered ephemeralities. **1878** *Fraser's Mag.* XVII. 530 Ephemerality? Is not the glory of even the Prime Minister, in most cases, but a passing brilliancy?

ephemeraliˈzation. [f. EPHEMERAL *a.* + -IZATION.] The practice or process of rendering (more) ephemeral; *spec.* Buckminster Fuller's word for the production or evolution of machinery smaller and lighter than that previously used for the same purpose (see also quot. 1972).
1960 R. W. MARKS *Dymaxion World of B. Fuller* 151/4 This process of doing more with less may be capsuled as 'ephemeralization'. The more ephemeralization advances the more flyable becomes any one cargo. **1962** R. B. FULLER *Epic Poem on Industrialization* p. x, The 'ephemeralization' of motive power has taken place under our eyes. A freight locomotive weighs 100 pounds per horsepower delivered at the track. An automobile engine weighs 13 pounds per horsepower. **1972** *N.Y. Times Bk. Rev.* 16 Jan. 4 'Ephemeralization' is the key word in Buckminster Fuller's bulging lexicon. To him it means increasing the obsolescence rate of all goods in order to speed up the recycling of elements. The corollary is 'regenerative' or inflamed consumerism.

†**eˈphemeran**, *a.* and *sb. Obs.* [f. EPHEMERA + -AN.] **A.** *adj.* = EPHEMERAL 1 a. **B.** *sb.* = EPHEMERAL B.
1643 *True Informer* 13 It was rather an Embryo of a Parliament, an Ephemeran of 20 dayes. *c* **1645** HOWELL *Lett.* (1650) I. 363 Methought, it was a strange opinion of our Aristotle to hold, that the least of those small insected ephemerans should be more noble than the sun, because it had a sensitive soul in it. **1727** BRADLEY *Fam. Dict.* s.v. *Fever*, The Ephemeran Fever is so call'd, because it lasts but one Day.

†**epheˈmerean**, *a. Obs. rare.* = EPHEMERAL.
1804 *Miniature* No. 4 (1806) I. 57 Celestial Peacock.. Whose conscious plumes diffuse a herd Of ephemerean dyes!

†**epheˈmerian**, *a. Obs.* [f. EPHEMERI-S + -AN.] 'Belonging to a journal, register or day-book' (Bailey 1736).

eˈphemeric, *a.* [f. EPHEMER-A + -IC.] = EPHEMERAL.
1755 in JOHNSON. **1847** in CRAIG; and in mod. Dicts.

ephemerid (ɪˈfɛmərɪd). [ad. mod.L. *Ephēmeridæ*, f. *ephēmera.*] An insect belonging to the group *Ephemeridæ*: see EPHEMERA[2]. Also *fig.*
1872 NICHOLSON *Palæont.* 186 The *Haplophlebium Barnesii* must have attained a size much larger than that of any recent Ephemerids. **1874** FARRAR *Christ* 65 The ephemerid that buzzes out its little hour in the summer noon. **1879** *Daily Tel.* 17 Oct., This gossamer nothing, this aerial ephemerid, paralyses the intellect.

†**eˈphemerid**, *a. rare.* [f. L. *ephēmerid-*, stem of *ephēmeris*: see EPHEMERIS.] = EPHEMERAL.
1804 MITFORD *Harmony* 91 The ephemerid fashion of orthography.
So †**ephemeridal.**
1795 tr. Mercier *Fragm. of Politics & Hist.* II. 444 These sons of fortune, these ephemeridal giants who threatened to swallow up every thing.

†**ephemeˈridian**, *a. Obs.* [f. L. *ephēmerid-*, stem of *ephēmeris* + -IAN.] Of or pertaining to an ephemeris.
1656–81 in BLOUNT *Glossogr.* **1721–1800** in BAILEY.

‖**ephemeris** (ɪˈfɛmərɪs). Pl. **ephemerides** (ɛfɪˈmɛrɪdiːz), formerly often used as a *sing.* [mod.L. *ephēmeris*, a. Gr. ἐφημερίς diary, calendar, f. ἐφήμερος daily: see EPHEMERA.]
†**1. a.** A record of daily occurrences; a diary, journal. *Obs.*
1591 LAMBARDE *Arch.* (1635) 168 The Bookes of Entries kept there; which is a true Ephemeris or Iournall of the Acts of the Court. **1629** DONNE *Serm.* xxiv. 240 God sees their sins..and in his Ephemerides—his Journals, he writes them downe. *a* **1682** SIR T. BROWNE *Chr. Mor.* 22 Register not only strange, but merciful occurrences; let ephemerides, not olympiads, give thee account of His mercies.
b. *pl.* for *sing.*
1613 JACKSON *Creed* I. xvii. Wks. I. 119 His written oracles ..an absolute ephemerides of all things that had been since the first moment of time. **1642** FULLER *Holy & Prof. St.* V. iv. 371 Having kept an exact Ephemerides of all actions for more then five thousand years together. **1650** R. STAPYLTON *Strada's Low C. Warres* x. 16 Set downe in a Diary (or Ephemerides).
2. a. A table showing the predicted (rarely the observed) positions of a heavenly body for every day during a given period. †Also, in *pl.* the tabulated positions (of a heavenly body) for a series of successive days.
1551 RECORDE *Cast. Knowl.* (1556) 283 Many eclipses of the sonne and moone also are not noted in the common Ephemerides and Almanachs. **1601** HOLLAND *Pliny* I. 188 Among the Babylonians there were found Ephemerides containing the obseruation of the stars, for 720 yeares. **1664** *Phil. Trans.* I. 3 The Ephemerides of the Comet. **1668** *Ibid.* III. 688 Tables of the Motion of the Satellits of Jupiter, with an Ephemeris of the same for this present Year. **1874** MOSELEY *Astron.* lxxxviii. (ed. 4) 232 The Nautical Almanac for 1835 contained ephemerides of two of them. **1880** *Academy* No. 440. 262 The following ephemeris..will be serviceable in searching for the comet.
†**b.** *pl.* As the title of a collection of such tables. Often used as sing. = 3 a. *Obs.*
1559 CUNINGHAME *Cosm. Glas* 95, I find in an Ephemerides the sonne to be in the firste Digree of Aries. **1594** BLUNDEVIL *Exerc.* I. xxviii. (ed. 7) 77 An example used by Stadius in the 115 Page of his Ephemerides. **1618** WITHER *Juvenil. Motto* (1633) 543 Be slaves unto an Ephemerides. **1635** N. CARPENTER *Geog. Del.* I. xi. 241 You may [know] by an Ephemerides at what houre an Eclipse shall happen.

fig. **1686** W. DE BRITAINE *Hum. Prud.* §21. 99 You must be careful to keep an Ephemerides, to know how the great Orbs of the Court move.

3. a. A book in which the places of the heavenly bodies and other astronomical matters are tabulated in advance for each day of a certain period; an astronomical almanac.

1647 *Almanak for* 1386, Astron. App. (1812) 61 An ephemeris..is a book giving the true places of the planets. **1796** HUTTON *Math. Dict.* s.v., The Nautical Almanac, or Astronomical Ephemeris, published in England by the Board of Longitude..which commenced with the year 1767. **1833** HERSCHEL *Astron.* v. 204 The equation of time is calculated and inserted in ephemerides for every day of the year. **1874** MOSELEY *Astron.* xlv. (ed. 4) 147 These quantities..are stated..in the tables of the Nautical Almanac, and other ephemerides.

b. ephemeris time, a uniform time scale used in astronomy, defined in terms of the orbital motions of the moon and planets and taking as the fundamental unit the **ephemeris second**, equal to a certain fraction of the tropical year 1900 (see quot. 1966).

1950 *Colloques Internat. du C.N.R.S.* XXV. Constantes Fondamentales de l'Astronomie..129 The Conference recommends that, in all cases where the mean solar second is unsatisfactory as a unit of time by reason of its variability, the unit adopted should be the sidereal year at 1900.0; that the time reckoned in these unit [*sic*] be designated Ephemeris Time. **1964** R. H. BAKER *Astron.* (ed. 8) iii. 78 The *American Ephemeris and Nautical Almanac* and the British *Astronomical Ephemeris*..tabulate the fundamental positions of the sun, moon, and planets at intervals of ephemeris time. *Ibid.*, In the present century, ephemeris time has been gaining on universal time and in 1960 was ahead by 35 seconds. **1966** KAYE & LABY *Tables of Physical & Chem. Constants* (ed. 13) 8 Since 1956 the ephemeris second, defined as the fraction 1/31 556 925.974 7 of the tropical year for 1900 January 0 at 12^h ET, has been adopted as the fundamental invariable unit of time by the International Committee of Weights and Measures.

†**4. a.** In wider sense: An almanac or calendar of any kind; in early use *esp.* one containing astrological or meteorological predictions for each day of the period embraced; also, a calendar of saints' days. Also *pl.* in same sense, sometimes used as sing. *Obs.*

In bibliographical works (e.g. in the *Brit. Mus. Cat.*), 'Ephemerides' is still used as a general heading for Almanacs, Calendars, etc.

1597 BP. HALL *Sat.* II. vii. 6 Why can his tell-troth Ephemerides Teach him the weathers state so long beforne. **1605** BACON *Adv. Learn.* I. i. §3 That Kalendar or Ephemerides which he maketh of the diversities of times and seasons for all actions and purposes. **1610** B. JONSON *Alch.* IV. iv, Cures Plagues, piles, and pox, by the ephemerides. *a* **1661** FULLER *Worthies, Flintshire* IV. 39 He ..wrote an Ephemeris of the Irish Saints. **1796** MORSE *Amer. Geog.* I. 45 Several Ephemerides or Almanacks are annually published.

fig. **1649** G. DANIEL *Trinarch., Hen. IV*, ccclii, Hee who had read the Ephemerides Of Fate; and could repeat his owne, by roat. **1796** BURKE *Regic. Peace* Wks. (1812) IX. 105, I think this can hardly have escaped the writers of political ephemerides for any month or year.

†**b.** *pl.* The appointed daily order of religious services. *Obs.*

1650 ELDERFIELD *Tythes* 117 How their ephemerides for divine services should be performed.

¶**5.** *catachr.* = EPHEMERA² 1 and 2.

1820 SHELLEY *Sens. Pl.* 49 The beamlike ephemeris Whose path is the lightning's. **1841-4** EMERSON *Ess., Self-reliance* Wks. (Bohn) I. 25 Honour is venerable to us because it is no ephemeris.

†**e'phemerist.** *Obs.* [f. EPHEMER-IS + -IST.] One who uses or makes an ephemeris.

1656-81 BLOUNT *Glossogr., Ephemerist*, one that registreth daily actions, or Nativities, with the help of an Ephemerides; a maker of an Ephemerides. *a* **1666** HOWELL (J.), He was discoursing of..the art of foolish astrologers and genethliacal ephemerists. **1706** PHILLIPS, *Ephemerist*, a maker of Ephemerides, Almanacks, etc. **1736** in BAILEY.

ephemeromorph (ɪˈfɛmərəʊˌmɔːf). *Biol. rare.* [f. Gr. ἐφήμερο-ς (see EPHEMERA) + μορφ-ή form.] Used by Bastian as a general name for the lowest forms of life, which cannot be assigned definitely to either the animal or vegetable kingdom. Hence **eˌphemeroˈmorphic** *a.*

1874 BASTIAN in *Contemp. Rev.* XXIII. 708 The song of the Ephemeromorphs might be, in the words of Ovid, 'Corpora vertantur; nec quod fuimusve, sumusve, Cras erimus'. **1876** —— in *Ibid.* Jan. 243 These creatures of circumstances, which become metamorphosed in a most striking and apparently irregular manner, I have proposed to include under the general designation of 'Ephemeromorphs'. **1880** —— *Brain* i. 6 The ephemeromorphic assemblage of vital forms.

ephemeron (ɪˈfɛmərən). *Pl.* 7-9 **ephemera**, 9 **ephemerons**. [a. Gr. (ζῷον) ἐφήμερον (Aristotle *H.A.* I. v.), neut. of ἐφήμερος: see EPHEMERA².]

1. An insect, which, in its winged state, lives but for a day. Cf. EPHEMERA².

1626 BACON *Sylva* (1677) §697 There are certain Flies that are called Ephemera that live but a day. **1710** HEARNE *Collect.* (Oxf. Hist. Soc.) III. 30 The Ephemeron, a Fly that lives but five Hours. **1845** R. CHAMBERS *Vest. Creat., Hypoth. Devel.*, An ephemeron, hovering over a pool for its one April day of life. **1884** G. F. BRAITHWAITE *Salmonidæ Westmorld.* vi. 26 The most beautiful species of our ephemera, the green and grey drakes, must not be forgotten.

2. *fig.* A short-lived person, institution, or production.

1771 *Bachelor* (1773) I. No. 38. 254 Unnotic'd, dull invective lyes, A mere Ephemeron it dyes, Or but provokes a jest. **1787** BECKFORD *Italy* (1834) II. 78 All the human ephemera of Lisbon. **1796** MORSE *Amer. Geog.* II. 371 This political ephemeron [constitution formed by the National Assembly in 1791]. **1837** HT. MARTINEAU *Soc. Amer.* III. 208 Every ephemeron of a tale-writer, a dramatist, etc. **1859** FAIRHOLT *Tobacco* (1876) 61 Samuel Rowlands, a prolific writer of ephemera. **1878** MORLEY *Carlyle* 173 A cloud of sedulous ephemera still suck a little spiritual moisture.

‖**3.** A plant described by ancient writers. *Obs.*

Some ancient authors distinguish two plants called *ephemeron*: one so named because springing up and dying in one day, the other as being a poison that causes death within a day.

1578 LYTE *Dodoens* II. xlv. 204 If it be Ephemeron as it seemeth to be, then it is good for the teeth. **1616** HAYWARD *Sanct. Troub. Soul* II. (1620) To Rdr. ¶9 Many writings are like the plant Ephemeron; which springeth, flourisheth, and fadeth in one day. **1661** LOVELL *Hist. Anim. & Min.* 35 It [goat's milk] helps against the ephemeron or cantharides [mistranslates *contra cantharidas et contra ephemeri potum* Plin. *N.H.* XXVIII. xlv].

4. *attrib.*

a **1735** DERHAM (J.), Swammerdam observes of the ephemeron-worms, that their food is clay. **1751** CHAMBERS *Cycl.* Travellers into Arabia tell us of several ephemeron-trees. *a* **1791** WESLEY *Serm.* Wks. 1811 IX. 115 An Ephemeron Fly lives six hours. **1796** D'ISRAELI *Lit. Recreat.* 115 Several singular coincidences alone gave the ephemeron critic his temporary existence. **1802** PALEY *Nat. Theol.* xxiii. (1826) 345 An ephemeron fly [produces] a cod-bait maggot.

ephemerous (ɪˈfɛmərəs), *a.* [f. EPHEMER-ON + -OUS.] Having the nature of, or resembling, an ephemeron; transitory.

a **1660** HAMMOND 19 *Serm.* vi. Wks. 1684 IV, Our ephemerous wishes, that no man can distinguish from true piety, but by their sudden death. **1790** BURKE *Fr. Rev.* 282 The ephemerous tale that does its business and dies in a day. **1872** DARWIN *Orig. Spec.* xiv. 386 A certain ephemerous insect during its development, moults..above twenty times.

Ephesian (ɪfiːʒən), *a.* and *sb.* [f. L. *ephesi-us* (ad. Gr. ἐφέσιος, f. Ἔφεσος) + -AN.]

A. *adj.* Of or pertaining to Ephesus.

B. *sb.*

1. An inhabitant of Ephesus.

1388 WYCLIF *Ephes.* Prol., Effesians [**1382** Ephecyes] ben of Asie. **1876** HUMPHREYS *Coin Coll. Man.* vi. 53 The money of the Ephesians bore a stag.

†**2.** A boon companion. *Obs.* Cf. the use of *Corinthian* in Shakspere, etc.

1597 SHAKS. *2 Hen. IV*, II. ii. 164 *Prin.* Where suppes he? .. What Company? *Page.* Ephesians, my Lord, of the old Church. **1598** —— *Merry W.* IV. v. 19 It is thine Host, thine Ephesian cals.

Ephesine (ˈɛfɪsɪn), *a.* [ad. L. *Ephesīnus*, f. *Ephesus*.] Of or pertaining to Ephesus; chiefly *Eccl.* with reference to the Third General Council, held there A.D. 431, or to certain liturgical uses supposed to have emanated from Ephesus.

1579 FULKE *Heskins' Parl.* 188 The Epistle of the Ephesine Counsell vnto Nestorius. **1664** EVELYN *Sylva* (1776) 339 The Ephesine temple. **1839** YEOWELL *Anc. Brit. Ch.* xi. (1847) 109 The Ephesine fathers had determined the Cyprian church to be independent of the bishop of Antioch. **1850** C. WORDSWORTH *Theoph. Angl.* 166 What is the tenor of the Ephesine Canon? **1882-3** A. F. MITCHELL in Schaff *Encycl. Relig. Knowl.* II. 1236 The Scottish fragment in the Book of Deer, the Irish fragments..of distinctly Ephesine character.

ephesite (ˈɛfɪsaɪt). *Min.* [f. *Ephes-us*, near which it was found + -ITE.] A pearly-white lamellar mineral, closely related to margarite.

1851 *Amer. Jrnl. Sc.* Ser. II. XI. 59 Ephesite [a new species]. **1873** *Proc. Amer. Phil. Soc.* XIII. 387 Ephesite, a mineral of..lamellar structure..resembles white cyanite.

†**e'phestian**, *a. Obs. rare*$^{-1}$. [f. Gr. ἐφέστι-ος of the house or family (f. ἐπί upon + ἑστία hearth) + -AN.] Domestic, as opposed to *foreign*.

1652 URQUHART *Jewel* Wks. (1834) 275 That the state [government] of this Isle, without regard to Ephestian or exotick country..should consider of men according to the fruits, whether good or bad.

ephete (ˈɛfiːt). *rare.* [ad. Gr. ἐφέτης, agent-n. f. ἐφιέναι to impose, command, etc., f. ἐπί (see EPI-) + ἱέναι to send.] In *pl.* The members of a body of magistrates at Athens. More commonly in L. form *ephetæ*.

1839 THIRLWALL *Greece* II. 19 He [Draco] introduced some changes in the administration of criminal justice, by transferring causes of murder, or of accidental homicide, from the cognizance of the archons to the magistrates called ephetes; though it is not clear whether he instituted, or only modified or enlarged, their jurisdiction.

So **e'phetic** *a.* [see -IC.] (See quot.)

1849 GROTE *Greece* II. x. (ed. 2) III. 107 *note*, Plato copies to a great degree the arrangements of the ephetic tribunals, in his provisions for homicide.

ephialtes (ɛfɪˈæltiːz). [a. Gr. ἐφιάλτης.

Usually believed to be agent-n. f. *ἐφιάλλεσθαι, var. of ἐφάλλεσθαι to leap upon, f. ἐπί on + ἅλλεσθαι to leap. But the phonological difficulties are considerable (cf., however, ἐφίορκος = ἐπίορκος, f. ἐπί + ὅρκος); and the synonymous ἠπιαλής, ἐφέλης, etc. suggest that the word may have been affected by popular etymology.]

A demon supposed to cause nightmare; nightmare itself.

1601 HOLLAND *Pliny* II. 214 The diseases called Ephialtes or Incubus, i.e. the night-Mare. **1646** SIR T. BROWNE *Pseud. Ep.* v. xxi. §21. 272 To prevent the Ephialtes or night-Mare we hang up an hallow stone in our stables. **1656** CULPEPPER *Eng. Physic.* 296 Such as in their sleep are troubled with the Disease called Ephialtes or Incubus. **1777** BRAND *Pop. Antiq.* 324 Ephialtes, or Night Mare is called by Common People Witch-riding.

ephippial (ɛˈfɪpɪəl), *a. Anat.* and *Zool.* [f. EPHIPPI-UM + -AL¹.] Of or pertaining to the ephippium.

1835-6 TODD *Cycl. Anat.* I. 738/1 Its corners are bounded by the ephippial..processes. **1841-71** R. JONES *Anim. Kingd.* (ed. 4) 455 The development of the ephippial eggs takes place at the posterior part of the ovaries.

†**e'phippiate**, *v. Obs.*$^{-0}$ [f. L. *ephippi-um* saddle + -ATE.] To harness or saddle.

1656-81 in BLOUNT *Glossogr.* **1704** in COCKER.

‖**ephippium** (ɛˈfɪpɪəm). [L. *ephippium* horse-cloth, saddle, ad. Gr. ἐφίππιος adj. 'that is for putting on a horse', f. ἐπί upon + ἵππος horse.]

1. *Anat.* A saddle-shaped depression of the sphenoid bone.

1842 DUNGLISON *Medical Lex.* s.v.

2. *Zool.* The envelope enclosing the winter ova of the Daphniidæ (a genus of the Crustaceans), which is situated between the back of the animal and the carapace, and probably is a development from the latter. It is shed with the carapace.

1841-71 T. R. JONES *Anim. Kingd.* (ed. 4) 455 As winter approaches, however, the Daphnia may be seen with a dark opaque substance within the back of the shell, which has been called the ephippium, from its resemblance to a saddle ..The ephippium is really only an altered part of the carapace. **1877** HUXLEY *Anat. Inv. An.* vi. 287 The ephippium sinks to the bottom, and, sooner or later, its contents give rise to young *Daphniæ*.

ephod (ˈɛfɒd). Also 4 **ephoth**. [Heb. *ēphōd*, f. *āphad* to put on.]

1. A Jewish priestly vestment, without sleeves, slit at the sides below the armpits, fastened with buckles at the shoulders, and by a girdle at the waist. The high-priest's ephod was of 'gold, purple, scarlet and fine-twined linen (byssus)'; that worn by others was of linen.

1382 WYCLIF *Ex.* xxv. 7 Gemmes to anowrn ephoth, that is, a preestis ouermest clothing, that we cleepen a coope. **1611** BIBLE *2 Sam.* vi. 14 Dauid was girded with a linnen Ephod. **1770** CHATTERTON *Happiness*, The bloody son of Jesse.. made himself an ephod to his mind. **1856** STANLEY *Sinai & Pal.* iv. (1858) 205 *note*, 'Bring hither the Ephod,' the priestly cape, dressed in which the High-priest delivered the oracle.

2. *transf.* A typical priestly garment; †hence used symbolically for 'the priestly office', 'clerical influence'.

1603 DRAYTON *Bar. Wars* IV. (R.) The holy ephod made a cloak for gain. **1649** SELDEN *Laws Eng.* I. v. (1739) 13 What the Ephod could not, the Sword wrapt up therein should. **1854** THACKERAY *Newcomes* I. 44 Many a good dinner did Charles Honeyman lose by assuming that unlucky ephod [i.e. wearing the surplice in the pulpit].

ephor (ˈɛfə(r)). Also used in L. pl. form **ephori**. [ad. Gr. ἔφορος (= Epic ἐπίουρος) overseer, overlooker, f. ἐπί upon + root *ϝορ, as in ὁράειν to see. Also used in L. pl. form *ephori*, whence app. the form *ephories* in 16-17th c.]

1. The title given to certain magistrates in various Dorian states, *esp.* at Sparta, where the five ephors, appointed annually by popular election, exercised a controlling power over the kings.

1586 T. B. *La Primaud. Fr. Acad.* I. (1589) 547 To content the people, they appointed five Ephories who were chosen out of the people, as Tribunes to keep away tyranny. **1594** *Mirr. Policy* (1599) B, Those which are good, would curbe and bridle him. As the Ephori did the Kings of Lacedemonia. **1602** L. LLOYD *Confer. Lawes* 43 The Areopagites in Athens..the Ephories in Sparta..the Amphictions at Trozaena. **1642** *Coll. Rights & Priv. Parl.* 10 At Lacedemonia, the Ephors; at Athens, the Demarches. **1689** *Def. Liberty agst. Tyrants* 76 The Ephores or Controllers of the Kings. **1835** THIRLWALL *Greece* I. 321 Before the ephors made an exception, every one rose at his [the king's] approach.

†**b.** *transf. Obs. rare.*

1647 CLARENDON *Hist. Reb.* (1703) II. VI. 5 Mr. Hollis, Sr. Walter Earl, and other ephori. **1732** WOGAN *Let.* in *Swift's Wks.* (1824) XVII. 485 Their [kings' of England] inherent rights..were but mere feathers, the sport of every wind that blew from the ephori of the people.

2. In modern Greece: An overseer, superintendent of public works.

1890 *Athenæum* 15 Mar. 252/1 The excavations at Lycosoura..will now be resumed, under the direction of the Ephor, B. A. Leonardos.

Hence **ˈephoral**, *a.*, of or pertaining to the ephors. **ˈephoralty**, the office of ephor; also, the body of ephors. **ˈephorate**, = EPHORALTY in both senses. **eˈphoric** *a.* = EPHORAL. †**ˈephorism**, *nonce-wd.*, a tribunal resembling

that of the ephors. †'ephorize *v. Obs.*, to exercise a controlling influence over; to overrule as the ephors did. **'ephorship**, the term of office as ephor. †**'ephory** [cf. Gr. ἐφορεία], the body of ephors.

1836 LYTTON *Athens* (1837) I. 209 Aristotle paints the evil of the *ephoral magistrature, but acknowledges that it gave strength and durability to the state. **1844** LD. BROUGHAM *Brit. Const.* i. (1862) 18 It was not till above a century after his decease that the Ephoral power became any protection to the people. **1833** LEWIS in *Philol. Museum* II. 49 Dr. Arnold then proceeds to describe the *Ephoralty as a magistracy contrived for the purpose of, etc. **1869** RAWLINSON *Anc. Hist.* 267 At the same time he abolished the Ephoralty. **1841** W. SPALDING *Italy & It. Isl.* III. 42 An *ephorate or court of supreme revision for laws and magistracies. **1897** *Daily News* 26 Apr. 8/6 The two native bodies, the Athenian Ephorate and the Society of Antiquities. **1923** W. W. TARN in J. B. Bury et al. *Hellenistic Age* 134 Then, having captured the ephorate, they were able to prevent him [*sc.* Agis] carrying out both his proposals together. *Ibid.* 135 He [*sc.* Cleomenes] also abolished the ephorate. **1846** GROTE *Greece* (1862) II. vi. 144 The annual *ephoric oath of office. **1633** JAMES in Hearne *Collect.* (Oxf. Hist. Soc.) I. 9 Thrice I have bin hal'd before Our *Ephorismes of state. **1647** WARD *Simp. Cobler* 50 These Essentially, must not be *Ephorized or Tribuned by one or a few Mens discretion. **1850** GROTE *Greece* II. lxii. VIII. 31 In this 13th year of the reign of Darius, and in the *ephorship of Alexippidas at Lacedæmon. **1689** tr. *Buchanan's De Jure Regni* 42 Upbraiding him that by adding the *Ephory he [Theopompus] had diminished the Power of his Authority.

Ephthalite ('ɛfθəlaɪt), *sb.* (and *a.*) [ad. late Gr. Ἐφθαλῖτος.] = *White Hun* s.v. WHITE *a.* 11 e. Also as *adj.*

[**1781** GIBBON *Decl. & F.* II. xxvi. 584 They preserved the name of Huns, with the epithet of Euthalites or Nepthalites. **1838** H. H. MILMAN *Gibbon's Decl. & F.* IV. xxvi. 351 The Armenian authors often mention this people under the name of Hepthal. St. Martin considers that the name Nephthalites is an error of a copyist. In Procopius they are Ἐφθαλῖται.] **1882** *Encycl. Brit.* XIV. 59/2 This white race.. around the Caspian and the Euxine.. appear in European history as White Huns (Ephthalites), White Ugrians.. White Bulgarians. **1920** in H. G. Wells *Outl. Hist.* xxxi. 397/1 Some state under Ephthalite dominion. **1957** *Encycl. Brit.* XII. 160/1 Under Skandagupta (455–470) the [Gupta] empire was successfully defended.. and the Ephthalite invasions postponed for nearly 50 years. **1965** [see *White Hun* s.v. WHITE *a.* 11 e]. **1973** L. DUPREE *Afghanistan* xv. 301 The early phases of the Kushano-Sasanian period in Afghanistan lasted until about the mid-fifth century A.D. with the arrival of the Hephthalites (or Ephthalites).

ephydriad (ɛ'fɪdrɪæd). *rare.* [ad. Gr. ἐφυδριάς, -άδος, f. ἐπί upon + ὕδωρ water.] A water-nymph.

1832 L. HUNT *Poems* 201 'Tis there the Ephydriads haunt.

‖**ephymnium** (ɛ'fɪmnɪəm). Also -ion. [ad. Gr. ἐφύμνιον the burden of a chorus or hymn.]

a. *Antiq.* In Poetry, a refrain, a short colon subjoined to a strophe. **b.** In some Eastern Churches, a refrain to a hymn; an antiphonal refrain.

[**1853** H. BURGESS *Sel. Metr. Hymns & Homilies of Ephraem Syrus* p. liv, These ἐφύμνια, or supernumerary verses, have a pleasing effect.] **1910** *Encycl. Brit.* XIV. 182/2 When a strophe contained five lines, the fifth was generally an 'ephymnium', detached in sense, and consisting of a prayer, invocation, doxology or the like, to be sung antiphonally, either in full chorus or by a separate part of the choir. **1931** *Ess. & Stud.* XVI. 21 The main Ode, which consists of four pairs of strophes or stanzas in various rhythms, the first three pairs being divided by ephymnions or refrains. **1949** *Oxf. Class. Dict.* 568/1 In an *Ephymnion* (refrain) words, as well as metrical form, are repeated: e.g. Aesch. *Supp.* 117–75.

ephyra ('ɛfɪrə), **ephyrula** (ɛ'fɪrjʊlə). *Zool.* [mod.L. (F. Peron 1809, in *Ann. du Muséum d'Hist. naturelle* XIV. 354), f. Gr. Ἐφύρα, Ionic -η, L. *Ephyrē*, name of a Nereid and of an Oceanid. *Ephyrula* is a diminutive.] A larval jellyfish, after separation from the scyphistoma.

1861 J. R. GREENE *Man. Anim. Kingdom* II. ii. 66 Each Ephyra soon acquires a nutritive system. **1897** PARKER & HASWELL *Text-bk. Zool.* I. iv. 161 The saucer-like bodies separate from one another, and each, turning upside down, begins to swim about as a small jelly-fish called an *Ephyrula*. .. The umbrella of the ephyrula is divided into eight long bifid arms. **1898** A. SEDGWICK *Student's Text-bk. Zool.* I. iv. 166 In rare cases (*Pelagia*) the development is simplified, and the larva passes directly into the *Ephyra*. **1916** H. S. PRATT *Man. Invertebr. Anim.* 125 Each disc is called an ephyra.. and is a young medusa or jellyfish, which on becoming free grows in time to be a sexual animal. **1940** L. H. HYMAN *Invertebrates* I. vii. 507 This [*sc.* the scyphistoma] is often followed by a young, free-swimming medusan stage, the *ephyra* (or *ephyrula*). **1967** P. A. MEGLITSCH *Invert. Zool.* vi. 153 (*caption*) Scyphistomae live for several years.. producing larval medusae known as ephyrae by transverse fission.

epi-, *prefix*, repr. Gr. ἐπι- (before an unaspirated vowel usually ἐπ-, before an aspirated vowel ἐφ-, represented in Eng. by EP-, EPH-), used in prepositional and advb. senses, 'upon, at, or close upon (a point of space or time), on the ground or occasion of, in addition'.

1. In words derived from compounds which either were, or might legitimately have been, formed already in Greek. Also in mod. scientific terms after the analogy of words derived from Gr.; chiefly with sense 'placed or resting upon', as in *epicalyx*, *epicorolline*.

2. a. In mod. Chemistry employed in the names **epibromhydrin**, **epichlorhydrin**, **epicyanhydrin**, **epiiodohydrin**, denoting substances of analogous composition belonging respectively to the bromhydrin, chlorhydrin, etc. series. They contain one equivalent of a salt-radical with 3 of carbon, 5 of hydrogen, and 1 of oxygen.

1857 W. A. MILLER *Elem. Chem.* III. 382 Epichlorhydrin ($C_6H_5O_2Cl$).. is a limpid oil. **1910** *Encycl. Brit.* I. 532/2 It [*sc.* acrolein] is also produced by the action of sodium on a mixture of epichlorhydrin and methyl iodide. **1956** *Nature* 21 Jan. 122/1 A polymer of repeating unit.. which may be prepared from 4,4'-dihydroxydiphenoxyethane and epichlorhydrin in the presence of sodium hydroxide.

b. [a. G. *epi-* (E. Votoček 1911, in *Ber. d. Deut. Chem. Ges.* XLIV. 360).] Occas. prefixed to the name of a sugar or sugar derivative to indicate that a second compound, bearing the prefix, is an epimer of the first.

1911 [see EPIMER]. **1932** H. PRINGSHEIM *Chem. Monosaccharides & Polysaccharides* iii. 38 Mannose might be termed 'epiglucose'. **1963** K. MAYER tr. *Staněk et al. Monosaccharides* xviii. 507 The term epi-glucosamine is today reserved for D-mannosamine (2-amino-2-deoxy-D-mannose).

3. In Mineralogy prefixed to the names of certain minerals to form names of other minerals closely resembling them in composition, as in **epibou'langerite**, a sulphantimonide of lead resulting from the decomposition of boulangerite. **epi'chlorite**, a hydrous silicate of aluminium, iron, and magnesium. **epi'diorite**, a mineral differing from diorite in that the hornblende it contains is fibrous. **epi'stilbite**, a zeolitic mineral, a hydrous silicate of aluminium, calcium, and sodium.

1872 DANA *Min.*, *1st App.* 5 *Epiboulangerite*. **1850** DANA *Min.* 263 Epichlorite.. fuses only in thin fibres and with difficulty. **1879** RUTLEY *Study Rocks* xiii. 245 The viridite (chlorite, epichlorite, or chloritic matter). **1887** DANA *Manual Min.* 482 Epidioryte consists of plagioclase with hornblende, some quartz, a little orthoclase, and some pyroxen. **1826** *Edin. Jrnl. Sc.* IV. 286 The cleavage of epistilbite is quite perfect.

epialid: see HEPIALID *a.* and *sb.*

epibasal (ɛpɪ'beɪsəl), *a. Bot.* [f. EPI- + BASAL *a.*] The distinctive epithet of the upper of the two cells in the oösphere of certain cryptogams. (See quot.)

1882 VINES *Sachs' Bot.* 375 The oospore is first of all clothed with a cell-wall, continues to grow considerably, and is then divided by a horizontal or slightly oblique wall (basal wall). The lower (hypobasal) of these two cells.. contributes but little to the formation of the embryo. The upper (epibasal) cell gives rise to the capsule and the seta.

epibiont (ɛpɪ'baɪɒnt). [f. EPI- + Gr. βιουντ- pr. pple. stem of βιοῦν to live, f. βίος life.] An organism that lives on the surface of another, esp. one that is not normally parasitic on it.

1949 W. C. ALLEE et al. *Princ. Animal Ecology* xvii. 244/1 Representatives of many different phyla grow as epicoles (epibionts) on the shells or the skin of others without becoming noticeably parasitic. **1951** *Arch. Néerlandaises de Zool.* X. 38, I found no evidence that any of the epibionts can be considered as true parasites feeding on the living tissues of the oyster itself. **1957** *New Biol.* XXIII. 62 An epibiont is an organism which lives on the surface of another organism, without causing any direct harm. **1961** J. GREEN *Biol. Crustacea* vii. 104 Sometimes one finds that there is competition for space on the surface of a popular host. The epibionts, which are the organisms living on the surface, of *Daphnia*, show this rather well. **1965** [see EPIBIOTIC *a.* and *sb.* 2].

epibiotic (ɛpɪbaɪ'ɒtɪk), *a.* and *sb.* [f. EPI- + Gr. βιωτικ-ός pertaining to life, f. βίος life.]

1. a. *adj.* Designating one of a few isolated plants or animals that are members of an otherwise extinct population of a species. **b.** *sb.* An epibiotic organism.

1930 H. N. RIDLEY *Dispersal of Plants* p. xviii, A number of.. plants of limited area, however, are the relics of an earlier flora which has nearly disappeared from change of climate or environment. These are known as *Epibiotics*, or survivors. *Ibid.*, Many plants.. become scarce, then Epibiotic, then perhaps disappeared entirely. **1947** R. F. DAUBENMIRE *Plants & Environment* x. 377 A species may suffer one or more catastrophes which destroy all but a fragment of the total population. The remnants are called relics, epibiotics, or depleted species.

2. *adj.* (See quot. 1960.)

1960 I. F. & W. D. HENDERSON *Dict. Sci. Terms* (ed. 7) 165/1 *Epibiotic*,.. growing on the exterior of living organisms. **1965** V. A. DOGIEL *Gen. Protozoology* (ed. 2) x. 574 The great majority of Protozoa of the plankton are free-living. Among them only a few epibionts belonging to the Suctoria lead an attached mode of life... The total number of such epibiotic forms is limited to a few dozen. **1967** *Oceanogr. & Marine Biol.* V. 518 The most characteristic species may be the following..: the sponge *Thenea muricata* (with its epibiotic zoanthid *Parazoanthus marioni*); [etc.].

epiblast ('ɛpɪblɑːst, -blæst). [f. EPI- + -BLAST.]

1. *Bot.* (See quot.)

1866 *Treas. Bot.*, *Epiblast*, a small transverse plate (a second cotyledon), found on the embryo of some grasses.

2. *Biol.* The outermost of the three layers constituting the wall of the blastoderm when fully formed.

1875 [see HYPOBLAST 2]. **1877** HUXLEY *Anat. Inv. An.* i. 50 The inner wall of the sac is the hypoblast (endoderm of the adult), the outer the epiblast (ectoderm). **1881** MIVART *Cat* 319 The epiblast investing the whole ovum within the vitelline membrane.

So **epi'blastic** *a.*

1887 A. C. HADDON *Introd. Study Embryol.* ii. 36 The blastoderm of a newly-laid egg.. consists of a definite epiblastic layer and an inferior irregular mass of rounded cells. **1893** A. M. MARSHALL *Vert. Embryol.* 371 The small epiblastic villi of the lower pole of the vesicle. **1921** A. KEITH *Hum. Embryol.* (ed. 4) i. 12 An epiblastic or ectodermal set [of cells].

‖**epiblema** (ɛpɪ'bliːmə). *Bot.* [mod.L., a. Gr. ἐπίβλημα that which is thrown over, f. ἐπί upon + βάλλειν to throw.] (See quot.)

1870 BENTLEY *Bot.* 48 The roots of plants are invested by a modified epidermal tissue to which the term Epiblema has been given by Schleiden.

epiboly (ɛ'pɪbəlɪ). *Embryol.* Also epibole (-əliː). [Gr. ἐπιβολή a throwing or laying on.] The inclusion of one set of segmenting cells within another by reason of the more rapid division of the latter. Hence **epibolic** (ɛpɪ'bɒlɪk) *a.*

1875 E. R. LANKESTER in *Q. Jrnl. Microsc. Sci.* XV. 163 Embolé and epibolé are but two extreme forms of one and the same process. *Ibid.* 165 (*heading*) Epibolic invaginate Planulæ. **1877** T. H. HUXLEY *Man. Anat. Invertebr. Anim.* xii. 683 The process of inclusion of the hypoblast within the epiblast may have the appearance of the growth of the latter over the former, or what is termed epiboly. **1887** A. C. HADDON *Introd. Study Embryol.* ii. 33 The gastrula in the Frog is thus formed partly by invagination (*embolé*), partly by overgrowth (*epibolé*). **1897** PARKER & HASWELL *Text-bk. Zool.* I. iv. 205 The stage has been produced, not by a process of invagination or tucking-in, but by one of epiboly or overgrowth. *Ibid.* v. 257 The process by which the germinal layers have become formed is.. a process of epibolic gastrulation. **1914** [see ENDODERM]. **1956** K. F. LAGLER *Freshwater Fishery Biol.* (ed. 2) vi. 97 When epiboly is about half completed in the Atlantic salmon, a few pairs of body segments (somites) are already visible. **1966** Epibolic [see EMBOLIC *a.* 2].

epibranchial (ɛpɪ'bræŋkɪəl), *a.* (and *sb.*) *Zool.* [See EPI-.] Of or belonging to the segment next below the pharyngobranchial in a branchial arch. As *sb.*, this segment.

1846 [see *pharyngo-branchial* (PHARYNGO-)]. **1877** HUXLEY & MARTIN *Elem. Biol.* (ed. 4) 119 Two lamellae united by their ventral edges and enclosing a central cavity which opens into a chamber (*epibranchial*) above. **1892** C. S. MINOT *Hum. Embryol.* 651 A chain of epibranchial organs. **1893** A. M. MARSHALL *Vert. Embryol.* 40 Along the mid-dorsal line of the pharynx is a deep epibranchial groove.., lined by a single layer of long columnar ciliated cells. **1921** A. KEITH *Hum. Embryol.* (ed. 4) 243 At the upper end of each cleft depression there develop remarkable sense-organs, known as the epibranchial placodes. **1929** *Q. Jrnl. Microsc. Sci.* LXXII. 152 Epibranchial flaps eventually grow downward over the gill-slits of both sides to form the belated atrium. **1946** *Nature* 12 Oct. 524/1 They open posteriorly at the basal portion of the vertical tube referred to above, which communicates between the epibranchial chamber and the exhalant chamber.

epic ('ɛpɪk), *a.* and *sb.* Also 6–9 epick, 7 epique, (epik). [ad. L. *epicus*, a. Gr. ἐπικός, f. ἔπος word, narrative, song. Cf. Fr. *épique*.]

A. *adj.*

1. Pertaining to that species of poetical composition (see EPOS), represented typically by the Iliad and Odyssey, which celebrates in the form of a continuous narrative the achievements of one or more heroic personages of history or tradition.

Epic dialect: that form of the Greek language in which the epic poems were written.

1589 PUTTENHAM *Arte Eng. Poet.* (Arb.) 176 Harding a Poet Epick or Historicall. **1644** MILTON *Educ.* (1738) 139 Teaches what the Laws are of a true Epic Poem. **1666** DRYDEN *Ann. Mirab.*, *Let. Sir R. Howard*, The same images serve equally for the Epique Poesie, and for the Historique and Panegyrique. **1710** STEELE *Tatler* No. 106 ¶1 Three and twenty Descriptions of the Sun-rising that might be of great Use to an Epick Poet. **1752** JOHNSON *Rambler* No. 202 ¶6 To be poor, in the epick language, is only not to command the wealth of nations. **1819** BYRON *Juan* I. cc, My poem's Epic, and is meant to be Divided in twelve books. **1841–4** EMERSON *Ess. Poet* Wks. (Bohn) I. 165 The epic poet.. must drink water out of a wooden bowl. **1879** B. TAYLOR *Stud. Germ. Lit.* 73 Tennyson has endeavored to imitate the old epic simplicity.

absol. *a* **1637** B. JONSON *Discoveries* (1641) 132 The best masters of the Epick, Homer and Virgil.

2. Such as is described in epic poetry; *epic theatre*, a play or plays characterized by realism and an absence of theatrical devices.

1731 A. HILL *Advice to Poets* 35 Then, might our great, Third Edward's awful Shade.. Pale, from his Tomb, in Epic Strides, advance. **1847** TENNYSON *Princ.* Prol. 219 Some great Princess, six feet high, Grand, epic, homicidal. **1935** *Life & Letters To-day* Sept. 74 This method of theatrical presentation was dubbed by Brecht the 'epic' as opposed to the 'dramatic' style. **1957** R. HOGGART *Auden* 15

In some of their techniques for presenting social problems and for obtaining a sense of urgent participation from the audience they seemed to have learned something from the early 'epic theatre' of the German Communist playwright Bertolt Brecht.

B. *sb.*

†**1.** An epic poet. *Obs.*

a **1637** B. JONSON *Horace's Art Poet* (1640) 5 Now to like of this, lay that aside, the Epic's office is.

2. a. An epic poem.

1706 A. BEDFORD *Temple Mus.* ii. 33 One of them was the Goddess of Elegies..and another of Epicks. **1789** J. CAMPBELL *Eccl. & Lit. Hist. Irel.* 170 (T.) He [Mr. M'Pherson] brought forward his counterfeit epicks (the alleged poems of Ossian). **1833** COLERIDGE *Table-t.* 23 Oct., The Homeric epic, in which all is purely external and objective, and the poet is a mere voice. **1876** GREEN *Short Hist.* viii. 583 The most popular of all English poems has been the Puritan epic of the 'Paradise Lost'.

b. *transf.* A composition comparable to an epic poem.

The typical epics, the Homeric poems, the Nibelungenlied, etc., have often been regarded as embodying a nation's conception of its own past history, or of the events in that history which it finds most worthy of remembrance. Hence by some writers the phrase ***national epic*** has been applied to any imaginative work (whatever its form) which is considered to fulfil this function.

1840 CARLYLE *Heroes* (1858) 267 Schlegel has a remark on his Historical Plays, *Henry Fifth* and the others, which is worth remembering. He calls them a kind of National Epic. **1869** FREEMAN *Norm. Conq.* (1876) III. xiv. 328 To turn from the glowing strains of the Norwegian prose epic. **1916** A. HUXLEY *Let.* 19 Mar. (1969) 95, I want very much to see the *Birth of a Nation*, which is said to be a really great film, an epic in pictures. **1940** M. GORELIK *New Theatres for Old* ix. 412 An 'epic' is a large-scale film in which the events, usually historical, take precedence over the 'love interest'. **1957** N. FRYE *Anat. of Crit.* IV. 314 *Ulysses*, then, is a complete prose epic. **1965** *Movie* Spring 36/1 The budget was supposed to have guaranteed an action-packed epic.

3. *fig.* A story, or series of events, worthy to form the subject of an epic.

1831 LYTTON *Godolph.* lxiii, This starry and weird incident in the epic of life's common career. **1866** MOTLEY *Dutch Rep.* VI. vii. 898 That life was a noble Christian epic.

epicacuana, illiterate var. IPECACUANHA.

epical ('ɛpɪkəl), *a.* [f. EPIC *a.* and *sb.* + -AL[1].]

1. Characteristic of an epic; resembling the style or the subjects proper to epic poetry.

1827 HARE *Guesses* Ser. I. (1873) 224 The simple epical accumulation of sentences. **1838** EMERSON *Addr. Camb. Mass.* Wks. (Bohn) II. 204 The Hebrew and Greek Scriptures contain immortal sentences..But they have no epical integrity. **1853** F. W. NEWMAN *Odes of Horace* 27 The rhythm is vigorous and simple, in some sense epical. **1877** MRS. OLIPHANT *Makers Flor.* Introd. 14 The great figure of the Poet..and the equally remarkable Preacher..give a certain historical and epical form to the narrative.

2. Of the nature of an epic, or of epic poetry: cf. EPIC *a.* 1.

1845 MAURICE *Mor. & Met. Philos.* in *Encycl. Metrop.* II. 565/1 The Epical poetry of the Hebrews. **1850** BLACKIE *Æschylus* I. Pref. 32 A high-toned epical narrative. **1882** A. W. WARD in *Macm. Mag.* XLVI. 425 A form of poetry more elastic than either the epical or the dramatic.

Hence '**epically** *adv.*, in an epical manner; in the style of an epic poem.

1863 *Athenæum* 8 Aug. 176/3 We have seen Milton's vision of Eden treated in fond fancy epically..by a small versifier. **1882** STEVENSON in *Longm. Mag.* I. 73 Typical incidents, epically conceived, fitly embodying a crisis.

epicalyx (ɛpɪ'kælɪks, -'keɪlɪks). *Bot.* [f. EPI- + CALYX.] A whorl of leaf-like organs surrounding the true calyx in some plants.

1870 BENTLEY *Bot.* 221. **1882** VINES *Sachs' Bot.* 540 In *Malope trifida*..the three parts of the epicalyx represent a sub-floral bract with its two stipules.

epicanthus (ɛpɪ'kænθəs). *Anat.* [f. EPI- + CANTHUS. Cf. Gr. ἐπικανθίς = ENCANTHIS.] A downward fold of skin which sometimes covers the inner angle or canthus of the eye, esp. in Mongols. Hence **epi'canthic** *a.*

1865 DUNGLISON *Dict. Med. Sci.* (rev. ed.) 355/1 Epicanthis, epicanthus. **1913** A. KEITH *Hum. Embryol.* (ed. 3) 196 The curious epicanthic fold..is represented in all races during foetal life. *Ibid.* 197 (*caption*) The epicanthic or Mongolian fold. **1936** *Jrnl. R. Anthrop. Inst.* LXVI. 37 The presence or absence of an epicanthic fold is not recorded. **1961** *Listener* 31 Aug. 317/1 He gave me a sidelong, rather quizzical glance from his dark epicanthic eyes. **1964** S. DUKE-ELDER *Parsons' Dis. Eye* (ed. 14) xxxi. 509 Epicanthus is a semilunar fold of skin, situated above and sometimes covering the inner canthus.

epicardium (ɛpɪ'kɑːdɪəm). Pl. -ia. [f. EPI-, after PERICARDIUM.] **1.** *Anat.* The innermost layer of the pericardium, closely investing the heart.

1865 in DUNGLISON *Dict. Med. Sci.* (ed.). **1894** D. J. CUNNINGHAM *Man. Pract. Anat.* II. I. 35 The investing part [of the pericardium] which covers the heart is called the visceral part or the epicardium. **1962** *Gray's Anat.* (ed. 33) 730 The visceral portion, or epicardium, covers the heart and the great vessels, and from the latter it is reflected to form the parietal layer, which lines the fibrous pericardium.

2. *Zool.* In certain ascidians, each of two hollow outgrowths from the pharynx, connected with the process of budding.

1893 *Q. Jrnl. Microsc. Sci.* XXXV. 125 The perivisceral cavity of Ciona corresponds to the epicardium of Clavellina. **1914** E. W. MACBRIDE *Text-bk. Embryol.* I. xvii. 626 The conjoined inner walls of the epicardia form a kind of visceral peritoneum, enwrapping heart, pericardium, and intestine. **1929** *Q. Jrnl. Microsc. Sci.* LXXII. 158 Pharynx produced behind the endostyle into a pair of diverticula ('epicardia'). **1950** J. Z. YOUNG *Life of Vertebrates* iii. 62 The situation is complicated by the presence of a pair of outpushings from the pharynx, the epicardia, or perivisceral sacs.

Hence **epi'cardiac, epi'cardial** *adjs.*

1893 *Q. Jrnl. Microsc. Sci.* XXXV. 123 Two tubes are first formed as outgrowths of the pharynx [in Clavellina], called by van Beneden and Julin [1887] the 'epicardiac tubes'. **1908** *Practitioner* Nov. 638 In the first group of cases there is simple adhesion between the peri- and epicardial layers. **1911** *Encycl. Brit.* XXVII. 390/1 There are..two main types of budding [in compound Ascidians]... There is first the 'stolonial' or 'epicardiac' type. **1914** E. W. MACBRIDE *Text-bk. Embryol.* I. xvii. 626 The epicardial tubes or epicardia. **1962** *Lancet* 29 Dec. 1373/1 The infection was cured without removing the electrode, which was left in the ventricle until the insertion of epicardial wires 10 days later.

epicarp ('ɛpɪkɑːp). *Bot.* [f. Gr. ἐπί (see EPI-) + καρπ-ός fruit.] In fruits: The outermost layer of the pericarp; the peel, rind, or skin. Cf. ENDOCARP.

1835 LINDLEY *Introd. Bot.* (1848) II. 3 In the apple and pear the epicarp is formed by the cuticle of the calyx, in the peach the separable skin is the epicarp.

epicay, var. of EPIKY, *Obs.*

epicede ('ɛpɪsiːd). *arch.* Also 7 **epiced.** Anglicized form of EPICEDIUM.

1549 BALE *Ded. of Leland's Itin.* (T.), His worthy works.. with hys epigrams and epicedes. **1613-6** W. BROWNE *Brit. Past.* I. v. (1772) 141 To heare the swan sing her oune epiced. **1654** VILVAIN *Epit. Ess.* VI. 99 Ausonius made many Epiceds. **1848** *Blackw. Mag.* LXIV. 228 He had hastily flattered Richard Cromwell's brief authority by an epicede on Oliver.

epi'cedial, *a. arch.* [f. EPICEDI-UM + -AL[1].] Of or pertaining to an epicedium; elegiac.

1654 VILVAIN *Epit. Ess.* VI. 50, 2 Epicedial Distichs. **1824** CARLYLE *Richter* Misc. (1869) 4 Some of them far exceed anything we English can exhibit in the epicedial style. **1828** —— in *For. Rev.* II. 461 In epicedial language, it may be said ..that his country mourned for him.

epicedian (ɛpɪ'siːdɪən), *a.* and *sb.* Also 7 **epecedean.** [f. as prec. + -AN.]

A. *adj.* Elegiac; funereal.

1623 COCKERAM II. s.v. *Song*, A Song sung ere the corse bee buried, Epicedian-Songe [*printed* Epiodian]. **1881** LD. LYTTON in *19th Cent.* Nov. 783 Epicedian strains.

†**B.** *sb. Obs.* = EPICEDIUM.

1606 MARLOW & CHAPMAN *Hero & Leander* IV, The.. black-ey'd swans Did sing..woful epicedians. **1662** TATHAM *Aqua Tri.* 3 Swans are said to sing a little before they die..an Epecedean, or Funerall Song.

†**epicedion.** *Obs.* = next.

1612 J. TAYLOR (Water P.) *Gt. Brit. in Black* (1872) 13 May thy Age never see An Epicedion in sculp't for thee.

‖**epicedium** (ɛpɪ'siːdɪəm, -siː'daɪəm). *Pl.* epicedia, -ums. [L. *epicēdīum*, a. Gr. ἐπικήδειον, neut. of ἐπικήδειος pertaining to funeral rites, f. ἐπί upon + κῆδος care, *esp.* funeral observance.] A funeral ode.

1587 FLEMING *Contn. Holinshed* III. 1375/2 In memorie of whom (but not as an epicedium, nor yet as an epitaph) these verses..may well be vsed. **1690** TEMPLE *Ess. Heroic Virtue* Wks. 1731 I. 214 That Song or Epicedium of Regnor Ladbrog. **1706** in PHILLIPS, *Epicedium*, a Funeral Song, or Copy of Verses in praise of the Dead. **1828** CARLYLE *Misc.* (1857) I. 163 Epithalamiums, epicediums, by which the dream of existence may be..embellished. **1838-9** HALLAM *Hist. Lit.* III. III. v. 276 The epicedia or funeral lamentations. **1882** CHILD *Eng. & Sc. Pop. Ballads* I. 33/1 He..whips off his 'brother-in-law's' head, with this epicedium: 'Lie there, thou head, and bleed'.

epicene ('ɛpɪsiːn), *a.* and *sb.* Also 6 **epysyn,** 7 **epicen,** 7-9 **epicœne.** [ad. L. *epicœnus*, a. Gr. ἐπίκοινος, f. ἐπί (see EPI-) + κοινός common.]

A. *adj.*

1. *Gram.* In Lat. and Gr. grammar, said of nouns which, without changing their grammatical gender, may denote either sex. Hence (improperly) ***epicene gender***. In Eng. grammar the term has no proper application, but is loosely used as a synonym of *common*.

c **1528** *Impeachm. Wolsey* in Furniv. *Ballads fr. MSS.* I. 356 Wherefor all gendyrs dysconte[nt] be..The dubyum & the epysyn Also. **1612** BRINSLEY *Pos. Parts* (1669) 8 *Q.* Is the Epicene Gender a Gender properly? *A.* No. **1865** *Sat. Rev.* 25 Mar. 348 'Boy' of course is to be understood as an epicene term. **1880** I. PITMAN *Argt. agst. Spelling Reform* 4, I use this word [persons] not invidiously, but as of the epicene gender.

quasi-*sb.* **1612** BRINSLEY *Pos. Parts* (1669) 89 But how shall the gender be known in Epicenes?

2. *transf.* and *fig.* (often with humorous allusion to 1). **a.** In humorous uses of the phrase ***epicene gender***; also of persons, their employments, characters, etc.: Partaking of the characteristics of both sexes.

1601 BP. BARLOW *Eagle & Body* (1609) B ij a, A Prey to the Eagles of the Epicene gender, both Hees and Shees. *a* **1637** B. JONSON *Masques* (T.), Of the epicene gender, hees, and shees, Amphibion Archy is the chief. **1644-58** CLEVELAND *Gen. Poems* (1677) 87 Her Head is Epicene. **1709** STEELE *Tatler* No. 27 ¶4 All Inamaratoes, or Persons of the Epicene Gender. **1823** *Monthly Rev.* CII. 541 The fables concerning this epicene Pope [Pope Joan]. **1830** COLERIDGE *Let.* 26 July, The mysterious epicene relation in which poor Miss Johnston stood to him. **1876** T. HARDY *Hand. Ethelb.* I. 43 What had at first appeared as an epicene shape, the decreasing space resolved into a cloaked female.

b. Adapted to both sexes; worn or inhabited by both sexes.

1624 MIDDLETON *Game at Chess* I. i, 'Stead of an alb, An epicene casible. *a* **1661** FULLER *Worthies, Lincolnsh.* II. 154 The Founder of those Epicœne, and Hermaphrodite Convents, wherein Monks and Nuns lived together. **1866** HOWELLS *Venet. Life* 25 With tatters of epicene linen.

c. *fig.*; often in the sense of 'effeminate'.

1633 T. ADAMS *Exp. 2 Peter* i. 4 Epicene and bastard phrases. *a* **1637** B. JONSON *Underwoods* Wks. (1692) 566 And in an Epicœne fury can write news. **1863** MRS. C. CLARKE *Shaks. Char.* vii. 170 In his code of morality we have no epicene or doubtful virtues. **1881** BLACK *Sunrise* 28 An epicene creature, a bundle of languid affectations.

B. *sb.* One who partakes of the characteristics of both sexes.

1609 B. JONSON (*title*), Epicene, or The Silent Woman. **1831** H. NEELE *Romance Hist.* I. 227 He has gone to take leave of his Epicene. **1873** E. H. CLARKE *Sex in Educ.* 44 [Arrest of development] .. substitutes .. a wiry .. masculineness..making her an epicene.

Hence '**epice,nism.** *nonce-wd.*

1850 *Fraser's Mag.* XLI. 331 Even Shakspere sometimes slides into the temptation which this epicenism [the performance of female parts by male actors] presents to unlicensed wit.

epicentral (ɛpɪ'sɛntrəl), *a.* [f. Gr. ἐπίκεντρ-ος (see EPICENTRUM, which in sense 2 is the immediate source) + -AL[1].]

1. Situated upon a (vertebral) 'centrum'. Also quasi-*sb.* (see quot.)

1866 OWEN *Anat.* I. 43 These 'scleral' spines [of fishes] are termed, according to the vertebral element they may adhere to, 'epineurals', 'epicentrals', and 'epipleurals'..In Esox..the..epicentral spines are present.

2. Of or pertaining to an epicentrum.

1887 *Science* (U.S.A.) 20 May 495/1 The determination of the epicentral tract.

epicentre ('ɛpɪ,sɛntə(r)). Anglicized f. next. Also *fig.*

1887 *Science* (U.S.A.) 20 May 495/1 The distance from the epicentre to the point where the rate of decline of the intensity is greatest. **1905** *Westm. Gaz.* 15 Feb. 2/1 The Ischian shock was chosen because of its relations to volcanic action; that of Charleston because of the discovery of the double epicentre. **1937** WOOLDRIDGE & MORGAN *Physical Basis Geogr.* v. 58 In the region of the epicentre (the point, or small area, immediately above the focus) actual waves or swells occur, which..are responsible for most of the damage. **1955** *Times* 21 June 10/2 A 'severe' earthquake, with its epicentre probably located either in the Aleutian Islands off Alaska, or in Siberia. **1970** *Times* 10 Apr. 3/1 It has been a good year for the Maltings. Those at Snape, epicentre of the Aldeburgh Festival, have been lovingly rebuilt after last year's fire.

‖**epicentrum** (ɛpɪ'sɛntrəm). [mod.Lat., a. Gr. ἐπίκεντρον, neut. of ἐπίκεντρος *adj.*, 'situate upon a centre', f. ἐπί upon + κέντρον CENTRE.] The point over the centre: applied in *Seismology* to the outbreaking point of earthquake shocks.

1879 LE CONTE *Elem. Geol.* 100 The point of first emergence (epicentrum). **1887** *Science* (U.S.A.) 20 May 495/2 Along this line there are three points, each of which has all the characters of an epicentrum, determined by as many distinct shocks, each having a focus of its own.

†**epice'rastic,** *a. Obs. rare.* [ad. Gr. ἐπικεραστικός, f. ἐπικεραννύναι to temper, f. ἐπί + κεραννύναι to mix.] Tempering the acrimony of the humours; emollient. Also as *sb.* in *pl.*

1684 tr. *Bonet's Merc. Compit.* VI. 232 An epicerastick Vomit may be made of Chicken-broth, etc. *Ibid.* IX. 317 The Vomits must be very gentle and epicerastick, as Warm-water. **1721-1800** BAILEY, *Epicerasticks.* **1847** in CRAIG; and in mod. Dicts.

epicerebral (ɛpɪ'sɛrɪbrəl), *a. Anat.* [f. EPI- + CEREBRAL.] Situated upon the brain.

epicerebral space: 'A space said by His to exist between the pia mater and the surface of the brain' (*Syd. Soc. Lex.*).

‖**epicheirema** (,ɛpɪkaɪ'riːmə). Also 8 **epichirema.** [mod.L., a Gr. ἐπιχείρημα lit. 'an attempt', f. ἐπιχειρέειν to undertake, f. ἐπί upon + χείρ hand.] (See quots.)

Aristotle used the word to denote 'an attempted proof, such as is used in Dialectic, being something short of a demonstrated conclusion' (Liddell & Scott); the use defined below is due to a misunderstanding of his meaning.

1721 in BAILEY. **1724** WATTS *Logic* III. ii. §6 Epichirema is a Syllogism which contains the Proof of the major or minor, or both, before it draws the Conclusion. **1837-8** SIR W. HAMILTON *Logic* xix. (1866) I. 365 A syllogism is now vulgarly called an Epicheirema, when to either of the two premises, or to both, there is annexed a reason for its support. **1870** JEVONS *Elem. Logic* xviii. 155 The peculiar name Epicheirema is given to a syllogism when either premise is proved or supported by a reason implying the existence of an imperfectly expressed prosyllogism.

epichile ('ɛpɪkaɪl). *Bot.* [ad. mod.L. *epichīlium*, f. Gr. ἐπί upon + χεῖλος lip, rim.] 'The upper half of the lid of an orchid, when that organ is once jointed or strangulated' (*Treas. Bot.*).

epichlorhydrin, -chlorite: see EPI- *pref.*

epichordal (ɛpɪˈkɔːdəl), *a. Anat.* [f. EPI- + CHORD + -AL^1.] Situated upon or about the intercranial part of the notochord: applied to certain segments of the brain.

epichorial (ɛpɪˈkɔərɪəl), *a.* [f. Gr. ἐπιχώρι-ος in or of the country (f. ἐπί + χώρα country) + -AL^1.] Proper or peculiar to a particular country or district.

1840 De Quincey *Mod. Superstition* Wks. III. 334 The local or epichorial superstitions from every district of Europe. **1842** *Blackw. Mag.* LII. 159 This adornment is quite epichorial; we never saw it out of the Veronese.

epichristian (ɛpɪˈkrɪstjən), *a. rare.* [f. EPI- + CHRISTIAN *a.*] Pertaining to the age not long after Christ. (App. invented by De Quincey, who explains that he uses it 'of all agencies that belonged to the primary movements of Christianity'.)

1840 De Quincey *Essenes* Wks. IX. 268 During the whole of this noviciate for Christianity, and, in fact, throughout the whole Epichristian era, etc. **1860** *Guardian* 20 June, The loss of the epichristian Hindu literature, no less than that of still greater antiquity, has been very considerable.

epicism (ˈɛpɪsɪz(ə)m). *rare.* [f. EPIC + -ISM.] The mental habit characteristic of the epic poet.

1878 T. Sinclair *Mount* 166 But the lyricism and the balance of epicism in his nature saved him.

epicist (ˈɛpɪsɪst). [f. EPIC + -IST.] A writer of epic poetry.

1853 Kingsley *A. Smith & A. Pope* Misc. I. 272 As the Greek epicists and Virgil copied Homer; as all succeeding Latin epicists copied Virgil. **1878** T. Sinclair *Mount* 60 His placing of Cervantes as the greatest epicist.

epiclastic (ɛpɪˈklæstɪk), *a. Geol.* [f. EPI- + CLASTIC *a.*] Designating rocks which are formed by the breaking up of pre-existing rocks upon the earth's surface.

1887 J. J. H. Teall in *Geol. Mag.* IV. 493 Some modification in the use of the term clastic is rendered necessary... I venture to suggest that it should be applied to all rocks which consist largely of mineral fragments and that we should distinguish between the three types of clastic rocks..by using the terms epiclastic, cataclastic, and pyroclastic. *Epiclastic*—Rocks formed of fragments resulting from the breaking up of older rocks occurring *upon* the earth's surface.

epiclesis (ɛpɪˈkliːsɪs). *Liturgiology.* Also epiklesis. [Gr. ἐπίκλησις, f. ἐπικαλεῖν to call upon, invoke.] A part of the prayer of consecration in which the presence of the Holy Spirit is invoked to bless the eucharistic elements, or the communicants, or both.

[**1832** W. Palmer *Orig. Liturg.* II. 134 The immediate or proper prayer of consecration..may be divided into two particulars: first, the prayer itself, or ἐπίκλησις, in the language of the primitive church; and secondly, the commemoration of our Lord's deeds and words at the last supper.] **1878** *Encycl. Brit.* VIII. 653/2 In Quæstio 107 it is laid down that immediately on the pronunciation of the *Epiclesis*, transubstantiation takes place. **1912** [see ANAMNESIS b]. **1925** *Contemp. Rev.* Oct. 426 Many Anglo-Catholics desire the introduction of the *Epiklesis*, or Invocation of the Holy Spirit, at the time of the consecration of the elements. **1959** J. Gill *Council of Florence* viii. 272 The problem as to whether it is the dominical words or the *epiclesis* in the Liturgy that should be deemed to effect the mystery. **1966** *Cath. Dict. Theol.* II. 226/2 There are *epikleses* with a similar drift in old Gallican liturgies.

epiclinal (ɛpɪˈklaɪnəl), *a. Bot.* [f. Gr. ἐπί (see EPI-) + κλίν-η couch + -AL^1.] 'Placed upon the disk or receptacle of a flower' (*Treas. Bot.*).

epicly (ˈɛpɪklɪ), *adv. rare.* [f. EPIC *a.* + -LY^2.] In an epic manner or style; EPICALLY.

1831 *Blackw. Mag.* XXX. 480 Poems in which are pictured and narrated, epicly, national characters and events. **1839** *Ibid.* XLVI. 121 It had been sung..lyrically, narratively, dramatically, and epicly.

epicœle (ˈɛpɪsiːl). [f. EPI- + Gr. κοιλ-ία the cavity of the belly.] (See quot. and ATRIUM.)

Hence **epiˈcœlous** *a.*, having an epicœle.

1877 Huxley *Anat. Inv. An.* xi. 653 In the Tunicata, the atrium is a kind of 'perivisceral cavity', which is formed by an invagination of the ectoderm, in which case it may be termed an epicœle.

epicolic (ɛpɪˈkɒlɪk), *a. Anat.* [f. EPI- + Gr. κόλον COLON. Cf. F. *épicolique.*] Of or pertaining to the region of the body which is over, or in the course of, the colon.

epicondyle (ɛpɪˈkɒndaɪl). *Anat.* [a. Fr. *épicondyle* (mod.L. *epicondylus*), formed by Chaussier *c* 1820: see EPI- and CONDYLE.

As Chaussier applied the name condyle to what is now called the 'radial head' of the humerus, *epicondyle* meant 'the process situated above the condyle'.]

The external condyle of the humerus.

1836–9 Todd *Cycl. Anat.* II. 161 It [*i.e.* the process] should be designated epicondyle. **1840** G. Ellis *Anat.* 304 Semiflex the elbow joint, and the prominences of the external or epicondyle on the outer side, and of the internal condyle or epitrochlea on the inner, will be rendered evident.

ˌepicontiˈnental, *a. Geol.* [f. EPI- + CONTINENTAL *a.* 1.] (See quot. 1905.)

1905 Chamberlin & Salisbury *Geol.* I. 11 Those shallow portions of the sea which lie upon the continental shelf, and those portions which extend into the interior of the continent with like shallow-depths, such as the Baltic Sea and the Hudson Bay, may be called epicontinental seas, for they really lie *upon* the continent, or at least upon the continental platform. **1935** *Geogr. Jrnl.* LXXXVI. 498 An epicontinental embayment of the Pacific. **1959** *New Biol.* XXIX. 8 There is plenty of evidence..that at various times nearly all the continents have been submerged by such 'epicontinental' seas.

epicoracoid (ɛpɪˈkɒrəkɔɪd), *a.* and *sb.* [f. EPI- + CORACOID.]

A. *adj.* The designation of a bone, or a pair of bones, found in reptiles, etc., and forming a continuation of the coracoid. **B.** *sb.* The epicoracoid bone.

1839–47 Todd *Cycl. Anat.* III. 377/1 The epicoracoids.. are wanting in the bird. **1873** Mivart *Elem. Anat.* iv. 158 An additional flat bone placed in front of the inner end of the coracoid called the epicoracoid. **1875** Blake *Zool.* 78 The clavicle is single, and, unlike that in the Monotremata, is not associated with an epicoracoid bone.

epicoracoidal (ɛpɪˌkɒrəˈkɔɪdəl), *a.* [f. prec. + -AL^1.] = prec.

1871 Huxley *Anat. Vert.* 256 [In Crocodilia] the pectoral arch has no clavicle, and the coracoid has no distinct epicoracoidal element.

epicormic (ɛpɪˈkɔːmɪk), *a. Forestry.* [f. EPI- + CORM^2 + -IC.] Of a shoot or branch: growing from a dormant bud which has been suddenly exposed to the light and air.

1909 P. T. Maw *Pract. Forestry* 149 With some trees, especially Oak and Chestnut, an unduly thick canopy will often cause..the flushing of latent buds along the stem, and epicormic branches will be thrown out. **1921** R. C. Hawley *Silviculture* 135 The isolated position of the standards with full light from all sides..often results in the formation of epicormic branches on trees which have not an adequate crown development. **1953** *Brit. Commonw. For. Terminol.* I. 44 *Epicormic branch*, a branch originating from a dormant or adventitious bud arising on the trunk or an older branch.

epicorolline (ɛpɪˈkɒərɒlɪn, -aɪn), *a. Bot.* [f. EPI- + COROLLA + -INE.] Inserted in or upon the corolla.

epicotyl (ɛpɪˈkɒtɪl). *Bot.* [f. EPI- + Gr. κοτύλ-η: see COTYLEDON.] (See quot.)

1880 C. & F. Darwin *Movem. Pl.* 5 The stem immediately above the cotyledons will be called the epicotyl or plumule.

epicotyˈledonary, *a. Bot.* [f. EPI- + COTYLEDON + -ARY.] Situated immediately above the cotyledons.

1884 Bower & Scott *De Bary's Phaner. & Ferns* 246 The bundles of the trace of the first epicotyledonary leaves insert themselves on the cotyledonary bundles at or close below the cotyledonary node.

epicranial (ɛpɪˈkreɪnɪəl), *a. Anat.* [f. EPICRANI-UM + -AL^1.] Pertaining to the epicranium. ***epicranial suture***: in insects (see quot. 1888).

1831 R. Knox *Cloquet's Anat.* 774 Epicranial Lymphatics. They are distributed on all sides beneath the skin of the cranium. **1856** Todd & Bowman *Phys. Anat.* II. 67 Three muscles..arising from the epicranial aponeurosis. **1888** Rolleston & Jackson *Anim. Life* 140 Its dorsal surface or Epicranium is convex, and is marked by a Y-shaped epicranial suture.

†ˌepiˈcranidal, *a. Obs. rare.* [f. Gr. ἐπικρανίς, ἐπικρανίδ-ος the membrane of the cerebellum (see EPICRANIUM).] Belonging to or situated in the cerebellum.

1684 tr. *Agrippa's Van. Artes* lii. 135 Eratistratus [places the Soul] in the Epicranidal Membrane.

‖epicranium (ɛpɪˈkreɪnɪəm). *Anat.* [mod.L., f. Gr. ἐπί (see EPI-) + κρανίον CRANIUM.] **a.** All that overlies the cranium or skull; the scalp. **b.** In insects: The upper surface of the head.

1888 [see EPICRANIAL].

‖epiˈcrasis. *Obs. Med.* [mod.L. *epicrăsis*, a. Gr. ἐπικρᾶσις, f. ἐπικρα-, ἐπικεραννύναι: see EPICERASTIC.] The process of 'tempering acrid humours'; the use of epicerastics.

1621 G. Hakewil *King David's Vow* 290 In such a case.. a skilfull Physician will use Epicrasis, as they call it, labouring to bring the body to a better temperature.

epicritic (ɛpɪˈkrɪtɪk), *a. Psychol.* [f. Gr. ἐπικριτικός adjudicatory.] An epithet used to designate the finer discriminations of the senses, particularly of touch, as contrasted with *protopathic.* In terms of behaviour, sometimes used to refer to emotional and instinctive forms, as opposed to rational.

1905 H. Head et al. in *Brain* XXVIII. 107 To this form of sensibility we propose to give the name 'epicritic', since it is peculiarly associated with the localisation and discrimination of cutaneous stimuli. **1920** W. H. R. Rivers *Instinct & Unconscious* iv. 23 Epicritic sensibility may be only a greater perfection of protopathic sensibility. **1920** *Discovery* Nov. 340/1 From a physiological aspect, the distinction of protopathic from epicritic sensibility is, so far, devoid of neurological basis. **1942** *Brit. Jrnl. Psychol.* July 61 Head..stipulates expressly that the elaboration of spatial schemata depends upon processes occurring only at the level of *epicritic* integration. **1966** B. Haigh tr. *Luria's Higher Cortical Functions* II. 146 A lesion of these cortical areas causes the most persistent disturbances of complex epicritic sensation.

epicure (ˈɛpɪkjʊə(r)), *sb.* Also 6 epecur. [perh. an appellative use of *Epicure* (cf. Fr. *Épicure*, It. *Epicuro*), ad. L. *Epicūrus* (as pr. name now used in Lat. form), a. Gr. Ἐπίκουρος, the name of an Athenian philosopher *c* 300 B.C. It may, however, be ad. late L. *epicūrius* (= L. *epicūrĕus*) Epicurean, f. *Epicūrus*; cf. *Vergyle, Ovyde*, ad. L. *Vergilius, Ovidius.* See EPICUREE, EPICURY.

It does not appear that *epicure* as a common noun was ever current in Fr.; a single instance (pl. *epicures*, in sense 2) is cited by Godef. from the *Tresor* of Brunetto Latino (13th c.), who in an identical passage in one of his Italian works uses *epicuri.* The Italian lexicographers, however, suggest that the form *epicuri*, both in this case and in the two or three instances of 14–15th c. in which it is used for 'Epicureans', is a scribal error for the more usual *epicurei* or *epicurii.*]

†1. (With capital initial.) A disciple or follower of Epicurus; = EPICUREAN B. 1. **a.** A philosopher of the school of Epicurus. *Obs.*

The distinctive doctrines of Epicurus were, 1. That the highest good is pleasure, which he identified with the practice of virtue. 2. That the gods do not concern themselves at all with men's affairs. 3. That the external world resulted from a fortuitous concourse of atoms.

[**1548** R. Hutten *Sun of Divin.* R v b, To confyrme oure myndes against Epicures opinions. **1589** Cooper *Admon.* 118 The schoole of *Epicure*, and the Atheists, is mightily increased in these dayes.] **1547** Bauldwin *Mor. Philos.* 20 a, Scholers of every secte became Epicures, but none of the Epicures became of other sectes. **1599** Davies *Immort. Soul* (1876) I. 26 Epicures make them swarmes of atomies. **1627–77** Feltham *Resolves* I. lxii. 96, I care not for the planed Stoic, there is a Sect between him and the Epicure. **1772** Fletcher *Wks.* (1795) I. 70 Unrenewed Man has imagined with the Epicure, a careless God.

†b. *loosely.* One who disbelieves in the divine government of the world, and in a future life; one who recognizes no religious motives for conduct.

1545 Joye *Exp. Dan.* xii. [xi.] 222 He describeth the furye of the Epicures..euen to contempne the very god. **1549** Latimer *Serm. bef. Edw. VI* (Arb.) 54 Or els beleue (as yᵉ Epecurs do) that after this life ther is neither hel nor heauen. **1633** G. Herbert *Temple, Ch. Porch* x, Were I an Epicure, I could bate swearing. **1691** Wood *Ath. Oxon.* I. 819 A professed unpreaching Epicure and Arminian.

†2. One who gives himself up to sensual pleasure, *esp.* to eating; a glutton, sybarite.

1565 in Strype *Ann. Ref.* I. xlv. 498 He marvelled why Feckenham should call him epicure [because he did not fast]. **1575** T. Rogers *Sec. Coming Christ* 12/2 Least happely by possessing much they..fal into ryotousnesse, and so become Epicures. **1605** Shaks. *Macb.* v. iii. 8 Then fly, false Thanes, And mingle with the English Epicures. **1675** Traherne *Chr. Ethics* App. 573 An epicure is for his wine or women or feasts continually. **1768–74** Tucker *Lt. Nat.* (1852) I. 270 Nobody was less of an epicure than Epicurus himself. **1774** Goldsm. *Nat. Hist.* (1776) V. 154 The poultry kind may be considered as sensual epicures, solely governed by their appetites.

3. (The current sense.) One who cultivates a refined taste for the pleasures of the table; one who is choice and dainty in eating and drinking.

1586 T. B. tr. *La Primaud. Fr. Acad.* (1589) I. 210 Let us ..forsake the discipline and life of Epicures, and beware that our pallate..be not moore sensible than our hart. *a* **1639** W. Whateley *Prototypes* II. xxxiv. (1646) 165 Such an epicure was Potiphar..to please his tooth and pamper his flesh with delicacies. **1662** Stillingfl. *Orig. Sacr.* III. i. §18 More sweetness in knowledge, than the little Epicure, the Bee, tasts in his choicest flowers. **1756–82** J. Warton *Ess. Pope* II. x. 130 Our author himself was a great Epicure. **1814** Scott *Wav.* xxix, As an epicure protracts, by sipping slowly, the enjoyment of a delicious beverage. **1872** Yeats *Growth Comm.* 61 Lucullus, a more refined epicure.

b. *transf.*

1670 G. H. *Hist. Cardinals* I. II. 49 The Cardinals..play the Epicures with Musick as well as Meat. **1798** Ferriar *Illustr. Sterne* ii. 47 This is excellently calculated to excite the appetite of literary epicures. **1823** Chalmers *Serm.* I. 382 Your epicures of feeling who riot in all the luxury of theatrical emotion. **1872** O. W. Holmes *Poet Breakf.-t.* ii. 54, I am afraid I am becoming an epicure in words.

4. *attrib.* and *Comb.*

1589 Greene *Menaphon* (Arb.) 70 Democles..spent his time Epicure-like in all kinde of pleasures. **1593** Nashe *Christ's T.* 89 b, Like one of Rome's Epicure Emperors. **1661** Pepys *Diary* 3 May, The exceeding unmannerly and epicure-like palate of Mr. Creed. **1852** Dickens *Bleak H.* vi, I have the epicure-like feeling.

†ˈepicure, *v. Obs. rare.* [f. prec. sb.] *trans.* To indulge as an epicure; in quot. *refl.*; also, *to epicure it* = to play the epicure.

1627–47 Feltham *Resolves* I. xli. 132 It [the body] would complain of loathing and satiety, and so would the soul if it did ever epicure itself in joy. **1655** Fuller *Hist. Camb.* ii. §48 They did Epicure it in daily exceedings.

†epicuˈreal, epiˈcurial, *a. Obs.* [f. L. *epicūrē-us, epicūri-us* (see next), + -AL^1.]

a. Characteristic of the Epicurean philosophy. **b.** Characteristic of a votary of sensual pleasure.

a **1555** Bradford *Wks.* 228 Take from us our.. hypocritical, and epicureal hearts. **1591** Harington *Orl. Fur.* 30 *note*, Epicuriall and idle life. **1607** Topsell *Four-f. Beasts* (1673) 103 Baked in Pasties, for his liquorous

Epicureal appetite. **1621** BURTON *Anat. Mel.* II. v. I. v, But these are Epicureall tenents, tending to looseness of life. **1630** BRATHWAIT *Eng. Gentl.* (1641) 88 Whose Epicureall mindes are only set upon prodigall expence. **1681** P. RYCAUT *Critick* 174 In making an epicurial pleasure the ultimate term. **1727** *Philip Quarll* 10 These provisions being something too Epicurial for an Hermit.

epicurean (ˌɛpɪkjʊˈriːən), *a.* and *sb.* Also in 6 epicureane, 7 epicurian. [f. L. *epicūrē-us*, late L. *epicūrius* (ad. Gr. ἐπικούρειος, f. Ἐπίκουρος Epicurus) + -AN. Cf. Fr. *Épicurien.*]

A. *adj.*

1. (With capital initial.) Of or pertaining to Epicurus, or to the ethical and physical system of philosophy taught by him.

1586 T. B. *La Primaud. Fr. Acad.* I. (1584) 442 Fortune being an Epicurian worde, rather than an Heathenish. **1621** BURTON *Anat. Mel.* II. iii. III. (1676) 205/2 It was no Epicurean speech of an Epicure. **1662** STILLINGFL. *Orig. Sacr.* III. ii. §11 The Atomical or Epicurean Hypothesis. **1741** MIDDLETON *Cicero* III. XII. (1742) 378 That chief good of an Epicurean life, his private ease and safety. **1861** MILL *Utilit.* ii. 11 There is no known Epicurean theory of life which does not assign to the pleasures of the intellect..a much higher value as pleasures than to those of mere sensation.

2. Devoted to the pursuit of pleasure; hence, luxurious, sensual, gluttonous. Now chiefly: Devoted to refined and tasteful sensuous enjoyment.

1641 MILTON *Ch. Discipl.* II. (1851) 66 Warming their Palace Kitchins, and from thence their unctuous, and epicurean paunches. **1656** COWLEY *Poems, Grasshopper*, Voluptuous, and Wise withal, Epicurean Animal! **1850** CARLYLE *Latter-d. Pamph.* vi. (1872) 192 No longer an earnest Nation, but a light epicurean one. **1868** TENNYSON *Lucretius* 215 Nothing to mar the sober majesties Of settled, sweet, Epicurean life.

b. Suited to the taste of an epicure.

1606 SHAKS. *Ant. & Cl.* II. i. 24 Epicurean Cookes, Sharpen with cloylesse sawce his Appetite.

B. *sb.* (With capital initial.) 1. A disciple of Epicurus; one who holds views similar to his.

1605 BACON *Adv. Learn.* II. xiv. §9 Velleius the Epicurian needed not to have asked, why God should have adorned the heavens with stars. **1698** NORRIS *Pract. Disc.* (1707) IV. 101 He may think with the Epicurean, that God is an idle, unactive Being. **1732** BERKELEY *Alciph.* IV. §16 The very Epicureans allowed the being of gods. **1856** R. VAUGHAN *Mystics* (1860) I. 60 The Epicureans and the Stoics..came forward to supply that moral want.

2. One who makes pleasure the chief object of his life.

*a*1572 KNOX *Hist. Ref.* Wks. (1846) I. 236 Symon Preastoun..a right Epicureane. *a*1652 J. SMITH *Sel. Disc.* i. 25 Those poor brutish Epicureans have nothing but the mere husks of fleshly pleasure to feed themselues with. **1825** SCOTT *Talism.* x, He was a voluptuary and an epicurean. **1866** MOTLEY *Dutch Rep.* II. i. 131 A horde of lazy epicureans, telling beads and indulging themselves in luxurious vice.

epicureanism (ˌɛpɪkjʊˈriːənɪz(ə)m). [f. EPICUREAN + -ISM.]

1. (With capital initial.) The philosophical system of Epicurus.

*a*1751 BOLINGBROKE *Ess. Hum. Reason* (R.), He that should take all his notions of..Epicureanism from Balbus. **1829** I. TAYLOR *Enthus.* iv. (1867) 78 The modern Stoic (or Antinomian)..borrows the practical part of Epicureanism.

2. Adherence to the principles of Epicurus, or to what are commonly understood as such; hence, devotion to a life of ease, pleasure, and luxury. Also *transf.*

1847 LEWES *Hist. Philos.* (1867) I. 376 That pensive epicureanism which gives so peculiar a character to his poems. **1855** MACAULAY *Hist. Eng.* IV. 250 His dislike of the Puritans..sprang, not from bigotry, but from Epicureanism. **1872** MINTO *Eng. Lit.* II. x. 611 This literary epicureanism (or rather gluttony).

epicuˈreanize, *v.* *nonce-wd.* [f. EPICUREAN + -IZE.] *trans.* To render epicurean or pleasure-loving.

1827 HARE *Guesses* (1859) 314 These naturally tend to enervate and epicureanize men's minds.

†**ˈepicuree.** *Obs.* In 4, 6 *pl.* epicureis, -ees. See also EPICURY. [ad. L. *epicūrē-us* (see EPICUREAN); cf. *Pharisee.*] = EPICUREAN B. 1.

(In the first quot. *epicureis* appears to be the Lat. pl. *epicurei* with an Eng. pl. ending; cf. *ephories* and similar formations common in 16–17th c.)

1382 WYCLIF *Acts* xvii. 18 Forsothe summe Epicureis and Stoycis..disputiden..with him. **1535** COVERDALE *ibid.*, Certayne Philosophers of yᵉ Epicurees & Stoikes.

†**ˈepicurely,** *adv.* *Obs.* *rare*⁻¹. [f. EPICURE + -LY².] After the manner of an epicure; luxuriously.

1599 NASHE *Lenten Stuffe* (1871) 109 His horses..are provendered epicurely.

†**epiˈcureous, -ious,** *a.* *Obs.* [f. L. *epicūrē-us*, late L. *epicūri-us*, + -OUS.] = EPICUREAN *a.*

1553 BALE *Gardiner's Obed.* Pref. A ij, The double-faced epicurious biteshepe of Couentrye and Lichefelde. **1606** *Choice, Chance, & C.* (1881) 56 Another out of his epicurious humor, made a kind of oration in the praise of a goose pie. **1615** HIERON *Wks.* I. 661 That epicureous and desperat speech..'Let vs eate and drinke, for to morrow we shall die'.

epicurial, -an: see EPICUREAL, -AN.

†**epiˈcurical,** *a.* *Obs.* *rare.* [f. EPICUR-US + -IC + -AL¹.] = EPICUREAN *a.*

1591 R. TURNBULL *S. James* 144 S. James [had to do] with Epicuricall professours.

ˈepicurish, *a.* *rare.* [f. EPICURE + -ISH.] Of the nature of an epicure; sensual, voluptuous.

1553 BALE *Vocacyon* in *Harl. Misc.* (Malh.) I. 340 Many abhominable ydolatryes mainteined by the epicurysh prestes. **1601** BP. BARLOW *Def. Prot. Rel.* 152 This is an Epicurish securitie. *a*1623 W. PEMBLE *Salomon's Recant.* (1628) 14 Brutish, sensual and epicurish.

Hence **epiˈcurishly** *adv.*

1834 WILSON in *Blackw. Mag.* XXXV. 1004 Gluttonously or epicurishly inclined.

epicurism (ˈɛpɪkjʊˌrɪz(ə)m). Also 6–7 epicurisme, 7–8 epicureism. [Two formations: (1) f. *Epicūrus*, after mod.L. type *Epicūrismus*; cf. Fr. *Épicurisme* (perh. the immediate source), It., Sp. *Epicurismo*. (2) f. EPICURE + -ISM.

As the sb. *epicure* long continued to be used with distinct consciousness of its connexion with the name of the philosopher, the two formations cannot be accurately distinguished exc. in recent examples. The accentuation shown above belongs properly to the second formation (sense 3); in the now rare sense 1 most persons would prob. say *epiˈcurism* (as in Johnson). Bailey (1736) places the accent on 2nd syllable, as app. in Shaks. *Lear* I. iv. 165; cf. the verse quots. s.v. EPICURIZE. The 17–18th c. *epicureism* is perh. strictly f. L. *epicūrē-us*: cf. Ger. *epikuräismus*.]

1. (With capital initial.) The philosophical system of Epicurus; doctrines regarded as analogous to that system; attachment to such opinions. Now *rare*; more commonly EPICUREANISM.

1575 FULKE *Confut. Doct. Purgatory* (1577) 444 Epicureisme and Saduceisme is more common at Rome then Christianitye. *a*1593 H. SMITH *Arrow agst. Atheists* (1622) 49 There seemeth small difference betweene Epicurisme, Atheisme, and Mahometisme. **1862** MERIVALE *Rom. Emp.* (1865) VI. liii. 327 They had resigned themselves to Epicurism..or had cultivated Stoicism.

†2. Practical conformity to the (supposed) principles of Epicurus; the pursuit of pleasure; sensuality. *Obs.*

1586 FERNE *Blaz. Gentrie* 20 Not the notes of Nobilitie, but the marks of Epicurisme, and companions to effeminacie. **1605** SHAKS. *Lear* I. iv. 265 Epicurisme and Lust Make it [our Court] more like a Tauerne, or a Brothell Than a grac'd Pallace. **1691–8** NORRIS *Pract. Disc.* 138 Nothing but meer Sensuality and Epicurism. **1775** BURKE *Corr.* (1844) II. 18 This general affection to religion..will make a common cause against Epicurism.

†b. Excess in eating; gluttony. *Obs.*

1586 COGAN *Haven Health* ccxii. (1612) 190 That Epicurisme, which is too much vsed in England, and especially of Merchants..to sit eating..for the space of three or four hours. **1613** MIDDLETON *Triumphs of Truth*, First then I banish from this Feast of Joy, All Excesse, Epicurisme, both which destroy The Healths of Soule and Body. **1614** T. ADAMS *Devil's Banquet* 291 Poysoning to Italie, Drunkennesse to Germanie, Epicurisme to England.

3. The disposition and habits of an epicure; cultivated taste in the pleasures of the table.

*a*1619 FOTHERBY *Atheom.* I. (1622) 116 Yea, and euen Salomon obserueth the same kind of Epicurisme. **1665** PEPYS *Diary* (1879) III. 226 Captain Cocke, for whose Epicurisme a dish of partridges was sent for. **1752** JOHNSON *Rambler* No. 206 ⁋13 He is venerated by the professors of epicurism, as the only man who understands the niceties of cookery. **1823** LAMB *Elia* (1860) 130 The heats of epicurism put out the gentle flame of devotion. **1830** M. DONOVAN *Dom. Econ.* I. 197 The epicurism of consumers of malt liquors.

b. *transf.* (Cf. EPICURE 3 b.)

1655 FULLER *Ch. Hist.* II. ii. §18 But such is the epicurism of modern times to addulce all words to the ear that, etc. **1661** PEPYS *Diary* 23 Sept., I never did pass a night with more epicurism of sleep. **1675** TRAHERNE *Chr. Ethics* App. 573 A vertuous man is..more prone to celestial epicurisme, if I may so speak, than all the world besides. **1860** SMILES *Self-Help* x. 272 Much of our reading is but the indulgence of a sort of literary epicurism.

†**epicurist.** *Obs.* [f. *Epicur-us* + -IST.] = EPICUREAN *sb.*

1610 HEALEY *St. Aug. Citie of God* 729 Were not the Epicurists in great accoumpt at Athens.

†**epiˈcurity.** *Obs.* *rare.* [f. EPICURE + -ITY.] Luxurious living; sensual indulgence.

1575 FENTON *Gold. Epist.* (1577) 26 The houses of good knights ought to bee as schooles of instruction to youth, and not Tauerns to professe epicuritie. *Ibid.* 41.

†**eˈpicurize,** *v.* *Obs.* [f. *Epicur-us* (or EPICURE) + -IZE; cf. late L. *epicūrizāre* (5th c.).]

1. *intr.* To profess or practise the doctrine of Epicurus; *esp.* to live luxuriously.

1621 BURTON *Anat. Mel.* Democr. (1676) 35/2 Let them tyrannize, epicurize, oppress, luxuriate, consume themselves with factions, etc. *a*1688 [see EPICURIZING *ppl. a.*].

2. To play the epicure; to feast daintily or luxuriously. Const. *on*. Also *fig.*

1634 BRERETON *Trav.* (1844) 18 The English burgomaister..was also epicurizing at this time, as the day before at Scedam. **1672** MARVELL *Reh. Transp.* 84 That Fellow..epicurizes upon burning Coals. **1678** CUDWORTH *Intell. Syst.* I. v. 8 These evil Demons therefore did as it were deliciate and epicurize in them.

fig. **1642** FULLER *Holy & Prof. St.* v. xvii. 426 Spending them [men's lives] by degrees and epicurizing on their pain. *a*1688 T. FLATMAN tr. *Ovid's Ep. Laod. to Prot.* 19 My greedy Eyes epicuriz'd on thine. *a*1711 KEN *Edmund* Poet. Wks. 1721 II. 269 He and th' infernal Powers epicuris'd, That Tobroc murder'd was while unbaptis'd.

Hence **ˈepicuˌrizing** *vbl. sb.* and *ppl. a.*

1652 GAULE *Magastrom.* 4 Let it..be interpreted..of their epicurizing, or their sacrificing to the stars. *a*1688 CUDWORTH *Serm.* 87 (T.) Epicurizing philosophy, Antinomian liberty.

†**ˈepicury,** *a.* *Obs.* *rare*⁻¹. [ad. late L. *epicūri-us* (= *epicūrēus*), f. *Epicūr-us*.] = EPICUREAN *a.*

[*c*1430 *Pilgr. Lyf Man.* III. xl. (1869) 156 Who ben, quod j, Epicurie? It ben, quod she, a folk that of here persede sak maken a god.] **1545** JOYE *Exp. Dan.* xii. [xi.] 222 Seinge this epicury godles furye be so horrible a sinne agayenst gods highe maiesty. *Ibid.* 222 b, These epicurye opinions.

epicuticle (ˈɛpɪkjuːtɪk(ə)l). Also epicuˈticula. [f. EPI- + CUTICLE.] The outer layer of a cuticle.

a. The thin outermost waxy covering on an insect or other arthropod.

1929 [see ENDOCUTICLE a]. **1934** A. D. IMMS *Gen. Textbk. Entomol.* (ed. 3) I. 7 In most insects a very thin stratum or epicuticula (less than 1 μ in thickness) is present outside the exocuticula. **1957** *Encycl. Brit.* XII. 417 F/1 Outside this [*sc.* the exocuticle of insects] there is an extremely thin layer, the 'epicuticle', which contains no chitin. **1967** P. A. MEGLITSCH *Invert. Zool.* xvi. 676 Three distinct layers can be recognized in the cuticle. A thin outermost layer of tanned proteins, waxes, and other fatty compounds makes up the epicuticle.

b. A thin outer membrane surrounding animal fibres or hairs, etc.

1949 J. LINDBERG et al. in *Textile Research Jrnl.* XIX. 674/1 Proceeding from the outside of the fiber inward..the following have been described: (*a*) a very thin *epicuticular membrane*..forming the external surface of the fiber, (*b*) an *exocuticle* layer and (*c*) an *endocuticle*... The epicuticle, as seen in the electron microscope, appears as a thin, uniformly thick..film falling easily into folds. **1956** *Nature* 18 Feb. 319/1 An interesting suggestion was that in human hair.. the epicuticle seems to be tucked in beneath the scale which it is covering; this feature is less obvious in wool fibres. **1962** W. J. ONIONS *Wool* ii. 16 The epicuticle, a membrane about 100 Å thick (i.e. about 1/100th of the thickness of the total cuticle in wool) was isolated..by treating wool with a solution of sodium sulphide.

Hence **epicuˈticular** *a.*

1939 V. B. WIGGLESWORTH *Princ. Insect Physiol.* ii. 20 The unicellular glands are lined only by the epicuticular cuticulin. **1945** *Ann. Reg. 1944* 376 The insecticidal action of chemically inert dusts which abrade the epicuticular wax film and so cause the insect's death.

epicycle (ˈɛpɪsaɪk(ə)l), *sb.* Forms: (4 episicle, 5 epicikle, epycikle), 6–7 epicicle, (7 epycycle), 7– epicycle. [ad. L. *epicyclus*, a. Gr. ἐπίκυκλος, f. ἐπί upon + κύκλος circle.]

1. A small circle, having its centre on the circumference of a greater circle. Chiefly *Astron.*

In the Ptolemaic system of astronomy each of the 'seven planets' was supposed to revolve in an epicycle, the centre of which moved along a greater circle called a deferent. This conception, though superseded as a physical explanation, describes with approximate correctness the relative motion of a planet when the earth is assumed as fixed; and it is therefore still occasionally used for this purpose by modern astronomers.

*c*1391 CHAUCER *Astrol.* II. §35 The Moone Moeuyth the contrarie from othere planetes as in hire Episicle. **1413** LYDG. *Pilgr. Sowle* v. i. (1859) 70 In the circumference of eueriche of these cercles, was sette a lytel Cercle..which Cercle is cleped of Astronomyens the Epicikle. **1561** EDEN *Arte of Nauig.* I. xx. 22. **1571** CAMPION *Hist. Irel.* II. vii. (1633) 97 The sun..standing still in his epicycle the space of three hours. **1613** M. RIDLEY *Magn. Bodies* 41 The needle ..doth turne himselfe twise about, and make two whole circles, or epicicles in this voyage. **1670** WALLIS in *Phil. Trans.* V. 2070 The Earth describes a small Epicycle about the Common Center of Gravity of the Earth and Moon. **1726** tr. *Gregory's Astron.* I. 194 Such..as still maintained, that the Earth was Immovable, made Mercury and Venus move in Epicycles round the Sun. **1860** GEN. P. THOMPSON *Audi Alt.* III. cxxii. 68 Copernicus or whoever..scattered the cycles and epicycles which had gone before.

fig. **1643** SIR T. BROWNE *Relig. Med.* I. §6, I love to.. follow the great wheele of the Church, by which I move, not reserving any proper poles or motion from the epicycle of my owne brain. **1831** CARLYLE *Sart. Res.* (1858) 157 What infinitely larger Cycle (of causes) our little Epicycle revolves on.

2. In mod. *Astron.* sometimes used for: The curve described by a planet moving in an epicycle, *i.e.* its geocentric path.

1854 MOSELEY *Astron.* liv. (ed. 4) 170 The path of the planet..will be a curve, called an Epicycle accurately.

†**ˈepicycle,** *v.* *Obs.* *rare*⁻¹. [f. prec. sb.] *trans.* To cause to move in an epicycle.

1652 BENLOWES *Theoph.* VII. xli, Thy Law..Does epicycle their obliquely gliding Cars.

epicyclic (ɛpɪˈsɪklɪk), *a.* (and *sb.*) [f. prec. + -IC.] Of or pertaining to epicycles; applied esp. to the gear of motor vehicles. Also as *sb.* *epicyclic train*: one in which the axes of the wheels revolve around a common centre.

1837 WHEWELL *Hist. Induct. Sc.* III. iv. §2 I. 197 The supposition of uniform circular motions, on which the epicyclic hypothesis proceeds. **1878** NEWCOMB *Pop. Astron.* Introd. 5 The theory of the epicyclic motions of the planets. **1881** PROCTOR *Poetry Astron.* viii. 277 Those points of its

[the moon's] epicyclic orbit about the earth where it is at its nearest to us. **1902** H. STURMEY in A. C. Harmsworth *Motors* x. 197 A Crypto or epicyclic gear..consists of two gear wheels, a small one A, with external teeth, and a large one B arranged on the outside of it with internal teeth. **1906** *Daily Chron.* 9 June 3/5 Another kind of gear, known as the epicyclic, its principle resembling that of the differential. **1907** *Westm. Gaz.* 13 Nov. 9/1 Three-speed epicyclic gear. **1910** *Ibid.* 1 Feb. 4/2 Many of the old epicyclics failed solely for the reason that their designers were too niggardly with the wearing surfaces. **1937** *Times* 13 Apr. p. xv/4 The manufacture of epicyclic gears is highly specialized work. **1948** *Autocar Handbk.* (ed. 20) vi. 120 The Wilson gear box ..uses epicyclic or 'planetary' gears.

Hence **epi'cyclical** *a.* = EPICYCLIC *a.*

1837 WHEWELL *Hist. Induct. Sc.* III. iv. §6 I. 217 The epicyclical theory. **1854** MOSELEY *Astron.* liv. 170 With respect to Venus, an analogous Epicyclical path..will be found.

epicycloid (ɛpɪˈsaɪklɔɪd). [f. EPICYCLE + -OID.] A curve generated by a point in the circumference of a moveable circle, which revolves on that of a fixed circle; in accurate phraseology the term is now limited to the case in which the moveable circle rolls on the exterior of the other (formerly ***exterior epicycloid***); the name *hypocycloid* being employed for what was formerly called the ***interior epicycloid***.

c **1790** IMISON *Sch. Art* I. 36. **1816** J. SMITH *Panorama Sc. & Art* I. 356 The acting faces of the leaves of the pinion should be parts of an interior epicycloid..and the acting surfaces of the teeth of the wheel should be portions of an exterior epicycloid. **1884** F. BRITTEN *Watch & Clockm.* 289 The action should be confined as nearly as possible to the epicycloid on the wheel.

epicycloidal (ˌɛpɪsaɪˈklɔɪdəl), *a.* [f. prec. + -AL[1].] Of the form or nature of an epicycloid.

1812 WOODHOUSE *Astron.* xvi. 172 The true pole..will describe an epicycloidal curve. **1837** WHEWELL *Hist. Induct. Sc.* III. iv. §3 I. 205 The epicycloidal form of her orbit. **1884** F. BRITTEN *Watch & Clockm.* 292 The pinion..must have the epicycloidal addendum to secure proper action.

epicyte (ˈɛpɪsaɪt). *Biol.* [f. EPI- + CYTE.] The investing membrane of a cell.

1900 in DORLAND *Med. Dict.* **1903** E. A. MINCHIN in E. R. Lankester *Zool.* I. i. 179 The cuticle or epicyte [in Gregarines] is a membrane secreted by the ectoplasm, usually of some thickness.

Epidaurian (ɛpɪˈdɔːrɪən), *sb.* and *a.* [f. Gr. Ἐπίδαυρος, L. *Epidaurus* (see below) + -IAN.]

A. *sb.* A native or inhabitant of the ancient city of Epidaurus, a centre for the cult of Asclepius, in the north-east Peloponnese. **B.** *adj.* Of or pertaining to Epidaurus or its inhabitants.

1589 *Almond for Parrat* sig. E2 The Epidaurians provident subtiltie. **1608** TOPSELL *Serpents* 157 The Epidaurian dragons..were dedicated to Aesculapius. **1631** JONSON *Barth. Fair* II. i. 16 Faine would I meet the Linceus now, that Eagles eye, that peircing Epidaurian serpent. **1794** T. TAYLOR tr. *Pausanias' Descr. Greece* I. II. xxvi. 209 About Lessa, the borders of the Epidaurians join with the land of the Argives. **1830** W. M. LEAKE *Trav. Morea* II. 426 Strabo..describes the Epidaurian sanctuary as 'a place renowned for the cure of all sorts of diseases, and always full of invalids'. **1856** W. SMITH *Dict. Gr. & Roman Geogr.* I. 842/1 The worship of Asclepius by the Epidaurians. **1976** *Classical Q.* XXVI. 263 Even for the Argives the principal object of the Epidaurian war was perhaps to bring enough pressure to bear on Corinth to force her into the alliance. **1984** F. W. WALBANK in *Cambr. Anc. Hist.* (ed. 2) VII. I. xii. 473 At Olympia the Eleans set up a statue representing Antigonus and Philip, crowned, and at Epidaurus the Epidaurians raised an altar to him.

epideictic, -ktic (ɛpɪˈdaɪktɪk), *a.* Also 8 epidictic. [ad. Gr. ἐπιδεικτικ-ός, f. ἐπί + δεικνύναι to show.]

a. Adapted for display or show-off; chiefly of set orations.

1790 V. KNOX *Winter Even.* (ed. 2) II. 197 Eloquence of that kind, which the ancient rhetoricians denominated the epidictic. **1795** *Charac.* in *Ann. Reg.* 20/1 Philosophic dialogues and epideiktic orations. **1874** FARRAR *Christ* (ed. 2) II. xxxv, He would not work any epideictic miracle at their bidding.

b. *spec.* in *Ornith.*: applied to collective displays and other conventional behaviour regarded by some as having evolved from the need to control the distribution of population.

1959 V. C. WYNNE-EDWARDS in *Ibis* CI. 440 There is a very large class of social phenomena in animals which partake of this character... In birds they usually involve collective displays, singing, aerial acrobatics and the like: the so-called 'crow's parliament' of Rooks and Jackdaws..is a familiar example in this country. They may be designated as *epideictic* demonstrations. **1962** —— *Anim. Dispersion* i. 16 Epideictic displays are especially evolved to provide the necessary feed-back when the balance of population is about to be restored... They generally involve conventions that have evolved away from the direct primitive contest. **1966** D. LACK *Population Stud. Birds* 311 Most of the behaviour considered epideictic by Wynne-Edwards can be satisfactorily interpreted in other ways, and no positive evidence has been presented for an epideictic function.

Hence **epi'deictical** *a.*

†**epi'demial**, *a. Obs.* [a. OF. *epidemial*, f. *épidémie* (see EPIDEMY).] = EPIDEMIC *a.* A. I.

1607 DEKKER *Knts. Conjur.* (1842) 76 Barbarisme was now growne to be an epidemiall disease. **1627** BP. WREN *Serm.* 15 The Epidemiall prophanation of our times. *a* **1641** BP. MOUNTAGU *Acts & Mon.* (1642) 184 To cure diseases epidemiall. **1710** T. FULLER *Pharm. Extemp.* 94. **1809** PEARSON in *Phil. Trans.* XCIX. 317 That very common and extensively epidemial disease of our climate, the *winter cough*.

†**epi'demian**, *a. Obs. rare.* [f. EPIDEMY + -AN.] = prec.

1599 T. M[OUFET] *Silkwormes* 56 That strange and Epidemian sweate.

epidemic (ɛpɪˈdɛmɪk), *a.* and *sb.* [ad. Fr. *épidémique*, f. *épidémie* (see EPIDEMY).]

A. *adj.*

1. Of a disease: 'Prevalent among a people or a community at a special time, and produced by some special causes not generally present in the affected locality' (*Syd. Soc. Lex.*).

1603 LODGE *Treat. Plague* B ij b, Epidemick..common vnto all people, or to the moste part of them. **1622** BACON *Hen. VII.* 6 It was conceived not to be an epidemick disease, but to proceed from a malignity in the constitution of the air. **1783** COWPER *Lett.* 29 Sept., The epidemic fever..has prevailed much in this part of the kingdom. **1798** MALTHUS *Popul.* (1817) II. 123 The endemic and epidemic diseases in Scotland fall chiefly, as is usual, on the poor. **1871** TYNDALL *Fragm. Sc.* (ed. 6) II. xii. 280 Reproductive parasitic life is at the root of epidemic disease.

fig. **1642** *Vind. King* p. iii, The Epidemicke trouble of our age. **1703** ROWE *Fair Penit.* v. i. 1921 Contagious Fury And Epidemick Madness. **1823** SCOTT *Peveril* xxxv, Influenced with..the epidemic terror of an imaginary danger. **1868** M. PATTISON *Academ. Org.* §5. 133 The mania for prize scholarships, then epidemic, infected the curators.

¶ *nonce-use.* Affected with an epidemic.

1781 COWPER *Conversation* 391 We next enquire..Of epidemic throats.

†**2.** In more extended sense: Wide-spread, widely prevalent, universal. *Obs.*

1643 MILTON *Divorce* II. xiv. (1851) 97 A toleration of epidemick whordom. **1667** WATERHOUSE *Fire Lond.* 110 That Epidemique mercy that he hath obliged all by. *a* **1745** SWIFT *Wks* (1841) II. 222 The trade of universal stealing is not so epidemic there as with us.

¶ **3.** ? That is a product of a particular region; cf. EPICHORIAL. *Obs.*

1634 SIR T. HERBERT *Trav.* 150 They have Arack or Usquebagh, distilled from Dates or Rice, both which are Epidemick, in their mirth and Festivals.

B. *sb.* An epidemic disease.

1799 *Med. Jrnl.* II. 468 He observed the variolous epidemic among a flock of sheep. **1861** FLOR. NIGHTINGALE *Nursing* ii. 11 There are schools..where 'children's epidemics' are unknown.

fig. **1757** BURKE *Abridgm. Eng. Hist.* II. ii. Wks. (1812) 267 An epidemick of despair. **1856** SIR B. BRODIE *Psychol. Inq.* I. i. 26 There are epidemics of opinion as well as of disease.

epidemical (ɛpɪˈdɛmɪkəl), *a.* Also 7 epidimicall. [f. prec. + -AL[1].]

1. Of diseases: of an epidemic character.

1621 BURTON *Anat. Mel.* Democr. (1676) 35/1 Cure us of our Epidemical diseases. **1669** WORLIDGE *Syst. Agric.* (1681) 297 Still and quiet Summers being the most..subject to Pestilential and Epidemical Diseases. **1728** MORGAN *Algiers* I. iv. 98 Their [camels'] epidemical Distemper is the Mange. **1751** *Phil. Trans.* XLVII. lxiii. 385 The plague.. has been mostly sporadic, seldom epidemical. **1816** F. H. NAYLOR *Hist. Germany* II. xxii. 316 An epidemical malady had raged among the cattle. **1881** *Sat. Rev.* 5 Feb. 172 Colds were epidemical; there were choruses of coughing.

fig. *a* **1640** JACKSON *Wks.* II. 380 This hypocrisie.. epidemical to this nation. *c* **1680** in Somers *Tracts* II. 321 Let such a Prince beware of epidemical Discontents. **1720** WELTON *Suff. Son of God* I. vi. 107 Those Vices, which are most prevalent and epidemical in the World. **1780** COWPER *Lett.* 5 Oct., That bashful and awkward restraint, so epidemical among the youth of our country. **1818** HALLAM *Mid. Ages* (1872) I. 35 Every means was used to excite an epidemical frenzy.

b. Pertaining to, characterized by an epidemic or epidemics.

1798 MALTHUS *Popul.* (1817) II. 186 The common epidemical years which are interspersed throughout these tables.

†**2.** General, prevalent, universal; that is to be found everywhere; = EPIDEMIC A. 2. *arch.* or *Obs.*

1628 PYM *Sp.* in Rushw. *Hist. Coll.* (1659) I. 600 Wedded to the love of epidemical and popular errors. *a* **1658** CLEVELAND *Rebel Scot* iii, Scotland's a National Epidemical. **1774** J. BRYANT *Mythol.* I. 131 He had great knowledge; yet could not help giving way to this epidemical weakness. **1836** SPARKS *Biog., Mather* VI. vii. 329 Contrary to the epidemical expectation of the country.

†**b.** *nonce-use.* ? Belonging to the whole people.

1642 HOWELL *For. Trav.* (Arb.) 76 That great Epidemicall Counsell [Parliament] wherein every one from the Peere to the Plebeian hath an inclusive Vote.

3. quasi-*sb. pl. rare*[−1]. Epidemical diseases.

1802 *Med. Jrnl.* VIII. 281 What candour and ability in his History of Epidemicals!

Hence **epi'demically** *adv.*, in an epidemic manner: (*a*) like an epidemic disease; (*b*) in a widespread manner, generally, universally. **epi'demicalness**, the state of being epidemic.

1641 *Frogs of Egypt* 2 They were heretofore so Epidemically strict. **1657** G. STARKEY *Helmont's Vind.* 29 The disease was epidemically malignant. *a* **1691** BOYLE *Wks.* VI. 372 An ingredient should be generally friendly, before it be entertained epidemically in our daily diet. **1845** STOCQUELER *Handbk. Brit. India* (1854) 380 Cholera and small-pox generally make their appearance epidemically once or twice a year. **1646** W. PRICE *Mans Delinquencie* 4 The Epidemicalnesse and spreading universality [of iniquities and trespasses].

epidemicity (ˌɛpɪdɪˈmɪsɪtɪ). [f. EPIDEMIC + -ITY.] The quality of being epidemic.

1880 SIR J. FAYRER in *Nature* XXI. 229/1 Not..that our enquiries should be restricted to mere epidemicity alone.

epidemiographist (ˌɛpɪˌdiːmɪˈɒgrəfɪst). [f. next + -IST.] A writer on epidemiography.

1885 C. CREIGHTON tr. *Hirsch's Handbk. Geog. & Hist. Pathol.* I. 140 Its everyday occurrence..weakened the interest of the epidemiographists towards it.

epidemiography (ˌɛpɪˌdiːmɪˈɒgrəfɪ). [f. Gr. ἐπιδήμιο-ς + -γραφία writing.] A treatise upon, or history of, epidemic diseases.

In mod. Dicts.

epidemiological (ɛpɪˌdiːmɪɒˈlɒdʒɪkəl), *a.* [f. as next + -IC + -AL[1].] Of or pertaining to epidemiology. Hence **epidemio'logically** *adv.*, in an epidemiological manner or way.

1881 M. KNAPP *Disasters* 23 This is a new etiological fact for epidemiological societies to consider. **1883** *Fortn. Rev.* 1 Aug. 183 The pathological, and epidemiological ideas that were current. **1882** COBBOLD in *Linn. Soc. Jrnl.* XVI. 187 Epidemiologically speaking.

epidemiologist (ɛpɪˌdiːmɪˈɒlədʒɪst). [f. next + -IST.] One who studies epidemic diseases.

1880 J. FAYRER in *Nature* XXI. 230 The most important ..information to the epidemiologist. **1883** *Fortn. Rev.* 1 Aug. 181 An outbreak which epidemiologists have always been unable to explain.

epidemiology (ɛpɪˌdiːmɪˈɒlədʒɪ). [f. Gr. ἐπιδήμιο-ς epidemic + -λογία discoursing (see -LOGY). Cf. Fr. *épidémiologie*.] That branch of medical science which treats of epidemics.

1873 J. P. PARKIN (*title*), Epidemiology, or the Remoter Causes of Epidemic Diseases. **1883** *Fortn. Rev.* 1 Aug. 176 It is just here the student of epidemiology comes in with his 'Distinguo'.

†**epidemy.** *Obs.* Forms: 5 epi-, epydemye, impe-, ipydymye, ipedemye, 8–9 epidemy. [a. OF. *ypidime*, *impidemie*, Fr. *épidemie*, ad. late L. *epidemia*, *epidimia*, Gr. ἐπιδημία prevalence of an epidemic, f. ἐπιδήμι-ος, f. ἐπί + δῆμος people.] An epidemic disease, *esp.* the plague. Also *attrib.*

1472 SIR J. PASTON in *Paston Lett.* No. 703 III. 59 Many off the sowders that went to hym into Bretayne been dede off the fflyxe, and other ipedemye. **1483** CAXTON *Gold. Leg.* 22/1 A grete pestelence whiche was called the botch of impedymye. **1494** FABYAN V. cxxxv. 121 In the yere folowyng dyed of the epedemye sikenesse, the holy abbesse of Ely. *Ibid.* VII. 612 And there also they dyed sore of yᵉ sykenesse of ipydymye. **1809** *State Paper* in *Ann. Reg.* 853/2 However this destructive epidemy originated. **1809** PEARSON in *Phil. Trans.* XCIX. 321 That constant epidemy of the British islands, the winter chronical pneumonia.

fig. **1813** *Examiner* 15 Feb. 103/1 We discover this withering epidemy.

epidendral (ɛpɪˈdɛndrəl), *a. Bot.* [f. EPI- + Gr. δένδρ-ον tree + -AL[1].] That grows upon trees.

1882 VINES *Sachs' Bot.* 838 Aërial roots of epidendral Orchids.

epidendric (ɛpɪˈdɛndrɪk), *a. Bot.* [f. as prec. + -IC.] = prec.

1880 A. R. WALLACE *Isl. Life* 307 Epidendric orchids. **1885** H. O. FORBES *Nat. Wand.* VI. iii. 463 The epidermis of an epidendric orchid.

epidendrum (ɛpɪˈdɛndrəm). Also -dendron. [mod.L. (C. Linnæus *Genera Plantarum* (1737) 272), f. Gr. ἐπί upon + δένδρον tree. Cf. EPIDENDRAL, -IC *adjs.*] Any of various chiefly epiphytic orchids of the genus so named, native to the western hemisphere (esp. tropical America).

1791 W. JONES *Let.* 18 Oct. (1821) II. 155 The most lovely *epidendrum* that ever was seen..grew on a lofty *amra*. **1842** *Florist's Jrnl.* (1846) III. 212 A fine orchidaceous plant, with the habit of an Epidendron. **1890** WATSON & BEAN *Orchids* xxxi. 237 The list of useful garden Epidendrums is a fairly long one. **1910** C. H. CURTIS *Orchids* 100 All Epidendrums are evergreen. **1951** *Dict. Gardening* (R. Hort. Soc.) II. 749/1 The so-called true Epidendrums have cylindric reed-like, often slender, stems. **1955** E. POUND *Classic Anthol.* I. 30 Feeble as a gourd stalk (epidendrum).

epiderm (ˈɛpɪdɜːm). [ad. F. *épiderme*, ad. mod.L. *epidermis*, *epiderma*.] = EPIDERMIS in its various senses.

1835–6 TODD *Cycl. Anat.* I. 349/1 An intermediate layer of unhardened epiderm. **1845** LINDLEY *Sch Bot.* x. (1858) 163 Leaves are expansions of bark..enclosed in a skin or epiderm. **1887** BLACKMORE *Springhaven* (ed. 4) II. xvi. 226 He would not have imperilled the gloss of his epiderm.

‖**epi'derma.** *Obs.* [mod.L. *epiderma*; see prec.] = EPIDERMIS.

1582 HESTER *Secr. Phiorav.* III. xxxviii. 54 Many tymes moste of them doe chaunge that subtill skinne called of the Doctours Epiderma.

epidermal (ɛpɪˈdɜːməl), *a.* [f. EPIDERM + -AL[1].] Of or pertaining to the epidermis, whether in animals or plants.

1816 KIRBY & SP. *Entomol.* (1843) II. 385 Its usual plan is to insinuate itself between the epidermal membranes of

the leaf. **1835** LINDLEY *Introd. Bot.* (1848) I. 146 The last cyto-blasts which the epidermal tissue forms. **1854** OWEN in *Circ. Sc.* (*c.* 1865) II. 69/2 The thick epidermal scutes called 'tortoise-shell'. **1873** MIVART *Elem. Anat.* vii. 238 Snakes cast off the entire epidermal investment at once.

epidermatoid (ɛpɪˈdɜːmətɔɪd), *a.* [f. as next + -OID.] Resembling an epidermis.
In mod. Dicts.

epidermatous (ɛpɪˈdɜːmətəs), *a.* [f. EPI- + Gr. δερματ-, stem of δέρμα skin + -OUS.] Pertaining to the epidermis.
1854 MOSELEY *Astron.* iv. (ed. 4) 24 That train of epidermatous calamities.

epidermeous (ɛpɪˈdɜːmɪəs), *a.* [f. EPIDERM + -(E)OUS.] = EPIDERMIC.
In mod. Dicts.

epidermic (ˌɛpɪˈdɜːmɪk), *a.* [f. EPIDERM + -IC; cf. F. *épidermique*.] Of or pertaining to the epidermis; of the nature of an epidermis.
1830 R. KNOX *Béclard's Anat.* 54 Some physiologists still place the horny or epidermic substance among the primitive fibres. **1836–9** TODD *Cycl. Anat.* II. 127/1 In the Trematode worms epidermic spines are seldom developed. **1872** HUXLEY *Phys.* i. 9 The razor ought only to cut epidermic structures.

†**epidermical** (ɛpɪˈdɜːmɪkəl), *a. Obs.* [f. as prec. + -AL[1].] = prec. Hence **epiˈdermically** *adv.*, by the epidermic method; by means of the epidermis; upon the outer skin.
1693 J. BEAUMONT *On Burnet's Th. Earth* II. 79 Any Dissolution of such a pitiful Epidermical covering. **1852** *Fraser's Mag.* XLVI. 93 To fasten on a fillet of the raw fish epidermically. **1854** BADHAM *Halieut.* 459 By applying it epidermically.

epidermidal (ɛpɪˈdɜːmɪdəl), *a.* [f. Gr. ἐπιδερμιδ-, stem of ἐπιδερμίς + -AL[1].] = EPIDERMAL.
In mod. Dicts.

epidermis (ɛpɪˈdɜːmɪs). [a. mod.L. *epidermis*, a. Gr. ἐπιδερμίς, f. ἐπί upon + δέρμα skin.]
1. *Anat.* The outer (non-vascular) layer of the skin of animals; the cuticle or scarf-skin.
1626 BACON *Sylva* §297 They never infect, but by such a Touch..as cometh within the Epidermis. **1650** BULWER *Anthropomet.* 156 They remain like peel'd Ewes, until their Faces have recovered a new Epidermis. **1774** GOLDSMITH *Nat. Hist.* (1862) I. xi. 215 The blackness lay in the epidermis, or scarf-skin. **1813** SIR H. DAVY *Agric. Chem.* (1814) 57 The epidermis is not vascular, and it merely defends the interior parts from injury. **1842** BARHAM *Ingol. Leg.*, *St. Medard*, It fail'd..to raise on the tough epidermis a lump or bump! **1860** EMERSON *Cond. Life* Wks. (Bohn) II. 311 A squint, a pug-nose, mats of hair, the pigment of the epidermis, betray character.
transf. **1850** LEITCH tr. *Müller's Anc. Art* §310. 353 The epidermis of the ancient statues is formed of the smearing with wax. **1819** SYD. SMITH *Wks.* (1859) I. 260/2 The epidermis of the country has hardly as yet been scratched.
b. = ECTODERM or EPIBLAST.
1877 HUXLEY *Anat. Inv. An.* i. 55 From the epidermis all cuticular and cellular exoskeletal parts, and all the integumentary glands are developed.
2. *Conch.* The outer animal integument of a shell.
1755 *Gentl. Mag.* XXV. 32 Epidermis, the marine covering, or incrustation, which is taken off to shew the native beauty of the shell. **1828** STARK *Elem. Nat. Hist.* I. 110 Shell..with a wrinkled brown or chestnut epidermis, and glossy white within. **1858** GEIKIE *Hist. Boulder* v. 91 The perfect shell..displayed its russet epidermis.
3. *Bot.* 'The true skin of a plant below the cuticle' (*Treas. Bot.*).
1813 SIR H. DAVY *Agric. Chem.* (1814) 178 Wheat, oats, and many of the hollow grasses, have an epidermis principally of siliceous earth. **1880** GRAY *Struct. Bot.* iii. §iv. 89. **1870** BENTLEY *Bot.* 37 Tabular parenchyma is found in the epidermis.

epidermoid (ɛpɪˈdɜːmɔɪd), *a.* [f. EPIDERM + -OID.] Of the nature of epidermis.
1835–6 TODD *Cycl. Anat.* I. 385/1 A cuticular or epidermoid covering cannot be detected in health. **1853** KANE *Grinnell Exp.* xxx. (1856) 263 A clean screen between my epidermoid and seal-skin integuments. **1876** GROSS *Dis. Bladder* 48 Epithelial hyperplasm, with epidermoid transformation.
Hence **ˌepiderˈmoidal** *a.* = prec.
1830 LINDLEY *Nat. Syst. Bot.* 290 Translucent cellular plants, destitute of stomata, having no epidermoidal layer. **1876** tr. *Wagner's Gen. Pathol.* 466 On this border the epidermoidal layer extends and divides, becoming, as it were, fan-shaped.

epidermolysis (ɛpɪdəˈmɒlɪsɪs). *Path.* [G. (H. Köbner 1886, in *Deut. Med. Wochenschr.* 14 Jan. 21/1), f. Gr. ἐπιδερμίς EPIDERMIS + -O + λύσις a loosening or releasing.] A loosened state of the epidermis, giving rise to large blisters with little or no external cause.
1894 GOULD *Illustr. Dict. Med.* 433/2 *Epidermolysis*, Acantolysis bullosa; Dermatitis bullosa; a rare skin-disease in which bullæ form upon the slightest pressure. **1897** *Brit. Jrnl. Dermatol.* IX. 301 (*title*) Epidermolysis bullosa. *Ibid.* 313 In Haemophilia bleeding occurs, in Epidermolysis exudation. **1909** W. BATESON *Mendel's Princ. Heredity* I. xii. 220 In epidermolysis transmission through unaffected persons occurred in some of the strains. **1922** R. C. PUNNETT *Mendelism* (ed. 6) 202 Epidermolysis bullosa, a disease in which the skin rises up into numerous bursting blisters. **1966** WRIGHT & SYMMERS *Systemic Path.* II. xxxix. 1463 Epidermolysis bullosa is a rare dermatosis affecting both sexes.

epidermose (ˌɛpɪdɜːˈməʊs). *Chem.* [f. EPIDERM + -OSE.] (See quot.)
1847–9 TODD *Cycl. Anat.* IV. 166/2 A small quantity of insoluble matter [in the epidermis] which he [Bonchardat] calls epidermose.

epidiascope (ɛpɪˈdaɪəskəʊp). [f. EPI- + DIA-[1] + -SCOPE.] A magic lantern made to project images of both opaque and transparent objects. Hence **epidiaˈscopic** *a.*
1903 *Nature* 19 Feb. 376/1 The epidiascope, a new optical lantern,..is primarily intended for the projection on the screen of opaque bodies, such as insects, coins, fossils, diagrams, &c., in their natural colours. It is equally serviceable for projection of transparent objects. **1907** *Practitioner* Dec. 860 An epidiascopic demonstration. **1927** *Brit. Jrnl. Photogr. Alm.* 345 The Ica Hand Epidiascope. **1940** *Geogr. Jrnl.* XCV. 73 Being printed on one side only the plates are readily adaptable for wall illustration and use in the epidiascope.

†**ˌepiˌdiaˈtessaron.** *Music. Obs.* [f. Gr. ἐπί upon + διατεσσάρων the interval of a fourth.] (See quot.)
1597 MORLEY *Introd. Mus.* 98 This waye, some terme a Fuge in epidiatessaron, that is in the fourth above.

epidictic, obs. form of EPIDEICTIC.

epididymal (ɛpɪˈdɪdɪməl), *a.* [f. EPIDIDYMIS + -AL[1].] Pertaining to the epididymis.
a **1693** URQUHART *Rabelais* III. xxxii. 274 The Epididymal Store-house of Man.

epididymectomy (ˌɛpɪdɪdɪˈmɛktəmɪ). *Surg.* [f. EPIDIDYM(IS + -ECTOMY.] Excision of the epididymis.
1900 GOULD *Pocket Med. Dict.* (ed. 4) 236. **1903** *Jrnl. Trop. Med.* 15 Jan. 25/1 The operation of epididymectomy can have only a very limited application in Egypt, owing to the late stages at which the disease is met with. **1938** *Brit. Jrnl. Urol.* X. 129 *Epididymectomy* is the operation of choice in tuberculous epididymitis.

epididymis (ɛpɪˈdɪdɪmɪs). *Anat.* Also 7 epididimis, -damies. [a. Gr. ἐπιδιδυμίς, f. ἐπί upon + δίδυμοι testicles.] 'A long, narrow structure attached to the posterior border of the adjoining outer surface of the testicle, and consisting chiefly of coils of the efferent duct, which emerge from it as the vas deferens' (*Syd. Soc. Lex.*).
1610 B. JONSON *Alch.* III. iii, Shee must milke his Epididimis, Where is the Doxie? *a* **1652** BROME *Court Beggar* IV. iii, To save his Epididamies. **1768–74** TUCKER *Lt. Nat.* I. 480 Animalcules..being never found, unless in the cellules producing them, in the epididymis, the vas deferens and the vesicles. **1870** ROLLESTON *Anim. Life* 134 A convoluted epididymis-like mass of a yellowish colour.
Hence **ˌepididyˈmitis**, *Path.* [see -ITIS], inflammation of the epididymis.
1849–52 TODD *Cycl. Anat.* IV. 991/1 A lad..affected with epididymitis. **1874** BUREN *Dis. Genit. Org.* 63 In this way epididymitis may sometimes be averted.

epiˈdidymo-, used as comb. form of EPIDIDYMIS, = 'pertaining to the epididymis and', as ***epididymo-orchitis***.
1897 *Ann. Surg.* XXV. 309 Those adhesions which are found in gonorrhoeal epididymo-orchitis are entirely wanting. **1963** *Lancet* 12 Jan. 95/1 In torsion of the fully descended testis the signs and symptoms resemble those of epididymo-orchitis.

epidiorite: see EPI- *prefix*.

epidosite (ɛˈpɪdəsaɪt). *Petrogr.* [ad. G. *epidosit* (L. Pilla 1845, in *Neues Jahrb. f. Min., Geognosie, Geol.* 64), altered form of EPIDOTE: cf. Gr. ἐπίδοσις a free or additional giving, and see -ITE[1].] A rock composed chiefly of granular or fibrous epidote with some quartz.
1863 *Rep. Progress Geol. Survey Canada* xvii. 497 In many parts occur buds which are entirely made up of quartz and epidote... This rock..is the epidosite of some lithologists. **1866** S. H. LAWRENCE tr. *Cotta's Rocks* 355 Epidosite, or pistacite rock.—Epidote usually combined with some quartz. **1868** J. D. DANA *Syst. Min.* (ed. 5) 284 [Epidote] sometimes forms with quartz an epidote rock, called epidosyte. **1880** —— *Man. Geol.* (ed. 3) 75 Epidosyte.—Pale green to pistachio-green. Consists of epidote mixed with quartz. **1893** A. GEIKIE *Text-bk. Geol.* (ed. 3) II. vii. 183 Epidote-Rocks.—Epidosite (Pistacite-rock)—an aggregate of bright green epidote with some quartz, occurs with chlorite-schist (Canada), with granite and serpentine (Elba), and with syenite. **1937** A. JOHANNSEN *Descr. Petrogr.* III. 211 With sufficient iron, the final product of alteration may be a mixture of epidote and quartz, producing the rock called epidosite, which has been described..as derived from various rocks—augiteporphyries, diabases, åkerites, etc.

epidote (ˈɛpɪdəʊt). *Min.* [a. Fr. *épidote*, f. as if on Gr. *ἐπιδοτός, f. ἐπιδιδόναι to superadd, f. ἐπί upon + διδόναι to give.
First used in Fr. by Haüy, who explains it as meaning lit. 'qui a reçu un accroissement' (*Minéralogie* 1801. III. 112), and as denoting a great additional length in the base of the crystal as compared with that of certain allied minerals with which it was previously confused.]
A mineral common in many crystalline rocks, consisting largely of the silicate of iron and lime. It usually takes the form of flattened needles, and has a peculiar yellowish-green colour.
1808 T. ALLAN *Minerals* 2 Akanticone or Thallite, Epidote. **1879** RUTLEY *Study Rocks* x. 127 Epidote seldom gives direct evidence of its derivation from pyroxenic minerals.
Hence **epiˈdotic** *a.*, pertaining to or resembling epidote, containing epidote. **ˌepidoˈtiferous** *a.*, bearing or containing epidote.
1849 DANA *Geol.* (1850) 565 The granitic and epidotic veins. **1862** —— *Man. Geol.* 76 An epidotic gneiss. **1884** *Harper's Mag.* 159/2 Veins of..epidotiferous quartz.

epidotized (ˈɛpɪdəʊtaɪzd), *ppl. a.* [f. EPIDOTE + -IZE + -ED.] Altered metamorphically into epidote. So **ˌepidotiˈzation**.
1888 J. TEALL *Brit. Petrography* 150 The epidotisation of the felspar is an alteration process. **1890** [see CHLORITIZATION]. **1930** PEACH & HORNE *Geol. Scotl.* 79 Beds with abundant pebbles of epidote and epidotized felspar. **1941** *Proc. Prehist. Soc.* VII. 58 The rock is identical with the epidotised tuffs. *Ibid.*, It is only however near the rhyolite that they exhibit..epidotization. **1965** G. J. WILLIAMS *Econ. Geol. N.Z.* x. 158/2 All rocks are hydrothermally altered, resulting in uralitization and ch[l]oritization of pyroxene, saussuritization of felspar, and epidotization of the rock as a whole. *Ibid.* xii. 181/2 Hutton, McCraw (1950) reported chalcopyrite as scattered grains in epidotized breccia in greywacke and argillite in the Takitimu Mountains, Southland.

epidural (ɛpɪˈdjʊərəl), *a.* and *sb. Anat.* [f. EPI- + DURA (MATER) + -AL[1].]
A. *adj.* Situated upon or outside, or affecting, the dura mater.
1882 E. A. SCHÄFER in *Quain's Elem. Anat.* (ed. 9) II. 374 The spaces between the fibrous trabeculæ..can be injected from the epidural space where this exists, and the injecting fluid can be forced along them..into the subdural space. **1895** *Buck's Handbk. Med. Sci.* Suppl. 68/2 There are two layers of dura [in the spine], an ectal (periosteal) and an ental (myelic), the interval between them constitutes an epidural space. **1902** CUNNINGHAM *Text-bk. Anat.* 558 The spinal dura mater..is separated from the walls of the spinal canal by an interval, the epidural space, which is occupied by soft fat and a plexus of thin-walled veins. **1968** *Guardian* 12 Sept. 1/1 Epidural analgesia—a procedure which means a mother can get continuous pain-relief throughout her confinement without any loss of clarity or consciousness. A cocaine derivative is passed into the membrane surrounding the fluid round the spinal cord.
B. *sb. Med.* An injection of anæsthetic into the epidural space, used esp. to control pain during childbirth by producing a loss of sensation below the waist without affecting consciousness.
1970 *Guardian* 7 Apr. 9/3 If I was in a lot of pain I would be offered an 'epidural'. **1977** *Daily Mail* 25 Jan. 13/4 Complain if there are not facilities for epidurals at your hospital. **1981** S. KITZINGER *Experience of Childbirth* (ed. 4) viii. 180 An epidural, in expert hands, can achieve complete relief from pain, while leaving the woman fully conscious and alert. **1985** *Times* 1 Feb. 11/3 As epidurals have spread from the teaching centres to general use there has been no central monitoring of epidural disasters.

epifauna (ˈɛpɪfɔːnə). [a. Da. *epifauna* (C. G. J. Petersen 1913, in *Beretn. f. d. Danske biol. Station* XXI (in *Fiskeri-Beretn. 1912*). 15), f. EPI- + FAUNA.] A collective term for the animal life of a region that lives on the surface of a marine deposit or another animal or plant.
1914 C. G. J. PETERSEN in *Rep. Danish Biol. Station 1913* XXI. 16, I would therefore propose, that..we can distinguish between an In-fauna, which is connected with the ordinary, level, uniform sea-bottom,..and various On-faunas (epifaunas), which occur in connection with such objects on the sea-bottom as stones, piles, shells, rocks or plants; the occurrence of such epifaunas is dependent on the distribution of these objects in the bottom. **1951** *Arch. Néerlandaises de Zool.* X. 38 Many members of the oyster's epifauna find their food on the shell itself. **1959** H. BARNES *Oceanogr. & Marine Biol.* I. 46 For the animals living on the surface or on other animals, the so-called epifauna, the material must be 'scraped' off the bottom and when the animals are relatively sparsely distributed a considerable amount of ground may have to be covered. **1964** *Adv. Marine Biol.* II. 172 Nearly every type of marine deposit..is inhabited by an assemblage of animals, some of which live on the surface (the so-called 'epifauna'), while others (the 'infauna') burrow or lie buried beneath the surface.
Hence **epiˈfaunal** *a.*, pertaining to, having the characteristics of, epifauna.
1960 *McGraw-Hill Encycl. Sci. & Technol.* I. 340/2 Caprellids commonly occur on epifaunal growths in shallow water. **1969** *Science* 28 Mar. 1419/2 In the past most deep-sea collections were made with coarse-meshed trawls which collected predominately larger epifaunal organisms.

epifocal (ɛpɪˈfəʊkəl), *a. Geol.* [See EPI- I.] Situated above the focus of an earthquake.
1898 J. MILNE *Seismology* x. 195 Mallet's well known method..might..outside an epifocal area, be equally well used for the..determination of the maximum slopes of surface waves. **1902** *Encycl. Brit.* XXVII. 608/1 Causes which should produce magnetic effects within an epifocal district. **1910** *Ibid.* VIII. 817/2 (*Earthquake*) That part of the surface of the earth which is vertically above the centre is called the *epicentre*; or, if of considerable area, the epicentral or epifocal tract.

epigæous, variant of EPIGEOUS.

epigamic (ɛpɪˈgæmɪk), *a. Zool.* [f. Gr. ἐπί upon + γάμος marriage + -IC. Cf. Gr. ἐπίγαμος marriageable.] Relating to the mating of animals and the characteristics of colour, etc., which serve to attract the opposite sex during courtship.

1890 E. B. POULTON *Colours of Animals* xvii. 338 Epigamic Colours. Colours displayed in courtship. **1926** J. S. HUXLEY *Ess. Biologist* (ed. 3) iv. 135 The human species..has epigamic characters of both kinds. Some, like voice and moustache, are different in the two sexes, others, such as colour of eyes and lips,..are common to both. **1959** *Chambers's Encycl.* II. 328/2 The principal types of display are epigamic, or display in which a sexual element is involved; aposematic or threat display; and distraction or diversionary display.

†**epiˈgaster.** *Obs.* [ad. Fr. *épigastre.*] = EPIGASTRIUM.

1653 URQUHART *Rabelais* I. xxvii, A smart souse on the Epigaster.

epigastrial (ɛpɪˈgæstrɪəl), *a.* [f. EPIGASTRIUM + -AL[1].] = next.

1767 A. CAMPBELL *Lexiph.* (ed. 4) 130 Get me a feather, that I may..resuscitate the convulsive motion of his epigastrial regions.

epigastric (ɛpɪˈgæstrɪk), *a.* [f. EPIGASTRIUM + -IC.]

Of or pertaining to the epigastrium. *epigastric speech* (nonce-use): ventriloquism.

1656–81 BLOUNT *Glossogr.* s.v. *Vein*, Epigastrick veins. **1678** in PHILLIPS. **1798** in *Phil. Trans.* LXXXVIII. 349 The heart..appeared to be situated in the epigastric region of the abdomen. **1804** ABERNETHY *Surg. Observ.* 214 To avoid the epigastric artery. **1852** JAMES *Pequinillo* III. 93 A gentle glow..was comforting the epigastric region. **1860** MILNES in *Edin. Rev.* Jan. 191 Sidney Rigdon, a man..subject to the strange phenomena of spiritual epilepsy and epigastric speech. **1877** HUXLEY *Anat. Inv. An.* vi. 343 The latter is again subdivided into two epigastric lobes.

†**epiˈgastrical,** *a. Obs.* [f. as prec. + -AL[1].] = prec.

1623 HART *Arraignm. Ur.* ii. 4 The eight epigastricall muscles. **1650** BULWER *Anthropomet.* 182 The congress of the Mamillaries descendent, with the Epigastrical ascendent.

epigastriocele (ɛpɪˈgæstrɪəʊ,siːl). *Path.* [f. Gr. ἐπιγάστριο-ς + κήλη tumour.] An abdominal hernia near the epigastrium.

‖**epigastrium** (ɛpɪˈgæstrɪəm). *Anat.* [mod.L., ad. Gr. ἐπιγάστριον, neut. of ἐπιγάστριος, f. ἐπί upon + γαστήρ stomach. Cf. F. *épigastre.*] 'That part of the abdomen which is immediately over the stomach' (*Syd. Soc. Lex.*).

1681 tr. *Willis' Rem. Med. Wks.* Voc., *Epigastrium*, the same with abdomen, or the outward part of the belly. **1767** GOOCH *Treat. Wounds* I. 375 The upper part of the Abdomen is called Epigastrium. **1877** ROBERTS *Handbk. Med.* (ed. 3) I. 41 Ice..may be usefully applied to..the chest or epigastrium.

epigeal (ɛpɪˈdʒiːəl), *sb.* [f. Gr. ἐπίγειο-ς: see EPIGEE + -AL[1].]

a. = EPIGEOUS.

In mod. Dicts.

b. Of cotyledons: borne above ground after germination.

1861 R. BENTLEY *Man. Bot.* 773 They burst through the coats, and rise out of the ground in the form of green leaves ..,in which case they are epigeal. **1884** A. HENFREY *Elem. Bot.* (ed. 4) 652 The seed-leaves..are pushed up above ground, and become epigeal. **1909** W. BATESON *Mendel's Princ. Heredity* 31 In *Phaseolus* hypo-geal cotyledons are dominant to epi-geal. **1964** A. J. BROOK *Living Plant* i. 13 Because they are raised above the soil on germination, these cotyledons..are termed *epigeal*.

epigee (ˈɛpɪdʒiː). [ad. Gr. ἐπίγειον (Ptolemy), neut. of ἐπίγειος adj. f. ἐπί upon, near to + γῆ earth.] = PERIGEE.

In mod. Dicts.

epigene (ˈɛpɪdʒiːn), *a.* [a. Fr. *épigène*, ad. Gr. ἐπιγενής, f. ἐπί upon, after + -γενής born, originating.

The Gr. word occurs with sense 'arising subsequently (to birth)', said of a disease, in opposition to 'congenital'. This use seems to be the source of sense 1; in sense 2 the prefix is taken as = 'upon', 'above'.]

1. *Crystallogr.* See quot. 1823. By some writers used for *pseudomorphous*.

1823 H. J. BROOKE *Introd. Crystallogr.* 93 To one class of these [crystals] the Abbé Haüy has applied the name of Epigene, where a chemical alteration has taken place in the substance of the crystal subsequently to its formation. **1851** RUSKIN *Stones Ven.* (1874) I. 2nd Pref. p. xiii, The epigene crystal, formed by materials of one substance modelled on the perished crystals of another.

2. *Geol.* Produced on the surface of the earth: opposed to *hypogene*.

1880 GEIKIE in *Nature* XXIII. No. 575. 4 The whole epigene army of destructive agencies, air, rain, frost, etc. **1882** —— *Text-bk. Geol.* III. I. 196 Epigene or Surface Action—the changes produced on the superficial parts of the earth. *Ibid.* III. II. 316 The word epigene may be suggested as..antithetical to hypogene.

epigenesis (ɛpɪˈdʒɛnɪsɪs). *Biol.* [f. Gr. ἐπί upon + γένεσις generation: see GENESIS. The word is used by W. Harvey, *Exercitationes* 1651, p. 148, and in the English *Anatomical Exercitations* 1653, p. 272. It is explained to mean 'partium super-exorientium additamentum', 'the additament of parts budding one out of another'.] The formation of an organic germ as a new product; *theory of epigenesis*: the theory that the germ is brought into existence (by successive accretions), and not merely developed, in the process of reproduction. Also *fig.*

The opposite theory was formerly known as the 'theory of evolution'; to avoid the ambiguity of this name, it is now spoken of chiefly as the 'theory of preformation', sometimes as that of 'encasement' or 'emboîtement'.

1798 A. F. M. WILLICH *Elem. Crit. Philos.* 156 Epigenesis of pure Reason has been called the Kantian explanation concerning the coincidence of the pure intellectual conceptions..with the objects of experience. **1807** *Edin. Rev.* XI. 81 The Epigenesis..is what most physiologists now assume as the only true theory of generation. **1831** *Blackw. Mag.* XXIX. 68 The two styles of conversation corresponded to the two theories of generation—one (Johnson's) to the theory of Preformation (or Evolution)—the other (Burke's) to the theory of Epigenesis. **1847** LEWES *Hist. Philos.* (1867) Proleg. §3 With Mind, as with Body, there is not preformation or pre-existence, but evolution and epigenesis. **1879** tr. *Haeckel's Evol. Man* I. ii. 40 Caspar Friedrich Wolff..with his new Theory of Epigenesis gave the death-blow to the entire Theory of Preformation.

Hence **epiˈgenesist**, one who holds the theory of epigenesis.

1816 KEITH *Phys. Bot.* II. 364 This is the theory of the epigenesists.

epigenetic (,ɛpɪdʒɪˈnɛtɪk), *a.* and *sb. pl.* [f. EPIGENESIS, on the analogy of GENETIC.]

A. *adj.* **1.** Of or pertaining to, or of the nature of, epigenesis.

1883 W. ARTHUR *Fernley Lect.* 160 Epigenetic progress from germ to organ. **1887** *Mind* Oct. 629 He..contends for an 'epigenetic' as distinguished from an evolutionary view of the origins of civilisation.

2. *Phys. Geogr.* and *Geol.* (*a*) Of a natural drainage system, = SUPERIMPOSED *ppl. a.* 1 b (*Cent. Dict.* Suppl., 1909); (*b*) applied to a deposit of later origin than the rocks among which it occurs (opp. SYNGENETIC *a.* 2).

[**1886** F. RICHTHOFEN *Führer f. Forschungsreisende* vi. 174 Man kann die hier dargestellten Bildungen als *epigenetische Erosionsthäler* bezeichnen.] **1905** J. GEIKIE *Struct. & Field Geol.* xvi. 233 *Epigenetic Ore-Formations.* The formations included under this head are of later age than the rocks with which they are associated or in which they occur. **1914** *Min. Mag.* XVII. 72 'Epigenetic'..still is used antithetically to the term 'syngenetic' by writers on ore deposits, to describe a deposit the age of which is subsequent to that of the rocks in which it occurs. **1937** WOOLDRIDGE & MORGAN *Phys. Basis Geogr.* xiv. 205 Such a drainage system is called *superimposed* or *epigenetic*. *Ibid.* xxii. 401 'Epigenetic gorges' through ridges, due to superimposition of drainage. **1965** [see AUTORADIOGRAPH *sb.*].

B. *sb. pl.* (See quot. 1942.)

1942 C. H. WADDINGTON in *Endeavour* Jan. 18/2 The.. more important part of the task is to discover the causal mechanisms at work, and to relate them as far as possible to what experimental embryology has already revealed of the mechanics of development. We might use the name 'epigenetics' for such studies, thus emphasizing their relation to the concepts, so strangely favourable to the classical theory of epigenesis, which have been reached by the experimental embryologists. **1952** —— (*title*) The epigenetics of birds. *Ibid.* (title-p.), 'Epigenetics'. The science concerned with the causal analysis of development.

Hence **epigeˈnetically** *adv.*

epigenic (ɛpɪˈdʒɛnɪk), *a.* [f. Gr. ἐπιγεν-ής (see EPIGENE) + -IC.] Originating above the surface of the earth.

1882 *Athenæum* 28 Oct. 566/3 Great changes which are being wrought upon the surface of the earth..partly by epigenic forces working from above.

epigenist (ɪˈpɪdʒɪnɪst). [f. Gr. ἐπί + γεν- (see EPIGENESIS) + -IST.] = EPIGENESIST.

1875 tr. *Schmidt's Desc. & Darw.* 45 The vehement dispute..between Evolutionists and Epigenists.

epigenous (ɪˈpɪdʒɪnəs), *a. Bot.* [f. as prec. + -OUS.] 'Growing upon the surface of a part, as many fungals on the surface of leaves' (*Treas. Bot.* 1866).

epigeous (ɛpɪˈdʒiːəs), *a. Bot.* [f. Gr. ἐπίγει-ος (f. ἐπί upon + γῆ earth) + -OUS.] Of plants: Growing close upon the earth. = EPIGEAL *a.* b.

1835 LINDLEY *Introd. Bot.* (1848) II. 380. **1847** J. LINDLEY *Elem. Bot.* p. xxxvi/2 *Epigeous*, growing close upon the earth. **1866** *Treas. Bot.*

†**ˈepiglot.** *Obs.* [cf. OF. *epiglote.*] Anglicized form of EPIGLOTTIS.

1547 BOORDE *Brev. Health* ccxxvi. 77 The longes, the midryffe, the arter trache, the Epiglote. **1578** BANISTER *Hist. Man* II. 39 The Epiglot..ought of right to be Gristely, that it might without hurt admitte continuall mouying. **1594** T. B. tr. *La Primaud. Fr. Acad.* II. 107 Another little instrument, called epiglot..like to a little tongue.

epiglottic (ɛpɪˈglɒtɪk), *a.* [f. EPIGLOTT(IS + -IC.] Of or pertaining to the epiglottis.

1887 *Pall Mall G.* 11 Nov. 7/1 Œdematous swelling of the arytæno-epiglottic folds. **1888** SIR M. MACKENZIE *Fredk. the Noble* 23, I found the left ary[teno]-epiglottic fold..a good deal congested.

epiglottidean (,ɛpɪglɒˈtɪdɪən), *a.* [f. mod.L. *epiglŏttide-us* (f. Gr. ἐπιγλωττιδ-, stem of ἐπιγλωττίς EPIGLOTTIS) + -AN.] = EPIGLOTTIC.

1840 G. ELLIS *Anat.* 268 A mass of yellowish fat, named the epiglottidean gland. **1844** J. WILKINSON tr. *Swedenborg's Anim. Kingd.* II. ii. 39 There are also glands termed arytænoid and epiglottidean.

epiglottiditis (,ɛpɪglɒtɪˈdaɪtɪs). *Path.* [f. Gr. ἐπιγλωττίδ-, ἐπιγλωττίς epiglottis + -ITIS.] = EPIGLOTTITIS.

1864 G. D. GIBB *Dis. Throat & Windpipe* (ed. 2) i. 63 A severe instance of acute epiglottiditis..occurring in a man.. in whom the epiglottis could be felt as a hard solid ball, filling up the lower end of the pharynx. **1901** P. W. WILLIAMS *Dis. Upper Respiratory Tract* (ed. 4) viii. 165 Local variations in the character and distribution of the inflammatory changes have been distinguished by the terms *epiglottiditis, arytenoiditis*, or *chorditis*.

epiglottis (ɛpɪˈglɒtɪs). [a. Gr. ἐπιγλωττίς, f. ἐπί upon + γλῶττα (γλῶσσα) tongue; cf. GLOTTIS.] 'The erect, leaf-like cartilage at the root of the tongue, which during the act of swallowing is depressed, and forms a lid, or cover for the glottis' (*Syd. Soc. Lex.*).

1615 CROOKE *Body of Man* 971 The cauity giues way to the Epiglottis to open and lift it selfe vp. **1646** SIR T. BROWNE *Pseud. Ep.* (ed. 2) 169 Birds have no Epiglottis. **1746** R. JAMES *Introd. Moufet's Health Impr.* 4 The Aliment to be swallowed presses upon the Epiglottis. **1847** YOUATT *Horse* ix. 217 The Epiglottis is a heart-shaped cartilage. **1884** BRISTOWE *Med.* 389 Such swelling..may affect mainly the epiglottis.

epiglottitis (,ɛpɪglɒˈtaɪtɪs). *Path.* [f. EPIGLOTT(IS + -ITIS.] Inflammation of the epiglottis.

1830 *London Med. Gaz.* VI. 314/2 Epiglottitis, though rare in its simple form, may nevertheless be frequently present in combination with inflammation of the neighbouring parts. **1888** *Brit. Med. Jrnl.* 15 Sept. 618/2 Before the invention of the laryngoscope, independent inflammation of the epiglottis was recognised and classified as epiglottitis. **1958** *New Eng. Jrnl. Med.* CCLVIII. 874/2 Acute epiglottitis is a serious and often fatal condition that, although infrequently recognized, lends itself to accurate bedside diagnosis.

epigon (ˈɛpɪgɒn). More recent form of EPIGONE[1].

1890 J. H. STIRLING *Philos. & Theol.* xii. 231 Any true follower of Hume, any genuine aufgeklärt *epigon* of his. **1890** W. CORY *Lett. & Jrnls.* (1897) 553 Anglo-Catholics, a second crop, the Epigons, started vestments. **1926** *Contemp. Rev.* July 22/1 The epigons of the fighters for freedom.

epigone[1] (ˈɛpɪgəʊn). *rare.* [In pl. a. Fr. *épigones*, ad. L. *epigonī*, a. Gr. ἐπίγονοι, pl. of ἐπίγονος born afterwards, f. ἐπί upon, after + -γονος, f. root of γίγνεσθαι to be born.

The designation οἱ ἐπίγονοι (L. *Epigoni*) was applied esp. to the sons of the seven heroes who led the war against Thebes; the mod. use is in allusion to this.]

One of a succeeding generation. Chiefly in *pl.* the less distinguished successors of an illustrious generation. Also in L. form (chiefly with initial capital) **eˈpigoni.**

1865 *Athenæum* No. 1989. 799/1 Epigones in the land of Erasmus. **1884** R. T. ELY *Pol. Econ.* 9 That economic system which the epigones in political economy contemplate with awe. **1937** H. READ *Art & Society* 257 That task may perhaps be left to future epigoni. **1964** F. H. BLUM in I. L. Horowitz *New Sociology* 162 Unlike the *epigoni* of his time ..Mills grasped this problem in its totality.

epigone[2] (ˈɛpɪgəʊn). *Bot.* [ad. mod.L. *epigonium*, f. Gr. ἐπί upon + γονή, γόνος seed.] The membranous bag or flask which encloses the spore-case of a liverwort or scale-moss when young. Also the nucule of a *Chara*.

1866 in *Treas. Bot.* **1870** BENTLEY *Bot.* 367 The case of the archegonium is called the epigone.

epigram (ˈɛpɪgræm). Also 6–7 epigramme, (6 epigrame, 7 epigramm). [ad. F. *épigramme*, ad. L. *epigramma*, Gr. ἐπίγραμμα, f. ἐπιγράφειν, f. ἐπί upon + γράφειν to write.]

†**1.** An inscription, usually in verse: = EPIGRAPH 1.

1552 HULOET, *Epigrame* or superscription. **1567** DRANT *Horace' Epist.* I. vii. D iij, Led by pompe wyth Sergeaunts sad the Epigrammes to graue. **1606** HOLLAND *Sueton.* Introd. 4 The Epigramme of the former is extant among the Antiquities of Rome citie. **1699** BENTLEY *Phal.* xviii. 528 The Epigram, that was written upon the public Sepulchre at Athens. **1782** V. KNOX *Ess.* I. 264 Inscriptions, for such are epigrams according to the original meaning. *a* **1876** M. COLLINS in *Pen Sketches* I. 246 What the Greeks meant by an epigram was simply an inscription, and its primary use was funereal.

2. A short poem ending in a witty or ingenious turn of thought, to which the rest of the composition is intended to lead up.

1538 LELAND *Itin.* VI. 59 If it be so I must amend my Epigramme of it. **1607** TOPSELL *Serpents* (1653) 756 Some

learned Writers..have compared a Scorpion to an Epigram..because as the sting of the Scorpion lyeth in the tayl, so the force and vertue of an Epigram is in the conclusion. **1876** GREEN *Short Hist.* ix. §3. 617 Even Rochester in his merciless epigram was forced to own that Charles 'never said a foolish thing'.

b. loosely used for a laudatory poem.

1872 ELLACOMBE *Bells of Ch.* ix. 493 This epigrame [of date 1558], as it is called, consists of sixty-four lines in English verse in praise of the said Robert Palmer and his sons, and other friends, skilled in ringing changes.

3. A pointed or antithetical saying.

1796 BURKE *Regic. Peace* iv. Wks. IX. 51 A short, affected, pedantick, insolent, theatrick laconism: a sort of epigram of contempt. **1884** CHURCH *Bacon* iii. 60 He liked..to generalise in shrewd and sometimes cynical epigrams.

b. Epigrammatic expression.

18.. LD. BROUGHAM *Dk. Bedford* Wks. 1872 I. 393 The morbid taste for slander steeped in epigram. **1877** E. CONDER *Bas. Faith* i. 35 Epigram is one thing, definition is another.

†**'epigram**, *v. Obs. rare*$^{-1}$. [f. prec. sb.] *intr.* To write an epigram.

1627-77 FELTHAM *Resolves* I. lxxi. 110 For this, does Martial Epigram upon it.

†**,epigramma'tarian**. *Obs.* [f. late L. *epigrammatāri-us* (f. *epigrammat-*: see next) + -AN.] A writer of epigrams.

1597 BP. HALL *Sat.* I. ix, Our epigrammatarians, old and late, Were wont be blamed for too licentiate. **1607** TOPSELL *Four-f. Beasts* (1673) 485 In the words of an Epigrammatarian in our age.

epigrammatic (,ɛpɪgrə'mætɪk), *a.* [f. L. *epigrammat-*, Gr. ἐπιγραμματ-, stem of ἐπίγραμμα (see EPIGRAM) + -IC.] Of or pertaining to epigrams; of the nature, or in the style, of an epigram; concise, pointed.

a **1704** T. BROWN *Praise of Poverty* Wks. 1730 I. 94 An epigrammatick poem is more charming than Homer or Virgil. **1750** H. WALPOLE *Lett. H. Mann* (1834) II. No. 213. 335 The sting is very epigrammatic. **1796** MORSE *Amer. Geog.* II. 674 Martial, of Spain, the epigrammatic poet. **1817** COLERIDGE *Biog. Lit.* I. i. 18 The logic of wit, conveyed in smooth and strong epigrammatic couplets. **1841-4** EMERSON *Ess.* xvi. *Manners* Wks. (Bohn) I. 217 Scott's..lords brave each other in smart epigrammatic speeches. **1876** BANCROFT *Hist. U.S.* V. xli. 4 He wrote with vivacity and sometimes with epigrammatic terseness.

epigra'mmatical, *a.* [f. as prec. + -AL^1.] = prec.

1605 CAMDEN *Rem.* (1637) 327 If you will reade carping Epigrammaticall verses of a Durham Poet against Ralfe the Prior. *a* **1623** —— (J.), Our good epigrammatical poet, old Godfrey of Winchester. **1711** ADDISON *Spect.* No. 74 ¶2 Epigrammatical Turns and Points of Wit.

epigrammatically (,ɛpɪgrə'mætɪkəlɪ), *adv.* [f. prec. + -LY^2.] In an epigrammatic manner; with the terseness and 'point' befitting an epigram.

1823 *Edin. Rev.* XXXVIII. 59 Who makes it almost a rule to say every thing epigrammatically. **1837** DICKENS *Pickw.* xv, 'Person's a waitin',' said Sam, epigrammatically. **1882** J. HAWTHORNE *Fort. Fool* I. xx, To put it epigrammatically—if you were to leave me a thousand pounds as a legacy, I would chuck it into the fire.

epigrammatism (ɛpɪ'græmətɪz(ə)m). [f. L. *epigrammat-* (see EPIGRAMMATIC) + -ISM.] Epigrammatic style.

1813 JANE AUSTEN *Let.* 4 Feb. (1870) The playfulness and epigrammatism of the general style. *a* **1849** POE *F.S. Osgood* Wks. 1865 III. 95 A rich tint of that epigrammatism for which the poetess is noted.

epigrammatist (ɛpɪ'græmətɪst). [ad. late L. *epigrammatist-a*, ad. Gr. ἐπιγραμματιστής, f. ἐπιγραμματίζειν (see next).] A maker of epigrams.

1589 PUTTENHAM *Eng. Poesie* I. xi. (Arb.) 41 Others..in short poemes vttered pretie merry conceits, and these men were called Epigrammatistes. **1598** MARSTON *Pygmal.* 136 Now by the whyps of Epigramatists, Ile not be lasht for my dissembling shifts. **1622** PEACHAM *Compl. Gentl.* x. (1634) 89 In Martiall you shall see..a true Epigrammatist. **1756-82** J. WARTON *Ess. Pope* (1782) II. xii. 355 [Donne's] grandfather on the mother's side was Heywood the epigrammatist. **1814** D'ISRAELI *Quarrels Auth.* (1867) 385 This familiar comparison of a MS with a squeezed orange provoked the epigrammatists. **1873** BLACK *Pr. Thule* ii. 17, I shouldn't advise a young man to marry an epigrammatist.

epigrammatize (ɛpɪ'græmətaɪz), *v.* [ad. Gr. ἐπιγραμματίζειν, f. ἐπίγραμμα (see EPIGRAM).]

1. *intr.* To compose epigrams; to speak or write in the epigrammatic style.

1811 *Ann. Reg.* 40 They may pun and epigrammatise. **1872** LIDDON *Elem. Relig.* vi. 210 Men do not..epigrammatize with the bitterness of Voltaire.

2. *trans.* To express in the form of an epigram, or with epigrammatic brevity and point.

1691 WOOD *Ath. Oxon.* I. 125 These answers are Epigrammatiz'd by an admired Muse of our Nation. **1864** LOWELL *Fireside Trav.* 318 Voltaire..epigrammatized the same thought when he said, *Le superflu, chose très-nécessaire.*

3. To make the subject of an epigram.

1862 THORNBURY *Turner* I. 9 Voltaire was epigrammatized by Young.

Hence **epi'grammatizer**, one who epigrammatizes; **epi'grammatizing** *vbl. sb.*

1870 LOWELL *Study Wind.* (1886) 363 He was..the condenser and epigrammatiser of Bolingbroke. **1872** HINDLEY in *J. Taylor's* (*Water Poet*) *Wks.* p. vii, His poetizing, epigrammatizing, and anagrammatizing on passing events.

‖**épigramme** (epigram). *Cookery.* [Fr.; app. a fanciful use of *épigramme* = EPIGRAM.] A name given to small cutlets of mutton, veal, etc. dressed in a particular manner.

1736 BAILEY, *Epigramme.* **1825** T. LISTER *Granby* vii. (1836) 40 The very eider-down of eatables! Oh, it was quite like eating air! And then, his epigrammes!

†**epi'grammical**, *a. Obs. rare.* [f. EPIGRAM + -IC + -AL^1.] = EPIGRAMMATICAL.

1606 *Choice, Chance, &c.* (1881) 66, I wrote a kind of epigrammicall sonnet in this manner.

†**'epigrammist**. *Obs. rare.* [f. EPIGRAM + -IST. Cf. It. *epigrammista.*] = EPIGRAMMATIST.

a **1635** NAUNTON *Fragm. Reg.* (1870) 35 There is an Epigrammist that saith, that Art and Nature had spent their excellencies in his fashioning.

epigraph ('ɛpɪgrɑːf, -æ-). Also 7 **epigraphe**. [ad. Gr. ἐπιγραφή inscription, f. ἐπιγράφειν to write upon, f. ἐπί upon + γράφειν to write. In Fr. *épigraphe.*]

1. An inscription; *esp.* one placed upon a building, tomb, statue, etc., to indicate its name or destination; a legend on a coin.

1624 FISHER in *White's Repl. Fisher* Pref. v, These words..which should serue as an Epigraph vpon all their houses. **1662** EVELYN *Diary* (1818) 3 Oct., Dr. Meret..shew'd me..the statue and epigraph under it of that renowned physitian Dr. Harvey. **1697** —— *Numism.* iii. 99 And this Epigraph, *Quid me Persequeris.* **1794** SULLIVAN *View Nat.* V. 90 The epigraph on the face, instead of the exurgue, is the precise Oriental custom of this day. **1832** THIRLWALL in *Philol. Mus.* I. 495 The epigraph of the thousand citizens who fell..at Chæronea. **1866** *Reader* 28 July 684 The oldest Samaritan epigraph now existing, which had been found immured in the wall of a mosque.

†**2.** The superscription of a letter, book, etc.; also, the imprint on a title-page. *Obs.*

1633 T. ADAMS *Exp. 2 Peter* i. 1 Our apostle puts in two words into the epigraph of this epistle, which he left out in the former. **1642** SIR E. DERING *Sp. on Relig.* 14 Dec. v. 20 You shall find it..in the Epigraphe of the Canons and Decrees. *a* **1734** NORTH *Exam.* III. vi. §116. 503 As he fronts it in the brazen Epigraph of his new Work. **1812** *Monthly Rev.* LXVII. 145 Geneva was adopted for the epigraph of the title-page. **1826** SOUTHEY *Lett. to Butler* 217 He was of opinion that a diviner impulse had led him to chuse that epigraph [the title of a book].

3. A short quotation or pithy sentence placed at the commencement of a work, a chapter, etc. to indicate the leading idea or sentiment; a motto.

1844 MRS. BROWNING *Sonnets from Portuguese* xlii. Wks. (1869) III. 229 And write me new my future's epigraph. **1860** S. LOVER *Leg. & Stor.* (ed. 10) i, The beautiful ballad whence the epigraph of this story is quoted. **1874** LEWES *Probl. Life & Mind* I. 123 That phrase which is placed as an epigraph to this chapter.

transf. **1858** CARLYLE *Fredk. Gt.* I. III. v. 171 The Epigraph and Life-motto which John the Steadfast had adopted.

epigraph ('ɛpɪgrɑːf, -æ-), *v.* [f. prec. sb.] *trans.* To furnish with an epigraph.

1860 MOTLEY *Netherl.* (1867) I. 526 *note*, Also a paper epigraphed: 'Lo que dijo J. B. Piata a Don Juan de Indiaquez,' 24 June, 1586.

epigrapher (ɪ'pɪgrəfə(r)). [f. EPIGRAPH-Y + -ER^1.] = EPIGRAPHIST.

1887 *Contemp. Rev.* LI. 562 It is a new doctrine that the most meritorious field-work will make a man a linguist, an epigrapher, and an historian.

epigraphic (ɛpɪ'græfɪk), *a.* and *sb.* [f. EPIGRAPH + -IC.]

A. *adj.* Of or pertaining to inscriptions, or to epigraphy.

1858 M. PATTISON *Ess.* (1889) II. 341 To bring up a loose analogy of this sort against epigraphic evidence is simply childish. **1881** R. LANCIANI in *Athenæum* 9 Apr. 498/3 Being mostly formed of a single letter, they escape an epigraphic reconstruction. **1883** I. TAYLOR *Alphabet* I. 266 Unsuitable for an epigraphic alphabet.

B. *sb.* In *pl.* The science of inscriptions.

In mod. Dicts.

Hence **epi'graphical** *a.* = EPIGRAPHIC *a.* **epi'graphically** *adv.*, in an epigraphic manner; from the point of view of epigraphic science.

1881 SAYCE in *Athenæum* 13 Aug. 208/3 Skill in reading Talmudic literature does not necessarily imply epigraphical skill as well. **1884** *Athenæum* 13 Sept. 344/1 The author summed up the existing records..annalistic, literary, and epigraphical. **1884** *Christian Treas.* Feb. 118/1 This epigraphical silence of the Holy Land. **1883** I. TAYLOR *Alphabet* I. 133 Epigraphically of the same age.

epigraphist (ɪ'pɪgrəfɪst). [f. EPIGRAPH-Y + -IST.] A student of, or authority on, inscriptions.

1865 MERIVALE *Rom. Emp.* VIII. lxvii. 300 Borghesi, the great epigraphist. **1869** J. BALDWIN *Preh. Nations* iv. 170 Epigraphists..use a method that is much too convenient.

epigraphy (ɪ'pɪgrəfɪ). [f. EPIGRAPH; see -GRAPHY.]

1. Inscriptions collectively.

1851 D. WILSON *Preh. Ann.* (1863) II. IV. ii. 215 Its philological features appear to be foreign to Irish epigraphy. **1877** J. NORTHCOTE *Catacombs* I. vi. 113 The language of Christian epigraphy was not created in a day. **1882** *Contemp. Rev.* Dec. 921 *note*, The records of epigraphy constitute a fair test of the progress of Christianity as far as the upper classes are concerned.

2. The science concerned with the interpretation, classification, etc. of inscriptions. Often in narrower sense: The palæography of inscriptions.

1863 *Sat. Rev.* 18 July 95 The science of epigraphy..seems still, as far as Britain is concerned, to be quite in its infancy. **1885** *Athenæum* No. 2985. 45 Aramaic epigraphy has made startling progress in the course of the year.

epigyne ('ɛpɪdʒaɪn). *Zool.* [ad. mod.L. *epigynum*, f. Gr. ἐπί EPI- + γυνή woman, female. Cf. EPIGYNOUS *a.*] The ovipositor in arachnids; the external genital plate in spiders. Also in mod.L. form **epigynum** (ɛpɪ'dʒaɪnəm).

1875 *Encycl. Brit.* II. 273/1 These [*sc.* ovaries] have a common exterior orifice (vulva)..and connected with this opening there is frequently an epigyne, or ovipositor. **1892** *Trans. Linnean Soc.* Zool. V. 297 The epigynum or external genital plate..entirely closes the genital aperture. **1900** *Proc. Zool. Soc.* 387 The under surface of the body is whitish except the small yellow-brown epigyne. **1916** H. S. PRATT *Man. Invertebr. Anim.* 415 Between them [*sc.* the lung spiracles] is the genital pore which, in the female, is covered by a plate..called the epigynum. **1951** LOCKET & MILLIDGE *Brit. Spiders* I. iii. 24 The term 'epigyne' (or 'epigynum') has been used in slightly different ways. In the present work it will be applied to..the general appearance of the female genital area from the outside, when the spider is viewed ventrally.

epigynous (ɪ'pɪdʒɪnəs), *a. Bot.* [f. EPI- + *gyn-* (in *Bot.* used for 'female organ, pistil'; a. Gr. γυν-ή) + -OUS.] That is placed upon the ovary; growing upon the summit of the ovary. Said of the stamens or corolla; hence of plants in which these are so placed.

1830 LINDLEY *Nat. Syst. Bot.* Introd. xxvii, [The Stamens] appear to proceed from the apex of an inferior ovarium, in which case they are named epigynous. **1882** VINES *Sachs' Bot.* 559 The flower finally is epigynous when it possesses an actually inferior ovary.

So **e'pigyny**, the character or quality of being epigynous.

1887 *Athenæum* 10 Dec. 787/3 The shortening of the axis within the flower itself, giving the transition from hypogyny through perigyny to epigyny.

epihyal (ɛpɪ'haɪəl), *a. Anat.* [f. EPI- + HY(OID) + -AL^1.] That is placed upon the hyoid bone. Applied to the upper part of the hyoid arch; also, to a bone found in certain fishes.

1854 OWEN *Skel. & Teeth* (1855) 17 the hæmapophysis is a broader, slightly arched bone; the upper division is called epihyal. **1880** GUNTHER *Fishes* 58 It consists of three segments, the epihyal, ceratohyal, which is the longest and strongest piece, etc. **1881** MIVART *Cat* 78 To the end of this is again annexed another long bone, called the epihyal.

epiklesis, var. EPICLESIS.

†**'epiky**. *Obs.* Also 6 **epicay**, **-cheia**. [ad. Gr. ἐπιείκεια, f. ἐπιεικής reasonable, f. ἐπί according to + εἰκός likely, reasonable. Cf. OF. *epyeykie* (14th c.).] Reasonableness, equity, as opposed to rigid law.

1508 FISHER 7 *Penit. Ps.* in Wks. I. 261 Epicheia whiche is proprely the mynde of the lawe. **1531** *Dial. Laws Eng* I. xvi. (1638) 28 His equity or Epicay. **1549** LATIMER *Serm.* v. O iiij, For auoydyng disturbaunce in the communewealth, such an epiky and moderacion maye be vsed in it [this law].

epilate ('ɛpɪleɪt), *v.* [f. Fr. *épil-er* (f. *é-* for *es-* L. *ex* out + *pil-us* hair) + -ATE^3.] *trans.* To pull out or eradicate (hair).

1886 FRAZER in *N. & Q.* 7th Ser. II. 298/2, I have by epilating such [white] hairs and stimulating the part succeeded in, etc.

epilation (ɛpɪ'leɪʃən). [a. Fr. *épilation*, f. *épiler* (see prec.).] The action of pulling out or eradicating hair.

1878 DUHRING *Dis. Skin* 281 Epilation is recommended strongly by Hebra and others.

†**'epilency**. *Obs.* Also 4 **epilence**, **-cye**. [ad. late L. *epilencia*, *-lensia*, *-lempsia*, a. Gr. *ἐπιληψία, var. of ἐπιληψία: see EPILEPSY.] = EPILEPSY.

[**1398** TREVISA *Barth. De P.R.* VII. x. (1495) 229 Epylencia lettyth but the pryncypal chambres of the brayne.] *Ibid.* 230 They that haue..Epylencye thei fele not toforhonde whan they shal falle. *Ibid.*, Pyany born and dronken helpith moche ayenst Epylence. [**1540** BOORDE *The Boke for to Lerne* C iij b, The fallyng sycknes called Epilencia.]

†**epi'lentic**, *a. Obs.* In 4 **epulentyk**, **epylentyk**, 6 **epilentycke**. [a. OF. *epilentic*, ad. late L. *epilenticus*, *epilemticus*, Gr. *ἐπιλημπτικός, var. of ἐπιληπτικός: see EPILEPTIC.] = EPILEPTIC.

1398 TREVISA *Barth. De P.R.* V. iii. (1495) 106 Lunatyk and epulentyk men. **1542** BOORDE *Dyetary* xxxii. (1870) 294 Venson, hare-flesshe..be not good for Epilentycke men. quasi-*sb.* **1398** TREVISA *Barth. De P.R.* VII. x. 230 The Epylentyk, that is hym that hathe the fallynge euyll.

Hence †**epi'lentical**, *a.* = EPILEPTICAL.

1483 CAXTON *Gold. Leg.* 409/3 After this machomete fyl ofte be thepylentycal passyon.

† 'epileny. *Obs. rare*⁻¹. [ad. Gr. ἐπιλήνιον (μέλος) (song) of the vintage, f. ἐπί + ληνός wine-vat.] A song in praise of wine; a drinking song.
1708 MOTTEUX *Rabelais* v. xlv, Then she..made him sing an Epileny, inserted in the Figure of the Bottle.

† **'epilepse.** *Obs. rare*⁻¹. [ad. Gr. ἐπιληψία.] = EPILEPSY.
1804 J. WHITEHOUSE *To Febris* in *Poet. Register* 92 That hideous choir, Marasmus, Epilepse, and Frenzy dire!

† **epi'lepsian,** *a. Obs. rare*⁻¹. [f. EPILEPSY + -AN.] = EPILEPTIC.
1627 H. BURTON *Baiting Pope's Bull* 43 So his epilepsian or comitial fit, but a trance, wherein he talked with his Angel Gabriel.

epilepsy ('ɛpɪlɛpsɪ). *Path.* Also 6–8 epilepsie. See also EPILENCY. [a. OF. *epilepsie*, ad. L. *epilēpsia*, a. Gr. ἐπιληψία, f. ἐπιλαμβάνειν to take hold of, f. ἐπί upon + λαμβάνειν to take.] A disease of the nervous system, characterized (in its severer forms) by violent paroxysms, in which the patient falls to the ground in a state of unconsciousness, with general spasm of the muscles, and foaming at the mouth. The Eng. name is *falling sickness* (now little used).
1578 LYTE *Dodoens* 35 The same..is good for the Epilepsie, or falling sicknesse. **1604** SHAKS. *Oth.* IV. i. 51 My Lord is falne into an Epilepsie; This is his second Fit. **1658** J. R. tr. *Mouffet's Theat. Ins.* 1098 By their smell the Epilepsie that ariseth from the strangling of the Mother, is discussed. **1757** BURKE *Abridgm. Eng. Hist.* Wks. (1812) X. 196 The epilepsy was by the Romans..called Morbus Sacer. **1843** LEVER *J. Hinton* xxxiv. (1878) 232 His features worked like one in a fit of epilepsy. **1850** W. IRVING *Mahomed* vi. (1853) 32 Some of his adversaries attributed them to epilepsy.

epileptic (ɛpɪ'lɛptɪk), *a.* and *sb.* Also 7 epileptique, -ticke. See also EPILENTIC. [a. F. *épileptique*, ad. L. *epilēpticus*, a. Gr. ἐπιληπτικός, f. ἐπιλαμβάνειν (see prec.).]
A. *adj.* 1. Of or pertaining to epilepsy; of the nature of epilepsy.
1608 L. MACHIN *Dumbe Knight* III, But Ile forestall thine Epileptique fits, And by my plots breed thy destruction. **1651** BIGGS *New Disp.* 190 ¶592 The epileptick fumes shall come that way out of the brain. **1794–6** E. DARWIN *Zoon.* I. 325 It appears..that reverie is a disease of the Epileptic or Cataleptic kind. **1840** BARHAM *Ingol. Leg., Pass. in Life H. Harris* A formidable epileptic attack. **1878** A. HAMILTON *Nerv. Dis.* 103 Epileptic coma can hardly be mistaken for that of cerebral hemorrhage. **1889** F. CLARK *Papers on Surg.*, He had two epileptic fits.
2. Affected with epilepsy.
1605 SHAKS. *Lear* II. ii. 87 A plague vpon your Epilepticke visage. **1655** JER. TAYLOR *Of Repentance* vi. §7 An epileptick son doth often come from an epileptick father. **1681** COLVIL *Whigs Supplic.* (1751) 81 Till through his epileptic mouth Those following speeches fierce and loud Burst out. **1806** *Med. Jrnl.* XV. 335 In Russia, Denmark, and Sweden, millions of children become epileptic from the breast. **1875** B. RICHARDSON *Dis. Mod. Life* 44 In the olden times..to be epileptic or insane was, to be possessed of an evil spirit.
B. *sb.* 1. An epileptic person. Cf. A. 2.
1651 HOBBES *Leviath.* III. xxxiv. 211 Epileptiques..they esteemed..Dæmoniaques. **1732** ARBUTHNOT *Rules of Diet* (R), Epilepticks ought to breathe a pure air. **1864** *Reader* No. 94. 485/1 Epileptics and idiots.
2. In *pl.* Medicines given to cure or mitigate epilepsy.
1721 in BAILEY; and in mod. Dicts.

epileptical (ɛpɪ'lɛptɪkəl), *a.* [f. as prec. + -AL¹.]
1. = EPILEPTIC A. 1.
1621 BURTON *Anat. Mel.* I. iii. II. i, Headache followes; and as Salust Salvianus..found, epilepticall, with a multitude of humours in the head. **1656** H. MORE *Enthus. Tri.* 21 That he was Melancholy his Epilepticall fits are one argument. **1727** LARDNER *Wks.* (1838) I. 487 It was a sad epileptical disease. **1819** BYRON *Juan* II. l, A kind of wild and horrid glee, Half epileptical, and half hysterical.
2. *fig.* Spasmodic; inconstant: also, hard to hold or retain.
1646 SIR T. BROWNE *Pseud. Ep.* II. vi. §3. 99 Did they answer their promise which are so commended, in Epilepticall intentions, wee would abate these qualities. **1646** EVANCE *Noble Ord.* 9 It is this that makes the state of honour so epilepticall, so slippery.

epileptically (ɛpɪ'lɛptɪkəlɪ), *adv.* [-LY².] As if affected with epilepsy; because of epilepsy.
1883 E. C. MANN *Man. Psychol. Med.* xxv. 483 There are on record many homicides committed by epileptically insane persons. **1912** KIPLING *Diversity of Creatures* (1917) 211 The House sang at the tops and at the bottoms of their voices,..epileptically beating with their swelled feet. **1929** D. H. LAWRENCE *Pansies* 128 Dostoevsky..With his sham christianity Epileptically ruined The last bit of sanity..Of the Russian nobility.

epileptiform (ɛpɪ'lɛptɪfɔːm), *a.* [f. EPILEPTI-C + -FORM.] Resembling epilepsy.
1861 WYNTER *Soc. Bees* 479 These fits were of an epileptiform character. **1876** BARTHOLOW *Mat. Med.* (1879) 544 Epileptiform convulsions is a constant phenomenon in animals bled to death.

epilepto'genic, epilep'togenous, *adjs. Path.* [See -GENIC and -OUS.] Producing epileptic attacks.
1885 *Alienist & Neurologist* (St. Louis) VI. 449 Seppilli..believes..that basilar motor centers..may acquire..the epiloptogenous property by exaggerating their proper function. **1889** *Cent. Dict.* II. 1970/2 Epileptogenic. **1908** *Practitioner* Sept. 466 The fits re-appear after a time, because the scar itself becomes in turn an epileptogenous centre. **1949** H. W. FLOREY *Antibiotics* II. xxxvii. 1215 Their critical epileptogenic dose. **1961** *Lancet* 22 July 179/2 Electroencephalographic examination..showed multiple epileptogenic areas.

epileptoid (ɛpɪ'lɛptɔɪd), *a.* [f. EPILEPT-IC + -OID.] Resembling epilepsy; of the nature of epilepsy.
1866 A. FLINT *Princ. Med.* (1880) 825 Mild attacks having an evident relationship to ordinary epilepsy..may be called epileptoid attacks. **1876** BARTHOLOW *Mat. Med.* (1879) 392 Epileptoid seizures, due to tumor or other coarse organic lesion of the brain.

epilimnion (ɛpɪ'lɪmnɪən). Pl. epilimnia. [f. EPI- + Gr. λιμνίον, dim. of λίμνη lake.] The upper, uniformly warm layer of water in a stratified lake: cf. HYPOLIMNION. Hence **epilim'netic** [cf. Gr. λιμνήτης living in marshes], **epi'limnial** *adjs.*, situated in or relating to the epilimnion.
1910 E. A. BIRGE in *Trans. Wisc. Acad. Sci., Arts & Lett.* XVI. II. 1005, I employ two new words in this paper... These terms are *epilimnion*, for the upper warm layer of water..and *hypolimnion*, for the lower colder water. **1936** *Nature* 5 Dec. 971/1 The result of this warming is that, in summer, a warm upper layer of less dense water, the epilimnion, comes to lie over a cold deeper water mass, the hypolimnion. **1940** *Ibid.* 24 Aug. 255/1 The epilimnial current..opposes the hypolimnial current, causing turbulence at the thermocline. **1957** G. E. HUTCHINSON *Treat. Limnol.* I. vii. 447 In the former case, the 15-m. depth was evidently ordinarily epilimnetic, in the latter case metalimnetic. **1959** J. CLEGG *Freshwater Life* (ed. 2) ii. 38 The epilimnion..is well lighted, warm and well oxygenated, and..a wealth of minute plants is able to thrive. **1959** *Times* 20 June 9/3 They [*sc.* tench] have been termed 'epilimnion feeders'.

epilobe ('ɛpɪləʊb). *Bot.* [ad. mod.L. *epilobium*, f. Gr. ἐπί upon + λοβ-ός lobe of the ear, in plants the capsule or pod, the name referring to the position of the corolla.] A plant of the genus *Epilobium* (N.O. *Onagraceæ*): e.g. the *Epilobium angustifolium* or Willow-herb. Also in mod.L. form **epi'lobium.**
1775 T. BLAIKIE *Diary Scotch Gardener* (1931) 5 July 49 Found several plants on the channells of the Lake [of Geneva] especially the new sort of *Epellobium*..with a strong root deep in the hand gravell... Most of the other *Epellobiums*..in general has creaping roots. **1809** SMITH & SOWERBY *Eng. Bot.* XXVIII. 2000 Epilobium alsinifolium. .. This *Epilobium* was gathered on the Cheviot hills by Mr. Winch, who rightly judges it to be the plant of Ray, always mistaken for *alpinum*. **1861** BARNES in *Macm. Mag.* June 133 The bush, or ditch-guarded epilobium. **1864** THOREAU *Maine W.* iii. 167 A spike as big as an epilobium. **1883** G. ALLEN in *Knowledge* 6 July 1/1 The epilobes and the St. John's worts are coming out in blossom again.

† **e'pilogate,** *v. Obs. rare*⁻¹. [f. Fr. *épilog-uer* + -ATE³.] *trans.* To speak the epilogue of (a play).
1652 URQUHART *Jewel* Wks. (1834) 232/1 Did..present himself to epilogate this his almost extemporanean comedie.

† **epilo'gation.** *Obs.* In 4–5 epilogacyon, -ion. [a. OF. *epilogacion*, f. *epiloguer* (see prec.).] A summing up by way of conclusion.
1474 CAXTON *Chesse* IV. viii, The epylogacion and recapytulacion of this book. **1502** *Ord. Crysten Men* (W. de W. 1506) II. xv. 121 Here foloweth the epylogacyon or shorte repytycyon of this seconde partye. *a* **1529** SKELTON *Col. Cloute* 521 Some make epylogacyon Of hyghe predestynacyon. *a* **1547** T. KEY *Erasm. Par., Mark* (1548) 21 a, By waye of epilogacion and gatheryng of the whole matter into a brief summe.

epilogic (ɛpɪ'lɒdʒɪk), *a.* [f. EPILOG-UE + -IC.] Pertaining to, or resembling, an epilogue.
So **epi'logical** *a.*
In mod. Dicts.

† **epilogism.** *Obs.* [ad. Gr. ἐπιλογισμός f. ἐπιλογίζεσθαι of twofold sense and formation (1) to reckon over or in addition, f. ἐπί over + λογίζεσθαι to reckon; (2) see EPILOGIZE.]
1. a. Calculation, computation; *concr.* number reckoned. b. Excess in reckoning.
1646 J. GREGORY *Notes & Observ.* (1850) Pref. 2 But the Hellenists or Græcists..added what is supernumerary to these Epilogismes. —— *Posthuma De Æris* (1650) 156 But where to begin or end this Epilogism, is the Vexata Quæstio. *Ibid.* 171 It cannot bee but that this Epilogism must bee detracted from the Hebrew.
2. Something said by way of epilogue.
1671 H. STUBBE *Reply* 47 Had he been such a Proficient.. he would never have..concluded a Discourse of this Nature, with this Epilogism.

epilogist (ɪ'pɪlədʒɪst). [f. EPILOG-UE + -IST.] The writer or speaker of an epilogue.
1716 M. DAVIES *Ath. Brit.* III. *Dissert. Drama* 5 The Prologist and Epilogist [in a certain drama]. **1885** *Times* 17 Dec. 9 The epilogist [to a play] is sometimes our political remembrancer. **1887** CHEYNE *Job & Solomon* 234 A warning is given to the disciple of the Epilogist 'to cast away the thirst for books'.

epilogistic (ˌɛpɪləʊ'dʒɪstɪk), *a.* [f. prec. + -IC.] Of the nature of an epilogue.
a **1790** WARTON *Milton's Sm. Poems* (T.), These lines are an epilogistic palinode to the last elegy.

epilogize (ɪ'pɪlədʒaɪz), *v.* [ad. Gr. ἐπιλογίζεσθαι, f. ἐπίλογος EPILOGUE.] *intr.* a. To serve as an epilogue. b. To write or speak an epilogue. c. *trans.* To put an epilogue to. Hence **e'pilogizing** *ppl. a.*
1623 COCKERAM, *Epilogize*, to make a conclusion, or end. *c* **1665** R. CARPENTER *Pragm. Jesuit* 65/2 Summe up the lies that will Epilogize to the Epilogue of this Comedy. **1834–43** SOUTHEY *Doctor* (1849) xl. i. 96 [Prayers] with which the so called Evangelical Clergymen..think proper sometimes to prologise and epilogize their grievous discourses. **1881** HALES in *Athenæum* 24 Dec. 851/2 He [Gower] epilogizes in these Latin lines.
transf. **1681** COLVIL *Whigs Supplic.* (1751) 120 When thumb or hammer of a clock Gives the epilogizing stroak.

‖ **e'pilogo.** *Obs. rare*⁻¹. Sp. form of next.
1588 R. PARKE tr. *Mendoza's Hist. China* 363 It shall seeme rather an Epilogo, then a new relation.

epilogue ('ɛpɪlɒg), *sb.* Also 6 epiloge. [a. F. *epilogue*, ad. L. *epilogus*, a. Gr. ἐπίλογος the peroration of a speech, f. ἐπί in addition + λόγος speech.]
† 1. *Rhet.* The concluding part or peroration of a speech. *Obs.*
1644 BULWER *Chiron.* 48 Commended the use and signification of this gesture; but in Epilogue onely.
† b. A summary. *Obs.*
1646 F. HAWKINS *Youth's Behav.* (1663) 24 If any one come on a suddain whil'st thou talk'st..it is seemly to make a little Epilogue, and brief collection of what thou deliverest.
2. The concluding part of a literary work; an appendix.
1564 *Brief Exam.* ****** iiij, Now at length are you come to the Epiloge (as it were) or full conclusion of your worke. **1651** HOBBES *Leviath.* III. xxxiii. 202 A Preface in the beginning, and an Epilogue in the end. **1704** in *Phil. Trans.* XXV. 1610 To this Book he subjoyns an Epilogue, containing some general Corollaries. **1875** JOWETT *Plato* (ed. 2) I. 191 The epilogue or conclusion of the Dialogue has been criticised.
transf. **1657** G. STARKEY *Helmont's Vind.* 230 For an epilogue of his Feaver, contracts a Chronick disease. **1882–3** SCHAFF *Encycl. Relig. Knowl.* 560 The fifth œcumenical council..is generally considered as a mere epilogue to the Council of Chalcedon.
3. A speech or short poem addressed to the spectators by one of the actors after the conclusion of the play.
1590 SHAKS. *Mids. N.* V. i. 362 No Epilogue, I pray you; for your play needs no excuse. **1616** BEAUM. & FL. *Cust. Country* Epil., Why there should be an epilogue to a play, I know no cause. **1719** YOUNG *Busiris* Epil., The race of critics, dull, judicious rogues, To mournful plays deny brisk Epilogues. **1756** J. WARTON *Ess. Pope* (1782) II. viii. 50 His epilogue to the Tartuffe. *Mod.* The Epilogue to the Westminster Play appears in the *Times* of to-day.
transf. and *fig.* **1645** QUARLES *Sol. Recant.* x. xiii, Folly brings in the Prologue with his tongue, Whose Epilogue is Rage and open wrong. *c* **1788** BURKE *W. Hastings* Wks. XIV. 204 You have heard as much of the drama as I could go through..Mr. Larkins's letter will be the epilogue to it.
4. *attrib.*
1654 GAYTON *Pleas. Notes* IV. viii. 220 The Hostesse..ran after the Epilogue-speaker.

epilogue ('ɛpɪlɒg), *v.* [f. prec. sb.] *trans.* To put an epilogue to.
1602 WARNER *Alb. Eng.* x. lix. 261 To epilogue our Tragedie, now Adoniah acts. **1758** *Monthly Rev.* 621 The whole being epilogued with a most delectable poem. *a* **1834** LAMB *Final Mem.* viii. 277 Knowles' play..epilogued by me. **1889** *Sat. Rev.* 21 Dec. 705/1 Mr. Dobson..prologues and epilogues the selection with charming verses of his own.

† **epiloguize** (ɪ'pɪləgaɪz), *v. Obs.* [f. EPILOGUE *sb.* + -IZE.] a. *intr.* To deliver an epilogue, to speak as one who is delivering an epilogue.
b. *trans.* To put an epilogue to. Cf. EPILOGIZE.
1634 MILTON *Comus* 976 The dances ended, the Spirit epiloguizes. **1651** BIGGS *New Disp.* 115 ¶158 Doth epiloguise and confesse, that, etc. *a* **1652** BROME *City Wit* Epil., Now let me Scholastikewise For us all Epiloguise. **1656** S. HOLLAND *Zara* 164 Nothing appears but a thick Stage and a thin-jaw'd Poet, who thus Epiloguizes.
transf. **1750** *Student* I. 143 (T.), The laugh of applause, with which the charming companion of my new acquaintance was epiloguising his witty raillery.
Hence † **e'piloguizer**, one who speaks or writes an epilogue.
1748 J. HOADLEY *Epil. to Shaks. I Hen. IV*, Go to, old lad, 'tis time that thou art wiser; Thou art not fram'd for an epiloguizer.

† **epi'loimic,** *a. Obs.*⁻⁰ [f. EPI- + Gr. λοιμ-ός pestilence + -IC.] 'Good against the Plague or Pestilence' (Phillips 1678).

† **epimace.** *Obs. rare*⁻¹. (See quot.)
1541 R. COPLAND *Guydon's Quest. Chirurg.*, The dysease of epimace, or apostumes of the rybbes.

e'pimacus. *Her.* An alleged synonym of OPINICUS, an imaginary beast resembling a griffin.
1830 in ROBSON *Brit. Her. Gloss.* **1889** in ELVIN.

epimedium (ɛpɪ'miːdɪəm). *Bot.* [mod.L. (Linnæus *Systema Naturæ* (1735)), f. L. *epimēdion*, Gr. ἐπιμήδιον.] Any plant of the genus of hardy perennial herbs so named.
1798 SMITH & SOWERBY *Eng. Bot.* VII. 438 Epimedium alpinum, *Barren-wort*... Dr. Withering has lately

introduced the *Epimedium* into his work on the authority of Dr. Richardson, who is said in Blackstone's *Specimen Botanicum* to have found it in Bingley Woods, Yorkshire. **1900** J. M. ABBOTT in W. D. Drury *Bk. Gard.* ix. 293 Epimediums are useful plants for shady positions. **1901** *Cassell's Dict. Gard.* 321/2 The Epimediums will thrive well in shady places, and even under trees. **1961** *Amat. Gardening* 2 Dec. 19 A plant of epimedium. This is a hardy herbaceous plant which does well in a rock garden.

epimer ('ɛpɪmə(r)). *Chem.* [a. G. *epimer*, pl. *epimere* (E. Votoček 1911, in *Ber. d. Deut. Chem. Ges.* XLIV. 360), f. EPI- + -MER.] Either of two isomers differing in the configuration of the atoms about a single asymmetric carbon atom in a compound containing other asymmetric carbon atoms; orig. in a more restricted sense (see quot. 1948¹). Hence **epi'meric** *a.*, of, having the qualities of, or standing in relation to another compound as, an epimer; **e'pimerism** [ad. G. *epimerie* (E. Votoček 1911, *loc. cit.*): see -ISM], the fact or condition of having epimers.

1911 *Chem. Abstr.* V. 1606 It is proposed that sugars which are related in the same manner as is glucose..to mannose..should be distinguished by prefixing epi- to the name of 1 member of the pair. The relationship itself should be termed epimerism; the 2 related compds. would then be called epimers. *Ibid.* 1607 Epimeric aldoses give the same osazone. **1948** W. W. PIGMAN *Chem. Carbohydrates* ii. 26 In the sugar series, substances which differ only in the configuration of the carbon atom immediately adjacent to that carrying the carbonyl or carboxyl group are known as epimers. *Ibid.*, It may be well to extend the definition of epimers to mean any pair of stereoisomers that differ solely in the configuration of a single asymmetric carbon atom. **1962** E. L. ELIEL *Stereochem. Carbon Compounds* iv. 40 Diastereoisomers that differ in configuration at only one asymmetric center are sometimes called 'epimers'; thus menthone and isomenthone are epimers. **1965** K. MISLOW *Introd. Stereochem.* ii. 91 The diastereomeric ephedrines and pentaric acids are necessarily epimeric.

epimeral (ɛpɪ'mɪərəl), *a. Anat.* [f. EPIMERON + -AL¹.] Of or pertaining to the epimeron.

1835-6 TODD *Cycl. Anat.* I. 781/2 A hole pierced in the epimeral piece near to its inferior edge. **1877** HUXLEY *Anat. Inv. An.* vi. 317 The line at which the epimeral is reflected into the pleural membrane.

quasi-*sb.* **1852** [See EPISTERNAL 2.]

epimerite (ɛ'pɪməraɪt). *Zool.* [f. Gr. ἐπί EPI- + μέρος part + -ITE¹.] (See quots.)

1885 *Encycl. Brit.* XIX. 854/1 (*Gregarinidea*) There is frequently if not always present, either in early growth or more persistently, an anterior proboscis-like appendage (the epimerite) growing from the protomerite. **1921** PARKER & HASWELL *Text-bk. Zool.* (ed. 3) I. ii. 85 Sometimes the protomerite is produced in front into a process ending in a rounded enlargement, the epimerite, which may be provided with radiating spine-like projections. **1961** MACKINNON & HAWES *Introd. Study Protozoa* III. 169 The Cephalina, which are gut parasites in which the body is typically divided into different regions, of which the anterior develops an organ of fixation called the epimerite.

epimerization (ɛ,pɪməraɪ'zeɪʃən). *Chem.* [f. EPIMER + -IZATION.] The conversion of one epimer into the other. Hence **e'pimerize** *v. trans.*, to convert (one epimer) into the other; **e'pimerizing** *vbl. sb.*

1929 *Jrnl. Chem. Soc.* I. 345 The authors have effected the epimerisation of several methylated lactones. **1930** *Ibid.* II. 2623 This is epimerised to tetramethyl glucose by alkali. **1956** L. F. & M. FIESER *Org. Chem.* (ed. 3) xiv. 361 A sugar carrying a methoxyl group at the 2-position is epimerized by alkali at C_2 with deuterium exchange at this position. **1959** *Jrnl. Chem. Soc.* I. 637 Titanium chloride is a powerful epimerising agent. **1965** G. HALLAS *Org. Stereochem.* ii. 43 In both cases, epimerization takes place by enolization.

‖**epimeron** (ɛpɪ'mɪərən). *Anat.* Pl. epimera. [f. Gr. ἐπί upon + μηρός thigh.] That part of the lateral wall of a somite of a crustacean which is situated between the articulation of the appendage and the pleuron. Also in Insecta (see quot. 1964).

[**1869** A. S. PACKARD *Guide to Study of Insects* 9 The episternum is situated between the epimerum and sternum.] **1872** NICHOLSON *Palæont.* 146 The superior arc is completed by two lateral pieces..which are termed the 'epimera'. **1880** HUXLEY *Cray Fish* iv. 143. **1895** J. H. & A. B. COMSTOCK *Man. Study of Insects* xxi. 502 The first of these [sclerites] is the episternum, the second is the epimeron. **1925** A. D. IMMS *Gen. Textbk. Ent.* I. 23 The pleuron consists of an anterior sclerite or episternum and a posterior sclerite or epimeron. **1964** R. M. & J. W. FOX *Introd. Compar. Ent.* ii. 53 The principal pleural sclerites of each segment are the episternum, lying anterior to the legs, and the epimeron, above and behind the leg bases.

epimyth ('ɛpɪmɪθ). [ad. Gr. ἐπιμύθ-ιον the moral, neut. of ἐπιμύθιος, f. ἐπί upon + μῦθος fable.] The moral of a fable or story.

[**1721-1800** BAILEY, *Epimythium*, the Moral of a Fable.] **1866** *Sat. Rev.* 24 Mar. 364 They [certain fables] go upon almost 'total abstinence' principles as regards moral and epimyth. **1869** *Ibid.* 13 Feb. 223 The way of putting it is so neat as to require no epimyth.

epinastic (ɛpɪ'næstɪk), *a. Bot.* [f. EPINAST-Y + -IC.] Of the nature of, or influenced by, epinasty.

1880 C. & F. DARWIN *Movem. Pl.* 262, So young that their epinastic growth..overpowered every other kind of movement. **1882** VINES *Sachs' Bot.* 857 As long as the organ grows most rapidly on the dorsal side, it may be termed, after de Vries, hyponastic; afterwards, when it grows most rapidly on the inner or upper side, epinastic.

epinasty ('ɛpɪnæstɪ). *Bot.* [f. EPI- + Gr. ναστός (f. νάσσειν to squeeze close) + -Y³.] (See quot.)

1880 C. & F. DARWIN *Movem. Pl.* 5 The term epinasty is now often used in Germany, and implies that the upper surface of an organ grows more quickly than the lower surface, and thus causes it to bend downwards. **1882** VINES *Sachs' Bot.* 859 Geotropism will act in the former in opposition to epinasty.

epinephrine (ɛpɪ'nɛfrɪn). *Chem.* Also -in. [f. Gr. ἐπί upon + νεφρός kidney + -INE⁵.] = ADRENALINE.

1899 *Jrnl. Chem. Soc.* LXXVI. I. 395 Epinephrine, the active material of suprarenal capsules. **1900** DORLAND *Med. Dict.*, Epinephrin. **1908** *Practitioner* Mar. 422 The active principle from the medulla of the suprarenal capsule is now generally known as adrenalin, though other terms have been applied, such as suprarenin, epinephrin. **1949** H. W. FLOREY et al. *Antibiotics* II. xxxviii. 1234 The use of propylene glycol with penicillin, epinephrine hydrochloride, and arachis oil. **1962** A. HUXLEY *Island* xiv. 250 Their pink epinephrin, my visions; their white epinephrin, my crimes. **1963** H. BURN *Drugs, Med. & Man* (ed. 2) ii. 23 Most people have heard of the substance adrenaline, which is called epinephrine in the United States Pharmacopoeia.

epineural (ɛpɪ'njʊərəl), *a. Anat.* [f. EPI- + NEURAL.]

1. Situated upon a neural arch, as a spine of a fish's backbone. Also quasi-*sb.*

1866 [see EPICENTRAL].

2. *Zool.* Lying over and parallel to a nerve. Said of various processes in echinoderms, etc.

1906 *Cambr. Nat. Hist.* I. xviii. 515 In Echinoids the ambulacral groove has become converted into a canal called the 'epineural canal'. **1914** E. W. MACBRIDE *Text-bk. Embryol.* I. viii. 254 The epineural sinus..derives its name from the circumstance that it lies above the rudiments of the ganglia of the ventral nerve cord. *Ibid.* xvi. 495 Epineural flaps. *Ibid.*, The epineural roof which covers in each radial nerve cord of the adult. *Ibid.* 514 The epineural ridges. *Ibid.*, These epineural canals meet in a central epineural space, roofed over by a membrane termed the epineural veil. **1955** L. H. HYMAN *Invertebrates* IV. xv. 140 To the outer side of the radial nerve lies a cavity, the epineural canal or sinus.

‖**epinglette.** [F. *épinglette*, dim. of *épingle* pin.] 'An iron needle with which the cartridge of any large piece of ordnance is pierced before it is primed' (Stocqueler).

†**epi'nicial**, *a. Obs. rare*⁻¹. [f. as next + -AL¹.] = EPINICIAN.

1774 WARTON *Hist. Eng. Poetry* Diss. i. (1840) I. p. xlii. note, These [spoils won in battle] were carried in triumph, while an epinicial song was chanted.

epinician (ɛpɪ'nɪsɪən), *a.* Also 9 epinikian. [f. EPINICI-ON + -AN.] Celebrating victory.

1652 BENLOWES *Theoph.* VI. xlviii, The Laureate King.. Warbles This Epinician Canzon to his Lyre. **1850** GROTE *Greece* II. lv. VII. 75 *note*, Alkibiadês obtained from Euripidês the honour of an epinikian ode, or song of triumph, to celebrate this event. **1873** SYMONDS *Grk. Poets* v. 120 The Epinikian Ode was the most costly and splendid flower in the victor's wreath.

epinicion (ɛpɪ'nɪsɪən). Also 7, 9 epinikion, 7 (in Lat. form) epinicium. [a. Gr. ἐπινίκιον song of victory, neut. of ἐπινίκιος adj., f. ἐπί upon + νίκη victory.] In Greece, an ode sung in honour of a victor in the games; a song of triumph generally.

1613 DAY *Day's Dyall* (1614) 106 That Creed..is called Epinicium by Erasmus, that is, a song of Triumph. *a* **1667** JER. TAYLOR *Serm.* (1678) 243 An Epinicion, and Song of eternal Triumph. **1698** [R. FERGUSON] *View Eccles.* Pref., He..Sung an Epinikion..too soon over his fancied Achievements. **1782** WARTON *Enq. Rowley's Poems* 69 (T.) A triumphal epinicion on Hengist's massacre. **1816** G. S. FABER *Orig. Pagan Idol.* I. 349 The sublime epinicion of Isaiah.

†**epi'nyctal**, *a. Obs. rare.* [f. Gr. ἐπινύκτ-ιος by night, nightly, f. ἐπί upon + νύξ, νυκτός night + -AL¹.] Nightly.

1600 TOURNEUR *Transf. Met.* Ded., To thee this Epinyctall register.

‖**epinyctis** (ɛpɪ'nɪktɪs). *Med. Obs.* [mod.L., a. Gr. ἐπινυκτίς, f. ἐπί + νύξ night.] A pustule, or an eruption, which appears only at night.

1676 R. WISEMAN *Chirurg. Treat.* I. viii. 44 Epinyctis and Terminthus; a couple of angry Pustules affecting the Skin in the Arms, Hands, and Thighs.

epiotic (ɛpɪ'ɒtɪk), *a. Anat.* [f. Gr. ἐπί upon + οὖς, ὠτ-ός ear + -IC.] Situated above the ear; the distinctive epithet of one of the three bones which together form the periotic bone. Also quasi-*sb.*

1870 ROLLESTON *Anim. Life* 44 The uppermost of these, a forked bone, [in the perch] suspends the arch to the squamosal and epiotic bones. **1878** BELL *Gegenbauer's Comp. Anat.* 452 The epiotic forms a second piece.

epipalæolithic (,ɛpɪpæliːə'lɪθɪk), *a. Archæol.* [ad. Sp. *epipaleolítico* (H. Obermaier *El Hombre Fósil* (1916) x. 314), f. EPI- 1 + PALÆOLITHIC, PALEO- *a.* (*sb.*).] Belonging to the period or cultural stage between the end of the palæolithic and the beginning of the mesolithic; formerly = MESOLITHIC *a.*

1921 R. A. S. MACALISTER *Textbk. Europ. Archæol.* x. 549 The 'Epipalaeolithic' Azilian. **1924** C. D. MATTHEW tr. *Obermaier's Fossil Man in Spain* x. 323 The final phase of the Capsian, the Tardenoisian, the Azilian, and the northern Maglemose industries are the posthumous descendants of the Palæolithic, on which account we have adopted for the group the name of 'Epipalæolithic'. **1928** V. G. CHILDE *Most Anc. East* ii. 33 Others [*sc.* rock-paintings] belong to the immediately succeeding epipalæolithic period. **1936** *Discovery* Aug. 262/2 Some would regard it [*sc.* the period between the Old and New Stone Ages] as a continuation in attenuated form of activities fundamentally developed by palaeolithic man. They, therefore, prefer to term it 'epi-palaeolithic'. Others regard it as essentially transitional, and call it 'mesolithic'. **1970** D. A. ROE *Prehistory* iii. 91 Between the fully Upper Palaeolithic Cultures..and the fully Mesolithic ones..there are cultures which are not clearly either one or the other, and the sensible name of 'epi-palaeolithic' is sometimes given to them. *Ibid.* 95 The various epi-palaeolithic cultures may be regarded as ending with the close of Late Glacial conditions and the beginning of the Pre-Boreal phase.

epipastic (ɛpɪ'pæstɪk), *a.* and *sb. Med.* [f. Gr. ἐπίπαστ-ος sprinkled over (f. ἐπιπάσσειν, f. ἐπί upon + πάσσειν to sprinkle) + -IC. Cf. F. *épipastique.*]

A. *adj.*

1860 MAYNE *Exp. Lex.*, *Epipastic Silk*, a term for vesicatory silk.

B. *sb.* A blister or vesicatory.

1710 T. FULLER *Pharm. Extemp.* 44 By plentiful.. Epipasticks..appease the angry rage of the Spirits.

†**,epipe'dometry.** *Obs.*⁻⁰ [f. Gr. ἐπίπεδ-ος (f. ἐπί upon + πέδον the ground), in *Geom.* = plane, superficial + -μετρία measurement.] Explained in Dicts. as 'The measurement of figures that stand on the same base'.

Etymologically the word can only mean 'measurement of plane surfaces', though some Fr. dicts. explain *épipédométrie* as 'measurement of solids'.

1706 in PHILLIPS. **1721-1800** in BAILEY. **1847** in CRAIG; and in mod. Dicts.

epiperipheral (,ɛpɪpə'rɪfərəl), *a.* [f. EPI- + PERIPHER-Y + -AL¹.] (See quot.)

1870 H. SPENCER *Princ. Psychol.* (ed. 2) I. II. vii. 250 Sensations..externally initiated or epi-peripheral.

epipetalous (ɛpɪ'pɛtələs), *a. Bot.* [f. EPI- + PETAL *sb.* + -OUS.] (See quots.)

1845 LINDLEY *Sch. Bot.* i. (1858) 15 If [the filaments grow] upon the sides of the corolla, they are *epipetalous.* **1870** BENTLEY *Bot.* 351 The stamens may be united separately to the corolla, when they are said to be epipetalous.

epiphanous (ɪ'pɪfənəs), *a. nonce-wd.* [f. Gr. ἐπιφαν-ής resplendent + -OUS: formed with allusion to next.] Resplendent.

1823 LAMB *Elia* Ser. II. xx. (1865) 373 Twelfth Day.. came..all royal, glittering and epiphanous.

Epiphany¹ (ɪ'pɪfənɪ). *Eccl.* Also 4-7 **epyphany(e, epiphanie,** (4 **the pyffanie** = th' **epyffanie**). [a. OF. *epiphanie* = Pr., It. *epifania*, ad. late L. *epiphania* neut. pl. (but often used as fem. sing.), a. late Gr. ἐπιφάνια (neut. pl. of adj. *ἐπιφάνιος), f. ἐπιφαίνειν to manifest, f. ἐπί to + φαίνειν to show.]

The festival commemorating the manifestation of Christ to the Gentiles in the persons of the Magi; observed on Jan. 6th, the 12th day after Christmas.

a **1310** in Wright *Lyric P.* 96 The thridde joie of that levedy, That men clepeth the Epyphany. **1389** *Eng. Gild* 45 þe thred shal bene þe soneday aftir þe fest of Epiphanie. **13**.. *Ibid.* 103 Ye sunday nest aftere the pyffanye. *c* **1410** LOVE *Bonavent. Mirr.* viii. (ed. Pynson) C vj, Of the Epyphanye to saye the open shewynge of oure lorde Jhesus. **1549** *Bk. Com. Pr.* xix b, The firste Sonday after the Epiphanye. **1661** USSHER *Power Princes* II. (1683) 225 The sixth day of January, which we call the Epiphany. **1782** PRIESTLEY *Corrupt. Chr.* II. VIII. 133 The Epiphany..is observed in the East.

attrib. *c* **1450** *Life St. Cuthb.* (Castle Howard MS.) 1747 þan come þe Epiphany day. **1876** GRANT *Burgh Sch. Scotl.* II. v. 183 The morning after Epiphany day. **1884** A. J. BUTLER *Coptic Churches Egypt* I. i. 22 The large Epiphany tank..forms a regular part of a Coptic church.

b. *transf.*

1647 CRASHAW *Poems* 166 May the great time in you still greater be, While all the year is your Epiphany.

epiphany² (ɪ'pɪfənɪ). [ad. Gr. ἐπιφάνεια manifestation, striking appearance, *esp.* an appearance of a divinity (in N.T. applied to the advent or 'appearing' of Christ), f. ἐπιφανής manifest, conspicuous, related to ἐπιφαίνειν: see prec.]

1. A manifestation or appearance of some divine or superhuman being.

a **1667** JER. TAYLOR *Serm.* III. ix. (R.), Him..they beheld transfigured, and in a glorious epiphany on the mount. **1677** GALE *Crt. Gentiles* II. III. 193 The Grecians in commemoration of these epiphanies or apparitions of their gods instituted certain Festival-dayes. **1826** E. IRVING *Babylon* II. VI. 121 The second coming of Christ; the glorious Epiphany of God our Saviour. **1847** GROTE *Greece* II. xxx. (1849) IV. 141 Probably all..sincerely believed in

the epiphany of the goddess. **1870** F. HALL in Wilson's tr. *Vishnu-purána* v. 3 The first definition of Hayagríva makes him an epiphany of Vishńu. **1879** FARRAR *St. Paul* I. 164 Transported beyond all thought of peril by that divine epiphany, he [Stephen] exclaimed, etc.

2. *transf.* and *fig.*

1840-1 DE QUINCEY *Style Wks.* XI. 257 There had been two manifestations or bright epiphanies of the Grecian intellect. **1881** BLACKIE *Lay Serm.* v. 186 The statesman has yet to make his epiphany who, etc.

epipharyngeal (ˌɛpɪfəˈrɪndʒɪəl), *a.* [f. Gr. ἐπί upon + φάρυγξ, φάρυγγ-ος + -(E)AL.] Situated above the pharynx.

1871 HUXLEY *Anat. Vert.* iii. 57 The uppermost articulations [of the branchial arches]..form the epipharyngeal bones.

epipharynx (ɛpɪˈfærɪŋks). *Zool.* [f. EPI- 1 + PHARYNX b.] In insects, a membranous lining (see quot. 1826); esp. in Diptera, a piercing organ (see quot. 1897); also in Arachnida, a chitinous plate (see quot. 1909).

1826 KIRBY & SPENCE *Introd. Entomol.* III. xxxiii. 359 Epipharynx (the Epipharynx). A small valve under the Labrum, that in many Hymenoptera closes the Pharynx, and is an appendage of its upper margin. **1897** PARKER & HASWELL *Text-bk. Zool.* I. xi. 592 A projection of the roof of the mouth cavity (epipharynx) is present in some Insects. **1909** *Cambr. Nat. Hist.* IV. xviii. 459 In those free living Mites which have undergone no great modification of the mouth parts two other portions can be distinguished, the upper lip or 'epipharynx', and the 'lingua'. **1957** RICHARDS & DAVIES *Imms's Textbk. Ent.* (ed. 9) III. 589 (*Diptera*) The labrum..is dorsally well sclerotized but ventrally more membranous, this surface sometimes being termed the epipharynx. *Ibid.* 669 (*Siphonaptera*) The epipharynx is a long slender organ which is ventrally grooved. *Ibid.* 676 (*Hymenoptera*) An epipharynx is well developed and trilobed in the higher forms, the median lobe being pointed and projecting. **1962** *Science Survey* XVII. 273 The flow of air passes between the floor of the pharynx and the little flap-like epipharynx, and is interrupted by movements of the latter.

epiphenomenal (ˌɛpɪfɪˈnɒmɪnəl), *a.* [f. EPIPHENOMEN(ON + -AL.] Of the nature of an epiphenomenon; relating to epiphenomena.

1899 J. WARD *Naturalism & Agnosticism* II. xiv. 100 From the standpoint of naturalism a world described in such terms is epiphenomenal. **1924** *Glasgow Herald* 29 Aug. 10 He maintained that mind was not epiphenomenal. **1929** C. S. MYERS *Psychol. Conceptions* 22 The old view expressed by Spencer..was that consciousness has arisen as an 'epiphenomenal' product of living matter when physiological processes became too complex to work automatically. **1943** A. M. FARRER *Finite & Infinite* ix. 99 'Beauty' has been regarded as a quality epiphenomenal upon sense-data. **1957** G. E. HUTCHINSON *Treat. Limnol.* I. i. 3 To the geologist the dam therefore is an epiphenomenal afterthought, while to the limnologist it makes all the difference in the world.

epipheˈnomenalism. [f. prec. + -ISM.] The theory that consciousness is an epiphenomenon, i.e. a secondary result and by-product of the material brain and nerve-system. So **epipheˈnomenalist**, one who holds this theory; also as *adj.*

1899 J. WARD *Naturalism & Agnosticism* II. xii. 34 Doctrine of conscious automatism or psychical epiphenominalism examined. **1903** A. E. TAYLOR *Elem. Metaphysics* 317 The epiphenomenalist theory is largely adopted by the workers in the physical sciences. **1915** G. F. STOUT *Man. Psychol.* (ed. 3) 98 Perhaps the word which best characterises the general position is epiphenomenalism. Consciousness is regarded as a superfluous apparition or phenomenon which unaccountably crops up at a certain stage in the course of material processes. **1922** W. R. INGE *Outspoken Ess.* 2nd Ser. 6 Not only does epiphenomenalism (as Plotinus said long ago) 'make soul an affection, or disease, of matter'. **1949** *Mind* LVIII. 124 Epiphenomenalism has outstanding merits, heuristic and educational. It teaches the student to take very seriously indeed the search for the neural correlates of his mental processes. *Ibid.*, It is refreshing..to read a clear defence of a frankly epiphenomenalist position.

epiphenomenon (ˌɛpɪfɪˈnɒmɪnən). *Path.* Pl. **epiphenomena.** [f. EPI- + PHENOMENON.]

a. Something that appears in addition; a secondary symptom. Also *transf.*

1706 in PHILLIPS. **1731-1800** in BAILEY. **1874** VAN BUREN *Dis. Genit. Org.* 93 Stricture is only an epiphenomenon, and not the disease itself. **1876** BRISTOWE *Theory & Pract. Med.* (ed. 2) 105 Fever is always secondary to some specific or other disease of which it is a mere epiphenomenon or symptom. **1882** *Nature* XXVI. 640 Trombes and tornadoes are short epiphenomena of cyclones.

b. *spec.* in *Psychol.* Applied to consciousness regarded as a by-product of the material activities of the brain and nerve-system.

1890 W. JAMES *Princ. Psychol.* I. v. 129 But this would be a quite autonomous chain of occurrences, and whatever mind went with it would be there only as an 'epiphenomenon', an inert spectator. **1899** J. WARD *Naturalism & Agnosticism* II. 37 The newly coined phrase *epiphenomenon* (or, as the Germans say, *Begleiterscheinung*). **1913** J. M. BALDWIN *Hist. Psychol.* II. iv. 60 This charge [of materialism] is frankly accepted..by those, such as Maudsley, who accept the 'epiphenomenon' theory of consciousness; to them consciousness is merely a by-product, a spark thrown off by the engine, the brain. **1952** W. SPROTT *Social Psychol.* 208 Marxists have never taken ideas as mere epi-phenomena. **1965** H. KUHLENBECK in J. R. Smythies *Brain & Mind* 156 Yet, in this respect, consciousness remains either an 'epiphenomenon' or a parallel, not 'causally' involved phenomenon... The term 'epiphenomenon' stresses the 'vectorial' or one-way, open transformation from public physical space-time into private perceptual space-time.

epiphloem (ɛpɪˈfləʊɛm). *Bot.* Also **-phlœum.** [f. Gr. ἐπί upon, EPI- + φλόος = φλοιός bark: see PHLOEM.] The outermost or corky bark.

1839 J. LINDLEY *Introd. Bot.* (ed. 3) I. 89 When the substance called *cork* is formed, the epiphlœum consists of polyhedral cells. **1866** LINDLEY & MOORE *Treas. Bot.* 1109/2 *Suber*.., cork. The epiphlœum of bark, when it acquires an elastic soft texture, and is preternaturally enlarged. **1900** B. D. JACKSON *Gloss. Bot. Terms*, Epiphloem.

‖**epiphonema** (ˌɛpɪfəʊˈniːmə). [L. *epiphōnēma*, a. Gr. ἐπιφώνημα, f. ἐπιφωνέειν to call to, f. ἐπί upon + φωνέειν to speak out, f. φωνή voice.]

1. *Rhet.* An exclamatory sentence or striking reflection, which sums up or concludes a discourse or a passage in the discourse.

1579 E. K. *Gloss. Spenser's Sheph. Cal.* May 304 *Such end*, is an Epiphonema, or rather the moral of the whole tale. **1622** PEACHAM *Compl. Gentl.* 80 What excellent Allegories ..what Epiphonema's. **1659** HAMMOND *On Ps.* cxlv. 17 *annot.*, Witness that solemn Epiphonema, His mercy endureth for ever. **1727** POPE, etc. *Art Sinking* 115 The epiphonema or exclamation [may be learned] frequently from the bear-garden. **1870** tr. *Lange's Comm. Song of Sol.* iii. 5 The epiphonema to the daughters of Jerusalem has a subordinate significance as a refrain.

b. *transf.*

1664 EVELYN *Sylva* (1776) 649 Those who may take these wonders for a florid Epiphonema only of this work.

2. (See quots.)

1654 L'ESTRANGE *Chas. I* (1655) 99 The House gave their Epiphonema and applause at every close and period. **1657** J. SMITH *Myst. Rhet.* 143 Epiphonema..Acclamation, or a shouting of the voyce. **1678-96** in PHILLIPS.

Hence ˌ**epiˌphoneˈmatical** *a.*, of the nature of an epiphonema. ˌ**epiˌphoneˈmatically** *adv.*, in the manner of an epiphonema.

a **1617** BAYNE *Diocesan's Trial* (1621) 3 Christ in his Epiphonematicall conclusion..doth speake of the same. **1644** JESSOP *Angel of Eph.* 12 The Epiphonematicall sentence which is added at the end of each Epistle. **1605** T. HUTTON in *Hieron's Def.* (1607) I. 161 Taking the word Iacob nominatively, vocatively, or epiphonematically.

†ˌ**epiˈphoneme.** *Obs.* Also 6 **epyphoneme**, 7 **epiphonemy.** Anglicized form of prec.

1589 PUTTENHAM *Eng. Poesie* II. xi. (Arb.) 125 The wise man..in th'ende cryed out with this Epyphoneme, *Vanitas vanitatum et omnia vanitas.* **1594** J. KING *On Jonah* (1618) 395 The last thing I proposed is the sentence or Epiphoneme, concluding the conclusion. **1636** J. COLE in *Ann. Dubrensia* (1877) 55 To whom Fame sounds an Epiphonemy. **1637** HEYWOOD *Dialogues* ii. 123 'Tis a short song, and hath as short a theme, And yet it bears a long Epiphoneme.

‖**epiphora** (ɛˈpɪfərə). [L. *epiphora*, a. Gr. ἐπιφορά a bringing to or upon, f. ἐπιφέρειν, f. ἐπί upon + φέρειν to bring.]

1. A sudden afflux of humours; *esp.* 'a superabundant flow of tears, or of an aqueous or serous humour from the eyes' (*Syd. Soc. Lex.*).

1657 *Phys. Dict.*, *Epiphora*, involuntary weeping. **1721-1800** in BAILEY. **1875** H. WALTON *Dis. Eye* 144 It displaced the lower eyelid together with the punctum, and produced epiphora. **1878** T. BRYANT *Pract. Surg.* I. 348 If accompanied by troublesome watering of the eye, epiphora.

2. *Rhet.* (See quots.)

1678 PHILLIPS, *Epiphora*, Force or Impression, a figure in Rhetorick, in which one word is repeated at the end of several Sentences, but differs from Epistrophe, in that it hath respect chiefly to the Matter. **1721-1800** BAILEY.

3. *Logic.* The conclusion of a syllogism or consequent of an hypothesis.

1721 in BAILEY; and in mod. Dicts.

epiphragm (ˈɛpɪfræm). [ad. mod.L. *epiphragma*, Gr. ἐπίφραγμα lid, f. ἐπιφράσσειν, f. ἐπί upon + φράσσειν to fence.]

1. *Zool.* The secretion with which a snail closes the aperture of its shell during hybernation.

1854 WOODWARD *Mollusca* II. 162 The epiphragm is a layer of hardened mucus, sometimes strengthened with carbonate of lime: it is always minutely perforated opposite the respiratory orifice.

2. *Bot.* A membrane closing the mouth of the spore-case in urn-mosses and fungi.

[**1830** LINDLEY *Nat. Syst. Bot.* 323 The membrane, or epiphragma, which occasionally closes up the orifice of the theca.] **1882** VINES *Sachs' Bot.* 341 As the Fungus matures, the upper part of the peridium becomes stretched and flat, forming the Epiphragm.

†**epiˌphylloˈspermous,** *a. Bot. Obs.* [f. EPI- + Gr. φύλλο-ν leaf + σπέρμ-α seed + -OUS.] Having the seeds on the back of the leaves. Cf. DORSIFEROUS.

1704 HARRIS *Lex. Techn.*, Epip[h]yllospermous Plants. **1706** in PHILLIPS. **1760** J. LEE *Bot.* (1776) 150 (Jod.) Such plants as are dorsiferous..have been called also epiphyllospermous. **1828** in WEBSTER; and in mod. Dicts.

epiphyllous (ɛpɪˈfɪləs), *a. Bot.* [f. EPI- + Gr. φύλλ-ον leaf + -OUS.] That grows upon a leaf: predicated **a.** of parasitical fungi; **b.** of stamens inserted upon the perianth; **c.** of flowers growing on the surface of a leaf.

1835 LINDLEY *Introd. Bot.* (1848) II. 380 Epiphyllous; inserted upon the leaf. **1872** OLIVER *Elem. Bot.* I. v. 51 There are [in Daffodil] six stamens, inserted upon the perianth (epiphyllous). **1874** M. COOKE *Fungi* 128 The epiphyllous Coniomycetes.

epiphysary (ɪˈpɪfɪsərɪ), *a. Anat.* [f. EPIPHYS-IS + -ARY².] = EPIPHYSEAL.

1861 BUMSTEAD *Ven. Dis.* (1879) 680 Such productions are often, for a time at least, movable upon the bone beneath, and are then called epiphysary exostoses.

epiphyseal (ɛpɪˈfɪzɪəl), *a. Anat.* Also **epiphysial.** [irreg. f. EPIPHYSI-S + -AL¹.] Pertaining to, or of the nature of, an epiphysis.

1842 *Penny Cycl.* XXIII. 135/2 Between the posterior extremity of the ilia and the first three caudal vertebræ, a distinct epiphyseal piece of bone is wedged in. **1854** OWEN *Skel. & Teeth* (1855) 227 These surfaces..are developed on separate epiphysial plates, which coalesce in the course of growth with the rest of the centrum. **1871** J. ASHHURST *Princ. & Pract. Surg.* xxiii. 418 The epiphyseal cartilages (cartilages of conjunction) become enlarged. **1908** *Practitioner* Oct. 531 The slightest tap on the point of either of these fingers gave her intense pain, referred to a spot corresponding with the epiphyseal line. **1964** L. MARTIN *Clinical Endocrinol.* (ed. 4) iii. 124 Radiological examination will show the characteristic changes of epiphyseal dysgenesis.

‖**epiphysis** (ɛˈpɪfɪsɪs). *Anat.* Pl. **epiphyses.** Also 7 **epiphise, -yse.** [a. Gr. ἐπίφυσις, f. ἐπί upon + φύσις growth. Cf. F. *épiphyse*; also used in English in 17th and 18th c.]

1. An extremity or other portion of a long bone which has originated in a centre of ossification distinct from the rest. Opposed to APOPHYSIS.

1634 T. JOHNSON *Parey's Chirurg.* VI. xxvi. (1678) 147 The wand hath two Epiphyses, or Appendices, the one at the upper end, the other at the lower. **1688** MOULEN in *Phil. Trans.* XVII. 714 The Cartilage had generally an Epiphise or two. **1741** MONRO *Anat.* (ed. 3) 39 An Epiphyse might be mistaken for a Fracture. **1854** OWEN in *Circ. Sc.* (*c* 1865) II. 47/1 These separately ossified ends being termed 'epiphyses'. **1872** MIVART *Elem. Anat.* ii. 23.

2. *abstr.* The process of developing such a growth.

1862 SIR H. HOLLAND *Ess., Hum. Longevity* 108 This period of Epiphysis or completion of bony union.

3. The pineal body of the brain. In full ***epiphysis cerebri.***

1882 A. THOMSON in *Quain's Elem. Anat.* (ed. 9) II. 831 (*heading*) Pineal gland. Epiphysis cerebri... This body is formed by an out-folding from the back part of the inter-brain roof, at a place where the opposite sides remain united by nervous matter afterwards giving rise to the pineal peduncles. **1887** A. C. HADDON *Introd. Study Embryol.* 199 Vertebral epiphyses are peculiar to Mammals. **1889** *Buck's Handbk. Med. Sci.* VIII. 175/1 The *epiphysis* (pineal gland) is not regarded as an important neural ingredient of the brain. **1951** O. LARSELL *Anat. Nerv. Syst.* (ed. 2) xiv. 349 The pineal body or epiphysis..is considered by many students of the brain as a vestigial organ, related to the parietal eye of lower vertebrates.

4. In sea-urchins, a calcareous piece attached to each half of an alveolus.

1906 *Cambr. Nat. Hist.* I. 526 [Echinus] Each tooth is firmly fixed by a pair of ossicles.—Their upper ends are connected by a pair of ossicles called 'epiphyses'. These two epiphyses meet in an arch above. **1959** *Chambers's Encycl.* I. 592/2 The divergent ends of the limbs of each jaw are bridged by ossicles called epiphyses.

epiphysitis (ɛpɪfɪˈsaɪtɪs). *Path.* [-ITIS.] Inflammation of an epiphysis (sense 1) or of the cartilage which separates it from the main bone.

1874 in DUNGLISON *Dict. Med. Sci.* (new ed.). **1889** *Buck's Handbk. Med. Sci.* VIII. 346/1 The most common disease of the hip joint is tubercular epiphysitis, occurring in the growing bone of children. **1908** *Practitioner* Apr. 507 The left elbow was swollen, and the condition was thought to be an epiphysitis. **1970** PASSMORE & ROBSON *Compan. Med. Stud.* II. xxi. 20 Syphilitic infection of growing bones takes the form of epiphysitis and perichondritis.

epiphytal (ɛpɪˈfaɪtəl), *a. Bot.* [f. EPIPHYSIS + -AL¹.] Having the distinctive property of an epiphyte.

1854 HOOKER *Himal. Jrnls.* I. i. 24 Additional epiphytal orchidaceous plants. **1872** OLIVER *Elem. Bot.* II. 266 Many of the tropical species [of Orchids] are called 'air-plants', from their being epiphytal.

epiphyte (ˈɛpɪfaɪt). [f. Gr. ἐπί upon + φυτόν plant.]

1. *Bot.* A plant which grows on another plant; usually restricted to those which derive only support (and not nutrition) from the plants on which they grow.

1861 MISS PRATT *Flower. Pl.* III. 385 Mosses, lichens.. are termed false parasites or epiphytes. **1874** COUES *Birds N.W.* 181 The true epiphytes, like the mistletoe, drawing sap directly from the other plants upon which they fix. **1879** *Cassell's Techn. Educ.* I. 91/2 The Vanilla is an epiphyte, or air-plant.

fig. **1878** M. & F. COLLINS *Vill. Comedy* II. viii. 91 She, a fragile epiphyte, unable to exist alone, fell into the hands of an adroit unscrupulous villain.

2. *Path.* A vegetable parasite on the surface of an animal body.

1847-9 TODD *Cycl. Anat.* IV. 144/1 Gruby detected epiphytes in sycosis.

epiphytic (ɛpɪˈfɪtɪk), *a.* [f. as prec. + -IC.]
1. *Bot.* = EPIPHYTAL.
1830 LINDLEY *Nat. Syst. Bot.* 264 Of the epiphytic class, one only is found so far north as South Carolina. **1874** COUES *Birds N.W.* 197 The nest was hung in a bunch of the Arceuthobium Oxycedri, an abundant epiphytic plant. **1879** WALLACE *Australasia* xi. 222 Epiphytic orchids.
2. *Path.* Of disease: Caused by epiphytes or vegetable parasites.
1869 E. A. PARKES *Pract. Hygiene* (ed. 3) 63 Scabies, and the epiphytic affections especially.

epiphytical (ɛpɪˈfɪtɪkəl), *a. Bot.* [f. as prec. + -AL¹.] = prec.
1861 *Athenæum* 29 June 862 An epiphytical plant..the leaves of which..were filled with pure water. **1880** BALL *Jungle Life Ind.* i. 41 The natives apply the term *banda*, meaning slave, to all parasitical and epiphytical plants.

epiphytically (ɛpɪˈfɪtɪkəlɪ), *adv. Bot.* [f. prec. + -LY².] In the manner of an epiphyte.
1854 HOOKER *Himal. Jrnls.* I. i. 22 On which a species of grass grew epiphytically. **1875** GRIFFITH & HENFREY *Microsc. Dict.* s.v. *Calicium*, Growing..epiphytically on other Lichens.

epiphytous (ɪˈpɪfɪtəs), *a. Bot.* [f. EPIPHYTE + -OUS.] = EPIPHYTAL.
1816 KIRBY & SP. *Entomol.* (1843) I. 385 Regarded by some of our first botanists as an epiphytous fungus, but proved on dissection to be a true gall. **1863** BATES *Nat. Amazon* ii. (ed. 2) 29 The air-roots of epiphytous plants which sit on the stronger boughs of the trees above.

epiplankton (ɛpɪˈplæŋktɒn). *Zool.* [EPI- I.] That portion of the plankton occurring from the surface of the sea to a depth of about one hundred fathoms. Hence ˌ**epiplankˈtonic** *a.*
1898 *Proc. Zool. Soc.* 13 Dec. 1024 As the *Collozoum* occurred in 30% of the Epiplankton hauls..I think we are justified in regarding it as essentially epiplanktonic. **1923** W. A. HERDMAN *Founders Oceanogr.* viii. 231 Epi-, Meso- and Bathy-plankton. **1967** *Oceanogr. & Marine Biol.* V. 320 The animal in question has a larval stage, or by epiplanktonic drift, in which mature stages are carried across the ocean adhering to floating material.

epiplasm (ˈɛpɪplæz(ə)m). *Biol.* [f. EPI- + PLASM.] Protoplasm remaining over after the formation of spores. Hence **epiˈplasmic** *a.*
1887 GARNSEY & BALFOUR tr. *A. de Bary's Compar. Morphol. Fungi* iii. 77 After the orientation of the spores the protoplasm of the ascus shows the characters of a substance, for which I formerly proposed the name of epiplasm. **1906** *Cambr. Nat. Hist.* I. 96 (*Sporozoa*) Some of the cytoplasm of the original cells remains over unused, as 'epiplasm', and ultimately degenerates. **1947** *Nature* 11 Jan. 64/1 When the cytoplasm is cut off from the nuclear vacuole by the spore wall, volutin accumulates in the epiplasm.

†**epiˈplectic**, *a. Obs. rare*⁻¹. [ad. Gr. ἐπιπληκτικός given to rebuking, f. ἐπιπλήσσειν: see EPIPLEXIS.] Of the nature of epiplexis.
1652 URQUHART *Jewel* Wks. (1834) 292 Instruments of elocution..attended on each side respectively with an epiplectick and exegetick modification.

‖**epiplerosis** (ˌɛpɪplɪəˈrəʊsɪs). [mod.Lat., a. Gr. ἐπιπλήρωσις overfilling, f. ἐπιπληρόειν, f. ἐπί + πληρόειν, f. πλήρης full.] (See quot.)
1847 CRAIG, *Epiplerosis*, in Pathology, overfilling, extensive distension, as of the veins or arteries with blood.

epipleural (ɛpɪˈplʊərəl), *a. Anat.* [f. Gr. ἐπίπλευρ-ος (f. ἐπί upon + πλευρά rib, side) + -AL¹.] Situated upon a rib. Also quasi-*sb.*
1866 OWEN *Anat. Vertebr.* I. 43 These 'scleral' spines are termed..'epineurals', 'epicentrals', and 'epipleurals', according to the vertebral element they may adhere to. **1870** ROLLESTON *Anim. Life* 20 Each rib..has an epipleural process. **1880** GUNTHER *Fishes* 77 The abdominal vertebræ have parapophyses developed with epipleural spines.

‖**epiplexis** (ɛpɪˈplɛksɪs). *Rhet.* [L. *epiplēxis*, Gr. ἐπίπληξις, f. ἐπιπλήσσειν, f. ἐπί upon + πλήσσειν to strike.] (See quot.)
1678 PHILLIPS, *Epiplexis*, A figure in Rhetorick which by an elegant kind of upbraiding, indeavours to convince. **1721–1800** in BAILEY; and in mod. Dicts.

‖**epiploce** (ɛˈpɪpləsiː). *Rhet.* [mod.L., a. Gr. ἐπιπλοκή plaiting together, f. ἐπιπλέκειν, f. ἐπί upon + πλέκειν to plait, twine.] 'A figure of rhetoric, by which one aggravation, or striking circumstance, is added in due gradation to another'. (J.)
1678–1706 in PHILLIPS. **1721–1800** in BAILEY. **1828** in WEBSTER; and in mod. Dicts.

epiplocele (ɛˈpɪpləsiːl). *Path.* Also 8 epiploocele. [ad. Gr. ἐπιπλοκήλη, f. ἐπίπλοον (see EPIPLOÖN) + κήλη rupture.] A hernia or rupture in which a portion of the omentum is protruded.
1721–1800 BAILEY, *Epiploocele.* **1758** J. S. *Le Dran's Observ. Surg.* (1771) Dict., *Epiplocele.* **1849–52** TODD *Cycl. Anat.* IV. 986/2 An epiplocele..might readily be mistaken for an additional testicle.

epiploic (ɛpɪˈpləʊɪk), *a. Anat.* [f. next + -IC.] Of or pertaining to the epiploön or omentum.
1656–81 BLOUNT *Glossogr.* s.v. *Veine*, Dexter Epiploick veine, the second branch of the spleen veine. **1731–6** in BAILEY. **1830** R. KNOX *Béclard's Anat.* 98 Examples of those prolongations are seen in the omentum and epiploic appendages.

epiploön (ɛˈpɪpləʊɒn). Also 6 epipleon. [mod.L., a. Gr. ἐπίπλοον, f. ἐπιπλέειν to sail or float on; the epiploön floating as it were on the intestines.]
1. The caul or omentum, a fatty membrane enwrapping the intestines.
1541 R. COPLAND *Guydon's Quest. Chirurg.*, What is Epypleon, and wherof is it composed? **1667** *Phil. Trans.* II. 552 The Epiploon, or the Double Membrane, which covers the Entrals of Animals, and is fill'd with Fat. **1870** ROLLESTON *Anim. Life* 4 The curtain-like omentum or epiploon.
2. *Entom.* (See quots.)
1826 KIRBY & SP. *Entomol.* IV. 115 What some regard as a real liver, others look upon as an epiploon or caul. *Ibid.* (1828) IV. xliv. 219 Chiefly the epiploon or fat of the larva. **1834** McMURTRIE *Cuvier's Anim. Kingd.* 322 The epiploon or *corps graisseux*.

epiploscheocele (ˌɛpɪˈplɒskɪəʊˌsiːl). *Path.* [f. Gr. ἐπίπλο-ον (see prec.) + ὄσχεο-ν scrotum + κήλη rupture.] A hernia or rupture in which a portion of the omentum descends into the scrotum.
In mod Dicts.

epipod (ˈɛpɪpɒd). *Zool.* Shortened form of EPIPODITE.
1893 T. R. R. STEBBING *Hist. Crustacea* 41 Huxley supposes that this valve may represent the epipod. **1911** *Encycl. Brit.* XVII. 457/1 In the maxillipeds and the trunk-legs it is common to find..a seven-jointed stem, the endopod, from which may spring two branches, the epipod from the first joint, the exopod from the second.

epipodial (ɛpɪˈpəʊdɪəl), *a.* [f. EPIPODI-UM + -AL¹.] Pertaining to or resembling the epipodium.
1877 HUXLEY *Anat. Inv. An.* viii. 510 There are very large epipodial lobes, by the aid of which some species propel themselves like Pteropods. **1878** BELL *Gegenbauer's Comp. Anat.* 337 The epipodial gill is arranged circularly in the Placophora.

epipodite (ɛˈpɪpədaɪt). *Anat.* [f. EPIPOD-IUM + -ITE.] A long, curved appendage to the basal joint or coxopodite of the anterior ambulatory limbs of some Crustacea.
1869 NICHOLSON *Zool.* 176 The protopodite bears a process which serves to keep the gills apart, and is termed the epipodite. **1877** HUXLEY *Anat. Inv. An.* vi. 328 Each epipodite is, in fact, expanded at its upper extremity into a broad bilobed membrane.
Hence **eˌpipoˈditic** *a.*, resembling an epipodite.
1877 HUXLEY *Anat. Inv. An.* vi. 364 The branchiæ..resemble not a little the epipoditic branchiæ of Astacus.

epipodium (ɛpɪˈpəʊdɪəm). *Pl.* -a. [mod.L., ad. Gr. ἐπιπόδιον, neut. of ἐπιπόδιος, f. ἐπί upon + πούς, ποδ-ός foot.]
1. *Zool.* A muscular lobe developed from the lateral and upper surfaces of the foot of some molluscs.
1877 HUXLEY *Anat. Inv. An.* viii. 503 Near its extremity are two lateral fleshy lobes which perhaps correspond with the epipodia of other Mollusks.
2. *Bot.* A form of disc consisting of glands upon the stipe of an ovary. Also the stalk of the disc itself.
1866 in *Treas. Bot.*

epipolic (ɛpɪˈpɒlɪk), *a. Physics.* [f. Gr. ἐπιπολ-ή surface + -IC.] **a.** Of or pertaining to the surface; taking place on the surface. **b.** Of or pertaining to epipolism. ***epipolic dispersion***: Herschel's term for the dispersion of light on the surface of a body; = FLUORESCENCE.
1845 HERSCHEL in *Phil. Trans.* CXXXV. 147 This singular mode of dispersion..which..I shall venture to call epipolic, from ἐπιπολή, a surface. **1848** W. GROVE *Contrib. Sc.* in *Corr. Phys. Forces* 349 Epipolic actions will..assume a much more important place in physics. *c* **1865** J. WYLDE in *Circ. Sc.* I. 54/1 Epipolic Dispersion. We have..noticed the epipolic appearance whilst pouring semi-congealed oil from a glass bottle.

epipolism (ɪˈpɪpəlɪz(ə)m). *Physics.* [f. EPIPOLIC + -ISM.] Epipolic dispersion; FLUORESCENCE.

epipolize (ɪˈpɪpəlaɪz), *v. Physics.* [f. EPIPOLIC + -IZE.] *trans.* To change into the epipolic condition; to cause to exhibit the phenomena of fluorescence.
Hence **eˈpipolized** *ppl. a.*, **eˈpipolizing**.
1845 HERSCHEL in *Phil. Trans.* CXXXV. 148 An epipolized beam of light (meaning thereby a beam which has been transmitted through a quiniferous solution and undergone its dispersing action) is, etc. *Ibid.* 153 An epipolizing surface. *c* **1865** J. WYLDE in *Circ. Sc.* I. 54/1 The passage of the epipolised rays is completely stopped.

epipteric (ɛpɪpˈtɛrɪk), *a. Anat.* [f. Gr. ἐπί upon + πτερόν wing + -IC.] ***epipteric bone*** or ***ossicle***, a small Wormian bone sometimes found between the parietal and the great wing of the sphenoid. Also as *sb.* = epipteric bone.
1879 W. H. FLOWER *Catal. Osteology* I. p. xi, The small supplementary ossifications at the upper end of the alisphenoid, which may be called epipterics. **1884** *Jrnl. Anat. & Physiol.* 219 Professor Flower has drawn attention to the fact, that..where the frontal and squamosal bones articulate..the union is brought about by means of a Wormian bone..uniting with the frontal or squamosal, this intercalary ossicle he termed the epipteric bone. **1902** CUNNINGHAM *Text-bk. Anat.* 127 They [*sc.* Wormian bones] occur commonly about the pterion, and in this situation are called epipteric bones (Flower). **1967** *Gray's Anat.* (ed. 34) 375 One or more [sutural bones], the pterion ossicles or epiteric [*sic*] bones, sometimes exist between the sphenoidal angle of the parietal bone and the greater wing of the sphenoid bone.

epipterous (ɪˈpɪptərəs), *a. Bot.* [f. Gr. ἐπί upon + πτερόν wing + -OUS.] Of seeds: Bearing wings at the summit.
1866 in *Treas. Bot.*

epipterygoid (ɛpɪpˈtɛrɪgɔɪd). *Anat.* [EPI- I.] A slender vertical bone which is situated above the pterygoid in the skull of certain living reptiles and of primitive tetrapods. Also *attrib.* or as *adj.*
1897 PARKER & HASWELL *Text-bk. Zool.* II. 297 Extending nearly vertically downwards from the prootic to the pterygoid is a slender rod of bone, the epipterygoid. **1912** J. S. KINGSLEY *Compar. Anat. Vertebr.* 82 An 'ascending process' which reaches the upper margin of the trabecula, and which, in many reptiles, often ossifies as the epipterygoid bone. **1956** A. S. ROMER *Osteol. Reptiles* iii. 64 The epipterygoid extends as a rodlike structure toward the skull roof.

epipubic (ɛpɪˈpjuːbɪk), *a. Anat.* [See next.] Situated on the pubis; of the nature of an epipubis; = MARSUPIAL A. *adj.* 2 b.
1897 PARKER & HASWELL *Text-bk. Zool.* II. 162 [Elasmobranchii] In some cases a median epipubic process projects forwards from the pelvic arch. *Ibid.* 489 [Marsupials, Echidna] With the anterior border of the pubes are articulated a pair of large epi-pubic or 'marsupial' bones. **1951** G. R. DE BEER *Vert. Zool.* (ed. 2) xli. 390 Nearly all Marsupials have a marsupial pouch in the female and epipubic bones in both sexes.

epipubis (ɛpɪˈpjuːbɪs). *Anat.* [EPI- I.] A cartilage or bone in front of the pubis in amphibians, marsupials, or reptiles.
1897 PARKER & HASWELL *Text-bk. Zool.* II. 282 Attached to the anterior border of the pubic region there occurs in many Urodela and in Xenopus, a rod of cartilage, forked in front, the epipubis. **1942** L. H. HYMAN *Compar. Vertebr. Anat.* (ed. 2) iv. 57 [In marsupials] this pouch..is supported by a V-like pair of marsupial bones (epipubes) projecting forward from the anterior end of the pelvic girdle.

epirhizous (ɛpɪˈraɪzəs), *a. Bot.* [f. Gr. ἐπί upon + ῥίζ-α root + -OUS.] Growing on a root.
1866 in *Treas. Bot.*

epirot (ɪˈpaɪrət). Also (sense b) Epirote (ɪˈpaɪrəʊt). [ad. Gr. ἠπειρώτης, f. ἤπειρος mainland, inland of a country as opposed to the coast.]
†**a.** One who dwells inland. *Obs. rare*⁻¹.
1660 JER. TAYLOR *Duct. Dubit.* II. i, The Greek and the barbarian, the epirot and the maritime.
b. (With capital initial.) A native or inhabitant of ancient or modern Epirus in north-western Greece and southern Albania; also as *adj.*
[**1642** HOWELL *For. Trav.* (1868) x. 50 You must go amongst the Mountaines and places of fastnesse, as the Epirotiques in Greece, the Heylanders in Scotland, the Brittaines in Wales.] **1835** W. M. LEAKE *Trav. N. Greece* ii. 68 The Epirotes seem to have been quite prepared to receive the Roman yoke. **1844** G. FINLAY *Greece under Romans* iv. 411 Carians, Paionians, Epirots, and Macedonians. *Ibid.* 435 The slave population of Attica and Laconia were replaced by tribes of Epirot or Albanian peasants. **1915** J. BUCHAN *Thirty-Nine Steps* i. 21 He has a bodyguard of Epirotes that would skin their grandmothers. *Ibid.* iv. 82 Epirote guards. **1932** G. N. CROSS *Epirus* i. 5 Theopompus ..speaks of fourteen Epirot tribes. *Ibid.* ii. 20 In the days of King Pyrrhus..the Epirots were a united people. **1957** D. M. NICOL *Despotate of Epiros* i. 15 The native Epirotes.. were a warlike people. *Ibid.* 17 The possession of most of the Epirote and Albanian coast-line and islands..had been granted to Venice.

epirrhema (ɛpɪˈriːmə). *Antiq.* [ad. Gr. ἐπίρρημα, f. ἐπί upon, after + ῥῆμα word, saying.] In the Attic Old Comedy, a speech addressed by the Coryphæus to the audience after the Parabasis. Hence **epirrheˈmatic** *a.*
1835 W. R. HAMILTON tr. *Süvern's Ess. Birds Aristoph.* 96 The second epirrhematic parabasis. **1887** *Amer. Jrnl. Philol.* VIII. 183 His [*sc.* Zielinski's] theory of the original 'epirrhematic' composition of a comedy as compared with the 'epeisodic' of a tragedy.

episcleral (ɛpɪˈsklɪərəl), *a. Anat.* [f. EPI- + Gr. σκληρ-ός hard + -AL¹.] Belonging to, or placed upon, the sclerotic or hard outer coat of the eye.
1861 BUMSTEAD *Ven. Dis.* (1879) 703 Some of the infiltrations..which have been described as belonging to the conjunctiva proper, have had their origin in the episcleral tissue. **1879** P. SMITH *Glaucoma* 22 Engorgement of episcleral vessels.

episcleritis (ˌɛpɪsklɪəˈraɪtɪs). *Path.* [f. as prec. + -ITIS.] An inflammation of the connective tissue covering the sclerotic coat of the eye.
1861 BUMSTEAD *Ven. Dis.* (1879) 702 Episcleritis begins commonly as a small hyperæmic spot, usually about a line from the margin of the cornea. **1878** T. BRYANT *Pract. Surg.* I. 320 Episcleritis is a somewhat rare disease.

episcopable (ɪˈpɪskəpəb(ə)l), *a.* [f. L. *episcop-us* bishop + -ABLE.] Qualified for appointment as a bishop.
1676 MARVELL *Gen. Councils* Wks. 1875 IV. 132 The deacons..would prick on to render themselves capable and episcopable, upon the first vacancy. **1680** HOBBES *Considerations* 43 The rest of the Clergy, Bishops and Episcopable men. **1884** *Pall Mall G.* 31 May 12/1 The Prime Minister has taken four years to discover that episcopable men exist outside his own ecclesiastical party.

episcopacy (ɪˈpɪskəpəsɪ). [f. late L. *episcopātus* the office or dignity of a bishop. See EPISCOPAL and -ACY.]
†**1.** Oversight; ecclesiastical authority. *Obs.*
1659 GAUDEN *Tears Ch. Eng.* 23 First three, afterward five Patriarchs had the general Episcopacy..over all the Christian World.
2. Government of the church by bishops; the system of church government which comprises three distinct orders, bishops, presbyters or priests, and deacons.
1647 CLARENDON *Hist. Reb.* I. (1843) 35/2 There was little more than the name of episcopacy preserved in that church. **1691** WOOD *Ath. Oxon.* I. 248 He was never a cordial friend to Episcopacy, but rather a patron of the Non-conformists. **1790** BURKE *Fr. Rev.* 80 Is the house of lords to be voted useless? Is episcopacy to be abolished? **1860** FORSTER *Gr. Remonstr.* 87 In the year 1570, the institution of episcopacy in the Protestant church was openly assailed by the Lady Margaret's professor of divinity at Cambridge.
3. The position or office of bishop. *rare.*
1685 A. LOVELL tr. *Simon's Crit. Hist. Relig.* 23 They observe not exactly the Age that is required for Priesthood and Episcopacy. **1869** LECKY *Europ. Mor.* (ed. 2) 86 Priests who attained the episcopacy.
4. The period during which a bishop holds his office; = EPISCOPATE. Now *rare.*
1660 JER. TAYLOR *Duct. Dubit.* II. iii. §11 By their differing presidencies or episcopacies. **1816** C. SHARP *Hist. Hartlepool* 20 During the episcopacy of Bishop Poor. **1844** LINGARD *Hist. Anglo-Sax. Ch.* (1858) II. xi. 171 Aldhelm died..in the fifth year of his episcopacy.
5. *concr.* The body of bishops in the aggregate.
1757 BURKE *Abridgm. Eng. Hist.* Wks. X. 38 Long may we enjoy our Church under a learned and edifying episcopacy. **1885** *Manch. Exam.* 10 Jan. 5/2 A usurping priesthood and an aggressive episcopacy. **1889** *Standard* 14 Sept. 5/3 The Episcopacy are still active in the preliminaries of the Electoral campaign.

episcopal (ɪˈpɪskəpəl), *a.* and *sb.* [a. Fr. *épiscopal*, ad. late L. *episcopālis*, f. *episcopus* BISHOP.]
A. *adj.*
1. Of or pertaining to a bishop or bishops.
1485 *Act 1 Hen. VII*, c. 4 Archbishops and Bishops, and other Ordinaries, having Episcopal jurisdiction. **1675** OGILBY *Brit.* 4 A City..Dignified with an Episcopal See. **1765** BLACKSTONE *Comm.* I. ii. (R.), The usual mode of elevating to the episcopal chair. **1877** W. JONES *Finger-ring* 210 The episcopal ring..was considered a symbol of sacerdotal authority.
2. Pertaining to, or of the nature of, episcopacy. †Formerly also of persons: Advocating or supporting episcopacy.
1651 BAXTER *Inf. Bapt.* 145 The Episcopall Party are far more confirmed in their way by it. *a***1674** CLARENDON *Hist. Reb.* IX. (1843) 592/2 The maintenance and support of the episcopal government in England. **1692** LUTTRELL *Brief Rel.* (1857) II. 379 By removing diverse of the kirk party and putting in episcopall men. **1704** NELSON *Fest. & Fasts* (1739) 530 The Christian Church..gives full Testimony in behalf of Episcopal Government.
3. Of a church: Constituted on the principle of episcopacy. Often *spec.* (with initial capital) of the Anglican Church, of which in Scotland and the United States it is the ordinary designation; also with prefixed adj. in the names of certain other religious bodies, as ***Methodist Episcopal***, ***Reformed Episcopal***. Hence of buildings used for worship, clergy, forms of service, etc.: Belonging to such a church.
In U.S. sometimes of persons, = EPISCOPALIAN *a.* 1.
1752 HUME *Ess. & Treat.* (1777) I. 69 The established clergy were episcopal. **1806** *Gazetteer Scotl.* 277 The episcopal chapel. *a***1831** A. KNOX *Rem.* (1844) I. 59 The distress of the English Episcopal Church during the Usurpation. **1844** S. WILBERFORCE *Hist. Prot. Episc. Ch. Amer.* (1846) 437 It would be difficult to find, in the whole Episcopal communion throughout America, one specimen, etc.
†**B.** *sb.* An adherent of episcopacy; one belonging to the Episcopal church; = EPISCOPALIAN.
1708 SWIFT *Sacram. Test.* Wks. 1755 II. I. 137 The dissenting episcopals. **1716** M. DAVIES *Ath. Brit.* II. 310 Twenty Episcopals perchance to one Kirker of the Calvinistical Order. **1823** *Blackw. Mag.* XIV. 181 Good episcopal as I am, you have sickened me.

episcopalia (ɪpɪskəˈpeɪlɪə), *sb. pl.* [neut. pl. of late L. *episcopālis* EPISCOPAL.] Episcopal belongings, e.g. vestments, buildings.
1865 BRANDE & COX *Dict. Sci.* (ed. 3) I. 798/1 *Episcopalia* or *Onera Episcopalia*, in ecclesiastical history, synodals or other customary payments from the clergy to their bishop. **1903** *Daily Chron.* 23 Jan., To St. Joseph's College at Mill-hill testator left his episcopal vestments and other episcopalia. **1914** W. E. BEET *Med. Papacy* 13 Symmachus was a busy builder, and in his erection of *episcopalia* over against the vestibule of St. Peter's may be seen the first beginnings of the Vatican.

episcopalian (ɪˌpɪskəʊˈpeɪlɪən), *a.* and *sb.* [f. late L. *episcopāli-s* (see EPISCOPAL *a.* and *sb.*) + -AN.]
A. *adj.*
1. Belonging to an episcopal church, *esp.* (usually with initial capital) to the Anglican Church.
1768 in Chauncy *Lett.* 66 The numbers and size of episcopalian churches. **1796** MORSE *Amer. Geog.* I. 454 The Episcopalian churches are respectable. **1840** SIR J. STEPHEN *Eccl. Biog.* (1850) II. 405 A long line of episcopal and episcopalian successors. **1844** S. WILBERFORCE *Hist. Prot. Episc. Ch. Amer.* (1846) 440 In New York, where the Episcopalian body is possessed of endowments, free churches have been opened for the poor.
2. Of an episcopal character. *rare.*
1822 *Blackw. Mag.* XI. 431 A wig, the episcopalian dimensions of which were reduced to suit it the better to the climate. **1822** T. L. PEACOCK *Maid Marian* ix, The departure of king Richard from England was succeeded by the episcopalian regency of the Bishops of Ely and Durham.
B. *sb.* **a.** An adherent of episcopacy. **b.** (Usually with initial capital.) One who belongs to an episcopal church; *esp.* a member of the Anglican Church.
1738 NEAL *Hist. Purit.* IV. 77 The Episcopalians were at this time excepted from a legal toleration. **1764** SECKER *Answ. Mayhew's Observ.* (R.), We are considered as..professed episcopalians. **1824** COLERIDGE *Aids Refl.* (1848) I. 7 The diffusion of light and knowledge through this kingdom..by Episcopalians and Puritans, from Edward VI. to the Restoration, was as wonderful as it is praiseworthy. **1825** LD. COCKBURN *Mem.* 305 Our episcopalians used to be so few that, etc. **1844** S. WILBERFORCE *Hist. Prot. Episc. Ch. Amer.* (1846) 98 They would not hear of granting to Episcopalians the most ordinary toleration.
Hence **Episco'palianism**, the principles distinctive of an Episcopalian. **Episco'palianize** *v.*, to make (a person) an Episcopalian. **Episco'palianized** *ppl. a.*
1846 *Eclectic Rev.* Feb. 233 Is not episcopalianism itself brought into question? **1865** WRIGHT *Hist. Caricat.* xxi. (1875) 360 The Puritans..looked upon Episcopalianism as differing in little from popery. **1886** *Pall Mall G.* 30 Mar. 11/1 The Presbyterian religion..would have suited the people..much better than our Episcopalianism. **1837** J. LANG *New S. Wales* II. 258 The Episcopalianized Scots Presbyterian.

episcopalism (ɪˈpɪskəpəˌlɪzm). [f. EPISCOPAL + -ISM.] That theory of church polity which places the supreme authority in the hands of an episcopal or pastoral order; if this authority is in practice exercised by any recognized head of the church it is only as the delegate of this order as a whole, and with their consent. Held in the Church of Rome by the Gallicans (but dogmatically rejected by the Vatican Council), and in various Reformed churches. Distinguished from *territorialism*, and COLLEGIALISM, q.v.

episcopality (ɪˌpɪskəˈpælɪtɪ). [f. EPISCOPAL + -ITY.] In various nonce-uses: †**a.** That which constitutes episcopacy. †**b.** The office or dignity of a bishop. **c.** The quality appropriate to a bishop; a bishop-like bearing.
*c***1618** E. BOLTON *Hypercritica* ii. §3 Enemies of Ecclesiastical Episcopality. **1636** PRYNNE *Unbish. Tim.* 158 Those Lordly Pontificians..will needs claime all their Episcopalities by a divine right. **1647** *16 New Quaeres to Praelates* Ded. 2 These Quaeres will proove fatall to your Popedomes, Episcopalities, etc. **1885** OXENHAM *Stud. Eth. & Relig.* 16 There is a sort of episcopality about them—if one may be permitted to coin the word.

episcopalize (ɪˈpɪskəpəlaɪz), *v. rare.* [f. as prec. + -IZE.] *trans.* To attribute an episcopal position to (a person); to speak of as a bishop.
1823 *New Monthly Mag.* VIII. 245 To episcopalize Saint Lazarus is quite as anachronismatical a sin as clapping the tiara upon the unconscious head of Saint Peter.

episcopally (ɪˈpɪskəpəlɪ), *adv.* [f. as prec. + -LY².] In an episcopal manner: **a.** In the rank of a bishop; as a bishop is or does. **b.** With reference to ordination: By the hands of a bishop. **c.** On the basis of episcopal government.
1680 *Answ. Stillingfleet's Serm.* 27 A Minister..ordained (and so Episcopally or Classically approved in his abilities for that function). **1702** *Lond. Gaz.* No. 3853/4 A French Minister, who is Episcopally Ordained. **1782** BURKE *Corr.* (1844) II. 464 To conclude episcopally, I heartily pray God Almighty to prosper your administration. **1785** COWPER *Tiroc.* 365 The father who designs his babe a priest, Dreams him episcopally such at least. **1804** *Ann. Rev.* II. 206 Some displeasure arose that Wesley should act thus episcopally. **1862** *Pall Mall G.* 8 Oct. 2 An episcopally ordained priest. **1882–3** S. M. HOPKINS in Schaff *Relig. Encycl.* III. 2554/2 Prescribed forms of prayer became characteristic of episcopally constituted churches.

†**e'piscopant.** *Obs.* [ad. med.L. *episcopant-em*, pr. pple. of *episcopāre* to hold a bishopric, f. *episcopus.*] One who holds a bishopric; a bishop.
1641 MILTON *Prel. Episc.* (1851) 90 Their usurping and over provender'd Episcopants.

†**episco'parian,** *a.* and *sb. Obs.* [f. L. *episcop-us* bishop + *-āri-us* (see -ARY) + -AN.]
A. *adj.* = EPISCOPAL A. 2.
1691 WOOD *Ath. Oxon.* II. 305 The episcoparian government then lately thrown out of doors.
B. *sb.* = EPISCOPALIAN B. a.
1649 NEEDHAM *Case Commw.* 89 Prudent Toleration of opinions in matters of Religion could never be proved yet, by any of our Episcoparians and Presbyterians..to be repugnant to the Word. **1671** H. STUBBE *Reply* 31, I most associated my self with the Episcoparians. **1691** WOOD *Ath. Oxon.* II. 316 As for his railing at the Episcoparians, all readers of his books..may..behold [it]. **1721–1800** in BAILEY; and in mod. Dicts.

episcopate (ɪˈpɪskəpət), *sb.* [ad. L. *episcopātus*, f. *episcopus* bishop.]
1. The office or dignity of a bishop.
1641 HEYWOOD *Priest, Judge, & P.* 1 The late firme scite of our Episcopate. **1744** ARNALD *Comm. Bk. Wisdom* Ded. (T.), These great qualities at length conducted you so deservedly to the episcopate. **1782** PRIESTLEY *Corrupt. Chr.* II. x. 251 [They] endeavoured to make the episcopate..a higher degree. **1833** CRUSE *Eusebius* VI. xxx. 249 Honoured with the episcopate in the churches of Pontus.
2. An episcopal see, a bishopric.
1807 G. CHALMERS *Caledonia* I. III. v. 357 Bede, who gave the history of that episcopate. **1847** DISRAELI *Tancred* II. v, The Church Temporalities' Bill in 1833..suppressed ten Irish episcopates. **1861** STANLEY *East. Ch.* vii. (1869) 227 The Episcopate of Egypt had but a doubtful existence in early times.
3. The period during which a bishop holds office.
1868 FREEMAN *Norm. Conq.* (1876) II. ix. 416 In the third year of his episcopate he was driven out. **1885** *Manch. Courier* 16 June 4/7 That was the 123rd church he had consecrated during the 15 years of his episcopate.
4. The bishops regarded as a collective body.
1842 PUSEY *Crisis Eng. Ch.* 140 First as to the Episcopate, the Evangelic Bishops in Germany are a creation of the state. **1859** *Lit. Churchm.* V. 117/2 The Committee advise the increase of the Episcopate. **1865** MAFFEI *Brigand Life* II. 98 The instructions to the Neapolitan episcopate.

†**e'piscopate,** *v. Obs.* [f. med.L. *episcopāt-* ppl. stem of *episcopāre*, f. *episcopus* bishop.]
a. *intr.* To act as a bishop; to become a bishop. **b.** *trans.* To make (a person) a bishop.
1641 MILTON *Ch. Govt.* ii. (1851) 106 There he [S. Peter] commits to the Presbyters only full authority both of feeding the flock, and Episcopating. *a***1661** FULLER *Worthies* (1840) II. 379 Though all the rest were episcopated, doctor Fulke was but doctor Fulke still. **1705** WYCHERLEY 7 Apr. in *Pope's Lett.* (1735) I. 9 A Bishop gains his Bishoprick by saying he will not Episcopate.

episcopation (ɪpɪskəˈpeɪʃən). [f. L. *episcopus* + -ATION.] The action of making a person a bishop; the fact of becoming a bishop.
1872 M. COLLINS *Pr. Clarice* II. xviii. 213 Her [a bishop's wife's] quasi-episcopation can hardly be expected to affect you. *a***1876** —— in *Pen Sketches* (1879) I. 251 The story of the episcopation of the saintly Ken.

e'piscopature. ? *nonce-wd.* = EPISCOPATE 4.
1884 *Macm. Mag.* July 184 Our Episcopature will soon owe it only to the actor's forbearance that he does not deny Christian burial to bishops.

episcope (ˈɛpɪskəʊp). [f. EPI- + -SCOPE.] A magic lantern for projecting images of opaque objects. So **episcopic** (-ˈskɒpɪk) *a.* (see quot. 1911).
1909 in *Cent. Dict.* Suppl. **1911** *Encycl. Brit.* XVI. 186/1 If the light traverses the object, the projection is said to be diascopic, if by reflected light, episcopic. **1922** *Nature* CIX. 56/1 The episcope, shown by Newton and Co., is a marked improvement on forms previously seen, and should come into more general use for the projection on screens of opaque objects. **1937** [see DIASCOPE].

episcopé (ɪˈpɪskəpɪ): see EPISCOPY.

†**e'piscopiˌcide.** *Obs. rare.* In 8 episcopacide. [f. L. *episcop-us* bishop + -(I)CIDE 2.] The crime of murdering a bishop.
1692 in COLES. **1708** J. CHAMBERLAYNE *St. Gt. Brit.* I. II. vii. (1743) 66 The Law of England..made the offences of Parricide & Episcopacide equal. **1751** CHAMBERS *Cycl.*, *Episcopacide*, the crime of murdering a bishop by one of his own clergy.

eˌpiscopi'zation. *rare.* [f. next + -ATION.] The action of making (a person) a bishop.
1861 *Sat. Rev.* XI. 337/2 The episcopization of Deans.

episcopize (ɪˈpɪskəpaɪz), *v.* [f. L. *episcop-us* bishop + -IZE.]
1. *trans.* To make or consecrate (a person) a bishop. Also *absol.*
1649 SELDEN *Laws Eng.* II. xxvii. (1739) 127 The course of Episcopizing continued the same as formerly it had been. **1820** SOUTHEY *Wesley* II. 407 There seems reason to believe that Wesley was willing to have been episcopized upon this

occasion. **1832** WILSON in *Blackw. Mag.* XXXI. 286 The very first act of the Devil's own reign Would episcopize Cobbett, and canonize Paine.

2. To rule as a bishop. Also *to episcopize it.*
1679 PRANCE *Addit. Narr. Pop. Plot* 46 Sent over into England by the Pope to Episcopize it over all English Catholicks. *a* **1745** W. BROOME *Poems, Death J. Shute* (R.), By whom he's prelated above the skies, And then the whole world's his t' episcopise.

b. *intr.* To assume the character of a bishop.
1820 SOUTHEY *Wesley* II. 310 An inclination to episcopize was evidently shown in this language.

3. To bring under episcopal government; also, to render episcopalian.
1767 CHAUNCY *Let.* (1768) 37 Their main view was to episcopise the Colonies. **1769** *Public Advertiser* 3 June 4/1 Mr. Apthorpe's Scheme of episcopizing America. **1868** *Lessons Mid. Age* 176 Not..free to use any active means for episcopising the Church of Scotland.

Hence **e'piscopizing** *vbl. sb.*; also *attrib.*
1768 W. LIVINGSTON *Let. Bp. Llandaff* 19 The episcopising of dissenters. **1768** in Chauncy *Let.* 45 The episcopising plan is of a very interesting nature. **1840** *Tait's Mag.* VII. 71 The mission of the apostles was not an episcopizing of geographical dioceses. **1881** BLACKIE *Lay Serm.* viii. 247 His father's episcopising schemes and theories.

†e,piscopo'factory. *Obs. rare*$^{-1}$. The making of bishops.
1649 SELDEN *Laws Eng.* II. xxxvi, The King himself had a power of Episcopofactory, without Conge d'eslire.

episcopolatry (ɪ,pɪskəʊ'pɒlətrɪ). *rare.* [f. Gr. ἐπίσκοπος bishop + λατρεία worship.] 'Worship' of bishops.
1867 *Ch. & State Rev.* 9 Mar. 224 The practical danger of episcopolatry is less imminent than might be supposed. **1882** *Ch. Times* 22 Dec. 915 Those Englishmen who, in the violence of their recoil from Presbyterianism and Congregationalism, have cherished proclivities in the direction of Episcopolatry.

episcopy (ɪ'pɪskəpɪ). Also episcopé. [ad. Gr. ἐπισκοπή watching over, f. ἐπί over + σκοπή watch.]
1. Survey; superintendence; *spec.* (in form *episcopé*) of pastoral government.
1641 MILTON *Ch. Govt.* II. iii. (1851) 158 The censor in his morall episcopy. **1957** *Relations betw. Anglican & Presb. Churches* 20 Among the functions of the ordained ministry ..is..that of exercising oversight or 'episcopé'. Apostolic mission and authority continue to be exercised through this 'episcopé', which includes pastoral care, the continuance of the ordained ministry through ordination, and the guardianship of truth and exclusion of error. **1963** R. S. LOUDEN *True Face of Kirk* iv. 39 In Presbytery..there has been gathered up this apostolic authority to ordain and induct—the oversight of the flock of God (*Episcopé*), regularly continued from Christian generation to generation, is corporately exercised and transmitted through Presbytery, in good church order.

†2. Government of the church by bishops. *Obs.*
1660 JER. TAYLOR *Duct. Dubit.* I. iv. §9 It was the universal doctrine of the Church of God for many ages..that episcopy is the divine, or apostolical institution.

3. *concr.* The body or bench of bishops. *rare.*
1874 DIXON *Two Queens* III. XVIII. iii. 337 A view supported by the English episcopy.

episcotister (ɛpɪskə'tɪstə(r)). [f. Gr. ἐπισκοτίζειν to throw a shadow or darkness over, f. ἐπί upon + σκότος darkness: see -IST and -ER[1].] An apparatus for admitting light into a darkened room by means of adjustable discs.
1905 TITCHENER *Exper. Psychol.* II. 80 The episcotister is placed as close as possible to the screen. **1939** *Brit. Jrnl. Psychol.* Oct. 140 Adjustment of the variable episcotister aperture.

episematic (ɛpɪsiː'mætɪk), *a. Biol.* [f. EPI- + SEMATIC *a.*] Designating natural colours, markings, etc., which serve to assist animals of the same species to recognize each other. (Opp. to APOSEMATIC *a.*)
1890 E. B. POULTON *Colours of Animals* xvii. 337 Recognition Markings..assist an individual of the same species, and are termed Episematic. *a* **1908** —— *Ess. Evol.* 357 Episematic Colours are the logical antithesis of Aposematic, their object being to assist in keeping friends together instead of keeping enemies at a distance. **1926** A. S. PEARSE *Animal Ecol.* ix. 299 Epigamic..might have been considered the same as episematic colors if they had not been believed to be concerned with..appreciation of beauty. **1934** J. S. HUXLEY in *Proc. 8th Internat. Ornith. Congr.* (1938) 454 Episematic function can also in many cases among birds be readily deduced for certain colour-patterns. **1959** VAN TYNE & BERGER *Fund. Ornith.* iii. 102 A means (especially in gregarious birds) of attracting the attention of other individuals of the same species... ('Episematic' colors and patterns.).

episepalous (ɛpɪ'sɛpələs), *a.* [f. EPI- + SEPAL + -OUS.] Growing upon the sepals of the calyx.
1882 VINES *Sachs' Bot.* 627 The epipetalous and episepalous position of the stamens.

episiorrhaphy (,ɛpɪsaɪ'ɒrəfɪ). [f. Gr. ἐπίσειον the region of the pubes + -ραφία, f. ῥάπτειν to sew.] An operation for the relief of prolapsus uteri by a suture.
1872 F. THOMAS *Dis. Women* 176 Closure of the vagina may be accomplished by two operations, episiorrhaphy and obliteration of the canal.

episiotomy (ɛpɪsɪ'ɒtəmɪ). *Surg.* [f. Gr. ἐπίσιον pubic region + -TOMY.] Incision of the vulval orifice to facilitate parturition; an operation of this kind.
1878 A. E. BROOMALL in *Amer. Jrnl. Obstetrics* XI. 524 In 56 cases, when the perineum was unyielding,..I incised the vaginal orifice, and in nearly all of these cases I demonstrated..that episiotomy saved the perineum. **1953** CARTER & DODDS *Dict. Midwifery* 166/1 A midwife may perform an episiotomy if she considers it to be in the interest of her patient. **1954** G. I. M. SWYER *Repr. & Sex* xi. 127 A properly timed and executed episiotomy will nearly always prevent a third degree tear.

episkeletal (ɛpɪ'skɛlɪtəl), *a. Anat.* [f. EPI- + SKELET-ON + -AL[1].] Of muscles: Situated upon the skeleton, *i.e.* lying above the horizontal plane of the vertebral axis.
1871 HUXLEY *Anat. Vert.* ii. 45 The episkeletal muscles are developed out of the protovertebræ.

episodal ('ɛpɪsəʊdəl), *a.* [f. next + -AL[1].] Of the nature of an episode; = EPISODIAL, EPISODIC.
1876 *Macm. Mag.* XXXIV. 200 He replaces such passages and semi-cadences by novel episodal matter.

episode ('ɛpɪsəʊd). Also 7-8 episod. [a. Gr. ἐπεισόδ-ιον, neut. of ἐπεισόδ-ιος coming in besides, f. ἐπί in addition + εἴσοδος entering, f. εἰς into + ὁδός way. Cf. Fr. *épisode.*]
1. In the Old Greek Tragedy, the interlocutory parts between two choric songs, because these were originally interpolations.
1678 T. RYMER *Trag. Last Age* 12 Thespis introduc'd the Episods, and brought an Actor on the stage. **1762** J. BROWN *Poetry & Mus.* iv. (1763) 42 Not only the Part of the tragic Choir, but the Episode or interlocutory Part would be also sung. *a* **1789** BURNEY *Hist. Mus.* (ed. 2) I. viii. 146 The custom of setting the Episodes as the acts of a play.

2. An incidental narrative or digression in a poem, story, etc., separable from the main subject, yet arising naturally from it.
1679 DRYDEN *Dram. Wks.* 369 The happy Episode of Theseus and Dirce. **1780** JAS. HARRIS *Wks.* (1841) 423 The dry didactic character of the Georgics [of Virgil] made it necessary they should be enlivened by episodes and digressions. **1839** THIRLWALL *Greece* II. 183 Herodotus introduces an episode, which..seems..at first sight strangely misplaced. **1865** TYLOR *Early Hist. Man.* i. 11 Familiar episodes, belonging to the medieval 'Reynard the Fox'.

3. *transf.* An incidental 'passage' in a person's life, in the history of a country, the world, an institution, etc.
1773 GOLDSM. *Stoops to Conq.* II. i, The terrors of a formal courtship, together with the episode of aunts, grandmothers and cousins. **1818** COBBETT *Pol. Reg.* XXXIII. 100 To answer..a hundred letters in a week, by way of episode in your other labours. **1875** LYELL *Princ. Geol.* (ed. 10) I. I. x. 203 Like the Glacial episode before mentioned. **1855** MILMAN *Lat. Chr.* (1864) V. IX. vii. 368 The conquest of Constantinople by the Latins, that strange and romantic episode in the history of the Crusades.

4. *Mus.* (See quot.) Also in other musical forms (see quot. 1947[1]).
1869 OUSELEY *Counterp.* xxii. 169 In ordinary fugues..it is usual to allow a certain number of bars to intervene from time to time, after which the subject is resumed..The intervening bars thus introduced are called Episodes. **1947** *Penguin Music Mag.* Dec. 29 *Italian Symphony.* A fresh subject (in technical language an 'episode') is introduced. **1947** A. EINSTEIN *Mus. Romantic Era* xvii. 311 It might even be called a rondo with varied theme and alternating episodes.

episodial (ɛpɪ'səʊdɪəl), *a.* [f. Gr. ἐπεισόδι-ος (see prec.) + -AL[1].] = EPISODIC.
1857 *Fraser's Mag.* LVI. 336 One of the most attractive of the episodial chapters.

episodic (ɛpɪ'sɒdɪk), *a.* [f. EPISODE + -IC.] Of or pertaining to, or of the nature of, an episode; incidental, occasional.
1711 SHAFTESB. *Charac.* (1737) III. 268 The same Episodick Liberty..which we have maintain'd in the preceding Chapters. **1725** POPE *Odyss.* XII. *note* (R.), This episodic narration gives the Poet an opportunity to relate, etc. **1856** MASSON *Ess., Story Year* 1770. 257 Such incidents as these, episodic as they were to the two great topics of Wilkes and the Constitution and the growing disaffection of the American colonies. **1879** GEO. ELIOT *Theo. Such* vi. 123 His episodic show of regard.

b. Also, of a literary work: Characterized by the frequent introduction of episodes.
1866 FELTON *Anc. & Mod. Gr.* I. iv. 68 It [the Mahabharata] is more episodic than the other [the Ramayana].

episodical (ɛpɪ'sɒdɪkəl), *a.* [f. as prec. + -AL[1].]
1. = EPISODIC.
1667 DRYDEN *Ess. Dram. Poesie* Wks. 1725 I. 23 Or the episodical ornaments, such as descriptions, Narrations, and other beauties, which are not essential to the Play. *a* **1720** SHEFFIELD (Dk. Buckhm.) *Wks.* (1753) II. 222 The bas-reliefs and little squares above are all episodical paintings of the same story. **1810** *Edin. Rev.* XV. 297 There are..no episodical conversations. **1837** MISS SEDGWICK *Live & Let Live* (1876) 12 One of those episodical reforms that occur in every drunkard's life.

2. *transf.* Of persons: Coming like an episode; casual, irregular.
1824 SCOTT *St. Ronan's* xvii, And in a short time lost all recollection of his episodical visitor. **1888** P. THORNE in *Advance* (Chicago) 9 Aug., The episodical people have become episodical once more in their attendance, and only the faithful few are left.

Hence **epi'sodically** *adv.*, in an episodical manner; by way of episode.
1753 CHESTERF. *Lett.* III. ccci. 29 There he gives episodically the best account I know of the customs and manners of the Turks. **1835** SOUTHEY *Life Cowper* I. vii. 201 Mr. Newton's life is too remarkable..to be treated episodically. **1868** E. EDWARDS *Raleigh* I. xii. 239 Sir Walter has told the story himself (episodically, and as illustrating.. a topic).

episome ('ɛpɪsəʊm). *Genetics.* [f. EPI- + -SOME[4].]
a. A small particle which together with a larger 'protosome' was postulated to constitute a gene, and which by its absence was held to cause gene mutation. (No longer current.)
1931 D. H. THOMPSON in *Genetics* XVI. 268 The gene [is pictured] as consisting of a main particle firmly anchored in the chromosome with varying numbers of one or more kinds of other particles attached. The main particle is called the protosome and the attached particles the episomes. **1966** E. A. CARLSON *Gene* xiii. 111 Using the position effect hypothesis with Thompson's protosome-episome chain theory of the gene, Dobzhansky tried to account for the various Bar mutations and their reversions.

b. [ad. F. *épisome* (Jacob and Wollmann 1958, in *Compt. Rend.* CCXLVII. I. 154).] A particle sometimes found in cells, esp. in bacteria, which has a genetic function and which can either exist and multiply as an independent unit or become attached to a chromosome and multiply with it. Hence **epi'somal** *a.*, pertaining to or having the character of an episome; **epi'somally** *adv.*, by means of or as a result of episomes.
1960 *Bacteriol. Rev.* XXIV. 209/1 For genetic factors that are additions to..the genome,..Jacob and Wollman..have proposed the term 'episomes'. **1962** *New Scientist* 6 Sept. 514/3 An episome is a genetically active particle which can exist in two alternative forms. *Ibid.*, These ideas have led Jacob and Wollman to propose the 'episome' hypothesis of extra-chromosomal inheritance. Some examples of episomally controlled inheritance..would be those controlling non-essential cell functions. *Ibid.*, The episomal determinants of bacteria. **1965** *Times* 26 Feb. 15/4 They are known collectively as episomes, a term which conveys merely that they are particles additional to the chromosome. **1968** J. A. SERRA *Mod. Genetics* III. xix. 24 Certain properties in bacteria are transmitted by the type of particle called an episome. *Ibid.* xxiii. 643 Variable location of the sex locus is better explained in terms of transposition of an episomal element, as in the dipteran *Megaselia scalaris.*

epispastic (ɛpɪ'spæstɪk), *a.* and *sb. Med.* [ad. mod.L. *epispasticus*, a. Gr. ἐπισπαστικός, f. ἐπισπάειν, f. ἐπί towards + σπάειν to draw.]
A. *adj.* Drawing out humours; blistering.
1657 *Phys. Dict.*, *Epispastick*, blistering plaisters, or any other strong drawing plaister. **1861** HULME tr. *Moquin-Tandon* II. III. iii. 133 Vinegar of Cantharides (Epispastic).

B. *sb.* A blister; a substance used for blisters.
1675 GREW *Anat. Plants* (1682) 286 A Blister..the common Effect of Fire, or any strong Epispastick. **1748** RICHARDSON *Clarissa* (1811) VIII. 253 Thy Epispastics may strip the parchment from thy plotting head. **1830** LINDLEY *Nat. Syst. Bot.* 7 Ranunculus flammula and sceleratus are powerful epispastics. **1876** BARTHOLOW *Mat. Med.* (1879) 536 An epispastic is a remedy which excites inflammation and vesication.

episperm ('ɛpɪspɜːm). *Bot.* [f. Gr. ἐπί upon + σπέρμα seed: see EPI- and SPERM *sb.*] The exterior covering of a seed. Hence **epi'spermic** *a.*
1819 J. LINDLEY tr. *Richard's Observ. Fruits & Seeds* 17 The covering or integument peculiar to the seed being the most exterior of its constituent parts, I give it the name of Episperm. *Ibid.* 32 If..the entire kernel..is immediately covered over by the episperm, it is called epispermic. **1861** R. BENTLEY *Man. Bot.* 337 The terms most frequently used, are *testa* or *episperm* for the outer coat.

epispore ('ɛpɪspɔə(r)). [f. EPI- + SPORE. In mod.L. *episporium.*]
1. The outer membrane or covering on the spore of a lichen or fern.
1835 LINDLEY *Introd. Bot.* (1848) II. 128 The membrane by which it [the spore] is covered..soon distends into a transparent Epispore. **1874** COOKE *Fungi* 60 This rosy colour..accumulating exclusively upon the epispore.

2. *Zool.* In Sporozoa (see quot.).
1903 E. R. LANKESTER *Zool.* I. II. 189 The spore-envelope or sporocyst [in Gregarines] consists of two layers, an outer clear and delicate epispore, and an inner refringent and tough endospore.

epistal, obs. var. of EPISTYLE.

epistasis (ɛ'pɪstəsɪs). [Gr. ἐπίστασις a stopping, stoppage, (also) scum on urine, f. ἐφιστάναι to stop, check.]
1. *Med.* **a.** The checking of any discharge, as of blood or menses. **b.** A pellicle that forms on the surface of urine after it has stood. *rare*$^{-0}$
[**1849** F. ADAMS *Genuine Wks. Hippocrates* II. Aphorisms vii. no. 35 When the scum on the surface is fatty and copious, it indicates acute diseases of the kidneys. [*Note*] It appears from Galen, that in some copies he found *epistasis*, and in others *hypostasis*; the one evidently referring to the scum on the surface, and the latter to the sediment: he favours the former reading, and understands it to refer to melting of the fat in the neighbourhood of the kidneys.]

1807 MORRIS & KENDRICK *Edin. Med. & Physical Dict.* II. Gloss., *Epistasis*, see Epischesis [= 'a suppression of excretions']. Also the substance on the surface of the urine. **1848** in DUNGLISON. **1889** in *Cent. Dict.* **1934** in WEBSTER; and in mod. med. dicts.

2. *Genetics.* [Back-formation from EPISTATIC *a.*] The expression of one hereditary character to the exclusion of another when the two are controlled by alleles of different genes; also more widely, any interaction of non-allelic genes.

1917 *Genetics* II. 613 (*index*) Epistasis. **1932** SINNOT & DUNN *Princ. Genetics* (ed. 2) v. 82 Epistasis..is similar to dominance except that it occurs between different factors instead of between the two members of an allelomorphic pair. **1965** J. A. SERRA *Mod. Genetics* I. iii. 63 Some of the most striking examples of inhibitor-type epistasis are provided by genes which control pigmentation in animals or plants. **1966** *McGraw-Hill Encycl. Sci. & Technol.* II. 327 Each gene may have favorable effects in some combinations and unfavorable effects in others, such as over-dominance and many kinds of epistasis, so that its average effect may be small.

epistasy (ɛ'pɪstəsɪ). *Genetics.* [ad. Gr. ἐπιστασία dominion: see -Y³ and cf. prec.] = EPISTASIS 2.

1918 R. A. FISHER in *Trans. R. Soc. Edin.* LII. 404 A similar deviation from the addition of superimposed effects may occur between different Mendelian factors. We may use the term Epistacy [*sic*] to describe such deviation. **1949** DARLINGTON & MATHER *Elem. Genetics* vii. 157 Epistasy comes in at all stages of development, early and obvious or late and inferential.

‖**e'pista,tes.** *Obs.* [mod.L. *epistatēs*, a. Gr. ἐπιστάτης one who is set over, f. ἐπί over + στα- stem of ἱ-στάναι to set; in Athens, the president of the ἐκκλησία or assembly.] An overseer, a superintendent.

1651 BIGGS *New Disp.* 41 Where Reason sits sole Epistates. **1731** BAILEY vol. II, *Epistates*, a commander or person who has the direction and government of a people.

epistatic (ɛpɪ'stætɪk), *a. Genetics.* [prob. f. EPI- + Gr. στάσις standing, position, state, after HYPOSTATIC *a.*, HYPOSTASIS; but cf. Gr. ἐπιστάτης one who is set over (see EPISTATES), ἐπιστασία dominion; a derivation directly from ἐπιστάτικος of government, (also) standing still, or from ἐπίστασις EPISTASIS is unlikely.] Of, exhibiting, or caused by epistasis (sense 2). Const. *to, on, over.* (Opp. to HYPOSTATIC *a.* 3.)

1907 W. BATESON in *Science* 15 Nov. 653/2 Till lately we spoke of the relations between the gray color of the mouse to the black color in terms of dominance. Those terms, strictly speaking, should only be applied to members of the same allelomorphic pair. We can perhaps best express the relation between the gray and the black by the use of the metaphor 'higher and lower', and I therefore suggest the term *epistatic* as applicable to characters which have to be, as it were, lifted off in order to permit the lower or *hypostatic* character to appear. **1909** —— *Mendel's Princ. Heredity* ii. 41 (*Primula*). The magenta shades have a factor epistatic to crimson and pink. *Ibid.* v. 98 The pale ivory is due to a factor epistatic on the bright yellow. **1910** L. DONCASTER *Heredity* vi. 75 The presence of a higher member of the series obscures or prevents the development of the lower. This is expressed by saying that grey is 'epistatic' over black and chocolate, and black over chocolate. **1949** DARLINGTON & MATHER *Elements of Genetics* vii. 157 A gene removing an organ is.. obviously epistatic to one modifying that organ. **1968** M. W. STRICKBERGER *Genetics* xv. 239 Epistatic or interaction effects are also known..in which the phenotypic expression caused by one pair of genes depends upon alleles at another gene pair.

‖**epistaxis** (ɛpɪ'stæksɪs). [mod.L., a. Gr. ἐπίσταξις, f. ἐπιστάζειν to bleed at the nose, f. ἐπί upon + στάζειν to let fall in drops.] Bleeding from the nose.

1793 T. BEDDOES *Let. Darwin* 8 The blood, discharged by Epistaxis. **1866** A. FLINT *Princ. Med.* (1880) 264 Epistaxis is the most common form of hemorrhage.

episteler, obs. variant of EPISTLER.

episteme (ɛpɪ'stiːmɪ). *Philos.* [Gr. ἐπιστήμη knowledge.] Scientific knowledge, a system of understanding; *spec.* Foucault's term for the body of ideas which shape the perception of knowledge at a particular period. Cf. EPISTEMOLOGY.

[**1856** W. E. JELF *Note to Aristotle's Ethics* II. vi. 39 Ἐπιστήμη, here used loosely for 'system', which proceeds on rules, as distinguished from empiricism, which acts without rules. **1907** R. D. HICKS *Aristotle's De Anima* 307 The student who has a capacity for learning, has only potential knowledge when compared with one who has gone through a course of study. Here ἐπιστήμη is related to ἄγνοια as actual to potential. **1961** in WEBSTER. **1966** M. FOUCAULT *Mots & Choses* 13 Ce qu'on voudrait mettre au jour, c'est le champ épistémologique, *l'épistémè* [sic] où les connaissances, envisagées hors de tout critère se référant à leur valeur rationnelle ou à leurs formes objectives, enfoncent leur positivité et manifestent ainsi une histoire qui n'est pas celle de leur perfection croissante, mais plutôt celle de leurs conditions de possibilité.] **1967** P. P. HALLIE in *Encycl. Philos.* VIII. 368/2 There is *episteme* or science, when all our firmly certain conceptions combine into a system. **1970** tr. *M. Foucault's Order of Things* x. iii. 365 The 'sciences of man' are part of the modern *episteme* in the same way as chemistry or medicine or any other such science; or again, in the same way as grammar and natural history were part of the Classical *episteme.* **1972** A. M. S. SMITH tr. *M. Foucault's Archaeol. Knowledge* IV. vi. 191 The analysis of discursive formations, of positivities, and knowledge in their relations with epistemological figures and with the sciences is what has been called, to distinguish it from other possible forms of the history of the sciences, the analysis of the *episteme.* **1979** N. C. GILLESPIE *Charles Darwin & Probl. Creation* i. 1, I make no claim to embrace all of Foucault's profound, if sometimes extravagant, ideas about 'epistemes',—i.e., the communal presuppositions about knowledge and its nature and limits. **1982** M. M. SLAUGHTER *Universal Lang. & Sci. Taxon. in 17th Cent.* III. 187 (*heading*) The end of the taxonomic episteme.

epistemic (ɛpɪ'stɛmɪk, -'stiːmɪk), *a. Philos.* [f. Gr. ἐπιστήμη knowledge + -IC.] Of or relating to knowledge or degree of acceptance. Hence **epi'stemically** *adv.*

1922 W. E. JOHNSON *Logic* II. p. xix, The charge of circularity or petitio principii is epistemic. **1933** *Mind* XLII. 82 Proof of the actual existence of a material world epistemically depends on just these elements of confusedness and involuntariness characteristic of our sense-awareness. **1936** *Mind* XLV. 270 The analysis of propositions so as to exhibit their reference to the qualitative continuum is called *epistemic* reduction. **1953** K. BRITTON *J. S. Mill* vi. 188 The Experience Philosophy arranges judgements in an 'epistemic order'.

epistemics (ɛpɪ'stiːmɪks), *sb. pl.* (const. as *sing.*). *Philos.* [f. EPISTEMIC *a.*: see -IC.] The scientific (as opp. to philosophical) theory or study of the processes of knowledge (see quot. 1969).

1969 *Guardian* 22 Nov. 9/1 Edinburgh University has just founded a school of epistemics... It has taken the trouble to explain what epistemics is. Or are. 'The word "epistemics"', the university journal explains, 'implies an intention to reformulate some of the key questions about knowledge and to construct formal models of the processes —perceptual, inferential, and linguistic—whereby we may be led to an understanding of the nature of thought.' **1977** C. LONGUET-HIGGINS in Bullock & Stallybrass *Fontana Dict. Mod. Thought* 209/2 Epistemics..signifies the scientific study of knowledge... A more extended definition of epistemics is 'the construction of formal models of the processes—perceptual, intellectual, and linguistic—by which knowledge and understanding are achieved and communicated'. **1979** A. FLEW *Dict. Philos.* 109/1 *Epistemics*, a term coined in Edinburgh University in 1969 to label a new school dedicated to the scientific, as opposed to the philosophical, study of knowledge.

epistemological (ˌɛpɪstiːməʊ'lɒdʒɪkəl), *a.* [f. EPISTEMOLOGY + -ICAL.] Pertaining to EPISTEMOLOGY.

1882 *Mind* VII. 533 What—using a convenient, though hardly current, term—I will distinguish as an *epistemological* doctrine. **1887** *Mind* Jan. 128 Prof. Volkelt expressly declines, as not forming part of the epistemological problem, the inquiries into the metaphysical nature of this relation. **1895** W. JAMES *Coll. Ess. & Rev.* (1920) 399 No conventional restrictions *can* keep metaphysical and so-called epistemological inquiries out of the psychology books. **1955** *Sci. Amer.* Apr. 100/3 This epistemological problem is best solved by following the classical dictum, 'If you can't beat 'em join 'em'.

epistemo'logically, *adv.* [-LY².] In an epistemological manner; with reference or in regard to epistemology.

1882 *Mind.* VII. 535 Epistemologically irrelevant. **1906** *Westm. Gaz.* 9 June 3/2 Epistemologically..Von Hartmann is a transcendental realist who ably defends his views. **1919** *Mind* Jan. 4 There is nothing which I believe to be epistemologically more unsound than this identification of the knower's knowledge or experience with the reality of the object he knows. **1963** J. LYONS *Structural Semantics* iii. 43 A psychologically and epistemologically satisfying theory of our understanding of other languages.

epistemologist (ˌɛpɪstiː'mɒlədʒɪst). [-IST.] One who is versed in epistemology.

a **1897** W. WALLACE *Lect. Nat. Theol.* (1898) 36 The epistemologist..examines the history of our ordinary physical knowledge. **1902** *Encycl. Brit.* XXXII. 55/2 It is only epistemologists, and notably Kant, who so describe individual experience. **1925** J. E. TURNER *Theory Direct Realism* 34 This systematic connection is ignored by Stout, as also by epistemologists in general. **1964** E. A. NIDA *Toward Sci. Transl.* iii. 33 A problem with which epistemologists since Descartes have continued to wrestle.

epistemology (ˌɛpɪstiː'mɒlədʒɪ). [f. Gr. ἐπιστημο-, comb. form of ἐπιστήμη knowledge + -λογία discoursing (see -LOGY).] The theory or science of the method or grounds of knowledge.

1856 FERRIER *Inst. Metaph.* 48 This section of the science is properly termed the Epistemology..It answers the general question, 'What is Knowing and the Known?' or more shortly, 'What is Knowledge?' **1883** *Athenæum* 20 Oct. 492/3 He divides his work into four sections, dealing with epistemology, ontology, anthropology, and ethics.

†ˌ**episte'monical**, *a. Philos. Obs. rare*⁻¹. [f. Gr. ἐπιστημονικ-ός capable of knowledge, f. ἐπιστήμων knowing, f. ἐπιστήμη knowledge + -AL¹.] ? Capable of becoming an object of knowledge.

a **1688** CUDWORTH *Immut. Mor.* IV. v. §5 No Man ever was or can be deceived in taking that for an Epistemonical Truth which he clearly and distinctly apprehends.

episternal (ɛpɪ'stɜːnəl), *a. Anat.* [f. EPISTERN-UM (or its elements) + -AL¹.]

1. Situate upon the sternum or breast-bone. Also, pertaining to the episternum; of the nature of an episternum. ***episternal granules***: 'the rudiments of the omosternal bones' (*Syd. Soc. Lex.*).

1839–47 TODD *Cycl. Anat.* III. 838/1 This central piece [in Chelonia] is bounded anteriorly by the episternal bones. **1859** *Ibid.* V. 259/1 The..left carotid arteries [in man] leaving the chest through the episternal notch. **1872** MIVART *Elem. Anat.* 65 The 'episternal granules' occasionally present in man are replaced in some mammals by considerable horn-like processes.

2. quasi-*sb.*

1852 DANA *Crust.* I. 26 Beyond the episternals, the epimerals normally come next in order.

episternum (ɛpɪ'stɜːnəm). *Anat.* [f. EPI- + STERNUM.] In mammals, the upper part of the sternum or breast-bone; in other animals, applied variously to certain structures adjoining the breast.

1855 OWEN *Skel. & Teeth* 39 The long stem of the episternum covers the outer part of the groove, where it represents the keel of the sternum in birds. **1872** NICHOLSON *Palæont.* 369 Clavicles were present, as well as an interclavicle (episternum).

‖**epis'thotonos.** [erroneously formed after the analogy of OPISTHOTONOS.] = EMPROSTHOTONOS.

1811 HOOPER *Med. Dict., s.v.*, A spasmodic affection of muscles drawing the body forwards. **1847** in CRAIG; and in mod. Dicts.

epistides, -ites, -rites, var. ff. HEPHÆSTITIS.

epistilbite: see EPI- *pref.*

epistle (ɪ'pɪs(ə)l), *sb.* Forms: 1, 5–6 epistole, (5 -toll), 4–5 epistel(l(e, 4–6 episti(l, (4 apistille), 6 epystole, epystle, 3– epistle. [a. OF. *epistle*, *epistole* (mod.F. *épître*), ad. L. *epistola*, a. Gr. ἐπιστολή, f. ἐπιστέλλειν, f. ἐπί on the occasion of + στέλλειν to send. The OE. *epistole* was directly ad. Lat. See PISTLE.]

1. A communication made to an absent person in writing; a letter. Chiefly (from its use in translations from L. and Gr.) applied to letters written in ancient times, *esp.* to those which rank as literary productions, or (after the analogy of 2) to those of a public character, or addressed to a body of persons. In application to ordinary (modern) letters now used only rhetorically or with playful or sarcastic implication.

In the A.V. the word does not occur in the O.T. (but occas. in the Apocrypha); in the N.T. it appears only in sense 2 or analogous uses, *letter* being employed in other cases. Until the present century it was common to speak, *e.g.*, of Cicero's or Pliny's 'epistles'; but *letters* is now the usual word in such cases.

c **893** K. ÆLFRED *Oros.* III. xi. 144 Eall heora ȝewinn awæcnedon ærest from Alexandres epistole. *c* **1374** CHAUCER *Troylus* III. 502 For there was some epistle hem betwene. **1382** WYCLIF *1 Macc.* xv. 1 The kyng Antiochus ..sente epistilis..to Symont. **1432–50** tr. *Higden* (Rolls) I. 111 But truly Seynte Ierom in his epistole to Eugenius expressethe. **1477** EARL RIVERS (Caxton) *Dictes* 43 a, And he wrotte an epistoll to Alexandre. **1529** MORE *Heresyes* I. Wks. 121/1 Holye sainct Austyn in an epystle of hys whyche he wrote to the clargy and the people. **1601** SHAKS. *Twel. N.* II. iii. 169, I will drop in his way some obscure Epistles of loue. *c* **1645** HOWELL *Lett.* IV. i, Epistles, or (according to the word in use) Familiar Letters, may be call'd the larum bels of Love. **1681–6** J. SCOTT *Chr. Life* (1747) III. 426 That there was..a Bishop in Philadelphia, is abundantly evident from Ignatius's Epistle to that Church. **1706** J. LOGAN in *Pa. Hist. Soc. Mem.* X. 165, I was so jaded with long epistles. **1781** GIBBON *Decl. & F.* II. 129 In the epistle or manifesto which he [Julian] himself addressed to the senate and people of Athens. **1839** LYTTON *Richelieu* II. i, Wide flew the doors ..lo, Messire de Beringhen, and this epistle! **1870** E. PEACOCK *Ralf Skirl.* III. 143 It was no uncommon thing for the epistles to lie many days in the post-office window.

b. A literary work, usually in poetry, composed in the form of a letter.

c **1385** CHAUCER *L.G.W.* 305 Prol. (Camb. MS. *c* 1430) What seyth also the epistelle of Ouyde. **1460** CAPGRAVE *Chron.* 81 Ambrose..that wrot many notabel bokes and episteles. **1614** BP. HALL *Epist.* Ded., Further..your Grace shall heerein perceive a new fashion of discourse, by Epistles; new to our language. **1697** DRYDEN *Æneid* Ded. (R.), Horace, in his first epistle of the second book. **1714** *Spect.* No. 618 ⁋3 Let our Poet, while he writes Epistles, though never so familiar, still remember that he writes in Verse. **1751** CHAMBERS *Cycl. s.v.*, The term epistle is now scarce, but for letters wrote in verse, and letters dedicatory.

†**c.** A preface or letter of dedication addressed to a patron, or to the reader, at the beginning of a literary work. *Obs.* See DEDICATORY.

1605 VERSTEGAN *Dec. Intell.* (1628) Pref. Ep., To beginne his Epistle (to a huge Volume) with Constantine the great, etc. **1637** *Decree Star Chamb.* §2 in Milton *Areop.* (Arb.) 10 All and euery the Titles, Epistles, Prefaces, Proems, Preambles, etc. **1653** WALTON *Angler* Ep. Ded. 6, I shall not adventure to make this Epistle longer.

2. *spec.* A letter from an apostle, forming part of the canon of Scripture.

[*a* **1200** *Vices & Virtues* 31 Sanctus Paulus us takð on his pisteles.] *a* **1225** *Ancr. R.* 8 In sein Iames canoniel epistle. *c* **1380** WYCLIF *Serm.* Sel. Wks. II. 277 Poul tellip in þis epistle of fredom of Cristene men. **1432–50** tr. *Higden* (Rolls) I. 149 To whom Paule did wryte an epistole. **1578** *Gude & Godlie Ball.* (1868) 63 The Lordis Supper, as it is writtin in the first Epistil to the Cor. xj. Chap. **1695** LOCKE *Reas. Chr.* (R.), I answer, that the epistles were written upon several occasions. **1704** NELSON *Festiv. & Fasts* vii. (1739)

95 The Epistle..is..an excellent Antidote against the Poison of Gnostick Principles. **1882** FARRAR *Early Chr.* II. 483 Eusebius and Origen seem to have regarded the Epistles [John I, II, III] as genuine.

3. *Eccl.* ***the Epistle***: The extract from one of the apostolical Epistles read as part of the Communion Service.

c **1440** *Gesta Rom.* liv. 373 (Add. MS.) The bere seid the masse: The asse redde the apistille; The Oxe redde the gospell. **1548–9** (Mar.) *Bk. Com. Prayer* 122 b, The priest, or he that is appointed, shall reade the Epistle. **1578** *Gude & Godlie Ball.* (1868) 63 Ane Ballat of the Epistill on Christinmes Euin. **1662** *Bk. Com. Prayer, Communion,* Immediately after the Collect the Priest shall read the Epistle. **1721** BAILEY, *Epistler,* he who reads the Epistles in a Cathedral Church. **1877** J. D. CHAMBERS *Div. Worship* 326 The other Clergy may sit during the Epistle.

4. *attrib.* and *Comb.*, as ***epistle-book***; also **epistle-side** (of the altar), the south side, from which the epistle is read.

1555 EDEN *Dec. W. Ind.* III. IX. (Arb.) 178 My epistell booke whiche I sente vnto yowre holynes. **1885** *Pall Mall G.* 2 Apr. 10/2 The Epistle side of the altar.

epistle (ɪˈpɪs(ə)l), *v.* [f. prec. sb.]

†1. *trans.* To write as a preface or introduction. *Obs. rare*⁻¹.

1671 MILTON *Samson* Pref., In behalf of this tragedy.. thus much beforehand may be epistled.

2. †a. To write a letter to (a person). **b.** To write (something) in a letter. *rare*⁻¹.

1741 MRS. FOLEY in *Mrs. Delany's Corr.* (1861) II. 164 If your fair sister don't epistle me this post. **1852** *Meanderings of Mem.* I. 35 'Tis noted down—Epistled to the Duke.

epistler (ɪˈpɪstlə(r)). Also 7 episteler. [f. as prec. + -ER¹. Cf. EPISTOLER.]

1. The writer of an EPISTLE.

1610 BP. HALL *Apol. Brownists* §13 Let this ignorant epistler teach his censorious answerer. **1657** HOBBES *Absurd Geom.* Wks. 1845 VII. 379 The best of your half-learnt epistlers. **1670** EACHARD *Cent. Clergy* 37 (T.) The young epistler is yours to the antipodes. **1876** M. ARNOLD *Lit. & Dogma* 277 So our Epistler says, 'God is love'.

2. *Eccl.* = EPISTOLER 2.

16.. *Canons Ch. Eng.* xxiv. (T.), The principal minister using a decent cope, and being assisted with the Gospeller and Epistler. **1641** *Life & Death Wolsey* in *Select. Harl. Misc.* (1793) 102 A gospeller and epistler of the singing priests. **1667** *Answ. West to North* 9 Gospelers, Epistelers, Virgers. **1721–1800** in BAILEY; and in mod. Dicts.

†eˈpistling, *vbl. sb. Obs.* [f. EPISTLE *v.* + -ING¹.] *concr.* Epistolary matter, correspondence.

1596 NASHE *Saffron Walden* F., Heere's a packet of epistling as bigge as a packe of woollen cloth.

†eˈpistolar, *sb. Obs.* In 6 apistiller. [ad. med.L. *epistolāre, -ārium.*] The book from which the 'epistle' is read.

c **1530** in Gutch *Coll. Cur.* II. 340 Two Claspes for the great Apistiller of silver and gilte.

†epistolar (ɪˈpɪstələ(r)), *a. Obs.* Also 6 epistolare. [ad. L. *epistolār-is,* f. *epistola*: see EPISTLE.] = EPISTOLARY in various senses.

1579 TWYNE *Phisicke agst. Fortune* II. Ep. Ded. 153 a, The Epistolare Preface of Fraunceis Petrarche. **1649** BP. HALL *Cases Consc.* II. ii. (1654) 81, I have long agoe spent my opinion upon this point, in a large epistolar discourse. **1681** H. MORE *Exp. Dan.* Pref. 50 The third is of the Epistolar Prophecy in the Apocalypse. **1715** M. DAVIES *Ath. Brit.* I. 49 His Epistolar Stile..was rather copious than eloquent.

epistolarian (ɪˌpɪstəʊˈlɛərɪən), *a.* and *sb.* [f. L. *epistola,* after *antiquarian,* etc.]

A. *adj.* Addicted to or occupied in letter-writing.

1838 GRANT *Sk. Lond.* 7 The admirable tactics of these epistolarian impostors.

B. *sb.* A letter-writer.

1807 ANNA PORTER *Hungar. Bro.* ii. (1832) 27 I'll maintain this sweet sermonising epistolarian to be a woman.

epistolarily (ɪˈpɪstələrɪlɪ), *adv.* [f. EPISTOLARY + -LY².] In an epistolary manner, by letter.

1854 THACKERAY *Newcomes* I. 28 Our friendship carried on epistolarily as it has been.

†eˈpistolarly, *adv. Obs.* [f. EPISTOLAR + -LY².] = prec.

1693 W. FREKE *Sel. Essays* xxxiii. 207, I will not say, that ..we may not justly write Epistolarly to a Church.

epistolary (ɪˈpɪstələrɪ), *a.* [ad. F. *épistolaire,* ad. L. *epistolāris,* f. *epistola* EPISTLE.]

1. Of or pertaining to letters or letter-writing.

1656 BLOUNT *Glossogr.* **1682** DRYDEN *Relig. Laici* Pref., The style of them [the verses] is, what it ought to be, epistolary. **1709** STEELE *Tatler* No. 87 ⁋2 The Rules of Epistolary Writing. **1730** *Swift's Corr.* Wks. 1841 II. 636, I seek no epistolary fame. **1780** COWPER *Lett.* 16 Mar., I saw the reason of your epistolary brevity. **1852** MISS MITFORD in L'Estrange *Life* III. xiii. 231 My excellent little maid..has every talent except the talent epistolary.

b. *absol.*

1812 *Examiner* 30 Nov. 753/1 Your Royal Highness stands upon record for your love of the epistolary.

2. Contained in letters; of the nature of letters; carried on by letters.

1706 H. DODWELL *(title),* An Epistolary Discourse, proving from the Scriptures..that the Soul is a Principle naturally Mortal. **1712** ADDISON *Spect.* No. 511 ⁋1, I do intend to continue my epistolary correspondence with thee. *a* **1826** T. JEFFERSON in *Sir J. Sinclair's Corr.* (1831) II. 48, I recall..the days of our former intercourse, personal and epistolary. **1880** E. WHITE *Cert. Relig.* 52 In the epistolary portions of the New Testament, written by the Apostles.

3. Of or pertaining to an 'epistle dedicatory'.

1681 T. MANNINGHAM *Disc.* 63 (T.) Scarce allowing the author one epistolary compliment. *a* **1764** LLOYD *Poems, On Rhyme,* Or with epistolary bow, Have prefac'd, as I scarce know how.

4. Pertaining to 'the epistle' read in the Communion Service.

1722 *Enq. Complutens. Ed. New Test.* in Somers *Tracts* II. 490 The Church of England has..prescrib'd the publick Reading of it in one of her Epistolary Sections.

eˈpistolatory, *a. arch.* [Erroneous formation.] = prec.

1715 M. DAVIES *Ath. Brit.* I. Pref. 24 Of the same Epistolatory kind. **1757** GOLDSM. *Misc. Writings* (1837) III. 466 The next ensuing eight [volumes] contain this lady's epistolatory Correspondence. **1856** *Sat. Rev.* II. 506/1 Admirable, also, are the remarks on epistolatory literature.

epistole, obs. var. of EPISTLE.

epistoˈlean. *rare*⁻¹. A writer of epistles or letters; a correspondent.

18.. MRS. C. CLARKE (Worcester *Suppl.*), He has been a negligent epistolean as well as myself.

epistoler (ɪˈpɪstələ(r)). Also 9 epistoller. [ad. F. *epistolier,* ad. L. *epistolāris,* f. *epistola* EPISTLE.]

1. A letter-writer; = EPISTLER 1.

1637 ABP. WILLIAMS *Holy Table* 136 Whether the Epistoler likes it or no. **1648** C. WALKER *Hist. Independ.* I. 112 A Preamble of great respect and love born to him by the Epistoler. **1880** SAINTSBURY in *Academy* 10 July 20 Or in those [letters] written by epistolers of recognised fame. **1881** *Sat. Rev.* 9 July 41/2 These two great epistolers and speakers.

2. *Eccl.* One who reads the 'epistle' in the Communion Service; = EPISTLER 2.

1530 PALSGR. 217/1 Epystoler at the masse. **1671** H. STUBBE *Reply* 30 But when a greater Man then this Epistoler made me the like Threat, I laugh'd thereat. **1732** NEAL *Hist. Purit.* I. 202 The principal ministers shall wear a Cope, with Gospeller, and Epistoler. **1859** *Lit. Churchm.* V. 69/2 To act as gospeller, epistoler, deacon, subdeacon, etc. **1862** J. SKINNER *Let.* in *Life* xi. (1884) 210, I gospeller, Serjeant epistoller.

epistolet (ɪˈpɪstəlɪt). *nonce-wd.* [f. L. *epistol-a* + -ET¹. Cf. It. *epistoletta.*] A small epistle.

1824 LAMB *Lett.* xiv. *Bernard Barton* 134 You see thro' my wicked intention of curtailing this epistolet.

†epiˈstolic, *a. Obs.* [a. Gr. ἐπιστολικ-ός, f. ἐπιστολή: see EPISTLE.] **a.** = EPISTOLOGRAPHIC. **b.** = EPISTOLARY.

1741 WARBURTON *Div. Legat.* II. 97, Three sorts of letters, the Epistolic, the Hieroglyphic, and the Symbolic. **1760** *Antiq.* in *Ann. Reg.* 156/1 The epistolic [writing], composed of alphabetic characters. **1777** JOHNSON *Let. Mrs. Thrale* 27 Oct., To make a letter..without news, and without a secret, is doubtless, the great epistolick art.

†epiˈstolical, *a. Obs.* [f. as prec. + -AL¹.] = EPISTOLARY.

1655 *Let. Hartlib.* in *Ref. Commonw. Bees* 30 A large Epistolical discourse. **1670** *Let.* in Fox Bourne *Locke* (1876) I. v. 253 You cannot be better pleased with our epistolical converse than I am. *a* **1742** BENTLEY *Lett.* 154 (R.) An epistolical dissertation on John Malelas.

†eˈpistolist. *Obs.* [f. L. *epistol-a* EPISTLE + -IST.] One who writes epistles.

1743 MISS CARTER *Lett.* (1809) I. 28, I am extremely obliged to you..for your account of the Italian epistolists. **1819** SOUTHEY *Lett.* (1856) III. 146 Detestable Dapple; Evil Epistolist; False Fellow. **1853** MIALL *Bases of Belief* IV. §10 (1861) 230 These New Testament epistolists.

eˈpistolizable, *a.* [f. as next + -ABLE.] That may form the subject of a letter.

1827 WHEWELL in Todhunter *Acc. W's Writ.* (1876) II. 87 If any epistolizable matter occurs to me, I will make a shot at him.

epistolization (ɪˌpɪstəlaɪˈzeɪʃən). *rare.* [f. EPISTOLIZE + -ATION.] The writing of letters.

1802 SOUTHEY *Lett.* (1856) I. 195 Remembrances that I always choose to forget in my epistolisation.

epistolize (ɪˈpɪstəlaɪz), *v.* Also 9 epistlize. [f. L. *epistol-a* EPISTLE + -IZE.]

1. *intr.* To write a letter.

c **1645** HOWELL *Lett.* I. I. i, There are some who..Preach when they should Epistolize. **1828** SOUTHEY *Lett.* (1856) IV. 117 This may stand over..till I epistolize again. *a* **1834** LAMB *Final Mem.* viii. 278 Very very tired! I began this epistle, having been epistolising all the morning.

2. *trans.* To write a letter to (a person).

1739 MRS. DELANY *Autobiog. & Corr.* (1861) II. 50 It is not always in my power to do what I like best, or you would have been epistolized much sooner. **1773** GIBBON *Misc. Wks.* (1814) II. 112 Forgive and epistolize me. **1789** COWPER *Let.* 23 June, I hope it will be long before I shall have occasion to epistolize thee again. **1810** BYRON *Let. H. Drury* 3 May, St. Paul need not trouble himself to epistolise the present brood of Ephesians. **1829** WHEWELL in Todhunter *Acc. W's Writ.* (1876) II. 101, I epistolize you in preference to, etc. **1835** *Tait's Mag.* II. 92 He thus retrospectively epistlized his friend.

Hence **eˈpistolizer,** a writer of letters. **eˈpistolizing** *vbl. sb.*

1634 W. WOOD *New Eng. Prosp.* Ded. Note, I should take upon me the usuall straine of a soothing Epistolizer. **1760** STERNE *Let.* 3 Aug. Wks. 1819 IV. 194 A fine set essay in the style of your female epistolizers, cut and trimm'd at all points. **1856** *Chamb. Jrnl.* V. 66 That production so dear to the feminine epistoliser—a crossed letter. *a* **1645** HOWELL *Lett.* I. III. xxxvii, Cryptology, or Epistolizing in a Clandestin way. **1715** tr. *Pancirollus, Rerum Mem.* II. xiv. 364 This way of Epistolizing made use of no Notes. **1804** SOUTHEY *Lett.* (1856) I. 283 Do you admire the catechistical form of epistolizing?

epistolographic (ɪˌpɪstələʊˈgræfɪk), *a.* [ad. Gr. ἐπιστολογραφικ-ός, f. ἐπιστολή (see EPISTLE + γράφ-ειν to write.] Used in the writing of letters. Applied *esp.* to the form of the ancient Egyptian character so employed: called also DEMOTIC and ENCHORIAL. (The Gr. word is thus applied by Clement of Alexandria and Porphyry.)

1699 GALE *Crt. Gentiles* I. I. xi. 64 The method of al Egyptian Leters, which is called Epistolographic. **1862** H. SPENCER *First Princ.* (1870) 349 The hieratic and the epistolographic or enchorial.

So **eˌpistoˈlographer, eˌpistoˈlographist,** a writer of letters. **eˌpistoˈlography,** letter-writing.

1824 DIBDIN *Libr. Comp.* 579 Marcus Tullius Cicero, at once an orator, a philosopher and epistolographer. **1822** *New Monthly Mag.* VI. 20 Your kinsman and epistolographist, Numenius. **1888** M. ARAGNOS in *Amer. Annals of Deaf* Apr. 102 Epistolography amounts almost to a passion with Helen.

epistom(e (ˈɛpɪstɒm, ˈɛpɪstəʊm). *Zool.* The Latin form **epistoma** is also used. [ad. mod.L. *epistoma,* f. Gr. ἐπί upon + στόμα mouth.] An appendage in front of the mouth in Crustacea and certain insects. Also applied to similar parts in arachnids, molluscs, etc.

1852 DANA *Crust.* I. 25 The base of the antennæ is thus cut off from the rest of the epistome. **1860** MAYNE *Expos. Lex.* Add. 1491/2 *Epistoma, epistomis, epistomium,* names for the space between the buccal cavity and origin of the intermediary *antennæ* in the *Crustaceæ Maxillares*; also for the hood of the *Condylopa.* **1878** BELL *Gegenbauer's Comp. Anat.* 160 The mouth..is in one division overhung by a movable process—the epistom. **1880** T. H. HUXLEY *Crayfish* 155 In front of the mouth, the sternal region which appertains, in part, to the antennæ, and, in part, to the mandibles, is obvious as a broad plate..termed the *epistoma.* **1897** PARKER & HASWELL *Text-bk. Zool.* I. 328 (Molluscs), A small lobe—the epistome..—overhangs the mouth and lies between it and the anus. *Ibid.* 499 The head exhibits no segmentation: its sternal region is formed largely by a shield-shaped plate, the *epistoma,* nearly vertical in position. **1909** *Cambr. Nat. Hist.* IV. 291 In *Pterygotus* there is a well-developed epistome..between the mouth and the front margin of the carapace. **1957** RICHARDS & DAVIES *Imms's Textbk. Ent.* III. 587 In holoptic flies... The epistoma is the distal border of the face. *Ibid.* 752 Among Curculionoidea the reduced fronto-clypeal region is often termed the epistoma.

‖**epistrophe** (ɛˈpɪstrəfiː). [mod.L., a. Gr. ἐπιστροφή, f. ἐπί upon + στροφή a turning, f. στρέφειν to turn.]

1. *Rhet.* A figure of speech in which each sentence or clause ends with the same word.

1647 SPRIGGE *Anglia Rediv.* (1854) Addr. 8 Feigned speeches, prosopopeias and epistrophes. *a* **1679** HOBBES *Rhet.* IV. v. 149 Repetition of the same sound in the end is called Epistrophe, a turning to the same sound in the end. **1706** A. BEDFORD *Temple Mus.* v. 95 Epistrophe's, or Endings of the Verses in the same Words. **1845** J. W. GIBBS *Philol. Studies* (1857) 207 Epistrophe..is the repetition of a word at the end of successive clauses; as, 'we are born to sorrow, pass our time in sorrow, end our days in sorrow'.

2. *Philos.* (See quot.)

1856 R. VAUGHAN *Mystics* (1860) I. 72 That doctrine of the Epistrophe—the return of all intelligence by a law of nature to the divine centre.

3. *Bot.* (See quot.)

1882 VINES *Sachs' Bot.* 750 In one mode, which he calls Epistrophe, the protoplasm and chlorophyll-granules collect on the free cell-walls.

epistrophy (ɪˈpɪstrəfɪ). *Bot.* = EPISTROPHE 3.

epistyle (ˈɛpɪstaɪl). *Archit.* Also 7 epistal. [ad. L. *epistȳlium,* Gr. ἐπιστύλιον, f. ἐπί upon + στῦλος pillar.] = ARCHITRAVE.

[**1563** SHUTE *Archit.* C j b, Vpon the Capitall shalbe layde or set Epistilium. *a* **1623** W. PEMBLE *Exp. Zachary* (1629) 160 Pillars of Stone, whose Epistylia or Chapiters were wrought about in fashion of a Crowne. **1721–1800** in BAILEY.] **1615** G. SANDYS *Trav.* 287 The walls and pauement of polished marble..with pillars, and Epistals of like workmanship. **1860** LEWIN *Jerusalem* 224 Which would yield about 23 feet for..each epistyle measured from the centres of the columns.

Hence **epiˈstylar** *a.*, belonging to the epistyle.

1849–50 WEALE *Dict. Terms* s.v. *Epistylium,* Epistylar arcuation is the system in which columns support arches instead of horizontal architraves and entablatures.

episuperˈstruction. *nonce-wd.* [f. EPI- + SUPERSTRUCTION.] Additional superstruction.

1840 DE QUINCEY *Wks.* x. 190 By superstruction and *epi*-superstruction it is gradually reared to a giddy altitude.

episyllogism (ɛpɪˈsɪlədʒɪz(ə)m). *Logic.* [ad. mod.L. *episyllogismus*: see EPI- and SYLLOGISM.] (See quot.)

1837–8 W. HAMILTON *Logic* (1860) I. 364 That syllogism which contains the consequent of another, is called an

Episyllogism. **1851** H. L. MANSEL *Proleg. Logica* 218 The subsequent consequence is related as an episyllogism. **1860** ABP. THOMSON *Laws Th.* § 111. 207. **1884** tr. *Lotze's Logic* 95 Every conclusion of a syllogism may..become the major premiss of another syllogism; the first is then called the *prosyllogism* of the second, and each one that follows the episyllogism of the one which preceded it.

Hence **episyllo'gistic** *a.*, pertaining to or characterized by an episyllogism.

1886 P. K. RAY *Text-bk. Deductive Logic* (ed. 2) III. vi. 216 The first form is called Synthetic, Progressive, or Episyllogistic. **1896** J. WELTON *Man. Logic* (ed. 2) I. 391 The progress of thought has been from prosyllogism to episyllogism. Such a demonstration is called *Progressive, Episyllogistic*, or *Synthetic*.

epitactic (ɛpɪ'tæktɪk), *a.* [ad. Gr. ἐπιτακτικ-ός, f. ἐπιτάσσειν to enjoin, f. ἐπί upon + τάσσειν to appoint.] Of the nature of an injunction.

1845 WHEWELL *Elem. Morality* Pref. 16 The categorical form involves an epitactic meaning.

epitaph ('ɛpɪtɑːf, -æ-), *sb.* Forms: α. (4 epithphy) 5 epytaphy, (6 epetaphy), 5–6 epitaphye, -taphie. β. 5–6 epitaphe, (5 epythaphe, epithaphe, epetaph, epitaff, 7– epitaph. [ad. L. *epitaphium*, a. Gr. ἐπιτάφιον, neut. of ἐπιτάφιος adj. (spoken) on the occasion of a burial, (written) upon a tomb, f. ἐπί upon + τάφος sepulture, tomb. The β forms prob. a. Fr. *épitaphe*.]

1. An inscription upon a tomb. Hence, occasionally, a brief composition characterizing a deceased person, and expressed as if intended to be inscribed on his tombstone.

α. [**1387** TREVISA *Higden* (Rolls) I. 225 þis geauntes *epitaphium*, þat is, þe writynge of mynde of hym þat lay þere, was suche.] *Ibid.* VII. 149 His epithphy—þat is, writynge on his grave. *c* **1470** HARDING *Chron.* XCVII. xv, Yᵉ bishop of Rome..on his tombe set his epitaphye. **1520** *Test. Ebor.* (Surtees) V. 123 Such a epitaphie as shall be devised by me or my executours. **1538** LELAND *Itin.* II. 49 A rich Tumbe of Alabastre..having this Epitaphie on it.

β. **1393** GOWER *Conf.* III. 326 Her epitaphe of good assise Was write about. **1430** LYDG. *Chron. Troy* II. xx, An Epythaphe anone he dyd do graue In his honour. *c* **1532** DEWES *Introd. Fr.* in *Palsgr.* 1032 (*title*) An epitaphe made upon the deth of Frenche. **1583** (*title*), A Booke of Epitaphes made upon the Death of Sir William Buttes. **1621** BURTON *Anat. Mel.* II. iii. 111, For all Orations..Epitaphes, herses ..he dies like a hog. **1711** ADDISON *Spect.* No. 25 ¶ 5 An Italian Epitaph written on the Monument of a Valetudinarian. **1816** SCOTT *Old Mort.* i, They belong, we are assured by the epitaph, to the class of persecuted Presbyterians. **1849** LYTTON *Caxtons* 103 But no epitaph tells their virtues.

b. *transf.* and *fig.*

1847 EMERSON *Repr. Men, Goethe* Wks. (Bohn) I. 382 The rolling rock leaves its scratches on the mountain..the fern and leaf their modest epitaph in the coal. **1860** FARRAR *Orig. Lang.* i. 26 That gigantic and mysterious epitaph of humanity.

2. *Comb.*

1709 STEELE *Tatler* No. 99 ¶ 5 What will become of your Embalmers, Epitaph-Mongers, and Chief Mourners?

epitaph ('ɛpɪtɑːf, -æ-), *v.* [f. prec. sb.]

1. *trans.* **a.** To describe in an epitaph; with *compl.* **b.** To write an epitaph upon.

1592 G. HARVEY *Four Lett.* 19 Let mee rather be Epitaphed, the Inuentour of the English Hexameter. **1818** J. BROWN *Psyche* 114 Epitaph'd an honest man. **1865** *Athenæum* No. 1992. 929/1 Proudly entombed and epitaphed.

†**2.** *intr.* To speak or write as in an epitaph; *impers.* in *pass.* Also, *to epitaph it. Obs.*

1627 BP. HALL *Heaven on Earth* § 18 The commons..in their speeches epitaph vpon him as on that Pope, 'He lived as a wolfe, and died as a dogge'. **1633** T. ADAMS *Exp. 2 Peter* ii. 15 (1865) 511 But many a man may say of his wealth, as it was epitaphed on that pope. *a* **1661** FULLER *Worthies* (1840) I. 211 The poet thus epitapheth it.

epitapher ('ɛpɪ,tɑːfə(r)). *rare.* [f. EPITAPH *v.* or *sb.* + -ER¹.] The writer of an epitaph.

1589 NASHE in *Greene's Menaphon* (Arb.) 14 Epitaphers, and position Poets haue wee more than a good many. **1883** *American* VI. 231 Of whom the epitapher wrote.

epitaphial (ɛpɪ'tæfɪəl), *a. rare.* [f. Gr. ἐπιτάφι-ος (see EPITAPH) + -AL¹.] Contained in sepulchral inscriptions.

1862 LOWELL *Biglow P.* Ser. II. 96, I cannot conceive that the epitaphial assertions of heathens should be esteemed of more authority.

So **epi'taphian** *a.*, †(*a*) (of a speech) delivered on the occasion of a funeral (*obs.*); (*b*) pertaining or appropriate to an epitaph.

1641 MILTON *Animadv.* Wks. (1847) 64/2 To imitate the noble Pericles in his Epitaphian speech..falls into a pittifull condolement. **1852** *Blackw. Mag.* LXXI. 724 But now to Vincent Bourne's epitaphian conciseness.

Also **epi'taphic, epi'taphical,** *adjs.*, pertaining to, or of the nature of, an epitaph. **'epitaphist**, a writer of epitaphs. **'epitaphize** *v. trans.*, to write an epitaph upon. **'epitaphless** *a.*

1883 *St. James's Gaz.* 15 Feb. 5 The death of Wagner has given occasion to some startling *epitaphic passages in the German papers. **1577–87** HOLINSHED *Chron.* III. 1243/2, I will here deliuer such *epitaphicall verses as I haue found touching king Edward the first. **1883** *Sat. Rev.* LVI. 108 After some preliminary praise, the *epitaphist works himself up to a grand effort, thus. *a* **1843** SOUTHEY *Comm.-pl. Bk.* Ser. II. (1849) 210 The Conde de Salinas *epitaphized him. **1883** P. ROBINSON *Some Poets' Dogs*, Cowper..epitaphises Sir John Throckmorton's pointer. *a* **1839** GALT *Demon Dest.* II. (1840) 10 The *epitaphless pyramids.

epitaphy: see EPITAPH.

‖**epitasis** (ɛ'pɪtəsɪs). Also 6 **epitazis.** [mod.L., a. Gr. ἐπίτασις, f. ἐπιτείνειν to intensify, f. ἐπί upon + τείνειν to stretch.] 'That part of a play where the plot thickens' (Liddell and Scott).

The Alexandrian grammarians regarded a dramatic work as consisting of three parts, the *protasis* or introduction, the *epitasis*, in which the action begins, and the *catastrophe*. Cf. CATASTASIS and quots. under that word.

1589 GREENE *Menaphon* (Arb.) 50 To make a more pleasing Epatazis, it fell out amongst them thus. *a* **1626** BP. ANDREWES *Serm.* (1856) I. 95 Being in the theatre all the while from the epitasis to the very catastrophe. **1759–67** STERNE *Tr. Shandy* (1802) II. v. 159 This matter..may make no uninteresting underplot in the epitasis and working-up of this drama. **1815** *Hist. J. Decastro* I. 259 The epitasis thereof, that is to say, the bustle, comes next.

†**epi'tatical**, *a. Obs. rare.* [f. Gr. ἐπιτατικ-ός, f. ἐπιτείνειν to exaggerate, intensify (see prec.) + -AL¹.] Intensive. Hence †**epi'tatically** *adv.*, in an intensive manner.

1652 URQUHART *Jewel* Wks. (1834) 292 Either epitatically or hypocoristically, as the purpose required.

epitaxy (ɛpɪ'tæksɪ, 'ɛpɪtæksɪ). Also in mod.L. form **epi'taxis.** [ad. F. *épitaxie* (L. Royer 1928, in *Bull. de la Soc. française de Min.* LI. 8), f. EPI- + Gr. τάξις arrangement: see -Y³.] The growth of crystals on a crystalline substrate that determines their orientation; the orientation of crystals so grown.

[**1929** *Mineral. Abstr.* IV. 175 'Épitaxie' is possible when the reticular distances are approximately identical only in two dimensions and not in three.] **1931** *Ibid.* 566 (*index*) Epitaxy. **1934** *Ibid.* V. 495 For epitaxy there is required both geometrical agreement and similarity of polarity between particles which replace one another at the points of union. **1949** *Proc. Physical Soc.* LXIIA. 344 (*heading*) The structure and epitaxy of lead chloride deposits formed from lead sulphide and sodium chloride. **1951** H. E. BUCKLEY *Crystal Growth* x. 382 The formation of small crystal elements of the impurity growing, on account of dimensional similarity, in parallel position on the plane in the host crystal (epitaxis). **1961** *New Scientist* 26 Oct. 244/1 Epitaxis. This is the latest weapon in the semiconductor engineers' armoury.

Hence **epi'taxial** *a.* [-AL], grown by, characterized by, or resulting from epitaxy: used of crystals, crystal growth, and crystal orientation; **epi'taxially** *adv.*, so that epitaxy occurs; by an epitaxial process.

1949 *Proc. Physical Soc.* LXIIA. 352 When strong epitaxial orientation occurs there are..usually two or more lattice row types which are parallel in the substrate and overgrowth crystals. **1960** *Proc. IRE* XLVIII. 1642/1 Epitaxial Diffused Transistors. This letter describes diffused base transistors, the structures of which incorporate thin semiconductor layers epitaxially deposited on low-resistivity substrates of the same semiconductor. **1960** *New Scientist* 25 Aug. 504/3 Epitaxial crystal growth (in which the growing crystal has the same orientation as the 'seed'). **1962** L. P. HUNTER *Handbk. Semiconductor Electronics* (ed. 2) iv. 46 The transistors currently referred to as 'epitaxial' are diffused junction transistors made on epitaxially deposited material. **1966** *New Scientist* 30 June 848/1 It is now also possible to grow epitaxial silicon crystal layers on to a single-crystal silicon substrate.

epithalamial (,ɛpɪθə'leɪmɪəl), *a.* [f. EPITHALAMI-UM + -AL¹.] Of the nature of an epithalamium.

1879 *Encycl. Brit.* IX. 162/1 He [Filelfo] wrote epithalamial and funeral orations. **1884** SYMONDS *Shaks. Predecessors* ix. 347 The epithalamial hymns of Catullus.

epitha'lamiast. *rare.* [f. EPITHALAMI-UM after *encomiast*, etc.] A composer of an epithalamium.

1846 LANDOR *Wks.* (1853) I. 515 Are not they rather the pale-faced reflections of some kind epithalamiast from Livonia or Bessarabia?

epithalamic (,ɛpɪθə'læmɪk), *a.* [f. EPITHALAM-IUM + -IC.] Of or pertaining to an epithalamium.

1756 TOLDERVY *Hist. Two Orphans* IV. 200 The youths and maids..performed this epithalamic ode. **1796** BURNEY *Mem. Metastasio* II. 390 Both the Epithalamic Psalm and the Cantata or Eunosto. **1846** GROTE *Greece* (1862) I. i. 50 The 'Sacred Wedding'..was familiar to epithalamic poets. **1884** STOCKTON *Lady or Tiger* 12 Dancing maidens.. treading an epithalamic measure.

‖**epithalamium** (,ɛpɪθə'leɪmɪəm). *Pl.* epithalamiums, -ia. Also 6–7 **epithalamion**, 7 **epythalamium.** [L. *epithalamium*, a. Gr. ἐπιθαλάμιον, neut. of ἐπιθαλάμιος, f. ἐπί upon + θάλαμος bride chamber.] A nuptial song or poem in praise of the bride and bridegroom, and praying for their prosperity.

1595 SPENSER (title) Epithalamion. *c* **1600** *Timon* III. v. (1842) 54 Sing us some sweete epithalamion. **1607** MARSTON *What You Will* II. i, Epythalamiums will I singe. **1653** *Cloria & Narcissus* I. 81 To sing Epithalamions to our marriage Feasts. **1684** T. BURNET *Th. Earth* II. 168 The 45th psalm..is an epithalamium to Christ and the Church. **1739** MELMOTH *Fitzosb. Lett.* (1763) 339 Give me timely notice of your wedding day, that I may be prepared with my Epithalamium. **1828** CARLYLE *Misc.* (1857) I. 163 Epithalamiums, epicediums. **1859** HOBHOUSE *Italy* II. 210 The Epithalamiums of Catullus and of Statius. **1860** ADLER *Fauriel's Prov. Poetry* iv. 67 The epithalamia belonged likewise to the popular class of poetry.

attrib. **1621** QUARLES *Argalus & P.* (1678) 102 Meanwhile, a dainty warbling Brest..presents this Epithal'mion Song.

Hence **epi'thalamize** *v. trans.*, to compose an epithalamium for.

1802 T. TWINING in *Sel. Papers Twining Family* (1887) 243 He will epithalamise you in person, I suppose.

epithalamus (ɛpɪ'θæləməs). *Anat.* [f. EPI- 1 + THALAMUS (sense 1).] A part of the diencephalon (see quot. 1962).

1902 CUNNINGHAM *Text-bk. Anat.* 501 The epithalamus, which comprises the pineal body and the habenular region. **1921** A. KEITH *Hum. Embryol.* (ed. 4) 103 In the upper region will be differentiated the optic thalamus, the epithalamus (the pineal body with its ganglia and commissures) and the metathalamus or geniculate bodies. **1962** *Gray's Anat.* (ed. 33) 1033 The epithalamus comprises the trigonum habenulae, the pineal body, and the posterior commissure.

†**epi'thalamy.** Also 7 **epithalmie.** Anglicized form of EPITHALAMIUM.

1589 PUTTENHAM *Eng. Poesie* I. xxvi. (Arb.) 65 And they were called Epithalamies as much to say as ballades at the bedding of the bride. **1652** SPARKE *Prim. Devot.* (1663) 64 Angels and men with combin'd harmony, Contend to sing this epithalamy. **1655** tr. *Hist. Francion* V. 21, I was resolved to have her Epithalamy sung by the Musicians of the New bridge. *Ibid.* VI. 11 Understanding that he was to marry, he offered to make the Epithalamy.

epithallus (ɛpɪ'θæləs). *Bot.* [f. EPI- 1 + THALLUS.] (See quots.)

1879 W. A. LEIGHTON *Lichen-flora Gt. Brit.* (ed. 3) 510 *Epithallus*, cortical layer. **1911** *Encycl. Brit.* XVI. 579/1 (Lichens), The term *epithallus* is sometimes applied to the superficial dense portion of the cortical layer.

So **epithalline** (ɛpɪ'θælaɪn) *a.*, situated or growing upon the thallus.

1943 AINSWORTH & BISBY *Dict. Fungi* 112 *Epi-thalline*, of a falsely thalline apothecial edge in lichens.

‖**epitheca** (ɛpɪ'θiːkə). *Zool.* [L. *epitheca*, Gr. ἐπιθήκη, f. ἐπί upon + θήκη case.] A continuous layer surrounding the thecæ in some corals.

Hence **epi'thecal** *a.*, of, or pertaining to, an epitheca. **epi'thecate** *a.*, provided with an epitheca.

1861 J. R. GREENE *Man. Anim. Kingd.* II. *Cœlent.* 190 The development..of an epitheca, cœnenchyma, and other similar structures. **1877** W. THOMSON *Voy. Challenger* II. i. 51 The external surface of the calicle is covered with a glistering epitheca. **1883** *Athenæum* 24 Nov. 673/3 The majority of the corallites of the colony arise from this basal epithecate structure.

epithecium (ɛpɪ'θiːʃɪəm). *Bot.* [mod.L., f. EPI- 1 + THECIUM.]

The surface layer of the fruiting body in certain lichens and fungi. So **epi'thecial** *a.*

1879 W. A. LEIGHTON *Lichen-flora Gt. Brit.* (ed. 3) p. ix, The *paraphyses* are slender filaments..which, by their close proximity, constitute the disk or *epithecium*. **1921** A. L. SMITH *Lichens* iv. 158 In some genera [of lichens] there is a profuse branching of the paraphyses to form a dense protective epithecium. **1952** C. J. ALEXOPOULOS *Introd. Mycology* xii. 290 In some apothecia, the paraphyses..have their tips united above the asci, forming a layer we call the epithecium. **1967** V. AHMADJIAN *Lichen Symbiosis* ii. 17 Some lichens have algal cells within their fruiting tissues.. either hymenial or epithecial algae, depending on their location within the fruiting body.

epithelial (ɛpɪ'θiːlɪəl), *a.* [f. EPITHELI-UM + -AL¹.] Of or pertaining to the epithelium; of the nature of epithelium: **a.** in animals; **b.** in plants.

a. 1845 TODD & BOWMAN *Phys. Anat.* I. 90 A pavement of nucleated epithelial particles. **1859** CARPENTER *Anim. Phys.* i. (1872) 42 The epithelial layer of the mucous membranes. **1872** HUXLEY *Phys.* ii. 36 An internal membranous and epithelial lining, called the endocardium.

b. 1862 H. MACMILLAN in *Macm. Mag.* Oct. 464 Numerous epithelial scales may be observed. **1884** BOWER & SCOTT *De Bary's Phaner. & Ferns* 447 A special layer, often consisting of numerous small epithelial cells.

epitheliate (ɛpɪ'θiːlɪeɪt), *v.* [f. EPITHELI-UM + -ATE³.] *intr.* To become covered with epithelium, as a wound when beginning to heal.

1887 *Brit. Med. Jrnl.* No. 1357. 13/2 It was beginning to epitheliate.

epithelioid (ɛpɪ'θiːlɪɔɪd), *a.* [f. as prec. + -OID.] Resembling epithelium.

1878 T. BRYANT *Pract. Surg.* I. 139 Cells of a more or less epithelioid type are packed together.

‖**epithelioma** (ɛpɪ,θiːlɪ'əʊmə). *Path.* Pl. **-mata.** [mod.L. f. *epithēlium*, after *carcinoma*, etc.] (See quot. 1878.)

1872 F. THOMAS *Dis. Women* 555 Cancer may affect the lining membrane in the form of vegetating epithelioma. **1876** tr. *Wagner's Gen. Pathol.* 465 Rindfleisch calls them cicatrical epitheliomata. **1878** T. BRYANT *Pract. Surg.* I. 124 Epithelioma and epithelial cancer are terms given to a form of cutaneous cancer from its similarity in structure to the epithelial elements of the natural skin.

epitheliomatous (ˌɛpɪθiːlɪ'əʊmətəs), *a. Path.* [-OUS.] Pertaining to, or of the nature of, epithelioma.

1881 *Trans. Obstetr. Soc. Lond.* XXII. 7 The disease was an ordinary epitheliomatous cervix. **1908** *Practitioner* Sept. 355 A squamous-celled epitheliomatous ulcer.

‖**epithelium** (ɛpɪ'θiːlɪəm). [mod.L. *epithēlium*, f. Gr. ἐπί upon + θηλή teat, nipple.]

1. *Anat.* A non-vascular tissue forming the outer layer of the mucous membrane in animals.

1748 HARTLEY *Observ. Man* I. ii. 117 The Impressions can easily penetrate the soft Epithelium. **1842** PRICHARD *Nat. Hist. Man* (1845) 87 The different appearances of the epithelia or outer membranous linings of all the surfaces. **1872** MIVART *Elem. Anat.* 237 The superficial layer of the skin so reflected inwards is termed epithelium, which is thus but a modified epidermis.

2. *Bot.* An epidermis consisting of young thin-sided cells, filled with homogeneous transparent colourless sap. (*Treas. Bot.*)

1870 BENTLEY *Bot.* 49 The canal of the style, and the stigma of Flowering Plants are also covered by a modified epidermis.. to which the name of Epithelium has been given by Schleiden.

epithem ('ɛpɪθəm), *sb. Med.* Also 6–7 epitheme, (6 epythyme, 7 epithyme). [ad. Gr. ἐπίθεμα, f. ἐπιτιθέναι, f. ἐπί upon + τιθέναι to place.] 'Any kind of moist, or soft, external application' (*Syd. Soc. Lex.*).

1559 MORWYNG *Evonym.* 37 They make no epithem or outward medicine at this day, but they put roosewater in it. *c* **1570** THYNNE *Pride & Lowl.* (1841) 81 Here is described an Epythyme [4 syll.]; Warm it and lappe it close unto thy brest. **1621** BURTON *Anat. Mel.* II. v. I. v, Bruel prescribes an Epitheme for the heart of Buglosse, Borage, etc. **1651** DAVENANT *Gondibert* II. II. lxx, With cordial epithems they bathed her breast. **1816** L. TOWNE *Farmer & Grazier's Guide* 19 Rub the Epithem thoroughly on the Part. **1863** READE *Very Hard Cash* in *All Y. Round* 11 July 458/1 The treatment hitherto has been hot epithems to the abdomen.

† **'epithem,** *v. Obs.* [f. prec. sb.] *trans.* To put an epithem upon.

1543 TRAHERON *Vigo's Chirurg.* II. i. 49 Let the head be epithemed in the place where the aquositie or watriness is.

‖ **ˌepithe'mation** (-'æʃɪən). *Obs.* Also 7 epithymation. [late L. *epithemation*, Gr. *ἐπιθεμάτιον, dim. of ἐπίθεμα: see EPITHEM.] A small plaister.

1615 CROOKE *Body of Man* 242 To this day we vse to apply Epithymations to them. **1715** KERSEY, *Epithemation*, a Plaister, Salve, or Ointment, to be laid upon a Sore.

‖ **epithesis.** [Gr. ἐπίθεσις placing upon, addition, f. ἐπί upon + τιθέναι to place; but Tourneur's sense is obscure.]

1600 TOURNEUR *Transf. Met.* xxxiv, And make his heart Epithesis of sinne.

epithet ('ɛpɪθɛt), *sb.* Forms: 6–7 epithete, -thite, epethite, (6 epithat, epythite, -the), 6– epithet. [ad. L. *epitheton*, a. Gr. ἐπίθετον adj., neut. of ἐπίθετος attributed, f. ἐπιτιθέναι, f. ἐπί upon + τιθέναι to place. Cf. Fr. *epithète*.

The Gr. word was used by grammarians for 'adjective', but they did not distinguish between adjs. and descriptive sbs. in apposition with a name.]

1. An adjective indicating some quality or attribute which the speaker or writer regards as characteristic of the person or thing described.

1588 FRAUNCE *Lawiers Log.* Ded., Your two last Epithetes wherein you disgrace the law with rudenesse and barbarisme. **1612** DEKKER *If it be not good, etc.* Wks. 1873 III. 305 T'expresse.. whose vilenes, there's no epithite. *a* **1661** FULLER *Worthies* (1840) II. 240 His epithets were pregnant with metaphors. **1718** LADY M. W. MONTAGUE *Lett.* II. xlix. 56, I admired the exact geography of Homer .. almost every epithet he gives to a mountain or plain is still just for it. **1788** REID *Aristotle's Log.* iv. §6. 95 The epithets of pure and modal are applied to syllogisms as well as to propositions. **1839** THIRLWALL *Greece* I. 173 The term barbarous.. in Homer.. is only used as an epithet of language. **1863** GEO. ELIOT *Romola* I. v, Hollow, empty—is the epithet justly bestowed on Fame.

¶ **b.** *nonce-use.* That which gives an epithet *to*.

1615 CHAPMAN *Odyss.* I. 154 To Sparta, then, and Pylos, where doth beat Bright Amathus, the flood, and epithet To all that kingdom.

2. A significant appellation.

(A spurious word '*Epithite*, a plotter, traitor', given in mod. Dicts., originated in a misunderstanding of quot. 1607.)

1579 G. HARVEY *Letter-bk.* (1884) 61 Christen them by names and epithites nothing agreable or appliante to the thinges themselves. **1607** G. WILKINS *Miseries Inforst Marriage* F iij, *Sir Will.* Like to a swine. *Lord Faulconb.* A perfect Epythite: hee feeds on draffe, And wallowes in the mire. **1634** W. WOOD *New Engl. Prosp.* I. v, Many of these trees.. have epithites contrary to the nature of them as they grow in England. **1683** PETTUS *Fleta Min.* II. 2 Before we fix our Title or Epithite to the Master of this Science. **1728** MORGAN *Algiers* I. vi. 201 He assumed the proud Epithet of Sultan or Monarch of Tunis and all Barbary. **1862** SIR B. BRODIE *Psychol. Inq.* II. iv. 129 We.. employ the French term of ennui, for want of an equally appropriate epithet in English.

† **3.** Used for: A term, phrase, expression. *Obs.*

1599 SHAKS. *Much Ado* v. ii. 67 Suffer loue! a good epithite; I do suffer loue indeede; for I loue thee against my will. **1604** —— *Oth.* I. i. 14 A bumbast Circumstance Horribly stufft with Epithites of warre.

4. *attrib.*

1874 SAYCE *Compar. Philol.* vi. 227 The epithet-period points to a vast series of bygone ages. **1884** *Manch. Exam.* 26 May 3/1 To increase the epithet power of our tongue in coining adjectives.

epithet ('ɛpɪθɛt), *v.* [f. prec. sb.] *trans.* †**a.** To add (a word) as an epithet (*obs.*). **b.** To apply an epithet to. **c.** To term, entitle.

1628 WALTON in *Reliq. Wotton* (1672) 566 Never was a town better Epithited. **1637** H. SYDENHAM *Serm.* II. 136 Ecclesiasticall honour (Episcopall he epithetes). **1650** FULLER *Pisgah* IV. Ep. Ded., Francis your Avus, whose death I would epithete Untimely. **1659** —— *Appeal* li. 7 Mr. Fox hath now the casual favour of my Pen to be epithited Reverent. **1698** *Christ Exalted* 88 Here are Whisperings, Surmises, Slanders and Reproaches, and these epethited with being private, evil, insinuated and clandestine. **1882** G. MACDONALD in *Sunday Mag.* XI. 80/2 Woeful Miss Witherspin, as Mark had epitheted her.

epitheted ('ɛpɪθɛtɪd), *ppl. a. rare.* [f. EPITHET *sb.* or *v.* + -ED.] **a.** Abounding with epithets. **b.** Designated by epithets.

1808 WOLCOTT (P. Pindar) *One more Peep at R. Acad.* Wks. 1812 V. 361 Doctor Darwin won a name By glittering tinsel, epitheted rhyme. **1880** *World* 10 Nov. 6/2 The profusely epitheted horse.

c. Designated by an epithet too coarse or violent to repeat. *jocular.*

1896 *Punch* 21 Nov. 241/2 Mr. Jones's compliments, Sir, and *when the epitheted substantive* is this noise going to stop? **1905** *Daily Chron.* 1 July 4/4 No London fire engine has such precedence as the 'Varsity boat. If you make it 'easy all' with your epithetted clumsiness in a boat—it is ten-and-sixpence.

epithetic (ɛpɪ'θɛtɪk), *a.* [ad. Gr. ἐπιθετικός, f. ἐπιτιθέναι (see EPITHET).]

†**a.** Abounding with epithets (*obs.*). **b.** Pertaining to, or of the nature of, an epithet.

a **1764** LLOYD *Poems, On Rhyme* 178 Verse.. which flows In epithetic measured prose. **1868** ARBER in *Sidney's Apol. Poetrie* Introd. 12 The epithets and epithetic phrases. **1874** SAYCE *Compar. Philol.* vi. 223 A language in which we may well expect to find general epithetic terms.

Hence **epi'thetical** *a.* = EPITHETIC. **epi'thetically** *adv.*, in an epithetic manner.

1715 M. DAVIES *Icon Libell.* I. 10 Some other Epithetical Term or Additional Word. **1837** DICKENS *Pickw.* xl, Sam, after bandying a few epithetical remarks with Mr. Smouch, followed at once. **1841** D'ISRAELI *Amen. Lit.* (1867) 557 Shakespeare bears away the prize among these epithetical allotments. **1857** F. HALL in *Jrnl. Asiat. Soc. Bengal* (1859) XXVII. 223 The word for 'sun'.. is, in the original, represented epithetically by a compound signifying 'the not cold-rayed'. **1868** —— *Benares Anc. & Mod.* 20 At least thirty or forty epithetical designations of Benares are scattered, etc.

† **'epithetish,** *a. Obs. rare*⁻¹. [f. EPITHET *sb.* + -ISH.] Inclined to the use of epithets.

1777 WOLCOTT (P. Pindar) in Polwhele *Trad. & Recoll.* (1826) I. 49 You were too epithetish.

'epitheˌtize, *v. rare.* [f. as prec. + -IZE.] *trans.* To apply an epithet *to*.

1716 M. DAVIES *Ath. Brit.* II. 214 The forementioned very false Son of the Church, that dar'd Epithetize him with that insolent Character. **1809** *Month. Mag.* XXVIII. 189 The images of (as he epithetizes them) scabby Job, blind Tobit, etc.

‖ **e'pitheton.** *Obs.* Also 6 apathaton, epithetone, 7 epithiton. [late L. *epitheton*, Gr. ἐπίθετον: see EPITHET *sb.*]

1. What is ascribed to a person; an attribute.

1547 HOOPER *Answ. Bp. Winchester's Bk.* Wks. (Parker Soc.) 124 This is properly the Epitheton of God to be of nothing but of himself.

2. = EPITHET 1 and 2.

1563–87 FOXE *A. & M.* (1684) III. 621 Alter the Epithethons, and I will subscribe. **1570–87** HOLINSHED *Scot. Chron.* (1806) II. 361 The rebellious faction (for by that name and epitheton doth Buchanan always term those that took the queens part). **1609** BIBLE (Douay) *Ps.* cxliv. comm., King, is the proper epitheton of Christ, the Sonne of God. **1611** SPEED *Hist. Gt. Brit.* v. ii. §4 The worthy Epitheton of King Edgar. *c* **1720** GIBSON *Farrier's Dispens.* (1734) 197 His Cordial powder, which he says has not that Epitheton for nought.

† **'epithyme.** *Bot. Obs.* Also 6 epithime. [ad. L. *epithymon*, Gr. ἐπίθυμον, f. ἐπί upon + θύμον thyme.] The *Cuscuta Epithymum* or Dodder, a parasitic plant growing on thyme, etc.

[*c* **1265** *Voc.* in Wr.-Wülcker 557 *Epitime*, epithimum, fordboh.] **1585** LLOYD *Treas. Health* v, Take violettes.. time, and epithime, ana ʒii. **1621** BURTON *Anat. Mel.* II. iv. I. v, Thyme and Epithyme, Hops, Scolopendria, Fumitory. **1725** BRADLEY *Fam. Dict.* s.v. *Saxifrage*, The second is Branch'd and like Epithyme.

epithymetic (ˌɛpɪθɪ'mɛtɪk), *a.* Also 7 epithumetik(e, 9 -ic. [ad. Gr. ἐπιθυμητικ-ός, f. ἐπιθυμέειν to desire, f. ἐπί upon + θυμός soul, appetite.] Connected with desire or appetite.

1631 R. H. *Arraignm. Whole Creature* xiii. §1. 175 No faculty of the Soule so represents Gods Infinite, as that which Philosophy calls Epithumetike; the burning appetite, or desire of the Soule. **1822** T. TAYLOR *Apuleius* 357 Receptacles of the epithymetic part. **1885** J. MARTINEAU *Eth. Theory* I. 77 The lowest (or epithumetic) part of human nature.

Hence † **epithy'metical,** *a. Obs.* in same sense.

1646 SIR T. BROWNE *Pseud. Ep.* v. xxi. §13. 267 By the girdle the heart and parts which God requires are devided from the inferiour and epithumeticall organs. **1847** in CRAIG.

† **e'pithymy.** *Obs. rare*⁻¹. [ad. Gr. ἐπιθυμία desire.] Desire; lust.

1600 TOURNEUR *Transf. Met.* xxxviii, Pan, that was once a cleere Epitimie, Is now transform'd to hot Epithymie.

epitimesis (ˌɛpɪtɪ'miːsɪs). [a. Gr. ἐπιτίμησις, f. ἐπιτιμάειν to rebuke.] Castigation, censure.

1678–1706 in PHILLIPS. **1721–1800** in BAILEY.

† **e'pitimy.** *Obs. rare*⁻¹.

1600 [See EPITHYMY.]

† **'epitoge.** *Obs.*⁻⁰ [a. Fr. *épitoge*, ad. L. *epitogium*, f. Gr. ἐπί + *toga* the Roman upper garment.] 'A Cassock, or long Garment worn loose over other Apparel, the habit of a Graduat in the University' (Blount *Glossogr.*).

1656–81 in BLOUNT. **1692** in COLES. **1678–1706** in PHILLIPS.

epitokous (ɛ'pɪtəʊkəs), *a.* [ad. G. *epitok* (E. Ehlers *Die Borstenwürmer* (1868) I. 453), f. Gr. ἐπίτοκος fruitful, bearing offspring, f. ἐπί EPI- + τόκος birth.] Of or relating to the **epitoke**, the posterior sexual part of the body of certain polychætous worms.

1896 W. B. BENHAM in *Cambr. Nat. Hist.* II. x. 276 Polychaeta... The immature forms may become ripe and lay eggs while still retaining the 'Nereid' characteristics, or these immature forms may become 'Heteronereids'... Ehlers employed the term 'epitokous', whilst he called the 'Nereid' phase 'atokous'. **1902** *Boston Soc. Nat. Hist.* XXIX. 399 The Heteronereis (epitokous form of Ehlers) is not uncommon. **1911** J. A. THOMSON *Biol. Seasons* III. 261 In some of our British shore-worms.. a remarkable change occurs in the body at the breeding season. So striking is the transformation in some instances, that the breeding ('epitokous') phase has been mistaken for a distinct species. **1916** H. S. PRATT *Man. Invertebr. Anim.* 283 In many (Polychæta) the anterior part of the body is sexless and is called the atoke, while the hinder part is sexual and is called the epitoke. **1963** R. P. DALES *Annelids* viii. 165 Durchon has shown that immature worms are prevented from metamorphosing into epitokous individuals by inhibitory hormones produced in the brain.

† **e'pitomate,** *v. Obs.* [f. L. *epitomāt-* ppl. stem of *epitomā-re* to abridge, f. *epitomē*: see EPITOME.] = EPITOMIZE.

1702 W. WOTTON in *Evelyn's Mem.* (1857) III. 384 His works have been epitomated by Mr. Bolton after a sort.

eˌpito'matic, *a. rare.* [Badly f. EPITOM-E, after *symptomatic*, etc.] Pertaining to, or of the nature of, an epitome.

1860 WESTCOTT *Introd. Study Gosp.* vi. (1881) 331 *note*, The style: vv. 9–20 are epitomatic, and wholly alien from S. Mark's general manner.

epitomator (ɪ'pɪtəˌmeɪtə(r)). [agent-n. f. L. *epitomāre*: see EPITOMATE.] One who writes an epitome of a larger work.

1621 BP. R. MOUNTAGU *Diatribæ* 420, I dare not utterly therefore condemne Epitomators. **1801** *Month. Mag.* XII. 574 To cleanse the Augean stable of ancient chronology is not the proper office of an epitomator. **1860** WESTCOTT *Introd. Study Gosp.* vii. (ed. 5) 367 St. Mark was regarded as a mere epitomator of the other synoptists. **1875** POSTE *Gaius* I. comm. (ed. 2) 113 The epitomator of Gaius.

e'pitomatory (ɪ'pɪtəʊmətərɪ), *a. rare.* [f. prec., as if ad. L. **epitomātōrius*.] Characterized by epitomizing; having the character of an epitome.

1860 WESTCOTT *Introd. Study Gosp.* vii. (ed. 5) 362 The erroneous views commonly held as to the epitomatory nature of St. Mark's Gospel.

epitome (ɪ'pɪtəmiː), *sb.* Also 7–8 epitomy, 6 epitomie, 6 *aphet.* (? *humorously*) pitomie. [a. L. *epitomē*, a. Gr. ἐπιτομή, f. ἐπιτέμνειν to make an incision into, abridge, f. ἐπί upon + τέμνειν to cut.]

1. A brief statement of the chief points in a literary work; an abridgement, abstract.

1529 FRITH *Antithesis* 299 A little treatise, after the manner of an epitome, and short rehearsal of all things that are examined more diligently in the aforesaid book. **1534** LD. BERNERS *Gold. Bk. M. Aurel.* (1546) B v. b, The wrytynges of theim.. semethe rather epitomes, than histories. **1589** 'MARPREL.' *Hay any Work* 35, I haue onely published a Pistle, and a Pitomie. **1612** *Drayton's Polyolb.* A iij, The common printed Chronicle.. is indeed but an Epitome or Defloration made by Robert of Lorraine. **1698** FRYER *Acc. E. India & P.* in *Phil. Trans.* XX. 347 'Tis very difficult to give an Abstract or Epitomy of them. **1751** JOHNSON *Rambler* No. 145 ⁋12 Some delight in abstracts and epitomes. *a* **1822** SHELLEY *Ess. Def. Poetry* (Camelot ed.) 9 Epitomes have been called the moths of just history; they eat out the poetry of it. **1856** MACAULAY *Biog.* (1867) 68 In general nothing is less attractive than an epitome: but the epitomes of Goldsmith.. are always amusing.

b. A summary or condensed account of anything; a compendium of a subject.

1621 SCLATER *Tythes* (1623) 183 This age is strangely in loue with Epitomees, if faith it selfe shall bee drawne to her compendium. **1645** W. BALL *Sphere Govt.* 12 Magna Charta .. is.. an Abridgement or Epitome of the liberties and rights of the Subjects of England. *c* **1665** MRS. HUTCHINSON *Mem. Col. Hutchinson* (1846) 24 To number his virtues is to give an epitome of his life. **1728** MORGAN *Algiers* I. Pref. 24 The

Introduction or Epitome of the Country I treat of.. is a mere work of Supererogation. **1755** *Mem. Capt. P. Drake* To Rdr., It may not be improper to furnish the Reader with an Epitomy of that Character. **1883** FROUDE *Short Stud.* IV. I. iii. 36 The articles in the text are an epitome of those which the Church found most objectionable.

2. *transf.* Something that forms a condensed record or representation 'in miniature'.

1607 SHAKS. *Cor.* v. iii. 67 This is a poore Epitome of yours, Which by th' interpretation of full time, May shew like all your selfe. **1628** EARLE *Microcosm., Pauls Walke* (Arb.) 73 Pauls Walke is the Lands Epitome, or you may call it the lesser Ile of Great Brittaine. **1666** J. SMITH *Old Age* (1752) 43 That world's epitomy, man. **1760** R. GRAVES *Euphrosyne* (1776) I. 124 Prepar'd to see A palace in epitome. **1773** BRYDONE *Sicily* xxxvii. (1809) 355 No less an epitome of the whole earth in its soil and climate, than in the variety of its productions. **1868** M. PATTISON *Academ. Org.* §2. 30 Congregation has been.. an epitome of Convocation. **1874** RUSKIN *Stones Ven.* I. Pref. 13 The Church of St. Mark .. is an epitome of the changes of Venetian architecture from the tenth to the nineteenth century.

†**b.** In depreciatory sense: Something that is reduced to insignificant dimensions. *Obs.*

a **1593** H. SMITH *Wks.* (1866–7) I. 282 When the hours of sleep.. of youth, and.. of sorrow are taken away, what an epitome is man's life come to. **1601** WEEVER *Mirr. Mart.* C ij, These were the worlds first youthfull progenie, To these our men are an Epitomie.

3. *in epitome*: **a.** in the form of a summary; **b.** in a diminutive form.

1649 G. DANIEL *Trinarch., Henry V*, cxiii, The fantasies .. Might have resolv'd this, in Epitomie. **1682** WHELER *Journ. Greece* 325 Snow, which this poor Hermite's aged Head seemeth, in epitome, to resemble. **1759** DILWORTH *Pope* 101 A description, calculated to contain in epitome the principles of a farther taste for magnificence. **1849** THOREAU *Week Concord Riv.* Saturday 26 The characteristics and pursuits of various ages and races of men are always existing in epitome in every neighborhood.

†**e'pitome**, *v. Obs.* [f. prec. sb.] *intr.* To make an epitome or summary; in quot. *pass. impers.*

1602 WARNER *Alb. Eng.* XII. lxx. (1612) 293 Of Northerne Regions partly is Epitomed before.

epitomic (ɛpɪ'tɒmɪk), *a.* [f. EPITOME *sb.* + -IC.] Of the character of an epitome.

1636 BRATHWAIT *Rom. Emperors*, Ep. Ded., Being all brought into the straights of this epitomicke volume.

epitomical (ɛpɪ'tɒmɪkəl), *a.* [f. prec. + -AL¹.] Of the nature of an epitome.

1609 HOLLAND *Amm. Marcell.* Annot. D ij b, Of her [Zenobia's].. skill in languages, writing of an Epitomicall Hystorie, and training up of her children in learning, read, etc. **1660** S. FISHER *Rusticks Alarm* Wks. (1679) 61 A kind of Epitomical Repetition. **1842** MRS. BROWNING *Grk. Chr. Poets* 188 Our literature is rich in ballads, a form epitomical of the epic and dramatic.

epitomist (ɪ'pɪtəmɪst). [f. as prec. + -IST.] One who writes an epitome.

1611 BIBLE *Transl. Pref.* 2 An Epitomist, that is, one that extinguished worthy whole volumes, to bring his abridgements into request. **1670** MILTON *Hist. Eng.* I. Wks. (1851) 22 Britomartus, whom the Epitomist Florus and others mention. **1880** MUIRHEAD tr. *Instit. Gaius* Introd. 15 The design of the epitomist.. having been to exclude what had become obsolete.

epitomization (ɪ,pɪtəmaɪ'zeɪʃən). [f. next + -ATION.] The action of epitomizing.

1805 *Ann. Rev.* III. 649 All such literary tautologists are proper objects of epitomization.

epitomize (ɪ'pɪtəmaɪz), *v.* [f. EPITOME *sb.* + -IZE.]

1. *trans.* To make an epitome of; to abridge.

1599 SANDYS *Europæ Spec.* (1632) Pref. 2 The same Booke was but a spurious stolne Copy, in part epitomized.. from the Authors Originall. **1644** MILTON *Jdgm. Bucer* (1851) 341 Thus far Martin Bucer, whom.. I deny not to have epitomiz'd. **1783** JOHNSON *Lett. Mrs. Thrale* 13 June, Mrs. Dobson.. epitomised a very bulky French Life of Petrarch. **1830** D'ISRAELI *Chas. I*, III. vi. 92 He was accustomed to epitomise Hooker, and others, on the present subject. **1868** PEARD *Water-Farm.* xii. 118 For the benefit of our readers, we will epitomise the pamphlet.

absol. **1861** PEARSON *Early & Mid. Ages Eng.* 119 He epitomizes, as if he were giving the pith of a paragraph.

b. To summarize; to give a concise account of; to state the essence of (a matter) briefly.

1624 CAPT. SMITH *Virginia* v. 172 Thus have you briefely epitomized Mother Natures benefits. **1683** tr. *Erasm. Moriæ Enc.* 65 They all would not suffice Folly in all her shapes to epitomise. **1728** MORGAN *Algiers* II. v. 321 Hassan Aga, whose Life I had begun to epitomize. **1856** FROUDE *Hist. Eng.* I. 123, I shall however in a few pages briefly epitomize what passed. **1877** E. CONDER *Bas. Faith* Pref. 11 Exhaustively to epitomise the evidence of Theism.

2. a. To contain in a small compass; to comprise in brief the sum of. **b.** To put into a small compass; to concentrate.

a. 1628 WITHER *Brit. Rememb.* IV. 1711 For, God in this one single Plague, comprised Those other Judgements, all, epitomized. **1634** SIR T. HERBERT *Trav.* 149 A Carpet, a Pan, and a Platter, epitomizes all their Furniture. **1868** STANLEY *Westm. Ab.* v. 416 In some respects it [the Chapter House] epitomises the vicissitudes of the Abbey itself.

b. 1635 AUSTIN *Medit.* 129 Hee himselfe epitomized those ten into two. **1654** COKAINE *Dianea* I. 51 In whom it appeared that Nature and Fortune had Epitomized all the wonders of the World. *a* **1763** SHENSTONE *Ess.* 106 Art, indeed, is often requisite to collect and epitomize the beauties of nature. **1857** WILLMOTT *Pleas. Lit.* xxi. 126 We have all the wilfulness of Cleopatra epitomized when, etc.

†**3.** To reduce to a smaller scale. *Obs.*

1612 WOODALL *Surg. Mate* Wks. (1653) Pref. 19 A Surgeons Chest epitomized. **1630** DRAYTON *David & Goliah* (R.), All those rare parts that in his brothers were Epitomiz'd, at large in him appear. **1660** FULLER *Mixt Contempl.* (1841) 258 Our standing army shall be epitomized to a more moderate proportion. **1713** *Guardian* No. 108 We should, in a little time, see mankind epitomized, and the whole species in miniature.

epitomized (ɪ'pɪtəmaɪzd), *ppl. a.* [f. prec. + -ED¹.] Presented in the form of an epitome; abridged, condensed, summarized.

1630 BRATHWAIT *Eng. Gentlew.* (1641) 283 An epitomized confection of all [nations]. **1866** LIVINGSTONE *Jrnl.* (1873) I. x. 254 It affords an epitomised description of his late travels.

epitomizer (ɪ'pɪtə,maɪzə(r)). [f. as prec. + -ER.] One who epitomizes; in the senses of the vb.

1615 CROOKE *Body of Man* 37 After Galens time, and his Epitomizer, Oribasius, who liued but in the next age. **1636** G. WILLIAMS in Spurgeon *Treas. Dav.* Ps. lv. 23 Sin is an epitomiser or shortener of everything. **1741** WARBURTON *Div. Legat.* II. 441 *note*, An epitomizer of one Jason of Syrene. **1809** COLEBROOKE *Ind. Divis. Zodiack* in *Asiat. Res.* IX. 349 The armillary sphere, described by the Arabian epitomiser, differs, therefore, from Ptolemy's.

epitomy, obs. var. of EPITOME.

epitonic (ɛpɪ'tɒnɪk). [f. Gr. ἐπίτονος on the stretch, f. ἐπιτείνειν to put a strain upon, f. ἐπί upon + τείνειν to stretch + -IC.] Overstrained.

1879 G. MEREDITH *Egoist* II. xi. 246 From the epitonic, the overstrained.

epitoxoid (ɛpɪ'tɒksɔɪd). [EPI- 1.] A toxoid which has less affinity than the toxin for the corresponding antitoxin.

1900 in DORLAND *Med. Dict.* **1903** [see TOXOID].

epitrichium (ɛpɪ'trɪkɪəm). *Anat.* [mod.L., f. Gr. ἐπί upon + τρίχιον, dim. of θρίξ hair.] A thin cellular membrane which overlies the epidermis and hair during fœtal life, usually disappearing before birth. Hence **epi'trichial** *a.*

1882 *Proc. Boston Soc. Nat. Hist.* XXI. III. 301 The surface is covered by a thin 'epitrichial' layer of large, flat, polygonal cells more or less granular, with inconspicuous nuclei. **1885** *Science* VI. 226/1 A new membrane of the human skin, which he homologizes with the epitrichium of the lauropsida. **1887** A. C. HADDON *Introd. Study Embryol.* 100 The epidermis of Amphioxus permanently remains as a single layer. In all other embryo Vertebrates, the epiblast, from being single, becomes double layered, owing to the primitive epiblast giving rise to a layer of flattened epithelial cells, the epitrichial layer. **1913** A. KEITH *Hum. Embryol.* (ed. 3) 451 The epitrichium,.. so named because the hairs are developed beneath it, and when they grow out in the sixth month this surface layer of flat epithelium is shed. **1962** *Gray's Anat.* (ed. 33) 138 The ectoderm at first consists of a single stratum of cells, but in the sixth week two strata can be recognised, a superficial, named the epitrichium, consisting of flat cells, the nuclei of which stain readily, and a deep, named the stratum germinativum.

epitrite ('ɛpɪtraɪt), *a.* and *sb. Pros.* Also 9 epitrit. [ad. L. *epitritos*, a. Gr. ἐπίτριτος amounting to one third more than the unit, f. ἐπί in addition + τρίτος the third.]

†**A.** *adj.* In the ratio of 4 to 3; *spec.* in ancient music: see quot.

1609 DOULAND *Ornith. Microl.* 65 The sesquitertia Proportion, which they call Epitrite.. Musically, when 4 Notes are sounded against 3, which are like themselues.

B. *sb. Prosody.* A foot consisting of three long syllables and one short one, and called first, second, third, and fourth epitrite, according as the short syllable stands first, second, third, or fourth respectively.

1678–1708 in PHILLIPS. **1749** *Power Pros. Numbers* 31 The first Epitrite.. a Close which Tully much delights in. **1819** H. BUSK *Vestriad* II. 183 Thro' the trite epitrite, when billows roar, Reader and sailor feel themselves ashore. **1821** *Blackw. Mag.* X. 388 The third foot of the major ionic tetrameter, we are told, may be a second epitrit, which is merely impossible. **1879** FARRAR *St. Paul* I. 167 The solemn rhythmical epitrite.

†**e'pitrochasm.** *Rhet.* Erron. -ism. [ad. late L. *epitrochasmus*, a. Gr. ἐπιτροχασμός, f. ἐπιτροχάζειν to run swiftly over.] A hurried accumulation of several points.

1652 URQUHART *Jewel* Wks. (1834) 292 There is neither definition, distribution, epitrochism, increment. **1721–1800** BAILEY, *Epitrochism.*

epitrochoid (ɛpɪ'trɒkɔɪd). *Math.* [f. Gr. ἐπί upon + τροχός wheel + -OID; after analogy of *epicycloid.*] The curve described by a point rigidly connected with the centre of a circle which rolls on the outside of another circle. Cf. EPICYCLOID.

1843 *Penny Cycl.* XXV. 284/2. **1879** THOMSON & TAIT *Nat. Phil.* I. I. §94.

Hence **epitro'choidal** *a.*, of or pertaining to an epitrochoid.

1800 *Phil. Trans.* XC. 149 Epitrochoidal curves, formed by combining a simple rotation or vibration with other subordinate rotations or vibrations. **1843** *Penny Cycl.* XXV. 284/2 Every direct-epicycle planetary system is both epitrochoidal and externally hypotrochoidal. **1959** *Times* 15 Dec. 7/1 The shape of the bore in which the triangular rotor revolves is described as epitrochoidal: the shield-shaped piston moves round the inside of a cavity like the hollow skin of an Edam cheese. **1969** *Observer* (Colour Suppl.) 23 Mar. 27/1 Take the revolutionary Wankel engine. Twin rotors in an epitrochoidal bore. That's two rotors going round and round, instead of four or more pistons going up and down.

‖**epitrope** (ɛ'pɪtrəpiː). *Rhet.* [L. *epitrope*, a. Gr. ἐπιτροπή, f. ἐπιτρέπειν to give up, yield, ἐπί upon + τρέπειν to turn.] (See quot.)

1657 J. SMITH *Myst. Rhet.* 131 Epitrope.. a figure when we either seriously or ironically permit a thing, and yet object the inconveniency. **1678–1706** in PHILLIPS. **1721–1800** in BAILEY. **1844** J. W. GIBBS *Philol. Stud.* (1857) 217 Epitrope.. is a figure of rhetoric by which a permission, either seriously or ironically, is granted to an opponent, to do what he proposes to do.

epitympanic (,ɛpɪtɪm'pænɪk), *a. Anat.* [f. EPI- + Gr. τύμπαν-ον drum + -IC. Cf. TYMPANIC.] Pertaining to or forming the uppermost subdivision of the tympanic pedicle which supports the mandible in fishes. Chiefly quasi-*sb.*

[**1856–8** W. CLARK *Van der Hoeven's Zool.* II. 61 The tympanicum, epitympanicum, and præoperculum.] **1849–52** TODD *Cycl. Anat.* IV. 941/2 The uppermost piece, the epitympanic, articulates by a diarthrodial joint with the mastoid. **1880** GÜNTHER *Fishes* 55.

‖**epizeuxis** (ɛpɪ'zjuːksɪs). *Rhet.* [mod.L., a. Gr. ἐπίζευξις a fastening upon, f. ἐπιζευγνύναι, f. ἐπί upon + ζευγνύναι to yoke.] A figure by which a word is repeated with vehemence or emphasis.

1589 PUTTENHAM *Eng. Poesie* III. xix. 167 Ye have another sort of repetition, when.. ye iterate one word without any intermission, as thus—It was Maryne, Maryne, that wrought mine woe.. The Greekes call him, *Epizeuxis*, the Latins *Subiunctio.* **1657** J. SMITH *Myst. Rhet.* 89. **1678–1706** in PHILLIPS. **1845** J. W. GIBBS *Philol. Stud.* (1857) 206.

epizoal (ɛpɪ'zəʊəl), *a.* [f. EPIZO-ON + -AL¹.] Of or pertaining to epizoa.

So **epi'zoan**, *a.* [see -AN] in same sense.

In mod. Dicts.

epizoic (ɛpɪ'zəʊɪk), *a.* and *sb.* [f. EPIZO-ON (or its elements) + -IC.]

A. *adj.* **a.** Of or pertaining to epizoa. **b.** Of plants: Living upon animals.

1857 BERKELEY *Cryptog. Bot.* 235 Fungi were defined as hysterophytal or epiphytal mycetals, (more rarely epizoic or inhabitants of inorganic substances). **1877** HUXLEY *Anat. Inv. An.* vi. 276 The parasite so common on the Stickleback, .. one of the most curious modifications of the epizoic type.

transf. **1872** O. W. HOLMES *Poet at Breakf.-t.* vi. 179 Our epizoic literature is becoming so extensive that, etc.

B. *sb.* An epizootic disease; = EPIZOOTIC B.

1879 JEFFERIES *Wild Life in S. Co.* 186 A kind of epizoic seems to seize them [little mice], and they die in numbers.

‖**epizoon** (ɛpɪ'zəʊən). *Zool.* Pl. epizoa. [mod.L., f. Gr. ἐπί + ζῷον animal.] A parasitic animal that lives on the exterior of the body of another animal. Opposed to ENTOZOON.

1836–9 TODD *Cycl. Anat.* II. 116/2 The Epizoa, or the external Lernæan parasites of Fishes. **1866** A. FLINT *Princ. Med.* (1880) 95 The parasites.. inhabiting the exterior of the body are called epizoa. **1876** BENEDEN *Anim. Parasites* 35 The Balatro calvus of Claparède, lives as an epizoon.

epizootic (,ɛpɪzəʊ'ɒtɪk), *a.* and *sb.* [ad. Fr. *épizootique*, f. *épizootie*: see next. In sense 2 taken as f. ἐπί (with interpretation 'subsequent to') + ζῷον animal.]

A. *adj.* **1.** Of diseases: Temporarily prevalent among animals; opposed to *enzootic.* Cf. EPIDEMIC.

1790 *Gentl. Mag.* June 496/2 Diseases are not so prevalent amongst our cattle (at least *epizo-otic* diseases are not)... Epizo-otic diseases are, in the brute creation, what epidemic diseases are in men. **1865** *Reader* 12 Aug. 178/3 A new epizootic disease has broken out among the horned cattle. **1880** *Times* 15 Sept. 7/6 Epizootic pleuro-pneumonia.

†**2.** *Geol.* Used by Kirwan as an epithet of 'secondary' mountains, to denote 'their posteriority to the existence of organized substances'.

1799 KIRWAN *Geol. Ess.* 161. **1840** HUMBLE *Dict. Geol. & Min.*, *Epizootic*, containing animal remains, as epizootic hills, or epizootic strata.

B. *sb.* An epizootic disease; a plague among cattle.

1748 SHORT in Chambers *Dom. Ann. Scotl.* II. 437, *note*, This epizootic raged also in England and other countries. **1827** DE QUINCEY *Last Days Kant* Wks. III. 124 Cats being so eminently an electric animal.. he attributed this epizootic to electricity. **1882** *Jrnl. Linn. Soc.* XVI. 187 All epizootics of this character are immediately due to excessive multiplication of worms.

epizooty (ɛpɪ'zəʊətɪ). [ad. Fr. *épizootie*, irreg. f. Gr. ἐπί upon + ζῷον animal.] An epizootic disease.

1781 *Projects* in *Ann. Reg.* 102/1 The report of an Epizooty is often spread. **1798** MALTHUS *Popul.* (1817) I. 251 Great and wasting epizooties are frequent among the cattle. **1867** RUFFINI *Quiet Nook in Jura* 274 And fears were entertained of a coming epizooty. **1882** *Jrnl. Linn. Soc.* XVI. 188 This ostrich epizoöty is a kind of strongylosis.

epoch ('ɛpɒk, 'iːpɒk). Forms: α. 7–9 epocha. β. epoche. γ. 7– epoch. [ad. late L. *epocha*, ad. Gr.

ἐποχή stoppage, station, position (of a planet), fixed point of time, f. ἐπέχειν to arrest, stop, take up a position, f. ἐπί + ἔχειν to hold. Cf. Fr. *époque*, It. *epoca*.]

I. A fixed point in the reckoning of time.

1. *Chron.* The initial point assumed in a system of chronology; *e.g.* the date of the birth of Christ, of the Hegira, of the foundation of Rome, etc.; an ERA. Also, in wider sense, any date from which succeeding years are numbered. Now *rare*.

α. **1614** SELDEN *Titles Hon.* 6 The residue will fall neer the first yeer of the Chaldæan Epocha. *a* **1638** MEDE *Wks.* III. ix. 599 The Times of the Beast and the Woman's being in the Wilderness have the same Epocha and beginning. **1726** tr. *Gregory's Astron.* I. 252 The Epocha of the Olympiads, of all Profane ones, is the most Ancient.

β. *a* **1658** CLEVELAND *Inund. of Trent* 138 Since we're deliver'd let there be, From this Flood too another *Epoche*.

γ. **1658** USSHER *Ann.* Ep. Rdr. (R.), In divers times and ages, divers epochs of time were used, and several forms of years. **1677** HALE *Prim. Orig. Man.* II. iii. 148 The pretended Epoch of the Babylonians. **1758** SWINTON in *Phil. Trans.* L. 801 On the Greek brass coins of Sidon.. both these epochs seem to have been used.

2. a. The beginning of a 'new era' or distinctive period in the history of mankind, a country, an individual, a science, etc. Phr., ***to make an epoch***.

α. **1673** [R. LEIGH] *Transp. Reh.* 55 Men that mark out Epocha's are not born in many revolutions. **1756** *Gentl. Mag.* XXVI. 415 Botany.. from hence boasts a new epocha. **1783** *Phil. Trans.* LXXIII. 360 The congelation of mercury ..must be allowed to form a very curious and important epocha in the history of that metal. **1827** SIR J. BARRINGTON *Own Times* (1830) I. 18 *note*, A circumstance which the.. Irish.. considered as forming an epocha.

β. **1824** D'ISRAELI *Cur. Lit.* (1859) II. 382 Every work which creates an epoch in literature is one of the great monuments of the human mind. **1841–4** EMERSON *Ess. Spir. Laws* Wks. (Bohn) I. 68 The epochs of our life are not in the visible facts.. but in a silent thought by the wayside. **1864** BURTON *Scot Abr.* I. v. 280 Luther's Bible makes an epoch in the formation of the German language.

†**b.** The date of origin of a state of things, an institution, fashion, etc.; occasionally, an event marking such a date. *Obs.*

α. **1659** PEARSON *Creed* (1839) 281 Nor need we be ashamed that the Christian religion, which we profess, should have so known an Epocha, and so late an original. **1788** PRIESTLEY *Lect. Hist.* v. li. 390 Great fisheries have always been epocha's of a great trade and navigation. **1789** *Hist.* in *Ann. Reg.* 14 The present crisis would become the epocha of a new splendor to the French monarchy. **1795** in Wythes *Decis. Virginia* 41 Whether the time of the settlement were the epocha of the title will be enquired. **1824** E. NARES *Heraldic Anom.* (ed. 2) II. 307 The year 1629 is reckoned the epocha of long perukes.

β. **1654** L'ESTRANGE *Chas. I* (1655) 156 The Epoche, the Nativity day from whence all the series of this kings troubles are to be computed.

γ. *a* **1716** SOUTH (J.), The year sixty; the grand epoch of falsehood. **1761** HUME *Hist. Eng.* I. xii. 290 This period.. the epoch of the house of commons in England.

3. In wider sense: A fixed point of time.

a. The date, or assigned position in chronological sequence, of a historical event.

Now less precise than *date*, which indicates a particular year or smaller division of time.

β. **1661** DRYDEN *Astræa Redux* 108 Such, whose supine felicity but makes In story chasmes, in epoche's [*in some later edd.* epocha's, epocha] mistakes.

γ. **1697** EVELYN *Numism.* v. 186 Epochs are sometimes noted in words at length. **1841** ELPHINSTONE *Hist. Ind.* I. 209 The date of his appearance.. the middle of the sixth century before Christ.. an epoch which, etc.

b. [= Fr. *époque*.] A precise date; the exact time at which an event takes place or is appointed to take place. Formerly *gen.*; now only with reference to natural phenomena (cf. 4 a).

α. **1761** *State Papers* in *Ann. Reg.* 258/2 An offer to treat about these epochas.

γ. **1786** T. JEFFERSON Wks. (1859) I. 570 To inform him what other numbers [of arms] you expect to deliver, with the epochs of delivery. **1794** BURKE *Pref. Brissot's Addr.* Wks. VII. 312 To foresee them [the designs of the court] so well, as to mark the precise epoch on which they were to be executed. **1838** DE MORGAN *Ess. Probab.* (Cabinet Cycl.) 123 When once the notion is obtained that a change of weather will follow that of the moon, the epoch is watched.

c. A point of time defined by the occurrence of particular events or the existence of a particular state of things; a 'moment' in the history of anything.

It is often uncertain whether a writer meant the word to be taken in this sense or in 5, since a given portion of time may be regarded either as a mere date or as a period.

α. **1728** MORGAN *Algiers* I. iii. 73 Not long before this Epocha so calamitous to that unhappy Country. **1777** G. FORSTER *Voy. round World* II. 103 In a warm climate.. the epocha of maturity seems to happen at a much earlier age than in colder countries. **1791** BURKE *Let. Member Nat. Assembly* Wks. VI. 9, I well remember, at every epocha of this wonderful history. **1801** HELEN WILLIAMS *Sk. Fr. Rep.* I. viii. 76 At the epocha of the [French] revolution. **1807** SOUTHEY *Espriella's Lett.* (1814) III. 74 The invention of the steam-engine, almost as great an epocha as the invention of printing. **1824** *Hist. Gaming* 26 At one of those epochas the Earl married a Countess in her own right. **1830** GODWIN *Cloudesley* I. xiii. 213 From this epocha there was a perpetual struggle in Cloudesley's mind.

γ. **1823** J. BADCOCK *Dom. Amusem.* Introd. 5 Davey and Brewster.. sustain that character at the present epoch of Science. **1838** CARLYLE *Chartism* (1858) 3 At an epoch of history when the 'National Petition' carts itself in waggons along the streets. **1841–71** T. R. JONES *Anim. Kingd.* (ed. 4) 510 At this epoch.. the polyp presents two cavities distinct from each other. **1845** MCCULLOCH *Taxation* II. v. (1852) 220 After the last-mentioned epoch.. the production of beet-root sugar began rapidly to increase. **1875** SCRIVENER *Lect. Text N.T.* 7 Those noted up to the present epoch. **1882** MRS. PITMAN *Mission L. Greece & Pal.* 190 It was an epoch never to be forgotten in her life, when she commenced labouring in Joppa.

4. *Astron.* The point of time at which any phenomenon takes place; an arbitrarily fixed date (often the first day of a century or half-century) for which the elements necessary for computing the place of a heavenly body are tabulated. Also, the heliocentric longitude of a planet at such a date (more fully, ***the longitude of the epoch***).

α. **1726** tr. *Gregory's Astron.* I. 466 Their Mean Motions made between the said Epocha and the Time propos'd, being equated. **1789** HERSCHEL in *Phil. Trans.* LXXX 20 I followed the shadow of the satellite.. up to the center, in order to secure a valuable epocha. **1795–8** T. MAURICE *Hindostan* (1820) I. I. iv. 128 By astronomers the word epocha is used to denote that particular point of the orbit of a planet, wherein that planet is, at some known moment of mean time, in a given meridian.

γ. **1790** HERSCHEL in *Phil. Trans.* LXXX. 488 Epochs of the mean longitude of the satellites. **1834** *Nat. Philos. Astron.* ix. 191/2 (Usef. Knowl. Soc.), The longitude of the sun, at some one time, which is called the epoch. **1858** HERSCHEL *Outlines Astron.* iv. (ed. 5) 168 They would be found.. to differ by the exact difference of their local epochs.

II. A period of time. (Cf. similar use of *era*, *term*).

5. a. In early use, a chronological period dated from an 'epoch' in sense 1. In later use, a period of history defined by the prevalence of some particular state of things, by a connected series of events, or by the influence of some eminent person or group of persons.

α. **1628** EARLE *Microcosm, Sordid Rich Man* (Arb.) 99 His clothes were neuer young in our memory: you might make long Epocha's from them. **1662** STILLINGFL. *Orig. Sacr.* II. vii. §8 They make three Epocha's, before the Law, under the Law, and the coming of the Messias. *c* **1720** PRIOR *Solomon on Van. World* III. 758 Scenes of war, and epochas of woe. **1794** SULLIVAN *View Nat.* II. 201 Chronologers have divided the age of the world into six different epochas. **1824** L. STANHOPE *Greece* 4 The most shining epocha of her history.

γ. *c* **1800** K. WHITE *Time* 385 Ages and epochs that destroy our pride. **1875** STUBBS *Const. Hist.* II. xvi. 486 A period of eight years of peace between two epochs of terrible civil discord. **1883** *Harper's Mag.* Feb. 467/2 'Ah, that indeed is a letter,' sighs the lover of the Addisonian epoch.

b. A period in an individual's life, or in the history of any continuous process.

α. **1768** STERNE *Sent. Journ.* (1775) II. 132 There are three epochas in the empire of a Frenchwoman. She is coquette —then deist—then *devote.* **1771** GOLDSM. *Hist. Eng.* III. 372 This is one of the most extraordinary epochas in English history. **1788** HOLCROFT *Life & Adv. Baron Trench* I. xiv, The second great and still more gloomy epocha of my life.

γ. **1853** ROBERTSON *Serm.* Ser. III. xx. 256 God's treatment of the penitent divides itself in this parable into three distinct epochs. **1865** DRAPER *Intell. Devel. Europe* i. 9 We express our surprise when we witness actions unsuitable to the epoch of life.

c. *Geol.* A period or division of the history of the formation of the earth's crust.

Chiefly used indiscriminately for any distinct portion of geological time. The International Congress of 1881 proposed to use the terms *era, period, epoch, age* to denote successively smaller divisions; but this has not been generally followed.

α. **1802** PLAYFAIR *Illustr. Hutton. Th.* 123 The most ancient epocha of which any memorial exists in the records of the fossil kingdom.

γ. **1850** LYELL *2nd Visit U.S.* II. 247 The language of those who talk of 'the epoch of existing continents'. **1871** TYNDALL *Fragm. Sc.* (ed. 6) I. viii. 268 But this would not produce a glacial epoch.

6. *Physics.* (See quots.)

1879 THOMSON & TAIT *Nat. Phil.* I. I. §54 The Epoch in a simple harmonic motion is the interval of time which elapses from the era of reckoning till the moving point first comes to its greatest elongation in the direction reckoned as positive, from its mean position or the middle of its range. **1882** MINCHIN *Unipl. Kinemat.* 9 The maximum excursion of the harmonic vibration $x = a \cos\left(\frac{2\pi t}{T} + \alpha\right)$ is *a*... The angle α is called the epoch angle, or simply the epoch.

7. *Comb.* [Perhaps after the equivalent compounds in German.] ***epoch-forming*** adj.; **epoch-making** *a.*, orig. said chiefly of scientific discoveries or treatises; now extended to designate any remarkable or sensational event, publication, etc.; **epoch-marking** *a.*, journalistic alteration of *epoch-making*.

1816 COLERIDGE *Lay Serm.* 313 All the epoch-forming revolutions of the Christian world. **1863** *Athenæum* July 9/1 He has produced what the Germans call an *epoch-making* book. **1874** H. REYNOLDS *John Bapt.* ii. 64 Epoch-making men.. of human history. **1881** W. R. SMITH *Old Test. in Jew. Ch.* iii. 56 This work of Ezra, and the covenant.. were of epoch-making importance. **1895** *Westm. Gaz.* 15 Jan. 2/2 Every author of an epoch-making or epoch-marking book is liable to pass through two stages. **1919** J. L. GARVIN *Econ. Found. Peace* 272 Consent by the United States to administer Constantinople and the Straits, Armenia and Palestine, would be an epoch-marking step in itself. **1923** *Daily Mail* 16 Jan. 7 This epoch-marking experiment. **1928** R. CAMPBELL *Wayzgoose* ii. 59 He produced an epoch-making article. **1940** GRAVES & HODGE *Long Week-End* vi. 93 Most of these inventions, all described as 'epoch-making', were never heard of again after the first news-thrill. **1963** *Times Lit. Suppl.* 4 Jan. 6/2 The evil of the Fulton speech.. was not that it was 'epoch-making' but that it was 'epoch-marking'.

epochal ('ɛpɒkəl), *a.* [f. EPOCH + -AL[1].]

1. Of or pertaining to an epoch or epochs.

1685 H. MORE *Paralip. Prophetica* 376 If the Epochal note should fall out either before the beginning of the first Semitime, etc. **1827** A. & J. HARE *Guesses* Ser. II. (1873) 355 Shakespeare has given such a national tinge and epochal propriety to his characters. **1847** J. HARE *Vict. Faith* 67 We ..hear the striking of one of its [Time's] epochal hours. **1865** DRAPER *Intell. Devel. Europe* xxvi. 617 The three distinct modes of life occur in an epochal order.

2. Of the nature of an epoch; forming an epoch; epoch-making.

1857 M. PATTISON *Ess.* (1889) II. 416 The.. epochal crises of affairs. **1866** ALGER *Solit. Nat. & Man* II. 80 [David Hume's] place in the history of philosophy is of epochal importance. **1877** DAWSON *Orig. World* VI. 127 Warring.. has suggested that the Mosaic days are epochal days.

'epochate. *nonce-wd.* [f. EPOCH + -ATE[1].] The position of being the 'epoch' of a computation.

1685 H. MORE *Paralip. Prophetica* 4 Four Decrees, but only two of them Competitors for the Epochate.

epochism ('ɛpəkɪz(ə)m). [f. as prec. + -ISM.] The practice of dividing time into epochs.

1865 *Athenæum* No. 1970 140/1 Chronological epochism.

Epochist ('ɛpɒkɪst). [Two formations: 1. f. Gr. ἐποχ-ή suspension of judgement, f. ἐπέχειν (see EPHECTIC) + -IST; 2. f. EPOCH + -IST.]

†**1.** A philosopher of the Ephectic School. *Obs.*

1603 FLORIO *Montaigne* II. xii. (1632) 280 Pyrrho and other Sceptikes, or Epochistes.

2. One who holds the theory that the 'days' of creation in *Genesis* signify epochs.

1888 CAVE *Inspir. O.T.* iii. 129 The Epochists.. regard the days as epochs.

epocryte: see HYPOCRITE.

epode ('ɛpəʊd). Also 7 epod. [a. OF. *epode* ad. L. *epōdos*, a. Gr. ἐπῳδός after-song, incantation, f. ἐπᾴδειν, f. ἐπί upon, after + ᾄδειν, ἀείδειν to sing.]

1. a. A kind of lyric poem, invented by Archilochus, in which a long line is followed by a shorter one, of metres different from the elegiac; used by Horace in his 5th Book of Odes. **b.** An incantation. **c.** A poem of grave character.

1598 FLORIO, *Epodo*, a kinde of verses, hauing the first verse longer then the second. **1616** B. JONSON *Forest* x, Now my thought takes wing, And now an Epode to deep ears I sing. **1647** CRASHAW *Music's Duel* Poems, 90 She qualifies their zeal With the cool epode of a graver note. **1655–60** STANLEY *Hist. Philos.* 410/1 Pythagoras made use of Epodes. **1656–81** BLOUNT *Glossogr.*, *Epod.* **1693** DRYDEN *Juvenal* Ded. (R.) Horace seems to have purged himself from those splenetic reflections in those odes and epodes. **1721–1800** in BAILEY. **1847** in CRAIG. And in mod. Dicts.

2. The part of a lyric ode sung after the strophe and antistrophe.

1671 MILTON *Samson* Pref., Strophe, Antistrophe, or Epode.. were a kind of Stanzas framed only for the music then used with the Chorus that sung. **1847** GROTE *Greece* II. xxix. (1862) III. 67 Choric compositions, containing not only a strophê and antistrophê, but also a third division or epode succeeding them.

Hence **e'podic** *a.*, pertaining to, or of the nature of, an epode.

1866 FELTON *Anc. & Mod. Gr.* I. ix. 152 A series of iambic and epodic invectives.

epoist ('ɛpəʊɪst). *rare.* [badly f. Gr. ἔπο-ς EPOS + -IST.] A writer of epic poetry.

1842 MRS. BROWNING *Grk. Chr. Poets* 22 Apollinarius, an epoist, dramatist, lyrist. **1863** BROWNING *Sordello* headline, Wks. III. 418 Successively that of epoist, dramatist, or analyst.

epomania (ɛpəʊ'meɪnɪə). *nonce-wd.* [f. Gr. ἔπο-ς EPOS + μανία madness.] A rage for the writing of epics.

1800 SOUTHEY in C. Southey *Life* II. 121 My Joan of Arc has revived the Epomania that Boileau cured the French of 120 years ago.

‖**éponge** (epɔ̃ʒ). [Fr., = sponge.] Sponge cloth (cf. RATINE).

1928 *Daily Express* 11 July 5/5 For a bathing-coat try to find flowery éponge or any other bright fabric. **1952** C. W. CUNNINGTON *Eng. Wom. Clothes Pres. Cent.* 294 *Éponge*, a soft, loose fabric of cotton, wool or silk; similar to ratine.

eponomy, variant of EPONYMY.

eponychium (ɛpəʊ'nɪkɪəm). *Anat.* [mod.L., f. Gr. ἐπί upon + ὄνυξ nail.] **a.** The horny embryonic structure whence the nail is developed. **b.** A film of epidermis covering the dorsal part of the nail; = QUICK *sb.*[1] 4.

1885 tr. P. G. Unna in H. Ziemssen *Handbk. Dis. Skin* i. 23 A trace of the horny layer of the first foetal months remains only on the ungual phalanx till a later period, and to this.. I have given the name 'eponychium'. **1892** C. S. MINOT *Hum. Embryol.* 555 The epitrichial layer over the area has received the special name of *eponychium* from Unna. **1902** CUNNINGHAM *Text-bk. Anat.* 734 The part [of

the epitrichium] which persists over the root of the nail is termed the eponychium, and covers the proximal part of the lunula. **1968** BLOOM & FAWCETT *Textbk. Histol.* (ed. 9) xxii. 495 Under the proximal fold, the horny layer spreads onto the free surface of the nail body as the eponychium.

eponym (ˈɛpənɪm). [ad. Gr. ἐπώνυμ-ος (*a.*) given as a name, (*b.*) giving one's name to a thing or person, f. ἐπί upon + ὄνομα, Æol. ὄνυμα name.]

1. One who gives, or is supposed to give, his name to a people, place, or institution; *e.g.* among the Greeks, the heroes who were looked upon as ancestors or founders of tribes or cities. Also in Lat. form **eponymus**.

1846 GROTE *Greece* I. vii. (1869) I. 150 Pelops is the eponym or name-giver of the Peloponnesus. **1851** D. WILSON *Preh. Ann.* (1863) I. II. vii. 481 The legendary eponymus of the district. **1877** MERIVALE *Rom. Triumv.* ii. 35 An ancient patrician race, which claimed as its eponym, Julus, the son of Æneas. **1883** *Q. Rev.* Apr. 297 The eponymus of which [Skinner's Horse] was his bosom friend.

b. *transf.* One 'whose name is a synonym for' something.

1873 SYMONDS *Grk. Poets* x. 306 Theocritus, Bion and Moschus are the Eponyms of Idyllic poetry. **1875** MERIVALE *Gen. Hist. Rome* ii. (1877) 7 Saturn becomes the eponym of all useful and humane discovery. **1875** BRYCE *Holy Rom. Emp.* xi. (ed. 5) 177 Charles [the Great]..had become, so to speak, an eponym of Empire.

2. *Assyriology.* A functionary (called *limu* in Assyrian) who, like the ἄρχων ἐπώνυμος at Athens (see EPONYMOUS 2), gave his name to his year of office. Also *attrib.*, as in ***eponym-list***, ***-year***; **eponym-canon**, the record which gives the succession of these officers.

1864 RAWLINSON *Anc. Mon.* II. viii. 261 The list of eponyms obtained from the celebrated 'Canon'. **1886** C. R. CONDER *Syrian Stone-Lore* ix. 325 The Sabeans also adopted the Assyrian system of eponyms to mark the year.

3. [ad. Gr. ἐπώνυμον an additional designation, cognomen] A distinguishing title.

1863 MISS YONGE *Chr. Names* II. 264 Jarl..was a favourite eponym. **1881** *Fair Trade Cry* 11 We are the modern Phœnicians, or to take a lower eponym, the Pickfords of the world.

Hence **epoˈnymic** *a.*, of or pertaining to an eponym; that is an eponym. **eˈponymism**, the practice of accounting for names of places or peoples by referring them to supposed prehistoric eponyms. **eˈponymist** = EPONYM I. **eˈponymize** *v. trans.*, to serve as eponym to.

1851 D. WILSON *Preh. Ann.* (1863) II. IV. i. 179 The young strength of the eponymic colonists. **1871** TYLOR *Prim. Cult.* I. 7 Eponymic myths which account for the parentage of a tribe by turning its name into the name of an imaginary ancestor. **1883** *Sat. Rev.* 23 June 784 Its patron saint or eponymic hero. **1858** GLADSTONE *Homer* I. 347 The foregoing sources of eponymism. *Ibid.* I. 85 Nor does he establish any relation whatever between any of the four races and any common ancestor or eponymist. **1862** ANSTED *Channel Isl.* 320 The eponymist of St. Helier's was confounded with Hilarius Bishop of Poitou. **1866** J. ROSE tr. *Ovid's Fasti* Notes 236 Pallas herself eponymizes the Pali fire-worshippers.

eponymous (ɛˈpɒnɪməs), *a.* [f. Gr. ἐπώνυμ-ος (see prec.) + -OUS.]

1. That gives (his) name to anything; said *esp.* of the mythical personages from whose names the names of places or peoples are reputed to be derived.

1846 GROTE *Greece* I. iv. I. 111 The eponymous personage from whom the community derive their name. **1874** SAYCE *Compar. Philol.* ix. 379 Eponymous heroes. **1889** SWINBURNE *B. Jonson* 27 The eponymous hero or protagonist of the play.

2. Giving his name to the year, as did the chief archon at Athens.

1857 BIRCH *Anc. Pottery* (1858) I. 195 Inscribed with the name of the eponymous magistrate.

eponymy (ɛˈpɒnɪmɪ). Also 9 **economy**. [ad. Gr. ἐπωνυμία, f. ἐπώνυμος: see EPONYM.]

1. a. = EPONYMISM. **b.** Eponymic nomenclature.

1865 MCLENNAN *Prim. Marriage* vii. 150 The universal tendency of rude races to eponomy. **1880** *Athenæum* 2 Oct. 425/3 Known..after the fashion of eponymy so prevalent among Asiatic nomads, as Nogais or Nogai Tartars.

2. The year of office of an (Assyrian) eponym.

1875 G. SMITH *Assyrian Eponym Canon* 193 The earlier and correct Text..has the eponymy of Assur-banai-uzur two years earlier. **1883** I. TAYLOR *Alphabet* I. 254 The first is dated in the eponymy of Sin-sarra-uzur.

epoophoron (ɛpəʊˈɒfərɒn). *Anat.* [mod.L., f. EP- + *oophoron* ovary (f. Gr. ᾠόν egg + -φόρος bearing, bearer).] = PAROVARIUM.

1883 FOSTER & BALFOUR *Elem. Embryol.* (ed. 2) 224 The sexual part becomes in the cock the after-testes or coni vasculosi... In the hen it forms part of the epoophoron of Waldeyer, and is composed of well-developed tubes with yellow pigment. **1887** *Buck's Handbk. Med. Sci.* V. 520/2 The parovarium (Syn., paroöphoron, epoöphoron, corpus pampiniforme (Wrisberg), organ of Rosenmüller) in the human female, is a structure having a vertical diameter of 15 to 25 mm. **1962** *Gray's Anat.* (ed. 33) 1538 The epoöphoron lies in the lateral part of the mesosalpinx between the ovary and the uterine tube.

epopee (ˈɛpəʊpiː). Now somewhat *rare.* Also 8–9 -pée. [a. F. *épopée*, ad. mod.L. *epopœia*; q.v.]

1. An epic poem (= EPIC B.). Usually the epic poem generically; the epic species of poetry.

1697 DRYDEN *Æneid* Ded., Both of them abhor strong metaphors, in which the epopee delights. **1768–74** TUCKER *Lt. Nat.* (1852) I. 23 The action of the drama or epopee.. must be one and entire. **1823** tr. *Sismondi's Lit. Eur.* (1846) I. xvi. 465 The discovery of the comic epopee.. The origin of the mock epopee. **1846** GROTE *Greece* II. xxi. 234 The age of the epos is followed by that of the epopee.

2. *transf.*

1846 GROTE *Greece* (1862) II. iii. 54 They may be said to constitute a sort of historical epopee. **1855** MILMAN *Lat. Chr.* (1864) IX. XIV. iii. 163 The Imitatio Christi is an epopee of the internal history of the human soul.

epoˈpœan, *a. rare.* [f. Gr. ἐποποι-ός (see next) + -AN.] Befitting an epic poet.

1819 H. BUSK *Vestriad* I. 18 Rouse my bold muse with epopœan rage, A hero's rise to sing.

epopœia (ɛpəʊˈpiːə). *arch.* In 8 epopea, -œa, 9 epopeia. [a. mod.L. *epopœia*, a. Gr. ἐποποιΐα the making of epics, f. ἐποποιός maker of epics, f. ἔπος (see EPOS) + -ποιος maker.] = EPOPEE I.

1749 HURD *Horace's Art Poetry* Wks. 1811 I. 67 It being more glaringly inconsistent with the genius of the drama to admit of foreign..ornaments, than of the extended *Episodical Epopœia.* **1756–82** J. WARTON *Ess. Pope* I. III. 126 That the action of the epopea be one great and entire. **1782** V. KNOX *Ess.* II. 384 [Stesichorus] gave to lyric poetry all the solemnity of the Epopœa. **1798** W. TAYLOR in *Monthly Rev.* XXVI. 248 He also wrote a tedious epopea, of which Belisarius is the hero. **1822** SCOTT *Nigel* Introd. Ep., The plot of a regular and connected epopeia.

epopœist (ɛpəʊˈpiːɪst). [f. prec. (or f. Gr. ἐποποι-ός) + -IST.] One who writes epic poetry.

1840 *Tait's Mag.* VII. 411 The historian is merely a more modern name for the Epopœist. **1850** BLACKIE *Æschylus* I. 7 Those who are familiar with the productions of the great Ionic Epopœist.

ˌepo-ˈpoet. [f. EPO-S + POET.] An epic poet.

1800 W. TAYLOR in Robberds *Mem.* I. 357 The taking of Seringapatam is a good subject for you epo-poets.

epopt (ˈɛpɒpt). [ad. late L. *epopta*, ad. Gr. ἐπόπτης, agent-n. f. ἐποπ- (f. ἐπί upon + root ὀπ- to see), serving as the base of certain tenses of ἐφοράειν to look upon, behold.] A 'beholder'; in *Gr. Antiq.* a person fully initiated into the Eleusinian mysteries. Also *transf.*

1696 TOLAND *Christianity not Myst.* 167 The right of seeing every thing, or being Epopts. **1798** W. TAYLOR in *Monthly Mag.* VI. 552 Those..who obtained the insight of these revelations, called themselves Epopts, Seers, or the Initiated. **1833** *Brit. Mag.* III. 48 That which has made us in some sort epopts of those mysteries which are between this world and the next. **1850** GROTE *Greece* II. lviii. (1862) V. 183 Addressing his companions as Mysts and Epopts.

Hence **eˈpoptic** *a*, of or pertaining to an epopt. **epoptics** *sb. pl.*, **eˈpoptist** = EPOPT.

1770 LANGHORNE *Plutarch's Lives, Alexander* ed. Tegg) 467 Those more secret and profound branches of science, which they call acroamatic and epoptic. **1711** tr. *Werenfel's Disc. Logom.* 99 Aristotle's Books of deep Learning, his Acroamaticks, Esotericks, Epopticks, and mysterious Writings. *a* **1652** J. SMITH *Sel. Disc.* i. 10 Hidden mysteries in divine truth..which cannot be discerned but only by divine Epoptists.

‖**epos** (ˈɛpɒs). [L. *epos*, a. Gr. ἔπος word, song, f. ἐπ- stem of εἰπεῖν to say.]

1. a. A collective term for early unwritten narrative poems celebrating incidents of heroic tradition; the rudimentary form of epic poetry. **b.** An epic poem: = EPIC B., EPOPEE. **c.** Epic poetry.

a. 1839 THIRLWALL *Greece* II. xii. 124 The epos..in this respect appears to have adhered to the model of the ancient hymnody. **1846** GROTE *Greece* II. 234 The age of the epos is followed by that of the epopee. **1883** H. KENNEDY tr. *Ten Brink's E.E. Lit.* 148 The ancient Epos hardly survived.

b. 1855 BROWNING *Men & Wom.* II. *Cleon* 172 That epos on thy hundred plates of gold Is mine. **1856** MRS. BROWNING *Aur. Leigh* v. 155 Every age..expects a morn And claims an epos. **1858** TRENCH *Parables* 45 The action, gradually unfolding itself of an Epos.

c. 1835 J. B. ROBERTSON tr. *Schlegel's Philos. Hist.* (1846) 6 The author next passes in review the Hesiodic epos, the middle epos, or the works of the Cyclic poets. **1850** CARLYLE *Latter-d. Pamph.* viii. (1872) 285 Almost rises into epos and prophecy.

2. *transf.* A series of striking events worthy of epic treatment.

1848 W. H. KELLY tr. *L. Blanc's Hist. Ten Y.* I. 234 All these episodes of the great epos [the insurrection of Paris] were similar in character, and imbodied the same lessons. **1872** GEO. ELIOT *Middlem.* (1878) Prel. 2 She found her epos in the reform of a religious order.

[**eposculation**, given in some Dicts., is app. a misprint for EXOSCULATION.

1563 BECON *Displ. Pop. Mass* Wks. III. 52a Your inspirations and eposculations, your benedictions and humiliations.]

†**epoˈtation.** *Obs.* [n. of action f. *ēpōtāre*: see next.] The action of drinking up or off.

1627–77 FELTHAM *Resolves* I lxxxiv. 128 The Epotations of dumb liquor damn him. **1660** *Charac. Italy* 55 There is by their epotation laid the seed of all future maladies.

†**eˈpote**, *v. Obs.* [ad. L. *ēpōt-āre*, f. *ē* out + *pōtāre* to drink.] *trans.* To drink; to drink up.

1657 TOMLINSON *Renou's Disp.* 297 The decoction of the root epoted, cures convulsions.

†**epouˈventable**, *a. Obs.* In 5 epoventable, 6 epouventabl, *Sc.* espoventabill, appoventabyll. [a. OF. *espouventable* (mod.F. *épouvantable*, corresp. to Pr. *espaventable*), f. *espouventer* (mod.F. *épouvanter*, Pr. *espaventar*), f. L. *expavent-em*, f. *ex* out + *pavē-re* to be in a fright.] Frightful, terrible.

1475 CAXTON *Jason* 67 The grete epouentable dragons. **1552** LYNDESAY *Monarchy* (1883), With horrabyll sound appouentabyll [*ed.* **1592** espouuentabill]. **1588** A. KING tr. *Canisius' Catech.* 92 The dreidful and epouuentabl rigor of Gods terrible iudgment.

epoxide (ɪˈpɒksaɪd). *Chem.* [f. EPI- + OXIDE.] A chemical compound the molecules of which contain an oxygen atom attached to two carbon atoms directly or indirectly bonded to one another; a cyclic ether. Also *attrib.*, as ***epoxide resin*** = *epoxy resin.*

1930 [see EPOXY *prefix* and quasi-*adj.*]. **1938** ALLEN & BLATT in H. Gilman *Org. Chem.* I. vi. 545 Peracetic acid and perbenzoic acid form epoxides by addition of an atom of oxygen to ethylenic linkages. **1950** *Chem. Abstr.* XLIV. 3298 *Epoxide resins*... Products for enamels, paints, adhesives, films, molded articles, etc. **1958** *Engineering* 31 Jan. 7/3 (Advt.), The epoxy or epoxide resins are among the newest and most versatile modern plastics.

Hence **epoxiˈdation**, the formation of an epoxide by the addition of an atom of oxygen to two doubly bonded carbon atoms; **eˌpoxiˈdizable** *a.*, capable of undergoing epoxidation; **eˈpoxidize** *v.*, to convert into an epoxide by means of epoxidation; so **eˈpoxidized**, **eˈpoxidizing** *ppl. adjs.*

1944 *Jrnl. Amer. Chem. Soc.* LXVI. 1927/2 The epoxidation of oleic acid. **1945** *Ibid.* LXVII. 414/2 Epoxidized oils, a new class of chemical reaction products from triglycerides, have been prepared. **1946** *Ibid.* LXVIII. 1507/2 The same olefins were epoxidized with peracetic acid in acetic acid solution. **1958** *Industrial & Engin. Chem.* June 873/1 Use of this versatile peracetic acid as the epoxidizing agent results in greater freedom from undesirable side reactions. **1960** J. G. WALLACE in Kirk & Othmer *Encycl. Chem. Technol.* Suppl. II. 327 Epoxides may be produced by decomposing the hemiperoxyacetate in the presence of an epoxidizable olefin. *Ibid.* 329 Epoxides..may also be obtained by reactions not involving epoxidation. **1963** W. R. MOORE *Introd. Polymer Chem.* vi. 178 New epoxy resins have recently been produced in which the epoxide groups are obtained by epoxidation of a carbon-carbon double bond.

epoxy (ɪˈpɒksɪ), *prefix* and quasi-*adj. Chem.* [f. EPI- + OXY-.] **A.** *prefix.* An element used in the names of chemical compounds that are epoxides. **B.** Hence as quasi-*adj.*: pertaining to or deriving from an epoxide; containing the ring structure characteristic of epoxides; **epoxy resin**, any of various synthetic polyether resins that contain epoxy groups and benzene rings, are usu. made by polymerizing an epoxide, and are convertible into a thermoset form.

1916 *Chem. Abstr.* X. 3400/2 Epoxy,—O—(to different atoms). **1930** *Jrnl. Amer. Chem. Soc.* LII. 1191 The epoxides of oleic and elaidic acids have been obtained in crystalline form... Three directions in which these epoxy acids decompose on heating have been discussed. **1945** *Ibid.* LXVII. 412/1 Peracetic acid functions as an oxidizing agent ..to yield epoxy compounds, but..in acetic acid solution the epoxy ring is opened and mixtures of hydroxy-acetoxy compounds are obtained. **1950** S. O. GREENLEE *U.S. Pat.* 2,494,295 5 The complex epoxides are in general resinous in character... The complex epoxy resins are soluble, unless too highly polymerized, in solvents such as acetone. **1960** 'A. BURGESS' *Doctor is Sick* viii. 58 If only the head could be, perhaps painlessly, severed and then, with some epoxy resin or other, fitted back. **1960** *Handbk. Chem. Soc. Authors* iii. 108 Oxygen linked, in a chain of carbon atoms, to two of these atoms will be denoted by the prefix epoxy in all cases where it would be unprofitable to name the substance as a cyclic compound. Examples: ethylene oxide = epoxyethane. **1966** *McGraw-Hill Encycl. Sci. & Technol.* X. 469/1 The epoxy resins form a relatively new class of cross-linked polyethers characterized by excellent chemical resistance, adhesion to glass and metals, electrical insulating properties, and ease and precision of fabrication. **1969** *Jane's Freight Containers 1968–69* 21 (Advt.), An extensive range of abrasion resistant phenolic, vinyl and epoxy linings with non-toxic, odourless and tasteless characteristics.

Hence as *v. trans.*, to glue with epoxy resin.

1974 *Sci. Amer.* Jan. 117 (*caption*), ¼" nut for traverse screw epoxied to aluminum backplate. **1982** *Guardian* 26 Oct. 8/6 With the buck-jaw, there is the ear that is epoxyed to the shoulder and the frantic lever-type action that finds the hair being constantly flipped back.

‖**épris** (epri), *a.* fem. éprise (-z). [Fr.] Enamoured.

1793 DR. BURNEY *Let.* May in *Diary Mme. d'Arblay* (1842) V. 426, I have for some time seen..that you are *éprise.* **1848** THACKERAY *Van. Fair* lxi. 555 That Major seems to be particularly *épris.* **1850** C. M. YONGE *Kenneth* viii. 90 You are quite *épris* with those children. **1893** BEERBOHM *Let.* 13 Oct. (1964) 75 Nor need you have said that you have been *épris* of little artistes yourself. **1917** A. HUXLEY *Let.* 22 Nov. (1969) 138 Who is Flora Fo[r]ster? I am so much épris with her poem that I shall write to her. **1949** 'C. HARE' *When Wind Blows* 54 As if anybody else

could not see that Mr. Ventry is *épris* of Nicola. **1949** A. WILSON *Wrong Set* 155 He would have felt it necessary to come to my defence, he was so completely *épris*.

EPROM (ˈiːprɒm). *Computing.* Also **eprom.** [Acronym f. *e*rasable *p*rogrammable *ROM*: see *ROM* s.v. R II. 2a.] A read-only memory whose contents can be erased by a special process (e.g. irradiation with ultraviolet light) and replaced.

1977 *Sci. Amer.* Sept. 147/2 (*caption*) The program is stored in an erasable and reprogrammable read-only memory (EPROM)... The program is erased by exposing the circuit to ultraviolet radiation, which causes the electric charges stored in the EPROM to leak away. **1983** RALSTON & REILLY *Encycl. Computer Sci.* (ed. 2) 971/2 PROMs and EPROMs can be written slowly by a series of high-voltage, short-duration electrical pulses. **1985** *Acorn User* Feb. 36/2 Several BBC Basic programs can be entered on one eprom. **1986** *Keyboard Player* Apr. 39/3 The System 360 MIDI Bass.. provides.. four sampled bass sounds. There is a whole library being built up which are fitted simply by inserting new EPROMS.

‖**eprouvette** (epruvɛt). [Fr. *éprouvette*, f. *éprouver* to try, to test.]

1. An apparatus for testing the strength of gunpowder. Also *attrib.*

1781 THOMPSON in *Phil. Trans.* LXXI. 298 All the eprouvettes, or powder-triers, in common use are defective. **1839** *Sat. Mag., Supp.* Jan. 40/1 Another form of éprouvette was devised by the late Dr. Hutton. **1846** GREENER *Sc. Gunnery* 37 Where experiments are conducted.. with moveable *eprouvettes*, a certain loss is sustained. **1874** KNIGHT *Dict. Mech.* s.v. *Eprouvette-gun*, The éprouvette-mortar of the British service is 8 inches in diameter.

2. A spoon used in assaying metals.

1874 KNIGHT *Dict. Mech.*, *Éprouvette*, a flux spoon. A spoon for sampling an assay.

eps, obs. form of ASP[1].

epsilon (ɛpˈsaɪlən). [Gr. ἐ ψιλόν, lit. 'bare e', i.e. 'e and nothing else', = short e written ϵ and not αι.] The fifth letter of the Greek alphabet (*E*, ϵ):

1. *Astr.* Denoting the fifth brightest star in a constellation.

c **1400** MAUNDEV. (1839) iii. 20. **1842** *Penny Cycl.* XXII. 448/2 The following stars, γ Leonis, ϵ Bootis, ζ Herculis, δ Serpentis, and γ Virginis, were made out to be revolving double stars, by W. Herschel, in 1803. **1930** A. J. QUIRKE *Forged, Anon. & Suspect Docs.* v. 77 Affectation of letter-forms of unconventional type... A typical example is the use of the Greek 'epsilon' for small *e*. *Ibid.* vii. 100 Examination of small 'e'... If Greek 'epsilon' form is used, [etc.]. **1931** *Times Lit. Suppl.* 1 Jan. 10/3 The epsilon-shaped E [i.e. ϵ]. **1959** *Listener* 3 Dec. 971/1 An interesting system is that of Epsilon Lyræ.

2. a. An examiner's fifth-class mark.

1907 [see ALPHA 4].

b. A person of low intelligence.

1932 A. HUXLEY *Brave New World* i. 15 'In Epsilons,' said Mr. Foster very justly, 'we don't need human intelligence.' *Ibid.* iv. 69 The liftman was a small simian creature, dressed in the black tunic of an Epsilon-Minus Semi-Moron. **1958** *Listener* 11 Sept. 374/2 With the people down below—'the epsilons'—enjoying very little—do you think this kind of situation can long endure?

Epsom (ˈɛpsəm). The name of a town in Surrey.

1. *attrib.* and *Comb.*, as **Epsom-water**, the water of a mineral spring at Epsom; **Epsom-salt** (*colloq.* **-salts**), originally the salt (chiefly composed of magnesium sulphate) obtained from this water; now the popular name of magnesium sulphate however prepared.

1770 tr. *Cronstedt's Min.* 137 This may be called English or Epsom salt. **1811** A. T. THOMSON *Lond. Disp.* II. (1818) 245 First artificially obtained in England in 1675, from the evaporation of the water of the Epsom spring: whence it was named Epsom salt. **1876** PAGE *Adv. Text-bk. Geol.* xv. 282 The manufacture of magnesia and Epsom salts.

2. Short for *Epsom salt*.

1803 *Ann. Rev.* I. 871/1 Even allowing Mr. K. the use of the term epsom, instead of sulphat of magnesia. **1854** *Pharmac. Jrnl.* XIII. 622 The sulphate of magnesia forming the 'rough Epsoms' of the alum-maker.

3. The racecourse on Epsom Downs in Surrey, where the Derby and the Oaks are run; the principal race-meeting held there.

c **1810** W. HICKEY *Mem.* (1960) 326 We all went.. to Epsom races. **1827** P. EGAN *Anecdotes Turf* 53 A young man had once the ambition of riding over Epsom against Dick. **1838, 1867** [see DERBY 1 b]. **1880** TROLLOPE *Duke's Children* I. xvii. 202 It was impossible that Lord Silverbridge should separate himself from the Major,—at any rate till after the Epsom meeting.

epsomite (ˈɛpsəmaɪt). *Min.* [f. *Epsom* + -ITE.] Native magnesium sulphate.

1814 T. ALLAN *Min. Nomencl.* 42 Natural Epsom Salt, Epsomite. **1878** LAWRENCE tr. *Cotta's Rocks Class.* 44 Epsomite occurs as an efflorescence from marshy ground.

Epstein-Barr virus (ɛpstaɪnbɑː). *Med.* [f. the names of M. A. *Epstein* (b. 1921), British virologist, and Y. M. *Barr* (now Balding) (b. 1932), Irish-born virologist.] An enveloped DNA herpes virus which causes infectious mononucleosis and is associated with Burkitt's lymphoma and nasopharyngeal carcinoma.

1968 *Biol. Abstr.* XLIX. 6557/1 Specific immunofluorescence test for the herpes-type EB (Epstein-Barr) virus of Burkitt lymphoblasts. **1970** *New Scientist* 22 Oct. 162 Added to the evidence linking the Epstein-Barr virus with Burkitt's lymphoma,.. this result will strengthen the growing conviction that viruses are an essential causal determinant for human cancer. **1985** *Sci. Amer.* Dec. 76/3 Infection with hepatitis *B*, Epstein-Barr virus or cytomegalo-virus is common among several of the groups at risk from AIDS.

ept (ɛpt), *a.* [Back-formation f. INEPT *a.*] Used as a deliberate antonym of 'inept': adroit, appropriate, effective.

1938 E. B. WHITE *Let.* Oct. (1976) 183, I am much obliged .. to you for your warm, courteous, and ept treatment of a rather weak, skinny subject. **1966** *Time* 30 Sept. 7/1 With the exception of one or two semantic twisters, I think it is a first-rate job—definitely ept, ane and ert. **1976** *N.Y. Times Mag.* 6 June 15 The obvious answer is summed up by a White House official's sardonic crack: 'Politically, we're not very ept.'

Hence **ˈeptitude**; **ˈeptly** *adv.*

1967 *New Yorker* 11 Mar. 133/1 At the start of a season, the custom milliners are always full of ertia and eptitude —an attitude that I parage. **1970** *Guardian* 3 Nov. 11/1 The Foreign Secretary has a deserved reputation for being an accident prone speechmaker, and his eptitude—if that is a word—is sometimes questionable. **1974** *New Yorker* 29 Apr. 129/1 Five masked instrumentalists visit, play a sort of march, exchange instruments and play it again, necessarily rather less eptly. **1978** *Observer* 29 Jan. 4/8 The affair.. has contributed to what has been called his 'eptitude problem': his ability, when he is wrong-footed, to extricate himself cleanly from the resulting mess.

eptagon, obs. form of HEPTAGON.

epulary (ˈɛpjʊlərɪ), *a.* [ad. L. *epulāris*, f. *epulum* feast.] Of, pertaining to, or having to do with, a feast or banquet.

1678 PHILLIPS, *Epulary*, belonging to a Banquet. **1721–1800** in BAILEY. **1839** G. RAYMOND in *New Monthly Mag.* LVII. 407 The hum of epulary commerce resounded on every side. **1856** SMYTH *Rom. Fam. Coins* 296 The corporation of Bedford, a body which had not quite lost its epulary renown when Oliver Goldsmith publicly complimented its manducatory energies.

epulation (ɛpjuːˈleɪʃən). Now *rare.* Also 6 epulacion, -cyon. [ad. L. *epulātiōn-em*, f. *epulārī* to feast, f. *epulum* feast.] The action of feasting or indulging in dainty fare. Also *fig.*

1542 BOORDE *Dyetary* ix. (1870) 250 As it is taken by epulacyon, of eatynge of crude meate. **1569** NEWTON *Cicero's Olde Age* 31 b, Neither did I take delectation in these banquettes and epulacions. **1646** SIR T. BROWNE *Pseud. Ep.* (1650) 324 When he [Epicurus] would dine with Jove, and pretend unto epulation, he desired no other addition than a piece of Cytheridian cheese. **1819** H. BUSK *Banquet* II. 617 To make your epulation quite complete, One thing you need. **1835** HOGG in *Fraser's Mag.* XI. 517 Such love.. 'Twas love's luxuriant epulation.

epulentic, var. of EPILENTIC *a. Obs.*

‖**epulis** (ɛˈpjuːlɪs). *Path.* [mod.L. *epūlis*, a. Gr. ἐπουλίς, f. ἐπί upon + οὖλον gum.] (See quots.)

1859 J. TOMES *Dental Surg.* 518 Tumours springing up from the margin of the gums.. usually receive the designation, epulis. **1878** T. BRYANT *Pract. Surg.* I. 537 Under epulis are included, rightly or wrongly, most of the tumours of the gums.

†**ˈepulose**, *a. Obs. rare*⁻⁰. [f. L. *epul-um* + -OSE, as if ad. L. **epulōs-us*.] Feasting to excess. Hence †**epuˈlosity**, a feasting to excess.

1731 in BAILEY vol. II. **1847** in CRAIG; and in mod. Dicts.

epulotic (ɛpjuːˈlɒtɪk), *a.* and *sb. Med.* [ad. Gr. ἐπουλωτικ-ός, f. ἐπουλόεσθαι to be scarred over, f. ἐπί upon + οὐλή scar.]

A. *adj.* Having power to cicatrize.

1761 W. LEWIS *Mat. Med.* (ed. 2) 160 s.v. *Calaminaris*, The officinal epulotic cerate. **1787** C. B. TRYE in *Med. Commun.* II. 154 The common epulotic dressings. **1832** in WEBSTER; and in mod. Dicts.

B. *sb.* in *pl.* Medicines or ointments that induce cicatrization, and heal wounds or sores.

1634 T. JOHNSON tr. *Parey's Chirurg.* XXVI. xvi. (1678) 639 We use Epuloticks when as the ulcer is almost filled up, and equal to the adjacent skin. **1751** DEBENHAM in *Phil. Trans.* XLVII. 94 The wound was.. by the use of epulotics, completely cicatrized. **1832** in WEBSTER; and in mod. Dicts.

Hence †**epuˈlotical** *a. Path. Obs.* = prec. adj.

1615 CROOKE *Body of Man* 86 The flesh is softned and dryed by Epulotical medicines as they call them. **1657** TOMLINSON *Renou's Disp.* 107 A slash or skar of a wound is closed with an Epulotical Powder.

†**ˈepulous**, *a. Obs. rare*⁻⁰. [f. L. *epul-um* + -OUS: see EPULOSE.] = EPULOSE.

1692–1732 in COLES.

ˈepurate (ˈɛpjʊəreɪt), *v. rare.* [f. F. *épur-er* to purify: see -ATE 6.] *trans.* To purify. *lit* and *fig.*

1799 *Hist.* in *Ann. Reg.* 474 The departmental administration, which having been long before epurated, was in the secret of the revolution. **1801** W. TAYLOR in *Monthly Mag.* XII. 581 As the evaporation of water in the sunshine epurates the atmosphere. **1813** —— *Monthly Rev.* LXXII. 473 With a diction epurated at Paris in royal times, she [Mde. de Genlis] is still not a classical writer.

Hence **ˈepurated** *ppl. a.*

1815 W. TAYLOR in *Monthly Rev.* LXXVI. 501 An epurated Christianity.

epuration (ɛpjʊˈreɪʃən). [a. F. *épuration*, f. *épurer*: see prec.] The action or process of purifying: purification; *esp.* (usu. in Fr. form *épuration* (epyrasjɔ̃)): the removal of politicians or officials from office, or their prosecution (in France); a purge.

1800 W. TAYLOR in *Monthly Mag.* X. 8 These opinions may require further epuration. **1825** *Ann. Reg.* 175 Epuration or investigation of the characters of official persons. **1883** *Sat. Rev.* 20 Oct. 489/1 There is.. no reason to suppose that any section of the French people.. has been offended by.. the *épuration* of its magistracy. **1948** W. STEVENS *Let.* 7 Jan. (1967) 573 The *épuration* has always been something that I have not been able to follow very attentively... I have always thought that Petain.. was quite badly treated.

epyllion (ɛˈpɪlɪən). Pl. **epyllia** (-ɪə). [Gr. ἐπύλλιον dim. of ἔπος EPOS.] In classical use: see quot. 1949. Also applied to post-classical poems of short or moderate extent resembling an epic in style or matter; a miniature epic.

The word seems to have been revived by German scholars in the mid-19th c.: see *Class. Jrnl.* XLIX (1953–4), 111 ff.

1876 R. ELLIS *Commentary Catullus* 228 Unfortunately the contemporaneous epyllia, the Io of Calvus, the Smyrna of Cinna, the Glaucus of Cornificius, have perished. **1890** A. S. WILKINS *Rom. Lit.* 75 The fashion at this time was to substitute for long and tedious epics brief and highly finished pictures of episodes or idylls (*epyllia*). **1895** J. W. MACKAIL *Latin Lit.* II. i. 104 Pieces in hexameter verse, belonging broadly to the class of the *epyllion*, or 'little epic', which was invented as a convenient term to include short poems in the epic metre that were not definitely pastorals either in subject or treatment. **1931** M. M. CRUMP (*title*) The epyllion from Theocritus to Ovid. **1949** *Oxf. Class. Dict.* 335/1 *Epyllion*, a literary type popular from Theocritus to Ovid, was a narrative poem of about 100 to 600 hexameters; the subject was usually taken from the life of a mythical hero or heroine, the love motif being prominent in later epyllia. **1952** C. S. LEWIS *Hero & Leander* 24 Marlowe's success is most easily seen if we compare him with other sixteenth-century specimens of the erotic epyllion.

equability (iːk-, ɛkwəˈbɪlɪtɪ). Forms: 6 equabilite, 6–7 equabilitie, 7 aequability, 6– equability. [ad. L. *æquābilit-ās*, f. *æquābili-s* EQUABLE: see -ITY.]

1. The quality of being equable or uniform; evenness of mind, temper, or behaviour; freedom from fluctuation or variation in condition, rate of movement, degree of intensity, etc.

1531 ELYOT *Gov.* III. xxi, There is also moderation in tolleration of fortune of euerye sorte, which of Tulli is called equabilite. **1577–87** HOLINSHED *Chron.* I. 21/2 He would not have beene led with such an equabilitie of mind. **1656** TRAPP *Comm. Matt.* vi. 22 Uniformity, equability, ubiquity, and constancy of holiness. **1692** RAY *Dissol. World* ii. (1732) 87 The Equability of the Sun's diurnal Motion. **1692** BENTLEY *Boyle Lect.* v. 160 Where is that æquability of nine months warmth to be found? **1711** ADDISON *Spect.* No. 68 ⁋3, I should join to these other Qualifications a certain Æquability or Evenness of Behaviour. **1713** ADDISON *Guardian* No 119 The equability of his numbers.. cloyed and satiated the ear for want of variety. **1762** J. FOSTER *Essay Accent & Quantity* 8 A monotony and æquability in the voice. *a* **1832** BENTHAM *Princ. Penal Law* Wks. 1843 I. 456 In respect of equability, these punishments [by disgrace] are really more defective than at first sight they might appear. *a* **1834** COLERIDGE *Shaks. Notes* 39 The security and comparative equability of human life. **1854** HOOKER *Himal. Jrnls.* I. vii. 169 The humidity, and equability of the climate. **1882** *Med. Temp. Jrnl.* I. 104 The excessive sensitiveness and want of equability of which so many complain.

†**2.** Capability of being regarded as equal, or of being compared on equal terms. *Obs.*

1581 J. BELL *Haddon's Answ. Osor.* 35 May any equabilitie seeme to bee betwixt them? either in the excellencie of the holy Ghost? or in sinceritie of Lyfe? **1631** R. BYFIELD *Doctr. Sabb.* 183 You that make the servant.. but as the Oxe and Asse is.. have utterly destroyed this equability. *a* **1652** BROME *Love-sick Court* IV. i, Their merits bear no æquability With mine. **1817** COGAN *Ethical Quest.* v. (R.), Bodies seem to act mutually upon each other, with a kind of equability in power.

†**3.** Due or just proportion; well-balanced condition. *Obs.*

1576 NEWTON *Lemnie's Complex.* (1633) 9 If he finde the plight and state of his body to be in equability and perfect temperatenesse, it shall be good to cherish and preserve it with his like. **1605** TIMME *Quersit.* II. iv. 116 The perfect combination, adequation, equabilitie of elements, etc.

equable (ˈiːk-, ˈɛkwəb(ə)l), *a.* Also 7–8 æquable. [ad. L. *æquābilis*, f. *æquāre* to make level or equal, f. *æquus* equal.]

1. Uniform, free from fluctuation or variation.

a. Of motions or continuous phenomena: Maintaining a constant level of speed or intensity. †Also of periods of time: uniform in duration.

1677 HALE *Prim. Orig. Man.* II. ix. 224, 25 Apocatastases annorum, which amounted to 36525 equable Years. **1726** *tr. Gregory's Astron.* I. III. 405 The apparent Motion of the Sun will be equable. **1799** *Med. Jrnl.* I. 279 The pulse slower, more uniform and equable. **1808** J. WEBSTER *Nat. Phil.* 29 Its parallels express the equable time of motion. **1811** A. T. THOMSON *Lond. Disp.* (1818) Introd. 28 Mercury is the liquid best adapted for thermometers; its expansion being most equable. **1812** WOODHOUSE *Astron.* xviii. 188 Kepler's discovery of the equable description of areas. **1850** GROTE

Greece II. lvi. (1862) V. 72 The slow, solemn, and equable march of the troops.

b. Of temperature: Free from extremes (or sudden changes) of heat and cold.

1807 *Med. Jrnl.* XVII. 292 Those parts of the kingdom where they may enjoy the most equable state of temperature. **1860** MAURY *Phys. Geog. Sea* xvii. §728 Thus the equable climates of Western Europe are accounted for.

c. Of the feelings, mind, temper, etc.: Even, not easily disturbed. Of a course of events: Free from vicissitudes, tranquil. Of literary style: Maintaining a constant level, uniform.

1796 BURKE *Regic. Peace* Wks. 1842 II. 341[Military ardour] is a cool, steady, deliberate principle, always present, always equable. **1814** WORDSW. *Laodamia* xvii, In worlds whose course is equable and pure. **1836** J. H. NEWMAN *Par. Serm.* (1837) III. xxiii. 375 A calm and equable piety. **1855** MACAULAY *Hist. Eng.* III. 468 His oratory was more correct and equable than theirs. **1875** JOWETT *Plato* (ed. 2) I. Introd. 12 It [a translation] should be ..equable in style. **1876** BLACK *Madcap V.* xvi. 140 An equable temper is the greatest gift a man can possess.

2. Free from inequalities; uniform throughout its extent or range of operation; equally proportioned.

1692 BENTLEY *Boyle Lect.* viii. Wks. 1838 III. 193 They would have the vast body of a planet..to be every where smooth and equable. **1812** SIR H. DAVY *Chem. Philos.* 233 Elastic fluids have a tendency to rapid equable mixture. **1838** THIRLWALL *Greece* V. xlii. 205 A new valuation..with a view to a more equable system of taxation. **1845** CARLYLE *Cromwell* II. viii. 69 A more equable division of representatives. **1847** DISRAELI *Tancred* III. iv, A rich subdued and equable tint overspread this visage. **1854** RONALDS & RICHARDSON *Chem. Technol.* (ed. 2) I. 205 A channel of equable diameter.

†**3.** Characterized by justice or fairness; = EQUITABLE. *Obs.*

1643 SIR T. BROWNE *Relig. Med.* II. §13 Becomming equable to others, I become unjust to myself. [Cf. quot. 1839 s.v. EQUABLY.]

equableness (ˈiːk-, ˈɛkwəb(ə)lnɪs). [f. prec. + -NESS.] The condition or quality of being equable; EQUABILITY, in various senses.

1641 SYMONDS *Serm. bef. Ho. of Com.* C b, We..should walk towards God with truth, æquablenesse, and certainty. **1736** in BAILEY. **1877** E. CONDER *Bas. Faith* iv. 163 Smoothness (that is, equableness of surface). **1880** *Nature* XXIII. No. 582. 184 A like equableness from year to year characterises the temperature and rainfall of the climate.

equably (ˈiːk-, ˈɛkwəblɪ), *adv.* [f. as prec. + -LY[2].] In an equable manner; uniformly, regularly; justly, fairly; calmly, tranquilly.

1726 tr. *Gregory's Astron.* I. III. 417 The Sun..mov'd both equably and in the Equator. *a* **1743** CHEYNE (J.), If bodies move equably in concentrick circles, etc. **1798** MALTHUS *Popul.* (1806) II. III. x. 238 The wealth of the civilized world will..be..more equably diffused. **1839** THIRLWALL *Greece* III. 61 The..cultivation of their fertile and equably divided territory. **1873** BLACK *Pr. Thule* xi. 172 Equably confessing her ignorance on all such points.

equacion, -cioun, obs. ff. of EQUATION.

equæval (ɪˈkwiːvəl), *a.* Also equiæval. [f. L. *æquæv-us* (f. *æquus* equal + *ævum* age) + -AL[1].] Of equal age; belonging to the same period.

1867 STUBBS *Pref. Benedict's Chron.* (Rolls) 24 A small folio, written in double columns, in a variety of equæval hands. **1881** W. PALGRAVE in *Macm. Mag.* XLV. 21 Her Capitol was equiæval with her birth.

†**eˈquævous,** *a. Obs.* [f. as prec. + -OUS.] = prec. (Const. *to.*)

1658 W. BURTON *Itin. Anton.* 173, I cannot think therefore of anything else proceeding from the Roman times here or Equaevous to their greatness..except it be the Thames.

equal (ˈiːkwəl), *a.* and *sb.* Forms: ? 4 *pl.* equals, -les, 6–7 æqual(l, equall, 6 equale, 6– equal. See also EGALL. [ad. L. *æquālis*, f. *æqu-us* level, even, just.

As the form of the L. *æquus* does not permit it to be directly anglicized without the addition of a suffix, the Eng. *equal* represents the senses of that word as well as those of its derivative *æquālis*. The OF. *equal* (orig. a literary adaptation of the L. word, the regular phonetic descendant of which, *ewel, ivel*, was in popular use) does not seem to have been adopted in Eng.; but its later form *egual* (*esgal*), *egal* became Eng. in 14th c. (see EGALL), and did not become wholly obs. until the 17th c.]

A. *adj.* **1. a.** Of magnitudes or numbers: Identical in amount; neither less nor greater than the object of comparison. Of things: Having the same measure; identical in magnitude, number, value, intensity, etc. Const. *to*, †*with*.

(In this and the next sense often with latent notion of 'at least equal'; hence *not equal to* means usually 'less than', 'inferior to'.)

c **1391** CHAUCER *Astrol.* I. §16 A smal croys..aboue the south lyne, þat shewith the 24 howres equals [Lat. *æquales*] of the clokke. *Ibid.* II. §8 To turn the howres in-equales in howres equales [*Ad conuertendum horas in-equales in horas equales*]. **1568** GRAFTON *Chron.* II. 676 Three hils, not in equall distaunce, nor yet in equall quantitie. **1587** GOLDING *De Mornay* xiv. 212 Yᵉ three inner angles are equal with the two right angles. **1598** BARNFIELD *Compl. Poetrie* xxxviii, The wiues of Troy for him made æquall mone. **1628** DIGBY *Voy. Medit.* (1868) 3 Then to shewe three lightes of aequall height fore and aft. *a* **1631** DONNE *Poems* (1650) 8 When with my browne, my gray haires equall be. **1697** DRYDEN *Virg. Georg.* III. 477 Hairy Goats of equal Profit are With Woolly Sheep. **1747** WESLEY *Prim. Physic* (1762) 116 Flower and fine Sugar equal quantities. **1776** WITHERING *Brit. Plants* (1796) III. 523 Stamens half as long again as the blossom, nearly equal. **1816** J. SMITH *Panorama Sc. & Art* I. 398 The actions of bodies on each other are always equal. **1818** CRUISE *Digest* (ed. 2) II. 223 He had equal equity with the mortgagee for 700*l.* **1838** T. THOMSON *Chem. Org. Bodies* 656 The number of atoms of hydrogen and oxygen, must..be equal both in amidin and amylin. **1846** G. DAY tr. *Simon's Anim. Chem.* II. 237 In both cases they occur in nearly equal ratios. **1858** LARDNER *Hand-bk. Nat. Phil., Hydrost.* 132 If the velocity of the float boards were equal to that of the water.

b. phr. ***other things being equal***: transl. mod.L. *ceteris paribus*.

1848 MACAULAY *Hist. Eng.* I. 386 All other circumstances being supposed equal. **1889** *Sat. Rev.* 16 Mar. 318/1 Other things being equal, the chances of any man being hit in action vary..with the rate of fire to which he is exposed.

†**c.** Equally reciprocated.

c **1540** tr. *Pol. Vergil's Eng. Hist.* (Camd.) I. 68, I nothinge desired more ardentlie than the æqual amitte of the Romains.

2. a. Possessing a like degree of a (specified or implied) quality or attribute; on the same level in rank, dignity, power, ability, achievement, or excellence; having the same rights or privileges. Const. *to, with.*

1526 *Pilgr. Perf.* (W. de W. 1531) 13 Where he is now resydent, equall in glory to the father. **1593** SHAKS. *2 Hen. VI.* v. i. 89 Vnloose thy long imprisoned thoughts, And let thy tongue be equall with thy heart. **1605** BACON *Adv. Learn.* I. iii. §9 The ancient custom was to dedicate them [books] only to private and equal friends. **1611** BIBLE *2 Macc.* viii. 30 And made the maimed, orphanes, widowes, yea, & the aged also, equal in spoils with themselves. —— *John* v. 18 Making himselfe equall with God. *a* **1631** DONNE *Paradoxes* (1652) 45 We deny soules to others equall to them in all but in speech. **1667** MILTON *P.L.* IX. 823 The more to draw his Love, And render me more equal. **1725** POPE *Odyss.* I. 383 For the chaste Queen select an equal Lord. **1818** CRUISE *Digest* (ed. 2) VI. 432 He meant his children to be all equal. **1834** *N.Y. Evening Post* 4 Apr. 2/2 A war of exclusive privileges against equal rights. **1878** JEVONS *Prim. Pol. Econ.* 56 All men are born free and equal. **1889** C. M. YONGE in *Monthly Packet* Christmas No., 31 It was of no use to talk to an old wretch like that about social movements and equal rights. **1923** *Management Engin.* IV. 343/2 *Equal Pay*, a principle whereby, given a specific occupation, the rate of pay should be the same for both sexes, output being the same. **1956** *Ann. Reg. 1955* 3 On 25 January Mr. Butler announced that an agreed basis had been found for the introduction of 'equal pay' (for both sexes) in the non-industrial civil service.

b. *Music.* ***equal voices***: voices either all male or all female.

†**c.** Equivalent; serving the same purpose. Const. *as, with. Obs. rare.*

1677 YARRANTON *Eng. Improv.* 10 Paper in Holland is equal with Moneys in England. *Ibid.* 13 A Ticket upon such Lands given to the Merchant would be equal to him as ready money.

3. a. Adequate or fit in quantity or degree. Now only const. *to*; formerly also *simply*.

a **1674** CLARENDON (J.), The Scotts trusted not their own numbers as equal to fight with the English. **1700** DRYDEN *Fables* Ded., To make my commendations equal to your merit. **1719** WATTS *Hymns* I. lxiii, What equal Honours shall we bring To Thee, O Lord. **1791** HAMPSON *Mem. J. Wesley* II. 28 Of the conduct of the magistrates..it is impossible to speak in equal terms of severity and indignation.

b. Adequately fit or qualified. Of persons: Having strength, endurance, or ability adequate *to* some requirement. Phrase, ***equal to the occasion.***

1697 DRYDEN *Virg. Georg.* II. 304 The Soil..Is..equal to the Pasture and the Plough. **1769** *Junius Lett.* iii. 17 The part you have undertaken is at least as much as you are equal to. **1796** JANE AUSTEN *Pride & Prej.* vii, She was not equal, however, to much conversation. **1816** *Remarks Eng. Mann.* 20 He did not feel equal to receiving the congratulations of the company. **1827** SOUTHEY *Hist. Penins. War* II. 124 They were not equal to contend with disciplined troops. **1872** LIDDON *Elem. Relig.* i. 4 Schemes of independent morality ..are not equal to resisting the impetuosities of passion. **1878** BOSW. SMITH *Carthage* 163 Gescon was equal to the emergency.

4. a. Of distribution, mixture, etc.: Evenly proportioned. Of rules, laws, conditions, processes, or actions (hence of agents): Affecting all objects in the same manner and degree; uniform in effect or operation (often passing into 5).

1661 MORGAN *Sph. Gentry* I. i 4 Consisting of the equallest mixture or temper of the four elements. **1676** H. PHILLIPS *Purch. Patt.* A v b, Though this way of valuing the ground be as equal and general a rule as can be; yet, etc. **1696** WHISTON *Th. Earth* I. 36 The equaller Division of the Year allow'd for. **1781** GIBBON *Decl. & F.* II. xxxiii. 251 The army dreaded his equal and inexorable justice. **1836** GEN. P. THOMPSON *Exerc.* (1842) IV. 80 If the Irish were refused equal laws, they would demand the dissolution of the Union. **1840** GLADSTONE *Ch. Princ.* 187 The Church contemplates with equal eye the whole of God's ordinances.

b. Of a contest: Evenly balanced.

1653 HOLCROFT *Procopius* I. 22 Two thirds of the day were past, and the fight yet equall.

†**c.** phr. ***it is equal to me*** (***whether***): = 'it makes no difference', 'it is all the same'. *Obs.* Cf. Fr. *c'est égal*, Ger. *es ist mir gleich.*

1705–15 CHEYNE *Philos. Princ. Relig.* (J.), They..may let them alone, or reject them; it is equal to me. **1746** *Col. Rec. Penn.* V. 57 The Governor said it was equal to him when they adjourn'd. **1749** CHESTERF. *Lett.* II. cxcvi. 237 Whether along the coast of the Adriatic, or that of the Mediterranean, it is equal to me. **1769** GOLDSM. *Rom. Hist.* (1786) II. 206 It was equal to him whether he fell by his enemies in the field, or by his creditors in the city.

d. ***equal opportunity***, the opportunity or right to be employed or considered for employment without prejudice or discrimination on the grounds of race, gender, physical or mental handicap, etc. In earlier wider use: see ***equality of opportunity*** s.v. OPPORTUNITY 2 c. Also ***equal opportunities*** and as attrib. phr.; ***equal-opportunity employer*** (orig. *U.S.*), one who professes not to discriminate against applicants or employees on such grounds.

1925 D. H. LAWRENCE *Refl. Death Porcupine* 155 They talk about 'equal opportunity': but it is bunk, ridiculous bunk. It is the old fable of the fox asking the stork to dinner. **1963** *N.Y. Times* 22 July 14/5 Mr. Screvane proposed to the Board of Estimate that $3,400,000,000 in city pension funds be invested only in securities of equal-opportunity employers. **1972** *Ibid.* 3 Nov. L/9 N.Y. Hilton..An equal opportunity employer. **1973** *Black Panther* 3 Mar. c/2 Those racist tenant businesses located at the Port of Oakland can and must be..made to apply the 'equal opportunity' and 'affirmative action' guidelines. **1977** B. PYM *Quartet in Autumn* ix. 79 'Equal opportunities!' said Norman. 'That's one of the things we men prefer to leave to the ladies.' **1979** *Tucson* (Arizona) *Daily Citizen* 3 Oct. 17A/1 (Advt.), We are an Equal Opportunity Employer M/F. **1984** *Times Educ. Suppl.* 30 Nov. 11/2 It may also recommend giving one governor on each body special responsibility for equal opportunities.

†**5.** In sense of L. *æquus*: Fair, equitable, just, impartial. *Obs.*

1535 STEWART *Cron. Scot.* II. 503 Equale in justice but partialitie. **1545** LELAND in Strype *Eccl. Mem.* I. App. cxviii. 332 My great labours..have profyted the studyous, gentyl, and equal reders. **1592** GREENE *Groatsw. Wit* (1617) 42 Equal heauen hath denied that comfort. **1641** 'SMECTYMNUUS' *Answ.* §5 (1653) 22 This had been no more rationall or equall then the former. **1656** BRAMHALL *Replic.* iv. 188 Is it equall that the Court of Rome themselves should be the Judges? **1681** *Relig. Clerici* To Rdr. 1 To the equal Reader. **1769** ROBERTSON *Chas. V*, III. XI. 354 Proposals of peace which were equal and moderate.

6. Of surfaces: Level, on the same level (*arch.*). †***equal to***: level with.

a **1649** DRUMM. OF HAWTH. *Jas. V.* Wks. 116 The most part of the church was made equal to the ground. **1715** LEONI *Palladio's Archit.* (1742) I. 27 All the Rooms..of the same Story, may have their Floor or Pavement equal. **1850** MRS. BROWNING *Poems* I. 156 The equal plains of fruitful Sicily.

†**7. a.** Uniform throughout in appearance, dimensions, or properties *Obs.*

1663 GERBIER *Counsel* 50 A rooff covered with them is of an equall colour. **1686** AGLIONBY *Painting Illustr.* iii. 107 The Painter must observe an equal Air, so as not to make one part Musculous and Strong, and the other Soft and Tender. **1691** T. H[ALE] *Acc. New Invent* 98 A Sheet of their full length equal within one pound in ten quite through. **1726** LEONI *Alberti's Archit.* II. 18 a, Large Stones, sound, equal, handsome and rare. **1793** SMEATON *Edystone L.* §246 That the building should be a column of equal strength, proportionate in every part to the stress it was likely to bear.

b. *Bot.* Symmetrical, having both sides alike.

1876 BALFOUR in *Encycl. Brit.* IV. 110 When the parenchyma is developed symmetrically on each side of the midrib or stalk, the leaf is *equal*.

8. Of movements, pressure, heat, light, etc.: Even, free from fluctuation in rate or intensity. *rare.* (With this and the next sense cf. EQUABLE 1.)

1626 BACON *Sylva* (1677) §392 Try them by boiling upon an equal fire. **1691** RAY *Creation* I. (1704) 71 These Revolutions..are as exactly equal and uniform as the Earth's are. **1761** EARL PEMBROKE *Mil. Equitation* (1778) 63 Even or equal trot. **1821** SHELLEY *Prometh. Unb.* III. iv. 88 Thy chaste sister Who guides the frozen and inconstant moon Will look on thy more warm and equal light.

9. Of the mind, temper, demeanour, tone of voice: Even, tranquil, undisturbed, unruffled. *arch.*

1680 OTWAY *Orphan* II. vii. 759 Who can hear this and bear an equal mind? *a* **1700** DRYDEN (J.), An equal temper in his mind he found, When fortune flatter'd him, and when she frown'd. **1781** GIBBON *Decl. & F.* III. 9 He proceeded, in a firm and equal tone, to offer Theodosius the alternative of peace, or war. **1821** SCOTT *Kenilw.* xxii, He addressed him in a tone tolerably equal. **1832** TENNYSON *Lotos-Eaters* 153 Let us swear an oath, and keep it with an equal mind.

†**10.** Of numbers: Even. *Obs. rare.* Cf. L. *par.*

1806 G. GREGORY *Dict. Arts & Sc.* s.v. *Bridge*, The piers of stone bridges should be equal in number, that there may be one arch in the middle.

†**11.** quasi-*adv.* Equally. *Obs.*

1613 SHAKS. *Hen. VIII*, I. i. 159 He is equall rau'nous As he is subtile. **1623** MASSINGER *Dk. Milan* II. i, Thou art A thing, that, equal with the devil himself, I do detest. **1633** P. FLETCHER *Purple Isl.* IV. xv, Therefore obtain'd an equall distant seat. **1659** DRYDEN *Cromwell* v, Where all the parts so equal-perfect are.

12. *Comb.* **a.** parasynthetic derivatives, as ***equal-armed, -blooded, -eyed -headed, -limbed, -sided, -souled.*** Also ***equal-handedness.*** **b.** adverbial, as ***equal-balanced, -poised, -suited.***

1833 J. HOLLAND *Manuf. Metal* II. 286 The *equal-armed balance, so commonly seen in this country. **1881** *Athenæum* 23 Apr. 567/1 At the top is an equal-armed cross. **1678** NORRIS *Coll. Misc.* (1699) 312 If the Good and the Evil be *equal-ballanc'd. **1764** CHURCHILL *Ep. Hogarth* Poems II. 135 Thou *equal-blooded judge. **1876** SWINBURNE *Erechth.* (ed. 2) 677 Toward good and ill, then, *equal-eyed

of soul. **1830** GEN. P. THOMPSON *Exerc.* (1842) I. 280 A government of so much benevolence and *equal-handedness. **1889** G. FINDLAY *Eng. Railway* 42 In 1837 the double and *equal-headed reversible rail was originated by Joseph Locke. **1855** MILMAN *Lat. Chr.* (1864) IX. XIV. viii. 278 The short *equal-limbed Greek cross. **1635** SWAN *Spec. M.* (1670) 170 The rising and falling of an *equal-poised balance. **1850** TENNYSON *In Mem.* lxxxv, O friendship, equal-poised control. **1807** T. THOMSON *Chem.* (ed. 3) II. 571 Four-sided prisms, terminated by *equal-sided pyramids. **1876** SWINBURNE *Erechth.* (ed. 2) 676 Nor thine nor mine, but *equal-souled are they. **1590** GREENE *Orl. Fur.* Wks. (1861) 102 The lilies and the native rose Sit *equal-suited with a blushing red.

B. *sb.*

1. One who is equal to another:

a. in rank or standing.

1573 G. HARVEY *Letter-bk.* (Camden Soc.) 4 M. Nevil hath shown himself disdainful towards his æquals and superiors too. **1599** SHAKS. *Much Ado* II. i. 171 She is no equall for his birth. **1614** JOHN DAY *Festivals* (1615) 322 First, that they match with their Equals as neere as may be, both in Condition or State of Life, as also in Yeers. *a* **1640** EARL STIRLING *Jonathan* (R.), You (though subjects) may my equals make. **1754** CHATHAM *Lett. Nephew* v. 38 Towards equals, nothing becomes a man so well as well-bred ease. **1844** H. H. WILSON *Brit. India* II. 468 The Governor-General, whom, as exercising a delegated authority only, he refused to recognise as the equal of a king. **1877** MOZLEY *Univ. Serm.* ix. 194 Humility is much more tried by equals than it is by inferiors.

b. in power or achievement, or in any specified quality; a 'match'.

1607 SHAKS. *Cor.* I. i. 257 Was euer man so proud as is this Martius? He has no equall. **1667** MILTON *P.L.* VI. 248 Satan ..Prodigious power had shewn, and met in Armes No equal. **1792** *Anecd. W. Pitt* IV. App. 270 A minister who never had his equal..for wisdom and integrity. **1875** FORTNUM *Maiolica* iv. 43 Orazio had no equal in the execution of his paintings.

†**c.** in age: (*a*) One who has lived as long; (*b*) A contemporary. Cf. L. *æquālis*. *Obs.*

1596 HARINGTON *Metam. Ajax* (1814) 110 That I may now deal with my ancients and not with my equals. **1611** BIBLE *Gal.* i. 14 And profited in the Iewes Religion, aboue many my equals in mine owne nation. **1678** CUDWORTH *Intell. Syst.* I, iv. 443 A Sophist Plutarch's equal.

2. abstr. ***an equal***: a state of equality; an equal footing. *Obs.* exc. *dial.*

1596 SPENSER *F.Q.* V. ii. 34 Thou that presum'st to weigh the world anew, And all things to an equall to restore. *Mod.* (Derbysh.) He talks to me as if we were on an equal.

equal ('iːkwəl), *v.* [f. prec.; cf. Fr. *égaler*.]

1. To make equal, equalize; to bring to the same level. Const. *with*, or simply. *arch.*

1594 DANIEL *Cleopatra* Ded, Wherby great Sidney & our Spencer might, With those Po singers being equalled, Enchant the world. **1611** BIBLE *2 Sam.* xxii. 34 He maketh my feet like [*marg.* equalleth] hinds' feet. **1667** MILTON *P.L.* I. 248 Him.. Whom reason hath equald, force hath made supream Above his equals. *Ibid.* III. 33 Those other two equal'd with me in Fate. **1687** DRYDEN *Hind & P.* I. 456 Rebellion equals all. **1705** STANHOPE *Paraphr.* I. 52 Persons equalled in the Favour of God. **1868** WHITTIER *Among the Hills* xvii, The fair democracy of flowers That equals cot and palace.

†**b.** To proportion. *Obs.*

1618 LATHAM *2nd Bk. Falconry* (1633) 24 Compare or equall so your meat with the length or shortnesse of time, as that she shall neuer be ouer emptie, yet, etc.

†**c.** To make (ground) level: to level (a building) *to*, *with the ground*; to make (a ditch) level by filling up. *Obs.*

1629 R. HILL *Pathw. Piety* (1849) II. 45 The goodliest cities have been equalled with the ground. *a* **1649** DRUMM. OF HAWTH. *Jas. III.* Wks. 39 The fortress..is demolished and equal'd with the ground. **1681** R. KNOX *Hist. Ceylon* (1817) 89 He employs his people..equalling unequal grounds. **1715** LEONI *Palladio's Archit.* (1742) II. 61 Equalling Ditches with raised or even Ground.

†**2.** To consider or represent as equal; to liken, compare. *Obs.*

1586 T. ROGERS *39 Art.* 78 To them, which with Gods word do equal their own doctrines, etc. **1635** PAGITT *Christianogr.* I. iii. (1636) 89 Their Dogmaticall Traditions, which they Equall with the holy Scriptures. *a* **1672** STERRY *Freed. Will* (1675) 150 As equalling God in savage cruelness to the most arbitrary Tyrants. **1751** JOHNSON *Rambler* No. 114 ¶9 To equal robbery with murder, is to reduce murder to robbery. **1799–1805** S. TURNER *Anglo-Sax.* I. IV. iii. 282 Not content with equalling the pleasures of war to social festivity.

3. *trans.* To be or become equal to; to 'come up to', match, rival.

1590 MARLOWE *2nd Pt. Tamburl.* V. iii, Let earth and heaven his timeless death deplore, For both their worths will equal him no more. **1594** SHAKS. *Rich. III*, I. ii. 249 On me [Richard], whose All not equals Edwards Moytie? **1611** BIBLE *Job* xxviii. 17 The golde and the chrystall cannot equall it. **1667** MILTON *P.L.* I. 40 He trusted to have equal'd the most High, If he oppos'd. **1792** *Anecd. W. Pitt* IV. App. 268 He came very young into Parliament, and..soon equalled the oldest and ablest actors. **1812** SIR H. DAVY *Chem. Philos.* 106 The weight of the carbonic acid gas exactly equals the weight of carbonic oxide and the oxygene gas. **1826** SCOTT *F.M. Perth* xxxiv, There are enough of brave men around me, whom I may imitate if I cannot equal. **1876** GREEN *Short Hist.* vii. 355 The courage of the Queen ..was only equalled by her terrible revenge. **1880** HAUGHTON *Phys. Geog.* vi. 281 They nearly equalled the elephant in size.

4. To produce or achieve something equal to, to match. †Also *intr.* To cope on equal terms *with* (*obs. rare*).

1597 SHAKS. *2 Hen. IV*, I. iii. 67, I thinke we are a Body strong enough (Euen as we are) to equall with the King. *c* **1610** *Women Saints* (1886) 154 It is a difficult matter, to equall my sisters vertues with my speache. *a* **1745** W. BROOME *To Pope* 26 A rival hand recalls from ev'ry part Some latent grace, and equals art with art. *a* **1832** MACKINTOSH *Machiavel* Wks. 1846 II. 480 Historical genius had risen..to a height which has not been equalled among the same nation in times of greater refinement.

b. To reciprocate in equal measure.

1697 DRYDEN, tr. Virgil *Æneid* VI. 641 [She] sought Sicheus, through the shady grove, Who answer'd all her Cares, and equal'd all her Love. **1749** FIELDING *Tom Jones* XIII. ix, The ardent passion..the extreme violence of which if he failed to equal, etc.

†**e'qualiform**, *a.* *Obs. rare*$^{-1}$. In 7 æq-. [f. L. *æquāli-s* equal + -FORM.] Having equal forms.

1655–60 STANLEY *Hist. Philos.* (1701) 379/2 It is all one amongst them if it be called biform, or æqualiform, or diversiform.

†**e'qualify**, *v.* *Obs. rare*$^{-1}$. [f. EQUAL *a.* + -(I)FY.] *trans.* To make equal.

1679 G. R. tr. *Boyastuau's Theat. World* III. 223 When he begins to equalify himself with his God, and to make comparisons with him.

equalist ('iːkwəlɪst). *rare.* [f. EQUAL + -IST.] One who asserts the equality of certain (contextually indicated) persons or things.

1661 *Origen's Opin.* in *Phœnix* (1721) I. 13 We can find nothing (according to the Hypothesis of the Equalists) why one [Hypostasis] should be called Father or Son rather than another. **1880** P. GREG *Acr. Zodiac* I. 133 The Equalists were driven from one untenable point to another.

equalitarian (iːˌkwɒlɪ'tɛərɪən), *a.* and *sb.* [f. EQUALIT-Y: cf. *humanitarian*, etc.]

A. *adj.* Pertaining to, or connected with, the doctrine of the equality of mankind. **B.** *sb.* An adherent of this doctrine.

1799 SOUTHEY *Lett.* (1856) I. 83 We were talking upon the equalitarian doctrines of the gospel. **1837** *Blackw. Mag.* XLI. 21 We, who are neither republicans nor equalitarians. **1883** STEVENSON in *Longm. Mag.* II. 295 These equalitarian plainnesses leave an open field for the insolence of Jack-in-office.

equali'tarianism. [-ISM.] Belief in the natural equality of mankind.

a **1866** J. GROTE *Moral Ideals* (1876) 409 The saying that the happiness of each *man* is to be consulted alike..: we will call it *equalitarianism*. **1920** H. G. WELLS *Outl. Hist.* 512/2 The dominant liberal ideas were freedom and a certain vague equalitarianism. **1921** *Q. Rev.* July 140 In fifth-century Athens, where equalitarianism ran to such a ridiculous extreme that gradually all civil offices were distributed among the citizens by lot. **1922** G. M. TREVELYAN *Brit. Hist. 19th Cent.* v. 84 Equalitarianism on board ship is proverbially dangerous.

equality (ɪ'kwɒlɪtɪ). Forms: 4–6 **equalite**, (5 **equalyte, eqwalyte**), 6 **equaltie, equalitie, -llitie**, (6 **æqualitie**, 7 **-ty**,) 6– **equality**. See also EGALITY. [a. OF. *équalité* (mod.Fr. *égalité*), ad. L. *æquālitāt-em*, f. *æquālis* EQUAL.] The quality or condition of being equal.

1. a. The condition of being equal in quantity, amount, value, intensity, etc.

c **1400** *Beryn* 2734 Of hete & eke of coldnes of oon equalite. **1530** PALSGR. 217/1 Equalite, *egallité*, evynnesse. **1555** EDEN *Decades W. Ind.* III. III. (Arb.) 147 The equalitie of the daye and nyght. **1635** N. CARPENTER *Geog. Del.* II. xiv. 221 Reduce to any shadow of Æquality. **1657** EARL MONM tr. *Paruta's Pol. Disc.* 200 God, by whom..the earth it self is sustained and held up with a miraculous equality of weight. **1791** COWPER *Iliad* xx. 572 Pleading equality of years. **1831** BREWSTER *Optics* ii. 19 In approaching the mirror, the image and object approach to equality. **1860** TYNDALL *Glac.* II. iii. 245 Will the exhausting of the tube disturb the equality? **1870** ROLLESTON *Anim. Life* 122 The ganglia do not maintain the same numerical equality.

b. *esp.* in *Math.* The exact correspondence between magnitudes and numbers in respect of quantity, the existence of which is sometimes expressed by the sign =.

1570 BILLINGSLEY *Euclid* I. def. 32. 5 This figure [rhombus] agreeth with a square, as touching the equallitie of lines. **1772** J. H. MOORE *Pract. Navig.* (1828) 4 = The Sign of Equality; it shews that the numbers or quantities placed before it are equal to those following it. **1846** MILL *Logic* I. iii. §11 Equality; which is but another word for the exact resemblance commonly called identity, considered as subsisting between things in respect of their quantity.

2. a. The condition of having equal dignity, rank, or privileges with others; the fact of being on an equal footing.

c **1425** WYNTOUN *Cron.* I. Prob. 60 Suppos hys Lordschype lyk noucht be Tyl gret statys in eqwalyte. **1526** *Pilgr. Perf.* (W. de W. 1531) 199 But all iii persones one god, of one substaunce, & of inseperable equalite. **1606** SHAKS. *Ant. & Cl.* I. iii. 47 Equality of two Domesticke powers, Breed scrupulous faction. **1667** MILTON *P.L.* XII. 26 Not content With faire equalitie, fraternal state. **1710** STEELE *Tatler* No. 225 ¶3 Equality is the Life of Conversation. **1794** SOUTHEY *Wat Tyler*, Ye are all equal; nature made you so. Equality is your birth-right. **1874** MICKLETHWAITE *Mod. Par. Ch.* 30 The feeling of perfect equality inside the church.

b. The condition of being equal in power, ability, achievement, or excellence. Also (*rarely*), the condition of being 'equal to an emergency'.

1595 SHAKS. *John* II. i. 327 The on-set and retyre Of both your Armies, whose equality By our best eyes cannot be censured. **1817** COLERIDGE *Biog. Lit.* (1882) 16 The confidence of his own equality with those whom he deemed most worthy of his praise. **1828** SCOTT *F.M. Perth* xxxiv, They fought with an equality. **1879** G. W. CURTIS *Sp. New Eng. Soc. Dinner*, With their equality to the emergency the Pilgrim Fathers would have lived in the best houses.

†**3. a.** In persons: Fairness, impartiality, equity. **b.** In things: Due proportion, proportionateness.

1447 BOKENHAM *Seyntys* (1835) 12 Shap and colour and eche feture Were comproporcyond in swych equalyte. **1552** HULOET s.v., Equalitie of lawes, wher thei be to al degrees indifferente. **1556** J. HEYWOOD *Spider & F.* lvi. 44 In hering of him what equaltie ye show. **1692** RAY *Dissol. World* 232 The breaking of order and equality in the world. **1845** MCCULLOCH *Taxation* (1852) Introd. 18 Equality is of the essence of such taxes.

4. Evenness of surface; uniformity of size or shape; level position. Also of movements or processes: Evenness, regularity, uniformity in rate or degree. Now somewhat *rare*.

1398 TREVISA *Barth. De P.R.* XIII. xxiii. (Tollem. MS.), The see is calde 'equor', and haþ þat name of equalite, evennesse. **1590** SIR J. SMYTH *Disc. Weapons* 4 b, All the points of the Piques of everie rancke carrying one equalitie. **1656** RIDGLEY *Pract. Physick* 172 Sometimes a Bone, so pressed down, settles to his natural equality. **1664** POWER *Exp. Philos.* I. 25 The equality of its Motion..without any fits or starts. **1691** T. H[ALE] *Acc. New Invent.* 95 The Plumber's vain pretence to near Equality, and endeavour to cast as equal as he can. **1834** HT. MARTINEAU *Farrers* iv. 73 The equality of wear of a piece of gingham or calico.

†**5.** *fig.* Of the body: An even condition or temper. Of the mind: Evenness, equability. *Obs.*

1460–70 *Bk. Quintessence* II. 20 It consumeth the corrupt superflue humouris, and reducit nature to equalite. **1647** CHARLES I. *Decl. Jan.* 18 Wks. (1662) 281 Patience and a great Equality of Mind. **1711** STEELE *Spect.* No. 143 ¶4 To enjoy Life and Health as a constant Feast, we should.. arrive at an Equality of Mind. *a* **1762** LADY M. W. MONTAGUE *Lett.* lxxiv. 121 You would find an easy equality of temper you do not expect.

6. Equality State, popular name in the U.S. for Wyoming, the first state to introduce women's suffrage.

1891 M. F. SWEETSER *King's Handbk. U.S.* 904 The Commonwealth [*sc.* Wyoming] has been called the equality state, because ever since its organization men and women have been accorded equal rights to vote. **1963** R. I. MCDAVID JR. *Mencken's Amer. Lang.* x. 700 Wyoming is the *Equality* or *Suffrage State*, so called because its Territorial Legislature made the first grant of the suffrage to women voters in 1869.

equalization (ˌiːkwəlaɪ'zeɪʃən). [f. next + -ATION.] The action or process of equalizing; the condition of being equalized.

1793 ANTHONY PASQUIN (John Williams) *Calm Exam.*, Upon the basis of necessary equalization and reciprocity. **1794** J. HUTTON *Philos. Light, etc.* 91 An opposite source of equalization, tending to restore that equilibrium which is also continually lost. **1806** HERSCHEL in *Phil. Trans.* XCVI. 210 A certain equalization, or approach to equality may be obtained between the motions of the stars. **1852** MCCULLOCH *Taxation* II. v. (ed. 2) 221 In August 1848, the nominal equalisation of the duties was effected. **1852** D. MITCHELL *Batte Summer* 283 Alas, for the happy equalization which our Republic was to effect.

equalize ('iːkwəlaɪz), *v.* Also 7–8 equallize, (7 egalise). [f. EQUAL + -IZE. Cf. Fr. *égaliser*.]

I. To equal, match.

†**1.** *trans.* To be or become equal to; to come up to, match, rival; = EQUAL *v.* 3. *Obs.*

15.. *Tom Thumb* 136 in Hazl. *E.P.P.* II. 239 Sir Tom Thomb, for thy fame, None can thee equalize. **1590** SPENSER *F.Q.* III. ix. 44 But a third kingdom..Both first and second Troy shall dare to equalise. **1595** *Locrine* IV. i. 169 The Scythians..Do equalize the grass in multitude. **1626** L. OWEN *Spec. Jesuit.* (1629) 19 In all seauen, equalizing the number of the Planets. **1634** SIR T. HERBERT *Trav.* 53 The order and scituation of this Fort and Fabricke, equalizing if not preceding any other in Persia. **1701** tr. *Le Clerc's Prim. Fathers* 68 The Elegancy and Nobleness of their Style which never any Philosopher could equalize. **1703** MOXON *Mech. Exerc.* 84 Fur..ought to have a greater Substance to equallize the strength of Oak. **1725** COLLIER *Disc. Pract. Subj.* 346 For by affecting to equalize a superior wealth, they are apt to make their own Figure too large. **1774** PENNANT *Tour Scotl.* 326 A spot equalized by few in picturesque and magnificent scenery. **1826** T. J. WHARTON in *Pa. Hist. Soc. Mem.* I. 112 His great house, that equalizes (if not exceeds) any I have ever seen.

†**2.** To reciprocate in equal degree; = EQUAL 4 b. *Obs.*

1598 MARSTON *Pygmal.* xxiv, Instill into her some celestiall fire That she may equalize affection.

II. To make equal.

†**3.** To regard, represent, or treat as equal; to place on an equality. *Obs.* Also (*rarely*), to regard as contemporary *with* (cf. EQUAL B. 1 c). Const. *to*, *with*.

1599 *Broughton's Lett.* vii. 22 There be that equalize some of them with S. Paul his time. **1621** R. JOHNSON *Way to Glory* 16 Doest [thou] ..equalize them [my writings] with the text of the canonicall Scriptures? **1664** H. MORE *Antid. Idolatry* v. 65 The Virgin..they do at least equallize to Christ. **1751** ORRERY *Remarks Swift* xxii. (R.), The..Poem ..which we equalize, and perhaps would willingly prefer to the Iliad, is void of those fetters [rhyme].

4. a. To make equal in magnitude, number, degree of intensity, etc. Const. *to*, *with*.

1622 MALYNES *Anc. Law-Merch.* 57 Equalizing the said Custome of Cloth, with the Custome of Wooll. **1634** SIR T. HERBERT *Trav.* 136 Intending to equalize it [Babel] with the Starres. **1646** SIR T. BROWNE *Pseud. Ep.* VI. vi. 301 Notwithstanding to equalize accounts, we will allow three hundred yeares. **1791** BOSWELL *Johnson* 2 June an. 1781 *note*, To show the propriety of equalising the revenues of bishops. **1794** J. HUTTON *Philos. Heat, &c.* 88 Their temperatures..must be always changing, and always tending to be equalised. **1825** BENTHAM *Ration. Rew.* 58 The emoluments of peace and war were, therefore, equalized by attaching a fixed salary to the office. **1837** HT. MARTINEAU *Soc. Amer.* III. 39 The despotism that would equalise property arbitrarily. **1871** B. STEWART *Heat* §43 Thus to equalize the distances.

b. *absol.* To make the score (in Football, etc.) equal to that of the opponent.

1925 S. J. SOUTHERTON in Marshall & Tosswill *Football* (rev. ed.) xviii. 318 Soon after half-time Millington should have equalised from a penalty kick. **1937** *Times* 15 Feb. 7/3 The South were not long in equalizing.

5. To make equal in condition, dignity, power, or character.

1634 SIR T. HERBERT *Trav.* 102 That they would not equallize him, in the manner of his death, to abject dogs. **1790** BURKE *Fr. Rev.* 72 Those who attempt to level, never equalize. **1803** JANE PORTER *Thaddeus* xxx. (1831) 266 A young woman of fashion..equalising herself with a creature depending on his wits for support. *a* **1859** MACAULAY *Hist. Eng.* V. 166 Office of itself does much to equalise politicians. *a* **1862** BUCKLE *Misc. Wks.* (1872) I. 164 The invention of gunpowder equalised all men on the field of battle.

†6. To level, bring to one level. *Obs.*

1596 SPENSER *F.Q.* v. ii. 38 These towring rocks..I will..equalize againe. **1632** LITHGOW *Trav.* i. 11 The Gothes..subuerted their pallaces, equalizing the walles with the ground. **1653** GATAKER *Vind. Annot. Jer.* 64 All alike eaven, as corn cut down and eqalised [*sic*] by the harvest mans hand.

7. a. To render (a movement, process, or condition) uniform.

1822 IMISON *Sc. & Art* (ed. Webster) I. 452 Fly wheels are employed to equalize the motion of a machine. **1825** J. NICHOLSON *Operat. Mechanic* 189 Contrivances for equalizing the action in Mr. Watt's patent of 1782. **1878** K. JOHNSTON *Africa* ii. 26 The rich forest lands of the Atlas slopes, which equalise the temperature.

b. To bring to an average level, compensate (an inequality).

1866 ROGERS *Agric. & Prices* I. xxix. 692 Equalizing the scarcity of one region by the plenty of another.

c. *Electr. trans.* To correct or modify (a signal or frequency response) by the use of an equalizer. Also *intr.*, to provide compensation (in the shape of an equalizer) *for*.

1928 STERLING & KRUSE *Radio Man.* xi. 385 These circuits are good for equalizing frequencies up to 3000 and 5000 cycles respectively. **1943** F. E. TERMAN *Radio Engineers' Handbk.* III. 244 For most purposes it is sufficient to equalize only for attenuation. **1958** *Van Nostrand's Sci. Encycl.* 606/1 The equalizer shows a frequency response which is the inverse of the system it is intended to equalize so the result..is to restore the overall response to a flat characteristic. **1962** A. NISBETT *Technique Sound Studio* iv. 80 When the high frequency losses are progressive, measures may be taken to equalize for them.

8. *intr.* To become equal.

1906 *Amer. Naturalist* June 427 The temperature in the outer and inner layers had equalized to a large extent. **1971** M. G. SCROGGIE *Found. Wireless & Electronics* xix. 324 These pressures tend to equalize.

Hence **'equalized** *ppl. a.*, **'equalizing** *vbl. sb.* (also *attrib.*) and *ppl. a.*

1657 S. W. *Schism Dispatch't* 450 He hath not shown us..one equalizing word of this power to counterpoise the many particularizing terms objected by us. **1703** MOXON *Mech. Exerc.* 85 This equallizing of strength must be referred to the Judgment of the Operator. **1790** BURKE *Fr. Rev.* 257 The utter subversion of your equalising principle. **1844** UPTON *Physioglyphics* 115 Equalized energy. **1844** CAROLINE FOX *Mem. Old Friends* (1882) 196 He talked of the national character of the French, and their equalizing methods of education. **1874** KNIGHT *Dict. Mech. Equalizing-saw*, a pair of saws on a mandrel at a gaged distance apart, and used for squaring off the ends of boards and bringing them to dimensions. **1875** HAMERTON *Intell. Life* I. iv. 22 The equalizing influence of the outside world.

equalizer ('iːkwəˌlaɪzə(r)). [f. as prec. + -ER¹.]

a. One who, or that which, makes equal; *spec.* an appliance for equalizing the speed of a machine, or the power used to drive it.

1792 MISS BURNEY *Diary* (1842) V. 351 [The Duke's] deportment is quite noble and in a style to announce conscious rank even to the most sedulous equaliser. **1792** SIR B. THOMPSON in *Phil. Trans.* LXXXII. 79 The ocean may be considered as the great reservoir and equalizer of heat. **1853** LEWES *Goethe* I. 233 The forest is the great equaliser of temperature in Nature. **1870** RUSKIN *Lect. Art* i. 5 Education..is not the equalizer, but the discerner of men. **1874** KNIGHT *Dict. Mech., Equalizer*, an evener or whiffletree to whose ends the swingle-trees or single-trees of the individual horses are attached. **1882** *Bazaar, Exch. & M.* 15 Feb. 174 The Otto Power Equaliser.

b. *Electr.* A passive network designed to modify the frequency response of a circuit (as a transmission line or an amplifier), esp. in order to compensate for frequency-dependent attenuation or phase shifts.

1928 STERLING & KRUSE *Radio Man.* vi. 222 The equalizer is employed to correct the frequency characteristic of the telephone line by forming a shunt which affords a variable impedance for different frequencies. **1930** *Bell Syst. Techn. Jrnl.* IX. 587 Since the amplifier has a flat gain characteristic, an attenuation equalizer is called for to correct the distortion introduced by the cable. **1943** F. E. TERMAN *Radio Engineers' Handbk.* III. 244 A phase equalizer is an all-pass filter designed to introduce a desired phase shift as a function of frequency in the load current. **1958** *N.Z. Listener* 26 Sept. 9/2 Here also are the variable equalisers that compensate for the frequency losses in the lines to the recording centre from outside points. All the lines come to the central rack and the equalisers there, except the fixed programme lines which go to fixed equalisers in the main equipment room. **1958** [see prec. 7 c].

c. *Football.* A goal that equalizes (cf. EQUALIZE *v.* 4 b).

1930 *Daily Express* 9 Sept. 12/2 Wednesday were playing very well..and Rimmer headed the equaliser just inside half an hour. **1960** *Times* 25 Jan. 16/5 Jackson scored a scrambling equalizer.

d. A revolver. Also, a cosh; (occas.) some other weapon. *slang* (orig. *U.S.*).

1931 D. RUNYON *Guys & Dolls* (1932) iv. 89 He outs with the old equalizer and starts blasting away. **1954** WODEHOUSE *Jeeves & Feudal Spirit* xvi. 162, I reached a hand into my pocket and got a firm grasp on the old Equalizer. **1958** B. HAMILTON *Too Much of Water* xi. 252, I..got..my little equalizer... I gave him a very sound bang, and he just slithered down. **1961** I. JEFFERIES *It wasn't Me!* xi. 157 He just thought anybody running about with a nasty look and an equalizer was a foreigner.

†'equallable, *a. Obs. rare.* [f. as next + -ABLE.] That can be equalled.

1621 LADY M. WROTH *Urania* 552 Ouercome (cryd hee) by the power not equallable of a Shepherdesse, etc.

'equaller. *rare.* [f. EQUAL *v.* + -ER¹.] One who, or that which, makes equal.

c **1630** DRUMM. OF HAWTH. *Poems* Wks. 26 Death..Impartial equaller of all with dust.

equalling ('iːkwəlɪŋ), *vbl. sb.* [f. EQUAL *v.* + -ING¹.] The action of the vb. EQUAL. In quot. used *attrib.*

1880 TURNER *Catal. Tools Sheffield* 72 s.v. *Files*, Equalling and Cotter Files.

equally ('iːkwəlɪ), *adv.* Also 6 **equallie, (equaly).** [f. EQUAL *a.* + -LY².]

1. To an equal degree or extent; as much in one case as in another. Const. *with*; sometimes *as*.

1634 SIR T. HERBERT *Trav.* 215 It is doubtfull whether it [Saint Helena] adhere to America or Afrique, the vast Ocean bellowing, on both sides, and almost equally. **1668** J. MALL *Offer of F. Help* 113 They all flow equally from the sovereignty of God. **1692** O. WALKER *Hist. Illustr.* 291 He was equally Learned as Warlike. **1701** DE FOE *True-born Eng.* II. 6 And equally of Fear and Forecast void. **1736** BUTLER *Anal.* I. i. Wks. 1874 I. 25 It is said these observations are equally applicable to brutes. **1791** MRS. RADCLIFFE *Rom. Forest* xvii, You and Clara shall be equally my daughters. **1848** MACAULAY *Hist. Eng.* II. 146 His presence and his absence were equally dreaded by the lord lieutenant. **1853** F. W. NEWMAN tr. *Odes Horace* 7 Being the inventor of the lyre, he [Hermes] is patron of poets equally as Apollo. **18..** T. ARNOLD *Wyclif's Sel. Wks.* III. Introd. p. x, This work is equally one-sided and uncompromising with Wyclif's tracts.

2. In equal shares.

c **1386** CHAUCER *Sompn. T.* 529 Ther nys no man can deme..If that it were departed equally. **1594** SHAKS. *Rich. III*, v. iii. 294 My Foreward..Consisting equally of Horse and Foot. **1695** LD. PRESTON *Boeth. Life* 15 Equally sharing with him his Labours and Victories. **1818** CRUISE *Digest.* (ed. 2) II. 25 To her other sisters equally between them. **1827** J. POWELL *Devises* II. 181 The said legacy should be divided equally between them that were alive.

3. According to one and the same rule or measure. Formerly also, impartially, equitably, justly.

1526 *Pilgr. Perf.* (W. de W. 1531) 110 Deale equally, without parcialite. **1597** DANIEL *Civ. Wares* v. (R.), The equally respecting eye Of pow'r looking alike on all deserts. **1605** SHAKS *Lear* v. iii. 45 So to vse them, As we shall find their merites, and our safety May equally determine. **1651** HOBBES *Leviath.* I. xv. 77 If a man..judge between man and man, it is a precept..that he deale Equally between them. **1702** *Eng. Theophrast.* 3 To enter equally into the genius of both nations. **1860** RUSKIN *Mod. Paint.* V. IX. i. 204 You say it is dealing equitably or equally.

†4. On a level with regard to height; uniformly with regard to direction; in a line *with*. *Obs.*

1599 HAKLUYT *Voy.* II. II. 69 Yet are they [the bridges] equally built, no higher in the middle then at either ende. **1660** BARROW *Euclid* I. Def. iv, A Right Line is that which lies equally betwixt its Points. **1721** STRYPE *Eccl. Mem.* II. I. i. 3 The nurse went equally with him that supported the train.

5. Uniformly; in uniform degree or quantity; in the same relative proportion.

1664 EVELYN *Kal. Hort.* (1729) 235 Distributing the Air ..more equally thro' the House. **1690** LOCKE *Hum. Und.* II. xiv. §22 Being constantly equally swift. **1735** BERKELEY *Querist* §214 Seed equally scattered produceth a goodly harvest. **1793** SMEATON *Eddystone L.* §242 The wedges and trenails..were every where equally applied. **1796** NELSON 5 June in Nicolas *Disp.* (1846) VII. Introd. 81, I know of none so equally good. **1825** J. NICHOLSON *Operat. Mechanic* 351 The thickest wires receive the strongest heat; therefore, the whole is equally heated in the same space of time. **1854** H. MILLER *Sch. & Schm.* xiii, The population, formerly spread pretty equally over the country.

equalness ('iːkwəlnɪs). *rare* in mod. use. [f. as prec. + -NESS.]

1. The state or fact of being equal in magnitude, number, condition, etc.; = EQUALITY 1, 2.

1530 PALSGR. 217/1 Equalnesse, *equiperation*. **1547–64** BAULDWIN *Mor. Philos.* (Palfr.) IV. iii, Friendship ought to be engendred of equalnes, for where equalitie is not, friendship cannot long continue. **1551** RECORDE *Pathw. Knowl.* I. xvi, The profe of yᵉ equalnes of this likeiam vnto the triangle, dependeth of the thirty and two Theoreme. **1660** *Trial Regic.* 25, I am sure, I am no waies able to Plead equalness, in point of Law, with those noble Gentlemen. **1726** LEONI *Alberti's Archit.* I. 53 The equalness of their weight. **1864** SPENCER *Illustr. Univ. Progr.* 170 There was some appreciation of the equalness of men's liberties to pursue the objects of life.

†2. Fairness, equity. *Obs.*

1548 R. HUTTEN *Sum Diuinitie* P viij a, To iudge accordyng vnto ryght and equalnes. **1556** J. HEYWOOD *Spider & F.* xxxvii. 34 Where reason and equalnesse be giders.

†3. a. Of movements, processes, etc.: Uniformity in rate or degree. **b.** Of the mind, temper, etc.: Evenness, equability, equanimity. *Obs.*

1545 ASCHAM *Toxoph.* (Arb.) 35 Softly exercisynge euery parte with equalnesse. **1675** TEMPLE *Let. Lockhart* Wks. 1731 II. 333 With so great Equalness of Temper, and Constancy of Mind. **1741** RICHARDSON *Pamela* (1824) I. xiii. 251 To bear the honour..with equalness of temper. **1799** SOUTHEY *Lett.* (1856) I. 81 His equalness and kindness of character.

equanimity (iːkwə'nɪmɪtɪ). Also 7 **æqu-.** [ad. Fr. *equanimité*, ad. L. *æquanimitas*, f. *æquanimis* having an even mind, f. *æquus* even + *animus* mind.] The quality of having an even mind.

†1. Fairness of judgement, impartiality, equity.

1607 *Schol. Disc. agst. Antichr.* II. v. 18 The third goodnes ..is that equinanimitie, which..accepteth a iust excuse. **1658** MILTON *Lett. State* Wks. (1851) 417 Your far celebrated Equanimity encourag'd us to recommend this Cause to your Highness. **1752** FIELDING *Amelia* v. v, You have the equanimity to think so.

2. Evenness of mind or temper; the quality or condition of being undisturbed by elation, depression, or agitating emotion; unruffledness.

1663 PEPYS *Diary* 8 Mar., I cannot but remember my Lord's equanimity in all these affairs with admiration. **1710** *Tatler* No. 242 ⁋1 This Quality [Good-Nature] keeps the Mind in Equanimity. **1785** BURKE *Sp. Nabob Arcot's Debts* Wks. IV. 238 These gentlemen have borne all the odium of this publication..with..unexampled equanimity. **1814** SCOTT *Wav.* lxv, The quiet equanimity with which the Baron endured his misfortunes, had something in it venerable and even sublime. **1859** GEO. ELIOT *A. Bede* 61 Mrs. Poyser has not yet recovered her equanimity on the subject.

b. *pl.* (*nonce-use.*) Seasons of equanimity.

1663 BUTLER *Hud.* I. iii 1020 Perturbations that possess The Mind or Æquanimities.

equanimous (iː'kwænɪməs), *a.* Also 7 **æquanimous.** [f. L. *æquanim-is* (see prec.) + -OUS.]

1. Even-tempered; not easily elated or depressed.

1656 TRAPP *Comm. Matt.* v. 16 [A minister must be] patient, or equanimous, easily parting with his right for peace sake. **1660** GAUDEN *Sacrilegus* 14 That the Reverend Bishops..may not seem less equanimous and condescending. **1721–1800** in BAILEY. **1865** *Pall Mall G.* 30 Aug. 3/2 It required all the splendour of the day..to make me equanimous on discovering the postmaster's audacious cheat.

†2. Impartial. *Obs.*

1670 MAYNWARING *Vita Sana* xv. 128 That æquanimous distribution of her [the Soul's] energy into the Members and Parts of the Body.

Hence **e'quanimously** *adv.*, with equanimity. **e'quanimousness**, the quality of being equanimous.

1652 GAULE *Magastrom.* 132 Disposing equanimously to all accidents. **1849** THACKERAY *Pendennis* III. iii. 41 Pendennis, in reality, suffered it very equanimously. **1736** BAILEY, *Equanimousness*, evenness of mind, contentedness. **1775** in ASH.

equant ('iːkwənt), *a.* and *sb. Astr. Obs.* exc. *Hist.* Also 7 **æquant.** [ad. L. *æquant-em*, pr. pple. of *æquā-re* to make equal, f. *æquus* equal.]

A. *adj.* That equalizes. ***equant circle*** [med.L. *circulus æquans*], a circle imagined by the ancient astronomers for the purpose of reducing the planetary movements to consistency with the hypothesis that celestial motion must be uniform in velocity. Also *fig.* **B.** *sb.* = *equant circle*.

1621 BURTON *Anat. Mel.* II. ii. III. 324 Excentricke, concentricke, circles æquant, etc., are absurd. *Ibid.* III. i. III. iii. (1676) 267/1 Love is the circle equant of all other affections. **1796** in HUTTON *Math. Dict.* **1834** *Nat. Philos., Hist. Astron.* vi. 31/1 (Usef. Knowl. Soc.) He [Ptolemy] was compelled to suppose that..the centre of the equant..revolved in a small circle round the centre of the excentric.

¶ Erroneously used for 'centre of the equant'.

1837 WHEWELL *Hist. Induct. Sc.* III. iv. §7 I. 221 About another point, the equant.

† **'equat(e**, *pa. pple. Obs.* [ad. L. *æquāt-us*, pa. pple. of *æquā-re* (see prec.).] Equivalent to the later EQUATED. **a.** *Astrol.* **b.** Made level, levelled.

1430 LYDG. *Chron. Troy* I. vi, In houre chosen equat for the nones. **1533** BELLENDEN *Livy* I. (1822) 39 At last, baith thir pepill war brocht undir ane communite to leif in Rome, and the ciete Alba equate..to the ground. **1536** —— *Cron. Scot.* (1821) II. 161 Nevir to sever fra this town, quhill the wallis thairof wer equate to the ground.

equatable (iː'kweɪtəb(ə)l), *a.* [f. EQUAT(E *v.* + -ABLE.] Capable of being equated.

1893 R. H. I. PALGRAVE *Dict. Pol. Econ.* I. 581/2 Difficulty of attainment experienced by the purchaser is equateable with the difficulty of production. **1935** G. K. ZIPF *Psycho-Biol. Lang.* 236 A corresponding degree of crystallization of the configuration, which is equatable with relative frequency of occurrence. **1967** *Technology Week* 23 Jan. 26/1 (Advt.), This is typical of the growing number of space guidance..assignments..in 'controlled software',..the establishment of equatable simulations for various missions.

equate (ɪ'kweɪt), *v.* Also 7 æquate. [f. L. *æquāt-* ppl. stem of *æquā-re*: see EQUAT(E *pa. pple.*]

† **1.** *trans.* To make (bodies) equal; to balance. *Obs. rare.*

1530 PALSGR. 539/1 They were nothyng egall, but he hath nowe equated them. **1755** B. MARTIN *Mag. Arts & Sc.* 394 The Guinea and large Piece of Cork..seem not to be nicely equated in Weight.

† **2.** To take the average of. *Obs.*

14.. *Mann. & Househ. Exp.* (1841) 439 Mete fyrst how many roddes that one ende is over thwart, and in lyke wyse mete that other ende. Than equate that.

b. *Astr.* To reduce to an average; to make the allowances necessary for bringing observations to a common standard, or for obtaining a correct result.

1633 T. JAMES *Voy.* Q ij, The Declination was not equated. **1677** R. CARY *Chronol.* I. I. I. xii. 44 With some other Epagomenae at the end of the Year, or in a short period of Years fit to equate the Motion of the Sun. **1751** CHAMBERS *Cycl.* s.v., To Equate solar days, that is to convert apparent into mean time, and mean into apparent time. **1833** HERSCHEL *Astron.* iv. 174 This last process is technically termed correcting or equating the observation for nutation.

3. *Math.* To state the equality of (one quantity) *to* or *with* (another); to state the equality between (two quantities); to put in the form of an equation.

1779 HUTTON in *Phil. Trans.* LXX. 9 The fluxion of this expression being equated to 0. **1806** —— *Course Math.* I. 229 By equating the terms which contain like powers of *z*. **1846** RUSKIN *Mod. Paint.* I. II. IV. iii. §24 It is not to be chipped out by the geologist or equated by the mathematician. **1883** *Nature* XXVII. 225 By equating the computed difference to the actual difference.

4. *transf.* and *fig.* To treat, regard, or represent as equivalent.

18.. DE QUINCEY *Philos. Herod.* Wks. 1862 VIII. 211 Three generations were equated to a century. **1840** GLADSTONE *Ch. Princ.* 399 The danger of confounding true and false by equating them [forms of religion] all. **1877** SKEAT *Piers Plowm.* Notes 460 Marlow uses the word 'chary' rather artfully, so that it may be equated either to 'dearly' or 'carefully'. **1882** J. RHYS *Celtic Brit.*, App. 278 Boudicca might perhaps be equated..with such a Latin name as Victorina. **1885** *Ch. Q. Rev.* Oct. 95 In the Book of Leinster thirty four foreign saints are equated with natives.

Hence **e'quated** *ppl. a.*, **e'quating** *vbl. sb.*

1633 H. GELLIBRAND in T. James *Voy.* R ij, The Æquated Anomaly of the ☾ orbe. **1691** WOOD *Ath. Oxon.* II. 338 He divulged his invention of the equating of a streight line to a crooked or parabole. **1694** E. HALLEY in *Phil. Trans.* XVIII. 251 When the æquated Number II. is less than 113. **1790** HERSCHEL *ibid.* LXXI. 122 The clock altered to true equated time. **1817** H. T. COLEBROOKE *Algebra, etc.* 312 The mean or equated depth. **1870** BOWEN *Logic* vi. 160 It makes no difference which of the equated quantities is placed first.

equation (iː'kweɪʃən, -ʒən). Also 4 equacion, equacioun, 6–7 æquation. [ad. L. *æquātiōn-em*, f. *æquā-re*: see EQUANT.] The action of equalling.

I. The action of making equal.

† **1.** *spec.* in *Astrol.* Equal partition. ***equations of houses***: the method of dividing the sphere equally into 'houses' for astrological purposes. *Obs.*

c **1386** CHAUCER *Frankl. T.* 551 And hise proporcioneles conuenientz ffor hise equacions in euery thyng. *c* **1391** —— *Astrol.* I. §22 With the smale point of the forseide label, shaltow kalcule thyne equaciouns in the bordure of thin Astrolabie. **1393** GOWER *Conf.* III. 67 He loketh his equacions And eke the constellacions.

2. *gen.* The action of making equal or balancing; the state of being equally balanced, equilibrium, equality. Now chiefly in phrases like *equation of demand and supply*, *equation of trade*, etc.

1656 BLOUNT *Glossogr.*, *Equation*, making equal, even or plain. **1677** HALE *Prim. Orig. Man.* II. ix. 216 The very Redundance it self of Mankind seeming by a natural consecution to yield and subminister this Remedy, for its Reduction and Equation. **1718** ROWE tr. *Lucan* II. (R.), Again the golden day resum'd its right, And rul'd in just equation with the night. **1726** SHELVOCKE *Voy. round World* 140 It would be difficult to determine the different values of the dollars and the candlesticks, so as to come to a nice equation of the matter. **1848** MILL *Pol. Econ.* III. xxi. §1 (1876) 375 An excess of imports over exports, arising from the fact that the equation of international demand is not yet established. **1850** GROTE *Greece* II. lx. VII. 481 If his personal suffering could..be..set in equation against the mischief brought by himself both on his army and his country. **1876** FAWCETT *Pol. Econ.* III. vii. 399 These prices would adjust the equation of international trade.

II. Reduction to a normal value or position.

3. a. *Astr.* The action of adding to or subtracting from any result of observation or calculation such a quantity as will compensate for a known cause of irregularity or error. Chiefly *concr.* the quantity added or subtracted for this purpose.

annual equation: see ANNUAL 2 b.

equation of the centre: the difference between the mean and the true anomaly of a heavenly body.

†***eccentric equation***: = *equation to the centre*.

equation of the equinoxes: the difference between the mean and apparent places of the equinoxes, arising from the phenomenon known as *precession of the equinoxes*.

equation of time: the difference between the time shown by a clock (mean time) and that shown by a sundial.

personal equation: the correction required in astronomical observations in consequence of greater or less inaccuracy habitual to individual observers. Also *transf.*

1666 EVELYN *Mem.* (1857) II. 11 To the Royal Society, where one Mercator. produced his rare clock, and new motion to perform the equations. **1726** tr. *Gregory's Astron.* I. III. 421 When both these Causes of the Equation of Time hold. **1812** WOODHOUSE *Astron.* xxxiv. 320 Corrections, or, as they are astronomically called, equations. **1834** *Nat. Philos., Astron.* x. 193/1 (Usef Knowl. Soc.) The equation of the centre [of the sun] is subject to a very slow secular variation. **1845** *Penny Cycl.* Suppl. I. 535/2 If A and B are severally in the habit of noting events 3-tenths of a second after and 4-tenths of a second before they take place, their personal equations may be described as being + 0^s.3 and 0^s.4. **1853** LARDNER *Handbk. Astron.* §3200 If we suppose an imaginary moon to move from perihelion through aphelion back to perihelion, with a uniform angular velocity..the distance between this imaginary moon and the true moon is called the *equation of the centre*. **1854** MOSELEY *Astron.* xxi. (ed. 4) 96 The difference between true and mean solar time ..is called the equation of time. **1865** BRANDE & COX *Dict. Sci.* (ed. 3) I. 800/2 The term personal equation has of late been introduced into Astronomy. **1881** LOCKYER in *Nature* No. 614. 318 Photography has no personal equation. **1881** *New York Nation* XXXII. 430 The scientific genealogists of the more advanced school, who settle the problem off-hand, often in accordance with their personal equation.

b. ***human equation***: *transf.* sense from *personal equation*.

1938 *Reader's Digest* Apr. 77/2 The Oakland Bridge suffers from such a simple, unpredictable human equation as the preference of truck drivers to loaf on a ferry. **1964** F. BOWERS *Bibliogr. & Textual Criticism* III. ii. 71 We must throw out the human equation as much as we can in our search to find an explanation for seeming aberrancies.

4. ***equation of payments***: the process of finding a mean time for the equitable payment in one amount of several sums due at different times.

1677 COCKER *Arith.* xxix. 309 Equation of payments is that Rule..whereby to reduce the times for payment of several sums of money to an equated time for payment of the whole debt without dammage to the Debtor or Creditor.

III. Statement of equality.

† **5.** *Math.* The action of stating the identity in value of two quantities or expressions. *Obs.*

1570 DEE *Math. Pref.* 6 That great Arithmeticall Arte of Æquation: commonly called..Algebra. **1579** DIGGES *Stratiot.* 44 Æquation is nothing else but a certain conference of two numbers being in value Equal, and yet in multitude and Denomination different. **1664** POWER *Exp. Philos.* III. 187 Thus came they to upbraid..Algebra with the Æquation of three discontinued Numbers. **1673** KERSEY *Algebra* I. xi. 51 An Equation in the Algebraical Art is a mutual comparing of two equal Quantities or Things of different Denominations.

6. a. *concr.* A formula affirming the equivalence of two quantitative expressions, which are for this purpose connected by the sign =.

The two chief kinds of equations are: (1) Those which contain symbols denoting one or more unknown quantities; to discover the numerical values of these is called 'solving' the equation; the numbers which will 'satisfy' an equation, i.e. which may be substituted for the symbol of unknown quantity without rendering the statement incorrect, are called its 'roots'. (2) Those which indicate a constant relation existing between variables; as *equation to a curve*, an equation expressing a relation between coordinates or the like, which is constant for every point in the curve; *equation of motions*, etc. Equations are distinguished as *simple, quadratic, cubic, biquadratic*, etc. (or as of the 1st, 2nd, 3rd, 4th, etc. degree) according to the highest power which they contain of any unknown or variable.

1570 BILLINGSLEY *Euclid* II. Introd 60 Many rules..of Algebra, with the equations therein vsed. **1657** HOBBES *Absurd Geom.* Wks. 1845 VII. 366 You mean that..the lowermost to the lowermost in the first equation are equal. **1750** *Phil. Trans.* XLVII. 62 Mr. de Buffon mention'd..we should..resolve the equation. **1807** HUTTON *Course Math.* II. 322 The equation to the curve being $ax = y^2$. **1816** PLAYFAIR *Nat. Phil.* II. 227 This method of determining the co-efficients of a given function, or correcting them from observation, by means of what are called Equations of Condition, is said to have been invented by Tobias Mayer of Göttingen. **1838** DE MORGAN *Ess. Probab.* 29 An investigation of the method of solving an equation. **1853** SIR H. DOUGLAS *Mil. Bridges* (ed. 3) 11 Hence there is obtained the following equation of motion: $a\,V^2 = g \sin. \theta$. **1871** B. STEWART *Heat* §62 From this equation we derive at once the relation between the temperature and the density of air. **1879** THOMSON & TAIT *Nat. Phil.* I. I. §191 What is called the 'equation of continuity' [for fluids], an unhappily chosen expression.

b. *transf.*

1860 ABP. THOMSON *Laws Th.* §68. 110 Every affirmative judgment may be regarded as an equation of subject and predicate.

c. A formula which represents a chemical reaction by stating the equality between the symbols representing the original and those which represent the resulting substances.

1807 T. THOMSON *Chem.* (ed. 3) II. 132 We have therefore this equation, Carbon 28 + Oxygen 72 = Carb. Ox. 69 + Oxygen 31. **1844–57** G. BIRD *Urin. Deposits* (ed. 5) 245 In the following equation this decomposition of the allantoin is assumed to have occurred. **1853** W. GREGORY *Inorg. Chem.* (ed. 3) 90 The following equation explains the change. $(KO,NO_5) + 2\,(HO,SO_3) = (KO,HO,_2SO_3) + (HO,NO_5)$.

7. equation box = *equational box* (see next); **equation table**, a table showing the time a clock should indicate when the sun is on the meridian.

1893 *Funk's Stand. Dict.* s.v. *Equational*, Equation box. **1731** (*title*) An explanation of the nature of equation of time, and use of the equation table for adjusting watches and clocks to the motion of the sun. **1850** DENISON *Clock & Watch-m.* 19 This [sundial]..with the equation-table will give the means of correcting a clock on any fine day.

equational (ɪ'kweɪʃənəl), *a.* [f. prec. + -AL[1].]

1. Pertaining to, or involving the use of, equations.

1864 W. HIPSLEY (*title*), Equational Arithmetic: Questions of Interest, Annuities, &c. **1880** *Athenæum* 13 Nov. 636/3 A further theoretical aid in equational logic.

2. *Mech.* Of gearing, etc.: equalizing, adjusting; ***equational box*** (see quot.).

a **1877** KNIGHT *Dict. Mech.* I. 807/2 *Equational box*... A differential gearing used in the bobbin and fly machine for the adjustment of different degrees of twist, for different yarns.

3. *Biol.* [tr. G. *aequationstheilung* 'equation division' (A. Weismann *Ueber die Zahl der Richtungskörper* (1887) ii. 42).] Of a division of the chromosomes in a cell: taking place longitudinally and resulting in two equal segments that are incorporated into the daughter nuclei.

1920 W. E. AGAR *Cytol.* 50 Now in a meiosis with tetrad formation of the Copepod type it follows that if both the joints represent division planes, one division must be longitudinal (or *equational*, since the resulting daughter chromosomes receive similar sets of chromatin elements), and the other division must be transverse (or *reductional*, since each resulting daughter chromosome receives only one half of the set of chromatin elements). **1949** DARLINGTON & MATHER *Elem. Genetics* ii. 52 The distribution of the chiasmata in the pairing segment relative to the centromere and the differential segments then decides whether the first division is reductional for these segments or equational.

4. *Gram.* Of a sentence or phrase (see quots.).

1933 BLOOMFIELD *Lang.* xi. 173 The equational type [of sentence] was less common [in Latin] than in Russian: *beātus ille* 'happy (is) he'. **1961** R. B. LONG *Sentence & its Parts* v. 115 The common-voice forms of *be* are reversible when *be* is a true equational verb. The worst thing is the lights. **1964** *Language* XL. 272 'Equational sentence' is a good term for a sentence containing a copula. **1964** R. H. ROBINS *Gen. Ling.* vi. 234 In some languages a favourite, productive, sentence type is found beside those containing a verb, namely a noun + noun or a noun + adjective structure, with no verb required to complete it. This type, which is sometimes labelled equational, is found in Russian.

Hence **e'quationally** *adv.*, in an equational form; by the use of equations.

1881 JEVONS in *Nature* XXIII. 487 They [secondary propositions] obey exactly the same formal laws as primary propositions, and are of course expressed equationally.

equationism (iː'kweɪʃənɪz(ə)m). [f. as prec. + -ISM.] Also **e'quationist** [+ -IST.] (See quots.)

1871 W. G. WARD *Ess. Theism* (1884) II. 247 The principle of 'equationism'; the principle..of effecting an 'equation' between the strength of his convictions and the amount of proof on which they respectively rest..The objection of equationists..can be otherwise met.

equative (iː'kweɪtɪv), *a.* [f. EQUAT(E *v.* + -IVE.] Used to denote identity or degree of comparison.

1913 J. M. JONES *Welsh Gram.* 241 The adjective in Welsh has four degrees of comparison, the positive, the equative, the comparative, and the superlative. **1926** *Glasgow Herald* 24 June, The difficulty of equative terms in dealing with matters of religious belief. **1965** *Language* XLI. 72 An equative clause. **1966** G. N. LEECH *Eng. in Advertising* ii. 18 Semantically, it [*sc.* apposition] signifies an equative or attributive relation.

equator (ɪ'kweɪtə(r)). Also 7–8 æquator. [a. late L. *æquātor* one who makes equal, hence in late L. (*circulus*) *æquator diei et noctis* 'the equalizer of day and night' (cf. *equinoctial*), f. *æquāre* to make equal, f. *æquus* equal.]

1. *Astr.* A great circle of the celestial sphere, whose plane is perpendicular to the axis of the earth. (When the sun is in the equator, day and night are equal in length: hence the name.) Commonly called the EQUINOCTIAL.

c **1391** CHAUCER *Astrol.* I. §17 The middel cercle..is cleped also the weyere, equator of the day. **1594** J. DAVIS *Seaman's Secr.* II. (1607) 2 When the Sunne cometh vpon the Equator, then the daies and nights are of one length through the whole worlde. **1682** SIR T. BROWNE *Chr. Mor.* 121 The time might come when capella..would have its motion in the æquator. **1726** tr. *Gregory's Astron.* I. II. 295 The beginning of the Equator, from whence the Right Ascension of the Stars is reckoned, is where it intersects the

Ecliptic. **1837** WHEWELL *Hist. Induct. Sc.* III. i. §8. I. 144 The circle which divided the sphere [of the heavens] exactly midway between these poles was called the equator.

2. *Geog.* A great circle of the earth, in the plane of the celestial equator, and equidistant from the two poles.

1612 BREREWOOD *Lang. & Relig.* xiv. 149 That the Earth on the South side of the Æquator, should be of a more ponderous disposition then on the North. **1646** SIR T. BROWNE *Pseud. Ep.* II. ii. 61 The Northern pole of the Loadstone attracteth a greater weight then the Southerne on this side the Equator. **1727** THOMSON *Summer* 647 Mountains big with mines, That on the high equator ridgy rise. **1774** GOLDSM. *Nat. Hist.* (1776) I. 11 A polar prospect, and a landscape at the equator, are as opposite in their appearances as in their situation. **1856** EMERSON *Eng. Traits, Voy. Eng.* Wks. (Bohn) II. 12 The sea-fire shines in her wake ..Near the equator, you can read small print by it.

fig. *a* **1631** DONNE *Select.* (1840) 105 A Christian hath no solstice..much less hath he any equator, where days and nights are equal, that is, a liberty to spend as much time ill, as well. *a* **1661** FULLER *Worthies* I. 39 It [the Reformation] is as it were the Æquator, or that remarkable Line, dividing between Eminent Prelates, Learned Writers, and Benefactors to the Publick, who lived Before or After it.

3. a. *transf.* A similarly situated circle on any heavenly (or, occasionally, any spherical) body.

1746 J. PARSONS *Hum. Physiognomy* i. 14 Because Santorini, in his Figure of the Face, makes the Eye-lids meet upon the very Equator of the Eye-ball. **1834** *Nat. Philos., Astron.* iii. 83 (Usef. Knowl. Soc.) The great circle perpendicular to the axis of the moon, is called for a similar reason the equator of the moon. **1839** G. BIRD *Nat. Phil.* 351 In a sphere of quartz..at the equator. **1868** LOCKYER tr. *Guillemin's Heavens* (ed. 3) 37 The rapidity of this movement varies regularly with their [Sun-spots'] distance from the solar equator.

b. ***magnetic equator***, an irregular line, passing round the earth in the neighbourhood of the equator, on which the magnet has no dip; = *aclinic line* (see ACLINIC). ***thermal equator***, the imaginary line on the earth's surface which denotes the location of highest mean air temperature for a particular period.

1832 *Nat. Philos., Magnetism* iii. §98 (Usef. Knowl. Soc.) The magnetic equator. **1849** MRS. SOMERVILLE *Connex. Phys. Sc.* xxx. 342 A line encircling the earth, called the magnetic equator. **1930** *Meteorol. Gloss.* (ed. 2) 172. **1945** E. BENNETT-BREMNER *Front-line Airline* x. 65 Making due allowance for south-easterly winds to the inter-tropical front which lies on the thermal equator.

c. ***equator of the magnet*** (see quots.).

1635 N. CARPENTER *Geog. Del.* I. iii. 60 The Magnet..is separated or diuided by a middle line or Æquator. **1837** BREWSTER *Magnet.* 251 It is obvious..that the magnetic intensity increases from the equator to the poles. **1871** TYNDALL *Fragm. Sc.* (ed. 6) I. xv. 416 Hold the needle over the equator of the magnet. **1885** S. THOMPSON *Electr. & Magn.* ii. §78 The portion of the magnet which lies between the two poles is apparently less magnetic..This region Gilbert called the equator of the magnet.

d. *Aeronautics.* 'The line along which the plane of the maximum horizontal section cuts the envelope of an aerostat' (W. B. Faraday *Gloss. Aeronaut. Terms* 1919).

1784 *New Review* July 61, 64 men who kept the machine in by ropes fixed to its equator. **1815** J. SMITH *Panorama Sci. & Art* (1826) II. 151 From this equator proceeded ropes, by which was suspended a car in the form of a boat, a few feet below the balloon. **1838** M. MASON *Aeronautica* 268 An opening, however, of about four feet in length which appeared above the equator of the balloon, soon brought it down again. **1900** *Westm. Gaz.* 1 May 2/1 A balloon loses but little of its lifting power if a rent is made below the equator.

e. *Biol.* The plane of division of a cell or nucleus lying midway between the poles and perpendicular to a line joining them.

1888 [see POLE *sb.*[2] 7]. **1896** [see EQUATORIAL *a.* 3]. **1908** J. A. THOMSON *Heredity* (*caption facing* p. 51) The nucleus spindle has at its equator four groups of tetrads. **1913** J. W. JENKINSON *Vertebr. Embryol.* 95 The structure and symmetry of the egg, its axis, poles, and equator. **1961** M. J. D. WHITE *Chromosomes* (ed. 5) v. 83 If there is a considerable distance between the chiasmata and the centromeres..the centromeres will be attached to the spindle about midway between the equator and the poles.

4. *attrib.* and *Comb.*, as ***equator-sun***; **equatorwards** *adv.*, towards the equator.

1735 THOMSON *Liberty* IV. 413 Those [paths of the sea] that, profuse Drunk by Equator-Suns, severely shine. **1875** CROLL *Climate & T.* x. 187 The pressure..impels the bottom-water equatorwards. **1884** *Daily News* 2 Aug. 5/4 To continue the voyage equatorwards.

equatorial (iːkwəˈtɔərɪəl, ɛkwə-), *a.* and *sb.* Also 7–8 æquatorial, 8–9 equatoreal. [f. L. *æquātor* (see prec.) + -(I)AL; in Fr. *équatorial*.]

A. *adj.*

1. a. Of or pertaining to the equator; situated or existing on or about the equator.

1713 DERHAM *Phys.-Theol.* II. i. *note* 1 (R.), A prolate sphæroid, making the polar about 34 miles shorter than the equatorial diameter. **1789** HERSCHEL *Saturn* in *Phil. Trans.* LXXX. 16 The arrangement of the belts..has always followed the direction of the ring, which is what I have called being equatorial. **1794** G. ADAMS *Nat. & Exper. Philos.* III. xxxii. 334 Their surfaces will be higher..in the equatoreal, than in the polar regions. **1860** MAURY *Phys. Geog. Sea* v. §296 Panama is in the region of equatorial calms. **1870** YEATS *Nat. Hist. Comm.* 65 Equatorial grains are maize and rice.

b. Pertaining to the 'equator' of a magnet, or of any spherical or spheroidal body.

1664 POWER *Exp. Philos.* III. 168 Those aequatorial parts of the Magnet, which before respected the East. **1837** BREWSTER *Magnet.* 268 The middle of a copper wire..was applied to the equatorial groove. **1861** J. R. GREENE *Man. Anim. Kingd., Cœlent.* 227 In Cestum..these [a pair of symmetrical tentacles] do not..issue from the equatorial region, thence turning away from the mouth.

c. Pertaining to the equator of a balloon (cf. prec. 3 d).

1838 M. MASON *Aeronautica* 30 In shape it [*sc.* a balloon] somewhat resembles a pear; its upright or polar diameter exceeding the transverse or equatorial by about one-sixth.

2. ***equatorial instrument*** or ***telescope***: an apparatus consisting essentially of a telescope attached by an arm to an axle revolving in a direction parallel to the plane of the equator. By a uniform motion given to this axle (in large instruments by clockwork) the telescope follows the diurnal apparent motion of any point in the heavens to which it is directed. ***equatorial circle***: a graduated circle (otherwise called *hour-circle, right-ascension-circle*) revolving in a plane parallel to the equator, forming part of the equatorial instrument.

1791 JEFFERSON in *Harper's Mag.* (1885) Mar. 535/2 He is to pay for equatorial instrument. **1793** SIR G. SHUCKBURGH *Equator. Instr.* in *Phil. Trans.* LXXXIII. 72 The idea of an equatorial telescope was again renewed by three several artists in this kingdom. **1868** AIRY *Pop. Astron.* ii. 39 For causing the Equatoreal instrument to revolve uniformly.

3. *Biol.* (Cf. prec. 3 e.) ***equatorial plate*** [tr. F. *plaque équatoriale* (E. van Beneden 1875, in *Bull. de l' Acad. R. d. Sci. de Belg.* (*Classe des Sciences*) 2me Sér. XL. 733)], in mitosis and meiosis, the position occupied by the chromosomes when arranged in the equatorial plane of the spindle during metaphase.

1887 A. C. HADDON *Introd. Study Embryol.* ii. 19 At the stage when the chromatin is equatorially situated (the 'equatorial plate', which is the equivalent of the wreath and aster stage), the achromatin forms a well-marked spindle-shaped bundle of fibres. **1896** E. B. WILSON *Cell* ii. 49 The chromosomes group themselves in a plane passing through the equator of the spindle, and thus form what is known as the equatorial plate. **1913** J. W. JENKINSON *Vertebr. Embryol.* iii. 40 The plane at right angles to the axis and including the centre of the egg is equatorial. **1952** A. HUGHES *Mitotic Cycle* iv. 116 During metaphase the chromosomes move from random positions into the 'equatorial plate'. **1958** C. P. SWANSON *Cytol. & Cytogenetics* iii. 52 The spindle..serves to bring the chromosomes onto the metaphase, or equatorial, plate. **1960** L. PICKEN *Organization of Cells* x. 501 Either before fertilization or at the eight-cell stage, an equatorial separation of the two halves of the egg gives rise to qualitatively different larvae.

B. *sb.* **a.** = *equatorial instrument*: see A. 2.

1793 SIR G. SHUCKBURGH *Equator. Instr.* in *Phil. Trans.* LXXXIII. 84 The equatorial is a machine calculated to observe the heavenly bodies in every part of the hemisphere. **1847** WHEWELL *Hist. Induct. Sc.* VII. vi. §1 (ed. 2) Transit instruments, equatorials, heliometers. **1879** LOCKYER *Elem. Astron.* vi. 224 An equatorial.

b. *attrib.* in ***equatorial clock***, a clock for driving an equatorial.

1884 BRITTEN *Watch and Clockm. Hand-bk.* 66, 102.

equatorially (iːkwəˈtɔərɪəlɪ, ɛkwə-), *adv.* [f. prec. + -LY[2].] In an equatorial direction or position.

1802 PALEY *Nat. Theol.* viii, It is occasionally requisite, that the object-end of the instrument be moved up and down, as well as horizontally or equatorially. **1868** LOCKYER *Elem. Astron.* 224 An eight-inch telescope, equatorially mounted. **1870** R. M. FERGUSON *Electr.* 41 Some arranged themselves axially, others equatorially. **1875** CROLL *Climate & T.* vi. 113 The cool and heavy water of the polar basin.. would flow equatorially with equal velocity. **1889** BURDON-SANDERSON in *Nature* 26 Sept. 529 Suppose that..the catalyzable material..is accumulated equatorially.

†**eque.** *Sc. Obs.* A balanced account; an acquittance, receipt. 'So called from the phrase, *et sic æque*, which was written at the foot of an account when it was closed or settled.' (Jam. *Suppl.*)

1636 *Rec. Burgh Glasg.* (1876) II. 41 Supplicatiounes to the exchequer annent our eque. **1637** *Rec. Burgh Aberdean* (1871) I. 118 The tounes eque wpoun the payment of thair burrow mailles.

equerry (ˈɛkwərɪ, ɪˈkwɛrɪ). Forms: *α.* 6 esquiry(e, 7 escuirie, 8 escurie. *β.* 6 equirrie, 7 equerie, 7–9 equery, 7– equerry. *γ. aphet.* 6–8 query, -rry, quiry, -rry. [ad. F. *écurie*, earlier *escurie* (also *escuierie*, by erroneous association with *escuyer* ESQUIRE), med.L. *scūria* stable, f. OHG. *scûr* shed, shelter (whence *sciura*, MHG. *schiure*, mod.G. *scheuer* barn). The surviving Eng. form is due to an erroneous idea of some connexion with L. *equus* horse; the accentuation on the first syll., favoured by most Dicts. of the present century, is due to the same cause.]

†**1.** The stables belonging to a royal or princely household; the body of officers in charge of the stables. *Obs.*

α. **1552** HULOET, Esquirye, equitium. **1595** in Spottiswood *Hist. Ch. Scotl.* (1677) VI. 413 His Majesties house and esquiry and stable. **1603** HOLLAND *Plutarch's Mor.* 84 The keeping of an escuirie or stable of horses.

β. **1600** *Gowrie Conspir.* in *Select. Harl. Misc.* (1793) 190 His hienes being now come downe by the equerie. *a* **1691** BOYLE *Wks.* VI. 354 (R.), Sir R. P., that is, (in the ear) Sir Robert Pye of the equerry. **1731** in BAILEY vol. II. **1800** COLERIDGE *Piccolom.* I. ix, There is brought to me from your equerry A splendid..hunting dress.

γ. **1611** SPEED *Hist. Gt. Brit.* IX. xxiv. (1632) 1183 He hauing familiar acquaintance in the Quirry. **1633** FORD *Love's Sacr.* I. ii, There's not a groom o' the query could have match'd The jolly riding man. **1719** *Glossogr. Angl. Nova* s.v. *Querry*, A Gentleman of the Querry.

2. [Short for 'gentleman of the equerry', 'groom of the equerry'; cf. AF. *esquire de qurye*, OF. *escuyer d' escuyrie.*] †**a.** A groom (*obs.*). **b.** An officer in the service of a royal or other exalted personage, charged with the care of the horses. At the English Court, an officer of the royal household, charged with the duty of occasional attendance on the sovereign.

α. **1708** CHAMBERLAIN *State Gt. Brit.* I. II. xii. (1743) 100 The constable hath also the power of escuries & pages.

β. **1591** HORSEY *Trav.* (1857) 197 At Yeraslaue another equirrie of the stable mett him. **1679–88** *Secr. Serv. Money Chas. & Jas.* (1851) 151 In repayring of his house as one of the equerys. **1708** *Lond. Gaz.* No. 4464/4 One Equery, two Pages of Honour, and the Gentleman Usher in waiting, in Her Majesty's Leading Coach. **1756–7** tr. *Keysler's Trav.* (1760) III. 255 Attended..by the Roman emperors..as if they were equerries or grooms of the holy see. **1813** *Examiner* 3 May 280/2 His Royal Highness..left Carlton House..accompanied by Captain Portier, his Equery. **1839** tr. *Lamartine's Trav. East* 41/1 The equerry of Lady Stanhope, who is at the same time her physician. **1865** MAFFEI *Brigand Life* II. 18 The equerries and militia of the barons.

γ. [**1526** *Househ. Ord.* 172 The Master of the Horse..to have sitting with him at his table the Esquires de Qurye and the Avenor.] *Ibid.* 206 The Master of the Horses doe appoint all such Querries, Officers, and Keepers as, etc. **1591** SYLVESTER *Du Bartas* I. vii. (1641) 61/2 As skilfull Quirry, that commands the Stable Of some great Prince. [**1603** FLORIO *Montaigne* I. ix. (1632) 17 A Gentleman.. serving the King in place of one of the Quiers of his Quierie.] **1608** BP. HALL *Epist.* I. vi, Francesco del Campo (one of the Arch-Dukes Quiryes). **1693** LUTTRELL *Brief Rel.* (1857) III. 165 Mr. Charles Turner..querrie to King James. **1763** MRS. E. STANLEY *Prince Titi* 14 The Querry or Riding-Master..beat down a poor ancient Woman into a very miry Place.

Hence **ˈequerryship**, the office or position of an equerry.

β. **1787** MISS BURNEY *Diary* (1842) III. 426 Her husband's Equerryship. **1882** *Standard* 13 Nov. 5/3 Colonel M'Neill has held for the last eight years an Equerryship to the Queen.

γ. **1611** COTGR., *Escuyrie*, a Querry ship. **1681** BLOUNT *Glossogr.*, Querryship.

equestrial (ɪˈkwɛstrɪəl), *a.* Now *rare.* [f. as next + -AL[1].] = EQUESTRIAN.

1553 GRIMALD tr. *Cicero's Duties* (c. 1600) 99 b, It was wont to bee done abroad by vs of the Equestriall order. **1607** TOPSELL *Four-f. Beasts* (1673) 232 The sight of one of these is nothing inferiour to the equestrial party coloured caparisons. **1611** CORYAT *Crudities* 289 One hundred and sixty fiue marble statues of worthy personages, partly equestriall, partly pedestriall. **1719** OZELL tr. *Misson's Trav. Eng.* 309 (D.), Two others of the same King, one equestrial, and most furiously ugly. **1883** C. BEARD *Reformation* iii. 96 The equestrial portrait which represents him triumphing over the Protestants on the battle-field of Mühlberg.

equestrian (ɪˈkwɛstrɪən), *a.* and *sb.* [f. L. *equestri-s* belonging to a horseman (f. *eques* horseman, f. *equ-us* horse) + -AN.]

A. *adj.*

1. Of or pertaining to horse-riding. Also of persons: Skilled in horse-riding.

1656–81 BLOUNT *Glossogr.*, *Equestrian*, pertaining to a Horse-man, Knight, or Gentleman, or to an Horse. **1711** STEELE *Spect.* No. 104 ⁋1, I should be glad if a certain Equestrian Order of Ladies..would take this Subject into their serious Consideration. **1741** MIDDLETON *Cicero* (1742) I. IV. 273 The Equestrian races of the Circus. **1758** JOHNSON *Idler* No. 6 ⁋4 Future candidates for equestrian glory. **1838** LYTTON *Alice* II. vi. 81 Evelyn's inexperience in equestrian matters. **1866** EDGAR *Runnymede* (1870) 80 Their mettled palfreys, and their equestrian grace.

2. Mounted on a horse. Also of a portrait or statue: Representing a person on horseback.

1711 ADDISON *Spect.* No. 59 ⁋4 The Antique Equestrian Statue of Marcus Aurelius. **1711–14** *Spectator* (J.), An equestrian lady appeared upon the plains. **1791** COWPER *Odyss.* III. 22 Advance at once to the equestrian chief. **1840** DICKENS *Barn. Rudge* x, To sit for an equestrian portrait.

3. *Rom. Ant.* Of or pertaining to the order of *Equites* or Knights.

1696 KENNETT *Rom. Antiq.* II. III. i. 97 One that had Four hundred [sestertia] might be taken into the Equestrian Order. **1781** GIBBON *Decl. & F.* III. 241 Whatever might be the numbers, of equestrian, or plebeian rank, who perished in the massacre of Rome. **1879** FROUDE *Cæsar* viii. 78 Cicero challenged his opponents..to find a single instance in which an Equestrian Court could be found to have given a corrupt verdict.

transf. **1791** BURKE *App. Whigs* Wks. 1808 VI. 237 A middle sort of men; a sort of equestrian order.

b. *Hist.* Of or pertaining to the 'knightly order' in the states of the Holy Roman Empire.

1684 *Scanderbeg Rediv.* iv. 64 Next day the Equestrian Order went to the House of Senators. **1711** *Lond. Gaz.* No. 4930/1 The Deputies of the Equestrian Order, were to meet there. **1845** S. AUSTIN *Ranke's Hist. Ref.* III. 617 The bishop, chapter and equestrian order, or nobles (Ritterschaft).

B. *sb.* **a.** One who rides on horseback. **b.** One who publicly performs on horseback.

1791 'G. GAMBADO' *Ann. Horsem.* v. (1809) 87 Many of his Majesty's faithful subjects, whose occupations oblige them daily to figure as equestrians. **1818** SCOTT *Hrt. Midl.* xiii, He stopped..internally wishing no good to the panting equestrian. **1840** BARHAM *Ingol. Leg., Spectre Tappington* (1882) 336 Mr. Peters..indifferent as an equestrian, had acquired some fame as a whip. **1860** EMERSON *Cond. Life, Fate* Wks. (Bohn) II. 328 As the equestrians in the circus throw themselves nimbly from horse to horse. **1873** H. SPENCER *Study Sociol.* x. 243 The tracts for equestrians having been from time to time increased.

Hence †**equestri'ana** ? *nonce-wd.* [f. as if Lat.], a female equestrian. **e'questria,nism**, the art or practice of riding on horseback. **e'questrianize** *v. intr.*, to act as an equestrian. **e'questria,nizing** *vbl. sb.*

1825 C. M. WESTMACOTT *Eng. Spy* I. 197 See Mrs. M. a superb equestriana. **1872** *Globe* 5 Aug., Dislike of equestrianism. **1881** *Morning Post* 29 Sept. 5/4 Schule Reiterei..or riding school equestrianism. **1887** *Boston* (Mass.) *Jrnl.* 28 Nov. 2/1 Senator—and his daughters equestrianize about Washington daily. **1886** BLACKIE in *Cassell's Fam. Mag.* Feb. 151 This habit of bracing equestrianising.

equestrienne. [pseudo-Fr. fem. of EQUESTRIAN.] A horsewoman, female equestrian.

1864 in WEBSTER. **1888** G. C. BOASE *Ducrow* in *Dict. Nat. Biog.* XVI. 97/1 A well-known equestrienne.

equi- ('iːkwɪ-, ɛkwɪ-), repr. L. *æqui-*, combining form of *æquus* equal, prefixed originally to words of Latin origin, as *equiangular*, but occasionally to those from other sources, as *equi-balance*. The majority of the words so formed are adjectives; these are chiefly parasynthetic derivatives f. sbs. after the analogy of the simple adjs.; in other instances the prefix has the advb. sense 'equally, in an equal degree'. Less frequently the prefix forms verbs and substantives.

,equianhar'monic *a.* (see quot.); hence **,equianhar'monically** *adv.* **,equiar'ticulate** *a.*, having equal joints with another. **equi'balance** *sb.* = EQUILIBRIUM. †**equi'balance** *v. Obs.*, to counterpoise, to constitute an equivalent to. **,equibi'radiate** *a.*, having two equal rays. **equi'cellular** *a. Biol.*, made up of similar cells. **equi'changeable** *a.*, equally varying. †**equi'cheapness**, *Obs.* the quality of being equally cheap. **equicohesive temperature** *Metall.* (see quot. 1917). **equicon'tinuous** *a. Math.* [tr. It. *egualmente continuo* (C. Arzelà 1895, in *Mem. d. R. Accad. d. Sci. dell'Ist. di Bologna* V. 226)], of a set of functions $f_i(x)$: having the property that for all x_1 and all $\epsilon > 0$ there corresponds a $\delta > 0$ such that, if $|x - x_1| < \delta$, $|f_i(x) - f_i(x_1)| < \epsilon$ for all *i*. **equi'convex** *a.*, having two convex surfaces presenting equal curves. **equi'crescent** *a.*, increasing by equal amounts, having equal increments. †**equi'curve** *a. Obs.*, having an equal curve *to* (some other line). **,equidi'agonal** *a.*, having the diagonals equal. **,equidi'urnal** *a. nonce-wd.*, transl. Gr. ἰσημερινός (see quot.). †**,equidi'vision**, *Obs.*, equal division. †**,equi'durable** *a. Obs.*, equally durable. **equi'excellency**, the being equally excellent. **equi'graphic**, *a.* (see quot.). **equi'lobate** *a.*, equally lobate, having equal lobes. †**equi'lucent** *a. Obs.*, shining with equal or even light. **equi'molar** *a.* = *equimolecular* (*b*). **equimo'lecular** *a.*, (*a*) having an equal number of molecules; (*b*) having an equal number of moles (cf. MOLE *sb.*[7]). **,equimo'mental** *a. Physics*, having equal moments of inertia about parallel axes. †**equi'necessary** *a. Obs.*, needful in an equal degree. †**equi'numerally** *adv. Obs.*, in equal, *i.e.* corresponding, numbers or feet. †**equi'numerant** *a. Obs.*, having the same number, consisting of the same number. †**,equiom'nipotent** *a. Obs.*, equally all-powerful. **equi'pensate** *v. Obs.*, to weigh equally; to esteem alike. **,equiperi'odic** *a.*, having equal periods. **equi'probabilism**, the doctrine of the equiprobabilists. **equi-'probabilist** (see quot.). **equipro'ducing** *a.*, equally producing; producing an equal amount or crop. **equi'radial** *a.*, having equal radii. **equi'radical** *a.*, 'equally radical' (W.). **,equiseg'mental** *a. Math.*, having equal segments. **equi'signal** *a. Aeronaut.*, of a radio beacon or guidance system of overlapping zones (see quot. 1951). **equi'sized** *a.*, equally sized, of equal size. †**equisu'fficiency** *nonce-wd.*, the being equally sufficient. **,equitan'gential** *a.*, having a tangent equal to a constant line; said of a certain curve. †**equitempo'raneous** *a. Obs.*, performed in equal lengths of time. †**equi'valiant** *a. Obs.*, equally valiant; of sufficient prowess. **equi'value** *v. trans.*, (*a*) to value equally, put on a par; (*b*) to equal in value. **'equivalved** *a. Conch.* (see quot.). †**,equive'locity**. *Obs.*, equality in velocity. **equi'vote**, the event of an equal number of votes having been given on either side.

1885 LEUDESDORF *Cremona's Proj. Geom.* 55 If two ranges, each of four points, are projective, they..are *equianharmonic. **1852** DANA *Crust.* II. 1131 The accessory branch is but little the shorter, nearly *equi-articulate. **1841** *Blackw. Mag.* XLIX. 372 The sphere of Coreggio..exemplified the attempt to create an *equi-balance of the great elements of the constitution of man. **1665** MANLEY *Grotius' Low C. Warres* 916, 500 Foot, or so many Ships, as should equi-ballance that Number. **1675** J. SMITH *Chr. Relig. Appeal* 48 (L.), In Mahomet..the passions of amorousness and ambition were almost equibalanced. *a* **1678** WOODHEAD *Holy Living* (1688) 110 Equiballancing to the other. **1890** E. R. LANKESTER in *Encycl. Brit.* XXIV. 810/2 The unicellular or *equicellular Protozoa. **1800** SIR W. HERSCHEL in *Phil. Trans.* XC. 536 The proportional elevations which a set of *equi-changeable thermometers would experience. **1612** STURTEVANT *Metallica* (1854) 85 Equi-sufficiencie, *Equi-cheapness, Equi-excellency [are the lesser vertues of a deriuatiue Inuention]. **1917** Z. JEFFRIES in *Jrnl. Amer. Inst. Metals* Dec. 300 (*title*) The Amorphous Metal Hypothesis and *Equi-Cohesive Temperatures. *Ibid.* 311 There must be some intermediate temperature in any given metal at which the cohesion of the amorphous and crystalline phases is the same. I will refer to this temperature as the 'Equi-Cohesive Temperature'. **1959** *Jrnl. Iron & Steel Inst.* CXCI. 208/2 The author first describes methods for determining equicohesive temperature and for ascertaining its dependence on grain size, strain and strain rate. **1926** E. W. HOBSON *Theory Functions* (ed. 2) II. ii. 168 In case the family of continuous functions is such that, for each value of ε, a single set of sub-intervals or sub-cells can be so determined that, for every function $f(x)$ of the family, the fluctuation in a sub-interval, or a sub-cell, of a set, is less than ε, the family is said to consist of **equi-continuous* functions. **1959** G. & R. C. JAMES *Math. Dict.* 21/1 *Ascoli's theorem.* From any set of uniformly bounded functions equicontinuous on a bounded closed (compact) set (such as a closed interval) it is possible to select an infinite sequence which converges uniformly to a limit function which is also continuous. **1857** B. PRICE *Infinitesimal Calculus* I. 89 This variable..I have ventured to call *Equicrescent. **1726** tr. *Gregory's Astron.* I. 1. 47 The Proportions..agree..to this Curve, to which the Circle is *equicurve. **1762** tr. *Busching's Syst. Geog.* I. Pref. 39 The radius of a circle æquicurve to the meridian. **1817** H. T. COLEBROOKE *Algebra* 58 *Equidiagonal tetragons. **1858** WHEWELL *Nov. Org.* 262 (L.), The circle which the sun describes in his diurnal motion, when the days and nights are equal, the Greeks called the *equidiurnal. **1633** AMES *Agst. Cerem.* II. 174 That doeth not hinder a superdivision, or *æquidivision, into common and speciall. **1686** GOAD *Celest. Bodies* II. viii. 256 To ascribe a durable Constitution, or State of Air, to an *Equi-durable mover. **1612** [see quot. for *equicheapness*] *Equiexcellency. **1866** PROCTOR *Handbk. Stars* 22 The homolographic (or, as I prefer to call it, the *equigraphic) projection of maps: that is of the construction of maps in which all areas shall be correctly given. **1872** NICHOLSON *Palæont.* 325 Ganoids with heterocercal *equilobate tails. **1608** SYLVESTER *Du Bartas* 767 Bee't Cloudy, cleer, Eclipse, or night, or day, His lovely browes are *equilucent ay. **1946** *Nature* 14 Dec. 877/1 Carré and Libermann have shown..that it is of great advantage to use *equimolar quantities of acid, pyridine, and thionyl chloride. **1961** *Lancet* 2 Sept. 566/2 The solution contained equimolar amounts of α-ketobutyric acid and sodium hydroxide. **1909** J. W. JENKINSON *Exper. Embryol.* iii. 140 *Equimolecular solutions of monobasic lithium salts. **1922** F. W. ASTON *Isotopes* 19 Solutions of two different compounds of lead in equimolecular proportions. **1963** A. J. HALL *Textile Sci.* ii. 72 An equimolecular mixture of the two monomers. **1881** J. LARMOR in *Nature* XXIV. 605 The well-known property of *equi-momental ellipses. **1663** BUTLER *Hud.* I. iii. 1034 For both to give blows and to carry, In fights are *equenecessary. **1640** J. GOWER (*title*), Ovid's Festivalls, or Romane Calendar; translated into English Verse *equinumerally. **1705** ARBUTHNOT *Coins* (J.), This talent of gold, though not *equinumerant, nor yet equiponderant, as to any other; yet was equivalent to some correspondent talent in brass. **1797** J. LAWRENCE in *Monthly Mag.* (1818) XLVI. 214 That even abstract power appears to be limited by *equiomnipotent absurdity. **1692–1732** COLES, **Equipensate*, weigh or esteem alike. **1882** MINCHIN *Unipl. Kinemat.* 10 Superposed *Equiperiodic Rectilinear Vibrations. **1817** H. T. COLEBROOKE *Algebra* 74 Also in an *equi-perpendicular tetragon..to find the area. **1888** *Dublin Rev.* Jan. 219 The contest between probabilism and *æquiprobabilism has not been touched at all. **1882** LITTLEDALE in *Encycl. Brit.* XIV. 636 s.v. *Liguori*, *Equiprobabilists, who teach that in a balance of opinion the less safe opinion may be lawfully followed, provided it be as probable, or nearly as probable, as its opposite. **1846** GROTE *Greece* II. vi. II. 537 Something approaching to *equi-producing lots for all. **1817** COLERIDGE *Biog. Lit.* 130 If we affirm of a circle that it is *equi-radial. **1931** P. V. H. WEEMS *Air Navig.* xiv. 273 A radio beam is broadcast by transmitters known as *equi-signal beacons. Transmitters employ two cross-loops, radiating a characteristic dot-and-dash signal. **1936** *Jrnl. R. Aeronaut. Soc.* XL. 172 The system of directional equi-signal beacons established to mark the chain of air routes throughout the U.S.A. **1951** *Gloss. Aeronaut. Terms (B.S.I.)* III. 31 *Equi-signal zone*, a zone within which, with an overlapping signal pattern system, indication is given that an aircraft is on a track. **1889** *Evening Post* 25 Jan. 1/4 The lady's bicycle, which is built..with *equi-sized wheels. **1612** [see quot. for *equicheapness*] *Equi-sufficiency. **1715** DE MOIVRE in *Phil. Trans.* XXIX. 334 The Curve *A C B* may..be call'd the *Equitangential Curve. **1871** OLNEY *Geom.* xiii. 172 The..Equitangential Curve is generated by the motion of a weight, etc. **1709** F. HAUKSBEE *Phys. Mech. Exper.* v. (1719) 197 Galileo's famous Proposition, about the *Equitemporaneous Descents of heavy Bodies in the Chords of a Circle. **1579** J. STUBBES *Gaping Gulf* D ij b, The daughter..shal haue much adoe to find *equiualiant champions. **1803** W. TAYLOR in Robberds *Mem.* I. 470 He has the fault of all our antiquaries, to *equivalue the noble and the rabble of authorities. **1865** F. HALL in *Reader* 14 Jan. 43/1 Anything adequate mounts up to; whereas that which is adequative simply equivalues. **1836** TODD *Cycl. Anat.* I. 711 In a considerable number of species the two valves are alike, when the shell is said to be *equivalved. **1662** STILLINGFL. *Orig. Sacr.* III. ii. §16 The *æqui-velocity of the motion of all Atoms..which he likewise asserted. **1745** *Revised Charter Yale Coll.* in *Catal. Yale Univ.* (1886) 20 Where an *Equivote happens, the President shall have a casting Vote. **1888** A. P. FOSTER in *Advance* (Chicago) 1 Mar. 132 In an equi-vote the question shall determine on that side on which the presiding member shall have voted.

equiæval: see EQUÆVAL.

†**equi'angle**, *a.* and *sb. Obs.* [a. Fr. *équiangle*, f. *équi-* EQUI- + *angle* ANGLE.]

A. *adj.* Having equal angles: = EQUIANGULAR.

1570 BILLINGSLEY *Euclid* IV. ii. 111* To describe a triangle equiangle vnto a triangle geuen. **1571** DIGGES *Pantom.* (1591) 5 They are termed Equiangle Polygons. **1611** COTGR., *Icosaëdre*..consists of twentie equiangle triangles.

B. *sb. pl.* Equal angles. ***by equiangles***: at right angles.

1593 NORDEN *Spec. Brit., M'sex.* I. 10 It cutteth the same also by equiangles.

†**equi'angled**, *a. Obs.* Also 7 æqui-. [f. as prec. + -ED[2]; cf. ANGLED.] = EQUIANGULAR.

1660 T. WILLSFORD *Scales of Commerce* 182 A triangle, equiangled with that of the Turrets shadow. **1672** BOYLE *Orig. Gems* Wks. 1772 III. 534 Twelve æquilateral and æquiangled Pentagons. **1695** ALINGHAM *Geom. Epit.* 75 The triangles..are equiangled.

equiangular (iːkwɪ'æŋgjʊlə(r)), *a. Geom.* [f. EQUI- + ANGULAR.] Having equal angles.

a. Having all its angles equal. **b.** Having angles respectively equal with those of another figure, or making equal angles with a line. ***equiangular spiral*** (see quot. 1884).

1660 BARROW *Euclid* I. def. 28 b, An Equiangular or equal-angled figure is that whereof all the angles are equal. **1721–1800** in BAILEY. **1756** SIMPSON *Euclid* (Jod.), A circle may be inscribed in a given equilateral and equiangular quindecagon. **1786** *Phil. Trans.* LXXVI. 21 The method employed to make the threads of the screw equiangular with the axis. **1840** LARDNER *Geom.* 119 Mutually equiangular, and..therefore similar. **1854** WOODWARD *Mollusca* II. 223 Beak prominent, area equiangular. **1884** B. WILLIAMSON *Diff. Calculus* xii. 223 In the logarithmic spiral..the angle between the radius vector and the tangent is constant. On account of this property the curve is also called the equiangular spiral.

equiangularity (,iːkwɪ,æŋgjuː'lærɪtɪ). [f. prec. + -ITY.] The condition or fact of being equiangular.

1855 H. SPENCER *Princ. Psychol.* (1873) II. 54 The equilateralness of a triangle is known from its equiangularity.

equianharmonic, -articulate: see EQUI-.

equiaxe ('iːkwɪæks), *a. Crystallogr.* [a. Fr. *équiaxe*, f. L. *æqui-* (see EQUI-) + *axis* AXIS.] Having equal axes.

1810 J. T. in *Risdon's Surv. Devon* Introd. 15 Some in equiaxe crystals have..been found. **1817** R. JAMESON *Char. Min.* 222 *Equiaxe*, when it has the shape of a rhomboid, in which the axis is equal to that of the primitive rhomboid.

equiaxed ('iːkwɪækst), *a.* = prec.

1869 PHILLIPS *Vesuv.* x. 272 Five types..all parts of one equi-axed system.

equibalance, -biradiate: see EQUI- *pref.*

equicellular, -changeable, -cheapness, -cohesive, -continuous, -convex, -crescent: see EQUI- *pref.*

†**'equicerve.** *Obs.* [ad. late L. *equicervus*, f. L. *equus* horse + *cervus* stag.] (See quots.)

[**1398** TREVISA *Barth. De. P.R.* XVIII. cx. (1495) 851 In the londe of Perthes is a wylde cowe that hathe heer in her necke as an horse and is of the quantyte of an harte and therfore many men calle that cowe Equiceruus and suche a cowe is wythout hornes.] **1572** BOSSEWELL *Armorie* II. 57 The fielde is Mercury, an Equicerve, of the Moone. **1688** R. HOLME *Armoury* II. 174/1 An Equicerve, or a Deer-Horse..is a Beast in the Oriental Countreys having the body of a Horse with outward bended horns.

equicrural (,iːkwɪ'krʊərəl), *a.* Also 7–8 æqui-. [f. L. *æquicrūr-us* (see next) + -AL[1]; cf. Fr. *équicrural.*] Of a triangle: Having legs of equal length; isosceles. Of a cross: Having equal arms.

1650 SIR T. BROWNE *Pseud. Ep.* (ed. 2) 233 Draw lines from angle to angle, untill seven equicrural triangles be described. **1656–81** in BLOUNT *Glossogr.* **1762** HAMILTON in *Phil. Trans.* LIII. 119 Let the æquicrural triangle A, B, C, represent a wedge. **1843** *Fraser's Mag.* XXVII. 716 Pieces of masonry, in the form of an equicrural cross.

†**'equicrure**, *a. Obs.* [ad. late L. *æquicrūr-us*, *æquicrūr-ius*, f. *æqui-* (see EQUI-) + *crūs, crūr-is* leg.] = prec.

1644 DIGBY *Nat. Bodies* ix. (1658) 88 Let the Equicrure triangle be A B C: and from the point A, etc. *Ibid.* ix, (R.), Consider the increase of an equicrure triangle. **1775** in ASH. **1847** in CRAIG; and in mod. Dicts.

equicurve: see EQUI- *pref.*

equid ('ɛkwɪd). [ad. mod.L. *equidæ*, f. *equus* horse.] A member of the family Equidæ, which embraces horses, asses, mules, zebras, and certain extinct ungulates with undivided hoofs.

1889 in *Cent. Dict.* **1928** V. G. CHILDE *Most Anc. East* ii. 25 The zebra, and perhaps another equid. **1932** *Antiquity* VI. 254 The calm, conventional figures of equids from Gross Spitzkopje. **1937** *Proc. Prehistoric Soc.* III. 185 A naturalistic engraving of an equid covered by the archaeological deposit. **1968** A. S. ROMER *Procession of Life* xvi. 252 In the equids the front foot, like the hind, eventually became monodactyl.

equidifferent (i:kwɪ'dɪfərənt), *a.* Also 8 æquidifferent. [f. EQUI- + DIFFERENT.]

1. Having equal differences; arithmetically proportional.

1695 HALLEY *Easy Demonstr. Log. Tangents* in *Misc. Cur.* (1708) II. 31 The Secants of æquidifferent Arches. **1827** HUTTON *Course Math.* I. 227 A Series of equidifferent Terms.

2. Said of a crystal in which the numbers of the faces presented severally by the prism and by each summit, form a series in arithmetical progression, as 6, 4, 2.

1817 R. JAMESON *Char. Min.* 208 Equidifferent basaltic hornblend is a six-sided prism.

equidistance (i:kwɪ'dɪstəns). [a. Fr. *équidistance*, f. *équidistant*: see next.] The fact of being equidistant. Also in phrase *at equidistance* = at equal distances.

1629 LIGHTFOOT *Misc.* 11 (T.), From the equidistance of the letters and vowel, they gather the distinction of the persons. **1649** BP. HALL *Cases Consc.* (1650) 334 The collaterall equidistance of cousens german from the stock whence both descend. *a* **1721** KEILL tr. *Maupertuis' Diss.* (1734) 35 The gravity of Bodies..at equidistance from the Center of the Earth, is as their quantities of Matter. **1873** BROWNING *Red. Cott. Night-c.* 417 There lie, out-spread at equidistance, thorpes And villages and towns along the coast.

equidistant (i:kwɪ'dɪstənt), *a.* [a. Fr. *équidistant*, ad. late L. *æquidistant-em*, f. *æqui-* (see EQUI-) + *distant-em* standing apart, DISTANT.]

1. Separated by an equal distance or equal distances. Also *fig.*

1593 FALE *Dialling* 14 Draw the line H. I. equidistant from A. B. or K. L. **1613** DONNE *Elegy Pr. Henry* Poems (1650) 240 Quotidian things, and equidistant hence, Shut in, for man, in one circumference. **1646** SIR T. BROWNE *Pseud. Ep.* 293 They would be equidistant from that Tropick. **1796** MORSE *Amer. Geog.* I. 590 The situation of this metropolis is..equi-distant from the northern and southern extremities of the Union. **1817** COLERIDGE *Biog. Lit.* I. x. 178 My opinions..were almost equi-distant from all the three prominent parties. **1869** OUSELEY *Counterp.* xii. 54 The (4) parts should be kept..equidistant.

2. Always preserving the same distance (from another line, etc.); parallel.

1570 BILLINGSLEY *Euclid* I. def. 35 Parallel or equidistant right lines. **1635** N. CARPENTER *Geog. Del.* I. ix. 208 It is contained betwixt two equidistant circles. **1657** S. PURCHAS *Pol. Flying-Ins.* 195 The back..hath several semicircular equidistant strakes down to the belly. **1805** REPTON *Landsc. Gardening* 88 The banks of a natural river are never equidistant. **1848** W. BARTLETT *Egypt to Pal.* xi. (1879) 240 I..found the two lines everywhere equidistant.

3. *equidistant projection*: a mode of mapping a sphere, where the 'centre of projection' is one reached by producing the diameter by a line equal to half the chord of a quadrant of the sphere.

1866 PROCTOR *Handbk. Stars* 20 The equidistant projection. **1867** DENISON *Astron. without Math.* 13.

Hence **equi'distantly** *adv.*, so as to be equidistant, at an equal distance. †**equi'distantness**, = EQUIDISTANCE.

1571 DIGGES *Pantom.* I. Def. B iij a, Two right lines.. equedistantly placed. **1646** SIR T. BROWNE *Pseud. Ep.* IV. v. 188 The Liver..doth equidistantly communicate its activity unto either arme. **1859** TODD *Cycl. Anat.* V. 598/2 These parts..when spread out equidistantly from each other. **1873** FERGUSSON in Tristram *Land of Moab* 377 The heads of the arches spaced equidistantly with those on the flanks. **1736** BAILEY, *Equidistantness*, a being equidistant.

equidiurnal, -division, -durable, -excellency: see EQUI- *pref.*

equiform ('i:kwɪfɔ:m), *a.* [ad. L. *æquiformis* uniform, f. *æquus* equal + *forma* shape, figure.] Having one and the same shape or form.

In mod. Dicts.

equiformal (i:kwɪ'fɔ:məl), *a.* [f. L. *æquiformis* (see prec.) + -AL[1].] = prec.

1883 E. R. LANKESTER in *Encycl. Brit.* XVI. 660 The teeth being equi-formal.

†**equi'formity**. *Obs.* [f. EQUIFORM + -ITY.] Uniformity.

1646 SIR T. BROWNE *Pseud. Ep.* 191 There being in them [the heavens]..a simplicity of parts, and equiformity in motion continually succeeding each other. **1721-1800** in BAILEY. **1847** in CRAIG; and in mod. Dicts.

equigraphic: see EQUI- *pref.*

equijacent, *a.* [f. EQUI- + L. *jacentem*, pr. pple. of *jacēre* to lie.]

1662 SALUSBURY *Math. Coll. & Trans.* II. 334 All these parts of the Water are Equijacent, as being all equidistant from the Center of the World.

†**equi'later**, *a.* and *sb. Obs.* Also 6 equilatre, 7 æquilater. [ad. Fr. *equilatere*, ad. late L. *æquilater-us*, f. *æqui-* (see EQUI-) + *latus, later-is* side.]

A. *adj.* Having equal sides.

1570 BILLINGSLEY *Euclid* I. def. 24 An equilatre triangle is that, which hath three equall sides. **1589** PUTTENHAM *Eng. Poesie* II. xi. (Arb.) 113 Of the square or quadrangle equilater. **1621** BURTON *Anat. Mel.* III. i. III. i. 520 Faith and Hope, which with this our loue make..an Æquilater Triangle. **1661** S. PARTRIDGE *Double Scale Proport.* 50 To find the side of an Equilater triangle. **1715** DE MOIVRE in *Phil. Trans.* XXIX. 335 Let *A H h* be an Equilater Hyperbola.

B. *sb.* **a.** *Geom.* A square or cube. **b.** *Arith.* A square or cube number.

1614 T. BEDWELL *Nat. Geom. Numbers* i. 4, 4 is a figurate equilater, and the side or roote of it is 2. **1636** HARTWELL in Record *Gr. Artes* 560 An æquilater plaine is a number made by two equall sides, or by any number multiplyed by it selfe. It is vulgarly called a square or quadrat. *Ibid.* 570 An Equilater, is a number made by three equall sides, or by any number multiplyed by it selfe, and that product againe by the foresaid number. It is called an Equilater..or Cube.

equilateral (i:kwɪ'lætərəl), *a.* Also 6-7 equilaterall, (7 æqui-). [ad. late L. *æquilaterālis*, f. *æqui-* (see EQUI-) + *latus, later-is* side + -AL[1].]

Having all the sides equal.

equilateral arch: an arch, in which the chords of the sides form with the base an equilateral triangle. ***equilateral hyperbola***, one whose axes are equal. ***equilateral shell***, one in which a transverse line drawn through the apex of the umbo divides the valve into two equal and symmetrical parts.

1570 BILLINGSLEY *Euclid* I. i. 10 How to describe an equilaterall triangle redily and mechanically. **1634** SIR T. HERBERT *Trav.* 112 The Sepulchre of Maleck Bahamans beloued Queene..'tis of foure Æquilaterall squares, eleuated eight yards high of stone. **1727** SWIFT *Gulliver* III. ii. 185 A shoulder of mutton, cut into an equilateral triangle. **1824** SCOTT *St. Ronan's* xv, A cocked hat of equilateral dimensions. **1848** RICKMAN *Archit.* 88 The principal moulding of these doors has generally an equilateral arch. **1851** RICHARDSON *Geol.* viii. 232 The shell is consequently equilateral. **1869** DUNKIN *Midn. Sky* 21 Denebola, Arcturus and Spica form very nearly an equilateral triangle. **1880** C. TAYLOR *Anc. & Mod. Geom. Conics* vi. 167 The Equilateral Hyperbola is..also called Rectangular. **1885** LEUDESDORF *Cremona's Proj. Geom.* 269 If the hyperbola is equilateral.. the asymptotes are the only pair of tangents which cut at right angles.

Hence **equi'laterally** *adv.*, in an equilateral manner or form.

1852 DANA *Crust.* II. 704 The posterior [epimeral] equilaterally triangular.

equilenin (i:kwɪ'li:nɪn). Also -ine. [ad. F. *équilénine* (A. Girard et al. 1932, in *Compt. Rend.* CXCV. 981), f. EQUILIN + infixed *-en-*.] A sex hormone, $C_{18}H_{18}O_2$, present in the urine of pregnant mares.

1933 *Chem. Abstr.* XXVII. 1929 Besides folliculin, $C_{18}H_{22}O_2$, 2 new hormones have been isolated from pregnant urine. Equilenine $C_{18}H_{18}O_8$..was obtained in a 1·50 g. quantity from 52 tons of urine. **1943** *Endeavour* Jan. 29/1 Analogy for aromatization of the hydrogenated ring system is provided by the oestrus-producing hormone equilenin. **1958** *Sci. News* XLVII. 88 Two other closely related oestrogens, produced by the equine species, are equilin and equilenin.

equilibrant (i:'kwɪlɪbrənt). *Physics.* [a. Fr. *équilibrant*, f. *équilibrer*, f. *équilibre*, ad. L. *æquilībrium*.] (See quot.)

1883 THOMSON & TAIT *Nat. Phil.* §558 Any system of forces which if applied to a rigid body would balance a given system of forces acting on it is called an equilibrant of the given system.

†**equi'librate**, *a. Obs.* [ad. L. *æquilībrāt-us* in equilibrium, pa. pple. of **æquilībrāre*, f. *æqui-* (see EQUI-) + *lībra* balance.] Equally balanced.

1693 *Phil. Trans.* XVII. 810 Next for the Earth, Plato says it was equilibrate without Inclination.

equilibrate (i:kwɪ'lɪbreɪt, -'laɪ-, -'kwɪlɪ-), *v.* Also 8 æquilibrate. [f. late L. *æquilībrāt-* ppl. stem of **æquilībrāre*: see prec.]

1. *trans.* To bring into or keep in a state of equipoise or equilibrium; to balance. Also const. *with.*

1635 N. CARPENTER *Geog. Del.* I. iii. 67 An iron-wire or needle, first equilibrated, and then stirred vp by the loadstone. **1713** DERHAM *Phys. Theol.* v. ii. 327 The Shoulders, Arms, and Sides æquilibrated on one Part. **1733** ARBUTHNOT *Air* (J.), The bodies of fishes are equilibrated with the water in which they swim. **1844** DE QUINCEY *Logic Pol. Econ.* 230 To equilibrate the supply with the demand. **1860** ADM. FITZ-ROY in *Merc. Mar. Mag.* VII. 356 It must go to equilibrate the atmosphere. **1872** *Contemp. Rev.* XX. 99 He may wisely try to equilibrate his impulses.

2. To be in equilibrium with; to counterpoise, balance.

1829 *Nat. Philos., Mechanics* III. ii. 10 (Usef. Knowl. Soc.), The weight which equilibrates that of the body. **1865** *Spectator* 4 Feb. 117 The excise duty on English malt is supposed to equilibrate the import duty on foreign malt. **1870** R. M. FERGUSON *Electr.* 122 The two forces would equilibrate each other.

3. *absol.* and *intr.* To be in a state of equilibrium; to balance. Const. *with.*

1829 *Nat. Philos., Mechanics* III. ii. 10 (Usef. Knowl. Soc.), This weight will equilibrate with that of the body. **1830** KATER & LARDN. *Mech.* x. 129 The forces neutralise each other and mutually equilibrate. **1862** F. HALL *Hindu Philos. Syst.* 17 When virtue and sin equilibrate, one inherits humanity. **1882** E. A. DOUGLAS in *Nature* XXV. 504 In order that solar gravity and centrifugal force may equilibrate.

Hence **equilibrated, equilibrating** *ppl. adjs.*

1664 POWER *Exp. Philos.* III. 161 It will acquire so strong a Magnetism..that it will..turn an equilibrated Needle. **1816** J. SMITH *Panorama Sc. & Art* I. 230 To explain the nature of the equilibrated arch. **1761** EARL PEMBROKE *Equitation* (1778) 26 By a proper equilibrating position of the body. **1797** T. JEFFERSON *Writ.* (1859) IV. 156 An equilibrating power against the fecundity of generation. **1882** MINCHIN *Unipl. Kinemat.* 25 An equilibrating system of forces.

equilibration (i:kwɪl(a)ɪ'breɪʃən). Also 7-8 æquilibration. [f. as prec.: see -ATION.] The action of bringing into or keeping in equilibrium; the state or condition of being evenly balanced. Applied both to material and immaterial things. Const. *to, with.* ***arch of equilibration*** (see quot.).

1612 BREREWOOD *Lang. & Relig.* xiv. 149 And so the opposite halfs of the earth..be brought on all sides, about the center, unto a perfect equilibration. **1625** JACKSON *Creed* v, vii. Wks. IV. 60 Simple Atheism consists in an equilibration of the mind. **1664** POWER *Exp. Philos.* II. 102 It comes to an æquilibration with those circumjacent Bodies. **1751** JOHNSON *Rambler* No. 111 ⁋3 Drowsy equilibrations of undetermined counsel. **1772** HUTTON *Bridges* 16 ABCD shall be an arch of equilibration, or be in equilibrium in all its parts. **1819** PLAYFAIR *Nat. Phil.* I. 147 An arch, of which the parts balance one another in this manner [by their weight only], is called an Arch of Equilibration. **1869** TYNDALL in *Fortn. Rev.* Feb. 228 The position of every atom..is determined by the equilibration of these two forces.

equilibrator (i:'kwɪlɪbreɪtə(r)). [f. EQUILIBRATE *v.* + -OR.] A device for maintaining or restoring equilibrium, as in an aircraft, or between the primary and secondary currents in a phototelegraphic apparatus.

1908 *Westm. Gaz.* 18 Aug. 4/2 All flying-machines..are liable to be brought more or less suddenly to earth by a wrong movement given to the equilibrator. **1909** *Ibid.* 11 Mar. 4/2 The pilot..might..by skilful manipulation of the equilibrator, succeed in recovering his equilibrium.

equilibratory (i:kwɪ'l(a)ɪbrətərɪ), *a.* [f. as EQUILIBRATION + -ORY.] Tending to produce equilibrium.

1875 JEVONS *Money* (1878) 139 A compensatory or, as I should prefer to call it, equilibratory action, goes on under the French currency law.

†**equi'libre**. *Obs.* Also 8 equiliber. [a. F. *équilibre*, ad. L. *æquilībrium*: see EQUILIBRIUM.]

1. = EQUILIBRIUM.

1621-31 LAUD *Serm.* (1847) 104 The earth itself, that hath but one 'pillar', and that is the poise and equilibre of the centre. **1761** EARL PEMBROKE *Equitation* (1778) 17 The true principles of equilibre and ease. **1772** BARRINGTON in *Phil. Trans.* LXII. 326 She at last taught herself the proper equilibre of the body. **1777** SIMPSON *Baratariana* (ed. 3) 25 *note*, The power a bird has of preserving its equiliber in the air. **1802** PALEY *Nat. Theol.* ix. (1819) 111 It is by the equilibre of the muscles..that the head maintains its erect posture.

2. A balancing feat.

1769 *Public Advertiser* 13 Mar. 4/2 The amazing Monkey ..that goes thro' his Equilibres on the tight..Rope.

equilibrial (i:kwɪ'lɪbrɪəl), *a.* [f. EQUILIBRIUM + -AL[1].] Of or pertaining to equilibrium; constructed on the principle of equilibrium.

1772 HUTTON *Bridges* 79 The elliptical arch seems..fittest to be substituted instead of the equilibrial one.

equilibriate (i:kwɪ'lɪbrɪeɪt), *v.* [f. as prec. + -ATE[3].] = EQUILIBRATE. Hence **equi'libriated** *ppl. a.*

1649 G. DANIEL *Trinarch., Rich. II*, cxxx, T' Equilibriate his Fame To all the Glories of his Crowne and Name. **1870** E. L. GARBETT in *Eng. Mech.* 11 Mar. 624/2 An equilibriated earth would have..a permanent high water. **1882** *Knowledge* 4 Aug. 161 If one be at a higher potential than the other, a current will pass through the conductor, and so equilibriate the two potentials.

equilibrious (i:kwɪ'lɪbrɪəs), *a.* Also 7-8 æquilibrious. [f. EQUILIBRI-UM + -OUS.] That is in a state of equilibrium; evenly balanced. Also const. *to.*

1643 *Oath Pacif.* 29 Our successe hath hitherto been so equilibrious, that we have no reason to presume. **1653** H. MORE *Conject. Cabbal.* (1662) 116 The Bodies of the Inhabitants are æquilibrious to the Region, and do not sink by any ponderosity. **1703** S. MORLAND in *Phil. Trans.* XXIII. 1326 A sort of Æquilibrious disposition of the Fluids, and Muscular parts. **1795** WYTHES *Decis. Virginia* 48 The evidence of priority had seemed otherwise equilibrious.

Hence †**equi'libriously** *adv. Obs.*, in an equilibrious or well-balanced manner.

1664 H. MORE *Myst. Iniq.* 313 At first he might wear his Horns somewhat equilibriously. **1682** SIR T. BROWNE *Chr.*

Mor. (1756) 58 Wherein falsehood and truth seem almost æquilibriously stated. **1847** in CRAIG; and in mod. Dicts.

equilibrist (iːˈkwɪlɪbrɪst, ? iːkwɪˈlɪbrɪst). [a. F. *équilibriste*, f. *équilibre*: see EQUILIBRE.] One who is skilled in feats of 'balancing'; *esp.* a rope-walker, acrobat.

1760 *Monthly Rev.* Aug. 163 Qualifications..judged necessary to constitute an equilibrist. **1801** STRUTT *Sports & Past.* III. v. 200 A monkey has lately performed there, both as a rope-dancer and an equilibrist. **1841** CATLIN *N. Amer. Ind.* (1844) II. li. 138 If he be not an experienced equilibrist, he is sure to get two or three times soused. **1861** *Illust. Lond. News* 24 Aug. 193/3 The daring equilibrist began her exhibition of skill.

Hence ˌ**equiliˈbristic** *a.*, of, pertaining to, or characteristic of, an equilibrist.

1882 *Standard* 14 Jan., Equilibristic performances. **1884** *L'pool Mercury* 22 Oct. 5/8 Miss Henriette on a single wire gives a clever 'equilibristic' entertainment.

equilibrity (iːkwɪˈlɪbrɪtɪ). [ad. L. *æquilībritas*, f. *æquilībris* equally balanced, f. *æquus* equal + *lībra* balance.] The state or condition of being equally balanced; equilibrium.

1644 DIGBY *Nat. Bodies* xix. (1658) 209 The weight of the other side..drew it the other way, and in this manner kept it in equilibrity. **1721–1800** in BAILEY. **1847** in CRAIG; and in mod. Dicts.

equilibrium (iːkwɪˈlɪbrɪəm). Also 7–9 æquilibrium. [a. L. *æquilībrium*, f. *æquus* equal + *lībra* balance.]

1. a. In physical sense: The condition of equal balance between opposing forces; that state of a material system in which the forces acting upon the system, or those of them which are taken into consideration, are so arranged that their resultant at every point is zero.

A body is said to be in *stable* equilibrium, when it returns to its original position after being disturbed; in *unstable* when it continues to move in the direction given to it by the disturbing force; in *neutral*, when it remains stationary in its new position.

1660 BOYLE *New Exp. Phys. Mech.* i. 36 The pressure on all hands being reduced as it were to an Æquilibrium. **1697** *Phil. Trans.* XIX. 446 The Fluids, pressing equally and easily yielding to each other, soon restore the Æquilibrium. **1796** ATWOOD *Floatation* ibid. LXXXVI. 51, 1st. The equilibrium of stability..2dly. The equilibrium of instability..3dly. The equilibrium of indifference. **1830** HERSCHEL *Stud. Nat. Phil.* 222 Thereby to maintain equilibrium. **1838** J. GRANT *Sk. Lond.* 299 Trying how fast they could run down [the hill] without losing their equilibrium. **1860** MILL *Repr. Govt.* (1865) 6/1 A government so situated is in the condition called in mechanics unstable equilibrium, like a thing balanced on its smaller end. **1879** tr. *De Quatrefages' Hum. Species* 4 In the crystal once formed, the forces remain in a state of stable equilibrium.

b. *equilibrium of temperature*: see quot.

1794 J. HUTTON *Philos. Light, etc.* 91 The supposed state of a perfect equilibrium, or equal temperature among bodies. **1871** B. STEWART *Heat* §12 Two bodies may be said to be in a state of equilibrium of temperature with each other when if shaken together they neither change their state with respect to heat, nor, etc.

2. a. The state of equal balance between powers of any kind; equality of importance or effect among the various parts of any complex unity.

1677 *Govt. Venice* 80 So to balance their [the Spaniard and the French] Power, as to keep both in an Equilibrium. **1741** MIDDLETON *Cicero* (1742) I. Pref. 38 [The two Gracchi] had in great measure overturned that æquilibrium of power in the Republic, in which its peace and prosperity depended. **1773** *Observ. State Poor* 80 A destruction of the equilibrium of population, by a defection of inhabitants from one county to another. **1840** MACAULAY *Ranke* Ess. 1851 II. 144 The war which followed was a war for the equilibrium of Europe. **1871** R. F. WEYMOUTH *Euph.* 4 Of such equilibrium and symmetry in antithesis every page of the Euphues furnishes examples.

b. The condition of suspense or uncertainty produced by equality in the force of opposing influences; neutrality of judgement or volition.

1685 SHARP *Doubting Conscience* 4 There is an end of the Doubt or Æquilibrium. **1754** EDWARDS *Freed. Will* I. i. 4 Where there is absolutely no preferring or chusing, but a perfect continuing Equilibrium there is no Volition. **1794** PALEY *Evid.* III. viii. (1817) 372 That indifferency and suspense, that waiting and equilibrium of the judgement. **1876** E. WHITE *Life in Christ* I. vii. 74 This is the infidelity of persons..who pass their lives in a state of equilibrium or indifference.

c. Well-balanced condition of mind or feeling.

1608 J. KING *Serm. St. Mary's* 26 Salomon a man in the perfit æquilibrium and stablest state of his age. **1874** FARRAR *Christ* II. 45 In this outward activity, she lost the necessary equilibrium of an inward calm. **1875** HAMERTON *Intell. Life* x. ix. 384 It is best to preserve our minds in a state of equilibrium.

3. The Lat. *in æquilibrio* 'in equilibrium' appears usually with anglicized spelling (*equi-*). (The Latin ablative in this phrase was formerly sometimes treated as an Eng. word; hence such expressions as *in perfect equilibrio.*)

1650 BULWER *Anthropomet.* 229 When the body is erect and in equilibrio. **1683** PETTUS *Fleta Min.* I. (1686) 150 Weigh it..until the Ballance standeth even in Æquilibrio. **1709** PRIOR *Poems, Ladle* 45 Is it in equilibrio, If deities descend or no? Then let the affirmative prevail, As requisite to form my tale. **1755** *Gentl. Mag.* XXV. 164 Being at the vernal equinox in an equilibrio. **1798** T. JEFFERSON *Writ.* (1859) IV. 231 The fate of Sprigg's resolutions seems in perfect equilibrio. **1868** ROGERS *Pol. Econ.* xv. (ed. 3) 209 These bills..may exactly balance between country and country. In such a case, the trade between the two countries is said to be in equilibrio.

4. *attrib.* **equilibrium diagram**, a diagram representing the limits of temperature and composition within which the various phases or constituents of an alloy system are stable; a constitutional diagram; **equilibrium moisture content** (see quot. 1966).

1874 KNIGHT *Dict. Mech.*, *Equilibrium-valve*..having a pressure nearly equal on both sides. **1880** HAUGHTON *Phys. Geog.* iii. 92 The point of equilibrium temperature, which is the Fahrenheit zero. **1925** *Jrnl. Iron & Steel Inst.* CXII. 345 In the equilibrium diagram of the iron-carbon system..the A2 line is shown by a dotted line. **1934** WEBSTER, Equilibrium moisture content. **1948** *New Biol.* IV. 91 Wood being a hygroscopic material adjusts itself to the moisture condition of its surroundings by losing or absorbing moisture until an equilibrium moisture content is attained. **1966** A. W. LEWIS *Gloss. Woodworking Terms* 27 *Equilibrium moisture content*, normal stable state of timber when its moisture content corresponds with the humidity of the air.

equilibrize (iːˈkwɪlɪbraɪz), *v.* [f. EQUILIBRIUM + -IZE.] *trans.* To bring to an equilibrium; to balance, counterpoise. Hence **eˈquilibrized** *ppl. a.*, well-balanced, tranquil.

1833 *New Monthly Mag.* XXXVII. 139 The fear of loss in one quarter should be equilibrized by the certainty of gain in another. **1889** *Blackw. Mag.* CXLVI. 742/1 The horde of savages who broke in upon her equilibrised society.

†**equiˈlibrous.** *Obs.* [f. L. *æquilībris* (see EQUILIBRITY) + -OUS.] = EQUILIBRIOUS.

1652 SPARKE *Prim. Devot.* (1663) 434 In matters of moment that are æquilibrous. **1658** J. ROBINSON *Eudoxa* viii. 46 In some [bodies], there need but a small moment to make them equilibrous with the Water.

equilin (ˈiːkwɪlɪn). Also -ine. [ad. Fr. *équiline* (A. Girard et al. 1932, in *Compt. Rend.* CXCIV. 911), f. L. *equ(īnus* (see EQUINE *a.*) + *follicu)line*.] A sex hormone, $C_{18}H_{20}O_2$, present in the urine of pregnant mares.

1932 *Chem. Abstr.* XXVI. 4090 The other 2 fractions on being extd. with ether yielded a new cryst. substance with chem. and phys. properties very similar to those of folliculin... The name equilin is suggested for this new hormone. **1958** [see EQUILENIN].

equilobate, -lucent, -molar, -molecular, -momental: see EQUI-.

equimultiple (iːkwɪˈmʌltɪp(ə)l), *a.* and *sb.* [ad. mod.L. *æquimultiplex*, f. *æqui-* (see EQUI-) + *multiplex* MULTIPLE.]

†**A.** *adj.* That contains a number or quantity the same number of times that a third quantity contains a fourth. *Obs.*

1656 HOBBES *Six Lessons* Wks. 1845 VII. 240 The antecedents are of their consequents..equimultiple.

B. *sb.* One of a set of numbers or quantities which each contain some other number or quantity the same number of times. Chiefly *pl.*

[**1570** BILLINGSLEY *Euclid* II. i. 63 Numbers that are equemultiplices to one and the selfe same number.] **1660** BARROW *Euclid* v. iv, Take I and K the equimultiples of E and F. **1793** T. BEDDOES *Math. Evid.* 78 Take certain equimultiples of the first and third. **1817** H. T. COLEBROOKE *Algebra* 162 The quotient will be an equimultiple of the dividend. **1878** GURNEY *Crystallogr.* 19 Magnitudes and their equimultiples have the same ratios to one another.

†**eˈquinal,** *a. Obs.* Also 7 equinall. [f. L. *equīnus* (see EQUINE) + -AL¹.] = EQUINE.

1609 HEYWOOD *Brit. Troy* XV. xxxiii, Chalchas deuisede the high Equinall pile. **1635**—— *Hierarch.* III. 139 The Shape Equinall doth his speed imply. **1839** J. TAYLOR *Poems & Transl.* 201 The Quirinal Feasts (the Equirinal, Equinal or Horse Festival) were in honour of the constellation Pegasus.

equine (ˈiːkwaɪn, ɛ-), *a.* and *sb.* [ad. L. *equīnus*, f. *equus* horse.] **a.** *adj.* Of, pertaining to, or resembling a horse.

1778 *Learning at a Loss* II. 7, I..made some feeble Efforts towards entering into an equine Conversation. **1801** J. BARROW *Trav. S. Africa* I. iv. 260 It [the gnoo] partakes of the horse, the ox, the stag, and the antelope: the shoulders, body, thighs, and mane, are equine; the head completely bovine. **1850** L. HUNT *Autobiog.* II. x. 41 His laugh was equine. **1862** LOWELL *Biglow P.* Ser. II. 55 The mule is apt to forget all but the equine side of his pedigree. **1879** G. MACDONALD *Sir Gibbie* II. xiii. 230 It brought a lusty equine response from the farm.

b. *sb.* A horse. Also, an equid.

1883 *Harper's Mag.* Nov. 904/2 The contests were..more tightly fought out than by the trotting equines. **1909** *Westm. Gaz.* 25 Mar. 4/2 One of the essential differences between the engineer's horse-power and the equine's effort is that a properly made engine..will give off its maximum effort for prolonged periods; but..this cannot be done by a horse. **1947** J. STEVENSON-HAMILTON *Wild Life S. Afr.* i. 9 The curious striped equines, known as zebras.

equinecessary: see EQUI- *pref.*

equinely (ˈiːkwaɪnlɪ), *adv.* [f. EQUINE *a.* + -LY².] In an equine manner; like a horse.

1899 *Pearson's Mag.* Apr. 395/1 At the end of this course a man is supposed to be entirely at home on his horse, and with it to do everything that is humanly and equinely possible. *a***1910** 'O. HENRY' *Trimmed Lamp* (1916) 86 The chestnut, approving his new rider, danced and pranced, reviling equinely the subdued bays.

equinity (ɪˈkwɪnɪtɪ). *rare.* [f. EQUINE *a.* + -ITY.] Equine nature or character.

1829 LANDOR *Imag. Conv.* (1846) II. 18 He also pricked up his ears, and gave sundry other tokens of equinity. **1899** *Westm. Gaz.* 29 Aug. 3/1 The femininity of other animals in proportion to their caninity, or felinity, or equinity.

equinoctial (ɛk-, iːkwɪˈnɒkʃəl), *a.* and *sb.* Forms: 4–7 equinoctiall, (4 equynoxial, 5 equinoccialle, 6 -ccyall, 6–8 æquinoctial(l, 7, 9 equinoxial(l, 6– equinoctial. [ad. L. *æquinoctiālis*, f. *æquinoctium* EQUINOX. Cf. Fr. *équinoxial.*]

A. *adj.* **1.** Pertaining to a state of equal day and night. ***equinoctial line***, ***circle*** (in Milton ***equinoctial road***), the celestial or terrestrial equator. Cf. B. 1 and 2. ***equinoctial point*** = EQUINOX 2.

*c***1391** CHAUCER *Astrol.* II. §25 Tak his nethere elongacioun lengthing fro the same equinoxial lyne. *c***1511** *1st Eng. Bk. Amer.* (Arb.) Introd. 29/2 So haue we sayled ouer yᵉ linie equinocciall. **1549** *Compl. Scot.* vi. (1872) 49 There is ane vthir circle of the spere, callit the circle equinoctial. **1551** ROBINSON tr. *More's Utop.* (Arb.) 31 For vnder the line equinoctiall..lyeth..great, and wyde desertes. **1656** tr. *Hobbes' Elem. Philos.* (1839) 428 The diurnal revolution is from the motion of the earth, by which the equinoctial circle is described about it. **1667** MILTON *P.L.* x. 672 Som say the Sun Was bid turn Reines from th' Equinoctial Rode. **1726** tr. *Gregory's Astron.* I. II. 305 To determine the Places of the Stars in respect of the Equinoctial and Solstitial Points. **1818** JAS. MILL *Brit. India* I. II. ix. 420 The origin of the Indian zodiac did not coincide with the equinoxial point. **1837** BREWSTER *Magnet.* 238 The magnetic equator will meet the equinoctial line only in two points.

2. Pertaining to the period or point of the equinox. ***equinoctial colure***: see COLURE. †***equinoctial day***: a normal day of 12 hours. †***equinoctial hour***: an hour of normal length. ***equinoctial month***: a month which includes one of the equinoxes. †***equinoctial spring***: the vernal equinox.

1570–87 HOLINSHED *Scot. Chron.* (1806) II. 58 After the equinoctiall spring. **1594** BLUNDEVIL *Exerc.* II. (ed. 7) 116, Six houres, which is the one halfe of an Equinoctiall day. **1635** N. CARPENTER *Geog. Del.* I. v. 104 The excesse of the greatest and longest day aboue the equinoctiall day. **1646** SIR T. BROWNE *Pseud. Ep.* VI. vii. 309 Marcus Varro.. exposeth his farme unto the equinoxiall ascent of the Sunne. **1775** ADAIR *Amer. Ind.* 77 The two Jewish months just mentioned, were æquinoctial.

b. Happening at or near to the time of the equinox; said *esp.* of the 'gales' prevailing about the time of the autumnal equinox.

1792 *Anecd. W. Pitt* III. xliii. 151 At last will come your equinoctial disappointment. **1795** LD. LYNDHURST *Let.* in Sir T. Martin *Life* 38 Many vessels have lost their anchors in this, I may call it, equinoctial gale. **1811** WELLINGTON in Gurw. *Disp.* VIII. 269 Till the equinoctial rains have filled the Tagus. **1865** LIVINGSTONE *Zambesi* xix. 369 And the equinoctial gales made it impossible for us to cross to the eastern side.

3. Of or pertaining to the equinoctial (see B. 1, 2); = EQUATORIAL. **a.** Pertaining to, or having reference to, the equator as a circle of the celestial or terrestrial sphere. ***equinoctial dial***: see quot. 1751. **b.** Pertaining to the regions adjacent to the terrestrial equator.

1594 J. DAVIS *Seaman's Secr.* (1607) 3 Therefore those that trauail must either vse the Globe or an Equinoctiall diall. **1667** MILTON *P.L.* II. 637 As when farr off at Sea a Fleet descri'd Hangs in the Clouds, by Æquinoctial Winds Close sailing from Bengala. **1684** T. BURNET *Th. Earth* 169 The polar parts sinking into the abyss, the middle or æquinoctial parts still subsisted. **1703** MOXON *Mech. Exerc.* 319 The Center of the Equinoctial Semi-circle. **1751** CHAMBERS *Cycl.* s.v. *Dial*, Equinoctial Dial is that described on an equinoctial plane, or a plane representing that of the equinoctial. **1770** GOLDSM. *Des. Vill.* 419 Where equinoctial fervours glow. **1816** KIRBY & SP. *Entomol.* (1843) I. 209 The warmer parts of equinoctial America. **1860** tr. *Hartwig's Sea & Wond.* i. 13 The equinoctial ocean.

B. *sb.* **1.** The celestial equator: so called because, when the sun is on it, the nights and days are of equal length in all parts of the world.

*c***1386** CHAUCER *Nun's Pr. T.* 36 By nature knew he ech ascencioun Of equinoxial. **1527** R. THORNE in Hakluyt *Voy.* (1589) 252 All other lands that are vnder and neere the Equinoctiall. **1646** SIR T. BROWNE *Pseud. Ep.* II. iii. 70 He affirmeth that Biarmia..hath the pole for its Zenith and Equinoctiall for the Horizon. **1774** GOLDSM. *Nat. Hist.* (1862) I. xvi. 92 At Tonquin..there is no tide at all, when the moon is near the equinoctial. **1833** HERSCHEL *Astron.* i. 58 They term the equator of the heavens the equinoctial. **1854** MOSELEY *Astron.* ix. (ed. 4) 43 The distance of the star from the equinoctial..is called the Declination of the star. **1869** DUNKIN *Midn. Sky* 133 The Ecliptic is inclined to the equinoctial at an angle of 23° 28′.

2. The terrestrial equator. Now *rare.*

1584 *Calendar St. Papers* 103–4 Any parts between the Equinoctial and the North Pole. **1634** SIR T. HERBERT *Trav.* 5 Nor is this weather rare about the Æquinoctiall. **1657** EVELYN *Mem.* (1857) I. 336 Born in the Caraccas, 1000 miles south of the equinoctial. **1784** BURKE *Sp. agst. W. Hastings* Wks. XIII. 155 As if, when you have crossed the equinoctial, all the virtues die. **1813** EUSTACE *Classical Tour* (1821) III. 130 Cities that lie between them and the equinoctial.

b. *transf.* and *fig.* (humorously.)

1601 SHAKS. *Twel. N.* II. iii. 24 Passing the Equinoctial of Queubus. **1609** DEKKER *Gull's Horne-bk.* 127 If he sit but one degree towards the equinoctial of the saltcellar. **1713** BIRCH *Guardian* No. 36 Started a conceit at the equinoctial, and pursued it through all the degrees of latitude.

†**3.** = EQUINOX. *Obs.*

1432-50 tr. *Higden* (Rolls) I. 325 From the equinocciалle of Ver on to the equinoccialle of herveste. **1549** *Compl. Scot.* vi. (1872) 56 Quhen ther multipleis ane grit numir of sternis in the equinoctial of Libra..at that tyme ther occurris grit tempestis. **1665** MANLEY *Grotius' Low C. Warres* 413 There are scarce fifty dayes of ours, at the greatest time of heat, before the latter Equinoctial.

fig. **1618** DONNE *Serm.* cxlv. V. 591 This day was a holy Equinoctial and made the day of the Jews and the day of the Gentiles equal.

4. An equinoctial gale.

1748 RICHARDSON *Clarissa* (1811) VIII. 260 The equinoctials fright me a little. **1880** BLACK *White Wings* II. 70 It is a shame he should be cheated out of his thunderstorm. But we have the equinoctials for him, at all events.

equinoctially (ɛk-, iːkwɪˈnɒkʃəlɪ), *adv.* In 7 æquinoxially. [f. as prec. + -LY².] In the direction of the equinoctial or equator.

1646 SIR T. BROWNE *Pseud. Ep.* II. ii. 60 Æquinoxially, that is toward the Easterne or Westerne points.

†**equiˈnoctian.** *Obs. rare.* In 7 æq-. [? f. as prec. + -AN; but cf. next.] = EQUINOX I.

1627 MAY *Lucan* x. 264 Nor is [Nile] confin'd within his bankes againe Till the Autumnal æquinoctian.

†**equiˈnoction.** *Obs.* In 5 equinoccion. [a. OF. *equinoction*, as if ad. L. **æquinoctiōn-em* = *æquinoctium.*] = EQUINOX I.

1483 *Cath. Angl.* 116 Equinoccion, *equinoctium, equidium.*

†**equiˈnoctional,** *a.* [as if f. L. **æquinoctiōn-em* (see prec.) + -AL¹.] = EQUINOCTIAL. Hence **equiˈnoctionally** *adv.*, in the direction of the equinoctial.

1658 SIR T. BROWNE *Hydriot. & Gard. Cyrus* 61 The floure twists Æquinoctionally from the left hand to the right, according to the dayly revolution.

‖**equinoctium.** *Obs. rare.* Pl. equinoctia, -ums. Also 5 equenoxium, 6-7 æquinoctium. [L. *æquinoctium*, f. *æquus* equal + *nox, noctis* night.] Equinox; (the original form in which the word was adopted).

c **1400** MAUNDEV. xvii. (1839) 183 [At Jerusalem]..a spere that is pight in to the erthe, vpon the hour of mydday whan it is Equenoxium..scheweth no schadwe. **1563** SHUTE *Archit.* B iij b, He should directly know..that, whiche they call Equinoctium, and Solsticium. **1607-12** BACON *Ess. Sedit. & Troub.* (Arb.) 390 Natural Tempestes are greatest about the æquinoctia. *a* **1625** FLETCHER *Nice Valour* I. i, Give me a man..Has a good stroke at tennis..Can play at æquinoctium with the line. **1688** R. HOLME *Armoury* II. 16 The Colure of the Equinoctiums or equinoxes.

equinox (ˈiːk-, ˈɛkwɪnɒks). Also 6-7 equinoxe, 6 æquinoxe, 7-8 æquinox. [ad. (directly or through OF. *equinoxe*) L. *æquinoctium* (in the Middle Ages spelt *equinoxium*) equality between day and night, f. *æqui-* (see EQUI-) + *noct-* stem of *nox* night.

The late L. *æquinox* adj. (f. as *æquinoctium*) used also as sb. in the sense 'equinoctial point or sign', though not the source of the word as now used, seems to occur in the quot. from Chaucer under 2.]

1. One of the two periods in the year when the days and nights are equal in length all over the earth, owing to the sun's crossing the equator. Hence, the precise moment at which the sun crosses the equator.

The vernal or spring equinox is at present on the 20 March, and the autumnal on the 22 or 23 September. Just before the reformation of the calendar they were 11 days earlier.

1588 A. KING tr. *Canisius' Catech.* H j, To tak away yᵉ ten dayes quhairby yᵉ æquinoxe of springe tyme had passeit yᵉ dew tyme. **1664** POWER *Exp. Philos.* III. 149 It is eight dayes more from the Vernal to the Autumnal Aequinox, then it is from the Autumnal to the Vernal again. **1692** BENTLEY *Boyle Lect.* 261 The months of March and September, the two æquinoxes of our year, are the most windy and tempestuous. **1726** tr. *Gregory's Astron.* I. 246 That he might..bring the Equinox to its former place, ten Days were suppressed in the Month of October, in the Year 1582. **1789** T. JEFFERSON *Writ.* (1859) III. 88, I should put off my departure till after the equinox. **1838** EMERSON *Milton* Wks. (Bohn) III. 296 He believed his poetic vein only flowed from the autumnal to the vernal equinox. **1842** TENNYSON *Will Waterproof* xxx, Live long, nor feel in head or chest Our changeful equinoxes. **1849** MRS. SOMERVILLE *Connex. Phys. Sc.* xiii. 105 At the time of the equinoxes..the sun's declination is zero.

attrib. **1643** LIGHTFOOT *Glean. Ex.* 20 That began..from the Equinox day.

b. The condition of having the days and nights of equal length. Also *fig.*

1604 SHAKS. *Oth.* II. iii. 129 [His vice is] to his vertue, a iust Equinox, The one as long as th' other. **1696** WHISTON *Th. Earth* I. (1722) 58 There must be a perpetual Equinox, or equality of Day and Night, through the whole Planet. **1698** KEILL *Exam. Th. Earth* (1734) 229 Then the Earth had a perpetual Equinox and unity of Seasons.

2. One of the two points at which the sun's path crosses the Equator, described technically as the first points in Aries and Libra. Formerly also used loosely for the region of the ecliptic adjacent to these points. ***precession of the equinoxes*** (see PRECESSION).

c **1391** CHAUCER *Astrol.* I. §17 And ther-fore ben thise two signes [Aries & Libra] called the equinoxiis [*ed.* **1560** equinoctes]. **1594** BLUNDEVIL *Exerc.* 149 a, The beginning of Aries, which is called the vernal Equinoxe. **1635** N. CARPENTER *Geog. Del.* I. v. 105 If..in any oblique Horizon, there should bee an equinoxe, it could no wise bee in the middle time betwixt the two Solstices. **1726** tr. *Gregory's Astron.* I. 418 The true and imaginary Sun will be equally distant from both Equinoxes.

†**3.** = *equinoctial line* or EQUATOR. *Obs.*

1579 FENTON *Guicciard.* VI. (1599) 252 The Iles of Cape Verde..are distant fourteene degrees from the Equinox. **1697** DAMPIER *Voy.* (1698) I. iv. 90 To the North of the Equinox..in these Seas, I never saw any [Seals]. **1728** EARBERY tr. *Burnet's St. Dead* II. 45 The true Fertility that brings Corn to a Masculine Perfection is in Countries far from the Equinox.

†**4.** An equinoctial gale. *Obs. rare.*

1687 DRYDEN *Hind & P.* III. 504 The wind, 'tis true, Was somewhat high, but that was nothing new, Nor more than usual equinoxes blew.

equinumerally, -numerant, -omnipotent: see EQUI- *pref.*

equip (ɪˈkwɪp). *v.* Also 6 eskippe, esquippe, 7 equippe, (8 acquip), 8 *aphet.* ˈquip. [a. Fr. *équipe-r, esquipe-r* (whence Sp., Pg. *esquipar*), prob. ad. ON. *skipa* to man (a vessel), fit up, arrange, prob. f. *skip* = SHIP.

The Fr. word in the sense 'to equip' is app. not recorded before 16th c.; but it must have existed much earlier, at least in AFr. and Norman Fr.; cf. AF. *eskipeson* equipment (14th c.) and med.L. *eschipāre* to man a vessel (M. Paris 13th c.). The OF. *esquiper, eschiper* 'to put or go on board a ship', 'to put out to sea', is perh. a different word, but must ultimately be f. ON. or OS. *skip* ship.]

1. *trans.* To fit out (a ship).

1580 BARET *Alv.* E 340 *Esquippe*, or furnishe ships with all ablements. **1583** STANYHURST *Æneis* I. (Arb.) 36 Ile ye man, esquipping youre ships with furniture aptlye. **1698-9** LUDLOW *Mem.* I. 335 (R.) The States General gave orders for equipping a considerable fleet. **1748** *Anson's Voy.* II. x. 246 Equipping the ship for these two different voyages. **1837** THIRLWALL *Greece* IV. xxxi. 184 Antiphon..had equipt two galleys at his own expense.

2. In wider sense: 'To furnish for service' (T.); to provide with what is requisite for efficient action, as arms, instruments, or apparatus of any kind. Hence *fig.* to furnish with the physical or mental qualifications necessary for any task. Const. *with*. Also of things: to constitute the equipment of.

1523 WOLSEY in Fiddes *Wolsey* II. 107, 50,000 soldiers largelie and plentifullye furnished eskipped and trymed. **1605** VERSTEGAN *Dec. Intell.* (1634) 205 A principall Courtier writing from London, to a personage of Authority ..willed him among other things to 'equippe' his Horses. **1727** *Philip Quarll* 183 The Pens, Ink, and Parchment have acquip'd me to keep a Journal. **1742** FIELDING *Jos. Andrews* III. viii, Can..any drugs equip disease with the vigour of that young man? **1793** SMEATON *Edystone L.* Pref. 6 Being so slenderly equipped as a writer. **1839** H. ROGERS *Ess.* I. iii. 107 How various..are the powers which must equip the truly great orator. **1856** FROUDE *Hist. Eng.* (1858) I. i. 60 Every man was ready equipped at all times with the arms which corresponded to his rank. **1872** YEATS *Growth Comm.* 151 Biörkö, one of the island cities, could equip an army of fourteen thousand burghers. **1879** M. ARNOLD *Democracy* Mixed Ess. 3 My aim is..not to set on foot and fully equip a new theory. **1881** *Chicago Times* 16 Apr., These lines [of railway] are all equipped in the best possible manner. **1885** *Manch. Exam.* 16 Mar. 5/2 A power of analysis equal to that which would equip a mathematician.

b. To supply with the pecuniary resources needful for any undertaking. Formerly also in slang or jocular use, to present *with* a sum of money.

c **1690** B. E. *Dict. Cant. Crew*, The Cull equipt me with a brace of Meggs. **1762** GOLDSM. *Nash* 18 His companions agreed to equip him with fifty guineas. **1829** LYTTON *Disowned* 69 We must equip you by a mortgage on Scarsdale.

3. a. To array, dress up, rig out. Also with the thing worn as subj. **b.** With some notion of 2 (chiefly *refl.*): To dress, accoutre, fit out (*for* a journey).

a. 1695 BLACKMORE *Pr. Arth.* IX. 304 A Cap of Crimson did his Head equip. **1711** ADDISON *Spect.* No. 129 ¶2 Equipped in a ridiculous Habit, when they fancy themselves in the Height of the Mode. **1741** RICHARDSON *Pamela* I. 49, I had better get myself at once 'quipt in the Dress that will become my Condition. **1815** SCOTT *Guy M.* iv, Equipt in a habit which mingled the national dress of the Scottish common people with something of an Eastern costume. **1836** W. IRVING *Astoria* III. 239 Chinook warriors, all painted and equipped in warlike style.

fig. **1725** *Wodrow Corr.* (1843) III. 210 Buchanan equipt them [epistles] with a French dress.

b. 1762-71 H. WALPOLE *Vertue's Anecd. Paint.* (1786) V. 72 It is Dr. Donne, equipped for the expedition to Cales. **1841** LANE *Arab. Nts.* I. 4 He equipped himself for the journey. **1879** JENKINSON *Guide to Lakes* 236 The tourist will do well to equip himself with good strong boots.

†**ˈequipace.** *Obs.* [f. EQUI- + PACE.] Equal step; regular marching order. ***in equipace***, in equal step. Cf. EQUIPAGE 14.

1600 J. LANE *Tom Tel-troth* 120 They strive to keep in equipace. **1619** HALES *Gold. Rem.* (1688) 456 Millenius, who goes in æquipace with Gomorus in Learning, etc. *Ibid.* 59. **1627** DRAYTON *Miseries Q. Margaret* xix, Twelve barons in their equipace, and twenty bishops.

equipage (ˈɛkwɪpɪdʒ), *sb.* Also 7 æquipage, equippage, 8 ecquipage. [a. F. *équipage*, f. *équiper*: see prec. and -AGE. (The Sp. *equipaje*, It. *equipaggio*, are ad. Fr.)]

I. The action or process of equipping; the state or condition of being equipped.

†**1.** The action or process of fitting out (a ship), of providing (a soldier) with accoutrements, etc.

1598 CHAPMAN *Iliad* I. 65 And ruled the equipage Of th' Argive fleet to Ilion. **1654** tr. *Scudery's Curia Politiæ* 69 After the compleate Equipage of this mighty royall Navy. **1656** BLOUNT *Glossogr.*, *Equipage*, a dighting or setting forth of a man, horse, or ship-furniture. **1684** *Lond. Gaz.* No. 1926/1 Count Vecchi hastens the Equipage of the Galleys and other small Vessels.

†**2.** The state or condition of being equipped; equipment. *Obs.*

c **1600** SHAKS. *Sonn.* xxxii, To march in ranckes of better equipage. *c* **1645** HOWELL *Lett.* II. lxiii, It cost Sir Walter Rawleigh much more to put himself in equipage for that long intended voyage. **1649** MILTON *Eikon.* Pref. (1851) 331 The force and equipage of whose Armes they have so oft'n met victoriously. **1652** NEEDHAM tr. *Selden's Mare Cl.* 209 A Fleet which attended in gallant Equipage to back his Forces. **1658** CLEVELAND *Rustick Ramp.* Wks. (1687) 420 Their Equipage and Order were not comely.

II. All that is needed for military operations, travelling, a domestic establishment, etc.

3. Apparatus of war, artillery, stores, and means of transport; tackle of a ship. ***camp equipage***: tents and furniture required for encampment. ***field equipage***: whatever is required to facilitate the movements of an army. ***siege equipage***: the train of battering guns, with ammunition, etc.

1579 FENTON *Guicciard.* I. (1599) 28 By reason of which great equipage..the army departed out of Naples, with great hope of the victory. *c* **1652** MILTON *Sonn.* xvii, To advise how war may..Move..In all her equipage. **1683** *Brit. Spec.* 98 Having with this Equipage crossed the Channel, he directly joyned Plautius. **1790** BEATSON *Nav. & Mil. Mem.* I. 30 With the guns, sails, rigging, and other equipage. **1810** SYD. SMITH *Wks.* (1859) I. 192/1 To provide himself with camp equipage. **1849-50** ALISON *Hist. Europe* III. xiii. 40 The superb siege equipage..was sent on to Valenciennes. **1853** SIR H. DOUGLAS *Mil. Bridges* (ed. 3) 139 An equipage of 20 boats was also collected. **1867** SMYTH *Sailor's Word-bk.* s.v., Camp equipage consists of tents, furniture, cooking utensils, etc.

†**4.** Military garb, uniform, accoutrements, trappings. *Obs.*

1633 SHIRLEY *Yng. Admiral* III. i, Put thy body in equipage, and beg of the princess to be one of these brave fellows. **1647** CLARENDON *Hist. Reb.* VI. (1843) 320/1 All the trained bands of London [were] led out in their brightest equipage upon the heath next Brentford. **1672** MARVELL *Reh. Transp.* I. 269 There a Don Quixot in an equipage of differing pieces. **1818** SCOTT *Leg. Montr.* ii, The equipage of a well-armed trooper of the period.

†**b.** Apparel, attire, costume, dress, 'get up'.

c **1645** HOWELL *Lett.* (1655) I. 265 He never saw.. Gentlemen..in a neater equipage. **1646** F. HAWKINS *Youth's Behav.* (1663) 62 Commanding the common Hangman to do his office in that Equipage [yellow starch'd Bands and Cuffs]. **1794** GODWIN *Cal. Williams* 255 It is unnecessary to describe the particulars of my new equipage. **1823** LAMB *Elia* Ser. I. xviii. (1865) 140 He never dressed for a dinner party but he forgot his sword..or some other necessary part of his equipage.

fig. **1653** H. COGAN tr. *Pinto's Trav.* xxvi. 100 They which came to fetch water, seeing us set there in so sad an equipage, returned. **1662** STILLINGFL. *Orig. Sacr.* I. vi. §5 Published them in the equipage they are in. **1665** J. MALL *Offer of F. Help* 111 You see the compleat Christian in his equipage for sufferings. **1732** POPE *Ess. Man* II. 44 Strip off all her equipage of pride.

5. Outfit for a journey, expedition, etc.

1616 BULLOKAR, *Equipage*, furniture or provision for horsemanship, especially in triumph, or tournaments. **1647** CLARENDON *Hist. Reb.* I. (1843) 6/1 Such an equipage..as might be fit for the Prince of Wales. **1727** SWIFT *Gulliver* II. viii. 173 The Queen had ordered a little equipage of all things necessary for me. **1820** SCOTT *Monast.* xxii, A small scrip and bottle..with a stout staff in his hand, completed his equipage. **1858** HAWTHORNE *Fr. & It. Jrnls.* (1872) I. 34 A few carpet-bags and shawls, our equipage for the night.

6. Small articles of domestic furniture, *esp.* china, glass, and earthenware. ***breakfast-, tea-equipage***: a breakfast-, tea-service. *arch.*

1672 CROWNE *City Politics* I. i, That Rogue! my patch upon my nose, my pillow and sick equipage, quickly. **1709** STEELE *Tatler* No. 86 ¶3, I had no sooner set Chairs..and fixed my Tea-Equipage, but, etc. **1724** *Lond. Gaz.* No. 6297/2 A Toilet Equipage of Plate for his Lady. **1756** NUGENT *Gr. Tour, Germany* II. 195 A tea-table, and all its equipage of solid gold. **1776** ADAM SMITH *W.N.* I. I. xi. 174 Household furniture, and what is called Equipage. **1825** MRS. SHERWOOD *Lady of Manor* I. (ed. 2) v. 149 The tea-equipage which they were then using..was convenient and genteel. **1833** DE QUINCEY *Wks.* XIV. 297 The whole breakfast equipage..set out..for no greater personage than myself. **1888** *Durham Univ. Jrnl.* 24 Mar. 36 The 'tea equipages' might be cleared away during the dinner hour.

7. Articles for personal ornament or use; a collection of such articles.

1716 LADY M. W. MONTAGUE *Basset-Table* 29 Behold this Equipage, by Mathers wrought. **1741** RICHARDSON *Pamela* II. 349 My Lady's..fine Repeating-Watch and Equipage. **1840** DICKENS *Barn. Rudge* xv, Without the aid of dressing case and tiring equipage. **1846** MRS. SHERWOOD *Fairchild*

Family II. 17 An equipage was a little case which held a thimble, scissors, a pencil, and other such little matters, and ..hung to the girdle to balance the great watches worn by the grandmothers and great grandmothers of people now living.

†**8.** Apparatus in general. *lit.* and *fig. Obs.*

1648 H. G. tr. *Balzac's Prince* 118 That long equipage of Debauchery, which the Voluptuous leade after them. **1677** GALE *Crt. Gentiles* II. III. 180 The Papists have transferred to their Saints al the equipage of the Pagan Gods. **1707** *Curios. in Husb. & Gard.* 249 All the Equipage of Substantial Forms and of Qualities. **1734** tr. *Rollin's Anc. Hist.* (1827) II. 353 By all the appurtenances and equipage of a voluptuous and effeminate life.

b. (See quot.)

1825 J. NICHOLSON *Operat. Mechanic* 146 The weight of the upper mill-stone..joined to the weight of the spindle.. and the trundle..(the sum of which three numbers is called the equipage of the turning mill-stone), should never be less than 1550 pounds avoirdupois.

III. The appurtenances of rank, office, or social position.

†**9.** Formal state or order; ceremonious display; the 'style' of a domestic establishment, etc.

1612 HEYWOOD *Apol. Actors* Author to Rk. 3 The earth a stage, Kings have their entrance in due equipage. **1633** FLETCHER *Purple Isl.* I. xii, Marching in Tragic State, and buskin'd equipage. **1682** BUNYAN *Holy War* 167 They perceived in what equipage, and with what honour they were sent home. *a* **1714** BURNET *Own Time* (1766) I. 239 She made an equipage far above what she could support. **1756** NUGENT *Gr. Tour, Netherl.* I. 273 Here are also sharpers.. with greater equipage than the sharpers in England.

†**10.** What is required to maintain an official establishment. Also *attrib.*, as in *equipage-money*.

1668 TEMPLE *Let. Sir J. Temple* Wks. 1731 II. 122 They ..brought down the Equipage Money of Ambassadors from three thousand Pounds..to 1500 Pounds. **1679–88** *Secr. Serv. Money Chas. & Jas.* (Camden Soc.) 149 To Sr John Trevor, Speaker of the House of Com'ons, bounty, for his equipage. **1769** *Junius Lett.* xxiii. 110 *note*, He received three thousand pounds for plate and equipage money.

†**11.** Train of retainers or attendants, retinue, following. *Obs.*

1579 SPENSER *Sheph. Cal.* Oct. 114 Teache her [the Muse] tread aloft in buskin fine, With queint Bellona in her equipage! **1600** FAIRFAX *Tasso* IX. xliv, With you take some part Of these braue Soldiers of mine equipage. **1641** EVELYN *Mem.* (1857) I. 16 On the 27th April, came over..the young Prince of Orange, with a splendid Equipage. *a* **1661** FULLER *Worthies, Cambridgesh.* I. 150 Dido had a piece of State in her Court peculiar to her self..an Equipage indeed..a hundred servants in ordinary attendance all of the same age. **1731** SWIFT *Corr.* Wks. 1841 II. 648 How many days will you maintain me [Swift] and my equipage?

transf. and *fig.* **1599** T. M[OUFET] *Silkwormes* 34 Their seuerall parts and feates thereon to play Amidst the rest of natures equipage. **1712** STEELE *Spect.* No. 472 ¶4 Distinct Suns, and their peculiar Equipages of Planets. **1806** WORDSW. *Ode on Intim. Immortal.* 106 The Persons..That Life brings with her in her equipage.

12. A carriage and horses, with the attendant servants; in later use sometimes applied to a carriage alone.

1721–1800 BAILEY, *Equipage*..is frequently used for a Coach and Number of Footmen. *a* **1762** LADY M. W. MONTAGUE *Lett.* lxxvii. 126 All the fine equipages that shine in the ring. **1765** in *Ld. Malmesbury's Priv. Lett.* I. 158 As for an equipage, I should do well..[if Mr. Walpole has not sold his] to buy it; otherwise to make an English chariot here. **1787** 'G. GAMBADO' *Acad. Horsem.* (1809) 44 A waggon or any tremendous equipage. **1811** L. HAWKINS *C'tess & Gertr.* I. 78 Her equipage was a travelling postchaise with one pair of horses. **1848** MACAULAY *Hist. Eng.* I. 377 The frequent mention of such equipages [a coach and six] in old books is likely to mislead us. **1860** HAWTHORNE *Marb. Faun* xii, Here..roll and rumble all kinds of equipages.

IV. †**13.** Transl. of Fr. *équipage*, the crew of a ship. *Obs. rare.*

1728 MORGAN *Algiers* II. ii. 221 When got to Sea, he opened his Mind to the Chiefs of his Equipage. *Ibid.* II. iv. 261 Her Equipage might have been all saved had they held out till the storm abated. **1751** CHAMBERS *Cycl.* s.v., *Equipage*, in navigation. See Crew.

†**V. 14.** In the phrase *to go* (*march, walk*) *in equipage*, the original sense was prob. 'to walk in military array *with*' (cf. 2); but in our examples (all *fig.*) the sense is 'to keep step *with*', so that the sb. becomes synonymous with EQUIPACE. Hence the word *equipage* was in 17th c. often supposed to be formed with the prefix *equi-*, and in many passages it occurs in the sense: Equality of position, rank, or importance.

[**1589** NASHE in *Greene's Menaphon* (Arb.) 14 Whose Amintas, and translated Antigone may march in equipage of honour, with any of our ancient Poets. **1600** (see 2).] **1607** *Schol. Disc. agst. Antichr.* I. i. 37 As the Papists are in equipage with former Pagans so likewise with all moderne aliens. **1613–6** W. BROWNE *Brit. Past.* I. ii, His worke, not seeming fit To walke in equipage with better wit. **1631** R. H. *Arraignm. Whole Creature* Ep. Ded. 4 That your vertue and goodnes might march in æquipage with your State and Authority. **1635** SWAN *Spec. M.* vii. §3 (1643) 322 According to..the best Authours, and nearest equipage to truth, the starres are called lights. **1655** SANDERSON *Serm.* II. Pref. 7 Nor doth it sound well, that the examples of men ..should..stand in so near equipage with the commands of God.

†**ˈequipage**, *v. Obs.* [f. prec. sb.]

1. *trans.* To furnish with an equipage, accoutrements, or outfit; to array; to furnish.

1590 SPENSER *F.Q.* II. ix. 17 A goodly traine Of Squires and Ladies equipaged well. **1623** WODROEPHE *Fr. & Eng. Gram.* 214 Wee shal all be mounted, equipaged, and in better order to morrow. **1651** tr. *Don Fenise* 276 Leon was equipaged in such manner, that he might be well taken for a thiefe. *a* **1711** KEN *Sion* Poet. Wks. 1721 IV. 328 Of sacred Hymn I strait made choice, With Organ equipaged, and Voice. **1784** COWPER *Task* III. 98 Well dress'd, well bred, well equipaged, is ticket good enough.

2. a. *trans.* To rank. **b.** *intr.* To stand in rank; to take rank. Cf. EQUIPAGE *sb.* 14.

1624 HEYWOOD *Gunaik.* II. 109 They all equipage together as being by the Poets never separate. *Ibid.* VIII. 396 This incomparable Ladie I know not where to equipage, or in what ranke to place.

Hence **ˈequipaged** *ppl. a.*, in senses of the vb.

1598 FLORIO Ep. Ded., The Vniuers containes all things, digested in best equipaged order. **1775** ASH, *Equipaged*, accoutred, attended, having a splendid retinue. **1847** in CRAIG.

†**equiparable**, *a. Obs.* Also 7 æquiparable. [a. Fr. *équiparable*, ad. L. *æquiparābilis*, f. *æquiparāre* to put on an equality, compare, liken, f. *æquipar* perfectly alike or equal, f. *æquus* equal + *par*.] Equal in comparison, equivalent.

1611 SPEED *Hist. Gt. Brit.* IX. xiii. §116 The childe or insipient (which are with him æquiparable) drinketh the sweet and delicious words vnaduisedly. **1695** WESTMACOTT *Script. Herb.* 152 The want of a competent heat, that is lasting and equiparable to the heat of the climate. **1721–66** in BAILEY; and in mod. Dicts.

†**eˈquiparance.** *Obs. rare.* In 7 æquiparance. [ad. late L. *æquiparantia* comparison, f. *æquiparant-em*: see next.] Equivalence.

1624 F. WHITE *Repl. Fisher* 520 There is proportion of Equalitie, or æquiparance.

†**eˈquiparant**, *a. Obs.* [ad. L. *æquiparant-em*, pr. pple. of *æquiparāre*: see EQUIPARABLE.] Equivalent, of equal value or importance.

c **1630** JACKSON *Creed* v. xlii. Wks. IV. 357 Her title of Lady is equiparant to His title as Lord.

†**eˈquiparate**, *a. Obs.* [ad. L. *æquiparāt-us*, pa. pple. of *æquiparāre*: see EQUIPARABLE.] Of equal weight or importance; equivalent. Const. *to*.

1654 L'ESTRANGE *Chas. I* (1655) 63 Princes desires are equiparate to commands. *Ibid.* 113 [Certain reprisals were] some satisfaction..but, though almost two for one, not equiparate to the merit of that nations cruelty.

†**eˈquiparate**, *v. Obs.* In 7 æquiparate, equiparat. [f. L. *æquiparāt-* ppl. stem of *æquiparāre*: see EQUIPARABLE.] *trans.* **a.** To reduce to a level; to level. **b.** To regard or treat as on the same level.

1632 VICARS *Æneid* xii, King Latines throne this day I'le ruinate And houses tops to th' ground æquiparate. **1671** *True Nonconf.* 163 Then you may equiparat them in the point of abuse.

equiparation (iːˌkwɪpəˈreɪʃən). [ad. L. *æquiparātion-em* equalizing, comparison, f. *æquiparāre*: see EQUIPARABLE.] **a.** The action of placing on an equality, or on an equal footing. †**b.** The action of comparing; *concr.* a parallel.

1615 A. STAFFORD *Heav. Dogge* 32 Yet thy felicity admits no equiparation, nay, hardly a comparison. **1623** COCKERAM, *Equiparation*, a comparison made with another. **1657** REEVE *God's Plea* 112, I would willingly..not only set forth a representation, but find an equiparation. **1886** MUIRHEAD in *Encycl. Brit.* XX. 714 The equiparation of legacies and singular trust-gifts.

†**ˈequipare**, *v. Obs. rare.* [a. Fr. *equipare-r*, ad. L. *æquiparāre*: see EQUIPARABLE.] Only in pa. pple. used as adj. = EQUIPARATE; equivalent, 'just like'.

1490 CAXTON *Eneydos* xxii. 84 The first lettres came out of fenyce equypared to purpre coloure. *Ibid.*, The grete trybulacion of Elysse is equypared to that of horrestes.

equipartition (ˌiːkwɪpɑːˈtɪʃən). *Physics.* [f. EQUI- + PARTITION.] In full *equipartition of energy*. A principle of thermodynamics which states that when a system is in thermal equilibrium the kinetic energy is equally divided amongst the degrees of freedom.

Earlier called 'the law of equal partition', 'the law of partition of kinetic energy', etc.

1902 *Phil. Mag.* IV. 385 The object of the present paper is, firstly, to give a proof of Boltzmann's Theorem on the Equipartition of Energy from a somewhat new point of view; and, secondly, to examine what are the precise conditions under which equipartition will take place, and whether these conditions..will occur in an actual gas. **1905** *Nature* 18 May 54/2 Equipartition of energy is supposed to establish itself within a small fraction of a second. **1929** LOWRY & SUGDEN *Physical Chem.* 19 According to Maxwell's principle of equipartition of energy, each degree of freedom calls for an equal increment of internal energy. **1957** *Encycl. Brit.* XIII. 386/2 According to a famous principle known as the equipartition of energy, when a dynamical system is in statistical equilibrium at a given temperature..the same amount of average kinetic energy is associated with each degree of freedom. **1962** W. B. THOMPSON *Introd. Plasma Physics* iii. 25 At the same time, collisions between the original and secondary electrons result in an equipartition of energy, so that the electrons acquire a roughly Maxwellian distribution at some temperature T_{-}. **1966** K. MENDELSSOHN *Quest for Absolute Zero* vi. 114 Another aspect of this picture which will later acquire great significance is the so-called 'law of equipartition'. This says that the energy will be distributed over all degrees of freedom.

‖**équipe** (ekip). Also equipe. [Fr., 'group, team'.] In motor-racing: = STABLE *sb.*[1] 3 c. Also in other sports and *fig.*

[**1935** EYSTON & LYNDON *Motor Racing* ii. 20 The *scuderia* Ferrari. This Italian team finds its equivalent in the French *équipe*, or our own 'stable' and the formation of such teams amongst racing men is a development of very recent years.] **1937** G. FRANKAU *More of Us* xiii. 134 And Venus knows how we had steered, or where, Manned by an équipe less misogynistic. **1956** G. HUNTINGTON *Madame Solario* xiii. 143 He led the Russian équipe at the Horse Show last spring. **1961** *Times* 5 May 5/6 The works teams of Cooper, Lotus and B.R.M. will be there in force as well as the private 'equipes' of Yeoman Credit, [etc.]. **1979** *Times* 16 Nov. (Obituaries Suppl.) p. iii/7 His circle of academic advisers was every whit as distinguished..as those of the equipe Kennedy. **1983** *N.Y. Times* 23 Apr. 8/1 Tino Buggio, the sous-chef at Maison Blanche, thinks he has put together an équipe that can whip not only the international bankers but even the Soviet Embassy squad [at soccer].

equipedal (iːkwɪˈpiːdəl), *a.* [f. L. *æquiped-us* (see next) + -AL[1]; cf. PEDAL.] Having equal feet. **a.** Said of the two equal sides of an isosceles triangle. **b.** *Zool.* Having the pairs of feet equal.

In mod. Dicts.

equipede (ˈiːkwɪpiːd), *a.* and *sb. Zool.* [ad. L. *æquiped-us* or *æquipēs, -pedis*, f. *æquus* equal + *pes* foot.] **A.** *adj.* Having legs of equal length. **B.** *sb.* See quot.

1835 KIRBY *Hab. & Inst. Anim.* II. xvi. 67 The *Æquipedes*, so called because all their legs, except the last pair, are nearly equal in length..The equipede Chilopodans.

†**equiˈpendence.** *Obs.* [f. EQUI- + PENDENCE.] The state of hanging in equilibrium.

1627 JACKSON *Creed* VI. i. vii. Wks. 1673 II. 39 Let Mathematicians imagine what rules or reasons of equipendence they list.

†**equiˈpendency.** *Obs.* [f. next: see -ENCY.] The state or condition of hanging in equipoise. In quot. *fig.*

1662 SOUTH *Serm. Gen.* i. 27 (1715) IV. 59 The Will of Man in the State of Innocence, had an entire Freedom, a perfect Equipendency and Indifference to either Part of the Contradiction..to accept, or not accept the Temptation. **1775** in ASH. **1847** in CRAIG; and in mod. Dicts.

†**equiˈpendent**, *a. Obs.* [f. EQUI- + PENDENT.] Hanging in equipoise; evenly balanced.

a **1640** JACKSON *Creed* XI. xxvi. Wks. 1673 III. 550 If the Scales be even or equipendent. **1681** MANTON *Serm. Ps.* cxix. 105 Wks. 1872 VIII. 74 If the balance be not equipendent, wrong may be done.

[In mod. Dicts.]

equipensate, -periodic: see EQUI- *pref.*

equipment (ɪˈkwɪpmənt). [f. EQUIP *v.* + -MENT. Cf. Fr. *équipement*.]

1. a. The action or process of equipping or fitting out. **b.** The state or condition of being equipped; the manner in which a person or thing is equipped. Also *fig.*

a. 1748 *Anson's Voy.* I. i. 5 The equipment of the squadron was still prosecuted with as much vigour as ever. **1809** *Hist. Europe* in *Ann. Reg.* 33/1 Lord Liverpool also defended the equipment of the expedition to Portugal. **1875** WHITNEY *Life Lang.* ii. 19 Mental training..as well as mental equipment. **1886** *Pall Mall G.* 14 Dec. 9/1 For the endowment and equipment of a Chair of Anatomy.

b. 1793 SMEATON *Edystone L.* §123 Its equipment might suit the purposes of a Store-Vessel for our building service. **1841** ELPHINSTONE *Hist. Ind.* II. x. iii. 423 An army which seemed irresistible from its numbers and equipment. **1856** EMERSON *Eng. Traits, Ability* Wks. (Bohn) II. 38 The admirable equipment of their Arctic ships carries London to the pole. **1863** BURTON *Bk. Hunter* 261 The institution did not spring in full maturity and equipment, like Pallas from the brain of Jove.

2. *concr.* Anything used in equipping; furniture; outfit; warlike apparatus; necessaries for an expedition or voyage. Used in the *pl.* to indicate the articles severally, in the *sing.* collectively.

1717 L. HOWELL *Desiderius* (ed. 3) 14 See my Crook, my Scrip, Box and other Parts of my equipment. **1793** SMEATON *Edystone L.* §275 To forward our equipments for rendering the house habitable. **1801** STRUTT *Sports & Past.* II. i. 46 The hunting equipments of the female archers. **1813** WELLINGTON in Gurw. *Disp.* X. 479 When you shall be in possession of your equipment of ordnance, etc. **1870** HOWSON *Metaph. Paul* i. 16 The helmet is..the brightest.. part of the soldier's equipment. **1873** *Act 36 & 37 Vict.* c. 88 Sched. 1, Equipments which are primâ facie evidence of a Vessel being engaged in the Slave Trade. **1879** *Cassell's Techn. Educ.* III. 264, I include under the general term equipment all that must be actually present with the fighting portion of an army at any one moment.

b. *fig.* Intellectual 'outfit'.

1841 MYERS *Cath. Th.* III. xliii. 165 A valuable portion of a student's [of the Bible] equipment. **1873** M. ARNOLD *Lit. & Dogma* 342 A hardly less grotesque object in his intellectual equipment for his task than in his outward attire. **1885** M. PATTISON *Mem.* 306 Our naive assumption that

classical learning was a complete equipment for a great university.

equipoise ('i:kwɪpɔɪz), *sb.* Also 7 æquipoiz, 8 æquipoise. [f. EQUI- + POISE *sb.*[1], replacing the phrase *equal poise.*]

1. Equality or equal distribution of weight; a condition of perfect balance or equilibrium.

a. in material things.

[**1635** N. CARPENTER *Geog. Del.* I. iv. 74 The least weight whatsoever added or subtracted would turne it from its Equall-poyze.] **1665** GLANVILL *Sceps. Sci.* xiv. 82 And even in the temperate Zone of our life, there are few bodies at such an æquipoiz of humours. **1713** DERHAM *Phys. Theol.* 14 *note*, An æquipoise of the Atmosphere produceth a Calm. **1787** 'G. GAMBADO' *Acad. Horsem.* 39 In your eagerness to mount, you may, by over-exerting yourself, lose your equipoise. **1822** IMISON *Sc. & Art* (ed. Webster) I. 34 If the arms of a balance be unequal, the weights in equipoise will be unequal in the same proportion. **1833** MARRYAT *P. Simple* xx, O'Brien..kept his left arm raised in equipoise. **1857** H. REED *Lect. Eng. Poets* vii. 257 The beam of the balance will scarcely be moved to recover its equipoise.

b. in immaterial things; *esp.* intellectual, moral, political, or social forces or interests.

1658 J. ROBINSON *Stone to the Altar* 83 If between the weight of two equal Senses, there be an indistinguishable Equipoise. **1678** NORRIS *Coll. Misc.* (1699) 117 So great reason..to lay the foundation of his [Des Cartes'] Philosophy in an equipoise of mind. **1759** JOHNSON *Idler* No. 83 ¶4 Sim Scruple..lives in a continual equipoise of doubt. **1822** DE QUINCEY *Confess.* (1862) 197 Opium on the contrary communicates serenity and equipoise to all the faculties. **1858** LONGF. *Birds of Passage, Haunted Houses*, Our little lives are kept in equipoise By opposite attractions and desires. **1885** STEVENSON in *Contemp. Rev.* Apr. 550 Between the implication and the evolution of the sentence there should be a satisfying equipoise of sound.

2. A counterpoise; a balancing or equivalent force. Chiefly *fig.*

1780 SIR J. REYNOLDS *Disc.* x. (1876) 6 One side making almost an exact equipoise to the other. **1847** DE QUINCEY *Sp. Mil. Nun* §20 (1853) 65 Some sort of equipoise to the wealth which her daughter would bring. *a* **1862** BUCKLE *Civiliz.* (1869) III. i. 43 The equipoise to the clergy [*i.e.* the aristocracy] being removed, the Church became so powerful.

equipoise ('i:kwɪpɔɪz), *v.* Also 7 equipoyse, æquipoise. [f. prec. sb.]

1. *trans.* To serve as an equipoise to; to counterbalance.

1664 POWER *Exp. Philos.* II. 105 A Cylinder of that weight does just æquipoise the Elastic power of the Ayr without. **1755** B. MARTIN *Mag. Arts & Sc.* 264, I see they just equipoize each other. **1816** SOUTHEY in *Q. Rev.* XVI. 228 An opposition, which, till then, had nearly equipoised the weight of the ministry. **1856** LANDOR *Ant. & Octav.* v. 39 No Praise Can equipoise his virtues. **1868** R. BUCHANAN *Trag. Dramas Hist., Wallace* I. vi, On yonder bier Lies one whose worth to equipoise thy master..Were gossamer to gold.

2. To place or hold in equipoise; to hold (the mind) in suspense.

a **1764** LLOYD *Poems, Actor*, A whole minute equipois'd he stands. **1804** *Med. Jrnl.* XII. 343 Regulating, and equipoising the various functions of the animal economy. **1823** D'ISRAELI *Cur. Lit.* (1858) III. 355 He had to equipoise the opposite interests of the Catholics and the Evangelists. **1887** J. W. GRAHAM *Neæra* II. xxiv. 361 Suspicion and dissimulation equipoised the Imperial mind [Tiberius].

†**3.** *intr.* To balance *with. Obs. rare*$^{-1}$.

1647 WARD *Simp. Cobler* (1843) 85 Where upper things will not With nether equipoyse.

Hence **'equipoised** *ppl. a.*, **'equipoising** *vbl. sb.*

a **1685** *Let. to Dk. York* in 5th *Coll. Papers Pres. Affairs* (1688) 38, I am a dutiful and hearty Lover of Monarchy..when establish'd on such an Equi-pois'd Basis of Wisdom as ours is. **1832** CARLYLE *Jas. Carlyle* 45 Mallets and irons hung in two equipoised masses over the shoulder. **1854** SCOFFERN in *Orr's Circ. Sc.* Chem. 6 The beam of an equipoised balance. *c* **1790** IMISON *Sch. Art* I. 166 By its [the air's pressure]..equipoising..29 and a half inches of mercury.

† **'equipoisure.** *Obs. rare*$^{-1}$. [f. prec. + -URE.] A state of being evenly balanced.

1683 PETTUS *Fleta Min.* II. 10 By standing in an Equipoisure or not, it [the tongue of this Ballance] doth..tell you the difference or certainty of the Weights.

† **'equipolle**, *a. Obs. rare*$^{-1}$. [a. OF. *equipol*, shortened form of *equipollent*: see EQUIPOLLENT.] = EQUIPOLLENT; equivalent.

c **1430** *Pilgr. Lyf Manhode* I. cxxi. (1869) 64 The whiche seyinge in singuler may wel be seid equipolle to a plurelle.

equipollence (i:kwɪ'pɒləns). Also 5 equipolence, 8-9 æquipollence. [a. OF. *equipolence*, mod.Fr. *équipollence*, ad. L. *æquipollentia*, f. *æquipollent-em* EQUIPOLLENT.] The quality of being equipollent.

1. Equality of force, power, or signification.

c **1430** *Pilgr. Lyf Manhode* IV. xlix. (1869) 199, I shal fynde in þis place countrepeis and equipollence of þe hegge of penitence. *a* **1528** SKELTON *Poems* 173 That in his equipollence He judgeth him equivalent With God Omnipotent. **1610** HEALEY *St. Aug. Citie of God* 242 Our Commentators missed to make a large discourse of æquipolences in this place. **1647** *Power of the Keys* iii. 35 The equipollence of the word Sacerdos and Episcopus being observed. *a* **1691** BOYLE *Wks.* III. 612 These phænomena do much depend upon a mechanical æquipollence of pressure. **1867** EMERSON *Progr. Culture* Wks. (Bohn) III. 228 There is also an equipollence of individual genius to the nation which it represents.

2. *Logic.* An equivalence between two or more propositions. Cf. EQUIPOLLENT 3 c.

c **1400** *Rom. Rose* 7078 Late hym study in equipolences. **1563-87** FOXE *A. & M.* (1596) 1008/1 So that *non omnis*, after the rule of equipollence, should be taken for as much as *nullus.* **1655-60** STANLEY *Hist. Philos.* (1701) 313/2 Of Reciprocation there are three kinds..the third..equipollence. **1725** WATTS *Logic* II. ii. §4 The Conversion and Opposition, and Equipollence of these modal Propositions. **1851** MANSEL *Proleg. Log.* vi. (1860) 220 The equipollence in some cases can only be determined materially.

equipollency (i:kwɪ'pɒlənsɪ). Also 7 æq-, equipollencie, 9 æquipollency. [f. EQUIPOLLENT: see -ENCY.]

1. Equivalence in signification, authority, efficacy, virtue, etc. Cf. EQUIPOLLENCE 1.

1623 ROWLANDSON *God's Bless.* 5 They have an equipollency, or equall weight, with the plainest precepts. *a* **1638** MEDE in Spurgeon *Treas. Dav.* Ps. xl. II. 273 What equipollency can be in sense between these two? *a* **1691** BOYLE *Wks.* (1772) III. 606 The endeavours of the one and the other were reduced to an equipollency. **1869** M. ARNOLD *Cult. & An.* 183 The notion of this sort of equipollency in man's modes of activity.

2. *Logic.* = EQUIPOLLENCE 2.

1652 URQUHART *Jewel* Wks. (1834) 199 The equipollencie and opposition both of plaine and modal enunciations. **1788** REID *Aristotle's Log.* i. §4. 15 The equipollency of propositions both pure and modal. **1846** MILL *Logic* II. i. §2 Examples of æquipollency or equivalence of propositions.

equipollent (i:kwɪ'pɒlənt), *a.* and *sb.* Also 5-7 equipolent, (5-6 equypolent, 8 equippolent), 6-7 æquipol(l)ent. [a. OF. *equipolent* (mod.F. *équipollent*), ad. L. *æquipollent-em* of equal value, f. *æquus* equal + *pollentem*, pr. pple. of *pollēre* to be strong.]

A. *adj.*

†**1.** Of persons: Possessed of equal power, authority, influence, rank, or personal capacity. *Obs.*

a **1420** HOCCLEVE *De Reg. Princ.* 2108 They wolden waite to be equipolent, And somewhat more, unto her husbondes. *c* **1460** FORTESCUE *Abs. & Lim. Mon.* (1714) 68 Ther may no gretter Perill growe to a Prince, than to have a Subgett equipolent to himself. **1548** HALL *Chron.* (1809) 163 Fewe princes..be to hym comparable or equipollent. **1581** W. STAFFORD *Exam. Compl.* i. (1876) 22 Being in capacity and memory both els equipolent. **1824-9** LANDOR *Wks.* (1846) I. 393 A maritime power..equipollent on the sea with France.

2. Of things, forces, or agencies: Equal in power, effectiveness, or validity.

a **1420** HOCCLEVE *De Reg. Princ.* xii. 5 The thoughtfulle wight is vesselle of turment, There is no greef to hym equipollent. **1471** RIPLEY *Comp. Alch.* VII. v. in Ashm. (1652) 170 After thyne Elements be made equypolent. **1513** BRADSHAW *St. Werburge* I. 291 Saynt Mylgyde the thyrde, of vertu equypolent. **1607-12** BACON *Ess. Custom & Educ.* (Arb.) 368 Votarie resolucion is made equipollent to Custome. **1686** BOYLE *Enq. Notion Nat.* 143 The Pressure of the Atmospheere, and the resistence of the Bubble [were] by Accident..near æquipollent. **1802** PALEY *Nat. Theol.* ix. (1819) 111 By the aid of a considerable and equipollent muscular force. **1873** M. ARNOLD *Lit. & Dogma* Introd. 28 To regard the Bible..as a sort of talisman..with all its parts equipollent.

3. Identical in effect or result; practically equivalent.

1664 POWER *Exp. Philos.* III. 165 To find the Longitude of any place, or some thing æquipollent thereunto. *c* **1730** BERKELEY in Fraser *Life* v. 180 The divine conservation is equipollent to..a continued repeated creation. **1790** WILDBORE *Spher. Motion* in *Phil. Trans.* LXXX. 530 An equipollent parallelopipedon which shall move in the very same manner as the body. **1837-9** HALLAM *Hist. Lit.* I. I. viii. 435 A uniformity of measure, which the use of nearly equipollent feet cannot..be thought to impair. **1846** SIR W. HAMILTON *New Anal. Log. Forms* in *Logic* II. (1860) 260 The equipollent forms of Limitation or Inclusion, and Exception. **1874** SAYCE *Compar. Philol.* vii. 292 Equipollent conceptions could be placed side by side in apposition.

b. Of expressions or symbols: Equivalent in meaning.

1577-87 HOLINSHED *Chron.* II. 13/1 The Greeke word ἀπειρόκαλος is equipollent to *Ineptus.* *a* **1619** FOTHERBY *Atheom.* II. iii. §1 (1622) 212 Two Philosophicall termes, in sense æquipollent vnto the very name of God. **1760** SWINTON *Coin* in *Phil. Trans.* LI. 865 The characters..were not precisely the same with those of the equipollent letters used in Umbria. **1858** TRENCH *Synon. N.T.* (1876) 299 Ὑπέρ shall be accepted as equipollent with ἀντί.

c. In *Logic.* Said *esp.* of propositions which express the same thing, notwithstanding formal diversity.

1642 SIR E. DERING *Sp. on Relig.* xv. 66 Indefinite propositions are æquipollent to uniuersall. **1656** tr. *Hobbes' Elem. Philos.* (1839) 40 Equipollent propositions..that may be reduced purely to one and the same categorical proposition. **1822** T. TAYLOR tr. *Apuleius* 381 Every proposition likewise, if it assumes in the beginning a negative particle, becomes its equipollent contradictory. **1846** MILL *Logic* II. i. §2 The original proposition..is first changed into a proposition æquipollent with it.

B. *sb.* Something that has equal power, weight, effect, importance, or significance; an equivalent.

1611 SCLATER *Key* (1629) 337 Are they not equipollents? **1612** —— *Ministers Portion* 13 In the Apostles Logicke, a Priest and receiver of tithes are equipollents. **1671** *True Nonconf.* 280 Because we exactly and fully do the equipollent. **1676** MARVELL *Mr. Smirke* 30 What is Declared..is the very Equipollent of what the Author had said. **1819** *Blackw. Mag.* IV. 723 'Choice set terms', for which there is absolutely no equipollent in any of the other languages of Europe. **1858** GLADSTONE *Homer* I. 420 The word Ἀχαιοί is used..as the simple equipollent of Greek. **1870** BOWEN *Logic* v. 136 Its logical equipollent.

Hence **equipollentness** = EQUIPOLLENCE 2.

1736 in BAILEY.

equipollently (i:kwɪ'pɒləntlɪ), *adv.* [f. prec. + -LY[2].] **a.** With equal force or significance; synonymously. †**b.** Virtually; by means of equivalent expressions; cf. EQUIVALENTLY 2, 3.

1642 J. EATON *Honey-c. Free Justif.* 68 Both expresly and equipollently..he sees no sin in his justified children. *Ibid.* 282 Evident and plaine, both expresly and equipollently by many places of Scripture. *a* **1677** BARROW *Wks.* (1686) II. 498 Both phrases [the spirit of God and the power of God] Saint Paul doth equipollently express by the power of the Holy Ghost. **1817** G. S. FABER *Eight Dissert.* (1845) II. 197 Using the two terms, Persians and Barbars, equipollently.

equiponderance (i:kwɪ'pɒndərəns). [f. EQUIPONDERANT: see -ANCE. Cf. Fr. *équipondérance.*] Equality of weight; equilibrium.

1775 in ASH. **1822** *Blackw. Mag.* XI. 155 Being, as it were, originally balanced to a sort of equiponderance. **1833** J. HOLLAND *Manuf. Metals* II. 287 The equiponderance of the scales may remain unaffected.

equiponderancy (i:kwɪ'pɒndərənsɪ). [f. EQUIPONDERANT: see -ANCY.] = prec.

1710 *Brit. Apollo* III. No. 56. 2/1 An Equiponderancy will be..caused. **1820** in JODRELL; and in mod. Dicts.

equiponderant (i:kwɪ'pɒndərənt), *a.* and *sb.* Also 7 equiponderent, 7-9 æquiponderant. [ad. med.L. *æquiponderant-em*, pr. pple. of *æquiponderāre*: see next vb. Cf. Fr. *équi pondérant.*]

A. *adj.*

1. †**a.** Having its weight equally distributed; evenly balanced. †**b.** Of equal specific gravity. **c.** Of equal weight.

a. 1646 SIR T. BROWNE *Pseud. Ep.* II. ii. 61 If the needle be not exactly equiponderant, that end which is a thought too light, if touched becommeth even.

b. 1691 RAY *Creation* (1714) 26 May serve to render their Bodies equiponderant to the water. **1766** AMORY *Life J. Buncle* (1770) IV. 100 To make gold, other metals must be rendered equiponderant to it.

c. 1660 BOYLE *New Exp. Phys. Mech.* xxxvi. 291 The quantity of Air to a quantity of Water equiponderant thereto, is as 1300 to 1. **1777** SHUCKBURGH in *Phil. Trans.* LXVII. 557 The proportional gravity of quicksilver to air will express inversely the length of two equiponderant columns of these fluids. **1821** J. Q. ADAMS in C. Davies *Metr. Syst.* III. (1871) 95 The silver penny..to which 32 kernels of wheat were equiponderant was equal to 22½ grains troy.

2. Of immaterial things: **a.** Of equal weight, importance, force, or influence. **b.** Evenly balanced.

c **1630** JACKSON *Creed* VI. xi. Wks. 1844 V. 290 In a measure equiponderent to their weight upon our souls. **1747** JOHNSON *Plan Eng. Dict.* Wks. IX. 172 The equiponderant authorities of writers alike eminent for judgment and accuracy. **1833** *Q. Rev.* XLIX. 550 The theory of three distinct and equiponderant estates. **1882** SYMONDS *Animi Figura* 127 Equiponderant strife 'twixt good And evil.

B. *sb. pl.* Things of equal weight.

1852 SIR W. HAMILTON *Discuss.* 326 The Treatise on Æquiponderants by Archimedes.

†**equi'ponderate**, *ppl. a. Obs.* [ad. med.L. *æquiponderāt-us*, pa. pple. of *æquiponderāre*: see next.] Equal in weight; in a state of equilibrium. Const. *to, with.*

1646 SIR T. BROWNE *Pseud. Ep.* II. ii. 58 Iron and steel..in long wires equiponderate with untwisted silke and soft wax. **1674** PETTY *Disc. Dupl. Proportion* 49 If 1728 Mice were equiponderate to one Horse.

fig. **1814** SCOTT *Wav.* xlvi, Which is equiponderate with our vernacular adage.

equiponderate (i:kwɪ'pɒndəreɪt), *v.* [f. med.L. *æquiponderāt-* ppl. stem of *æquiponderāre*, f. *æquus* equal + *ponderāre* to weigh.]

†**1.** *intr.* To be in a state of equipoise. Const. *to, with. Obs.*

1641 WILKINS *Math. Magick* I. iv. (1648) 21 The power that doth equiponderate with any weight. **1672** —— *Nat. Relig.* 11 The evidence on each side doth equiponderate. **1682** *Weekly Mem. Ingen.* 355 When bodies do equiponderate to the bulk of water equal to them. **1710** *Brit. Apollo* III. No. 56. 2/1 They Equiponderate. **1822** IMISON *Sc. & Art* (ed. Webster) I. 20 The point about which they would equiponderate or rest in any position.

2. *trans.* To counterpoise, counterbalance.

1661 BOYLE *Spring of Air* II. ii. (1682) 26 Till it is come to equiponderate a cylinder of Mercury of that height. **1673** WALKER *Educ.* 20 To equiponderate the prejudices of pleasure and interest. **1766** AMORY *Life J. Buncle* (1770) IV. 102 Both equiponderate (a pound suppose) in air. **1853** DE QUINCEY *Autobiog. Sk.* Wks. I. 162 *note*, Countervailing claims..had far more than equiponderated the declension.

3. *trans.* To put into a well-balanced condition.

1810 (see quot. for EQUIPONDERANT).

Hence **equi'ponderated**, **equi'ponderating** *ppl. adjs.*

1810 A. KNOX in *Bp. Jebb's Corr.* (1834) II. 404 In this obviously measured and equiponderated speech. **1691** ED. TAYLOR *Behmen's Theos. Philos.* 163 The Mean of Equiponderating Solemnity of Humane Creatures. **1879** G. MACDONALD *Sir Gibbie* III. x. 167 His equiponderating description of the place of misery.

equiponderation (ˌiːkwɪpɒndəˈreɪʃən). [n. of action f. med.L. *æquiponderāre*: see prec. and -ATION.] The action or process of making equally balanced, or putting in equipoise; the state or condition of being in equipoise.

1656 tr. *Hobbes' Elem. Philos.* (1839) 351 Equiponderation is when the endeavour of one body, which presses one of the beams, resists the endeavour of another body pressing the other beam, so that neither of them is moved. **1784** J. BARRY *Lect. Art* iii. (1848) 129 The anatomy of the human body.. the equiponderation of its parts. **1874** *Edin. Rev.* No. 285. 175 Equiponderation, or the relation of equipoise and balance.

†**equiˈponderous**, *a.* *Obs.* Also 7 æquiponderous. [f. EQUI- + L. *pondus, ponder-is* weight + -OUS.] Of equal weight or specific gravity; *fig.* of equal authority.

1656–81 in BLOUNT *Glossogr.* **1664** POWER *Exp. Philos.* 96 Being.. æquiponderous to a Mercurial Cylinder of 28 Inches. **1691** T. H[ALE] *Acc. New Invent.* p. xxvi, His Character justly renders him æquiponderous to them in Moral.. Knowledge. **1729** H. DE SAUMAREZ in *Phil. Trans.* XXXVI. 54 To make it equiponderous with the Water.

Hence **equiˈponderousness**.

1736 in BAILEY.

†**equiˈpondious**, *a.* *Obs. rare*$^{-1}$. [f. L. *æquipondi-um* equality of weight (f. *æquus* equal + *pond-us* weight.) + -OUS.] Having equal weight on both sides; nicely-balanced.

1661 GLANVILL *Vanity Dogm.* 228 The Scepticks affected an indifferent equipondious neutrality. **1775** in ASH. **1846** in WORCESTER; and in mod. Dicts.

†**eˈquipotency**. *Obs. rare.* [f. next: see -ENCY.] The condition of being equally powerful.

1658 *Fulness of Christ* 137 The union is not by means of exequation or equipotency [*printed* equipatency].

equipotent (iːˈkwɪpətənt), *a. rare.* [f. EQUI- + POTENT.] Equally powerful.

1875 *Contemp. Rev.* XXVII. 85 Nor am I speaking of cases where it is clear that one of the qualities has over-powered the other, but of instances where they appear equipotent.

equipotential (ˌiːkwɪpəʊˈtɛnʃəl), *a.* [f. EQUI- + POTENTIAL.]

†**1.** Of equal power or authority. *Obs.*

a **1678** WOODHEAD *Holy Living* (1688) 56 Not equipotential, or independent one of another.

2. *Physics.* Of points: In which the potential of a force is the same. Of lines, surfaces, etc.: In which the potential is constant at all points. *equipotential function*: one which expresses the conditions of equality of potential.

1865 BRANDE & COX *Dict. Sci.* (ed. 3) I. 804/1 Equipotential surface. **1879** *Encycl. Brit.* VIII. 25/2 A surface constructed so that the potential at every point of it has the same value is called an equipotential or level surface. **1880** *Nature* XXI. 361 A disk, through which an electric current was passing until two nearly equipotential points were found. **1880** *Athenæum* 13 Nov. 644/1 Equipotential lines in a plate. **1881** MAXWELL *Electr. & Magn.* I. 14 When a potential function exists, surfaces for which the potential is constant are called Equipotential surfaces. **1882** MINCHIN *Unipl. Kinemat.* 228 Equipotential and flow functions.

3. *Biol.* Of a germ or embryo: having equal potentialities (see quot. 1920). Hence ˌ**equipotentiˈality**.

1908 H. DRIESCH *Sci. & Philos. Organism* I. 83 Though ectoderm and endoderm have their potencies equally distributed amongst their respective cells, they possess different potencies compared one with the other. And the same relation is found to hold for all cases of what we may call elementary organs: they are 'equipotential', as we may say, in themselves, but of different potencies compared with each other. **1909** J. W. JENKINSON *Exper. Embryol.* 282 This conception, of the absolute equipotentiality of the parts, as we have already had occasion to remark, is erroneous. **1920** L. DONCASTER *Introd. Cytol.* 118 It is maintained by Driesch and others that eggs of this type are equipotential systems, that is to say, they are not differentiated before fertilisation into regions of different potentiality, and any part of the egg is capable of giving rise to any part of the embryo. **1964** M. CRITCHLEY *Developmental Dyslexia* xiii. 77 The frequent occurrence of cortical equipotentiality.

equipped (ɪˈkwɪpt), *ppl. a.* [f. EQUIP *v.* + -ED[1].] In senses of the vb.

1838 LYTTON *Leila* II. ii, The best equipped was conducted by the Marquess de Villena. **1866** ALGER *Solit. Nat. & Man* II. 69 The penalty affixed to supremely equipped souls.

†**equippee**, *a. Her. Obs.* Also 8 equippé. [ad. F. *équipé*, pa. pple. of *équiper*. See EQUIP *v.*] (See quots.)

1731 BAILEY vol. II. *Equippé* signifies a knight equipped, i.e. armed at all points. **1751** in CHAMBERS *Cycl.* **1775** ASH, *Equippee.*

equipper (ɪˈkwɪpə(r)). [f. as prec. + -ER[1].] One who equips; one who fits out (a ship, etc.).

1864 LD. BRAMWELL in *Morning Star* 12 Jan., The misdemeanour is committed.. according to the intent, not of the equipper, but of his customer.

equipping (ɪˈkwɪpɪŋ), *vbl. sb.* [f. as prec. + -ING[1].] The action of the vb. EQUIP.

1704 *Collect. Voy.* (Churchill) III. 740/1 The Governour was busy in equipping of Men of War. **1790** BEATSON *Nav. & Mil. Mem.* I. 337 The equipping of two such armaments, did not escape the notice of the British Ministry. **1799** NELSON 28 Nov. in Nicolas *Disp.* (1845) IV. 118 Our Ships off Malta.. will want a complete equipping.

¶ Used gerundially with omission of *in*.

1681 *Lond. Gaz.* No. 1677/1 The rest of the Ships that are Equipping at Thoulon. **1772–84** COOK *Voy.* (1790) I. Introd. 11 The Endeavour was equipping for a voyage to the South Seas. **1810** *Naval Chron.* XXIII. 113 In the basin.. were seven two-deckers equipping.

equiprobabilism, -producing, -radial, -radical: see EQUI- *pref.*

equiprobability (iːkwɪprɒbəˈbɪlɪtɪ). [f. next + -ITY.] The characteristic of being equally probable.

1921 J. M. KEYNES *Treat. Probability* iv. 41 The discovery of a rule, by which equiprobability could be established, was, therefore, essential. **1937** *Mind* XLVI. 485 In any actual case the evidence for equi-probability is always empirical. **1958** *Oxf. Mag.* 1 May 408a/2 This conclusion.. does not rest.. on any gratuitous equiprobability assumption; the only equiprobability postulate is [etc.].

equiprobable (iːkwɪˈprɒbəb(ə)l), *a.* [f. EQUI- + PROBABLE *a.*] Equally probable.

1921 J. M. KEYNES *Treat. Probability* v. 65 A set of exclusive and exhaustive *equiprobable* alternatives. **1937** *Mind* XLVI. 485 No-one imagines that he can tell *a priori* what are the probabilities of the various alternatives when they cannot be seen to be equi-probable. **1949** W. KNEALE *Probability* 151 Even in games of chance we do not know *a priori* that the various alternatives are equiprobable. **1953** J. B. CARROLL *Study Lang.* vii. 200 There are thirty-two characters.. which can be transmitted; if these characters are regarded as equiprobable, the transmission of one character represents five units of information, five being the logarithm of 32 to the base 2.

equirotal (iːkwɪˈrəʊtəl), *a.* [f. EQUI- + L. *rota* wheel + -AL[1].]

1. Having the fore and hind wheels of equal diameter.

1839 *Sat. Mag. Suppl.* Aug. 88/1 The first equirotal carriage thus made was a phaeton. **1843** *Jrnl. R. Agric. Soc.* IV. II. 492 His spring-waggon on the equirotal cross-lock principle. **1884** *Health Exhib. Catal.* 103/2 Ambulance wagon, complete with new pattern stretchers, equirotal, lockunder, converted.

2. 'Having equal rotation.'

In mod. Dicts.

equisegmental: see EQUI- *pref.*

equisetaceous (ˌɛkwɪsɪˈteɪʃəs), *a. Bot.* [f. mod.L. *equisētāce-æ* + -OUS: see EQUISETUM and -ACEOUS.] Belonging to the order *Equisetaceæ*.

1867 J. HOGG *Microsc.* I. ii. 133 Siliceous crystals in the epidermis of equisetaceous plants.

equisetic (ɛkwɪˈsiːtɪk), *a. Chem.* [f. EQUISETUM + -IC.] Derived from Equisetum. *equisetic acid*, obtained from *Equisetum fluviatile*, is now known to be identical with ACONITIC acid.

1838 T. THOMSON *Chem. Org. Bodies* 54 When malic acid is distilled at the temperature of 349°, it is resolved into water, and two pyro-acids, which are isomeric. These acids have been distinguished by the names of equisetic or maleic, and fumaric or paramaleic acid. **1876** HARLEY in *Royle's Mat. Med.* 771 Aconitia is combined in the root with aconitic or equisetic acid.

equisetiform (ɛkwɪˈsiːtɪfɔːm), *a. Bot.* [f. EQUISET-UM + -(I)FORM.] Having the form of an Equisetum.

1847 in CRAIG; and in mod. Dicts.

equisetum (ɛkwɪˈsiːtəm). *Bot.* Pl. equisetums, -a. [a. L. *equisētum* (more correctly *equisætum*), f. *equus* horse + *sæta* bristle.] A genus of plants called popularly Horsetail or Mare's-tail; the typical genus of the N.O. *Equisetaceæ*.

1830 LYELL *Princ. Geol.* I. 101 The fossil ferns, equiseta, and other plants of the coal strata. **1847** DARWIN in *Life & Lett.* (1887) I. 360 His oolitic upright Equisetums are dreadful for my submarine flora. **1873** DAWSON *Earth & Man* vi. 129 Mares' Tails or Equisetums.

equisignal, -sized: see EQUI- *pref.*

†**ˈequison**[1]. *Obs. rare.* In 7 æquison. [ad. L. *æquison-us* adj, f. *æqui-* (see EQUI-) + *-son-us* sounding.] (See quot.)

1609 DOULAND *Ornith. Microl.* 79 Aequisons are those [notes], which being stroke together, make one sound of 2.

equison[2]. *nonce-wd.* [ad. L. *equisōn-em* groom, stable-boy, f. *equus* horse.] A groom; a horse-jockey.

1824–8 LANDOR *Imag. Conv.* (1846) I. 13 Newmarket, the competitors at its games, their horses, their equisons and colours.

equisonance (iːkwɪˈsəʊnəns). *Ancient Music.* [f. as next: see -ANCE; cf. Fr. *équisonnance.*] The fact of being equisonant; the concord of octaves.

1819 In REES *Cycl.* **1838** In SMART; and in mod. Dicts.

equisonant (iːkwɪˈsəʊnənt), *a. Ancient Music.* [f. EQUI- + SONANT; after L. *æquisonus*: see EQUISON[1].] Consonant in the octave.

In mod. Dicts.

equisufficiency: see EQUI- *pref.*

equitable (ˈɛkwɪtəb(ə)l), *a.* [a. Fr. *équitable*, f. *équité* EQUITY.]

1. Characterized by equity or fairness. **a.** Of actions, arrangements, decisions, etc.: That is in accordance with equity; fair, just, reasonable.

1646 SIR T. BROWNE *Pseud. Ep.* To Rdr. a 5 b, The equitable considerations and candour of reasonable mindes. **1649** CROMWELL *Lett.* 15 Apr. (Carlyle), Both my paper.. and yours of the 28th do in all literal and all equitable construction agree. **1654** *True State Commonw.* 11 To interpose upon the same equitable grounds. **1769** ROBERTSON *Chas. V*, III. XI. 306 He might compel Charles to accept of an equitable peace. **1818** JAS. MILL *Brit. India* II. IV. v. 466 To take the lands.. under an equitable valuation. **1856** FROUDE *Hist. Eng.* (1858) I. iv. 296 Their punishment, if tyrannical in form, was equitable in substance.

b. Of persons: Guided by principles of equity, displaying a spirit of equity; unbiased, impartial, candid. Now *rare*.

1682 BURNET *Rights Princes* viii. 296 Equitable Judges would acknowledg that he had reason of his side. **1690** BOYLE *Chr. Virtuoso* I. Pref. 2, I hope the Equitable Reader will not expect to find every Subject.. fully Treated of. **1793** T. BEDDOES *Math. Evid.* 153 Nor will any equitable critic.. dwell a moment upon this charge. **1875** MANNING *Mission H. Ghost* vi. 165 The more severe we are to our own faults, the more gentle and equitable we shall be to the faults of others.

2. Pertaining to the department of jurisprudence called EQUITY. Of rights, claims, etc.: Valid in 'equity' as distinguished from 'law'.

a **1720** SHEFFIELD (Dk. Buckhm.) *Wks.* (1753) II. 105 They could make me no legal title.. and I have only an equitable one to depend on. **1818** CRUISE *Digest* I. 225 A trust estate.. is good as an equitable jointure. **1845** POLSON in *Encycl. Metrop.* 856/1 In Demerara, Berbice, the Cape of Good Hope, etc... the supreme courts are courts of equitable as well as legal jurisdiction. **1876** DIGBY *Real Prop.* vii. §4. 337 The legal estate is vested in the trustee, in trust for the cestui que trust, who has the equitable estate.

equitableness (ˈɛkwɪtəb(ə)lnɪs). [f. prec. + -NESS.] The quality of being equitable.

1643 NETHERSOLE *Proj. for Peace* (1648) 5 The justice or equitablenesse of any.. Article of the Project. **1797** *Hist.* in *Ann. Reg.* 74/2 The public would give them credit for its equitableness. **1882** MISS BRADDON *Mt. Royal* III. iv. 77 He was so thoroughly assured as to the perfect equitableness of the transaction.

equitably (ˈɛkwɪtəblɪ), *adv.* [f. as prec. + -LY[2].] In an equitable manner; according to the rules of equity, in a spirit of fairness.

1663 CHARLETON *Chor. Gigan.* 7 And equitably examined the probability. **1736** BUTLER *Anal.* II. vi. Wks. 1874 I. 232 No more [will] be required of any one, than what might have been equitably expected of him. **1839** JAMES *Louis XIV*, III. 343 Acting equitably towards the unoffending peasantry of another nation. **1872** YEATS *Growth Comm.* 249 He.. distributed the imposts more equitably.

equitangential: see EQUI- *pref.*

equitant (ˈɛkwɪtənt), *a.* [ad. L. *equitant-em*, pr. pple. of *equitāre* to ride, f. *equit-em* (nom. *eques*) horseman, f. *equus* horse.]

†**1.** Riding on horseback. *Obs.*$^{-0}$

1840 in SMART.

2. (See quot. 1880.)

1830 LINDLEY *Nat. Syst. Bot.* 260 Crocus leaves are not equitant. **1880** GRAY *Struct. Bot.* iv. 136 Equitant, where leaves override, the older successively astride the next younger.

†**equitate** (ˈɛkwɪteɪt), *v. rare*$^{-1}$. *bombastic.* [f. L. *equitāt-* ppl. stem of *equitāre*: see prec.] *intr.* To ride.

1708 MOTTEUX *Rabelais* (1737) V. 232 To which we equitate with Maturation.

equitation (ɛkwɪˈteɪʃən). Also 6 equitacion. [ad. L. *equitātiōn-em*, n. of action f. *equitāre*: see EQUITANT. Cf. Fr. *équitation.*] The action, art, or habit of riding on, or as on, horseback; horsemanship.

1562 BULLEYN *Sicke Men* 67 b, Equitacion.. must be used upon a soft easie goyng horse. **1771** GIBBON *Let.* Misc. Wks. 1796 I. 443, I have got a droll little poney, and intend to renew the long forgotten practice of equitation. **1833** *Regul. Instr. Cavalry* I. 39 Military Equitation may be divided into three parts. **1845** STOCQUELER *Handbk. Brit. India* (1854) 32 Witching the world with noble equitation. **1870** LOWELL *Among my Bks.* Ser. I. (1873) 116 Broomsticks.. the canonical instruments of their nocturnal equitation.

b. An excursion, a ride on horseback.

1728 *Let.* in Nichols *Illustr. Lit. Hist.* IV. 497 (L.), I have lately made a few rural equitations to visit some seats, gardens, etc. **1851** CARLYLE *Sterling* III. ii. (1872) 179 Sterling was at his poetisings and equitations again.

equitative (ˈɛkwɪteɪtɪv). [f. L. *equitāt-* (see EQUITATE) + -IVE.] Of or pertaining to equitation.

1855 *Chamb. Jrnl.* IV. 35 A whole legion of spectacles, warlike, gymnastic, legerdemain, equitative, and equivocal.

equitemporaneous: see EQUI- *pref.*

equity ('ɛkwɪtɪ). Forms: 4-6 equite, -yte, (4 equitee, -ytee, -ytie, 5 eqwyte), 4-7 equitie, (6 æquitie, -ity), 6 equity. [a. OF. *equité* = Pr. *equitat*, Sp. *equidad*, It. *equità*, ad. L. *æquitāt-em*, f. *æquus* even, fair.]

I. In general.

1. The quality of being equal or fair; fairness, impartiality; evenhanded dealing.

The L. *æquitas* was somewhat influenced in meaning by being adopted as the ordinary rendering of Gr. ἐπιείκεια (see EPIKY), which meant reasonableness and moderation in the exercise of one's rights, and the disposition to avoid insisting on them too rigorously. An approach to this sense is found in many of the earlier Eng. examples.

c **1315** SHOREHAM 154 Thet hys hys pryvete Of hys domes in equyte. **1382** WYCLIF *Mal.* ii. 6 In equitee he walkide with me. *c* **1425** WYNTOUN *Cron.* VII. x. 491 Be justys he gave and eqwyte Til ilke man, þat his suld be. **1477** EARL RIVERS (Caxton) *Dictes* 6 a, He [God] shal juge you in equite. **1535** COVERDALE *Job* xxix. 14 Equity was my crowne. **1588** J. UDALL *Diotrephes* (Arb.) 19 Weigh it in the ballance of equitie. **1611** BIBLE *Transl. Pref.* 10 They can with no show of equity challenge vs for changing and correcting. **1660** JER. TAYLOR *Duct. Dubit.* III. vi. §1. 399 Not to punish any man more than the law compels us; that's equity. **1673** *Rules of Civility* (ed. 2) 141 The person of honour is in equity to go in first. **1759** ROBERTSON *Hist. Scot.* II. VIII. 32 These princes readily acknowledged the equity of his claim. *a* **1832** MACKINTOSH *Revol.* Wks. 1846 II. 158 Those principles of equity and policy on which religious liberty is founded. **1870** LOWELL *Among my Bks.* Ser. I. (1873) 257 There is a singular equity and absence of party passion.

2. *concr.* What is fair and right; something that is fair and right. *rarely* in *pl.*

c **1374** CHAUCER *Boeth.* IV. vi. 144 Amonges þise þinges sitteþ þe heye makere.. to don equite. **1377** LANGL. *P. Pl.* B. XIX. 305 He dede equite to alle euene forth his powere. **1483** CAXTON *Cato* A viij, That he may do equyte and justyce. **1875** MANNING *Mission H. Ghost* x. 267 The equities which we owe to our neighbour.

II. In Jurisprudence.

3. The recourse to general principles of justice (the *naturalis æquitas* of Roman jurists) to correct or supplement the provisions of the law. ***equity of a statute***: the construction of a statute according to its reason and spirit, so as to make it apply to cases for which it does not expressly provide.

1574 tr. *Littleton's Tenures* 6 a, They bee taken by the equitie of the statute. **1642** PERKINS *Prof. Bk.* iv. §270. 120 Such Assetts are not taken by the equitie of the Statute of Gloucester. **1858** LD. ST. LEONARDS *Handy Bk. Prop. Law* ii. 3 Chancellors.. moderated the rigour of the law according.. to equity.

4. a. In England (hence in Ireland and the United States), the distinctive name of a system of law existing side by side with the common and statute law (together called 'law' in a narrower sense), and superseding these, when they conflict with it.

The original notion was that of sense 3, a decision 'in equity' being understood to be one given in accordance with natural justice, in a case for which the law did not provide adequate remedy, or in which its operation would have been unfair. These decisions, however, were taken as precedents, and thus 'equity' early became an organized system of rules, not less definite and rigid than those of 'law'; though the older notion long continued to survive in the language of legal writers, and to some extent to influence the practice of equity judges. In England, equity was formerly administered by a special class of tribunals, of which the Court of Chancery was chief; but since 1873 all the branches of the High Court administer both 'law' and 'equity', it being provided that where the two differ, the rules of equity are to be followed. Nevertheless, the class of cases formerly dealt with by the Court of Chancery are still reserved to the Chancery Division of the High Court.

1591 LAMBARDE *Arch* (1635) 46 And likewise in his Court of Equitie he doth.. cancell and shut up the rigour of the generall Law. *Ibid.* 58 The Iustices should informe him [the King] of the Law, and the Chancellor of Equitie. **1745** *De Foe's Eng. Tradesman* II. xxxix. 116 He will always have the worst of it in equity, whatever he may have at common law. **1765-9** BLACKSTONE *Comm.* (J.), In the court of Chancery, there are two distinct tribunals; the one ordinary, being a court of common law; the other extra-ordinary, being a court of equity. **1832** AUSTIN *Jurispr.* (1879) I. 40 Equity sometimes signifies a species of law. **1853** WHARTON *Pa. Digest* 708 Equity will grant relief when.. a contract is made under a mistake. **1858** LD. ST. LEONARDS *Handy Bk. Prop. Law* ii. 3 There are settled and inviolable rules of equity, which require to be moderated by the rules of good conscience.

b. Defined so as to include other systems analogous to this; *e.g.* the *prætorium jus* of the Romans.

1861 MAINE *Anc. Law* ii. (1870) 28 What I call equity.. any body of rules existing by the side of the original civil law, founded on distinct principles and claiming incidentally to supersede the civil law in virtue of a superior sanctity inherent in those principles.

5. a. An equitable right, i.e. one recognizable by a court of equity. Often in *pl.*

a **1626** BACON *Max. & Uses Com. Law* 65 Upon which agreement in Writing, there ariseth an Equitie or Honestie, that the land should goe according to those agreements. **1826-30** KENT *Comm.* II. 118 The wife's equity to a suitable provision for the maintenance of herself and her children. **1844** WILLIAMS *Real Prop.* (ed. 12) 177 Incidental equities are also to be recognized by the courts respectively and every judge thereof. **1883** SIR E. E. KAY in *Law Times Rep.* XLIX. 77/2 It was hardly said that he was entitled to any charge, or lien, or equity on this particular fund.

b. ***equity of redemption***: the right which a mortgagor who has in law forfeited his estate has of redeeming it within a reasonable time by payment of the principal and interest. ***equity to a settlement***: a wife's equitable right to have settled upon her any properties coming to her after marriage.

1712 ARBUTHNOT *John Bull* 67 But has not Esquire South the equity of redemption? **1767** BLACKSTONE *Comm.* II. 159 This reasonable advantage, allowed to mortgagors, is called the equity of redemption. **1858** LD. ST. LEONARDS *Handy Bk. Prop. Law* xiv. 92 Twenty years' adverse possession, by a person claiming the equity of redemption, will bar the rightful owner.

c. (See quot. 1966.) orig. *U.S.*

1904 E. S. MEADE in *Pol. Sci. Q.* Mar. 50 Its preferred stock is quoted at.. prices which indicate a general conviction that the equity in the company is worth little. **1928** *New Statesman* 28 July, Finance Suppl. p. vi, Out of the combined issued capital of £16,629,000 the public put up 93 per cent. of the cash required, but received only 21.8 per cent. of the equity—that is the balance of profits remaining after the fixed dividends have been paid on the Preferred capital. **1930** *Times* (Financial Rev.) 11 Feb. p. iii/2 It was widely imagined that more money was to be made in high pressure equities than in anæmic mortgages. **1966** A. GILPIN *Dict. Econ. Terms* (1967) 72 *Equities*, the ordinary shares of a limited company. They carry the right to the residue of a company's assets after it has paid all its creditors, and share in the distribution of profits, if any, after interest has been paid to preference share-holders and debenture holders each year. **1969** *Times* (Suppl.) 5 May p. iii/1 The shift in portfolio preferences of institutional investors from bonds to equities.. is even more rapid.. than the statistics suggest. **1970** *Money Which?* Sept. 143/2 The ordinary shares of companies (also called equities) are bought and sold on a Stock Exchange.

attrib. **1930** *Daily Express* 8 Sept. 10/2 Purchasers of equity securities of the speculative type. **1931** *Ibid.* 16 Oct. 14/5 To pay 5 per cent. on the equity shares and meet the preferential and debenture interests, a trading profit of £111,000 is necessary. **1953** *Economist* 4 Apr. 18/2 Canadian tax practice.. has made loan finance more attractive to corporations than equity finance. **1965** *McGraw-Hill Dict. Mod. Econ.* 181 *Equity capital*, the total investment in a business by all its owners.

6. *attrib.* and *Comb.*, as ***equity-bar***, ***court***, ***-judge***, ***-lawyer***. Also **equity-draughtsman**, a barrister who draws pleadings in equity.

a **1832** BENTHAM *Justice & Codific. Petit.* Wks. 1843 V. 484 Turn first to the self-styled equity courts.

† **'equivale**, *v. Obs.* [ad. Fr. *équival-oir*, ad. late L. *æquivalē-re*, f. *æquus* equal + *valē-re* to be strong.] *trans.* **a.** To provide an equivalent for. **b.** To be equivalent to. *rare.*

1608 [S. HIERON] *Defence* III. 30 Sociall admission to the Lords table.. is equivaled & sufficiently supplyed, in that.. ye partake of the deinties. **1659** FULLER *App. Inj. Innoc.* II. 98 Such participles equivale infinitives. **1695** KENNETT *Par. Antiq.* App. 685 The English addition Field equivaling the Greek Νίκη.

equivalence (ɪ'kwɪvələns), *sb.* Also 7 æquivalence. [a. F. *équivalence*, ad. med.L. *æquivalentia*, f. *æquivalent-em* EQUIVALENT.]

1. a. The condition of being equivalent; equality of value, force, importance, significance, etc.

a **1541** WYATT *Poet. Wks.* (1861) 203 When he weigheth the fault and recompense, He.. findeth plain Atween them two no whit equivalence. **1590** GREENE *Fr. Bacon* Wks. (ed. Dyce) 173/2 Have you courted and found Castile fit To answer England in equivalence? **1652** WADSWORTH tr. *Sandoval's Civ. Wars Spain* 212 In satisfaction or equivalence thereof, hee might allow a pension or stipend to, etc. **1655-60** STANLEY *Hist. Philos.* (1701) 467/1 Æquivalence we call an equality as to Belief or Unbelief. **1677** HALE *Prim. Orig. Man.* I. ii. 53 No Organs.. which are wanting in the constitution of the humane Body, at least in substance and equivalence. **1690** NORRIS *Beatitudes* (1694) I. 214 Tho there be no Proportion of Equivalence between our best Works and the Rewards of Heaven. **1847** LEWES *Hist. Philos.* (1867) I. Introd. 63 The whole stress of Verification consists in reducing propositions to identity or equivalence. **1870** BOWEN *Logic* viii. 250 It brings to light very clearly the virtual equivalence of those moods in the several Figures. **1890** *Times* 4 Jan. 9/2 Gold and silver will.. assume equivalence at the ratio the Act names.

b. *Physics.* Equality of energy or effect.

1842 GROVE *Corr. Phys. Forces* (ed. 6) 61 The relation is not a relation of simple mechanical equivalence. **1878** TAIT & STEWART *Unseen Univ.* iii. 112 But the exact and formal enuntiation of the equivalence of heat and work.. was given by Davy in 1812.

c. ***equivalence of force***: the doctrine that force of one kind becomes transformed into force of another kind of the same value. Cf. *conservation of energy*, ENERGY 6.

1871 TYNDALL *Fragm. Sc.* (ed. 6) II. xiv. 348 No engine.. can evade this law of equivalence, or perform on its own account the smallest modicum of work. **1863** B. STEWART *Conserv. Force* viii. 205 The doctrine called the correlation, persistence, equivalence, transmutability, indestructibility of force.

d. ***principle of equivalence***: one of the fundamental postulates of the general theory of relativity, which states that at any point of space-time the effects of a gravitational field cannot be experimentally distinguished from those due to an accelerated frame of reference. Also ***equivalence principle***.

The principle was proposed by Einstein in *Ann. d. Physik* (1911) XXXV. 898-908, and was first called *äquivalenzprinzip* by him in *Ibid.* (1912) XXXVIII. 360, 443.

1918 A. S. EDDINGTON *Rep. Relativity Theory Gravitation* ii. 19 The hypothesis that gravitation may be of essentially the same nature as the geometrical forces introduced by the choice of co-ordinates.. which was put forward by Einstein, is called the Principle of Equivalence. **1955** O. KLEIN in W. Pauli *Niels Bohr* 99 In a generalized quantum-relativity theory, comprising also electromagnetism and perhaps meson fields corresponding to the nuclear forces, there would probably be some kind of generalized equivalence principle.

2. *Chem.* The doctrine that differing fixed quantities of different substances are 'equivalent' in chemical combinations.

1880 tr. *Wurtz' Atom. Th.* 76 He mentions polybasic acids as forming an exception to the theory of equivalence.

† **equivalence**, *v. nonce-wd.* [f. prec. sb.] *trans.* To balance, serve as equipoise to.

1646 SIR T. BROWNE *Pseud. Ep.* I. i. 3 Whether the resistibility of his reason did not equivalence the facility of her seduction.

equivalency (ɪ'kwɪvələnsɪ). [ad. L. *æquivalentia*: see EQUIVALENCE *sb.* and -ENCY.]

1. = EQUIVALENCE 1.

1535 BP. SALISBURY in Strype *Eccl. Mem.* I. App. lxi. 150 Your letter.. having the equivalency of a inhibition. **1614** SELDEN *Titles Hon.* 199 Dux and Comes Britanniæ, of whose equiualencie in ancient time, alreadie. **1674** PETTY *Disc. Dupl. Proportion* 38 The one to measure the velocity of the Wind, and the other its Power or Equivalency to Weight. *a* **1677** BARROW *Serm.* (1810) I. 159 We have redemption through his blood, the forgiveness of Sins; which argueth the equivalency of these terms. **1737** L. CLARKE *Hist. Bible* (1740) II. v. 126 He promises them the reward of an hundredfold by way of comfort and equivalency. **1803** *Edin. Rev.* III. 237 Money only serves as a measure of equivalency, not as a medium of exchange. **1821** *Ibid.* XXXV. 432 By means of which alone the equivalency of dactyls and spondees could ever be established. **1864** HUXLEY *Compar. Anat.* v. 85 Leave aside altogether the question of the equivalency of these groups.

b. *Physics.* = EQUIVALENCE 1 b.

1866 *Intell. Observ.* No. 54. 454 This equivalency of heat and mechanical force.

2. *Chem.* = EQUIVALENCE 2.

1869 MRS. SOMERVILLE *Molec. Sc.* I. iii. 106 And thus chemical equivalency extends to them.

3. *Geol.* Of strata: Correspondence in serial order and characteristics.

1853 G. TATE *Addr. Berwick. Naturalists' Club*, Fossiliferous beds.. furnish interesting evidence as to age and equivalency. **1862** DANA *Man. Geol.* 203 (*title*) Reality of the Primordial or Potsdam Period in America, and its equivalency with the European.

†**4.** An equivalent, a substitute. *Obs.*

1698 NORRIS *Pract. Disc.* (1707) IV. 84 A Vicarious Punishment, not a rigid Satisfaction, but an Equivalency. **1705** *Col. Rec. Penn.* II. 195 Will prove a sufficient Equivalency.

equivalent (ɪ'kwɪvələnt), *a.* and *sb.* Forms: 6-7 eque-, equivolent(e, 6 equyvalent, 7-8 æquivalent, 5- equivalent. [ad. late L. *æquivalent-em*, pr. pple. of *æquivalēre*, f. *æquus* equal + *valēre* to be powerful, to be worth. Cf. Fr. *équivalent*.]

A. *adj.* Equal in value, power, efficacy, or import. Const. *to*, †*with*, †*for* or *simply*.

†**1.** Of persons or things: Equal in power, rank, authority, efficacy, or excellence. *Obs.*

c **1460** FORTESCUE *Abs. & Lim. Mon.* (1714) 67 The Kyng of Scotts.. put out of the.. Lond, the Erles Dowglas, whose Lyvelood and Myght was nerehand equivalent to his owne. **1513** BARDSHAW *St. Werburge* I. 803 Euyqualent to Ruth she was in humylyte. **1531** ELYOT *Gov.* I xiv, At the laste we shulde haue.. publike weale equiualent to the grekes or Romanes. **1568** GRAFTON *Chron.* II. 437 The Duke of Burgoyn.. thinking no man eyther in aucthoritie or blood equyvalent to himselfe.. tooke upon him the whole rule and governaunce of the realme. **1597** BACON *Coulers Good & Evill* v. (Arb.) 146 Fraunce.. was equiualent with them all, and beside more compacted and vnited. **1601** HOLLAND *Pliny* II. 161 The oile of the Lentiske.. were æquiualent euery way to oile-rosat, but that it is found to be more astringent. **1608** SHAKS. *Per.* v. i. 92 Ancestors Who stood equivalent with mighty kings. **1655** *Let.* in Hartlib *Ref. Commonw. Bees* 25 As to Medicinal virtue æquivalent, if not exceeding the other. **1657** *Burton's Diary* (1828) II. 88 Certainly their authority was equivalent with yours. **1667** MILTON *P.L.* IX. 609 No Fair to thine Equivalent or second. *a* **1687** PETTY *Pol. Arith.* i. (1691) 1 A small Country and few People may be equivalent in Wealth and Strength to a far greater People and Territory.

†**2.** Occasional uses. **a.** Of songs: ? Concordant. **b.** Correspondent, proportioned to. *Obs.*

1513 BRADSHAW *St. Werburge* I. 3107 Syngynge full swetely theyr songes equyualent. **1560** ROLLAND *Crt. Venus* I. 703 It is Equiualent To all ressoun.. That thy mater.. I tak on hand.

3. a. Equal in value. Now only in more restricted uses: (*a*) of things regarded as mutually compensating each other, or as exchangeable; (*b*) of things of which one serves as a measure of value for the other.

1591 HORSEY *Trav.* (Hakluyt Soc.) App. 301 The gayne.. wold be at the leaste equevolente with the comodytyes the marchantes should reape therby. **1639** FULLER *Holy War* IV.

xviii. (1647) 198 Tarqueminus reserving his person [King Louis] as an equivalent ransome. *c* **1720** PRIOR *1st Hymn Callimachus* 70 Things of moment well nigh equivalent, and neighbouring value, By lot are parted. **1769** GOLDSM. *Hist. Rom.* (1786) I. 210 The lives of those men were not equivalent for those of an army. **1818** JAS. MILL *Brit. India* II. v. ii. 372 To pay an equivalent penalty, in case she failed in the proof of her charges. **1848** MACAULAY *Hist. Eng.* II. 251 Thirty thousand pounds may be considered as equivalent to a hundred and fifty thousand pounds in the nineteenth century. **1858** BRIGHT *Sp. India* 24 June, Taxation equivalent to 300,000,000*l.*

b. Of weights, measures, numerical expressions: Equal in quantitative 'value'.

1806 HUTTON *Math.* I. 56 Reduce $\frac{9}{40}$ to its equivalent number. To reduce a whole number to an equivalent fraction. **1825** NICHOLSON *Operat. Mech. Gloss.* 780 *Quintal*, a French or Spanish weight equivalent to 100 lbs. of those respective nations.

4. Having equal or corresponding import, meaning, or significance: chiefly of words and expressions.

1529 MORE *Heresyes* IV. Wks. 280/1 It is now all one to cal him a Lutherane or to call him an heretike, those two wordes being in maner equiualent. **1530** LYNDESAY *Test Papyngo* 786 Doctryne and deid war boith equeuolent. **1614** SELDEN *Titles Hon.* 169 With them *Princeps* alone was equiualent with the name of Emperor. **1668** WILKINS *Real Char.* 369 That double Letter in the Hebrew (צ)..is by some accounted equivolent to this. **1749** *Power Pros. Numbers* 61 Furnish yourself with a Copia of Equivalent Words. **1832** LEWIS *Use & Ab. Pol. Terms* vii. 63 Here he makes a republic equivalent to a democracy. **1846** MILL *Logic* I. v. §7 Let us substitute for the word virtue an equivalent but more definite expression. **1886** F. W. MAITLAND in *Law Q. Rev.* Oct. 481 The further back we trace our legal history the more perfectly equivalent do the words *seisin* and *possession* become.

5. a. That is virtually the same thing; identical in effect; tantamount.

1639 FULLER *Holy War* III. xx. (1647) 144 Who knoweth not, but such a witnesse is equivalent to a generall consent? **1698** KEILL *Exam. Th. Earth* (1734) 99 The centrifugal force ..is equivalent..to two forces. **1751** JOHNSON *Rambler* No. 153 ¶4 The contrariety of equal attractions is equivalent to rest. **1772** *Junius Lett.* lxviii. 346 Being taken with vert or venison was declared to be equivalent to indictment. **1842** LYTTON *Zanoni* 28 A whisper against his honour and repute will, in future, be equivalent to an affront to myself. **1865** S. AUSTIN *Ranke's Hist. Ref.* III. 237 His presence..would be equivalent to an army of ten thousand men. **1885** WATSON & BURBURY *Math. Th. Electr. & Magn.* I. 145 The system is therefore equivalent to a complete sphere charged to unit potential.

b. *Optics.* ***equivalent focal length*** (see quots.).

1867 SUTTON & DAWSON *Dict. Photogr.* (ed. 2) 116 Suppose that a lens..when presented towards a distant object, renders the image of it a certain size upon the ground glass. Then the 'equivalent focal length' of that lens..is equal to the principal focal length of a single lens, having a small stop in close contact with its central portion, which gives the same sized image of that object, when taken from the same point of view. **1961** A. L. M. SOWERBY *Dict. Photogr.* (ed. 19) 335 The focal length, or equivalent focal length, of a lens is defined as the distance from the node of emission, to the position at which the lens forms a sharp image of a distant object.

c. *Electr.* ***equivalent circuit***: an electric circuit consisting usually of resistance, inductance and capacitance and having characteristics equivalent to those of other electric circuits or apparatus.

1920 in R. E. Neale *Whittaker's Electr. Engin. Pocket-Bk.* 242 When speaking of the constants of a transformer, it is permissible to consider an equivalent circuit, the impedance of which is such that the same current at the same power-factor would flow if the same pressure were applied to it as to the primary of the transformer. **1943** *Electronic Engin.* XVI. 149 It is convenient to consider an equivalent circuit composed of pure reactances and resistances. **1962** SIMPSON & RICHARDS *Junction Transistors* v. 75 These usually take the form of equivalent circuits which can be used to represent the transistor under different circuit conditions.

6. Having the same relative position or function; corresponding.

1634 BRERETON *Trav.* (Chetham Soc.) 8 Burgomaisters.. are equivalent to our bailiffs of cities or towns corporate. **1796** MORSE *Amer. Geog.* II. 583 The Cadi, or some equivalent officer. **1807** J. E. SMITH *Phys. Bot.* 7 Perhaps in the fossil kingdom heat may be equivalent to a vital principle. **18..** DANA (W.), The equivalent strata of different countries. **1882** VINES *Sachs' Bot.* 152 The underground hairs of Mosses and the true roots of vascular plants are physiologically equivalent.

7. *Chem.* Of a quantity of any substance: Equal in combining value to a (stated) quantity of another substance. Also, of elements: Having the same degree of quantivalence.

1850 DAUBENY *Atom. Th.* ix. (ed. 2) 280 *note*, Otto employs the term equivalent volume instead of atomic volume. **1869** ROSCOE *Elem. Chem.* 172 The elements belonging to one class are equivalent. **1873** WILLIAMSON *Chem.* §85 One atom of oxygen takes the place of two atoms of chlorine, and it is spoken of as equivalent to two atoms of chlorine. **1880** tr. *Wurtz' Atom. Th.* 33 The atoms of simple bodies are equivalent to each other.

B. *sb.*

1. a. Something equal in value or worth; said *esp.* of things given by way of exchange or compensation; also, something tantamount or virtually identical.

1502 *Ord. Crysten Men* (W. de W. 1506) IV. vii. 185 By delyberacyon and fully consentynge or equyualent trespasseth ony of the x. commaundementes. *a* **1616** ROGERS (J.), A regular obedience to one law will be a full equivalent for their breach of another. **1672** MARVELL *Reh. Transp.* I. 234 You may well think we expected no less an equivalent. **1722** *Wodrow Corr.* (1843) II. 678 I'll remit the money to you as you direct, or send you equivalents. **1760** GOLDSM. *Cit. W.* xxvii, For every dinner..they returned an equivalent in praise. **1771** —— *Hist. Eng.* IV. 270 This, however, was considered as no equivalent to the damages that had been sustained. **1792** *Anecd. W. Pitt* II. xxiii. 52 Belleisle alone..was a sufficient equivalent for Minorca. **1828** LD. GRENVILLE *Sink. Fund* 9 Those quantities of money and of bread are equivalents. **1841** LANE *Arab. Nts.* I. 18 To be paid in kind, or in money, or other equivalent. **1855** BAIN *Senses & Int.* III. iii. (1864) 567 The existence of a plurality of weak resemblances will be the equivalent of a single stronger one. **1872** YEATS *Techn. Hist. Comm.* 159 Thus a white weasel's skin was an equivalent for eleven sheepskins.

b. ***the Equivalent*** in *Eng. Hist.*: a sum of money ordered, by the Act of Union of 1707, to be paid to Scotland as a set-off against additional excise duties, loss on coinage, etc.

1706 *Articles of Union* xv, The sum of 398,085*l.* 10*s.*.. being the equivalent to be answered to Scotland for such parts of the said customs and excises, etc. The said commissioners..shall keep books containing accounts of the amount of the equivalent. **1707** LUTTRELL *Brief Rel.* VI. 181 Most of the Scotch commissioners for the equivalent are gone for that kingdom. **1708** *Lond. Gaz.* No. 4419/6 A.. quantity of arms..belonging to the Commissioners of the Equivalent.

†**c.** An equal part. *Obs. rare.*

c **1590** MARLOWE *Faust.* vii. (1878) 12 The streets straight-forth..Quarter the town in four equivalents.

2. A word, expression, sign, etc., of equivalent meaning or import.

1651 HOBBES *Govt. & Soc.* ii. 32 The words themselves.. have in them the very essence of an Oath, to wit, so God help me, or other equivalent. **1862** H. SPENCER *First Princ.* II. iii. (1875) 158 Appearance, which is its [Phenomenon's] verbal equivalent. **1865** TYLOR *Early Hist. Man.* v. 96 Wrote down the pictured equivalents for these words. **1876** FREEMAN *Norm. Conq.* II. App. 683, I have not found any English equivalent for that title.

3. In various scientific uses: **a.** *Chem.* = ***equivalent proportion*** (see quot and A. 7.).

1827 FARADAY *Chem. Manip.* xxii. 554 The term chemical equivalent may therefore be used to imply that proportion of a body which is necessary to act upon another body. **1881** WILLIAMSON in *Nature* No. 618. 416 The term equivalent was subsequently introduced to indicate the proportional weights of analogous substances found to be of equal value in their chemical effects.

b. That which corresponds in relative position or function (see A. 6); in *Biol.* said of analogous and homologous structures; in *Geol.* of a stratum or formation in one country answering to one in another country.

1839 MURCHISON *Silur. Syst.* I. iii. 33 The English equivalents of the Keuper. **1856** WOODWARD *Mollusca* 48 The univalve shell is the equivalent of both valves of the bivalve.

c. *Physics.* ***mechanical equivalent***: the amount of mechanical effect resulting from the operation of a force. ***mechanical equivalent of heat***: conventionally, the amount of mechanical energy required to raise 1 lb. of water through 1° C.; cf. JOULE; ***mechanical equivalent of light***: the amount of radiant flux that corresponds to unit luminous flux (or, in quot. 1908, that is emitted by a source of unit luminous intensity), usu. expressed in watts per lumen.

1842 GROVE *Corr. Phys. Forces* 19 Where both lose, then an equivalent of heat results. **1845** *Rep. Brit. Assoc.* II. 31 (*heading*) On the Mechanical Equivalent of Heat. **1860** TYNDALL *Glac.* II. xix. 329 This force is the mechanical equivalent of the heat generated. **1863** —— *Heat* ii. (1870) 39 He first calculated the mechanical equivalent of heat. **1862** H. SPENCER *First Princ.* II. iii. (1875) 165 An equivalent of the pressure we consciously exert. **1876** TAIT *Rec. Adv. Phys. Sc.* vi. 137 For a quantity of heat represents its equivalent of work. **1908** *Proc. R. Soc.* A. LXXX. 19 The labours of workers in Germany and in the United States [have not]..sufficed to permit of definite values being adopted for..the mechanical equivalent of light. *Ibid.* 22 The mechanical equivalent of light $M = \frac{4\pi p}{I} = \frac{Wr}{Kf}\left(\frac{d}{D}\right)^2$, giving the mechanical equivalent in watts per candle. **1959** W. S. SHARPS *Dict. Cinemat.* 110/2 The reciprocal of the luminous efficiency of radiant energy is often termed, the 'mechanical equivalent of light'.

fig. **1878** SEELEY *Stein* II. 17 Napoleon..had tried to find the Mechanical Equivalent of Catholicism.

4. *Comb.* **equivalent-money** (see 1 b); **equivalent number** (*Chem.*), atomic weight.

1707 LUTTRELL *Brief Rel.* (1857) VI. 189 The remainder of the equivalent money for Scotland is to be sent thither next Tuesday in specie and bank bills. **1715** *Lond. Gaz.* No. 5307/2 Commissioners for disposing so much of the Equivalent Mony payable to Scotland as remains yet unapplied. **1826** HENRY *Elem. Chem.* I. 629 The equivalent number, or weight of the atom, of alumina, has been less satisfactorily determined than that of most of the earths.

equivalently (iː'kwɪvələntlɪ), *adv.* [f. prec. adj. + -LY².]

1. To an equivalent amount, in an equivalent degree.

a **1528** SKELTON *How Dk. Albany, &c.* 403 His grace to magnify and laude equivalently. **1786** T. JEFFERSON *Writ.* (1859) I. 598 He must lessen equivalently his consumption of some other European articles in order to pay for his coffee and sugar. **1842** GROVE *Corr. Phys. Forces* (ed. 6) 171 Each force is..equivalently convertible into each other.

2. As an equivalent term, or in equivalent terms, with equivalent force or signification.

1545 UDALL *Erasm. Par. Luke* (1548) Pref. 5 b, Whose full importyng cannot with one mere Englishe worde equiualently be interpreted. **1631** J. BURGES *Answ. Rejoined* 201 The termes..are not vsed disiunctiuely but equiualently. **1805** H. TOOKE *Purley* (1840) 265 *Certain is* was used in the same manner equivalently to *certes*.

†**3.** Virtually, in effect. (In 17th c. often opposed to ***expressly, formally.***) *Obs.*

1644 HUNTON *Vid. Treat. Monarchy* iv. 30 When the promise or Oath..amounts either expressely or equivalently to a relaxation of the bond of subjection. **1648** J. GOODWIN *Right & Might*, Either formally or equivalently the same. **1652** L. S. *People's Liberty* viii. 14 The major part of the suffrages is equivalently the whole number. **1655** FULLER *Ch. Hist.* Index, Athelwolphus Monarch of the Saxons maketh (equivalently) a Parliament act for the paying of Tithes. *a* **1677** BARROW *Wks.* (1687) I. 285 We seldom, in kind or equivalently, are our selves clear of that which we charge upon others. **1689** *Treat. Monarchy* II. i. 37 By the Grant of the former Laws..he did equivalently put himself into the State of Legal Monarchs.

equivaliant: see EQUI- *pref.*

†**e'quivalize**, *v. Obs. rare*⁻¹. [f. EQUIVALENT + -IZE.] In phrase, ***to equivalize account***: to amount.

1647 M. HUDSON *Div. Right. Govt.* Ep. Ded. 10 The summa totalis of my ability did never equivalize account to one hundred pence.

equivalue: see EQUI- *pref.*

equivalve ('iːkwɪvælv), *a. Zool.* [f. EQUI- + VALVE *sb.*¹ 2.] Of a bivalve mollusc: having both valves alike in shape and size.

[**1856** P. H. GOSSE *Man. Marine Zool.* II. 51 Shell oval or oblong, equal-valved.] **1862** J. G. JEFFREYS *Brit. Conchol.* I. 28 Shell equivalve, oblong, inequilateral. **1897** PARKER & HASWELL *Text-bk. Zool.* I. xii. 650 (Pelecypoda), As a general rule the right and left valves are alike, or nearly so, the shell being therefore equivalve. **1968** N. F. MCMILLAN *Brit. Shells* 17 Equivalve. Where the two valves of a bivalve are similar.

†**e'quivocacy.** *Obs. rare.* [f. L. *æquivoc-us* (see next) + -ACY: cf. Browne's *univocacy.*] Equivocal character.

1646 SIR T. BROWNE *Pseud. Ep.* III. vii. 120 Againe, it is unreasonable to ascribe the equivocacy of this forme unto the hatching of a Toade. **1847** in CRAIG; and in mod. Dicts.

equivocal (ɪ'kwɪvəkəl), *a.* and *sb.* Also 7 equi-, æquivocall, 7–9 æquivocal. [f. late L. *æquivoc-us* ambiguous (f. *æquus* equal + *voc-āre* to call) + -AL¹.] **A.** *adj.*

†**1.** Equal or the same in name (with something else) but not in reality; having a name, without the qualities it implies; nominal. *Obs.*

1643 SIR T. BROWNE *Relig. Med.* I. §12 This visible world is but a picture of the invisible, wherein, as in a pourtract, things are not truely, but in equivocall shapes. **1661** USSHER *Power Princes* I. (1683) 34 They being subject to the over-sight..of the Ephori, were but equivocal Kings, such in name, but not in deed. **1744** BERKELEY *Siris.* §210 From the sun's light, which is corporeal, there springs forth another equivocal light which is incorporeal.

2. Of words, phrases, etc.: Having different significations equally appropriate or plausible; capable of double interpretation; ambiguous.

1601–2 FULBECKE *1st Pt. Parall.* 68 Your libel..should be certaine, and without ambiguous or equiuocall tearmes. **1604** SHAKS. *Oth.* I. iii. 217 These Sentences, to Sugar, or to Gall, Being strong on both sides, are Equiuocall. **1656** COWLEY *Pindar. Odes* Note 47 These vast accounts arose from the æquivocal term of a Year among them. **1712** F. T. *Shorthand* 25 Even in Long-Hand oftentimes equivocal Abbreviations are often written. **1756–7** tr. *Keysler's Trav.* (1760) IV. 208 He..takes care that his answers be so equivocal as always to secure him a retreat. **1818** CRUISE *Digest* (ed. 2) VI. 187 There was perhaps no word in the language of more equivocal effect than the word *or.* **1868** GLADSTONE *Juv. Mundi* vii. (1870) 184 To say..that the Greek religion as it grew old improved..would be to use equivocal and misleading language.

b. Of evidence, manifestations, etc.: Of uncertain bearing or significance.

1769 *Junius Lett.* xxvii. 126 Some..less equivocal proofs of his munificence. **1794** SULLIVAN *View Nat.* V. 87 No very equivocal symptom of antiquity. **1842** H. ROGERS *Ess.* I. i. 3 An equivocal indication of merit.

c. *nonce-use.* Of a person: Expressing himself in equivocal terms.

1601 SHAKS. *All's Well* v. iii. 249 As thou art a knaue and no knaue, what an equiuocall Companion is this?

3. Of uncertain nature; not admitting of being classified, 'nondescript'. ***equivocal generation***: the (supposed) production of plants or animals without parents; spontaneous generation.

1658 SIR T. BROWNE *Hydr. & Gard. Cyrus* 51 The Æquivocal production of things under undiscerned principles, makes a large part of generation. **1662** STILLINGFL. *Orig. Sacr.* I. iv. §9 Born by the same æquivocall generation that mice and frogs are from the impregnated slime of the earth. **1677** HALE *Prim. Orig. Man.* IV. ii. 306 Whether those imperfect or equivocal Animals were created or no, it is not altogether clear. **1724** SWIFT *Drapier's Lett.* vii, If any new ones [party and faction] spring up, they must be of equivocal generation, without any seed. **1772–84** COOK *Voy.* (1790) I. 29 The sea was tinged..with these equivocal substances. **1796** C.

MARSHALL *Garden*. ii. 16 Equivocal generation we reject. **1830** SCOTT *Demonol.* v. 143 The equivocal spirits called fairies. **1863** LYELL *Antiq. Man* xx. 391 The old doctrine of equivocal or spontaneous generation.

b. Of sentiments, etc.: Undecided, not determined to either side. Chiefly in negative sentences.

1791 BURKE *Corr.* (1844) III. 219, I am sure the sentiments of London were not equivocal. **1845** S. AUSTIN *Ranke's Hist. Ref.* I. 139 The equivocal and half hostile attitude he had assumed.

c. *Music. equivocal chord*: one which may be resolved into different keys without changing any of its tones.

4. Of advantages, merits, etc.: Dubiously genuine, questionable.

a **1797** H. WALPOLE *Mem. Geo. III* (1845) I. ii. 19 A Churchman.. whose sanctity was as equivocal as their own. **1846** PRESCOTT *Ferd. & Is.* II. xix 191 In the sciences their success was more equivocal. **1847** DISRAELI *Tancred* II. vii, Without that equivocal luxury, a great country-house. **1878** BOSW. SMITH *Carthage* 159 To set against this equivocal gain, the Romans had lost 700 ships.

5. Of persons, callings, tendencies, etc.: Doubtful in character or reputation; liable to unfavourable comment or description; questionable; suspicious.

1790 BURKE *Fr. Rev.* Wks. V. 247, I shall always.. consider that liberty as very equivocal in her appearance, which has not wisdom and justice for her companions. **1831** LYTTON *Godolph.* 12 The equivocal mode of life he had entered upon. **1863** GEO. ELIOT *Romola* II. xxi, The preparations for the equivocal guest.

†**B.** *sb.* An equivocal word or term; a homonym.

1653 URQUHART *Rabelais* I. ix, Æquivocals so absurd and witlesse that, etc. **1668** WILKINS *Real Char.* 17 Great variety of Equivocals. So the word Bill signifies both a Weapon, a Bird's Beak, and a written Scroul. **1715** BENTLEY *Serm.* x. (1735) 360 The scandalous shifts of Equivocals and Mental Restrictions. *a* **1734** DENNIS (J.), Shall two or three wretched equivocals have the force to corrupt us? **1775** in ASH; and in mod. Dicts.

equivocality (iːˌkwɪvəʊˈkælɪtɪ). [f. prec. + -ITY.] The quality or condition of being equivocal; also *concr.* Something which is equivocal; an equivoque.

1734 tr. *Rollin's Anc. Hist.* (1827) I. 58, I repeat it in Latin because the equivocality.. will not subsist. **1830** GALT *Lawrie T.* VI. i. (1849) 254 They interpreted her equivocalities, as she intended they should. **1847** *Fraser's Mag.* XXXVI. 560 The conduct of Lady Hamilton and Nelson was.. guaranteed against equivocality by the fact of Sir William Hamilton's station in life. **1881** *Contemp. Rev.* June 889 Suggesting ideas by such equivocalities.

equivocally (iːˈkwɪvəkəlɪ), *adv.* Also 6–7 æq-. [f. as prec. + -LY².] In an equivocal manner.

†**1.** So as to have the name without the properties implied in the name; nominally. Cf. EQUIVOCAL I. *Obs.*

1579 FULKE *Heskins' Parl.* 208 By flesh and bloud æquiuocally, he vnderstandeth the sacrament of the flesh and bloud of Christe. *a* **1619** FOTHERBY *Atheom.* I. xiv. §4 (1622) 152 Which whosoeuer lacketh, he is not properly, but equiuocally, a man. *a* **1716** SOUTH (J.), Words abstracted from their proper sense and signification, lose the nature of words, and are only equivocally so called.

2. By equivocal generation. See EQUIVOCAL *a.* 3.

1645 WITHER *Gt. Assises Parnass.* 31–3 Reptiles, which are equivocally bred. **1828** MACAULAY *Misc. Writ.* (1860) 419 Those foul reptiles.. of filth and stench equivocally born.

3. a. So as to admit of a twofold or manifold application. **b.** So as to convey a double meaning, ambiguously.

a. 1630 BRATHWAIT *Eng. Gentl.* (1641) 70 Vocation may be taken equivocally or univocally. *c* **1790** REID *Let.* in *Wks.* I. 75/2 The same word may be applied to different things in three ways.. equivocally, when they have no relation but a common name.

b. 1660 R. COKE *Just. Vind.* 39, I forgive Grotius in this, not having defined anything less equivocally. *a* **1720** SHEFFIELD (Dk. Buckhm.) *Wks* (1753) II. 153 She spoke equivocally. **1818** JAS. MILL *Brit. India* II. v. v. 551 They [the instructions] were so equivocally worded.

eˈquivocalness. [f. as prec. + -NESS.] The quality or condition of being equivocal.

1647 *Power of the Keys* vi. 131 This is a mistake, arising from the equivocalnesse of the word. **1724** WATERLAND *Athan. Creed* 122 The equivocalness of the title gave a handle to those that came after to understand it of a form of faith composed by Athanasius. **1760** C. JOHNSTON *Chrysal* (1822) I. 30 The equivocalness of my character. **1878** F. TAYLOR in Grove *Dict. Mus.* I. 19 This method of writing merely substitutes a greater equivocalness for a less.

†**eˈquivocant,** *a. Obs.* [ad. L. *æquivocant-em*, pr. pple. of *æquivoc-āre*: see EQUIVOCATE.] Speaking equivocally.

1609 HOLLAND *Amm. Marcel.* XXIII. iv. 224 An answere by Oracle.. no lesse ambiguous and equivocant.

†**equivocas.** *Obs.* [perh. the L. (*verba*) *æquivoca* 'equivocal words', with an Eng. pl. ending.]

c **1400** *Test. Love* III. (1561) 317/2 Thus maie wille by terme of equivocas in three waies been understonde. **1775** ASH, *Equivocas*, an equivocation, *Chaucer*.

equivocate (iːˈkwɪvəkət), *sb. rare.* [ad. L. *æquivocāt-um*, neut. pa. pple. of *æquivocāre*: see next.] A word identical in form but not in meaning.

1881 *Pall Mall G.* 11 June 21/1 The comic confusion made by the translator between the Latin *algeo* and its Greek equivocate.

equivocate (iːˈkwɪvəkeɪt), *v.* [f. low L. *æquivocāt-* ppl. stem of *æquivocā-re* to call by the same name, f. late L. *æquivoc-us*: see EQUIVOCAL. Cf. It. *equivocare*, Fr. *équivoquer*.]

†**1.** *intr.* To have the same sound *with*. *Obs.*

1611 COTGR. s.v. *Promesse*, The words *fol lie* equivocate vnto *folie*. *Ibid.* s.v. *Sens*, This word [*Sens*].. equivocates with *Cent*, a hundred.

†**2.** *trans.* To resemble so closely as to occasion mistake. *Obs.*

1681 P. RYCAUT *Sp. Critick* 120 Making Hell with these Sports and Pastimes equivocate a Paradise. *Ibid.* 158 Such twins both in colour and bigness, that one equivocates the other.

†**3.** *intr.* To use a word in more than one application or sense; to use words of double meaning; to deal in ambiguities. *Obs.*

1613 R. C. *Table Alph.* (ed. 3), *Equivocate*, to speake doubtfully. **1635** AUSTIN *Medit.* 98 Hee doth not equivocate: but his meaning is, etc. **1685** BAXTER *Paraphr. N.T.* 1 Cor. xv. Annot., To.. place those with the blessed Spirits, is but to equivocate, and not to use the Words univocally. **1681–6** J. SCOTT *Chr. Life* (1747) III. 37 Either .. he meant according to the common Sense, or.. he intended to equivocate.

†**b.** *trans.* To misapprehend through ambiguity of language. *Obs.*

1665 J. SERJEANT *Sure-footing* 207 To put the point of Faith out of danger of being equivocated.

4. *intr.* In bad sense: 'To mean one thing and express another' (J.); to prevaricate.

1590 SANDYS *Europæ Spec.* (1632) 102 Making it lawfull for them to æquivocate with their adversaries in their answeres. **1727** DE FOE *Syst. Magic* I. iii. (1840) 84 It is enough if he does but equivocate, and tacitly grant it. **1832** HT. MARTINEAU *Ireland* v. 88 By equivocating, hesitating, and giving ambiguous answers, she effected her purpose. **1848** MACAULAY *Hist. Eng.* II. 379 The witness shuffled, equivocated, pretended to misunderstand the questions.

†**5.** *trans.* **a.** To insinuate by equivocation. **b.** To evade (an oath, a promise) by equivocation.

1626 L. OWEN *Spec. Jesuit.* (1629) 20 To equiuocate and falsie their oaths and faiths. **1645** T. HILL *Olive-br. Peace* (1648) 14 Though you will not swear (perhaps), God knows whether you will not equivocate a lye in your Trading. **1646** SIR G. BUCK *Rich. III*, 142 He equivocated his Vow by a Mental Reservation. *a* **1649** DRUMM. OF HAWTH. *Wks.* (1711) 201 When an oath.. should oblige you to arise in arms.. ye.. endeavour now to make evasions and equivocate it.

equivocating (iːˈkwɪvəkeɪtɪŋ), *vbl. sb.* [f. prec. + -ING¹.] The action of the verb EQUIVOCATE; prevarication.

1606 *St. Trials, H. Garnet* (R.), This equivocating and lying is a kind of unchastity. *a* **1714** BURNET *Own Time* (1766) I. 146 An æquivocating.. that did not become a Prince.

eˈquivocating, *ppl. a.* [f. as prec. + -ING².] That equivocates, in senses of the verb.

1645 MILTON *Tetrach.* Introd. (1851) 140 A late equivocating Treatise. **1659** T. PECKE *Parnassi Puerp.* 155 Equivocating Fortune gave the Day To Cæsar in the large Pharsalia. **1707** (*title*), The Church of England not in Danger and What a Bifarious, equivocating, sort of Cant does Mr. Higgins employ. **1881** MISS BRADDON *Asph.* III. 300 Her equivocating answer.

Hence **eˈquivocatingly** *adv.*

1652 GAULE *Magastrom.* 289 He answered æquivocatingly, that, etc. **1884** A. FORBES *Chinese Gordon* ii. 92 Bailey replied, equivocatingly, that he had heard so.

equivocation (iːˌkwɪvəʊˈkeɪʃən). Forms: 4–6 equivocacion(e, (4 equivocacoun, 5 equyocacion), 6–7 æquivocation, 6– equivocation. [ad. late L. *æquivocātiōn-em*, f. *æquivocāre*: see EQUIVOCATE. Cf. Fr. *équivocation*, Pr. *equivocatio*, Sp. *equivocacion*, It. *equivocazione*.]

†**1.** The using (a word) in more than one sense; ambiguity or uncertainty of meaning in words; also [cf. Sp. *equivocacion*], misapprehension arising from the ambiguity of terms. *Obs.*

c **1380** WYCLIF *Serm.* Sel. Wks. I. 61 Bi þis may we se hou argumentis gone awei bi equivocacion of wordis. **1413** LYDG. *Pilgr. Sowle* v. i. (1859) 73 Ye clepe seculum the world here abouen. what mene ye by this equyocacion of that name? **1432–50** tr. *Higden* (Rolls) I. 327 The oon of theyme is callede Tilis, and that other is callede Tile, leste equiuocacion of the names deceyve hym. **1532** MORE *Confut. Tindale* Wks. 537/2 Here Tindall runneth in iuglinge, by equiuocacion of thys worde church. **1606** HOLLAND *Sueton.* Annot. 10 Playing upon the æquivocation or double sense of the word Dialis. **1656** BEN ISRAEL *Vind. Jud.* in *Phenix* (1708) II. 1409 That because of the Equivocation of the Word, they should change it for another. **1738–41** WARBURTON *Div. Legat.* III. App. Wks. (1811) III. 337 The second.. receives all its strength from an equivocation in the term, *good*. **1809–10** COLERIDGE *Friend* (1865) 23 It hides its deformity in an equivocation, or double meaning of the word truth.

b. *Logic.* As the equivalent of Gr. ὁμωνυμία: The fallacy which is committed when a term has different senses in the different members of a syllogism.

1605 BACON *Adv. Learn.* II. xiv. §7 The great sophism of all sophisms being equivocation or ambiguity of words and phrase. **1646** SIR T. BROWNE *Pseud. Ep.* I. iv. 13 The fallacie of Æquivocation and Amphibologie, which conclude from the ambiguity of some one word, or the ambiguous sintaxis of many. **1870** JEVONS *Elem. Logic* xx. 171.

2. The use of words or expressions that are susceptible of a double signification, with a view to mislead; *esp.* the expression of a virtual falsehood in the form of a proposition which (in order to satisfy the speaker's conscience) is verbally true. Also *concr.*

1605 SHAKS. *Macb.* v. v. 43, I.. begin To doubt th' Equiuocation of the Fiend. **1609** BIBLE (Douay) *1 Kings* xi. Comm., The men of Iabes deluded their enemies by æquivocation. **1627** P. FLETCHER *Locusts* II. vi, His matter fram'd of slight equivocations, His very form was form'd of mentall reservations. *a* **1634** RANDOLPH *Poems* (1652) 51 That can the Subtle difference descry Betwixt Æquivocation and a Lye. **1741** RICHARDSON *Pamela* (1824) I. 113 You won't tell a downright fib for the world; but for equivocation! no jesuit ever went beyond you. **1856** FROUDE *Hist. Eng.* (1858) I. iii. 250 The Bishop.. stooped to an equivocation too transparent to deceive any one.

b. *transf.*

1642 R. CARPENTER *Experience* III. vii. 76, I see there may be an equivocation committed, as well in manners as in words. **1681** COLVIL *Whigs Supplic.* (1751) To Rdr. 8 They eluded my vow by equivocation putting gold unawares in the neck of my doublet.

equivocator (iːˈkwɪvəkeɪtə(r)). [a. late L. *æquivocātor*, agent-n. f. *æquivocāre*: see EQUIVOCATE and -OR.] One who equivocates.

1599 SANDYS *Europæ Spec.* (1632) 102 The Iesuites are noted.. to be too hardie æquivocators. **1621** BURTON *Anat. Mel.* I. ii. I. ii. (1676) 26/2 The second rank is of Lyars, and Æquivocators, as Apollo Pythius, and the like. **1691** WOOD *Ath. Oxon.* I. 304 He was.. a Sycophant, an Equivocator. **1741** RICHARDSON *Pamela* (1824) I. xv. 25 You little equivocator! What do you mean by *hardly*? **1864** J. H. NEWMAN *Apol.* App. 76 But an equivocator uses them in a received sense, though there is another received sense.

equivocatory (iːˈkwɪvəkəˌtərɪ), *a.* [f. EQUIVOCATE *v.*: see -ORY.] Indicating, or characterized by, equivocation.

1821 *New Monthly Mag.* II. 326 The laugh obligato or forced.. the laugh reluctant or equivocatory. **1847** in CRAIG.

†**ˈequivoce,** *a. Obs.*⁻⁰ [ad. late L. *æquivoc-us*: see EQUIVOCAL.] = EQUIVOCAL.

1483 *Cath. Angl.* 116 Equivoce; *equivocus*.

†**eˈquivocous,** *a. Obs.* [f. late L. *æquivoc-us* (see EQUIVOCAL) + -OUS.] = EQUIVOCAL.

1701 G. KEITH *Plain Discov. Falseh.* 42 Many Sophisms are built on that very fallacy of equivocous Terms.

†**eˈquivocy.** *Obs. rare*⁻¹. [f. late L. *æquivoc-us* EQUIVOCAL: see -Y.] = EQUIVOCATION.

1630 in T. Westcote *Devon.* 142 Thus Satan doth decieve us with equivocy.

equivoˈluminal, *a. Physics.* [See EQUI-.] Having an equal unchanging volume (see quot.).

1899 KELVIN in *Phil. Mag.* XLVII. 480 On the Application of Force within a Limited Space, required to produce Spherical Solitary Waves, or Trains of Periodic Waves, of both Species, Equivoluminal and Irrotational, in an Elastic Solid. *Note*, By 'equivoluminal' I mean every part of the solid keeping its volume unchanged during the motion.

equivoque, -voke (ˈiːkwɪ-, ˈɛkwɪvəʊk), *a.* and *sb.* Forms: (4 equivoc, 6 -ocke, equyuoke, 7 equivok), 7–8 æquivoque, (7 -voc, -voke), 7– equivoke, -que. [ad. L. *æquivocus*: see EQUIVOCAL.]

†**A.** *adj.* = EQUIVOCAL in various senses. *Obs.*

1388 WYCLIF *Prol.* 59 Wordis equiuok, that is, that hath manie significacions vndur oo lettre. **1574** *Life 70th Abp. Canterb.* To Rdr. D vij, Which name [*fora*], I thincke, is therefore equiuocke to a Market and courte, because in both all things are to be solde euen as in Rome. *c* **1650** BROME *Agst. Corrupted Sack* (R.), Thou.. art a bastard got by th' town By equivoque generation.

†**b.** quasi-*sb.* with pl. ending: Things (specified) which are equivocal. *Obs.*

1541 R. COPLAND *Guydon's Quest. Chirurg.*, *Manner Exam. Lazars* Q ij, They that ought to iudge and approue them shulde ryght dylygently beholde theym & considre the vnyuoke sygnes and equyuokes also.

B. *sb.*

†**1.** A thing which is called by the same name as something else. *Obs.* [after Gr. ὁμώνυμον].

1599 BLUNDEVIL *Logic* 13 Equiuokes be such things as haue one selfe name, and yet be diuers in substance or definition: as a naturall dogge and a certaine starre in the firmament are both called by one name in Latine, *Canis*, yet they be nothing like in substance, kind, or nature. **1655–60** STANLEY *Hist. Philos.* (1701) 120/2 There is a treatise of Æquivokes under Xenophon's name.

2. An expression capable of more than one meaning; a play upon words, often of a humorous nature, a pun; word-play, punning.

1614 SELDEN *Titles Hon.* 72. **1619** DRUMM. OF HAWTH. *Conv. B. Jonson* Wks. 226 W. Alexander.. hath sextains.. echoes and equivoques, which he [Petrarch] hath not. **1729** SWIFT *Corr.* II. 632 Beyond the power of conception.. or, to avoid an equivoque, beyond the extent of my ideas. *a* **1734** NORTH *Exam.* II. v. §47. (1740) 343 Here's his old Equivoque; by Papists, he means the King, Ministry and Loyal Party. **1824** DIBDIN *Libr. Comp.* 589 Who mistook

equivoque, abuse, and impudence, for wit. **1834** *Gentl. Mag.* CIV. I. 219 The dialogue is..enlivened by much facetious and amusing equivoque. **1866** Felton *Anc. & Mod. Gr.* II. xi. 476 The Greeks consoled themselves as well as they could by the equivoque of the Bavarian and Barbarian.

3. Ambiguity of speech; double meaning in words or phrases used. Also *transf.*

1809-10 Coleridge *Friend* (ed. 3) I. 202 The equivoque between an action and a series of motions. **1833** Herschel *Astron.* xiii. 415 Confusion, owing to the equivoque between the lunar and calendar month. **1847** Lewes *Hist. Philos.* (1867) I. Introd. 23 And to avoid equivoque I shall use the words Metaphysical Philosophy. **1878** F. Harrison in *Fortn. Rev.* Nov. 700 Right is perhaps that idea which has led to the greatest amount of sophism and equivoque.

4. The use of words in a double meaning with intent to deceive; = EQUIVOCATION. *rare.*

1616 B. Jonson *Devil an Ass* (1692) III. iii, What do you value this at, thirty Pound? *Gui.* No, sir, he cost me forty ere he was set. *Mer.* Turnings you mean? I know your Equivokes. **1877** Morley *Crit. Misc.* Ser. II. 152 Every man ..is called upon to keep himself clear from mendacity and equivoke.

equivorous (ɪ'kwɪvərəs), *a. rare.* [f. L. *equus* + *-vor-us* devouring + -OUS: see -VOROUS.] Feeding on horseflesh.

1828 Webster quotes *Q. Rev.*, Equivorous Tartars.

equivote: see EQUI- *pref.*

†**er**, *conj. Obs.* [contracted f. ME. *eðer*, *eiðer*, OE. *ǽȝðer* EITHER. Cf. OR.] = OR.

c **1220** *Rel. Ant.* I. 211 Fare he norð, er fare he suð leren he sal his nede. *Ibid.* 219 On stede er on stalle stille er lude in mot er in market er oni oðer wise. **1389** in *Eng. Gilds* 31 Qwat brother or syster, be goddis sonde, falle in mischefe er mys-ese..he schal han Almesse.

er (ɜː(r)). Used to express the inarticulate sound or murmur made by a hesitant speaker. Also, preceded by *Mr.* (or *Miss*, etc.), used in place of a name of which the speaker is uncertain. Also as *v. intr.*

1862 *St. James's Mag.* Mar. 481 Oh!—er—Well I think it was a—er—little fête at—at—Dear me—where was it? **1878** *Porcupine* XX. 681/2 Those ladies and gentlemen..who have had the advantage of—er—being—er—confined in Newgate prison. **1904** V. L. Whitechurch *Canon in Residence* i. 9 Mr. Smith said, 'Er, can I have a bed?' **1912** R. W. Wright-Henderson *Annabel* i. 9, I think, Mr. Buckle, if you would slightly modulate—er—that is—. *Ibid.* viii. 122 Have you decided yet what—er—. **1924** R. Macaulay *Orphan Island* xxi, Grandmamma's—er—adultery (if you will pardon the crude word). **1931** *Time & Tide* 12 Sept. 1057 He ahs and ers, and hums and hawes his way through an incredibly fatuous pronouncement. **1935** Marsh & Jellett *Nursing-Home Murder* viii. 116 That's what makes it so dreadful, Mr.—er—I never could have believed it. **1940** 'N. Blake' *Malice in Wonderland* ix. 129 You sound quite breathless, Miss Er. **1958** *Aspects of Translation* 37 The really astute Englishman..must feign a certain diffident hesitation, put in a few well-placed —ers. **1967** R. Rendell *Wolf to Slaughter* vi. 56, I happened to see your advert in Grover's window, Mrs. Er..?

er, obs. form of ERE before, sooner.

er, obs. form of ARE: see BE *v.*

-er, *suffix*[1], ME. *-er(e*, *-ar(e*, OE. *-ęre* (ONorthumb. often *-are*), forming sbs., represents WGer. *-âri*:—OTeut. *-ârjo-z*, whence OHG. *-âri* (MHG. *-ære*, mod.G. *-er*), and (with change of declension) ON. *-ari* (OIcel. *-are*, later *-ari*, Sw. *-are*, Da. *-ere*). The related and functionally equivalent WGer. *-ari* (OS. *-eri*, Du. *-er*, OHG. *-ari*, *-eri*, MHG. *-ere*) = Goth. *-areis*:—OTeut. type *-arjo-z* (which by phonetic law would prob. have become in OE. *-erȝe*, in ON. *-ri*) has in OE. coalesced with this. The phonological relation between OTeut. *-ărjo-z* and L. *-ārius* is obscure: Möller *Zur ahd. Alliterationspoesie* (1888) 142 argues that *-ârjo-z* originated in words adopted from Lat. words in *-ārius*, and that *-ărjo-z* is either an accentual variant of this, or (possibly) represents an OAryan type *-orios*.

1. In its original use the suffix *-ărjo-z* was added (like L. *-ārius*) to sbs., forming derivative sbs. with the general sense 'a man who has to do with (the thing denoted by the primary sb.)', and hence chiefly serving to designate persons according to their profession or occupation; e.g. Goth. *dômareis*, ON. *dômari* judge, f. OTeut. **dômo-* judgement, DOOM; Goth. *bôkareis*, OE. *bócere* scribe, f. OTeut. **bôk-* BOOK; OHG. *sangâri* (mod.G. *sänger*), ON. *sǫngare*, OE. *sangere* (ME. *songere*) singer, f. OTeut. **sangwo-* SONG. Of this type there are many specially Eng. formations, e.g. *hatter*, *slater*, *tinner*. Where the primary sb. ends in *-w*:—ME. *-ȝe*:—OE. *-ȝe*, the suffix assumes the form *-yer* (in ME. *-iere*, *-yere*), as in *bowyer*, *lawyer*, *sawyer*; and, either after the analogy of these or by assimilation to Fr. derivatives in *-ier* (see -ER[2]), it appears as -IER in certain other words of ME. date, as *brazier*, *clothier*, *collier*, *glazier*, *grazier*, *hosier*. The Eng. words of this formation not referring to profession or employment are comparatively few: examples are *bencher*, *cottager*, *outsider*, *villager*. With these may be compared a class of words chiefly belonging to mod. colloquial language, and denoting things or actions, as *header*, *back-hander*, *fiver*, *out-and-outer*, *three-decker*. A special use of the suffix, common to the mod. Teut. langs. though scarcely to be found in their older stages, is its addition to names of places or countries to express the sense 'a native of', 'a resident in', e.g. *Londoner*, *New Yorker*, *Icelander*. With similar notion, derivatives in *-er* have been formed upon certain Eng. adjs. indicating place of origin or residence, as *foreigner*, *northerner*, *southerner*.

2. Most of the sbs. which in early Teutonic gave rise to derivatives in *-ărjo-z*, also gave rise to wk. vbs. in *-jan* or *-ôjan*, to which the former stood related in sense as agent-nouns; thus Goth. *dômareis* judge, served as the agent-noun to *dômjan* to judge. Hence, by analogy, the suffix came to be regarded as a formative of agent-nouns, and with this function it was added to verbal bases both of the weak and the strong conjugation. Many derivatives of this type existed already in OE., and many more have been added in the later periods of the language. In mod.Eng. they may be formed on all vbs., excepting some of those which have agent-nouns ending in *-or*, and some others for which this function is served by sbs. of different formation (e.g. *correspond*, *correspondent*). The distinction between *-er* and *-or* as the ending of agent-nouns is purely historical and orthographical; in the present spoken language they are alike pronounced (ə(r)), except that in law terms and in certain Lat. words not fully naturalized, *-or* is still sounded (ɔː(r)). In received spelling, the choice between the two forms is often capricious, or determined by other than historical reasons. The agent-nouns belonging to vbs. f. L. ppl. stems, and to those formed with -ATE, usually end in *-or*, being partly adoptions from Lat., and partly assimilated to Lat. analogies. But when the sense is purely agential, without any added notion such as that of office, trade, or profession, function, etc., *-er* is often used; cf. *inspector*, *respecter*; *projector*, *rejecter*. In a few instances both forms of the agent-noun are still in current use, commonly without any corresponding distinction in sense, as *asserter*, *assertor*; sometimes with a distinction of technical and general sense (often however neglected) as *accepter*, *acceptor*. The Romanic *-our*, *-or* of agent-nouns has been in most cases replaced by *-er* where the related vb. exists in Eng.; exceptions are *governor*, *conjuror* (for which *-er* also occurs); in special sense we have *saviour*, but in purely agential sense *saver*. In *liar*, *beggar*, the spelling *-ar* is a survival of the occasional ME. variant *-ar(e*. The agent-nouns in *-er* normally denote personal agents (originally, only male persons, though this restriction is now wholly obsolete); many of them, however, may be used to denote material agents, and hence also mere instruments; e.g. *blotter*, *cutter*; *poker*, *roller*, etc.

3. In several instances *-er* has the appearance of being an unmeaning extension of earlier words ending in *-er* denoting trades or offices. Most of these words are of Fr. origin, as *caterer*, †*cytolerer* (= CITOLER), †*fermerer*, †*feuterer*, *fruiterer*, *poulterer*; an analogous case in a native word is *upholsterer*. The real formation of these words is obscure: some are prob. from vbs., while in other cases formation on words in *-ery* may be conjectured.

4. After the analogy of ASTROLOGER, ASTRONOMER (q.v.), the suffix *-er* is used to form sbs. serving as adaptations of L. types in *-logus*, *-graphus*; e.g. *chronologer*, *philologer*, †*theologer*; *biographer*, *geographer*, *orthographer*.

Philosopher (in Chaucer and Gower always *philo'sophre*) is perh. not a formation of this kind, as the *r* may be merely excrescent. In *chorister*, *sophister*, *barrister* (cf. ME. *legistre*) the *-er* is not a suffix, but results from an AF. substitution of *-istre* for *-iste*, perh. on the analogy of *ministre*.

-er[2], *suffix*, of various origin, occurring in sbs. and adjs. adopted from OF.

1. ME. *-er*, repr. OF. *-er*:—L. *-ārem*, *-ar*: see -AR. Nearly all the ME. words ending in *-er* of this origin have been refashioned after Lat., so that the suffix is now written *-ar*: see examples under -AR. The older form of the suffix is retained in *sampler*.

2. ME. *-er*, a. AF. *-er* (OF. *-ier*) in sbs. which descend from L. forms in *-ārius*, *-ārium* (see -ARY), or which were formed in Fr. after the analogy of those so descending. Where the L. type of the suffix is the masc. *-ārius*, it has usually the sense 'a person connected with', and the words are designations of office or occupation, as *butler*, *carpenter*, *draper*, *grocer*, *mariner*, *officer*. (So also in a few ME. adoptions of OF. fem. sbs. in *-iere*:—L. *-āria*, as *chamberer*, *lavender*.) Where the suffix represents the L. neuter *-ārium*, the sense is 'a thing connected with', 'a receptacle for', as in *antiphoner*, *danger*, *garner*, etc.

3. In mod.Eng. *-er* appears as a casual representative of various other suffixes of OF. origin which have been weakened in pronunciation to (ə(r)); thus in *border*, *bracer*, it stands for OF. *-ëure* (:—L. *-ātūram*), commonly represented by -URE; in *laver* it stands for OF. *-ëor*, now *-oir* (:—L. *ātōrium*), in ME. rendered -OUR. The agent-suffix -OUR (OF. *-ëor*:—L. *-ātōrem*) is now very often replaced by *-er*; it can seldom be determined whether this is due to phonetic weakening, or to the substitution of -ER[1] for its Romanic synonym. Where the same word had in 14th c. the two forms *-our* and *-er(e*, as *chaungeour*, *changer*, the former supposition is excluded; but the forms in *-er(e* may possibly sometimes be a. OF. nominative forms in *-ere*:—L. *-'ātor*.

-er[3], *suffix*, the formative of the comparative degree in adjs. and advbs.

A. In *adjs.* ME. *-er*, *-ere* (*-ore*, *-ure*), *-re*, OE. *-ra* (fem., neut. *-re*) represents two different suffixes used in OTeut. to form the compar., viz.: *-izon-* (Goth. *-iza*, OHG., OS. *-iro*, ON. *-ri* with umlaut), and *-ôzon-* (Goth. *-ôza*, OHG. *-ôro*, ON. *-ari*). These OTeut. suffixes are f. the adverbial *-iz*, *-ôz*: see B. In OE. only a few comparatives retained the umlaut which phonetic law requires in the *-izon-* type; in mod.Eng. no forms with umlaut remain, except *better*, *elder* (OE. *bętera*, *ięldra*), the comparatives being ordinarily formed by adding *-er* to the positive. The 'irregular comparatives' *worse* (OE. *wiersa* = Goth. *wairsiza*) and *less* (OE. *lǽssa*) contain the suffix *-izon* in a disguised form, and the analogy of other comparatives has given rise to the extended forms *worser* and *lesser*. In mod.Eng. the comparatives in *-er* are almost restricted to adjs. of one or two syllables; longer adjs., and also disyllables containing any suffix other than *-y* or *-ly*, having the periphrastic comparison by means of the adv. *more*. Earlier writers, however, have *beautifuller*, *eminenter*, *slavisher*, etc.; a few modern writers, *e.g.* Carlyle, affect the same method. The periphrastic form is admissible (esp. in predicative use) for all adjs., even monosyllables, which are not extremely common colloquially.

2. In *hinder*, *inner*, the comparative suffix, though in WGer. and ON. formally coincident with that treated above, is quite distinct in origin, repr. OTeut. *-eron-*, f. OAryan *-ero-*.

B. In *adverbs.* The OE. form of the comparative suffix was *-or*, corresp. to OS., OHG. *-ôr*, Goth. *-ôs*:—OTeut. *-ôz*. OTeut. had also a suffix *-iz* with the same function, corresponding to L. *-is* in *magis*, *nimis*, and cogn. with L. *-ior* of adjs.; it is represented by Goth. *-is*, ON. *-r* with umlaut; in OE. by the umlaut in monosyllabic comparatives like *lęng*:—**langiz* longer, *bęt*:—**batiz* better, which died out in early ME., being superseded by the adj. forms. The relation between the two OTeut. suffixes is much disputed: a widely-held hypothesis is that *-ôz* is f. *-ô* adverbial suffix + *-iz*. The advbs. which take *-er* in the comparative are chiefly those which are now identical in form with adjs. (either repr. OE. advbs. in *-e*, or modern adverbial uses of the adj.): e.g. 'to work *harder*', 'to stand *closer*'. Exceptional instances are *oftener*, *seldomer*, *sooner*. The advbs. in -LY[2] are now compared periphrastically with *more*, though in earlier writers the inflexional comparison is common, e.g. *easilier* = more easily, ME. *entierlocure* = more entirely; in poetry it still occurs, as in *keenlier* (Tennyson).

-er, *suffix*[4], the ending of certain AF. infinitives used substantively as law terms, e.g. *cesser*,

disclaimer, *misnomer*, *trover*, *user*, *waiver*. Of similar origin is the ending in *dinner*, *supper*, a. OF. *disner*, *soper*.

-er, *suffix*[5], forming frequentative vbs. The vbs. of this formation which can be traced in OE. have the form *-rian* (:—OTeut. *-rôjan*); e.g. *clatrian* CLATTER, *flotorian* FLUTTER. The other Teut. langs. have many vbs. of this type, denoting repeated action; often they are f. verbal bases, as MHG. *wanderen* = OE. *wandrian* WANDER, f. OTeut. **wandjan* WEND *v.*, ON. *vafra* WAVER, f. *vafa* = WAVE *v.*; sometimes app. on onomatopœic bases, as OHG. *zwizarôn* = TWITTER. Further examples in Eng. are *batter*, *chatter*, *clamber*, *flicker*, *glitter*, *mutter*, *patter*, *quaver*, *shimmer*, *shudder*, *slumber*.

-er, *suffix*[6]. Also **-ers**. Introduced from Rugby School into Oxford University slang, orig. at University College, in Michaelmas Term, 1875; used to make jocular formations on sbs., by clipping or curtailing them and adding *-er* to the remaining part, which is sometimes itself distorted. Among the earliest instances are FOOTER *sb.*[1] 3b (= football) (1863), RUGGER[2] (1893), SOCKER (1891); TOGGER (1897), TOSHER[3] (1889); BONNER, BREKKER (1889), DIVVERS, EKKER (1891).

Other familiar examples are BEDDER[3], *bed-sitter* = bed-sittingroom, *collekkers* = collections (see COLLECTION 8), CUPPER[2], and (formerly) *rudders* = rudiments (of divinity), *stragger* = stranger. Examples of proper names are *Adders* = Addison's Walk, *Bodder* = Bodleian, *Jaggers* = Jesus (College), *Quaggers* = The Queen's College. (Cf. F. Madan *Oxford outside the Guidebooks*, 1923.)

1892 *Isis* 8 June 26/1 At the close of the Lancashire match we heard one man ejaculate..'This is breath-ers'... This..is all that remains of the..expression 'breathless excitement'. **1899** *Daily Tel.* 14 Aug. 9/5 The triumph of this jargon was reached when some one christened the Martyrs' Memorial the 'Martyrs' Memugger'. **1903** D. F. T. COKE *Sandford of Merton* ii. 10 'Wagger-pagger-bagger' for the receptacle of torn-up letters and the like. **1904** *Daily Chron.* 25 Mar. 4/7 Mr. Gladstone was 'the Gladder'. An undergraduate left his 'bedder' in the morning to eat his 'brekker' in his 'sitter'; later he attended a 'lecker', and in the afternoon he might run with the 'Toggers' (torpid races) or take some other form of 'ecker'. **1912** *Tatler* 23 Oct., Suppl. 40 The 'Pragger-Wagger', it should be explained, is the new name given to the Prince of Wales. **1914** D. O. BARNET *Lett.* (1915) 13 The P-Wagger came to see us yesterday. I met him coming off parade, and threw a hairy salute. **1914** C. MACKENZIE *Sinister St.* II. III. 517 'They say we shall all have to interview the Warden tomorrow.' 'They say on Sunday afternoon the Wagger makes the same speech to the freshers that he's made for twenty years.' *Ibid.* 543 'You'd better let me put your name down for the Ugger'. 'The what?'..'The Union.' **1963** *Sunday Times* 22 Sept. 18/4 The twenties were the age of the 'er' at Repton. The changing-room was the chagger and a sensation a sensagger. A six at cricket was a criper.

era ('ɪərə). Also 7-9 **æra**. [a. late L. *æra* fem. sing. 'a number expressed in figures' (see Forcellini, s.v.), prob. f. *æra* counters used in calculation, pl. of *æs* brass, money

The chronological use of the word appears to have originated in Spain; where (as also in Southern Gaul and North Africa) it is found in inscriptions prefixed to the number of years elapsed since 38 B.C., the selection of which as an initial year has not been satisfactorily explained. (Isidore of Seville in the 6th c. says that this was the year in which Augustus first ordered the taxation of Spain.) Thus 'æra (oftener written *era*) DXXXVIII' (= 'No. 538') meant the year 500 A.D. This method of reckoning was in use from the 5th to the 15th century, and Spanish Latin writers employed the word *æra* as its specific designation. The phrase *æra Hispanica*, 'Spanish æra', suggested to the scholars of the Renascence the parallel expressions *æra Christiana*, *æra Varroniana*, etc., in which the sb. had the generalized sense 'a reckoning of time from a particular epoch', for which no term had previously existed in Latin.]

1. A system of chronological notation, characterized by the numbering of years from some particular point of time; e.g. the ***Christian***, ***Common***, or ***Vulgar era*** (see CHRISTIAN 7); ***era of the Hegira*** (***Hijrah***), the Mohammedan era, reckoned from the year of Mohammed's flight from Mecca; ***era of Nabonassar***, a Babylonian era, employed in astronomy, commencing 747 B.C., etc., etc. These phrases are also frequently employed in sense 2.

a **1646** J. GREGORY *Learned Tracts* (1649) 164 Dionysius the Abbot..brought in the Æra of Christ's Incarnation, so that..the Christians did not use to reckon by the years of Christ, until the 532 of the Incarnation. **1650** Row *Hist. Kirk* (1842) 504 They would begin their epocha or æra from his coming to Jerusalem. **1658** USSHER *Ann.* Ep. Rdr. That midnight which began the first day of the Christian æra. **1716** PRIDEAUX *Connect. O. & N.T.* I. I. 1 The vulgar era, by which we now compute the years from his incarnation. **1796** MORSE *Amer. Geog.* II. 658 The computing of time by the Christian æra is introduced by Dionysius the monk. **1840** CARLYLE *Heroes* (1858) 223 In the year 570 of our Era..the man Mahomet was born. **1861** F. HALL in *Jrnl. Asiat. Soc. Bengal* 149 A few words on the vexed subject of the Gupta era.

2. The initial point assumed in a system of chronology; also, any date from which succeeding years are numbered; = EPOCH 1.

1615 BEDWELL *Arab. Trudg.*, Tarich..is the same that *Epocha* is to the Greeks: or *Æra* to the Latines. **1657** WHARTON *Wks.* 49 The Greek Church numbereth from the Creation to Christ's Æra, 5508 compleat years. **1704** HEARNE *Duct. Hist.* (1714) I. 6 Æra is the same with Epocha, signifying..a fixed point among Historians whence to begin to reckon the Years. **1748** HARTLEY *Observ. Man* II. ii. 116 When we come still farther to the Aera of Nabonassar. **1777** ROBERTSON *Hist. Amer.* I. I. 10 About six hundred and four years before the Christian æra. **1816** SINGER *Hist. Cards* 13 The 7th century before the present æra. **1853** HERSCHEL *Pop. Lect. Sc.* v. §12 (1873) 187 Some three centuries before our era.

3. a. A date, or an event, which forms the commencement of a new period in the history of a nation, an institution, individual, art or science, etc.; a memorable or important date. Cf. EPOCH 2.

1703 ROWE *Fair Penit.* II. i. 488 From this sacred Æra of my Love A better order of succeeding Days Come smiling forward. **1765** T. HUTCHINSON *Hist. Col. Mass.* I. 90 [The earthquake of 1638] was a remarkable æra. **1787** J. BARLOW *Oration 4th July* 6 This single circumstance..will..mark it [the American revolution] as a distinguished æra in the history of mankind. **1851** DIXON *W. Penn* xxiv. (1872) 210 The landing of this English Governor was an era in their lives. **1867** FREEMAN *Norm. Conq.* (1876) I. vi. 419 This same year a Witenagemot was held, which marks an æra in the reign of Cnut.

†**b.** Date of origin; = EPOCH 2b.

1646 SIR T. BROWNE *Pseud. Ep.* IV. ix. 199 And it will evidently appeare, that custome hath an elder Æra then this Chronologie affordeth.

4. a. A historical period; a portion of historical time marked by the continuance throughout it of particular influences, social conditions, etc. Cf. EPOCH 5.

1741 MIDDLETON *Cicero* I. I. 12 This æra of joy. **1758** H. WALPOLE *Catal. Roy. Authors* (1759) I. Advt. 2 The polished æra of Queen Anne! *a* **1789** BURNEY *Hist. Mus.* (ed. 2) IV. i. 21 The beginning of this century (1600) was the æra of musical recitation on the public stage at Florence. **1809** PINKNEY *Trav. France* 106 Gallantry is..as much in fashion..as in the most corrupt æra of the monarchy. **1858** KINGSLEY *Lett.* (1878) I. 399, I cannot but hope that a better intellectual era is dawning for the working men.

b. A period in an individual's life, or in the history of any continuous process; = EPOCH 5b. In *Geology* sometimes with more specific sense: see EPOCH 5c.

1796 MORSE *Amer. Geog.* I. 341 In autumn, after harvest, that gladsome era in the husbandman's life. **1809** CRABBE *Tales* 63 Felt the new æra of her changeful life. **1839** MURCHISON *Silur. Syst.* I. Introd. 11 The æra when the newly-raised surface was first occupied by lakes. **1870** F. WILSON *Ch. Lindisf.* 95 It belongs to the worst era of architecture.

c. ***era of good feeling***(***s***, in U.S. Hist., a period during the presidency of Monroe (1817–24), when there was virtually only one political party. Also *transf.*

1817 *Columbian Centinel* 12 July (Th.) (*heading*) Era of Good Feelings. **1851** H. A. GARLAND *Life J. Randolph* II. 278 During the 'era of good feelings', and the undisturbed repose of Mr. Monroe's administration, [these ideas] had been widely disseminated. **1904** *N.Y. Herald* 22 Sept. 4 The nomination was made unanimously, and the era of good feeling continued throughout the naming of the rest of the ticket. **1945** *Chicago Daily News* 16 Aug. 10/2 We do not wish to disturb the new 'Era of Good Feeling' in traction. **1948** *Pennsylvania Mag. Hist.* Apr. 113 The era of the 1820's—the so-called but ludicrously named 'Era of Good Feeling'. **1951** G. DANGERFIELD (*title*) The Era of Good Feelings.

5. The portion of historical time to which an event is to be assigned; the approximate date, 'period', 'epoch' of an event, of a monument, etc.

1714 MANDEVILLE *Fab. Bees* (1733) II. 132 Many useful arts and sciences, of which the beginnings are of uncertain æra's. **1774** J. BRYANT *Mythol.* I. 261 The pillar stands..its parts..betray a difference in their æra. **1819** BYRON *Juan* I. cxxi, 'Twas in November, but I'm not so sure About the day—the era's more obscure.

6. *attrib.*, as ***era-date***; **era-making** *a.* = *epoch-making*.

1758 W. THOMPSON *Hymn to May* 242 Ne rueful murder stain thy æra-date. **1894** J. MILLAR tr. *Weizsäcker's Apostolic Age* I. II. iii. 188 The era-making significance of the treaty. **1929** R. A. CRAM *Cath. Ch. & Art* iv. 53 The great monastic sovereignty..that had grown out of the first and era-making beginnings at the hands of St. Benedict. **1965** *Times Lit. Suppl.* 27 May 438/3 We recognize easily enough in the history of cultures how era-making an invention writing has been.

erable, var. of EARABLE *a.*, *Obs.*, arable.

erace, obs. variant of ERASE.

†**e'racinate**, *v. Obs. rare*$^{-1}$. [f. OF. *er-*, *esraciner* (f. *es-* (see ES-) + *racine* root) + -ATE. See -ATE[3] 6.] *trans.* To root out; to remove.

1758 J. S. tr. *Le Dran's Observ. Surg.* (1771) 201 The whole Piece was eracinated.

†**e'rade**, *v. Obs.* [ad. L. *ērādĕre* to scrape off, f. *ē* out + *rādĕre* to scrape, scratch. Cf. ERASE.] *trans.* To scrape off.

1657 TOMLINSON *Renou's Disp.* 85 Then must the scum be ..eraded and separated.

eradiate (ɪ'reɪdɪeɪt), *v.* [f. L. *ē* out + RADIATE.]

1. *intr.* To shoot forth, as rays of light.

1647 H. MORE *Song of Soul* Notes 139/2 A kind of life eradiating and resulting both from Intellect and Psyche. **1828** in WEBSTER; and in mod. Dicts.

†**2.** *trans.* To give forth like rays, or in rays.

1678 CUDWORTH *Intell. Syst.* 252 Proclus concludes, that the World was..always Generated or Eradiated from God, and therefore must needs be Eternal. **1694** NORRIS *Refl. Ess. Hum. Und.* 24 Let him..tell me how any Body can eradiate such an inconceivable Number of these Effluvias. **1794** J. HUTTON *Philos. Light, etc.* 87 Bodies, far below the heat of incandescence, eradiate a species of light.

eradiation (ɪˌreɪdɪ'eɪʃən). Also 7 **erradiation**. [f. prec.: see -ATION.]

1. The action or process of eradiating or shining forth; the emission of rays of light or heat.

1633 T. ADAMS *Exp. 2 Peter* iii. 18 The first eradiation of this light, like some flash of lightning, breaks the stone in the heart. **1686** GOAD *Celest. Bodies* II. xii. 331 Neither must we Imagine his Erradiation to be Idle. **1794** SULLIVAN *View Nat.* I. 139 But, whether it comes directly from the sun, by successive emissions or eradiations, etc. **1865** F. P. B. MARTIN *MS. Lect. Geol.*, The attraction of the sun increases the Eradiation of the Earth.

b. *transf.* and *fig.*

a **1630** HALES *Gold. Rem.* (1673) I. 288 He first supposeth some eradiation and emanation of Spirit..to be directed from our bodies to the blood dropped from it. **1678** CUDWORTH *Intell. Syst.* 252 They will not understand what manner of making or production the world had—to wit, by way of effulgency or eradiation from the Deity.

2. *concr.*

1678 CUDWORTH *Intell. Syst.* 744 As if they were a kind of Eternal Effulgency, Emanation or Eradiation from an Eternal Sun. **1691-8** NORRIS *Pract. Disc.* (1711) III. 172 He is in his proportion..an Effulgency, an Eradiation of God's Glory. **1855** MILMAN *Lat. Chr.* (1864) I. I. i. 51 All the rest acknowledged some Deity, some efflux, eradiation, emanation of the primal Godhead.

eradicable (ɪ'rædɪkəb(ə)l), *a.* [f. L. *ērādīc-āre* (see ERADICATE *v.*) + -ABLE.] Capable of being eradicated.

1847 in CRAIG. **1865** *Cornh. Mag.* XI. 547 Even rage and hate..are eradicable, as most systems of ethics have assumed.

†**e'radicat**(**e**, *pa. pple. Obs.* [ad. L. *ērādīcātus*, pa. pple. of *ērādīcāre*: see next.] Equivalent to the later ERADICATED.

1533-4 *Act 25 Hen. VIII*, c. 14 Heresie, shulde..vtterly be abhorred, detested, and eradicate. **1556** LAUDER *Tractate* 124 And ȝour successioun thay sall be Eradicat frome ȝour ryngs [= reigns, kingdoms].

eradicate (ɪ'rædɪkeɪt), *v.* Also 7 **irradicate**. [f. L. *ērādīcāt-* ppl. stem of *ērādīcāre*, f. L. *ē* out + *rādīc-em*, nom. *rādix* root.]

1. *trans.* To pull or tear up by the roots; to root out (a tree, plant, or anything that is spoken of as having 'roots').

1564-78 BULLEYN *Dial. agst. Pest.* (1888) 48 And to the places aboute the rootes of the carbuncle round about it, this is good both to eradicate & defend the same. **1599** A. M. tr. *Gabelhouer's Bk. Physicke* 44/2 Till such time, as they [hayre] be wholye eradicated, and rootede out. **1635** NABBES *Hannibal & Sc.* (1637) Kiij, Okes eradicated By a prodigious whirlwind. **1664** EVELYN *Kal. Hort.* (1729) 213 Cauly-flowers over-speeding to pome and lead..should be quite eradicated. *a* **1674** CLARENDON *Surv. Leviath.* (1676) 111 To demolish all Buildings, eradicate all Plantations. **1725** BRADLEY *Fam. Dict.* s.v. *Infirmities of Trees*, Such [Weeds] as can be eradicated must be diligently pluck'd up by the Hands. **1860** tr. *Hartwig's Sea & Wond.* vi. 73 Huge weapons, fit for eradicating trees. **1871** DARWIN *Desc. Man* II. xix. 348 The Indians of Paraguay eradicate their eyebrows and eyelashes.

2. To remove entirely, extirpate, get rid of.

1647-8 COTTERELL *Davila's Hist. Fr.* (1678) 35 To see the seeds of those discords eradicated. **1656** EARL MONM. *Advt. fr. Parnass.* 49 Totally to irradicate all vertue from out his subjects souls. **1658** A. FOX *Wurtz' Surg.* III. viii. 240 Without Chymical preparations congealed bloud will not be eradicated out of the body. **1784** COWPER *Task* v. 437 That man should thus encroach on fellow man..Eradicate him..Moves indignation. **1788** REID *Act. Powers* III. III. iii, All desires and fears, with regard to things not in our power, ought to be totally eradicated. **1857** HUGHES *Tom Brown* Pref. (1871) 13 By eradicating mercilessly the incorrigible. **1869** LECKY *Europ. Mor.* II. i. 102 Laws of the most savage cruelty were passed in hopes of eradicating mendicancy.

†**3.** *Math.* To extract the (square) root of (a number). *Obs.*

1610 W. FOLKINGHAM *Art of Survey* II. viii. 61 Eradicate the ductat of the said mediatie and remainders.

¶ Misused for IRRADICATE.

1657 TOMLINSON *Renou's Disp.* 14 Seeds and plants sown and eradicated in the ground.

eradicated (ɪ'rædɪkeɪtɪd), *ppl. a.* [f. prec. + -ED[1].] Rooted out.

1661 MORGAN *Sph. Gentry* I. viii. 118 Assailing him with Firre-Trees eradicated. **1775** in ASH.

b. *Her.* (See quot. 1864.)

1708 J. CHAMBERLAYNE *St. Gt. Brit.* II. III. x. (1743) 429 A large square plate of silver enamelled azure into an oak-

tree eradicated and fructed. **1809** J. HOME in *Naval Chron.* XXIV. 193 On oak tree vert, eradicated proper. **1864** BOUTELL *Heraldry Hist. & Pop.* xi. 70 [Trees] if having their roots exposed [are] eradicated.

eradicating (ɪˈrædɪkeɪtɪŋ), *vbl. sb.* [f. as prec. + -ING[1].] The action of the verb ERADICATE.

a **1660** HAMMOND *Wks.* IV. 589 (R.) The eradicating of any other enemies of God. **1664** EVELYN *Pomona* vi. (1729) 69 Sudden irradicating of Trees for an early Transplantation.

eradicating (ɪˈrædɪkeɪtɪŋ), *ppl. a.* [f. as prec. + -ING[2].] That eradicates, extirpates, etc.

1628 LAYTON *Syons Plea* (ed. 2) Ep. Ded., Consultation.. can do no good without reall and in some things eradicating Reformation. **1667** WATERHOUSE *Fire Lond.* 4 Greater and more eradicating judgements. **1775** in ASH. **1879** ESCOTT *England* II. 498 The convict taint has outlived the eradicating influences of education.

eradication (ɪˌrædɪˈkeɪʃən). Also 6 -cion. [ad. L. *ērādīcātiōn-em*, n. of action f. *ērādīcāre*. See ERADICATE *v.*] The action of pulling out by the roots; total destruction; extirpation.

1548 LD. SOMERSET *Epist. Scots* 239 The finall eradicacion of your nacion. **1614** RALEIGH *Hist. World* II. 479[A] warrant..had been given to Jehu..for the eradication of Ahab's house. **1646** SIR T. BROWNE *Pseud. Ep.* II. vi. 95 The roots of Mandrakes doe make a noyse..upon eradication. **1751** JOHNSON *Rambler* No. 183 ¶10 The eradication of envy from the human heart. **1825** T. JEFFERSON *Autobiog.* Wks. 1859 I. 38 This stopped the increase of the evil by importation, leaving to future efforts its final eradication.

eradicative (ɪˈrædɪkətɪv), *a.* and *sb.* [f. L. *ērādīcāt-* (see ERADICATE *v.*) + -IVE.]

A. *adj.* Tending or having the power to root out or expel (disease, etc.). Const. *of.*

†*eradicative cure*: orig. the 'curative' treatment of disease, as opposed to *palliative*. In later use the phrase occurs with *cure* taken in the mod. sense.

1543 TRAHERON *Vigo's Chirurg.* 43 b, We wyll speake of his cure aswel eradicatyue as palliatyue. **1684** tr. *Bonet's Merc. Compit.* VI. 217 A certain Sweat..had been plainly critical and eradicative of the whole Disease. *a* **1691** BOYLE *Wks.* V. 386 (R.) Copious evacuations eradicative of the morbific matter. **1711** F. FULLER *Med. Gymn.* (1718) 143 To effect a compleat and Eradicative Cure of this Distemper. **1828** in WEBSTER; and in mod. Dicts.

†**B.** *sb.* An eradicative medicine.

1654 WHITLOCK *Zootomia* 88 Sometimes Eradicatives are omitted in the beginning. **1731–1800** in BAILEY. **1828** in WEBSTER. **1847** in CRAIG; and in mod. Dicts.

eradicator (ɪˈrædɪkeɪtə(r)). [agent-n. f. ERADICATE after Lat. analogies: see -OR.]

a. One who, or that which, roots up or removes utterly. **b.** An agricultural or horticultural implement for uprooting.

1659 R. GELL *Amendm. Bible* 58 Sihon is eradicator, that evil spirit that endeavours to root up all the plants of righteousness. **1807** A. YOUNG *Agric. Essex* (1813) I. 148 Eradicator..an implement. **1881** *Salem* (U.S.) *Gaz.* 10 June 1/4 Fogg's iron rust eradicator.

eradicatory (ɪˈrædɪkətərɪ), *a.* [f. as prec. + -ORY.] Tending to eradicate, root out, or destroy.

1801 W. TAYLOR in *Monthly Mag.* XII. 578 Unfeelingly eradicatory of the domestic charities.

†**er-ˈaftur**, *conj. Obs.* [? f. *er* = EVER + AFTER.] According as.

1370–80 in *O.E. Misc.* App. 225 Lasse or more schal he be deruet Er-aftur he haþ heer deseruet.

eral (ˈɪərəl), *a. rare.* [f. ERA + -AL[1].] Of or pertaining to an era.

1861 F. HALL in *Jrnl. Asiat. Soc. Bengal* 16 No Hindu date, unintegrated by the particularity at last amended, is available for eral determination.

†**ˈerament.** *Obs.* [ad. L. *ærāment-um* that is prepared from copper or bronze.] Copper.

1623 in COCKERAM.

[**eranc**, error or misprint for *cranoc* CRANNOCK.

1610 HOLLAND *Camden's Brit.* II. 167; cf. 175.]

erand(e, obs. form of ERRAND.

erane, variant of ARAIN, *Obs.*, spider.

eranist (ˈɛrənɪst). [ad. Gr. ἐρανιστής, f. ἔρανος a meal to which each contributes his share, a contribution, also a club.] In Greece: A member of an ἔρανος or club.

1825 *New Monthly Mag.* XIII. 220 Eranists, who might be called joint-stock companies for trade. **1873** *Contemp. Rev.* XXI. 569 By partaking of the banquets of the eranists a man rendered himself..a member of a brotherhood.

‖**eranthemum** (ɛˈrænθɪməm). *Bot.* [mod.L., ad. Gr. ἠράνθεμον (Dioscor.), f. ἦρ = ἔαρ spring + ἄνθεμον blossom, flower.]

†**1.** 'The Herb Camomile' (Kersey 1715). *Obs.*

2. 'A widely distributed genus of *Acanthaceæ*, containing nearly 50 species' (*Treas. Bot.*).

1882 *Garden* 21 Jan. 37/2 Much resembling some of the Eranthemum, and, like them, flowering during winter.

erany(e, var. of ARAIN, *Obs.*, spider.

erasable (ɪˈreɪsəb(ə)l, -z-), *a.* [f. next + -ABLE.] That can be erased or obliterated.

1849 *Fraser's Mag.* XL. 516 Not so easily erasable from thy heart.

erase (ɪˈreɪs, -z), *v.* Also (5 irrase, 7 ereaze), 7–8 erace, -aze. [f. L. *ērās-* ppl. stem of *ērādĕre*, f. *ē* out + *rādĕre* to scrape, scratch. (In some early examples perh. a variant of ARACE to uproot.)]

1. a. *trans.* To scrape or rub out (anything written, engraved, etc.); to efface, expunge, obliterate.

1605 CAMDEN *Rem.* (1637) 154 The names were ereazed out of the publick Records. **1632** G. FLETCHER *Christ's Vict.* I. vii, Lest it should quite erace That from the world, which was the first world's grace. **1762–71** H. WALPOLE *Vertue's Anecd. Paint.* (1786) V. 130 Lombart afterwards erased the face, and inserted that of Cromwell. **1778** BP. LOWTH *Isa.* Notes (ed. 12) 340 A letter is erased at the end of the word. **1826** SCOTT *Woodst.* i, Erasing, as far as they could be erased, all traces of its ancient fame. **1858** GREENER *Gunnery* 248 Every person fraudulently erasing..from any barrel, any mark. **1863** H. COX *Instit.* I. vi. 57 James I..erased from the journals of the House of Commons an obnoxious protestation.

transf. **1860** TYNDALL *Glac.* I. xxvii. 198 The snow had practically erased it [the road].

¶ In quasi-*passive* use.

1837 CARLYLE *Fr. Rev.* III. I. vi, Things, which lie very black in our Earth's Annals, yet which will not erase therefrom.

b. *Electr.* To remove the recorded signals from a magnetic tape or medium.

1945 *Sci. News Let.* 9 June 363 Any part of the wire can be erased without harm to the sound recorded on adjacent parts. **1949** FRAYNE & WOLFE *Elem. Sound Recording* xxix. 592 Magnetic media..that require high magnetizing forces to produce saturation are more difficult to erase. **1962** *Gloss. Terms Autom. Data Proc.* (*B.S.I.*) 68 *Erase*, in a magnetic store, to obliterate stored data by returning the magnetic state of a cell to a uniform null condition.

2. *fig.* To efface, obliterate from the mind or memory.

1695 LD. PRESTON *Boeth.* I. 37 My Griefs have dulled my Memory, and eras'd almost every thing out of it. **1792** S. ROGERS *Pleas. Mem.* I. 275 Though the iron school of War erase Each milder virtue. **1856** SIR B. BRODIE *Psychol. Inq.* I. ii. 58 The effect of a blow..has been..to erase from the memory the events which immediately preceded the accident. *a* **1862** BUCKLE *Civiliz.* (1869) III. v. 318 Erasing from his view of human nature those premisses which he had already handled.

3. *transf.* To destroy utterly. *rare.*

1728 R. MORRIS *Ess. Anc. Archit.* 9 He..left it quite ruin'd and eras'd. **1855** SINGLETON *Virgil* I. 376, I have not with the Greeks at Aulis sworn To erase the Trojan nation.

erase (ɪˈreɪz), *sb.* = ERASING *vbl. sb.* c. Also *attrib.*, as ***erase head***, etc.

1948 WIEGAND & ZENNER in *Trans. Amer. Inst. Electr. Engin.* LXVII. 507 (*title*) A turn-in-gap erase head for magnetic recorders providing intense high-frequency fields. **1949** FRAYNE & WOLFE *Elem. Sound Recording* xxix. 593 The equipment required for such erase is very simple. **1952** *Gramophone* Aug. 68 The Tape-desk..contains..an erase unit. **1954** *Electronic Engin.* XXVI. 294 The erase head consists of a specially designed permanent magnet which subjects the individual elements of the tape to reversing magnetic fields. **1957** *Encycl. Brit.* X. 618/2 The erase and re-use features of magnetic recordings are important economic advantages in many commercial applications [of tape recorders]. **1962** A. NISBETT *Technique Sound Studio* 273 *Tape recording amplifier* differs from an ordinary amplifier in that it includes an oscillator for bias and erase.

erased (ɪˈreɪst, -zd), *ppl. a.* [f. ERASE *v.* + -ED[1].]

1. In senses of the verb.

1848 W. H. KELLY tr. *L. Blanc's Hist. Ten Y.* I. 331 Dupont de l'Eure..repaired to the king, and told him if the erased passages were not restored he would resign.

2. *Her.* †**a.** (see quot.). *Obs.*

1486 *Bk. St. Alban's, Her.* D ij b, Certan armys..ar called quarterit armys irrasit, for the colouris be rasit owt as oon coloure in rasyng ware take away from an othir.

b. Of the head, body, or other part of an animal: Represented with a jagged edge, as if torn violently off.

1572 BOSSEWELL *Armorie* II. 117, Iij Griphons heades erased de Argent. **1677** *Lond. Gaz.* No. 1208/4 Three Bears heads erased in Chief. **1823** RUTTER *Fonthill* p. xxii, A Wolf's head erased at the neck, Argent.

transf. **1678** BUTLER *Hud.* III. iii. 214 Drag'd out through straiter Holes by th' Ears, Eras'd, or Coup'd for Perjurers.

erasement (ɪˈreɪsmənt). [f. as prec. + -MENT.] The action of erasing; obliteration; total demolition (of cities).

1721 BAILEY, *Erasement*, a blotting or dashing out. **1753** WARD *Rom. Inscr.* in *Phil. Trans.* XLVIII. 345 There are.. no traces of the word *sua* now remaining;..which makes me suspect, there has been an erasement. **1769** *Gentl. Mag.* Jan. 52/1 The Grand Jury's erasement of the words aiding and assisting. **1812** BARCLAY, *Erasement*, applied to buildings and cities, entire destruction and demolition. **1837** *Blackw. Mag.* XLII. 749 Not on Russia alone does the guilt of her erasement from the book of nations rest.

eraser (ɪˈreɪsə(r), -z-). [f. as prec. + -ER[1].] One who, or that which, erases; any instrument used to erase written characters, blots, etc. Cf. *ink-eraser*.

In mod. Dicts.

erasing (ɪˈreɪsɪŋ, -z-), *vbl. sb.* [f. as prec. + -ING[1].] **a.** The action of the verb ERASE. **b.** *Her.* See quot. and ERASED.

1610 GUILLIM *Her.* III. xiii. 125 When any part is thus born with ligges, like peeces of the flesh or skinne, depending, it is termed *erasing*. **1775** in ASH.

c. *Electr.* The action of the verb ERASE 1 b. Also *attrib.*

1949 FRAYNE & WOLFE *Elem. Sound Recording* xxix. 580 The recording material first passes over an erasing magnet or head to eliminate any previous recording. **1950** G. A. BRIGGS *Sound Reprod.* (ed. 2) xx. 139 A combined head for recording, reproducing and erasing has been designed. *Ibid.*, The operations of erasing and re-recording are likely to be carried out only at infrequent intervals. **1959** W. S. SHARPS *Dict. Cinemat.* 94/1 An erasing head is a device for obliterating any previous recordings on magnetic media. **1960** H. CARTER *Dict. Electronics* 94 *Erasing*, the process of demagnetizing the tape used in a tape recorder.

erasion (ɪˈreɪʒən). *rare.* [n. of action f. L. *ērās-*: see ERASE and -ION[1].] **a.** The action of erasing; **b.** an instance of it.

1790 PORSON *Lett. to Travis* 388 Such a piece of fraud as the erasion of the three witnesses. **1886** *Athenæum* 11 Sep. 334 A freer use of erasion in quoting from local reports is strongly recommended. **1889** *Catholic Union Gaz.* Dec. 96 The rules revised, in which occur the erasions we complain of.

eˈrasive, *a. rare*[−1]. [f. as ERASE + -IVE.] That tends to erase or obliterate.

1657 TOMLINSON *Renou's Disp.* 298 A cyperus, which..is erasive, if illited on a place.

Erasmian (ɪˈræzmɪən), *a.* and *sb.* [f. *Erasm-us* the literary name of an eminent scholar of the 16th c. + -IAN.]

A. *adj.* Pertaining to, or after the manner of, Erasmus.

1881 POTTER in *Critic* 10 Sept. 240 Daudet listened to Erasmian stories while the mistral rushed howling through the belfry.

B. *sb.* A follower of Erasmus; one who holds the views of Erasmus. **b.** One who follows the system of ancient Greek pronunciation advocated by Erasmus: opposed to *Reuchlinian*.

1883 A. F. MITCHELL in Schaff *Encycl. Relig. Knowl.* II. 935 At this date he [Patrick Hamilton] was probably more of an Erasmian than a Lutheran.

Hence **Eˈrasmianism**, the doctrines or religious system of Erasmus.

1758 JORTIN *Erasm.* I. 616 Here and there he smells a little of Erasmianism.

erast, obs. form of ERST.

Erastian (ɪˈræstɪən), *a.* and *sb.* [f. *Erast-us* + -IAN.]

A. *adj.* Of or pertaining to Erastus or his doctrines, characterized by or embodying the tenets attributed to Erastus.

Erastus, or Liebler, was a physician of Heidelberg in the 16th cent., to whom has been attributed the theory of State supremacy in ecclesiastical affairs. His actual efforts were mainly directed against the use of excommunication, which was exercised tyrannically by the Calvinistic churches.

1837–9 HALLAM *Hist. Lit.* III. ii. §49 This is the full development of an Erastian theory. **1865** *Englishm. Mag.* Jan. 14 The predominance of the wordly and Erastian element in the Church consequent on the secession of the Non-jurors. **1876** GLADSTONE in *Contemp. Rev.* June 4, I take no notice of the system termed Erastian.

B. *sb.* An adherent of the (supposed) doctrines of Erastus; one who maintains the complete subordination of the ecclesiastical to the secular power.

1651 BAXTER *Inf. Bapt.* 228 He was far from being an Erastian. **1661** *Serm. Coronat. Chas. II* in *Phenix* I. 256 Erastians are more dangerous Snares to Kings than Sectaries..and are Great Enemies to Presbyterian Government. **1721–1800** in BAILEY. **1876** GLADSTONE in *Contemp. Rev.* June 4 Many most respectable persons have been..Erastians.

Hence **Eˈrastianism**, the theory or system of Erastus. **Eˈrastianize** *v.* (*a*) *trans.* To organize (a church) on Erastian principles. (*b*) *intr.* To incline to Erastian principles. **Eˈrastianizing** *ppl. a.*

1681 BAXTER *Acc. Sherlocke* iii. 181 Many were inclined to Erastianism hereby. **1761–2** HUME *Hist. Eng.* (1806) V. lxvi. 49 Their submission..was stigmatised as erastianism. **1856** FROUDE *Hist. Eng.* II. 309 The theory of an Anglican Erastianism found favour with some of the higher church dignitaries. **1850** J. H. NEWMAN *Diffic. Anglic.* 153 Its Erastianizing Bishops.

erasure (ɪˈreɪʒə(r)). [f. as ERASE + -URE.]

1. a. The action of erasing or obliterating.

1755 YOUNG *Centaur* vi. Wks. 1757 IV. 277 The desperate erasure of his Christian name. **1817** W. SELWYN *Law Nisi Prius* II. 825 The devise to the trustees was not revoked by the erasure. **1836** J. GILBERT *Chr. Atonem.* ii. (1852) 31 To select a part [of a book] which we may happen to approve, and by evasive arts to effect the erasure of the other part. **1861** MAY *Const. Hist.* (1863) I. i. 24 The erasure of his name from the list of privy councillors.

b. An instance of erasing or obliterating.

1734 tr. *Rollin's Anc. Hist.* (1827) I. II. 239 A good performance is not to be expected without many erasures and corrections. **1817** COLERIDGE *Biog. Lit.* 183 If the number of these fancied erasures did not startle him. **1858** LD. ST. LEONARDS *Handy Bk. Prop. Law* xix. 146 The

erasure was not made by the testator with an intention to revoke his will.

c. *Electr.* = ERASING *vbl. sb.* c.

1950 G. A. BRIGGS *Sound Reproduction* (ed. 2) xx. 139 Thorough erasure of the tape or wire is necessary before it passes over the recording head. **1962** A. NISBETT *Technique Sound Studio* 252 *Erasure*, the removal of recorded signals from a tape so that it is ready to re-use. **1967** *Electronics* 6 Mar. 79/2 (Advt.), Complete, gradual or selective erasure is possible.

2. *concr.* The place where a word or letter has been erased or obliterated.

a **1891** *Mod.* The word was written over an erasure.

3. Total destruction; 'wiping out'. *rare.*

a **1794** GIBBON (O.), Erasure of cities. **1851** D. WILSON *Preh. Ann.* II. IV. iv. 267 Repeated destruction of the settlements and erasure of the accompanying progress of arts.

erayne, var. of ARAIN, *Obs.*, spider.

erbage, erbare, obs. ff. HERBAGE, ARBOUR.

erbbe, erbe, obs. forms of HERB.

erber, early form of ARBER, *Obs.*

erber, obs. form of ARBOUR.

erbia ('ɜːbɪə). *Chem.* [mod.Lat., f. last two syllables of *Ytterby*, the locality of gadolinite, in which it occurs.] One of the three earths formerly confounded under the general name YTTRIA.

1869 'URBAN' in *Eng. Mech.* 10 Dec. 303/3 Erbia..is a brown powder, discovered by Mosander, 25 years back, in gadolinite. **1873** WATTS *Fownes' Chem.* 382 Erbia, obtained by ignition of erbium nitrate or oxalate, has a faint rose colour.

erbigage, obs. form of HARBOURAGE.

erbium ('ɜːbɪəm). [mod.Lat., f. ERBIA, as *sodium* f. *soda*, etc.] The metallic radical of erbia.

1843 *Chemist* I. 446 [Mosander's] close examination of Yttria has led him to discover..two oxides, to which he has given the names terbium and erbium. **1873** WATTS *Fownes' Chem.* 382 Erbium and yttrium, are again precipitated by oxalic acid.

erbswurst ('ɜːbzwɜːst). [G.] Seasoned pease-flour compressed into sausage shape and used for making soup (see also quot. 1885).

1885 J. NIXON *Compl. Story Transvaal* x. 180 Twice a week we had 'erbswurst', or dried beans. **1890** KIPLING *Life's Handicap* (1891) 36 Erbswurst, tinned beef..and meat-biscuits may be nourishing but,..Thomas Atkins needs..bulk. **1913** W. LEE WHITE in F. H. Harris *Dartmouth out o' Doors* 117 With erbswurst and beef tablets for a base [of a soup]. **1941** V. NABOKOV in *Atlantic Monthly* Nov. 619/2 This churlish, heavy man, who fed mainly on *Erbswurst* and boiled potatoes.

ercebishop, -dekne, obs. ff. ARCHBISHOP, -DEACON.

erch, *v.*[1] *Obs.*, var. *ergh*, ARGH *v. Sc.* to be unwilling, hesitate.

1584 J. CARMICHAEL *Lett.* in *Wodr. Soc. Misc.* (1844) 428 Paul Methven heard him, and came not to the ministers while Thursday at morn, and erched to tell them that.

†**erch**, *v.*[2] *Obs. rare*⁻¹.

1601 HOLLAND *Pliny* IX. xx. I. 247 Lampries..erch forward like as Serpents doe vpon the earth.

erche-, obs. form of ARCH-.

†**erche'vesque.** *Obs. rare*⁻¹. [a. OF. *archevesque* (mod.F. *archevêque*), repr. late L. *archiepiscopus*.] = ARCHBISHOP.

?*a* **1400** *Morte Arth.* 67 At Carlelele a Cristynmese he haldes..Wyth erles and ercheuesqes and other ynowe.

Ercles ('ɜːkliːz), Bottom's pronunciation of 'Hercules'; 'Ercles vein' is a stock quotation. (See *Mids. N.D.* I. ii. 31, 42.)

1898 G. F. R. HENDERSON *Stonewall Jackson* II. xv. 100 Even the Northern press made sport of Pope's "Ercles vein', and the Confederates contrasted his noisy declamation with the modesty of Lee and Jackson. **1901** *Standard* 9 Apr. 4/7 Mr. J. B. Glacier, in his opening speech, was in the Ercles vein, and dwelt on perils overcome and triumphs gained. **1922** J. BUCHAN *Huntingtower* ii. 36 The Ercles vein—'God's in His Heaven, all's right with the world.' No good, Mr McCunn. **1927** T. S. ELIOT in T. Newton tr. *Seneca's Trag.* I. p. xxxiii, This is the proper Ercles bombast, ridiculed by Shakespeare, Jonson, and Nashe.

†**erd**, *sb. Obs.* Forms: 1–2 **eard**, 2–4 **erd(e**, 3 **ærd, ard, eærd**, 3–4 **herd**, 4 **ertd**. [OE. *eard* masc. is cogn. w. OS. *ard* masc. 'dwelling', OHG. *art* fem. 'ploughing', ON. *örð* fem. 'harvest':—OTeut. **ardu-z, ardâ*, prob. f. WAryan root **ar* to plough. For the sense cf. OE. *búan* to cultivate, inhabit.]

1. The land where one dwells; native land, home; a region, country.

Beowulf 2654 (Gr.) We rondas beren eft to earde. *c* **1000** *Ags. Ps.* ciii. 11 [civ. 12] (Gr.) Ofer þan heofonfuȝelas healdað eardas. *c* **1175** *Lamb. Hom.* 13 Eower burh heo forbernað..and eard heo amerrað. *c* **1205** LAY. 29175 Inne France wes his ærd. *c* **1250** *Gen. & Ex.* 210 Paradis, An erd al ful of swete blis. *a* **1300** *Cursor M.* 12382 (Cott.) Til þai had geten þair herd a-gain. *c* **1340** *Gaw. & Gr. Knt.* 1808, I am here [on] an erande in erdez vncouþe.

2. In OE.: ? State, condition. Hence (in ME.), disposition, temper.

With the ME. use cf. MHG. *art* masc., fem., mod.G. *art* fem. 'manner, disposition', which, however, Kluge regards as prob. of distinct etymology.

a **1000** *Hymns* vii. 97 (Gr.) þar man us tyhhað on dæg tweȝen eardas. Drihtenes ær oðð e deofles þeowet. *c* **1314** *Guy Warw.* (A.) 2988 Wiþ þat come forþ an amireld, A Sarrazin of wicked erd. *c* **1340** *Cursor M.* 11973 (Fairf.) Ihesus þat was meke of erde kepped noȝt to make his moder ferde.

3. *Comb.* †**erd-folk**, people of the land.

c **1250** *Gen. & Ex.* 1880 God sente on ðat erdfolc swilc dred.

erd(e, etc., obs. forms of EARTH, etc.

†'**erde**, *v. Obs.* Forms: 1 **eardian**, 2–3 **erde(n**. [OE. *eardian* (= OHG. *artôn* to inhabit), f. *eard*, ERD *sb.*]

1. *intr.* To dwell, live.

c **893** K. ÆLFRED *Oros.* I. i. 18 On þæm morum eardiað Finnas. *c* **1000** *Ags. Gosp.* Matt. ii. 23 And he com þa and eardode on þære ceastre ðe is ȝenemned nazareth. *c* **1175** *Lamb. Hom.* 89 Trowfeste men of elchere þeode þet under heofene erdeden. *c* **1230** *Hali Meid.* 43 Ha ne muhen nawt somen earden in heuene. *a* **1300** *E.E. Psalter* xxi. 4 [xxii. 3] þou soth-lik in haligh wel Erdest, loof of Israel. *c* **1400** *Destr. Troy* 4233 To the yle þere Appolyn erdis with in.

b. To be or to be found; to exist in a certain place, or in a certain condition.

c **1400** *Destr. Troy* 923 þis stone..Is erdand in Judé. *Ibid.* 7128 Folk..entryd full Esely, erdyng in sorow.

2. *trans.* To inhabit.

Beowulf 2590 (Gr.) Se mæra maȝa Ecȝðeowes sceolde..wic eardian elles hwerȝen. *a* **1300** *E.E. Psalter* xxiv. [xv.] 13 His sede erde þe land sal swa.

erdene, obs. form of ERRAND.

†'**erding**, *sb. Obs.* Also 1 **earding**. [f. ERDE *v.* + -ING[1].] Abode, dwelling. Also in *comb.* **erding-stow**, dwelling-place.

a **1000** *Ags. Ps.* cvi. 3 [cvii. 4] (Gr.) Ne meahton ceastre weȝ cuðne mittan, þe hi eardunge on ȝenaman. *c* **1000** *Ags. Gosp.* Matt. xvii. 4 Drihten..ȝyf þu wylt, uton wyrcean her þreo eardung-stowa. *c* **1200** *Trin. Coll. Hom.* 159 Ure louerd iesu crist giue hem..echeliche erding and blisse on heuene. *a* **1250** *Owl & Night.* 28 On old stoc..was thare ule earding-stowe.

erdne, obs. form of ERRAND.

ere, *sb. pseudo-arch. rare*⁻¹. (See quot.)

1866 SIR G. W. DASENT *Gisli* 23 They went out of their booth to the point of the 'ere' [*footnote*, 'Ere' old English for a sandy spit of land; from the Icelandic eyri].

ere (ɛə(r)), *adv.*, *prep.* and *conj.* Forms: α. 1–3 **ær**, (3 **ære**), 1–6 **er**, 3–4 **her**, (3 **heer**), 4–5 **eer(e**, (3 **eær**, 4 **eir**, 5 **eyer**), 2–6 **ear(e**, 8–9 *Sc.* **ear**, 3–6 **ar(e**, 4 **aar**, 4–5 **ayr(e**, 4–9 *Sc.* **air(e** (see AIR *adv.*), (8 *erron.* **e'er**), 4– **ere**. β. 3–7 (9 *arch.*) **or**, 3–5 **ore**. γ. 4–5 **ȝer(e**, 6–7 **yeer**, **yer**. [OE. *ǽr*, corresp. to OFris., OS. *êr* (MDu. *eer*, *êre*, *ee*, Du. *eer*), OHG. *êr* (MHG. *êr*, *ê*, mod.G. *eher*, *ehe*), Goth. *airis*:—OTeut. **airiz*, compar. degree of **air* (Goth. *air*, ON. *ár*) adv., early. Some have suggested ultimate connexion with Gr. ἠρι- early in the morning. See also ERER and ERST.

The ME. spellings *ar(e* and *or(e* partly represent ON. *ár* (or an unrecorded OE. **ár* without umlaut), and partly arise from *ǽr* through loss of stress.]

A. *adv.*

1. Used as positive. **a.** in OE. (late WS.): Early, at an early hour; **b.** since 15th c. only *Sc.* (forms *air*, *ear*): Early, soon: opposed to *late*.

a **1000** *Guthlac* 816 (Gr.) Hy to ær aþreat, þæt hy waldendes willan læsten. *c* **1000** *Ags. Gosp.* Mark xvi. 2 And swyðe ær anum reste-dæȝe comon to þære byrȝene. *c* **1200** ORMIN 6246 Beon ar & late o ȝunnkerr weorrc. *c* **1225** *Ancr. R.* 338 Ich hit do ungledliche, oðer to er, oðer to leate. *a* **1340** *Cursor M.* 25419 (Gött.) Are and late i will ȝu mon. *c* **1425** WYNTOUN *Cron.* VII. xxxiii. 143 Come I are; come I late. **1474** in *Househ. Ord.* (1790) 28 To be ere at his supper. **1578** *Scot. Poems 16th C.* II. 152 Thow art keiper lait and aire. **1795** MACNEILL *Will & Jean*, Baith ear' and late, Will in briny grief lay steeping. **1879** G. MACDONALD *Sir Gibbie* I. iv. 46 'Ye michtna be up ear eneuch to get yer-self shaved afore kirktime.'

†**2.** Sooner, at an earlier time. *Obs.*

α. *a* **900** *Charters* in *O.E. Texts* 445 Gif he ȝewite er ðonne hia. *c* **1000** *Ags. Gosp.* John i. 15 Se ðe to cumenne is æfter me..wæs ær þonne ic. *c* **1400** *Ywaine & Gaw.* 1061 Bitwene this and the thrid night, And ar if that it are myght be. **1465** *Paston Lett.* No. 518 II. 218, I received the box..on Friday last and non er. *c* **1650** *Merlin* 2094 in Furniv. *Percy Folio* I. 487, & thou had comen eare, indeed, thou might haue found him in that stead.

β. **1526** TINDALE *John* i. 15 He that commeth after me, was before me because he was yer than I.

†**3.** Sooner, rather, in preference. *Obs.*

α. *c* **1200** [see C 2].

β. *c* **1300** [see C 2].

γ. *a* **1536** TINDALE *Wks.* II. 235 The flesh..would be exalted and lift up on high, yer than cast down.

†**4.** Before, formerly, at a former time, on a former occasion; often preceded by *ever*, *never*. Also, A little while ago, just now.

α. *c* **825** *Vesp. Hymns* in *O.E. Texts* 419 Ðæt mon ðu alesdes ðone ær soðlice ȝehiowades. *a* **900** *Martyrol.* ibid. 178 Fyr of heofonum..forbernde..alle ða ðe..ær tintersȝedon ðone halȝan wer. *a* **1000** *Elene* 1285 Worda..eallra unsnyttro ær ȝesprecenra. *a* **1123** *O.E. Chron.* an. 1101 And þæt ealle þa on Engle lande heora land onȝean heafdon, þe hit ær þurh þone eorl forluron. *c* **1175** *Lamb. Hom.* 5 Ȝe iherden er on þe godspel hu, etc. *c* **1200** ORMIN 2349 Forr nass þat næfre fundenn æ r Amang wimmenn onn erþe. *c* **1275** LAY. 6626 Ne cnew hine no man þat hine heer hi-sehȝe hadde. *c* **1300** *Harrow. Hell* 222 That y seyde er the to. **1375** BARBOUR *Bruce* IX. 442 Thai..war eir pouer and bare. *c* **1430** *Pilgr. Lyf Manhode* I. c. (1869) 54, I se blood shed on þe scrippe þat neuere er j apperceyuede. **15..** *Kyng & Hermit* 40 in Hazl. *E.P.P.* (1864) 14 Sych one saw I never are. **1557** *Myliner of Abyngton* 82 ibid. III. 103 He myght not do as he dyd are. **1647** R. STAPYLTON *Juvenal* 259 A beane-hull, ere the praise of all The neigh'bring village.

β. *c* **1340** *Cursor M.* 1402 (Trin.) þo he [Adam] lowȝe but neuer ore. *Ibid.* 12147 (Trin.) Ȝe wondir on þat I seide ore. **15..** *Childe of Bristowe* 342 in Hazl. *E.P.P.* I. 123 Into the chamber he went that tide, and knelid, as he dud ore.

γ. *c* **1420** *Chron. Vilod.* 147 By conselle of Elmestone as I sayde ȝere. *c* **1450** *Guy Warw.* (C.) 60 Soche a mayde was neuer ȝere. *a* **1612** HARINGTON *Epigrams* III. (1633) 42 Chaste Linus, but as valiant as a gander, Came to me yer,..Lamenting that I raised on him a slander.

b. First; before something else, or before anything else is done.

α. *c* **1000** *Ags. Gosp.* Matt. v. 24 Gang ær and ȝesybsuma wið þinne broðer.

β. *c* **1250** *Gen. & Ex.* 88 Fro ðat time we tellen ay, Or ðe niȝt and after ðe day. *c* **1300** *Havelok* 728 But or he hauede michel shame.

B. *prep.*

1. Before (in time). Also in *comb.* †**ere-yesterday**, the day before yesterday.

α. ?*a* **735** (*MS. a* **900**) *Bede's Death Song* ibid. 149 Aer his hin iongae. *c* **825** *Vesp. Psalter* liv. 20 [lv. 19] in *O.E. Texts* 263 God..se is ær weorulde and wunað in ecnisse. *c* **1000** *Ags. Gosp.* Matt. xxiv. 38 Swa hi wærun on þam daȝum ær þam flode. *c* **1175** *Lamb. Hom.* 17 þet he icherre from þan uuelnesse ear his ende dei. *a* **1300** *Cursor M.* 11383 (Gött.), A tuelmoth are þe natiuite. *c* **1300** *K. Alis.* 344 Aboute mydnyght, ar the day..Scheo saw..a dragon adoun lyght. **1413** LYDG. *Pilgr. Sowle* IV. xxii. (1483) 69 Yf thou er this tyme haddest done right. **1465** *Paston Lett.* No. 505 II. 194 Yf ye send to me contrary comaundement er that tyme. **1583** GOLDING *Calvin on Deut.* clxxiii. 1076 Ere three dayes to an end he had quite forgotten. **1647** CLARENDON *Hist. Reb.* (1702) I. v. 456 E're that time. **1649** LOVELACE *Poems* 22 Could you ascend yon Chaire of State e're him? **1678** DRYDEN *All for Love* I. i, Our fruitful Nile Flow'd ere the wonted Season. **1819** BYRON *Juan* I. i, Sent to the devil somewhat ere his time. **1884** W. C. SMITH *Kildrostan* 45 He Nigh lost his wits ere morning.

β. *c* **1250** *Gen. & Ex.* 47 Or ani werldes time boren. *c* **1400** *Destr. Troy* 114 A broþer of birþe born or hym-seluyn. **1439** R. ROCHEFORT in *E.E. Wills* (1883) 123 If..Margarete his wyff decesse or tyme Rauf his son comme at full age. *a* **1533** LD. BERNERS *Huon* lxxxvi. 273 Though he haue or this tym sufferyd greate trauayle.

γ. *c* **1430** *Freemasonry* 160 Ȝe mowe hyt knowe long ȝer nyȝht. **1535** COVERDALE *Gen.* xxxi. 2 And Iacob behelde Labans countenaunce, & beholde, it was not towarde him as yesterdaye and yeryesterdaye.

b. In preference to, more than.

β. **1377** LANGL. *P. Pl.* B. xv. 502 þe red noble Is reuerenced or þe Rode.

2. In the advb. phrases †*ere þon*, *ere then*, *ere this*, etc. (OE. *ǽr ðon*, *ǽr ðissum*), before then, before this. Also ERELONG, ERENOW, EREWHILE.

α. *c* **897** K. ÆLFRED *Gregory's Past.* 7 Sio lar Lædenȝeðiodes ær ðissum afeallen wæs ȝiond Angelcynn. *c* **1175** *Lamb. Hom.* 3 Moni of þan floc manna þe earþon fulieden ure drihten. *Ibid.* 11 We maȝen..ibeten ure sunne þet we abbet idon erþisse. **1297** R. GLOUC. (1724) 501 Thou sedest vs ar this The priuete of thin herte. *c* **1315** SHOREHAM 121 Thet unicorn..That erthange [*read* erthanne] was so wylde. *c* **1340** *Cursor M.* 9830 (Trin.), More selcouþe herde we neuer ar þis. *c* **1430** *Chev. Assigne* 70 As I haue holde her er þis 'our lorde so me helpe'. **1594** PLAT *Jewell-ho.* I. 59 We should haue had a sufficient ear this. **1667** MILTON *P.L.* IV. 970 Ere then Farr heavier load thyself expect to feel. *Ibid.* x. 240 If mishap [had attended him], Ere this he had return'd. **1776** GIBBON *Misc. Wks.* (1814) II. 173 You have ere this heard of the..accident. **1826** SCOTT *Woodst.* ii, I trust the King is ere this out of their reach. **1884** PAE *Eustace* 28, I should ere this have shaped into words the warm affection which..existed in my heart.

γ. **1598** HAKLUYT *Voy.* I. 6 They might very well, yer this, haue surpassed..any particular Monarchie els.

C. *conj.* (or as part of conjunctional phrase).

1. Of time: Before.

†**a.** in conjunctional phrases, consisting (*a*) of the adv. with *than*; (*b*) of the prep. with pronominal regimen (OE. and early ME. *þam þe*, *þon þe*, *þam*, *þan*, *þon*; subsequently *that*). *Obs.*

α. *a* **1000** *Judith* 252 in Sweet *Ags. Rdr.* (1884) 165 Ær ðon ðe him se eȝesa on ufan sæte Mæȝen Ebrea. *a* **1000** *Happy Land* 38 ibid. 170 Næfre brosniað Leaf under lyfte..ær ðon edwenden Worulde ȝeweorðe. *c* **1000** *Ags. Gosp.* Matt. v. 18 An prica ne ȝewit fram þære æ ærþam [*c* **1160** *Hatton* ær þan] ealle þing ȝewurþan. *Ibid.* vi. 8 Eower fæder wat hwæt eow þearf ys ær þam þe ȝe hyne biddað. *c* **1200** ORMIN 9351 Ær þann þe Laferrd Jesu Crist Bigann owwþerr to donne. *c* **1200** *Trin. Coll. Hom.* 37 Er þonne þet child beo ifulȝed hit is þes deofles. *a* **1225** *Ancr. R.* 296 Cwench hit..er þen hit waxe. *c* **1290** *Lives Saints* (1887) 52 Are þat heo were ded. *a* **1300** *Havelok* 229 'In manus tuas, lou[er]de, ' he seyde, Her þat he þe speche leyde. *c* **1325** *Chron. Eng.* in Ritson *Met. Rom.* II. 270 This lond wes cleped Albyon, Er then Bruyt from Troye com. *c* **1386** CHAUCER *Frankl. T.* 895 Now telleth me er that ye ferther wende. **1483** *Vulgaria abs Terentio* 24 a, Night cam vpon me er than j myght com hydere a geyne. **1559** BALDWIN in *Mirr. for Mag.* (1563) H i a, Wherof she warnd prepared a myghty power, And ere that myne were altogether redy, Came swyft to Sandale and besieged my bower.

β. *c* **1250** *Gen. & Ex.* 2435 Or ðan he [Abraham] wiste off werlde faren, He bade hise kinde to him charen.

γ. **1526** TINDALE *Gal.* ii. 12 Yerre that certayne cam from James he [Peter] ate with the Gentyls.

b. hence as simple *conj. arch.* and *dial.*

α. *Beowulf* 2019 (Gr.) Oft hio beah wriðan secʒe [sealde] ær hie to setle ʒeong. **971** *Blickl. Hom.* 47 On niht ær he ræste. *c* **1175** *Lamb. Hom.* 9 Heo weren strongliche ibunden er ure drihten come to þisse liue. *a* **1225** *Leg. Kath.* 1393 To beon i-fulhtnet..ear we faren henne. **1340** HAMPOLE *Pr. Consc.* 1051 Bot of þe mare world yhit wil I mare say, Ar I pas fra þis matir away. **1393** LANGL. *P. Pl.* C. IV. 303 Thei asken hure hyure er þey hit haue deserued. **1430** LYDG. *Chron. Troy* I. v, Ar Titan his bemes reyse agayne We shall departe. **1483** *Act I Rich. III*, c. 8 Pream., Clothes so shorn er they be wette. **1581** MULCASTER *Positions* xxxiv. (1887) 122 Ear they entered into their exercise, and..ear they went to meat. **1611** BIBLE *John* iv. 49 The noble man saith vnto him, Syr, come downe ere my child die. **1664** EVELYN *Kal. Hort.* (1729) 190 It will be a long Time e'er your Graff produce any Fruits considerable. **1762–71** H. WALPOLE *Vertue's Anecd. Paint.* (1786) IV. 76 These promising abilities were cut off e'er they had reached their maturity. **1810** SCOTT *Lady of L.* I. ii, Ere his fleet career he took, The dew-drops from his flanks he shook. **1870** E. PEACOCK *Ralf Skirl.* II. 22 It was very late ere the party broke up.

β. *c* **1250** *Gen. & Ex.* 649 Or he [noe] was on werlde led, His kinde was wel wide spred. *c* **1340** *Cursor M.* 710 (Fairf.) Al þinges..ware of gretter strenȝt and piþ, or adam had fordone þe griþ. **1476** *Paston Lett.* No. 771 III. 152, iiij howrs or he dyed. *c* **1570** *Moral Play Wit & Sc.* (Shaks. Soc.) 3 Wherfore, or I pas hens, now must I See thys same token heere. [Still very common *dial.*]

γ. **1526** TINDALE *Rom.* ix. 11 Yeer the children were borne. **1563–87** FOXE *A. & M.* (1596) 109/1 The king laie after long sicke yer he were healed. **1609** HOLLAND *Amm. Marcel.* xxx. i. 379 He might be intercepted yer he was aware.

†**c.** with a redundant *ere* (in sense A. 4 b), or some equivalent word, belonging to the principal clause, though occasionally standing in the subordinate.

α. *c* **1200** ORMIN 12694 Ær þann þe Laferrd fullhtnedd wass Ær wass he wunedd offte To cumenn till þe flumm. **1297** R. GLOUC. (1724) 207 Ar hii come vpe þys hul, arst he wass ycome. *a* **1300** *K. Horn* 546 Mid spere ischal furst ride ..Ar ihc þe ginne to woȝe. **1377** LANGL. *P. Pl.* B. v. 468, I shal seke treuthe arst ar I se Rome!

β. *c* **1250** *Gen. & Ex.* 658 Nine hundred ȝer and fifti told, or or he starf, noe was old. *c* **1330** R. BRUNNE *Chron.* (1810) 74 Or Roberd wist, or þouht on suilk a dede, Ore was his hous on fire. *c* **1400** MAUNDEV. (1839) viii. 83 Before or þei resceyue hem, þei knelen doun. *c* **1460** *Towneley Myst.* 131 Myn dede ere shuld I dyght, Or it were so.

d. with the addition of *ever*.

α. *c* **1325** *E.E. Allit. P.* A. 328 Schal I efte forgo hit er euer I fyne? **1529** MORE *Comf. agst. Trib.* III. Wks. 1212/2 Before a gret storm the sea begynneth..to worke..ere euer the windes waxe boistous. *c* **1630** DRUMM. OF HAWTH. *Poems* Wks. 12 Er e're she was, weep that day's wheel was roll'd.

β. **1605** SHAKS. *Lear* II. iv. 289 This heart shal break into a hundred thousand flawes Or ere Ile weepe. **1611** BIBLE *Dan.* vi. 24 The Lyons..brake all their bones in pieces or euer they came at the bottome of the den. **1883** SWINBURNE *Cent. Roundels* 23 These, or ever man was, were.

2. Of preference: Sooner than, rather than. Sometimes with correlative adv. as in 1 c.

α. *Beowulf* 1371 (Gr.) Ær he [*sc.* heorot] feorh seleð..on ofre, ær he in wille hafelan [hydan]. *c* **1200** ORMIN 6316 Forr ær þeȝȝ wolldenn þolenn dæþ Ær þann þeȝȝ wolldenn gilltenn ohht Onnȝæness Godess wille. *c* **1230** *Hali Meid.* 45 Hu ha..þoleden stronge pines ear ha walden nimen ham. *c* **1330** *King of Tars* 44 Rather wolde i spille my blod..Ar heo scholde wedde a Sarazyn. **1393** LANGL. *P. Pl.* C. IV. 157 Er ich wedde such a wif, wo me by-tyde.

β. *a* **1300** *Cursor M.* 9815 (Gött.) Or aght his herte brest o thrinne, Or fra his comandementis tuinne. **1375** BARBOUR *Bruce* IX. 594 In auenture till de He vald him put, or he vald fle.

†**D.** *adj.* Only in late OE. and ME.

1. The compounds in which OE. *ǽr-* has an adjectival force = 'early', 'former' (see E. 1) were occasionally resolved, so that the first element was treated as a real adj., and inflected as such. For examples see E. 1.

2. Hence, rarely, the adjectival use occurs where it does not originate directly from composition.

a **1400** *Isumbras* 520 To mende hir are mysdede.

E. *Comb.*

1. With adjectival force, as OE. **ǽrdæʒ** (see DAY), early day, beginning of the day, also pl. *ǽrdaʒas* (in ME. as phrase ***are dawes***), former days; OE. **ǽrdǽd** (see DEED), in ME. *erdede*, a former deed; OE. **ǽrmorʒen** (see MORN, MORROW), early morning, in phrase ***on ǽrmorʒen***, ME. *on armorowe*, also (with adjectival flexion of the first element) OE. ***on ǽrne morʒen***, ME. *on erne marȝen*, *on arnemorwe*; also ARETHEDE.

Beowulf 253 Mid *ær-dæʒe. *a* **1000** *Andreas* 220 (Gr.) Scealtu æninga mid ærdæʒe..Ceol ʒestiʒan. *a* **1000** *Hymns* iii. 25 (Gr.) þu eart se æðela, þe on ærdaʒum ealra fæmnena wyn fæʒere akende on Bethleem. *c* **1300** *Havelok* 27 It was a king bi are dawes. *c* **1000** *Ags. Gosp.* Luke xxiii. 41 And wyt witodlice be uncer *ærdædum on-foð. *c* **1200** *Trin. Coll. Hom.* 153 Ech man shal understonden mede of his er-dede. *c* **1205** LAY. 8745 Nu þu scalt adreden for þine ær dæden [*c* **1275** for þine erdede]. *a* **1400** *Octouian* 1808 Clement was made a knyght For hys er dedes. *a* **1000** *Ps.* lxii[i]. 6 (Gr.) Ic ..on *ærmerʒen on þe eac ʒewene. *c* **1000** *Ags. Gosp.* Matt. xx. 1 Gelic þam hiredes ealdre þe on ærne merʒen ut-eode. *c* **1175** *Lamb. Hom.* 115 þa aldormen etað on erne marȝen ulaȝeliche. *c* **1300** *K. Alis.* 5458 The oost arist on erne morowe. *c* **1314** *Guy Warw.* (A.) 3391 An armorwe erliche þemperour aros, sikerliche. *Ibid.* 5164 On anemorwe þan come we.

2. With prepositional force: see ERELONG, ERENOW, EREWHILE; also *ere-yesterday* in B 1.

ere, var. of EAR obs. to plough.

1621 BOLTON *Statutes Irel.* 10 Labourers..to ere the ground.

ere, obs. f. *are*: see BE *v.*; also of EVER.

'ere (ɪə(r)), *adv.* Also **ere**. Non-standard var. of HERE *adv.*

1837 [see WATER-CART b]. **1862** R. H. NEWELL *Orpheus C. Kerr Papers* 1st Ser. 231 One of the fellers on the middle seat ..when he spied them butes, he winked to me, and sung out: 'Gheewhillikins! who owns these ere big trotters?' **1886** BAUMANN *Londinismen* 49/2 This 'ere chum o' mine. **1898** G. B. SHAW *Candida* II. 114 Ow long ave you known my son-in-law James ere? **1955** 'MISS READ' *Village School* x. 85 This 'ere 'eathen-jelly..took his tracts and that round to the building site. **1976** *Daily Mirror* 17 Mar. 24/4 'Ere Wellington..a couple of weeks ago you were pluggin' St. David.

ereable, obs. form of EARABLE, arable.

†**erean**, *a.* *Obs.*$^{-0}$ [f. L. *ære-us* brazen (f. *æs, æris* brass) + -AN.] Made of brass or copper, brazen.

1656–81 in BLOUNT. **1775** in ASH.

erear, var. of AREAR *v.* *Obs.*

Erebus ('ɛrɪbəs). *Myth.* Also 6 erron. **erobus.** [a. L. *Erebus*, a. Gr. Ἔρεβος; ? cogn. with Goth. *riqis* darkness.] The proper name of 'a place of darkness, between Earth and Hades' (Liddell and Scott); often used in phrase ***dark as Erebus***.

1596 SHAKS. *Merch. V.* v. i. 87 His affections [are] darke as Erobus. **1667** MILTON *P.L.* II. 883 Harsh Thunder..the lowest bottom shook Of Erebus. **1839** MARRYAT *Phant. Ship* x, The night was dark as Erebus.

Comb. **1815** *Scribbleomania* 169 The pow'r that impell'd thee was Erebus bred.

erect (ɪ'rɛkt), *a.* and *sb.* [ad. L. *ērect-us*, pa. pple. of *ērigĕre* to set up, f. *ē* out + *regĕre* to direct.]

A. *adj.*

1. Upright, in an upright posture; not bending forward or downward. Of straight lines and plane surfaces: Vertical. ***erect vision***, the fact that we see objects 'the right way up', notwithstanding the inverted position of the retinal image. ***erect dial***: see DIAL.

c **1386** CHAUCER *Man of Law's T.* 9 The schade of every tree Was in the lengthe the same quantite That was the body erecte, that caused it. **1514** BARCLAY *Cyt. & Uplondyshm.* (Percy Soc.) p. lvi, Whether that thy lord sit or yet stande erect Stil must thou stande. **1593** FALE *Dialling* 3 When the plat standeth upright, it maketh a right angle with the Horizon and is called Erect. **1646** SIR T. BROWNE *Pseud. Ep.* IV. i. 180 Birds..are so farre from this kinde of pronenesse, that they are almost erect. **1697** DRYDEN *Virg. Georg.* III. 666 A Snake..in his Summer Liv'ry rouls along: Erect, and brandishing his forky Tongue. **1726** tr. *Gregory's Astron.* I. 362 The erect or vertical Diameter of the Luminary seems contracted. **1799** J. WOOD *Elem. Optics* vii. (1811) 148 An erect image of the figure intended to be represented. **1841** BREWSTER *Mart. Sc.* III. ii. (1856) 184 He ascribed erect vision to an operation of the mind. **1863** FR. KEMBLE *Resid. Georgia* 42 The figures of some of the women are handsome ..erect and good. **1872** BLACKIE *Lays Highl.* 89 Erect with majesty severe The Buchail More upshoots his Titan cone.

b. Used *Bot.* and *Her.* in general sense.

1688 R. HOLME *Armoury* II. 115/1 Erect Flowers [are] such as grow upright without hanging the head. **1766–87** PORNY *Heraldry* Gloss., *Erect or Erected*.. said of any-thing upright, or perpendicularly elevated. **1811** A. T. THOMSON *Lond. Disp.* (1818) 256 The stamens are erect, and longer than the corolla. **1880** GRAY *Struct. Bot.* vi. §8. 277 Ovules are erect, when they rise from the very bottom of the cell. **1882** CUSSANS *Heraldry* vi. 95 Erect, when used in blazoning wings, signifies that the principal wing feathers make nearly a right angle with the back of the bird.

c. *fig.*

1672 CAVE *Prim. Chr.* II. vii. (1673) 195 A mind erect amongst the Ruines of a tottering Age. *a* **1735** GLANVILLE (J.), Stand erect, and sound as loud as fame. **1837** THIRLWALL *Greece* IV. xxxiii. 321 A spirit as erect as the king's tiara. **1878** MORLEY *Carlyle* 175 Here was a way of erect living within.

2. Chiefly participial: †**a.** Of the countenance: Not downcast, unabashed. *Obs.* **b.** Of the hands: Uplifted. **c.** Of the hair, tail of animals, etc.: Set up, rigid, bristling.

1618 CHAPMAN *Hesiod.* II. 542 Not..with face erect, Against the Sun, but, sitting. **1687** DRYDEN *Hind & P.* I. 394 Her front erect with majesty she bore. **17..** PHILIPS (J.), Vows, and plaints, and suppliant hands to Heav'n erect. **1735** SOMERVILLE *Chase* II. 91 With Ears And Tail erect, neighing he paws the ground. **1796** BURKE *Regic. Peace* Wks. 1842 II. 326 It is an erect countenance, it is a firm adherence to principle..that assert our good faith and honour. **1870** BRYANT *Iliad* II. XXIV. 403 With hair erect He stood, and motionless.

†**3.** *fig.* Of the mind: Uplifted, directed upwards; alert, attentive. *Obs.*

1544 *Litany* in *Priv. Prayers* (1851) 570 Having their minds erect to Almighty God. **1626** BACON *Sylva* (1637) §266 It conduceth much to haue the Sense Intentiue, and Erect. **1756** BURKE *Subl. & B.* I. xv, Just at the moment when their minds are erect with expectation.

†**B.** *sb.* *Obs. rare.*

In order to facilitate the attainment of uniformity in type-founding, Moxon proposed to divide the square of the height of each kind of type into smaller squares by 42 vertical lines (*erects*) and 42 horizontal lines (*parallels*).

1676 MOXON *Print Lett.* 7 The Divisions that are imagined to be made between the Left Hand and the Right are called Erects. *Ibid.* 20 Set your Compasses to 9..placing one Foot in Parallel 21, Erect 9.

erect (ɪ'rɛkt), *v.* Also 6 *Sc.* **ereck**, 5–6 *pa. pple.* **erect(e.** [f. L. *ērect-* ppl. stem of *ērigĕre*: see prec.]

†**I.** *trans.* To elevate in direction or position.

†**1.** To direct upwards; to lift up (the eyes, hands, etc.). Also ***to erect up***. *Obs.*

1609 *Man in Moone* (1849) 39 Erect thy countenance, like a man. **1635** PAGITT *Christianogr.* I. ii. (1636) 61 The Bishop ..erecting his hands stood all the while with his face to the Altar. *a* **1634** CHAPMAN *Revenge Hon.* Wks. 1873 III. 337 Good sir, erect your looks. **1704** SWIFT *T. Tub* Wks. 1760 I. Introd. 26 To stand with their mouths open, and erected.

fig. **1548** GEST *Pr. Masse* 117 Having our mindes erected up into heaven. **1629** H. BURTON *Babel no Bethel* 4 Wee erect our best attention to this motion. **1690** NORRIS *Beatitudes* (1694) I. 54 The Minds of Men began to be more generally erected towards Heaven.

†**b.** To put up on high; to lift up (the head); also, to hoist up. *Obs.*

1552 ABP. HAMILTON *Catech.* (1884) 52 Moyses..made & ereckit a brassin ymage of a serpent. **1567** *Trial Treas.* in Hazl. *Dodsley* III. 273 That thou are nat erected, in faith, it is pity, As high as three trees and a halter will reach. **1611** CORYAT *Crudities* 9 A little chappell..wherein is erected the picture of Christ and the Virgin Mary. **1696** TATE & BRADY *Ps.* xxiv. 7 Erect your Heads, eternal Gates. **1767** *Babler* I. 224 However we may erect the crest upon the superior dignity of manhood.

†**2.** To exalt in consideration or dignity; to raise to eminence or importance; elevate to office; in earlier use, to raise *to* (a kingdom); to set up *for*, *to be* (an emperor, king, etc.). Also ***to erect up***.

1432–50 tr. *Higden* (Rolls) I. 283 Grete Charles..was erecte to the kyngedome of Fraunce after the dethe of his fader. **1549–62** STERNHOLD & H. *Ps.* lxxxix. 20 A man of might I have erect your king and guide to be. **1583** *Exec. for Treason* (1675) 27 Bishops, who in the Popes name had erected him up. *a* **1592** GREENE *Jas. IV*, Wks. (1861) 198 He shall erect your state and wed you well. **1611** SPEED *Hist. Gt. Brit.* VI. xlii. 3 The Ægyptians erected one Saturninus a Captaine..for Emperour. *a* **1631** DONNE in *Select. fr. Donne* (1840) 16 Thou shalt find..as many records of attainted families..as of families newly erected and presently celebrated. **1656** BRAMHALL *Replic.* vi. 238 Lawfull for the King and Church of England..to have erected a new Primate. **1709** STEELE *Tatler* No. 130 ¶2 We have seen.. Monarchs erected and deposed.

†**b.** To elevate *into* or *unto* (a specified condition). *Obs.*

1508 FISHER *Wks.* 254 They were erecte vnto eternal lyfe. **1589** R. ROBINSON in Farr *S.P. Eliz.* (1845) II. 364 Erect my spirite into thy blisse.

II. To raise to an upright position.

3. To raise, set upright (the body, oneself, etc.); to rear (a standard). Also *fig.*

1573 TUSSER *Husb.* (1878) 5 Erecting one most like to fall. **1602** MARSTON *Ant. & Mel.* II. Wks. 1856 I. 25 Ladie, erect your gratious simmetry. **1646** SIR T. BROWNE *Pseud. Ep.* II. iii. 74 If unto the powder of Loadstone or Iron we admove the North pole of the Loadstone, the powders or small divisions will erect and conforme themselves thereto. **1730** A. GORDON *Maffei's Amphith.* 93 The Charioteers sometimes bowed to the Ground, then erected themselves on high. **1750** JOHNSON *Rambler* No. 6 ¶3 The necessity of erecting our-selves to some degree of intellectual dignity. **1774** GOLDSM. *Nat. Hist.* (1776) VII. 49 The muscle..is capable of erecting itself on an edge. **1818** JAS. MILL *Brit. India* II. IV. iii. 97 Erected against Aliverdi the standard of revolt. **1877** MRS. OLIPHANT *Makers Flor.* xiii. 325 His weak frame erected itself.

b. *Optics.* To restore (an inverted optical image) to an upright position.

1831 BREWSTER *Newton* (1855) I. x. 245 Without using two glasses, the object may be erected.

†**c.** *intr.* for *refl.* To straighten oneself, assume an upright position.

1626 BACON *Sylva* (1631) §827 By Wet, Stalkes doe erect, and Leaues bow downe.

4. To set upright (a member of the body); to prick up (the ears); also *Phys.* (chiefly in pass.), to render turgid and rigid any organ containing erectile tissue.

1626 BACON *Sylva* (1637) §266 You..erect your Eare, when you would heare attentiuely. **1718** ROWE tr. *Lucan* I. 540 At ev'ry Shout [the horse] erects his quiv'ring Ears. **1796** BURKE *Regic. Peace* Wks. VIII. 318 That this faction.. does erect its crest upon the engagement, there can be little doubt.

†**5.** *fig.* from 3, 4. To rouse, stir up, excite, embolden (the mind, oneself). *Obs.*

a **1568** COVERDALE *Treat. Death* I. xvi, We ought to erect and comfort ourselves with the resurrection. **1605** BACON *Adv. Learn.* II. iv. §2 It doth raise and erect the mind. **1654** R. CODRINGTON tr. *Hist. Ivstine* 314 With this Victory the courages of the Sicilians were erected. **1665** J. SERGEANT *Sure-footing* 201 His Book coming forth..my Expectation was now erected. *a* **1668** DENHAM (J.), Why should not hope As much erect our thoughts, as fear deject them? *a* **1734** NORTH *Lives* (1826) II. 131 He found his spirits low, and thought to..erect them by a glass or two of sherry.

†**b.** *occas.* To stimulate (in a physical sense).

1620 VENNER *Via Recta* (1650) 273 It..erecteth the digestive faculty of the stomack.

†**6.** To elate with pride. *Obs.*

1631 R. H. *Arraignm. Whole Creature* 137 Least..the contemplation of their proud plumes and feathers too much erect them and puffe them up.

III. To set on a foundation, construct, establish.

7. To set up (a building, statue, framework, etc.); to rear, build. Also † *to erect up*.

1417 in Ellis *Orig. Lett.* II. 19. I. 59 He hath erected a new tower upon the same for a warde. **1555** EDEN *Decades W. Ind.* I. IV. (Arb.) 80 The inhabitantes sawe newe buyldynges to bee dayly erected. **1570** ABP. PARKER *Corr.* (1853) 372 Intending..to erect up certain iron mills. **1593** SHAKS. *2 Hen. VI*, III. ii. 80 Erect his Statue, and worship it. **1664** EVELYN *Kal. Hort.* (1729) 229 Erect on the out-side Wall your Stove..of Brick. **1692** O. WALKER *History Illustrated* 288 Gallus lamented much his death, and erected him a Sepulchre. **1701** DE FOE *True-born Eng.* I. 1 Where-ever God erects a House of Prayer The Devil always builds a Chappel there. **1796** H. HUNTER tr. *St. Pierre's Stud. Nat.* (1799) I. 446 He erects trophies. **1825** J. NICHOLSON *Operat. Mechanic* 190 An engine was erected in the vicinity of Bath ..on this principle. **1848** MACAULAY *Hist. Eng.* II. 16 A more peaceful class erected silk manufactories in the eastern suburb of London. **1856** FROUDE *Hist. Eng.* (1858) II. ix. 382 The scaffold had been awkwardly erected.

¶ To build (a vessel).

1650 SIR J. BURROUGHS in *Wealth of Gt. Brit.* (1749) 33 By erecting two hundred and fifty busses..there will be employment for one thousand ships.

b. *fig.* To build up (a theory, conclusion, etc.), set up (a pretension). Also *absol.*

1646 SIR T. BROWNE *Pseud. Ep.* I. vii. 25 Our advanced beliefs are not to be built upon dictates, but..[we] are to erect upon the surer base of reason. *a* **1704** LOCKE (J.), Malebranche erects this proposition, of seeing all things in God, upon their ruin. **1818** JAS. MILL *Brit. India* II. v. ii. 350 The pretension erected by Mr. Hastings..would destroy one great source of the evidence. **1864** J. H. NEWMAN *Apol.* 195 It was necessary for us to have a positive Church theory erected on a definite basis.

8. a. *Geom.* To set up or draw (a perpendicular to a given line); †to construct (a triangle, etc. upon a given base). **b.** *Astrol.* and *Astron.* To 'set up' (a figure of the heavens).

a **1646** J. GREGORY *Assyr. Mon.* in *Posth.* (1650) 215 This was the figure of the Heavens..Astronomically calculated and erected according to Tycho's tables. **1660** BARROW *Euclid* I. x, Upon the line given AB erect an equilateral triangle. *a* **1672** WOOD *Life* (1848) 73 After Lillie (the astronomer) had erected his figure, he told her, etc. **1715** KERSEY, *To Erect a Figure*, to divide the 12 Houses a-right. **1815** SCOTT *Guy M.* iv, He accordingly erected his scheme, or figure of heaven. **1828** J. H. MOORE *Pract. Navig.* 44 On B erect the perpendicular BA. **1887** T. B. REED *O.E. Lett. Found* 182 He [Moxon] professes to be able to erect in any other square..the same letter.

†**9.** To set up, establish, found (an office, court of justice, corporation, institution, etc.); to initiate, set on foot (a project, scheme). *Obs.* or *arch.* exc. in *Law*.

1565 CALFHILL *Answ. Treat. Crosse* (1846) 24 A pilgrimage in Wales was straight erected. **1570** in Strype *Ann. Ref.* I. lvii. 626 The Divinity lecture, erected by the noble lady Margaret. **1602** WARNER *Alb. Eng.* x. lviii. (1612) 254 This League was halowed..gainst all That worke the gospell to erect. **1651** HOBBES *Leviath.* I. xv. 73 There is no Civill Power erected over the parties promising. **1663** MARVELL *Corr.* Wks. 1872–5 II. xl. 88 Courts of Merchants to be erected in some..ports of the nation. **1683** *Royal Proclam.* in *Lond. Gaz.* No. 1856/1 The Office of Post-Master General hath been Erected by Act of Parliament. **1743** TINDAL tr. *Rapin's Hist. Eng.* II. 151 *note*, This year Queen Elizabeth erected the East-India Company. **1761–2** HUME *Hist. Eng.* II. xli. 415 The Jesuits, a new order of regular priests erected in Europe. **1792** CHIPMAN *Amer. Law Rep.* (1871) 12 The statute has erected a summary jurisdiction. **1818** JAS. MILL *Brit. India* II. v. ix. 702 The ministerial board erected by Mr. Pitt. *a* **1862** BUCKLE *Civiliz.* (1869) III. iii. 125 Two Courts of High Commission were erected. **1865** H. PHILLIPS *Amer. Paper Curr.* II. 56 Congress resolved to erect a lottery.

†**b.** To raise (an armed force); to form (a nation). *Obs.*

1480 CAXTON *Chron. Eng.* III. (1520) 24/2 These two erected an hoost ayenst Hanyball. **1598** BARRET *Theor. Warres* II. i. 20 When a Companie is newly leuied and erected, etc. *a* **1618** RALEIGH (J.), He suffers seventy-two distinct nations to be erected out of the first monarchy under distinct governours. **1680** HICKES *Spir. Popery* 71 The Cess ..for erecting and maintaining the foresaid additional Forces. **1698** J. CRULL *Muscovy* 123 A new Body of Militia should be erected in their stead.

10. *to erect into* [cf. Fr. *ériger en*]: to constitute or form into (*e.g.* an organization, municipality, territorial division, etc.); to set up as (a rule or precedent); to invest with the rank or character of; †to represent as.

1670–98 LASSELS *Voy. Italy* Pref. 1, I had not the least thought..of erecting my self into an Authour. **1710** STEELE *Tatler* No. 56 ¶1 For the Sharpers..are by Custom erected into a real and venerable Body of Men. **1718** *Col. Rec. Penn.* III. 58 The sd. town might be Erected into a Borough by a Charter, etc. *a* **1768** ERSKINE *Inst. Law Scotl.* (1773) 345 By secularizing, or, in our law-style, erecting most of the monasteries into temporal lordships. **1796** H. HUNTER tr. *St. Pierre's Stud. Nat.* (1799) III. 455 The Officers of an inferior order..erected themselves into seignorial proprietors. **1818** JAS. MILL *Brit. India* II. v. viii. 669 He could erect every interference in that sovereignty into an act of guilt. **1821** SCOTT *Kenilw.* vii, Her majesty was minded to erect the town into a staple for wool. **1822** M. A. KELTY *Osmond* I. 158 You..erect him into a standard of right and wrong. **1839** YEOWELL *Anc. Brit. Ch.* xi. (1847) 110 Valentia ..was erected into a province. **1860** MILL *Repr. Govt.* (1865) 54/2 That portion..whom the institutions of the country have erected into a ruling class.

¶**11.** ? Used for ARRECT, DIRECT.

1526 SKELTON *Magnyf.* 2507 Unto me formest this processe is erectyd. **1655** M. CARTER *Hon. Rediv.* (1660) Ep. Ded., No more then the Subject of it [*i.e.* Honour] erects.

erectable (ɪˈrɛktəb(ə)l), *a.* [f. ERECT *v.* + -ABLE.] Capable of being erected.

1802 G. MONTAGU *Ornith. Dict.* (L.), These erectable feathers..are scarcely longer than the rest.

erected (ɪˈrɛktɪd), *ppl. a.* [f. ERECT *v.* + -ED¹.]

†**1.** Having an upward direction. Of the eyes, face, etc.: Uplifted. Of motion: Directed upwards. *fig.* Of the mind: Active, attentive. *Obs.*

1581 SIDNEY *Apol. Poetrie* (Arb.) 26 Our erected wit, maketh vs know what perfection is. **1593** DRAYTON *Eclog.* x. 26 Th' erected eyes (Of a poore Wretch with miseries oppresť). **1659** *Instruc. Oratory* 16 He..proceeds to a new subject with a more erected attention. **1668** CLARENDON *Ess.* Tracts (1727) 92 An erected face toward heaven. **1682** SOUTHERNE *Loyal Bro.* I. i, My erected head was rais'd to give A fuller majesty to crowns. **1697** DRYDEN *Virg. Georg.* I. 499 Herons..mounting upward with erected Flight.

†**2.** Elevated, exalted; aspiring, high-souled, noble. *Obs.*

1580 SIDNEY *Arcadia* I. (T.) High erected thoughts seated in a heart of courtesy. **1601** CORNWALLYES *Disc. Seneca* (1631) 68 Men of the highest erected states have dyed. **1611** SPEED *Hist. Gt. Brit.* IX. xx. (1632) 963 [They] march with erected courages against King Henry. **1631** T. MAY tr. *Barclay's Mirr. Mindes* ii. 65 Pride adorned with the name of an erected manly nature. **1667** MILTON *P.L.* I. 679 Mammon, the least erected Spirit that fell.

3. †**a.** Set upright, or in a perpendicular position. **b.** Of hair, etc.: Bristling. Of ears: Pricked up.

1603 B. JONSON *Entertainm. Jas. I* Wks. (1838) 530/2 This erected and broad-spreading tree. **1610** GUILLIM *Heraldry* III. xv. (1611) 138 A sleeping lion which did not shew his rage with his erected Shagge. **1663** J. SPENCER *Prodigies* (1665) 165 The falling of an erected Staff this way or that. **1675** DRYDEN *Arungz.* v. i. 2566 The Golden Serpents bear Erected Crests alike. **1707** E. WARD *Hud. Rediv.* (1715) I. ix, The Teacher..Rose from his Seat, and stood erected. **1782** COWPER *Charity* 516 'Tis called a satire, and the World appears Gathering around it, with erected ears.

4. Built up; up-reared. Also *fig.* of a kingdom: Established.

1603 KNOLLES *Hist. Turks* (1638) 29 The disquieting of the state of that new erected kingdom. **1625** S. D'EWES in Ellis *Orig. Lett.* I. 322 III. 218 Going from this erected stage downe into St. Edwards Chappel. **1880** *Daily Tel.* 30 Apr., An erected bridge is subjected to great lateral pressure.

5. See ERECT *v.* 9. also 10.

1754 ERSKINE *Princ. Sc. Law* 229 Having by their grants the same title to the erected benefices, that the monasteries had formerly.

erecter: see ERECTOR.

†**e'rectify**, *v. Obs.* [f. ERECT *a.* + -(I)FY, after the analogy of *rectify*; cf. *edify*.] *trans.* To build. Implied in **e'rectifying** *ppl. a.*

1627 SPEED *England* xxx. §6 Vpon whose desolations that erectifying Lady Edelfled cast her eyes of compassion.

erectile (ɪˈrɛktaɪl, -ɪl), *a.* [a. F. *érectile*, f. L. *ērect-*: see ERECT *v.*] Capable of being erected or set upright.

1834 MᶜMURTRIE *Cuvier's Anim. Kingd.* 155 Chauna.. Chaïa of Paraguay..whose occiput is ornamented with a circle of erectile feathers. **1858** O. W. HOLMES *Aut. Breakf.-t.* i. 3 The men of genius that I fancy most have erectile heads. **1869** GILLMORE *Reptiles & Birds* ii. 78 Viperine Snakes..have a long, perforated, erectile fang on the maxillary bone.

b. *erectile tissue*: a kind of tissue found in various parts of animals, capable of being distended under excitement, and consequently of becoming rigid; also, a similar tissue in vegetables.

1830 R. KNOX *Béclard's Anat.* 188 The erectile tissue is of very large dimensions in the organs of copulation. **1861** H. MACMILLAN *Footn. Page Nat.* 200 An elongation of the erectile tissue of the plant. **1874** VAN BUREN *Dis. Genit. Org.* 2 The Corpus Spongiosum Urethræ is also composed of erectile tissue.

Hence **erec'tility**, the quality of being erectile or capable of erection.

1860 WORCESTER cites Dr. Dix; in mod. Dict.

erecting (ɪˈrɛktɪŋ), *vbl. sb.* [f. ERECT *v.* + -ING¹.]

1. The action of the vb. ERECT, in various senses.

1553 T. WILSON *Rhet.* (1567) 23 b, No buildyng of pillers, no erecting of arches. **1649** SELDEN *Laws Eng.* I. (1739) 22 It seemeth to be done..after the erecting of the Bishoprick of Ely. **1776** G. SEMPLE *Building in Water* 67 A judicious erecting of the Sounding-boards.

2. *attrib.*, as in *erecting-eye-piece*, *-glass*, *-prism*: (see quots.)

1837 GORING & PRITCHARD *Microgr.* 144 No achromatic erecting eye-piece..can be made with so few as three lenses. **1874** KNIGHT *Dict. Mech.*, *Erecting eye-piece*, a combination of four lenses used for terrestrial telescopes, and so arranged as to exhibit the objects viewed in an erect position. *Ibid.*, *Erecting-glass*, a tube with two lenses, slipped into the inner end of the draw-tube of a microscope, serving to erect the inverted image. *Ibid.*, *Erecting-prism*, a contrivance of Nachet's for erecting the inverted image produced by a compound microscope, by means of a single rectangular prism placed over the eye-piece.

¶ Used gerundially with omission of *in*, *a*.

1654 EARL ORRERY *Parthen.* (1676) 562 She was ignorant of that fatal Theater which was erecting within sight of her Window. **1809** KENDALL *Trav.* II. lii. 216 One or two small salt-works are erecting in New Bedford.

erecting (ɪˈrɛktɪŋ), *ppl. a.* [f. as prec. + -ING².] That erects; in quot. stimulating.

1654 GAYTON *Pleas. Notes* III. i. 68 He is to be interdicted Oats and all Flatulent and erecting dyet for a Moneth.

erection (ɪˈrɛkʃən). Also 6 ereccion. [ad. late L. *ērectiōn-em*, n. of action f. *ērect-*: see ERECT *v.* Cf. F. *érection*.] The action of erecting, the condition of being erected.

†**1.** A lifting up (of the hands); also, an elevated condition; (of hills) elevation, altitude.

1584 R. SCOT *Discov. Witchcr.* xv. xxiv. 371 There must be erection of hands, confession. **1612** BREREWOOD *Lang. & Relig.* xiii. 138 We are not to consider only the erection of the hils. *a* **1649** WINTHROP *New Eng.* (1853) I. 136 The congregation testifying their consent by erection of hands. **1692** RAY *Dissol. World* iii. (1732) 32.

†**2.** Advancement in condition or dignity; elevation to office. *Obs.*

1503–4 *Act 19 Hen. VII*, c. 26 The seid Ereccion and Creacion to the Kinges seid sone made to hym as to the Duke of Yorke. **1528** in Strype *Eccl. Mem.* I. App. xxiii. 46 Synnes his erection to this dignitie, his Holynes, etc. **1661** USSHER *Power Princes* I. (1683) 47 God..knoweth when and in what place to appoint the Erection of Kings.

b. *concr.* in *Sc. Law.* A temporal lordship 'erected' out of a spiritual benefice.

1754 ERSKINE *Princ. Sc. Law* (1809) 244 That all the superiorities of erections..should be declared to be in the crown.

3. A setting upright; an upright position.

1622 SPARROW *Bk. Com. Prayer* (1661) 39 By the erection of our bodies, expressing the elevation..of our souls. **1691** RAY *Creation* (1714) 221 Of this Erection of the body of Man the ancients have taken notice. **1855** BAIN *Senses & Int.* II. i. §7. (1864) 86 The erections and bendings of the body are outlets for spontaneous activity.

4. *Phys.* The action of making rigid any bodily organ containing erectile tissue; the condition of being so erected; also, an instance of the same.

1594 PLAT *Jewell-ho.* I. 18 As to woorke an erection of those engendring parts. **1607** SHAKS. *Timon* IV. iii. 164 That your Actiuity may defeate and quell The sourse of all Erection. **1650** BULWER *Anthropomet.* 216 Which serve the erection to Coition. **1658** J. ROWLAND tr. *Moufet's Theat. Ins.* 1004 They are good for such as want erection. **1787** H. WATSON in *Med. Commun.* II. 158 His penis was in a state of erection. **1885** *Law Rep.* Appeal X. 176 The appellant had an erection on each of two unsuccessful attempts.

†**5.** Exaltation, excitement, invigoration (of the mind, spirits, etc.). *Obs.*

1580 SIDNEY *Arcadia* I. (1590) 88 a, Her peereles height my minde to high erection Drawes up. **1626** BACON *Sylva* (1631) §713 When a Man would listen suddenly to any Thing, he Starteth; For the Starting is an Erection of the Spirits to attend. **1651** CLARENDON *Contempl. Ps.* Tracts (1727) 542 It must be a wonderful erection of their spirits, to know that God will be a father of those fatherless.

6. The action of rearing (a building, column, etc.). Also *fig.*

1597 SHAKS. *2 Hen. IV*, I. iii. 44 When we see the figure of the house, Then must we rate the cost of the Erection. **1614** RALEIGH *Hist. World* (J.), Counting Seth to be an hundred years old at the erection of them [pillars]. **1664** POWER *Exp. Philos.* Pref. 20 In the erection of a more judicious and consistent Fabrick. **1786** W. THOMPSON *Watson's Philip III* (1839) 337 Prohibiting the erection of all Protestant fabrics on lands belonging to the church. **1825** J. NICHOLSON *Operat. Mechanic* 95 The erection of such mills is not to be recommended universally. **1844** H. H. WILSON *Brit. India* III. 187 Their respect for his memory was evinced by the erection of a monumental column.

b. *concr.* That which is built up or reared; a building, structure. *lit.* and *fig*

1609 *Manch. Crt. Leet Rec.* (1885) II. 242 Two small erections latelye adjoyned to the houses called the red houses. **1614** RALEIGH *Hist. World* II. 286 The English were driven to make such an erection upon a fable, or person fained. **1796** MORSE *Amer. Geog.* II. 164 There is in Perthshire a barrow which seems to be a British erection. **1831** BREWSTER *Newton* (1855) II. xxi. 253 It..is surmounted by a wooden erection said to have been Newton's private observatory.

7. *Astrol.* The construction of a scheme or figure of the heavens. *Obs.*

1610 B. JONSON *Alch.* IV. iv, By erection of her figure, I gest it.

8. a. Constitution or establishment (of an office, institution, etc.). **b.** Investment with a specified condition.

1508 FISHER *Wks.* 184 This mercyfull ereccion and buyldynge of crystes chirche. **1577–87** HOLINSHED *Chron. Scotl.* (1587) 68/1 After the first erection of the Scottish Kingdome. **1664** H. MORE *Myst. Iniq.* 506 Erection into life. **1701** BP. ATTERBURY *Serm.* (1740) I. vii. 255 From their [the Jews'] first Erection into a People, down to their final Excision. **1706** tr. *Dupin's Eccl. Hist. 16th C.* II. IV. iii. 406 The Bull of Erection [of Bishopricks] was despatched. **1796** BURKE *Regic. Peace* Wks. VIII. 187 Any capital innovation which may amount to the erection of a dangerous nuisance. **1863** H. COX *Instit.* I. x. 240 The statute..prohibits the erection of any such courts hereafter. **1885** *10th Rep. Hist. MSS. Comm.* 34 He consolidated his possessions by obtaining their erection into a barony.

erective (ɪˈrɛktɪv), *a.* [f. ERECT *v.* + -IVE.] Tending to erect or set upright.

? **1611** COTGRAVE, *Erectif*, erective. **1847** in CRAIG; and in mod. Dicts.

erectly (ɪˈrɛktlɪ), *adv.* [f. ERECT *a.* + -LY².] In an erect manner or posture.

In speaking of posture the sense is now commonly expressed by the adj., as *to walk erect.*

1646 SIR T. BROWNE *Pseud. Ep.* IV. i. 181 Birds.. generally carry their heads erectly like man. **1682** —— *Chr. Mor.* 99 Be not under any brutal metempsychosis while thou livest and walkest about erectly under the scheme of man. **1796** C. MARSHALL *Garden.* xii. (1813) 144 A weak tree is helped much by training it more erectly than usual. **1801** STRUTT *Sports & Past.* III. vi. 225 A goat walking erectly on his hinder feet. **1808** SCOTT *Marm.* II. xxxii, The locks, that wont her brow to shade, Start up erectly from her head. **1824-9** LANDOR *Imag. Conv.* (1846) II. 4 The Greeks were under disadvantages..yet they rose through them vigorously and erectly.

b. *Comb.* **erectly-spreading** *a. Bot.* 'between erect and spreading'.

1849 in PAXTON *Bot. Dict.*

erectness (ɪˈrɛktnɪs). [f. as prec. + -NESS.]

1. The quality or condition of being erect; an erect attitude.

1646 SIR T. BROWNE *Pseud. Ep.* 180 One kinde of Locust ..stands..in a large erectnesse..by Zoographers called *mantis.* **1662** STILLINGFL. *Orig. Sacr.* I. i, Persons [who] .. think not the erectness of man's stature a sufficient distinction of him from Brutes. **1748** RICHARDSON *Clarissa* (1811) IV. 208 The erectness of her mien. **1811** L. HAWKINS *C'tess & Gertr.* II. 379 For the use of these, he set up a perpendicular staff, as a standard of erectness. **1862** GEO. ELIOT *Romola* I. xv. (1863) III. 263 In the renunciation of her proud erectness, her mental attitude seemed changed.

fig.

1647 H. MORE *Song of Soul* Notes 164/1 The rightnesse of the angles, is a plain embleme of erectnesse or uprightnesse of mind. **1822** HAZLITT *Men & Mann., Knowl. World* (1852) 142 We should retain something of the erectness and openness of our first unbiassed thoughts. **1878** BAYNE *Purit. Rev.* ii. 47 A refreshing sense of moral erectness.

†**2.** Altitude. *Obs. rare*⁻¹.

1612 BREREWOOD *Lang. & Relig.* xiii. 134 The highest sort of them [mountains] pass not in perpendicular erectness 10 furlongs.

erectopatent (ɪˌrɛktəʊˈpætənt, ˈpeɪtənt), *a.* [f. *ērecto-* used as combining form of L. *ērectus* (see ERECT *ppl. a.*) + PATENT.]

a. *Bot.* Having a position intermediate between erect and spreading. **b.** *Entom.* 'When the primary wings of an insect at rest are erect and the secondary horizontal' (Maunder 1848).

1848 JOHNSTON in *Proc. Berw. Nat. Club* II. 290 Those on the back are capitate and barbed with numerous erecto-patent spinules. **1870** HOOKER *Stud. Flora* 18 *Fumaria densiflora*..pedicels erecto-patent.

erector (ɪˈrɛktə(r)). Also 6- erecter. [f. ERECT *v.* + -OR.] One who, or that which, erects.

1. a. One who erects or rears a building, statue, etc.

1538 LELAND *Itin.* III. 97 Richard Poure..first Erector of the Cathedral Chirch of New Saresbyri. **1563** *Homilies* II. *Peril Idol.* (1859) 239 Therefore woe be to the erecter, setter up, and maintainer of images in churches and temples. **1648** W. MOUNTAGUE *Devout Ess.* I. (T.), Rehoboam's young counsellors were, in some relation, the Erectors of Jeroboam's calves. **1823** SCOTT *Peveril* i, William Peveril.. the erector of that Gothic fortress. **1884** *Birmghm. Daily Post* 24 Jan. 3/5 Good Bridge Erectors and Carpenters.

b. *spec.* An engineer who works at the assembling of engines and other iron and steel structures.

1892 *Daily Chron.* 28 Apr. 9/2 Engineer, Fitter, or Erector. **1905** *Westm. Gaz.* 18 Dec. 7/1 Charles Grove, a foreman erector of steel work.

c. A machine used in erecting iron and steel structures.

1895 *Daily News* 31 Oct. 6/5 These 'erectors' are two hydraulic appliances for lifting up and fixing in position the ponderous segments of the iron ring constituting the exterior of the tunnel. **1909** *Daily Chron.* 19 May 3/4 The tunnel shield, complete, with hydraulic erector.

†**2.** One who institutes an office, rule, or practice; the founder of an institution; also, one who sets up a candidate or pretender. *Obs.* exc. as *fig.* of 1.

1548 in Stow *Surv.* (1754) I. III. v. 580/2 Their [the Hospitals'] chiefe Erector being dead. **1580** NORTH *Plutarch* (1676) 246 And for the holy Band..Gorgidas was the first erector of the same. **1609** *Man in Moone* (1849) 16 Idlenesse patrone, Pride's founder, Gluttonies erector. **1611** SPEED *Theat. Gt. Brit.* (1614) 66 The erectors of Lambert, a counterfet Warwick. **1648** *King's Messages for Peace* 73 The erectors and propugnators of the Presbyterian Discipline in Scotland. **1754** *Phil. Trans.* XLVIII. 463 Pherecydes was the original erecter of it. **1803** BINGHAM in *N. & Q.* Ser. III. III. 76 They were..simply the result of a fashion, or the taste, or means of the erecter. **1850** MRS. BROWNING *Poems* I. 153 How I, The erector of the empire in his hand,—Am bent beneath that hand.

3. *Optics.* = *erecting-glass* (see ERECTING *vbl. sb.* 2).

4. A term applied to certain muscles, from their office in causing erection in any part of the body. Also *attrib.*, as in *erector-muscle.*

1831 R. KNOX *Cloquet's Anat.* 187 The erector muscles of the spine. **1857** BULLOCK tr. *Cazeaux' Midwif.* 42 The clitoris..has..an erector muscle. **1876** DUHRING *Dis. Skin* 29 *Erectores pili* or erectors of the hair.

†**erege.** *Obs.* See also ERITE. [a. OF. *erege, herege* (corresp. to Pr. *heretge*, Sp. *herege*):—L. *hæreticus*: see HERETIC.] A heretic.

1340 *Ayenb.* 40 Verst huanne me draȝþ uoulliche þet bodi of oure lhorde aze doþ þe ereges. and þe wychen.

erelong (ɛəˈlɒŋ), *adv.* [f. ERE *prep.* + LONG *adv.*; sometimes written as two words.] Before long; before the lapse of much time; soon. Of future time; also (*arch.*) of past.

1577 HARRISON *England* III. viii. (1878) II. 52 Whereby he receiued a wound that yer long killed him altogither. *a* **1586** SIDNEY (J.), Erelong he had not only gotten pity but pardon. **1714** H. GROVE *Spect.* No. 635 ¶4, I..shall e'er long shoot away with the Swiftness of Imagination. **1777** SIR W. JONES *Pal. Fortune* 31 Erelong the damsel reach'd her native vale. **1809** SOUTHEY in *Q. Rev.* II. 60 English..will probably ere long be..blended with their language. **1850** MRS. BROWNING *Poems* I. 331 Erelong Ye brake off in the middle of that song.

‖**eremacausis** (ˌɛrɪməˈkɔːsɪs). *Chem.* [mod.L., f. Gr. ἠρέμα quietly + καῦσις burning, f. καίειν to burn; cf. Fr. *érémacause.*] 'A slow combustion taking place in presence of air and water, and accompanied by a kind of fermentation' (Watts).

1847 in CRAIG. *c* **1865** LETHEBY in *Circ. Sc.* I. 89/1 The phenomena termed *Eremacausis*, or slow burning.. witnessed in the glowing of phosphorus. **1881** *Academy* 12 Mar. 192 Their influence on eremacausis.

†**e'remigate**, *v. Obs.*⁻⁰ [f. *ērēmigāt-* ppl. stem of *ērēmigāre*, f. *ē* out + *rēmigāre* to row.] *trans.* To row or sail through or over; to navigate. Hence **eremi'gation.**

1623 in COCKERAM I. & II.

†**'eremitage.** *Obs.* Also 6 heremitage, -etage. [var. of HERMITAGE: see EREMITE and -AGE.]

1. The state or condition of a hermit.

1582 N. T. (Rhem.) *Luke* xxi. 1 *marg*, Solitarinesse or heremitage..is a goodly thing. **1619** SCLATER *Exp. 1 Thess.* (1630) 50 Iohn Baptist professed a kinde of Eremitage.

2. The dwelling of a hermit.

c **1400** MAUNDEV. viii. (1839) 93 There ben many.. hermytages where heremytes weren wont to duell. **1535** STEWART *Cron. Scot.* II. 301 The lordis..Decretit hes for Feachar his bruther To send richt sone..Far furth in France into ane heremetage. **1612** SHELTON *Quix.* I. IV. xxv. I. 572 A leaden Box, which as he affirmed was found in the ruines of an old Eremitage. **1847** in CRAIG.

3. The name of a wine (see HERMITAGE).

1796 MORSE *Amer. Geog.* II. 352 The best sorts of French wine are..muscat, frontigniac, eremitage.

eremital (ˈɛrɪmaɪtəl), *a.* Also 7 heremitall. [ad. F. *heremital*, f. late L. *(h)erēmīta*: see EREMITE and -AL¹.] Of or belonging to an eremite, characteristic of an eremite.

1613 WITHERS *Abuses Stript & Whipt* II. Sat. iii, Some hold them wise and vertuous that possesse An Heremitall solitarinesse. **1834-43** SOUTHEY *Doctor* (1849) lxviii. 146 An eremital way of life would have been more rational.

†**'eremiˌtary**, *a. Obs. rare*⁻¹. In 5 heremytarye. [ad. med.L. *h)erēmītārius*, f. *erēmīta*: see EREMITE and -ARY.] = prec.

1491 CAXTON *Vitas Patr.* (W. de W. 1495) II. 179 a/2 A hermyte..afore his professyon in the lyfe heremytarye.

eremite (ˈɛrɪmaɪt). Forms: 3 æremite, 3-7 heremite, -yte, 5 herimyte, 3- eremite. [ad. late L. *erēmīta* (med.L. *herēmīta*, ad. eccl. Gr. ἐρημίτης, f. ἐρημία a desert, f. ἐρῆμος uninhabited. In OF. the regular phonetic descendant of late L. *(h)erēmīta* was *(h)ermite* with loss of the middle syllable (see HERMIT); but the L. word was also adapted in OF. as *(h)eremite*, and this was taken into ME. Originally *h)eremite* and *h)ermit(e*, HERMIT, were employed indiscriminately; but from about the middle of the 17th c. they have been differentiated in use, *hermit* being the ordinary and popular word, while *eremite* (always spelt without the unetymological *h*) is used either poet. or rhetorically, or with special reference to its primitive use in Gr.]

1. One who has retired into solitude from religious motives; a recluse, hermit.

Said *esp.* of the Christian solitaries from the 3rd cent. onwards, as distinguished from the cœnobites, who, though withdrawn from the world, lived as members of a community.

c **1200** *Trin. Coll. Hom.* 85 Seint iohan baptist þe on his childhode bicom eremite. **1205** LAY. 18804 þene æremite [**1275** heremite] he iseh come. *a* **1340** HAMPOLE *Psalter* ci. 7 Heremytis..þat flees þe felaghshipe of men. **1387** TREVISA *Higden* (Rolls) V. 87 Paule þe firste heremyte. **1486** *Bk. St. Albans* F. vij a, An Obseruans of herimytis. **1586** J. HOOKER *Girald. Irel.* in *Holinshed* (1808) VI. 113 A Satyre in the wildernesse did talke with Antonie the heremite. **1667** MILTON *P.L.* III. 474 Embryo's and Idiots, Eremits and Friers. **1764** MACLAINE tr. *Mosheim's Eccl. Hist.* iii. §15 The Eremites..seem to have deserved no other reproach than that of a delirious and extravagant fanaticism. **1812** BYRON *Ch. Har.* I. iv, His native land..seemed to him more lone than Eremite's sad cell. **1874** H. REYNOLDS *John Bapt.* viii. 508 The law of the eremite and the cœnobite corresponds with the transitory dispensation of John.

b. *transf.* (By Milton used with allusion to the lit. sense 'desert-dweller'.)

1671 MILTON *P.R.* I. 8 Thou Spirit who ledst this glorious Eremite Into the Desert. **1832** LYTTON *Eugene A.* x, The twilight Eremites of books and closets. **1847** EMERSON *Woodnotes* Wks. (Bohn) I. 430 The little eremite Flies gaily forth, and sings in sight.

2. In the formal designation of certain monastic orders: e.g. ***Eremites (Hermits) of St. Augustine***, a branch of the Augustinian Friars.

1577-87 HOLINSHED *Chron.* III. 926/1 At Padua in the church of the heremites of saint Augustine. **1651** *Life Father Sarpi* (1676) 6 The mother begun to have almost a perpetual conversation among those immur'd Heremites of Saint Hermagora. **1773** NOORTHOUCK *Hist. Lond.* 600 The founder of the eremites of St. Anthony.

3. A (? quasi-religious) mendicant, a vagabond (see HERMIT).

1495 *Act 11 Hen. VII*, c. 2 §3 Every vagabounde heremyte or begger able to labre.

4. *attrib.*

1651 W. CARTWRIGHT *Ordinary* I. v. in Hazl. *Dodsley* XII. 231 Let us try To win that old eremite thing. **1816** SCOTT *Antiq.* xx, Like a grey palmer, or eremite preacher.. **1843** CARLYLE *Past & Pr.* (1858) 250 Eremite fanaticisms and fakeerings. **1861** J. SHEPPARD *Fall Rome* xi. 587 The eremite and monastic theory of the Christian life which was then almost universally held.

eremiteship (ˈɛrɪmaɪtʃɪp). [f. EREMITE + -SHIP.] The condition of being a hermit.

a **1603** T. CARTWRIGHT *Confut. Rhem. N.T.* (1618) 152 The Eremitship of Elias and Iohn Baptist.

eremitic (ɛrɪˈmɪtɪk), *a.* Also 5 **heremytyke.** [f. as prec. + -IC.] Of or pertaining to an eremite.

1483 CAXTON *Gold Leg.* 423/2, I do seke a place for to lede my lyf heremytyke and solytarylye. **1859** I. TAYLOR *Logic in Theol.* 170 The romance of the eremitic life must be abandoned as impracticable. **1864** LOWELL *Fireside Trav.* 75 The eremitic instinct is not peculiar to the Thebais.

eremitical (ɛrɪˈmɪtɪkəl), *a.* Also 6 **heremeticall**, 7-8 **-itical**, 6-8 **ermetical**(l. [f. prec. + -AL¹.]

1. Of or pertaining to an eremite; characteristic of or habitual to an eremite.

1577 HARRISON *Descr. Brit.* ix. in *Holinshed* (1807) I. 46 The heremeticall profession was onelie allowed of in Britaine. **1601** F. GODWIN *Bps. of Eng.* 497 Affecting much an Eremiticall and solitarie life. **1693** G. D'EMILIANNE *Hist. Monast. Ord.* xii. 101 That he might learn the Eremetical Trade. **1814** L. HUNT *Feast of Poets* (1815) Notes 97 The latter [Wordsworth]..nourishes that eremitical vagueness of sensation,—that making a business of reverie, etc. **1876** J. H. NEWMAN *Hist. Sk.* II. III. ii. 314 [An] opportunity of becoming acquainted with these..eremitical stations when he became their Bishop.

2. Of or pertaining to an order of Eremite friars. See EREMITE 2.

1756-7 tr. *Keysler's Trav.* (1760) III. 401 The church of St. Philip and St. James belongs to the eremetical fathers of St. Augustine. **1762** tr. *Busching's Syst. Geog.* I. 324 Here formerly stood the only Eremitical convent in the whole kingdom. **1857** MISS WINKWORTH tr. *Tauler's Life & Serm.* 89 The eremitical Cœlestines..seem also to have been offshoots from these Spiritual Franciscans.

eremitish (ˈɛrɪmaɪtɪʃ), *a.* [f. EREMITE + -ISH.] Resembling an eremite; befitting an eremite.

1608-11 BP. HALL *Medit. & Vows* I. 90 Christian good-fellowship better than an eremitish and melancholike solitarinesse. **1833** T. MEDWIN in *Shelley Papers* 61 The Guiccioli..seemed by no means to admire Milord's eremitish diet. **1880** L. WALLACE *Ben-Hur* 213 A priest.. never being more perfectly eremitish.

eremitism (ˈɛrɪmaɪtɪzm). [f. EREMITE + -ISM.] The state of a hermit; a living in seclusion from social life.

In mod. Dicts.

eremurus (ɛrɪˈmjʊərəs). *Bot.* [mod.L. (F. A. Marschall von Bieberstein *Centuria Plantarum* (1818) 61), f. Gr. ἐρῆμος solitary + οὐρά tail.] A hardy herbaceous perennial plant of the genus of Liliaceæ so named, native to west and central Asia, and cultivated for its dense racemes of white, yellow, or reddish flowers.

1829 LOUDON *Encycl. Plants* 278 *Eremurus*... Its long spikes of yellow flowers may be easily imagined to merit such an appellation. **1855** *Curtis's Bot. Mag.* LXXXI. 4870 (*caption*) Showy Eremurus. **1900** W. D. DRURY *Bk. Gard.* x. 325 Eremuri are noble plants. **1901** *Cassell's Dict. Gard.* I. 323/1 A good but not too heavy soil suits the Eremuruses. **1962** *Amat. Gardening* 17 Mar. 4/2 One of the most effective spike plants is probably the eremurus, often called Foxtail Lily.

erende, etc. obs. form of ERRAND, etc.

†**'erendrake.** *Obs.* Forms: 1 ǣrendwreca, érendwrica, érendwreca, ǣrendraca, ǣryndraca, 2 erndraca, ærndrache, 3 erndrake, ærendrake, (herindrak), 2-3 erendrake. [OE. *ǣrendwreca* (= ON. *eyrindreki*), f. *ǣrende* ERRAND + *wrecan* to tell. The form *-raca* perhaps represents a different ablaut-grade of the same root.] A messenger, ambassador.

c **825** *Vesp. Psalter* lxvii[i]. 32 Cumað erendwrecan of Ægyptum. *c* **890** K. ÆLFRED *Bæda* v. xxi, Sende he ærendracan. *c* **900** *Bede Glosses* 10 *Legatis*, erendwrica. *c* **1000** *Ags. Gosp.* Luke xiv. 32 He sent ærynd-racan [*c* **1160** *Hatton* erendraken] and bitt sibbe. *a* **1175** *Cott. Hom.* 231 þa

sende se King his aerndraches of fif ceðen to alle his underþeoden. *c* **1200** *Trin. Coll. Hom.* 31 On holie erndrake brohte þe holie godspelle fram heuene. *c* **1205** LAY. 660 Heo nomen ænne ærendrake [*c* **1275** herindrak].

erenow (ɛəˈnaʊ), *adv.* Forms: see ERE and NOW; often as two words. Before this time.

c **1340** *Cursor M.* 2982 (Trin.) She is clene as she was ar now. *Ibid.* 17785 (Fairf.) Ye wold nevir yt leve or now. **1393** LANGL. *P. Pl.* C. VIII. 181 Ich seyh neuere palmere with pyk ne with scrippe Asken after hym, er now in þys ilke place. **1553** T. WILSON *Rhet.* (1567) 47 b, He hath made suche shiftes for money ere-now, that, etc. **1577** tr. *Bullinger's Decades* (1592) 258 The very same words, that other before me.. haue vsed yer now. **1673** DRYDEN *Conq. Granada* (J.), My father has repented him erenow. **1774** GOLDSM. *Nat. Hist.* (1776) II. 384 The whole species would have ere now been extinguished. **1828** HAWTHORNE *Fanshawe* viii. (1879) 140, I have done enough, erenow, to insure its heaviest weight.

erepsin (ɪˈrɛpsɪn). [a. G. *erepsin* (O. Cohnheim 1901, in *Zeitschr. f. physiol. Chem.* XXXIII. 460), f. L. *eripere* to take away, f. Gr. ἐρείπειν + PE)PSIN.] Name given to a mixture of enzymes in the intestinal juice.

1902 *Jrnl. Chem. Soc.* LXXXII. II. 93 Erepsin has no action on ordinary proteid, but only on peptone, and on a part of the proteoses. **1940** *Thorpe's Dict. Appl. Chem.* (ed. 4) IV. 325/1 The early literature refers to an enzyme 'intestinal erepsin' able to hydrolyse polypeptides, peptones, etc... The term is now abandoned in favour of polypeptidases. **1961** *Brit. Med. Dict.* 513/1 *Erepsin*, a mixture of enzymes, chiefly polypeptidases, present in the intestinal mucosa and capable of converting polypeptides into amino acids.

† **eˈrept,** *ppl. a. Obs.*—⁰ [ad. L. *ērept-us*, pa. pple. of *ēripĕre*, f. *ē* out + *rapĕre* to snatch.] Snatched away.

1736 in BAILEY.

erept (ɪˈrɛpt), *v. rare.* [f. L. *ērept-* (see prec.).] *trans.* To snatch away, carry off.

1865 *Athenæum* No. 1951. 376/3 Pluto erepts Proserpine.

† **erepˈtation.** *Obs.*—⁰ [agent-n. f. L. *ēreptāre* to creep forth.] 'A creeping forth.'

1736 in BAILEY. **1775** in ASH.

ereption (ɪˈrɛpʃən). [ad. L. *ēreptiōn-em*, n. of action f. *ēripĕre*.] The action of snatching or taking away.

1633 BP. HALL *Hard Texts* 341 The suddaine and inexpected ereption of Isaac from that his imminent and intended death. **1721–1800** in BAILEY. **1875** POSTE *Gaius* II. (ed. 2) 246 The recovery of the civil inheritance by *hereditatis petitio* might be rendered unavailing by ablation or ereption for *Indignitas*.

† **ˈerer,** *a.* and *adv. Obs.* Forms: *adj.* 1 ǽrra (m.), ǽrre (f. and n.), 2 ærra, (2 erra, 3 earre, eror, errure, 4 erore); *adv.* 1 ǽror, -ur, (3 ærer, erur, arer, -ure), 4–6 *Sc.* erar(e, (4 errar), 5 erer, (6 earar). [The OE. adj. *ǽrra* corresponds to OHG. *êriro*, Goth. *airiza*:—OTeut. **airizon-*, f. **airiz* adv.: see ERE. The OE. adv. *ǽror* is a new formation after the analogy of advb. comparatives in *-or* (:—OTeut. *-ôz*); the OE. *ǽr* (:—**airiz*), owing to the loss of the suffix, not being distinctly shown by its form to be a comparative. Cf. OHG. *êror* of similar formation.]

A. *adj.* Former.

c **888** K. ÆLFRED *Boeth.* xxxv. §6 Þonne forlyst he eall his ærran god. *a* **1000** *Elene* 305 (Gr.) Se þe of deaðe sylf woruld awehte.. in þæt ærre lif. *c* **1175** *Lamb. Hom.* 95 Þe þet on þam erran [*MS.* ercan] to-cume liðegedde þan sunfullen to þere godnesse. *c* **1230** *Hali Meid.* 7 Hire latere were.. lesse haueð þen hauede ear hire earre. **1297** R. GLOUC. (1724) 324 Of þe kunde he was of Denemarch, of þe eror wyf y bore. *a* **1300** *Relig. Songs* (Percy Soc.) v. 79 Of alle hire errure freond nu nafdh heo non. *c* **1305** *St. Kenelm* 290 in *E.E.P.* (1862) 55 & for þe erore miracle of þe toun þe whatlokere þerto hi come. *c* **1380** *Sir Otuel* 46 Otuwel thoute on errore deede.

B. *adv.*

1. Before, formerly, at a former time.

Beowulf 810 Se þe fela æror, modes myrðe manna cynne fyrene ȝefremede. *a* **1000** *Cross* 108 (Gr.) Swa he him ærur her on þyssum lænum life ȝeearnað. *c* **1200** *Trin. Coll. Hom.* 183 Uncuðe men fon to þe aihte þe arure his waren. *c* **1205** LAY. 17459 Mærlin heom gon ræren alse heo stoden ærer. *a* **1250** *Owl & Night.* 1736 Al swo hit was erur bi-speke. **14**.. *Pol. Rel. & L. Poems* 221 And of þat erer was his Nou shal he hauen mys.

2. Sooner, rather, in preference; also with *than*.

1375 BARBOUR *Bruce* I. 458 Thai war sum tyme erar may then les. *c* **1425** WYNTOUN *Cron.* VII. Prol. 32 Swa erare will I now ches me To be reprowyd of sympilnes, Ðan blame to thole of wnkyndnes. **1513–75** *Diurn. Occurr.* (1833) 93 Erar to hasert the samyn vpoun the chance of battell, than continwalle to be in feir of thair life. **1552** ABP. HAMILTON *Catech.* (1884) 30 He chesit earar to thoile ane cruel deid. **1560** ROLLAND *Crt. Venus* I. 527 He wald preuaill the erar I assure.

eresie, obs. form of HERESY.

† **eresop.** *Obs.* Also ersope. [? f. EAR *sb.* + SOAP.] App. = Ear-wax: see quots.

[*c* **1225** JOHN DE GARLANDE in Wright *Vocab.* 121 Duo cornua, quibus vicine sunt aures, per quas colera expurgatur.] *c* **1450** *Nominale* in Wr.-Wülcker 676 *Hec colera*, the ersope. *c* **1475** *Pict. Voc.*, ibid. 748 *Hec colera* [MS. *tolera*], a eresope. [*a* **1500** *Nominale*, ibid. 676 *note*, *Colera*, arwax.]

erest, var. of ERST.

† **eret,** *v. Obs.* [var. of ARET.] = ARET *v.* I.

1574 tr. *Littleton's Tenures* 53 a, It shalbe eretted the foly of the elder sister that shee wolde agree to the particion.

erethic (ɪˈrɛθɪk), *a.* [f. ERETH(ISM + -IC.] = ERETHISMIC *a.*

1888 *Amer. Jrnl. Psychol.* I. 375 My mental make-up is inherited mostly from the paternal side and is erethic in quality. **1894** [see SPURTY *a.*].

erethism (ˈɛrɪθɪz(ə)m). *Path.* [ad. Fr. *éréthisme*, ad. Gr. ἐρεθισμός, f. ἐρεθίζειν to irritate.

(A misspelling *erythism*, due to false etymology, occurs in many medical books.)]

Excitement of an organ or tissue in an unusual degree; also *transf.* morbid over-activity of the mental powers or passions.

1800 *Med. Jrnl.* IV. 370 Producing.. a very useful perspiration, without augmenting the irritation or erethism in those parts. **1833** *Cycl. Pract. Med.* II. 104 Mercurial erethism. The word erethismus.. has hitherto been almost exclusively confined to that species of erethism which sometimes arises from the use of mercury. **1836–7** SIR W. HAMILTON *Metaph.* xliii. (1870) II. 456 The powers are in excessive vigour,—at least in excessive erethism or excitation. **1847** TODD *Cycl. Anat.* III. 56/2 His stomach was in a continued state of erethism. **1859** BUCKNILL in *Sat. Rev.* Sept. 288 A fancy usually so cold and impassive, but now in agonising erethism.

erethismic (ɛrɪˈθɪzmɪk), *a.* [f. prec. + -IC.] Resembling or of the nature of erethism.

1846 G. DAY tr. *Simon's Anim. Chem.* II. 257 An erethismic type of fever.

erethistic (ɛrɪˈθɪstɪk), *a.* [ad. Gr. ἐρεθιστικός, f. ἐρεθίζειν to irritate.] Relating to erethism.

In mod. Dicts.

eretike, -yck, obs. forms of HERETIC.

erew, obs. var. of ARGH.

† **ˈereward,** *sb. Obs.* Also 3 erward. [ME. *ereward*, OE. *ęrfe-weard*, f. *ęrfe* (*iędrfe*, *yrfe*) inheritance + *weard* keeper, lord.] An heir. Also in *comb.* **ereward-riche** [+ ME. *riche*, OE. *rice* dominion], inheritance.

c **975** *Rushw. Gosp.* Matt. xxi. 38 Þis se erfe-weard. *c* **1000** *Ags. Gosp.* Luke xx. 14 Her ys se yrfe-weard. *c* **1250** *Gen. & Ex.* 934 Of ðe self sal ðin erward ten. *Ibid.* 1512 Two doles of ereward riche auen.

† **ˈereward,** *adv. Obs. rare.* In 5 erward. [f. ERE *adv.* + WARD.] Before, previously.

14.. *Tundale's Vis.* 1844 Within that wall come they sone As they hadon erward done.

erewhile (ɛəˈhwaɪl), *adv.* Forms: see ERE and WHILE. A while before, some time ago, formerly.

a **1300** *Cursor M.* 20304 Me com tiþand arquil fra heuen. *c* **1305** *St. Andrew* 91 in *E.E.P.* (1862) 100 Ic iseo mie swete louerd: and erwhile ic iseȝ þat abydeþ me til ic come. *c* **1440** *Gesta Rom.* iv. 10 (Harl. MS.) Sir, I seide to you erwhile, þat, etc. **1526** TINDALE *John* ix. 27, I tolde you yerwhile, and ye did nott heare. **1595** *Locrine* II. v. 154, I, that erewhile did scare mine enemies.. Must now depart. *a* **1678** MARVELL *Wks.* III. 522 The tree erewhile fore-shortned to our view. **1724** RAMSAY *Tea-t. Misc.* (1733) II. 129 Forth that foam'd and roar'd erewhile Glides calmly down. **1810** SCOTT *Lady of L.* II. iii, Remember then thy hap erewhile. **1870** MORRIS *Earthly Par.* I. II. 461 The faces weeping lay That erewhile laughed the loudest.

So † **ereˈwhiles,** *adv.* [see WHILES].

1584 R. SCOT *Disc. Witchcr.* 550 The Pneumatomachi.. did erwhiles ioine themselues to those that were sound of iudgement. **1598** *Mucedorus* in Hazl. *Dodsley* VII. 211 Erewhiles assaulted with an ugly bear: Fair Amadine in company all alone. **1635** J. HAYWARD tr. *Biondi's Banished Virgin* 26 The very same you saw me with erewhiles. **1755** in JOHNSON.

Erewhonian (ɛrɪˈwəʊnɪən), *a.* and *sb.* [f. *Erewhon*, title of a book (partial reversal of *Nowhere*) by Samuel Butler, published 1872 and describing a form of utopia: see -IAN.] **A.** *adj.* Of, belonging to, or characteristic of the book *Erewhon*, the utopia described in it, or the principles inculcated therein. **B.** *sb.* An inhabitant of Erewhon.

1897 *Daily News* 16 June 5/2 The Erewhonian plan of counting disease as a crime. **1900** *Ibid.* 10 Dec. 9/6 The Erewhonian Professors, Hanky and Panky. **1921** *Edin. Rev.* July 28 The exhortation which persuaded Samuel Butler's Erewhonians to destroy all their machines. *Ibid.* 36 The Erewhonian policy of breaking up the machines is manifestly impossible in this country. **1927** *Observer* 25 Sept. 16/6 The Erewhonian paradox of imprisoning the invalid is not wholly a barren one. *a* **1930** D. H. LAWRENCE *Collier's Friday Night* (1934) ii. 49 *Beatrice*:.. But was it the Gypsy, or the Athletic Girl that does Botany? *Ernest* (*shaking his head*): No. It was an Erewhonian. **1954** P. CAPON *Down to Earth* iv. 68 The Antigeosians had an almost Erewhonian attitude to physical disabilities... Illness was not something that could be talked about without shame.

ereyne, var. of ARAIN, *obs.*, spider.

† **erf**¹. *Obs.* Also 2–3 erfe, (*Orm.* errfe), erve. [Common Teut.: OE. *ęrfe*, *iędrfe*, *yrfe*, corresp. to OFris. *erve* (Du. *erf*), OHG. *erbi*, *arbi* (MHG. and Ger. *erbe*), Goth. *arbi*:—OTeut. **arbjo(m* neut. 'inheritance' (ON. has *arfr* masc., whence Sw. *arf*, Da. *arv*), related to Gr. ὀρφανός orphan, L. *orbus* bereft. Cf. ORF¹.]

For the specially Eng. development of meaning, cf. *cattle*.

1. Cattle.

1154 *O.E. Chron.* an. 1125 Hunger and cwealm on men and on erue. *c* **1200** *Trin. Coll. Hom.* 39 Ðese fower mannisshe.. beð þat erf þe þo herdes ouer wuakeden. *c* **1200** ORMIN 1068 Off þatt errfe þatt tæ r wass Drihhtin to lake ȝarrkedd. *c* **1250** *Gen. & Ex.* 2750 Moyses.. wattrede here erue eueril on. *Ibid.* 3018 Egyptes erf sal al for-faren. *a* **1300** *E.E. Psalter* cxlviii. 10 Bestes and alle erfes ma.

2. *Comb.* † **erfe-blood,** blood of animals; † **erf-kin,** the race of animals, cattle.

c **1200** ORMIN 1788 þatt allterr þatt tatt errfe blod Wass eȝȝwhær strennkedd onne. *c* **1250** *Gen. & Ex.* 3177 Al erf-kin hauen he ut-led.

erf² (ɜːf). Pl. erfs, erven; †erbes. [a. Du. *erf* in same sense, orig. 'inheritance': see prec.] In South Africa: 'A garden plot, usually containing about half-an-acre' (Webster). Also *attrib.*, as *erf-holder*, *-licence*.

1812 A. PLUMPTRE tr. *M. K. H. Lichtenstein's Trav.* I. xxiii. 335 The proposal, that instead of extensive farms, it should be divided into small parcels of land, or *erbes*. **1818** C. I. LATROBE *Jrnl. Visit S. Afr. 1815–16* xvi. 262 His industry put him in possession of this *erf*, a name given to a small lot of ground, not being a complete farm. **1851** J. J. FREEMAN *Tour S. Afr.* viii. 184 The party came to Buxton on Thursday morning, when burning commenced immediately, and no entreaties of erf-holders, tears of mothers and children, availed. **1887** in *Barker's Trade & Finance* 23 Mar. 3. **1902** *Westm. Gaz.* 14 Apr. 10/1 The erven (acres) in question were granted to these Reservists by the Government. **1947** *Cape Argus* 11 Jan. 6/4 Erfs were allocated. **1948** *Cape Times* 26 Mar. 3/2, 21 erfholders who dwell on the mainland but till their land on the island. **1959** *Star* (Johannesburg) 12 Jan. 20/3 We will sell by Public Auction the following:.. Five Erven.. Certain Erf No. 136 situate on Olive Avenue.

erfeth, etc., var. ff. ARVETH, etc. *Obs.*

erg¹ (ɜːg). *Physics.* Also ergon. [ad. Gr. ἔργ-ον work.]

1. A unit of work or energy; the amount of work done when a force of one dyne moves its point of application one centimetre in the direction of the force.

1873 *Brit. Assoc. Rep.* 224 We propose to denote it [the C.G.S. unit of work] by some derivative of the Greek ἔργον. The forms *ergon*, *ergal* and *erg* have been suggested.. We propose, for the present, to leave the termination unsettled; and we request that the word *ergon* or *erg* be strictly limited to the C.G.S. unit of work, or what is for purposes of measurement, equivalent to this the C.G.S. unit of energy. **1874** MAXWELL in *Life* (1882) 632 Your sum of Vital energy Is not the millionth of an erg. **1875** GARNETT *Elem. Dynamics* (1889) §63 The C.G.S. unit of work is that done by a dyne in working through a centimetre and is called an erg.

2. *Comb.* as **erg-nine, erg-ten,** the product of an erg multiplied respectively by 10^9 and 10^{10}.

1873 *Brit. Assoc. Rep.* 224 One horse-power is equal to three quarters of an erg-ten per second. More nearly, it is 7·46 erg-nines per second.

‖ **erg**² (ɜːg). Pl. areg, ergs. [Fr. (E. Fromentin *Un été dans le Sahara* (1857),) f. N. Afr. Arabic *ʿirj*, of Berber origin.] A type of desert area in the Sahara consisting of shifting sand dunes.

Fromentin's book appeared in serial form in the *Revue de Paris* 1854.

1875 *Encycl. Brit.* I. 250/1 The most truly desert region of the Sahara is an irregular belt of shifting sand dunes, the 'Erg' or 'Areg'. **1937** WOOLDRIDGE & MORGAN *Physical Basis Geogr.* xx. 301 The sand areas of the Old World deserts ('Erg' of the Sahara, 'Koum' of Asia). *Ibid.* 319 It was at a later date.. that the red Kalahari sands extended widely in South Africa. They appear to represent an 'erg phase'. **1943** *Algeria* (Naval Intelligence Div.) I. ii. 27 The sand-dune areas are called *ergs*. *Ibid.* v. 155 Two fairly distinct types [of sand desert] can be distinguished: the *nebkas* or small areas of sand,.. and the erg (pl. areg) or large dune system... The erg consists of drinn steppe with a drought-resisting grass as the dominant species. **1950** G. BRENAN *Face of Spain* ix. 195 He.. had spent his life among the sand *ergs* and *ashab* pastures of the Sahara.

ergastic (ɜːˈgæstɪk), *a. Cytol.* [ad. G. *ergastisch* (A. Meyer 1896, in *Bot. Zeitung* I. 212), f. Gr. ἐργαστικός able to work.] Of or pertaining to the non-living products of the cell.

1902 E. B. WILSON *Cell* (ed. 2) i. 30 The passive energid-products (ergastic structures..) are formed as enclosures.. or excretions. **1935** *Nature* Suppl. 9 Mar. 378/2 Plastids, Golgi material, chondriosomes and ergastic substances. **1957** *Encycl. Brit.* XVIII. 7/1 All living cells in plants contain variable amounts of non-living materials that are collectively designated as inclusions or ergastic substances... One of the most common examples of ergastic substances is the cell sap.

ergastoplasm (ɜːˈgæstəʊplæz(ə)m). *Biol.* [ad. F. *ergastoplasme* (C. Garnier 1897, in *Bibliographie Anat.* V. 288), f. as prec. +

PLASM.] (See quot. 1925.) Hence **ergasto'plasmic** *a.*

1902 E. B. WILSON *Cell* (ed. 2) vi. 322 The 'ergastoplasmic' (Garnier) fibrillæ of gland-cells. *Ibid.*, The conception of a dominating or 'superior' cytoplasm (including 'archoplasm', 'kinoplasm', 'ergastoplasm'). **1903** *Nature* 12 Mar. 455/2 (*title*) On the structure of the tracheal cell of the gad-fly, and on the origin of the ergastoplasmic formations. **1925** E. B. WILSON *Cell* (ed. 3) iv. 264 The term 'ergastoplasm', originally applied by Garnier and Bouin to the basophilic fibrillar formations in certain types of cells.. has recently been resuscitated..as a non-committal term applied to strongly basophilic cytoplasmic material. **1964** G. H. HAGGIS et al. *Introd. Molecular Biol.* i. 12 Two differentiated regions of the cytoplasm can be recognized in the microscope—one being usually called the Golgi region, the other the ergastoplasm. *Ibid.* v. 137 The ergastoplasm or rough-surfaced endoplasmic reticulum.

ergastulum (ɜːˈgæstjʊləm). *Rom. Antiq.* Pl. **-ula** (-jʊlə). [L.] A prison-like building on a large estate, used for housing slave workers (in quot. 1891, an urban prison for slaves).

1833 W. BLAIR *Inquiry into Slavery amongst Romans* v. 100 When Columella wrote, some distinction appears to have existed between the *ergastulum* for ordinary workmen, and that for ill-behaved slaves, as he directs the latter to be built under ground. **1865** BRANDE & COX *Dict. Sci.* I. 808/2 *Ergastulum*, a workhouse, or a dwelling place for the slaves. **1885** R. S. STORRS *Div. Orig. Christianity* v. 159 As workers on farms, they [*sc.* slaves]..slept at night in the cells of the ergastula, under-ground. **1891** F. W. FARRAR *Darkness & Dawn* I. xxxi. 303 The ergastulum is half-subterranean. Its windows are narrow, and high above our heads.

†**'ergasy.** *Obs. rare*$^{-1}$. [ad. Gr. ἐργασία working, production, f. ἐργάζεσθαι to work, f. ἔργον work.] A literary production, a treatise.

1637 R. HUMPHREY tr. *St. Ambrose* Pref., Ending the whole ergasie or tractate with it.

ergate (ˈɜːgeɪt). *Ent.* Also in mod.L. form **ergates** (ˈɜːgətiːz). [ad. Gr. ἐργάτης workman.] The worker ant.

1901 W. M. WHEELER in *Amer. Nat.* XXXV. 877 (*title*) The parasitic Origin of Macroërgates among Ants. **1910** —— *Ants* 97 The worker (ergates) is characterized by the complete absence of wings.

So **erga'tandromorph** [Gr. ἀνήρ, ἀνδρός man, -μορφος -form], an ant that combines worker and male characters; **'ergata,ner** (-ɪə(r)) [Gr. ἀνήρ man], a male ant resembling a worker; **'ergato,gyne** [Gr. γυνή woman], a worker-like ant with female characters; **'ergatoid** *sb.*, a wingless sexually competent ant, as an ergatogyne; also as *adj.*; **,ergato'morphic** *a.*, worker-like; **,ergato'telic** *a.* (see quot.).

1899 *Cambr. Nat. Hist.* VI. 140 The adult, sexually capable, though wingless forms, are called ergatoid, because they are similar to workers. **1901** *Amer. Nat.* XXXV. 885 The *fusca* workers attempt to change worker larvæ of Polyergus into queens but succeed only in producing the wingless ergatoids. **1910** W. M. WHEELER *Ants* vi. 94 The *ergatanēr*, ergatomorphic, or ergatoid male resembles the worker in having no wings and in the structure of the antennæ. *Ibid.* 96 The ergatogyne, ergatomorphic, or ergatoid female, is a worker-like form, with ocelli, large eyes, and a thorax more or less like that of the female, but without wings. *Ibid.* 99 The ergatandromorph..is an anomaly similar to the [gynandromorph] but having worker instead of female characters combined with those of the male. *Ibid.* vii. 120 In these [*sc.* honey-bees] only the secondary instincts are manifested in the queen, while the worker retains the primary series in full vigor and thus more clearly represents the ancestral female of the species. This type may therefore be called ergatotelic. **1915** H. ST. J. K. DONISTHORPE *Brit. Ants* 114 Wasmann records a mixed ergatandromorph with only the colour of the head like that of the worker. **1927** *Glasgow Herald* 16 July 4 The ergatoids can reproduce ergatoids, besides workers and soldiers. **1970** BROWN & TAYLOR in *Insects of Australia* (C.S.I.R.O.) xxxvii. 952/2 Various wingless intermediates between queens and workers occur in some species. These are the *ergatogynes* (ergatoids).

ergative (ˈɜːgətɪv), *a. Gram.* [f. Gr. ἐργάτης workman + -IVE.] In full ***ergative case.*** A term used of a grammatical case marking the subject of a transitive verb in languages such as Eskimo, Basque, and some others. Also *ellipt.*

1943 J. MAROUZEAU *Lexique Terminol. Linguistique* (ed. 2) 89 Ergatif (Ergativ, Ergative). Cas désignant l'agent dans les langues comme le basque. **1950** *Archivum Linguisticum* II. II. 100 In syntactically transitional types of language like Georgian and Laz..the ergative and nominative are found side by side. **1964** E. PALMER tr. *Martinet's Elem. Gen. Ling.* vi. 179 This ending..was necessarily the morpheme of an 'ergative' case. **1968** J. LYONS *Introd. Theoret. Ling.* viii. 352 The term..for the syntactic relationship that holds between (1) [*the stone moved*] and (3) [*John moved the stone*] is 'ergative': the subject of an intransitive verb 'becomes' the object of a corresponding transitive verb, and a new ergative subject is introduced as the 'agent' (or 'cause') of the action referred to.

Hence **erga'tivity**, the state or condition of being ergative.

1968 J. LYONS *Introd. Theoret. Linguistics* viii. 342 This syntactic parallelism between the 'goal' of a transitive verb and the subject of an intransitive verb is generally referred to as 'ergativity'. **1978** *Language* LIV. 216 Ergativity, accusativity, and other case phenomena. **1983** *Canad. Jrnl. Linguistics* XXVIII. 182 His proposal is..unable to provide a uniform treatment of ergativity.

ergatocracy (ɜːgəˈtɒkrəsɪ). [f. Gr. ἐργάτης workman: see -OCRACY.] Government by the workers. So **ergato'cratic** *a.* (in example *fig.*).

1920 E. & C. PAUL (*title*) Creative revolution. A study of Communist ergatocracy. **1920** *Glasgow Herald* 28 Oct. 4 So far from Bolshevism being an experiment in democracy, or even in..ergatocracy, it is a reversion to the crudest oligarchy. **1944** G. BARKER *Eros in Dogma* 33 The common growing that gives the grass its ergatocratic green.

ergh, dial. form of ARGH.

‖**ergo** (ˈɜːgəʊ), *adv. Logic.* [L. *ergo* therefore.] A word used (like Eng. 'therefore') to mark the conclusion of a syllogism.

? *a* **1400** *Chester Pl.* (Shaks. Soc.) II. 45 Ergo, a kinge thou arte or was. **1503** HAWES *Examp. Virt.* v. 52 Ergo my labour was not in vayn. **1562** COOPER *Answ. Priv. Masse* (1850) 108 Ergo it ought to remain indifferent. **1625** W. PEMBLE *Justification* (1629) 131 To rebell against the Law is sinne. Ergo, To haue a rebellious inclination is sinne likewise. **1780** COWPER *Lett.* 23 June, Ergo (I have reached the conclusion at last) I did not mean to flatter you. **1846** GREENER *Sc. Gunnery* 343 'Ergo' says one, if a 56lb. ball can be thrown 3¼ miles, certain a 68lb. ball can be thrown further, for 'weight is power'.

†**'ergo,** *sb. Obs.*

1. The adverb *ergo* used as a name for itself; *hence*, a conclusion, a conclusive authorization.

1589 R. HARVEY *Pl. Perc.* 20 Such a quoile about *pro* and *con*, such vrging of *Ergoes*. *a* **1613** OVERBURY *A Wife* (1638) 125 The currant of his speech is clos'd with an Ergo. **1654** R. WHITLOCK *Zootomia* 259 We come not to the Ergo of our knowledge untill we come to the conclusion of our daies. **1655** FULLER *Ch. Hist.* IX. vi. §25 No conclusive argument could then be framed without the Ergo of the Royall assent. **1867** J. R. LOWELL *Fitz Adam's Story* in *Poems* (1912) 569 His fancy's thrall, he drew all ergos thence, And thought himself the type of common sense.

2. *nonce-use.* A 'logic-chopper'.

1597 *1st Ret. Parnass.* III. i. 979, I reward the poor ergoes most bountifullie, and send them away.

†**'ergo,** *v. Obs.* [f. ERGO *adv.*; cf. ERGOT *v.*] *intr.* To use the term *ergo*. In quot. quasi-*trans.*

1589 *Pappe w. Hatchet* (1844) 14 He will ergo Martin into an ague.

ergocornine (ɜːgəˈkɔːniːn, -ɪn). *Chem.* [ad. G. *ergocornin* (Stoll & Hofmann 1943, in *Helv. Chim. Acta* XXVI. II. 1570), f. ERGO(T + CORNIN + *-e.*] An alkaloid derived from ergot, $C_{31}H_{39}N_5O_5$.

1944 *Chem. Abstr.* XXXVIII. 2957 Alkaloids of the ergotoxine group—ergocristine, ergocryptine and ergocornine. **1963** *New Scientist* 21 Feb. 389/1 The alkaloid drug, ergocornine,..stops the production of the progesterone hormone.

ergodic (ɜːˈgɒdɪk), *a. Math.* [ad. G. *ergoden* (L. Boltzmann 1887, in *Jrnl. f. d. reine und angewandte Math.* C. 208), f. Gr. ἔργον work + ὁδός way + -IC.] Of a trajectory in a confined portion of space: having the property that in the limit all points of the space will be included in the trajectory with equal frequency. Of a stochastic process: having the property that the probability of any state can be estimated from a single sufficiently extensive realization, independently of initial conditions; statistically stationary. Also, of or pertaining to this property.

1928 tr. *E. Schrödinger's Coll. Papers Wave Mech.* 143 The 'ergodic hypothesis' (Boltzmann) is what Maxwell called the 'principle of continuity of path'. **1931** G. D. BIRKHOFF in *Proc. Nat. Acad. Sci.* XVII. 651, I propose.. to establish a general recurrence theorem and thence the 'ergodic theorem'. **1947** COURANT & ROBBINS *What is Mathematics?* (ed. 4) vii. 354 A rectangular box..leads in general to an ergodic path; the ideal billiard ball going on for ever will reach the vicinity of every point, except for certain singular initial positions and directions. **1962** E. PARZEN *Stochastic Processes* iii. 74 In general, a stochastic process is said to be ergodic if it has the property that sample (or time) averages formed from an observed record of the process may be used as an approximation to the corresponding ensemble (or population) averages. **1967** CONDON & ODISHAW *Handbk. Physics* (ed. 2) v. ii. 19 The justification for the use of this ensemble would be a consequence of an ergodic theorem; that is, a theorem which states that almost all systems in the ensemble spend the same amount of time in any regions of the same (nonvanishing) area on the constant energy surface.

Hence **ergo'dicity**, the quality or property of being ergodic.

1949 W. FELLER *First Berkeley Symposium on Math. Statistics & Probability* 418 What ergodicity might possibly mean in practice may be illustrated by the much discussed Pareto law of income distribution. **1960** G. HERDAN *Type-Token Math.* xx. 296 Under certain circumstances a system will tend in probability to a limiting form which is independent of the initial position from which it started. This is the Ergodicity Property.

ergogram (ˈɜːgəgræm). [f. Gr. ἔργον work + -GRAM.] A record made by an ergograph.

1904 G. S. HALL *Adolescence* I. 150 Endurance as measured by ergograms. **1918** C. S. MYERS *Present-Day Applic. Psychol.* 8 After sufficient rest, complete recovery occurs, so that a second ergogram equal to the first is obtainable. **1948** A. G. BILLS in T. G. Andrews *Methods of Psychol.* 469 The pattern of the ergogram, which was long considered typical for the fatigue of all isolated muscle groups.

ergograph (ˈɜːgəgrɑːf, -æ-). [ad. It. *ergografo* (A. Mosso 1888, in *Atti d. R. Accademia d. Lincei* 4th Ser. V. 411), f. Gr. ἔργον work: see -GRAPH.] An instrument which measures and records the work done by particular groups of muscles. Hence **ergo'graphic** *a.*, **er'gography**.

1892 *Sat. Rev.* 9 Apr. 430/2 The action of the brain on the muscles, as demonstrated by experiments made with the ergograph. **1897** E. W. SCRIPTURE *New Psychol.* 230 The ergograph..consists of a rest in which the arm is fixed so that the middle finger can be moved alone without involving any of the others. **1898** *Daily News* 25 Nov. 6/3 His ergographic curves, and his abdominal respiratory curves, are duly recorded. **1909** C. S. MYERS *Text-bk. Exper. Psychol.* xiv. 184 Ergography.—The work performed by an active muscle..may be best determined by means of graphic records. *Ibid.* 186 An ergographic record. *Ibid.* 383 The ergograph..is especially adapted for the study of simple movements in which very few muscles are involved. **1948** A. G. BILLS in T. G. Andrews *Methods of Psychol.* 468 The most widely used type of ergograph is that invented by Mosso... Its purpose is to force an isolated muscle group.. to work against strong resistance repeatedly until a point of apparent exhaustion is reached. **1953** F. BARTLETT in Floyd & Welford *Sympos. Fatigue* i. 2 The model for the experimental study of muscle fatigue in the intact organism: some form of ergographic technique.

ergoism (ˈɜːgəʊɪz(ə)m). [f. as ERGO *v.* + -ISM.] Pedantic adherence to logically constructed rules.

1864 BURTON *Scot Abr.* II. 262 All [Law's] suggestions were subject to that 'ergoism', as it is aptly termed, of the French.

ergometer (ɜːˈgɒmɪtə(r)). [f. Gr. ἔργο-ν work + μέτρον measure.] An instrument for measuring work or energy.

1879 in THOMSON & TAIT *Nat. Phil.* I. I. §436. **1884** *Nature* XXX. 3 July 220 Work measuring dynamometers, or ergometers, as the author terms them.

ergometrine (ɜːgəˈmɛtriːn, -ɪn). *Biochem.* [f. ERGO(T + Gr. μή τρ(α- womb + -INE^5.] An amide of lysergic acid, $C_{19}H_{23}N_3O_2$, which is one of the most powerful alkaloids present in ergot and is used as an oxytocic.

1935 DUDLEY & MOIR in *Brit. Med. Jrnl.* 16 Mar. 520/2 In 1932 one of us (C.M.) drew the conclusion..that the characteristic and traditional effect of ergot was caused..by a substance still unidentified... We are now..reporting the isolation of the substance to which ergot rightly owes its long-established reputation as the '*pulvis parturiens*'. We propose to call it 'ergometrine'. **1937** GWYNNE-VAUGHAN & BARNES *Struct. & Devel. Fungi* (ed. 2) 253 The sclerotia.. contain a number of alkaloids one of which, ergometrine, causes rapid contraction of the uterus. **1961** *New Scientist* 2 Nov. 278/2 They isolated ergometrine from ergot, simultaneously with American workers, who called it ergonovine. **1963** *Lancet* 19 Jan. 139/1, 0.5 mg. of ergometrine maleate was given intravenously and intramuscularly, and the drip was discontinued. **1970** J. CROSSLAND *Lewis's Pharmacol.* (ed. 4) xvi. 428 Ergometrine is responsible for the abortions seen in ergotism.

†**'ergonist.** *Obs. rare*$^{-1}$. [? f. ERGO + -IST, after *Platonist*, etc.] ? One who is fond of saying 'ergo'; a wrangling logician.

1593 NASHE *Four Lett. Confut.* 32 This I will iustifie against any Dromidote Ergonist whatsoeuer.

ergonomics (ɜːgəˈnɒmɪks). [f. Gr. ἔργον work: see ECONOMICS.] The scientific study of the efficiency of man in his working environment. Hence **ergo'nomic** *a.*, of or pertaining to ergonomics; **ergo'nomically** *adv.* Also **er'gonomist**, one who is skilled in ergonomics.

1950 *Lancet* 1 Apr. 645/2 In July, 1949, a group of people decided to form a new society for which the name the 'Ergonomics Research Society' has now been adopted. **1952** *Oxf. Mail* 2 July 2/5 He [*sc.* K. F. H. Murrell] found it necessary to invent the word 'ergonomics' to cover the kind of work he and other people are doing in studying work in relation to environment. **1954** W. E. LE GROS CLARK in Floyd & Welford *Sympos. Human Factors in Equipment Design* ii. 5 A man and his machine may be regarded as the functional unit of industry, and the aim of ergonomics is the perfection of this unit so as to promote accuracy and speed of operation, and at the same time to ensure minimum fatigue and thereby maximum efficiency. *Ibid.*, Anatomists have not given so much attention as other groups of workers to the application of their studies to ergonomic problems. **1958** *Engineering* 21 Feb. 226/2 This attempt to promote the study of ergonomics, that is, the study of the interaction of men and their environment (now usually with special reference to the machine environment) deserves every success. **1958** *Archit. Rev.* CXXIV. 42/2 The design of an instrument to be gripped by such a diversity of hands must be an ergonomic compromise, but on the whole the new G.P.O. model achieves a fairly satisfactory balance between function and aesthetics. **1959** *Daily Tel.* 8 Apr. 16/3 (*heading*) Ergonomists seek easier design for working. **1961** *Engineering* 6 Oct. 432/3 The keyboard has been ergonomically designed and is contoured..to make every key more accessible to the typist's fingers. **1969** *Times* 5 May 23/5 A seat designed by the one car-maker with an ergonomics department. **1970** *Sci. Jrnl.* Apr. 28/2 The whole subject [of absenteeism] indeed is of interest..to sociologists and ergonomists (industrial psychologists and work physiologists).

ergonovine (ɜːgəˈnəʊviːn, -ɪn). *Biochem.* [a. It. *ergonovine* in *Boll. Soc. Ital. Biol. Sper.* (1937)

XII. 232–4, f. ERGO(T + L. *nov(us* NEW *a.* + -INE[5].] = ERGOMETRINE.
1938 *Chem. Abstr.* XXXII. 303 (*heading*) The determination of ergonovine in ergot preparations... The ergonovine content is detd. by the intensity of coloration. **1955** *Sci. News Let.* 30 July 71/3 The radioactive fungus ergot, and the drugs ergotamine and ergonovine to be extracted from it. **1957** *Encycl. Brit.* VIII. 683/2 Ergonovine is used widely in obstetrical practice in the management of the placental stage in the prevention of excessive blood loss. **1961** [see ERGOMETRINE].

ergophobia (ɜːgəˈfəʊbɪə). *jocular.* [f. Gr. ἔργον work + -PHOBIA.] Fear of work. Hence **ergoˈphobic** *sb.*, one who fears work.
1905 W. D. SPANTON in *Brit. Med. Jrnl.* 11 Feb. 300/2 He has discovered that it often pays better to idle and loaf about than to work, and the consequence is that a new disease has been engendered, which I have termed 'ergophobia'. **1905** *Daily Chron.* 26 May 5/7 Ergophobia.. means a hatred or terror of work... It is a new disease which a medical paper has recently called attention to. **1921** *19th Cent.* Dec. 986 Ergophobia—a recognised if not a notifiable disease. **1960** *Daily Mail* 24 Nov. 10 (*headline*) Ergophobics? *Ibid.* 10/3 Boys suffering from ergophobia (the dilemma of having to choose between working and stealing).

ergosome (ˈɜːgəsəʊm). *Biochem.* [f. Gr. ἔργον work + RIBO)SOME.] (See quots.)
1963 F. O. WETTSTEIN et al. in *Nature* 2 Feb. 434/2 In this article we have described a novel ribosomal particle which appears to be the functional unit of protein synthesis and which we therefore propose to call 'ergosome'. **1964** *Inst. Biol. Jrnl.* II. III. 94 *Ergosome*, an aggregate of ribosomes which is active in the synthesis of proteins. Same as polysome.

ergosterol (ɜːˈgɒstərɒl). *Biochem.* [f. ERGO(T + -STEROL.] A steroid alcohol, $C_{28}H_{44}O$, present esp. in ergot and in many yeasts and fungi, and productive of vitamin D_2 under ultraviolet irradiation. Also earlier **ergosterin** [ad. F. *ergostérine* (C. Tanret 1889, in *Compt. Rend.* CVIII. 98); cf. CHOLESTERIN].
1889 *Jrnl. Chem. Soc.* LVI. 408 Ergosterin.. is completely dissolved by sulphuric acid without discoloration. **1906** *Ibid.* XC. II. 202 As obtained by Bömer's method.. from the fat of rye, ergosterol contains a small amount of a product which forms small, white flocks melting at 60–61° and is non-saponifiable, but the nature of which is unknown. **1927** *Nature* 24 Sept. 440/2 Irradiated ergosterol possesses extraordinarily potent anti-rachitic activity. **1928** A. B. CALLOW *Food & Health* 51 Ergosterol.. was present in minute quantities in what was formerly thought to be pure cholesterol... When ergosterol is irradiated it acquires the property of preventing or curing rickets, that is to say, it becomes vitamin D. **1934** *Nature* 2 June 838/1 Irradiated ergosterol determines the fixation of calcium in the animal organism, and hence induces good ossification... These ergosterol-containing oils readily become rancid. **1963** D. KRITCHEVSKY in Florkin & Stotz *Comprehensive Biochem.* X. i. 14 Ergosterol.. was isolated initially from ergot but.. also occurs in most fungi, including yeast, in lichens, algae and some vegetable oils.

ergot (ˈɜːgət), *sb.* [a. Fr. *ergot*, OF. *argot* cock's spur: see ARGOT[1].]
1. A diseased transformation of the seed of rye and other grasses, being really the *sclerotium* or hardened *mycelium* of a fungus (*Claviceps purpurea*), in colour dark-violet, and in form resembling a cock's spur; hence the name. Also, the disease consisting in this transformation.
1683 *Weekly Mem. Ingen.* 151 That malignity.. breeding in the ears of corn certain black grains called in Sologne, Ergots. **1762** BONES in *Phil. Trans.* LII. 533 The gentle-men of the academy were of opinion, that the disease.. was produced.. by bread, in which there was a great quantity of ergot. **1793** T. BEDDOES *Calculus, etc.* 209 The disease of rye called ergot is exactly analogous to the scurvy in animals. **1838** T. THOMSON *Chem. Org. Bodies* 879 We give to the seeds of rye altered by this disease, the name of ergot of rye. **1863** *N. Brit. Rev.* May 379 An extraordinary disease, called ergot, occurs on wheat and rye.
b. The diseased seed of rye used medicinally.
1860 TANNER *Pregnancy* v. 266 The ergot of rye will often excite contractions, and cause the uterus to empty itself. **1876** HARLEY *Mat. Med.* 365 Ergot seems to have been first used as a medicine by the profession in France and the United States. **1880** N. KERR in *Mech. Temp. Jrnl.* July 151 Half a drachm of the ergot was given every fifteen minutes.
¶ **c.** (See quot.)
1764 BAKER in *Phil. Trans.* LV. 107, I observed a disease mentioned under the appellation of Ergot, a name borrowed from its supposed cause, viz. vitiated rye.
2. *Farriery.* 'A small horny capsule on each side of the claw or horny envelope of the digits in Ruminants and Pachyderms' (*Syd. Soc. Lex.*). Cf. ARGOT[1].
3. *Anat.* (See quot.)
1840 G. ELLIS *Anat.* 41 The *hippocampus minor* or 'ergot' is a projection in the floor of the posterior extremity or cornu of the lateral ventricle [of the brain].
Hence **ˈergoted** *ppl. a.*, tainted with ergot.
1841 *Jrnl. Royal Agric. Soc.* II. I. 16 A poor man.. ventured to make bread of some ergotted rye. **1869** E. A. PARKES *Pract. Hygiene* (ed. 3) 222 Flour.. may be ergoted or grown and fermenting.

† **ˈergot**, *v. Obs. rare.* Also 7 ergat. [a. F. *ergoter* 'to rise on his toes, wrangle' (Cotgr.), f. *ergot* (cf. ARGOT[1]) the spur of a cock; but the word was associated both in Fr. and Eng. with ERGO.] *intr.* To argue, wrangle.
1653 URQUHART *Rabelais* I. xvii, After they had well ergoted pro and con, they concluded in Baralipton, that, etc. *a* **1658** HEWYT *Serm.* (1658) 178 Little doth it concern us what the school-men ergat in their schools.

ergotamine (ɜːˈgɒtəmiːn, -ɪn). *Biochem.* [ad. G. *ergotamin* (Spiro & Stoll 1921, in *Actes Soc. Helv. Sci. Nat. 1920* 235), f. ERGOT + AMINE.] An alkaloid, $C_{33}H_{35}O_5N_5$, present in some kinds of ergot and used chiefly in the treatment of migraine. Hence **ergoˈtaminine** [ad. G. *ergotaminin* (Spiro & Stoll 1921, in *Actes Soc. Helv. Sci. Nat. 1920* 236), f. ERGOT + AMIN(E + -INE[5]], a physiologically inactive ergot alkaloid, isomeric with ergotamine.
1921 *Brit. Pat. 170, 302* The principal alkaloid of ergot in the pure crystallised state.. has since been designated.. by the scientific name of 'ergotamine'. **1922** *Jrnl. Chem. Soc.* A. CXXII. I. 47 Ergotamine, obtained in crystallisable form from ergot, on treatment with methyl alcohol gives a new, less active alkaloid, *ergotaminine*. **1952** L. MARION in Manske & Holmes *Alkaloids* II. 376 Ergotamine and ergotaminine do not seem to occur in rye ergot, but are found in other ergots such as that growing.. on marrom grass. **1955** [see ERGONOVINE]. **1961** *New Scientist* 2 Nov. 278/2 The first pure ergot alkaloids were obtained by Stoll in 1920, namely the pharmacologically-active compound ergotamine and the inactive mirror-image molecule ergotaminine. **1964** S. DUKE-ELDER *Parsons' Dis. Eye* (ed. 14) xxiv. 362 Rest, warmth, and sleep are the best measures to combat the attacks [of migraine]; they can sometimes be warded off or alleviated by ergotamine tartrate. **1968** J. H. BURN *Lect. Notes Pharmacol.* (ed. 9) 75 Ergotamine has now lost much of its importance since the discovery of ergometrine (ergonovine).

† **ergoˈteer**, *v. Obs.* [as if f. **ergoteer* sb., f. ERGO (confused with ERGOT *v.*) + -EER[1]. Cf. next.] *intr.* To argue, wrangle.
Hence **ergoˈteerer**, a wrangler. **ergoˈteering** *vbl. sb.*, wrangling.
1687 STILLINGFL. *Vind. Answ. Papers conc. Authority Cath. Ch.* 104 They are a sort of Ergoteerers, who are for a Concedo rather than a Nego. *Ibid.* 109 This Gentleman sets himself to Ergoteering.

‖ **ergoteur** (ɛrgɔtœr). [Fr. *ergoteur*, agent-n. f. *ergoter*: see ERGOT *v.*] = prec.
1881 *19th Cent.* Sept. 325 Mr. Gladstone and this famous ergoteur are the only people living who have boundless faith in reasoning.

ergotic (ɜːˈgɒtɪk), *a.*[1] [f. ERGOT *sb.* + -IC.] Of or pertaining to ergot; resulting from the action of ergot.
ergotic acid, 'a volatile acid said to exist in Ergot of rye' (*Syd. Soc. Lex.*).
1875 H. WOOD *Therap.* (1879) 546 It is.. very doubtful whether the ergotic spasm is local in its origin.

† **erˈgotic**, *a.*[2] *Obs.*[−0] In 7 -ique. [a. Fr. *ergotique*; cf. ERGOT *v.*] Sophistical, cavilling, full of conclusions.
1681 in BLOUNT *Glossogr.*

ergotine (ˈɜːgətɪn). [f. ERGOT *sb.* + -INE.] The active principle of ergot of rye.
1851 R. HUNT in *Art Jrnl. Catal. Gt. Exhib.* IV. p. xv*/1 Sardinia contributes many chemical products.. amongst others.. ergotine. **1875** H. WOOD *Therap.* (1879) 543 In the frog the injection of a gramme of ergotin caused a diastolic arrest of the heart.
Hence **erˈgotinine** *Chem.* [+ -INE.], 'an unstable alkaloid existing in very small quantity in ergot' (Watts).
[**1875** C. TANRET in *Compt. Rend. Acad. Sci.* LXXXI. 896 Un alcaloïde nouveau.. Je propose de l'appeler *ergotinine*]. **1875** H. WOOD *Therap.* (1879) 541 Of all the substances named, the crystallizable ergotinine of Tauret [*sic*] seems most promising. **1940** *Thorpe's Dict. Appl. Chem.* (ed. 4) IV. 329/1 The first alkaloid ergotinine isolated by Tanret.. was inert.

ergotism[1] (ˈɜːgətɪz(ə)m). [f. ERGOT *sb.* + -ISM.]
1. The disease (in grasses) consisting in the formation of ergot.
1853 *Pharmaceut. Jrnl.* XIII. 13 Mr. Blyth drew attention to the subject of the ergotism of grasses.
2. The disease produced by eating bread made from flour affected by ergot.
1869 E. A. PARKES *Pract. Hygiene* (ed. 3) 222 The most important disease connected with flour is.. ergotism. **1876** BARTHOLOW *Mat. Med.* (1879) 289 Chronic ergotism.. exists in two forms, the convulsive and gangrenous.
3. The use of ergot for poisoning animals.
1884 A. WILLOWS in *Australasian* 8 Nov. 875/4 The special claims of ergotism.. are its cheapness, etc.

ergotism[2] (ˈɜːgətɪz(ə)m). [a. Fr. *ergotisme*, f. L. *ergo*, associated with *ergoter*: see ERGOT *v.*]
a. Arguing, quibbling, wrangling. **b.** Logical conclusions.
1656–81 BLOUNT *Glossogr.* **1682** SIR T. BROWNE *Chr. Mor.* (1756) 60 States are not governed by ergotisms. **1685** COTTON *Montaigne* I. 269, I think these lowsy ergotismes and little sophistry.. are the cause. **1775** in ASH. **1847** in CRAIG; and in mod. Dicts.

† **ˈergotist.** *Obs.* [a. Fr. *ergotiste* (Montaigne): cf. prec.] A quibbler, pedantic logician.
1739 tr. *Algarotti on Newton's Theory* (1742) I. 188 Declaiming.. against the ancient Philosophy.. stigmatizing those who profess it with the Title of Ergotists.

ergotization (ˌɜːgətaɪˈzeɪʃən). [f. next + -ATION. See -ATION.] The action or process of poisoning by ergot of rye.
1886 *Brit. Med. Jrnl.* 30 Jan. 198/1.

ergotize (ˈɜːgətaɪz), *v.*[1] [f. ERGOT *sb.* + -IZE.] *trans.* To affect with or transform into ergot.
Hence **ˈergotized** *ppl. a.*
1860 *Gard. Chron.* 29 Sept., The formidable consequences of ergotized corn, when eaten. **1875** H. WOOD *Therap.* (1879) 552 When the summer is wet and cold, the rye becomes very extensively ergotized. **1884** *Pall Mall G.* 12 Sept. 2/1 Some fifteen outbreaks of foot-rot, the result of eating ergotized rye.

ergotize (ˈɜːgətaɪz), *v.*[2] [f. ERGO: cf. ERGOTISM and -IZE.] *intr.* To quibble, wrangle.
1883 STEVENSON *Treasure of Franchard* vi, He uses it [the word *ratiocinate*].. in the sense of *to ergotise*, implying as it were.. a vein of sophistry.

ergotoxine (ɜːgəˈtɒksiːn, -ɪn). *Biochem.* [f. ERGO(T + TOX(IN + -INE[5].] A mixture of three similar alkaloids present in ergot and used as an oxytocic, formerly thought to be a single compound; also, any of the alkaloids of this mixture.
1906 BARGER & CARR in *Chem. News* XCIV. 89/2 The crystalline alkaloid ergotinine was obtained from ergot by Tanret more than thirty years ago... We have now obtained the second alkaloid in a state of chemical purity, and suggest for it the name *ergotoxine*. **1937** GWYNNE-VAUGHAN & BARNES *Fungi* (ed. 2) 253 Owing to the presence of ergotoxine the sclerotia, if included in the grain used for bread, give rise to serious disease. **1952** L. MARION in Manske & Holmes *Alkaloids* II. 377 This anomaly.. has recently been explained away by the discovery that ergotoxine is not homogeneous, but a complex mixture. **1958** FRUTON & SIMMONDS *Gen. Biochem.* (ed. 2) xxxiii. 862 Ergot contains the pharmacologically active alkaloids ergometrine, ergotamine, and several ergotoxines.

‖ **erh hu** (ɜː huː). Also ellhwu, erh-hu, erhu. [Chinese *èrhú*, f. *èr* two + *hú* foreign; cf. *huqin* a generic term for a bowed stringed instrument.] A Chinese two-stringed fiddle (see quots. 1975).
1908 *Jrnl. North-China Branch R. Asiatic Soc.* XXXIX. 125 Êrh Hu (Eul Hou)... This differs from the *Ssŭ Hu*.. in having one pair of strings instead of two... At Peking, where it is not common, it is called *Êrh Ku tzŭ*. **1917** S. COULING *Encycl. Sinica* 389/1 *Mabillon* quotes *Fétis* as saying that the *Erh hu* was derived from a Cingalese violin. **1954** *Grove's Dict. Mus.* (ed. 5) II. 246/1 Liou also left a number of compositions for the *ellhwu* and was himself an outstanding executant on this instrument. **1954** *Folk Arts of New China* 15 One or two manipulated the dolls... Two others sang and declaimed, the rest provided the music on drums and cymbals, *erh hu* (Chinese violin) and flute. **1964** S. MARCUSE *Mus. Instruments* 174/2 *Erh hu*, spike fiddle of China, a hu ch'in with small hexagonal body of wood, snakeskin belly, 2 strings looped to the handle and tuned a 5th apart, and a tubular neck that pierces the belly... The bow passes between the strings, thus causing them to sound simultaneously. **1975** C. P. MACKERRAS *Chinese Theatre in Mod. Times* 22 Although the *hu-ch'in* and the *erh-hu* are often played simultaneously, the former is normally allowed to dominate when accompanying the singers of male roles; the latter, when accompanying the singers of female roles. **1986** J. TRENHAILE *Mahjong Spies* v. 101 The clash of gong and cymbals.. yielding to the more melodious strains of the erhu.

eri, obs. form of EERIE *a.*

eria (ˈɪərɪə). Also eri. [Assamese *eriya*, adj. f. *era* the castor-oil plant.] In ***eria silk***: see quot. 1881; ***eria worm***: the silkworm that produces this silk, *Attacus ricini*. Also ***eria cocoon, moth***.
1837 *Jrnl. Asiatic Soc. Bengal* VI. 23 The *eria* worm and moth differ from the mulberry worm or moth in every respect. **1866** *Chambers's Encycl.* VIII. 724/1 The 'Eria', or 'Arrindy' silkworm, native of India. **1868** WOOD *Homes without H.* xiv. 282 The well known Eria silk of India is produced by an insect closely allied to the Atlas Moth. **1881** HUNTER in *Encycl. Brit.* XII. 752 s.v. *India*, Eria silk is obtained from the cocoons of *Phalæna Cynthia*, and the worm is fed.. upon the leaves of the castor-oil plant. **1887** *Ibid.* XXII. 60/2 The eria or arrindi moth of Bengal and Assam, *Attacus ricini*, which feeds on the castor-oil plant. **1909** H. MAXWELL-LEFROY *Indian Insect Life* 479 Moths reared from true eri cocoons cultivated in Assam proved to be the latter [sc. *Attacus ricini*]. **1923** *Nature* CXI. 411/2 It appears that all the recognised diseases are prevalent, and those of the mulberry, muga, and eri worms are the same. **1944** *Indian Farming* V. 365/1 The rearing of *eri* is much easier than that of any other silk worm. *Ibid.* 365/2 There is a large trade in silk and the *eri* cocoons. **1956** W. J. B. CROTCH *Silkmoth Rearer's Handbk.* (ed. 2) x. 128 Philosamia Grote (Eri Silkmoth).

Erian (ˈɪərɪən), *a. Geol.* [f. *Erie*, name of the lake + -IAN.] A synonym of DEVONIAN: see quots.
1873 DAWSON *Earth & Man* v. 84 The Devonian, or, as it may be better called in America, from the vast development of its beds on the south side of Lake Erie, the Erian formation. **1877** —— *Orig. World* 380 Erian and Carboniferous plants.

‖**eric** (ˈɛrɪk). *Hist.* Forms: 6 eriach, earike, erycke, 7 erick(e, 8– eric. [Ir. *eiric.*] (See quots.)

1586 [see EARIK]. **1596** SPENSER *State Irel.* Wks. (1862) 504/2 In the case of Murder..the malefactor shall give unto them [the friends], or to the child, or wife of him that is slain a recompence, which they call an Eriach. **1612** DAVIES *Why Ireland, etc.* (1747) 111 The killing of an Irishman was.. punished..by a fine or pecuniary punishment which is called an Ericke. *Ibid.* (1787) 126 Your Sheriff..shall be welcome to me, but let me know his erick aforehand. *a* **1849** J. C. MANGAN *Poems* (1859) 389 All the dead Heaped on the field..Were scarce an eric for his head. **1885** R. BAGWELL *Irel. under Tudors* I. 11 This blood-fine, called an eric, was an utter abomination to the English of the sixteenth century.
attrib. **1875** MAINE *Hist. Inst.* vi. 170 'Eric'-fines or pecuniary compensation for violent crime.

‖**Erica** (ɪˈraɪkə, ˈɛrɪkə). *Bot.* [L. *erīca*, ad. Gr. ἐρείκη heath.] The botanical name of the genus of plants called in Eng. HEATH. (In quot. used affectedly as an Eng. word.)

1826 CARRINGTON *Dartmoor* 37 Th' undaunted race Contented on the rude Erica sink To balmy sleep.

ericaceous (ɛrɪˈkeɪʃəs), *a. Bot.* [f. mod.L. *ericāce-æ* + -OUS: see prec. and -ACEOUS.] Belonging to the natural order *Ericaceæ*, of which the *Erica* or heath is the typical genus.

1882 *Garden* 7 Oct. 323/2 Other Ericaceous plants are represented admirably.

ericetal (ɛrɪˈsiːtəl), *a. Bot.* [as if f. L. **ericēt-um* place where heaths grow (f. *erīca* heath) + -AL[1].] Of the type characteristic of heathy regions; moorland.

1876 G. W. LATHAM in *Encycl. Brit.* V. 589 The botany of the high-lands east of Macclesfield is nearly ericetal in its nature.

ericineous (ɛrɪˈsɪnɪəs), *a. Bot.* [f. mod.L. *ericine-æ* (a synonym of *ericāce-æ*), f. *erīca*, on analogy of *grāmineæ*, etc.] = ERICACEOUS.

1852 TH. ROSS *Humboldt's Trav.* I. xiii. 425 The shrubs of the family of the ericineous plants..do not find the cold climate which is necessary for their development.

ericoid (ˈɛrɪkɔɪd), *a. Bot.* [f. ERIC(A: see -OID.] Resembling or belonging to a plant of the genus *Erica*, the family Ericaceæ, or the subfamily Ericoideæ.

1900 B. D. JACKSON *Gloss. Bot. Terms* 92/2 *Ericoid*, used of leaves which are like those of heaths. **1954** *Proc. Prehist. Soc.* XX. 234 Beaulieu IX..appears to be the oldest, though it actually shows a higher quantity of ericoid pollen than Beaulieu VI. **1965** *Jrnl. Linn. Soc. Bot.* LIX. 119 (*heading*) The Ericoid Group... If we ignore *Calluna*, the floral and fruit characters used by Drude are correlated with the presence of the characteristic 'ericoid' habit.

ericolin (ɛˈrɪkəlɪn). *Chem.* [f. ERICA + -OL + -IN.] A resinous substance found in several plants of the ericaceous order.

1876 HARLEY *Mat. Med.* 530 Ericolin is obtained from the mother-liquor from which the arbutin has crystallised.

erie, obs. form of AERIE.

†**eˈriferous**, *a. Obs.* [f. L. *ærifer* (f. *æri-* combining form of *æs*, *æri-s* brass + *-fer* producing) + -OUS.] Containing or yielding brass or copper.

1681 BLOUNT *Glossogr.*

†**eriff.** *Obs.* [Of unknown etymology; the forms *eiress*, *eress*, *eriss*, in Dicts. appear to represent the same word.]

1. A canary-bird two years old.

c **1690** B. E. *Dict. Cant. Crew.* **1727** BRADLEY *Fam. Dict.* s.v. *Canary Bird*, Those that exceed two, are named Erisses. **1736** BAILEY, *Erisses, eresses.*

2. 'A rogue just initiated'. (*New Cant. Dict.* 1725.)

eriff, dial. form of HAIRIF.

1796 *Agric. Surv. Staffordsh.* 95 Eriff, *Galium Aparine.*

erigant, error for *erigaut*, var. of HERIGAUT.

‖**eˈrigeron.** [Gr. ἠριγέρων, f. ἦρι early + γέρων old man. Cf. L. *senecio*, f. *senex* old man.]

†**a.** The Gr. name of the Groundsel: see quots. In botanical Latin the name of an allied genus. *Obs.*

1601 HOLLAND *Pliny* II. 238 The Greekes imposed that name Erigeron, because in the Spring it looketh hoarie, like an old gray beard. **1666** J. SMITH *Old Age* (ed. 2) 163 This is the true Erigeron, that early in the Spring-time bears the representation of Old Age.

b. [Linnæus *Hortus Cliffortianus* (1737) 407, from a name used by Theophrastus for a similar plant.] A hardy herbaceous annual, biennial, or perennial plant bearing daisy-like flowers and belonging to the large genus so called, of the family Compositæ.

1815 *Bot. Reg.* I. 10 (*caption*) Fordyce's Erigeron. **1900** J. M. ABBOTT in W. D. Drury *Bk. Gard.* viii. 270 Erigerons are summer-flowering composites with beautiful star-shaped flowers. **1901** *Cassell's Dict. Gard.* I. 325/2 Snails and slugs are frequently very destructive to Erigerons in late autumn. **1922** *Glasgow Herald* 16 Dec. 8 Mauve erigerons, scarlet geums, arabis. **1964** M. FISH *Ground Cover Plants* xi. 82 For years I have grown a low, fleshy erigeron..and nothing could make better ground cover for a bank or wall. **1969** HAY & SYNGE *Dict. Garden Plants* 295/1 A wide range of hybrid erigerons have been raised in England and in Germany.

†**eˈright**, *v. Obs.* [? var. of ARIGHT *v.*] *trans.* ? To invest with a right.

1556 J. HEYWOOD *Spider & F.* xx, Or by sine of purpose craftely clokte To possession here any flie erighting.

erigible (ˈɛrɪdʒɪb(ə)l), *a.* [f. L. *ērig-ĕre* (see ERECT *v.*) + -IBLE.] Capable of being erected or set in an upright position.

a **1803** G. SHAW *Zool.* IV. II. 378 A very strong spine, which..is erigible at the pleasure of the animal. **1847** in CRAIG; and in mod. Dicts.

†**erimites:** app. mistake for ERMINITES.

1577 STANYHURST *Descr. Irel.* in *Holinshed* II. 105/1 His signet..hauing powdred erimites ingrailed in the seale.

erinaceous (ɛrɪˈneɪʃəs), *a. Zool.* [f. L. *ērināce-us* hedgehog + -OUS.] Pertaining to the hedgehog family; of the nature of a hedgehog. See also HERINACIOUS.

In mod. Dicts.

erinde, obs. form of ERRAND.

erineum (əˈrɪnɪəm). *Bot.* [mod.L. (C. H. Persoon *Mycologia Europaea* (1822) I. 2), f. Gr. ἐρίνεος woolly, f. ἔριον wool.]

A pathological growth of the epidermis of plants caused by mites of the family Eriophyidæ. Hence **eˈrineal** *a.*

Formerly supposed to be caused by a fungus to which *Erineum* was given as the generic name.

1889 *Cent. Dict.* III. 1994/2 The erinea were formerly considered to constitute a genus of fungi. **1901** H. M. WARD *Disease in Plants* xxiii. 214 In true galls the hypertrophy may consist merely in the enlargement of cells already present.. e.g...the hairy outgrowths of the epidermis known as *Erineum.* **1916** H. S. PRATT *Man. Invertebr. Anim.* 438 A fuzzy spot or erineum is a dense mass of twisted hairs, among which the mites live. **1937** F. D. HEALD *Introd. Plant Path.* ii. 16 An abnormal development of hairs or trichomes from the surfaces of leaves giving feltlike patches, first believed to be of fungous origin and named *erineum*, but now known to be caused by parasitic mites and designated *erinose.* **1964** M. S. MANI *Ecol. Plant Galls* iii. 50 Erineal galls with papillate hairs are not uncommon. **1969** N. W. HUSSEY et al. *Pests of Protected Cultivation* vi. 223 *Aceria lycopersici* (Wolffenstein), known as the tomato erineum mite, causes white and densely hairy patches on the stems and petioles.

eringo, var. form of ERYNGO.

erinite (ˈɛrɪnaɪt). *Min.* [f. *Erin* the ancient name of Ireland + -ITE.] A green arseniate of copper found in Cornwall and in some parts of Ireland.

1828 *Phil. Mag.* Ser. II. IV. 155 The colour of erinite is a beautiful emeral green. **1843** PORTLOCK *Geol.* 221 Erinite occurs in small nodules in a soft wacke at Ballintry. **1887** DANA *Manual Min.* 153 Erinite occurs in emerald-green mammillinated coatings.

Eˈrinnic, *a. rare*[−1]. [f. L. *Erinn-ys*, *Erīnys*, Gr. Ἐρῖνύς a Fury + -IC.] Characteristic of a Fury.

1827 SOUTHEY in *Q. Rev.* XXXVI. 345 Even their [the cats'] cries, erotic or erinnic..could neither dismay nor disturb her.

So †**Eˈrinnical**, *a. Obs.*

1613 SIR E. HOBY *Counter-snarle* 67 Vexed with their Erynnical libels.

erinose (ˈɛrɪnəʊs, -z). *Bot.* [f. as ERINEUM see -OSE.] = ERINEUM. Freq. *attrib.*

[**1910** G. MASSEE *Dis. Cultivated Plants & Trees* 541 Vine erinosis.—This disease is caused by *Eriophyes vitis.*] **1926** F. D. HEALD *Man. Plant Dis.* xvi. 416 Erinose spots are always convex above. **1937** —— *Introd. Plant Path.* ii. 16 Erinose spots on grapes are white at first. **1951** *Dict. Gardening* (R. Hort. Soc.) II. 772/1 Erinose often follows an attack of Red Spider on Cinerarias, Pelargoniums, and Vines.

eriometer (ɛrɪˈɒmɪtə(r)). [f. Gr. ἔριον wool + μέτρον measure.] An instrument for measuring by optical means the diameter of small fibres, such as wool, cotton, or flax.

1829 *Nat. Philos., Optics* xv. 27 (Usef. Knowl. Soc.) By means of an instrument which he [? Dr. Young] calls an Eriometer, he was enabled to measure the size of minute particles or fibres. **1836** TODD *Cycl. Anat.* I. 406/2 The results..having..been come to by the aid of the eriometer.

eristic (ɛˈrɪstɪk), *a.* and *sb.* [ad. Gr. ἐριστικ-ός, f. ἐρίζειν to wrangle, f. ἔρις strife.]

A. *adj.* Of or pertaining to controversy or disputation; adapted for or disposed to controversy.

1637 GILLESPIE *Eng. Pop. Cerem.* Ord. C iij, Polemicke and Eristicke discourses. **1655–60** STANLEY *Hist. Philos.* (1701) 145/1 A Sect..called..Eristick from the Litigious Sophistical Nature thereof. **1710** W. HUME *Sacred Success.* 28 The controversie among our eristick divines. **1850** GROTE *Greece* II. lxvii. VIII. 540 *note*, Euthydemus and Dionysodorus..applied themselves to the eristic or controversial dialogue. *a* **1852** MOORE *Devil among the Schol.* 72 He fought the combat syllogistic With..skill and art eristic.

B. *sb.*

1. One given to disputation, a controversialist. *the Eristics*: philosophers of the Megarian school.

1659 GAUDEN *Tears Ch.* 93 Fanatick Errour and Levity would seem an Euchite as well as an Eristick. **1875** JOWETT *Plato* (ed. 2) I. 481 You would not confuse the principle and the consequences in your reasoning, like the Eristics. **1965** *Times Educ. Suppl.* 26 Mar., Arrogance characterized the eristic while humility marked the heuristic.

2. = Gr. ἡ ἐριστική (τέχνη), the art of disputation.

1866 MILL in *Edin. Rev.* CXXIII. 314 Real Dialectic contrasted with Eristic. **1875** JOWETT *Plato* (ed. 2) I. 183 The art of Eristic, or fighting with words.

†**eˈristical**, *a. Obs.* [f. as prec. + -AL[1].] = prec.

1624 BP. MOUNTAGU *Gagg* Pref. 2 Eristicall discourses. **1654** TRAPP *Comm. Job* xxiii. 32 Some are so eristical and teasty, that they will not hear the adverse party. **1673** BP. PARKER *Reproof of Reh. Transp.* 125 (L.) To what purpose should he or any man write eristical books?

†**ˈeritage**, *v. Obs. rare.* [f. *eritage*, obs. form of HERITAGE.] *trans.* **a.** To inherit. **b.** To give as a heritage.

1382 WYCLIF *Ps.* xxxvi[i]. 11 The debonere forsothe shuln eritagen the erthe [**1388** enerite the lond]. —— *Ecclus.* xvii. 9 The lawe of lif he eritagede [**1388** enheritide] them.

eritage, obs. form of HERITAGE.

†**erite.** *Obs.* [a. OF. *herite* app. a back formation from L. *hæret-icus.*] A heretic.

c **1175** *Lamb. Hom.* 143 þe forsworene, þe heðene, þe erites sculen beon iwarpen ine eche pine.

erith, obs. var. of HARIFF, Goosegrass.

1601 HOLLAND *Pliny* II. 174 Erith or Goose grasse..is by some called in Greeke *Aparine.*

†**erivate**, *v. Obs.*[−0] [f. L. *ērīvāt-* ppl. stem of *ērīvā-re*, f. *ē* out + *rīvus* brook.] *trans.* To draw out, draw off.

1656–81 in BLOUNT *Glossogr.*

erk (ɜːk). *slang.* Also **irk.** [Of obscure origin.] **a.** A naval rating. **b.** An aircraftman, esp. an A.C.2. **c.** *transf.* Used as a term of contempt.

1925 FRASER & GIBBONS *Soldier & Sailor Words* 89 *Erk*, a rating. (Navy). Lower deck colloquialism for any 'rank' not that of an officer. **1928** T. E. LAWRENCE *Let.* 20 Jan. (1938) 570 Cranwell, which was a home from home, for the irks. **1940** *Reader's Digest* May 31/2 The aviators..call their mechanics *erks*, apparently a corruption of A.C., the abbreviation for aircraftsman. **1943** P. BRENNAN et al. *Spitfires over Malta* iii. 65 The erks came running up to tell us that..the 109 had been diving down. **1944** E. PARTRIDGE in *19th Cent.* Apr. 182 An *erk*, now used for an A.C.2.. meant an air mechanic. This odd word is, the writer believes, a shortened pronunciation of the italicised letters in *air mechanic* (perhaps in the form of 'air mech')... Some airmen less convincingly maintain that it comes from 'lower-deck hand'. **1959** I. & P. OPIE *Lore & Lang. Schoolch.* x. 175 Somebody they dislike..may be called.. erk, gawp, kid.

erke, obs. form of IRK.

Erlang (ˈɜːlæŋ). The name of a Danish mathematician, Agner Krarup *Erlang* (1878–1929).

1. Used to designate various formulæ, functions, etc., derived by him or arising out of his work; as ***Erlang('s) distribution***, a distribution function of the time required for the occurrence of *n* random events (see quot. 1960[1]); also, an Erlang loss formula; ***Erlang('s) formula***, a formula giving the probability that a given number of lines in a communication system are occupied; *spec.*, ***Erlang('s) congestion*** (or ***B-*** or ***first loss***) ***formula***, a formula giving the probability of congestion assuming that calls finding all lines occupied are cleared; ***Erlang('s) delay*** (or ***second loss***) ***formula***, a formula giving the probability of congestion assuming that such calls are delayed until a line is available. Hence **Erˈlangian** *a.* [-IAN].

1918 *Post Office Electr. Engin. Jrnl.* XI. 151 These durations are very far from complying with either of Mr. Erlang's distribution laws, yet the results agree closely with the theoretical curve. I think, therefore, Mr. Erlang's formula can be looked upon as being of quite general application. **1920** *Ibid.* XIII. 215 Erlang's formula states that if the average number of simultaneous calls is *A*, the probability of exactly *r* switches being engaged if the total number of switches is *x*, is $(A^r/r!)/(1 + A + A^2/2! + .. + A^r/r! + .. + A^x/x!)$. **1948** *Bell Syst. Techn. Jrnl.* XXVII. 425 The..assumption underlying the Erlang B formula is that of no delay. A call which encounters *all trunks busy* is cleared out. **1953** *Ann. Math. Statistics* XXIV. 339 We may also mention an intermediate type of input: E_k (Erlangian). **1954** A. JENSEN *Distribution Model* v. 16 Erlang's distribution corresponds to Poisson's distribution just as that of Pascal corresponds to the binomial distribution. **1960** R. SYSKI *Congestion Theory Teleph. Syst.* iv. 139 One has: $f_n(t)dt = (n\mu t)^{n-1}e^{-\mu nt}n\mu dt/(n-1)!$, $t \geq 0$ where μ is a positive constant. This form is known as the Erlang distribution... In several cases, the Erlang distribution is the only one which yields explicit solutions to congestion problems. *Ibid.* v. 252 The famous Erlang's loss formula (his B-formula—denoted usually by $E_n(A)$)..serves as the basis of traffic calculations for most telephone administrations. **1968** P. A. P. MORAN *Introd. Probability Theory* ii. 87 We can also truncate the Poisson distribution on the other tail and obtain a bounded distribution

$$p_n = \ldots = \lambda^n \Big/ \Big\{ n! \sum_{j=0}^{N} \lambda^j (j!)^{-1} \Big\},$$

$n = 0, 1, \ldots, N$. This is also known as 'Erlang's distribution' and arises in the theory of telephone traffic.

2. A unit of the intensity of traffic in a communication system (see quot. 1960).

1947 *Post Office Electr. Engin. Jrnl.* XXXIX. 174/2 The proposal by the Swedish Administrations to use the name 'erlang' for the unit of intensity of traffic was adopted [by the 6th and 7th Commissions de Rapporteurs of the C.C.I.F.]. **1948** E. Brockmeyer et al. *Life & Wks. A. K. Erlang* 20 The name of 'Erlang' has been used in the Scandinavian countries to denominate the unit of traffic since the beginning of 1944. **1951** *Jrnl. R. Statistical Soc.* B. XIII. 153 A parameter of special importance is the traffic-intensity $\rho \equiv b/a$; in a long period of time, T, there will be approximately T/a calls for service, each of mean length b, and so ρ is the expected service demanded per unit of time, in 'erlangs'... (Properly it is not a unit at all, but an indication of how the preceding figure has been calculated; in this respect it resembles the octave, the decibel and the stellar magnitude.) **1960** *Gloss. Terms Telecomm. & Electronics* (*B.S.I.*) 216 *Erlang*, the unit of traffic flow... An Erlang is..equivalent to the traffic flow in one circuit continuously occupied.

erld, erldom, erle, obs. ff. EARL, EARLDOM.

erlish (ˈɜːlɪʃ), *a.* *rare*⁻¹. [var. of *elrish*, ELDRITCH.] = ELDRITCH.

a **1802** *Yng. Tamlane* xlix. in Child *Eng. & Sc. Pop. Ballads* II. (1884) 355/2 Up there raise an erlish cry.

erl-king (ˈɜːlˈkɪŋ). [transl. Ger. *erl-könig* (lit. alder-king), an erroneous rendering by Herder of the Danish *ellerkonge*, *ellekonge*, i.e. *elverkonge*, *elvekonge* king of the elves. Cf. ELLE-MAID.]

1797 Scott tr. *Goethe's Erl King* Pref. Poet. Wks. (1848) The Erl-King is a goblin that haunts the Black Forest, in Thuringia.

erm, var. of ARM *a. Obs.* poor.

c **1175** *Lamb. Hom.* 113 Moni mon..is erm for worlde · and uniseli for gode. *Ibid.* 115 Ðet is kinges rihtwisnesse þet he mid wohȝe ne of-sitte ne ermne ne eadine.

†**erme**, *v. Obs.* [OE. *yrman*, *ięrman* (Anglian *ęrman), f. *earm* miserable.] **a.** *trans.* To make miserable, grieve, harass, vex. **b.** *intr.* for *refl.* To grieve, be sorry.

c **897** K. Ælfred *Gregory's Past.* xvii. 121 Ic mæȝ slean and ierman mine [h]eafodȝemæccan. *a* **1000** *Boeth. Metr.* ix. 45 He [Nero] hæfde him to gamene..hu he eorþcyningas yrmde and cwelmde. *c* **1386** Chaucer *Pard. Prol.* 26 But weel I wot thou dost myn herte erme. **1481** Caxton *Reynard* (Arb.) 48 Thenne departed he fro the kynge so heuyly, that many of them ermed.

Hence **ˈerming** *vbl. sb.*, grieving, sadness.

c **1300** *K. Alis.* 1525 Theo bysschop wep for ermyng.

ermelin (ˈɜːməlɪn). Now *arch.* or *poet.* Also 6–7 **armelin(e, ermilin, h)ermeline**, (7 **armlin**), 6 **ermly**. [The immediate source is uncertain: the word appears in most of the Romanic langs.; It. *armellino*, *ermellino*, Sp. *armelina*, Fr. *hermeline* (Boiste), *armeline* (Cotgr.), med.L. *armelinus* (in Fr. documents of 13th c.).

The ulterior etymology shares in the uncertainty belonging to that of the synonymous ERMINE. If the latter be of Teut. origin, the Romanic forms above cited must be regarded as ad. MHG. *hermelîn* (mod.G. *hermelin*), dim. of *harme*:—OHG. *harmo* (see ERMINE). If the alternative view be correct, the med.L. type *armelīnus* must be a diminutive or adjectival formation on *armenius*, and the MHG. *hermelîn* an adoption from Romanic, though perh. influenced by association with the native word.]

1. The animal called ermine; = ERMINE 1.

1555 Eden *Decades W. Ind.* (Arb.) 323 Sables, Marternes, Hermelines. **1590** Greene *Never too late* (1600) 34 Adamants that will draw youth as..yᵉ sight of the Panther, the Ermly. **1596** Spenser *F.Q.* III. ii. 25 And on his shield enueloped seuenfold He bore a crowned little Ermelin. **1607** Topsell *Four-f. Beasts* (1673) 405 The Armelins are called Alpine Mice. *c* **1630** Drumm. of Hawth. *Poems* Wks. 3 Fair yokes of ermelines, whose colour pass The whitest snows. **1742** Shenstone *Schoolmistr.* 171 Fair as the furry coat of whitish ermilin.

2. The skin or fur of this animal.

1555 Eden *Decades W. Ind.* (Arb.) 311 Furres which wee caule Armelines. **1818** Milman *Samor* 38 Of silver and of stainless ermelin The bright caparisons. **1831** *Fraser's Mag.* IV. 549 Who she that, in the ermelin involved, Rests on the hastening car? *Ibid.* IV. 550 O thou, involved in ermelin!

ermight. ?

c **1435** *Torr. Portugal* 1008 Let thy beytyng and thy Ermyght be.

ermine (ˈɜːmɪn), *sb.* Forms: 3–7 **ermin, -yn(e**, (4–7 **hermin, -yn**, 5–7 **armin, -yn(e, -yon**, 6 **ermion, emerine**), 3– **ermine**. [a. OF. *(h)ermine* (mod.F. *hermine*), cogn. with Pr. *ermini*, Sp. *armiño* (Minsheu). The remoter etymology is disputed.

Some scholars (including Kluge and Skeat) think that the Romanic word is ad. OHG. *harmîn* adj., 'belonging to the ermine', f. *harmo* ermine, stoat, weasel, corresp. to the synonymous OE. *hearma* (glossed 'megale' = *mygale* Wr.-Wülck. 32) and Lith. *szermů̄* (OAryan type *k'ormon-, -en-*).

A different hypothesis (favoured by Littré, Paul Meyer, and others) is that the Romanic words represent L. *Armenius* Armenian. The *mus Ponticus*, 'Pontic rat', mentioned by Pliny as a fur-bearing animal, is commonly supposed, though without actual proof, to be the ermine; and as Pontus and Armenia were conterminous, it has been suggested that an alternative name for the animal may have been *mus Armenius*. That *some* animal was known by this designation in the second century is rendered probable by a passage in Julius Pollux (*circa* A.D. 180), who (*Onomast.* VII. 60) gives μυωτός as the name of an Armenian garment, and, amongst other conjectures as to the origin of the word, suggests that this article of dress may have been so named because made of the skins of 'the mice (or rats) of that country'. The belief that the ermine derived its name from Armenia was common in the 14th c., and the supposition accounts quite satisfactorily for the Romanic forms of the word. If this view be correct, it involves the consequence that the resemblance in sound between *ermine* and OHG. *harmîn* was merely accidental; there may however have been an early confusion between two distinct words of similar sound and meaning.]

1. An animal of the weasel tribe (*Mustela Erminea*), an inhabitant of northern countries, called in England a *stoat*, whose fur is reddish brown in summer, but in winter (in northern regions) wholly white, except the tip of the tail, which is always black.

a **1200** *Moral Ode* in *Lamb. Hom.* 181 Ne scal þer beo fou ne grei · ne cunig ne ermine. *c* **1450** *Guy Warw.* (C.) 9085 Owt of hys mowþe wente a þynge Also whyte, as any armyne. **1530** Palsgr. 217/1 Ermyne, a beest, *ermyne*. **1555** Eden *Decades W. Ind.* (Arb.) 326 *marg.*, The skynnes of sables and Ermynes. **1601** Holland *Pliny* I. 307 The rats and mice in the country of Pontus, namely Hermins, & such like. **1655** Gurnall *Chr. in Arm.* xxv. §4 (1669) 322/1 The Ermine..will dye before she will be got into the dirt to defile her beautiful skin. **1744** Thomson *Winter* 812 Fair ermines, spotless as the snows they press. **1774** Goldsm. *Nat. Hist.* (1776) III. 354 The weasel may be easily distinguished from the ermine by the tip of the tail, which in the latter is always black. **1835** Sir J. Ross *N.W. Pass.* xv. 228 An ermine came on board, quite starved. **1863** Miss Yonge *Chr. Names* II. 82 The pretty tale of the spotless ermine, that took refuge under his shield.

2. The fur of the ermine, often having the black tails (formerly pieces of black lamb's-wool) arranged upon it, at regular intervals, for the sake of effect. The whiteness of ermine is often referred to in poetry as an emblem of purity.

1297 R. Glouc. (1724) 191 Noble men, y cloþed in ermyne echone. *c* **1400** *St. Alexius* (Laud 622) 398 Pelured wiþ Ermyne & wiþ grijs. *a* **1450** *Knt. de la Tour* (1868) 30 Hodes & cotes furred with ermyn. *a* **1500** *Flower & Leaf* xxxv, With cloth of gold, and furred with ermine Were the trappoures of their stedes strong. **1587** Holinshed *Chron. Irel.* an. 1568 (R.) Princelie robes of crimson veluet doubled or lined with ermin. **1628** Wither *Brit. Rememb.* Pref. 159 From the Fox-fur, to the spotted Ermine. **1719** D'Urfey *Pills* (1872) I. 13 Her skin by nature, No Ermin better. **1795** Macneill *Will & Jean* IV, Strips thee of thy robes of ermine (Emblems of thy spotless life). **1855** Longf. *Hiaw.* xi, Shirt of doeskin..fringed with ermine.

b. *pl.* Trimmings, or garments, made of this fur. †Formerly also used, as in the sing. (see prec.), as a name for the material (cf. *sables*).

1474 Caxton *Chesse* 16 A mantel aboue furrid with ermynes. **1523** Ld. Berners *Froiss.* I. cxxv. 151 Robes of scarlet, furred with Armyns. *c* **1530** —— *Arthur* (1814) 273 Riche aparayle of emerines lay abrode in euery wyndowe. **1579** Spenser *Sheph. Cal.* Apr. 58 Yclad in Scarlot..And Ermines white. **1639** Massinger *Unnat. Combat* III. ii, I've charged thro' fire that would have singed your sables, Black fox, and ermines. *a* **1700** Dryden (J.), A lady's honour.. nice as ermines, will not bear a soil. **1732** Lediard *Sethos* II. VII. 32 Having nothing on his body but some ermins. **1756** Nugent *Gr. Tour, France* IV. 81 His habit of ceremony is a violet-coloured gown with a mantle of ermins.

3. *fig.* With reference to the use of ermine in the official robes of judges and the state robes of peers.

1794 Godwin *Cal. Williams* 261 Reluctant to fix an unnecessary stain upon the ermine of their profession. **1836** Lytton *Duch. de la Vallière* IV. iv, This garb of serge Dares speech that daunts the ermine. **1850** Whipple *Ess. & Rev.* (ed. 3) I. 21 The purity of the critical ermine, like that of the judicial, is often soiled by contact with politics. **1856** Emerson *Eng. Traits, Aristocr.* Wks. (Bohn) II. 79 Skilful lawyers..were rewarded with ermine.

4. *Her.* A heraldic fur; white marked with black spots of a particular shape.

1562 Leigh *Armorie* (last page), *Ermyn*, white poudered wᵗ Black. **1655** M. Carter *Hon. Rediv.* (1660) 99 If..it be white powdred with black, it is Ermin..if white with black, and one red hair, Erminites. **1766–87** Porny *Heraldry* 25 Ermine is a Field Argent, with small points or spots Sable, in the form of little Triangles, which in Heraldry are generally called Powdering. **1864** Boutell *Heraldry Hist. & Pop.* iv. (ed. 3) 20 Ermine, Black spots on a White field.

5. *attrib.* and *Comb.* **a.** simple *attrib.* in senses 1–4. †*ermine cross*: = cross ERMINEE.

c **1450** *Guy Warw.* (C.) 8425 Veire and gryce and pylches armyne And clothys of sylke and of satyne. **1486** *Bk. St. Albans* (Her.) D j, Ermyn cros. **1627** Drayton *Agincourt* 15 The men of Rutland..In their rich Ensigne bear an Ermine Ram. **1649** Lovelace *Poems* 63 Grieve not pretty Ermin Cabinet [a Lady's glove]. **1742** Mrs. Delany *Autobiog.* (1861) II. 199 My lady..was in dark green velvet trimmed with ermine, and an ermine petticoat. **1768** Pennant *Zool.* I. 85 Easily distinguished from the other in the ermine state by the tail. **1832** G. Downes *Lett. Cont. Countries* I. 50 The ermine mantle wherein the female is robed. **1864** Boutell *Heraldry Hist. & Pop.* xxx. 454 The practice of..artists..in representing ermine-spots.

b. quasi-*adj.* White as ermine.

1610 G. Fletcher *Christ's Vict.* in Farr *S.P.* (1847) 62 What should I here depaint..her ermine breast. **1821** Shelley *Prometh. Unb.* IV. i. 287 Vapours clothe earth's monarch mountain-tops With kingly, ermine snow.

c. *Comb.*, as ***ermine-hunter***; also **ermine white** *a.*, white as ermine; **ermine moth** [cf. Fr. *hermine*, 'Bombyx herminea' (Littré)] (*Hyponomeuta padellus*), a moth with white wings spotted with black.

1580 Sidney *Arcadia* III. 399 The Ermion whitest skin, spotted with nought. **1859** W. S. Coleman *Woodlands* (1866) 76 The pretty little Ermine Moth commits great ravages on the leaves of the Apple Tribe. **1865** Burritt *Walk Land's End* 194 Ermine-hunters have always had a harder time of it than even the Honiton lace-workers.

ermine (ˈɜːmɪn), *v.* [f. prec. sb.] *trans.* To clothe as if with ermine; to make white as ermine.

1825 *New Monthly Mag.* XIII. 63 It [snow] ermined all the dark-brown moor. **1870** H. Macmillan *Bible Teach.* xiv. 269 The glistening beach, ermined by the surf.

ermined (ˈɜːmɪnd), *ppl. a.* [f. as prec. + -ED².]

†**1.** Having white feathers spotted with black.

1486 *Bk. St. Albans* A viij b, Bot and a sparehawke be so Ermyned vppon the brayles.

¶ Perh. the designation *almond tumbler* is a corruption of this: see quot. below.

1735 J. Moore *Columbarium* 39 There is a Mixture of three Colours, vulgarly call'd an Almond, perhaps from the Quantity of Almond-coloured Feathers that are found in the Hackle: Others call it an Ermine, I suppose from the black Spots that are generally in it.

2. Lined or trimmed with ermine; made to resemble ermine.

c **1485** *Digby Myst.*, *Mor. Wisd.* i. (1882) 139 *heading*, With a mantyll..ermyned within. **1814** *Hist. Univ. Oxf.* II. 261 The ermined hood..is the peculiar badge of the Proctor's office. **1842** Barham *Ingol. Leg.*, *Auto-da-fé*, He wipes his eyes with his ermined sleeve. **18..** Longf. *Renouveau* i, Now Time throws off his cloak again of ermined frost.

fig. **1715** M. Davies *Ath. Brit.* I. 185 The collateral scenes of those Dialogues are freez'd or ermin'd sideward.

3. Robed in ermine; advanced to the dignity of wearing ermine, *i.e.* made a judge or a peer.

1735 Pope *Ep. Lady* 7 Arcadia's countess, here, in ermined pride. **1777** W. Whitehead *Goat's Beard* (R.), Regal robe, Which rules, in ermin'd state the globe. **1837** Lockhart *Scott* (1839) V. 47 Certain ermined sages of his own acquaintance. **1857** Whittier *Lines* Poet. Wks. (1882) 201 Give ermined knaves their hour of crime. **1869** *Globe* 13 Nov. 4 The ten newly ermined members of the Liberal party.

fig. *c* **1749** W. G. Hamilton in *Parl. Logick* (1808) 204 Thy balm-distilling sweets alone To ermin'd Innocence are known.

4. ? = ERMINE 5 a (*Her.*) or 5 b.

1823 Rutter *Fonthill* 50 The ermined cinque-foil upon a crimson ground.

erminee (ˈɜːmɪniː), *a.* *Her.* [a. heraldic Fr. *(croix) erminée*, f. *ermine*.] (A cross) composed of four ermine spots placed in the form of a cross.

1736 in Bailey. **1775** in Ash.

ˈermines. *Her.* Also 6 **ermynes, ermins**, 7 **ermyness.** [In some way connected with ERMINE; possibly a. OF. *herminès*, pl. of *herminet*, dim. of *hermine*.] A 'fur' forming the reverse of ERMINE, *i.e.* with white 'spots' on a black ground.

1562 Leigh *Armorie* (last page), *Ermines*, Black powdred whight. **1572** Bossewell *Armorie* II. 129 b, He beareth Or, a Cheuron Checkey Ermin and Ermins. **1677** Plot *Oxfordsh.* 179 The skins of black Grey-hounds powdered with white, or made Ermyness. **1751** Chambers *Cycl.*, *Ermines* is used by some English writers for the reverse of ermine, i.e. for white spots on a black field. **1864** Boutell *Heraldry Hist. & Pop.* iv. (ed. 3) 20.

erminites (ˈɜːmɪnaɪts). *Her.* [ad. Fr. *herminite.*] A heraldic fur, similar to ermine, with the addition of a red hair on each side of the 'spots'.

1562 Leigh *Armorie* 130 b. **1610** Guillim *Heraldry* I. v. (1611) 16 That being called Ermine, and this Ermynites. **1655** [see ERMINE *sb.* 4]. **1731–1800** Bailey, *Erminites*, A white Ground powder'd with Black, to which a red Hair is added. **1868** Cussans *Hand-bk. Her.* iii. 53 Erminites [is] sometimes included amongst the Furs.

erminois (ɜːmɪˈnɔɪz). [a. OFr. *(h)erminois*, f. *hermine* ERMINE.] A heraldic fur, Or with Sable 'spots'.

1562 Leigh *Armorie* 130 b, The fift doubling is Or, poudred with Sable, and must bee called properly Erminoys. **1610** Guillim *Heraldry* I. iv. (1660) 23 Ermynois whose ground or field is yellow, and the Poulderings black. **1775** in Ash. **1864** Boutell *Heraldry Hist. & Pop.* xvii. 281 A griffin per fesse erm. and erminois.

ermit(e, ermitage, obs. ff. HERMIT, -AGE.

ermlic, var. of ARMLICH *a. Obs.* pitiable.

c **1175** *Lamb. Hom.* 115 Þenne bið hit ermlic · ȝif he bið unrihtwis.

ermodattil, obs. form of HERMODACTYL.

†**ermth(e.** *Obs.* Forms: 1 **ęrmþ(u, ięrmþ(u, yrmþ(u**, 3 **ærmðe**, (2 **ermde**), 2–3 **ermðe**. [OE. *ęrmþu*, repr. OTeut. type **armiþâ*: see ARM *a.* and -TH¹. Also without umlaut: see ARMTH(E.] Poverty; wretchedness.

Beowulf 1259 (Gr.) Grendles moder..yrmþe ȝemunde. *c* **888** K. Ælfred *Boeth.* xxxviii. ii, To sellenne witu & ermþa þam yfelum monnum. *a* **1000** *Ags. Ps.* civ. 14 [cv. 16] Cwom

ofer eorþan ermþu. *c* **1175** *Lamb. Hom.* 113 He..nule on his ermðe edmodnesse halden. *c* **1205** LAY. 87 Eneas þe duc mid ermden at-wond. *Ibid.* 16143 þurh þe muclen ærmðe & þurh þene mucle hærm.

ermytage, ermyte, obs. ff. HERMIT, -AGE.

†**ern,** *v. Obs.* Forms: 1 irnan, *pa. t.* arn, 4–5 erne(n, -yn, 5 eerne. [ME. *ernen,* OE. *irnan,* by metathesis for *rinnan* to run.] *intr.* To run. Of water, a river: To flow.

c **893** K. ÆLFRED *Oros.* I. i. §8 Seo ea Danai irnð þonan suðryhte. *c* **1000** ÆLFRIC *Gen.* xviii. 7 He arn him sylf to his hryðera falde. *c* **1300** *K. Alis.* 5003 Every wilde dere astore, Hy mowen by cours ernen tofore. **1377** LANGL. *P. Pl.* B. xix. 376 Water for wikked werkes Egerlich ernynge out of mennes yeen. *c* **1440** *Promp. Parv.* 142 Ernyn, as horse [*MS.* P. eerne], *cursito.* *a* **1600** in Pinkerton *Anc. Scott. Poems* 217 (Jam.) Nor hare, befoire the ernand grew-hounds face, With speid is careit so.

ern, obs. form of *are*: see BE *v.*

ern, dial. form of IRON.

ern, dial. form of EARN (see EARN *v.*[1] 3). So **ernes** *sb. pl.* (see quot.)

1695 KENNETT *Par. Antiq.* Gloss., *Ernes,* the loose scattered ears of corn that are left on the ground after the binding or cocking of it.. Hence to *ern* is in some places the same as to glean. **1726** *Dict. Rust.* (ed. 3) s.v. *Ernes.*

-ern, *suffix,* in the adjs. *eastern, northern, southern, western,* represents OTeut. *-rônjo-,* f. *-ro-* thematic suffix in **austro-*, etc. + *-ônjo-* = L. *-āneus.*

†**ernde,** *v. Obs.* Forms: 1 ǽrendian, 3 arndi-en, erendi-en, erndi-en, 5 ernde-n. [OE. *ǽrendian,* f. *ǽrende*: see ERRAND. Cf. OHG. *ârundjan,* MHG. *ernden.*] **a.** *trans.* To treat for, obtain by intercession. **b.** *intr.* To intercede. Const. *to* and *dat.* of indirect obj.

c **890** K. ÆLFRED *Bæda* II. xii, Ða ærendracan, ðe his cwale ærndedon. *c* **1205** LAY. 23315 He..bad heom arndien him to hæhʒen þan kingen. *a* **1225** *Juliana* 78 Heo us erndi to godd þe grace of him seoluen. **1225** *Leg. Kath.* 2157 Eadi meiden! ernde me to þi leoue lauerd. *a* **1310** in Wright *Lyric P.* xxi. (Percy) 62 Ernde us hevene lyht.

†'**ernding,** *sb. Obs.* Forms: 3 ernding(e, -unge, h)erendinge. [OE. *ǽrendung,* n. of action f. *ǽrendian* (see prec.).] Intercession.

a **1000** *Benedictine Rule* (Schröer) xxvi, Oðþe þurh æniʒe spræce oðþe þurh æniʒes oþres mannes ærendunʒe. *a* **1225** *St. Marher.* 23 þat we bituhen þe engles þurh hire erndunge moten ʒet iseon hire. *c* **1275** *Doomsday* 86 in *O.E. Misc.* 168 For hire herendinge þat heo ure sawle to heouerige bringe. *a* **1310** in Wright *Lyric P.* xviii. (Percy Soc.) 58 Thourh ernding of the hevene quene.

erne (ɜːn), *sb.* Forms: 1 earn, 3 ærn, 3–4 arn(e, 3–6 ern, (4 eerne, 4–6 eren), 8–9 earn, 4– erne. [OE. *earn,* corresp. to MLG. *arn* (Du. *arend*), ON. *ǫrn* str. masc.:—OTeut. **arnu-z.* OTeut. had also a synonymous **aron-* wk. masc., whence OHG. *aro* (MHG. *are,* mod.G. *aar*), ON. *ari,* Goth. *ara.* Cf. OSlav. *orilŭ,* Lith. *erelis* eagle, Gr. *ὄρνις* bird.]

1. An eagle; in mod. use chiefly the *golden eagle* or the *sea-eagle* (see EAGLE).

a **1000** *Elene* 29 (Gr.) Urigfeðera earn sang ahof. *c* **1000** *Ags. Gosp.* Matt. xxiv. 28 Swa hwær swa hold byð, þæder beoð earnas ʒegaderude. *c* **1200** ORMIN 6056 Forr ærn maȝȝ fleȝhenn i þe lifft Full heȝhe towarrd heoffne. *a* **1225** *Ancr. R.* 196 Vre widerwines beoð swifture þen þe earnes. *a* **1300** *Cursor M.* 13444 (Cott.) For-þi to þe arn lickest es he. *c* **1325** *Chron. Eng.* 156 in Ritson *Meir. Rom.* II. 276 Ther spac an ern [a] prophecie. *c* **1380** WYCLIF *Sel. Wks.* III. 35 As þe eerne clepynge hise briddis. *a* **1455** *Houlate* xxv, Ernes ancient of air kingis that croond is. **1513** DOUGLAS *Æneis* XII. v. 64 For Jovis foule, the ern, com sorand by. **1555** EDEN *Decades W. Ind.* (Arb.) 315 Erens or eagles. **1565** GOLDING *Ovid's Met.* VI. (1593) 144 The scarefull erne With hooked talents trussing up a hare among the ferne. **1744** PRESTON *Zetland* in *Phil. Trans.* XLIII. 62 There are very large Eagles, which they call Earns. **1813** HOGG *Queen's Wake* 97 He saw.. A sight that scared the erne away. **1869** FREEMAN *Norm. Conq.* (1876) III. xiv. 344 Men told.. how.. ravens and ernes sat on the stern of every ship.

2. *Comb.* **erne-fern,** the Brake (*Pteris aquilina*); **erne-hued** *a.,* having the colour of an eagle; **erne-stone** = AETITES.

c **1325** *E.E. Allit. P.* B. 1698 Erne hwed he watz & al ouerbrawden. **1587** HARRISON *England* III. xii. (1878) II. 79 At this season there are found in England the Aetites (in English called the ernestone).

erne, obs. form of EARN *v.*[2]

c **1175** *Lamb. Hom.* 157 Ure erde is in houene, if we þer efter erneð. **1526** *Pilgr. Perf.* (W. de W. 1531) 205 Harde herted art thou yf thyne herte erne not ne melte in suche remembraunce.

ernes(se, -st(e, -xst, -ys(t, obs. ff. EARNEST.

Ernestine ('ɜːnɪstaɪn), *a. Hist.* [f. *Ernest,* proper name = G. *Ernst.*] Designating the elder or electoral line of the house of Frederick of Saxony, originating from his son Ernest (1441–86).

1841 *Penny Cycl.* XX. 493/2 Albert and Ernest, who were the founders of the Albertine and Ernestine lines. **1866** *Chambers's Encycl.* VIII. 515/2 The Ernestine, which was also the elder or electoral line. **1904** *Westm. Gaz.* 23 Nov. 2/3 The Ernestine line of the House of Saxony to which the late Prince Consort belonged. **1911** *Encycl. Brit.* XXIV. 270/1 This deed transferred the electoral title.. from the Ernestine to the Albertine branch of the house. **1943** A. J. GRANT *Hist. Europe 1494–1610* (ed. 3) i. 5 The electoral title went with the Ernestine line. **1962** R. A. G. CARSON *Coins* 366 In the original partition the electorate of Saxony was in the portion of Ernest but was transferred from the Ernestine line to the Albertine by the emperor Charles V in 1547.

Ernie ('ɜːnɪ). [f. *e*lectronic *r*andom *n*umber *i*ndicator *e*quipment.] Name given to the device for drawing the prize-winning numbers of premium bonds.

1956 *Electronic Engin.* XXVIII. 400 It has been decided that the only feasible method of making the draw is by electronic means. For this purpose an Electronic Random Number Indicator Equipment (ERNIE) has been evolved. **1957** *Times* 1 June 4/1 Ernie here is a pleasant enough fellow and.. will be a lot more efficient at picking winning premium bonds. **1966** C. BERMANT *Diary of Old Man* 115 He won the premium bonds once, I know that for sure. We were sitting in the library and he was going over the Ernie numbers with a magnifying glass when he gave a sudden loud whoop. **1970** 'A. GILBERT' *Death wears Mask* ix. 137, I might have come from Ernie, to tell him he's won £25,000 in the draw.

ernute, -tte, obs. ff. of EARTH-NUT.

erode (ɪ'rəʊd), *v.* [a. Fr. *érode-r,* ad. L. *ērōd-ĕre,* f. *ē* out + *rōdĕre* to gnaw.] To gnaw away.

1. a. *trans.* Of the action of acids, canker, ulceration, etc.: To destroy by slow consumption.

1612 [see ERODING *ppl. a.*]. **1626** BACON *Sylva* (1627) §983 It hath beene anciently received that the Sea Hare hath an Antipathy with the Lungs..and erodeth them. **1650** BULWER *Anthropomet.* 187 The blood.. becoming sharp, doth easily erode the vessels. **1762** *Gentl. Mag.* 274 A thick yellowish matter, which eroded everything near it. **1811** A. T. THOMSON *Lond. Disp.* (1818) 432 Liquid muriatic acid.. erodes animal and vegetable substances. **1836** TODD *Cycl. Anat.* I. 232/2 The process of ulceration.. eroding the middle coat [of the vessel]. **1878** HUXLEY *Physiogr.* 119 All natural waters can dissolve carbonate of lime.. and thus erode the limestone rocks.

†**b.** *transf.* of a personal agent. *rare.*

1781 E. DARWIN *Bot. Gard., Econ. Vegetation* II. Notes, Hannibal was said to erode his way over the Alps by fire and vinegar.

2. *Geol.* Of the action of currents, glaciers, etc.: **a.** To wear away; to eat out. **b.** To form (a channel, etc.) by gradual wearing away. **c.** *intr.* To undergo erosion. Also *fig.*

a. 1830 LYELL *Princ. Geol.* I. 223 The river has filled the lake, and partially cut through the barrier, which it is still gradually eroding to a greater depth. **1871** TYNDALL *Fragm. Sc.* (ed. 6) I. vi. 214 The adjacent land seemed eroded in a remarkable manner.

b. 1830 LYELL *Princ. Geol.* I. 170 The materials through which the channel is eroded. **1859** R. F. BURTON *Centr. Afr.* in *Jrnl. Geog. Soc.* XXIX. 122 Cups, and basins, eroded by the friction of the gravelly waters. **1872** W. S. SYMONDS *Rec. Rocks* vi. 166 Before the Lugg had eroded the track in which it now flows.

c. 1862 DANA *Man. Geol.* 636 The stream.. commences to erode laterally during freshets. **1867** MURCHISON *Siluria* xx. (ed. 4) 492 The deep ocean never erodes. **1969** *Daily Tel.* 15 Oct. 16 (*heading*) Are the joys of canal boating to erode away? **1970** *Ibid.* 14 Oct. 17/2 Over the years their power has eroded considerably.

3. In etymological sense (see quot.).

1816 KIRBY & SP. *Entomol.* (1843) I. 328 The stone-eating caterpillars are now found to erode the walls.. solely for the purpose of forming their cocoons.

eroded (ɪ'rəʊdɪd), *ppl. a.* [f. prec. + -ED[1].]

1. In the senses of the vb.

1741 MONRO *Anat.* (ed. 3) 17 The eroded Cells of the Bone. **1880** HAUGHTON *Phys. Geog.* iii. 78 The upturned and eroded edges of the Azoic strata.

2. *Bot.* Having the edge irregularly jagged. 'Used to express a particular kind of irregular denticulation' (Loudon); = EROSE.

erodent (ɪ'rəʊdənt), *a.* and *sb.* [ad. L. *ērōdent-em,* pr. pple. of *ērōdĕre* to ERODE.]

A. *adj.* 'Applied to medicines which cause erosion' (*Syd. Soc. Lex.*). **B.** *sb.* A substance which erodes.

In mod. Dicts.

eroding (ɪ'rəʊdɪŋ), *vbl. sb.* [f. ERODE *v.* + -ING[1].] The action of the vb. ERODE; in quot. *attrib.*

1862 DANA *Man. Geol.* 639 The eroding action of water during freshets becomes immense. **1865** LIVINGSTONE *Zambesi* xxviii. 577 It is a kind of clay on which the eroding power of water has little effect.

e'roding, *ppl. a.* [f. prec. + -ING[2].] That erodes.

1612 S. H. *Enchir. Med.* II. 84 This infirmitie proceedeth from gnawing and eroding humours. **1741** MONRO *Anat.* (ed. 3) 37 The Effects of eroding acrid Matter. **1803** *Med. Jrnl.* IX. 558 Eroding ulcerations in the neck. **1870** TYNDALL in *Times* 15 Sept. 7/6 The eroding forces of the atmosphere had weathered and decomposed the molten rocks.

†'**erogate,** *ppl. a. Obs.* [ad. L. *ērogāt-us,* pa. pple. of *ērogā-re*: see next.] Equivalent to the later *erogated.* Distributed.

1583 STUBBES *Anat. Abus.* II. 23 That some of our superfluitie might be erogate to them.

†'**erogate,** *v. Obs.* [f. L. *ērogāt-* ppl. stem of *ērogā-re* to pay out, f. *ē* out + *rogāre* to ask, the orig. sense being to pay out public money after *asking* the consent of the Roman people.] *trans.* To pay out, expend; to distribute. Also *absol.*

1531 ELYOT *Gov.* II. viii, Aristotle defineth a liberal man to be whiche doth erogate accordinge to the rate of his substance. **1550** VERON *Godly Sayings* (1846) 72 They thought that he should erogate and part his body emonge them. **1692** BP. OF ELY *Answ. Touchstone* 119 No Man can Supererogate till he have first erogated. **1828** in WEBSTER; and in mod. Dicts.

†**ero'gation.** *Obs.* [ad. L. *ērogatiōn-em,* n. of action f. *ērogāre*: see prec.] The action of the vb. EROGATE; expenditure, *esp.* in the bestowal of gifts, almsgiving; *concr.* in *pl.* money expended.

1531 ELYOT *Gov.* II. viii, Some thinke suche maner of erogation nat to be worthy the name of liberalitie. **1563** FOXE *Life Latimer* in *Serm. & Rem.* (1845) p. xii, Works of erogation, foundations, oblations. *c* **1645** HOWELL *Lett.* IV. xlvii. (T.), Touching the wealth of England, it never also appeared so much by publick erogations and taxes, which the Long Parliament raised. **1652** URQUHART *Jewel* Wks. (1834) 254 He.. whose literate erogations reach to this and after ages. **1677** HALE *Pomponius Atticus* 204 His greatest Bounty and Erogations commonly employed upon those that were not in any likelihood of making him any return.

ero'genic, *a. Phys.* [f. Gr. *ἔρω-ς* sexual love + -GENIC: after Fr. *érogénique.*] That gives rise to sexual desire.

1887 *Binet & Féré's Anim. Magnetism* 152 In the case of some hysterical subjects there are regions in certain parts of the body termed by Chambard erogenic zones.

erogenous (ɛ'rɒdʒɪnəs), *a.* [f. as EROGENIC *a.* + -OUS.

Both words are incorrectly formed.]

= EROGENIC *a.* Usu. collocated with *zone.*

1889 in *Cent. Dict.* **1905** H. ELLIS *Stud. Psychol. Sex* IV. I. i. 9 In some hysterical subjects there are so-called 'erogenous zones' simple pressure on which suffices to evoke the complete orgasm. **1915** C. R. PAYNE tr. *Pfister's Psychol. Method* 155 Those places which are important for the gaining of sexual pleasure, we call erogenous zones. **1925** C. FOX *Educat. Psychol.* 237 Any portion of the skin or mucous membrane which yields a feeling of pleasure when stimulated is described as an erogenous zone. **1949** G. BATESON in M. Fortes *Soc. Structure* 38 All the modes associated with the erogenous zones.. define themes for *complementary* relationship. **1967** G. STEINER *Lang. & Silence* 90 Once the maximum number of erogenous zones of the maximum number of participants have been brought in contact.. there is not much left to do or imagine.

eromancy, bad form of AEROMANCY.

1608 DAY *Law Trickes* IV. ii, Deep Eromancy, or the pretious soule Of Geomantique spells and Characters. **1623** COCKERAM, *Eromancie,* divination by things in the ayre.

eron, obs. pl. of EGG *sb.*

c **1450** *Two Cookery-bks.* (1888) 82 And then make faire bater of rawe yolkes of eron.

-eroo, factitious slang suffix as in BOOZEROO, *brusheroo* (BRUSH *sb.*[2] 8 b), FLOPPEROO.

U.S. formations in *-eroo, -aroo* (e.g. BUCKAROO) are discussed in *Amer. Speech* (1942) XVII. 10f, and in T. Pyles *Words & Ways Amer. Eng.* (1952) 199.

1964 *Guardian* 8 July 7/6 Those jerkeroos feel embarrassed.

erore, variant of ERER. *Obs.*

Eros ('ɪərɒs). Pl. Erotes (ɛ'rəʊtiːz); Eroses ('ɪərɒsɪz). [L. *Erōs,* a. Gr. *ἔρως.*]

1. Love, the god of love, or a representation of him: = CUPID.

[*c* **1386** CHAUCER *Knt.'s T.* 1374 Nat oonly lik the loueris maladye of Hereos but rather lyk Manye]. **1671** PHILLIPS *New World of Words* (ed. 3), *Eros,* according to the *Ethnic* Poets the God of Love, who in Latin is commonly called *Cupido* also the name of *Mark Anthony's* servant who killed himself.. the word in Greek signifying Love. **1775** J. BRYANT *Mythol.* I. 510 Under this characteristic they represented an heavenly personage, and joined her with Eros, or divine Love. **1817** BYRON *Manfred* II. ii. 35 He from out their fountain dwellings raised Eros and Anteros. **1864** TENNYSON *Enoch Arden, etc.* 157 A bevy of Eroses apple-cheek'd. **1870** S. H. HODGSON *Theory of Practice* I. 196 Love.. in this sense should be called Eros... The resulting Eros will be felt in strength proportional to the combined intensity of these two constituents. **1877** PATMORE (*title*) The Unknown Eros and other Odes. **1888** A. H. SMITH *Catal. Engr. Gems Brit. Mus.* 127 Silenus.. threatening to flog Eros, who is held up by two other Erotes. **1896** L. R. FARNELL *Cults Gk. States* II. xxi. 625 The only ancient centres of Eros-worship were Thespiae and Parion, where he was regarded probably not merely as the personification of human love, but as a physical and elemental force, a divinity of fertility. **1904** BUDGE *3rd & 4th Egypt. Rooms Brit. Mus.* 229 Erotes, or Cupids, holding grapes and thyrsus with wreath. **1928** *Times* 14 Dec. 10/4 Mr. John Murray's suggested new site for the Shaftesbury memorial.. would be an excellent one but for the fact that 'Eros' would then be lost to view from the principal approach roads to Piccadilly-circus. **1960** V. NABOKOV *Invitation to Beheading* xiv. 139 We were discussing.. the pleasures of life, and had just examined Eros in a general way.

b. *spec.* in Freudian Psychology: the urge towards self-preservation and sexual pleasure. Also, in recent Christian writings, earthly or sexual love, contrasted with AGAPE 2.

1922 C. J. M. HUBBACK tr. *Freud's Beyond Pleasure Principle* vi. 64 Thus the Libido of our sexual instincts would coincide with the Eros of poets and philosophers, which holds together all things living. *Ibid.* 67 We are the more compelled now to accentuate the libidinous character of the self-preservative instincts, since we are venturing on the further step of recognising the sexual instinct as the Eros, the all sustaining. **1932** A. G. HEBERT tr. *Nygren's Agape & Eros* vii. 166 Eros is longing and desire; but God can have no unsatisfied needs. *Ibid.* 167 Eros-love is the movement of man to God, whereby man's need seeks to find its satisfaction in the Divine fullness and blessedness. *Ibid.* 175 Eros-religion is always æsthetic. **1940** W. EMPSON *Gathering Storm* 29 The Freudians regard the death-wish as fundamental, Though 'the clamour of life' proceeds from its rival 'Eros'. **1955** [see AGAPE 2]. **1960** C. S. LEWIS *Four Loves* v. 106 That sexual experience can occur without Eros, without being 'in love', and that Eros includes other things besides sexual activity, I take for granted. **1967** A. EHRENZWEIG *Hidden Order of Art* xiii. 219 Both phenomena have their common source in a more fundamental rhythm that may be associated with the interaction of the life instincts, Eros and Thanatos.

2. *Astr.* An asteroid discovered by Witt at Berlin in 1898.

1900 *Ann. Reg. 1899* II. 102 Dr Witt, exercising a discoverer's right, has named the new planet Eros. **1901** G. C. COMSTOCK *Observations of Eros* 3 The following observations of Eros were made with the 40-cm. (Clark), equatorial telescope of the Washburn Observatory. **1926** H. MACPHERSON *Mod. Astron.* 92 Eros..comes at perihelion within the orbit of the Earth, from which it is then distant but thirteen million miles. **1959** SPITZ & GAYNOR *Dict. Astron.* 29 *Eros*, 20 mi. in diameter comes within 14 million miles, every 44 years.

erose (ɪ'rəʊs). *Bot.* and *Zool.* [ad. L. *ērōs-us*, pa. pple. of *ērōdĕre*: see ERODE.] Having the margin irregularly incised or indented, as if bitten by an animal.

1793 T. MARTYN *Lang. of Bot.*, *Erosum folium*, an erose or gnawed leaf. **1852** DANA *Crust.* I. 208 Hand and carpus unarmed, above minutely erose. **1870** HOOKER *Stud. Flora* 237 Sepals and petals erose obtuse.

erose, var. of ÆROSE (*Syd. Soc. Lex.*).

erosion (ɪ'rəʊʒən). Also 6 eroysion. [a. Fr. *erosion*, a. L. *ērōsiōn-em*, n. of action f. *ērōdĕre*: see ERODE.]

1. a. The action or process of eroding; the state or fact of being eroded. *spec.* in *Geol.*: cf. ERODE *v.* 2.

1541 R. COPLAND *Guydon's Quest. Chirurg.* 2 A iij b, Holowe vlceres..procede of two causes, that is to wete of excysyon and of eroysion. *Ibid.* 2 A iij b, Erosion. **1612** WOODALL *Surg. Mate* Wks. (1653) 383 By extream erosion or corrosion of Caustick Medicines. **1753** TORRIANO *Sore Throat* 60 The Erosion or Rupture of the Vessels. **1774** GOLDSM. *Nat. Hist.* (1862) I. xiv. 75 Bounds are thus put to the erosion of the earth by water. **1813** THOMSON *Lect. Inflamm.* 369 The phenomena which it [ulcerative absorption] exhibits were denominated erosion by Galen. **1836** TODD *Cycl. Anat.* I. 450/2 The erosion or absorption of the cartilages. **1851–9** DARWIN *Geol.* in *Adm. Man. Sci. Enq.* 294 Where ranges of cliffs exist the marks of the erosion of the waves may sometimes be expected to occur. **1854** WOODWARD *Mollusca* iv. (1856) 41 We can often recognise fresh-water shells, by the erosion of those parts where the epidermis was thinnest.

b. An instance of erosion.

1710 T. FULLER *Pharm. Extemp.* 133 It [*i.e.* the Electuary] is very profitable against..erosions of the Mouth. **1725** BRADLEY *Fam. Dict.*, *Ulcer*, a Solution of Continuity made by an Erosion of the soft Parts. **1744** BERKELEY *Siris* §21 Ulcerous erosions of the inward parts. **1880** KINGLAKE *Crimea* VI. viii. 184 The tumours, the erosions of the gums.

2. *transf.* and *fig.* Also *concr.*

1804 W. TAYLOR in *Ann. Rev.* II. 352 The expenders of rents are the most unproductive and useless class of citizens; their income is a fairer object of erosion, than that of the industrious..classes. **1817** H. T. COLEBROOKE *Algebra* 311 The erosion being subtracted from both diameters, etc. **1889** *Sat. Rev.* 23 Mar. 331/1 About twenty per cent. of the Government majority has disappeared by the natural erosion of bye-elections.

3. *attrib.*, as ***erosion cycle, territory***; ***erosion theory***: the theory which regards the contour of the land as due to superficial denudation rather than to subterranean agencies.

1879 LE CONTE *Elem. Geol.* 251 Erosion inequalities, once commenced, tend to increase. **1937** *Geogr. Jrnl.* XC. 376 Erosion-territory of the Great Ice sheet. **1946** L. D. STAMP *Brit. Struct. & Scenery* v. 37 It may be said that land-forms depend..thirdly on the phase or stage within the erosion cycle.

erosional (ɪ'rəʊʒənəl), *a.* [f. EROSION: see -AL.] Caused by erosion.

1903 *Science* 2 Jan. 26/2 The terraced character of the outlet at Horseheads was also described, and the opinion expressed that the broader terrace is an erosional and not a constructional..feature. **1947** *Endeavour* V. 43 That stratified rocks are the sands and muds of bygone ages and have been thus formed out of the erosional debris of pre-existing land masses began to be appreciated at the end of the eighteenth century. **1963** D. W. & E. E. HUMPHRIES tr. *Termier's Erosion & Sedimentation* i. 17 Heavy erosional phases represented by conglomeratic deposits of 'molasse' type. **1969** *Nature* 11 Oct. 164/1 Such streams are usually associated with extensive flood-plains leading out from upland V-shaped erosional valleys.

erosionist (ɪ'rəʊʒənɪst). [f. EROSION + -IST.] One who upholds the erosion theory in Geology.

1864 *Reader* No 94. 482/1 The erosionists allow the opportunities of ages. **1881** GEIKIE in *Macm. Mag.* XLIV. 230 The Erosionists, or upholders of the efficacy of superficial waste.

erosive (ɪ'rəʊsɪv), *a.* [f. L. *ērōs-* ppl. stem of *ērōdĕre* (see ERODE) + -IVE.] Having the property of eroding.

1830 LYELL *Princ. Geol.* I. 181 Should the erosive action not be accelerated in future, it will require upwards of thirty thousand years for the falls to reach Lake Erie. **1851** RICHARDSON *Geol.* x. 376 The erosive power of the water has been aided by the proneness of the volcanic rocks to decomposition. **1871** TYNDALL *Fragm. Sc.* (ed. 6) I. ix. 297 Proving its impotence as an erosive agent.

eroso- (ɪ'rəʊsəʊ-), combining form of L. *ērōsus* (see EROSE) in **e͵roso-'dentate** *a. Bot.* and *Zool.* (see DENTATE), toothed irregularly, as if bitten (*Treas. Bot.*). **e͵roso-den'ticulate** *a. Zool.* (see DENTICULATE).

1848 DANA *Zooph.* 270 The upper margin of the coral is very fragile and eroso-dentate. *Ibid.* 261 Lamellæ finely eroso-denticulate.

erostrate (iː'rɒstreɪt). *Bot.* [f. E- *pref.*[3] + L. *rostr-um* beak + -ATE.] Not having a beak.

1866 in *Treas. Bot.*

‖**ero'tema.** *Rhet. Obs.* [mod.L., a. Gr. ἐρώτημα, f. ἐρωτάειν to question.] = next.

1589 PUTTENHAM *Eng. Poesie* III. xix. (Arb.) 220 Erotema ..This figure I call the Questioner. **1678–1706** in PHILLIPS. **1721–1800** in BAILEY.

‖**erotesis** (ɛrəʊ'tiːsɪs). *Rhet.* [mod.L., a. Gr. ἐρώτησις, f. ἐρωτάειν to question.] (See quot. 1845.)

1657 J. SMITH *Myst. Rhet.* 136. **1678–1706** in PHILLIPS. **1721–1800** in BAILEY. **1845** J. W. GIBBS *Philol. Stud.* (1857) 206 Erotesis..is a figure of speech by which a speaker, in the form of an interrogation, boldly asserts the opposite of what is asked; as 'Creditis avectos hostes?'

erotetic (ɛrəʊ'tɛtɪk), *a.* [ad. Gr. ἐρωτητικός, f. ἐρωτάειν to question.] Pertaining to questioning; interrogatory.

1848 HAMPDEN *Bampt. Lect.* (ed. 3) 59 The erotetic method by which the Greek sage used to extort the truth from his reluctant opponent. **1853** H. ROGERS *Ecl. Faith* 96, I have no skill in that erotetic method.

erotic (ɛ'rɒtɪk), *a.* and *sb.* [ad. Gr. ἐρωτικ-ός, f. ἔρως, ἔρωτ-ος sexual love. Cf. Fr. *érotique*.]

A. *adj.* Of or pertaining to the passion of love; concerned with or treating of love; amatory.

1651 CHARLETON *Ephes. & Cimm. Matrons* II. Pref., That Erotic passion is allowed by all learned men to be a species of Melancholy. *a* **1789** BURNEY *Hist. Mus.* (ed. 2) I. v. 61 These modes had other..dependent on them, such as the Erotic or amorous. **1823** tr. *Sismondi's Lit. Eur.* (1846) I. xvi. 448 The lyric and erotic poets of his country. **1850** SIR J. STEPHEN *Eccl. Biog.* I. 158 Arising from these erotic dreams, he suspended at her shrine his secular weapons. **1865** HOOK *Lives Abps.* III. i. §9. 101 The common language of civility, as addressed to a lady, was erotic.

B. *sb.* **a.** An erotic or amatory poem. **b.** [after sbs. in -IC, repr. Gr. -ική (τέχνη).] A 'doctrine' or 'science' of love.

1858 *Sat. Rev.* V. 266/1 A lecture on popular erotics from the authoress. **1862** *Sat. Rev.* 8 Feb. 150 Religious erotics are something worse than an offence against taste. **1872** M. COLLINS *Plunges for Pearl* III. viii. 193 Instruction in the famous science of erotic. **1888** *Athenæum* 18 Aug. 214/2 A strange doctrine of 'spiritual wives'—a mystical erotic. *Ibid.* 215/1 The sublime erotic, free from all passional instincts.

Hence †**e'rotical**, *a. Obs.*, of the nature of, or pertaining to, sexual love. **e'rotically** *adv.*, in an erotic manner; in an erotic sense. **e'roticism** [+ -ISM], erotic spirit or character; also = EROTISM sense a.

1621 BURTON *Anat. Mel.* III. ii. I. ii, Jason Pratensis writes copiously of this Erotical love. **1882–3** SCHAFF *Encycl. Relig. Knowl.* I. 398 Others [understand it (Song of Solomon)] erotically. **1881** *Sat. Rev.* 9 July 53/1 The religious eroticism of Redi. **1885** *Ibid.* 11 Apr. 483/1 This martyr [Mme. de Montifaud] to eroticism.

erotica (ɛ'rɒtɪkə). [a. Gr. ἐρωτικά, neut. pl. of ἐρωτικός amatory, f. ἐρωτ-, ἔρως love.] Matters of love; erotic literature or art (freq. as a heading in catalogues).

1854 (*title*) Erotica. The Elegies of Propertius. **1913** H. JACKSON *Eighteen Nineties* v. 122 The romance,..in its unexpurgated form, suggests deep knowledge of that literature generally classed under *facetiæ* and *erotica* by the booksellers. **1956** K. CLARK *Nude* viii. 323 Supplied the Court with presentable *erotica*. **1957** N. FRYE *Anat. Criticism* ii. 110 The silly ones [*sc.* studies], which simply project the author's own erotica. **1960** *Spectator* 21 Oct. 595 In 1939, Girodias took over the erotica industry. **1961** *Ibid.* 3 Mar. 296 The artist had drawn the erotica. **1967** G. STEINER *Lang. & Silence* 91 Above the pulp-line..lies the world of erotica, of sexual writing with literary pretensions or genuine claims.

eroticize (ɛ'rɒtɪsaɪz), *v.* [f. EROTIC *a.* and *sb.* + -IZE.] *trans.* To make erotic; to stimulate sexually.

1914 GEDDES & THOMSON *Sex* vi. 122 At the time of sexual maturity, according to Steinach, the brain is greatly influenced by the internal secretions, it is 'eroticised'. **1915** E. POUND *Let. c* 7 Sept. in *Lett. J. Joyce* (1966) II. 366 Bed rooms [*sic*] scenes where the audience can be tittivated, eroticised. **1955** H. MARCUSE *Eros & Civilization* (1956) ii. 39 Their unrepressed development would eroticize the organism. **1970** *Jrnl. Gen. Psychol.* Apr. 154 More women [than men] were embarrassed by eroticized stories and would not attend a sexy show if they could avoid it.

erotism ('ɛrətɪz(ə)m). [f. Gr. ἔρως, ἔρωτ-ος + -ISM. Cf. Fr. *érotisme*.] *Path.* Sexual excitement. **b.** = EROTICISM. *rare.*

1849 *Lancet* I. 538/2 The erotism is excited by..the medical practitioner. **1875** H. WOOD *Therap.* (1879) 563 The general perturbation too great, for erotism to be induced. **1888** *Athenæum* 18 Aug. 220/3 The love sonnets.. are free alike from erotism and from mawkishness.

erotize ('ɛrətaɪz), *v.* [f. Gr. ἐρωτ-, ἔρως love + -IZE.] *trans.* To transform (an emotion, etc.) into sexual feeling.

1936 *Brit. Jrnl. Psychol.* Jan. 288 The erotizing of aggressive impulses is a remarkably general process which accounts for much of the complexity of life. **1966** *New Statesman* 23 Sept. 441/1 The key could well be the primate and human capacity for erotising experience.

erotogenic (ɛ͵rəʊtəʊ'dʒɛnɪk), *a.* [f. Gr. ἐρωτο-, ἔρως love + -GENIC.] = EROGENIC *a.*

1909 in *Cent. Dict.* Suppl. **1922** J. RIVIERE tr. *Freud's Introd. Lect. Psycho-analysis* 264 The gratification obtained can only relate to the region of the mouth and lips; we therefore call these areas of the body *erotogenic zones*. **1924** J. RIVIERE et al. tr. *Freud's Coll. Papers* II. 39 A certain degree of directly sexual pleasure is produced by the stimulation of various cutaneous areas (erotogenic zones). **1955** H. MARCUSE *Eros & Civilization* (1956) ii. 39 The pleasure of the proximity senses plays on the erotogenic zones of the body. **1968** *Economist* 25 May 25/3 Libido transcends beyond the immediate erotogenic zones.

erotogenous (ɛrə'tɒdʒɪnəs), *a.* [f. as prec.: see -GENOUS.] = EROTOGENIC *a.*

1928 H. ELLIS *Studies Psychol. Sex* VII. ii. 116, I adopted the term 'erogenous zones' or, as I now prefer, 'erogenic zones'. The English psycho-analysts have sometimes put forward the form 'erotogenous'.

erotology (ɛrəʊ'tɒlədʒɪ), [f. as EROTISM + Gr. -λογία discoursing: see -LOGY.] The 'science' of love.

1886 (*title*), The Perfumed Garden of the Cheikh Nefzaoui, a Manual of Arabian Erotology.

erotomania (ɛ͵rəʊtəʊ'meɪnɪə). *Path.* [f. as prec. + Gr. μανία madness.] **a.** Melancholy or madness arising from passionate love; **b.** (see quot. 1884).

1874 VAN BUREN *Dis. Genit. Org.* 464 Erotomania is a species of insanity. **1877** WOODMAN & TIDY *Forensic Med.* 726 Extreme sexual passion is called erotomania in both sexes. **1884** *Syd. Soc. Lex.*, *Erotomania.* By some authors the term is restricted to those cases in which the imagination alone is affected; by others the grosser forms nympho-mania and satyriasis are included.

eroto'maniac. [f. EROTOMANIA: see MANIA.] One affected by erotomania. Also *attrib.* or *adj.*

1858 BUCKNILL & TUKE *Man. Psychol. Med.* 212 The erotomaniac is..the sport of the imagination. **1895** *Contemp. Rev.* Apr. 494 The impudences..of the erotomaniacs. *Ibid.* 496 Erotomaniac literature. **1895** *Church Times* 5 Apr. 398/1 This kind of erotomaniac fiction. **1897** WILDE *Let.* 10 Aug. (1962) 631 He is the most learned erotomaniac in Europe. **1921** *Spectator* 16 Apr. 497/1 Outside an asylum for erotomaniacs, the world is not governed by perpetual storms of unrestrainable animal passion. **1967** *Listener* 30 Nov. 723/1 The erotomaniac gleam at the tip of the phallic cigar [of Groucho Marx].

erpetology, -ist: see HERP-.

err (ɜː(r)), *v.*[1] Forms: 4–7 erre, (4 erry, 7 arre), 4– err. [ME. *erre*, a. Fr. *erre-r*, Pr. and Sp. *errar*, It. *errare*, L. *errāre*:—prehistoric **ersāre*, cogn. with Goth. *aírzjan* trans. to lead astray, OHG. *irrōn* trans. and intr. (Ger. *irren*).]

†**1.** *intr.* To ramble, roam, stray, wander. *Obs.*

c **1374** CHAUCER *Troylus* IV. 274 O wery ghost, that errest to and fro. **1382** WYCLIF *Gen.* xxxvii. 15 A man fonde hym in the feelde erryinge. **1481** CAXTON *Myrr.* III. xv. 169 He erred so ferre by strange londes that he passed the flood of Ganges. **1549–62** STERNHOLD & H. *Ps.* cvii. 40 And likewise caused them to erre Within the wildernesse. **1601** JONSON *Poetaster* I. i, In no labyrinth can I safelier err, Than when, etc. **1697** DRYDEN *Virgil* (J.), A storm of strokes.. errs about their temples, ears, and eyes.

2. To go astray; to stray *from* (one's path or line of direction). Chiefly *fig.* and now *arch.*

1303 R. BRUNNE *Handl. Synne* 9517 Lewede men þat erre ful moche oute of the weye. *c* **1340** HAMPOLE *Prose Tr.* 17 Whoso myghte by þe grace of Godd go þis way he sulde noghte erre. **1382** WYCLIF *Isa.* liii. 6 Alle wee as shep erreden. *c* **1440** *Gesta Rom.* 330 (Add. MS.) Vayn, waveryng, and erryng fro the faithe. **1552** *Bk. Com. Prayer, Gen. Conf.*, We haue erred and strayed from thy wayes, lyke loste shepe. **1678** R. BARCLAY *Apol. Quakers* 15 He that Errs in the Entrance, is not so easily reduced again into the Right Way. **1812** BYRON *Juan* II. xciv, Probably it [a bird] might have err'd Upon its course. **1832** J. C. HARE in *Philol. Museum* I. 645 Indeed in this, as in every other practical

question, there are two extremes, into which one may err. **1850** TENNYSON *In Mem.* lxxiii, Nothing is that errs from law.

b. To fail, miss; also, *to err from* (a mark or proposed end): to miss, fail to strike. *rare.*

c **1430** LYDG. *Bochas* II. xxiii. (1554) 60a, Kynd in her forge list nothing to erre. **1538** STARKEY *England* I. i. 19 Erryth not from the end. **1703** POPE *Thebais* 772 On me, on me, let all thy fury fall, Nor err from me, since I deserve it all. **1732** —— *Ess. Man* I. 142 But errs not Nature from this gracious end, From burning suns when livid deaths descend. **1801** SOUTHEY *Thalaba* I. xlii, The Arrows..err not from their aim.

c. ? quasi-*trans.* (But perh. *way* is the object of *leading*: 'I shall not err if thou lead the way'.)

1667 MILTON *P.L.* x. 266, I shall not lag behinde, nor erre The way, thou leading.

3. To go wrong in judgement or opinion: to make mistakes, blunder. Of a formula, statement, etc.: To be incorrect.

1303 R. BRUNNE *Handl. Synne* 473 Ȝif þou telle hem [*sc.* dremys] þan mayst þou errre. *c* **1380** WYCLIF *Sel. Wks.* III. 342 Petre suffride mekeli at Poul snybbide him whanne he erride. **1477** EARL RIVERS (Caxton) *Dictes* 9b, Whan thy frende erreth or mystaketh him agenst the. **1552** ABP. HAMILTON *Catech.* (1884) 43 Quhasaever doutis or erris in the faith. **1591** HARINGTON *Orl. Fur.* VII. l, By dreames, by oracles that never arres. **1650** JER. TAYLOR *Holy Living* (J.), Possibly the man may err in his judgement of circumstances. **1784** COWPER *Task* I. 662 Fancy..Perhaps errs little, when she paints thee thus. **1811** A. T. THOMSON *Lond. Disp.* (1818) 478, Both the above formulæ err in this particular. **1856** SIR B. BRODIE *Psychol. Inq.* I. ii. 42 It seems to me that the best writers..have erred in considering the mind too abstractedly.

†**b.** quasi-*trans.* with cognate object.

1656 *Handsom. Artif.*, Those that are so subject to erre customary errors in greater matters. **1659** BP. GAUDEN *Tears Ch.* 281 In this it seems to have erred a Catholick errour. *Ibid.* 285 Not once erring so Catholick and great an errour. **1674** HICKMAN *Quinquart. Hist.* (ed. 2) 194 They erre as bad an errour as the Pelagians do.

4. To go astray morally; to sin.

c **1315** SHOREHAM 164 God wyste wel that man schold erry. *a* **1340** HAMPOLE *Psalter* x. 8 He suffirs wrecched men to erre in thoght & word & dede. **1450-1530** *Myrr. our Ladye* 22 They erre greatly that hastely..say these holy houres. **1482** *Monk of Evesham* (Arb.) 109 The perels of hem that offendyn and erryn. **1611** BIBLE *2 Chron.* xxxiii. 9 So Manasseh made Iudah, and the inhabitants of Ierusalem to erre. **1645** WALLER *Poet. Wks.* (J.), The Muses' friend.. With silent pity looks on all that err. **1871** B. TAYLOR *Faust* (1875) I. Prol., While Man's desires and aspirations stir He cannot choose but err.

†**b.** *trans.* (*nonce-use.*) To make (a person) sin.

1621 BURTON *Anat. Mel.* I. iv. I. ii, The Lord of lies.. tempts by covetousness, drunkenness, pleasure, pride, etc., errs, dejects, saves, kills..some men.

†**5.** *trans.* To do (a thing) wrongly or sinfully; to make a mistake or commit a fault in. Chiefly *pass. Obs.*

a **1340** HAMPOLE *Psalter* 497, I will amend þat i hafe errid. **1340** —— *Pr. Consc.* 5733 For ilka thyng þat erred es..Man ..sal be ledde To þe dome. **1527** R. THORNE in Hakluyt *Voy.* (1589) 257 In this little Card I think nothing be erred touching the situation of the lande. **1644** MILTON *Areop.* (Arb.) 79 To redresse willingly and speedily what hath bin err'd.

†**err**, *sb. Obs.* In 6 erre. [f. prec. vb.] An error, fault; also, erroneous belief, heresy.

1509 FISHER *Wks.* I. 260 A londe without erre. *c* **1511** *1st Eng. Bk. Amer.* (Arb.) Introd. 30/2 They haue a great erre for they saye, etc.

errability (ɛrəˈbɪlɪtɪ). [f. ERRABLE: see -ITY.] Liability to err.

1705 HICKERINGILL *Priest-cr.* II. i. 8 How durst Church of England..confess Errability and Fallibility? **1850** D. THOMAS *Crisis of Being* vi. 101 Errability is an attribute of our common nature.

errable (ˈɛrəb(ə)l), *a. arch. rare.* [f. ERR *v.* + -ABLE.] Fallible, liable to err.

1665 J. SERGEANT *Sure-footing* 217 Experience teaching that men..are errable. **1705** HICKERINGILL *Priest-cr.* IV. (1721) 219 The punishment of Schismaticks, that are Deserters from an errable Church, is unaccountable nonsense. **1715** M. DAVIES *Athen. Brit.* I. Pref. 8 Very errable and uninspir'd Penman. *a* **1718** PENN *Tracts, Wks.* (1726) I. 604 Man is Errable. **1741** BERKELEY *Let.* 7 June Wks. 1871 IV. 272 We hold all mankind to be peccable and errable, even the Pope himself. **1839** J. ROGERS *Antipopopr.* II. ii. 116 Errable, liable to mistake.

Hence †ˈ**errableness**, *Obs.*, liability to error.

1653 W. MOUNTAGUE *Devout Ess.* iv. §4 Considering the errableness of our judgments, when extended to foreign and remote subjects. **1667** *Decay Chr. Piety* xvii. (1683) 355 The errableness of our nature. **1775** in ASH. **1828** in WEBSTER; and in mod. Dicts.

errable, -bull, obs. forms of EARABLE.

errabund (ˈɛrəbənd), *a.* *rare*$^{-1}$. [ad. L. *errābund-us* wandering to and fro, wandering about, f. *errā-re*: see ERR.] Erratic, random.

1834-43 SOUTHEY *Doctor* Interch. xiii. (1848) 248 With your errabund guesses, veering to all points of the literary compass.

errancy (ˈɛrənsɪ). Also 7 errancie. [f. ERRANT *a.*: see -ANCY.] The condition of erring or being in error.

1621 W. SCLATER *Tythes* (1623) 161 In the Infancie, and as I may terme it, Errancie of the Church. **1811** *Monthly Mag.* XXXII. 143 The more remarkable cases of credulity, superstition, errancy of idea, etc. **1854** W. WATERWORTH *Orig. Anglicanism* 4 The Catholic Church..denies the fact of the errancy of the Church. **1864** *Ch. & State Rev.* No. 26/2 Mr. Gladstone's errancy has continued longer..than that of any other politician.

errand (ˈɛrənd). Forms: 1-2 ærende, 3-5 ærnde, erende, ernde, errnde (*Orm.*), arunde, (3 earende, erinde, erd(e)ne), 4 arende, arnd, erned, 5 erunde, 4-6 erand(e, errande, (4 eraunt, -ond(e, herand(e, 5 -end, ardene, arend, eraunde, erdon, ernedde, erundi, herunde, heyrne, 6 haraunte, arande, arnede), 6-7 arrant(e, 7 arrand, -end, earrant, earande, 6-8 errant, (8 *dial.* arnt), 4- errand. [OE. *ǽrende* str. neut., corresp. to OS. *ârundi*, OHG. *ârunti, âronti, ârandi* (MHG. *erende*), ON. *eyrindi, örindi, erindi* neut. (Da. *ærinde, ærend*, Sw. *ærende*). The ulterior etymology is obscure: the OS. and OHG. forms seem to point to an OTeut. type *ǣrundjo-(m, and the ON. forms to *ărundjo-m neither of which is easy to reconcile with the otherwise plausible (and generally accepted) connexion with Goth. *áirus*, ON. *árr*, OS. *êru*, OE. *ár* messenger; if any relation exists, the *ai* of OTeut. *airus must be due to epenthesis.]

†**1. a.** A message, a verbal communication to be repeated to a third party. *Obs.*

c **890** K. ÆLFRED *Bæda* II. ix, He his hlafordes ærende secȝan sceolde. *a* **1000** *Guthlac* 696 (Gr.) Bartholomeus aboden hæfde godes ærendu. *c* **1200** ORMIN *Ded.* 159 Goddspell onn Ennglissh nemmnedd iss..God errnde. *c* **1290** *Lives Saints* (1887) 25 And seiden him þe erende. *c* **1325** *E.E. Allit. P.* C. 72 Now sweȝe me þ ider swyftly & say me þis arende. **1393** LANGL. *P. Pl.* C. XIV. 41 The messager.. with hus mouth telleþ Hus erande, and hus lettere sheweþ. *c* **1440** *York Myst.* xx. 233 To þam youre herand for to say. **1535** COVERDALE *1 Sam.* xi. 5 So they tolde him [Saul] the Earande of the Men of Iabes. **1571** CAMPION *Hist. Irel.* II. ix. (1633) 116 They pressed him sore with a trayterous errant, sent by his daughter the Lady of Slahe, to all his brethren. **1583** STANYHURST *Æneis* I. (Arb.) 22 Tel your King, from me, this errand. **1725** DE FOE *Voy. round World* (1840) 93 The second messenger came in, and delivered his part of the errand. **1754** SHERLOCK *Disc.* (1759) I. iv. 153 Preachers of the Gospel were sent..and the Errand was worthy of Him who sent them.

b. In religious language: A petition or prayer presented through another (the Virgin Mary).

c **1200** *Trin. Coll. Hom.* 167 Ure lafdi Seinte Marie bere ure arende to ure louerd ihesu crist. *c* **1440** *Bone Flor.* 1857 Lady Mary free..Here my errande, as thou well may. *c* **1460** *Emare* 8 Mary, hevyn qwene, Bere our arunde..To thy sone. **1849-53** ROCK *Ch. of Fathers* III. ix. 341 The 'handmaid of the Lord' was looked upon as one among the appointed bearers of our errands unto heaven.

2. A going with a message or a commission:

a. In an elevated or dignified sense: A mission, embassy, an expedition for a specific purpose. Now *arch., poet.*, or *rhetorical.*

a **1000** *Andreas* 215 (Gr.) Ne mæȝ þæs ærendes ylding wyrðan. **1065** *O.E. Chron.*, Hig læȝ don ærende on hine to þam cyninge Eadwarde. **1683** TEMPLE *Mem.* Wks. 1731 I. 477, I never obey'd the King so unwillingly in my Life; both upon Account of an Errand so unnecessary, and, etc. **1744** THOMSON *Summer* 526 Immortal forms, On gracious errands bent. **1837** W. IRVING *Capt. Bonneville* II. 257 They met the guide returning from his secret errand. **1856** KANE *Arct. Expl.* II. xxi. 207 The scene..impressed my brother when he visited it on his errand of rescue.

b. In mod. colloquial language, *esp.*: A short journey on which an inferior (*e.g.* a servant, a child) is sent to convey a message or perform some simple business on behalf of the sender. Phrases, *to run* (*on*) *errands, to go* (*on*) *an errand.*

1642 CHARLES I *Declar.* 12 Aug. 13 Attending the doores of both Houses to be employed in their errants. **1859** DICKENS *T. Two Cities* II. i, He was never absent during business hours, unless upon an errand.

c. Phrases, *a fool's errand*: a profitless undertaking. †*a sleeveless errand*: see SLEEVELESS.

1705 HICKERINGILL *Priest-cr.* I. (1721) 20 Did not the Pope send all the Princes of Christendom upon a Fool's Errand, to gain the Holy Land? **1840** MARRYAT *Poor Jack* viii, The doctor's come on a fool's errand. **1884** *Century Mag.* Nov. 59/1 He was only going on a fool's errand again.

3. The business on which one is sent; in wider sense, the object of a journey, a purpose, intention.

a **1225** *Ancr. R.* 246 Clene bone..cumeð in biuoren Almihti God, & deð þe erinde..wel. *c* **1250** *Gen. & Ex.* 1402 Eliezer..tolde hem..And for quat erdene he ðider nam. *c* **1340** *Gaw. & Gr. Knt.* 257 To wone any quyle in þis won, hit watz not myn ernde. *a* **1400** *Cov. Myst.* (1841) 282, I come ageyn Fulleche myn Erdon for to spede. *c* **1400** *Destr. Troy* 522 The woman..vnder shadow of shame shewid forth hir ernd. **1432-50** tr. *Higden* (Rolls) I. 243 To exercise theire causes and erneddes. **1483** CAXTON *Gold. Leg.* 263/4 Gotard..for certeyne necessitees and erandes retorned into placence. **1484** *Paston Lett.* No. 881 III. 314 Your sunne dede hese heyrne ryght wele as ye shal her aftyr this. **1598** YONG *Diana* 24, I..tooke out before me a few goates.. bicause I would not goe without some errant. **1609** SKENE *Reg. Maj.* 179 Commissions of Justitiarie, suld nocht be granted..for langer space nor the earand in hand may be conveniently perfited. **1610** T. LORKIN in Ellis *Orig. Lett.* II. 251 III. 221 The chief errand of my last Letters was to let you understand of our safe comming hither. **1699** BENTLEY *Phal.* 70 He had another errant to Persia, than buying of Slaves. **1790** PALEY *Horæ Paul.* Rom. i. 9 The errand which brought him to Jerusalem. **1883** OUIDA *Wanda* I. 3 This errand was distasteful.

4. *to make an errand*: **a.** (cf. 2) to make a short journey; **b.** (cf. 3) to find a pretence for going.

c **1400** *Rom. Rose* 2513 If thou..any errand mightest make Thider, for thy loves sake. **1491** *Act 7 Hen. VII*, c. 22 Pream., Y made myn errand unto you for seyng of evydence. **1549** EDWARD VI *Jrnl.* in *Rem.* (1857-8) 249 Guidotty made divers harauntes from the constable of Fraunce to make peace with us. **1580** NORTH *Plutarch* 729 (R.) He himself made an errand home to fetch such things as he lacked. **1589** NASHE *Anat. Absurditie* 13 Women..will not stick to make an errant ouer the way. **1850** MRS. STOWE *Uncle Tom's C.* xxvii, Tom..after vainly waiting for him to come out, determined, at last, to make an errand in.

5. *attrib.* and *Comb.*, as *errand-bearer, -bringer, -cart, -goer, -porter*; *errand-bearing* adj.; also, †**erindebere**, ME., = *errand-bearer*; **errand-boy**, a boy kept to run on errands; so **errand-girl, lad**; †**erendes-man**, ME., an ambassador; **errand-making**, *a.*, that finds an excuse for accosting or intruding upon a person. Also ERENDRAKE.

a **1225** *Ancr. R.* 60 Þe liht eie..is ase *erindebere [*C.* erende beorere] of þe lihteheorte. *a* **1300** *Cursor M.* 3226 (Cott.) Apon his kne he did him suere þat he suld be lel errand berer. **13..** *Interloc. Poem* in *Rel. Ant.* I. 146 Thu salt be my herand-bere. **1765** *Minute Bk. St. Anne's Sch., Blackfriars* in D. Owen *Eng. Philanthropy* (1965) I. i. 25 [The Mother] suffering her said Boy to go from Place to Place as *Errand-boy instead of keeping him at School. **1815** TWEDDELL *Remains* lxviii. 300 (Jod.) Savoyard [a term] for chimney-sweeper and errand-boy at Paris. **1838** DICKENS *O. Twist* x, The tradesman leaves his counter..the errand boy his parcels, the schoolboy his marbles. **1879** 'E. GARRETT' (Mrs. Mayo) *House by Wks.* I. 66, I will send the errand boy with thee to carry a note. **1720** OZELL *Vertot's Rom. Rep.* I. IV. 235 The Consuls..ordered that *Errand-bringer of theirs to be driven away ignominously. **1810** *Edin. Rev.* XV. 342 Who employs the drivers of *errand-carts to distribute them indiscriminately to travellers. **1782** F. BURNEY *Diary* 28 Dec. (1842) II. 220 The green-woman..sent her own *errand-girl. **1860** C. M. YONGE *Hopes & Fears* II. v. 100 Augusta will be ready to take her in—she is pining for an errand girl. **1933** D. L. SAYERS *Murder must Advertise* ii. 31 'And who do you think I am,' I said, 'the errand-girl?' **1865** DICKENS *Mut. Fr.* I. v, He was *errand-goer by appointment to the house at the corner. **1887** *Pall Mall G.* 29 June 13/2 Here, too, were *errand lads, shop lads, clerks. **1599** *Warn. Faire Wom.* I. 355 These *errand-making gallants are good men, That cannot pass, and see a woman sit..But they will find a 'scuse to stand and prate. *c* **1205** LAY. 24862 Nu ha man demen *erendes-mon [*c* **1275** heren-drake] to dæðen. **1818** SCOTT *Hrt. Midl.* xxi, A tattered cadie, or *errand-porter..exclaimed in a strong north-country tone.

Hence †**erranˈdeer** [+ -EER[1]] (see quot.). ˈ**errander** [+ -ER[1]]. *rare.* One who goes on an errand. ˈ**errandry** [+ -RY] = ERRAND.

1736 BAILEY, *Errandeer*, a scout at Oxford. **1803** G. STEPHENS *Bugge's N. Mythol.* 41 A shrub forgotten by the erranders. **1834** DISRAELI *Rev. Epick* I. xxxi. 44 Swift Tomorrow [is] but a truant hind, That lags upon a graceless errandry.

errant (ˈɛrənt), *a.* (*sb.*) Also 4-5 erraunt(e, errawnt(e, 7 errand. See also ARRANT. [a. Fr. *errant*, originally two distinct words, which, however, were to some extent confused in Fr. In the senses represented by branch I it is pr. pple. of OF. *errer* (pr. t. *oirre*), also written *esrer*, earlier *edrer*:—vulgar L. *iterāre* (= literary late L. *itinerāre, -āri*) to journey, travel, f. *iter* journey. In the senses represented by branch III it is ad. L. *errant-em* pr. pple. of *errāre*, (Fr. *errer*, of learned origin) to stray, wander, ERR. The primary notion in branch II is uncertain; it seems natural to interpret *thief errant* as 'vagrant' thief, and so to refer it to *errare*; but if Romanic scholars be right in referring *juif errant* (see 3) to *iterāre*, this derivation may be correct here; or perh. the two words were already confused when the phrase arose.]

I. Itinerant, travelling.

1. [after Fr. *chevalier errant*; cf. 'ensemble oirrent li chevalier' quoted in Godef.] Said of knights who travelled about in quest of adventure. See KNIGHT-ERRANT.

[*c* **1340** *Gaw. & Gr. Knt.* 810 Knyȝt erraunt.] **1470** MALORY *Arthur* IV. xii. 134 Here maye ye see what auentures befallen oftyme of erraunte knyghtes. **1596** SPENSER *F.Q.* v. vi. 6 Now she deuiz'd, amongst the warlike rout..to seeke her errant Knight. **1629** MASSINGER *Picture* III. v, I have read the tales of errant Knighthood. **1663** BUTLER *Hud.* I. i. 21 Chief of Domestick Knights and Errant, Either for Chartel or for Warrant. **1813** SCOTT *Trierm.* I. x, He journey'd like errant knight the while.

b. *transf.* (often as pr. pple.): Travelling, roaming (in quest of adventure, or like a knight-errant). *poet.* or quasi-*arch.*

? *a* **1634** CHAPMAN & SHIRLEY *Ball* IV, We bee no Ladies errant. **1805** WORDSW. *Prelude* III. (1850) 466 Boys and youths Forsook their homes..errant in the quest Of Patron. **1834** SIR H. TAYLOR *Artevelde* II. v. iii. (1849) 256 Errant for geste and enterprise. **1858** MRS. OLIPHANT *Laird of Norlaw* I. 289 Thinking of that ship, or of the sons of other mothers who were errant in her. **1858** *Sat. Rev.* V. 61/2 That same lady-errant who, etc.

c. That is in the spirit of a knight-errant; also, with notion of 9, erratic, 'quixotic'.

1822 B. CORNWALL *Ep. to Sir J. Lawrence* in *Misc. Poems*, With pleasure which rewards mine errant pains. **1874** T. HARDY *Madding Crowd* I. xxviii. 306 Her temerity in such an errant undertaking.

d. *sb.* A knight-errant; one who travels in the manner or spirit of a knight-errant.

a **1643** W. CARTWRIGHT *Lady Errant* IV. i. (1651) 50 Truth is the essence of our Order, we Who are errants cannot deceive and be. **1689** EVELYN *Mem.* (1857) III. 309 Isaac [Vossius] was invited thither [to Sweden] by the heroic and royal errant. **1811** SHELLEY in Hogg *Life* I. 414 If we were errants, you should have the tilting all to yourself.

†**2.** ***pawn errant*** [OF. *paonnet errant* (*Rom. Rose*)]: in chess, a travelling pawn, one that has been advanced from its original square.

c **1369** CHAUCER *Dethe Blaunche* 661 Fortune seyde ..'mate' in mid pointe of the chekkere With a powne erraunt.

†**3.** ***Errant Jew*** [Fr. *juif errant*]: the 'Wandering Jew'; in quot. *transf.*

? *a* **1400** *Morte Arth.* 2895 Thus es þe geante for-juste, that errawnte Iewe.

†**4.** In the designations of certain English legal functionaries: **baliff-errant** (see BAILIFF 4) [AF. *baillif errant*, 14 Edw. III, st. I. c. 9]; **justice-errant** [AF. *justice-erraunt*, Britton *c* 1290; in Anglo-Lat. always *justiciarius itinerans*], a justice who travels on circuit.

1502 ARNOLDE *Chron.* (1811) 3 Our lord the Kynge.. shall not assigne Justicis wythin the cite.. other than Justicis errauntis to the tour of London, etc. **1574** tr. *Littleton's Tenures* 105 a, The original and the processe were sente beefore Justices errantes, where the parties came. **1641** *Termes de la Ley* 141 Justices that goe circuit, and Bailiffes at large.. are therefore called Justices Errants and Bailiffes Errants.

5. Said *gen.* of itinerant functionaries, offices, or jurisdictions.

1638 *Penit. Conf.* ix. (1657) 292 Whether every errant Priest is so furnished, that comes unto them in that name? **1874** HELPS *Soc. Press.* iv. 60 All the funtionaries of government were more errant. **1887** GORE in *Expositor* June 417 We find.. side by side with.. the local ministry of Bishops and Deacons, a still general or errant ministry.

II. In senses of ARRANT 2–6.

†**6.** In phrase ***thief errant***, ***errant*** (***arrant***) ***thief***: in Chaucer, the leader of a band of robbers; subsequently, a notorious, 'common' thief. *Obs.* exc. in form ARRANT.

c **1386–1822** [See ARRANT 2.]

†**7.** Used as an intensive with sbs. of reproachful sense: Thoroughgoing, 'unmitigated': see ARRANT 3, 3 b.

1393–1538 [see ARRANT 3]. **1619** W. WHATELY *Gods Husb.* i. (1622) 76 Thou art an errand grosse hypocrite. **1719** [see ARRANT 3]. *a* **1720** SHEFFIELD (Dk. Buckhm.) *Wks.* (1753) II. 131 Doing a thing in one Parliament, and ordering it to be no precedent to another, is an errant bull. **1776** [see ARRANT 3 b]. **1840** SMART says that *errant* is 'often wrongly used for *arrant*'.

†**8.** Without opprobrious sense: Thorough, downright absolute, unquestionable. *Obs.*

1644 MILTON *Areop.* (Arb.) 63 Protestants and professors, who live and dye in as errant and implicit faith, as any lay Papist of Loretto. *c* **1698** LOCKE *Cond. Underst.* (1781) 20 A country gentleman who.. can away with no company whose discourse goes beyond what claret and dissoluteness inspire. To such a one truly an ordinary coffee-house gleaner is an errant statesman. **1703** MRS. CENTLIVRE *Love's Contriv.* v, I shall become as errant a husband as you'd wish. **1710** CROMWELL *Let.* 5 Nov. in *Pope's Wks.* V. 99 He is so errant a whig, that he strains even beyond his author, in his passion for liberty.

†**b.** as *pred.* ? Unquestionable.

1653 HALES *Brevis Disq.* in *Phenix* (1708) II. 333 Unless we take that for errant which is in question.. Whether the Pope be the infallible Judg of Controversies.

III. Straying, wandering, erring.

9. Astray, wandering, roving; straying from the proper course or place; having no fixed course.

(In first quot. used as a mere pple.)

14.. *Circumcision* in *Tundale's Vis.* (1843) 97 To bryng the lost schepe ageyn.. That was eraunt ydyl and in vayne. **1590** SPENSER *F.Q.* III. viii. 6 A shady glade.. to her reveald By errant Sprights, but from all men conceald. **1606** SHAKS. *Tr. & Cr.* I. iii. 9 As knots.. Infect the sound Pine, and diuerts his Graine Tortiue and erant from his course of growth. *a* **1720** SHEFFIELD (Dk. Buckhm.) *Wks.* (1753) II. 7 The Lord Rochester at the place appointed, who.. brought an errant life-guard man. **1828** SCOTT *F.M. Perth* xix, When he has seen the errant damsel safe home, it will be time enough to claim his reward. **1861** TEMPLE & TREVOR *Tannhäuser* 21 With errant foot He wander'd on to Hörsel. **1865** DICKENS *Mut. Fr.* II. vi, With an errant motion of his hands as if he could have torn himself.

†**b.** Said of the planets (L. *stellæ errantes* = Gr. ἀστέρες πλανῆται) as opposed to the fixed stars. *Obs.*

1616 R. C. *Times' Whis.* 146 Astronomers that can foretell eventes.. By errant planettes & by fixèd starres. **1646** SIR T. BROWNE *Pseud. Ep.* IV. xii. 210 There are just seven Planets or errant Starres in the lower orbs of heaven. **1646** G. DANIEL *Poems* Wks. 1878 I. 17 Tis but her Errant motion; Hee, the Same Light, to the world. [**1860** EMERSON *Cond. Life* viii. Wks. (Bohn) II. 428 He heard a voice none else could hear From centred and from errant sphere.]

†**c.** In the classification of diseases; = ERRATIC.

1621 BURTON *Anat. Mel.* I. i. I. ii, Diseases.. Errant, Fixed, Simple, etc.

10. Erring in opinion, conduct, etc.; deviating from the correct standard.

1609 G. CHAPMAN *End Learn.* in Farr *S.P. Jas. I.* (1848) 253 Skill, that doth produce But tearmes and tongues, and parroting of arte, Without that powre to rule the errant part. **1676** EVELYN *Diary* 6 Sept., The famous beauty and errant lady the Dutchesse of Mazarine. **1881** G. F. WATTS in *19th Cent.* Mar. 452 Correcting errant taste in dress. **1883** *Brit. Q. Rev.* July 4 To counteract an errant condition by another condition which is itself errant.

b. Used as *sb. rare.*

1839 J. ROGERS *Antipopopr.* vi. 219 Oh lunacy, insanity, madness.. Oh papal errant, how great is your error!.. how ridiculous your creed!

'errant, *v. nonce-wd.* [f. prec.] *intr.* To travel abroad (like a knight errant).

1807 SIR R. WILSON *Jrnl.* 14 Nov., The British soldier.. has the advantage of erranting for his service. He seeks his glory abroad.

erranteer, var. of ERRANDEER.

1736 in BAILEY.

†**e'rrantic**, *a. Obs.* [f. ERRANT *a.* + -IC.] Of, pertaining to, or characteristic of, knights errant. So **e'rrantical** *a.*

1654 GAYTON *Pleas. Notes* III. ii. 73 Presented ten thousand whirlygigs, Windmils, and Turne-pikes to his errantick soule. *Ibid.* IV. xxv. 283 They have been rid many hundred of more then errantick miles. **1612** SHELTON *Quix.* I. I. vii. 47 The errantical Knighthood ought to bee againe renewed. **1654** GAYTON *Pleas. Notes* I. viii. 29 For Sancho having now two capacities, the one personall, and the other Squire erranticall, etc. *Ibid.* II. v. 57 For the Don.. sets her out in her erranticall titles.

errantly ('ɛrəntlɪ), *adv.* [f. ERRANT *a.* + -LY².] Wanderingly, at random; without definite purpose.

1831 CARLYLE *Sart. Res.* (1858) 168 Into how many strange shapes, of Superstition and Fanaticism, does it not tentatively and errantly cast itself. **1859** *Chamb. Jrnl.* XI. 349 The images flit.. so errantly and transiently.

'errantness. *rare*⁻⁰. [f. as prec. + -NESS.] The state or fact of being errant.

1730–6 BAILEY (folio), *Errantness*, wandering faculty.

errantry ('ɛrəntrɪ). [f. ERRANT + -RY.] The condition of being errant; the condition of a knight-errant; conduct or notions characteristic of a knight-errant. See also KNIGHT-ERRANTRY.

1654 GAYTON *Pleas. Notes* I. i. 2 As appeares by his Errantry, which is but a neater word for wandring. **1661** K. W. *Conf. Charac.* (1860) 20 He sends so many St. Georges to an eternal errantry never to returne to his burnt bottometh pocked. **1733** FIELDING *Quix.* I. v, I should not have followed his errantries so long. **1825** A. W. FONBLANQUE in *West. Review* IV. 398 Sheridan's part in this affray was considered by the shrewder observers as a ridiculous piece of errantry. **1881** DUFFIELD *Don Quix.* Pref. 35 On the return home from their errantries.

†**'errantship.** *Obs.* (*nonce-wd.*) [f. ERRANT *sb.* + -SHIP.] The personality of a (knight-) errant.

1654 GAYTON *Pleas. Notes* IV. xix. 265 When Maritornes and his Errant-ship were imbracing.

†**errat(e.** *Obs.* Anglicized f. ERRATUM.

1548 HALL *Chron.* (1809) Introd. 12 For what young man .. when he cometh to more ripenes of yeres.. doth not amend and change into better, his old errates and wanton actes. **1654** VILVAIN *Epit. Ess.* Pref. B. iv. b, Verses with sundry Errats are distended.

errata: see ERRATUM.

erratic (ɛ'rætɪk), *a.* and *sb.* Forms: 4 erratike, -tyk, 6 erratik, -tycke, 7 erratique, 7–8 erratick(e, 6– erratic. [ad. L. *errātic-us*, f. *errāre* to wander, ERR. Cf. Fr. *erratique.*]

A. *adj.* Wandering; prone to wander.

1. First used in certain special applications:

†**a.** ***erratic star***: a planet. *Obs.*

c **1374** CHAUCER *Troylus* v. 1824 He saw with full avisement The erratike sterres, herkening armonie. **1413** LYDG. *Pilgr. Sowle* v. i. 70 The seuene name couthe planetes, that ben cleped of clerkes sterres erratiks. **1549** *Compl. Scot.* vi. (1873) 47 Cosmaghraphie.. sal declair the mouyng.. of the sternis fixt, and sternis erratic. **1655–60** STANLEY *Hist. Philos.* (1701) 187/2 The Erratick [stars] are seven. **1774** J. BRYANT *Mythol.* II. 32 If.. these.. stones related to the seven erratic bodies in our spheres [i.e. the planets].

b. Said of pains, or diseases which are not fixed, but move from one part to another, as gout, rheumatism, etc.

1547 BOORDE *Brev. Health* cxlviii. 54 The Erratycke and commyxt fever. **1651** BIGGS *New Disp.* 178 Materiall cause of all erratick pains. **1725** N. ROBINSON *Th. Physick.* 154 Costiveness, succeeded with a slow Erratic Fever. **1748** tr. *Vegetius' Distemp. Horses* 12 This Ailment, because it is erratick, all of a sudden removes to the other foot.

†**c.** ***erratic poppy***: transl. L. *papaver erraticum* (Pliny), identified by Eng. writers with the Wild or Corn Poppy (*Papaver Rhœas*).

1661 LOVELL *Hist. Anim. & Min.* 193 Endive, roses, and erratick poppies. **1672** JORDAN *London Triumph.* in Heath *Grocers' Comp.* (1869) 494 A wreath about her head, consisting of variety of grain.. intermingled with.. erratick Poppies.

†**2.** Wandering from place to place; vagrant; nomadic. *Obs.*; shading off into 4.

1656 BLOUNT *Glossogr.*, *Erratique*, that wanders or creeps this way and that way. **1725** POPE *Odyss.* XII. 74 Through the vast waves the dreadful wonders move, Hence named Erratic by the gods above. **1751** JOHNSON *Rambler* No. 141 ¶10 When fortune did not favour my erratick industry, I gleaned jests at home. **1757** BURKE *Abridgm. Eng. Hist.* Wks. X. 539 This erratick justice [when the courts travelled with the kings] must have been productive of infinite inconvenience to the litigants. **1808** PIKE *Sources Mississ.* II. 175 Those savages although erratic must remain long enough in one position to cultivate this grain. **1816** SCOTT *Old Mort.* Introd., No entreaty could induce him to alter his erratic way of life. **1816** G. S. FABER *Orig. Pagan Idol.* II. 220 At this period Delos was supposed to have floated in an erratic state on the surface of the waters.

b. *Biol.*

1857 WOOD *Com. Obj. Sea-shore* 99 They are rather migratory in their habits, but not erratic, for they seem to go over the same course week after week. **1871** T. R. JONES *Anim. Kingd.* (ed. 4) 286 The first period of their existence, during which they lead an erratic life, then closes.

3. ***erratic blocks***, ***boulders***, in *Geol.*: stray masses of rock, foreign to the surrounding strata, that have been transported from their original site, apparently by glacial action.

a **1828** W. PHILLIPS *Treat. Geol.* (Humble), The magnitude of the transported rocks is such as to deserve the name of erratic blocks. **1849** MURCHISON *Siluria* i. (1867) 19 To the unskilled eye Russia presents only monotonous undulations, chiefly covered by mud, sand, and erratic blocks. **1859** DARWIN *Orig. Spec.* xii. (1873) 330 Erratic boulders and scored rocks plainly reveal a former cold period. **1871** TYNDALL *Fragm. Sc.* (ed. 6) I. viii. 270 We crossed Creag Dhubh, and examined the erratic blocks upon its sides.

4. Irregular or uncertain in movement; having no fixed course.

1841 CATLIN *N. Amer. Ind.* (1844) II. xlvii. 97 My erratic wanderings. **1854** MOSELEY *Astron.* lxxviii. (ed. 4) 218 The attraction of Jupiter.. upon this erratic comet. **1879** G. W. CABLE *Old Creole Days* 150 Short remnants of the wind now and then came down the narrow street in erratic puffs.

5. Irregular or eccentric in conduct, habit, or opinion.

1841 DISRAELI *Amen. Lit.* (1867) 623 The genius of Dee was as erratic as the course of life he shortly fell into. **1876** M. DAVIES *Unorth. Lond.* 23 To gather up those erratic spirits that now stand aloof from any religious school. **1885** MISS BRADDON *Wyllard's Weird* I. 17 He did not appear at luncheon, but.. he is always erratic.

B. *sb.*

1. An erratic person: †**a.** A vagabond (*obs.*). **b.** One who is eccentric in modes of action, etc.

1623 COCKERAM, *Erraticke*, a Rogue. **1669** GALE *Crt. Gentiles* I. II. iii. 35 Euripides cals the Bacchic Priests.. Erratics, or wanderers. **1816** G. S. FABER *Orig. Pagan Idol.* III. 340 The canonized erratic vouchsafed to inform Eadmer that he disapproved of returning to his old station. **1835** *Fraser's Mag.* XII. 274 It is.. only by following the erratics through their concentric courses that we can trace out the manifold ways and vices of man.

†**2.** An erratic star, a planet. *Obs. rare.*

1714 DERHAM *Astro-Theol.* II. ii. (1769) 74 Our Sun doth [warm] the erratcks encompassing it.

3. *Geol.* An erratic block.

1849 MURCHISON *Siluria* xx. 505 The huge erratics of the later cold period. **1882** DAWKINS in *Nature* XXVI. 436 Icebergs, melting as they passed southwards, deposited.. erratics.

b. *Comb.*

1881 G. M. DAWSON in *Nature* XXIII. 281 The drift-covered and erratic-strewn character of the country.

erratical (ɛ'rætɪkəl), *a.* and *sb.* [f. prec. + -AL¹.]

1. Wandering.

1620 BP. HALL *Hon. Mar. Clergy* 200 This man's wit wanders with his erraticall synode. **1646** J. MAINE *Agst. False Proph.* 31 Those erraticall, uncertain, wandring night-fires.. which shine only to lead Travellers out of the way. **1650** FULLER *Pisgah* IV. ii. 20 The Midianites especially led erraticall lives. **1721–1800** in BAILEY.

2. †**a.** Deviating from a given type. **b.** Guided by no rule, capricious, irregular, strange.

1646 SIR T. BROWNE *Pseud. Ep.* II. vi. 95 And therefore come not forth in generations erraticall, or different from each other. **1698** W. CHILCOT *Evil Thoughts* iv. (1851) 48 Unhappy conjunctions oftentimes prove the consequence of such erratical motions. **1854** RUSKIN *Two Paths* ii. 70 And enough bad teaching, to bring out very erratical results.

†**B.** *sb.* = ERRATIC B. 2. *Obs.*

1647 LILLY *Chr. Astrol.* clxxxv. 796 Were the scurvy position of ♄ in ♒ seconded with other malignant positures of the Erraticals.

Hence **e'rratically** *adv.*, in an erratic manner; irregularly, capriciously. **e'rraticalness.**

1613 M. RIDLEY *Magn. Bodies* 99 Varieth their direction diversely, and erratically. **1775** in ASH. **1861** WILSON & GEIKIE *Mem. E. Forbes* xii. 427 The remainder of this year was spent somewhat erratically. **1862** LYTTON *Str. Story* I. 166 The needle stirred, indeed, but erratically. **1884** H. STURMEY *Tricyclist's Indispens. Ann.* 12 The machine is made to steer very erratically. **1730–6** BAILEY (folio), *Erraticalness*, wandring faculty.

erraticism (ɛ'rætɪsɪz(ə)m). [see -ISM.] Erratic tendencies.

1889 E. DOWSON *Let.* 14 July (1967) 92, I discovered the erraticism of the Sunday posts. **1907** *Daily Chron.* 18 Jan. 9/6 Pronounced Erraticism [in golf-play]. **1920** *19th Cent.* July 6 In various ways his erraticism threatened actual danger to the allied cause. **1925** DREISER *Amer. Trag.* II. II. xlvi, (Strange, equivocal, frivolous erraticism of his in this instance) the tripod of a recently purchased camera [etc.]. **1928** T. C. CHAMBERLIN *Two Solar Families* p. xxi, Their courses were all-wayward. And yet their erraticisms are accompanied with spectacular brilliancy.

†**'erratile**, *a. Obs. rare.* [ad. L. *errātilis*, f. *errāre*.] **a.** Of a star: Wandering. **b.** Erroneous, mistaken.

1652 GAULE *Magastrom.* 66 To..note all the stars (both fixed and erratile) under which one is born, and that without any errour or erratile apprehension in himself.

†**e'rration.** *Obs.*$^{-0}$ [ad. L. *errātiōn-em*, n. of action f. *errāre* to wander.]

1623 COCKERAM, *Erration*, a wandring to and fro. **1730–6** in BAILEY (folio). **1832** in WEBSTER.

erratum (ɛ'reɪtəm, -'rɑ:-). Pl. **errata.** [a. L. *errātum*, neut. pa. pple. of *errāre*: see ERR.]

1. An error in writing or printing; *chiefly*, an error noted in a list of corrections attached to a printed book.

1589 *Marprel. Epit.* G b, Errata, or faults escaped. **1632** QUARLES *Div. Fancies* IV. xxxv. (1660) 151 The World's a Book..'Tis falsly printed, though divinely penn'd, And all th' Errata will appear at th' end. **1691** NORRIS *Pract. Disc.* 247 God..upon a Solemn Review of his Works..found not one Erratum in the whole Book of Nature. **1714** *Spect.* No. 579 ¶1 The Company of Stationers..made a very remarkable Erratum or Blunder in one of their Editions [of the Bible]. **1756** C. LUCAS *Ess. Waters* I. Pref., The long Catalogue of errata that disfigures this work. *c* **1817** HOGG *Tales & Sk.* II. 234 An erratum to a volume. **1824** J. JOHNSON *Typogr.* II. vi. 142 The errata are put immediately before the body of the work, or at the end of it. **1875** JOWETT *Plato* (ed. 2) I. p. vii, I have inserted as corrections under the head of errata.

b. *transf.*

1771 FRANKLIN *Autobiog.* Wks. 1840 I. 26 This I therefore reckon one of the first errata of my life.

¶**2. a.** Like other plurals in *-a*, *errata* often appears in 17–18th c. with the addition of *-'s* or *-es* without alteration of sense. **b.** At the same period, *errata* occurs as a *sing.*, = 'list of errata', and in that sense takes *-es* in *pl.*

a. 1644 QUARLES *Sheph. Orac.* xi, Hee's a page Fill'd with Errata's of the present age. **1678** *Yng. Man's Call.* 53 Look back upon time past..that the former errata's and miscarriages of life may be henceforth corrected. **1727** SWIFT *Further Acc. E. Curll*, Resolved, That a number of effective errata's be raised out of Pope's Homer.

b. 1635 T. LAMBARDE *To Rdr.* in *W. Lambarde's Archeion*, Those that..swallow the Errours for Errataes. **1650** EARL MONM. tr. *Senault's Man become Guilty* A. 4 a, I have made an Amends by printing an Errata. **1659** HEYLIN *Examen Hist.* II. 150 Such Misnomers are so frequent in him, as might make a sufficient Errata at the end of his History. **1663** GERBIER *Counsel* 105 The Errataes at the end of books.

3. *attrib.* in pl.

a **1852** MOORE *Devil among Schol.* 35 In whom the dear errata column Is the best page in all the volume!

eraunt, obs. form of ERRANT.

erre, var. of ARR, *Obs.*, wound, scar.

a **1340** HAMPOLE *Psalter* xxxvii. 5 Myn erres..þat is þe wondes of my synnes. *c* **1450** *Mirour Saluacioun* 265 Shewing his woundes errys. **1562** BULLEYN *Bk. Simples* 14 a, Anoint the faces of children, that haue the small Pockes, when the said Pockes be ripe, to kepe them from pittes or erres.

erre, var. of IRRE, *Obs.*, wrath.

c **1450** MYRC 1225 Hast thow had enuye and erre To hym that was thyn ouer herre.

erred (ɜ:d), *ppl. a. rare.* [f. ERR + -ED[1].] Used erroneously; misapplied.

1602 WARNER *Alb. Eng.* IX. xlix. (1612) 226 Catholiques (that erred name doth please the Papists).

†**'erres.** *Obs. pl.* [a. OF. *erres* pl.: see ARLES.] Earnest-money; an earnest.

c **1425** *Leg. Rood* (1871) 217 To bye hys chaffare þe child payed erres.

†**'errevous,** *a. Obs. rare*$^{-1}$. [f. *erre*, IRRE, anger, after *plentevous*, *bountevous*, etc.] Wrathful.

a **1420** HOCCLEVE *De Reg. Princ.* 84 Alle his angre and his erreuous [*printed* errenous] talent Refraynede he.

errhine ('ɛraɪn), *sb.* (and *a.*) *Med.* Also 7 errhin. [ad. mod.L. *errhīnum*, ad Gr. *ἔρρῑν-ον*, f. *ἐν* in + *ῥίν* nostril. Cf. Fr. *errhin* adj.]

1. 'A medicine which when applied to the mucous membrane of the nose increases the natural secretions and produces sneezing' (*Syd. Soc. Lex.*).

1626 BACON *Sylva* 1631 §38 Powders.. (which the Physitians call Errhines) put into the Nose, draw Flegme, and water from the Head. **1634** T. JOHNSON tr. *Parey's Chirurg.* XXVI. xxxv. (1678) 654 Drie Errhines are to be blown into the nose with a pipe or quill. **1710** T. FULLER *Pharm. Extemp.* 151 Errhines are to be us'd cheefly in the Morning. **1875** H. WOOD *Therap.* (1879) 557.

†**2.** A plug of lint steeped in such a medicine for insertion in the nose. *Obs.*

[**1611** COTGR., *Errhine*, a tent-like medicine applyed vnto, or put into, the nose, etc.] **1601** HOLLAND *Pliny, Explan. Words of Art*, Errhines be deuises made like tents, sharper at one end than the other, to bee put vp into the nose. **1758** J. S. *Le Dran's Observ. Surg.* (1771) *149, I hooked it with an Errhine, and divided the Skin with a Bistoury.

3. as *adj.* Having the action of an errhine (*Syd. Soc. Lex.*).

1876 HARLEY *Mat. Med.* 380 Externally it is rubefacient and errhine.

erring ('ɜ:rɪŋ), *vbl. sb.* [f. ERR *v.* + -ING[1].] The action of the verb ERR; †an instance of the same, a fault.

1483 *Cath. Angl.* 117 An Errynge, *erratus, error.* **1649** H. LAWRENCE *Some Consid.* 38 Two sorts of errings. **1654** E. JOHNSON *Wond.-wrkg. Provid.* 175 Yet have they their errings as well as others. **1699** POMFRET *Love Triumph. over Reason*, There's no erring twice in Love and War. **1727** HARTE *To Pr. Orange* (R.), Isis, whose erring on the modest side Th'unkind and ignorant mistake for pride.

erring ('ɜ:rɪŋ), *ppl. a.* [f. ERR *v.* + -ING[2].] That errs in senses of the vb.: †wandering, roaming (*obs.*); deviating from the right or intended course, missing the mark; that is in error, or commits errors in opinion or conduct.

a **1340** HAMPOLE *Psalter* xiii. 1 Delite of synn egges errand men to ween God noght to be. *c* **1400** *Lay Folks Mass-bk.* App. v. 394 As a Errynge pylgrym in the seruyse of the myghty and dredful god of loue, how many perylous passages and wayes that I ha passyd by. **1602** SHAKS. *Ham.* I. i. 154 Th' extrauagant, and erring Spirit, hyes To his Confine. **1623** WHITBOURNE *Newfoundland* Pref. 14 This Ship was intercepted by an English erring Captaine. **1651** HOBBES *Leviath.* III. xlii. 319 Danger..may arise to Religion, by the Subjects tolerating of an..Erring Prince, etc. **1697** DRYDEN *Æneid* (T.), He all those erring parts described so well, That Theseus conquer'd, and the monster fell. **1715–20** POPE *Iliad* v. 24 His sounding spear, Which..spent in empty air its erring force. **1836** J. GILBERT *Chr. Atonem.* ii. (1852) 39 Still to erring, wilful man, the way to life is strait. **1875** JOWETT *Plato* (ed. 2) I. 173 The erring act which is done without knowledge is one in ignorance.

†**b.** *erring star* = planet. *Obs.*

c **1449** PECOCK *Repr.* v. i. 480 Erring sterris. **1647** H. MORE *Song of Soul* II. III. III. xv, So doth the Earth one of the erring Seven Wheel round the fixèd sunne. **1697** DRYDEN *Virg.* (J.), Fix'd and erring stars dispose their influence.

erringly ('ɜ:rɪŋlɪ), *adv.* [f. prec. + -LY[2].] In an erring manner, in the senses of the verb.

1815 WORDSW. *Wh. Doe* Ded., He serves the Muses erringly and ill, Whose aim is pleasure light and fugitive. **1835** *New Monthly Mag.* XLIV. 69 That army, like a rudderless bark, floats erringly. **1841** D'ISRAELI *Amen. Lit.* (1867) 131 A standard from which the prevalent style of its contemporaries has erringly diverged.

erriwig, -wiggle, dial. form of EARWIG *sb.*

1830 FORBY *Norf. & Suffolk Voc.* 106 *Erriwiggle*, an earwig. **1879** MISS JACKSON *Shropsh. Word-bk.* 134 Looks like a throttled erriwig.

errone'osity. ? *nonce-wd.* [f. ERRONEOUS, after the analogy of *curiosity*, etc.] = Erroneousness.

1840 *New Monthly Mag.* LIX. 501 All his opinions..were founded on 'erroneosity'.

erroneous (ɛ'rəʊnɪəs). Forms: 4–7 erronious(e, 5–6 erronyous(e, (5 arronious, eronyous, 6 erreoneous, ironyos, 7 erroneus), 4– erroneous. [? ad. OF. *erroneus*, f. L. *errōneus* (whence mod.F. *erroné*) vagrant, wandering (post-class. also 'erroneous'), f. *errōn-em* vagabond, f. *errāre* to wander: see -OUS.]

†**1.** Wandering, roving; moving aimlessly, vagrant. Also quasi-*adv.* *Obs.*

1460 CAPGRAVE *Chron.* 252 The bischoppis..opened no mouth to berk ageyn these erroneous doggis. **1667** MILTON *P.L.* VII. 20 On th' Aleian Field I fall Erroneous, there to wander and forlorne. **1704** NEWTON *Optics* (1721) 91 This Circle, by being placed here, stopped much of the Erroneous Light. *a* **1777** FAWKES tr. *Halley's Eulogy on Newton*, With what proportion'd force The Moon impels, erroneous in her course, The refluent main.

†**b.** Straying from the proper course. *Obs. rare.*

1731 ARBUTHNOT *Aliments* 165 An erroneous Circulation (that is, when the Blood strays into the Vessels destin'd to carry Serum or Lymph).

†**2.** Straying from the path of right or virtue, morally faulty, criminal. *Obs.* or *arch.*

1593 SHAKS. *3 Hen. VI*, II. v. 90 What Stragems? how fell? how Butcherly? Erreoneous, mutinous, and vnnaturall. **1634** SIR T. HERBERT *Trav.* 55 The Prophet used to lay this stone on the shoulders of the erronious. **1777** DODD in Boswell *Johnson* (1848) 542 My life for some few unhappy years has been dreadfully erroneous. *a* **1797** H. WALPOLE *Mem. Geo. II* (1845) I. vii. 95 The probability was, that himself had been erroneous. **1819** BYRON *Juan* III. xii, Shut The book which treats of this erroneous pair.

†**3.** Straying from the ways of wisdom or prudence; under the influence of error, misguided. *Obs.* or *arch.*

1512 *Act 4 Hen. VIII*, c. 19 Pream., The seid Frensche kyng..abydyng in his..erronyous mynde. **1526** *Pilgr. Perf.* (W. de W. 1531) 55 He..sleeth by confessyon the wormes of the scrupulous and erronyous conscience. **1594** SHAKS. *Rich. III*, I. iv. 200 Erroneous Vassals. **1640** *Lond. Petit.* in Rushw. *Hist. Coll.* (1692) I. 94 The great encrease of..Ignorant and Erroneous Men in the Ministry. **1684** BUNYAN *Pilgr.* II. 64 *marg.*, 'Tis difficult getting of good Doctrine in erroneous Times. **1685** BAXTER *Paraphr. N.T.* (1701) Matt. vi. 22 If thy judgment then be blind which must guide thee, what a miserable erroneous wretch wilt thou be. **1759** GOLDSMITH *Miscell. Wks.* (1837) III. 246 Leibnitz..being very erroneous himself, cannot be expected to have bequeathed precision to his followers. **1775** JOHNSON *Tax. no Tyr.* 87 That erroneous clemency. **1810** CRABBE *Borough* xx, And should have strengthened an erroneous heart. **1829** SOUTHEY *Sir T. More* I. 133 He who shows himself grievously erroneous upon one important point must look to have his opinions properly distrusted upon others.

absol.

1601 CORNWALLYES *Ess.* II. xxix. (1631) 42 He will never instruct the erronious for a frowning reply quailes him. **1649** *Alcoran* 188 God prolongeth the life of the erroneous.

4. Of doctrines, opinions, statements, etc.: Containing errors; of the nature of error; incorrect, mistaken, wrong.

c **1400** *Test. Love* I. 277/2 See ye not everie wight that to these erronious opinions were assentaunt. **1494** FABYAN *Chron.* VII. 539 [The] erronyouse opynyons of yᵉ sayd heresy [Wyclif's]. *c* **1530** MORE *Answ. Frith* Wks. (1557) 833/1 A letter of sir Thomas More knight impugning the erroniouse wryting of John Frith agaynst the blessed sacrament of the aulter. **1556** *Chron. Gr. Friars* (1852) 63 What an ironyos oppynyone is this unto the leye pepulle. **1667** MILTON *P.L.* x. 969 How little weight my words with thee can find, Found so erroneous. **1711** J. GREENWOOD *Eng. Gram.* 246 Mr. Ray says this spelling is erroneous and that..*flood* and *blood*.. ought to be written *flud*, *blud*. **1757** BURKE *Abridgm. Eng. Hist.* Wks. (1842) II. 529 His astronomy is..imperfect and grossly erroneous. **1822** IMISON *Sc. & Art* II. 2 But modern chemistry has shown that this was an erroneous supposition. **1845** BUDD *Dis. Liver* 53 The erroneous impression that abscesses exist in the liver only.

b. Of a legal proceeding: Faulty in law, irregular; chiefly, vitiated by 'error' in the technical sense: see ERROR 4 c.

1495 *Act 11 Hen. VII*, c. 59 Pream., For so muche as the same utlagarie is arronious. **1601–2** FULBECKE *1st Pt. Parall.* 58 Otherwise the iudgment is erronious. **1818** CRUISE *Digest* (ed. 2) V. 109 The same lands were granted to two different persons, which was repugnant and erroneous. **1848** WHARTON *Law Lex* 226/2 Any matter appearing on the face of the record, which shews the judgment to be erroneous.

erroneously (ɛ'rəʊnɪəslɪ), *adv.* [f. ERRONEOUS + -LY[2].] In an erroneous manner:

†**a.** In an erratic or wandering manner. **b.** In a misguided manner, under the influence of error. **c.** Otherwise than is the fact; incorrectly.

a. 1528 ROY *Sat.* (1845) 111 We wander in darcknes With out light erroniously.

b. 1512 *Act 4 Hen. VIII*, c. 19 Pream., Erronyously defendyng and maynteynyng his seid obstynate opynyons. **1655** FULLER *Ch.-Hist.* I. 2 They who erroneously conceive one God too little, will find two too many. **1726–7** SWIFT *Gulliver* (J.), I..conceived it, perhaps, erroneously, rather to be rigorous than gentle. **1855** MACAULAY *Hist. Eng.* IV. 330 They erroneously imagined that there was an exact analogy between, etc.

c. 1578 LYTE *Dodoens* II. xliv. 203 This flowre is called Affodillus..but very erroniously. **1646** SIR T. BROWNE *Pseud. Ep.* III. xviii. 153 If vision..receive its objects erroneously, [it is called] Hallucination. **1675** OGILBY *Brit.* 17 It is computed, but erroneously, mid-way between Durham and Newcastle. **1751** JOHNSON *Idler* No. 100 ¶1 Which produce very mischievous mistakes when they are erroneously interpreted. **1879** J. GRANT in *Cassell's Techn. Educ.* IV. 382/2 Hitherto been set down most erroneously in all maps.

erroneousness (ɛ'rəʊnɪəsnɪs). [f. as prec. + -NESS.] The quality of being erroneous.

1624 A. WOTTON *Runne from Rome* 68, I haue alreadie.. discouered and proued the erroneousnesse of the faith of that Church. **1748** HARTLEY *Observ. Man* I. iii. 391 The Erroneousness of the Judgment in Children and Idiots. **1818** HALLAM *Mid. Ages* (1872) III. 299 The erroneousness of this religion. **1854** TOULM. SMITH *Parish* (1857) 11, I shall show the erroneousness of the..notion.

†**'erronist.** *Obs. rare*$^{-1}$. [f. L. *errōn-em* vagabond (cf. ERRONEOUS) + -IST.] ? A teacher of false doctrine.

1654 E. JOHNSON *Wonder-wrkg. Provid.* 98 These Erronists..Cry out against a learned Presbitery.

error ('ɛrə(r)). Forms: 4 erur, errur(e, 4, 6 erroure, 4–8 errour, (4–5 arrour, -owre, errowre, 5–6 errore, 6 erore), 4– error. [a. OF. *error*, *errur*, *errour* (mod.Fr. *erreur*) = Pr. and Sp. *error*, It. *errore*:—L. *errōr-em*, f. *errāre* to wander, ERR. (Some of the early forms may be due to the influence of OF. *erreüre*:—Lat. type **errātūram*).

Down to the end of the 18th c. the prevailing form was *errour*, which is the form given by Johnson and by Todd (1818); Bailey's Dict. introduces *error* in 1753, and this spelling is now universal. (In words which have *-rr-* before the suffix, as *horror*, *terror*, *mirror*, the spelling of *-or* for an older *-our* is accepted by British as well as American writers.)]

I. 1. The action of roaming or wandering; hence a devious or winding course, a roving, winding. Now only *poet.*

The primary sense in Latin; in Fr. and Eng. it occurs only as a conscious imitation of Lat. usage.

1594 DANIEL *Compl. Rosamond* Wks. (1717) 50 Intricate innumerable Ways, With such confused Errors. **1610** GUILLIM *Heraldry* xvi. (1660) 201 Being by error lost, they [dogs] have refused meat. **1636** B. JONSON *Discov.* Wks. (ed. Rtldg.) 765/1 His error by sea, the sack of Troy, are put not as the argument of the work. **1654** R. CODRINGTON tr. *Ivstine* 318 But Archagathus was taken by them, who had lost his Father in the error of the night. **1667** MILTON *P.L.* IV. 239 The crisped Brooks, Rowling..With mazie error under pendant shades. **1673** *Lady's Call.* I. iv. ¶13. 30 [The moon] has a kind of certainty even in her planetary errors. **1743** R. BLAIR *Grave* 99 Where the..stream has slid along In grateful errors through the underwood. **1720** GAY *Poems* (1745) I. 13 If an enormous salmon chance to spy The wanton errors of the floating fly. **1872** TENNYSON *Gareth & Lynette* 1183 The damsel's headlong error thro' the wood.

II. †**2.** Chagrin, fury, vexation; a wandering of the feelings; extravagance of passion. *Obs.*

[A common use in OF.; cf. IROUR, a. OF. *irour* anger, which may have been confused with this word.]

c 1320 *Sir Beues* 1907 Tho was Beues in strong erur. c 1325 *Coer de L.* 5937 Kyng Richard pokyd [? þo kyd] gret errour, Wrathe dede hym chaung colour. c 1450 *Merlin* xx. 318 A-boute his herte com so grete errour that it wete all his visage with teeres of his yien. 1460 *Lybeaus Disc.* 1081 The lord wyth greet errour Rod hom to hys tour.

III. The action or state of erring.

3. a. The condition of erring in opinion; the holding of mistaken notions or beliefs; an instance of this, a mistaken notion or belief; false beliefs collectively. Phrases, ***to be, stand in, lead into error***; † ***without error*** = 'doubtless'.

a 1300 *Cursor M.* 16900 (Cott.) Þan sal rise mar þan beforn errur of vr fai. c 1340 *Ibid.* 25225 (Cott. Galb.) All men þat in errure iss for to be broght vnto þi blis. c 1340 HAMPOLE *Prose Tr.* 9 Astronomyenes.. þeyre errowre es reproffede of haly doctours. 1340 —— *Pr. Consc.* 4277 Þus sal þai bring þe folk in errour Thurgh þair prechyng. c 1400 MAUNDEV. xxxiv. (Roxb.) 155 To mayntene þam in þaire mawmetry and þaire errour. 1450 MYRC 63 Forsakest [thou] alle heresies and arrours. 1475 CAXTON *Jason* 84 The king Serath confessid thenne openly that without errour appollo was a god. c 1500 *Pol. Rel. & L. Poems* 44 And if sche wot nat whoo it is, bute stonde in erore. 1548–9 (Mar.) *Bk. Com. Prayer* 127 We are brought out of darkness and error. 1596 SHAKS. *Merch. V.* III. ii. 78 In Religion, What damned error, but some sober brow Will blesse it? 1646 SIR T. BROWNE *Pseud. Ep.* I. iii. 8 For Error, to speake strictly, is a firme assent unto falsity. 1756 C. LUCAS *Ess. Waters* I. 33 The general notion, that springs are colder in summer and warmer in winter, is but a vulgar error. 1776 GIBBON *Decl. & Fall* I. xv. 340 The paths of error are various and infinite. 1830 V. KNOX *Béclard's Anat.* 194 This circumstance has led those into error. 1860 TYNDALL *Glac.* II. iv. 249 Let us here avoid an error which may readily arise out [of] the foregoing reflections. 1875 JOWETT *Plato* (ed. 2) V. 136 Actions done in error are often thought to be involuntary injustice.

b. *personified.*

1590 SPENSER *F.Q.* I. i. 167 God help the man so wrapt in Errours endless train. 1601 SHAKS. *Jul. C.* v. iii. 69 O Error soone conceyu'd, Thou.. kil'st the Mother that engendred thee. 1646 J. HALL *Horæ Vac.* 6 Though error bee blinde, shee sometimes bringeth forth seeing Daughters. 1738 WESLEY *Psalms* LXXX. xv, And Error in ten thousand Shapes Would every gracious Soul beguile.

†**c.** A delusion, trick. *Obs. rare.*

c 1320 *Seuyn Sag.* (W.) 2353 So longe thai vsed this errour Thai were richcher than th' emperour.

4. a. Something incorrectly done through ignorance or inadvertence; a mistake, *e.g.* in calculation, judgement, speech, writing, action, etc. Phrase, ***to commit an error***. ***clerical error*** (see CLERICAL).

a 1340 HAMPOLE *Psalter* Comm. 45 Errour in hit is ther non. c 1425 WYNTOUN *Cron.* v. xii. 286 Huchowne bath and þe autore Gyltles ar of gret errore. 1483 CAXTON *Cato* 3, I.. byseche all suche that fynde faute or errour that of theyr charyte they correcte and amende hit. 1538 STARKEY *England* 116, I wyl confesse thys to be a grete errore in our commyn wele. 1590 SHAKS. *Mids. N.* v. i. 250 This is the greatest error of all the rest; the man should be put into the Lanthorne. 1651 HOBBES *Leviath.* I. iv. 15 For the errours of Definitions multiply themselves. 1710 H. BEDFORD *Vind. Ch. Eng.* 182 With all the Errors of the Press corrected in it with a Pen. 1781 COWPER *Friendship* iv, Boys care but little whom they trust, An errour soon corrected. 1816 PLAYFAIR *Nat. Philos.* 323 The first solution of the problem of the Precession.. given by Newton.. is not free from error. 1855 MACAULAY *Hist. Eng.* III. 125 He could hardly fail to perceive that he had committed a great error.

†**b.** A mistake in the making of a thing; a miscarriage, mishap; a flaw, malformation. ***nature's error*** = *lusus naturæ*. *Obs.*

1398 TREVISA *Barth. De P.R.* v. i. (1495) 101 This wonderfull errour [abortion] happyth moost in shepe and geete. 1413 LYDG. *Pilgr. Sowle* IV. xxx. (1483) 78 Hit behoueth.. that it [a statue] be fourged right withoute ony errour. 1697 DRYDEN (J.), He look'd like Nature's errour, as the mind And body were not of a piece design'd. 1791 BOSWELL *Johnson* (1816) I. 87 Sure, thou art an errour of nature.

c. *Law.* A mistake in matter of law appearing on the proceedings of a court of record. ***writ of error***: a writ brought to procure the reversal of a judgement, on the ground of error. By the Judicature Act of 1875 writs of error are limited to criminal cases; in civil cases appeal is substituted. ***plaintiff, defendant in error***: the parties for or against whom the writ of error is used. ***court of error*** (U.S.), a court of appeal in cases of error. †***clerk of the errors*** (see quot. 1706).

1495 *Act 11 Hen. VII*, c. 59 §2 The seid utlagaries.. were reversed by meane of errour aftir the due order of your lawes. 1641 *Termes de la Ley* 142 Errour is a fault in a judgement, or in the processe, or proceeding to judgment, or in the execution upon the same in a Court of Record. 1663 BUTLER *Hud.* I. II. 163 Lawyers.. Do stave and tail with Writs of Error. 1699 LUTTRELL *Brief Rel.* (1857) IV. 505 The place of clerk of the errors, worth £400 per annum. 1706 PHILLIPS, *Clerk of the Errours*, an Officer of the Common-Pleas, whose Business it is to Copy out and Certifie the Tenour of the Records of a Cause or Action, upon which the Writ of Errour is brought into any of those Courts. 1775 SHERIDAN *Rivals* Prol. i. 31 No writ of error lies—to Drury Lane! 1817 W. SELWYN *Law Nisi Prius* II. 1121 If the defendant avow for so much rent arrear, part whereof is not due at the time of the distress, and enters judgment for the whole, it will be error. 1821 MARSHALL *Const. Opin.* (1839) 239 The counsel for the defendant in error. 1827 HALLAM *Const. Hist.* (1876) II. xii. 418 During the fifteenth and sixteenth centuries writs of error from inferior courts to the house of lords became far less usual.

d. *Math.* The quantity by which a result obtained by observation or by approximate calculation differs from an accurate determination. ***error of a planet***: the difference between its observed place and that indicated by calculation. ***error of a clock***: the difference between the time which it indicates and that which it ought to indicate. ***law of error, random error*** (see quots.). ***probable error, standard error*** (see under the first element).

1726 tr. *Gregory's Astron.* I. 123 All the Errors of the Body *L*, arise from the Forces represented by the Right lines *AM*, *MN*. 1833 HERSCHEL *Astron.* iii. 136 By applying its [clock's] error and rate.. he can correct its indications. 1838 DE MORGAN *Probab.* 135 The number of positive and negative errors will in the long run be equal. 1875 F. GALTON in *Phil. Mag.* 4th Ser. XLIX. 37 The law of frequency of error says that 'magnitudes differing from the mean value by such and such multiples of the probable error, will occur with such and such degrees of frequency'. 1876 Law of error [see DISPERSION 6]. 1878 TAIT & STEWART *Uns. Univ.* iii. 123 The same law as that of the Probability of error. 1910 *Encycl. Brit.* IX. 754/2 In mathematics, 'error' is the deviation of the observed or calculated quantity from its true value. The calculus of errors leads to the formulation of the 'law of error', which is an analytical expression of the most probably true value of a series of discordant values. 1936 *Jrnl. R. Aeronaut. Soc.* XL. 77 The distribution of the components of the velocity fluctuation at any given point appears to follow the 'random error law'. 1951 M. JAHODA et al. *Res. Methods Social Rel.* I. IV. 100 Random error is due to those transient aspects of the person, of the situation of measurement, of the measurement procedure, etc., which are likely to vary by chance from one measurement to the next. 1959 *Chambers's Encycl.* VIII. 220/1 The component of molecular velocity along any chosen direction is distributed according to the so-called 'error law', i.e. the number of molecules whose component velocity u lies between narrow limits u and $u + du$ is proportional to $e^{-Au^2}du$.

5. A departure from moral rectitude; a transgression, wrong-doing.

In mod. use conveying the notion either of something not wholly voluntary, and so excusable, or of something imprudent as well as blameable. Cf. 4.

c 1330 R. BRUNNE *Chron.* (1810) 78 William the Conqueror changis his wikked wille, Out of his first errour. 1393 GOWER *Conf.* I. 21 Where lawe lacketh errour groweth. 1477 EARL RIVERS (Caxton) *Dictes* 11 That they shuld escheue al errours & applye them to all good dedis. 1535 COVERDALE *Wisd.* i. 12 O seke not youre owne death in yᵉ erroure of youre life. 1611 BIBLE *Heb.* ix. 7 Blood, which he offered for himselfe, and for the errors of the people. 1713 BERKELEY in *Guardian* No. 8 Allusions to the errors of a very wild life. 1792 BURKE *Corr.* (1844) III. 407 It is an error, not of the head, but of the heart. 1800 MRS. HERVEY *Mourtray Fam.* II. 261 Capital vices? Say, rather, fashionable errors. 1851 KINGSLEY *Lett.* (1878) I. 252 Every error must in God's universe, bring down on itself.. some cognate misery.

6. *Comb.*, as ***error-blasted, -darkened, -free, -proof, -stricken, -tainted, -teaching***, adjs.; ***error-analysis, -holder***; ***error-correcting, -detecting*** vbl. sbs. (so ***error-correction, -detection***); **error box** *Astr.*, a quadrilateral area of sky whose dimensions correspond to the uncertainty of a measured position inside it.

1963 P. STREVENS *Papers in Lang.* (1965) i. 8 The study of *error-analysis. 1968 FOX & MAYERS *Computing Methods for Scientists & Engineers* V. 119 Wilkinson (1963) also gives more details in a reasonably elementary way, of the error analysis for matrix problems. 1647 WARD *Simple Cobler* 16 A.. minde.. *Error-blasted from Heaven and Hell. 1968 *Space Sci. Rev.* VIII. 536 The source *error box is defined only by the errors in the more accurately known radial (frequency) determinations. 1974 *Nature* 20 Dec. 661/1 We call attention here to the existence of a rich Abell cluster of galaxies in the error box of the Uhuru high galactic latitude source 3U1706 + 32. 1978 *Sci. News* 5 Aug. 88 X-ray observing equipment characteristically locates a source within a certain 'error box' that may contain several candidates for visual identification, and the task is to make the error box smaller or pick the likeliest candidate. 1962 *Gloss. Terms Automatic Data Processing* 22 **Error correcting code*, an error detecting code which uses additional code elements so that for certain errors the mutilated representation resembles more closely the original than any other valid representation. 1965 *Math. in Biol. & Med.* (*Med. Res. Council*) III. 124 The similarity to, and the difference from, either the 'substantialization' of sign-sequences or error-correcting codes may be noted. 1964 T. W. MCRAE *Impact of Computers on Accounting* vi. 164 These *error-correction procedures are very complicated indeed. 1657 S. W. *Schism Dispach't* 558 The obscurity of ambiguities is most proper and least offensive to his *errour-darkned eyes. 1927 J. ADAMS *Errors in School* 236 Applying the parallel to *error-detecting. 1962 *Gloss. Terms Automatic Data Processing* 22 *Error detecting code*, a code in which each representation of a character conforms to specific rules of construction, so that for certain errors the mutilated representation corresponds to no valid character. 1927 J. ADAMS *Errors in School* 248 Responsibility of *error-detection. *Ibid.* 38 *Error-free material. 1964 C. DENT *Quantity Surveying by Computer* iii. 32 Checking devices to ensure error-free tapes. 1577 *Vicary's Anat.* To Rdr. 9 They are.. condemned for ignoraunt men, and *errour-holders. 1646 SHIRLEY *To Stanley*, Let me deal plainly with your youth, Not *error-proof yet. 1871 E. BURR *Ad Fidem* iv. 63 Bring truth home, to *error-stricken souls. 1657 S. W. *Schism Dispach't* 239 The poison of heresy and *error-tainted opinions. 1853 G. S. FABER *Recapit. Apostasy* 72 Giving heed to *error-teaching spirits and to doctrines concerning demons.

error (ˈɛrə(r)), *v. Law.* [f. prec. sb.] *trans.* To determine or decide to be erroneous (a decision of a court).

1828 in WEBSTER; and in mod. Dicts.

errorful (ˈɛrəfʊl). [f. ERROR *sb.* + -FUL.] Erroneous, faulty.

1563–87 FOXE *A. & M.* 990 Brought in by errorfull custome.

†**eˈrrorious**, *a. Obs.* In 5 **herrorious.** [f. ERROR + -(I)OUS.] ? Holding erroneous tenets.

1543 HARDING *Chron.* ccxi. fol. ccviii, Then fled the lorde Cobham herrorious [*v.r.* erronyouse] To Wales, so with lollers many one.

errorist (ˈɛrərɪst). [f. ERROR + -IST.] One who is inclined to error; one who encourages and propagates error.

1647 WARD *Simple Cobler* 17 Prudent men.. should doe well not to ingage themselves in conference with Errorists. 1849 *Blackw. Mag.* LXV. 537 Our feelings are with such errorists. 1874 J. H. BLUNT *Dict. Sects* 4 Adalbert an errorist of the eighth century.. was opposed to St. Boniface Winfred.

errorless (ˈɛrəlɪs). [f. ERROR + -LESS.] Without error; free from fault or mistake.

1856 RUSKIN *Mod. Paint.* III. IV. viii. §18 It.. brings out the positive creature, errorless, unquestionable. 1868 GEO. ELIOT *Sp. Gipsy* 234 Shipwrecked man.. Sees that full light is errorless despair. 1878 P. BAYNE *Purit. Rev.* viii. 338 His Satan incarnates with errorless accuracy the Puritan conception of superlative sin.

Hence **ˈerrorlessness**, the state or condition of being free from error.

1875 HOLYOAKE *Co-op. Eng.* I. 244 Sincerity does not connote or imply errorlessness.

†**ˈerrorous**, *a. Obs.* In 7 **errourous.** [f. ERROR + -OUS.] = ERRONEOUS.

1633 AMES *Agst. Cerem.* I. 62 By reason of an errourous conceit.

†**ers.** ? *Obs.* [a. Fr. *ers* = Pr. *ers*, app. cogn. with Cat. *er*, Sp. *yero*, *yervo*, It. *ervo*:—L. *ervum.*] The Bitter Vetch (*Ervum Ervilia* L.).

1578 LYTE *Dodoens* IV. xxiv. 482. 1879 PRIOR *Plant-n.* s.v.

ers(e, obs. ff. ARSE, q.v. *Comb.* **ersgerdyll** (= **arse-girdle*); **erswort** (= **arse-wort*), some plant (see quot.).

1438 *E.E. Wills* (1882) 110 To Edmond of Cornewayle an ersgerdyll of siluer. a 1400 *Sloane MS.* 10 b/1 *Pilosella*.. [French] *pilocelle*.. lambestounge *uel* erswort.

ersatz (ˈɜːzæts, ǁˈɛrzats). [G., = compensation, replacement.] A substitute or imitation (usually, an inferior article instead of the real thing). Also *attrib.* or *adj.*, and *fig.*

1875 *Encycl. Brit.* II. 594/2 (German army), Those who are exempted.. are passed into the *Ersatz* reserve. 1892 J. ROYCE *Let.* 17 Oct. in R. B. Perry *Tht. & Char. of W. James* (1935) I. 803 To me he is a great comfort, although.. no *Ersatz* for the aforesaid condition of my heart. 1910 *Pedagogical Seminary* 305 When names are forgotten owing to such a disturbance, an *Ersatz* name appears. 1919 *War Terms* in *Athenæum* 1 Aug. 695/1 Another word not seldom met with is 'ersatz'. It is the German 'substitute'. 1927 *Daily Express* 30 Sept. 1/1 It will merely be an imitation Parliament, an 'Ersatz' Parliament, designed to fulfil the immediate needs of the Dictatorship. 1928 T. S. ELIOT *For Lancelot Andrewes* 89 Of course Mr. Shaw and Mr. Wells are also much occupied with religion and *Ersatz-Religion*. 1930 *Observer* 9 Mar. 12 The coffee.. will be.. tempered with a judicious mixture of 'ersatz'. 1938 *Jrnl. R. Aeronaut. Soc.* XLII. 919 The problem of 'Ersatz' materials is well considered and modern aeronautical materials (like plastics, compressed wood, resin glues, etc.) are described. 1939 *Punch* 22 Nov. p. vii/2 (Advt.), A *real* tobacco. There is no Ersatz in Four Square. 1940 *Nature* 13 Jan. 60/1 Present-day brands of margarine cannot be considered in any way *Ersatz* butter. 1942 L. B. NAMIER *Conflicts* 58 This set a high premium on Hitler's jack-boots and *ersatz* uniforms. 1944 E. H. W. MEYERSTEIN *Let.* 24 Nov. (1959) 297 He [*sc.* Swinburne] went now and then to places where women beat him, which must have been a wretched ersatz for the sort of thing he wanted, e.g. to be flogged by the Duke of Wellington. 1949 F. MACLEAN *Eastern Approaches* III. v. 362 A breakfast of black bread and captured ersatz coffee made from roasted grain. 1950 *Mind* LIX. 20 Propositions regarded as *ersatz* facts or quasi-things. 1952 H. READ *Philos. Mod. Art* I. iii. 69 All we can create in that way is an *ersatz* culture, the synthetic product of those factories we call variously universities, colleges or museums. 1956 C. WILSON *Outsider* v. 133 Kant, with his *ersatz* morality, is a special target.

Erse (ɜːs), *a.* Forms: 4 **Erische, Erysche,** 4–7 **Ersch(e,** 7 **Erish,** 8 **Earse,** 8– **Erse.** [An early Sc. variant of IRISH; either repr. OE. *Īrisc*, or ON. *Írskr*, or possibly descending from a parallel form retaining the vowel of OIr. *Ériu* Ireland.]

†**1.** In early Sc. use: = IRISH.

c 1375 BARBOUR *Bruce* XIV. 123 The erische [*v.r.* ersch] kyngis. *Ibid.* XVI. 309, XVIII. 115.

2. Applied by Sc. Lowlanders to the Gaelic dialect of the Highlands (which is in fact of Irish origin), to the people speaking that dialect, to their customs, etc. Hence in 18th c. *Erse* was used in literary Eng. as the ordinary designation of the Gaelic of Scotland, and occasionally extended to the Irish Gaelic; at present some

writers apply it to the Irish alone. Now nearly *Obs.*

c **1375** [Implied in Barbour's use of ERSHRY: see below]. *c* **1470** HENRY *Wallace* I. 217 Thow Scot, abyde.. Ane Ersche mantill it war thi kynd to wer. [But perh. this belongs to I.] **1500–20** DUNBAR *Dance Sev. Deadly Sins* 116 Thae tarmegantis, with tag and tatter, Fful lowd in Ersche begowth to clatter. **1769** *De Foe's Tour Gt. Brit.* IV. 236 Though the Inhabitants of Inverness speak English, yet there are scarce any who do not understand the Erse or Irish. **1773** BOSWELL *Johnson* 15 Oct., Miss M'Lean produced some Erse poems by John M'Lean, who was a famous bard in Mull. **1777** JOHNSON in *Boswell* Apr., The Erse dialect of the Celtick language has, from the earliest times, been spoken in Britain. **1782** SHAW *Authentic. Ossian* 14 The Earse dialect of the Gaelic was never written nor printed until Mr. Macfarlane.. published, in 1754, a translation of Baxter's Call to the Unconverted. **1785** BURNS *Addr. to Deil* xix. **1796** MORSE *Amer. Geog.* II. 209 The language, which is called the Manks, is radically Erse, or Irish. **1823** BYRON *Juan* VIII. xxiii, He was what Erin calls, in her sublime Old Erse or Irish. **1838** *Penny Cycl.* XI. 32. s.v. *Gaelic.* The language spoken by the Scottish Highlanders is familiarly known among the Lowlanders by the name of the Erse, or according to the more usual pronunciation the Ersh, that is plainly the Eirish or Irish. **1864** I. TAYLOR *Words & Places* (1873) 129 The Erse of Ireland, the Gaelic of the Scotch Highlands, and the Manx of the Isle of Man.

Hence † **'Erseman,** *Obs.*, a man who is Erse by birth or descent. † **'Ershry,** the Gaelic-speaking inhabitants of Ireland and Scotland: see IRISHRY.

1500–20 DUNBAR *Dance Sev. Deadly Sins* 113 Ffar northwart in a nuke Be he the correnoch had done schout, Erschemen so gadderit him abowt, In Hell grit rowme thay tuke. **1375** BARBOUR *Bruce* XVIII. 443 All the erischry.. of Argyle and the Ilis alsua. **1425** *Sc. Acts Jas. I*, §61 (1814) II. 11 Ande for twa causis ande principaly sene þe kingis notourus rebellouris ar reset in Erschry [ed. **1597** Irishrie] of Yrelande.

ersh: see EARSH *dial.*, eddish.

erst (ɜːst), *a.* and *adv.* Forms: 1–3 **ǽrest, ǽrost, ǽrst,** 2–4 **erest,** 3–4 **arst,** (4 ? **eroust,** 5 **erast, eerst),** 3–7 **earst,** (3 **earest),** 4–6 **erste,** (6 **ierst,** 6, 7 **yerst),** 4– **erst.** [OE. *ǽrest*, superl. of *ǽr* (see ERE); repr. OTeut. **airisto-*, whence OHG. *êrist* (MHG. *êrist*, mod.G. *erst*), OS. *êrist* (Du. *eerst*).]

A. *adj.*

† **1.** First in time or serial order. *Obs.*

a **1000** *Guthlac* 408 (Gr.) Wæs seo æreste earmra gæsta costung ofercumen. *c* **1175** *Lamb. Hom.* 75 Ec of heom wrat þer his uers and sancte peter wrat þet ereste. *c* **1205** LAY. 2646 þes wes þe æreste [*c* **1275** ereste] king þe ferde vt to ræuing. *a* **1225** *Leg. Kath.* 885 þes alre schafte schuppent, Schawde ure eareste aldren.. þe wit & te wei of lif. *a* **1225** *Ancr. R.* 10 Powel þe erest ancre.

† **2.** *absol.* in advb. phrases. ***now*** (***then***) ***at erst***: now (then) and not sooner; cf. Ger. *erst dann.* (App. through misunderstanding of this, Spenser has *at erst* = 'as soon as possible, at once'.) ***on erst*** (only early ME.; also ***on alre erst***): in the first place, at first.

a **1225** *Ancr. R.* 264 þeonne on erest biginneð þe deoflen to weden. *a* **1225** *St. Marher.* 14 þenne þudde ich in ham lueliche þohtes, on earst hare unþonckes. *c* **1230** *Hali Meid.* 17 þat is on alre earst þe stude & te time. *c* **1300** *Havelok* 2688 Tho tarst [= at arst] bigan Godrich to go Vpon the Danshe. *c* **1374** CHAUCER *Boeth* III. xi. 95 But þan atte arst ben þei verray good. *c* **1386** —— *Sec. Nun's T.* 151 And thanne at erst thus to him sayde sche. **1430** LYDG. *Chron. Troy* I. vi, And than at erst fro hense will I wynde. **1475** *Bk. Noblesse* 6 Now at erst the irness be brennyng hote. **1579** SPENSER *Sheph. Cal.* Sept. 6 And now at earst the dirke night doth hast. **1596** —— *F.Q.* (J.), Abandon this forestalled place at erst.

B. *adv.*

† **1.** Earliest, soonest, first in order of time.

Beowulf 616 þa freolic wif ful ȝesealde ærest east dena eþelwearde. *c* **1000** ÆLFRIC *Gen.* xix. 53 And eode seo yldre swystor ærost to his bedde. *c* **1230** *Hali Meid.* 15 þ urh ure lafdi meidenhad þat hit bigon earst þe meiden Marie. **1362** LANGL. *P. Pl.* A IV. 29 Bote Concience com arst to Court bi A Myle. **1377** *Ibid.* B. XIV. 216 Arst in þe Maister þan in þe man. *c* **1400** *Destr. Troy* 7233 But Ector the honerable erst was on fote.

† **2.** In the first place, before something else is or was done; in preference to doing something else. (Sometimes pleonastically before *ere.*) *Obs.*

c **1260** *Ballad* in *Rel. Ant.* I. 101 Arst we sullen scinin him ay rowe. *c* **1300** *K. Alis.* 6480 Ac arst mony of his knyghtis gode Loren theo balles in heore hode. **1362** LANGL. *P. Pl.* A. IV. 5 Bote Reson Rede me þer-to Arst wol I dye! **1377** —— *P. Pl.* B. v. 468, I shal seke treuthe arst ar I se Rome. *c* **1380** *Sir Ferumb.* 1281 Ac arst þow schalt sykery me.. þat þou, etc. **1483** CAXTON *Gold. Leg.* 258/4 Why hast not thou erst taken awey the sowle fro my body. **1535** JOYE *Apol. Tindale* (Arb.) 30 He shuld haue erst proued his parte trw and myn false. **1578** *Chr. Prayers* in *Priv. Prayers* (1851) 511 Having erst uttered the bowels of thy mercy, thou gavest up the ghost. **1587** M. GROVE *Pelops & Hipp.* (1878) 13 Earst t'obtaine that still, Which they perceiue doth please the flesh. **1587** TURBERV. *Trag. T.* (1837) 276 And ierst with sodaine feare Lepte of the bed.

† **3.** At first, as opposed to *afterwards. Obs.*

a **1175** *Cott. Hom.* 229 Aceas he him leorninchnihtes erest twelf.. siððan twa and sefentiȝe. *c* **1205** LAY. 27456 Ærst [*c* **1275** earest] heo lette fleon to feondliche swiðe flan.. Seoð-ðen speren chrakeden. **1297** R. GLOUC. (1724) 389 Luþer he was arst ynou, & wel wors he was þo. *c* **1330** *Arth. & Merl.* 8497 Taurus hit [= hight] Wawain arst. *a* **1541** WYATT *Poet. Wks.* 4 Which comforts the mind, that erst for fear shook. **1605** ROWLANDS *Hell's Broke Loose* 34 Tamberlaine Was earst a Sheepheard ere he play'd the King.

† **4.** Sooner, earlier; before a specified time or event: *esp.* with negatives; ***not erst***: not before, not till then. *Obs.*

c **1330** *Florice & Bl.* 799 Arst ne schal hit neuer bi do. **1387** TREVISA *Higden* (Rolls) III. 337 þanne þe money schal be payde and nouȝt arst. *c* **1449** PECOCK *Repr.* 405 Bi sentence of the iuge.. and not erst, neither other wise. **1475** CAXTON *Jason* 26 b, The wedowes bewailled gretly because he was not erst comen. **1588** *Liturg. Serv. Q. Eliz.* (1847) Of thy most singular bounty, and never yerst seen care.

† **b.** conjunctional phrases, ***erst than, that*** = BEFORE C. *Obs.*

? *a* **1400** *Arthur* 291 Now, erst þan we goo ferþer Every man þat ys here Sey a Pater noster. **1523** SKELTON *Garl. Laurel* 1032 Far may be sought Erst that ye can finde, etc.

5. Before the present time:

a. Referring to a remoter past: 'Once upon a time', formerly, of old. *arch.* or *poet.*

14.. *Songs & Carols* (Warton Club) 22 That ilke blys That arte [? *read* arste] haȝt ben, and alwey is. **1663** BUTLER *Hud.* I. i. 917 As erst the Phrygian Knight, So ours.. did smite His Trojan Horse. **1729** T. COOKE *Tales, etc.* 185 To Strains which erst the brave Tyrtæus sung. **1789** COLERIDGE *Anthem Chr. Hosp.* Let full gratitude now prompt the tear Which erst did sorrow force to flow. **1808** WORDSW. *Inscript. Coleorton*, The ivied ruins of forlorn Grace Dieu; Erst a religious House. *a* **1839** PRAED *Poems* (1864) II. 48 Count o'er the friends whom erst you knew.

¶ Misused as *prep.* = BEFORE.

1839–48 BAILEY *Festus* x. 109 Erst all time And all incarnate emanations.

† **b.** Referring to a recent past: Not long ago, a little while since. Often in Spenser and Milton.

1480 CAXTON *Chron. Eng.* ccxxxii. 250 That ferefull company, that I spak of eerst. **1581** J. BELL *Haddon's Answ. Osor.* 153 But a litle earst ye confessed the thyng, which ye do now deny. **1590** SPENSER *F.Q.* I. v. 9 The armes that earst so bright did show. **1606** WARNER *Alb. Eng.* XV. xcv. 381 The vgliest was this Plot, Preuented earst miraculously. **1663** BUTLER *Hud.* I. iii. (1694) 179 Meanwhile the other Champions, yerst In hurry of the fight disperst, Arriv'd. **1671** MILTON *Samson* 1543 This.. horrid spectacle, Which erst my eyes beheld, and yet behold. **1791** COWPER *Retired Cat* 100 Forth skipped the cat, not now replete As erst with airy self-conceit.

6. In comb. with adjs. and ppl. adjs.

1594 J. DICKENSON *Arisbas* (1878) 33 Wherewith Flora had in plentie poudred the freshnesse of her earst-green hue. **1602** CAREW *Cornwall* 100 a, The earst remembered Sir Ric.. entertained at one time.. the admirals of the English, Spanish, and Netherland fleets. **1740** SOMERVILLE *Hobbinol* (1749) 135 All but the stout And erst unconquer'd Hildebrand.

Hence **'erstly** *adv.*, in the first place.

1600 *Chester Pl.* Proem (Shaks. Soc.) 3 Their fore be boulde Erstelye to playe the same.

erstwhile ('ɜːsthwaɪl), *adv.* and *a.* [f. ERST + WHILE *adv.* (The stress is variable.)]

A. *adv.* Some while ago, formerly. *arch.* Also † **'erstwhiles** [see WHILES], in same sense.

1569 SPENSER *Sonn.* ix. in *Van der Noodt's Theatre for Worldlings*, Which erstwhile [*later edd.* earst] so pleasaunt scent did yelde. **1584** R. SCOT *Discov. Witchcr.* III. xix. 56 They resist the truth erstwhile by them professed. **1599** SANDYS *Europæ Spec.* (1632) 184 Those very same minds, wherein they were erst-whiles enshrined with all devotion. **1624** GATAKER *Transubst.* 209 Which our adversarie also Earstwhiles confessed. **1662** GLANVILL *Lux Orient.* 180 Those thick and clammy vapours which erstwhile ascended in such vast measures.. must.. descend again. **1881** DUFFIELD *Don Quix.* II. 407 During that year the clouds erstwhile had withheld their dew from the earth.

B. *adj.* = former. (Cf. *whilom.*) *literary.*

1903 'A. MCNEILL' *Egregious English* iii. 31 The erstwhile portly mother of daughters. **1909** *Westm. Gaz.* 21 Aug. 13/1 A tottering pleasure-resort, whose erstwhile patrons look more longingly every year at the pretty and easily reached villages of Normandy and Brittany. **1925** L. HOUSMAN *Odd Pairs* i. 24 Her erstwhile rival.

ert, obs. form of *art*: see BE *v.*

† **ert,** *v. Obs.* [prob. a. ON. *erta* to taunt, tease; but cf. ART *v.*[1]]

1. *trans.* **a.** To incite, urge on, encourage. Const. *on, to, till,* and *to* with *inf.* Also with *on.* **b.** To irritate, provoke.

c **1325** *Metr. Hom.* Prol. 5 That thai mai her and hald in hert, Thinge that thaim til God mai ert. *Ibid* 19 Quen Crist cumes intil our hertes, To lef sin he us ertes. *c* **1400** *Destr. Troy* 4857 We haue ournyt hym with angur, ertid hym mykill. *Ibid.* 12326 To ert hym on exile euer of the londe. *c* **1440** *Promp. Parv.* 142 Ertyn, *irrito.* **1789** D. DAVIDSON *Seasons* 24 (Jam.) The herd.. now and then Erts on the tir'd tike with 'Sheep awa, a, a!'

absol. c **1400** *Destr. Troy* 2725 Envy, þat Euermore ertis to skathe.

2. *intr.* To be eager, prone; to hurry.

c **1400** *Destr. Troy* 264 He ertide to an ende egerly fast.

Hence † **'ertand** *ppl. a.*, pressing on, ambitious. † **'erter,** one who provokes. † **'erting** *vbl. sb.*, the action of the vb. ERT.

c **1440** *Gaw. & Gol.* xxxi. Schir Gawyne.. Egir, and ertand, and ryght anterus. *c* **1440** *Promp. Parv.* 142 Ertare, *irritator, irritatrix. Ibid.* 142 Ertynge, *irritacio.*

Ertebølle (ɜːtə'bœlə). Also Ertebölle, Ertebolle. [Place-name in Jutland, Denmark.] An early Danish culture illustrated by remains found at Ertebølle. Also *attrib.*

1927 PEAKE & FLEURE *Hunter & Artists* vii. 109 This period, known as the Littorina period, is the time of the 'kitchen-middens' or shell-mounds... Two phases of this culture are usually recognised... The second or chief phase .. is called the Ertebölle phase. **1933** *Antiquity* VII. 47 Sites of the Ertobolle cultures which are in the Atlantic period and correspond roughly to the Litorina maximum. **1948** A. L. KROEBER *Anthropol.* (ed. 2) xvi. 670 *Ertebølle*, first called Kjøkkenmødding, then kitchen-midden culture. Type site in Denmark, distribution northern. Time, late Mesolithic.. 5000–3000 B.C. **1954** S. PIGGOTT *Neolithic Cultures* iii. 84 Bone combs.. occur in the Ertebølle culture. **1959** *Chambers's Encycl.* V. 453/2 The Ertebölle culture is well known from the extensive middens formed of the shells of the molluscs on which the people largely lived.

erth, -en, obs. forms of EARTH, EARTHEN.

erthe, ? var. of ERD *v. Obs.* to dwell.

c **1300** *Havelok* 739 Bigan he there for to erthe.

ertu, obs. f. *art thou*: see BE *v.* and THOU.

erubescence (ɛruː'bɛsəns). *rare.* [a. F. *érubescence*, ad. late L. *ērūbēscentia*, f. *ērūbēscent-em*: see next and -ENCE.] Erubescent quality or state.

1736 in BAILEY. **1775** in ASH. **1823** *New Monthly Mag.* VII. 143 He.. sent forth blood of a brilliant erubescence. **1886** *Academy* 31 July 66/3 To describe as the 'law of erubescence' the fact, etc.

So **eru'bescency.**

1656 in BLOUNT *Glossogr.* **1736** in BAILEY. In mod. Dicts.

erubescent (ɛruː'bɛsənt), *a.* [ad. L. *ērūbēscent-em*, pr. pple. of *ērūbēscĕre* to blush, f. *ē* out + *rūbēscĕre* to redden. Cf. F. *érubescent.*] Reddening, blushing.

1736 in BAILEY. **1775** in ASH. **1849** THACKERAY *Pendennis* liii, The Major erubescent confounded the impudence of the young folks.

¶ quasi-*sb.* = RUBEFACIENT.

1823 H. H. WILSON *Ess. on Sansk. Lit.* (1864) I. 383 Besides these we have thread, leaves, bandages, pledgets, heated metallic plates for erubescents, etc.

erubescite (ɛruː'bɛsaɪt). *Min.* [f. L. *ērūbēscĕre* (see prec.) + -ITE.] A copper sulphide, purple copper.

1850 DANA *Min.* 511 Massive varieties of erubescite are found in the U.S. **1882** WATTS *Dict. Chem.* II. 501 *Erubescite*, Purple copper.

‖**eruca** (ɪ'ruːkə). *rare.* See ERUKE. [L. *ērūca* caterpillar.] The larva of a butterfly or such like insect; a caterpillar. Hence **eruca-like** *a.*

[**1609** BIBLE (Douay) *Joel* i. 4 *Comm.*, Eruca, a worme that destroyeth herbes and fruictes.] **1691** RAY *Creation* (1701) 136 May be observed in the production of silk worms, yea all other eruca's, and many insects more! *a* **1839** GALT *Demon Dest.* III. (1840) 22 Eruca-like they rise, As bright aurelias in the summer's shine.

erucic (ɪ'ruːsɪk), *a. Chem.* [f. L. *erūca* a kind of cabbage + -IC.] Of or pertaining to *eruca.* **erucic acid,** 'an acid ($C_{22}H_{42}O_2$) obtained by the saponification of the fixed oil of white mustard (Sinapis alba)' (Watts *Dict. Chem.*).

1869 ROSCOE *Elem. Chem.* 390 Erucic acid is contained in rapeseed oil.

eruciform (ɪ'ruːsɪfɔːm), *a. Ent.* [f. L. *ērūca* caterpillar: see -FORM.] Resembling a caterpillar.

1874 LUBBOCK *Orig. & Met. Ins.* v. 88 [Two types of Larvæ] Packard has named Leptiform and Eruciform.

eruct (ɪ'rʌkt). [ad. L. *ēruct-āre*, f. *ē* out + *ructāre* to belch, emit. Cf. It. *eruttare*, Sp. *erutar.*]

1. *intr.* **a.** To void wind noisily from the stomach through the mouth. † **b.** To rise in eructation.

1666 G. HARVEY *Morb. Angl.* iv. 46 By force of these torrid streams eructing into several parts.. those flushings.. are produced. **1755** SMOLLET *Quix.* (1803) IV. 40 Beware.. of chewing on both sides of your mouth, as well as eructing before company.

2. *trans.* **a.** To emit (fumes) by eructation; = BELCH 3. **b.** Of a volcano; = BELCH 5.

1774, 1869 [see ERUCTED *ppl. a.*].

eructate (ɪ'rʌkteɪt), *v.* Now *rare.* [f. L. *ēructāt-* ppl. stem of *ēructāre* (see prec.).] **1.** *trans.* To belch, vomit forth. Chiefly *transf.* and *fig.*

1638 ROUSE *Heav. Univ.* iv. (1702) 34 This affection doth eructate.. hidden truths. *c* **1645** HOWELL *Lett.* (1650) I. 44 That Ætna in times past hath eructated such huge gobbets of fire. **1655** MILTON *2nd Defence* 264 You have begun to eructate the rage of your apostacy. **1782** V. KNOX *Ess.* I. 42 Though he should.. daily eructate his invectives against the most respectable men. **1828** in WEBSTER; and in mod. Dicts.

2. *intr.* = ERUCT I.

1774 JOEL COLLIER [J. L. Bicknell] *Mus. Trav.* (1775) 93 After this, he successively coughed, sneezed, hiccupped, eructated, squeaked, etc.

'eructated, *ppl. a.* [f. ERUCTATE *v.* + -ED[1].] Vomited.

1869 C. L. BRACE *New West* i. 13 The reeling staterooms, smelling of oil, bilgewater and eructated dinner.

eructation (ˌiːrʌkˈteɪʃən). Also 6 **eructuacyon**. [ad. L. *ēructātiōn-em*, n. of action f. *ēructāre*: see ERUCT.]

1. The action of voiding wind from the stomach through the mouth; belching.

1533 ELYOT *Cast. Helthe* (1541) 41 b, The savour of his meate by eructation ascendeth. **1542** BOORDE *Dyetary* viii. (1870) 247 Lest that the meate which is in your stomacke, thorow eructuacyons..ascend. **1612** WOODALL *Surg. Mate* Wks. (1653) 71 Ginger..preventeth sowre eructation. **1699** EVELYN *Acetaria* 17 Cabbage..is greatly accus'd for lying undigested in the Stomack and provoking Eructations. **1847** YOUATT *Horse* xiv. 300 The animal has no power to expel this dangerous flatus by eructation. **1869** E. A. PARKES *Pract. Hygiene* (ed. 3) 67 Dyspepsia..attended with..enormous eructations after meals.

†**b.** *fig. Obs.*

1647 H. MORE *Poems* 235 Oft the soul lets flie Such unexpected eructations. **1683** *Argt. for Union* 22 They have Mental Prayer, and..Spiritual Eructations.

2. The eruptive action of a volcano; violent emission (of flames, etc.). Also *fig.*

1652 J. HALL *Height Eloq.* 65 The Ætna, whose eructations throw whole stones from its depths. **1678** MARVELL *Def. John Howe* Wks. (1875) IV. 234 But a perpetual eructation there is of humane passions. **1692** RAY *Phys. Theol. Disc.* (1713) 19 The mountain Ætna, at the last Eructation..disgorged..a Flood of melted Materials. **1783** *Phil. Trans.* LXXIII. 161 The eructation of elastic vapour from below. **1862** G. P. SCROPE *Volcanoes* 24 The column of ashes projected becomes gradually shorter, the eructations less frequent.

3. *concr.* That which is belched forth. Also *fig.*

1607 *Schol. Disc. agst. Antichr.* I. iii. 161 What is it else, but an eructation of the minde? **1664** POWER *Exp. Philos.* III. 155 The grosser Steams..are the fuliginous Eructations of that internal Fire which constantly burns within us. **1701** tr. *Le Clerc's Prim. Fathers* 104 One (Philogonius Bishop of Antioch) said, 'That the Son was an Eructation'.

†**eructator.** *Obs. rare*$^{-1}$. [f. ERUCTATE + -OR.] One who 'eructates'.

1767 A. CAMPBELL *Lexiph.* (1774) 34 The former was assisted by the auxiliar virtues and subsidiary aids of patriots, anterior eructators.

eructed (ɪˈrʌktɪd), *ppl. a.* [f. ERUCT *v.* + -ED^{1}.] Thrown up by eructation.

1774 STRANGE *Basaltine Columns* in *Phil. Trans.* LXV. 20 Vesuvius, Ætna..and such like eructed piles. **1869** E. A. PARKES *Pract. Hygiene* (ed. 3) 67 The eructed gas had a strong smell of sulphuretted hydrogen.

eruction (ɪˈrʌkʃən). *rare.* [n. of action f. ERUCT: see -TION.] The action of eructing. *lit.* and *fig.*

1623 COCKERAM, *Eruction*, Belking. **1837** *Fraser's Mag.* XV. 586 They are utterly insensible to any eruction of generosity. **1842** *Tait's Mag.* IX. 723 Bonfires of immense eruction Fling abroad their gorgeous rays.

erudit (ˈɛruːdɪt). *rare.* [a. Fr. *érudit*, = next.] = ERUDITE *sb.*

1800 *Monthly Mag.* VIII. 600 The Jesuits certainly have deserved..much admiration for the classical learning which their erudits displayed. **1872** *Daily News* 2 May 2/7 [Lord Alwyne Compton denied] that the intelligence of the country was against the creed, and its supporters only Oxford and Cambridge erudits.

erudite (ˈɛrədaɪt), *a.* and *sb.* [ad. L. *ērudīt-us*, f. *ērudīre* to instruct, train, f. *ē* out + *rudis* rude, untrained.]

A. *adj.*

1. Of persons and their faculties: †**a.** Trained, well-instructed (*obs.* or *arch.*); **b.** Learned, scholarly. (Now somewhat rare exc. in sarcastic use.)

1432–50 tr. *Higden* (Rolls) I. 231 A man callede Nanus, erudite in the arte of nigromancy. **1539** J. FOSTER in Ellis *Orig. Lett.* I. 141 II. 112 The Kyngys erudyte jugementt, with all hys cowncell temperall and spyrytuall hathe stableschyd a contrary order. **1598** MARSTON *Pygmal.* Sat. IV. 153 Would ever any erudite Pedant Seeme in his artles lines so insolent? *a* **1773** LD. CHESTERFIELD (T.), Your Latin lecture is as good Latin as the erudite Germans speak or write. **1791** D'ISRAELI *Cur. Lit.* (1858) I. 3 Having chosen the erudite Varro for its librarian. **1823** LAMB *Elia* Ser. I. ii. (1865) 15 Those variæ lectiones, so tempting to the more erudite palates. **1849** LYTTON *Caxtons* I. 24 Before I was six years old, I was erudite in that primitive literature. **1875** HAMERTON *Intell. Life* XI. ii. 408 The remarkably skilful man is not likely to be the erudite man.

2. Of literary productions, etc.: Characterized by erudition.

1533 MORE *Apol.* v. Wks. 854/1 Shewed in his most erudite famous booke agaynst Luther. *a* **1667** JER. TAYLOR (W.), Erudite and metaphysical theology. **1715** M. DAVIES *Athen. Brit.* I. 6 The fore-mentioned Treasuries of Erudite Pamphlet-tracts. **1820** W. IRVING *Sketch Bk.* II. 95 A most erudite sermon on the rites and ceremonies of Christmas. **1861** GEO. ELIOT *Silas M.* 16 Some erudite research, some ingenious project.

B. *sb.* [So Fr. *érudit.*] An erudite person, a scholar. *rare.*

1865 GROTE *Plato* I. iv. 141 These laborious and useful erudites. **1888** *Pall Mall G.* 6 Sept. 3/1 There are to be found, in and out of America, women citizens of that great country..female would-be erudites.

Hence **ˈeruditely** *adv.*, in an erudite manner, learnedly, skilfully. **ˈeruditeness**, the quality or condition of being erudite. **eruˈditical** *a. rare*, characterized by, or laying claim to, erudition.

1529 MORE *Supplic. Soulys* Wks. 331/1 Theyr holy workes eruditely written. **1736** in BAILEY. **1811** BYRON *Hints fr. Horace* 433 Who eruditely know To separate the elegant and low. **1862** LYTTON *Str. Story* II. 68 The truth which you so eruditely insinuate to be a fable. **1818** COLERIDGE *Lit. Rem.* (1836) I. 160 Some meritorious modern poets..attempt an eruditeness. **1832** *Fraser's Mag.* VI. 107 Edinburgh, the most eruditical city in Christendom. **1838** GALT in *Tait's Mag.* V. 43 There is no saying how eruditical I became.

erudition (ɛruːˈdɪʃən). Forms: 5–6 **erudicioun(e**, 6 **erudician, -ion, -yon, erudycyon, -ditioun, -dytion**, 5– **erudition**. [ad. L. *ērudītiōnem*, n. of action f. *ērudīre*: see prec. Cf. F. *érudition.*]

†**1.** The action or process of training or instructing; instruction, education. *Obs.*

c **1400** *Beryn* 1428, I seyd a word or to..Ffor thyne erudicioune. **1483** CAXTON *Cato* 2 For the erudition of my lord Bousher. **1533** BELLENDEN *Livy* III. (1822) 268 Commoun skulis war devisit for erudicioun of young persouns. *a* **1626** BACON *Max. & Uses Com. Law* xviii. 67 Hee had contracted for his owne aliments and erudition. **1749** FIELDING *Tom Jones* I. vi, This gift Jenny had..improved by erudition.

†**2.** *concr.* Imparted instruction, teaching; also a doctrine, maxim. *Obs.*

1528 ROY *Sat.*, Doinge after the apostles erudicion..I..will not be negligent to put my brethren in remembraunce. **1567** *Trial Treas.* in Hazl. *Dodsley* III. 300 Let all men consider this good erudition. **1574** tr. *Littleton's Tenures* 77 b, It is a common erudicion and learning that a man, etc.

3. †**a.** The state or condition of being trained or instructed; const. *in*, *of* (*obs.*). **b.** In later use: Acquired knowledge, *esp.* in languages, literature, antiquities, etc.; learning, scholarship.

1530 PALSGR. *Introd.* 6 Your noble graces other manyfolde sortes of excellent erudytion and lytterature. *a* **1533** FRITH *Another Bk. agst. Rastell* (1829) 210 More and Rochester were men of..singular erudition in all kind of learning. **1536** BELLENDEN *Cron. Scot.* (1821) I. p. xviii, Howbeit they had na sicker cognosance and ful erudition of al thingis. *a* **1639** WOTTON (J.), The Earl was of good erudition, having been placed at study in Cambridge very young. **1718** *Freethinker* No. 18. 110 Madam Dacier has the Advantage in Point of Erudition. **1796** MORSE *Amer. Geog.* II. 65 She had a romantic taste for classical erudition. **1860** MACAULAY *Biog.* (1867) 13 Exhibiting a little erudition in such a manner as to make it look like a great deal. **1862** GOULBURN *Pers. Relig.* I. (1873) 3 Some Monks and Priests..represented all the erudition of their times.

†**4.** Of a coin: Perfect workmanship, finish. *Obs. rare.*

1702 ADDISON *Dial. Medals* Wks. 1721 I. 437 The intrinsic value of an old coin does not consist in its metal but its erudition. It is the Device that has raised the species. **1747** DINGLEY *Gems* in *Phil. Trans.* XLIV. 506 The Merit both of Intaglio's and Cameo's depends on their Erudition, on the Goodness of the Workmanship, and on the Beauty of their Polish.

Hence **eruˈditional** *a.*, of or pertaining to erudition, †educational, disciplinary. **eruˈditionist**, one who devotes himself to erudition or training.

1657 M. LAWRENCE *Use & Pract. Faith* 245 A conditional speech is but an eruditional speech, to warn us of our weakness. **1805** W. TAYLOR in Robberds *Mem.* II. 107 The poem struck me as..having lyrical and eruditional merit. **1836** CHALMERS *Mor. & Mental Philos.* Wks. V. 57 They never fully grappled with the question as eruditionists.

†**ˈerugate**, *ppl. a. Obs.*$^{-0}$ [ad. L. *ērūgāt-us*, pa. pple. of *ērūgā-re* to remove wrinkles, f. *ē* out + *rūga* wrinkle.] Having the wrinkles rubbed out, smooth.

1840 in SMART. **1859** in WORCESTER; and in mod. Dicts.

†**ˈerugate**, *v. Obs. rare.* [f. L. *ērūgāt-* ppl. stem of *ērūgāre* (see prec.).] *trans.* To remove wrinkles from; to smooth.

1656 in BLOUNT *Glossogr.* **1657** TOMLINSON *Renou's Disp.* 397* Chian Earth..erugates the face, makes it splendid and deleates scars.

†**eruˈgation.** *Obs.*$^{-0}$ [f. as prec.: see -ATION.] A taking away of wrinkles.

1736 in BAILEY.

†**eˈruginary**, *a. Obs.* [f. L. *ærūgin-em* rust of copper, verdigris + -ARY.] = next.

1681 *Phil. Trans.* XII. 77 Another kind of Eruginary Stone, which yields a vitriolate and stiptick efflorescence.

†**eˈruginous**, *a. Obs.* [ad. L. *ærūginōsus*, f. *ærūgin-em*: see prec.] Partaking of the nature or substance of verdigris, or of copper itself; resembling verdigris.

1646 SIR T. BROWNE *Pseud. Ep.* VI. xii. 336 Artificiall copperose..is a rough and acrimonious kinde of salt drawn out of ferreous and eruginous earths. **1666** G. HARVEY *Morb. Angl.* (J.), Agues depend..upon an adust stibial or eruginous sulphur.

erugo: see ÆRUGO.

eruh, var. of ARGH *a. Obs.*

a **1225** *Ancr. R.* 296 Ne ȝif him neuer inȝong: auh tep him oðe schulle, uor he is eruh ase beore þeron.

†**eˈruke.** *Obs.* [Anglicized form of ERUCA.] A caterpillar.

1382 WYCLIF *Joel* i. 4 A locust ete the residue of eruke, that is, a worme of bowis. **1609** BIBLE (Douay) *ibid.*, The residue of the eruke hath the locust eaten. [**1711** J. GREENWOOD *Eng. Gram.* 190 Eruke from Eruca, this some turn to Ear-Wig, as if it took its Name from the Ear.]

†**eˈrumnate**, *v. Obs.*$^{-0}$ [f. L. *ærumn-a* + -ATE^{4}.] *trans.* To impoverish, make miserable.

1692–1732 in COLES. **1775** in ASH.

†**eˈrumny.** *Obs.* [ad. L. *ærumna* of same meaning; after the supposed analogy of *calumny*, etc.] Calamity, hardship.

1657 TOMLINSON *Renou's Disp.* 148 That God might free man from those erumnies and egritudes wherewith he is..pestered. **1657** *Phys. Dict.*, *Erumnies*, griefs, miseries.

†**eˈrump**, *v.* [ad. L. *ērump-ĕre*: see next.] *intr.* To break out as an eruption.

1657 TOMLINSON *Renou's Disp.* 658 Oyl of Myrtles..emends biles, or lumps erumping.

erumpent (ɪˈrʌmpənt), *a.* [ad. L. *ērumpentem*, pr. pple. of *ērumpĕre*, f. *ē* out + *rumpĕre* to burst forth.] That bursts forth.

1650 BULWER *Anthropomet.* 131 The Masculine..faculty..either erumpent, and progredient, or consumed. **1857** BERKELEY *Cryptog. Bot.* 313 This genus..seems to me essentially innato-erumpent. **1871** COOKE *Fungi* (1875) 197 The erumpent ostiola of the perithecia of Melanconis stilbostoma.

†**eˈruncate**, *v. Obs. rare*$^{-1}$. [f. L. *ēruncāt-* ppl. stem of *ēruncāre*, f. *ē* out + *runcāre* to weed.] *trans.* To weed out, extirpate.

1651 BIGGS *New Disp.* 197 Those tares, enormities..are with ease eruncated.

Hence **erunˈcation**, a taking away of weeds.

1678–1706 in PHILLIPS.

erupt (ɪˈrʌpt), *v.* [f. L. *ērupt-* ppl. stem of *ērumpĕre* to break out, burst forth: see ERUMPENT. The transitive senses have been developed under the influence of the sb. ERUPTION.]

1. *intr.* To burst forth in the process of growth. Now only of the teeth: To break through the skin of the gums.

1657 TOMLINSON *Renou's Disp.* 223 Its roots..from which some sprigs erupt. **1878** L. P. MEREDITH *Teeth* 44 Sometimes the process of absorption in the roots of the temporary teeth fails to be brought about, and the permanent teeth erupt in front of or behind them.

b. *trans.* To force (teeth) through the gums.

1859 J. TOMES *Dental Surg.* 53 The incisors and first temporary molars have been erupted. **1883** W. WHITEHOUSE in *Standard* 25 Jan. 6/3 The four teeth stated to have been extracted never were erupted.

2. *intr.* Of a volcano, geyser, etc.: To break out in eruption, be in a state of eruption. (Perhaps often felt as an absol. use of 2 b.). Also of volcanic masses or showers: To burst forth.

1770 HAMILTON *Soil Naples* in *Phil. Trans.* LXI. 12 Strabo, Dio, Vitruvius, all agree, that Vesuvius, in their time, shewed signs of having formerly erupted. **1786** *Ibid.* LXXVI. 379 Suppose Mount Etna to have ceased erupting for many ages. **1861** E. T. HOLLAND in *Peaks, Passes & Glac.* Ser. II. I 10 A treatment under which this fountain can generally be made to erupt. **1866** ANSTED in *Intell. Observ.* No, 52. 270 The showers continued to erupt. **1879** LE CONTE *Elem. Geol.* 81 Volcanoes which have not been known to erupt during historic times are said to be extinct. *fig.* **1881** W. SIMPSON in *Academy* 8 Jan. 22/5 Our modern Proteus..'erupts' in an entirely new direction.

b. *trans.* Of a volcano, geyser, or any subterranean force: To throw out in an eruption.

1769 HAMILTON *Etna* in *Phil. Trans.* LX. 17 I found, with respect to the matter erupted, nothing on Mount Etna that Vesuvius does not produce. **1833** LYELL *Princ. Geol.* III. 183 The volcanic rocks of Tuscany..have been chiefly erupted beneath the sea.

3. *intr.* Of a river: To burst forth.

1864 S. F. SURTEES *Waifs & Strays N. Humber Hist.* 86 The Don..erupts into what has evidently been a large inland lake.

Hence **eˈrupted**, **eˈrupting** *ppl. a.*

1769 HAMILTON *Etna* in *Phil. Trans.* LX. 17 A much greater variety in the erupted matter and lavas. **1797** HOLCROFT *Stolberg's Trav.* (ed. 2) IV. xciv. 293 The erupting floods of fire. **1824** *Blackw. Mag.* XVI. 704 Visions of erupted embers. **1870** PROCTOR *Other Worlds* i. 17 *note*, Vomited forth by the erupting mountain.

eruption (ɪˈrʌpʃən). [ad. L. *ēruptiōn-em*, n. of action f. *ērumpĕre*: see ERUMPENT. Cf. Fr. *éruption.*]

1. The bursting forth (of water, fire, air, etc.) from natural or artificial limits.

1555 EDEN *Decades W. Ind.* III. VIII. (Arb.) 173 Eruptions of the springes owte of the montaines. **1605** VERSTEGAN *Dec. Intell.* iv. (1628) 100 The great harmes that these parts haue heretofore by eruption of the sea sustained. **1669** BOYLE *Contn. New Exp.* II. (1682) 128 The compressed air suddenly finding out a way of eruption. **1725** DE FOE *Voy. round World* (1840) 243, I sat up..staring out from the window at the eruption of fire upon the hills. **1774** PENNANT *Tour Scotl. in 1772*, 19 Pelling Moss, which made an eruption similar to Solway. **1819** G. S. FABER *Dispensations* (1823) I. 106 During the whole sixteen centuries which intervened between the sentence of Cain and the eruption of the deluge. **1830** LYELL *Princ. Geol.* I. 287 One of the most memorable eruptions occurred in 1421, where the tide..burst through a dam..and overflowed twenty-two villages.

¶ Used for: The bursting (of a gun). *rare*$^{-1}$.

1660 T. WILLSFORD *Scales Commerce* 192 All guns..perpetrated with cold and frosty weather are most subject to an eruption at the first shot.

b. *concr.* That which bursts forth; a sudden rush of flame, smoke, water, etc.

1699 GARTH *Dispens.* 6 From the Vulcano's gross eruptions rise. **1717** BERKELEY in Fraser *Life* 581 The streets of Naples..paved with the matter of eruptions. **1728** MALLET *Excursion* 42 With black Eruption in foul Storm A Night of Smoke..Rolls forth. **1774** PENNANT *Tour Scotl. in 1772*, 67 The eruption burst from the place of its discharge, like a cataract.

2. An outbreak of volcanic activity; the ejection of solid or liquid matter by a volcano, of hot water from a geyser, etc.

[**1603** HOLLAND *Plutarch's Mor.* 1190 The breakings forth and eruptions of fire out of a mountaine.] **1740** GRAY *Let.* in *Poems* (1775) 94 A Roman town that..was overwhelmed by a furious eruption of Mount Vesuvius. **1794** SULLIVAN *View Nat.* II. 133 Iceland chronicles give a list of 63 eruptions at Heckla. **1857** DUFFERIN *Lett. High Lat.* (1867) 87 Our principal object in coming..was to see an eruption of the Great Geysir. **1876** PAGE *Advd. Text-bk. Geol.* iii. 50 Consolidated products of volcanic eruption.

3. Of persons: The action of breaking forth, of issuing suddenly and violently from within boundaries; *e.g.* the sallying forth of armed men from a stronghold, or of a horde of barbarians from their own country, the forcible escape of a prisoner, etc. *rare* in recent use.

1615 G. SANDYS *Trav.* 43 Two hundred and fourteene years after their eruption out of Scythia. **1623** TH. AILESBURY *Sermon* (1624) 17 In that eruption of the Prodigall sonne from his Father. **1638** HEYWOOD *Rape Lucr.* Wks. 1874 V. 205 The enemie is pounded fast In their owne folds..There's no eruption to be feared. **1652** NEEDHAM tr. *Selden's Mare Cl.* 262 Danegeld for the pay of those that should be imploied to hinder the eruption of Pirates. *a* **1677** BARROW *Pope's Suprem.* (1687) 181 The eruptions of Barbarians, the straits of Emperours..&c. did all turn to account for him. **1775** JOHNSON *Tax no Tyr.* 18 Of this kind were the eruptions of those nations. **1822** *Q. Rev.* XXVII. 377 Securing to them the benefits of prison-discipline, by providing against furtive or forcible eruptions.

4. *fig.* In many obvious applications of the sense 'outbreak': An outbreak of disease, war, calamity, or evil of any kind; an outburst of passion, eloquence, or merriment; a 'sally' of wit. Now *rare*, except with distinct allusion to sense 2.

1588 SHAKS. *L.L.L.* v. i. 121 The Curate and your sweet self are good at such eruptions, and sodaine breaking out of myrth. **1602** —— *Ham.* I. i. 69 This boades some strange erruption to our State. **1656** OWEN *Mortific. Sin* (1668) 47 A man may be sensible of a lust, set himself against the eruptions of it. **1680** *Life Edw. II.* in *Select. Harl. Misc.* (1793) 33 The archbishop of York..resolves to oppose this over-daring and insolent eruption. **1762–71** H. WALPOLE *Vertue's Anecd. Paint.* (1786) V. 107 Before the eruption of the civil war. *a* **1847** MRS. SHERWOOD *Lady of Manor* III. xviii. 32 There is nothing which retards the progress of the Gospel so much as the remaining eruptions of sin among the rulers of the Church. **1883** G. A. MACDONNELL *Chess Life-Pictures* 8 The twirling of that ornament in his hand..portended an anecdotal or jocose eruption.

5. †**a.** In plants: The bursting forth from the bark of buds, leaves, offshoots, roots, etc.; also *concr.* an excrescence. *Obs.* **b.** Of the teeth: The action of breaking out from the gums, in the process of 'cutting the teeth'.

a. 1626 BACON *Sylva* (1631) §588 When they [the branches] make an Eruption, they breake forth casually, where they finde best way in the Barke or Rinde. **1660** SHARROCK *Vegetables* 142 Both buds and leaves, and all eruptions..on every vegetable. **1671** GREW *Anat. Plants* I. 27 The place of their [Trunk-roots'] Eruption is sometimes all along the Trunk; as in Mint. **1713** DERHAM *Phys.-Theol.* x. i. 447 The Art in Folding up the leaves before their eruption out of their Gems, etc. is incomparable.

b. 1859 J. TOMES *Dental Surg.* 104 The relations of the eruption of the permanent teeth to the age of the individual. **1863** HUXLEY *Man's Place Nat.* ii. 83 The order of eruption of the permanent teeth is different.

6. *Path.* **a.** A breaking out of a rash, or of pimples on the skin. (In early use with notion of a 'breaking out' of latent disease or of 'peccant humours'.)

1596 SHAKS. *1 Hen. IV*, III. i. 27 Diseased Nature oftentimes breakes forth In strange eruptions. **1674** *Gov. Tongue* vi. (ed. 2) 102 When there is an eruption of Humor in any part, tis not cured meerly by outward applications. **1731** ARBUTHNOT *Aliments* 172 Some Sorts of cutaneous Eruptions are occasion'd by feeding much on acid unripe Fruits. **1799** *Med. Jrnl.* I. 322 An eruption of pimples on that day, which disappeared on the next.

b. The skin affection itself; an efflorescence, rash.

1770 *Junius Lett.* xxxix. 203 No man regards an eruption upon the surface, when he feels a mortification approaching to his heart. **1802** *Med. Jrnl.* VIII. 147 The matter..scarcely ever afforded any eruptions like the small-pox. **1846** J. BAXTER *Libr. Pract. Agric.* (ed. 4) II. 156 A scaly eruption appears, attended by extreme itching. **1882** SQUIRE in Quain *Med. Dict.* 927 The declining rash of measles leaves a mottling of the skin, not unlike the mulberry eruption of typhus.

Hence **e'ruptional** [+ -AL], *a.*, of or pertaining to volcanic eruption.

1858 G. P. SCROPE *Geol. & Volcanoes Centr. Fr.* (ed. 2) 212 It may have sustained considerable absolute elevation..during its eruptional era. **1883** PROCTOR in *Knowledge* 30 June 384/2 When there are few spots or none on the sun's surface, the eruptional or jet prominences are not seen.

eruptive (ɪˈrʌptɪv), *a.* [a. Fr. *éruptif, -ive*, f. *ērupt-* ppl. stem of *ērumpĕre*: see ERUPT and -IVE.]

1. Bursting forth; inclined or accustomed to break out from restraint, or to burst into violent action.

1646 SIR T. BROWNE *Pseud. Ep.* 143 All which is perverted in this eruptive generation. **1744** THOMSON *Summer* 1132 The sudden glance [lightning] Appears far south eruptive through the cloud. **1865** M. ARNOLD *Ess. Crit.* 65 The eruptive and the aggressive manner in literature. **1873** BROWNING *Red Cott. Night-c.* 117 Hell, eruptive and fuliginous, Sickens to very pallor.

2. Of or pertaining to volcanic eruption; tending to or engaged in eruption; of the nature of or characterized by eruption. Of rocks: Formed or forced up by eruption, showing traces of eruption.

1799 KIRWAN *Geol. Ess.* 288 Into these errors Mr. Whitehurst was betrayed by his fondness for the eruptive or plutonic theory. **1819** BYRON *Proph. Dante* III. 187 The volcano's fierce eruptive crest. **1849** MURCHISON *Siluria* v. 92 Crystalline rock, both eruptive and metamorphic. **1869** PHILLIPS *Vesuv.* iii. 79 Within the crater was found a round and small actively eruptive cone. **1878** NEWCOMB *Pop. Astron.* III. ii. 262 The eruptive protuberances.

quasi-*sb.* **1884** IRVING in *Amer. Jrnl. Sc.* Ser. III. (1885) XXIX. 241 The gneisses..forming our supposed eruptives, are if eruptive, manifestly not to be compared with the lavas of modern times.

3. *Path.* Attended with or producing eruption or efflorescence.

1790 SIR W. FORDYCE *Virtues Mur. Acid.* 1 The striking effects produced by the spirit of sea-salt in all our putrid diseases..I mean the Eruptive fevers. **1796** BURKE *Regic. Peace* Wks. (1842) II. 279 It is in the nature of these eruptive diseases in the state to sink in by fits, and re-appear. **1834** *Penny Cycl.* II. 207/2 Antimony is also used in some eruptive or exanthematous fevers. **1852** MISS YONGE *Cameos* (1877) III. v. 41 A serious attack of illness of an eruptive kind.

b. *transf.* (*humorous.*)

1848 THACKERAY *Bk. Snobs* xxxiii, Thomas wears a page's costume of eruptive buttons.

Hence **e'ruptively** *a.*, in an eruptive manner. **e'ruptiveness**, the quality of being eruptive. **erup'tivity** = ERUPTIVENESS.

1869 *Daily News* 1 July, The candlesticks all over knobs and excrescences as if eruptively affected. **1885** G. MEREDITH *Diana Crossw.* I. i. 19 They create by stoppage a volcano, and are amazed at its eruptiveness. **1882** GEIKIE *Text-bk. Geol.* IV. VII. 537 They possess likewise various values as marks of eruptivity.

†**erup'turient,** *a. Obs.* [f. L. *ērupt-* ppl. stem of *ērumpĕre*, after the analogy of words derived from desiderative vbs., e.g. *esurient.*] Ready to burst forth, on the point of bursting forth.

1664 POWER *Exp. Philos.* 138 You shall perceive a greater protrusion of your finger by the erupturient quicksilver. **1685** H. MORE *Para. Prophet.* 388 Something akin to actual Persecution, which was erupturient all the while. **1721–61** in BAILEY. **1775** in ASH.

†**erup'turive,** *a. Obs.*$^{-0}$ [badly f. L. *ērupt-*: see ERUPT *v.*] 'Breaking forth'.

1782–90 in BAILEY.

erur, obs. form of ERER, ERROR.

eru'scation. Ignorantly used for CORUSCATION.

1653 A. WILSON *Jas. I*, 64 Some eruscations and lightnings of joy appeared in her Countenance.

†**erustate,** *v. Obs.*$^{-0}$ [Error for **eruscate*, f. late L. *æruscāt-* ppl. stem of *æruscāre*, glossed '*æs undique colligere*'.]

1623 COCKERAM II, Getting Mony by all means. *Erustating.*

erve, var. of ERF, *Obs.*, cattle.

erven, pl. of ERF^{2}.

ervest, obs. form of HARVEST.

erveth, -lich(e, var. of ARVETH, -LICH(E, *Obs.*

†**'ervil.** *Obs.* Anglicized form of L. *ervilia* 'the bitter vetch' (L. and Sh.).

1551 TURNER *Herbal* I. K iij a, Theophrastus rekeneth *cicerculam* among eruilles and peese. **1601** HOLLAND *Pliny* II. 9 Madder of Italie..is sowed besides of seed, and set of slips in manner of Eruile.

ery, obs. form of EERY and EVERY.

-ery, *suffix*, ME. *-erie*, forming *sbs.*, first occurs in words adopted from Fr., and after the analogy of these has been extensively used as an Eng. formative.

1. The Fr. *-erie* is of two distinct origins: **a.** Representing a com. Romanic *-a'ria* (Pr. *-aria*, It. *-eria*, Sp. *-ería*), produced by the addition of the suffix *-'ia* (Fr. *-ie*, -Y^{3}) to sbs. or adjs. formed with the L. suffix *-ārio-* (Fr. *-ier, -er*). A large proportion of the Fr. sbs. in *-ier, -er* (see -ER^{2}) are designations of persons according to occupation or office; their derivatives in *-erie* denote sometimes the class of goods in which these persons deal, as *draperie* drapery, f. *drapier* draper; sometimes their employment or art, as *archerie* archery, f. *archer* archer; sometimes the place where their occupation is carried on, as *boulangerie* bakery, f. *boulanger* baker. After the analogy of these, many Fr. words were formed with *-erie* from sbs. and adjs. without the intervention of a derivative in *-ier*. Examples of the varying force of the suffix are *soierie* silk goods, f. *soie* silk; *niaiserie* foolish conduct, f. *niais* foolish; *juiverie* Jewry, f. *juif* Jew. **b.** Resulting from the addition of the suffix *-ie* to agent-nouns in OF. *-ere, -eor* (mod.F. *-eur*):—L. *-ātor, -ātōrem*. After the analogy of words thus formed, the suffix *-erie* was used to form derivatives immediately from verb-stems. Of the Fr. sbs. in *-erie* derived from vbs. (either through an agent-noun or directly) some denote a class of actions, as *tromperie* deceit, f. *tromper* to deceive; others an occupation, art, etc., as *confiserie* the business of a confectioner, f. *confire* to preserve fruits, etc.; others the place where an occupation is carried on, as *brasserie* brewery, f. *brasser* to brew.

2. a. Of the Eng. words ending in *-ery* many are adoptions from Fr., as *battery, bravery, cutlery, nunnery, treachery*. Many others are formed on sbs. in *-er*, and are properly examples of the suffix -Y^{3}; but in individual instances it is often uncertain whether a word was originally formed on an agent-noun in *-er* or directly on the verb. The derivatives of sbs. in *-er* and of verbs for the most part denote the place where an employment is carried on, as *bakery, brewery, fishery, pottery*; occasionally they denote classes of goods, as *confectionery, ironmongery, pottery*; after the analogy of such words, the suffix is added to sbs. with a general collective sense (= '*-ware*', '*-stuff*', or the like) as in *crockery, machinery, scenery*. The words formed by adding *-ery* to sbs. sometimes (though rarely) signify a state or condition, as *slavery*; oftener the force of the suffix is 'that which is characteristic of, all that is connected with', in most cases with contemptuous implication, as in *knavery, monkery, popery*; another frequent use is to denote the place where certain animals are kept or certain plants cultivated, as *piggery, rookery, swannery, vinery*. During the last century this suffix in pl. form has been rather extensively used in the coinage of jocular nonce-words; the Fisheries Exhibition held at South Kensington in 1883 having been colloquially known as 'the Fisheries', the name 'Healtheries' was commonly given to the succeeding Health Exhibition, and the Colonial and Indian Exhibition was called 'the Colinderies'; an exhibition of bicycles and tricycles was called 'the Wheeleries'. These formations are often imitated colloquially. Cf. 'The Dukeries' (after the analogy of 'The Potteries') as a name for the tract of country occupied by the great ducal estates in Notts. and North Derbyshire.

b. In modern, chiefly U.S., use, after *bakery* (= baker's shop or works), and similar words, this suffix has gained considerable currency in denoting 'a place where an indicated article or service may be purchased or procured', as *beanery, bootery, boozery, breadery, cakery, carwashery, drillery, drinkery, eatery, hashery, lunchery, mendery, toggery, wiggery*.

3. In many words this suffix has now the contracted form -RY, q.v.

erye, obs. form of EAR *v.* to plough.

eryness, obs. form of EERINESS.

1375 BARBOUR *Bruce* II. 295 Sum men for eryness will trymbill.

[**erynet,** mistake for *crynet*, CRINET.

1688 R. HOLME *Armoury* II. 237/1 Of a Hawk..the Erynets are the little Feathers under the eyes, or hairs about the Sear.]

†**e'rynge.** *Obs. rare.* [ad. L. *ēryngion*: see ERYNGO.] = ERYNGO 1 b.

1578 LYTE *Dodoens* IV. lviii. 519 Plinie calleth it also Eryngе; the writers of our time cal it *Eryngium marinum*. **1601** HOLLAND *Pliny* II. 119 As for the white Erynge, our countrymen call it in Latine Centum-capita.

eryngium (ɪˈrɪndʒɪəm). [mod.L., f. L. *ēryngion*, a. Gr. ἠρύγγιον: see ERYNGO. Adopted by Linnæus (*Systema Naturæ* 1735) and earlier botanists as a genus name.] A hardy herbaceous perennial plant of the genus so called, belonging

to the family Umbelliferæ, and bearing blue or white flowers.

[**1548** [see SEA-HOLLY].] **1578** H. LYTE tr. *Dodoen's Herb.* IV. 518 Two kindes of Eryngium, the one called the great Eryngium, or Eryngium of the Sea, and the other is called but Eryngium onely. **1616** SURFL. & MARKH. *Country Farme* 203 Eringium groweth in an vntilled, rough, and drie ground. **1626** BACON *Sylva* (1631) §53 Some few Slices of Eryngium Roots. **1861** MISS PRATT *Flower Pl.* III. 4 Eryngium (Eryngo). Flowers in a dense prickly head. **1899** G. JEKYLL *Wood & Garden* xi. 138 Sometimes a Poppy or an Eryngium comes up with one thick root, impossible to divide. **1900** W. D. DRURY *Bk. Gard.* 270 Eryngiums are handsome plants with.. large branching heads of Thistle-like flowers. **1962** *Amat. Gardening* 17 Mar. 5/3 Echinops and eryngiums.. are others which need little attention.

eryngo (iː'rɪŋgəʊ). Also 6–8 eringo, 6–7 *aphet.* ringo. [Immediate source uncertain: perhaps a corrupt adoption of It. or Sp. *eringio*, ad. L. *ēryngion*, a Gr. ἠρύγγιον, dim. of ἤρυγγος the name of this plant, also a goat's beard.]

1. †**a.** The candied root of the Sea Holly (*Eryngium maritimum*), formerly used as a sweetmeat, and regarded as an aphrodisiac. *Obs.* **b.** In later use, the plant itself, or any other of the same genus. (In this sense the L. *eryngium* was used by earlier writers.)

a. 1598 SHAKS. *Merry W.* v. v. 23 Let it.. haile kissing Comfits, and snow Eringoes. **1599** MARSTON *Sco. Villanie* I. iii. 181 Camphire and Lettuce chaste Are clean casheird, now Sophi Ringoes eate. **1616** R. C. *Times' Whis.* VI. 2771 Candid eringoes, and rich marchpaine stuff. *c* **1630** RISDON *Surv. Devon* §277 (1810) 288 Sea-holly groweth plentifully, whose roots are called eringo. **1681** OTWAY *Soldier's Fort.* v, Here child, here's some Ringoes. **1709** POPE *Jan. & May* 377 Satyrion near, with hot Eringo's stood.

b. 1668 WILKINS *Real Char.* II. iv. §4. 94 Eringo, an Herb. **1695** BLACKMORE *Pr. Arth.* v. 439 In verdant Samphire and Eringo drest. **1718** QUINCY *Compl. Disp.* 120 Eryngo grows in sandy places, and near the Sea-Shore. **1798** CANNING *New Morality* in *Anti-Jacobin* No. 36 (1852) 212 Eringoes o'er the hallow'd spot shall bloom. **1861** [see ERYNGIUM].

2. *attrib.*, esp. ***eryngo-root.***

1634–5 *Althorp MS.* in Simpkinson *Washingtons* (1860) p. lxix, For ashen keyes and eringo rootes. **1656** EVELYN *Mem.* (1857) I. 332 Colchester.. is also famous for oysters and Eringo root. **1709** PRIOR *Paulo Purganti* 72 One might see Eringo Roots and Bohé Tea. **1848** C. A. JOHNS *Week at Lizard* 283 Candied Eryngo-root.

†**ˌeryˌsipe'laceous,** *a. Obs. rare.* [f. ERYSIPEL-AS + -ACEOUS.] = ERYSIPELATOUS.

1684 tr. *Bonet's Merc. Compit.* VI. 191 In a very vehement and urgent Inflammation, as an Erisipelaceous one.

erysipelas (ɛrɪ'sɪpɪləs). *Path.* Forms: 4 herisipila, 6 herisipelas, erisipila, 6–7 erisipelas, -ilas, -ylas, erisypelas, erysipilas, -iles, -ely, (eresipyla, iresipilis, 9 earisiply), 7– erysipelas. [a. Gr. ἐρυσίπελας (Hippocrates), of doubtful etymology. Commonly regarded as f. *ἔρυσι-ς reddening (:—OAryan **rudhti-s*, f. root **reudh*, whence Gr. ἐρυθρός red) + πελ- in πέλλα skin (cogn. with L. *pellis* and FELL); but the formation appears abnormal. For the first element cf. ἐρυσίβη red blight on corn.]

A local febrile disease accompanied by diffused inflammation of the skin, producing a deep red colour; often called St. Anthony's fire, or 'the rose'.

1398 TREVISA *Barth. De P.R.* Add. MS. 27944 fo. 63 As it farep of hem þat haue an euel þat hatte herisipla. **1527** ANDREW *Brunswyke's Distyll. Waters* H iij b, Hous-leke.. is good agaynst the sore called Erisipila. **1543** TRAHERON *Vigo's Chirurg.* II. iii. 37 You must beware, that Herisipelas retourne not. **1635** BRATHWAIT *Arcad. Pr.* 173 This Erysipelas or wilde fire being once kindled, the flame is not so soon to be quenched. **1693** Q. MARY *Let.* (1886) 107, I so heated my blood that I had an iresipilis upon on arm. **1736** BAILEY *Househ. Dict.* 268 Erysipelas or St. Anthony's fire. **1769** W. BUCHAN *Dom. Med.* (1790) 251 It is common to bleed in the erysipelas. **1826** J. WILLIAMS *Last Legacy* 10 For the Earisiply, or St. Anthony's Fire. **1872** DARWIN *Emotions* xiii. 325 Erysipelas of the head commonly induces delirium.

Hence **ˌeryˌsipe'latic** *a.* [see -IC], of the nature of erysipelas; resembling erysipelas. **ˌerysi'pelatoid** *a.* [see -OID], resembling erysipelas. †**ery'sipelous** *a.* [+ -OUS] = ERYSIPELATOUS. †**ˌerysi'pelaˌtose** *a.* [see -OSE] = ERYSIPELATOUS.

1883 *Standard* 3 Jan. 3/2 Wide-spread inflammation of an erysipelatic character. **1710** T. FULLER *Pharm. Extemp.* 283 It is a useful thing.. for Erysipelatose Affections. **1786** COWPER *Let.* Aug. 9 An eresypylatose [*sic*] eruption.

erysipelatous (ˌɛrɪsɪ'pɛlətəs), *a.* [f. Gr. ἐρυσιπελατ- stem of ἐρυσίπελας (see prec.) + -OUS: cf. Fr. *érysipélateux.*] Pertaining to, or of the nature of, erysipelas; affected with erysipelas.

1646 SIR T. BROWNE *Pseud. Ep.* IV. iii. 182 An Inflammation.. Oedematous, Schirrous, Erisipelatous according to the predominancy of melancholy, flegme, or choler. **1769** BUCHAN *Dom. Med.* liv. (1826) 269 Erysipelatous redness in the skin. **1814** COLERIDGE in Cottle *Remin.* (1837) 357 An erysipelatous complaint. **1861** HULME tr. *Moquin-Tandon* II. v. ii. 264 Erysipelatous spots. **1871** NAPHEYS *Prev. & Cure Dis.* III. xiv. 1094 An erysipelatous patient.

erysipeloid (ɛrɪ'sɪpɪlɔɪd). *Path.* [a. G. *erysipeloid* (Rosenbach 1887, in *Arch. f. klin. Chir.* XXXVI. 346), f. ERYSIPEL(AS + -OID. J. Daudé (*Traité de l'érysipèle épidémique* (1867) II. 128) had earlier used *érysipéloïde* as the name of some skin diseases that he distinguished from erysipelas and from erythema, but this is not the source of the mod. sense.] Dermatitis of the hands due to infection with the bacillus causing swine erysipelas *Erysipelothrix rhusiopathia.*

[**1882** A. STILLÉ in J. Ashhurst jr. *Internat. Encycl. Surg.* I. 181 The nature of most of these recurrent cases is open to question, and.. not a few of them seem to have been instances of erythema rather than of erysipelas, or, as they have been called by Daudé, erysipeloids.] **1888** *Jrnl. Cutaneous & Genito-Urinary Dis.* VI. 13 Rosenbach describes Erysipeloid as being a form of wound infection. **1955** G. O. DAVIES in Gaiger & Davies *Vet. Path. & Bacteriol.* (ed. 4) xv. 319 Swine erysipelas infection sometimes occurs in man from handling infected pigs and is spoken of as erysipeloid. **1961** *Lancet* 2 Sept. 530/1 Does penicillin cure erysipeloid in a few days? **1969** *New Scientist* 13 Feb. 349/1 Infections including.. erysipeloid in Man—a wound infection especially common in veterinarians.

erysy, erytage, obs. ff. HERESY, HERITAGE.

erythema (ɛrɪ'θiːmə). *Path.* [a. Gr. ἐρύθημα (stem ἐρυθηματ-), f. ἐρυθαίνειν to be red, f. ἐρυθ-ρός red.] A superficial inflammation of the skin, showing itself chiefly in rose-coloured patches.

1766–83 W. CULLEN *First Lines Phys.* §274 Wks. 1827 II. 23 When the disease is an affection of the skin alone.. I shall give the disease the name of Erythema. **1811** ABERNETHY *Surg. Wks.* I. 198 A Burgundy pitch plaster causes extensive erythema. **1855** *Lancet* 11 July 79/2 A fugacious roseola or erythema.

Hence **e'rythemal** *a.* [-AL], of, pertaining to, or causing erythema; **ˌerythe'matic** *a.* [+ -IC], of, pertaining to, or of the nature of erythema. **ery'thematous** *a.* [+ -OUS] = prec.

1940 *Jrnl. Appl. Physics* June 422 Other emissivities such as an erythemal emissivity might be defined. **1961** *Lancet* 26 Aug. 449/1 Other spectral regions—e.g., 260–320 mμ produced normal erythemal responses. **1962** H. C. WESTON *Sight, Light & Work* (ed. 2) v. 156 The amount of erythemal .. ultra-violet radiation emitted by fluorescent tubes.. is about the same.. as that which accompanies noon sunlight. **1766–83** W. CULLEN *First Lines Phys.* §385 Wks. 1827 II. 71 The inflammation of the stomach is of two kinds, Phlegmonic, or Erythematic. **1842** T. H. BURGESS tr. *Cazenove's Dis. Skin* 130 This erythematous ring is often the seat of small vesicles. **1861** T. GRAHAM *Pract. Med.* 667 Surrounded by an erythematous efflorescence.

erythism, erroneous spelling of ERETHISM.

erythræmia (ɛrɪ'θriːmɪə). *Path.* Also erythremia. [mod.L., ad. G. *erythrämie* (W. Türk 1904, in *Wiener klin. Wochenschr.* 18 Feb. 192/1), f. Gr. ἐρυθρός red + αἷμα blood.] An excess of red cells in the blood; any disease so characterized, esp. polycythæmia vera.

[**1860** MAYNE *Expos. Lex.* Add. 1493/1 *Erythræmia*, term for the full preparing of arterial blood in the lungs.] **1908** W. OSLER in *Lancet* 18 Jan. 145/1 For the recognition of the disease a blood count is necessary, not simply a blood examination, as in cases of leukæmia. The essential feature, the polycythæmia, the erythræmia, can be determined only by counting the number of red blood corpuscles in a cubic millimetre. **1968** PASSMORE & ROBSON *Compan. Med. Stud.* I. xxvi. 3 The red cell mass is naturally low in anaemia; when it is raised the patient is said to have erythraemia.

Hence **ery'thræmic** *a.*, characterized by or characteristic of erythræmia.

1938 HARROP & WINTROBE in H. Downey *Handbk. Hematol.* IV. xxxiv. 2378 Many members of such families may possess the 'erythremic constitution'. **1962** *Lancet* 1 Dec. 1140/2 Acute erythræmic myelosis, or acute immature-cell erythræmia, has become well known since its original description by Di Guglielmo (1928).

erythric (ɛ'rɪθrɪk), *a. Chem.* [f. Gr. ἐρυθρ-ός red + -IC.] ***erythric acid:*** †**a.** (see quot. 1840); **b.** = ERYTHRIN.

1840 HENRY *Elem. Chem.* II. 415 An acid has also been obtained by Brugnatelli, by acting on uric acid with nitric acid, which he has proposed to call erythric acid. **1861** MACMILLAN *Footn. Page Nat.* 117 Schunk.. discovered [in rock-moss or cudbear] a colourless crystalline acid, called erythric acid.

erythrin (ɛ'rɪθrɪn). *Chem.* [f. as prec. + -IN.] 'An acid ($C_{20}H_{22}O_{10}$) discovered by Heeren in *Roccella tinctoria*; it appears also to be contained in most of the lichens from which archil is prepared' (Watts *Dict. Chem.* 1882).

1838 T. THOMSON *Chem. Org. Bodies* 385 The erythrin.. undergoes a notable change, for it is insoluble in water.

‖**Erythrina** (ɛrɪ'θraɪnə). [mod.L., f. Gr. ἐρυθρ-ός red.] The Coral-tree, a genus of tropical trees (N.O. *Leguminosæ*) bearing clusters of blood-red flowers.

1865 PARKMAN *Huguenots* iv. (1875) 58 The coral blossoms of the erythrina glow in the shade beneath. **1871** MATEER *Travancore* 100 The flaming Erythrina, or coral tree. **1875** MISS BIRD *Sandwich Isl.* (1880) 69 The surf-board.. is usually made of the erythrina, or the breadfruit tree.

erythrine (ɛ'rɪθraɪn). *Min.* [f. Gr. ἐρυθρ-ός red + -INE.] = COBALT-BLOOM.

1837 ALLAN *Phillips' Min.* 289 *Cobalt Bloom*.. Erythrine. **1882** WATTS *Chem. Dict.* s.v.

erythrism ('ɛrɪθrɪz(ə)m). [f. Gr. ἐρυθρός red + -ISM.] Abnormal or excessive redness (in the plumage of birds or hair of mammals); a red variety (of some recognized species).

1886 *Proc. Zool. Soc. Lond.* 77 Erythrism is particularly common among the Mungooses. **1893** *Athenæum* 28 Jan. 124/3 Mr. Hose thought that this species might possibly be only an erythrism of *S[emnopithecus] chrysomelas.* **1908** *Zoologist* Apr. 136 A good example of the same erythrism was that by Mr. McLean in the summer of 1906. **1930** E. W. HENDY *Wild Exmoor* 297 Erythrism, or excess of red colouration, may be produced.. by feeding birds upon red pepper. **1962** *New Scientist* 9 Aug. 284/2 All examples of albinism (whitening),.. xanthism (yellowing) or erythrism (reddening) are throwing light on genetic divergence.

Hence **ery'thristic** *a.*, exhibiting erythrism.

1910 *Encycl. Brit.* V. 489/1 A third colour-phase, the 'erythristic' or red, is represented by the sandy cat. **1923** *Glasgow Herald* 17 Mar. 6 The variety, technically called 'erythristic', occurs among ferrets as well as among polecats. **1936** *Discovery* Feb. 57/1 Another collector kicked guillemots' eggs into the sea in the hope that subsequent layings might produce the erythristic eggs for which he was looking. **1953** BANNERMAN *Birds Brit. Isles* II. 11 (Calandra lark), Erythristic eggs occur.

erythrite (ɛ'rɪθraɪt). Also 9 erithrite. [f. as ERYTHRINE + -ITE.]

1. *Min.* **a.** = COBALT-BLOOM. **b.** 'A flesh-coloured feldspar, containing 3 per cent. magnesia, found in amygdaloid' (Watts *Dict. Chem.* 1882).

1844 DANA *Min.* 351 The Erythrite of Thomson.. is a flesh colored feldspar. **1868** *Ibid.* 559 Erythrite when abundant is valuable for the manufacture of smalt.

2. *Chem.* An organic substance obtainable from erythrin.

1865 WILLIAMSON *Chem. for Students* li. §312 The formula of erithrite is $C^4H^{10}O^4$. **1869** ROSCOE *Elem. Chem.* 391 The only tetravalent alcohol as yet known is erythrite.

erythritol (ɛ'rɪθrɪtɒl). *Chem.* [f. ERYTHRITE + -OL.] A tetrahydric alcohol, 1,2,3,4-butanetetrol, occurring chiefly in lichens and algæ, and obtainable by reduction of erythrose.

1891 *Jrnl. Chem. Soc.* LX. 657 (*heading*) Alkaline derivatives of erythritol. *Ibid.*, Cold concentrated solutions of erythritol and sodium hydroxide were mixed.. and the solution was allowed to evaporate. **1900** *Jrnl. Chem. Soc.* LXXVIII. I. 579 The algæ *Trentepholia Jolithus*.. when extracted with ether, yields erythritol. **1923** J. J. SUDBOROUGH *Bernthsen's Org. Chem.* (new ed.) viii. 210 Erythritol (Butane-tetrol) occurs in the free state in *Protococcus vulgaris.* **1968** *New Scientist* 30 May 445/1 Certain tissues in the foetus, but not in the adult, contain erythritol, which stimulates the growth of *Brucella abortus.*

erythro- (ɛ'rɪθrəʊ-) (before a vowel *e'rythr-*), combining form of Gr. ἐρυθρό-ς red, in several compounds occurring in Chemistry, with a few in Mineralogy, etc.

e'rythro-ben'zene (see quot.). **e'rythroblast** [G. (M. Löwit 1886, in *Sitzungsber. d. Akad. d. Wissenschaften in Wien* 3rd Ser. XCII. 56)], any of the normal series of nucleated cells recognizable as precursors of erythrocytes; hence **erythro'blastic** *a.* **e'rythrocyte,** a red blood corpuscle; also *attrib.*; hence **erythro'cytic** *a.* **eˌrythrocy'thæmia** = ERYTHRÆMIA. **eˌrythrocy'tosis,** erythræmia, esp. when a secondary condition resulting from some other disturbance. **ery'throlein** [see OLEIN]. **eˌrythro'litmin** [see LITMUS and -IN], 'red substances obtained from litmus' (Watts *Dict. Chem.* 1882). **eˌrythrome'lalgia,** dilatation of the arteries of the extremities, esp. the feet. **eˌrythro'phobia,** (*a*) fear of blushing; (*b*) hypersensitivity to the colour red. **e'rythrophyll,** *Chem.* [Gr. φύλλ-ον leaf], the red colouring matter of leaves in autumn. **eˌrythro'phyllin,** *Chem.* [see prec. and -IN] = prec. **eˌrythro'phytoscope** [Gr. φυτό-ν plant + -σκοπος observer] = ERYTHROSCOPE. **eˌrythro'plastid** = *erythrocyte.* **eˌrythro'protid** [see PROTEID or PROTIDE], 'a red extractive matter obtained by Mulder from albumin and allied substances'. **ery'thropsia** [Gr. -οψια seeing], a form of chromatopsia in which all objects appear red. **eˌrythro'retin,** *Chem.* [see RET-ENE and -IN], 'a resinous constituent of rhubarb-root, soluble with purple-red colour in alkalis' (Watts *Dict. Chem.* 1882). **e'rythroscope** [Gr. -σκοπος observer], an optical contrivance, by which the green of foliage is caused to appear red, while all other green objects retain their natural hue (see quot.). **eˌrythro'siderite,** *Min.* [Gr. σίδηρ-ος + -ITE], a hydrous chloride of potassium and iron formed by sublimation in the lavas of Vesuvius. **e'rythrozyme,** *Chem.*

[Gr. ζύμη leaven], 'an azotised substance which exists in madder root, and gives rise to a peculiar transformation of rubian' (Watts *Dict. Chem.* 1882).

1879 WATTS *Dict. Chem.* VI. 583 **Erythrobenzene*, a red colouring matter prepared from nitrobenzene by leaving 12 pts. of that substance in contact with 24 pts. of fine iron filings and 6 pts. strong hydrochloric acid, for 24 hours at ordinary temperatures. **1890** BILLINGS *Med. Dict.*, *Erythroblasts. **1898** *Allbutt's Syst. Med.* V. 651 None of the leucocytes of the blood becomes transformed into red corpuscles, these being formed from special cells—'erythroblasts'—in the bone-marrow. **1908** OSLER & MCCRAE *Syst. Med.* IV. 600 A considerable number of the immature cells of the adult marrow, including many of the erythroblasts, possess a considerable degree of affinity for basic coloring matters. **1968** H. HARRIS *Nucleus & Cytoplasm* iv. 86 An electron microscopic study of nuclear elimination from the late erythroblast. **1908** *Practitioner* Feb. 239 The *erythroblastic tissues of the marrow. **1908** OSLER & MCCRAE *Syst. Med.* IV. 679 The disease is due to a primary hyperplasia of the erythroblastic bone-marrow. **1894** G. M. GOULD *Illustr. Dict. Med.* 441/1 **Erythrocyte*, a red blood-corpuscle. **1908** OSLER & MCCRAE *Syst. Med.* IV. 600 We speak of the..blue-stained erythrocyte as polychromatophilic. **1946** *Nature* 30 Nov. 793/1 Regular erythrocyte counts and hæmoglobin determinations were done in a drop of blood. **1961** *Lancet* 2 Sept. 522/2 The erythrocyte-sedimentation rate was 35 mm. in the 1st hour. **1905** OSLER *Princ. Med.* (ed. 6) 748 An increase in the number of the red blood-corpuscles—*erythrocythæmia. **1908** *Practitioner* Feb. 234 According to the degree in which the parent cell has developed along the leucocytic or *erythrocytic route. **1946** *Nature* 16 Nov. 707/2 Therapeutic potency..is apparent not only against the erythrocytic but also against the exo-erythrocytic forms of the malaria parasite. **1908** *Practitioner* Feb. 238 It would almost seem better to bring the nomenclature of this new disease into line with that adopted to describe an increase of the various forms of leucocytes, and to call it polycythæmia rubra, *erythrocytosis, or, better still, erythrocythæmia. **1966** WRIGHT & SYMMERS *Systemic Path.* I. iv. 175 The number of red cells in the blood is seldom as large in erythrocytosis as in polycythæmia vera. **1882** *Ibid.* III. 731 *Erythrolitmin forms crystalline grains of a fine deep red colour, coloured blue by potash. **1878** S. W. MITCHELL in *Amer. Jrnl. Med. Sci.* July 17 The foot and hand disorder I am about to describe may be conveniently labelled *Erythromelalgia. **1956** *New Gould Med. Dict.* (ed. 2) 419/2 *Erythromelalgia*... Also called acromelalgia, Mitchell's disease. **1894** G. M. GOULD *Illustr. Dict. Med.* 441/2 **Erythrophobia*, morbid intolerance of red colors: sometimes observed after operations for cataract. **1936** *Mind* XLV. 389 They are then 'neurotic' symptoms..(neurotic vomiting.. blushing and erythrophobia, [etc.]). **1947** P. L. HARRIMAN *Dict. Psychol.* 126 *Erythrophobia*, morbid fear of blushing; also, hypersensitivity to reds, a symptom reported as occurring in some patients who have had cataracts removed. **1960** KOESTLER *Lotus & Robot* II. viii. 213 In this is included fear of blushing when appearing before a person, or erythrophobia. **1875** BENNETT & DYER tr. *Sachs' Bot.* 686 *Erythrophyll group. **1884** BOWER & SCOTT *De Bary's Phaner. & Ferns* 66 Cell-sap..tinted with dissolved pigments (Erythrophyll, &c.). **1876** *S. Kens. Museum Catal.* No. 3702 *Erythrophytoscope. **1921** A. KEITH *Hum. Embryol.* (ed. 4) xxi. 336 At every period of life the red blood corpuscles (*erythroplastids) arise from erythroblasts. **1845** G. DAY tr. *Simon's Anim. Chem.* I. 29 Glutin and water may be supposed to be formed from protid and *erythroprotid by the ammonia. **1852-9** TODD *Cycl. Anat.* IV. 164/2 Erythroprotid, when pure, is of a fine red colour. **1885** *Boston Med. & Surg. Jrnl.* 24 Dec. 615/2 The patient reported the appearance of the red vision in four months after having had the cataract extracted... It came on at bedtime... The *erythropsia had gone on the following morning. **1964** S. DUKE-ELDER *Parsons' Dis. Eye* (ed. 14) xxiv. 363 *Erythropsia* (red vision) occurs particularly after cataract extraction if the eyes are exposed to bright light. **1876** HARLEY *Mat. Med.* 466 Rhubarb contains 3 resins, aporetin phœoretin, and *erythroretin. **1876** *S. Kens. Museum Catal.* No. 3700 *Erythroscope. **1879** ROOD *Chromatics* vii. 83 Simler has constructed a simple.. apparatus, based on the singular property which living leaves have of reflecting abundantly the extreme red rays of the spectrum: it is called an erythroscope. **1875** DANA *Min.* App. ii. 19 *Erythrosiderite..Color red. Very soluble. **1876** tr. *Schützenberger's Fermentation* 24 In the fermentation of sugar by means of *erythrozyme.

erythroblastosis (ɛˌrɪθrəʊblæˈstəʊsɪs). *Path.* [ad. G. *erythroblastose* (H. Rautmann 1912, in *Beitr. z. Path. Anat.* LIV. 347), f. *erythroblast*: see prec. and -OSIS.] The presence of erythroblasts in the blood; *esp.* hæmolytic disease of the newborn, erythroblastosis fœtalis, a severe anæmia that results when the mother develops antibodies against the blood of the fœtus. Hence **eˌrythroblaˈstotic** *a.*

1931 *Amer. Jrnl. Path.* VII. 293 Erythroblastosis may occur without edema. **1938** *Nature* 29 Jan. 202/2 Researches aiming at investigating the nature of the virus of aviary erythroblastosis. **1957** *Encycl. Brit.* I. 863/1 Once a woman has borne an erythroblastotic infant, she is likely to bear others. **1964** M. HYNES *Med. Bacteriol.* (ed. 8) xxv. 404 Erythroblastosis from rhesus incompatibility.

erythrogen (ɛˈrɪθrəʊdʒɛn). [mod. f. Gr. ἐρυθρο- ERYTHRO- + -GEN² 'producer'.]

1. *Bot.* 'A term for a variety of the supposed colouring matter of vegetables, called Chromogen, because it produces a red colour with acids'. (*Syd. Soc. Lex.*)

2. *Chem.* 'A crystalline, fatty substance obtained from diseased bile; so called from the reddish or purple color of some of its compounds' (Watts *Dict. Chem.* 1882).

1846 WORCESTER cites *Penny Cyclop.*; and in mod. Dicts.

Hence **eˌrythroˈgenic** *a.*, (*a*) producing a sensation of redness; (*b*) pertaining to the production of erythrocytes; (*c*) causing redness of the skin.

1902 C. L. FRANKLIN in Baldwin *Dict. Philos.* II. 780/2 *Colour* should be used in its subjective sense,..and *erythrogenic radiations* should be substituted for the physical cause of colour. **1951** WHITBY & HYNES *Med. Bacteriol.* (ed. 5) xi. 158 Only streptococci of Lancefield's Group A produce the erythrogenic toxin. **1951** [see ERYTHROPOIESIS].

erythroid (ˈɛrɪθrɔɪd), *a.* [mod. f. Gr. ἐρυθρ-ος (see ERYTHRO-) + -OID.]

1. Of a red colour, reddish.

1847 in CRAIG; and in mod. Dicts.

2. Of or pertaining to erythrocytes.

1927 SABIN & DOAN in *Proc. Soc. Exper. Biol. & Med.* XXV. II. 122 In the new-born rabbit the erythroid-myeloid ratio of the bone marrow is nearly the reverse of that of the adult. **1961** *Lancet* 26 Aug. 491/1 Moderate to severe folic-acid deficiency existed in the absence of megaloblastic characteristics in the erythroid or myeloid series of the blood and marrow.

erythrol (ˈɛrɪθrɒl). *Chem.* [f. ERYTHR(ITE + -OL.] **1.** = ERYTHRITOL.

1879 *Jrnl. Chem. Soc.* XXXVI. 664 *Erythrol* (erythrite) mixed with hay-water yielded a trace of alcohol. **1910** *Practitioner* Feb. 277 Erythrol tetranitrate is said to have less effect than liquor trinitrini. **1940** A. J. CLARK *Appl. Pharmacol.* (ed. 7) xxi. 402 Organic nitrates, such as nitro-glycerine and erythrol tetranitrate, act like nitrites.

2. (See quot. 1908.) (Disused.)

1900 in DORLAND *Med. Dict.* **1908** *Practitioner* Feb. 279 For butyric fermentation, is used erythrol, a red powder insoluble in water, which is a double iodide of bismuth and cinchonidine.

erythromycin (ɛˌrɪθrəʊˈmaɪsɪn). *Med.* [f. ERYTHRO-: see -MYCIN.] An antibiotic isolated from *Streptomyces erythreus.*

1952 *Antibiotics & Chemotherapy* II. 279 The announcement..of the discovery of erythromycin (Ilotycin), a new broad spectrum antibiotic..emphasizes again the extensive efforts necessary to isolate an antibiotic. **1960** M. E. FLOREY *Clinical Appl. Antibiotics* IV. ii. 36 Like erythromycin, the antibiotic carbomycin..was isolated in 1952 and has similar antibacterial properties. **1962** *Lancet* 24 Nov. 1096/1 Erythromycin has an antibacterial range somewhat similar to that of penicillin. **1967** *New Scientist* 5 Oct. 35/2 The extremely useful macrolide group of antibiotics, which includes erythromycin and oleandomycin.

erythronium (ɛrɪˈθrəʊnɪəm). [mod.L. (Linnæus *Systema Naturæ* 1735), ad. Gr. σατύριον ἐρυθρόνιον, Dioscorides' name for the red SATYRION, referring to the colour of the flowers of the European species.] A member of the genus of ornamental bulbous plants so called, native to North America, Europe, Russia, and Japan, and belonging to the family Liliaceæ.

1797 *Encycl. Brit.* VI. 722/1 *Erythronium*, dog's-tooth violet. **1868** *Curtis's Bot. Mag.* XCIV. 5714 It would appear that the species or forms of West American *Erythronia* retain their colours over considerable areas. **1900** W. D. DRURY *Bk. Gard.* x. 326 Erythroniums range between 6 in. and 9 in. in height. **1961** *Amateur Gardening* 30 Dec. 5 Erythroniums like a good loam to which the peat and leaf mould has been added.

erythropoiesis (ɛˌrɪθrəʊpɔɪˈiːsɪs). *Physiol.* [f. ERYTHRO- + Gr. ποίησις creation.] The production of red blood cells (erythrocytes).

1918 *Amer. Jrnl. Anat.* XXIV. 24 In the liver..and the omentum, erythropoiesis has been repeatedly described as taking place extravascularly. **1941** *Lancet* 23 Aug. 208/2 A scheme of normal and pathological erythropoiesis is proposed which shows that disease may cause changes in the development of the normoblastic group of cells or maturation may be deflected to a megaloblastic group. **1951** G. H. BOURNE *Cytol. & Cell Physiol.* (ed. 2) x. 432 Perhaps the most favourable material for observing the details of erythropoiesis in living tissue is provided by small explants of the presumptive erythrogenic mesoderm of an early chick blastoderm... The erythrogenic cells rapidly disintegrate into small, almost spherical primitive blood cells.

eˌrythropoiˈetic, *a.* [f. ERYTHRO- + POIETIC *a.*] Of or pertaining to the production of erythrocytes.

1908 *Practitioner* Apr. 457 The bone-marrow of dogs which have developed a polycythæmia from being kept at high altitudes, has been..found to give abundant evidence of increased erythropoietic activity. **1949** FLOREY & JENNINGS in H. W. Florey *Antibiotics* II. xxxvii. 1209 Harmlessness to the erythropoietic tissues was an important desideratum for penicillin. **1966** *Lancet* 24 Dec. 1416/2 Iron utilisation is a marker of bone-marrow erythropoietic activity.

eˌrythroˈpoietin. [f. ERYTHROPOIET(IC *a.* + -IN¹.] A protein formed in the kidney that stimulates the formation of red blood cells (erythropoiesis).

1948 *Acta Physiol. Scand.* XVI. 152 Our present knowledge of the formation of erythropoietins and their role in anoxic conditions is limited. **1958** *Nature* 31 May 1537 Recently the presence of a substance capable of stimulating erythropoiesis (erythropoietin) in the peripheral blood of man and anæmic animals has been demonstrated repeatedly by a variety of assay methods. **1963** *Lancet* 12 Jan. 89/2 He supports the suggestion that there is a single erythropoietin produced or activated by the kidney.

erythrose (ɛˈrɪθrəʊz, ˈɛrɪθrəʊz, -s). *Chem.* [f. ERYTHR(ITE + -OSE².] A tetrose sugar, $CHO{\cdot}[CH(OH)]_2{\cdot}CH_2OH$, isolated as a liquid and existing in two molecular configurations; it differs from threose in having the hydroxyl groups on the second and third carbon atoms on the same side of the carbon chain.

1900 *Jrnl. Chem. Soc.* LXXVIII. I. 139 *d*-Erythrose.. shows mutarotation, and has an approximate maximum specific rotation $[\alpha]_D - 14.5°$ at 20°. **1963** E. PERCIVAL in Florkin & Stotz *Comprehensive Biochem.* V. i. 11 The simplest sugars are the tetroses D- and L-erythrose..and D- and L-threose.

erythrosin (ɛˈrɪθrəsɪn). *Chem.* Also -ine. [irreg. f. Gr. ἐρυθρός red + -IN¹.] A red colouring matter obtained from fluorescein by the action of iodine, used in photography and as a histological stain.

1884 *Photogr. Jrnl.* Dec. 52 Each of the following colouring matters was found to exercise a sensitizing action ..for the extreme red rays of the solar spectrum. Iodine green,..erythrosin, pyrosin. **1891** *Jrnl. Camera Club* V. 123-7. **1892** *Photogr. Ann.* II. 72 Plates sensitised with erythrosin and erythrosin silver. **1908** *Jrnl. Chem. Soc.* XCIV. I. 669 When silver nitrate is added to an excess of a dilute solution of erythrosin, a much more intensely colloidal solution of the silver salt of erythrosin is obtained. **1926** *Encycl. Brit.* Suppl. III. 133/2 Erythrosine, that is the tetra-iodo derivative of fluorescein, was found by Eder to be the most suitable dye for sensitising in the green and yellow. **1968** *Brit. Corrosion Jrnl.* III. 31/1 The fruit salad contained a few cherries dyed with erythrosin.

erytyke, obs. form of HERETIC.

†**es**, *sb. Obs.* Also 4 **hes**, 5 **ese**. [OE. *ǣs*, corresp. to OHG. *âs*, MDu. *aes* (mod.Ger., Du. *aas*):—OTeut. **ǣsso(m*, f. *ǣt-* ablaut-form of root **et-* to EAT.] Carrion; also carrion used as bait, a bait.

Beowulf (Gr.) 1331 Atol æse wlanc eft siðas teah fylle ȝefræȝnod. **975** *O.E. Chron.*, Letan him behindan..þane hasewan padan earn æftan hwit æses brucan. *c* **1175** *Lamb. Hom.* 123 Þenne bið he ȝredi þes eses and forswoleȝeð þene hoc forð mid þan ese. **1340** *Ayenb.* 55 Yerne to þe mete ase deþ þe hond to þe hes. *c* **1450** *Lat. & Eng. Voc.* in Wr.-Wülcker 579 *Edia*, ese.

es, *pers. pron. Obs.* [phonetic variant of *hes*, *his*; often attached to the vb. of which it is the obj.: see HIS *pron.*², and cf. † AS *pron.*]

a. Them (*acc. pl.*). **b.** Her, it (*acc. fem. sing.*).

a **1200** *Moral Ode* 55 Þe þet echte wile habben wel hwile þe he muȝe es welden. Giue hies for godes luue: þenne deþ hes wel ihalden. *c* **1250** *Gen. & Ex.* 135 He knowned [*read* knoweð] one ilc sterre name, He settes in ðe firmament. *c* **1300** *Havelok* 970 He bouthe him boþe hosen and shon, And sone dide him dones on. *c* **1314** *Guy Warw.* (A.) 3850 He oxed his armes hastiliche And men es him brouȝt sikerliche.

es, obs. form of HIS *pron.*¹

a **1300** *Cursor M.* 4641 (Cott.), I wat nour quar es mak. *Ibid.* 4677 Depe selers..Thoru es aun scel-wis red, He fild wit wines, quite and red.

es, obs. form of *is*: see BE *v.* A. 1.

es, obs. var. of *are*: see BE *v.* A. 1 ¶.

es-, *prefix*, occurring in adoptions of OF. words beginning with *es-*:—L. *ex-* out. A few of these words survive with the prefix unchanged, as *escape*, *escheat*; a few others have been refashioned with *ex-*, after Latin, as *esample*, now *example*, *eschange*, now *exhange*; but the much larger number of them are obsolete. Before *ch* this prefix was in 14-15th c. occasionally written *ep-*. A frequent variant of *es-* is *a-*: see A- *pref.* 9.

¶The examples of the prefix *es-* must be distinguished from those of the euphonic *e* prefixed in OF. (as in Pr., Sp., Pg.) to an initial *s* followed by a consonant, e.g. *especial*, *esquire*.

Esalen (ˈɛsələn). [ad. *Esselen*, the name of an extinct American Indian people of the Californian coast.] An alternative philosophy and technique intended to heighten individual self-awareness and 'human potential' by psychological and physiotherapeutic means, such as group therapy, psychodrama, etc.: developed at the Esalen Institute in California. Freq. *attrib.*

1966 *Look* 28 June 33/2 (*caption*) Jubilant Michael Murphy, president of the Esalen Institute at Big Sur Hot Springs, acts as a catalyst for a growing company of scientists, educators and religious leaders who feel that the abilities of the average human being can be vastly broadened. **1967** *N.Y. Times Mag.* 31 Dec. 8/3 Esalen..is concerned with those who are too well-adjusted, too tight and controlled. It attempts to release them for growth and greater integration. **1968** *Daily Tel.* (Colour Suppl.) 20 Dec. 16/1 What is the Esalen method? Well, one of its manifestations is the power of touching. It also means acting naturally and loosening up with members of your particular group. **1969** *Jrnl. Contemp. Psychotherapy* Summer 57 To many, Esalen means Fritz Perls' gestalt therapy and the crusading spirit of Michael Murphy. To others it is William Schutz's encounter groups, George Brown's gestalt

awareness training, Bernard Gunther's sensory awareness, George Bach's marital couples workshop. **1976** [see SILVA].

‖**'esalon.** *Obs. rare.* Also 6 **easalon.** Misspelling of Lat. *æsalon* [ad. Gr. αἰσάλων], the name of a bird of prey, 'the rust-kite or moor-buzzard' (Lewis and Short), 'the merlin' (Liddell and Scott); in context of first quot. it is said to be the smallest of the buzzard kind.

1572 BOSSEWELL *Armorie* III. 27 Enemye to them [Ravens] is a lyttle Byrde called Easalon, which breaketh theire egges. **1651** J. F[REAKE] *Agrippa's Occ. Philos.* 40 There is..a bitter enmity betwixt the litle bird called Esalon, and the Asse.

Esau ('iːsɔː). Name of the elder of the twin sons of the patriarch Isaac, who sold his birthright to his brother Jacob for 'a mess of pottage' (Gen. xxv. 25 ff.), used symbolically for: one who prefers present advantage to permanent rights or interests.

1662 T. BROOKES *Crown & Glory of Christianity* 82 He that is a Cato without, and a Nero within; a Jacob without, and an Esau within..is ripened for the worst of torments. **1822** *Nat. Intelligencer* (Washington) 14 Feb. 2/3 The elder brethren of the confederacy—the political Esaus of our tribe. **1845** BROWNING *Flight of Duchess* xvii, Smooth Jacob still robs homely Esau. **1859** KINGSLEY *Misc.* II. 240 Esau is a dumb soul, especially here in England; but he has as deep a heart in him as Jacob. **1859** THACKERAY *Virginians* II. xxxvi. 297, I turned from Esau, and I clung to Jacob. And now I have my reward, I have my reward! **1888** STEVENSON *Master of Ballantrae* iv. 105 'Ah! Jacob', says the Master. 'So here is Esau back.' **1923** D. L. SAYERS *Whose Body?* ii. 26 It's no good talking as if you were announcing dinner—you're spilling the brandy. The voice is Jacob's voice, but the hands are the hands of Esau.

†**es'batement.** *Obs.* [a. OF. *esbatement*, mod.Fr. *ébattement*, f. *(s')ébattre* to divert (oneself) = Pr. *esbatre*, It. *sbattere*:—late L. type **exbattĕre*, f. *ex* out + *battĕre* to beat. Cf. ABATE.] Amusement, diversion; an amusement. Cf. ABATEMENT 2 b.

1475 CAXTON *Jason* 119 The daye passed and the feste in daunces, carolles and esbatements. **1483** —— *G. de la Tour* xxiii, These wordes are but sport and esbatement of lordes. **1531** ELYOT *Gov.* I. x, If he haue pleasure in wrastling.. where shall he se any more plesant esbatementes than that.

†**esbay,** *v. Obs. rare.* Also 6 **esbaie.** [a. OF. *esbaï-r*, mod.Fr. *(s')ébahir*: see ABASH, of which this is a variant.] *trans.* To cow, dismay.

1480 CAXTON *Ovid's Met.* XIII. xvii, I was moche esbayed and wondred what this might be. **1531** ELYOT, *Gov.* III. xix, Wherwith [the letter of Parmenio] he [Alexander] beinge nothing esbaied, helde in his handes the letter..and dranke also the medicine.

†**esbrandill,** *v. Obs. rare*⁻¹. [ad. Fr. **esbrandeler* (now *ébranler*), f. *es-* (see ES-) + *brandeler*, now *branler* to shake.] *trans.* To shake.

1588 Q. ELIZABETH *Let. to Jas.* 8 Oct. (1849) 159 Never shall dread of any mans behaviour cause me doo ought that may esbrandill the seat that so well is settled.

†**'escal,** *a. Obs.*⁻⁰ [ad. L. *escāl-is*, f. *esca* food.] Pertaining to food; fit to be eaten.

1656–81 in BLOUNT *Glossogr.*; **1775** in ASH.

escalade (ɛskə'leɪd), *sb.* Also 8 **escallade.** [a. Fr. *escalade*, ad. Sp. *escalada* = It. *scalata*, f. It. and med.L. *scalāre* to scale, f. L. *scāla* ladder. Cf. SCALADE, SCALADO.]

1. The action of scaling the walls of a fortified place by the use of ladders; also *transf.* and *fig.*

1598 FLORIO, *Scalada*, an escalade, a scaling of a wall with ladders. **1672** MARVELL *Reh. Transp.* I. 60 He must raze the Fort of S^t. Katherine, and attempt..a second Escalade. **1712** *Lond. Gaz.* No. 5026/5 Two thousand of the Enemy attempted..to take Arrouches by Escallade. **1790** BEATSON *Nav. & Mil. Mem.* I. 180 He prepared ladders for an escalade. **1824** WIFFEN *Tasso* XII. iii, Whilst I..with distant shafts but checked Their eager escalade. **1832** SOUTHEY *Hist. Penins. War* III. 416 Had they been aware how little it [the fort] was injured, they would not have recommended the escalade so soon. **1884** STEVENSON *New Arab. Nts.* 107 The wall had been protected against such an escalade by.. old bottles.

¶**2.** ? *erroneous use.* A series of terraces one above the other, like a staircase. Hence the same writer forms **esca'laded** *a.* [-ED²], formed into an 'escalade'.

1853 KANE *Grinnell Exp.* vi. (1856) 46 The washings of the melted snows had accumulated, in little escalades or terraces, a scanty mould. **1856** —— *Arct. Expl.* II. xiv. 148 The escaladed structure of the Arctic glacier.

escalade (ɛskə'leɪd), *v.* [f. prec. sb.] *trans.* To climb up and get over or enter (a wall, rampart, etc.) by means of ladders; to scale.

1801 WELLINGTON in Gurw. *Disp.* I. 361 They might escalade the outer wall, taking care to carry over some ladders for the purpose of escalading the inner wall. **1839** ALISON *Hist. Europe* (1849) I. iv. 535 A..multitude had already begun..to escalade the parapets.

Hence **esca'lader,** one who escalades. **esca'lading** *vbl. sb.*, in quot. *attrib.*

1849 GROTE *Greece* II. xli. V. 157 The successful escaladers opened the gates to the entire Persian host. **1863** THORNBURY *True as Steel* III. 105 The escaladers were then to advance. **1839–42** ALISON *Hist. Europe* (ed. 8) III. xviii. 557 A loud shout..announced the success of the escalading party.

escalado (ɛskə'lɑːdəʊ). *arch.* Also 6–7 **escalada.** [a. Sp. *escalada* (see ESCALADE); first used in correct form, afterwards with the usual perversion of Sp. *-ada* into -ADO².] = ESCALADE *sb.*

1598 BARRET *Theor. Warres* Gloss. 250 *Escalada*..is the skaling of a wall or fort with ladders. **1600** HOLLAND *Livy* XLII. lxiii. 1152 The Consull..purposed to invest the citie round about with the Escalado. **1625** BACON *Consid. War Spain* (1629) 51 That..we should..haue wonne one Toune of importance by Escalada. **1641** BAKER *Chron.* 67 Using all meanes possible, by Escalado, Battery, and burning the gates, to enter the City. **1859** THACKERAY *Virgin.* lxxii, Tragedies, intrigues, serenades, escaladoes.

escalate ('ɛskəleɪt), *v.* [Back-formation f. ESCALATOR.] **1. a.** *trans.* To climb or reach by means of an escalator. **b.** *intr.* To travel on an escalator.

1922 *Granta* 10 Nov. 93/2, I dreamt I saw a Proctor 'escalating', Rushing up a quickly moving stair. **1927** *Atlantic Monthly* Jan. 48/1 With almost incredible ingenuity we ward off the bumps, plane the sharp corners, 'escalate' the heights. **1959** *Observer* 21 June 14/6 Why does other people's luggage always look so neat and articulate as it comes escalating along at the airport?

2. *fig.* (*trans.* and *intr.*). To increase or develop by successive stages; *spec.* to develop from 'conventional' warfare into nuclear warfare.

1959 *Manch. Guardian* 12 Nov. 1/1 The possibility of local wars 'escalating into all-out atomic wars'. **1961** *Economist* 28 Oct. 317/2 Using tactical nuclear weapons which would be likely to escalate hostilities into a global nuclear war. **1962** *Listener* 29 Mar. 543/2 To keep the Communists from escalating the war to a stage in which they are capable of..taking over the reins of local government themselves. *Ibid.* 549/1 Something short of a deliberate Soviet attack, some sort of accident, some sort of border incident, will escalate so rapidly into nuclear war that we shall be unable to stop it. **1963** *Horizon* (U.S.) July 37/1 The wish of the author to magnify or escalate (favorite new word in Washington) the importance of a trivial utterance by grandiloquent terminology. **1963** *Oxf. Mail* 26 July 6/9 Peace as well as war, can escalate. **1966** *Punch* 28 Sept. 482/2 The animal book boom is terrific and still escalating. **1967** *Listener* 3 Aug. 131/3 Only a tiny percentage of cannabis-smokers escalate to heroin. **1970** *Guardian* 4 June 12/1 The National Council has before it a demand to 'escalate Palestinian action in all fields'.

escalation (ˌɛskə'leɪʃən). [f. ESCALATE *v.* + -TION.] **a.** The act or process of increasing armaments, prices, wages, etc. **b.** An increase or development by successive stages; *spec.* the development of 'conventional' warfare into nuclear warfare, or the use of successively more powerful types of weapons in war.

1938 *Kansas City Star* 29 Mar. 2/4 *Escalation* means the building of bigger battleships when other nations do so. **1947** *Times* 14 Feb. 8/3 Mr. Dalton said that the report [of the War Damage Commission] did advise a certain escalation. **1949** *N.Y. Times* 14 Aug. III. 1/1 Sales contracts permit upward adjustment through 'escalation' as a result of wage increases granted by the vendors. **1959** W. YOUNG *Strategy for Survival* iii. 32 The main argument against this policy is the danger of what strategists call *escalation*, the danger that the size of the weapons used would mount up and up in retaliation until civilization is destroyed. **1959** *New Statesman* 5 Dec. 784/2 The risk of starting the process of escalation towards total war. **1960** *Guardian* 14 Dec. 8/1 The 'escalation' of a minor conventional war into a major nuclear one. **1962** H. KAHN *Thinking about Unthinkable* vi. 185 There is a tendency for each side to counter the other pressure with a somewhat stronger one of its own. This increasing pressure step by step is called 'escalation'. **1964** *Ann. Reg. 1963* 136 In addition both leaders..were anxious to check the increasingly painful escalation of defence costs. **1964** *Financial Times* 23 Mar. 14/3 Shell Oil Company and the Moonie Oil Group have agreed on a price of $2.83 a barrel for Moonie oil without an escalation clause. **1965** *Spectator* 12 Feb. 187/3 A conviction that President Johnson would not risk escalation. **1967** *Ibid.* 21 July 87/1 The case for liberalising the law re marihuana seems almost proven... The doubts remaining are..that it may produce escalation to hard drugs.

escalator ('ɛskəleɪtə(r)). orig. *U.S.* [f. ESCALADE *v.*, after ELEVATOR.]

1. (Orig. a trade-name.) A moving staircase made on the endless-chain principle, so that the steps ascend or descend continuously, for carrying passengers up or down.

1900 *N.Y. Jrnl.* 25 Nov. 59/2 The escalator..is a movable stairway built by the Otis Elevator Company for the use of passengers of the Manhattan Elevated Railway. **1904** *Daily Chron.* 21 Nov. 5/5 [New York] There are to be four elevator shafts, besides stairways and 'escalators'. *a* **1910** 'O. HENRY' *Trimmed Lamp* (1916) 131 You will perceive that the Bee-Hive was not a fashionable department store, with escalators and pompadours. **1910** *Daily News* 2 July 10 In the course of the hearing counsel referred to a proposed moving staircase as an 'escalator'. **1911** *Engineer* 6 Oct. 356/3 The escalator or moving stairway connecting the 'Piccadilly' and District Railway. **1923** *Spectator* 29 Sept. 411/2 Three escalators will serve the Bakerloo Tube. **1968** *Listener* 20 June 817/1 A counterblast to the prurience of *Playboy* and the escalator ads.

b. *fig.*

1927 *British Weekly* 14 Apr. 38/2 The mechanism of a great social 'escalator' whereby the 'down and outs' of Manchester have restored to them the loving ministry of Christian service. **1927** L. MACNEICE in *Oxf. Poetry* 18 And watching the Before become Beyond Down the escalator shifting of the Past. **1943** J. D. HICKS *Short Hist. Amer. Democracy* xxxv. 729 He climbed aboard the political escalator in 1899 when he became a councilman. **1950** *Economist* 9 Dec. 1003/1 Prices and wages are fellow-travellers on the same upward escalator. **1967** D. BOULTON *Objection Overruled* i. 20 The Serbian assassin's shot..put the world on an irreversible escalator to multiple war.

2. *attrib.*, esp. designating a clause, contract, agreement, or the like, that provides for an increase (occas., a decrease) in prices, wages, armaments, etc., to meet specified contingencies.

1930 *N.Y. Times* 18 Apr. 2/1 The so-called safeguarding, or contingency, clause, sometimes referred to as the escalator provision. **1930** *Times* 1 May 16/3 The existence and implications of the 'contingent' or 'escalator' clause of the Treaty are naturally of importance from the American point of view. **1932** *Daily Express* 1 July 9/1 France..wants an 'escalator' clause inserted in the agreement which would link up the war debts to America with this proposed fund. **1948** *Time* 7 June 5/3 Labor leaders have never liked cost-of-living 'escalator' contracts, on the grounds that they tie the worker to a fixed standard of living. **1960** *Farmer & Stockbreeder* 23 Feb. 7/2 Cattle prices are subject to escalator adjustment. **1963** *Economist* 5 Jan. 50/1 'Escalator' mortgages, which deliberately bunch repayment towards the end of the life of the mortgage.

'escaˌlatory, *a.* [f. ESCALATE *v.* + -ORY².] Tending to escalate or increase by successive stages, esp. of the development of nuclear weapons; characteristic of or conducive to escalation.

1965 H. KAHN *On Escalation* xii. 230 A situation is made largely escalatory or de-escalatory by the net balance of these elements. **1968** *N.Y. Times* 13 Mar. 46 These escalatory measures may be necessary, it is argued, in order to strengthen our increasingly difficult position in South Vietnam. **1980** *Sci. Amer.* Apr. 42/2 NATO's chemical weapons would add little to the deterrence of chemical warfare unless the retaliation threatened were highly escalatory. **1983** *Times* 8 Jan. 7/6 What factor, other than any proposed by CND, has a good chance of changing the escalatory effect of Russian/American insistence that new weaponry is justified because it will enable the possessor to negotiate reduction from strength?

†**e'scale,** *v. Obs. rare*⁻¹. [var. of SCALE *v.*]

1579 FENTON *Guicciard.* VI. 301 Vsing the seruice of eskaling ladders, they commaunded the wall.

†**escaline.** *Obs.* [ad. F. *escalin*, ad. Du. *schelling*, Ger. *schilling* SHILLING.] A Flemish coin.

1674 *Lond. Gaz.* No. 904/4, 2 or 300 Lewises of Gold, 32 Escalines of Gold.

escalion (ɛ'skæliən). *rare.* = SCALLION.

1847 GOSSE *Birds of Jamaica* 312 They are fond of picking about the beds of shallots and escalions.

‖**Escallonia** (ɛskə'ləʊnɪə). [mod.Lat. f. *Escallon* the name of the discoverer.] A genus of flowering shrubs (N.O. *Saxifragaceæ*) found in the temperate parts of South America.

1882 *Garden* 29 Apr. 292/1 Escallonias are useful. **1884** *Daily News* 2 Sept. 2/1 Looking on a summer sea from.. terraces lined with laurel, fuchsia, and escalonia.

escallop (ɛ'skæləp). Also 7 **escollop,** 7–8 **escalop.** [a. OF. *escalope* shell, an adoption from some Teut. lang.; cf. MDu. *schelpe* (mod.Du. *schelp*) shell. The variant SCALLOP is found much earlier, and is still in use.]

1. A bivalve mollusc of the genus *Pecten*; = SCALLOP 1.

1610 GUILLIM *Heraldry* III. xxiii. (1660) 238 The Escallop (according to Dioscorides) is engendred of the Dew and Ayre. **1677** PLOT *Oxfordsh.* 78 The stone is stuck full of Cockles, Escallops, and Oysters. **1886** *Daily News* 24 Dec. 2/6 Escallops, 6d. per dozen.

2. *Her.* = ESCALLOP-SHELL.

1671 J. WEBSTER *Metallogr.* i. 21 Shillings marked with an Escalope. **1708** J. CHAMBERLAYNE *St. Gt. Brit.* II. III. x. (1743) 429 The point of the sword [is] formed like an escalop flourished. **1864** BOUTELL *Heraldry Hist. & Pop.* xv. (ed. 3.) 184 Three escallops or.

3. One of a series of segments of circles forming a 'scalloped' edge. More usually SCALLOP.

1691 RAY *Creation* (1714) 102 The figure of the leaves.. divided into so many jags or Escallops.

4. *Comb.* **escallop-basin,** a basin made in the form of an escallop shell.

1644 EVELYN *Mem.* (1819) I. 44 Before this grotto is a long poole into which ran divers spouts of water from leaden escollop basins.

escalloped (ɛ'skæləpt), *ppl. a.* [f. **escallop* vb. (= SCALLOP *v.*) + -ED¹.] An alternative (but now less frequent) form of SCALLOPED.

1. Having the border or edge cut in 'scallops' or segments of circles; = SCALLOPED 1.

1611 SPEED *Hist. Gt. Brit.* IX. xii. §82 Now Burgundians scorne their Fliece of Gold; The French, th' Escalopt Collar set with grace. **1672** GREW *Idea Philos. Hist. Plants* (1682) 3 Leaves are Long or Round, Even-edg'd or Escallop'd, and many other ways different. **1842** *Blackw. Mag.* LI. 727 They only succeed..by cross beams and escalloped wedges jambed in between them and their coronets. **1885** R. HEATH in *Mag. Art.* Sept. 481/2 The ladies wore escalloped laced 'heads', mostly English.

b. *Her.*

1720 STRYPE *Stow's Surv.* II. v. xiv. 320/2 His robe turned down about his neck Azure, Escaloped.

2. Of oysters: = SCALLOPED 2. *rare.*

1880 HOWELLS *Undisc. Country* 14 A person you might help to escalloped oysters or ice-cream at an evening party.

e'scallop-'shell. = SCALLOP-SHELL.

1. The shell of the escallop, usually a single valve of the shell.

Pilgrims returning from the shrine of St. James at Compostella were accustomed to wear an escallop-shell found on the Galician shore; hence, this shell (in ecclesiastical symbolism used as the emblem of the apostle) is often referred to as the distinctive badge of a pilgrim.

1628 COKE *On Litt.* Pref., The Senators of Rome did weare bracelets of Escalop shelles about their armes. **1634** PEACHAM *Gentl. Exerc.* II. iv. 116 Upon her [Thetis'] head a Coronet of Periwinkle and Escallop shelles. **1644** EVELYN *Mem.* (1857) I. 101 The piazza..being made with descending steps, much resembles the figure of an escalop-shell. **1835** KIRBY *Hab. & Inst. Anim.* I. viii. 254 None are more beautiful..than.. Escallop shells or Comb shells. **1846** PRESCOTT *Ferd. & Is.* I. vi. 283 The escallop-shell, the device of St. James, was adopted as the universal badge of the palmer.

2. An imitation of a scallop shell used for ornamental purposes; *esp.* in the collar of the order of St. Michael.

1664 EVELYN *Acc. Architects* (R.), With such ornament and decoration as best becomes them: as to Nymphs.. escalop-shells. **1864** J. WOODWARD in *N. & Q.* V. 184 The collar of this order was composed of escallop shells.

3. *Her.* The figure of an escallop borne as a charge.

1610 GUILLIM *Heraldry* III. xxiii. (1611) 171 He beareth Argent, an Escallop shell gules by the name of Prelate. **1628** COKE *On Litt.* Pref., A Cheuron betwene three Escalop shelles Sable. **1766–87** PORNY *Heraldry* 175 Three Escallop-shells Pearl. **1864** BOUTELL *Heraldry Hist. & Pop.* xv. 192 The escallop shells appear again upon the shield of De Bigot.

escalope ('ɛskələʊp). Also escalop, escallope. [OF. *escalope* shell: see ESCALLOP.] Thin slices of boneless meat (occas. of fish), prepared in various ways; *esp.* a special cut of veal taken from the leg.

1828 LYTTON *Pelham* III. viii. 128 You have neither applauded my jokes, nor tasted my *escallopes*. **1845** BREGION & MILLER *Pract. Cook* 41 *Escalopes*, small pieces of meat cut in the form of some kind of coin. **1877** E. S. DALLAS *Kettner's Book of Table* 179 Many cooks here..begin to speak of escalopes of veal and of other meat. **1894** C. RANHOFER *Epicurean* 690 Escalops of tenderloin of beef with truffles. **1900** S. BEATY-POWNALL *'Queen' Cookery Bk.* IV. ii. 16 These [entrées]..are also termed *escalopes*,.. *médaillons*, &c... These latter terms are nowadays more frequently applied to beef or veal, or even fish, than to mutton. **1956** R. FROST in J. C. Trewin *Plays of Year 1955* XIII. 154 It says here that this is an escalope of veal Viennoise. In the appalling bilingual jargon of small hotels that means to say that it's a Wiener Schnitzel. **1959** R. POSTGATE *Good Food Guide* 97 One member notes for special praise the escalope Holstein at 6/-. **1963** *Listener* 24 Jan. 187/2 The veal escallops are cooked in cider for half an hour.

†e'scandalize, *v. Obs.* In 6 -ise. [ad. Sp. *escandalizar*:—late L. *scandalizāre*.] = SCANDALIZE.

1574 HELLOWES *Gueuara's Fam. Ep.* 242 Before they..do justice they shall escandalise the common wealth. **1640** R. BRATHWAIT *Boulster Lect.* 100 By jesting I have many times escandalized another.

escapable (ɛ'skeɪpəb(ə)l), *a.* [f. ESCAPE *v.* + -ABLE.] That can be escaped.

1864 in WEBSTER; and in mod. Dicts.

escapade (ɛskə'peɪd). [a. Fr. *escapade*, ad. Sp. or Pr. *escapada*, f. *escapar*: see ESCAPE *v.*]

1. An act of escaping from confinement or restraint; a runaway excursion.

1653 URQUHART *Rabelais* I. iv, I wish your bum-gut [may] fall out and make an escapade. **1815** SCOTT *Guy M.* xxxvi, His second escapade was made for the purpose of visiting the field of Rullion-green. **1868** E. EDWARDS *Raleigh* I. iv. 74 He tried..an escapade to the Low Countries..in a ship which lay..at Sandwich.

b. *fig.* A breaking loose from restraint or rules; a flighty piece of conduct.

1814 SCOTT *Wav.* xxxiv, A youthful escapade, which might be easily atoned. **1827** A. FONBLANQUE *Eng. under Seven Administr.* (1837) I. 80 A young nobleman..commits an escapade (the name given to the offences of persons of quality). **1862** MRS. H. WOOD *Mrs. Halib.* II. xxiii, Anna could have died rather than suffer her escapade to reach the ears of home. **1885** *Manch. Exam.* 15 May 5/3 Lord R. Churchill's latest escapade..is the theme of general remark.

†2. Of a horse: A throwing off of control; a fit of plunging and rearing. *Obs. rare.*

1673 DRYDEN *Conq. Granada* I. i, His fiery Arab..Sprung loose, and flew into an Escapade.

‖escapado[1] (eska'pado). [Sp.; pa. pple. of *escapar* to ESCAPE.] An escaped prisoner.

1881 MAYNE REID *Free Lances* I. ix. 94 The retaken escapadoes had been brought back.

esca'pado[2]. *rare*$^{-1}$. Pseudo-foreign form of ESCAPADE.

1849 JAMES *Woodman* xxxvi, Know you aught of this escapado, Signor Chartley.

†e'scapal. *Obs. rare.* [f. ESCAPE *v.* + -AL[1].] An escape.

1634 W. WOOD *New Eng. Prosp.* II. i. 58 [He] fled through the woods and came to his native home where he still lives to rehearse his happie escapall.

escape (ɪ'skeɪp), *sb.*[1] Also 4–5 eschap(e. [f. ESCAPE *v.*; cf. OF. *eschap* (perh. the source in 14th c.), Sp. *escape*.]

1. a. The action of escaping, or the fact of having escaped, from custody, danger, etc.; *spec.* in *Law*: see quot. 1641.

α. *c* **1300** *K. Alis.* 4287 For that eschape they beon anoyed sore. **1375** BARBOUR *Bruce* II. 65 He wes off his eschap sary. **1417** BP. CLIFFORD in Ellis *Orig. Lett.* II. 29. I. 90 Foryevyng me graciously the eschapes of the clerkes convictes out of my prison of Storteford.

β. **1596** SHAKS. *Tam. Shr.* I. i. 235 Your fellow Tranio.. Puts my apparrell..on, And I for my escape haue put on his. **1611** BIBLE *Ps.* lv. 8, I would hasten my escape from the windie storme, and tempest. **1614** B. JONSON *Barth. Fair* IV. iv, What, has he made an escape! which way? follow, neighbour Haggise. **1641** *Termes de la Ley* 142 Escape is where one that is arrested commeth to his liberty before that he be delivered by award of any Justice, or by order of Law. **1659** HAMMOND *On Ps.* lxviii. 20. Paraphr. 330 To him we owe all our escapes. **1698** LUDLOW *Mem.* I. 221 No sooner was the King's Escape taken notice of by the Guards. **1713** ADDISON *Guardian* (J.), Men of virtue have had extraordinary escapes out of such dangers as have enclosed them. **1769** BLACKSTONE *Comm.* III. 415 When a defendant is once in custody upon this process [*ca. sa.*]..if he be afterwards seen at large, it is an *escape*. **1777** PRIESTLEY *Matt. & Spir.* (1782) I. xx. 267 An igneous substance, which..makes its escape at death. **1848** MACAULAY *Hist. Eng.* II. 171 His escape was attributed partly to his own singular equanimity, and partly to, etc. **1878** BROWNING *La Saisiaz* 65 Yet is..forbidden premature escape from time.

b. *fig.* Mental or emotional distraction, esp. by way of literature or music, from the realities of life.

1853 DICKENS in *Househ. Words*, extra Xmas no. 35/2 Labouring people..in need of mental refreshment and recreation... Come! Amuse me harmlessly, show me something, give me an escape! **1919** *English Rev.* Mar. 183 It has been said by Mr. Arthur Symons that 'all art is a mode of escape'. **1923** *Time* 14 Apr. 14/3 For the cities are saturated with the literature of escape. **1933** *Amer. Speech* VIII. III. 34/1 Those who use drugs merely as an escape-mechanism while incarcerated. **1934** *Punch* 18 Apr. 440/1 *Libel* makes no pretence to belong to any other class than it is now the contemptuous fashion to call the literature of escape. **1942** *Sphere* 25 July 120/1 Music always enjoys a boom in wartime. It acts as a magic carpet, as an escape. **1954** M. F. RODELL *Mystery Fiction* (ed. 2) ii. 4 Mysteries belong to the vast category of escape fiction. **1969** *Islander* (Victoria, B.C.) 16 Nov. 16/3 But far from being escape reading, these fantasties often make more penetrating comments on the 'real' world than realistic fiction does.

c. The action of escaping from the region where the gravitational force of a planet is predominant. Usu. *attrib.* (See 8 below.)

1947 *Jrnl. Aeronaut. Sci.* XIV. 471 (*heading*) The problem of escape from the earth by rocket.

2. *concr.* **a.** A plant that has 'escaped' from cultivation, a garden plant growing wild.

1870 HOOKER *Stud. Flora* 16 *Chelidonium majus*..in the S. of England, elsewhere an obvious escape. **1887** W. R. HAYWARD *Botanist's Pocket-bk.* Pref. (ed. 5) 4 In many cases they [alien plants] are escapes from gardens.

b. *U.S.* An escaped person, a fugitive.

1881 *Philada. Record* No. 3464. 4 All the Chinese in this country, excepting officials, were escapes.

c. A bird that has escaped from captivity.

1937 *Brit. Birds* XXXI. 27 There is no reason to think this bird an escape as the place is very remote. **1953** D. A. BANNERMAN *Birds Brit. Isles* I. 108 There is a doubt as to whether they were genuine wild birds or merely 'escapes' from captivity.

3. A means of escape. In FIRE-ESCAPE; and short for that word.

1810 *Trans. Soc. Arts* XXVIII. 177 If every parish would provide one of these escapes..it would lessen the many accidents which occur by fire. **1887** *Daily News* 16 May 6/2 The fire brigade ran out a couple of their escapes.

4. a. The escaping of water, gases, etc. from confinement; in recent use *esp.* a leakage of gas, electricity, etc.

1874 KNIGHT *Dict. Mech.* I. 808 *Escape* (*Telegraphy*), leakage of current from the line-wire to the ground, caused usually by defective insulation and contact with partial conductors. *a* **1891** *Mod.* There is an escape of gas in the kitchen.

†b. *euphemistically.* (More commonly SCAPE.)

1599 HARSNET *Agst. Darell* 41 Hee meeting Alice Goodridge in a Coppice did Let an Escape (as the book termeth it) which shee taking to be done in her contempt, etc.

c. An outlet for a liquid; *esp.* a sluice or gate for the outlet of surplus water in a canal. Also *attrib.*, as ***escape drain, head, water.***

1889 W. WILLCOCKS *Egypt. Irrig.* ii. 80 The Ibrahimia Canal regulator lock works except when silt deposit interferes. The escape headlock does not work. **1891** *Daily News* 31 Oct. 6/4 The Koshesha Escape, or Barrage... The escape is constructed to discharge 2,000 million cubic metres in twenty days in good Nile years. **1893** *Pall Mall Gaz.* 30 Jan. 3/1 The revolution of these caps whips the skim-milk through a broad escape. **1907** W. G. BLIGH *Irrig. Wks.* x. 274 In places on a canal where an Escape or a Branch takes off, a regulating bridge across both works is generally necessary. *Ibid.* 280 An Escape Head should, if practicable, be combined with a fall. **1911** W. WILLCOCKS *Irrig. Mesopot.* 27 Every canal system needs its escapes. **1913** WILLCOCKS & CRAIG *Egypt. Irrig.* (ed. 3) II. viii. 465 The escape waters of the canals and larger water-courses should be allowed to enter the escape-drain by means of regulators at the tails of the canals.

†5. An involuntary outburst of feeling; a sally of wit. *Obs.*

1603 SHAKS. *Meas. for M.* IV. i. 63 Thousand escapes of wit Make thee the father of their idle dreame, And racke thee in their fancies. **1670** COTTON *Espernon* III. XII. 623 Excusing himself for that little escape of his resentment. **1796** BURKE *Regic. Peace* Wks. 1842 II. 314 Their views were only discovered now and then, in heat and as by escapes, but on this occasion they exploded suddenly.

†6. a. An inadvertence, blunder, mistake; *esp.* a clerical or printer's error. *Obs.*

1563–87 FOXE *A. & M.* (1684) II. 469 The book itself sheweth the escape and biddeth instead of four to read three. **1590** SWINBURNE *Testaments* Epil., There be sundrie escapes in the print. **1642** JER. TAYLOR *Episc.* To Rdr., The Printer thinkes it the best instance of pardon if his Escapes be not laid upon the Author. **1680** R. FILMER *Patriarcha* ii. §1 This negligence, or wilful escape of Lambine, in not translating a word. **1721** *Wodrow Corr.* (1843) II. 613 There are several other variations between the 8vo and the quartos; but they seem literal escapes. **1786** COWPER *Wks.* (1837) XV. 187 Some escapes will happen in so long a work. **1803** S. PEGGE *Anecd. Eng. Lang.* (1844) 134 Many grammatical escapes and errors. **1844** DARWIN in *Life & Lett.* (1887) II. 30 Now you may quiz me for so foolish an escape of mouth.

†b. An unstudied or artless peformance.

1667 DRYDEN *Sir Mart. Mar-all* II. i, I am wholly ignorant of painting, music, and poetry; only some rude escapes.

†7. An inconsiderate transgression; a peccadillo, venial error. (In Shaks. with different notion: an outrageous transgression.) Applied *esp.* to breaches of chastity. *Obs.*

1576 WOOLTON *Chr. Manual* (1851) 74 Yet God, such is his goodness, winketh (as it were) at such escapes. **1588** SHAKS. *Tit. A.* IV. ii. 113 Rome will despise her for this foul escape. **1596** LODGE *Marg. Amer.* 37 The escapes of Jupiter, the wanton delights of Venus, and the amorous deceits of Cupid. **1611** COTGR., *Peccadille*, an escape, little sinne, small fault, venial offence. **1614** WITHER *Sat. to King* Juvenilia (1633) 339 If her escapes I had not chanced to tell. **1678** BARCLAY *Apol. Quakers* 468 O! how will they insult, and make more noise of the escape of one Quaker, than of an hundred among themselves.

8. *Comb.* **escape clause**, a clause in a formal or legal document that specifies the conditions under which a contracting party is free from obligations; **escape-cock** (see quot.); **escape committee**, a group of prisoners that plans and co-ordinates escapes from a prisoner-of-war camp, prison, etc.; **escape hatch**, an emergency exit in a ship, submarine, or aircraft; also *fig.*; **escape-pinion**, the pinion on the escape-wheel arbor; **escape-pipe**, the pipe through which steam passes from an escape-valve; **escape rocket** (see quots.); **escape-shaft**, a shaft provided for the escape of miners in case of the ordinary shaft becoming blocked; **escape-valve**, a valve fitted to the boiler, cylinder, or other part of a steam-engine, to provide for the exit of steam or water when necessary; **escape velocity** (of space vehicles, etc.), a speed sufficient to overcome the gravitational force of a planet; also ***escape speed***; **escape-warrant**, a process addressed to all sheriffs, etc. throughout England, to retake an escaped prisoner, even on a Sunday, and commit him to proper custody (Wharton); **escape-wheel**, the wheel that forms part of the escapement in a watch, called also *escapement-wheel.*

1945 *Time* 5 Nov. 29 These prohibitive terms were eased a bit..by an *escape clause under which interest could be postponed in years when Britain had an unfavorable balance of trade. **1948** *Ann. Reg. 1947* 72 There were so many necessary 'escape clauses' that the importance of a permanent organisation to supervise the working of them was apparent. **1966** M. R. D. FOOT *SOE in France* xi. 363 He was given a long list of instructions to carry out in France, but a pair of escape clauses let him omit any that were inconvenient. **1971** *Where* Sept. 279/1 Pretty well all universities and colleges have some escape clause in their entrance regulations by which they can avoid having to turn away somebody they wish to admit merely because of a lack of formal qualifications. **1884** F. J. BRITTEN *Watch & Clockm.* 62 *Escape cock is the bracket that supports the upper end of the escape wheel and pallet staff arbors. [**1946** BRICKHILL & NORTON *Escape to Danger* xxvii. 238 An escape assistance committee was set up in the first few days at North Compound.] **1952** M. GILBERT *Death in Captivity* ii. 32 Colonel Baird was head of the *Escape Committee. **1974** *Times* 21 Jan. 12/3 The Provisionals long ago set up an escape committee with a representative in each detainee's compound. **1925** *Sci. Amer.* Dec. 373 The submarine.. carried four torpedo tubes at the forward end of the torpedo room, which was provided with an *escape hatch. **1940** *Flight* 17 Oct. 332/1 He could have followed the rear gunner through the bottom escape hatch. **1948** R. DE KERCHOVE *Internat. Maritime Dict.* 244/1 *Escape hatch*, 1. A small hatch ..in a 'tween-deck or weather deck for the safe exit of men engaged in trimming or stowing coal or grain. **1955** *Sci. News Let.* 6 Aug. 86/1 The continuous reconnaissance of people and traffic, preferably from the air for maximum scanning of 'escape hatches'. **1962** W. NOWOTTNY *Lang. Poets Use* iv. 84 These crucial words..may serve as escape-hatches from conceptual terms. **1884** F. J. BRITTEN *Watch & Clockm.* 68 When the verge has an *escape pinion of 6, use an escape pinion of 7. **1817** COLERIDGE *Lay Serm.* 425 Superfluous steam ejected by the *escape pipes..of a self-regulating machine. **1878** HUXLEY *Physiogr.* 39 The dense

clouds of steam which roll forth from..the escape-pipe of a steam-engine. **1951** *Flight* 3 Aug. 141/2 The propellant thus assembled, being stored at a high fraction of escape velocity, will represent a substantial energy potential and its transfer into a single '*escape rocket' will mean that this vehicle supports itself only from the time it leaves the terminal orbit. **1963** M. Caidin *Man-in-Space Dict.* 76/2 *Escape rocket*, a rocket used in a system to ensure the escape of an astronaut from a booster in the event of malfunctioning. **1889** *Pall Mall G.* 22 Apr. 3/1 A cube shaft fulfils the requirements of the Act as an *escape shaft. **1951** *Tuscaloosa News* 16 Oct. 4/6 The problem of reaching the moon is basically that of getting rockets to fly fast enough to attain an '*escape' speed—an escape speed being about 23,000 miles an hour—sufficient to escape from the pull of the earth's gravity. **1850** Mrs. Stowe *Uncle Tom's C.* xxiii, Fasten down the *escape-valve, and sit on it, and see where you'll land. **1934** *Space* (Cleveland) I. iv. 1 The equation for *escape velocity is derived from the equation for the orbital velocity of a particle about a mass. **1945** H. S. Zim *Rockets & Jets* 207 Calculations based on the law of falling bodies indicate that a speed of about seven miles per second or 25,000 per hour is essential before 'escape velocity' is attained. **1954** Escape velocity [see astronaut 2]. **1959** *Listener* 22 Jan. 161/1 The Moon has a diameter of only 2,160 miles, and an escape velocity of one and a half miles per second. **1751** Smollett *Per. Pic.* (1779) IV. xcvi. 184, I kept snug and laughed at his *escape-warrant. **1884** F. J. Britten *Watch & Clockm.* 58 The *escape wheel is of hard hammered brass.

escape (ɪ'skeɪp), *sb.*² *Arch.* [a. Fr. *escape*, earlier *escappe* (Godef.), ad. L. *scapus*: see scape².] Properly, the shaft of a column; but (through confusion with escape *sb.*¹) explained in Dicts. as = apophyge.

1846 Parker *Gloss. Archit.* (1875) 109 *Escape*, term used sometimes for the Apophyge. **1850** Weale *Dict. Terms*, *Escape*, the scape of a column in architecture.

escape (ɪ'skeɪp), *v.* Forms: α. 4–5 **eschape**, 6 *Sc.* **eschaip**, **echap**. See also achape, aschape, chape, schape. β. (4 **esscape**, ? 5 **eskepe**, 6 **eskape**), 4– **escape**. See also ascape, atscape, ofscape, scape. [ME. *eschape* is a. Central OF. *eschaper* (mod.F. *échapper*), and ME. *escape* is a. ONF. *escaper* (mod. Picard *écaper*), corresp. to Pr., Sp., Pg. *escapar*, It. *scappare*:—late L. type **excappāre*, f. *ex* out + *cappa* cloak. (For the sense, Diez compares Gr. ἐκδύεσθαι to put off one's clothes, to escape.) The earliest forms recorded in Eng. appear to be ascape (after the ONF. variant *ascaper*) and the aphetic scape, which occur in 13th c.; the former survived until 16th c.; the latter continued in ordinary use until 17th c., and as a poetic archaism (often written '*scape*) is still employed. In 14th c. the forms of Central Fr. origin, *eschape*, aschape, achape, aphetically schape, chape, are of frequent occurrence, esp. in northern writers, while in southern use the forms from Northern Fr., *escape*, ascape, scape, were more common. After 15th c. the former type is found only in Sc. writers, finally disappearing in 17th c. The forms atscape, ofscape, occasional in 13–14th c., appear to be due to a confusion of the initial *a-* in *ascape* with the prepositional prefix in synonymous Eng. vbs.

In Fr. the vb. *échapper* has always remained intransitive. The development of the trans. senses in Eng. was assisted by the formal coincidence of the dative and the accusative; cf. also such constructions as 'to be banished the country'. Formerly the vb. was often conjugated with *be*, not only when intrans. (as still sometimes *arch.*) but also when transitive.]

1. a. *intr.* To gain one's liberty by flight; to get free from detention or control, or from an oppressive or irksome condition. Const. *from*, †*of*, *out of*.

α. [**1292** Britton 27 Si il le face si negligaument garder qe il eschape]. *c* **1340** *Cursor M.* 5277 (Fairf.) Vnneþe eschaped I [Joseph, from the pit]. **1490** Caxton *Eneydos* xxxii. (1890) 120 And alle thus eschaped dedalus oute of the pryson of Mynos kynge of Crete.

β. *c* **1330** R. Brunne *Chron.* (1810) 201 Þat of his anguys grim so lightly was escaped. *c* **1385** Chaucer *L.G.W.* 2643 *Hypermestre*, Thow nescapist nought Out of my paleis, or that thou be deed. *c* **1392** —— *Compl. Venus* 50 For tescape [MS. *T.* teschape] oute of youre lace. **1529** More *Comf. agst. Trib.* iii. Wks. 1243/1 Such sure watch layd vpon him that he cannot eskape. **1598** Shaks. *Merry W.* iv. ii. 73 He might put on a hat, a muffler, and a kerchiefe, and so escape. **1722** Wollaston *Relig. Nat.* ix. 216 That it once had an inhabitant, and that he is escaped out of it. **1828** Scott *F.M. Perth* xx, How we shall prevent the guilty person from escaping in the interim. **1841** Lane *Arab. Nts.* I. 91 The beast also escaped from before his eyes in the desert.

b. Of organisms, fluids, etc.: To issue, find egress, from some confining envelope or enclosure.

c **1450** *Castle Hd. Life St. Cuthb.* (Surtees) 4263 All þe bolnyng was eschaped. **1825** Nicholson *Operat. Mechanic* 159 There is a cloth hood..to prevent the finer particles of flour from escaping. **1839** Todd *Cycl. Anat.* II. 409/2 The young escape fully formed through stomachal orifice. **1849** Mrs. Somerville *Connex. Phys. Sc.* xxxii. 362 Common electricity escapes when the pressure of the atmosphere is removed. **1882** *Garden* 18 Mar. 189/2 At the time of flowering the leaves are only escaping from their buds.

c. Of time: To slip away. *rare.*

1836 Marryat *Japhet* lxxix, After two delightful hours had escaped, I returned home to the hotel.

d. *fig.* To avoid or retreat from the realities of life. (Cf. escape *sb.*¹ 1 b.)

1939 *Punch* 20 Dec. 675/2 Many a publisher has had the good idea of advising you to escape really thoroughly by way of an eight hundred-and-fifty page novel about family life in the Victorian era.

e. Of a space-craft: to attain sufficient velocity to enable it to overcome the gravitational force of a planet.

1947 *Jrnl. Aeronaut. Sci.* XIV. 471/1 The problem of imparting to a..pay load the..velocity to escape from the earth is re-examined. **1949** *Jrnl. Brit. Interplanetary Soc.* VIII. 79 A spaceship will escape from Earth at 11·2 kilometres a second.

†**2. a.** *trans.* To effect one's flight from (prison); to free oneself from (a person's grasp or control); to get safely out of (painful or dangerous conditions).

α. **1340** Hampole *Pr. Consc.* 2678 Þan may he eschape and passe lightly þe bitter payn of purgatory. **1375** Barbour *Bruce* ii. 64 Thai tauld the king than hale the cas, And how that he eschapyt was.

β. **1393** Gower *Conf.* II. 36 How they the prison might escape [in which they were then confined]. *c* **1430** *Syr Gener.* (Roxb.) 593 Suffre he shal grete travaile, And wele escape it he shal. **1664** Evelyn *Kal. Hort.* (1729) 228 The most tender..Plants did outlive and escape those rigorous seasons. **1667** Milton *P.L.* iii. 14 Thee I re-visit now with bolder wing, Escap't the Stygian Pool.

b. To issue unawares or involuntarily from (a person, his lips); to be uttered inadvertently by.

Perhaps the obj. was originally dative, in which case this use belongs historically to sense 1. Cr. Fr. *il lui est échappé une sottise*.

α. ? *a* **1400** *Morte Arth.* 1020 That the no wordez eschape, whate so be-tydez.

β. **1823** Lamb *Elia* Ser. ii. xix. (1865) 372 But his sea songs seldomer escape him. **1836** J. Grant *Random Recoll. Ho. Lords* xv. 366 Never did personality, or anything calumniatory of an opponent escape his lips. **1846** Ruskin *Mod. Paint.* I. i. i. i. §5 The feeling and fondness which I have for some works of modern art escape me sometimes where they should not. **1870** E. Peacock *Ralf Skirl.* III. 191 No word of courtesy escaped his lips.

3. a. *intr.* To get off safely when pursued or imperilled; to avoid capture, punishment, or any threatened evil; to go unhurt or unpunished.

α. *c* **1400** Maundev. (Roxb.) xxxi. 139 Þai eschape withouten harme of body. **1588** A. King tr. *Canisius' Catech.* 36 Quha can eschaip? *Ibid.* 143 Præsumption of gods mercie to echap for sinne vnpunished.

β. *c* **1330** R. Brunne *Chron.* (1810) 122 ȝif any lewed man laid hand opon clerk..He suld not escape. *c* **1340** *Cursor M.* 23322 (Fairf.) Þai ar escapid of þat care. *c* **1386** Chaucer *Monk's T.* 654 But swich a reyn doun fro the welkne shadde That slow the fyr and made hym to escape. **1398** Trevisa *Barth. De P.R.* ix. xxv. (1495) 362 Whan nyght comyth vpon theim that ben in peryll of wracke, vnethe they may escape. **1541** *Act 33 Hen. VIII*, c. 12. §1 Somtime their offences..escape vnpunished. **1590** Spenser *F.Q.* iii. v. 14 Yet not escaped from the due reward Of his bad deedes, which daily he increast. **1611** Bible *Acts* xxvii. 44 They escaped all safe to land. **1618** Donne *Serm.* cxliii. V. 560 He may escape with his life. **1651** Hobbes *Leviath.* ii. xxvii. 155 Death, from which he sees not how to escape. **1725** Watts *Logic* (J.), Laws are not executed, men of virtue are disgraced, and murderers escape. **1881** P. Brooks *Candle of Lord* 270 There are many troubles from which it is better for a man not to escape than to escape wrongly.

†**b.** To recover from dangerous sickness. *Obs.*

Cf. Fr. *échapper*, 'se tirer d'une maladie, guérir' (Littré).

1464 *Paston Lett.* No. 490 II. 160 He is ded, or ellys ryght seke and not lyke to eskape. **1479** *Ibid.* No. 836 III. 251 My grandam is dyssessed..Myn uncle had a messenger ȝesterday that she shuld not escape.

4. *trans.* To get clear away from (pursuit or a pursuer); to elude (a person's grasp); to succeed in avoiding (anything painful or unwelcome).

α. *a* **1340** Hampole *Psalter* xxxiii. 14 Turnynge fra ill eschapis dampnacioun. **1450** Somner in *Four C. Eng. Lett.* 4 If he myght eschape the daunger of the Towr he should be saffe. **1549** *Compl. Scot.* Prol. (1873) 17, I hef rehersit thir vordis, in hope to eschaipt the detractione of invyful gramariaris. **1552** Abp. Hamilton *Catech.* (1884) 25 That ye may eschaip the dangerous thirldome and captivite of the devil.

β. **1393** Gower *Conf.* III. 35 He may nought the deth escape. **1514** Barclay *Cyt. & Uplondyshm.* (Percy Soc.) p. lv, If the court were close continually Some men should escape great payne and misery. *a* **1547** Surrey *Æneid* ii. 1054 Thrice did my hands vain hold th' image escape. **1559** *Mirr. Mag.*, *Worcester* xi, Shall not eskape Gods vengeaunce. **1578** Timme *Calvin on Gen.* 205 They might know that they were escaped a thousand deaths. **1597** Daniel *Civ. Wares* (1609) vii. 16 His owne person eagerly pursu'd Hardly (by Boate) escap't the multitude. **1669** Sturmy *Mariner's Mag.* C iiij, In a Work of this Nature it is impossible to escape Mistakes. **1751** Johnson *Rambler* No. 96 ¶14 Truth was easily escaped by the oblique and desultory movements..which Falsehood always practised. **1751** Jortin *Serm.* (1771) I. iii. 45 He seems to have escaped suspicion. **1870** L'Estrange *Miss Mitford* I. v. 120 They cannot expect to escape being laughed at.

5. a. To elude (observation, search, etc.); to elude the notice of (a person). Also *absol.*

1594 Hooker *Eccl. Pol.* ii. vii. (1611) 72 Many things escape them. *a* **1668** Denham (J.), 'Tis still the same, although their airy shape All but a quick poetick sight escape. **1670** Cotton *Espernon* Pref., This History may suffer..by the Faults escap'd the Press. **1698** Ludlow *Mem.* I. 122 Things..so well conceal'd that they escaped the Search of the Enemy. **1711** Addison *Spect.* No. 129 ¶3, I..have leisure to make many Observations that escape the Notice of my Fellow-Travellers. **1821** J. Q. Adams in Davies *Metr. Syst.* iii. (1871) 174 It cannot escape observation, that, etc. **1847** L. Hunt *Jar Honey* Pref. 12 How came Shakspeare to let such a subject escape him? **1860** Tyndall *Glac.* ii. xxxii. 416 A fact, the significance of which had previously escaped me.

b. To elude (a person's recollection).

1696 Hope tr. *Solleysel's Mareschal* 4 Lest it might have escaped my memory, I here set it down. **1865** Dickens *Mut. Fr.* i. ii, The name of which escapes me. *Mod.* The matter quite escaped my memory.

escapee (ɛskə'piː, ɛ'skeɪpiː). [f. escape *v.* + -ee.] One who has escaped; *esp.* (*a*) an escaped convict from a penal settlement; (*b*) an escaped military or political prisoner.

1875–6 W. Whitman *Mem. War* 40 Southern Escapees. **1880** *Melbourne Argus* 22 July 2/3 The 10 New Caledonia escapees..are to be handed over to the French consul. **1884** *Manch. Guard.* 9 Sept. 5 Some of the worst crimes have been committed in the colonies by escapees. **1902** *Westm. Gaz.* 21 Aug. 3/1 The military watched him in his home in Middelburg as a cat watches a mouse, and..traps in the way of sham rebels and escapees were laid for him. **1945** *News Chron.* 20 Apr. 4/4 A large number of the escapees were members of air crews who had baled out over France. **1954** Koestler *Invisible Writing* iv. xxxix. 421 The five of us, plus some fifty other escapees.

escapeful (ɪ'skeɪpfʊl), *a.* [f. escape *sb.* or *v.* + -ful.] Giving a chance of escape.

1883 *Longm. Mag.* Aug. 367 Is there no help at all..and no escapeful way?

escapeless (ɪ'skeɪplɪs), *a.* [f. as prec. + -less.] Without escape; that cannot be escaped.

1855 *Tait's Mag.* XXII. 552 It presses with all the weight of an escapeless fate. **1856** Ruskin *Mod. Paint.* III. iv. xv. §5 A chasm as utterly hopeless and escapeless as any into which Dante gazed.

escapement (ɪ'skeɪpmənt). See also scapement. [f. escape *v.* + -ment; app. first in sense 2 after Fr. *échappement*.]

1. a. The action of escaping. *rare.*

1824 Hood *Two Swans* iv, Hope can spy no golden gate For sweet escapement. **1864** Sala in *Daily Tel.* 19 Oct., Wilmington, the last avenue of escapement left open to the beleaguered South.

b. A means of escape; an outlet.

1856 Froude *Hist. Eng.* (1858) I. iv. 327 He allowed her to go her own way, as the best escapement of a frenzy. **1857** Livingstone *Trav.* iii. 67 This little arm would prove a convenient escapement to prevent inundation. **1876** Geo. Eliot *Dan. Der.* I. xi. 209 The archery ball..was not an escapement for youthful high spirits.

2. a. *Watch and Clock-making.* In a watch or clock, the mechanism which intervenes between the motive power and regulator, and which alternately checks and releases the train, thus causing an intermittent impulse to be given to the regulator.

Escapements are of various kinds, as the *anchor-*, *chronometer-*, *crown-*, *dead-beat-*, *lever-*, etc., *escapement*.

[The Fr. *échappement* (in quot. 1801 anglicized as *echapement*) occurs, as a current term in a paper dated 1716 printed in *Machines approuvées par l'Académie* (1735) III. 93; the etymological reference is to the regulated 'escape' of the toothed wheel from its detention by the pallet. The earliest instances of the word in Eng. are in the form scapement, though at the period to which they belong the verb scape was already archaic in general sense.]

[**1739** *Phil. Trans.* XLI. 126 The teeth of the swing wheel would scape free of the pallets. **1755** *Bosley's Patent* No. 698, 4 Scapement. **1766** Cumming *Clockmaking* Index, *Scapement* is the means by which the action of the wheels is applied to maintain vibration.] **1779** Chambers *Cycl.* (ed. Rees), *Escapement*, see Scapement. **1801** J. Jones tr. *Bygge's Trav. Fr. Rep.* xvi. 384 Breguet, the famous watch-maker, has discovered a new echapement. **1825** J. Nicholson *Operat. Mechanic* 514 From the..description of the several parts of the escapement..it will be easy to see the mode of its action. **1880** S. P. Thompson in *Nature* XXI. 398 Models of every form of escapement.

transf. **1858** O. W. Holmes *Aut. Breakf.-t.* (1865) 73 Death alone can..silence at last the clicking of the terrible escapement we have carried so long beneath our wrinkled foreheads.

b. *attrib.*, as in ***escapement-wheel***.

1830 Kater & Lardner *Mech.* xiv. 194 From the action of the pallets in checking the motion of the wheel and allowing its teeth alternately to escape, this has been called the escapement wheel.

3. In a pianoforte (see quot. 1896).

1896 A. J. Hipkins *Pianoforte* 114 *Escapement*, a space that is left between the hammer at its full rise and the strings, necessary for the strings to vibrate and to prevent jarring. **1961** C. Clutton in A. Baines *Mus. Instruments* 89 The essentials of the modern pianoforte action:..double action, a check, an escapement, and an *una corda* mechanism.

escaper (ɪ'skeɪpə(r)). [f. escape *v.* + -er¹.] One who escapes.

1611 Bible *2 Kings* ix. 15 *marg.*, Let no escaper goe. **1849** Lytton *K. Arthur* v. ci, The bright escaper from a world of grief. **1890** *Temple Bar* July 331 He dropped his robe and veil, and appeared before them as the famed escaper.

escaping (ɪ'skeɪpɪŋ), *vbl. sb.* [f. escape *v.*] The action of the vb. escape. Also *attrib.*

c **1325** *Coer de L.* 2122 The messengers went out ful swythe; Of their escaping they were blithe. **1571** Golding *Calvin on Ps.* v. 9 That God should..open him an escaping place. **1650** Bp. Jer. Taylor *Fun. Sermon* 14 Such escapings we must reckon to be an extraordinary fortune. **1856** Mrs. Browning *Aur. Leigh* v. 20 The great escaping of ecstatic souls.

escaping (ɪ'skeɪpɪŋ), *ppl. a.* [f. as prec. + -ING².] That escapes; in the senses of the vb.

1870 *Daily News* 15 Nov., I have not heard of the escaping English. **1884** *Pall Mall G.* 6 Sept. 10/1 They were deluged by the escaping water.

Hence **e'scapingly** *adv.*, in an escaping manner; evasively.

a **1631** DONNE *Paradoxes* (1652) 63 To Speak Oraculously, whisperingly, generally, and therefore Escapingly.

escapism (ɪ'skeɪpɪz(ə)m). [f. ESCAP(E *sb.*¹ 1 b + -ISM.] The tendency to seek, or the practice of seeking, distraction from what normally has to be endured.

1933 *Encycl. Social Sci.* IX. 533/1 The bibulous, aphrodisiac lyrics strummed out by Anacreon of Teos at the banquets of Polycrates, tyrant of Samos, are an example of escapism, comparable to the songs of Alcaeus and Sappho in strife ridden Mytilene. **1935** L. MACNEICE *Poems* 26 This escapism of yours is blasphemy. **1937** H. READ *Art & Society* 260 Many of the critics of abstract art..dismiss it as the most evident byzantinism, escapism, absolutism. **1940** L. D. WEATHERHEAD *This is Victory* ix. 188 Religion that was mere escapism. **1946** J. CARY *Moonlight* 16 Was she, after all, an escapist? Amanda had a great contempt for escapism. **1954** *Essays in Criticism* IV. 50 He is not entering a plea for mere 'escapism' in literature.

escapist (ɪ'skeɪpɪst). [f. ESCAP(E *sb.*¹ + -IST.]

1. One who escapes, or who tries to escape, from captivity, prison, etc. Cf. ESCAPEE.

1934 in WEBSTER. **1938** *Punch* 22 June 700/2 Escapists... The efforts of these nefarious ruffians to dodge the police. **1943** *Hutchinson's Pict. Hist. War* May–Aug. 43 Pantellaria was the destination of these rubber dinghy escapists, but they were rounded up by the Royal Navy. **1958** *Times* 22 Mar. 7/4 He rushed out of court before he could be stopped, whereupon the judge..fined the escapist £20.

2. *fig.* Esp., one who seeks distraction from reality or from routine activities. Cf. ESCAPISM.

1933 C. S. LEWIS *Pilgrim's Regress* VI. iii. 125 'And you have never heard Mr. Halfways either.' 'Never. And I never will. Do you take me for an escapist?' **1937** *Essays & Studies* XXII. 148 The satirist is a kind of escapist. **1942** E. WAUGH *Put out more Flags* 252 Turning their backs on the world of effort and action. Fortunate islanders [*sc.* the Irish],.. happy, drab escapists. **1946** [see ESCAPISM]. **1958** *Spectator* 6 June 738/1 Both Hawthorne and Henry James were censured as escapists.

Hence *attrib.* or as *adj.*, that provides escape from reality or routine; pertaining to escapism.

1930 J. C. RANSOM *God without Thunder* 178 It is much more likely that they betoken a defeated and escapist people. **1933** *Archit. Rev.* LXXIII. 206/2 Those great pioneers of the past..took up the escapist attitude of William Morris. **1940** W. EMPSON *Gathering Storm* 62 A critic like Dr. Leavis can speak with the same tone of moral outrage about an Escapist (sentimental) novel as a customs official would about *Lady Chatterley's Lover*, say. **1959** *Manch. Guardian* 15 Aug. 3/6 The escapist peace of a nudist camp.

escapologist (ɛskə'pɒlədʒɪst, ɛskeɪp-). [f. ESCAP(E *sb.*¹ + -OLOGIST.] A performer skilled in extricating himself from knots, handcuffs, confinement in a box, etc. Also *transf.* and *fig.* (= ESCAPIST 1, 2).

1926 *Glasgow Herald* 1 Oct. 6 An Australian 'Escapologist'..gave a demonstration of his powers to a private audience at the London Coliseum yesterday. **1936** C. BELFRAGE (*title*) Away from it all. An escapologist's notebook. **1943** A. R. D. FAIRBURN *Strange Rendezvous* (1952) 16 Philosophers, sportsmen, and men who are very busy about their own and other people's business are three kinds of escapologists. **1946** G. MILLAR *Horned Pigeon* vii. 81 Cram was an escapologist. He had already escaped once, from a transit camp in Palermo. **1955** J. THOMAS *No Banners* x. 85 On Christmas night the [Madrid] Embassy threw a party for the 'escapologists', mostly R.A.F. and B.E.F. personnel. **1958** *Times* 22 Oct. 6/2 Randi, the Canadian escapologist who recreates a number of famous Houdini tricks. **1970** *Daily Tel.* 22 Sept. 12/4 Yesterday's edition included an escapologist who freed himself from a mail bag and manacles inside a locked chest.

So **esca'pology**, the methods and technique of escaping, esp. from captivity or danger; the calling of an escapologist.

1939 T. KOEVES *Timetable for Tramps* 22 At the higher escapology, the escape from reality by the use of the imagination aided by fashionable dopes, I had found myself to be a duffer. **1959** *Times* 29 Dec. 6/6 This was P—'s seventeenth escape from prisons and approved schools... At his trial..he was described as 'a past master in the art of escapology'. **1965** *Spectator* 12 Mar. 341/3, I carefully read all the books in the library about disasters by sea, fire, earthquake..and marked those passages which seemed to contain some lesson in escapology. **1966** *Daily Tel.* 19 Dec. 14 (*caption*) Escapology adviser to the musical, 'Man of Magic'.

escar(e, obs. form of ESCHAR.

escarbuncle (ɪ'skɑːbʌŋk(ə)l). *Her.* Also 6 escarboucle. [a. OF. *escarbuncle*, Fr. *escarboucle*: see CARBUNCLE.] = CARBUNCLE 2.

1572 BOSSEWELL *Armorie* II. 26 b, Beareth quarterly Golde, and Gules, an Escarboucle Pomettè. **1610** GUILLIM *Heraldry* III. vi. (1660) 126 The Escarbuncle is of most use in Armes. **1688** R. HOLME *Armoury* II. 39/1 An Escarbuncle..is a kind of precious Stone. **1864** BOUTELL *Heraldry Hist. & Pop.* xix. §4. 304 Badges: Henry II..an Escarbuncle.

‖**e'scargatoire.** *Obs. rare*⁻¹. [Misspelling of F. *escargotière*, (or a dial. synonym), f. *escargot* snail.] A place for rearing snails.

1705 ADDISON *Italy* 473 Escargatoire..a square Place boarded in, and filled with a vast quantity of large Snails. **1755** in JOHNSON; and in mod. Dicts.

‖**escargot** (ɛskargo). [Fr.] An edible snail.

1892 in T. F. GARRETT *Encycl. Pract. Cookery* I. viii. 575/1. **1926** *Glasgow Herald* 26 Mar. 10 I've savoured an escargot. **1960** *Times* 30 Jan. 9/6 The increase in appreciation of food, that has called forth *escargots* in Inverness.

†**e'scarmouche**, *sb. Obs.* Forms: 5 escarmissh, 6 escharmouch, -mousch, 9 (*Scott*) escaramouche. [a. Fr. *escarmouche* = Pr. *escarmussa*, Sp. *escaramuza*, It. *scaramuccia*; see SKIRMISH.] A skirmish; also *fig.* a fit of anger.

1475 *Bk. Noblesse* 13 After many assautes and grete escarmisshes. **1549** *Compl. Scot.* ix. (1872) 79 The atheniens and ther allya..assailȝet the persans be escharmouchis and incursions. **1579** TOMSON *Calvin's Serm. Tim.* 843/1 What shall wee say when a man is olde, and shoulde haue passed all those escharmouches. **1820** SCOTT *Monast.* xxxvii, Such of the men as have escaped this escaramouche.

†**e'scarmouche**, *v. Obs.* Also 6 escharmousch. [a. Fr. *escarmoucher*, f. *escarmouche*: see prec.] **a.** *intr.* To skirmish. **b.** *trans.* To skirmish with; to engage.

1549 *Compl. Scot.* ix. (1872) 78 Leonides.. escharmouschit xerxes gryt armye, and sleu tuenty thousand persuns. **1560** DAUS tr. *Sleidane's Comm.* 258 He had hearde only of a fewe Spaniardes, that laye therin garrison, and them wold he haue prouoked to escarmouche.

escarole ('ɛskərəʊl). *U.S.* Also escarolle. [a. Fr., f. It. *scariola*, *scarola* chicory, endive, f. late L. *escariola*, *scariola*.] A variety of endive with broad, frilled leaves, used in salads. Cf. SCARIOLE.

[**1877** E. S. DALLAS *Kettner's Bk. of Table* 171 The broad-leaved or Batavian endive, always known in France as the escarole.] **1897** H. A. DREER *Open-Air Vegetables* xxiv. 122 Broad-leaved Batavian Endive is sometimes called Escarolle. **1937** M. HILLIS *Orchids on your Budget* vi. 103 A mixed green salad bowl with lettuce, chicory, escarole, watercress, celery, shredded cabbage, diced carrots, tomatoes and cucumbers. **1971** *Daily Colonist* (Victoria, B.C.) 23 Jan. 2/3, I love greens..and..dandelion greens, escarole and endive. **1979** *Arizona Daily Star* 1 Apr. (Parade Suppl.) 10/1 Check your market—or your own garden—for sharp young mustard greens, tender spinach leaves, long celery-shaped Chinese cabbage, tangy escarole (or endive), chewy chicory.

escarp (ɪ'skɑːp), *sb. Fortif.* [a. Fr. *escarpe*, ad. It. *scarpa*. Cf. SCARP.]

1. 'A steep bank or wall immediately in front of and below the rampart..generally the inner side of the ditch' (Adm. Smyth).

1688 J.S. *Fortification* 27 The Escarpe or Slope of the Ditch next to the wall. **1811** WELLINGTON in Gurw. *Disp.* VIII. 12 The enemy had cleared the rubbish from the bottom of the escarp. **1853** SIR H. DOUGLAS *Mil. Bridges* 338 The crest of the exterior slope, or escarp.

2. *transf.* A natural formation of a similar kind.

1856 KANE *Arct. Expl.* II. vii. 81 These shelves.. presented distinct and recognisable embankments or escarps of elevation. **1868** SIR R. NAPIER *Disp. on Capture of Magdala* 12 May, Sir Charles Staveley effected an entrance..through a difficult crevice in the rocky escarps.

escarp (ɪ'skɑːp), *v.* [ad. Fr. *escarper*, f. *escarpe*: see prec. The aphetic form SCARP is the more usual.] *trans.* To make into an escarp, to cut or form into a steep slope; to furnish with scarps.

1728 G. CARLETON *Mem.* 100 The Glacis was all escarp'd upon the live Rock. **1852** LEVER *Daltons* II. 265 Carried along the mountain-side by a track escarped in the rock itself. **1855** BAILEY *Mystic* 69 The angels wrought the mountains, bulk by bulk, And chain by chain, serrated or escarped. **1884** *World* 27 Feb. 6/2 Billows of land, washed and escarped by ancient seas.

Hence **e'scarped** *ppl. a.*, cut out in the form of an escarp.

1853 KANE *Grinnell Exp.* vi. (1856) 48 The dike..rising up..into escarped terraces nearly 1400 feet high. **1859** JEPHSON *Brittany* v. 47 The escarped rock upon which they were constructed.

escarpment (ɪ'skɑːpmənt). [ad. Fr. *escarpement*, f. *escarper*: see prec.] The condition of being escarped; hence *concr.*

1. Ground cut into the form of an escarp for the purpose of fortification.

1802 C. JAMES *Mil. Dict.*, *Escarpment*: see Declivity. **1847** DISRAELI *Tancred* VI. i, The living rock..formed the impregnable bulwarks and escarpments. **1860** RUSSELL *Diary India* 1858–9 I. 82 The old Porto Batavo walls still surround the town, with moat and escarpments. **1882** *Luck of Ladysmede* I. 93 From which a natural escarpment swept down towards the river.

2. *Geol.* 'The abrupt face or cliff of a ridge or hill range' (Page). Also *attrib.*

1813 BAKEWELL *Introd. Geol.* (1815) 70 It is only on the sides of the nearly perpendicular peaks and escarpments that the bare rock is visible. **1845** DARWIN *Voy. Nat.* viii. (1852) 165 The view is generally bounded by the escarpment of another plain. **1870** YEATS *Nat. Hist. Comm.* 23 Plains of New Red Sandstone and Lias, succeeded by two great escarpments, the edges of table-lands. **1880** HAUGHTON *Phys. Geog.* v. 216 The western, or Libyan chain, is merely the escarpment edge of the plateau of the Sahara.

b. *transf.*

1853 KANE *Grinnell Exp.* viii. (1856) 56 A naked escarpment of ice, twelve hundred feet high. **1856** WHITTIER *Panorama* 2 [The] long escarpment of half-crumbled wall.

†**escarteled, escartelee**, *a. Her. Obs.* [ad. and a. OF. *escartelé*, pa. pple. of *escarteler* (mod.F. *écarteler*) to break into quarters = Pr. *esquartelar*, f. *es-* (:—L. *ex* out) + med.L. *quartellus*, dim. of *quartus* fourth.]

1. Quartered or quarterly.

1730–6 BAILEY (folio) *Escartelé*. **1775** in ASH. **1889** in ELVIN *Dict. Her.*

¶**2.** Having a square notch.

[This sense is app. due to a misunderstanding of some sort. The Fr. writers on heraldry (*e.g.* Palliot 1664) recognize *croix escartelée* only as meaning a cross divided by lines along the middle of each arm: this is substantially = sense 1.]

1688 R. HOLME *Armoury* I. iii. 19 *Escartelee*, that is, when the streight line is cut off in the middle with a perfect Square. *Ibid.* 21 A Chief Escartelee. *Ibid.* I. v. 47 Some call it a cross escartalled, couped: as if it had only a nick or notch ..sawed into the four ends of it. *Ibid.* I. ix. 92 A Cross Patee escarteled. [Hence in mod. Dicts.]

-escence, *suffix*, forming sbs. corresponding to adjs. in -ESCENT, as *effervescence*, *iridescence*.

-escent, *suffix*, forming adjs., repr. L. *-escentem*, the ending of pr. pples. of vbs. in *-ēscĕre*, chiefly inceptives, f. vbs. of state in *-ēre*. Primarily occurring in words ad. L. pples., as *deliquescent*, *effervescent*, *obsolescent*, *putrescent*, where the general sense is 'beginning to assume a certain state'. Hence in recent times the suffix has been used (both in Eng. and in other European langs.) to form adjs. upon sbs., as in *alkalescent* (? after *acescent*), and in several words referring to play of light or colour, as *flourescent*, *iridescent*, *opalescent*, *phosphorescent*.

esch, obs. Sc. form of ASH *sb.*¹

1513 DOUGLAS *Æneis* XI. iii. 80 The hie eschis soundis thare and here, For dyntis rude of the scharp stelyt ax.

‖**esch.** The German name for the grayling; in some Dicts. treated as Eng.

1658 HOOLE *Comenius' Vis. World* xxxiv. 71 Others of this sort are..the Barbel, the Esch [orig. *der Esch*], the Trout. **1753** CHAMBERS *Cycl. Supp.*, *Esch*..a name given, by Hildegard and others, to the fish we call the grayling. [In some mod. Dicts.]

eschalot (ɛʃə'lɒt). [ad. Fr. *eschalotte* (now *échalotte*), dim. of *eschaloigne* SCALLION.] = SHALLOT.

1707–12 MORTIMER *Husb.* (J.), Eschalots are now from France become an English plant. **1750** E. SMITH *Compl. Housewife* (ed. 14) 37 Take some horse radish, one or two eschalots, etc. **1755** JOHNSON, *Eschalot*. Pronounced *shallot*. **1858** GLENNY *Gard. Every-day Bk.* 48/1 Eschalots may still be planted, if not already in the ground.

eschange: obs. var. EXCHANGE.

†**eschansonnery.** *Obs.* [a. OFr. *eschansonnerie*, f. *eschanson*:—med.L. *scanciōn-em*, ad. Teut. **skankjon-* cupbearer, butler (= OE. *scęnca*).] The butlery.

1514 *Rutl. Papers* (Camden) 26 Eschansonnery celler. In wyn iiij septiers.

‖**eschantillon.** *Obs. rare*⁻¹. [F. *eschantillon* (now *échantillon*); cf. SCANTLING.] A fragment, diminutive specimen.

1720 POPE *Let. R. Digby* 20 July, Lady Scudamore, whose short Eschantillon of a letter (of a quarter of a page) I value.

eschar ('ɛskɑː(r)). *Path.* Forms: 6–7 **asker**, (6 **ascher, askar**), 6–8 **escar(e**, 6 **eschare, eskarre**, 7 **escarre**, (**esker**), 7– **eschar**. [ad. (partly through Fr. *eschare*) L. *eschara*, a. Gr. ἐσχάρα lit. 'hearth', hence mark of a burn. The Fr. word was at an earlier period adopted aphetically as *scarre*, SCAR¹.]

'A brown or black dry slough, resulting from the destruction of a living part, either by gangrene, by burn, or by caustics' (*Syd. Soc. Lex.*).

[*c* **1430** tr. *Gul. de Saliceto* in *MS. Sloane* 277 fo. 49 Þe remeuynge of þe escara or cruste.] **1543** TRAHERON *Vigo's Chirurg.* II. ix. 23 After that the malignite is taken awaye, ye muste cause the eschare to fal awaye. **1582** HESTER *Secr. Phiorav.* I. vii. 8 You maie not take awaie yᵉ Askar, vntill such tyme as it falleth out of hymself. **1607** TOPSELL *Four-f. Beasts* (1673) 313 Bind it thereto for three days, in which space you shall see a white asker on the sore. **1655** CULPEPPER, etc., *Riverius* IV. vii. 119 When the Eschar falls off, they will bleed again. *c* **1720** W. GIBSON *Farrier's Guide* II. xlviii. (1738) 182 It does not form anything like an Escar. **1755** *Phil. Trans.* XLIX. 50 The tongue alone was the seat of the gangrenous eschar. **1807** *Med. Jrnl.* XVII. 223, I cauterized the wound by means of burning tinder..until an eschar was produced about the size of a shilling. **1874** H. ROGERS *Orig. Bible* 286 In the eschar produced by cautery no nerve thrills.

†**b.** *transf. Obs.*

1709 *Phil. Trans.* XXVI. 379 The Flame of common Fire ..is able to reduce it [Iron] to an Eschar or sort of Rust. **1727** BRADLEY *Fam. Dict.* s.v. *Ant*, Insects..cause so many Escars, that the Leaves cannot avoid circling.

†**escharbon.** *Obs. rare*⁻¹. [Cf. OF. *escarboton, escharbote*, It. *scarbone*, f. Vulgar L. *scarab-us* (L. *scarabæus*) beetle.] A beetle.

1480 CAXTON *Ovid's Met.* xv. iv, Escharbons ben born & norysshid of dede horses.

escharotic (ɛskəˈrɒtɪk), *a.* and *sb.* Also 7 escarotick, 7-8 escharotick. [ad. late L. *escharōtic-us*, a. Gr. ἐσχαρωτικός, f. ἐσχάρα: see ESCHAR. Cf. Fr. *escharotique*.]

A. *adj.* Fitted or tending to form an eschar, caustic.

1612 WOODALL *Surg. Mate* Wks. (1653) 305 Put never one Caustick or Escarotick medicine after another too soone. **1655** CULPEPPER, etc. *Riverius* IV. vii. 119 Burnt Vitriol.. besides its Escharotick quality, is good to stanch blood. **1718** QUINCY *Compl. Disp.* 80 Its hot escharotick Quality makes it very hurtful to Sheep.

B. *sb.* An escharotic drug; a powerful caustic.

1655 CULPEPPER, etc. *Riverius* IV. vii. 119 Escharoticks.. by burning the mouths of the Veins, produce a Scab. **1791** *Edin. New Disp.* 118 Verdegris applied externally proves a gentle detergent and Escharotic. **1875** H. WALTON *Dis. Eye* 139 An escharotic will suffice to remove all small warts.

So †**eschaˈrotical,** *a. Obs.*

1651 BIGGS *New Disp.* 173 An escharoticall caustick.

†**ˈescharous,** *a. Obs.* Also 6 escarous. [f. ESCHAR + -OUS.] Full of eschars; resembling an eschar; scabby.

1543 TRAHERON *Vigo's Chirurg.* II. x. 23 Yf the ulceration shulde come of fier..it is escarous. **1562** BULLEYN *Dial. Soarnes & Chir.* 17a, You maie..often applie the same, untill the same come to an escharous crust or scabbe.

eschatocol (ˈɛskətəʊkɒl). [G. *eschatokoll* (It. *escatocollo*, F. *eschatocole*), f. Gr. ἔσχατος last + κόλλα glue. Cf. πρωτόκολλον PROTOCOL. Martial (II. vi. 3) has ἐσχατοκόλλιον end of a papyrus roll.] The concluding section of a charter, containing the attestation, date, etc.; a concluding clause or formula.

1897 F. W. MAITLAND *Domesday Bk.* 247 Such words as a charter has about 'consent'..may occur in the eschatocol, the clause which deals with the execution and attestation of the instrument. **1904** *Eng. Hist. Rev.* Jan. 152 In regard to the dating we find originally a separation, the year going into the protocol, the month and regnal year into the eschatocol. But by the middle of the twelfth century the whole date is put into the eschatocol.

eschatological (ˌɛskətəʊˈlɒdʒɪkəl), *a.* [f. ESCHATOLOGY + -IC + -AL¹.] Of or pertaining to eschatology.

1854 *Fraser's Mag.* XLIX. 713 Many of these poems touch on eschatological questions. **1863** *Jrnl. Sacr. Lit.* Jan. 295 Eschatological notions, which he [Paul] is supposed to have borrowed at first from Judaism. **1881** E. WILSON *Egypt of the Past* in *Nature* 24 Nov. 75 The eschatological notions of the period differed exceedingly from those of subsequent periods.

eschatoˈlogically, *adv.* [f. ESCHATOLOGICAL *a.* + -LY².] In relation to eschatology.

1910 W. MONTGOMERY tr. *Schweitzer's Quest Historical Jesus* xix. 349 The eschatological school itself..represents Jesus as thinking and speaking eschatologically in some of the most important passages of His teaching. **1922** A. E. GARVIE *Beloved Disciple* ix. 199 Whether we interpret these functions spiritually or eschatologically. **1934** *Theology* XXVIII. 153 The Holy Spirit is present in us eschatologically. **1963** AUDEN *Dyer's Hand* 78 Today, Christian and Atheist alike are eschatologically minded.

eschatologist (ɛskəˈtɒlədʒɪst). [f. ESCHATOLOGY + -IST.] One who studies or treats of eschatology.

1877 M. ARNOLD *Last Ess. Ch.* Pref. 29 The ideas of the great prophets..are more true than the ideas of the eschatologist of the book of Daniel.

eschaˈtologize (-dʒaɪz), *v.* [See -IZE.] *trans.* To give an eschatological character to.

1919 S. C. CARPENTER *Christianity acc. S. Luke* vii. 101 The first Evangelist has 'eschatologized' an originally non-eschatological saying.

eschatology (ɛskəˈtɒlədʒɪ). *Theol.* [f. Gr. ἔσχατο-ς last + -λογία discourse: see -LOGY; cf. F. *eschatologie*.]

a. The department of theological science concerned with 'the four last things: death, judgement, heaven, and hell'.

1844 G. BUSH *Anastasis* (1845) Pref. v, Scriptural Eschatology. **1858** J. MARTINEAU *Stud. Chr.* 228 The Eschatology of the Apocalypse and the Epistles. **1879** BALDW. BROWN in *Chr. World* 24 Dec. 825/3 Eschatology, the science of the last things, is, as a science, one of the most baseless.

b. In recent theological writing, esp. as 'realized eschatology' (see quot. 1957), the sense of this word has been modified to connote the present 'realization' and significance of the 'last things' in the Christian life.

1950 *Scottish Jrnl. Theol.* III. 90 Correspondingly for Christians..eschatology is being anticipated in the here and now, and the glory of the parousia throws its light backwards into the present life of the Church. **1957** *Oxf. Dict. Chr. Ch.* 462/1 In modern Protestant theology eschatology has been given a new meaning, esp. through the studies of A. Schweitzer... Acc. to him, primitive Christianity was exclusively an eschatological preaching of judgement and salvation. Eschatological considerations are also a dominant factor of the teaching of K. Barth and his school..which sees the life of the individual Christian and of the Church as a series of 'decisions' invested with an eschatological character... Recently many attempts have been made to draw out the present and abiding significance of future eschatological happenings, e.g. by C. H. Dodd in his conception of 'realized eschatology'.

‖**eschaton** (ˈɛskətɒn). *Theol.* [a. Gr. ἔσχατον, neut. of ἔσχατος last.] (See quots.)

1935 C. H. DODD *Parables of Kingdom* vi. 193 The *eschaton*, the divinely ordained climax of history, is here. **1936** —— *Apostolic Preaching* 199 In prophecy and apocalypse alike, the divine event, the *eschaton*, is always 'round the corner'. The prophet never conceives himself as standing midway in the course of history. *Ibid.* 210 For the New Testament writers in general, the *eschaton* has entered history. **1950** *Scottish Jrnl. Theol.* III. 301 Behind the parable, or rather beside it, there is the kingdom which has broken into the midst, the *eschaton* which is here and now.

†**eˈschaufe,** *v. Obs.* Also 4-5 eschauffe, eschawfe. [a. OFr. *eschaufe-r, eschauffe-r*: see ACHAFE.] *trans.* To heat, warm; also *fig.* to heat with passion, inflame, excite. Also *refl.* to become hot.

c **1374** CHAUCER *Boeth.* I. v. 22 Þe sedes..ben waxen hey[e] cornes whan þe sterre sirius eschaufeþ hym. **1413** LYDG. *Pilgr. Sowle* I. xxvii. (1859) 32 Fyre warmeth and eschaufeth tho that stonde nye. *a* **1450** *Knt. de la Tour* 164 To eschauufe and to draw the man or woman by sum falce delite vnto synne. *c* **1475** *Partenay* 969 Wine..wold eschawfe the braines appetite. **1530** PALSGR. 539/2 By that tyme your horse be a lytle eschaufed, he wyll go well ynoughe.

Hence †**eˈschaufed,** *ppl. a.* †**eˈschaufing** *vbl. sb.*

c **1374** CHAUCER *Boeth.* IV. vi. 142 Þei wexen eschaufed in to hat[e] of hem þat anoien hem. *c* **1386** —— *Pars. T.* ¶916 Euere the gretter merite shal he han, that moost restreyneth the wikkede eschawfynges of the ordure of this synne.

eschaunge, obs. var. of EXCHANGE.

†**esˈchay.** *Obs. Sc.* [? repr. some deriv. of OF. *escheoir*: see ESCHEAT; and cf. Fr. 'la terme échoit à la Saint-Jean'.] Expiry, termination.

1488 *Act. Dom. Conc.* (1839) 113/2 To complett fiftene ȝeris, quhilk beand completit was in the ȝere of God lxxxiiii ȝeris; and the eschay of his terme at witsounday.

esche, obs. form of ASH¹, ASK.

escheat (ɛsˈtʃiːt), *sb.* Forms: 4-7 eschet(e, (4 echete, escheyte, 5 eshete, eþchete), 5-7 escheate, 6-7 *Sc.* escheit(te, 6-7 excheat(e, -chete, 6- escheat. See also CHEAT *sb.* [ME. *eschete*, a. OF. *eschete, eschaete, escheoite*, n. of action (orig. fem. pa. pple), f. OF. *escheoir* (mod.F. *échoir*):—late L. **excadēre* (class. L. *excidĕre*) to fall to a person's share, f. L. *ex* out + *cadēre* (vulg. L. *cadēre*, OF. *cheoir*) to fall. In continental OF. the sb. meant succession, inheritance, *esp.* collateral inheritance; in England the etymological sense received a different application. As in many other words (cf. *exchange*) the prefix *es-* was in the 16-17th c. often replaced by *ex-* after L. analogies.]

I. *Law.*

1. An 'incident' of feudal law, whereby a fief reverted to the lord when the tenant died without leaving a successor qualified to inherit under the original grant. Hence, the lapsing of land to the Crown (in U.S., to the state), or to the lord of the manor, on the death of the owner intestate without heirs.

As an attainted person, according to the doctrine of 'corruption of blood' (see ATTAINDER), could have no legal heir, his property suffered escheat. This 'escheat by corruption of blood', theoretically distinct from the 'forfeiture' inflicted as a penalty for treason and felony, was abolished together with the latter by the Felony Act, 1870.

[**1292** BRITTON 69 Queus demeynes nous tenoms..de eschete et de purchaz.] *c* **1380** WYCLIF *Sel. Wks.* III. 307 Many londis schulde falle into þe kyngis [hondis] bi eschet. *c* **1430** *Syr Gener.* (Roxb.) 2190 A rich erle-dam..to him of Eshete late cam. *c* **1460** FORTESCUE *Abs. & Lim. Mon.* (1714) 77 By Eschetes, ther may not so mich Land fall to any Man as to the Kyng by cause no man hath so many lordshippes as he. **1533** MORE *Debell. Salem* Wks. 977/1 Swering a mans death, and winning a mans lande by eschete. **1649** SELDEN *Laws Eng.* I. lxiv. (1739) 130 He forbad the study of the Law, that so it might die without heir, and he have all by Escheat. **1765** BLACKSTONE *Comm.* I. II. vi. 69 Escheats are equally incident to tenure in socage. *a* **1862** BUCKLE *Misc. Wks.* (1872) I. 353 Escheats were frequent in England, because there was no power of willing away land.

transf. **1658-9** *Burton's Diary* (1828) III. 183 The right did revert by escheat to the people upon the great change.

b. In Scotland in wider sense, including: Confiscation or forfeiture of property, real or personal. ***simple escheat***: the absolute forfeiture of a person's estate; opposed to ***liferent escheat***, the forfeiture of the profits accruing during his lifetime.

1457 *Sc. Acts Jas. II* (1597) §71 That na woman cum to kirk..with hir face mussalled, or covered that scho may not be kend, vndir the pane of escheit of the courchie.

2. *concr.* Property, real or personal, falling by escheat to the lord, king, or state. In quot. 1330 *eschete* may be pa. pple.

c **1330** R. BRUNNE *Chron.* (1810) 244 Ilk castelle and toure To þe kyng is eschete, als to chefe of alle. **1393** LANGL. *P. Pl.* C. v. 169 Thorȝ ȝoure lawe, ich leyue ich lese menye escheytes. **1474** *Ld. Treas. Acc. Scotl.* 11 The eschaeatis.. of thaim that [wer] at the slauchter of Thome of Prestone. **1577-87** HOLINSHED *Chron.* III. 1073/2 As well in prouiding excheats and wards for their children and kinsfolks. **1600** HOLLAND *Livy* 39 Suffering himselfe and all that he had to fall into the king's hands as an escheat. **1637-50** ROW *Hist. Kirk* (1842) 37 Such as is put to the horn for Ministers stipends, their escheits shalbe uplifted. **1841** ELPHINSTONE *Hist. Ind.* I. 41 Escheats for want of heirs have been mentioned as being his [the King's]. **1875** STUBBS *Const. Hist.* I. xiii. 607 Not even the tenants of a great escheat in the royal hands escaped the obligation.

transf. **1590** SPENSER *F.Q.* III. viii. 16 To leave to him that lady for excheat.

†**b.** *collect.* The fund or possession formed by escheated estates. *Obs.*

c **1330** R. BRUNNE *Chron.* (1810) 247 Þe dettes þat men þam auht..Wer taxed & bitauht to þe eschete of þe kyng.

3. The right of appropriating property subject to escheat.

1570-6 LAMBARDE *Peramb. Kent* (1826) 496 But as touching the Lande, he shall neither have the Eschete of it. **1609** SKENE *Reg. Maj.* 3 The Baron sall haue the escheit of the gudes pertening to the malefactor. **1759** STERNE *Tr. Shandy* I. 18 Reversions, services, annuities..views of frank-pledge, escheats, etc. **1844** WILLIAMS *Real Prop.* (1877) 127 A right of escheat seldom accruing.

†**4.** A writ (AF. *bref de eschaete*) now abolished, to recover escheats from the person in possession.

[**1292** BRITTON 54 Voloms nous qe teles alienaunces soint repellables par les chiefs seignurs des feez par nos brefs de Eschaete.] **1672** in COWEL *Interpr.* s.v. *Eschete*, Escheat is used for a Writ which lyeth, where the Tenant having Estate in Fee-simple in any Lands or Tenements holden of a superior Lord, dyeth seised without Heir general or special. **1842** BARHAM *Ingol. Leg.*, *Sir Rupert*, Away went 'cognovits,' 'bills,' 'bonds,' and 'escheats.'

†**5.** (See quots.) *Obs.*

1672 COWEL *Interpr.* s.v. *Eschete*, Escheat is also used sometimes for the Place or Circuit within which the King, or other Lord hath Escheats of his Tenants. **1736** in BAILEY. **1751** in CHAMBERS *Cycl.*; and in mod. Dicts.

II. 6. The levying of contributions, plunder; *concr.* in *pl.* booty, spoil. Cf. CHEAT 2.

1577-87 HARRISON *Descr. Brit.* x. 37 in *Holinshed*, For their wares, whereof they [pirates] make good peniworths, as theeves commonlie doo of such pieces as they get by like Escheat. **1590** SPENSER *F.Q.* I. v. 25 To make one great by others losse is bad excheat. **1609** HOLLAND *Amm. Marcel.* XXVI. viii. 299 Commanded the house of Arbetio, full (as it was) by reason of those inestimable escheats..to be rifled and ransacked cleane.

escheat (ɛsˈtʃiːt), *v.* Forms: see the sb. *Pa. pple.* Sc. 6 escheit, 8-9 escheat. (See also CHEAT *v.*) [f. prec. sb.; cf. OF. *eschaeter*.]

1. *trans.* To make an escheat of, confiscate; to hand over as an escheat *to* or *into*. (Some apparent examples of the pass. may belong to the *intr.* sense 2.)

1382 WYCLIF *3 Esdras* vi. 32 And the goodis ofhem to the king be eschetid [**1388** ethchetid]. **1474** *Ld. Treas. Acc. Scotl.* 67 His schip and gudis..was escheit as the kings eschete. **1548** BODRUGAN (Adams) *Epit. King's Title* 251 Locrine herupon seazed Albania..as excheated wholy to hymself. **1574** tr. *Littleton's Tenures* 12a, If it [lande] be escheted unto the king. **1641** A. MERVIN in Rushw. *Hist. Coll.* III. (1692) I. 216 Their Primitive and Genuine Tenures escheated by Acts of State, and strangled by Monopolies. **1687** *Assur. Abb. Lands* 40 It was the Opinion of the Justices that they were Escheated to the Lords of the Fee. **1855** MILMAN *Lat. Chr.* (1864) V. IX. v. 275 He.. escheated their estates into the hands of laymen. **1873** DIXON *Two Queens* VI. ix, His honours lost, his lands escheated, and his liberty restrained.

b. *transf.* and *fig.*

1589 WARNER *Alb. Eng.* v. xxviii. (1612) 141 And to his Coffres did escheate a world of wealth. *a* **1643** W. CARTWRIGHT *On Christ Ch. Building*, As doubtful whether 't should escheated be To ruine, or redeem'd to majesty.

2. *intr.* To become an escheat; to revert by escheat to the superior lord, king, or state; const. *to* or *simply*. Also *fig.*

1531 *Dial. Laws Eng.* I. vii. (1638) 13 The land shall escheat to the Lord of whom the Land is holden. **1596** SPENSER *State Irel.* Wks. (Globe) 657/2 Landes..which should otherwise have escheated to her majestie. **1633** T. STAFFORD *Pac. Hib.* xiv. (1821) 639 His Land should haue excheated unto her. **1698** SIDNEY *Disc. Gov.* i. §19 (1704) 42 A Kingdom so gotten may escheat for want of an Heir. **1761** HUME *Hist. Eng.* I. viii. 168 All baronies which escheated to the Crown were under his administration. **1848** MILL *Pol. Econ.* I. 261 The property in case of intestacy should escheat to the state.

fig. **1850** H. COLERIDGE *Poems* II. 13 Great nature's waif, that must by law escheat To the liege-lord Corruption.

†**3.** *trans.* To forfeit. *Sc. Obs.*

1513-75 *Diurn. Occur.* (1833) 83 All thair movabill guidis decernit to be escheit, at the mercat croce of Edinburgh. **1514** BARCLAY *Cyt. & Uplondyshm.* (Percy Soc.) p. lii, His shirt, his doublet, or bonet to excheate. **1752** J. LOUTHIAN *Form of Process* 151 All their moveable Goods and Gear, to be escheat and in-brought to his Majesty's Use. **1816** SCOTT *Old Mort.* xxxvi, His moveable goods and gear escheat..to his majesty's use. **1876** GRANT *Burgh Sch. Scotl.* I. i. 49 In

1509 persons were prevented from importing.. Books under penalty of escheating the same.

¶ 4. Used (after Fr. *échoir*) for: To 'fall' to a person by inheritance.

1603 FLORIO *Montaigne* III. ix. (1632) 541 Those that have beene hereditarily escheated unto them.

escheatable (ɛs'tʃiːtəb(ə)l), *a.* [f. prec. + -ABLE.] Liable to escheat.

1611 COTGR., *Escheable*, escheatable. *a* **1626** BACON *Max. & Uses Com. Law* 49 The Customes of Kent is that Gauilkind land is not forfeitable nor Escheatable for Felonie. **1828** in WEBSTER; and in mod. Dicts.

escheatage (ɛs'tʃiːtɪdʒ). [f. ESCHEAT *sb.* or *v.* + -AGE.] The right of succeeding to an escheat.

1611 COTGR., *Escheatage*, the right which a Lord hath in the land of his tenant, dying without heires of his bodie, or bloud. **1756** NUGENT *Montesquieu's Spir. Laws* II. XXI. xiii. 54 In those times were established the ridiculous rights of escheatage and shipwrecks. **1779** *State Papers* in *Ann. Reg.* 435/2 Exempt from the right of escheatage. **1828** in WEBSTER; and in mod. Dicts.

escheated (ɛs'tʃiːtɪd), *ppl. a.* Also 6 Sc. escheit. [f. as prec. + -ED.] Of land, etc.: That has reverted by escheat to the superior lord, the king, or the state.

1551 *Sc. Acts, Mary* c. 7 The saidis escheit gudis. **1607** DAVIES *1st Let. Earl Salisb.* (1787) 233 To enquire of all escheated and concealed lands in that county. **1623** SIR T. CREW in Rushw. *Hist. Coll.* (1659) I. 118 You have made these ample Endowments of Churches out of your own Excheated Revenue. **1860** FORSTER *Gr. Remonstr.* 30 The lesser proprietors whom grants of escheated honours might newly have created.

es'cheating, *vbl. sb.* [f. as prec. + -ING¹.] The action of the vb. ESCHEAT; in quot. = Forfeiting.

c **1575** SIR J. BALFOUR *Practicks* (1754) 37 It is statute and ordanit.. that thair be na mercattis nor fairis haldin upon halie dayis.. under the pane of eschetting of the gudis.

es'cheatment. [f. ESCHEAT *v.* + -MENT.] Forfeiture or lapsing by escheat.

1869 BLACKMORE *Lorna D.* I. xxiv. 283 On pain of a heavy fine or escheatment. **1919** E. MACNEILL *Phases Irish Hist.* xi. 312 The new grants were not preceded.. by.. any escheatment or invalidation of the existing contract.

escheator (ɛs'tʃiːtə(r)). Forms: 5-6 eschetour(e, eschetour, -er, 5-7 escheatour, -etor, exchetor, (5 echetour, eshetour, 7 excheator), 7-8 escheater, (7 eschaetor), eþcheitour, 7- escheator. [ME. *eschetour*, a. AF. *eschetour*, f. *eschete*: see ESCHEAT *sb.*] An officer appointed yearly by the Lord Treasurer to take notice of the escheats in the county to which he is appointed, and to certify them into the Exchequer. ***escheator-general***: a superintendent or chief of escheators.

The office having practically fallen into disuse, procedure in cases of escheat, is now regulated by the Escheat Procedure Act, 1887.

[**1292** BRITTON I. ii. §2 En office de nos Eschetours, et en presence de nous devaunt noster Seneschal.] **1398** TREVISA *Barth. De P.R.* XIX. cxxviii. (1495) 934 Fiscus is a comyn sacke or a bagge in whiche the Eschetour and rente gaderers put the comyn dette and custome that is payed to kynges. **1463** *Mann. & Househ. Exp.* (1841) 187 Edward be the grace of God Kyng of Yngland.. to alle sryftes, mayrys, escheatours, etc. **1500** *Plumpton Corr.* 147 Ralfe Sauchevereth of Hopwell is eschetour of Notinghamshire and Derby. **1593** NORDEN *Spec. Brit. M'sex & Herts.* II. 1 It [Herts.] was annexed to Essex. And one Sheriffe supplied both Counties, and did also one Eschetor. **1667** E. CHAMBERLAYNE *St. Gt. Brit.* I. II. ix. (1743) 78 The Lord Treasurer hath the nomination of the Escheators in every county. **1755** CARTE *Hist. Eng.* IV. 375 He had got into the service of one Kenny escheator general of the kingdom [of Ireland]. **1827** HALLAM *Const. Hist.* (1876) I. i. 15 The King's title was to be found by the inquest of a jury, summoned at the instance of the escheator.

Hence **es'cheatorship**, the office of escheator.

1570 *Act. 13 Eliz.* c. 4. §13 His Office of Sheriffwick, Escheatorship or Bailiffwick. **1887** *19th Cent.* XXII. 789 When he applied for the escheatorship, he informed Lord Castlereagh that he intended to have his seat transferred to Mr. Balfour.

eschecker, -cheker(e, obs. ff. EXCHEQUER.

eschel ('ɛʃəl). [a. Ger. *eschel*, dim. of *esche* ashes.] †**a.** (See quot. 1753.) *Obs.* **b.** The third quality of powder blue.

[**1726** LINCKIUS in *Phil. Trans.* XXXIV. 202 Tum ad separationem pulveris illius cinerei albicantis levioris, quem Eschel appellant.] **1753** CHAMBERS *Cycl. Supp.*, *Eschel*, a term used by the smalt workers, to express a sort of grey substance resembling ashes, which is usually mixed with the smalt when in fusion. This is carefully separated from it, before it is powdered for use, otherwise it would debase the colour. **1875** URE *Dict. Arts* 874 s.v. *Cobalt*, In commerce, smalts are classified both according to their contents in cobalt, and the size of the grain, the following being the chief marks.. [*e.g.*] O.E. Ordinary Eschel. Ordinary indicates the relative quantity in cobalt.. Eschel the state of division.

†**eschele.** *Obs.* Also 4 eschel, 5 eschelle. [a. OF. *eschele* (mod.F. *échelle*), *eschiele*, believed to be an altered form of *eschiere*, corresp. to It. *schiera*, of Teut. origin: cf. OHG. *skara* (MHG. *schar*, Ger. *schaar*).] A troop, squadron (of soldiers); rarely a company (of travellers).

c **1330** *Arth. & Merl.* 7580 With xv thousand in on eschele. **1375** BARBOUR *Bruce* VIII. 218 In twa eschelis ordanit he had The folk that he had in leding. *c* **1425** WYNTOUN *Cron.* VIII. xl. 155 Þe worthy men Ðare Folk.. arayid þen, And delt þame in-til Eschelis thre. *c* **1460** *Towneley Myst.* 47 (Jacob *loq.*) Rachelle, stand thou in the last eschelle.

†**eschellett.** *Obs.* Also 6 eschellit. [a. OF. *eschellette*, mod.F. *échelette*, dim. of *échelle* ladder.] A small ladder.

1578 in T. Thomson *Inventories* (1815) 256 (Jam.) Ane eschellit schod with yron without ane bolt. *Ibid.* 258 Ane eschellett schod without ane bolt.

†**eschend,** pa. pple. of *ȝe-schenden*: see SHEND *v.*¹

c **1375** *XI Pains of Hell* 343 in *O.E. Misc.* 221 Cursid dedis makis men al day eschend.

eschenite, var. form of ÆSCHYNITE.

eschequer, obs. form of EXCHEQUER.

eschete, obs. form of ESCHEAT.

†**e'scheve,** *v.* *Obs.* Forms: 4-6 eschew(e, escheve, (4 escheffe, 6 esschef). [a. OF. *escheve-r*, corrupt form of *achever*: see ACHIEVE.]

1. *trans.* To bring to a successful issue, accomplish; = ACHIEVE 1.

1375 BARBOUR *Bruce* III. 283 Gret thingis eschewyt he [Cesar], As men may in his story se. *c* **1500** *Lancelot* 2229 Aduentur is non so gret to pref.. nor ȝhe sal it esschef. *a* **1533** LD. BERNERS *Huon* xx. 57 God ayde you to eschew & to fornyshe thys grete besynes.

2. To succeed in gaining; to gain; = ACHIEVE 5 a.

1520 *Calisto & Melibæa* in Hazl. *Dodsley* I. 77 To enjoy your youth.. For that time pleasures are most escheved.

3. *intr.* To gain one's end; const. *of* or *simply*; = ACHIEVE 6.

c **1375** *Sc. Leg. Saints, Mathou* 321 To sanct mathow son went he, Wenand be hym wele til eschewe. *Ibid., Eugenia* 533 He had eschewit of his wil, Or ony helpe had cumyne hir til. ? *a* **1400** *Morte Arth.* 2301 Lappede them in lede, lesse that they schulde Chawnge or chawffe, ȝif þay myghte escheffe.

†**eschevin.** *Obs.* Variant of ECHEVIN, q.v.

1670 COTTON *Espernon* I. II. 49 The Eschevins of Paris. **1756** NUGENT *Gr. Tour, Netherl.* I. 85 The eschevins or aldermen form a court of justice here as in every town.

†**es'chew,** *sb.* *Obs.* [f. ESCHEW *v.*¹; cf. OF. *escheu*, *eschui* of similar formation.] The action of keeping clear; avoidance (of danger).

a **1541** WYATT *Poet. Wks.* (1861) 158 So fareth love.. The first eschew is remedy alone.

†**es'chew,** *a.* *Obs.* Also 4 eschiewe, 4-5 eschu(e. [a. OF. *eschieu* (nom. *eschif*), corresp. to Pr. *eschiu*, Sp. *esquivo*, It. *schivo*:—Com. Romanic **skivo*, of Teut. origin: cf. OHG. **sciuh* (MHG. *schiech*, mod.Ger. *scheu*), OE. *scéoh* SHY.]

1. Disinclined, loth, unwilling. Const. *of* or *to* with *inf.*

c **1386** CHAUCER *Pars. T.* ¶ 897 He þat ofte falleth in synne .. is the moore eschew [*v.r.* eschewe, eschue, eschiewe] for to shryuen hym. *c* **1386** —— *Merch. T.* 568 To eten hem alle he nas no thyng eschu [*v.r.* eschewe, eschwe]. **1393** GOWER *Conf.* II. 286 She is escheue of bothe two. *a* **1420** HOCCLEVE *De Reg. Princ.* 136 Vertu So excellent, that to feble is my witte To expresse it; wherfore I am eschu To medle, or make a long sermoun of itte.

2. ? Objectionable, to be avoided.

c **1420** *Pallad. on Husb.* I. 528 Dounge of foules is ful necessarie To lond tillynge; yit gooses dounge eschew is. *Ibid.* IV. 586 Her taste is eke eschewe In places weet.

eschew (ɛs'tʃuː), *v.*¹ Forms: 4-6 escheve (? escheue), eschewe, (4 ech-, esshue, etchewe, isschewe, 4-5 eschef, eschiewe, -uwe, eþchewe, 5 escheu, eshew, 6 escue, estchue, as-, estew(e, -iew), exchew(e, (4 exschew, 6 exchue, -tue), 4-7 eschu(e, 4- eschew. [a. OF. *eschiver*, *eschever* (also in other conjugations, as *eschevoir*, *eschivir*, *eschivre*), corresp. to Pr., Sp., Pg. *esquivar*, It. *schivare* (whence prob. mod.F. *esquiver* to dodge, the retention of the *s* being otherwise anomalous):—Common Romanic **skivāre*, f. **skivo*: see prec.; cf. OHG. *sciuhen*, MHG. *schiuhen*, *schiuwen*, mod.Ger. *scheuen* to dread, avoid, shun; also Eng. SHY *v.*]

1. *trans.* To avoid, shun.

†**a.** To avoid, keep clear of, escape (a danger or inconvenience). Rarely with clause as obj.

c **1375** *Sc. Leg. Saints, Mathias* 205 [A sone] þat scho, til eschewe destiny, Ine a cophyne kest ine þe se. *c* **1460** FORTESCUE *Abs. & Lim. Mon.* (1714) 105 To eschewe thees two Harmes, hyt may than be advised, etc. **1514** BARCLAY *Cyt. & Uplondyshm.* (Percy Soc.) 1 Pastoures.. drawe to cotes for to eschewe the colde. **1526** TINDALE *2 Cor.* viii. 20 Thus we eschue thatt eny man shulde rebuke us in this aboundance. *c* **1530** LD. BERNERS *Arth. Lyt. Bryt.* (1814) 17 To exchewe therby the displeasure of my lorde. **1598** SHAKS. *Merry W.* v. v. 251 What cannot be eschew'd, must be embrac'd. **1671** J. WEBSTER *Metallogr.* iv. 61 To eschew tediosness, [I] shall transcribe what Dr. Jorden hath written. **1721** *St. German's Doctor & Stud.* 60 To eschew that in-convenience that Statute was made.

†**b.** To 'fight shy of', avoid (a place); to stand aloof from (a person). *Obs.*

1377 LANGL. *P. Pl.* B. VI. 55 Suche men eschue. **1413** LYDG. *Pilgr. Sowle* IV. iii. (1483) 59 The quene of Saba.. eshewed it [that brydge] and took another wey. *c* **1450** *Castle Hd. Life St. Cuthbert* (Surtees) 160 Fra þen forthe sho forhewed þe kynges presence, and it eschewed. **1553** T. WILSON *Rhet.* 2 Beware.. of straunge woordes, as thou wouldest take hede and eschewe greate rockes in the sea. **1621** BURTON *Anat. Mel.* III. ii. VI. iii. (1651) 564 A woman a man may eschue, but not a wife.

c. To abstain carefully from, avoid, shun (an action, a course of conduct, an indulgence, an article of food or drink, etc.). The current sense: †Formerly with obj.-inf. preceded by *to*.

JOHNSON 1755 notes the word as 'almost obsolete'; it is now not uncommon in literary use.

1340-70 *Alex. & Dind.* 1001 But al þat badde is for a burn here abouen erþe, Huo so haþ chaunce to echue & chese the betture. *c* **1375** *Lay Folks Mass-bk.* (MS. B.) 358 Gyue me grace for to etchewe to do þat þing þat me shuld rewe. **1388** WYCLIF *2 Tim.* ii. 16 Eschewe thou vnhooli and veyn spechis. *c* **1450** MYRC 28 Grete othes thow moste enchewe. **1509** HAWES *Joyful Medit.* 20 They may extue For to do wronge. **1535** COVERDALE *Ps.* xvii. 23, I.. will eschue myne owne wickednes. **1637** EARL STIRLING *Doomesday* 9th Hour (R.), These curious doubts which good men doe eschew Make many atheists. **1656** RIDGLEY *Pract. Physick* 22 Fat things must be eschewed. *a* **1707** BEVERIDGE *Serm.* II. lxxxiii. (R.), They must not only eschew evil but do good in the world. **1801** WORDSW. *Cuckoo & Night.* xxiii, For every wight eschews thy song to hear. **1848** THACKERAY *Van. Fair* xlv, He has already eschewed green coats, red neckcloths, and other worldly ornaments. **1855** MACAULAY *Hist. Eng.* IV. 693 Observers.. thought that capitalists would eschew all connection with what must necessarily be a losing concern. **1876** BLACKIE *Songs Relig. & Life* 228 Eschew the cavilling critic's art, The lust of loud reproving.

absol. **1621** BURTON *Anat. Mel.* I. i. II. viii. (1651) 25 The power to prosecute or eschue.

†**2.** *intr.* To get off, escape. *Obs.*

1375 BARBOUR *Bruce* XI. 391 Thai sall nocht weill eschew foroutyn fall. *c* **1450** *Castle Hd. MS. Life St. Cuthb.* (Surtees) 2525 And þat he couet to eschew. **1560** ROLLAND *Crt. Venus* IV. 441 Grant him his life.. And I promit.. That he sall not eschew away, nor fle.

†**3.** *trans.* To rescue. *Obs. rare.* [So Fr. *eschiver*.]

c **1500** *Melusine* 170 þey recouered there six of theire galeyes, & eschiewed þem fro the fyre.

Hence **es'chewal**, an eschewing, a keeping clear of (evil). **es'chewance**, the action of eschewing; avoidance. **es'chewer**, one who eschews, avoids, shuns. **es'chewing** *vbl. sb.*, the action of the vb. ESCHEW in various senses. **es'chewment**, the action of eschewing.

1583 BABINGTON *Commandm.* vii. (1590) 278 Things which keepe chastitie vncorrupted.. sobrietie, labour.. & *eschewall [ed. **1637** eschewing] of oportunitie. **1656** JEANES *Mixt. Scho. Div.* 22 The bare eschewall of an evill is sufficient for the denomination of feare. **1841** G. S. FABER *Prov. Lett.* (1844) I. 182 The convenient negative process of an eschewal of all cross-questioning. **1842** JAMES *Morley Ernstein* xv, With that careful *eschewance of all listening ears.. that gentleman remained bowing in silence till the waiter was out of the room. **1578** *Ch. Prayers* in *Priv. Prayers* (1851) 460 Give them such judges, as are .. *eschewers of all partiality. **1621** DK. BUCKHM. in *Life Bacon* xxii. (1861) 501 A messenger of good news to you and an eschewer of evil. **1825** COLERIDGE *Aids Refl.* (1848) I. 188 These eschewers of mystery. *c* **1374** CHAUCER *Boeth.* III. xi. 99 The ferme stablenesse of pedurable dwellynge and ek the *eschuynge of destruccyoun. **1563** in *Vicary's Anat.* (1888) App. iii. 164 Theschuynge of the greate Daunger & perill of the.. plage. **1864** WEBSTER, **Eschewment* (rare).

†**es'chew,** *v.*² *Obs. rare*⁻¹. [ad. OF. *escheu*, pa. pple. of *eschoir* (mod.Fr. *échoir*): see ESCHEAT.] *intr.* To fall out, fall to one's lot, befall.

? *a* **1400** *Morte Arth.* 2957 This chekke hyme eschewede be chauncez of armes.

eschin, obs. form of ESHIN, *dial.*

‖**es'choppe.** *Obs. rare*⁻¹. [Fr. *eschoppe* (now *échoppe*), OFr. *eschople*, *escopre*, corresp. to Sp. *escoplo*, Pg. *escopro*:—L. *scalprum*.] A steel-pointed tool for engraving on copper; a graver.

1662 EVELYN *Chalcogr.* 126 Bosse's invention of the Eschoppe does render the making of this Sulcus much more facile. *Ibid.* 97 His points and eschoppes.

‖**eschscholtzia** (ɛ'ʃɒltsɪə). Also eschscholzia. [mod.L.; the name was given in 1821 by A. v. Chamisso (*Hor. Phys. Berol.* 73) in compliment to J. F. v. Eschscholtz, one of his colleagues in the Romanzoff exploring expedition.] A Californian genus of herbaceous plants (N.O. *Papaveraceæ*); *E. californica*, the best known species, has finely divided glaucous leaves, and large bright yellow flowers, saffron-coloured in the centre. Also *attrib.*

1857 HENFREY *Bot.* 232 *Eschscholtzia*, a Californian genus, is now found in every garden. **1870** MISS BROUGHTON *Red as Rose* I. 73 Pulling the green nightcaps off the escholtzia [*sic*] buds.

eschutcheon: obs. var. ESCUTCHEON.

escien, obs. form of ASK.

escimuz, corrupt form of ECHENEIS.

1481 CAXTON *Myrr.* II. ix. 87 Ther is another manco of ffyshe in this see [of ynde], whiche ben named escimuz, whiche.. haue such strengthe that in contynent that they touche a ship one of them only reteyneth hym stylle.

esclaircisment, -issement, obs. forms of ECLAIRCISSEMENT.

1730-6 in BAILEY (folio). **1775** in ASH.

‖**esclandre** (ɛsklɑ̃dr). [Fr. *esclandre*, later form of OF. *escandre, escandle*:—L. *scandalum*: see SCANDAL and SLANDER.] Unpleasant notoriety; an occurrence which gives rise to it; a disturbance, scene.

1832 GREVILLE *Mem.* 1 June (1874) II. xviii. 306 Threatening to make an *esclandre* and leave the château. **1855** THACKERAY *Newcomes* (F. Hall). **1857** KINGSLEY *Two Y. Ago* xi. II. 11 Scoutbush, to avoid ésclandre and misery ..paid her her dividends as usual. **1881** LADY HERBERT *Edith* 18 Since the last 'esclandre' he had held little or no communication with her. **1882** J. C. MORISON *Macaulay* 55 An esclandre of any kind, cannot be associated even in imagination with his name.

†**e'sclare,** *v. Obs. rare*⁻¹. [a. OF. *esclare-r, esclarier* (mod.F. *éclairer*), corresp. to Pr. *esclairar*:—L. *exclār-āre* (rare), f. *ex-* out + *clārus* bright.] *trans.* To make clear, clear up.

1655 DIGGES *Compl. Ambass.* 318 We think it now reason that the matter of Religion be first esclared.

†**e'sclarish,** *v. Obs.* Also 6 esclarissh. [ad. OF. *esclariss-* lengthened stem of *esclarir*:—late L. type **exclārīre*, f. L. *ex-* out + *clār-us* clear, bright.] *trans.* To make clear or bright; to bring to light; to render illustrious.

1546 *St. Papers Hen. VIII*, XI. 16 This amitie and peax, which is now nuely esclarisshed and confirmed. **1566** PAINTER *Pal. Pleas.* 259 b, Which singuler perseueration in defence of her charitie..esclarisheth to the whole flocke of womankynde the bright beames of wisedome.

†**e'sclarishment.** *Obs.* In 6 esclerishement. [ad. OF. *esclerissement*, var. of *esclarissement*, f. *esclarir*: see prec.] A clearing up, explanation.

1549 in Strype *Eccl. Mem.* II. App. CC. 102 By the former treaty with th' esclerishement joynt hostility is not entred.

‖**esclavage** (ɛsklavaʒ). *Obs.* [Fr. *esclavage* (lit. 'slavery', f. *esclave* slave) used in same sense.] A necklace composed of several rows of gold chains, beads, or jewels, so called from its resemblance to the fetters of a slave.

1758 MRS. DELANY *Autobiog.* (1861) III. 478 All the bougets, esclavages, earrings and knots. **1766** COLMAN & GARRICK *Clandestine Marr.* 1, How d'ye like the Style of this Esclavage? **1834** PLANCHÉ *Brit. Costume* 323.

†**e'sclavish,** *v. Obs. rare.* [ad Fr. *esclaver* to enslave, on the analogy of *cherish*, etc.] *trans.* To enslave. Hence **esclavishing** *vbl. sb.*

1583 T. STOCKER *Hist. Ciu. Warres lowe C.* II. 32 To our vtter esclauisshyng and destruction for euer.

†**'escle.** *Obs.* [ad. L. *æsculus.*] (See quot.)

1577 B. GOOGE *Heresbach's Husb.* (1586) 106 The Escle is a kind of Oke, called..in Latine Esclus.

esclepis, obs. form of ECLIPSE.

‖**esclopette.** *Obs.* [var. of ESCOPETTE: for the form cf. med.L. *sclopētum.*] (See quot.)

1824 S. R. MEYRICK *Anc. Armour* Gloss., *Sclopus*, the esclopette or hand-gun. **1830** —— *Illust. Anc. Arms & Armour* Plate cxix, Fig. 4. A short wheel-lock esclopette of the time of Charles I..It is..intended to be carried in a holster in the same manner as a long pistol.

escocheon, obs. form of ESCUTCHEON.

‖**escoinçon.** *Arch.* [OF. *escoinçon* (mod. *écoinson.*] A stone which forms the upper part of an arched window. In quot. *attrib.*

1867 H. T. ELLACOMBE in *Trans. Exeter Archit. Soc.* I. Ser. II. 98 The jambs of these windows are splayed on the inside, and surmounted by escoinçon arches.

†**escompesall.**

1486 *Bk. St. Albans* C iij, Put in the wonde Escompesall unto tyme the dede flesh be wastyde.

†**esconduy,** *v. Obs. rare*⁻¹. [ad. OF. *escondui-re* (mod. *éconduire*), in this sense a pseudo-etymological perversion of earlier *escondire*, corresp. to Pr. *escondire*:—**excondīcĕre*, f. *ex-* out + *con* (= *cum*) with + *dīcĕre* to say.] *trans.* To give (a person) a denial *of* (something).

a **1450** *Knt. de la Tour* (1868) 85 Euery woman that disobeyed or esconduyed her husbonde of ani thinge that he comaunded her..she shulde be mued alle a yere.

†**escondyte,** *v. Obs. rare*⁻¹. [f. OF. *escondite* refusal, f. *escondire*: see prec.] *intr.* To give a refusal *to.*

1510-20 *Compl. too late maryed* (1862) 8 She wolde to no maner a man escondyte.

escopette (ɛskəʊ'pɛt). *U.S.* Also 9 escopate, -et. [ad. Sp. *escopeta* (assimilated to Fr. *escopette*) musket, ad. It. *schioppetto, scoppietto*, f. *schioppo* (by metathesis *scoppio*) noise, explosion, L. *sclopus, stlopus* the noise produced by a blow on the inflated cheek (in med.L. 'a gun').] A sort of carbine, used chiefly in Mexico and the adjoining parts of the U.S.

1805 PIKE *Sources Mississ.* II. (1810) 201, 50 dragoons and 50 mounted militia of the province, armed in the same manner, viz., Lances, escopates and pistols. **1850** B. TAYLOR *Eldorado* xxxiii. (1862) 336 A ranchero, carrying an escopette and three turkeys..offered his horse in exchange. **1851** MAYNE REID *Rifle Rangers* xx, A dozen..men were..firing their escopettes and pistols as they came down.

esco'petto. = prec.

1854 BARTLETT *Mex. Boundary* I. ii. 29 The Mexican beat him upon the head with the butt of his escopetto.

†**e'scorse,** *v. Obs.* [ad. OF. *escorce-r, escorcher* (mod.Fr. *écorcher*), corresp. to Pr. *escorgar, escortegar*:—med.L. *excorticāre*, f. *ex* out + *cortic-em* bark.] *trans.* To skin, flay. In quot. *fig.*

1546 *St. Papers Hen. VIII*, XI. 112 So..that they wer not escorsed and fleen to the bones.

escort ('ɛskɔːt), *sb.* Also 6 eskert (eskart), 8 escorte. [a. Fr. *escorte*, ad. It. *scorta*, f. *scorgere* to conduct:—late L. type **excorrigĕre*, f. *ex* out + *corrigĕre* to set right.]

1. a. *Mil.* A body of armed men accompanying a traveller or travellers (whether for protection or surveillance, or as a mark of honour), or serving as a guard or convoy for baggage, provisions, treasure, etc.

1579 FENTON *Guicciard.* XVIII. 1077 The bands..had ouerthrowen the eskert [*ed.* **1599** eskart] or garde [orig. *scorta*] of victuals. **1708** *Lond. Gaz.* No. 4458/2 The Horses and Waggons..began their March with an Escorte of 2000 Foot and 800 Horse. **1802** C. JAMES *Mil. Dict.*, *Escort of Deserters* consists..of a corporal and three rank and file. **1810** WELLINGTON in Gurw. *Disp.* VI. 470 And Colonel Trant with his division attacked the escort of the military chest. **1867** FREEMAN *Norm. Conq.* (1876) I. vi. 496 Not with an army but with a mere escort of strangers.

b. *Naut.* A warship, or group of warships, accompanying merchant ships or other vessels for protection. Also used of aircraft in a similar role. Freq. *attrib.*, as ***escort carrier, destroyer, vessel***; so ***escort duty, work.*** Also with defining word, as ***convoy escort, surface escort.***

1914 *Sphere* 31 Oct. 121/2 Numerous letters have now been received from men in the torpedo boat destroyers. One writes: 'We are doing patrolling duties...' Another says: 'After a period as escorts for transports we are now having a change.' **1918** *Ibid.* 9 Mar. 223 (*caption*) Some British battleships at sea with their escort of protecting destroyers. *Ibid.* 30 Mar. 273 (*caption*) A convoy escort returning to port. *Ibid.* 29 June 234/2 Two British destroyers..which formed the anti-submarine escort, at once engaged the enemy vessels. **1919** L. FREEMAN *Sea-Hounds* v. 129 As I heard one of the men put it, it was the 'bruisiest' bit of escort-work they had ever been..called upon to face. **1923** W. S. CHURCHILL *World Crisis* I. xxi. 496 The First Cruiser Squadron..had been..employed on escort duties at sea. **1938** *Jane's Fighting Ships* p. v, The heavily armed escort vessel *Egret* obviously designed to protect convoys against air attack. **1944** *Jane's All World's Aircraft 1943-44* 25a/2 The new class of Escort Carriers..adapted for flying operations by installing a 'flat top' deck. **1948** *Jane's Fighting Ships 1947-48* 222 New Construction Programme, 1948-50. Six escort destroyers to be laid down. **1954** S. W. ROSKILL *War at Sea 1939-1945* I. xvii. 358 The tactical employment of air escorts was now being improved steadily. *Ibid.*, Aircraft employed as convoy escorts or on anti-submarine patrols. *Ibid.*, Surface escorts..were being formed into Escort Groups in the Western Approaches Command. *Ibid.* xxi. 464 It was now possible to provide convoys with an average strength of five anti-submarine escorts.

c. *Aeronaut.* A fighter aircraft used to accompany bombers; usu. *attrib.*, as ***escort fighter.***

1946 A. LEE *German Air Force* i. 11 Messerschmitt 110.. As a long-range day escort fighter it was to fail. **1965** *New Statesman* 30 Apr. 690/3 The rapid conversion of the Mustang into a long-range escort.

2. *transf.* **a.** A number of persons, or often a single person, accompanying any one on a journey for the purpose of protection or guidance, or for courtesy's sake.

1745 *Fortunate Orphan* 33 Five Women, who had no other Escorte than a Recollet, this Jeweller, and a Youth of sixteen. **1754** RICHARDSON *Grandison* (1760) V. 61, I could not be so welcome to you as your escorte, as..I should be to Miss Byron and her friends, as her guest. **1847** JAMES *J. Marston Hall* xii, The encounter with the courier and his escort had taken place. *a* **1860** WRAXALL tr. *R. Houdin* xviii. 263 The ladies in waiting and the lady patronesses formed the royal escort.

b. A person (usu. a man) accompanying a woman to a dance, party, etc.

1936 *Lit. Digest* 12 Dec. 29/1 The escort merely announces himself downstairs at the client's address and presently she appears. **1946** K. TENNANT *Lost Haven* (1947) xvii. 267 Miss O'Shea was drinking ginger-beer and her escort had a shandy. **1955** T. STERLING *Evil of Day* viii. 95 The forget-me-not corsage..she had bought for herself, explaining to her escort that gardenias gave her a headache. **1955** J. P. DONLEAVY *Ginger Man* (1956) xi. 95 I've just walked into a bar, and I was frightened to death that the barman would tell me that women without escorts couldn't come in.

3. *abstr.* Attendance in the capacity of an escort.

1833 HT. MARTINEAU *Loom & Lugger* II. v. 97 To make him desire Cooper's escort. **1858** J. MARTINEAU *Studies Chr.* 221 The elder deities were compelled to..attend in escort to the Eastern idol.

escort (ɛ'skɔːt), *v.* [f. prec. sb.; cf. Fr. *escorter*, It. *scortare.*] *trans.* To act as escort to. **a.** *Mil.* of armed men; *Naut.* of a convoy. **b.** In wider sense: To accompany for the purpose of protecting or conducting, or of showing civility.

a. 1708 *Lond. Gaz.* No. 4478/3 Yesterday the Troops that escorted our Foragers, met with several of the Enemy's Parties. **1761-2** HUME *Hist. Eng.* (1806) IV. lx. 539 The herring busses were escorted by twelve men of war. **1855** MACAULAY *Hist. Eng.* III. 636 He was escorted by a body-guard under the command of Sarsfield.

b. 1742 DUNKIN in Francis *Horace's Sat.* I. ix, In private haunt, in public meet, Salute, escort him through the Street. **1754** RICHARDSON *Grandison* II. iv. 50 To escorte and guide me through this wood. **1828** SCOTT *F.M. Perth* xxxi, Catharine, escorted by old Henshaw and a groom of the Knight of Kinfauns. **1888** MISS BRADDON *Fatal Three* I. ii, He had escorted her to the first of her parties.

c. To 'keep company' or 'walk out' with (a woman). *U.S.*

1890 *Harper's Mag.* Oct. 716/2 A whisper also went the rounds that Dick Jones was escorting Miss Turner.

Hence **e'scorting** *ppl. a.*, that escorts. **e'scortment,** the action of escorting.

1870 *Pall Mall G.* 7 Nov. 7 The official list of the escorting officers. **1775** ADAIR *Amer. Ind.* 303 One of the warriors was sent to accompany me..by way of escortment.

escortage (ɛ'skɔːtɪdʒ). *U.S.* [f. ESCORT *v.* + -AGE.] The action of escorting.

1894 P. L. FORD *Hon. Peter Stirling* xxvii. 153 She likes my company, and finds my escortage very convenient. **1911** H. S. HARRISON *Queed* xiii. 146 At nine, as it chanced, she was to go out under the escortage of Charles Gardiner West.

e'scot, *sb.* [A Fr. form of SCOT (as in *scot and lot*); cf. OF., Pr. *escot* (mod.F. *écot*), It. *scotto.*] (See quot.; it does not appear where Johnson found the word.)

1755 JOHNSON, *Escot*, a tax paid in boroughs and corporations towards the support of the community, which is called scot and lot.

†**e'scot,** *v. Obs.* [a. OF. *escot-er*, f. *escot* (mod.F. *écot*): see prec.] *trans.* To pay a reckoning for, maintain.

1602 SHAKS. *Ham.* II. ii. 362 What are they Children? Who maintains 'em? How are they escoted? **1775** in ASH.

†**e'scout,** *sb. Obs.* [a. OF. *escoute* fem. (mod.F. *écoute*) act of listening, also sentinel, SCOUT, f. *escouter* (mod. *écouter*) to listen.]

1. Look-out, watch. [Cf. OF. *se mettre aux escoutes.*]

1630 HAYWARD *Edw. VI*, 29 They were well entrenched, having good escout abroad and sure watch within.

2. A SCOUT, spy.

1560 DAUS tr. *Sleidane's Comm.*, The escoutes that were sent out to knowe whiche waye the Emperour went, brought contrary reportes. **1600** HOLLAND *Livy* XXII. xxviii. 449 Intelligence given him..by meanes of his owne escouts and spies. **1603** —— *Plutarch's Mor.* 1329 Those be the Dæmons which are their [the gods'] espies and escouts.

†**e'scout,** *v. Obs. rare*⁻¹. [a. OF. *escout-er* (mod.F. *écouter*) = Pr. *escoutar*, Cat. *escoltar*, It. *ascoltare*:—L. *auscultāre* to listen.] *intr.* To act as a scout, explore, reconnoitre.

1600 HOLLAND *Livy* XXII. xv. 441 Having sent out to escout and espie 400 horsemen of confederats.

escribe (iː'skraɪb), *v.* [f. E- *pref.*³ + L. *scrībĕre* to write.]

†**1.** *trans.* To write or copy out. (More commonly EXSCRIBE.) *Obs.*

1558 in Picton *L'pool Munic. Rec.* (1883) I. 30 An old book of Precedences which was escribed, extracted out of the elder Precedences of the town.

2. *Math.* To describe (a circle) so as to touch one side of a triangle exteriorly, and the productions of the other two sides. (Cf. EXSCRIBE.) Hence **e'scribed** *ppl. a.*

1870 W. CHAUVENET *Geom.* II. 87 The three circles which lie without the triangle have been named escribed circles. **1881** J. CASEY *Seq. Euclid* 54 If the circle touch..the sides *AB, AC* produced; that is if it be an escribed circle.

†**e'scrime.** *Obs. rare*⁻¹. [a. Fr. *escrime*, f. *escrimer* to fence.] The art of fencing, *esp.* with sabre or sword.

1652 URQUHART *Jewel* Wks. (1834) 220 The most skilful teachers of Escrime, and fencing-masters of Italy.

†**e'scrimer.** *Obs.* In 6 eskrymeur. [a. Fr. *escrimeur*, f. *escrimer* to fence.] One who practises fencing; a fencer, a swordsman.

1572 SIR T. SMITH in Ellis *Orig. Lett.* II. 191 III. 21 The duke..provided..some eskrymeurs to shew us pastyme.

†**'escript.** *Obs.* Also 6 escripte. [a. OF. *escript*, semi-learned spelling of *escrit* (mod.F. *écrit*):—L. *script-um* neut., pa. pple. of *scrībĕre* to write.] A written document, a writing; *spec.* a written decree or mandate, a 'writ'.

1483 *Plumpton Corr.* p. xcv, We award that all such evidences, escripts, or muniments be delivered..afore the feast of St. John Babtist next coming. **1563** FOXE *A. & M.* 776/2 All and euery such proces, writings and escriptes as haue passed and bene don in this matter. **1590** T. FENNE *Fruits* 75 Those escripts and appointments which seemed so difficult and almost unpossible to be brought to passe. **1649**

SELDEN *Laws Eng.* II. iv. (1739) 21 Amongst other of the King's Escripts, it formed Writs remedial, for such as had received wrong. **1686** *Royal Proclam.* 10 Mar. in *Lond. Gaz.* No. 2120/2 And also Excepted, all Offences of Perjury.. Forging or Counterfeiting any Deeds, Escripts. **1724** *Col. Rec. Penn.* III. 245 The Governour proposed to send the following Escript by way of amendment.

†**e'scripture.** *Obs.* [a. OF. *escripture* (mod.F. *écriture*) = Pr. *escriptura*, Sp. *escritura*, It. *scrittura*:—L. *scrīptura* writing.] = SCRIPTURE.
1489 CAXTON *Faytes of A.* I. i. 4 The holy escripture saith of god that he is fiers.

escritoire (ɛskriːˈtwɑː(r), ˈɛskrɪtwɔː(r)). Forms: 8 escrutore, 8–9 escrutoire, escritoir, (8 escretore, -critore, 9 -cretoire), 8– escritoire. [a. F. *escritoire* (now *écritoire*) writing-case, writing-desk:—late L. *scrīptōrium* apparatus or place for writing, f. *scrībĕre* to write.
The aphetic forms *scritore*, SCRUTOIRE, occur in 17th c.]
A writing-desk constructed to contain stationery and documents; in early use, often one of a portable size; more recently, chiefly applied to a larger piece of furniture, a bureau or secretary.
[**1611** COTGR., *Escriptoire*, a penner.] **1706–7** FARQUHAR *Beaux' Strat.* v. iv, Captain Gibbet..had made bold..with your Study and Escritore. **1720** STRYPE *Stow's Surv.* (1754) I. III. vi. 598/2 Chests of drawers, Escrutores, Tables, and such like Joinery Wares. **1742** FIELDING *J. Andrews* III. iii. She..accordingly departed herself, having first broken open my escrutore. **1756** NUGENT *Gr. Tour, France* IV. 115 The escrutore, in the middle of this chamber, contains a most magnificent collection of antient and modern medals. **1848** THACKERAY *Van. Fair* xxiv, In the large shining mahogany escrutoire Mr. Osborne had a drawer especially devoted to his son's affairs and papers. **1882** MISS BRADDON *Mt. Royal* ix, An escritoire in the Sherraton style.
attrib. **1849** DICKENS *Dav. Copp.* xvii, There was a chest of drawers with an escrutoire top.
Hence **escri'torial** *a. nonce-wd.*, of or pertaining to an escritoire.
1785 COWPER *Let. Newton* Wks. 1837 XV. 163 One more circumstance..will impress upon you..a sense of the value we set upon its escritorial capacity.

†**escri'vain.** *Obs. rare*⁻¹. [a. OF. *escrivain* (mod.F. *écrivain*) = Pr. *escriban*, Sp. *escribano*, It. *scrivano*:—late L. *scrībānus*, f. L. *scrība* scribe.] A clerk.
a **1734** NORTH *Lives* (1826) II. 399 Servants, escrivains and other attendances at a great expense.

†**escri'van.** *Obs. rare*⁻¹. [ad. Pg. *escrivão*: see prec.] A clerk on board a ship, a supercargo.
1726 SHELVOCKE *Voy. round World* 341 The Escrivan of the said ship..desir'd we would sell him the Jesus Maria.

†**e'scroc,** *v. Obs.* [f. F. *escroc* swindler: cf. Fr. *escroquer* to swindle.] *trans.* To gain by swindling.
1738 *Com. Sense* (1739) II. 45 Employing Tricks to escroc all they could for the Civil List, etc. *Ibid.* II. 183 Occasions are laid hold of to escroc more and more from the Publick.

escrod (ɛˈskrɒd). A small fresh cod broiled; = SCROD.
18.. D. WEBSTER (Webster), That morsel for Monica, an escrod. In mod. Dicts.

‖**escroeles,** *sb. pl. Obs. rare*⁻¹. In 5 *erron.* escroceles. [OF. *escroelles* fem. pl. (mod.F. *écrouelles*):—late L. *scrofellas*, dim. of *scrofulæ*: see SCROFULA.] Scrofula.
1483 CAXTON *Gold. Leg.* 372/2 A maide..had her throte gretely swollen of a maladye called the escroceles.

escroll (ɛˈskrəʊl). Forms: 6–7 escrowle, 7–8 escrol(e, -olle, 7– escroll. [ad. OF. *escroele*, dim. of *escroe*: see next and SCROLL.]
†**1.** *Law.* = ESCROW. *Obs.*
1622 MALYNES *Anc. Law-Merch.* 102 To deliuer a Writing, or a Bill as an Escroll is vnknowne vnto all Merchants there. **1642** PERKINS *Prof. Bk.* i. §9. 5 If..shee deliver the same deed unto a stranger as an Escrowle, upon condition that, etc. **1736** CARTE *Ormonde* I. 569 They signed the instrument of the peace to agree it might lie as an escroll in the hands of the Marquis of Clanricarde.
2. *Her.* = SCROLL.
1610 GUILLIM *Heraldry* III. xx. (1611) 160 With one Escrole hauing this Motto *Ich Dien.* **1706** HEARNE *Collect.* 25 Mar. (Oxf. Hist. Soc.) I. 209 Underneath there is this Escrolle, *Memoria pij æterna.* **1807** G. CHALMERS *Caledonia* I. III. x. 463 Ancient families converted their war-cries into mottos, which they placed upon escrols above their crests. **1868** *Regul. & Ord. Army* 8 The Motto 'Virtutis fortuna comes' in an Escrole above.

escrow (ɛˈskrəʊ). *Law.* [a. AF. *escrowe*, *escrouwe*, OF. *escroe*, *escroue* scrap, shred, strip of parchment, scroll (mod.F. *écroue* entry of a name in a jail register):—med.L. type **scrōda*, of Teut. origin: cf. OHG. *scrôt* scrap, fragment:—OTeut. **skraudo-* (whence Eng. SHRED).]
a. (See quots.)
1598 KITCHIN *Courts Leet* (1675) 449 It was delivered as an Escrow upon condition. **1708** *Termes de la Ley* 306 An Escrow is a Deed delivered to a third person to be the Deed of the party upon a future condition. **1885** *Law Times Rep.* LI. 663/1 The part signed by the defendant was only an escrow in the hands of her solicitor, and not to take effect until the other part was signed by the plaintiff.
b. A deposit held in trust or as security; ***in escrow***, phr. used of money, etc., so held. *N. Amer.*
1888 *Boston* (Mass.) *Jrnl.* 17 Oct. 1/7, $800,000 is held in escrow to pay off unmatured bonds. **1932** *Amer. Mercury* May 44/2 Ralston now had in his possession diamonds believed to be worth at least $1,500,000, ample security for the $300,000 which had been placed in escrow, and which he immediately paid over to the prospectors. **1957** *Economist* 30 Nov. 777/2 About $100 million in fees from the disputed area of Louisiana have been put in escrow pending the court's decision. **1967** WODEHOUSE *Company for Henry* i. 27 'I am temporarily not in possession of a watch.' 'Pawned it?' 'It is for the moment in escrow.'

escrutoire, obs. form of ESCRITOIRE.

†**e'scry,** *sb. Obs.* [f. ESCRY *v.* See the variant forms ASCRY, SCRY.] **a.** Outcry, exclamation; notoriety. **b.** Battle-cry. *lit.* and *fig.*
1483 CAXTON *G. de la Tour* L v, Suche dishonour and escry is not soone put oute. **1489** —— *Faytes of A.* I. xxiv. 75 The lasse bolde are wont for to gyue vp the escrye by-fore that the bataylle be bygonne. **1515** BARCLAY *Egloges* IV. (1570) Dj/1 Faynt cowarde mindes soone at the first escry Of sturdie labour, fall to the grounde as lame. **1538** LELAND *Itin.* VI. 66 Gaspar..durst not welle land for Escryes that were made when he proferid to the Shore.

†**e'scry,** *v. Obs.* Forms: 5–6 escrye, 7 escrie. [a. OF. *escrie-r*, f. *es*:—L. *ex* out + *crier* to CRY. The earlier Eng. form from 13th c. was ASCRY, prob. representing an AF. *ascrier*; and there was an aphetic SCRY, q.v.]
1. *intr.* To cry out, exclaim.
1483 CAXTON *Gold. Leg.* 84/1 Thenne one of them escryed and said, etc. *a* **1533** LD. BERNERS *Huon* lv. 185 He escryed a hye & sayd 'Syr Kynge', etc.
2. *trans.* To call out to, hail; also, to call upon, invoke.
1483 CAXTON *Gold. Leg.* 121/2 Put out thy voys and escrye hym frely. **1485** —— *Chs. Gt.* 77 He..began to escrye the holy trynyte. *c* **1530** LD. BERNERS *Arth. Lyt. Bryt.* (1814) 112 He spurred horse and escryed the senesshall.
b. ***to escry him, them,*** etc. ***to*** or ***unto death,*** used to translate Fr. *lui, leur escrier 'à mort!'* or *'à la mort!'*
1475 CAXTON *Jason* 8b, And syn they escried alle the dronken centauris unto the dethe. **1523** LD. BERNERS *Froiss.* I. ccclxxxvi. 659 They were enclosed with the gauntoyse, who escryed them to dethe.
3. *trans.* = DESCRY: to cry out upon on discovering; *hence* to espy, discover. Also, with *out.*
1581 J. BELL *Haddon's Answ. Osor.* 100 Vouchsafe therefore a good felowshyp (Osorius) to escry out one safe Haven for us. **1581** J. STUDLEY tr. *Seneca's Medea* III. Cho. 127b, Some travelers shall the Countreys farre escrye Beyond small Thule, Knowen furthest at this day. **1598** HAKLUYT *Voy.* I. 596 (R.) At the same time the Spanish fleet was escried by an English Pinasse. **1625** PURCHAS *Pilgrims* II. 775 From hence you may plainly escrie the promontory of Azaphi.

‖**e'scu.** [Fr.; older form of *écu*: see ÉCU.]
c **1663** F. WILLUGHBY in *Ray's Philos. Lett.* (1718) 11 At the expence of an Escus for a Guide. **1731** in BAILEY vol. II. **1775** in ASH.

escuage (ˈɛskjuːɪdʒ). *Feudal Law. Obs.* exc. *Hist.* [a. AF. *escuage*, f. OF. *escu* (mod.F. *écu*):—L. *scūtum* shield. Cf. SCUTAGE.]
†**1.** The chief form of feudal tenure (*lit.* shield-service), personal service in the field for a period of forty days in each year. *Obs.*
1513 BRADSHAW *St. Werburge* II. 1773 Many helde their landes..with seruice de chiualere and some by escuage. **1592** WYRLEY *Armorie* 19 Euery tenant that held lands by a knights fee was tied to do his Lord escuage or shield seruice. **1695** TEMPLE *Hist. Eng.* (1699) 171 Those Authors.. pretend this Duty of Escuage..to have come over in this Reign. **1766** BLACKSTONE *Comm.* II. v. 74 This kind of tenure was called *scutagium* in Latin..or *servitium scuti*..in our Norman French *escuage.*
b. *transf.*
1605 SYLVESTER *Du Bartas* II. ii. III. (1605–7) I. 454 Our Grand-sires..euen in Age Could render duly Venus Escuage. **1623** COCKERAM, *Venus-escuage*, wanton fleshlinesse.
2. A money payment in lieu of military service; = SCUTAGE.
1577–87 HOLINSHED *Chron.* an. 1214. 184/1 The king demanded escuage of them that refused to go with him into Poictow. **1641** W. HAKEWIL *Libertie of the Subject* 17 Every man that by his tenure is bound to serve the King in his warres, and faileth, is to pay..a fine by the name of Escuage. **1679** BLOUNT *Anc. Tenures* 95 When escuage is assessed throughout the land..the said Sir Philip shall pay, etc. **1738** *Hist. Crt. Excheq.* ii. 23 The Baron appearing in the Host had Escuage on his own Tenants that made Default.

‖**escudero** (eskuˈdero). [Sp.; f. *escudo* shield: see ESQUIRE.] A shield-bearer; an esquire; hence, an attendant; a lady's page.
a **1637** B. JONSON (Webster). **1865** T. B. ALDRICH *Knt. of Aragon* Poems 113 His escuderos rode in front, His cavaliers behind.

escudo (ɛˈskjuːdəʊ). [Sp., Pg.:—L. *scūtum* shield. Cf. ÉCU, SCUDO.] A Portuguese silver coin, originally of the value of a crown. Also applied to other former coins, gold or silver, in Spain, Portugal, and Spanish America.
1821 P. KELLY *Universal Cambist* (ed. 2) II. 281 *Escudo*,.. a gold coin of Portugal and Spain. **1914** E. C. HARGROVE *Progressive Portugal* 262 In 1913, the Portuguese Authorities altered the denomination of the coinage from milreis and reis to escudos and centavos. **1920** *Chambers's Jrnl.* 404/2 The escudo, which normally..is of the value of nearly four shillings and sixpence. **1925** *Glasgow Herald* 14 Aug. 6 The paper escudos nominally equivalent to a French franc. **1957** *New Statesman* 2 Nov. 554/1 Scruffy black-marketeers..offered me wads of *escudos* for my ticket.

Esculapian, var. of ÆSCULAPIAN.

esculate, var. form of ÆSCULATE.

†**'esculency.** *Obs. rare*⁻¹. [f. next: see -ENCY.] The quality of being esculent or eatable.
1651 BIGGS *New Disp.* 197 Though lesse commodious for esculency.

esculent (ˈɛskjʊlənt), *a.* and *sb.* [ad. L. *esculent-us*, f. *esca* food.]
A. *adj.*
1. Suitable for food, eatable.
1626 BACON *Sylva* §630 A Number of Herbs are not Esculent at all. **1756** C. LUCAS *Ess. Waters* III. 238 The gardens afford good supplies of the best esculent vegetables. **1813** BINGLEY *Anim. Biog.* (ed. 4) III. 471 Esculent Snail. **1816** KIRBY & SP. *Entomol.* x. (1828) I. 310 The order Aptera does not much more abound in esculent insects than the Diptera. **1866** ROGERS *Agric. & Prices* I. iv. 66 Onions and cabbage appear to have been the only esculent vegetables.
¶ *confused use.*
1813 BINGLEY *Anim. Biog.* (ed. 4) II. 212 The Esculent Swallow. The nest of this bird is edible.
2. *absol.* quasi-*sb.*
1626 BACON *Sylva* (1631) § 474 In Plants, where the Root is the Esculent, as Radish, and Parsnips.
B. *sb.* Anything that is eatable, or fit for food; *esp.* vegetables.
1625 MASSINGER *New Way* IV. ii, A piece of Suffolk cheese, or gammon of bacon, Or any esculent, as the learned call it. **1725** BRADLEY *Fam. Dict. Esculents*, by which is to be understood Plants for Food. **1754** DODSLEY *Agric.* ii, His various esculents, from glowing beds Give the fair promise of delicious feasts. **1863** BALL in *N. & Q.* Ser. III. IV. 193 The 4th of August was the period when the juicy esculent could be first enjoyed. **1872** YEATS *Growth Comm.* 25 The varieties of palm furnished..an esculent something like the cabbage.

esculic, -in(e, var. forms of ÆSCULIC, -IN.

†**e'scume.** [a. OF. *escume* (mod.F. *écume*): see SCUM.] Froth.
1527 ANDREW *Brunswyke's Distyl. Waters* Piij, Escume made of this herbe [radish] used in vaperous bathes dystroyeth age.

E'scurialize, *v. nonce-wd.* [f. *Escurial* (better *Escorial*), the name of the chief palace of the Spanish kings, about 30 miles from Madrid.] *trans.* To subject to influences like those which prevailed at the Escurial.
1843 *Tait's Mag.* X. 617 Kings and queens are no longer ..puppets to be played with by dexterous mountebanks, or Escurialized into idiotism.

escurie: see EQUERRY.

escuse, obs. form of EXCUSE *sb.* and *v.*

escutcheon (ɛˈskʌtʃən). Forms: (5 escochon, 6 escuchon), 7, 9 escocheon, (7 eschoch-, eschucheon, -ion, escochion, escotch-, escucheon, -tchion, -tcheer), 8 eschutcheon, 6– escutcheon. See also SCUTCHEON. [a. ONF. *escuchon* (central OF. *escusson*, mod. *écusson*):—late L. type **scūtiōn-em*, f. *scūtum* shield.]
JOHNSON **1755** has only the form *eschutcheon.*
1. a. *Her.* The shield or shield-shaped surface on which a coat of arms is depicted; also in wider sense, the shield with the armorial bearings; a sculptured or painted representation of this.
1480 *Wardr. Acc. Edw. IV* (1830) 131 Escochons of papir in colours of the armes of Lorde George Ver. **1594** *Mirr. Policy* (1599) M iij, And from that time the use of Escuchons and Armory was found out, as a witnesse of their Nobility. **1610** HOLLAND *Camden's Brit.* I. 405 Their Eschocheon Gules with sixe escallops argent. **1679** PLOT *Staffordsh.* (1686) A, The figures on the right hand each Escocheon, shewing what Armes belong to the Houses. **1774** WARTON *Hist. Eng. Poetry* III. (R.), The addition of the escutcheon of Edward the Confessor..was a sufficient foundation for an impeachment of high treason. **1815** SCOTT *Guy M.* xli, The carved stone escutcheon of the ancient family..was hung diagonally beneath the helmet and crest. **1846** PRESCOTT *Ferd. & Is.* I. vi. 277 They were prohibited from quartering the royal arms on their escutcheons. **1885** MISS BRADDON *Wyllard's Weird* ii, Gray granite pillars, each crowned with the escutcheon of the Heathcotes.
b. *fig.*; esp. in phrases like ***a blot on an escutcheon*** = a stain on a person's reputation.
1697 DRYDEN *Virgil* (1806) II. 175 Ded., The banishment of Ovid was a blot in his escutcheon. **1848** R. W. HAMILTON *Disq. Sabbath* v. 180 We are not ashamed of our [Puritan] fathers..The escocheon of their virtues is our proudest heraldry. **1862** SHIRLEY *Nugæ Crit.* x. 444 The people of Edinburgh were eager to remove an unseemly stain from the escutcheon of their city. **1868** FREEMAN *Norm. Conq.* (1876) II. vii. 45 A dark blot on the escutcheon of the House of Godwine.

c. *escutcheon of pretence*: the small escutcheon bearing the arms of an heiress placed in the centre of her husband's shield. Cf. INESCUTCHEON.

1677 *Lond. Gaz.* No. 1208/4 Upon an Escutcheer of Pretence, a Chevern between three Birds. **1766–87** PORNY *Her.* 123. **1823** RUTTER *Fonthill* p. xxiv, Mervyn quartering Squire, and on an escutcheon of pretence, Green, etc.

†**2.** A hatchment. (More fully ***funeral escutcheon***.) *Obs.*

a **1672** WOOD *Life* (1848) 40 Escocheons which he had got by burying several persons of quality. **1688** R. HOLME *Armoury* I. 4/1 Every Gentleman..was interr'd with Funeral Escochions. **1722** DE FOE *Col. Jack* (1840) 347 Mrs. Veal was..dead, and her escutcheons were making. **1750** JOHNSON *Rambler* No. 73 ¶7 At last the eldest fell ill..I dreamed every night of escutcheons and white gloves. **1820** W. IRVING *Sketch-bk.* II. 183 Several ancient monuments.. over some of which hang funeral escutcheons.

3. Anything shaped like, or resembling, an escutcheon: **a.** *gen.* (see quot.)

1602 PLAT *Delightes for Ladies* xviii, Of..Marchpane paste..our comfit makers..make..Armes, escocheons, beasts, birds, and other fancies.

b. *Arch.* A shield-shaped ornament, chiefly in Gothic buildings, carved on the bosses of ceilngs, at the ends of weather-mouldings, etc.

1875 PARKER *Gloss. Goth. Archit.*

c. A key-hole plate, a name plate, etc.

1655 MRQ. WORCESTER *Cent. Inv.* §72 An Escocheon to be placed before any of these locks. **1879** GWILT *Archit.* Gloss., *Escutcheon*..a plate for protecting the keyhole of a door; or one to which the handle of a door is attached.

d. *Horticulture.* A shield-shaped portion of a branch, containing a bud, cut for use as a graft.

1658 EVELYN *Fr. Gard.* (1675) 61 Cut your escutcheon long enough..that it may derive nourishment.

e. *Naut.* (see quot.)

1867 SMYTH *Sailor's Word-bk.*, *Escutcheon*, the compartment in the middle of the ship's stern, where her name is written.

f. *Zool.* (see quots.)

1854 WOODWARD *Mollusca* II. 947 The lunule..is an oval space in front of the beaks [of bivalves]..When a similar impression exists behind the beaks, it is termed the escutcheon. *Ibid.* (1856) 305 Meroe..Shell oval, compressed..ligament in a deep escutcheon.

g. = *milk escutcheon* (MILK *sb.* 10).

1847 tr. *F. Guenon's Treat. Milk Cows* 33 Cows of each class have their print or escutcheon marked by the hair, which starting first from the middle of the four teats, as the center, extends under the belly... It may be said in general, that the cows whose escutcheon is formed of the finest hair, are the best. **1881** [see *milk-escutcheon*]. **1912** F. T. BARTON *Cattle, Sheep & Pigs* i. 18 The escutcheon may extend over the whole of the hind quarters and the udder.

4. *Comb.* **escutcheon grafting** (see 3 d).

1727 BRADLEY *Fam. Dict.* s.v. *Grafting*, They will thrive.. well upon the Quince tree by Escutcheon grafting.

Hence **e'scutcheoned** *ppl. a.*, furnished or decorated with escutcheons.

1742 YOUNG *Nt. Th.* II. 356 What..is this escutcheon'd world, Which hangs out Death in one eternal night? **1822** BYRON *Werner* v. i, Our banner'd and escutcheon'd gallery. **1843** CARLYLE *Past & Pr.* (1858) 298 Doggeries never so escutcheoned must take the fate of such.

-ese, *suffix*, forming adjs., is ad. OF. *-eis* (mod.F. *-ois*, *-ais*):—Com. Romanic *-ese* (It. *-ese*, Pr., Sp. *-es*, Pg. *-ez*):—L. *ēnsem*. The L. suffix had the sense 'belonging to, originating in (a place)', as in *hortēnsis*, *prātēnsis*, f. *hortus* garden, *prātum* meadow, and in many adjs. f. local names, as *Carthāginiēnsis* Carthaginian, *Athēniēnsis* Athenian. Its representatives in the Romanic langs. are still the ordinary means of forming adjs. upon names of countries or places. In Eng. *-ese* forms derivatives from names of countries (chiefly after Romanic prototypes), as *Chinese*, *Portuguese*, *Japanese*, and from some names of *foreign* (never English) towns, as *Milanese*, *Viennese*, *Pekinese*, *Cantonese*. These adjs. may usually be employed as sbs., either as names of languages, or as designations of persons; in the latter use they formerly had plurals in *-s*, but the pl. has now the same form as the sing., the words being taken rather as adjs. used *absol.* than as proper sbs. (From words in *-ese* used as pl. have arisen in illiterate speech such sing. forms as *Chinee*, *Maltee*, *Portugee*.) A frequent mod. application of the suffix is to form words designating the diction of certain authors who are accused of writing in a dialect of their own invention; e.g. *Johnsonese*, *Carlylese*. On the model of derivatives from authors' names were formed *Americanese*, *cablese*, *headlinese*, *journalese*, *newspaperese*, *novelese*, *officialese*, etc.

1898 F. HARRISON in *19th Cent.* June 941 As Mat Arnold said to me..'Flee Carlylese as the very devil!' Yes! flee Carlylese, Ruskinese, Meredithese, and every other *ese*. **1899** *Golf Illustr.* 14 July 134 American 'golfese'. **1906** *Daily Chron.* 2 Aug. 3/2 Deplorable guide-bookese. **1935** E. E. CUMMINGS *Let.* 11 Mar. (1969) 140 Am fighting..to retranslate 71 poems out of typewriter language into linotype-ese. **1951** *Amer. Speech* XXVI. 172 (*heading*) Washingtonese.

ese, eseliche, esement, obs. ff. EASE, etc.

esee, -i, -ie, -y(e, obs. forms of EASY.

esemplastic (ɛsɛmˈplæstɪk), *a.* [f. Gr. ἐς into + ἕν, neut. of εἷς + πλαστικ-ός, f. πλάσσειν to mould: a word irregularly formed by Coleridge, and probably suggested to him by the Ger. *ineinsbildung* forming into one.] Having the function of moulding into unity; unifying.

1817 COLERIDGE *Biog. Lit.* 139 On the imagination, or esemplastic power. **1827** HARE *Guesses* Ser. I. (1873) 220 Nor I trust will Coleridge's favorite word esemplastic..ever become current. **1879** FARRAR *St. Paul* II. 488 The unifying—or if I may use the expression, esemplastic—power of the imagination over the many subordinate truths.

esemplasy (ɛˈsɛmpləsɪ). [f. as prec. + Gr. πλάσις moulding + -Y.] (See quot.)

1852 *Fraser's Mag.* XLVI. 65 Neither of them possessed that gift, which Schelling endeavoured to express by the term Eseinsbildung [*sic*; *read* ineinsbildung], and Coleridge by the term esemplasy—the power, that is, of infusing into the various parts of a subject an ever-present unity.

esen, pl. of *ease*, obs. form of EAVES.

eserine (ˈɛsəraɪn). *Chem.* [a. Fr. *ésérine*, f. *éséré*, the native name of the plant; see -INE.

(First used in Fr. by Vée *Recherches chimiques sur la fève du Calabar* 1865).]

A crystalline alkaloid obtained from the Calabar bean, the fruit of *Physostigma venenosum*, employed in solution in medicine to produce contraction in the pupil of the eye.

1879 P. SMITH *Glaucoma* 153 Eserine lowers the tension of the glaucomatous eye. **1888** *Edin. Rev.* Oct. 507 Eserine or physostigmine.

†**esguard.** *Obs.* [a. OF. *esgard* (mod.F. *égard*) 'tribunal des chevaliers de Malte', lit. 'look, attention', corresp. to It. *sguardo*: see ES- and GUARD.] A tribunal existing among the knights of St. John, to settle differences between members of the order.

1616 BEAUM. & FL. *Knt. of Malta* v. ii, Proceed to th' ceremony:—one of our Esguard Degrade Mountferrat first.

esh, -en, dial. forms of ASH, ASHEN.

1512 *Northumb. Househ. Bk.* 354 To gyf yerely as many eshen cuppis. **1808** R. ANDERSON *Cumbld. Ball.*, *Our Jwohny*, I cowr'd my ways down, ahint our young eshes.

†**eshen, eshime.** *Obs.* Some precious stone.

1613 PURCHAS *Pilgrimage, Descr. India* (1864) 38 Of Eshime, which stone comes from Cataya, one Batman. *Ibid.* 42 Lignum aloes, Eshen and Corall.

'eshin. *dial.* Also 6 **eschin, eshen, -yne, ession, esshon, -en**, 7 **eshon.** [Etymology uncertain; ? var. of ASHEN (vessel); cf. ON. *eski* ashen box, mod.Icel. *askja* box generally.] A wooden pail or shallow tub.

1547 *Lanc. & Chesh. Wills* (Chetham Soc.) I. 109, V milke trowhgs and v essions xxd. **1558** *Ibid.* (1884) 20 Fyve loomes for Ale..and iiij Esshons. **1573** *Ibid.* III. 60 Sex eshens or skales. **1688** R. HOLME *Armoury* III. 335/1 Of some Milk-Maids..I have heard..a Milk Pail called..a Cruck, an Eshon, of others a Bouk. **1691** RAY *N.C. Words*, *Eshin*, a pail or kit. **1775** in ASH. **1884** *Cheshire Gloss.*, *Eshin*, a large can for carrying milk from the shippon to the house.

eshlar (ˈɛʃlə(r)), var. of ASHLAR *sb.*

1847 in CRAIG.

esi(e, esili, obs. forms of EASY, EASILY.

esil(e, var. forms of EISELL.

eskanted, variant of ASKANTED, *Obs.*

eskart, ? obs. form of ESCORT.

esker (ˈɛskə(r)). *Geol.* Also 9 **escar, eskar, -ir.** [a. Ir. *eiscir.*] 'The name given in Ireland to the elongated and often flat-topped mounds of post-glacial gravel which occur abundantly in the greater river-valleys of that country' (Page); (not now restricted to Ireland or to Irish usage). Also in *comb.*, as *esker-like*.

1852 E. FORBES in Wilson & Geikie *Life* xiv. 505 The top of Headon Hill is capped by a great esker of gravel. **1865** PAGE *Hand-bk. Geol.*, *Eskirs* or Escars. **1882** GEIKIE *Text-bk. Geol.* VI. v. i. §1. 892 Ridges, known in Scotland as kames, in Ireland as eskers, and in Scandinavia as ösar. **1882** O'DONOVAN *Merv Oasis* I. iii. 55 Towards sunset we neared the flank of a long escar-like sand ridge. **1917** *Nature* 2 Aug. 441/2 He considers that the ice-barrier tongues from the Antarctic glaciers are afloat and do not rest on esker-like embankments built of their moraines and subglacial gravels. **1955** *Sci. Amer.* Sept. 85 Winding across the center [of the Tasnuna Valley, Alaska] is an esker, a narrow ridge of gravel left by a stream that ran through the glacier. **1966** *Times* 28 Feb. (Canada Suppl.) p. xvi/2 Frozen lakes, eskers and beaches permit the landing of heavily loaded machines for six months of the year.

eskert, obs. var. ESCORT.

esk-ien, obs. form of ASK *v.*

Eskimo (ˈɛskɪməʊ), *sb.* and *a.* Also **Esquimaux** (6–8 **Eskemo, Esquimaw, Esquimo**, etc.). Pl. **-oes, -os** (-əʊz), **-aux** (-əʊ). [a. Da. *Eskimo* (Sw. *Eskimå*), ad. F. *Esquimaux* pl., from some Algonquian Indian language; cf. Proto-Algonquian **ašk-* raw, **-imo* eat, Abnaki *askimo* (pl. *askimoak*), Eskimo, eaters of raw flesh.]

A. *sb.* **1.** A member of a widely spread people inhabiting the Arctic from Greenland to Eastern Siberia. (Their own name for themselves is INNUIT.) Used as sing. and pl.

1584 HAKLUYT *Disc. Western Planting* (1877) xiii. 88 The more northerly partes of the lande amonge the Esquimawes of the Grande Bay. *c* **1685** P. E. RADISSON *Voyages* (1885) 260 Wee put into Harbour..to take in fresh Water..at the Coast of the Indians called Esquimos. **1689** H. KELSEY *Jrnl.* 5 July in *Kelsey Papers* (1929) 27 Not suffering me to speak aloud in pretence yͤ Eskemoes would hear us. **1792** G. CARTWRIGHT *Labrador* 7 The Esquimaux from Ice and snow now free, In Shallops and in Whale-boats go to Sea. **1850** *Eskimaux & Eng. Vocab.* p. vii, If the extent of country be considered, the Innuit or Eskimaux is one of the most widely spread nations on the globe. **1850** R. G. LATHAM *Nat. Hist. Var. Man* I. F. 290 The Eskimo is essentially a Mongol in physiognomy. **1895** KIPLING *2nd Jungle Bk.* 145 Kadlu was an Inuit—what you call an Esquimau. **1915** *Lit. Digest* 16 Jan. 130/1 A month in the land of Gold, Glaciers, Totems, and Esquimos. **1936** *Discovery* July 200/2 According to his view the eastern or Caribou Eskimo are neither original nor degenerate, but represent a fusion of Eskimo and Indian cultures. **1965** R. F. SPENCER et al. *Native Americans* 119 Even though the territorial expanse covered by the Eskimo is tremendous, there is a remarkable unity to Eskimo culture.

2. Any of the several languages of this people, of which one set of dialects or languages, also called Inupik, is spread from Norton Sound, Alaska, to Greenland, and another set, also called Yupik, is in southwest Alaska and the eastern tip of Siberia. These languages, together with those of the Aleut, form the *Eskimo-Aleut*, *-Aleutian* family. Also applied to a jargon used in intercourse between Eskimos and persons of European origin, consisting mainly of Eskimo words.

1819 J. ROSS *Voy. Discovery* v. 80 A reply was again made in the Eskimaux. **1850** R. G. LATHAM *Nat. Hist. Var. Man* I. F. 290 From the grammar of Fabricius, the Eskimo was soon known to be a language of long compound words. **1916** E. W. HAWKES *Labrador Eskimo* 6 Lieut. Lucas, who had acquired a knowledge of Eskimo. **1921** E. SAPIR in *Science* LIV. 408 (*heading*) Eskimo-Aleut. **1932** W. L. GRAFF *Lang. & Langs.* xi. 405 A common Uralian language with which also Eskimo-Aleutian appears to be related. **1939** L. H. GRAY *Found. Lang.* xiii. 374 Eskimo-Aleut has been regarded by highly competent authorities as ultimately cognate with Altaic. **1958** C. F. HOCKETT *Course in Mod. Ling.* 260 In Eskimo..ordinary nouns have a case system of the ergative type. **1964** M. SWADESH in Jennings & Norbeck *Prehist. Man in New World* 531 The last extant language to enter the New World was apparently the forerunner of Eskimo-Aleutian.

3. = *Eskimo dog.*

1856 KANE *Arct. Expl.* I. xiv. 163 My dogs,..the nine splendid Newfoundlanders and thirty-five Esquimaux.., had perished. **1872** W. F. BUTLER *Great Lone Land* (ed. 2) xxii. 339 The other two [dogs] were a curious compound of Esquimaux and Athabascan. **1909** W. T. GRENFELL *Adrift on Ice-Pan* (1910) 3 'Sue', a large, dark Eskimo, the image of a great black wolf, with her sharp-pointed and perpendicular ears. **1948** C. L. B. HUBBARD *Dogs in Britain* xvii. 178 The Husky Proper..has long been officially recognised..as a show dog, under the name of Eskimo.

4. = *Eskimo pie.*

1922 *Glasgow Herald* 11 Oct. 8 Chocolate eggs filled with ice-cream and known as 'Eskimos'.

B. *adj.* **1.** Of or pertaining to this people or their language.

1744 A. DOBBS *Hudson Bay* 49 The East Main... Here the Nodway or Eskimaux Indians live. *Ibid.* 203 A vocabulary of English and Eskima words. **1770** G. CARTWRIGHT *Jrnl.* 6 Dec. (1792) I. 66 A very imperfect vocabulary of the Esquimaux language. **1791** J. LONG (*title*) Voyages and travels of an Indian interpreter... To which is added..a list of words in the Iroquois, Mohegan, Shawanee, and Esquimeaux Tongues. **1845** YOUATT *Dog* iii. 56 The Esquimaux Indian goes in pursuit of the seal. **1850** R. G. LATHAM *Nat. Hist. Var. Man* I. F. 289 The difficulties presented by the Eskimo language. **1875** H. RINK *Tales & Trads. Eskimo* p. viii, Words..peculiar to Eskimo life. **1918** [see ESKIMOID *a.*]. **1965** *North* (Ottawa) Nov.–Dec. 12 Letters from the children written in English and Eskimo script.

2. ***Eskimo dog***, a large, powerful dog used in the Arctic to draw sledges and for hunting.

1774 B. LA TROBE *Acc. Mission Esquimaux Indians* 29 The great number of Esquimaux dogs..tear out and devour the fish. **1845** YOUATT *Dog* iii. 55 The Esquimaux Dog is a beast of burden and of draught. **1909** W. T. GRENFELL *Adrift on Ice-Pan* (1910) 38, I determined..to kill a big Eskimo dog.

3. ***Eskimo curlew*** (see quots.). *U.S.*

1813 A. WILSON *Amer. Ornith.* VII. 22 The Esquimaux Curlew..is called by our gunners on the sea-coast, the Short-billed Curlew. **1870** *Amer. Naturalist* III. 83 Esquimaux Curlew (*Numenius borealis*) breeds near Fort Benton. **1921** *Outing* (U.S.) May 65/1 The passenger pigeon, the great auk.., the Eskimo curlew are no more. **1966** *New Statesman* 11 Nov. 710/3 The Eskimo curlew.. winters in Patagonia..and then flies the whole length of the two continents to breed inside the Arctic Circle.

4. ***Eskimo pie*** (proprietary name), a bar of ice cream coated with chocolate. Chiefly *U.S.*

1928 TURNBOW & RAFFETTO *Ice Cream* 57 Chocolate-coated ice cream bars were introduced in 1921 as 'Eskimo Pies'. **1937** L. BROMFIELD *Rains Came* I. i. 13 The cries of vendors of eskimo pies and *pan*. **1970** D. M. DAVIN *Not Here, Not Now* IV. i. 219 'Let's bring her back some Eskimo pies,' Martin said. 'I haven't had one since I was at school.'

5. ***Eskimo roll***: in Canoeing (see quots.).
1946 P. W. Blandford *Canoeing To-Day* 4 In them [*sc.* folding canoes] experts are able to perform the 'Eskimo roll' — a complete rollover, under the water and return to upright at the opposite side. **1965** *Clarendonian* XIX. iii. 116 There are one or two gymnastic exercises that canoeists like to perform. The most famous is the so-called 'Eskimo roll' for which there are at least three possible paddle strokes. **1968** W. Warwick *Surfriding in N.Z.* 10/2 When you have to paddle out through larger waves, over about 8 ft., it is safest to use the Eskimo roll, as a means of getting past a broken wave.

Eskimoid ('ɛskɪmɔɪd), *a.* [f. Eskimo *sb.* + -oid.] Eskimo-like; similar in racial type to the Eskimo; resembling an Eskimo. Also as *sb.*
1918 E. A. Hooton in *Amer. Jrnl. Phys. Anthropol.* I. 53 (*title*) On certain Eskimoid characters in Icelandic skulls. *Ibid.* 54, I have ventured to call these 'Eskimoid characters', because they occur in association predominantly in Eskimo skeletons. **1939** *Peking Nat. Hist. Bull.* XIII. 172 An Eskimoid skull very similar to that of the Upper Cave [in China] is, for instance, represented among the remains of the pre-Columbian Indians from South Western Texas. **1946** F. E. Zeuner *Dating the Past* viii. 272 Three different racial elements, best to be classified as primitive Mongoloid, Melanesoid and Eskimoid. *Ibid.* ix. 300 Another [racial] type...that of Chancelade, supposed to have eskimoid affinities.

eskip, obs. form of equip.

†**e'skirmish.** *Obs.* [ad. F. *escarmouche*: see escarmouche and skirmish.] = skirmish.
1581 Styward *Mart. Discipl.* i. 1, In marching, incamping, approch, eskirmish, camisado, or retraite.

Esky ('ɛskɪ). *Austral.* Also **esky**. [Proprietary: perh. f. Esk(imo *sb.* and *a.* + -y⁶.] A proprietary name for a portable, insulated container, used esp. to keep food or drink cool.
1962 *Austral. Official Jrnl. Patents* 13 Sept. 1997/2 Class 11. *Esky*..2nd Nov., 1961. Cooling apparatus and equipment inclusive of portable ice boxes. Malleys Ltd.. 128 Rothschild-avenue, Rosebery, New South Wales, Australia, manufacturers. **1965** E. Brown *Big Man* xiii. 110 That indispensable addition to Australian motoring, an 'Esky' ice-box. Captain Barnes noticed him staring at the 'Esky' and its contents. **1971** *Telegraph* (Brisbane) 10 Nov. 26/4 The bulk of the kidneys were being freighted in 'common old eskies'. **1975** *Times* 8 Jan. 11/1 The Hill [at Sydney] is..for taking as many cans of beer as an 'esky' (a portable icebox) can carry. **1980** *Listener* 23 Oct. 524/3 People clutching their 'Eskys'—plastic picnic hampers which keep the food fresh. **1983** *Age* (Melbourne) 2 Nov. 3/2 Those who had thought they could go straight from the station platform into a car park for Esky entertainment were soon disappointed. Police politely stopped and told them they could not go through the gates with liquor.

†**e'slake.** *Obs.* [var. of aslake or y-slake.] = slake.
1514 Barclay *Cyt. & Uplondyshm.* (Percy Soc.) p. xxxvi, No drop thou gettest for to eslake thy lust.

eslar, obs. Sc. form of ashlar *sb.*

†**e'slarge**, *v.* *Obs.* [a. OF. *eslarg-ir*: see next.] *trans.* = next.
a **1450** *Knt. de la Tour* (1868) 132 He his stered vnto myse and eslargithe his pitee vpon hem.

†**e'slargish**, *v.* *Obs.* In 5 eslargys(s)he. [a. OF. *eslargiss-* lengthened stem of *eslargir* (mod.F. *élargir*), f. *es-*:—L. *ex* + *large*: see large.]
a. *trans.* To extend the range or scope of; = enlarge 3 b. **b.** *refl.* To set (oneself) at large; to free (oneself) from restraint. Cf. enlarge 6.
1483 Caxton *G. de la Tour* F iiij b, Ye may eslargysshe yourself to say or do your wylle. *Ibid.* I ij, God..moueth hym self to pyte and eslargyssheth his misericorde.

eslier, obs. var. ashlar *sb.*
15.. in Raine *Auckland Cas.* (1852) 64 *note*, Eslier worke.

eslior, eslisor, obs. ff. elisor.

esloign, -oin(e, -oyne, obs. ff. eloin.

eslonge, var. form of elong *v.* *Obs.*
c **1500** *Melusine* xxi. 133 Within a short while they eslongyd ferre one fro other.

†**e'smarvel**, *v.* *Obs.* Forms: 5 esmervail, -vayll, 6 esmarveyl. [ad. OF. *esmerveill-er*, f. *es-*:—L. *ex-* out + *merveill-er* to wonder, marvel. See also amarvel.] *trans.* **a.** To astonish. **b.** To wonder at, admire.
1475 Caxton *Jason* 98 Jason was moche esmeruailled thenne whan he understod the hyghe mysteres that hym behoued to make. **1502** *Ord. Crysten Men* (W. de W. 1506) iv. xxix. 341 Contemple, and esmarueyll the grete & incomprenable dyfference. **1509** Hawes *Past. Pleas.* (Percy Soc.) 189 Thus al esmarveyled we dyd then awake.

†**e'smay**, *v.* *Obs.* See also amay, asmay. [a. OF. *esmaie-r* to trouble = Pr. *esmagar, esmaiar*, It. *smagare*:—med.L. **exmagāre*, f. *ex-* out + *-mag-* (whence **dismagāre*: see dismay), usually believed to be of Teut. origin; cf. OHG. *magan* to be able: see may *v.*] *trans.* and *refl.* = dismay.
1393 Gower *Conf.* I. 281, I am..so distempred and so esmaied. *Ibid.* II. 239 But Jason wolde him nought esmaie. **1475** Caxton *Jason* 76 Appollo on this..began to rise abasshed and esmayed of this werke. **1483** —— *Gold. Leg.* 153/2 But he was gretely esmayed how he myght burye the body.

e'smayle, emayle. *Obs. rare.* [ad. OF. *esmail*, F. *émail*: see amel.] Enamel.
1589 Puttenham *Eng. Poesie* iii. xix. (Arb.) 242 Set rich rubie to red esmayle. **1594** Nashe *Terrors of Night* D iij. (D.), No wine but was turned to red emayle as soon as euer it came amongst them [Icelanders].

†**e'smeute.** *Obs.* [a. Fr. *esmeute*, older form of *émeute*.] = emeute.
1652 Needham tr. *Selden's Mare Cl.* 469 And an Esmeute of their people who are all interested in that Question.

esmint, obs. form of easement.

†**e'smove, e'smeve**, *v.* *Obs. rare.* [a. OF. *esmover* (accented stem *esmeuv-*, whence a later inf. form *esmevre*):—late L. *exmovēre*, f. *ex-* out + *movēre* move.] *trans.* To move strongly, excite.
1474 Caxton *Chesse* iii. v. G viij, As sone as she sawe hym she was soe smoued wyth Joye that she deyed tofore hym. **1475** —— *Jason* 12/2 He was so esmeuid..with loue that, etc. *Ibid.* 78/2 Their aduersaires..were so esmeuyed upon them that, etc.

†**esne** ('ɛzniː). *Obs.* exc. *Hist.* [OE. *ęsne* = Goth. *asneis*:—OTeut. **asnjo-z* harvestman, f. **asano-z* harvest.] The OE. designation of a class of domestic slaves.
c **950** *Lindisf. Gosp.* Matt. x. 24 Ne is ðegn ofer ðone laruu nec ðea vel esne ofer hlaferde his. *c* **975** *Rushw. Gosp.* John iv. 51 Esnas ȝiurnon togægnes him. **1820** Scott *Ivanhoe* xxxii, Theow and Esne art thou no longer. **1861** Pearson *Early & Mid. Ages Eng.* 201 The..esnés or day-labourers, were the lowest. **1875** Stubbs *Const. Hist.* I. v. 78 The esne or slave who works for hire.

†'**esnecy.** *Obs.* [ad. med.L. *æsnecia*, latinized form of OF. *ainsneece* (mod.Fr. *aînesse*) position of elder brother or sister, ad. med.L. **antenātitia*, f. *antenātus* one born before another, f. *ante* before + *nātus* born.] 'A private prerogative allowed to the eldest coparcener, where an estate is descended to daughters for want of an heir male, to choose first after the inheritance is divided' (Wharton).
1607 in Cowel *Interpr.* **1641** in *Termes de la Ley* 144. **1721** in Bailey. **1823** in Crabbe *Techniol. Dict.*; and in mod. Dicts.

eso- ('ɛsəʊ-), *prefix* [Gr. ἔσω within], employed in a few compounds of modern formation from words of Greek origin, as **esoente'ritis**, *Path.* [see enteritis], inflammation of the intestinal mucous membrane. **esoga'stritis**, *Path.* [see gastritis], inflammation of the mucous lining of the stomach. **eso'narthex** [see narthex], the inner vestibule of a Greek church (cf. exonarthex). **eso'neural** *a.* [see neural], operating within the nerves. **eso'scopic** *a. rare* [Gr. -σκοπ-οα watching + -ic], (see quot.).
1847 Craig **Esoenterites. Ibid.* **Esogastrites.* **1850** Neale *East. Ch.* I. 245 The *esonarthex opens on to the church by nine doors, to the exonarthex by five. **1851** H. Mayo *Pop. Superst.* (ed. 2) 73 The mental forces, or operations of a living human being, may be conceived to be essentially *esoneural. **1816** Bentham *Chrestom.* Wks. (1838–43) VIII. 94 Division of Politics and Government into *Esoscopic, i.e. internal or interior-concerns-regarding, viz. Internal Government, and Exoscopic.

esodic (ɛ'sɒdɪk), *a.* [f. Gr. ἔσ-ω within + ὁδ-ός way + -ic.] Of nerves: Proceeding to or into the spinal marrow; afferent.
1850 M. Hall *Diastaltic Nervous Syst.* 6 [Section headed 'New Terms Proposed.'] *Esodic* (εἰς) will express the action *into*; *exodic* the action out of, etc. **1850** Barnes in *Lancet* II. 84/1 This paralyzing effect on the extremities of the esodic nerves. **1852** G. Wilson *Life J. Reid* 92 The sensific nerves have also been named esodic (ingoing).

esophageal, esophagus, etc.: see œs-.

esophoria (ɛsəʊ'fɔːrɪə). *Ophthalmology.* [f. eso- + *-phoria* ad. Gr. φέρειν to bear.] A latent convergent strabismus of the eyes.
1886 [see *exophoria* s.v. exo-]. **1891** R. J. McKay in *Trans. Amer. Ophthalmol. Soc.* VI. 136, I put a dark red glass in front of one eye..and see whether there is diplopia, hyperphoria, esophoria, or exophoria. **1906** S. Theobald *Prevalent Dis. Eye* xii. 473 In the causation of esophoria hypermetropia and hypermetropic astigmatism play even a more important rôle than myopia does in that of exophoria. **1964** S. Duke-Elder *Parsons' Dis. Eye* (ed. 14) xxx. 472 If the latent deviation is one of convergence the condition is called *esophoria*, of divergence *exophoria*, if vertical, *hyperphoria*.

esoteric (ɛsəʊ'tɛrɪk, iːsəʊ-), *a.* and *sb.* [ad. Gr. ἐσωτερικ-ός, f. ἐσωτέρω, compar. of ἔσω within.
The Gr. word occurs first in Lucian, who ascribes to Aristotle a classification of his own works into 'esoteric' and 'exoteric'. (Cic. *De Fin.* v. §5 recognizes such a classification but uses only the term 'exoteric', leaving the opposite class undesignated; Aristotle himself merely uses ἐξωτερικός in the sense of 'popular, untechnical'.) By later writers the word was employed to designate the secret doctrines said to have been taught by Pythagoras to a select few among his disciples.]
A. *adj.*
1. Of philosophical doctrines, treatises, modes of speech, etc.: Designed for, or appropriate to, an inner circle of advanced or privileged disciples; communicated to, or intelligible by, the initiated exclusively. Hence of disciples: Belonging to the innner circle, admitted to the esoteric teaching. Opposed to exoteric.
Esoteric Buddhism: a system of 'theosophical' doctrines, alleged by its adherents to have been handed down by secret tradition among an initiated class of Buddhists.
1655–60 Stanley *Hist. Philos.* (1701) 372/1 The Auditors of Pythagoras..were of two sorts, Exoterick and Esoterick; the Exoterics were those who were under probation, which if they well performed, they were admitted to be Esotericks. **1738** Warburton *Div. Legat.* iii. §2 (1755) 98 The exoteric teaching [of the Pythagoreans] admitted fable and falsehood ..the esoteric only what the teacher believed to be true. *a* **1754** Fielding *Comm. Bolingbroke's Ess.* Wks. 1784 X. 310 In rescuing the esoteric purity of his doctrines from that less amiable appearance in which their exoteric garb represents them. **1768–74** Tucker *Lt. Nat.* (1852) II. 677 These two classes [the adept and the vulgar] must be addressed in two different languages, the esoteric and the exoteric. **1817** Coleridge *Biog. Lit.* I. x. 200, I considered..the Trinity.. entitled to the rank of an esoteric doctrine of natural religion. **1837** Hallam *Hist. Lit.* I. i. iii. §90. 204 A hidden stream of esoteric truth was supposed to flow beneath all the surface of Scripture. **1883** Sinnett (title), *Esoteric Buddhism.*
b. *absol.* (quasi-*sb.*) = 'Esoteric sense'. *rare.*
1842 Mrs. Browning *Grk. Chr. Poets* (1863) 52 The esoteric of the most suspicious turnings of his phraseology is 'Glory to the true God'.
2. *transf.* **a.** Of motives, purposes, etc.: Not openly avowed. **b.** Pertaining to a select circle; private, confidential. **c.** Qualifying a personal epithet: That is esoterically such.
1866 W. Thornbury *Greatheart* III. 176 He had two motives in his visit, an exoteric and an esoteric motive. **1859** Macaulay *Hist. Eng.* V. 206 His esoteric project was the original project of Christopher Columbus. **1876** Black *Madcap V.* xliii, How could he aid in this esoteric interview? **1876** Fairbairn *Strauss* 11, Strauss had hardly the stuff in him to be an exoteric Conservative while an esoteric Radical. **1881** *Nature* XXIV. 578 There is nothing to hinder them having also more esoteric meetings at stated intervals.
3. *Phys.* (In etymological sense): 'Applied to things which relate to, or have origin within the organism' (*Syd. Soc. Lex.*).
1860 in Mayne *Exp. Lex.*
B. *sb.*
1. *pl.* (after Gr. τὰ ἐσωτερικά.) Esoteric doctrines; esoteric treatises.
1711 tr. *Werenfels' Disc. Logomachys* 99 Aristotle's Books of deep Learning, his Acroamaticks, Esotericks, Epopticks, and mysterious Writings. **1768–74** Tucker *Lt. Nat.* (1852) I. 430 Our predecessors had their esoterics and exoterics. **1809** Knox & Jebb *Corr.* I. 488 Alexander complained to Aristotle, that he had done ill to give the world his esotericks. **1821** S. Parr *Wks.* (1828) viii. 353 I must, in my esoterics, stand aloof from all controversies.
2. One initiated in esoteric doctrines.
1655–60 [see A. 1].

esoterica (ɛsəʊ'tɛrɪkə, iːsəʊ-), *sb. pl.* [mod.L., f. Gr. ἐσωτερικ-ός (see esoteric *sb.*).] Esoteric objects or products; esoteric details; = esoteric *sb.* 1; pornography.
c **1929** O. Nash *Coll. Verse* (1961) 107 The postal authorities of the United States of America Frown on Curiosa, Erotica and Esoterica. **1950** A. Lomax *Mr. Jelly Roll* (1952) 78 He..can bore you to death with the esoterica of forgotten bands. **1958** *Spectator* 13 June 770/2 In Soho it is usually possible to get esoterica such as passion fruit, mangoes, [etc.]. **1958** *Times Lit. Suppl.* 31 Oct. 629/4 A collection of oddments..on Jungian esoterica, on sex, on dreams and nightmares.

esoterical (ɛsəʊ'tɛrɪkəl, iːsəʊ-), *a.* [f. esoteric *a.* + -al¹.]
1. = esoteric *a.*
1850 L. Hunt *Autobiog.* I. iii. 128 This was his [Coleridge's] esoterical opinion of him. **1876** Birch *Rede Lect. Egypt* 42 Walls covered with mythological representations and esoterical texts, explanatory of the old religion.
2. In etymological nonce-use: (see quot.)
1850 Maurice *Mor. & Met. Philos.* I. i. §3. 27 When by esoterical we mean that which concerns the inner man.

esoterically (ɛsəʊ'tɛrɪkəlɪ, iːsəʊ-), *adv.* [f. prec. + -ly².] In an esoteric manner.
1738 Warburton *Div. Legat.* iii. §2 III. (1811) 27 Exoterically..of the national Gods; esoterically..of the first Cause of all things. **1836** *Fraser's Mag.* XIV. 4 It essentially and esoterically preserves its separateness. **1873** Whitney *Orient. Stud.* 87 While oral tradition continued to be the exoteric practice, writing might still be resorted to esoterically.

esotericism. [f. esoteric + -ism.] = next. Also, a tendency toward esoteric thought or language, obscurity; an example of such thought or language.
1846 Worcester cites *Christian Observer*. Hence in later Dicts. **1885** Mrs. H. Ward tr. *Amiel's Jrnl.* II. 315 Yes, but still a certain esotericism [*orig.* ésotérisme] is inevitable, since critical, scientific, and philosophical culture is only attainable by a minority. **1923** J. M. Murry *Pencillings* 1 One of the most peculiar features of literature during the last thirty or forty years has been the steady movement of a part of it towards esotericism. **1955** *Essays in Criticism* V. 421 Yeats's intellectual esotericisms (such as the phrase 'perne in a gyre' in *Sailing to Byzantium*). **1963** *Times* 14 Mar. 16/2

It is still possible to write..without code words or esotericism.

So **eso'tericist**, one who holds esoteric doctrines. Also **'esoterist** (*Funk's Stand. Dict.* 1893).

1891 *Review of Rev.* 15 June 522/2 She [*sc.* Madame Blavatsky] made all her 'esotericists', as she called them, send her their photographs. **1892** *Ch. Times* 1 Apr. 337/1 Further on the esotericist is identified with the Rationalist. **1954** W. Y. Evans-Wentz *Tibetan Bk. Great Liberation* 33 The Christian esotericists, derived largely from uncultured slave populations, inaugurated a religious revolution against the Christian esotericists, the cultured and well-born followers of the Gnosis.

esoterism (ɛ'sɒtərɪz(ə)m, iːsəʊ-). [f. Gr. ἐσωτέρ-ω (see ESOTERIC) + -ISM.] The holding of esoteric doctrines; the habit of regarding knowledge as the property of the few.

1835 Maurice *Let. to Acland* 12 Mar. in *Life* (1884) I. 171 A dangerous tendency [in Alex. Knox] to esoterism and exclusiveness. **1871** Farrar *Witn. Hist.* ii. 62 Its perfect openness rebuked their esoterism. **1884** *Syd. Soc. Lex.*, *Esoterism, medical.* Simon's term for the mystery which some medical men think themselves bound to adopt towards their patients by reason of their prejudices and ignorance.

e'soterize, *v. rare.* [f. as prec. + -IZE.] *intr.* To hold esoteric doctrines.

1842 G. S. Faber *Provinc. Lett.* (1844) II. 21 Unlike the Esoterising Exclusiveness of Pagan Philosophy.

esotery ('ɛsəʊtərɪ). [f. as prec. + -Y³.]

(An irregular formation; in first quot., from which Todd obtained the word, *esoteries* may be mispr. for *esoterics*.)]

Esoteric doctrine, secret lore. Also *pl.*

1763 Tucker *Freewill* 172 *note*, Reserving their esoteries for adepts, and dealing out exoteries only to the vulgar. **1828** Webster, *Esotery*, mystery; secrecy. (*Little used.*) **1879** G. Meredith *Egoist* II. i. 7, I seem to be instructed in one of the mysteries of erotic esotery, yet on my word I am no wiser.

esoundir(e, obs. var. ASUNDER.

a **1400-50** *Alexander* 510, 3977.

‖**esox** ('iːsɒks). Also 6 ezox. [L. *esox*, a Gaulish word: cf. Welsh *ëog*, Ir. *iach* salmon.] The name of a large fish mentioned by Pliny (in first quot. app. identified with the Sturgeon); the Corpus Glossary (*a* 800) renders the name by *lax*, i.e. salmon. In mod. Ichthyology used as the generic name of the Pike.

c **1520** L. Andrewe *Noble Lyfe* in *Babees Bk.* 234 Ezox is a very grete fisshe in that water danowe be the londe of hungarye, he is of suche bygnes that a carte with iiij horses can nat cary hym awaye..he hath swete fisshe [? flesh] lyke a porke. **1706** Phillips, *Esox*, a great Fish in the River Rhine; a Lax. **1774** Goldm. *Nat. Hist.* (1862) II. III. i. 303 The Esox or Pike. **1854** Badham *Halieut.* 296 Pliny's esox (a name which modern ichthyology has imposed upon the pike) is evidently a misnomer.

esp(e, obs. form of ASP¹.

E.S.P.: see EXTRA-SENSORY *a.*

†**espace.** *Obs.* [a. F. *espace*:—L. *spatium*: see SPACE.] = SPACE.

1483 Caxton *Gold. Leg.* 340/3 In that espace of tyme the kynge and mo than lx thousand men were baptysed. *c* **1490** —— *Blanchardyn* 146 We..haue ben a longe espace wyth hym.

espacement (ɪ'speɪsmənt). *Arch.* [a. F. *espacement*, f. *espacer* to space out.]

1. The action of spacing, or of placing at suitable distances.

1867 A. Barry *Life Sir C. Barry* iv. 95 The espacement of the windows.

2. *Forestry* and *Agriculture*. The distance at which trees or crops are set apart when planted.

1934 *Forestry* VIII. 21 Corsican pine is usually planted in this country at an espacement of 4 feet 6 inches or 5 feet. **1950** *Q. Jrnl. Forestry* XLIV. 13 In order to economize in the number of trees per acre, espacements of less than 5 ft. have seldom been adopted.

‖**espada** (ɛ'spɑːda). Also erron. espardo. [Sp., = It. *spada*, Fr. *épée* sword.] = MATADOR 1.

1882 [see MATADOR 1]. **1893** [see CUADRILLA]. **1902** *Encycl. Brit.* XXVI. 460/1 Two *matadors* or *espardos* are engaged in each day's fight. **1923** Ld. Curzon *Tales Trav.* 215 Just as the *espada* lunged with the sword..the bull..was upon him. **1926** *Blackw. Mag.* Sept. 290/2 Bull-fighting requires great courage in the bull-fighters from the espada to the mozo.

‖**espadon.** [a. F. *espadon*, app. a. Sp. *espadon*, augmentative of *espada* sword: cf. It. *spadone*.] A long two-handed sword used in 15–17th c.

1846 Fairholt *Costume* 494 *Espadon*, a long sword of Spanish invention. **1881** *Blackw. Mag.* May 565 The horseman's huge espadon of six feet long.

espadrille (ɛspə'drɪl). Also -illo. [Fr., ad. Prov. *espardillo*, f. *espart* ESPARTO.] A canvas shoe with soles of twisted rope, originally worn in the Pyrenees.

[**1865** M. Eyre *Lady's Walks* xxiv. 263 The Spaniards..wear..the *espartilla*, or hempen sandal.] **1892** *Daily News* 16 June 5/4 'Espadrilles', or shoes with woven rope soles, are likely to come into favour with running men. **1905** W. J. Locke *Morals M. Ordeyne* I. xii. 146 The bathing hour, when she..divests her of *peignoir* and *espadrilles*. **1907** Baring-Gould *Bk. Pyrenees* vii. 123 Mauléon..has become the centre of manufacture of the espadrillos. **1923** *Blackw. Mag.* Aug. 162/1, I crept through the thickets in my rope-soled espadrilles. **1941** A. Christie *Evil under Sun* iv. 61 Over it [*sc.* bathing dress] she flung on a bath-robe and laced espadrilles on her feet. **1945** E. Bowen *Coll. Impressions* (1950) 230 *Their* sons and daughters wanted something more *plage-y*: shorts, espadrilles, the drink after the swim.

‖**espagnole** (ɛspaɲɔl). [Fr., lit. = Spanish.] In full *espagnole sauce*, a simple brown sauce.

1845 E. Acton *Mod. Cookery* iii. 88 (*heading*) Espagnole (Spanish sauce.) (A highly flavoured Gravy.) **1846** 'A Lady' *Jewish Man.* iv. 58 A little Espagnole sauce heightens the flavour. **1951** *Good Housek. Home Encycl.* (1956) 397/2 A tablespoonful of chopped mushrooms..may be added to the Espagnole sauce. **1961** *Harper's Bazaar* Feb. 72/2 The basic brown sauce—*espagnole*.

‖**espagnolette.** [Fr. *espagnolette*, f. *espagnol* Spanish.] The fastening of a French window; also *attrib.*

1870 *Daily News* 20 Dec., Had he fallen it might have been the better for him; but the neckcloths and the espagnolette held fast and prevented him. **1876** Gwilt *Encycl. Archit.* 687 For French casements, what is called the Espagnolette bolt is now in use. **1887** *Pall Mall G.* 19 Sept. 5/2 Paris has espagnolette windows opening like doors.

espaire, var. form of ESPEIRE. *Obs.*

espalier (ɪ'spæljə(r)), *sb.* Also 7 espaliere. [a. F. *espalier*, ad. It. *spalliera* 'wainscot work to lean the shoulders against' (Florio), hence, stakes of the same height, f. *spalla* shoulder. Cf. Sp. *espalera*, *espaldera*, of same meaning.]

1. A kind of lattice-work or frame-work of stakes upon which fruit trees or ornamental shrubs are trained; also the stakes individually.

1741 *Compl. Fam. Piece* II. iii. 356 Repair your Espaliers, and fasten your Fruit-trees thereto. **1754** Dodsley *Agriculture* II. (R.), His ripening fruits Display their sweet temptations from the wall, Or from the gay espalier. **1816** Kirby & Spence *Entomol.* xiv. (1828) I. 436 The upright putrescent espaliers of vine-props. **1862** Ansted *Channel Isl.* II. viii. 168 The willow..is much used, its young shoots being employed to tie up the fruit trees to the espaliers.

2. A fruit-tree trained on a lattice, usually of woodwork, or on stakes.

1662 Evelyn *Kal. Hort.* (1729) 223 Plant your fairest Tulips..under Espaliers. **1731** Pope *Ep. Burlington* 78 Behold Villario's ten years toil compleat, His Quincunx darkens, his Espaliers meet. **1796** Morse *Amer. Geog.* I. 541 Espaliers of European grapes in gardens have long ago been introduced. **1833** Tennyson *Blackbird*, The espaliers and the standards all Are thine.

†**3.** A row of trees so trained. *Obs.*

1712 J. James tr. *Le Blond's Gardening* 3 A Fruit-Garden planted..in long Espaliers. **1725** Bradley *Fam. Dict.* s.v. *Batardier*, Fruit-Trees..placed in Espaliers or elsewhere, instead of a dead Tree.

4. *attrib.* and *Comb.*, chiefly simple *attrib.*; also **espalierwise** *adv.*, in the form of an espalier.

1717 Berkeley *Tour Italy* 16 Jan., Espalier hedges..make the ornaments of this place. **1727** Bradley *Fam. Dict.* s.v. *Garden Fences*, The Horse-Chestnut..will bear forming Espalierwise. **1806** Miss Mitford in L'Estrange *Friendship* (1882) I. 20 One of the espalier apple-trees in the garden is a perfect picture. **1858** Glenny *Gard. Everyday Bk.* 102/1 Espalier Trees may be much more easily cleaned of vermin.

espalier (ɛ'spæljə(r)), *v.* [f. prec. sb.] *trans.* **a.** To train as an espalier. **b.** To furnish or surround with an espalier.

1810 Bp. Copleston *Repl. to Edin. Rev.* in *Mem.* (1851) 329 We want not men who are clipped and espaliered into any form which the whim of the gardener may dictate. **1846** in Worcester; and in mod Dicts.

Hence **e'spaliered** *ppl. a.*, **e'spaliering** *vbl. sb.*

1856 Ruskin *Mod. Paint.* IV. v. xi. §9 Latticed and espaliered cottages. **1865** Miss Braddon *Doctor's Wife* iii, There were roses and sweet-brier, espaliered apples. **1882** *Jrnl. Derbysh. Archæol. Soc.* IV. 154 He appears to be engaged in that form of training trees called espaliering.

†**E'spanolize.** *v. Obs. rare.* [f. Sp. *español* Spanish + -IZE; cf. Fr. *espagnoliser*.] *trans.* To make Spanish; to naturalize in Spain.

1630 Wadsworth *Sp. Pilgr.* 1 The life of the English Espanoliz'd trauailer. **1658** Osborn *Jas. I* (1673) 477 Gondomar and our Espanolized English took this last advantage.

esparagrass, obs. corruption of ASPARAGUS.

1711 *Life & Char. R. Thornhill* 6 To suck two or three Esparagrass's.

†**e'sparcet.** *Obs.* [a. F. *esparcet*, *esparcette*; cf. Sp. *esparceta*.] (See quot.)

1669 Worlidge *Syst. Agric.* (1681) 31 Esparcet is a kind of St. Foyn, and by some judged to be the same. So **1708** Mortimer *Husb.* (ed. 2) I. 36. **1736-1800** in Bailey; and in mod. Dicts.

†**e'sparse**, *v. Obs.* [ad. OF. *esparse-r*, f. *espars* (mod.F. *épars*):—L. *spars-us*, pa. pple. of *spargĕre* to scatter.] *trans.* To scatter.

1625 Lisle *Du Bartas, Noe* 181 Into th' esparsed pipes o' th' Sommier thorow bored.

esparto (ɪ'spɑːtəʊ). Also 6, 8 sparto. [a. Sp. *esparto*:—L. *spartum*, ad. Gr. σπάρτον a rope made of σπάρτος, either the same plant or Spanish Broom (*Spartium junceum*).] A kind of rush (*Macrochloa* or *Stipa tenacissima*), called by some Spanish grass, imported from Spain and the north coast of Africa, for manufacture into paper. In ancient times it was, and in Spain is still, made into cordage, shoes, and other articles. Also called **esparto grass**.

[**1591** Percivall *Sp. Dict.*, *Esparto*..a kinde of tree whereof they make fraile*s*. **1779** H. Swinburne *Trav. Spain* 6 Making ropes, baskets, and shoes, of a small rush or reed called *esparto*.] **1868** *Q. Rev.* No. 248. 356 Printed upon paper made from esparto alone. **1883** *Pall Mall G.* 11 Sept. 9/1 At Lloyd's paper mills, Sittingbourne, the..cover of a boiler used for boiling esparto and straw blew off.

attrib. **1791** J. Townsend *Journ. Spain* III. 130 The esparto rush makes good mats for houses. **1878** Hooker & Ball *Marocco* 335 Large bales of esparto grass..from the adjoining province of Haba. **1888** *Pall Mall G.* 27 Oct. 9/1 An esparto boiler burst in the North of Ireland Paper Mills.

espathate (iː'speɪθeɪt), *a. Bot.* [f. E- *pref.*³ + L. *spātha* SPATHE + -ATE².] Not having a spathe (1866 *Treas. Bot.*).

†**espaut.** *Obs. rare*⁻¹. [ad. F. *espeautre* (now *épeautre*):—L. *spelta* SPELT.] Millet or spelt.

a **1682** Sir T. Browne *Tracts* (1684) 22 For Milium is more agreeable unto Spelta or Espaut [than unto Rye], as the Dutch and others still render it.

†**e'speccion.** *Obs. rare*⁻¹. [as if a. OF. *especcion, repr. L. *spectiōnem* looking, f. *specĕre* to look.] Looking, beholding.

14.. *Epiph.* in *Tundale's Vis.* (1843) 112 And ever the more they loked besyly The more thei lyked in especcyon.

†**e'spece.** *Obs.* See also ESPICE. [a. Fr. *espece*, corresp. to Pr. *e)specia*, It. *specie*:—L. *species*.

In OF. the normal phonetic representative of L. *species* was *espice* (mod. *épice* SPICE); the form *espece* (mod. *espèce*) is influenced by Lat., Pr. or It.]

Kind, species.

1602 Segar *Hon. Mil. & Civ.* I xxv. 32 The Romanes vsed diuers Especes..of Cassing. **1659** Macallo *Can. Physick* ii. 3 It rests to find out the Espece or kind of the disease.

†**especial**, *sb.* [Corruption of *espial*, due to the influence of L. *specĕre* to look, or possibly to confusion with next.] = ESPIAL 1 and 2a.

a **1500** *Chaucer's Friar's T.* 23 [*MS. Petworth* especiale, *MSS. Corpus, Lansd.* especiaile; *other MSS. have the correct reading* espiaille]. **1548** Hall *Chron.* (1809) 283 His especials and Explorators declared and accompted to hym that all the Realme was up. **1555** Eden *Decades W. Ind.* II. II. (Arb.) 112 One of their coompanye standynge vppon the toppe of a hyghe rocke of especiall..beganne to crye Lynnyn sayles.

especial (ɪ'spɛʃəl), *a.* Forms: 4 especiale, 4-7 -all(e, 5-6 especyal(l, (5 aspeciall, 5-6 asp-, espesyal(l, 6 especcial, 6-7 aspeciall, 7 especil, -shal, -tial(l), 4- especial. [a. OF. *especial* (mod.F. *spécial*, assimilated to the L. form), ad. L. *speciālis* (see SPECIAL) belonging to or concerned with a particular species, special as opposed to general (in med.L. current in legal and philosophical use), f. *species* SPECIES. Cf. Pr., Sp. *especial*, It. *speziale*. (Lat. words with initial *sp*, *st*, *sc*, adopted into Fr. before 15th c. usually assumed a euphonic *e*.)

In OF. the word had developed the secondary sense 'pre-eminent, important' (for the transition cf. *particular*). In Eng. the two forms *especial* and *special* differ materially in use; the latter (owing perh. to its closer relation to the L. etymon) is preferred in applications arising proximately from the primary sense, while the former is chiefly confined to the derivative sense. The distinction is still more marked in the advs. *especially*, *specially*.]

1. In senses now commonly expressed by SPECIAL: **a.** Special as opposed to general (*arch.*); also in Law †*especial pleading, especial tail.* †**b.** Particular, individual, 'specific' (*obs.*). †**c.** Provided for a particular purpose (*obs.*).

c **1400** *Rom. Rose* 6717 Lo heere the caas especial. **1574** tr. *Littleton's Tenures* 103 b, By especial pleading he may be barred of the action that he sueth. **1604** Shaks. *Oth.* IV. ii. 225 There is especiall Commission come from Venice. **1614** Markham *Cheap Husb.* I. xi. (1668) 49 Spoyling an especial member by some strange contraction. **1628** Coke *On Litt.* 26 In this case the husband hath an estate in especiall taile. **1754** Richardson *Grandison* (1781) I. xxvi. 189, I shall dispatch what I shall farther write..by an especial messenger. **1824** Byron *Juan* XV. xxv, And rend'ring general that which is especial.

2. Pre-eminent, exceptionally distinguished. Formerly often in phrase (*my*) *especial friend* (cf. 3). Now chiefly of feelings, qualities, or attributes: Exceptional in degree. (*Obs.* in predicative use.)

In examples of 2 and 3 *special* may commonly be substituted with little change of meaning.

c **1386** Chaucer *Melibeus* ¶200 First schul ye clepe to youre conseil a fewe of youre frendes that ben especial. **1494** Fabyan II. xxx. 22 He had hym in shorte whyle in especiall fauoure. **1594** Hooker *Eccl. Pol.* I. x. (1611) 29 Causeth them to haue especiall respect in making lawes. **1603** Knolles *Hist. Turks* Ep. Ded., My most especiall good friend Sir Peter Hamond Knight of the Bath. *c* **1630** Risdon *Surv. Devon* §28 (1810) 34 It is one of the especialest fisher towns of this shire. **1841** Lane *Arab. Nts.* I. 95 And among my books is one of the most especial value. **1860** Tyndall *Glac.* II. xxviii. 397 One fact of especial importance is to be borne in mind.

3. Belonging pre-eminently to a particular person or thing; pertaining chiefly to one particular case.
1855 MILMAN *Lat. Chr.* (1864) II. III. vii. 152 Every passion, every vice had its especial demon. **1868** M. PATTISON (*title*), Suggestions on Academical Organization, with especial reference to Oxford. **1875** JOWETT *Plato* (ed. 2) I. 233, I must repeat one thing..for your especial benefit.

4. *in especial*, also rarely *by especial*: in particular; especially; particularly. *Obs.* exc. *arch.* (Occas. written as one word; cf. INESPECIALLY.)
c **1390** CHAUCER *Truth* 25 And in especial Drawe unto hym and pray in general. *c* **1430** *Pilgr. Lyf Manhode* I. xxi. (1869) 15 þilke he wolde bi especial weren ministres and serueres to him. **14..** *Pol. Rel. & L. Poems* (1866) 49 At thys parlament most in Asspeciall. **1475** *Bk. Noblesse* 20 In divers regions, and inespecialle in Fraunce and Normandie. **1477** EARL RIVERS *Dictes* (Caxton) 74 a, He wold haue reserued them inespeciall in his sayd dictes. **1540** COVERDALE *Old Faith* Wks. (Parker Soc.) I. iii. 21, I will now speak of every word in especial. **1828** SCOTT *F.M. Perth* xxix, His word, which he addressed to me in especial. **1860** J. KENNEDY *Swallow B.* 14 In especial, I had fallen into some unseemly prejudices. **1881** S. COLVIN *Life Landor* 187 Whether it was of these four dramas and of Count Julian in especial, or of all Landor's dramatic..writings together, that, etc.

†**5.** quasi-*sb.* An especial point, a 'particular'.
1633 D. ROGERS *Treat. Sacram.* I. 173 In this conceive these sixe especialls..breefely. 1. The excellencie of the gift ..6. The manner of exhibiting.

†**6.** quasi-*adv.*
1591 F. SPARRY tr. *Cattan's Geomancie* 123 It is especiall good to goe to dwell with great Princes and Lordes.

†**e'speciality.** *Obs.* [f. prec. + -ITY.] An especial point or detail.
c **1460** FORTESCUE *Abs. & Lim. Mon.* (1714) 52 Noble and grete Costs..of which it is not now possible to the Writer herof, for to remember the Especialities.

especially (ɛ'spɛʃəlɪ), *adv.* [f. as prec. + -LY².] In an especial manner; principally, chiefly. Also in phr. †*in especially* (see also INESPECIALLY). In later use also with adjs.: In an especial degree.
?*a* **1400** *Chester Pl.* (1843) I. 105 Sybbell, I praye thee especiallye, etc. **1509** HAWES *Past. Pleas.* v. iii, Evander.. dyd well abounde In many vertues, especially in lernyng. **1557** NORTH tr. *Guevara's Diall. Pr.* 92 a/1 The women, & in especially greate ladies, know not, etc. **1581** MARBECK *Bk. of Notes* 685 And then the Priest prayed in generall for all estates and degrees, and for increase of grace, and in especially if neede required. **1640** in *Hamilton Papers* (Camden Soc.) App. 259 Hereof he was especially advertised by the Hammiltons. **1677** JOHNSON in *Ray's Corr.* (1847) 127 Great shoals of salmon..often take in at the mouths of our rivers, especially if the north bar be open. **1747** WESLEY *Prim. Physic* (1762) 30 It sometimes cures an Ague especially in Children. **1834** NEWMAN *Par. Serm.* (1837) I. IV. 61 Unless they are especially watchful. **1863** LYELL *Antiq. Man* 9 Around the borders of the bogs..lie trunks of trees, especially of the Scotch fir. **1875** JOWETT *Plato* (ed. 2) IV. 130 Two points in his criticism are especially deserving of notice.

especialness (ɪ'spɛʃəlnɪs). [f. as prec. + -NESS.] The state of being especial.
1611 W. LOE *Blisse Brightest Beautie* (1614) 25 (R.) Your precious diamond in especialness. **1828** in WEBSTER. **1846** in WORCESTER; and in mod. Dicts.

†**e'specialty.** *Obs.* [ad. OF. *especialté*, AF. *especiaulté* (in *especiaulté d'escrit* special mention in writing; cf. sense 2), f. *especial*: see ESPECIAL.]
1. An especial degree (of anything).
1606 J. KING *4th Serm. Hampt. Crt.* 41 In time of persecution the especialty and difference of honour might bee allotted to such men.
2. *Law.* A contract by deed; = SPECIALTY.
1576 LAMBARDE tr. *Customal* in *Peramb. Kent* 426 The chartre of the King of this especialtie is in yᵉ custodie of Sir Jhon of Norwood. **1588** J. MELLIS *Brief Instr.* F vj, Your especialties, as are billes of hande. **1602** FULBECKE *2nd Pt. Parall.* 65 It is an inconuenience in reason, that an especialtie sealed and solempnlie deliuered, should be auoyded by the bare agreement of the parties. **1641** *Termes de la Ley* 239 It behooveth to him that bringeth the Writ to shew forth an Especialty.

espede, var. of EXPEDE *v. Obs.* to dispatch.
1558 *Sc. Acts Mary* (1814) 507/1 All signatouris, letteris of gift, and all vthiris letteris ellis esped.

†**e'speire, e'spoire.** *Obs.* Also 4 espeir, espeyre, 5 espaire, espoyr 4 *aphet.* speire. [a. OF. *espeire* fem., *espeir* masc., mod.F. *espoir*, f. *esperer* to hope. Cf. Pg. *esper* masc., Sp. *espera* fem.] Hope, expectation.
1393 GOWER *Conf.* I. 211 To putten Rome in full espeire [*v.r.* espeyre]. *Ibid.* III. 33 And as the plover doth of aire, I live and am in good espeire. *c* **1400** *St. Alexius* (Laud 622) 1030 To þi comyng was al my speire, To haue ymade of þee myne eire. *c* **1400** *Test. Love* II. (1560) 287/1 The good were weived and put out of espoire of the knot. *c* **1450** *Castle Hd. Life of St. Cuthbert* (Surtees) 2671 And asked him with gude espaire. **1475** CAXTON *Jason* 7 b, The foundement upon whiche my total espoyr and hope resteth.

†**'espelers,** *sb. pl. Obs.* Snags or dentelations on the hinder edge of the palm or broad upper part of a buck's horn; = SPILLER.
1486 *Bk. St. Albans* E iiij, He most haue..xxiiij espelers and then ye may hym call..a grete Bucke. **1692–1732** in COLES. **1715** KERSEY, *Espelers*, the third Branch of the Harts Horn.

†**'esperance.** *Obs.* Also 5–6 esperaunce, 6 espirance. [a. F. *esperance* = Pr. *esperansa*, Sp. *esperanza*, It. *speranza*:—late L. **spērantia*, f. *spērāre* to hope.] Expectation, hope.
c **1430** *Pilgr. Lyf Manhode* I. civ. (1869) 56 þe burdoun hatteth esperaunce. **1474** CAXTON *Chesse* 51 Made hym to sitte besyde hym for to geue hym good esperaunce. *a* **1508** HENRYSON *Gamut Good Ladies* viii, in Gilfillan *Spec. Brit. Poets* (1861) I. 58 Her sleeves should be of esperance To keep her from despair. **1552** LYNDESAY *Monarche* IV. 5632 On the left hand of that gret Iuge; But espirance to gett refuge. **1605** SHAKS. *Lear* IV. i. 4 The lowest and most deiected thing of Fortune, Stands still in esperance. *a* **1651** CALDERWOOD *Hist. Kirk* (1842–6) III. 9 In assured hope and esperance to recover his oun rowme.
b. Used as a watchword or battle-cry.
1596 SHAKS. *1 Hen. IV*, v. ii. 97 Now Esperance Percy, and set on. **1649** G. DANIEL *Trinarch., Hen. IV*, ccc, Esperance! Noe, the word is, face about.

Esperanto (ɛspə'ræntəʊ). [Orig. the pen-name (Dr. *Esperanto* = Dr. Hoping-one) used by the inventor on the title-page of his book *Langue internationale; préface et manuel complet*, 1887.] An artificial language invented for universal use by Dr. Ludovik Lazarus Zamenhof, a Polish physician. Its vocabulary consists of roots common to the chief European languages, with endings normalized. Also *attrib.*, *fig.*, and *transf.*
[**1888** 'J. ST.' (title) Dr. Esperanto's International Tongue... Edited for Englishmen.]. **1892** *Science* XIX. 32/1 Esperanto's grammatic rules are few in number, for they are all gathered upon four pages only. **1898** R. H. GEOGHEGAN (*title*) The International Language 'Esperanto'. **1903** *Daily Chron.* 13 Jan. 5/2 Esperanto is, in fact, a vocal international shorthand. **1905** *Westm. Gaz.* 22 Sept. 2/1 Latin, the Esperanto of the Middle Ages and Renaissance. **1907** *Daily Chron.* 23 Oct. 4/6 If this Esperanto sort of spirit could be extended to the coinage, how easy would holiday-making become! **1922** C. R. BUXTON *In Russian Village* xvi. 70 Petrov..called himself by the Esperanto name, 'Pečnego'. **1936** [see ESTABLISHMENT 8 b]. **1958** *Times Lit. Suppl.* 17 Jan. 29/2 The promise not to use 'technical jargon or the special esperanto of *ciné-club* experts'. **1960** KOESTLER *Lotus & Robot* I. i. 37 It is true that there were a few huge concrete blocks in the usual Esperanto architecture. **1968** *Listener* 19 Dec. 814/2 The way in which we are less and less able to understand what is said or done to us unless we can readily translate it all into the Esperanto of common pragmatism.
Hence **Espe'rantic** *a.*, resembling Esperanto; **Espe'rantist**, one who is versed in Esperanto; an advocate of the spread of Esperanto as a world-language; also *attrib.*
1905 *Westm. Gaz.* 4 May 10/2 The Congress of Esperantists. **1909** M. L. JONES *Advantages of Esperanto* 2 (*dedication*) To my Esperantist friends of the Yorkshire Federation. **1909** 'IAN HAY' *Man's Man* vii, He first of all abused them with all the resources of an almost Esperantic vocabulary. **1916** H. G. WELLS *Mr. Britling* I. v. 164 'Just Esperantists,' said Teddy. **1922** C. R. BUXTON *In Russian Village* xvi. 70 He was a fluent Esperantist. **1955** *Times* 13 Aug. 5/5 Economists, students, or esperantists.

†**'esperate.** *Obs.* [?; cf. ESPARCET.]
1626 A. SPEED *Adam out of E.* v. (1659) 38 The Country where Esperate or Clovergrass is most in use at this day is Daphine towards the quarter of Day.

†**esperduct.** *Obs.* [altered form (after Latin) of OF. *esperduite* fem.:—L. **experducta*, fem. of *experductus*, pa. pple. of *experdūcere*, f. *ex* out + *per* through + *dūcere* to lead.] A portion of steel drawn out to a certain length; a rod.
1866 ROGERS *Agric. & Prices* I. xix. 472 Steel [in 13th c.] is generally sold by the garb or sheaf, containing thirty esperducts or gads.

†**esperite.** *Obs.* [a. OF. *esperite* (mod.F. *esprit*): see ESPRIT, ESPRITE.] = SPIRIT.
1475 CAXTON *Jason* 94 b, Your esperite is trauailled with newe fantasies. **1481** —— *Myrr.* II. xxiv. 117 Of this Ayer the euyl esperites take their habyte and their bodyes.

†**esperon.** *Fortif. Obs.* [a. OF. *esperon* (mod.F. *éperon*) in same sense (lit. 'spur').] A work projecting beyond the line of the ramparts; a SPUR.
1598 IVE *Fortif.* 21 The wall and it esperons or counterfeit being laid out, begin to raise of the same.

esperver, var. SPARVER *Obs.* sparrow-hawk.

espial (ɪ'spaɪəl). Forms: 4 espi-, espyaile, -lle, (expyayle), 4–7 espiall(e, 6–7 espyal(l, 5– espial. [a. OF. *espiaille* the action of spying (concr. in pl. 'spies'), f. *espier*, mod.F. *épier*: see ESPY *v.*]
1. The action of espying or spying.
a. The acting as a spy; the action of keeping watch; observation. Also *attrib.*
c **1386** CHAUCER *Melibeus* ¶353 Thanne schal ye evermore counterwayte embusshementz and alle espiaille. **1393** GOWER *Conf.* III. 56 For espiall and mistrowinges They dide thanne suche thinges, That every man might other knowe. **1477** EARL RIVERS (Caxton) *Dictes* 11 a, Be ware well that thou be not supprised by thin ennemyes, for lakke of wache and good espial. **1552** HULOET, *Espiall place*, or corner to spye out of. **1612–15** BP. HALL *Contempl. O.T.* XIX. ix, There are spies upon him, whose espials have moved their anger. **1848** DICKENS *Dombey* 256 The Captain..cut a small hole of espial in the wall. **1876** MISS BRADDON *J. Haggard's Dau.* I. 73 A little room next the hall-door, a closet of espial.
†**b.** Detection, discovery. *Obs.*
a **1557** G. CAVENDISH *Life Wolsey* (T.), After the espial of this boy my lord revealed the same unto the Council.
c. The action of espying or catching sight of anything; the fact of being espied.
1580 BABINGTON *Exp. Lord's Prayer* (1596) 212 A true espiall of sanctification of life in our selues. **1683** tr. *Erasm. Moriæ Enc.* 24 They are as Eagle-sighted as may be in the espial of others faults. **1814** BYRON *Corsair* I. xvii, Conrad's prow pass'd by, Screen'd from espial by the jutting cape. **1830** HOOD *Haunted House* I. ix, Roses with thistles struggled for espial.
†**2.** *concr.* A body of spies; hence (chiefly in *pl.*) a spy, scout. *Obs.*
c **1386** CHAUCER *Friar's T.* 23 Ful prively he had his espiaile. **1531** ELYOT *Gov.* III. vi, Dauid by an espiall knewe that they were all faste on slepe. *a* **1572** KNOX *Hist. Ref.* Wks. 1846 I. 452 The Quene had amangis us her assured espiallis. **1577–87** HOLINSHED *Chron.* I. 174/2 His [Harold's] vnskilfull espials tooke the Normans for priests. **1649** JER. TAYLOR *Gt. Exemp.* v. §31 Our Judge stands as an espial and a watch over our actions. **1653** HOLCROFT *Procopius* II. 51 The espialls returning assured him, there would bee no invasion.
transf. **1607** TOPSELL *Serpents* (1608) 644 Bees..when the flowers are spent neer their lodgings, send out their espials to look for more in places further distant.

†**e'spice.** *Obs.* [a. OF. *espice* (mod.F. *épice* in sense 2):—L. *species*: see SPECIES, SPICE.]
1. A species, kind. In 14–15th c. also SPICE.
c **1386** CHAUCER *Parson's T.* ¶374 The especes [*v.r.* espices] that sourden of pride. **1502** *Ord. Crysten Men* (W. de W. 1506) IV. vi. 181 The maners and dyuers espyces, the whiche may be in one self synne.
2. An aromatic drug; now SPICE.
1483 CAXTON *Gold. Leg.* 112/4 Yf all the espyces of the world had ben stamped to gydre it shold not haue smellyd so well.

‖**espiègle** (ɛspjɛgl), *a.* [F. *espiègle*, ? corruption of Ger. *Eulenspiegel*, the name of a personage of fiction, renowned for his practical jokes.] Frolicsome, sprightly, roguish.
1816 SCOTT *Old Mort.* xxxvii, Features, originally sly and espiegle in expression. **1819** BYRON *Juan* XVI. lxv, Her black, bright, downcast, yet espiègle eye Had gather'd a large tear into its corner.

‖**espièglerie** (ɛspjɛgləri). [F. *espièglerie*, f. *espiègle.*] Frolicsomeness, roguishness.
1816 SCOTT *Antiq.* vi, A pretty young woman..with an air of *espièglerie* which became her very well. **1852** SMEDLEY *L. Arundel* xxxviii, Which act of un-*English*-woman-like *espièglerie* must be set down to the score of a foreign education.

espier (ɪ'spaɪə(r)). Forms: 4 aspier, 4–5 espi-, espyour, 6– espier. [f. ESPY *v.* + -ER¹.] One who espies or spies out; †a spy.
1382 WYCLIF *Hebr.* xi. 31 She [Raab] takynge, or receyuynge, the aspiers with pees. *c* **1430** *Pilgr. Lyf Manhode* II. xii. (1869) 79 A cherl, shrewede, prowd, and daungerous..hath maad him an espyour of weyes. **1587** J. HARMAR tr. *Beza's Serm.* 175 (T.) Ye crafty espiers of the necessity of your poor brethren. **1860** PUSEY *Min. Proph.* 58 Ephraim..would himself be a seer, an espier of future events. **1886** BURTON *Arab. Nts.* (abr. ed.) I. 146 Not an inhabited house appeared to the espier.

espiery (ɪ'spaɪərɪ). *rare.* [f. prec. + -Y.] The action or habit of espying. Const. *of.*
1845 R. W. HAMILTON *Pop. Educ.* ix. (ed. 2) 224 The espiery of the letter's confidence at home.

†**espi'nel.** *Obs.* [ad. F. *espinelle* (Cotgr.), later *spinelle.*] A kind of ruby; = SPINEL.
1595–6 BUREL in Watson *Collect* II. 11 (Jam.) The Espinell, a precious stane. **1677** SIR T. HERBERT *Trav.* (ed. 4) 359 Here [at Pegu] is store of Gold, Silver..Espinels, and Cats-eyes.

†**espi'nette.** *Obs.* [a. OF. *espinete* (mod.F. *épinette*).] = SPINET.
1668 PEPYS *Diary* 15 July, At noon is brought home the espinette I bought the other day of Haward.

espionage ('ɛspɪənɑːʒ, 'ɛspɪənɪdʒ). Also espionnage. [ad. F. *espionnage*, f. *espionner*, f. *espion* spy: see ESPIOUN.] The practice of playing the spy, or of employing spies.
1793 LD. AUCKLAND *Corr.* (1861) II. 500 Military preparations, *espionages*, consultations, conferences, etc. **1825** BENTHAM *Ration. Rew.* 100 To the word espionage a stigma is attached. **1856** FROUDE *Hist. Eng.* (1858) I. iv. 368 The system of espionage with which they [the ecclesiastical courts] had saturated English society. **1870** DEUTSCH *Lit. Rem.* (1874) 283 The Dominicans..were especially singled out for the function of holy espionage.

†**espiot.** *Obs. rare*⁻¹. In 5 espyotte. [a. OF. *espiot*, ? a. Pr. *espiaut* SPIT.] A spear.
1490 CAXTON *Eneydos* I. (1890) 143 Eneas..launched at hym his grete espyotte or spere.

†**e'spioun.** *Obs.* [a. F. *espion*, prob. ad. It. *spione*, of Teut. origin: cf. OHG. *spehan* to look out.] A spy, scout.
1636 E. DACRES tr. *Machiavel's Disc. Livy* III. x. 502 And then keepe good espiouns, so that if hee chance to bend towards thee, thou maist avoyd him at leysure.

†**espiouress.** *Obs.* [f. *espiour* (see ESPIER) + -ESS.] A female espier.
c **1430** *Pilgr. Lyf Manhode* II. cli. (1869) 136 Bi hire j am deliuered to these old theeues, espyowresses of pilgrimes.

espire, obs. var. of EXPIRE.
1483 CAXTON *Gold. Leg.* 131/2 He espyred and deyed in grete payne.

espire. ? Mistake for *enspire* = INSPIRE.
c **1430** LYDG. *Min. Poems* (Percy Soc.) 62 Whan [= *whom* (sc. the Virgin Mary)] the holigost, with his swete brethe, Gan to espiren as for his chosen place.

†**e'spiritual,** *a. Obs.* In 4–5 espirituel(l, 5 -alle. [a. OF. *espirituel* (mod.F. *spirituel*):—L. *spīrituāl-em*.] = SPIRITUAL in various senses.
c **1386** CHAUCER *Parson's T.* ¶79 Manye been the weyes espirituels that leden folk to oure Lord Ihesu Crist. *c* **1400** —— *Rom. Rose* 650 So faire it was, that trusteth well, It semed a place espirituell. *Ibid.* 672 As angels doon espirituell. **1477** EARL RIVERS (Caxton) *Dictes* 71 b, He that multiplieth his temporall goodes dyminueth his espiritualles [*printed* espûalles].

esplanade (ɛsplə'neɪd). Also 7 *aphet.* **splanade.** [a. F. *esplanade*, ad. Sp. *esplanada* (corresp. to It. *spianata*), f. *esplanar*:—L. *explānāre* to level, f. *ex* out + *-plānus* level, PLAIN.]

I. *Fortif.* **a.** The glacis of the counterscarp, or the sloping of the parapet of the covered way toward the country.
1696 in PHILLIPS. **1755** H. T. CROKER *Orlando Fur.* XIV. cxxix, The Pagan forces.. by ladders different essay'd Upon the second esplanade to creep. **1811** WELLINGTON in Gurw. *Disp.* VII. 331 There was a heavy fire of musketry on the Esplanade: so that the enemy are not in the covered way.

b. 'An open, level space of ground, separating the citadel of a fortress from the town' (Stocqueler *Mil. Encycl.*).
1708 KERSEY, *Esplanade*.. is now chiefly taken for the void Space between the Glacis of a Citadel, and the first Houses of a Town. **1736** in BAILEY. **1763** SCRAFTON *Indostan* iii. (1770) 72 The fort was a regular square.. no glacis; and but a small esplanade of about two hundred and fifty yards. **1824** SCOTT *St. Ronan's* xvii, The esplanade in the front of the old castle. **1855** MOTLEY *Dutch Rep.* (1861) II. 455 Throwing up a breastwork.. upon the esplanade, between the citadel and the town.
transf. **1817** M. KEATINGE *France & Sp. to Mor.* I. 166 [Spain] to be effectually defended on this side, the state must always be prepared to evacuate and make an esplanade of her territory, to the Sierra Morena; which thus would be the line of defence to her capital, Seville.

2. A levelled piece of ground; often, such a space intended to serve as a public promenade.
1682 WHELER *Journ. Greece* I. 31 A large place, which they call the Splanade. **1726** CAVALLIER *Mem.* I. 96 A fine Walk, call'd the Esplanade, without the Town. **1788** *Gentl. Mag.* LVIII. I. 69/2 An esplanade.. on which.. the foundations of a regular street were laid. **1805** G. ROSE *Diaries* (1860) II. 199, I went on the esplanade [at Weymouth] early in the morning. **1823** HEBER *Narr. of a Journey* (1828) I. 28 Behind the [Calcutta] esplanade, however, are only Tank-square, and some other streets occupied by Europeans. **1831** CARLYLE *Sart. Res.* (1858) 12 The Palace esplanade, where music plays while Serene Highness is pleased to eat his victuals. **1863** KINGLAKE *Crimea* (1876) I. xiv. 296 The Esplanade of the Invalides.

b. *transf.* A level open space.
1681 BLOUNT *Glossogr.*, *Esplanade*, a plain open ground. **1702** W. J. tr. *Bruyn's Voy. Levant* v. 13 Upon the mountain we met with an Esplanade of a considerable Bigness. **1768** STERNE *Sent. Journ.*, *The Dwarf*, At the end of the orchestra, and betwixt that and the first side-box, there is a small esplanade left. **1823** SCOTT *Quentin D.* iii, An open esplanade, devoid of trees. **1868** MILMAN *St. Paul's* i. 2 No eminence.. could compare with the spacious esplanade on which St. Paul's stands.

c. 'In modern gardening, a grass plot' (T.).
1818 in TODD. **1828** in WEBSTER; and in mod. Dicts.

esplees (ɛ'spli:z), *sb. pl. Law.* [ad. AF. *esplez*, *espletz*, pl. of OF. *esplet*, *espleit*, *esploit* revenue:—L. *explicitum*, neut. pa. pple. of *explicāre* to unfold, in vulg. Lat. to develop, extract, accomplish. Cf. EXPLOIT, which is ultimately the same word.] The products which ground or land yield; as the hay of meadows, herbage of pasture, corn of arable, rents, services, etc.; also, the lands, etc. themselves. (Wharton.)
1598 KITCHIN *Courts Leet* (1675) 252 It behoveth to lay the Esplees in his court. **1613** SIR H. FINCH *Law* (1636) 357 The demandant must alledge the taking of the profits, we call it esplees, in the declaration. **1865** NICHOLS *Britton* II. 135 Inasmuch as he never took esplees in full seisin before the death of the grantor.

espleit(e, esploit(e, obs. ff. of EXPLOIT.

espoire, var. of ESPEIRE, *Obs.*, hope.

†**e'spontoon.** *Obs.* [ad. Fr. *esponton* (cf. Sp. *esponton*), ad. It. *spuntone*: SPONTOON.] A half pike carried by an infantry officer; = SPONTOON.
1772 SIMES *Mil. Guide*, s.v. **1815** SOUTHEY in *Q. Rev.* XII. 339 Capt. Lewis slipped and.. recovered himself by means of his espontoon. **1838** SPARKS *Biog. W. Eaton* ii. IX. 173 Was met in his advance by the other, with his espontoon.

†**e'spousage.** *Obs.* Also 6 **esposage.** See SPOUSAGE. [a. OF. *esposage*, *espousage*, f. *esposer*, *espouser* to ESPOUSE.] **a.** The action of espousing or betrothing. **b.** The condition of being espoused or married, spousehood, wedlock.
1549 LATIMER *1st Serm. bef. Edw. VI.* (Arb.) 34 To.. leade hys life in pure and chaste esposage. **1599** R. GREENHAM *Wks.* 288 There was a solemne promise to bee made of the parties that should be maried before they were to be ioyned in marriage, and that was called their espousage.

espousal (ɪ'spaʊzəl), *sb.* (*a.*) Forms: 4–5 **espousaile,** 5–7 **espousel, -elle,** (5 **espoisalle, espousayl(l)e),** 6–7 **espousall,** 6– **espousal.** Also SPOUSAL. [a. OF. *espousailles* (mod.F. *épousailles*), corresp. to Pr. *esposalhas*, Cat. *esposallas*, OSp. *esponsalias*:—L. *sponsālia*, neut. pl. of *sponsālis* adj., f. *sponsus*: see ESPOUSE *v.*]

1. In *plural*, formerly also in *sing.* The formal 'plighting of troth' between a man and a woman; the whole of the ceremonies constituting or accompanying this. **a.** The celebration of a marriage; nuptials, a wedding. **b.** The celebration of a betrothal.
Now merely literary and somewhat archaic. It seems probable that the sense 'marriage' was the original one in Eng., and that the sense 'betrothal' arose at a late date through the influence of L. *sponsus* and its derivatives, especially as used in Canon Law.
a. [*c* **1330** R. BRUNNE *Chron.* (1810) 308 Þe courte of Rome had ordeynd þat spousale. **1382** WYCLIF *Gen.* xxix. 26 It is not of custom in oure place, that the lesse bifore we taken to sposeyls.] **1485** CAXTON *Chas. Gt.* I. I. iii. 15 The fyrst nyght after the espousaylles.. Clotyldis.. said to the kyng. **1523** *Act 14 & 15 Hen. VIII*, c. 8 Euery of them so maryed maye haue.. their said office.. as they did.. before the sayd espouselles. **1641** *Termes de la Ley.* 39 Though it [the childe] were borne but one day after the espousels solemnized. **1643** MILTON *Divorce* x. (1851) 48 His naming of a meet or like help in the first espousall instituted. **1719** YOUNG *Revenge* I. i, Is not the day then fix'd for your espousals? **1848** MACAULAY *Hist. Eng.* I. 251 The multitude.. drank in eagerly the tale of the secret espousals and the black box.
b. **1637** HEYWOOD *Dial.* 311 My espousals remaine in my Fathers power, and not mine. *c* **1645** HOWELL *Lett.* I. III. xxvi. (1655) I. 146 In the interim the Earl was commanded not to deliver the aforesaid Proxy of the Prince for the desponsorios or espousall untill Christmas. **1726** AYLIFFE *Parerg.* 246, I shall here.. define Espousals to be a mutual Promise of a future Marriage. **1828** SCOTT *F.M. Perth* ix, After the espousals of the Duke of Rothsay with the Earl of March's daughter, Douglas entered the lists to break off the contract. **1846** MASKELL *Mon Rit.* I. p. ccxxii, Lyndwood tells us the distinction which there is between espousals and matrimony. 'Stunt etiam Sponsalia repromissio futurarum nuptiarum,' etc.

c. *fig.* esp. in spiritual sense, of the 'marriage' of the soul or the church to God or Christ.
[**1450–1530** *Myrr. our Ladye* 138 The spousayle that ys betweene oure Lorde Iesu Cryste and holy chyrche.] *a* **1450** *Knt. de la Tour* cix. (1868) 147 Where as was made the espoisalle, and the alyaunce, and knyttynge of the godhede vnto the manhode. **1611** BIBLE *Jer.* ii. 2. **1738** WESLEY *Hymn*, *'Jesus, Thou everlasting King'* ii, Let every Act of Worship be Like our Espousals, Lord, to Thee. **1849** ROBERTSON *Serm.* Ser. I. iii. (1866) 44 In the first espousals of the soul. **1850** MRS. JAMESON *Leg. Mon. Ord.* Introd. (1863) 22 To solemnise the espousals of sanctity and poverty. **1855** J. H. NEWMAN *Callista* xix, We have possession of Him [Christ]. It is an espousal for eternity.

†**2.** In phrases ***to break one's espousal(s*** (= †'*to break spouse*'), ***to hold espousal***, to violate, be faithful to, the marriage vow. Also (*sing.* and *pl.*), the married state. *Obs.*
[**1303** R. BRUNNE *Handl. Synne* 1621 Grete mede he getyþ.. þat wele wil holde his spousayle. *c* **1340** *Cursor M.* 7849 (Trin.) Isaac his son in spousaile was.] **1393** GOWER *Conf.* II. 322 [He] had his espousaile broke. **1545** UDALL *Erasm. Par.* (1548) Pref. 15 b, Estate and dignitie of espousall and mariage. **1549** LATIMER *1st Serm. bef. Edw. VI.* (Arb.) 36 He [King Lewis] had rather be sycke euen vnto death then he wold breake his espousals. **1574** tr. *Littleton's Tenures* 8 b, The thirde parte of the tenementes, which were her husbandes duringe the espousels.

3. [With sense as if f. the vb.; cf. *arrival*, *withdrawal*, etc.] In *sing.* only. The action of espousing. Const. *of*. **a.** *lit.*
In mod. Dicts.

b. *fig.* [cf. ESPOUSE *v.* 4] The 'espousing' a cause, a principle, etc.; †the taking up the defence (of a person). Now somewhat *rare*.
1674 *Ch. & Court of Rome* 34 The espousal and owning of this bloody Fact, after its execution. **1681** in *Select. Harl. Misc.* (1793) 466 They reckoned they had wrought him to such an espousal of his brother, etc. **1683** *Addr. fr. Carmarthen* in *Lond. Gaz.* No. 1856/5 The Fanaticks pious pretences in the espousals and pursuits of the most Barbarous Villanies. *a* **1716** SOUTH *Serm.* VIII. vii. (R.), The scene.. is properly private revenge, not a zealous espousal of the publick injuries. *a* **1797** H. WALPOLE (T.), Political reasons forbid the open espousal of his cause.

4. *concr.* An espoused person, a husband or wife.
c **1470** HARDING *Chron.* Proem xiii, To his espousaile, The dukes doughter of Melayn. **1611** SPEED *Hist. Gt. Brit.* IX. xxi. §67, I neither will nor intend to consent.. vnto the said Lady Katherine as my espousall and wife. **1620** SHELTON *Quix.* III. xxi. 146 Therefore, said Basilius, take me and I deliver myself as thy Espousal.

5. *attrib.*
1598 YONG *Diana* 392 We concluded that the espousall rites should bee solemnized in the citie of Lysbone. **1622** BACON *Hen. VII*, 80 Maximilians Ambassadour.. put his Legge.. betweene the Espousall Sheets. **1649** BP. HALL *Cases Consc.* 348 A mutuall engagement of both parties that they will marry each other; which is most properly an espousall-contract. **1877** W. JONES *Finger-ring* 107 The espousal-ring of King Hydaspes.

¶**6.** Used as *adj.* Cf. SPOUSAL *a.*
1773 J. ROSS *Fratricide* II. 716 To whom thus Eve.. Fraught with espousal tenderness replies.

†**e'spouse,** *sb. Obs.* Also 5–6 **espowse.** See also SPOUSE *sb.* [a. OF. *espos*, *espus*, *espous* (mod.F. *époux*) masc., *espuse*, *espouse* (mod. *épouse*) fem., corresp. to Pr. *espos*, Sp., Pg. *esposo*, It. *sposo*:—L. *sponsus*: see ESPOUSE *v.*]

1. a. A betrothed person of either sex; also a newly-married person, a bride or bridegroom.
c **1475** *Partenay* 954 The Erle the espouse courtoisly forth lad. *c* **1534** tr. *Pol. Verg. Eng. Hist.* I. 141 The good virgin Alfreda, knowinge the deathe of her espowse.. convayed herselfe into a place named Crolande. **1594** R. PARSONS *Confer. Success* I. vi. 133 The heyre apparent (which be-fore was but espouse,) is made now the true king and husband of the commonwealth. **1603** HOLLAND *Plutarch's Mor.* 464 Hee would not allow that the new married bride-grome should lie with his espouse.

b. A husband or wife.
1490 CAXTON *Eneydos* xviii. (1890) 68 My true husbande & espouse. **1530** PALSGR. Ep. 4 Charles Brandon duke of Suffolke, her moost worthy espouse. **1642** W. BIRD *Mag. Honor* 111 The King's Espouse is a free person, exempted by the Common Law. **1654** tr. *Scudery's Curia Politiæ* 153 Immodest and vicious Messalina was the espouse and wife of dull and ignoble Claudius.

2. *fig.*
1483 CAXTON *Gold. Leg.* 92/2 Thou shalt haue me thyn espowse in the Royaume of heuen. *a* **1555** RIDLEY in Foxe *A. & M.* (1684) III. 364 Christ, who is the most loving spouse of his espouse the Church.

espouse (ɪ'spaʊz), *v.* Also 7 **expouse.** See also SPOUSE *v.* [a. OF. *espouse-r* (mod.F. *épouser*), corresp. to Pr. *espozar*, Cat. *esposar*, It. *sposare*:—L. *sponsāre*, f. *sponsus*, pa. pple. of *spondēre* to betroth. Cf. SPOUSE *v.*]

†**1.** *trans.* To contract or betroth (*gen.* a woman) *to*, †*with* another; also *simply*. Usually said of the parents, or those standing *in loco parentis*, rarely of the bridegroom. *Obs.*
1605 CAMDEN *Rem.* (1637) 414 Two Lovers who being espoused, dyed both before they were married. **1611** BIBLE *2 Sam.* iii. 14 Deliuer mee my wife Michal, which I espoused to mee. —— *Luke* i. 27 To a virgine espoused to a man whose name was Ioseph. *a* **1626** BACON (J.), He had received him as a suppliant.. and espoused him with his kinswoman.

†**b.** *fig.* To pledge, commit, engage. *Obs.*
1605 BACON *Adv. Learn.* II. xxiii. §6 Those that will espouse us to many factions and quarrels. **1654** WHITLOCK *Zootomia* 225, I will.. look on all the changes of Common-wealths.. without espousing my reason so to any one, as, etc. *Ibid.* 253 To espouse our selves.. to one part of truth.

2. To take (a person) as spouse; to marry. Said chiefly of the man, occas. of the woman. Also of the father: To give in marriage *to*.
1475 CAXTON *Jason* 8 And this day Pyrithyon espoused the fayr Ypodame. **1511–12** *Act 3 Hen. VIII*, c. 18 Pream., Richarde.. whose dowghter & heyre the seid Syr John Rysley espoused & maryed. **1594** SHAKS. *Rich. III*, IV. v. 18 The Queene hath heartily consented He should espouse Elizabeth hir daughter. **1613** PURCHAS *Pilgr.* (1626) 201 He which shall espouse a woman bringeth witnesses. **1642** PERKINS *Prof. Bk.* v. §439. 190 If a man assigne unto his wife when he espouses her, at the Church doore [etc.]. **1725** POPE *Odyss.* II. 130 If her [Penelope's] sire approves, Let him espouse her to the Peer she loves. **1768** H. WALPOLE *Hist. Doubts* 40 Before Edward had espoused the lady Grey, he had been contracted to the lady Eleanor Butler. **1860** MOTLEY *Netherl.* (1868) I. ii. 55 The Duke of Savoy was himself to espouse the Infanta.

b. *transf.* and *fig.*
1615 G. SANDYS *Trav.* 2 On Ascension Day the Duke [of Venice] is towed thither [to the sea] in the Bucentoro.. where he solemnly espouseth the sea. *a* **1711** KEN *Psyche* Poet. Wks. 1721 IV. 236 Sweet Jesus to espouse your Spirit deigns. **1802** WORDSW. *On Extinction Venet. Republic*, And when she [Venice] took unto herself a mate, She must espouse the everlasting Sea. **1860** PUSEY *Min. Proph.* 8 God.. Who now vouchsafes to espouse.. and unite with Himself.. our sinful souls.

†**3.** To unite in marriage. Const. *to*, also *simply*. *lit.* and *fig. Obs.*
1593 SHAKS. *2 Hen. VI*, I. i. 9 In presence of.. twenty reuerend Bishops I.. was espous'd. —— *Lucr.* 20 Kings might be espoused to more fame. **1599** —— *Hen. V*, IV. vi. 26 And so, espous'd to death, with blood, he seal'd A Testament of Noble-ending-loue.

†**b.** *absol.* with reciprocal sense.
a **1700** DRYDEN (J.), They soon espous'd; for they with ease were join'd; Who were before contracted in the mind.

4. *trans.* To choose, attach oneself to (any object); to take to oneself, make one's own (a cause, quarrel, etc.); to become a supporter of (a party); to adopt, embrace (a doctrine, opinion, theory, profession, mode of life). [So Fr. *épouser*.]
1622 BACON *Hen. VII* (J.), In gratitude unto the duke of Bretagne.. he espoused that quarrel, and declared himself in aid of the duke. **1655** GURNALL *Chr. in Arm.* xxix. §5. (1669) 333/1 The Mariners needle espousing the North point rather than any other. **1667** DRYDEN *Ess. Dram. Poetry* in Arb. *Garner* III. 531 And by that means, expouse the interest of neither. **1672** CAVE *Prim. Chr.* I. ii. (1673) 18 You ought not.. to espouse barbarous and foreign Rites. **1711** ADDISON *Spect.* No. 1. ¶6, I never espoused any Party with Violence. **1759** ROBERTSON *Hist. Scot.* I. IV. 265 He espoused, for this reason, the cause of the Scottish queen. **1782** PRIESTLEY *Corrupt. Chr.* I. III. 307 The protestants

espoused..the doctrine of Austin. **1789** T. JEFFERSON *Writ.* (1859) II. 555 The Parliaments..were led..to espouse, for the first time, the rights of the nation. **1814** WORDSW. *White Doe* II. 208 Espouse thy doom at once, and cleave To fortitude without reprieve. **1825** LYTTON *Falkland* 16 [They] looked to my support in whatever political side they had espoused. **1854** BALFOUR *Bot.* 130 Many travellers have espoused the vertical theory of wood formation.

espoused (ɪˈspaʊzd), *ppl. a.* [f. prec. + -ED¹.] In senses of the verb. Also quasi-*sb.*

1611 BIBLE *Luke* ii. 5 To be taxed with Mary his espoused wife. **1660** GLANVILL *Vanity Dogmat.* xiii. 120 The beloved Opinion being..wedded to the Intellect; the case of our espoused self becomes our own. **1667** MILTON *P.L.* IV. 710 With Flowers, Garlands, and sweet-smelling Herbs Espoused Eve deckt first her Nuptial Bed. **1701** LADY M. W. MONTAGUE *Lett.* II. xlvii. 46 The espoused never see one another till three days after their marriage. **1791** COWPER *Iliad* I. 138 My own first espoused. **1828** D'ISRAELI *Chas. I*, I. iii. 39 The female..was still more actively propagating the espoused doctrines.

‖**espouˈsee.** In 5 espowsee. [OF. *espousee* (mod.F. *épousée*) fem., pa. pple. of *espouser* (*épouser*): see ESPOUSE *v.*] A bride.

1480 CAXTON *Ovid's Met.* XI. viii, They were parents and of kynne to the espowsee.

†**eˈspousement.** *Obs.*⁻⁰ [a. OF. *espousement*, f. *espouser* to ESPOUSE.] The action of espousing or marrying; espousal, marriage.

1847 in CRAIG; and in mod. Dicts.

espouser (ɪˈspaʊzə(r)). [f. ESPOUSE *v.* + -ER¹. Cf. Fr. *épouser*.] One who espouses.

1. †**a.** One who brings about a betrothal or marriage. *Obs.* **b.** One who makes a contract of marriage with (a woman). *rare.*

1653 GAUDEN *Hierasp.* 156 As Woers and Espousers..to make up..Espousals, between Christ and the Church. **1828** in WEBSTER. **1884** C. READE *Picture* I. ii. in *Harper's Mag.* Mar. 634/2 'You have accepted me publicly as your betrothed.' 'Say *my espouser*,' said she, calmly.

2. One who takes up the cause of (a person, party, etc.); one who adopts (an opinion, system, etc.); a partisan, supporter, upholder.

1654 HAMMOND *Answ. Animadv. Ignat.* iii. §4. 79 They shew themselves far from passionate espousers of Episcopacy. *a* **1687** H. MORE *Answ. Psychop.* 109 He seems to be an Espouser of this Opinion. **1738** WARBURTON *Div. Legat.* I. 33 Mr. Bayle, the last Espouser of this Paradox. **1741** MIDDLETON *Cicero* I. VI. 519 The most factious espouser of a Dictator. **1761** ALLEN *Serm. Univ. Oxf.* 11 (T.) The espousers of that unauthorised and detestable scheme. **1828** in WEBSTER; and in mod. Dicts.

†**eˈspousess.** *Obs. rare*⁻¹. In 6 espowzes. [f. ESPOUSE *sb.* + -ESS. Cf. SPOUSESS.] A bride.

1597 J. PAYNE *Royal Exch.* 43 So gloriouse and Princely a spowze, to theire espowzes..so poore and meane an espowzes.

eˈspousing, *vbl. sb.* Also 6 espousein. [f. ESPOUSE *v.* + -ING¹.] The action of the vb. ESPOUSE in various senses.

1531 *Dial. on Laws Eng.* II. xxv. (1638) 106 A Man hath two sons, one borne before espousein, and the other after espousels. **1632** SHERWOOD, An espousing, *mariement.* **1687** BP. CARTWRIGHT in *Magd. Coll.* (Oxf. Hist. Soc.) 188 The espousing of your cause.

†**espred,** *pa. pple. Obs.* [for YSPRED, pa. pple. of SPREAD *v.*]

1587 *Mirr. Mag.* (N.), He layde him then downe by the altars side Upon the white hindes skin espred therefore.

‖**espressivo** (espresˈsivo), *adv. Mus.* [It. *espressivo* expressive.] With expression.

espresso (ɛˈsprɛsəʊ). Also **expresso.** [It. *caffè espresso*, lit. 'pressed-out coffee'.] Coffee made under steam pressure; the apparatus used for making this; a coffee-bar where it is sold. Also *attrib.*

1945 'A. BOUCHER' in M. & G. Gordon *Pride of Felons* (1964) 80, I was drinking a caffé espresso, a strong, bitter, steamed coffee. **1955** *N.Y. Times* 13 Mar. x. 11/5 Also new are the numerous small Coffee Expresso Snack Restaurants off Dublin's Grafton Street. **1955** *20th Cent.* June 549 The brittle conversation of the Espresso Cafés. **1957** A. WILSON *Bit off Map* 137 The even more degrading swamps of espresso bar rebellion. **1957** *Observer* 3 Nov. 18/2 The piece on lunch-time in an espresso. **1958** M. SPARK *Robinson* xii. 186 When I am walking down the King's Road or sipping my espresso in the morning. **1958** *Spectator* 22 Aug. 248/3 And what about changes in fashionable pronunciation, from taytable to espresso usage. *Ibid.* 7 Nov. 611/1 It was not easy to accept a character like the expresso poet with his impeccable Oxford accent, grovelling in dirt. *Ibid.* 21 Nov. 700/2 The rise of the expresso with its skiffle groups. **1958** *Times* 23 Oct. 16/1 An espresso machine. **1967** 'J. CROSS' *To Hell for Half-a-Crown* iii. 50 The waiter came in with a pot of espresso and a bottle of fifteen-year-old Meukouw.

espringal. *Obs.* exc. *Hist.* Also 7 espringold; and see SPRINGALD. [ad. OF. *espringale* (mod.F. *espringale*), perh. f. Ger. *springen* SPRING *v.* Cf. Pr. *espingala*, Sp. and Pg. *espingarda.*] A mediæval military engine or catapult for throwing stones, bolts, or other missiles.

1605 CAMDEN *Rem.* (1657) 206 Some kind of bricol.. which the English and Scots called an espringold. **1795** SOUTHEY *Joan of Arc* VIII. 250 Some the mangonels supply ..or in the espringal Fix the brass-winged arrows. **1840** L. RITCHIE *Windsor C.* 215 The espringal, which threw darts that had brass plates instead of feathers, to render their flight steady.

†**eˈsprise,** *v. Obs.* [f. OF. *espris*, pa. pple. of *esprendre* (mod.F. *éprendre*) in same sense, f. *es-*:—L. *ex-* + *prendre* to take.] *trans.* chiefly *pass.* To set on fire, enkindle, inflame (with love, etc.); also *lit.* (with flame).

1474 CAXTON *Chesse* II. ii. (1860) B. vij, She was esprysed and taken with his loue. **1483** —— *Gold. Leg.* 29/2 Whiche thyng the holy ghoost maketh whan he espriseth hym of hys love. **1491** —— *Vitas Patr.* (W. de W. 1495) I. 206 b/2 The faces of the other semed as they had be esprysed with a dredefull flamme. **1567** DRANT *Horace' Epist.* xv. E vj, Wyne that will make my paramour Esprysed on my face.

b. To kindle (a passion).

1490 CAXTON *Eneydos* xiv. (1890) 50 The grete furour enflammed wyth brennyng desire of loue esprysed wythin her sinewes.

‖**esprit** (ɛspri). [Fr., corresp. to Pr. *esperit*, *sperit*, Sp. *espiritu*, Pg. *espirito*, It. *spirito*, ad. L. *spīrit-us* SPIRIT.] In Fr. primarily 'spirit, mind'. Hence used in many derivative senses; those occurring in Eng. writers are the following:

1. Sprightliness, vivacious wit in conversation or composition (see Littré, *Esprit* 15). Formerly in wider sense: Cleverness, 'brains', 'nous' (see Littré, *Esprit* 13).

1591 F. SPARRY tr. *Cattan's Geomancie* 103 If the man be of a good esprit and vnderstanding. **1659** *Gentl. Call.* iv. §19. 406 They inscribe upon these poisons the inviting names of ingenuity and 'esprit'. **1777** DR. JEANS in *Priv. Lett. 1st Ld. Malmesbury* I. 353 He has certainly more esprit than the rest, because he knows how to save himself in good time. **1788** *Walpoliana* cix. 45 Wit, or even what the French term esprit, seems little compatible with feeling. **1851** MAYNE REID *Scalp Hunt.* xx, Frenchmen..singing their boat songs with all the esprit of their race. **1867** PARKMAN *Jesuits N. Amer.* xix. (1875) 285 The French conceived that they had to do with a man of esprit.

2. In Fr. phraseological combinations.

a. esprit de corps (ɛspri də kɔr). [*corps* body] Also erron. **esprit du corps.** The regard entertained by the members of a body for the honour and interests of the body as a whole, and of each other as belonging to it.

1780 H. WALPOLE *Let.* 27 Sept. (1904) XI. 285 How *l'esprit du corps* absorbs all feelings! **1790** W. MACLAY *Jrnl.* 12 Feb. (1890) 195 This I considered as something in the taste of *esprit de corps*, for he is a lawyer. **1814** JANE AUSTEN *Mansf. Park* I. v. 94 Well done, sister! I honour your *esprit du corps.* **1827** BENTHAM *Ration. Evid.* Wks. 1843 VI. 155 A particular community..such as that of divines, lawyers, merchants, etc., has its *esprit de corps*, its corporate affections, and other interests. **1873** H. SPENCER *Stud. Sociol.* x. 242 *Esprit de corps*..in each specialized part of the body politic, prompts measures to preserve the integrity of that part in opposition to other parts. **1955** *Times* 15 Aug. 11/3 All observers expressed high praise for the esprit de corps and élan of the infantrymen.

b. esprit fort (ɛspri fɔr). Pl. *esprits forts.* [Fr. *fort* strong.] A 'strongminded' person; usually, one who professes superiority to current prejudices, *esp.* a 'freethinker' in religion.

1750 *Chesterf. Lett.* ccxii. (1792) II. 311 Whenever you happen to be in company with those pretended *Esprits forts.* **1765** HARRIS [Lord Malmesbury] *Priv. Lett. 1st Ld. Malmesbury* I. 163 To pass for an esprit fort is all their ambition. **1800** MAR. EDGEWORTH *Belinda* xvii, She next tried what could be done by talking to her as an esprit fort.

c. esprit de l'escalier (ɛspri də lɛskalje), **esprit d'escalier** [Diderot, *Paradoxe sur le Comédien*: F. *escalier* staircase], a retort or remark that occurs to a person after the opportunity to make it has passed.

1906 H. W. & F. G. FOWLER *King's Eng.* i. 32 No one will know what *spirit of the staircase* is who is not already familiar with *esprit d'escalier.* **1911** BEERBOHM *Zuleika D.* xvi. 248 He prayed, as he followed the victorious young woman downstairs, that *l'esprit de l'escalier* might befall him. **1936** A. HUXLEY *Eyeless in Gaza* xxi. 305 One might be allowed a bit of poetic licence—make the *esprit d'escalier* happen at the same time as the romantic affair. **1959** *Listener* 15 Jan. 121/3 The ripostes which come so readily to their lips..smell slightly of *l'esprit de l'escalier.* **1964** S. BELLOW *Herzog* (1965) 325 This mixture of clairvoyance and spleen, *esprit de l'escalier*, noble inspirations, poetry and nonsense.

†**esprite.** *Obs.* [a. Fr. *esprit*: see prec. Cf. ESPERITE, SPRITE.] Mind, SPIRIT.

Hence **esprited** *a.* [+ -ED²], in *dull-esprited* = dull-spirited.

1591 F. SPARRY tr. *Cattan's Geomancie* (1599) 229 A man diligent and of a vigilant esprite. *Ibid.* 107 The partie is dull esprited, and hath but small vnderstanding. *Ibid.* 149 The good esprites vnto whome this my Booke may come.

†**eˈsprove,** *v. Obs.* [ad. OF. *esprove-r* (mod.F. *éprouver*), f. *es-*:—L. *ex-* out + *prouver* to prove. Cf. Pr. *esproar.*] *trans.* (*refl.*) To make trial of (oneself, one's strength).

1480 CAXTON *Ovid's Met.* x. viii, Yf ye wil have worship or loos..esprove you agaynst me. *c* **1500** *Melusine* 224 Somme castyng the barre of yron, other held theire spere & shild and esprouued them self that one on þat other.

†**eˈspy,** *sb. Obs.* Also 5 esspie, 3-5 ASPY. See also SPY. [a. OF. *espie*, f. *espier*: see ESPY, SPY *vbs.* Cf. Sp. *espia*, It. *spia.*]

1. The action of espying; espial, espionage.

c **1386** CHAUCER *Melibeus* ¶ 60 In such a wyse that thou ne wante noon espye ne wacche thy body for to save. *c* **1430** *Syr Gener.* (Roxb.) 2588 Of here espie no thing thei wist. **1598** HAKLUYT *Voy.* I. 203 Of these he made subtile inuestigation Of his owne espie, and other mens relation. **1607** TOPSELL *Serpents* (1653) 712 The Eagle..Sharp war..did prepare Gainst Serpent..after espy.

b. In Wyclif the form *aspye* occurs often in the sense 'snare, ambush'.

[*c* **1380** WYCLIF *Serm.* Sel. Wks. II. 363 Aspies þat þe fend haþ leid. **1382** —— *Ex.* xxi. 13 If eny man of avysement sle his neiȝbour and by aspyes. **1388** —— *Gen.* iii. 15 Thou schalt sette aspies to hir heele.]

2. *concr.* [cf. *sentinel*, *watch*, etc.] A spy.

c **1450** *Merlin* xxviii. 575 The saisnes it wisten by theire esspies that thei hadde through the countrey. **1564** HAWARD *Eutropius* II. 14 Hee had apprehended the espyes of Pirrhus. **1598** BARCKLEY *Felic. Man* II. (1603) 111, I am indeede an espie of thy covetousnesse and madnesse. **1624** CAPT. SMITH *Virginia* VI. 235 [He] sent his wife as an espy to see. **1656** HOBBES *Liberty, Necess., & C.* (1841) 112 This argument was sent forth only as an espy, to make a more full discovery.

espy (ɪˈspaɪ), *v.* Forms: 4-7 **espie, -ye,** 5- **espy.** Also ASPY. [a. OF. *espie-r* (mod.F. *épier*), corresp. to Pr. and Sp. *espiar*, It. *spiare*:—Com. Romanic **spiāre*, ad. OHG. *spehôn* (Ger. *spähen*) to SPY. Cf. L. *specĕre*, Gr. σκέπτεσθαι to look.]

†**1.** *trans.* To act as a spy upon, to watch (a person); to inspect as a spy (sometimes with *out*); to examine closely. Also, to watch for, look out for. *Obs.*

[*c* **1330** R. BRUNNE *Chron.* (1810) 37 Tille wikked men scho spak, Edward to aspie.] *c* **1420** *Pallad. on Husb.* I. 105 But thicke and drie [*sc.* land] espie [*printed* espy]. **1480** CAXTON *Chron. Eng.* II. (1520) 10 b/1 Brute anone sende of his men to lande for to espye the maner of the countree. **1552** HULOET, Espye or waite a time, *aucupari tempus.* *a* **1555** LATIMER *Serm. & Rem.* (1845) 304 To espy and search his land. **1588** SHAKS. *Tit. A.* II. iii. 48 Now question me no more, we are espied. **1590** GREENE *Fr. Bacon* Wks. (ed. Rtldg.) 154/2 Espy her loves, and who she liketh best. **1611** BIBLE *Josh.* xiv. 7 Moses..sent me from Kadesh Barnea, to espie out the land. *a* **1667** JER. TAYLOR (Ogilvie), He sends angels to espy us in all our ways.

b. *absol.* or *intr.* To look steadily, watch, keep a look out; to act as a spy. *arch.*

c **1386** CHAUCER *Knt's T.* 254 With that word Arcite gan espye Wher as this lady romed to and fro. **1513** DOUGLAS *Æneis* VIII. iii. 134 Evander..espying wyth his sicht. **1565-73** COOPER *Thesaurus, Episcopius*, a brigantine or ship sent out to espie. **1611** BIBLE *Jer.* xlviii. 19 Stand by the way and espie. **1846** KEBLE *Lyra Innoc.* (1873) 42 [He] on the dark edge stands..and downward dares espy.

†**c.** (*trans.* In ME. form ASPY: To lie in wait for; also *absol.*)

c **1225** *Ancr. R.* 196, I ðe wildernesse heo aspieden us to slean. **1382** WYCLIF *Acts* xxiii. 21 More than fourty men of hem aspien him [Vulg. *insidiantur ei*].

2. *trans.* To discover by spying or by looking out; to catch sight of; to descry, discern, discover (what is distant or partly hidden); to detect (a fault, flaw, etc.); to discern (a convenient time or opportunity). †Formerly sometimes with *out.* †Also, to discern *from.*

c **1320** *Seuyn Sag.* (W.) 1796 Yif thou dost a folie, Thi louerd hit wil sone espie. *c* **1384** CHAUCER *H. Fame* II. 198 [It were impossible] How that..he [Fame] shulde here al this Or they [his spies] espie hyt. *c* **1460** *La Belle Dame sanz mercy* 88 in *Pol. Rel. & L. Poems* (1866) 55 But tweyne þat were my frendis here before had me espied. **1486** *Bk. St. Albans* D ij, She [the hawk] espith theym and commyth couerte her selfe. **1531** ELYOT *Gov.* I. xiii, He sone espiethe good herbes from nettiles. **1543-4** *Act. 35 Hen. VIII*, c. 5 A time may be espied to haue them..by malice conuicted. **1581** J. BELL *Haddon's Answ. Osorius* 462 Whose prophane blasphemy some merry conceited man espyeng out, opened the Caskett privily. **1666** BUNYAN *Grace Ab.* 24 If I could in any place espy a word of promise. **1726** SWIFT *Gulliver* I. i. 21 The seamen espied a rock within half a cable's length of the ship. **1788** WESLEY *Wks.* (1872) VI. 375 These skilful wrestlers espy the smallest slip we make. **1817** COLERIDGE *Sibyl. Leaves* (1862) 280 Can she the bodiless dead espy? **1847** L. HUNT *Jar Honey* ix, We all, like Moses, should espy, Ev'n in a bush, the radiant Deity. **1877** BLACK *Green Past.* xliii, Who was trying to espy a squirrel.

b. To perceive by chance or unexpectedly.

1483 CAXTON *Gold. Leg.* 373/3 A man came for to take water & espyed the deed chylde. **1551** ROBINSON tr. *More's Utop.* I. (Arb.) 29, I chaunced to espye this foresayde Peter. **1588** SHAKS. *Tit. A.* II. iii. 194 Where I espy'd the panther fast asleep. **1611** BIBLE *Gen.* xlii. 27 As one of them opened his sack, he espied his money. **1634** SIR T. HERBERT *Trav.* 196 Espying me, hee blest him selfe and suddenly began to mutter his prayer to Mahomet.

†**c.** To observe, perceive (a fact); with clause as *obj.* *Obs.*

c **1374** CHAUCER *Anel. & Arc.* 67 Creon gan espie how that the blode riall was brought adoun. **1413** LYDG. *Pilgr. Sowle* IV. xx. (1483) 66 Seem..hyled his fader Noe When he espyed that naked soo was he. **1461** *Paston Lett.* No. 399 II. 24, I can espye some of his meny was grete cause of T.D. deth. **1526** *Pilgr. Perf.* (W. de W. 1531) 129 Yf..they espye in the soule..ony feare to ryse. **1551** T. WILSON *Logike* II. 73 b, The hontesman..will sone espie, when he seeth a hole, whether it be a foxe borough or not. **1581** J. BELL *Haddon's answ. Osorius* 463 [A supposed 'portion of Peters Brayne']..afterwardes being more narrowlye examined and viewed, was espyed to be a very pumeyse.

e'spying, *vbl. sb.* Also 4–5 **aspying**. [f. prec. + -ING¹.] The action of the vb. ESPY. In Wyclif, lying in wait; a snare. Also *attrib.*

1340 *Ayenb.* 117 Þet he him delyuri of þe kueade and of his aspiinges. **1388** WYCLIF *Prov.* xi. 6 Wickid men shulen be taken in her aspyingis [Vulg. *insidiis*]. **1486** *Bk. St. Albans* A ij b, It hade need to be died other green or blwe for espieng of thee hawke. **1580** BARET *Alv.* E 337 An espying place, *specula.* **a1693** URQUHART *Rabelais* III. xxxiii. 281 A suspicious espying and prying into the.. Deportments of their Wives.

e'spying, *ppl. a.* [f. as prec. + -ING².] That espies. Hence †**e'spyingly** *adv.* (in 4 *aspyingly, aspiendeli*), in a spying manner; insidiously.

1382 WYCLIF *2 Kings* x. 19 Forsothe Hieu dydde this aspyingly. —— *Ecclus.* xxxii. 19 [15] Who secketh the lawe, shal be fulfild of it; who aspiendeli doth, shal be sclaundrid in it. **1580** HOLLYBAND *Treas. Fr. Tong, En espiant,* espyingly.

†**espyne**. *Sc. Obs.* Also 4 **aspine, -yne, hespine**. [a. ON. *espingr* (Sw. *esping*).] A long boat.

1375 BARBOUR *Bruce* XVII. 719 The gynour Hit in ane espyne [*v.r.* aspine, aspyne, hespyne] with a stane.

esq., esqr., abbreviations of ESQUIRE, appended to a name.

†**e'squadron**. *Obs.* [a. OF. *esquadron* (mod.F. *escadron*); see SQUADRON.] = SQUADRON.

1579 FENTON *Guicciard.* II. (1599) 80 The Italians.. had spred vpon the shoare of the riuer their esquadrons and rancks prepared to the battell. *Ibid.* (1618) 357 An esquadron of Turks payed by them. **1738** [G. SMITH] *Curious Relat.* II. 363 An Esquadron of the Guard du Corps.

†**e'squaymous**, *a. Obs.* [var. of SQUEAMOUS; in AF. *escoymous* (Bozon).] Squeamish.

1303 R. BRUNNE *Handl. Synne* 7249 Many one are.. oute of mesure esquaymous.

-esque, *suffix*, forming adjs., represents Fr. *-esque*, ad. It. *-esco*:—med.L. *-iscus* in words adopted from Teut.; cf. OHG. *-isc* (mod.G. *-isch*):—OTeut. *-isko-*: see -ISH. Occurring in many words coming through Fr. from It., as in *arabesque, burlesque, Dantesque, grotesque, romanesque*, where the suffix has the sense 'resembling the style partaking of the characteristics of'. In Ital. derivatives in *-esco* are formed *ad libitum* on names of artists, and Fr. and Eng. writers on art have imitated this practice. The words formed with this suffix on Eng. sbs. are chiefly nonce-words of a jocular character, as *cigaresque*. Other formations separately noticed include *Audenesque, Bramantesque, Browningesque, Caravagg(i)esque, Carlylesque, Chaplinesque, Dantonesque, Dickensesque, Disneyesque, Macaulayesque, Turneresque*.

†**esquele**. *Obs.* [ad. OF. *escuele* (mod.F. *écuelle*), corresp. to Pr. *escudella*, It. *scodella*:—L. *scutella*, dim. of *scuta, scutra* dish.] A platter, porringer.

1371 in Riley *Lond. Mem.* (1868) 350, 48 esqueles.. 3 dozens of esqueles. **1601** F. TATE *Househ. Ord. Edw. II*, §53 (1876) 37 The silver vessel.. that is to saile [*sic*; ? saie] chargeours and esqueles.

esquiller, esquillery, obs. ff. SQUILLER, scullion, and SCULLERY.

1601 F. TATE *Househ. Ord. Edw. II*, §49 (1876) 32 An other vallet shalbe Ewer, who shal receve the kitchen vessel by indenture of the Esquiller. *Ibid.* §53. The Esquillerye.

e'squillous, *a. rare.* [ad. Fr. *esquilleux*, f. *esquille* 'small fragment of a fractured bone' (Littré).] Of fracture: Splintery.

1853 TH. ROSS *Humboldt's Trav.* III. xxix. 168 The serpentine is sometimes of an esquillous, sometimes of a conchoidal fracture.

esquinancy, obs. f. QUINSY; see SQUINANCY.

1751 in CHAMBERS. **1775** in ASH.

esquippe, obs. form of EQUIP.

esquire (ɪ'skwaɪə(r)), *sb.*¹ Forms: 5–7 esquier, -yer, (5 esqwyer, 6 esquior, -yor, 6–7 escuir, -ier), 6– esquire. [a. OF. *esquier* (mod.F. *écuyer*), corresp. to Pr. *escuier, escudier, escuder*, Sp. *escudero*, Pg. *escudeiro*, It. *scudiere*, lit. 'shield-bearer':—L. *scūtārius*, f. *scūtum* shield. See also SQUIRE, which in our quotations appears much earlier.

In Fr. the use of the word has been influenced by a mistaken association with *écurie* (OF. *escurie*), see EQUERRY. Some traces of this confusion appear in English use.]

1. a. *Chivalry.* A young man of gentle birth, who as an aspirant to knighthood, attended upon a knight, carried his shield, and rendered him other services. (Now only *arch.*, the form SQUIRE being commonly used *Hist.*) Cf. ARMIGER, PAGE.

1475 CAXTON *Jason*, Ther ne abode knight ne esquyer in the sadyl. **1601** F. TATE *Househ. Ord. Edw. II*, §1 (1876) 6 If he be but an ordinari knight.. he shal have diet for two esquiers. **1656** COWLEY *Davideis* IV. 849 This saw, and heard with joy the brave Esquire.. fill'd with his Masters fire. **1852** MISS YONGE *Cameos* II. xviii. 193 Hard work the good esquire seems to have had.

†**b.** As a rendering of L. *armiger* armour-bearer, Gr. ὑπασπιστής shield-bearer. *Obs.*

1553 BRENDE *Q. Curtius* 172 (R.) Alexander.. willed a weapon to be deliuered to hys hands, as other esquiers vsed. **1603** HOLLAND *Plutarch's Mor.* 427 His [Epaminondas'] esquire or shield-bearer had received a good piece of money for the ransome of a prisoner. **1609** BIBLE (Douay) *1 Macc.* iv. 30 Jonathas Sauls sonne, and.. his esquyer.

c. Applied to various officers in the service of a king or nobleman, as ***esquire for*** (or ***of***) ***the body, esquire of the chamber, esquire of the stable*** [cf. EQUERRY, which was sometimes confused with this], ***carving esquire***, etc.

1495 *Act 11 Hen. VII*, c. 32 §7 David Philippe, Esquyer for the body of oure Sovereign Lord the Kyng. **1587** FLEMING *Contn. Holinshed* III. 1381/2 Chiefe escuir of the kings escuir, and the other escuires of the escuir togither. **1601** F. TATE *Househ. Ord. Edw. II*, §26 (1876) 18 The kinge shall have.. an esquier to carve before the kinge.

2. A man belonging to the higher order of English gentry, ranking immediately below a knight.

Of esquires, legally so called, there are, according to some authorities, five classes: '(1) younger sons of peers and their eldest sons; (2) eldest sons of knights, and their eldest sons; (3) chiefs of ancient families (by prescription); (4) esquires by creation or office, as heralds and sergeants of arms, judges, officers of state, naval and military officers, justices of the peace, barristers-at-law; (5) esquires who attend the Knight of the Bath on his installation—usually two specially appointed' (*Encycl. Brit.*, s.v.). The correctness of this enumeration, however, is greatly disputed; it would be impossible here to state the divergent views on the subject. In heraldic Latin the equivalent of *esquire* was *armiger*, properly = 'armour-bearer', but often taken in the sense 'one bearing (heraldic) arms'; hence, in 16th and 17th c. *esquire* was sometimes explained as meaning a man entitled to coat-armour; but by accurate writers this is condemned as involving the confusion between 'esquire' and 'gentleman'.

*c***1460** FORTESCUE *Abs. & Lim. Mon.* (1714) 41 His Highness schal then have.. aboute his Persone.. Lords, Knights, and Esquyers. **1535** WRIOTHESLEY *Chron.* (1875) I. 27 A jurie of esquiers and gentlemen of Middlesex were sworne to passe on them. **1577** HARRISON *England* II. v. (1877) I. 127 Esquire (which we call commonlie Squire) is a French word.. and such are all those which beare armes.. testimonies of their race. **1793** BLACKSTONE *Comm.* I. ix. (ed. 12) 352 The statute 13 Ric. II. c. 7 orders them [justices of the peace] to be of the most sufficient knights, esquires, and gentlemen of the law. **1818** CRUISE *Digest* (ed. 2) III. 265 The second sort of persons were those who had titles, as esquires, etc.

b. A landed proprietor, (country) 'squire'. *arch.*

1597 SHAKS. *2 Hen. IV*, III. ii. 63, I am Robert Shallow (Sir) a poore Esquire of this Countie, and one of the Kings Justices of the Peace. **1827** LYTTON *Pelham* xii, There was, indeed, a motley congregation; country esquires; extracts from the universities; half-pay officers, [etc.]. **1848** MACAULAY *Hist. Eng.* iii. (L.), An esquire passed among his neighbours for a great scholar, if, etc.

3. As a title accompanying a man's name. Originally applied to those who were 'esquires' in sense 2; subsequently extended to other persons to whom an equivalent degree of rank or status is by courtesy attributed.

a. Following the surname preceded by the Christian name. In formal documents written in full; elsewhere commonly abbreviated ***Esq.*** or ***Esqr.*** (In ceremonious use, *e.g.* in legal writings or in genealogy, when the name of the person's estate or of his place of residence is given, the title is, by English custom, placed last, as 'A.B., of C., Esquire'; in Scotland, on the contrary, the title immediately follows the surname. Similarly, in England the title 'esquire' traditionally follows the designation 'Junior' or 'The Younger', but in Scotland precedes it.)

The designation of 'esquire' is now commonly understood to be due by courtesy to all persons (not in clerical orders or having any higher title of rank) who are regarded as 'gentlemen' by birth, position, or education. It is used only on occasions of more or less ceremonious mention, and in the addresses of letters, etc.; on other occasions the prefix 'Mr.' is employed instead. When 'esquire' is appended to a name, no prefixed title (such as 'Mr.,' 'Doctor,' 'Captain,' etc.) is used. In the U.S. the title belongs officially to lawyers and public officers.

1552–3 *Inv. Ch. Goods, Staffs.* in *Ann. Litchfield* IV. 46 Walter Wrotcheley & Edward Lyttylton, esquyors, by vertue of the kynges majesties comyssion. **1599** SHAKS. *Hen. V.* IV. viii. 109 Davy Gam, esquire. **1655** FULLER *Ch. Hist.* IX. vi. §2 Anthony Brown at Tolethorp in Rutland Esquire. **1709** STEELE *Tatler* No. 19 ⁋2 If you read the superscriptions to all the offices in the kingdom, you will not find three letters directed to any but esquires. **1711** BUDGELL *Spect.* No. 150 ⁋7 My Banker.. writes me Mr. or Esq.; accordingly as he sees me dressed. **1711** HEARNE *Collect.* (Oxf. Hist. Soc.) III. 111, I shall be glad to know.. whether he be Esqʳ. that I may give him his true Title when I reprint the List. **1867** MISS MULOCK *Two Marriages* I. 42 'Jane, wife of Mr. John Bowerbank' (he was not *Esquire* then). **1887** *Scott. Leader* 12 May 6 The Clerk said that some letters were addressed Esquire and some not.

†**b.** Preceding the surname. *Obs.* (Cf. the similar use of SQUIRE.)

1710 *Lond. Gaz.* No. 4761/4 Stolen.. out of Esquire Chester's Stables.. a.. Horse. **1712** ARBUTHNOT *John Bull* (1755) 1 His cousin esquire South. **1730** SOUTHALL *Bugs* 17 Esquire [*ed.* 2 (1793) Mr.] Pitfield and Mr. White.

4. [transf. use of 1.] A gentleman who attends or escorts a lady in public. Cf. SQUIRE.

1824 BYRON *Juan* XVI. ci, Their docile esquires also did the same. **1875** W. S. HAYWARD *Love agst. World* 13 'Come on, my brave esquire,' said Florence.

5. *Comb.* Only appositive; chiefly in sense 1 c. Also ***esquire bedel***: see BEADLE 3.

*c***1600** *Epitaph* in Strype *Stow's Surv.* (1754) I. III. i. 535/1 Esquire-Joyner to our Queen. **1601** F. TATE *Househ. Ord. Edw. II*, §14 (1876) 13 This esquier fruiterer shal take every night for his coch, a galon of beare. **1797** T. JOHNES tr. *La Brocquière's Trav.* 48 Among them was his [Duke Philip le Bon's] first esquire carver La Brocquière.

esquire (ɪ'skwaɪə(r)), *sb.*² *Her.* Also 6 equire; and see SQUIRE². [app. a. OF. *esquire* (mod.F. *équerre*) square (now only mason's square, but formerly also the geometrical figure).

Perhaps *based esquire* may represent OF. *bas d'esquire*, bottom of a square. Guillim and R. Holme use *squire* both in the sense explained below and for a figure of a mason's square; the latter is the sense of *équerre* in Fr. heraldry.]

a. ***esquire based***: used by Leigh for the lower of the halves into which a canton is divided diagonally. **b.** Apparently by misunderstanding of this use, *esquire* is esplained by later writers as a synonym of GYRON, or as a bearing somewhat resembling the gyron, but ending elsewhere than in the centre of the shield.

1562 LEIGH *Armorie* 154 Thre pallets between ij Equires [ed. **1597** Esquires] bast dexter and sinister of the second. [**1610** GUILLIM *Heraldry* 61 A Canton parted trauerse-waies, whether it be from the Dexter corner or from the Sinister, doth make two Base Squires.] **1889** ELVIN *Dict. Her., Esquire*, Similar to the Gyron; it may extend across the shield; termed also a Base Esquire.

esquire (ɪ'skwaɪə(r)), *v. rare.* [f. ESQUIRE *sb.*¹] *trans.* **a.** To raise to the rank of esquire. **b.** To address as 'Esquire'. **c.** To attend (a lady) as a 'squire'. Hence **e'squired** *ppl. a.*

*a***1652** BROME *City Wit* IV. i, By'r Lady a match for my Esquir'd Son and heire. **1786** MISS BURNEY *Diary* III. 240 He proposed that the Colonel and himself should esquire me. **1796** *Ibid.* VI. 60 M. d'Arblay again ventured to esquire me to the rails round the lodge. **1824** BYRON *Juan* XVI. lxix, All country gentlemen, esquired or knighted, May drop in without cards. **1887** *Scott. Leader* 12 May 6 The Rev. Mr. Cameron, of Farnell.. asked why one elder was 'Esquired' and another not.

esquiredom (ɪ'skwaɪədəm). [f. as prec. + -DOM.] **a.** The status or dignity of an esquire. **b.** The body of esquires; esquires collectively.

1863 SALA *Capt. Dang.* II. iii. 107 Mr. Pinchin, whose Esquiredom.. I may now as well drop. **1864** BURTON *Scot Abr.* I. i. 38 The flower of the chivalry and esquiredom.

esquirehood (ɪ'skwaɪəhʊd). [f. as prec. + -HOOD.] = prec. b.

1864 H. R. LUARD *Pref. to Ann. Monastici* I. 31 The 'Communitas bacheleriæ Angliæ', i.e., the esquirehood of England.

esquireship (ɪ'skwaɪəʃɪp). [f. as prec. + -SHIP.] The position or dignity of an esquire. The service of an esquire or escort.

?**16..** *Time's Storehouse* (L.), They make the dignitie of esquireship successorie. **1650** B. *Discollim.* 48 If I be an Esquire, I will sell my Esquireship to any honest man for a good People-ship. **1783** MISS BURNEY *Diary* II. 282, I most gladly accepted and almost asked his 'squireship. **1843** *Fraser's Mag.* XXVII. 667 He had attained the envied esquireship, and its further appendage of R.A.

esquiress (ɪ'skwaɪərɪs). [f. as prec. + -ESS¹.] A female esquire.

1596 FOSBROKE in J. Smyth *Lives Berkeleys* 211 The principall mournuresse apparelled as an Esquieresse. **1630** J. TAYLOR (Water P.) *Praise Clean Linen* Ded. Wks. II. 164 Martha Legge, Esquiresse.. Laundresse to the Right worshipfull and generous the Innes of Court. **1864** R. BURTON *Dahome* II. 79 An esquiress at arms, generally a small slave girl, carrying the musket.

†**esquiry**, *sb. Obs.*⁻⁰ Also SQUIRY. [? a. OF. *escuierie*, f. *escuier*: see ESQUIRE *sb.*¹] The position or dignity of an esquire.

1681 in BLOUNT *Glossogr.* **1775** in ASH.

esquiry(e, obs. form of EQUERRY.

‖**esquisse**. [Fr. *esquisse*, ad. It. *schizzo*: see SKETCH.] The first slight sketch of a picture, the first thought of a design drawn loosely with a crayon.

1731–6 in BAILEY, (folio). **1775** in ASH.

†**es'rache**, *v. Obs. rare*⁻¹. [ad. OF. *esrachier*: see ARACHE.] *trans.* To pull up by the roots.

1475 CAXTON *Jason* 102 b, He retourned to the dragon and esrached out of his hedde xii tethe.

esraj (ɛs'rɑːdʒ). [Bengali.] An Indian musical instrument with three or four strings, and extra sympathetic strings.

1921 H. A. POPLEY *Music of India* 109 The *Esrāj* is the Bengal variety of the sārangī. It is a little smaller than the latter, and uses all wire strings instead of gut... This is the common instrument that one finds to-day in the houses of cultured people in Bengal. It is played with a bow like the

sārangī. **1952** A. DANIELOU *Catal. Indian Mus.* 32 The Esrāj. A long and narrow bowed string instrument used mainly in Bengal to accompany singing. **1957** O. GOSVAMI *Story Indian Mus.* xxvii. 305 The difference between Esraj and Dilruba is that the latter is a little bigger. **1966** *Daily Tel.* 13 Aug. 10/4 Four leading folk singers of Bengal and the Punjab.. will be travelling from India for the Festival and will be accompanied by stringed instruments like the esraj.

ess. The name of the letter S; anything in the shape of an S. Pl. **esses**; also 6 **esces**. *collar of esses*: see COLLAR. Also in *Comb.*, **es-hook, es-link**, *dial.* (see quots.)

1540 in Ellis *Orig. Lett.* III. 364 (1846) III. 283 The reste of the players whiche represented the three esces. **1579** in T. Thompson *Inventories* (1815) 293 A chayn.. with essis of gold emaillit reid. **1587** FLEMING *Contn. Holinshed* III. 1299/2 The bow with two esses, all cleane wrought. **1610** GUILLIM *Heraldry* IV. v. (1611) 199 He beareth Gules, three text Esses or.. by the name of Kekir-more. **1681** OTWAY *Soldier's Fort.* IV. i, *Sir Jol.* O here are the Esses; let me consider now--Sapho? *Cour.* No, Sir. *Sir Jol.* Selinda? *Cour.* Neither. **1865** LE FANU *Guy Dev.* II. xvii. 179 There's an ornament of scrowl-work.. shaped like letter esses. **1879** MISS JACKSON *Shropsh. Word-bk.*, *Es-hook*, a hook at the extremity of a waggon-horse's traces, in the form of the letter S. **1884** *Chesh. Gloss.*, *Es-link*, a small piece of iron shaped like a letter S, used for mending a broken chain.

ess, obs. and dial. form of ASH *sb.*[1] ashes.

-ess, *suffix*[1], forming sbs. denoting female persons or animals, is a. Fr. *-esse*:—Com. Romanic *-essa*:—late L. *-issa*, a. Gr. *-ισσα* (:—*-ikyā*: cf. the OE. fem. agent-suffix *-icge*:—*-igjôn-*) occurring in class. Gr. only in *βασίλισσα* queen (f. *βασιλ-εύς* king), but after the analogy of this employed in several late formations, as *βαλάνισσα* bathing-woman, *πανδόκισσα* female innkeeper. A few of these (notably *διακόνισσα*, L. *diaconissa* deaconess) were adopted into late L. together with their correlative masculines, and many new derivatives of the same pattern were formed in Latin, whence they descended into the Romanic langs.; *e.g.* from *abbātem* abbot, was formed *abbātissa*, whence Fr. *abbesse* ABBESS. On the analogy of these the suffix became in Romanic the usual means of forming feminine derivatives expressing sex. In ME. many words in *-esse* were adopted from Fr., as *countess, duchess, hostess, lioness, mistress, princess*, and several which were formed on sbs. in *-ëor*, *-ier* (see -ER[2]), as †*devoureresse, enchantress*, †*espyouresse, sorceress*. In imitation of these the suffix was in 14th c. appended to Eng. agent-nouns in *-er*, as in Wyclif's *dwelleresse, sleeress* (f. *sleer* = SLAYER), and to other native words, as in *goddess*. In 15th c. derivatives in *-er* + *-ess* gradually superseded the older Eng. fem. agent-nouns in -STER (OE. *-estre*), which no longer had an exclusively feminine sense; subsequently the sbs. in *-ster* (exc. *spinster*) came to be regarded as properly masc., and new feminines in *-ess* were formed on them, as *seamstress, songstress*. By writers of 16th and succeeding centuries derivatives in *-ess* were formed very freely; many of these are now obsolete or little used, the tendency of mod. usage being to treat the agent-nouns in *-er*, and the sbs. indicating profession or occupation, as of common gender, unless there be some special reason to the contrary. Of the words of Eng. formation still in current use, examples are *authoress, giantess, Jewess, patroness, poetess, priestess, quakeress, tailoress*. In Eng. the suffix is not used to form feminines of names of animals: *lioness, tigress* being adoptions from Fr. When *-ess* is added to a sb. in *-ter*, *-tor*, the vowel before the *r* is usually elided, as in *actress, doctress, protectress, waitress*; the derivatives with ending *-tress*, f. L. agent-nouns in *-tor*, have in most cases been suggested by, and may be regarded as virtual adaptations of, the corresponding Fr. words in *-trice*:—L. *-trīcem*. The substitution of *governess* (already in Caxton) for the earlier *governeresse* f. *governor* was perh. due to false analogy with pairs of words like *adulter-er, -ess, cater-er, -ess, sorcer-er, -ess*; in *conqueress, murderess, adventuress* the similar phenomenon is sufficiently explained by phonetic reasons. The existence of such words, in which *-ess* has the appearance of being added directly to vbs., gave rise in the 17th. c. to formations like *confectioness, entertainess, instructess*; but none of these obtained general currency.

-ess, *suffix*[2], ME. *-esse*, in sbs. a. Fr., represents OF. *-esse, -ece*, = Pr. *-ezza, -eza*, Sp. *-eza*, It. *-ezza*:—L. *-itia*, appended to adjs. to form nouns of quality; examples are *duress*, †*humblesse, largess, prowess*, †*richesse* (now *riches*). These words have been imitated in the pseudo-archaic *idlesse*, but otherwise the suffix scarcely occurs as an Eng. formative.

†**e'ssamplerie.** *Obs.* [See ENSAMPLER, EXEMPLARY, *sbs.*] Example.

1393 GOWER *Conf.* III. 163 But yet men sene thessamplerie Of Aristippe is well received.

essart (ɛ'sɑːt), *sb.* [a. OF. *essart*: see ASSART *sb.*] = ASSART *sb.* 1.

1851 SIR F. PALGRAVE *Norm. & Eng.* (1864) III. 258 The essarts still constitute the prominent features of the pleasant region. **1875** STUBBS *Const. Hist.* II. 36 *note*, The essarts and purprestures made in the forests of Hampshire.

essart (ɛ'sɑːt), *v.* [a. OF. *essart-er*: see ASSART *v.*] *trans.* = ASSART *v.*; also *absol.*

1721 BAILEY, *Essart*, to extirpate or clear the ground of shrubs. **1839** STONEHOUSE *Axholme* 10 The process of essarting. **1857** SIR F. PALGRAVE *Norm. & Eng.* II. 435 The Forêt de Bichoul, of which the greater portions have long since been essarted.

essay ('ɛseɪ), *sb.* In 7 *pl.* **essaies, -yes.** [a. OF. *essai, essay*: see ASSAY *sb.* For several of the senses see also SAY.

In 18th c. the accent. was sometimes on the 2nd syll.]

I. The action or process of trying or testing.

†**1.** A trial, testing, proof; experiment; = ASSAY *sb.* 1, 3. *Obs.*

c **1600** SHAKS. *Sonn.* cx, Worse essays proved thee my best of love. **1605** BACON *Adv. Learn.* II. vii. §7 Democritus.. attributed the form thereof [of the ' frame of things'] able to maintain itself to infinite essaies or proofs of nature. **1631** HEYLIN *St. George* 247, I will make bold to venture on it, by way of tryall and essay. **1648** *Eikon Bas.* 26 It was the first overt Essay to be made, how patiently I could bear the loss of my kingdoms. **1660** SHARROCK *Vegetables* Ep. Ded., You were pleased to judge me able, and.. to propose.. that I should make an essay of that ability. **1704** ADDISON *Italy* (1733) 195 After having made Essays into it, as they do for Coal in England. **1745** *De Foe's Eng. Tradesman* I. xii. 98 He has made an essay by which he knows what he can, and cannot do. **1812** J. HENRY *Camp. agst. Quebec* 28 From the essays made, it seemed to me that, etc.

†**b.** *spec.* The trial of metals; = ASSAY 6. *Obs.*

1668 in *Phil. Trans.* III. 821 The Ore being ground.. they divide it in several heaps, and then by lesser Essays, they find out how much silver is contained in every heap. **1731-6** in BAILEY (folio).

†**2.** A trial specimen, a sample, an example; a rehearsal. Cf. ASSAY 17. *Obs.*

1614 SELDEN *Titles Hon.* 22 An essay also of that age's vnhappie affectation of Greek patch. **1656** BLOUNT *Glossogr.*, *Essay*, a flourish or preamble. **1659** HAMMOND *On Ps.* cvi. 16-18 *Paraphr.* 532 Two terrible essayes of God's wrath were here shewed. *a* **1674** CLARENDON *Hist. Reb.* (1704) III. xv. 498 A small essay of my zeal for.. your Majesty. **1684** T. BURNET *Th. Earth* II. 55 These are lesser essays or preludes to the general fire. **1734** tr. *Rollin's Anc. Hist.* (1827) VII. XVI. §9. 110 Gave an essay in this first action of what might be expected one day from his valour and bravery.

†**3.** *Venery.* **a.** = ASSAY 9. In phrase *to take essay.* **b.** *concr.* The part of a deer in which trial was made of the 'grease'; the breast or brisket.

1611 COTGR., *Foulz*.. cut out from betweene the necke, and the essay of a Deere. **1658** PHILLIPS s.v. *Essay*, The Essay of Deer is the breast or brisket.. in French *la hampe.* **1694** *Acct. Denmark in 1692* (ed. 3) 160 One that is likeliest to give a good Gratuity to the Huntsman, is invited to take Essay.

†**4.** A taste, or first taste, of food or drink presented to a great personage; = ASSAY 12. *Obs.* exc. *Hist.*

1598 in FLORIO s.v. *Fare la credenza.* **1632** in COTGR. **1682** G. ROSE *Instr. Officers of the Mouth* 16 The Master Cook is desired not to forget his Larding-pricks, nor the Master-Butler his Essay. *Ibid.* 94 Let him [the Royal Butler] bring in his Wine, present his Bason and Ewer to wash, take his Essay both of Wine and Water. **1708** J. CHAMBERLAYNE *St. Gt. Brit.* I. III. iii. (1741) 168 A Viscount may have a Cover of Essay holden under his Cup, while he drinks, but no Essay taken as Dukes, Marquises and Earls may have.

II. A trying to do something.

5. An attempt, endeavour. Const. *after, at*, †*of, on, towards*, and *to* with *inf.*

1598 YONG *Diana* 77 They were all but papers of essaies Of that. *a* **1652** J. SMITH *Sel. Disc.* vii. (1821) 364 Languishing creatures.. we are, in our essays after heaven. **1682** DRYDEN *Satyr* 3 Whose first Essay was in a Tyrants praise. **1738** *Col. Rec. Penn.* IV. 316 Essays.. to encourage the raising some of these Commodities. **1762** J. BROWN *Poetry & Mus.* (1763) 74 The first rude Essays towards an expressive Melody in barbarous Countries. **1778** SIR J. REYNOLDS *Disc.* viii. (1876) 447 An artist, in his first essay of imitating nature. **1820** W. IRVING *Sketch Bk.* II. 325 Our first essay was along a mountain brook. **1853** C. BRONTË *Villette* viii, Is this your first essay at teaching? **1860** TYNDALL *Glac.* I. xxvii. 206 Making a preliminary essay upon the glacier. **1865** LIVINGSTONE *Zambesi* Introd., I am now in this my second essay at authorship.

b. *concr.* The result of an attempt. *nonce-use.*

1697 DRYDEN *Virg. Past.* vii. 42 These Branches of a Stag, this tusky Boar (The first essay of Arms untry'd before).

†**6.** A hostile attempt. *Obs.*

c **1640** J. SMYTH *Lives Berkeleys* (1883) I. 229 The King at Canterbury grants him a generall protection from all Essayes for a year following.

†**7.** A first tentative effort in learning or practice; = ASSAY 16. *Obs.*

1656 COWLEY *Pindar. Odes* Pref., This Essay is but to try how it [Pindar's Poetry] will look in an English Habit. **1663** J. SPENCER *Prodigies* Pref. B., Admiration is.. an Essay to knowledge. **1665-9** BOYLE *Disc. Occas. Medit.* Wks. 1772 II. 356 The green and immature essays of early Writers. **1700** DRYDEN *Fables* (1773) Pref., The first of Homer's Iliads (which I intended as an Essay to the whole work). **1723** SHEFFIELD (Dk. Buckhm.) *Wks.* (1753) I. 64 My hand is yet untaught to write to men; This is th' essay of my unpractis'd pen. **1734** tr. *Rollin's Anc. Hist.* (1827) I. 377 These were considered only as essays preparatory to the great design.

b. A rough copy; a first draft.

1656 J. HARRINGTON *Oceana* (1700) 174 The List.. enter'd in the Parish Book, and diligently preserv'd as a Record, call'd the first Essay. **1793** GOUV. MORRIS in Sparks *Life & Writ.* (1832) I. 417, I have made an essay of a letter.

8. A composition of moderate length on any particular subject, or branch of a subject; originally implying want of finish, 'an irregular undigested piece' (J.), but now said of a composition more or less elaborate in style, though limited in range.

The use in this sense is app. taken from Montaigne, whose *Essais* were first published in 1580.

1597 BACON (*title*) Essayes. **1607-12** —— *Essays, Ded. Prince Henry* (Arb.) 158 For Senacaes Epistles.. are but Essaies—that is dispersed Meditations.. Essaies. The word is late, but the thing is auncient. **1665** GLANVILL *Sceps. Sci.* Addr. 16 No higher title, then that of an essay, or imperfect offer at a Subject. *c* **1700** *Poem to Roscommon* (J.), Yet modestly he does his work survey, And calls his finish'd poem an essay. **1712** ADDISON *Spect.* No. 476 ¶1 The Wildness of those Compositions which go by the Names of Essays. **1764** REID *Inquiry* Ded., This leaves me no room to doubt of your favourable acceptance of this essay. **1782** V. KNOX *Ess.* (1819) I. i. 1 Essays.. may now convey the idea of regular treatises. **1843** MACAULAY (*title*) Critical and Historical Essays. **1865** DICKENS *Mut. Fr.* II. i, She could write a little essay on any subject.

III. 9. Phrase, *in all essays*: under all circumstances. *Obs.* Cf. ASSAY 21, 22.

1669 STURMY *Mariner's Mag.* 20 And so likewise I have shown you thus much of the Practick part of Navigation, in which you may perceive that I have wrought the Ship in all Essays, in Words and proper Sea-Phrases; and if I was at Sea, I should perform it both in Word and Deed.

10. *attrib.* and *Comb.*, as *essay-weaver, -writer*; also **essay-hatch** (see quot.); **essay-scale**, a test-scale.

1721-1800 BAILEY, *Essay Hatch, [among Miners] a Term for a little Trench or Hole which they dig to search for Oar. **1684** R. WALLER *Nat. Exper.* 149 Putting in the *Essay-Scales two Steel Wires of equal Weight. **1884** *Punch* 16 Feb. 84/1 And twaddling *essay-weavers, mild boilers-down of Lamb! **1711** SHAFTESB. *Charac.* (1737) III. 97 We *essay-writers are of the small-craft, or galley-kind. **1851** HELPS *Friends in C.* I. 29 The fault into which you essay-writers generally fall.

essay (ɛ'seɪ), *v.* [refashioned form of ASSAY, after Fr. *essayer*: see ASSAY.]

1. *trans.* To put to the proof, try (a person or thing); to test the nature, excellence, fitness, etc. of; = ASSAY *v.* 1. Also to practise (an art, etc.) by way of trial; = ASSAY 8.

1483 CAXTON *G. de la Tour* G ij b, I wold also ye knew the tale of the Squyer whiche essayed his wyf. **1593** *Prodigal Son* I. 92 It is a fine thing for a young man who goes to essay the world, to travel and see much. **1738** GLOVER *Leonidas* II. 436 None more willing to essay thy force. *a* **1744** POPE *Epistle* v, She.. No arts essay'd, but not to be admir'd. **1848** MACAULAY *Hist. Eng.* II. 109 A youth whose great powers, first essayed in this conflict, etc. **1856** MRS. STOWE *Dred* II. xxxiii. 326 The last boat was essayed.

†**b.** with *object clause.* *Obs.*

1483 CAXTON *Gold. Leg.* 376/4 Willyam.. wold preue and essaye yf there were ony elacion.. in his corage. **1684** R. BERKELEY in Evelyn *Mem.* (1857) III. 273 It would be soon essayed with Mr. Boyle's pump, whether or no it may give such a vacuum as to preserve fruit.

†**2.** To test the composition of (an ore, metal, salt, etc.) by chemical means; = ASSAY 4. *Obs.*

1691 LOCKE *Lower. Interest* Wks. 1727 II. 94 Whether.. Goldsmiths.. will not take what is by the free Labour of the Mint ready essay'd and adjusted to their use. *a* **1704** —— (J.), The standard in our mint being now settled, the rules and methods of essaying suited to it should remain unvariable. **1739** *Joe Miller's Jests* No. 207 The seven Golden Candlesticks were sent to be essay'd in the Tower. **1816** ACCUM *Chem. Tests* (1818) 93 The salt to be essayed is covered with sulphuric acid.

†**3.** To try by tasting; = ASSAY 5. *Obs.*

1598 YONG *Diana* 164 If wormewood in his drinke he hath essaied.

4. To attempt; to try to do, effect, accomplish, or make (anything difficult); = ASSAY 16.

1641 R. BROOKE *Eng. Episc.* II. vi. 97 In our Gracious Kings Reigne, they have.. essay'd many Soule-Schismes. *a* **1661** FULLER *Worthies* (1662) I. 129 He also.. directed the standers by to fetch him a great hollow-stone for a font, which sundry of his father's servants essayed in vain. **1712** BLACKMORE *Creation* I. 14 While I this unexampled Task essay. **1805** WORDSW. *Waggoner* I. 99 And now the conqueror essays The long ascent of Dunmail-raise. **1876** LOWELL *Among my Bks.* Ser. II. (1873) 257 His method leads to most unhappy results when essayed by men to whom nature has denied a sense of what the picturesque really is. **1882** A. W. WARD *Dickens* vii. 213 He never even essayed the picture of an artist devoted to art for her own sake.

†**b.** To attempt to show or prove. *Obs.*

1656 [J. SERJEANT] tr. *White's Peripat. Instit.* 337 (*title*) A Theologicall Appendix.. Wherein 'tis essay'd how subservient Philosophy is to Divinity. **1674** N. FAIRFAX *Bulk & Selv.* 194 The worthy Doctor More has suprizingly essay'd the infinity or boundless manifoldness of worlds from the Head of lightsomness.

5. with *inf.* To set oneself, undertake, try (*to do* something). Also *absol.*; = ASSAY 17.

c 1530 *Hickscorner* in Hazl. *Dodsley* I. 181 Therefore in thy conceit essay To axe God mercy. **1641** MILTON *Ch. Govt.* Wks. 1738 I. 40 This I shall essay to prove, can be no other than that of Presbyters and Deacons. *a* **1762** LADY M. W. MONTAGUE *Lett.* I. xxxvii. 143 Apelles is said to have essayed, by a collection of the most exact features, to form a perfect face. **1781** COWPER *Table Talk* 182 Not Brindley nor Bridgewater would essay, To turn the course of Helicon that way. **1820** SCOTT *Monast.* vii, I will essay, reverend Father. **1879** M. ARNOLD *Ess., Fr. Crit. on Goethe* 276 So dense is the cloud of error here that the lover of truth will hardly even essay to dissipate it.

6. *intr.* To make an attempt.

1715 M. DAVIES *Ath. Brit.* I. 233 Doctor Bray has lately essay'd with a large scope towards a more Comprehensive Martyrologe.

essayal (ɛ'seɪəl). [f. prec. + -AL[1].] Attempt, trial.

1837 *New Monthly Mag.* LI. 186, I knew them [the roads] and could make essayal of at least one of them.

essayer (ɛ'seɪə(r)). [f. ESSAY *v.* + -ER.]

1. In various senses of the vb.; = ASSAYER 1, 2, 3.

1611 COTGR., *Credentier*, a Princes Taster, Essayer, Cup-bearer. **1663** BLAIR *Autobiog.* iii. (1848) 57 The long-rested land yielded such plentiful harvests that many followed the first essayers. **1870** J. ROSKELL in *Eng. Mech.* 18 Mar. 647/2 The centre, which the essayer calls the *eye*.

†**2.** One who 'essays' a certain form of composition, or attempts to treat a certain subject; in later use = ESSAYIST. *Obs.*

1664 H. MORE *Myst. Iniq.* 353 As a late Essayer upon the Apocalyps imagines. **1711** ADDISON *Spect.* No. 68 ¶2 He [Tully] hath been followed by all the Essayers upon Friendship, that have written since his time. **1711** DENNIS *Refl. on Pope's Essay on Criticism*, He was, like this Essayer, a very indifferent poet. **1712** HUGHES *Spect.* No. 525 ¶3 The Essayers in Lampoon and Satyr.

essayette (ɛseɪ'ɛt). [f. ESSAY *sb.* + -ETTE.] A short essay.

1877 C. GIBBON in *Casquet Lit.* I. 182/1 We take the following essayette. **1886** TUPPER *My Life as Author* 160 The book includes a hundred and thirty original fables, essayettes, anecdotes, tirades, songs, and musings. **1890** *Glasgow Herald* 26 May 7/2 The eight or nine pages of Mr. Armstrong's interesting essayette.

'essayfy, *v.* [f. as prec. + -FY.] *intr.* To write essays.

1815 J. GILCHRIST *Labyrinth Demol.* 11, I am essayfying or speechifying..instead of prefacing.

essayical (ɛ'seɪɪkəl), *a.* Also essaical. [f. as prec. + -IC + -AL[1].] Of the nature of an essay.

1860 DICKENS *Lett.* 25 Sept., Remarks..a little too essayical for this purpose. **1875** F. ARNOLD *Our Bps. & Deans* I. 21 The idea was that a sermon should be made brief, dry, essaical, moral or mystical.

essaying (ɛ'seɪɪŋ), *vbl. sb.* [f. ESSAY *v.* + -ING[1].] The action of the vb. ESSAY; also *concr.* Also (*nonce-use*) the writing essays.

1861 in *Macm. Mag.* IV. 43 It might have been much better..if they had left essaying and reviewing alone. **1869** *Spectator* 1 May 539/1 To..watch the reception given to his essayings without throwing his own shadow on the page. **1882** *Spectator* No. 2804 They are the presomnial essayings of a man who has to be up by times in the morning.

e'ssaying, *ppl. a.* [f. ESSAY *v.* + -ING[2].] That essays or attempts.

1715–25 POPE *Odyss.* XXI. 445 From his essaying hand the string let fly.

essayish ('ɛseɪɪʃ), *a.* [f. ESSAY *sb.* + -ISH.] Of the nature of an essay.

1863 PATON *Wilson the Ornithologist* 9 It is a fair specimen of that essayish style of letter writing which characterised the epistles of Burns.

essayism ('ɛseɪɪz(ə)m). [f. as prec. + -ISM.]

a. The practice of writing essays. **b.** The quality that constitutes an 'essay'.

1821 *New Monthly Mag.* II. 301 Cant is the epidemic of periodical essayism. **1822** *Ibid.* V. 141 My talents..were.. frittered in periodical writing and common-place essayism. **1887** *Sat. Rev.* 24 Sept. 412 That mysterious literary essence known as essayism which pervades all literature.

¶ About 1862 occas. used for: The theological doctrines taught in the book called *Essays and Reviews*.

1862 *Lit. Churchm.* VIII. 4/1 A medium between Essayism and Evangelicism. *Ibid.* 458/1 If Essayism has been effectually rebuked.

essayist ('ɛseɪɪst). [f. ESSAY *sb.* and *v.* + -IST.]

1. One who essays, one who makes trials or experiments. Const. *of*. Now *rare*.

1736 in BAILEY. **1794** BURKE tr. *Pref. Brissot's Address* Wks. VII. 313 All the essayists and novices of revolution in 1789, that could be found, were promiscuously put to death. **1815** W. H. IRELAND *Scribbleomania* 80 The panegyric may prompt such unfortunate essayists to consult the productions of the personage so extolled. **1868** MRS. H. WOOD *Red Court Farm* ix, The mistakes made by both essayists kept the platform in a roar.

2. A writer of essays.

1609 B. JONSON *Sil. Wom.* II. iii, Meere Essaists! a few loose sentences, and that's all. *a* **1774** GOLDSM. *Reverie* (R.), I am not to have admittance as an essayist. **1791** BOSWELL *Johnson* (1831) I. 211 A cessation..of any exertion of his talents as an essayist. **1829** MACAULAY *Misc. Writ.* (1860) I. 311 The conclusion at which the essayist arrives. **1884** J. W. EBSWORTH in *Roxb. Bal.* II. Pref. p. viii, He was a brilliant historical Essayist.

essay'istic, *a.* [f. ESSAY *sb.* + -ISTIC.] In the style of a literary essay, or of an exposition; discursive, informal; essay-writing.

1862 *Independent* (N.Y.) 29 May 3/6 Good specimens of De Quincey's writings—autobiographical, narrative, critical, and essayistic. **1895** *Thinker* VIII. 404 The young pastor thinks himself obliged by the weight of custom to press much that is humanistic and essayistic into the ministrations of the truth. **1935** *Times Lit. Suppl.* 9 Nov. 768/4 It is as difficult to predict for him an essayistic future as it is for Mr. James Laver. **1936** WIRTH & SHILS tr. *Mannheim's Ideology & Utopia* i. 47 This essayistic-experimental attitude in thought also explains why here and there repetitions have not been eliminated. **1960** K. AMIS *New Maps of Hell* (1961) iv. 88 Even at his most essayistic, Wylie shows none of that complacent indifference to his reader.

essayistical (ɛseɪ'ɪstɪkəl), *a.* [f. ESSAYIST + -IC + -AL[1].] Resembling the work of an essayist.

1863 *Scotsman* 7 May, The Victoria Magazine..a story-telling, essayistical..miscellany.

essaykin ('ɛseɪkɪn). *nonce-wd.* [f. ESSAY *sb.* + -KIN.] A little essay.

1860 THACKERAY *Round. Papers* 134 In these humble essaykins I have taken leave to egotize.

essaylet ('ɛseɪlɪt). [f. as prec. + -LET.] = prec.

1872 *Temple Bar* July 550 Literary sandwiches, tales, sketches and essaylets. **1874** HELPS *Soc. Press.* xii. (1875) 153 The essaylet, if I may so coin a word. **1886** *Jrnl. Education* 1 Sept. 378 This is a book of miscellaneous essaylets.

Ess Bouquet (ɛs bu:'keɪ). [Short for F. *essence de bouquet*.] The trade name of a perfume. Also *ellipt.* as *Ess*.

1855 G. W. S. PIESSE *Art of Perfumery* vi. 118 'Ess' Bouquet..is but a mere contraction of 'essence' of bouquet. **1875** BROWNING *Inn Album* 11, With nose in want of snuff Rather than Ess or Psidium. **1892** G. W. ASKINSON tr. *Furst's Perfumes* 175 The title Ess. Bouquet is an abbreviation of the full name given above [*i.e.* Essence des Bouquets]. **1905** *Westm. Gaz.* 8 Aug. 10/1 Queen Alexandra ..has recently abandoned her favourite Ess Bouquet to some extent and taken to Sweet Pea. **1920** A. H. J. KEANE tr. *Deite's Man. Toilet Soap-Making* (ed. 2) 222 'Ess-Bouquet' Soap. **1926–7** *Army & Navy Stores Catal.* 487/1 Bayley's Ess Bouquet—bot. 4/6.

esscheker, obs. form of EXCHEQUER.

‖**esse** ('ɛsi:). [L. *esse* to be, inf. of *sum*, but used by the schoolmen as a sb.]

1. In med.L. phrase ***in esse***, in actual existence; opposed to *in posse*, in potentiality.

1592 *Nobody & Some-b.* 1299 Like a king in Esse..this night, Lets make a hostile uprore in the Court. **1597** HOWSON *Serm.* 31 Our spirituall preferments in *esse* and in *posse*. **1767** BLACKSTONE *Comm.* II. 169 Some one, that may by common possibility..be *in esse* at or before the particular estate determines. **1818** CRUISE *Digest* VI. 19 All natural persons who are *in esse* at the time when a will is made.

2. a. Essence, essential nature.

1642 SIR E. DERING *Sp. on Relig.* 14 Dec. v. 16 The very *esse* of every Synod doth subsist in a double foundation. **1736** BAILEY, *Esse* [in the school philosophy] is used in the same sense with essence; principally for that which is actual, or actually existing. **1920** *Life of Faith* 23 June 619/2 The great missionary meeting on the Saturday morning..is not the *esse* of the movement. **1929** I. M. CLARK *Hist. Ch. Discip. in Scot.* 208 Some form of law will be necessary to regulate her [*sc.* the Church's] life and protect that distinctive character which is her *esse*.

b. Esp. in contrast with *bene esse*. Cf. WELL-BEING *vbl. sb.*

1621 BURTON *Anat. Mel.* I. ii. Mem. 3 Subs. 15 p. 170 How many poore Schollers haue lost their wits..neglecting all worldly affaires, and their owne health, wealth, *esse*, and *benè esse* to gaine knowledge? **1899** *Daily News* 21 Oct. 7/1 So long as your clergy believe that Episcopacy is essential not only to the bene esse, but to the esse of the Church. **1958** *Listener* 12 June 977/1 No Anglican could possibly dream of claiming that Establishment..is of the *esse* of the Church. Our question is simply whether it is of its *bene esse*.

esse, obs. var. ASK *v.*, EASE *sb.*; also of *is*: see BE *v.*

†**essed, essede.** *Obs.* [ad. L. *essed-um* (a Gaulish word).] A kind of war-chariot used by the Gauls.

1656–81 in BLOUNT *Glossogr.*; and in mod. Dicts.

†**essedary.** *Obs.* [ad. L. *essedārius*, f. *essedum*: see prec. and -ARY.] A fighter in a (Gaulish) war-chariot.

a **1470** TIPTOFT *Caesar* iv. (1530) 4 Theyr essedaryes..be men of armys fighting uppon charyotts. **1656–81** in BLOUNT *Glossogr.* **1775** in ASH.

†**Essee.** *Obs.* Also 4 Essey, 7 Hessee, 4–6 *pl.* Esseis. [ad. L. *Essæ-i* pl., Gr. 'Εσσαῖ-οι. (The pl. *Esseis* is app. formed on L. pl. *Essæi* taken as a sing.; Wyclif's *Essey* is prob. the L. plural misspelt. Cf. EPICUREE.] = ESSENE.

c **1380** WYCLIF *Wks.* (1880) 2 Pharisees, Saduces, and Esseis. —— *Sel. Wks.* II. 36 Essey, Saducey, and Pharisey. *a* **1570** BECON *Christ's Chron.* (1844) 546, The Essees..not altogether unlike to monks in life. **1607** T. ROGERS *39 Art.* (1854) 353 Of another mind were the Esseis. **1613** PURCHAS *Pilgr.*, (1617) 147 Essees, Essens, or Hessees.

†**essefirme.** *Obs. rare.* [? some compound of *-ess*, name of the letter S.]

1600 *Queen's Wardrobe* in Nichols *Progr. Q. Eliz.* III. 510 The sleeves..garnished with a lace of Venice sylver, like essifirmes. *Ibid.* 511 Brodered upon with essefirmes and other knotts of seede pearle.

†**'essel.** *Obs. rare*[−1]. [a. OF. *aissel*, *essel* (now *essieu*):—L. *axiculus*, dim. of *axis* axle-tree.] A beam or bar of wood or iron.

c **1205** LAY. 18992 Vndo þis ȝæt essel; þe eorl is icumen here.

†**'essell.** *Obs.* Also 6 esele. [ad. med.L. *esula*.] A sort of spurge.

[**14..** *Alphita* (Anecd. Oxon.) 60 Esula quedam species est titimalli, gallice yesele.] **1527** L. ANDREW *Brunswyke's Distyl. Waters* Ciij, *Esula*, essell. **1567** MAPLET *Gr. Forest* 41 b, Esele of some is taken for Eiebright; this hath his leafe verie thinne and plaine.

essence ('ɛsəns), *sb.* Also 4 in med.Lat. form essencia, 6 assence. [a. Fr. *essence*, ad. L. *essentia*, f. **essent-em*, fictitious pr. pple. of *esse* to be, in imitation of Gr. οὐσία being, f. ὀντ-, stem of pr. pple. of εἶναι to be. Cf. Pr. *essentia*, Sp. *esencia*, It. *essenza*.]

†**1. a.** Being, existence, viewed as a fact or as a property possessed by something. *Obs.*

1576 FLEMING *Panop. Ep.* 284 Nature hath not given unto men their essence and being, to be..in idlenesse..but..still to bee doinge. **1579** LYLY *Euphues* (Arb.) 166 How canst thou abide his presence, that beleevedst not his essence? **1605** SYLVESTER *Du Bartas* I. i. Argt. (1605–7) I. 1 World not eternall.. But of meere Nothing God it Essence gaue. **1622** FLETCHER *Sp. Curate* IV. iv, I would resign my Essence, that he were As happy as my Love cou'd fashion him. *a* **1688** CUDWORTH *Immut. Mor.* (1731) 2 None of these things have in Nature any Essence of their own.

¶ **b.** The kind of being distinctive of animals; animal life. *Obs. rare*[−1].

1633 EARL MANCH. *Al Mondo* (1636) 35 Of creatures, the lowest ranke have no life, the next no essence, the third no reason; none but man hath grace.

2. a. *concr.* Something that *is*; an existence, entity. Now restricted to spiritual or immaterial entities.

1587 GOLDING *De Mornay* iv. 43 Man is an essence subiect to time, place and accidents. **1602** MARSTON *Antonio's Rev.* IV. i, There is no essence mortal, That I can envie, but a plumpe cheekt foole. **1604** SHAKS. *Oth.* IV. i. 16 Her honor is an Essence that's not seene. **1643** SIR T. BROWNE *Relig. Med.* I. §31 Those noble essences in heaven beare a friendly regard unto their fellow nature on earth. **1667** MILTON *P.L.* I. 138 All this mighty Host In horrible destruction laid thus low, As far as Gods and Heav'nly Essences Can Perish. **1742** YOUNG *Nt. Th.* IX. 2303 Through radiant ranks of essences unknown. **1796** BURKE *Regic. Peace* i. Wks. VIII. 79 Commonwealths are not physical but moral essences. **1824** W. IRVING *T. Trav.* I. 72 Fanciful speculations on spiritual essences. **1833** TENNYSON *Poems* 77 All nature widens upward: evermore The simpler essence lower lies. **1836** EMERSON *Nature, Spirit* Wks. (Bohn) II. 166 Of that ineffable essence which we call Spirit, he that thinks most will say least. **1847** J. WILSON *Chr. North* (1857) I. 257 The immortal essence enshrined within.

†**b.** 'Species of existent being' (J.); an element. Chiefly in phrase, ***fifth essence***, transl. of L. *quinta essentia*: see QUINTESSENCE.

The 'fifth essence' was a supposed substance distinct from the recognized four elements. What this fifth essence was, and where existing, was much disputed. Originally, it seems to have been the material of the starry heaven, as conceived by those who hesitated to identify it with 'fire'. Among the alchemists, it was usually supposed to be latent in all bodies, and to be capable of being extracted from them by distillation or some more recondite process; many thought that alcohol was one of its forms. Others regarded the discovery of the 'fifth essence' as one of the unrealized aims of science, and attributed to the hypothetical substance all sorts of miracle-working properties. Hence *fifth essence* or *quintessence* was used loosely in the various senses 'highly refined extract or essence' and 'universal remedy'.

1582 HESTER tr. *Phioravanti's Secretes* III. liv, The Quintaessence..is an essence aboue the fower elements. *a* **1626** BACON (J.), Here be four of you, as differing as the four elements..as for Eupolis..he may be the fifth essence. **1662** R. MATHEW *Unl. Alch.* 20 An Universal Medicine, or fifth Essence. **1817** BYRON *Manfred* I. i, Ye, who do compass earth about, and dwell In subtler essence. **1837** WHEWELL *Hist. Induct. Sc.* (1857) I. 41 There is some essence of body, different from those of the four elements.

c. 'Constituent substance' (J.).

1398 TREVISA *Barth De P.R.* II. ii. (1495) 28 The essencia of angels is symple and vnmateryal, pure, dystyngt and discrete. **1599** DAVIES *Nosce Teipsum* 10 The Elements conspire, And to her [soul's] Essence each doth give a part. **1667** MILTON *P.L.* I. 425 Spirits..Can either Sex assume, or both; so soft And uncompounded is their Essence pure. **1801** SOUTHEY *Thalaba* III. i, Those Beings Through whose pure essence as through empty air The unaided eye would pass.

†**3. a.** Specific being, manner of existing, 'what a thing is'; nature, character. *Obs.*

c **1532** DEWES *Introd. Fr.* in Palsgr. 920 Thre thynges dothe cause the essence of whythnesse. **1588** GREENE *Pandosto* (1843) 20 The god Apollo, who by his devine essence knew al secrets. **1603** SHAKS. *Meas. for M.* II. ii. 120 Man..Most ignorant of what he's most assured, His glassy essence..Plays such fantastic tricks, etc. **1620** MELTON *Astrolog.* 37 By the fourth House, you will judge of the essence of the Child that is borne, how long it shall liue, and how well. **1626** BACON *Sylva* (1631) §287 Eccho..is a great Argument of the Spirituall Essence of Sounds. **1664** POWER *Exp. Philos.* III. 184 The numerous Rabble that seem to have

the Signatures of Man in their faces..have nothing of the nobler part that should denominate their Essences.

†**b.** *by essence* in *Path.*: idiopathically: cf. ESSENTIAL 1 d. Opposed to *by sympathy*. *Obs.*

1656 RIDGLEY *Pract. Physick* 74 The part that principally offends must be cured. If it be by essence, opening a Vein is good. *Ibid.* 185 It [head-ach] is either by essence or by sympathy with the stomach, etc.

4. a. 'Substance' in the metaphysical sense; the reality underlying phenomena; absolute being.

1646 SIR T. BROWNE *Pseud. Ep.* I. x. 38 The substraction of that essence, which substantially supporteth them. **1871** R. H. HUTTON *Ess.* II. 188 But belief in a universal essence gave no solidity to the order of the world.

b. *Theol.* A synonym of 'substance', as denoting that in respect of which the three persons in the Trinity are one.

The L. *essentia* literally renders Gr. οὐσία, the technical word in this sense. The alternative rendering, *substantia*, substance, corresponds literally to Gr. ὑπόστασις, which however in theological use meant not 'substance' but 'person'.

1398 TREVISA *Barth. De P.R.* I. (1495) 6 Thise thre persones be not thre goddes, but one very god, one essence or one beyng. **1481** CAXTON *Myrr.* III. xii. 160 [Plato and Aristotle] fonde by their wysedom and connyng thre persones in one essence. **1538** BALE *Thre Lawes* 37 All-one with the sonne, and holy ghost in essence. **1552** LYNDESAY *Monarche* IV. 6146 Augustyne sayis, he had leuer tak on hand To be in Hell, he seyng the assence Off God, nor be in Heuin, but his presence.

5. That by which anything subsists; foundation of being.

c **1585** *Answ. to Cartwright* 35 Christ being the essence and life of the Church. **1591** SHAKS. *Two Gent.* III. i. 182 Shee [Siluia] is my essence, and I leaue to be; If I be not by her faire influence Foster'd. **1793** HOLCROFT *Lavater's Physiogn.* iii. 25 There is a tranquil strength the essence of which is immobility. **1841** MYERS *Cath. Th.* III. §6. 20 Of Him who was The Truth—its author and its essence. **1884** H. JENNINGS *Phallicism* iv. 41 The Hindoos holding Fire to be the essence of all active power in nature.

†**6.** Essentiality, importance. Cf. OF. *de grant essence* (Godef.).

1605 BACON *Adv. Learn.* II. xv. §1 A matter of great use and Essence in studying. **1652** SHIRLEY *Brothers* IV. 46 Ther's something Of Essence to my life, exacts my care.

7. That which constitutes the being of a thing; that 'by which it is what it is'. In two different applications (distinguished by Locke as ***nominal essence*** and ***real essence*** respectively):

a. of a conceptual entity: The totality of the properties, constituent elements, etc., without which it would cease to be the same thing; the indispensable and necessary attributes of a thing as opposed to those which it may have or not. Also, in narrower sense, those among the indispensable attributes which involve all the rest by logical consequence, and are sufficient for a valid definition; the 'connotation of the class-name'.

a **1600** HOOKER (J.), Those things, which supernaturally appertain to the very essence of Christianity. **1610** BP. HALL *Apol. Brownists* 20 [It] will proue but an appendance of an externall forme, no part of the essence of a true Church. **1690** LOCKE *Hum. Und.* II. xxxii, The Essence of a Triangle, lies in a very little compass..three Lines meeting at three Angles, make up that Essence. **1714** J. FORTESCUE-ALAND *Pref. to Fortescue's Abs. & Lim. Mon.* 6 We may exactly know the several Ideas that go to make each Law-term, and so their real Nature and Essence may be known. **1841** MYERS *Cath. Th.* III. §39. 140 To confound the transitory and special form with the characteristic and permanent essence. **1870** BOWEN *Logic* iv. 74 Logic considers the Essence of a Concept to be the aggregate of its Marks.

b. of a real entity: Objective character, intrinsic nature as a 'thing-in-itself'; 'that internal constitution, on which all the sensible properties depend'.

1667 H. MORE *Div. Dial.* I. xxiv. 93 I might believe its [a spirit's] Existence, without meddling at all with its Essence. **1725** WATTS *Logic* I. vi. §2 In defining the Name there is no Necessity that we should be acquainted with the intimate Essence or Nature of the Thing. **1739** HUME *Hum. Nat.* I. Introd., The essence of the mind being equally unknown to us with that of external bodies. **1777** PRIESTLEY *Matt. & Spir.* (1782) I. xii. 139 In fact, we have no proper idea of any essence whatever. **1808** J. WEBSTER *Nat. Phil.* 16 We clearly view the effects of attraction..but human ingenuity has not been able to fathom its principle or essence. **1856** FERRIER *Inst. Metaph.* IX. xi. 251 With the old philosophers the essence of things was precisely that part of them of which a clear conception could be formed.

8. *loosely.* The most important indispensable quality or constituent element of anything; the specific difference. ***of the essence*** (*of*): indispensable (to). (Cf. F. *de l'essence de.*)

1656 tr. *Hobbes' Elem. Philos.* (1839) 117 The accident which denominates its subject, is commonly called the essence thereof. **1754** CHATHAM *Lett. Nephew* iv. 27 The essence of religion is, a heart void of offence towards God and man. **1841–4** EMERSON *Ess., Friendship* Wks. (Bohn) I. 92 The essence of friendship is entireness. **1843** MILL *Logic* I. vii. §5. I. 172 It is said that genus and species must be of the essence of the thing. **1873** *Act 36 & 37 Vict.* c. 66 §25 (7) Stipulations..as to time or otherwise, which would not before the passing of this Act have been deemed to be or to have become of the essence of such contracts in a Court of Equity. **1876** FREEMAN *Norm. Conq.* V. xxiv. 452 It is the essence of the modern Jury that they should..give their verdict according to the evidence. **1931** *Morn. Post* 21 Aug. 8/2 While time is of the essence of the contract to retrieve the situation, discussion still proceeds. **1936** WODEHOUSE *Laughing Gas* iii. 37 It seemed to me that pomposity was of the essence... You can't tick a bloke off properly unless you come over a bit mid-Victorian. **1958** *Listener* 30 Oct. 677/2 The only way for the workers to defend themselves in such a case is by immediate action. Time is of the essence.

9. a. An extract obtained by distillation or otherwise from a plant, or from a medicinal, odoriferous or alimentary substance, and containing its characteristic properties in a concentrated form. In pharmacy chiefly applied to alcoholic solutions containing the volatile elements or 'essential oil' to which the perfume, flavour, or therapeutic virtues of the substance are due. ***essence of Venus*** = *ens Veneris*: see ENS 2 b.

[This sense is common to all the Romanic langs., its general currency being prob. due to its use by Paracelsus. It is in part a development of 8, perh. suggested by the older *fifth essence* (see 2 b), which had assumed a nearly similar meaning.]

1660 BOYLE *New Exp. Phys. Mech.* xxv. 195 Very small Viols, such as Chymical Essences..are wont to be kept in. **1662** R. MATHEW *Unl. Alch.* 177 The true preparation of the Essence of Venus. **1744** THOMSON *Spring* 509 Bees..with inserted tube Suck its pure essence. **1838** T. THOMSON *Chem. Org. Bodies* 459 It comes to us from the South of Europe under the name of essence of lemons. **1842** BARHAM *Ingol. Leg., Babes in the Wood* iv, Mind Johnny's chil-blains are rubb'd Well with Whitehead's best essence of mustard.

b. *fig.*

1798 FERRIAR *Illustr. Sterne, Eng. Historians* 252 The essence of history..is always apt to evaporate in the moment of enjoyment. **1816** BYRON *Ch. Har.* III. lxxviii, His love was passion's essence. **1836** MARRYAT *Midsh. Easy* xxii, It was a perfect love-letter, that is to say, it was the essence of nonsense. **1841** MYERS *Cath. Th.* III. §14. 53 Truth cannot be given us in essence.

c. Name of a variety of Tokay wine.

1773 [see TOKAY[1]]. **1862** C. TOVEY *Wine & Wine Countries* v. 208 Until recently, the only wine known in England as the produce of Hungary, was the *Imperial Tokay*, or Tokay essence. **1872** THUDICHUM & DUPRÉ *Treat. Orig. Wine* xix. 629 *Tokay.*—1. *Essence*: very sweet. **1911** *Encycl. Brit.* XXVIII. 728/1 The most precious variety of Tokay is the so-called *essence.*

10. *spec.* A fragrant essence; a perfume, scent. Somewhat *arch.*

1627–77 FELTHAM *Resolves* II. lxiii. 293 It sinks as essence does in cotton till all becomes a Fragrancy. **1712–4** POPE *Rape Lock* II. 94 To save the powder from too rude a gale, Nor let th' imprison'd essences exhale. **1841** JAMES *Brigand* xv, A toilet table covered with all the most costly essences and perfumes which could be procured from the four quarters of the globe. **1855** TENNYSON *Maud* I. xiii, His essences turn'd the live air sick.

fig. **1768** STERNE *Sent. Jour., Riddle Explained*, Delicious essence! how refreshing art thou [flattery] to nature!

11. *attrib.* and *Comb.* (chiefly sense 10). **essence-peddler** *U.S.*, (*a*) a pedlar of medicines; (*b*) *transf.*, a skunk.

1659 BOYLE *Exper. Spring of Air* xxv. Wks. 1772 I. 59 We prosecuted the experiment so long, without seeing any effect wrought upon the essence-bottles, that, etc. *Ibid.* Essence-glass. **1777** SHERIDAN *Trip Scarb.* III. i, Thou essence-bottle, thou musk-cat! **1838** HAWTHORNE *Note-Bks.* (1868) I. 119 He was not exclusively an essence-peddler. **1849** J. R. LOWELL *Let.* 9 Mar. (1894) I. 170 A skunk was shot in our back-kitchen this morning. There were two of these '*essence-peddlers*', as the Yankees call them, gambolling there the night before. **1860** *Knickerbocker* Apr. 361 It is a vulgar mistake that the porcupine has the faculty of darting his quills to a distance, as the essence-peddler has of scattering his aromatic wares. **1862** LOWELL *Biglow P.* 2nd Ser. II. 77 With means about 'em (Like essence-peddlers) thet'll make folks long to be without 'em. **1886** *Pall Mall G.* 27 Aug. 3/2 The essence-steeped fur of a glove. **1890** E. B. CUSTER *Following Guidon* xiv. 200 As soon as that essence-peddler saw fit to move on, the major-general commanding would issue his order to march. **1944** E. A. HOLTON *Yankees were like This* 179 Who later established some of the best known shops in the county; the tin peddler; the essence peddler.

essence ('ɛsəns), *v.* [f. prec. sb.] *trans.* **a.** To pour like an essence (in quot. *fig.*). **b.** To furnish or perfume with an essence. **c.** *nonce-use.* To compress the essence of (a book) *into*.

a. 1635 QUARLES *Embl.* I. v. (1718) 22 Love essenc'd in the hearts of men.

b. 1675 [see next]. **1735** POPE *Donne Sat.* IV. 232 [Ladies] Painted for sight, and essenced for the smell. **1784** COWPER *Task* II. 227 A girl, all essenced o'er With odours. **1823** [see next].

c. 1888 *Punch* 1 Dec. 257/2 *Diamonds Led* is a three-volume novel essenced into five pages.

essenced ('ɛsənst), *ppl. a.* [f. as prec. + -ED[1].] Perfumed with 'essences', scented.

1675 WYCHERLEY *Country Wife* Epil., You essenced boys, both old and young, Who would be thought so eager, brisk, and strong. **1698** VANBRUGH *Æsop* v. i, An essenc'd Peruke, and a sweet handkerchief. **1823** PRAED *Poems, Troubadour*, There were brooks of essenced waters.

†**essencificate**, *v. Obs.* [f. ESSENCE *sb.* after the analogy of *amplificate*, etc. Cf. ESSENTIFICATE.] *trans.* To imbue with an essence.

1657 G. STARKEY *Helmont's Vind.* 321 These elixerated Oyls and essencificated Salts.

†**essencify**, *v. Obs. rare*⁻¹. [f. ESSENCE *sb.* + -(I)FY.] *trans.* = prec.

1707 *Curios. in Husb. & Gard.* 330 Salt..continuing always essencify'd with the same Qualities and Virtues, as the Plant from which it is extracted.

†**e'ssencion** *Obs.* [f. ESSENCE *sb.* + -ION[1], ? confused with *ascension*.] = ESSENCE.

? *a* **1400** *Chester Pl.* (Shaks. Soc.) I. 8 The wholle foode of paternite Is sette in my [God's] essencion.

†**'essency.** *Obs.* [ad. L. *essentia*: see ESSENCE.] = ESSENCE in various senses. ***fifth essency*** = QUINTESSENCE.

1460–70 *Bk. Quintessence* I. 11 The science in þe extracciour of þe 5 essencie from blood, and fleisch, and eggis. **1570** LEVINS *Manip.* 96 Essencie, *essentia.* **1647** H. MORE *Song of Soul* II. iii. III. xii, One steddy Good, centre of essencies. **1648** *Royalist's Def.* 114 The essency of a House of Parliament doth not consist meerly in the legall assembling of the Members.

Essene (ɛ'siːn). Also 6 **essen.** [ad. L. *Essēn-i* pl., a. Gr. Ἐσσηνοί; presumably of Heb. or Aramaic origin, but the etymology is disputed. See the 19 different suggestions in Ginsburg *The Essenes* (1864) 27–30.] One of an ancient Jewish sect, characterized by certain mystical tenets and ascetic practices, and by a cenobitical life.

1553 T. WILSON *Rhet.* 33 The Essens, of whom Josephus speaketh that thei wil neither haue wyfe nor servauntes. **1587** GOLDING *De Mornay* xxv. 392 It wil not be amiss to rehearse this record of Porphyrius, yᵗ the Religious sect of the Essens among yᵉ Iewes..made a profession of Prophesying. **1748** HARTLEY *Observ. Man* II. iv. 390 Many, as the Pharisees and Essenes, had recourse to this great Source of Comfort. **1841–4** EMERSON *Ess.* Ser. II. viii. 197 Why so impatient to baptize them Essenes, or Port-Royalists, or Shakers.

Hence **E'ssenian** *a.*, also 8 -ien, pertaining to, or resembling, the Essenes. **E'ssenic, E'ssenical** *adjs.*, of the nature of Essenism. **'Essenism,** (*a*) the doctrine and practice of the Essenes; (*b*) a leaning to the doctrine of the Essenes. **'Essenize** *v.*, to assert or favour the tenets of the Essenes; also **'Essenizing** *ppl. a.*

1878 *N. Amer. Rev.* CXXVII. 496 The survivors..were half Christian and Essenian. **1832–4** DE QUINCEY *Caesars* (1862) IX. p. ix, The two codes of practical doctrine—Christian and Essenic. **1879** FARRAR *St. Paul* II. 542 The Essenic elements which were destined to ripen into Gnosticism. *a* **1641** BP. MOUNTAGU *Acts & Mon.* (1642), This Essenicall piety in observing the Sabbath. **1852** GEO. ELIOT *Let.* 21 Jan. in J. W. Cross *Life* (1884) I. v. 218 He..traces Essenism back to Egypt, and thence to India. **1875** LIGHTFOOT *Comm. Col.* (ed. 2) 419 The deliverance of the individual in the shipwreck of the whole..was the plain watchword of Essenism. **1882** FARRAR *Early Chr.* II. 18 Critics have spoken of the Essenism and the Ebionism of the Epistle [of St. James]. **1875** LIGHTFOOT *Comm. Col.* (1886) 352 Ewald..points out..an Essenizing Sibylline poem.

‖**essenhout** ('ɛsənhəʊt). *S. Afr.* [Afrikaans, ad. MDu. *eschenhout*, f. *esch* ash + *hout* wood.] = ESSENWOOD.

[**1789** W. PATERSON *Narr.* 80 A tree very useful in making waggons, which the Dutch call Essen, or Ash.] **1819** *Account Colony Cape Good Hope* 71 Essenhout. **1950** *Cape Argus* (Mag. Section) 18 Mar. 7/7 The Cape ebony, white stinkwood, flatcrown, essenhout and umzimbiti, trees that yield beautiful timber for furniture-making, grow in profusion in every kloof. **1961** PALMER & PITMAN *Trees S. Afr.* 277 The essenhout or dog plum is a medium sized tree found in most of the forests of the country.

essential (ɪ'sɛnʃəl), *a.* and *sb.* Forms: 4–6 essenciall(e, -yal(l, (4 escencyalle, 6 assencial), 6–7 essentiall, 6– **essential.** In B 2 also *aphet.* sensual. [ad. late L. *essentiālis*, f. *essentia* ESSENCE: cf. Pr. *essencial*, Sp. *esencial*, It. *essenziale*.]

A. *adj.*

1. In various senses related to ESSENCE *sb.* 1–4.

a. That is such by essence, or in the absolute or highest sense.

c **1340** HAMPOLE *Prose Tr.* (1866) 16 þe soueravne and þe escencyalle joy es in þe lufe of Godd by hymselfe and for hym-selfe, and þe secundarye es in, etc. **1817** COLERIDGE *Biog. Lit.* I. i. 22 The poem..to which we return..claims the name of essential poetry. **1877** SPARROW *Serm.* xv. 203 As the love of God is essential happiness, sin, which is enmity to him, is essential misery, eternal misery.

†**b.** Having existence, real, actual. Also, identical with what now exists. *Obs.*

1535 *Act 27 Hen. VIII*, c. 27 Monasteries..which the kinges maiestie..shall declare and limittee to continue and be in their assencial estate. *Ibid.* c. 28 §3 As if the same monasteryes..hadde contynued in ther essencyall bodyes and states that thei now be or were in. **1552** *Bk. Com. Prayer, Communion*, Anye reall and essenciall presence. *a* **1635** CORBET *Poems* 62 Was his essential table full and free As boasts and invitations used to be?

†**c.** Relating to position in the scale of being. *Obs. rare.*

1677 HALE *Prim. Orig. Man.* I. vi. 122 The production of Creatures of various degrees of essential perfection.

†**d.** Dependent on the intrinsic character or condition of anything, not on extraneous circumstances. Of diseases: Idiopathic (cf. ESSENCE 3 b). ***essential merit*** (*Theol.*) = 'merit of condignity', the merit belonging to good works in proportion to their intrinsic excellence; so ***essential reward.***

1502 *Ord. Crysten Men* (W. de W. 1506) IV. iv. 172 He shall not be rewarded of meryte essencyall for those werkes done in deedly synne. **1560** tr. *Fisher On Prayer* D viij, Euerie merit.. whiche is recompensed by essentiall rewarde

(as they call it) in heauen. *a* **1654** J. WEBSTER (Webster), Is it true, then, that thou art but a name, And no essential thing? **1875** LYELL *Princ. Geol.* I. I. iii. 28 Mountains are formed, he [Avicenna] says, some by essential, others by accidental causes. **1884** *Syd. Soc. Lex.*, *Essential disease*, a disease complete in itself, and not depending on, or symptomatic of another.

e. ***essential debility***, ***dignity*** (*Astrol.*): see the sbs.

†**f.** With descriptive sbs.: Thorough, entire.

1604 DEKKER *Honest Wh.* Wks. 1873 II. 31 Oh he's a most essentiall gentleman, coz. **1721** CIBBER *Woman's Wit* III, Dear Ladies, your most essential humble Servant.

2. Of or pertaining to essence, specific being, or intrinsic nature. ***essential difference*** (*Logic*): = 'specific difference', DIFFERENTIA. ***essential character***: in scientific classification, the marks which distinguish a species, genus, etc. from the others included with it in the next superior division. ***essential proposition*** (*Logic*): one which predicates of a subject something that is implied in its definition. †***essential name*** (*Theol.*): see quot. 1398. ***essential form*** (*Metaph.*): see FORM.

1398 TREVISA *Barth. De P.R.* I. (1495) 7 The names signyfienge or betokenynge the dyuyne essence or beynge ben callid names essencialles. **1590** MARLOWE *2nd Pt. Tamburl.* IV. ii, The essential forme of Marble stone, Temper'd by science metaphysical. **1594** HOOKER *Eccl. Pol.* I. ii. (1611) 4 In which essentiall vnitie of God. **1605** BACON *Adv. Learn.* I. iv. §8 Deceit or untruth..doth destroy the essential form of knowledge, which is nothing but a representation of truth. **1628** T. SPENCER *Logick* 4 [The copula] signifies an essentiall attribution (that is) that, the latter part of the definition doth giue being vnto the former. **1656** BRAMHALL *Replic.* i. 3 Rationability..is a substantiall part of a man, because it is a part of his definition or his essentiall difference. **1687** *Death's Vis.* vii. *note* (1713) 6 Essential Forms I say, rather than Substantial. **1736** BUTLER *Anal.* I. iii. 63 Its [Virtue's] having in the essential nature of the thing a tendency to produce them [Superiority and Advantages]. **1776** WITHERING *Brit. Plants* (1796) I. 212 The nectary gives the essential character. **1846** MILL *Logic* I. vi. §4 An essential proposition then, is one which is purely verbal. **1875** JOWETT *Plato* (ed. 2) I. 178 The desire to ascertain..the essential nature of virtue.

3. Constituting, or forming part of, the essence of anything; belonging to a thing by virtue of its essence; necessarily implied in its definition; indispensably entering into its composition.

1546 LANGLEY *Pol. Verg. De Invent.* IV. i. 82 His only begotten son equal to him in essential power. **1596** SPENSER *Hymn Heav. Beauty* xvi, Those essentiall parts of his, His truth, his love, his wisedome, and his blis. **1661** BRAMHALL *Just Vind.* vii. 225 By the Law of Nature as an essential right of Soveraignty. **1690** LOCKE *Hum. Und.* III. vi. (1695) 246 The thought of any thing essential to any of them, instantly vanishes. **1705** STANHOPE *Paraphr.* I. 54 The Glory of God is so exquisite in itself and so Essential to Him, that, etc. **1862** SIR B. BRODIE *Psychol. Inq.* II. i. 9 The desire of reputation..is an essential part of human nature. **1878** TAIT & STEWART *Unseen Univ.* i. 23 In the essential immortality of the soul.

b. Affecting the essence of anything; 'material', important.

1770 *Junius Lett.* xli. 209 You have done essential service to the cause. **1781** GIBBON *Decl. & F.* III. 44 The piercing eye of the founder of the republic must have discerned two essential imperfections. **1794** BURKE *Rep. Lords' Jrnls.* Wks. 1842 II. 617 To have adopted the civil law with no very essential variation. **1871** BLACKIE *Four Phases* I. 142 It is not in the nature of things that a better man should receive essential harm from a worse.

4. Absolutely necessary, indispensably requisite.

essential vows: the three vows (of chastity, poverty, and obedience) indispensable to the monastic life.

1526 *Pilgr. Perf.* (W. de W. 1531) 151 b, The lyfe of religyous persones, that professeth the thre essencyall vowes. **1612** BP. HALL *Pref. to Brinsley's Lud. Lit.*, Those sciences which are so Essentiall to the Spirituall house of God. **1662** GERBIER *Princ.* 4 The first and essential point of Building, (to wit, Solidity with Ornament and Conveniency). **1712** ADDISON *Spect.* No. 279 ¶8 That serious Air which seems essential to the Magnificence of an Epic Poem. **1807** T. THOMSON *Chem.* (ed. 3) II. 85 Silica.. is an essential ingredient in mortar. **1858** BUCKLE *Civiliz.* (1873) II. viii. 425 Propositions which I hold to be most essential for a right understanding of history. **1874** MICKLETHWAITE *Mod. Par. Churches* 223 The essential quality of a monument is permanence.

b. *Music.* ***essential chord***, in early use = ***common chord***; in later use = FUNDAMENTAL, opp. to ***accidental*** (see quot. 1806). ***essential harmony*** (see quot. 1851). ***essential notes***: the 1st, 3rd, and 5th notes of a chord. ***essential sharps*** and ***flats*** (see quot. 1806).

1721 A. MALCOLM *Treat. Mus.*, Of the natural Notes of every Mode or Octaue, Three go under the Name of the essential Notes, in a peculiar Manner, viz. the Fundamental, the 3d, and 5th. **1806** CALCOTT *Mus. Gram.* (1817) 55 Sharps or flats..which occur in the course of the Movement ..are termed accidental, to distinguish them from those of the Signature, which are essential to the Scale of the original key note. *Ibid.* 202 His [Kirnberger's] arrangement of Chords, into essential and accidental. **1851** WARNER tr. *Weber's Th. Composition* 258 There are only certain particular harmonies, which belong to any one particular key..These are called the Essential harmonies of the key. **1880** GROVE *Dict. Mus.* I. 679/1 s.v. *Harmony*, The use of preliminary notes a semitone above or below any note of an essential chord.

5. That is of the nature of, or resembles, an essence or extract (see ESSENCE 10); that is in a state of essence.

1641 FRENCH *Distill.* v. (1651) 113 This Spirit contains in it..essentiall Sulphur. **1673** GREW *Anat. Plants* II. i. v. §16 In the Vessels, a more Essential Liquor..in the Fibres a more simple and Essential Aer. **1751** JOHNSON *Rambler* No. 120 ¶2 They filled his apartments with alexipharmics, restoratives, and essential virtues. **1832** WORDSW. *Devot. Incitements*, From humble violet—modest thyme—Exhaled, the essential odours climb.

b. ***essential oil***, a volatile oil, obtained by distillation, and marked by the characteristic odour of the plant or substance from which it is extracted; as the oil of laurel, oil of turpentine, etc. Now often as a synonym of 'volatile oil'.

1674 GREW *Anat. Plants* Lect. i. (1682) 237 Having.. made mention of the preparation of Essential Oyls. **1732** BERKELEY *Alciphr.* vi. §14 The soul of any plant..is neither more nor less than its essential oil. **1813** SIR H. DAVY *Agric. Chem.* (1814) 102 Volatile oil, likewise called essential oil, differs from fixed oil, in being capable of evaporation by a much lower degree of heat. **1859** GULLICK & TIMBS *Paint.* 208 The Volatile or Essential Oils are destitute of the strength of the fixed oils. **1867** J. HOGG *Microsc.* I. iii. 205 Sections of woods..containing gum, resin, etc., should be soaked in essential oil, alcohol, or ether.

†**c.** ***essential salt*** (see quot.). *Obs.*

1715 in KERSEY. **1718** QUINCY *Compl. Disp.* 9 The essential salt is that which is obtain'd by Chrystallization from the Juices of Plants. **1800** tr. *Lagrange's Chem.* II. 181 What the first chemists called, in general, the Essential Salts of Vegetables.

6. quasi-*adv.* = ESSENTIALLY.

1827 POLLOK *Course T.* x, His face with clouds Of glory circled round, essential bright.

B. *sb.*

†**1.** What exists; existence, being. *Obs.*

1667 MILTON *P.L.* II. 93 His utmost ire..Will..quite consume us, and reduce To nothing this essential.

2. Something belonging to the essence of a thing; an indispensable element or adjunct; also, in weaker sense, a chief or leading point. Orig. only in *pl.*; in later use, occas. *sing.* †**b.** *pl.* = *essential vows*; see A 4.

1513 BRADSHAW *St. Werburge* 2372 Euer after to obserue the essencyals thre. *Ibid.* 1913 The sensuals thre. *a* **1619** FOTHERBY *Atheom.* I. iv. §3 (1622) 23 Vowes, and invocations, and other the Essentials of religion. **1750** HARRIS *Hermes* Wks. (1841) 167 These matters..being rather among the elegancies, than the essentials of language. **1793** SMEATON *Edystone L.* §266 If..all our essentials had duly performed their duties, we could have reaped little advantage from them. **1815** SCOTT *Guy M.* xxxiii, 'Well, well', said Glossin, 'no occasion to be particular, tell the essentials'. **1848** MILL *Pol. Econ.* I. vii. §1 Natural motive powers..are a help, but not an essential of production. **1850** MRS. JAMESON *Leg. Monast. Ord.* (1863) 230 The distinction between the Franciscans and Dominicans lay not in essentials, but merely in point of discipline. **1860–1** FLO. NIGHTINGALE *Nursing* ii. 7 The first essential to the patient, without which all the rest..is as nothing. **1873** H. SPENCER *Study Sociol.* v. 111 A tendency..to be blinded by exterior trivialities to interior essentials.

†**3.** *pl.* Inmost nature; 'vitals'. *Obs. rare.*

a **1716** SOUTH (J.), The plague of sin has even altered his nature, and eaten into his very essentials.

essentialism (ɪˈsɛnʃəlɪz(ə)m). [f. ESSENTIAL *a.* and *sb.* + -ISM.]

1. *Educ.* A theory advocating the teaching, on traditional lines and to everyone, of certain ideas and methods supposed to be essential to the prevalent culture (opp. to PROGRESSIVISM).

1939 J. S. BRUBACHER *Mod. Philos. Educ.* xiv. 336 Over against the philosophy of progressive education..stands that of essentialism or traditionalism. **1950** T. BRAMELD *Patterns Educ. Philos.* vii. 211 What then is the central outlook of essentialism?.. It views the established beliefs and institutions of our modern heritage as not only real but true, and not only true but good.

2. *Philos.* The belief in real essences of things, esp. the view that the task of science and philosophy is to discover these and express them in definitions.

1945 K. R. POPPER *Open Society* I. iii. 26 Methodological essentialism, i.e. the theory that it is the aim of science to reveal essences and to describe them by means of definitions. **1948** *Mind* LVII. 302 Essentialism is not only deep-rooted in men's thought habits—or linguistic habits; as it penetrates different departments of human thought it works on these. **1957** K. R. POPPER *Poverty of Historicism* i. 27 This 'realist' theory has also been called 'idealist'. I therefore propose to rename this antinominalist theory 'essentialism'.

b. [tr. F. *essentialisme.*] The doctrine that essence is prior to existence (opp. to EXISTENTIALISM).

1949 E. L. MASCALL *Existence & Analogy* i. 11 However much vestigial Platonic essentialism there may have been in the thought of the great Greek father [*sc.* St. John of Damascus], St. Thomas interprets him in the most existential manner possible.

e'ssentialist, *sb.* and *a.* [f. ESSENTIAL *a.* and *sb.* + -IST.]

A. *sb.*

†**1.** The name given to a Nonjuror who held that the 'usages' which were omitted from the Second Prayer-book of Edward VI were 'essential'. *Obs.*

1719 (*title*), A Dialogue in Vindication of our present Liturgy and Service; between Timothy a Churchman and Thomas an Essentialist.

2. One who follows or advocates essentialism.

1945 K. R. POPPER *Open Society* I. iii. 25 These methodological essentialists also agreed with Plato.

B. *adj.* Of or relating to essentialism (in its various senses).

1938 *Newsweek* 14 Mar. 26 (*heading*) Essentialist group urges pupils be coddled less and taught more. **1943** P. WYNDHAM LEWIS *Let.* 17 Aug. (1963) 365, I have been hearing a lot of talk about what appears to me a most promising movement in American education: namely the socalled 'essentialist', as opposed to the 'progressive' principle. **1945** K. R. POPPER *Open Society* I. iii. 27 The problems of the social sciences..are still..treated by essentialist methods. **1948** *Mind* LVII. 302 Nineteenth century Idealist theories..are vitiated through and through by the 'essentialist fallacy'. **1949** E. L. MASCALL *Existence & Analogy* ii. 19 A typical Thomist statement..tells us that in God essence and existence..are identical. Understood from the essentialist standpoint, this statement simply affirms that existence is analytically contained in the notion of God's essence.

essentiality (ɪˌsɛnʃɪˈælɪtɪ). [f. as prec. + -ITY.]

1. The quality or fact of being essential.

1640 GOODWIN *Justifying Faith* I. i. (R.), The substantialness and essentiality of a promise relates to the actual execution of it. **1646** SALTMARSH *Some Drops* ii. 32 The onenesse, Entirenesse, indivisibility and essentiality of the Truth. **1874** CARPENTER *Ment. Phys.* I. viii. (1879) 351 There are many upon whom the essentiality of Intellectual and Moral discipline will..impress itself.

2. Essential character or nature; essence.

1616 R. C. *Times' Whis.* I. 122 The mistery Of searching his [God's] essentialitie. **1647** JER. TAYLOR *Dissuas. Popery* II. I. §4 (R.) This faith is perfected, as to the essentiality of it, in the death and resurrection of Christ. **1683** PORDAGE *Myst. Div.* 79 Love's Eternal Essentiality is that out of which all pure simplified Spirits were brought forth. **1866** CARLYLE *Edw. Irving* Misc. (1881) I. 229 This 'noble lady' was in essentiality an artist.

3. An essential quality (*rare*); also *pl.* essential points or elements; essentials. Cf. ESSENTIAL B. 2.

1649 J. ECCLESTON tr. *Behmen's Epist.* I. 9 This essentiality is called Sophia, being the essentiall wisedome, or the body of Christ. **1710** SWIFT in *Examiner* No. 32 ¶3 The French ..whose essentialities are generally so very superficial. **1821** *Blackw. Mag.* X. 322 When priests..shall forget the solemn essentialities of their office. **1858** CARLYLE *Fredk. Gt.* II. IX. iii. 425 In all the essentialities of it, there had not been..the least flaw.

e'ssentialize, *v.* In 7 essentialise. [f. as prec. + -IZE.]

†**a.** *trans.* To make essential; to give essence or being to. *Obs.*

1669 GALE tr. *Plato* in *Crt. Gentiles* I. III. iii. 325 The Divine Opificer, by whose..effective word, althings were essentializ'd.

b. To formulate in essential form, to express the essential form of.

1913 *Westm. Gaz.* 22 Feb. 5/1 Its difficulties and restrictions, instead of essentialising his thought, have frustrated it. **1922** *Times Lit. Suppl.* 5 Jan. 10/1 A poet [*sc.* Dante] in whom the manifold passions and cultural movements of his time were essentialized and ennobled into the highest poetical utterance. **1923** *Glasgow Herald* 19 Apr. 4 The essentialising flame of Rembrandt's genius. **1923** A. HUXLEY *On Margin* 153 That consolation and strength.. essentialized and distilled in the form of art. **1930** N. SHEPHERD *Weatherhouse* x. 181 Garry went drunk to bed, but not with whiskey. Again he had seen life essentialised.

Hence **e'ssentializer**.

1669 GALE *Crt. Gentiles* I. III. iii. 320 The first fabricator, perfector, essentialiser of Beings or he that gives Essence to Beings.

essentially (ɪˈsɛnʃəlɪ), *adv.* [f. as prec. + -LY².] In an essential manner.

1. *fig.* In essence; with respect to essence; as an essential attribute or constituent.

1398 TREVISA *Barth. De P.R.* III. xiv. (1495) 58 A myȝte of yᵉ soule essenciably [? *read* essencialli] yeue to werke and doo his dedes in yᵉ body. **1534** MORE *Answ. Poysoned Bk.* Wks. 1121/1 The glory of his godhed is, to be present and to fill al places at ones assencially. **1597** HOOKER *Eccl. Pol.* v. lxviii. (1611) 367 They define not the Church by what the Church essentially is. *a* **1631** DONNE *Serm.* i. (1634) 7 To see that God essentially and face to face. *a* **1680** GLANVILL (J.), Body and spirit are essentially divided, though not locally distant. **1715** DE FOE *Fam. Instruct.* I. i. (1841) I. 20 Jesus Christ is essentially God, though in a second person. **1835** FOSTER in *Life & Corr.* (1846) II. 301 Principles which are essentially inherent in your institution.

†**b.** On the ground of (one's) actual nature.

1593 SHAKS. *2 Hen. VI*, v. ii. 39 He that loues himselfe, Hath not essentially, but by circumstance The name of Valour. **1624** GATAKER *Transubst.* 4 In like manner is the bread said to be the Body of Christ..not really or essentially, but typically and sacramentally.

†**c.** In fact, really. *Obs.*

1602 SHAKS. *Ham.* III. iv. 187 That I essentially am not in madnesse, But mad in craft.

d. In respect of the essential points, materially, substantially.

1774 BURKE *Corr.* (1844) I. 483 My opinion..does not.. essentially differ from that of your lordship. **1823** LAMB *Elia* Ser. II. xxiv. (1865) 405 A form of words—literally false, but essentially deceiving no one. **1856** KANE *Arct. Expl.* I. xxiii. 304 Its food is essentially marine, the acalephæ, etc. **1875** BRYCE *Holy Rom. Emp.* v. (ed. 5) 56 The impression which the three narratives leave is essentially the same. **1879** J.

TIMBS in *Cassell's Techn. Educ.* IV. 7/1 She [*i.e.* a steamship] was, as a whole, essentially completed.

e. In the proper or essential function.

1609 DOWLAND *Ornith. Microl.* 51 Rests are placed in songs after three manners.. Essentially when they betoken silence.

2. a. Indispensably.

1757 FOOTE *Author* I, I believe her Brother's consent essentially necessary. **1812** WELLINGTON in Gurw. *Disp.* IX. 122 Some supplies essentially necessary to both armies.

b. In a marked or eminent degree; eminently.

1593 DRAYTON *Past. Eclog.* VIII. (R.), None are so essentially high As those that on her [Wisdom's] bounty do rely. **1713** ADDISON in *Guardian* No. 3 ¶4 Knowledge.. truly and essentially raises one man above another. **1869** *Mem. J. Grey* 100 That blessed union.. has contributed so essentially to the.. prosperity of both countries.

essentialness (ɪ'sɛnʃəlnɪs). [f. as prec. + -NESS.] The quality or fact of being essential.

1640 LD. DIGBY *Sp. conc. Trien. Parl.* 12 The Essentialnes Sir of frequent Parliaments to the happinesse of this Kingdome. *a* **1699** BONNELL in W. Hamilton *Life* II. (1703) 175 Each endeavouring.. to pretend them to be of more Essentialness and Weight in Religion, than indeed they are. **1736** in BAILEY. **1854** RUSKIN *Lect. Archit.* Add. 120 A confusion of the idea of essentialness.. with the idea of nobleness.

† **e'ssentiate,** *ppl. a. Obs.* [as if ad. L. **essentiāt-us*; see next.] = ESSENTIATED. In quot. *sb.*

1630 G. WIDDOWES *Schysmat. Puritan* A iij b, The scriptures deduceable sence in Essentials, Essentiates, Efficients, Finals, Subiects, Effects, and their Modalities,.. confounds this Professor.

† **e'ssentiate,** *v. Obs. Pa. pple.* in 6 **essentiate.** [f. as if on L. **essentiāt-* ppl. stem of **essentiāre*, f. *essentia*: see ESSENCE.]

1. *trans.* To make into an essence or being; to form or constitute the essence or being of.

1561 T. NORTON *Calvin's Inst.* I. 39 For whosoeuer sayth that the Sonn was essentiate or made to be of his Father, denieth that he is of himself. **1647** SALTMARSH *Sparkl. Glory* (1847) 66 That which forms, essentiates, or constitutes the true Christian, is the Spirit of Jesus Christ. **1680** BAXTER *Answ. Stillingfl.* 8 A Church as well as a Kingdom, is essentiated by a *pars regens*, and *pars subdita*. **1687** *Death's Vis.* Pref. 4 Those turns of Fancy and Wit, that almost Essentiate a Poem.

b. *to essentiate together*: to unite in essence; to make into one essence or being.

1593 NASHE *Christ's T.* 9 b, What is a man, if the parts of his body be disparted, and not incorporated and essentiate together?

2. *intr.* To become essence; to be assimilated or converted into a being or body.

1599 B. JONSON *Ev. Man out of Hum.* V. iv, What comes nearest the nature of that it feeds, converts quicker to nourishment, and doth sooner essentiate.

3. *trans.* To refine into an 'essence' or subtle extract. (See ESSENTIATED *ppl. a.*)

Hence **e'ssentiated** *ppl. a.* **e'ssentiating** *vbl. sb.* and *ppl. a.* **e'ssentiator,** he that 'essentiates'.

1656 H. MORE *Antid. Ath.* (1662) 14 A rabble of Self-essentiated and divided Deities. **1675** EVELYN *Terra* (1778) 170 Essentiated Spirits.. are as pernicious to them [plants] as brandy and hot waters to men. **1736** BAILEY, *Essentiated*, made or brought into essences, or essential spirits. **1635** MONTAGUE in *Hammond's Wks.* (1684) II. 701 If it were simply necessary to the essentiating of a church. **1681** BAXTER *Acc. Sherlocke* v. 204 A Constitutive Cause in the common sense of Logicians, signifieth the Essentiating Cause. **1689** in *6th Coll. Papers Pres. Affairs* 15 One Corporation made up of three Constituent Essentiating Parts, King, Lords and Commons. **1561** T. NORTON *Calvin's Inst.* I. 38 That he [the Father] is the onely essentiator or maker of the essence. **1677** GALE *Crt. Gentiles* II. IV. 249 He who is the first independent Essence and Essentiator of althings can be but one.

† **essentie.** *Obs. rare*⁻¹. [ad. L. *essentia.*] = ESSENCE, ESSENCY.

1552 HULOET, *Essentye* or substance compacted of matter and shape.

† **essen'tifical,** *a. Obs.* [f. L. *essenti-a* being or essence + -FIC + -AL[1] (after mod.L. *essentificus*).] Forming or producing the essence of a thing.

1656 [J. SERJEANT] tr. *White's Peripat. Instit.* 210 Now, naturall Things are naturall parts of the world, unerringly flowing from the Essentificall Idea's. **1662** J. CHANDLER *Van Helmont's Oriat.* 144 Although the formall light doth shine; yet its act is not terminated in shining, but in an essentificall thingliness.

† **essen'tificate,** *v. Obs.* [f. as prec. + -ATE[3]. Cf. *essencificate.*] *trans.* To make into an essence. Hence **essen'tificated** *ppl. a.*

1660 tr. *Paracelsus' Archidoxis* I. v. 74 Take Mercurie Essentificated, the which separate from all its Superfluities. **1736** in BAILEY. **1775** in ASH.

essenwood ('ɛsənwʊd). [Partial transl. of Afrikaans *essenhout*: see ESSENHOUT.] **a.** The South African ash, *Ekebergia capensis.* **b.** Cape mahogany, *Trichilia roka* (*emetica*).

1891 R. M. SMITH *Great Gold Lands S. Afr.* xx. 179 Essen-wood, the South African ash (*Ekebergia capensis*). **1910** J. BUCHAN *Prester John* vi, We took a path up the Berg among groves of stinkwood and essenwood.

† **essera.** *Path. Obs.* Also 8 essere, -rs. [med.L. *essera, essere*, ad. Arab. *sharā*, with the art. *ash-sharā*: see Avicenna *Canon* IV. iii. cap. 13 in the orig. and in the Lat. version of 1483. Cf. Fr. *essère.*] 'Old term for a cutaneous eruption attacking the face and hands, resembling that caused by the sting of nettles, but the spots not elevated, and usually unattended by fever' (*Syd. Soc. Lex.*); a variety of nettle-rash.

1706 PHILLIPS, *Essere.* **1721–1800** BAILEY, *Essers.* **1744** MITCHELL *Colours of People* in *Phil. Trans.* XLIII. 108 Cutaneous Diseases, as the Itch, prickly Heat or Essere. **1782** W. HEBERDEN *Comm.* iii. (1806) 14 The attacks of the essera or nettle-rash. **1811** in HOOPER *Med. Dict.* **1847** in CRAIG; and in mod. Dicts.

essew, obs. form of ISSUE.

Essex ('ɛsɪks). The name of an English county, occurring attrib. in ***Essex board*** (see quot. 1933); ***Essex calf***, properly a calf reared in Essex, but often used as a contemptuous designation for the natives of that county; hence, punningly, † ***Essex-growth***, growth in the 'calf' of the leg; ***Essex pig*** (also ***Black Essex*** and *absol.*), a pig of a kind bred originally in Essex. Hence † **'Essexed** *a.*

1573 G. HARVEY *Let.-bk.* (1884) 135 Will you haue all in a worde and a halfe, Foes must be frende, quoth an Essex kalfe. **1630** J. TAYLOR (Water P.) *Wks.* II. 165 A good Legge is a great grace if it be discreetly essex'd in the calfe, and not too much spindled in the small. **1659** *Lady Alimony* v. v. in Hazl. *Dodsley* XIV. 361 You would wish that his puny baker-legs had more Essex growth [*i.e.* more calf] in them. *a* **1661** FULLER *Worthies* (1840) I. 497 A Cumberland cow may be bought for the price of an Essex calf in the beginning of the year. **1838** *Penny Cycl.* X. 19/2 Essex has been long noted for a superior breed of pigs... The common Essex pigs have long ears. **1861** MRS. BEETON *Bk. Househ. Managem.* 365 Varieties of the Domesticated Hog.. *Native*—Berkshire, Essex, York, and Cumberland. **1877** F. D. COBURN *Swine Husbandry* 83 The Essex are so very similar to the Suffolk, in nearly every respect except color... Their skin, from its color, affords them one advantage over the Suffolks. **1897** S. SPENCER *Pigs* i. 15 The Small Black or Suffolk, or again, as it is styled in the States, the Essex,.. and a few other breeds brought the Small Black pig within measurable distance of perfection. **1906** J. LONG *Bk. Pig* (ed. 2) i. 6 (*caption*) Neapolitan.. a black race of pigs.. crossed with the old Black Essex with excellent results. *Ibid.* 7 The Essex and the Dorset.. although still recognized by farmers and breeders in their particular districts, are not recognized by experts and the agricultural societies as special breeds. **1911** *Encycl. Brit.* XXI. 595/1 The *Small Black* or *Black Suffolk* was produced from the old Essex pig by crossing with the Neapolitan. **1933** C. W. GLOVER *Pract. Acoustics for Constructor* 429 Essex Board... Composition—compressed fibre in plies, bound together by strong, fire-resisting cement. **1954** I. MURDOCH *Under Net* xii. 170 It's only made of plastic and Essex board. **1960** *Farmer & Stockbreeder* 22 Mar. 85/1 Demand was keen for all four breeds—Large Whites, Essex, Wessex Saddlebacks and Landrace.

essign, obs. form of ASSIGN.

essive ('ɛsɪv). [ad. Finn. *essiivi*, f. L. ESSE, with termination ad. L. *-īvus*: see -IVE.] The designation of one of the fifteen cases of Finnish, a declension expressing a continuous state of being, existence in a specified state or capacity.

1890 [see ADESSIVE *a.*]. **1905** JESPERSEN in *Englische Studien* XXXV. 9 Essive, indicating the state in which anybody or anything is. **1924** —— *Philos. Gram.* xiii. 183 In Finnish the predicative is.. in the essive to denote the state in which the subject is at a given time.

essoin, essoign (ɛ'sɔɪn), *sb. Law.* Forms: 4–7 essoyn(e, 4 essonie, *Sc.* essonȝe, 5 esson, 6–9 essoine, 7–8 essoign(e, 7 (*Sc.*) essonȝie, 6– essoin, 7– essoign. See also ASSOIN *sb.* [a. OF. *essone, essonie, essoine, essoigne, essoyne* (mod.F. *exoine*), vbl. sb. f. *essoigner*: see next.]

1. *Law.* The allegation of an excuse for non-appearance in court at the appointed time; the excuse itself. Also in phrases ***to cast, make, challenge essoin. day of essoin***: the day when excuses were received, the first day of term.

Essoins were admitted on various grounds, pilgrimage, the king's service, illness, etc. The practice is now obsolete.

c **1330** R. BRUNNE *Chron.* (1810) 249 Þat non eft mad essoyn, þe kynges right to clame. *Ibid.* 291, I may not cast essoyn, bot felow my somons. **1483** *Act 1 Rich. III*, c. 3 §1 Non esson or proteccion be allowed in any suche accion. **1514** FITZHERB. *Just. Peas* (1538) 89 b, No protection, essoyne, nor wager of lawe to be allowed. **1612** DRAYTON *Poly-olb.* xvii. Notes 270 The xl daies in the essoine of childbirth allowed by the Norman customs. **1620** J. WILKINSON *Hundred Crt.* 169 Whosoever will cast any essoine in these courts, he must come at the beginning of the court. **1702** *Royal Proclam.* 29 Mar. in *Lond. Gaz.* No. 3797/2 The First Day of the said *Quindena Paschæ*, commonly called the Day of Essoigns. **1713** SWIFT *Cadenus & Van.* Wks. 1824 XIV. 475 But, with.. Demur, imparlance, and essoigne The parties ne'er could issue join. *a* **1734** NORTH *Ld. Guildford* in Ld. Campbell *Chancellors* (1857) IV. xciv. 284 He reasoned the court by their pence for essoines. **1885** L. O. PIKE *Year-bks.* 12 & 13 *Edw. III*, Introd. 31 The essoin was fraudulently cast without his knowledge.

b. ***clerk of the essoins***: 'an officer of the Common Pleas, who keeps the Essoin-rolls, delivers them to every officer, and receives them again when they are written' (Phillips 1678–1706).

1657 HOWELL *Londinop.* 368 The Officers of this Court [Common Pleas] are many; viz. *Custos Brevium*, three Protonotaries, Clerk of the Essoins [etc.]. **1678–1706** in PHILLIPS. **1721–1800** in BAILEY; and in mod. Dicts.

2. *In general.* An excuse, exemption, making of conditions, parleying, delay; also in phr. ***without essoin.***

c **1330** R. BRUNNE *Chron.* (1810) 136 He gaf a þousand mark, withouten essoyne. *c* **1375** *Sc. Leg. Saints, Julian* 181 To fynd sume essonȝe for-quhy þai mycht frely pase forby. *c* **1470** HARDING *Chron.* CCXXVI. ii, The duke then of Burgoyn, Kepte Fraunce full well without any essoyn. **1590** SPENSER *F.Q.* I. iv. 20 From everie worke he chalenged essoyne, For contemplation sake.

¶ **3.** The alleged sense 'one who is excused' (= ESSOINEE) is app. due to a misunderstanding, Cowell's explanation of AF. *essonié* having been taken by later lexicographers as referring to *essoin.*

(If the sense were authenticated, the word as so used would be a distinct sb., repr. AF. *essoinié*, as ASSIGN *sb.*[2] represents AF. *assigné.*)

1607 COWELL *Interpr.*, Essoine (*Essonium*) cometh of the French *Essonié* or *exonnié* .i. *causarius miles*, he that hath his presence forborne or excused vpon any iust cause.. It signifieth in our common lawe an alledgement of an excuse.

4. *Comb.* **essoin-day** (see quot.); **essoin-roll,** the list containing the names of the essoinees.

1679 *Trials of White, etc.* 8 Monday is the Essoign Day. **1765–9** BLACKSTONE *Comm.* III. xviii. (1783) 278 Thereon the Court sits to take essoigns.. wherefore this is usually called the essoign day of the term. **1848** WHARTON *Law Lex. s.v.*, Formerly the first general return day of the term was called essoign day, because the court sat to receive essoigns.

essoin (ɛ'sɔɪn), *v. Law.* Forms: 5–7 essoyne, 6–8 essoign(e, 6–7 essoine, 7 (*Sc.*) essonyie, -zie, 7– essoin. See also ASSOIN *v.* [a. OF. *essoignier, essoinier, essoyner*, f. *essoyne*:—med.L. *exsoniāre*, f. *ex* out + *sonia, sunnis* lawful excuse, f. OHG. *sunna, sunnia*, corresp. to OS. *sunnea* doubtfully explained as 'want, lack', ON. *syn* refusal, denial; the OTeut. type coincides in form with that of Goth. *sunja* truth; the OHG. sense must have existed in Goth., which has the derived vb. *sunjôn* to excuse.]

1. *trans.* To offer an excuse for the non-appearance of (a person) in court; to excuse for absence. Also, ***to essoin one's attendance.***

1495 *Act 11 Hen. VII*, c. 5 The defendaunt.. be not essoyned. **1607** COWELL *Interpr. s.v.*, The causes that serue to Essoine any man summoned be diuers and infinite: yet drawne to fiue heads. **1609** SKENE tr. *Acts Will.* (an. 1165) c. 26 §1. 7 Gif ane man is essonyied at the fourt day, be reason of seiknes.. or being beȝond Forth: he sall have respit, or ane continuation of fourtie days. **1642** PERKINS *Prof. Bk.* xi. 332 The Plaintiffe is essoined so that I cannot answer unto him. **1651** tr. *Kitchin's Courts Leet* 272 The Tenant was Essoyned and at the day made default. **1738** *Hist. Crt. Excheq.* ii. 23 They might excuse or essoign their Attendance, and attend by Deputy. **1885** L. O. PIKE *Year-bks.* 12 & 13 *Edw. III*, Introd. 30 The tenant.. caused himself to be essoined.

2. To accept an excuse from, let off (a person).

1620 QUARLES *Jonah* Div. Poems (1717) 30 Away with wings of time, (I'll not essoin thee).

essoinee (ɛ,sɔɪ'niː). *Law.* [a. AF. *essoignié* (Britton), pa. pple. of *essoignier*: see ESSOIN *v.*] A person excused for non-appearance in court.

[**1607** See ESSOIN *sb.* 3.] **1642** W. BIRD *Mag. Honor* 162 It shall rest upon the credit and integrity of the Essoinee. **1865** NICHOLS *Britton* II. 351 If the essoinee does not.. appear to warrant the essoiner.

essoiner (ɛ'sɔɪnə(r)). Also 7 (*Sc.*) essonyier, -zier. [ad. AF. *essoigniour* (Britton), f. *essoignier*: see ESSOIN *v.*] One who essoins; one who offers an excuse for the absence of another.

1609 SKENE *Reg. Maj.* 111 b, It behoues the essonzier to name his awin name, and the name of him that is essonzied. **1651** tr. *Kitchin's Courts Baron* 374 The Name of the Essoyner shall be put in. **1671** F. PHILLIPS *Reg. Necess.* 397 An Essoin de Service le Roy was challenged, for that the Essoiner was under age. **1889** *Univ. Rev.* Nov. 436 In the High Court of Night Be thou essoiner for us unto Death.

essoinment (ɛ'sɔɪnmənt). [f. ESSOIN *v.* + -MENT.] The action of essoining.

† **e'ssome,** *v. Obs. rare*⁻¹. [a. OF. *essome-r*, var. of *asomer* (mod.F. *assommer*) to knock down.] *trans.* To confound, confuse.

1660 BURNEY Κέρδ. Δῶρον (1661) 99 Mahumetane juglings, to essome their spectators in this lower world.

† **esso'menic,** *a. Obs. rare.* [f. Gr. ἐσσόμεν-ος, fut. pple. of εἶναι to be + -IC.] (See quot.)

1771 P. PARSONS *Newmarket* I. 123 Another kind of mirror .. the Essomenic.. which has the singular power of representing things and persons in future times. *Ibid.* 124 It has all the qualities of the other two kinds, but the Essomenic is peculiar to itself.

essonite, var. of HESSONITE, cinnamon-stone.

esssse, obs. form of ASHES.

essue, obs. form of ISSUE.

essurine, var. form of ESURINE.

e'ssuyance. Also **assuyance.** [as if a. F. **essuyance* f. *essuyer* to wipe.] (See quot.)

1646 BUCK *Rich. III*, I. 27 Holding a Cloth of Plaisance (or rather of Essuyance) for her [the Queen's] Cup. *Ibid.* I. 157 Cloth of assuyance, Towel or napkin that wait on the cup.

est (ɛst). [Acronym f. the initial letters of *E*rhard *S*eminars *T*raining.] An alternative philosophy and technique intended to raise self-awareness and 'human potential', involving philosophical and psychological means, including motivational theories from the business world, devised in California by Werner Erhard (J. P. Rosenberg, b. 1935). Freq. *attrib.*

[**1970** L. C. STEVENS *Est* 34 Complete representatives of the Electronic Social Transformation, they are the people of the EST.] **1973** *Bull. San Francisco Med. Soc.* Sept./Oct. 40/2 The male graduate of the *est* training is more willing to assume responsibility for himself. **1976** L. RHINEHART *Book of Est* p. xii, *Est* is not a religion, not a therapy, not an academic course, not a belief system. It might best be described.. as theater—..as encounter theater. **1979** *Brit. Med. Jrnl.* 15 Dec. 1558/1 For Appelbaum Gestalt therapy, 'est', bioenergetics, transcendental meditation, primal screaming, and yoga all constitute elements of the 'human potential' movement. **1983** *Listener* 23 June 14/1 More clients are going to naturopaths, chiropractors and faith healers, or are trying fashionable psychological health movements, such as dianetics and est.

est, dial. form of NEST; cf. *adder* for *nadder*.

est, obs. var. of EAST.

est, var. of ESTE, *Obs.*, delight, favour.

-est, *suffix*, forming the superl. deg. of adjs. and advbs., represents two forms originally distinct: (1) OE. *-ost-*, *-ust-*, *-ast-*, corresp. to OFris., ON. *-ast-*, OS., OHG., Goth. *-ôst-*:—OTeut. *-ôsto-*; (2) OE. *-est-*, *-st-*, with umlaut, corresp. to OFris., OS., OHG., Goth. *-isto-*:—OTeut. *-isto-*. These OTeut. suffixes are combinations of the two comparative suffixes *-ôz-*, *-iz-* with OAryan *-to-*; similar formations in other Aryan langs. are Gr. -ιστο-, Skr. *ishtha-*. In OE. the two suffixes were already confused, so that *-ost-* occasionally appears with umlaut of the root-vowel, and conversely *-est-* without umlaut; a few umlaut forms survived into early ME., as *lengeste* longest; the only examples now remaining are *best*, *eldest*. In OE. (as in Gothic) the suffix *-isto-* was added to the stems of certain older superlatives formed with the suffix *-m-*; the resulting OE. ending *-mest-* was in later Eng. confused with the adv. *most*: cf. *forma*, *fyrmest*, *foremost*; *innema*, *innemest*, *inmost*: see -MOST. (For the relation in historical and present usage between the inflexional comparison in *-er*, *-est*, and the periphrastic comparison with the advbs. *more*, *most*: see -ER[3].)

†**e'stable**, *v. Obs.* Also 6 astable, -bill, estabill. [ad. F. *establ-ir* (mod.F. *établir*) = Pr. *establir*, *stablir*, It. *stabilire*:—L. *stabilīre*, f. *stabilis* STABLE *a.* See also STABLE *v.*] *trans.* = ESTABLISH in various senses. To make stable; to settle, fix permanently; to secure, confirm; to decree; to make steady, support, calm (the mind).

[**1377** LANGL. *P. Pl.* B. I. 120 God of his goodnesse gan stable..þe heuene.] *c* **1386** CHAUCER *Melib.* ¶102 Be it so that youre emprise be establid and ordeyned by gret multitude of people. **1481** CAXTON *Myrr.* I. i. 7 He [God] is establed without ony meuyng. **1496–7** *Act 12 Hen. VII*, c. 8 §1 The Kynge..enactith, ordeyneth and estableth that, etc. *c* **1510** BARCLAY *Mirr. Good Mann.* (1570) D. iij, This answere besemed..a man establed in magnanimitie. **1513** DOUGLAS *Æneis* X. iv. 74 To comfort and astabill Hys hevy amorus thochtis ennoyus. *Ibid.* XIII. vi. 36 Thair myndis mesys and estabillis he. **1533** BELLENDEN *Livy* I. xvi. (1822) 74 Quhill he micht, under his name, etabill the kingdome of Romanis to him.

establish (ɪ'stæblɪʃ), *v.* Forms: 4 **establisse-n**, 5 **astabilishe, establisch, -ysch, -issh**, 6 **astablese, establyshe**, 4- **establish**. See also STABLISH. [ME. *establisse-n*, a. OF. *establiss-* lengthened stem of *establir*: see prec.]

1. To render stable or firm. †**a.** To strengthen by material support (*obs.*). †**b.** To ratify, confirm, validate (*obs.*). **c.** To confirm, settle (what is weak or wavering); to restore (health) permanently; to give calmness or steadiness to (the mind). †**d.** *catachr.* To calm (anger), to settle (doubts).

[**1375** BARBOUR *Bruce* X. 303 His land first [weill] stablist he.] **1477** EARL RIVERS (Caxton) *Dictes* 10 a, Establisshe and ease thyn ire with thy pacience. **1524** CDL. WOLSEY in Strype *Eccl. Mem.* I. iv. 53 This small number of halbardiers were appointed..to establish every captain of your archers. **1533** FRITH *Answ. More* 34 b, I shall establyshe his wordes by S. Austen. **1537** in Wright *Monast. Lett.* 154 To conferme, ratefie and astabilishe this my deyd [of surrender of Furness Abbey]. **1558** KENNEDY *Compend. Tract.* in *Wodr. Soc. Misc.* (1844) 108 The onelie jugis appoyntit be God, to establische all doutis. **1611** BIBLE *Numb.* xxx. 13 Euery vow..her husband may establish it, or her husband may make it voyd. —— *Rom.* iii. 31 Doe we then make void the lawe through faith? God forbid; yea, we establish the Law. **1623** J. WINTHROP *Let.* in *Hist. New Eng.* (1853) I. 407, I pray continually, that God will please to establish your heart. **1664** EVELYN *Kal. Hort.* (1729) 211 Supports, Cradles, Canes or Hoofs, to establish them [Carnations, etc.] against Winds. **1708** *Lond. Gaz.* No. 4439/2 The great Pensioner's Health seems to be Establish'd. **1815** JANE AUSTEN *Emma* I. viii. 56 Harriet's cheerful look and manner established hers.

2. a. To fix, settle, institute or ordain permanently, by enactment or agreement. Sometimes with obj. clause. †Also (rarely) to impose (something) *upon*.

c **1374** CHAUCER *Boeth.* I. iv. 311 Coempcioun þat is to seyn commun achat or bying to-gidere þat were establissed vpon poeple by swiche a manere imposicioun as, etc. *c* **1386** —— *Parson's T.* ¶155 The peynes that been establissed and ordeyned for synne. **1588** A. KING tr. *Canisius' Catech.* H v b, Yᵉ beginning of yᵉ monethes was swa astablesed. **1611** BIBLE *Gen.* ix. 9 And I, behold, I establish my couenant with you. **1660** CHAS. II. *Declar. Eccl. Affairs* in Cobbett *Parl. Hist.* (1808) IV. 139 We shall use our best endeavour that such laws may be established, as may best provide for the peace of the church and state. **1700–1** *Act Settlement* 12–13 *Will. III*, c. 2. §2 Subject to such Incapacities, as.. are by the said recited Act provided, enacted, and established. *a* **1714** SHARP *Wks.* I. vi. 177 The standing public methods which God hath established in the church. **1793** SMEATON *Edystone L.* §283 Having first established, that they should quit the work at nights. **1801** STRUTT *Sports & Past.* Introd. 42 This edict was established, for the regulation of the Christian army..during the Crusade. **1884** GLADSTONE in *Standard* 29 Feb. 2/6 We establish in Irish counties, as in Scotch and English counties..the lodger franchise.

†**b.** To secure or settle (property, privileges, etc.) *to* or *upon* persons. *Obs.*

c **1460** FORTESCUE *Abs. & Lim. Mon.* (1714) 139 To establisch..the same Lyvelood to his Crowne. **1605** SHAKS. *Macb.* I. iv. 37 We will establish our estate upon Our eldest Malcolm. **1665** WALTON *Life Hooker* 33 Destroying what was by those known laws happily establisht to them and their posterity.

†**c.** To impute (guilt) *to*. *Obs.* [Cf. 'ne statuas illis hoc peccatum,' *Acts* vii. 30 in Vulgate.]

1483 CAXTON *Gold. Leg.* 99/1 He cryed with an hye voys and said 'lord establysshe not to theym thys synne'.

3. To set up on a secure or permanent basis; to found (a government, an institution; in mod. use often, a house of business).

c **1460** FORTESCUE *Abs. & Lim. Mon.* (1714) 103 It schal be good that an honorable..Conceile be establischid. **1509** HAWES *Past. Pleas.* (1554) XXVII. I. xxi, Knighthode, he sayed, was first established The commen wealthe in right to defende. **1670** TEMPLE *Let.* in *Wks.* (1731) III. 227 A Government is never well established but in the Hearts of the Subjects. **1863** P. BARRY *Dockyard Econ.* xii. 261 The manufactory of Messrs. —— was first established towards the end of the last century. **1867** SMILES *Huguenots Eng.* xi. (1880) 183 They succeeded in establishing many important and highly flourishing colonies. **1867** FREEMAN *Norm. Conq.* (1876) I. vi. 433 The throne of Cnut, established by wasting wars.

4. a. To place in a secure or permanent position; to install and secure in a possession, office, dignity, etc.; to 'set up' (a person, oneself) in business; to settle (a person) in or at a place; *refl.* to obtain a secure footing; also in weaker sense, to take up one's quarters. †Also *intr.* for *refl.* To 'settle'.

1557 *Order Hospitalls* B v, To deliuer unto such [Bedells] as then remayne, their Staves, and again astablishe them. **1601** SHAKS. *Jul. C.* I. iii. 86 The senators to-morrow Mean to establish Cæsar as a king. **1677** *Govt. Venice* 102 Since the Turks established in Europe. **1770** LANGHORNE *Plutarch* (1879) I. 73/2 Numa..with a view to establish himself in the people's good graces..attempted to soften them. **1793** SMEATON *Edystone L.* §298 The workmen being established in the house..every one went to the occupation allotted. **1815** *Scribbleomania* 96 If a writer be desirous of establishing himself as a candid censor of literature. **1840** THIRLWALL *Greece* VII. lvii. 205 His first object was to establish Eumenes in his satrapy. **1867** LADY HERBERT *Cradle L.* iii. 92 The gentlemen of the party..established themselves in very comfortable rooms. **1874** GREEN *Short Hist.* ii. 83 The Jewish traders..were enabled by the royal protection to establish themselves in separate quarters.

†**b.** To provide for the maintenance of (persons). *Obs.* Cf. *settle*.

1644 CHAS. I. in Clarendon *Hist. Reb.* VIII. (1843) 514/1 [He appointed them] to consider..in what manner his family should be established. **1872** H. LAWRENNY in *Fortn. Rev.* Mar. 313 Heads of families ceased..to dower and 'establish' the daughters of the house.

5. a. To set up or bring about permanently (a state of things); to 'create' (a precedent); to introduce and secure permanent acceptance for (a custom, a belief). Also, to secure for oneself, gain permanently (a reputation, a position).

1597 SHAKS. *2 Hen. IV*, IV. i. 86 But to establish here a peace indeed. **1814** *Stock Exchange Laid Open* 5 It establishes a price in the market. **1826** F. COOPER *Mohicans* ii, The most confirmed gait that he could establish was a Canterbury gallop with the hind legs. *a* **1832** MACKINTOSH *Causes Revolution* Wks. 1846 II. 164 He had established, by his own sole authority, the most unbounded liberty of worship. **1861** TULLOCH *Eng. Purit.* ii. 177 In the remaining years of Milton's academic career, he established a high reputation for scholarship. **1865** DICKENS *Mut. Fr.* I. vi, It has been hard work to establish order here. **1885** *Manch. Exam.* 13 July 5/3 The French troops have pretty well established their ascendency in the capital.

b. To erect *into* (a rule, etc.). †Also (with *complement*), to secure in a certain condition.

1795 T. JEFFERSON *Writ.* (1859) IV. 113 Emergencies which threatened our country with slavery, but ended in establishing it free. **1855** J. S. C. ABBOT *Napoleon* II. i. 17 If such a tyranny is allowed to be established into a principle, etc.

c. *Card-playing.* ***to establish a suit*** (see quot.).

1862 'CAVENDISH' *Whist* (1879) 56 Twos and threes may become quite as valuable [as higher cards] when the suit is established. **1876** A. CAMPBELL-WALKER *Correct Card* Gloss. 11 A suit is said to be established when you have exhausted all the best cards in it which were against you.

d. *Cinemat.*, etc. To introduce and secure the identity or position of (a character, set, etc.).

1948, etc. [see ESTABLISHING *ppl. a.*]. **1960** O. SKILBECK *Film & TV Working Terms* 48 Artists, or items in sets, are said to be established once they have been photographed. From then on, their positions must be held. **1962** A. NISBETT *Technique Sound Studio* 252 *Establishing an effect.* Allowing it sufficient time (and volume, which may be greater than that subsequently used) for it to register in the listener's mind. **1966** *Listener* 22 Sept. 426/3 Lillian Hellman's screenplay..deserves credit for the swiftly efficient manner in which the numerous main characters are established.

6. a. To place beyond dispute; to prove (a proposition, claim, accusation); rarely with personal obj. and complement.

a **1704** T. BROWN *Sat. Antients* Wks. 1730 I. 21 He has establish'd..five or six essential differences between those two poems. **1767** GOOCH *Treat. Wounds* I. 134 This doctrine Cæsar Magatus and Belloste have taken great pains to establish. **1802** MAR. EDGEWORTH *Moral T.* (1816) I. 224 If he fail to establish in your minds the innocence of the count. **1867** FREEMAN *Norm. Conq.* (1876) I. App. 659 His great point he seems to me fully to establish. **1873** BROWNING *Red. Cott. Nt.-cap* 266 Some better theory Than would establish him participant In doings yonder. **1885** SIR C. P. BUTT in *Law Times Rep.* LIII. 61/1 It is..extremely difficult to establish a case of negligence against the steamer.

b. To affirm judicially the validity of (a disputed will).

1818 CRUISE *Digest.* (ed. 2) VI. 311 Upon a bill to establish this will..Sir Joseph Jekyll declared that, etc.

7. From 16th c. often used with reference to ecclesiastical ceremonies or organization, and to the recognized national church or its religion; in early use chiefly *pass.* in sense 2 (esp. in phrase ***by law established***, i.e. 'prescribed or settled by law'), but sometimes with mixture of senses 3–5. Hence in recent use: To place (a church or a religious body) in the position of a national or state church.

1558 *Act 1 Eliz.* c. 2. §27 Laws wherein..any other service is limited, established, or set forth to be used within this realm. **1592** *Sc. Acts 12 Parl. Jas. VI*, §114 The trew and halie Kirk, presentlie established within this Realme. **1642** *King's Protest.* 19 Sept. in Rushw. *Hist. Coll.* (1721) V 21, I will..defend and maintain The True Reformed Protestant Religion established in the Church of England. **1660** CHAS. II *Declar. Eccl. Affairs* 25 Oct. 8 The..esteem we have for the Church of England, as it is established by Law. **1731** CALAMY *Life* (1830) I. i. 73 Opposition to the church by law established. **1731** SWIFT *Presbyterian's Plea Merit* Wks. 1776 IV. 260 Which [Presbyterian] sect was..established in all its forms by..an ordinance of the lords and commons. **1838** GLADSTONE *State in Rel. Ch.* 108 What is established is by the very force of the term likewise endowed.

e'stablishable, *a.* [f. prec. + -ABLE.] That can be established or made secure.

1667 WATERHOUSE *Fire Lond.* 115 Establishable against a relapse only from him. **1918** E. HOLLOWAY in W. P. Trent et al. *Hist. Amer. Lit.* II. III. i. 259 The facts of his biography which are well established or establishable. **1940** W. FAULKNER *Hamlet* I. iii. 48 A thick squat soft man of no establishable age between twenty and thirty. **1964** R. H. ROBINS *Gen. Linguistics* v. 194 They are equally well establishable in unwritten languages.

established (ɪ'stæblɪʃt), *ppl. a.* [f. as prec. + -ED[1].] In senses of the vb. ***Established Church***: see CHURCH 5 c, and ESTABLISH *v.* 7. ***established clerk***, ***servant***, etc.: one on the 'establishment', in permanent employ. ***established list***, the list of those in permanent employ.

1642 T. LECHFORD (*title*) Plain Dealing..A short view of New-Englands present Government..compared with the ..Established Government of England. **1672–5** COMBER *Comp. Temple* (1702) 81 All Establisht Protestant Churches do approve, and use prescribed Forms. **1682** CLAVERHOUSE in M. Morris *Life* vi. (1888) 93 [The king] was relenting nothing of his..care of maintaining the established government. **1753** SMART *Power Supreme Being* (R.), Rul'd by establish'd laws and current nature. **1790** BURKE *Fr. Rev.* 135 We are resolved to keep an established church, an established monarchy, an established aristocracy, and an established democracy. **1824** L. MURRAY *Eng. Gram.* (ed. 5) I. 5 They respect some of the established principles and arrangements of the language. **1849** RUSKIN *Sev. Lamps* vii. 186 The architecture of a nation is great only when it is as universal and as established as its language. **1865** EARLE *Sax. Chron.* Notes 340 One of the established sensation scenes of history. **1888** *Pall Mall G.* 25 April 10/2 A return of the number of established and unestablished servants [in the Post Office.]

establisher (ɪ'stæblɪʃə(r)). [f. as prec. + -ER[1].] One who establishes (in senses of vb.).

a **1600** HOOKER *Eccl. Pol.* (1617) 613 The first founders and establishers of them. *a* **1677** BARROW Wks. (1741) II. xx. 215 God being the author and establisher of nature. **1812** *Examiner* 14 Sept. 577/2 Luck..was the establisher of his greatness. **1824–9** LANDOR *Imag. Conv.* (1846) I. 93 That the *foudre* is rather a destroyer than an establisher.

establishing (ɪˈstæblɪʃɪŋ), *vbl. sb.* [f. as prec. + -ING¹.] The action of the vb. ESTABLISH in its various senses.

c **1400** *Rom. Rose* 6371 No prelate may done so, But it the pope be..That made thilk establisshing. **1413** LYDG. *Pilgr. Sowle* IV. xxx. (1483) 80 In the election and establysshynge of chyuetayns ther may be founden errour. **1660** MILTON *Free Commw.* 451 When we have our Forces..in our hands, to the firm establishing of a Free Common-wealth. **1846** TRENCH *Mirac.* vi. (1862) 188 The words are for the establishing of his trembling faith.

eˈstablishing, *ppl. a.* [f. as prec. + -ING².] That establishes; sustaining, supporting; *spec.* (*Cinemat.*) in ***establishing shot.*** (Cf. ESTABLISH *v.* 5 d.)

1667 FLAVEL *Saint Indeed* (1754) 52 This heart reviving and establishing doctrine of the dominion of our Father. **1948** E. LINDGREN *Art of Film* 205 *Establishing shot*, long shot introduced at the beginning of a scene to establish the inter-relationship of details to be shown subsequently in nearer shots. **1953** K. REISZ *Technique Film Editing* 280 *Establishing shot*, shot (usually long shot) used near the beginning of a scene to establish the inter-relationship of details to be shown subsequently in nearer shots. **1959** W. S. SHARPS *Dict. Cinemat.* 94/1 *Establishing shot.* This is usually a long shot for establishing a mood or location and so tying together the separate parts of the scene or sequence. **1961** J. MCCABE *Laurel & Hardy* (1962) viii. 159 Some idiotic fool comes along and cuts the film up... Continuity, establishing shots—most of them gone. The pictures just don't make sense on television. **1962** *Listener* 13 Dec. 1025/1 Most of the blame must attach to the director..whose long establishing tours..managed to create an edgy tedium without ever really conveying the curious characteristic atmosphere.

establishment (ɪˈstæblɪʃmənt). [f. as prec. + -MENT. Cf. OF. *establissement* (late AF. *establisement*), Fr. *établissement*.]

I. Action or means of establishing.

1. The action of establishing; the fact of being established: in various senses of the vb.

1596 J. NORDEN *Progr. Pietie* (1847) 117 An establishment of concord amongst ourselves [is] to be sought and heartily prayed for. **1688** *Col. Rec. Penn.* I. 226 That such Sanction and Establishment may be as Effectual and binding as any Law. **1739** BUTLER *Serm.* Wks. (1874) II. 225 The bare establishment of Christianity in any place..is a very important and valuable effect. **1788** W. GORDON (*title*) The History of the rise, progress and establishment of the United States of America. **1851** D. WILSON *Preh. Ann.* (1863) II. IV. i. 192 The establishment of Christianity in Scotland. **1871** *Figure Training* 38 A most awkward and clumsy figure is in a fair way towards formation and permanency of establishment. **1875** FORTNUM *Maiolica* 37 The establishment of the ducal court at Urbino.

2. *esp.* The 'establishing' by law (a church, religion, form of worship). (See ESTABLISH *v.* 7.) †**a.** In early use, the settling or ordering in a particular manner, the regulating and upholding of the constitution and ordinances of the church recognized by the state. †**b.** In 17th–18th c. occasionally the granting of legal status to (other religious bodies than that connected with the state). **c.** Now usually, the conferring on a particular religious body the position of a state church.

a. 1640–1 LD. DIGBY *Sp.* in Rushw. *Hist. Coll.* (1721) IV. 172 A Man..that made the Establishment by Law the Measure of his Religion. **1706–7** *Act 5 Anne* c. 5 *Securing Ch. Eng.*, Acts of Parliament now in Force for the Establishment and Preservation of the Church of England.

b. 1731 E. CALAMY *Life* (1830) I. v. 401 The allowance of the law is of necessity a sufficient establishment [of dissenting worship]. **1792** COKE & MOORE *Life Wesley* II. iv. (ed. 2) 355 Mr. Wesley's great desire to remain in union with the Church of England..would not allow him to apply for a legal establishment.

c. 1662–3 *Addr. of Commons to King* 27 Feb. in Cobbett *Parl. Hist.* (1808) IV. 262 In time, some prevalent sect will ..contend for an establishment. **1788** PRIESTLEY *Lect. Hist.* v. lvii. 449 There is no place where there are more forms of religion openly professed, and without the establishment of any of them than Pennsylvania. **1792** BURKE *Let. Sir H. Langrishe* Wks. VI. 318 The perpetual establishment of the confession of Faith, and the Presbyterian church government. **1813** MRQ. LANSDOWNE in *Ho. Lords* 8 Mar., They [Catholic Petitioners of City of Limerick] asked for no establishment of their own Church. *a* **1832** MACKINTOSH *Causes Revol.* Wks. 1846 II. 227 Toleration..was sometimes sought by Dissenters as a step to-wards establishment. **1886** EARL SELBORNE *Def. Ch. Eng.* I. iv. 77 All such relations of the Church to the State as those which are summed up in the term 'Establishment'.

†**3. a.** Established or stable condition; settlement, permanence; also, settled condition of mind, calmness, confidence. *Obs.*

1561 T. NORTON *Calvin's Inst.* I. 15 For it is merueilous, how great establishment groweth hereof. **1641** J. JACKSON *True Evang. T.* III. 228 A succession of three good Princes together doth notably contribute to establishment, and felicity of a Kingdome. *a* **1674** CLARENDON *Hist. Reb.* XVI. (1704) III. 603 If God shall be pleased to add Establishment and Perpetuity to the Blessings he then Restored. **1674** OWEN *Holy Spirit* (1693) 69 Our Permanency and Establishment in the Truth. **1777** PRIESTLEY *Mart. & Spir.* (1782) I. Introd. 6 Truth will..gain a firm establishment in the minds of all men.

†**b.** Manner in which anything is established; organization, 'footing'. *Obs.*

1799 WELLINGTON in Owen *Disp.* 106 The improved establishment on which he had placed their garrisons.

†**4.** A means of establishing; something that strengthens, supports, or corroborates. *Obs.*

1561 T. NORTON *Calvin's Inst.* I. 17 So many and so notable miracles..are euen as many establishments of the law. **1581** MARBECK *Bk. of Notes* 210 Truth is the piller and establishment of the church. **1646** SIR T. BROWNE *Pseud. Ep.* III. xx. 155 Their hornes..being a weake and hollow body, require some inward establishment, to confirme the length of their advancement.

5. a. Settlement in life; formerly often (now rarely) in the sense of marriage.

1684 PRIDEAUX *Lett.* 12 Nov. (1875) 138, I..wish with that you had all the other satisfactions you can desire, especially a good establishment in England. **1734** tr. *Rollin's Anc. Hist.* IV. IX. 345 You owe..to them, birth, nurture, education and establishment. **1769** ROBERTSON *Chas. V*, III. XI. 365 To acquire an establishment of such dignity and value for one of his sons. **1800** MRS. HERVEY *Mourtray Fam.* I. iii. 259 Her chief solicitude was to procure an affluent establishment for her daughter. **1815** JANE AUSTEN *Emma* II. vi. 173 Whenever he were attached, he would willingly give up much wealth to obtain an early establishment. **1825** LYTTON *Falkland* 16, I saw in the notes of the mothers their anxiety for the establishment of their daughters.

b. Settled income, provision for a livelihood.

1727 SWIFT *Gulliver's Travels* (1731) 104 His Excellency, who had the sole Disposal of the Emperor's Revenue, might easily provide by gradually lessening your establishment. **1776** GIBBON *Decl. & F.* I. xviii. 484 For each of these princes a suitable establishment was provided. **1776** COWPER *Wks.* (1837) XV. 34 It will afford me some sort of an establishment, at least for a time. **1832** HT. MARTINEAU *Life in Wilds* vii. 94 Providing a permanent establishment for the captain as their chief magistrate.

6. ***establishment of a port*** [Fr. *établissement d'un port*]: (see quot.).

1833 HERSCHEL *Astron.* xi. 337 That deviation of the time of high and low water at any port or harbour, from the culmination of the luminaries..which is called the 'establishment' of that port. **1875** BEDFORD *Sailor's Pocket-bk.* v. (ed. 2) 168 The time of high water at any particular place is the same on the days both of New and Full Moon, and is termed the 'Establishment of the Port'. **1886** GODFRAY *Astron.* App. (ed. 4) 200 The interval between the instant of the moon's transit across the meridian on the day of new or full moon, and the subsequent high water, is called the vulgar establishment of the port.

II. Something that is established.

†**7. a.** A settled arrangement; a settled constitution or government. Also, a legal enactment. *Obs.*

1481 CAXTON *Godfrey* (E.E.T.S.) 42 Helde a counseyl..of the prelates of ytalye at playsance, where he made.. establischemens tamende the maners of the Clergye. **1596** SPENSER *State Irel.* (J.), Bring in that establishment by which all men should be contained in duty. **1605** VERSTEGAN *Dec. Intell.* iii. (1628) 63 Aduanced to the honourable titles of Earles and Lords, with Establishment for the continuall remaining of these titles. *a* **1655** VINES *Lord's Supp.* (1677) 418 Not that I would encourage any man to break a wholsom order or establishment. **1714** *Fr. Bk. of Rates* 5 That so much talk'd of Establishment, call'd the Tariff of 1664. **1793** SMEATON *Edystone L.* §134 Our establishment respecting seamen was as follows.

b. *spec.* in Fr. Hist. (transl. of Fr. *établissement*).

1818 HALLAM *Mid. Ages* (1872) I. 244 When St. Louis enacted that great code which bears the name of his Establishments. **1873** G. W. KITCHIN *Hist. France* I. III. viii. 343 The royal 'Establishments' or codes of law.

†**c.** The 'estimates' for public expenditure. *Obs.*

1672 EARL ESSEX in *Essex Papers* 31 Aug., Upon the closing of the Establishment for this Kingdome [Ireland], five hundred Pounds a year were reserved with intention that if I should find cause to move the King in behalf of this City of Dublyn, it should be restored to them agen..I desire that I may have an order to insert them [the £500] into the Establishment.

8. a. The ecclesiastical system established by law; more fully ***Church Establishment.*** Hence ***the Establishment*** often occurs as a distinctive name for the established church (esp. of England, Scotland, formerly Ireland), in contradistinction to the non-established churches or sects.

[**1667** J. CORBET *Disc. Relig. Eng.* 28 The Setling of a Nation may be made up of an Establishment, a Limited Toleration, and a Discreet Connivence, etc.] **1731** E. CALAMY *Life* (1830) I. v. 469 There was a variety of sentiments amongst those out of the Establishment, as well as those under it. **1786** W. PITT in Ld. Stanhope *Life* (1879) I. 252 It is certainly a delicate thing to meddle with the Church Establishment in the present situation of Ireland. **1795** J. AIKIN *Manchester* 241 Chaderton came a chapel of the establishment. **1806–31** A. KNOX *Rem.* (1844) I. 93 These teachers have generally been found..within Establishments. **1824** SYD. SMITH *Wks.* (1859) II. 51/1 America..has no Establishment. **1829** GEN. P. THOMPSON *Exerc.* (1842) I. 22 Half the people in England dislike the church establishment. **1869** *Times Ann. Summary* 306 The Irish Church Establishment has been abolished.

b. Esp. as ***the Establishment***: a social group exercising power generally, or within a given field or institution, by virtue of its traditional superiority, and by the use esp. of tacit understandings and often a common mode of speech, and having as a general interest the maintenance of the *status quo.* Also *attrib.* Hence ***establishment-ˈminded*** adj., ***-ˈminded-ness.*** Cf. *anti-Establishment* (ANTI-¹ 4).

Quot. 1955 is the *locus classicus* for this modern sense though occasional earlier uses are recorded.

1923 R. MACAULAY *Told by an Idiot* II. xiv. 117 The moderns of one day become the safe establishments of the next. **1936** H. PEARSON *Labby* x. 260 They spoke the common language, the Esperanto, of the Establishment. **1945** D. GOLDRING *Nineteen Twenties* I. viii. 110 It was a head-on collision between two acknowledged leaders of the literary avant-garde and the powerful forces of what Ford Madox Ford used to call the Establishment. **1955** H. FAIRLIE in *Spectator* 23 Sept. 380/1 By the 'Establishment' I do not mean only the centres of official power—though they are certainly part of it—but rather the whole matrix of official and social relations within which power is exercised. **1957** LD. ALTRINCHAM in *National & Eng. Rev.* Sept. 108/2 He delivered his well-known attack on 'the Establishment', a term generally taken to denote those elements in society and politics which are self-satisfied and opposed to all radical change. **1958** *Times Lit. Suppl.* 17 Jan. 26/3 Sir Maurice Bowra, in his dexterous résumé of what might be called the Establishment view of the ancient Greek world. **1958** *Listener* 6 Nov. 716/1 In Russia, Mr. Khrushchev has been trying with some success to shake up an ossified Communist Establishment. **1958** C. P. SNOW *Conscience of Rich* xxxiv. 254 'That gang' meant the people who had the real power, the rulers, the establishment. **1959** *Encounter* Dec. 57/1 The charge of being Establishment-minded. **1959** C. HOLLIS in H. Thomas *Establishment* 181 The power of the Establishment..comes..from the fact that there is in all of us a degree of establishment-mindedness—that we feel it right that the opinions of such persons should have attention paid to them. **1962** *Listener* 8 Feb. 269/1 Always ready for a dig at the musical establishment. **1969** *Mind* LXXVIII. 26 Where scepticism is thorough and pervasive it is usually directed against some entrenched intellectual Establishment. **1969** *Oz* May 19/1 The Establishment is IBM, Xerox, the Kennedys, the London and New York Times, Harvard University, LSE, the Courts.

9. a. An organized body of men, maintained at the expense of the sovereign or of the state for a specific purpose; *orig.* said of the military service, but applied also to the naval and civil. **b.** The quota of officers and men in a regiment, ship, etc., complement. Also in ***peace, war establishment***; cf. 3 b.

1689 LUTTRELL *Brief Rel.* (1857) I. 518 What forces shall be sent to the Low Countries..shall be continued in English pay, and on the English establishment. **1796** MORSE *Amer. Geog.* I. 266 The support of the civil, military and naval establishments. **1800** DUNDAS in Owen *Wellesley's Disp.* 558 The establishment does not seem to have exceeded eighty thousand men. **1828** J. M. SPEARMAN *Brit. Gunner* (ed. 2) 69 The usual establishment of officers for ships of the same class. **1848** MACAULAY *Hist. Eng.* I. 295 These gallant brigades..had been placed on the English establishment. **1853** STOCQUELER *Mil. Encycl.*, *Peace Establishment* is the reduced condition of an army suited to a time of peace. *War Establishment* is the augmentation of regiments to a certain number..to meet war exigencies. **1884** *Pall Mall G.* 12 Sept. 10/2 Lieutenant-Colonel —— formerly H.E.I.C.S., Bengal establishment.

10. An organized staff of employés or servants, often including, and sometimes limited to, the building in which they are located: **a.** A public institution, a school, factory, house of business, etc.

establishment hand (colloq. *stab hand*): among printers, an employé on weekly wages as distinguished from one on piece-work.

1832 G. DOWNES *Lett. Cont. Countries* I. 188, I now perceived..the high road passed close to the establishment [Pestalozzi's schools]. **1838** DICKENS *Nich. Nick.* iv, We don't consider the boys' appetites at our establishment. **1842** BISCHOFF *Woollen Manuf.* II. 33 The British manufacturers..have been compelled to seek markets, and form establishments in..the most distant parts of the globe. **1845** STOCQUELER *Hand-bk. Brit. India* (1854) 74 Of these establishments the Bishop's College Press, at Calcutta, unquestionably stands at the head. **1851** D. WILSON *Preh. Ann.* (1863) II. IV. i. 192 The religious establishment founded at Iona. **1873** *Act 36 & 37 Vict.* c. 76. §6 The.. insufficiency of the establishment for working such railway.

b. A household; a family residence.

separate establishment: a phrase often used when it is indicated that a married man maintains a paramour.

1803 *Mod. Paris*, Two or three families long connected with mine, have still establishments here. **1828** D'ISRAELI *Chas. I*, II. i. 3 Even long after this period, the poverty of the royal establishment was observed. **1856** FROUDE *Hist. Eng.* (1858) II. vii. 174 Her establishment was broken up, and she was sent to reside..in the household of the Princess Elizabeth. **1862** TROLLOPE *Orley F.* i, His wealth would have entitled him to the enjoyment of a larger establishment. *a* **1891** *Mod. Newspaper*, Everybody but his wife seems to have known that he had a separate establishment.

establishmentarian (ɪˌstæblɪʃmənˈtɛərɪən), *a.* and *sb.* [f. prec. + *-arian*.]

A. *adj.*

1. a. Advocating the principle of an established church; characteristic of those who advocate this principle. **b.** That adheres to or favours a church for the reason that it is established.

1847 *Ecclesiologist* VII. 173 The old establishmentarian leaven is not worked out, far from it. **1858** *Sat. Rev.* V. 387/1 The analogous form of this faith..has taken an Erastian and Establishmentarian turn. **1875** GLADSTONE *Glean.* VI. lv. 171 The prosecutors..are strongly (to use a barbarous word) establishmentarian. **1878** G. A. DENISON *Notes of My Life* (ed. 2) 79 The Church Corporate cannot be said to be in substance other than Establishmentarian.

2. Belonging to the Established Church.

1849 *Fraser's Mag.* XXXIX. 128 Children of Methodist, Baptist..and Establishmentarian parents.

B. *sb.* One who supports the principle of an 'Establishment' or an Established Church. Also, an adherent of the Established Church.

1846 Hook *Educ. People* 37 Those who, like myself, are called High Churchmen, have little or no sympathy with mere Establishmentarians. **1862** *Sat. Rev.* XIV. 417/2 They [Baptists and Independents] were all generally Establishmentarians; but they could make no other claim to be established than that of numbers and power. **1879** *Daily News* 28 June 6/1 The Nonconformists have made inroads on the ranks of the Establishmentarians.

Hence **establishmen'tarianism**, the tenets of an establishmentarian; attachment to the principle of a State Church.

1873 F. Hall *Mod. Eng.* 44 Establishmentarianism was wont to roll over the prelatial [Abp. Trench's] tongue. **1876** *Tinsley's Mag.* XVIII. 386 The days of Establishmentarianism would be numbered.

e'stablishmentism. [f. ESTABLISHMENT + -ISM.] The principle of a State Church.

1851 J. H. Newman *Cath. in Eng.* 54 Establishmentism is the very life of Protestantism.

‖**esta'cade.** *Mil.* Also 8 erron. estocade. [Fr., ad. Sp. *estacada*, f. *estaca* stake; sense 2 arises from a confusion with It. *steccata* (which has this sense), f. *stecca* lath.]

1. A dike constructed of piles in the sea, a river, or a morass, to check the approach of an enemy. Cf. STOCKADE.

1663 Gerbier *Counsel* C viij b, The Town had held out till the Sea overturned the Ditch and the Estacade. **1755** Carte *Hist. Eng.* IV. 194 Beyond that a third of ships sunk forming an estocade. **1777** Watson *Philip II* (1793) II. xiii. 171/2 He formed in the most shallow parts an estacade, a work of prodigious labour. **1847** in Craig.

b. An arrangement of stakes for defence.

1827 Southey *Penins. War* II. 715 The Spaniards made every exertion to defend it [a breach in the Baluarte del Rey] with sacks of earth, estacades, and whatever other obstacles they could oppose to the enemy.

2. A raft made of balks of timber, fastened together with chains, used to block up a channel or harbour-mouth.

1670 Cotton *Espernon* II. viii. 393 He propounded..a Machine, which was an Estacade, or kind of floating Fort.

‖**esta'cado.** *rare*⁻¹. [see -ADO.] = prec.

1810 tr. *Le Moniteur* in *Naval Chron.* XXIII. 137 An estacado has been established, which secured our gunboats from fire-ships.

‖**estafette** (ɛstafɛt). [Fr. *estafette*, ad. It. *staffetta*, dim. of *staffa* stirrup, f. OHG. *stapho* step.] A mounted courier.

1792 Boothby *Burke's App. Whigs* 84 *note*, An estafette was despatched on the part of our Ministers at the Hague, requiring Marshal Bender to suspend his march. **1812** Wellington in Gurw. *Disp.* VIII. 649 They can secure the services of the Estafette..only by placing him in the centre of the escort. **1858** Carlyle *Fredk. Gt.* (1865) II. v. ii. 77 Diplomatic correspondence, carried once by breathless estaffettes.

Hence **esta'fetted** *ppl. a.*, provided with estafettes; in quot. app. taken as 'provided with arrangements for posting'.

1837 Palgrave *Merch & Friar* (1844) 18 The best estafetted road, the road to Rome.

estait, Sc. form of ESTATE.

†**'estal**, *sb. Obs. rare*⁻¹. [a. OF. *estal* (mod. Fr. *étal*), corresp. to Pr. *estal*, OSp. *estalo*, It. *stallo*, ad. OHG. *stal.* Cf. STALL.] A place post.

1480 Caxton *Ovid's Met.* xiii. ii, None..durst hold, ayenst the noble Hector, ony estal.

†**e'stale**, *v. Obs.* In 5 astale. [ad. OF. *estaler* (mod.Fr. *étaler*) to display.] *trans.* To bespread, to hang (with drapery).

c **1440** *Gaw. & Gol.* v, Syne hynt to ane hie hall, That was astalit with pall.

†**e'stall**, *v. Obs.* Also STALL. [app. ad. OF. *estaler* to place, fix; cf. INSTALL.] *trans.* To arrange the payment of (a debt, sum of money) by instalments. Hence **e'stallment** (see quot.; also STALMENT).

1577–87 Holinshed *Chron.* III. 1142/2 That debt is estalled, and is according to that estallment trulie answered. **1643** *Sc. Acts* (1814) VI. 38/1 Some wther way how satisfactioune..may be made..by estalment at four equall payments. **1738** *Hist. Crt. Excheq.* v. 100 An Estallment, which is an Assizing or Establishing the Times of Payments of such Debtors.

estamin ('ɛstəmɪn). Also 8 **estemine, estamina**, 9 **estamene** (see below). See also ETAMINE. [a. Fr. *estamine* (now *étamine*), corresp. to Sp. *estameña*, Pg. *estamenha*, It. *stamigna*:—late L. **stāminia*, L. *stāminea*, fem. of *stāmineus* made of thread, f. *stāmen* warp, thread. The form *estamina* is perh. a. Sp.]

An open woollen fabric, used for making sieves, etc.; see quot. 1883. In 18th c. also applied to some silk fabric, presumably of similar texture. Also spelt **estamene**, as the name of a woollen cloth for dresses.

1701 *Lond. Gaz.* No. 3701/4 All sorts of Mercery Goods, viz... Estemines, Russels..Rashes..Antharines..will be sold by Auction. **1750** Beawes *Lex. Mercat.* (1752) 693 Woollens, such as Estaminas, Druggets, Serges, Flannels, Crapes. *Ibid.* 704 From England..Estaminas wide and well calendered, brown and green. *Ibid.* 706 Silk Estaminas from Italy. **1862** *Illustr. Catal. Internat. Exhib.* II. xxi. No. 4019 (*heading*) Elworthy, W. & T., Wellington, Somersetshire.—Serges, blankets, yarn, &c. The following goods, of which samples are exhibited, are manufactured by this firm, viz. Serges, estamenes, long ells for China, and swanskins for Newfoundland, &c. **1883** Simmonds *Dict. Trade, Estamin*, a woollen stuff made in Prussia, used for cartridges, sack-cloth, plush caps, etc. **1897** *Daily News* 8 Apr. 8/5 Estamene serges with their diagonal ribs or plain woolly surface.

‖**estaminet** (ɛstaminɛ). [Fr. *estaminet*, Wall. *staminet*, of unknown etym., by some connected with OFr. *estamine*: see prec.] A café in which smoking is allowed. Now, any small establishment selling alcoholic liquor. Also *attrib.*

1814 G. W. Bridges *Alpine Sks.* ii. 47 A delightful shade of oak and elm, beneath which are numerous *estaminets* and *restaurateurs.* **1848** Thackeray *Van. Fair* lxiv, Frequenters of billiard-rooms and estaminets. **1867** Dixon *New Amer.* II. v. 42 The rascal would..play his game of dominoes at the estaminet door. **1883** *Pall Mall G.* 13 July 4/1 The few buildings that..form a scattering suburb—estaminets, chiefly. **1915** W. H. L. Watson *Adv. Despatch Rider* ii. 19 We..had some coffee at a little *estaminet.* **1955** J. Thomas *No Banners* i. 15 The brothers went into the *estaminet*, hoping to find a bottle of wine or something to eat.

†**e'stamp**, *v. Obs.* [ad. Fr. *estamp-er* to STAMP.] *trans.* To stamp; to pound. Hence **e'stamped** *ppl. a.*, pounded.

1648–60 Hexham *Dutch Dict.*, *Gestampte spijse*, estamped meate. **1658** Bp. Reynolds *Lord's Supp.* vi, The very presence of a dying man estamps on the minde an affection of fear and aw.

estampage (ɛ'stæmpɪdʒ, ‖ɛstɑ̃pɑʒ). *Archæol.* [Fr., f. *estamper* to stamp.] A squeeze or impression on paper of an inscription.

1887 *Academy* 24 Dec. 427/3, I made complete estampages..of the Asoka inscription at Kâlsi. **1888** *Epigraphia Indica* I. 1 Methods of taking direct inked impressions from stone, also, have been devised; and *estampages* can thus be taken, having the advantages of presenting a direct reading of the inscription on the inked face and a mould from it on the back, so that the slightest scratch on the stone is retained on a carefully-taken impression. **1904** M. de Z. Wickremasinghe *Epigraphia Zeylanica* I. p. iii, From these estampages..it was arranged that I should edit the texts for publication. As to the scrupulous care taken in the preparation of ink-estampages there need not be the slightest doubt.

estampede (ɛstæm'piːd), *sb. rare.* See STAMPEDE. [ad. Sp. *estampido* a sudden crash, report of a gun.] A sudden fright seizing upon large bodies of cattle and horses, causing them to run wildly to great distances; hence, any sudden rush caused by panic.

So **estam'pede** *v. trans.*, to frighten (cattle, etc.) away; to drive off. ‖**estampe'dero** [Sp. *estampidero*], an animal under the influence of stampede; a runaway. **estam'pedo** *v.* [f. Sp. *estampido* sb.: cf. STAMPEDO, *intr.*] (of cattle, etc.) to rush off in a panic.

1843 Marryat *M. Violet* xx, Oxen..have been known, when under the influence of the estampede..to run forty miles without ever stopping. *Ibid.* xxvi, Pawnee hunters had had their horses estampeded one night, by some hostile Indians. *Ibid.* xx, We..then watched the singular and ridiculous movements of this estampedero. *Ibid.* xxix, The animals had estampedoed the whole distance at the utmost of their speed.

‖**estancia** (ɛ'stansɪə, in Sp. -θia). [Sp. *estancia*, lit. station = OF. *estance*, med.L. *stantia*, f. *stāre* to stand.] A cattle-farm in Spanish America.

1704 *Collect. Voy.* (Churchill) III. 19/2 These they call *Estancia's.* **1845** Darwin *Voy. Nat.* iv. (1873) 64 Every estancia or farming estate has a corral attached to it.

‖**estanciero** (estanθi'ero). [Sp., f. *estancia*: see prec.] The keeper of an estancia; a cattle-farmer (in Spanish America).

1845 Darwin *Voy. Nat.* viii. (1873) 149 An estanciero told me. **1890** G. Stables in *Boy's Own Paper* 1 Feb. 278/1 We were old estancieros.

†**estandard**, obs. var. of STANDARD [a. OF. *estandart*].

1586 Ferne *Blaz. Gentrie* ii. *Lacies Nobil.* 24 The Asirian Emperours, did beare in their estandarde the Eagle. **1656–81** Blount *Glossogr.*, *Standard* or Estandard..the principal or standing measure of the king, to the scantling whereof, all the measures throughout the Land are, or ought to be framed. **1676–1706** in Phillips. **1721–1800** in Bailey.

†**e'stang.** *Obs.* Also 7 estangue. [a. OF. *estang* (mod.F. *étang*).] A pool, fishpond.

1628 Coke *On Litt.* 53 a, Tenant of a warren, park, estangues and the like. **1673** Ray *Journ. Low C.* (1738) I. 395 The bath is not above two flight-shots distant from the estang.

†**e'stantion.** [app. a confusion of Sp. *estacion* (STATION) and ESTANCIA.] A cattle-farm. Also *attrib.* (The quots. relate to Central America and Mexico.)

1697 Dampier *Voy.* I. vi. 157 Where we went ashore to a Beef Estantion or Farm. *Ibid.* ix. 250 The Carrier before-mentioned was lying at the Estantion-house. **1699** L. Wafer *Voy.* (1729) 312 Estantions or farm-houses for the managing their cattle. **1707** Funnell *Voy.* (1729) 59 The Main here is full of Cocoa walks with Estantions or Farms of Beeves.

†**e'stap.** *Obs. rare.* [ad. OFr. *estape*, *estappe* (mod.F. *étape*), *estaple* market (see STAPLE 2), night-quarters for troops on the march, where rations were supplied.] A day's rations for troops; in quot. *attrib.* Also ***by estap***: by fixed stages of march.

1755 *Mem. Capt. P. Drake* I. xvii. 196 Our Estap Allowance was to each Man, three Pounds of Bread, etc. *Ibid.* II. ii. 12 We..continued our March by Estap to Abbeville.

‖**e'staple.** *Obs.* [OF. *estaple*: see prec. and STAPLE.] A market. ***Estaple of Calais***: the market held there for the sale of English wool.

1550 J. Coke *Eng. & Fr. Herald.* (1877) 115 The ryght worshypful company of marchauntes adventurers, and the famous felyshyp of the Estaple of Calais.

estate (ɪ'steɪt), *sb.* Forms: 3 **aestat**, 4–6 **astat(e**, 4–5 **estat**, (4 **astaat(e**, **-tait**, **estaat(e**, 6 **estat**, **estatt**, 6–7 *Sc.* **estaite**, **-tte**), 4– **estate**; *pl.* 3 **astaz**, **aestaz**. Cf. ASTATE and STATE. [a. OF. *estat* (= Pr. *estat*, Sp. and Pg. *estado*, It. *stato*), ad. L. *status* STATE, f. *stā-re* to stand.]

1. a. State or condition in general, whether material or moral, bodily or mental. In ME. occas.: Constitution, nature. *arch.*; now almost exclusively in Biblical phrases.

c **1230** *Hali Meid.* 13 þis mihte..i þis deadlich lif scheaweð in hire estat of þe blisse undeadlich. *c* **1340** *Cursor M.* 1587 (Trin.) þat god not myȝt Brynge mon..Into þe astate þat he had tynt. *c* **1374** Chaucer *Boeth.* v. vi. 171 Lat vs loken now as we mowen whiche þat þe estat is of þe deuyne substance. **1395** *E.E. Wills* (1882) 4 In hool estat of my body. **1486** *Bk. St. Albans* C j a, Sum put hawkys in mew at high estate. *Ibid.* C iij a, Ye se yowre hawke may not endew her meete nor remounte her astate. **1490** Caxton *Eneydos* xiv. 50 Alle the werkes are taryed and lefte in the astate of inperfection. **1519** *Interl. Four Elements* in Hazl. *Dodsley* I. 11 Each element I reduce to his first estate. **1549** Thomas (*title*), The History of Italye..because it intreateth of the astate of many and divers commonweales. **1563** Shute *Archit.* D iv a, In Italie are these pillers founde standing in good estate. **1605** *Lond. Prodigal* I. i. 224, I hope he died in good estate. **1614** Raleigh *Hist. World* v. i. §10. 574 He arrives in safety at Carthage, and makes them know the estate of Lilybæum. **1624–47** Bp. Hall *Rem. Wks.* (1660) 2 A Physician..enquiring of her estate. **1630** Earl Dorchester in Ellis *Orig. Lett.* ii. 268. III. 262 The Queene..is in good estate. **1662** *Bk. Com. Prayer* (Pickering 1844) 56 We pray for the good estate of the Catholick Church. **1676** Grew *Anat. Plants, Lect.* ii. (1682) 241 There is some kind of Alkaline Salt in Plants even in their natural estate. **1794** S. Williams *Vermont* 154 The savages of North America were sunk into the lowest estate of filth. **1844** Kinglake *Eöthen* xxvi. (1878) 341 Their second estate would be worse than their first. **1868** Freeman *Norm. Conq.* (1876) II. ix. 402 The wall, in its first estate, seems to have been merely a dyke of earth and rough stones. **1873** Browning *Red Cott. Nt.-c.* 219, I am forty-three years old; In prime of life, perfection of estate.

b. A special state or condition; a condition of existence. Also ***in estate*** = in existence. *Obs.* exc. in ***man's***, ***woman's estate*** = manhood, womanhood, and (*arch.*) in ***the (holy) estate of matrimony***.

a **1225** *Ancr. R.* 178 Sik mon haueð two swuðe dredfule aestaz: þet on is hwon he ne iveleð nout his owune sicknesse. *c* **1385** Chaucer *L.G.W.* 125 Prol., Fforgetyn hadde the erthe his pore estat O wyntyr. **1483** Caxton *Gold. Leg.* 374/1 She was in the estate of vyrgynyte, in estate of maryage, in estate of wydowhede. **15..** *Adam Bel & Clym of Clough* 665 in Ritson *Anc. Pop. Poetry* 30 When he commeth to mannes estate. **1541** R. Copland *Galyen's Terap.* 2 C j, The fyrste..doth away the dysease that is present. And the other wᵗstandeth the dysease that is nat yet in estate. **1594** Hooker *Eccl. Pol.* i. xv, In regard of a future estate hereafter necessary to be knowne. **1744** E. Heywood *Female Spect.* (1748) II. 23 A gentleman in the western parts of England had two daughters at marriage estate.

†**c.** ***in estate*** [= Fr. *en état (de)*]: in a position, able (*to* do something). *Obs. rare.*

1651 *Hist. Don Fenise* 40 She took Felix by the hand, and put him in estate to come to the point of his desires.

†**d.** Good or normal condition. ***in his estate***: just as he was. ***out of estate***: 'out of condition'.

c **1400** *Rom. Rose* 4675 Thou Art so anguisshous and mate, Disfigured oute of astate. **1447–8** Shillingford *Lett.* (Camd. Soc.) 37 Stondyng yn his astate ayenst the fire. *c* **1460** *Towneley Myst.* 104 My belly farys not weylle, it is out of astate. **1578** Lyte *Dodoens* i. lxi. 88 The floures do not lightly perishe or vade, but may be kept a long time in their estate, and colour. **1587** Fleming *Contn. Holinshed.* III. 1351/2, I found the good prince laid in his estate.

†**e.** ? State of privilege or advantage. *Obs.*

1628 Wither *Brit. Rememb.* ii. 119 Knew I not the Christian Man's estate Extended further than to contemplate. **1633** G. Herbert *Temple* 54 Mans whole estate Amounts (and richly) to serve thee.

†**f.** An account of the state or condition of anything; a 'statement' of particulars. *Obs.*

1474 *Househ. Ord.* 22 For the contentement of his household royal and creditors thereof, as is expressed before in the estate of this seyd court for the yere, xiii Mˡ [*i.e.* 13,000*l.*]. **1484** *Paston Lett.* No. 880 III. 311 The seid John requerith an astate to be takyn in those londys lymyted to William the sone for deffaut off issue off Clement Paston. **1502** Arnolde *Chron.* (1811) 285 The sayd Cardinal hath yow bounde aparte to make him a sure astate of alle the said landes, by Ester next comyng.

2. a. Condition with respect to worldly prosperity, fortune, etc. Cf. 12. *arch.*

a 1300 *Cursor M.* 17321 (Cott.) Do hym by kept in presoners estate Till yt be past our sabate. c 1386 CHAUCER *Knt.'s T.* 68 Noon estat [*v.r.* astate, estaat, estate] assureth to be weel. ? 1370 *Robt. Cicyle* 54 Hym to brynge to lowar estate. a 1400 *Cov. Myst.* 61 A ryght pore man.. Of sympyl astat in clothis rent. 1447 BOKENHAM *Seyntys* (Roxb.) 9 In poure astate and in low degre. a 1535 MORE *De quat. Noviss.* Wks. 86/1 Yet thou wouldest not greatly enuy his estate, if thou thoughteste, etc. 1662 *Bk. Com. Prayer* (Pickering 1844) 56 Any ways afflicted or distressed in mind, body, or estate. 1671 tr. *Frejus' Voy. Mauritania* 7 Made a slave.. and detained in that estate till our arrival. 1846 KEBLE *Lyra Innoc.* (1873) 192 From ox and ass that wait Here on His poor estate. a 1862 BUCKLE *Civiliz.* (1869) III. i. 1 One of the greatest nations of the earth, was broken, and cast down from its high estate.

†b. ? Means, ability, opportunity. In phrase, ***after (one's) estate***. *Obs.*

c 1380 WYCLIF *Sel. Wks.* II. 409 þei shulen lyve as þe world axiþ and take gladnesse of þe world aftir her astaat. c 1430 *Syr Tryam.* 469 Every man lovyd hym aftur ther estate. c 1510 *Virgilius* in Thoms *Prose Rom.* 21 Remus toke with hym manye folke after his estate. 1545 BRINKLOW *Lament.* (1874) 88 Thou must be diligent dayley to helpe thyne neyghbour acordinge to thyne estate.

3. a. Status, standing, position in the world; degree of rank; *esp.* exalted rank or dignity. Also in phr. ***man***, etc. ***of estate***. *arch.*

a 1225 *Ancr. R.* 160 Ant te eadie Johan in onliche stude, þer ase he was, þeos þreo astaz of-earnede him one. c 1340 *Cursor M.* 6949 (Trin.) His fadris astate he [eliazar] bere Til Iosue we speke of here. c 1368 CHAUCER *Compl. Pite* 41 Wisdome, estaat, drede and gouernaunce. 1413 LYDG. *Pilgr. Sowle* IV. xxix. (1859) 61 Of this statua or ymage it is, that men of hyhe power ben cleped men of estate. 1432 *Paston Lett.* No. 18 I. 34 Suche persones as for.. their estate, owe of reson to be suffred to speke with the king. c 1450 *Bk. Curtasye* 276 in *Babees Bk.*, 3e be bothe of on astate. 1483 CAXTON *Gold. Leg.* 201/3, I had the estate of a clerke in the chyrche. c 1500 *Lancelot* 543 So cam ther in an agit knyght, and hee Of gret esstat semyt for to bee. 1531 ELYOT *Gov.* I. i, All the inhabitantes of a realme.. of what astate or condition so euer they be. 1596 SHAKS. *Merch. Ven.* II. ix. 41 O, that estates, degrees, and offices, Were not deriu'd corruptly. 1611 BIBLE *Transl. Pref.* 1 If any man conceit, that Princes are priuiledged by their high estate, he is deceiued.

†b. A definite position in life; an occupation. *Obs. rare.* [A usual sense of Fr. *état*.]

1685 PETTY *Will* p. xi, Those who have been bred to no calling nor estate.

†c. *ellipt.* = *person* or *persons of estate*. *Obs.* (Cf. similar use of *dignity*.)

1399 LANGL. *Rich. Redeles* Prol. 82 þe story is of non estate þat stryuen with her lustus. a 1483 *Liber Niger* in *Househ. Ord.* 32 Knyghts or other wurshypfull astate for the towell. 1509 FISHER *Wks.* 144 The crummes that fall vnder the bordes of lordes or grete estates. 1530 *Proper Dyaloge* (1863) 9 Bothe comones and estates none excepte. 1611 BIBLE *Mark* vi. 21 Herod.. made a supper to his lords, high captaines, and chiefe estates of Galilee. 1634 R. H. *Salerne Regim.* 88 Let them [eels] be drest with Galendine.. as great Estates Cookes are wont to doe.

†4. a. Outward display of one's condition; grandeur, pomp, STATE. *Obs.* exc. *arch.* (*poet.*)

c 1385 CHAUCER *L.G.W.* 1034 *Dido*, This frosche lady.. Stod in the temple in hire estat ryal. c 1386 —— *Sqr.'s T.* 18 And kepte alwey so wel roial estat. 1393 GOWER *Conf.* III. 299 He.. cast about his eye, And sigh the lordes in estate. a 1483 *Liber Niger* in *Househ. Ord.* 19 In the festyvall dayes or when astate should be shewed. c 1489 CAXTON *Sonnes of Aymon* xxiii. 495 Soo shall I gyve theym landes ynoughe for to mayntene theyr astate. 1870 MORRIS *Earthly Par.* I. I. 384 Thou.. by my side shalt sit in such estate That, etc.

†b. Retinue. *Obs.*

c 1500 *Melusine* 50 Honourably might a kinge with alle his estate haue be Receyued therat.

c. ***cap of estate*** (*Her.*): see CAP *sb.*[1] 4 f (*c*). †***chair, cloth, cup, horse, place, robe, throne***, etc. ***of estate*** = *chair*, etc. of STATE. *Obs.*

1423 JAS. I *Kingis Q.* xciv, In a cheire of estate besyde.. There sawe I sitt the blynde god Cupide. 1555 *Fardle Facions* I. v. 56 [The Kinge] put on some robe of estate. 1579 GOSSON *Sch. Abuse* (Arb.) 33 He.. gaue him wine to drink in cups of estate. 1586 MARLOWE *1st Pt. Tamburl.* v. ii, Mount up your royal places of estate. 1599 HAKLUYT *Voy.* II. 62 His imperiall throne of estate. 1632 LITHGOW *Trav.* IV. 140 Who inthronized himself, in the Persian Chair of Estate, Anno 1030. 1653 H. COGAN tr. *Pinto's Trav.* lx. 246 Covered overhead with three cloths of Estate. 1662 OGILBY *King's Coronation* (1685) 2 The Duke of Albemarle, Master of the Horse, on Horseback, leading a Horse of Estate. 1844 DISRAELI *Coningsby* I. iv, There he stood.. in his robes of estate. 1864 BOUTELL *Heraldry Hist. & Pop.* xxiv. 413 Ensigned by a cap of estate of very large dimensions.

†d. *ellipt.* A canopy, chair, dais, fold of 'state'. ***to lay, make (an) estate***: to make a fold of the cloth, in token of respect, opposite the king's seat.

c 1460 J. RUSSELL *Bk. Nurture* 192 in *Babees Bk.*, Ley estate with the vpper part [of the cloth] þe brede of half fote is greable. 1494 *Househ. Ord.* 119 On that side make an estate with his rodd; & then goeing before the kinge doeing his reverence, & soe make another estate on the other side of the king. 1513 *Bk. Keruynge* in *Babees Bk.* 268 And laye estat with the vpper parte halfe a fote brode. 1587 FLEMING *Contn. Holinshed* III. 1490/1 My lord before the estate of his majestie knighted a Dutch gentleman, called Sir Martin Shinke. 1603 DRAYTON *Bar. Wars* VI. lv, The Queen.. sat under an Estate of Lawne. 1605 *Journ. Earl Nottingh.* in *Harl. Misc.* (Malh.) I. 560 The two virgins near her, and the other six upon the degrees at the foot of the estate. 1607 TOPSELL *Four-f. Beasts* (1673) 128 Princes.. sitting upon their estate.

†5. A class, order, rank in a community or nation. ***all estates***: all sorts of people. *Obs.*

1530 PALSGR. Introd. 1 Unto the nobilite.. and.. unto all other estates of this my natyfe countrey. 1577 NORTHBROOKE *Dicing* (1843) 36 Vice raigneth too, too much amongst al estates and degrees. 1590 RECORDE, etc. *Gr. Artes* (1646) 183 This Rule is.. profitable for all estates of men. 1594 SHAKS. *Rich. III*, III. vii. 213 We know your tendernesse of heart.. to all Estates. 1601 HOLLAND *Pliny* I. 126 A fit estate there is besides in great request, and namely of Philosophers and Religious. 1643 MILTON *Divorce* Introd. (1851) 3 Filling each estate of life and profession, with abject and servil principles.

6. a. An order or class regarded as part of the body politic, and as such participating in the government either directly or through its representatives.

The number of 'estates' in most of the nations of Christendom has usually been three (exceptionally four, as in Sweden and Aragon), but the specific enumeration has varied considerably. In England the 'estates' as represented in Parliament were originally 1. Clergy; 2. Barons and Knights; 3. Commons; after various fluctuations, the final arrangement was 1. Lords Spiritual; 2. Lords Temporal; 3. Commons. In France the three estates were 1. Clergy; 2. Nobles; 3. Townsmen. The Scottish estates were at first 1. Prelates; 2. Tenants in Chief; 3. Townsmen; after 1428 they were 1. Lords, lay and clerical; 2. Commissioners of Shires; 3. Burgesses. For a full account of the matter see Stubbs *Const. Hist.* xv.

third estate was formerly common (now much less so) as a designation of the English 'commons' or (transl. Fr. *tiers état*) the French bourgeoisie before the Revolution. The other two 'estates' are seldom spoken of numerically.

[c 1380 WYCLIF *Sel. Wks.* III. 184 þer ben in þe Chirche þre states þat God haþe ordeyned, state of prestis and state of knyȝtis, and þe þridd is staat of comunys.] 1425 *Sc. Acts Jas. I* (1597) 7 It is ordaned be the King, be consent and deliuerance of the three Estaites, that, etc. c 1460 FORTESCUE *Abs. & Lim. Mon.* (1714) 73 The Gabell of the Salte, and the Quaterymes of the Wynys, war granted to the Kyng, by the three Estats of Fraunce. 1489 CAXTON *Faytes of A.* I. v. 10 He shal assemble to counseil the foure estates of his contree. 1494 FABYAN VII. 500 The thre astates of his realme, that is to meane the spiritualtie, the lordes and nobles, and the hedes or rulers of cyties. 1547 J. HARRISON *Exhort. Scottes* F iij b, This was done in Parliamente, by consente of the thre estates. 16.. *Proclam. Jas. I* in *Examiner* 5 Oct. (1812) 626/2 A sufficient and well composed House, such as may be worthy to be a representative of a third estate of our kingdom. 1681 NEVILE *Plato Rediv.* 98 Which Deputies are now called the third Estate. 1765 T. HUTCHINSON *Hist. Col. Mass.* iv. 419 Any step towards forming themselves into a church estate. 1794 J. GIFFORD *Reign Louis XVI*, 350 The instructions of the clergy coincided with those of the nobility and Third Estate. 1827 HALLAM *Const. Hist.* (1876) I. ii. 73 The fall of the mitred abbots changed the proportions of the two estates which constitute the upper house of parliament. 1850 GLADSTONE *Glean.* (1879) V. xx. 185 The concessions of the spiritual estate of the realm. 1875 STUBBS *Const. Hist.* II. xv. 184 It was not by any means clear, at the end of the reign of Edward I, that they [the smaller land-owners] might not furnish a fourth estate of Parliament.

b. *pl.* An assembly of the governing classes or their representatives. ***estates-general*** (in France): see *States-General*.

1603 KNOLLES *Hist. Turks* (1621) 1326 The Estates of the united Provinces.. resolved to make a league with the Turke. 1628 tr. *Camden's Hist. Eliz.* II. (1688) 226 The Estates camp at Rimenant. 1684 *Scanderbeg Rediv.* iii. 44 The Estates being Assembled in the Castle of Warsaw. 1827 SCOTT *Napoleon* Introd., The Estates-General of France met at Versailles on the 5th May, 1789. 1845 S. AUSTIN *Ranke's Hist. Ref.* I. 359 The emperor could come to no agreement with the Estates. 1875 STUBBS *Const. Hist.* II. xv. 163 An assembly of Estates is an organised collection, made by representation or otherwise, of the several orders, states or conditions of men who are recognised as possessing political power.

¶ 7. a. ***the (three) estates of the realm*** (see 6) has often been misused to denote the three powers whose concurrence is necessary for legislation, viz. the Crown, the House of Lords, and the House of Commons.

Perh. Aylmer (quot. 1559) took the word in sense 8, as he argues that the three forms of government, monarchy, aristocracy, and democracy, are united in the English constitution.

1559 BP. J. AYLMER *Harb. Faithf. Subjects* H iij, In the parliament hous.. you shal find these 3 estats. The king or Queene which representeth the Monarchie. The noble men which be the Aristocratie. And the Burgesses and Knights the Democratie. 1648 DK. ORMOND *Let.* in Milton *Observ. Art. Peace*, The three estates of king, lords, and commons, whereof in all ages parliaments have consisted. a 1745 SWIFT *Lett.* (1768) IV. 279 An assembly of the three estates is not properly of Gothick institution. 1769 *Lett. Junius* xvii. 75 Not.. any one, or any two, of the three estates have power to make a new law, without the concurrence of the third. 1819 SYD. SMITH *Wks.* (1859) I. 282/1 The king, four aristocratical assessors, and the assembly of captains, are the three estates of the Ashantee government. 1887 *Pall Mall G.* 8 June 3/2 Mr. Bryce's accuracy is at fault when he tells us that the Canadian Parliament, 'like its model in Westminster, is made up of the three estates, the Queen and the two Houses'.

b. ***the fourth estate***: (*a*) formerly in various jocular applications (see quots.); (*b*) now appropriated to the Press.

We have failed to discover confirmation of Carlyle's statement (quot. 1841) attributing to Burke the use of this phrase in the application now current. A correspondent of *Notes & Queries* (1st Ser. XI. 452) states that he heard Brougham use it in the House of Commons in 1823 or 1824, and that it was at that time treated as original.

1752 FIELDING *Covent-Garden Jrnl.* 13 June No. 47 Wks. (1806) X. 80 None of our political writers.. take notice of any more than three estates, namely, Kings, Lords, and Commons.. passing by in silence that very large and powerful body which form the fourth estate in this community.. The Mob. *Ibid.* 83 Nor hath this estate.. been unknown to the other three. 1821 HAZLITT *Table Talk* vi. 115 He [Cobbett] is a kind of fourth estate in the politics of this country. 1837 CARLYLE *Fr. Rev.* I. VI. v, A Fourth Estate, of Able Editors, springs up. 1841 —— *Hero-worship*, Lect. v, Burke said there were three Estates in Parliament, but in the Reporters' Gallery.. there sat a fourth Estate more important far than they all. 1854 KNIGHT *Once upon a Time* II. 20 Hackney-chairman.. belonged to what Fielding termed 'The Fourth Estate'. That dignity is now assigned to the Press. 1870 SIR H. LYTTON BULWER *Life Palmerston* II. IX. 119 *note*, At that period the 'Times' constituted a fourth estate of the realm. 1885 *Harper's Mag.* Mar. 647/1 A power which calls itself the Fourth Estate of the realm.

c. ***the fifth estate***: in various applications (see quots.).

1932 *Times Educ. Suppl.* 7 May 157/2 Small wonder that radio has been called 'the fifth estate'. 1955 *Times* 14 July 8/1 Unions were now the fifth estate of the realm, Mr. Tiffin continued, and when they wanted a shorter week they would go to the employers and tell them to give it to them.

†8. Political constitution, form of government. [Cf. *état* 8 in Littré.] *Obs.*

1559 [see 7]. 1603 KNOLLES *Hist. Turks* (1621) 76 The whole estate of that great empire.. was almost utterly subverted. 1614 RALEIGH *Hist. World* II. 493 Alcamenes governed Sparta; after whom the Estate changed, according to Eusebius. [Often in Raleigh.] 1670 MILTON *Hist. Eng.* v. (1851) 190 When God hath decreed servitude on a sinful Nation, fitted by their own vices for no condition but servile, all Estates of Government are alike unable to avoid it.

†9. Administration of government; in phrases, ***affairs***, etc. ***of estate***, ***Secretary of Estate***. *Obs.* Now STATE.

1599 HAKLUYT *Voy.* II. 175 Our Secretarie of estate. 1605 BACON *Adv. Learn.* I. ii. 9 Such Popes.. proceed vpon truer principles of Estate than those which haue ascended to the Papacie from an education and breeding in affairs of Estate. 1651 *Reliq. Wotton.* 360 The Cavalier Vieta, his principall Secretary of Estate. 1679 EVERARD *Prot. Princes Europe* 26 That which.. did happen upon this Error of Estate to the Imperial House of Austria.

†10. A body politic, a kingdom or commonwealth; = STATE. *Obs.*

1605 BACON *Adv. Learn.* I. vii. 33 Then should people and Estates be happy when either Kings were Philosophers, or Philosophers Kings. 1750 BEAWES *Lex Mercat.* (1752) 7 The merchants which trafficked in the interior parts of their estates.

11. *Law.* **a.** The interest which any one has in lands, tenements, or any other effects; often with qualifying words or phrases, as an ***estate upon condition, in fee, for life, of inheritance, tail, from year to year, at will***, etc. ***real estate***, an interest in landed property; ***personal estate***, an interest in movables; but the phrases are often regarded as signifying the respective kinds of property. See also FEE, TAIL, etc.

1439 *E.E. Wills* (1882) 119 They that haue.. estate in my land to the execucion of this my last will. c 1462 *Paston Lett.* No. 461 II. 114 Your seid besecher had non astate in the seid maners. 1592 W. WEST *Symbol.* B iiij §39 *An Estate*.. is that right and power whereby we haue the propertie or possessions of things. 1650 *Bury Wills* (1850) 226 My brother Butts Bacon, whom I haue intrusted with the estate of the house or cottage in which the said Norton now liveth. 1756 W. TOLDERVY *Two Orphans* IV. 265 The good gentleman at the Abbey, who has left you his real estate. 1793 SMEATON *Edystone L.* §75 Her estate in the Lighthouse was only for life. 1818 CRUISE *Digest* (ed. 2) I. 70 All inferior estates and interests in land are derived out of the fee simple. 1845 POLSON in *Encycl. Metrop.* 829/1 An estate from year to year may arise.. from that general letting heretofore held to constitute an estate at will. 1876 DIGBY *Real Prop.* i. 43 The tenant is conceived as having only an estate in the lands—an interest which.. was some-thing short of absolute ownership.

†b. ***to make an estate of (a thing) to (a person)***: to give an interest in, a legal right or title to. *Obs.*

1415 *E.E. Wills* (1882) 25, I wolle that my feoffes mak estat to.. my sone, of Thattely and Farley. 1520 SIR R. ELYOT *Will* in *Elyot's Gov.* (1883) I. App. 314 To make astate in fee to two other discrete persones. 1588 *Wills & Inv. N.C.* (1860) II. 256 *note*, Whereas I haue made an estatt unto Robert Selbye.. of my tenement or burgage. 1621 BOLTON *Stat. Irel.* 400 (Act 28 Eliz.), The rebels.. did make ..secret and fraudulent estates and conveyances of their lands. a 1626 BACON *Max. & Uses Com. Law* 56 Where a man maketh an estate of his land to others, by fine, feofment, or recovery.

12. a. Property, possessions, fortune, capital. Cf. 2. *arch.* in gen. sense.

1563 *Homilies* II. *Agst. Wilful Rebell.* II. (1859) 565 Hazarding the whole estate of our Country. 1596 SHAKS. *Merch. V.* I. i. 43 Nor is my whole estate Vpon the fortune of this present yeere. 1627–77 FELTHAM *Resolves* I. xxxi. 54 What do we, but like foolish merchants, venture all our estate in a bottom? 1644 EVELYN *Mem.* (1857) I. 90 The marchands.. have.. little or no extent of ground to employ their estates in. c 1665 MRS. HUTCHINSON *Mem. Col. Hutchinson* 14 The large estate he reaped by his happy industry. 1690 LOCKE *Govt.* I. iv. §42 'Twould always be a Sin in any Man of Estate, to let his Brother perish. 1697 POTTER *Antiq. Greece* III. xviii. (1715) 142 It was frequent for Men of Estates to rig out Ships at their own Expence. 1730 YOUNG *Ep. to Pope* I. (R.), One loses his estate, and down he sits, To show (in vain) he still retains his wits. 1762 J. BROWN *Poetry & Mus.* viii. (1763) 161 The Bards had estates settled on them, that they might be free from worldly Cares. 1847 EMERSON *Repr. Men, Napoleon* Wks. (Bohn) I. 381 France served him with life, and limb, and estate. 1848 MACAULAY *Hist. Eng.* I. 308 The greatest estates in the

kingdom then very little exceeded twenty thousand a year. **1878** OUIDA *Friendship* I. vii. 70 They were very poor and of no great estate.

b. *Accounts.* The collective assets and liabilities of a person (*esp.* of a deceased person, a bankrupt, a *cestui que trust*) viewed as an entity capable of owing or being entitled to money, of being solvent or insolvent. Phrase, ***to wind up an estate.*** (By accountants often used in somewhat wider sense: The 'affairs' of a client so far as the accountant is concerned with them.)

Possibly this sense may be historically connected with 1 f, a 'ledger account' being spoken of in book-keeping as a creditor or debtor; but evidence is wanting.

1830 MCCULLOCH *Princ. Pol. Economy* (ed. 2) 268 The bankrupt is entitled to a reasonable allowance out of his effects.. if his estate pay 10*s.* in the pound, he is to be allowed 5 per cent. *Mod. Newspaper* It takes 10‰ of the assets of a fifty-pound estate to pay for the Board of Trade stamps.

13. a. A landed property; usually, one of considerable extent. (Now the commonest sense.) *spec.* a property on which a crop, as rubber, tea, etc., is cultivated; also, a vineyard. Freq. preceded by a defining word.

1760–72 tr. *Juan & Ulloa's Voy.* (ed. 3) I. VI. 311 When the wind blows from that quarter the weather is so sharp, that the rich families.. retire to their estates, situated in a warmer air. **1772** *Ann. Reg.* 177/2 Her Ladyship had 10,000*l.* left her by her father, and an estate of 700*ol.* per annum. **1784** COWPER *Task* III. 755 Estates are landscapes, gazed upon awhile, Then advertised, and auctioneered away. **1794** MRS. RADCLIFFE *Myst. Udolpho* i, And retired to a small estate in Gascony. **1847** JAMES *J. Marston Hall* x, He intended to send some one to his estates in Brittany. **1848** MACAULAY *Hist. Eng.* I. 151 The public charges can no longer be borne by the estates of the crown. **1851** C. REDDING *Hist. Mod. Wines* (ed. 3) vi. 158 The value of wine estates is very considerable in this department [*sc.* the Gironde]. **1855** TENNYSON *Maud* I. I. v, Lord of the broad estate and the Hall. **1862** in C. TOVEY *Wine & Wine Countries* iv. 142 That wine is.. possessed of *finesse, delicatesse,* and *bouquet,* which are quite peculiar to the estate. **1878** E. MONEY *Cultiv. & Manuf. Tea* (ed. 3) i. 2 Making.. 1,000 acres the outside area.. that should ever have been purchased for any one estate. *Ibid.* ii. 11 Coolies are well treated on Tea estates. **1911** *Encycl. Brit.* XXVI. 480/1 The finest teas are produced at high elevations in Darjeeling and Ceylon.. but the quality from individual estates varies much from season to season. *Ibid.* XXVIII. 721/2 The yield of the principal estates of the Médoc are kept distinct and reach the consumer as the products of a particular growth and of a particular year. **1911** STEVENS & BEADLE *Rubber* ii. 13 Sometimes the rubber plants are set amongst matured coffee or tea, with the idea of.. gradually transforming a tea or coffee estate into a rubber estate. **1916** P. SCHIDROWITZ *Rubber* (ed. 2) iv. 26 The *working expenses* of an estate containing say 10,000 to 15,000 trees. **1921** A. L. SIMON *Wine & Wine Trade* vii. 86 All Clarets which have a claim to a more or less high degree of excellence are too proud of their birthright not to go into the world under their own name—the name of the estate or château whence they came. **1965** T. EDEN *Tea* (ed. 2) i. 3 From the progeny of the plants thus raised the first estate was planted in 1869. *Ibid.*, In 1924 a commercial estate was established near Tukuyu. *Ibid.* vii. 69 The ideal conditions on a tea estate would be to have no bare soil but a moderate growth of weeds. **1968** KRUG & DE POERCK *World Coffee Survey* v. 374 The Coffee Board annually collects data from a representative set of estates.

b. = *housing estate.*

[**1906** W. A. HARVEY *Model Village* 13 Nearly all the old trees and woodland on the Estate have been preserved. *Ibid.* 68 The planning and working out of the Bourneville Estate.] **1915** G. CADBURY *Town Planning* iv. 68 In laying out estates it is advisable to plan the roads so that they do not form through routes for traffic. *Ibid.*, Other road problems are practically confined to estate development. **1923** E. BOWEN *Encounters* 142 Their house was among the first two or three on a new estate. **1939, 1958** [see *council (housing) estate* s.v. COUNCIL 17]. **1960** C. S. LEWIS *Studies in Words* i. 13 When I was a boy *estate* had as its dominant meaning 'land belonging to a large landowner', but the meaning 'land covered with small houses' is dominant now. **1970** *Woman* 14 Nov. 76/4 Till my Dad died we lived in a council house, but then we moved into a larger estate house and my mother became very snobbish.

14. *attrib.* and *Comb.*: *estate-owner*; **estate agent**, one who acts as steward or manager of a landed estate; one who conducts business in the sale of houses and land; hence *estate agency*; **estate-bottled** *a.*, (of a wine) bottled at the vineyard of its growth; **estate car**, a light saloon motor car spec. constructed or adapted to carry both passengers and goods; also *ellipt.*; **estate duty**, a graduated charge levied by the State on real or personal property at the death of the owner; **estate management**, the art of administering an estate (sense 13 or 13 b); hence ***estate-manager***; **estate wagon** = *estate car.*

1912 *Estate Agents, Architects & Surveyors* (*Pitman's Shorthand*) 5 The *Estate Agency profession. **1880** *Harper's Mag.* Sept. 565 '*Estate agent?' he next asked. **1884** *The 'Estate Agent'* 3 House and Estate Agents. **1886** S. W. MITCHELL *R. Blake* xx. 188 It seemed to her natural that an unknown Yankee estate-agent should wish to marry a woman of assured social place. **1940** H. J. GROSSMAN *Guide to Wines* 378/2 **Estate-bottled,* wine bottled by the vineyard owner or producer. **1959** *Times* 21 Sept. 13/2 High prices for estate-bottled wines. **1950** *Motor Industry* July 118/2 (*heading*) Latest car price list... Standard... Vanguard saloon.. *Estate car. **1958** *Times* 1 July 6/6 The Hillman Minx.. has its own estate car version. **1961** *Ibid.* 5 Oct. 11/4 Enter the swish new Anglia Estate. **1966** *Guardian* 19 Oct. 9/3 Both the saloon and the estate carry 5 in comfort. **1889** *Act 52 Vict.* c. 7 §5, *Estate Duty on personal property passing by will or on intestacy. **1896** *Act 59 & 60 Vict.* c. 28 §16 The estate duty payable in respect of any annuity. **1915** G. CADBURY *Town Planning* v. 89 Town Planning is ..*estate management on a large scale. **1921** in Jeffery & Neville *House Property* 92 The London University now grants a Degree in Estate Management. **1937** *Discovery* Sept. 268/1 Industrial management needs sound traditions just as much as estate management or the professions. **1962** H. R. LOYN *Anglo-Saxon England* iv. 146 A little treatise on eleventh-century estate management. *Ibid.* ix. 370 *Estate-managers to look after the lands of the church. **1937** *Discovery* May 164/1 Rich *estate owners in Brazil, Peru and Nicaragua. **1962** H. R. LOYN *Anglo-Saxon England* i. 16 Their eponymous Gallo-Roman estate-owners. **1959** M. STEEN *Tower* I. vii. 91 There was an *estate wagon and a couple of big private cars.

estate (ɪˈsteɪt), *v.* [f. prec. sb.]

1. *trans.* To put (a person) into an estate; to give (a person) an estate or possession, or a secured position, *in* (a thing); to endow *with* (possessions). Rare in mod. use.

1609 G. BENSON *Serm.* 26 Salomons outlandish women.. so much estated themselves in the bosom of the king, that they drew him and his people to idolatry. **1611** DEKKER *Roaring Girle* Wks. 1873 III. 225 Estate him In those possessions, which your loue and care Once pointed out for him. **1639** J. MAYNE *City-Match* v. v, I have estated her in all I have. **1670** WALTON *Lives* I. 22, [I] will quit my Benefice, and estate you in it. **1823** LAMB *Let. to Southey* xiii. 125 In what possession has not this last name alone estated me. **1859** TENNYSON *Lancelot & Elaine* 1312 Then would I.. Estate them with large land and territory. **1887** *Sat. Rev.* 24 Sept. 413 His country seat at Wootton, wherein Mr. Zabriskie has surely estated Rousseau somewhat at the cost of one Mr. Davenport.

†**2.** To furnish with an estate or property. *lit.* and *fig.* *Obs.* See also ESTATED *ppl. a.*

1625 DONNE *Serm.* cl. VI. 63 And in the Resurrection [we are] Estated and put in possession of his Kingdom. **1625** FLETCHER *Fair Maid Inn* III. i, This puppy being left well estated, comes to Florence. **1646** BUCK *Rich. III,* II. 55 Cruell Lords estated onely by their unjust Armes. **1653** BP. HALL *Christ Mysticall* §2. 6 Our faith.. must shew us.. how royally we are allied, how gloriously estated.

†**3.** To bestow or settle as an estate *on* or *upon* (also rarely *unto*) a person. Also, *to estate out*: to let out. *Obs.*

1590 SHAKS. *Mids. N.* I. i. 98 And all my right of her, I do estate vnto Demetrius. **1622–62** HEYLYN *Cosmogr.* II. (1682) 88 There was nothing left of the ancient Saxony to be estated upon Bernard of Anhalt. *Ibid.* III. (1673) 211 1 The whole Land being also his, he estates it out for no term certain. *a* **1669** BP. KING *Poems* III. xv. (1843) 109 Till he estate his vertue on his son.

†**4.** To put into a certain state or condition. Sometimes with allusion to sense 1. *Obs.*

1605 HEYWOOD *If you know not me* Wks. 1874 I. 238 Convert her foes; estate her in true peace. *a* **1626** BP. ANDREWES *Serm.* (1641) 389 Hee liveth.. to estate us in this life in the hope of a reversion. **1640** FULLER *Joseph's Coat* (1867) 66 By faith and repentance we are first estated in God's favour. **1701** BEVERLEY *Glory of Grace* 16 It cannot be suppos'd such High Angelical Beings.. should be so Estated in him and by him, under an Ignorance of him.

estated (ɪˈsteɪtɪd), *ppl. a.* [f. ESTATE *sb.* and *v.* + -ED.] Furnished with an estate, possessed of 'means' or property; in later use, *esp.* of landed property.

1607 TOPSELL *Serpents* To Rdr., Because we were not so throughly estated, as to maintain a sufficient Scholar to attend only upon the Presse. **1615** MANWOOD *Lawes Forest* xx. §8 173 A Pourallee man that may keepe greyhounds must be a man estated according to this law of 1 Iac. **1729** SWIFT *Let. to Dublin Weekly Jrnl.*, Look upon the poor starving in your streets, while the rich and estated men live in pomp. **1758** *Herald* No. 18. II. 40 The estated and labouring parts of the people. **1774** GEN. LEE in *Burke's Corr.* (1844) I. 509 Men, from the first estated gentleman to the poorest planters. **1861** MAINE *Anc. Law* 299 This system was.. especially disadvantageous to one class of estated proprietors. **1877** *Hon. Miss Ferrard* I. ii. 56 The estated heretic who drives his carriage and pair.

†**eˈstately**, *a.* and *adv.* *Obs.* Also 4 estatelich(e, estatly. [f. ESTATE + -LY[1] and [2].]

A. *adj.* Dignified, majestic, stately. **B.** *adv.* In a stately manner.

c **1374** CHAUCER *Troylus* v. 823 She sobre was, ek symple, and wyse withalle.. Charytable, estateliche, lusty, and fre. *c* **1386** —— *Monk's T.* 722 Julius.. well loved estatly honesté. **14..** (*title*) A Noble Boke off Cookry ffor a Prynce Houssolde or eny other Estately Houssolde (ed. A. Napier 1882). *c* **1430** LYDG. *Min. Poems* (1840) 4 Sergeauntes and other officeres, Estatly horsed.

estatesman (ɪˈsteɪtsmən). [f. ESTATE *sb.* + MAN; = estate's man; cf. *beadsman, craftsman,* etc.] An etymologizing perversion of STATESMAN, a Cumberland or Westmoreland yeoman.

1820 WORDSW. *Scen. Lakes* (1823) 85 The family of each man, whether estatesman or farmer, formerly had a two-fold support. *Ibid.* 86 The lands of the estatesmen being mortgaged.. they fall into the hands of wealthy purchasers.

†**eˈstatute.** *Obs.* [f. OF. *estatut* (Littré), ad. L. *statūtum*: see STATUTE.] = STATUTE. **a.** A law, ordinance. **b.** A bond, security.

a. *a* **1514** *Act 6 Hen. VIII*, c. 13 Pream., Shoting in long bowes is the lesse used and diverse good estatutes for reformacion of the same have ben made. **1574** tr. *Littleton's Tenures* 48 b, An ordynaunce that is entred in the auncient estatuts. **1587** HARRISON *England* II. iii. (1877) I. 77 Without all respect of order or estatutes devised by the founders [of colleges]. **1610** in Picton *L'pool Munic. Rec.* (1883) I. 122 All Acts and Estatutes made by the Quene's highnes. [**1731** BAILEY cites CHAUCER.]

b. **1584** LODGE *Alarum* 64 You will seale me an estatute for my mony.

estcheker, obs. form of EXCHEQUER.

†**este**, *sb.* *Obs.* Forms: 1 ést, 2–3 este (*Orm.* esste), 5 est. [OE. *ést* fem. (:—prehistoric **ôsti*), corresp. to OFris. *êst, enst,* OS., OHG. *anst,* ON. *ást,* Goth. *ansts*:—OTeut. **ansti-z*; also late OE. (in sense 3) *ést* masc. (pl. *éstas*); f. root of UNNE, to grant. Cf. OHG. *unst,* mod.G. *g-unst,* Sw. *ynnest,* Da. *yndest,* f. *un-* weak grade of the same root.]

1. Good pleasure, favour, grace (*esp.* of God). In OE. also: Bounty, munificence.

Beowulf 3074 (Gr.) He.. hæfde ꝫarendes est ær ꝫesceawod. *a* **1000** *Andreas* 1217 (Gr.) Ne moton ofer mine est þinne lichoman lehtrum scyldiꝫe deaðe ꝫedælan. *c* **1430** *Syr Tryam.* 1416 As y yow say, be Goddys est! *a* **1440** *Sir Eglam.* 904 Make we mery for Goddys est.

2. Pleasure, delight, luxury.

c **1000** *Ags. Gosp.* Luke vii. 25 þa ðe synt on deorwurþum reafe & on estum [*c* **1160** *Hatton* esten; Vulg. *deliciis*]. *a* **1175** *Cott. Hom.* 241 Mine esten beoð wunian mid mannen bearnen. *a* **1240** *Ureisun* in *Cott. Hom.* 201 Ne wene nomon to stihen wið este to þe steorren. *a* **1240** *Sawles Warde* ibid. 257 Meaðful in alles cunnes estes. *a* **1250** *Owl & Night.* 1504 Thu miȝt mid wlate the este bugge.

3. Dainty food; also *pl.* dainties.

c **1000** ÆLFRIC *Voc.* in Wr.-Wülcker 152 *Dapes,* kininga wist, *uel* estas. *a* **1200** *Moral Ode* 359 Ne scal þer ben bred ne win. ne oþer cunnes este. *c* **1200** *Trin. Coll. Hom.* 99 þis dai is cleped estre dai þat is estene da, and te este is husel. *c* **1200** ORMIN 7542 & ȝiff we wolldenn shunenn aȝȝ To fillenn uss wiþþ esstess. *a* **1250** *Owl & Night.* 353 Mid este thu the miȝt over-quatie.

4. In *Comb.*, which did not survive beyond early ME.: **ˈestdede** [see DEED], deed of kindness; **ˈestful** *a.*, dainty, fastidious, luxurious; hence **ˈestfullness**, daintiness; **ˈestlich** *a.* [see -LY[1]], dainty, luxurious; **ˈestliche** *adv.* [see -LY[2]], daintily, luxuriously; **ˈestmete** = 3.

c **1250** *Gen. & Ex.* 2758 And ietro geld it him in *estdede. *a* **1000** *Ags. Gloss.* in Wr.-Wülcker 218 *Deliciosa,* *estful. *a* **1225** *Ancr. R.* 108 Estful is þeos ancre, ant muchel is þet heo bit. *c* **1340** *Cursor M.* App. i. (Edin. MS.) 23750 þe fleis es ai to flihtis fus, þe werd estful and couaitus. *a* **1000** *Voc.* in Wr.-Wülcker 220 *Deuotio,* *estfulnes. *a* **850** *Kentish Gloss.* ibid. 84 *Delicatæ,* *estelice. *c* **1200** *Trin. Coll. Hom.* 179 þe riche habbeð of here [underlinges] swinche.. estliche metes and drinkes. *c* **1000** *Andreas* 292 (Gr.) We þe *estliche mid us willað feriꝫan. *a* **1225** *Ancr. R.* 204 þe Suwe of ȝiuernesse þet is, Glutunie, haueð pigges þus inemned. To Erliche hette þet on: þet oðer to Estliche. *c* **1000** ÆLFRIC *Gram.* ix. (Z.) 54 *Hæc daps,* þeos sund oððe *estmete. *c* **1200** *Trin. Coll. Hom.* 37 þe est metes and drinkes [he] ut speweð. *c* **1200** ORMIN 829 Nass nan essteмete þær þatt follȝheþþ gluternesse.

†**este**, *a.* *Obs.* Also 3 *north.* eist. [OE. *éste* (**anstjo-*), f. *ést*: see ESTE *sb.*] **a.** Of persons: Gracious, kind, bountiful. **b.** Of things: Agreeable, pleasant, savoury.

Beowulf 945 (Gr.) þæt hyre eald Metod este wære bearnꝫebyrdo. *a* **1000** *Cædmon's Gen.* 1509 (Gr.) Ðæt he him ealra wæs ara este. *a* **1250** *Owl & Night.* 997 That lond nis god, ne hit nis este. *a* **1300** *Cursor M.* 3610 (Cott.), If þou mai bring me any beist þou graith me ful fair and eist. *a* **1300** *Prov. Hendyng* xiii, Este bueth oune brondes.

esteem (ɪˈstiːm), *sb.* Forms: see the vb. [f. next: cf. Fr. *estime* (perh. the source), Sp., Pg. *estima,* It. *stima.*]

†**1. a.** Estimate, valuation, in phr. ***to make an esteem.*** **b.** Estimated value, valuation. **c.** ***to put, set (an) esteem, a high, low esteem upon***: to set a value upon, cause to be esteemed (highly, etc.).

a **1528** SKELTON *Vox Populi* 672 Of the substance of your realme.. I wyll make an esteame. **1601** SHAKS. *All's Well* v. iii. 1 We lost a Iewell of her, and our esteeme Was made much poorer by it. **1660** WEBSTER & ROWLEY *Cure for Cuckold* II. ii, I will deliver you in ready Coin the full and dearest esteem of what you crave. **1662** J. BARGRAVE *Pope Alex. VII* (1867) 123 But they put an esteem upon them, and I [was] made pay dear for them. **1665** MANLEY *Grotius' Low-C. Warres* 677 Here may be a Reason why valiant men should set a light esteem thereon. *a* **1672** WILKINS *Nat. Relig.* II. vi. (1693) 363 Every one who will act rationally.. must proportion his esteem of things, according to the real value of them. *a* **1680** BUTLER *Rem.* (1759) I. 21 The World, that never sets Esteem On what Things are, but what they seem.

2. Estimation, opinion, judgement. Somewhat *arch.*

1588 SHAKS. *L.L.L.* II. i. 4 Yourself, held precious in the worlds esteeme. **1640** FULLER *Joseph's Coat* viii. (1867) 185 The good esteem which foreigners have conceived of the piety and learning of the Geneva ministers. **1667** MILTON *P.L.* IX. 328 Our Foe.. affronts us with his foul esteem Of our integritie. **1675** TRAHERNE *Chr. Ethics* II. 19 Perfect righteousness is a full and adequate esteem of all the value that is in things. **1836** J. GILBERT *Chr. Atonem.* vi. (1852) 162 In the Divine esteem, the law was not more excellent after than before atonement.

3. Favourable opinion; regard; respect. ***in (much) esteem***: in favour. (*obs.* or *arch.*)

1611 BIBLE *Transl. Pref.* 1 [It] deserueth certainly much respect and esteeme. **1650** BULWER *Anthropomet.* Pref., A Camoyse Saddle-nose is in esteem. **1697** DRYDEN *Æneid*

(J.), Who can see, Without esteem for virtuous poverty, Severe Fabritius. **1700** —— *Fables* Pref., Both those poets lived in much esteem with good and holy men in orders. **1738–9** W. RICHARDSON in *Swift's Lett.* (1768) IV. 219, I am ever, dear Sir, with the highest esteem and respect, etc. **1800** COGAN *Philos. Treat. Passions* II. iii. (1802) 151 Esteem is the commencement of affection. **1823** LAMB *Elia* (1867) 43 Whist had engaged her maturer esteem. **1841–4** EMERSON *Ess. Self-Reliance* Wks. (Bohn) I. 37 They measure their esteem of each other by what each has, and not by what each is. **1861** GEO. ELIOT *Silas M.* 26 He was banished for ever from the sight and esteem of Nancy Lammeter.

†**4.** Account, worth; reputation; also, *man*, etc. *of* (*great*, etc.) *esteem*. *Obs.*

a **1450** *Knt. de la Tour* 179, I hold them of none extyme. **1483** CAXTON *Esope* (E.E.T.S) 144 Of the which wordes the labourer made lytyl extyme. **1591** SHAKS. *1 Hen. VI*, III. iv. 8 Fiue hundred Prisoners of esteeme. *Ibid.* V. v. 27 Your Highnesse is betroath'd Vnto another Lady of esteeme. **1604** ROWLANDS *Looke to it* 42 Earth's delightes shall be of no esteeme. **1634** SIR T. HERBERT *Trav.* 106 A drowsy Oracle, long time of divine Æsteam among them. **1642** FULLER *Holy and Prof. St.* III. iii. 158 Others..boast of their robberies, to usurp the esteem of valour. **1673** TEMPLE *Observ. United Prov.* Wks. 1731 I. 34 Men..who have pass'd through most of the Employments of State, with the Esteem of Prudence and Integrity. **1712** HEARNE *Collect.* (Oxf. Hist. Soc.) III. 311 Whatsoever is of any Esteem with Men. **1762** J. BROWN *Poetry & Mus.* iv. (1763) 44 The Profession of Bard or Musician would be held..of high Esteem. **1824** W. IRVING *T. Trav.* II. 90 All these were of precious esteem, being family reliques.

esteem (ɪ'stiːm), *v.* Forms: 5–6 **es-, extyme**, 5–7 **esteme**, 6–7 **esteeme**, (6 **æsteme, extime, exsteme, esteam**, 7 **æsteam, estime**, 8 **esteam**), 5– **esteem**. Also 5 *aphet.* **stime**. [ad. OF. *estimer* (often spelt *extimer*), ad. L. *æstimāre*, of which ESTIMATE is the direct representative. Cf. Pr., Sp. and Pg. *estimar*, It. *stimar*.

The regular phonetic representative of L. *æstimāre* in OF. was *esmer* AIM *v.* For the phonology in Eng. cf. *redeem*, ad. L. *redim-ĕre*; the sound (ɪ) under some undefined circumstances became in late ME. (eː) afterwards passing regularly into the modern (iː).]

I. To estimate value; to value.

†**1.** *trans.* To estimate the value of, assign (a value) to; to value, assess, appraise. Const. *at*. In later use only *fig.*, to assign the degree of merit of *Obs.*

1475 CAXTON *Jason* 65 b, Ye are in valewe moche more thenne I can exteme. *a* **1533** LD. BERNERS *Huon* cxxiii. 440 The bed that Huon lay on..no humayne tonge can esteme the valewe therof. **1551** BIBLE *Lev.* xxvii. 17 Hys land..shalbe worthe accordinge as it is estemed. **1581** LAMBARDE *Eiren.* IV. v. (1588) 496 So of Charters..their value cannot be esteemed. **1611** SHAKS. *Cymb.* I. iv. 85 What do you esteeme it at? **1621** AINSWORTH *Annot. Pentat.* Lev. v. 13 The priest..was to esteeme and value all holy things. **1711** ADDISON *Spect.* No. 257 ¶8 No other Being can..esteem us according to our Merits. **1776** SIR J. REYNOLDS *Disc.* vii. (1876) 422 It is the duty of the connoisseur to know and esteem..every part of painting.

2. To attach value (subjectively) to.

a. In neutral sense, qualified variously by adverbs (*highly*, *lightly*, *little*, *well*, etc.) or phrases: To hold in (favourable or unfavourable) estimation.

In mod. use *highly*, *little*, are merely intensive or the reverse, the verb having the sense b. In the archaic *to esteem lightly* the original sense remains.

1532 MORE *Confut. Barnes* VIII. Wks. 810/2 Suche apostasye..is in oure wretched dayes..little estemed. **1538** STARKEY *England* I. i. 22 Hys vertue schold have byn otherwyse extymyd. **1590** SHAKS. *Com. Err.* v. i. 4 *Mar.* How is the man esteem'd heere in the Citie? *Gold.* Of very reuerent reputation sir. *a* **1600** HOOKER (J.), They..esteem highly profound wisdom. *c* **1600** SHAKS. *Sonn.* xcvi, On the finger of a throned Queene The basest Jewell wil be well esteem'd. **1772** SIR W. JONES *Ess.* i. (1777) 184 Yet Sadi's poems are highly esteemed at Constantinople. **1783** COWPER *Lett.* 12 May, If I can tell you no news I can tell you at least that I esteem you highly.

b. In favourable sense: To regard as valuable; to think highly of; to feel regard for, respect (persons or their qualities; now chiefly with reference to moral characteristics).

1530 PALSGR. 540/1 Wene you that men shall estyme you for your fayre eyes. **1620** SHELTON *Quix.* IV. ii. 11 Every Man bears with the rich man's Follies..have much and thou shalt be esteem'd much. *a* **1704** T. BROWN *Sat. Antients* Wks. (1730) I. 24 All this does not hinder me from esteeming the great men that live now. **1772** SIR W. JONES *Ess.* i. (1777) 183 Those authors who are generally esteemed in Persia. **1815** JANE AUSTEN *Emma* I. viii, If he had never esteemed my opinion before, he would have thought highly of me then. **1863** FAWCETT *Pol. Econ.* III. v. 350 Gold and silver have always been sufficiently rare to be esteemed for their scarcity.

†**c.** To think much of, regard as important. *Obs.*

1570 ASCHAM *Scholem.* Pref. (Arb.) 23, I..shall not moch æsteme the misliking of any others. **1631** T. MAY tr. *Barclay's Mirr. Mindes* I. 202 They can also entertaine long friendship, and, where they truely loue, esteeme no dangers in respect of that sacred league.

†**d.** *intr.* To have a (more or less favourable) opinion *of* (*on*). *Obs.*

1583 W. HUNNIS *Seven Sobs* 5 We little doo esteeme thereof. **1585** ABP. SANDYS *Serm.* (1841) 315 This were a cause sufficient to esteem of marriage highly. **1589** SPENSER *Let. to Raleigh* Wks. (Globe) 3 Seeing..nothing esteemed of, that is not delightfull and pleasing to commune sence. **1612** WOODALL *Surg. Mate* Wks. (1653) Pref. 13 He that light thereof esteems May leave the book unbought. **1648** E. CALAMY *Pref. to Roberts' Clavis Bibl.* 6 The Author of it is ..well known, and very well esteemed on in this famous City. **1670–98** LASSELS *Voy. Italy* I. 19 They esteem very much of Chesnuts roasted. **1697** POTTER *Antiq. Greece* II. *Index*, Self-murder, how esteem'd of.

II. To estimate generally; to deem, think.

†**3.** *trans.* To estimate; to form or pronounce a (usually approximate) judgement respecting the number, quantity, or magnitude of (anything). Const. *at*, *to* (an amount); also *simply*. See ESTIMATE *v.* 2. *Obs.*

c **1460** FORTESCUE *Abs. & Lim. Mon.* (1714) 42 The expensys of which Houshold may sone be estemyd by thes, which of old time have byn Officers theryn. **1481** CAXTON *Myrr.* III. xv. 170 A place..so ful of spyrites..that they coude not be nombred ne estemed. *c* **1500** *Melusine* 117 They extimed them þat had lodged there to the nombre of xxx thousand men. **1523** LD. BERNERS *Froiss.* I. clv. 187 The finance to pay the wages of so many men of warre was estemed to l. M. *li.* parisiens. **1559–66** *Hist. Estate Scot. Wodr. Soc. Misc.* (1844) 58 The brethren who came to Lt. Johnstone were esteemed to four or five thousand men.

†**b.** with the amount as complement, or introduced by *to be*. *Obs.*

a **1512** FABYAN *Chron.* (1811) Pref. 8 Suche money as shall remayn..I estyme to be every yere xiid. **1612** BREREWOOD *Lang. & Relig.* iii. 17 A learned man hath esteemed them [the inhabitants of Rome]..to have been no less then three or four millions. **1673** RAY *Journ. Low C.* 109 The Citizens [Ausburgh] are divided between Papists and Lutherans, these latter being esteemed double the number of the former. **1696** WHISTON *Th. Earth.* IV. (1722) 334, I esteem the Upper Crust to be not above 50 or 100 miles deep. **1717** BERKELEY *Jrnl. Tour Italy* Wks. 1871 IV. 589 The great torrent in the widest part 3 miles broad esteemed.

†**4.** In wider sense: To judge of; to form an opinion of. Also with obj. sentence. *Obs.*

1534 LD. BERNERS *Gold. Bk. M. Aurel.* viii, For to esteme the thyng that he had doone, and to puruey for that he had to do. **1535** E. HARVEL in Ellis *Orig. Lett.* II. 115 II. 71 By al the next monith I stime that his labor shal take end. **1551** ROBINSON tr. *More's Utop.* II. (Arb.) 124 Al the resydewe of the woomans bodye beinge couered with cloothes, they esteme her scaselye be one handebredeth. **1592** WEST *Symbol.* I. I. §12 It is to be esteemed whether they may be said to be Contracts named or un-named. **1624** BEDELL *Lett.* iv. 79 What anger and shame this was to the Popish faction, I leaue it to you to esteeme.

5. To account, consider, think, hold (a thing to be so and so). With simple complement; less frequently with *as* or *to be*; rarely const. †*for*.

1526 *Pilgr. Perf.* (W. de W.) 211 The people esteme & take vs as the mynistres of Chryst. **1530** PALSGR. 539/2, I esteme my selfe better than I am. **1534** WHITTINTON *Tullyes Offices* I. (1540) 1 Nor I wolde thou shulde exteme this to be sayd of arrogaunce. **1538** STARKEY *England* I. i. 13 Lawful increse of the pepul ys, among al men..estymyd vertue and honesty. **1590** SHAKS. *Mids. N.* III. ii. 353 This their iangling I esteeme a sport. **1628** HOBBES *Thucyd.* (1822) 104 Esteeming these virtues to be in me. **1667** PEPYS *Diary* (1879) IV. 348 To have all that I shall buy, or do, esteemed as got by the death of my uncle. **1671** H. M. tr. *Erasmus' Colloq.* 453 Wouldest thou not esteem that Alchymist for a god, who were able, etc. **1708** J. CHAMBERLAYNE *St. Gt. Brit.* II. I. i. (1743) 290 St. Patrick is esteemed to have been made the first bishop of the Scots. **1739** HUME *Hum. Nat.* I. Introd., To hope we shall arrive at it [truth] without pains ..must certainly be esteemed sufficiently vain. **1790** GIBBON *Misc. Wks.* (1814) V. 171 The small islands of the ..Pacific..may be esteemed as some of the most agreeable spots on the globe. **1818** JAS. MILL *Brit. India* II. v. ii. 374 The majority of the Council esteemed the evidence of the charge complete. **1845** S. AUSTIN *Ranke's Hist. Ref.* II. 299 The imperialists..esteemed themselves happy to escape without a beating.

†**b.** *intr.* To account *of*, have (such or such) an opinion *of*. *Obs.* Cf. 2 c.

1576 FLEMING *Panopl. Ep.* 268 Know you that I esteeme of him, as of my friend. **1590** GREENE *Orpharion* 47 Avicen said that love was a fury: how didst thou esteeme of this but as an axiome? **1611** SHAKS. *Wint. T.* II. iii. 149 We haue alwayes truly seru'd you, and beseech' So to esteeme of vs. **1633** BP. HALL *Hard Texts N.T.* 111 Esteem of things as they really are.

c. With *subord. clause*. To think, be of opinion, suppose *that*.

1548 R. HUTTEN *Sum of Diuinitie* E 4 a, We esteme verely that we haue the benifytes of the gospel for hys sake. **1645** USSHER *Body Div.* (1647) 138 Their blindnesse..esteemed that the shaddow or thicknesse of trees would hide them from the face of God. **1654** EARL ORRERY *Parthenissa* (1676) 305 Which blemish the King esteem'd the Marriage would deface. **1765** BLACKSTONE *Comm.* Introd. 4 Esteeming, that the best return..for your favourable opinon..will be, etc.

†**6.** To purpose, aim, intend. *Obs. rare.*

1534 LD. BERNERS *Gold. Bk. M. Aurel.* (1539) 4 a, This Emperoure estemed to haue the knowlage of payntyng..He trauayled also to knowe the arte of Nygromancye. **1557** NORTH *Gueuara's Dial. Pr.* 229 b/1 The noble and valiaunt hartes do not esteme to lose the rewarde of their laboure.

†**e'steemable,** *a. Obs.* [f. ESTEEM *v.* + -ABLE.] = ESTIMABLE.

c **1460** [see ESTIMABLE A. 1]. **1614** SPEED *Theat. Gt. Brit.* xliii. 85/2 Were it not for the antiquity that makes it [Apelby] the more esteemable..it would be little better in account than a village. **1661** FELTHAM *Resolves* II. lv. 298 If we would be prevalent and esteemable, we ought..to preserve that interest, which never can, but by our own neglect, be lost. **1715–20** POPE *Iliad* VI. note xxxiii, Homer does not paint him [Paris] and Helen..like Monsters..but allows their Characters esteemable Qualifications. **1720** WELTON *Suffer. Son of God* II. xiv. 375 The Lowest Places ..are not less..Esteemable in the Eye of God, than the most Elevate. **1752** HUME *Ess. & Treat.* (1777) II. 366 That the esteemable qualities alone..are entitled to the appellation of virtues. **1761** FRANCES SHERIDAN *Sidney Bidulph* III. 185 A man..every way esteemable in his character. **1828** in WEBSTER; and in mod. Dicts.

esteemate: see ESTIMATE.

esteemed (ɪ'stiːmd), *ppl. a.* [f. ESTEEM *v.* + -ED[1].] Held in esteem, valued, respected. Much in vogue as a complimentary epithet in commercial correspondence.

1549 CHEKE *Hurt Sedit.* C iij b, What an hynderaunce is it, to haue a good garmente hurte..or anye estemed thyng to be decaied. **1647–8** COTTERELL *Davila's Hist. Fr.* (1678) 8 A man of subtil wit, and esteemed valour. **1781** J. MOORE *View Soc. It.* (1790) II. lxxviii. 450 Ornamented with some highly esteemed sculpture in wood. **1828** SCOTT *F.M. Perth* xviii, According to the esteemed qualities of the time. **1871** CARLYLE in *Mrs. Carlyle's Lett.* I. 247 An esteemed tutor in noble families. **1903** *Daily Chron.* 25 Feb. 7/2 Sir, yours of even date to hand. If you can make it convenient, we should be glad if you could come on Wednesday morning to try on your esteemed favour. **1905** H. G. WELLS *Kipps* I. ii. 37 He [*sc.* a draper] never acknowledged an order that was not an esteemed favour.

esteemer (ɪ'stiːmə(r)). [f. as prec. + -ER[1].] One who esteems, prizes, or respects; a valuer, judge. *Obs.* exc. const. *of*.

1551 ROBINSON tr. *More's Utop.* II. (Arb.) 99 A wise and indifferent estimer of thynges will not greatlye marueill. **1587** *Misfort. Arthur* I. iii. in Hazl. *Dodsley* IV. 271 Grief is no just esteemer of our deeds. **1607** HIERON *Wks.* I. 375 The base esteemers, and carelesse respecters of these seruices. **1664** H. MORE *Synopsis Proph.* 453 Boasters of the certainty of their knowledge in the divinest matters, and great esteemers thereof. **1675** L. ADDISON *State of Jews* 14 Rabbi Aaron Ben-Netas..wanted nothing but Christianity to render him acceptable to equal esteemers. *c* **1698** LOCKE *Cond. Underst.* §3 This might instruct the proudest esteemer of his own parts how useful it is to talk and consult with others. **1775** in ASH; and in mod. Dicts.

e'steeming, *vbl. sb.* [f. as prec. + -ING[1].]

a. The action of the vb. ESTEEM. **b.** Estimation, value, worth.

1530 PALSGR. 217/2 Estemyng, *estimation*. **1561** T. NORTON *Calvin's Inst.* Pref., It thinketh them to be holy prelates of religion, whom it seeth to be heads ouer great cities: Away therfore with such foolishe estemyng. *c* **1600** SHAKS. *Sonn.* cii, That love..whose rich esteeming The owners tongue doth publish every where. **1617** COLLINS *Def. Bp. Ely* II. ix. 351 *Venerari* implies no worship..but onely reuerent esteeming. **1633** P. FLETCHER *Elisa* II. xxxix, Such is the world..This base and scorned; that great, in high esteeming. **1672** WILKINS *Nat. Relig.* I. xii. (R.), By love, I mean an esteeming of him [God] and a seeking after him as our only happiness.

e'steeming, *ppl. a.* [f. as prec. + -ING[2].] Hence †**e'steemingly** *adv.*; so as to express esteem; appreciatively.

1775 ASH, *Esteeming*. **1653** BAXTER *Worc. Petit. Def.* 7, I doubt you would fain partake your selves more of such profits, that you speak so esteemingly of them.

†**este'llation.** *Obs.* In 4 **-cioun**. [f. L. *stella*: see -ATION and cf. OF. *estellement*.] Astrology.

c **1300** *K. Alis.* 589 Wiser clerk no lyved non..In art of estellacioun.

estend, obs. form of EXTEND.

ester ('ɛstə(r)). *Chem.* [G. (L. Gmelin *Handb. d. Chemie* (1848) IV. 161), prob. f. *essig* vinegar + *äther* ether.] A derivative of an acid in which one or more acidic hydrogen atoms are replaced by an alkyl, aryl, or similar group; **acrylic ester** (see quot. 1951). Also *attrib.* and *Comb.*; **ester gum** (see quot. 1940).

[**1852** H. WATTS tr. *Gmelin's Hand-bk. Chem.* VII. 190 *Ethers du troisième genre.* I formerly distinguished these compounds by the name of Naphthas produced by oxygen-acids (*Naphthen durch Sauers*[*t*]*offsäuren erzeugt*); but I now propose for them the term *Ester*.] *Ibid.* 215 Compound Ethers formed by Oxygen-acids (Ester). **1889** MUIR & MORLEY *Watts's Dict. Chem.* II. 466 A compound ether (or ester) is a hydrogen salt in which the typical hydrogen has been displaced by an alkyl. **1899** E. F. SMITH tr. *von Richter's Org. Chem.* I. 139 Just as salts result from the union of metallic hydroxides with acids, so esters are formed by the combination of alcohols with acids. **1904** [see THION-]. **1906** *Practitioner* Nov. 593 The rapidly fermentable fruit and malt sugars, esters, and higher alcohols. **1907** *Jrnl. Chem. Soc.* XCII. I. 383 Ester-Acids of Sulphur-substituted Carbonic Acids with Aliphatic Hydroxy-Acids. **1921** *Jrnl. Soc. Dyers & Colourists* XXXVII. 288/1 Acetyl silk, the new ester-silk. **1930** *Flight* 17 Jan. 134/2 Dope is a solution of cellulose esters in various solvents and diluents. **1940** *Chambers's Techn. Dict.* 309/2 *Ester gums*, rosin or gums which have been esterified with glycerine; raw material for varnishes. **1946** *Nature* 28 Dec. 930/2 It may conveniently be obtained by direct esterification of the glycol or by catalysed ester-interchange between the glycol and dimethyl terephthalate. **1951** *Gloss. Terms Plastics* (*B.S.I.*) 9 *Acrylic ester*, an ester of acrylic acid, or of a structural derivative of acrylic acid. **1958** *Engineering* 28 Feb. 281/3 The production of cross links of the ester type formed by the introduction of the COOH and OH groups. **1965** *Nomencl. Org. Chem.* (I.U.P.A.C.) c. 126 Neutral esters of carboxylic acids, *etc.*, are named in the same way as their neutral salts except that (*a*) the name of the alkyl or aryl, *etc.*, radical replaces the name of the cation and (*b*) a periphrase such as '(alkyl or aryl) ester' replaces '(metal) salt'.

Hence **e,sterifi'cation**, the process of forming an ester; the conversion of an acid into its ester; **e'sterify** *v.* [-FY], to convert into an ester.

1898 *Nature* 6 Jan. 239/1 The authors have made experiments on the esterification of many cinnamic acids.

1903 *Rep. Brit. Assoc.* (1902) 586 The rate of esterification of methyl hydrogen succinate. **1907** *Practitioner* June 864 Arhovin..is a product of diphenylamin and the esterified thymol-benzoic acid. **1920** CROSS & BEVAN *Paper-Making* (ed. 5) 27 Esterifying reagents. **1940** Esterify [see above]. **1946** Esterification [see above]. **1956** *Nature* 24 Mar. 575/2 Vitamin A is absorbed through the lymphatic system mostly in the esterified form and is stored in the liver predominantly as ester. **1966** *Lancet* 24 Dec. 1421/2 The galactose is esterified with the sulphate at position 6.

Ester, -ne, obs. forms of EASTER.

esterase (ˈɛstəreɪs, -z). *Biochem.* [f. ESTER + -ASE.] An enzyme which brings about the hydrolysis of an ester into the corresponding acid and alcohol.

1916 A. E. PORTER in *Biochem. Jrnl.* X. 523 (*title*) The distribution of esterases in the animal body. *Ibid.*, Esterases such as cholesteryl esterases and wax-splitting ferments, that is ferments which are able to split the esters of higher alcohols. **1949** H. W. FLOREY et al. *Antibiotics* II. xxxi. 1076 The blood of the mouse, rat and guinea-pig was shown to contain an esterase which hydrolysed the methyl and benzyl esters. **1956** *Nature* 28 Jan. 185/2 The esterase activity was expressed as the amount of carbon dioxide evolved from the bicarbonate buffer by the acid formed during the enzymatic hydrolysis of acetylthiocholine.

esterling, var. form of EASTERLING, *Obs.*

†**estery feather.** *Obs. rare.* App. = *estridge* (ostrich) feather; applied to some peculiarity in the coat of a horse.

1685 *Lond. Gaz.* No. 2524/4 A bright Bay Horse with a Bob Tail, and three Estery Feathers, one at his breast, and one at each side of his Neck. *Ibid.*, A brown Roan Mare.. the hair curleth almost like an Estery Feather.

†**estew.** *Obs.* [var. of STEW; cf. OF. *estuver* to stew.] A dish of stewed meat, a stew.

1566 WARDE tr. *Alexis' Secr.* III. I. 28 b, We make..an estewe or Bayne wherin hath bene sodden some Ieniper.

esteward(e, obs. form of EASTWARD.

estful: see ESTE *sb.* 4.

Esth (ɛsθ, ɛst), *a.* and *sb.* [G. *Esth, Ehst.*] = ESTONIAN *a.* and *sb.* Now *rare.*

1868 *Fraser's Mag.* LXXVIII. 535/1 The Esths..speak a language closely allied to the Finnish. *Ibid.* 536/1 The poem was published in Esth, with a translation into German. *Ibid.* 542/2 Turja is the Esth name for Norway. **1910** *Encycl. Brit.* IX. 798/1 The Esths, Ehsts or Esthonians. **1920** *Glasgow Herald* 28 Dec. 4 Warsaw expects an attack at any moment, the Esths and Letts in February. **1935** HUXLEY & HADDON *We Europeans* vii. 221 The Esths have reddish-flaxen hair, blue eyes and a cephalic index of 79.

esthete, -ic, var. ff. ÆSTHETE, -IC.

†**esthiomene.** *Path. Obs.* [a. Fr. *esthiomène*, ad. Gr. ἐσθιόμενος, pr. pple. pass. or middle of ἐσθίειν to eat.] A gangrenous sore.

1541 R. COPLAND *Galyen's Terap.* 2 Fj b, In al Esthiomenes [*printed* Eschirmenes] that is to say that are eaten and reade. **1541** —— *Guydon's Quest. Chirurg.*, Auycen in his fourth boke commaundeth them to be done rounde aboute the estiomenes [*printed* estionoenes] sores.

estile, obs. form of ESTOILE, *Her.*

estimable (ˈɛstɪməb(ə)l), *a.* and *sb.* See also ESTEEMABLE. [a. Fr. *estimable*, ad. L. *æstimābilis*, f. *æstimāre*: see ESTEEM, ESTIMATE, *vbs.*]

A. *adj.*

†**1.** Capable of being estimated, valued, or appraised. *Obs.*

c **1460** FORTESCUE *Abs. & Lim. Mon.* vi. (1885) 122 The kepynge off the see I reken not amonge the ordinarie charges ..bi cause it is not estimable [*ed.* 1714 estemable]. *Ibid.* xvii. (1885) 151 It is not lyghtly estymable [*ed.* 1714 estemable], what myght þe kynge may haue off is officers. **1638** SANDERSON *Serm.* vii. (1673) 99 These precious Souls..not estimable with any other thing than with the precious blood of God. *a* **1805** PALEY (cited by Webster 1828).

†**2.** Valuable, worth a great price; of worth. *Obs.*

1596 SHAKS. *Merch. V.* I. iii. 167 A pound of mans flesh.. Is not so estimable, profitable neither As flesh of Muttons, Beefes, or Goates. **1791** BOSWELL *Johnson* I. Advt., His Contributions to my Collection are highly estimable. **1796** C. MARSHALL *Garden.* xix. (1813) 376 The colchicums are pretty plants for the end of the flowery season (October) which makes them estimable objects near the house. **1803** JANE PORTER *Thaddeus* xi. (1831) 97 All that rendered existence estimable.

3. Of persons and their attributes: Worthy of esteem or regard.

a **1698** TEMPLE (J.), A lady said of her two companions, that one was more amiable, the other more estimable. **1759** HURD *Dial.* 8 (R.) The more estimable, nay the most accomplished characters, that have been formed among ourselves. **1796** BURKE *Regic. Peace* iv. Wks. IX. 67 A Tartar believes, when he has killed a man, that all his estimable qualities pass with his clothes and arms to the murderer. **1831** SIR J. SINCLAIR *Corr.* II. 346, I do not recollect having met with a more estimable character than Count Itzenplitz. **1860** TYNDALL *Glac.* I. xxiv. 170 So determined a climber and so estimable a man.

†**4.** Of things: Worthy of consideration; of considerable importance. *Obs.*

1570–6 LAMBARDE *Peramb. Kent* (1826) 131 The Towne was long since somewhat estimable. **1741** MIDDLETON *Cicero* II. XI. 583 These letters still more estimable.

†**B.** *sb. pl.* Things estimable. *Obs. rare*⁻¹. Cf. *valuables.*

a **1682** SIR T. BROWNE *Tracts* (1684) 50 The Queen of Sheba..brought some plants of the Balsam Tree, as one of the peculiar estimables of her Country.

ˈestimableness (ˈɛstɪməb(ə)lnɪs). [f. prec. + -NESS.] The quality of being estimable, or of deserving esteem or regard.

1730–6 in BAILEY (folio). **1777** BRAND *Pop. Antiq.* (1849) I. 229 The estimableness of the characters of their neighbours. **1828** WEBSTER cites R. NEWTON.

ˈestimably, *adv.* [f. as prec. + -LY².] In an estimable manner.

1847 in CRAIG; and in mod. Dicts.

estimate (ˈɛstɪmət), *sb.* [ad. L. *æstimāt-us* (only in abl.), vbl. sb. f. *æstimāre*: see ESTEEM, ESTIMATE, *vbs.*]

†**1. a.** The action of valuing or appraising; a valuation; *lit.* and *fig. to make no estimate of*: to make no account of, not to value. **b.** The price at which anything is rated; *fig.* attributed value. *Obs.*

Shakspere's *to have estimate in* (quot. 1601), seems to mean 'to have a claim to be considered in the valuation of'.

1563 GOLDING *Cæsar* VI. 158 They make an estimate of their own goods and lay so muche in valew therevnto. **1594** SOUTHWELL *M. Magd. Fun. Teares* 92 Love..doubleth the estimate of things that are precious. **1600** DEKKER *Gentle Craft* 33 Of my love he makes no estimate. **1601** SHAKS. *All's Well* II. i. 183 Thy life is deere, for all that life can rate Worth name of life, in thee hath estimate. **1607** —— *Timon* I. i. 14 If he will touch the estimate. **1611** COTGR. s.v. *Donner*, Hee that giues quickly..Doubles th' estimate of his gift. **1622** CALLIS *Stat. Sewers* (1824) 26 My Ship..is returned to your Shores, furnished..with Merchandize of several estimates. **1630** J. TAYLOR (Water P.) *Wks.* I. 106/2 They are of farre more estimate and price Than th' Estrich, or the bird of Paradise. *a* **1674** CLARENDON *Surv. Leviath.* (1676) 227 The high estimate they have made of the joies of Heaven. **1677** HALE *Contempl.* II. 90 They will soon lose their Estimate and Delight.

†**c.** Repute, reputation. *Obs.*

1593 SHAKS. *Rich. II*, II. iii. 56 There stands the Castle.. And in it are the Lords of Yorke, Barkely, and Seymor, None else of Name, and noble estimate. **1607** —— *Cor.* III. iii. 114 My deere Wiues estimate. **1657** J. PETTUS in *Loveday's Lett.* (1663) A 4 a, Seneca's and Cicero's Epistles have escap'd: may Loveday's have the same success and estimate.

2. An approximate judgement based on considerations of probability, respecting the number, amount, magnitude, or position of anything; the quantity assigned by such a judgement.

1630 PAGITT *Christianogr.* I. ii. (1636) 38 There was an old estimate made of Germany..that..there was not past one twelfth part of it remaining Catholicke. **1669** BOYLE *Contn. New Exp.* I. xxxiv. (1682) 118 Drawn up (by our æstimate) about two inches and a half. **1702** R. NELSON in *Pepys' Diary* VI. 256 There is a design of building a Church..which by estimate will cost [etc.]. **1709** BERKELEY *Th. Vision* §3 The estimate we make of the distance of objects. **1846** MCCULLOCH *Acc. Brit. Empire* (1854) II. 523 In forming any estimate of the total or yearly value of lands and houses. **1860** MAURY *Phys. Geog. Sea* v. §294 This estimate as to the quantity of rain in the two hemispheres.

b. *the estimates*: accounts presented annually to Parliament, showing the probable amount of expenditure on the several administrative departments for the current year.

1732 *Gent. Mag.* II. 881 The Accounts for the Year 1731 and Estimates of Charges on the Articles therein mention'd for the present Year. **1740** LD. BALTIMORE *Ibid.* X. 586 The Estimate of the Navy..is lower..than that which was laid before us the last Session. **1851** HT. MARTINEAU *Hist. Peace* (1877) III. IV. xi. 87 The estimates were reduced half a million. **1887** *Daily News* 25 July 5/2 The Estimates, in fact, should have a fixed appendix.

c. A statement furnished by a builder, contractor, or other tradesman, of the sum for which he is prepared to undertake the execution of a specified piece of work.

1796 *Hull Advertiser* 14 May 2/2 Estimates to be given in on or before the 25th of May. **1829** C. WELCH *Wesl. Polity* 158 The various candidates for a contract deliver in estimates **1857** W. COLLINS *Dead Secret* (1861) 60, 'I wish he had sent the estimate with it' said Rosamond. **1878** *Print. Trades Jrnl.* xxv. 5 The proprietor of a..weekly newspaper sought estimates for its cheaper production.

3. A judgement formed or expressed respecting the character or qualities of a person or thing, or respecting a state of affairs, etc.

1589 NASHE *Pref. Greene's Menaphon* (Arb.) 7 Well may the Adage, *Nil dectum quod non dictum prius*, bee the most iudiciall estimate, of our latter Writers. *a* **1704** L'ESTRANGE (J.), A true estimate upon the odds betwixt a publick and a private life. **1711** ADDISON *Spect.* No. 257 ¶9 Outward Actions can never give a just Estimate of us. **1816** J. SCOTT *Vis. Paris* (ed. 5) 270 The estimate of the French character and condition, given in this volume, is an unfavourable one. **1858** FROUDE *Hist. Eng.* IV. xviii. 31 This estimate both of interest and fitness varied from day to day.

b. Estimation; manner in which things are viewed.

1637 R. HUMFREY tr. *S. Ambrose* Pref., What is reputed good in the estimate of the world. **1856** EMERSON *Eng. Traits, Aristocr.* Wks. (Bohn) II. 84 The English barons, in every period, have been brave and great, after the estimate and opinion of their times. **1863** GEO. ELIOT *Romola* III. xxv, He was not unaware that he had sunk a little in the estimate of the men who had accepted his services.

estimate (ˈɛstɪmeɪt), *v.* Forms: 5–6 **estymat(t,** 7 **æstimate, estimat,** 6– **estimate.** [f. L. *æstimāt-* ppl. stem of *æstimāre*, in class. L. = sense 1; in late L. also as in 1 b, 2–4. Cf. ESTEEM.]

†**1.** *trans.* To assign a value to; to appraise, assess; to fix proportionately (penalties, wages, etc.). Const. *at. Obs.*

1611 BIBLE *Lev.* xxvii. 14 As the Priest shall estimate it, so shall it stand. **1646** SIR T. BROWNE *Pseud. Ep.* v. xiv. 255 If she were between the age of five and twenty, shee was to be estimated but at ten shekels. *a* **1704** LOCKE (J.), It is by the weight of silver.. that men estimate commodities. **1710** PRIDEAUX *Orig. Tithes* ii. 68 The wages are to be estimated according to the qualifications which are necessary in the person. **1751** JOHNSON *Rambler* No. 118 ¶9 To..estimate securities, and to engage for mortgages.

b. To value (subjectively); to attribute value to; to appreciate the worth of; to esteem, hold in (higher or lower) estimation.

1597 DANIEL *Civ. Wares* IV. iii, Their wisedome..Liuedogges before dead Lyons estimates. **1651** JER. TAYLOR *Clerus Dom.* 6 Saul's messengers and Saul himselfe turned Prophets, that they might estimate the place and preserve its priviledge. **1751** JOHNSON *Rambler* No. 172 ¶8 It is difficult not to estimate what is lately gained above its real value.

2. To form an approximate notion of (the amount, number, magnitude, or position of anything) without actual enumeration or measurement; to fix by estimate *at.* Also with clause as obj.

1669 STURMY *Mariners' Mag.* I. 157 The Error is to be imputed..to the judgment in estimating the Distance run, in making it too little. *a* **1687** PETTY *Pol. Arith.* (1690) 82 Some have estimated that there are not above Three hundred Millions of People in the whole World. **1765** MATY in *Phil. Trans.* LV. 308 The difference of declination was only estimated. **1774** GOLDSM. *Nat. Hist.* (1776) III. 143 By the rule of proportion, we may estimate his size at eight or nine feet. **1828** J. H. MOORE *Pract. Navig.* 16 Estimate 8 parts out of 20 of the next smaller division. **1848** W. BARTLETT *Egypt to Pal.* xiii. (1879) 286 One of our number ..estimated that this valley would pasture a thousand cattle three months. **1855** PRESCOTT *Philip II*, I. II. xii. 278 The amount of injury inflicted during this dismal period, it is not possible to estimate. **1885** *Manch. Exam.* 6 July 4/7 The prosecutors estimate the defalcations at about 1,800*l.*

†**3.** To esteem, consider, judge (a thing to be so and so); with simple complement, or *as. Obs. rare* = ESTEEM *v.* 5.

c **1532** DEWES *Introd. Fr.* in Palsgr. 1066 We may make no greatter honour to God than to estymat him trew..nor greatter dishonour than to mystrust hym. **1654** tr. *Scudery's Curia Politiæ* 69 Those who are interested will estimate us as their Liberators. **1794** S. WILLIAMS *Vermont* 153 This may properly be estimated as a part of the Indian dress.

4. To gauge; to judge of, form an opinion of.

1651 HOBBES *Leviath.* III. xliii. 327 This article [that Jesus is the Christ] is the measure and rule by which to estimate, and examine all other Articles. **1665** BOYLE *Occas. Refl.* III. vii, In estimating a Man's condition, we should not only consider what Possessions he has, but what Desires. **1692** LOCKE *3rd Let. Toleration* Wks. 1765 V. 215 The measure of punishments being to be estimated..by the length of their duration. **1768** JOHNSON *Pref. to Shaks.* Wks. IX. 240 While an author is yet living, we estimate his powers by his worst performance. **1794** GOUV. MORRIS in Sparks *Life & Writ.* (1832) III. 50 If it be just to judge a private man by his friends, it is not amiss to estimate a public officer by his foes. **1837** LANDOR *Pentameron* Wks. 1846 II. 258 Bacon and Hooker could not estimate Shakespeare. **1878** MORLEY *Carlyle* Crit. Misc. Ser. I. 201 To estimate the intention and sincerity of a movement.

†**ˈestimate,** *pa. pple. Obs. rare.* In 5 **estymatt,** 6 **esteemate.** [ad. L. *æstimāt-us*, pa. pple. of *æstimāre*: see ESTEEM.] Used as pa. pple. of ESTEEM or ESTIMATE.

c **1425** tr. *T. à Kempis' Consol.* II. xi, Lete him not pondre gret, all þat may be estymatt gret. **1635** BARRIFFE *Mil. Discip.* cx. (1643) 337 A Jem, more prizable and esteemate, then the best Armours of proofe.

estimation (ɛstɪˈmeɪʃən). Forms: 4–6 **estim-, estymacion, -oun, -yon(e,** 4 **extymacion,** 5–6 **estymation, -oun,** (6 **estymacon, esteemation,** 7 **æstimation),** 6– **estimation.** [ME. *estimacion, -cioun*, a. OF. *estimacion* (mod.F. *estimation*, corresp. to Pr. *estimatio, estimacion*, Sp. *estimacion*, It. *stimazione*), ad. L. *æstimātiōn-em*, f. *æstimāre*: see ESTEEM, ESTIMATE.] The action of estimating or esteeming.

†**1.** The action of appraising, assessing, or valuing; statement of price or value; valuation.

1382 WYCLIF *Ex.* xxii. 5 If eny man harme feeld..what euer best thing he hath in his feeld..he shal restore for estymacioun of the harm [Vulg. *pro damni æstimatione*; **1388** the valu of harm]. **1413** LYDG. *Pilgr. Sowle* IV. ix. (1483) 62 The prys of myn Appel is of suche valewe that it passeth the estymacion of ony creature. **1523** LD. BERNERS *Froiss.* I. xiii. 13 They had syluer for theyr horses..at theyre owne estymation, without any grudgyng. **1609** BIBLE (Douay) *1 Kings* viii. 5 They immolated sheepe and oxen without estimation and number. **1667** E. CHAMBERLAYNE *St. Gt. Brit.* I. III. ii. (1743) 158 Silver and gold have been chosen to be the Instruments of Exchange and Estimation of all Things. **1776** ADAM SMITH *W.N.* I. i. 190 In the household book of Henry..there are two different estimations of wheat. **1792** A. YOUNG *Trav. France* 499 The Bureau de la Balance du Commerce at Paris..is beyond all

comparison more accurate in its estimations [than the English Custom-house.]

†**b.** Estimated value; *concr.* something which one values. *Obs.*

1551 ROBINSON tr. *More's Utop.* II. (Arb.) 155 They be wrought so fynely and conningelye..that the estimation of no costely stuffe is hable to counteruaile the price of the worke. **1611** SHAKS. *Cymb.* I. iv. 99 Your Ring may be stolne too, so your brace of vnprizeable Estimations, the one is but fraile, and the other Casuall. **1631** T. MAY tr. *Barclay's Mirr. Mindes* I. 245 The earth in the bowels of it hath many metalls, both of different natures and estimations. **1775** JOHNSON *Tax. no Tyr.* 41 For some thing, in their opinion, of more estimation.

2. a. Appreciation, valuation is respect of excellence or merit; esteem considered as a sentiment. Phrase, ***to have or hold in estimation.***

1530 PALSGR. 34 If he desyre that his wrytynges shulde be had in any estymacion. *a* **1535** MORE *De quat. Noviss.* Wks. 82/2 As rising of an hie estimacion of our self. **1576** FLEMING *Panopl. Ep.* 268 So farre from having monie in estimation.. I have cast it away from me. *a* **1680** BUTLER *Rem.* (1759) II. 17 He holds it a kind of Self-Preservation to maintain a good Estimation of himself. **1712** STEELE *Spect.* No. 456 ¶5 Mens Estimation follows us according to the Company we keep. **1787** CANNING in *Microcosm* No. 18 Wishing to know in what estimation he was held by man-kind. **1796** C. MARSHALL *Garden.* i. (1813) 1 The degree of estimation that the art of gardening is worthy of. **1848** DICKENS *Dombey* 273 Mr. Dombey is so generous in his estimation of any trivial accomplishment. **1882** PEBODY *Eng. Journalism* xxi. 156 The Provincial Press of Great Britain never stood higher in public estimation than it stands to-day.

†**b.** The condition of being esteemed; 'account' or worth in the opinion of others; esteem considered passively; repute. Of places: Importance, consequence. Phrases, ***to be in estimation, to grow out of estimation.*** *Obs.*

1530 PALSGR. 300 Any auctour of estymation. **1531** ELYOT *Gov.* I. xiii, The frute..leseth his verdure and taste, and finally his estimation. **1569** J. ROGERS *Gl. Godly Loue* 185 How in estimacion a chaste life is. **1570–6** LAMBARDE *Peramb. Kent* (1826) 159 The name of Hyde..led me to thinke that it had been of more estimation in time past. **1571** GOLDING *Calvin on Ps.* lxxi. 6 Gods miracles growe out of estimacion with us by custome. **1593** NASHE *Four Lett. Confut.* 14 His brother..indeuord to take from mee all estimation of Arte or witte. **1612** BRINSLEY *Lud. Lit.* xxiv. (1627) 268 To avoide carefully..whatsoever may diminish his estimation and authority. **1764** FRANKLIN *Ess.* Wks. 1840 II. 349 Gold and silver have..universal estimation. **1792** BURKE *Let. Sir H. Langrishe* Wks. 1842 I. 544 A miserable populace, without property, without estimation, without education. **1824–8** LANDOR *Imag. Conv.* (1846) 51 The family of every criminal is a loser in estimation..by his punishment, however just. **1828** SCOTT *F.M. Perth* xxv, The sole virtue of our commonweal, its strength, and its estimation, lay among the burgher craft of the better class.

3. The process of forming an approximate notion of (numbers, quantities, magnitudes, etc.) without actual enumeration or measurement.

c **1400** MAUNDEV. v. (1839) 41 That Tour..was of 25 myle in cyrcuyt of the Walles..as Men may demen by estymatioun. **1424** *Paston Lett.* No. 4. I. 12 To the noumbre of four score and more by estimacion. **1473** WARKW. *Chron.* 5 A blasynge sterre..iiij. fote highe by estimacyone. **1558** in *Vicary's Anat.* (1888) App. v. 182 Three..parcells of pasture grounde..conteyning by estimacion eighteene acres. **1669** STURMY *Mariner's Mag.* I. 160 If a ship sail 8 Miles South in an Hour, by Log or Estimation. **1772** HUTTON *Bridges* 86 The proper estimation of the expence. **1786** *Phil. Trans.* LXXVI. 9 The distance of the nearest threads became a very visible space, answerable to one minute each, and therefore capable of a much further subdivision by estimation. **1838** DE MORGAN *Ess. Probab.* 128 That which we call estimation means guess formed by a person whose previous habits and experience are such as to make it very likely that he can tell nearly true that which would require instruments to obtain with great approach to accuracy.

†**b.** Estimated number. *Obs.*

1513 *Bk. Keruynge* in *Babees Bk.* 274 There shall be set brede, trenchours, and spones, after the estymacyon of them that shall syt there.

4. Manner of estimating or judging; opinion, judgement.

c **1374** CHAUCER *Boeth.* IV. iv. 125 þou hast quod she þe ry3t estimacioun of þis. *c* **1400** *Test. Love* I. (Chalm. *Poets*) 474/1 Thestimacion of the enuious people, ne loketh nothing to desertes of men..but onely to the auenture of fortune. **1447** BOKENHAM *Seyntys* Introd. (Roxb.) 6 Be the blyssyd medyacyoun Of this virgyne aftyr my estimacyoun. **1560** DAUS tr. *Sleidane's Comm.* 21 a, Reuchline in the defence of his estimation, aunswereth him [Phefercorn] with another. *a* **1677** BARROW *Wks.* (1741) I. v. 45 He that walketh uprightly..is sure not to come off disgracefully..in the estimations of men. **1790** BURKE *Fr. Rev.* 39 The crown ..in the..estimation of law..had ever been, perfectly irresponsible. **1841** LANE *Arab. Nts.* I. 88 The dearest of men in my estimation. **1864** I. TAYLOR *Words & Places* 469 In popular estimation, idle and vagabond habits were acquired by those who made the pilgrimage to the..Holy Land.

†**b.** Conjecture, guessing. *Obs. rare*$^{-1}$. Cf. 3.

1596 SHAKS. *1 Hen. IV*, I. iii. 273, I speake not this in estimation, As what I thinke might be, but what I know Is ruminated, plotted, and set downe.

†**5.** 'Judgement' as a mental faculty. *Obs.* Cf. ESTIMATIVE.

1398 TREVISA *Barth. De P.R.* III. xi. (1495) 55 Proprely to speke a hound vsyth no reason but he vsyth a besye and stronge estymacyon. **1509** HAWES *Past. Pleas.* XXIV. ii, These are the v. wyttes..Fyrst, commyn wytte..Fantasy, and estymacyon truely.

estimative ('ɛstɪmətɪv), *a.* [ad. late L. *æstimātīv-us*, f. *æstimāre*: see ESTIMATE and -IVE.]

1. Adapted for estimating; having the power of estimating. †**a.** ***estimative faculty, virtue***, etc.: the faculty of 'judgement' (*obs.*). **b.** ***estimative art*** [after Gr. στοχαστικὴ τέχνη].

1398 TREVISA *Barth. De P.R.* III. xi. (1495) 55 The vertue estimatiue and the ymagynatyf ben comyn to vs and to other beest. **1548–77** VICARY *Anat.* iv. (1888) 31 In the middest sel or ventrikle [of the brain] there is founded..the Cogitatiue or estimatiue vertue. **1606** *Sir G. Goosecappe* I. iv. in Bullen *O. Pl.* III. 22 To..make my estimative power believe, etc. **1666** J. SMITH *Old Age* (1752) 37 The fancy both estimative and cogitative. *a* **1691** BOYLE (J.), The errour is not in the eye, but in the estimative faculty. **1859** *Encycl. Brit.* XVII. 567/2 Mr. Combe..and others acknowledge that applied phrenology is an estimative art only.

†**2. a.** Based upon estimation or approximate calculation. **b.** Imputed, due to estimation. *Obs.*

1618–29 *Charges agst. Dk. Buckhm.* in Rushw. *Hist. Coll.* (1659) I. 346 This he delivered as a Sum Estimative. *a* **1640** WANDESFORDE *Instruct. to his Son* (1777) §83 A Jewel of that unvaluable Richness, not estimative but intrinsicall. **1651** CULPEPPER *Astrol. Judgem. Dis.* (1658) 151 It anticipates the time estimative but 10. min.

Hence †**'estimatively** *adv. Obs.*, in an estimative manner; by way of esteem or respect.

1633 T. ADAMS *Exp. 2 Peter* iii. 1 Our spiritual parents are more to be loved estimatively; our natural, more intensively.

estimator ('ɛstɪmeɪtə(r)). Also 8 **-er.** [a. L. *æstimātor*, agent-n. f. *æstimāre*: see ESTIMATE *v.* and -OR.] One who estimates.

a **1665** J. GOODWIN *Filled w. the Spirit* (1867) 406 Our Saviour..was the best estimator concerning matters of profit. **1768–74** TUCKER *Lt. Nat.* (1852) I. 363 We are very bad estimaters of happiness. **1861** *Lond. Rev.* 20 Apr. 434/2 They are by no means the keenest estimators.

estimatory ('ɛstɪmətərɪ), *a.* [ad. L. *æstimātōrius*, f. *æstimātor*: see prec.] (See quots.)

1736–1800 BAILEY, *Æstimatory*, of or belonging to pricing or valuing; for a price or estimation. **1818** COLEBROOKE *Oblig. & Contracts* I. 18 Estimatory contract (binding in the alternative to sell for a fixt price or return the goods).

estime, -er, obs. ff. ESTEEM, -ER.

estin, Sc. form of EASTEN *a. Obs.*

‖**estivage.** [Fr. *estivage*, f. *estiver*, ad. It. *stivare* = Pr. *estipar*, Sp. and Pg. *estivar*:—L. *stipāre* to pack close.] A mode of stowing or trimming vessels by pressing or screwing the cargo into the vessel by means of a capstan machinery, practised in American or Mediterranean ports. (Ogilvie.)

estival, var. form of ÆSTIVAL.

estivate, *v.* An occasional spelling of ÆSTIVATE, to spend the summer; *esp.* of animals, to spend the summer in a state of torpor.

1656–81 in BLOUNT *Glossogr.* **1854** THOREAU *Walden* xvi. (1863) 317 As if he had a design to estivate with us. **1883** *Sunday Mag.* 676 The unfortunate reptile was estivating exactly under the spot where the fire had been made.

estivation, var. of ÆSTIVATION.

estivator ('ɛstɪveɪtə(r)). [f. ESTIVATE *v.* + -OR.] An animal that estivates or passes the summer in a state of torpor.

1883 *Sunday Mag.* 674 They search the dry bed of the river, dig up the buried estivators, and live on them.

estive, var. form of ÆSTIVE *a. Obs.*, of or belonging to summer.

†**'estivous,** *a. Obs.* [f. L. *æstīv-us* + -OUS.] Of or pertaining to summer, summer-like.

c **1420** *Pallad. on Husb.* IV. 580 In landes that beth estyvous for heete.

estlande, obs. form of EASTLAND.

estlar, -er, obs. Sc. forms of ASHLAR *sb.*

estmast, obs. form of EASTMOST.

‖**estoc** ('ɛstɒk). [F. *estoc* = Pr. *estoc*, Sp. and Pg. *estoque*, It. *stocco*.] A kind of sword; the name was variously applied at different times: see quots.

1830 JAMES *Darnley* xxvii, A good downright blow of estoc at a fair gentleman's head. **1834** PLANCHÉ *Brit. Costume* 138 The scabbard of his estoc or small stabbing-sword. **1860** FAIRHOLT *Costume in Eng.* (ed. 2) 440 *Estoc*, a short sword, worn at the girdle by soldiers.

†**esto'cade.** *Obs.* Also 6 **estockado.** [a. F. *estocade*, f. *estoc*: see ESTOC; cf. Sp. *estocada*, It. *stoccata*, and see -ADE[1] and -ADO[2].] A thrust with an estoc; in quots. the weapon itself.

1579 FENTON *Guicciard.* II. 104 Rodolphe Gonzague.. was so hurt in the face with an estockado by a french man. *Ibid.*, Euery one beganne..to lay handes vpon their masses, estokados, and other short weapons.

estocade: erron. f. ESTACADE.

estoil(e (ɪ'stɔɪl). *Her.* Also 7 **estile.** [a. OF. *estoile*, mod.F. *étoile*.] A common charge in the form of a star with wavy points or rays.

1572 BOSSEWELL *Armorie* II. 114 Three cressants and as many Estoiles montans of the seconde: borne by the name of Dillon. *a* **1661** FULLER *Worthies* (1840) II. 79 His [John Gwillim's] industry..about stars (but here we must call them estoiles). **1688** R. HOLME *Armoury* II. 16/2 A Star..is better in Blazon to be termed an Estile or Estoile. **1763** *Brit. Mag.* IV. 303 A chevron between three estoils, sable. **1864** BOUTELL *Heraldry Hist. & Pop.* ix. 47 The Mullet essentially differs from the Estoile the rays of which are always wavy.

estoilée (ɪ'stɔɪleɪ), *a. Her.* [a. OF. (*croix*) **estoilé(e*, f. *estoile* (mod.F. *étoile*) star.] (See quot.)

1730–6 BAILEY (folio), *Estoillée* as a Cross Estoilleé signifies a star with only 4 long rays in form of a cross, and so broad in the centre, and ending in sharp points. **1847** in CRAIG; and in mod. Dicts.

Estonian (ɛ'stəʊnɪən), *a.* and *sb.* Also **Esthonian.** [f. mod.L. *Est(h)oni(a*, f. ESTH *a.* and *sb.*, after *Saxonia*, etc. + -AN.] **A.** *adj.* Of or belonging to Estonia (native name *Eesti*), since 1940 a constituent republic of the U.S.S.R., stretching along the south coast of the Gulf of Finland. **B.** *sb.* **1.** A native or inhabitant of Estonia. **2.** The Finno-Ugrian language of Estonia.

1795 in W. Tooke *Varieties of Literature* I. 23 Esthonian poetry. *Ibid.*, The Esthonians..have an extremely soft, delicate, and tender articulation. **1841** LADY EASTLAKE *Resid. Shores Baltic* II. xvi. 62 Nothing can exceed the hospitality of the Estonians. **1863** R. G. LATHAM *Nationalities of Europe* I. xii. 129 *Ma*, in Estonian, means *land*. *Ibid.* 132 The Estonian instrument is the harp. **1874** A. H. SAYCE *Princ. Compar. Philol.* 322 *Wanna Issi* in Esthonian means 'the old father'. **1894** W. F. KIRBY *Hero of Esthonia* I. p. xvi, The Finns, the Esthonians, and the Lapps ..speak very similar languages. **1925** O. RUTTER *New Baltic States* xi. 199 Estonian folklore owes something to the Finnish. **1941** J. H. JACKSON *Estonia* i. 20 The Soviets.. were asking for naval bases on Estonian territory. *Ibid.* iii. 58 One of the eight chairs on the original foundation was a professorship in the Estonian language. **1948** A. ORAS *Baltic Eclipse* i. 20 The Estonian shipyards, railway works, plywood factories. **1952** E. UUSTALU *Hist. Estonian People* v. 82 These tax and work registers, or 'Vakus-books', as they were called in Estonian.

e'stonied, obs. var. of ASTONIED *ppl. a.*, struck with consternation, dismayed.

1581 MARBECK *Bk. of Notes* 362 Manie men shall be estonied when they shall see Christ our sauiour.

estop (ɪ'stɒp), *v.* Also 5–7 **estopp(e.** [a. OF. *estoper*, *estouper* (sense 1), and AF. *estopper* (sense 2), f. OF. *estoupe* (mod.F. *étoupe*) = Pr. and Sp. *estopa*, It. *stoppa*:—L. *stuppa* tow. Cf. STOP *v.*]

1. *trans.* To stop with or as with a dam, plug, or bar: to fill up (a pool). *arch.*

[**1292** BRITTON I. xxx. §8 Devises remuez, chemins et euwes estopez.] *a* **1420** HOCCLEVE *De Reg. Princ.* 63 For God estopped eke the concepcioun Of every woman of his [Pharaoh's] mansioun. **1586** FERNE *Blaz. Gentrie* 61 A barre to estop..the mouthes of the people. **1621** BOLTON *Stat. Irel.* 51 (*Act 8 Hen VII.*) They have estopped both parts of the Podell. **1860** RUSSELL *Diary India* II. 109 The road.. winds along the side of a barren mountain..till it appears to be estopped by a high cliff.

2. *Law.* To stop, bar, hinder, preclude. Chiefly *refl.* and in *pass.*, to be precluded by one's own previous act or declaration from doing or alleging something. Const. †*of*, *to* with *inf.* [= AF. *estopper à* with *inf.*], and in recent use *from*; also *simply*.

1531 *Dial. on Laws Eng.* I. xix. (1638) 34 The law in such cases giveth no remedy to him that is estopped. **1594** WEST *Symbol.* II. *Chancerie* §37 A man may not deny..that whereof he wilfully estopped or excluded himselfe by deed indented. **1598** KITCHIN *Courts Leet*, (1675) 303 He is estopped to say contrary. **1654** *Burton's Diary* (1828) I. Introd. 31 An indenture can estopp only such as are parties, and where an interest is also conferred. **1767** BLACKSTONE *Comm.* II. 295 And therefore a man shall always be estopped by his own deed, or not permitted to aver or prove anything in contradiction to what he has once so solemnly and deliberately avowed. **1818** HALLAM *Mid. Ages* (1872) I. 201 The lord who had granted the charter of franchise was estopped from claiming him again. **1884** *Law Times Rep.* 16 Feb. 773/1 L. had sworn that the lights in question were not ancient, and was therefore estopped from alleging..that they were ancient.

b. *gen.* To stop, prevent. *rare.*

1876 BRET HARTE *G. Conroy* III. iii. 101 An event to be expected, feared, and if possible, estopped by fasting and prayer.

3. To cease from, stop. *rare.*

1796 [C. ANSTEY] *Pleaders' Guide* (1803) 121 Nor would the Fates estop their task, To help thee over Quinden' Pasch.

e'stop, *sb.* [f. prec. verb.] A stop or stoppage.

1884 A. A. WATTS *Life Alaric Watts* I. 127 An untimely estop was put upon all this prosperity by an article in the *Quarterly* which..denounced it [a book] as a catchpenny.

estoppage (ɪ'stɒpɪdʒ). [f. ESTOP *v.* + -AGE.]

a. The action of the verb ESTOP; = STOPPAGE. **b.** *Law.* The condition of being estopped.

1701 BEVERLEY *Apoc. Quest.* 42 And though there was the Roar of Judahs Lyon, and the Utterances of the Thunders,

yet they were Seald by the Estoppage of the Effects. **1890** *Daily News* 2 Apr 2/5 The defendants' counsel urged that this doctrine of estoppage was being carried further than had ever been known before.

estoppel (ɛ'stɒpəl). Forms: 6–7 **estople, -pel, -ppell,** 7–8 **estopple,** (9 **estoppal**), 6– **estoppel.** [app. ad. OF. *estoupail, estouppail* bung or cork, f. *estouper*: see ESTOP. Cf. STOPPLE.]

† **1.** An obstruction (to a watercourse) whether natural or artificial. *Obs.*

1608 NORDEN *Surv. Dial.* (N.), But estoples of water courses doe in some places grow by such meanes, as one private man or two cannot by force or discretion make remedie. **1638** EARL CORK *Diary* in *Lismore Papers* Ser. I. (1886) V. 44, I sent him 5 Indictments and orders for removing the weares and other estopels.

2. *Law.* An impediment or bar to a right of action arising from a man's own act, or where he is forbidden by law to speak against his own deed. (Wharton.)

1531 *Dial. on Laws Eng.* II. xliv. (1638) 141 Without it be by such a matter that it worke by way of conclusion or estoppell. **1645** MILTON *Colast.* (1851) 376 This shall be an Estoppel to him in an Assise from the recovering his own Land. **1667** E. CHAMBERLAYNE *St. Gt. Brit.* I. II. ii. (1743) 47 No estoppel can bind the king. **1794** MATHIAS *Purs. Lit.* (1798) 377 He may take advantage of the estoppel, for it runs with the land. **1818** CRUISE *Digest* (ed. 2) VI. 538 Executory interests..may be passed at law by deed, fine, and common recovery, by way of estoppel. **1853** WHARTON *Pa. Digest* 783 Estoppel rests on the principle that every man is presumed to speak and act according to the truth and fact of the case.

† **b.** *gen.* Stoppage, prohibition. *Obs.*

1583 T. STOCKER *Civ. Warres Low C.* II. 5 b, Accordyng to the full rate of the tyme of the saied Estoppell.

estorax, obs. form of STORAX.

1714 *Fr. Bk. of Rates* 383 Estorax in Grain.

† **estoure.** *Obs.* Also 5 **estowr.** See STOUR. [a. AF. *estor.*] Stir, tumult, war.

1481 CAXTON *Myrr.* II. viii. 83 Fayr ladyes whiche in batayiles and in estowrs vse alle their Armes of syluer for lacke of yron. **1490** —— *Eneydos* xxxix. (1890) 129 There was grete effort made, & bigge estoure, after that Eneas was come there.

estovers (ɪ'stəʊvəz), *sb. pl. Law.* [a. OF. *estover, estovoir,* subst. use of *estovoir* to be necessary. Cf. STOVER.] 'Necessaries allowed by law' (J.). In various specific applications: *esp.* Wood which a tenant is privileged to take from his landlord's estate so far as it is necessary for repairing his house, hedges, implements, etc.; alimony for a widow or for a wife separated from her husband; maintenance for an imprisoned felon. (See quots. Cf. BOOT *sb.*[1] 5 b.)

[**1292** BRITTON III. vii. §5 La value de renables estovers en autri soil.] **1594** WEST *Symbol.* II. §55 Housebote, haibote, and plowbote may be demanded by the name of estovers. **1641** *Termes de la Ley* 147 Estovers..Bracton used it for such sustenance as a man taken for Felony is to have forth of his lands or goods for himselfe and his family during his imprisonment. And the Statute of 6 Ed. 1 cap. 3. useth this for allowance in meate or cloth. **1642** PERKINS *Prof. Bk.* i. §104. 46 Estouers granted to be burnt in a house certaine. **1741** T. ROBINSON *Gavelkind* II. vi. 243 Estovers in meat or clothes. **1765** BLACKSTONE *Comm.* I. 441 Alimony to the [divorced] wife..is sometimes called her estovers. **1818** CRUISE *Digest* (ed. 2) III. 89 Estovers for the building of new houses. **1876** DIGBY *Real Prop.* iii. 116 She [a widow] shall have in the meantime her reasonable estovers of the common.

b. *common of estovers*: a liberty of taking necessary wood, for the use or furniture of a house, or farm, from off another's estate. (Wharton.)

1523 FITZHERB. *Surv.* 7 The Lord may gyue or selle the resydewe of the sayde woodes or wastes, Excepte that a manne haue commen of Estouers. **1594** WEST *Symbol.* II. *Chancerie* §141 All..common, aswell of estovers and pastures, as all other commons. **1765** BLACKSTONE *Comm.* I. II. iii. 27 Common of estovers..is a liberty of taking necessary wood. **1879** MISS BRADDON *Vixen* xxviii, The piled-up logs testified to the Tempest common of estovers.

estrada (ɛ'strɑːda). [Pg.:—L. *strāta* (see STREET *sb.*).] In the Brazilian rubber trade, a winding path or road connecting a series of trees. Also in Fr. form **estrade.**

1906 *Westm. Gaz.* 12 July 9/3 The estradas (or roads) which are being worked produce at least 250 kilos of rubber per harvest. **1913** R. H. LOCK *Rubber* 20 To each seringueiro or collector are assigned from 100 to 150 trees, which are connected by a winding path, or *estrade,* cut through the undergrowth... Beginning at sunrise the seringueiro makes two rounds of his estrade. **1921** *Glasgow Herald* 3 May 10 From one estrada in six months about one ton of rubber may be obtained.

estrade (ɪ'strɑːd). [a. F. *estrade* fem., ad. Sp. *estrado* masc.: see ESTRADO.] A slightly raised platform; a dais.

1696–1706 PHILLIPS *Estrade* the one half of an Alcove or Chamber rais'd with Boards and rail'd in, more richly furnish'd and adorn'd for the reception of Persons of Quality. **1718** OZELL *Tournefort's Voy.* I. 372 On the Estrade is spread but one carpet for the officers to sit upon. **1851** SIR F. PALGRAVE *Norm. & Eng.* I. 208 Upon the highest step of the estrade. **1866** MRS. H. WOOD *Elster's Folly* I. 227 He was standing on the sort of estrade which abutted on the river. **1880** J. G. FITCH *Lect. Teaching* 69 The teacher..should have his desk on a mounted estrade or platform.

estradiol, var. ŒSTRADIOL.

† **e'stradiot.** *Obs.* Also STRADIOT. [a. F. *estradiot* = It. *stradiotto,* f. Gr. στρατιώτης soldier.] One of a class of light cavalry, originally raised in Greece and Albania, who served in the Venetian and other armies during the 15th and 16th centuries.

1577–87 HOLINSHED *Chron.* III. 822/1 The French were discomfited: for those that were behind saw..their Estradiots also. **1579** FENTON *Guicciard.* (1618) 264 Many bands of Estradiots leuied in the kingdome of Naples. **1596** DANETT tr. *Comines* 330 Crossebowe men on horsebacke, Estradiots, and footemen.

‖ **estrado** (e'strado). [Sp. *estrado* the carpeted part of a room, drawing-room, reception-room, corresp. to Pg. *estrado,* It. *strato*:—L. *strātum* neut., pa. pple. of *sternĕre* to spread (with carpets).]

a. In Sp. sense: see quot. 1748. **b.** = ESTRADE.

1588 R. PARKE tr. *Mendoza's Hist. China* 47 Then doth hee cause them to sit in an Estrado, or rich pallet, gallantly dressed and furnished in one of the three halles. **1748** *Earthquake of Peru* i. 12 Carpets..to spread on the Estradoes, or places where the Women sit on Cushions. **1838** LYTTON *Leila* II. vii, At the upper part of the space was an estrado, or platform.

estrager, var. of (? or error for) *ostreger,* AUSTRINGER.

1472 *Paston Lett.* No. 708 III. 68.

† **e'strain,** *v. Obs. rare*⁻¹. In 5 **estrayn.** [ad. OF. *estrain-dre*: see STRAIN.] *trans.* To bind tightly.

1483 CAXTON *Gold. Leg.* 363/4 She remembryd how Jhesus in that hour was taken, estrayned, haled forth, and mocked.

† **e'strait,** *v. Obs.* [f. OF. *estreit* adj. (mod.F. *étroit*): see STRAIT.] *trans.* To enclose within narrow bounds, to restrict.

1529 MORE *Heresyes* IV. Wks. 277/2 At this daie the Turke hath estraited vs verye nere, and brought it in within a right narow compace.

† **e'straiten,** *v. Obs.* [var. of STRAITEN.] *trans.* To confine in a narrower space, to restrict.

1598 MANWOOD *Lawes Forest* xxiv. §5 (1615) 248 b Estraitening the Kings Deere from the Forest, to the hurt of the owners.

estrama'zone. [var. of STRAMAZON; cf. Fr. *estramaçon.*] A slashing cut in fencing.

1820 SCOTT *Monast.* xxvii, Being eager to punish him, I made an estramazone.

† **e'strange,** *a.* and *sb. Obs. rare.* Also 4–6 **estraunge.** [a. OF. *estrange*: see STRANGE.]

A. *adj.* **1. a.** Distant, reserved. **b.** Strange, unusual, wonderful.

a. *c* **1374** CHAUCER *Troylus* I. 1084 [1077] His hieghe porte and his manere estraunge. [So *MSS. Harl.* 2280 and *Campsall*; *Harl.* 3943 straunge.]

b. **1549** SIR T. CHALONER tr. *Erasm. Moriæ Enc.* M j a, I maie adde here to their sentences or sawes whiche are so estraunge. **1587** HOLINSHED *Discov. Irel.* iv. (R.), You tell vs of manie gugawes and estrange dreams.

2. *Law.* Not privy or party *to.*

1721 *St. German's Doct. & Stud.* 195 The entry..is void in law, because he is estrange to the deed.

B. *sb.* A stranger, foreigner.

1384 in Arnolde *Chron.* 39 Y^r non estraunges bey or selle w^t any od' estraunges any maner marchandises wythyn ye fraunches of ye same cite.

estrange (ɪ'streɪndʒ), *v.* Also 6 **astrange, -aunge,** 6–7 **estraunge.** [ad. OF. *estranger* (mod.F. *étranger*), corresp. to Pr. *estranhar,* Cat. *estranyar,* Sp. *estrañar,* Pg. *estranhar,* It. *stranare, straniare*:—L. *extrāneāre,* f. *extrāneus*: see STRANGE.] To cause to be strange, or a stranger, or as a stranger (to).

1. *trans.* To remove (permanently or for a length of time) from an accustomed abode, haunt, association, or occupation; to keep apart from experience of or acquaintance with anything. Const. *from.* Somewhat *arch.*

1485 CAXTON *Paris & V.* (1868) 68 He wold estrange hym fro that contree of genes. **1579** E. K. *Gloss. Spenser's Sheph. Cal.* Ep. Ded. §4 Thus much haue I aduentured vpon his frendship, himselfe being for long time furre estraunged. **1612** T. WILSON *Chr. Dict.,* To abstain from sig[nifieth] To seperate or estrange, and turne our mind from a thing. **1665** GLANVILL *Sceps. Sci.* xiv. 80 We must endeavour to estrange our assent from every thing, which is not clearly evidenc'd to our faculties. **1713** *Guardian* No. 5. ¶2 The..lady..has for some time estranged herself from Conversation. **1718** ROWE tr. *Lucan* I. (R.), None shall ask if guiltily I fled, Or thy command estrang'd me from thy bed. **1731** POPE in *Swift's Corr.* II. 648 My lord is as much estranged from politics as I am. **1841** D'ISRAELI *Amen. Lit.* (1867) 59 Edward, long estranged from his native realm. **1864** BROWNING *James Lee's Wife* i, The world has changed! The sun's away, And the bird estranged. **1871** B. TAYLOR *Faust* (1875) II. II. i. 88 The room Waits for its master long estranged.

† **b.** To make (a person) a stranger *to* (a condition or place). *Obs.*

1725 POPE *Odyss.* XIX. 697 To rest and joy Estrang'd since dear Ulysses sail'd to Troy! **1738** THOMSON *Autumn* 1158 A solid Life, estrang'd To Disappointment, and fallacious Hope. **1767** H. BROOKE *Fool of Qual.* II. 152 (D.) Mr. Meekly had long estranged himself to Enfield.

† **c.** To withhold *from* a person's perception or knowledge. *Obs.*

1611 SPEED *Hist. Gt. Brit.* X. i. (1632) 1251 The designe being so estranged from the conceit of man. **1614** EARL STIRLING *Doomesday, 10th Hour* (R.), Their faults are told, Which had been still estrang'd from them before. **1677** HALE *Prim. Orig. Man.* IV. v. 338 None of which ways are estranged from the knowledge of those experienced Spirits.

2. To render alien; to regard or treat as alien; to sever from a community; to remove (possessions, subjects) from the ownership or dominion of any one. *arch.*

1523 *Act 14–15 Hen. VIII,* c. 4 §1 They..estraunge theimselfe from the kynges obeysaunce. **1548** UDALL, etc. *Erasm. Par. Eph.* ii. 12 You wer vtterly astraunged from the title and felowship of the nation of Jewes. **1577** HANMER *Anc. Eccl. Hist.* (1619) 92 He should not estrange or cut off all the Churches of God which retained the tradition of old custome. *a* **1600** HOOKER (J.), For conversion of infidels estranged from the house of God. **1611** BIBLE *Jer.* xix. 4 They haue forsaken mee, and haue estranged this place, and haue burnt incense in it vnto other gods. **1872** BROWNING *Fifine* lviii, I say, I cannot think..such gain Can ever be estranged.

† **b.** To put away from oneself, eschew. *Obs. rare.*

1613–6 W. BROWNE *Brit. Past.* I. v, God will be seene his sentence changing, If he behold thee wicked wayes estranging.

† **c.** To render 'foreign' or dissimilar in character. *Obs.*

1727 POPE, etc. *Art Sinking* 108 Technical terms, which estrange your style from the great and general ideas of nature.

3. To alienate in feeling or affection. Const. *from,* or *simply.*

1494 FABYAN VII. 644 The duke of Brytayne began to estrange hym from the Kyng and refusyd to come vnto his presence. **1561** T. NORTON *Calvin's Inst.* II. ii. (1634) 119 The wicked..which are altogether estranged from God. **1570** *Act 13 Eliz.* c. 2. §1 Minding..to estrange and alienate the Minds and Hearts of sundry her Majestys Subjects from their dutiful Obedience. **1606** HOLLAND *Sueton.* 91 With Ivlia he lived at the first in great concord and mutuall love; but afterwardes hee began to estraunge himselfe. **1681** FLAVEL *Right Man's Ref.* 271 It is therefore his great Design, to estrange and alienate the Saints from their God. **1722** DE FOE *Moll Fl.* (1840) 93, I was quite estranged from him in affection. **1768** BEATTIE *Minstr.* I. xviii, His heart from cruel sport estranged, would bleed To work the wo of any living thing. **1780** BURKE *Sp. Econ. Ref.* Wks. 1842 I. 253 You are going to estrange his majestys confidence from me. **1878** GLADSTONE *Prim. Homer* 106 To direct them towards good persons..and to estrange them from the bad.

† **b.** *intr.* for *refl.* To become alienated in feeling. *Obs. rare.*

1649 SELDEN *Laws Eng.* II. xxvii. (1739) 126 Perswading the King, that Foreign Princes estranged from him..for some apprehensions they had of his departure from that way of Religion.

† **4.** To change, render remote from one's accustomed or normal condition; to make unlike oneself; hence, to put beside oneself, madden. *Obs.*

1547 J. HARRISON *Exhort. Scottes* G j b, So farre did we estraunge our selfes, that wee could finde in our hartes to become seruile..to a forrein nacion. **1577** HANMER *Anc. Eccl. Hist.* (1619) 86 Being mad and sodainly estranged and bereft of his wits. **1598** BARRET *Theor. Warres* I. ii. 10 They sawe their souldiers so estranged from their former valour. **1622** WITHER *Mistr. Philar.* (1633) 687 That neither wasting Cares..Might from what she is estrange her.

5. To render strange or unfamiliar in appearance; to disguise. *arch.*

a **1637** B. JONSON *Challenge at Tilt,* Sure they are these garments that estrange me to you. **1875** [see ESTRANGING *ppl. a.*].

† **6.** *pass.* To be astonished. *Obs. rare.* [Cf. Sp. *estrañarse.*]

1658 A. FOX tr. *Wurtz' Surg.* III. xxi. 284 At which [prunella in throat] some Surgeons are estranged [orig. *het welck sommige voor een wonder..achten*] and others do slight it.

estranged (ɪ'streɪndʒd), *ppl. a.* [f. ESTRANGE *v.* + -ED[1].]

1. In various senses of the verb. Now chiefly: Alienated in feeling or affection. Of manner, look, etc.: Indicating estrangement.

1552 HULOET, Estraunged, aliened, or put awaye, *alienatus, a, um.* **1630** LORD *Banians* Introd., A countenance shy and somewhat estranged. **1643** SIR T. BROWNE *Relig. Med.* I. §46. 108, I beleeve that our estranged and divided ashes shall unite againe. **1650** BULWER *Anthropomet.* 171 These therefore, who are so salvage and far estranged from humane life. **1667** MILTON *P.L.* IX. 1132 Adam estrang'd in look and alter'd style. **1826** MILMAN *A. Boleyn* (1827–52) Nor passion..nor the love Of kindred touch this earth-estranged heart. **1837** LYTTON *E. Maltrav.* 27 His last words had been uttered in estranged tones. **1860** PUSEY *Min. Proph.* 448 An estranged dress betokened an estranged heart.

absol. **1877** SPARROW *Serm.* xiii. 180 The estranged are reconciled, man is brought nigh to God.

† **2.** Foreign. *Obs.*

1615 LATHAM *Falconry* (1633) 36 These kindes of hawkes do leaue these countries, and all other estranged places.

estrangedness (ɪˈstreɪndʒɪdnɪs). [f. prec. + -NESS.] The state or condition of being estranged; alienation in feeling or affection.

1645 PRYNNE *Vind. Four Questions* 2 (L.) The greatest token of estrangedness or want of familiarity one with another. **1662** EARL ORRERY *State Lett.* (1743) II. 434 The estrangedness of the Irish papists. *a* **1677** BARROW *Serm.* (1716) I. 60 Instead of a suspicious estrangedness..will spring up an humble confidence. **1825** COLERIDGE *Aids Refl.* (1848) I. 96 By estrangedness and distance from God. **1869** S. WILBERFORCE *Oxf. Lent Serm.* I The long Gentile estrangedness.

† **e'strangeful,** *a. Obs.* [f. ESTRANGE *v.* + -FUL.] Foreign in appearance, strange.

1613 CHAPMAN *Masque Inns of Court* Plays 1873 III. 92 Buskins embrodered with gould, and enterlac't with rewes of fethers; Altogether estrangfull and Indian like.

‖ **Estrangelo, Estranghelo** (ɛsˈtræŋgɪləʊ). Also 8 Estrangel, 9 Estrangela. [Syriac *estrangelō*: Nöldeke accepts the view of Assemani that the word is a. Gr. στρογγύλος rounded] An archaic form of the Syriac alphabet. Also *attrib.*

1730–6 BAILEY (folio), *Estrangel*, the Estrangelus character, a particular species or form of Syriack letter serving as capitals. **1751** CHAMBERS *Cycl.* s.v., The Abyssinians..still occasionally use the estrangel character. **1853** H. BURGESS *Hymns Ephraem Syrus* Introd. 93 The four gospels in the Estrangelo character. **1883** *Palæogr. Soc. Facsimiles*, Orient. Ser. VIII. Pl. xcix, A small, elegant Estrangela. *Mod.* The Estrangelo Syriac version of the Gospels.

estrangement (ɪˈstreɪndʒmənt). [f. as prec. + -MENT.] The action of estranging; the condition of being estranged; separation, withdrawal, alienation in feeling or affection.

1660 JER. TAYLOR *Duct. Dubit.* III. ii. (R.), If excommunication be incurred..he that is guilty..is bound to submit to estrangements and separations. **1736** BERKELEY *Disc. Magistrates* Wks. 1871 III. 429 The prevailing contempt of God's word, and estrangement from his house. **1738–41** WARBURTON *Div. Legat.* v. §1. Wks. 1811 V. 10 Moses, to prevent any such estrangement..was careful to acquaint the chosen Family..of their descent from one man and woman. **1818** JAS. MILL *Brit. India* II. v. v. 496 Apprehending a greater estrangement of the mind of the Nizam. **1848** MACAULAY *Hist. Eng.* II. 261 The estrangement between the King of England and the Prince of Orange became daily more complete. **1883** H. DRUMMOND *Nat. Law in Spir. W.* v. (1884) 169 The estrangement of the soul from God.

† **e'strangeness.** *Obs. rare*⁻¹. [f. ESTRANGE *a.* + -NESS.] = STRANGENESS.

1549 CHALONER *Erasm. Moriæ Enc.* N iv a, The hearer, mervailyng at the estrangenesse of the devise.

estranger¹ (ɪˈstreɪndʒə(r)). [f. as prec. + -ER¹.] One who or that which estranges, parts asunder, or causes estrangement.

1623 DRUMM. OF HAWTH. *Cypress Grove* Wks. 117 Death is the violent estranger of acquaintance. **1850** MRS. BROWNING *Poems* I. 130 What estranger, What ill most strong in evil, can be thrust Between the faithful Father and the Son.

† **e'stranger**². *Obs.* Also 5–6 estraunger. [a. OF. *estranger* (mod.F. *étranger*): see STRANGER.]

1. a. One belonging to another nation; an alien, foreigner. **b.** One belonging to another family or district; a stranger.

1471 *Paston Lett.* No. 664. II. 421 The Kyngs gret enemys and rebellis acompanyed with enemys estrangers be nowe aryved. **1550** J. COKE *Eng. & Fr. Herald.* §59 (1877) 75 Notwithstandyng this excedynge power of Estraungers, Heralde the usurper fought the battayle to th' utteraunce. **1586** FERNE *Blaz. Gentrie* 297 That none of the family might alienate the coatearmor of their house, to the bearing of an estranger. **1641** *Termes de la Ley* 148 *Estrangers* are.. sometimes they that be borne beyond the sea. **1721–1800** in BAILEY.

2. *Law.* One who is not privy or party to an act, contract, title, etc.; = STRANGER.

1594 WEST *Symbol.* II. §36 Any act..to be done or performed..by any estranger or estrangers to this present submission. **1622** CALLIS *Stat. Sewers* (1647) 183 There be two Joyntenants, and an estranger do disseise the other. **1714** SCROGGS *Courts-leet* (ed. 3) 90 If the Beasts of another Man are..agisting my Land..and are taken by an Estranger, I shall have a Replevin. **1721–1800** in BAILEY.

e'stranging (ɪˈstreɪndʒɪŋ), *vbl. sb.* [f. as prec. + -ING¹.] The action of the vb. ESTRANGE.

1574 tr. *Marlorat's Apocalips* 43 The death of yᵉ soule.. is an vtter estranging of the soule from God. **1607** HIERON *Wks.* I. 406 Ordinary estranging in body breedeth strangenesse in affection. *a* **1677** HALE *True Relig.* III. (1684) 38 There arise Schismes, Factions..and studied estrangings of Professors of Christianity.

e'stranging, *ppl. a.* [f. as prec. + -ING².] That estranges: cf. ESTRANGE *v.* 5.

1775 in ASH. **1870** MORRIS *Earthly Par.* II. III. 59 The image of cold death, With his estranging agonies. **1875** HOWELLS *Foregone Concl.* viii. 119 The four stood in the pale, estranging moonlight.

† **e'strangle,** *v. Obs.* [ad. OF. *estrangler* (mod.Fr. *étrangler*): see ASTRANGLE, STRANGLE.] *trans.* = STRANGLE *v.*: in quot. to choke.

1483 CAXTON *Gold. Leg.* 134/2 A woman..had a sone deying in whos throte was a bone of a fysshe thwart whyche estrangled him.

estrapade (ɛstrəˈpeɪd). [a. Fr. *estrapade* (cf. Sp. *estrapada*), ad. It. *strappata*, f. *strappare* to pull tight; app. of Teut. origin; cf. Ger. (Swiss) *strapfen* to draw, Ger. *straff* drawn tight.]

1. The attempt of a horse to get rid of his rider by rearing and kicking.

1730–6 in BAILEY (folio). **1828** in WEBSTER. In mod. Dicts.

2. *Hist.* A torture consisting in attaching a person's hands and feet to a rope, drawing him up by them to a great height, and then letting him fall suddenly; = STRAPPADO.

1856 FROUDE *Hist. Eng.* I. 404 He [Francis] could ill afford to forsake a religion which allowed him so pleasantly to compound for his amatory indulgences by the estrapade. *Ibid.* (1858) I. v. 423 The estrapade was an infernal machine introduced by Francis into Paris for the better correction of heresy.

estray (ɪˈstreɪ), *sb.* and *a.* [a. AF. *estray*, vbl. sb. (taken *concr.*) f. *estraier* to stray: see ASTRAY.]

A. *sb.* **a.** *Law.* A stray animal; 'any beast not wild, found within any Lordship, and not owned by any man' (Cowell).

[**1292** BRITTON I. xviii. § 3 Weyf ou estray nent chalengez de eynz le an et le jour si soit al seignur de la fraunchise.] **1594** WEST *Symbol.* ii. *Chancerie* §37 The like is it of an Estray or a Deodand. *c* **1640** J. SMYTH *Lives Berkeleys* (1883) I. 334 All such Estrays and Cumelings as..should be taken or found upon the Abbots demesnes. **1714** SCROGGS *Courts-leet* (ed. 3) 105 The Estray shall be proclaimed in the two next Market Towns. **1765** BLACKSTONE *Comm.* I. 298 Any beast may be an estray, that is by nature tame or reclaimable. **1776** in Stonehouse *Axholme* (1839) 145 The Lord's Bailiff, or receiver of estrays. **1850** LONGF. *By Fireside, Pegasus in Pound* vi, The..village crier..proclaiming there was an estray to sell.

b. *transf.*

1581 LAMBARDE *Eiren.* (1602) 589 Many things haue escaped me vnseen..and it shall not bee harde for him that meeteth with such Estrais to take and lodge them in their right Titles here. **1741** RICHARDSON *Pamela* 1824 I. lxxvii. 432 This happy estray, thus restored, begs leave by me to acknowledge its lovely owner. **1853** KANE *Grinnell Exp.* xxxviii (1856) 350 This poor little wanderer was an estray from his fellows. **1881** E. C. STEDMAN in *Scribn. Mag.* Oct. 817 How he seizes on some promising estray.

B. *adj.* Of an animal: That is astray. Also *transf.* Chiefly *U.S.*

1789 *Kentucky Gaz.* (Lexington, Ky.) 28 Mar. 1/3 All persons shall have access to the Estray-book, without paying any fee therefor. **1865** NICHOLS *Britton* I. 216 Things found, which do not belong to anybody, as wreck of sea, beasts estray [orig. *estravagauntes*] rabbits, hares, etc. **1876** *Rep. Vermont Board Agric.* III. 426 Many..of these new varieties of grain are not new... They are old varieties estray ..from remote quarters..of the globe. **1889** *Harper's Mag.* June 158/2 A farmer living near a middle Georgia town, one day found an estray cow in his pasture.

estray (ɪˈstreɪ), *v. arch.* [ad. OF. *estrai-er*: see ASTRAY *v.*] *intr.* To STRAY. *lit.* and *fig.*

1572 R. H. tr. *Lauaterus' Ghostes* (1596) 199 If the auncient Fathers had so doone, they had not estrayed so farre from the Apostles simplicitie. **1600** TOURNEUR *Transf. Met.* I. The lambes that sometime did estray. **1602** DANIEL *Hymen's Tri.* IV. iii, This nymph one day..Estrays apart, and leaves her Company. **1660** tr. *Amyraldus' Treat. Relig.* II. ix. 289 How could it be that men should so prodigiously neglect the glory of God, unless they were estrayed from their end, since they were made for it? **1855** SINGLETON *Virgil* I. 44 One of the sisters led Gallus estraying by Permessus' streams To th' Aon mountains. *a* **1864** HAWTHORNE *Eng. Note-bk.* (1879) I. 261 Just estraying a little way.

Hence **e'strayed** *ppl. a.*, that has strayed. **e'straying** *vbl. sb.*

1535 *Act 27 Hen. VIII*, c. 7 §5 Estraied cattell claimed and proued by the owners. **1580** SIDNEY *Arcadia* III. (1622) 310 The sweete touch of that hand seemed to his estrayed powers so heauenly a thing, etc. **1598** YONG *Diana* 318 But euermore despaire..From former course of minde doth cause estraying. **1620** J. WILKINSON *Cor. & Sheriffs, Crt. Leets* 140b, And likewise you shall present all such cattel estraied as shall usually come within your office. **1883** W. R. WILLIAMS in *Butler's Bible-Wk.* I. 366 The shepherd seeking his estrayed sheep.

estrayte, obs. form of ESTREAT.

† **'estre.** *Obs.* Also 3 eastre, 4 ester(e, hestre, 5 esture, estyr. [a. OF. *estre* being, condition (in pl. = sense 2), orig. a subst. use of *estre* (mod.F. *être*) to be. In sense 2 b this was in Fr. already confused with another word, = Pr. *estra* fem., of unknown etymology.]

1. Condition of being, way of life, position, circumstances; also, a state of things.

c **1300** *K. Alis.* 5467 To wite of Alisaundres estre..Grete wille had Porus the kyng. *c* **1314** *Guy Warw.* (A.) 4563 Siker þou be þat al mi pine & alle mine estris ichil telle þe. *c* **1330** R. BRUNNE *Chron.* (1810) 94 He told him of alle þe estere, þat him mette þat nyght. **1393** GOWER *Conf.* I. 272 What shall I telle unto Silvestre Or of your name or of your estre. *a* **1400** *Sir Perc.* 1559 Thay..talked and tolde Off othir estres fulle olde.

2. *concr.* **a.** A place; places generally; hence the parts about a country; localities, a region; also an estate, dominions.

c **1205** LAY. 3583 Leir is an is londe, icume ouer sæ streme to isen is eastress. **1303** R. BRUNNE *Handl. Synne* 10586 So long he [Tumna] leuede yn þat estre þat for hys name he hyȝt Tuncestre. *c* **1330** —— *Chron.* (1810) 891 To Wales is William schaken, estres to spie. *Ibid.* 145 He bouht Two maners tille his estre. *Ibid.* 212 Jon regned in þis estre kyng auhten ȝere. *c* **1430** LYDG. *Bochas.* III. v. (1554) 74 a, He gan espie thestres of the place. *c* **1440** *Bone Flor.* 293 He toke hym come To spere the estyrs of Rome. **1480** CAXTON *Chron. Eng.* ccxxiii. 221 The noble baron of stafford priked hir hors vp and doune by the hylles for to kepe the estres [*ed.* **1520** estrees] of the countrey.

b. Chiefly *pl.* Apartments, dwellings, quarters; the inner rooms in a house, divisions or alleys in a garden, etc.

a **1225** *Ancr. R.* 296 Brouhte o brune alle hire huses [*v.r.* eastres.] *a* **1300** *Cursor M.* 2252 (Cott.) His esters sal we see ful suyth. *c* **1300** *K. Alis.* 7611 Y wol sende hire lovedrewry, And hire hestris eke aspye. *c* **1330** *Arth. & Mer.* 816 At hir dore and hir fenester Hadde y blisced and ech ester. *c* **1350** *Will. Palerne* 1768 ȝede a grom of grece in þe gardyn to pleie to bi-hold þe estres & þe herberes so faire. *c* **1385** CHAUCER *L.G.W.* 1711 *Lucrece*, The husbonde knew the estris wel & fyn. *c* **1400** *Beryn* 556 For thow knowest better then I, al the estris of this house, go vp thy selff and spy. *c* **1400** *Rom. Rose* 1448, I wente.. Aboute the place; it was not left, Tyl I hadde all the gardyn bene In the estres that men might sene. **1470–85** MALORY *Arthur* XIX. vii, Pleaseth it yow to see the estures [*printed by Caxton* eftures] of this castel. **1775** in ASH.

3. App. used for: Fruit, produce.

a **1300** *E.E. Psalter* lxiv [lxv.] 11 Fele falde his estres in þe land [Vulg. *multiplica genimina ejus* (sc. *terræ*)].

estreat (ɪˈstriːt), *sb. Law.* Forms: 6 estrayte, -eyt, 6- estreat. Also 5–7 *aphet.* strete, (5 streete). [a. AF. *estrete*, OF. *estraite* (in law Lat. *extracta*), fem. sb. from pa. pple. of *estraire* to extract:—L. *extrahĕre*, f. *ex* out + *trahĕre* to draw. Cf. Fr. *extrait* EXTRACT.]

1. 'The true extract, copy. or note of some original writing or record, *esp.* of fines, amercements, etc., entered on the rolls of a court to be levied by the bailiff or other officer'. (Wharton.)

[**1292** BRITTON I. xxii. §7 Qi..ount..plus levé qe contenu ne fust en les estretes de noster Escheker.] *c* **1440** *Promp. Parv.* 480 Streete, catchepol['s] bok to gader by mercymentys. **1479** in *Eng. Gilds* (1870) 421 The seide Toune clerk to make vp his Stretys vnto the Baillifs. **1514** FITZHERB. *Just. Peas* (1538) 137 b, Shall be bounde and shall make theyr Estraytes. **1601** F. TATE *Househ. Ord. Edw. II*, §24 (1876) 17 The clarke of the market..shal deliver..the stretes into the warderobe. **1641** *Termes de la Ley* 178 Greene waxe..signifies the estreats of issues, fines, and amercements. **1679–88** *Secr. Serv. Money Chas. & Jas.* (Camden Soc.) 160 To supply the estreats of the patents in the 16th year of King Ch. 2ᵈ. **1857** TOULM. SMITH *Parish* 107 Estreats—that is copies—of all the fines and forfeitures imposed. **1875** STUBBS *Const. Hist.* II. xvi. 452 *note*, The estreats or rate rolls of the general taxation.

transf. **1625** LISLE *Du Bartas, Noe* 158 What are they but estreats of those originals? Wherof th' Almighty word engroue the portrature.

b. ***Clerk of the Estreats*** (see quot.).

1667 E. CHAMBERLAYNE *St. Gt. Brit.* I. II. xiii. (1743) 120 The office of the Clerk of the Estreats is to receive every term the estreats or extracts out of the office of the Remembrancer. **1721–1800** in BAILEY. **1833** CRABB *Technol. Dict.*

†**2.** *transf.* in *pl.* The fines themselves and other payments enforced by law. *Obs.*

c **1550** *Plumpton Corr.* 255 He did receive xiˢ..over and above your rents and your estreats. **1630** in Nichols *Churchw. Acc. St. Margarets Westm.* (1797) 40 John Fennell and Ralph Atkinson collectors of the estreats for repair of Brentford Bridge and Knightsbridge. **1640** *Order Ho. Commons* in Rushw. *Hist. Coll.* III. (1692) I. 154 The said Clerks Wages, and the several Fines and Estreats.

estreat (ɪˈstriːt), *v.* [f. prec. sb.]

1. *trans.* To extract or take out the record of (a fine, bail, recognizance, etc.) and return it to the court of exchequer to be prosecuted.

1523 FITZHERB. *Surv.* 28 The issues and profytes of them are estreyted by the sayd iustices, and returned in to the kynges escheker. **1649** SELDEN *Laws Eng.* II. xi. (1739) 59 If they were not arrayed, then the Recognizances of such as undertook the work, are estreated. **1737** *Col. Rec. Penn.* IV. 256 Lest their Recognizances should be estreated. **1827** HALLAM *Const. Hist.* (1876) III. xiii. 8 The fines thus imposed upon jurors had been estreated into the exchequer. *Mod.* The recognizances were ordered to be estreated.

2. *loosely.* To exact (a fine); to enforce forfeiture of (anything).

1647 BOYLE *Agst. Swearing* Wks. 1772 VI. 24 The poor.. seem to have a title..to the amerciaments that are estreated upon trespasses against their Lord. **1843** LEVER *J. Hinton* xix, The old farmer saw his tricks confiscated, and his games estreated.

estreg, var. of ESTRICHE, *Obs.*

estren, obs. form of EASTERN.

estrepe (ɪˈstriːp), *v. Law.* [ad. OF. *estrepe-r* = Pr. *estrepar*:—L. *exstirpāre* to root up (see EXTIRPATE).] *trans.* (See quot.)

1672 COWELL *Interpr., Estrepe*, to make Spoil by a Tenant for Life in Lands or Woods, to the prejudice of him in the Reversion. **1721–1800** in BAILEY. In mod. Dicts.

estrepement (ɪˈstriːpmənt). Forms: 6 estreppement, 7 estrepment, -ipament, 7–8 estrepament, 8– estrepement. Also 7 *aphet.* strepment. [a. AF. *estrepement*, f. *estreper*: see prec.]

1. 'Wasting' of lands, *esp.* 'Any spoil or waste made by tenant for life, upon any lands or woods, to the prejudice of him in reversion; also, making land barren by continual ploughing' (Wharton). ***writ of estrepement*** (see quot. 1768: this was abolished by 3 and 4 Will. IV. c. 27).

1503 *Will of Copynger* (Somerset Ho.), Wᵗ oute eny estreppement or wast. **1607** COWELL *Interpr.*, Estrepement or Estripament. **1736** BAILEY, *Estrepament.* **1741** T. ROBINSON *Gavelkind* II. i. 151 Without doing any Estrepement, Waste, or Exile. **1768** BLACKSTONE *Comm.* III. 225 And the writ of estrepement lay at the common law ..to stop any waste which the vanquished party might be tempted to commit. **1847** in CRAIG; and in mod. Dicts.

†**2.** (See quot.) *Obs.*

In cases of felony and Petit Treason the king had the right of estrepement, i.e. of enjoying the felon's lands for a year and 'wasting' them to his heart's content. This being to the injury of the lord of the fee, it became customary to compound with the king for the right of estrepement, which came to be represented merely by a fine.

c **1640** J. SMYTH *Lives Berkeleys* (1883) II. 435 Estrepments, goods of fugitives and of convict, attainted, outlawed, and wayved persons.

†**eˈstrete.** *Obs. rare.* [a. OF. *estraite* in same sense:—L. *extracta*: see ESTREAT.] Extraction, origin; hence, nature.

1393 GOWER *Conf.* I. 87 Toward this vice of which we trete There ben yet tweie of thilke estrete.

ˈestrich, ˈestridge. [var. of OSTRICH, q.v.; and cf. Pr. *estruz*.]

†**1.** = OSTRICH. *Obs.*

c **1450** *Voc.* in Wr.-Wülcker 585 *Fungus*, a ffynch [*vel* an Estrich, *secundum quosdam*]. *a* **1528** SKELTON *Phyllyp Sparowe* 478 The estryge, that wyll eate An horshowe. **1579** LYLY *Euphues* (Arb.) 124 The Estrich disgesteth harde yron to preserue his health. **1606** SHAKS. *Ant. & Cl.* III. xiii. 197 To be furious, Is to be frighted out of feare, and in that moode The Doue will pecke the Estridge. *a* **1653** G. DANIEL *Idyll* iv. 7 The Estrich may digest A Broken Rocke, and on a Plough-Share feast. **1687** A. LOVELL tr. *Bergerac's Com. Hist. Moon* II. 72 A kind of Estridge.

2. (See quot.)

1842 BRANDE *Dict. Sc.*, *Estrich*, the commercial name of the fine down of the ostrich. **1858** SIMMONDS *Dict. Trade. Estridge*, the fine soft down which lies under the feathers of the ostrich.

3. *attrib.* and *Comb.*

1460 *Will of Tame* (Somerset Ho.), Ciphum cum esterigefeders. *a* **1528** SKELTON *Speke Parrot* 80 *Ic dien* serueth for the erstrych fether. **1613** S. ROWLANDS *Paire of Spy-Knaves* B iij a, Point the Feather-maker not to faile To plume my head with his best Estridge tayle. *a* **1634** RANDOLPH *Muses Looking-gl.* III. iii, He shall eat something else too that rides here; Ile try his estridg stomack. **1634** S. R. *Noble Soldier* IV. i. Bullen *O. Pl.* I. 307 Taught me Estridge-like, To digest Iron and Steele. **1649** G. DANIEL *Trinarch., Hen. V*, cxcvii, Everie Bow..May weare a Scarfe, each Shaft, an Estrich Plume. **1685** [see ESTERY FEATHER]. **1715** tr. *Pancirollus' Rerum Mem.* II. i. 276 This Tree bears a Flower..about the bigness of an Estrich-Egg. **1812** J. SMYTH *Pract. of Customs* 255 Ostrich, or Estridge wool, is used as a substitute for beaver.

†**ˈestriche.** *Obs.* Also 1 éast-ríce, 5 austridge, est(e)rych(e, 8 estreg. [f. EAST + RICHE; cf. -RIC.]

1. a. An eastern kingdom or country. **b.** In OE. *spec.* The East-Frankish kingdom.

893 *O.E. Chron.* (Parker MS.), Her on þysum ȝeare for se micla here..eft of þæm east rice westweard. *a* **1200** *Trin. Coll. Hom.* 45 Þe þre kinges þe comen of estriche.

2. *attrib.* ***estrich board***: applied to timber coming from Norway or the Baltic.

[It is not quite certain that this is rightly placed here; cf. Ger. *estrich* floor (which however strictly means a *plaster* floor). But the similar use of *estlande* (see EASTLAND) strongly supports the view here adopted.]

1350 *Proclam.* in Riley *Mem. Lond.* (1868) 261 Divers boards of estrichesborde..*6l. 12s. 4d.* **1354** *Mem. Ripon* (Surtees) III. 91 In xiij bord. de Estriche emp. pro feretro Beati Wilfridi exaltando *2s. 2d.* **1459** *Bury Wills* (Camden Soc.) 242 Duo scabella de estryche board. **1481–90** *Howard Househ. Bks.* (Roxb.) 23, Xij austrige bourde, and viij. other boordes. **1514** *Inv. Goods* in *Gentl. Mag.* (1834) CIV. I. 47 In the parlour, a table of Estriche bourde with ij tristells. **1706** PHILLIPS, *Estreg bords*, Boards, Deal or Firr, brought from the Eastern Parts. **1715** in KERSEY. **1866** ROGERS *Agric. & Prices* I. xx. 489 The better kinds [of boards] were called estrich and wainscot.

estrin, obs. form of EASTERN.

estrin, estriol, varr. ŒSTRIN, ŒSTRIOL.

‖**ˈestro.** [It. *estro* 'poetic rage' (Baretti), ad. L. *œstrus* in same sense, lit. gadfly.] Inspiration, irresistible impulse.

1606 MARSTON *Parasitaster* II. D iij, With..this same Estro, or Enthusiasme..Will we goe rate the Prince. **1817** BYRON *Let.* 2 Jan. (1830) II. 70, I have not done a stitch of poetry since I left Switzerland, and have not at present the *estro* upon me. **1849** ROSSETTI *Let.* 18 Oct. (1965) I. 81 The verse gets its measure of *estro* accordingly.

estrogen, estrogenic, estrone, estrous, varr. ŒSTROGEN, etc.

†**ˈestuance.** *Obs.* [f. as next: see -ANCE.] Heat, warmth.

1818 in TODD [with quot. from Sir T. Browne; the passage occurs in *Pseud. Ep.* v. xxi, but edd. 1646, 1650, 1658, 1672, 1686 read *æstuation*.] Hence in later Dicts.

†**ˈestuant,** *a. Obs.* Also 7 ÆSTUANT. [ad. L. *æstuant-em*, pr. pple. of *æstuāre* to boil, be inflamed.] Boiling hot.

c **1420** *Pallad. on Husb.* XI. 434 Yit leve a litel hool oute atte to brethe, Thaire heetes estuant forto alethe. **1633** [see ÆSTUANT].

estuarial (ɛstjuːˈɛərɪəl), *a.* [f. L. *æstuāri-um* + -AL¹.] Of or pertaining to an estuary. So **estuˈarian** *a.*

1883 *Standard* 12 May 3/5 The construction of the estuarial works. **1880** WEBSTER *Suppl.*, *Estuarian.*

estuarine (ˈɛstjuːəraɪn), *a.* [f. ESTUARY or L. *æstuāri-um*, after analogy of *mar-ine*, *lacustr-ine*: see -INE.] Of or belonging to an estuary; *esp.* of strata, etc. formed or deposited in an estuary.

1849 MURCHISON *Siluria* xii. 297 The lowest estuarine zone of Scotland. **1858** GEIKIE *Hist. Boulder* x. 193 The remains of..estuarine..organisms. **1880** A. R. WALLACE *Isl. Life* vi. 102 Clearly marked shore and estuarine deposits.

estuary (ˈɛstjuːərɪ). Forms: 6 **estuarie,** (7 **estuar**), 6– **estuary**; also ÆSTUARY. [ad. L. *æstuāri-um*, prop. adj. 'tidal', hence a tidal marsh or opening, f. *æstus* heat, boiling, bubbling, tide.]

1. *gen.* A tidal opening, an inlet or creek through which the tide enters; an arm of the sea indenting the land. *rare* in mod. use.

1538 LELAND *Itin.* V. 29 A greate Sande with a shorte Estuary into the Lande. **1665** MANLEY *Grotius' Low C. Warres* 219 Two Castles..sufficiently defended..by the Estuary of the Sea. **1782** W. GILPIN *Wye* (1789) 128 The finest estuary [Cardiff] we had seen in Wales. **1825** HEBER *Jrnl.* (1828) II. xxi. 389 The country resembled extremely a large aestuary, but studded with rocky islands. **1839** STONEHOUSE *Axholme* 53 The word Fleet means an estuary or arm of the sea. **1880** HAUGHTON *Phys. Geog.* v. 238 The La Plata..is rather an estuary of the sea than a river.

2. *spec.* The tidal mouth of a great river, where the tide meets the current of fresh water.

15.. STOW *Annales* (1615) 3 The Riuer of Taus..breaketh into the German sea, and at yᵉ mouth forceth great estuars or armes of the sea. **1798** SKRINE *Tour S. Wales* (T.), The river swells into a great estuary, and in sight forms the Bristol Channel. *a* **1804** W. GILPIN (T.), Among the solitary birds, which frequent the estuaries of rivers. **1830** LYELL *Princ. Geol.* I. 265 Estuaries (a term which we confine to inlets entered both by rivers and tides of the sea). **1853** PHILLIPS *Rivers Yorksh.* i. 1 Estuaries worthy of such tributaries. **1878** HUXLEY *Physiogr.* 212 Upraised deposits of silt..skirt the estuary of the Clyde.

†**3.** A place where liquid boils up. *Obs.*

1684 BOYLE *Wks.* (1772) IV. 799 Whether..over the æstuary..there arise any visible mineral fumes.

transf. **1825** *New Monthly Mag.* XVI. 50 Bacon was accustomed to take a draught of March-beer towards bedtime, to settle this æstuary of his mind.

†**4.** A vapour-bath. *Obs.*

1657 TOMLINSON *Renou's Disp.* 189 Chirurgions have invented a certain Æstuary..like a bird-cage. **1706** PHILLIPS, *Æstuary*.

5. *attrib.* (sometimes quasi-*adj.* = ESTUARINE).

1832 LYELL *Princ. Geol.* II. 280 Estuary shells are more frequently liable..to be intermixed with the exuviæ of pelagic tribes. **1845** DARWIN *Voy. Nat.* vii. (1852) 129 My reasons for considering the Pampæan formation to be an estuary deposit were, etc. **1884** *Daily News* 7 Oct. 6/1 While the estuary fishermen have reaped a remunerative harvest, the rod men have had little or no fishing.

estuate, -ation, var. ff. ÆSTUATE, -ATION.

†**eˈstudiant.** *Obs.* [a. OFr. *estudiant*, pr. ppl. of *estudier*: see ESTUDY *v.* Cf. STUDIANT.] A student.

1481 CAXTON *Myrr.* III. vii. 142 Seynt dionyse..beyng an estudyaunt in grece. **1494** FABYAN, VII. 526 They sent yᵉ estudyauntys of yᵉ lawe, canon & cyuyle.

†**eˈstudy,** *v. Obs.* Forms: 3 astudie, 5–6 estudie, -ye. [a. OF. *estudier* (mod.F. *étudier*) ad. late L. *studiāre*, f. *studium* STUDY. Cf. Pr. and Sp. *estudiar*, Pg. *estudar*, It. *studiare*.] = STUDY *v.*, *trans.* and *intr.*

c **1225** *Ancr. R.* 200 Auh abuten þeos, þencheð & astudieð wel swuðe. **1474** CAXTON *Chesse* II. iii. (1860) B viij b, Theyr offyce is..to estudye diligently in such wyse..so that they be not founde corupt. **1491** —— *Vitas Patr.* I. vii. 10 b, He taughte hem to do wel, to estudie, etc. **1550** J. COKE *Eng. & Fr. Herald.* §203 (1877) 116 The great nombre of gentilmen ..alwayes estudyeng the lawes of the realme.

Hence **eˈstudied** *ppl. a.*, learned.

1550 J. COKE *Eng. & Fr. Herald.* §167 (1877) 107 The most parte of them be wel estudied in the lawes of God.

†**eˈstudy,** *sb. Obs.* [a. OF. *estudie* STUDY, f. L. *studium*.] Care, desire, zeal; = STUDY *sb.*

1483 CAXTON *Cato* E iij, They dyd put all theyr estudye for to knowe the faytes or dedes of thauncientes. **1483** —— *Golden Leg.* 221/3 They bothe were of one loue, of one estudye and of one wylle.

‖**estufa** (ɛˈstuːfə). *U.S.* [Sp. *estufa*, heated room, vapour bath, corresp. to It. *stufa*, OF. *estuve* (mod.F. *étuve*); of Teut. origin: cf. OHG. *stupa* (Ger. *stube* room): see STOVE.] An underground chamber, in which a fire is kept constantly burning; used by the Pueblo Indians of Spanish North America as a place of assembly.

1844 J. GREGG *Commerce of Prairies* I. 271 The famous *estufas*, or subterranean vaults. **1875** PARKMAN in *N. Amer. Rev.* CXX. 45 Estufas, or subterranean chambers..where the men of the community meet for social, deliberative, and religious purposes. **1876** L. H. MORGAN *ibid.* CXXIII. 83 Circular estufas found in connection with the new Mexican pueblos. **1881** —— *Contrib. Amer. Ethnol.* 148 The regular time for meeting in the estufa is the last day of December.

†**estuˈosity.** *Obs.* [f. L. *æstuōs-us* (see ÆSTUOUS) full of heat, f. *æstus* heat + -ITY.] A heated state or condition.

1657 TOMLINSON *Renou's Disp.* 222 It..tempers the estuosity of the blood. **1710** FULLER *Pharm. Extemp.* 158 A Refrigerating Expulsion..tempers flatulent Estuosities of the Hypochondria. **1730** *Ibid.* (ed. 4) 153 Heat, Estuosity, Erosions of the Stomach, and Thirst.

esture, var. form of ÆSTURE, *Obs.*

1615 CHAPMAN *Odyss.* XII. 111 The seas retain..their outrageous esture there. **1782–1800** in BAILEY; **1828** in WEBSTER; and in mod. Dicts.

estward(e, obs. form of EASTWARD.

estyme, obs. form of ESTEEM.

estynct, var. of EXTINCT *v. Obs.*

esundire, obs. form of ASUNDER.

a **1400–50** *Alexander* 338 He had gedird his grese & grune paim esundire.

†**ˈesure.** *Obs. rare*⁻¹. [f. *ēs-* ppl. stem of *edĕre* to eat + -URE.] The process of eating.

1657 TOMLINSON *Renou's Disp.* 338 More suave and wholsome both for medicinall uses and esure.

†**eˈsurial,** *a. Obs. rare*⁻¹. [ad. L. *ēsuriālis*, f. *ēsuriēs* hunger.] Pertaining to hunger, given up to fasting.

1656–81 in BLOUNT *Glossogr.* **1708** MOTTEUX *Rabelais* v. i, These esurial idle Days [Fr. *feries esuriales*].

†**eˈsuriate,** *v. Obs.* [f. L. *ēsuri-ēs* hunger + -ATE³.] *intr.* To hunger.

1623–6 COCKERAM, *Essuriate* [sic].

esurience (iːˈsjʊərɪəns). [f. L. *ēsurient-em*. pr. pple. of *ēsurīre*: see ESURIENT and -ENCE.] The state of being esurient; hunger, appetite; 'neediness and greediness'.

1825 COLERIDGE *Lit. Rem.* (1836) II. 338 Esurience..the origin and interpretation of whose name is found in the Hebrew root signifying hunger, and thence capacity. **1851** CARLYLE *Sterling* I. viii. (1872) 53 A ray of empyrean light; —but imbedded..in such indolences and esuriences as had made strange work with it. **1889** SWINBURNE *Study Ben Jonson* 40 No pretext beyond the fact of esurience..is suggested for the villainy of Subtle.

esuriency (iːˈsjʊərɪənsɪ). [f. as prec. + -ENCY.] The quality or state of being esurient; fondness for eating.

1819 L. HUNT *Indicator* No. 12 (1822) I. 91 His third era of esuriency takes place in the house of a Spanish gentleman. **1833** *New Monthly Mag.* XXXVIII. 223 That were as endless as Mr. Dando's infinite esuriency. **1886** W. S. LILLY *Chapt. Europ. Hist.* I. 30 The eye speaks of nothing but dull esuriency.

esurient (iːˈsjʊərɪənt), *a.* [ad. L. *ēsurient-em*, pr. pple. of *ēsurīre* to be hungry, desiderative vb. f. *ēs-* ppl. stem of *edĕre* to eat.]

A. *adj.* **1.** Hungry: in early use chiefly *fig.* Now humorously pedantic in lit. sense, or (with reminiscence of Juvenal's *Græculus esuriens*) in the sense 'impecunious and greedy'.

a **1672** WOOD *Life* (1848) 107 He [A. Wood] might advance his esurient genie in antiquities, especially in those of the said universitie. **1691** —— *Ath. Oxon.* II. 867 He was as esurient after fame as Tom Coryate. **1790** J. WILLIAMS *Shrove Tuesday* (1794) 32 Esurient Ruin shall be taught to spare Those altars congregated Virtues rear. **1833** LAMB *Elia, Pop. Fallacies*, To sit esurient at his own table, and commend the flavour of his venison upon the absurd strength of his never touching it himself. **1837** CARLYLE *Fr. Rev.* I. IV. iv, He is an esurient, unprovided Advocate; Danton by name. **1854** BADHAM *Halieut.* 476 Juvenal's picture of an esurient Greek. **1858** *Sat. Rev.* VI. 559/2 The English Cabinet annually avails itself of the delightful facility thus afforded to esurient ichthyophagi. **1881** *Spectator* 15 Jan. 81 Untrustworthy, esurient, broken attorneys.

b. *transf.*

1710 FULLER *Pharm. Extemp.* (1730) 156 Calcin'd Hartshorn..must needs..leave its Pores empty and esurient.

¶**2.** *catachr.* Pertaining to appetite or the love of eating; gastronomic.

1821 *New Monthly Mag.* I. 438 Esurient and bibulous reminiscences ooze from its surface. **1852** *Blackw. Mag.* LXXI 749 Let them..extend the esurient knowledge of their race..inculcate educational cookery.

B. *sb.* A greedy person.

1691 WOOD *Ath. Oxon.* (1817) III. 965 An insatiable esurient after riches and what not.

Hence **eˈsuriently** *adv.*, hungrily.

1883 G. A. MACDONNELL *Chess Life Pict.* 106, I..was waiting esuriently the appearance of the committee in order to commence our refection.

†**esurine**, *a.* and *sb. Obs.* Also 7 essurine. [ad. mod.L. *ēsurīn-us*, app. irreg. f. *ēsuriēs* hunger; used by Paracelsus in the sense 'promoting appetite', with reference to medicaments of an acid nature; subsequently (in pre-scientific chemistry) used as the distinctive epithet of mineral acid salts, and sometimes interpreted as 'eating, corrosive'.]

A. *adj.* **a.** Promoting appetite; also, inclined to eat; (of the appetite) voracious. **b.** Having the nature of a mineral acid; corrosive. ***esurine salts***: ' such as are of a fretting or eating quality' (Bailey).

[*a* **1541** PARACELSUS *Buch v. den Tartarischen Kranckh.* (1589) 246 Nuhn ist Esurinum Acetosum ein Artzney die von ihrer Natur den Magen so hungerig machet dass er begert zu essen vnessentliche Speiss, und aber was er begert das verzehrt er. *a* **1644** VAN HELMONT *Paradoxa* III. §10 Wks. (1704) 650 Sal quoddam hermaphroditicum metallorum, quod defectu nominis esurinum sive acetosum re et nomine vocari cœpit.] **1651** BIGGS *New Disp.* 218 Digestible, esurine, and depascent ferment. **1652** FRENCH *Yorksh. Spa* vi. 55 By esurine salt I understand..a certain acid vapour applicable to all Metals and Minerals. **1662** H. STUBBE *Ind. Nectar* vii. 156 Whatever will saturate that esurine [*printed* esurive] Humour upon the Stomach. **1669** W. SIMPSON *Hydrol. Chym.* 2 Every vitriol is made of an essurine salt. *c* **1676** WISEMAN (J.), The air of Hampstead in which..there is always something esurine and acid. **1687** P. MADAN *Tunbr. Waters* in *Harl. Misc.* I. 591 If at dinner you have an esurine appetite, take care not to eat too much.

†**B.** *sb. Obs.* A medicine which provokes appetite or causes hunger.

1775 in ASH; hence in mod. Dicts.

†**e'surion.** *Obs.* [ad. L. *ēsuriōn-em* in same sense, f. *ēsurīre*: see ESURIENT.] A hungry fellow.

1656 in BLOUNT *Glossogr.* **1704** in COCKER. **1775** in ASH.

†**esu'rition.** *Obs.* [f. L. *ēsurīre*: see ESURIENT and -TION.] The state or condition of being hungry.

1678–96 in PHILLIPS; **1775** in ASH.

et, ME. variant of AT *prep.*

et, obs. form of EAT.

-et, *suffix*[1], forming diminutives from sbs., represents OF. *-et* masc., *-ete* (mod.F. *-ette*) fem., corresp. to Pr. *-et*, *-eta*, Sp. *-ito*, *-ita* (also *-ete*, *-eta* in adopted words), It. *-etto*, *-etta*:—Com. Romanic *-itto*, *-itta*, of unknown (? non-Latin) origin. In Eng. the suffix occurs chiefly in Fr. words adopted into ME., as *basnet*, *bullet*, *crotchet*, *fillet*, *gullet*, *hatchet*, *mallet*, *pocket*, *pullet*, *sonnet*, *tablet*, *turret*, etc.; most of these are now used without any consciousness of their original diminutive sense. The distinction in form between the masc. and fem. suffixes was not often observed even in ME.; the spelling *-ete* however occasionally occurs for OF. *-ete*, as in *polete* PULLET; in adoptions from mod.F. in 16th and 17th c. *-et* represented Fr. *-ette* as well as *-et* (e.g. in *facet*, *islet*); in more recent adoptions the latter usually remains as -ETTE. The suffix has been little used as an English formative, though words like *riveret* are found in 17th c. writers. Certain Fr. diminutives formed with *-et* on sbs. ending in *-el* (either diminutive or adjectival) have been adopted into Eng., and have given rise to the suffix -LET, which has been largely employed to form diminutives in Eng.

-et, *suffix*[2], forming neuter verbal and denominative sbs., represents OE. *-et(t* (= Goth. *-iti*, OHG. *-izzi*), as in *thicket*.

-et, *suffix*[3], representing the 3rd pers. sing. pres. tense ending of Latin verbs of the second conjugation, as *scilicet*, *tenet*.

eta[1] ('iːtə, 'eɪtə). [a. Gr. ἦτα (see ETACISM).] The name of the seventh letter (*H*, *η*) of the Greek alphabet, corresponding to English *e*.

c **1400** in MAUNDEVILLE *Trav.* (1839) iii. 20. **1642** [see UPSILON 1]. **1883** I. TAYLOR *Alphabet* II. vii. 85 The Latin H and the Greek *eta* are identical in form and in alphabetic position, though not in value.

eta[2] ('iːtə). In full, ***eta palm***. = ITA-PALM.

1769 E. BANCROFT *Ess. Nat. Hist. Guiana* 61 The Eta Tree is of the same species with the foregoing [*sc.* cabbage tree], but smaller. **1866** G. W. BENNETT *Illustr. Hist. Brit. Guiana* 228 The Eta Palm (*Mauritia flexuosa*) is a beautiful tree and is adored by the Indians for the numerous uses to which it can be applied. **1922** *Blackw. Mag.* July 6/1 The road used to end..before a great eta-palm swamp.

Eta, eta[3] ('ɛtə). [Jap.] A member of a class of Japanese outcasts. Also *collect.* and *attrib.*

1897 A. M. KNAPP *Feudal & Modern Japan* I. v. 173 The cause of the intense repulsion and contempt with which the Japanese have regarded the *eta* class is unknown. *Ibid.*, No pariah class of any nation has ever been under a greater ban of disdain and contempt than have the *eta* of Japan. *Ibid.* 174 The spot where an *eta* has been standing must be sprinkled with salt if a Japanese would tread there without contamination. **1906** *Westm. Gaz.* 28 July 12/2 Hoshiko, eta though she be, full of the supreme devotion. **1955** *Times* 14 July 11/4 He visited the Ainu,..the Etas (those mysterious out-castes), and strip-tease shows. **1958** *Ibid.* 9 Sept. 9/7 The pitiable existence of many people of *eta* origin..has hampered their emancipation. **1960** KOESTLER *Lotus & Robot* II. vi. 176 The eta—the sweepers, scavengers and tanners—ceased to be untouchables. **1969** *Daily Tel.* 6 Mar. 16/5 The continuation of a practice in Japan..which permits 3,000,000 people known as 'eta' or 'the untouchables' to live in 6,000 outcast hamlets isolated from the people by centuries-old discrimination.

etacism ('eɪtəsɪz(ə)m). [f. Gr. ἦτα, *ēta*, the name of the letter *η*, after the analogy of LAMBDACISM (Gr. λαμβδακισμός).] The 'Erasmian' pronunciation of the Greek letter *η* as (eː) or (ɛː) as distinguished from the 'Reuchlinian' or modern Greek pronunciation (iː). Cf. ITACISM. So **'etacist**, one who practises or upholds etacism.

1833 E. ROBINSON tr. *Buttmann's Gr. Gram.* 23 note, The Erasmian [mode of pronunciation] is also called Etacism (*e* like *a* in *hate*).

etærio (ɛ'tɪərɪəʊ). *Bot.* Also rarely hetærio. [ad. F. *etairion*, *etairium* (C.F.B. de Mirbel 1813, in *Nouveau Bulletin des Sciences, par la Société Philomatique* III. 317), f. Gr. ἑταιρεία association.] An aggregate fruit, like that of the buttercup, strawberry, or raspberry.

The form *hetærio* never attained wide currency.

1832 LINDLEY *Introd. Bot.* I. ii. 176 The parts of an Etærio are Achenia. **1861** R. BENTLEY *Man. Bot.* iv. 316 When the achænia borne by a single flower are so numerous that they form more than a single whorl or series, they constitute collectively an *etærio*. **1866** *Treas. Bot.* 471/2 *Etærio*..such a kind of aggregate fruit as that of the *Ranunculus* or strawberry. **1870** BENTLEY *Bot.* 308 In the Raspberry and Bramble we have a kind of etærio formed of a number of little drupes, or drupels. **1896** G. HENSLOW *Wild Flowers* 102 The cluster of drupels is called an etaerio. **1956** *Dict. Gardening* (R. Hort. Soc.) Suppl. 204/1 Etaerio or Aetaerio. An aggregate fruit made up of drupes or achenes as in the Strawberry or Blackberry.

‖**étagère** (etaʒɛr). [Fr. *étagère*, f. *étage* shelf, story.] A piece of furniture having a number of shelves or stages, one above another, for receiving articles of elegance or use.

1858 SIMMONDS *Dict. Trade*, *Etagere*, a piece of cabinet furniture; a what-not, side-board, dumb-waiter or set of shelves. **1884** *New York Herald* 27 Oct. 1/4 Etageres.

‖**et al.** (ɛt æl), *phr.* [Abbrev. of L. *et alii* (masc.), *et aliæ* (fem.) or *et alia* (neut.), 'and others'.] And others. (Used esp. to avoid giving a list of authors, etc., in full.)

1883 in S. FALLOWS *Handbk. Abbrevs.* 10/2. **1907** W. JAMES *Let.* 13 Sept. in R. B. Perry *Tht. & Char. of W. J.* (1935) II. 482 As overcomer of Baumgarten, Crusius *et al.*, he [*sc.* Kant] was no doubt great. **1959** *Listener* 13 Aug. 256/2 He relegates Hamilton *et al.* to a prologue and epilogue. **1962** G. K. HUNTER *John Lyly* ii. 39 Lyly no doubt completed his school career..having read, construed and explicated innumerable passages of Ovid, Cicero, Virgil, *et al.*

‖**étalage** (etalaʒ). [Fr., f. *étaler* to display.] A display.

1900 *Daily News* 4 Sept. 4/7 A constant étalage of jewellery. **1925** *Blackw. Mag.* Oct. 493/2 The *étalage* in the window betrayed a small grocer's shop. **1953** B. CAMPBELL *Finding Nests* ii. 22 Artifact arrangements of the vegetation, for example the étalage of leaves at the entrance to many robins' nests,..cannot easily be seen from above.

étalon, etalon (‖etalɔ̃, 'ɛtəlɒn). [F. *étalon* (Fabry & Pérot 1902, in *Ann. de Chimie et Physique* XXV. 107), lit. 'a standard (of weights, measures, etc.)':— OF. *estalon*, *estelon* prob. of Gmc. origin: see STALLION.] A device used to produce interfering beams of light, consisting essentially of two plane parallel reflecting plates of fixed separation and (in some kinds) adjustable orientation.

1905 E. C. C. BALY *Spectroscopy* ix. 302 Fabry and Perot, profiting by their experience with their interferometer, have adopted fixed air layers as interference apparatus, the widths of which are determined once and for all. They call these apparatus standards (*étalons*). **1914** *Astrophysical Jrnl.* XXXIX. 185 Interferometer, echelon grating, parallel interference-plates, etalon, etc. **1934** *Discovery* July 184/1 The interferometer..is of the type known as the Fabry-Perot étalon, and in this particular form it consists of a metal tube having extremely flat and parallel end surfaces, to which are contacted polished flat plates of glass or natural quartz. **1963** R. W. DITCHBURN *Light* (ed. 2) ix. 358 A determination of the length of the shortest etalon in terms of the wavelength of the cadmium red line.

'etamine. Also 8 etamin. Also in Fr. form étamine. [a. Fr. *étamine*: see ESTAMIN.]

†**a.** = ESTAMIN (*obs.*). **b.** (see quot. 1884.)

1714 *Fr. Bk. of Rates* 378 Etamins fine..Etamins common. **1759** W. VERRAL *Cookery* p. xxviii, An etamine or two for the straining your thick soups, cullies or creams. **1794** A. YOUNG *Trav.* (ed. 2) I. xix. 552 Here are etamines, linen, stockings, bleach-grounds, &c. **1884** *West. Daily Press* 13 June 7/6 Etamine, a sort of embroidered canvas..likely to be worn at spas. **1886** *Pall Mall G.* 3 June 8/1 A..dainty chemiset of cream étamine. **1966** *Harper's Bazaar* Sept. 50 Evening dress..in bougainvillia pink étamine.

‖**étang** (etɑ̃). [Fr., ad. OF. *estanc*: see STANK *sb.*] A shallow pool or small lake, esp. one of the type found along the French coast and resulting from the blocking of streams by sand dunes.

c **1845** C. BRONTË *Professor* (1857) II. xxi. 109 Near it [*sc.* a place of public resort in the outskirts of Brussels] were several of those lakelets called étangs; and there was one étang, larger than the rest, where..people were accustomed to amuse themselves by rowing round it. **1879** *Encycl. Brit.* X. 265/2 The dunes travel inland in parallel, irregular, and often confluent ridges, between which rain-water is sometimes arrested to form pools (*étangs* of the French coasts), where formations of peat occasionally take place. **1940** M. SADLEIR *Fanny by Gaslight* 10 One of the several solitary and reed-grown *étangs* which occur..in the forest above Les Yvelines. **1960** W. W. WILLIAMS *Coastal Changes* ii. 38 Probably the most important effect of eustatic and isostatic movements..is the part that they play in the formation of many coastal features, notably..bars like those which lie between the *étangs* and the sea in the South of France. **1969** *Daily Tel.* (Colour Suppl.) 10 Jan. 32/1 There is a bit of French Provincial between Nantes and Bordeaux, which soon fades into the bleak pine barren of Landes and the sinister *étangs* of the sandy wastes to the south.

etaoin shrdlu ('ɛtəɔɪn 'ʃɜːdluː). The letters set by running a finger down the first two vertical banks of keys on the left of the keyboard of a Linotype machine, used as a temporary marking slug but sometimes printed by mistake; any badly blundered sequence of type. Also *ellipt.* **etaoin.** Cf. SHRDLU.

1931 J. THURBER *Owl in Attic* III. vii. 135 The author sends in a manuscript without exclamation marks. The linotyper puts them in, the author takes them out in proof, the linotyper puts them back in, together with a couple of etaoins. **1967** *Listener* 15 June 793/2 What I love about newspapers is their etaoin shrdl. **1983** *Daily Tel.* 13 Sept. 12/4 'Lot of pleasure but also a lot of pleasure but also a lot of anxiety and heart-searching.' etaoinshrdlu cmfwyp shrdlu cd showed that cinema and per- Mrs Nissel said that the study forming arts ticket prices had more or less remained in line with the Retail Price Index up to 1975/76.

eta patch. *Aeronaut.* [f. Gr. ἦτα, the name of the Greek letter *η*; it was the designation of the first airship, built in 1913 at the Royal Aircraft Factory, Farnborough, to have this means of attachment.] (See quot. 1919.)

1918 W. E. DOMMETT *Dict. Aircraft* 25 *Goosefoot*, a method of attaching the rigging on the envelope, often called an 'Eta Patch'. **1919** W. B. FARADAY *Gloss. Aeronaut. Terms* 57 *Eta patch*, a means of attaching rigging to the envelope consisting of a large fan-shaped patch made up of several thicknesses of fabric and reinforced with webbing bands and terminating in a metal ring. **1955** *Aeroplane* LXXXIX. 51/1 Because her suspension was distorting the envelope, 'Eta' patches were introduced, and cured the trouble.

‖**étatisme** (etatizm). Also **etatism.** [Fr., f. *état* STATE *sb.* + *-isme* -ISM.] Extreme development of the power of the State over the individual citizen.

1923 *Contemp. Rev.* Aug. 195 What one might almost call the fetishism of the State, an extreme form of *étatisme*. **1926** *Spectator* 2 July 6/2 That hideous thing which later the French called *Etatisme* produced a social and political atmosphere in which a free man could hardly breathe. *Ibid.* 24 July 122/2 It must not be thought that we should like to see the British spirit of individual liberty subjected to any such trial of extreme *étatisme*. **1952** V. A. DEMANT *Relig. & Decline of Capitalism* ii. 57 Absolute individualism or absolute *étatisme*. **1960** *Encounter* Mar. 63/2 He denounces the over-mighty Communist states because he is opposed to all *étatisme*. **1960** *Spectator* 2 Dec. 889 The excessive economic control and 'Etatism' of the Populist regime.

‖**état-major** (etamaʒɔr). *Obs.* [Fr., f. *état* state + *major*, major, adjutant; cf. Sp. *estado mayor*.] The staff of an army, regiment, etc.; = STAFF *sb.*[1] 21. Also *transf.*

1805 *Wynne Diaries* 1 Dec. (1940) III. vii. 220 Fremantle had still on board Villeneuve's état major (who he says divert him greatly with their gasconnades). **1830** HAZLITT *Life Nap. Buonaparte* IV. xlviii. 29 Lorence, general-in-chief of the *état-major*, ordered several Jews to be brought before him. **1848** THACKERAY *Van. Fair* lxv. 591 The second floor apartments occupied by the *état major* of the gambling firm. **1890** [see TYPICALITY].

etc., an abbreviation of ET CETERA.

et cetera, etcetera (ɛt 'sɛtərə). Also et cætera; often abbreviated as etc., &c. [a. L. *et cētera* (*et* and + *cētera*, often written *cætera*, the rest, neut. pl. of **cēterus* the other).]

1. As phrase: And the rest, and so forth, and so on (cf. Gr. καὶ τὰ λοιπά, Ger. *und so weiter*), indicating that the statement refers not only to the things enumerated, but to others which may be inferred from analogy. Occasionally used when the conclusion of a quotation, a current formula of politeness, or the like, is omitted as being well known to the reader. Also ***Yours etc.***, used as an ending in letters.

A custom formerly common, but now nearly disused except in certain government offices, is to write '&c., &c.' in the addresses of letters, as a substitute for the titles of office or dignity affixed to the name of the person addressed.

1418 *E.E. Wills* (1882) 37 Also a gowne..in ward, &c. *a* **1450** *Knt. de la Tour* cxiii. 154 Not to foryete the countesse moder unto the erle et cetera. **1532** More *Confut. Tindale* Wks. 612/1 The woordes of saynt Paule, It is impossible that they whiche haue once been illumined, &c. **1640** in Rushw. *Hist. Coll.* III. II. 1186, I *A.B.* do swear, That I do approve the Doctrine and Discipline..established in the Church of England..nor will I ever give my Consent to alter the Government of this Church by Archbishops, Bishops, Deans, and Archdeacons, &c. **1745** J. Elton in Hanway *Trav.* (1762) I. v. lxvii. 306, I beg you will not lose one single thought upon me. I am, &c. **1825–6** Dickens *Let.* (1965) I. 1 Cheaper in comparison than a Leg. Yours &c *C Dickens.* **1860** *All Y. Round* No. 47. 497 In the name of the indigent classes themselves..et cetera. **1920** F. W. Crofts *Cask* xi. 124 An unexpected call to England prevented me ordering this in person. Yours, etc., *Leon Felix.* **1970** *Times* 13 Nov. 11/4 He came..from Italy. Yours, &c., *F. Bennett.*

2. As *sb.* Also pl. **etceteras. a.** The phrase as a name for itself. Also *attrib.*, as in ***Etcetera Oath***, a form of oath which the convocation of 1640 attempted to impose on the English clergy: see quot. 1640 in 1.

1597 Shaks. *2 Hen. IV*, II. iv. 198 Come wee to full Points here, and are et cetera's nothing. **1640** in Rushw. *Hist. Coll.* (1721) III. II. 1206 This Clause is administer'd with an &c. which we conceive was never tendered in any Oath before now. **1640** Ld. Digby *Sp.* 9 Nov. *ibid.* IV. III. 31 Besides the bottomless Perjury of an Et cætera. **1640** Sir J. Culpepper *ibid.* IV. III. 33 Besides the Et cætera Oath. **1656** Heylin *Extr. Vapulans* 208, I thought our Author had been such an enemy to all *etcæteras*, because of the mysterious import.. which they carry with them. **1681** *Ess. Peace & Truth Ch.* (Fly Leaf), The Year 1640, when the Et cætera Oath was imposed. **1709** Addison *Tatler* No. 133 ⁋7, I have by me an elaborate Treatise on the Aposiopesis call'd an Et cætera. **1761** Hume *Hist. Eng.* III. liii. 147 An oath which contained an *et cætera* in the midst of it. **1853** *Brimley Ess.* 24 Sept. 293 Even then, a comprehensive et cætera would be needed for supernumeraries. **1898** *Daily News* 15 July 6/2 Colonial affairs..formed a sort of etcetera department of the War Office. **1900** *Ibid.* 23 May 6/3 The nickname, Etcetera Department, sometimes given to the English Home Office.

b. as substitute for a suppressed substantive, generally a coarse or indelicate one. *spec.* (*pl.*), trousers.

1592 Shaks. *Rom. & Jul.* II. i. 38 (Qq.). **1611** Cotgr. s.v. *Bergamasque*. **1643** *Myst. Iniq.* 43 It is concluded..betwixt the two *Etcætera's*, that a Cessation of Armes..should bee agreed on. **1794** Scott *Let.* 5 Sept. (1932) 36 A pair of new boots & Buckskin &c's in which the soldier is to be equipt. **1843** J. R. Planché *Fortunio* I. i. 8 Hush! hush! for up I go, To put a light Silk pair of tight Etcæteras on below. **1937** E. Pound *Fifth Decad Cantos* xlii. 7 And how this people can in this the fifth et cetera year of the war, leave that old etcetera up There on that monument! **1942** J. Cary *To be a Pilgrim* xix. 36 'All the things you silly geese have muddled up till you don't know your etc. from an etc.' A very coarse comparison, such as never before..had I used to a woman.

c. A number of unspecified things or (improperly) persons.

1656 Cowley *Misc.*, *The Chron.* x, A pretty Thomasine, And then another Katherine, And then a long *Et cætera.* **1746** *Brit. Mag.* 331 A Gardner, and a long &c. of Heroes fell for our Sakes. **1824** Miss Ferrier *Inher.* ix, Milton, Spenser, and a long et cetera of illustrious names. **1868** M. Pattison *Academ. Org.* ii. 37 The powers..conferred on the Chancellors, including an etc. of consuetudinary privileges. *Mod. Newspaper*, There were present Messrs. A., B., C., &c.

d. *pl.* only: Things usually included under the phrase *etcetera*; usual additions, extras, 'sundries'.

1817 Keatinge *Trav.* I. 232 Various fanciful forms of puddings, forced meats, minced meats, and indescribable et-ceteras. **1838** Dickens *Nich. Nick.* xxvi, Fifty guineas a-year without the et-ceteras. **1862** *Gifts & Graces* v. 62 The thousand little etceteras which had to be done the day before the move. **1884** *Bazaar* 22 Dec. 664/2 These et-ceteras, by the by, must be much in the children's way.

¶ **3.** as *vb.* (cf. 2 b).

1867 H. Kingsley *Silcote of Sil.* lxi, I am etcetera'd if I stand it.

Hence various whimsical nonce-words, as **et'ceterarist, et'ceteraize** *v.*, **et'ceteraly** *adv.*

1822 *Blackw. Mag.* XII. 56 To write critically, scientifically..etceteraly. **1831** *Fraser's Mag.* III. 67 He.. sowed his wild oats of course—soberized—etceteraized. **1834–37** Southey *Doctor* clxxvi. (1848) 462 The benevolent and erudite etceterarist of Bealings.

etch (ɛtʃ), *sb.*[1] [contracted form of eddish.]

1. a. = eddish 2 a; **b.** = eddish 2 b.

a. **1573** Tusser *Husb.* (1878) 85 Eat etch er ye plow, with hog, sheepe and cow. **1669** [see eddish 2].

b. **1727** Bradley *Fam. Dict.* s.v. *Corn*, Let the Dung be laid upon the Etch, and sow it with Barley. **1795** *Scots Mag.* LVII. 817/1 We observe wheat sowing after wheat, and likewise upon weak barley and oat etches. **1846** J. Baxter *Libr. Pract. Agric.* II. 209 Left foul after a crop of white grain..the stubble or etch is shallow ploughed.

2. *attrib.*, as *etch-crop* (see quots.).

1707 Mortimer *Husb.* (J.), When they sow their etch crops, they sprinkle a pound or two of clover on an acre. **1727** Bradley *Fam. Dict* s.v. *Corn*, The next Crop, which they call the Etch-crop, [they sow it] with Oats, Beans, Pease, &c. **1806–7** A. Young *Agric. Essex* (1813) I. 206 Every where you hear a condemnation of all etch or after crops, such as clover, pease, beans, tares, or oat.

etch (ɛtʃ), *sb.*[2] [f. etch *v.*[2]] The action or process of etching. Freq. *attrib.* and *Comb.* (see etch *v.*[2] 4).

1896 *Amer. Bookmaker* Mar. 81/1 After the first etch the plate should be perfectly cleaned. **1967** E. Chambers *Photolitho-Offset* x. 142 After 30 sec. immersion in the etch-bleach bath, the room light (white light) is switched on permanently. **1967** *Times* 23 Nov. 4/7 (*heading*) Improved etch for integrated circuits. *Ibid.*, The new development is called an anisotropic etch, which ensures that the slot does not get wider as it gets deeper.

†**etch,** *v.*[1] *Obs.* or *dial.* [f. etch *sb.*[1]] *intr.* To sow an after-crop.

Hence **'etching** *vbl. sb.*

1806–7 A. Young *Agric. of Essex* (1813) I. 210 Crops and fallow is better than etching.

etch (ɛtʃ), *v.*[2] [a. Du. *etsen*, a. Ger. *ätzen* to etch:—MHG. *etzen, atzen*:—OHG. *ezjan, azjan* to cause to eat or to be eaten = Goth **atjan* (in *fra-atjan* to distribute for food):—OTeut. **atjan*, causative of **etan* to eat.]

1. a. *trans.* To engrave (metals, sometimes glass, stone) by 'eating away' the surface with acids or other corrosives; chiefly, to engrave by this process (a copper or other metal plate) for the purpose of printing from it. Hence, to produce (figures), copy or reproduce (pictures, drawings, etc.), represent or portray (subjects) by this method.

In etching plates to be printed from, the metal is covered with a protective varnish called the ground, and the lines of the design are drawn through this substance with an 'etching-needle'; the acid is then poured over the ground, and acts on the plate only where its surface has been exposed by the needle. The vb. is also used of the production of designs on polished metal, *esp.* steel, by means of acids, the designs 'etched' appearing dead or clouded; also of the similar ornamentation of glass, the agent in this case being fluorine.

1634 J. B[ate] *Myst. Nat.* 140 Thereupon must be pounced, drawne, or traced, the thing that you are to etch. **1662** Evelyn *Chalcogr.* 72 The incomparable Landskips set forth by Paul Brill (some of which have been Etched in Aqua fortis by Nieulant). *a* **1691** Boyle *Wks.* (1772) III. 459, I have very seldom seen lovelier cuts..than I have seen made on plates etched, some by a French and others by an English artificer. **1781** W. Gilpin in *Mrs. Delany's Corr.* Ser. II. III. 38 A nephew of mine..thinks he has skill enough in his art to etch the drawings in aqua tinta. **1799** G. Smith *Laborat.* I. 231 To etch 100 or more Knife-blades at once. **1854** J. Scoffern in *Orr's Circ. Sc.* Chem. 370 The piece of glass to be etched. **1857** Mrs. Jameson *Sacr. & Leg. Art* (ed. 3) Pref., All the Illustrations, which were formerly etched on copper, have been newly etched on steel.

b. *transf.* and *fig.*

1768 Sterne *Sent. Journ.*, *Captive*, With a rusty nail he was etching [upon a stick] another day of misery. **1851** Longf. *Gold. Leg.* I. *Crt.-yard of Castle*, The swift and mantling river..Etched with the shadows of its sombre margent. **1863** Hawthorne *Old Home, Lond. Suburb* (1879) 244 Hours of Sabbath quietude, with a calm variety of incident softly etched upon their tranquil lapse. **1870** Lowell *Study Wind.* 54 The shadows..of the bare boughs etched with a touch beyond Rembrandt.

2. *absol.* and *intr.* To practise the art of etching.

1634 J. B[ate] *Myst. Nat.* 134 It is impossible for one ever to Grave or Etch well except he can draw well with the pen. *Ibid.* 140 The Plate you are to etch upon..[must be].. ouerlaid..with a ground made for the purpose. **1662** W. Faithorne (*title*), The Art of Graving and etching. **1768** W. Gilpin *Ess. on Prints* 150 Swanevelt..etched in the manner of Waterlo. **1807** T. Thomson *Chem.* (ed. 3) II. 199 The property which this acid has of corroding glass, has induced several ingenious men to attempt, by means of it, to..etch upon glass. **1854** J. Scoffern in *Orr's Circ. Sc.* Chem. 370 The operation of etching upon glass.

3. To corrode. ***to etch out***: to eat out (by an acid, etc.).

1664 Power *Exp. Philos.* II. 90 The cylinder of Quicksilver will seem cragged and itch'd [*in Errata* etch'd], and never purely smooth and polished. **1875** Sir J. W. Dawson *Life's Dawn* 101 By acting on the surface with a dilute acid we etch out the calcareous part.

4. *Comb.*, **etch figure** [tr. G. *aetzfigur* (H. A. Baumhauer 1869, in *Ann. d. Physik und Chem.* CXXXVIII. 563)], a depression on the face of a crystal caused by the action of a solvent; also ***etch pit***; **etch-water**, the acid used in etching.

1879 *Jrnl. Chem. Soc.* XXXVI. 439 '*Etch-figures' on quartz crystals. *Ibid.* 440 Different 'etch-figures' are produced by acids upon the octohedral faces from those produced by the action of water upon those faces. **1922** A. E. H. Tutton *Crystallography* (ed. 2) II. III. liii. 1200 These etch-figures in every case are symmetrical to the single plane of symmetry. **1923** Glazebrook *Dict. Appl. Physics* V. II. 376/2 The etched facets on crystal surfaces..appear as more or less isolated markings on the crystal surface. In the latter case they exhibit the typical geometrical characteristics of the crystal, and are known as 'etch figures'. **1950** *Sci. News* XV. 67 The *etch pits are seen to go down in a series of terraces like Dante's Inferno. **1959** *Jrnl. Inst. Metals* LXXXVII. 376/1 A knowledge of the factors that influence the formation and distribution of etch pits is of primary importance, since these factors govern the validity of the etch-figure technique as a method of determining the distribution of dislocations in a material. **1799** G. Smith *Laborat.* I. 230 To prepare the *etch-water.

Hence **etched** (ɛtʃt), *ppl. a.* ***etched figure*** = *etch figure* above.

1847 (*title*), Sixty Etched Reminiscences of the Models in the University Galleries, Oxford, by Sir F. Chantrey. **1876** *Jrnl. Chem. Soc.* II. 273 (*heading*) Etched figures on cubes of rock-salt. **1877** Kate Thompson *Handbk. Picture Gall.*, His etched works, which are so numerous and well-known. **1902** H. A. Miers *Min.* I. v. 112 Etched figures are of the greatest possible value in indicating the true symmetry of a mineral. *Ibid.* 113 A closer study of the etched figures upon various minerals shows that they are of two sorts; some faces of the crystal become covered with minute depressions or pits, others with minute elevations.

†**etch,** *v.*[3] [? var. of edge *v.*[1]] = edge *v.*[1] 6.

1691 Ray *Creation* II. (1701) 245 Without shifting of sides or at least etching this way and that way more or less.

etch, *v.*[4] var. of eche *v.* *Obs.* ***to etch out***, to eke out. See eke *v.* 3.

1682 D'Urfey *Butler's Ghost* 73 And none like him had e're the skill To etch and lengthen out a Bill. *c* **1698** Locke *Cond. Underst.* (1813) §29 Terms..found in some learned writers, to which they had recourse to etch out their systems.

etchant ('ɛtʃənt). [f. etch *v.*[2] + -ant[1].] A corrosive agent used for etching. Also *attrib.*

1930 *Engineering* 26 Sept. 388/2 Dr Voce had used the term 'etchant' in his paper, instead of writing the words 'etched by', and he would like to protest against the use of such an unpleasant word. **1950** *Jrnl. Iron & Steel Inst.* CLXVI. 270/1 A list of ten etchants for revealing austenitic grain size. **1960** *New Scientist* 11 Aug. 391/1 The tests will obviously have to be extended to different compositions, etchant concentrations and temperature regimes. **1968** *Ibid.* 1 Aug. 241/3 The clue that led to the development of the new technique which may eventually replace acid etchants.

etcher ('ɛtʃə(r)). [f. etch *v.*[2] + -er[1].] One who etches.

1662 Evelyn *Chalcogr.* 56 Giovanni Maggi was an excellent Painter and Etcher. **1713** *Guardian* No. 1 ⁋1 Engravers, artists by way of mezzo-tinto, etchers, and the like. **1851** Ruskin *Stones Ven.* I. Pref. 10 A carefully penned outline for the etcher. **1862** Thornbury *Turner* I. 245 Vivares, a Frenchman..a beautiful etcher of trees..was born 1709. **1870** *Illust. Lond. News* 29 Oct. 446 The Queen ..is an accomplished etcher.

etching ('ɛtʃɪŋ), *vbl. sb.* [f. as prec. + -ing[1].]

1. The action of the vb. etch; the art of the etcher.

1634 J. B[ate] *Myst. Nat.* 140 Etching is an imitation of Engraving, but more speedily performed. *a* **1691** Boyle *Wks* (1772) III. 459 The art of etching, whereby copper and silver plates may be enriched with figures. **1762** Hume *Hist. Eng.* lxxi. §27 Prince Rupert..was the inventor of etching. **1845** J. Pye *Patron. Brit. Art* ii. 50 Etching is not my profession.

2. a. *concr.* A copy or representation produced by the process of etching; an impression from an etched plate.

1762–71 H. Walpole *Vertue's Anecd. Paint.* (1786) I. 244 His etchings for Aesop's fables and view of Bruges were much esteemed. **1783** Cowper *Lett.* Wks. (1876) 127, I have an etching of the late Chancellor hanging over the parlour chimney. **1860** C. Sangster *Sonn.* 161 These leaves are merely etchings of the artist.

b. *transf.*

1765 Sterne *Tr. Shandy* VII. xxxii, Never is my imagination so busy as in framing his responses from the etchings of his countenance.

3. *attrib.*, as ***etching-club, -needle, -printing, -varnish, -wax***; **etching figure, pit** = *etch figure, pit* (s.v. etch *v.*[2] 4); **etching-ground,** the composition with which the metal plate, etc. is covered preparatory to etching.

1878 Hamerton *Engraving* in *Encycl. Brit.* VIII. 444/2 *Etching clubs, or associations of artists for the publication of original etchings. **1877** E. S. Dana *Textbk. Min.* II. i. 118 Analogous to the *etching-figures are the figures produced on the faces of some crystals by the loss of water. *c* **1790** Imison *Sch. Art* II. 51 Take a copper plate prepared as before..lay the *etching ground upon it, and etch the outlines of your design. **1821** Craig *Lect. Drawing* vii. 374 The use of such a cushion has..been generally laid aside, since the *etching-needle has been employed. **1925** *Jrnl. Iron & Steel Inst.* CXI. 588 Deep etching with picric or nitric acid fails to develop *etching pits. **1935** A. Sauveur *Metallogr. & Heat Treatment* (ed. 4) ii. 17 The figures thus outlined, in reality small cavities, are often called 'etching pits' or 'etching figures'. **1885** *Bookseller* 5 Mar. 311 *Etching Printing has recently received especial care and attention. **1860** Piesse *Lab. Chem. Wonders* 162 *Etching varnish is made of virgin wax and asphaltum. **1875** Ure *Dict. Arts* II. 298 One process of engraving on glass is carried out by covering the glass with an *etching wax, etc.

etchist ('ɛtʃɪst). [f. as prec. + -ist.] A jocular synonym for etcher.

1888 *Punch* 16 June 282/2 James the First, Etchist, is no longer President of the R.S.B.A.

ete, obs. form of eat.

eteliche, var. ateliche *adv.* *Obs.*, grievously, cruelly.

c **1175** *Lamb. Hom.* 123 He hit forgulte eteliche þa þe he tuhte and spuhte þet folc to cristes cwale.

†**'eten, 'ettin.** *Obs.* Forms: 1 eoten, eten, 3 eatand(e, -ante, eotand, -end, -ind, ȝeten, 4 eten(e, -in, yhoten, 4–5 etayn(e, 6 *Sc.* eitin, etin, eyttyn, 7 ettin. [OE. *eoten, eten* = ON. *ιǫtunn* (Sw. *jätte*, Da. *jette*):—OTeut. **ituno-z.*] A giant.

c **1205** Lay. 1801 Heo funden i þon londe twenti eotandes [*c* **1275** eatantes] stronge. *Ibid.* 17275 Hit hatte þere Eotinde King. *c* **1250** *Gen. & Ex.* 545 Of hem woren ðe ȝetenes borne, Miȝti men, and fiȝti. *a* **1300** *E.E. Psalter* xviii. 6 [xix. 5] He gladed als yhoten to renne his wai. *c* **1325** *Leg. Rood* (1871) 118 Quen dauid faȝt againe þat etin has he noȝt his staf for-ȝetin. *c* **1340** *Gaw. & Gr. Knt.* 723 He werrez.. Boþe wyth bullez & berez, & borez oþer-quyle, & etaynez. *c* **1380** Wyclif *Serm.* Sel. Wks. II. 111 No man is an etene to fede him þus bodili of Crist. *c* **1440** *MS. Lincoln* A. I. 17. f. 128 (Halliw.) Fy, he said, thou foule! thou etayne! Alle my knyghtes thou garte be slayne. **1528** Lyndesay *Dream* Ep. to King 45 Off the reid Etin [*v.r.* Eitin] and the gyir carlyng.

1549 *Compl. Scot.* 63 The taiyl of the reyde eythyn vitht the thre heydis. **1611** BEAUM. & FL. *Knt. Burning Pestle* I. ii, They say the King of Portugal cannot sit at his meate but the Giants and the Ettins will come and snatch it from him.

†'**etenish.** *Obs.* Forms: 1 eoten-, etonisc, 3 ȝeteniss. [f. ETEN + *isc*, -ISH.] Gigantic.

a **1000** *Beowulf* 1559 He..ȝeseah on searwum siȝe eadiȝ bil eald sweord eotenisc. *Ibid.* 2616 And his maȝum atbær brun faȝne helm hringde byrnan eald sweord etonisc. *c* **1250** *Gen. & Ex.* 3715 Ȝetenisse men ben in ebron.

Eteocretan (ˌiːtɪəʊˈkriːtən, ˌɛtɪəʊ-), *a.* and *sb.* [f. Gr. Ἐτεόκρης lit. 'true Cretan', f. ἐτεό-ς true + Κρητ-, Κρής Cretan, + -AN.] **A.** *adj.* Of, pertaining to, or designating a pre-Greek people of Crete or their language. **B.** *sb.* **1.** A member of this people or linguistic group. **2.** The language of this people.

1615 CHAPMAN tr. *Homer's Odysses* XIX. 245 There [*sc.* in Crete] Greekes suruiue, There the great-minded Eteocretans liue. **1895** A. J. EVANS *Cretan Pictographs* 85 The language here found represents that of the Eteocretans of whom, as we know, Praesos was a principal stronghold. *Ibid.* 86 It is possible that in the early period during which the indigenous Cretan script, both pictographic and linear, seems to have taken its origin the sole or preponderating element in the island may have been the 'Eteocretan'. **1904** *Ann. Brit. School at Athens 1901–2* VIII. 155 Messapian and Illyrian are clearly related to Venetic, a language to which we have found certain resemblances in Eteocretan. **1939** J. D. S. PENDLEBURY *Archæol. of Crete* v. 270 Of the famous post-Minoan 'Eteocretan' inscriptions from Praisos it is again unsafe to say anything with certainty. **1962** *Daily Tel.* 4 Apr. 15/3 Prof. Cyrus H. Gordon..claimed..'Linear A' ..and also 'Eteo-Cretan', long taken to be the pre-Greek speech of Crete, are both actually Phoenician. The Eteo-Cretan is written with the Greek alphabet. **1962** *Listener* 10 May 810/2 The Eteocretans of Homer.

†**ete'ostic, ete'ostichon.** *Obs. rare.* [f. Gr. ἔτεο-ς, gen. of ἔτος year + στίχ-ος row.] = CHRONOGRAM.

a **1637** B. JONSON *Execr. Vulcan* 36 Had I..pump'd for those hard trifles, Anagrams, Or Eteostics. **1882** J. HILTON *Chronograms* 378 A book..contains this eteostichon, said to be the cemetery of St. Severin [Paris].

-eteria: see -TERIA.

†**e'terminable,** *a.* *Obs.* *rare*$^{-1}$. Also etermynable. [f. E- *pref.*^{3} (here = IN-) + TERMINABLE.] That cannot be terminated; without termination or end; eternal.

a **1528** SKELTON *Death Earl Northumbld.* 199 Bring unto thy joye eterminable The soull of this lorde. **1847–78** HALLIWELL, *Etermynable*, interminable.

†**e'ternable, æ'ternable,** *a.* *Obs.*$^{-0}$ [ad. L. *æternābilis*, f. *æternāre* to make perpetual, f. *æternus*: see ETERNE.] Capable of being made eternal or everlasting.

1730–6 BAILEY (folio), *Æternable*: So **1775** in ASH.

eternal (iːˈtɜːnəl), *a.* and *sb.* Forms: 4 eternale, -eel, (5 eternaile *Sc.*), 5–7 eternall(e, 6 æternall, 4– eternal. [a. OF. *eternal*, *-el* (mod. F. *éternel*) = Pr. and Sp. *eternal*, It. *eternale*, ad. late L. *æternālis*, f. *ætern-us*: see ETERNE and -AL^1.

In philosophical and theological uses the word is the representative of Gr. αἰώνιος, f. αἰών age, ÆON.]

A. *adj.*

1. a. Infinite in past and future duration; without beginning or end; that always has existed and always will exist: *esp.* of the Divine Being.

c **1470** HENRY *Wallace* II. 180 Eternaile God, quhy suld I thus wayis de. **1524** ABBOT MALVERN in *R. Glouc.* (1724) 584 The Eternall King..shall reward everychone, Which..this wretched world doth despise. **1526** *Pilgr. Perf.* (W. de W. 1531) 2 b, We shall se the father of heuen and..his eternall sone our lord Jesu chryst. **1611** BIBLE *Deut.* xxxiii. 27 The eternall God is thy refuge, and vnderneath are the euerlasting armes. **1667** MILTON *P.L.* I. 25 That to the highth of this great Argument I may assert th' Eternal Providence. *a* **1729** CLARKE *Serm.* I. iv. (R.), The eternal, supreme cause, has..a perfect.. comprehension of all things. *a* **1800** BLAIR *Serm.* III. xix. (R.), The ancient philosophers..maintained the eternal existence of matter. **1847** EMERSON *Repr. Men, Goethe* Wks. (Bohn) I. 392 The old Eternal Genius who built the world.

b. By those who hold that time, *i.e.* the relation of succession, pertains merely to things as viewed by finite intelligence, and not to absolute reality, the word as used of God or His actions is interpreted in the sense: Not conditioned by time; not subject to time relations.

Phrases in which the word has properly this sense are, however, often used in religious language without any definite recognition of the metaphysical theory which they imply, being taken as figurative expressions of the divine omniscience.

1651 HOBBES *Leviath.* 20 Names that signifie nothing..as ..*eternal—Now*, and the like canting of Schoolemen. **1793** T. TAYLOR *Sallust* xiii. 64 *note*, The *eternal* (τὸ αἰώνιον) says Olympiodorus, is a total now, exempt from the past and future circulations of time, and totally subsisting in a present abiding now; but the *perpetual* (τὸ ἀΐδιον) subsists indeed always, but is beheld in the three parts of time, past, present, and future. *a* **1834** COLERIDGE, This eternal (*i.e.* timeless) act [the sacrifice of Christ] He manifested in time. **1875** JOWETT *Plato* (ed. 2) III. 620 The past and future are created species of time, which we unconsciously but wrongly transfer to the eternal essence; for we say indeed that he was, he is, he will be, but the truth is that 'he is' alone truly expresses him.

2. Infinite in past duration; that has always existed.

1690 LOCKE *Hum. Underst.* IV. x. §10 If we suppose bare matter without motion, eternal; motion can never begin to be. **1707** *Curios. in Husb. & Gard.* 245 Asserting the World to be Eternal, in Contradiction to the express Texts of the Holy Scripture.

3. a. Infinite in future duration; that always will exist; everlasting, endless.

c **1386** CHAUCER *Sec. Nun's T.* 34 Thy maydens deeth, that wan thurgh hire merite The eterneel lyf. **1526** TINDALE *2 Cor.* iv. 18 For thinges which are sene, are temporall: but thynges whiche are not sene, are eternall. **1552** ABP. HAMILTON *Catech.* (1884) 3 All levand in ane hoip of the eternal glore. **1579** SPENSER *Sheph. Cal.* Dec. 90 The power of herbs..which be wont to work eternall sleep. **1660** JER. TAYLOR *Worthy Commun.* I. iv. 74 Christ was..admitted to the celestial and eternall priesthood in heaven. **1752** HUME *Pol. Disc.* x. 155 There is very little ground..to conclude the universe eternal or incorruptible. **1827** POLLOK *Course T.* x, To the evil..Eternal recompense of shame and woe. **1834** J. H. NEWMAN *Par. Serm.* (1839) I. ii. 18 Judgment upon the eternal soul. **1850** MRS. STOWE *Uncle Tom's C.* xl, An eternal, inexorable lapse of moments is ever hurrying the day of the evil to an eternal night, and the night of the just to an eternal day.

¶ The New Testament expressions *eternal life, death, punishment*, etc. are here referred to sense 3, this being the sense in which the adj. in such contexts is ordinarily taken. Other meanings have, however, been assigned to it: (*a*) Some theologians interpret it in the etymological sense, which is also that of Gr. αἰώνιος, 'lasting for an age or ages'; (*b*) others regard the adj. as expressive of a notion of *quality* in the conditions which it designates, either in addition to, or instead of, the notion of endless duration (cf. 1 b).

1853 MAURICE *Theol. Essays* (ed. 2) 451 Knowledge constitutes Eternal Life, and..the loss of it is Eternal Death. **1882** FARRAR *Early Chr.* II. 366 The word eternal, far from being a mere equivalent for 'everlasting', never means 'everlasting' at all, except by reflexion from the substantives to which it is joined. **1885** T. C. FINLAYSON *Biol. Relig.* 87 A human soul might be immortal..and yet might never have what is distinctively called 'eternal life'—the true spiritual life of fellowship with God.

b. *transf.* Pertaining to eternal things; having eternal consequences.

1605 SHAKS. *Ham.* I. v. 21 This eternall blason must not be To eares of flesh and bloud. **1732** LAW *Serious C.* iii. (ed. 2) 44 He has liv'd without any reflection..in things of such eternal moment.

4. a. *rhetorically*. Said of things to which endless continuance is ascribed hyperbolically or in relative sense. ***Eternal City*** (L. *urbs æterna*): a designation of Rome, occurring in Ovid and Tibullus, and frequent in the official documents of the Empire.

c **1460** FORTESCUE *Abs. & Lim. Mon.* (1714) 84 Their Renowne wol be eternal. **1555** EDEN *Decades W. Ind.* (Arb.) 49 An eternal testimonie of absolute glory. **1609** HOLLAND *Amm. Marcel.* XXII. ix. 202 A certain region or quarter of that eternall citie [*urbis æternæ*] Rome. **1697** DRYDEN *Virg. Past.* x. 71 To..climb the frozen Alps, and tread th' eternal Snow. **1789** WOLCOTT (P. Pindar) *Subjects for Painters, Song to Delia*, O nymph, th' eternal tear shall flow; The sigh unceasing breathe of thee. **1792** BURKE *Pres. State Affairs* Wks. VII. 106 These accounts..tend to make an eternal rupture between the powers. **1793** *Trial T. Muir at Edinb. for Sedit.* 33 The Lord Advocate..declared that his imprisonment would be eternal. **1823** LAMB *Elia* Ser. I. xiii. (1865) 106 Delightful eternal commonplaces, which 'having been will always be'. **1844** *Mem. Babylonian P'cess* II. 301 Hours..passed in the bosom of the eternal mountains. **1850** ALISON *Hist. Europe* IX. lvii. 5 Stupendous mountains, whose summits..wrapped in eternal snow, almost overhang the lake. **1869** 'MARK TWAIN' *Innoc. Abr.* (1870) xxvii. 218 Michael Angelo..designed the Eternal City. **1876** FREEMAN *Norm. Conq.* V. xxiv. 390 At no moment..has the Parliament..ever given up its eternal right to regulate the royal succession at its will. **1887** STEVENSON *Underwoods* I. xxxv. 69 Eternal granite hewn from the living isle.

b. Familiarly, implying weariness or disgust: That seems to be going on for ever; perpetual, incessant, always recurring.

1787 T. JEFFERSON *Writ.* (1859) II. 164 My answers to the eternal applications I receive. **1825** COBBETT *Rur. Rides* (1885) I. 374 Respecting whose proceedings we read eternal columns in the broad-sheet. **1837** THACKERAY *Ravenswing* i, Mrs. C. was sipping her eternal tea. **1884** DUNCKLEY in *Manch. Exam.* 26 May 6/2 Perhaps more serious reading would then dethrone the eternal novel.

c. *nonce-use*. Having an 'eternal' resolve.

1606 SHAKS. *Tr. & Cr.* V. ii. 166 Never did young man fancy With so eternal and so fix'd a soul.

d. ***eternal triangle***: see TRIANGLE *sb.*

5. Of truths, principles, divine or natural laws, etc.: Valid through all eternity, immutable, unalterable. Esp. in phr. ***eternal truths*** or ***verities***, necessary truths, as being valid at all times.

[**1604** HOOKER *Eccl. Pol.* I. §2 The law wherby he [God] worketh is eternall, and therfore can have no shew or colour of mutabilitie.] *a* **1688** CUDWORTH (*title*) A Treatise concerning Eternal and Immutable Morality. **1690** LOCKE *Hum. Und.* IV. xi. 323 Propositions that are once true, must needs be eternal Verities. **1694** *Ibid.* (ed. 2) IV. xi. 366 Propositions are therefore call'd *Eternal Truths*, not because they are Eternal Propositions actually formed... But because being once made..they will, whenever they can be supposed to be made again at any time..always actually be true. *a* **1700** DRYDEN (J.), Hobbes believed the eternal truths which he opposed. **1791** BURKE *Let. to Memb. Nat. Assembly* Wks. VI. 64 It is ordained in the eternal constitution of things, that men [etc.]. **1847** EMERSON *Repr. Men, Napoleon* Wks. (Bohn) I. 381 It was the nature of things, the eternal law of man..which baulked and ruined him. **1855** BRIMLEY *Ess., Tennyson* 82 To exhibit some of the eternal elements of tragedy still in operation among us. **1883** F. H. BRADLEY *Logic* II. II. i. 289 No vehicle conveys the eternal verities half so well as does the labyrinth of a fantastic genealogy. **1900** B. RUSSELL *Philos. of Leibniz* ii. 18 The eternal truths, he says, are all hypothetical. **1960** K. AMIS *Take a Girl like You* xxvi. 301 'Do you think it's right to give up your principles for somebody you're in love with?' 'I say, we are getting down to the eternal verities, aren't we?'

6. ***eternal flower***, a name for the *Xeranthemum*; also called 'everlasting'.

1794 MARTYN *Rousseau's Bot.* xxvi. 388 Eternal Flower has an imbricate calyx with the inner scales membranaceous.

7. 'Used to express extreme abhorrence' (Schmidt). Now *vulgar* or *dial.*

1601 SHAKS. *Jul. C.* I. ii. 160 There was a Brutus once, that would haue brook'd Th' eternall Diuell to keepe his State in Rome. **1604** —— *Oth.* IV. ii. 130, I will be hang'd, if some eternall Villaine Haue not deuis'd this Slander. *a* **1825** FORBY *Voc. E. Anglia*, *Eternal*, infernal, damned..'Oh, he is an eternal rogue'!

8. quasi-*adv.*

1611 SHAKS. *Wint. T.* I. ii. 64 We were.. Two Lads, that thought there was no more behind, But..to be Boy eternall. **1614** ROWLANDS *Fooles Bolt* 36 Such sable colours should be worne, for them that do eternall mourne. **1671** MILTON *P.R.* IV. 391 What kingdom, Real or allegoric, I discern not; Nor when: eternal sure—as without end, Without beginning.

B. quasi-*sb.* and *sb.*

1. ***the Eternal***: God, the Deity. Cf. Fr. *l'Eternel* (transf. Heb. *yhwh* JEHOVAH).

1582 NORTH tr. *Gueuara's Diall Princes* 189 The eternall [ed. **1557** eternal creator] created this world in short space. **1591** SHAKS. *Two Gent.* V. iv. 81 By Penitence th' Eternalls wrath's appeas'd. **1594** HOOKER *Eccl. Pol.* I. i. (1611) 3 The lawe whereby the Eternall himselfe doth worke. **1667** MILTON *P.L.* II. 46 His trust was with th' Eternal to be deem'd Equal in strength. **1724** T. RICHERS *Royal Geneal. Spain* 200 Having been summon'd to appear before the Tribunal of the Eternal.

†**2.** = ETERNITY. Chiefly in phrase ***from eternal*** = L. *ab æterno*. *Obs.*

1622 S. WARD *Life of Faith in Death* (1627) 29, I was from eternall a sheepe destined to the slaughter. **1633** W. STRUTHER *True Happiness* 65 Albeit we be in God from eternall. **1742** YOUNG *Nt. Th.* III. 34 Eternal is at Hand, To swallow Time's Ambitions.

3. *pl.* Eternal things.

1649 ROBERTS *Clavis Bibl.* 391 These temporals, spirituals, and eternals..must be prudently distinguished. **1652** GAULE *Magastrom.* 154 Angells..administring not only in temporalls and in spiritualls, but likewise to eternalls. **1742** YOUNG *Nt. Th.* II. 340 All God-like Passion for Eternals quench'd; All Relish of Realities expir'd. **1840** DE QUINCEY *Essenes* Wks. X. 265 A body of men so truly spiritual in the eternals of their creed, whatever might be the temporals of their practice. **1885** J. MARTINEAU *Ethical Th.* I. 6 A certain stock of eternals transmigrates through various forms.

e'ternalism. *rare.* [f. prec. + -ISM.] The condition of being eternal; an eternal character or nature.

1889 BOYD CARPENTER *Bampton Lect.* Pref. xvii, Religion gives a sort of Eternalism to Righteousness.

†**e'ternalist.** *Obs. rare.* [f. as prec. + -IST.] One who believes in the eternal duration of the world.

1684 T. BURNET *Th. Earth* III. 23 Porphyry..had the same principles with these æternalists in the text..and thought the world never had, nor ever would undergo any change. *Ibid.* III. 42 Those eternalists that denyed the doctrine of the change and revolutions of the natural world. **1721–1800** in BAILEY. **1828** in WEBSTER; and in mod. Dicts.

eternality (iːtəˈnælɪtɪ). [f. as prec. + -ITY.] The condition or quality of being eternal; eternalness.

a **1400** *Cov. Myst.* 288 O! fili Altissimi! clepyd by eternalytè! **1532** MORE *Confut. Tindale* Wks. 438/1 Christes satisfaccion also for theternalitie of the payne, and full restitucion to Goddes fauoure. **1548** UDALL, etc. *Erasm. Par. John* viii. 66, I am that I am: sygnifiyng an eternalitie, and a nature that cannot chaunge. **1925** A. N. WHITEHEAD *Sci. & Mod. World* (1926) 121 Every scheme for the analysis of nature has to face these two facts, change and endurance. There is yet a third fact to be placed by it, *eternality*, I will call it.

eternalize (iːˈtɜːnəlaɪz) *v.* [f. as prec. + -IZE.]

1. *trans.* To render eternal in duration or character.

1847 A. J. DAVIS in *Fraser's Mag.* XXXVII. 134 It contains truth eternalised. **1850** R. MONTGOMERY *God & Man* 314 If the body of Jesus is thus substantially eternalised so will the bodies of the righteous be. **1890** J. MARTINEAU *Seat Authority in Relig.* IV. iii. 507 His personal manifestation of what God is and loves and eternalizes.

b. *hyperbolically*. To prolong indefinitely, perpetuate.

1808 *Ann. Reg. 1806*, 717 The second form of negotiation would eternalize the war. **1855** M. ARNOLD *Consolation* 63 The hour, whose happy Unalloy'd moments I would eternalize. **1859** GEN. P. THOMPSON *Audi Alt.* II. c. 92 The grandest move..ever made towards eternalizing the supremacy of money at elections.

†**2.** To make eternally famous; to immortalize.

1620 SHELTON *Quix.* II. xliv, And so with his burnt ashes ..Don Quixotes valour is eternalized. **1663** ROLLOCK in *Mrq. Worcester's Water-Comm. Engine* 9 This [the Water-Engine] alone were enough to eternalize his Name to all Ages. **1702** C. MATHER *Magn. Chr.* IV. iv. (1852) 112 The deaths of the heroes whose lives they have eternalized. **1822** T. MITCHELL *Aristoph.* I. 112 The gratitude of the Athenians..eternalized the circumstance in songs.

Hence **e'ternalized** *ppl. a.*

1830 *Fraser's Mag.* II. 267 We..have thus, in an article, placed some of the unfortunate gentleman's productions in an eternalized form. **1884** *Congregational Year-bk.* 78 It is but His eternalized action.

eternally (iːˈtɜːnəlɪ), *adv.* [f. as prec. + -LY².] In an eternal manner.

1. Chiefly with reference to God: 'From everlasting and to everlasting'.

a **1385** CHAUCER *L.G.W.* 2226 *Philomene*, Thow..that hast wrought This fayre world, & bar it In thyn thought Eternaly [*v.r.* eternally] er thow thyn werk beganne. **1594** HOOKER *Eccl. Pol.* I. xvi, The lawe which God with himselfe hath eternally set downe. **1677** HALE *Prim. Orig. Man.* I. iii. 86 If it were eternally altered, or eternally corrupted, then it was eternally, and eternally was not; it was eternally without alteration, and eternally altered. **1839** BAILEY *Festus* (1852) 344 What comes before and after the great world..God alone knows eternally.

2. a. Without end; for ever; throughout eternity.

c **1393** CHAUCER *Scogan* 2 To-brokene ben þe statutis in heuene þat creat were eternally [*v.r.* eternaly] to dure. *c* **1430** *Syr. Gener.* (Roxb.) *ad fin.*, To heven blis forto wende Eternallie there to be. **1549** *Bk. Com. Prayer, Burial of Dead*, Whosoeuer liueth, and beleueth in hym, shal not dye eternallye. **1595** W. C. CLARKE in *Shaks. C. Praise* 15 Bartasse, eternally praiseworthie for his weeks worke. **1654** EARL ORRERY *Parthenissa* (1676) 575 Then the survivor, fetching two or three groans over his dead enemy, fell down eternally by his side. **1746-7** HERVEY *Medit.* (1818) 76 Would they not bless the grave..and wish to lie eternally hid in its deepest gloom?

b. *hyperbolically.*

1664 SIR C. LYTTELTON in *Hatton Corr.* (1878) 43 Yrs, eturnally. **1850** W. R. RYAN *Upper & Lower California* I. 310 If you'll sell it me..I'll be etarnally obliged to you.

3. With perpetual recurrence; continually, constantly, incessantly.

1670 COTTON *Espernon* Pref., The Duke himself being so eternally upon the Scene of Action, that we shall seldom find him retir'd. **1712** ARBUTHNOT *John Bull* (1755) 31 The other was eternally drunk. **1793** SMEATON *Edystone L.* §246, I found it eternally rung in my ears from all quarters. **1884** F. M. CRAWFORD *Rom. Singer* I. 14 Nor is he eternally pulling a pair of monstrous white cuffs over his hands.

4. Immutably, unalterably.

a **1716** SOUTH (J.), That which is morally good..must be also eternally and unchangeably so. **1878** HOPPS *Princ. Relig.* viii. 26 There is such a thing as the eternally right and the unchangeably good.

eternalness (iːˈtɜːnəlnɪs). [f. as prec. + -NESS.] The state or condition of being eternal.

1730-6 BAILEY (folio), *Eternalness*, the being eternal. **1862** F. HALL *Hindu Philos. Syst.* 65 The texts of scripture declaratory of the eternalness of the Vedas. **1885** G. MEREDITH *Diana Crossw.* III. x. 197 Her still-flushed senses protested on behalf of the eternalness of the passion.

eterne (iːˈtɜːn), *a. Obs.* exc. *arch.* (*poet.*) Also 6-9 **etern**, 7-9 **ætern(e**. [a. OF. *eterne*, ad. L. *ætern-us*, for *æviternus*, f. *ævum* age.]

1. = ETERNAL *a.*

c **1366** CHAUCER *A.B.C.* 56 To stink eterne he wol my gost exyle. *c* **1374** —— *Boeth.* v. vi. 171 Þe comune iugement of alle creatures resonables than is þis þat god is eterne. **1413** LYDG. *Pilgr. Sowle* v. ix. (1483) 100 By the kynge eterne the raunson fully shalle be payd for man. **1423** JAS. I. *Kingis Q.* cvii, The effectis of my bemes schene Has thaire aspectis by ordynance eterne. *c* **1470** HARDING *Chron.* CXV. xi, Saynt Edmonde..dyed, and made his fare To blysse eterne. **1534** LD. BERNERS *Gold. Bk. M. Aurel.* (1546) K vij b, Other thynges I fynd in the saied annales worthie of etern memorie. **1605** SHAKS. *Macb.* III. ii. 38 Banquo and his Fleans liues. But in them, Natures Coppie's not eterne. **1647** H. MORE *Song of Soul* I. II. lii, Straight he to higher pearch, like bird in cage, Did skip, and sang of etern Destiny. **1683** E. HOOKER *Pref. Pordage's Mystic Div.* 101 An Ætern Beeing of Beeings. **1773** J. ROSS *Fratricide* (MS.) VI. 281 On him shall fall Retaliation sevenfold and eterne. **1820** KEATS *Hyperion* I. 117 Open thine eyes eterne. **1856** MRS. BROWNING *Aur. Leigh* III. 754 An individualism of the Infinite, Eterne, intense, profuse. **1877** M. ARNOLD *Balder Dead* 89 The prophetesses, who by rite eterne On Frea's hearth feed high the sacred fire.

2. *absol.* †**a.** In phrase *fro eterne* (= L. *ab æterno*), from eternity (*obs.*). **b.** *the eterne*: that which is eternal. **c.** *the Eterne*: the Eternal, God.

c **1374** CHAUCER *Boeth.* v. ii. 153 Þe deuyne purueaunce ..þat alle þinges byholdeþ and seeþ fro eterne. **14..** *Circumcis.* in *Tundale's Vis.* (1843) 91 The name of names sacryd from eterne. **1613** W. BROWNE *Brit. Past.* I. iv, O thou Eterne! by whom all beings move. **1839-48** BAILEY *Festus* Proem (ed. 3) p. vi, And in the vast conditions of the eterne The possible, the probable.

†**3.** quasi-*adv. Obs.*

c **1590** *Howers Blessed Virg.* 97, I verily think and beleeve surely, That my Redeemer is eterne on live.

†**e'terne,** *v. Obs. rare.* [f. ETERNE *a.*] *trans.* To make eternal; to eternize.

1598 SYLVESTER *Du Bartas* II. ii. II. *Babilon*, Whose happy Labours haue your laudes eterned. **1606** *Ibid.* II. iv. I. *Trophies*, O Verse right-worthy to bee ay eterned! —— *Wks.* (1621) 1118 Your name already is eterned In Memory's fair Temple.

†**e'ternify,** *v. Obs.* [f. ETERNE + -(I)FY.] *trans.* To make eternal. Hence the pa. pple. is used to translate Gr. ἀμβρόσιος.

1610 *Mirr. Mag., Winter's Nts. Vis.* Induct., True Fame ..by her power eternifies the name. **1615** CHAPMAN *Odyss.* I. 162 Her wing'd shoes..Formed all of gold, and all eternified. **1818** in TODD; and in mod. Dicts.

†**e'ternish,** *v. Obs.* Also 6 *pa. pple.* **eternest**. [f. ETERNE *a.*, or ad. F. *éterniser*: see -ISH.] *trans.* **a.** To make eternal or perpetual. **b.** To make eternally famous, to immortalize.

1579 LYLY *Euphues* (Arb.) 126 If this order had not bene in our predecessors..they had neuer bene eternished [ed. **1636** eternized] for wise men. **1589** GREENE *Menaphon* (Arb.) 56 The angrie heauens..haue eternisht thy exile. **1594** *First Pt. Contention* (1843) 72 Shall be eternest in all age to come. **1594** MARLOWE *Dido* I, A princess-priest.. Shall yield to dignity a double birth, Who will eternish Troy in their attempts.

†**eterni'tarian,** *sb. Obs.* [f. as next: cf. *trinitarian.*] A believer in the eternity (of the soul). Implied in **anti-eternitarian**, one who opposes this doctrine.

1746 ELIZA HEYWOOD *Female Spectator* (1748) IV. 221 Whether you read the works of these anti-eternitarians, or hear their discourse on that subject, etc.

e'ternitize, *v. nonce-wd.* [f. ETERNIT-Y + -IZE.] = ETERNALIZE.

a **1713** ELLWOOD *Elegy* in *Autobiog.* 208 Eternitiz'd be that right worthy Name.

eternity (iːˈtɜːnɪtɪ). Forms: 4 **eternite**, 4-5 **-yte(e**, 6 **-itie**, 6-7 **æternitie**, **-y**, 6- **eternity**. [ME. *eternite*, a. Fr. *eternité*, ad. L. *æternitāt-em*, f. *æternus*: see ETERNE. Cf. Pr. *eternitat*, Sp. *eternidad*, It. *eternità*.]

1. a. The quality, condition, or fact of being eternal (see the adj.); eternalness; eternal existence.

c **1374** CHAUCER *Boeth.* v. vi. 171 God is eterne..lat vs considere þan what is eternite. **14..** *Inholders* in *York Plays* 515 Euer withoutyn ende With the to reyne in thyne eternyte. **1447** BOKENHAM *Seyntys* Introd. (Roxb.) 8 To magnyfye God in hys blysful eternyte. **1578** T. N. tr. *Conq. W. India* Pref. 8 Giving them knowledge of the eternitie, and holy trinitie in unitie. **1607** SHAKS. *Cor.* v. iv. 25 He wants nothing of a god but Eternity. **1653** WALTON *Angler* i. 15 God injoyes himself only by Contemplation of his Goodness, Eternity, Infiniteness and Power. **1707** *Curios. in Husb. & Gard.* 246 There should always have been a preexisting Matter, to establish his Opinion concerning Eternity. **1831** BREWSTER *Newton* (1855) II. xvii. 125 An argument..to prove the eternity of the world.

b. *hyperbolically.* Perpetual or indefinite continuance; *esp.* 'immortality' of fame.

c **1420** *Pallad. on Husb.* IV. 476 Thus maketh thai of thaire fertilitee In helping nature a feire eternytee. **1606** HOLLAND *Sueton.* 208 A desire he had..of æternity and perpetuall fame. **1611** CORYAT *Crudities, Orat. in praise of travel*, Hercules..purchased himselfe eternity of name. **1611** TOURNEUR *Ath. Trag.* I. i, Here are my Sonnes—There's my eternitie. My life in them And their succession shall for euer liue. **1726** LEONI tr. *Alberti's Archit.* I. 28 b, The Vine exceeds even the Eternity of Time itself. **1877** MRS. OLIPHANT *Makers Flor.* xi. 277 That eternity is brief which hangs upon the sentiments of any multitude.

c. as a title: cf. 'Your Majesty, Grace', etc.

1791 D'ISRAELI *Cur. Lit.* (1834) I. 264 Their [Eastern Emperors'] subjects address them by the titles of 'Your Perpetuity, your Eternity.'

d. *the eternities*: (in vaguely concrete sense) things eternal; the eternal truths or realities. Frequent in Carlyle, and often cited (sometimes derisively) as characteristic of his style.

1843 CARLYLE *Past & Pr.* Wks. 1858 IX. 253 Truly, if a man cannot get some glimpse into the Eternities, looking through this portal,—through what other need he try it? **1878** MORLEY *Carlyle* 165 We begin with introspection and the eternities, and end in blood and iron.

2. Infinite time. The total eternity, which has neither beginning nor end, may be regarded as divided by any moment into two eternities: the past eternity (in scholastic language *æternitas a parte ante*), and the future eternity (*æternitas a parte post*). Hence the applications of the word in this sense may be classed as follows:

a. Absolute eternity, having neither beginning nor end.

1587 GOLDING *De Mornay* i. 6 The eternitie hath not any thing either afore or after it. **1667** MILTON *P.L.* II. 148 Those thoughts that wander through Eternity. **1802** PALEY *Nat. Theol.* xxiv. (1819) 396 Eternity is a negative idea, clothed with a positive name. **1856** DOVE *Logic Chr. Faith* III. 132 Infinite time is called eternity.

b. The two 'eternities'.

1656 COWLEY *Pindar Odes, The Muse* Notes 25 There are two sorts of Eternity; from the Present backwards to Eternity, and from the Present forwards. **1678** CUDWORTH *Intell. Syst.* 119 The Ancient Atheists..did at once deny both Eternities to the World: Past and Future. **1850** MRS. STOWE *Uncle Tom's C.* xxii, The soul awakes..between two dim eternities—the eternal past, the eternal future. **1874** H. REYNOLDS *John Bapt.* ii. 63 The introduction of the first man into the world..was a dividing line between the eternities.

c. The past eternity.

1651 HOBBES *Leviath.* II. xxvi. 148 'Natural' are those which have been Lawes from all Eternity. **1812** COGAN *Theol. Disq.* I. i. (R.), A first cause; who, being uncaused, must exist from eternity.

d. The future eternity; time without end.

c **1374** CHAUCER *Boeth.* II. vii. 58 Þou wilt maken comparisoun to þe endeles space of eternite. **1667** MILTON *P.L.* XII. 556 Beyond [time] is all abyss, Eternitie, whose end no eye can reach. **1713** ADDISON *Cato* v. i, Eternity, thou pleasing, dreadful thought..Through what new scenes and changes must we pass! **1801** SOUTHEY *Thalaba* IX. xiv, They, with their Leader, through eternity, Must howl in central fires. **1827** POLLOK *Course of T.* VI, Slowly numbers o'er The mighty cycles of eternity.

3. Hyperbolical uses of 2: A space of time felt as 'endless'; a term indefinitely remote.

1703 MOXON *Mech. Exerc.* 239 Those Grey Kentish Bricks..will last to Eternity. **1703** MAUNDRELL *Journ. Jerus.* (1732) 90 With such absolute firmness as if it had been design'd for Eternity. **1813** BYRON *Giaour* 272 Tho' in Time's record nearly nought, It was Eternity to thought. **1856** H. MILLER *Test Rocks* ix. (1857) 354 A few more worlds..to which the destroying flood does not reach, save once or twice in an eternity or so.

4. In expressed or implied contrast with *time*.

a. In metaphysical sense (cf. ETERNAL 1 b): Timelessness; existence with reference to which the relation of succession has no application.

1662 HOBBES *Consid.* (1680) 50 Eternity is a permanent Now. **1853** MAURICE *Theol. Essays* (ed. 2) 450 Eternity, in relation to God, has nothing to do with time or duration.

b. Opposed to 'time' in its restricted sense of duration measured by the succession of physical phenomena. Hence, the condition into which the soul enters at death; the future life. Also, eternal welfare.

1602 SHAKS. *Ham.* I. ii. 73 All that liues must dye, Passing through Nature to Eternity. *a* **1650** CRASHAW *Death Herrys*, Weak time shall be pour'd out Into eternity. **1691** T. H[ALE] *Acc. New Invent.* p. xciv, Most grave..Citizens, are put to it by a promissory Oath to stake their Eternities, and in effect to invocate God. **1785** *Gentl. Mag.* Aug. 658/2 Just as they were going to be launched into eternity.

5. *nonce-uses.* Viewed imaginatively as an agent or a person.

1509 HAWES *Past. Pleas.* XLIV. ix, I [Time] am the lode-starre to dame Eternitie. **1818** BYRON *Ch. Har.* IV. lxxi, It comes like an eternity, As if to sweep down all things in its track.

6. In *plural* (cf. 1 d, 2 b): Eternity viewed as consisting of 'ages'.

1382 WYCLIF *Pref. Ep. Jerome* iv. 64 Thoo that techen many men to rightwisnes [shulen shyne] as sterres into perpetuel eternytees [**1388** euerlastyngnessis]. **1609** BIBLE (Douay) *Dan.* xii. 3 They that instruct many to justice [shal shine] as starres unto perpetual eternities. **1856** MRS. BROWNING *Aur. Leigh* v. 566 Like a clock Which strikes the hours of the eternities. **1858** SEARS *Athan.* III. i. 256 To unfold through the ages, yea, through the eternities. **1871** R. H. HUTTON *Ess.* I. 247 The throne of heaven is to them a lonely one. The solitude of the eternities weighs upon their imaginations.

7. *attrib.*, as **eternity ring** (see quots.).

1939-40 *Army & Navy Stores Catal.* 449/1 Diamond and Platinum Eternity Ring from £10 10 0. **1950** 'P. WENTWORTH' *Eternity Ring* iv. 30 'You know the kind of ring they call an eternity ring?' She smiled. 'An old fashion which has come back—a circle of small stones set continuously.' **1960** H. HAYWARD *Antique Coll.* 112/1 *Eternity ring*, a ring in the form of a plain circle symbolising eternity, often set with a single row of stones.

eterni'zation. [f. next + -ATION.] The action of eternizing; immortalization.

1864 in WEBSTER; whence in later Dicts.

eternize (iːˈtɜːnaɪz, ˈiːtənaɪz), *v.* Also 6-7 **æternise**, 7 **-ize**. [a. Fr. *éternise-r*, ad. med.L. *æternizāre*, f. *ætern-us*: see ETERNE.

Both the accentuations above noted are frequent in poetry; Shaks. has *e'ternize*, which is now the more usual stress.]

1. *trans.* To make eternal, i.e. everlasting or endless; to give endless nature or duration to.

1580 C'TESS. PEMBROKE *Ps.* lxix. (1823) 123 There his name who love and prize, Stable stay shall eternize. **1610** HEALEY *St. Aug. Citie of God* 481 His [God's] holy will..can eternize creations. **1667** MILTON *P.L.* XI. 60 That [happiness] fondly lost, This other [immortality] serv'd but to eternize woe. *a* **1711** KEN *Imitat.* Poet. Wks. 1721 IV. 534 Assur'd to reunite on high And eternize their sacred Tie. **1740** CHEYNE *Regimen* 14 The most perfect Cherubim in Heaven, to perpetuate and eternise its Happiness, must [etc.] **1839** BAILEY *Festus* iv. (1848) 30 The mortal soul Shall be divinised and eternised.

2. To prolong indefinitely (a state or condition); to prolong indefinitely the existence of (a thing).

1601 HOLLAND *Pliny* (1634) I. 522 By this meanes they take order to eternise their Oliues. **1633** *Battle of Lutzen* in *Harl. Misc.* (Malh.) IV. 197 A truce which..they wished had been a peace, whereby their repose might be eternised. **1681** NEVILE *Plato Rediv.* 35 Force or Fraud may alter a Government; but it is Property that must Found and Eternise it. **1716** LADY M. W. MONTAGUE *Lett.* I. vi. 18 Perpetual quarrels which they take care to eternise, by leaving them to their successors. **1847** EMERSON *Repr. Men, Swedenborg* Wks. (Bohn) I. 327 An attempt to eternize the fireside and the nuptial chamber. **1879** CHR. ROSSETTI *Seek and F.* 236 Their first stage is transitory: eternize that first stage, and it would become penal.

b. *esp.* To make lasting, perpetuate (fame, memory, praise, etc.).

1568 NORTH tr. *Gueuara's Diall Princes* IV. II. 104 The memory of you shall remain eternized to your Successors for euer. **1589** NASHE *Anat. Absurditie* Epist., My tongue is too to base a Tryton to eternise her praise. **1605** *Play Stucley* in

Sch. Shaks. (1878) 266 Our fame Shall be eterniz'd in the mouths of men. **1628** R. B[ELING] *Contn. Sidney's Arcadia* VI. 487 To eternise the famous memorie..of his deceased Mistris Hellen. **1683** *Apol. Prot. France* iii. 10 The famous Act of Parliament at Paris has eternized the Memory of this Execrable Attempt. *a* **1711** KEN *Hymnotheo* Poet. Wks. 1721 III. 211 His Favours eternizing their Renown. **1773** BRYDONE *Sicily* xix. (1809) 198 Horses..had magnificent monuments erected to eternize their memory. **1866** FELTON *Anc. & Mod. Greece* I. xii. 490 An art which eternizes the memory of the human race.

3. To make eternally or perpetually famous; to perpetuate the fame or memory of; to immortalize.

1610 *Mirr. Mag.* 869 Cadiz..Where great Alcides..Did fixe his pillars t'eternize his name. **1665** J. WEBB *Stone-Heng* Ded. (1725) 1 Trajan, Adrian are Eternized for practising all liberal Sciences. **1746** SMOLLETT *Reproof* 113 Did not his virtues eterniz'd remain. **1818** BENTHAM *Ch. Eng.* 153 What might be..eternized in glass by Mr. Pearson. **1853** BRIGHT *Sp. Peace* 13 Oct., Marble monuments to eternise the men who have thus become great. **1862** R. H. PATTERSON *Ess. Hist. & Art* 107 To see helpless and unbeauteous agony eternised in stone. **1876** BLACKIE *Songs Relig. & Life* 148 Monuments..to eternise Lawyers with supple conscience, and glib tongue.

e'ternized, *ppl. a.* [f. as prec. + -ED[1].] Immortalized.

1603 H. PETOWE *Eliza's Fun.* in *Harl. Misc.* X. 334 To live againe in glory with his æternized sister, divine Eliza. **1610** HEALEY *St. Aug. Citie of God* 38 Rome amongst all her..eternized spirits cannot shew one better than hee was. **1627** SPEED *England* ix. §4 That eternized Queene Elizabeth of euerlasting memory. **1632** LITHGOW *Trav.* I. 34 To welcome thy hellish eternized guests.

†**e'ternizement.** *Obs.* [f. as prec. + -MENT.] The condition or state of being eternized; immortal fame.

1595 CHAPMAN *Ovid's Banq. Sence* (1639) 39 But give thy bounty true eternizement.

†**e'ternizer.** *Obs.* [f. as prec. + -ER[1].] One who eternizes.

1593 NASHE *Christ's T.* (1613) 54 Admirable Italian teare-eternizers, Ariosto, Tasso, and the rest. **1636** W. AMBROSE in *Ann. Dubrensia* (1877) 38 This epitaph his noble Vrne shall cover, Cotswolds Eternizer, Robert Dover.

eternizing (iːˈtɜːnaɪzɪŋ), *vbl. sb.* [f. as prec. + -ING[1].] The action of the vb. ETERNIZE.

1591 SPENSER *Ruines of Time* Ded., Intended.. to the eternizing of some of the chiefe of them. **1847** LD. COCKBURN *Jrnl.* II. 170 Nothing can justify the eternising of individual caprice over the fixed national property.

e'ternizing, *ppl. a.* [f. as prec. + -ING[2].] That eternizes.

1659 PEARSON *Creed* (1741) 100 Their eternal and eternizing oil lost long before. **1705** *Phil. Trans.* XXIV. 1104 Wishes her Dead Companion to share in her then present felicity, by virtue of eternizing Monuments.

†**e'ternness.** *Obs. rare.* Also eterneness. [f. ETERNE *a.* + -NESS.] = ETERNITY 1 and 2.

1606 *Sir G. Goosecappe* II. i. in Bullen *O. Pl.* III. 29 What Eternesse is, The World, and Time, and Generation. **1608** CHAPMAN *Trag. Byron* Plays 1873 II. 311 What impossible mixtures? vice and vertue, Corruption and eternnesse.

etesian (ɛˈtiːʒɪən), *a.* (*sb.*) [f. L. *etēsi-us*, a. Gr. ἐτήσιος, lit. 'annual', f. ἔτος year + -AN.]

1. a. *properly*, The distinctive epithet of certain winds in the region of the Mediterranean, blowing from the NW. for about 40 days annually in the summer.

†**b.** Hence, occasionally, applied to winds annually blowing from a particular quarter in other parts of the world, as the trade-winds, monsoons, etc.

1601 HOLLAND *Pliny* I. 473 The Ides of Iuly, which are forerunners of the Etesian winds. **1635** N. CARPENTER *Geog. Del.* II. vi. 102 The Etesian winde, which is obserued to blow euery yeere from the Northeast about the rising of Dog-starre. **1704** SWIFT *Batt. Bks.* (1711) 257 A sheet of Lead, which an Etesian Wind blows suddenly down from the Roof of some Steeple. **1775** R. CHANDLER *Trav. Asia M.* (1825) I. 21 Vessels find shelter in its port..during the etesian or contrary winds. **1828** *Lempriere's Classical Dict.* (ed. Barker) 304 Those winds are properly Etesian which blow from that part of the horizon which is beneath the north and west. **1853** GROTE *Greece* II. lxxxiv. XI. 123 A gentle and steady Etesian breeze carried them across.

fig. **1858** DE QUINCEY *Parr* Wks. V. 52 Had Dr. Bridges happened to be a vulgar sectarian..those etesian gales or annual monsoons would have been hailed by Parr as the harbingers of a triumph in reversion.

†**2.** quasi-*sb. Obs.*

1658 USSHER *Ann.* 346 Whom they nicknamed the Etesian, because he continued in the place but 45 dayes. **1675** EVELYN *Terra* (1729) 45 The Protection of a thin Hedge or Canvas Curtain..defend them from our too constant and rigorous Etesians. **1684** *Phil. Trans.* XIV. 561 These Eastern Winds (which I call our English Etesians).

etfleon, -fluwen, -foran, etc.: see ATFLEE, -FORE.

eth, var. EDH.

eth- (ɛθ-). *Chem.* The first syllable of ETHER, employed as a radical to form names for the typical members of the bi-carbon or ETHYL series of hydro-carbons and their compounds.

eth(e, obs. forms of EATH.

ethal (ˈɛθəl). *Chem.* [f. ETH- + -AL[1].] The same as *cetyl* or *cetylic alcohol* (see CET-). Hence **e'thalic** *a.*, as in **ethalic acid** = *cetylic acid.*

1839 TODD *Cycl. Anat.* II. 234/1 Ethal is a solid transparent..fatty matter. **1877** WATTS *Fownes' Chem.* II. 160 Ethal is obtained from spermaceti.

ethane (ˈɛθeɪn). *Chem.* [f. ETH- + -ANE.] The paraffin or saturated hydrocarbon, C_2H_6, forming the second member of the series C_nH_{2n+2}; also called *ethyl hydride* and *di-methyl*; a colourless inodorous gas.

1873 WATTS *Fownes' Chem.* (ed. 11) 545 We may take the formation of ethane from ethyl iodide. *Ibid.* (1877) II. 50 Ethane and propane..are given off from it [American petroleum] as gas at ordinary temperatures.

‖**Ethanim** (ˈɛθənɪm). [Heb. (*yéraḥ hā-*)*ēthānīm*, interpreted by Gesenius as 'month of swollen streams'.] The seventh month (Sept.-Oct.) of the Jewish ecclesiastical year, the first of the civil year, afterwards called by the Babylonian name Tisri.

[**1382** WYCLIF *1 Kings* viii. 2 Bethanym.] **1535** COVERDALE *1 Kings* viii. 2 In the moneth Ethanim, that is yᵉ seuenth moneth. **1876** M. DAVIES *Unorth. Lond.* 395 It was celebrated on..the 7th month, called in the Old Testament Ethanim, but by the Jews in later times Tisri.

ethanol (ˈɛθənɒl). *Chem.* = *ethyl alcohol.*

1900 *Jrnl. Chem. Soc.* A. LXXVIII. I. 618 Ethanol mercury salts in alkaline solution yield no precipitate with potassium sulphide. **1946** *Nature* 23 Nov. 744/2 A solution of the substance in 10 per cent aqueous ethanol gave no coloration with ferric chloride. **1964** N. G. CLARK *Mod. Org. Chem.* viii. 125 The first three alkanols are methanol, ethanol, propanol.

ethanolamine (ɛθəˈnɒləmiːn). *Chem.* [f. prec. + AMINE.] Any of three compounds in which one or more of the hydrogen atoms in ammonia is replaced by a group CH_2CH_2OH, which are viscous, high-boiling liquids usu. manufactured from oxirane (ethylene oxide) and ammonia with extensive industrial uses; *spec.* 2-aminoethanol, $H_2NCH_2CH_2OH$; also, any other amino alcohol structurally related to ethyl alcohol.

1897 *Jrnl. Chem. Soc.* LXXII. I. 313 (*heading*) Amido-ethylic alcohol (1:2-ethanolamine). **1950** KIRK & OTHMER *Encycl. Chem. Technol.* V. 855 The ethanolamines, combined with fatty acids, yield soaps that are extensively used in industry as emulsifiers and detergents. **1951** C. R. NOLLER *Chem. Org. Compounds* xxxiv. 694 Ethanolamine and its trimethylammonium salts, the cholines.., constitute a portion of an important class of biological substances known as the phospholipids. **1959** *Times* 1 Apr. 7 (Advt.), Even the photograph was processed with the help of *Shell* ethanolamines.

ethbete: see EATH C. 1.

†**ethe,** *v.*[1] *Obs.* In 1 éðian, 3 eði. [OE. *éðian*:—OTeut. type **anþjôjan*, related to ANDE.] *intr.* To breathe.

a **1000** *Greg. Dial.* IV. iii. (Bosw.), Hy ealle eðiaþ [L. *spirant omnia*]. *a* **1225** *St. Marher.* 13 Leowse þi fot of mi necke..eadiest þæt ich eði mahe.

†**ethe,** *v.*[2] *Obs.* [repr. OE. **ǽþan*, f. *áþ* OATH. Cf. MHG. *eiden.*] *trans.* To ask with an oath; to adjure.

c **1340** *Gaw. & Gr. Knt.* 379 Fyrst I eþe þe, haþel, how þat þou hattes, þat þou me telle truly. *Ibid.* 2467 Þerfore I eþe þe, haþel, to com to þy naunt. *a* **1400-50** *Alexander* 340 Þe ious out he wrengis, Erne till exorzise & ethis euer elike, þat it suld worthe as he wald.

†**ethecke.** *Obs. rare*[−1]. [ad. L. *etheca*, ad. Heb. *attīq* (only in this chapter); the sense is uncertain: Gesenius suggests 'pillar', others 'gallery, portico'.]

1609 BIBLE (Douay) *Ezek.* xli. 15 And he measured the length of the building against the face of that, which was separated at the backe: the etheckes on both sides of an hundred cubits.

†'**ethel,** *sb. Obs.* exc. *Hist.* Also 1 éðel, œ́ðel, 1-3 eðel, æðel, 3 aðel. [Common Teut.: OE. *œ́ðel*, *éðel* = OS. *ōðil*, OFris. *éthel*, *óthol*, OHG. *uodil*, ON. *óðal*, f. stem **ôþ-*, ablaut-derivative of **aþ-*: see ATHEL.] Ancestral land or estate, patrimony; native land.

c **888** K. ÆLFRED *Boeth. Metr.* xxiv. 99 Þis is eallunga min agen cyð eard and eþel. *c* **1000** *Ags. Gosp.* Luke iv. 24 Nan witega nis andfenge on his eþele [*Lindisf.* on oeðel his, *Rushw.* on oedle his.] *c* **1160** *Hatton Gosp.* ibid., On his æðele. *c* **1175** *Lamb. Hom.* 113 We ne maȝen habben þene heouenlichen eþel butan we beon clene from alle sake. *c* **1205** LAY. 16289 Min æðel to biwinnen. *Ibid.* 20201 þat aðel wes his aȝene. **1875** STUBBS *Const. Hist.* I. v. 75 An 'ethel', an inherited or otherwise acquired portion of original allotment.

†'**ethel,** var. form of ATHEL *a. Obs.*

1. = ATHEL A. 2.

c **1200** *Trin. Coll. Hom.* 5 [We] understonden him on ure eðele bede. *Ibid.* 125 To bisechen..mid eðele worde and edie. *a* **1225** *Ancr. R.* 172 Þeos þrelles beoð hire eðele vif wittes.

2. *Comb.*, as **ethelborn** *a.*, nobly born (*Hist.* after OE. phrase *æþele ȝeboren*).

1844 LINGARD *Anglo-Sax. Ch.* (1858) II. App. 359 The prejudices of the ethelborn Saxons. **1844** LD. BROUGHAM *Brit. Const.* x. (1862) 140 An ethel born or noble woman.

etheling, obs. form of ATHELING.

†'**ethem.** *Obs.* Forms: 1 ǽðm, éðm, 2 eþem. [Com. WGermanic: OE. *ǽðm*, *éðm*, cogn. w. OFris. *êthma*, OS. *áðom* (Du. *adem*), OHG. *âtam* (MHG. *âtem*, Ger. *athem*), f. Teut. root **ǣþ-*, OAryan **ēt-* to breathe.] Vapour, breath.

Beowulf 2593 (Gr.) Hreðer æðme weoll. *a* **1000** *Cædmon's Christ & Satan* (Gr.) 704 Hu sid se swarta eðm [swol-] seo. *c* **1175** *Lamb. Hom.* 43 Heore eþem scean swa deð þe leit a-monge þunre.

ethen, var. form of HETHEN *a.*, *Obs.* hence.

ethene (ˈɛθiːn). *Chem.* [f. ETH-YL + -ENE.] A fatty hydrocarbon, C_2H_4, forming the second member of the series C_nH_{2n}: known also as ethylene, olefiant gas, or heavy carburetted hydrogen. Also *attrib.*, as in ***ethene bromide, chloride, iodide***, etc.

1873 WATTS *Fownes' Chem.* 554 Ethene is formed by the action of nascent hydrogen upon ethine or acetylene. *Ibid.* 619 Ethene Iodide is a colourless, crystalline, volatile substance, of penetrating odour. *Ibid.* (1877) II. 56 Ethene ..is most easily prepared by heating strong alcohol with three or four times its weight of strong sulphuric acid.

ethene, obs. form of HEATHEN.

ethenoid (ˈɛθɪnɔɪd), *a. Chem.* [f. ETHEN(E + -OID.] Resembling ethylene in structure or properties; ethylenic.

1907 *Jrnl. Chem. Soc.* XCII. I. 307 The interaction of ethenoid compounds and bromine in solution is of the second order. **1932** *Canad. Jrnl. Research* VII. 475 The bromine absorption of the polymers is very small but.. measurable. This fact might be taken to prove the existence of an open-chain structure with an ethenoid linkage. **1951** *Gloss. Terms Plastics (B.S.I.)* 7 *Ethenoid plastics*, a class generally understood to comprise the acrylic, vinyl and styrene groups of plastics.

ether (ˈiːθə(r)). Also æther. [a. L. *æther*, ad. Gr. αἰθήρ (in senses 1-3 below), f. root of αἴθ-ειν to kindle, burn, shine; cf. αἶθρα fair weather, f. same root.

The spelling *æther* is still not uncommon in senses 1-3, and occasionally occurs in sense 5. In the chemical sense 6 *ether* is the only form recognized by good authorities.]

I. Senses adopted from Greek (orig. through Latin; but now often used with direct reminiscence of passages in Gr. classic authors).

1. a. The clear sky; the upper regions of space beyond the clouds; the medium filling the upper regions of space, as the air fills the lower regions. Now *poet.* or *rhetorical.*

1587 GOLDING *De Mornay* ix. 122 What will he answere to Plato, who saith that the Heauen or Skye is called Aether. **1718** POPE *Iliad* XVI. 361 All the unmeasured aether flames with light. **1790** COWPER *Iliad* XIX. 431 Through ether down she darted. **1813** SCOTT *Trierm.* III. xxv, The wizard song at distance died, As if in ether borne astray. **1855** LONGF. *Hiaw.* XVII. 236 The people..saw the wings of Pau-Puk-Keewis flapping far up in the ether. **1871** R. ELLIS *Catullus* lxiv. 206 The Ocean shook, and stormy the stars 'gan tremble in ether.

b. As the element breathed by the gods; 'diviner air'.

1733 POPE *Ess. Man* III. 115 Whate'er of life all-quickening æther keeps..one nature feeds the vital flame. **1840** CLOUGH *Amours de Voy.* I. 4 A land wherein gods of the old time wandered, Where every breath even now changes to ether divine.

2. In ancient cosmological speculation conceived as an element filling all space beyond the sphere of the moon, and as the constituent substance of the stars and planets and of their spheres. The earliest Eng. use; now only *Hist.*

It was variously regarded as a purer form of fire or of air, or as differing in kind from all the 'four elements'. By some it was supposed to be the constituent substance, or one of the constituents, of the soul.

1398 TREVISA *Barth. De P.R.* VIII. v. (Addit. MS. 27944 fol. 107) Isidor seiþ þe ouere parties of fuyre & of ayer hatte Ether. **1678** CUDWORTH *Intell. Syst.* 16 From the æther was made the heavens. *Ibid.* 493 The Pagans answer thus..we call God in the Æther Jupiter. **1695** BP. PATRICK *Comm. Gen.* i. 7 The thinner parts..made the æther, or higher firmament, wherein the sun and the planets are seated.

3. Air; respirable fluid.

1713 *Guardian* No. 44 They sucked-in so condensed and poisonous an Aether. **1809** PINKNEY *Trav. France* 277 His senses are hailed..by the freshness of a pure æther.

II. Senses of modern development.

†**4.** As a general name for extremely subtle fluids, the existence of which was imagined or inferred; = AURA 2, 3. *Obs.*

1691 ED. TAYLOR *Behmen's Theos. Philos.* xvi. 22 The Elements themselves pass into their Ethers. **1757** DARWIN *Vapour* in *Phil. Trans.* L. 252 There was no real opposition in the electric æther of glass, and that from wax.

fig. **1791** BOSWELL *Johnson* 1 July an. 1763, My mind was ..strongly impregnated with the Johnsonian æther.

5. a. *Physics.* A substance of great elasticity and subtilty, formerly believed to permeate the

whole of planetary and stellar space, not only filling the interplanetary spaces, but also the interstices between the particles of air and other matter on the earth; the medium through which the waves of light are propagated. Formerly also thought to be the medium through which radio waves and electromagnetic radiations generally are propagated. Sometimes called ***the luminiferous ether***. Also *attrib.*, as in ***ether-strain, -vibration, -wave***.

Later views of the ether were that it provided a frame of reference for the universe, with respect to which Maxwell's equations of electromagnetism or other field equations are valid, but that it possibly lacked any material properties. Following the special theory of relativity, which assumed that there is no absolute frame of reference and which explained why the Michelson–Morley experiment failed to detect an 'ether wind', the concept was gradually discarded in scientific thought, and has received little support since the 1920s.

1644 DIGBY *Nat. Bodies* xxxii. (1658) 342 The Ether..like an immense Ocean, tossed with all varieties of motion. **1692** BENTLEY *Boyle Lect.* 226 These phænomena are produced either by the intervention of air or æther or other such medium, that communicates the impulse from one body to another. **1704** NEWTON *Opticks* (J.), Ether, like our air, may contain particles which endeavour to recede from one another. **1778** *Dict. Arts & Sc.*, *Æther*, an imaginary fluid, supposed by several authors, both ancient and modern, to be the cause of gravity, heat, light, muscular motion, and, in a word, of every phænomenon in nature..Perrault represents it as 7200 times more rare than air; and Hook makes it more dense than gold itself. **1831** BREWSTER *Newton* (1855) I. vi. 134 Descartes was the first philosopher who maintained the existence of an ether, a medium more subtle than air, filling the interstices of air. **1872** HUXLEY *Phys.* ix. 219 The vibrations of ether..constitute the physical basis of light. **1878** B. TAYLOR *Deukalion* III. iii. 109 Our dark orb Drinks light from ether till it grows a star. **1924** H. L. BROSE tr. *Born's Einstein's Theory Relativity* iv. 75 So far as this conception of the ether is still used nowadays it is taken to mean nothing more than empty space associated with certain physical states or 'fields'. **1935** A. S. EDDINGTON *New Pathways in Sci.* ii. 39 Some distinguished physicists maintain that modern theories no longer require an aether. .. I think all they mean is that, since we never have to do with space and aether separately, we can make one word serve for both; and the word they prefer is 'space'. **1951** E. T. WHITTAKER *Hist. Theories Aether & Electricity* (ed. 2) I. p. v, It seems absurd to retain the name 'vacuum' for an entity so rich in physical properties, and the historical word 'aether' may fitly be retained. **1961** M. ČAPEK *Philos. Impact Contemp. Physics* xiv. 251 There are even now physicists who are looking hopefully toward aether as a clue to the explanation of micro-physical phenomena. **1965** J. D. NORTH *Measure of Universe* iii. 30 It was not long before attempts were being made to design an aether suitable for the representation of (Newtonian) gravitation. **1967** CONDON & ODISHAW *Handbk. Physics* (ed. 2) vi. 158 It is not profitable to identify the mechanical ether of the eighteenth and nineteenth centuries with the 'polarizable vacuum' of modern quantum field theories.

attrib. **1879** G. ALLEN *Col. Sense* i. 2 We must find out how the various modes of æther-waves..came originally to be distinguished from one another. **1884** tr. *Lotze's Metaph.* III. iii. 475 We cannot conceive any reason why a soul that feels ether-waves as colours must, in consistency, perceive air-waves as sounds. **1925** O. LODGE *Ether & Reality* ii. 42 Fearfully rapid tremors or ether vibrations which can be excited electrically in a form which we know as X-rays. **1926** B. RUSSELL *ABC of Relativity* iii. 31 If there is an aether wind, it is clear that, relatively to an observer on the earth, light-signals will seem to travel faster with the wind than across it.

b. *fig.*

1831 CARLYLE *Sart. Res.* (1858) 33 We are—we know not what;—light-sparkles floating in the æther of Deity! **1835** I. TAYLOR *Spir. Despot.* viii. 352 Measures which would have reduced the papal authority out of Italy to a thin ether visible to none but the clergy. *a* **1849** POE *Poems, Ulalume*, She rolls through an ether of sighs.

c. Hence *colloq.*, wireless, 'the radio'.

1899 *Daily News* 26 May 5/1 An age of ether-wave telegraphy and the Röntgen rays. **1923** *Daily Mail* 22 Jan. 7 The climax of an entrancing week of ether-borne opera... She possesses the real 'wireless voice'. **1930** J. S. HUXLEY *Bird-Watching* p. vii, A..request I made over the ether for more information. **1933** *Discovery* Sept. 280/1 The Babel of a thousand languages will soon assail him on the ether. **1961** G. MILLERSON *T.V. Production* ii. 20 This interlacing method of scanning effectively saves 'etherspace', allowing more stations to work in any band. **1968** *Listener* 4 July 26/1 The authentic atmosphere, the enthusiasm, ease and élan, can be felt over the ether, but it's even better on TV.

6. *Chem.* **a.** The colourless, light, volatile liquid, ($C_4H_{10}O$) resulting from the action of sulphuric acid upon alcohol, whence it was also known as ***sulphuric, phosphoric***, etc. ***ether***. In popular and commercial use the incorrect name 'sulphuric ether' is still common, and the term 'ether' without prefixed word is ordinarily understood to refer to this substance, which in technical nomenclature is now distinguished as ***common, ethylic***, or ***vinic ether***, or ***ethyl oxide***. It is an anæsthetic, and capable of producing extreme cold by its evaporation. The mod. systematic name is ***diethyl ether***, usu. given as ***ethyl ether***; *ethoxyethane* is occas. used. Also *attrib.* (Cf. ETHERICAL *a.* sense.)

1757 LEWIS in *Phil. Trans.* L. 161 The subtile fluid, prepared from vinous spirits with the vitriolic acid, called by the chemists æther. **1794** PEARSON *ibid.* LXXXIV. 389 Fifty grains of white lac readily dissolved in 500 grains measure of sulphuric æther. **1860** PIESSE *Lab. Chem. Wonders* 82 A solution of gold in æther applied to the surface of fine polished steel instruments gilds them. **1875** URE *Dict. Arts* II. 309 s.v., A duty of 1*l.* 5*s.* per gallon was fixed on sulphuric ether on the 25th September 1862. **1877** ROBERTS *Handbk. Med.* (ed. 3) I. 63 Ether dissolves the fat and brings the striæ again into view.

attrib. **1872** H. SPENCER *Princ. Psychol.* I. v. x. 611 Æther-narcosis produces the loss of 1. The local sensibility of extreme parts..2. The intellectual powers. **1873** J. P. COOKE *New Chem.* 18 And the globe will hold just as much ether-vapor as if neither of the other two were present. **1879** H. SPENCER *Data of Ethics* x. §64. 177 By ether-spray it [an external part of the body] is made very cold.

†**b.** Any of various compounds analogous to ethyl ether, formed by the reaction of ethyl alcohol and either an acid (other than sulphuric acid) or a salt and sulphuric acid. *Obs.*

The compounds were named according to the acid or salt from which they were derived: e.g. nitrous acid gave ***nitrous ether*** (now called ethyl nitrite, $C_2H_5NO_2$). The extension of meaning of the word *ether* thus took place in two stages, the first including other acids in the preparation, the second other alcohols (giving sense 6 c).

1796 R. HERON tr. *Fourcroy's Elem. Chem. & Nat. Hist.* III. 424 The nitric æther obtained by these processes is a yellow fluid, equally volatile and susceptible of evaporation with sulphuric æther. *Ibid.* 427 M. de la Planche, apothecary, has proposed the preparing of muriatic æther, by pouring..sulphuric acid and alcohol upon decrepitated muriate of soda. *a* **1797** *Encycl. Brit.* IV. 475/2 With the nitrous acid and spirit of wine, may also be made an exceedingly volatile liquor, called nitrous ether, to distinguish it from the vitriolic above mentioned. **1833** *Penny Cycl.* I. 158 The acids which occasion the formation of the æthers already described do not enter at all into their composition. **1867** C. L. BLOXAM *Chem.* 522 Acetic ether.. has a share in the perfume of cider, perry, vinegar, and of many wines. **1962** M. P. CROSLAND *Hist. Stud. Lang. Chem.* v. i. 289 The authors [of the *Méthode de nomenclature chimique* (1787)] had decided that each of the aetherial compounds obtained by the reaction of alcohol with various acids should be known as 'ether' qualified by an adjective according to the acid used to prepare it, e.g. *éther acétique* (i.e. ethyl acetate). Most of these 'ethers' were what we should now call esters.

c. Hence by extension, the generic name of a large class of compounds, formed by the action of acids upon alcohols, divided into (1) *simple ethers*, of which the above Common Ether is the type, and which comprise the oxides, sulphides, chlorides, etc. of alcohol radicals. (2) *compound ethers*, in which the hydrogen of the hydroxyl of an alcohol is replaced by an acid-radical. In mod. use, *ether* is restricted to compounds of the type R_2O (*simple ethers*) and ROR′ (*mixed ethers*), where R, R′ are organic groups (other than acyl groups and their analogues) linked directly to the oxygen by a carbon atom; ***compound ethers*** are now known as ESTERS.

1838 T. THOMSON *Chem. Org. Bodies* 324 Sulphuric ether ..possesses the characters of a base, being capable of neutralizing various (probably all) acids..These new compounds are at present very inaccurately termed ethers. **1850** DAUBENY *Atom. Th.* viii. (ed. 2) 257 An ether..bearing the same relation to fusel oil, which sulphuric ether does to alcohol. **1852** *Rep. Brit. Assoc. 1851* I. 129 Chemists..seem to consider it sufficient to place all those bodies, the basis of which is an ether, under the head of compound ethers. *Ibid.* 130 If the term, compound ether, be retained at all, it should be restricted to bodies..in which a simple ether is united with an ether radical, as the oxide of ethyl with methyl or with amyl. **1877** WATTS *Fownes' Chem.* II. 110 In the polyatomic alcohols, two hydroxyl groups may also be replaced by one atom of oxygen, giving rise to another class of oxygen ethers. The replacement of the hydrogen of the hydroxyl in an alcohol by acid radicles produces ethereal salts or compound ethers. **1950** L. F. & M. FIESER *Org. Chem.* (ed. 2) vi. 134 Ethers are regarded more appropriately as derivatives of alcohols, from which they usually are prepared. **1964** N. G. CLARK *Mod. Org. Chem.* viii. 142 The ethers are all colourless, neutral, inflammable compounds, sparingly soluble in and less dense than water. **1966** *McGraw-Hill Encycl. Sci. & Technol.* V. 85 The names of the ethers correspond to the hydrocarbon groups present. Thus, CH_3-O-CH_3 is methyl ether, rarely dimethyl ether, and $C_6H_5-O-CH_3$ is phenyl methyl ether.

ether, var. of EDDER.

1649 R. HODGES *Plain. Direct.* 28 You must either take out of the hedg the ether or the stake.

ether, obs. form of EITHER.

etherate ('iːθəreɪt). *Chem.* [f. ETHER + -ATE¹.] Any compound whose molecule contains an ether molecule, esp. $(C_2H_5)_2O$.

1904 *Jrnl. Chem. Soc.* LXXXVI. I. 215 Etherates of Haloid Compounds of Magnesium... The author has determined the solubilities in ether at different temperatures of the compounds $MgBr_2,2Et_2O$ and $MgI_2,2Et_2O$.., to which he gives the name of 'dietherates'. **1973** I. L. FINAR *Org. Chem.* (ed. 6) I. vii. 197 Ethers.. readily form co-ordination complexes (etherates) with Lewis acids. **1976** H. CAMPION et al. in B. E. C. Nordin *Calcium, Phosphate & Magnesium Metabolism* xii. 454 Acids, and especially Lewis acids (for example, boron trifluoride etherate) caused isomerization of previtamin D. **1984** [see ACETYLIDE].

†'**etherated**, *ppl. a. Obs.* [f. ETHER + -ATE³ + -ED¹.] Combined with ether; = ETHERIZED.

1802 *Med. Jrnl.* VIII. 190 The author..had concluded.. that the fulminating mercury was composed in 100 parts, 21,28 of oxalic acid, 64,72 of mercury, and 14 of etherated nitrous gas, and of a surplus of oxygen.

ethercap, obs. form of ETTERCAP.

ethereal, etherial (iː'θɪərɪəl), *a.* and *sb.* Also 6–9 æthereal(l. [f. L. *ætheri-us* or *æthere-us* (ad. Gr. αἰθέρι-ος) + -AL¹.

The uncertainty of the spelling began in Latin, the orig. *ætherius* from the Gr. being often written *-eus* after the ordinary Latin adj. ending, as in *ciner-eus, lign-eus*, etc.; this spelling is however generally rejected by mod. scholars. The spelling *-eal* is now perhaps the more common in Eng. Cf. *aereal, aerial*.]

1. Of the nature of, or resembling the idea of, the ether or lightest and most subtle of elements; light, airy, attenuated.

1598 BARCKLEY *Felic. Man* (1631) 366 In the world wherewith we are environed [there is a continual ascending] from the elements and compound things, by the Æthereall substance to Heaven. **1638** WILKINS *New World* I, The Elementary and Æthereal..doth not belong to the present Question, but of the Sea and Land, etc. **1857** WOOD *Com. Obj. Sea-shore* 27 In the kingdom of Ocean, water is the atmosphere, and, like its more ethereal relative, is ever rolling.

2. Heavenly, celestial. Chiefly *poet.*

1667 MILTON *P.L.* VIII. 646 Go, heavenly Guest, Ethereal Messenger. **1697** DRYDEN *Virg. Georg.* III. 56 Heroes, whose Etherial Root Is Jove himself. **1702** ROWE *Amb. Step-Moth.* I. i, Nor could the Breath of Art kindle again Th' Etherial Fire. **1743** J. DAVIDSON *Æneid* VII. 192 Steeds of Etherial Breed. *c* **1820** S. ROGERS *Italy, Meillerie* 75 Bright and unsullied lives the ethereal flame. **1840** BARHAM *Ingol. Leg., Nurse's Story*, Ethereal Spirits, gentle and good, Aye weep and lament o'er a deed of blood.

3. Of or pertaining to the material heaven, or highest region of the atmosphere.

1513 DOUGLAS *Æneis* XII. Prol. 41 Phebus..Defundand from hys sege etheriall Glaid influent aspectis celicall. **1530** RASTELL *Bk. Purgat.* III. ix, Pure regyon ethereall where the sonne & the other sterres renne. **1610** HEALEY *Vive's Comm. St. Aug. Citie of God* (1620) 354 Porphyry reckneth gods that are either heavenly, etherall, ayery, watry, earthly, or infernall. **1638** WILKINS *New World* xiv. (1707) 115 The extreme Coldness of the Æthereal Air. **1744** AKENSIDE *Pleas. Imag.* I. 42 There to breathe at large Ætherial Air. **1821** SHELLEY *Prometh. Unb.* I. 275 Mischiefs sent To blast mankind from yon ethereal tower.

b. Pertaining to the terrestrial atmosphere, in opposition to the lower regions. So occasionally L. *ætherius*.

1697 DRYDEN *Virg. Georg.* IV. 706 Near the Confines of Etherial Light..Th' unwary Lover cast his Eyes behind.

4. Spirit-like, impalpable; of unearthly delicacy and refinement of substance, character, or appearance.

1647 H. MORE *Immort. Soul* I. II. xxiv, Ethereall corporeity, Devoid of heterogeneall organity. **1722** WOLLASTON *Relig. Nat.* ix. 199 The soul may be also perceptive of finer impressions and ethereal contacts. **1802** SYD. SMITH *Wks.* (1859) I. 8 It is not possible to endure the draggling and the daubing of Dr. Rennel, after the ethereal touches of Mr. Burke. **1810** SOUTHEY *Kehama* II. i, Only Kehama's powerful eye beheld The thin etherial spirit. **1847** DISRAELI *Tancred* II. xv, Her ethereal nature seemed to shrink from coarse reality. **1872** BLACK *Adv. Phaeton* xxi. 299 The far and ethereal masses of the Langdale Pikes. **1873** MAX MÜLLER *Sc. Relig.* 365 As men, we only know of embodied spirits, however ethereal their bodies may be conceived to be. **1879** W. J. LOFTIE *Ride in Egypt* 150 A faith which is so wholly ethereal as to be independent of facts.

5. *Physics.* Of, pertaining to, or having the nature of 'ether'. See ETHER 5. In early use nearly = 1.

1692 BENTLEY *Boyle Lect.* 206 An æthereal subtile matter ..may penetrate and pervade the minutest and inmost cavities of the closest bodies. **1810** VINCE *Astron.* xxiii. 252 Beyond the atmosphere of the comet, the ætherial air..is extremely rare. **1816** J. SMITH *Panorama Sc. & Art* II. 328 All the substances in nature..may be considered either as solid, fluid, aëriform, or ethereal. **1863** E. V. NEALE *Anal. Th. & Nat.* 159 That which propagates movement, the ethereal atoms. **1873** H. SPENCER *Study Sociol.* xvi. (1877) 402 Millions of such etherial waves must successively make infinitesimal additions to its motion. **1878** TAIT & STEWART *Unseen Univ.* iii. §114. 126 Something analogous to ethereal friction.

6. *Chem.* Of or pertaining to the liquid called 'ether' (see ETHER 6); resembling ether or its qualities.

1800 tr. *Lagrange's Chem.* II. 321 Ethereal tinctures are prepared in pharmacy. **1807** T. THOMSON *Chem.* (ed. 3) II. 414 A combination of two parts of sulphuric acid and one of alcohol..emits a smell perceptibly ethereal. **1818** FARADAY *Exp. Res.* viii. 24 Substituting a stream of æthereal vapour for the wick. **1838** T. THOMSON *Chem. Org. Bodies* 306 To distinguish acetal from acetic ether and other etherial liquids. **1844–57** G. BIRD *Urin. Deposits* (ed. 5) 414 The ethereal solution of fat. **1870** SIR J. Y. SIMPSON *Anæsthesia* Wks. 1871 II. 23 As early as 1805, Dr. Warren of Boston employed ethereal inhalation.

7. ***ethereal oil.*** **a.** = essential or volatile oil (see quot.).

1694 SLARE in *Phil. Trans.* XVIII. 210 Some [Essential Oyls] are lighter than the best rectified Spirit of Wine.. which has made our Chymists call them Æthereal Oyls. **1751** CHAMBERS *Cycl.* s.v. *Ætherial oil*, The pure liquor rising next after the spirit, in the distillation of turpentine, is called the æthereal oil of turpentine. **1799** *Med. Jrnl.* I. 503 The water..was previously impregnated with as great a portion of ethereal oil as it was capable of holding in solution. **1811** HOOPER *Med. Dict.*, *Etherial oil*, Any highly rectified essential oil may be so named. **1884** BOWER & SCOTT *De Bary's Phaner. & Ferns* 69 Drops of resin and ethereal oil in increasing quantity. **1887** *Pall Mall G.* 4 July 7/1 Absinthe..contains several ethereal oils.

b. In *Pharmacy* (see quot.).

1860 MAYNE *Exp. Lex.* 803/2 *Oleum Æthereum*, Etherial oil: a name for a sulphate of ether used only for the preparation of the compound spirit of sulphuric ether.

B. *absol.* and *sb.*

a. *absol.* The ethereal principle, the spirit or essence. b. *sb.* An ethereal being, a spirit, an immortal.

1661 EVELYN *Fumifugium* Misc. Writ. I. (1805) 215 The Ætherial, which is a certain Aer of Plato's denomination. **1748** RICHARDSON *Clarissa* (1811) IV. 356 There is no sex in etherials. **1854** SYD. DOBELL *Balder* xxiv. 154 A spirit Unseen, nor having organs to discourse The rare ethereal of its too divine And necessary beauty.

Hence **e'therealism**, the state or quality of being ethereal.

In mod. Dicts.

ethereality, etheriality (iːˌθɪərɪ'ælɪtɪ). [f. ETHEREAL (or -IAL) + -ITY, after analogy of *equal-ity*, *real-ity*, etc.] **a.** The quality or state of being ethereal or incorporeal, or of being beyond material grasp or analysis. **b.** *concr.* Something that is ethereal.

1827 LYTTON *Pelham* lxxiii, Dismount me, and I become a mere clod of the earth.. fire, energy, ethereality have departed. **1850** L. HUNT *Autobiog.* II. xvi. 223 A good natured wizard.. able to conjure his etherealities about him in the twinkling of an eye. **1859** G. WILSON *Gateways Knowl.* (ed. 3) 48 A certain etheriality thus belongs preeminently to music. **1871** TYLOR *Prim. Cult.* I. 412 Among rude races, the original conception of the human soul seems to have been that of ethereality, or vaporous materiality.

c. *nonce-use.* As a mock form of address.

1806-7 J. BERESFORD *Miseries Hum. Life* (1826) VII. Introd., If your Etheriality can condescend to take any interest in such earthly stuff.

etherealization, etherialization (iːˌθɪərɪəlaɪ'zeɪʃən). [f. next + -ATION.] The action or process of etherealizing or making ethereal in various senses. Also *concr.*

1867 J. H. STIRLING tr. *Schwegler's Hist. Philos.* (ed. 8) 115 He [Aristotle] conceives the moral element.. as etherealization, spiritualization of the physical. **1873** PATER *Renaissance* iv. 53 The wasting and etherealisation of Death. **1886** MISS BRADDON *One Thing Needful* xxii, She has dedicated herself to.. the etherialisation of humanity.

etherealize, etherialize (iː'θɪərɪəlaɪz), *v.* Also æther-. [f. ETHEREAL (or -IAL) + -IZE.] *trans.* To make or render ethereal: **a.** To refine, exalt, or spiritualize, by removing all that is material or corporeal; also *absol.* **b.** To bring out the spirit or spiritual conception of. **c.** To give an ethereal appearance to.

1829 WILSON in *Blackw. Mag.* XXV. 389 Every breath of air we draw is terrestrialized or etherealized by imagination. **1833** LYTTON *England* IV. ii. (1840) 435 Wordsworth's poetry is of all existing in the world the most calculated to refine, to etherealise, to exalt. **1850** HAWTHORNE *Scarlet L.* xxiii. (1879) 283 So etherealized by spirit as he was. **1852** —— *Blithedale Rom.* viii. (1885) 78 The clods of the earth.. were never etherealized into thought. **1856** *Chamb. Jrnl.* VI. 263 All silvered over and etherealised by moonlight. **1876** GLADSTONE *Synchr. Homer.* 192 Difficult.. to accept as history, or to etherialize and translate as myth. **1879** GEO. ELIOT *Coll. Breakf. P.* 796 Art's creations.. etherialized To least admixture of the grosser fact. **1882** A. AUSTIN *Canons Poet. Crit.* II. 41 If ever Thought was etherialized.. it is in the foregoing passage.

etherealized, etherialized (iː'θɪərɪəlaɪzd), *ppl. a.* Also æther-. [f. prec. + -ED¹.] Made or rendered ethereal; exalted, refined, spiritualized.

*a***1850** JANE PORTER in Spurgeon *Treas. Dav.* Ps. xcii. 4 Half-mortal, half-etherealized. **1851** RUSKIN *Mod. Paint.* II. III. I. xiii. §15 Age of expanded and ætherialized moral expression. **1863** MRS. C. CLARKE *Shaks. Char.* iv. 104 Ariel was the etherealised impersonation of swift obedience. **1872** LIDDON *Elem. Relig.* ii. 42 The religion of the future—an etherialized abstraction. **1874** M. ARNOLD in *Contemp. Rev.* Oct. 811 Angels, etherialized men.

ethereally, etherially (iː'θɪərɪəlɪ), *adv.* Also 7 etherealie. [f. ETHEREAL (or -IAL) + -LY².] In an ethereal manner; celestially, spiritually; with extreme delicateness or purity.

1616 J. LANE *Sqr.'s T.* x. 256 Still iustelie live theie whoe deigne iustice raise etherealie enshrind in mortal claies. **1816** SHELLEY *Alastor* 585 Leaves.. Red, yellow, or etherially pale. **1865** DICKENS *Mut. Fr.* I. xii, It was not Gentle spring ethereally mild. **1875** HAMERTON *Intell. Life* XI. v. 425 Absolutely and ethereally pure.

etherealness (iː'θɪərɪəlnɪs). [f. as prec. + -NESS.] The quality of being ethereal.

1730-6 BAILEY (folio), *Etherealness.* **1832** MARRYAT *N. Forster* xl, All his etherealness departs.

etherean, etherian (iː'θɪərɪən), *a. rare.* In 6, 9 ætherean, -ian. [f. L. *æthere-us* or *ætherius* + -AN] = ETHEREAL. **a.** Heavenly, refined. **b.** Of a colour: Delicate.

1651 LENNARD tr. *Charron's Wisd.* II. Pref. (1670) 208 But my hope is, that the simple and debonaire, the Ætherian and sublime spirits will judge indifferently. **1881** *Gard. Chron.* XVI. 780 The sepals and petals are milk-white, with an ætherean hue of orange.

etherene ('iːθəriːn). *Chem.* Also 9 -ine. [f. ETHER + -ENE.] 'A synonym of ETHYLENE' (Watts).

1850 DAUBENY *Atom. Th.* v. (ed. 2) 147 Protoxide and peroxide of iron will bear the same relation one to the other, as methylene and etherene do amongst organic compounds. *c* **1865** LETHEBY in *Wylde's Circ. Sc.* I. 116/1 *Etherene* (C_8H_8), or the volatile gas of Faraday.. [is] met with in most of the illuminating gases of commerce.

ethereous, etherious (iː'θɪərɪəs), *a.* [f. L. *æthere-us* + -OUS.] Composed of, or of the nature of ether, or of the upper element of the universe.

1667 MILTON *P.L.* VI. 473 The bright surface Of this Ethereous mould whereon we stand. **1677** GALE *Crt. Gentiles* II. IV. 465 The Ethereous Heaven, where the Sun and Stars are. **1775** ASH, *Etherious*, formed of ether, celestial. **1814** J. GILCHRIST *Reason* 85 Perhaps it is ethereous meat or drink of gods. In mod. Dicts.

etheric ('iːθərɪk), *a.* [f. ETHER + -IC.] Of or pertaining to ether (see ETHER 5).

1878 G. M. BEARD in *Pop. Sc. Monthly* XIII. 331 The 'etheric force' of Mr. T. A. Edison was primarily a question of physics. **1889** *Forum* (N.Y.) Feb. 662 The mode of vibration of the etheric particles.

etherical (iː'θɛrɪkəl), *a.* In 7 ætherical. [f. as prec. + -ICAL.] Of, pertaining to, or of the nature of, ether.

1655-60 STANLEY *Hist. Philos.* (1701) 329/1 Possidonius defineth a Star, a Divine Body, consisting of ætherical fire. **1920** *Conquest* May 317/2 The plant.. responds to different rays of the vast etherical spectrum, from the extreme ultra-violet to the longest wireless electrical waves.

†**ethe'ricity.** *Obs. rare*⁻¹. [f. ETHER + -IC + -ITY.] A proposed name for electricity, implying the view that its phenomena were caused by an 'ether' (see ETHER 4).

1748 *Lond. Mag.* 256 Electricity.. ought much more properly to be called ethericity.

etherification (ˌiːθərɪfɪ'keɪʃən). [f. ETHERIFY: see -FICATION.] The action or process of converting alcohol into ether. Also *attrib.*

1805 C. HATCHETT in *Phil. Trans.* XCV. 220 [Phenomena] attendant on etherification. **1833** *Penny Cycl.* I. 157/1 s.v. *Æther*, During the etherification of the alcohol the sulphuric acid plays an active part. **1869** ROSCOE *Elem. Chem.* 324 This process is called the continuous etherification process. **1881** WATTS in *Nature* XXV. 50 The experiments of Williamson on Etherification.

etheriform ('iːθərɪfɔːm), *a.* [f. ETHER + -(I)FORM.] Having the form of ether: see ETHER 5.

1885 *Science* V. 432 The author believes that the original etheriform mass of our solar system condensed to cosmical clouds.

etherify ('iːθərɪfaɪ), *v.* [f. ETHER + -(I)FY.] *trans.* To make or convert into an ether.

1857 W. A. MILLER *Elem. Chem.* III. §990. 161 Various salts are.. capable of etherifying alcohol, if heated strongly with it under pressure. **1875** URE *Dict. Arts* II. 309 s.v. *Ether*, The stronger mineral acids etherify the alcohols.

etherin ('iːθərɪn). *Chem.* [f. ETHER + -IN.] (See quot.)

1882 WATTS *Dict. Chem.* II. 507 s.v. When heavy oil of wine.. is warmed with water, a light oily liquid rises to the surface, which is a mixture of two substances, both polymeric with ethylene, viz. etherin and etherol.

ethering, *Sc.* **etherins,** var. forms of EDDERING: see EDDER.

1691 RAY *S. & E. Country Words*, *Vrith*, Eththerings or windings of Hedges.

etherism ('iːθərɪz(ə)m). *Med.* [f. ETHER + -ISM; cf. *alcoholism.*] **1.** 'The successive phenomena developed in the animal body by the administration of the vapour of ether.' (*Syd. Soc. Lex.*).

2. Addiction to taking ether; cf. next, sense 2.

1888 N. KERR *Inebriety* vii. 108 Etherism is the antipodes of opiumism.

etherist ('iːθərɪst). [-IST.]

1. One who administers ether to a patient.

1884 H. THOMPSON *Tumours of Bladder* 25 If the etherist permits the patient any power of resisting with the abdominal muscles, the effort is hopeless.

2. One who is addicted to taking ether as a stimulant or intoxicant.

1888 N. KERR *Inebriety* vii. 109 At first he took chloral and opium, then he devoted himself to ether, and has been an etherist for some four years.

etherization (ˌiːθəraɪ'zeɪʃən). Also 9 æther-. [f. next + -ATION.] **a.** The administration of ether as an anæsthetic or narcotic; also *fig.* **b.** The process of becoming, or condition of being, etherized.

1851 H. MAYO *Pop. Superstit.* (ed. 2) 138 A sketch.. of the phenomena of etherisation. **1873** LOWELL *Among my Bks.* Ser. II. 117 The etherization of excitement and the magnetism of crowds. **1875** H. C. WOOD *Therap.* (1879) 274 Chloral administered shortly before etherization. **1884** W. S. LILLY *Anc. Relig. & Mod. Thought* 318 The phenomena of ætherisation are certainly very curious.

etherize ('iːθəraɪz), *v.* [f. ETHER + -IZE. Cf. Fr. *éthériser.*]

1. *trans.* To convert (alcohol, etc.) into ether.

1828 in WEBSTER. **1847** in CRAIG; and in mod. Dicts.

2. To mix or compound with ether.

1800–1876 [see ETHERIZED].

3. To put (a patient) under the influence of ether. Also *transf.*

1864 LOWELL *Fireside Trav.* 145 Gradually the mind was etherized to a like dreamy placidity. **1879** J. TIMBS *Chloroform* in *Cassell's Techn. Educ.* IV. 107/1 A patient.. was etherised, and had a limb amputated.. without the infliction of any pain. **1881** *Philada. Telegraph* XXXVI. No. 33. 2 After the morning bulletin was issued he was etherized.

†**4.** = ELECTRIFY *v.*

1748 *Lond. Mag.* 255 Besides being constantly electeriz'd or rather etheriz'd by the earth.

Hence **'etherized** *ppl. a.*, in senses 2 and 3 of the vb. †***etherized nitrous gas.*** **'etherizer**, an apparatus for administering ether. **'etherizing** *ppl. a.*, in sense 3 of the vb.; in quot. *fig.*

1800 *Phil. Trans.* XC. 219 The gas.. into which the nitrous etherized gas can be resolved, by treatment with dilute sulphuric acid. **1807** T. THOMSON *Chem.* (ed. 3) II. 421 When equal parts of alcohol and nitric acid are mixed, a violent effervescence takes place.. owing to the emission of a gas.. a compound of nitrous gas and ether. It has been termed for that reason etherised nitrous gas. **1848** SIR J. Y. SIMPSON in *Monthly Jrnl. Med. Sc.* IX. 211 When the patient was in an etherized state. **1876** tr. *Schutzenberger's Ferment.* 28 The etherized alcoholic liquid is distilled in a retort.

etherol ('iːθərɒl). *Chem.* [f. ETHER + -OL.] (See quot. for ETHERIN and cf. *glycerin*, *glycerol.*)

1876 HARLEY *Mat. Med.* 334 When boiled with water it is resolved into sulphæthylic acid and ætherol.

etheromania (ˌiːθərəʊ'meɪnɪə). *Path.* [f. ETHER + -O + -MANIA.] A morbid addiction to the consumption of ether as a stimulant or intoxicant. So **ˌethero'maniac**, an ether addict.

1889 N. KERR *Inebriety* (ed. 2) vii. 122 Etheromania has been a contributory cause of insanity in cases treated at asylums in the North of Ireland. **1894** *Ibid.* (ed. 3) viii. 138 A gentleman aged 35, had been an etheromaniac for 3 years. **1909** *Westm. Gaz.* 13 Feb. 14/3 Etheromania is largely on the increase in South-west Russia.

etherous ('iːθərəs), *a.* [f. ETHER + -OUS.] Savouring of ether, ether-like.

1863 B. TAYLOR *H. Thurston* II. 283 Impregnated with a pungent etherous smell.

ethic ('ɛθɪk), *a.* and *sb.* Forms: 4-5 etik(e, -yk, 4-7 ethique, 5 etique, (ethyque, etick, eytike), 6-9 ethick(e, 7 æthique, 7- ethic. [ad. L. *ēthic-us*, Gr. ἠθικός, f. ἦθος character, *pl.* manners. Cf. Fr. *éthique.*]

A. *adj.* (Now usually ETHICAL.)

1. Relating to morals.

1581 SIDNEY *Apol. Poetrie* (Arb.) 30 The Ethicke and politick consideration, with the end of well dooing and not of well knowing onely. **1644** BULWER *Chiron.* 25 The Æthique precepts and the lawes of civil conversation. **1698** F. B. *Modest Censure* 12 What! nothing but Ethick and Oeconomick Strictures, and such like Documents? **1735** SAVAGE *Progress of a Divine* 363 N'er let your doctrine ethic truth impart. **1871** TYNDALL *Fragm. Sc.* (ed. 6) II. xi. 249 Who.. find the ethic life of their religion unimpaired.

2. Of an author or literary work: Treating of moral questions, and of ethics as a science.

1589 PUTTENHAM *Eng. Poesie* I. iv. (Arb.) 25 Therefore were they [Poets] the first Philosophers Ethick. **1732** POPE (*title*) An Essay on Man, Being the First Book of Ethic Epistles. **1791** BOSWELL *Johnson* an. 1749, But 'The Vanity of Human Wishes' is.. as high an effort of ethick poetry as any language can show. **1796** MORSE *Amer. Geog.* II. 185 Dr. Hutcheson is the principal Ethic writer of this country [Ireland]. **1814** CARY *Dante* 33 Thy ethic page describes Three dispositions adverse to Heav'n's will. **1815** *Edin. Rev.* XXV. 355 In some of his odes and ethic exhortations.

3. Characterized by 'ethos.' (See ETHOS 2).

1848 WORNUM *Lect. on Paint. by R.A.* 355 *note*, The style of Polygnotus was strictly ethic.

4. *Gram.* ***ethic dative***: = 'ethical dative': see ETHICAL 3.

1867 FARRAR *Gr. Syntax* (1870) 80 To this dative of reference belongs what is called the ethic (i.e. emotional) dative.

B. *sb.*

I. *sing.* **1.** [after Fr. *éthique*, It. and Sp. *etica*, ad. L. *ēthicē*, Gr. ἡ ἠθικὴ (τέχνη).] **a.** The science of morals; cf. 2. **b.** A scheme of moral science.

1387 TREVISA *Higden* (Rolls) III. 363 Ethik [*v.r.* etyk] þat is þe sciens of þewes. *c* **1400** *Lanfranc's Cirurg.* (MS. *A.*) 9 So cloþe he him wiþ vertues, þat of him mai arise good fame & name: & þis techiþ etik. **1632** LITHGOW *Trav.* (1682) VIII. 327 As for the Science Practick, it doth first imbrace.. Ethick, that doth form the Manners. **1875** CLIFFORD *Ess.*, *Basis of Morals* (1879) II. 106 By Morals or Ethic I mean the doctrine of a special kind of pleasure or displeasure which is felt by the human mind in contemplating certain courses of conduct, whereby they are felt to be right or wrong, and of a special desire to do the right things and avoid the wrong ones. **1886** *Athenæum* 17 July 73 In.. Mr. Spencer's 'Data of Ethics'.. an attempt to construct an ethic apart from theology is regarded as practicable.

attrib. **1778** J. JAMES in *Lett. Radcliffe & James* 53 Not a book, beyond a logic or ethic compend, is recommended.

II. *pl.* **ethics.** **2.** (after Gr. τὰ ἠθικά). The science of morals; the department of study concerned with the principles of human duty.

In this sense now usually construed (like other words of like formation) as *sing.*; formerly as *pl.*

1602 WARNER *Alb. Eng.* XII. lxxv. (1612) 313 Nor wanted thear..that did relye On Physickes and on Ethickes, and..a God deny. *a* **1677** BARROW *Serm.* vi. Wks. 1741 I. 48 Out of them [St. Paul's writings] might well be compiled a body of ethicks. **1691** WOOD *Ath. Oxon.* I. 258 He was made Professor of Eloquence and Ethicks in the Universitie of Ingolstade. *a* **1700** DRYDEN (J.), Persius professes the stoick philosophy; the most generous amongst all the sects who have given rules of ethicks. **1789** BENTHAM *Princ. Legisl.* xix. §11 Ethics at large may be defined, the art of directing men's actions to the production of the greatest possible quantity of happiness. **1836** EMERSON *Nature, Idealism* Wks. (Bohn) II. 164 Ethics and religion differ herein; that the one is the system of human duties commencing from man; the other, from God. **1889** BOYD CARPENTER *Bampton Lect.* vii, Religion without ethics seems little else than irreligious religion.

b. A treatise on the science; *spec.* that of Aristotle.

c **1430** *Pilgr. Lyf Manhode* I. cxxxvi. (1869) 71 This is that Aristotle seith in etiques. **1483** CAXTON *Cato* A vij, The phylosopher sayeth in the viii book of ethyques that, etc. **1646** SIR T. BROWNE *Pseud. Ep.* III. iv. 112 The same is touched by Aristotle in his Ethicks. **1769** *Junius Lett.* xxix. 131 If this gentleman will go back to his Ethics. **1837–9** HALLAM *Hist. Lit.* (1847) I. 343 Edward himself..read the ethics of Aristotle in Greek.

†**c.** As discrete plural: Ethical maxims or observations. *Obs. rare.*

1678 R. L'ESTRANGE *Seneca's Mor.* To Rdr., I have reduc'd all his scatter'd Ethiques to their proper Heads.

3. In narrower sense, with some qualifying word or phrase: **a.** The moral principles or system of a particular leader or school of thought.

1651 BAXTER *Inf. Bapt.* 288 God's laws, standing at the top of our Ethicks. **1692** BENTLEY *Folly of Atheism* 31 If the Atheists would but live up to the Ethics of Epicurus himself. **1791** BURKE *Let. to Memb. Nat. Assembly* Wks. VI. 34 This philosophical instructor [Rousseau] in the ethicks of vanity. **1855** H. REED *Lect. Eng. Lit.* vii. 232 [The Spectator's] morality..is not a very high order of Christian ethics. **1869** LECKY *Europ. Mor.* II. i. 1 The Ethics of Paganism were part of a philosophy. **1869** J. MARTINEAU *Ess.* II. 94 It lifts you ..from the zoölogical ethics of Combe.

b. The moral principles by which a person is guided.

1837 M. DONOVAN *Dom. Econ.* II. 47 It is not the province of man to pronounce judgment on the ethics of his fellow-creature, in the last extremities of starvation.

c. The rules of conduct recognized in certain associations or departments of human life.

1789 BENTHAM *Princ. Legisl.* xviii. §46 Now to instruct each individual in what manner to govern his own conduct in the details of life, is the particular business of private ethics. **1864** BURTON *Scot Abr.* II. 279 Sea rights, and sea ethics were by no means so distinctly defined as they are now. **1870** R. W. DALE *Week-day Serm.* vii. 137 The ethics of dining. **1876** MOZLEY *Univ. Serm.* ix. 185 The peculiar scope of our Church ethics for the last thirty years has been the culture of works of compassion. **1884** *Syd. Soc. Lex., Ethics, medical*, the laws of the duties of medical men to the public, to each other, and to themselves in regard to the exercise of their profession.

4. In wider sense: The whole field of moral science, including besides Ethics properly so called, the science of law whether civil, political, or international.

1690 TEMPLE *Ess. Heroic Virtue* Wks. 1731 I. 200 The Sum of his [Confutius'] Writings seems to be a Body or Digestion of Ethicks, that is, of all Moral Virtues, either Personal, Oeconomical, Civil or Political. **1793** BLACKSTONE *Comm.* (ed. 12) 27 Jurisprudence..is the principal and most perfect branch of ethics.

ethical (ˈɛθɪkəl), *a.* [f. prec. + -AL¹.]

1. a. Of or pertaining to morality or the science of ethics.

1607 TOPSELL *Serpents* (1653) 639 It remaineth to discourse of the Politick, Ethical, and Oeconomick vertues and properties of them [bees]. **1652** EVELYN *State of France* Misc. Writ. (1805) 47 This ethicall and morall part of travel ..embellisheth a gentleman. **1830** MACKINTOSH *Eth. Philos.* Wks. 1846 I. 63 The ethical principles of Hobbes, are completely interwoven with his political system. **1860** MANSEL *Prolegom. Logica* Pref. (ed. 2) 8 The value of every ethical system must ultimately be tested on psychological grounds. **1876** tr. *Haeckel's Hist. Creat.* I. ii. 36 Moral, or ethical materialism, is something quite distinct from scientific materialism.

b. Pertaining to 'ethos' as opposed to 'pathos': see ETHOS.

a **1626** BP. ANDREWES *Serm.* (1856) I. 445 Rather in pathetical than in ethical terms.

2. Of an author or literary work: Treating of the science of ethics, or of questions connected with it.

1665 BOYLE *Occas. Refl.* (1675) 16 From Ethical or Theological Composures, to take out Lessons that may improve the Mind. **1756–82** J. WARTON *Ess. Pope* (T.), He [Pope] is the great Poet of reason, the first of ethical authors in verse. *a* **1845** BARHAM *Ingol. Leg., Bro. Birchington*, A metaphor taken out of an ethical work by the Stagyrite. **1870** RUSKIN *Lect. Art* i. (1875) 7 Ethical and imaginative literature.

3. *Gram.* *ethical dative*: the dative when used to imply that a person, other than the subject or object, has an indirect interest in the fact stated.

1849 L. SCHMITZ *Lat. Gram.* 212 This kind of dative, which occurs still more frequently in Greek, is called the Ethical Dative.

4. *Med.* Of a medicine or drug: advertised only in the professional press, not to the general public, and often available only on a doctor's prescription (see quots.). Hence as *sb.*, such a medicine.

1935 *Lancet* 24 Aug. 463/2 Ethical Pharmaceuticals Association (E.P.A.). A number of firms representing manufacturers of ethical pharmaceutical preparations—i.e., preparations not advertised to the public—have formed themselves into an association. **1952** MERKER & WHALE in Kirk & Othmer *Encycl. Chem. Technol.* X. 229 The term *ethical* generally refers to a drug which is dispensed on the prescription of a physician and administered under his direction. **1962** *Which?* Jan. 21/1 The second group are often known as ethical proprietary preparations. They are branded and advertised to the medical profession through their journals and through the mail, but are not advertised to the general public. *Ibid.* 21/2 Many ethicals are well known to the general public. **1963** *Times Rev. Industry* July 10/2 There are 250 companies manufacturing prescription or 'ethical' drugs in this country. **1968** D. E. ALLEN *Brit. Tastes* v. 114 Sales of medicines only to be obtained on prescriptions ('ethicals') are reported to be unduly low here.

ethicalism (ˈɛθɪkəlɪz(ə)m). [f. ETHICAL *a.* + -ISM.] Devotion to ethical ideals.

1892 A. B. BRUCE *Apologetics* II. ii. 192 The ethical monotheism of Hebrew prophecy has for one of its necessary presuppositions the intense ethicalism of the prophets themselves. **1953** *Theology* LVI. 209 The all-too-human ethicalism of a progressive movement asserting a brotherhood of men.

ethicality (ɛθɪˈkælɪtɪ). [f. ETHICAL *a.* + -ITY.] Ethical quality, behaviour, or principles.

1890 J. H. STIRLING *Philos. & Theol.* v. 89 Ethicality is the right doing according to the conscience of the State, of the community, while morality is right doing according to the conscience of the individual. **1934** *Punch* 19 Sept. 314/3 But when it came to the discussions of what one team was going to do to another I was unable to distribute marks for ethicality quite so freely. **1965** M. BRADBURY *Stepping Westward* vii. 333 Froelich..was a man beyond outmoded ethicalities.

ethically (ˈɛθɪkəlɪ), *adv.* [f. ETHICAL *a.* + -LY².] In an ethical manner; according to the principles or rules of ethics; from an ethical point of view.

1649 BULWER *Pathomyot.* Pref. 12 Those also that shall hereafter Physically and Ethically handle the Doctrine of humane affections. **1674** *Govt. Tongue* ix. §2. 150 Besides my subject leads me not to discourse ethically, but Christianly of the faults of the tongue. **1861** *Sat. Rev.* 21 Dec. 636 Little can be said ethically, and nothing prudentially, for foolish things written. **1874** SPURGEON *Treas. Dav.* Ps. xcii. 1 It is good ethically, for it is the Lord's right.

ethicalness (ˈɛθɪkəlnɪs). [f. as prec. + -NESS.] The quality of being ethical.

1678 CUDWORTH *Intell. Syst.* I. v. 890 The foundation whereof..has not so much as one of the least seeds either of Politicalness or Ethicalness at all in it. **1886** W. J. LILLY in *Fortn. Rev.* 591 How can we predicate ethicalness or unethicalness of a thing?

ethician (ɛˈθɪʃən). *rare.* [f. L. *ēthic-us*: see -IAN.] A writer on ethics; one versed in ethics.

1889 WALDSTEIN in *Harper's Mag.* Feb. 406 Between the priest..and the theoretical ethician..lies the activity in the sphere of sociology and economics of writers like Ruskin.

ethicism (ˈɛθɪsɪz(ə)m). [-ISM.] Devotion to ethics or ethical ideals; tendency to moralize.

1895 *Harper's Mag.* Nov. 867/2 Their art..was marred by the intense ethicism that pervaded the New England mind for two hundred years. **1900** *Daily News* 12 Nov. 7/4 A scientific theory of social duty,..ethicism founded on a solid and comprehensive science of man. **1908** *Mod. Philol.* V. 623 This means that he..rejected ethicism, declamation, narration, and description.

ethicist (ˈɛθɪsɪst). [f. as ETHICIAN + -IST.] = ETHICIAN. Also, one who supports ethics or morality in opposition to religion.

1891 *Monist* I. 556 A scientific ethicist has to proceed like any other naturalist. **1905** *Daily Chron.* 29 Nov. 3/3 Able to make their understanding 'issue in act', as the Oxford ethicists used to say. **1907** H. BEGBIE *Vigil* xix. 307 He would play the part of ethicist and point people to the highest example of human perfection. **1908** *Lit. Guide* 1 Aug. 121/1 A Rationalist or an Ethicist can seldom get credit for what he does, however good his intentions. **1964** P. MEADOWS in I. L. Horowitz *New Sociology* 446 Among the ethicists..the new technological age was seen as a function of an immanent axiological model.

ethicize (ˈɛθɪsaɪz), *v.* [f. as prec. + -IZE.]

1. *intr.* To discuss ethics; to speak or write on morals, moralize. *rare.*

1816 G. COLMAN *Br. Grins, Fire* xix, They criticize, chop logic, ethicize, philosophize.

2. *trans.* To make ethical; to invest with an ethical element.

1885 J. MARTINEAU *Types Ethical Th.* (1889) II. 424 By naturalizing Ethics [the school of Herbert Spencer] reverses the idealizing process which rather ethicizes nature. **1889** BOYD CARPENTER *Bampton Lect.* vii. 276 The creed..becomes ethicized.

ethico- (ˈɛθɪkəʊ-), repr. Gr. ἠθικο-, combining form of ἠθικός: see ETHIC. Occurring in a few compound adjs.; as **ethico-physical, -political, -religious, -social**, partaking of the nature of or pertaining jointly to ethics, and physics, politics, religion, or society.

1667 H. MORE *Div. Dial.* (1713) 565 The Bereshith of Moses bears a triple meaning..viz. Ethico-political, Physico-theosophical, and Literal. **1847** DE QUINCEY *Milton* Wks. (1863) VI. 318 For what may properly be called the Ethico-physical Sublime there is but one great model surviving in the Greek poetry. **1868** BAIN *Ment. & Mor. Sc., Ethics* (1875) 535 The philosophical system of Neo-Platonism was throughout ethical or ethico-religious in spirit. **1905** *Spectator* Lit. Suppl. 28 Jan. 119/1 Modern ethico-social guides, such as Stevenson, Whitman, and Maeterlinck. **1920** *Red Triangle* May 352/2 Every Church is trying to overcome every danger which is trying to destroy its ethico-social being. **1924** W. B. SELBIE *Psychol. Relig.* 102 The social element in these early forms of ritual..points to a tribal consciousness which has in it at least the beginnings of an ethico-social outlook.

ethide (ˈɛθaɪd). *Chem.* [f. ETH- + -IDE.] A compound formed by the union of an element or a radical with the monad radical ethyl.

1865 ODLING in *Athenæum* No. 1944. 131/1 Aluminium ethide, and methide. **1880** *Libr. Univ. Knowl.* VIII. 593 The action of carbonic acid on ethyde of sodium [will produce ketones].

ethike, obs. form of HECTIC.

ethimologise, obs. form of ETYMOLOGIZE.

ethine (ˈɛθaɪn). *Chem.* [f. ETH- + -INE.] The systematic name (see -INE) of the gaseous hydrocarbon C_2H_2, the bi-carbon member of the series C_nH_{2n-2}, called also ACETYLENE.

1877 WATTS *Fownes' Chem.* II. 61 When an electric arc from a powerful voltaic battery passes between carbon poles in an atmosphere of hydrogen, the carbon and hydrogen unite in the proportion to form ethine.

ethine: see HETHING, *Obs.*, contempt, scorn.

ethinylœstradiol (ˌɛθɪnɪlˌiːstrəˈdaɪɒl). Also **ethinyl estradiol, œstradiol**. [f. ETHINE + -YL + ŒSTRADIOL.] A synthetic œstrogen, $C_{20}H_{24}O_2$.

1939 *Chem. Abstr.* XXXIII. 3465 (*title*) The action of ethinylestradiol, a derivative of follicular hormone, given by mouth. **1963** H. BURN *Drugs, Med. & Man* (ed. 2) xv. 156 A pill has now been accepted by the US Food and Drug Administration as an oral contraceptive which contains 9.85 milligrams of norethynodrel, and 0.15 milligram of an oestrogen ethinyl oestradiol 3-methyl ether. **1964** L. MARTIN *Clinical Endocrinol.* (ed. 4) viii. 244 Ethinyl œstradiol is a modification of the natural hormone. *Ibid.* 253 Norethisterone given with ethinylœstradiol to maintain the endometrium.

ethionamide (ɛθɪˈɒnəmaɪd). *Pharm.* [Blend of ETHYL and THION- + AMIDE.] An antibiotic, $C_8H_{10}N_2S$, which is active against mycobacteria and has been used to treat tuberculosis.

1960 *Tubercle* XLI. 367 Ethionamide..is given orally in small bulk, is highly effective and is of low toxicity. **1974** [see PYRAZINAMIDE]. **1983** *Oxf. Textbk. Med.* I. v. 254/1 The use of ethionamide and prothionamide..is limited by their adverse effects, notably gastrointestinal irritation. **1984** *Brit. Med. Jrnl.* 25 Aug. 496/1 It is difficult to establish whether liver damage has been due to rifampicin or one of its companion drugs (such as isoniazid and ethionamide), which may form potentially hepatotoxic combinations with rifampicin.

ethionic (iːθɪˈɒnɪk), *a.* *Chem.* [f. E(THER) + Gr. θεῖον sulphur + -IC.

Formed by Magnus in 1833, in imitation of the terms *proto-, deuto-, trito-œnothionic* [Gr. οἶνος wine], introduced by Sertuernor (1818) to designate three acids, one of which Magnus supposed to have been identical with ethionic acid.]

ethionic acid: $C_2H_6S_2O_7$ (Watts *Dict. Chem.*) produced by the action of water on *ethionic anhydride*, $C_2H_42SO_3$, formerly called *sulphate of carbyl* (Watts *Dict. Chem.*), which is obtained by bringing together olefiant gas and vapour of sulphuric anhydride in a tube.

1838 T. THOMSON *Chem. Org. Bodies* 190 Of Ethionic Acid. **1877** WATTS *Fownes' Chem.* II. 174 Ethionic Anhydride.

ethionine (iːˈθaɪənɪn, -iːn). *Chem.* [f. ETH- + *-ionine* as in METHIONINE.] A crystalline amino-acid that is the ethyl homologue of methionine and inhibits growth.

1938 H. M. DYER in *Jrnl. Biol. Chem.* CXXIV. 519 We have for convenience called the S-ethylhomocysteine ethionine. **1955** *Jrnl. Exper. Med.* CII. 151 (*title*) Effect of ethionine-induced pancreatic damage on iron absorption. *Ibid.*, Rats were fed diets containing *dl*-ethionine (α-amino-γ-(ethylmercapto)-butyric acid) in quantities sufficient to damage the exocrine cells of the pancreas. **1966** *New Scientist* 17 Mar. 708/3 A medium containing puromycin or ethionine, both of which cause almost complete inhibition of protein synthesis in these cells.

Ethiop (ˈiːθɪɒp), *sb.* and *a.* *arch.* Also: 4–7 ethiope, (5 ethyope), 6–9 æthiop(e. [ad. L. *Æthiops*, gen. *Æthiop-is*, ad. Gr. Αἰθίοψ, Αἰθίοπος, 'Ethiopian', commonly believed to be f. αἴθ-ειν to burn + ὤψ face, and to mean primarily 'burnt-face' (cf. αἴθοψ 'fiery-looking', later 'sunburnt', f. same or cognate elements); the formation is however not clear, and some have supposed the

word to be an etymologizing corruption of a foreign ethnic name.

The 'Ethiopians' are mentioned by Homer as a people dwelling in the far east and the far west; in later Gr. the name was applied chiefly to the inhabitants of Africa south of Egypt, but also to peoples of swarthy complexion in other parts of the world.]

A. *sb. lit.* = ETHIOPIAN; hence, usually, a person with a black skin, a blackamoor. Phrase, ***to wash an*** (or ***the***) ***Ethiop*** (***white***): to attempt the impossible.

1382 WYCLIF *Jer.* xiii. 23 Yf chaunge mai an Ethiope his skyn. **1490** CAXTON *Eneydos* xxiii. (1890) 84 Vpon his last part of therth there habitable where conuerse thethyopes. **1509** HAWES *Past. Pleas.* XXXVII. x, Out there flew, ryght blacke and tedyous, A foule Ethyope. **1599** SHAKS. *Much Ado* v. iv. 38 Ile hold my minde, were she an Ethiope. **1660** HICKERINGILL *Jamaica* (1661) 106 The truth whereof many an Æthiope hath now unwillingly asserted. *a* **1688** VILLIERS (Dk. Buckhm.) *Ep. to Julian*, As sure to miss, As they, that wash an Ethiope's Face. **1775** SHERIDAN *Rivals* III. ii, Though I were an Æthiop. *a* **1791** WESLEY *Serm.* lxviii. (1825) II. 158 In the most elegant language, she labours to wash the Æthiop white.

B. *attrib.* and *adj.*

1. = ETHIOPIAN. †***Ethiop line*** (Milton): ? the equator.

1667 MILTON *P.L.* IV. 282 By som suppos'd True Paradise under the Ethiop Line By Nilus head.

2. Of the hue of an Ethiop; black.

1600 SHAKS. *A.Y.L.* IV. iii. 35 Ethiop vvords, blacker in their effect Then in their countenance. **1635** [GLAPTHORNE] *Lady Mother* v. ii. in Bullen *O. Pl.* II. 193 To hang this matchless diamond in the eare Of Ethiope Death. **1812** HEBER *Transl. Pindar* II. 155 Aurora's knight of Ethiop hue. **1818** KEATS *Endymion* II. 413 The ivy mesh, Shading its Æthiop berries.

†**Ethiopesse.** *Obs.* Also **Æthiopesse.** [f. prec. + -ESS, after L. *Æthiopissa* (Vulg. *Num* xii.), Gr. *Αἰθιόπισσα* (LXX.).] A female Ethiopian.

[**1382** WYCLIF *Numb.* xii. 1 The Ethiopis his wijf.] **1614** RALEIGH *Hist. World* I. 126 Josephus his Tale of an Ethiopesse, wife of Moses. **1640** HARSNET *God's Summ.* 272 Moses..married an Æthiopesse, yet could hee not change her hue.

Ethiopian (iːθɪˈəʊpɪən), *a.* and *sb.* Also 6–7 **æthiopian,** 7 **ethiopean.** [f. ETHIOP or *Ethiopia*: see -IAN, -AN.]

A. *adj.* **1. a.** Of or belonging to Ethiopia (in the various historical uses of the name), or to the peoples known to the ancients as *Æthiopes*. Often used (now only humorously) as = 'negro'. ***Ethiopian serenader***: a 'nigger' minstrel, a musical performer with face blackened to imitate a negro.

1684 *Friendly Advice Planters E. & W. Indies* III. (*title*) Dialogue between an Ethiopean or Negro Slave, and a Christian. **1697** DRYDEN *Virg. Georg.* IV. 413 The teeming Tide..pouring down from Ethiopian Lands. **1838** LYTTON *Leila* IV. i, The Ethiopian guards..marched slowly in the rear. **1861** MAYHEW *Lond. Labour* III. 190 There are [in London] 50 Ethiopian serenaders.

†**b.** *absol.* with pl. sense. *Obs.*

1635 PAGITT *Christianography* (1646) 107 The Ethiopian and Moscovites doe baptize in the Church porch.

c. in proper names of various plants. ***Ethiopian sour gourd*** = BAOBAB.

1578 LYTE *Dodoens* II. xcviii. 281 The seconde Seseli.. hath leaues like Juye..The stalk is blackishe..And this is counted to be the Ethiopian Seseli. **1597** GERARD *Herbal* II. lxi. 347 In English we have thought good to call it the Aethiopian Apple. **1640**, etc. [see *sour gourd* s.v. SOUR *a.* 11]. **1884** S. J. CAPPER in *Chr. World* 31 July 575/4 Ethiopian lilies, which are exquisitely beautiful.

2. a. *Anthropology.* Used by some as the distinctive epithet of one of the races into which the human species is divided. **b.** *Biol.* The distinctive epithet of one of the biological 'regions' of the earth's surface.

1861 HULME tr. *Moquin-Tandon* I. vi. 36 In the kingdom which he [Man] constitutes (Hominal) there is but one genus (Homo), and in this genus but one species (Sapiens). This species presents three varieties or principal races.. Caucasian, Mongolian, and Ethiopian. **1880** A. R. WALLACE *Isl. Life* 53, *Region*, Ethiopian..*Geographical Equivalent*, Africa (south of the Sahara) with Madagascar.

c. Of or pertaining to Ethiopianism.

1904 H. O. DWIGHT et al. *Encycl. Missions* (ed. 2) 8/1 The seceders [from Wesleyan Methodist Society churches in the Transvaal] formed a new body which adopted the name, 'Ethiopian Church'. The movement was..a protest against a color line in the churches of Africa. **1911** *Encycl. Brit.* XVIII. 593/1 The South African governments foresaw dangerous developments in the Ethiopian movement. **1915** J. HASTINGS *Encycl. Relig. & Ethics* VIII. 736/2 *S. Africa.* .. The racial factor is especially in evidence in the 'Ethiopian Movement', composed of groups of congregations who in 1892 formally seceded from their missionary connections.

B. *sb.* **a.** A native of Ethiopia; †a negro, blackamoor.

1552 HULOET, *Ethiopians.* **1598** SHAKS. *Merry W.* II. iii. 28 Is he dead, my Ethiopian? **1611** —— *Wint. T.* IV. iv. 375 This hand..as white as..Ethyopians tooth. **1686** BUNYAN *Book for Boys & Girls* (Repr.) 42 Moses was a fair and comely man, His wife a swarthy Ethiopian. **1727** DE FOE *Syst. Magic* I. iii. (1840) 63 Ethiopians of Arabia Felix, which they call the South; and who, though Arabians, are called Ethiopians in Scripture. **1737** [see ABYSSINIAN *sb.*]. **1884** A. H. SAYCE *Fresh Light from Anc. Monuments* vi. 153 Tirhakah the Ethiopian, whom the Assyrians had driven out, invaded it from the south. **1935** *Times* 17 Oct. 10/4 The Pope has to consider whether such action would do anything to help the Ethiopians. **1946** *Times Lit. Suppl.* 15 June 278/4 It is the fashion.. to complain of the backwardness of the Ethiopians.

b. An 'Ethiopian serenader'. See A. 1.

1861 MRS. CARLYLE *Lett.* III. 81 The brass band is succeeded by a band of Ethiopians.

c. An advocate or supporter of Ethiopianism.

1911 *Encycl. Brit.* XVIII. 593/1 Each bishop [in S. Africa] now deals with the Ethiopians in his own diocese. **1948** B. G. M. SUNDKLER *Bantu Prophets* ii. 53 As *Ethiopians* I classify such independent Bantu Churches as have (*a*) seceded from White Mission Churches chiefly on racial grounds, or (*b*) other Bantu Churches seceding from the Bantu leaders classified under (*a*). **1961** *Listener* 30 Nov. 918/1 The term 'Ethiopian' was first employed by the African secessionists themselves, who took it from the Authorized Version of the Bible, in which Africa and black men are usually called vaguely 'Ethiopia' and 'Ethiopians'.

Ethiopianism (iːθɪˈəʊpɪənɪz(ə)m). [-ISM.] An African nationalist movement in South Africa (see quot. 1961).

1906 *Daily Chron.* 13 Feb. 5/4 The rising in Natal is now officially declared..to be the result of the teaching of Ethiopianism, namely 'South Africa for the Black races'. **1910** J. BUCHAN *Prester John* vii. 131 It is what they call 'Ethiopianism', and American negroes are the chief apostles. **1936** *Times Lit. Suppl.* 28 Mar. 252/4 So-called Ethiopianism appears to have been started in South Africa by various disgruntled native ministers of the Gospel. **1961** *Listener* 30 Nov. 918/1 The term 'Ethiopianism', then, is properly applied to early religio-political manifestations of African nationalism in South Africa..from the eighteen-nineties to about the nineteen-twenties.

Ethiopic (iːθɪˈɒpɪk), *a.* [ad. L. *æthiopic-us*: see ETHIOP and -IC.]

1. Of or belonging to Ethiopia. Now only with reference to language, denoting the ancient language of Abyssinia, or to the church using this language in its services.

1659 HAMMOND *On Ps.* lxxii. 9 Annot. 350 The Æthiopick sea. **1732** LEDIARD *Sethos* II. 4 The Phœnicians pass'd from the Eastern or Ethiopick sea. **1774** GOLDSM. *Nat. Hist.* (1776) II. 62 The characters of an Ethiopic manuscript. **1882–3** SCHAFF *Encycl. Relig. Knowl.* 1842 In the Ethiopic church he [Pilate] is a saint.

2. *absol.* The Ethiopic language.

1867 WHITNEY *Lang. & Study of Lang.* 299 The ancient tongue of Abyssinia, the Ethiopic or Geëz, has a literature. *attrib. a* **1891** *Mod.* A good Ethiopic scholar.

†**'ethiops.** *Obs.* Also **æthiops.** [a. L. *æthiops* lit. 'ETHIOP, negro,' by mediæval chemists used in this sense.]

A name given to certain black or dark-coloured compounds of metals. ***ethiops martial, martial ethiops*** (L. *æthiops martialis*): the black oxide of iron. ***ethiops mineral*** (L. *æ. mineralis*): the black sulphide of mercury, prepared by triturating mercury and sulphur together. (*Ethiops* without adj. usually = *ethiops mineral.*)

1706 PHILLIPS, *Æthiops mineral.* **1753** CHAMBERS *Suppl. s.v.*, A new preparation of Æthiops is given by Cruger. **1770** *New Disp.* 538/2 The sulphur..and the mercury..remain at the bottom..united into an ethiops. **1794** G. ADAMS *Nat. & Exp. Philos.* I. xi. 474 The whole wire is consumed..the globules of iron will be found in that state called Martial Ethiops. **1837** BREWSTER *Magnet.* 304 The powder which formed the basis of this paste was..martial Ethiops. **1854** J. SCOFFERN in *Orr's Circ. Sc.* Chem. 500 Sulphuret of mercury is obtained in the condition of black powder, formerly known by the appellation Ethiop's mineral.

ethisterone (ɛˈθɪstərəʊn). [f. ETHI(NE + TESTO)STERONE.] A synthetic hormone similar to progesterone (see quots.).

1947 *Brit. Chem. Abstr.* A III. 224 (*heading*) Biological properties of ethinyl testosterone (ethisterone). *Ibid.*, Ethisterone has the following testosterone-like effects: it causes growth of the sex organs in the normal or hypophysectomised castrated immature male rat. **1948** *Brit. Pharmacopœia* 44 Ethisterone. *Synonyms.* Pregneninolone: Anhydrohydroxyprogesterone: Ethinyltestosterone... Ethisterone is 17-ethinyl-Δ^4-androsten-17-ol-3-one. **1962** *Lancet* 25 Aug. 406/2 Amenorone..contains 10 mg. ethisterone (17-α-ethinyl testosterone) and 0.01 mg. œstradiol. **1964** L. MARTIN *Clinical Endocrinol.* (ed. 4) viii. 246 Ethisterone, a synthetic compound very similar to progesterone, is active by sub-lingual administration but, owing to its feeble progesterone-like action, comparatively large doses must be given.

ethize (ˈɛθaɪz), *v. rare.* In 9 ethise. [ad. Gr. *ἐθίζειν* to accustom, use.] *trans.* (See quot.)

1876 GROTE *Eth. Fragm.* v. 153 All legislators try to ethise—to create habits among—the citizens for the purpose of making them good.

ethlete, ethluke: see EATH C. 1.

ethmo- (ˈɛθməʊ-), combining form of Gr. *ἠθμός* sieve, in a few compounds of mod. formation, occurring in anatomy, with general sense 'pertaining jointly to the ethmoid bone and some other part of the skull', *e.g.* **ethmo-frontal** *a.* [see FRONTAL], pertaining to the ethmoid and frontal bones: as the ***ethmo-frontal notch.*** **ethmo-maxillary** *a.* [see MAXILLARY], pertaining to the ethmoid and to the maxillary bones: as ***ethmo-maxillary suture.*** **ethmo-nasal** *a.* [see NASAL], pertaining to the ethmoid and to the nasal bones: as ***ethmo-nasal suture.*** **ethmo-presphenoidal** *a.* [see PRESPHENOIDAL], of or pertaining to the ethmoid and to the presphenoid bone: as ***ethmo-presphenoidal suture*** (Huxley). **ethmo-turbinal** (plates) or **ethmo-turbinals** [see TURBINAL], the lateral masses of the ethmoid bone, connected horizontally with each other at the upper surface by the cribriform plate. **ethmo-vomerine** (***plate***) (see quot.).

1875 BLAKE *Zool.* 46 The olfactory chamber of the nasal cavity..contains a series of simple, longitudinally placed ethmoturbinals. **1872** MIVART *Elem. Anat.* 94 This prolongation forwards..forms a median plate (termed Ethmo-vomerine). **1881** —— *Cat* 337 A cartilaginous expansion called the ethmo-vomerine plate.

ethmoid (ˈɛθmɔɪd), *a.* and *sb. Anat.* Also 9 erron. **æthmoid.** [ad. Gr. *ἠθμοειδής* sieve-like, 'cribriform' (Galen has *ἠθμοειδὲς ὀστοῦν* ethmoid bone), f. *ἠθμός* sieve: see -OID. Cf. Fr. *ethmoïde.*]

A. *adj.* Sieve-like, finely perforated. ***ethmoid bone***: a square-shaped cellular bone, situated between the two orbits, at the root of the nose, containing many perforations, through which the olfactory nerves pass to the nose.

1741 MONRO *Anat.* (ed. 3) 80 Joined to the Ethmoid Bone. **1831** R. KNOX *Cloquet's Anat.* 583 It dives into the posterior ethmoid cells. **1854** OWEN in *Circ. Sc.* (*c* 1865) II. 90/1 Parts of the olfactory capsules..forming the compound bone called 'æthmoid.'

B. quasi-*sb.* passing into *sb.* = *ethmoid bone.*

1842 COL. H. SMITH *Nat. Library* xiii. 87 The cranium.. may be subdivided into three compartments, the anterior containing the two frontal bones and the æthmoid. **1851** RICHARDSON *Geol.* viii. 313 The 3rd the ethmoid with the two frontal. **1858** GEIKIE *Hist. Boulder* vii. 121 The eye orbits seem to have been at the corners of the intermaxillary, circumscribed by the sub-orbitals and the ethmoids.

Hence **eth'moidal** *a.* (*a*) Of or pertaining to the ethmoid bone. (*b*) = ETHMOID.

a. 1741 MONRO *Anat.* (ed. 3), The *Ethmoidal* and *Sphenoidal* [Sutures] surround the Bones of these Names. **1831** R. KNOX *Cloquet's Anat.* 47 On each side of the ethmoidal notch, there is observed a triangular concave surface. **1842** E. WILSON *Anat. Vade-m.* 281 Ethmoidal arteries pass through the ethmoidal foramina.
b. 1764 HADLEY in *Phil. Trans.* LIV. 4 The superior maxillary, sphenoïdal and ethmoïdal bones were broken away. **1849** E. BLYTH *Cuvier's Anim. K.* 39 The cranium subdivides into three portions: the anterior is formed by the two frontal and the ethmoidal bones.

ethmose (ɛθˈməʊs). *Phys.* [f. Gr. *ἠθμ-ός* sieve + -OSE.] A name given to cellular tissue.

In mod. Dicts.

ethnagogue (ˈɛθnəgɒg). [f. Gr. *ἔθν-ος* nation + *ἀγωγ-ός* leader.] A leader of a nation.

1889 GLADSTONE in *19th Cent.* Jan. 152 If I may coin a word for the occasion, he [O'Connell] was an ethnagogue.

ethnarch (ˈɛθnɑːk). [ad. Gr. *ἐθνάρχ-ης*, f. *ἔθν-ος* nation + *-αρχος* ruler.] A governor of a nation or people; a ruler over a province.

a **1641** BP. MOUNTAGU *Acts & Mon.* 95 They [the Jews] had their Ethnarchs, Toparchs, high-Priests, Rulers, Princes, and some sometimes Kings of their owne. **1692** WASHINGTON tr. *Milton's Def. Pop.* iv, Cæsar..did not appoint a King over them [the Jews], but a Governour, whom they called an Ethnarch. **1778** APTHORPE *Preval. Chr.* 210 Julius Cæsar..authorized Hyrcanus and his children to be ethnarchs of the Jews. **1879** C. GEIKIE *Christ* 30 Pompey set up Hyrcanus as high priest and ruler, under the title of ethnarch.

ethnarchy (ˈɛθnɑːkɪ). [ad. Gr. *ἐθναρχία*, f. *ἐθνάρχης*: see prec.] **a.** The dignity or office of an ethnarch. **b.** The dominion of, or province ruled by, an ethnarch.

1612 HEYWOOD *Apol. Actors* 26 They divided their dominions and contryes into principalities; some into provinces..others into ethnarchyes. **1643** *Subject of Suprem.* 68 Antipater..deposeth him of his Ethnarchie. **1862** MERIVALE *Rom. Emp.* (1865) V. xlvi. 417 Syria..was still skirted by several tributary kingdoms or ethnarchies.

ethnic (ˈɛθnɪk), *a.* and *sb.* Forms: 4–6 **ethnyke,** 5–7 **ethnik(e,** 6–8 **ethnick(e,** (6 **æth-, ethenicke, etneke**), 7 **ethnique,** (**ethnycke**), 6– **ethnic.** [ad. Gr. *ἐθνικ-ός* heathen, f. *ἔθνος* nation; in the LXX, hence in N.T. and the Fathers, *τὰ ἔθνη* = the nations, Gentiles (rendering Heb. *gōyīm*, pl. of *gōy*, nation, esp. non-Israelitish or 'Gentile' nation).

The Gr. *ἔθνος* was formerly often imagined to be the source of Eng. HEATHEN; hence the confused forms *hethnic*, HEATHENIC, which might be regarded as corrupt variants of this word.]

A. *adj.*

1. Pertaining to nations not Christian or Jewish; Gentile, heathen, pagan.

c **1470** HARDING *Chron.* Printer's Pref. ix, The bible bookes of Iudges and Kynges..farre surmounting all ethnike dooynges. **1545** UDALL *Erasm. Par.* Pref. 3 An ethnike and a pagane kyng. **1581** MARBECK *Bk. of Notes* 61 That all composition is against the nature of God even the Ethnicke Philosophers perceived. **1611** SPEED *Hist. Gt. Brit.* VI. xlix. §171 Professing himselfe to be a Christian, and

withall protesting that he would not be a soueraigne ouer an Ethnike Empire. **1651** HOBBES *Leviath.* III. xlii. 281 Exhorted their Converts to obey their then Ethnique Princes. **1804** MOORE *Epist.* III. iii. 45 All the charm that ethnic fancy gave To blessed arbours o'er the western wave. **18..** LONGF. *Drinking Song* vii, These are ancient ethnic revels Of a faith long since forsaken. **1851** CARLYLE *Sterling* I. vii. (1872) 45, I find at this time his religion is as good as altogether Ethnic, Greekish. **1873** LOWELL *Among my Bks.* Ser. II. 107 There is first the ethnic forecourt, then the purgatorial middle-space.

2. a. Pertaining to race; peculiar to a race or nation; ethnological. Also, pertaining to or having common racial, cultural, religious, or linguistic characteristics, esp. designating a racial or other group within a larger system; hence (*U.S. colloq.*), foreign, exotic.

1851 D. WILSON *Preh. Ann.* (1863) I. ix. 229 That ethnic stock which embraced all existing European races. **1865** *Reader* 11 Feb. 163/1 The slight development of ethnic peculiarities in childhood. **1875** LIGHTFOOT *Comm. Col.* (1886) 133 Heresies are at best ethnic: truth is essentially catholic. **1935** HUXLEY & HADDON *We Europeans* iv. 136 Nowhere does a human group now exist which corresponds closely to a systematic sub-species in animals, since various original sub-species have crossed repeatedly and constantly. For existing populations, the noncommittal term *ethnic group* should be used. *Ibid.* vi. 181 The special type of ethnic grouping of which the Jews form the best-known example. **1936** *Discovery* June 167 [In Africa] linguistic divisions are a very fair indication of ethnic groups. **1939** C. S. COON *Races of Europe* xi. 444 The Jews are an ethnic unit, although one which has little regard for spatial considerations. Like other ethnic units, the Jews have their own standard racial character. **1964** *Listener* 6 Feb. 233/2 There are many groupings of people, ethnic units, population aggregates—call them what you will—that may be distinguished from each other. **1965** *Sun* 6 Dec. 7/6 Ethnic.. has come to mean foreign, or un-American or plain quaint. **1969** *New Yorker* 30 Aug. 76/2 Its hopelessly reactionary nature is best exemplified not.. even by the ethnic comedians. **1970** *Daily Tel.* 16 Apr. 18 The situation is fast becoming greatly complicated by the presence in Cambodia of large numbers, put at 400,000 to 500,000, of 'ethnic' Vietnamese.

b. ***ethnic minority (group)***, a group of people differentiated from the rest of the community by racial origins or cultural background, and usu. claiming or enjoying official recognition of their group identity. Also *attrib.*

1945 *Amer. Sociol. Rev.* X. 481 (*heading*) Status and housing of ethnic minorities. **1964** GOULD & KOLB *Dict. Social Sci.* 244/1 R. E. Park and his students have done outstanding research work into the patterns of adjustment, accommodation, and assimilation of ethnic minorities. **1968** [see BILINGUALITY]. **1974** *Educ. & Community Rel.* Jan. 1, Primary and secondary schools were included which were in areas of ethnic minority group settlement but had no ethnic minority group children in the school. **1976** *Equals* Oct./Nov. 1/1 An all-out campaign against both racial hatred and the discrimination and disadvantages facing ethnic minorities in Britain has been launched by the Trades Union Congress. **1984** *Guardian* 20 Nov. 8/7 Ethnic minorities will hopefully be tempted into the force by the fact that a black and female PC is given a starring role in the film.

B. *sb.* †**1.** One who is not a Christian or a Jew; a Gentile, heathen, pagan. *Obs.*

c **1375** *Sc. Leg. Saints, Barnabas* 161 A part of It [the temple] fel done & mad a gret distruccione Of ethnykis. *c* **1534** tr. *Pol. Verg. Eng. Hist.* (Camd. Soc.) I. 169 Beinge on all sides beesett with the Tracherie of these rude æthenickes, hee was sodainlie slayne. **1588** ALLEN *Admon.* 37 Yf he.. heare not the Churche, let him be taken for an Ethnike. **1625** B. JONSON *Staple of N.* II. iv, A kind of Mule! That's half an Ethnick, half a Christian! **1664** EVELYN *Sylva* (1776) 614 The Ethnics do still repute all great trees to be divine. **1728** MORGAN *Algiers* I. iv. 77 They look upon them [the Jews] as several degrees beneath.. Heathens, Ethnicks, Pagans, and Idolaters.

2. *Greek Antiq.* An epithet denoting nationality, derived from or corresponding to the name of a people or city [= ἐθνικόν (Steph. Byz.)]. Also *gen.*

1828 J. A. CRAMER *Anc. Greece* III. Index p. i, The Greek ethnic of each town or place has been subjoined where there was authority for it. **1902** D. G. HOGARTH *Nearer East* 194 Where the 'Arab' (to use the ethnic widely) lives under conditions similar to the Greek, he resembles him. **1921** C. T. SELTMAN *Temple Coins Olympia* 103 The dies.. upon which the full ethnic *ΓΑΛΕΙΩΝ* appears. **1921** *Brit. Mus. Return* 79 The ethnics of Damastium and Pelagia. **1959** A. G. WOODHEAD *Study Gk. Inscriptions* 44 Sometimes the single name, without further elaboration, sometimes with patronymic and demotic or ethnic, or with one of the two.

3. A member of an ethnic group or minority. orig. *U.S.*

1945 WARNER & SROLE *Social Syst. Amer. Ethnic Groups* (Yankee City Ser. III) v. 68 The Irish.. had their origins largely in the peasant stratum... The Jews were of the burgher class... These differences in the ethnics' social-class backgrounds will be seen later to have important bearing on their adaptation. *Ibid.* 93 The ethnics have conspicuously succeeded in 'getting ahead' in the Yankee City social hierarchy. **1961** *Times Lit. Suppl.* 17 Nov. 828/4 The former 'ethnics', a polite term for Jews, Italians, and other lesser breeds just inside the law. **1963** T. & P. MORRIS *Pentonville* iii. 62 It is the general view of the prison staff that the majority of 'coloureds' and 'ethnics' are West Indians. **1964** S. M. MILLER in I. L. Horowitz *New Sociology* 297 As the white ethnics—first the Irish, later the Jews, and still more recently the Italians.. gained strength.

ethnical ('ɛθnɪkəl), *a.* [f. prec. + -AL[1].]

†**1.** Of an ethnic nature or character; heathenish.

1547 BP. HOOPER *Declar. Christ* v. Diij, What.. blasphemy of God, and Et[h]nycall idolatrie is this. **1577** NORTHBROOKE *Dicing* (1843) 67 Ethnicall sportes and pastimes. **1634** SIR T. HERBERT *Trav.* 195 The Religion of the Peguans is Ethnicall, knowing many but false Gods. **1702** C. MATHER *Magn. Chr.* III. II. xx. (1852) 447 The custom of preaching at funerals may seem ethnical in its origin.

†**b.** Pagan; = ETHNIC A. 1. *Obs.*

a **1638** MEDE *Wks.* III. viii. 643 The Woman which escaped the fury of the Ethnical Dragon. **1659** W. BROUGH *Sacr. Princ.* 548 Should not.. Ethnical Rome be lesse Babylon then the Christian. **1762** J. BROWN *Poetry & Mus.* xiii. (1763) 237 The Subjects of the narrative.. may be drawn.. either from ethnical or sacred Story.

2. Of or pertaining to race or races, their origin, and characteristics. Cf. ETHNIC A. 2.

1846 GROTE *Greece* II. i. II. 308 Purely upon geographical not upon ethnical considerations. **1871** FREEMAN *Hist. Ess.* Ser. I. iii. 58 As far as ethnical connexion is concerned, this analogy will hold good.

3. Pertaining to the science of races; = ETHNOLOGICAL 2.

1862 D. WILSON *Preh. Man* i. (1865) 4 Here then are materials full of promise for the ethnical student. **1884** *Publisher & Bookbuyer's Jrnl.* 15 Nov. 11/2 The confused character of the prevailing ethnical literature dealing with the Sudan.

ethnically ('ɛθnɪkəlɪ), *adv.* [f. prec. + -LY[2].]

†**1.** In an 'ethnical' or heathenish manner. *Obs.*

1563–87 FOXE *A. & M.* (1596) 117/2 This pope.. mainteined the filthie idolatrie of images.. commanding them most ethnicallie to be incensed.

2. As regards race; 'racially'.

1847 GROTE *Greece* II. xxii. III. 464 The Œnotrians were ethnically akin to the primitive population of Rome. **1876** GLADSTONE *Synchr. Homer.* 65 No one can suppose Trojan and Hellene to have been.. ethnically one, though both were probably of the Aryan stock.

ethnicism ('ɛθnɪsɪz(ə)m). [f. ETHNIC + -ISM.]

†**a.** Heathenism, paganism; heathenish superstition; an instance of this (*obs.*). **b.** In mod. use without reproachful implication: The religions of the Gentile nations of antiquity; the common characteristics of these as contrasted with Hebraism and Christianity.

1613 PURCHAS *Pilgr.* IX. v. §3 (R.) Certaine Brasilians.. had set vp a new sect of Christian ethnicisme, or mungrell-Christianity. **1625** JACKSON *Orig. Vnbeliefe* xxiii. 226 Feigned relations of a new starres appearance or other like Ethnicismes. **1667** WATERHOUSE *Fire Lond.* 111 In darkness of errour and in the shadow of death through Ethnicism. **1849** tr. *Nitzsch's Chr. Doctr.* Pref. 7 The two great directions of religio-historical development, Ethnicism and Revelation. **1851** CARLYLE *Sterling* I. ix. (1872) 54 A mind.. occupied.. with mere Ethnicism, Radicalism and revolutionary tumult.

ethnicist ('ɛθnɪsɪst). *rare.* [f. as prec. + -IST.] = ETHNOLOGIST.

1846 *Times* 15 May 4/5 'Smith' has been proved by.. an American ethnicist and philologist to be nothing more nor less than Shemita, or a descendant of Shem.

eth'nicity. [f. as prec. + -ITY.]

†**1.** Heathendom, heathen superstition. *Obs. rare.*

1772 NUGENT tr. *Hist. Friar Gerund* I. 332 From the curling spume of the celebrated Egean waves fabulous ethnicity feigned Venus their idolatress conceived.

2. Ethnic character or peculiarity.

1953 D. RIESMAN in *Amer. Scholar* XXIII. I. 15 The groups who, by reason of rural or small-town location, ethnicity, or other parochialism, feel threatened by the better educated upper-middle-class people. **1964** P. WORSLEY in I. L. Horowitz *New Sociology* 384 Existing barriers of ethnicity imported into office could thus be removed. **1970** *Oxf. Univ. Gaz.* C. Suppl. VI. 14 In Hilary Term Dr. Leslie Palmier.. gave a series of lectures entitled 'Ethnicity in Indonesia'.

†**'ethnicize,** *v. Obs. rare*[−1]. [f. as prec. + -IZE.] *intr.* To act, speak, etc. like an 'ethnic' or heathen.

1663 J. SPENCER *Prodigies* (1665) 247 Whereas both Tacitus and Josephus relate the sudden opening of the doors of the Temple, etc... they appear to me very much to Ethnicize in all these stories.

†**'ethnish,** *a. Obs.* [f. Gr. ἔθνος (see ETHNIC) + -ISH.] = HEATHENISH.

1550 BECON *Fortr. Faithful* Prol., Walowing in al kind of wealthe like Ethnysh Epicures. **1563** *Homilies* II. *Idolatry* (1859) 187 Helene.. worshipped the King, and not the wood .. for that is an ethnish error.

ethnize ('ɛθnaɪz), *v. rare.* [f. Gr. ἔθν-ος (τὰ ἔθνη the nations, Gentiles: see ETHNIC) + -IZE.] *intr.* To favour Gentile or heathen views or practices. Hence **'ethnizing** *vbl. sb.*, in quot. *attrib.*

1847 BUCH tr. *Hagenbach's Hist. Doctr.* I. 42 The earliest heresies of which we have any trustworthy account, appear either as judaizing, or as ethnizing (hellenizing) tendencies.

ethno- (ɛθnəʊ, ɛθnɒ), mod. combining form of Gr. ἔθνος nation (first recorded in ETHNOGRAPHY) in words relating to the study of peoples or cultures, attached to (*a*) endings (as *-graphy, -logy*, etc.), and (*b*) nouns (as *botany, psychology*, etc.), or derivatives of these.

ethnoarchæology (ˌɛθnəʊɑːkiː'ɒlədʒɪ). [f. ETHNO- + ARCHÆOLOGY.] The study of the relationship between the social and economic operation of modern societies and the durable evidence left by these societies, in order to attempt to reconstruct human behaviour patterns in a former society in the light of its material remains.

1969 *Plateau* XLII. 27 It appeared to be an excellent area in which to test some of the problems of ethno-archaeology. **1973** *Amer. Antiquity* XXXVIII. 122/1 Only with the data of ethnography and ethno-archaeology can we merge archaeology and cultural anthropology. **1980** R. A. GOULD *Living Archaeol.* 3 Termed ethnoarchaeology in most quarters, this approach represents an attempt by archaeologists to overcome the limitations of their data in interpreting past human behavior. **1984** *Nature* 1 Mar. 88/3 He.. draws upon ethnography, ethnoarchaeology and nutritional research to build a case for nutritionally conditioned selectivity on the part of the bison hunters.

Hence **ˌethnoarchæo'logical** *a.*; **ˌethno-archæ'ologist.**

1968 J. D. CLARK in Lee & DeVore *Man the Hunter* xxx. 278/2 This emphasizes the urgent need for 'ethnoarchaeological' studies of such extant 'Stone Age' groups while they still exist. **1980** *Nature* 20 Mar. 215/2 Other ethnoarchaeological work has examined in detail the processes of fragmentation and preservation of animal bone. **1981** *Sci. Amer.* May 34/3 These days it appears probable that time devoted to econometrics, statistics and materials science repays a working ethnoarchaeologist much sooner than time spent with the philosophers, old or new.

ethnobotany (ɛθnəʊ'bɒtənɪ). orig. *U.S.* [f. Gr. ἔθνο-ς nation + BOTANY.] The traditional knowledge and customs of a people concerning plants; the scientific study or description of such knowledge and customs. Hence **ˌethno-bo'tanical** *a.*, **ethno'botanist.**

1896 J. W. HARSHBERGER in *Bot. Gaz.* XXI. 146 The study of ethno-botany aids in elucidating the cultural position of the tribes who used the plants for food, shelter or clothing. **1899** *Smithsonian Rep.* 65 Dr. Walter Hough was detailed to carry on ethno-botanical researches in Mexico. **1934** *N. & Q.* CLXVII. 129/1 The importance of ethno-botany has long been understood by systematic anthropologists. *Ibid.*, An ethno-botanical note on *Datura Metel.* **1934** WEBSTER, Ethnobotanist. **1955** *Times* 3 Aug. 7/4 Its distinguished American ethnobotanist.

ethnocentric (ɛθnəʊ'sɛntrɪk), *a.* [f. Gr. ἔθνο-ς nation + CENTRIC *a.*] Regarding one's own race or ethnic group as of supreme importance. So **ethno'centrism, ˌethnocen'tricity.**

1900 W. J. MCGEE in *Ann. Rep. Bur. Amer. Ethnol. 1897–98* 831 In primitive culture the epocentric and ethnocentric views are ever-present and always-dominant factors of both mentation and action. **1907** W. G. SUMNER *Folkways* i. 13 *Ethnocentrism* is the technical name for this view of things in which one's own group is the center of everything, and all others are scaled and rated with reference to it. *Ibid.* 15 The state.. became the object of that group vanity and antagonism which had been ethnocentric. **1951** E. E. EVANS-PRITCHARD *Social Anthrop.* vi. 127 This ethnocentric attitude has to be abandoned if we are to appreciate the rich variety of human culture and social life. **1957** W. S. ALLEN *Ling. Stud. Lang.* 8 Mar. 7 A familiarity with many languages.. may do much to reduce the ethnocentrism with which, as native speakers of a language, we are inevitably burdened. **1959** *Listener* 1 Jan. 27/2 Is it really necessary to resuscitate the white man's burden at the very time when so much depends upon our getting rid of this form of ethnocentricity? **1964** I. L. HOROWITZ *New Sociology* 34 The present ethnocentricity reflects a fascination with machines at the expense of minds. **1964** M. CRITCHLEY *Developmental Dyslexia* xii. 70 The age at which a child normally begins to read with facility is also the age at which.. he turns from an autistic, egocentric individual, to a societal, ethnocentric being.

ethnocide ('ɛθnəʊsaɪd). [f. ETHNO- + -CIDE 2.] The deliberate and systematic destruction of the culture of an ethnic group, esp. within a larger community.

1974 *Ann. Reg. 1973* 382 The Central Committee of the World Council of Churches in May.. criticized 'the policy of extermination, ethnocide and exploitation of the Indian people continuously practised in the United States', with special reference to riots at Wounded Knee. **1980** *Daily Tel.* 10 Sept. 17/7 They are guilty of ethnocide: destruction of the Indians' tribal identities and thus of their ability to live. **1984** *Times* 28 Aug. 11/7 India can do things differently—by acting now to prevent the ethnocide of the Madia Gonds.

ethnodicy (ɛθ'nɒdɪsɪ). *rare.* [mod. f. Gr. ἔθνο-ς nation + δικία administration of justice, f. δίκη justice.] Comparative jurisprudence as a branch of ethnology.

1889 *Athenæum* 21 Sept. 391/3 The labours of the [Ethnographical] Congress are organized in six sections, viz. general ethnology; ethics, ethnodicy, and sociology.

ethnogenesis (ˌɛθnəʊ'dʒɛnɪsɪs). [f. ETHNO- + GENESIS 4; cf. F. *ethnogénie* (A. C. Moreau de Jonnès *Ethnogénie caucasienne* (1861) 13).] The formation or emergence of an ethnic group within a larger community.

1962 L. SINGER in *Social Research* XXIX. 423 Following Emancipation, the group-forming process moved with much greater speed and intensity than before. I propose that this formative process be referred to as 'ethnogenesis', meaning by this term the process whereby a people, that is an ethnic group, comes into existence. **1965** G. WHEELER *Mod. Hist. Soviet Central Asia* i. 8 They have traced the

ethnogenesis of each people much farther back. **1983** *Trans. Philol. Soc.* 163 At some time there was contact, but this must have been in the Indo-European period before the ethnogenesis of either group.

ethnogenic (ɛθnəʊˈdʒɛnɪk), *a.* [f. next + -IC.] Pertaining to ethnogeny.

ethnogeny (ɛθˈnɒdʒɪnɪ). [mod. f. Gr. ἔθνο-ς nation + -γένεια birth.] That branch of ethnology which treats of the origin of races, nations, and peoples.

In mod. Dicts.

ethnographer (ɛθˈnɒgrəfə(r)). [f. ETHNOGRAPH-Y (or Gr. ἔθνο-ς nation + -γραφ-ος writer) + -ER[1].] One who treats descriptively of the races of mankind; one who is versed in the science of ethnography.

1854 H. MILLER *Sch. & Schm.* x. (1857) 202 An evidence, the ethnographer might perhaps say, of its purely Celtic origin. **1865** TYLOR *Early Hist. Man.* viii. 202 The Ethnographer, who has studied the stone implements of Europe. **1884** A. M. FAIRBAIRN in *Congregationalist* Apr. 280 The greatest ethnographers, that is, the men who have most extensively studied the customs, the manners, the beliefs of men.

ethnographic (ɛθnəʊˈgræfɪk), *a.* [f. as prec. + -IC.] Of or pertaining to ethnography.

1836 CDL. WISEMAN *Sc. & Relig.* II. vii. 46 Nor is this confined merely to the members of the same ethnographic family. **1852** TH. ROSS *Humboldt's Trav.* III. xxvi. 87 The ethnographic document called *El Auto de Figueroa*, is one of the most curious records of the barbarism of the first *conquistadores*. **1878** GLADSTONE *Prim. Homer* 103 These Iaones . . represent the Javan of the great ethnographic document, chap. x. of the Book of Genesis.

ethno'graphical, *a.* [f. prec. + -AL[1].] = prec.

1842 PRICHARD *Nat. Hist. Man* 473 The ethnographical outline which I have now concluded. **1876** *N. Amer. Rev.* CXXIII. 150 Ethnographical studies have made some progress in these later days. **1879** FARRAR *St. Paul* I. 391 *note*, Galatia had two meanings—the first ethnographical, the second political.

ethnographically (ɛθnəʊˈgræfɪkəlɪ), *adv.* [f. prec. + -LY[2].] In an ethnographical manner; from an ethnographical point of view.

1839 *Fraser's Mag.* XX. 712 Which, contemplated . . ethnographically . . holds out . . abundant matter. **1869** RAWLINSON *Anc. Hist.* 9 Ancient History may be mapped out . . ethnographically, according to states and nations.

ethnographist (ɛθˈnɒgrəfɪst). [f. ETHNOGRAPH-Y + -IST.] = ETHNOGRAPHER.

1880 *Libr. Univ. Knowl.* V. 560 Ethnographists deal with tribes, and with particular institutions and . . customs.

ethnography (ɛθˈnɒgrəfɪ). [mod. f. Gr. ἔθνο-ς nation + -γραφία writing.] The scientific description of nations or races of men, with their customs, habits, and points of difference.

1834 *Penny Cycl.* II. 97 The term ethnography (nation-description) is sometimes used by German writers in the sense which we have given to anthropography. **1857** DE QUINCEY *China* Wks. 1871 XVI. 233 The Englishman . . of Chinese ethnography has not a house, except in crevices of rocks. **1868** GLADSTONE *Juv. Mundi* vii. (1870) 206 It is in truth a main key to the ethnography of the poems. **1878** RECLUS in *Encycl. Brit.* VIII. 613 *s.v.*, Ethnography embraces the descriptive details, and ethnology the rational exposition, of the human aggregates and organizations.

ethnohistory (ɛθnəʊˈhɪstərɪ). [f. Gr. ἔθνο-ς nation + HISTORY *sb.*] The study of the history of races or cultures, esp. non-Western races or cultures. So ˌ**ethnohi'storian**, a student or expert in ethnohistory; ˌ**ethnohi'storical** *a.*, of or pertaining to ethnohistory.

1936 *Times Lit. Suppl.* 2 May 378/2 Each of us must have within reach five hundred ethnohistorians. **1936** L. P. WEAVER tr. *Székely's Cosmos, Man & Soc.* 12 Hitherto ethnohistorical research has depended on three sources: archæological documents, linguistic documents and authentic writing. **1952** *Amer. Anthropologist* LIV. 331 Ethnohistory is blessed with an abundance of source materials. **1965** *Language* XLI. 203 Evidence that the ethnohistorian must use. **1966** *New Statesman* 13 May 710/2 (Advt.), The study . . of internal change within the non-Western societies (i.e. ethnohistory).

ethnolinguist (ɛθnəʊˈlɪŋgwɪst). [f. ETHNO- + LINGUIST 2; see ETHNOLINGUISTIC *a.*] A student of ethnolinguistics.

1957 *Publ. Amer. Dial. Soc. 1956* XXVI. 13 It is the *ethnolinguist* who will have to bring the answer to the question of the social circumstances under which the learning of the second language occurs. **1971** *Amer. Psychologist* XXVI. 871/1 The work of contemporary sociologists and ethnolinguists seems conclusively to demonstrate the presence of complex contingent thinking in situations that are all too often characterized by psychologists as consisting of syncretic, affective interactions.

ethnolinguistic (ˌɛθnəʊlɪŋˈgwɪstɪk), *a.* [f. Gr. ἔθνο-ς nation + LINGUISTIC *a.*] Of or pertaining to ethnolinguistics.

1920 B. MALINOWSKI in *Bull. School of Oriental & Afr. Studies* I. IV. 69 There is an urgent need for an Ethnolinguistic theory. **1950** D. L. OLMSTED *Ethnolinguistics So Far* iv. 10 The frequency of morphemes in a given ethnolinguistic situation is of importance in determining the relations between talk and action. **1964** E. A. NIDA *Toward Sci. Transl.* vii. 148 One important element in this ethnolinguistic model of translation is the nature of the response implied.

ethnolinguistics (ˌɛθnəʊlɪŋˈgwɪstɪks). [f. as prec.] The study of the relations between linguistic and cultural behaviour.

1947 *Amer. Anthropologist* XXXXIX. 589 Synchronic ethno-linguistics has so far been either particularistic or programmatic. **1950** D. L. OLMSTED *Ethnolinguistics So Far* 1 The word *ethnolinguistics* has been used in a number of contexts by social scientists. **1964** R. H. ROBINS *Gen. Linguistics* ix. 352 The specific study of the interdisciplinary links . . between anthropology and linguistics has been called *ethnolinguistics*.

ethnologer (ɛθˈnɒlədʒə(r)). [f. ETHNOLOG-Y + -ER[1].] = ETHNOLOGIST.

1850 MERIVALE *Rom. Emp.* (1865) I. v. 222 The Iberi, whom modern ethnologers represent as belonging to a distinct family. **1881** FREEMAN *Hist. Geog. Europe* I. iii. 57 It is from Caesar, ethnologer as well as conqueror, that we get our chief knowledge of the country as it was in his day.

ethnologic (ɛθnəʊˈlɒdʒɪk), *a.* [f. as prec. + -IC.] = next.

1864 H. SPENCER *Illust. Univ. Progr.* 31 Progress of every kind—astronomic, geologic, organic, ethnologic, social.

ethnological (ɛθnəʊˈlɒdʒɪkəl), *a.* [f. as prec. + -ICAL.] Of or pertaining to ethnology.

1849 FREEMAN *Archit.* 18 Others . . belong rather to the ethnological and philological inquirer. **1858** GLADSTONE *Homer* I. 284 The ethnological formation of the different communities. **1861** GEN. P. THOMPSON *Audi Alt.* III. clxiv. 184 If our Ethnological Societies cannot otherwise be contented, they must, etc. **1873** *Daily News* 19 Sept. 1/2 A collection of ethnological curiosities from New Guinea.

ethnologically (ɛθnəʊˈlɒdʒɪkəlɪ), *adv.* [f. prec. + -LY[2].] In an ethnological manner; from an ethnological point of view.

1861 G. MOORE *Lost Tribes* 4 A circumstance, ethnologically considered, of much interest and importance. **1867** FREEMAN *Norm. Conq.* (1876) I. ii. 36 Lothian was politically as well as ethnologically English.

ethnologist (ɛθˈnɒlədʒɪst). [f. ETHNOLOG-Y + -IST.] One who is engaged or versed in the study of ethnology.

1842 PRICHARD *Nat. Hist. Man* xv. (1843) 132 Every new ethnologist subdivides the nations which his predecessor had connected. **1878** W. H. DALL *Later Preh. Man* 4 The ethnologist . . may rifle their burial places. **1881** *Atlantic Mag.* XLVII. 232 The ethnologist, who deals with skulls and statures and complexions.

ethnologize (ɛθˈnɒlədʒaɪz), *v.* [mod. f. as prec. + -IZE.] *intr.* To speculate on ethnological questions.

1873 WHITNEY *Orient. Stud.* 224 If our author will not allow the etymologists to ethnologize, etc.

ethnology (ɛθˈnɒlədʒɪ). [f. Gr. ἔθνο-ς nation + -λογία discourse: see -LOGY.] The science which treats of races and peoples, and of their relations to one another, their distinctive physical and other characteristics, etc.

1842 PRICHARD *Nat. Hist. Man* 132 The history of nations termed ethnology, must be mainly founded on the relations of their languages. **1847** *Proc. Amer. Phil. Soc.* IV. 358 Dr. Bethune made some remarks on ethnology, a term he preferred to ethnography. **1878** LUBBOCK *Preh. Times* Pref. 9 Ethnology in fact is passing at present through a phase from which other sciences have safely emerged.

ethnomaniac (ɛθnəʊˈmeɪnɪæk). [f. Gr. ἔθνο-ς nation + MANIAC.] One who is crazy about the rights of 'nationalities'.

1863 S. EDWARDS *Poles Captivity* II. 140 The political ethnomaniacs to be consistent ought to propose the annexation of Alsace to some German state.

quasi-*adj.* **1886** *Sat. Rev.* 16 Jan. 69 The game, from the ethnomaniac point of view, may be regarded as won.

ethnomethodological (ˌɛθnəʊmɛθədəˈlɒdʒɪkəl), *a.* *Sociol.* [f. ETHNOMETHODOLOGY: see -ICAL.] Of or pertaining to ethnomethodology.

1967 H. GARFINKEL *Stud. Ethnomethodol.* p. v, Ethnomethodological studies analyze everyday activities as members' methods for making those same activities visibly-rational-and-reportable-for-all-practical-purposes, i.e., 'accountable', as organizations of commonplace everyday activities. **1973** *Social Sci. Q.* LIII. 905 From an ethnomethodological perspective, the Mexican American is seen as any other societal member who encounters, knows, and sees the social order . . as consisting of normal courses of action that are dealt with in routine ways. **1976** *Human Relations* XXIX. 195 Ethnomethodological investigation purports to have no purpose except that of revealing the purpose of those exposed by it. **1984** *Lang. & Communication* IV. I. 72 The ethnomethodological concern to analyse 'real' data in 'real' situations is revealing in this respect.

ethnomethodologist (ˌɛθnəʊmɛθəˈdɒlədʒɪst). *Sociol.* [f. ETHNOMETHODOLOGY + -IST.] A student or practitioner of ethnomethodology.

1967 *Social Problems* XIV. 427/1 The present paper represents an attempt to combine the two approaches by applying methods developed by the ethnoscientists to a problem conceptualized in terms relevant to an ethnomethodologist. **1972** *Science* 12 May 627/3 He does not interview people (as cognitive psychologists and ethnomethodologists do). **1975** *Brit. Jrnl. Sociol.* XXVI. 139 By the ethnomethodologists' own admission . . Schutz, in recommending a clarification of methods, only pointed the way. **1984** *Lang. & Communication* IV. I. 73 This approach is essentially the one adopted by ethnomethodologists and exponents of the analysis of 'interactive discourse'.

ethnomethodology (ˌɛθnəʊmɛθəˈdɒlədʒɪ). *Sociol.* [f. ETHNO- + METHODOLOGY.] A style of sociological analysis associated with H. Garfinkel (b. 1917), which seeks to expose and analyse the methods by which participants in a given social situation construct their commonsense knowledge of the world.

1967 H. GARFINKEL *Stud. Ethnomethodol.* i. 11, I use the term 'ethnomethodology' to refer to the investigation of the rational properties of indexical expressions and other practical actions as contingent ongoing accomplishments of organized artful practices of everyday life. **1974** R. TURNER (*title*) Ethnomethodology. **1975** *Brit. Jrnl. Sociol.* XXVI. 139 Schutz is . . presented as providing the driving force for . . ethnomethodology. **1978** M. DOUGLAS *Cultural Bias* i. 5 Not surprisingly, sociology finds even Cicourel's cogent form of ethnomethodology difficult to accept. **1984** *Rev. Eng. Stud.* XXXV. 428 For him, however, this work has left sociological positivism undisturbed at heart, and so has ethno-methodology.

ethnomusicology (ˌɛθnəʊmjuːzɪˈkɒlədʒɪ). [f. Gr. ἔθνο-ς nation + MUSICOLOGY.] The scientific study of the music of a culture or sub-culture, considered either as a combination of sounds or as an aspect of socio-cultural behaviour; also, the comparative study of the music of more than one culture. Hence ˌ**ethnomusico'logical** *a.*, pertaining to this study; ˌ**ethnomusi'cologist**, a student of or expert in ethnomusicology.

1950 J. KUNST *Musicologica* Pref., It is intended as a general introduction to ethno-musicology, before going on to the study of the forms of separate music-cultures. **1951** *Africa* Jan. 319 This work fulfilled a long-standing need by ethnomusicologists. **1958** *Listener* 15 May 824/3 The book reflects the present state of ethnomusicological studies. **1959** *Times Lit. Suppl.* 5 June 332/1 The new subject of ethnomusicology has emerged in no more than a generation to put system into a mass of authentic material gathered from all parts of the globe. **1967** W. P. MALM *Music Cultures of Pacific* i. 9 An ethnomusicologist should be a man of many viewpoints if he is to appreciate fully the meaning of music in a given culture. **1970** *Daily Tel.* 30 Sept. 10/5 Dr Frank Harrison, Reader in the History of Music at Oxford University . . , has been appointed to the Chair of Ethnomusicology at Amsterdam University.

ethnonym (ˈɛθnəʊnɪm). *Anthropol.* [f. ETHNO- + *-nym*, as in HOMONYM, PSEUDONYM; app. a. Russ. *étnonim* (cf., for example, *Sovetskaya Étnografiya* (1946), IV. 34); also *étnonimika* 'ethnonymics', the study of ethnonyms (1939).] A proper name by which a people or ethnic group is known; *spec.* one which it calls itself.

1964 tr. *Levin & Potapov's Peoples of Siberia* 761 The Chinese knew the Oroks as 'Oron'cho'. The etymology of this and related ethnonyms is probably derived from the Manchu and Tungus word for the domesticated reindeer—oro or oron. Names with this root usually mean 'reindeer people' or 'reindeer breeders'. **1966** Y. MALKIEL in *Current Trends in Linguistics* III. 360 Refractory ethnonyms fell into desuetude in Romance. **1974** Y. V. BROMLEY in Grigulevich & Koslov *Races & Peoples* 34 A peculiar but . . essential distinctive ethnic feature is ethnic consciousness, i.e., the awareness by members of a given ethnos of their affinity to it, this awareness being . . manifested first of all by a common ethnonym. **1980** —— in E. Gellner *Soviet & Western Anthropol.* III. 155 An ethnic community proper or ethnos in the general sense . . may be defined as an historically formed aggregate of people who share relatively stable specific features of culture (including language) and psychology, an awareness of their unity and their difference from other similar groups, and an ethnonym which they have given themselves. **1983** D. L. GOLD in *Comments on Etym.* XII. 26 Some Hebrew-speakers interpret the informal Israeli Hebrew ethnonym *yeke* (which is clearly from Eastern Yiddish *yeke*) as being from (Heb.) *yehudi Keshe-havana* 'Jew [who is] hard of understanding' (Heb. *yeke* is spelled *yod-kof-he*).

ethnophaulism (ɛθnəʊˈfɔːlɪz(ə)m). [f. ETHNO- + *-phaulism*, f. Gr. φαύλισμα disparagement, contempt, f. φαυλίζω to hold cheap.] A contemptuous expression for (a member of) a people or ethnic group; an expression containing a disparaging allusion to another people or ethnic group.

1944 A. A. ROBACK *Dict. Internat. Slurs* 13, I can visualize, however, a future edition which would contain more extended inventories of the foreign disparaging allusions (or as I have named them, 'ethnophaulisms') in a score of languages. **1962** E. B. PALMORE in *Amer. Jrnl. Sociol.* Jan. 442 (*title*) Ethnophaulisms and ethnocentrism. **1963** R. I. MCDAVID *Mencken's Amer. Lang.* vi. 367 The English have fewer strangers within their gates, and hence their native armamentarium is smaller, and not a few of the achthronyms (or ethnophaulisms) they use come from the United States. **1977** H. GILES et al. in H. Giles *Lang., Ethnicity & Intergroup Relations* xiii. 342 The use of spoken ethnophaulisms is also . . a common tactic used by dominant groups in order to demean members of subordinate groups. **1980** *Logophile* IV. I. 15/2 Gillian Edwards examined . . a range of ethnophaulisms . . from 'Greek trust' (no trust at all) to 'Dutch courage'.

ethnopsychology (ˌɛθnəʊsaɪˈkɒlədʒɪ). [f. Gr. ἔθνο-ς nation, people + PSYCHOLOGY.] The

investigation of the psychology of races and peoples.

1886 LANG in *19th Cent.* XIX. 58 For this method [philological] we propose to substitute..the method of Völkerpsychologie..or ethnopsychology.

Hence **ˌethnopsychoˈlogical** *a.*, of or pertaining to ethnopsychology.

1885 C. LOWE *Bismarck* II. 131 *note*, The ethnopsychological problem which lies concealed in the nature of the Oriental.

ethnoscience (ɛθnəʊˈsaɪəns). [f. Gr. ἔθνο-ς nation + SCIENCE.] The study of races or cultures; ethnography.

1964 E. A. NIDA *Toward Sci. Transl.* iii. 38 B. N. Colby in an unpublished paper, entitled 'Eidos, Semantics and Ethnoscience', has dealt extensively with a number of these approaches to studies of semantic fields. **1964** *Language* XL. 230 The terminology which is now appearing in anthropological literature devoted to ethnoscience.

ethnosemantic (ˌɛθnəʊsɪˈmæntɪk), *a.* [f. ETHNO- + SEMANTIC *a.*: see next.] Of or pertaining to ethnosemantics.

1967 *Word* XXIII. 219 In the 'ethnosemantic' school of contemporary American anthropology, the analysis of whole semantic regions..in terms of combinations of recurrent features has come to be called a paradigm. **1983** *Anthropol. Linguistics* XXV. 316 Before revealing these connections, we come to the issue of ethnosemantic misinterpretation. *Ibid.* 322 The phenomenon of persistence of myth in such diverse form confirms, finally, the ethnosemantic interpretation of the charm.

ethnosemantics (ˌɛθnəʊsɪˈmæntɪks), *sb. pl.* (const. *sing.*). [f. ETHNO- + *semantics* (see SEMANTIC *sb.* 1): see prec.] The study of how members of a speech community categorize their experience, esp. by analysing the semantic organization of the vocabulary of the community.

1968 M. HARRIS *Rise Anthropol. Theory* xx. 585 Since much of the terminological data which provides the basis for the ethnosemantics of kinship derives from fieldwork that can no longer be repeated, there is little hope of correcting for overagreement in the formal accounts. **1975** *Gen. Systems* XX. 108/2 Ideological-sector enthronement is also misplaced... Its recent resurgence in the movement of ethnosemantics (cf. 'ethnoscience') is blasted. **1978** *Social Sci. & Med.* XII. 185 Dorothy Clement reports the use of ethno-semantics for opinion survey, finding, for example, that Navajos wished their community center to bear mirror-windows rather than two-way glass. **1984** *Dictionaries* VI. 8 The cataloguing/cognitive role of lexical items as organizers of a community's universe of experience and imagination (focal object of analysis in German field theory and American ethnosemantics) must be distinguished from their role as carriers of linguistic constraints..about their uses in utterance and in context.

et hoc genus omne: see HOC GENUS OMNE.

ethogram (ˈiːθəʊgræm). *Zool.* [f. Gr. ἦθος (see ETHOLOGY 4) + -GRAM.] (A catalogue of) all the different kinds of behaviour or activity exhibited by an animal.

1936 *Ardea* XXV. 60 An attempt has been made to give an exhaustive description of the habits (an ethogram) of the European Avocet. **1964** *Oceanogr. & Marine Biol.* II. 457 Behaviour is observed..and the various elements or movements of the behaviour are carefully described. In this way an ethogram, or catalogue of the behavioural repertoire, of the species is obtained, and names can be assigned to the various components. **1977** SAVAGE & RUMBAUGH in D. M. Rumbaugh *Lang. Learning by Chimpanzee* xvi. 291 Such approaches presume that the set of all behavioral events (i.e., the ethogram) is equal to the total uncertainty in the situation. **1983** *New Scientist* 24 Mar. 793/1 Before we can begin to understand social interaction we must have a sound descriptive data-base: an 'ethogram' or compendium of all the behaviours an animal typically performs, how often they are performed, with whom and to whom.

ethography (iːˈθɒgrəfɪ). [mod. f. Gr. ἦθο-ς character + -γραφία writing.] 'The description of the morals and characteristics of man'.

1878 in KRAUTH *Vocab. Philos. Sc.*

ethologic (iːθəʊˈlɒdʒɪk), *a.* [f. ETHOLOG-Y + -IC.] = next.

1864 in WEBSTER; and in mod. Dicts.

ethological (iːθəʊˈlɒdʒɪkəl), *a.* [f. as prec. + -AL[1].]

1. Pertaining to 'ethology'. **a.** According to the Dicts.: Pertaining to ethics. **b.** After J. S. Mill: Pertaining to the science of human character.

1730–6 in BAILEY (folio). **1775** in ASH. **1843** MILL *Logic* VI. v. §6 The ethological consequences of particular circumstances of position. **1883** W. MINTO in *Academy* 29 Dec. 425 The son is sufficiently candid for the most exacting student of ethological truth.

2. Pertaining to the scientific study of customs.

1865 MAX MÜLLER *Chips* (1880) II. xxv. 266 What may be called ethological as distinguished from ethnological researches.

3. Of or pertaining to ETHOLOGY 4.

1908 *Westm. Gaz.* 1 Aug. 15/2 Animal psychology in France is no longer the quoting of instances of the supernatural intellectual qualities of the tame dog... The ethological method has sprung into existence. **1959** *Ibis* No. 101, p. 357 (*heading*) The ethological analysis of incubation behaviour. **1959** *New Biol.* XXVIII. 71 The reproductive segregation which it brings about is commonly called ethological isolation.

ethologist (iːˈθɒlədʒɪst). [f. L. *ētholog-us*, Gr. ἠθολόγ-ος (f. ἦθο-ς character + -λογος one who discourses) + -IST.]

†**1.** [= Gr. ἠθολόγος] One who portrays character by imitative gestures and facial expression; a mimic. *Obs.*$^{-0}$

1730–6 in BAILEY (folio). **1775** in ASH.

2. One who treats of, or is versed in, the science of ethology; a writer on ethics.

1828 in WEBSTER; and in mod. Dicts.

3. One who is engaged or versed in the study of ETHOLOGY 4.

1953 *New Biol.* XIV. 7 Contemporary study of vertebrate behaviour is increasingly influenced by the school of ethologists, led by Nils [*sic*] Tinbergen and Konrad Lorenz. **1964** *Language* XL. 215 Ethologists find little novelty in the proposal that there is a qualitative difference between human and nonhuman cognitive faculties. **1966** R. ARDREY *Territorial Imperative* (1967) i. 27 Ethologists have assumed that there must be a neurological foundation in the central nervous system providing an anatomical switchboard for handling messages.

ethology (iːˈθɒlədʒɪ). [ad. L. *ēthologia*, a. Gr. ἠθολογία, f. ἠθολόγ-ος: see prec. and -LOGY.]

†**1.** The portrayal of character by mimic gestures: mimicry. *Obs.*$^{-0}$

1656–81 in BLOUNT *Glossogr.* **1721–1800** in BAILEY.

†**2.** According to the Dicts.: The science of ethics; also, a treatise on manners or morals. *Obs.*

1678–1706 in PHILLIPS. **1721–1800** in BAILEY.

3. After J. S. Mill: The science of character-formation.

1843 MILL *Logic* VI. v. §4 The laws of the formation of character..are to be obtained by, etc. A science is thus formed, to which I would propose to give the name of Ethology, or the science of character.

4. *Zool.* [Gr. ἦθος nature or disposition of animals; in pl., customs, haunts.] That branch of Natural History which deals with the actions and habits of animals, and their reaction to their environment; esp. the study of instinctive animal behaviour.

[**1859** I. GEOFFROY SAINT-HILAIRE *Histoire Naturelle Gen. des Règnes Organiques* II. 285 C'est à l'éthologie.. qu'appartient l'étude des relations des êtres organisés..dans *l'agrégat* et *la communauté.*] **1897** PARKER & HASWELL *Zool.* I. 9 The whole question of the relation of the organism to its environment gives us a final and most important branch of Natural History which has been called Ethology or Bionomics. **1910** W. M. WHEELER *Ants* viii. 124 Their ethology, that is, their functional aspect (physiology and psychology). **1956** O. L. ZANGWILL in A. Pryce-Jones *New Outl. Mod. Knowl.* 170 A new type of behaviour study which endeavours to combine the rigours of scientific materialism with genuine understanding of the ways of animals..has been christened *ethology*. **1962** *Listener* 9 Aug. 207/1 Ethology is a method developed for studying automatic behaviour in animals, by looking at their movements and postures, but it can also be applied to man.

‖**ethoˈpœia.** *Obs. rare.* [L. *ēthopœia*, a. Gr. ἠθοποιία, f. ἦθο-ς character + ποιία representation.] Delineation of character; moral portraiture. Also *Rhet.* (see quot. 1678).

1659 *Instruct. Oratory* 74 Examples of such Descriptions and Histories of things under which I comprehend Ethopoeas. **1678–1706** PHILLIPS, *Ethopœa*, a figure of Rhetorick in which there is a feigning of certain words accommodated to certain persons, either to their praise or reproach. **1721–1800** in BAILEY.

†**ˌethoˈpoetic,** *a.* *Obs. rare*$^{-1}$. [ad. Gr. ἠθοποιητικ-ός, f. ἦθο-ς character + ποιητικός, f. ποιέειν to make, represent.] Intended to represent character or manners.

1652 URQUHART *Jewel* Wks. (1834) 228 [Crichtoun] begun to prank it *a la Venetiana*, with such a flourish of mimick and ethopoetick gestures.

‖**ethos** (ˈiːθɒs). [mod.L., a. Gr. ἦθος character, a person's nature or disposition. Used by Eng. writers in certain particular applications.]

1. [After Arist. *Rhet.* II. xii–xiv.] The characteristic spirit, prevalent tone of sentiment, of a people or community; the 'genius' of an institution or system.

1851 SIR F. PALGRAVE *Norm. & Eng.* v. 691 The Romanized Danes conformed to the ethos of the Carlovingian monarchy. **1859** W. F. WINGFIELD *Tour in Dalmatia* 27 This prevalence of the Italian language and ethos exists..not only in the maritime cities, etc. **1882** *Contemp. Rev.* Aug. 245 The ethos of Catholic sacerdotal life is altogether different.

2. In reference to ancient æsthetic criticism and rhetoric.

Aristotle's statement that Polygnotus excelled all other painters in the representation of 'ethos' app. meant simply that his pictures expressed 'character'; but as Aristotle elsewhere says that this painter portrayed men as nobler than they really are, some mod. writers have taken *ethos* to mean 'ideal excellence.' The opposition of *ethos* and *pathos* ('character' and 'emotion'), often wrongly ascribed to Aristotle's theory of art as expounded in the *Poetics*, really belongs only to Greek rhetoric.

1875 A. S. MURRAY in *Encycl. Brit.* II. 359 s.v. *Archæology*, By ethos, as applied to the paintings of Polygnotus, we understand a dignified bearing in his figures, and a measured movement throughout his compositions. **1881** *Q. Rev.* Oct. 542 The real is preferred to the ideal, transient emotion to permanent lineaments, pathos to ethos.

†**ethroclyte,** *sb.* Var. of HETEROCLITE: here used *transf.* in pl. for: Perplexed condition, state of frenzy. (See Du Cange s.v. *Diversiclinium.*)

1485 CAXTON *Chas. Gt.* 154 Thadmyral..beyng in the ethroclytes in his entendement, cryed and sayd.

ethyl (ˈɛθɪl, ˈiːθaɪl). Also † **ethule, 9 ethyle.** [a. G. *ethyl* (J. Liebig 1834, in *Ann. d. Pharm.* IX. 18), f. ETH(ER: see -YL.] The univalent hydrocarbon radical C_2H_5-, either as a group in an organic compound or as a short-lived free radical; ***ethyl acetate*** $CH_3COOC_2H_5$, ***ethyl acetoacetate*** $CH_3COCH_2COOC_2H_5$, ***ethyl alcohol*** C_2H_5OH, ***ethyl chloride*** C_2H_5Cl, ***ethyl ether*** = ETHER 6 a, ***ethyl formate*** $HCOOC_2H_5$, ***ethyl iodide*** C_2H_5I, ***ethyl iodoacetate*** $CH_2I.COOC_2H_5$ (a kind of teargas), ***ethyl nitrite*** $C_2H_5NO_2$.

1838 *Penny Cycl.* X. 49/2 Ethereum (as it is termed by Dr. Kane, and *ethule* by Berzelius). **1840** *Proc. Amer. Phil. Soc.* I. 311 Mr. Boyè read a communication entitled 'On the Perchlorate of the Oxide of Ethule.' **1850** DAUBENY *Atom. Th.* vii. (ed. 2) 219 If we suppose then a body to exist, consisting of C_4H_5..it has been proposed to designate it by the term ethyle. **1862** SIR H. HOLLAND *Ess., Mod. Chem.* 450 Ethyl..the radical of the numerous class of ethers. **1869** ROSCOE *Elem. Chem.* (1875) 295 Alcohol may be regarded as water in which one atom of hydrogen has been replaced by ethyl.

Comb. **1874** *Index to Jrnl. Chem. Soc. 1848–72* 144/2 *Ethyl acetate, action of sodium and isopropylic iodide on. **1940** *Chambers's Techn. Dict.* 310/1 *Ethyl acetate*,.. colourless liquid of fruity odour, used as a lacquer solvent and in medicine. **1874** *Jrnl. Chem. Soc.* XXVII. 883 The complicated changes involved in all previous processes are at once simplified if *ethyl acetoacetate, $CH_3.CO.CH_2.CO.OC_2H_5$, be taken as the starting point. **1964** B. G. CLARK *Mod. Org. Chem.* xv. 292 Ethyl acetoacetate, or ethyl β-ketobutyrate, is the most important of the β-keto-esters. The free acid occurs in the urine of uncontrolled sugar diabetics. **1869** ROSCOE *Elem. Chem.* 310 *Ethyl alcohol, known as spirits of wine. **1878** *Jrnl. Chem. Soc.* XXXIV. 1065/1 *Ethyl ether, brominated. **1885** I. REMSEN *Introd. Study Compounds of Carbon* iv. 42 Ethyl ether, $C_4H_{10}O$ = $(C_2H_5)_2O$.— This is the substance commonly known simply as *ether*, or *sulphuric ether*. **1868** *Jrnl. Chem. Soc.* XXI. 528/1 *Ethyl formate. **1960** A. E. BENDER *Dict. Nutrition* 46/2 *Ethyl formate*, $H.COOC_2H_5$. Fumigant used against raisin moth..etc... Chemical intermediate—in synthesis of B_1, sulphadiazine, etc. **1877** WATTS *Fownes' Chem.* II. 47 Ethane..is formed..by the action of zinc and water on *ethyl iodide. **1905** *Jrnl. Chem. Soc.* LXXXVII. 483 *Ethyl iodoacetate, ethyl bromoacetate, and methyl bromoacetate interact at 25° with one equivalent of sodium thiosulphate. **1932** A. HUXLEY *Brave New World* iii. 54 Phosgene, chloropicrin, ethyl iodoacetate. **1870** *Jrnl. Chem. Soc.* XXIII. 455/1 *Ethyl nitrite, action of sulphurous acid on. **1961** *Brit. Med. Dict.* 523/2 *Ethyl nitrite*, $C_2H_5.O.NO$, a compound which, dissolved in alcohol.., has been used in angina pectoris with limited effect.

Hence many derivatives, names of compounds containing ethyl, as **ˈethylaˌmine**, a compound ($NH_2C_2H_5$) of the ammonia type in which one of the hydrogen atoms of ammonia is replaced by ethyl. **ˈethylate** *sb.*, a salt of the radical ethyl, in which ethyl takes the place of the oxygenated group in a metallic salt. **ˈethylate** *v. trans.*, to convert into an ethyl compound, to introduce ethyl into; also ***ethylated*** ppl. adj., ***ethylating*** vbl. sb. **ˌethylˈbenzene**, a hydrocarbon, C_8H_{10}, usually made from ethylene and benzene. **ˌethylhydroˈcuprein(e**, a derivative of quinine having various bactericidal uses. **ethylia**, a synonym of *ethylamine*; now disused. **eˈthylic** *a.*, of ethyl; = ETHYL, used attributively, as in ***ethylic cyanate*** = ethyl cyanate. **ethylˈmorphine**, a toxic homologue of morphine, $C_{19}H_{23}NO_3$.

1850 DAUBENY *Atom. Th.* viii. (ed. 2) 239 *Ethylamine.. where it [1 atom of hydrogen] is replaced by ethyle. **1875** URE *Dict. Arts* II. 309 Several alkaloids existing in the animal and vegetable kingdom afford ethylamine on distillation with potash. **1864** *Athenæum* No. 1937. 788/3 The *ethylate of acetyl. **1880** *Med. Temp. Jrnl.* July 165 Report on the use of Ethylate of Sodium (Sodium Alcohol). **1850** *Phil. Trans. R. Soc.* CXL. 110, I have not attempted to *ethylate this compound any farther. **1920** *Chemical Age* III. 557/2, I have to learn, for example, how to ethylate *alpha*-naphthylamine [*printed* naphthalymine] very expeditiously at 100° C. on a commercial scale by means of ethyl chloride. **1850** *Phil. Trans. R. Soc.* CXL. 110 In..the other *ethylated bases, the properties of the mother-compound are only slightly modified. **1861** G. FOWNES *Man. Elem. Chem.* (ed. 8) 607 (*heading*) Methylated and ethylated derivatives of natural bases. **1920** *Jrnl. Soc. Chem. Industry* XXXIX. T1/1 Although English manufacturers of ethylated products are persistently demanding ethyl sulphate and other *ethylating agents, none of these can compete with ethyl chloride. *Ibid.* 3/1 As to the method of ethylating amino compounds with ethyl chloride, it is.. impossible to generalize. **1873** *Jrnl. Chem. Soc.* XXVI. 1028 (*title*) Action of bromine on boiling *ethylbenzene. **1934** *Jrnl. R. Aeronaut. Soc.* XXXVIII. 315 In addition to benzene and toluol derived from coal tar, higher aromatic hydrocarbons such as ethyl-benzene, pseudo-cumene and mesitylene have been synthesised and used..as fuel for aviation engines. **1964** N. G. CLARK *Mod. Org. Chem.* xix. 376 The first homologue is methylbenzene, $C_6H_5.CH_3$, known as 'toluene', which is followed by ethylbenzene,

$C_6H_5.C_2H_5$, and higher alkylbenzenes. **1913** THRON & FREUND *U.S. Pat. 1,062,203* 2/2 We claim.. the process of producing *ethyl-hydrocupreine which comprises treating hydrocupreine with an ethylating agent. **1914** *Chem. Abstr.* 2756 In human syphilis marked effect was obtained with.. injection of ethyl hydrocuprein. **1925** C. H. BROWNING *Bacteriology* xi. 252 But, so far, the only success obtained in generalised infections due to the ordinary bacteria is the cure of pneumococcal infection in mice by means of Morgenroth's 'optoquine' (ethyl-hydrocuprein, a derivative of quinine). **1873** WILLIAMSON *Chem. for Stud.* 241 This remarkable base was called ethylamine by Würtz, its discoverer, but is now more commonly called *Ethylia. **1869** *Eng. Mech.* 26 Nov. 255/3 Circumstances lead the operator to suspect that hydro-carbon to be *ethylic hydride. **1873** WATTS *Fownes' Chem.* 580 Ethylic ether is also called common ether, or simply ether. **1912** *Jrnl. Chem. Soc.* CII. I. 797 *(heading)* *Ethylmorphine and ethylmorphine hydrochloride (Dionine). **1964** S. DUKE-ELDER *Parsons' Dis. Eye* (ed. 14) 564 Therapeutic preparations. Eye-drops. Ethylmorphine (Dionene).

ethylene ('ɛθɪliːn). *Chem.* [f. ETHYL + -ENE.]
1. The diatomic hydrocarbon or olefine of the ethyl series, C_2H_4; also known as ethene, an important constituent of coal gas.

1852 H. WATTS tr. *Gmelin's Hand-bk. Chem.* VII. 32 Ethylene (olefiant gas) = C^4H^4. **1869** ROSCOE *Elem. Chem.* 358 Ethylene, known as olefiant gas, has already been mentioned. **1878** A. GREEN *Coal* vi. 207 One of the most important of these hydro-carbons is known as ethylene or ethene. **1881** *Athenæum* 26 Feb. 303/1 By heating glycol with an excess of fuming hydrochloric acid in a sealed tube to 100°, the author has converted this substance into ethylene dichloride.

2. The bivalent hydrocarbon radical $-CH_2CH_2-$. So **ethylene'diamine**, a viscous, strongly alkaline liquid, $C_2H_4(NH_2)_2$, that acts as a chelating agent in the formation of complexes and is used industrially; **ethylenediamine tetra-acetic acid**, $[-CH_2N(CH_2COOH)_2]_2$, a compound widely used, esp. in the form of its salts, as a chelating and sequestering agent in industry, biology, and medicine; abbrev. *EDTA*; **ethylene glycol**, a sweet-tasting liquid, $HOCH_2CH_2OH$, used chiefly in anti-freezes; **ethylene oxide**, the simplest epoxide, $(CH_2)_2O$, a colourless gas used chiefly as a chemical intermediate and fumigant.

1966 *Nomencl. Org. Chem.* (*A & B*) (I.U.P.A.C.) (ed. 2) 16 The names of bivalent radicals derived from normal alkanes by removal of a hydrogen atom from each of the two terminal carbon atoms of the chain are ethylene, trimethylene, tetramethylene, etc. **1861** G. FOWNES *Man. Elem. Chem.* (ed. 8) 606 *(heading)* *Ethylene-diamine and diethylene-diamine. **1967** *Martindale's Extra Pharmacopoeia* (ed. 25) 252 Ethylenediamine hydrate is used in the manufacture of aminophylline and in the preparation of aminophylline injections. **1942** *Brit. Chem. Abstr.* A1. 334 *(heading)* Copper, nickel, and uranyl compounds of *ethylenediaminotetra-acetic acid. **1959** *Sci. News* LII. 7 The degree of hardness of water.. could be measured precisely by an elegant titration with an organic compound then mainly used as a textile auxiliary, ethylene diamine tetra-acetic acid (usually abbreviated to EDTA). **1964** S. DUKE-ELDER *Parsons' Dis. Eye* (ed. 14) xxvi. 378 Irrigation with.. a solution of the sodium salt of ethylene-diamine tetra-acetic acid.. diminishes scarring in lime burns. **1964** L. MARTIN *Clinical Endocrinol.* (ed. 4) iv. 158 Edetic acid (ethylenediamine-tetra-acetic acid, EDTA) is a chelating agent which reduces the amount of ionized calcium in the blood. **1901** *Jrnl. Chem. Soc.* LXXX. I. 307 The boiling points of *ethylene glycol under varying pressures have been determined. **1959** Ethylene-glycol [see ANTI-FREEZE *a.* and *sb.*]. **1898** *Jrnl. Chem. Soc.* LXXIV. I. 399 *Ethylene oxide reacts vigorously with ethylamine. **1933** *Discovery* Aug. 250/2 Control [of the Cacao moth] can also be exercised by vacuum fumigation with ethylene oxide. **1962** *Listener* 20 Sept. 430/1 Another method of sterilization [of a space capsule] is to use the gas known as ethylene oxide.

Hence **ethylenic** (-'liːnɪk) *a.*, containing, derived from, or characteristic of ethylene; used spec. of a double bond between two carbon atoms.

1880 *Jrnl. Chem. Soc.* XXXVIII. 604 *(heading)* Heats of combustion of glycerol and of ethylenic glycol. **1946** *Nature* 14 Dec. 876/2 The lachrymatory activity of some ethylenic compounds. **1964** N. G. CLARK *Mod. Org. Chem.* ii. 14 The pair of valency bonds.. which is the essential feature of the olefins and upon which their chemical properties depend, is referred to as an ethylenic or olefinic bond.

ethylidene (ɛ'θɪlɪdiːn). *Chem.* Also 9 -den. [f. ETHYL + -ID(E + -ENE.] The bivalent hydrocarbon radical $CH_3CH=$.

1859 H. WATTS tr. *Gmelin's Hand-bk. Chem.* XIII. 451 Bromide of ethylidene. $C^4H^4Br^2$. *Ibid.* 453 The term *ethylidene* is applied to a radical (C^2H^4), supposed to exist in a series of compounds derived from aldehyde, and isomeric with the ethylene-compounds. **1952** MORTON & HOGGARTH in E. H. Rodd *Chem. Carbon Compounds* IB. xiv. 903 Ethylideneditrethane, $CH_3CH(NH{\cdot}CO_2Et)_2$, m.p. 126°, from urethane and acetaldehyde.

etic ('ɛtɪk), *a.* [f. PHON)ETIC *a.* Coined by K. L. Pike.] Describing a generalized, nonstructural approach to the description of language and behaviour. Cf. EMIC *a.*

1954 K. L. PIKE *Language in Rel. Human Behavior* I. ii. 8/1 In.. the *etic* approach to the data, an author is primarily concerned with generalized statements about the data. *Ibid.* 8/2 The etic approach is comprised of a complex of goals and procedures. **1965** *Language* XLI. 95 His concern is primarily with the etic-emic dichotomy. **1969** *English Studies* L. 586 One person will shake hands with you by lifting your hand up to about shoulder height and then drop it, another will move your hand less high and then down again, a third will 'pump' it up and down two or three times; in Western culture these may be called *etic* differences and can be viewed as various realizations of the one *emic* element: 'shaking hands'.

etik(e, obs. forms of HECTIC.

etin, var. of ETEN, *Obs.*, giant.

-etin, *suffix. Chem.* Forming the names of aglycones, esp. those not chemically characterized when discovered and named, usually by replacing *-in* in the name of the glycoside from which the aglycone is obtained; so FRAXETIN, PHLORETIN, QUERCETIN.

etine, -un, -yn, obs. ff. pa. pple. of EAT.

etiolate ('iːtɪəʊleɪt). [f. Fr. *étioler* (see -ATE[3] 6), of dialectal origin from Norm. (*s'*)*étieuler* to grow into haulm, f. *éteule*, OF. *esteule*, *esteulle*:—L. *stipula* straw.]
1. *trans.* To render (a plant) pale or colourless by excluding the light from it; to blanch.

1791 E. DARWIN *Bot. Gard.* I. 45 *note*, Celery blanched or etiolated for the table by excluding the light from it. **1822** IMISON *Sc. & Art* II. 34 Plants that grow in darkness are pale and without colour, and.. are said to be etiolated, or blanched. **1833** WHEWELL *Astron.* (Bridgew. Treat.) I. xiii. 99 Celery is in this manner blanched or etiolated. **1879** *Syd. Soc. Lex.* s.v. *Albino*, No chlorophyll is formed, and they [Albino plants] are said to be etiolated.

2. *transf.* To give a pale and sickly hue to (a human being or his skin).

1842 PRICHARD *Nat. Hist. Man* 78 The skin is also white, or etiolated. **1864** R. F. BURTON *Dahome* II. 66 *note*, We may etiolate them [females] as in New England.

3. *fig.* (See next, *ppl. a.*)

4. *intr.* To become white or whiter; to blanch; to be whitened by exclusion of sunlight, as plants.

1828 in WEBSTER; and in mod. Dicts.

etiolated ('iːtɪəʊleɪtɪd), *ppl. a.* [f. prec. + -ED[1].] Blanched, pallid, colourless. Also *fig.*

1799 SIR H. DAVY in Beddoes *Contrib. to Phys. & Med. Knowledge* 186 The whiteness of etiolated vegetables is occasioned by the deficiency of light. **1848** C. BRONTË *J. Eyre* (1857) 146, I.. left a bullet in one of his poor etiolated arms. **1852** TH. ROSS *Humboldt's Trav.* II. xxii. 359 It is caoutchouc in a particular state, I may almost say an etiolated caoutchouc. **1857–81** O. W. HOLMES in *Old Vol. of Life* (1883) 60 This poor human weed, this dwarfed and etiolated soul. **1866** *Reader* 15 Dec. 1005 Examples of the kind of etiolated theology. **1879** A. MONGREDIEN *Free Trade & Eng. Comm.* (ed. 4) 26 These industries.. are for the most part sickly, nerveless, and etiolated.

etiolation (iːtɪəʊ'leɪʃən). [f. ETIOLATE *v.*: see -ATION.] The action of etiolating; the process of becoming, or the condition of being, etiolated.

1799 SIR H. DAVY in Beddoes *Contrib. to Phys. & Med. Knowledge* 188 Plants, in the process of etiolation, lose the light combined with their leaves, and become white. **1816** KEITH *Phys. Bot.* II. 498 Etiolation may also ensue from the depredation of insects. **1844** *N. Brit. Rev.* II. 81 Newton smoked himself into a state of absolute etiolation. **1845** CARLYLE *Cromwell* (1873) I. i. 9 This is the collapse, the etiolation of human features into mouldy blank. **1882** VINES *Sachs' Bot.* 754 It is remarkable that etiolation does not extend to the flowers.

etiolin ('iːtɪəlɪn). [f. ETIOL-ATE + -IN.] A yellow modification of chlorophyll formed in plants growing in the dark.

1882 VINES *Sachs' Bot.* 747.

etiolize ('iːtɪəlaɪz), *v. rare.* [f. Fr. *étiol-er* + -IZE.] *trans.* = ETIOLATE. Hence **etio'lized** *ppl. a.*

1884 *Trans. Victoria Institute* 40 The young shoots, pale, etiolised, and delicate from the hour they show their tiny leaves.

etiological, var. of ÆTIOLOGICAL.

1834 J. FORBES *Laennec's Dis. Chest* (ed. 4) 451 Our etiological researches. **1862** LEWIS *Astron. Ancients* i. 4 An etiological legend.

etiologically, var. ÆTIOLOGICALLY *adv.*

1905 *Daily Chron.* 23 Aug. 3/1 It is an effort to show etiologically, with cold-blooded impartiality and freedom from partisanship, how [etc.]. **1956** *Nature* 14 Jan. 90/1 Both a virus and pleuro-pneumonia-like organisms have been etiologically implicated.

etiologist (iːtɪ'ɒlədʒɪst). [f. next + -IST.] One who studies etiology or the science of causes.

1830 R. KNOX *Béclard's Anat.* 174 One of the points of minute anatomy that have most exercised.. the imagination of etiologists. **1866** *Times* 17 Aug. 10/3 The etiologist will be the better enabled to estimate aright the influence of other insanitary elements.

etiology, var. of ÆTIOLOGY.

1656–81 BLOUNT *Glossogr.*, *Etiology*, a rendering of a cause, a shewing of reason. **1832** LYELL *Princ. Geol.* II. 240 The etiology of our science. **1861** T. GRAHAM *Pract. Med.* 26 The etiology of disease. **1881** M. L. KNAPP *Disasters* 7 Astronomical etiology.

etiquette ('ɛtɪkɛt). [a. Fr. *étiquette* (:—OF. *estiquette*). The primary sense in Fr. is represented by Eng. TICKET (an adoption either of the word or the synonymous *étiquet*:—*estiquet*): in OF. the word chiefly denotes a soldier's billet. The transition from the sense 'ticket, label' to that of 'prescribed routine' presents no intrinsic difficulty, but its actual history in Fr. is not very clear; the other mod. Romanic langs. have adapted the word from Fr. in the secondary sense; It. *etichetta*, Sp. *etiqueta* ('a book of ceremonies hid in the king's palace', Del Pino *Sp. Dict.* 1763).]

1. a. The prescribed ceremonial of a court; the formalities required by usage in diplomatic intercourse. **b.** The order of procedure established by custom in the army or navy (*esp.* with reference to promotion), in parliament, etc. **c.** The conventional rules of personal behaviour observed in the intercourse of polite society; the ceremonial observances prescribed by such rules. **d.** The unwritten code of honour by which members of certain professions (*esp.* the medical and legal) are prohibited from doing certain things deemed likely to injure the interests of their brethren, or to lower the dignity of the profession.

a. 1750 CHESTERF. *Lett.* 19 Mar., Without hesitation kiss his [the Pope's] slipper or whatever else the *étiquette* of that court requires. *Ibid.* (1792) IV. 187 Over head and ears engaged in ceremony and *étiquette*. **1797** BURKE *Regic. Peace* iii. Wks. VIII. 329 Etiquette.. had it's original application to those ceremonial and formal observances practised at Courts.. The term came afterwards.. to signify certain formal methods used in the transactions between sovereign States. **1865** LIVINGSTONE *Zambesi* v. 110 They keep perfect time in this species of court etiquette.

b. 1818 JAS. MILL *Brit. India* II. v. v. 512 It was to him that, in etiquette, the command of the expedition belonged. **1848** MACAULAY *Hist. Eng.* II. 667 A proceeding, conducted.. with such minute attention to prescriptive etiquette. **1867** SMYTH *Sailor's Word-bk.*, *Etiquette*, naval or military observances, deemed to be law. **1875** STUBBS *Const. Hist.* III. xx. 459 The later etiquette of procedure on money bills, will be sought in vain in the rolls of the mediæval parliaments.

c. 1768 STERNE *Sent. Journ.*, *The Letter*, I was not altogether sure of my etiquette, whether I ought to have wrote or no. **1779** J. MOORE *View Soc. Fr.* II. li. 21 For all etiquette of this nature is waved even in Germany at the tables d' Hôtes. **1800** MRS. HERVEY *Mourtray Fam.* IV. 10 A formal dinner; which, according to his ideas of etiquette, he thought himself obliged to give. **1851** ROBERTSON *Serm.* Ser. I. xviii. (1866) 301 Man is.. a slave.. to etiquette. **1876** MISS BRADDON *J. Haggard's Dau.* II. 164 After tea.. the bondage of etiquette was loosened.

pl. **1859** THACKERAY *Virgin.* xxiii. 181 A little place with its pompous ways, small etiquettes and punctilios.

d. 1868 ROGERS *Pol. Econ.* ii. (1876) 15 The etiquette of certain professional functions prescribes that a service should be divided. **1888** BRYCE *Amer. Commonw.* III. 382 A code of etiquette forbids them [lawyers] to undertake certain sorts of work.

†**2.** A rule of etiquette; an observance prescribed by etiquette. Chiefly *pl. Obs.*

1771 *Junius Lett.* xlii. 225 *note*, This diplomatic lord has spent his life in the study and practise of etiquettes. **1779** BURGOYNE *Let. to Constituents* (ed. 3) 7 A court etiquette was invented.. viz. that the persons whose conduct was so put in question, should not appear at Court pending the enquiry. **1807** COGAN *Eth. Treat. Passions* I. ii. (R.), Ludicrous offences against the laws of custom, or the etiquettes of fashion. **1812** *Edin. Rev.* XX. 76 Some of the etiquettes known in our legal and parliamentary oratory. **1816** KEATINGE *Trav.* I. 277 Some of the etiquettes of his majesty's court are rather whimsical.

3. In the primary Fr. sense: A label. *rare.*

1867 VCT. POLLINGTON *Half round Old World* 121 German matches.. with the remarkable lines, 'If you want a light, I'll shine so bright,' printed on the etiquette.

4. *attrib.* and *Comb.*, as ***etiquette-book***; ***etiquette-bound*** adj.

1881 'MARK TWAIN' *Lett. to Publishers* (1967) 133 Send me a collection of *etiquette books. **1952** *N.Y. Hist. Soc. Q.* XXXVI. 226 Etiquette books of various years yield information concerning mourning cards and notices. **1954** *Neuphilologische Mitteilungen* LV. 26 The rules laid down in the etiquette books need not always be strictly observed. **1902** *Westm. Gaz.* 28 May 2/1 It is many weary months before the small English lady—*etiquette-bound as the most world-worn *mondaine*—is at home in foreign 'Society'.

Hence **'etiquetted** *ppl. a.*, given up to etiquette.

1861 H. A. TILLEY *Japan* 385 The contrast altogether between them and the etiquetted ladies of Europe.

etiquettical (ɛtɪ'kɛtɪkəl), *a.* [-ICAL.] Pertaining to etiquette.

1838 J. PARDOE *River & Desart* II. iv. 33 Death.. has resumed its etiquettical observances. **1887** MRS. CUSTER *Tenting on Plains* (1889) ii. 66 It was too much for his etiquettical instincts. **1900** G. SWIFT *Somerley* 107 We shouted directions at one another, and, in the interest of the moment, forgot the 'Miss' and 'Mr.' and other etiquettical matters.

†**'etisie, 'etisis.** *Obs.* [cf. Fr. *étisie*; app. irreg. f. med.L. *etica*, L. *hectica* (see HECTIC *sb.*) on analogy of *phthisie*, *phthisis*.] = HECTIC *sb.*

1527 ANDREW *Brunswyke's Distyll. Waters* clxxviii. M ij b, For the Ptisicis and etisis, and for the consumynge sekenesse of the longues. **1582** HESTER *Secr. Phiorav.* III. ii. 6 It helpeth muche against the Etisie, and against all sortes of Catarres.

ˈ**etist.** *rare.* [f. Gr. ἦτ-α the name of the letter η + -IST.] One who pronounces the Greek letter η as (eɪ), not (iː); = ETACIST.
1839 HALLAM *Hist. Lit.* v. I. §25 Distinguished from the Etists of Erasmus's party.

etna (ˈɛtnə). Also 9 **ætna.** [f. the name of the volcano.] A vessel (in the form of an inverted cone placed in a saucer) for heating a small quantity of liquid by burning some kind of spirit.
1832 *Athenæum* 9 June 375 (*Advt.*), Jones's Ætnas for boiling half a pint of water in three minutes. **1870** *Eng. Mech.* 18 Mar. 659/1, I have an Etna with which I can produce a pint of boiling water in eight minutes. **1880** M. COLLINS *Th. in Garden* II. 263 Ask my *placens uxor* to mull some claret in the etna.

‖**etoile** (ɪˈtɔɪl, etwal). [a. Fr. *étoile* star.]
† **1.** *Fortif.* A small fort or redoubt in the shape of a star. *Obs.*
1730–6 BAILEY (folio), *Etoile*, a small fort or work of 4, 5, or 6, or more points, a star redoubt. **1775** in ASH.
2. *Her.* A heraldic charge consisting of a star with wavy points or rays. Cf. ESTOILE.
1766 PORNY *Heraldry Gloss., Etoile*, the French word for a Star. **1882** CUSSANS *Heraldry* 103 Étoile is represented with six wavy points.
3. *Comb.*
1789 MRS. PIOZZI *Journ. France* II. 287 The public walks and drives..are formed etoile-wise.

Eton (ˈiːt(ə)n). The name of a college, the largest of the ancient English public schools, founded by Henry VI on the Thames opposite Windsor, used *attrib.* or *Comb.* **a.** ***Eton boy***, a pupil at Eton College.
1842 T. MORTON (*title*) The Eton boy. **1883** [see POINT *sb.*[1] 13 b]. **1929** D. H. LAWRENCE *Assorted Articles* (1930) 40 What could be more uncanny than the present pattern of the Eton-boy girl with flower-like artificial complexion?
b. ***Eton jacket***, a short black broadcloth jacket, with an open front and broad lapels, pointed at the back and cut square at the hips, formerly worn by the younger boys at Eton (and elsewhere); also a garment of similar cut worn by women; hence ***Eton-jacketed*** adj. So ***Eton suit***, a suit consisting of an Eton jacket with trousers and waistcoat; also, a woman's suit with a similar jacket and a skirt. Often ellipt. *Eton* (and in pl.).
1881 *Punch* 15 Oct. 170/3 The coat having no tails, could serve as an Eton jacket to a growing youth. **1882** 'F. ANSTEY' *Vice Versâ* ii, Two small boys..in Eton jackets and broad white collars. **1883** *Graphic* 14 Apr. (Advt.), Eton suit, 32/6, 37/6. **1892** [see TOREADOR c]. **1892** *Queen* 28 May 888 'With a stout heart', published in 1874,..delighted an Eton-jacketed public. **1894** *Million* V. 377/2 Among the ladies riding was Lady ——, in an Eton suit and blue sailor hat. **1899** *Westm. Gaz.* 6 Jan. 3/2 The natty little Eton that in the South so often replaces the coat in the *costume tailleur*. **1900** *Daily News* 8 Sept. 6/3 Two-thirds of the smart dresses are now made with an Eton or bolero over a more or less ornamental front. **1900** *Captain* III. 405/2 The spectacle of Jim in Fourth Form Etons would have been too entrancing a sight. **1913** C. MACKENZIE *Sinister Street* I. I. viii. 124 A new Eton suit well became him. **1918** —— *Early Life Sylvia Scarlett* I. ii. 68 Sylvia was wearing Etons at Monkley's suggestion. **1925** *Blackw. Mag.* July 80/2 The Eton jacket (or 'tum-coat') was reserved for Sundays.
c. ***Eton blue***, a light blue adopted as the school colour.
1883 J. BRINSLEY-RICHARDS *Seven Yrs. at Eton* 306 A birch tied with Eton blue ribbon and rosettes. **1899** T. M. ELLIS *Three Cat's-eye Rings* 93 Looking at her wonderingly from his wide Eton-blue eyes. **1899** *Captain* II. 14/2 A very gorgeous equipage, with much Eton blue about it. **1963** *Harper's Bazaar* Feb. 74/2 Eton-blue water.
d. ***Eton collar***: a broad stiff white collar formerly worn outside the jacket by Eton boys (and others); also, a similar collar as part of a woman's dress or jacket. Also *ellipt.*
1887 *Army & Navy Stores Catal.* 1095 Boys' Collars and Cuffs. The Eton. **1895** *Ibid.* 1160 Boys' front with Eton collar. **1925** *Queen* 22 Apr. 11 Its prim Eton collar, its daintiness of finish with its jabot and cuffs of pleated lawn. **1955** C. S. LEWIS *Magician's Nephew* i. 7 In those days, if you were a boy you had to wear a stiff Eton collar every day.
e. In the phrases ***Eton-and-Harrow***, ***Eton-and-Oxford***, used (chiefly *attrib.*) to designate a person who has been at Eton or Harrow, or Eton and Oxford, or the characteristic manner, speech, behaviour, etc., of such a person.
[**1824** SOUTHEY *Let.* 7 Oct. (1965) II. 268 He is an excellent scholar, thoroughly bred at Eton and at Oxford.] **1894** MRS. H. WARD *Marcella* I. II. iii. 271 The young Eton and Oxford athlete, just home for his Christmas vacation. **1915** J. BUCHAN *Thirty-nine Steps* i. 18 An elegant young man who talks Eton-and-Harrow English. **1931** WODEHOUSE *If I were You* iii. 38 He may be a bit Eton and Oxford, but he's working in your best interests. **1952** R. KNOX *Hidden Stream* xii. 110 It is possible to regard the Crusades as a kind of vast Eton-and-Harrow, in which both sides rallied to their respective ties by instinct, rather than by reasoned preference. **1962** 'A. GILBERT' *No Dust in Attic* xiv. 186 Every man for himself, none of the old Eton-and-Harrow spirit.
f. ***Eton crop***, a style of cutting women's hair close to the head all over. Hence ***Eton cropped*** ppl. adj.
1926 E. WALLACE *Square Emerald* 9 The masculinity of the powerful face was emphasized by the grey hair cut close in an Eton crop. **1927** A. MONKHOUSE *Alfred the Great* 248 Maud was a trim, competent schoolgirl, long-legged, Eton-cropped. **1930** *Punch* 29 Jan. 126/1 A young thing whose essential plainness is emphasised rather than concealed by an Eton crop. **1958** B. NICHOLS *Sweet & Twenties* 137 She is an..Eton-cropped..mannish young woman.

Etonian (iːˈtəʊnɪən), *sb.* [f. *Eton* + -IAN.] One educated at Eton College.
c **1770** GEORGE III in *Etoniana* v. 81 You were an Etonian. **1844** DISRAELI *Coningsby* I. xi, The Lord of the equipage.. as an old Etonian, placed in the hands of the Albanian his contribution.

Etonian (iːˈtəʊnɪən), *a.* [f. as the sb.] Of, pertaining to, or characteristic of Eton College.
1749 FIELDING *Tom Jones* V. XIII. i. 6 O Learning..in thy favourite Fields, where the..Thames washes thy Etonian Banks. **1841** LADY STANLEY *Let.* in N. Mitford *Ladies of Alderley* (1938) 11 Etonian ways have no charm for him. **1883** J. BRINSLEY-RICHARDS *Seven Yrs. at Eton* 321 It held a quart of beer, and the ceremony of drinking out of it constituted an initiation into the higher circle of Etonian swelldom. **1931** T. H. PEAR *Voice & Personality* 75 There is an Etonian voice, the soft cultured drawl.

‖**étourderie** (eturdəri). [Fr.] Thoughtlessness, carelessness, blundering.
1763 D. HUME *Let.* 24 Feb. in Boswell *London Jrnl.* (1950) 206 By this *étourderie*, to give it the lightest name, you were capable of making a quarrel between me and that irascible little man. **1814** JANE AUSTEN *Mansf. Park* III. xv. 276 Henry is blameless, and in spite of a moment's *etourderie* thinks of nobody but you. **1886** T. HARDY *Mayor Casterbr.* I. xxii. 279, I ought to endeavour to disperse the shade which my *étourderie* flung over my name, by asking you to carry out your promise to me. **1958** I. MURDOCH *Bell* vii. 101 His love affairs appeared as the *étourderies* of a much younger man.

‖**étourdi** (eturdi), *a.* Also (fem.) **étourdie.** [Fr.] Thoughtless, irresponsible, flighty. Also as *sb.*, a thoughtless irresponsible person.
1688 T. BROWN *Reasons of Mr. Bays* 11 The first that I begin with shall be that *etourdy bete*, that humble admirer of Jest and Quibble, the Melancholy Clergyman. **1750** CHESTERFIELD *Lett.* 26 Apr. (1774) II. 3 All those French young fellows are excessively *étourdis*, be upon your guard against scrapes and quarrels. **1794** in G. C. Paget *One-Leg* (1961) 45, I must begin this letter by owning that I am the greatest *Etourdi* that ever lived yet that I am always lucky enough to get well out of every Scrape. **1828** C. H. PHIPPS *English in France* II. 347 Had she but the animal spirits to be *étourdie*, she would be so. **1848** THACKERAY *Van. Fair* vi. 45 'I beg a thousand pardons..,' said the young *étourdi*, blushing. **1905** MRS. H. WARD *Marriage W. Ashe* ii. 29 What a little *étourdie*! How lacking in the reserves, the natural instincts and shrinkings of the well-bred English girl!

‖**et patati et patata** (e patatɪ e patata), *phr.* [Fr.] And so on and so forth; = ET CETERA I.
1904 M. BEERBOHM in *Sat. Rev.* 14 May 619/2 Vanity of actor-managers, intolerable attempts to stifle honest criticism, shall such things be? et patati, et patata. **1920** F. M. FORD *Let.* 19 Sept. (1965) 128 We have pulled this house to pieces a good deal and successfully—et patati et patata! **1929** R. ALDINGTON *Death of Hero* I. i. 38 'We have brought you up to be a God-fearing Christian man..' *et patata et patati.*

‖**étrenne** (etrɛn). [Fr., older *estreine*:—L. *strena*.] A New Year's gift; a Christmas box, gift.
1802 C. WILMOT *Let.* 3 Jan. in *Irish Peer* (1920) 31 A hundred whimsical little 'bon bons', I have been given by 'Monsieur et Madames' as 'Étrennes' or New Year's gifts. **1834** K. H. DIGBY *Mores Cath.* v. vii. 234 The faithful were forbidden to give etrennes. **1880** DISRAELI in Buckle *Life* (1920) VI. 505 Osborne has sent me, as an *étrenne* a most beautiful book. **1883** *Sat. Rev.* 24 Mar. 377/1 Mme. de Witt's magnificent volume belongs to the class of *étrennes*. **1928** *Observer* 29 Jan. 12/3 The concierges..demand..the abolition of their étrennes.

‖**étrier** (etrije). *Mountaineering.* Also etrier(s. [a. Fr. *étrier* stirrup.] A short rope ladder with two or three wooden or metal rungs (see quots.). Also *attrib.*
1955 J. E. B. WRIGHT *Technique Mountaineering* iv. 64 Etriers are rope steps usually of one or two rungs. *Ibid.* v. 82 *Etrier steps.* Etrier-stirrups are generally used in pairs and each consists of one to four light alloy rungs placed a foot or so apart and fastened to two short pieces of rope. The result is a short portable ladder which can be hung from pitons on rock or ice pitches. **1956** C. EVANS *On Climbing* iii. 53 Étriers ..are small two- or three-rung rope-ladders, clipped to pitons. **1970** *Daily Tel.* (Colour Suppl.) 27 Mar. 42/1 He had left his etriers (a little three-rung rope ladder) hooked on to a piton a few feet below.

Etrurian (iːˈtrʊərɪən), *a.* and *sb.* Also 7 **Hetrurian.** [f. *Etruria* + -AN.] **A.** *adj.* Of or belonging to Etruria. **B.** *sb.* A native of Etruria.
1623 COCKERAM III, *Decii*, the Sonne [vowed himself] against the Hetrurians. **1653** URQUHART *Rabelais* I. i, Hetrurian Letters. **1667** MILTON *P.L.* I. 303 In Vallombrosa, where th' Etrurian shades High overarch't imbowr. **1842** LYTTON *Zanoni* 23 As old as Greek or Etrurian fable.

Etruscan (iːˈtrʌskən), *a.* and *sb.* Also 8 **Hetruscan.** [f. L. *etrusc-us* + -AN.]
A. *adj.* **1.** Of or belonging to ancient Etruria or its people; *absol.* the language of the Etruscans (in quot. 1817 jocularly used for 'Tuscan').
1706 HEARNE *Collect.* 14 Dec. (Oxf. Hist. Soc.) I. 312 The Hetruscan inscription. **1773** MONBODDO *Lang.* (1774) I. III. xii. 580 The Latin and Hetruscan. **1817** BYRON *Beppo* xxxi, For few Italians speak the right Etruscan. **1882** OUIDA *Maremma* I. 17 His name was the old Etruscan name.
2. Designating encaustic pottery made by Josiah Wedgwood and his followers in imitation of ancient pottery discovered in Etruria. Also *ellipt.* as *sb.*, a vase of this kind.
1768 J. WEDGWOOD *Let.* 21 Nov. (1965) 69 Mr Cox is as mad as a march Hare for Etruscan Vases. **1769** *Ibid.* 6 Feb. 70 Three vases, one of them the large blue.., the other two Etruscans at a Guinea each. **1875** E. METEYARD *Wedgwood Handbk.* 264 The body used for the larger portion of the Etruscan painted vases was basaltes. **1957** MANKOWITZ & HAGGAR *Eng. Pottery & Porcelain* 233/2 The first day's production consisted of six Etruscan ware vases.
3. Designating a style of decorative bookbinding (see quots.).
1835 'J. A. ARNETT' *Bibliopegia* II. 98 *Etruscan.* This style is, where, instead of covering with gold, the book is ornamented with gothic or arabesque compartments, or imitations of Greek borders and Etruscan vases, in their proper colours. *Ibid.* 210 Etruscan style of binding. **1893** S. T. PRIDEAUX *Hist. Sketch Bkbinding* i. 134 John Whitaker initiated the style termed Etruscan, in which designs from the decoration of Etruscan vases were copied in colours. **1907** C. DAVENPORT *Book* viii. 201 Such books are known as 'Etruscan', because many of the designs are of classical feeling.
B. *sb.* One belonging to the Etruscan nation.
1841 W. SPALDING *Italy & It. Isl.* I. 44 The Etruscans, a separate race, whose origin is still quite uncertain.

Etruscology (iːtrʌˈskɒlədʒɪ). [f. L. *Etrusc(us* ETRUSCAN + -OLOGY.] The study of Etruscan history and antiquities. Hence **Etruˈscologist**, one versed in Etruscology.
1889 *Archæol. Rev.* III. 376 The melancholy career, not progress, of Etruscology during the last 150 years. *Ibid.* 377 Two other Etruscologists remain to be noticed. **1928** *Times* 7 June 12/3 The International Congress recently held at Florence demonstrated the great interest taken in the science of Etruscology. **1963** *Punch* 22 May 755/1 Etruscologists..have been overcome by gloomy feelings.. and..projected those feelings on to the Etruscans.

etslopen, -stand, -stent, -stunt: see AT-.

-ette, *suffix.* **1.** Forming diminutive sbs., represents OF. *-ette*, the fem. form corresponding to the masc. *-et*: see -ET[1]. In early Eng. use the Fr. *-et* and *-ette* (OF. *-ete*) were not clearly distinguished, and in 15th c. *-ette* is a mere variant spelling of *-et*; *e.g.* the OF. *basinet* occurs sometimes in Eng. as *basinette*. The older adoptions of Fr. words in *-ette*, so far as they survive, are now written with -ET[1]; the spelling *-ette* belongs chiefly to words introduced since 17th c., as *chemisette*, *cigarette*, *eprouvette*, *etiquette*, *pipette*, *serviette*. During the present century a few words have been formed by the addition of *-ette* to Eng. sbs.; most of these, as *leaderette*, *sermonette*, *essayette*, can scarcely be said to be in good use, though often met with in newspapers; *wagonette*, however, is well established. Formations of this kind are very common in the names given by manufacturers to materials intended as imitations of something else: one such word which has come into general use is *leatherette*.
1849 J. WILSON in *Blackw. Mag.* LXVI. 19 This side of the glen..is known to be a descent but by the pretty little cataractettes playing at leap-frog. **1887** *Mod. Newspaper*, Great sale of Brussellette carpets. Messrs. ——'s plushettes.
2. Used to denote a female, as in MAJORETTE, SUFFRAGETTE, USHERETTE.
1921 H. L. MENCKEN *Amer. Lang.* (ed. 2) vi. 187 The wide use of the suffix *-ette* in such terms as *farmerette*, *conductorette*,..*usherette* and *huskerette*, is due to the same effort to make one word do the work of two. **1939** *New Yorker* 11 Nov., The girls employed to annoy visitors to some kind of Chamber of Commerce festival in Southern California will be called welcomettes. **1942** in *Amer. Speech* (1943) XVIII. 147 Roosevelt Signs 'Sailorette' Bill... Usherette in the..movie theater... Chicago tries 'Copettes'. **1970** *Women Speaking* Apr. 5/2 Female teams are called Rockettes, Mercurettes, Atomettes.

ettercap (ˈɛtəkæp). *Sc.* Also 8 **ethercap.** [var. form of ATTERCOP.]
1. A spider; = ATTERCOP I.
2. *fig.* An ill-humoured person; = ATTERCOP 2.
1725 RAMSAY *Gentle Sheph.* IV. i, 'Tis dafter like to thole An ether-cap like him to blaw the coal! *c* **1750** A. ROBERTSON in Scott *Wav.* lxiv, A fiery etter-cap, a fractious chiel. **1820** *Blackw. Mag.* VIII. 15 That ettercap..is flying through the town like a shunky. **1840** *Fraser's Mag.* XXII. 478 A cool temper..I'm sure yon fiery ettercap has not.
Hence **ettercapped**, *ppl. a.*, inflicted by a spider.
1721 RAMSAY *Poems, To Gay* xii, Ye may smile at ethercopit stings With careless pride.

etterlin (ˈɛtəlɪn). In 9 **etterling.** 'A cow which has a calf when only two years old' (Jam.).
1863 *N. Brit. Daily Mail* 5 May, Among the live stock, some very fine etterlings brought over 12*l.* a head.

ettick, obs. form of HECTIC.

ettin, var. form of ETEN, *Obs.*, giant.

ettle ('ɛt(ə)l), *v.* Since 14th c. only *north. dial.* Forms: 3 atli-en, 3–5 atle, 3–4 *north.* (h)aght-, eghtel, -il, 4–5 attel(e, -y, attle, ettill(e, (4 aghli, ahtil, atyle, eitle, ettele, -elle, -ylle, 5 attel(l, atthill, ettil, 6 attile), 4–6 etle, (7 attill, 7–9 *dial.* eckle), 3– ettle. [a. ON. *ætla* (also *etla, atla*) to think, conjecture, purpose, destine, apportion:—prehistoric **ahtila*, **ehtla* (whence some of the ME. forms), f. OTeut. **ahtâ* (OE. *eaht*, OHG. *ahta*, mod.G. *acht*) consideration, attention, f. root of Goth. *aha* 'νοῦς', understanding, *ahma* soul. From the same nominal base without *-l-* suffix are OE. *eahtian*, OHG. *ahtôn* (mod.G. *achten*) to esteem, consider.]

I. To purpose (and senses derived from this).

1. *trans.* a. With *inf.* as obj. (usually preceded by *to*); To intend, purpose, plan; to make it one's object, to endeavour. (In most instances this may be taken as *intr.* with inf. of purpose; hence the vb. was occas. followed by *thereto* referring to an inf. in context.)

c **1200** *Trin. Coll. Hom.* 79 Wolde him seluen wreke gif he mihte and þerto ettleð and abit his time. *a* **1300** *Cursor M.* 16384 (Cott.) O yur king þat es in hand, quat aghtel yee do þan? **1340** HAMPOLE *Pr. Consc.* 5784 A doghter..þe whilk he luved specialy And eghtild to mak hir qwene of worshepe. *c* **1340** *Gaw. & Gr. Knt.* 27 An aunter in erde I attle to schawe. *c* **1375** *Sc. Leg. Saints, Magdalena* 279 þi husband eitlise þare-to..To helpe þe puyre of his riches. ?*a* **1400** *Morte Arth.* 520 Syr Arthure es thyne enmye fore ever, And ettelles to bee overlynge of þe empyre of Rome. *c* **1400** *Destr. Troy* 2965 Hit were..semly for wemen, þaire houses to haunt &..þere onesty attell to saue. *a* **1400–50** *Alexander* 15, I forwith 3ow all ettillis to schewe Of ane Emperoure. **1674** RAY *N.C. Words* 16 *Eckle* or *Ettle*, to aim, intend, design. **1808** J. MAYNE *Siller Gun* IV, To bell the cat wi' sic a scrow, Some swankies ettled. **1863** J. NICHOLSON *Poems, The Burnie*, So bent on the bauble we ettle aye to win, The best o' life's blessings we lee far behin'.

b. With *sb.* (or *pron.*) as obj.: To purpose, seek to bring about (a result).

1513 DOUGLAS *Æneis* XII. xiii. 14 Quhat purposis or etlis thou now? lat see. **1774** C. KEITH *Farmer's Ha'* 35 They wad think it a braw scheme..Mischief to ettle.

c. *refl.* To intend (= ON. *ætlask*).

?*a* **1400** *Morte Arth.* 554, Bee Estyre..I ettylle my selfene, To hostaye in Almayne. *a* **1400–50** *Alexander* 2829 (Dublin MS.) þou..ettlys þe [*Ashm. MS.* etils to] sir Alexander efte to assayle.

2. To destine, ordain, assign. Const. *dat.* of persons, *for, to*: also *simply*, and with complement or complemental inf.

a **1300** *Cursor M.* 9426 (Cott.) Qua herd euer spek o mare bliss, þan aghteld [*Trin.* ordeyned] was adam and his? *Ibid.* 21759 Godd þat haghtils ilkin stat. *c* **1400** *Destr. Troy* 394 She was eldist and heire etlit to his londes. *Ibid.* 6775 Pepull, þat by ordynaunse of Ector was etlit to hym. **1513** DOUGLAS *Æneis* I. i. 30 This Goddes etlit..This realme to be.. mastres To all landis. **1818** SCOTT *Rob Roy* xxxiv, 'He drees the doom he ettled for me'. **1832–53** A. LAING in *Whistle-binkie* (Sc. Songs) Ser. III. 29 I'll bless the doom I hae to dree That ettled her, my Highland maid, To dwell in Borristoun wi' me!

3. To direct (speech or actions) to an object; *esp.* to aim (a blow or missile) *at* a person or a mark (also *fig.*); *absol.* or *intr.* to take aim (*at*).

c **1400** *Destr. Troy* 6399 He auntrid vpon Ector, atlit hym a dynt. *a* **1400–50** *Alexander* 2322 To all you of atthenys þus atthill I my sawes. *c* **1470** HENRY *Wallace* VIII. 269 Bot Wallace..Folowed on him, and a straik etlyt fast. *a* **1500** *Eger & Grine* 992 in Furniv. *Percy Folio* I. 385 Grine.. attilde him a dint that bote full well. **1513** DOUGLAS *Æneis* V. ix. 37 Mynestheus..Onto the heid has halit wp on hie, Baith arrow and ene etland at the merk. **1830** GALT *Lawrie T.* I. i. (1849) 3 To ettle at butts. **1862** HISLOP *Prov. Scot.* 7 Aft ettle, whiles hit.

fig. **1830** GALT *Lawrie T.* II. IV. xi. 90, I was persuaded he had something to ettle at me.

b. *intr.* To direct one's course.

c **1205** LAY. 25996 Hete we nu þene eotend bi-lafuen and atlien [*c* **1275** go we] to þan kinge. **1340–70** *Alex. & Dind.* 15 þat Alixandre wiþ his ost atlede þidire. *c* **1400** *Destr. Troy* 7424 Ector eftirsons ettlyt on Achilles. *Ibid.* 8989 Eneas afterward etlit anone. **1513** DOUGLAS *Æneis* IX. ix. 66 Quhayr thikkest was the pres thar etlis he. **1876** *Whitby Gloss.*, 'Ill ettle for yam', Ill turn my steps homeward.

c. To aim *at* (a thing); to make an effort *at*.

1725 RAMSAY *Gentle Sheph.* I. ii, When a they ettle at—their greatest wish Is to be made o' and obtain a kiss. **1820** SCOTT *Monast.* xvii, They that ettle at the top of a ladder will at least get up some rounds. **1873** F. K. ROBINSON in *Gloss. W. Riding Yorksh.* (E.D.S.) s.v. *Ettle*, I've been ettling after a new place.

4. To arrange, set in order, range; to prepare.

a **1310** in Wright *Lyric P.* ix. 35 Hire teht aren..Evene set ant atled al. *c* **1400** *Destr. Troy* 2376 Arowes and other geire atled I anon.

b. *refl.* To prepare oneself. Cf. 1 c.

a **1400–50** *Alexander* 1157 þan etils him sir Alexander. **1515** *Scot. Field* 180 Our english men ful merrilye attilde them to shoote. *Ibid.* 318 Soe eagerly with Ire attilld them to meete.

II. 5. *trans.* To guess, conjecture, divine. Also *absol.*

c **1205–75** [cf. ETTLING *vbl. sb.*]. *c* **1350** *Will. Palerne* 813 Alisaundrine anon atteled þat time, & knewe wel bi hire craft. *Ibid.* 941 Alysaundrine anon attlede alle here þou3tes.

Hence **'ettlement**, intention. **'ettler**, a schemer, an aspirant.

1787 GROSE *Provinc. Gloss.*, *Ettlement*, intention. **1825–79** JAMIESON, *Ettlement*, intention. **1823** GALT *R. Gilhaize* II. xxx, His father, through all the time of the first king Charles, an eydent ettler for preferment.

ettle ('ɛt(ə)l), *sb.*[1] [f. ETTLE *v.*]

1. Aim, intent, purpose.

1790 BURNS *Tam o' Shanter* 213 Nannie..flew at Tam wi' furious ettle. **1832–53** *Whistle-Binkie* (Sc. Songs) Ser. II. 51 Ill tarry nane to tell..The ettle o' my eeran.

2. Chance, opportunity.

1768 ROSS *Helenore* III. But fainness to be hame, that burnt my breast, Made me to tak the ettle when it keest.

'ettle, *sb.*[2] Dial. form of NETTLE; cf. *adder* for *nadder*, etc.

1688 *Churchw. Acc. Minchinghampt.* in *Archæol.* XXXV. 451 For cutting of ettles. **1842** AKERMAN *Wiltsh. Gloss.*, *Ettle*, a nettle. **1884** *Upton-on-Severn Gloss.*, *Ettles*, nettles.

'ettling ('ɛtlɪŋ), *vbl. sb. Obs.* exc. *north.* [f. ETTLE *v.* + -ING[1].] The action of the vb. ETTLE.

1. Intention, purpose; also, endeavour.

c **1325** *E.E. Allit. P.* B. 688, & alle myne atlyng to Abraham vn-haspe bylyue. **1375** BARBOUR *Bruce* I. 587 Off hys etlyng rycht swa It fell, As I sall eftirwartis tell. *c* **1375** *Sc. Leg. Saints, Magdalena* 564, & sowne þai arywinge mad In þe porte quhare þai etline had. *c* **1470** HENRY *Wallace* x. 166 For charge off nan, bot it had ben his king At mycht that tym bryng him fra his etlyng. **1822** GALT *Steam-Boat* 125 (Jam.) But there was an ettling beyond discretion perhaps in this.

†2. Conjecture, estimation. *wiðuten eni etlunge* (early ME.): without any guessing, unquestionably. *Obs.*

c **1205** LAY. 25761 Bi atlinge [*c* **1275** hatling] heom þuhte þritti uoðere. *c* **1230** *Hali Meid.* 39 Muche mare he haueð wiðuten eni etlunge at halden to him seluen. *a* **1240** *Sawles Warde* in *Cott. Hom.* 263 Wið uten ei etlunge þen of his ahne gleadunge.

†3. Preparation. *Obs.*

1340–70 *Alisaunder* 266 Redy too fight With atling of are-blast & archers ryfe.

†**ettouch**, *v. Obs.* [? ad. OF. *estachier, etachier* (with assimilation to TOUCH).] *trans.* To attach, fasten, fix.

1483 CAXTON *Gold. Leg.* 17/1 Chirographe or oblygacion the which Jhesu Cryst bare and ettouchyd it to the crosse.

‖**étude** (etyd). *Mus.* [Fr.] = STUDY *sb.* 11.

1837 J. A. HAMILTON *Dict. Mus. Terms* (ed. 4) 31 *Etude* (French), a study. **1855** CHOPIN (*title*) Grand Study, extracted from the 24 Etudes for the Pianoforte. **1882** *Pall Mall Gaz.* 22 Dec. 20/1 A fantasia on opera airs or an impromptu or an étude. **1947** A. EINSTEIN *Mus. in Romantic Era* xv. 223 Alkan..wrote..an étude 'The Railroad'. **1962** A. HARMAN et al. *Man & his Music* 810 The justly celebrated melody of the E major Etude..has the external features of Bellinian *bel canto*, while being unmistakably Chopin in that its rise and fall reflects the sensuously fluctuating tensions of the harmony.

etui, etwee (ɛ'twiː). Forms: 7 estuife, estwefe, ettuy, ettwee, *pl.* etweese, 8 etuis, etuy, 7– etwee, 8– etui. [a. Fr. *étui*, OF. *estui* = Pr. *estui, estug* (med.L. *estugium*, 1231, Du Cange), according to M. Paul Meyer a vbl. sb. f. F. *estuier*, Pr. *estuiar, estugar* (:—late L. type **stugāre*) to keep, guard, hold in custody. (The Pr. form is inconsistent with the commonly assumed identity with the synonymous Sp. *estuche*, It. *astuccio*.) Cf. TWEEZE *sb.*

In the forms *estuife, estwefe* in Florio the *f* may be a misprint for *s*; if not, these forms suggest some sort of association with *huswife* subsequently used in the same sense.]

A small case, usually ornamental, for small articles, as bodkins, needles, toothpicks, etc.; formerly also a case for surgical instruments.

1611 FLORIO, *Astuccio*, an estuife, a pocket cace or little sheath with cizers, bodkin, penknife..in it. —— *Stucchio*, an estwefe, etc. **1611** COTGR., *Estui*, an Ettwee. —— *Pennarol de Chirurgien*, a Chirurgians Case or Ettuy; the box wherein he carries his Instruments. **1657** R. LIGON *Barbadoes* (1673) 27 Our Knives, Etweese, Keys, Needles. **1710** STEELE *Tatler* No. 245 ¶2 Gold Etuys for Quills, Scissars, Needles, Thimbles. *a* **1763** SHENSTONE *Wks.* (1764) I. 299 The gold etwee, With all its bright inhabitants, shall waste Its melting stores. **1771** SMOLLETT *Humph. Cl.* II. 10 June, He presented..me with a gold etuis. **1811** PINKERTON *Petral.* II. 112 It is used..in making boxes, socles, handles of knives, etuis, etc. **1859** THACKERAY *Virgin.* xlii, The pearl necklace and the gold etwee. **1883** *Fisheries Exhib. Catal.* 78 Travelling Bags, Razor Cases, Etuis, etc.

attrib. **1828** WEBSTER s.v. *Etwee-case*, a case for pocket instruments.

-etum ('iːtəm), *suffix*, from Latin *-ētum*, neut. of *-ētus, -tus* (see -ED[2]), is appended to names of trees or other plants, (*a*) to designate a collection or plantation of various species of a single genus or group of plants, as in L. *arboretum* and *pinetum* (see ARBORETUM, PINETUM); (*b*) in *Ecology*, to designate an association dominated by the species or genus named, as in *characetum, ericetum, salicornietum*.

1688 EVELYN *Diary* 28 Mar. (1955) IV. 576 We went to Kew, to Visite Sir Hen: Capels, whose Orangerie & Myrtetum, are most beautifull. **1905** F. E. CLEMENTS *Res. Methods Ecology* iv. 299 The suffix -etum is used to designate a consocies of a formation, e.g. *Picetum, Caricetum*, etc. **1939** *Geogr. Jrnl.* XCIII. 403 The termination -etum in ecological studies denotes an association. The suffix is added to the root of the name of the dominant species. **1964** V. J. CHAPMAN *Coastal Veg.* i. 11 It is convenient to recognize such communities [*sc.* associations] by use of the termination -etum. Thus for a community dominated by species of *Salicornia* one refers to the Salicornietum.

'etym. *rare.* = ETYMON.

1847 H. F. TALBOT *Eng. Etymologies* 470, *Thing.* I have already given an etym of this word.

etymic (ɛ'tɪmɪk), *a.* [f. ETYM-ON + -IC.] Of or pertaining to the etymon or primitive form of a word.

In some mod. Dicts.

ety'mography. *nonce-wd.* [f. Gr. ἔτυμο-ς true (see ETYMON) + -γραφια writing; after *etymology*.] Historical accuracy of spelling.

1886 F. HARRISON in *19th Cent.* Jan. 103 It is as vain to ask us, in the name of etymography, to turn that name [Shakespeare] into Shakspere, as it would be to ask us, in the name of etymology, to turn 'Tragedy' into Goat-song.

†**e'tymologe**, *v. Obs. rare.* [ad. Gr. ἐτυμολογ-έειν, f. ἐτυμολόγ-ος etymologer, f. ἔτυμον ETYMON + -λογος one who discourses.]

trans. a. To give an etymological signification to. b. To trace the etymology of; to derive.

1586 FERNE *Blaz. Gentrie* 50 Which word [Musicke].. hath been etymologed for the signification of the studies of humanitie and chiefly of poetry. **1611** SPEED *Hist. Gt. Brit.* VII. ii. (1632) 198 Whose originall Name..some will have Etymologed from *Saxum* a Stone.

etymologer (ɛtɪ'mɒlədʒə(r)). [f. Gr. ἐτυμολόγ-ος (see prec.) + -ER[1].] One who traces etymologies; = ETYMOLOGIST.

1650 MASSEY *Glasse for Worldlings* 10 With the Etymologer tis..water hardened by extream cold. **1660** M. GRIFFITH *Fear of God & King* 82 (T.) '*Lex à ligando*', saith the etymologer: it is called a law from binding. **1816** J. GILCHRIST *Philos. Etym.* 160 A plain, blunt etymologer may take the liberty of putting the extinguisher or monk's hood on his shallow, misty notions. **1880** J. A. H. MURRAY *Addr. Philol. Soc.* 36 The fancies of..monkish etymologers.

etymologic (ˌɛtɪməʊ'lɒdʒɪk), *a.* [ad. L. *etymologic-us*, a. Gr. ἐτυμολογικ-ός, f. ἐτυμολογία ETYMOLOGY.] = next.

1813 W. TAYLOR *Eng. Synonyms* (1856) Introd. xix, I have habitually endeavoured, by etymologic investigation, to ascertain of every analyzed word the primary sense. **1886** *Athenæum* 7 Aug. 165/1 Without help from etymologic or other record we may safely go back ages further. [In mod. Dicts.]

etymological (ˌɛtɪməʊ'lɒdʒɪkəl), *a.* [f. as prec. + -AL[1].] Of, or pertaining to, etymology; based upon, or in accordance with, etymology.

1592 tr. *Junius on Rev.* ix. 11 This name belongeth unto the Etymological interpretation of Hildebrand. **1612** DRAYTON *Poly-olb.* i. Notes 20 Take largest etymologicall liberty and you may have it from ' Ellan-ban i.e. the white Isle'. *c* **1620** A. HUME *Brit. Tongue* (1865) 11 It wer more etymological to wryt montan, fontan, according to the original. **1688** R. HOLME *Armoury* II. 9/2 Peruse, for a farther Description..Francis Holyoke, his Etymological Dictionary. **1747** JOHNSON *Plan Dict.* Wks. IX. 183 Its [arrive's] original and etymological sense. **1769** in Grant *Burgh Sch. Scotl.* II. xiii. (1876) 355 The Etymological part of the rudiments of the Latin grammar. **1824** L. MURRAY *Eng. Gram.* (ed. 5) I. 331 Specimens of etymological Parsing. **1865** MAX MÜLLER *Chips* (1880) I. vi. 130 A meaning that..can..be defended on..etymological grounds.

b. *nonce-use.* Engaged in the study of etymology.

1856 R. A. VAUGHAN *Mystics* (1860) I. 15 So, we are to be etymological to night, exclaimed Gower.

etymologically (ˌɛtɪməʊ'lɒdʒɪkəlɪ). *adv.* [f. prec. + -LY[2].] In an etymological manner; according to or as regards etymology; on etymological principles.

1730–6 in BAILEY (folio), *Etymologically*, by way of etymology. **1798** W. TAYLOR in Robberds *Mem.* I. 229, I try ..to use no words of which I cannot etymologically defend the application. **1809** SYD. SMITH *Wks.* (1859) I. 169/1 Latin and Greek have now mixed themselves etymologically with all the languages of modern Europe. **1860** PUSEY *Min. Proph.* 522 The Devil, etymologically, the accuser. **1878** FOSTER *Phys.* III. i. 390 Such a use of the word is.. etymologically incorrect. **1883** SIR J. C. DAY in *Law Rep. Q. Bench* XII. 206 Etymologically considered, a journeyman is one who is employed by the day.

‖**etymologicon** (ˌɛtɪməʊ'lɒdʒɪkən). [mod.L., a. Gr. ἐτυμολογικόν, neut. of ἐτυμολογικός: see ETYMOLOGIC.] A work in which the etymologies of words are traced; an etymological dictionary.

1645 MILTON *Tetrach.* (1851) 238 They who are so exact for the letter, shall be dealt with by the Lexicon, and the Etymologicon too if they please. **1753** in CHAMBERS *Cycl. Supp.* **1862** MARSH *Eng. Lang.* iii. 49 No English dictionary at all fulfils the requisites either of a truly scientific or of a popular etymologicon.

etymologist (ɛtɪ'mɒlədʒɪst). [f. ETYMOLOGY + -IST.] One who treats of, or is versed in, the

science of etymology; one who searches into the history and origin of words.

1635 N. CARPENTER *Geog. Del.* II. xiii. 216 The Greeke Etymologists ridiculously draw it from many other originalls. **1679** PLOT *Staffordsh.* (1686) 240 This I take but for the imagination of some fond Etymologist. **1747** JOHNSON *Plan Dict.* Wks. IX. 177 In exhibiting the descent of our language, our etymologists seem to have been too lavish of their learning. **1774** WARTON *Hist. Eng. Poetry* xx. (1840) II. 268 Chaucer, Gower, and Occleve..are supposed by the severer etymologists, to have corrupted the purity of the English language. **1841–4** EMERSON *Ess., Poet* Wks. (Bohn) I. 162 The etymologist finds the deadest word to have been once a brilliant picture. **1879** FROUDE *Cæsar* iv. 38 Etymologists could arrive at no conclusion as to the origin of the name.

etymologi'zation. *rare.* [f. next + -ATION.] The action of etymologizing.

a **1831** BENTHAM *Logic* Wks. 1838–43 VIII. 245 By etymologization I..mean..the exposition of inflected words and conjugates by the exhibition of the root from which they are derived.

etymologize (ɛtɪ'mɒlədʒaɪz), *v.* Also 6 **ethimologise,** 7 **æ-, etimologise, -ize,** 9 **etymologise.** [ad. late L. *etymologizāre* (spelt *ethimologisare*), f. *etymologia* ETYMOLOGY: see -IZE and cf. Fr. *étymologiser*.]

1. *trans.* To give the etymology or derivation of; to trace the etymology of; to invent or suggest an etymology for.

c **1530** *Remedie of Love* 301 (T.), The first parte of this name we have yfounde, Let us ethimologise the secounde. **1599** B. JONSON *Cynthia's Rev.* IV. i, *Pha.* Breeches, *quasi* Beare-riches; when a gallant beares all his Ritches in his Breeches. *Amo.* Most fortunately etymologized. *c* **1645** HOWELL *Lett.* II. lxxxvii. (1753) 464 Langûedoc..Scaliger would etymologize from *'langue d'ouy'*. **1726** AMHERST *Terræ Fil.* App. 325 Having started the conceit of an undergraduate's being like an apprentice, (which you etymologize in a very accurate manner). **1816** KEATINGE *Trav.* I. 117 Even the word *merino* is not altogether etymologized. **1862** F. HALL *Hindu Philos. Syst.* 191 With this in view, the first portion of *Brahma* is etymologized as follows. **1871** TYLOR *Prim. Cult.* I. 147 The habit of etymologizing words off-hand from expressive sounds.

†**b.** To denote etymologically. *Obs. rare.*

1634 SIR T. HERBERT *Trav.* 12 And indeed the Analogie of the word induces me to imagine, some adventrous Cambrian first arrived here, memorizing it by this name *Pengwin* in the British Tongue, Etymologizing so much. **1661** MORGAN *Sph. Gentry* I. 45 The field is argent, a Mullet sable, by the name of Aston, as if it did Etymologize a stone.

2. *intr.* To study etymology; to search into the origin of words; to invent or suggest etymologies for words.

1652 GAULE *Magastrom.* 145, I rejoyce not much in etimologizing. **1816** J. GILCHRIST *Philos. Etym.* 83 It would not be proper to etymologise too much or too minutely on some words. **1851** TRENCH *Study of Words* vii. (1869) 266 How perilous it is to etymologize at random. **1877** PEILE *Primer Philol.* i. 16 We etymologise as if each man were a standard to himself.

Hence **ety'mologizing** *vbl. sb.* and *ppl. a.*

1771 *Antiq. Sarisb.* 5 A rational employment..is etymologizing. **1880** S. R. DRIVER *Hebrew Tenses* App. iii. 251 Reckless etymologizing is to be avoided. **1882** *Athenæum* 23 Dec. 844/1 Man is, as Mr. Palmer says, an etymologizing animal, and abhors an unmeaning word.

etymology (ɛtɪ'mɒlədʒɪ). Forms: [4 with Latin termination **ethimolegia**], 5–6 **ethi-, ethymologie, -y(e,** (5 **ethimilogie**), 6–7 **ætym-, etim-, etymologie, -y(e,** 6– **etymology.** [a. OF. *ethimologie*, mod.F. *etymologie*, ad. L. *etymologia*, a. Gr. ἐτυμολογία, f. ἐτυμολόγ-ος: see ETYMOLOGE.]

1. a. The process of tracing out and describing the elements of a word with their modifications of form and sense.

1588 FRAUNCE *Lawiers Log.* I. xii. 51 Notation or Etymologie is the interpretation of the word. **1725** WATTS *Logic* I. iv. §1 This tracing of a word to its original, (which is called etymology), is sometimes a very precarious..thing. **1786** H. TOOKE *Purley* (1798) I. ix. 456 The explanation and etymology of those words..require a degree of knowledge in all the antient northern languages.

¶ With explanation drawn from the Gr. derivation. (Cf. L. *veriloquium*, by which Cicero renders the Gr. word.)

1613 R. C. *Table Alph.* (ed. 3), *Etymologie*, true expounding. **1681** tr. *Willis' Rem. Med. Wks.* Voc., *Etymology*, the true exposition or interpretation of a thing.

b. An instance of this process; an account of the formation and radical signification of a word.

1460 CAPGRAVE *Chron.* 34 As Ysider tellith in the third book of Ethimilogies. **1575** TURBERV. *Falconrie* 204 So that the etymologie of the name proceedeth all upon one cause. **1611** SPEED *Hist. Gt. Brit.* v. ii. 8 Neither let this Etymologie of Britaines seeme to be either harsh or absurd, seeing the very words sound alike, etc. **1665** BOYLE *Occas. Refl.* v. i. (1675) 296 Critical Inquiries into Obsolete Rites, or Disputable Etymologies. **1755** JOHNSON *Pref. Dict.* Wks. IX. 201 For the Teutonick etymologies, I am commonly indebted to Junius and Skinner. **1845** STODDART in *Encycl. Metrop.* (1847) I. 166/1 A little investigation will show this etymology [of *since*] to be entirely erroneous.

c. The facts relating to the formation or derivation (of a word). (In 16–17th c. occur confused expressions such as 'the etymology comes from,' 'to derive the etymology from'.)

[**1398** TREVISA *Barth. De P.R.* III. ii. (1495) 50 What is the menynge of the Ethimolegia and the settyng of this name?] **1447** BOKENHAM *Seyntys* (Roxb.) 46 Yf we them dewly kun applye And ordenelly aftyr the ethimologye. **1581** MARBECK *Bk. of Notes* 276 Dagon..as maie be iudged by the Etimologie of the word, was some God of the Sea. For *Dag* in Hebrue signifieth a fish. **1583** FULKE *Defence* (1843) 267 The etymology of this English word 'priest' cometh from presbyter. **1631** WEEVER *Anc. Fun. Mon.* 683 Heralt..is meerely a Teutonic or Duytch word, and in that tongue and no other, the true Ætymologie thereof is onely to be found. **1651** HOWELL *Venice* 34 Som derive the Etimologie of this rare Cittie from Venetia, which is old Latin signifieth the frothing or seething of the Sea. **1666** G. HARVEY *Morb. Angl.* (J.), Consumption is generally taken for any universal diminution and colliquation of the body, which acceptation its etymology implies. **1725** WATTS *Logic* I. iv. §1 If the meaning of a word could be learned by its derivation or etymology, yet, etc. **1865** MAX MÜLLER *Chips* (1880) II. xxv. 260 The etymology of a word can never give us its definition.

transf. **1864** KIRK *Chas. Bold* I. ii. 48 Those distinctions of origin, habits, dialect, and history which constitute what may be termed the etymology of the nation.

†**d.** Etymological sense, original meaning. *Obs.*

a **1592** GREENE *Jas. IV*, I. ii, *Ateu.* What's thy name? *Nano.* Nano. *Ateu.* The etymology of which word is a dwarf. **1631** BRATHWAIT *Eng. Gentlew.* (1641) 332 This name [widowes]..hath received one constant Etymology; 'deprived' or 'destitute'. **1711–14** ADDISON *Spect.* (J.), Pelvis is used by comick writers for a looking-glass, by which means the etymology of the word is visible.

2. That branch of linguistic science which is concerned with determining the origin of words.

1646 SIR T. BROWNE *Pseud. Ep.* II. vi. 93 Others have better observed the laws of Etymology, and deduced it from a word of the same language. **1797** GODWIN *Enquirer* I. vi. 44 The science of etymology has been earnestly recommended. **1862** MARSH *Eng. Lang.* iii. 48 Etymology, is the study of the primitive, derivative, and figurative forms and meanings of words. **1864** MAX MÜLLER *Sc. Lang.* Ser. II. vi. (1868) 242 As long as etymology was carried on on such principles it could not claim the name of a science.

3. *Gram.* That part of grammar which treats of individual words, the parts of speech separately, their formation and inflexions.

1592 WEST *Symbol.* §100 The rules of Grammar, touching eyther the Ætymologie or Syntaxis thereof. **1612** BRINSLEY *Lud. Lit.* ix. (1627) 127 For the Etymologie, all the difficulty is in these three parts of Speech, Nownes, Verbs, and Participles. **1669** MILTON *Accedence* Wks. (1847) 457/1 Etymology, or right wording, teacheth what belongs to every single word or part of speech. **1748** HARTLEY *Observ. Man* I. iii. 304 Etymology and Syntax, as Grammarians call them. **1824** L. MURRAY *Eng. Gram.* (ed. 5) I. 60 The second part of grammar is etymology.

‖**etymon** ('ɛtɪmən). [L. *etymon*, a. Gr. ἔτυμον (orig. neut. of ἔτυμος true): (1) the 'true' literal sense of a word according to its origin; (2) its 'true' or original form; (3) hence, in post-classical grammatical writings, the root or primary word from which a derivative is formed.

According to Brugmann, ἔτυμος is for a prehistoric **s-etumo-s*, f. *'s* weak grade of OAryan **es* to be + suffixes.]

†**1.** The primitive form of a word; the word or combination of words from which it has been corrupted. Sometimes nearly = ETYMOLOGY 1 b, 1 c.

1570–6 LAMBARDE *Peramb. Kent* (1826) 477 Thus much then concerning the Etymon of this woorde Gavelkinde. **1606** PEACHAM *Graphice* (1612) 83 Blew hath his Etymon from the high Dutch Blaw. **1651** H. MORE *Second Lash* in *Enthus. Triumph* (1656) 227 For the word must so signifie, as I did above prove, both from Testimony, and might also from the Etymon of the word. **1678** CUDWORTH *Intell. Syst.* 451 The true Etymon of Jupiter..being..not Juvans Pater, but Jovis Pater. **1768** SWINTON in *Phil. Trans.* LVIII. 239 The etymon laid down here seems more apposite and natural than that obtruded upon the learned world by Bochart. **1793** PINKERTON in D'Israeli *Cur. Lit.* (1866) 129/2 Of the etymon of pamphlet I know nothing.

2. The primary word which gives rise to a derivative.

1659 T. PECKE *Parnassi Puerp.* 58, *Nummus* denotes Money told out; Upon This Fancy, Number, will give Etymon. **1811** PINKERTON *Petral.* I. 429 Greek etymons have become universal in the science. *a* **1834** LAMB *Lett. to Manning* v. 48 Logic is nothing more than a knowledge of words, as the Greek etymon implies. **1873** WHITNEY *Orient. Stud.* 210 Enabling them [the roots] to stand as etymons of almost any given word. **1882** *Edin. Rev.* July 114 The name has an evidently Norman etymon.

†**3.** Original or primary signification. *Obs. rare.*

1619 *Sacrilege Handl.* App. 43 Take him in his true Etymon, and Morall will be, but, whatsoeuer concerneth Manners. **1626** W. SCLATER *Exp. 2 Thess.* (1629) 223 Ἄτακτοι, those are to them after the Grammer Etymon, men of no setled abode; vaguing, or vagabond Iewes. *a* **1634** R. CLERKE in Spurgeon *Treas. Dav.* Ps. cxxii. 6 Peace denominates Jerusalem, 'tis the etymon of the word. *a* **1834** COLERIDGE (Webster), The import here given as the etymon or genuine sense of the word.

†**4.** The true name of a thing. *Obs.*

1651 BIGGS *New Disp.* 67 ¶ 106 Neither dare they call their ..medicines by their proper Etymon; that is to say they hide Scammony under the name of *diagredium.*

Hence **ety'monic** *a. rare*$^{-1}$. Pertaining to the etymon; etymological.

1813 W. TAYLOR *Eng. Synonyms* (1856) 128 The application of the word anterior to time only is neither based on ancient practice nor etymonic necessity.

eu, obs. var. of YEW.

eu-, *prefix*, repr. Gr. εὐ-, combining form of ἐΰς good, used in neut. form εὖ as adv. = well. In Gr. the words with this as first element are primarily adjs. (often used as sbs., and in many instances giving rise to derivative sbs. or vbs.). Of these many are parasynthetic f. sbs., as εὔστομος having a good mouth, f. στόμ-α mouth, εὐσχήμων having a good form, f. σχῆμ-α form. In others the second element is a verbal root or a verbal adj. in -τος; the sense of the compound varies (often in the same word) between active and passive; in those that are active the prefix has the force of 'well'; in those of passive signification its sense is sometimes 'well', more commonly 'easily': thus, εὐλαβής 'taking good hold', 'easy to take hold of', f. λαβ- 'to take'; εὔπρᾱκτος 'doing well, prosperous', 'easy to do', f. πρᾱκ- (πρᾱ́σσειν) to do; εὐποίητος well made, f. ποιεῖν to make. In Eng. the prefix occurs almost exclusively in words of Gr. derivation, as *eulogy*, *euphemism*, or formed on Gr. elements, as *eucalyptus*; the few exceptions are terms of mod. scientific classification.

In late L. the *u* in this prefix when occurring before vowels was consonantized (i.e. became *v*), and in order to preserve the traditional quantity of the syllable the *ĕ* was made long, as in *ēvangelium*. The derivatives and cognates of *evangelium* are almost the only words current in Eng. with the *ev-* form of the prefix; in Fr. it is much more common, being used even in recent formations from Gr. elements.

eubacterium (ju:bæk'tɪərɪəm). *Bacteriol.* [mod.L. (A. Janke 1930, in *Zent. f. Bakt.* II Abt. LXXX. 490; A.-R. Prévot 1938, in *Ann. Inst. Pasteur* LX. 294), f. EU- + BACTERIUM.] A genus of bacteria of the order Eubacteriales, comprising Gram-positive anaerobic bacilli found in the intestines of vertebrates and in soil and water; formerly a subgenus (see quot. 1939).

1939 D. H. BERGEY et al. *Man. Determ. Bacteriol.* (ed. 5) 29 Janke..1930..proposes an outline which is slightly modified... Two new generic terms are used, *Anaerobacillus* and *Eubacterium*. *Ibid.* 30 Genus I. *Bacterium* Sub-genus..b. *Eubacterium*. **1946** [see BACTERIOLYTIC *a.*]. **1957** G. E. HUTCHINSON *Treat. Limnol.* I. xi. 715 In extreme cases, another iron eubacterium, *Ochrobium teetum* occurred at slightly lower levels.

eubages: see EUHAGES.

Euboic (ju:'bəʊɪk), *a.* [ad. L. *Euboïcus*, Gr. Εὐβοϊκός, f. Εὔβοια Eubœa, the island now called Negropont.] Belonging to Eubœa; *esp.* in ***Euboic talent***, a weight in use at the time of the Persian war. (Some authors write *Eubœan* in this as in other uses.)

1667 MILTON *P.L.* II. 546 And [Alcides] Lichas from the top of Oeta threw Into th' Euboic Sea. **1771** RAPER *Anc. Coins* in *Phil. Trans.* LXI. 486 The Euboïc Talent certainly came from Asia.

eubruche, var. of EAUBRUCHE, *Obs.*, adultery.

eucaine (ju:'keɪn). *Pharm.* [f. EU-, after COCAINE.] A synthetic compound, $C_{15}H_{21}NO_2$, used as a local anæsthetic.

1896 *Chemist & Druggist* XLVIII. 597 Eucaine is employed like cocaine as a hypodermic solution of the hydrochloride. **1897** *Jrnl. Chem. Soc.* LXXII. I. 499 Eucaine,..whose chloride is used in commerce as a substitute for cocaine. **1907** *Practitioner* Apr. 473 Under eucaine, combined with a very little general anaesthetic, the abdomen was quickly opened. **1950** T. LONGSTAFF *This my Voyage* vi. 117 A hypodermic injection of eucaine accomplished the magic.

eucairite (ju:'kɛəraɪt, ju:'kaɪraɪt). *Min.* Also **eukairite.** [f. Gr. εὔκαιρ-ος well-timed, opportune (f. εὐ- EU- + καιρός time, season) + -ITE: see quot.] A mineral, consisting principally of selenium, copper, and silver.

1822 CLEAVELAND *Min.* 539 Eukairite..was discovered about the time Berzelius completed his examination of the new metal Selenium. **1844** DANA *Min.* 487 Eucairite.

eucalyn ('ju:kəlɪn). *Chem.* [f. EUCALY-PTUS + -(I)N.] 'A saccharine substance, produced in the fermentation of melitose (the sugar of the eucalyptus), under the influence of yeast' (Watts *Dict. Chem.*).

1864 H. SPENCER *Biol.* I. 11 Starch, sugar, eucalyn, sorbin [etc.], are polymeric. **1878** KINGZETT *Anim. Chem.* 404.

eucalypsinthe (ju:kə'lɪpsɪnθ). [f. EUCALYPTUS, after *absinthe*.] (See quot.)

1875 H. C. WOOD *Therap.* (1879) 88 Under the name of Eucalypsinthe, a liquor distilled from its leaves [those of *Eucalyptus globulus*] has appeared in European commerce.

'eucalypt. Anglicized form of EUCALYPTUS.

1877 F. VON MÜLLER *Botanic Teachings* i. 7 The vernacular name of Gum-trees for the Eucalypts. **1880** T. W. NUTT *Melbourne Palace Ind.* 11 Stems of the soaring Eucalypts that rise Four hundred friendly feet to glad blue skies. **1885** F. VON MÜLLER (*title*), Eucalyptographia: A Descriptive Atlas of the Eucalypts of Australia. **1893** D. C. MURRAY *Time's Revenges* vii, A forest of eucalypt closed in

the band. **1898** *Queens-land Year Bk.* 96 Great eucalypts spread their huge arms overhead. **1953** A. Upfield *Murder must Wait* xx. 179 Bark shed by the eucalypt instead of its leaves. **1970** *Daily Tel.* 10 Jan. 8/6 Dense forests of the ubiquitous eucalypt.

attrib. and *Comb.* **1956** *Nature* 3 Mar. 417/1 Sylvicultural research in Cyprus..on eucalypt forests. *a* **1963** J. Fountain in B. James *Austral. Short Stories* (1963) 268 A forest of spindly eucalypt-suckers pressing in darkly from either side. **1965** G. McInnes *Road to Gundagai* iii. 40 Lonely eucalypt-clad valleys. *Ibid.* x. 172 The eucalypt-scented darkness.

eucalyptian (juːkəˈlɪptɪən), *a.* (*sb.*) [See -ian.] Belonging to the genus *Eucalyptus*. Also as *sb.*, a tree of this genus. Also **euca'lyptic** *a.*

1870 A. L. Gordon *Bush Ballads* Ded. 8 The gnarl'd knotted trunks Eucalyptian. **1873** J. B. Stephens *Black Gin* 6 This eucalyptic cloisterdom. **1901** *Harper's Mag.* CII. 708/1 The huge, white-armed eucalyptians overhead.

‖**eucalyptus** (juːkəˈlɪptəs). Pl. -i, -uses. [mod.Lat., as if f. Gr. *εὐκάλυπτος, f. εὐ- (see eu-) + καλυπτός covered, f. καλύπ-τειν to cover. The name, first given by L'héritier in 1788, was intended to mean 'well-covered' (cf. the Ger. name *schönmütze*); the flower before it opens being protected by a sort of cap ('calyptra obverse hemisphærica', L'héritier).]

a. A genus of plants of the Nat. Order *Myrtaceæ*; the Gum-tree of Australia and the neighbouring islands; an individual tree of this kind.

1809 *Naval Chron.* XXII. 388 The Thelaleuca, Casuarina, Eucalyptus. **1823** Syd. Smith *Botany Bay* Wks. 1859 II. 22/1 A London thief..lodged under the bark of the dwarf eucalyptus, and keeping sheep..is not an uninteresting picture. **1875** H. C. Wood *Therap.* (1879) 89 Upon the lower mammalia the oil of Eucalyptus appears to act precisely as it does on man. **1879** *Temple Bar* Oct. 237 The sombre eucalypti..interspersed here and there by their dead companions.

attrib. **1875** Ure *Dict. Arts* II. 309 s.v., Gas extracted from eucalyptus leaves. **1884** *Syd. Soc. Lex.*, Eucalyptus oil.

b. Used *ellipt.* for *eucalyptus oil*, any of many essential oils distilled from the leaves of eucalypts and used medicinally and industrially.

1885 *Buck's Handbk. Med. Sci.* I. 262/2 Odor and expense serve to tell against eucalyptus preparations. **1895** *Lancet* 3 Aug. 268 The soap is pleasantly medicated with 'sanitas' and eucalyptus. **1970** J. Crossland *Lewis's Pharmacology* (ed. 4) xxviii. 832 Cough stimulants are many in number... They include tolu, menthol, eucalyptus, guaiacol, terpin hydrate, benzoin and oil of turpentine.

Hence are formed the names of various products; as, **euca'lyptene** [+ -ene]. **euca'lyptin** [+ -in]. **euca'lyptol** [+ -ol]. (See quots.)

1879 Watts *Dict. Chem.* VII. 2nd Suppl. 494 s.v., Eucalyptol heated with phosphoric anhydride gives up water, and yields *eucalyptene, $C^{12}H^{18}$. **1853** *Pharmac. Jrnl.* XIII. 79 Kino consists principally of a peculiar substance (*eucalyptin) analogous..to pectin. **1879** Watts *Dict. Chem.* VII. 2nd Suppl. 493 **Eucalyptol*, this compound is contained in large quantity in the volatile oil of *Eucalyptus globulus*. **1884** *Pall Mall G.* 28 July 12/2 Any preparation from which the slightest odour of eucalyptol is diffused.

Eucarist, obs. form of Eucharist.

eucaryon, etc.: varr. eukaryon, etc.

euch, obs. form of each.

eucharis (ˈjuːkərɪs). *Bot.* [a. Gr. εὔχαρις pleasing, f. εὐ- (see eu-) + χάρις grace.] A South American bulbous plant (N.O. *Amaryllidaceæ*) bearing white bell-shaped flowers, much in request for bouquets, etc. Also *attrib.*

1866 *Treas. Bot.* 473/1 s.v. **1882** *Garden* 7 Jan. 10/3, I have several large pots of Eucharis in and coming into flower. **1882** *Daily News* 30 Dec. 2/2 Beyond where the palms live, are eucharis, with their great starry flowers. **1884** *Pall Mall G.* 10 July 8/2 Each bridesmaid carried a bouquet of eucharis lilies and maidenhair ferns. **1885** *Athenæum* 24 Jan. 126/1 Dahlia and eucharis bulbs.

Eucharist (ˈjuːkərɪst). Forms: *α.* 5 **eukaryste**, 6 **eucarist**, **-chariste**, **euchrist**, 6– **eucharist**; *β.* 6 **eucharistie**, 8 **eucharisty**. [a. OF. *eucariste* (cf. mod.F. *eucharistie*), ad. late L. *eucharistia*, a. Gr. εὐχαριστία thanksgiving, hence the Lord's Supper, f. εὐχάριστος grateful, f. εὐ- (see eu-) + stem of χαρίζεσθαι to offer willingly. The *β* forms may either be ad. L. or a. mod.F.]

I. 1. *Eccl.* The sacrament of the Lord's Supper; the Communion.

a **1400** *Relig. Pieces fr. Thornton MS.* (1867) 37 Þe brede of eukaryste, þat es þe grace in þe sacrament of þe autere. **1509** Barclay *Shyp of Folys* (1570) 174 Eucharist..is the priestes seruice and busynes. *a* **1535** More *On the Passion* Wks. 1338/2 This blessed sacrament is also called Eucharistia. *a* **1600** Hooker (J.), Himself did better like of common bread to be used in the eucharist. *a* **1638** Mede *Wks.* I. li. 287 Our Sacrament of Peace is called the Eucharist. **1712** Sir G. Wheler *Liturgy after Model of Ancients* (MS.) 195 The importance of the Holy Eucharisty is so great that they did..give a general Scheme, how it shou'd be celebrated. **1786** W. Thomson *Watson's Philip III* (1839) 335 Sigismond..allowed them [the Hussites] the cup in the sacrament of the eucharist. **1845** S. Austin *Ranke's Hist. Ref.* I. 255 It was not denied that the efficacy of the Eucharist in both kinds was more complete.

2. The consecrated elements, *esp.* the bread. Phrases, ***to give, receive***, etc. ***the Eucharist***.

1536 Bellenden *Cron. Scot.* (1821) II. 401 Thay spulyeit the eucarist out of the cais of silver. **1579** Fulke *Heskins' Parl.* 82 A..priest sent to Serapion a little portion of the Eucharistie. **1644** Evelyn *Mem.* (1857) I. 103 The Emperor, Henry VII, who was..poisoned with the Holy Eucharist. **1660** R. Coke *Power & Subj.* 162 At no time a Priest is worthy to celebrate Mass, who hath not received the Eucharist. **1772** Priestley *Inst. Relig.* (1782) II. 352 Giving the eucharist to children was..finally abolished. **1861** Hook *Lives Abps.* I. vi. 323 The corporal presence of our Lord in the Eucharist. **1875** W. Smith *Dict. Chr. Antiq.* I. 625 Clement of Alexandria (*Strom* i. §5. p. 318) speaks of ministers distributing the eucharist (τὴν εὐχαριστίαν διανείμαντες) *i.e.* the elements, to the communicants.

†**3.** The box or closed vessel containing the consecrated bread; the pyx. *Obs.*

1535 Stewart *Cron. Scot.* III. 255 The siluer euchrist be ane cord..that hang..Tha pluckit doun. **1560** *St. Giles Charters* (1859) p. xlviii, Ane rownd eucharist, ane chalece, ane plate. *Ibid.* p. xlvii, The pece of gold that held the breid within the eucharist.

II. 4. Thanksgiving.

1613 R. C. *Table Alph.* (ed. 3), *Eucharist*, a thanksgiuing. **1644** Jer. Taylor *Apol. Liturgy* §38 For which ability they should do well to pay their eucharist to the Holy Ghost. **1691–8** Norris *Pract. Disc.* 225 The Second calls for our Praise and Eucharist. *a* **1716** South *Serm.* (1744) VII. 12 He ..is..led through a vale of tears to the region of eucharist and hallelujahs. **1879** Farrar *St. Paul* II. 80 Adding their Amen to the voice of Eucharist.

Eucharistial (juːkəˈrɪstɪəl). [f. L. *eucharisti-a* + -al[1].] A vessel intended to hold the bread consecrated for use at the Eucharist.

1844 Lingard *Anglo-Sax. Ch.* (1858) II. i. 35 The eucharistial, or 'new sepulchre of the body of Christ,' in which was reserved the eucharist under the form of bread. *Ibid.* II. 42 The rubric ordered that the housel..should be kept..under the kind of bread in a vessel called the eucharistial.

Eucharistic (juːkəˈrɪstɪk), *a.* and *sb.* [f. Eucharist + -ic; cf. Fr. *eucharistique*.]

A. *adj.*

1. Of or pertaining to the Eucharist.

1664 H. More *Myst. Iniq.* xiii. 42 The belief of the Eucharistick Bread being the real Body of Christ. *a* **1711** Ken *Psyche* Poet. Wks. 1721 IV. 242 Invites her to the Eucharistick Feast. **1847** Disraeli *Tancred* v. vi, The ceremony..eternally invested with eucharistic grace. **1869** Haddan *Apost. Succ.* viii. (1879) 232 Poison administered in the Eucharistic cup.

b. Of the nature of, or resembling, the Eucharist.

1860 Westcott *Introd. Study Gosp.* vi. (ed. 5) 335 In this connexion the eucharistic meal at Emmaus gains a new meaning. **1877** Sparrow *Serm.* xii. 161 The taking of food, if sanctified by religion, is eucharistic.

2. Of or pertaining to thanksgiving (occasionally with mixed notion of 1).

1678 Cudworth *Intell. Syst.* 401 He [Socrates] would have an Eucharistick Sacrifice offered to him [Æsculapius] in his behalf, as having now cured him at once of all diseases by Death. *a* **1711** Ken *Edmund* Poet. Wks. 1721 II. 372 They sang new Eucharistick Strains To glorious God. **1853** J. Brown in Spurgeon *Treas. Dav.* Ps. xviii. I. 280 It is a magnificent eucharistic ode. **1882** Farrar *Early Chr.* I. 443 *note*, The meat-offerings were eucharistic, and the sin-offerings expiatory.

†**B.** *sb.* = Eucharist 4. *Obs.*

1623 Cockeram, *Eucharisticke*, a giuing of thankes. **1709** Strype *Ann. Ref.* I. vii. 107 *marg.*, An eucharistic of the exiles to Jesus Christ.

Eucharistical (juːkəˈrɪstɪkəl), *a.* [f. as prec. + -ical.]

1. = Eucharistic A. 1.

1534 More *On the Passion* Wks. 1342/1 The eucharisticall bread vpon which thankes bee giuen. **1612** Brerewood *Lang. & Relig.* Pref. 7 The eucharistical elements are not naked and empty signs. **1686** Horneck *Crucif. Jesus* xviii. 521 The Deacon.. poured some drops of the Eucharistical wine into her mouth. **1725** tr. *Dupin's Eccl. Hist. 17th c.* I. v. 128 That after the Memory of the Passion is finish'd, this Eucharistical Body is not destroyed. **1799** V. Knox *Nat. Lord's Supper* Pref. (R.), Those who understand them of the eucharistical bread and wine. **1842** Manning *Serm.* (1848) I. xiv. 187 They..offered the eucharistical sacrifice in their upper chambers.

2. = Eucharistic A. 2.

1548 R. Hutten *Sum of Diuinitie* 66 b, Whiche be sacrifices Eucharisticall, or of prayse? **1558** Bp. Watson *Sev. Sacram.* xiii. 79 Then the priest begynneth the Eucharisticall sacryfyce of geuing thankes..before the consecration. *c* **1645** Howell *Lett.* (1650) II. 106 You should do well to intersperse among them som eucharisticall ejaculations. **1795** Mason *Ch. Mus.* ii. 123 The music..was originally set to a Eucharistical Hymn of Thanksgiving.

Hence **Eucha'ristically** *adv.*, in a Eucharistic manner.

1639 W. Sclater *2nd Worthy Commun. Rewarded* 46 No more is Christ offered up (save onely Eucharistically, and commemoratively). **1710** W. Hume *Sacred Success.* 260 They might find some way to communicate eucharistically.

Eucharistize (juːkəˈrɪstaɪz), *v.* [f. Eucharist + -ize; suggested by Gr. εὐχαριστεῖν.] *trans.* A rendering of Gr. εὐχαριστεῖν (classically only *intr.* to give thanks), as used for the nonce by Justin Martyr: To affect (the elements of the Lord's Supper) by an act of thanksgiving.

1714–7 J. Johnson *Unbloody Sacrif.* (1724) 198 Our Saviour blessed or Eucharistized the Bread and Wine. **1737** Waterland *Eucharist* (ed. 2) 134 Justin Martyr speaks of the Elements being Eucharistized or blessed by the Prayer of the Word. **1876** J. H. Blunt *Annot. Bk. Com. Prayer* (ed. 7) 174 The bread and wine..to be by Him eucharistized to the higher sphere and purpose of the new creation.

Hence **Eucha'ristized** *ppl. a.*, **Eucha'ristizing** *vbl. sb.*

1737 Waterland *Doct. Eucharist* v. 128 Justin Martyr.. calls the consecrated Elements by the Name of Eucharistized Food which looks as if he thought that the Thanksgiving was the Consecration: But yet, etc. **1714** Johnson *Unbloody Sacrif.* (1724) 198 The Blessing, or eucharistizing, terminates on the Bread.

Euchite (ˈjuːkaɪt). Also 7 **euchet**. [ad. late L. *euchīta*, *euchēta*, ad. Gr. εὐχίτης (misspelt εὐχήτης), f. εὐχή prayer.] One of a sect which arose in the fourth century, taking its name from a belief that perpetual prayer was the only means of salvation. The name was also applied to later sects holding similar views.

1585 Abp. Sandys *Serm.* (1841) 263 Give ourselves only to prayer. That is the error of the Euchites. **1621** J. Mayer *Eng. Catech.*, It [the Christian soule] will rather become an Euchet, by being continually lifted up in prayer. **1730–6** in Bailey (folio). **1882–3** Schaff *Encycl. Relig. Knowl.* II. 1478 Massalians, a Christian sect, which soon obtained other names,—Euchites.

†**eu'chlore**, *a.* *Obs.* [f. Gr. εὐ- (see eu-) + χλωρός green.] 'Of a distinct green colour; said of certain minerals'.

1847 in Craig; and in mod. Dicts.

†**eu'chloric**, *a.* *Obs.* [f. as next + -ic.] ***euchloric gas*** = euchlorine.

(The explanation in Craig and mod. Dicts. 'Having a distinct green colour' represents the meaning intended by Davy; but the adj. seems to occur only in this connexion.)

1811 *Edin. Rev.* XVIII. 480 The new compound..may be denominated from its peculiarly bright green, euchlorine or euchloric gas.

euchlorine (juːˈklɔərɪn). *Chem.* [f. Gr. εὐ- (see eu-) + χλωρός green + -ine. Formed by Davy on the analogy of chlorine, a word introduced by himself a few months earlier.] 'A gaseous mixture of chlorine and oxide of chlorine, obtained by the action of hydrochloric acid on chlorate of potassium' (Watts *Dict. Chem.*).

1812 Sir H. Davy *Chem. Philos.* 238, I discovered this elastic substance..in January 1811, and gave to it the name of Euchlorine [*note*, Ευ and χλωρος] from its bright yellow-green colour. **1823** Faraday *Exp. Res.* xxi. 92 Fluid euchlorine was obtained by enclosing chlorate of potash and sulphuric acid in a tube. **1873** Watts *Fownes' Chem.* 187 The euchlorine of Davy, prepared by gently heating potassium chlorate with dilute hydrochloric acid.

euchlorite (juːˈklɔəraɪt). *Min.* [f. Gr. εὐ- + χλωρός (cf. prec.) + -ite.] A variety of magnesia mica of a deep green colour, found at Chester (Mass.) in 1876.

1876 *Amer. Jrnl. Sc.* Ser. iii. XII. 231 Euchlorite. Massive, in coarse elongated scales. **1879** Watts *Dict. Chem.* VIII. 3rd Suppl. i. 762.

‖**euchologion** (juːkəʊˈləʊdʒɪɒn). Also 8 in Latin form **-um**. [ad. Gr. εὐχολόγιον prayer-book, f. εὐχή prayer + λογ- ablaut stem of λέγειν to say.] A collection of prayers; a prayer-book; also, a book of ritual, primarily that of the Greek Church.

1651 Jer. Taylor *Holy Dying* v. §7 (1680) 261 A Prayer taken out of the Euchologion of the Greek Church. **1751** Chambers *Cycl.* s.v., The *euchologium* is properly the Greek ritual. **1876** *Prayer-bk. Interleaved* 211 Forms by Basil and Chrysostom are given in the euchologion.

†**'euchologue.** *Obs.* [ad. Gr. εὐχολόγιον (see prec.), assimilated to *epilogue*, etc.] = prec.

1646 J. Gregory *Notes & Observ.* (1650) 169 This Recollection out of their own Euchologues. Pater noster qui es in Cœlis, etc. *Ibid.* 171 So the order in the Euchologue βαπτίζει αὐτὸν ὁ ἱερεύς. **1700** Sir H. Chauncy *Hist. Herts* 47 'Tis farther observ'd by the Euchologue of the Greek Church, that the Bishop having his formalities upon him fumeth the Groundwork or Foundation, with his Incense circular wise.

euchology (juːˈkɒlədʒɪ). Anglicized form of euchologion.

1659 Gauden *Tears Ch.* i. xii. 93 Fanatick Errour.. insinuating it self..in Prayers, Sacraments, and Euchologies. *a* **1710** Bp. G. Bull *Wks.* II. 556 He..took out of the ancient euchologies, or prayer-books of the Jews, what was good and laudable in them. **1735** Johnson tr. *Lobo's Voy. to Abyssinia* 369 Father Goar..has observ'd, in his Notes on the Euchology, etc. **1843** J. H. Newman *Miracles* 129 To introduce a prosaic phraseology into..the lessons of the Euchology.

Hence **eucho'logical** *a. rare*, of or pertaining to euchologies.

1844 Lingard *Anglo-Sax. Ch.* (1858) II. App. 414 The liturgical and euchological forms of her worship.

euchre (ˈjuːkə(r)), *sb.* Formerly also **uker**, **yuker**, **eucre**. [Of uncertain etymology.

As bower *sb.*[3], one of the terms used in this game, is of Ger. origin, it has often been supposed that the word *euchre* is also from German, but no probable source has been found in that lang. Can it be a Sp. *yuca*, in the phrase *ser yuca*, given by Caballero as an American expression for 'to be cock of the walk, to get the best in anything' (*ser el gallito en alguna cosa, sobresalir en algo*)?]

1. A game at cards, of American origin, played by 2, 3, or 4 persons, with a pack of 32 cards (the 2, 3, 4, 5, 6 of each suit being rejected). A player may, if he pleases, 'pass' or decline to play, but if he undertakes to play, and fails to take 3 tricks, he or his side is said to be 'euchred' and the other side gains two points.

The highest cards at Euchre are the knave of trumps and the other knave of the same colour (see BOWER *sb.*[3]); the other cards used rank as in whist. There are various modifications of the game, as ***Railroad Euchre***, played with the usual 32 cards and an extra blank card called 'the joker', or 'imperial trump', which is superior to all; ***French Euchre***, played with 24 cards; and others.

1846 in Smedes & Marshall *Rep. High Court App. Mississippi* (1847) 60 No matter whether defendants played at pool, whist, uker, poker, etc. *Ibid.*, Whist, yuker, brag, etc. **1850** (*title*), The game of Euchre, with its Laws. **1856** MAYNE REID *Quadroon* xlvii, The thing was impossible, as I had never played euchre. **1863** DICEY *Federal St.* II. 57 The men..played the mysterious game of 'euchre.' **1870** B. HARTE *Heathen Chinee* 21 We had a small game, And Ah Sin took a hand: It was euchre. The same he did not understand. **1872** MARK TWAIN *Roughing It* xxiii, At night, by the camp-fire, we played euchre and seven up, to strengthen the mind. **1889** *Pall Mall G.* 27 Feb. 3/2 Euchre was probably acclimatised on the Mississippi by the Canadian voyageurs, being a form of the French game of triomphe.

2. An instance of 'euchreing' or being 'euchred'.

1880 *Amer. Hoyle* 75 No. 1 deals, but..fearing a euchre, he turns down the trump.

Hence **'euchreist**, a player at euchre.

1861 W. H. RUSSELL in *Times* 10 July, The sentry tells his captain, who is an euchreist, that 'It's all right,' and resumes his seat and his cigar.

euchre ('juːkə(r)), *v.* [f. prec. sb.] *trans.* At euchre: To gain the advantage over (an adversary) by his failure to take three tricks: see the sb. Hence *transf.* to outwit, 'do', 'best'. Also, *to euchre* (a person) *out of* (a thing).

c **1866** B. HARTE *Tennessee's Partner* Wks. 1880 II. 141 'Euchred, old man!' said Tennessee smiling. **1880** in WEBSTER (Suppl.) **1887** *Concord* (N. Hamp.) *Monitor* 23 Mar., The stockholders..have been euchered out of their investments in Vermont railroads.

Euchrist, obs. form of EUCHARIST.

euchroite ('juːkrəʊaɪt). *Min.* [f. Gr. εὔχρο-ος well-coloured, f. εὐ- (see EU-) + χροά colour + -ITE.] A hydrous arsenate of copper of a bright emerald-green colour.

1825 W. HAIDINGER *Mohs' Min.* III. 94. **1835** SHEPARD *Min.* I. 189 Euchroite..was discovered at Libethen in Hungary.

euchromatic (juːkrəʊ'mætɪk), *a. Cytology.* [f. next + -IC.] Of chromosome material: staining normally throughout the nuclear cycle.

1936 *Biol. Abstr.* X. 1620/2 Chromosome I (X) is heterochromatic from the proximal end to almost the exact centre; from here to the distal end euchromatic. **1942, 1951** [see HETEROCHROMATIC *a.* 2]. **1968** H. HARRIS *Nucleus & Cytoplasm* iv. 75 It is probable that other highly condensed heterochromatic or heteropyknotic regions in interphase nuclei also synthesize very much less RNA than the euchromatic regions.

euchromatin (juː'krəʊmətɪn). *Cytology.* [a. G. *euchromatin* (E. Heitz 1928, in *Jahrb. f. wissenschaftliche Botanik* LXIX. 764), f. EU- + CHROMATIN.] Euchromatic chromosome material.

1932 *Biol. Abstr.* VI. 347/1 Chromosomes are composed of sections of heterochromatin and of euchromatin attached end to end. **1942** *Nature* 17 Jan. 67/1 In the euchromatin the regions between the chromomeres contain globulin-type proteins. **1951** [see HETEROCHROMATIN]. **1960** DARLINGTON & LA COUR *Handling of Chromosomes* (ed. 3) 67 Heterochromatin is a part of the chromosome which is out of step with the major bulk of the euchromatin. **1961** *Lancet* 26 Aug. 463/1 The synthesis of desoxyribose nucleic acid in heterochromatin and in euchromatin.

euchromocentre (juː'krəʊməsɛntə(r)). *Biol.* [a. F. *euchromocentre* (V. Grégoire 1931, in *Académie Royale de Belgique: Bulletins de la Classe des Sciences* 5th Ser. XVII. 1435), f. EU- + CHROMOCENTRE.] (See quot. 1968.)

1934 L. W. SHARP *Introd. Cytol.* (ed. 3) iii. 57 In many nuclei there are at certain stages one or more conspicuous masses of karyotin at several points in the reticulum. Of the many terms applied to these the most suitable seems to be *chromocenters*... In some cases it has been shown that they represent definite chromosomal regions which remain condensed and highly chromatic... These *euchromocenters* appear to correspond in part to the 'prochromosomes'. **1937** *Nature* 22 May 889/2 During prophase, in addition to the euchromocentres, the nucleolus and nuclear sap also stain faintly with Feulgen. **1968** R. RIEGER *Gloss. Genetics & Cytogenetics* 152 *Euchromocenter*, in interphase nuclei, a chromocenter which consists of the heterochromatic segments..located on both sides of the centromere.

euchromosome (juː'krəʊməsəʊm). *Biol.* [f. EU- + CHROMOSOME.] = AUTOSOME.

1914 C. E. MCCLUNG in *Jrnl. Morphology* XXV. 697 The word 'euchromosome' I shall employ to distinguish those without any marked peculiarities of form or behavior... 'Heterochromosome' might advantageously be used as an antonym. **1925** E. B. WILSON *Cell* (ed. 3) xi. 839 The autosomes or euchromosomes..include those [*sc.* chromosomes] of the more normal type.

†**eu'chymous**, *a. Obs.* [f. mod.L. *euchȳm-us*, (ad. Gr. εὔχυμος, f. Gr. εὐ- EU- + χυμ-ός CHYME) + -OUS.] Conducive to a healthy condition of the blood or other fluids of the body.

1651 BIGGS *New Disp.* 195 Whatsoever is pleasant to the tongue..nor very harsh to the stomack, that is cried up as euchymous, sound and wholesome.

So †**'euchymy** [ad. Gr. εὐχυμία]. *Obs.* A good state of the blood and other fluids of the body.

1678–96 in PHILLIPS. **1721–1800** in BAILEY. **1860** in MAYNE.

†**euchy'siderite.** *Min. Obs.* [f. Gr. εὐ- (see EU-) + χύ-σις melting (f. χέ-ειν to melt) + σίδηρ-ος iron + -ITE.] A variety of augite; = PYROXENE.

1823 W. PHILLIPS *Min.* 62 Euchysiderite..may be considered as an augite, of which iron enters into the composition in an uncommon degree.

euclase ('juːkleɪs). *Min.* [a. Fr. *euclase*, f. Gr. εὐ- (see EU-) + κλάσ-ις breaking, f. κλά-ειν to break; so called on account of its easy cleavage.] A silicate of aluminium and glucinum occurring in light-green, transparent crystals.

1804 FOURCROY *Chem.* II. 412 The primative form of euclase is a right rectangular prism. **1822** IMISON *Sc. & Art* II. 93 Glucina..has been procured from..the euclase. **1868** DANA *Min.* 380 Euclase receives a high polish, but is useless as an ornamental stone on account of its brittleness. **1874** WESTROPP *Man. Prec. Stones* 25 The euclase is also of the same chemical composition as the emerald.

Euclid ('juːklɪd). [ad. Gr. Εὐκλείδης.] A mathematician of Alexandria who flourished about 300 B.C.: hence, **a.** the works of Euclid, *esp.* the Elements (cf. ELEMENTS); **b.** a copy of the same.

1581 MULCASTER *Positions* xli. (1887) 241 [He] gave them a number of Euclides of his owne coast. **1665** J. SERGEANT *Sure-footing* 163 To study my Book with that severity as they would do an Euclid. **1845** STODDART in *Encycl. Metrop.* (1847) I. 42/1 When we read Euclid, we find neither first person nor second in any part of his whole Work. *Mod.* We don't approve of symbolical Euclids. They were examined in Algebra and Euclid.

Euclidean (juː'klɪdɪən, juːklɪ'diːən), *a.* Also Euclidian. [f. L. *Euclīdē-us*, Gr. Εὐκλείδειος (f. *Euclīd-ēs*, Εὐκλείδης Euclid) + -AN.] Of or pertaining to Euclid; that is according to the principles of Euclid.

By recent writers ***Euclidean geometry*** has been used as the distinctive name of the geometry based on an acceptance of the axioms laid down by Euclid, as distinguished from the systems (constructed e.g. by Lobatchewsky, Grassmann, Riemann) which develop the consequences that would follow from the rejection of some of these. So also ***Euclidean space***: the kind of space actually known to us, for which these axioms are valid, as opposed to hypothetical kinds of space for which one or more of the axioms would be false.

1660 BARROW *Euclid* Pref. (1714) 2 The whole Euclidean work. *c* **1865** in *Wylde's Circ. Sc.* I. 551/2 Euclidean geometry tolerates no such imperfections. **1883** *Standard* No. 18464. 5 This abstruse discourse on Euclidian space and magnitudes of four dimensions. **1883** *American* VII. 75 This would be their Euclidian geometry.

†**'Euclionism.** *Obs. rare*[−1]. [f. *Euclīōn-em*, the name of a miser, the chief character in Plautus' *Aulularia* + -ISM.] Stinginess.

1599 NASHE *Lenten Stuffe* 3 Those grey beard Huddled-duddles..were strooke with such stinging remorse of their miserable Euclionisme and snudgery.

eucnemic (juːk'niːmɪk), *a. nonce-wd.* [f. Gr. εὐκνήμ-ις well-greaved (an epithet of Homeric heroes), f. εὐ- (see EU-) + κνημίς greave + -IC.] Well-greaved; hence belonging to ancient Greece.

1851 *Fraser's Mag.* XLIII. 249 The existence of togate and eucnemic proficients in the art of angling is competently attested.

eucnemidal (juːk'niːmɪdəl), *a. nonce-wd.* [f. Gr. εὐκνημιδ- stem of εὐκνήμις (see prec.) + -AL[1].] Pertaining to a well-greaved man; hence quasi-*sb. pl.*: Stout leggings.

1839 *New Monthly Mag.* LVI. 30 A collection of weather clothing, contemporary with, and equally efficacious as, the eucnemidals before alluded to.

eucolite ('juːkəlaɪt). *Min.* Also **eukolite, -yte.** [f. Gr. εὔκολ-ος easily satisfied (f. εὐ- (see EU-) + κόλον food) + -ITE. The name is founded on the fact that it contains less zirconia than wöhlerite does.] A variety of eudialyte.

1847 SCHEERER in *Pogg. Ann.* 565 [Explains that he gave this name to the mineral 'because it *contented itself*, so to speak, with iron oxide in default of zirconia']. **1849** *Amer. Jrnl. Sc.* Ser. II. VIII. 126 On Eukolite, a new Mineral. **1868** DANA *Min.* 249 Eucolite is from islands of the Langesund fiord in Norway. **1882** WATTS *Dict. Chem.* II. 605 Eukolyte is distinguished by the presence of cerium.

eucomis (juː'kəʊmɪs). *Bot.* [mod.L. (C. L. L'Héritier *Sertum Anglicum* (1788) 17), ad. Gr. εὐκόμης fair-haired, beautiful-headed, f. εὐ- (see EU-) + κόμη hair.] A plant of the liliaceous genus so named, comprising certain bulbous plants native to southern and tropical Africa, having a crown of large leaves on the flower-spike.

1804 H. ANDREWS *Botanist's Repos.* VI. Pl. 369 *Purple-stalked Eucomis*... Eucomis, with a clavated scape, leaves pointing many ways expanded orbicular-spatula-shaped. **1884** [see *pineapple flower* s.v. PINEAPPLE 3 b]. **1966** *House & Garden* Dec. 61/1 (*caption*) The delicate Eucomis, from South Africa, raises its splendid head of flower. **1966** E. PALMER *Plains of Camdeboo* xvii. 283 The other green or green and white flowers of the veld, such as the Eucomis.. which bears a great tuft of leaves above its greenish inflorescence.

eucone ('juːkəʊn), *a. Ent.* [a. G. *eucone* (H. Grenacker 1877, in *Klin. Monatsblätter f. Augenheilkunde* Suppl. XV. 18), f. EU- + CONE *sb.*[1]] Of the eyes of certain insects: having a well-developed or true cone (see quots.).

1885 S. J. HICKSON in *Q. Jrnl. Microsc. Sci.* XXV. 230 The crystalline cone of the 'eucone eyes'. **1888** ROLLESTON & JACKSON *Forms Anim. Life* 502 The vitreous cells..are reduced to feeble remnants inclosing a solid crystalline cone composed of 2–5 parts, the eucone eyes of other Insecta... In pseudocone and eucone eyes the seven cells are grouped round a central axis. **1957** A. D. IMMS *Gen. Textbk. Ent.* (ed. 9) 104 *Eucone eyes.* In eyes of this type each ommatidium contains a true crystalline cone, which is a hard refractive body formed as an intracellular product of the cone cells.

eucrasy ('juːkrəsɪ). Also 7 eucracy, 8 **euchrasy.** [ad. Gr. εὐκρᾱσί-α good temperature, f. εὔκρᾱτος well-tempered, f. εὐ- (see EU-) + κρᾱ-, κεραννύναι to mix.] Such a due or well-proportioned mixture of qualities as constitutes health or soundness.

1607 WALKINGTON *Opt. Glass* xv, In this eucrasy there is an absolute *symmetriè*. **1642** W. PRICE *Serm.* 39 Of this Eucracy, this healthfull temper and constitution, the City once was. **1670** MAYNWARING *Vita Sana* vi. 79 It is some dayes before the stomach recover its eucrasy, and perform its office well. **1719** QUINCY *Med. Dict.*, *Euchrasy.* Hence in mod. Dicts.

†**eu'cratic**, *a. Obs. rare*[−1]. [f. Gr. εὔκρᾱτ-ος (see prec.) + -IC.] (See quot.)

1795 tr. *Mercier's Fragments* I. 56 A state truly eucratic.. where good and ill are intermingled, but where the good preponderate.

†**euctical** ('juːktɪkəl), *a. Obs.* [f. Gr. εὐκτικ-ός pertaining to prayer (f. εὔχεσθαι to pray) + -AL[1].] Pertaining to prayer; supplicatory.

a **1638** MEDE *Wks.* x. xlix, Eucharistical Offerings are such whose end is Thanksgiving to God..Euctical..such as are made to God..when we come to pray before him. **1745** BP. E. LAW *Theory Relig.* 227 Hence was the Origin of Sacrifices, as they are distinguished into expiatory, euctical, and eucharistical.

Hence **'euctically** *adv.*

a **1638** MEDE *Wks.* I. li. 291 The Heave-offering..was as it were an Offering of his own, and therefore he applieth it Euctically.

eucyclic (juː'saɪklɪk), *a. Bot.* [ad. G. *eucyclisch* (A. Braun 1858, in *Jahrb. f. wissenschaftliche Botanik* I. 367), f. EU- + CYCLIC *a.*] Cyclic with alternate isomerous whorls (see quots.).

1875 BENNETT & DYER tr. *Sachs's Text-Bk. Bot.* II. v. 524 Braun calls those flowers *eucyclic* in which the members of all the whorls are equal in number and alternate. It also happens however that members of the same kind arise subsequently between those of a whorl already formed; as.. in many eucyclic flowers with ten stamens. **1878** HENFREY & MASTERS *Elem. Bot.* (ed. 3) I. ii. 91 A flower thus presenting all the whorls is called complete or eucyclic. **1910** *Encycl. Brit.* X. 560/1 When a flower consists of parts arranged in whorls it is said to be *cyclic*, and if all the whorls have an equal number of parts and are alternate it is *eucyclic*.

eu,daimo'nology. *rare*[−1]. [f. Gr. εὐδαίμων, εὐδαίμον-ος fortunate, happy + -(O)LOGY.] (See quot.) Hence **eu,daimono'logian.**

a **1832** BENTHAM *Deontology* I. xx. 320 The employment of the word Eudaimonology, to represent the utilitarian doctrines, and Eudaimonologians its professors.

eudemon, -dæmon (juː'diːmən). [a. Gr. εὐδαίμων fortunate, happy, f. εὐ- (see EU-) + δαίμων guardian, genius. Sense 2 is of mod. origin, and not according to Gr. idiom.]

1. *Astrol.* (See quot.)

1706 PHILLIPS (ed. Kersey), *Eudæmon*, the Eleventh House of a Celestial Figure, so call'd by Astrologers, upon account of its good and prosperous Significations. **1730–6** in BAILEY (folio). **1819** JAS. WILSON *Dict. Astrol.* 94 Eudemon, the good demon, the 11th house, so called because it is the source of as many good things as the 12th house is of evil.

2. A good angel; = AGATHODEMON.

1629 H. BURTON *Babel no Bethel* Ep. to Cholmley 1 For the style..I tooke it to bee some Iesuites, some Eudemon's, or Cacodaemon's, or the like. **1730–6** in BAILEY (folio). **1834–43** SOUTHEY *Doctor* (1848) 672/1 The simple appendage of a tail will cacodemonise the Eudæmon.

eudemonic, -dæmonic (juːdɪ'mɒnɪk), *a.* [ad. Gr. εὐδαιμονικ-ός, f. εὐδαιμονία happiness.]

1. Conducive to happiness; viewed as conducive to happiness.

1865 J. GROTE *Treat. Mor. Ideas* vi. (1876) 72 The former of these is the eudæmonic worth of actions.

2. *pl.* **a.** (after Gr. τὰ εὐδαιμονικά) (see quot. *a* 1832). **b.** (*nonce-use*) Appliances for comfort, means of happiness.

a **1832** BENTHAM *Logic* Wks. (1838–43) VIII. 289 Eudæmonics, or the art of applying life to the maximization of wellbeing. **1865** J. GROTE *Treat. Mor. Ideas* ii. (1876) 13 Eudæmonics however has generally been, and is likely to be, exceedingly ideal. **1883** BURTON & CAMERON *To Gold Coast for Gold* I. iv. 137 Bright sun and pure air..better eudæmonics than purple and fine linen.

So **eude'monical** *a.*

1865 J. GROTE *Treat. Mor. Ideas* i. (1876) 8 The axiom might be very sterile in results without eudæmonical observation to give us particulars about the pain.

eudemonism, -dæmonism (juːˈdiːmən ɪz(ə)m). Also 9 **eudaimonism.** [f. Gr. εὐδαιμονία happiness (f. εὐδαίμων happy, f. εὐ- EU- + δαίμων guardian genius: see DEMON¹) + -ISM.]

That system of ethics which finds the foundation of moral obligation in the tendency of actions to produce happiness.

1827 DE QUINCEY *Last Days Kant* Wks. 1862 III. 101 *note*, Ethics, braced up into stoical vigour by renouncing all effeminate dallyings with Eudæmonism. **1839** *Blackw. Mag.* XLV. 845 In England men were satisfying themselves.. with the unveiled eudæmonism of Paley. **1866** FERRIER *Grk. Philos.* I. xi. 277 Eudaimonism, or the philosophy of happiness. **1876** M. ARNOLD *Lit. & Dogma* 47 We English are taunted with our proneness to an unworthy eudæmonism.

eudemonist, -dæmonist (juːˈdiːmənɪst). Also **-daimonist.** [f. as prec. + -IST.] One who believes in eudemonism.

1818 COLERIDGE in *Lit. Rem.* (1836) I. 273 Yet this is the common *argumentum in circulo* in which the eudæmonists flee and pursue. **1840** *Q. Rev.* LXV. 494 The enlightened Eudæmonist..by his first maxim necessarily excludes the idea of a divine revelation. **1866** FERRIER *Grk. Philos.* I. xi. 292–3 The utilitarians or Eudaimonists define the good as centring in happiness. **1872** MINTO *Eng. Lit.* I. i. 48 He [De Quincey] described himself as a Eudæmonist.

Hence **eudemo'nistic** *a.*, of or pertaining to eudemonism. **eudemo'nistical** *a.* = prec.

1855 *Ess. Intuitive Morals* 67 Whence come these religious considerations which are so completely to modify our Eudaimonistic ethics. **1866** FERRIER *Grk. Philos.* I. xi. 283 Socrates..had strong utilitarian, even eudaimonistic, tendencies. **1881** *Mod. Rev.* Oct. 718 We reject the Israelitish morals as eudæmonistical.

eudemonize, -dæmonize (juːˈdiːmənaɪz), *v.* *rare*⁻¹. [ad. Gr. εὐδαιμονίζ-ειν, f. εὐδαίμων happy.] *trans.* To consider happy.

1876 GROTE *Eth. Fragm.* v. 154 No person is entitled to be called happy, whom the intelligent and reflective observer does not macarise (or eudæmonise).

eu'demony, -'dæmony. *rare.* [ad. Gr. εὐδαιμον-ία, f. as prec.] Happiness, prosperity.

1730–6 in BAILEY (folio). **1885** J. MARTINEAU *Types Eth. Theory* (1886) II. II. iii. 509 The best defence of the invariable eudaemony of Virtue proceeds from Shaftesbury.

eudialyte (juːˈdaɪəlaɪt). *Min.* Also erron. **eudyalite** [f. Gr. εὐδιάλυτος easily dissolved, f. εὐ- (see EU-) + διαλύειν to dissolve (see DIALYSE); the name refers to the solubility of the mineral in hydrochloric acid.] A vitreous bisilicate of zirconium, iron, calcium, sodium, and other elements, occurring in rhombohedral crystals, rose pink or brownish red; first found at Kangerdluarsuk in Greenland. Cf. EUCOLITE.

1837 *Penny Cycl.* X. 64/2 Eudyalite. **1887** DANA *Man. Min.* (ed. 4) 275 Eudialyte.

eudiometer (juːdɪˈɒmɪtə(r)). [f. Gr. εὔδιο-ς clear (weather) (f. εὐ- EU- + διϝ- stem of Ζεύς, Διός the god of the sky and the atmosphere) + μέτρον measure.]

An instrument for testing the purity of the air, or rather the quantity of oxygen it contains.

Various kinds have been in use, but the commonest is that invented by Dr. Ure, consisting of a tube closed at one end, in which certain quantities of hydrogen and atmospheric air are exploded over water by an electric spark. From the rise of the water in the tube inferences are drawn as to the amount of oxygen that was present. The apparatus is also, and now chiefly, employed in the analysis of gases.

1777 DE MAGELLAN (*title*), Glass apparatus for making mineral waters..with the description of some new Eudiometers. **1792** A. YOUNG *Trav. France* 153 He has a large course of eudiometrical experiments going on at present, particularly with Fontana's and Volta's eudiometers. **1807** PEPYS *Eudiometer* in *Phil. Trans.* XCVII. 249 Known quantities of the air to be tried, and of nitrous gas being mixed, were admitted..into a graduated tube, which he [Priestley] denominated a eudiometer. **1825** FARADAY *Exp. Res.* xxx. 161 Seven volumes of this mixture were detonated in a eudiometer tube by an electric spark. **1877** W. THOMSON *Voy. Challenger* I. i. 28 The eudiometer has the legs of glass united by an india-rubber tube of suitable length.

Hence **eudio'metric** *a.*, of, pertaining to, or requiring the use of the eudiometer or eudiometry. **eudio'metrical** *a.* = prec. **eudio'metrically** *adv.*, in a eudiometric way; by the use of a eudiometer. **eudi'ometry**, the art or practice of using the eudiometer either for ascertaining the purity of the air, or in the analysis of gases.

1854 SCOFFERN in *Orr's Circ. Sc.* Chem. 321 The analysis ..may be..effected by the *eudiometric method. **1859** TODD *Cycl. Anat.* V. 378/1 The eudiometric researches of a number of observers. **1792** [see EUDIOMETER]. **1794** G. ADAMS *Nat. & Exp. Philos.* I. xi. 437 Graduated glass tubes for *eudiometrical experiments. **1852** TH. ROSS *Humboldt's Trav.* I. v. 173 The absorption of two gases in a eudiometrical tube. **1808** HENRY in *Phil. Trans.* XCVIII. 290 After trying, *eudiometrically, the quality of an aliquot part of the gas in the receiver. **1881** W. CROOKES in *Nature* XXIII. 423 Collecting samples [of gas] and analysing them eudiometrically. **1800** HENRY *Epit. Chem.* (ed. 5) 159 The application of nitrous gas to the purpose of *eudiometry. **1826** —— *Elem. Chem.* I. 237 Platinum in this form becomes, therefore, a most useful agent in eudiometry. **1853** W. GREGORY *Inorg. Chem.* (ed. 3) 82 When it is required to ascertain the exact proportion of oxygen in any specimen of air..The operation is called eudiometry, and the instruments employed eudiometers.

eudipleural (juːdɪˈplʊərəl), *a.* [f. Gr. εὐ- (see EU-) + δί-ς twice + πλευρ-ά the side + -AL¹.] Having two equal and symmetrical halves.

1878 BELL *Gegenbauer's Comp. Anat.* 128 The radiate form of body..is replaced [in the Vermes] by the eudipleural form.

eue, obs. f. EWE and YEW.

†**eu'ectic.** *Obs.* Spelt **evectic** in Dicts. [ad. Gr. εὐεκτικ-ή (τέχνη), fem. of εὐεκτικός pertaining to a good habit (of body), f. phrase εὖ ἔχειν to be well (εὖ well, ἔχειν lit. to have): see EU- and HECTIC.] (See quot.)

1574 J. JONES *Nat. Beginning Grow. Things* 45 Three partes of the Arte curative: First Euectick, whose scope is to keep the helthie in the same State. [**1706** PHILLIPS, *Euectica* (Gr.), that part of Physic which shews how to get a good habit of Body.] **1721** BAILEY *Evectick.*

Hence in same sense **eu'ectics** *pl.* [after *mathematics*, *optics*, etc.]

1823 CRABB *Technol. Dict.*, *Evectics.* So in mod. Dicts.

Euemerism, etc., obs. f. EUHEMERISM, etc.

euer, obs. var. EWER.

euerose, var. of EWROSE, *Obs.*, rose-water.

†**eu'forbe, eu'forbie.** *Obs.* Anglicized form of EUPHORBIUM.

1436 *Pol. Poems* (1859) II. 173 Wee shulde have no nede to skamonye, Turbit, euforbe, etc. **1460–70** *Bk. Quintessence* 16 A litil of euforbie, or turbit, or sambucy. **1541** R. COPLAND *Guydon's Quest. Chirurg.*, Water in the whiche is steped and dyssolued the vertue of Euforbie.

euforbium, obs. form of EUPHORBIUM.

eufrage, obs. var. of EUPHRASY, eyebright.

euge (ˈjuːdʒiː). [a. L. *euge*, a. Gr. εὖγε well done!] An exclamation of *Euge!*; approval, commendation.

1655 GURNALL *Chr. in Arm.* 14 x. §1 (1669) 40/1 To give you the Euge of a Faithful servant. **1692** J. EDWARDS *Remarkable Texts* 256 To look for the euge's of angels, and the applause of Heaven. **1798** ROOT in *Amer. Law Rep.* I. 1 Happiness consists primarily in..the pleasing anticipation of a final euge of well done good and faithful servant.

eugenesic (juːdʒɪˈnɛsɪk), *a.* [f. next + -IC.] Capable of breeding freely; applied *esp.* to those hybrids that are fertile.

1864 *Reader* No. 94. 476/3 An eugenesic progeny (i.e. a progeny every generation of which is perfectly fruitful). **1878** BARTLEY tr. *Topinard's Anthrop.* II. vii. 369 Eugenesic.

eugenesis (juːˈdʒɛnɪsɪs). *Biol.* [f. Gr. εὐ- (see EU-) + -γένεσις generation: see GENESIS.] The quality of breeding well or freely; the production of young by the union of individuals of different species or stocks.

In mod. Dicts.

eugenetic (juːdʒɪˈnɛtɪk), *a.* [f. EUGENESIS, after GENETIC.] Of or pertaining to eugenesis, favourable to the production of healthy offspring.

1887 *Athenæum* 5 Nov. 607/3 These tendencies towards deterioration are to be met by endeavours..to encourage marriage only under eugenetic conditions.

Eugenia (juːˈdʒiːnɪə). *Bot.* [mod.Lat.: the name was given in 1729 by Micheli in honour of Eugene, Prince of Savoy.] A genus of tropical trees (N.O. *Myrtaceæ*), mostly found in America and the West Indies, of which the most important is *E. Pimenta* or Allspice Tree.

1775 ASH, *Eugenia*, a genus of plants, the silver tree. **1875** MISS BIRD *Sandwich Isl.* (1880) 81 The great glossy-leaved Eugenia—a forest tree as large as our largest elms.

Hence **eu'genic (acid)** [+ -IC], $C_{10}H_{12}O_2$, oxidized essence of cloves. **'eugenin** [+ -IN], clove-camphor; a crystalline substance deposited from water which has been distilled from cloves. **'eugenol** [+ -OL] = eugenic acid.

1838 T. THOMSON *Chem. Org. Bodies* App. 1057 Oil of cloves, or eugenic acid. **1882** WATTS *Dict. Chem.* II. 604 Eugenic acid, when exposed to the air, quickly assumes a darker colour and becomes resinous. **1847** CRAIG, *Eugenin.* **1886** *Sci. American* 25 Sept. 196 Eugenol represents the strength of the essential oil of cloves.

eugenic (juːˈdʒɛnɪk), *a.* and *sb.* *Biol.* [f. Gr. εὐ- (see EU-) + root γεν- to produce (Gr. had εὐγενής well-born) + -IC.]

A. *adj.* Pertaining or adapted to the production of fine offspring, *esp.* in the human race.

1883 F. GALTON *Hum. Faculty* 24 Various topics more or less connected with that of the cultivation of race, or as we might call it, with 'eugenic' questions. **1886** G. ALLEN in *Fortn. Rev.* 1 Oct. 458 The result..would be as bad..if he made the choice [of a wife] himself on abstract biological and 'Eugenic' principles.

B. *sb.* in *pl.* [after analogy of *economics*, *politics*, etc.] The science which has this for its object.

1883 F. GALTON *Hum. Faculty* 44 The investigation of human eugenics, that is, of the conditions under which men of a high type are produced. **1890** *Univ. Rev.* May 54 People will fall in love, in spite of your eugenics.

eugenically (juːˈdʒɛnɪkəlɪ), *adv.* [f. EUGENIC: see -ICALLY.] In regard to eugenics; from a eugenic point of view.

1912 *Q. Rev.* July 65 The propagation of the eugenically fit. **1922** *Edin. Rev.* July 46 It is eugenically bad, making early marriage impossible, or encouraging the dysgenic art of fortune hunting. **1928** *Daily Express* 1 June 10/4 Wondering why he has not gone in for the great adventure. .. Is he eugenically unfit?

eugenism (ˈjuːdʒɪnɪz(ə)m). [f. as EUGENIC *a.* + -ISM.] (See quot.)

1887 *Athenæum* 31 Dec. 897/3 'Eugenism,' the word suggested by him [Mr. Galton] some time ago..to express the aggregate of the most favourable conditions for healthy and happy existence.

eugenist (ˈjuːdʒɪnɪst, juːˈdʒiːnɪst, -ˈdʒɛn-). [f. EUGENIC: see -IST.] A student or advocate of eugenics. Also *attrib.* or as *adj.*

1908 C. W. SALEEBY *Health, Strength & Happiness* xxiv. 420 There is thus..a quasi-fatalistic element with which the hygienist, as well as the *eugenist*—to coin a word now necessary—must reckon. **1921** W. R. INGE *Lay Thoughts* (1926) 247 Prudent eugenists are in no hurry to advocate legislation. **1921** W. McDOUGALL *Nat. Welfare* p. vii, This great gap in the eugenist argument. **1928** *Daily Express* 16 Jan. 8/7 Candidates for marriage..may be faced..with a searching Eugenist standard of physical fitness. **1959** B. WOOTTON *Soc. Sci.* ii. 55 This multiplicity of their social irregularities which first evoked the interest of the eugenists in these families.

eugeogenous (juːdʒiːˈɒdʒɪnəs), *a.* *Geol.* [ad. F. *eugéogène* (J. Thurmann *Essai de Phytostatique* (1849) iv. 95), f. EU- + GEO- + -GENOUS.] Of rock: that readily decomposes into detritus and is therefore able to form good soil. Opp. to *dysgeogenous*.

1850 *Phytologist* III. 918 The subjacent rocks, with reference to their mode of disintegration, their power of absorption, and their permeability, are divisible essentially into *eugeogenous* and *dysgeogenous*. The eugeogenous rocks produce an abundant detritus. When it is of a clayey (*pélique*) nature, it makes humid stations that are often inundated... The dysgeogenous rocks produce a scanty detritus, sometimes sandy, usually clayey, and always making stations more dry than those of the eugeogenous rocks. **1863** J. G. BAKER *North Yorkshire* 152 They are due south of the hills of the eugeogenous range and based upon their slope. **1903** *Geogr. Jrnl.* Aug. 151 Eugeogenous..rocks ..yield a plentiful detritus, and the overlying soils are cool and moist.

eugh, eughen, obs. ff. YEW, YEWEN *a.*

euglenoid (juːˈgliːnɔɪd), *a.* and *sb.* *Biol.* [f. mod.L. *Euglena* (C. G. Ehrenberg 1830, in *Ann. d. Physik und Chem.* XCIV. 507), f. EU- + Gr. γλήνη pupil of the eye + -OID.]

A. *adj.* Resembling *Euglena*, a member of the genus of single-celled aquatic flagellates so called, which are treated as either protozoa or algæ. **B.** *sb.* An organism of this kind.

1885 *Encycl. Brit.* XIX. 852/2 The movements now become neither vibratile nor amœboid but definitely restrained, and are best described as 'euglenoid'. *Ibid.* 857/1 Euglenoidea... Fam. 6. Astasina. Colourless, metabolic, or stiff Euglenoids. **1888** ROLLESTON & JACKSON *Forms Anim. Life* 843 Chromatophores..are numerous, small, round, or oval in Euglenoids. **1906** *Cambr. Nat. Hist.* I. 124 *Euglena* ..shows a peculiar wriggling motion, waves of transverse constriction passing along the body from end to end... Such motions are termed 'euglenoid'. **1955** *New Biol.* XIX. 114 Organisms..of euglenoid affinities. *Ibid.* 119 In euglenoids without the stigma, this phototactic response does not occur.

euglobulin (juːˈglɒbjʊlɪn). *Biochem.* [f. EU- + GLOBULIN (F. Hofmeister 1899, in *Beitr. z. chem. Physiol.* (1901) I. 361).] The name of one of the fractions into which serum globulin is divided, so called because of its true globulin properties; it is insoluble in pure water but soluble in saline solutions and is precipitated by half-saturation with ammonium sulphate. Also *attrib.*

1905 W. B. HARDY in *Jrnl. Physiol.* XXXIII. 333 Englobulin [*sic*] itself may be merely a step in a series of proteid compounds. **1907** *Jrnl. Biol. Chem.* III. 233 The two serum globulin fractions of the Hofmeister classification

..the lower or euglobulin fraction (2·9 to 3·4 saturated) comprises diphtheria and tetanus antitoxin. *Ibid.* 235 The repeatedly precipitated euglobulin..contained..10 per cent of the antitoxin. **1962** *Lancet* 22 Dec. 1302/1 The euglobulin lysis-time..will probably have to serve..as a measure of fibrinolytic activity.

‖**eu'hages, eu'bages,** *sb. pl. Celtic Antiq.* [Lat., occurring twice in a passage of Ammianus Marcellinus; the form *eubages* in one of the places is a scribal error. The better form *euhages* is evidently due to a misreading of Gr. οὐατεῖς, Strabo's spelling of a Gaulish word = L. *vātes* prophet; Ammianus must have read εὐαγεῖς, and taken this for the pl. of εὐαγής pure, holy. Cf. OVATE.] (See quot.)

1609 HOLLAND *Amm. Marcel.* xv. ix, The Eubages.. searching into the highest altitudes of nature's worke, endevoured to lay open and declare the same. **1751** CHAMBERS *Cycl.*, *Eubages*, an order of priests, or philosophers, among the antient Celtæ, or Gauls. **1809** KENDALL *Trav.* II. xlv. 124 The euhages cultivated what they called natural philosophy. **1827** G. HIGGINS *Celtic Druids* 275 The Eubages or prophets were the third order.

euharmonic (juːhɑːˈmɒnɪk) *a.* [f. Gr. εὐ- (see EU-) + ἁρμον-ία harmony + -IC.] Producing perfect harmony. In ***euharmonic organ***: see quots.

1811 LISTON *Perfect Intonation* 27 The Euharmonic Organ is contrived..to enable the musician..to produce harmony absolutely perfect, while the keyboard remains the same as before. **1876** J. W. MOORE *Dict. Mus. Inf.*, *Euharmonic Organ*, invented by Joseph Alley and H. W. Poole at Newbury Port, Mass., 1848. It gives all the tones of the ancient enharmonic scale.

euhedral (juːˈhiːdrəl, -ˈhɛdrəl), *a.* [f. EU- + HEDRAL *a.*] = IDIOMORPHIC *a.*

1906 J. P. IDDINGS *Rock Minerals* ii. 64 *Euhedral*, well faced, completely bounded by crystal planes, automorphic, idiomorphic. **1913**, etc. [see ANHEDRAL *a.*].

Euhemerism (juːˈhiːmərɪz(ə)m). Also 9 Euemerism. [f. L. *Euhēmer-us*, Gr. Εὐήμερος (see below) + -ISM.] The method of mythological interpretation which regards myths as traditional accounts of real incidents in human history.

Euhemerus, a Sicilian (*c* 316 B.C.) was the author of a book called Ἱερὰ Ἀναγραφή, in which he maintained that the deities of Hellenic mythology were deified men and women, and pretended to cite authentic records of their lives.

1846 GROTE *Greece* I. xvi. I. 596 In regard to the Thracian god Zalmosis, the Hellespontic Greeks interpreted his character and attributes according to the scheme of Euemerism. **1864** MAX MÜLLER *Sc. Lang.* Ser. II. ix. (1868) 397 Euhemerism has become the recognized title of that system of mythological interpretation which..reduces the gods of old to the level of men.

So **Eu'hemerist** [+ -IST], one who follows the method of Euhemerus; also *attrib.* (quasi-*adj.*). **Euheme'ristic** *a.* [f. prec. + -IC], (*a*) of persons: Inclined to euhemerism; (*b*) of things: Of the nature of or resembling euhemerism. **Eu'hemerize** *v.*, (*a*) *trans.* To subject to euhemeristic interpretation; also, ***to euhemerize into*** or ***out of***. (*b*) *intr.* To follow the method of Euhemerus. **Eu'hemerized,** *ppl. a.* **Eu'hemerizing** *vbl. sb.* (in quot. *attrib.*).

1856 MAX MÜLLER *Chips* (1880) II. xvi. 115 It is easier to answer these German than the old Greek *euhemerist. **1871** TYLOR *Prim. Cult.* I. 252 The modern 'euhemerists'..in part adopted the old interpretations. **1884** *Academy* 22 Mar. 205 Saxo..treats Odin and Baldr in euhemerist fashion. **1856** MAX MÜLLER *Chips* (1880) II. xvi. 115 *Euhemeristic critics. **1876** H. SPENCER *Princ. Sociol.* (1877) I. 232 This interpretation will be called Euhemeristic. **1847** J. W. DONALDSON *Vind. Protestant Princ.* 140 One of its [Genesis'] editors **euhemerized* into spurious narratives some of the deep symbolism of the original vaticination. **1881** *Fraser's Mag.* Mar. 355 To euhemerise, rationalise and etherialise them [nursery heroes] out of existence. **1887** I. TAYLOR in *Academy* 3 Sept. 143/2 The legend of Semiramis was a *euhemerised version of the story of Istar. **1871** FARRAR *Witn. Hist.* ii. 57 He did but extend to the New Testament the *Euhemerising principles which Eichhorn had applied to the Old.

eukairite: see EUCAIRITE.

eukaryon (juːˈkærɪən). *Biol.* Also **-caryon.** Pl. **eukarya.** [f. Gr. εὐ- EU- + κάρυον nut, kernel: cf. PROKARYON, EUKARYOTE.] The highly organized nucleus, bounded by a nuclear membrane, that is characteristic of a eukaryotic cell.

1957 [see PROKARYON]. **1967** *Jrnl. Med. Lab. Technol.* XXIV. 261 *Eucaryon*, the highly organized nucleus characteristic of higher organisms.

eukaryote (juːˈkærɪət). *Biol.* Also **-caryote.** [a. F. *eucaryote* (É. Chatton 1925, in *Ann. des Sci. Nat.: Zool.* VIII. 76), f. as prec. + Gr. -ώτ-ης.] A eukaryotic organism. Opp. PROKARYOTE.

1961 in WEBSTER. **1963**, **1967** [see PROKARYOTE]. **1969** *New Scientist* 14 Aug. 327/2 The oldest rocks in which eucaryotic fossils are known are about 1.2 to 1.4 aeons old, although eucaryotes may have made their debut before this. **1977** *Sci. Amer.* July 28/3 The paleontological record suggests that prokaryotes existed on the earth for a billion or more years before the more complex eukaryotes arrived on the scene. **1983** *Nature* 21 July 211/1 Many sexually reproducing species of lower eukaryotes are not differentiated into males and females. **1984** J. W. KIMBALL *Cell Biol.* (ed. 3) iii. 72/1 (*caption*) Electron micrograph..of a blue-green alga. Although internal membranes are found in this prokaryote, these are not organized into the membrane-bounded organelles characteristic of eukaryotes.

eukaryotic (juːkærɪˈɒtɪk), *a. Biol.* Also **-caryotic.** [f. EUKARYOT(E + -IC.] (Of a cell) characterized by a nuclear membrane and organelles; (of an organism) composed of such cells, belonging to the group which includes all higher organisms and some lower ones; of or pertaining to such a cell or organism. Opp. PROKARYOTIC *a.*

1957, etc. [see PROKARYON]. **1969** *New Scientist* 14 Aug. 327/1 The presence of free oxygen..was presumably followed by the evolution of the eucaryotic cell, with nuclear wall, well-defined chromosomes, mitotic cell division, and the capacity for sexual reproduction and genetic recombination as the usual mode of replication. **1973** R. G. KRUEGER et al. *Introd. Microbiol.* ii. 18/1 As our knowledge of microorganisms has progressed the differences between the procaryotic bacteria and blue-green algae and eucaryotic organisms including..algae, fungi, and protozoa..have become more apparent. **1977** *N.Y. Rev. Bks.* 27 Oct. 18/3 Eukaryotic DNA is the DNA of organisms, such as animals and higher plants, in which genetic material is marshaled and structurally organized in the form of chromosomes, the nucleic acid being combined with a basic protein to form a salt-like compound. **1982** ARMS & CAMP *Biology* (ed. 2) iv. 51 Prokaryotic cells are simple in structure, and for this reason are believed to be evolutionarily more primitive than eukaryotic cells.

eukolite, -yte: see EUCOLITE.

eulachon (ˈjuːləkɒn). Also **ulikon, ulicon, ulken**; and OOLAKAN, -CHAN, etc. [ad. Chinook jargon *ulâkân*.] A small fish of the northwestern parts of North America, ascending the rivers in immense numbers to spawn; the candle-fish.

1807 P. GASS *Jrnl.* 187 In the afternoon some of the natives came to visit us, and brought some of the small fish, which they call Ulken... At noon our fishermen returned with some ulken and sturgeon. **1866** J. K. LORD *Naturalist in Vancouver Isl.* I. 88 A fish..called by the natives *Eulachon* or Candle-fish. **1880** *Libr. Univ. Knowl.* (N.Y.) I. 205 All the early navigators and explorers..have spoken of the immense numbers of salmon, cod, halibut, mullet, ulicon, etc. **1885** SIMMONDS *Animal Food Resources* ix. 318 The ulikon or oulachan (*Thaleichthys pacificus*, Gerard)..has long been an ichthyological curiosity... It is a small silvery fish, averaging about fourteen inches long, and in general appearance much resembling a smelt. **1888** GOODE *Amer. Fishes* 476 They [*sc.* trout] are taken in Frazer River at the time of the eulachon run, but they probably then ascend the river to feed upon the eulachon, and not for spawning purposes. **1955** *Sci. News Let.* 3 Jan. 32/1 The candlefish, or eulachon, of America's north Pacific coast is prized by Indians as food and for its oil.

Euler (ˈɔɪlə(r)). The name of Leonard Euler (see EULERIAN *a.*) used *attrib.*, in *Comb.*, or in the possessive to designate principles, effects, etc., discovered by him or arising out of his work.

1847 *Phil. Mag.* 3rd Ser. XXX. 424 Recent researches.., in reference to the new analytical theory of imaginary quantities, have revived attention to Euler's theorem, that the sum of four squares multiplied by the sum of four squares produces the sum of four squares. **1889** *Cent. Dict.*, *Euler's numbers*, the numbers E_2, E_4, etc., which occur in the development of sec x by Maclaurin's theorem: namely, sec $x = 1 + E_2x^2/2! + E_4x^4/4! +$ etc. *Ibid.*, *Euler's solution*, a solution of a biquadratic after the second term has been got rid of. **1940** *Jrnl. R. Aeronaut. Soc.* XLIV. 43 The term quasi-Euler is used to distinguish the failure which occurs by buckling over the greatest wave length which the supports allow from the corrugated failure fixed by the minimum condition. Although the skin fails in an Euler curve it is not a true Euler effect. **1947** COURANT & ROBBINS *What is Math.?* (ed. 4) v. 240 On the basis of Euler's formula it is easy to show that there are no more than five regular polyhedra. **1953** W. RUDIN *Princ. Math. Anal.* viii. 163, $1 + \frac{1}{2} + \ldots + (1/n) - \log n$..converges. (The limit, often denoted by γ, is called Euler's constant. Its value is 0·5772. ..) **1961** *New Scientist* 16 Mar. 698/3 The result $V + F - E = 2$ was originally derived for polyhedra: this is the *Euler-Descartes relation*, known to Descartes but first explicitly proved by Euler.

Eulerian (juːˈlɪərɪən), *a.* [f. *Euler*, the name of a celebrated Swiss mathematician (1707–83) + -IAN.] Of, pertaining to, or discovered by, Euler; as ***Eulerian constant, function, integral.***

1882 MINCHIN *Unipl. Kinemat.* 139 In the first case what we have done for the fixed-space point P we imagine to be done for all fixed-space points; and in the second case we imagine our record to be similarly kept for every individual fluid particle..They are..often called the Eulerian and the Lagrangian methods, respectively. **1886** TODHUNTER *Integral Calculus* 249 We shall now prove an important equation which connects the two Eulerian integrals. *Ibid.* 255 The quantity C is called Euler's constant.

euloge, obs. f. EULOGY.

‖**eulogia** (juːˈləʊdʒɪə). [Eccl. Lat., a. Gr. εὐλογία in N.T. 'blessing': see EULOGY.] **a.** A name applied by the early Christians to the Eucharist. **b.** A portion of the consecrated bread reserved for those who were not present at the communion. **c.** In the Greek church, the unconsecrated bread remaining after communion, blessed by the priests and given to the non-communicants; also bread, sweetmeats, etc. blessed and distributed as tokens of mutual love. See EULOGY 2.

1751 in CHAMBERS *Cycl.* **1849** ROCK *Ch. of Fathers* I. 137 This holy loaf or eulogia was meant to be an emblem of.. brotherly love. **1883** ADDIS & ARNOLD *Cath. Dict.* s.v. *Eulogiæ*, The Eulogia, then, was a substitute—though of course a most imperfect one..for Holy Communion, whence the Greek name, ἀντίδωρον.

†**eulo'giacal**, *a. Obs. rare*$^{-1}$. [f. EULOGI-UM + -ACAL.] = next.

1654 VILVAIN *Epit. Ess.* VI. 34 Eulogiacal Elegies.

eulogic (juːˈlɒdʒɪk), *a. rare.* [f. EULOGY + -IC.] Pertaining to eulogy; containing praise; commendatory.

1753 CHAMBERS *Cycl. Supp.* s.v. *Æolic*, Æolic verse..is otherwise called *eulogic*. **1831** *Fraser's Mag.* III. 563 Passing by numerous passages that are too unintelligible..even for the eulogic commentaries of his sworn admirers.

†**eu'logical**, *a. Obs.*$^{-0}$ [f. as prec. + -AL[1].] **a.** = prec. ¶**b.** (See quot. 1656–81.)

1656–81 BLOUNT *Glossogr.*, *Eulogical* well spoken. **1692–1732** in COLES. **1818** TODD, *Eulogical*, commendatory, containing praise. In mod. Dicts.

Hence **eu'logically** *adv.*, by way of eulogy.

1634 SIR T. HERBERT *Trav.* 161 Magnifying eulogically their great Mahumed. **1818** in TODD. In mod. Dicts.

eulogious (juːˈləʊdʒɪəs), *a. rare.* [f. EULOGIUM + -OUS.] Full of eulogy; eulogistic.

1887 *Sat. Rev.* 3 Dec. 768 Méry wrote lengthy prefaces and eulogious introductions. **1890** *Harper's Mag.* Mar. 562/1 To detain the reader with eulogious phrases.

eulogism (ˈjuːlədʒɪz(ə)m). [f. EULOG-Y + -ISM.] A eulogistic speech; eulogistic language.

1761 *London & Environs* IV. 143 (Jod.) The pompous eulogisms bestowed on this bridge. **1853** FELTON *Fam. Lett.* xxiii. (1865) 195 Passing a glowing eulogism on her enlightened policy. **1864** *Realm* 30 Mar. 4 The eager eulogism which the Ministers of Queen Victoria accord to the conspirators against her Imperial ally.

eulogist (ˈjuːlədʒɪst). [f. as prec. + -IST.] One who eulogizes; one who speaks or writes in commendation of a person or thing.

1808 HAN. MORE *Cœlebs* I. iv. 41 The eulogist of the L'Almanac des Gourmands. **1853** C. BRONTË *Villette* xix. (1876) 133, I must not from the faithful narrator degenerate into the partial eulogist. **1876** BANCROFT *Hist. U.S.* IV. li. 289 Franklin, when he died, had..the great and the good throughout the world as his eulogists.

eulogistic (juːləʊˈdʒɪstɪk), *a.* [f. prec. + -IC.] Pertaining to or expressive of eulogy; of the nature of eulogy; commendatory, laudatory. Const. *of*.

1825 SYD. SMITH *Wks.* (1859) II. 71 Some adjunct of the eulogistic cast, such as moderate..or practical. **1827** BENTHAM *Rationale Evid.* Wks. 1843 VII. 224 Scotch lawyers..do not plaster over the foulness of their system with eulogistic daubings. **1848** H. MILLER *First Impr.* vi. (1857) 95 The inscription is eulogistic of the poet's character.

Hence **eulogistical** *a.* = prec.

In mod Dicts.

eulo'gistically *adv.*, in a eulogistic manner.

1831 CROKER in *Boswell's Johnson* 20 July an. 1763 *note*, To talk thus eulogistically of 'the very spirited exertions' of a piratical bookseller. **1848** *Fraser's Mag.* XXXVIII. 501 He writes..too eulogistically for a critic.

eulogium (juːˈləʊdʒɪəm). *Pl.* **eulogiums**; also 8 **eulogia.** [a. med.L. *eulogium*, app. formed by a confusion between *ēlogium* (see EULOGIUM) and *eulogia* (see EULOGY), being used in both senses.]

A laudatory discourse; a formal expression of praise; = EULOGY 1.

1706 PHILLIPS, *Eulogium*, an Elogy, a praising or speaking well of. **1711** ADDISON *Spect.* No. 68 ¶2 He..falls into a general eulogium of friendship. **1789** BENTHAM *Princ. Legisl.* xiii. §6 Allowing nothing to approach the throne but mercenary eulogiums. **1808** *Med. Jrnl.* XIX. 464 Just eulogia on the Navy and Army practitioners. **1838** DICKENS *Nich. Nick.* xxv, These remarks put a termination to Mr. Crummles's eulogium. **1848** H. MILLER *First Impr.* ii. (1857) 20, I realized..the justice of the eulogium of Thomson on the art of the architect.

b. Eulogistic speaking; = EULOGY 1 b.

1802 *Paris as it was* II. lxviii. 334 A master-piece of art, which is above all eulogium. **1862** TROLLOPE *Orley F.* vi, They are very nice..How can he avoid eulogium?

eulogize (ˈjuːlədʒaɪz), *v.* [f. EULOG-Y + -IZE.]

1. *trans.* To pronounce a eulogy upon; to speak or write in commendation of; to extol, praise.

a **1810** HUDDESFORD *Satir. Poems* (T.), Those Who eulogize their country's foes. **1815** W. H. IRELAND *Scribbleomania* 25 Rhymsters who..meanest actions eulogize. **1865** LECKY *Ration.* II. v. 200 He eulogised constitutional government as immeasurably superior to despotism.

¶**2.** Used to represent Gr. εὐλογεῖν in sense 'to bless'.

1885 E. S. FFOULKES *Prim. Consecr.* ix. 419 What our Lord had effected by blessing and giving thanks..by eulogising them, as S. Cyril has it.

Hence **'eulogizer**, one who eulogizes; a eulogist.

1837 *New Monthly Mag.* XLIX. 341 The eulogizers of the wisdom of our ancestors. **1866** ALGER *Solit. Nat. & Man* IV. 200 An atheistic eulogizer of nothingness.

eulogo'mania. *nonce-wd.* A mania for eulogy.
1802 SYD. SMITH *Wks.* (1859) I. 4/2 Why should Dr. Parr confine this eulogomania to the literary characters of this island alone?

eulogy ('juːlədʒɪ). Forms: (? 5 **wloge**, 6–7 **eulogie**, 7–8 **euloge**, 7– **eulogy**. [In sense 1 prob. anglicized form of EULOGIUM: but the ulterior source is Gr. εὐλογία praise, in N.T. blessing (f. εὐ- + -λογία speaking, after phrase εὖ λέγειν to speak well of), of which the word in sense 2 is an adaptation.]

1. A speech or writing in commendation of the character and services of a person, or the qualities of a thing; *esp.* a set oration in honour of a deceased person.
[**14..** *E.E. Misc.* (Warton Club) 18, I wylle apposse Thin wlogé, yf hit do the apleyse.] **1591** SPENSER *Tears of Muses* 372 And Eulogies turne into Elegies. **1611** SPEED *Hist. Gt. Brit.* v. vii. 38 In a soile whereof we finde this Euloge. **1667** PEPYS *Diary* (1877) V. 216 Every body..came to me..with such eulogys as cannot be expressed. **1752** HUME *Ess. & Treat.* (1777) I. 25 If our constitution does in any degree deserve these eulogies. **1818** HALLAM *Mid. Ages* (1872) I. 13 His greatest eulogy is written in the disgraces of succeeding times. **1830** LYELL *Princ. Geol.* 27 Fontenelle..pronounced his eulogy more than fifty years afterwards. *a* **1839** PRAED *Poems* (1864) II. 323 Thy portrait and thine eulogy Traced by some artist hand.

b. Eulogistic speaking; commendation, praise.
1725 BRADLEY *Fam. Dict.* s.v. *Nitre*, All the pompous Eulogie, made from Time to Time to celebrate the Excellency of Salt. **1791** MACKINTOSH *Vind. Gall.* Wks. 1846 III. 17 *note*, The commercial abilities of Mr. Eden.. were the theme of profuse eulogy. **1827** HALLAM *Const. Hist.* (1876) I. i. 36 Some mention Henry VIII after his death in language of eulogy. **1873** SYMONDS *Grk. Poets* vi. 169 Pindar..knew how to mingle eulogy with admonition.

†**2.** *Eccl.* In the senses of EULOGIA, which is now more common in historical use.
1709 J. JOHNSON *Clergym. Vade-m.* II. 100 That the Holy Mysteries be not carried into other parishes on the Feast of Easter, by way of Eulogies. **1725** tr. *Dupin's Eccl. Hist. 17th C.* I. v. 209 The things upon which these Invocations were made, were afterwards consider'd as holy and sacred things, and call'd..the Eucharist, Eulogy, and Praise. **1730–6** in BAILEY (folio). **1751** CHAMBERS *Cycl.* s.v., These pieces of bread they call eulogies..The wine sent as a present, was also held an eulogy. Bollandus remarks..that the eucharist itself was called eulogy. **1782** PRIESTLEY *Corrupt Chr.* II. VI. 16 Some churches substituted what they called eulogies, or holy bread for the bread of the Lord's Supper.

†**3.** = ELOGY 3. *Obs. rare.*
1703 W. WOTTON in *Evelyn's Mem.* (1857) III., What countryman? What his employment? in short, a short eulogy of him..with an account of the time of his death.

eulysite ('juːlɪsaɪt). *Min.* Also **-yte**. [f. Gr. εὐλυσία easy solubility (f. εὔλυτος see next) + -ITE.] 'A granular mixture of augite, garnet, and nearly 50 per cent. of a mineral allied to olivine' (Watts *Dict. Chem.*).
1868 DANA *Min.* 259 It [Iron-Manganese Chrysolite] occurs in a gneissoid rock called Eulysyte. **1879** RUTLEY *Study Rocks* xiii. 263 Eulysite occurs in a very thick bed in the gneiss of Tunaberg in Sweden.

eulytin ('juːlɪtɪn), *Min.* Also **-ine**. [f. Gr. εὔλυτος easily dissolved (f. εὐ- EU- + λυτός soluble, f. λύειν to loose, dissolve) + -IN.] Native silicate of bismuth, usually occurring in brownish crystals with a resinous lustre.
1850 DANA *Min.* 413 Bismuth Blende, Eulytine. **1882** WATTS *Dict. Chem.* II. 606 *Eulytin*. Silicate of Bismuth. Bismuth-blende.—A rare mineral, occurring at Schneeberg in Saxony.

eulytite ('juːlɪtaɪt). *Min.* = prec.
1868 DANA *Min.* 391 Eulytite..Silicate of Bismuth.

eumorphous (juː'mɔːfəs), *a. rare.* [f. Gr. εὔμορφος, f. εὐ- (see EU-) + μορφή form + -OUS.] Well-shaped.
1859 R. F. BURTON *Centr. Afr.* in *Jrnl. Geog. Soc.* XXIX. 315 The skeleton is of eumorphous proportions.

eunomia (juː'nəʊmɪə). = EUNOMY.
1861 MILL *Repr. Govt.* x. 195 The ballot..conduced to the Eunomia by which Athens was distinguished among the ancient commonwealths. **1952** A. R. RADCLIFFE-BROWN *Struct. & Function Prim. Soc.* ix. 182 They conceived..the eunomia of a society as being in each instance a condition of the harmonious working together of its parts.

Eunomian (juː'nəʊmɪən), *sb.* (*a.*) *Ch. Hist.* [See -AN.] A follower of Eunomius, bishop of Cyzicus in the 4th century A.D., who developed Arianism to an extreme form; an Anomœan. Also as *adj.* Hence **Eu'nomianism**.
c **1449** PECOCK *Repr.* v. iii. 499 The sect of Acyanys and of Ennomynyarys [*sic*]. **1559** ABP. HEATH *Speech* 30 Jan. in *Cobbett's Parl. Hist.* (1806) I. 645 Damase, then bishop of Rome.., did give sentence against the heretics, Macedonians, Sabellians and Eunomians. **1577** [see MACEDONIAN *a.*[2] and *sb.*[2]]. **1607** T. ROGERS *39 Art.* i. 6 Some thinke there be three Gods..not distinguished onely, but divided also, as did the Eunomeans, and Tretheites. **1780** A. BUTLER *Lives Saints* (ed. 2) VII. 109 The sixth Volume [*sc.* of St. Ephrem's writings] gives us ninety other polemical *Discourses* against the Arian and Eunomian heretics. **1788** GIBBON *Decl. & F.* IV. xli. 205 Theodosius had been educated in the Eunomian heresy. **1880** E. VENABLES in W. Smith *Dict. Chr. Biogr.* II. 288 Eunomianism, as a cold, logical system, wanted the elements of vitality. **1893** W. M. RAMSAY *Church in Empire* xviii. 448 Did the Eunomian differ from the Catholic only in point of doctrine? **1959** *Chambers's Encycl.* V. 433/2 An extreme 'Eunomian' party of the Arians. *Ibid.*, After his death the Eunomians..broke completely with the orthodox church.

eunomic (juː'nɒmɪk), *a.* [f. EUNOM(Y + -IC.] Law-abiding; (socially) well adjusted or ordered.
1952 A. R. RADCLIFFE-BROWN *Struct. & Function Prim. Soc.* ix. 182 Whether a given society at a given time is normal or pathological, eunomic or dysnomic. **1957** R. K. MERTON *Social Theory* (ed. 2) II. v. 166 The behavior of 'anomic' and 'eunomic' *individuals* within groups having a designated degree of objective anomie could be systematically compared.

eunomy ('juːnəmɪ). *rare.* [ad. Gr. εὐνομία, f. εὐ- (see EU-) + νόμος law.] A political condition of good law well-administered.
1721–1800 BAILEY, *Eunomy*, a Constitution or Ordination of good Laws. **1846** GROTE *Greece* II. vi. II. 454 The state of 'eunomy' and good order which that constitution [*sc.* Lycurgus'] brought about.

eunuch ('juːnək), *sb.* Forms: [4 **eunuchus**], 5 **enuke**, 6–7 **eunuche**, 6– **eunuch**. [ad. L. *eunūchus*, a. Gr. εὐνοῦχος, f. εὐνή bed + -οχ- ablaut-stem of ἔχειν to keep; the literal sense is thus a bedchamber guard or attendant.]

1. a. A castrated person of the male sex; also, such a person employed as a harem attendant, or in Oriental courts and under the Roman emperors, charged with important affairs of state. Also *fig.* (freq. preceded by a descriptive adj.).
c **1430** LYDG. *Bochas* III. xxv. 96 a, Whan the Enukes to y[e] King her brought She was accepted. **1590** NASHE *Anat. Absurd* B ij a, Speaking..of whoredome, as though they had beene Eunuches from theyr cradle. **1593** SHAKES. *2 Hen. VI* IV. ii. 175 Lord Say hath gelded the Commonwealth, and made it an Eunuch. **1601** —— *All's Well* II. iii. 94 And they were sons of mine..I would send them to'th Turke to make Eunuches of. *a* **1616** BEAUMONT *Poems, The Glance*, Throw Those flakes upon the eunuch's colder snow. **1642** FULLER *Holy & Prof. St.* III. xxi. 210 Those who are born Eunuchs deserve no such great commendation for their chastity. **1701** W. WOTTON *Hist. Rome* i. 462 He had a mortal Aversion to Eunuchs, that third Species of Mankind. **1781** GIBBON *Decl. & F.* II. 51 The private apartments of the palace were governed by a favourite eunuch. **1807** ROBINSON *Archæol. Græca* v. xiii. 472 The first that made eunuchs was Semiramis. **1819** BYRON *Don Juan* Ded. in *Wks.* (1833) XV. 105 The intellectual eunuch Castlereagh. **1819** SHELLEY *Peter Bell 3rd* IV. xi, But from the first 'twas Peter's drift To be a kind of moral eunuch. **1867** LADY HERBERT *Cradle L.* viii. 224 Achill Aga, offered to show the ladies his harem; and a black eunuch was summoned to escort them. **1871** R. ELLIS *Catullus* lxiii. 34 Thither hie the votaress eunuchs with an emulous alacrity. **1963** *Times* 18 Jan. 9/5 It seems that in Rhodesia one cannot remain neutral, that after all one is provoked to react, or become a political eunuch.

¶ In the LXX. and the Vulgate the Gr. εὐνοῦχος, L. *eunūchus*, following the corresponding Heb. *sārīs*, sometimes designate palace officials who were not 'eunuchs', *e.g.* Potiphar (*Gen.* xxxix. 1, where A.V. has 'officer'). Hence the Eng. word has occas. been similarly used in discussions of passages in which the meaning of the word is disputed.
[**1387** TREVISA *Higden* (Rolls) II. 305 Putyphar þat was eunuchus..Eunuchus is he þat is i-gilded, and suche were somtyme i-made wardeynes of ladyes in Egipt.] **1557** N. T. (Genev.) *Acts* viii. 27 *note*, Noble men were called Eunuehes, although they were not gelded.

b. A male singer, castrated in boyhood, so as to retain an alto or soprano voice. Cf. CASTRATO.
1732 LD. LANSDOWNE *Charac. Wycherly* Wks. 1736 II. 112 Our modern writers..like Eunuchs..sacrifice their Manhood for a Voice, and reduce Poetry, like Echo to be nothing but Sound. **1738** JOHNSON *London* 59 Let such.. With warbling eunuchs fill a licenc'd stage. **1761** CHURCHILL *Rosciad* Poems (1763) I. 35 Never shall a truly British Age Bear a vile race of Eunuchs on the Stage.

c. Used as *adj.*: Emasculated. *rare*[−1].
1817 GODWIN *Mandeville* III. 96 He had a mind wholly eunuch and ungenerative in matters of literature and taste.

2. *attrib.* and *Comb.* Also *fig.* **eunuch flute**, a type of mirliton (see quot. 1928).
[**1635** M. MERSENNE *Harmonicorum Libri* II. ii. 79 De Instrumentis Harmonicis... *Fleuste Eunuque.* Fistula monofora.] **1666** DRYDEN *Ann. Mirab.* xl, That eunuch guardian of rich Holland's trade, Who envies us what he wants power to enjoy. **1739** P. WHITEHEAD *Manners* 8 What sing-song Riot, and what Eunuch-squawling. **1826** DISRAELI *Viv. Grey* III. vi, Bright moon! sultana of the soul! the Passions are thy eunuch slaves. **1849–50** ALISON *Hist. Europe* VIII. l. §37. 157 Liberty..expired amidst eunuch servility and Eastern adulation. **1928** E. W. NAYLOR *Poets & Music* v. 97 The 'eunuch' flute..is not a flute at all, but a tube covered at the small end with a thin membrane. The performer sings, or rather hums, through a hole in the side, near the membrane. **1961** A. BAINES *Mus. Instruments* 19 The Eunuch Flute, and the Bumbass.

†**'eunuch**, *v. Obs.* [f. prec. sb.] *trans.* To make a eunuch of, castrate; also *fig.*
a **1658** CLEVELAND *Gen. Poems* (1677) 15 Give me a Lover bold and free, Not Eunuch'd with Formality; Like an Embassador that beds a Queen. **1682** CREECH *Lucretius* (T.), They eunuch all their Priests.

Hence **'eunuched** *ppl. a.*, emasculated.
1627 MAY *Lucan* x. 156 Th' vnhappy strength-robb'd company, The Eunuch'd youths.

eunuchal ('juːnəkəl), *a.* [f. as prec. + -AL[1].] Of or pertaining to a eunuch; emasculate; effeminate.
1878 A. CAMERON in *N. Amer. Rev* CXXVI. 489 Manly forgiveness becomes eunuchal sentimentality.

†**'eunuchate**, *v. Obs.* [f. L. *eunūchāt-* ppl. stem of *eunūchāre*, f. *eunūchus*: see EUNUCH.] *trans.* To make a eunuch of, castrate; to deprive of virility or generative power.
1646 SIR T. BROWNE *Pseud. Ep.* III. iv. 113 To eunuchate or castrate themselves. *Ibid.* ii. vii. 115 That Camphire Eunuchates or [*printed* or Eunuchates] begets in men an impotency unto venery, observation will hardly confirm. **1721–1800** in BAILEY; hence in ASH, etc.

eunuchism ('juːnəkɪz(ə)m). Also 7 **eunochisme**, **-ucisme**. [f. EUNUCH *sb.* + -ISM.] The process or custom of making eunuchs; the condition of being a eunuch; emasculation.
1620 BP. HALL *Hon. Mar. Clergy* I. §7 Neither doe we thinke that the earth affords any thing more glorious then eunuchisme for the kingdome of heauen. **1650** BULWER *Anthropomet.* xx. 202 To introduce Eunochisme, and this way of degrading men from their manhood. *Ibid.* 204 Eunucisme. **1688** W. PAYNE *Texts of Papists conc. Celibacy Exam.* II. 782 (T.) This voluntary eunuchism is not to be understood literally, as it was by Origen. **1718** (*title*), Eunuchism Display'd, describing all the different Sorts of Eunuchs, etc. **1875** J. DAVENPORT *Curios. Erot. Physiol.* Essay v. (*title*) Eunuchism.

eunuchize ('juːnəkaɪz), *v.* Also 7 **eunuchise**. [f. EUNUCH *sb.* + -IZE.] *trans.* To reduce to the condition of a eunuch; to emasculate; *lit.* and *fig.*
1632 BROME *Novella* IV. ii, If I worship any of 'hem more ..let me be eunuchiz'd. **1634** SIR T. HERBERT *Trav.* 99 The King having at that instant, a Knife in his hand, gives it the poore Father and bids him Eunuchize him. **1847** MEDWIN *Life Shelley* II. 209 Moore..asterized and eunuchized his [Byron's] pages so barbarously. **1887** tr. *V. Hehn's Wanderings Plants & Anim.* 79 Apollonius said that the emperor spared men but eunuchized the earth.

eunuchoid ('juːnəkɔɪd), *a.* (*sb.*) [See -OID.] Resembling, or characteristic of, a eunuch. Also as *sb.* Hence **'eunuchoidism**.
1906 *Rep. Brit. Assoc.* 703 (*heading*) Observations made on an 'Eunuchoid' Subject in the Cambridge Anatomy School. **1925** W. J. H. SPROTT tr. *Kretschmer's Physique & Char.* 26 A growth in length which indicates eunuchoidism. *Ibid.* 73 Disposition of fat according to the eunuchoid plan. *Ibid.* 86 Schizophrenes and eunuchoids. **1928** *Cowdry's Spec. Cytology* 1231 Eunuchoid conditions. **1959** *Times* 3 Apr. 14/6 Farinelli..looks down..slightly eunuchoid in shape under his smart cerise frockcoat. **1970** *New Yorker* 3 Oct. 36/1 The eunuchoid subtleties of a well-trained choirboy.

'eunuchry. *rare.* [f. as EUNUCHIZE *v.* + -RY; in Fr. *eunuquerie*.] The state of being a eunuch.
1864 R. F. BURTON *Dahome* 43 *note*, M. Wallon..says that these horns are a sign of eunuchry, but they are not so.

euodic (juː'əʊdɪk), *a.* [f. Gr. εὐώδ-ης (f. εὖ well + ὠδ- ablaut-stem of ὄζειν (perf. ὄδωδα) to smell + -IC.] Aromatic, fragrant; used *Chem.* in the name ***euodic aldehyde*** (see quot.).
1873 WATTS *Fownes' Chem.* 749 Euodic aldehyde is the essential constituent of oil of rue. **1876** HARLEY *Mat. Med.* 680 Oil of Rue is composed chiefly of euodic aldehyd.

euonymin (juː'ɒnɪmɪn). *Pharm.* Also **-ine**. [f. EUONYM(US + -IN[1].] A crude extract of the bark of *Euonymus atropurpureus* (see quot. 1912).
1862 W. T. WENZELL in *Amer. Jrnl. Pharmacy* XXXIV. 390 The bitter taste of the principle Euonymin. **1886** *Jrnl. Chem. Soc.* L. 72 The bark of *Euonymus europæus* contains no euonymin. **1912** *Jrnl. Chem. Soc.* CI. 1041 A crude, resinous product, as well as an alcoholic extract of the drug, has met with somewhat extended use under the name of 'Euonymin', and this appellation has also been given to various other substances obtained from the bark, all of which, however, appear to have been of a very indefinite character. **1967** T. E. WALLIS *Textbk. Pharmacognosy* (ed. 5) vii. 84 Euonymin (the powdered extract) is an hepatic stimulant, direct cholagogue, and mild cathartic.

euonymous (juː'ɒnɪməs), *a.* [f. Gr. εὐώνυμος (see next) + -OUS.] Well or felicitously named.
1864 *Sat. Rev.* XVII. 613/1 The Peace Society and its euonymous president, Mr. Pease.

euonymus (juː'ɒnɪməs). *Bot.* Also 8 **euonymous**. [ad. L. *euōnymos* (Plin. XIII. xxxviii. §118), subst. use of Gr. εὐώνυμος of good name, lucky, f. εὐ- (see EU-) + ὄνομα, in Æolic ὄνυμα name.

Pliny says that the flowering of the euonymus was a presage of pestilence; hence it seems probable that the name 'lucky' was given with euphemistic intention.]

A genus of shrubs (N.O. *Celastraceæ*), of which many species are now cultivated as ornamental plants. The only British species is the Spindle-tree, otherwise known as the *peg-*, *prick-*, *skewerwood* from the uses to which its wood is applied.
1767 J. ABERCROMBIE, *Ev. Man his own Gard.* (1803) 180 Deciduous flowering shrubs..such as..candleberry, myrtle, dog-wood, or euonymus. *a* **1775** SIR J. HILL *Hist. Plants* 239 (Jod.) Euonymous with broad, lanceolated, and serrated leaves, Virginian spindle-tree. **1785** J. M. MASON *Notes on Shaks.* 349 The euonymus, of which the best

skewers are made, is called Prick-wood. **1882** *Garden* 21 Jan. 37/1 Many varieties of the Euonymus are finely variegated.

b. U.S. *Pharmacopœia.* The bark of an American species (*E. atropurpureus*), called also the Wahoo-tree.

1876 BARTHOLOW *Mat. Med.* (1879) 484 Euonymus possesses cathartic properties similar to rhubarb.

euosmite (juːˈɒzmaɪt). [f. Gr. εὔοσμ-ος sweet-smelling (f. εὐ EU- + ὀσμή smell) + -ITE.] A fossil resin, looking much like pitch, of a brownish-yellow colour, and giving an aromatic odour when burned.

1868 DANA *Min.* 743 Euosmite..dissolves easily in cold alcohol or ether.

Eupad (ˈjuːpæd). *Pharm.* [f. the initials of *E*dinburgh *U*niversity *P*athological *D*epartment (where the mixture was invented) with jocular reference to EU- and PAD *sb.*[3], quasi 'good pad'.] A mixture of chlorinated lime and boric acid, used as an antiseptic dry dressing.

1915 J. L. SMITH et al. in *Brit. Med. Jrnl.* July 129/1 For convenience we have given the name 'Eupad' to a powder consisting of equal weights of finely ground bleaching powder and powdered boric acid intimately mixed. **1920** MARTINDALE & WESTCOTT *Extra Pharmacop.* (ed. 17) I. 56 A large boil on the leg..was opened and a drain of gauze powdered with Eupad inserted. **1967** *Martindale's Extra Pharmacopoeia* (ed. 25) 313/2 Eupad... A mixture of equal parts of finely ground chlorinated lime (dry) and boric acid, containing about 15% of available chlorine.

eupathy (ˈjuːpəθɪ). [ad. Gr. εὐπάθεια happy condition of the soul, f. εὐπαθής, f. εὐ- (see EU-) + πάθος state of feeling, condition.]

Ancient Stoical Philos. (See quots.)

1603 HOLLAND *Plutarch's Mor.* 74 They do terme those joies, those promptitudes of the will, and warie circumspections by name of Eupathies, i.e. good affections. **1655-60** STANLEY *Hist. Philos.* (1701) 321/1 There are three kinds of good affections of the Mind, called Eupathies, or Constancies; Joy, Caution, Will. **1744** HARRIS *Three Treat.* III. xlviii. 329 *note*, In Laertius we read..that..the Virtuous [had] his Εὐπαθείαι, his Eupathies, or Well-feelings. **1834-43** SOUTHEY *Doctor* lxxvi. (1862) 160 The Stoics who called our good affections eupathies, did not manage those affections as well as they understood them. **1837** —— in C. Southey *Life & Corr.* VI. 346 Our affections, our eupathies, our capacities of happiness and of improvement.

¶ Wrongly explained.

1730-6 BAILEY (folio), *Eupathy*, an easiness, or patience in bearing of sufferings or afflictions.

eupatorine (juːˈpætəraɪn). *Chem.* Formerly also eupatorin, and in L. form **eupatorina**. [f. *eupator-ium* + -INE[4].] (See quot.)

1838 T. THOMSON *Chem. Org. Bodies* 294 Eupatorina..is said to have been discovered by M. Righini in the flowers and leaves of the *Eupatorium cannabinum*, or hemp agrimony. **1882** WATTS *Dict. Chem.* II. 606 s.v. *Eupatorium*, The water-hemp, *Eupatorium cannabinum*, contains, according to Righoni, an alkaloïd, called eupatorine.

‖**Eupatorium** (juːpəˈtɔərɪəm). [mod.L., a. Gr. εὐπατόριον, *Agrimonia Eupatorium*, so called from Mithridates Eupator (Gr. Εὐπάτωρ), king of Pontus, who first used it.] A genus of the Nat. Order *Compositæ*, abundant in America; only one species, *E. cannabinum*, Hemp Agrimony, being British. Also an individual plant of the same.

[**1578** LYTE *Dodoens* I. xxxix. 57 Agrimonie is called..in Latine Eupatorium, and Hepatorium: in shoppes Agrimonia.] *Ibid.* I. xl. 59 The male Bastarde Agrimonie, is called in Shoppes Eupatorium. **1664** EVELYN *Kal. Hort.* (1729) 219 September ..Flowers in Prime or yet lasting.. Eupatorium of Canada. **1741** *Compl. Fam. Piece* II. iii. 380 Eupatoriums, Asphodels, Phalangiums. **1863** B. TAYLOR *H. Thurston* III. 54 Late flowering grasses..and the eupatoriums in the meadows.

†**ˈeupatory.** *Obs.* Also 6-7 eupatorie. [Anglicized form of prec.] Hemp Agrimony; but applied in Dicts. to Liverwort. Cf. AGRIMONY 2.

1542 BOORDE *Dyetary* xxv. 289 These thynges folowyng do purge color: Fumytory..Eupatory..& the whay of butter. **1568** TURNER *Herball* III. 29 The flowres of Eupatorie of Mesue are longe or somethinge longe. **1578** LYTE *Dodoens* III. xxvi. 352 The same boyled with..bastard Eupatory healeth the Jaundise. **1656** RIDGLEY *Pract. Physick* 97 To the straind liquor add syrup Bizantine, or Eupatory. **1678-96** in PHILLIPS. **1732** in COLES.

eupatrid (juːˈpætrɪd, ˈjuːpətrɪd). *Pl.* **eupatrids**; also (sense 1 a) in Lat. form **eupatridæ**. [ad. Gr. εὐπατρίδ-ης person of noble ancestry f. εὐ- (see EU-) + πατήρ father.]

1. a. One of the hereditary aristocracy of Athens; a member of the first of the three orders in the early Athenian constitution. **b.** Hence (rarely) *gen.* One who is of noble descent, a 'patrician'.

1836 THIRLWALL *Greece* II. 41 It [the Four Hundred] was a popular body, as compared with an assembly of the eupatrids. **1838** F. A. PALEY tr. *Schömann's Assembl. Ath.* 342 Clisthenes.. abolished the ancient division of tribes, as the most effectual means of reducing the power of the Eupatridæ. **1862** F. HALL in *Jrnl. As. Soc. Bengal* 205 *Amushyáyana*, 'son of somebody', an hidalgo, a eupatrid. **1863** *Blackw. Mag.* Sept. 290 The Greek Eupatrid or the Roman Patrician. **1864** R. F. BURTON *Dahome* I. 251 The big eupatrid is of somewhat offensive presence.

2. *attrib.* (quasi-*adj.*)

1833 J. KENRICK in *Philolog. Museum* ii. 368 A proof of Athenian blood and citizenship, not of Ionian and eupatrid extraction. **1847** GROTE *Greece* II. x. III. 107 This eupatrid oligarchy and severe legislation. **1866** FELTON *Anc. & Mod. Gr.* I. xi. 206 He [Æschylus] belonged to a distinguished eupatrid family probably descended from Codrus.

‖**eupepsia** (juːˈpɛpsɪə). [mod.L., a. Gr. εὐπεψία good digestion, f. εὔπεπτος (see EUPEPTIC).] = next.

1706 in PHILLIPS. **1847** in CRAIG. **1883** GOLDW. SMITH in *Contemp. Rev.* Dec. 807 Here was bigness, strength, heartiness, eupepsia in perfection.

eupepsy (ˈjuːpɛpsɪ, juːˈpɛpsɪ). [Anglicized form of prec.] Healthy action of the digestive organs; good digestion.

1721-1800 in BAILEY. **1860** MAYNE *Exp. Lex.*, *Eupepsia*, old term for good digestion: eupepsy.

eupeptic (juːˈpɛptɪk), *a.* and *sb.* [f. Gr. εὔπεπτ-ος easy of digestion, having a good digestion (f. εὐ- EU- + πέπ-τειν to digest) + -IC.]

A. *adj.*

†**1.** Promoting 'eupepsy,' assisting digestion. *rare.*

1699 EVELYN *Acetaria* 89 Those [herbs] that are Eupeptic, and promote concoction.

2. Having a good digestion.

1831 CARLYLE *Schiller* Misc. Ess. (1888) III. 87 The perennial never-failing joys of a digestive apparatus thoroughly eupeptic. **1848** CLOUGH *Bothie* III. 10 E'en after dinner, eupeptic, would rush yet again to his reading.

absol. **1883** *Times* 8 Mar. 9/3 City dinners may be an excellent form of amusement for the eupeptic and robust.

3. Of or pertaining to 'eupepsy' or good digestion; characteristic of, or resulting from, good digestion.

1845 CARLYLE *Cromwell* (1871) IV. 241 A massiveness of eupeptic vigour. **1859** LEWES *Phys. Com. Life* I. 137 Persons ..living in that happy eupeptic ignorance which only knows Digestion as a name. **1866** CARLYLE *Remin.* (1881) I. 172 At length his faculties were getting hebetated, wrapt in lazy eupeptic fat.

4. *nonce-use.* Studious of what conduces to good digestion.

1871 COLLINS *Mrq. & Merch.* III. ii. 60 Terrell, never scientifically eupeptic, went in for a couple of dozen [oysters].

5. Easy of digestion; easily digested.

1864 in WEBSTER; and in mod. Dicts.

†**B.** *sb.* (cf. *tonic, sudorific*, etc.) *Obs.*$^{-0}$

1731 BAILEY vol. II, *Eupepticks*, medicines, or other things that promote concoction.

Hence **eupepˈticity**, the state or condition of feeling resulting from good digestion.

1849 CARLYLE *Irish Journ.* 152 Simplicity, energy, eupepticity; a right healthy thick-sided Irish soul. **1865** —— *Fredk. Gt.* V. XIII. vii. 77 No man..has swum through such seas of transcendent eupepticity.

eupeptically (juːˈpɛptɪkəlɪ), *adv.* [f. EUPEPTIC *a.* + -AL + -LY[2].] In a eupeptic manner; so as to assist digestion.

1939 *Scrutiny* Mar. 403 Eupeptically gay composers like Virgil Thomson. **1966** *New Statesman* 7 Oct. 522/3 A eupeptically progressive consideration of human affairs.

euphausiacean (juːfɔːzɪˈeɪʃən). [f. mod.L. *Euphausiacea*, f. Gr. εὐ- EU- + φα- root of φαίνειν to show + οὐσία substance + -ACEA.] A member of the order Euphausiacea of shrimp-like planktonic crustaceans. So **euˈphausian**, a member of the genus *Euphausia* of crustaceans; loosely, a euphausiacean; **euˈphausid, -idian, -iid**, a member of the family Euphausiidæ. Also **euphausid** *a.*

1885 G. O. SARS in *Challenger Reps.* (*Zool.*) XIII. 63 In regard to the capture of Euphausidians..scarcely a single haul failing to yield some of the forms comprised in this group. **1893** *Funk's Stand. Dict.*, Euphausiid. **1893** T. R. R. STEBBING *Hist. Crustacea* xviii. 265 The Euphausid larva. **1909** W. T. CALMAN in R. Lankester *Treat. Zool.* VII. 245 Order *Euphausiacea*... The phosphorescence of certain Euphausians was first observed by J. V. Thompson. **1924** W. M. TATTERSALL in *Brit. Antarctic* (*Terra Nova*) *Exped.* (*Zool.*) VIII. 1 The Euphausians in this collection were provided entirely by the tow nettings and other plankton gatherings. **1928** RUSSELL & YONGE *Seas* v. 117 Euphausiids ..are about an inch and a half in length, but are so abundant that they form a large part of the food of many of the northern fishes. **1934** *Geogr. Jrnl.* LXXXIV. 126 Thousands of the Euphausid, *Thyanoessa inermis.* **1950** J. S. COLMAN *Sea & its Mysteries* v. 106 The animals that make up the krill belong to the group of crustacea known as Euphausians. **1956** A. C. HARDY *Open Sea* ix. 171 The Euphausiaceans..have..a wonderful set of luminous organs. **1959** H. BARNES *Oceanogr. & Marine Biol.* 93 Planktonic organisms, such as the shrimp-like Euphausids, are responsible for this deep scattering layer. **1965** *New Scientist* 1 July 41/1 The euphausiaceans..are characterized by possessing well developed light-producing organs. **1968** *Ibid.* 24 Oct. 205/1 Whales feed on krill, composed largely of planktonic, relatively large, shrimp-like creatures known as euphausids.

euˈphemian (juːˈfiːmɪən), *a. rare.* [f. as next + -IAN.] = EUPHEMISTIC.

1820 W. TOOKE tr. *Lucian* I. 550 *note*, An euphemian turn, to avoid directly saying that something dreadful would befall them.

euphemious (juːˈfiːmɪəs), *a. rare.* [f. Gr. εὔφημ-ος fair of speech, also well reputed (f. εὐ- EU- + φήμη speaking, fame) + -(I)OUS.]

a. = EUPHEMISTIC. **b.** That has a reputable name.

1867 L. CAMPBELL tr. *Plato's Polit.* Introd. 50 He may have recourse to the more 'euphemious' plan of emigration.

Hence **euˈphemiously** *adv.* = EUPHEMISTICALLY.

1853 *Fraser's Mag.* XLVII. 683 The 'poets' had 'mounted their horse', as getting drunk was euphemiously called by that polite people. **1884** B. NICHOLSON in *Athenæum* 28 June 824/3 It is euphemiously said to be a 'change of three letters'.

euphemism (ˈjuːfɪmɪz(ə)m). [ad. Gr. εὐφημισμός, f. εὐφημίζειν to speak fair, f. εὔφημος: see prec.]

1. *Rhet.* That figure of speech which consists in the substitution of a word or expression of comparatively favourable implication or less unpleasant associations, instead of the harsher or more offensive one that would more precisely designate what is intended.

1656-81 BLOUNT *Glossogr.*, *Euphemism*, a good or favourable interpretation of a bad word. **1678-96** in PHILLIPS. **1721-1800** in BAILEY. **1793** BEATTIE *Moral Sc.* §866 Akin to it [Litotes] is Euphemism. **1879** M. D. CONWAY *Demonol.* I. III. vi. 348 Serpent-worship in India was developed by euphemism.

2. An instance of this figure; a less distasteful word or phrase used as a substitute for something harsher or more offensive.

1793 BEATTIE *Moral Sc.* §866 The euphemism ['he fell asleep'] partakes of the nature of metaphor. **1860** FROUDE *Hist. Eng.* VI. 27 *foot-n.*, A shorn crown..a euphemism for decapitation. **1865** TYLOR *Early Hist. Man.* vi. 143 The euphemism of calling the Furies in the Eumenides. **1877** E. COUES *Fur Anim.* vii. 216 The Skunk yields a handsome fur, lately become fashionable, under the euphemism of 'Alaska Sable'.

†**3.** (See quot.) *Obs.*$^{-0}$

1678-96 PHILLIPS, *Euphemism*, a setting forth any ones good fame. **1721-1800** in BAILEY. **1828** in WEBSTER.

‖**euphemismus** (juːfiːˈmɪzməs). Now *rare.* [late L., ad. Gr.; see prec.] = prec.

1599 *Broughton's Lett.* 19 *Commilitones*..is giuen by an *Euphemismus* of Captaines to their Souldiers. **1657** J. SMITH *Myst. Rhet.* 224 Euphemismus..a good change of a word, or a fair kind of speech. **1706** in PHILLIPS. **1836** SIR H. TAYLOR *Statesman* xii. 85 Adherence to system or precedent, called by euphemismus adherence to principle.

euphemist (ˈjuːfɪmɪst). *rare*$^{-0}$. [f. Gr. εὔφημ-ος + -IST.] One who uses euphemisms.

1860 WORCESTER cites CARLYLE.

euphemistic (juːfɪˈmɪstɪk), *a.* [f. Gr. εὔφημ-ος (see EUPHEMIOUS) + -IST + -IC.] Pertaining to euphemism; of the nature of a euphemism; containing a euphemism.

1856 *Sat. Rev.* II. 265/2 He is entitled to claim, or to negotiate, or to arrange—or whatever euphemistic phrase may be more suitable—for a retiring competency, etc. **1876** FREEMAN *Norm. Conq.* V. 18 The euphemistic spirit goes so far..that the Norman owner is spoken of as the 'heir' of the Englishman who had been turned out. **1877** *Outl. Hist. Relig.* 149 Rudra..under his euphemistic name of Siva.

Hence **eupheˈmistical** *a.* = prec. Also **eupheˈmistically** *adv.*, by way of euphemism.

1879 M. ARNOLD *Ess.*, *Falkland* 220 Such is Clarendon's euphemistical phrase for poor and proud men of letters. **1860** in J. A. Hessey *Notes Bampton Lect.* 473 Whisky, (euphemistically termed refreshment). **1874** DEUTSCH *Rem.* 365 R. Joseph bar Chama, the Blind, euphemistically called the clear-sighted.

euphemize (ˈjuːfɪmaɪz), *v.* [ad. Gr. εὐφημίζειν to speak fair, use auspicious words, f. εὔφημος: see EUPHEMIOUS.] **a.** *trans.* To express by a euphemism; to speak of euphemistically. **b.** *intr.* To speak euphemistically; to make use of euphemisms.

1857 SIR F. PALGRAVE *Norm. & Eng.* II. 1 The agreeable cheat we pass upon ourselves by euphemizing sins. **1872** LEVER *Ld. Kilgobbin* lxiii, What Sheil used to euphemize as 'the wild justice' of noble spirits. **1880** *Blackw. Mag.* Feb. 253 Euphemise and moralise as our humanitarian sophists may. **1888** *Standard* 24 Feb. 5/2 They euphemise gambling bargains as 'special transactions'.

euphemizer (ˈjuːfɪmaɪzə(r)). [f. EUPHEMIZE *v.* + -ER[1].] One who speaks euphemistically.

1890 C. MARTYN *Wendell Phillips* 186 He was the one outspoken man in a nation of euphemizers.

euphemous (ˈjuːfɪməs), *a. rare.* [f. Gr. εὔφημ-ος (see EUPHEMIOUS) + -OUS.] = EUPHEMISTIC.

1859 *Times* 15 Mar. 9/3 The name of this noisy bustling quarrelsome discontented and insalubrious little island [Hong Kong] may..be used as a euphemous synonym for a place not mentionable to ears polite.

euphemy (ˈjuːfɪmɪ). *rare.* [ad. Gr. εὐφημία, f. εὔφημος: see EUPHEMIOUS.] = EUPHEMISM 2.

1857 I. TAYLOR *World of Mind* 629 In human nature, love is more than a euphemy for selfism.

euphenics (juːˈfɛnɪks). *Biol.* [f. Gr. εὐ- EU- + φαίν-ειν to show, appear + -ICS.] A practice analogous to eugenics in which physical improvement of man is sought through the modification and control of his development (as by chemical or surgical means).

1963 J. LEDERBERG in *Nature* 4 May 428/2, I propose the term 'euphenics' as the counterpart of 'eugenics', in the same sense that 'phenotype' is opposed to 'genotype'. **1965** *New Scientist* 9 Dec. 714/2 By 'cultural euphenics'..one could make revolutionary changes in a generation. **1967** *Technology Week* 23 Jan. 50/3 Euphenics [is] the modification of his [*sc.* man's] biological development.

‖**euphonia** (ˌjuːˈfəʊnɪə). [late Lat., a. Gr. εὐφωνία: see EUPHONY.] = EUPHONY.

1591 PERCIVALL *Sp. Dict.* B ij, Pleasantnes or easines of sound or vtterance, called Euphonia. **1602** CAREW *Cornwall* 120 a, *g* for Euphonias sake being turned into *n.* **1706** in PHILLIPS. **1736** in BAILEY. **1814** SCOTT *Wav.* liv, Seven Highland ladies..screamed the company deaf, with examples of Celtic euphonia. **1824** *Blackw. Mag.* XV. 144 So much for exordium and euphonia!

euphoniad (juːˈfəʊnɪæd). *Mus.* [irreg. f. prec.] (See quot.)

1854 J. W. MOORE *Encycl. Mus.* s.v., This instrument was invented by P. L. and G. Grosh, of Petersburg, Pa. They claim that it..combines in its tones those of the organ, clarinet, horn, bassoon, and violin. **1864** Hence in WEBSTER.

euphonic (juːˈfɒnɪk), *a.* [f. EUPHON-Y + -IC; cf. Fr. *euphonique.*]

1. †**a.** Well sounding, agreeable to the ear; = EUPHONIOUS. *Obs.* **b.** Conformable to the laws of euphony.

1814 SCOTT *Wav.* i, The most sounding and euphonic surname that English history or topography affords. **1851** SIR F. PALGRAVE *Norm. & Eng.* I. 276 Under the more euphonic denomination of Arsenius. **1876** BIRCH *Egypt* 30 The Greek Sesoosis, or Setesura, made euphonic as Sesostris.

2. Of or pertaining to euphony.

1816 J. GILCHRIST *Philos. Etym.* p. xviii, The consonants, have been as in a kind of euphonic spite gnawed down into musical notes. **1875** WHITNEY *Life Lang.* vii. 128 Purely euphonic influences. **1879** F. HARRISON *Choice Bks.* (1886) 28 *note*, To English hexameters there are euphonic obstacles which seem to be insuperable.

3. as *sb.* in *pl.* Euphonious expressions. *nonce-use* (ironical).

1850 L. HUNT *Autobiog.* I. v. 191 It was curious to hear him..urge on his horses with the other customary euphonics of his tribe.

euˈphonical (juːˈfɒnɪkəl), *a.* [f. as prec. + -AL[1].] = prec. Hence **euˈphonically** *adv.*; **euˈphonicalness**, the quality of being euphonical.

1668 WILKINS *Real Char.* III. xiv. 381 Our English hath what is comely and euphonical in each of these. **1674** PETTY *Disc. Dupl. Proportion* Ep. Ded., Grandisonous or Euphonical Nonsense. **1824** *Blackw. Mag.* XVI. 58 With a grand euphonical sentence..I concluded. **1860** TYAS *Wild Fl.* 11 *Sow-Bread.*—How euphonical is the name. **1884** *Bath Jrnl.* 25 Oct. 6/2 The contest over what is euphonically called 'the City Staff'. **1668** WILKINS *Real Char.* Contents D j b, A comparison of the Language here proposed, with fifty others, as to the facility and Euphonicalness of it.

euphonion, an early form of EUPHONIUM.

1862 *Catal. Internat. Exhib., Brit.* II. No. 3377, An Euphonion or solo bass in B flat.

euphonious (juːˈfəʊnɪəs), *a.* [f. as EUPHONICAL *a.* + -OUS.] Full of or characterized by euphony; pleasing to the ear. (Often used ironically.)

1774 JOEL COLLIER *Mus. Trav.* (1775) 5, I chose to change my name from Collier to Coglioni or Collioni, as more euphonious. **1797** W. TAYLOR in *Monthly Mag.* III. 337 Those hexameters are most euphonious whose feet are interwoven. **1836** W. IRVING *Astoria* II. 68 Restoring the Indian names, wherever significant and euphonious. **1865** *Reader* 26 Aug. 224/2 Is it grammatical, even if it were euphonious, to say, etc. **1872** JENKINSON *Guide Eng. Lakes* (1879) 189 A lane, bearing the euphonious cognomen of Spooney Green.

Hence **euˈphoniously** *adv.*, in a euphonious manner, with pleasant sounds.

1836 JAS. GRANT *Recoll. Ho. Lords* xv. 368 His language sounds most euphoniously in your ears. **1856** KANE *Arct. Expl.* II. xii. 125 Thus euphoniously solicited, the Upernaviks sat down and ate. **1867** MILL *Subj. Women* (1869) 22 They euphoniously paraphrase it.

euphonism (ˈjuːfənɪz(ə)m). Also 8 in Latin form **euphonismus.** [f. as prec. + -ISM.] The habit of using well-sounding words or names; a well-sounding combination or expression.

1774 *Westm. Mag.* II. 567 The metaphor and digression, the allegory and euphonismus. **1820** *Blackw. Mag.* VII. 664 This elaborate system of euphonism. **1847** in OSWALD *Etym. Dict.*

euphonistic (juːfəˈnɪstɪk), *a.* [f. as prec. + -IST + -IC.] Chosen with regard to euphony; aiming to be euphonious.

1837 LYTTON *E. Maltrav.* IX. iv, [Her] words were not euphonistic, nor her voice mellifluous. **1856** *Sat. Rev.* II. 220/2 Among the Greeks, the Furies had an especially euphonistic appellative. **1876** MRS. HOPKINS *Rose Turq.* I. i. 3 The euphonistic but somewhat fictional language of domestic life.

euphonium (juːˈfəʊnɪəm). *Mus.* [as if Lat., f. Gr. εὔφων-ος: see EUPHONY.] 'A name given to the bass instrument of the Saxhorn family, usually tuned in B♭ or C. It only differs from the barytone Saxhorn in the larger diameter of its bore, which thus produces a longer and somewhat deeper quality of tone' (Grove). Also *attrib.*

1865 *Reader* No. 139. 244/2 The bass duet..upon a couple of euphoniums. **1879** STAINER *Music of Bible* 27 The construction of a harmonium..accordion, or euphonium. **1888** *Daily News* 3 Sept. 3/3 The death is also announced of the popular euphonium player Mr. A. J. Phasey.

euphonization (juːfənaɪˈzeɪʃən). [f. next: see -ATION.] The action of rendering euphonious.

1890 F. HALL in *Nation* (N. York) LI. 361/2 Pinkerton's egregious attempt, in 'Thea Visiona of Mirza', at the euphonization of English.

euphonize (ˈjuːfənaɪz), *v.* [f. EUPHON-Y + -IZE.] *trans.* To render euphonious, impart euphony to; to alter (a word) for the sake of euphony.

1774 MITFORD *Harm. Lang.* 172 The spreading of classical learning had not at first that general effect in euphonizing our language which might have been expected. **1832** *Blackw. Mag.* XXXII. 972, I am now in the heart of Nadoly, or, as we euphonize it, Natolia. **1840** BARHAM *Ingol. Leg., Leech Folkest.*, A row of houses then denominated 'Frog-hole'. Modern refinement subsequently euphonized the name into 'East-street'.

euphonon (juːˈfəʊnən). *Mus.* [ad. Gr. εὔφωνον, neut. of εὔφωνος: see EUPHONY.] A musical instrument (see quot. 1842) which resembled the upright piano in form and the organ in tone.

1824 *Specif. Patent* No. 4994 These said frames are to be placed as nearly as possible to the strings of the pianofortes and the euphonons. **1842** A. SAVAGE in *Mech. Mag.* XXXVII. 563 When describing the claviol I ought to have mentioned..the euphonon. In this instrument the strings are of steel wire..put into vibration by an endless band, acting as a bow, one band to each string.

euphonous (ˈjuːfənəs). [f. Gr. εὔφωνος see next + -OUS.] = EUPHONIOUS.

1805 W. TAYLOR in *Ann. Rev.* III. 651 He is a great artist ..full of dexterities, various and euphonous. **1827** *Blackw. Mag.* XXII. 593 That euphonous compliment devoted by Irish patriots and mob-orators to slavery and oppression. **1834** SIR H. TAYLOR *Artevelde* Wks. (1864) I. 301 *note*, I have adopted this..very euphonous epithet from a little poem called 'The Errors of Ecstacie'.

euphony (ˈjuːfənɪ). Also 7 euphonie. [a. F. *euphonie*, ad. Gr. εὐφωνία, f. εὔφωνος well-sounding, f. εὐ- (see EU-) + φωνή voice, sound.]

a. The quality of having a pleasant sound; the pleasing effect of sounds free from harshness: chiefly with reference to combinations of words in sentences, or of phonetic elements in spoken words. **b.** In recent philological use often: The tendency to greater ease of pronunciation, as shown in those combinatory phonetic changes formerly ascribed to an endeavour after a pleasing acoustic effect.

1623 COCKERAM, *Euphonie*, accent in words. **1680** DALGARNO *Didascol.* 114 (T.), Had the Grecians been as careless of euphony..in the terminations, as they have been in the initial syllables. **1727** *Art of Speaking in Publick* (ed. 2) 99 'Tis the same in speaking, as in Musick; Words for the Euphony of the one, and Notes for the Harmony of the other. **1773** W. KENRICK *Rhet. Gram.* i. §4. 13 (Jod.) The euphony of speech frequently interferes with the rules, founded solely on its significancy. **1822** EUSTACE *Tour Italy* (ed. 6) III. 18 Epopeus, now for euphony softened into Epomeo. **1865** TYLOR *Early Hist. Man.* iv. 71 Their voices lose all cheerfulness and euphony. **1874** HELPS *Soc. Press.* xii. 161 Euphony then is the mother of many lies. **1885** PERRY *Sanskr. Primer* §38 The rules of Sanskrit euphony affecting this sound.

‖**Euphorbia** (juːˈfɔːbɪə). *Bot.* Also 4 euforbia. [a. L. *euphorbea*, f. *Euphorbus*, the name of a physician to Juba king of Mauritania.] The Latin and botanical name of the Spurge genus (N.O. *Euphorbiaceæ*), comprising many species, which vary from a herbaceous plant in temperate regions, to a tree-like growth in warm climates. They are marked by two almost constant characteristics, the secretion of a viscid milky juice, and the peculiar inflorescence of having a number of stamens round a stalked and three-celled ovary. Some of the species, as *E. punicea*, are cultivated for the beauty of their involucre, the bracts of which are a brilliant scarlet, with the appearance of a real flower. Cf. SPURGE.

1398 TREVISA *Barth. De P.R.* xv. xciii. (1495) 524 In Mauritanea groweth an herbe callyd Euforbia..the whyte juys therof is wonderly praysyd in clerenesse of sight. **1601** HOLLAND *Pliny* II. 222 Iuba king of Mauritania, found out the herb Euphorbia, which he so called after the name of his own Physitian Euphorbus. **1794** MARTYN *Rousseau's Bot.* xx. 281 Euphorbia has a corolla of four and sometimes of five petals. **1813** SIR H. DAVY *Agric. Chem.* (1814) 147 Different species of Euphorbia emit a milky juice. **1834** PRINGLE *Afr. Sk.* vi. 209 The lofty candelabra-shaped euphorbias towering above the copses of evergreens. **1878** H. M. STANLEY *Dark Cont.* I. vi. 139 The villages..are surrounded by hedges of euphorbias, milk-weed.

Hence ˌ**euphorbiˈaceous** *a.* [+ -ACEOUS], of the Natural Order *Euphorbiaceæ*. **euˈphorbial** *a.* [+ -AL[1]] = prec.

1852 TH. ROSS *Humboldt's Trav.* II. xvi. 52 *note*, The juice of a euphorbiaceous plant (*Sapium aucuparium*)..is so glutinous that it is used to catch parrots. **1863** BATES *Nat. Amazon* iv. (1864) 86 The tree which yields this valuable sap [India-rubber] is the Siphonia Elastica, a member of the Euphorbiaceous order. **1864** WEBSTER, *Euphorbial*, citing OGILVIE; and in mod. Dicts.

†**euphorbine**[1]. *Obs.* In 4 euforbine [f. L. *euphorbea* (see prec.).] Some product of the euphorbia.

c **1400** *Lanfranc's Cirurg.* (MS. A.) 104 Anoynte..his necke wiþ hoote oynementis, as with oile of nardine, euforbine, oile of rue.

euphorbine[2] (juːˈfɔːbaɪn). *Chem.* [f. EUPHORBIA + -INE[4].] (See quots.)

1838 T. THOMSON *Chem. Org. Bodies* 792 This is the substance which M. Ricord-Madianna has called euphorbin. **1882** WATTS *Dict. Chem.* II. 607 The milky juice of *E. myrtifolia*..contains, according to Ricord-Madianna, a non-volatile poisonous principle, euphorbine.

‖**Euphorbium** (juːˈfɔːrbɪəm). Also 4 euf-, eufforbium. [a. L. *euphorbeum* = *euphorbea.*]

†**1.** = EUPHORBIA. *Obs.*

1607 SYLVESTER *Du Bartas* II. iv. II. (1605–7) III. 67 His Shield..freng'd about with sprigs of Scammonie, And of Euphorbium, forged cunningly. **1626** BACON *Sylva* (1631) §639 Euphorbium also hath a Milke..not very white, which is of a great Acrimony. **1712** E. COOK *Voy. S. Sea* 326 The Trees I observ'd here, were Lignum Vitæ, Birch.. Euphorbium. **1767** J. ABERCROMBIE *Ev. Man his own Gard.* (1803) 130 Succulent kinds..such as..euphorbiums.

2. A gum resin obtained from certain succulent species of *Euphorbia*. It is an extremely acrid substance, formerly used as an emetic and purgative. The powder causes violent sneezing.

c **1400** *Lanfranc's Cirurg.* (MS. A) 43 To drie bodies he muste be medlid wiþ a litil euforbium [printed *enforbium*]. *c* **1530** *Hickscorner* in Hazl. *Dodsley* I. 178 He..spake To a prentice for a penny-worth of euphorbium. **1653** URQUHART *Rabelais* II. xvi, Another [pocket] he had all full of Euphorbium very finely pulverised..shaking it [his handkerchief] hard at their nose [he] made them sneeze for foure hours without ceasing. **1760** WILLIS in *Phil. Trans.* LI. 663 She took..two ounces of the tincture of euphorbium. **1860** SIR W. HOOKER & ARNOTT *Brit. Flora* 291 *Euphorbia officinarum, antiquorum* and *canariensis* give the euphorbium of the shops.

euphorbone (juːˈfɔːbəʊn). *Chem.* Also euphorbon. [f. prec. + -ONE.] (See quots.)

1876 HARLEY *Mat. Med.* 437 According to Flückiger, 100 parts [of Euphorbium] contain..22 of Euphorbon. **1889** MUIR & MORLEY *Watts' Dict. Chem.* II, *Euphorbone*, $C_{20}H_{36}O$. Extracted from Euphorbium by light petroleum at 70° and crystallised from alcohol-ether.

euphoria (juːˈfɔərɪə). Also 7–8 in Anglicized form **euphory**, chiefly in sense 1. [ad. Gr. εὐφορία, f. εὔφορος well-bearing, f. εὖ well + φέρειν to bear.]

†**1.** *Path.* (See quot.) *Obs.*

1684 tr. *Bonet's Merc. Compit.* XIX. 674 The most certain rule for the quantity [of mineral waters] is the Euphory or well-bearing [of the patient]. **1706** PHILLIPS (ed. Kersey), *Euphoria*, the well bearing of the Operation of a Medicine, *i.e.* when the Patient finds himself eas'd or reliev'd by it.

2. *Path.* 'A word used to express well-being, or the perfect ease and comfort of healthy persons, especially when the sensation occurs in a sick person' (*Syd. Soc. Lex.*). Now freq. in non-technical contexts: a state of cheerfulness or well-being, esp. one based on over-confidence or over-optimism.

1727–51 in CHAMBERS *Cycl.* **1882** W. JAMES *Let.* 2 Nov. (1920) I. 211 Having taken the plunge, the cutaneous glow and 'euphoria' (*vide* dictionary) succeeded. **1922** R. S. WOODWORTH *Psychol.* vii. 120 The warmed-up person *feels* ready for business, full of 'ginger' or 'pep'—in short, full of life. The name 'euphoria', which means about the same as 'feeling good', is given to this condition. **1927** F. BRETT YOUNG *Portrait of Clare* 607 In this detached euphoria she began to approve of Dr. Boyd. **1939** A. HUXLEY *After many a Summer* I. iii. 37 The delightful condition of euphoria into which those poor kids and Clancy's good news had plunged him. **1954** A. W. FIELDING *Hide & Seek* 215 In this abnormal silence, which only intensified our state of euphoria, we settled down to sleep. **1960** AUDEN *Homage to Clio* 89 Good Queen Victoria, In a fit of euphoria, Commanded Disraeli To blow up the Old Bailey. **1964** *Ann. Reg. 1963* 9 But this euphoria was not to last. **1971** *Physics Bull.* Apr. 216/1 In the post war euphory, it was easy to obtain support for fundamental research.

euphoriant (juːˈfɔːrɪənt), *a.* and *sb. Med.* [f. EUPHORI(A + -ANT[1].] **A.** *adj.* Of drugs: inducing euphoria or an exaggerated feeling of well-being. **B.** *sb.* A drug with this property.

1947 *Brit. Med. Jrnl.* 28 June 919/1 The ideal euphoriant for clinical use..must induce a high degree of euphoria, must be stable and fully active by the oral route. *Ibid.*, There is a common and widespread belief that all euphoriant drugs are necessarily habit-forming, whereas this is in fact not the

case. **1957** H. McIlwain *Chemotherapy & Central Nervous System* x. 243 Synhexyl proved euphoriant, producing drowsiness, lightheadedness, and feelings of strangeness and of floating. **1965** J. Pollitt *Depression & its Treatment* iv. 48 Treatment with drugs may be indicated in certain cases, either in the form of sedatives, tranquillisers or euphoriants. **1968** A. Goldstein et al. *Princ. Drug Action* ix. 592 Although..the narcotics produce similar actions in all animal species, the euphoriant actions can be observed directly only in man.

euphoric (juːˈfɒrɪk), *a.* and *sb.* [f. EUPHORIA: see -IC.] **A.** *adj.* Pertaining to, characteristic of, or characterized by euphoria. Hence, characterized by a feeling of well-being, cheerful; also, producing or causing cheerfulness.

1888 *Amer. Jrnl. Psychol.* I. 361 Dr. Battaglia produced [by hashish] a great variety of symptoms with great uniformity, but never the commonly reported euphoric apathy. **1925** W. McDougall *Introd. Soc. Psychol.* (ed. 2) 394 When we have laughed, we commonly experience..its pleasing euphoric effects. **1947** Auden *Age of Anxiety* (1948) ii. 53 Come, peregrine nymph, display your warm Euphoric flanks in their full glory Of liberal life. **1951** R. Hoggart *Auden* vi. 196 Behind the slightly glittering euphoric exterior; the misery of a whole society. **1957** *Times Lit. Suppl.* 12 July 426/4 The euphoric pipe-smoking President. **1958** A. Wilson *Middle Age of Mrs Eliot* II. 271 It seemed impossible that she could truly be as euphoric as she seemed. **1959** *Listener* 20 Aug. 296/2 Two criminal alcoholics, one desperate, the other euphoric.

B. *sb.* A drug, etc., which produces a sense of euphoria; = EUPHORIANT *sb.*

1934 in Webster. **1951** A. Burger *Medicinal Chem.* ii. 9 The South American Indians..chewed coca leaves as a stimulant and euphoric. **1958** A. Huxley *Brave New World Revisited* (1959) viii. 102 The classical euphoric, alcohol..in excessive doses, causes illness and addiction.

Hence **euˈphorically** *adv.*, in a euphoric manner; cheerfully.

1958 *Observer* 8 June 15/6 The picaresque Sgt. Bilko has been crackling on ingeniously and euphorically now for week after week after week. **1963** *Times* 15 Jan. 11/2 The euphorically minded husband.

euphory: see EUPHORIA.

euphotic (juːˈfəʊtɪk), *a.* [f. EU- + PHOTIC *a.* b.] Pertaining to or designating the upper layer of the photic zone in sea-water where sufficient light penetrates to permit photosynthesis.

1909 Groom & Balfour tr. *Warming's Oecol. Plants* IV. xxxvi. 150 *Euphotic* vegetation, which receives an abundance of light. **1959** *New Scientist* 1 Oct. 586/1 Only a relatively thin surface layer of the ocean, the 'euphotic layer', is illuminated, and so only in this layer can photosynthesis and primary production of organic matter take place. **1964** *Oceanogr. & Marine Biol.* II. 360 The observation at 70m represents the luminescent activity of euphotic zone inhabitants plus that of scattering layer organisms. **1970** *Nature* 25 July 375/1 The flux of organic carbon from the euphotic zone (0–100 m) into the deep sea and into the bottom sediments.

euphotide (juːˈfəʊtaɪd). *Geol.* [a. Fr. *euphotide*, f. Gr. εὐ- (see EU-) + φῶς, φωτ-ός light.] 'A crystalline rock consisting essentially of Labrador felspar and diallage, with subordinate intermixtures of hornblende and augite' (Page). Called also GABBRO, q.v. Also *attrib.*

1836 Macgillivray tr. *Humboldt's Trav.* xxi. 301 The secondary formations..are pierced by syenitic and euphotide rocks. **1865** Lyell *Elem. Geol.* 750. **1879** *Spectator* 21 June 785 Blocks of diorite, of serpentine, and of euphotide.

‖**Euphrasia** (juːˈfreɪzɪə). Also 8 **euphragia**. [L. form of next.]

1. *Bot.* = EUPHRASY 1.

1706 Phillips (ed. Kersey), *Euphragia* or Euphrasia, the Herb Eye-bright. **1865** Tylor *Early Hist. Man.* vi. 123 The Euphrasia, or eye-bright, was, and is, supposed to be good for the eyes.

2. In etymological sense: Cheerfulness.

1882 T. Ribot *Dis. Memory* II. 109 An organic lesion.. may transform the cœnæsthesis..producing undue joyousness..of which the most striking example is seen in the euphrasia of the dying.

euphrasy (ˈjuːfrəsɪ). Also 5 **heufrasy**, 6–7 **euphrasie**, 7 **eufrage**. [ad. med.L. *euphrasia* (incorrectly *eufragia*), a. Gr. εὐφρασ-ία, lit. 'cheerfulness', f. εὐφραίνειν to cheer, f. εὐ- (see EU-) + φρήν mind. Cf. Fr. *eufraise*.]

1. *Bot.* A plant, *Euphrasia officinalis* (N.O. *Scrophulariaceæ*), formerly held in high repute for its medicinal virtues in the treatment of diseases of the eye; = EYE-BRIGHT. Also *fig.*

c **1475** *Pict. Voc.* in Wr.-Wülcker 787 *Hec eufrasia*, a heufrasy. **1503** *Sheph. Kalender* xxviii, Salendin, eufrage, pimpernell. **1577** Frampton *Joyful News* 43 b, Euphrasie, otherwise called eye-bright. **1667** Milton *P.L.* XI. 414 Michael..purg'd with Euphrasie and Rue The visual Nerve. **1742** Shenstone *Schoolmistr.* xii. 100 Euphrasy.. That gives dim eyes to wander leagues around. **1816** Southey *Poet's Pilgr.* I. 40 Reason when the props of flesh gave way Purged as with euphrasy the mortal eye. **1865** Gosse *Land & Sea* (1874) 15 The little euphrasy derives its name of eyebright..from its old reputation for 'making old eyes young again'.

b. *fig.*

1838 S. Bellamy *Betrayal* II. 45 The early zephyr from the Orient breath'd And rent the curtain'd sky..The euphrasy of dawn. **1848** H. Miller *First Impr.* xvii. (1857) 308 The eye purged and strengthened by the euphrasy of science. **1860** Faber *Bethlehem* vi. (1865) 353 Eyes which have been touched with the special euphrasy of heaven.

¶**2.** In pseudo-etymological sense: Fine phrasing. *rare*$^{-1}$.

[A Gr. *εὐφρασία in this sense might have been f. εὐ- + φράζειν to speak, but it is not actually found.]

1833 *Fraser's Mag.* VII. 216 His former volumes abounded in..affected idioms, and constant attempts at euphrasy.

Euphratean (juːˈfreɪtɪən), *a.* [f. *Euphrates* + -AN.] Of, pertaining to, or bordering on the river Euphrates.

1877 J. W. Dawson *Origin of World* xii. 253 This primitive Cushite empire called Ethiopia..occupied the Euphratean valley. **1902** D. G. Hogarth *Nearer East* 220 Trade between east and west has deserted the painful Euphratean routes. *Ibid.* 222 The route taken by the Persian *haj*, after visiting the Euphratean shrines. **1934** A. Toynbee *Study Hist.* II. 385 The Nilotic and Euphratean jungle-swamps.

euphroe (ˈjuːfrəʊ). *Naut.* Also **uphroe, uvrou, uvrow**. [a. Du. *juffrouw*, also *juffer* dead-eye, lit. 'maiden'; the equivalent Ger. *jungfer*, Da. *jomfrue*, Sw. *jungfru* are used in same sense.] A crow-foot dead-eye; see quot.

1815 Falconer *Marine Dict.* (ed. Burney), *Uphroe. Ibid.* s.v. *Dead-eye*, Crowfeet Dead-Eyes..generally termed an euphroe. **1867** Smyth *Sailor's Word-bk.* s.v. *Dead-eye*, The crowfeet dead-eyes are long cylindrical blocks with a number of small holes in them, to receive the legs or lines composing the crowfoot. Also called *uvrows*. *Ibid.*, *Euphroe, Uphroe, Uvrou*. **1874** Knight *Dict. Mech.* s.v., The euphroe (or uphroe) and its pendent cords form a crowfoot.

†**ˈeuphue**, *v. Obs. rare.* [f. next.] *trans.* = EUPHUIZE.

1592 G. Harvey *Pierce's Super.* 70, I cannot stand nosing of candlesticks or euphuing of similes. *Ibid.* 138 Stationers ..finde more gaine in the lillypot blanke then in the lillypot Euphued.

Euphues (ˈjuːfjuːiːz). [Gr. εὐφυής well-endowed by nature, f. εὐ- (see EU-) + φυή growth, f. φύειν to produce, in *pass.* to grow.

The adoption of this word by Lyly as the name of a personage of fiction was suggested by the passage of Ascham quoted below.]

The name of the chief character in John Lyly's two works, *Euphues, The Anatomy of Wit* (1578), and *Euphues and his England* (1580). Hence **a.** The book bearing that name. †**b.** *to speak Euphues*: to talk the dialect of 'Euphues', to 'parley Euphuism' (see EUPHUISM).

[**1570** Ascham *Scholem.* (Arb.) 38 Εὐφυής is he that is apte by goodnes of witte, and appliable by readines of will, to learning, hauing all other qualities of the minde and partes of the bodie that must another day serue learning, not troubled, mangled, and halfed, but, etc.] *a* **1613** Overbury *A Wife* (1638) 88 And speaks Euphues, not so gracefully as heartily. **1613** Beaum. & Fl. *Honest Man's Fort.* v. iii, The courtier..has nothing in him but a piece of Euphues, And twenty dozen of twelvepenny ribband.

euphuism (ˈjuːfjuːɪz(ə)m). Also 6–7 **euphueisme**, 9 **-eism**. [f. prec. + -ISM.]

1. Properly, the name of a certain type of diction and style which originated in the imitation of Lyly's *Euphues* (see prec.), and which was fashionable in literature and in the conversation of cultivated society at the end of the 16th and beginning of the 17th c. Hence applied to any similar kind of affectation in writing or speech, and (loosely) to affectedly periphrastic or 'high-flown' language in general.

The chief features of 'euphuism' in the proper sense are: the continual recurrence of antithetic clauses in which the antithesis is emphasized by means of alliteration; the frequent introduction of a long string of similes all relating to the same subject, often drawn from the fabulous qualities ascribed to plants, minerals, and animals; and the constant endeavour after subtle refinement of expression. The sense in which (exc. in books on literary history) the word is now commonly used, is chiefly suggested by the absurd bombast which Scott puts into the mouth of Sir Piercie Shafton (who is described as a 'Euphuist') in *The Monastery*: this caricature, however, bears very little resemblance to the genuine 'euphuism'. Some loose uses of the word can hardly be accounted for exc. by supposing that the writers (recognizing the familiar prefix *eu-*) had the notion that its etymological sense was 'fine talking' or something equivalent.

1592 G. Harvey *Third Let.* 34 What hee is improued since, excepting his good olde *Flores Poetarum*, and Tarletons surmounting Rhetorique, with a little Euphuisme, and Greenesse inough. **1632** E. Blount *Lyly's Six Crt. Comedies* Ep. to Rdr., All our Ladies were then his Schollers; And that Beautie in Court, which could not Parley Euphueisme, was as little regarded; as shee which now there, speakes not French. **1820** Scott *Monast.* xiv, When euphuism is out of fashion. **1841–4** Emerson *Ess.*, *Nature* Wks. (Bohn) I. 227 As soon as men begin to write on nature, they fall into euphuism. **1852** Lever *Daltons* I. xxvii. 225 Her perfumed little notes, written in a style of euphuism all her own. **1874** Green *Short Hist.* vii. 427 The Pedantry of Euphuism was giving way to the pedantry of Scriptural phrases.

¶ *transf.* Affected elegance in dress, etc.

This curious use is found also in Fr.; see Littré.

1824 *New Monthly Mag.* X. 493 Their own frippery euphueism of dress and manner.

2. An instance of euphuism; a euphuistic phrase or composition.

1871 R. F. Weymouth *Euph.* 13, I take a euphuism..as signifying a particular form of expression characteristic of Lilie's prose. **1884** E. P. Hood in *Chr. World* 21 Aug. 629/2 Hymn-writers..whose frigid euphuisms have found their names in Mr. Miller's large catalogue.

¶ Erroneously for EUPHEMISM.

1865 Mrs. Gaskell *Wives & Dau.* in *Cornh. Mag.* Aug. 139 'If anything did—go wrong, you know', said Cynthia, using an euphuism for death. **1866** Geo. Eliot *F. Holt* (1868) 63 Those are your roundabout euphuisms that dress up swindling till, etc.

Euphuist (ˈjuːfjuːɪst). [f. as prec. + -IST.] An imitator of the style of expression characteristic of Lyly's *Euphues*; one whose writing or speech is characterized by EUPHUISM.

1820 Scott *Monast.* xv, There he found the Euphuist in the same elegant posture of abstruse calculation which he had exhibited on the preceding evening. **1828** Macaulay *John Dryden* It is needless to mention Sidney and the whole tribe of Euphuists. **1871** R. F. Weymouth *Euph.* 3 Shakespeare does not call Don Adriano a euphuist; nor is he such. **1874** Green *Short Hist.* vii. 392 Elizabeth was the most affected and detestable of Euphuists.

euphuistic (juːfjuːˈɪstɪk), *a.* [f. prec. + -IC.] Tending to or resembling euphuism; of the nature of euphuism; characterized by euphuism. Chiefly in inaccurate sense: Abounding in 'highflown' or affectedly refined expression.

1828 Carlyle *Goethe's Helena* Misc. Ess. (1888) I. 157 If indeed it is not a little euphuistic. **1842** Lytton *Zanoni* 21 Ears grown nice and euphuistic in the..dulcet melodies of the day. **1863** Mrs. C. Clarke *Shaks. Char.* xvii. 448 He was intended to be a satire upon some euphuistic and bombastious characters..found in other plays of his time. **1871** R. F. Weymouth *Euph.* 3 The most important element by far in the euphuistic style is antithesis. **1876** E. A. Abbott *Bacon* in *Contemp. Rev.* June 154 The..antithetical euphuistic prose of Essex.

So **euphuˈistical** *a.* = prec. **euphuˈistically** *adv.*

1823 *Blackw. Mag.* XIV. 521 Making an agreeable and euphuistical alliteration. **1856** R. A. Vaughan *Mystics* (1860) II. 5 A poem, most euphuistically entitled The Cherubic Wanderer. **1874** Motley *Barneveld* II. xxi. 391 The Advocate had, as it was euphuistically expressed, been looking towards the enemy.

†**ˈEuphuize**, *v. Obs.* [f. EUPHU-ES + -IZE.]

a. *intr.* To talk like Euphues. **b.** *trans.* To fashion after the model of Euphues. Hence **ˈEuphuized** *ppl. a.*

1609 Dekker *Gull's Horne-bk.* vi. (Nares), When the Arcadian and Euphuis'd gentlewomen have their tongues sharpened to set upon you. *a* **1627** Middleton *Father Hubburd's T.* Wks. V. 561 For if thou Euphuize..I'll say thou borrow'st and condemn thy style.

euphyllite (juːˈfɪlaɪt). *Min.* [f. Gr. εὔφυλλ-ος well-leafed (f. εὐ- EU- + φύλλον leaf) + -ITE: see quot. 1849.] A hydrous silicate, micaceous in structure, and of a white colour.

1849 *Amer. Jrnl. Sc.* Ser. II. VIII. 383 The beautiful foliae [*sic*] of this pearly white mineral have suggested the name Euphyllite. **1873** *Proc. Amer. Phil. Soc.* XIII. 391 Euphyllite accompanied by tourmaline and zirsite is a very rare associate of corundum. **1882** Watts *Dict. Chem.* II. 608.

eupione (ˈjuːpɪəʊn). *Chem.* Also 9 **eupion**. [a. Gr. εὐπίων very fat, f. εὐ- (see EU-) + πίων fat; later assimilated to derivatives in -ONE.] A volatile, oily liquid obtained by the distillation of wood, tar, etc.

1838 T. Thomson *Chem. Org. Bodies* 701 Eupion is a colourless limpid liquid. *c* **1865** J. Wylde *Circ. Sc.* I. 420/2 *Eupione* is another product of wood-tar. **1873** Watts *Fownes' Chem.* 549 The liquid compounds of the paraffin series, known in commerce as paraffin oil, photogene, solar oil, eupione, etc. **1882** —— *Dict. Chem.* II. 608.

euplastic (juːˈplæstɪk), *a.* and *sb.* [f. Gr. εὔπλαστ-ος easy to mould (f. εὐ- EU- + πλαστός, f. πλάσσειν to form, mould) + -IC.]

A. *adj.* That is easily formed into an organic tissue: see quot. 1884.

1847 Todd *Cycl. Anat.* III. 754/1 Between the..euplastic and the..aplastic deposits the gradations are almost insensible. **1860** in Mayne *Exp. Lex.* **1884** *Syd. Soc. Lex.*, *Euplastic*. Lobstein's term for morbid deposits of plastic lymph which are of perfect structure and of easy organisation, as well as for healthy blastema in general.

B. *sb.* Euplastic matter.

1864 in Webster; and in mod. Dicts.

euploid (ˈjuːplɔɪd), *a.* *Biol.* [a. G. *euploid* (G. Täckholm 1922, in *Acta Horti Berg.* VII. 234), f. EU- + -PLOID.] Of a cell, an organism, or tissue: having each of the different chromosomes of the set in equal numbers; having an exact multiple of the haploid chromosome number. So **ˈeuploidy**, the condition or state of being euploid.

1926 L. W. Sharp *Introd. Cytol.* (ed. 2) xvii. 385 When the total number [of chromosomes] is..an exact multiple of the fundamental haploid number the term *euploid*..may be employed. *Ibid.* 387 (*caption*) The diploid chromosome complements of various species of *Rosa*, illustrating

euploidy. **1933** *Times Lit. Suppl.* 9 Nov. 779/1 Euploidy (regular multiplication of the basic chromosome number) is characteristic of cultivated apples. **1956** *Nature* 25 Feb. 384/2 By developing more constant euploid (or polyploid) cells.

‖**eupnœa** (ju:p'ni:ə). *Path.* [mod.L., a. Gr. εὔπνοια, f. εὔπνοος breathing easily, f. εὖ well + πνέ-ειν to breathe.] Natural or normal breathing; easy respiration.

1706 in PHILLIPS. **1721-1800** in BAILEY. **1847** in CRAIG. **1876** FOSTER *Phys.* II. ii. (1879) 354 The different conditions of the respiratory centre during apnœa, normal breathing or eupnœa, and dyspnœa.

eupnoic (ju:p'nəʊɪk), *a.* [f. Gr. εὔπνο-ος (see prec.) + -IC.] Relating to eupnœa; breathing easily and freely.

1884 in *Syd. Soc. Lex.*

‖**eu'poria** (ju:'pɔərɪə). [mod.L., a. Gr. εὐπορία an easy way (of doing a thing), f. εὔπορος easily done, f. εὐ- (see EU-) + πόρος way.] (See quot.)

1706 PHILLIPS (ed. Kersey), *Euporia*, a readiness in preparing Medicines, or the easiness of their Working. **1753** CHAMBERS *Cycl. Supp.* (citing Blancard). **1775** in ASH.

†**eupo'ristical**, *a. Obs. rare*$^{-1}$. [f. as next + -IC + -AL^1.] Of a kind to be easily procured.

1657 TOMLINSON *Renou's Disp.* 711 There is not amongst..euporistical medicaments, one more frequent or simple.

‖**eupo'riston.** *Obs.* Pl. **euporista.** [a. Gr. εὐπόριστον, neut. of εὐπόριστος easy to procure (τὰ εὐπόριστα (sc. φάρμακα) common family medicines, title of a work by Dioscorides), f. εὐ- (see EU-) + πορίζειν to procure.] A common medicine; a medicine that may be easily procured.

1706 PHILLIPS, *Euporista.* **1710** T. FULLER *Pharm. Extemp.* 420 This Euporiston doth..melt down, and draw forth tough Phlegm. **1775** in ASH.

†**'eupory.** *Obs.*$^{-0}$ [Anglicized form of EUPORIA.]

1721-1800 in BAILEY.

eupractic (ju:'præktɪk), *a. rare.* [f. Gr. εὖ well + πρᾶκ-, πράσσειν to do, act: cf. PRACTIC.] Inclined to act rightly.

1833 CARLYLE *Diderot* Misc. (1857) III. 215 An easy laconic gentleman..good-humoured, eupeptic, and eupractic.

†**eu'praxy.** *Obs. rare*$^{-1}$. [ad. Gr. εὐπραξία well-doing, f. εὖ well + πρᾶκ-, πράσσειν to act.] Well-doing; right action.

1675 BAXTER *Cath. Theol.* I. II. 5 That Liberty and Eupraxy or Obedience are all one.

†**eu'pyrion.** *Obs.* [f. Gr. εὐ- (see EU-) + πυρεῖον firestick, f. πῦρ fire.] The name given by the inventor to a contrivance for obtaining a light instantaneously; see quot. 1827. Also *fig.*

1827 FARADAY *Chem. Manip.* i, Hertner's Eupyrion..consists of a very small bottle half filled with asbestus..moistened with very concentrated sulphuric acid..The matches are small slips of wood tipped with sulphur..dipped into a mixture of chlorate of potash, and starch or sugar. *Ibid.* i. 22 An eupyrion should always be conveniently placed in the laboratory. **1827** HOOD *Bianca's Dream* i, Each eye of hers had Love's Eupyrion in it, That he could light his link at in a minute.

Eurafrican (jʊə'ræfrɪkən), *a.* and *sb.* [f. EUR(OPEAN + AFRICAN *sb.* and *a.*]

1. *Anthrop.* Designation of a dark-skinned race which inhabited regions on both sides of the Mediterranean.

1890 D. G. BRINTON *Races & Peoples* iv. 105 The white race is..an *African* race. I have calculated..the area of its control of the three continents... These figures vindicate for the race the title I have given it—Eurafrican. **1899** A. H. KEANE *Man: Past & Present* 444 The right of citizenship is to be withdrawn from such time-honoured names as 'Hamitic', 'Semitic'..in favour of 'Mediterranean', 'Eurafrican', and other upstarts. **1910** *Encycl. Brit.* XIV. 217/1 Whether this type is more conveniently designated by the word *Iberian*, or by some other name ('Eur-african', 'Mediterranean', &c.). **1928** V. G. CHILDE *Most Anc. East* ii. 39 The so-called Eurafrican, Mediterranean, or Brown race.

2. Pertaining to or involving both Europe and Africa, or their peoples together.

1909 in *Cent. Dict.* Suppl. **1957** *Time* 18 Feb. 18/2 Pineau said..'[France] would like to promote the formation of a Eurafrican whole.' **1958** *Economist* 25 Jan. 286/2 A Eurafrican bargain [i.e. between France and Algeria]. **1962** *Ibid.* 23 June 1192/1 The 'Eurafrican' negotiations at Brussels.

3. Designation of the 'Coloured People' of S. Africa, descendants of the native peoples with white admixture.

1922 S. G. MILLIN *Adam's Rest* II. v. 156 Frances no longer looked as if she might be a beautiful Spaniard or Italian. She was obviously a Eurafrican. **1927** W. M. MACMILLAN *Cape Colour Question* 288 All recent restrictive legislation, designed for the 'segregation' of the Natives, classes the 'Eurafricans' with the Europeans. **1927** *Times* (weekly ed.) 24 Nov. 586/1 The coloured or Eurafrican workers.

‖**euraquilo** (jʊə'rækwɪləʊ). Also **Euroaquilo.** [L. *Euraquilo* (in Gr. form Εὐρακύλων), *Euroaquilo* (Vulg.), f. L. *Eur-us* east-wind + *Aquilo* north-wind.] A stormy wind from the NE. or NNE. blowing in the Levant. Cf. EUROCLYDON.

1582 N. T. (Rhem.) *Acts* xxvii. 14 A tempestuous vvinde that is called Euro-aquilo [**1611** Euroclydon. **1881** *(Revised)* Euraquilo].

Eurasian (jʊə'reɪʃən), *a.* and *sb.* [f. *Eur-ope* + *Asia* (in sense A. 1 f. the compound *Eurasia*) + -AN.] **A.** *adj.*

1. Of or pertaining to Eurasia, *i.e.* to Europe and Asia considered as forming in reality one continent. Cf. EURASIATIC.

1868 HAYDN *Dict. Dates* (ed. 13), *Eurasian-plain*, the great central plain of Europe and Asia.

2. Of mixed European and Asiatic (*esp.* Indian) parentage. (The earlier designation was EAST INDIAN.)

1844 J. M. *Local Sketches* (Calcutta) in *N. & Q.* Ser. vi. XII. 177 The Eurasian Belle. **1858** *Calcutta Rev.* XXXI. 96 East Indian subscribers to the Fund are a very superior class to the mixed Eurasian population we see around us. **1860** *S. Times* 26 Aug. 4/2 The term Eurasian is applied to the offspring of a European father and a Hindoo or Mussulman woman in India. **1870** KAYE *Sepoy War* II. 291 The families also of European or Eurasian merchants and traders were gathered there [at Cawnpore] in large numbers. **1881** G. A. MACKAY *Tour Sir Ali Baba* 121 The Eurasian girl is often pretty and graceful.

B. *sb.* 'A modern name for persons of mixt European and Indian blood' (Col. Yule). See CHEE-CHEE.

1845 STOCQUELER *Handbk. Brit. India* (1854) 30 Eurasians, a term invented by the late Marquis of Hastings, conventionally accepted as embracing all the progeny of white fathers and Hindoo or Mahometan mothers. **1869** E. A. PARKES *Pract. Hygiene* (ed. 3) 461 Eurasians (that is the mixed race of British, Portuguese, Hindoo, Malay, blood mixed in all degrees). **1880** G. A. MACKAY *Tour Sir Ali Baba* 123 The shovel-hats are surprised that the Eurasian does not become a missionary or a schoolmaster.

Eurasiatic (jʊəreɪʃɪ,ætɪk), *a.* (*sb.*) [f. as prec. + -ATIC.] Of or pertaining to Eurasia; see prec. A. 1. Also as *sb.*, a person of Eurasiatic origin.

1870 HUXLEY in *Contemp. Rev.* XIV. 519 Spreading over the great Eurasiatic plains. **1883** G. ALLEN *Colin Clout's Gard.* xxiv, In the colder parts of the Eurasiatic continent. **1935** [see ALPINE *sb.* 2]. **1944** J. S. HUXLEY *On Living in Revol.* 175 The French claimed that the Aryan language and..civilization came into Europe with the Alpines (Eurasiatics).

Euratom (jʊə'rætəm). [Shortened f. *European Atomic Energy Community.*] An international organization set up in 1958 to co-ordinate the development and use of nuclear energy in Europe; since 1967, administratively merged with the EEC. Also *attrib.*

1956 *Times* 7 Jan. 7/2 The O.E.E.C. plan would leave purely national uses of atomic energy, including warlike uses, uncontrolled, whereas Euratom could not. **1958** *Economist* 5 Apr. 11/1 The newly-created six-nation Euratom community..has great military significance. **1961** *Daily Tel.* 14 Dec. 22/6 Euratom is sure to want to increase its budget as soon as Britain is among its contributors. **1962** *Ibid.* 3 July 29/4 The British negotiators may ask for assurances on the regulations authorising Euratom inspectors to check on stocks of fissionable material in member States. **1969** *Times* 2 May 27/1 One more attempt to get Euratom..on the road again has been made by the commission with a proposal for a five-year programme. **1974** *Encycl. Brit. Micropædia* III. 999/3 A major incentive for the creation of Euratom was to facilitate the establishment of a nuclear energy industry on a European..scale. **1986** *Financial Times* 12 Feb. II. 28/4 Euratom..is also raising LuxFr 300m with a bond maturing in 1992.

†**eure**, *sb. Obs.* Also 4-6 ure, 5 ewre. [a. OF. *eure, heur, aür*, Walloon *aweure* = Pr. *agur, augur, auguri*, Sp. *agüero*, It. *augurio*:—L. *augurium* augury, omen; cf. F. *bonheur.*] Destiny, fate, whether good or evil; luck.

1375 BARBOUR *Bruce* I. 312 Tak the vre that god wald send. **1430** LYDG. *Chron. Troy* I. v, As the goddes in this myne auenture Lyst to ordeyne for my fatall eure. *c* **1440** *Generydes* 2788 Bothe on thei rode to knowe what was ther vre. **1477** EARL RIVERS (Caxton) *Dictes* 119 The moste and grettest ewre or happe of aman is to have a good felawe. *c* **1525** SKELTON *Col. Cloute* 1003 He hath good ure Which can hymselfe assure How fortune wyll endure.

†**eure**, *v. Obs.* [f. prec. sb.] *trans.* To destine; to invest *with*, as by the decree of fate.

1428 *Will Flore* (Somerset Ho.), If god eure him to dye. **1440** DK. GLOUC. *Manifesto, Patent Roll 18 Hen. VI.* pt. III, The worship that God so long hath eured him with. **1526** SKELTON *Magnyf.* 6 Men nowadayes be so unhappely ured That nothynge than welth may worse be endured.

Eureka (jʊə'ri:kə), *int.* (*sb.*) [Gr. εὕρηκα, 1st pers. sing. perf. of εὑρίσκειν to find. The correct spelling *heureka* is rare.]

1. The exclamation ('I have found it') uttered by Archimedes when he discovered the means of determining (by specific gravity) the proportion of base metal in Hiero's golden crown. (See Vitruvius *Arch.* IX. iii, Plutarch *Mor.* (Didot) 1338.) Hence *allusively*, an exulting exclamation at having made a discovery.

[**1570** DEE *Math. Pref.*, For this, may I (with ioy) say ΕΥΡΗΚΑ.] **1603** HOLLAND *Plutarch's Mor.* 590 [Archimedes] crying out, *Heureca.* **1658** tr. *Porta's Nat. Mag.* XVIII. viii. 384 We have gone beyond Archimedes his *Eureka.* **1742** FIELDING *J. Andrews* II. xiii. (ed. 2) 267 Adams..returned overjoyed..crying out 'Eureka' [ed. 1 (1742) *Ευρηκα*; ed. 3 (1743) Heureka.] **1818** BYRON *Ch. Har.* IV. lxxxi, We clap Our hands, and cry 'Eureka!' **1862** BURTON *Bk. Hunter* I. 34 A triumphant cry of Eureka! calls me to his place of rest. **1877** FARRAR *My Youth* viii. 73 That great Eureka,—'We have found the Messiah'.

2. A discovery justifying self-congratulation. Often used *attrib.* by advertising tradesmen in the names given to special articles of manufacture.

1853 *Advt.* in *Athenæum* 29 Jan. 151 Eureka shirts. **1854** BADHAM *Halieut.* 233 A recent addition to the long list of modern Mediterranean eurekas.

3. The proprietary name of an alloy of copper and nickel used for electrical filament and resistance wire. Also *attrib.*

1914 *Trade Marks Jrnl.* 21 Jan. 85 *Eureka.* Electric Conduits and Union Joints and Fittings therefor... John Birch & Sons..Manufacturers. **1915** *Phil. Mag.* XXIX. 368 Of the following metals and alloys all..gave a positive emission..platinoid, eureka, tinned copper, and 'galvanized' iron. **1930** *Engineering* 28 Nov. 672/1 Winding, for which 47-gauge Eureka wire is used. **1939** *Trade Marks Jrnl.* 2 Aug. 1070 *Eureka...* Uncovered copper-nickel electrical resistance wire. The London Electric Wire Company and Smiths Limited..Manufacturers. **1943** *Electronic Engin.* XVI. 78 The heater wire is generally made of eureka or a copper nickel alloy.

eurhythm ('ju:rɪθ(ə)m). [ad. Gr. (τὸ) εὔρυθμον, neut. of εὔρυθμος: see below.] = EURHYTHMY 1.

1831 *Fraser's Mag.* IV. 279 They pretend to feast our eyes with symmetry, proportion, eurythm [*sic*], harmony.

eurhythmic (ju:'rɪθmɪk), *a.* and *sb. pl.* [f. next + -IC.] **A.** *adj.* **1.** Of or pertaining to well-arranged proportion, *esp.* in architecture.

1831 *Fraser's Mag.* IV. 287 Each [design]..is exceedingly funny in its way..with regard to 'tactic efficiency', 'eurythmic [*sic*] diathesis'..and every other imaginable kind of diathesis. **1855** LEWES *Goethe* (1864) 177 Owing to some eurhythmic tendency in the construction of Greek plays.

2. Of or pertaining to eurhythmics (see below).

1921 H. F. RUBINSTEIN tr. *Jaques-Dalcroze's Rhythm, Music & Educ.* 196 Eurhythmic exercises enable the individual to feel and express music corporally.

B. *sb. pl.* A system of rhythmical bodily movements, *esp.* dancing exercises, with musical accompaniment, freq. used for educational purposes.

1912 *Standard* 27 Nov., Eurythmics [*sic*] is no longer a mysterious art—it is the new craze. Eurythmics is a word which Professor Jacques-Dalcroze has invented to describe his 'rhythmic gymnastics'. **1920** *Challenge* 21 May 44/3 In the Eurythmics of M. Jacques Dalcroze..the dancer expresses by improvized postures the emotions aroused by music. **1925** C. FOX *Educat. Psychol.* 84 Dancing and eurhythmics in school.

Hence **eu'rhythmical** *a.*, **eurhyth'mician**, **eu'rhythmist.**

1921 H. F. RUBINSTEIN tr. *Jaques-Dalcroze's Rhythm, Music & Educ.* 195 The art of the Eurhythmist is self-sufficient. *Ibid.* 206 Eurhythmicians watching exercises performed by fellow-students. **1923** *Daily Mail* 17 Mar. 10 An eurhythmical display under the command of M. Jaques-Dalcroze. **1924** J. J. FINDLAY in V. Davis *Modern Teaching* (1928) 101 The eurhythmist does not neglect or despise the body; he accepts the counsel of the trainer, but he leads his pupils to fix their attention on rhythmic values.

eurhythmy (ju:'rɪθmɪ). Forms: 7 **eurythmie**, 8-9 **eurithmy, -ythmy.** Also 8-9 in L. form **eurythmia.** [ad. L. *eur(h)ythmia* (Vitruv.) proportion, a. Gr. εὐρυθμία, f. εὔρυθμος well-proportioned (f. εὐ- (see EU-) + ῥυθμός proportion, RHYTHM); cf. Fr. *eurhythmie.*]

1. *Archit.* Harmony in the proportions of a building.

1624 WOTTON *Archit.* 118 Eurythmia is that agreeable Harmony, betweene the breadth, length and height of all the Roomes of the Fabrique..which suddenly..taketh euery Beholder. **1721-1800** in BAILEY. **1847** LEITCH tr. *Müller's Anc. Art* §118 As well as the law of symmetry and eurhythmy. **1876** GWILT *Archit.* Gloss. s.v.

2. *Path.* Regularity of the pulse.

1721-1800 BAILEY, *Eurithmy*, an excellent Disposition of the Pulse. **1884** *Syd. Soc. Lex.*, *Eurythmia*, regularity in beat of the pulse.

3. In wider senses of Gr. εὐρυθμία:

a. Rhythmical order or movement; **b.** a graceful proportion and carriage of the body.

1706 in PHILLIPS. **1721-1800** in BAILEY. **1844** BECK & FELTON tr. *Munk's Metres* 1 The artistic figure, as well as the artistic rhythm, must be beautiful. In this case we say the artistic figure has symmetry, and the artistic rhythm has eurhythmy.

†**eu'ripe.** *Obs.* [a. F. *euripe*, ad. L. *eurīpus*, a. Gr. εὔριπος: see EURIPUS.] = EURIPUS.

1600 HOLLAND *Livy* XLIIII. xi. 1177 On the other side there is an Euripe or arm of the sea. **1621** BURTON *Anat. Mel.* III. iv. I. i, A sea full of shelves and rocks, sands, gulfes, Euripes and contrary tides. *a* **1649** DRUMM. OF HAWTH. *Cypress Grove* Wks. 119 What Euripe..doth change so often as man? **1656-81** BLOUNT *Glossogr.*, *Euripe*, any strait, fret or Channel of the Sea, running between two shoars. *fig.* **1646** SIR T. BROWNE *Pseud. Ep.* VII. xiii. 366 Nor can he [a man] ever perish but in the Euripe of Ignorance.

Euripidean (juːˌrɪpɪˈdiːən), *a.* [f. L. *Eurīpidēus*, ad. Gr. Εὐριπίδειος, f. Εὐριπίδης (see def.).] Of, pertaining to, or characteristic of Euripides, the Athenian tragic poet, or his works, style, etc.
1821 *Q. Rev.* XXIV. 369 The prefatory narrative, which forms..an Euripidean prologue to Miss Austin's novels. **1871** Browning *Balaustion's Adv.* 168 So might..no Euripidean pathos plague Too much my critic-friend of Syracuse. **1924** E. B. Osborn *Our Debt to Greece & Rome* vi. 93 In the Euripidean drama..the chorus merely provides charming interludes of song and dance.

†ˈ**euripize**, *v. Obs. rare*$^{-1}$. [ad. Gr. (δι-)ευριπίζειν (Arist. *Probl.* §25); if not a misreading, it is f. Εὔριπος (see next), with sense 'to change like the tides of the Euripus'.] *intr.* (See quot.)
1646 Sir T. Browne *Pseud. Ep.* vii. xiii. 366 Aristotle.. seems to borrow a Metaphor from Euripus; while..he enquireth, why in the upper parts of houses the ayre doth Euripize, that is, is whirled hither and thither. [Hence in Blount *Glossogr.*, and in later Dicts.]

Euripus (jʊəˈraɪpəs). *Pl.* euripi. [L., a. Gr. εὔριπ-ος, f. εὐ- (see eu-) + ῥιπή rush.]
1. In ancient Geography, the proper name of the channel between Eubœa (Negropont) and the mainland, celebrated for the violence and uncertainty of its currents. Hence *gen.* a strait or sea-channel, *esp.* one having these characteristics.
1601 Holland *Pliny* I. 82 From thence [Hellespontus] there is extended a small Euripus or arme of the sea for 86 miles. **1630** *R. Johnson's Kingd. & Commw.* 643 That Euripus..by reason of his..violent course is never frozen. The other Euripus on the backside of Groneland heth three inlets..Betweene these two raging Euripi lyeth an Iland.. the habitation..of the Pigmies. **1751** Chambers *Cycl.*, *Euripus* has since become a general name for all streights where the water is in great motion or agitation.
fig. *a* **1797** Burke (T.), The provision of this establishment ..should not fluctuate with the Euripus of funds and actions. **1884** *Pall Mall G.* 16 Feb. 2/1 Although all nations are nowadays more or less unquiet, Paris seems to lie in a very Euripus of change.
2. *transf.*
1766 Smollett *Trav.* II. xxxii. 131 (Jod.) The euripus, or canal, made by order of Julius Cæsar to contain crocodiles and other aquatick animals which were killed occasionally. **1849–50** Weale *Dict. Terms*, *Euripus*, any artificial canal or water-course.

eurite (ˈjʊəraɪt). *Min.* [a. Fr. *eurite*, f. Gr. εὔρυτος (recorded in sense 'flowing plentifully'), f. εὖ well + ῥέειν to flow.
D'Aubuisson, who gave the name in 1819, states (*Géognosie* II. 119) that he meant it to denote 'the principal characteristic of the rock, viz. its melting when exposed to fire'.]
'A variety of syenite occurring near Christiania, of a blue colour and stratified'. (Watts.)
1847 Craig, *Eurite*, White-stone, the Weiss-stein of Werner. A variety of granite, in which felspar predominates. **1852** Th. Ross tr. *Humboldt's Trav.* I. xv. 490 *note*, Talkschiefer of Werner, without garnets or serpentine; not eurite or weisstein. **1879** Rutley *Study Rocks* xii. 214 The eurites proper are more easily fusible than the felstones.
Hence **euˈritic** (jʊəˈrɪtɪk), *a.*, pertaining to or consisting of eurite.
1844 Darwin *Geol. Observ.* ii. xix. (1876) 470 Near the Pacific, the mountain-ranges are generally formed of syenite or granite, or an allied euritic porphyry. **1879** Rutley *Study Rocks* x. 152 A globular condition of silica..occurring in the euritic porphyries of Les Settons.

euro (ˈjʊərəʊ). *Austr.* Also uroo, yuro. [Native name (also *uroo*, *waroo*).] A species of kangaroo. Also *attrib.*
186. Waterhouse in R. P. Whitworth *Bailliere's S. Austral. Gazetteer* (1866) 165 The uroo kangaroo was occasionally seen in the same localities. **1876** —— in Harcus *S. Austral.* 284 *Osphranta crebescens.* Uroo kangaroo. **1885** Mrs. Praed *Head Station* II. 256 Cliffs, with ledges and crannies that afforded foothold only to yuros and rock-wallabies. **1898** Morris *Austral Eng.* 140/1 *Euro*, one of the aboriginal names for a Kangaroo; spelt also *Yuro*. **1931** I. L. Idriess *Lasseter's Last Ride* (1933) iii. 22 Wallaby, euro, and dingo tracks showed how popular this cool rock-hole was. *Ibid.* iv. 32 They found the hills alive with euros and wallabies. **1934** *Bulletin* (Sydney) 17 Jan. 20/4 Winnie, our pet euro (Westralian rock kangaroo), had a liking for softgoods. **1944** *Living off Land* ii. 27 A number of men are required to capture the wallaby or the euro (hill kangaroo). **1950** 'N. Shute' *Town like Alice* 81 You'll find little diggings all over in the sand, where the kangaroos and euros have dug for water.

Euro- (jʊərəʊ), combining form of *Europe*.
1. General uses. (Often *spec.* with reference to Western Europe.) **Euro-African** *a.*, = Eurafrican 2, 3; **Euro-American** *a.*, pertaining to both Europe and America; = western *a.* 4 a; also as *sb.* = western *sb.* 1; **Euro-Asiatic** *a.*, = Eurasiatic *a.*; **Eurocentric** *a.* = Europocentric *a.*; hence **Eurocentricity, -centrism, Eurocentrist; Eurocheque**, a collaborative arrangement among banks in a number of European countries, enabling cheque-account holders from one country to encash cheques or make purchases in another participating country; a cheque or cheque-guarantee card issued under this system; freq. *attrib.*; **Eurocontrol**, an organization for the co-operative control of civil and military air traffic in the upper airspace over Europe; also called the European Organization for the Safety of Air Navigation; **Eurocrat** [-crat] (see quot. 1962); **Euro-dollar** (see quot. 1965); **Eurogroup**, an informal subgroup within NATO, comprising most of its European members and aiming to agree on European defence policy; **Euromissile**, a medium-range nuclear weapon deployed in Europe; **Eurostrategic** *a.*, relating to defence strategy in Europe; *spec.* of nuclear weapons: designed for deployment and use in Europe, having a strike capability limited to the continent of Europe; **Eurovision** [after television], television of European range (see quot. 1951).
1952 B. Davidson *Rep. S. Afr.* i. iv. 53 The *Euro-African, or Coloured, rate of increase. **1958** *Optima* Mar. 25/2 A Euro-African market, which would, as its name implies, favour trade and exchanges between the two continents. **1963** *Guardian* 7 Jan. 5/7 The school's Provisional Committee of nine Africans and three Euro-Africans. **1928** *Critical Crown* I. 28 Economists lose even the shade of the 'economic man' as they contemplate cultures other than the *Euro-American. **1949** M. Mead *Male & Female* ii. 27 Hygienic fears with which most Euro-Americans surround themselves in native villages. **1961** *New Left Rev.* July–Aug. 10/2 A vast..Euro-American entity. **1935** *Discovery* Oct. 293/1 The *Euro-Asiatic origin of Man. **1963** *Economist* 30 Nov. 902/2 If General de Gaulle had any illusions about converting his guest to his *Eurocentric ideas, Herr Erhard dispelled them. **1984** *Times* 17 Feb. 7/8 They have become less eurocentric in their approach and pay more attention to Third World issues. **1975** *Austral. Outlook* XXIX. 287 Until the late 1960s New Zealand's foreign policies seemed characterised by *Eurocentricity. **1985** *Listener* 24 Jan. 11/3 Those days of Eurocentricity are now gone. Chinese civilisation has at least been touched on in recent years and Africa got its own TV series more recently. **1974** J. White tr. *Poulantzas's Fascism & Dictatorship* 12 Throughout its existence..the Comintern was confronted with fascism in Europe. This, together with its characteristic *Eurocentrism, means that its policy towards fascism is a good indication of the wider theory and practice it adopted. **1984** *Times Lit. Suppl.* 24 Aug. 948/1 There is the danger of Eurocentrism... To determine the meaning of myth for the modern world is not ..to determine the meaning of myth for Western man. **1985** *Times* 10 May 5/8 The tension persists between the Atlanticists, who see the unity of Western Europe as part of a wider partnership with the United States, and *Eurocentrists, who believe that the unity of Western Europe requires it to be distinct from the United States. **1969** *Daily Tel.* 11 Apr. 3/3 The service will be known as '*Eurocheque' and banks taking part will show the 'Eurocheque' blue and red sign. **1976** *Ibid.* 13 Nov. 21/1 Under the Eurocheque system the Briton travelling abroad can get up to the equivalent of £30 in cash from a Continental bank. **1985** *Financial Times* 1 June (Weekend Suppl.) p. v/1 Eurocheques are now available from Midland, Lloyds and Natwest banks... As well as paying.. for the Eurocheque guarantee card, you will be charged.. each time you write a cheque. **1960** *Aeroplane* XCIX. 757/2 Mr. Rankin asked for more information about the main provisions of *Eurocontrol. **1974** *Encycl. Brit. Macropædia* XVIII. 643/2 In Europe, the many national boundaries make the need [for integration] greatest. This situation has led to the formation of Eurocontrol, a supranational authority. **1985** *Interavia Air Let.* 29 Apr. 2 Eurocontrol.. has clarified the situation concerning..forthcoming air traffic control (ATC) arrangements. **1961** *Economist* 29 July 449/1 These new '*Eurocrats' are worth watching. **1962** *Britannica Bk. of Year 1961* 546/1 *Eurocrats*, administrative staff of the various European organizations such as the European Economic Community. **1968** *New Scientist* 14 Nov. 386/3 Eurocrats and au pair girls, bankers from Basle ..all are examined. **1960** *Times* 24 Oct. (Financ. Rev.) p. viii/3 London became..the most active dealer in the so-called '*Euro-dollar'. **1965** *Economist* 19 June p. xiii/1 Euro-dollars are deposits of United States dollars with banks outside the United States. The overseas banks need not be in Europe. **1969** *Guardian* 12 Feb. 3/4 (Advt.), When you want Euro-dollars, or any other Euro-currency, a Chaseman can get them for you in minutes rather than hours. **1971** *Listener* 7 Jan. 15/3 The *Euro-Group of Ministers. **1972** *Times* 24 May 6/4 The Eurogroup started at dinner party level in 1968 but became more formalized in 1970. **1984** *Listener* 24 May 6/3 NATO, with its plethora of groups: its Eurogroup, its Nuclear Planning Group, its Special Consultative Group, its Defence Planning Committee, and so on. **1979** *Summary of World Broadcasts* (B.B.C.) 21 Apr. SU/6097/A1/3 New medium-range missiles..are the '*Euromissiles', which the NATO leaders want to impose on the West European countries. **1983** *U.S. News & World Rep.* 13 June 27 The President's performance at the Williamsburg summit convinced skeptics that Reagan is on track in his strategy to *limit Euromissiles on both sides.* **1977** *Guardian Weekly* 27 Feb. 15/3 This class of regional, or '*Eurostrategic' arms is composed of a disparate group of weapons—NATO and Warsaw Pact nuclear-capable strike aircraft, Soviet medium-range bombers, Soviet IRBM and the British and French submarine-launched missiles. **1979** *Economist* 6 Oct. 49/3 The question..of stationing in Europe of Euro-strategic weapons so that there is a Euro-strategic balance, not just one covered by an inter-continental balance. **1982** *Christian Science Monitor* 15 Jan. b-6/2 'The dawn of the eighties,' Mr. Churchill writes, 'ushered in an era in which every one of NATO's offsetting advantages in the field of nuclear weapons—at strategic, Euro strategic and battlefield level—has been lost.' **1951** *Evening Standard* 5 Nov., What is *Eurovision? A system of collaboration among the West European countries including Britain by which television programmes will become interchangeable. **1954** *N.Y. Times* 6 June 85/3 Europe's leading television engineers will twirl dials with crossed fingers tomorrow when they tune in the first eight-nation 'Eurovision' hook-up through Lille. **1958** *Listener* 13 Nov. 796/1 Millions more saw the coronation..on television, through the Eurovision link. **1965** *BBC Handbk.* 39 Twenty-three television organizations in eighteen Western European countries..make up 'Eurovision'. **1968** *Guardian* 22 Aug. 6/5 Czech television screened the invasion... Austrian television was able to pick up the pictures and send them to Britain via Eurovision.

2. With specific reference to the European Economic Community (cf. Europe). **a.** Of or relating to the EEC in general, as ***Euro-executive, -farmer, -quango***; **Eurocrat**: see sense 1; **Euro-fanatic**, one who is excessively enthusiastic about (membership of) the EEC; **Euromarket**, the Common Market of the European Economic Community; also, **Euromart; Euronet**, the name of a scientific and technical data-sharing computer network sponsored by the EEC for the benefit of its member countries; **Eurospeak** [-speak], jargon used in EEC documents, statements, etc.; **Eurosummit**, a summit meeting of EEC heads of government.
1970 *Times* 18 Aug. 21/6 So much for the *Euro-executive's remuneration; but what of the way he has to work in order to gain it? **1985** *Financial Times* 6 Mar. i. 4/7 Such VAT-exempt goods as wedding presents, company cars and the household belongings of mobile Euroexecutives. **1967** *Guardian* 19 May 10/6 Those *Euro-fanatics in the Cabinet who persist in seeking to join the Common Market on humiliating terms. **1981** *Economist* 3 Jan. 17/1 M is permanently at loggerheads with Peter's eurofanatics. **1965** *Economist* 13 Mar. 1164/2 (*caption*) *Eurofarmer: catching up with the townies? **1983** *Financial Times* 6 Oct. iii. 40/5 It seems a combination of poor harvest and what Euro-farmers would consider a severe price cut is the immediate solution in the U.S. **1957** *N.Y. Times* 14 July iv. 4/6 (*heading*) Vote on *Euromarket and Euratom. **1963** N. Freeling *Gun before Butter* ii. 82 The great difference in the fixed retail price..is one of the complex anomalies that the Euromarket has not yet abolished. **1957** *Birmingham* (Alabama) *News* 14 Feb. 46/1 The plan, nicknamed '*Euromart', has yet to be ratified by these six nations. **1976** *Times* 17 Feb. 16/2 Implementation of the proposed *Euronet computer network has got under way. **1985** *Financial Times* 25 Mar. ii. 15/8 The best known [data base] of this type is the Diane network operated by Euronet. **1982** M. Fallon *Rise of Euroquango* iv. 17 *Euroquangos have been the vehicle by which national trade unions..have gained power in Community decision-making. **1985** *English Today* Apr. 38/2 Euro-MPs are not against the Euro-quango as such. **1979** *Sunday Tel.* 8 July 8/1 Mrs. Thatcher is particularly severe on the rubbish-jargon of *Eurospeak. **1984** *N.Y. Times* 9 Dec. iv. 5/1 IMP's—in Eurospeak, the community jargon, the acronym for agricultural subsidies known as Integrated Mediterranean Programs. **1979** *Economist* 12 May 63/1 EEC leaders told the community's finance ministers to study the problem and come up with ideas before the next *Euro summit, in Strasbourg next month. **1985** *Financial Times* 28 Oct. 21/2 It is still too early to predict how far they will get by the next Euro-summit in five weeks' time.

b. Of or relating to the European Parliament, its members or elections, as ***Euro-candidate, -constituency, -election, -poll***; **Euro-campaign**, a campaign for election to the European Parliament; hence as *v. intr.*, to take part in such a campaign; **Euro-MP**, a member of the European Parliament (cf. M.E.P.); **Europarliament**, the European Parliament (see European *a.* 2); also *transf.*; **Euro-seat**, a seat in the European Parliament.
1979 *Economist* 16 June 30/3 Germany's *Euro-campaign never really managed to stop looking like a giant party. **1984** *Financial Times* 14 June i. 11/4 His more serious message about jobs and disarmament..showed why he has been such a star of the Euro-campaign. **1984** *Southern Rag* No. 22. 20/2 He was recently Euro-campaigning in his Leeds constituency when he came across two people busking. **1976** *Glasgow Herald* 26 Nov. 8/4 (*heading*) £1000 deposit plan for *Euro candidates. **1984** *Daily Tel.* 11 June 14/1 In justice to the Euro-candidates, some of them have tried to address themselves to these detailed, boring matters. **1976** *Jrnl.* (Newcastle) 26 Nov. 6/6 The boundaries of the *Euro-constituencies have yet to be drawn up. **1984** *Which?* June 265/2 Each of our Euro-constituencies is roughly the size of eight Westminster constituencies. **1979** *Economist* 30 June 20/2 Mr Edward Heath, who canvassed in 41 constituencies during the *Euro-election. **1985** *Financial Times* 14 May i. 2/3 The distribution of Spain's seats will later be adjusted as soon as the country stages direct Euro-elections. **1975** *Economist* 20 Dec. 37/2 All Danish *Euro-MPs will also be members of the Danish parliament. **1977** *Belfast Tel.* 27 Jan. 10/1 For the future three Euro-MPs from the province it will not only be a step into the 'big time' of pay scales but also a new setting with linguists, headphones and even TV cameras. **1982** *Daily Tel.* 14 Sept. 2/8 Euro-MPs voted by 82 votes to 45 in favour of a resolution recommending the progressive reduction in the manufacture and sale of war toys. **1962** *Punch* 21 Nov. 741/2 Today's debate in *Europarliament at Bournemouth. **1977** *Time* 27 June 13/1 Europe's leaders agreed to proceed with the directly elected Europarliament as stipulated in the Treaty of Rome in 1957. **1984** *Daily Tel.* 19 June 14/1 The second Euro-parliament to emerge from direct suffrage seems doomed to lack more credibility even than its predecessor. **1976** *Jrnl.* (Newcastle) 26 Nov. 6/6 (*heading*) £1,000 needed in *Euro-poll. **1984** *Daily Tel.* 19 June 14/2 The increase in Labour's vote in the Euro-poll would still leave the Conservatives with a comfortable majority there. **1977** *Times* 16 Apr. 12/8 Proportional representation in the election to the so-called *Euroseats. **1984** *Daily Tel.* 19 June 14/2 A second and less

obvious gain for Labour was its ability to take second place from the Alliance in 18 of the 32 Euro-seats.

c. In a number of ad-hoc formations: conforming to or resulting from EEC standards, regulations, etc., as ***Euro-bottle*, *-code*, *-plug***, etc.

1962 *Economist* 19 May 708/2 It will be open to European inventors to apply for the Euro-patent or national patents for both will co-exist. **1965** *Daily Tel.* 1 June 14/1 Studies are being made aimed at agreeing on common electrical standards throughout Europe... A common electric plug has been devised... It is called the 'Europlug'. **1967** *Economist* 5 Aug. 523/3 Germany's second biggest [brewery]..will spend about £600,000 to £700,000 on changing over from the conventional flip top bottle to the 'euro bottle', a Brussels invention. **1977** *Sunday Times* 23 Jan. 13/6 The new Euro-pass is introduced by means of a simple agreement, made in Brussels... Not even the design of the new passport is likely to come under the scrutiny of Parliament. **1985** *Times* 28 Jan. 4 Marking animals with a Eurocode so that their owners can identify them.

3. With reference to the 'European' money market, international trade in currencies or securities that have been deposited outside their country of origin, although not necessarily in Europe. **a.** Of money used in this way: collectively, as ***Euro-currency*, *-money***; also, in the names of individual currencies, as ***Euro-dollar*** (see sense 1 above), ***-mark*, *-sterling*, *-yen***, etc.

1962 *Economist* 17 Mar. 1045/1 The high rates being paid for sterling deposits in Paris ('Eurosterling'). **1963** *Ibid.* 25 May 797/1 The frictions and imperfections..that lie behind the Euro-currencies. **1964** *Statist* 7 Feb. 423/1 The market in euro-Swiss francs, or Euro-Deutschmarks is relatively small. **1970** *Daily Tel.* 27 Jan. 19/7 The newest exciting arrival on the international currency scene looks like being the 'Euroyen'. **1970** *Times* 24 June 29/7 The defence possibilities in line with the market are much more favourable owing to the attraction of the Euromoney market. **1972** *Ibid.* 19 Dec. 15/5 (Advt.), We have a vacancy for a Senior Euro-currency Deposit Dealer. **1974** M. Mayer *Bankers* xvii. 475 Since the late 1960s, some of the loans that would once have been made in Eurodollars have been made instead in Euromarks, Euroyen, Eurosterling, and Euro (Swiss) francs. **1979** *Economist* 31 Mar. (Survey) 28/3 The Eurocurrency market has become a borrowers' one. **1980** *Harper's Mag.* Feb. 48/1 Even when..the various Euroyen, Eurofrancs, Euromarks, and so forth are subtracted, there exists no reasonable external source for these funds. **1985** *Times* 1 June 25 In Japan investment will be Samurai (Government) bonds, Euroyen bonds and convertibles.

b. Of loans and securities in this market, as ***Euro-credit*, *-debt*, *-deposit*, *-loan***; **Eurobond**, an international bond issued outside the country in whose currency it is denominated; **Euro-issue**, a loan issued outside its home market; **Euronote**, a financial note issued for the European money market.

1966 *Economist* 2 Apr. 74/1 Prices of *Euro-bond issues have at last turned upward. **1969** *Times* 5 May (Suppl.) p. xiii/3 The investor in Eurobonds has shown a good appetite for the issue that is geared to Wall Street for its growth. **1979** D. Meiring *Foreign Body* xiv. 144 [He] was carrying on abrasively about the Ministry of Finance's failure to send him Eurobond interest rates in time. **1985** Eurobond [see *Euro-credit* above]. **1975** *Economist* 23 Aug. 64/3 According to the World Bank, *Eurocredits in the April–June quarter totalled nearly $5 billion. **1985** *Amer. Banker* 4 Dec. 37/4 London..is regarded as the center of Eurobond and Eurocredit offerings. **1976** *Daily Beacon* (Univ. of Tennessee) 23 July 6/3 The rub is that nobody knows how much *Eurodebt is floating around the world. **1982** *Financial Times* 4 May (World Banking Survey) p. i/5 In a couple of years up to 30 per cent of all outstanding Eurodebt will have to be rescheduled. **1971** *Amer. Banker* 6 Jan. 16/3 Wanted funds at the short end of the market caused *Eurodeposit rates to close firm. **1974** M. Mayer *Bankers* ix. 219 Eurodeposits were forty-four negative. **1966** *Economist* 3 Sept. 947/3 In 1965, total '*Euro-issues'—that is, loans denominated in currencies other than that of the market in which they were floated—reached well over $1 billion. **1982** *Financial Times* 1 Mar. 15/7 Short—usually 5-year—maturities are the norm for Euro-issues. **1972** *New Yorker* 22 Apr. 57/1 (Advt.), We make loans to customers who've never had *Euro-loans before. And we invent unusual forms for Euro-loans. **1985** *Financial Times* 4 Dec. I. 6 Reserves stood..well above the average level..because of the boost received in October by the Government's $2.5 bn floating rate Euroloan. **1977** *Business Week* 14 Nov. 196/2 It is this real..penalty..that is leading Reynolds to get out of its mark debt by refinancing it with U.S. dollar *Euronotes. **1979** *Wall St. Jrnl.* 20 Aug. 19/1 The first Euronote [issue] to be denominated in Canadian dollars in three months was badly received. **1985** *Amer. Banker* 20 Dec. 2/3 Euronote issuance activity has expanded because borrowers have been eager to replace syndicated loans with the more flexible, cheaper Euronote issuance facilities.

c. Of institutions and services connected with this market, as ***Eurobank(ing)*, *-finance*, *-lending***; **Euroclear**, a clearance service for Euro-currency transactions; **Euromarket**, the European money market in general; a particular Euro-currency market.

1972 *Times* 24 May (Banking in Europe Suppl.) p. xii/2 It is not only American companies which obtain finance from *Eurobanks. **1982** *Atlantic Monthly* Aug. 13/1 In *Eurobanking, there is no deposit insurance. **1969** *Times* 5 May (Suppl.) p. xiii/4 Morgan Guaranty of Brussels.. introduced its *Euroclear which is an attempt to bring some organization into the market. **1970** *Times* 1 June 22 Euroclear is based in Brussels and already has some 164 members. **1985** *Financial Times* 6 Dec. 31/4 Euroclear, the Brussels-based Eurobond clearing house, is to begin providing a same-day issuance and settlement service. **1968** *Amer. Banker* 2 July 1/1 The American Banker Today begins a new weekly column..entitled *Eurofinance. **1985** *Ibid.* 20 Dec. 2/3 New financing techniques came fast and furiously to the Eurofinance markets in 1985. **1976** *Economist* 14 Feb. (Survey) 10/3 True, after soaring to a record of more than $29 billion in 1974, syndicated medium-term *Eurolending totalled little over $20 billion last year. But that drop was in itself a sign of the return to normality. **1985** *Financial Times* 2 Dec. 22/4 The big expansion of Eurolending business is a thing of the past. **1963** *Statist* 5 Apr. 37/2 This short description of the '*Euro' markets. **1971** *Amer. Banker* 14 Sept. 18/1 The latest push in the Euromarket is developing through commercial paper. **1985** *Financial Times* 19 Dec. II. 31/1 Yields in the Euromarkets have looked too high against New York yields to attract borrowers.

euro-aquilo: see euraquilo.

† euro-boreal, *a. Obs.* [f. late L. *Euro-*, a. Gr. Εὐρο- combining form of Εὖρος (see eurus) + boreal.] North-easterly.

1664 Evelyn *Sylva* (1776) 285 In Cheshire.. Cumberland and Anglesey and several of our Euro-boreal tracts.

euroclydon (jʊə'rɒklɪdən). [a. Gr. εὐροκλύδων (if genuine, only in *Acts* xxvii. 14, where the better attested reading is εὐρακύλων: see euraquilo), f. εὖρος east wind + κλύδων wave, billow.] A stormy wind mentioned in the *Acts of the Apostles*: see euraquilo. Hence occas. with allusion to this, a 'tempestuous wind' in general. Also *fig.*

1611 Bible *Acts* xxvii. 14 There arose against it a tempestuous winde called Euroclydon. **1667** Waterhouse *Fire Lond.* 3 Men are so variously acted in this Euroclydon of Providence. **1676** I. Mather *Hist. Wars* (1862) 162 It.. continued a cold Euroclidon, or, North-East storm all that day and night. **1767** J. Bryant (*title*) Observations and Inquires relating to various parts of Ancient History, containing Dissertations on the Wind Euroclydon. **1839** Longf. *Midn. Mass for Dying Year*, The storm-wind from Labrador, The wind Euroclydon. **1870** Lowell *Study Wind.*, *Good Word for Winter*, Euroclydon..bellows down the chimney.

Eurocommunism (jʊərəʊ'kɒmjuːnɪz(ə)m). *Pol.* Also **Euro-communism, -Communism.** [f. Euro- + communism: see also Fr. *Eurocommunisme*, It. *Eurocommunismo*, and quot. 1977².] The communism of Western European Communist parties; used esp. of a movement among certain European communists that arose in the mid-1970s, emphasizing acceptance of democratic institutions and the rights of individual parties to independence from Soviet influence.

1976 *Survey* Spring 129 The Soviet leaders are perfectly conscious that Euro-communism represents a danger for them. **1977** *Ann. Reg.* *1976* 117 Kádár caused some surprise by denying that he regarded Eurocommunism as a form of anti-sovietism. **1977** *N.Y. Times* 10 Oct. 27 The word 'Eurocommunism'..was coined by a Yugoslav named Franj Barberi..in one of his articles in Milan's Il Giornale. **1979** *Dædalus* Winter 133 We can..single out the three parties which have given rise to the notion of Eurocommunism (the Italian, the Spanish, and the French). **1982** *Christian Science Monitor* 15 Jan. 12 Enrico Berlinguer, leader of the PCI and founder of Eurocommunism, this week repeated earlier statements that the situation in Poland is unacceptable. **1986** *N.Y. Times* 3 Feb. A1/5 A new doctrine called Eurocommunism, which pledged respect for parliamentary democracy.

Hence ˌ**Euro'communist** *sb.* and *a.*

1976 *Survey* Summer–Autumn 91 The fact that a challenge to the 'Soviet model' is issued by Euro-Communists is undeniable. **1976** *Harper's Mag.* Oct. 22/3 To the foreign journalists who waited up with prepared copy about democracy in peril or a Euro-Communist triumph, the results may have seemed anticlimactic. **1977** *Time* 4 July 7/1 French Party Boss Georges Marchais, striving to burnish his image as a moderate Eurocommunist, announced that he 'did not need to see Brezhnev every time he comes to Paris'. **1979** *Dædalus* Winter 114 The Eurocommunists are getting more distant from Moscow at the same time as Moscow is getting closer to Europe. **1982** *N.Y. Times* 14 Nov. vii. 7/3 Hostility at authentic non-alignment or even at Eurocommunist autonomy. **1986** *Ibid.* 3 Feb. A1/5 The Italians are increasingly toying with a new term, Euroleft, to replace Eurocommunist.

Europæo-, -eo- (jʊərəʊ'piːəʊ-), combining form of L. *Eurōpæus* European in **Euroˌpeo-A'merican** *a.*, pertaining jointly to Europe and America. **Euroˌpeo-Asi'atic** *a.* (see quot.). **Euroˌpæo-Si'berian** *a.*, comprising most of Siberia and a large part of Europe.

1841 Sterling *Russia* 153 The idea of an Asiatic balance of political power, as well as a Europeo-American one, etc. **1853** Gen. P. Thompson *Audi Alt.* (1858) I. xv. 52 A Europeo-Asiatic power will probably at some time give the signal for a break-up. *c* **1860** G. Bentham *Notes on Compositæ* 542 Under the name of Europæo-Asiatic or North temperate and Mountain region. **1877** Bennett tr. *Thomé's Struct. Bot.* (1878) 438 The Europæo-Siberian Forest Region [One of Griesbach's 24 phytogeographical regions of the earth.]

Europe. [See European *a.* and *sb.*] Used ellipt. and allusively with reference to membership of the European Economic Community (the Common Market).

1957 *Times* 8 Oct. 11/7 The defeat shortly after this success of the plan for a European Defence Community was a setback for 'Europe'. **1962** *Listener* 8 Feb. 240/1 The decision to go into Europe. **1970** *Guardian* 28 Nov. 5/8 Mr. Shore scornfully dismissed the arguments of those who feared there was no future for Britain outside Europe. **1977** [see *Europarliament* s.v. Euro- 2b]. **1980** B. Castle *Castle Diaries* 160 It isn't only Europe. It is a question of whether this country is going to cut itself off from the Western Alliance and go isolationist.

European (jʊərəʊ'piːən), *a.* and *sb.* Also 7 Europian, -æan. [ad. Fr. *européen*, f. L. *eurōpæus*, *f. Eurōpa*, a. Gr. Εὐρώπη Europe.]

A. *adj.*

1. a. Belonging to Europe, or its inhabitants.

In India, *European* (not 'English' or 'British') was the official designation applied to the troops sent from the United Kingdom, as distinguished from the native soldiers.

1603 Knolles *Hist. Turks* (1638) 152 At such time as he was by the Europian Tartars deliuered. **1624** Bedell *Lett.* iv. 78 On the Christian and Europæan side, was the word, *Et erunt Reges nutritij tui.* **1632** Massinger *Maid of Honour* i. i, England, The empress of the European isles. **1702** Rowe *Tamerl*, i. i, Polish'd Arts of Europæan Courts. **1862** Dana *Man. Geol.* 559 The European Caves were mostly Caves of Bears. **1878** Morley *Carlyle* Crit. Misc. Ser. i. 198 Spain was finally thrust from among the efficient elements in the European State-system.

b. Taking place in, or extending over, Europe.

1665 Manley *Grotius' Low C. Warres* 675 Their Ancestors..were not content with European Victories. **1837** Lockhart *Scott* (1839) IX. 359 The popularity of Sir Walter Scott, European and more than European as it was. *Mod.* A scholar of European celebrity.

c. Used in the names of certain economic and defence organizations or unions of western European countries.

1952 *Ann. Reg. 1951* 164 Signature on 18 April in Paris of the treaty establishing a European Coal and Steel Community among the six participating countries. *Ibid.*, The..project for a European Defence Community was the subject of intensive negotiations. **1955** *Times* 30 July 5/3 The council of the Organization for European Economic Cooperation to-day approved the plans that had been submitted to it for renewing for a year the European Payments Union. **1957** *Times* 8 Oct. 11/1 The European Common Market now being organized by the 'Six'—France, Germany, Italy, and Benelux. **1958** *Spectator* 7 Feb. 184/3 The Common Market Treaty, laying down the conditions under which the European Economic Community..is to be established, came into force on 1st January 1958. **1961** *Listener* 17 Aug. 252/1 Britain's application to join the European Community. **1969** *Times* 6 Jan. 7/7 It may be rather less pressing in Britain than in the European Economic Community, where the cost of financing the mounting butter surplus has threatened the whole structure with collapse.

2. *Comb.* ***European-built*, *-minded*, *-style*** adjs.; **European corn-borer** *U.S.*, the larva of the moth *Pyrausta nubilalis*, which attacks maize and other crops; **European Court**, (*a*) (in full: ***European Court of Human Rights***) the Court of Human Rights in Strasbourg, established under the European Convention on Human Rights in 1958; (*b*) (in full: ***European Court of Justice***) the Court of Justice of the European Economic Community, the European Coal and Steel Community (ECSC), and Euratom in Luxembourg, established in 1958 and superseding the Court of Justice of the ECSC; **European Parliament**, the principal representative and consultative body of the European Economic Community, the ECSC, and Euratom, originally set up (as the European Parliamentary Assembly) under Article 138 of the Treaty of Rome, and since 1979 elected by direct universal suffrage throughout the EEC; cf. *Europarliament* s.v. Euro- 2b; **European plan** *U.S.*, the method or practice at a hotel of charging for lodging and service without inclusion of meals (opp. *American plan*).

1725 De Foe *Voy. round World* (1840) 63 They had five or six *European-built ships. **1920** G. W. Herrick *Insects of Economic Importance* 122 The *European Corn Borer..has lately been discovered in the United States. **1955** *Sci. News Let.* 10 Sept. 164/1 European corn borers and boll weevils appear to be causing the nation's farmers the greatest losses at present. [**1958** *Times* 8 Oct. 9/2 (*heading*) European Communities Court of Justice.] **1959** *Times* 18 Sept. 9/7 Lord McNair..has been confirmed as president of the newly established *European Court of Human Rights at Strasbourg. **1961** *Whitaker's Almanack 1962* 966/2 The European Court superseded the Court of Justice of ECSC and is common to the three European Communities. **1973** *Times* 3 Jan. 4/4 It was not abnormal for member countries to be taken to the European Court. **1985** R. C. A. White *Admin. Justice* i. i. 8 It is possible, and sometimes obligatory, for questions on the interpretation of the treaties establishing the European Communities..to be referred to the European Court from an English court. **1986** *Financial Times* 28 Feb. i. 12/2 The Government is urgently considering legislation to comply with the ruling of the European Court..that Britain's different retirement ages for men and women breach EEC directives. **1932** Hemingway *Death in Afternoon* xix. 268 *European-minded politicians. **1961** A. Wilson *Old Men at Zoo* vii. 312 A literary critic of that older, more European-minded school. [**1959** A. H. Robertson *Europ. Institutions* v. 124 The new European Parliamentary Assembly..first met on March 19, 1958, and became the parliamentary organ of all

three Six-Power Communities.] **1961** *Ann. Reg. 1960* 170 On 17 May..the European Parliamentary Assembly.. adopted a draft convention on the election of a *European parliament by direct universal suffrage. **1976** *Times* 21 May 4/3 Parliament can debate direct elections to the European Parliament before the European summit meeting discusses the subject. **1983** *Listener* 6 Jan. 4/1 The directly elected European Parliament will have a special role to play. **1834** *Sun* (N.Y.) 26 May 2/1 The hard times did not warrant his taking board on the '*European Plan'. **1889** *Harper's Mag.* Aug. 484/3 Is this hotel on the European plan? **1914** [see *American plan* s.v. AMERICAN *a.* 3]. **1907** *Daily Chron.* 24 July 3/3 A prosperous *European-style city. **1957** P. WORSLEY *Trumpet shall Sound* vi. 115 He..had built himself a European-style house.

B. *sb.* **1.** A native of Europe.

1632 MASSINGER *City Madam* III. iii, You are learned Europeans, and we worse Than ignorant Americans. **1649** G. DANIEL *Trinarch., Hen. IV*, ccciv, Iudging Soules (Europeans are soe) Laught at them afeard. **1692** in COLES. **1721–1800** in BAILEY. **1844** H. H. WILSON *Brit. India* III. 360 Europeans in India rarely possessing..the inclination to invest capital in landed property. **1858** J. B. NORTON *Topics* 64 He had saved the lives of three Europeans.

2. A person of European extraction who lives outside Europe; hence, a white person, esp. in a country with a predominantly non-white population.

1696 J. OVINGTON *Voy. to Suratt* 79 She takes her liberty with Subject or Foreigner, African or European at her will. *Ibid.* 87 The more wary Europeans, who traffick with these People. **1791** G. CARTER *Narr. Loss of Grosvenor* xli. 154 This party or detachment consisted of one hundred Europeans, and three hundred Hottentots. **1832** A. EARLE *Narr. Residence N.Z.* 73 Several Europeans who had accompanied various tribes to battle. **1857** LIVINGSTONE *Missionary Trav. S. Afr.* v. 104 By Griquas is meant any mixed race sprung from natives and Europeans. **1905** W. B. *Where White Man Treads* 286 In fact, that no 'native'..may bequeath or divert his land to a European without valuable consideration. **1913** W. W. THOMPSON *Sea Fisheries Cape Col.* ii. 42 At Somerset West Strand the industry is carried on by Malays and coloured men with a few Europeans; at Hermanus and East London nearly all those engaged in boat fishing are Europeans. **1954** R. ST. JOHN *Through Malan's Africa* I. i. 12 'European' in the South African lexicon, means anyone whose skin appears to be white, regardless of where he may have been born or brought up and what his parents may have been. **1959** *Cape Argus* 23 Jan. 4/3 More and more the landladies of London are talking of 'Europeans' when they mean people of white skin. **1961** *Observer* 19 Mar. 23/3, I, a 'European' from Canada, listened to an African Sunday orator in Trafalgar Square.

3. A member(-country) of the European Economic Community; a person who advocates membership thereof.

1959 *Listener* 31 Dec. 1142/2 By 'convinced Europeans' I mean those who are consciously constructing a new European entity... 'Europeans'..feel that the Community of the Six is still very fragile. **1962** *Ibid.* 8 Feb. 241/2, I am also worried that perhaps the Europeans do not value the adhesion of Britain sufficiently. **1963** *Guardian* 21 Jan. 9/2 'Europeans' of the five countries feel it is of the utmost importance to make this combined stand..against the French boycott of further meetings with the British. **1970** *Daily Tel.* (Colour Suppl.) 20 Feb. 7/1 As a dedicated European of long standing I must now face the plain fact that the Common Market is in a mess.

Europeanism (jʊərəʊˈpiːənɪz(ə)m). [f. prec. + -ISM.] **1. a.** Tendency to adopt what is European; *e.g.* European ideas, manner of living, systems of government, etc. **b.** Anything peculiar to or characteristic of Europe or Europeans. **c.** The modes of living, thought, etc. current in Europe.

1828 *Blackw. Mag.* XXIV. 67 Orientals drawn by an European are always likely to have an unnatural tinge of Europeanism, in their modes of thought and action. **1864** SALA in *Daily Tel.* 13 Oct., To eat alone and *à la carte* is known as living on 'the European system', and you are mulcted for your Europeanism accordingly. **1865** *Cornh. Mag.* Oct. 512 The Maories are suffering now from a surfeit of Europeanism. **1887** *Pall Mall G.* 23 July 3/1 For a European to write of modern Hinduism is much as though a native of India were to write of modern Europeanism or modern Christianity.

2. (Support for or promotion of) the ideal of unifying western Europe politically and economically; *spec.* support for the European Economic Community (see EUROPE).

[**1926** tr. *Coudenhove-Kalergi's Pan-Europe* v. 82 Pan-Americanism has a tremendous head-start on Pan-Europeanism.] **1961** in WEBSTER. **1962** *Queen's Q.* (Canada) Spring 2 Whatever one's apprehensions about.. Europeanism, it is necessary to recognise..an inclination to reconciliation. **1966** *New Society* 23 June 6/3 Those in favour of joining [the EEC] were then asked..why they wanted to join... 'Europeanism' was specified by only 6 per cent. **1970** G. COCHRANE *Big Men & Cargo Cults* ix. 151 The movements were anti-European... In some cases Europeanism is rejected. **1972** *Times* 4 Aug. 2/2 Few Westminster politicians believe Mr. Taverne could win Lincoln on Europeanism in a by-election. **1984** *Listener* 2 Aug. 34/1 Why now, with Europeanism at such a low ebb, and the Common Market so afflicted with economic blight?

Hence **Euroˈpeanist** *sb.* and *a.*, (one) expressing support for Europe or the EEC.

1962 *Queen's Q.* (Canada) Spring 1, There are Europeanists who interpret the purposes of the Treaty of Rome in terms of a rapid advance to federation. **1967** *Economist* 28 Jan. 312/1 Europeanists will no doubt continue to reproach Mr Wilson with his lack of commitment to their own burning ideals. **1970** *Times* 30 June 6/8 Men under the age of 50 are more likely to be Europeanist than men over 50. **1985** *N.Y. Times* 17 Jan. A22/4 American policy makers have been more Europeanist than most Europeans.

Europeˈanity. *rare.* [f. as prec. + -ITY.] The quality or fact of being European.

1805 W. TAYLOR in *Monthly Mag.* XIX. 657 Madoc would soon have surpassed in Europeanity of reputation the pretended works of Ossian.

Europeanization (jʊərəʊ,piːənaɪˈzeɪʃən). [f. next + -ATION.] The process of Europeanizing.

1882 E. DICEY in *19th Cent.* Aug. 169 The gradual Europeanisation of Egypt. **1886** *Academy* 11 Dec. 401 The process of Europeanisation in Japan.

Europeanize (jʊərəʊˈpiːənaɪz), *v.* [f. EUROPEAN *a.* + -IZE.] *trans.* To make European in appearance, form, habit, or mode of life.

1857 *Sat. Rev.* IV. 459/2 To suppose that India can be Europeanized through the pressure exerted by a mass of settlers. **1870** J. MACGREGOR *Rob Roy on Jordan* viii. 121 This is the only piece of real carriage-way in all Syria, and its presence..at once Europeanises the scene. **1880** K. JOHNSTON *Lond. Geog.* 82 In Japan 'everything is being rapidly Europeanised'.

b. To make coextensive with Europe.

1857 T. E. WEBB *Intellect. Locke* i. 8 The reaction thus originated in Germany was..Europeanized by France.

Hence **Euroˈpeanized** *ppl. a.* **Euroˈpeanizing** *vbl. sb.*; also *attrib.*

1849 CURZON *Visits Monast.* 72 The natty vessels which were more Europeanised and quicker than mine. **1874** SAYCE *Compar. Philol.* iv. 140 The most Europeanised of the Turanian tongues. **1888** BRYCE *Amer. Commw.* III. VI. cxiii. 626 In the Eastern cities the upper class is more Europeanized in its code of etiquette. **1887** *Athenæum* 14 May 634/3 Ismail Pasha's Europeanizing policy.

Euroˈpeanly, *adv.* [-LY².] In a European way or style.

1902 S. LANE-POOLE *Story of Cairo* i. 27 Mean and uneven offices and tenements, neither Europeanly regular nor Orientally picturesque. **1935** E. WEEKLEY *Something about Words* 41 We are told nowadays to think internationally, or at any rate Europeanly. **1958** *Times Lit. Suppl.* 24 Jan. 48/2 The Europeanly aesthetic meaningfulness of certain pictures by Van Eyck, Brueghel and Rembrandt.

europium (jʊəˈrəʊpɪəm). *Chem.* [mod.L. *europium* (E. Demarçay 1901, in *Compt. Rend. Acad. Sci.* CXXXII. 1485), f. *Europe* + -IUM.] A metallic element of the rare-earth group, symbol Eu, atomic number 63.

1901 *Jrnl. Chem. Soc.* LXXX. II. 511 The oxide of the new element *europium*..has been obtained so pure that it does not give any indication of the samarium spectra. **1938** *Nature* 24 Sept. 579/2 Comparison of the lattice constants with those of strontium and barium fluorides shows that in this respect europium compounds approximate more closely to strontium than to barium compounds. **1967** [see BASTNÄSITE].

Europocentric (jʊərəʊpəˈsɛntrɪk), *a.* [f. *Europe* + -O + -CENTRIC.] Having or regarding Europe as its centre; presupposing the supremacy of Europe and Europeans in world culture, etc. Cf. *Eurocentric* a. s.v. EURO- 1.

1934 in WEBSTER. **1958** B. MAGEE *Go West, Young Man* 251 Young men..have a real need to get outside Europe, to stop thinking in a Europocentric way, to learn at first hand about the Great Powers who now make the running in the world. **1969** *New Scientist* 27 Feb. 473/2 How far Marx's nineteenth century europocentric vision is..applicable to the second half of the twentieth century is debatable. **1977** G. CLARK *World Prehist.* (ed. 3) p. xv, Greater efforts have been made to avoid viewing prehistory from a Europocentric point of view. **1980** *Dædalus* Spring 80 If one were to brand an age as inward-turning and Europocentric, the Reformation and the Enlightenment are possibly better candidates than the Middle Ages. **1982** *Times Lit. Suppl.* 18 June 673/2 Reaction to the Europocentric writing of African history which was common up to twenty years ago.

Hence **Europoˈcentrism**, the idea or practice of placing Europe at the centre of one's world-view.

1960 *Times Lit. Suppl.* 1 July 422/4 Professor Hall briefly indicates the kind of work which is needed to avoid 'Europocentrism'. **1974** *Times* 16 Apr. 7/3 The *People's Daily* today sharply attacked 'Europocentrism' and the idea that Greek and Roman classical culture are at the root of modern thinking. **1979** I. BERLIN *Against Current* 354 This wellnigh universal Europocentrism may at least in part account for the fact that the vast explosion..of anti-imperialism..remained so largely unpredicted.

eurose, var. f. EWROSE, *Obs.*, rose-water.

†**ˈeurous,** *a. Obs.* Also 5 eureux, ewrous, 6 eurouse. [a. AF. *eürous*, OF. *eüreux* (mod.F. *heureux*), f. *eur*: see EURE *sb.*] Lucky, prosperous, successful.

c **1430** LYDG. *Thebes* 1267 Tidyus Eurous in Armes, and manly in workyng. **1473** EDW. IV. *Proclam. 10 Nov., Patent Roll* 13 Edw. IV. pt. 1, In this world to be therefore the more eureux and fortunate. **1474** CAXTON *Chesse* III. iii. F iv b, As long as a man is ewrous and fortunat he hath many frendes. *c* **1510** BARCLAY *Mirr. Good Mann.* (1570) A iv, More eurouse or happy..Then if the whole world by him were subiugate.

Eurovision: see EURO-.

‖**eurus** (ˈjʊərəs). *Obs.* [L. *Eurus*, a. Gr. Εὖρος the east wind (more correctly ESE.).] The east-wind, ESE. or SE.; the god of the east-wind. Now only *Mythol.* or in poet. personification.

c **1325** *E.E. Allit. P.* C. 133 Eurus & Aquiloun..Blowes bope at my bode vpon blo watteres. **1398** TREVISA *Barth. De P.R.* XI. iii. (1495) 386 Eurus that is the South este wynde. **1606** PEACHAM *Graphice* (J.), Eurus..must be drawn with blown cheeks, wings upon his shoulders, and his body the colour of the tawny moon. **1667** MILTON *P.L.* x. 705 Forth rush the Levant and the Ponent Winds, Eurus and Zephir. **1727** POPE, etc. *Art of Sinking* 120 Recipe for a tempest. Take eurus, zephyr, auster and boreas, and cast them together in one verse. **1775** in ASH. **1828** in WEBSTER; and in mod. Dicts.

eurybathic (jʊərɪˈbæθɪk), *a. Biol.* [f. Gr. εὐρύ-ς wide + βάθος depth.] Of aquatic life: able to live at varying depths.

1902 *Encycl. Brit.* XXXIII. 934/1 Similarly, in regard to depth, species have been classed as eurybathic and stenobathic. **1903** [see EURYTHERMAL *a.*]. **1942** H. U. SVERDRUP et al. *Oceans* xvii. 806 Many species are eurybathic, that is, they endure great ranges of depth. **1967** *Oceanogr. & Marine Biol.* V. 467 It is possible to suppose that eurybathic species may go down beyond the lower limit of the bathyal zone.

eurycephalic (jʊərɪsɪˈfælɪk), *a. Ethnol.* [f. Gr. εὐρύ-ς wide + κεφαλ-ή head + -IC.] *lit.* Broad-headed; applied to a subdivision of the brachycephalic or short broad-skulled races of mankind.

[**1866** HUXLEY *Preh. Rem. Caithn.* 85, I propose to subdivide the Brachycephali into Eurycephali, with the cephalic index ·80 to ·84, and Brachistocephali, with the cephalic index ·85 and above.] **1878** BARTLEY tr. *Topinard's Anthrop.* v. 176 Eurycephalic, large skull.

eurycerous (jʊəˈrɪsərəs), *a.* [ad. Gr. εὐρύκερ-ως, f. εὐρύ-ς broad + κέρ-ας horn + -OUS.] Having broad horns.

1836 in SMART; and in mod. Dicts.

eurygnathism (jʊəˈrɪgnəθɪz(ə)m). [See -ISM.] Eurygnathous character.

1890 H. ELLIS *Criminal* iii. 52 Microcephaly of the frontal region,..eurigmatism [*sic*; ed. 3 (1901) 50 eurignathism]. **1911** *Encycl. Brit.* XXII. 424/2 Eurygnathism..is the lateral projection of jawbones so characteristic of the Mongolic races.

eurygnathous (jʊəˈrɪgnəθəs), *a.* [f. Fr. *eurygnathe* (f. Gr. εὐρύ-ς broad + γνάθ-ος jaw) + -OUS.] Having a broad upper-jaw.

1878 BARTLEY tr. *Topinard's Anthrop.* II. i. 201 The second, a Mongolian, with the face broad, in consequence of the prominence of the cheek-bones (eurygnathous).

euryhaline (jʊərɪˈheɪlaɪn), *a.* [a. G. *euryhalin* (K. Möbius 1871, in *Jahresbericht der Commission zur wissenschaftlichen Untersuchung der deutschen Meere in Kiel* (1873) I. 139), f. Gr. εὐρύ-ς wide + ἅλινος of salt.] Able to tolerate a wide range of salinity.

1888 *Challenger Rep.: Zool.* XXIX. 421 All Baltic marine animals can live in water of varying saltness, and are therefore said to be *euryhaline*. **1964** J. A. LOVERN in *Oceanogr. & Marine Biol.* II. 169 Migratory, euryhaline or estuarine species are treated in full where appropriate.

euryphagous (jʊəˈrɪfəgəs), *a. Zool.* [f. Gr. εὐρύ-ς wide + -PHAGOUS.] (See quots.)

1926 A. S. PEARSE *Animal Ecol.* iii. 72 Animals that..eat a wide variety [of foods] are *euryphagous*. **1953** *New Biol.* XV. 23 Euryphagous predators (i.e. those which will eat a large number of different species), such as insect-eating birds.

eurypterid (jʊəˈrɪptərɪd). *Palæont.* [ad. mod.L. *Eurypteridæ* pl., f. *Eurypterus* name of the typical genus, f. Gr. εὐρύ-ς broad + πτερόν feather, wing.]

One of a group of fossil Crustacea, abundant in the Silurian and Devonian periods, some of which attained a large size. The name is due to a pair of broad swimming appendages, the hindmost of a series attached to the cephalo-thorax.

1871 HARTWIG *Subterr. W.* ii. 125 Contemporaneous with the Trilobites were the Eurypterids, which vary from one foot to five or six feet in length. **1873** DAWSON *Earth & Man* iv. 71 Eurypterids..with powerful limbs, long flexible bodies, and great eyes in the front of the head.

euryscope (ˈjʊərɪskəʊp). [f. Gr. εὐρύ-ς wide + -SCOPE.] A rapid rectilinear photographic lens of wide aperture. (*Disused.*)

1892 *Photogr. Ann.* II. p. v, The Rapidity of this series is equal to that of the Rapid Euryscopes. **1902** *Encycl. Brit.* XXXI. 694/2 Voigtländer's 'Euryscopes'..are..still largely in use. **1906** R. C. BAYLEY *Compl. Photographer* vi. 71 Many [rapid rectilinear lenses] have been made which could be used at F/6; these are known as 'Euryscopes'.

eurystomatous (jʊərɪˈstɒmətəs), *a.* [f. Gr. εὐρύ-ς broad + στόμα, στόματ-ος mouth + -OUS.] Wide-mouthed. Chiefly of serpents: Having a distensible mouth.

1878 BELL *Gegenbauer's Comp. Anat.* 463 The two halves of the jaw are movably connected together in the eurystomatous Ophidii.

eurythermal (jʊərɪˈθɜːməl), *a. Biol.* [ad. G. *eurytherm* (K. Möbius 1871, in *Jahresbericht der*

Commission zur wissenschaftlichen Untersuchung der deutschen Meere in Kiel (1873) I. 139), f. Gr. εὐρύ-ς wide + THERMAL *a.*] Able to tolerate a wide range of temperature. So **'eurytherm, eury'thermic, eury'thermous** *adjs.*

1881 [see *stenothermal* s.v. STENO-]. **1888** *Challenger Rep.: Zool.* XXIX. 421 Such animals are distinguished as *eurytherm*, in opposition to *stenotherm* animals, which can live only in warm or only in cold water. **1903** *Nature* 5 Nov. 23/2 Twelve [species] were eurythermic and eurybathic, ranging from the surface to 700 fathoms in both areas. **1940** *Chambers's Techn. Dict.* 311/2 Eurythermous. **1964** V. J. CHAPMAN *Coastal Veg.* iii. 73 *F[ucus] serratus*..can be regarded as a *eurythermal* species.

eurythm, etc.: see EURHYTHM, etc.

Eusebian (juː'siːbɪən), *a.* and *sb.* [ad. L. *Eusebiān-us*, f. *Eusebi-us.*] **A.** *adj.*

1. Of or pertaining to Eusebius.

a. A distinctive epithet applied in the 4th c. to the Arians, from their leader Eusebius, bishop of Nicomedia.

(Mod. writers have often regarded it as referring to his contemporary Eusebius of Cæsarea, whose theology was rather semi-Arian than Arian, and who formed no party.)

1882-3 SCHAFF *Relig. Encycl.* I. 161/2 Gregorius, a bishop of the Eusebian party.

b. Pertaining to Eusebius of Cæsarea, or the historical works written by him. ***Eusebian Canons***: an arrangement of the contents of the four Gospels into ten classes of passages, according as the passages occur in Matthew, Mark, Luke, or John alone, or in any one of the nine possible combinations of two or three out of the four. Numerals referring to these canons are often found in MSS. of the Greek N.T. and of the early versions.

1860 ANGUS *Bible Handbk.* 23 To these [Ammonian] sections Eusebius..adapted his tables of references, called from him the Eusebian Canons. **1870** BP. CHR. WORDSWORTH *N. Test.* I. xxv, The Eusebian Canons of the Four Gospels.

2. ***Eusebian pear***: (the original has *chrestien*: see *bon-christian* under BON.)

a **1693** URQUHART *Rabelais* III. xiii, You shall eat good Eusebian and Bergamot-Pears.

B. *sb.* A member of the Eusebian sect.

1730-6 BAILEY (folio), *Eusebians*, a sect of Arians, socalled on account of the favour shown them by Eusebius, bishop of Cæsarea. **1838** *Penny Cycl.* X. 95/1 s.v. *Eusebius*, The party to which he [Eusebius of Cæsarea] attached himself were called Eusebians, from their leader Eusebius of Nicomedia.

Hence **Eu'sebianize** *v. intr.*, to incline to Eusebian views. **Eu'sebianizing** *ppl. a.*

1888 T. W. ALLIES *Holy See* p. vi, The great letter of St. Julius to the Eusebianising bishops at Antioch in 342.

Euskarian (juː'skɛərɪən), *a.* and *sb.* [f. Basque *Euskara, Eskuara, Uskara*, the Basque language.] Basque; used by some ethnologists to designate that pre-Aryan element in the population of Europe, which they suppose to be typically represented by the Basques.

1864 I. TAYLOR *Words & Places* (1873) 113 The black-haired, short-statured race which is found..in parts of Wales is undoubtedly of Ugrian or Euskarian, not of Celtic blood. **1870** HUXLEY in *Contemp. Rev.* 519 The people of Spain and of Aquitaine at the present day must be largely 'Euskarian' by descent. **1882** *Cornh. Mag.* Dec. 733 The Portland of the earliest Celtic or Euskarian settlers. **1883** G. ALLEN *Colin Clout's Gard.* xxxix, The Euskarians are separated in our island from the Ango-Saxons and Danes by [a] long interval.

Eusol ('juːsɒl). *Pharm.* Also eusol. [f. initial letters of *E*dinburgh *U*niversity + SOL(UTION *sb.*: cf. EUPAD.] A solution of chlorinated lime and boric acid that is used as a general antiseptic.

1915 J. L. SMITH et al. in *Brit. Med. Jrnl.* July 129/1 The solution of free hypochlorous acid prepared in this way we have named 'Eusol'. *Ibid.* 134/2 The eusol treatment was kept up. **1920** MARTINDALE & WESTCOTT *Extra Pharmacop.* (ed. 17) I. 52 Eusol has been most extensively used to wounds. **1962** *Pharm. Jrnl.* 31 Mar. 270/2 Its instability in comparison with the more alkaline hypochlorite preparations has always been a serious disadvantage to the use of eusol.

Eustachian (juː'steɪʃən, -kɪən), *a.* *Anat.* [f. *Eustachi-us* name of a celebrated Italian anatomist (died 1574) + -AN.] Used as the distinctive epithet in the names of certain anatomical structures or organs which were discovered by Eustachius. †***Eustachian medulla***: the medullary portion of the kidneys. ***Eustachian tube*** (occas. *E. canal*): a canal leading from the upper part of the pharynx to the cavity of the tympanum, which it appears to supply with air; hence ***Eustachian catheter***, an instrument for inflating the Eustachian tube with air. ***Eustachian valve***: a membranous fold at the orifice of the vena cava inferior, which in the fœtus directs the current of blood from this vessel to the foramen ovale and left auricle.

1741 MONRO *Anat. Nerves* (ed. 3) 15 The Kidneys..have a reticulated Cortex of Vessels, from which the Eustachian or Bellinian Medulla, consisting of longitudinal Fibres and a few longitudinal Blood Vessels, proceeds. *Ibid.* 114 Part of the Eustachian Tube. **1755** WATHEN *Hearing* in *Phil. Trans.* XLIX. 215, I took that opportunity to examine the eustachian tube of each ear. **1831** R. KNOX *Cloquet's Anat.* 636 The..Eustachian Valve. **1870** T. HOLMES *Syst. Surg.* (ed. 2) III. 289 Recourse must be had to the Eustachian catheter. **1872** HUXLEY *Phys.* viii. 213 The function of the Eustachian tube is probably to keep the air in the tympanum ..of about the same tension as that on the outer side.

eustasy ('juːstəsɪ). *Physical Geogr.* [anglicized back-formation from next (see -Y³), after mod.L. *-stasis* sb. corresponding to *-static* adj.] A uniform change of sea-level throughout the world.

1946 F. E. ZEUNER *Dating the Past* iii. 47 Such movements of the sea-level are called eustatic, and the phenomenon, glacial eustasy. **1962** *New Scientist* 2 Aug. 243/1 If the whole level of the ocean has risen or fallen (we call it eustasy), then the total quantity of water in the ocean has been changed from time to time.

eustatic (juː'stætɪk), *a.* *Physical Geogr.* [ad. G. *eustatisch* (E. Suess *Das Antlitz der Erde* (1888) II. xiv. 680); see EU- and STATIC *a.*] Of, pertaining to, or caused by eustasy. Hence **eu'statically** *adv.*; **'eustatism** = EUSTASY.

1906 H. B. C. SOLLAS tr. *Suess's Face of Earth* II. III. xiv. 538 We must commence by separating from the various other changes which affect the level of the strand, those which take place at an approximately equal height, whether in a positive or negative direction, over the whole globe; this group we will distinguish as *eustatic movements*. The formation of the sea basins produces spasmodic eustatic negative movements. **1934** R. A. DALY *Changing World of Ice Age* vii. 226 Assume that in the last Inter-glacial stage, when sea level rose on the bank eustatically, a main atoll reef ..grew up. **1935** H. BAULIG *Changing Sea Level* 4 We have to consider..eustatic movements, resulting from changes in the capacity of the oceanic basins, a kind of eustatism which might be called deformational. **1935** *Nature* 28 Sept. 492/2 But the more recent the eustatic emergence, the fewer are the dangers of mistaking the traces of the corresponding strand-lines on the rocks of continents and islands. **1939** *Proc. Prehist. Soc.* V. 264 Sea-level..rose and fell eustatically in response to the melting and growth of ice-sheets. **1946** [see prec.]. **1954** W. D. THORNBURY *Princ. Geomorphol.* vi. 142 *Diastrophic eustatism* is change of sea level resulting from variation in capacity of the ocean basins, whereas *glacio-eustatism* refers to changes in sea level produced by withdrawal or return of water to the oceans. **1970** R. J. SMALL *Study of Landforms* xii. 425 Successive eustatic falls, independent of those attributable to glacial eustatism, occurred either as the ocean basins were deepened and/or the continental land areas raised *en masse*.

†**eusto'machic**, *a.* *Obs.* *rare*⁻¹. [f. Gr. εὐστόμαχ-ος good for the stomach (f. εὐ- EU- + στόμαχος stomach) + -IC.] Good for the stomach.

1661 LOVELL *Hist. Anim. & Min.* 242 Diphilus saith they are eustomachick, but preferreth the rosted before those that are boiled.

†**eusto'machical**, *a.* *Obs.* *rare*⁻¹. [f. as prec. + -AL¹.] = prec.

1657 TOMLINSON *Renou's Disp.* 208 Gentle Purgatives and eustomachical Medicaments..are assumed.

eu'stomachous, *a.* *rare.* [f. as prec. + -OUS.] 'Having a good digestion; easy of digestion' (*Syd. Soc. Lex.* 1884).

Euston Road ('juːstən 'rəʊd). The name of a road in London, site of a short-lived School of Drawing and Painting (1938–39), used *attrib.* or *absol.* to designate a group of English post-Impressionist realistic painters of the late 1930s or their type of art. Hence **Eu'stonian, 'Euston 'Roader**, a member or follower of this group.

1941 *Horizon* May 349 The painters of the Euston Road school resemble each other in that they all paint almost entirely from nature. **1945** P. NASH *Let.* 24 June in A. Bertram *Nash* (1955) ix. 264 The Euston Road boys, and their ruddy realism. **1945** C. BELL *V. Pasmore* 14/1 The Euston Road School was founding. In that school Pasmore was to be the principal teacher; yet he was and is far from being a typical Eustonian. Euston Road was a call to order and an antidote to the sensationalism and amateurism of the school of Paris. **1959** *Listener* 3 Dec. 981/3 The Euston Roaders owed a little to Tonks.

eustrydge, obs. form of OSTRICH.

eustyle ('juːstaɪl), *a.* and *sb.* *Archit.* [ad. L. *eustȳl-os*, a. Gr. εὔστυλος with pillars at the best distances, f. εὐ- (see EU-) + στῦλος pillar: cf. F. *eustyle*.]

A. *adj.* Of a building, colonnade, etc.: Having the space between each successive pair of columns equal to two diameters of a column and a quarter or half diameter. **B.** *sb.* The distance itself.

[**1563** SHUTE *Archit.* F j a, Eustylos..the distaunce betwen the . 2. pillers to be .2. Diameters & a quarter..but at the furdest .2. Diameters and a halfe or .3.] **1696** PHILLIPS, *Eustyle*, the order where Pillars are rightly placed; the Intercolumniations being two Diameters and a Quarter. **1775** R. CHANDLER *Trav. Asia M.* (1825) I. 152 The Temple was *in antis*, or of the eustyle species. **1832** GELL *Pompeiana* I. v. 80 The distance of two diameters and a half called the eustyle. **1876** GWILT *Archit.* 839 The diastyle and eustyle intercolumniations are very convenient in use.

eutaxite (juː'tæksaɪt). *Geol.* [f. Gr. εὐ- (see EU-) + τάξις arrangement + -ITE.

The name was given by Fritsch and Reiss, *Geol. Beschreibung Tenerife* (1868) 414.]

A rock consisting of layers of different kinds of lava lying regularly one above the other.

1879 RUTLEY *Study Rocks* xii. 233 The eutaxites of the Canary Islands..are agglomeratic and banded lavas.

Hence **euta'xitic** *a.*, of the nature of eutaxite.

1884 G. H. WILLIAMS in *Amer. Jrnl. Sc.* Ser. III. XXVIII. 261 The structure termed by Fritsch and Reiss 'Eutaxitic'.. observed in acid lavas like trachyte and phonolite.

†**eutaxy**. *Obs.* [a. F. *eutaxie*, ad. Gr. εὐταξία good arrangement, f. εὔτακτος well-arranged, f. εὖ well + τάσσειν to arrange.] Good or established order or arrangement.

1614 T. ADAMS *Devil's Banquet* 51 Let not Gods eutaxie, Order, by our friuolous scruples be brought to ataxie, Confusion. **1649** NEEDHAM *Case of Commw.* 18 Those two can never be secured, nor any politicall eutaxie, good Order, or Tranquillity maintained. **1675** R. BURTHOGGE *Causa Dei* 411 The Eutaxie and Goodly order of the World. **1677** GALE *Crt. Gentiles* II. IV. 159 Plato makes Justice to be the ευταξια, Eutaxie of moderate empire.

eutectic (juː'tɛktɪk), *a.* and *sb.* [ad. Gr. εὔτηκτος easily melting (f. εὐ- EU- + τήκ-ειν to melt) + -IC.]

A. *adj.* That is a eutectic; of or pertaining to a eutectic or its liquefaction or solidification; ***eutectic point***, the melting-point of a eutectic, or the point representing it in a constitutional diagram.

1884 F. GUTHRIE in *Phil. Mag.* 5th Ser. XVII. 462 The main argument..hinges upon the existence of compound bodies, whose chief characteristic is the lowness of their temperatures of fusion. This property..may be called Eutexia, the bodies possessing it eutectic bodies or eutectics (εὖ τήκειν)... It will, however, perhaps be better to make the term more useful by limiting its application. I shall use it.. for bodies made up of two or more constituents..in such proportion to one another as to give to the resultant compound body..a lower temperature of liquefaction than that given by any other proportion. **1885** *Nature* 5 Nov. 21/1 When metals do unite in atomic ratios the alloy produced is never *eutectic, i.e.*, having a minimum solidifying-point. Thus pure cast-iron is..an *eutectic* alloy of carbon and iron. **1902** [see B. *sb.* below]. **1910** *Encycl. Brit.* I. 705/2 The two sloping lines cutting at the eutectic point are the freezing-point curves of alloys. **1911** *Ibid.* XXI. 330/1 This mixture, which is known as the eutectic mixture, has the lowest melting-point of any which can be formed from these minerals. **1950** *Engineering* 16 June 672/2 Fusible plugs of eutectic alloys. **1967** A. H. COTTRELL *Introd. Metallurgy* xvi. 253 This is the ternary eutectic point at which the liquid is in equilibrium with all three solids *A*, *B* and *C*.

B. *sb.* **1.** A mixture which is distinguished from other mixtures of the same constituents in different proportions by having a single temperature at which it melts and freezes, this temperature being lower than the freezing-point of any of the constituents or of any other mixture of them. Also *fig.*

1884 [see A. *adj.* above]. **1884** *Asclepiad* Oct. App. 3 Eutexia..applies to compound bodies in chemistry 'whose chief characteristic is the lowness of their temperature of fusion.' They are henceforth to be called eutectics. **1885** *Athenæum* 28 Mar. 412/3 The temperature of liquefaction of a eutectic substance is lower than the temperature of either, or any, of the metallic constituents of an alloy. **1902** *Encycl. Brit.* XXVIII. 569/2 The eutectic F[reezing] P[oint] is of longer duration, but still at the same temperature. For an alloy of the composition of the eutectic itself there is no arrest until the eutectic temperature is reached. **1923** GLAZEBROOK *Dict. Applied Physics* V. II. 454/2 This most fusible alloy of a system is termed the 'eutectic' and its microscopic appearance is often characterised by fine laminations. **1926** AUDEN in *Oxford Poetry* 1 Love mutual has reached its first eutectic. **1948** GLASSTONE *Physical Chem.* (ed. 2) x. 750 Only a pure substance, or a mixture having the composition of the eutectic, melts sharply at a definite temperature. **1954** *Proc. Prehistoric Soc.* XX. 76 It is probably true that speculum is not very far removed from the eutectic of copper and tin. **1958** *Van Nostrand's Sci. Encycl.* (ed. 3), *Eutectic*... By a similar usage in petrology, a eutectic is a discrete mixture of two or more minerals, in definite proportions, which have simultaneously crystallized from the mutual solution of their constituents.

2. A eutectic point.

1940 GLASSTONE *Physical Chem.* x. 740 The temperature at which the first minute drops of liquid appear..is the eutectic for the given system. **1967** A. H. COTTRELL *Introd. Metallurgy* xiv. 210 Such a singular point of phase equilibrium is known as a eutectic or peritectic.

eutectiferous (juːtɛk'tɪfərəs), *a.* [f. EUTECT(IC + -IFEROUS.] Bearing or producing eutectics; of eutectic form or kind.

1925 P. HIDNERT *Thermal Expansion Aluminum* 715 Previous observers found that these alloys form a eutectiferous series with no chemical compounds. **1950** *Engineering* 3 Feb. 136/1 Cast irons are frequently described as eutectiferous alloys. **1953** *Sci. News* XXVIII. 111 In a simple 'eutectiferous' system the liquid breaks down into the elementary metals.

eutectoid (juː'tɛktɔɪd), *a.* and *sb.* *Metallurgy.* [f. EUTECT(IC *a.* and *sb.* + -OID.] **A.** *adj.* That is a eutectoid; of or pertaining to a eutectoid or its transformation; ***eutectoid point***, the transformation temperature of a eutectoid, or the point representing it in a constitutional

diagram. **B.** *sb.* A solid analogous to a eutectic, in which the high temperature phase is a solid solution instead of a liquid and the constituents separate out simultaneously when it is cooled to the transformation temperature.

1903 H. M. Howe *Iron, Steel, & Other Alloys* 440 The word 'eutectoid' occurred to me (June 7, 1903)... It suggests having the shape or other important properties of the 'eutectic', while the two words differ from each other enough to indicate that they refer to really distinct things. **1910** *Encycl. Brit.* XIV. 805/1 Excess of iron over this eutectoid ratio. *Ibid.*, Far below the freezing-point, transformations may take place in the solid metal, and follow a course quite parallel with that of freezing, though with no suggestion of liquidity. A 'eutectoid' is to such a transformation in solid metal what a eutectic is to freezing proper. **1925** *Jrnl. Iron & Steel Inst.* CXI. 584 The eutectoid occurring at 0·89 per cent. carbon theoretically should be regarded as a eutectoid of iron and a solid solution containing about 2·0 per cent of carbon. **1946** *Thorpe's Dict. Appl. Chem.* (ed. 4) VII. 596/2 In this case..it is the solid solution beta breaking down into the two solutions alpha and gamma, and the point P is known as a eutectoid point. **1950** *Engineering* 15 Dec. 492/3 Austenite in a plain eutectoid steel could decompose isothermally. **1961** J. N. Anderson *Appl. Dent. Mat.* (ed. 2) vi. 56 One such reaction ..is known as a eutectoid reaction. This involves the breakdown as a solid solution at a definite temperature to produce an intimate mechanical mixture of two solids.

eutelegenesis (juːtɛlɪˈdʒɛnɪsɪs). [mod.L., f. EU- + TELE- + -GENESIS.] (See quots.)

1935 H. Brewer in *Eugenics Rev.* XXVII. 123 For the process of reproduction from the germ cells of individuals between whom is no bodily contact, I propose the name telegenesis. The possible application of the process to the eugenic breeding of man may be termed eutelegenesis. **1936** *Nature* (Suppl.) 12 Sept. 447/2 Recent successful experiments with mammals in parthenogenesis and eutelegenesis. **1962** *Daily Tel.* 7 June 19/7 What is known as eutelegenesis, namely insemination by sperm from some admired donor to 'father' their children.

‖**Euterpe** (juːˈtɜːpiː). [mod.L., a. Gr. Εὐτέρπη the name of one of the Muses (goddess of music), f. εὖ well + τέρπ-ειν to please.]

1. *Bot.* A genus of palms of extremely graceful habit, sometimes measuring a hundred feet in height. (*Treas. Bot.* 1866.)

2. *Astron.* The 27th asteroid.

1867 Lardner & Dunkin *Handbk. Astron.* xv. (ed. 3) 224 The planet Euterpe was found on the evening of the 8th of November 1853, by Mr. Hind.

Euterpean (juːˈtɜːpɪən), *a.* [f. L. *Euterpē*, a. Gr. Εὐτέρπη (see prec.) + -AN.] Pertaining to the muse Euterpe, or to music.

Mod. A performance that would have been barely creditable to the 'Euterpean' or 'Philharmonic' Society of a country town.

eutexia (juːˈtɛksɪə). [a. Gr. εὐτηξία, f. εὐ- (see EU-) + τήκειν to melt.] The quality of melting easily, *i.e.* at a low temperature.

1884 [see EUTECTIC *sb.* 1]. **1885** *Athenæum* 28 Mar. 412/3 The phenomena of eutexia..as it has been named by Dr. Guthrie.

euthanasia (juːθəˈneɪzɪə, -sɪə). [a. Gr. εὐθανασία, f. εὐ- (see EU-) + θάνατ-ος death.]

1. A gentle and easy death.

1646 Bp. Hall *Balm Gil.* 337 But let me prescribe and commend to thee, my sonne, this true spirituall meanes of thine happy Euthanasia. **1709** *Tatler* No. 44 ¶3 Give me but gentle Death: Euthanasia, Euthanasia, that is all I implore. **1768** Burke *Corr.* (1844) I. 155 At her age, no friend could have hoped for your mother any thing but the Euthanasia. **1837** Carlyle *Fr. Rev.* II. v. v, Not a torture death, but a quiet euthanasia. **1875** H. C. Wood *Therap.* (1879) 239 It has been very largely employed to induce euthanasia in advanced stages of phthisis.

fig. **1813** T. Jefferson *Writ.* (1830) IV. 224 We must leave ..to others..to prepare this euthanasia for Platonic Christianity. **1844** Disraeli *Coningsby* VII. iii, This euthanasia of the day exercises a strange influence on the hearts of those who love.

2. The means of bringing about a gentle and easy death. Also *transf.* and *fig.*

1742 Hume *Essays* (1875) I. 120 Death is unavoidable to the political as well as to the animal body. Absolute monarchy..is the easiest death, the true *Euthanasia* of the British constitution. **1792** A. Young *Trav. France* (1794) I. II. xi. 414 If they [great cities] conduct easily to the grave, they become the best euthanasia of too much populousness. **1797** *Hist. Europe* in *Ann. Reg.* 257/1 Sir Francis Burdett.. said, that without a reform of Parliament corruption would become the euthanasia of the constitution. **1829** Gen. P. Thompson *Exerc.* (1842) I. 12 The true Euthanasia of religious dissension..is in the Thousand-and-One sects, whereof none shall be before or greater than another. **1862** Merivale *Rom. Emp.* (1865) III. xxviii. 335 The true euthanasia she discovered, it is said, in the bite of the asp.

3. In recent use: The action of inducing a gentle and easy death.

Used *esp.* with reference to a proposal that the law should sanction the putting painlessly to death of those suffering from incurable and extremely painful diseases.

1869 Lecky *Europ. Morals* I. xi. 233 An euthanasia, an abridgement of the pangs of disease. **1873** L. A. Tollemache in *Fortn. Rev.* Feb. 218 All persons who feel a lively interest in the mitigation of human suffering, should rejoice that the very interesting essay on Euthanasia..has been published in a separate form. **1873** —— in *Spectator* 22 Feb. 240 Euthanasia would be..no more demoralising than capital punishment.

Hence (*rare* or *nonce-wds.*) **euthaˈnasian** *a.*, of or pertaining to euthanasia. **euthaˈnasiast**, one who advocates euthanasia. (See EUTHANASIA 3.)

1873 *Contemp. Rev.* XXI. 706 Mankind at different stages of culture differ utterly as to the morality of suicide and 'euthanasian' homicide. **1884** L. A. Tollemache *Stones of Stumbling* 5 The Euthanasiasts must be admitted to have gained the day.

euthanasy (juːˈθænəsɪ). Now *rare*. [Anglicized form of EUTHANASIA. Cf. Fr. *euthanasie*.] = EUTHANASIA 1; also *fig.*

1633 Earl Manch. *Al Mondo* (1636) 164 Augustus Caesar..so often as he heard of a man that had a quicke passage, with little sense of paine, he wished for himselfe that Euthanasie. *a* **1637** B. Jonson *Underwoods, Eupheme* ix, Dare I profane so irreligious be, To greet or grieue her soft euthanasy. **1736** in Bailey (folio). **1775** in Ash. **1821** De Quincey *Confess.* (1862) 240 The practice..tends to a natural euthanasy. **1862** Syd. Dobell *Love*, The swift euthanasy of her last change.

euˈthanatize, *v. nonce-wd. trans.* To subject to 'euthanasia'.

1873 *Spectator* 22 Feb. 241/1, I saw a crab euthanatising a sickly fish, doubtless from the highest motives.

euthenics (juːˈθɛnɪks), *sb. pl.* [f. Gr. εὐθην-έειν to thrive, flourish + -ICS.] The science and art of improving the well-being of man by the betterment of the conditions of life.

1905 Mrs. E. H. Richards *Cost of Shelter* i. 12 The student of social ethics—Euthenics, or the science of *better* living—may well ask..Are the people growing more healthy ..stronger, happier? **1910** —— (*title*) Euthenics, the science of controllable environment; a plea for better living conditions as a first step toward higher human efficiency. **1926** *Daily Colonist* (Victoria, B.C.) 25 July 24/1 Euthenics as a word is comparatively young. Various definitions are given for it, the simplest being efficient living. **1967** *Technology Week* 23 Jan. 50/3 Euthenics [is] the amelioration of his [*sc.* man's] environmental opportunity, i.e., his education.

eutherian (juːˈθɪərɪən), *sb.* and *a. Zool.* [f. mod.L. *Eutheria* (T. N. Gill 1872, in *Smithsonian Misc. Coll.* XI. p. iii), f. Gr. εὐ- EU- + θηρία beasts.] **A.** *sb.* A member of the Eutheria, an infraclass which comprises the placental mammals. **B.** *adj.* Of or pertaining to this group.

1880 T. H. Huxley in *Proc. Zool. Soc.* 657 An undifferentiated Eutherian. *Ibid.* 658 Eutherian forms with deciduate placentation. **1894–5** [see METATHERIA *sb. pl.*]. **1950** J. Z. Young *Life of Vertebrates* xxi. 545 All the eutherians (placentals) have been derived from small, perhaps nocturnal, insectivorous or omnivorous animals. **1969** L. H. Matthews *Life of Mammals* I. ix. 197 The introduction of European eutherian predators..have [*sic*] played havoc with the metatherian fauna of Australia.

euthuˈtropic (juːθjuːˈtrɒpɪk), *a. Seismology.* [f. Gr. εὐθύ-ς straight + τρόπο-ς direction + -IC.]

1881 J. Milnes in *Nature* No. 632. 126 In other shocks normal or direct vibrations are the most prominent. These shocks might be called euthutropic.

†ˈ**euthymy**. *Obs.* Also 7 **euthymie**. [a. Gr. εὐθυμία, f. εὐ- (see EU-) + θυμός mind, mood.] Cheerfulness, tranquillity.

1623 Cockeram, *Euthymie*, Hearts-ease, quietnesse. **1671** H. M. tr. *Erasm. Colloq.* 221 Tranquillity, or, to speak in Greek..euthymie, or quietness of mind. **1730–6** Bailey (folio), *Euthymy*. **1775** in Ash.

euthyroid (juːˈθaɪərɔɪd), *a. Med.* [f. EU- + THYROID *a.*] Having a thyroid gland with normal function. So **euˈthyroidism**.

1924 J. Snowman tr. *F. de Quervain's Goitre* v. 43 The two opposing conditions, euthyroidism and athyroidism require no comment. **1932** C. A. Joll *Dis. Thyroid Gland* xii. 233 There are..certain cases on the borderline.. between diminished functional activity and the normal or euthyroid state. **1961** *Lancet* 2 Sept. 550/2 The patient was euthyroid. **1964** L. Martin *Clinical Endocrinol.* (ed. 4) iii. 110 Relapse does not take place after radioiodine treatment provided that euthyroidism has been attained.

Eutopia (juːˈtəʊpɪə). [f. Gr. εὐ- (see EU-) + τόπος place. First used by Sir T. More or his friend Peter Giles (see quot. 1516), with a play on UTOPIA (f. Gr. οὐ τόπος, and hence = 'no place, land of nowhere'), the name of the imaginary country described in More's famous book with that title. Some later writers have misused the word for *Utopia*, imagining the latter to be an incorrect spelling; others have correctly used the two words in an antithesis.] A region of ideal happiness or good order.

[**1516** Sir T. More or P. Giles *Hexastichon Anemolii Poete Laureati*, prefixed to *Utopia*, Vtopia priscis dicta ob infrequentiam, Nunc ciuitatis æmula Platonicæ..Eutopia merito sum vocanda nomine.] **1556** R. Robinson tr. *Hexastichon* in *More's Utopia* (ed. 2) S vij a, Wherfore not Utopie, but rather rightely My name is Eutopie, a place of felicitie. **1595** Sidney *Apol.* (1891) 19 Sir Thomas Moore's Eutopia. **1610** Th. Th[orpe] *Ded. Healey's St. Augustine's City of God*, Then [when Healey translated Hall's *Mundus Alter et Idem*, he treated] of a deuised Country scarse on earth, now of a desired Citie sure in heauen; then of Vtopia, now of Eutopia. *a* **1613** Overbury *A Wife* (1638) 255 Certain edicts from a Parliament in Eutopia. **1638** Featley *Strict. Lyndom.* II. 23 No more..than it will prove there is a Commonwealth in Eutopia.

eutraˈpelia. [f. as EUTRAPELY.] Wit, repartee; liveliness; urbanity; = EUTRAPELY.

1956 *Essays & Studies* IX. 65 The satire extends through sex, religion, politics: to the Statesman who is an 'easy' man (the overtones of that word are impossible to define; it is often something like *eutrapelia*). **1965** Battershaw & Quinn tr. Rahner (*title*) Man at play, or did you ever practise eutrapelia? *Ibid.* v. 95 The object of eutrapelia is play for the sake of seriousness.

†**euˈtrapelize**, *v. Obs.* [f. Gr. εὐτράπελ-ος (see next) + -IZE.] (See quots.)

1656–81 Blount *Glossogr.*, *Eutrapelize*, to treat civilly, or use courteously. **1775** Ash, *Eutrapelize*, to behave courteously, to use civility.

†**euˈtrapely**. *Obs. rare.* [ad. Gr. εὐτραπελία, f. εὐτράπελος pleasant in conversation, f. εὖ well + τρέπειν to turn.

The Gr. word is used by Aristotle for 'pleasantness in conversation' (one of the seven moral virtues enumerated by him); in the N.T. (*Eph.* v. 4) for reprehensible levity of speech (A.V. 'jesting'). The quots. below merely reflect these uses.]

1596 *Advice Gen. Assemb.* in *J. Melvill's Diary* (1842) 350 Aischrologie, eutrapelie, using vean and profane company. **1678** Phillips, *Eutrapely*, courtesie, urbanity. **1775** Ash, *Eutrapely*, courtesy.

eutrophic (juːˈtrɒfɪk), *a.* and *sb.* [f. next + -IC.]

A. *adj.* **1.** *Med.* Tending to promote nutrition.

2. Of a lake, swamp, etc.: (over-)rich in organic or mineral nutrients and having as a result an excessive growth of algæ and other plants, with depletion of oxygen and consequent extinction of animal life; *spec.* (see quot. 1931). Hence **eutrophiˈcation**, the process of becoming eutrophic.

1931 R. N. Chapman *Animal Ecol.* xvi. 305 The eutrophic type of lake is characterized by the paucity or absence of oxygen in the bottom waters. **1947** A. D. Hasler in *Ecology* XXVIII. 383/1 Enrichment of water, be it intentional or unintentional, is called eutrophication... In this paper eutrophication will be interpreted in the broadest sense; namely, lake enrichment owing to any and all nutritive substances. *Ibid.* 390/1 Eleven oligotrophic and dystrophic lakes have taken on eutrophic characteristics since comparatively recent times. Most rapid eutrophication has taken place in regions where there are deposits of postglacial clay;..the process has been accelerated by 'cultural influences' such as effluents from flax retting plants,.. barnyards, fertile soil, urban settlements. **1959** J. Clegg *Freshwater Life* (ed. 2) Pl. 2 (*caption*) An evolved lake in which eutrophic conditions occur. *Ibid.* xix. 317 Large reservoirs..exhibit all the characteristics of a typical eutrophic lake. **1967** *Technology Week* 23 Jan. 70/3 Lake Erie's eutrophication. **1968** *Observer* 17 Nov. 9/4 Decaying plant matter consumes all the oxygen in the water, which becomes lifeless... This process of 'eutrophication' (or over-fertilisation) has overtaken at least 40 lakes in Britain and the US. **1970** *Nature* 11 Apr. 101/1 The characteristic of a eutrophic lake is the way in which the bottom layers are depleted of oxygen during the summer as organic matter sinks to the bottom and decays. **1970** *Motor Boat & Yachting* 16 Oct. 25/1 Eutrophication (dense growth of weed) tends to occur in enclosed areas of water.

B. *sb.* A eutrophic medicine.

1884 *Syd. Soc. Lex.* s.v., The chief eutrophics are mercurials, the preparations of iodine, bromine, etc.

eutrophy (ˈjuːtrəfɪ). [ad. Gr. εὐτροφία, f. εὖ well + τρέφειν to nourish.] **1.** *Med.* Good nutrition.

1721 in Bailey; **1847** in Craig; hence in mod. Dicts.

2. The state of being eutrophic.

1947 A. D. Hasler in *Ecology* XXVIII. 392/1 Erosion has a two-fold effect..increasing sediment volume as well as contributing a higher flow of nutrients which promote eutrophy. **1967** *Oceanogr. & Marine Biol.* V. 284 Such ordination of communities, along a succession is similar to the delineation of freshwater communities along the line, eutrophy—oligotrophy.

Eutychian (juːˈtɪkɪən), *a.* and *sb.* Also 6 Eutichian, 6–7 -ean. [ad. L. *Eutychiān-us*, f. *Eutych-es* + -IAN.]

A. *adj.* Of, pertaining to, or adhering to the doctrine of Eutyches, a presbyter of Constantinople, in the 5th cent., who maintained that the human nature of Christ was lost in the divine. **B.** *sb.* A member of the Eutychian sect.

1556 J. Clement in Strype *Eccl. Mem.* III. App. lxi, 214 From all Arians, Eutichians..and all other heretikes. **1579** Fulke *Heskins' Parl.* 187 The Eutychian heresie..denyed the trueth of Christes body after the adunation therof to the Diuinitie. **1635** Pagitt *Christianogr.* I. ii. (1636) 176 The Armenians are iudged by manie to be Eutichean heretickes. **1724** Waterland *Athan. Creed* vii. 103 It cannot reasonably be set lower than the Eutychian times. **1882–3** Schaff *Encycl. Relig. Knowl.* I. 775 The measures which were employed against the Eutychians were rather harsh.

Hence **Euˈtychianism**, the Eutychian heresy.

1612 Brerewood *Lang. & Relig.* xxi. 186 Eutychianisme so mightily prevailed in those parts. **1846** G. S. Faber *Tractar. Secession* 192 The Eutychianism which Dr. Moehler would make the badge of..the Protestant System.

euxanthic (juːˈzænθɪk), *a. Chem.* [tr. G. *euxanthinsäure* euxanthic acid (O. L. Erdmann 1844, in *Jrnl. f. prakt. Chem.* XXXIII. 192), f. EU- + Gr. ξανθ-ός yellow + -IC.] ***euxanthic acid***: a glycoside, $C_{19}H_{16}O_{10}$, yielding

glucuronic acid and euxanthone on hydrolysis; purreic acid.

1852 [see PURREE]. **1943** *Thorpe's Dict. Appl. Chem.* (ed. 4) VI. 424/2 Euxanthic acid is isolated by digesting piuri with dilute hydrochloric acid. **1959** E. H. RODD *Chem. Carbon Compounds* IV. viii. 966 Xanthen derivatives have long been known and include euxanthic acid and the related euxanthone.

euxanthone (juːˈzænθəʊn). *Chem.* [ad. G. *euxanthon* (O. L. Erdmann 1844, in *Jrnl. f. Prakt. Chem.* XXXIII. 205), f. prec. + -ONE.] A yellow derivative of xanthone, $C_{13}H_8O_4$; purrenone; 1:7-dihydroxyxanthone.

1852, 1857 [see *s.v.* PURREE]. **1952** K. VENKATARAMAN *Chem. Synthetic Dyes* II. xxiv. 740 Euxanthone, found in the urine of cows fed on mango leaves, is 1,7-dihydroxyxanthone. **1959** [see prec.].

euxenite (ˈjuːksɪnaɪt). [f. Gr. εὔξεν-ος hospitable (f. εὐ- EU- + ξένος stranger) + -ITE.

So named by Scheerer in 1840 (*Pogg. Ann.* L. 153) 'on account of the many rare constituents which it harbours'.]

A mineral found in Norway, consisting mainly of niobate and titanate of yttrium.

1844 DANA *Min.* 436 Euxenite comes from Jölster in Norway. **1873** WATTS *Fownes' Chem.* 378 It [Thorium] has since been found in Euxenite.

euzeolite (juːˈziːəlaɪt). [f. EU- + ZEOLITE.] (See quots.)

1832 SHEPARD *Min.* 178 Heulandite..Euzeolite. **1868** DANA *Min.* 443 In 1817, Breithaupt separated the two zeolites..and called the latter euzeolite. In 1822 Brooke..named the other heulandite.

[**evacate**: a spurious word in Dicts; see EVOCATE.]

evacuant (ɪˈvækjʊənt), *a.* and *sb.* [f. L. *ēvacuant-em*, pr. pple. of *ēvacuāre*: see EVACUATE.]

A. *adj. Med.* That evacuates or tends to evacuate; promoting evacuation, cathartic, purgative.

1800 *Med. Jrnl.* IV. 214 Evacuant and debilitating remedies. **1818** A. T. THOMSON *Lond. Disp.* II. 41 Their general operation is evacuant, either by the stomach, the bowels, or the skin. **1881** tr. *Trousseau & Pidous' Treat. Therap.* 168 Evacuant treatment in general.

B. *sb.* **1.** *Med.* A medicine that promotes evacuation; as a purgative, emetic, diaphoretic.

1730-6 in Bailey (folio). **1732** *Hist. Litt.* IV. 9 Those stupendous Effects which vegetable Concretes excite in the Body, both as Evacuants and Alterants. **1753** TORRIANO *Sore Throat* 32 The Emetic repeated did not act as an Evacuant in the least. **1830** LINDLEY *Nat. Syst. Bot.* 73 Asarabacca is used by native practitioners in India as a powerful evacuant. **1876** BARTHOLOW *Mat. Med.* (1879) 2 To the class of evacuants belong emetics..and diuretics.

2. In *Organ-building*, a valve to let out the air from the bellows.

evacuate (ɪˈvækjuːeɪt), *v.* Also 6-7 evacuat. *Pa. pple.* 6-7 evacuat(e. [f. L. *ēvacuāt-* ppl. stem of *ēvacuā-re* (Pliny), f. *ē* out + *vacuus* empty. Cf. Fr. *évacuer*.

In class. L. *ēvacuāre* is found only in Pliny, with the sense 'to empty (the bowels)'. The Vulgate and later law-books have the fig. sense 'to make void, nullify', which is rather to be regarded as parallel with the older sense than as developed from it, being based on the fig. sense of *vacuus* 'void, null, of no validity'. The sense represented in branch II, where the obj. is the contents instead of the vessel or receptacle, is a development similar to that in *to empty*, Fr. *vider*; it occurs in med.L. in medical use (*evacuare humores*, etc), and hence in Fr. *évacuer*.]

I. To make empty.

* *To remove the contents of.*

1. a. *trans.* To empty, clear out the contents of (a vessel or receptacle). Chiefly in uses more or less technical: To empty (the stomach, bowels, or other bodily organ); to deplete (the body) by purging or vomiting (formerly also by bleeding, sudorifics, etc.); to exhaust (of air).

1542 BOORDE *Dyetary* viii. 248 After you haue euacuated your body, and trussed your poyntes, kayme your heade oft. **1601** HOLLAND *Pliny* XXXII. ix. 443 The broth of these fishes hath the name to evacuat both the bellie and the bladder. **1644** HAMMOND *Loyal Convert* 13 Physicians evacuate the Body, sometimes by Vomit, sometimes by Purge. *a* **1652** BROME *City Wit* III. ii, I will prefer thee to..make my Bed ..and evacuate my Chamberpot. **1660** BOYLE *New Exp. Phys. Mech.* To Rdr. (1682) 5 Evacuate such Receivers till there be no air left in them. **1710** STEELE *Tatler* No. 99 ¶3 Had detached all his Subjects and evacuated all his Stores. **1748** HARTLEY *Observ. Man* I. ii. 215 The Contraction of the Lacrymal Glands, whereby they are evacuated. **1875** BEDFORD *Sailor's Pocket Bk.* viii. (ed. 2) 305 In all cases of poisoning, the first step is to give the antidote..and then evacuate the stomach. **1883** *Standard* 31 Jan. 5/4 It is possible..to evacuate them by cutting trenches through which the black ooze drains.

b. *absol.* (In quot. †to let blood.)

1621 BURTON *Anat. Mel.* II. v. I1, If the malady continue, it is not amiss to evacuate in a part in the fore-head.

c. *fig.* in various senses. Const. *of*. In recent use *esp.* To deprive (a term, concept, etc.) *of* its contents or value. Cf. 4.

1594 HOOKER *Eccl. Pol.* IV. x. (1611) 147 By euacuating cleane, and emptying the church of euery such rite and ceremony. *a* **1653** S. WARD in Spurgeon *Treas. Dav.* Ps. xiii. 5 Hath it [faith] not sovereign virtue in it, to..evacuate the mind of all ill thoughts and passions. *a* **1734** NORTH *Lives* I. 8, I hope to evacuate my mind of every matter and thing I know..concerning his lordship. **1825** COLERIDGE *Aids Refl.* (1836) 150 They..evacuate the term [spirit] of all its proper meaning. **1836-7** SIR W. HAMILTON *Metaph.* xxxix. (1870) II. 384 Brown..evacuates the phænomenon of all that desiderates explanation. **1862** MERIVALE *Rom. Emp.* (1865) III. xii. 15 They sank into exhaustion, evacuated of all life and energy. **1869** HADDAN *Apost. Succ.* i. (1879) 15 To evacuate the sacraments of grace, and to regard them as merely acted prayers.

†**d.** *refl.* and *intr.* for *refl.* Of a body of water, etc.: To empty, discharge itself. Also *fig. Obs.*

1725 DE FOE *Voy. round World* (1840) 311 At the further end of the lake, they found that it evacuated itself into a large river. **1762** STERNE *Tr. Shandy* V. iii. 23 Such griefs evacuate themselves best by that particular channel. **1817** KEATINGE *Trav.* II. 265 Where the canal evacuates is placed a net to catch what would pass off and be lost.

†**2.** To clear (a place) of inmates, etc., (a country) of inhabitants, troops, wild beasts. Const. *of*.

1607 TOPSELL *Four-f. Beasts* (1673) 136 That the whole countrey might be evacuated and quite cleared from wolves. **1687** in *Magd. Coll.* (Oxf. Hist. Soc.) 81 To evacuate a whole College will be..scandalous. **1704** *Addr. Norfolk* in *Lond. Gaz.* No. 4068/2 A Great Monarch..evacuates whole Countries. **1708** *Ibid.* No. 4462/2 Evacuating the Kingdom of all Foreign Troops. **1751** JOHNSON *Rambler* No. 171 ¶14 In France they annually evacuate their streets, and ship their prostitutes and vagabonds to their colonies. **1753** SMOLLETT *Ct. Fathom* (1784) 34/1 Her room was no sooner evacuated of such troublesome visitants, than [etc.].

3. a. Of an army; To relinquish the occupation of (a country, fortress, town, position). Said also of the general in command, or of the authority that orders the withdrawal.

1710 STEELE *Tatler* No. 76 ¶5 The Army..had begun to repass the Mountains, and would shortly evacuate Savoy. *a* **1745** SWIFT (J.), The emperour..never effectually evacuated Catalonia. **1792** *Anecd. W. Pitt* III. xxxix. 35 The French forces who had invaded and seized Turks Island must immediately evacuate the same. **1840** MACAULAY *Clive* 21 The garrison, in a panic, evacuated the fort. **1863** KINGLAKE *Crimea* I. xxv. 433 She [Austria] summoned the Emperor Nicholas to evacuate the Principalities. **1887** *Spectator* 28 May 722/1 Egypt is to be evacuated within three years.

absol. **1881** DILLON in *Times* 5 Jan. 10/1 As soon as the army evacuates he can go back to his own home.

b. *gen.* To quit, withdraw from (a place or apartment). Also *absol.*

1809 W. IRVING *Knickerb.* (1861) 271 The burgomasters were not slow in evacuating the premises. **1830** GALT *Lawrie T.* VII. viii. (1849) 337 The other guests had evacuated the apartment. **1849** C. BRONTË *Shirley* xv. 226 Request your friend Mr. Donne to evacuate. **1877** FARRAR *My Youth* xxx. 303, I will evacuate it whenever you like.

** *To make void or worthless.*

†**4.** To make void, annul, deprive of force or validity. Chiefly in religious and legal phraseology. (The earliest recorded sense in Eng.) *Obs.*

1526 *Pilgr. Perf.* (W. de W. 1531) 5 Ceremonyes..whiche all were euacuate and made voyde by the passyon of our sauyour Jesu Chryst. **1548** LATIMER *Ploughers* (Arb.) 32 Thys is the marke at the whyche the Deuyll shooteth, to evacuate the crosse of Chryste. **1563** DAVIDSON *Answ. Kennedy* in *Wodr. Soc. Misc.* 257 To have evacuat the Reasonis of ȝour Buik. **1622** BACON *Hen. VII*, 81 Which defect..would not euacuate a Marriage after Cohabitation and Actual Consummation. *a* **1626** BP. ANDREWES *Serm.* (1856) I. 83 We evacuate the gift..if we vouchsafe not to accept of it. **1638** CHILLINGW. *Relig. Prot.* iv. § 45. 213 Words, which evacuate your objection. **1709** STRYPE *Ann. Ref.* I. ii. 62 Of which lands they had been thrown out in Queen Mary's reign, and their patents from king Edward evacuated. **1785** PALEY *Mor. Philos.* (1818) I. 141 A latitude, which might evacuate the force of almost all promises.

II. To empty out (the contents of anything).

†**5.** Of the action of a medicine, vomiting, etc. (rarely of a personal agent by means of medicine): To clear out, get rid of, remove (a disease or humour). Also *fig. Obs.* Cf. 1.

1533 ELYOT *Cast. Helthe* III. vii, Vnctions with oyles and oyntementes..do shortely euacuate the fulnesse. **1601** HOLLAND *Pliny* XXV. v. 217 The white [Ellebore purgeth] by vomit upward, and doth evacuat the offensive humours which cause diseases. **1671** SALMON *Syn. Med.* II. xlvi, 314 A perfect Crisis is that which evacuates all the vitious Matter. **1715** I. PETIVER in *Phil. Trans.* XXIX. 230 The Seed of this Plant evacuates yellow Choler. *a* **1716** SOUTH *Serm.* ix. 341 (T.) Fasting and humiliation is a sovereign remedy to evacuate all spiritual distempers. **1779** JOHNSON *L.P., Pope* Wks. IV. 85 Thomson declared his [Pope's] distemper to be a dropsy, and evacuated part of the water by tincture of jalap. **1790** W. BUCHAN *Dom. Med.* (ed. 11) 553 The principal intention..is to evacuate the offending matter.

6. a. To void, discharge (excrements, etc.) through 'any of the excretory passages' (J.); in mod. use only through the bowels or mouth.

1607 TOPSELL *Four-f. Beasts* (1673) 322 That part..will grow unto a head and break, evacuating great abundance of filthy matter. **1664** POWER *Exp. Philos.* I. 37 That round hole near her [Black Snail's] neck..out of which I have observed some salivous Matter to be evacuated. **1766** ALEXANDER in *Phil. Trans.* LVII. 68, I started up..made some efforts to vomit, but evacuated nothing. **1800** *Med. Jrnl.* IV. 386 About four pints of urine had been evacuated. **1865** BARING-GOULD *Werewolves* x. 173 He evacuated such floods of water that the mountain torrents were full.

absol. **1634** J. LEVETT *Ordering of Bees* 59 They haue no Intraylls or other inward Organs, by which either to retaine or evacuat. **1666** G. HARVEY *Morb. Angl.* (1672) 104 A man that doth feed upon one dish at a meal shall nothing near evacuate..so quick or readily as one that dines upon two or more. **1705** OLIVER in *Phil. Trans.* XXV. 2178 But no body ever saw him Eat or Evacuate.

b. In wider sense (partly *transf.* from the above): To discharge, throw off, vent. Also *fig.*

1622 HAWKINS *Voy. S. Sea* (1847) 146 Their houses are made..with a laver in the toppe to evacuate the smoake when they make fire. **1662** GERBIER *Princ.* 20 The Lime having evacuated its putrefaction. **1816** J. SCOTT *Vis. Paris* (ed. 5) 19 When a Margate hoy evacuates her cargo, the crowd on the pier is usually considerable. **1841** *Fraser's Mag.* XXIII. 511 Judging from sentiments which he has evacuated in some of his public spoutifications.

†**7. a.** To take out mechanically, leaving a vacuum or void; to pump out (water); to exhaust (air). Also *fig. Obs.* exc. in surgical use.

1719 DE FOE *Crusoe* II. i, Any one would have thought that the native Propensity to rambling..should be worn out, the volatile Part be fully evacuated. **1751** SMOLLETT *Per. Pic.* (1779) I. xiii. 115 The contents of his skull must have been evacuated. **1767** GOOCH *Treat. Wounds* I. 295 As much of the brain was evacuated, as wou'd fill a hen's eggshell. **1772** HUTTON *Bridges* 82 The water will ooze up..in too great abundance to be evacuated by the engines. **1781** COWPER *Lett.* 5 Mar., As much of the mould as can be taken out without disturbing the roots must be evacuated and its place supplied with fresh. **1794** G. ADAMS *Nat. & Exp. Philos.* I. iv. 137 The ascent of the quicksilver..is proportional to the quantity evacuated by each turn. **1797** M. BAILLIE *Morb. Anat.* (1807) 112 If..the pus be evacuated externally, there will be a scar in the neck. **1877** tr. *Ziemssen's Cycl. Med.* XII. 704 The contents of abscesses have been evacuated in the following directions.

b. *intr.* for *refl.*

1643 R. O. *Man's Mort.* iii. 13 A Vessell..so sollid every where, that the Aire could not possibly evacuate. **1707** *Curios. in Husb. & Gard.* 261 The Sap..turns aside and evacuates by this Aperture.

8. a. To clear out, remove (inhabitants, inmates, or troops). †Also *intr.* for *refl.* Cf. 2.

a **1639** WOTTON in Gutch *Coll. Cur.* I. 220 Action had pretty well evacuated the idle people, which are the stock of rapine. **1669** CHILD *Disc. Trade* (ed. 4) 233 The people that evacuate from us to Barbadoes. **1691** BEVERLEY *Thous. Years Kingd. Christ* 23 Nor can he cease to Reign, till They [his enemies] are so Evacuated. **1698** LUDLOW *Mem.* (1721) I. 179 The Garrison would be entirely evacuated before they could signify their Pleasure to the Army. **1872** *Daily News* 3 May 5/6 The wounded used to be stowed in it [the refreshment room at Meaux] till the time came conveniently to evacuate them. **1884** *Ibid.* 5 Mar. 5/7 He was evacuating the garrison and Egyptian inhabitants of that place [Tokar].

b. *spec.* To remove (inhabitants of an area liable to aerial bombing or other hazards) to safer surroundings. Also *transf.*

1938 *Times* 28 Oct. 15/2 Authorities of our large towns will wonder whether or not to evacuate more than children. **1940** *Ann. Reg. 1939* 87 Mr. Greenwood and others strongly appealed to the Prime Minister to evacuate children at once. **1941** *Essays & Studies* XXVI. 61 This statement it has proved impossible to check, as the Burney newspapers are evacuated and the journal is not at Bodley.

evacuated (ɪˈvækjuːeɪtɪd), *ppl. a.* [f. prec. + -ED[1].] In the various senses of the vb.

1684 R. WALLER *Nat. Exper.* 63 He [Boyle] mentions a Larks living in the Evacuated Receiver..about ten Minutes. **1762** CANTON in *Phil. Trans.* LII. 461 Within an evacuated glass ball. **1773** HORSLEY *ibid.* LXIV. 236 Columns of water, sustained in evacuated tubes of sufficient length. **1822** J. FLINT *Lett. Amer.* 236, I took this opportunity of reconnoitring the evacuated field. **1939** *Times* 28 Oct. 7/2 Parents of evacuated children should contribute to their maintenance. **1942** E. WAUGH *Put out more Flags* ii. 144, I am the district billeting officer. I'm looking for a suitable home for three evacuated children.

evacuating (ɪˈvækjuːˌeɪtɪŋ), *vbl. sb.* [f. as prec. + -ING[1].] In senses of the verb. Also *attrib.*

1594 PLAT *Jewell-ho.* I. 27 The euacuating thereof [the vaine of earth]. **1642** J. EATON *Honey-c. Free Justif.* 40 To the abolishing, evacuating, or utter vanishing away of sinne. **1660** BOYLE *New Exp. Phys. Mech.* xxiv. 188 Upon the evacuating of the Receiver. **1753** TORRIANO *Sore Throat* Pref. 15 For one Patient..that dies by this Method, five will die by the evacuating Method. **1875** W. HOUGHTON *Sk. Brit. Insects* 18 The evacuating ducts are constant.

evacuation (ɪˌvækjuːˈeɪʃən). [ad. late L. *ēvacuātiōn-em*, n. of action f. *ēvacuā-re*: see EVACUATE.] The action of evacuating; the condition of being evacuated.

1. *spec.* **a.** *Med.* The action or process of depleting (the body or any organ), or of clearing out (morbid matter, 'humours', etc.), by medicine or other artificial means. *rare* in recent use.

Before the present century the word was most frequently used with reference to bleeding; for this we have a large number of quotations.

c **1400** *Lanfranc's Cirurg.* (MS. A.) 100 Ofte tymes he haþ ..to myche evacuacioun of blood. **1533** ELYOT *Cast. Helthe* (1541) 53a, To expell the sayd excrementes are ix sundry kyndes of evacuation..abstinence, vomyte, purgation by siege, letting of bloude, etc. **1603** HOLLAND *Plutarch's Mor.* 1317 Evacuation, or clensing the body by clistre. **1621** BURTON *Anat. Mel.* II. v. II. (1651) 398 Bleed on..If the parties strength will not admit much evacuation in this kinde at once, it [bleeding] must be assayed again and again. **1651** BIGGS *New Disp* 136 One manner of evacuation of evil humours, purgation. **1748** SMOLLETT *Rod. Rand.* xxxv. (1804) 229, I prepared for this important evacuation [of blood]. **1790** W. BUCHAN *Dom. Med.* (ed. 11) 217 The patient exhausted by mere evacuations, sunk under the disease. **1805** W. SAUNDERS *Min. Waters* 467 This method

..seems to have a preference over actual evacuation by the lancet. **1836** TODD *Cycl. Anat.* I. 179/1 The evacuation of the contents of the rectum and bladder.

b. *Phys.* The process of discharging (waste matter, etc.) through the excretory organs (now *esp.* from the bowels); an instance of this process; a manner in which it takes place.

c **1532** DEWES *Introd. Fr.* in Palsgr. 1054 A body..may not grow by the vertue of such degestion without expulsion or evacuation. **1603** KNOLLES *Hist. Turks* (1638) 176 After many euacuations, sitting downe vpon an homely bed [he] died. **1643** R. O. *Man's Mort.* vii. 54 The evacuation of seed in carnall copulation. **1659** HAMMOND *On Ps.* cvi. 15 Annot. 537 Nature..seeks to discharge it selfe by the several evacuations. **1725** N. ROBINSON *Th. Physick* 73 This Evacuation [perspiration] is by far the greatest of any in the Body. **1727** POPE, &c., *Art of Sinking* 75 Has had some poetical evacuation, and no question was much the better for it in his health. **1748** HARTLEY *Observ. Man* I. iii. 399 The causes of it are..violent and long-continued Passions, profuse Evacuations. **1784** JOHNSON *Let.* 18 Mar. in *Boswell*, The dropsy..has now run almost totally away by natural evacuation. **1851** J. DAVIES *Manual Mat Med.* 375 To promote alvine evacuations. **1852** SIR W. HAMILTON *Discuss.* 247 Under the terms crudity, coction and evacuation, were designated [according to the Humoral Pathology] the three principal periods of diseases.

c. *concr.* Evacuated or excreted matter.

1625 HART *Anat. Ur.* II. viii. 100 Other euacuations, both vpwards and downwards, came. **1759** STERNE *Tr. Shandy* (1802) I. xxiii. 119 Others..will draw a man's character..merely from his evacuations. **1846** G. E. DAY tr. *Simon's Anim. Chem.* II. 384 Sometimes we find, in the deposit from these evacuations, small white or yellow masses.

2. a. *gen.* The action of emptying (a receptacle), or of removing (the contents of anything) so as to produce a vacancy; the depletion (of a treasury, one's resources, etc.). Sometimes with transf. notion of 1 a. Also *fig.*

1598 BARCKLEY *Felic. Man* (1631) 400 They [Lawyers & Physicions] have one common end, that is gaine, & the manner of both their proceedings..is—by evacuation! *a* **1600** HOOKER (J.), Popery hath not been able to re-establish itself in any place, after provision made against it by utter evacuation of all Romish ceremonies. **1640** J. DYKE *Worthy Commun.* Ep. to Rdr., The continuall effluences of vertue out of Him..is not the least evacuation at all unto Him. **1697** POTTER *Antiq. Greece* II. xix. (T.), Their treasury ..exhausted by so frequent evacuations. **1774** GOLDSM. *Nat. Hist.* I. 52 It is pretty evident that their [grottoes'] evacuation has been owing to waters. **1806** VINCE *Hydrostat.* vii. 79 The evacuation made by so swift a current. **1840** MACAULAY *Clive* 30 Not content with these ways of getting rid of his money, [he] resorted to the most speedy and effectual of all modes of evacuation, a contested election. **1869** PHILLIPS *Vesuv.* iii. 48 After the extraordinary evacuation of the large crateral space. **1877** tr. *Ziemssen's Cycl. Med.* XII. Index *s.v.*

†**b.** The quantity removed by 'evacuation'. *Obs.*

1794 G. ADAMS *Nat. & Exp. Philos.* I. iv. App. 136 The evacuations [*sc.* of air] and the remainders do both of them decrease in the same geometrical progression.

†**c.** A clearing out, depleting (of population, etc.). *Obs.*

1669–94 CHILD *Disc. Trade* (ed. 4) 201 And if that evacuation [of population] be grown to an excess. **1677** HALE *Prim. Orig. Man.* II. x. 238 Let us also consider the vast Evacuations of Men that England hath had by Forein Assistances lent to Forein Kingdoms. **1755** MRS. DELANY *Autobiog.* (1861) III. 362 There will be a great evacuation at Bath of fine folks.

3. *Mil.* †**a.** The clearing (a place) of troops (*obs.*). **b.** The withdrawal (by an army or commander) from occupation of a country, fortress, town, etc. **c.** The removal (of a garrison, the population of a place, etc.).

1710 *Lond. Gaz.* No. 4666/1 The Deputies..have insisted ..on the Evacuation of the Kingdom of all Foreign Troops. **1783** *Chron.* in *Ann. Reg.* 221 New York..the final evacuation of that city. **1796** BURKE *Corr.* IV. 354 An evacuation of the Mediterranean, as a preliminary to a war with Spain. **1839** THIRLWALL *Greece* IV. 125 They offered no concession beyond the evacuation of Decelea and the Attic territory. **1863** KINGLAKE *Crimea* (1876) I. xvii. 378 A declaration..which made the further continuance of peace dependent upon the evacuation of the Principalities. **1880** MCCARTHY *Own Times* III. xxxiv. 92 The time for the evacuation of the garrison came.

attrib. a **1854** G. FURMAN *Antiquities Long Island* (1875) 269 The Evacuation day..has been observed as a species of holiday on the west end of Long Island. **1880** WEBSTER (Suppl.), *Evacuation day*, the anniversary of the day on which the British army evacuated the city of New York, November 25, 1783. **1939** *Times* 2 Nov. 8/7 Parents should remember that such educational facilities as can be provided in the evacuation areas are not likely to be nearly so good as those available in the reception areas. **1940** *Archit. Rev.* LXXXVII. 101 (*title*) Evacuation camp. **1940** E. T. SETON *Trail of Artist-Naturalist* 241 Monday, which, being Evacuation Day, was a public holiday.

4. The action of making void and of no effect; cancelling, nullification. Cf. EVACUATE *v.* 4.

1650 *Vind. Hammond's Addr.* §66 The suspension of the latter, farre from including the evacuation, or cancelling of the former. **1691** BEVERLEY *Thous. Years Kingd. Christ* 21 Putting Them quite under his Feet, by that perfect distinguishing Catargesis, or Evacuation of All Power, Motion, or Action. **1750** JOHNSON *Rambler* No. 31 ⁋10 Sophisms tending to the confusion of all principles, and the evacuation of all duties.

evacu'ationist. *nonce-wd.* [f. prec. + -IST.] One who advocates the evacuation of (an occupied territory).

1884 J. MORLEY in *Macm. Mag.* July 230 There is no reason why annexationists and evacuationists should not continue their controversy on the floor of Parliament.

evacuative (ɪ'vækjuːətɪv), *a.* and *sb.* [a. F. *évacuatif, -ive*, f. *évacuer*, ad. L. *ēvacuāre*: see EVACUATE and -IVE.]

A. *adj.* That evacuates or empties (the bowels); cathartic, purgative, evacuant.

1611 COTGR., *Evacuatif*, euacuatiue; purgative. **1828** in WEBSTER; and in mod. Dicts.

B. *sb.* An evacuative medicine; an evacuant.

1656 RIDGLEY *Pract. Physick* 50 Palliative is made..by evacuatives and alteratives.

evacuator (ɪ'vækjuːeɪtə(r)). Also 7 -er. [f. EVACUATE + -OR.] One who or that which evacuates (in the senses of the verb).

1611 COTGR., *Vuideur*, a voyder, emptier, euacuater. *a* **1660** HAMMOND *Wks.* I. 175 (T.) Be not too busy..in excusing the great evacuators of the Law. **1696** EDWARDS *Demonstr. Exist. & Provid. God* II. 99 The ears are the evacuators of the bilious excrement that flows thither. **1718** QUINCY *Compl. Disp.* 63 The whole Materia Medica is certainly to be included under..Alteratives, Evacuators, and Restoratives. **1828** in WEBSTER; and in mod. Dicts.

†**e'vacuatory,** *a.* and *sb. Obs. rare.* [f. prec.; see -ORY.] = EVACUANT A. and B.

1704 *Gentleman Instr.* (1732) 309 (D.) An imposthume calls for a lance, and oppletion for unpalatable evacuatories. **1789** W. FALCONER *Ess. Health Pers. Agric.* 84 Medicines of the evacuatory kind.

†**e'vacue,** *v. Obs.* [a. F. *évacue-r*: see EVACUATE *v.*] In senses of EVACUATE *v.*

c **1400** *Lanfranc's Cirurg.* (MS. B.) 17 He moste kunne evacuen hym þat ys ful of euele humores. *Ibid.* 94 First euacue þe malancolient mater. **1541** R. COPLAND *Guydon's Quest. Chirurg.*, By the whiche incysyon the blode euacueth.

evacuee (ɪvækjuː'iː). Also ‖**évacué(e).** [ad. F. *évacué.*] A person who has been evacuated (see EVACUATE *v.* 8 b). Also *attrib.*

1934 WEBSTER, *Évacué* n. masc., *évacuée* fem. **1938** *Times* 24 Nov. 10/4 The Minister..will determine the number and type of evacuees and of residents in each area to be cared for. **1939** *Times Weekly* 1 Nov. 12 The embarcation of these, mostly unwilling, evacuees is illustrated. **1939** in *English Studies* (1940) XXII. 29 Some evacuee mothers have complained... Parents visited their evacuee children in the reception areas. **1950** E. HYAMS *From Waste Land* 11 There sprang up a gaudy and elaborate legend concerning the evacuees.

†**e'vacuity.** *Obs. rare*⁻¹. [f. E- *pref.*³ + VACUITY.] A vacuity, vacancy.

1655 FULLER *Ch. Hist.* XI. (1845) VI. 253 Fit it was therefore so many evacuities should be filled up.

evadable (ɪ'veɪdəb(ə)l), *a.* In Dicts. also **evadible.** [f. next + -ABLE.] That may be evaded.

1857 DE QUINCEY *Judas Iscar.* Wks. VII. 31 A piece of artillery..not evadable by any counter artifice of his opponents.

evade (ɪ'veɪd), *v.* Also *Sc.* 6 avaid, ev-, ewaid. [a. Fr. *évader*, ad. L. *ēvādĕre*, f. *ē* out + *vādĕre* to go. Cf. Pr. *evazir*, Sp. *evadir*, It. *evadere*. (The trans. use does not occur in Lat. or mod.F., but is found in Fr. of the 15th c.)]

1. *intr.* To get away, escape: const. *from, out of. rare* in mod. use.

1513 DOUGLAS *Æneis* II. viii. 102 All that fled war, and evadit Throw the dirk nycht. **1535** STEWART *Cron. Scot.* II. 661 That he micht nocht avaid out of thair handis. **1560** ROLLAND *Crt. Venus* II. 84 Gif ȝe wald fra this auenture ewaid. **1622** BACON *Hen. VII* (J.), His wisdom, by often evading from perils, was turned rather into a dexterity to deliver himself from dangers, than, etc. **1647** LILLY *Chr. Astrol.* lxvi. 403 He was brought to some trouble, but evaded. **1735** SOMERVILLE *Chase* I. 345 The serous particles evade Thro' th' open Pores. **1880** MRS. WHITNEY *Odd or Even* v. 33 The 'three of 'em', as they were always numerically reproached when..a fowl evaded.

†**b.** In a Lat. sense: To 'turn out' to be. *Obs.*

1677 GALE *Crt. Gentiles* II. IV. 29 Doth it [the soul] not evade altogether happy, being freed from Error?

2. *trans.* To escape by contrivance or artifice from (attack, pursuit, adverse designs; an assailant, pursuer, or adversary); to avoid, save oneself from (a threatened evil or inconvenience); to elude (a blow), avoid encountering (an obstacle).

1535 STEWART *Cron. Scot.* II. 246 No vther wa tha micht evaid his feid. **1607** SHAKS. *Cor.* III. iii. 2 If he euade vs there. **1632** MASSINGER *City Madam* IV. ii, You that..knew, in your accompts, To cheat my brother; if you can, evade me. **1646** SIR T. BROWNE *Pseud. Ep.* I. xi. 48 Hee might evade the accomplishment of those afflictions he now but gradually endureth. **1670** MILTON *Hist. Eng.* Wks. 1738 II. 16 Cæsar foreseeing that the Britains..would easily evade his Foot. **1703** POPE *Thebais* 680 The Nymph, her father's anger to evade, Retires from Argos to the sylvan shade. **1807** JAS. JOHNSON *Orient. Voy.* 218 Had we lain here..we should have evaded great part of the sickness. **1837** W. IRVING *Capt. Bonneville* III. 117 The Crows were not to be evaded. **1866** GEO. ELIOT *F. Holt* xxxvii, He evaded calamity by choosing privation. **1867** FREEMAN *Norm. Conq.* (1876) I. v. 384 The ships evaded the obstacle. **1885** *Manch. Exam.* 5 May 5/1 A thief could evade capture by slipping out of one parish into another.

3. In various applied or extended uses.

a. To contrive to avoid (doing something); to 'get out of' performing (a duty), making (a payment), etc.

1722 DE FOE *Moll Flanders* (1840) 133, I always found something or other to say to evade the thing. **1802** *Med. Jrnl.* VIII. 139 A design to evade the duties. **1832** HT. MARTINEAU *Ireland* 111 The people have discovered a method of evading the payment. **1858** FROUDE *Hist. Eng.* III. xiv. 265 Henry..desired at first to evade a duty in which he had little interest at any time. **1867** LADY HERBERT *Cradle L.* vii. 173 The sheykh evaded translating them.

b. To avoid giving a direct answer to (a question, request, charge); to put off (a questioner); to avoid or shirk the discussion of (an argument, a subject).

1604 SHAKS. *Oth.* I. i. 13 He (as louing his owne pride, and purposes) Euades them..with Epithites of warre. **1677** DRYDEN *State of Innoc.* III. i, Our question thou evad'st. **1771** *Junius Lett.* lxiii. 323 He evades the charge..by..poor contemptible quibbles. **1832** HT. MARTINEAU *Ella of Gar.* vi. 70 He evaded all inquiries as to his plans. **1846** TRENCH *Mirac.* xxxi. (1862) 437 Difficulties..such as we are bound to meet, and not to attempt to evade. *a* **1848** R. W. HAMILTON *Rew. & Punishm.* viii. (1853) 389 We have evaded no known argument and difficulty. **1855** MACAULAY *Hist. Eng.* III. 285 That question the Estates of Scotland could not evade.

c. To escape yielding to (an argument, claim, or obligation), admitting (a conclusion), acknowledging (a fact), by means of sophistry.

1630 PRYNNE *Anti-Armin.* 195 For fear our Arminians.. should euade its force. **1664** H. MORE *Myst. Iniq.* xii. 40 Nor can the demonstrativeness of this reason be eluded or evaded. *a* **1699** STILLINGFL. (J.), My argument evidently overthrows all that he brings to evade the testimonies of the fathers. **1729** BUTLER *Serm.* Wks. (1874) II. 89 Every moral obligation whatever may be evaded. **1754** SHERLOCK *Disc.* (1759) I. i. 14 Can this truth be evaded or denied? **1844** LD. BROUGHAM *Brit. Const.* xii. (1862) 172 Edward endeavoured ..to evade the force of the obligation.

d. To defeat the intention of (a law, stipulation, etc.), *esp.* by specious compliance with its letter.

1760 GOLDSM. *Cit. W.* lxxx, The same degree of cunning ..had taught the knave to evade the former statutes. **1815** ELPHINSTONE *Acc. Caubul* (1842) I. 285 Few decent Mussulmauns openly infringe a prohibition which it is so easy to evade. **1868** J. H. BLUNT *Ref. Ch. Eng.* I. 285 Processes..adopted for the sake of evading the principle. **1884** *Law Rep.* 25 Chanc. Div. 720 The object of the arrangement..was to evade the provisions of the Bankruptcy Act.

4. *absol.* or *intr.* To practise evasion.

a **1716** SOUTH (J.), The ministers of God are not to evade or take refuge in any of these two forementioned ways. **1818** JAS. MILL *Brit. India* II. v. iv. 429 They evaded, procrastinated, and withheld rather than refused compliance with his desire. **1825** MACAULAY *Milton* Ess. (1851) I. 17 He hesitates; he evades.

5. *trans.* Of things: To elude, baffle (efforts, vigilance, etc.).

a **1716** SOUTH (J.), A contingent event baffles man's knowledge, and evades his power. **1857** WHEWELL *Hist. Induct. Sc.* I. IV. i. 188 These assertions..long evaded refutation. **1869** J. MARTINEAU *Ess.* II. 76 Some offences evade definition.

6. *nonce-use.* To go out of. Opposed to *invade.*

1725 in Hearne *Langtoft's Chron.* II. 442 Julius Cæsar having once and againe audaciously envaded, and as shamefully evaded, Britaine.

Hence **e'vader,** one who evades; in the senses of the verb. **e'vading** *vbl. sb.* and *ppl. a.*; also *attrib.* **e'vadingly** *adv.*, in an evading manner, evasively.

1754 EDWARDS *Freed. Will* IV. i. 194 The Race is at an End, but the Evader is taken in his Flight. **1824–9** LANDOR *Imag. Conv.* (1846) II. 218 Evader!..glad am I that you have spoken the word. **1883** LD. BRABAZON in *19th Cent.* Nov. 802 Laws which can never be evaded without punishment swiftly falling on the head of the evader. **1669** in Magens *Insurances* (1755) II. 618 For the evading of all Collusion and Suspicion..it is stipulated that, etc. **1817** BYRON *Beppo* xcvii, However, he got off by this evading. **1657** J. SERGEANT *Schism. Dispach't* 256 To..leave an evading hole for the Dr. to say, afterwards, etc. **1646** SIR T. BROWNE *Pseud. Ep.* IV. xi. 206 The wary and evading assertor. **1858** CARLYLE *Fredk. Gt.* II. v. vii. 127 Wolf, with bows down to the ground, answered always evadingly.

evads: see I'VADS *int.*

evagation (iːvə'geɪʃən). Also 5 evagacion, -cyon. [First introduced in the fig. sense 2; a. F. *évagation*, L. *ēvagātiōn-em*, n. of action f. *ēvagārī*, f. *ē* out + *vagārī* to wander.]

1. The action of wandering away, or departing from a specified locality, prescribed course, etc.; rambling, roving; an instance of the same.

1691 RAY *Creation* (1714) 220 Long ridges..of mountains serve to stop the Evagation of the Vapours. **1713** DERHAM *Phys.-Theol.* (1727) 118 To Bridle the Evagation of the Sound. **1714** —— *Astro-Theol.* VI. iii. (1769) 154 The preventing the evagation of the Planets. **1785** LANDEN *Rot. Motion* in *Phil. Trans.* LXXV. 328 That evagation is caused by the motive forces urging the body to turn about *AB, AC, AD*, conjunctly. **1802** PALEY *Nat. Theol.* xxii. (1819) 355 If the prevailing law had transgressed the limits above assigned, every evagation [of a planet] would have been fatal.

b. In speech or discussion: A digression.

a **1656** HALES *Gold. Rem.* (1688) 571 They have held their Synod with delays, stays and evagations. **1887** *Blackw. Mag.* Oct. 504 Leading us, even though by very tedious evagations, up to a noble climax.

†2. Wandering of the mind, thoughts, spirit, etc. (Mentioned as one of the 'branches' of *Accidia* or Sloth, one of the seven mortal sins.)

c **1425** tr. *T. à Kempis' Consol.* III. xxvii, Restreyne all euel evagacions & all miȝty temptacions. **1502** *Ord. Crysten Men* (W. de W. 1506) II. vii. 102 Euagacyon of thought is to gyue & occupye himselfe with talkynge in folysshe and vayne langage. **1503** *Sheph. Kalender* vii. (ed. Paris) 51 Heyr.. followys the branchys of sweyrnes, qwych ar ewylthoght, enwy of good..ewagacyon [1508 Euagacyon], etc. **1526** *Pilgr. Perf.* (W. de W. 1531) 94 b, Euagacyon of mynde..is yᵉ doughter of slouth. **1607** *Schol. Disc. agst. Antichr.* I. iii. 161 That euagation of the soule..is not *ex fragilitate*. **1677** GALE *Crt. Gentiles* II. III. 63 The soul is..moved..even unto an ecstasie or divine evagation.

†3. A diversion. **b.** A departure from propriety, an extravagance. *Obs.*

1638 WALTON in *Reliq. Wotton.* (1672) 579 You married men are deprived of these evagations. **1649** J. HALL *Motion to Parl.* 8 Neither subject to these wilde evagations, nor savage rudenesses.

evaginable (ɪ'vædʒɪnəb(ə)l), *a.* [f. next + -ABLE.] Capable of being evaginated or unsheathed; protrusible.

evaginate (ɪ'vædʒɪneɪt), *v.* [f. L. *ēvagināt-* ppl. stem of *ēvagīnā-re* to unsheath, f. *ē* out + *vagina* sheath.] *trans.* †**a.** To unsheath. *Obs.*$^{-0}$ †**b.** To take grain out of the husk. *Obs.* **c.** *Phys.* To turn (a tubular organ) inside out; to protrude by eversion of a tubular sheath. Hence **e'vaginated** *ppl. a.*

1656–81 BLOUNT *Glossogr.*, *Evaginate*, to draw out of a sheath or scabberd. **1661** LOVELL *Hist. Anim. & Min.* 281 The greater lead, and the lesser evaginate the corne. **1877** HUXLEY *Anat. Inv. Anim.* iv. 210 The caecum is next evaginated or turned inside out, and the embryo has the form of a phial, of which the evaginated caecum is the neck.

evagination (ɪˌvædʒɪ'neɪʃən). [ad. L. *ēvāgīnātiōn-em*, n. of action f. *ēvāgīnā-re*: see prec.] **a.** The action or process of evaginating. **b.** *concr.* A result of this process.

1663–76 BULLOKAR, *Evagination*, an unsheathing, a drawing out of the sheath. **1721–1800** BAILEY, *Evagination*, an unsheathing, or drawing out of a Sheath or Scabbard. **1877** HUXLEY *Anat. Inv. Anim.* iii. 125 Very slight pressure causes the thread to be swiftly protruded, apparently by a process of evagination. **1889** *Athenæum* 30 Nov. 748/2 Evaginations of the walls of the oral groove.

†**e'vague**, *v. Obs.* In 6 *Sc.* evaig. [a. OF. *evague-r*, ad. L. *ēvagā-ri* to roam about, f. *ē* out + *vagāri* to wander.] *intr.* To wander about.

1533 BELLENDEN *Livy* II. (1822) 200 The Equis..sufferit thair enemyis to evaig [L. *vagari*].

eval ('iːvəl), *a. rare*$^{-1}$. [f. L. *æv-um* age + -AL¹; cf. COEVAL.] Of or pertaining to an age; age-long.

1791 *Addr. to Abp. Canterb.* 67 Αἰών age, and αἰώνιος, eval, improperly everlasting, do not convey the ideas of a proper eternity. **1818** in TODD; and in mod. Dicts.

evaluable (ɪ'væljuːəb(ə)l), *a.* [f. next; cf. *estimate*, *estimable*.] That can be evaluated.

1880 *Contemp. Rev.* XXXVII. 480 Love, delight, adoration are only scientifically expressed as unknown forces and quantities not at present evaluable.

evaluate (ɪ'væljuːeɪt), *v.* [f. Fr. *évalu-er* (see next *sb.*) + -ATE³.] *trans.* **a.** *Math.* To work out the 'value' of (a quantitative expression); to find a numerical expression for (any quantitative fact or relation). **b.** *gen.* To 'reckon up', ascertain the amount of; to express in terms of something already known.

1842 W. GROVE *Corr. Phys. Forces* (ed. 6) 61 An attempt to evaluate numerically the mechanical equivalent of the thermal unit. **1874** W. WALLACE *Hegel's Logic* 86 God.. must be known and evaluated in terms of thought. **1886** BALL *Story of Heavens* 527 No attempt can be made at present to evaluate the date of that epoch. **1890** *Athenæum* 29 Mar. 407/3 The method of evaluating the absorption of different thicknesses by comparison with a polarizing photometer.

evaluation (ɪˌvæljuː'eɪʃən). [a. Fr. *évaluation*, f. *évaluer*, f. *é-* = *es-* (:— L. *ex*) out + *value* VALUE.]

1. The action of appraising or valuing (goods, etc.); a calculation or statement of value; = VALUATION. Now *rare*.

1755 MAGENS *Insurances* II. 137 When a certain Evaluation is admitted in the Policy, no Premium can be demanded back. **1804** COLEBROOKE *Husb. & Commerce Bengal* (1806) 54 The usual evaluation of different articles of produce. **1850** MERIVALE *Rom. Emp.* (1865) I. ii. 58 The evaluation of his treasures has been preserved.

2. The action of evaluating or determining the value of (a mathematical expression, a physical quantity, etc.), or of estimating the force of (probabilities, evidence, etc.).

1779 INGENHOUSZ in *Phil. Trans.* LXIX. 395 This evaluation was made before the new discoveries upon the nature of nitre and charcoal. **1790** GIBBON *Misc. Wks.* (1814) III. 509 His evaluation [of the *mansus*] would produce two hundred, or more probably twenty thousand English acres. **1828** *Edin. Rev.* XLVIII. 511 The evaluation of certain sorts of evidence. **1846** MILL *Logic* III. xviii. §3 Before applying the doctrine of chances..the foundation must be laid for an evaluation of the chances. **1887** *Athenæum* 2 Apr. 452/1 The author's ..evaluation of some terms in the [lunar] theory..was thereby lost.

evaluative (ɪ'væljuːətɪv), *a.* [f. EVALUATE *v.* + -IVE.] Of, pertaining to, or tending to evaluation; appraisive, estimative.

1927 L. V. KOOS *Amer. Secondary School* vii. 221 Compilation and subsequent evaluative scrutiny of these claims. **1934** *Philos. Rev.* XLIII. 127 The expression of such feeling of life, and of our evaluative reactions, is.. admitted to be a legitimate and worth-while activity. **1939** *Mind* XLVIII. 469 It is only confusing to talk of a 'valuational logic' whose basic rule is that an evaluative conclusion cannot be deduced from non-evaluative premises. *Ibid.* 529 The existential transformation essential to inquiry is teleological and so evaluative. **1952** R. M. HARE *Lang. Morals* II. vii. 111 Two sorts of things that we can say ..about strawberries; the first sort is usually called *descriptive*, the second sort *evaluative*... Examples of the second sort of remark are 'This is a good strawberry' and 'This strawberry is just as strawberries ought to be'. **1964** E. A. NIDA *Toward Sci. Transl.* iii. 44 The intention may be described as evaluative or appraisive, that is to say, the source not only designates some referent, but also provides its own evaluation of it.

evanesce (ɛvə'nɛs), *v.* [ad. L. *ēvānescĕ-re*, f. *ē* out + *vānescĕre* to vanish, f. *vānus* empty, insubstantial, VAIN. Cf. EVANISH.] *intr.* To fade out of sight, 'melt into thin air', disappear; chiefly *fig.* Also in scientific use, To disappear, become effaced; said *e.g.* of markings or organs in plants, or of the edge of a polyhedron when two adjacent faces are made to rotate into one plane.

1822 DE QUINCEY *Confess.* (1862) 59 A single psychological discovery, therfore, caused my musical anticipations to evanesce. **1854** FABER *Growth in Holiness* xxiii. (1872) 472 As soon as these spiritual favours are known they will evanesce. **1857** WHEWELL *Hist. Induct. Sc.* III. 366 The intermediate corolla having evanesced. **1875** JOWETT *Plato* (ed. 2) I. 77 This general notion..evanesces before the dialectic of Socrates.

evanescence (ɛvə'nɛsəns). [f. EVANESCENT *a.*: see -ENCE.]

1. The process or fact of vanishing away.

1751 JOHNSON *Rambler* No. 156 ¶2 The great principles of truth..fade at last in total evanescence. *Ibid.* No. 163 ¶5 The sudden evanescence of his reward. **1789** PRIESTLEY in *Phil. Trans.* LXXIX. 149 The almost total evanescence of both of them [nitrous and dephlogisticated air], when they are very pure, and mixed in due proportions. **1833** BREWSTER *Nat. Magic* ii. 29 The circumstances under which these evanescences would take place. **1849** MRS. SOMERVILLE *Connex. Phys. Sc.* xxi. 201 Varying through all degrees of brightness down to total, or almost total evanescence. **1878** LECKY *Eng. in 18th C.* II. ix. 522 A great variety of causes had led to the gradual evanescence of dogmatic teaching.

2. The quality of being evanescent; tendency to vanish away.

18.. SMITH *Addr. Mummy* Poet. Wks. (1846) 15 Statue of flesh! Immortal of the dead! Imperishable type of evanescence. **1830** *Blackw. Mag.* XXVIII. 731 The shadowy and fleeting evanescence..of the regal office and functions. **1841–4** EMERSON *Ess.* Ser. II. ii. (1876) 46 This evanescence and lubricity of all objects..lets them slip through our fingers.

3. *concr.* An evanescent thing. *rare.*

1830 *Blackw. Mag.* XXVII. 848 That most celestial Evanescence—a Lunar Rainbow.

†**eva'nescency.** *Obs.* [see -ENCY.] = prec.

1664 H. MORE *Synopsis Proph.*, *Myst. Iniquity* 294 The bottomless pit; For so ἄβυσσος may signify as well as the Sea, or Abolition, or Evanescency.

evanescent (ɛvə'nɛsənt), *a.* [a. Fr. *évanescent*, ad. L. *ēvānescent-em*, pr. pple. of *ēvānescĕre* (see EVANESCE).]

1. That is on the point of vanishing or becoming imperceptible. In Mathematics, said of a diminishing quantity: That is at the instant of becoming zero; infinitesimal. Hence *transf.* of things: Imperceptibly minute, too small to perceive.

1717 J. KEILL *Anim. Œcon.* (1738) 41 The smallest Capillaries or evanescent Arteries. **1722** WOLLASTON *Relig. Nat.* i. 31 To render the crime evanescent or almost nothing. *a* **1761** J. CAWTHORN *Wit & Learn.* Poems (1771) 73 How the moon was evanescent, Was now an orb, and now a crescent? **1770** HORSLEY in *Phil. Trans.* LX. 437 *note*, The particles of light, which fall upon the evanescent zone..are as that evanescent annular space which they cover. **1811** WOOD *Optics* iv. 56 The limiting ratio of an evanescent arc to its sine is a ratio of equality. **1849** MRS. SOMERVILLE *Connex. Phys. Sc.* xxvi. 276 A quantity so evanescent that it is hardly possible to conceive a time when a change will become perceptible. **1882** PROCTOR *Fam. Sc. Studies* 29 Our knowledge..has in reality but an evanescent range.

2. That quickly vanishes or passes away; having no permanence. Said of appearances, conditions, impressions, etc.

1738 THOMSON *Spring* 148 The melting Pulp Of mellow Fruit, the nameless Nations feed[s] Of evanescent Insects. **1750** JOHNSON *Rambler* No. 60 ¶11 The incidents which give excellence to biography are of a volatile and evanescent kind. **1784** COWPER *Task* v. 167 A scene Of evanescent glory. **1816** R. JAMESON *Char. Min.* (1817) 301 Evanescent, when the colour remains as long as the mineral is in a state of fusion, but disappears on cooling. **1828** SCOTT *F.M. Perth* xxxi, The Duke of Rothsay, whose virtuous feelings were as easily excited as they were evanescent. **1836** HOR. SMITH *Tin Trump.* (1876) 271 [The] Pen which gives ubiquity of permanence to the evanescent thought of a moment. **1876** DUHRING *Dis. Skin* 41 Maculæ are evanescent or permanent according to their cause.

b. *Bot.* Of parts of plants: Not permanent.

1776 WITHERING *Brit. Plants* (1796) IV. 189 Curtain white, evanescent. **1870** HOOKER *Stud. Flora* 361 Liparis.. glands evanescent.

Hence **eva'nescently** *adv.*

1847 in CRAIG. **1865** BUSHNELL *Vicar. Sacr.* II. iv. 142 Evanescently dim to our feeling. **1873** *Argosy* XVI. 290 The colour flitted evanescently. **1881** *Daily News* 25 July 5/2 Kindliness, slightly and almost evanescently..tempered by a sort of indulgent scorn.

evanescing (ɛvə'nɛsɪŋ), *ppl. a.* [f. EVANESCE + -ING².] That passes quickly away.

1805 *Med. Jrnl.* XIV. 537 Symptomatic fever of a mild nature took place about the 9th day, and the usual evanescing course followed. **1847** EMERSON *Repr. Men, Swedenborg* Wks. (Bohn) I. 328 It is dangerous to sculpture these evanescing images of thought.

evangel¹, **evangile** (ɪ'vændʒəl, -ɪl). Now *arch.* or rhetorical. Forms: α. 4 **evangil**, 5 **evangille**, **-ylle**, 6 **ewangyle**, 4–7, 9 (*rare*) **evangile**. β. 4 *aphet.* **vangel** (*þe vangel* for *þ'evangel*), 5 **ewangel**, 6–7 **evangell**, 5–7, 9 **evangele**, 4– **evangel**. [ME. *evangile*, a. OF. *evangi(l)le* (mod.F. *évangile*), corresp. to Pr. *evangeli*, Sp., Pg. *evangelio*, It. *evangelio*, *evangelo* (aphet. *vangelio*, *vangelo*), repr. Eccl. Lat. *ēvangelium*: see EVANGELY. The β forms are due to the influence of the Lat. spelling.

In England the word was in 17th c. already archaic and purely literary, but in Scotland it remained in current use, as a synonym for *gospel*, until a still later period. At the present time it is chiefly used in transferred sense, or with allusion to the etymological meaning 'good news'. The prevailing form now is *evangel*; but a few writers of the present century have preferred *evangele*, *evangile*, either to distinguish the word from EVANGEL², or merely for archaistic effect.]

I. In various sense of GOSPEL.

1. The 'good news' of redemption to the world through Jesus Christ; the religious teaching contained in the New Testament; the Christian religion.

a **1340** HAMPOLE *Psalter* cxviii. 72 Laghe of godis mouth is þe vangel. *c* **1399** *Pol. Poems* (1859) II. 10 Crist bad him self, how that we schulden preche, And to the folk his evangile teche. *c* **1425** WYNTOUN *Cron.* VII. vii. 224 Nowcht be þe Lauche of þe Ewangyle. **1558** KNOX *First Blast* (Arb.) 31 And worthy is thy sonne Christ Iesus, to haue his Euangil and glorie aduanced. **1578** *Godly & Spirituall Songs* (1801) 183 Priests, take ȝour staffe And preich the euangell on ȝour feit. **1641** MILTON *Ch. Govt.* II. iii. (1851) 158 The heavenly ministery of the Evangel. **1655** GOUGE *Comm. Heb.* xiii. 9 An Evangile (as the Scots according to the Greek notation, term it), that is good or glad tidings. **1820** SCOTT *Abbot* ii, That worthy man..teacheth the Evangel in truth and sincerity. *Ibid.* xxii, Your ears..deceived you when they were closed against the preachers of the evangele. **1834** H. MILLER *Scenes & Leg.* viii. (1857) 107 All the other ministers of the Evangel. **1855** R. WILLIAMS *Rational Godl.* xiv. 207 The spirit of the Evangile. **1884** *Congregationalist* June 459 The gospel is the evangel.

b. The 'Gospel dispensation.'

1560 *Conf. Faith Kirk Scotl.* (1811), As the fatheris vnder the law..Sa..we now, in the tyme of the Euangell, haue twa cheif Sacramentis.

2. a. The record of Christ's life as contained in the Four Gospels.

1393 GOWER *Conf.* III. 34 How that this vice is for to drede In thevangile it telleth pleine. **1483** CAXTON *Gold. Leg.* 436/1 That our lord hath sayd in the holy euangyle. **1552** ABP. HAMILTON *Catech.* (1884) 35 Christ in the evangil ..confermis the same promis. **1588** A. KING tr. *Canisius' Catech.* 76 b, Yᵉ testimonies baith of Yᵉ Euangell and of yᵉ Apostle S. Paul ar verray plane. **1858** J. MARTINEAU *Studies Chr.* 273 The ground work..of the triple Evangile.

b. One of the 'Four Gospels'.

c **1400** MAUNDEV. (Roxb.) xv. 67 He made þe Ewangels, in þe whilk es helefull teching and sothefastnes. **1552** ABP. HAMILTON *Catech.* (1884) 25 The wordis writtin in S. Mathewis evangel. *a* **1631** DONNE *Let. to Sir G. Moore* Wks. (ed. Alford) VI. xcvi. 414 The Evangiles and Acts teach us what to believe, but the Epistles of the Apostles what to do. **1678** GALE *Crt. Gentiles* III. 60 Lukes Greek, both in his Evangel as also in the Acts of the Apostles, is most..eligant. **1828** LAMB in *Life & Lett.* xvi. 153 The Quakers are the only professors of Christianity as I read it in the Evangiles. **1866** NEALE *Sequences & Hymns* 39 Those infrangible Evangels, welded by the Holy Ghost.

3. *pl.* Copies of the Gospels; a book containing them, used to impart sanctity to an oath. Rare in *sing.*; *attrib.* in ***evangel-book***.

c **1386** CHAUCER *Man of Law's T.* 568 A Briton book, written with Euaungiles Was fet, and on this book he swoor anoon. **1489** CAXTON *Faytes of A.* III. viii. 184 He is bounde unto hym by othe upon the holy euangilles. **1535** STEWART *Cron. Scot.* III. 28 And swoir also vpoun the evangell buik. **1609** SKENE *Reg. Maj.*, *Sc. Act. Robt. II*, 51 The Earle of Carrik..made his aith the halie Eu-angellis being tuiched be him. **1886** BURTON *Arab. Nts.* (abridged) I. 233, I conjured him by the Evangel to alight at my house.

4. *transf.* †**a.** Something 'as true as gospel'.

1613 R. C. *Table Alph.* (ed. 3), *Euangell*, true expounding. **1622** BACON *Hen. VII.* 145 The Attaint upon a false Verdict between party and party, which before was a kind of Euangile, irremediable. **1639** DRUMM. OF HAWTH. *Consid. to Parl.* Wks. 186 That the covenant be..esteem'd in all times coming, the first evangel. **1681** COLVIL *Whigs Supplic.* (1751) 136 That..Merline's prophesies [are] evangels.

b. A doctrine or principle (pertaining *e.g.* to politics, social reform, or morals) to which

'saving' efficacy is attributed. Sometimes with some notion of the etymological sense 'good news'.

1831 CARLYLE *Sart. Res.* (1858) 109 *La carrière ouverte aux talens*.. which is our ultimate Political Evangel. **1865** *Sat. Rev.* XIX. 622/2 The law of trust is to be henceforth applied under the inspiration of this new evangele. **1879** *Contemp. Rev.* XXXVI. 290, I do not announce a new and perfect evangel to be ushered in by loud flourish of trumpets.

II. 5. In etymological sense: A message of glad tidings. Also (*nonce-use*), a song of joyful promise.

1842 LONGF. *Slave Singing at Midn.* vi, What holy angel Brings the slave this glad evangel? **1844** MRS. BROWNING *Drama of Exile* Poems I. 14 Our requiems follow fast on our evangels.

evangel² (ɪˈvændʒəl). [ad. Gr. εὐάγγελος bringing good news, f. εὖ well + ἀγγέλλειν to announce.] A proclaimer of the gospel; = EVANGELIST.

1593 [see below]. **1614** STIRLING *Doomsday 2nd Hour* xxxviii, When the Euangell most toyl'd Soules to winne. **1860** C. SANGSTER *Hesperus* 13 We heard the evangels relate the glad story. **1866** NEALE *Sequences & Hymns* 157 The great Evangel of Patmos. **1878** SYMONDS *Sonn. Campanella* xxxv, The true sons of perfidy.. Calling themselves evangels of the faith.

Hence †**e'vangelship**, the office of evangelist.

1593 BILSON *Govt. Christ's Ch.* 233 No part of their Euangelship.

evan'gelian, *a. Gr. Antiq. rare*⁻¹. [f. Gr. (τὰ) εὐαγγέλια (pl. of εὐαγγέλιον: see EVANGELY) + -AN.] ***evangelian sacrifice***: transl. of Gr. τὰ εὐαγγέλια, the sacrifice offered in token of gratitude on receipt of good news.

1808 MITFORD *Greece* xxxvii. §7. IV. 357 Twice had the evangelian sacrifice been performed, as if thanks were due to the gods for signal victories. **1832** WEBSTER *Evangelian*, rendering thanks for favors [*citing* Mitford].

So in later Dicts.

Evangeliar (iːvænˈdʒɛlɪɑː(r)). Also **Evangeliary** (-ɪərɪ) and in L. form. [ad. eccl. L. *ēvangeliārium*. Cf. OF. *evangelier*, mod.F. *évangéliaire*.] = EVANGELISTARY I.

1846 W. MASKELL *Monumenta Ritualia Ecclesiæ Anglicanæ* I. iv. p. lii, The 'Evangelistarium', 'Evangelium', or 'Evangeliarium', is not involved in so great difficulty. **1893** F. C. CONYBEARE in *Expositor* Oct. 244 The titles 'of Matthew', 'of Mark',.. in this Evangeliar at the heads of their respective Gospels. **1900** *Jrnl. Theol. Stud.* Apr. 453 As Mr. Kenyon points out, at least one Byzantine Evangeliarium was written in France, in 1022. *Ibid.*, The Evangeliary has no significance for the purpose in hand. **1953** P. D. RECORD *Summary Catal. Western MSS. in Bodl. Libr.* VII. 160/1 Evangeliary. Grk. (XII), 18406.

evangelic (iːvæn-, ɛvænˈdʒɛlɪk), *a.* and *sb.* Forms: 5–6 **evangelik(e, -yke**, 6–8 **-ick(e**, 7 **-ique**, 7– **evangelic**. [ad. late L. *ēvangelic-us*, a. Eccl. Gr. εὐαγγελικός, f. εὐαγγέλιον: see EVANGELY.]

A. *adj.*

1. Of or pertaining to the Gospel.

a. Of or pertaining to the Gospel narrative, or to the Four Gospels.

1594 CAREW *Huarte's Exam. Wits* xv. (1596) 332 That this doctrin is true and catholicke, the letter of the Euangelicke text prooueth. *a* **1711** KEN *Hymns Festiv.* Poet Wks. 1721 I. 393 His Evangelick Volume to compleat. *a* **1806** S. HORSLEY *Serm.* (1811) 313 The evangelic maxim, that 'no man can serve two masters'. **1858** SEARS *Athan.* II. x. 233 So we understand the Evangelic narrative. **1885** SALMON *Introd. N.T.* viii. 131 *note*, It is an arrangement of the Evangelic text in the form of a harmony.

b. Of or pertaining to the faith or precepts of the Gospel, or to the Christian religion; pertaining to, or characteristic of, the Gospel dispensation.

1502 *Ord. Crysten Men* (W. de W. 1506) III. ii. 143 Those yᵉ whiche haue auowed pouerte euangelyke. **1545** JOYE *Exp. Dan.* ii, In the tother parte (as it were with an euangelik sermone) he calleth them all and vs to the knowlege of cryste. **1569** J. SANFORD tr. *Agrippa's Van. Artes* 68 b, Farre from the Euangelicke doctrine and holy Canons. **1653** MILTON *Hirelings* Wks. 1738 I. 581 In the first Evangelic Times. **1790** BURKE *Fr. Rev.* Wks. V. 197 That primitive evangelick poverty. **1806** A. KNOX *Rem.* I. 12 His [Boethius'] book 'De consolatione Philosophiæ' is Platonic not evangelic. **1845** R. W. HAMILTON *Pop. Educ.* iv. (ed. 2) 64 Let the younger scholar be taught.. the grounds and motives of evangelic obedience. **1866** J. MARTINEAU *Ess.* I. 412 A Hebrew ode was made to yield evangelic dogma.

c. ***evangelic prophet***: see EVANGELICAL 1 c.

1683 E. HOOKER *Pref. Ep. Pordage's Mystic Div.* 14 Peruse that Vers of the Evangelic Prophet, if this iniquitie be purged from you, etc.

†**d.** In uncertain sense; perh. 'pious'. *Obs.*

1460–70 *Bk. Quintessence* I. 1 How þat olde euangelik men, and feble in kynde, myȝte be restorid, and haue aȝen her firste strenkþis of ȝongþe. *Ibid.* II. 15 To reduce an oold feble euangelik man to þe firste strenkþe of ȝongþe.

2. As the designation of a sect or party. (Now usually EVANGELICAL.) **a.** = EVANGELICAL 2 a.

1583 STOCKER *Civ. Warres Lowe Countries* I. 33 b, The Euangelike Churches both of hygh and lowe Germanie. *a* **1649** DRUMM. OF HAWTH. *Idea* Wks. 220 Two eminent religions.. the Roman, and that which is protestant or evangelick. **1758** *Hist. Europe* in *Ann. Reg.* 50/2 They had rather a contrary effect in rousing the whole evangelic body to a sense of their own danger. **1792** BURKE *Let. to Sir H. Langrishe* Wks. VI. 318 When the three religions were established in Germany, they were.. declared to be Evangelick, the Reformed and the Catholick.

b. = EVANGELICAL 2 b.

1812 J. JEBB *Corr.* (1834) II. 197 A far nearer approach to the genius of a hierarchy than we can at all discern in our evangelic churchmen. **1814** SCOTT *Wav.* xxx, I have never been able to discover which he belonged to, the evangelic, or the moderate party in the kirk. **1850** P. CROOK *War of Hats* 24 Why not excite petitions to proscribe The chapels of the evangelic tribe? **1874** SPURGEON *Treas. Dav.* Ps. lxxxv. Introd., The purely evangelic annotators [in contrast with the sceptical].

B. *sb.*

†**1.** The adj. used *absol.*: see A. 1 c. *Obs.*

a **1617** S. HIERON *Aaron's Bells* (1623) 11 Jerome sticks not to call hem [Esay] an Evangelicke.

†**2.** A Protestant; = EVANGELICAL B. 1. *Obs.*

1616 BRENT tr. *Sarpi's Council Trent* (1676) 387 The Protestants did increase in Germany, and the Evangeliques did multiply amongst the Suisses. **1660** BLOME *Fanat. Hist.* i. 5 They [the Anabaptists].. troubled the Evangeliques more than the papists. **1688** *True Spirit of Popery* 6 He made a Gaol of his own House, such was his inveterate Malice against the Evangelicks. **1709** STRYPE *Ann. Ref.* I. i. 41 Now did both the Evangelics and the Papalins bestir themselves for their parties. **1758** JORTIN *Erasm.* I. 442, I abhor the Evangelics.

†**3.** A member of the Evangelical party, *Obs.*; = EVANGELICAL B. 2.

1812 A. KNOX in *J. Jebbs's Corr.* (1834) II. 100 A good evangelic, mild and pious, rooted in the ways of worthy Wilberforce.

evangelical (iːvæn-, ɛvænˈdʒɛlɪkəl), *a.* and *sb.* [f. prec. + -AL¹.]

A. *adj.*

1. Of or pertaining to the Gospel.

†**a.** Of or pertaining to the Gospel narrative, or to the Four Gospels; contained or mentioned in the Gospels. *Obs.*; = EVANGELIC 1 a.

1553 T. PAYNELL (*title*) The Pandectes of the Euangelicall Lawe; comprisyng the whole Hystorie of Christes Gospell. **1583** STUBBES *Anat. Abus.* II. 90 Thorough the whole euangelicall historie. **1597** HOOKER *Eccl. Pol.* v. xl. §2 What disorder is it if these few Evangelical Hymns.. be.. every day rehearsed? **1660** BURNEY *Κέρδ. Δῶρον* (1611) 32 The King.. commissionates every active hand in Israel, like the Evangelical Centurion. *a* **1703** BURKITT *On N.T.* Luke i. 79 In this evangelical hymn there is a prophetical prediction. **1751** CHAMBERS *Cycl.* s.v. *Harmony*, Evangelical Harmony, is a title of divers books, composed to shew the.. agreement of the accounts given by the four evangelists.

b. Of or pertaining to, or in accordance with, the faith or precepts of the Gospel, or the Christian religion; pertaining to, or characteristic of, the Gospel dispensation.

1531 TINDALE *Exp. St. John* (1537) 92 He exhorteth them to procede constauntly in the euangelicall truth. **1581** J. BELL *Haddon's Answ. Osor.* 103 The Evangelicall Philosphye doth call us higher. **1619** W. PERKINS *Cases Consc.* 31 A stirring vp of the heart to Euangelicall sorrow. **1642** ROGERS *Naaman* 41 In legal, and evangelicall respects. **1699** BURNET 39 *Art.* x. (1700) 123 Faith.. separated from the other Evangelical Graces. **1730** BERKELEY *Serm.* Wks. 1871 IV. 641 Not lip-worship, nor will-worship, but inward and evangelical. **1782** PRIESTLEY *Corrupt. Chr.* I. II. 164 There is nothing evangelical; all is legal and carnal. **1839** YEOWELL *Anc. Brit. Ch.* ii. (1847) 10 He has taken away.. the legal priesthood, that he may establish.. the evangelical priesthood. **1858** MARSDEN *Early Purit.* 18 Their detestation of the papacy and their views of evangelical truth, were confirmed. **1875** MANNING *Mission H. Ghost* i. 13 The one great evangelical gift.. is the gift of the Holy Ghost.

c. ***evangelical prophet***: a designation of Isaiah, representing the view that his writings describe prophetically the life of Christ, and the state of things under the Gospel dispensation, and that they abound in anticipations of the doctrines revealed in the Gospel.

The idea is due to St. Jerome, in whose writings it frequently occurs in various forms: e.g. he says (*Ad Paulam*, Wks. 1575 III. 18) that Isaiah 'non tam propheta dicendus est quam evangelista.'

1547 *Homilies* I. *Falling from God* II. (1859) 85 The evangelical Prophet Esay.. doth teach us. **1585** ABP. SANDYS *Serm.* (1841) 8 Our evangelical prophet Esaias hath .. most lively described and set forth the nativity.. of our Saviour Christ to judge the quick and the dead. **1699** EVELYN *Acetaria* (1729) 168 The Evangelical Prophet adumbrating the future Glory of the Catholick Church. **1778** BP. R. LOWTH *Isaiah* Prelim. Diss. (ed. 12) 52 The sublime and spiritual uses to be made of this peculiarly evangelical Prophet. **1853** MAURICE *Proph. & Kings* xiii. 226 He [Isaiah] is often called the evangelical prophet; by which it is meant that he is especially the prophet of the Messiah.

d. Of a person: Imbued with the spirit of the Gospel. *rare.*

1768 STERNE *Sent. Journ.* (1775) 101, I am so evangelical in this, and have such a fellow-feeling for whatever is weak.

2. Since the Reformation adopted as the designation of certain theological parties, who have claimed that the doctrines on which they lay especial stress constitute 'the Gospel'. This claim is of course disallowed by their adversaries, but (as in the case of other self-assumed party names) the designation has received the sanction of general usage.

a. = PROTESTANT. Now only with reference to Germany and Switzerland, where its German and French equivalents are also applied in narrower sense to the Lutheran as distinguished from the 'Reformed' or Calvinistic Church. In the German Empire 'The Evangelical Church' was the official name of the established Protestant Church of Prussia, formed in 1817 by the union of the Lutheran and Reformed churches.

1532 MORE *Confut. Tindale* Wks. 353/2 Tindall himselfe woulde no lesse were done.. then would hys euangelical brother Barns. **1581** W. STAFFORD *Exam. Compl.* iii. (1876) 94 Every bishop should yerely keepe a sinode in his diocesse of all euangelicall persons. **1619** *Arraign. Barnevelt* §11 The reformed euangelicall religion. **1697** EVELYN *Numism.* viii. 265 The Evangelical Churches in Germany. **1786** W. THOMSON *Watson's Philip* III. (1839) 345 They should maintain two companies of evangelical soldiers. **1845** S. AUSTIN *Ranke's Hist. Ref.* III. v. iii. 109 The evangelical communes became aware of their superiority.

b. From 18th c. applied to that school of Protestants which maintains that the essence of 'the Gospel' consists in the doctrine of salvation by faith in the atoning death of Christ, and denies that either good works or the sacraments have any saving efficacy.

Other features more or less characteristic of the theology of this school are: a strong insistence on the totally depraved state of human nature consequent on the Fall; the assertion of the sole authority of the Bible in matters of doctrine, and the denial of any power inherent in the Church to supplement or authoritatively interpret the teaching of Scripture; the denial that any supernatural gifts are imparted by ordination; and the view that the sacraments are merely symbols, the value of which consists in the thoughts which they are fitted to suggest. As a distinct party designation, the term came into general use, in England, at the time of the Methodist revival;and it may be said, with substantial accuracy, to denote the school of theology which that movement represents, though its earlier associations were rather with the Calvinistic than the Arminian branch of the movement. In the early part of the 19th c. the words 'Methodist' and 'Evangelical' were, by adversaries, often used indiscriminately, and associated with accusations of fanaticism and 'puritanical' disapproval of social pleasures. The portion of the 'evangelical' school which belongs to the Anglican church is practically identical with the 'Low Church' party. In the Church of Scotland during the latter part of the 18th and the early part of the 19th c. the two leading parties were the 'Evangelical' and the 'Moderate' party.

[**1747** DODDRIDGE *Life Col. Gardiner* 162 It was his deliberate Judgment, that the Law should be preached, as well as the Gospel; and hardly any Thing gave him greater Offence, than the irreverent Manner in which some, who have been ignorantly extolled as the most zealous Evangelical Preachers, have sometimes been tempted to speak of the former.] **1791** HAMPSON *Mem. J. Wesley* III. 61 What are usually called evangelical views of religion. **1809** R. SOUTHEY in *Q. Rev.* I. 195 The Wesleyans, the Orthodox dissenters of every description, and the Evangelical churchmen may all be comprehended under the generic name of Methodists. **1825** LD. COCKBURN *Mem.* i. 43 The principles and feelings of the persons commonly called evangelical were the same then as they are now. **1842** DICKENS *Amer. Notes* (1850) 38/2 Evangelical ladies there are, likewise, whose attachment to the forms of religion, and horror of theatrical entertainments, are most exemplary. **1871** BLACKIE *Four Phases* I. 54 The sacred-sounding columns of an evangelical newspaper. **1889** *Dict. Nat. Biog.* XVII. 433 Erskine was.. devoted to the doctrines and aims of the evangelical party in the church.

3. Of or pertaining to an evangelist, or preacher of the Gospel. *rare.*

1651 HOBBES *Govt. & Soc.* xvii. §23. 321 The Apostolicall worke indeed was universall.. the Evangelicall to preach, or to be publishers of the Gospell among the infidels. **1794** GODWIN *Cal. Williams* 291 He [the vicar] condescended, with his evangelical hand, to guide the plough.

B. *sb.*

1. A Protestant; *esp.* a German Lutheran, or an adherent of the national church of the German Empire. See A. 2 a.

1532 MORE *Confut. Tindale* Wks. 352/1 Those euaungelicalles theimselfe cease not to pursue and punishe .. their euaungelicall bretherne. **1860** FROUDE *Hist. Eng.* V. 323 Clergymen professing to be Evangelicals held four or five livings, and officiated in none. **1878** in Grove *Dict. Mus.* I. 109 He [Veit Bach] is said.. to have moved into Hungary with many other Evangelicals for protection from persecution.

2. A member of the Evangelical party, *esp.* in the Church of England. Cf. A. 2 b.

1804 R. SOUTHEY in *Ann. Rev.* II. 189 The history of this society is truly characteristic of the Evangelicals. **1807** —— *Espriella's Lett.* (1814) II. 359 [Whitfield's] preachers were usually called by her [Lady Huntingdon's] name, which they have now dropt for the better title of Evangelicals. **1852** NEWLAND *Lect. Tractar.* 77 We claim the Evangelicals of the last generation as our fellow workers. **1865** PUSEY *Truth Eng. Ch.* 4 Ever since I knew them.. I have loved those who are called 'Evangelicals'. **1876** M. DAVIES *Unorth. Lond.* 374 Dr. Arnold defines the Evangelical to be 'a good Christian, with a narrow understanding'.

Hence **evan,geli'cality**, **evan'gelicalness** (*rare*), the quality or state of being evangelical; faithfulness to the Gospel.

1857 DE QUINCEY in H.A. Page *Life* (1877) II. xviii. 129 One of the Edinburgh Professors, and notorious for his evangelicality. **1645** J. GOODWIN *Innoc. & Truth Tri.* 63 Mr. Prynne by representing my Parish as divided, disordered by my Independent way, hath rather given testimony to the truth and evangelicalnesse of it. **1730–6** BAILEY (folio), *Evangelicalness*, the having evangelical quality.

evangelicalism (iːvæn-, ɛvænˈdʒɛlɪkəˌlɪz(ə)m). [f. prec. + -ISM.] The doctrines and modes of thought peculiar to the Evangelical party; adherence to that party.

1831 *Edin. Rev.* LIII. 305 We have always thought that the worst things about Evangelicalism were its exclusiveness, etc. **1871-2** GEO. ELIOT *Middlem.* xvi. (D.), Evangelicalism had cast a certain suspicion as of plague-infection over the few amusements which survived in the provinces. **1884** A. M. FAIRBAIRN in *Contemp. Rev.* Mar. 371 An age weary of a hard and pragmatic evangelicalism.

evangelically (iːvæn-, ɛvænˈdʒɛlɪkəlɪ), *adv.* [f. as prec. + -LY².] In an evangelical manner.

1. As the Gospel requires; in accordance with the spirit of the Gospel; from the point of view of the Gospel.

1624 GEE *Foot out of Snare* 14 The least sin, legally considered, is damnable; though evangelically, the greatest of all is pardonable. **1654** TRAPP *Comm. Nehemiah* i. 9 'And keep my Commandments'—Evangelically keep them: for with a legal obedience none can. **1673** *Lady's Call.* I. v. 32 Socrates has excellently (I had almost said evangelically) defin'd, the best way of worshipping God, to be the doing what he commands. **1772** FLETCHER *Logica Genev.* 63 Agreeably to that evangelically-legal proposition.

2. According to the principles of those called Evangelicals.

1532 MORE *Confut. Tindale* Wks. 639/2 When our euaungelical englishe heretiques fall in acquaintaunce.. with some of our marchauntes factours, they mylke them so euaungelically, that, etc. **1890** *Dict. Nat. Biog.* XXI. 14/2 His parents were.. by no means 'evangelically' religious.

evanˈgelican, *a.* and *sb.* [f. EVANGELIC + -AN.]
A. *adj.* = EVANGELICAL A. 2 b.

1847 DE QUINCEY *Protestantism* Wks. (1862) VII. 100 Distinguishing between the Romanist and the Newmanite, on the one hand, between the Calvinist and the Evangelican man, on the other.

B. *sb.* = EVANGELICAL B. 2.

1876 MIVART *Contemp. Evolution* 116 The heartfelt piety of the evangelican protest against the cold formalism of the established clergy of that time.

Hence **evanˈgelicanism** = EVANGELICALISM.

1887 BENHAM *Dict. Relig.* 412 Evangelicanism is essentially the theology of the inner life of the individual soul.

evanˈgelicism. *rare.* [f. EVANGELIC *a.* + -ISM.] = EVANGELICALISM.

1807 SOUTHEY in *Life* (1850) III. 92 In spite of his evangelicism, I always expected great things, from the proof he had given of very superior powers. **1864** *Sat. Rev.* XVIII. 490/1 The reign of Evangelicism had discountenanced debts incurred in this quarter.

evanˈgelicity. [f. as prec. + -ITY.] The quality of being evangelical.

18.. *Eclectic Rev.* (Ogilvie), A thorough earnestness and evangelicity. **1839** J. H. NEWMAN *Anglo-Amer. Ch. Essays* (1872) I. 365 Apostolicity.. is one side, one whole aspect of Christian truth, and Evangelicity is another side.

†evanˈgelicly, *adv.* *Obs.* = EVANGELICALLY.

1678 GALE *Crt. Gentiles* III. 15 Both are Evangelicly possible, through the habitual and actual assistances of the Spirit of Grace.

evangelism (ɪˈvændʒɪlɪz(ə)m). [f. EVANGEL + -ISM, as if ad. Gr. *εὐαγγελισμός, f. εὐαγγελίζεσθαι: see EVANGELIZE. Cf. F. *évangélisme.* In sense 2 f. EVANGEL-IC + -ISM.]

1. The preaching or promulgation of the Gospel; performance of the function of an evangelist.

a **1626** BACON *New Atl.* (1650) 10 Thus was this Land saved from infidelitie.. through the Apostolicall and Miraculous Evangelisme of S. Bartholomew. **1813** *Examiner* 18 Jan. 35/1 Evangelism or the Announcement of Good Tidings. **1857** T. B. BUNTING *Life J. Bunting* I. vii. 94 The Sunday School.. never to be entered.. in any spirit but that of an earnest evangelism.

2. a. Attachment to or profession of evangelical doctrines, *i.e.* = EVANGELICALISM (chiefly in derisive or hostile use). **b.** The faith of the Gospel. (*rare.*)

a. **1812** *Religionism* 26 But lectureship requires, Grave face, evangelism and curbed desires. **1831** *Blackw. Mag.* XXIX. 96 Attacking what it calls evangelism and puritanism. **1840** MRS. GORE in *New Monthly Mag.* LX. 52 Taking his sly aim from behind the whited wall of evangelism. **1876** MISS BRADDON *J. Haggard's Dau.* II. 95 Triumphant party cries and watch-words of evangelism.

b. **1842** FABER *Provincial Lett.* (1844) II. 13 The sure test ..of soul-preserving Evangelism or of soul-destroying Heresy. **1888** SPURGEON in *British Weekly* 3 Feb. 275 Here is an inner core of Evangelism in which all true believers are at one.

evangelist (ɪˈvændʒɪlɪst). Forms: 2-4 ewan(i)geliste, 3-8 evangelist(e, -yste, (4 euuan-, evaungelist, -istte), 4- evangelist. Also 4 aphet. (after *þe*) wangelist(e, -yst. [a. Fr. *évangéliste,* = Pr., Sp. and It. *evangelista,* ad. L. *evangelista,* ad. Gr. εὐαγγελιστής, agent-n. f. εὐαγγελίζεσθαι: see EVANGELIZE.]

1. One of the writers of the Four Gospels, Matthew, Mark, Luke, and John.

c **1175** *Lamb. Hom.* 81 Seint Iohan þe ewangeliste in apocalipsi. *c* **1225** *Juliana* 31 þe worldes wealdent þat wiste sein iuhan his ewanigeliste unhurt. **1297** R. GLOUC. (1724) 67 And sende Sent Mark þe euangelist in to Egypt. *a* **1300**

Cursor M. 13977 (Gött.) Als tellis luca þe wangeliste. *a* **1330** *Roland & V.* 153 Jones broþer, þe wangelist. **1377** LANGL. *P. Pl.* B. x. 243 Cryst clepid hym-self so þe ewangelistes bereth witnesse. **1480** CAXTON *Chron. Eng.* II. (1520) 14/2 This Asarias and his sone Joas and his nevewe Amasia Mathew the evangelist putteth not in the lyne of Cryst for theyr offences. **1561** T. NORTON *Calvin's Inst.* I. viii. (1634) 27 The three Evangelists write the Historie in base and simple speech. **1697** LOCKE *2nd Vind. Reas. Chr.* He is of opinion.. if we had nothing but the four Evangelists, we could not be sav'd. **1747** J. SCOTT *Chr. Life* III. 115 The same may be said of the three other Evangelists. **1833** CRUSE *Eusebius* VI. xxxi. 250 In this he most clearly establishes the consistency of two evangelists. **1845** CORRIE in *Encycl. Metrop.* 879/1 The Evangelist relates the circumstances attendant on the baptism of Christ.

transf. **1587** GOLDING *De Mornay* xxxiii. 534 He [Apollonius of Thyanie] fetched a yoong wench to life again, but yet his counterfeit Euangelist Philostratus durst not auowe that she was starke dead.

†2. The book of the Gospels; a copy of the Gospels. *Obs.* [A med.L. use of *evangelista*; cf. *apostolus* for a lectionary from the epistles.]

1523 LD. BERNERS *Froiss.* I. ccxii. 260 We swere on the holy euangelist, by vs corporally touched. **1618** *Barnevelt's Apol.* Fiij b, Let the Aduocate remember what Christ thunders out in the Euangelist. **1713** STEELE in *Guardian* No. 21 ¶8 To see a well dressed young man produce an evangelist out of his pocket.

3. a. *gen.* One who preaches the gospel.

1535 COVERDALE *Ps.* lxvii. 11 The Lorde shal geue the worde, with greate hoostes of Euangelistes. **1548** UDALL, etc. *Erasm. Par. John* 69 b, They [the Pharisees] were as blynde in soule as the beggar, beyng now an euangelyste, was before in body. **1559** in Strype *Ann. Ref.* I. App. vi. 11 A woman.. is not called to be an evangelist.

transf. **1790** BURKE *Fr. Rev.* 16 The new evangelists will, I dare say, disappoint the hopes that are conceived of them. **1840** CARLYLE *Heroes* (1858) 325 The French Revolution found its Evangelist in Rousseau. **1883** *Harper's Mag.* Sept. 559/1 Mr. Norman Shaw has been the chief evangelist of this strange revival.

b. One who evangelizes or brings the gospel to (a heathen nation, etc.); = APOSTLE 3 b.

Mod. St. Boniface the evangelist of Germany.

c. In the primitive Church, the designation given to a certain class of teachers, mentioned in *Eph.* iv. 11 after 'apostles' and 'prophets', and presumably having the function of preaching the gospel to the unconverted. The title has at various periods been revived, usually denoting an itinerant preacher having no fixed pastoral charge. At present, in the usage of various Protestant denominations, it means chiefly a layman commissioned to perform home missionary work.

1382 WYCLIF *Acts* xxi. 8 Philip euangelist. *Ibid., Eph.* iv. 11 He ʒaf ʒiftis to men.. And he ʒaf summe sotheli apostlis, summe forsoth prophetis, othere forsothe Euangelistis. **1526** *Pilgr. Perf.* (W. de W. 1531) 21 Many offices and dignytees of the chirche.. as apostles, prophetes, euangelistes, doctours. **1588** J. UDALL *Demonstr. Discipl.* (Arb.) 23 Timothie and Titus.. were Euangelists, a degree aboue ordinarie ministers. **1611** BIBLE *2 Tim.* iv. 5 Endure afflictions, do the work of an evangelist. **1681** BURNET *Hist. Ref.* II. 368 It was designed, that there should be in every diocese some who should go round a precinct, and preach like evangelists. **1732** NEAL *Hist. Purit.* I. 165 He [John Knox] was a sort of Evangelist over the whole kingdom. **1839** YEOWELL *Anc. Brit. Ch.* iv. (1847) 39 Evangelists, who appear to have acted as pioneers and forerunners of a stationary ministry. **1852** CONYBEARE & H. *St. Paul* (1862) I. xiii. 409 The term Evangelist is applied to those missionaries who.. travelled from place to place. **1881** BIBLE (Revised) *Eph.* iv. 11.

∥evangeliˈstarium. Also 9 evangelistarion. [a. med.L. *evangelistārium,* mod.Gr. εὐαγγελιστάριον, f. *evangelista* EVANGELIST.] = next.

1850 NEALE *East. Ch.* II. 903 note, I.. consult the Evangelistarium, to see what is the tone for the week. **1882** *Athenæum* 2 Dec. 737/1 A Greek Evangelistarium.. of the twelfth century.

evangelistary (ɪˌvændʒəˈlɪstərɪ). [ad. med.L. *evangelistāri-um* (see prec.).]

1. a. A book containing the portions of the Gospels that form part of the liturgy. **b.** A copy of the Four Gospels.

a. *a* **1646** J. GREGORY *Posthuma* (1649) 119 The Saxons had.. kept the daie, as it seemeth by their Evangelistarie, where the Rubrick to the Gospel is, þys Godspel sceal on cyldamasse daʒ. **1682** WHELER *Journ. Greece* iv. 323 An Evangelistary.. written in Capital Letters. **1790** PORSON *Lett. to Travis* 230 (T.) The evangelistaries and lectionaries have often transfused their readings into the other manuscripts.

b. **1865** *Reader* 29 Apr. 490/3 But attention was chiefly directed to an Evangelistary, which was exhibited at the meeting. **1873** HALE *In His Name* ii. 7 An Evangelistary, or copy of the Four Gospels, in Latin. **1882-3** SCHAFF *Encycl. Relig. Knowl.* I. 731 The Rushworth Gloss (in the Bodleian), an interlinear evangelistary.

†2. (See quots.: is the sense genuine?)

1656-81 BLOUNT *Glossogr., Evangelistary,* the Office of an Evangelist; also a Pulpit, or the place where the Gospel is delivered. **1692** in COLES. **1775** ASH, *Evangelistory.*

evangelistic (ɪˌvændʒəˈlɪstɪk), *a.* [f. EVANGELIST + -IC.]

1. Of or pertaining to the Four Evangelists.

1845 W. BROMET in *Archæol.* XXXI. 498 At the angles [of an Incised Slab] are the evangelistic symbols. **1850** NEALE *Med. Hymns* 108 These are they, the symbols mystic Of the forms Evangelistic. **1869** SPURGEON *Treas. Dav. Ps.* xxii.

7-8 The evangelistic narrative of the ridicule endured by the Crucified One.

2. Of or pertaining to preachers of the Gospel.

1860 ELLICOTT *Life Our Lord* vii. 281 The fulfilment of type and shadow of the hopes of patriarchs.. must be declared by the whole Evangelistic company. **1886** *Q. Rev.* CLXIII. 122 Apparatus, necessary for their [missionaries'] educational and evangelistic labours.

3. Pertaining to the Evangelical school.

1848 H. MILLER *First Impr.* viii. (1857) 129 The Voluntary controversy united Evangelistic Dissent and Roman Catholicism by the bonds of a common cause.

eˈvangelistship. [f. EVANGELIST + -SHIP.] The office, position, or dignity of an evangelist.

a **1603** T. CARTWRIGHT *Confut. Rhem. N.T.* (1618) 578 A full performance of his office of the Evangelistship. **1636** PRYNNE *Unbish. Tim.* (1661) 2 Can we.. conjecture, that Timothy would.. descend from an Evangelistship to a Bishoprick?

∥evangelium (iːvænˈdʒɛlɪəm). *Obs.* or *arch.* Also 6 **evangelion.** [L. *ēvangelium,* a. Gr. εὐαγγέλιον: see EVANGELY.] The GOSPEL (in various senses); a proclamation of the 'glad tidings' of the Gospel.

1541 COVERDALE tr. *Bullinger's Old Faith* (1624) iii, This is the first promise, and the first sure Evangelion. **1550** CROWLEY *Last Trump.* 359 If thy prince do commaunde the ought Against Goddes Evangelion, Then praye for him styl in thy thought. **1692-1732** COLES, *Evangelium.* **1850** MARG. FULLER *Life without & Life within* (1860) 18 If we can find out how much was given him, we are told, in a pure evangelium to judge.. how much shall be required.

evangelization (ɪˌvændʒəlaɪˈzeɪʃən). [f. EVANGELIZE *v.* + -ATION.]

1. The action or work of preaching the Gospel.

1651 HOBBES *Leviath.* III. xlii. 270 Evangelization, that is, a Proclamation of Christ. **1868** M. PATTISON *Academ. Org.* v. 122 Instead of holding up evangelisation—they make the cultivation of knowledge the business of the life.

2. The action or process of evangelizing, or bringing under the influence of the Gospel.

1827 G. S. FABER *Sacred Cal. Prophecy* (1844) I. 195 When this universal evangelisation shall have taken place. **1869** FARRAR *Fam. Speech* iii. (1873) 105 The Aryan should advance farther and farther to the civilisation.. the evangelisation of the whole habitable globe. **1879** MACLEAR *Celts* iii. 38 The most powerful influence in the gradual evangelization of the Celtic races. **1883** *Harper's Mag.* Sept. 498/2 The evangelization of the Dalecarlians.

b. The action of interpreting (heathen myths) in an evangelic or Christian sense.

1843 TURNER tr. *Geijer's Hist. Sweden* (L), The evangelization of the native superstitions was the first object of these latitudinarian missionaries.

3. The state or condition of being evangelized or converted to the Christian faith.

1870-4 ANDERSON *Missions Amer. Bd.* IV. xlvi. 481 The effect of the thorough evangelization of that community.

Hence **eˌvangeliˈzationer** (*nonce-wd.*), one engaged in evangelization.

1825 R. SOUTHEY in *Q. Rev.* XXXII. 26 One of these qualified evangelizationers has devised what he calls Church questions.

evangelize (ɪˈvændʒəlaɪz), *v.* [ad. Eccl. L. *ēvangeliz-āre,* ad. Gr. εὐαγγελίζεσθαι, f. εὐάγγελος: see EVANGEL².]

†1. *intr.* **a.** To bring or tell good tidings. **b.** To preach, proclaim the Gospel. Const. *to. Obs.*

a. **1382** WYCLIF *Isa.* xl. 9 Thou that euangelizist to Sion. **1609** BIBLE (Douay) *ibid.,* Thou that evangelizest to Sion.

b. **1382-8** WYCLIF *Ps.* Prol., [These things] Dauid.. so euydentli openede, that more be he seen to euangelisen than to profecien. **1582** N.T. (Rhem.) *2 Cor.* x. 16 For we are come as farre as you in the Gospel of Christ.. to evangelize. **1641** J. JACKSON *True Evang. T.* II. 116 S. Peter.. Euangelized abundantly with his tongue. **1666** J. SMITH *Old Age* 256 Conversant in the Word of God; and able to evangelize. *a* **1808** PORTEUS *Serm.* II. xii. (R.), Thus did our heavenly instructor most exactly fulfil the predictions of the prophets.. that he would evangelize to the poor.

†2. *trans.* To proclaim as glad tidings; to preach. Const. *to, unto. Obs.*

1382 WYCLIF *Luke* i. 19, I am sent to thee for to speke, and to euangelise or telle [*v.r.* or shewe] to thee thes thingis. —— *Acts* v. 42 Thei ceessiden not in the temple, and aboute housis, techinge and euangelisynge Ihesu Crist. **1579** J. KNEWSTUB *Confut. Heresies* 73 a, The mysterie of the heauenly trueth.. becommeth nowe.. euangelized and declared vnto you all. **1581** MARBECK *Bk. of Notes* 457 From that time the kingdome of God was evangelized. **1649** ROBERTS *Clavis Bibl.* 278 O all the earth sing praise alway.. Evangelize from day to day His glorious salvation. **1698** *Christ Exalted* 3, I evangelize to you great Joy, which shall be to all People.

3. To preach the Gospel to; to win over to the Gospel or the Christian faith; rarely, in etymological sense: To announce glad tidings to.

a **1652** J. SMITH *Sel. Disc.* vii. 349 There were amongst the Jews some that were evangelized. **1667** MILTON *P.L.* XII. 499 His [Messiah's] Apostles, whom he sends To evangelize the Nations. **1813** *Examiner* 3 May 283/1 Why go to India to 'evangelize' the natives? **1839** YEOWELL *Anc. Brit. Ch.* xiv. (1847) 165 Aidan, by whose self-denying labours Northumbria soon became evangelized. **1845** J. H. NEWMAN *Ess. Developm.* 385 Mary the Virgin, receiving faith and joy, when Gabriel the Angel evangelized her. **1867** FREEMAN *Norm. Conq.* (1876) I. v. 289 A zealous Christian, who evangelized his kingdom at the point of the sword. **1874** *Daily News* 14 Feb., Eight Incumbents.. have asked.. for..

lay churchmen to evangelise their parishes on Sunday evenings.

b. *absol.* or *intr.* To act as an evangelist.

1882 *Century Mag.* XXV. 77 Trading, manœuvering, lying, or evangelizing, as occasion required.

4. To imbue with the spirit of the Gospel; to interpret in an evangelical sense.

1677 GALE *Crt. Gentiles* II. IV. 94 The Divine Law.. evangelised and sweetned by evangelic grace. **1857** BADEN POWELL *Chr. without Judaism* 145 The spirit of allegorising and evangelising all parts of it [the Old Testament].

Hence **e'vangelized** *ppl. a.* **e'vangelizer**, one who evangelizes (in various senses of the vb.). **e'vangelizing** *vbl. sb.* and *ppl. a.* (in quot. 1382 *absol.* One who brings good tidings).

1816 FABER *Orig. Pagan Idol.* II. 212 He had become contemptible in the eyes of the evangelized Britons. **1819** —— *Dispensations* (1823) II. 150 When Christianity itself shall be added to evangelized Judaism. **1382** WYCLIF *Ps.* lxvii[i]. 11 The Lord shal ȝiuen a word, to the euangeliseris. **1883** JESSOPP *Coming of Friars* i. (1889) 49 The Friars were the Evangelizers of the towns of England for 300 years. **1862** GOULBURN *Pers. Relig.* i. (1873) 8 The evangelizing of the heathen. **1382** WYCLIF *Nahum* i. 15 Loo! on hillis the feet of euangelizinge and tellynge pees. **1631** R. H. *Arraignm. Whole Creature* xii. §5. 140 The Evangelizing Apostles, that in their Epistles writ as they preacht.

evangely (ɪ'vændʒəlɪ). *Obs.* or *arch.* Forms: 4–7 ev-, ewangeli(e, -ye, (5 evangilye), 4–5 evaungelie, -y, 5– evangely. Also 5 *aphet.* vangelye. [ad. Eccl. L. *ēvangelium*, ad. Gr. εὐαγγέλιον good tidings (in class. Gr. only 'reward for bringing good news,' and in pl. 'a sacrifice offered on receiving good news'), f. εὐάγγελος, f. εὖ well + ἀγγέλλειν to announce. Cf. EVANGEL[1].]

1. The 'good news' of redemption; the Gospel revelation, the faith of the Gospel; = EVANGEL 1.

1382 WYCLIF *Gal.* i. 7 Ther ben summe that.. wolen mysturne the euangelie of Crist. *c* **1450** LONELICH *Grail* lii. 969 [Piers] the holy vangelye gan him vndo. *c* **1540** in Prance *Addit. Narr. Pop. Plot* (1679) 36 To most notable slaunder of Christs Holy Evangely. **1590** SPENSER *F.Q.* II. x. 53 Christes Evangely. **1675** *Case of Quakers conc. Oaths def.* 47, I..submit myself principally to the Evangely of Jesus Christ. **1683** E. HOOKER *Pref. Ep. Pordage's Mystic Div.* 29 This Gospel is, this the Evangelie.

b. In etymological sense: Glad tidings.

c **1380** WYCLIF *Serm.* (Sel. Wks.) II. 339 Evangeli is seid as good typing of blis: and þus not oonly þes foure gospels but epistlis of Poul..ben clepid Evangelies. *c* **1449** PECOCK *Repr.* I. xi. 54 If oure Euangelie is couered.

2. The Gospel record; = EVANGEL[1] 2. Also a passage in the same.

1362 LANGL. *P. Pl.* A. I. 174 þeos beþ wordes I-writen In þe Ewangelye. *c* **1386** CHAUCER *Melib.* ¶ 113 As he him selfe recordeth in his Evaungelie. **1393** LANGL. *P. Pl.* C. XII. 204 For clergie seith þat he seih in the seynt euangelie, That, etc. *c* **1470** HARDING *Chron.* LXXXVII, Thou vnderstandest full litill theuangilye. **1483** CAXTON *G. de la Tour* L ij, Jhesus Cryst sayd in theuangely that, etc. **1583** STUBBES *Anat. Abus.* (1877–9) 120 Our Sauiour Christ Iesus..in his Euangely, the sixt of Mathew, saith.

b. One of the Four Gospels; = EVANGEL 2 b.

1393 LANGL. *P. Pl.* C. XVI. 45 þenne cam scripture, And serued hem þus sone of sondrie metes menie, Of austyn, [of] ambrosie, of all þe foure euangelies. ? *a* **1400** *Chester Pl.* 210 Austyne..his homilye upon Saynte John Evangelye. **1513** BRADSHAW *St. Werburge* I. 2854 Rehersed by Mathewe, in his evangely. **1529** LATIMER *1st Serm. on the Card* I. 5 Christ..left be hind for our safeguard..the evangelies, the sacraments, the commandments, and so forth. **1530** *Compend. Treat.* (1863) 53 That the Euangely off Jhon was drawen into Englishe by the forsayde Bede.

¶ App. taken to mean 'evangelist'. (The older texts have *euangelist, wangeliste.*)

c **1340** *Cursor M.* 13977 (Trin.) Als telleþ luke þe euangele.

3. As an object to swear upon. **a.** *pl.* A copy of the Four Gospels; cf. EVANGEL[1] 3. **b.** *sing.* used collectively: The Gospels.

1494 FABYAN VII. 548 And I swere vpon the holy Euaungelys here presentlye with my handys towchyd, that, etc. **1547** *Homilies* I. *Swearing* II. (1859) 79 Whosoever wilfully forsweareth himself upon Christs holy Evangely. **1577** HARRISON *England* II. v. (1877) I. 123 You shall..swear upon the holy evangelies by you bodily touched.

evanid (ɪ'vænɪd), *a. Obs.* or *arch.* Also 7 evanide. [ad. L. *ēvānid-us* vanishing, related to *ēvānescĕre*: see EVANESCE.]

1. Vanishing away; of short duration; evanescent, fleeting, transient.

1626 BACON *Sylva* (1631) §389 The Smell of the Flower is rather Euanide and Weaker than in the Leaues. **1664** EVELYN *Sylva* (1776) 372 This delicate and evanid flower [the Jasmine]. **1665** GLANVILL *Sceps. Sci.* xxii. 139 As great a difference..as between the Sun, and an unconcocted evanid Meteor. **1699** BURNET 39 *Art.* i. (1700) 35 Those Animal Spirits are of such an Evanid and Subtile Nature. *a* **1711** KEN *Edmund* Poet. Wks. 1721 II. 140 Ye trifling Honours..are th' evanid Bubbles of Mankind. **1751** CHAMBERS *Cycl.* s.v., Some authors..use the..term to express those flowers of plants whose petals fall off as soon as they are opened. **1835** W. A. BUTLER in *Blackw. Mag.* XXXVII. 857 That misty veil Evanid, disenshrouding field and grove, Left us, a mirror of each heavenly hue.

2. Faint, weak.

1646 SIR T. BROWNE *Pseud. Ep.* VI. xii. 338 The decoctions of simples..are dead and evanid without the commixtion of Alume Argol, and the like. **1765** WARBURTON *Div. Legat.* IV. vi. (ed. 4) 94 How evanid is it [Dr. Shuckford's reasoning], therefore, when applied to a prophet under the impulse of inspiration.

†**3.** = EMPHATICAL 5.

1663 BOYLE *Exp. on Colours* I. iv, A difference betwixt these apparent colours and those that are wont to be esteemed genuine, as to the duration, which has induced some learned men to call the former rather evanid than fantastical. **1751** CHAMBERS *Cycl.* s.v., Evanid colours are the same with those otherwise called fantastical, and emphatical colours.

Hence **e'vanidness**. *Obs.*

1659 H. MORE *Immort. Soul* (1662) 151 Fooleries..that pinch our Perception into such an intolerable evanidness, that, etc. **1731–6** in BAILEY. **1775** in ASH.

evanish (ɪ'vænɪʃ), *v.* Forms: 5–6 evanesch, -isch, *Sc.* evanis, 7– evanish. [a. OF. *evaniss-*, lengthened stem of *evanir*, corresp. to It. *svanire*:—popular L. **exvānīre* = class. L. *ēvānescĕre*: see EVANESCE.]

1. *intr.* To vanish out of sight, disappear from view: **a.** of objects present to the eye.

1432–50 tr. *Higden* (Rolls) I. 370 Then Criste euaneschede awey. **1536** BELLENDEN *Cron. Scot.* (1821) I. p. xxxiii, Thay [heryings] be now evanist, for offence that is maid aganis sum Sanct. **1753** MELVILLE in *Phil. Trans.* XLVIII. 268 A satellite, seen from the earth, ought to change its colour..and at last evanish in violet. *a* **1813** A. WILSON *Poems, Foresters*, At last the path evanishes from view. **1880** BROWNING *Dram. Idylls* Ser. II. *Muléykeh* 99 And a leap indeed gave she, and evanished for ever more.

b. of objects present only to the mind.

1599 JAMES I Βασιλ. Δωρον (1603) 104 The people will conceiue..præ-occupied conceits of the Kings inward intention: which although with time..it will euanish, by the euidence of contrary effects, yet *interim patitur iustus*. **1604** EARL STIRLING *Avrora*, li, My happinesse evanish'd with the sleepe. **1728** RAMSAY *Gent. Sheph.* Poems (1844) 43 And cares evanish like a morning dream. *a* **1813** A. WILSON *Poems, To T. Wotherspoon*, When all these evanished and horror distressed me.

2. To vanish out of existence; to die away; to become dissipated or dispelled: said of both material and immaterial objects. Also with *away*.

1597 LOWE *Chirurg.* (1634) 84 That [Carbuncle] which appeareth and evanisheth away, is mortall. **1604** JAMES I *Counterbl.* (Arb.) 109 All his members shall become feeble.. and in the end..he shall euanish in a Lethargie. **1629** RUTHERFORD *Lett.* No. 4 (1862) I. 44 A star, which going out of our sight, doth not die and evanish, but shineth in another hemisphere. **1639** J. CORBET *Ungird. Scot. Arm.* 6 If hee [the king] at the beginning had showne himselfe like a blazing Star, you had all evanished as smoak. **1790** H. BOYD *Ruins of Athens* in *Poet. Reg.* (1806–7) 75 Th' imperial bubble.. breaks Spontaneous, or..Evanishes to nothing. **1830** TENNYSON *Poems* 77 When thy light perisheth..Our life evanisheth. **1880** MUIRHEAD tr. *Instit. Gaius* II. §244 Servius holds..that the legacy evanishes if at the time it vests the legatee be still in *potestate*.

Hence **e'vanished** *ppl. a.*, that has vanished, in senses of the vb. **e'vanishing** *vbl. sb.*, the action of the vb. EVANISH; an instance of the same. **e'vanishing** *ppl. a.*, that vanishes or disappears. **e'vanishment**, the action of evanishing, the fact of having evanished, disappearance.

1818 COLERIDGE *Lit. Remains* (1836) I. 204 When.. convalescence has made its [the imagination's] chilled and evanished figures and landscape bud, blossom and live in scarlet, green and snow white. **1829** J. WILSON in *Blackw. Mag.* XXVI. 544 It hangs in the abyss of the evanish'd lake. **1853** G. TATE in Johnston *Nat. Hist. E. Bord.* I. 297 We shall now describe the forms of evanished animal life. **1633** W. STRUTHER *True Happiness* 38 The first is a vacuitie; the second is a weaknesse; and the third an evanishing. **1797** SIR W. SCOTT in Robberds *Mem. W. Taylor* (1843) I. 99 After the evanishing of the deer. **1872** M. COLLINS *Two Plunges for a Pearl* II. x. 176 Ianthe's evanishing caused the Earl of Chessington to be more in love than ever. **1629** SYMMER *Spir. Posie* I. i. 7 That evanishing shadow of seeming Charity. *a* **1649** DRUMM. OF HAWTH. *Bibl. Edin., Lectori* Wks. 222 Riches being momentary and evanishing. **1886** *Pall Mall G.* 14 July 1/1 He has pursued the rapidly evanishing phantom of a Home Rule majority. **1797** MRS. A. M. BENNETT *Beggar Girl* (1813) II. 174 On the evanishment of her ducal vision. **1836** T. HOOK *G. Gurney* viii, I contented myself with watching the evanishment of my bright star from the sphere which she adorned and illuminated. **1868** BROWNING *Ring & Bk.* VII. 1728 May my evanishment for evermore Help further to relieve the heart.

evanition (ɛvə'nɪʃən). *rare.* [f. EVANISH, after the analogy of *abolition*, etc.; cf. OF. *evanition.*] Evanishment, disappearance.

a **1797** H. WALPOLE *Geo. II* (1847) I. xii. 373 The numbness of that enchantment has been dispelled by the evanition of the talisman. **1817** T. JEFFERSON *Writ.* (1830) IV. 304 The evanition of party dissensions has harmonized intercourse.

evansite ('ɛvənzaɪt). *Min.* [f. (Brooke) *Evans* who brought it from Hungary in 1855 + -ITE.] A hydrous phosphate of aluminium occurring in white reniform masses.

1864 *Phil. Mag.* Ser. IV. XXVIII. 341. **1868** DANA *Min.* 585 Evansite..moistened with sulphuric acid colors the flame green.

evaporability (ɪ,væpərə'bɪlɪtɪ). [f. EVAPORABLE: see -ITY.] The quality of being evaporable.

1854 J. SCOFFERN in *Orr's Circ. Sc.* Chem. 150 The force of vapour from each liquid..is proportionate to its evaporability.

evaporable (ɪ'væpərəb(ə)l), *a.* [f. L. *ēvăpōrā-re* (see EVAPORATE *v.*) + -ABLE.] Capable of being evaporated.

1541 R. COPLAND *Guydon's Quest. Chirurg.*, They haue but lytell blode, and theyr flesshe is largely euaporable. **1635** PERSON *Varieties* II. 51 Not all subtile humidity is evaporable, but that of water only. *a* **1691** BOYLE *Effluviums* vi. Wks. 1772 III. 675 A far more evaporable and dissipable kind of bodies than minerals. **1758** FRANKLIN *Wks.* (1840) VI. 216 Drinking frequently of a thin evaporable liquor. **1831** BREWSTER *Optics* xii. 102 Placing a thick film of an evaporable fluid upon a clean plate of glass. **1881** *Standard* 18 Nov. 5/3 The frightful holocaust..at Abergele..was due to an oil by no means evaporable.

†**e'vaporate**, *pa. pple.* and *ppl. a. Obs.* [ad. L. *ēvăpōrāt-us*, pa. pple. of *ēvăpōrā-re*: see next.] = EVAPORATED.

1607 TOPSELL *Serpents* (1658) 599 All the humour acquired, is consumed into a loose and evaporate flesh. **1671** *True Nonconf.* 259 That both your Reason and Religion are evaporat. **1730** THOMSON *Autumn* 1210 The filmy threads Of dew evaporate.

evaporate (ɪ'væpəreɪt), *v.* Also 6 evaperatt, 7 -ourate. [f. late L. *ēvăpōrāt-* ppl. stem of *ēvăpōrā-re*, f. *ē-* out + *vapor, vapōr-is* steam, VAPOUR. Cf. Fr. *évaporer.*]

1. *trans.* To convert or turn into vapour; to convert from a solid or liquid into a gaseous state; to drive off in the form of vapour. Said both of natural and personal agents. *to evaporate* †*in* or *into*: to change by evaporation *into*.

1555 EDEN *Decades* 336 Euaporatynge the quickesyluer from it in a styllatory of glasse. **1604** JAMES I *Counterbl.* (Arb.) 104 The raynie cloudes are often transformed and euaporated in blustering winds. *a* **1648** DIGBY *Closet Open.* (1677) 18 Clove gilly flowers must never be boiled in the liquor: that evaporateth their spirits. **1794** J. HUTTON *Philos. Light, &c.* 193 When we expose such a body to a burning heat..the aqueous part is evaporated. **1813** SIR H. DAVY *Agric. Chem.* (1814) 64 In the leaves much of the water of the sap is evaporated. **1836** EMERSON *Nat., Commodity* Wks. (Bohn) II. 144 The wind sows the seed; the sun evaporates the sea. **1853** KANE *Grinnell Exp.* xxxvi. (1856) 325 The snow began to move, and fell, leaving a moist stain. This was either evaporated or frozen instantly.

b. *fig.*

1616 *Pasquil & Kath.* III. 250 Blacke sorrow, nurse of plaints..Euaporate my spirit with a sigh, That it may hurrie after his sweet breath. **1641** MILTON *Ch. Govt.* iii. (1851) 111 Evaporating and exhaling the internall worship into empty conformities and gay shewes. **1647** MAY *Hist. Parl.* I. vii. 73 They would evaporate and dis-spirit the power and vigour of Religion. **1877** L. TOLLEMACHE in *Fortn. Rev.* Dec. 846 Did the Jews..dream of spiritually evaporating the plain prediction about David?

2. *intr.* To become vapour; to pass off or become dissipated in vapour. Also †*to evaporate to.*

1567 MAPLET *Gr. Forest* 10 Being put into the fornace [this metal] doth not euaporate.. neyther doth it lesse of hys waight. **1601** HOLLAND *Pliny* XIII. i. (R.), The sweet odour ..would evaporate and soone be lost. **1683** PETTUS *Fleta Min.* I. (1686) 122 If such an earthen Jug should crack..the Quicksilver will be lost, and will evaporate to smoak. **1698** KEILL *Exam. Th. Earth* (1734) 155 They [animal liquors] must evaporate and be exhaled by the extreme heat. **1774** GOLDSM. *Nat. Hist.* (1776) I. 369 Water is known to evaporate more powerfully in the severest frost, than when the air is moderately warm. **1858** LARDNER *Hand-bk. Nat. Phil., Heat* 319 There is no temperature, however low, at which water will not evaporate.

3. *fig.* **a.** Of things: To pass off like vapour; to be wasted or dissipated. Const. *into*.

a **1631** DONNE in *Select.* (1840) 116, I shall have a joy, which shall no more evaporate, than my soul shall evaporate. **1649** SELDEN *Laws Eng.* II. xxxiii. (1739) 149 Much of the Riches of the Nation evaporated into the Wars both Civil and Foreign. *a* **1745** SWIFT (J.), The enemy takes a surer way to consume us, by letting our courage evaporate against stones and rubbish. **1781** GIBBON *Decl. & F.* (1869) II. xlii. 584 These hostile menaces evaporated without effect. **1833** LAMB *Elia* Ser. II. iv. (1865) 263 By this subtle vent half of the hatefulness of the character evaporates. **1862** BURTON *Bk. Hunter* 211 His memory has utterly evaporated with the departure of his own generation.

b. *humorously* of persons: To become missing, vanish from sight or existence.

1727 POPE, etc. *Art of Sinking* 119 Any other person [than the hero of the poem] who may be lost and evaporate in the course of the work. **1797** MRS. RADCLIFFE *Italian* vii, I would fain evaporate through that door myself. **1821** BYRON *Let. to Moore* 1 Oct., You should have more, if I evaporate [*i.e.* die] within a reasonable time. **1865** DICKENS *Mut. Fr.* I. vi, Bob and Jonathan with similar meekness took their leave and evaporated.

4. *trans.* To expose or subject to evaporation; to drive off the liquid part of; to reduce by evaporation *to* (a residuum, a denser state). Also *absol.*

1646 SIR T. BROWNE *Pseud. Ep.* II. iii. 68 If the menstruum or dissolvent be evaporated to a consistence. **1706** PHILLIPS (ed. Kersey), *To Evaporate to a Pellicle.* **1799** G. SMITH *Laborat.* I. 435 Evaporate to the consistence of honey. **1838** T. THOMSON *Chem. Org. Bodies* 536 Evaporate to dryness an alcoholic solution of the resin of guaiacum. **1877** W. THOMSON *Voy. Challenger* I. i. 33 For evaporating or heating in flasks or beakers a small sand-bath..has been found very useful.

5. *intr.* To exhale moisture; to part with liquid particles by evaporation.

1799 G. SMITH *Laborat.* I. 86 Let this solution evaporate over a fire until it becomes thickish. **1844–57** G. BIRD *Urin. Deposits* (ed. 5) 149 If a solution of it be allowed to evaporate spontaneously on a glass plate. **1869** ROSCOE *Elem. Chem.* 191 A substance..is dissolved in water, and the solution allowed gradually to evaporate.

†**6.** *trans.* To emit in the form of vapour; to give vent to, exhale; to lose (perfume, strength, etc.) by evaporation. Also *absol. Obs.*

1611 COTGR., *Spiracle*, a hole to let ayre..in and out; also, a hole that euaporates a strong or pestilent ayre. *a* **1631** DONNE in *Select.* (1840) 192 By long lying they have exhaled, and evaporated, and breathed out all their gross matter. **1646** J. HALL *Poems* 52 As flowers assoone as smelled at Evaporate, Even so this shadow, ere our eyes Can view it, flies. **1684** T. BURNET *Th. Earth* II. 67 After a gentle rain..the warmth of the sun makes them [flowers] evaporate more freely. **1702** W. J. *Bruyn's Voy. Levant* liv. 211 The Smoke of the Lamps is evaporated by three Funnels that are at the Roof. **1715** LEONI *Palladio's Archit.* (1742) I. 46 Having vents..through which the offensive smell is evaporated.

†**b.** *fig.* (Cf. Fr. *évaporer la bile*).

1591 HORSEY *Trav.* (Hakluyt Soc.) 188 His stomake full of their treasonable purposes, must evaperatt somwhat for revenge. **1650–3** tr. *Hales' Dissert. de Pace* in *Phenix* (1708) II. 370 Any one but him who..hath quite evaporated, and breath'd out all charity. **1651** *Reliq. Wotton.* (1685) 105 My Lord of Essex chose to evaporate his thoughts in a Sonnet. **1711** ADDISON *Spect.* No. 116 ¶8 It might conduce very much to evaporate the Spleen.

†**7.** *intr.* To be emitted in the form of vapour; to be exhaled. *Obs.*

1545 RAYNOLD *Byrth Mankynde* Y vj, Humors..the whiche daylye and hourely, by vnsensyble swettinge, euaporatith and yssueth furthe. **1622** VENNER *Via Recta* 2 Filthy vapours evaporating or breathing out of standing pooles. **1694** CROWNE *Regulus* I. 8 A ghost? a damp evaporates from the word Which sickens me to death. **1799** *Med. Jrnl.* I. 464 Rendering the syphilitic poison inert, the moment it begins to evaporate.

†**8.** *trans.* To subject to a vapour-bath; to steam. *Obs.* Cf. EVAPORATION 5.

1610 BARROUGH *Meth. Physick* III. liii. (1639) 186 Moreover the wombe must be evaporated and fomented with odoriferous things.

Hence **e'vaporated** *ppl. a.*

1846 G. E. DAY tr. *Simon's Anim. Chem.* II. 52 Residue of evaporated whey, 78·0. **1870** *Daily News* 23 Sept., The Swiss and American preparations of evaporated milk. **1875** H. SPENCER *First Princ.* II. iv. §52. 173 The evaporated water..may be brought by condensation to its original shape.

evaporate (ɪ'væpəreɪt), *sb. rare.* [f. the vb.] = EVAPORITE.

1920 A. W. GRABAU *Textbk. Geol.* I. x. 215 Such salts are called evaporation products, or briefly, evaporates. **1924** [see EVAPORITE].

e'vaporating, *vbl. sb.* [f. EVAPORATE *v.* + -ING[1].]

1. The action of the vb. EVAPORATE; *lit.* and *fig.*

1630 J. TAYLOR (Water-P.) *Wks.* II. 253/1 Let it bee a trade to practise..the gulpe, the euaporating or retention. **1663** J. SPENCER *Prodigies* Pref., The evaporating of Religion in the Doctrine thereof, into a multitude of perplext questions.

2. *attrib.*, as ***evaporating dish, furnace, power***; **evaporating cone**, an apparatus of Belgian invention, used in the sugar manufacture; **evaporating pan**, in sugar and salt manufacture, a large shallow iron vessel in which the juice of the sugarcane and the brine is evaporated.

1874 KNIGHT *Dict. Mech.*, **Evaporating-cone.* **1826** HENRY *Elem. Chem.* I. 3 A shallow kettle of water, in which is placed the *evaporating dish and its contents. **1800** tr. *Lagrange's Chem.* I. 27 The *evaporating furnace..serves not only for evaporation, but also for digestion, distillation, solutions, etc. **1862** M. HOPKINS *Hawaii* 14 A natural *evaporating pan for the production of salt. **1862** SMILES *Engineers* II. 78 The *evaporating power of different kinds of fuel.

evaporating (ɪ'væpəreɪtɪŋ), *ppl. a.* [f. as prec. + -ING[2].] That evaporates.

1597 *Pilgr. Parnass.* v. 576 Such an ayre as is wonte to proceede from an evaporatinge dunghill in a summers daye. **1796** MORSE *Amer. Geog.* I. 60 [Evaporation] is greatly increased by a current of air or wind flowing over the evaporating surface. **1860** MAURY *Phys. Geog. Sea* vii. §355 An evaporating region at sea.

evaporation (ɪ,væpə'reɪʃən). Also 4 -cion, 7 evaperation. [a. Fr. *évaporation*, ad. L. *ēvapōrātiōn-em*, n. of action f. *ēvapōrā-re*: see EVAPORATE *v.*]

1. The action or process of conversion into vapour; the action of passing off in vapour; an instance of this.

1398 TREVISA *Barth. De P.R.* XVI. vii. (1495) 556 Quycke syluer passyth out by euaporacion in sethyng and in smokynge. **1616** SURFL. & MARKH. *Country Farme* 480 The oyle also [is] kept the better from euaporation. **1799** KIRWAN *Geol. Ess.* 48 The great evaporation that took place soon after the creation, as soon as the solids began to crystallize. **1802** PALEY *Nat. Theol.* xxi. §1 (1819) 330 By evaporation, water is carried up into the air. **1813** SIR H. DAVY *Agric. Chem.* ii. (1814) 37 Cold is produced during evaporation. **1871** B. STEWART *Heat* §110 Evaporation, where a liquid is converted into a gas quietly, and without the formation of bubbles.

b. *fig.*

1824 BYRON *Juan* XVI. ix, The evaporation of a joyous day Is like the last glass of champagne. **1852** GLADSTONE *Glean.* IV. xliii. 174 It cannot be imposed upon the agent by a third party without the instant evaporation of all its savour.

2. The action or process of driving off the liquid part of a substance in the form of vapour, by means of heat; an instance of the same.

1718 QUINCY *Compl. Disp.* 32/2 The Solution..would part with its Salts but very sparingly, without Evaporation. **1838** T. THOMSON *Chem. Org. Bodies* 652 These alternate filtrations and evaporations. **1845** BUDD *Dis. Liver* 23 When obtained by evaporation from alcohol [Bilin] reddens litmus paper. **1854** RONALDS & RICHARDSON *Chem. Technol.* (ed. 2) I. 277 The most simple method of evaporation..is to place the liquid in a pan or vessel immediately over a fire. **1875** URE *Dict. Arts* III. 945 s.v. *Sugar*, The next process in sugar-refining is the evaporation of the clarified syrup to the granulating or crystallising point.

3. The action or process **a.** of exhaling moisture; †**b.** of emitting (breath, fire, etc.); †**c.** of perspiring insensibly. Also *fig.*

a. **1551** TURNER *Herbal* I. O iij b, If it [Daucus] be layde wythout it wyll greatly dryue furth by euaporation. **1669** BOYLE *Contn. New Exp.* I. (1682) 184 The great Evaporation I have observed even in Winter, of Fruits. **1807** J. E. SMITH *Phys. Bot.* 186 The use of a tin box..for the purpose of restraining the evaporation of plants. **1887** H. M. WARD tr. *Sachs' Phys. Plants* III. xxv. 227 Evaporation takes place through the leaves.

b. **1599** HAKLUYT *Voy.* II. II. 333 Euen in the sea are seen euaporations of fire. **1599** SANDYS *Europæ Spec.* (1632) 124 The best way..is to let the good men chide a while hartily together..so necessarie are these evaporations to the minds of the multitude. **1646** SIR T. BROWNE *Pseud. Ep.* III. xxi. 161 The fuligenous exhalations wanting evaporation recoyle upon the flame and choake it. **1754** JOHNSON *Adventurer* No. 137 ¶4 To reckon the hours laid out in these compositions as..suffered to fume away in useless evaporations.

c. **1626** BACON *Sylva* (1631) §968 So in Pestilent feuers, the Intention is to expell the Infection by Sweat and Euapouration. **1706** PHILLIPS (ed. Kersey), *Evaporation*.. In Physick, a discharging of Humours through the Pores of the Body. **1721–1800** in BAILEY.

4. *concr.* The product of the evaporating process; exhalation, fumes; the amount evaporated.

1533 ELYOT *Cast. Helthe* (1541) 35 b, Pollio prolonged his lyfe certayne dayes with the evaporation of honye. **1605** TIMME *Quersit.* III. 151 Such heates..doe proceed out of the spirits only, either niterous or sulphurus, lifted up into euaporations. **1664** POWER *Exp. Philos.* I. 57 The best Glasses..would not represent to me, the evaporations of Camphire. **1695** WOODWARD *Nat. Hist. Earth* (J.), Evaporations are at some times greater, according to the greater heat of the sun. **1794** SULLIVAN *View Nat.* I. 245 The nocturnal emanations of leaves, and continual evaporations of flowers and of fruits, do not diminish in quality in winter ..only in quantity. **1856** STANLEY *Sinai & Pal.* vii. (1858) 290 The lake, with the..mist of its own evaporations floating over its surface.

fig. **1606** *Proc. agst. Traitors* in *Harl. Misc.* (Malh.) III. 20 This letter should prove to be nothing but the evaporation of an idle brain. **1655** FULLER *Ch. Hist.* III. iv. §5 The vain evaporations of his discontentment.

†**5.** Medical treatment by means of vapour; *concr.* vapour, a vapour-bath. *Obs.*

[**1585** LLOYD *Treas. Health* F v, Euaporatio is when the diseased membre is holden in y[e] hote vapour of some decoctyon.] **1601** HOLLAND *Pliny* II. 424 Good it is to apply spunges to those accidents and infirmities of the body which require euaperation. **1610** BARROUGH *Meth. Physick* III. lxii. (1639) 198 If the evill be waxed old, you must use suffumigations, and evaporations made of aromatick things.

6. *attrib.*, as ***evaporation-gage***.

1874 KNIGHT *Dict. Mech.*, *Evaporation-gage*, a graduated glass measure..to determine the ratio of evaporation in a given exposure.

evaporative (ɪ'væpərətɪv), *a.* [f. EVAPORATE *v.* + -IVE; cf. Fr. *évaporatif, -ive*, late L. *ēvapōrātīv-us*.] **a.** Pertaining to or producing evaporation.

1668 WILKINS *Real Char.* 341. **1823** COLERIDGE *Rem.* (1836) II. 371 The evaporation..froze the fluid at the two ends, that is, at a given distance from the greatest intensity of the evaporative process. **1887** *Pall Mall G.* 7 Dec. 12/1 The average evaporative power of petroleum was found to be 9·82 lbs. of water per lb. of fuel.

b. ***evaporative cooling***: the cooling (of an engine) in which the heat is removed by the evaporation of a liquid coolant.

1931 A. H. R. FEDDEN in *Handbk. Aeronaut.* (R. Aeronaut. Soc.) vi. 450 The commonest methods of maintaining the cylinder temperatures within reasonable limits are by water cooling, air cooling, evaporative cooling and liquid cooling. **1934** *Aircraft Engineering* Nov. 290/3 In a system working on the evaporative cooling principle the water is introduced into the engine jackets at..boiling point.

evaporator (ɪ'væpəreɪtə(r)). [f. as prec. + -OR.]

1. One who or that which evaporates.

1883 CAIRD in *Scotsman* 23 Nov. 9/7 A scepticism which evaporates all thought, at the same time evaporates the sceptical evaporator.

2. *spec.* Any apparatus for evaporating solutions, drying fruits, etc.

1827 FARADAY *Chem. Manip.* xxiv. 629 A bent tube evaporator. **1850** *Nat. Encycl.* XI. 594/1 A series of evaporating coppers or pans..These evaporators are placed over a long flue, etc. **1888** *Pall Mall G.* 9 May 12/1 An evaporator..which, besides drying fruit, may be used to bake and roast.

evapo'rimeter. Also -ometer. [f. EVAPORATION + -(I)METER, Gr. μέτρον measure. Cf. Fr. *évaporomètre*.] An instrument for measuring the quantity of a liquid evaporated in a given time; an atmometer.

1828 WEBSTER cites *Jrnl. Science*, Evaporometer. **1876** *Catal. Sci. App. S. Kens.* 396 *Evaporimeter.* **1881** *Nature* XXIV. 387 An evaporimeter with constant level has been recently described by Professor Fornioni.

evaporite (ɪ'væpəraɪt). *Geol.* [f. EVAPOR(ATE *sb.*: see -ITE[1].] A deposit of sodium chloride or other salts resulting from the evaporation of a body of water.

1924 C. P. BERKEY in *Bull. N.Y. State Mus.* CCLI. 116 The genetic idea is carried better if the product of evaporation were called an *evaporate*, as Doctor Grabau does in his work on Salt Deposits, and the product of reaction by mixing were called a *reactionate*. Perhaps one could write them *evaporite* and *reactionite*. **1949** *Mineral. Mag.* XXVIII. 621 (*heading*) The lower evaporite bed. **1965** A. HOLMES *Princ. Physical Geol.* (ed. 2) iv. 78 Salt deposits (evaporites), such as are left behind when salt lakes dry up, or when enclosed bodies of sea water are strongly evaporated. **1967** *Oceanogr. & Marine Biol.* V. 131 Evaporite sediments of Mississippian age have caused similar uplift in nearby Nova Scotia.

Hence **evapo'ritic** *a.*, pertaining to, characteristic of, an evaporite.

1951 *Jrnl. Sedimentary Petrol.* XXI. 75/1 In the upper Gulf Coast area, evaporites occur in the Ferry Lake, with showings of gypsum and evaporitic dolomite on the outcrop near Austin. **1969** *Daily Tel.* 13 Jan. 10/7 An evaporitic area is an arid region where evaporation prevails.

evaporize (ɪ'væpəraɪz), *v.* [f. E- *pref.*[2] + VAPORIZE.] = EVAPORATE *v.* I. *lit.* and *fig.*

1832 H. H. WILSON *Ess. & Lect.* (1862) I. 351 Put water over the fire in a boiler, and the fire will evaporise the water. **1836** I. TAYLOR *Phys. Th. Another Life* (1858) 214 In worlds where our bodies would instantly congeal, or would as suddenly be evaporized.

†**e'vaporous**, *a. Obs.* [f. EVAPOR-ATE + -OUS.] Of the nature of an evaporation.

1694 E. HALLEY in *Phil. Trans.* XVIII. 184 The evaporous effluvia of Water.

evapotranspiration (ɪ,væpəʊtrɑːnspɪ'reɪʃən, -træns-). [f. EVAPO(RATION + TRANSPIRATION 2.]

The conversion of water to water vapour, from the soil by evaporation and from plants by transpiration; the amount of water so lost.

1948 *Geogr. Rev.* XXXVIII. 55 The combined evaporation from the soil surface and transpiration from plants, called 'evapotranspiration', represents the transport of water from the earth back to the atmosphere, the reverse of precipitation. **1958** *New Biol.* XXV. 52 The hydrologic cycle of an area of land receiving all its water as precipitation can be expressed by the equation P = E + R ± S where P = precipitation, E = evapotranspiration (interception by vegetation, evaporation from the soil and transpiration by plants), R = run-off and S = changes in water storage.

†**e'vapour**, *v. Obs.* In 6–7 evapore, 7 -oure. [a. Fr. *évapore-r*, ad. late L. *ēvapōr-āre*: see EVAPORATE *v.*]

1. *trans.* To send up in vapour; to emit.

1615 G. SANDYS *Trav.* (1632) 243 Ætna..black clouds euaporeth to skies.

2. *intr.* To be exhaled or given out like a vapour; = EVAPORATE *v.* 6 b.

1545 RAYNOLD *Byrth Mankynde* 38 The yealowisshe swet which euaporith continually from the skin of thinfant whylst it is in the womb. **1611** COTGR. s.v. *Eau* [as in Raynold]. **1612** STURTEVANT *Metallica* (1854) 96 No..unsauory smells euapoure out or presse through them.

†**3.** *trans.* To subject to a vapour bath; to steam. *Obs.*

1543 TRAHERON *Vigo's Chirurg.* II. xiii. 60 It sufficeth than to evapore the mattier by the decoction of thynges anodyne (that is to say) whiche take away payne.

evasible (ɪ'veɪsɪb(ə)l), *a.* [f. L. *ēvās-* ppl. stem of *ēvādĕre* to EVADE + -IBLE.] Capable of being evaded.

18.. OGILVIE cites *Eclectic Rev.*

evasion (ɪ'veɪʒən). Also 5 evasyown, 6 evacion, -tion. [a. Fr. *évasion*, ad. late L. *ēvāsiōn-em*, n. of action f. *ēvādĕre*: see EVADE.]

1. The action of escaping from confinement or danger; escape.

Now rare, exc. in writers influenced by Fr. usage.

1460 CAPGRAVE *Chron.* 306 Al that tyme fro his [Oldcastle's] evasion [from the Tower] about Myhilmesse onto the Ephihanie. **1601** BP. BARLOW *Def. Prot. Relig.* 175 By hope of euasion from Purgatorie in time. **1612** T. TAYLOR *Comm. Titus* iii. 4 In any miserie we shall haue assured felicitie..in temptation assurance of euasion. **1633** P. FLETCHER *Purple Isl.* III. xi, The next fair river..Topping the hill, breaks forth in fierce evasion. **1779** J. MOORE *View Soc. Fr.* II. lii. 29 Contemplating the happy evasion he had made from the cabinets at Frankfort. **1834** *Blackw. Mag.* XXXV. 618 An account of the evasion of Louis XVI, and the arrest of the unfortunate monarch at Varennes. **1871** H. AINSWORTH *Tower Hill* II. x, The plan of evasion was frustrated by the prisoner's irresolution.

†**b.** Means, opportunity, or way of escape. *Obs.*

1563–87 FOXE *A. & M.* (1684) III. 271 [God] in the midst of the Temptation will make such an evasion, as, etc. **1613** HEYWOOD *Brazen Age* Wks. 1874 III. 211 Ere you enwrap your selfe into these perils, Whence there is no euasion. **1650** *Sc. Metr. Ps.* lxxxviii. 8 So Shut up, that I find no evasion for me. **1734** tr. *Rollin's Anc. Hist.* (1827) IX. 250

The unhappy woman, who found herself without evasion or resource, swallowed the draught.

2. The action of avoiding or escaping (a blow, missile, pursuit, etc.) by artifice or contrivance.

1657 S. PURCHAS *Pol. Flying-Ins.* I I In a storm they [Bees] will help themselves by flying under the Lee-side of an hedge, [etc.]..But if it bee a plain Champaign Country, where evasions avail nothing; then, etc. **1822** FORSYTH *Roland's Mod. Art Fencing* 201 *Evasion* means to avoid being reached by a thrust, even when you are near enough to receive it.

3. The action of evading (a duty, law, requisition, an argument, charge, etc.); dodging, prevarication, shuffling. Also, an instance of this.

1603 SHAKS. *Meas. for M.* I. i. 51 No more euasion: We haue with leauen'd, and prepared choice Proceeded to you, therefore take your honors. **1672** MARVELL *Reh. Transp.* I. 139 Perhaps he said only for evasion. **1685** H. MORE *Paralip. Proph.* 447 There is no evasion from the strength of this Argument. **1711** HEARNE *Collect.* (Oxf. Hist. Soc.) III. 210 But this I looked on as Evasion. **1746** WESLEY *Princ. Methodist* 9, I have found this in many of you, i.e. much subtlety, much Evasion and Disguise. **1783** BURKE *Rep. Affairs India* Wks. XI. 53 He was ordered at once to furnish 5,000 horse..'on evasion' he was declared a violator of treaties. **1818** CRUISE *Digest* (ed. 2) V. 376 To do it..is artifice and evasion. **1846** PRESCOTT *Ferd. & Is.* I. vii. 326 If the prisoner..was suspected of evasion, he was subjected to the torture. *a* **1862** BUCKLE *Misc. Wks.* (1872) I. 71, I deem anonymous writing of every kind to be an evasion of responsibility. **1868** J. H. BLUNT *Ref. Ch. Eng.* I. 59 The king's licence for the evasion of the act.

b. The means of evading; an evasive argument, shuffling excuse, subterfuge.

c **1425** WYNTOUN *Cron.* VIII. i. 112 And be the text þai decerne all thai casis, but exceptyown: By that is nane evasyown. *a* **1533** FRITH *Disput. Purgat.*, I say that this their evasion is nothing worth. **1581** MARBECK *Bk. of Notes* 669 The prohibition goeth before the vowe, wherefore this euation can haue no place. **1621** BURTON *Anat. Mel.* I. ii. III. xiii. (1651) 118 The meaner sort have no evasion why they should not be counted mad. **1777** PRIESTLEY *Philos. Necess.* ii. 19 By such poor evasions do some persons think to shelter themselves from the force of conviction. **1845** S. AUSTIN *Ranke's Hist. Ref.* I. 451 A miserable evasion, which did not in the least touch the assertion of his adversary. **1874** GREEN *Short Hist.* iv. 171 The towns..could generally force the Crown by evasions and delays to a compromise.

4. In primary Latin sense: Going out, exit, sallying forth. *rare*.

a **1659** OSBORN *Queries* Wks. (1673) 605 And from this the whole World comes to be so universally Inhabited, Every Family seeking rest by Evasion. **1669** FLAMSTEED in Rigaud *Corr. Sc. Men* (1841) II. 81 In the eclipse he ought to observe the spurious and the true shades, and their evasions from the moon's superficies. **1837** DE QUINCEY *Revolt Tartars* Wks. IV. 144 If the Kalmuck evasion should prosper.

evasive (ɪˈveɪsɪv), *a.* [ad. Fr. *évasif, -ive*, f. L. *ēvās-* ppl. stem of *ēvādĕre* (see EVADE) + -IVE.]

1. Of persons: Seeking to evade; addicted to evasion, shuffling.

1725 POPE *Odyss.* I. 530 Thus he, though conscious of the ethereal guest, Answer'd evasive of the sly request. **1785** PALEY *Mor. Philos.* (1818) II. 404 The..honest workman will be employed, in preference to..the fraudulent, and evasive. **1794** BURKE *Sp. agst. W. Hastings* Wks. XV. 107 He had been dilatory, evasive, shuffling, and unwilling to pay that which, however unwilling, evasive, and shuffling, he did pay.

2. Of actions or utterances: Tending to evasion; containing or characterized by evasion. Const. *of*. Esp. in phr. (*to take*) ***evasive action***: of a pilot, (to take) action designed to avoid having his aircraft attacked; hence, in general use, (to take) action to avoid any kind of trouble or unpleasantness.

1744 BERKELEY *Siris* §107 Though evasive arts will, it is feared, prevail so long as distilled spirits of any kind are allowed. **1772** *Ann. Reg.* 20/2 Terms apparently inoffensive, and evasive of their real and essential meaning. **1777** SHERIDAN *Sch. Scand.* III. i, He has received nothing but evasive promises of future service. **1820** SCOTT *Monast.* xi, Objections which the Sub-Prior treated as evasive. **1848** MACAULAY *Hist. Eng.* II. 451 The president, completely taken by surprise, stammered out a few evasive phrases. **1940** *War Illustr.* 10 Feb. 124/1 The formation opens out and we do a bit of dodging. 'Evasive Action' they call it in the official reports. **1941** M. W. MONKS in Michie & Graebner *Lights of Freedom* iv. 58 Fighter pilots' combat reports include 'I took evasive action', and the W.A.A.F.s adopted it in describing their adventures on dates. **1961** J. HELLER *Catch-22* (1962) v. 49 There was no established procedure for evasive action. All you needed was fear.

3. Elusive, evanescent.

1881 C. DE KAY *Vision of Nimrod* vi. 113 Above the cities of the plain the tender Evasive strains dropt gently from the sky.

4. as *sb.* An evasive phrase or speech.

a **1734** NORTH *Exam.* (1740) 90 The Party..followed their Game full Cry..without much Trouble about Precautions and Evasives. *Ibid.* 399 What may not be said and wrote, if this Author's Evasives may pass such as—it seems, many believed?

Hence **e'vasively** *adv.*, in an evasive manner, by an evasion. **e'vasiveness**, the quality of being evasive.

1736 BAILEY (folio), *Evasively*, craftily, deceitfully. *a* **1804** J. BRYANT (T), I answered evasively, or at least indeterminately. **1848** MACAULAY *Hist. Eng.* II. 502 Searching questions were put, and were evasively answered. **1883** *Rules of Supreme Crt.* Order xix. I. 19 When a party..denies an allegation of fact..he must not do so evasively. **1730-6** BAILEY (folio), *Evasiveness*, evading quality. **1863** GEO. ELIOT *Romola* III. xxvii, That self-justifying evasiveness into which he was often hurried in public. **1877** MORLEY *Crit. Misc.* Ser. II. 288 Most recent controversies are marked by obliqueness, evasiveness, a shiftiness of issue.

†**eva'sorious**, *a.* *Obs. rare*$^{-1}$. [as if f. L. **ēvāsor*, agent-n. f. *ēvādĕre* (see EVADE) + -(I)OUS: cf. *censorious*.] = EVASIVE.

1687 H. MORE *Contn. Remark. Stor.* (1689) 439 The tergiversations of the Incredulous, and their evasorious Pretences.

eve (iːv), *sb.*[1] Forms: (3 heve, 4 ave), 6-7 eeve, (7 eave, yeave), 3- eve. [var. of EVEN *sb.* (orig. 2 syll.); for the loss of the final *n* cf. *morrow*.]

1. = EVENING *sb.*[1] *lit.* and *fig. poet.* or *rhetorical.*

a **1250** *Owl & Night.* 432 Thu singest from eve fort a morȝe. *c* **1300** *St. Brandan* 214 The foweles tho hit eve was, bigonne here evesong. **1393** LANGL. *P. Pl.* C. VI. 117 On saterday at eue. *c* **1430** LYDG. *Bochas* IX. xxvii. (1554) 209 a, The fayre day men do prayse at eue. **1632** MILTON *L'Allegro* 130 Such sights as youthful poets dream On summer eves by haunted stream. **1667** —— *P.L.* I. 743 From Noon to dewy Eve. **1642** HOWELL *For. Trav.* ix. (Arb.) 47 The yeaue of the Conquering of France, is the morning of the Conquest of England. **1728** THOMSON *Spring* 19 Winter oft at Eve resumes the breeze. **1801** SOUTHEY *Thalaba* VIII. ii, In the light of the setting eve. **1833** HT. MARTINEAU *Charmed Sea* i. 4 To tell the tale from eve to morning, and from morning to eve again.

2. The evening, and hence usually the day before a Saint's day or other church festival. Hence *gen.* the evening, or the day, before any date or event.

c **1290** *Lives Saints* (1887) 76 In þe monþe of Ieneuer: a-seint Fabianes eue. *c* **1330** *Arth. & Merl.* 5391 The king ther stode with his meine On a palmesonnes aue. **1480** CAXTON *Chron. Eng.* ccxxvi. 231 In the same yere (1340) on mydsomer eue kyng edward bygan to sayll toward fraunce. **1548** HALL *Chron.* 82 b, Christmas eve. **1571** HANMER *Chron. Irel.* (1633) 123, 23rd of August being Saint Bartholomewes Eeve. *a* **1662** BP. B. DUPPA *Rules to Devotion* (J.), Let the immediate preceding day be kept as the eve to this great feast. **1796** H. HUNTER tr. *St. Pierre's Stud. Nat.* (1799) III. 692 The tolling of bells..on the eve of the funeral, on the day of it, and the last day of the year. **1828** SCOTT *F.M. Perth* iii, A father's blessing and St. Valentine's, whose blessed eve this chances to be. **1852** MISS YONGE *Cameos* II. viii. 102 On the eve of the New Year 1370 he [Chandos] set forth to retake the town of St. Salvin. **1884** BLUNT *Annot. Bk. Com. Prayer* 118 All Festivals have Eves, including Sundays, but only some have Vigils.

fig. **1647** CLARENDON *Contempl. on Ps.* Tracts (1727) 497 Our time in this world is but a short eve to an everlasting holiday.

3. *transf.* The time immediately preceding some event, action, etc. Chiefly in phrase ***to be on*** or ***upon the eve of***.

1780 T. JEFFERSON *Corr.* Wks. 1859 I. 269 We are upon the eve of a new arrangement as to our commissary's and quarter-master's departments. **1793** SMEATON *Edystone L.* §253 Being now arrived at the eve of October. **1806** A. DUNCAN *Nelson* 165 The hull on the eve of sinking. **1818** MARRYAT in *Parl. Deb.* 642 It was proposed to pass this bill just when they were upon the eve of a general election. **1875** BRYCE *Holy Rom. Emp.* ix. (ed. 5) 150 These regions seemed on the eve of being lost to Christendom.

4. *attrib.* and *Comb.*, chiefly in sense 1, as ***eve-repast, -time***; also **eve-feast** a feast on the evening before a festival or holy day; **eve-of-poll** *a.*, of, pertaining to, or occurring in the period immediately preceding the polling in an election; **eve-tide** = EVENTIDE; **eve-weed** (see quot.). Also EVE-CHURR, -JAR, -SONG, -STAR.

1711 BUDGELL *Spect.* No. 161 ¶2 A Country Wake, which you know in most Parts of England is the *Eve-Feast of the Dedication of our Churches. **1960** D. POTTER *Glittering Coffin* Postscript, p. iii, The most savagely controversial *eve-of-poll issue. **1960** *Guardian* 26 Feb. 6/3 A parliamentary candidate dying..while actually making his eve-of-poll speech. **1970** *Ibid.* 5 Nov. 2/5 Arguments..forcefully delivered by Senator Muskie, on an eve-of-poll television appearance. **1725** POPE *Odyss.* xx. 466 They rise, and bid prepare An *everepast. **1382** WYCLIF *Job* xxxviii. 32 Thou bringist..the *euetid sterre [**1388** euene sterre] vp on the sones of the erthe. *c* **1460** in Hearne *R. Glouc.* (1724) II. 484 Quene Alionore..childed a sone..in the Christesmasse eue [*printed* ene] In whiche euetid [*printed* ene-] appered in the West ii sterres, of fuyry colour. **1482** *Monk of Evesham* (Arb.) 36 Y laye in the chaptur hows tyl the euetyde of saturday foloyng. *c* **1275** LAY. 12858 þo hit com to þan *eue-time. *Ibid.* 17860. **1878** BRITTEN & HOLLAND *Dict. Eng. Plant-n.*, **Eveweed, Hesperis matronalis*, a name apparently invented by Dr. J. Hill in Herb. Brit. 1769, in reference to the fragrance of the blossoms in the evening.

eve, *sb.*[2] *slang* or *dial.* (See quots.)

1725 *New Cant. Dict.*, *Eves*, Hen-Roosts. **1847-78** HALLIWELL, *Eve*, a hen-roost.

†**eve**, *v.*[1] *Obs. rare.* [f. EVE *sb.*[1]] *trans.* To be the EVE (sense 2) of; to immediately precede.

1639 W. BERKLEY *Lost Lady* I. ii. in Hazl. *Dodsley* XII. 557 The night that eves the day of marriage.

eve, *v.*[2] *dial.* [repr. *yeve*, the regular (now obs.) southern form of GIVE. In midl. dialects *give* is used in same sense.] *intr.* To become moist or damp (cf. quots).

1847-78 in HALLIWELL. **1863** W. BARNES *Dorset Gloss.* s.v., 'We shall ha' rain: the stwones do eve.' **1880** *E. Cornw. Gloss.* s.v., A stone floor is said to eve before wet weather.

eve, var. of EAVE.

1746 W. HORSLEY *Fool* (1748) I. 29 A Stone Cornice..which..would make a pretty Eve over the Kitchen Windows.

'eve-churr. Also 7 -churre, 8 -chair, -chier, -chur. [f. EVE *sb.*[1] + CHURR: see CHURR-WORM.]

†**1.** The Mole-Cricket; also called ***churr-worm, fen-cricket***. ? *Obs.*

1658 ROWLAND *Moufet's Theat. Ins.* 1018 Of the Fen-Kricket, the Eve-churre, or the Chur-worm..we may call it Gryllotalpa; a Mole-kricket. **1668** WILKINS *Real Char.* II. v. §2 Fen-Cricket, Evechurr, Churr-worm. **1721-1800** BAILEY, *Eve-churr*, a Worm. **1726** [see CHURR-WORM].

2. The Nightjar, *Caprimulgus europæus*. Cf. CHURN-OWL.

1837 MACGILLIVRAY *Hist. Brit. Birds* III. 633. **1885** SWAINSON *Provinc. Names Brit. Birds* (E.D.S.) 96. **1890** *Daily News* 15 July 5/1 He is still a bird of many names. Some, like nightjar, eve-churr..are suggestive of his voice.

†**'eveck.** *Obs.* Also 6 evecke, 6-7 evick(e. [Of unknown origin; not connected with L. *ibex*.

The Welsh *ewig*, earlier *ewic*, means a sort of deer; but Canon Silvan Evans informs us that it was sometimes used vaguely; if this word was adopted into Eng. Higgins may have been misled by the fancy of an etymological connexion with *ibex*.]

(See quots.)

1585 J. HIGGINS tr. *Junius' Nomenclator* 50 Ibex..a kind of wild goate, and supposed to be that which they call the euecke. **1601** HOLLAND *Pliny* VIII. liii. I. 231 Among them [the goats kind] you shall haue the roe bucke, the shamois, the wilde goat called the Eveck [L. *ibices*]. *c* **1611** CHAPMAN *Iliad* IV. 122 The evicke [αἶξ ἄγριος] skipping from a rock.

evecristen(e, var. f. EVEN-CHRISTIAN, *Obs.*

evectant (ɪˈvɛktənt). *Math.* [f. L. *ēvect-* (see EVECTOR) + -ANT.] A contravariant formed by operating upon an invariant or contravariant with an evector.

1876 SALMON *Higher Algebra* 295 The discovery of evectants is Hermite's (*Camb. & Dubl. Math. Jrnl.* vi. 292).

e'vected, *ppl. a. rare.* [f. L. *ēvect-* ppl. stem of *ēvehĕre* to carry out + -ED[1].] Of the edge of a tube: Turned outwards, trumpet-shaped.

1861 HULME tr. *Moquin-Tandon* II. III. ii. 85 The aperture [of a Roman Snail's shell]..is provided with an evected [Fr. *évasé*] margin.

evectic, a dictionary spelling of EUECTIC.

evection (ɪˈvɛkʃən). [ad. L. *ēvectiōn-em*, n. of action f. *ēvehĕre* to carry out, f. *ē-* out + *vehĕre* to carry.]

†**1.** A lifting up; elevation, exaltation (in quot. *fig.*). *Obs. rare*$^{-1}$.

1656 in BLOUNT *Glossogr.* **1659** PEARSON *Creed* (1839) 359 [Joseph's] evection to the power of Egypt next to Pharaoh.

2. *Astron.* **a.** An inequality in the moon's longitude (see quot. 1787).

1706 PHILLIPS (ed. Kersey), *Evection*, or Libration of the Moon [The explanation confuses a and b.] **1787** BONNYCASTLE *Astron.* 422 Evection, an inequality in the motion of the moon, by which, at her quarters, her mean place differs from her true one by about $2\frac{1}{2}$ degrees more than at her conjunction and opposition. **1834** *Nat. Philos., Hist. Astron.* ix. 45/1 (Usef. Knowl. Soc.), The evection discovered by Ptolemy is greatest in the quadratures. **1847** WHEWELL *Hist. Induct. Sc.* I. 229 Such is the announcement of the celebrated discovery of the moon's second inequality afterwards called by Bulhialdus evection. **1879** NEWCOMB & HOLDEN *Astron.* 163 The disturbing action of the sun [upon the moon] produces a great number of other inequalities, of which the largest are the evection and the variation.

†**b.** Alleged to have been used for LIBRATION.

1706 [see a]. **1796** HUTTON *Math. Dict.* I. 450 Evection is used by some astronomers for the Libration of the moon.

†**3.** ***evection of heat***: the diffusion of heated particles through a fluid in the process of heating it; convection. *Obs.*

e'vectional, *a.* [f. prec. + -AL[1].] Relating or belonging to the evection.

e'vector. *Math.* [Agent-n. from L. *ēvehĕre* (see EVECTION).] An operator formed by substituting the differential operators d/da_0, d/da_1, d/da_2, etc. for the coefficients a_0, na_1, $\frac{1}{2}n(n-1)\ a_2$, etc. of a binary quantic.

eve-dropper, obs. form of EAVES-DROPPER.

1704 *Gentleman Instr.* (1732) 181 (D.) Soldiers..may be as guilty of thefts as eve-droppers or cut-purses.

'eve-'eel. *dial.* (See quots.)

1831 *Agric. Survey Forfarsh.* (Jam.), Muraena conger; conger eel..the name seems familiar even to the common people; they call it Eve-eel. **1867** SMYTH *Sailor's Word-bk.*, *Eve-eel*, a northern name for the conger; from the Danish *hav-aal*, or sea-eel.

'Eveish, *a. nonce-wd.* [f. *Eve* the first woman + -ISH[1].] Like Eve; curious.

1754 RICHARDSON *Grandison* vi. 210 (D.), I saw it was a long letter; I felt very Eveish, my dear.

eve-jar. [f. EVE *sb.*[1] + JAR.] = EVECHURR 2.

1789 G. WHITE *Selborne* (1853) 356 A notion that the fern-owl or eve-jarr..is very injurious to weanling calves. **1883** *Hampsh. Gloss.*, *Eve-jar*, the goat-sucker.

evel, obs. form of EVIL.

eveles, var. form of EVILLESS, *a. Obs.*

‖**evelié**, *a. Obs. rare*⁻¹. [a. Fr. *éveillé*, f. *éveiller* to awake.] Wide awake, sprightly.

1676 ETHEREDGE *Man of Mode* IV. i, A pretty kind of young woman..more evelié than our English women commonly are.

'Eve-like, *a.* [f. *Eve* the first woman + LIKE *a.*] Resembling Eve, or her characteristics.

a **1711** KEN *Psyche* Poet. Wks. 1721 IV. 213 To all the Daughters of laps'd Eve, Eve-like Concupiscences cleave.

†**e'vell**, *v. Obs. rare*⁻¹. [ad. L. *ēvell-ĕre*, f. *ē-* out + *vellĕre* to pluck.] *trans.* To pluck, pick (a flower).

1657 TOMLINSON *Renou's Disp.* 500 The flowers being evelled, new ones grow not again that year.

evelles, var. form of EVILLESS, *Obs.*

evelong: see EVENLONG.

even ('iːv(ə)n), *sb.* Forms: 1 ǽfen, ǽfan, *Mercian* éfen, *Northumbr.* éfern, 2–3 æfen, 2 afen, 3 *Orm.* efenn, 3–6 eaven, (3 æven, aven, 5 evon, ȝeven, -yn), 4–6 evin, -yn, ewin, -yn, 6 (heven), eeven, (9 *dial.* eem), 3– even. Also contracted 7 eevn, ev'n, 9 *dial.* e'en. See also EVE. [OE. *ǽfen*, *éfen*, *éfern*, neut. and masc., cogn. with OFris. *ȧvond*, *êwnd*, OS. *âband* (Du. *avond*), OHG. *âband* (MHG. *âbent*, mod.G. *abend*) masc.; perh. also with the synonymous ON. *aptann*, *aftann* (Sw. *afton*, Da. *aften*), though this may be of different origin, cogn. with AFTER. The OE. forms appear to agree only in the root (OAryan *ēp* or *ēbh*) with the other Teut. forms: the OTeut. type of the OHG., OS., OFris. forms would be **ǣbando-*, that of the OE. *ǽfen*, *éfen* would be **ǣbinjo-* or **ǣbunjo-*. The ONorthumb. *éfern* is app. an alteration of *éfen(n*; cf. ONorthumb. *wœ́stern*, *festern* (= WS. *wésten*, *fæsten*), and OFris. forms like *epernia* to open.

One hypothesis as to the relation of the forms is that **ǣbando-* represents a pre-Teut. **ēpont-*, a pr. pple. act., and that derivatives of a corresponding passive pple. occur in ON. *aptann*:— **ēptono-*) and OE. *ǽfen* (:— **ǣbunjo-*:— **ēptṇyo-* or **ēpṇyo-*. The etymological sense is unknown; a not inappropriate meaning for the act. and pass. formations is suggested by Gr. ἤπιος, mild, gentle (sometimes used with reference to temperature) which may possibly belong to the same root.]

1. The latter part or close of the day; evening. Also in phrases ***even and (nor) morn***; ***at even and at prime***, at all times of the day; ***good even***, a salutation (see further GOOD, GOOD EVEN); ***yestereven*** (Sc. *yestreen*), yesterday evening (see YESTER). *Obs.* exc. *poet.* and *dial.*

Beowulf 1235 Ǽfen cwom and him Hroþgar ȝewat. *c* **950** *Lindisf. Gosp.* Mark vi. 47 Miððy efern woere wæs scip in middum sæes. *a* **1000** *Guthlac* 1216 (Gr.), Engel ufancundne, se mec efna ȝehwam..ȝesohte. *c* **1040** *Rule St. Benet* (ed. Logeman) 82 þæt þæt eis towyrcanne hi wyrcan oððe æfan. *a* **1123** *O.E. Chron.* an. 1106 On æfen ætywde an ..steorra. *c* **1200** ORMIN 1105 He wass all daȝȝ Unnclene anan till efenn. *c* **1205** LAY. 19570 þa hit wes eauen. *c* **1250** *Gen. & Ex.* 1675 Iacob wurð drunken, and euen cam. *c* **1340** *Cursor M.* 6385 (Fairf.), Fra heyuen þen come þaire fode.. euen & morne hit con falle. *c* **1430** LYDG. *Bochas* II. xxii. (1554) 58a, Socrates..wisest named at euen and at prime. *c* **1460** *Towneley Myst.*, *Oblacio Mag.* 125 We shalle not rest, even nor morne. **1535** COVERDALE *Ezek.* xii. 4 Thou thy self shalt go forth also at euen in their sight. **1538** BALE *Thre Lawes* 178 God geue ye good euen. **1591** SHAKS. *Two Gent.* v. ii. 42 She did intend confession At Patricks cell this even. **1600** —— *A.Y.L.* II. iv. 69 Peace I say; good euen to your friend. **1622** MAY *Virgil* (J.), The sun's orb both even and morn is bright. **1660** HOWELL *Dict.* s.v., Good even (or by contraction Goodeen). **1697** DRYDEN *Virg.* (J.), Th' unerring sun..declares, What the late ev'n or early morn prepares. **1759** JOHNSON *Rasselas* ii, From the dawn of morning to the close of even. **1816** J. WILSON *City of Plague* II. ii. 228 A plaintive tune..sung at fall of even. **1816** SCOTT *Old Mort.* x, 'My cousin winna stay ony langer, Mr. Halliday; sae, if ye please, gude-e'en t'ye.' **1826** DISRAELI *Viv. Grey* II. vi, Good even to you. **1843** BETHUNE *Sc. Fireside Stor.* 279 Daylight, done at four o'clock, Yields to the lang dark e'en.

2. The EVE of a holy day or church festival. Rarely in wider sense: The evening or the day before (a certain day or event). ***fastryn even*** (Sc.: now ***fastryn's e'en***) = SHROVE TUESDAY; ***the Kings' even*** = TWELFTH-NIGHT. *Obs.* exc. *dial.*

c **1330** R. BRUNNE *Chron.* (1810) 171 þe euen of þe Trinite vnder Acres R. gan aryue. **1375** BARBOUR *Bruce* x. 440 As apon fastryn even is The custom. **1398** TREVISA *Barth. De P.R.* IX. xxxi. (1495) 368 To Ester perteyneth the euyn therof that..is callyd..the holy Saterday. *c* **1420** *Chron. Vilod.* 1020 þe whiche in Mydwyntrus ȝevyn to þ'chirche dude gonne. **1463** *Bury Wills* (Camd. Soc.) 17 On the evyn [of the funeral] myn solempne dirige shalbe kept. **1483** CAXTON *G. de la Tour* D ij, Upon the vygyl or euen of our lady. *a* **1536** TINDALE *Prol. to Jonas* Wks. I. 450 The saints ..torment the souls in hell, if their evens be not fasted. **1549** CRANMER in Strype *Life* App. xl, Vigils, otherwise called Watchings, remain in the Calendars upon certain Saints' Evens. *a* **1572** KNOX *Hist. Ref.* Wks. 1846 I. 230 Upoun the Kinges Evin, when French men commonlie use to drynk liberallie. **1587** FLEMING *Contn. Holinshed* III. 1286/1 He died on Maie eeuen. **1623** MINSHEU s.v., An holy daies Euen. **1764** BURN *Poor Laws* 13 No labourer..shall take any hire..for the evens of feasts. **1855** ROBINSON *Whitby Gloss.*, *E'en*, Kessenmas e'en..Cannelmas e'en. *a* **1891** *Mod. dial.* (Sheffield), Christmas eem.

3. *attrib.* and *Comb.* (= 'evening'), as ***even-bell***, ***-blush***, ***-light***, ***-prayer***, ***-rising***, ***-time***; also **even-close**, the closing in of the evening; **even-fall**, the 'fall' or commencement of the evening; **even-fire**, evening gun; **evenglome** (*arch.*; revival of OE. *ǽfenglóm*), gloaming, twilight; **even-mete**, *arch.* (OE. *ǽfen-mete*), evening-meal, supper; †**even-while**, eventide, eventime. Also EVENSONG, EVEN-STAR, EVENTIDE.

a **1450** *Le Morte Arth.* 2236 By the tyme of *euyn belle. **1835** BROWNING *Paracelsus* Wks. I. 5 From *even-blush to midnight. **1845** HIRST *Poems* 23 Came *even-close And darkness; yet they turned not back. **1814** SOUTHEY *Paraguay* Ded., One thrush was heard from morn to *even-fall. **1859** W. H. GREGORY *Egypt* II. 200 Flamingoes..winging their rosy flight at evenfall across the bay. **1879** H. DUVAR *D'Anville's Fleet* in *Poems of Places*, *Brit. Amer.* 34 At *even-fire the bells were rung. *a* **1000** *Guthlac* 1265 (Gr.), From *æfenglome oðþæt eastan cwom..dægredwoma. **1871** M. COLLINS *Inn of Strange Meetings* 25 The robins singing in the evenglome. *Beowulf* 5014 Siððan *æfen-leoht under heofenes hador beholen weorþeð. *a* **1400** *MS. Cantab.* Ff. i. 6. f. 66 (Halliw.), Sche..sey it is ferr in the nyght, And I swere it is evenlight. *a* **1440** *Sir Degrev.* 1601 Syre Degrivaunt at evene-lyȝth Armede hym and hys knyȝth. *c* **975** *Rushw. Gosp.* Matt. xxvi. 26 Æt þæm *æfen-mete. **1848** LYTTON *Harold* xi. vii, The even-mete will summon thee soon. **1660** HOWELL *Dict.* s.v., Evensong, or *Even Prayer. **1601** HOLLAND *Pliny* I. 13 The planet Mercurie seldome hath his *euen rising in Pisces. *c* **1000** *Ags. Gosp.* Mark xi. 11 þa *æfen tima [*c* **1160** *Hatton* afen time] wæs he ferde to bethaniam. *c* **1205** LAY. 17860 A þan auen time. **1870** ROSSETTI *Dante at Verona* xxxiv, Flushed in the limpid eventime. *c* **1350** *Will. Palerne* 1747 To heiȝ vs hastily henne..euenly þis *euen while.

even ('iːv(ə)n), *a.* Forms: 1 ebn, efen, æfen, efn, emn, *in comb.* em-, 2–3 efn(e, æfne, *Orm.* efenn, effen, emne, 3–4 evene, 4–6 evin(e, -yn, ewyn(e, (5 evan, heven, 6 evne), 6–7 ea-, eeven, 4– even. [Common Teutonic: OE. *efen*, *efn*, by assimilation *emn* = OFris. *even*, *evin*, OS. *eban* (Du. *even*, *effen*), OHG. *eban*, *epan* (Ger. *eben*), ON. *iafn*, *iamn* (Da. *jevn*, Sw. *jemn*), Goth. *ibns*:—OTeut. **ebno-*.

The word has not yet been satisfactorily connected with any other Teut. or Aryan word; hence it is uncertain whether the primary sense was 'level' or 'equal, like'.]

1. a. Of a piece of ground, a country, etc.: Flat, plain, level, not hilly or sloping.

c **893** K. ÆLFRED *Oros.* I. ii. §4 Seo burg wæs ȝetimbred an fildum lande & on swiþe emnum. *c* **1400** *Destr. Troy* 2078 Set full sad on a soile euyn. **1605** SHAKS. *Lear* IV. vi. 3 *Glo.* Me thinkes the ground is eeuen. *Edg.* Horrible steepe. **1605** VERSTEGAN *Dec. Intell.* iv. (1628) 100 They are euen and plaine without any hilles or hilly grounds. **1692** BENTLEY *Boyle Lect.* 78 Our sight..would be terminated..in the largest and evenest plain by the very convexity of the earth. **1705** ADDISON *Italy* (1733) 175 The present Face of Rome is much more Even and Level than it was formerly. **1859** TENNYSON *Geraint & Enid* 239 At last they..climb'd upon a fair and even ridge.

b. Of uniform height.

1523 FITZHERB. *Husb.* §70 Beastes alone..wyll not eate a pasture euen, but leaue many tuftes and hygh grasse in dyuers places. **1593** SHAKS. *Rich. II*, III. iv. 36 All must be euen, in our Gouernment. **1601** B. JONSON *Poetaster* IV. ix, Both waies, I am too high; and thou, too lowe, Our Mindes are euen, yet. *a* **1626** DAVIES (J.), When he did set his foot in the middle, all the other parts lay flat and even.

c. In a level position; horizontal. *Obs.* exc. *Naut.* in phrase, ***(on) an even keel***.

1375 BARBOUR *Bruce* III. 136 He laid hym ewyn him beforn. *c* **1391** CHAUCER *Astrol.* II. §29 Lat thyn Astrelabie kowch adown evene upon a smothe grond. **1836** MARRYAT *Midsh. Easy* xxvi, The frigate was on an even keel. *c* **1850** *Rudim. Navig.* (Weale) 117 A ship is said to swim on an even keel when she draws the same quantity of water abaft as forwards. **1853** KANE *Grinnell Exp.* xxvi. (1856) 213, I wish it would give us an even keel.

2. Of surfaces or lines: Uniform, without inequality; smooth.

a **1225** *Ancr. R.* 2 þe on [riwle] riwleð þe heorte, þe makeð hire efne & smeðe, wiðute knotte & dolke of woh inwit. **1340** *Ayenb.* 151 Efterward he deþ al be reule, þet makeþ þane wal emne. *a* **1350** *Childh. Jesus* 1382 þis treo mot beo..At eithur ende euene and quarre. **1535** COVERDALE *1 Chron.* xiii. 15 The valleys were eauen both [Luther *dass alle Grunde eben waren*] towarde the East and towarde the West. **1552** ABP. HAMILTON *Catech.* (1884) 28 Ane biggare can nocht make ane evin up wal without direction of his lyne. **1577** B. GOOGE *Heresbach's Husb.* III. (1586) 141 b, Looke..that..the grounde bee made fayre and even, some thing hanging. **1580** BARET *Alv.* E 364 To make eeuen with the rule, *exæquare ad regulam*. **1664** EVELYN *Kal. Hort.* (1729) 202 Cut close and even. **1693** DRYDEN tr. *Persius* vi, To see a beggar's brat in riches flow, Adds not a wrinkle to my even brow. **1697** —— *Virg. Georg.* IV. 213 He knew to rank his Elms in even Rows. **1704** NEWTON *Optics* (J.), The superficies of such plates are not even, but have many cavities and swellings. **1712** J. JAMES tr. *Le Blond's Gardening* 34 Parterres..should be flat, eaven, and disengaged. *c* **1720** PRIOR *Poems*, *Charity*, Charity..Lays the rough paths of peevish nature even. **1781** COWPER *Anti-Thelyp.* 47 Smooth and even as an iv'ry ball. **1848** MACAULAY *Hist. Eng.* II. 486 The water in the bay was as even as glass. **1858** HAWTHORNE *Fr. & It. Jrnls.* I. 213 Hedges..as even as a brick-wall at the top and sides.

3. Uniform alike throughout (in colour, texture, consistency, quality, etc.).

1821 CRAIG *Lect. Drawing* vii. 406 Nor can it..produce a light even tint of any extent. **1846** TROTTER in *Baxter's Lib. Pract. Agric.* (ed. 4) II. 347 These last [turnips] are..the evenest and best crop..The whole field is an even piece, not having suffered from the fly. **1883** F. M. CRAWFORD *Dr. Claudius* viii, The sky was of an even lead colour.

†**4.** Of a path: Straight, direct. Of movements or speech: Direct, straightforward. Of a visible object: Directly in front. *Obs.*

c **1200** ORMIN 9214 þær shulenn beon..effne & smeþe weȝȝess. *c* **1325** *Metr. Hom.* 48, I bid you mac the gates euin To Crist. *c* **1470** HARDING *Chron.* LXII. v, Constantyne sawe a crosse..full euine. **1594** HOOKER *Eccl. Pol.* I. viii. (1611) 17 As the straight way is most acceptable to him that trauaileth ..so in action that which doth lye the euenest betweene vs and the end we desire. **1599** SHAKS. *Hen. V*, IV. viii. 114 In plaine shock, and euen play of Battaile. **1602** —— *Ham.* II. ii. 298 Be euen and direct with me, whether you were sent for or no.

5. a. Level *with* (†*to*); neither higher or lower. *arch.*

a **1300** *Cursor M.* 11688 þe tre it boued doune..þe crope was euen wid þe rote. **1420** *E.E. Wills* (1882) 52 A flate ston off marbill, ewyn with the grounde. **1579** LYLY *Euphues* (Arb.) 135 When Demetrius wonne the Citie, and made it euen to the ground. **1611** BIBLE *Luke* xix. 44 And shall lay thee euen with the ground. **1626** PURCHAS *Pilgr.* (ed. 4) 434 The nether part of the Sunne seeming iust and euen with it. **1653** H. COGAN tr. *Pinto's Trav.* xxxvi. 142 On the out-side about eight and thirty foot high above the water, and on the in-side even with the ground. **1698** FROGER *Voy.* 33 Waiting till the Fish swim even with the Surface of the Water.

b. In the same plane or line (*with*). Also (of a course, etc.) parallel; (of the two ends of an object) in line with the centre.

a **1350** *Childh. Jesus* 1425 Josep swiþe glad was þo þat euene weren þe endes two. **1586** A. DAY *Eng. Secretary* (1625) A iiij, I have applied a number of Figures..and Tropes in the margent of every Epistle, even with the places where they are used. **1603** SHAKS. *Meas. for M.* IV. ii. 83 His life is paralel'd Euen with the stroke and line of his great Iustice. **1663** GERBIER *Counsel* 22 The Chimney to be made even with the upright of the wall. **1712** F. T. *Shorthand* 11 Write the Consonant in an even line with the foregoing Consonant. **1726** LEONI tr. *Alberti's Archit.* I. 72 b, You may ..make a..foundation for every particular Peer..lying directly even with the current of the water. **1748** *Anson's Voy* II. ii. 127 A ship to leeward, with her courses even with the horizon.

6. Accurately coincident or accordant; exactly adjusted; *spec.* in type-setting, ***to make even***, ***make even lines***, or ***end even***: to space out the last few lines of copy, so as to make the last a full line.

c **1400** *Rom. Rose* 5821 We been at one, By even accord of everichone. **1577** B. GOOGE *Heresbach's Husb.* II. (1586) 73 b, Good Grafters, thinke it best to hold the Graffe even with both hands. **1597** MORLEY *Introd. Mus.* 89 The third is a driuing waie in two crotchets and a minime, but odded by a rest, so that it neuer commeth euen till the close. **1703** MOXON *Mech. Exerc.* 277 Lay the streight edge even upon the line AE.

†**7.** Of computed results, statements, etc.: Exact, precise. Also, '(The) exact' (place etc.).

c **1300** *Cursor M.* 20834 (Edinb.) Qua wel can caste sal finde it euin. **1393** LANGL. *P. Pl.* C. XXIII. 270 Hevene haueþ evene numbre, and helle is with-oute numbre. *a* **1470** TIPTOFT *Caesar* xiii. (1530) 18 Fewe or none of them [ships] came to the even port. **1551** RECORDE *Pathw. Knowl.* II. xliv, It maketh iust xxix, the euen halfe of fifty and eight. **1601** SHAKS. *All's Well* v. iii. 326 To make the euen truth in pleasure flow.

8. Of actions, movements, processes, continuous states: Uniform, free from fluctuations. Of the mind, temper, etc.: Free from variations, 'equal', equable, unruffled.

c **897** K. ÆLFRED *Gregory's Past.* xlii. 306 Ðæs wisan monnes mod bið suiðe emn. *a* **1240** *Sawles Warde* in *Cott. Hom.* 265 þole wið efne heorte þe dom of rihtwisnesse. **1297** R. GLOUC. (1724) 193 þer come in tuelf olde men myd euene pas þere. **1382** WYCLIF *Baruch* iv. 5 Thou peple of God, be of euener inwitt. *c* **1386** CHAUCER *Clerk's T.* 811 With euene herte I rede yow tendure This strook of ffortune or of auenture. *c* **1440** *Promp. Parv.* 143 Euen in meuynge [*printed* menynge] or clothynge. **1561** T. NORTON *Calvin's Inst.* I. To Rdr., That I may with euen sufferance continue in the course of his holy calling. **1613** SHAKS. *Hen. VIII*, III. i. 37, I know my life so euen. **1710** ADDISON *Tatler* No. 192 ¶5 Persons of even Tempers and uniform Dispositions. **1766** JOHNSON in Boswell Feb., Pope's [horses] go at a steady even trot. **1770** LANGHORNE *Plutarch* (1879) I. 177/2 Pericles acquired..a firm and even tone of voice. **1850** TENNYSON *In Mem.* lxxxv, My blood an even tenour kept. **1870** HUXLEY *Lay Serm.* xiv. 334 The even rhythm of the breathing of every one of us.

9. Equally balanced; in a state of equilibrium; 'not inclining to either side' (J.).

1579 GOSSON *Sch. Abuse* (Arb.) 39 Bearing her sword so euen, that neither the poore are trod vnder foote, nor the rich suffred to loke too hye. **1607** SHAKS. *Cor.* IV. vii. 37 He has A Noble seruant to them; but he could not Carry his honors eeuen. **1655–60** STANLEY *Hist. Philos.* (1701) 188/1 Its proper place..by reason of its even weight is the Centre. **1667** MILTON *P.L.* I. 349 In even ballance down they light. **1703** MOXON *Mech. Exerc.* 69 The Hand must be carried along the whole length..exactly even. **1742** YOUNG *Nt. Th.* VIII. 1180 An Eye impartial, and an even Scale. *c* **1819** BENTHAM *Wks.* (1843) II. 446 The balance is now restored. The two scales hang even. **1863** W. PHILLIPS *Speeches* vii. 155 He holds the scales of justice most exactly even. **1866** J. MARTINEAU *Ess.* I. 67 The balance cannot be expected to hang..even.

10. a. Of accounts, affairs, a reckoning: Having no balance or debt on either side; 'square.'

1551 T. WILSON *Logike* (1567) 2 b, Arithmetik by nomber can make Reckenynges to be euen. **1596** HARINGTON

Metam. Ajax Pref. (1814) 14 For a man to make even his reckonings. **1605** Bp. Hall *Medit. & Vows* B. 2 §4 It hath beene an olde and true Proverbe, Oft and even reckoninges make long friends. **1712** Arbuthnot *John Bull* (1755) 14 How is it possible for a man of business to keep his affairs even in the world at this rate? *a* **1716** South (J.), Even reckoning makes lasting friends.

b. *to be even*: to be square or quits; to have settled accounts. †*to make even*: to square accounts. †*to make even for*: to compensate for.

1511 *Plumpton Corr.* p. cxviii, Memor. That Sir Robert Plompton..is even for every thing to this present day of August. **1594** R. Haydocke tr. *Lomazzo* To Rdr., I haue bettered mine, or at the least made even for such other imperfections, as can hardly escape the best translators. **1618** Bolton *Florus* IV. ix. (1636) 308 By the slaughter of Pacorus, wee were even for Crassus overthrow. **1622** S. Ward *Christ All in All* (1627) 36 When he had distributed all he had to the poore, and made euen with his reuenues, etc. **1637** Rutherford *Lett.* No. 113 (1862) i. 283, I know that Christ and I shall never be Even: I shall die in His debt. **1661** Pepys *Diary* 25 June, I made even with my father and the two drapers for the cloths I sent to sea lately. **1780** Johnson *Let. to Mrs. Thrale* 21 June, I wish I had been with you to see the Isle of Wight; but I shall perhaps go some time without you, and then we shall be even.

c. *to be even* (†*evens*) *with*: to be quits *with*; to have one's revenge upon.

14.. *Merch. & Son* in Halliw. *Nugæ Poet.* 32 My fadur ys evyn wyth all the worlde. **1589** *Hay any Work* A ij b, Ile be euen with them to. **1626** *Buck. Imp.* (1889) 63 Wherre uppon hee vowed to bee even with our Inglish. **1655–60** Stanley *Hist. Philos.* (1701) 111/1, I will be even with you for this scorn. *a* **1719** Addison (J.), The publick is always even with an author who has not a just deference for them. **1752** A. Breck Stewart in *Scots Mag.* July (1753) 339/1 He would be evens with him. **1794** Mrs. Radcliffe *Myst. Udolpho* xxvii, I was determined to be even with Barnardine for refusing to tell me the secret. **1831** Lytton *Godolph.* 9 Come out, and I'll be even with you, pretty one. **1875** Jowett *Plato* (ed. 2) III. 264 Verily I would be even with thee, if I had the power.

d. *to get even* (*with*): to take one's revenge (on), to retaliate (against). orig. *U.S.*

1846 S. F. Smith *Theatr. Apprent.* 148, I took my seat with the hope of getting even. **1880** 'Mark Twain' *Tramp Abroad* I. xxv. 250 One should always 'get even' in some way, else the sore place will go on hurting. **1889** Barrère & Leland *Dict. Slang* I. 402/2 Those who think this country [*sc.* America] fails to get even with France for her unjust discrimination against American pork. **1906** F. H. Burnett *Shuttle* xxxiii. 330 There exists for people of a certain type a pleasure full-fed by the mere sense of having 'got even' with an opponent. Through-out his life he had made a point of 'getting even' with those who had irritatingly crossed his path. **1910** *Granta* 11 June 9, I feel that I can never get quite even with him again. **1923** L. J. Vance *Baroque* 40 Crooks ..blow the works to get even.

e. (*on*) *even terms* (see quots.). *Austral.* and *N.Z.*

1933 L. Acland in *Press* (Christchurch) 23 Sept. 13/7 *Cadet*, a young man working on a station to learn sheep-farming..often worked 'on even terms' but is now usually paid a low wage. **1941** Baker *Dict. Austral. Slang* 27 *Even Terms*, working for one's food.

11. That is a just mean between extremes; of proper magnitude or degree.

c **1386** Chaucer *Prol.* 83 Of his stature he was of evene lengthe. *c* **1470** Henry *Wallace* vi. 70 Be ewyn tyme off hyr age, A squier Schaw..hyr gat in mariage. **1577** B. Googe *Heresbach's Husb.* II. (1586) 80 b, There must be an even temperature amongest these extreamities. **1653** Urquhart *Rabelais* I. xxxiv, The rest of his traine came after him by even journeys [Fr. *a justes journées*] at a slower pace.

12. Of conduct, laws, and their administration: Equal towards all, just, impartial. †Also of weights and measures: Just, true.

c **1000** Ælfric *Lev.* xix. 36 Habbaþ..emne wæʒa and emne ʒemetu and sestras. **1382** Wyclif *Lev.* xix. 46 Riȝt balaunce, and euen ben the weiȝtis, ryȝt bushel, and euen sextarye. **1637** Earl Stirling *Doomsday, 6th Hour*, Yet were their aimes and ends in th'end not eaven. **1719** W. Wood *Surv. Trade* 17 The wisdom of the legislative Power consists in keeping an even hand to promote all. **1775** Johnson *Tax no Tyr.* 33 Though power has been diffused with the most even hand.

†**13. a.** Equal in rank, dignity, or power; in earlier use with *dat.* or with *til*, *to*; also *absol.* *Obs.*

c **1205** Lay. 22928 At þine borde..scal þe heh3e beon æfne [*c* **1275** efne] þan loȝe. *a* **1240** *Lofsong* in *Cott. Hom.* 209 Þe oli goste þet is efne wið þe and wið þin eadi feder. *a* **1340** Hampole *Psalter* ii. 7 Þe son is of his fadire..euen til hym in godhed. *c* **1380** Wyclif *Sel. Wks.* III. 341 Sum men seien þat he [the pope] is even wiþ the manheed of Crist. *c* **1400** *Apol. Loll.* 85 We awe not to arett..þingis formid of mannis craft, heyar nor euen to man in kynd. *a* **1450–1530** *Myrr. our Ladye* 103 These thre persones . were alyke euen in all thynges. **1565** Jewel *Repl. Harding* (1611) 333 The Figure may not be far off from the Truth: otherwise it were no Figure: Neither may it be euen, and one with the Truth. **1674** N. Fairfax *Bulk & Selv.* 117 Nevertheless, we may hold such a body to be even with another. **1720** Prior *For my Tombstone*, To me 'twas given to die: To thee 'tis given to live: alas one moment sets us even. **1754** Richardson *Grandison* I. xxxix. 297 Is there no way to be even with him in any one thing?

b. *to be even with*: to be on a par, on equal terms *with*.

1593 Nashe *Four Lett. Confut.* 86 You wil..imbrace anie religion which will be euen with the profession that fauors not you. **1633** Earl Manch. *Al Mondo* (1636) 24 For all this, man is even with Death. **1682** N. O. *Boileau's Lutrin* I. 250 We may with both in time be even. **1733** Fielding *Intrig. Chamberm.* i. v, I am not the first gentleman..who has been even with his master.

¶**c.** The *Combs.* of *even-* are sometimes resolved, so that the adj. in apparent syntactical concord expresses the sense of L. *co-*, Eng. *fellow-*, *joint-*.

a **1000** *Voc.* in Wr.-Wülcker 214 *Coheres*, efn yrfeweard. **1382** Wyclif *Ezek.* vii. 16 Thei shulen be in mounteyns as culueres of euyn valeys [Vulg. *convallium*]. **1482** *Monk of Evesham* (Arb.) 103 He..schalle be an euyn heyre with me eternaly. **1483** *Cath. Angl.* 118 Euen, *equus, co-, equalis*.

14. a. Equal in magnitude, number, quantity, etc. *even break*: see BREAK *sb.*[1] 18; *even chance*: an equal chance that something will or will not happen; *even money*: odds in betting that offer the gambler the chance of winning as much as he has staked; also sb. pl. *evens*.

c **1205** Lay. 29103 He hafde genge efne wið Gurmunde. *Ibid.* 30835 For his æfne wiht of golde. **1387** Trevisa *Higden* (Rolls) I. 325 Whan þe day and þe nyȝt beeþ euen. *c* **1420** *Pallad. on Husb.* I. 1121 Hardde pitche, and wex, take even weight. *c* **1449** Pecock *Repr.* III. i. 280 The north schal be eendid by euen terme. *c* **1450** *Castle Hd. Life St. Cuthb.* (Surtees) 931 With' childre of his euen elde. **1495** *Act 11 Hen. VII*, c. 39 The seid Edmond to pay yerely..CCCCli. at the same festis by evyn porcions. **1577** B. Googe *Heresbach's Husb.* III. (1586) 115 The legges and the thies.. ought to be even [L. *æqualia*], straight, and sound. **1660** Bloome *Archit.* A c, Three even parts. **1749** Fielding *Tom Jones* XII. v, Partridge..kept even pace with Jones. **1814** Scott *Ld. of Isles* III. xviii, Were my Monarch's order given, Two shafts should make our number even. **1816** Jane Austen *Emma* II. viii. 149 It was an even chance that Mrs. Churchill were not in health or spirits for going. **1834** T. Medwin *Angler in Wales* I. 85 It is wax and caoutchouck even quantities, melted together. **1891** N. Gould *Double Event* xxvii, The book-makers were roaring themselves hoarse. 'Even money Perfection, 3 to 1 Captain Cook.' **1907** *Westm. Gaz.* 25 June 10/2 Two even-money chances—Troutbeck and the White Knight—won. **1964** A. Wykes *Gambling* ix. 223 The Biarritz system is more for players who find the even-chance systems too slow and too tame. *Ibid.* 225 The *noir* is an even-money bet.

b. *of even date*: of the same date. (Common in U.S.; in England chiefly in legal language.)

1681 *Indenture* 10 Mar., Reciting an Indenture of even date therewith. **1885** *Weekly Notes* 142/1 By deed of even date he covenanted to pay all calls in respect of the shares.

c. *absol.* (See quot.)

1589 Puttenham *Eng. Poesie* III. xix. (Arb.) 222 Ye haue another figure [*marg.* Parison] which we may call the figure of euen, because it goeth by clauses of egall quantitie.

d. *even Stephen* (or *Steven*): a *colloq.* rhyming phrase used as an intensive for 'even' in various senses; *spec.* = FIFTY-FIFTY *adv.* and *a.*

[**1711** Swift *Jrnl. to Stella* 20 Jan. (1948) I. xiv. 171 Now we are even, quoth Stephen, when he gave his wife six blows for one.] **1866** C. H. Smith *Bill Arp* 64 Dick says you allowed the members to exchange two hundred dollars for two hundred dollars of State money, even steven. **1925** Wodehouse *Sam the Sudden* xiii. 96 Do you mean to say.. that if Soapy was sitting in with the Archbishop of Canterbury on a plan for skinning a sucker the archbish wouldn't split Even Stephen? **1939** C. Morley *Kitty Foyle* xxxi. 320 Some of his stories were a bit corny, but a few of Parry Berwyn's old Racquet Club favorites were even-Steven with his. **1955** R. Bradbury *October Country* (1956) 80 It's a fifty-fifty fight. Even Stephen. **1963** A. Prior *Z Cars Again* (1964) xi. 95 It's even-Steven we'll catch him at it. **1970** A. Draper *Swansong for Rare Bird* i. 10 It's even stevens I'll con my way out of it with no more than a big helping of porridge. *Ibid.* v. 32 He used to break even stephen though by helping himself from her purse.

15. a. Of numbers: Divisible integrally into two equal parts; opposed to *odd*. Of a dance: Performed by an equal number of persons.

1557 Recorde *Whetst.* A iij, Euen nombers are those, whiche maie be diuided into equalle halfes. **1577** B. Googe *Heresbach's Husb.* III. (1586) 138 b, He woulde your number should rather be odde then even. **1586** W. Webbe *Eng. Poetrie* (Arb.) 84 Then the daunce wyll be eune. **1603** Shaks. *Meas. for M.* III. i. 41 Death we feare That makes these oddes, all euen. **1650** Jer. Taylor *Holy Living* (J.), Let him tell me whether the number of the stars be even or odd. **1674** Playford *Skill Mus.* II. 103 An even number of Quavers or Semiquavers, as 2, 4, 6, or 8. **1759** Johnson *Rasselas* xlvii, The same number cannot be even and odd. **1801** Strutt *Sports & Past.* (1876) 414 The army that presents a front of even numbers is called even hoste. *a* **1839** Praed *Poems* (1864) II. 171 Death looks down with nods and smiles, And make the odds all even. **1875** Jowett *Plato* (ed. 2) I. 407 Three is an odd number and four is an even number.

b. Of objects in a series: Having a place marked by an even number. *even page*: the left-hand page of a printed book.

1646 Sir T. Browne *Pseud. Ep.* IV. v. 193 The laterall division of man by even and odde, ascribing the odde unto the right side, and even unto the left. **1684** Earl Roscom *Ess. Verse* (1709) 229 Accents regularly plac'd On even Syllables. **1824** L. Murray *Eng. Gram.* (ed. 5) I. 374 The accents are to be placed on even syllables.

c. †*even and odd*: all included, without exception. †*for even or odd*: for good and all. †*for odd nor for even*: on no account whatever. *evenly even*, *oddly even* (see quots.).

c **1440** *Boctus* in *Laud MS.* 559. 10 b, He shulde.. foryeven hym even and odde That he hadde doone. *c* **1450** *Castle Hd. Life St. Cuthb.* (Surtees) 4957 All' ȝone oste, bathe euen and od. *c* **1460** *Towneley Myst.* 170, I have sene the lamb of God..And towchid hym for even or od. *c* **1485** *E. Eng. Misc.* (Warton Club) 42 Loke thou lete, for oode ne for ewyne. **1557** Recorde *Whetst.* A iij b, Euen nombers euenly, are such numbers as maie bee parted continually into euen halfes, till you come to an vnitie. As for example, 32. **1676** tr. *Agrippa's Van. Arts* xii, Arithmetic treats of Numbers..which is evenly odde, and which odly even. **1796** Hutton *Math. Dict.* I. 450/1 *Evenly Even Number*, is that which an even number measures by an even number; as 16, which the number 8 measures by the even number 2.

†**d.** *even and* (*or*) *odd*: a game of chance; = *odd or even* (see ODD). Hence *to go even or odd*. *Obs.*

1580 Hollyband *Treas. Fr. Tong*, *Per ou nom per*..a play called *euen or odde*. **1598** Florio, *Pari dispari*, euen and odde, a kinde of play so called. **1681** W. Robertson *Phraseol. Gen.* (1693) 551 To play at even or odd. **1710** *Brit. Apollo* III. No. 5. 2/2 A..Challenges B. to go even or odd with him for a..Sum of Money. **1739** Cibber *Apol.* (1756) I. 16 Socrates cou'd take pleasure..in playing at Even or odd with his children.

16. Of sums of money, numbers, etc.: 'Round', expressible in integers, or in tens, scores, etc.; containing no fractions or 'odd' money.

1638 Penkethman *Artach.* C ij b, Beginning with an odde 6*d.* and ending with an even shillings. **1720** *Lond. Gaz.* No. 5877/3 That..no Stock be allowed but in even 5*l.* *Mod.* Of the price of bread, etc. Down again to even money.

17. †**a.** *absol.* in adverbial phrases: OE. *on efn*, *on emn* (see ANENT); ME. *an emne*, *an evene*, equally, quietly. *to bring til even*: to reconcile. *Obs.*

Beowulf 5798 Him on efn liȝeþ ealdor-ʒewinna. *a* **1000** *Byrhtnoth* 184 (Gr.), þa on emn hyra frean feorh ʒesealdon. *c* **1000** Ælfric *Gen.* xvi. 12 He ʒewislice arærð æfre his ʒeteld on emne his ʒebroþra. **1297** R. Glouc. (Rolls) 9567 King steuene Vor lute poer & feblesse huld him al an euene. *c* **1315** Shoreham 75 ȝyf bothe beth of god wylle, And of assent an emne. *c* **1330** R. Brunne *Chron.* (1810) 134 þan wer boþe þe kynges brouht alle tille euen.

b. quasi-*sb.* in various uses. †Of a person: One's like or equal. †*the even of it*: the plain truth, 'the long and short of it'. *Sporting*, something expressed in integers; *in evens*: of a hundred-yard run, done in ten seconds.

1393 Gower *Conf.* II. 240 Of beaute sigh he never her even. **1599** Shaks. *Hen. V*, II. i. 128 The King hath run bad humours on the Knight, that's the euen of it. **1889** *Boy's Own Paper* 14 Sept. 794/2 All the amateur records are 'evens.' **1920** *Baily's Mag.* May 238 He ran the hundred in 'evens' in 1904. **1955** *Times* 23 July 2/7 The Mill Hill schoolboy..rarely, if ever, fails to do the 100 yards in evens.

18. Combined in phrases with *hand*. †*at* (*of*) *even hand*: on equal terms; also, without either gain or loss. †*to go even hand*: to go 'in equipace' with. *to be even hands with*: (Sc.) = 'to be even with': see 10.

1576 Fleming *Panopl. Epist.* 363 The Muses..never flit, but followe thee, or rather, goe even hande with thee, and treade foote by foote? **1625** Bacon *Ess., Envy* (Arb.) 512 Who so is out of Hope to attaine to anothers Vertue, will seeke to come at euen hand, by Depressing an others Fortune. **1650** R. Gentilis *Consid. Alcibiades* 33 He contents not himselfe to come out of trouble at even hand, by onely remaining comforted. **1756** W. Toldervy *Two Orphans* I. 38 Certainly, if a man will keep but of even hand, his ordinary expences ought to be but to the half of his receipts. **1822** Hogg *Perils Man* I. 325 (Jam.), I's be even hands wi' them an' mair.

even ('iːv(ə)n), *adv.* Forms: 1–2 **efne, emne,** 3–5 **evene,** 4–7 **evin, -yn(e,** 4–5 **eeven,** (4 **ewyn,** 5 **evon, -un, ewene, eyven, hevene),** 4– **even.** Also contracted 6–7 **ene,** 6–9 **een, e'en, ev'n.** [OE. *efne*, by assimilation *emne*, *efen*, = OFris. *efne*, *ivin*, OS. *efno* (Du. *even*), OHG. *ebano* (MHG. *ebene*, Ger. *eben*):—OTeut. **ebnô*, f. **ebno-* EVEN *a.* (In literary use the contracted form *e'en* (iːn) now occurs only in verse, and in colloq. use it is rare exc. *north. dial.*)

The mod.Teut. langs. (exc. Scandinavian) have developed senses similar to those in branch II.]

I. In senses closely related to the adj. (Chiefly admitting of degrees of comparison.)

†**1.** Evenly, in an even manner; regularly, steadily, uniformly. *Obs.*

a **1000** Ælfric *Ps* cxviii. [cxix.] 77 (Gr.) Ic æ þine efnast healde. *a* **1250** *Owl & Night.* 313 Ich singe efne Mid fulle dreme and lude stefne. **1297** R. Glouc. (1724) 43 So euene hot þat lond ys, þat men durre selde Here orf in howse awynter brynge out of the felde. *a* **1310** in Wright *Lyric P.* ix. 35 Hire teht aren white ase bon of whal, Evene set ant atled al. *c* **1375** *Sc. Leg. Saints* Prol. 47 Demaying hire in althing ewine. *c* **1400** *Destr. Troy* 436 Mony proude rynges, Euyn set to þe sight. **1458** *MS. Christ's Hosp. Abingdon* in Turner *Dom. Archit.* III. 44 Now God geve us grace to folowe treuthe even. **1728** T. Sheridan *Persius* I. (1739) 17 That Poet of ours makes his Verses run as even as a Carpenter can draw his Line.

†**2.** In exact agreement. *to go even* (= Fr. *marcher d'accord*): to agree (*with*). *Obs.*

c **1330** R. Brunne *Chron.* (1810) 126 Henry and he euen acorded or þei went. *a* **1569** Kingesmyll *Comf. Afflict.* (1585) A vij, Behold how good a thing it is..for brethren to dwell even together. **1601** Shaks. *Twel. N.* v. i. 246 As the rest goes euen. **1611** —— *Cymb.* I. iv. 47, I..rather shun'd to go euen with what I heard. **1645** Fuller *Good Th. in Bad T.* (1841) 39 Both are for the privileges of parliament; can they come closer? Both are for the liberty of the subject; can they meet evener?

†**3.** Equally. **a.** In equal divisions or parts. **b.** In an equal degree. Also as quasi-*prep.* with *dat.*: Equally with. **c.** On equal terms. *Obs.*

a. *c* **888** K. Ælfred *Boeth.* xxxix. §13 Sio sunne and se mona habbaþ todæled butwuht him þone dæʒ and þa niht swiþe emne. *c* **1330** R. Brunne *Chron.* (1810) 51 Þe barons portiond þe lond euen þam bituene. **1393** Gower *Conf.* II.

46 Copes riche.. Departed even of white and blewe. *c* **1420** *Sir Amadace* (Camd.) lix, Take and dele hit Euun in toe.

b. *c* **1380** WYCLIF *Wks.* (1880) 310 Wheþer alle þese ordris ben euene goode. *c* **1380** *Sir Ferumb.* 2946 þat ech of ous.. do al þat a may, To helpe ys felawe euene him-selue; among our fon to day. *c* **1449** PECOCK *Repr.* III. vi. 313 In the same euen miche pouerte.. folewe in euen likenes. *c* **1450** *Castle Hd. Life St. Cuthb.* (Surtees) 4066 Edylwald was a man expert, Euen gyuen to god with cuthbert. *c* **1485** *E. Eng. Misc.* (Warton Club) 85 Alle in ewene warme water.

c. 1470–85 MALORY *Arthur* X. xlv, Neuer were there foure knyghtes euener matched. **1577** B. GOOGE *Heresbach's Husb.* III. (1586) 128 b, Be well assured that you bye them [draught oxen] even matched.

†**4.** In a just or proper degree. *Obs.*

c **1430** *Two Cookery-bks.* 12 Let boyle tylle the Onyonys an þe Brawn ben euyne sothyn, an nowt to moche. *Ibid.* 14 Take þe sylf brothe.. Make it euen Salt.

†**5.** Directly, straight; also of descent: In a direct line. *Obs.* See also EVEN-DOWN.

a **1300** *Cursor M.* 3105 (Cott.) It brend, þe reke raght vp euen. *c* **1340** *Ibid.* 3106 (Fairf.) þe smelle was squete and stode ful eyuen. **1375** BARBOUR *Bruce* I. 61 Ony male, [That were in lyne] ewyn descendand. *c* **1380** WYCLIF *Wks.* (1880) 334 He lediþ his soule eeuen to heuen by goddis lawe. *c* **1435** *Torr. Portugal* 2281 Into a lond bothe riche and good, ffulle evyn he toke the way. **1486** *Bk. St. Albans* E vij b, Ayen the Water his Way eeuen iff he hent.

†**b.** 'Due' (east, etc.); directly (contrary, etc.).

c **1300** *St. Brandan* 515 Hi wende evene south. *c* **1400** MAUNDEV. (Roxb.) xxxiii. 149 Beȝond þir ilez.. to ga euen est, es na land inhabited. **1480** CAXTON *Chron. Eng.* ccxxxv. 257 The wind was euen contrary vnto him. **1483** *Cath. Angl.* 118 Evyn agayn. ? *a* **1550** *Freiris of Berwik* 344 In the west he turnit him ewin about.

II. In weakened senses as an intensive or emphatic particle. (With 6–8 cf. similar uses of *just*.)

6. Exactly, precisely, 'just'. Now chiefly *arch.* after Bible use, and suggesting some notion of 9.

a. of manner; often followed by *as*, *thus*, *so*.

Beowulf 1571 Lixte se leoma efne swa of heofene hadre scineð rodores candel. *a* **1000** *Crist* 330 (Gr.), And efne swa ðec ȝemette meahtum ȝehrodene clæne and ȝecorene Crist almihtiȝ. **1340** HAMPOLE *Pr. Consc.* 4767 þe thred day, þe se sal.. And stand even in.. Als it stode first. **1398** TREVISA *Barth. De P.R.* XI. xiii. (1495) 398 Thonder smythth the ayre.. euyn soo that it.. sownyth.. in the manere of rollyng and hurlynge of whelys. *c* **1400** *Destr. Troy* 1633 Priam by purpos a pales gert make.. And euyn at his etlyng Ylion was cald. **1526** *Pilgr. Perf.* (W. de W. 1531) 2 b, Euen so man in the cage of this worlde. **1578** TIMME *Calvin on Gen.* 97 Even as if a Man should give a sword and buckler into the hands of another. **1594** SHAKS. *Pass. Pilgr.* xi, Even thus.. the warlike god embraced me. **1611** BIBLE *John* xvii. 18 Euen so haue I also sent them into the world. **1808** R. K. PORTER *Trav. Sk. Russ. & Swed.* (1813) I. i. 6 It was even as Saxo Grammaticus relates. **1816** SCOTT *Old Mort.* Introd., 'Even sae—even sae.'

b. of time: occas. quasi-*prep.* = at the same moment with. Often with *now* (see further under NOW, and cf. ENOW). †Formerly also *absol.* = 'just now', 'just then' (cf. *just* and Ger. *eben*).

c **1205** LAY. 25939 Efne [*c* **1275** eafne] þissen worden þa þat wif seide, Beduer heo gon hirten. **1297** R. GLOUC. (1724) 535 Euene as the ssire sat, [Sir Maci] to the toune's ende him drou. *c* **1325** *Poem temp. Edw. II* (Percy) lxxv, Euen upon the Monday. *c* **1400** *Destr. Troy* 1980 He.. Shoke euyn into ship, & the shalke leuyt. **1413** LYDG. *Pilgr. Sowle* v. xiv. (1859) 81 And euen with this word this Angel flewe his weye vp in to heuene. **15..** *Merch. & Son* 230 in Hazl. *E.P.P.* I. 148 Ryght evyn abowte mydnyght. *c* **1600** SHAKS. *Sonn.* lxxi, Let your love even with my life decay. **1611** —— *Cymb.* III. vi. 16 Euen before, I was At point to sinke, for Food. **1607** HIERON *Wks.* I. 399 The high priest will holde a councell, euen the dawning. **1612** R. SHELDON *Serm. St. Martin's* 48 Our most gratious Soueraigne being almost euen with the breaking vp of her [Q. Elizabeth's] ghost most ioyfully in this city proclaimed. **1703** MOXON *Mech. Exerc.* 30 These Shanks are to be rivetted (as you were taught even now). **1820** KEATS *St. Agnes* xxxv, But even now Thy voice was at sweet tremble in mine ear.

†**c.** of place. Also *absol.* = close at hand (cf. Ger. *n-eben*). *Obs.*

1340 HAMPOLE *Pr. Consc.* 5179 Even aboven þat vale namly, Whare al men sal se his body. **1393** LANGL. *P. Pl. C.* XX. 152 Ho so is hurt in þe hand, euene in þe myddes, He, etc. *c* **1489** CAXTON *Sonnes of Aymon* iii. 73 Of the other side it [the castell] had evyn at hande a grete wood. **1578** WHETSTONE *Promos & Cass.* II. ii. 2 *Ap.* Where dwels Lady Lamia? *Ros.* Even by, Syr.

†**d.** of shape. *Obs.*

c **1400** MAUNDEV. (Roxb.) xi. 43 þare was a table of gold, euen sqware. *c* **1400** *Destr. Troy* 1635 A clene wall clustrit with towres, Euyn round as a ryng richely wroght.

7. Quite, fully. Formerly often before numerals; now only *arch.* in *even to* (= L. *usque ad*), in which use it suggests some notion of sense 9.

c **897** K. ÆLFRED *Gregory's Past.* xli. 300 Crist.. hiene selfne ȝeeaðmedde emne oð ðone deað. *a* **1000** *Cædmon's Gen.* 1158 (Gr.) Cainan wintra hæfde efne hund-seofontiȝ ær him sunu woce. *c* **1205** LAY. 13924 He heom wes leof æfne al swa heore lif. *c* **1325** *Chron. Eng.* 938 in Ritson *Metr. Rom.* II. 309 He reignede her Evene five ant thritti yer. **1546** *Wyclif's Wycket* 1, In greate sufferance of persecution euen to the death. **1611** BIBLE *Ex.* xxvii. 5 That the net may bee euen to the midst of the Altar. **1646** F. HAWKINS *Youths Behav.* (1663) 4 Nor is it beseeming to stoop so low as even to crowching. **1653** H. COGAN tr. *Pinto's Trav.* xlvi. 180 Carried at the mercy of the Sea even until Sun-set. **1667** MILTON *P.L.* III. 586 His magnetic beam.. Shoots invisible vertue even to the deep.

8. Prefixed to a subject, object, or predicate, or to the expression of a qualifying circumstance, to emphasize its identity. *Obs.* exc. *arch.* Also in 16–17th c. (hence still *arch.* after Bible use) serving to introduce an epexegesis; = 'namely', 'that is to say'.

a **1000** *Guthlac* 946 Domes hleotan, Efne þæs ilcan, þe ussa yldran fyrn Frecne onfengon. *a* **1000** *Met. Boeth.* viii. 46 Efne sio ȝitsung. *c* **1489** CAXTON *Sonnes of Aymon* xii. 306, I shall smyte of your hede, evyn anone. **1535** COVERDALE *2 Chron.* vii. 22 Euen because they haue forsaken the Lorde God of their fathers. **1591** SHAKS. *Two Gent.* II. i. 49 *Speed.* She that you gaze on so... *Val.* Even she I meane. **1594** HOOKER *Eccl. Pol.* Pref. iii. §9 They imagined they even beheld as it were with their eyes. **1596** SHAKS. *Merch. V.* v. i. 242, I sweare to thee, euen by thine owne faire eyes. **1610** —— *Temp.* III. i. 14 These sweet thoughts, doe euen refresh my labours. **1611** BIBLE *Zech.* xi. 10, I took my staff, euen Beauty, and cut it asunder. *Ibid. John* viii. 25 Euen the same that I said vnto you from the beginning. **1820** KEATS *St. Agnes* xvii, I will, even in a moment's space, Awake.. my foemen's ears.

b. (Chiefly in colloq. form *e'en.*) Prefixed to verbs, with vague force expressible by 'just', 'nothing else but'; in early use sometimes with notion of 'to be sure', 'forsooth' (L. *scilicet*). Now *arch.* and *dial.*

a **1553** UDALL *Royster D.* III. iv. (Arb.) 52 If she despise you een despise ye hir againe. **1653** WALTON *Angler* 125 Come, now bait your hook again.. and we wil ev'n retire to the Sycamore tree. **1655** FULLER *Ch. Hist.* II. iii. §8 The beastly Monk.. had e'ne learned as far as Virgil's Æneids, whence he fetched the Platform of this pretty Conceit. **1686** P. HENRY *Diaries & Lett.* (1882) 353, I can buy them here for 2*s.* 10*d.*, which is e'en cheap enough. **1719** DE FOE *Crusoe* (1840) I. x. 172, I e'en let him out. **1741** RICHARDSON *Pamela* I. 178 E'en send to him to come down. **1802** BENTHAM *Let.* Wks. 1843 X. 384 As to the intrigue about the Institute, since it is begun, e'en let it take its course. **1821** MRS. WHEELER *Westmorl. Dial.* 26 Ise ean gang with yee.

9. Intimating that the sentence expresses an extreme case of a more general proposition implied (= Fr. *même*). Prefixed (in later use often parenthetically postfixed) to the particular word, phrase, or clause, on which the extreme character of the statement or supposition depends.

This use, now the prevailing one in Eng., is foreign to the other Teut. langs. It is rare in purely dialectal speech, and (though a natural development of 8) seems not to have arisen before the 16th c. Cotgrave 1611 does not give *even* among the equivalents of Fr. *mesme*. The phrase *not even* (= L. *ne.. quidem*) is rare in early use; Cooper *Lat. Dict.* 1572 renders *ne in publicis quidem* by 'no, not in common affaires' (though for *ne nunc quidem* he has 'no, not euen now': see 6 b); Walker *Dict. Particles* 1673 renders *ne.. quidem* only by 'no, not so much as'; the earliest Lat. Dict. that gives 'no, not even' is app. Ainsworth 1736.

a. Attached to the subj., agent, or object.

1607 SHAKS. *Timon* I. i. 82 Make sacred euen his styrrop. **1641** J. JACKSON *True Evang. T.* III. 209 In Warre, even the Conqueror is commonly a loser. **1697** DRYDEN *Virg. Georg.* III. 418 Ev'n the fearful Stag dares for his Hind engage. **1747** WESLEY *Prim. Physic* (1762) 117 This quickly heals even cut veins and Sinews. **1802** MAR. EDGEWORTH *Moral T.* (1816) I. x. 82 Even this stupid gardener.. is as useful to society as I am. **1821** KEATS *Lamia* 34 Jealousies Of the Wood-gods, and even the very trees. **1854** DORAN *Habits & Men* 176 He was in debt to no man, not even to his tailor. **1863** FR. A. KEMBLE *Resid. in Georgia* 11 The tone of insolent superiority assumed by even the gutter urchins. **1884** W. C. SMITH *Kildrostan* 88 A harp, even, blunts the finger-tips.

b. Attached to a word or clause expressing time, manner, place, or any attendant circumstance.

1577 B. GOOGE *Heresbach's Husb.* I. (1586) 36 The leafe.. turneth with the Sunne, whereby it sheweth to the husbande, even in cloudie weather, what time of the day it is. **1611** E. GRIMSTONE tr. *De Serres' Hist. France* 257 Fortune is a secret operation of the wisdome of God, alwaies iust, euen when it is most vnknown to vs. **1736** BUTLER *Anal.* I. i, A method of providential conduct, the like of which has been exercised even with regard to ourselves. **1782** GIBBON *Decl. & F.* I. xiii. (1828) 491 Even on that memorable occasion his stay did not exceed two months. **1818** HALLAM *Middle Ages* ix. (1869) 636 Even in Italy.. the domestic architecture of the middle ages did not attain any great perfection. **1881** BIBLE (Revised) *Mark* xiv. 59 And not even so [**1611** But neither so] did their witness agree together.

c. Attached to a hypothetical clause.

1697 DRYDEN *Virg. Georg.* III. 594 Ev'n though a snowy Ram thou shalt behold, Prefer him not in haste, for Husband to thy Fold. **1791** SHERIDAN *Pizarro* III. iii, Even though that moment lost your Elvira for ever. **1824** SCOTT *St. Ronan's* xxviii, For such evil bruits Mr. Touchwood cared not, even if he happened to hear of them. **1848** MACAULAY *Hist. Eng.* I. 175 Even if the king had been desirous to fulfil the promises which he had made to the Presbyterians. **1865** LUBBOCK *Preh. Times* 323 Even if the embankment had remained intact to this day. **1873** F. HALL *Mod. English* 36 Even suppose that these solecisms were collected. *Mod.* Even were there no other evidence, we should still be justified in assuming, etc.

d. Attached to the predicate (or any of its adjuncts), to emphasize the full extent of the statement (whether affirmative or negative).

1728 R. MORRIS *Ess. Anc. Archit.* 17 Such as these never arise even to the universal Knowledge of Order. **1779** HERVEY *Nav. Hist.* II. 335 These [conditions] the parliament disliked and even signified a disinclination to ratify. **1841** DICKENS *Old C. Shop* xlii, He maintained a strict reserve, and even shunned her presence. **1848** MACAULAY *Hist. Eng.* II. 111 Nor had they ever.. found England an agreeable, or even a safe, residence.

e. Emphasizing a comparative; 'still', 'yet'.

173. BUTLER *Serm.* xi, It will even more strongly be taken for granted that, etc. **1766** GOLDSM. *Vic. W.* i, The vanity and the satisfaction of my wife were even greater than mine. **1854** MRS. JAMESON *Bk. of Th.* (1877) 29 This advice is even more applicable to the painter.

even- (in early combs. repr. OTeut. stem **ebno-*, sometimes with adjectival, sometimes with adverbial force; in later use, combining directly as *adj.* or *adv.*). The forms are identical with those of the adj., but in ME. the *-n* was often omitted.

1. In various senses of the adj. Chiefly in parasynthetic derivatives, as †***even-carriaged***, ***-edged***, ***-handed***, ***-tempered***, ***-toed***, †***-wayed***; also in **even-aged** *a.*, of a forest: composed of trees that are of approximately the same age; **even-even** *a.*, of a nucleus: having an even number of both protons and neutrons; **even-odd** *a.*, of a nucleus: having an even number of protons and an odd number of neutrons; **even-wise** *adv.*, in like manner.

1905 *Terms Forestry* (*U.S. Dept. Agric.*) 9 *Even-aged forest. **1928** R. S. TROUP *Silvicultural Systems* ii. 23 Even-aged crops.. are more susceptible to damage by wind and snow than uneven-aged crops. **1962** *Times* 1 Jan. 6/4 Trees in even-aged woods had gone down in swathes. **1670** BROOKS *Wks.* (1867) VI. 342 Upright hearts in their constant course are *even-carriaged hearts. **1672** GREW *Anat. Plants, Idea Philos. Hist.* §6 Leaves, which are Long or Round, *Even-edg'd or Escallop'd. **1940** *Physical Rev.* LVIII. 104/1 States with higher angular momenta of the core alone (an *even-even nucleus) are known in many cases to be very close to the normal state. **1949** GAMOW & CRITCHFIELD *Theory Atomic Nucleus* iv. 93 An even-even nucleus can transform into another even-even nucleus of the same A only by simultaneous emission of two β-particles. **1955** J. A. WHEELER in W. Pauli *Niels Bohr* 167 Heavy even-even nuclei always have zero spin. *a* **1825** FORBY *Voc. E. Anglia* s.v., An *even-flavoured day of rain. **1605** SHAKS. *Macb.* I. vii. 10 This *euen-handed Iustice Commends th'Ingredience of our poyson'd Challice To our owne lips. **1879** FROUDE *Cæsar* xviii. 305 Pompey's justice was even-handed. **1849** J. F. JOHNSTON *Exper. Agriculture* 120 To the.. *even-numbered portions, nothing was applied. **1955** *U.N. Provisional Gloss. Atomic Energy* 82 *Even-odd nucleus. **1966** PHILLIPS & WILLIAMS *Inorg. Chem.* II. xxxv. 627 Two hundred and one beta-stable nuclides contain an even number of protons and an even number of neutrons, sixty-nine are even-odd, i.e. contain an even number of protons and an odd number of neutrons. **1875** FARRAR *Seekers* III. i. 267 Controlled, modest, faithful, and *even-tempered. **1854** OWEN in *Circ. Sc.* (*c* 1865) II. 79/2 This.. family of 'artiodactyle' or *even-toed beasts. **1670** NARBOROUGH in *Acc. Sev. Late Voy.* (1711) 64 These People.. are smooth and even toothed and close set and very white. **1645** QUARLES *Sol. Recant.* v. 84 This unlevells Thy *even-way'd Peace, with indigested evills. **1865** SWINBURNE *Poems & Bal., Two Dreams* 78 Love.. Tuned evenwise with colours musical.

†**2.** Prefixed to sbs. with the sense 'fellow-', L. *co-*, as in ***even-disciple***, ***-servant***, ***-worker***; **even-knight**, transl. of L. *commilito* fellow-soldier; **even-next**, 'neighbour' (in Biblical sense); **even-sucker**, a foster-brother; EVEN-CHRISTIAN. On the analogy of these, *even-* renders L. *co-* in **even-buying**, transl. of L. *coemptio* purchase. *Obs.*

This formation was common in OE.; examples of later origin chiefly occur in Wyclif.

1382 WYCLIF *2 Macc.* viii. 11 *Euyn byinge [**1388** euen-biyng] of boonde men of Jewis. —— *John* xi. 16 Thomas.. seide to *euen disciplis, And go we. —— *Phil.* ii. 25 Epaphrodite, my brothir and *euene worchere, and myn *euene knyȝt. *c* **1175** *Lamb. Hom.* 13 Uwil(c)mon scal his *euenexta beodan alswa he walde þet me him bude. **1382** WYCLIF *Rev.* xix. 10, I am thin *euen seruaunt, and of thi britheren. [**1388** Y am a seruaunt with thee]. —— *2 Macc.* ix. 29 Philip, his *euen souker [**1388** euene soukere] transferride the body.

3. In senses of the adv. †**a.** = 'Equally', 'similarly', as in *even-clad* ppl. adj., *even-high*, *-mighty*, *-rich*, *-right*, *-worth*, *-worthy* adjs.; also **even-eche** *a.*, co-eternal; EVENMETE, EVENOLD. **b.** = 'Evenly', as in *even-pleached*, *-set*, *-spun*. †**c.** With quasi-prepositional sense, in **even-deed** *adv.*, according to fact, indeed. **d.** Straight, directly; see EVEN-DOWN, -FORTH.

1622 T. SCOTT *Belg. Pismire* 81 The only glory is to be gay, and the greatest shame to be under-clad or *euen-clad to our callings. **1555** *Inst. Gentleman* (1568) I vij, He whyche is the rycher man doth seeme to dooe wronge vnto the other, although *euen deede he haue the wronge doone vnto hym. *a* **1000** *Crist* 465 (Gr.) Ær ðon up stiȝe ancenned sunu, *Efenece bearn aȝnum fæder. *c* **1000** ÆLFRIC *Hom.* (1846) II. 598 Ælmihtiȝa God, þu ðe þurh ðinum euenecum Wisdome mannan ȝesceope. *c* **1200** ORMIN 18582 He naffde nohht ben aȝȝ Hiss Faderr æfenneche. *a* **1000** *Dial. Devil & Recluse* in Kemble *Sal. & Sat.* (1848) 85 He dyde hine *efenheahne Gode. *c* **1200** ORMIN 15720 Crist iss Godess Sune.. & wiþþ hiss Faderr efennheh. *Ibid.* 18571 *Efennmahhtiȝ Godd wiþþ himm [þe Faderr]. **1599** SHAKS. *Hen. V*, v. ii. 42 Her [France's] Hedges *euen pleach'd.. Put forth disorder'd Twigs. *c* **890** K. ÆLFRED *Bæda* v. x, Wæron hi eft *efenrice. *c* **1200** ORMIN 11868 Teȝȝ shulenn wurrþenn þær Wiþþ enngless efennrike. **1382** WYCLIF *Ecclus.* xlix. 3 He is *euene riȝt [L. *directus*] godly in the penauance of folc. **1647** H. MORE *Song of Soul* I. II. lx, A lower rank on either side we saw Of lesser shrubs *even-set with artifice. **1645** QUARLES *Sol. Recant.* vi. 75 If the *even-spun Twine should be extended. **1388** WYCLIF *Job* xxviii. 19 Topasie of Ethiope schal not be maad *euene worth to wisdom. *c* **1380** —— *Serm.* Sel. Wks. II. 323 Suffringis of þis tyme ben not *even-worþi to þe glorie þat is to come. **1482**

Monk of Evesham (Arb.) 44 Y..dyd not for my synnys euynworthy penans.

even ('iːv(ə)n), *v.* Forms: 1 efnan, 2–3 efnen, (3 effnen), 3–4 evene(n, -yn, (4 emni, 6 evin), 6–7 eeven, 8 eaven, 4– even. [OE. *efnan*, also *ʒe-efn(i)an*, f. *efen*, EVEN *a.* Cf. OHG. *ebanôn* (Ger. *ebenen*), ON. *iafna*, Goth. *ga-ibnjan*.
The OE. *efnan*, *æfnan*, to accomplish, achieve, corresponding to ON. *efna* of same meaning, is wholly unconnected.]

I. To make even, level, or straight.

1. *trans.* **a.** To level (ground); to level, render plane or smooth (any surface); also *fig.* †**b.** To bring up or restore to a level, or to a straight line. **c.** *to even out*: to dispose evenly *into*; also, to make even or level. **d.** To fit (one thing) *to* (another).

a. *c* **1200** ORMIN 9207 All þatt ohht iss wrang & crumb Shall effnedd beon & rihhtedd. **1382** WYCLIF *Isa.* xxviii. 25 Whan he shal euenen therto his [the erthes] face, he shal sowe the sed gith. *c* **1400** *Lanfranc's Cirurg.* (MS. A.) 127 Whanne þou hast removed of þe boon þat schal be removed evene þe brynkis with schavynge. *c* **1420** *Pallad. on Husb.* VI. 39 And even the erthe above. **1581** SIDNEY *Apol. Poetrie* (Arb.) 54 Law, whose end is, to euen and right all things. **1662** MERRETT tr. *Neri's Art of Glass* 364 Scissers cut the Glass, and even it. **1686** AGLIONBY *Painting Illust.* I. 28 Upon a dry Wall, having first Evened it. **1712** J. JAMES tr. *Le Blond's Gardening* 118 The Line and Rake for eavening and smoothing the Ground. **1750** tr. *Leonardus' Mirr. Stones* 145 When the face of it is evened, it reflects images like a looking-glass. **1860** PUSEY *Min. Proph.* 309 The Good Shepherd..smoothed for them all rugged places, and evened them by His own steps. **1864** E. BURRITT *Lond. to John O' Groat's* 318 The tailor's shears, the mason's trowel, and the carpenter's edge, tools are evening everything in Christendom to one dead level of uniformity.

b. **1382** WYCLIF *1 Kings* xi. 27 Salomon beeldide Mello, and euenede the swelwʒ of the citee of Dauid. *c* **1440** *Promp. Parv.* 143 Evenyn, or make evyn. **1688** CAPT. J. S. *Art of War* 6 Even your Ranks, straiten your Files. *a* **1705** EVELYN (J.), Beat, roll, and mow carpet-walks..for now the ground is supple, and it will even all inequalities. **1849** *Sidonia Sorc.* II. 290 The Prussian government..desired the foundation to be evened, for it had sank in various places.

c. *c* **1674** N. FAIRFAX *Bulk & Selv.* 2 Those things that right reason..had evened out into ranks and kindreds by themselves, have been unhappily hudled and broken. **1931** *Economist* 18 July 127/2 Company practice may rightly go beyond the mere creation of secret reserves, and cover their employment to 'even out' fluctuations in earning power. **1962** A. NISBETT *Technique Sound Studio* v. 102 Volumes have to be controlled; they have to be evened out and held back.

d. **1530** PALSGR. 540/2 Even this lynyng to my gowne. **1659** HAMMOND *On Ps.* xviii. 33 Annot. 102 Evening or fitting [lit. tr. Heb. *meshavvēh*] my feet he makes them nimble.

†**2. a.** To level *to*, *with* (the ground, etc.). In OE. example: To throw (a person) down. *Obs.*

a **1000** *Riddles* xxviii. (Gr.), Ic..efne to eorðan hwilum ealdne ceorl. **1382** WYCLIF *Jer.* I. 12 Confoundid is ȝoure moder ful myche, and euened to pouder. **1559** SACKVILLE *Mirr. Mag.* Induct. lxii, Walls and towers flat evened with the soyle. **1591** RALEIGH *Last Fight Rev.* (Arb.) 21 Her vpper worke [was] rased, and..euened shee was with the water. **1632** HEYWOOD *2nd Pt. Iron Age* III. Wks. 1874 III. 393 Sees..The stately walls he reard, leuel'd and euen'd.

†**b.** To bring down to a specified level. *Obs.* exc. *dial.*

1636 RUTHERFORD *Lett.* No. 70 (1862) I. 183 He wd not even you to a gift of dirt and clay. **1650** H. BROOKE *Conserv. Health* H v, Evened my words to the meanest capacity. **1741** RICHARDSON *Pamela* I. 84 You do well, Sir, said I, to even your Wit to such a poor Maiden as me. **1880** *Antrim & Down Gloss.* s.v., I wouldn't even my wit to you.

†**3.** To make (a balance) even. *Obs.*

a **1618** RALEIGH *Prerog. Parl.* Ep. A iij b, The point of honour well weighed hath nothing in it to euen the ballance. **1638** CHILLINGW. *Relig. Prot.* iii. §86 Even the ballance, and hold it even. *a* **1718** PENN in *Pa. Hist. Soc. Mem.* I. 421 Prudence and proportion will more than even the scale.

4. a. To make (accounts, etc.) even; to balance, settle, square; to come to agreement upon (points of difference).

1536 BELLENDEN *Cron. Scot.* (1821) II. 65 Foure prudent men wer chosin, on ilk side, to evin all debatis betwix thame. **1619** SIR R. BOYLE in *Lismore Papers* (1886) I. 215 By my payment Mr. Dalton and I have evened all accompts. **1664** PEPYS *Diary* (1879) III. 11 He hath now evened his reckonings at the Wardrobe till Michaelmas last. **1719** W. WOOD *Surv. Trade* 90 The goods we send to that Country are by no means sufficient to even the account between us. **1745** *De Foe's Eng. Tradesman* (1841) II. xlii. 141 He has evened all his differences. **1856** MRS. BROWNING *Aur. Leigh* VIII. (1882) 349 To sorrow for mankind And even their odds. **1947** T. MAYNARD *Humanist as Hero* xiii. 158 He now had a wonderful chance to even old scores.

absol. **1667** PEPYS *Diary* 13 Oct., Evened with W. Hewer for my expenses upon the road.

b. *to even up*: to compensate exactly. Also, to make even or equal; to balance.

1865 BUSHNELL *Vicar. Sacr.* Introd. 16 They take..what he [Anselm] says of justice as if He [Christ] were engaged to even up the score of penalty. **1898** *Westm. Gaz.* 28 Feb. 7/1 So this morning a big collapse was provided to even things up. *Ibid.* 1 Nov. 9/1 When they return to-morrow it is quite possible that those who sold yesterday in order to even up their books may be again purchasers. **1908** *Daily Chron.* 9 Mar. 3/3 But all things are evened up in every age. **1958** R. WILLIAMS *Culture & Society* III. 307 The result of the new educational provision was in part..an evening-up between the fortunate places and the unfortunate.

†**c.** To make (a person) 'even' or quits *with* another. *Obs.*

1604 SHAKS. *Oth.* II. i. 308 Nothing..shall content my Soule Till I am eeuen'd with him.

†**d.** To bring into accord, reconcile. *Obs.*

1620 *Horæ Subseciuæ* 142 To euen and compound them [factions] in mutuall amity and agreement.

5. †**a.** To make equal. *Obs. rare.*

a **1225** *Ancr. R.* 182 Sicknesse þet God sent..efneð þene þolemode to martir. **1553** GRIMALDE *Cicero's Offices* 2 a, That diligently you read not onely my Orations, but these Bookes also of Philosophy, which now well nigh to those have euened themselues in quantitie.

b. To treat or represent as equal; to put on the same level; *refl.* to pretend to equality. Const. *to*, *with* (in ME. *ʒæn*). Also *absol. rare* in mod. use exc. *Sc.*

c **1200** ORMIN 1396 Enngless..wolldenn effnenn hemm ȝæn Godd. *Ibid.* 15979 For þatt teȝȝ Haliȝ Gastess mahht Effnenn wiþ þerþlic ahhte. **1340** *Ayenb.* 16 Liȝtbere..wolde by above þe oþre angeles, and him wolde emni to God. **1382** WYCLIF *Isa.* xlvi. 5 To whom licneden ȝee me, and eueneden and comparisounden me. *a* **1605** MONTGOMERIE *Sonn.* lxii, I think it scorne..To euin an ape with aufull Alexander. **1815** SCOTT *Guy M.* xi, They never thought..of evening themselves to the Ellangowans. **1824** —— *Redgauntlet* let. xii, 'Me and Miss Lilias even'd thegither! Na, na, lad—od, she is..four or five years younger.' **1830** GALT *Laurie T.* VI. i. (1849) 254 The idea of me evening myself in sincerity to their mother. **1881** *Sat. Rev.* No. 1323. 301 We disclaim the slightest idea of evening the two poets, which would be simply absurd. **1887** SAINTSBURY *Eliz. Lit.* 201 A touch of pathos, again to be evened only to Shakespere's.

c. *Sc.* 'To talk of one person as a match for another in marriage' (Jam.).

1823 LOCKHART *Reg. Dalton* III. 119 (Jam.), 'Would ony Christian even yon bit object to a bonny, sonsy, weel-faurd young woman like Miss Catline?'

d. *dial.* To treat as appropriate to (a person's character); chiefly in bad sense, to impute *to*.

1845 MRS. S. C. HALL *Whiteboy* I. iv. 58 It's long since I heard such a thing as that [having a nice cottage and some fields] evened to a poor man. **1853** READE *Chr. Johnstone* 261 'How daur ye even to me, that I'm seeking a lad?' **1880** *Antrim & Down Gloss.* s.v., Would you even the like of that to me. **1884** *Illust. Lond. News* 2 Feb. 114/3 I'd have knocked any one down that had evened Such a thing to you in my hearing.

6. To liken, compare. *Obs.* exc. *dial.*

c **950** *Lindisf. Gosp.* Matt. vii. 24 Ȝeefned biþ. *c* **1200** *Trin. Coll. Hom.* 161 Ðis woreldes biwest is efned to wastene. *a* **1225** *Ancr. R.* 132 Auh þe treowe ancren we efneð to briddes. *c* **1290** *Lives Saints* (1887) 62 For ore louerd euenede him-sulf to a lomb. **1860** READE *Cloister & H.* IV. 258 Would ye even a beast to a man? **1863** C. J. ATKINSON *Provinc. Danby*, *Even*, to compare, to liken.

II. To be or become even.

†**7.** *intr.* **a.** To be equal or comparable. Const. *to*, *with*. *Obs.*

c **1230** *Hali Meid.* 19 Hare weden ne mahen euenen to hare. *a* **1240** *Sawles Warde* in *Cott. Hom.* 251 Helle is..ful of brune uneuenlich, for ne mei nan eorðlich fur euenin þer towart. *c* **1325** *E.E. Allit. P.* A. 1072 What schulde þe mone þer compas clym..to euen wyth þat worþly lyȝt.

†**b.** To tally, agree *with*; also, to be in line *with*. *Obs.*

1602 CAREW *Cornwall* (J.), A redoubled numbering never eveneth with the first. **1663** PEPYS *Diary* 22 June, To Westminster, where all along I find the shops evening with the sides of the houses.

8. a. *trans.* To come up to, equal. *rare.*

1583 STANYHURST *Æneis* II. (Arb.) 58 A toure..that in altitud euened Thee stars. **1607** TOPSELL *Serpents* (1653) 647 In bignesse he [the Drone] eveneth, yea, surpasseth the King himself. **1639** FULLER *Holy War* 192 The English Earl ..conceived himself to even him in valour and martiall knowledge. **1886** BURTON *Arab. Nts.* (Abr. ed.) I. 177 A daughter who eveneth thee in beauty.

†**b.** To act up to, keep pace with. *Obs rare*⁻¹.

1611 SHAKS. *Cymb.* III. iv. 184 Wee'l euen All that good time will giue vs.

9. *to even out*: to become even or normal.

1950 A. L. ROWSE *England of Elizabeth* v. 158 Things were beginning to even out a little.

Hence '**evened** *ppl. a.*

1847 BUSHNELL *Chr. Nurt.* II. iii. (1861) 275 In the molds of a perfectly evened judgement.

†'**even-'Christian.** *Obs.* Forms: (see EVEN *a.* and CHRISTIAN). [f. EVEN- + CHRISTIAN: cf. OFris. *ivinkerstena*, OHG. *ebanchristani* (MHG. *ebenkristen*).] A fellow-Christian.

?*c* **1100** *Laws Edw. Conf.* §36 Fratrem suum..quod Angli dicunt his emcristen. *c* **1175** *Lamb. Hom.* 65 Luue þine euecristene. *Ibid.* 149 Reuþe for his emcristenes wawe. *c* **1340** HAMPOLE *Prose Tr.* 21 Envy and ire ayene thyne even cristene. *c* **1386** CHAUCER *Pars. T.* ¶521 Worschip of God, and helping of thin even cristen. **1450–1530** *Myrr. our Ladye* 99 Some longe to god, somme to oure selfe and some to our euen crysten. **1544** *Exhort.* in *Priv. Prayers* (1851) 568 Brotherly love..toward all our even Christen. **1552** LATIMER *Serm. Lord's Prayer* vii. 51 To hate his euen Christian or to do other manner of sinnes. **1602** SHAKS. *Ham.* v. i. 32 The more pitty that great folke should haue countenance..to drowne or hang themselues, more then their euen Christian.

'**evendown,** *adv.* and *a.* *north.* (Often hyphened, or as two words.) Also 4 evenden. [f. EVEN *adv.* (sense 5) + DOWN *adv.*]

A. *adv.*

†**1.** Straight down. *Obs.*

c **1340** *Gaw. & Gr. Kn.* 1345 So ryde þay of by resoun bi þe rygge bonez, euenden to þe haunche. *c* **1400** *Destr. Troy* 13285 Thai..derkon euon down on a depe slomur.

2. *dial.* = 'Downright'; quite, thoroughly.

1869 *Lonsdale Gloss.* s.v., 'He threaped ma evven-down' = He flatly contradicted me. **1876** *Whitby Gloss.* s.v., That's even-down just. **1877** *Holderness Gloss.* s.v., He's even-doon fond, is that lad.

B. *adj.* (*dial.*)

1. Coming straight down: said of rain.

1801 *Har'st Rig* lxxxiii. (Jam.), Now it turns an eident blast, An even-doun pour. **1822** GALT *Steam Boat* 258 An even-doun thunder-plump came on, that..drookit the Doctor to the skin. **1880** *Antrim and Down Gloss.* s.v., There was an even down pour.

2. a. Of persons, in a good sense: Upright, straightforward; in a bad sense: Downright, out and out. **b.** Of statements, etc.: Downright, direct. Of things: Downright, sheer; absolute.

1786 BURNS *Twa Dogs* 206 But Gentlemen, an' Ladies warst, Wi' ev'n doun want o' wark are curst. **1789** SILLAR *Poems* 186 It was a fiction, An ev'n doun perfect contradiction. **1818** SCOTT *Rob Roy* vi, To tell your honour the even down truth. **1823** *Petticoat Tales* I. 288 (Jam.) I may hae said that Andrew liked a drap drink, but that's no just an even doun drinker. **1826** J. WILSON *Noct. Ambr.* Wks. 1855 I. 63, I never heard such evendown nonsense.. in a' my born days. **1834** SIR H. TAYLOR *Artevelde* I. x. (1849) 33 In the even-down letter you are right. **1877** *N.W. Linc. Gloss.* s.v., He's a strange punct'al man, as even down to the ground as can be.

†'**evene,** *sb. Obs.* Also 3 efne, efene. [ME. *efne*, *evene*, ad. ON. *efni* material, *pl.* ability, OSw. *æfni* (Sw. *æmna* stuff, Da. *evne* ability).]

1. Material; subject-matter.

a **1300** *Cursor M.* 335 (Cott.) Of himself he toke his euen þat he of wroght bath erth and heuen. **1423** JAS. I *Kingis Q.* clxxxii, Quhat nedis me, apoun so litill evyn, To writt all this?

2. a. Nature; form or shape. **b.** Natural powers.

c **1200** *Trin. Coll. Hom.* 137 þe heuenliche þremnesse was mid him þo he fulcnede ure helende. þe fader on stefne. þe sunne on mannes efene. þe holi gost on culures hewe. *a* **1225** *Ancr. R.* 126 Ancre..ouhte leden herd lif, ase dude þe lefdi Iudit, efter hire efne. *a* **1225** *Leg. Kath.* 57 Euchan bi his euene..wurðschipede his maumez. *c* **1230** *Hali Meid.* 43 Ha cwikede of cleane cunde, as is in engles euene. *Ibid.* 43 A charbucle is betere þen a iacinct iþe euene of hare cunde. *a* **1240** *Ureisun* in *Cott. Hom.* 187 He mot scottin efne after his euene. *c* **1325** *Pol. Songs* (1839) 157 Somenours..Mys motinde men alle by here evene.

†**e'vene.** *v. Obs.* [ad. L. *ēven-īre* to come out, happen, f. *ē-* out + *venīre* to come.] *intr.* To come to pass, happen, result.

1654 tr. *Scudery's Curia Pol.* 106 He must necessarily have his particular interest, besides the publique, which cannot but evene and happen on many occasions. **1663** *Flagellum, or O. Cromwell* (1872) 89 The Scotch War now evening, the lucky minute was come. **1669** BOYLE *Contn. New Exp.* II. (1682) 57 To try whether the same success would evene with all unripe fruits. **1702** C. MATHER *Magn. Chr.* II. App. (1852) 210 God sometimes may suffer such things to evene.

†**e'venement.** *Obs. rare.* [a. F. *événement* event, occurrence: see prec. and -MENT.] An occurrence; an issue, result.

1660 tr. *Amyraldus' Treat. Relig.* I. i. 6 A Providence.. which disposes of all evenements of things agreeably to his will. **1677** GALE *Crt. Gentiles* III. IV. 524 God.. contemplates..in his own wil the efficient of al future evenements.

evener ('iːv(ə)nə(r)). [f. EVEN *v.* + -ER¹.] **a.** One who or that which makes even; *esp.* one who makes or is a party to an equal division of anything.

a **1400** *Hymn to Virgin* in Warton *Hist. Eng. Poetry* (1840) II. x. 109 Heil evenere of old lawe and of newe. **1889** *Dublin Rev.* Apr. 364 The 'Cattle Eveners' Pool' in Chicago was the result of a contract between the four federated railways leading thence eastward and three large dealers. *Ibid.* 364 The eveners agreed in return to divide the traffic according to the terms of the railway agreement.

b. In *Weaving*, 'an instrument used for spreading out the yarn on the beam' (Jam.).

c. An apparatus for giving an equal proportion of work to horses in pulling, drawing a load, etc.

1850 *Rep. Comm. Patents 1849* (U.S.) 371, I claim..the exclusive use of said spring rests and 'evener'. **1874** KNIGHT *Dict. Mech.*, *Evener*, a double or treble tree to 'even' or divide the work of pulling upon the respective horses.

†**even forth,** *adv.* and *prep.* *Obs.* Also EMFORTH. [f. EVEN *adv.* + FORTH.]

A. *adv.*

1. Straight on. [Cf. EVEN *adv.* 5.]

c **1394** *P. Pl. Crede* 163 þanne y entrid in and even-forþ went.

2. (Just so far. Hence) Equally (*with*). [Cf. OE. *swá forð swá* as far as.]

1377 LANGL. *P. Pl.* B. XIII 143 Lere þe to louye þine enemye..euene forth with þi-selue. **1430** [see EMFORTH.]

B. *prep.* To the extent of; in proportion to.

c **1314**, *c* **1374**, **1393** [see EMFORTH]. **1377** LANGL. *P. Pl.* B. XIX. 305 He dede equite to alle euene forth his powere. **1413** LYDG. *Pilgr. Sowle* I. xxx. (1859) 33 To amende and satysfy for his trespaas..euen forth his power.

†'**evenhead,** '**evenhood.** Forms: 4–5 evenhede, 5 evenhode, evynhede, -hoode. [OE. **efenhád* (cf. *efenháda bisceop* co-bishop), f. *efen* EVEN *a.* + *hád* rank: see -HEAD, -HOOD.]

1. Equality; position of equality; equal dignity or rank.

a 1340 HAMPOLE *Psalter* xviii. 7 He stegh in til heuen til þe euenhede and ioy of his fadere. *c* 1440 HYLTON *Scala Perf.* (W. de W. 1494) II. xxviii, He shal areyse hem aboue al other chosen soules to the euenhede of cherubyn & seraphyn. 1483 *Cath. Angl.* 118 An Evyn-hede, *equalitas.*

b. *concr.* One who is of equal rank; also something equivalent.

c 1330 R. BRUNNE *Chron.* (1810) 253 Sir Edward.. suilk on wild he take His euenhed in mariage. *c* 1380 WYCLIF *Serm.* Sel Wks. II. 361 þes þree vertues.. ben evenhed to Goddis witt. 1570 LEVINS *Manip.* 206 Euenheads, *coæquales.*

2. a. Impartiality, fairness, equity. **b.** Equilibrium, well-balanced state (of mind).

c 1330 R. BRUNNE *Chron.* (1810) 37 Boþe riche & pouere he ȝemed in euenhede. *a* 1340 HAMPOLE *Psalter* ix. 8 He sall deme þe world of þe erth in euenhed. *a* 1400 *Relig. Pieces fr. Thornton MS.* 11 Þat kepes vs fra owterage and haldes vs in evenhede [*printed* everhede]. *c* 1400 *Test. Love* III. (1560) 293/2 By evenhede profitably to rayne. 1496 *Dives & Paup.* (W. de W.) II. xviii. 130/2 Equyte.. ne euenhode in shyftynge and in demynge myght not entre.

† **e'veniency.** *Obs. rare*⁻¹. [f. L. *ēvenient-em*, pr. pple. of *ēvenīre* to happen: see -ENCY.]

Coming to pass.

1656 JEANES *Fuln. Christ* 341 The effects of Christs obedience transcend those of Adams disobedience, in regard of certainty of eveniency.

evening ('iːvnɪŋ), *sb.*[1] Forms: 1 æfnung, 3 eveningue, 4–6 evenyng(e, (7 *Sc.* e'ening), 3– evening. [OE. *æfnung*, verbal sb. f. *æfnian* 'to grow towards evening', f. *æfen* EVEN *sb.*

The vb. occurs in K. ÆLFRED tr. *Greg. Dial.* (Hatton MS.) I. x, þa þa se dæȝ æfnode. Also in tr. *Bæda de Temp., Sax. Leechdoms* III. 260.]

† **1.** The coming on of 'even', the process or fact of growing dusk; the time at which this takes place, the time about sunset. *Obs.*; merged in 2.

c 1000 ÆLFRIC *Gen.* viii. 11 Heo com ða on æfnunge eft to Noe. *c* 1205 LAY. 30419 Riht to þan euening þa fleh Cadwalan þe king. *c* 1290 *Lives Saints* (1887) 40 In þe eueningue riȝht Seint Ieme cam to him ride. 1382 WYCLIF *Matt.* xxvii. 57 Whanne the euenyng was maad, there came a riche man fro Armathia. *c* 1440 *Bone Flor.* 1458 To hyt drewe to the evenynge.

2. a. As a synonym of *even*, which it has now superseded in ordinary use: The close of the day; usually, the time from about sunset till bedtime.

c 1440 *Promp. Parv.* 144 Evenynge, þe laste parte of þe day. 1553 DUKE NORTHUMBLD. in *Four C. Eng. Lett.* 22 Wofull was the newes I receyved this evenynge. 1613 SHAKS. *Hen. VIII*, III. ii. 226, I shall fall Like a bright exhalation in the Euening. 1741 WATTS *Improv. Mind* I i. §9 The Pythagoreans.. every evening thrice run over the actions and affairs of the day. 1767–95 MACNEILL *Will & Jean* II, The tears that now ilk e'ening Bleach'd her lately crimson'd cheek. 1860 TYNDALL *Glac.* I. xviii. 122 On the evening of the same day. 1871 MORLEY *Voltaire* (1886) 111 People met.. at the supper at nine in the evening.

b. *transf.* and *fig.* The closing or declining period of a person's life, or of anything compared to a 'day'.

1614 RALEIGH *Hist. World* (J.), The long day of mankind drawing towards an evening. 1647 CLARENDON *Hist. Reb.* VI. (1843) 350/1 He was a person of great courage, honour, and fidelity, and not well known till his evening. 1725 POPE *Odyss.* IV. 116 The sad evening of a stormy life. 1812 SHELLEY *Addr. Irish People* 8 The king of Great Britain has arrived at the evening of his days. 1865 PUSEY *Truth Eng. Ch.* 3 To.. consecrate the evening of my life to the unfolding of some of the deep truths of God's Holy Word.

c. Afternoon. *dial.* and *U.S. local.*

1788 in G. F. Jackson *Shropshire Word-Bk.* (1879) 136 The meeting held on Monday evening last was adjourned to be holden to-morrow Evening at three of the Clock. 1790 *Pennsylv. Packet* 5 Jan. 3/1 It was.. dark from about two o'clock until about half after four in the evening. 1806 M. LEWIS in *Lewis & Clark Exped.* (1905) IV. 319 It was one in the evening before he returned. 1876 'MARK TWAIN' *Tom Sawyer* i. 3 He'll play hookey this evening. 1880 G. W. CABLE *Grandissimes* xiv. 94 This evening (the Creoles never say afternoon) about a half-hour before sunset. 1882 MRS. CHAMBERLAIN *West Worcs. Word* 10 A woman lately wished me 'good marnin'' at 1.30 p.m., then, having passed, turned back to apologize: '*Good evenin*' ma'am, I should 'a' said.' 1889 'C. E. CRADDOCK' *Broomsedge Cove* x. 177 Air ye obligated ennywise ter stan' in the middle o' this narrer bridge all evening? 1966 G. W. TURNER *Eng. Lang. in Austral. & N.Z.* viii. 164 In Queensland *evening* may be used to refer to anytime after midday.

d. *evenings*, in the evening; of an evening. Cf. NIGHTS *adv. colloq.* or *dial.* (chiefly *U.S.*).

1652, *c* 1740 [see MORNING *sb.* 3 c]. 1862 O. W. NORTON *Army Lett.* (1903) 40 We have rather dull times, but evenings we write letters or sing. 1885 *Century Mag.* XXXI. 35/1 We had some real good talks evenings down on the rocks. 1926 B. RUCK *Her Pirate Partner* xvi. 209 So, for all they keep you so close, you go out as you like, evenings! Every night of the week? 1968 *Globe & Mail* (Toronto) 17 Feb. 32 (Advt.), Evenings, there's dancing to do, nightclubs to visit.

e. *Ellipt.* for 'good evening'. *colloq.*

1912 MASEFIELD *Widow in Bye St.* IV. st. 17, 'Evening,' she said. 'Good evening.' 1965 I. FLEMING *Man with Golden Gun* v. 70 The eyes flirted. 'Evenin'.' 'Good evening. Could I have a Red Stripe?'

f. *Ellipt.* for *evening paper* (see 5 b below). *colloq.*

1961 'B. WELLS' *Day Earth caught Fire* vii. 109 The Covent Garden blaze had turned out to be a natural for the evenings, but even more so for the mornings. 1967 G. DOUGLAS *Death went Hunting* v. 36 We've missed the final edition of the local evening now.

3. An evening spent in a particular way; *esp.* an evening devoted to the reception and entertainment of friends. Cf. *soirée.*

1870 MRS. RIDDELL *Austin Friars* iv, Two or three friends were dropping in to supper; and occasional 'evenings out'. 1877 M. M. GRANT *Sun-Maid* xvii, He enjoyed those 'little evenings', as his aunt termed them. 1881 H. JAMES *Portr. Lady* xxxv, Mrs. Osmond having an 'evening'—she had taken the Thursday of each week. 1883 J. HATTON in *Harper's Mag.* Nov. 844/2 Smoking parties and weekly 'evenings'.

† **4.** *dial.* (See quot.; possibly this belongs to next word.) *Obs.*

1695 KENNETT *Par. Antiq.* Gloss., *Evenings*, the delivery at even or night, of a certain portion of grass or corn to a customary tenant, who performs his wonted service of mowing or reaping for his lord, and at the end of his day's work receives such a quantity of the grass or corn.. as a gratuity or encouragement of his bounden service. 1721–1800 in BAILEY; hence in mod. Dicts.

5. *attrib.* and *Comb.* **a.** Simple *attrib.* or quasi-*adj.* with sense 'pertaining to evening, occurring in the evening', etc.

1535 COVERDALE *Zech.* xix. 7 Aboute the euenynge tyme it shal be light. 1591 SHAKS. *Two Gent.* IV. ii. 17 Now must we.. giue some euening Musique to her eare. 1651 DAVENANT *Gondibert* II. i. (R.), Near to his evening region was the sun. 1677 GILPIN *Demonol.* (1867) 22 Knowledge.. from the effects of things; which, because it is more dark and obscure than that which ariseth from the causes of things, they [the schoolmen] termed evening knowledge. 1697 DRYDEN *Virg. Georg.* III. 521 The cool Evening-breeze the Meads renews. *Ibid.* IV. 628 A Shepherd's Groom Surveys his Ev'ning Flocks returning Home. 1704 POPE *Pastorals, Autumn* 40 The birds shall cease to tune their ev'ning song. *Ibid. Winter* 45 No grateful dews descend from ev'ning skies. 1711 SHAFTESB. *Charac.* (1737) II. 282 We took our evening-walk in the fields. 1712 ADDISON *Psalm* xix, Soon as the evening shades prevail. 1725 POPE *Odyss.* XIX. 83 A day-devourer, and an evening-spy! 1728 —— *Dunc.* II. 72 At early dawn to drop Her evening cates before his neighbour's shop. *a* 1763 SHENSTONE *Elegies* VIII. 5, I saw my friends in ev'ning circles meet. 1804 T. JEFFERSON *Writ.* (1830) IV. 19 My evening prospects now hang on the slender thread of a single life. 1870 DICKENS *E. Drood* iv, I have been.. wasting my evening conversation on the desert air. 1879 E. GARRETT *House by the Works* II. 188 Aunt Barbara.. took her to the evening classes of the Art School.

b. In various combinations of a more permanent character, chiefly simple *attrib.*, as ***evening-hymn***, †***-mass***, ***meal***, ***-prayer***, ***-sacrifice***, ***school***, ***-service***, etc.; also **evening-bird** (see quot.); **evening dress**, the costume prescribed by fashion to be worn in the evening; hence ***evening-dressed*** adj.; † **evening end**, app. the western end (of a mine work); **evening flower**, a genus of plants (*Hesperantha*, N.O. *Iridaceæ*) so called because its flowers expand early in the evening; † **evening glade**, ? some atmospherical phenomenon seen in the evening; **evening gun** (see quot.); **evening-lighted** *ppl. a.*, illuminated by the light of the evening; **evening paper**, a newspaper published later than a morning paper, usually so as to be on sale from about midday onward; **evening party**, a social gathering beginning some time in the evening (cf. 3); **evening primrose** (see quot. 1872); † **evening-song** = EVENSONG; **evening-star**, applied with definite article to Venus, with indef. art. also to Jupiter and Mercury, when seen in the west after sunset, also *fig.*; **evening suit**, a suit of formal clothes as prescribed by fashion to be worn in the evening; **evening-tide** = EVENTIDE.

1884 *Girl's Own Paper* Feb. 227/2 The gecko.. is sometimes known as the *'Evening Bird'. 1797 N. HEIDELOFF *Gallery of Fashion* Nov. in Jane Austen *Novels* (1926) I. 387 *Evening dresses. 1825 H. WILSON *Memoirs* I. 91 Ponsonby.. had put on an evening dress. 1863 MRS. GASKELL in *All Year Round* IX. 74/1 There stood Mrs. Forbes in her handsome evening dress. 1880 MRS. FORRESTER *Roy & V.* I. 11 'Have you no evening-dress' asks Netta. 1936 E. A. BAKER *Hist. Eng. Novel* VII. iii. 186 Evening dress in any colour that suited the fancy of the wearer was discarded for the black coat. 1970 *Times* 6 Nov. 1/5 News readers at B.B.C. Leeds have been told to wear evening dress at night. 1896 *Westm. Gaz.* 15 Feb. 3/2 An *evening-dressed audience. 1933 P. GODFREY *Back-Stage* xiv. 179 An evening-dressed gentleman. *Ibid.*, Comedy sketches which allowed of being evening-dressed were booked in preference to those which did not. 1684 *Copper Mines* ii. in *Phil. Trans.* XVII. 741 Which Seam or Vein did go from the *Evening-end to the Morning-end of the said Work. 1847 CRAIG, *Hesperantha*, The *Evening-flower. 1866 in *Treas. Bot.* 1714 *Phil. Trans.* XXIX. 66 In the next place he mentions the *Evening Glade. 1748 *Anson's Voy.* II. iii. 145 The Master of the Pink was prevailed on to omit firing the *evening gun. 1810 *Naval Chron.* XXIII. 121 The guard ship fires evening and morning guns. 1867 SMYTH *Sailor's Word-bk.*, *Evening Gun*, the warning-piece, after the firing of which the sentries challenge. 1832 TENNYSON *Margaret*, From the *evening-lighted wood. 1592 SHAKS. *Rom. & Jul.* IV. i. 38 Shall I come to you at *euening Masse? 1860 *Evening meal [see MEAL *sb.*[2] 2 a]. 1954 A. S. C. ROSS in *Neuphilologische Mitteilungen* LV. 43 U-speakers eat ..*dinner* in the evening; ..*Evening meal* is non-U. 1958 *Listener* 10 July 68/2 A time when many of us are either cooking or eating our evening meal. 1727–41 *Evening paper [see PAPER *sb.* 8]. 1857 DICKENS *Dorrit* II. xii. 419 The evening paper was full of Mr. Merdle. 1940 L. MACNEICE *Last Ditch* 24 Divided by the morning tea By the evening paper, By children and tradesmen's bills. 1816 JANE AUSTEN *Emma* II. xvi. 299 Dinner-parties and *evening-parties were made for him. 1871 *Temple Bar* May 229 In all places where Londoners do congregate, whether at dinner or evening parties. 1879 ROBINSON *Coward Consc.* II. vii, In true evening-party fashion. 1598 SHAKS. *Merry W.* II. ii. 100 A ciuill modest wife.. that will not misse you morning nor *euening prayer. 1806 SMITH & SOWERBY *Eng. Bot.* XXII. 1534 *Œnothera biennis.* Common *Evening-Primrose. 1872 OLIVER *Elem. Bot.* II. 172 The expansion of the flowers in the evening only, of Common Œnothera.. hence called Evening Primrose. 1882 *Garden* 22 July 64/3 The Evening Primrose covers the ground with large pale lemon flowers. 1535 COVERDALE *1 Esdras* viii. 72, I sat still full of heuines vntill the *euenynge sacrifice. 1822 *Missionary Herald* (Boston, Mass.) XVIII. 51 Avails of an *evening school. 1832 *Chambers's Edin. Jrnl.* I. 361/2 On the discovery of his literary taste, Mr. Laidlaw put him to an evening school. 1937 *Discovery* Sept. p. lxxxi, Evening Schools of History and Geography are specially arranged to meet the needs of Adult Students. 1794 MRS. RADCLIFFE *Myst. Udolpho* ii, St. Aubert read, in a low and solemn voice, the *Evening Service. 1634 CANNE *Necess. Separ.* (1849) 89 To use it as Papists did their matins and *evening song. 1660 JER. TAYLOR *Duct. Dubit.* II. ii. §61 Untill the Evening song be finished, for then the Ecclesiastical solemnity is over. *c* 1740 SHENSTONE *Rape Trap*, When the bell rung For evening song, His dinner scarce was ended. 1535 COVERDALE *Ps.* lxiv. [lxv.] 8 Thou makest both the mornynge and *euenynge starres to prayse yᵉ. 1667 MILTON *P.L.* VIII. 519 Till the amrous Bird of Night.. bid haste the Evening Starr On his Hill top. 1781 COWPER *Retirement* 46 Ere we yet discern life's evening star. 1812 WOODHOUSE *Astron.* xxiii. 240 Venus: This brilliant star when seen in the west setting soon after the sun, is known by the name of the Evening Star. 1819 BYRON *Juan* I. cxxii, 'Tis sweet to see the evening star appear. 1886 *Whitaker's Almanac* 17 Venus is an evening star in the first half of the month [February]. 1862 G. MEREDITH *Lett.* (1970) I. 166 If you want me to dine, know that I can only do so if you are absolutely *alone*, having no *evening suit. 1912 J. JOYCE *Let.* 11 Sept. (1966) II. 319 My evening suit is in the lower drawer of the wardrobe. 1915 D. H. LAWRENCE *Let.* 2 Mar. (1962) I. 328 Will you tell me if I must bring evening suit. 1552 HULOET, **Euenynge tyde*, or euen tyde. 1611 BIBLE *2 Sam.* xi. 2 It came to passe in an euening tide, that Dauid arose from off his bed. 1743 R. BLAIR *Grave* 716 Behold him in the evening-tide of life. *a* 1800 COWPER *Moralizer corrected* 12 To serious thought at evening-tide.

Hence (*nonce-wds.*) **'eveningless** *a.*, without an evening; **'eveningly** *adv.*, every evening.

1825 *Blackw. Mag.* XVIII. 441 And eveningless that sunny noon of heart. 1844 J. T. HEWLETT *Parsons & W.* xxviii, Daily, or more correctly, eveningly.

† **'evening**, *sb.*[2] *Obs.* [f. EVEN *v.* + -ING[1].]

1. The action of the vb. EVEN: **a.** the action of making even, level, or smooth; **b.** ? the action of comparing; hence, comparison (quot. 1230, which may belong to next word).

c 1230 *Hali Meid.* 7 Heouenliche luren.. passeð alle oðre wiðuten eueninge. 1511–2 *Act 3 Hen. VIII*, c. 6. §1 Suche byer.. may drawe and strayn them [clothes] for evenyng of them oonly. 1611 COTGR., *Vniement*, an euenning, equalling, planing. 1670 NARBOROUGH in *Acc. Sev. Late Voy.* I. (1711) 73, I saw where the Natives had been by the evening of the Grass.

2. The condition of being even; equality.

c 1400 *Destr. Troy* 3372 þi maister.. neuer yet of nobley An euenyng to me.

† **'evening**, *sb.*[3] and *a. Obs.* [a. ON. *iafning-i*, sb. f. *iafn* EVEN *a.* But possibly this may have blended with an adv. f. OE. *efen*, EVEN *a.* + *-inga*, *-unga* advb. suffix.]

A. *sb.* An equal, one of the same rank; a 'match'; a neighbour (in scriptural sense).

a 1200 *Moral Ode* 162 in *Lamb. Hom.* 169 þer sculen eueninges bon þe riche and the laȝe. *c* 1200 ORMIN 10702 Tatt tu wiþþ þin efenninng þe metelike lede. *a* 1225 *Leg. Kath.* 119 Heo.. undernam hit [lare] se wel þæt nane ne was hire euening. *c* 1325 *Chron. Eng.* 24 in Ritson *Metr. Rom.* II. 271 Geomagog hatte here Kyng, Me nuste no wer ys evenyng. *c* 1450 MYRC 1229 Hast thou enuyet thyn euenynge.

B. *adj.* ? or *adv.*

1. [The sb. or adv. used predicatively.] Equal; on a level; of the same rank. Const. *to*, *with.*

c 1200 *Ormin* 13674 þe laþe gast þatt wollde ben effninng wiþþ Godd. *a* 1225 *Ancr. R.* 334 Hwuche unðeauwes beoð efnunge to þeos. *a* 1300 *Cursor M.* 11688 (Cott.) þe crop was euening to þe rote. *Ibid.* 23392 þat ilk þan mai þe angels do þat þou sal euening þan be to. *c* 1400 *Destr. Troy* 2217 Of any erdyng in erthe euenyng to vs.

2. As *adv.* qualifying an adj.

c 1300 *Cursor M.* 28170 (Cott.) Of him þat was myn euening rike.

† **'evenkin**, *a. Obs. rare*⁻¹. [f. EVEN *a.* + KIN; cf. ALKIN.] Of the same kindred.

c 1450 *Lay Folks Mass-bk.* 72 We sal make a specialle prayer for.. all oure euenkyn saules.

† **'evenleche**, *v. Obs.* [OE. (*ȝe-*)*efenlǽcan*, f. *efen*, EVEN *a.* + *-lǽcan*, f. *-lác* (see -LOCK) used as suffix forming sbs. of quality.] *trans.* To imitate.

c 1000 *Ps.* lxxxviii. 7 (Lye). *c* 1000 ÆLFRIC *Hom.* II. 34 He [Stephanus].. Cristes.. ȝebysnunge ærfæstlice ȝeefenlæhte. *c* 1175 *Lamb. Hom.* 113 Soðliche nis nan mon wel cristene butan þe þe criste euenlecheð.

† **'evenlength.** *Obs.* In 3 **ȝevelengðhe.** [a. ON. *iafnlengd*, f. *iafn* equal, EVEN + *lengd* length.]

The time of year when the days and nights are of equal length; the equinox.

c **1250** *Gen. & Ex.* 147 In geuelengðhe worn it [ðe mones ligt] mad.

†**'evenless**, *a. Obs.* [f. EVEN *a.* + -LESS.] Without evenness; unrhythmical; awkward.
1652 ASHMOLE *Theat. Chem.* Proleg. 12 The slow and evenlesse Numbers of Prose.

†**even'lesten.** *Obs.* [OE. *efe(n)láste*, wk. fem.] Some plant. (Cockayne's rendering 'everlasting' is due to mistaken etymology.)
c **1000** *Sax. Leechd.* II. 78 Grudeswelȝe, hole cersan, weȝbræde, efelaste, ontre..wel on buteran eal togædere. *Ibid.* III. 2 With heafod wræce ȝenim hamorwyrt & efenlastan nyðowearde. *c* **1265** *Voc. Names Plants* in Wr.-Wülcker 559 Mercurialis, i. euenlesten, i. mercurial [*Evenlesten*, The herb mercury, Halliwell].

†**'evenlikly**, *adv. Obs. rare.* [f. ME. *evenlyk*, EVENLY *a.* + -LY².] **a.** Directly, in a direct line; **b.** exactly. Cf. EVENLY *adv.* 2.
c **1425** WYNTOUN *Cron.* IV. viii. 2 A thowsand a hundyr and fyfty And thre yhere thare-till ewynlykly. *Ibid.* VIII. iii. 113 Bot fra the stok down ewynlykly Discendand persownys lynealy.

†**'evenliness.** *Obs.* Also 1 efnlicnesse, emlicnes. [OE. *efnlicnesse*, f. *efnlic, efenlic*, EVENLY *a.* + -NESS.] The quality of being even; equality, evenness; adaptation, suitability.
c **897** K. ÆLFRED *Gregory's Past.* xvii. 122 Hie healdað ma ȝeferrædenne & efnlicnesse ðonne ealdordom. *a* **1000** *Eadwine's Cant. Psalt.* cxviii. [cxix.] 144 Emlicnes ȝewitnesse þin on ecnesse. **1674** N. FAIRFAX *Bulk & Selv.* 8 If we do but allow God to deal with us..in wayes bearing an evenliness with our kind.

†**'evenling.** *Obs.* Also 1 efnling, 1-2 efenling. [OE. *efenling*, f. *efen*, EVEN *a.* + -LING.] An equal, fellow-man, 'neighbour'.
a **1000** *Eadwine's Cant. Psalt.* xliv. 8 [xlv. 7] Foreðæn smirede ðe god god þin of ele blisse fore efnlinge þine. *c* **1175** *Lamb. Hom.* 57 Luuien þi cristen euenling Alswa þe seoluen in alle þing. *Ibid.* 67 Þin sunful efenling luue him for godes þing.

†**'evenlong**, *a.* and *adv. Obs.* Also evelong. [f. EVEN- + LONG *a.*
The etymological notion is obscure; perh. the adv. originated first, and the adj. use was developed from the sense 'straight along', with the help of some confusion with AVELONGE. In OE. *efelang* occurs once ('þæt cuðe hol..þæt he efelang ær ȝefylde' *Riddles* xlv. 7), with the sense 'of the same length', or perh. 'lengthwise'.]
A. *adj.* Oblong.
1387 TREVISA *Higden* (Rolls) I. 405 Butter, melk and chese I-schape euelong and cornered wise [*oblongus et tetragonus*]. **1398** —— *Barth. De P.R.* III. xvii. (Tollem. MS.), An euen longe tre meuid swyftly semeþ rounde. *Ibid.* v. ix. (1495) 115 Euenlonge browes wyth lytyll heer sygnefyeth cowardnesse. *c* **1430** *Two Cookery-bks.* 53 Take þe Stuffe of þe Porke, & putte it on euelong cofyn of fayre past. **1565** GOLDING *Ovid's Met.* VIII. (1593) 199 This brooke is woont..evelong stones [L. *obliqua saxa*] to carrie With hideous roring downe his streame.
B. *adv.* **a.** Straight along, in a line. **b.** In an oblong form.
1398 TREVISA *Barth. De P.R.* v. xxxvi. (1495) 148 The herte is euenlonge shapen as a toppe. **14..** *Porkington MS.* in Wright *Dict.* s.v., One the upper syde make holys evenelonge, as many as thou wylt.

†**evenly** ('iːv(ə)nlı), *a. Obs.* exc. *Sc.* Forms: see EVEN *a.* and -LY¹. [ME. *evenlich*, OE. *efenlic*, f. *efen*, EVEN *a.* + *-lic*, -LY¹. Cf. ON. *iafnligr*, Goth. *ibnaleiks*.]
1. Equal; of the same character, degree, rank, weight, etc. Of a date: The same (cf. EVEN *a.* 14 b).
a **1000** *Crist* 39 (Gr.) Næniȝ efenlic ðam ær ne siððan in worlde ȝewearð wifes ȝearnung. *c* **1200** ORMIN 1837 Michææl bitacneþþ uss..whillc iss wiþþ Godd all efennlic. *c* **1275** in *O.E. Misc.* 90 Haly thomas of heoueriche Alle apostles eueliche. *c* **1330** R. BRUNNE *Chron.* (1810) 318 Þe date was euenlik, a þousand þre hundred & tuo, Whan þe Erle of Karrik turned þe Scottis fro. *c* **1374** CHAUCER *Boeth.* III. ix. 88 Þou by euenlyk causes enhaunsest þe soules and þe lasse liues. *c* **1425** WYNTOUN *Cron.* VIII. iii. 77 Ȝhoure modyr and I in ewynlyk gre Discendand fra þe stok are we. **1513** DOUGLAS *Æneis* v. viii. 2 Eneas..Twa evinlie burdouns walit..And equale armour..On schulderis..buklis he.
†**b.** Equal to one's needs; moderate. *Obs.*
c **1200** *Trin. Coll. Hom.* 13 Ðet foremeste [Temperancia] is riht medeme mel..Ðat oder [Modica potio] is emliche drinke..for to beten his þurstes nede.
2. Even: **a.** Of persons: Fair, equitable, just, impartial.
c **1425** WYNTOUN *Cron.* v. x. 882 Sutyle off ingyne he was: and eloquent And ewynlyk in-till jugement. **1488** *Sc. Acts Jas. IV* (1814) 210/2 Personis..vnsuspect to his hienes, & evinly to all his liegis. **1494** *Act. Dom. Conc.* 361 (Jam.) The money..salbe layit in ane evinly manis hand. **1567** in G. Buchanan *Detect. Q. Mary* (1572) sig. X iij a, I desyre the mony to be consignit into an eueuly mans hand.
b. Of the ground, roads, etc.: Free from inequalities, level, smooth, uniform.
1721 RAMSAY *Poems, To R. Yarde*, Poets show'd these evenly roads That lead to dwellings of the gods. **1808-25** JAMIESON s.v., We speak..of an evinly course, both as respecting progress in a journey, and the tenor of one's conduct.

evenly ('iːv(ə)nlı), *adv.* [OE. *efenlíce*: see EVEN *a.* and -LY².] In an even manner or degree.
The physical senses are of late emergence, having in early use been expressed by EVEN *adv.*
1. So as to present an even or uniform surface or line; smoothly, without inequalities in level, form, texture, consistency, depth of tint, etc.
1634-5 BRERETON *Trav.* (1844) 49 The court..is most evenly paved with bricks. *a* **1639** WOTTON (J.) A palish clearness, evenly and smoothly spread..of a pretty solid consistence. **1755** in JOHNSON. **1879** G. GLADSTONE in *Cassell's Techn. Educ.* I. 151 The paste is spread evenly upon the table to an exact depth.
†**2.** In a straight line, directly. *Obs.*
1596 SHAKS. *1 Hen. IV*, III. i. 103 Here the smug and Siluer Trent shall runne, In a new Channell, faire and euenly. **1599** —— *Hen. V*, II. iv. 91 You find him euenly deriu'd From his most fam'd, of famous Ancestors.
b. In an even direction or position *with.*
1599 SHAKS. *Much Ado* II. ii. 7 Whatsoeuer comes athwart his affection, ranges euenly with mine. **1875** BEDFORD *Sailor's Pocket Bk.* iv. (ed. 2) 93 Looking carefully up the vernier, the third line above the figure 3 is seen to lie evenly with a line on the scale.
†**3.** Exactly; in exact coincidence or agreement.
c **1325** *Metr. Hom.* 96 The stern, that thaim the gat gan schawe..com euenlye Thar Crist was abowen. **1375** BARBOUR *Bruce* x. 228 Quhen it [the wain] wes set evinly Betuix the chekys of the ȝet. **1393** GOWER *Conf.* II. 179 He ..Let make of gold..A precious ymage riche After his fader evenliche. *c* **1449** PECOCK *Repr.* v. iii. 496 Euenlier and more accordingli. **1512** *Act. 4 Hen. VIII*, c. 19. §10 The hole some ..evenly agreable and concordaunte with the hoole some comprised in the seid endenture.
†**b.** At the very moment; immediately. *Obs.*
c **1350** *Will. Palerne* 1747 To heiȝ vs hastily henne..ich hope be þe best, euenly þis euen while. *Ibid.* 5338 Eche man was esed euenli at wille.
4. With reference to movement or action: Without fluctuations or variations; equably, uniformly.
1671 MILTON *Samson* 671 Thou towards him with hand so various..Temper'st thy providence through his short course: Not evenly, as thou rul'st The angelic orders. **1674** N. FAIRFAX *Bulk & Selv.* 117 A wheel of manifold rims.. would make out uneven bows of circles, in even shares of time, the whole wheel being evenly turned. *a* **1732** ATTERBURY *Serm.* (1740) I. vii. 251 We are so apt to forget God's administration of the great affairs below, when they go on evenly and regularly. *Mod.* The hind wheel of my bicycle doesn't run evenly.
b. With equanimity or evenness of mind; serenely, tranquilly.
a **1400** *Relig. Pieces fr. Thornton MS.* (1867) 11 Strenghe ..of herte and will euynly to suffire þe wele and þe waa. **1682** NORRIS *Hierocles* Pref. 19 That can look upon another man's Lands evenly and pleasingly as if they were his own. **1844** STANLEY *Arnold* (1858) II. x. 275 To be ready to bear evenly, not sullenly.
5. Without inclination to either side. **a.** In a state of equipoise; under even conditions; without manifest advantage on either side. **b.** Impartially, fairly, justly, equitably.
a **1250** *Prov. Alfred* 79 in *O.E. Misc.* 106 And þe clerek and þe knyht he schulle demen euelyche [*a* **1275** (*2nd text*) euenliche] riht. **1375** BARBOUR *Bruce* VII. 103, I trow he suld be hard to sla, And he war bodyn all evynly. **1424** *Sc. Acts Jas. I* (1597) §45 Gif the Iudge refusis to do the Law eavenlie, the partie compleinand sall haue recourse to the King. *c* **1470** HENRY *Wallace* VI. 53 He thinkis als luff did him hye awance, So evynly held he fauour the ballance. **1509** FISHER *Fun. Serm. C'tess Richmond* Wks. 297 [She] prouyded men lerned..euenly & indyfferently to here all causes. *a* **1626** BACON *Advice to Villiers* (J.), It behoves you to carry yourself wisely and evenly between them [the king and prince] both. *a* **1742** BENTLEY (J.), Being evenly balanced between infinite attractions. **1843** ARNOLD *Hist. Rome* III. 157 A single battle, evenly contested and hardly won. **1855** MACAULAY *Hist. Eng.* III. 255 The Sovereign.. had not the power to bear himself evenly between his large and his small kingdom. **1878** LECKY *Eng. in 18th C.* I. i. 118 The apparent wishes of the nation hung so evenly and oscillated so frequently.
6. Equally. †**a.** In an equal degree or proportion. Sometimes followed by *as. Obs.*
a **1000** tr. *Bæda's Eccl. Hist.* III. xxiii, Calin..wæs mæsse preost & efenlic Godes man. *c* **1374** CHAUCER *Boeth.* I. v. 25 Þou..compleinest þat gerdouns ne ben not euenliche ȝolde to þe desertes of folk. **1382** WYCLIF *Ezek.* xlvii. 14 Forsoothe ȝe shuln weelde it, eche euenly as his brother. *c* **1400** *Three Kings Cologne* xiv. 48 Þe sterre euenlich ȝede to-fore euery kyng and all her pepil. **1413** LYDG. *Pilgr. Sowle* IV. xxvi. (1483) 71 b, Theyr wyttes shold ben euen y lyke, and euenly shold they comprehenden.
b. In the same degree throughout. Cf. 1.
a **1613** BREREWOOD (J.), The upper face of the sea is known to be level by nature, and evenly distant from the centre. **1756** BURKE *Subl. & B.* (1759) 309 The liquor reflecting all the rays of its proper colour *evenly*.
c. In equal parts or shares; as much on one side as on the other.
1395 *E.E. Wills* (1882) 5, Cxx *li*, euenliche to be departed betwix ham thre. *c* **1420** *Pallad. on Husb.* I. 606 Hony, myxt with salt armonyake And comyn evenly, is goode therfore. **1471** *Act. Audit.* 18 One [= on] baith thair expensis evinly. **1574** tr. *Littleton's Tenures* 43 b, Gavel-kind whereby..the children males oughte evenly to inherit. **1614** RALEIGH *Hist. World* Pref. B iij, There is no great Art in deuiding euenly of those things, which are subiect to number and measure. **1885** *L'pool Daily Post* 30 June 5/6 The two parties in the borough are very evenly divided.
7. *evenly even, odd*: see EVEN, ODD.

†**even'mete**, *a. Obs.* Also 2 *Orm.* efennmete. [? OE. **efenmǽte*, f. *efen*, EVEN *a.* + *mǽte* (see MEET *a.*) of a certain measure, f. WGer. **mâta* measure. Cf. OHG. *ebenmâzi.*] Of the same measure or standing, co-equal.
c **1200** ORMIN 12365 Wiþþ enngless efennmete. *a* **1300** *E.E. Psalter* xlviii. 13 [xlix. 12] Til un-wise meres even-mete es he.

evenness ('iːvənnıs). [OE. *efenniss*: see EVEN *a.* and -NESS.]
1. The quality or state of being smooth or level; smoothness, levelness.
1580 BARET *Alv.* P 441 The plainenesse or euennesse of the sea. **1611** COTGR. s.v. *Limé*, Scraped, or shauen vnto a sleeknesse, or euennesse. **1644** EVELYN *Mem.* (1857) I. 91 For stateliness of the buildings, paving, and evenness of the street..far superior to any in Europe. **1714** DERHAM *Astro-Theol.* Prel. Disc. (1750) 33 The evenness of the surface of the lunar spots. **1885** *Manch. Weekly Times* Supp. 20 June 4/3 The paring down must..be done with great evenness and accuracy.
2. Uniformity in shape, texture, arrangement, etc.
1634 SIR T. HERBERT *Trav.* 182 Trees of admirable height and evennesse. **1684-5** BOYLE *Min. Waters* 69 The length and evenness of the stem. **1726** LEONI tr. *Alberti's Archit.* I. 27 b, The Sallow, the Hornbeam..and the Fig..by their Dryness and Evenness, are..wonderfully soft and easy under the Carver's Tool. **1878** L. P. MEREDITH *Teeth* 2 The evenness, the whiteness..in a beautiful set of teeth.
3. Of movement or action: Uniformity, freedom from fluctuations in speed or intensity; equability. Also of the mind, temper, etc.: Equability; calmness, equanimity.
1574 H. G. *Briefe Tables* G ij a, Thou, for to cause that the raye maye go with an euennesse, shalte cause this maniple to go by fiue in a rancke in breadth. **1655** JER. TAYLOR *Unum Necess.* iii. §5 (R.) A good man may..in a sudden anger go beyond the evenness of a wise Christian. **1683** TEMPLE *Mem.* Wks. 1731 I. 401 His Recovery..was owing to the great Evenness of his Temper. **1701** GREW *Cosm. Sacr.* (J.), The ether most readily yieldeth to the revolutions of the celestial bodies, and the making them with that evenness and celerity is requisite in them all. **1711** STEELE *Spect.* No. 147 ¶2 Evenness of Voice and Delivery. **1867** A. J. ELLIS *E.E. Pronunc.* I. iv. 331 The evenness with which a Frenchman pronounces the syllables.
†**4.** Balanced condition, equipoise. *lit.* and *fig.* Also, Equidistance from extremes: the just mean.
1398 TREVISA *Barth De P.R.* III. xxiii. (1495) 71 Some pulse hyght meane euyn and temperate. This meane and euinnes comyth of moche and lytyll. *a* **1420** HOCCLEVE *De Reg. Princ.* 140 He lucre & losse weiethe in evennesse. *a* **1600** HOOKER (J.), That so it [a crooked stick] may settle itself..in a middle estate of evenness. **1646** J. WHITAKER *Uzziah* 22 It [is] a difficulty for an unsteady paralyticall hand to carry a full cup with evennesse. **1653** ROUSE *Myst. Marr.* 316 The one are so ballanced with the other that the soul is kept in an evenness. **1660** *Andromania* I. i. in Hazl. *Dodsley* XIV. 200 See the ambassadors entertain'd With such an evenness as should be us'd to men We neither fear nor love.
5. Of the administration of justice: Equitableness, impartiality. †Formerly in wider use: Equity, righteousness.
c **1000** *Ags. Ps.* (Spelm.) cxviii [cxix]. 144 (Bosw.) Efennys ȝecyðnys ðin on ecnysse. *a* **1300** *E.E. Psalter* ix. 9 And als deme sal he World of erþe in evennesse. *c* **1430** *Pilgr. Lyf Manhode* I. xxviii. (1869) 19 To varie it at your wille..after that the cas asketh and right and euenenesse is. **1607** HIERON *Wks.* I. 138 Be carefull..in the duties of equity and euennesse amongst men, this is religion. **1679** BURNET *Hist. Ref.* Pref. 5 They have delivered things to posterity with.. much candour and evenness. **1866** KINGSLEY *Herew.* I. xvi. 302 Without it.. these noble knights had never known the evenness of Count Baldwin's justice.
¶*pl.* after the Vulgate and the Heb.: Right things.
a **1340** HAMPOLE *Psalter* xvi[i]. 2 Þin eghen se euenesses.
†**6.** Equality. *Obs.*
1398 TREVISA *Barth. De P.R.* III. xxiv. (1495) 73 The line of the euynesse of daye and nighte. **1530** PALSGR. 217/2 Evennesse, *equalité.* **1668** WILKINS *Real Char.* II. i. §4. 34 Evenness, Parity.

†**even-old**, *a.* and *sb. Obs.* Forms: (see EVEN *a.* and OLD). [OE. *efeneald*: see EVEN- and OLD.]
A. *adj.* Of the same age; co-eval. **B.** *sb.* One who is of the same age.
a **1000** *Widsith* 40 (Gr.) Nænig efen-eald him eorlscipe maran on-orette. *c* **1000** ÆLFRIC *Hom.* II. 134 (Bosw.) Pleȝende mid his efen-ealdum. *c* **1200** ORMIN 18605 Swa wass Crist..all wiþþ hiss Faderr efenald. **1382** WYCLIF *Dan.* i. 10 He shal see ȝour cheeris lener byfore other ȝunge men, ȝour euenelde. *c* **1440** *Promp. Parv.* 143 Eveneholde, or euenelde, *coevus.* **1483** *Vulgaria abs Terentio* 14 b, Lyke as I se my son do for his frende & euenȝelde.

evenomate (iː'vɛnəmeıt), *v. rare*⁻¹. [f. E- out + VENOM *sb.* + -ATE³.] *trans.* To take out the poison from (food, etc.).
a **1834** COLERIDGE *Lit. Rem.* (1836) III. 122 Purified from the poison of the practical Romish doctrine of works as the Mandioc is evenomated by fire.

†**'evens**, *adv. Obs.* [genit. of EVEN *sb.* used *advb.*] In the evening.
a **1400-50** *Alexander* 375 Folke was on þaire firste slepe & it was furth euyns.

evensong (ˈiːv(ə)nsɒŋ). [f. EVEN *sb.* + SONG.]

1. *Eccl.* The English name of the service (also called *vespers*) usually celebrated shortly before sunset, being the sixth of the seven 'canonical hours' of the Western Church. After the Reformation applied to the 'Evening Prayer' of the Church of England, which is 'an abridgement of the offices of Evensong and Compline as used before the Reformation' (Hook *Ch. Dict.*).

the Doleful Evensong: the 'Fatal Vespers' of 26 Oct. 1623, at which the greater part of a R.C. congregation lost their lives through the falling-in of a floor.

c **1000** *Canons of Ælfric* xix, þa seofon tid-sangas.. uhtsang ant þrim-sang.. non-sang ant æfen-sang. *c* **1040** *Rule St. Benet* (Logeman) 50 Æfensanc dæghwamlice mid feower sealmorum. *c* **1325** *E.E. Allit. P.* A. 528 At þe day of date of euen-songe, On oure byfore þe sonne go doun. **1389** in *Eng. Gilds* 17 Euery brother and sister.. shullen.. heren yᵉ seruice of bothe yᵉ euensonge & messe. **1462** in Ellacombe *Bells of Ch.* ix. (1872) 277 He schall helpe to ryng all in to Matens and Masse and evynsong with his felow. **1549** *Bk. Com. Prayer*, Table for the Ordre of the Psalmes, to be sayed at Matins and Euensong. *c* **1550** BECON *Treat. Fasting* in *Catechism* (1844) 533 Such should not be counted to fast that did eat before evensong was done. *a* **1613** OVERBURY *A Wife* (1638) 217 The country Lasses dance in the Church-yard after Even-song. **1691** WOOD *Ath. Oxon.* I. 427 He [John Gee] had been at the doleful Evensong in the Black-Friers in London, 26 Oct. 1623. **1735** POPE *Donne Sat.* II. 106 Doom'd to say his beads and Evensong. **1818** SCOTT *Rob Roy* xvii, 'I might hae gaen to evensong, and heard Daddy Docharty mumbling his mass'. **1882** SPURGEON *Treas. Dav.* Ps. cxix. 97 His matin prayer.. his evensong were all out of Holy Writ.

attrib. **1641** MILTON *Animadv.* ii. Wks. (1847) 61/1 To diet their ignorance.. with the limited draught of a matin, and evensong drench.

b. The time of evensong; the hour of sunset. *arch.* Also more fully † ***evensong time***.

a **1300** *Cursor M.* 25594 (Cott.) Suete iesu.. þou gaf sight o þi blod and flexs at euen-sanges time [*c* **1340** (Fairf.) euensange time]. *c* **1330** *Arth. & Merl.* 4800 Fram afternone to auensong. **1375** BARBOUR *Bruce* XVII. 450 Quhen that evynsang-tym ves neir. **1465** *Paston Lett.* No. 504 II. 191 On the same day at evyn-song time. **1486** *Bk. St. Albans* C v a, Let hir fast till euensong. **1523** LD. BERNERS *Froiss.* I. ccclxix. (R.), The yonge kyng entred into Reynes, the Saturday at euensongtyme. **1560–78** *Bk. Discipl. Ch. Scot.*, The Saterday, and other vigils to be holy daies from Evensong to Evensong. **1650** JER. TAYLOR *Holy Living* (J.), If a man were but of a day's life, it is well if he lasts 'till evensong. *a* **1700** DRYDEN *Poems* (J.), He tun'd his notes both evensong and morn. **1755** in JOHNSON. **1775** in ASH. **1865** SWINBURNE *Poems & Ballads, Before Dawn* 9 From evensong to day time.

†**c.** ***Sicilian evensong***: = 'Sicilian vespers': see VESPERS. *Obs.*

1586 T. B. *La Primaud. Fr. Acad.* I. (1589) 718 All the Frenchmen that were in the Ile of Sicilia.. upon Easter day, at the first peale to Evensong.. were al put to death.. whereupon this proverbe doth yet remaine amongst us, The Sicilian Evensong. *a* **1649** DRUMM. OF HAWTH *Irene* Wks. 168 Towns will close their gates upon you; and ye may some day expect a Sicilian even-song.

2. *gen.* (partly *transf.* from 1). A song sung in the evening.

c **1386** CHAUCER *Prol.* 830 If euen song and morwe song accorde Lat se now who shal telle the firste tale. **1632** MILTON *Penseroso* 64 Thee, chauntress, oft the woods among I woo, to hear thy even-song. **1647** CRASHAW *Poems* 176 Sit thee down, and sing thy evensong in the sad tree's shade. **1876** OUIDA *Winter City* xii. 373 Flocks of birds.. were singing their sweet shrill evensong.

†**even-star.** *Obs.* Also 5 -stern. [OE. *æfensteorra*, f. *æfen*, EVEN *sb.* + *steorra*, STAR; for *even-stern* cf. ON. *aptan-stiarn*.] Evening-star.

c **888** K. ÆLFRED *Boeth.* xxxix. §13 Se steorra ðe we hataþ æfensteorra. *c* **1220** *Bestiary* 766 For he is faier ouer alle men, so euen sterre ouer eððe fen. **1388** WYCLIF *Job* xxxviii. 32 Thou.. makist euene sterre.. to rise on the sones of erthe. **1483** *Cath. Angl.* 119 The Euenstern, *vesperus*. **1552** HULOET, Euen starre.. *vesper, vesperugo*.

event (ɪˈvɛnt), *sb.* Also 6 *Sc.* evend. [a. OF. *event*, ad. L. *ēvent-us* occurrence, issue, f. *ēvenīre* to come out, happen, result, f. *ē-* out + *venīre* to come.]

1. a. The (actual or contemplated) fact of anything happening; the occurrence *of*. Now chiefly in phrase ***in the event of***: in the case (something specified) should occur; also (*U.S.*) without *of*.

1602 FULBECKE *1st Pt. Parall.* Introd. 1, I could not but expect the euent of so good a thing. *Mod.* In the event of the earl's death, the title will lapse. **1835** DICKENS *Let.* 29 Oct. (1965) I. 84, I have instructed the Bearer to wait for an answer, in the event of your being at home. **1922** JOYCE *Ulysses* 404 The juridical and theological dilemma in the event of one Siamese twin predeceasing the other. **1966** *Publ. Amer. Dial. Soc.* 1964 XLII. 8 *Roll bar*, a metal tubular structure over the cockpit which protects the driver in the event the car overturns.

†**b.** ***in point of event***: in point of fact, as things have actually happened. *Obs.*

1676 ALLEN *Addr. Nonconf.* 29 And.. we find in point of event, that the ordinary way.. hath been, etc.

2. a. Anything that happens, or is contemplated as happening; an incident, occurrence. ***the course of events***: see COURSE.

1588 SHAKS. *Tit. A.* v. iii. 204 To Order well the State, That like Euents, may ne'er it Ruinate. **1632** LITHGOW *Trav.* IV. 140 The dangerous euents in darke and tempestuous nights, which happen there [in this sea]. **1650** CROMWELL *Lett.* 12 Sept. (Carlyle), [We do not think] of the hand of the great God in this mighty and strange appearance of His; but can slightly call it an 'event'! **1736** BUTLER *Anal.* Introd. Wks. 1874 I. 2 This observation forms.. a presumption.. that such event has or will come to pass. **1803** CAMPBELL *Lochiel's Warning*, Coming events cast their shadows before. **1828** SCOTT *F.M. Perth* xix, Her affection, awakened by the events of the morning. **1876** J. H. NEWMAN *Hist. Sk.* I. I. ii. 86 An utter change in the political events which came after.. would have been the result.

b. In various *spec.* uses (see quots.).

1919 A. N. WHITEHEAD *Enquiry Princ. Nat. Knowledge* II. vi. 72 The 'constants of externality' are those characteristics of a perpetual experience which it possesses.. when we apprehend it. A fact which possesses these characteristics, namely these constants of externality, is what we call an 'event'. **1920** A. S. EDDINGTON *Space Time & Gravit.* iii. 45 A point in this space-time, that is to say a given instant at a given place, is called an 'event'. An event in its customary meaning would be the physical happening which occurs at and identifies a particular place and time. However, we shall use the word in both senses. **1924** R. M. OGDEN tr. *Koffka's Growth of Mind* v. §10. 329 Here a process of uniting two event-configurations into one is indicated. The transference from a one-word to a many-word sentence is carried out. **1959** *Times* 13 Mar. 10/6 The site of a suspected 'event' (the technical term for a nuclear explosion). **1959** *Operations Research* VII. 649 An 'event', depicted by circled numbers in Fig. 1, is defined as a distinguishable, unambiguous point in time that coincides with the beginning and/or end of a specific task or activity in the R[esearch] and D[evelopment] process. **1963** J. LYONS *Structural Semantics* vi. 118 If the antecedent is an 'event'-'state' verb, then the aorist of the antecedent expresses the 'event' which issues in the 'state' expressed by the imperfective of the consequent. It follows.. that the consequent will be either an 'event'-'state' verb or merely a 'state' verb. **1964** K. G. LOCKYER *Introd. Critical Path Analysis* ii. 9 An arrow diagram is made up of only two basic elements—(i) *An event*, which must be 'of a definite recognizable nature and.. must be a point in time'.. (ii) *An activity*, which is the 'work' or 'job' which leads up to an event. *Ibid.* x. 100 This 'event-orientation' is quite common in PERT systems. **1968** *Gloss. Terms Project Network Anal.* (*B.S.I.*) 6 *Event*, a state in the progress of a project after the completion of all preceding activities but before the start of any succeeding activity. **1968** P. A. P. MORAN *Introd. Probability Theory* iv. 186 The σ-field and its corresponding measure is known as a 'probability space', and the sets, {A}, are 'events'.

c. *pl.* (without article) for 'the course of events'; also occas. in sing. ***the event***.

1719 DE FOE *Crusoe* (1840) I. xiv. 238, I resolved to put myself upon the watch to see them.. and leave the rest to the event. **1842** MIALL *Nonconf.* II. 1 Events have proved us right. **1879** DIXON *Windsor* II. xii. 130 Nature and events had made him king.

d. In mod. use chiefly restricted to occurrences of some importance; hence colloquial uses such as ***quite an event***. (Cf. Fr. *un véritable événement*.)

1883 MRS. BISHOP in *Leisure H.* 84/2 The first sight of a real mangrove swamp is an event.

e. In the doctrine of chances: (*a*) Any one of the possible (mutually exclusive) occurrences some one of which will happen under stated conditions, and the relative probability of which may be computed. ***compound event***: one that consists in the combined occurrence of two or more simple events. (*b*) Occasionally, a trial or hazard, which will result in some one of several different ways ('events' in the preceding sense).

1838 DE MORGAN *Ess. Probab.* 96 One of the events, A, B, C, &c. must happen at every trial, and each event brings with it a specified gain or loss. **1885** CROFTON in *Encycl. Brit.* (ed. 9) XIX. 771 Determination of the probabilities of Compound Events, when the probabilities of the simple events on which they depend are known. *Ibid.*, Let there be an event which must turn out in one of two ways, W and B.

f. In sporting language: Something on the issue of which money is staked; also, one of the items in a programme of sports.

1855 THACKERAY *Newcomes* II. 66 The young fellows were making an 'event' out of Ethel's marriage and sporting their money freely on it. **1865** TROLLOPE *Belton Est.* i. 4 Trusting to the next event at Newmarket to set him right. **1884** *Cyclist* 13 Feb. 247/2 The Amateur Athletic Association passed a rule prohibiting the holding of professional events at amateur athletic meetings. **1884** *Sat. Rev.* 12 July 50 Of the leading events Oxford, Cambridge, and Eton each won one.

3. a. That which follows upon a course of proceedings; the outcome, issue; that which proceeds from the operation of a cause; a consequence, result. ***in*** (***the***) ***event***: in (the) result.

1573 *Sempill Ball.* 187 Weill micht the counsals beir ane gude euend. **1570–6** LAMBARDE *Peramb. Kent* (1826) 247 Touching the originall, proceeding, and event of these wars I spare to speake much. **1611** HEYWOOD *Gold. Age* I. i, Causes best friended haue the best euent. **1612** T. TAYLOR *Comm. Titus* ii. 4 Too much indulgence.. is a cruell loue in the euent. **1645** FULLER *Good Th. in Bad T.* (1841) 24 His courtesy in intention proved a mischief in event. **1711** STEELE *Spect.* No. 113 ¶3 A beautiful Creature in a Widow's Habit sat in Court, to hear the Event of a Cause concerning her Dower. **1767** GOOCH *Treat. Wounds* I. 96 We have surprising accounts.. of the recovery of persons, without the least prospect of a favourable event. **1820** SCOTT *Ivanhoe* xiii, He then took his aim.. and the multitude awaited the event in breathless silence. **1848** MACAULAY *Hist. Eng.* II. 612 The event of his enterprise was doubtful. **1866** MOTLEY *Dutch Rep.* II. ii. 146 They openly, and in the event successfully, resisted the installation of the new prelate. **1875** JOWETT *Plato* (ed. 2) V. 53 There is no merit.. in learning wisdom after the event.

†**b.** Undesigned or incidental result. *nonce-use.*

1644 H. PARKER *Jus Pop.* 25 The Pilot wafts himself by event [Aristotle's κατὰ συμβεβηκός, *Phys.* II. 1], it being impossible that he should waft others, if hee were absent.

†**4.** What 'becomes of' or befalls (a person or thing); fate. *Obs.*

15.. MORE *Edw. V.* Ep. Ded. 2 The miserable and wretched end and event of the other. **1591** SPENSER *Teares Muses* 143 A ship in midst of tempest left.. Full sad and dreadfull is that ships event. **1611** BIBLE *Eccl.* ix. 2. **1674** OWEN *Holy Spirit* (1693) 129 They differ as unto the Event they may come unto.

5. Idiomatic phrases, with mixed notion of 2 and 3. ***at*** (or †***in***) ***all events***: whatever happens or happened; in any case, at any rate. † ***upon all events***: for every emergency.

1672 EVELYN *Mem.* (1857) II. 80, I had put all things in readiness upon all events. **1685** *Ibid.* II. 250 In all events.. the Church of England.. is the most primitive, apostolical, and excellent. [**1703** LD. HOLT in Raymond *Rep.* 909 He is bound to answer for the goods at all events but acts of God and the king's enemies.] **1761–2** HUME *Hist. Eng.* (1806) IV. li. 42 Civil war.. must in all events, prove calamitous to the nation. **1818** JAS. MILL *Brit. India* II. IV. ii. 73 Dupleix sent repeated orders that it [the reinforcement] might be intercepted at all events. **1857** BUCKLE *Civiliz.* I. x. 603 Berkstead was a pedlar, or at all events a hawker of small wares. **1875** JOWETT *Plato* (ed. 2) III. 35 Not this at all events, which is the opposite of truth.

6. Special Comb.: **event horizon** *Astr.*, a notional surface from beyond which no matter or radiation can reach an external observer; *spec.* the Schwarzschild sphere of a black hole; **event-particle**, one of the abstract minimal elements into which, according to A. N. Whitehead, space-time can be analysed.

1969 *Rivista del Nuovo Cimento* I. Suppl. 273 Have we any right to suggest that the *only* type of collapse which can occur is one in which the space-time singularities lie hidden, deep inside the protective shielding of an absolute *event horizon? **1977** J. NARLIKAR *Struct. of Universe* iv. 123 A stage will come when B will have moved so far that the signal sent at t'_1 will never reach B. When this stage comes B is said to have crossed beyond the event horizon of A. **1980** *Sci. Amer.* Apr. 101/2 The cosmological singularity is similar to the singularity in the event horizon of a black hole, the hypothetical surface in which matter and light rays are confined by gravity. **1919** A. N. WHITEHEAD *Enquiry Princ. Nat. Knowledge* III. x. 121 An *event-particle is an instantaneous point viewed in the guise of an atomic event. The punct which an event-particle covers gives it an absolute position in the instantaneous space of any moment in which it lies. **1920** —— *Concept of Nature* viii. 172 Thus we finally reach the ideal of an event so restricted in its extension as to be without extension in space or extension in time. Such an event is a mere spatial point-flash of instantaneous duration. I call such an ideal event an 'event-particle'. **1933** *Mind* XLII. 161 The instantaneous punctiform 'event-particles' of certain modern theories.

†**event**, *v.*[1] *Obs.* [f. L. *ēvent-* ppl. stem of *ēvenīre* (see EVENE *v.*) to happen, take place.] *intr.* To come to pass.

(An alleged transitive verb of this form in RICHARDSON and later Dicts. is based on a passage misquoted from T. Wilson *Rhet.* 6 b; edd. 1553 and 1580 have *invented*.)

1590 GREENE *Never too late* (1600) 13, An English History acted and euented in my Countrey of England. **1615** A. NICCHOLES *Marriage & Wiv.* xii, My Maid and I.. Will tell old Stories long ago evented To pass the Time. **1650** *Vind. Hammond's Addr.* §32 To teach their Disciples *apathy*, or courage against whatsoever events.

†**eˈvent**, *v.*[2] *Obs.* [ad. Fr. *éventer*, OF. *esventer*, f. *es-*:—L. *ex-* + *vent* wind; cf. AVENT.] **a.** *trans.* To expose to the air; hence, to cool. **b.** *intr.* for *refl.* To vent itself, find a vent.

1559 BALDWIN in *Mirr. Mag.*, *Clifford* viii, To euent the heat that had me nye vndoen. **1603** B. JONSON *K. Jas'. Entertainm. Coronat.*, Lest the fervour of so pure a flame As this my city bears, might lose the name Without the apt eventing of her heat. **1609** —— *Case is altered* v. iii, The place from whence that scalding sigh evented. **1606** CHAPMAN *Hero & Leander* III, Till he [Phœbus] find oppos'd A loose and rorid vapour that is fit T' event his searching beams.

event (ɪˈvɛnt), *v.*[3] *Equestrianism.* [Back-formation f. EVENTING.] **a.** *intr.* To take part in horse trials (one-, two-, or three-day events). **b.** *trans.* To enter or ride (a horse) in horse trials.

1970 BATCHELOR & LONGLAND *Horse Trials Horses* ix. 76 When she was only thirteen she was eventing with a horse called Foxtrot. **1975** *Cork Examiner* 30 May 21/1 (Advt.), Gelding, 6 years, hunted and evented. **1976** *Horse & Hound* 10 Dec. 71/1 (Advt.), T.B. chestnut gelding.. sound and with potential to point-to-point or event. **1985** *Times* 13 Apr. 29/1 If you can be fit at 40, there's no reason why you shouldn't event and enjoy it.

†**evenˈtation.** *Obs.* [a. F. *eventation*, f. *éventer*: see EVENT *v.*[2]] A letting out, a drawing (of blood).

1544 PHAER *Regim. Lyfe* (1560) O vj b, In suche cases a litle eventacion of the infected bloude, maye bee the saving of their lyves. [**1611** COTGR., *Eventation*, a venting; also, the opening of a veine.]

†**eˈventerate**, *v. Obs. rare*$^{-1}$. [irreg. f. L. *ē-* out + *venter* belly + -ATE[3]: cf. F. *éventrer*.
Prob. orig. a misprint in BROWNE for *exenterate*.]

a. *trans.* To open the bowels of; to disembowel. **b.** *intr.* 'To come out of the belly' (Blount *Glossogr.*, 1656). Hence †**evente'ration** *Obs.*$^{-0}$ = EVENTRATION.

1646 SIR T. BROWNE *Pseud. Ep.* III. vi. 116 In a Bear which the Hunters eventerated, I beheld the young ones with all their parts distinct. **1678** PHILLIPS, *Eventeration*, a taking out the belly of anything. **1692–1732** in COLES.

eventful (ɪ'vɛntfʊl), *a.* [f. EVENT *sb.* + -FUL. A word used once by Shakspere, whence Johnson's only quotation; not appearing otherwise in our quots. till after Johnson.]

1. Full of events; rich in striking occurrences.

1600 SHAKS. *A.Y.L.* II. vii. 164 Last Scene of all, That ends this strange euentfull historie. **1781** GIBBON *Decl. & F.* III. 252 The eventful story of her [Placidia's] life. **1848** MACAULAY *Hist. Eng.* I. 173 The changes which fourteen eventful years had produced. **1874** MOTLEY *Barneveld* I. i. 5 Barneveld's eventful life.

2. Fraught with important issues; momentous.

1773 LANGHORNE *Orig. Veil* (R.) The man of faith thro' Gerar doom'd to stray, A nation waiting his eventful way. **1797** MRS. RADCLIFFE *Italian* xii, A thousand times she turned about the eventful paper. **1801** SOUTHEY *Thalaba* VII. xiii, Thalaba..waited calmly for the eventful day. **1848** MACAULAY *Hist. Eng.* II. 591 The interval between the sitting of Saturday and the sitting of Monday was anxious and eventful.

3. = EVENTUAL 5.

1826 BENTHAM in *Westminst. Rev.* VI. 474 To levy..any part..not exceeding..for any child, a moiety of such his, her, or their then eventful portion or portions.

Hence **e'ventfulness**, eventful quality.

1866 *Contemp. Rev.* II. 592 What we miss in eventfulness is made up in descriptions, etc. **1884** CHURCH *Bacon* iv. 93 Bacon..saw..the critical eventfulness of the moment.

eventide ('i:v(ə)ntaɪd). Chiefly *arch.* [OE. *æfen-tíd*, f. *æfen*, EVEN *sb.* + *tíd* time, TIDE.]

a. The time of evening; evening. Also *fig.*

[*c* **950** *Lindisf. Gosp.*, Mark xi. 11 Miððy ʒee efrn wæs tid ʒefoerde on Bethania mið tuoelfum.] *a* **1000** tr. *Greg. Dial.* I. x. (Bosw.), Seo æfen-tid ðæs dæʒes. *a* **1225** *Ancr. R.* 404 Iðen ende of al his liue, þet was iðen euentid. **1388** WYCLIF *Gen.* i. 8. *c* **1430** tr. *T. à Kempis' Imit.* I. xix, In þe eventide discusse þe maner, what þou hast ben þis day in worde, worke, & þouȝt. **1578** *Chr. Prayers* in *Priv. Prayers* (1851) 447 This life hath not one hour certain, whensoever the eventide thereof cometh. **1611** BIBLE *Gen.* xxiv. 63. **1780** COWPER *Nighting. & Gloww.*, Nor yet at eve his note suspended, Nor yet when eventide was ended. **1851** LONGF. *Gold. Leg.* VI. *Castle Vautsberg*, Those same soft bells at eventide Rang in the ears of Charlemagne.

attrib. **1382** WYCLIF *Ps.* cxl. 2 Euentid sacrifise.

b. eventide home, a home for elderly persons (orig. one maintained by the Salvation Army).

1918 H. BARNETT *Canon Barnett* II. l. 317 An eventide-home for those who are near the end of their pilgrimage. **1959** J. FLEMING *Miss Bones* viii. 95 She was in touch with dozens of good causes, eventide homes, hostels for distressed gentlewomen. **1962** —— *When I grow Rich* x. 120 It looks like an Eventide Home for old liners.

†**e'ventilate**, *v. Obs.* [f. L. *ēventilāt-* ppl. stem of *ēventilā-re* to fan, f. *ē-* out + *ventilāre* to fan: see VENTILATE. Cf. OF. *eventiler.*]

1. *trans.* To expose to the wind or air; to fan; to winnow (corn); to aerate (blood).

1623 in COCKERAM. **1657** *Phys. Dict.*, *Eventilated*, fanned, cooled, or clensed by the wind. **1684** tr. *Bonet's Merc. Compit.* VI. 185 The Symptoms..were caused by Bloud fermenting too much, and not eventilated enough. **1706** in PHILLIPS; hence in ASH, etc.

2. *fig.* To lay open to discussion; to discuss; to VENTILATE.

1657 HOWELL *Londinop.* 377 It is nowhere so narrowly discussed and eventilated. **1669** *Addr. Yng. Gentry Eng.* 136 This is a subject so copiously and methodically elsewhere..eventilated.

b. (See quot.: not in the Law Dicts.)

1706 PHILLIPS (ed. Kersey), *Eventilate*..in a Law-sense, to estimate, prize, or value an Estate or Inheritance.

†**eventi'lation.** *Obs.* [f. prec.: see -ATION. Cf. It. *eventilatione* (Florio).]

1. a. The action of fanning, or of supplying fresh air. **b.** The action of winnowing; also of scattering to the winds. **c.** Aeration (of blood, humours, etc.).

a. **1643** J. H[OWELL] *Parables on Times* 15 Nothing could be..so directly opposite to his soft gentle breezes and eventilations. *c* **1645** HOWELL *Lett.* I. VI. xxxv, This heat is ..a generative gentle heat joyn'd with moisture, nor needs it ayr for eventilation. **1651** —— *Venice* 33 By reason of the fresh breezes and eventilations of the circumjacent Sea. **1721–1800** BAILEY, *Eventilation*, a Winnowing.

b. **1727** BRADLEY *Fam. Dict.* s.v. *Anemone*, Which, by means of that Eventilation, sends out the Seed in such a Manner as it is proper to be sown. **1767** A. CAMPBELL *Lexiph.* (1774) 109 My cudgel..shall soon disseminate, by a rapid eventilation, the brains in his pericranium.

c. **1684** tr. *Bonet's Merc. Compit.* VI. 161 Lest it should obstruct and hinder eventilation by its clamminess. *Ibid.* XI. 378 The Skull being carefully opened..he was recovered by the eventilation of his Brain. **1744** BERKELEY *Siris* §205 It [vital flame] requires constant eventilation, through the trachæa and pores of the body.

¶ Used for: What is 'vented' or belched forth.

1716 M. DAVIES *Athen. Brit.* 238 There remains scarce anything now of all their Factions and Frothy Eventilations or Productions of any kind.

2. The action of laying open to discussion; an examination, discussion.

c **1645** HOWELL *Lett.* (1650) III. 21 In the search and eventilation of naturall verities. **1651** —— *Venice* 148 After some Eventilations of the matters, this Answer was sent. **1706** PHILLIPS (ed. Kersey), *Eventilation*..a strict examining..or sifting of a Business. **1721–1800** in BAILEY.

e'venting. *Equestrianism.* [f. EVENT *sb.* (as in *three-day event* s.v. THREE *a.* and *sb.* III. 2) + -ING[1]: see also EVENT *v.*[3]] The act or practice of competing in horse trials (one-, two-, or three-day events).

1965 *Riding* May 179/1 Miss Anneli Drummond-Hay and Merely-a-Monarch made a triumphant return to their original sport of 'eventing'. **1972** *Observer* (Colour Suppl.) 3 Dec. 85/1 We have not found a less clumsy name than 'eventing' for that thrilling exercise in all-round horsemanship, the heart of which is a cross-country gallop. **1975** *Daily Tel.* 10 June 6/6, I suppose our sort of horse at the top of the market is sought for 'eventing'. **1982** BARR & YORK *Official Sloane Ranger Handbk.* 154/1 Sloane children belong to the Pony Club, and they go on to eventing. **1985** *Financial Times* 24 July 13/3 Working class families where grand-dad would have sneered at a pink coat follow show jumping and eventing as grand-dad once followed Tranmere Rovers.

Also **e'venter**, a horse or rider that takes part in horse trials.

1974 G. M. PHILLIPS *Horses in our Blood* 274 A horse.. likely to make an 'eventer'..needs to be a brilliant all-round athlete. **1982** BARR & YORK *Official Sloane Ranger Handbk.* 19/2 He's jolly good-looking and he's a top eventer. **1986** *Riding* May 12/3 Escapism..has proved himself as an eventer as well as a sire.

eventless (ɪ'vɛntlɪs), *a.* [f. EVENT *sb.* + -LESS; cf. *eventful.*] Without events; unmarked by noteworthy incidents.

1815 MAD. D'ARBLAY *Diary* (1842–6) VII. 231 Our journey was eventless. **1868** MORRIS *Earthly Par.* (1870) I. I. 72 So smoothly o'er our heads the days did flit, Yet not eventless either. **1878** H. M. STANLEY *Dark Cont.* x. 213 On the 21st we made a tedious eventless voyage. **1880** J. W. SHERER *Conjuror's Daughter* 225 The long eventless day was nearing to its close.

Hence **e'ventlessly** *adv.*, in an eventless manner. **e'ventlessness**, the condition of being eventless.

1888 G. E. POST *Lond. Miss. Conf.* I. 24 Her life goes on eventlessly year after year until she reaches the mature age of ten. **1872** HOWELLS *Wedd. Journ.* (1884) 309 He was pleased with the natural eventlessness of the whole adventure.

eventration (i:vɛn'treɪʃən). [a. Fr. *éventration*, f. *éventrer*, f. *é-* (*es-*:—L. *ex-*) out + *ventre* belly.]

1. The action of opening the belly (of an animal).

1875 MISS COBBE *False Beasts* 39 The animal's [camel's] provision of water, which his master could always reach..by the simple process of eventration.

2. a. The condition of a fœtus in which the abdominal viscera are extruded. **b.** In women: A pendulous condition of the lower abdomen. **c.** 'The condition of a large ventral hernia' (*Syd. Soc. Lex.* 1884). **d.** The escape of a large amount of intestines from an abdominal wound.

a. **1860** in MAYNE *Exp. Lex.* **1884** in *Syd. Soc. Lex.*
c. **1836** TODD *Cycl. Anat.* I. 508/1 The tumour formed by the protruding viscera is designated..eventration.
d. **1847** in CRAIG. **1884** in *Syd. Soc. Lex.*

†**e'ventriqueness.** *Obs. rare*$^{-1}$. [f. as if **eventric* (*-ique*) (f. *ē-* out + L. *ventr-em* belly + -IC) + -NESS.] Corpulence. In quot. *fig.*

1667 WATERHOUSE *Fire Lond.* 141 If London..must..be born with till its humors be sweetened, and its eventriqueness be reduced..then to no purpose is this waste of rage.

eventual (ɪ'vɛntjuəl), *a.* [ad. F. *éventuel*, f. as if ad. L. **ēventuāl-is*, f. *ēventu-s*: see EVENT.]

†**1.** Of or pertaining to events or occurrences; consisting in events; of the nature of an event. *Obs.*

1612–5 BP. HALL *Contempl.* XIV. i, There is nothing more dangerous than to make construction of God's purposes, out of eventuall appearances. **1656** *Artif. Handsom.* 50 To run counter to Gods providence, which is his reall word, and as it were an Eventuall Oracle. **1684** H. MORE *Answ. Remarks Exp. Apoc.* B iv a, The true Authentick eventual measure to compute the fulfilling of the Medial-Visions by.

†**2.** That happens to exist. *Obs.*

1752 FIELDING *Amelia* IX. x, By pride I mean that saucy passion which exults in every little eventual pre-eminence over other men. **1794** GODWIN *Cal. Williams* 158 In what manner I should prevent the eventual delay of twenty-four hours from becoming..a source of new calamity.

3. That will arise or take place in a particular contingency.

1767 LD. LYTTELTON *Hen. II*, I. (ed. 2) 86 William aspired to secure to himself the eventual succession to the crown of that kingdom [France], in case that Louis..should die before his father. **1785** BURKE *Sp. Nabob Arcot's Debts* Wks. IV. 279 Nothing is provided for it, but an eventual surplus to be divided with one class of the private demands. **1874** DEUTSCH *Rem.* 252 The Bishops will not have too much time to prepare their eventual opposition. **1874** GREEN *Short Hist.* ix. 623 He offered to admit England to a share in the eventual partition of the Spanish monarchy.

†**b.** Of stipulations: Conditional (cf. EVENTUALLY 1 b). Of an army: To be raised if required.

1683 TEMPLE *Mem.* Wks. 1731 I. 440 The Dutch began to talk of finishing an Eventual Treaty (as they call'd it) for themselves, as soon as the Acts about Powers were wholly dispatch'd. **1796** GOUV. MORRIS in Sparks *Life & Writ.* (1832) III. 98 The consideration of their services should be eventual, and depend on the success of their exertions. **1799** T. JEFFERSON *Writ.* (1859) IV. 279 A bill..authorizing the President in case of a declaration of war..by any European power, to raise an eventual army of thirty regiments.

4. Of the nature of an event or result.

1699 BURNET *39 Art.* xvii. (1700) 162 The Certainty of the Prescience is not antecedent or causal, but subsequent and eventual. **1755** JOHNSON, *Eventual*, happening in consequence of anything; consequential. **1810** BENTHAM *Packing* (1821) 134 Eventual vexation to persons liable to be called upon to serve in the capacity of special jurors. **1834** HT. MARTINEAU *Moral* III. 124 An aggression on the rights of industry, and an eventual injury to all concerned.

5. Ultimately resulting.

1823 FABER *Diffic. Infidelity* (1833) 3 The necessary consequence which it involves..an eventual denial of God's omnipotence. **1850** GLADSTONE *Gleanings* V. cxxxvi. 252 The silent decay and eventual overthrow of her natural defences. **1857** BUCKLE *Civiliz.* I. x. 618 As society advances, the eventual cessation of all such attempts is certain. **1868** J. H. BLUNT *Ref. Ch. Eng.* I. 437 Gradually moulded into their eventual form.

eventuality (ɪˌvɛntju:'ælɪtɪ). [f. prec. + -ITY: cf. F. *éventualité.*]

1. Something that may happen; a possible event or occurrence; a contingency.

1759 *Monthly Rev.* XX. 448 Our Historian [*sc.* W. Harte] ..uses..*eventualities*, where *contingencies*, or *contingent events*, would be as expressive. **1852** LEVER *Daltons* I. 123 Some experience had..trained him to a tactic of waiting and watching for eventualities. **1855** BROWNING *Men & Wom.* i. *Bp. Blougram's Apol.*, In that bewildering entanglement Of horrible eventualities. **1878** LADY HERBERT tr. *Hübner's Ramble* I. xii. 184 In certain eventualities this state of things might give rise to grave difficulties.

2. *Phrenology.* The faculty of observing and remembering the order of succession in events; the supposed 'organ' of this faculty.

1828 G. COMBE *Const. Man.* 72 Individuality and Eventuality, or the powers of observing things that exist and occurrences. **1859** R. F. BURTON *Centr. Afr.* in *Jrnl. Geog. Soc.* XXIX. 314 The forehead converges to a central protuberosity, where phrenologists locate eventuality.

eventually (ɪ'vɛntju:əlɪ), *adv.* [f. as prec. + -LY[2].]

1. In the event of something happening.

1830 FOSTER in *Life & Corr.* (1846) II. 164 Some eventually possible inconvenience.

†**b.** In order to provide against a contingency; in conditional terms. *Obs.*

1749 CHESTERF. *Lett.* II. cxcvi. 239 So many of my letters have miscarried..that I am forced to repeat the same thing over and over again eventually. **1752** *Ibid.* IV. 3, I am sensible that they can only be met with by great accident at family sales and auctions, so I only mention the affair to you eventually. [So often in CHESTERF.] **1785** BURKE *Sp. Nabob Arcot's Debts* Wks. IV. 271 Not conditionally and eventually, but positively and authoritatively.

†**2.** In result (as opposed to intention). *Obs.*

1660 BOYLE *Seraphic Love* Wks. 1772 I. 248, I..think that Hermione has but intentionally, not eventually disobliged you. **1706** DE FOE *Jure Div.* Pref. 20 King James was not deposed by those, otherwise than eventually: these were the Causes of all this. **1729** BUTLER *Serm.* Wks. 1874 II. 109 Other vices eventually do mischief: this alone aims at it as an end.

3. In the event, in the end, finally, ultimately.

a **1680** GLANVILL *Serm.* i. (1681) 80 If one that shall eventually be shut out, may do all this, what shall become of the generality of Religious men that never do so much? **1797** E. M. LOMAX *Philanthrope* 278 Seneca..endeavoured to employ every day of his life as if it eventually might be his last. **1843** MISS MITFORD in L'Estrange *Life* (1870) III. x. 179 Absentees..will doubtless eventually disappear from Ireland. **1879** PROCTOR *Pleas. Ways Sc.* v. 122 This line eventually became the brightest line of the whole spectrum.

eventuate (ɪ'vɛntjueɪt), *v.* [f. L. *ēventu-s* EVENT *sb.* + -ATE; cf. *actuate*. First used in U.S., and still regarded as an Americanism, though it has been employed by good writers in England.]

1. *intr.* To have a (specified) event or issue; to turn out (well or ill); to issue, result *in*.

1789 GOUV. MORRIS in Sparks *Life & Writ.* (1832) I. 313, I am sure it is wrong, and cannot eventuate well. **1835** M. SCOTT *Cruise Midge* xii, The squib had eventuated, as the Yankees say..in a zigzag or cracker. **1855** MILMAN *Lat. Chr.* (1864) IX XIV. iii. 151 The Schoolmen could not but eventuate in William of Ockham. **1873** SMILES *Huguenots Fr.* II. ii. (1881) 361 He heard..the discussions which eventuated in Acts of Parliament. **1877** A. J. ROSS *Mem. Bp. Ewing* xxxi. 536 The crisis had eventuated favourably.

2. To be the issue; to result, come about.

1834 DE QUINCEY *Coleridge* Wks. (1863) II. 93 In the upshot, this conclusion eventuated (to speak Yankeeishly), that, etc. **1876** M. DAVIES *Unorth. Lond.* I. 25 If So-and-so were condemned, a schism in the National Church would eventuate. **1884** *Law Times* 14 June 121/1 When there was danger of a war eventuating with America.

3. *trans.* To bring to the event or issue.

1837–40 HALIBURTON *Clockm.* (1862) 103 Yes, (to eventuate my story) it did me good.

eventuation (ɪˌvɛntju:'eɪʃən). [f. prec.: see -ATION.] The action of 'eventuating'; bringing or coming to an issue; realization; issue.

a **1848** R. W. HAMILTON (Ogilvie). **1876** *Overmatched* II. 196 Deputing to some good genius..the eventuation of his more dazzling hopes.

†'**ever**, *sb. Obs.* Forms: 1 eofer, eofor, efer, efor, 3 eaver, 4 ever. [OE. *eofer* = OHG. (and mod.Ger.) *eber*, ON. *iǫfurr*:—OTeut. **eƀuro-z*, allied to OSlav. *veprĭ*, L. *aper*.]

1. A wild boar.

c **1000** *Ags. Ps.* lxxix. [lxxx.] 13 Hine utan of wuda eoferas wrotað and wilde deor westað and frettað. *c* **1000** *Sax. Leechd.* II. 182 Sele þu him..flæsc eofores. *c* **1230** *Hali Meid.* 13 Ha in hare wurðunge as eaueres forroteden.

2. *Comb.* **ever-fern**: **a.** the Polypody, *Polypodium vulgare*; **b.** *Osmunda regalis.*

c **1000** *Sax. Leechd.* I. 188 Ðeos wyrt man..efor fearn nemneð. *c* **1000** ÆLFRIC *Gloss.* in Wr.-Wülcker 135 *Filix arboratica*, eferfearn. *c* **1050** *Ags. Voc.* ibid. 297 *Filix minuta*, eoforfearn. *c* **1325** *E.E. Allit. P.* C. 438 He busked hym a bour..Of hay & of euer-ferne & erbez a fewe. *a* **1387** *Sinon. Barthol.* (Anecd. Oxon.) 32 Osmunda, herba est, everferne. *a* **1400** *Sloane MS.* 5. 9b, Osmundo..eueruern. **14..** *Recipes* in *Rel. Ant.* I. 52 For the stane..tak everferne that grewes on the ake.

ever ('ɛvə(r)), *adv.* Forms: α. 1–3 æfre (*north.* æfra, 2 ævre, 3 ævere), 2–3 afre, efre, efer(e, 3 aver(e, avre, eur, 2–4 evr(e, evere, 3–4 hevere, 2–5 eaver, 2–6 evir, -yr, 9 *dial.* ivver, 2– ever. β. 3 ær, er, 4–7 ere, 6– e'er. Also α. 3 ȝavre, 6 yeffor. β. 4 yer. [OE. *ǽfre*. Not found in other Teut. langs.; the ulterior etymology is doubtful. Connexion of some kind with OE. *á*, AY is probable on account of the sense.

If it be a compound of *á*, the second element should begin with *f* or less probably with *b*, and contain the vowel (iː). The most plausible suggestion hitherto made is that of Cosijn (*Taalk. Bijdragen* II. 267), that it is equivalent to Goth. **aiw fairhwau* 'ever in life'; cf. the common OE. phrase *á tó feore* in similar sense; also OHG. *neonaltre* never, lit. 'never in life'. This is supported by the agreement of the final *-a* of the ONorthumb. *ǽfra* with the ending of the locative (dat.) of the *-u* declension, to which the sb. *feorh* life (:—**ferhwus*) originally belonged. The recorded forms of *feorh*, however, do not account for the umlaut; but cf. the cognate OE. *fíras*, OS. *firihôs*, ON. *fírar* 'men'. A different suggestion has been made by Prof. G. Hempl in *Mod. Lang. Notes* IV. (1889) 417, viz. that the word is an adverbial case of a subst. compound f. *á* + *byre* (:—*buri*) event, occasion. On this view its formation would be closely analogous to that of Ger. *jemals*. With regard to the umlaut Prof. Hempl compares *ǽrende*:—**árundi*; with regard to the *f* from *b* he compares *wéofod* for **wih-bed* (or *-béod*).]

I. Always, at all times; in all cases. (All these senses, exc. 1 b and 5 b, are now *arch.* or merely literary.)

1. a. Throughout all time, eternally; throughout all past or all future time; perpetually (often hyperbolically or in relative sense: throughout one's life, etc.). *arch.* Also strengthened ***ever and ever***, † ***ever ay***.

a **1000** CYNEWULF *Crist* 111 Ðu æfre wære. *c* **1175** *Lamb. Hom.* 57 Þet is and wes and efre scal beon iblecced ofer al. *c* **1200** ORMIN 206 Icc amm Gabriæl þatt æfre & æfre stannde Biforenn Godd. *c* **1200** *Trin. Coll. Hom.* 173 Þe endelese dai is afre abuten ende. *a* **1300** *Cursor M.* 13180 (Gött.) Þarfor euer ay worth hir wa! Þat god man dos wid tresun sla. **1340** *Ayenb.* 71 Þe oþre lyue þet eure wyþoute ende ssel yleste. **1500–20** DUNBAR *'Full oft I mus'* vi, The lyfe that evir dois lest. **1548–9** (Mar.) *Bk. Com. Prayer, Offices* 34 That wee may euer liue with thee in the worlde to come. **1551** ROBINSON tr. *More's Utop.* II. (Arb.) 73 It [the island] was not euer compassed about with the sea. **1610** SHAKS. *Temp.* IV. i. 123 Let me liue here euer. **1662** *Bk. Com. Prayer* (1844) 113 He liveth and reigneth ever one God. **1733** LD. MAYOR OF LONDON *Let.* 6 Aug. in *Swift's Lett.*, A set of great men, who will ever be an honour..to their country. **1831** CARLYLE *Sart. Res.* (1858) 152 Ever must the Sovereign of Mankind be fitly entitled King.

b. In sense limited by a following adv., prep., or conj., as in ***ever after(-ward)***, ***ever before***, ***ever since***, throughout all the time before or after a specified date.

α. *a* **1300** *Cursor M.* 3942 (Gött.) Euer siþen [*c* **1340** *Trin.* euer aftir] halted he. *c* **1380** WYCLIF *Sel. Wks.* III. 510 Hevere bifore and evere aftir. **1525** LD. BERNERS *Froiss.* II. clxxxvi [clxxxii]. 565 He hath assembled toguyder into his house..a great noumbre of menne, and hath kepte them there couertly euersyth the ferst of Whitsontyde. **1535** COVERDALE *Isa.* li. 9 Euer and sence the worlde beganne. **1714** ADDISON *Spect.* No. 556 ¶7 The Coffee-houses have ever since been my chief Places of Resort. **1782** PRIESTLEY *Corrupt. Chr.* I. I. 104 Ever after..the phraseology of the Greeks prevailed. **1865** H. KINGSLEY *Hillyars & B.* xxxv, It must have been raining cats and dogs ever since I had been out. **1875** JOWETT *Plato* (ed. 2) I. 364 This sign I have had ever since I was a child.

β. **1601** SHAKS. *Twel. N.* I. i. 23 My desires like fell and cruell hounds, Ere since pursue me.

c. ***Yours ever***: a phrase used in the subscription of a letter (cf. YOURS *poss. pron.* 1 c). Also *ellipt.* *ever*.

[**1601** R. LYTTON *Let.* 19 Sept. in S. Williams *John Chamberlain's Lett.* 118 And so, with the best wishes of an assured friend and loving kinsman, I committ you to God. Your ever soe, R. Lytton.] **1611** T. HEYWOOD *Golden Age* sig. A2, As this is received, so you shall find the rest: either fearefull further to proceede, or encouraged boldly to follow. Yours ever T.H. **1763** BOSWELL *Let.* 28 July (1924) I. 38 My kind service to Bob. Yours ever, with most sincere affection, James Boswell. **1807** BYRON *Let.* 6 Mar. (1898) I. 122 Poetic fame is by no means the 'acme' of my wishes.—Adieu. Yours ever, Byron. **1914** T. E. LAWRENCE *Lett.* (1938) 169 Yours ever, T. E. Lawrence. **1934** *Ibid.* 809 It's what I call making use of history. Ever, T. E. S. **1954** A. S. C. Ross in *Neuphilologische Mitteilungen* LV. 28 People who know each other really well..sign *Yours ever.*

2. a. At all times, on all occasions, on each occasion; = ALWAYS i. *arch.* and *north. dial.*

c **1040** *Rule St. Benet* (Logeman) 12 Myndiȝ siȝ [se abbod] æfre, þæt [etc.]. *c* **1175** *Lamb. Hom.* 9 Efere to þam setteres dei hes comen..to þan sinagoge. *c* **1205** LAY. 547 Brutus heom com æfter & æfer [*c* **1275** euere] he heom leide on. *a* **1325** *Prov. Hendyng* xxxiii, Ever out cometh evel sponne web. **1483** CAXTON *G. de la Tour* E v, Of euyll lyf cometh euer an euylle ende. **1523** LD. BERNERS *Froiss.* I. 748 As they passed by, ever the Parisyens enclyned themselfe to them. **1602** SHAKS. *Ham.* I. ii. 162 Your poore Seruant euer. **1632** LITHGOW *Trav.* II. 49 They were dayly molested and besieged, but the victory fell euer to the Christians. **1688** R. HOLME *Armoury* III. 54/1 The Prelate of the Garter..is ever the Bishop of Winchester. *a* **1718** PENN *Life* Wks. 1726 I. 137 Envy and Railing..almost ever follow. **1771** GOLDSM. *Hist. Eng.* IV. 378 He attacked the largest ships, and almost ever with success. **1812** WOODHOUSE *Astron.* ix. 70 Longitude is ever measured from the intersection of the equator and ecliptic. **1832** HT. MARTINEAU *Homes Abroad* viii. 113 The rude state which is ever the consequence of a scarcity of knowledge. **1885** *North Star* 1 July 3/2 Lord Randolph..has been a hard hitter, but he has ever hit fair.

b. Idiomatic phrases. † ***ever among*** (see AMONG B. 2); also in same sense † ***ever between***. ***ever and again***; ***ever and anon*** (see AGAIN 4 b, ANON 6 b). † ***ever and oft***(***e***(***n***: with constant reiteration, continually. † ***ever now and now***, ***ever now and then***, ***ever now and then among***: 'every now and then'. † ***ever umwhile*** (ME.): every now and then, from time to time. *Obs.*

1154 *O.E. Chron.* an. 1137. §3 Hi læiden gæildes o[n] þe tunes æureumwile. *c* **1230** *Hali Meid.* 27 Nawt ane on ende; ah eauer umbehwile. *a* **1300** *Cursor M.* 14336 (Cott.) Honurd be þou fader, euer and oft. **1387** TREVISA *Higden* (Rolls) VII. 7 Elsynus bisshop of Wynchestre evere among fondede to have þe see. **1470–85** MALORY *Arthur* VI. xviii, And euer now and now came alle the Knyghtes home. *Ibid.* x. lxxxviii, And euer bitwene, sir Tristram resorted vnto Ioyous gard. **1542** UDALL *Erasm. Apoph.* 250 b, Who when he had clene beggered hymself wᵗ expenses, would euer now and then thus saie vnto the birde [etc.]. **1581** J. BELL *Haddon's Answ. Osor.* 207 Besides these written ordinaunces of the law, he did ever now and then among, rayse uppe Prophetes unto them. **1590** SPENSER *F.Q.* II. ix. 41 And ever and anon, with rosy red, The bashful blood her snowy cheeks did dye. **1632** LITHGOW *Trav.* II. 46 Dalmatians..by Sea with Frigots and Brigantines did euer and often vexe the Venetian Commerce. **1687** A. LOVELL tr. *Bergerac's Comical Hist.* I. 71 Ever now and then I looked upwards. **1739** J. HUXHAM *Ess. Fevers* (1750) 312 A spoonful or two..should be given ever and anon. **1821** BYRON *Sardan.* II. i. 551 And ever and anon some falling bolt Proves his divinity. **1875** JOWETT *Plato* (ed. 2) I. 274 Ever and anon we are landed in particulars. **1883** P. ROBINSON *Fishes of Fancy* 90 Ever and again the husky voices of narwhal and shark..murmured, etc.

3. a. Constantly, incessantly, perpetually; with continual recurrence. *arch.* † ***ever forth*** (cf. Ger. *immerfort*): continually, constantly. † ***ever in one***: unchangingly. *Obs.*

a **1000** *Cædmon's Crist & Satan* 297 Æfre forth. *c* **1000** ÆLFRIC *Deut.* xxxi. 27 Æfer ȝe fliton onȝen God. *a* **1123** *O.E. Chron.* an. 1101 His men mycel to hearme æfre ȝedydon. *c* **1205** LAY. 1276 Þritti dawes & þritti night heo ferden efer [*c* **1275** efre] forð riht. *c* **1230** *Hali Meid.* 5 Babilones folc weorreð & warpeð eauer toward tis tur. *c* **1290** *Lives Saints* (1887) 33 Þis Abbod hire siwede euere forth. *c* **1386** CHAUCER *Clerk's T.* 546 But he neuer hir coude fynde But euer in oon ylyke sad and kynde. *c* **1430** LYDG. *Bochas* II. xxvii. (1554) 62 b, With these two vices, he brenneth euer in one. **1709** STEELE *Tatler* No. 17 ¶2 Pedants..will ever be carping. **1837** J. H. NEWMAN *Par. Serm.* (ed. 2) III. vii. 99 We are ever sinning, we must ever be renewing our sorrow. **1876** FREEMAN *Norm. Conq.* IV. xviii. 186 The same tale..we have ever to tell in the English history of these years.

b. With comparatives to mark a constant increase or decrease, *esp.* before the correlatives *the—the* (OE. *swá—swá*, ME. *se—se*, *þe—þe*).

α. **1154** *O.E. Chron.* an. 1137 Ðæt lastede þa xix wintre wile Stephne was king & æure it was uuerse & uuerse. *c* **1175** *Lamb. Hom.* 51 Þis fis is of swulc cunde þet euer se he mare strengðed him to sw[i]mminde mid þe watere se he mare swimmeð abac. *c* **1230** *Hali Meid.* 27, & eauer se hare murðe wes mare togederes; se þe sorhe is sarre at te twinninge. *a* **1300** *Cursor M.* 14441 (Gött.) And ȝeit troud noght þaa felun Bot eur mistroud mar and mare. *c* **1380** WYCLIF *Sel. Wks.* III. 173 Evere þe lenger þat þou lyfest to lyve bi Goddis lawe, evere þe harder it, etc. *c* **1440** *Ipomydon* 1833 (Weber) Euyr the fayrer that she spake, The fouler braydes gan he make. **1526** *Pilgr. Perf.* (W. de W. 1531) 144 He was euer more quyet & restfull in hymselfe. **1833** MRS. BROWNING *Prometh. Bd.* Poems 1850 I. 165 This wandering, everlonger, evermore Hath overworn me.

β. **1297** R. GLOUC. (1724) 110 Er þe lenger þe more. *c* **1400** *Apol. Loll.* 58 Þer þe more þat þey þole, ai þe more schal þe fendis torment.

†**c.** ***ever as*** (see AS): with varying force = 'as long as', 'as often as', 'whenever', 'wherever', 'always in proportion as'. *Obs.*

1297 R. GLOUC. (Rolls) 3974 Þe kynge..ȝef hom large ȝiftes, euere as hii worthe were. **1470–85** MALORY *Arthur* X. xxxvi, And euer as he smote doune knyghtes, he made them to swere, etc. **1529** RASTELL *Pastyme* (1811) 251 His armye ..euer as they went, won dyvers strange holdes and tounes. **1530** TINDALE *Exp. 1 Cor.* 308 And ever as he grew in promotions and dignity, so gathered he unto him of the most subtle-witted. **1571** CAMPION *Hist. Irel.* (1809) 71 He subdued the land through and through, ever as he went building up castles and fortresses. **1594** *2nd Rep. Faustus* in Thoms *Prose Rom.* (1828) 101 Ever as they came up to the breach, the cannon heaved them off. **1614** MARKHAM *Cheap Husb.* VII. xxiv. (1668) 126 Ever as you knead it, sprinkle into it the grains of small Chilter wheat. **1631** WEEVER *Anc. Fun. Mon.* 139 These..haue beene diuers times reformed, euer as they did degenerate from their primitiue sincerity.

†**4.** Prefixed to indefinite pronouns or advs. to impart to them a distributive sense; also, to distributive words in order to emphasize this function. ***ever all***: all and sundry. ***ever either*** (***outher***): each of the two respectively. ***ever aywhere***, ***ever where***: everywhere. *Obs.* For ***ever each***, ***ever ywhere***, see their mod. forms EVERY, EVERYWHERE.

a **1300** *Cursor M.* 13873 (Cott.) Iesus went him forth here and þar, And did meracles euer-ai-quar. *c* **1314** *Guy Warw.* (A.) 1084 Now we han ben her & tar, Þe pris y-wonne euer ay-war. **1382** WYCLIF *Prov.* xxii. 2 The werkere of euer either is the Lord. ?*a* **1400** *Chester Pl.* (Shaks. Soc.) 192 Prophescied..to ever all mankinde. *c* **1420** *Sir Amadace* (Camd.) xxxi, For ȝe moue haue maysturs euyrqware. **1444** *Close Roll 23 Hen. VI*, And euerawther of the said Priour and Geffrey..was bownden in £40. *c* **1449** PECOCK *Repr.* I. ii. 8 But if [= unless] euereither of the premissis be trewe the conclusion is not trewe.

¶ Giving a distributive sense to numerals. (A mere Germanism.)

1535 COVERDALE *Judg.* xv. 4 Samson..catched thre hundreth foxes..and put euer a fyre brande betwene two tayles [LUTHER, *einen Brand je zwischen zwei Schwänze*].

5. quasi-*sb.* use of 1. †**a.** In ME. phrase, ***long is ever*** (cf. 'long is ay'). *Obs.*

c **1205** LAY. 18848 Longe beoð æuere dæd ne bið he næuere. *c* **1325** *Metr. Hom.* 103 Ful lang es ever, lang es ever.

b. in phrases, ***for ever*** (sometimes, *esp.* in U.S., written FOREVER, q.v.): for all future time, for eternity, in perpetuity; hence (chiefly in colloq. use), incessantly, interminably. In proper sense often in strengthened forms, †***for all ever***, ***for ever and*** (***for***) ***ever***, ***for ever and ay*** (arch.), ***for ever and a day*** (? a corruption of prec.; also hyperbolically, (for) a very long time).

α. *a* **1300** *Cursor M.* 6218 (Cott.) Þis folk..þat suld vs serue for euer and ai. *c* **1330** R. BRUNNE *Chron.* (1810) 16 Tuo dukes & tuo bisshopes for euer toke þer leue. **1393** LANGL. *P. Pl.* C. v. 124 Non go to galys, bote it be for euere. *c* **1420** *Chron. Vilod.* 1011 We wylle..ben ȝowre servaundys for ever and hoo. **14..** *Tundale's Vis.* 1488 To that same peyn schuld y have goo And dwellyd ther in for ever and oo. **1549–62** STERNHOLD & H. *Ps.* lxxvii. 8 Is his goodnesse cleane decayd for euer and a day? **1583** GOLDING *Calvin on Deut.* ii. 9 The Doctrine which is set forth in the name of God, serueth not for our age onely, but for all euer. **1594** HOOKER *Eccl. Pol.* I. ii. (1611) 5 One onely God is to be blessed for euer. **1596** SHAKS. *Tam. Shr.* IV. iv. 97 Farewell for euer and a day. **1600** *A.Y.L.* IV. i. 145. **1627** DONNE *Serm.* clvii. VI. 276 New heavens and new earth for ever and ever and ever. **1697** DRYDEN *Virg. Georg.* IV. 719 For ever I am ravish'd from thy sight. **1712–4** POPE *Rape Lock* III. 153 The meeting points the sacred hair dissever From the fair head, for ever, and for ever! **1771** GOLDSM. *Hist. Eng.* III. 225 It was the fate of Charles, for ever to aim at projects which were..impracticable. **1794** MRS. RADCLIFFE *Myst. Udolpho.* i, Madame St. Anbert knew not that she left it for ever. **1817** W. SELWYN *Law Nisi Prius* (ed. 4) II. 1202 To him and his successors for ever. **1823** CARLYLE *Let.* 28 Sept. (1886) II. 225 One youth was to go to Germany, the other to Oxford, and I to take my leave I supposed for ever and a day. **1878** MORLEY *Carlyle* Crit. Misc. Ser. I. 201 Hitherto certainly, and probably it will be so for ever. **1934** J. O'HARA *Appointment in Samarra* (1935) i. 13 It was only a little after three o'clock, but the party had been going on for ever. **1966** J. AIKEN *Trouble with Product X* vii. 138 They [*sc.* traffic lights] always take for ever to change. **1967** *Listener* 18 May 656/3 How else can one explain why the Second Reform Bill of 1867 did not sweep the Conservatives from power for ever and a day?

β. *a* **1592** GREENE *Alphonsus* Wks. (1861) 241 Were banish'd both for e'er from Arragon.

†**6.** quasi-*adj.* uses of 1–3. Everlasting, constant, perpetual. Chiefly with agent-nouns or sbs. of action. *Obs.*

1550 VERON *Godly Sayings* (1846) 129 But ever fire of hel (yᵉ punishment of the devils) do hang over us. **1580** SIDNEY *Arcadia* (1622) 481 But the time of my euer farewell approcheth. **1605** VERSTEGAN *Dec. Intell.* Ded., I take my leaue, desiring Almightie God..to be your Maiesties euer protector. *Ibid.* ii. (1628) 42 They haue beene the onely and euer possessors of their countrey. **1607** ROWLANDS *Diog. Lanth.* 29, I know thy euer care For winters want..In Sommer doth prepare. **1609** *Epist. Shaks. Tr. & Cr.* (Qq. 1, 2) 179 A neuer writer, to an euer reader.

II. At any time (= L. *unquam*); whence: In any case, in any degree. Primarily in negative and interrogative sentences and in hypothetical and subordinate clauses.

7. a. At any time.

α. *a* **1000** *Cædmon's Crist & Satan* 171 Þat ic..ne sceal æfre ȝeheran þære byrhtestan beman stefne. *c* **1000** *Ags. Gosp.* Matt. xiii. 15 Þe læs hiȝ æfre [*c* **1160** *Hatton* afre] mid eaȝum ȝeseon. *c* **1200** *Trin. Coll. Hom.* 183 A weilewei þu fule hold, þat ich auere was to þe iteied. *a* **1225** *Ancr. R.* 230 Al þet euer dude Job, euer he nom leaue þerof et ure Louerde. *a* **1250** *Owl & Night.* 1178 Ich not ȝef thu were ȝavre prest. *c* **1300** *Thrush & Night.* 127 in Hazl. *E.P.P.* 55 Com thou heuere in here londe, Hy shulen don the in prisoun stronge. *c* **1340** *Cursor M.* 15116 (Trin.) Þei bicoom soriere þen euer eer þei were. **1375** BARBOUR *Bruce* I. 198 That Scottis men mycht do na thing That euir mycht pless to thar liking. **1382** WICLIF *John* i. 18 No man euere syȝ God, no but the oon bigetun sone. **1526** *Pilgr. Perf.* (W. de W. 1531) 3 b, More..pleasaunt to beholde than euer it was ..before. **1577** B. GOOGE *Heresbach's Husb.* IV. (1586) 165 b, Hortensus..was the first that ever killed Peacocke for the Table in Rome. **1600** SHAKS. *A.Y.L.* III. v. 28 If euer..You meet in some fresh cheeke the power of fancie. **1612** SHELTON *Quix.* III. viii. I. 187 Whence I have no hope ever to return. **1660** PEPYS *Diary* (1875) 156 The first time that ever I remember to have heard the..singing-men in

surplices in my life. **1662** Stillingfl. *Orig. Sacr.* iii. ii. §17 We deny that ever his Atoms with all their occursions would ever produce those things which are in the Universe. **1711** Addison *Spect.* No. 37 ⁋1 One of the prettiest Grotesque Works that ever I saw. **1837** Dickens *Pickw.* xi, For who could ever gaze on Mr. Pickwick's beaming face without [etc.]. **1888** Bryce *Amer. Commw.* III. xcix. 387 The criticisms of an outspoken press rarely assail their [English Judges'] ability, hardly ever their fairness.

β. *c* **1205** Lay. 14320 He wes þe bezste latimer þat ær com her. *c* **1400** *Apol. Loll.* 99 It is scham to hem to say þus, þat ere kirk erriþ, sin He & His kirk is o persone. **1591** Shaks. *Two Gent.* iv. ii. 141 It hath bin the longest night That ere I watch'd, and the most heauiest. **1692** tr. *Sallust* 28 For who..would ere endure, that they should wallow in wealth. ..while we are pinch'd?

¶**b.** ***seldom or ever***: confusedly used for 'seldom if ever', 'seldom or never'.

1771 *Contempl. Man* I. 83 All those people who were afflicted with any Illness, seldom or ever survived it. **1804** Syd. Smith *Mor. Philos.* v. (1850) 75 Dreamers..who walk in their sleep have seldom or ever the most distant recollections that they have been dreaming at all. **1809** —— *Two Vols. Serm.* I. 76 This plea is rarely or ever true.

c. Sometimes used pleonastically as in ***seldom ever***.

1813 J. C. Hobhouse *Journey* 78 The peasants seldom ever can get a farthing for their beasts. **1828** Carlyle in *Foreign Rev.* II. 460 And seldom ever can he succeed. **1857** Bagehot *Lit. Studies* (1879) II. 275 The words of a great poet, in our complex modern time, are rarely ever free from its traces.

d. In the (orig. intensive) colloq. phrase ***as ever is*** or ***was***.

1708 *Essex Inst. Hist. Coll.* X. 78 Bad riding as ever was. **1842** *Knickerbocker* XX. 96, I am seventy-two as ever was this very spring. **1850** Dickens *Dav. Copp.* xxi. 216 She has been as good a girl as ever was. **1890** S. Hale *Lett.* (1919) 248 Louis Church..a dear as ever was, aged twenty-one. **1919** F. M. Ford *Let.* 2 Sept. (1965) 98 If..you wd. care to adventure either next Week End as ever is or next but one, a train leaves Victoria at 3:40 p.m.

e. Colloq. phr. ***did you ever?*** = did you ever see or hear the like?, would you believe it? Similarly ***did anybody ever?***, ***if ever!***, ***was there ever?***, ***who'd ever?*** (Cf. *well I never*.)

1817 Byron *Beppo* xcii, Did I ever? No, I never Saw a man grown so yellow! **1825** J. Neal *Bro. Jonathan* I. 150 'My stars!—well, if ever!'—wiping her fat hands very carefully. **1828** T. Creevey *Let.* 6 Dec. in Gore *Creevey's Life & Times* (1934) xiii. 294 Lady Louisa..believed Papa would not have come..if I had not been coming. Was there ever? **1840** *Spirit of Times* 21 Nov. 447/3 What a fib! did you ever? well, I never did hear the beat of that. **1844** G. E. Jewsbury *Let.* 24 June (1892) 136 He..found that the surgery-boy had..given calomel instead of ipecacuanha! Did you ever? **1854** J. E. Cooke *Virginia Comedians* I. xiv. 77 'Did anybody ever!' said Miss Alethea. **1861** Reade *Cloister & H.* xliv, So then, if they take us to task we can say, alack we knew nought; we thought no ill; now, who'd ever? and so forth. **1892** *Peel City Guardian* 23 Jan. 3/3 'And where is she now?' 'In a studio.'..'Did you ever!' said Mrs. Fanshaw. **1909** Masefield *Tragedy of Nan* iii. 61 Fifty pou-und. Fifty pou-und. Did you ever.

f. Qualifying a superlative (usu. an adjective) = ever known, experienced, etc.; 'on record'. orig. *U.S.*

1906 'O. Henry' *Four Million* (1916) 71 Anna and Maggie worked side by side in the factory, and were the greatest chums ever. **1924** *Westm. Gaz.* 12 Aug., Mr. Coolidge is expected to reach the largest audience ever in his acceptance address as Republican candidate. **1955** *Times* 12 May 4/3 The last amateur side from the States..had proved in 1951 the first-ever to beat the A.B.A. in one of their own rings. **1958** *Listener* 17 July 94/3 Cambodia's first-ever seaport. **1960** *Sunday Express* 11 Sept. 1/4 Mr. Matthews had not expected to be able to see his son become the youngest-ever champion. **1969** *Guardian* 6 Sept. 9/1 The biggest ever postbag of telegrams.

g. Colloq. phr. ***if ever there*** (or ***if there ever***) ***was*** (***one***): an assertion that the person or thing referred to is a perfect or undoubted example of its kind.

1822 Carlyle *Let.* 12 Jan. (1886) II. 30 In composition with 'fence' to be sure, and not governing 'shrubs', but still a preposition if there ever was one. **1872** Hardy *Under Greenw. Tree* I. ii. v. 189 Geoffrey Day is a clever man if ever there was one. **1912** T. Dreiser *Financier* xix. 213 A great young man, if there ever was one. **1929** G. Goodwin *Conversations with G. Moore* xxvi. 161 Richard Wormald was..a large-hearted millionaire if ever there was one. **1969** *Guardian* 21 May 10/4 The Playboy Club—an example of how 'architecture can help to solve the social, visual, technical, and economic problems of the twentieth century' if ever there was one.

8. On any supposition, by any chance, at all.

a. †***ever any***: any at all (*obs.*). Also ***ever a(n***, ***e'er a(n*** (now *vulgar*, though *never a(n* is in good colloquial use: see the corrupt form arrow).

α. *a* **1067** *Charter of Eadweard* in *Cod. Dipl.* IV. 219 Ic nelle ðat efre ani bisscop ani þing him ðer on a ateo. *c* **1175** *Lamb. Hom.* 43 Heo wes wurse to þolien þenne efreni of alle þa oðre pine. *c* **1205** Lay. 15525 ȝif mon funde in auer æi londe. æuer æi cniht bærn. **1583** Rich *Phylotus & Emelia* (1835) 31 If there bee euer a Deuill of them bothe, I knowe it is she. **1612** T. Taylor *Comm. Titus* ii. 14 Here is policie, but pietie scarce euer a whit. **1769** *Fair Annie* in Herd *Sc. Songs*, Had ye ever a brother. **1879** Miss Jackson *Shropsh. Word-bk.* s.v., 'Drink or cider'..'ever-a-one', 'I dunna car w'ich'. **1884** *Chesh. Gloss.* s.v., Have you ever a shilling as you could lend me?

β. **1597** Shaks. *2 Hen. IV*, ii. iv. 295, I loue thee better, then I loue ere a scuruie young Boy of them all. **1611** —— *Wint. T.* iv. iv. 180. **1598** B. Jonson *Ev. Man in Hum.* iv. i, The should haue beene perboyl'd..e're they should ha' come in, e're a one of 'hem. **1653** H. Cogan tr. *Pinto's Trav.* xxxviii. 151 If there were ere a one amongst you that could find out any device or stratagem of war. **1657** Earl Monm. tr. *Paruta's Pol. Disc.* 200 Nor..have [they] made me ere a whit more happy then I was at first. **1706** Watts *Horæ Lyr.* i. '*Happy the hours*', Angels, assist my doleful song, If you have e'er a mourning string. **1746** W. Horsley *Fool* (1748) I. No. 33. 232 A Man of my Turn enjoys a Holiday with as high a Relish as e'er a Prentice-Boy..within the Bills of Mortality. **1802** Bentham *Wks.* (1843) X. 387, I don't know whether you have e'er an one.

b. In comparative clauses introduced by *as*, *than*; also in relative clauses introduced by *that* preceded by a superlative or by *all*, *the only*, etc.

α. **1523** Ld. Berners *Froiss.* I. 746 All that ever the kyng ..coude do coude never tourne them fro that opinyon. *c* **1530** —— *Arth. Lyt. Bryt* 468 Rode forthe as fast as ever they myght. *a* **1533** —— *Huon* l. 169 As naked as ever he was borne. **1583** Stubbes *Anat. Abus.* ii. 89 [They] runne.. from towne to towne..till they haue spent al that euer they haue. **1681** Dryden *Sp. Friar* (J.), As like him as ever he can look. **1776** G. Semple *Building in Water* 9 Piles..driven in as close together as ever they can stick. **1777** Johnson *Let.* 18 Feb. in *Boswell*, She will accommodate you as well as ever she can in the old room. **1835** Mrs. Carlyle *Lett.* I. 43 Try all that ever you can to be patient. **1859** G. W. Dasent *Pop. Tales Norse* 19 All she wanted was to get above ground as fast as ever she could. **1885** F. Anstey *Tinted Venus* 25 Can't you see I'm as anxious to get that statue again as ever you can be?

β. **1591** Shaks. *1 Hen. VI*, i. iii. 72 As lowd as e're thou canst, cry.

c. Added for emphasis to the conjunctions *as soon as*, *before*, *ere*, *or* (= *ere*). Also †***when ever*** = 'just as soon as'.

1325–1883 [see ere C. 1 d.]. **1632** Lithgow *Trav.* i. 38 Most part of all which M. Arthur and I saw, before euer we either eate, drunke, or tooke our lodging in Venice. **1655** *Francion* viii. 7 He gave me a good supper last night, when ever I came within his doors. *a* **1656** Bp. Hall *Occas. Medit.* §15 (1851) 20 So soon as ever he hears the noise of a fly afar off, how he hastens to his door! **1718** Hicks *J. Kettlewell* i. xxiii. 46 So soon as ever he commenced Master. **1844** Mrs. Browning *Drama of Exile* Poems I. 48 Or ever she [the Earth] knew sin! **1872** G. W. Dasent *Three to One* II. 256, I know what is to happen, before ever I get up-stairs.

d. Following interrogative pronouns, advs., etc. (*how*, *who*, *what*, *where*, *why*), to intimate that the speaker has no notion what the answer will be.

Sometimes these combinations are (improperly) written as single words: see however, whoever, etc.

1595 *World of Wonders* (1607) 240, I shal desire him to consider how ever it was possible to get from these priests.. a pertinent answer. **1859** G. W. Dasent *Pop. Tales Norse* 12 Where ever in the world have you been? *Ibid.* 163 The Troll began to wonder..how ever they could be rid of the lad. *Ibid.* 215, I wonder now what ever there can be inside this chest.

e. Appended to relative pronouns or advbs., and giving to them a generalized or indefinite force; = L. *-cumque*. These combinations are now always written as single words: see how(so)ever, who(so)ever, etc.

f. Used as a colloquial intensive, usu. to emphasize an exclamation. (Cf. sense 8d.) Chiefly *N. Amer.*

1934 F. Pickersgill *Let.* 29 May (1948) ii. 9 Was I ever glad to get off the beastly boat! **1945** S. Lewis *Cass Timberlane* (1946) vii. 46, I thought they were all so nice, and oh boy! are they ever learned! *Ibid.* xvi. 91 You're damn tootin'... Are we ever! Oh boy, I'll say we are! **1949** *Canadian Forum* Aug. 113/2 Do you remember it George?.. Do I ever!

9. In any degree. **a.** Prefixed to *the* followed by a comparative; = 'at all', 'any'. Now only *colloq.* (Cf. *never*, which in the parallel use is much more common).

α. **1622** Sparrow *Bk. Com. Prayer* (1661) 172 The Primitive Christians did not like the Jewish Rites ever the worse because they were Theirs. *a* **1656** Bp. Hall (J.), Let no man fear that harmful creature ever the less, because he sees the apostle safe from that poison. **1697** Collier *Ess.* (1703) I. 9 A Mine undiscovered, for which neither the Owner of the Ground or any Body else, are ever the Richer.

β. **1642** Rogers *Naaman* 364 For none are ere the wiser for them. *a* **1679** Hobbes *Absurd Geom.* Wks. 1845 VII. 386 Do you think..the opinion of your judgment would have been ere the less?

b. ***ever so***: prefixed in hypothetical sentences to adjs. or advbs., with the sense 'in any conceivable degree'. Sometimes *ellipt.* = 'ever so much'; also *dial.* in phrases like ***were it ever so***, = 'however great the need might be'. Similarly, ***ever such (a)***.

This expression has been substituted, from a notion of logical propriety, for *never so*, which in literary use appears to be much older, and still occurs *arch.*, though app. not now known in dialects. See never.

1690–2 Locke *Educ.* in T. Fowler *Locke* (1880) 6 Not to take an answer, though ever so full and satisfactory. **1741** Richardson *Pamela* II. 273 Let me..not be call'd down for ever so much. **1751** *Beau-Philosopher* 193 Was it to be attended with ever such difficult Circumstances, there is nothing that a great mind will not undertake. **1764** Reid *Inquiry* vi. §3 His eyes, though ever so perfect. **1777** Sheridan *Sch. Scand.* ii. ii, Though Sir Peter's ill humour may vex me ever so, it never shall provoke me to, etc. **1816** Kirby & Sp. *Entomol.* (1828) II. xix. 142 If ever so many queens are introduced into a hive. **1843** Thackeray *Jerôme Paturot* 349 If..the caricaturist had made fun of me ever so, I would..have put up with the insult. *a* **1850** Rossetti *Dante & Circ.* i. (1874) 173 Though of great heart and worthy everso, He shall be counted low. **1854** A. E. Baker *Gloss. Northants Words* 215 'I wouldn't do it if it were ever so,' *i.e.* nothing should induce me to do it. **1858** C. M. Yonge *Christmas Mummers* viii. 115, I couldn't lead the worship if it was ever so! **1882** *W. Worc. Gloss.* s.v., 'I wunt ax 'im for bread, not if it was ever so'.

c. Hence ***ever so*** is used in affirmative contexts as a vague intensive: 'vastly', 'immensely'.

1858 Hawthorne *Fr. & It. Jrnls.* (1872) I. 13 Ever so little to their credit. **1870** Mrs. Whitney *We Girls* i, Ever so many years ago. **1877** *N.W. Lincolnsh. Gloss. s.v.*, She fret ever so when Harry 'listed. **1885** F. Anstey *Tinted Venus* 79 Thank you ever so much, Leander dear!

III. Combinations.

10. a. When *ever* (in senses 1–3) qualifies an adj. or ppl. adj. used attributively, it is almost invariably hyphened, thus giving rise to an unlimited number of quasi-compounds, as ***ever-abiding***, ***-angry***, ***-blooming***, ***-changeful***, ***-dear***, ***-esteemed***, etc.

1570 T. Norton tr. *Nowel's Catech.* (1853) 152 The only holy and ever-increasing noble fountain. **1580** Sidney *Arcadia* (1622) 136 The euer-noble nature of Leonatus. **1586** T. B. *La Primaud Fr. Acad.* (1589) I. 47 Philosophie.. is..to lead us to the eternall fruition of our supreme and ever-abiding good. **1588** Shaks. *L.L.L.* i. i. 268 My euer esteemed dutie prickes me on. **1590** T. Watson *Poems* (1870) 159 Yee seaunfold flames, whose euer-circling fires maintain this earth. **1590** Spenser *F.Q.* i. i. 39 Cynthia still doth steepe In silver deaw his ever-drouping hed. **1599** T. M[oufet] *Silkwormes* 46 The Vulture gnawing stil That euer-dying euer-liuing wretch. **1604** Shaks. *Oth.* iii. iii. 463 Witnesse you euer burning Lights aboue. **1610** —— *Temp.* i. ii. 289 Thy grones Did..penetrate the breasts Of euer-angry Beares. **1612** Drayton *Poly-olb.* i. Notes 2 O euer-happie Iles..By Nature strongly fenc'd. *c* **1630** Drumm. of Hawth. *Poems* Wks. 32 Ethereal princes, ever-conquering bands. **1641** Milton *Ch. Govt.* i. vi, God..brought forth.. that beneficent and ever-distributing office of deacons. **1648** *Hamilton Papers* (1880) 174 My ever honored Lord. *a* **1650** Crashaw (J.), Panting murmurs, still'd out of her breast That ever-bubbling spring. **1659** (*title*) Golden Remains of the Ever Memorable John Hales. **1682** Dryden *Medal* 24 Oh, could the style that copied every grace..have formed his ever-changing will. **1685** —— *Misc.* ii. 72 To treat thy evercraving Mind With ev'ry Blessing. *a* **1687** Waller *Wks.* (1729) 183 (Jod.) What our earth, and what our heav'n denies, Our everconstant friend, the sea supplies. **1703** Rowe *Fair Penit.* ii. i, Oh! hear me, hear your ever faithful creature! *a* **1711** Ken *Hymnotheo* Poet. Wks. 1721 III. 74 Their drink from ever-dropping Trees is rain'd. **1712–4** Pope *Rape Lock* ii. 66 The skies, Where light disports in ever-mingling dyes. **1715** —— *Iliad* ii. (1019) The fierce Pelasgi..March from Larissa's ever-fertile Ground. **1741** Richardson *Pamela* (1824) I. 227 My ever-dear and ever-honoured father and mother. **1742** F. Blyth *Sermons* II. 281 The immense Sea of God's ever-flowing Mercy. **1744** Armstrong *Preserv. Health* iii. 427 (Jod.) Th' ever-varying circle of the day. **1744** Thomson *Autumn* 812 The melting snows, and ever-dripping fogs. **1786** Burns *Ded. to G. Hamilton*, O'er the harp pale Mis'ry moans, And strikes the ever-deep'ning tones. **1797** Mrs. Radcliffe *Italian* i, The City and Bay of Naples, an ever-moving picture. **1808** Han. More *Cœlebs* I. 401 (Jod.) Its versatile temper, and its evernew resources. **1812** Byron *Ch. Har.* i. l, The ball-piled pyramid, the ever-blazing match, Portend the deeds to come. **1822** Carlyle *Let.* 2 June (1886) 218 The minute and ever-present knowledge of his duties in every emergency. **1827** Keble *Chr. Y.* Quinquagesima i, Brightening in ever-changeful bloom. **1846** W. Hamilton in *Wks. of T. Reid* 798/2 No answer could be afforded to the ever-recurring questions. **1848** Mill *Pol. Econ.* II. iii. xxiv. §5.215 The ever growing attributions of the government. **1852** Tennyson *Wellington* 79 Ever-echoing avenues of song. **1855** A. L. Phillipps *Mahometanism* vi. 249 Anarchical and revolutionary outbreaks, that..have, with ever-increasing force, shaken..the civilized world. **1866** Kingsley *Herew.* II. xxii. 372 A life literally new, ever-renewing, ever-expanding and eternal. **1866** J. H. Newman *Gerontius* ii. 14 Fainter and more faint the accents come, As at an ever-widening interval. **1868** Darwin in *Life & Lett.* (1887) III. 75 My ever-recurrent uncomfortable sensations. **1901** W. James *Let.* 17 May (1920) II. 146 Plane rising behind plane of flat dark relieved against flat light in ever-receding gradation. **1909** E. Pound *Exultations* 39 This ever-flowing monotony. **1933** *Mind* XLII. 146 Immortality is of no value unless it is a ground for the experience of eternal life: 'the continuous enjoyment of an ever-present good'. **1937** R. H. Lowie *Hist. Ethnol. Theory* viii. 109 An ever-recurring principle. **1939** M. Spring Rice *Working-class Wives* iii. 50 Years of ever-increasing toil. **1957** P. Worsley *Trumpet shall Sound* ii. 39 These new wants attracted an ever-growing army of recruits. **1969** *Jane's Freight Containers 1968–69* 188/3 To speed the clearance and handling of the ever-increasing number of containers.

b. Occasionally prefixed to a passive inf. (preceded by *to*), forming an attrib. adj. Cf. never *adv.* 6c.

1778 F. Burney *Evelina* III. ii. 22 He wrote the ever-to-be-regretted letter. *Ibid.* xvii. 200 My ever-to-be-regretted mother. **1815** Mrs. Pilkington *Celebrity* II. 91 This dear and ever-to-be-lamented parent. **1815** Wordsworth *Poems* I. 366 If Names are more acceptable than images, where is the ever-to-be-honoured Chaucer?

c. Prefixed to sbs. denoting action or state. *rare*.

1665 J. Serjeant *Sure-footing in Chr.* 76 The Proper Cause must be an ever-delivery. *Ibid.* 106 The ever-continuance or uninterruptedness of Tradition.

11. Special Combinations: **ever-bearer**, a plant which bears flowers and fruits (sometimes simultaneously) for a long time; hence ***ever-bearing*** adj.; **ever-being** *a.*, that always is; hence †**everbeingness**; †**everbleving** *vbl. sb.* [f. *bleve*, beleave *v.*], everlastingness; **ever-bloomer** = *ever-bearer* (orig. applied to a rose); hence ***ever-blooming*** adj.; **everbrown** *sb.*, a plant always brown (humorously after

evergreen); †**ever-crescent** *a.*, ? growing in whatever place; †**ever-durable** *a.*, destined to last for ever; †**ever-glooming** *a.*, involved in perpetual gloom; †**ever-grow** (see quot.); **ever-loving** *a.*, that loves for ever; usu. as a stock colloq. epithet for a wife; hence as *sb.*, one's wife; **ever-ready** *a.*, always accessible or prepared; hence as *sb.*, a person or thing that is always ready; *spec.* (usu. with capital initials) a member of a territorial army or similar force that is liable to be mobilized at any time. See also the main-words EVER-BLESSED, -DURING, etc.

1929 WEAVER & CLEMENTS *Plant Ecology* xiii. 326 While.. most plants have a comparatively short period of flowering and fruiting each year..reproductive activity in some continues through several months. The latter are known as ever-bloomers or *ever-bearers. **1921** *Daily Colonist* (Victoria, B.C.) 13 Oct. 15/1 Evergreen blackberries and *everbearing strawberries are coming in but in small quantities. **1655** GOUGE *Comm. Heb.* i. 8 The greek word here translated ever, αἰῶνα, according to the notation signifieth *ever-being (ἀεὶ ὤν). **1674** N. FAIRFAX *Bulk & Selv.* 24 Gods whole eternity rightly taken..is..one only everbeing now. **1839** BAILEY *Festus* xx. (1848) 233 A bride of God, And handmaid of the Everbeing One. **1674** N. FAIRFAX *Bulk & Selv.* 13 Such words to set forth Gods *ever-beingness by, as may be sure to shut out formerness and afterness. **1340** *Ayenb.* 105 þet uerste word [Pater] ous sseweþ þe langnesse of his *eureblenge. **1887** *N.Y. Semi-Weekly Tribune* 3 May (Cent. Dict.), We have grown over sixty named *ever-bloomers or tea-roses. **1929** WEAVER & CLEMENTS *Plant Ecology* xiii. 326, Several species of plant.. show a tendency to exhibit the '*ever-blooming' or 'ever-bearing' habit, *i.e.* the ability to continue both vegetative and reproductive activities more or less successfully together. **1838** DICKENS *Nich. Nick.* ii, The scanty box, and stunted *everbrowns, and broken flower-pots..are scattered mournfully about. **1650** BULWER *Anthropomet.* 172 The Organs of the Practique Intellect are to rectifie and regulate the excrescent, supercrescent, and *ever-crescent parts. **1664** H. MORE *Myst. Iniq.* 386 A third Angel.. denounces most direfull and *ever-durable torments to those that worship the Beast and his Image. **1592** KYD *Sp. Trag.* I. in Hazl. *Dodsley* V. 9 Through dreadful shades of *ever-glooming night. **1676** GREW *Anat. Plants* IV. I. v. §1 And an *Evergrow, is a degree above an Evergreen: here, the Buds and young Sprigs, do only live; there, they grow and are put forth. **1931** D. RUNYON *Guys & Dolls* (1932) i. 26 Maud Milligan, who is well known to one and all as the *ever-loving doll of Big Nip. **1938** —— *Furthermore* v. 87 His ever-loving wife is passing a tambourine around. **1968** 'P. BARRINGTON' *Accessory to Murder* ii. 34 The old fool was devoted to his ever-loving. I reckon she was damn lucky. **1828** MILL in *Westm. Rev.* IX. 257 A summary appeal to that *ever-ready standard of comparison, English practice. **1842** MANNING *Serm.* (1848) I. xxiv. 354 They..declined also the ever-ready spirit of a Christian life. **1917** 'CONTACT' *Airman's Outings* iii. 60 That vindictive exponent of frightfulness, Archibald the Ever-Ready [*i.e.* an anti-aircraft gun]. **1936** C. DAY LEWIS *Friendly Tree* 15 An ever-ready, over-sweet smile. **1962** *Times* 21 Mar. 7/4 This [*sc.* the revival of National Service] is undesirable for a number of reasons. The purpose of the Ever-Readies is to avoid such a measure. **1966** *Guardian* 19 Aug. 1/8 The searchers.. included 190 'ever-readies' of the Metropolitan Police's Special Group.

ˌever-ˈblessed, *a.*

a. Always enjoying blessedness. **b.** Worthy to be always blessed or adored. Also *absol.* (quasi-*sb.*)

*a***1711** KEN *Hymnarium* Poet. Wks. 1721 II. 6 The thought..Which on their Spirits was impress'd, When they beheld the Ever-bless'd. *a***1711** —— *Hymnotheo*, ibid. III. 375 The Pray'r flew first of Mary ever-bless'd, Her Love invigorating all the rest. **1738** WESLEY '*All praise to Him*' v, And bless the Ever-bless'd. **1842** MANNING *Serm.* (1848) I. xiii. 179 The power of the ever-blessed Trinity.

everdamp (ˈɛvədæmp). [f. EVER *adv.* + DAMP *a.*] (See quot. 1968.)

1933 N. MONTAGUE in W. Atkins *Art & Practice Painting* III. vi. 43 'Everdamp' Transfer Paper. This paper, which, in addition to the composition, contains hygroscopic compounds (these keeping the paper moist) and requires no damping book, may be run on a dry plate... 'Everdamp' is an extremely useful paper. **1967** E. CHAMBERS *Photolitho-Offset* xvii. 258 Yellow everdamp can be purchased either smooth or slightly rough surfaced and embodies a thin non-dry coating. *Ibid.*, It is usual for a good conditioned everdamp paper to require no damping. **1968** *Gloss. Terms Offset Lithogr. Printing* (*B.S.I.*) 24 *Everdamp*, a type of transfer paper which remains limp by having a hygroscopic content in its coating.

ˌever-ˈduring, *a. arch.* [f. EVER *adv.* + DURING *ppl. a.*] Always enduring, everlasting.

1382 WYCLIF *Isa.* xxiv. 5 For thei..scatereden the euere durende [**1388** euerlastynge] bond. **1480** *Robt. Devyll* 1133 The paynes of hell, that ys euer durynge. **1541** COVERDALE tr. *Bullinger's Old Faith* xi. (1624) 91 This only true and everduring salvation. **1667** MILTON *P.L.* VII. 206 Heav'n op'nd wide Her everduring Gates. **1725–6** POPE *Odyss.* VII. 306 Let instant death surprize With ever-during shade these happy eyes! **1784** COWPER *Task* v. 710 Sculpture..Gives bond in stone and ever-during brass. **1847** MACAULAY *Misc. Poems* (1860) 432 The ever-during plant whose bough I wear. **1854** J. S. C. ABBOTT *Napoleon* (1855) I. xxiv. 391 That civil code..will remain an ever-during monument of his labors.

Hence **ever-ˈduringness**.

1867 BUSHNELL *Mor. Use Dark Th.* 327 The sense of our ever-duringness comes through no speculation about the matter of dateless continuance.

†**ˌeverˈeft**, *adv. Obs.* [f. EVER *adv.* + EFT *adv.*] Ever after; ever since, thenceforth. Also ***evereft afterward, evereft more.***

1297 R. GLOUC. (1724) 281 A uayre abbey..þat euereft aþ ylaste. *c***1290** *Lives Saints* (1887) 316 Eueref Aftur-ward.. Of þondre huy beoth so sore a-ferd. *c***1315** SHOREHAM 124 Evereft more a-lyve to ben, And nevere eft to deyȝe.

Everest (ˈɛvərɪst). [The name of the highest mountain in the world, on the frontier of Nepal and Tibet, f. the name of Sir George *Everest* (1790–1866), Surveyor-General of India.] Used *transf.* to designate the greatest conceivable achievement, spiritual height, difficulty, etc.

1929 R. ALDINGTON *Death of Hero* I. ii. 52 Isabel.. displayed signs of that..talent for violent invective she afterwards developed to such Everest peaks of unpleasantness. **1956** A. H. COMPTON *Atomic Quest* 346, I see him [*sc.* Jesus] as the Everest among the world's many high mountains. **1958** DUKE OF EDINBURGH in M. Holdgate *Mountains in Sea* p. v, Every man has to face his Everest some time during his life.

everglade (ˈɛvəgleɪd). *U.S.* [? f. EVER *adv.* + GLADE.

The formation is irregular, and the intended etymological sense uncertain; perh. *ever* was used to mean 'interminable'.]

A marshy tract of land mostly under water and covered in places with tall grass; chiefly in *pl.* as the name of a large swampy region of South Florida. Also *attrib.*, as ***everglade kite*** (*Rostrhamus sociabilis*), a bird inhabiting the everglades of Florida and other parts. ***Everglade State***, Florida.

1827 TANNER *Map Florida*, Extensive Inundated Region ..generally called the Everglades. **1837** J. L. WILLIAMS *Florida* 13 The back country presents a singular alternation of savannas, hammocks, lagoons, and grass ponds, called altogether the Everglades. **1841** in WEBSTER. **1841** CATLIN *N. Amer. Ind.* II. xxxvi. 33 Her [Florida's] swamps and everglades..gloom the thoughts of the wary traveller. **1856** OLMSTED *Slave States* 153 A very large purchase had been made by one company in the Florida everglades. **1860** DARWIN in *Life & Lett.* (1887) II. 300 All the pigs being black in the Everglades of Virginia.

evergreen (ˈɛvəˌgriːn), *a.* and *sb.* [f. EVER *adv.* + GREEN.] **A.** *adj.*

1. Always green.

[**1555** EDEN *Decades* 196 Certeyne trees which contynewe euer greene and neuer lose theyr leaues.] **1796** H. HUNTER tr. *St. Pierre's Stud. Nat.* (1799) III. 409 Magnificent coursers pasture..in the ever-green valleys. **1860** MAURY *Phys. Geog. Sea* x. §462 Were the sea fresh..Ireland would never have presented those ever-green shores.

b. *fig.* Always fresh, never-failing.

1871 *Echo* 13 Feb., One could not help being struck with the evergreen good humour of the French.

2. Of trees, shrubs, etc.: Having green leaves all the year round; opposed to *deciduous*.

In trees of this kind, the leaves of the past season remain on the tree, until the new ones are completely formed, as in the holly, holly-oak, pine, etc.

1671 MILTON *Samson* 1735 Shade Of laurel ever-green, and branching palm. **1712** J. JAMES tr. *Le Blond's Gardening* 186 When your Ever-green Trees and Shrubs are got to some Height. **1845** *Florist's Jrnl.* 156 It [Arctostaphylos nitida] forms a handsome evergreen shrub five or six feet high. **1884** BOWER & SCOTT *De Bary's Phaner. & Ferns* 535 The evergreen Jasmines.

b. Of leaves: Lasting till the next season.

1776 WITHERING *Brit. Plants* (1796) II. 211 Ilex. Leaves surrounded by a strong woody border; tough, shining, ever-green. **1861** MISS PRATT *Flower. Pl.* III. 357 Leaves, which are often rigid and evergreen.

B. *sb.* **1.** An evergreen tree or shrub. Cf. A. 2.

1644 EVELYN *Mem.* (1857) I. 87 The Isle of Corsica, and St. Remo, where the shore is furnished with evergreens, oranges, citrons, and date-trees. **1676** GREW *Anat. Plants* IV. I. v. §1 An Evergreen, is one degree above a Plant which is simply Perennial: of This, only the Trunk and Buds live all the Winter; of That, also the Expanded Leaves. *a***1711** KEN *Hymnotheo* Poet. Wks. III. 116 He to a Thicket lead, With ever-greens and downy Moss bespread. **1813** SIR H. DAVY *Agric. Chem.* (1814) 67 The cause of the preservation of the leaves of evergreens through the winter is not accurately known. **1828** SCOTT *Let. Ballantyne* Jan., in Lockhart, She has no business in a ball room but to be ranged against the wall as an evergreen. **1848** MACAULAY *Hist. Eng.* I. 162 Christmas had been..the season..when every house was decorated with evergreens.

fig. **1878** E. JENKINS *Haverholme* 98 Lady Willowgrove.. was an evergreen. She had been a distinguished figure in society for three generations.

2. *attrib.*

1825 J. NEAL *Bro. Jonathan* II. 31 The evergreen tribe. **1841** W. SPALDING *Italy & It. Isl.* III. 319 The peculiar tints of the evergreen region disappear. Deciduous oaks and horse-chestnuts become prevalent.

b. In names of various trees, shrubs, etc., as ***evergreen alkanet, magnolia, spurge laurel***; **evergreen oak**, the Holm Oak (*Quercus Ilex*).

*a***1682** SIR T. BROWNE *Tracts* 62 He found the Ilex, or Evergreen oak in many places. **1861** MISS PRATT *Flower. Pl.* IV. 51 Evergreen Alkanet..is a stout bristly plant..its leaves are of rich deep green colour. **1867** LADY HERBERT *Cradle L.* vii. 168 Terebinth or evergreen oak here and there gave a graceful shade. **1882** *Garden* 8 July 27/3 The Evergreen Magnolia..is too well known to need description.

Hence **ˈevergreenness**.

1882–3 W. E. BAXTER *Winter in India* vii. 68 The evergreenness of Indian trees is one of the most striking features of the country.

†**ˈevering.** *Obs.*

1641 BEST *Farm. Bks.* (1856) 107 These rammers are made of old everinges [*Glossary*, The rounds of a waggon], harrowe balls, or such like thinges as have holes.

†**everˈlastable**, *a. Obs.* [f. EVER *adv.* + LAST *v.* + -ABLE.] Capable of lasting for ever.

1548 GEST *Pr. Masse* 105 Christes churche is everlastable.

everlasting (ɛvəˈlɑːstɪŋ, -ˈlæst-), *a.* and *sb.* [f. EVER *adv.* + LASTING.] **A.** *adj.*

1. a. Lasting for ever; infinite in future duration; endless; = ETERNAL A. 3.

1340 *Ayenb.* 189 Guoþ ye acorsede in-to þe greate uere eurelestinde ine helle. **1509** *Paternoster, Ave, & Creed* A iij, I trowe in yᵉ..forgyuenes of synnes agen rysynge of flesshe, and euerlastynge lyf. **1552** LYNDESAY *Monarche* IV. 5145 Thay depart from cair and cummer..Tyll Ioy and euirlestand lyfe. **1605** SHAKS. *Macb.* II. iii. 22 Some..that goe the Primrose way to th' euerlasting Bonfire. *a***1668** DENHAM (J.), What a trifle is a moment's breath, Laid in the scale with everlasting death! **1758** S. HAYWARD *Serm.* i. 2 We are in danger of falling into everlasting misery. **1781** COWPER *Truth* 41 Too busy..to wait On the sad theme, their everlasting state. **1837** CARLYLE *Sart. Res.* II. ix, Love not pleasure; love God. This is the Everlasting Yea. **1838** LYTTON *Leila* I. v, I would all the gold of earth were sunk into the everlasting pit.

b. Extended to the full sense of the L. *æternus*, so as to imply past as well as future eternity; = ETERNAL A. 1. (In the examples following this sense is merely contextual; but cf. *from everlasting* in B. 1.)

1382 WYCLIF *Gen.* xxi. 33 Abraham..inwardli clepide.. the name of euerlastynge God. **1535** COVERDALE *ibid.*, And Abraham..called vpon the name of the Lorde yᵉ euerlastinge God. **1578** *Gude & Godlie Ball.* (1868) 127 Thow onlie Maker of all thing, Thou euerlastand licht. **1611** BIBLE *Isa.* ix. 6 The mightie God, The euerlasting Father.

2. a. Used hyperbolically or in relative sense. Cf. ETERNAL 4.

1382 WYCLIF *Ezek.* xxxv. 9, I shall bytake thee into wildernessis euerlastynge [*solitudines sempiternas*]. *c***1400** *Destr. Troy* 9569 Ye worship might haue, With a lose euer-lastond, when your lyff endis. *c***1460** FORTESCUE *Abs. & Lim. Mon.* (1714) 84 To make their Rewards, everlasting in ther Heyrs. *c***1532** DEWES *Introd. Fr.* in Palsgr. 1019 To.. Henry..kyng..of all Englande..be laude everlastyng, honour without ende. **1628** HOBBES *Thucyd.* (1822) 13 It [this history] is compiled rather for an everlasting possession than to be rehearsed for a prize. **1734** POPE *Ess. Man* IV. 284 See Cromwell, damn'd to everlasting fame! **1832** LYTTON *Eugene A.* I. x, The rivulet..descends from the everlasting mountains. **1839** DE QUINCEY *Recoll. Lakes* Wks. 1862 II. 217 These mighty gates of everlasting rock. **1873** *Slang Dict.* s.v., The barefooted children about Seven Dials..are said to wear everlasting shoes and stockings. *Everlasting staircase*, the treadmill. **1882** MISS BRADDON *Mnt. Royal* I. iii. 79 It is the most everlasting kind of beauty, is it not?

b. Constant, perpetual, unceasing. Often implying weariness or disgust: Interminable, endlessly recurring; = ETERNAL A. 4 b.

1688 S. PENTON *Guardian's Instruct.* 28 What..were the Occasions of the present great Contempt of Matrimony.. The everlasting Din of Mother-in-law. **1716** LADY M. W. MONTAGUE *Lett.* I. vi. 19 The foundation of these everlasting disputes turns entirely upon rank. **1725** DE FOE *Voy. round World* (1840) 269 It is never dark here, you are now come to the country of everlasting day. **1801** SOUTHEY *Thalaba* v. xxii, From Ait's bitumen-lakes..ascends That everlasting roar. **1833** HT. MARTINEAU *Brooke Farm* vii. 87 There was an everlasting boiling, of the kettle in the morning, the potatoes for dinner, and the kettle again in the afternoon. **1837** LYTTON *E. Maltrav.* 4 On which there hung an everlasting frown. **1838–9** HALLAM *Hist. Lit.* I. i. I. §38. 35 The tedious descriptions of spring, and the everlasting nightingale.

3. Indefinitely durable, that will 'never' wear out (see B. 3). ***everlasting trimming***: an embroidered edging for underclothing.

1590–1607 [see B. 3]. **1882** *Daily News* 4 Mar., The demand is fully maintained for everlasting trimmings. *Mod.* I can recommend this material; it's everlasting wear.

4. In various plant-names: **a.** Retaining shape and colour when dried; as in ***everlasting flower***, a name given to some species of cudweed (*Gnaphalium*), but more commonly to various species of *Helichrysum*; cf. Fr. *immortelle*; †***everlasting life***: 'American Cudweed' (*Antennaria margaritacea*). **b.** Perennial; as in ***everlasting pea*** (*Lathyrus latifolius* and other species), †***everlasting grass*** (*Onobrychis sativa*, sainfoin).

1677 PLOT *Oxfordsh.* 154 Commonly called Saintcfoin or Everlasting grass. **1705** TATE tr. *Cowley's Hist. Plants* (J.), Witness the everlasting-pease and scarlet bean. **1772–84** COOK *Voy.* (1790) II. 391 The everlasting-flower..when it is plucked it cannot be perceived to fade. **1783** AINSWORTH *Lat. Dict.* (Morell) I. s.v., *Life everlasting*, Gnaphalium Americanum. **1861** S. THOMSON *Wild Fl.* III. (ed. 4) 200 The yellow meadow vetchling, or everlasting pea. **1877** M. ARNOLD *Poems, Heine's Grave*, Crisp everlasting-flowers, Yellow and black, on the graves. **1882** *Garden* 25 Mar. 202/2 The Everlasting Flowers..are all beautiful border plants.

5. quasi-*adv.* = EVERLASTINGLY 2 and 4. †**a.** For ever, throughout eternity (*obs.*). **b.** *U.S. slang.* Very, exceedingly, excessively.

1482 *Monk of Evesham* (Arb.) 67 Some of hem contynued in euyll..and now they be euerlasting dampde. **1692** WASHINGTON tr. *Milton's Def. Pop.* x. (1851) 228 This

everlasting talkative Advocate of the King. ?**18..** 'MAJ. JACK DOWNING' *May Day in N. York* (in Bartlett *Dict. Amer.*), New York is an everlasting great concern. **1832** S. SMITH *Major Downing* 95, I had rather fight forty New Orleans battles than to govern this everlasting great country one year. **1848** LOWELL *Lett.* I. 136 It's everlasting hot to-day. **1903** K. D. WIGGIN *Rebecca* 262 She'd kick the ladder from out under her, everlastin' quick.

B. *absol.* (quasi-*sb.*) and *sb.*

1. *absol.* **a.** In phrases *for everlasting*: for all future time, in perpetuity. *to everlasting*: to all eternity. **b.** Subsequently with extension as in A. 1 b: *from everlasting*: from all eternity.

c **1340** *Cursor M.* 4188 (Fairf.) þai wille him lede in-to fer lande to be þair bonde for euer-lastande. **1535** COVERDALE *Ps.* xcii [xciii]. 2 From that tyme forth hath thy seate bene prepared, thou art from euerlastinge. *a* **1600** HOOKER (J.), We are in God through..the love which is born towards us, from everlasting. **1611** BIBLE *Ps.* xc. 2 Euen from euerlasting to euerlasting thou art God. **1715** DE FOE *Fam. Instruct.* I. i. (1841) I. 19 You will learn that God is from the beginning, and to the end, from everlasting to everlasting. **1719** WATTS *Ps.* xc., From everlasting thou art God To endless years the same. **1828** K. DIGBY *Broadst. Hon.* (1846) II. *Tancredus* 6 It [chivalry] is now enlisted in the cause of truth and goodness..to reign for everlasting. **1873** SYMONDS *Grk. Poets* x. 317 Love and beauty have belonged to men from everlasting.

2. *the Everlasting*: God, the Eternal.

1382 WYCLIF *Prov.* viii. 23 Of the euere lastende [? mistranslation of *ab æterno*] I am ordeyned..er the erthe shulde be maad [**1388** Fro with out bigynnyng; **1611** from everlasting]. **1602** SHAKS *Ham.* I. ii. 131 Oh..that the Euerlasting had not fix't His Cannon 'gainst selfe-slaughter.

3. *sb.* **a.** A material used in 16–17th c. for the dress of sergeants and catchpoles, app. identical with DURANCE. **b.** In later times, a strong twilled woollen stuff, called also LASTING: see quots.

The word in quots. 1590 and 1607 may possibly be adj.; the former app. identifies the material of the 'everlasting garment' with *buff*, but it is not clear whether this means buff leather or some woollen substitute for it.

1590 SHAKS. *Com. Err.* IV. ii. 33 *Adr.* Where is thy Master Dromio? *S. Dro.* A diuell in an euerlasting garment hath him..a fellow all in buffe. **1607** FLETCHER *Woman-Hater* IV. ii, Were't not for my smooth, soft, silken citizen, I would quit this transitory trade, get me an everlasting robe, sear up my conscience, and turn sergeant. **1738** J. MUNN *Observ. Brit. Wool & Manuf.* 5 Damasks, Russets, Everlasting, Cantiloons, Worsted Plush..with many other sorts of Plain and Figur'd Stuffs. **1754** *South Carolina Gaz.* 1 Jan. 4/2 Check mantuas and Irish stuffs, everlastings, bombazine. **1763** *Essex Inst. Hist. Coll.* XLIX. 142 Had on..either a pair of black Ever-lasting Breeches, or cloth colour'd Leather ones. **1822–35** D. BOOTH *Analyt. Eng. Dict.* I. 184 *Lasting*, or *everlasting*, is a stout closely-woven worsted stuff, dyed black and other colours, and very much used for ladies' shoes. **1837** HAWTHORNE *Twice-told T.* (1851) I. ii. 32 They [pantaloons] must have been made of the stuff called 'everlasting'. *a* **1845** BARHAM *Ingol. Leg., Jerry Jarvis' Wig*, A well-worn..jacket, of a stuff by drapers most pseudonymously termed 'everlasting'.

4. = *everlasting flower*. See A. 4.

1794 MARTYN *Rousseau's Bot.* xxvi. 387 There are several species both of yellow and white Everlastings. **1864** GILBERT & CHURCHILL *Excurs. Dolomite Mts.* 350 His hat was ornamented with yellow everlastings. **1871** RAMSAY *Remin.* (ed. 18) 17 Wreaths of 'everlasting' placed over graves as emblems of immortality.

ever'lastingly, *adv.* [f. prec. + -LY².]

1. Without end; for ever; throughout all future time. Also hyperbolically and in relative sense.

c **1450** *Mirour Saluacioun* 4174 To be qwene of alle heven now and eure lastyngly. **1526** *Pilgr. Perf.* (W. de W. 1531) 179 They..shall lyue euerlastyngly and neuer dye spiritually. **1593** SHAKS. *Rich. II*, III. ii. 207 Ile hate him euerlastingly That bids me be of comfort any more. **1631** GOUGE *God's Arrows* I. §34. 35 The favour which they primarily had with God is everlastingly confirmed. **1715** DE FOE *Fam. Instruct.* I. i. (1841) I. 12 He punishes them everlastingly in hell. *a* **1745** SWIFT (J.), Many have made themselves everlastingly ridiculous. **1804** WORDSW. *To the Supreme Being*, The fetters of my tongue do Thou unbind, That I may..sound thy praises everlastingly. **1865** E. C. CLAYTON *Cruel Fortune* III. 67 If you could lend me half a sov., I should be everlastingly obliged to you.

b. Through all past and future time, 'from everlasting to everlasting'. †Also, Throughout all past time (*obs.*).

1587 GOLDING *De Mornay* vii. 91 Againe, haue they [the two Sexes] bin euerlastingly but two, or euerlastingly mo than two? **1594** HOOKER *Eccl. Pol.* I. v. (1611) 11 God..who ..euerlastingly is whatsoeuer he may be. **1594** CAREW *Huarte's Exam. Wits* (1616) 90 God was not made at anie time, in as much as he is euerlastinglie vnbegotten. **1860** PUSEY *Min. Proph.* 428 God's ways are everlasting, ordered everlastingly, existing everlastingly in the Divine Mind.

2. With perpetual recurrence; continually, constantly, incessantly; = ETERNALLY 3.

1826 COBBETT *Rur. Rides* (1885) II. 104 They are everlastingly railing against the working people. **1856** LEVER *Martins of Cro' M.* 526 The rights of property everlastingly put in dispute. **1870** MISS BRIDGMAN *R. Lynne* I. vi. 93 Everlastingly running up and down from town.

3. Beyond measure; immeasurably, excessively. (Common in U.S. slang.)

everlastingness (ɛvəˈlɑːstɪŋnɪs, -ˈlæst-). [f. as prec. + -NESS.]

1. The quality, condition, or fact of being everlasting (see the senses of the adj.). **a.** In etymological senses: Endless existence; perpetual continuance; unlimited durability. **b.** In extended sense = ETERNITY 1: The having neither beginning nor end of existence.

a. **1398** TREVISA *Barth. De P.R.* VIII. ii. (1495) 300 The nobilyte of heuen..in purenesse and euerlastyngnes. *c* **1440** *Promp. Parv.* 144 Evyrlastyngnesse, *eternitas*. **1580** HOLLYBAND *Treas. Fr. Tong*, *Perpetuité*, euerlastingnesse. **1648** HERRICK *Hesper.*, *To Sir R. Stone*, No lesse Strong than the heavens for everlastingnesse. **1656** JEANES *Mixt. Schol. Div.* 50 A perswasion of the soules everlastingnesse is needfull. **1664** EVELYN *Sylva* (1776) 343 The everlastingness of the wood [Cypress]. **1730–6** BAILEY (folio) *Everlastingness*, durable nature. **1850** LYNCH *Theo. Trin.* ii. 20 He was meditating Christianity..and its everlastingness. **1865** PUSEY *Truth Eng. Ch.* 14 He affirmed the everlastingness of future punishment.

b. **1565** JEWEL *Repl. Harding* (1611) 225 [Our Lord] hath mingled the nature of his owne flesh to the nature of his euerlastingnesse vnder the Sacrament. **1587** GOLDING *De Mornay* iv. 44 He hath neither beginning nor end, which thing wee cal Euerlastingnes..And so Gods being is altogether at once, which is yᵉ peculiar propertie of euerlastingnesse. **1880** CHEYNE *Isaiah* I. 242 The idea of the Divine everlastingness is one of the primary notes of the prophecy.

2. Infinite time; = ETERNITY 2. **a.** *properly*, The future eternity; endless duration. Also *pl.* †**b.** In extended sense: The absolute eternity, without beginning or end, or the past eternity without beginning (*obs.*).

a. **1382** WYCLIF *Dan.* xii. 3 Thei that lemen, or enfourmen, manye to riȝtwisnesse [shuln shyne] as sterris in to euerlastyngnessis. —— *2 Pet.* iii. 18 To him [Crist] glory and now and in to the day of euerelastingenesse. **1577** tr. *Bullinger's Decades* (1592) 90 And that euerlastingnesse verily is perpetual and hath no end. *a* **1631** DONNE *Serm.* ciii. IV. 385 There cannot be two Everlastingnesses in the torments of Hell. **1655** GOUGE *Comm. Hebr.* 45 This extent of the promise to everlastingnesse.

b. **1388** WYCLIF *Isa.* lvii. 15 The Lord..that dwellith in euerlastyngnesse. **1535** COVERDALE *2 Esdras* viii. 20 Thou that dwellest in euerlastyngnesse. **1579** TOMSON *Calvin's Serm. Tim.* 1039 1 That life was giuen them before all euerlastingnesse. **1633** T. ADAMS *Exp. 2 Peter* i. 1 Future glory was from everlastingnesse prepared for those servants.

†**3.** Eternity as opposed to *time*; the future state; eternal welfare. *Obs.*

c **1430** tr. *T. à Kempis* 99 Not sekyng þo þinges þat are þyn ..ner in tyme, ner in euerlastingnes. **1560** DAUS tr. *Sleidane's Comm.* 240 Thys lyfe tyme is verey shorte and vncerten, therefore must they thinke of an euerlastingnes. **1650** BAXTER *Saints' R.* IV. v. §3 What a step is it from hence to Everlastingness? **1681** GLANVILL *Sadducismus* I. (1726) 46 If such can barter their souls for Trifles and sell Everlastingness for a Moment.

b. *fig.* regarded as an entity.

1627–47 FELTHAM *Resolves* I. lxiv. 197 [These] all prove it [a soul] a shoot of Everlastingness. **1655** H. VAUGHAN *Silex Scint.* I. 52 My conscience..felt through all this fleshly dresse Bright shootes of everlastingness. **1846** I. WILLIAMS *Baptistery, Voices of Dead* 175 Visiting with starlike gleams Of everlastingness.

†ˌ**ever'lastingty.** *Obs. rare.* [f. as prec. + -TY.] Eternity.

1382 WYCLIF *Isa.* lvii. 15 The heȝe Lord wonende the euerlastingte [Cf. prec. 2 b]. *c* **1449** PECOCK *Repr.* I. i. 7 Ysaie lvij where it is seid that God dwelling in euerlastingte dwellith with a meke..spirit.

ˌ**ever-'living**, *a.*

1. That lives or will live for ever.

1547 COVERDALE *Old Faith* x. Wks. (Parker Soc.) I. 73 Very God and man, the only and everliving Saviour. **1614** RALEIGH *Hist. World* (J.), The everliving subjects of his [God's] reward and punishment. **1704** NEWTON *Optics* (J.), The instinct of brutes and insects can be the effect of nothing else than the wisdom and skill of a powerful ever-living Agent. **1870** BRYANT *Iliad* II. xv. 77 She found the ever-living gods Assembled in the halls of Jupiter.

b. *fig.* Of a name, fame, etc.: Immortal.

1591 SHAKS. *1 Hen. VI*, IV. iii. 51 That euer-liuing man of Memorie, Henrie the fift. **1595** W. CLARKE in *Shaks. C. Praise* 15 Everliving praise to her loving Delia. *a* **1625** FLETCHER *Hum. Lieutenant* I. i, So many idle hours as here he loiters, So many ever-living names he loses. **1871** MORLEY *Voltaire* (1886) 4 The ever-living gifts of Grecian art and architecture and letters.

2. quasi-*sb.*

1601 BRETON *Blessed Heart* v. Wks. (Grosart) 15 While the hand of heauen is giuing Comfort from the euer-liuing?

†'**everly**, *adv. Obs.* or *Sc.* In 4 everliche, -lyche, evirly. [f. EVER *adv.* + -LY².] Always, continually.

c **1314** *Guy Warw.* (A.) 466 His care him neweth euerliche. **1375** BARBOUR *Bruce* II. 58 (ed. Innes 1856) He..Duelt in hys chambyr..With a clark with him evirly [ed. Skeat *reads* anerly].

†**ever'mo**, *adv. Obs.* [OE. phrase *ǽfre má* (see EVER and MO). In the OE. quots. the words have their ordinary sense, so that the phrase = 'any longer', 'ever again' (cf. EVERMORE 3 c); but prob. *má* was also used to emphasize *ǽfre* in the sense 'to all future time'; cf. Ger. *immer* always (:—OHG. *io-mêr*), *immermehr* evermore, Fr. *jamais* ever, never (:—vulgar Lat. *jam magis* 'now more').] = next.

[*c* **897** K. ÆLFRED *Gregory's Past.* lii. 405 Gif hwelc wif forlæt hiere ceorl, & nimð hire oðerne, wenestu recce he hire æfre ma? *a* **1000** *Cædmon's Crist & Satan* 140 (Gr.) Ne on þa beorhtan ȝescæft Ne mot ic æfre ma eaȝum starian.] *a* **1200** *Moral Ode* 106 To deþ idemet, and eure ma [*Trin. Coll. MS.* afremo] forlorene. *c* **1200** *Vices & Virtues* (1888) 35 Hie [karitas] scal æure mo ȝelasten, aiðer on ðessere woreld and ec on ðare oðre. **1297** R. GLOUC. (1724) 44 Londone he ys now y cleped, and worþ euermo. *c* **1380** *Sir Ferumb.* 2466 For þo was þe gurdel þat he com fore y-lost for euere-mo. *c* **1386** CHAUCER *Knt.'s T.* 174 In a tour, in anguish and in wo, Dwellen this Palamon and eke Arcite, For everemo. **1393** GOWER *Conf.* III. 25 For such a coke I may go fasting evermo.

evermore (ɛvəˈmɔə(r)), *adv.* For forms see EVER and MORE *adv.*; sometimes written as two words. [A later form of prec., *mo* being replaced by *more.*] An emphatic synonym of EVER.

In poetry the accentuation *'evermore* sometimes occurs.

1. For all future time. *Obs.* exc. *arch.*

c **1205** LAY. 31051 King Penda..ȝerneð þine ære nu and auere mære. *c* **1250** *Gen. & Ex.* 12 Blisse and soules reste[n] ðat him sal eauermor lesten. **1340** HAMPOLE *Pr. Consc.* 6838 It es right þat þai duelle þare, In þat hidus myrknes ever-mare. *c* **1440** *Gesta Rom.* i. 4 (Harl. MS.) He shalle dye in euermore lastynge dethe. *c* **1470** HENRY *Wallace* I. 13 Thai haff wrocht..To hald Scotlande at wndyr euirmar. **1592** W. WARNER in Farr *S.P. Eliz.* (1845) II. 379 Disable vs eremore. **1611** BIBLE *John* vi. 34 Lord, euermore giue vs this bread. **1791** BURNS *Lament Earl Glencairn*, Awake thy last sad voice, my harp!..Then sleep in silence evermair! *a* **1854** MONTGOMERY *O where shall rest be found*, Lest we be banished from thy face And evermore undone.

b. *for* (†*unto*) *evermore*.

c **1300** *Cursor M.* 23934 (Edin.) Leuedi..led me wit þe for þi son for euir mar wit him to won. **1375** BARBOUR *Bruce* I. 155 Gyff thou will hald in cheyff off me For euirmar. **1382** WYCLIF *Ecclus.* xlviii. 27 He..comfortede the weilende men in Sion, vnto euermor. **1555** *Act 2–3 Phil. & Mary* c. 20 §3 Leases..shall for evermore pass and be made under..the Seals of the said Duchy. **1622** S. WARD *Woe to Drunkards* (1627) 34 For euer and euer, and if it were possible for more than for euer, for euermore. *a* **1694** TILLOTSON (J.), Those pleasures which flow from the presence of God for evermore. **1850** TENNYSON *In Mem.* xxxiv, My own dim life should teach me this, That life shall live for evermore.

2. Always, at all times, constantly, continually.

c **1280** *A Sarmun* in *E.E.P.* (1862) 4 Of helle pine we aȝt be ware and euer more hit hab in þoȝt. **1393** LANGL. *P. Pl.* C. XVII. 3 Thei þat haue been hyre by-fore aren eueremore poure. **1486** *Bk. St. Albans* E iij a, He [the hare] fymaes and crotis and Roungeth euermoore. **1551** RECORDE *Pathw. Knowl.* II. xlvii, The line..dothe euermore run within the edge of the circle. **1594** HOOKER *Eccl. Pol.* II. vii. (1611) 73 The minde of man desireth euermore to know the truth. **1632** LITHGOW *Trav.* v. 209 Wilde Arabs..euermore annoy the Turkes. **1668** CULPEPPER & COLE *Barthol. Anat.* I. xviii. 48 These Vessels..are evermore found in all Bodies. **1801** SOUTHEY *Thalaba* XI. xxxvi, Yonder roar..evermore increasing, Still louder, louder, grows. **1850** LYNCH *Theo. Trin.* viii. 138 Lift your eyes unto the evermore silent heaven.

3. With negatives and expressions implying a negative: †**a.** In any degree. *Obs.* **b.** At any future time. **c.** (With the full sense of *more*: in this use better written as two words.) Ever again, any longer.

c **1380** WYCLIF *Serm.* Sel. Wks. I. 7 Heynes of state makiþ not a man evermore beter to God. *c* **1600** SHAKS. *Sonn.* xxxvi, I may not evermore acknowledge thee. **1832** HT. MARTINEAU *Hill & Vall.* vi. 85 This circumstance seemed to destroy the hope that the works..could evermore enjoy the prosperity which had been their lot. **1842** MRS. BROWNING *Grk. Chr. Poets* (1863) 139 Not in England evermore.

4. quasi-*sb.*

c **1850** F. T. PALGRAVE *O Light of Life*, Through heaven's great day of evermore.

†**e'verr**, *v. Obs.*⁻⁰ [a. L. *ēverr-ĕre* to sweep out, f. *ē-* out + *verrĕre* to sweep.] (See quot.)

1623–6 COCKERAM, *Euerre*, to sweepe the house.

†**e'verse**, *a. Obs.* [ad. L. *ēvers-us*, pa. pple. of *ēvertĕre* to overturn.] (See quot.)

1570 BILLINGSLEY *Euclid* v. Def. xvi. 134 Conuersion of proportion (which of the elders is commonly called euerse proportion, or euersion of proportion).

†**e'verse**, *v. Obs.* [f. L. *ēvers-* ppl. stem of *ēvertĕre*: see EVERT.] *trans.* To overturn, overthrow; = EVERT. Also *fig.*

c **1430** LYDG. *Bochas* III. v. (1554) 77 a, Many riche royall mighty towne Haue bene euersed..For sinne of princes which that wern lecherous. **1530** PALSGR. 540/2 Fortune hath eversed his chaunce upsyde downe. **1661** GLANVILL *Van. Dogm.* iv. 38 The foundation of which Principle..is totally evers't by the most ingenious Commentator.

Hence † **e'versed** *ppl. a.*

1584 R. SCOT *Discov. Witchcr.* XIII. xix. 316 Diuerse sorts of glasses..the cornerd, the inversed, the eversed..and blew glasses.

eversible (ɪˈvɜːsɪb(ə)l), *a.* [f. L. *ēvers-* ppl. stem of *ēvertĕre* (see EVERT) + -IBLE.] Capable of being everted or turned inside out.

1877 HUXLEY *Anat. Inv. Anim.* iv. 179 The penis is often eversible and covered with spines. **1878** BELL tr. *Gegenbauer's Comp. Anat.* 383 This latter appendage is eversible.

eversion (ɪˈvɜːʃən). [a. OF. *eversion*, ad. L. *ēversiōn-em*, n. of action f. *ēvertĕre*: see EVERT.]

†**1.** The action of overthrowing; the condition of being overthrown; an overthrow, overturning; *lit.* and *fig.* *Obs.*

c **1470** HARDING *Chron.* vii. (1812) 33 *note*, Iason at Troie first evercion Caste doun Ilion. **1536** BELLENDEN *Chron. Scot.* (1821) I. 58 This nobil realme..wes neir brocht to finall eversione. **1614** T. ADAMS *Devil's Banquet* 292 Their euersion is our conuersion. **1640** BP. HALL *Episc.* I. i. 15 The restauration of the English Church and eversion of Popery. **1678** WANLEY *Wond. Lit. World* I. xxxiv. §16. 55/2 I will take from Pollio all future occasion of falling into such

precipitant eversion of the mind. **1709** STRYPE *Ann. Ref.* I. lvii. 625 Disorderly preaching..tending to the eversion of good laws and orders ecclesiastical. **1801** FUSELI *Lect. Art.* i. (1848) 354 Scenes subsequent to the eversion of Troy. **1820** S. TURNER *Anglo-Sax.* (ed. 3) I. II. App. 545 The fate of the column of the image after its eversion.

†**b.** (See quot.) *Obs.*

1678–1706 PHILLIPS, *Eversion* in Rhetorick is the same figure, according to Ruffianus, with Epanodus.

2. †**a.** *gen.* The action of turning outwards; opposed to *inversion*. *Obs.*

1610 GUILLIM *Heraldry* III. xv. (1660) 197 The Eversion of the taile of the Lyon is an expresse token of his placabilitie or tractablenesse.

b. *Path.* and *Phys.* The action of everting or turning (an organ or structure) inside out; the condition of being everted. ***eversion of the eyelids*** = ECTROPION.

1751 SPRY in *Phil. Trans.* XLIX. 19 The conjunctive became greatly inflamed, with an eversion of the upper lid. **1866** HUXLEY *Preh. Rem. Caithn.* 100 The increased breadth at the latter spot being due to the well marked eversion of the tuberosities. **1872** DARWIN *Emotions* v. 121 Dogs, in their expressions of fondness, have a slight eversion of the lips. **1884** *Syd. Soc. Lex., Eversion*, in Botany, the external protrusion of organs from the cavity in which they are developed.

†**3.** ***eversion of proportion*** = *conversion of proportion*: see CONVERSION. *Obs.*

1570 [see EVERSE *a.*].

eversive (ɪˈvɜːsɪv), *a.* [f. L. *ēvers-* ppl. stem of *ēvertĕre* (see EVERT) + -IVE.] Tending to eversion or overthrow. Const. *of*.

1717 *Wodrow Corr.* (1843) II. 324 Changing that imposition to some other shape, as eversive of the rights of the Christian people. **1756** T. AMORY *Life J. Buncle* (1770) I. 216 Schemes..eversive of true knowledge. **1767** H. BROOKE *Fool of Qual.* (1792) III. 250 No man..can possibly be bound by any consents or contracts eversive of the laws of God and of their own nature. **1792** GEDDES *Bible* Ex. xi. (R. *Supp.*), A maxim eversive..of all justice and morality.

evert (ɪˈvɜːt), *v.* [ad. L. *ēvert-ĕre* to overturn, f. *ē-* out + *vertĕre* to turn.]

†**1.** *trans.* To turn upside down, upset. *lit.* and *fig. Obs. rare.*

1601 B. JONSON *Poetaster* IV. iv, The very thought Everts my soul with passion. **1620** VENNER *Via Recta* viii. 182 To end the meale with much drinke, doth by euerting the concoction, cause eructations. *a* **1693** URQUHART *Rabelais* III. Prol. 6 There did he..evert it [a tub], invert it, subvert it.

2. †**a.** To overthrow (a city, temple, enemy, etc.). Also *absol. Obs.*

1533 BELLENDEN *Livy* I. (1822) 53 Legiounis of futemen, to evert and cast doun the foresaid ciete to the ground. **1593** BILSON *Govt. Christ's Ch.* 311 It is easier to euert or disturbe, then to plant or establish. **1599** NASHE *Lenten Stuffe* 50 For feare after he had euerted their foes..hee woulde rauen vp them. **1730–1800** in BAILEY.

b. *fig.* To overthrow (an empire, government); to upset (a judgement, argument, doctrine, law, etc.); to frustrate (a purpose); rarely, to overthrow (a person) in argument. *Obs.* or *arch.*

1538 STARKEY *England* II. ii. 192 The suttylty of one sergeant schal euerte [*misprinted* enerte] and destroy al the jugementys of many wyse men before tyme receyuyd. *c* **1555** HARPSFIELD *Divorce Hen. VIII* (1878) 281 He began ..to evert his fathers..testament. **1563** *Homilies* II. *Idolatry* II. (1859) 211 And the noble Empire of Greece clean everted. **1581** SAVILE *Agric.* (1622) 189 And chiefly his great attempts against Germany turning to nothing, euerted that purpose. **1600** HOLLAND *Livy* VIII. xxx. 303 Then hath the master of horsemen..everted and overthrowne both Dictatours Majestie and Militarie discipline. *a* **1681** WHARTON *Fasts & Fest.* Wks. (1683) 11 Antiochus Epiphanes..everted the true worship of God. **1686** GOAD *Celest. Bodies* II. vii. 244 We have everted that Objection. **1726** AYLIFFE *Parerg.* 175 The Jurisdiction of the Judge is not yet everted and overthrown. **1849** J. WILSON in *Blackw. Mag.* LXVI. 652, I am overthrown—everted—subverted —the contradiction is flagrant. **1872** J. WALKER *Scot. Theol. & Theolog.* iv. (1888) 100 They clearly evert the fundamentals.

†**3.** To draw or turn out of the way; to turn aside. Also *fig. Obs.*

1578 BANISTER *Hist. Man* IV. 59 This muscle..hauying in office to euerte the foote to the interiour partes. **1650** BAXTER *Saints' R.* I. viii. (1662) 141 The Will is thus everted from the fore-mentioned Objects.

4. To turn the inner surface of (the eyelid, etc.) outwards; to turn inside out.

1804 [see EVERTED *ppl. a.*]. **1821** T. SANDWITH *Observ. Med. & Surg.* 99 The cheeks drawn downward in such a manner as to evert the lower eye-lids. **1839** TODD *Cycl. Anat.* II. 38/1 The gullet and part of the stomach [of starfish] are usually everted, protruded, and applied round the object to be swallowed. **1871** DARWIN *Desc. Man* II. xviii. 281 Muscles for everting the sack, and for closing or opening the orifice. **1879** HARLAN *Eyesight* v. 51 It is a very simple and easy thing to evert the eyelid.

evertebral (iːˈvɜːtɪbrəl), *a. Anat.* [f. E- *pref.*³ + L. *vertebr-a* + -AL¹; cf. VERTEBRAL.] Not vertebral; not of the nature of, or not connected with, the vertebral column.

1878 BELL *Gegenbauer's Comp. Anat.* 447 The anterior, or evertebral portion [of the cranium].

evertebrate (iːˈvɜːtɪbrət), *a.* and *sb. Zool.* [f. E- *pref.*³ + L. *vertebra* + -ATE²; cf. VERTEBRATE.] = INVERTEBRATE.

1883 A. LESLIE tr. *Nordenskiöld's Voy. Vega* 97 The dredging yielded..a large number of marine evertebrates.

evertebrate (iːˈvɜːtɪbreɪt), *v.* [f. as prec. + -ATE³.] *trans.* To deprive of the backbone.

1880 *Times* 28 Apr. 7/6 Professor Odling complained.. that the statute had been 'evertebrated and eviscerated'.

everted (ɪˈvɜːtɪd), *ppl. a.* [f. EVERT + -ED¹.] Turned outwards or inside out.

1786 R. SMITH in *Microcosm* No. 3 Even these [persons] would..be absolutely taken ill of an everted coal-box. **1804** ABERNETHY *Surg. Observ.* 83 And turns over the everted edges of the opening. **1836** TODD *Cycl. Anat.* I. 225/1 When cut longitudinally, the inner surface of the arteries does not become everted. **1859** R. F. BURTON *Centr. Afr.* in *Jrnl. Geog. Soc.* XXIX. 53 The lips are tumid and everted. **1866** HUXLEY *Preh. Rem. Caithn.* 130 The jugal arches of the European are hardly ever, if ever, so wide and everted as those of some Esquimaux. **1878** GROVE *Dict. Mus.* I. 210 *Bell*, the everted opening in which most wind instruments terminate.

e'verting, *vbl. sb.* [f. as prec. + -ING¹.] The action of the vb. EVERT; in quot. = 'throwing off'.

1611 SPEED *Hist. Gt. Brit.* IX. xi. (1632) 680 What will not money..doe; with corrupt dispositions, euen to euerting of all bands of either religious or ciuill duties.

Everton (ˈɛvətən). The name of a suburb of Liverpool, used *attrib.* in **Everton toffee,** (*a*) (see quot. 1951); (*b*) rhyming slang for 'coffee'.

1857 'DUCANGE ANGLICUS' *Vulgar Tongue* 7 *Everton toffee*, coffee. **1861** MRS. BEETON *Bk. Househ. Managem.* 800 (*heading*) To make Everton toffee. **1869** TROLLOPE *Phineas Finn* I. 93 His pockets were crammed full of gingerbread and Everton toffy. [**1907** *Vict. Hist. Count. Engl., Lancaster* III. 20/2 Molly Bushell's original manufactory of the sweet to which Everton has given a name was in Village Street... She was living in 1759.] **1951** *Good Housek. Home Encycl.* 456/2 *Everton toffee*, a brittle sweetmeat similar to butterscotch, but containing cream or evaporated milk. **1960** J. FRANKLYN *Dict. Rhyming Slang* 62/2 *Everton toffee*, coffee... Now obsolescent.

evertor (ɪˈvɜːtə(r)). *Anat.* [f. EVERT *v.* + -OR.] Any muscle which turns or rotates a part outward.

1903 *Lancet* 4 July 56/2 Either the evertor or invertor is out of use. **1967** *Gray's Anat.* (ed. 34) 717 When the foot is off the ground, it [*sc.* the peroneus longus] is an evertor.

every (ˈɛvərɪ, ˈɛvrɪ), *sb.* Also 4 eur. [Var. form of EAVER¹.] Rye grass (*Lolium perenne*).

14.. tr. *Higden* (Rolls) VII. 525 (*Harl. MS.* 1900) Of whete and of eur' that som men clepeth darnel. **1863** BARNES *Dorset Gloss.* (Philol. Soc.), *Every or ever-grass*.

every (ˈɛvərɪ, ˈɛvrɪ), *a.* (quasi-*pron.*) Forms: α. 1 æfre ælc, 2 efrec, 3 æver ælc(h, æfrech, ever ech, evreche, 3–6 everc, (5 evre). β. 3 ever ulc, 3–6 ev(e)rilc, -il(k(e, (3, 4–5 *north.* evere -ilc, -ilke). γ. 2 æv(e)ric, æwric, efri, 3 eaver euch, æv-, eavriche, a-, efri(c(h, æv-, av-, everihc, 3–6 everich(e, -yche, (4 evreich, everuch(e, 5 evirych, evyriche, 6 ewerik), 4–7 everi(e, -ye, (4 evri, 6 ewry), 4– every. Also 5 ery, 8 (in verse and colloq.) e'ery. [OE. *ǽfre ǽlc*, **ǽfre ylc*: see EVER *adv.* and EACH.

The OE. *ǽlc, ylc*, was a compound of *á*, synonymous with *ǽfre*; but, owing to umlaut and contraction, the etymological force of the word had become obscured, and *ǽfre* was prefixed in order to express more distinctly the original sense. Although the phrase was always written in OE. (as sometimes in ME.) as two words, it had in 10th c. already come to be felt as a compound, and when it is governed by a prep. this is placed before the first of the two words. The forms marked α descend from *ǽfre ǽlc*, and the β forms, including the mod. *every*, from *ǽfre ylc*. It does not appear that *ǽfre* was prefixed to the other two words, *ǽghwilc* and *ȝehwilc*, which enter into the history of EACH.]

I. As *adj.* used *attrib.*

1. Used to express distributively the sense that is expressed collectively by *all*.

Originally this sense was expressed by *each*, from which *every* differed only in emphasizing the element of universality in the signification. Thus Wyclif writes '*euery* langour and *eche* sekenesse,' it being unnecessary to repeat the emphasis. When *every* had ceased to be recognizable as a compound of *each*, the two words were at first often used somewhat indiscriminately, but their functions were gradually differentiated. In mod. usage, *every* directs attention chiefly to the totality, *each* chiefly to the individuals composing it. It may also be observed that *each* usually refers to a numerically definite group, in contrast to the indefinite universality expressed by *every*: thus 'Each theory is open to objection' relates to an understood enumeration of theories, but 'Every theory is open to objection' refers to all theories that may exist.

a. followed immediately by a sb., or by a sb. preceded by a descriptive adj.; occas. with vb. in *pl.*

WULFSTAN *Hom.* (Napier) 20 Ǽfre ælcne neode [Man] ȝeærnað to gode sylfum ymbe. *O.E. Chron.* an. 1014 And æfre ælcne Deniscne cyng, utlah of Engla lande ȝecwædon. *c* **1175** *Lamb. Hom.* 135 Æuriche sunendeie, and oðre heȝe daȝen. *Ibid.* 139 Efri cristenne Mon. *a* **1200** *Moral Ode* 65 (Trin. MS.) Africh man mid þat he haueð mai bugge heueriche. *c* **1205** LAY. 2378 For euer ulc [*c* **1275** euerech] god mon ah his lauerdes heste to do. *Ibid.* 25299 Æuer ælc swein. *a* **1225** *Ancr. R.* 4 Rihten hire and smeðen hire is..of efrich ordre þe god. *c* **1230** *Hali Meid* 13 Eauer euch wif is hire were þral. **1258** *Proclam. Hen. III*, And al on þo ilche worden is isend in to æurihce oþre shcire. *a* **1300** *Cursor M.* 3309 Euer ilk fote miht he noght blinne, To bihold þat fair maydene. *c* **1340** *Ibid.* 761 (Trin.) Wommon telle me whi þat ȝe eten not al comynly In paradis of euer vche tre? ? *a* **1400** *Morte Arth.* 212 In ever-ilk aperty pyghte with precyous stones. *c* **1400** *Beryn* 1779 The Burgeyse toke a-visement long on euery drauȝte. *c* **1450** *Merlin* IV. 65 Eueriche man to brynge with hym his wyf. **1500–20** DUNBAR '*Quhome to sall I complene my wo*' ix, Fra ever-ilk mowth fair wirdis proceidis. *a* **1535** MORE *On the Passion* Wks. 1299/1 Euery fynger shalbe a thombe. **1558** Q. KENNEDY *Compend. Tract.* in *Wodr. Soc. Misc.* (1844) 117 Bot everilk faithfull minister to bestowe the grace quhilk God hes gevin hym. **1588** J. HARVEY *Prophecies* 51 Every right woonder, such as Moises and Elisaeus used, were neither fained apparences, or, etc. **1606** G. W[OODCOCKE] tr. *Justin's Hist.* 16 a, Discending amongst euery private Captaine. **1610** SHAKS. *Temp.* I. i. 62 Hee'l be hang'd yet, Though euery drop of water sweare against it. *a* **1618** RALEIGH in Walton *Angler* (1653) 67 If all the world and love were young, And truth in every Shepherds tongue? **1711** E. WARD *Vulgus Brit.* VIII. 89 E'ery willing Hero. **1763** GARRICK in *Colman's Posth. Lett.* (1820) 249 They have dug up Every Utensil that were in use among the Romans. **1796** *Hist. Ned Evans* II. 105 Every inhabitant, male and female, young and old, was assembled. **1820** SOUTHEY *Life Wesley* I. 393 To see every person in his class at least once a week. **1848** MACAULAY *Hist. Eng.* I. 279 In every experimental science there is a tendency towards perfection. **1860** MRS. CARLYLE *Lett.* III. 34 Feeling better in every way. **1879** LOCKYER *Elem. Astron.* IX. l. 307 Every particle of matter attracts every other particle.

b. preceded by a possessive pronoun.

1588 SHAKS. *L.L.L.* IV. i. 87, I prophane my heart on thy euerie part. **1610** —— *Temp.* II. i. 257 A space whose eu'ry cubit Seemes to cry out, how, etc. **1611** —— *Cymb.* I. iv. 49 Then a young Traueller..in my euery action to be guided by others experiences. **1682** DRYDEN & LEE *Dk. Guise* II. ii, Your every Grace Will kill at least your thousand in a day. **1702** ROWE *Tamerl.* I. i, There my Thoughts my every Care is center'd. **1748** RICHARDSON *Clarissa* (1811) III. 97 Her every moment to find the moment critical. **1798** JANE AUSTEN *Northang. Abb.* (1866) 95. **1812** COLERIDGE in Southey *Omniana* II. 234 The ungrateful traitor, whose every measure has been to make them still more incapable. **1835** BECKFORD *Recoll.* 146 Anger pervaded his every look and gesture. **1870** LOWELL *Study Wind.* 87 The Americanism of his every thought, word and act. **1879** J. W. SHERER *Who is Mary?* 258 She turned her love over in its every aspect.

c. with a superl. adj. (preceded by *the*) interposed before the sb. *Obs.* or *arch.* (The sense would now be expressed by *even the least*, etc., treated as a parenthesis).

1620 J. KING *Serm.* 28 Euery the least remembrance. **1659** BP. WALTON *Consid. Considered* 73 In all the Copies extant..every the least iota and tittle is to be found. **1785** MRS. A. M. BENNETT *Juvenile Indiscr.* (1786) V. 117 Strict adherence to every the minutest part of their customs and religion. **1806–7** J. BERESFORD *Miseries Hum. Life* (1826) I. x, Every the most minute article. **1837–8** SIR W. HAMILTON *Logic* xv. (1866) I. 277 Every, the most complex, web of thought may be reduced to simple syllogisms.

†**d.** with *a* or *an* before the sb. *Obs.*

a **1300** *Cursor M.* 510 (Gött.) Iornays..fourti mile euerilk a day. *c* **1325** *Pol. Songs* (1839) 157 Everuch a parosshe heo polketh in pyne. **1352** MINOT *Poems* x. 51 God save sir Edward his right In everilka nede. *c* **1440** HYLTON *Scala Perf.* (W. de W. 1494) II. xli, Eueryche a soule resonable owyth for to coueyte..nyghynge to Jhesu.

e. (*a*) with sbs. referring to time, as *day*, *year*, etc. in advb. phrases indicating repetition (cf. EVERYDAY); also (*b*) before a cardinal numeral, to indicate successive groups of objects; (*c*) before an ordinal, successive intervals of action; so ***every other*** (***day***, etc.), where *other* = 'second'; also *attrib.*; †***every other while***: at alternate periods; every now and then; (*d*) ***every time***, on all occasions, without fail or exception, certainly; freq. used as an affirmative exclamation. *colloq.* (orig. *U.S.*).

(*a*) *c* **1205** LAY. 6034, & aure alche [*c* **1275** euereche] wintre inne Wales hev wuneden. *a* **1300** *Cursor M.* 19041 (Gött.) Arli þe apostlis euer-ilke day went to þe temple for to prai. *c* **1420** *Sir Amadace* (Camd.) xii, A marchand of this cite, Hade..euirych ȝere thre hundryth pownde. *c* **1440** *Promp. Parv.* 141 Eryday, or eueryday, *quotidie*. **1570** LEVINS *Manip.* 196 Eueryday, *quotidie*. **1652** NEEDHAM tr. *Selden's Mare Cl.* 23 The keeping of..greater Armadoes every day then other. **1697** DRYDEN *Virg. Georg.* III. 823 Tisiphone.. every Moment rises to the sight. **1732** BERKELEY *Alciphr.* II. §6 The world every day grows wiser. **1796** H. HUNTER tr. *St.-Pierre's Stud. Nat.* (1799) III. 41 The two tides of six hours re-appear every day equal.

(*b*) **1606** SHAKS. *Ant. & Cl.* V. ii. 278 In euery tenne [women] that they [the Gods] make, the diuels marre fiue. *a* **1626** BACON *New Atl.* (1629) 19 Euery twelue yeares ther should be set forth..two Ships. *a* **1716** LADY M. W. MONTAGUE *Let. to Mrs. S.* 5 Aug., Every twenty paces gives you the prospect of some villa, and every four hours a large town. **1848** MACAULAY *Hist. Eng.* I. 176 A parliament should be held every three years.

(*c*) *c* **1400** MAUNDEV. (1839) xvi. 174 At euery thrydde pas þat þei gon fro here hows þei knelen. *c* **1400** *Beryn* 1256 To clothe the al new, euerich othir day. **1517** TORKINGTON *Pilgr.* (1884) 20 Every yer or every other yer ys Chosyn a Duke. **1545** UDALL, etc. *Erasm. Par.* (1548) *Luke* IV. 98 a, An extreme tyrannous deiuill..dooeth euery other while soodainly take hym. **1597** SHAKS. *2 Hen. IV*, III. ii. 329 This same staru'd Iustice hath done nothing but prate to me.. and euery third word a Lye. **1829** BENTHAM *Wks.* (1843) XI. 18 The daily, more than the every other day, papers. **1884** M. E. WILKINS in *Harper's Mag.* Oct. 793/1 She stopped.. to kiss her..every other minute.

(*d*) **1865** *Trans. Ill. Agric. Soc.* V. 318, I advise everybody to plant it,..but always charge them to also plant Delaware

and Catawba without fail, 'every time'. **1925** *Times Lit. Suppl.* 16 July 469/2 The Americans, if only because they have twice the population, are bound to win every time. **1927** A. B. Cox *Mr. Priestley's Problem* ii. 30 'It could be done... What do you say, Doyle?'.. What he did say, tersely, was: 'Every time! Let's!' **1928** S. Lewis *Man who knew Coolidge* I. 41 If he'd study his mother and me a little more.. he'd be a lot better off! You bet! Every time! **1939** G. B. Shaw *Good King Charles* I. 50 Thats what I have done, and you havnt. And that puts me ahead of you with the British people every time.

f. Phrases, ***on every side***: everywhere, in every direction. In same sense, †***in*** or ***on every end***, ***on every half***. ***every man Jack***, ***every mother's son*** (*colloq.*): every single individual. ***every now and then***, ***every now and again***, ***every once in a while*** [corruption of *ever*, etc.]: at intervals, from time to time. ***every bit***, ***every whit***: altogether, entirely, quite. ***every here and there***: at various points or places. ***every last***: absolutely every (*colloq.*, orig. *U.S.*). ***every so often*** (or ***oft***): from time to time, at intervals. ***every which way*** (also ***ever(y) which a way(s)***): orig. and chiefly *U.S.*, everyway, in all directions; so ***every which***: whichever, every. Also EVERY-DEAL.

c **1205** Lay. 5883 On æuer alchere [*c* **1275** euereche] halue. *Ibid.* 10549 Folc hi wende an æuerælche [*c* **1275** euereche] ende. **1297** R. Glouc. (Rolls) 5952 The deneis.. in euerich ende Him worrede her & þer. *c* **1340** *Cursor M.* 1646 (Trin.) Couetise lecchery and pride Haþ spred þis world on euery syde. **1583** Stocker *Warres Lowe C.* i. 79 a, The Spaniardes murdered euery mothers sonne of them. **1700** S. Parker 6 *Philos. Ess.* 12 The Primæval Earth will be e'ery whit as ill shaped as that we poor Mortals inhabit. **1731** *Select fr. Fog's Wkly. Jrnl.* (1732) II. 255 The Doctor was every now and then confoundedly puzzled what to do with them. **1824** 'A. Singleton' *Lett.* 82 Children [in Virginia] learn from the slaves some odd phrases; as, every which way. **1833** Bp. Thirlwall in *Philol. Mus.* II. 240 The theory will every now and then become the foundation of the history. **1840** Dickens *Barn. Rudge* xxxix, 'Every one of 'em,' replied Dennis, 'Every man Jack'. **1844** 'J. Slick' *High Life N.Y.* I. iv. 39 He kept a flinging his arms about every which way. **1859** Dasent *Pop. Tales Norse* 347 Every man Jack of them are so sound asleep. **1860** Bartlett *Dict. Amer.* s.v., Every once in a while. **1872** Mark Twain *Roughing It* (in Farmer *Americanisms*), He put on the pack saddle.. and then wound a rope all over and about it and under it every which way. **1883** P. Robinson *Fishes of Fancy* 90 Every now and again the ear could catch the sudden splash of pike meeting pike. **1887** A. W. Tourgée *Button's Inn* 80 You've done.. more'n any other man would have done, working and contriving every which way. **1888** 'Mark Twain' in *Century Mag.* Jan. 460/2, I know it *is* with me—every last sentence of it. **1896** — *Tom Sawyer, Detective* (1897) xi. 117 He got that big di'mond out.. and let it flash and blaze and squirt sunlight everwhichaway. **1896** J. K. Snowden *Web of Old Weaver* x. 118 Every so oft I could hear him say a word or two. **1905** *Eng. Dial. Dict.* Suppl. 99/1 'Er goes charing at Mrs. Long's every so often. **1928** 'M. Chapman' *Happy Mountain* i. 8 [His hair] had a habit of sticking out every-which-a-ways. **1928** R. Frost *Let.* 11 Oct. (1964) 191 Thought on in these bookish ways our lives go everywhichway. **1931** D. Runyon *Guys & Dolls* (1932) iv. 89 Other coppers are coming from every which direction. *Ibid.* xi. 237 People running every which way. **1949** R. Harvey *Curtain Time* xiii. 128 Sleepily, monotonously, every so often, a drop would form, slide down the umbrella and fall with a soft plop on the floor. **1953** R. Graves *Poems* 29 From every-which-a-way, hot as a two-buck pistol. **1958** *Times Lit. Suppl.* (Suppl.) 15 Aug. p. x/2 Stacked-up copies of every-which volume published in Great Britain since the prosperous thirties. **1959** *Listener* 15 Jan. 115/1 The bullocks bellowed as one, and surged away in a great sea of cattle, every last 900 head of them. **1962** L. Deighton *Ipcress File* v. 30 Hemmed in every-which-way was Ross. **1965** *Listener* 3 June 836/3 As for driving a motor-car while looking every whichway and singing a duet, I hope that the Road Safety Council has already protested. **1968** J. Wainwright *Edge of Extinction* 200 Clear 'em out—every last one of 'em. **1970** *Sunday Times* 22 Nov. 35/5 Every so often we would hear the tender melancholy note of the horn.

†**2.** With plural sb. (chiefly with defining word interposed): All severally (cf. Gr. ἕκαστοι). *Obs.*

1558 Q. Eliz. in Strype *Ann. Ref.* I. App. i. 2 Subjects of every the said kingdomes. **1591** F. Sparry tr. *Cattan's Geomancie* 68 Of the head and of euery things therein contayned. **1610** Shaks. *Temp.* v. i. 249 I'le resolue you.. of euery These happend accidents. **1623** Bingham *Xenophon* 126 Taking Polycrates the Athenian Captaine with him, and a man from euery the Coronels. **1626** W. Sclater *Exp. 2 Thess.* (1629) 256 Wee.. owe him [God] obedience according to euery his morall commands. **1671** H. M. tr. *Erasm. Colloq.* 91 Every several Troups have their Ensignes.

3. With loss of distributive sense: = 'All possible', 'the utmost degree of'.

[**1783** Ld. Percy in *G. Rose's Diaries* (1860) I. 58 Every domestic ease.. that a mortal could enjoy.] *Mod.* I feel every respect for him. They showed him every consideration. There is every prospect of success.

4. In senses now commonly expressed by *each*.

a. In *every man*, used to distribute a plural. (*arch.*) †**b.** Each of two (*obs.* exc. *dial.*).

1526–34 Tindale *Matt.* xx. 9 They.. came and receaved every man a peny. [So in **1611** and *R.V.*] **1599** Thynne *Animadv.* (1875) 50 They dyd ryde one euerye syde of hym. **1632** Lithgow *Trav.* x. 455 The Sergeants, and the two slaues, thrust on euery ancle an heauy bolt. **1880** *Antrim & Down Gloss.* s.v., There's a chimley on every en' o' the house.

†**5.** = any; in sentences expressing possibility.

1552 Huloet s.v., Euerye man, *quilibet*. **1577** B. Googe *Heresbach's Husb.* iv. (1586) 180 b, When everie season suffereth them [bees] not to be abroad, they must at such times bee fedde. **1760** Goldsm. *Cit. W.* xxv, The weakness of the wall which every earthquake might overturn.

II. *absol.* (quasi-*pron.*)

†**6.** Everybody, every one. *Obs.*

a **1225** *Ancr. R.* 4 Vor euerich schal holden þe uttre efter þet þe licome mei best mid hire serui þe inre. *c* **1250** *Gen. & Ex.* 2355 Euerilc he kiste, on ilc he gret. *c* **1380** Wyclif *Sel. Wks.* III. 102 Fuyr schal preve þe werke of everyche. *c* **1386** Chaucer *Wife's Prol.* 103 Every hath of God a propre gifte, Som this, som that, as him likith. **1475** Caxton *Jason*, Euerich hadde well eten and dronken raysonably. **1502** Arnolde *Chron.* (1811) 4 That euerich admyttyd in to the lybarte of the cite be of certayn crafte or office.

7. a. Each, or every one, *of* (several persons or things). Formerly often with verb in pl. *Obs.* exc. in legal documents.

1388 Wyclif *Matt.* xx. 9 Thei token eueryche of hem a peny. **1398** Trevisa *Barth. De P.R.* iii. xii. (Tollem. MS.), þe wit þat takeþ hede to many þingis takeþ þe lasse hede to eueriche þerof. *c* **1430** *Cookery Bks.* 20 Temper it vppe wyth almaunde mylke, & do euery of hem in a potte. **1486** in *Surtees Misc.* (1890) 47 Hertly I pray you, and everych of you. **1512** *Act 4 Hen. VIII*, c. 10 All other thinges comprised in the same Indentures and letres patentes and in everych of them. **1578** Lyte *Dodoens* i. lxxviii. 116 Every of the sayde joyntes are of the quantitie of a wheate corne. **1658** Slingsby *Diary* (1836) 420 Promissing to them and every of them rewards and summes of money. **1665** J. Sergeant *Sure-footing in Chr.* 224 Every of whose Words and Actions were infinitely to be admir'd. **1722** De Foe *Plague* (1840) 41 Every of the said chirurgeons is to have twelvepence a body searched by them.

b. *esp.* in phrase ***all and every*** (= L. ***universi et singuli***). The phrase is also occas. used in concord with a sb. in sing. or pl.

1502 *Gt. Charter* in Arnolde *Chron.* (1811) 223 That the chartur aforsaid in alle and euerych her articles.. be obserued. **1526** *Pilgr. Perf.* (W. de W. 1531) 182 Let vs all & eueryche of vs in all our distresse.. ron to that trone of mercy. **1570** Grindal *Rem.* (1843) 149 That all and every of the said vicars have a Bible. **1655** Mrq. Worcester in Dircks *Life* (1865) 390 Use these seals to all and every of the purposes aforesaid. **1826** Bentham in *Westm. Rev.* VI. 473 To all and every the children and child of the said intended marriage. **1845** *Act 8 & 9 Vict.* c. 119 Sched. ii, The said covenantor, his heirs, executors, or administrators, and all and every other person whosoever.

†**c.** Each (of two). *Obs.*

c **1385** Chaucer *L.G.W.* 2378 *Philomene*, In armes everych of hem [Philomela and Progne] other taketh. **1393** Langl. *P. Pl.* C. xxi. 77 A cacchepol.. craked a-two here legges.. of euerich of þo þeoues. *a* **1502** in Arnolde *Chron.* (1811) 300 It was decreed by the sayd arbitrours, that eueryche off my Lordis of Glouceter and of Winchester shulde take ethir other by the hand. **1560** Frampton in Strype *Ann. Ref.* I. xx. 242 Two men covered with white canvas coats.. and every of them a vizard upon their faces. **1578** Lyte *Dodoens* v. ii. 547 There be two sortes of Blites.. and every of them is diuided againe into two kindes.

†**8.** Distributing a plural. *Obs.*; = each.

c **1300** *Beket* 671 Forto do everech his beste to wende ech in his side. *c* **1430** *Cookery Bks.* 27 Take a porcyon of pouder of Clowys, of Gyngere, of Graynys of Perys, of Euery a porcyon. *c* **1440** *Douce MS.* 55 xxxix, Cast.. broth and water and wyn of everiche a quantite. **1485** Caxton *Paris & V.* 16 Goo ye eueryche under that baner that he wyl mayntene.

III. Combinations.

†**9. every other.** = Each other: used as a reciprocal pronoun. (In early use *every* is subj. and *other* obj.; later the phrase appears as a compound.) *Obs.*

1154 *O.E. Chron.* an. 1135, Æuric man sone ræuede oþer þe mihte. *c* **1175** *Lamb. Hom.* 7 We luuien ure efrec oðer us bi-twenen swa we weren broðre. *c* **1385** Chaucer *L.G.W.* 719 *Tisbe*, The name of everych gan to othyr sprynge. *c* **1386** — *Pars. T.* 128 The lovyng children.. wolden everych of hem eten other if thay mighten. **1413** Lydg. *Pilgr. Sowle* v. xiv. (1483) 105 They saiden graces wonder ioyfully takyng eueriche other by the hand. **1594** Kyd *Cornelio* v. in Hazl. *Dodsley* V. 242 They ran at ever-each other hand and foot.

10. every one. (In 16–17th c. the form *everych one* was often divided *every chone*.)

†**a.** *adj.* = sense 1 a. *Obs.*

1548 Udall *Erasm. Par. Luke* 103 b, Euery one man ought to be neighbour to an other.

b. *adj. absol.* (ˌɛvrɪ ˈwʌn). With reference to a sb. or pron. going before, which it usually distributes; or followed by *of*. Often incorrectly with pl. vb. Sometimes = Each (of two things).

c **1225** *Ancr. R.* 18 Blescið ou mid euerichon of ðeos gretunges. *c* **1250** *Gen. & Ex.* 185 Ilk kinnes erf, and wrim, and der.. And euerilc on in kinde good. *c* **1320** R. Brunne *Medit.* 132 With hym þey ryse everyche-one. *c* **1380** Wyclif *Sel. Wks.* III. 502 Evere ilk one of þese parties is þo same Gods body. *c* **1430** *Hymns Virg.* (1867) 48 We schulen foonde euery-choon. *c* **1460** *Towneley Myst.* 121 He commaundes you everilkon, To hold no kyng bot hym alon. **1503** *Sheph. Kalender* xlvii, I shall them soon vanquish every chone. *a* **1535** More *On the Passion* Wks. 1389/1 To haue hadde theym taken and slayne euerye chone. **1588** King tr. *Canisius' Catech.* 216 The sinne of Adam.. is in al men, ane seueral and peculiar sinne in euerilk ane. **1607** Topsell *Four-f. Beasts* (1673) 223 The under lip five, every one of the cheeks ten. **1611** Bible *Num.* xvi. 3 All the Congregation are holy, euery one of them. *a* **1680** Butler *Rem.* (1759) I. 14 What we every one can swear. **1699** Bentley *Phal.* Pref. 89 Every one [of these Passages] are true.

c. *pron.* (ˈɛvrɪwən, ˈɛvrɪˌwʌn). Everybody; sometimes written as one word. The pron. referring to *every one* is often *pl.*: the absence of a sing. pron. of common gender rendering this violation of grammatical concord sometimes necessary.

a **1225** *Ancr. R.* 252 Muchel neod is þet euerichon holde mid oðer, mid bisie bonen. *c* **1340** *Cursor M.* 10047 (Trin.) þe chastite of þis lady Ouercomeþ.. Gredines of eueruchon. **1387** Trevisa *Higden* (Rolls) VII. 125 Euerichon loked to hym self. **1526** Skelton *Magnyf.* 1055 Cryst save everych-one. **1556** J. Heywood *Spider & F.* A iij, Tyll everie one had mocked everichone. **1695** Woodward *Nat. Hist. Earth* Pref., The Difficulties.. of every one. **1732** Berkeley *Alciphr.* iv. §21 Every one knows that analogy is a Greek word. **1735** Johnson tr. *Lobo's Voy.* 99 Every one Sacrifices a Cow or more, according to their different Degrees of Wealth or Devotion. **1870** Dasent *Eventful Life* (ed. 4) I. 1 Every one had made up their minds that I was to be one thing, and I came out another. **1875** Jowett *Plato* (ed. 2) I. 479 Those familiar words.. are in the mouth of every one. **1877** W. H. Mallock *New Repub.* (1878) 94 Everyone then looked about them silently, in suspense and expectation.

11. a. In parasynthetic derivatives, as ***every-coloured***.

1744 Thomson *Spring* 726 The Peacock spreads His every-colour'd Glory to the Sun.

b. every-nighter, one who attends every performance of a play, series of concerts, etc.

1905 G. B. Shaw in *Grand Mag.* Feb. 126 He specially appeals to those who have seen King Henry VI. five times.. to discontinue their visits... The every-nighters.. have no excuse for their selfishness. **1947** *Penguin Music Mag.* II. 35 The orchestral player will admit the strain.. and so will the most fanatical every-nighter after a few seasons.

12. Combined with adverbs, as everyhow, everywhere, etc., and with substantives, in which the combination is usually written as one word, the sense of the substantive being weakened; as everybody, everything, etc.

¶**13.** The form *ever each*, surviving in archaistic use till 16th c., was corrupted into *every each*, which often appears in late editions of 15th c. texts (where the originals had *evereche*, *everych*, or the like), and hence has occas. been used *arch.* by recent writers.

1430 Lydg. *Bochas* i. xix. (1554) 35 b, Sampson.. toke their [foxis] tailes knit them twein and twein And amid euery eche he set a fire-bronde. **1477** Norton *Ord. Alch.* i. in Ashm. (1652) 21 Everie each of Foure were Gold and like a Knight. **1567** Maplet *Gr. Forest* 29 And euery eche moment at death his nod and beck. **1607** Topsell *Four-f. Beasts* (1673) 375 Every each other day he suffereth one sickness or other. **1609** C. Butler *Fem. Mon.* vii. (1623) R iij, But for the most part they die everyeach one. **1634** *Malory's Arthur* i. xxvii. (1816) I. 49 Every each of them [**1470** everyche of hem] did him homage. **1864** Munby in *Once a Week* 26 Nov., Now every each hath pass'd the bar.

every, obs. var. of ivory.

everybody (ˈɛvərɪ-, ˈɛvrɪbɒdɪ, -bədɪ), *pron.* [Comb. of every and body *sb.* in the sense (now obs. in literary use) of *person*. Formerly written as two words: cf. anybody.] Every person, every one. ***everybody else***: every other person. Sometimes incorrectly with *pl. vb.* or *pron.*

c **1530** Ld. Berners *Arth. Lyt. Bryt.* 285 Every bodye was in theyr lodgynges. **1580** Sidney *Arcadia* ii. (1613) 156 Now this king did keepe a great house, that euerie body might come and take their meat freely. **1620** *Horæ Subsec.* 477 To take vpon him the disciplining of euery body for their errours. **1691** T. H[ale] *Acc. New Invent.* p. lxxxvii, That which is every body's work is no body's. **1710** Berkeley *Princ. Hum. Knowl.* §97 Time, place, and motion.. are what everybody knows. **1715** De Foe *Fam. Instruct.* i. i. (1841) I. 10 Do not everybody else love him? **1759** Bp. Warburton *Lett.* (1809) 280 Every body else I meet with are full ready to go of themselves. *c* **1817** Hogg *Tales & Sk.* II. 196 Gilbert was every body's body. **1820** Byron *Wks.* (1840) IV. 298 Every body does and says what they please. **1860** Tyndall *Glac.* i. xi. 72 What I suppose has been observed.. by everybody. **1866** Ruskin *Eth. Dust* v. (1883) 82 Everybody seems to recover their spirits. **1871** Morley *Voltaire* (1886) 119 He was ever on the alert.. to impart of it [knowledge] to everybody else.

everyday (ˈɛvərɪ-, ˈɛvrɪdeɪ, ˌɛvrɪˈdeɪ), *sb.* and *a.* [Combination of every and day.]

A. *sb.* †**a.** Each day in continued succession. **b.** *dial.* A week-day, as opposed to Sunday.

c **1374** Chaucer *Boeth.* ii. ii. 33 O þou man wher fore makest þou me gilty by þine euerydayes pleynynges. **1888** Elworthy *W. Somerset Word-bk.* s.v., Oh! I keeps they for Sundays, I don' put 'em on 'pon everydays. *Mod. Sc.* Ask him for an every-day, he cannot come on a Sunday. Sunday and every-day are alike to him.

B. *attrib.*, passing into *adj.*

1. Of or pertaining to every day, daily; also, pertaining alike to Sundays and week-days.

1647 Saltmarsh *Spark. Glory* (1847) 170 His fulness lives in an eternal every-day sabbath, while some live in little more than.. one day in the week. **1648** Hammond *Wks.* IV. (1684) 508 An every-day care for the drying up of the great fountain of Leprosie in the Heart. **1796** Lamb *Lett. to Coleridge* in *Life* ii. 16, I am heartily sick of the every-day scenes of life. **1804** Bp. Lincoln in G. Rose's *Diaries* (1860) II. 85, I do not doubt but you want constant every-day debaters. **1857** Livingstone *Trav.* Introd. 6 *note*, Make religion the every-day business of your life. **1861** Flo. Nightingale *Nursing* 95 The everyday management of a sick room. **1880** Muirhead tr. *Instit. Gaius* 591 Voluntary sale of a slave was of everyday occurrence. **1888** Elworthy *W. Somerset Word-bk.* s.v., An 'every-day horse' is one that can work all the week long.. not like a Parson's horse, which can only work on Sundays.

2. Of articles of dress: Worn on ordinary days or week-days, as opposed to Sundays or high-days. Also *fig.* ***every-day self***.

1632 Massinger *City Madam* I. i, Few great ladies going to a masque..outshine our's [fashions] in their every-day habits. **1824** Miss Mitford *Village* Ser. I. (1863) 215 The every-day ribbands were coloured. **1840** Dickens *Old C. Shop* xiii, Mr. Quilp invested himself in his every-day garments. **1883** H. H. Kane in *Harper's Mag.* Nov. 945/2, I seemed to have left my every-day self in the..vestibule.

3. To be met with every day; common, ordinary. Of persons and their attributes: Commonplace, mediocre, inferior. Also ***every-day-world*** adj.

a **1763** Shenstone (T.), Things of common concern.. make no slight impression on everyday minds. **1781** Johnson *L.P.*, *Akenside*, This was no every-day writer. **1791** Boswell *Johnson* (1831) IV. 19 Every-day knowledge had the most of his just praise. **1817** Coleridge *Biog.* 202 Persons of no every-day powers and acquirements. **1845** J. H. Newman *Ess. Developm.* 249 Her every-day name..was the Catholic Church. **1847** Alb. Smith *Chr. Tadpole* xxxii. (1879) 277 [She] had shrunk from the every-day people in the parlour of the public-house. **1862** Burton *Bk. Hunter* 5 The vulgar everyday-world way of putting the idea. **1868** Freeman *Norm. Conq.* (1876) II. viii. 287 Treason is spoken of as an everyday matter. **1871** *Mad. Simple's Invest.* iv, People who have a cook..ought not to dine like everyday folks.

Hence **everydayness**.

1840 Lowell *Love* Poet. Wks. (1879) 82 The every-dayness of this work-day world. **1876** Mrs. Whitney *Sights & Ins.* xxiv, Nice, jolly every-dayness. **1862** *Temple Bar* V. 263 The every-dayness, the common-placeness of life oppressed me. **1892** *Sat. Rev.* 26 Mar. 364/1 The everydayness of this nineteenth century. **1904** M. E. Durham *Through Lands of Serb* 289 Their dull 'everydayness'. **1954** L. MacNeice *Autumn Sequel* 19 The need for everydayness.

† '**everydeal.** *Obs.* [Combination of every and deal.]

1. as *sb.* Every part, the whole, every point in particular.

1297 R. Glouc. (1724) 35 For my god heo louede me, & now he habbeþ euery del. *c* **1330** R. Brunne *Chron.* (1810) 78 A message..Teld William eueridele of Malcolme robberie. **1413** Lydg. *Pilgr. Sowle* iv. xxxvi. (1483) 83 The feete ben the bases that beren euerydele. **1496** *Dives & Paup.* (W. de W.) I. xx. 54/2 As they saye one holy prayer may chaunge euery dele. **1531** Elyot *Gov.* I. xx, The straunge kynge..understode euery dele of the mater.

b. subjoined to a sb. or sb. pron.; emphasizing the totality of the object: Every whit, every part (of it); shading off into the advb. use 2.

c **1220** *Bestiary* 345 Forwerpen pride euril[c] del, so hert doð hise hornes. **1297** R. Glouc. (1724) 408 An quoynte tour hii lete make eueryldel of tre. *c* **1374** Chaucer *Boeth.* II. i. 31 She þat ȝit couereþ hir and wympleþ hir to oþer folk, haþ shewed hir euerydel to þe. **1483** Caxton *Gold. Leg.* 102/1 Thenne saynt Iohn toke the cuppe..and dranke it of euerydele. **1560** *School-ho. Women* 787 in Hazl. *E.P.P.* IV. 135 Thy beasts, thy goods and thy children all Be dead and brent now euery deale.

2. as *adv.* In every part, in every respect; entirely, wholly.

c **1375** *Lay Folks Mass-bk.* (MS. B.) 526 Make my loue, both day & nyght sykerly sett euerilk dele. *c* **1400** *Sowdone Bab.* 314, I have aspied everydele Howe thai shalle alle be betrayede. *c* **1475** *Partenay* 914 Ther coursers loged.. Insyde tentes ful fair eueridel. **1597** Bp. Hall *Sat.* III. vii. 49 If that semblance suite not euerie deale. **1714** Gay *Sheph. Week* v. 79 There ev'ry deale my Heart by Love was gain'd.

everyhow ('ɛvərɪ-, 'ɛvrɪhaʊ), *adv. rare.* [See every 12.] In every way.

1837 Hawthorne *Amer. Note-bks.* (1879) I. 102 Crags, all shattered and tossed about everyhow. **1880** *Athenæum* 24 Apr. 529 The walking tour was got through every how but on foot.

† **everylike,** *adv. Obs.* exc. *dial.* Also 5 **everelike, -yllyke, -ylyche.** [f. ever + elike, though probably looked upon as = every + like.] Ever in like fashion; continually; in later dialectal use, from time to time; at intervals.

a **1400-50** *Alexander* 340 þe ious out he wrengis, Erne till exorzise & ethis euer elike. *Ibid.* 727 (Dublin MS.) That oþer wy for hys werkez wepys eueryllyke. *c* **1420** *Chron. Vilod.* 2164 ȝet almys-dede and fastyng he dude everylyche continuelle. **1855** Robinson *Whitby Gloss.* s.v., They kept playing the music every like.

Everyman ('ɛvrɪmæn). [Name of the leading character in a 15th-c. morality play.] The ordinary or typical human being. Also *attrib.*

1906 (*title*) Everyman's Library. **1914** *Scotsman* 22 Oct. 1/2 The 'Everyman' Belgian Relief Fund. **1929** R. Bridges *Test. Beauty* IV. 1337 Nor might he escape the fall of Ev'ryman. **1930** *Ess. by Divers Hands* IX. 49 Everyman's rhyme—'Good friend, for Jesus sake forbear'—does well enough for Philip-sober. **1930** D. L. Morse-Boycott (*title*) God and Everyman. **1935** *Discovery* Mar. 74/2 A concession to the stumbling steps of Everyman, who knows nothing of biology. **1964** *English Studies* XLV. 354 He is not presenting us with an Everyman figure.

every one: see every 10.

everything ('ɛvər-, 'ɛvrɪθɪŋ), *pron.*

1. a. A combination of every (sense 1) and thing. As in *anything*, *something*, *nothing*, the subst. element has usually no definable meaning, the compound being equivalent to a neuter absol. use of the adj. The distributive sense etymologically belonging to the word is often absent, its force being merely collective; hence it is the current substitute for *all* (absol.), *all things*, which in most contexts are now somewhat formal. Often followed by adj., as ***everything good*** = 'all that is good'. Formerly written as two words; this is now rare, exc. where the two words are used without modification of sense.

c **1385** Chaucer *L.G.W.* 398 *Prol.*, In noble corage oghte been areste, And weyen eueryþing by equytee. *c* **1440** *Generydes* 4 Wyse and manly preuyd in euery thyng. **1567** J. Sanford tr. *Epictetus* 2 b, In euery thing..which thou louest, thou must diligently consider the qualitie. **1600** Shaks. *A.Y.L.* II. vii. 166 Sans teeth, sans eyes, sans taste, sans euery thing. **1672** Wilkins *Nat. Relig.* I. ii, Every thing is endowed with such a natural Principle, whereby it is necessarily inclined to promote its own preservation and well being. **1681** Dryden *Abs. & Achit.* I. 548 Zimri..was everything by starts and nothing long. **1751** Johnson *Rambler* No. 180 ¶8 Among the sons of learning, many seem to have thought of everything but themselves. **1796** Jane Austen *Pride & Prej.* xxvii, Every thing however went on smoothly. **1855** Macaulay *Hist. Eng.* IV. 567 She had not ..his partiality for everything Dutch and for everything Calvinistic. **1857** Buckle *Civiliz.* I. ix. 572 The government [in France] is believed to see every thing, know every thing, and provide for every thing. **1879** M. Arnold *Guide to Eng. Lit.*, Mixed Ess. 180 Everything, surely, depends upon what the lesson is.

b. as *predicate*, characterizing something as of supreme importance. *colloq.*

a **1891** *Mod.* Be sure you are in good time; that is everything.

c. Colloq. phr. ***to have everything***: to possess every kind of attraction, advantage, requirement, etc.

The early examples lack the colloq. flavour of the current phrase.

1845 Wellington *Let.* 25 Feb. (1890) 141, I was very sensible of your kind offer of Assistance—But he had everything. **1852** Mrs. Stowe *Uncle Tom's C.* x. 63/1 Mas'r George, you has everything,—l'arnin', privileges, readin', writin'. **1903** *Westm. Gaz.* 27 May 2/2 The little boy who, when told that if he did a certain thing he would not go to heaven, retorted that you couldn't have everything. **1921** R. Macaulay *Dangerous Ages* v. 95 She was to tell stories of Nan, who had everything. **1925** *New Yorker* 6 June 9/1 In the language of baseball, the fellow has everything. **1928** T. Wolfe *Let.* 21 May (1956) 135 I've got a *new* book in mind. .. I don't see how this one can fail—it has everything: rich people, swank, a poor but beautiful girl, romance, adventure, [etc.]. **1958** Wodehouse *Cocktail Time* xviii. 156 The Beetle and Wedge home-brew..touched the spot. It had everything. It ran like fire through Albert Peasemarch's veins and made a new man of him. **1969** *New Yorker* 20 Dec. 70/2 The latest expensive, worthless gift for the person who has everything.

2. *sb. rare* in *sing.*; in *pl. humorously*. Things of every kind. Also (nonce-use) quasi-*adj.*; and in comb., ***everything-maker***.

1797 Mrs. A. M. Bennett *Beggar Girl* (1813) V, Miss Walsingham was..the most accomplished, the most sensible, the most every thing woman could be. **1802** Bentham *Wks.* (1843) X. 390 It is against my habits, my principles, my everything, to propose it to him. *a* **1845** Hood *To Mr. Malthus* iii, There are..too many everything-makers. **1865** Dickens *Mut. Fr.* I. iii, But to be sure there were rum everythings. **1884** Ruskin in *Pall Mall G.* 3 Dec. 3/2 Patent everythings going of themselves everywhere.

everyway ('ɛvərɪ-, 'ɛvrɪweɪ), *adv.* [Cf. alway, anyway: sometimes written as two words.]

1. a. In every manner or way; in every direction. **b.** In every respect.

a. 1570 Levins *Manip.* 197 Eueryway, *omni modo, quauis.* **1580** Baret *Alv.* E 376 Square euerie way, *quo-quo versus quadratum.* **1774** Goldsm. *Nat. Hist.* (1776) I. 398 A Deity residing in the midst of an universe, infinitely extended every way. **1878** Browning *La Saisiaz* 34 The everyway external stream.

b. 1601 Shaks. *Jul. C.* IV. iii. 55 You wrong me every way: You wrong me Brutus. **1615** Bedwell *Moham, Imp.* II. §57 The contrary..opinion is euery way without any shew of probability. **1749** Fielding *Tom Jones* IV. ii, Her mind was every way equal to her person. **1828** Carlyle *Misc.* (1857) I. 169 A wide and everyway most important interval.

quasi-*adj.* **1628** Hakewill in *Ussher's Lett.* (1686) 399 Sir Thomas Bodley of whose..every way sufficiency, I have had a long trial.

2. *Comb.* (*nonce-wds.*)

1768-74 Tucker *Lt. Nat.* (1852) I. 475 A clock..with everyway-multiform-exquisitely-mechanical circumstances belonging to it. **1841** J. T. Hewlett *Parish Clerk* III. 320 Every-way-at-once-ish eyes.

Hence **everywayness** (*nonce-wd.*), the quality of extending in every direction.

1674 N. Fairfax *Bulk & Selv.* 103 His everywayness or immensity is the same.

† '**everyways,** *adv. Obs.* [every + *ways* advb. genitive. Cf. anyways.] In every direction.

1398 Trevisa *Barth De P.R.* IV. iv. (1495) 85 The bodies euery wayes ben grete hye and longe and brode.

everywhen ('ɛvərɪ-, 'ɛvrɪˌhwɛn), *adv.* [f. every + when; on analogy of *everywhere*.] At all times, always.

1843 Carlyle *Past & Pr.* (1858) 211 Everywhere and everywhen a man has to 'pay with his life'. **1850** Lynch *Theo. Trin.* xi. 208 Every when and every where Sweetest flowers welcome are. **1862** *Q. Rev.* Apr. 425 Religion..must be with us everywhere and everywhen.

everywhence ('ɛvərɪ-, 'ɛvrɪˌhwɛns), *adv. rare.* [f. every + whence on analogy of *everywhere*.] From every direction.

1890 Rossetti *Wks.* II. 458 They all come at his summoning Everywhence both far and near.

everywhere ('ɛvərɪ-, 'ɛvrɪhwɛə(r)), *adv.* [repr. two distinct ME. compounds. 1. *ever-ywhere*, f. ever + ywhere (OE. *ȝehwǽr*) anywhere, everywhere. 2. *every-where*, f. every (ME. *everilk*) + where. Formerly often written separately.]

1. In every place; also in narrower sense, in every part (of a limited space, of a book, an author's writings, etc.). Also, loosely: in many places; of frequent occurrence.

a **1225** *Ancr. R.* 200 Auh ȝe euerihwar, hwarse ich go swuðest forð, bileaue ȝe þe lengure. *a* **1225** *Leg. Kath.* 681 þi leofmon & ti lauerd..is mit te eauerihwer. *a* **1300** *Cursor M.* 5567 (Gött.) Ouer-all his kingriche euerilk-quar [*c* **1340** *Trin.* euery where]. *c* **1340** *Ibid.* 18001 (Trin.) What maner is þat ihesus þat euereþ on þe euerywhore. **1413** Lydg. *Pilgr. Sowle* III. x. (1483) 56 Suche noyse and crye euery where sownyd allas. *c* **1590** Marlowe *Faust.* Wks. (Rtldg.) 85/1, I may be here and there and everywhere. **1662** Stillingfl. *Orig. Sacr.* III. ii. §18 Motion..must be alike everywhere in it [matter]. **1692** E. Walker *Epictetus' Mor.* xiv, You'll find th' Avenues guarded ev'ry where. **1748** Hartley *Observ. Man* I. Introd., I every-where use these Words in the Senses here ascribed to them. **1850** McCosh *Div. Govt.* I. ii. (1874) 39 We discover everywhere signs of littleness and restlessness. **1860** Tyndall *Glac.* I. xix. 136 The horizontal stratification is everywhere beautifully shown. **1875** Jowett *Plato* (ed. 2) I. 116 Irresistible here, as everywhere in Plato, in his intellectual superiority. **1906** Mrs. Beeton *Bk. Househ. Managem.* lxix. **1811** Patent Carpet Sweepers..are in use everywhere. **1912** H. H. Munro *Unbearable Bassington* vii. 122 'Real country scenery; apple blossom everywhere.' 'Surely only on the apple trees,' said Lady Caroline. **1960** *News Chron.* 19 July 3/1 The Italian fashions are glitter, glitter, all the way... Lamé is everywhere.

† **2.** quasi-*adj.* All-pervading. *Obs. rare*⁻¹.

1674 N. Fairfax *Bulk & Selv.* 31 Eternity is said to be an everlasting now, and immensity as an every where cleavelesness.

3. As *sb.* All places or directions; ***the everywhere***, the infinite; omnipresent space.

a **1631** Donne *The Good Morrow* 11 in *Poems* (1633) 165 For love, all love of other sights controules, And makes one little roome, an every where. **1893** G. Macdonald *Poems* II. 158 Out of the everywhere into here. **1922** D. H. Lawrence *England, my England* 207 Everywhere seemed silent, but for the rattle of trains at the crossing.

Hence **everywhereness**, ubiquity, omnipresence. *rare.*

1674 N. Fairfax *Bulk & Selv.* 32 Neither of them would come any nearer to everlastingness, or everywhereness, than the shortest and the least do. **1839** Bailey *Festus* xx. (1848) 70/1 Poetry is not confined to books, For the creative spirit ..hath God's everywhereness.

everywheres, U.S. colloq. and dial. var. everywhere *adv.*

1865 'Mark Twain' *Sketches* (1872) 18 Fellers that had travelled and been every-wheres. **1876** —— *Tom Sawyer* vi. 66 He's been nearly to Coonville and most everywheres. **1957** B. & C. Evans *Dict. Contemp. Amer. Usage* 164/2 In the United States *everywheres* is often heard in the speech of well educated people, but it does not appear in print.

every while, whit: see while, whit.

everywhither ('ɛvərɪ-, 'ɛvrɪˌhwɪðə(r)), *adv.* [f. every + whither; in ME. perh. f. ever + ywhither.] In every direction.

1398 Trevisa *Barth. De P.R.* IV. iv. (1495) 85 The moost mater is obedyent that stretchyth itselfe euery whyther and moost vpwarde. **1851** Carlyle *Sterling* I. viii. (1872) 48 It was talk..spreading everywhither in inextricable currents. **1888** Talmage *Serm.* in *The Voice* (N. York) 28 June, A hymn has wings, and can fly everywhither.

‖**eveschie.** *Obs. rare*⁻¹. [OF. *eveschié* (mod.F. *évêché*) = Pr. *evescat*:—L. *episcopātus*, f. *episcopus* bishop.] A (French) bishopric.

1475 *Bk. Noblesse* 34 Withe thre eveschies clepid diocesis and citees in the saide duchie.

eves(e), obs. form of eaves.

† '**evese,** *v. Obs.* [OE. *efesian, efsian*, f. *efes*, eaves; the original sense must app. have been 'to cut the thatch at the eaves of a building' (cf. *eaves-knife*); but all the known OE. examples have the wider sense 'to clip'.] *trans.* To cut, clip (a person's hair, the coat of an animal, a tree, etc.); to cut short the hair of (a person).

c **1000** Ælfric *Gram.* xxvi. (Z.) 157 Ic efesige oð ðe ic scere scep oððe hors. *a* **1225** *Ancr. R.* 398 Absalones schene wlite, þet ase ofte ase me euesede him me solde his euesunge—þeo her þe me kerf of—uor two hundred sicles of seolure. *c* **1300** *Marina* 64 in Horstmann *Leg.* I. 172 A robe he dude hire apon, Ant euesede hire ase a mon. *c* **1325** *Gloss. W. de Biblesw.* in Wright *Voc.* 144 Monn top vus pri estancez [*Gloss.*, evese my cop]. *c* **1340** *Gaw. & Gr. Knt.* 184 Watz euesed al vmbe-torne, a-bof his elbowes. *c* **1394** *P. Pl. Crede* 166 Orcheȝardes and erberes euesed well clene.

evesing, var. form of eavesing, *Obs.*

† '**evesong.** *Obs.* [f. eve *sb.*¹ + song.]

1. = evensong 1 a; also *gen.* (perh. *transf.*) a song sung at eventide.

a **1225** *Ancr. R.* 22 Efter euesong anonriht siggeð ower Placebo. *c* **1290** *Lives Saints* (1887) 66 He bi-gan one saume of euesongue. *c* **1300** *St. Brandon* 214 The foweles tho hit eve was, bigonne here evesong. **1389** in *Eng. Gilds* (1870) 121 þe secunde belle of þe Euesong of seint Peter. **1455** E. CLERE in *Four C. Eng. Lett.* 5 He seith matyns of Our Lady and evesong.

2. Short for 'evensong-bell'.

1393 LANGL. *P. Pl.* C. VII. 396 Bargeynes and beuereges bygunne to aryse, And setyn so til euesong rang.

3. *attrib.*

c **1315** SHOREHAM 87 Of the crouche he was do At evesanges oure. **1387** TREVISA *Higden* (Rolls) VII. 243 þe bataille dured from underne of þe day to eue song tyme. **1460** *Lybeaus Disc.* (Kölb.) 1424 From þe our of prime Till hit was evesong time To fiȝte þey wer þro.

† **'evest.** *Obs.* Forms: 1 æfest, æfst, æfist, efest, 3 evest, -ist, ? eust, oust. Cf. EFT *sb.*² [OE. *æfest*, acc. to Sievers for **æfést*, f. *æf-* (= OF, Ger. *ab*) from, away from + *ést* (see ESTE *sb.*); cf. Ger. *abgunst*.] Envy, malice.

a **1000** CYNEWULF *Elene* 496 þæt hie for æfstum unscyldigne.. feore beræ ddon. *c* **1000** *Ags. Ps.* lxix. 4 Heora æfstu eac ealle sceamien. *a* **1300** *Cursor M.* 18552 (Gött.) þe princes als his ful fas wid eust [*printed* enst; Cotton, oust, *printed* onst] and nith again his ras. *Ibid.* 23138 (Edin. MS.) In niþe and euest [*printed* enest] and licheri. *Ibid.* 23279 (Edin.) þai þat war fild of enist [*printed* enist].

'eve-star. *Obs.* exc. *poet.* [f. EVE *sb.*¹ + STAR.] = *evening star*.

c **1374** CHAUCER *Boethius* I. v. 22 þe euesterre esperus.. is pale by þe morwe at þe rysynge of þe sonne. **1387** TREVISA *Higden* (Rolls) I. 301 This Spayne.. heet somtyme of Hespera, the eue sterre. *c* **1440** *Promp. Parv.* 144 Evesterre, *esperus, vesper*. **1878** BROWNING *Poets Croisic* xii, There peered May's earliest eve-star.

† **e'vestigate,** *v.* *Obs.*$^{-0}$ [f. L. *ēvestīgāt-us*, pple. f. *ē* out + *vestīgāre* to track, discover. Cf. INVESTIGATE.] *trans.* To seek out, search after, follow in the track of.

1656-81 in BLOUNT *Glossogr.* **1721-1800** in BAILEY; hence in CRAIG, etc.

Hence **e'vestigated** *ppl. a.* **e,vesti'gation**, a searching out, an investigation.

1775 ASH, *Evestigated*, searched out. **1658** PHILLIPS, *Evestigation*, an earnest seeking after. **1721-1800** in BAILEY.

evet(e, evett, obs. ff. EFT *sb.*

Évian (evjɑ̃). Also Evian. The name of a town in the department of Haute-Savoie in eastern France (in full, *Évian-les-Bains*), used *attrib.* and *ellipt.* to designate a mineral water obtained from springs there.

1857 R. M. GLOVER *Mineral Waters* III. xv. 308 *Evian* (*Savoy*). This is a water quite of a Malvern type, in one of the most charming sites in the world. **1865** E. LEE *Princ. Baths Switzerland & Savoy* 29 The Evian waters have great analogy with those of Contrexeville, though they are less exciting, and are consequently more applicable.. where there exists much irritability of the urinary passages. **1886** *Encycl. Brit.* XXI. 332/2 Mineral waters of various kinds abound (Amphion and Evian, chalybeate;.. La Caille, hot, sulphurous). **1908** *Practitioner* Sept. 468 Milk diet and water, alternating the glasses of milk with glasses of Evian-water. **1933** E. A. ROBERTSON *Ordinary Families* x. 230 Evian water, ryevita biscuits and cheese were laid out for him. **1936** 'R. WEST' *Thinking Reed* i. 12 André.. poured out a glass of Evian and sat back on the duchesse sofa. **1945** J. B. PRIESTLEY *Three Men in New Suits* v. 81 Markinch appeared to be dining on Evian, white tablets and cigarettes. **1970** *Time* 30 Nov. 40/2 Serving the teetotalers Vichy water instead of the first wine, Evian water instead of the second and ginger ale instead of champagne.

† **evibrate,** *v.* *Obs. rare.* [f. L. *ēvibrāt-* ppl. stem of *ēvibrāre*, f. *ē-* out + *vibrāre* to brandish: see VIBRATE.] **a.** *intr.* To shake, tremble. **b.** *trans.* To brandish (a sword); to hurl (a missile); in quot. *fig.*

1583 STUBBES *Anat. Abus.* 63 Doe not his handes and all his bodie euibrate, quauer, and shake. **1623-6** COCKERAM *Euibrate*, to shake. **1680** H. MORE *Apocal. Apoc.* 199 That wonderful contrition of heart, that the word of God makes, when it is sincerely and powerfully evibrated against the Enemies of his Kingdom.

Hence † **evi'bration** [see -ATION], the action of brandishing, a quick movement.

1644 H. VAUGHAN *Serm.* 20 Doth thou.. stay the loose evibrations and glances of the eye? **1656-81** in BLOUNT *Glossogr.* **1721-1800** in BAILEY.

evick(e, var. form of EVECK, *Obs.*

evict (ɪ'vɪkt), *v.* [f. L. *ēvict-* ppl. stem of *ēvincĕre*, f. *ē-* out + *vincĕre* to conquer.

The etymological senses of the Lat. word are 1. To conquer or overcome completely (*ē-* having merely an intensive force); 2. To obtain by conquering or overcoming; to recover by judicial means; to gain or accomplish in spite of obstacles; 3. To overcome and expel; to eject by judicial process; 4. To elicit by force of argument, to prove. See EVINCE.]

I. *Law.*

1. *trans.* To recover (property or the title to property) *of* or *from* any one by a judicial process, or in virtue of a superior title.

1503-4 *Act 19 Hen. VII*, c. 29 Indent., Yf the seid advouson.. after the seid.. appropriacion be evicted and taken from the seid Abbas and Convent. **1541-2** *Act 33 Hen. VIII*, c. 39. §54 If the said manours.. be recovered or euicted out of or from the possession of eny suche person.. by eny just or former title. **1577** HOLINSHED *Chron.* II. 145 Earle Hubert granted to the said John.. all the right that he had in the countie of Granople, and whatsoever might be got and evicted in the same countie. **1601** F. GODWIN *Bps. Eng.* 118 He euicted the same [the island of Seales] in law. *a* **1610** HEALEY *Theophrast.* (1616) To Rdr., If the thing bought bee euicted from the buyer, by reason the seller his possession was not good. **1635** SIR R. BOYLE *Diary* in *Lismore Papers* Ser. I. (1886) IV. 81 That [he].. should give sufficient securetie.. to answer all the mean profitts if by law I should evict his tytle. **1809** TOMLINS *Law Dict.* s.v. *Eviction*, If land is evicted, before the time of payment of rent on a lease, no rent shall be paid by the lessee. **1818** CRUISE *Digest* (ed. 2) IV. 434 If A. gives in exchange three acres to B. for other three acres, and afterwards one acre is evicted from B... the whole exchange is defeated.

† **b.** ? To vacate, retire from. *Obs. rare*$^{-1}$.

1530 in Rymer *Fœdera* (1712) XIV. 373 The same Lord Cardinall shall not Resign Leve Relese or otherwise Discharge or Evicte his Possession.

2. To expel (a person) by legal process †*of*, *from*, *out of* (land, etc.); also *simply*.

1536 HEN. VIII. in Ellis *Orig. Lett.* II. 124. II. 90 You have evictyd hym of the possessyon of the same. **1579** FENTON *Guicciard.* v. (1599) 199 They had no conscience to euict the iust owner out of the whole. *a* **1619** DANIEL *Coll. Hist. Eng.* (1626) 52 Being.. euicted by Law, of certayne other parcels of Land. **1720-54** *Apol. S.-Sea Direct.* in Strype *Stow's Surv.* (1754) II. v. xvii. 365/2 They had been evicted out of their estates however long enjoyed. **1767** BLACKSTONE *Comm.* II. 323 If, after an exchange of lands.. either party be evicted of those which were taken by him in exchange, through defect of the other's title. **1809** TOMLINS *Law Dict.* s.v. *Eviction*, If a widow is evicted of her dower or thirds, she shall be endowed in the other lands of the heir. **1845** M^cCULLOCH *Taxation* II. iv. §3 Should it be sold.. the purchaser may be evicted by the wife or children.

b. In recent popular use, *esp.* To eject (a tenant) from his holding.

1861 PEARSON *Early & Mid. Ages Eng.* xxxiv. 419 The great landowners evicted their tenantry, who were thus thrown upon the country, houseless and landless, but free. **1889** *Daily News* 8 May 5/7 Two of the principal tenants on the estate.. were evicted.

c. Hence *transf.* To eject (persons) forcibly from any position.

1876 WEISS *Wit. Hum. & Shaks.* i. 5 When a great freshet takes possession of a country and evicts the tenants of every hole, thicket, and burrow, there is an indiscriminate stampede of the animals. **1878** LADY HERBERT tr. *Hübner's Ramble* I. xii. 197 The new arrivals are the born antagonists of our enemies. They will evict them.

II. General senses.

† **3. a.** To conquer (a country, etc.); to obtain by conquest. *Obs.*

1560 *Cotton MS.* in Froude *Hist. Eng.* (1881) VI. 326 [The kingdom to be] evicted out of the hands of their own nation. **1602** WARNER *Alb. Eng.* Epit. (1612) 368 Edward.. euicted from the Danes the Prouince of East-Anglia.

† **b.** To overcome (an adversary, adverse circumstances, etc.) *Obs.*

1642 G. EGLISHAM *Forerun. Revenge* 7 Meanes may be had to resist or evict the most violent beast that ever nature bred. **1667** WATERHOUSE *Fire Lond.* 171 Their industry fortunated by God has made head against its misfortune, and evicted its cloud.

† **4.** To extort by force. *Obs.* Cf. EVINCE 3.

1631 CHAPMAN *Cæsar & Pompey* IV. i, Your happy exposition.. Euicts glad grant from me you hold a truth. **1648** G. DANIEL *Eclog.* v. 200 Rebell mouths (who speake noe truth, vnles Evicted 'bove their Rage) did then confesse Him master of ye feild.

† **5. a.** To vanquish in argument or litigation; to confute (a disputant), refute (an opinion or argument). **b.** To convict or convince (*of*). *Obs.*

1591 HORSEY *Trav.* (Hakluyt Soc.) App. 305 When by argumente they weare evicted, they pleaded mysunderstandinge of the interpretore or coruptyone in the translacion. **1594** T. B. *La Primaud Fr. Acad.* II. 585 Before hee coulde haue euicted Democritus of his foolish opinion. **1601** DENT *Pathw. Heaven* Pref. (1831) 77 This work doth sharply reprove and evict the world of sin. **1610** BARROUGH *Meth. Physick* I. xxx. (1639) 50 Therfore (as Johannicus saith) the eye hath seven coates.. But his opinion.. by sundry Anatomists hath been evicted, making but only six. **1611** SPEED *Theat. Gt. Brit.* vii. (1614) 13/2 Canute to evict his flatterers made triall of his Deitie. **1660** R. COKE *Justice Vind.* 5 He.. had need take great heed.. least instead of evicting his adversary, he only acquires the repute of a light and foolish man. **1730-6** BAILEY (folio), *Evict*, to convince by force of argument, etc.

† **6.** To establish by argument, to prove. With simple *obj.* or *obj.* sentence; also with *inf.* or *as* with complement. *Obs.* = EVINCE 4.

1584 FENNER *Def. Ministers* (1587) 126 There are wonderfull cunning men on your side, if they can euict this. **1610** C. HAMPTON *Serm.* 30 Which euicteth.. that there was one greater than the rest. **1614** BP. HALL *Epist.* v. ix, Let this stand evicted for the true and necessarie sense of the Apostle. **1650** BULWER *Anthropomet.* 221 That it is in its own nature laudable.. is by some evicted by the authority of the Ancients. **1715** CHEYNE *Philos. Princ. Relig.* I. (ed. 2) 306 This nervous Fluid has never been discovered in live Animals.. nor its necessity evicted by any cogent experiment. **1722** *Wodrow Corr.* (1843) II. 683 Unless your friend have more to evict them [papers] to be Mr. M'Ward's than Mr. Goodal's saying so.

† **b.** To settle (a controversy) by a decisive argument. *Obs.*

1581 J. BELL *Haddon's Answ. Osor.* 447 It might seeme that we had alleadged sufficiently for thys matter, and evicted the controversy throughly. **1660** JER. TAYLOR *Duct. Dubit.* I. II. vi. Whether.. that argument does evict the question.

Hence **'evict** *sb.* [cf. *convict*], **e,vic'tee**, an evicted tenant (*rare*). **e'victing** *vbl. sb.* (*attrib.*) and *ppl. a.*

1886 *Pall Mall G.* 10 Dec. 1/2 Not a penny of rent to be paid until the 'evicts' were reinstated. **1879** *Daily News* 31 Jan. 2/2 This I found tenanted by some people who.. were considerably above the rank of the evictees. **1889** *Daily News* 8 May 5/7, 130 police accompanied the evicting party. **1863** FAWCETT *Pol. Econ.* II. vii. 237 Assassination was the retribution with which the cottiers of Ireland not unfrequently punished an evicting landlord.

evicted (ɪ'vɪktɪd) *ppl. a.* [f. EVICT *v.* + -ED¹.] **a.** In various senses of the vb. **b.** Of a holding: From which the tenant has been evicted.

1604 J. BURGES in W. Covell *Answ.* (1606) 156 Farre be it from vs for any mans cause to maintaine an euicted errour. **1863** FAWCETT *Pol. Econ.* II. vii. 237 For the evicted tenant would only be replaced by another tenant of the same character. **1874** GREEN *Short Hist.* vii. 445 The evicted natives withdrew sullenly to the lands which had been left them by the spoiler. **1888** *Daily News* 26 Sept. 6/2 This staying of the evictor's hand was due.. to the boy cotting of evicted farms.

eviction (ɪ'vɪkʃən). [ad. L. *ēvictiōn-em*, n. of action f. *ēvincĕre*: see EVICT, EVINCE.] The action of evicting or †of evincing.

I. *Law.*

1. The action of recovering or taking possession of lands or property by legal process. Cf. EVICT *v.* I.

1583 STOCKER *Warres Lowe C.* II. 5 b, That reasonable satisfaction bee made.. to the buyers and sellers of the Possessions and Rentes aforesaied, in respect of their euiction. *a* **1610** HEALEY *Theophrast.* (1616) To Rdr., He is lyable to make good the euiction, who selleth for another as he who, etc. **1655** FULLER *Ch. Hist.* III. ix. §23 The Title of the Foundation thereof, with the land thereunto belonging, were.. subject to eviction. **1753** *Scots Mag.* Mar. 127/2 The eviction or destruction of a thing mortgaged, don't extinguish the debt. **1809** TOMLINS *Law Dict.*, *Eviction*, A recovery of lands, &c. by form of law. **1848** in WHARTON *Law Lex.*

2. The action of evicting or dispossessing a person of property, etc. In recent use, *esp.* the evicting a tenant from lands, houses, etc. Also *attrib.*

a **1626** BACON (J.), The pretorian court will set back all things, and no respect had to eviction or dispossession. **1818** CRUISE *Digest* (ed. 2) III. 322 A rent service is discharged by the eviction of the tenant out of the whole land. **1863** FAWCETT *Pol. Econ.* II. vii. 237 Neither could the landlord have recourse to eviction. **1884** PAE *Eustace* 69, I will get your father to order their eviction from the cottage. **1889** *Daily News* 8 May 5/7 An exciting eviction scene occurred to-day on the property of Lord Inchiquin.

fig. **1643** PRYNNE *Sov. Power Parl.* App. 159 On the contrary the people have a right of perpetuall eviction. **1691** BP. LLOYD *God's Disposing of Kingd.* I. 67 An eviction by the just sentence of God, who thus put's him out of a Trust that he abused.

II. *gen.*

† **3.** The action of conquering (a country, etc.), or of obtaining by conquest. *Obs.*

1602 WARNER *Alb. Eng.* Epit. (1612) 366 After the Euiction from the Scots of those Countries. **1611** SPEED *Hist. Gt. Brit.* IX. xx. §31 King Henry.. was not vnwilling, because.. Britaine seemed clearely past possibilitie of euiction.

† **4. a.** The action or process of vanquishing (a person) in argument, or of confuting (an opinion); an instance or a means of confutation; the condition of being confuted. **b.** Conviction (of an accused person). *Obs.*

1614 BP. HALL *Epist.* IV. v, He hath.. counsels for all doubts, evictions for all errours. **1615** G. SANDYS *Trav.* 62 All euictions there, as elsewhere, depend vpon witnesses. **1627** BP. HALL *Gt. Impostor* 509 Wise men.. whose wisedome is frequently imployed in the triall, euiction, dooming, of malefactors. **1649** —— *Cases Consc.* III. v, Meere error makes not an heretick.. eviction and contumacy must improve his error to be heretical. **1651** GATAKER in *Fuller's Abel Rediv.*, *Whitaker* 405 He grapled with.. Rainolds.. who had bin nibling.. at the Preface to his eviction of Sanders his Demonstration. **1703** T. N. *City & C. Purch.* Pref. 22 Upon Eviction I shall freely yield.

† **5.** The action or process of eliciting or establishing by argument; demonstration, proof. Also an instance or means of proving; an evidence, proof. *Obs.* Cf. EVICT *v.* 6, EVINCE *v.* 4.

1621 W. SCLATER *Tythes* (1623) A 1 b, Difficultie of euiction ariseth hence: first, that, etc. **1625** A. GIL *Disc. Trinity* 214 Faith is said to bee.. an eviction or proofe of things hoped for, though they be not seene. **1653** H. MORE *Conject. Cabbal.* (1713) 82 For further eviction, we may yet add, that, etc. **1678** CUDWORTH *Intell. Syst.* 875 That these two Circles should continue thus.. is a farther Eviction of a Providence also. **1692** L'ESTRANGE *Fables* 114 A Plurality of Voices.. carryes the Question in all our Debates, but rather as an Expedient for Peace than an Eviction of the Right. **1755** YOUNG *Centaur* i. 22 It has ever been prejudicial to the truth, to labour at rational evictions of sacred mysteries. **1776** G. CAMPBELL *Philos. Rhet.* (1801) I. I. iv. 82 The sole and ultimate end of logic is the eviction of truth.

† **e'victive,** *a.* *Obs. rare*$^{-1}$. [f. L. *ēvict-* (see EVICT *v.*) + -IVE.] Tending to evince or prove; demonstrative, conclusive.

1624 BP. MOUNTAGU *Gagg* x. 75 Your texts.. are not evictive, nor convincing.

evictor (ɪˈvɪktə(r)). Also evicter. [f. EVICT *v.* + -OR.] One who evicts.

a. One who expels the inhabitants from a country. **b.** One who evicts his tenants. **c.** A person employed to eject tenants from their holdings.

1816 KEATINGE *Trav.* I. 162 They [Moors of Spain] were as different too..from their conquerors and evictors as possible. **1865** PALL MALL G. 14 Oct. 5/2 One of the pitmen ..barricaded his door, and as the evictors had no warrant to force it open the proceedings were suspended. **1885** *Manch. Exam.* 20 Oct. 4/7 A crusade against those denounced as evicters and rackrenters. **1888** KENNY in *Times* 2 Oct. 5/6 The Plan of Campaign..is..their [the tenantry's] only.. protection against the hand of the evictor.

evidence (ˈɛvɪdəns), *sb.* Forms: 4–6 evi-, evydens, -nce, (5 hevydense, 6 esvedence, ewydence), 4– evidence. [ME. *evidence*, a. F. *évidence*, ad. L. *ēvidentia*, f. *ēvident-em*: see EVIDENT. Cf. Pr., Sp. *evidencia*, It. *evidenza*.]

I. 1. The quality or condition of being evident; clearness, evidentness.

1665 BOYLE *Occas. Refl.* V. iv. (1675) 310 Certain Truths, that have in them so much of native Light or Evidence..it cannot be hidden. **1665** BUNYAN *Holy Citie* Pref. Ep. A iij, I should not have been able to speak..so much as five words of truth with life, and evidence. **1677** HALE *Prim. Orig. Man.* I. ii. 63 They [our faculties] expand and evolve themselves into more distinction and evidence of themselves. **1721–1800** in BAILEY. **1882** MIVART *Nat. & Th.* (1885) 122 So evident that we require no grounds at all for believing them save the ground of their own very evidence.

b. *in evidence* [after F. *en évidence*]: actually present; prominent, conspicuous.

18.. *Blackw. Mag.*, The sister whose presence she had relied on was not in evidence. **1873** BROWNING *Red Cott. Nt.-cap* 479 The faithful of our province raised the sum.. And so, the sum in evidence at length, Next step was to obtain [etc.]. **1888** *Ch. Times* 28 Dec. 1153/3 The Broad Church school was more in evidence than at any previous Congress.

†**2.** Manifestation; display. *Obs.*

1382 WYCLIF *2 Macc.* iii. 24 The spirit of almiȝti God made grete euydence [Vulg. *evidentiam*] of his shewyng. *c* **1430** LYDG. in *Pol. Rel. & L. Poems* (1866) 45 Doblettes of glass yeue a gret euidence, Thyng countirfet wyl faile at assay. **1611** BIBLE *Transl. Pref.* 5 Which hee performed with that euidence of great learning.

II. That which manifests or makes evident.

3. An appearance from which inferences may be drawn; an indication, mark, sign, token, trace. Also † *to take evidence*: to prognosticate. *to bear, give evidence*: to afford indications.

a **1300** *Cursor M.* 4518 (Gött.) If ani man þer ware Coude telle to quat euidens it [Pharaoh's vision] bare. *c* **1391** CHAUCER *Astrol.* Prol. 1, I have perceived well by certeyne evidences theire ability to lerne sciences. **1393** GOWER *Conf.* I. 81 This horse..was to Troie an evidence Of love and pees for evermo. **1398** TREVISA *Barth. De P.R.* XVIII. xxxix. (1495) 800 Ofte men that shall fyght takyth euydence and diuineth..what shall befalle by sorowe othe by the joye that the horse makith. **1530** PALSGR. 217/2 Evydence, declaryng of a thynge. **1601** CORNWALLYES *Ess.* II. xxxi, The creatures that giue us earthly immortalitie [**1632** mortalitie], whose chosen evidence is beauty. **1644** CROMWELL in Ellis *Orig. Lett.* I. 362 III. 300 It had all the evidences of an absolute Victorie. **1681–6** SCOTT *Chr. Life* (1747) III. 263 A plain Evidence that this God and that Angel of Jehovah were the same Person. **1727** DE FOE *Syst. Magic* I. ii. (1840) 50, I give you this as an evidence of the difference in the kinds of magic. **1846** PRESCOTT *Ferd. & Is.* II. II. i. 243 She every where afforded the evidence of faculties developed by unceasing intellectual action. **1856** FROUDE *Hist. Eng.* (1858) II. vii. 221 An opportunity was offered them of giving evidence of their loyalty. **1860** TYNDALL *Glac.* I. xv. 99 A day..was spent in examining the evidences of ancient glacier action. **1867** LADY HERBERT *Cradle L.* vii. 167 The country they were traversing gave evidence of careful cultivation.

b. In religious language: Signs or tokens of personal salvation.

1758 S. HAYWARD *Serm.* xvi. 493 A person just entering upon eternity..with his evidences all dark.

†**4.** Example, instance (frequent in Gower). Also, *to take (an) evidence*. *Obs.*

a **1300** *Cursor M.* 2295 (Gött.) Þis euydens [*Cott.* forbisming] biheld þis oþer. *c* **1377** LANGL. *P. Pl.* B. xv. 429 Go bifore as a good baneoure, And hardy hem þat bihynde ben and ȝiue hem good euydence. **1393** GOWER *Conf.* I. 50 Whereof thou might take evidence To reule with thy conscience. *Ibid.* III. 270 By this evidence lerne, How it is good, etc.

5. Ground for belief; testimony or facts tending to prove or disprove any conclusion. Const. *for*, *of* (the thing to be proved), *from*, *of* (the source of testimony). † *to have evidence to say*, etc.: to have good grounds for saying, etc. (For *external*, *internal*, *moral*, *probable evidence*, see these adjs.)

c **1380** WYCLIF *Serm.* Sel. Wks. II. 107 Þe dedis þat Crist dide ben unsuspect evydence þat Crist is boþe God and man. —— *Sel. Wks.* III. 340 Þei shulden haue euydence to seie þat God haþ told þem þis. **1393** GOWER *Conf.* III. 87 Theology ..yiveth evidence Of thing, which is nought bodely. ? *a* **1400** *Morte Arth.* 286 Thus hafe we evydens to aske þe Emperour..whate ryghte þat he claymes. *c* **1425** WYNTOUN *Cron.* VIII. xv. 163 Ðis Kyng [Edwart] þan feyhnyd evydens As to declere hys Consciens..Quhat he in Scotland gert be dwne. **1480** CAXTON *Descr. Eng.* 18 He maketh non euidence for in neyther side he telleth what moeueth him so for to saye. **1530** *Compend. Treat.* (1863) 49 But it ought to be.. as we shall proue by open euidence thorough goddes helpe. **1594** HOOKER *Eccl. Pol.* I. iv. (1611) 10 Adoration, grounded vpon the euidence of the greatnesse of God. **1611** BIBLE *Heb.* xi. 1 Now faith is..the euidence [**1887** *Revised* assurance] of things not seen. **1662** STILLINGFL. *Orig. Sacr.* III. i. §7 Those who deny that there is a God, do assert other things on far less evidence of reason. **1736** BUTLER *Anal.* II. iii. Wks. 1874 I. 179 Its evidence not being so convincing and satisfactory, as it might have been. **1769** *Junius Lett.* v. 27 The plain evidence of facts is superior to all declarations. **1794** PALEY *Evid.* (1825) II. 285 There is no evidence that any forgeries were attempted. **1809** *Med. Jrnl.* XXI. 359 The truth..of which I can yet attest by living evidence. **1816** J. SMITH *Panorama Sc. & Art* I. 457 The evidence of sight is corrected by the judgment. **1846** MILL *Logic* III. xxi. §1 Evidence is not that which the mind does or must yield to, but that which it ought to yield to. **1878** HUXLEY *Physiogr.* 100 The weight of evidence appears strongly in favour of the claims of Cavendish.

†**b.** *an evidence*: something serving as a proof. *Obs.* Cf. 8.

1463 *Bury Wills* (Camd. Soc.) 19 Thinges wiche I graunte ..expressyd as folwith aftyr in writyng that here aftyr it may be knowe for an euydence in the seid tabyll. **1478** *Paston Lett.* No. 821 III. 234 Donne..ffounde that the Duke off Suffolk was verrye patrone, whyche was ffalse, yitt they ded it ffor an euydence. **1665** GLANVILL *Sceps. Sci.* Addr. 3, I took the boldness to borrow that deservedly celebrated Name, for an Evidence to my Subject. *a* **1704** LOCKE (J.), Cato Major..has left us an evidence, under his own hand, how much he was versed in country affairs.

c. *Evidence* or *Evidences of Christianity, of the Christian Religion*, or simply *The Evidences*.

[**1699** BP. S. BRADFORD (*title*) The Credibility of the Christian Religion, from its intrinsic Evidence.] **1729** ENTICK (*title*) The Evidence of Christianity asserted. **1730** (*title of posthumous work by Addison*) The Evidences of the Christian Religion. **1794** PALEY (*title*) Evidences of Christianity. **1859** MILL *Liberty* (1866) 63/2 There is no reasonable objection to examining an atheist in the evidences of Christianity. **1864** BOWEN *Logic* ix. 295 The other half [of the Fallacy is found] in a treatise on the Evidences.

III. Legal uses of 5.

6. Information, whether in the form of personal testimony, the language of documents, or the production of material objects, that is given in a legal investigation, to establish the fact or point in question. Also, *an evidence* = a piece of evidence. Phrases *to bear, give in, give evidence. to call in evidence*: to call as a witness. For *circumstantial*, *parole*, *presumptive*, *primâ facie*, *verbal*, etc. *evidence*, see these adjs.

1503–4 *Act 19 Hen. VII*, c. 4 The seid Justices shall awarde to the same persone so gevyng evydens xs. **1553** BRENDE *Q. Curtius* 114 Euery one of them geuing in euidence that they had spoken afore. **1594** DANIEL *Compl. Rosamond* xcii, The bed that likewise giues in euidence Against my soule. **1677** HALE *Prim. Orig. Man.* II. i. 130 The concurrent testimonies of many Witnesses..make an evideuce more concluded. **1683** DRYDEN *Ded. Plutarch's Lives* 20 They..transported their evidence to another [country] where they knew 'twas vendible. **1707** *Curios. in Husb. & Gard.* 343 To be call'd in Evidence concerning a Curiosity, that employ'd all the Great Men of his time. *a* **1714** BURNET *Own Time* I. III. 415 The person he had sent to Mitchell gave a full evidence of the promises he had made him: but Sharp denied them all. **1761–2** HUME *Hist. Eng.* App. i. I. 158 Want of discernment in judges, who could not discuss an intricate evidence. **1792** *Anecd. W. Pitt* I. iv. 58 To find proper evidence for convicting the offender. **1817** W. SELWYN *Law Nisi Prius* (ed. 4) II. 987 *Primâ facie* evidence of a publication by the bookseller. **1859** DICKENS *T. Two Cities* II. xii, There was no getting over his evidence. **1863** *Royal Charter* §16 in *Lond. Univ. Calendar* (1866) 25 Which Register shall be conclusive evidence that any person whose name shall appear thereon..is..entitled to vote.

transf. **1611** BIBLE *Transl. Pref.* 5 So S. Chrysostome, that liued in S. Hieromes time, giueth euidence with him. *a* **1719** ADDISON *Evid. Chr. Relig.* (1730) 23 They bear evidence to a history in defence of Christianity. **1875** SCRIVENER *Lect. Grk. Test.* 10 Their evidence is entirely independent of the later Greek copies.

b. *the evidence*: the testimony which in any particular cause has been received by the court and entered on its records. Similarly, *to be* or *produce in evidence*: to be a part, *or* to produce as a part, of the evidence before the court.

1817 W. SELWYN *Law Nisi Prius* (ed. 4) II. 959 The policy must be produced in evidence. **1860** DICKENS *Uncomm. Trav.* viii, The same incorrigible medical forefinger pointed out another passage in the evidence. *Mod.* The document is not in evidence.

c. Statements or proofs admissible as testimony in a court of law.

1817 W. SELWYN *Law Nisi Prius* (ed. 4) II. Index, Fleet books, not evidence. Where declaration of wife, and letters written by her, are evidence. *Mod.* What a witness states on hearsay is not evidence. My lord, I submit that this document is not evidence.

†**7.** One who furnishes testimony or proof; a witness. Sometimes *collect.* = 'witnesses.' *Obs.*

1593 SHAKS. *Lucr.* 1650 His scarlet lust came evidence to swear That my poor beauty had purloin'd his eyes. **1605** —— *Lear* III. vi. 37 I'll see their trial first: Bring in the evidence. **1681** *Trial S. Colledge* 72 And did not you come to me and tell me, there was a noise of your being an Evidence. **1731** *Gentl. Mag.* 218 The Lady Lawley was sentenced to be imprisoned one month for spiriting away an evidence. **1762** FOOTE *Orators* II. (1767) 50 Look upon this evidence, was he present at Mr. Parson's knockings. **1823** SCOTT *Peveril* xli, Two infamous and perjured evidences.. made oath to the prisoners' having expressed themselves interested in the great confederacy of the Catholics.

†**b.** *transf.* A spy. *Obs.*

1691 SOUTHERNE *Sir A. Love* v. i, Get you gone then, like an Evidence, behind the hangings.

c. *to turn King's* (*Queen's*, *State's*) *evidence* (formerly also † *to turn evidence*), said of an accomplice or sharer in a crime: to offer himself as a witness for the prosecution against the other persons implicated.

1722 DE FOE *Col. Jack* (1840) 79 One of the gang, to save his own life, has turned evidence. **1865** H. KINGSLEY *Hillyars & B.* iv, I hate a convict who turns Queen's evidence. **1886** *Science* (N.Y.) VIII. 603 Mr. Bartlett Channing Paine comes into court, and, as state's evidence, gives the following testimony.

transf. **1889** *Daily News* 25 Dec. 5/2 The Bishop might have been better employed than in turning King's evidence against the Sermon on the Mount.

†**8.** A document by means of which a fact is established (see quot. 1628); *esp.* title-deeds. (In 15–16th c. often in collective sense = 'documents'; sometimes with a numeral, as if mistaken for an actual plural. Cf. EVIDENT.) *Obs.* exc. *Hist.* and in legal formulæ.

a **1444** *Paston Lett.* No. 38 I. 51 The evidences..receyved of yow at your last beyng at Norwich. **1465** *Ibid.* No. 500 II. 179, I have put your evydens that com owte of the abbay in a seck and enseylyd hem under Ric. Call ys seall. **1465** *Mann. & Househ. Exp.* (1841) 175 The same day Brame toke to Thorneton sertene hevydense of myn, to take to James Hobard. **1501** *Plumpton Corr.* 151 All your new esvedence by your father to John Norton. **1505** in *Eng. Gilds* (1870) 327 A boxe wᵗ iiij ewydence wᵗ iij other wretynges. **1535** COVERDALE *Jer.* xxxii. 14, I charged Baruch..to take this sealed euydence with the copie. **1587** HOLINSHED *Chron.* III. 938 A poore woman..besought him to declare what he had doone with evidences of hirs. **1594** *Mirr. Policy* (1599) I ij, All the farmers..were murthered..their goods spoiled, their euidences burned, their houses raised. **1628** COKE *On Litt.* 283 a, Writings vnder seale, as Charters and Deeds, and other writings without seale, as Court Rolles, Accounts, and the like..are called Euidences. *a* **1672** WOOD *Life* (1848) 142 He began to peruse the evidences of Oriel coll. in their treasury. **1706** in PHILLIPS (ed. Kersey). **1818** CRUISE *Digest* (ed. 2) IV. 327 The next clause usually inserted..is, 'together with all deeds, evidences, and writings'. **1875** J. T. FOWLER *Ripon Ch. Acts* (Surtees) Pref. 5 A book of evidences relating to Obits kept in Ripon Minster.

9. *Comb.*

1827–8 BENTHAM *Wks.* (1843) X. 584 You might go on to examine evidence of the character of the evidence-giver. **1828** C. WORDSWORTH *K. Chas. I.* 103 A more visionary piece was never sketched by the pencil of a determined evidence-maker. **1832** R. SOUTHEY in *Q. Rev.* XLVII. 500 Jurymen are not the only persons who, upon occasion, can show themselves evidence-proof.

evidence (ˈɛvɪdəns), *v.* [f. prec. sb.]

1. *trans.* Of things: To serve as evidence for; to attest, prove. Rarely intr. *to evidence to.*

a **1619** FOTHERBY *Atheom.* II. xii. §2 (1622) 334 The testimonie of neither of them..doth so euidence the matter, as the things themselues doe. **1657** AUSTEN *Fruit Trees* I. 1 Worcestershire..Kent, and many other parts..can sufficiently evidence the profits of Orchards. **1690** PENN *Rise & Progr. Quakers* (1834) 57 His behaviour at Derby.. did abundantly evidence it. **1742** YOUNG *Nt. Th.* VII. 520 Fierce passions..presage a nobler flight, And evidence our title to the skies. **1859** HALLIWELL *Evid. Chr.* 97 Occurrences evidencing the divinity of Christ. **1875** LYELL *Princ. Geol.* (ed. 12) II. II. xxviii. 88 The Hillsides..were much shaken, as evidenced by the many bare patches with which they were chequered. **1885** CLODD *Myths & Dr.* I. iv. 68 The survival of grammatical forms common to the Aryan ancestors..evidenced to one parent primitive speech.

2. Of persons: To support by one's testimony, attest (a fact or statement).

a **1647** W. BRADFORD *Plymouth Plantation* (1856) 424 Yᵉ cause and passages..were clearly represented & sufficiently evidenced. **1667** E. CHAMBERLAYNE *St. Gt. Brit.* I. (1684) 336 No one Saint in all the Calendar (except those attested by Scripture) is better evidenced. **1721** SOUTHERNE *Disappointm.* III. ii, I invoke Heav'n, earth, and men to evidence my truth. **1826** DISRAELI *Viv. Grey* III. iv, The one [story] I am about to tell is so well evidenced that I think even Mr. Vivian Grey will hear it without a sneer. **1864** BOWEN *Logic* xiii. 422 This is no reason for doubting their reality, when they are evidenced by Intuition. **1886** BURTON *Arab. Nts.* (abridged) 163 If the truth of her story be evidenced I will exact retaliation.

†**3.** To establish by evidence; to make evident, demonstrate, prove. With simple *obj.*, *obj.* sentence, or *inf.* *Obs.*

1632 J. LEE *Short Survey Sweden* 53 How great forces.. this mighty Prince is able to bring into the field, may..by this late..expedition..easily be evidenced. **1648** CHAS. I in Neal *Hist. Purit.* III. 506 Until the same shall be evidenced to me to be contrary to the word of God. **1649** SELDEN *Laws Eng.* I. xvi. (1739) 31 This the words of the Historian do evidence. **1665–6** *Phil. Trans.* I. 244 Cassini pretends to evidence by his observations, that those spots were very large. **1673** TEMPLE *Ess. Irel.* Wks. 1731 I. 118 The Horses must be evidenced by good Testimonies to have been bred in Ireland. **1749** FIELDING *Tom Jones* XVIII. vii, Put together so many circumstances to evidence an untruth. **1793** T. JEFFERSON *Writ.* (1859) III. 550 Our laws..to evidence their right to this, permit them, etc. **1806–7** J. BERESFORD *Miseries Hum. Life* I. Introd., As I will evidence in a few instances already quoted.

4. With reference to legal evidence. †**a.** To give evidence against (a person). *Obs.*

1691 LUTTRELL *Brief Rel.* (1857) II. 190 Charles Edwards, who evidenc'd Mr. Arnold in 1683..hath made affidavit.. that what he swore against Mr. Arnold was false. **1695** *Remarks Late Serm.* (ed. 2) 6 One T.O..hath..Evidenc'd I know not how many to the Gallows.

†**b.** To disclose or relate as a witness. *Obs.*

1656–7 *Burton's Diary* (1828) I. 336 He evidenced two remarkable passages of her life. **1694** CROWNE *Regulus* III. ii, I have nothing to evidence. **1812** J. J. HENRY *Camp. agst. Quebec* 161 The wretch had evidenced all our proceedings minutely.

c. *intr.* To give evidence, appear as a witness.

1656 S. H. *Gold. Law* 19 His apparent perfections..spake and evidenced for him. **1692** ROCHESTER *Contriv. S. Blackhead* in *Select. Harl. Misc.* (1793) 511 One of the most graceless wretches, that ever yet entered upon the stage of evidencing. **1693** LUTTRELL *Brief Rel.* (1857) III. 185 Her maid..will evidence against her. **1887** *Scribn. Mag.* (Farmer *Americanisms*), I hadn' 'a' thought ye'd 'a evidenced agin me that-a-way.

5. To give evidence or indication of; to indicate, manifest. Const. with *sb.* or *refl. pron.* as *obj.*, also with complementary *inf.* or with *obj.* sentence.

*c***1610** SIR J. MELVIL *Mem.* (1735) 91 Thereby evidencing she did not stand upon Ceremonies. **1646** SIR T. BROWNE *Pseud. Ep.* IV. xiii. 225 Were there any such effectuall heat in this starre, yet could it but weakly evidence the same in Summer. **1659** HAMMOND *On Ps.* xxxiv. 20 Paraphr. 183 Evidenceth it selfe in a signal preservation of such. **1663** CHARLETON *Chor. Gigant.* 56 The ruines evidence themselves to be the effect. *a* **1729** CLARKE *On the Evidences* 331 (R.) The effect..evidenced itself in a..remarkable manner. **1788** W. TUDOR in Sparks *Corr. Amer. Rev.* (1853) IV. 230 A desire of evidencing that respect and gratitude which I..feel for you. **1863** MRS. C. CLARKE *Shaks. Char.* xii. 299 Her native hilarity of heart is evidenced constantly. **1872** BROWNING *Fifine* xliii, If somehow every face..Evidence..that warm Beneath the veriest ash, there hides a spark of soul. **1876** DIGBY *Real Prop.* viii. 349 The courts eagerly seized on any expressions evidencing this intention.

Hence **'evidencing** *ppl. a.* and *vbl. sb.* Also *attrib.*

1630 SANDERSON *Serm.* II. 253 For the farther evidencing of the necessity of which duty. **1654** EARL ORRERY *Parthen.* (1676) 170 By so evidencing a demonstration, it was impossible to separate us. **1682** *Abs. & Achit.* II. 74 Since our evidencing days began! **1774** GOLDSM. *Hist. Greece* I. 337 The most detested..part of the citizens, such as lived by evidencing and informing.

† **'evidenceable,** *a. Obs.* [f. prec. + -ABLE.] That may be evidenced; capable of being evidenced or proved.

1665 J. SERGEANT *Sure-footing in Chr.* 3 This must..be..easily evidenceable by other knowledges. **1668** HOWE *Bless. Righteous* (1825) 141 Wherein that necessity is evidenceable from the nature of this blessedness. **1687** *Relat. Eng. Reform.* 249 What is easily evidenceable to another, may happen not to be so to the Sovereign power.

Hence † **evi'denceableness.**

1665 J. SERGEANT *Sure-footing in Chr.* 55 To show the Evidenceableness of Tradition's Ruling Power.

† **'evidencer.** *Obs.* [f. as prec. + -ER[1].] One who gives evidence; a witness.

1593 NASHE *Christ's T.* (1613) 25, I, which am the Lord and Authour of life, must bee the Authour and Euidencer against thee of death. **1653** R. BAILLIE *Dissuasive Vind.* (1655) 27 The first evidencer of justification. *a* **1734** NORTH *Exam.* II. iv. (1740) 238 Oates wrought..to bring him into the Preferment of an Evidencer's Place.

† **'evidenceship.** *Obs.* [f. EVIDENCE *sb.* + -SHIP.] **a.** The office or function of an evidence (or witness). **b.** *humorously*, as a title (after *lordship*, etc.).

a **1734** NORTH *Lives* I. 315 And thereby gave so great offence to their evidenceships, the plot witnesses. **1748** RICHARDSON *Clarissa* (1811) IV. 338 That ingenious knack of forgery..and a detection since in evidenceship, have been his ruin.

evidencive ('ɛvɪdənsɪv), *a. rare.* [f. EVIDENCE *v.* + -IVE.] Giving evidence or indication; indicative. Const. *of.*

1848 LD. WODEHOUSELEE in *Ramsay's Wks.* III. App. 390 The most remarkable circumstance evidencive of his enthusiastic attachment.

† **evidency** ('ɛvɪdənsɪ). *Obs.* [ad. L. *ēvidentia*: see EVIDENCE and -ENCY.]

1. The quality or state of being evident or clear; clearness, evidentness; = EVIDENCE *sb.* 1.

1533 tr. *Erasmus' Com. Crede* 150 b, Payntyng setteth the thing forth to the eye..and perfourmeth that euidencie makynge the thynge manifeste. **1592** tr. *Junius on Rev.* xvii. 8 So I expound the words of the Apostle for evidency sake. **1611** BIBLE *Prov.* viii. Argt., The fame and euidencie of wisdome.

2. Indication, mark, sign, token; = EVIDENCE *sb.* 3.

1586 BRIGHT *Melanch.* xxxvi. 206 These things being matters of iudgement..& consisting of euidencie to be knowen of others. **1646** SIR T. BROWNE *Pseud. Ep.* III. xxv. 178 These are not dead when they cease to move or afford the visible evidencies of life. **1813** *Examiner* 26 Apr. 266/1 Surer evidencies of the immortality of man.

evident ('ɛvɪdənt), *a.* and *sb.* [ad. L. *ēvident-em*, in same sense, f. *ē-* out + *vident-em*, pr. pple. of *vidēre* to see. Cf. Fr. *évident.*

With the use of this active form in passive sense cf. 'to look (well or ill)', Ger. *aussehen* to appear, lit. 'to see out.' Late Lat. had the pass. *ēvidēri* to be evident.]

A. *adj.*

1. † **a.** Of physical objects: Distinctly visible; conspicuous (*obs.*). **b.** (With mixed notion of 2) of tokens, vestiges, etc., or of states or conditions: Obvious to the sight; recognizable at a glance.

1382 WYCLIF *Wisd.* xiv. 17 The euydent [**1388** opyn, **1611** expresse; Vulg. *evidentem*] ymage of the king, whom worshipen thei wolden, thei maden. *c* **1400** *Festivall* in Hearne *R. Brunne's Chron.* Pref. 198 Þat ylke white cerne [*printed* cerue] was an euydent tokon of her martirdome. *c* **1430** LYDG. *Thebes* III. (1500) Kiiij, The Grekes Dysesperyed Dempte playnly by tokens euydent. **1483** CAXTON *G. de la Tour* A v, He doth for them euydent myracles. **1570** DEE *Math. Pref.* 7 Make good euident markes, at euery inches end. **1598** DRAYTON *Heroic. Ep.* I. 68 Then doe I strive to wash it out with Teares, But then the same more evident appears. **1667** MILTON *P.L.* IX. 1077 Bad Fruit of Knowledge..Which leaves..in our Faces evident the signes Of foul concupiscence. **1669** STURMY *Mariner's Mag.* II. 79 At Shooting at a Ship in a River, he must put his Piece to some evident mark on the other side the River. *c* **1790** IMISON *Sch. Art* II. 65 Thin persons have the muscles of the neck much more evident than would be judicious to imitate [in painting]. **1806** *Med. Jrnl.* XV. 443 Of which [small-pox] she bore evident marks. **1820** KEATS *Hyperion* I. 338 Thou canst move about, an evident God. **1860** TYNDALL *Glac.* II. xvii. 320 The retardation of the ice is most evident near the sides.

2. Clear to the understanding or the judgement; obvious, plain. Const. *to.* † *(it) is evident to be...*: = 'it is evident that (it) is...'

1393 GOWER *Conf.* III. 221 Which in the bible is evident, How David in his testament, etc. **1541** R. COPLAND *Galyen's Terap.* 2 B iv b, It is euydent yᵗ none indication is taken of the cause. **1601** SHAKS. *Twel. N.* II. v. 128 Why this is evident to any formall capacitie. **1649** SELDEN *Laws Eng.* I. (1739) 202 It is evident to be nothing but a Temporal Monarchy. **1659** PEARSON *Creed* 4 Truths apparent in themselves..are not called Credible, but evident to the understanding. **1754** EDWARDS *Freed. Will* II. xii. 119 For a Thing to be certainly known to any Understanding, is for it to be evident to that Understanding. **1842** BISCHOFF *Woollen Manuf.* II. 360 The vast importance of sheep, with their constant increase, is most evident. **1874** MORLEY *Compromise* (1886) 209 That this distinction is as sound on the evolutional theory of society as on any other is quite evident.

† **b.** Occasional uses: Having preponderating evidence. Of a remark: Obviously true. *Obs.*

1711 SHAFTESB. *Charac.* III. §2 (1737) II. 417 Upon fair Conviction, to give our heart up to the evident side..is to help Reason heartily. **1722** DE FOE *Plague* (1840) 192 But this remark of my friend's appeared more evident in a few weeks more.

† **3.** Of a sign, testimony, etc.: Indubitable, certain, conclusive. *Obs.*

1529 MORE *Heresyes* I. Wks. 161/1 No scripture can be euident to proue any thing that he lyst to deny. **1571** GOLDING *Calvin on Ps.* xx. 20 He yeeldeth an evidenter witnesse of his trust. **1611** SHAKS. *Cymb.* II. iv. 120 Render to me some corporall signe about her More evident then this: for this was stolne. **1631** GOUGE *God's Arrows* I. §39. 61 We see how..evident the holy Scripture is in this principle of our Christian Faith. **1653** MILTON *Hirelings* Wks. (1847) 430/1 Where did he assign it [the tenth], or by what evident conveyance to ministers?

† **4.** quasi-*adv.* = EVIDENTLY. *Obs.*

1519 *Interl. Four Elements* in Hazl. *Dodsley* I. 38 One way it [the earth] is round, I must consent, For this man proved it evident.

B. *sb.* Something that serves as evidence; *spec.* in *Sc. Law*, a document proving a person's title to anything; usually in *pl.* title-deeds.

1424 *Sc. Acts Jas. I* (1597) §9 The King..may gar summond, all..his tennentes..to schaw their charters and evidentes. **1535** STEWART *Cron. Scot.* III. 247 His lordis all befoir him he [Robert the Bruce] gart caw, Thair euidentis of thair landis till schaw. **1678** in Burt *Lett. N. Scot.* (1818) I. 64 [Inscription in a house] 16 Christ is my life and rent 78 His promise is my evident. **1816** SCOTT *Antiq.* iv, It is written all these various ways in the old writings and evidents. **1868** *Act 31-32 Vict.* c. 101 §8 Absolute warrandice as regards the lands and writs and evidents.

† **'evident,** *v. Obs. rare*⁻¹. [f. prec.] = EVIDENCE *v.*

1643 PRYNNE *Sov. Power Parl.* II. 74 As all the old and new Acts..with other such aides in all our Kings Reignes, abundantly evident.

evidential (ɛvɪ'dɛnʃəl), *a.* [f. L. *ēvidenti-a* + -AL[1].]

1. a. Of or pertaining to evidence. **b.** Based or resting on evidence; relying on evidence; *esp.* the Evidences of Christianity, as in *evidential method, school, system.*

1654 W. SCLATER *Fun. Serm.* 20 No such evidentiall verity is demonstrated in Holy Writ, as of Absolute Necessity to be believed unto salvation. **1668** HOWE *Bless. Righteous* (1825) 204 It is a steady..direction of heart towards the future glory..that must be the evidential ground of thy hope to enjoy it. **1683** E. HOOKER *Pref. Ep. Pordage's Mystic Div.* 69 The firm and evidential Probation of invisibls, things out of sight. **1772** R. HILL in Fletcher *Logica Genev.* 58 You cannot suppose that..he intended to exclude good works in an evidential sense. **1865** MOZLEY *Mirac.* i. 7 The evidential function of a miracle is based upon the common argument of design. **1871** TYLOR *Prim. Cult.* I. 380 The basis of theological science must be historical as well as evidential. **1882–3** SCHAFF *Encycl. Relig. Knowl.* III. 2507/1 Whately was a genuine disciple of the 'evidential' school. Faith is to him the conclusion drawn from historical premises.

2. Furnishing evidence; having the nature of evidence; serving to attest. Const. *of.*

a **1641** BP. MOUNTAGU *Acts & Mon.* (1642) 198 Sight of all our senses is most active, penetrative, discerning, and evidential. **1701** FLEETWOOD *Miracles* 229 Those [miracles] should be Evidential ones, which God enables Men to work in order to gain belief. **1837** J. MACCULLOCH *Proofs Attrib. God* II. 431 Subjects evidential of the attributes of the Deity. **1839** *Blackw. Mag.* XLVI. 94 Evidential miracles..simply prove Christianity. **1879** FARRAR *St. Paul* I. 202 That Paul should have passed..from one direction of life to the very opposite is evidential of the power and significance of Christianity.

† **3.** Resting on documentary evidence. *Obs.*

(Folkingham explains that the 'evidential' character of a possession is that which is denoted by such terms as *feodum, allodium*, etc.)

1610 W. FOLKINGHAM *Art of Survey* III. i. 65 The Propriety of Possessions intimates their particular state and condition, and may be diuided into Vocall and Euidential. *Ibid.* III. ii. 66.

evidentially (ɛvɪ'dɛnʃəlɪ), *adv.* [f. as prec. + -LY[2].]

1. By means of evidence; as regards evidence; with regard to its value as evidence.

1654 EYRE in Warren *Unbelievers* B iij, Faith is from justification causally, and justification by faith evidentially. *a* **1734** NORTH *Lives* I. 362 It was believed, though not so soon evidentially discovered, that a rebellion was ready to break out. **1836** G. S. FABER *Answ. Husenbeth* 6 Any doctrine which can be shewn evidentially to have existed in the third century. **1886** GURNEY *Phantasms of Living* I. 35 Of the two series..the second is evidentially to be preferred.

† **2.** Intuitively. *Obs.*

a **1716** SOUTH *Serm.* IX. xi. 323 They [angels] do not fully and evidentially know them [the mysteries of God].

evidentiary (ɛvɪ'dɛnʃərɪ), *a.* [f. L. *ēvidenti-a* EVIDENCE + -ARY.]

1. Of or pertaining to evidence; = EVIDENTIAL 1 a.

1810 BENTHAM *Packing* (1821) 181 The clearing of his character..so far as concerns evidentiary trustworthiness. **1846** GROTE *Greece* I. xix. II. 56 An inscription..carries evidentiary value under the same conditions as a published writing on paper. **1879** CARPENTER *Ment. Phys.* I. ix. §2. 395 Through its power of modifying the relative force of different evidentiary considerations.

2. Furnishing evidence; having the nature of evidence. Const. *of.* = EVIDENTIAL 2.

1818 JAS. MILL *Brit. India* III. i. 32 The charges ought to be exhibited first; and no evidentiary matter granted, but, etc. **1827** BENTHAM *Ration. Evidence* Wks. 1843 VII. 20 To treat it upon the footing of an evidentiary act, with reference to the corresponding principal act. **1845** MILL *Ess.* II. 221 But they are evidentiary of a tone of thought which has prevailed so long among the superior intellects. **1875** *Contemp. Rev.* XXVI. 580 The upward slant..becomes an evidentiary fact of singular cogency. **1875** POSTE *Gaius* II. (ed. 2) 201 It is only the adventitious or accidental or evidentiary portion of the title in which they differ.

evidently ('ɛvɪdəntlɪ), *adv.* [f. EVIDENT *a.* + -LY[2].]

† **1.** So as to be distinctly visible or perceptible; with perfect clearness, conspicuously. Hence in active sense, with vbs. of perceiving, knowing, explaining, etc.: Without possibility of mistake or misunderstanding; clearly, distinctly. *Obs.* or *arch.*

c **1374** CHAUCER *Boeth.* III. xi. 101 Þanne alle the dyrknesse of his mysknowynge shal seen..euydently to [þe] syhte of his vndyrstondynge. **1477** EARL RIVERS (Caxton) *Dictes* 1 Whiche grace euidently to me knowen and understonde hath compelled me [etc.]. **1551** TURNER *Herbal* I. B viij a, It is evidently knowen that water will wexe thycke, if this roite be brused and put in it. **1584** FENNER *Def. Ministers* (1587) 39 We haue here most manifestlie & most euidentlie written the contrarie. **1594** HOOKER *Eccl. Pol.* I. viii. (1611) 21 Things which men by the light of their naturall vnderstanding euidently know. **1611** BIBLE *Gal.* iv. 1 O foolish Galatians..before whose eyes Jesus Christ hath been evidently [*Revised*, openly] set forth. **1725** DE FOE *Voy. round World* (1840) 277, I found the way go evidently down hill. **1776** GIBBON *Decl. & F.* xii. (1854) II. 41 An act ..which evidently disclosed his [Tacitus'] intention of transmitting the empire to his descendants. **1794** SULLIVAN *View Nat.* I. 435 All the substances hitherto examined..have evidently appeared to be compounded of one or more of these elementary principles. **1833** CRUSE *Eusebius* I. vi. 31 And this is evidently proved to have been fulfilled.

2. So that the fact predicated is evident; manifestly, obviously. Now chiefly *parenthetic*; = 'as manifestly appears', 'as may be clearly inferred'.

1690 LOCKE *Hum. Und.* II. xxix. §5 No Idea, therefore, can be undistinguishable from another..for from all other, it is evidently different. **1748** HARTLEY *Observ. Man* I. iii. 387 Those who walk and talk in their Sleep, have evidently the Nerves of the Muscles so free, as that, etc. **1761** HUME *Hist. Eng.* II. xxxvi. 292 Reason was so evidently on their side. **1839** THIRLWALL *Greece* VIII. 391 They evidently regarded Macedonia as a bulwark against the encroachments of Rome. **1860** TYNDALL *Glac.* I. xi. 71 The spirit and the muscles were evidently at war.

† **3.** *Sc. Law.* By evidence of a deed or document. *Obs.*

1609 SKENE *Reg. Maj., Forme of Proces* 118 Quhen the defender proves his exception, or duplie, be sic wreit, and evidently as said is, lib. I. c. 25. 12. quon attach. c. 81.

evidentness ('ɛvɪdəntnɪs). [f. as prec. + -NESS.] The quality or state of being evident; clearness, obviousness, plainness.

1552 in *Vicary's Anat.* (1888) App. xvi. 295 It behoueth first to vnderstande for the more evidentnesse of that that foloweth, that [etc.]. **1587** GOLDING *De Mornay* viii. 100 What euidentnesse or certeintie is there in the Greeke Histories. **1730–6** BAILEY (folio), *Evidentness*, plainness to be seen, perceived or understood. **1869** *Contemp. Rev.* XII. 120 There is a want..of evidentness of meaning.

†**e'vigilate**, *a. Obs.*−⁰ [f. L. *ēvigilāt-* ppl. stem of *ēvigilāre*, f. *ē-* out + *vigilāre* to watch, f. *vigil* awake.]

1730–6 BAILEY (folio), *Evigilate*, to watch diligently, to study hard. **1775** in ASH.

†**evigi'lation.** *Obs. rare*−¹. [ad. late L. *ēvigilātiōn-em*, n. of action f. *ēvigilāre*: see EVIGILATE.] Awakening. In Dicts. explained as 'a waking or watching'.

1720 S. PARKER *Biblioth. Biblica* I. 157 The Evigilation of the Animal Powers, when Adam awoke. **1832** in WEBSTER, etc.

evil ('iːv(ə)l), *a.* and *sb.* Forms: 1–2 yfel (in inflexions yf(e)l-), (2–4 ifel, 2 efel, yfell, 3 ywel(l, 2–3 ufel, 2–4 uvel(e, 2–5 ivel, (3 ȝevel, 4 ivil), 3–6 evel(l(e, (5 ewelle, hevelle, 6 ewil, yell), 4–6 evill(e, -yl(l(e, yvel(l(e, (6 yevill), 4– evil. [ME. *uvel* (*ü*), OE. *yfel* = OS. *ubil*, OFris., MDu. *evel* (Du. *euvel*), OHG. *ubil*, *upil* (Ger. *übel*), Goth. *ubils*:—OTeut. **ubilo-z*; usually referred to the root of *up*, *over*; on this view the primary sense would be either 'exceeding due measure' or 'overstepping proper limits'.

The form *evel*, whence the mod. form descends, appears in ME. first as west midland and Kentish, but in 15th c. had become general. The conditions under which early M.E. (i) or (y) became (eː), the antecedent of mod.Eng. (iː), are not clearly determined; the present word and *weevil* seem to be the only examples in which this change was other than local; obs. and dial. instances are *yeve* = 'give', *leve* = 'live', EASLE. (Other apparent examples are due to OE. forms with *eo*, resulting from *u-* or *o-* umlaut.)]

A. *adj.* The antithesis of GOOD in all its principal senses.

In OE., as in all the other early Teut. langs. exc. Scandinavian, this word is the most comprehensive adjectival expression of disapproval, dislike, or disparagement. In mod. colloquial Eng. it is little used, such currency as it has being due to literary influence. In quite familiar speech the adj. is commonly superseded by *bad*; the sb. is somewhat more frequent, but chiefly in the widest senses, the more specific senses being expressed by other words, as *harm*, *injury*, *misfortune*, *disease*, etc.

I. Bad in a positive sense.

1. Morally depraved, bad, wicked, vicious. Also *absol. Obs.* as applied to persons.

971 *Blickl. Hom.* 37 We sceolan..ure heortan clænsian from yflum ȝeþohtum. *Ibid.* 161 Hi cyningum & yfelum ricum ealdormannum wiþstandan mihtan. *c* **1200** ORMIN 1742 To bærnenn all þatt ifell iss Aweȝȝ inn hise þeowwess. *c* **1340** *Cursor M.* 8106 (Fairf.) Lothe is Eville mannys soule & body boþe. **1398** TREVISA *Barth. De P.R.* xv. cxvii. (1495) 532 Pentapol..hathe that name of 5 cytees of euel men that were dystroyed wyth fyre of heuen. *c* **1440** *Gesta Rom.* x. 31 (Harl. MS.) Ivel men, þe which neyþer lovith god, neyþer hire neghebowre. **1526** TINDALE *Matt.* xxi. 41 He will cruellye destroye those evyll persons. **1584** POWEL tr. *Lloyd's Cambria* 16 Sigebert..for his Euill behaviour was expelled. **1611** BIBLE *Gen.* viii. 21 The imagination of mans heart is euil from his youth. **1794** COLERIDGE *Relig. Musings* Wks. 1847 I. 94 She..from the dark embrace all evil things Brought forth and nurtured: mitred Atheism! **1817** W. SELWYN *Law Nisi Prius* (ed. 4) II. 1156 Imputing to a person an evil inclination. **1871** SMILES *Charac.* i. (1876) 10 Good deeds act and react on the doers of them; and so do evil.

absol. *c* **1200** *Trin. Coll. Hom.* 23 Alle men shullen cume to libben echeliche..þe gode on eche blisse..þ e uuele on eche wowe. *c* **1300** *Cursor M.* 25249 (Cott. Galba MS.) On domesday..þe euill sall fra þe gude be drawn. **1827** POLLOK *Course T.* x. 215 To the evil..Eternal recompense of shame and woe.

2. Doing or tending to do harm; hurtful, mischievous, prejudicial. Of advice, etc.: Misleading. Of an omen, etc.: Boding ill.

c **1175** *Lamb. Hom.* 3 Heo urnen on-ȝein him al þa hebreisce men mid godere and summe mid ufele þeonke. *c* **1205** LAY. 2541 Ah þa heora fader wes dæd þe sunen duden vuelne [*c* **1275** vuele] ræd. *a* **1225** *Ancr. R.* 52 Is hit so ouer vuel uor te toten utward? **1297** R. GLOUC. (1724) 593 Thurghe evelle conceille was slayne..the Erle of Arundelle. *c* **1340** *Cursor M.* 4635 (Fairf.) He prisoned was wiþ euel rede. *c* **1380** WYCLIF *Sel. Wks.* III. 330 Evyl ensaumple of opyn synne. *c* **1400** *Lanfranc's Cirurg.* (MS. A.) 41 It is not yvel to putte a litil opium to þe oile of þe rosis. *a* **1400–50** *Alexander* 703 þe euyll sterne of Ercules how egirly it soroȝes. *c* **1420** *Chron. Vilod.* 808 Hym shulnot harme non hevelle thyng. *c* **1449** PECOCK *Repr.* 4 Gouernauncis of the clergie whiche summe of the comoun peple..iugen to be yuele. **1530** PALSGR. 217/2 Evyll tourne, *maluais tour.* **1584** POWELL tr. *Lloyd's Cambria* 99 King Edward by Euill counsel banished Algar. **1587** MASCALL *Govt. Cattle, Oxen* (1627) 36 Yeugh is euill for cattell to eate. **1593** SHAKS. *3 Hen. VI*, v. vi. 44 The Owle shriek'd at thy birth, an euill signe. **1611** BIBLE *Gen.* xxxvii. 20 Some euill beast hath deuoured him. *a* **1649** DRUMM. OF HAWTH. Wks. 32 Weigh not how we, Evil to our selves, against Thy laws rebell. **1655** CULPEPPER *Riverius* I. xvi. 57 In a great Headach it is evil to have the outward parts cold. **1846** RUSKIN *Mod. Paint.* II. II. II. xv. §5 The neglect of art..has been of evil consequence to the Christian world. **1868** J. H. BLUNT *Ref. Ch. Eng.* I. 403 The evil system of pluralities.

3. Uses partaking of senses 1 and 2: **a.** ***evil will***: depraved intention or purpose; also, desire for another's harm; = ILL-WILL. *rare* in mod. use.

c **897** K. ÆLFRED *Gregory's Past.* xxi. 157 He of yfelum willan ne ȝesyngað. *a* **1300** *Cursor M.* 1065 (Cott.) For caym gaf him wit iuel will. **1340** *Ayenb.* 66 þe dyeuel beginþ þet uer of tyene and euel wyl uor to becleppe. **1377** LANGL. *P. Pl.* B. v. 121 For enuye and yuel wille is yuel to defye. **1523** LD. BERNERS *Froiss.* I. cxix. 142 The duke..pardoned them all his yuell wyll. **1540** COVERDALE *Fruitf. Less.* iii. Wks. (Parker Soc.) I. 370 Many afflictions, much evil-will..shall happen unto you. **1563** *Homilies* II. *Rogat. Week* III. (1859) 492 Cast we off all malice & all evil will. **1598** GRENEWEY *Tacitus' Ann.* III. ii. (1622) 65 He [Piso] increased the euill will of the people towards him.

b. ***evil angel, spirit***, etc. Also, ***the evil one*** (†Sc. ***the evil man***): the Devil.

c **950** *Lindisf. Gosp.* Matt. xiv. 26 Forðon yfel wiht is. **1555** EDEN *Treat. Newe Ind.* (Arb.) 27 Sundrie illusions of euyl spirites. **1601** SHAKS. *Jul. C.* IV. iii. 282 *Bru.* Speake to me, what thou art. *Ghost.* Thy euill Spirit, Brutus? **1611** BIBLE *Luke* vii. 21 Hee cured many..of euill spirits. **1648** *Acts Gen. Assemb.* 463 (Jam.) Whilest some fell asleep, and were carelesse..the evil man brought in prelacy. **1667** MILTON *P.L.* IX. 463 That space the Evil one abstracted stood From his own evil. **1681–6** J. SCOTT *Chr. Life* (1747) III. 347 The Ministry of the evil Angels to him. **1727** DE FOE *Syst. Magic* I. i. (1840) 24 They did not suppose those wise men..had an evil spirit. **1825** LYTTON *Zicci* 2 The Evil Spirit is pulling you towards him. **1841** LANE *Arab. Nts.* I. 117 Sakhr was an evil Jinnee. **1881** BIBLE (Revised) *Matt.* vi. 13 Deliver us from the evil one.

c. Of repute or estimation: Unfavourable. ***evil tongue***: a malicious or slanderous speaker. *arch.*

c **1330** R. BRUNNE *Chron.* (1810) 20 Of him in holy kirke men said euelle sawe. **1382** WYCLIF *2 Cor.* vi. 8 By yuel fame and good fame. *c* **1450** MYRE 58 Wymmones serues thow moste forsake, Of euele fame leste they the make. **1535** COVERDALE *Ecclus.* xxviii. 19 Wel is him that is kepte from an euell tonge. **1611** BIBLE *Deut.* xxii. 19 He hath brought vp an euill name vpon a virgine of Israel. *a* **1891** *Mod. Newspaper*, The defendant was arrested in a house of evil repute.

4. Causing discomfort, pain, or trouble; unpleasant, offensive, disagreeable; troublesome, painful.

a **1131** *O.E. Chron.* an. 1124 Se king let hine don on ifele bendas. **1577** B. GOOGE *Heresbach's Husb.* IV. (1586) 161 The berrie of..the wilde Vine..the evill taste wherof will cause them to loth Grapes. **1578** LYTE *Dodoens* I. lxxxviii. 130 The herbe..is of a very evill and strong stincking savour. **1690** LOCKE *Hum. Und.* II. xx. (1695) 121 We name that Evil, which is apt to produce or increase any Pain, or diminish any Pleasure in us. **1850** TENNYSON *In Mem.* lv, Are God and Nature then at strife That Nature lends such evil dreams?

†**b.** Hard, difficult. Const. *to* with *inf. Obs.*

c **1175** *Lamb. Hom.* 147 Hit is uuel to understonden on hwulche wise Mon mei him solf forsake. **1377** LANGL. *P. Pl.* B. xv. 63 Hony is yuel to defye and engleymeth þe mawe. **1523** LD. BERNERS *Froiss.* I. ccxxi. 286 It was yuell mountyng of yᵗ hyll. **1551** TURNER *Herbal* I. A iv b, Astriction..is ether very euyll to be founde, or els there is none to be founde at all.

†**5.** Of conditions, fortune, etc., also (rarely) of persons: Unfortunate, miserable, wretched. ***evil health***: misfortune (see HEALTH). *Obs.*

c **1175** *Lamb. Hom.* 33 Hwi beo we uule on þisse wrecche world. *a* **1300** *Floriz & Bl.* 441 Hi beden God ȝiue him uuel fin. *c* **1340** *Cursor M.* 7320 (Trin.) þei aske anoþer kyng þen me Euel hele þe tyme shul þei se. *c* **1450** *Merlin* i. 20 Thow toldest the person that thow were euel thereon. **1475** CAXTON *Jason* 30 Thenne cam agaynst him the king of Poulane, but that was to his euill helthe. *c* **1500** *Melusine* 78 He..after the dede & euylhap..fledd with all from þis land. **1530** PALSGR. 217/2 Evyll lucke, *malevr.* **1611** BIBLE *Ex.* v. 19 The officers..did see that they were in euill case. **1614** RALEIGH *Hist. World* v. iii. §15 So beaten and yn such euill plight.

b. Of periods of time: Characterized by misfortune or suffering, unlucky, disastrous. ***evil May-day***: see MAY-DAY¹.

1377 LANGL. *P. Pl.* B. IX. 120 Wastoures and wrecches out of wedloke..Conceyued ben in yuel tyme. *c* **1489** CAXTON *Sonnes of Aymon* iii. 107 Evyll daye gyve you, god. **1667** MILTON *P.L.* IX. 780 Her rash hand in evil hour Forth reaching to the Fruit. **1738** WESLEY *Psalms* iv, Help me in my Evil Day. **1806–7** J. BERESFORD *Miseries Hum. Life* (1826) IV. Introd., In an evil hour I..changed my lodgings. **1848** MACAULAY *Hist. Eng.* I. 280 In times which might by Englishmen be justly called evil times. **1878** BOSW. SMITH *Carthage* 186 The Boii..determined to anticipate the evil day.

6. ***evil eye.*** (Phrases, ***to bear, cast, look with, an evil eye.***) **a.** A look of ill-will.

c **1000** *Liber Scintillarum* xxvii. (1889) 102 Unclænnyss eage yfel [oculus malus] withersacung..gemænsumiaþ man. **1382** WYCLIF *Mark* vii. 22 Fro withynne, of the herte of men comen..vnchastite, yuel yȝe, blasphemyes. **1526–34** TINDALE *Matt.* xx. 15 Ys thyne eye evyll because I am good. **1611** BIBLE *Mark* vii. 22 Lasciuiousnesse, an euill eye [*Rev. V.* an evil eye], blasphemie. *a* **1639** W. WHATELEY *Prototypes* I. xx. (1640) 202 Why should wee..beare an evill eye towards them? **1645** QUARLES *Sol. Recant* x. 79 Let not thine eyes be evill. **1704** ADDISON *Italy* (1733) 58 They look with an evil eye upon Leghorne. **1875** JOWETT *Plato* (ed. 2) I. 394 Patriotic citizens will cast an evil eye upon you as a subverter of the laws.

b. A malicious or envious look which, in popular belief, had the power of doing material harm; also, the faculty, superstitiously ascribed to certain individuals, of inflicting injury by a look. Cf. Fr. ***mauvais œil***, It. ***malocchio***.

1796 *Statist. Acc. Scot.* XVIII. 123 The less informed..are afraid of their [old Women's] evil Eye among the cattle. **1797** DALLAWAY *Acc. Constantinople* 391 Nothing can exceed the superstition of the Turks respecting the Evil Eye of an enemy or infidel. **1834** LYTTON *Pompeii* I. iii, He certainly possesses the gift of the evil eye. **1871** READE *Terrible Tempt.* xxxiii, Or if you didn't kill him, you'd cast the evil eye on him. **1879** MISS JACKSON *Shropsh. Wood-bk.* s.v. *Evil*, 'E's a nasty downlookin' fellow—looks as if 'e could cast a nev'l-eye upon yo'.

II. Bad in a privative sense: Not good.

†**7. a.** Of an animal or vegetable growth or product, as a tree, fruit, the body, 'humours': Unsound, corrupt. Of a member or organ: Diseased. ***to have an evil head***: to be insane. **b.** Of air, diet, water: Wanting in the essentials of healthy nutrition; unwholesome. *Obs.*

c **1000** *Ags. Gosp.* Matt. vii. 17 Ælc yfel treow byrþ yfele wæstmas. *c* **1000** *Sax. Leechd.* II. 178 Gif of þære wambe anre þa yfelan wætan cumen. *c* **1200** *Trin. Coll. Hom.* 183 Gief þe licame beð euel, loð is heo þe sowle. *c* **1320** *Seuyn Sag.* (W.) 1878 Iuel blod was hire withinne. **1382** WYCLIF *Matt.* vii. 18 A good tree may nat make yuel fruytis, nether an yuel tree make good fruytis. *c* **1400** *Lanfranc's Cirurg.* (MS. A.) 38 Yvel fleisch growiþ in a wounde. *Ibid.* 80 If..þe eir be yvel, þe sike man schal be chaungid into good eyr. *a* **1450** *Knt. de la Tour* (1868) 20 A gentille man..was riotous..and hadd an evelle hede [Fr. *male teste*]. **1523** LD. BERNERS *Froiss.* I. xviii. 24 Beastis they..myght eate at their pleasure without bredde, whiche was an euyll dyette. **1555** LATIMER in Foxe *A. & M.* (1563) 1372/2, I am an old man and haue a verye euill backe. **1591** F. SPARRY tr. *Cattan's Geomancie* 199 I iudged that the horse had an euill foote and was worth nothing. **1594** SHAKS. *Rich. III*, I. i. 139 O he hath kept an euill Diet long. **1600** HAKLUYT *Voy.* (1810) III. 341 The water whereof was so evill. **1611** BIBLE *Jer.* xxiv. 3 Very euill [figs] that cannot be eaten, they are so euill.

†**8.** Inferior in quality, constitution, condition or appearance; poor, unsatisfactory, defective. *Obs.*

971 *Blickl. Hom.* 197 Heo [seo cirice] is eac on onsyne utan yfeles heowes. *c* **1300** *Cursor M.* 21805 (Edin.) þis tale queþir it be iuil or gode I fande it writin. **13..** tr. *Leges Burgorum* c. 63 in *Sc. Stat.* I. 345 And gif scho makis ivil ale and dois agane þe custume of þe toune..scho sall gif til hir mercyment viii s or..be put on þe kukstule. *c* **1400** *Rom. Rose* 4459 Whanne she wole make A fulle good silogisme..aftirward ther shal in deede Folwe an evelle conclusioun. *c* **1400** *Lanfranc's Cirurg.* (MS. B.) 8 Euyle maners beþ folwynge þe lyknesse of an yvele complexioun. **1561** in T. Thomson *Inventories* 141 Item, ane evill litle burdclaith of grene. **1576** GRINDAL *Let. Ld. Burleigh* Wks. (1843) 392, I pray your lordship, appoint when you come to take an evil dinner with me. **1583** BABINGTON *Commandm.* i. (1637) 7 If a man cut with an evill knife, he is the cause of cutting, but not of evill cutting. **1592** in *Vicary's Anat.* (1888) App. ix. 229 Vayns..gude to be opynd for..euyll sight. **1609** SKENE *Reg. Maj.* 142.

†**b.** Of a workman, work, etc.: Unskilful. *Obs.*

1513 MORE *Rich. III* (1883) 6 None euill captaine was hee in the warre. **1530** PALSGR. 416/1, I acloye with a nayle, as an yvell smythe dothe an horse foote. **1561** T. NORTON *Calvin's Inst.* IV. 85 He is an euell pyper but a good fiddler. **1577** B. GOOGE *Heresbach's Husb.* I. (1586) 36 An excellent good seede for an evyll husbande. **1799** S. FREEMAN *Town Off.* 146 Forfeit every hide marred or hurt by his evil workmanship.

B. *sb.*

I. The adj. used *absol.* That which is evil.

1. a. In the widest sense: That which is the reverse of good; whatever is censurable, mischievous, or undesirable. Also with adj.: ***moral, physical evil.***

c **1340** *Cursor M.* 939 (Fairf.) Y made eville & good to you knowen. **1382** WYCLIF *Gen.* iii. 5 ȝe shul ben as Goddis, knowynge good and yuel. **1559** *Bury Wills* (1850) 153, I, Sir Willm Paynter..wᵗ all vnderstanding of good and evell, make this my last will. **1611** BIBLE *Gen.* iii. 5. **1732** POPE *Ess. Man* I. 292 All Nature is but Art, unknown to thee..All partial Evil, universal Good. **1759** JOHNSON *Idler* No. 89 ¶4 Almost all the moral good which is left among us, is the apparent effect of physical evil. **1819** *Pantologia* s.v., The most serious difficulty lies in accounting for the permission of moral evil or guilt. **1846** TRENCH *Mirac.* xviii. (1862) 295 They [the Scriptures] ever recognize the reality of evil. **1860** PUSEY *Min. Proph.* 180 Evil is of two sorts, evil of sin, and evil of punishment. **1869** J. MARTINEAU *Ess.* II. 42 Moral evil is a broad black fact. **1878** TAIT & STEWART *Unseen Univ.* vii. 269 The greatest of all mysteries—the origin of evil.

b. What is morally evil; sin, wickedness.

c **1040** *Rule St. Benet* (Logeman) 3 Gecyr from yfele & do god. *a* **1175** *Cott. Hom.* 219 þat teonðe werod abreað, and awende on yfele. *c* **1200** *Trin. Coll. Hom.* 11 An wereȝed gost..him aure tacheð to ufele. **1413** LYDG. *Pilgr. Sowle* IV. xxv. (1483) 71 To..chesen the good fro euylle. **1596** RALEIGH in *Four C. Eng. Lett.* 37 Converting badd into yevill and yevill in worse. **1611** BIBLE *Prov.* iii. 7 Feare the Lord, and depart from euill.

c. What is mischievous, painful, or disastrous.

c **850** *Bede's Death-song* in Sweet *O.E. Texts* 149 To ymbhycgannae..huaet his gastae, godaes aeththa yflaes aefter deothdaeȝe doemid uueorthae. **971** *Blickl. Hom.* 115 Nu is æȝhwonon yfel and sleȝe. **1154** *O.E. Chron.* an. 1135 Al unfrið, & yfel, & ræflac. *c* **1250** *Gen. & Ex.* 788 Ðat ywel him sulde nunmor deren. *a* **1300** *Cursor M.* 7949 (Cott.) Iuel he sal apon þe rais. *c* **1380** WYCLIF *Serm.* Sel. Wks. II. 249 3elde to noo man yvel for yvel. *a* **1400–50** *Alexander* 1699 Depely þam playnt, Quat erroure of þis Emperoure & euill þai suffird. *c* **1450** *Nominale* in Wr.-Wülcker 709 *Morbosus*, full of ewylle. **1611** BIBLE *Job* ii. 10 Shall wee receiue good at the hand of God, and shall wee not receiue euil? **1789** BENTHAM *Princ. Legisl.* xviii. §17 *note*, It was the dread of evil, not the hope of good that first cemented societies together. **1850** TENNYSON *In Mem.* xcviii, Evil haunts The birth, the bridal.

2. ***to do***, †***say evil.*** (In post-inflexional Eng. hardly distinguishable from use of EVIL *adv.*) †***with evil***: with evil intention. †***to take in***, or ***to***, ***evil***: to take (a thing) ill; also, to be hurt by.

c **825** *Vesp. Psalter* xiv. [xv.] 3 Ne he dyde ðæm nestan his yfel. **971** *Blickl. Hom.* 51 He us þonne forgyldeþ swa we nu her doþ, ȝe godes ȝe yfeles. *c* **1000** *Ags. Gosp.* Matt. v. 11 Eadiȝe synt ȝe þonne hi wyriað eow and ehtað eow and secȝeað ælc yfel [Vulg. *omne malum*] ongen eow. —— John v. 29 þa þe gad worhton farað on lifes æreste, and þa þe yfel [Vulg. *mala*] dydon on domes æreste. *c* **1340** *Cursor M.* 23183 (Trin.) For good & euele þat þei dud ere. **1377** LANGL. *P. Pl.* B. VIII. 23 'And whoso synneth', I seyde 'doth yuel, as me þinketh'. *c* **1430** *Syr Gener.* (Roxb.) 2494 Mi lordes..Take it not in euel that I say here. *Ibid.* 3972 That stroke

Generides to yuel nam. c **1460** *Emare* 535 Another letter she made with evyll. c **1510** More *Picus* Wks. 15/2 If folk backbite us & saie euill of us: shal we so grevously take it, that lest they should begin to do yuel? **1570** Levins *Manip.* 127 To do Evil, *male facere.* **1611** Bible *Eccl.* v. 1 They consider not that they doe euill. **1842** Lytton *Zanoni* 29 He does no evil.

3. With defining word: That which is evil in some particular case or relation; the evil portion or element of anything. Also quasi-*abstr.* as in ***to see the evil of*** (a course of action).

c **897** K. Ælfred *Gregory's Past.* xxi. 157 Đu meaht ʒeseon eall ðæt yfel openlice ðæt ðærinne lutað. c **1400** *Solomon's Bk. Wisd.* 70 ʒif he wot any yuel by þe. **1523** Ld. Berners *Froiss.* I. cv. 127 So that all thynges consydred, the good and yuell, they yelded them to therle of Derby. **1590** Spenser *F.Q.* ii. viii. 29 The evill donne Dyes not, when breath the body first doth leaue. **1611** Bible *John* xvii. 15, I pray..that thou shouldest keepe them from the euill. **1651** Hobbes *Leviath.* ii. xxviii. 162 All evill..inflicted without intention..is not Punishment. **1667** Milton *P.L.* i. 163 If then his Providence Out of our evil seek to bring forth good. **1759** Johnson *Rasselas* xxix, To inquire what were the sources of..the evil that we suffer. **1877** Mozley *Univ. Serm.* ii. 34 The evil which is the excess of appetite and passion is not so bad as the evil which corrupts virtue.

II. A particular thing that is evil.

4. *gen.* Anything that causes harm or mischief, physical or moral. ***the social evil***: prostitution.

a **1300** *Cursor M.* 8108 (Cott.) Þir wandes thre wit-in þe rote Gains iuels all þai bar al bote. c **1325** *E.E. Allit. Poems* B. 277, & þenne euelez on erþe ernestly grewen. c **1450** *Castle Hd. Life St. Cuthb.* (Surtees) 3696 Of twa euels gif ʒe nede þe tane To chese. c **1500** *Melusine* 237 Of two euylles men ought to choose the lasse. **1539** Taverner *Erasm. Prov.* 39 A lytle euyll, a great good. **1577** B. Googe *Heresbach's Husb.* ii. (1586) 77 Among other evils, they [hop gardens] will be full of Woormes. **1611** Bible *Prov.* xxii. 3 A prudent man foreseeth the euill, and hideth himselfe. **1674** R. Godfrey *Inj. & Ab. Physic.* 94 We being admonisht by the vulgar proverb, To choose the least of Evils. **1793** Burke *Corr.* (1844) IV. 135 There are evils to which the calamities of war are blessings. **1835** Thirlwall *Greece* I. 305 Correcting an evil which disturbed the internal tranquillity of Sparta. **1848** Macaulay *Hist. Eng.* II. 136 One of the chief evils which afflicted Ireland. **1871** Morley *Voltaire* (1886) 13 A real evil to be combated. **1875** Jowett *Plato* (ed. 2) V. 75 We can afford to forgive as well as pity the evil which can be cured.

†**5.** A wrong-doing, sin, crime. Usually *pl. Obs.*

Beowulf 4194 [Ic] þam leod-scaðan yfla gehwylces hond-lean forgeald. c **1000** *Ags. Ps.* cv. 25 [cvi. 32] Þær Moyses wearð mæʒene ʒebysʒad for heora yfelum. c **1175** *Lamb. Hom.* 15 Þas þeues þet nulleð nu nefre swike heore uueles. a **1300** *E.E. Psalter* lxxiv. 5 [lxxv. 4], I said to wicke, Ivels wicli do þer forn. c **1374** Chaucer *Boeth.* iv. i. 109 Yif þat yuelys passen wiþ outen punyssheinge. c **1489** Caxton *Sonnes of Aymon* xxi. 465, I have don many grete evylles agenst my creatour. **1559** *Mirr. Mag., Worcester* xvii, King Edwardes evilles all wer counted mine. **1597** Shaks. *Rich. III*, i. ii. 76 (Qo.) Of these supposed evils [*Fo.* crimes]..to acquit myself. **1614** Bp. Hall *Contempl. O.T.* vi. ii, Men thinke either to patronize or mitigate evils, by their fained reasons.

†**6.** A calamity, disaster, misfortune. *Obs.*

a **1300** *E.E. Psalter* lxxxix. [xc.] 15 Yheres in whilke we segh ivels þus. c **1400** *Apol. Loll.* 41 He reprouid þe rych, and seid many iuel to cum to hem. c **1489** Caxton *Sonnes of Aymon* xix. 408 Grete evylles and harmes are happeth therby. **1535** Coverdale *Esther* viii. 6 How can I se the euell that shal happe vnto my people? **1590** J. Smythe in *Lett. Lit. Men* (Camden) 64 Ther may uppon dyvers accidents ensue such and so great evills unto your Majestie and Realme. **1667** Milton *P.L.* ii. 281 How in safety best we may Compose our present evils. **1791** Mrs. Radcliffe *Rom. Forest* i, With the additional evil of being separated from his family.

7. †**a.** *gen.* A disease, malady. *Obs.*

c **1205** Lay. 17598 Aurilie wule beon dæd. Þat ufel is under his ribben. c **1300** *Havelok* 114 Than him tok an iuel strong. **1340** Hampole *Pr. Consc.* 3001 Som..Sal haf als þe yuel of meselry. c **1400** Maundev. (Roxb.) viii. 29 A medicinal thing it [aloes] es for many euils. **1480** Caxton *Descr. Eng.* 25 The yelow euyll that is called the Jaundis. **1697** Dryden *Virg. Georg.* iii. 843 The slow creeping Evil eats his way. **1725** N. Robinson *Th. Physick* 280 It cannot be expected that..the feeling his Pulse..will remove the Evil he labours under.

fig. c **1400** *Rom. Rose* 3269 This is the yvelle that love they calle.

b. ***the Aleppo evil***: 'a disease, which first appears under the form of an eruption on the skin, and afterwards forms into a sort of boil' (*Penny Cycl.* XII. 12/2). †***the foul evil***: the pox. †***the falling evil***: = 'the falling sickness', epilepsy.

c **1340** *Cursor M.* 11831 (Trin.) Þe fallyng euel had he to melle. c **1400** Maundev. (1839) vi. 69 It heleth him of the fallynge Euyll. c **1475** *Pict. Voc.* in Wr.-Wülcker 791 *Hic morbus caducus*, the fallyn evylle. **1607** Topsell *Four-f. Beasts* (1673) 506 The bloud of a lamb mingled with wine doth heal..those which have the foul evil. **1869** E. A. Parkes *Pract. Hygiene* (ed. 3) 79 The Aleppo evil, the Damascus ulcer, and some other diseases.

c. Short for King's evil: scrofula. Also *attrib.* in †***evil gold***, the gold coin (see angel *sb.* 6) given by the king to those touched by him for 'the evil'.

[**1530** Palsgr. 182 *Les escrovelles*, a disease called the quynnancy or the kynges yvell.] **1605** Shaks. *Macb.* iv. iii. 146 *Macd.* What's the Disease he means? *Mal.* Tis call'd the Euill. **1667** *Lond. Gaz.* No. 154/4 There will be no farther Touching for the Evil till Michaelmas next. **1702** *Ibid.* No. 3814/4 Stolen..two Pieces of Evil Gold. **1737** Pope *Hor. Epist.* ii. ii. 219 When golden Angels cease to cure the Evil. **1751** Fielding in *Lond. Daily Advertiser* 31 Aug., Two of the most miserable Diseases..the Asthma and the Evil. **1868** Freeman *Norm. Conq.* (1876) II. App. 536 The first who undertook to cure the evil by the royal touch.

C. *Comb.*

1. Of the *adj.*, chiefly parasynthetic adjs., as ***evil-affected*** (hence ***evil-affectedness***), ***-complexioned***, ***-eyed***, ***-fortuned***, ***-headed***, ***-hearted***, ***-hued***, ***-mannered***, ***-minded*** (hence ***evil-mindedness***), ***-officed***, ***-qualitied***, ***-savoured***, ***-starred***, ***-thewed*** [see thew], ***-thoughted***, ***-tongued***, ***-weaponed***, ***-willed***; also †**evil-usage** = ill-usage. evil-favoured, etc.

1611 Bible *Acts* xiv. 2 Stirred vp the Gentiles, and made their mindes *euill affected against the brethren. **1670** Cotton *Espernon* i. iv. 154 The *evil-affectedness of the people. **1623** Drumm. of Hawth. *Cypress Grove* Wks. 121 If they were not distempered and *evil complexioned, they would not be sick. **1611** Shaks. *Cymb.* i. i. 72 You shall not finde me (Daughter) *Euill-ey'd vnto you. **1661** Pierce *Serm. 29 May* 35 Nor can you rationally hope to keep your Peace any longer, then whilest the evil-ey'd Factions want power to break it. **1872** Ruskin *Eagle's N.* §106 But to be evil-eyed, is that not worse than to have no eyes? **1490** Caxton *Eneydos* xxvi. 94 O fortune *euyll fortuned why haste thou not permytted me, etc. c **1583** Balfour *Practicks* 490 (Jam.) Gif the awiner of the beist..knew that he was *evil-heidit or cumbersom. **1832** Tennyson *Œnone* 49 *Evil-hearted Paris..Came up from reedy Simois all alone. a **1225** *Ancr. R.* 368 Me..tolde him þet his deore spuse..were..lene & *vuele iheowed. **1656** Trapp *Comm. Col.* ii. 20 The most uncivil and *evil-mannered..of all those who have borne the name of God upon earth. **1531** in *Vicary's Anat.* (1888) App. vii. 201 Opportunity was taken by the *evil-minded to worry alien Surgeons. **1687** Dryden *Hind & P.* ii. 689 Some evil-minded beasts might..wreak their hidden hate. **1817** Cobbett *Pol. Reg.* 8 Feb. 164 The endeavours which have recently been exerted..by designing and evil-minded men. **1884** J. Parker *Apost. Life* III. 144 We ourselves are..infinite in the variety of our *evil-mindedness. **1607** Tourneur *Rev. Trag.* ii. i, What makes yon *euill-offic'd man? **1613** *Life Will I* in *Select. Harl. Misc.* (1793) 12 His return was on foot, by reason of the *evil-qualitied ways. c **1400** *Rom. Rose* 4733 [Love is] Right *evelle savoured good savour. **1842** Tennyson *Locksley H.* 155 In wild Mahratta-battle fell my father *evil-starr'd. c **1400** *Beryn* 2177 Nevir thing so wild Ne so *evill thewid, as I was my selff. **1824** J. Symmons tr. *Æschylus' Agamem.* 11 Cure me of *evil-thoughted care. **1867** in *Deutsch's Rem.* 8 The *evil-tongued messenger arrived in the camp. **1645** Milton *Tetrach.* Wks. (1847) 218/1 Hemingius..writing of divorce..gives us six [causes thereof], adultery, desertion, inability, errour, *evil usage, and impiety. **1590** Sir J. Smyth *Disc. Weapons* Sig. ***, They have been contented to suffer their soldiers to goe *evill weaponed. **1393** Langl. *P. Pl.* C. ii. 189 Men of holy churche, Auerouse & *euel-willed whanne thei ben auaunsed. c **1400** *Apol. Loll.* 25 Who schal rise to gidre wiþ me aʒenis þe iuil willid. **1460–70** *Bk. Quintessence* (1889) 26 Saturn is a planete evel-willid and ful of sekenes. **1533** More *Answ. poysoned Bk.* Wks. 1054/2 His wisedome will not enter into an euil-willed heart.

2. Of the *sb.* **a.** objective with agent-noun, as ***evil-sayer***, ***-speaker***, ***-worker***; with vbl. sb. and pr. pple. forming adjectives and substantives, as ***evil-boding***, ***-saying***, ***-speaking***, ***-wishing***. **b.** instrumental, with pples., forming adjs., as †***evil-bicaught***, ***-impregnated***. Also **evil-proof** *a.*, proof against evil. evil-doer, -willer, etc.

c **1330** *Arth. & Merl.* 296 Thai weren sought and founde hem nought Tho he held hem *iuel bicought. **1833** Ht. Martineau *Manch. Strike* xi. 125 The *evil-bodings which a succession of Job's comforters had been pouring into her ears. **1855** Singleton *Virgil* I. 101 And evil-boding bitches, and ill-omened birds. **1855** *Woman's Devotion* II. 25 *Evil-impregnated air that seemed to surround Lady Jane, wherever she went. **1864** Skeat *Uhland's Poems* 63 Now, builder, finish the walls and roof, God's blessing hath made it *evil-proof. **1530** Palsgr. 217/2 *Evyll sayer, *maldisant.* **1526** *Pilgr. Perf.* (W. de W. 1531) 93 Detraccyon is a preuy & secrete *euyll sayenge of our neyghbour. a **1200** *Moral Ode* 274 Þeor beð naddren..þa tered and freteð þe *uuele speken. **1413** Lydg. *Pilgr. Sowle* iii. v. (1483) 53 Gladly heryng euery euel speker. **1611** Bible *1 Pet.* ii. 1 *Euill-speakings. **1705** Stanhope *Paraphr.* III. 495 Many good Men..look upon these Evil-speakings as a sort of Martyrdom. **1847** Grote *Greece* ii. xi. (1862) II. 339 [Solon] forbade absolutely evil-speaking with respect to the dead. a **1586** Sidney (J.), A country full of *evilwishing minds towards him. **1552** Abp. Hamilton *Catech.* (1884) 4 Behald the doggis, behald *ewil workeris. **1611** Bible *Phil.* iii. 2 Beware of euill workers.

†**'evil**, *sb.*² *Obs.* Meaning uncertain.

(Some commentators explain it as 'a jakes, privy'; there seems to be no ground for this exc. in the two passages themselves, where 'hovel' would suit equally well. But identity with prec. seems quite possible.)

1603 Shaks. *Meas. for M.* ii. ii. 172 Hauing waste ground enough, Shall we desire to raze the Sanctuary And pitch our euils there? **1613** —— *Hen. VIII*, ii. i. 67 Let 'em looke they glory not in mischiefe Nor build their euils on the graues of great men.

'evil, *sb.*³ *dial.* [The OE. word for 'fork' is *ʒeaful*; a parallel form **ʒifel* might give *evil* in dialects.] (See quot.)

1642 in Cotton *Barnstaple* (1890) 68 [The common sort] betooke themselves to armes..some with pikes, some with dunge Evells, some with great poles. **1863** Morton *Cycl. Agric.* (E.D.S.), *Evil*, three-pronged fork.

evil ('iːv(ə)l), *adv.* Forms: 1 yfele, yfle, 3–4 uvele, ufele, 4–6 evel(e, -el(l(e, yvel(e, -ell, (4 evyil, ivel, yvyl, yvle, 5 avell, ewell, yeffell), 4–7 evill(e, -yl(e, -yl(l(e, (6 ewill), 3– evil. [ME. *uvele* (*ü*), *ivele*, *evele*, OE. *yfele*, f. *yfel* = OS. *ubilo* (Du. *euvel*), OHG. *ubilo*, *upilo* (MHG. *übele*, Ger. *übel*):—OTeut. **ubilô*.] In an evil manner; ill.

†**1.** Wrongly, wrongfully, wickedly, ill; *esp.* with *to do*, *speak*, etc. *Obs.*; cf. evil *sb.* 2.

c **1000** *Ags. Gosp.* John xviii. 22 Gif ic yfele [**1160** *Hatton* efele] spræce cyð ʒewittnysse be yfele. c **1000** *Ags. Ps.* lxx[i]. 9 Oft me feala cwædon feondas yfele. a **1300** *Cursor M.* 6531 (Gött.) Sone herd he..þat his folk ful euil had don. c **1330** R. Brunne *Chron.* (1810) 147 Þe clergy Gaf a grete cursyng on whilk of þam..þat euelle bituex þam spak. c **1380** Wyclif *Wks.* (1880) 12 Þei coueiten euyle here neiʒ eboris goodis. c **1400** *Destr. Troy* 10493 Ector with envy evill he dyssayuet, Dang hym to dede. c **1440** *Gesta Rom.* xc. 413 (Add. MS.) The yonge sone..spendid Euyll the money that was take hym to the vse of the scole. **1541** R. Barnes *Wks.* (1573) 361/1 Man euill vsyng hys free-will, dyd both loose him selfe, and also his freewil. **1547** *Homilies* i. *Contention* ii. (1859) 138 If I be evil reviled, shall I stand still, like a goose or a fool? **1580** Baret *Alv.* E 388, It is euill done of you, *iniquè facis.* **1611** Bible *John* xviii. 23 If I haue spoken euill beare witnesse of the euill.

b. ***to speak evil*** (OE. *be*) ***of***: to speak maliciously, slanderously, abusively *of*; in later use perh. regarded as a *sb.*, but in OE. and ME. an *adv.*

c **1000** *Ags. Gosp.* Mark ix. 39 Nis nan þe on minum naman mæʒen wyrce & mæʒe raðe be me yfele sprecan. **1535** Coverdale *Ezek.* xxxvi. 23 My greate name..which amonge the Gentiles is euel spoken of. **1580** North *Plutarch* 740 [Alexander's friends] beganne..to speake euill of him. **1611** Bible *Mark* ix. 39 There is no man, which shall doe a miracle in my Name, that can lightly speake euill of me. c **1630** Drumm. of Hawth. *Poems* Wks. 45 Here Aretine lies..Who, whilst he liv'd spoke evil of all. a **1768** T. Secker *Serm.* (1775) lxxxix. III. 229 Whoever is..long evil spoken of, hath been faulty. **1841** Lane *Arab. Nts.* I. 91 That I should be his enemy, and speak evil of him.

†**c.** ***to hear evil***: to be evil spoken of; = L. *male audire.* Cf. *to hear ill. Obs.*

1584 *Forme of Prayer Ch. Scotl.* G 2b, If he haue..gouerned him selfe in suche sorte as the worde of God hath not hearde euill. **1590** Spenser *F.Q.* i. v. 23 O! what of gods then boots it to be borne, If old Aveugles sonnes so evill heare?

†**2.** Harmfully, injuriously, *esp.* in ***to evil entreat***; badly, severely, shamefully. *Obs.*

c **1205** Lay. 1903 Vfele [c **1275** vuele] he hine mærde. **1340** *Ayenb.* 239 He het þet ha wer riʒt wel ybeate and euele y-draʒe. c **1380** *Sir Ferumb.* 2557 Do make vp Seynt petris churche þat þe Sarsynz han yule arayd. c **1400** *Destr. Troy* 9685 The bodies on bent brethit full euyll. a **1450** *Knt. de la Tour* 23 They..plucked each other bi the here of the hede right evelle. **1485** Caxton *Paris & V.* 19 Geffroy went to therthe under hys hors ryght evyl hurte. **1562** *Act 5 Eliz.* c. 4. §35 If any such Master shall misuse or evil intreat his Apprentice. **1578** *Gude & Godlie Ball.* (1868) 133, I was..Euill totcheit and rockit. **1611** Bible *Deut.* xxvi. 6 The Egyptians euil intreated vs, and afflicted vs. **1693** *Mem. Ct. Teckele* ii. 89 More fit to ruine and evil entreat the Peasants..than to fight an Enemy. **1749** *Act 22 Geo. II* in Beawes *Lex Mercat.* (1752) 251 Pillaged, beaten, or evil-intreated.

†**3.** With difficulty, hardly. *Obs.*

1377 Langl. *P. Pl.* B. xii. 8 In pyne olde elde þat yuel can suffre Pouerte. c **1435** *Torr. Portugal* 81 Fulle evylle thow dourst hyme stond. **1470–85** Malory *Arthur* ii. viii, It is euyl sene said the knyghtes that thou art a true man that thou wolt not telle thy name. **1523** Ld. Berners *Froiss.* I. ccccxxxviii. 771 They shulde full yuell agone any farther to gette any forage. **1580** North *Plutarch* (1676) 819 Brutus could evil away with the tyranny.

†**4.** Badly, poorly, indifferently, insufficiently; not well. ***evil at ease*** = ill at ease. *Obs.*

a **1300** *Cursor M.* 16119 (Cott.) Mi wyf es sumquat iuel at ess. c **1340** *Ibid.* 4422 (Trin.) Alas Ioseph..Euel is þ e quit þi trewe seruyse. **1399** Langl. *Rich. Redeles* iv. 52 Euyll be we worthy to welden oure hire. c **1420** *Anturs of Arth.* ix, Alle bare was the body..in clething evyl clad. **1475** *Bk. Noblesse* 30 No cheveteyn can not have..good men of armes eville paied. c **1489** Caxton *Sonnes of Aymon* ix. 253, I am evyll contente. **1523** Ld. Berners *Froiss.* I. xviii. 21 With them came other folkis of the countrey..with brede euyll bakyn. *Ibid.* I. lxxxiii. 105 They were but yuell payed. **1563** *Homilies* ii. *Idolatry* ii. (1859) 197 The East and West Churches, which agreed evil before..fell to utter enmity. **1587** Harrison *England* ii. xxi. (1877) i. 332 Sicke and evill at ease. **1599** Hakluyt *Voy.* II. 129 Horses..very leane and evill appoynted for service.

†**5.** Badly, defectively; imperfectly, unskilfully; also, incorrectly, wrongly. *Obs.*

a **1000** *Riddles* xliv. 10 (Gr.) Gif se esne his hlaforde hyreð yfle. a **1250** *Owl & Night.* 1204 Ic wot if smithes sale vuele clenche. c **1300** *Beket* 404 So schal the pays of the londe wel uvele beon iholde. c **1340** *Cursor M.* 25828 (Fairf.) Qua-sim dos squa is iuel taʒt. c **1400** *Lanfranc's Cirurg.* (MS. A.) 93 Cankre..comeþ of a wounde yvel heelid. c **1450** *Merlin* iii. 46 Sirs ye knewe Merlin full euell. **1551** Robinson tr. *More's Utop.* Ded. Ep. (Arb.) 14 A good tale euel tolde. **1577** B. Googe *Heresbach's Husb.* i. (1586) 22 If it be shallowe in one place, and deepe in an other, it declares the grounde to be evill handled in the plowing. **1597** Morley *Introd. Mus.* 74 Shew me a reason why the Discord is euill taken here? **1629** Purchas *Pilgrims* II. 1032 These vessels are more wide than ours, being evil made.

†**6.** Badly, unfortunately, unhappily, unsuccessfully. *Obs.*

971 *Blickl. Hom.* 247 Þy læs wen sie þæt we yfele forweorþon. a **1000** *Cædmon's Gen.* 387 (Gr.) Ðæt sceolde unc Adame yfele geweorðan ymb ðæt heofonrice. c **1340** *Cursor M.* 18278 (Fairf.) Evylle hast þou done thy-self to spede. c **1400** *Rom. Rose* 1067 Yvel mote they thryve & thee..These losengers ful of envye! **1401** *Pol. Poems* (1859) II. 97 Evel mot he spede, that beggith of the puple more than is nede. **1795** *Robin Hood* (Ritson 1795) I. 83 Yeffell mot he the, Seche thre strokes he me gafe. **1611** Bible *1 Chron.* vii. 23 It went euill with his house.

†7. With *to become, like*, etc. *Obs.*

*c*1230 *Hali Meid.* 7 To don al & drehen þat him likeð ne sitte hit hire se uuele. *a*1300 *Cursor M.* 548 (Gött.) Of thing men likis, euil or wele. *c*1300 *Beket* 1179 Uvele bicom him to gon afote. 1540 COVERDALE *Fruitf. Less.* Pref. Wks. (Parker Soc.) I. 201 How evil doth it become a believer to be ireful and greedy of vengeance. 1593 SHAKS. *3 Hen. VI*, IV. vii. 84 How euill it beseemes thee, To flatter Henry.

8. *Comb.* **a.** With *agent-nouns*, forming sbs., as ***evil-liver, -looker***.

1846 TRENCH *Mirac.* xxxiii. (1862) 462 The ship of the Church,—encumbered with *evil-livers till it well nigh makes shipwreck altogether. 1887 LADY BELLAIRS *Gossips w. Girls* II. 64 Do not delude yourself that..you will be able to reform a lover who has been an evil liver. 1697 EVELYN *Numism.* IX. 302 Witches and *Evil-lookers as they call them.

b. With *pres. pples.*, forming adjs., as ***evil-smelling***; with *vbl. sbs.*, forming sbs., as ***evil-getting*** (*concr.*), ***-taking***. Also **evil-liking**, ill-favoured; **evil-sounding**, harsh-sounding; EVIL-WILLING.

1652 BP. HALL *Invis. World* III. §5 He [Satan] heartens us in *evil gettings under pretence of the opportunity of liberal almsgiving. 1535 COVERDALE *Joel* i. 18 The bullockes are very *euel likynge because they haue no pasture. 1881 BESANT & RICE *Chapl. Fleet* I. 187 They were here, crouched in this filthy, *evil-smelling place. 1552 HULOET *Euil soundynge, *absonus*. 1547 *Homilies* I. *Salvation* III. (1859) 32 To avoid *evil taking and misunderstanding.

c. With *pa. pples.*, forming adjs. (*a*) With sense 'wickedly, wrongly', as ***evil-disposed, -gotten, -won***. (*b*) With sense 'imperfectly, unskilfully' (= *mis-*), as ***evil-fashioned, -loved, -ordered, -pieced, -shaped, -shapen, -sown, -spun, -taught***. Also **evil-sained** [see SAIN], lit. 'ill-blessed' *i.e.* accursed.

1563 FOXE in *Latimer's Serm. & Rem.* (1845) p. xix, He was tossed and turmoiled by *evil-disposed persons. 1854 J. S. C. ABBOTT *Napoleon* (1855) I. xxxvii. 571, I should, on the contrary have created the Tribunate, had I been hypocritical or evil-disposed. 1483 in *Surtees Misc.* (1890) 28 Breyerton, talȝer, has an ewell dyspossid woman to hys wyff. *Ibid.* John Herrot has avell dyssposid chylld. *c*1496 *Serm. Episc. Puer.* (W. de W.) Biij, *Euyll-fasshened garmentes & deuyllysshe shoon & slyppers of frensmen. 1539 TAVERNER *Erasm. Prov.* 25 *Euyl gotten good go euyll awaye. 1552 HULOET *Euil loued, *antiphalus*. 1526 *Househ. Ord.* 235 That the napery be not torne nor rent or otherwise *evill-ordered. 1570–6 LAMBARDE *Peramb. Kent* (1826) 307 Friendship, that is but *evill peeced, will not ioine close, but falleth asunder againe. 1588 A. KING tr. *Canisius' Catech.* Kiv, Away with luther and Caluine and sic *euilsained sanctes. 1832 MOTHERWELL *Poems* (1847) 17 And sway to their purpose Each *evil-shaped mood. 1398 TREVISA *Barth. De P.R.* XII. xxxii. (1495) 432 The pecok hath an ..*euyll shapen heed. *a*1541 WYATT *Poet. Wks.* (1861) 170 The gain is hers, the loss is mine: Of *evil-sown seed such is the fruit. 1388 *Songs Costume* (Percy Soc.) 45 Ware of *evel-spon waste. 1377 LANGL. *P. Pl.* B. xx. 185 'Sire *euel-ytauȝte elde' quod I 'vnhende go with the'! 1583 *Semphill Ball.* 210 Ane carling of the Quene of Phareis, That *ewill win geir to elphyne careis.

†**'evil**, *v.*[1] *Obs.* Forms: 1 yfelan, -ian, 2 uvelien, 3 i-uvelen, 4 evel-, yl(en, 5 evel, -yl. [ME. *uvelien* (*ü*), OE. *yfelian*, f. *yfel*, EVIL *a.*]

1. *trans.* To do evil to; to harm or injure; to ill-treat; to affect with disease.

*c*1000 *Ags. Ps.* lxxxii[i]. 3 And ehtunga ealle hæfdon, hu hi þine halȝan her yfeladan. *Ibid.* cvi[i]. 38 Næs heora neata nan ȝeyfelad. *c*1175 *Lamb. Hom.* 15 Ne scal us na mon uuelien þer uore. *c*1205 LAY. 31774 Ær þe uisc i-eten weore i-uueled was þe king. *c*1435 *Torr. Portugal* 1843 Thou shalte lyve and wel fare, Yf the nothing evylle.

2. *intr.* **a.** To grow bad (morally). **b.** To fall ill; to be ill or sick.

1002–23 WULFSTAN *Addr. to Eng.* (ed. Napier) 156 Ðeos woruld..sceal..ær Antecristes tocyme yfeljan swiðe. 1303 R. BRUNNE *Handl. Synne* 8032 She euylde, And deyde sunner þan she wylde. 1387 TREVISA *Higden* (Rolls) I. 81 In Ynde beeþ men of fyue cubites long, þat eueleþ nouȝt, noþer ȝildeþ vp þe breeþ. 14.. tr. *Higden* (Rolls) VII. 516 (Harl. MS. 1900) The duke eueled so in the wey.

'evil-'doer. [f. EVIL *sb.* + DOER.] One who does evil; a malefactor.

1398 TREVISA *Barth. De P.R.* XII. xxxvii. 436 The herte of the lapwynge is gode to euyl doers. 1526–34 TINDALE *2 Tim.* ii. 9, I suffre trouble as an evyll doar even vnto bondes. 1611 BIBLE *1 Pet.* ii. 12 They speake against you as euill doers. 1736 BERKELEY *Disc. to Magistrates* Wks. III. 421 Punishments that await evil-doers. 1851 D. JERROLD *St. Giles* ix. 87 Those who were so sharp after evil-doers had commonly not the cleanest consciences themselves. 1864 BURTON *Scot Abr.* I. v. 248 The formidable Proctor, who is a terror to evil-doers.

'evil-'doing, *vbl. sb.* [f. EVIL *sb.* + DOING.] The action of doing evil.

1398 TREVISA *Barth. De P.R.* XII. xxxvii. (1495) 436 In theyr euyll doyng they vse theyr hertes. 1526–34 TINDALE *1 Pet.* iii. 17 It is better..that ye suffre for well doynge then for evyll doynge [1611 euill doing, 1881 (*Rev.*) evil doing]. 1682 *Sec. Plea Nonconf.* 59 His Approbation, which he never gave to Evil-doing. 1768–74 TUCKER *Lt. Nat.* (1852) I. 576 The penalties annexed to evil-doing.

†**'evilfare.** *Obs. rare*[−1]. [f. EVIL *sb.* + FARE *sb.*; cf. *welfare*.] Ill-success, misfortune.

1553 GRIMALDE *Cicero's Offices* II. (1558) 79 A great power ther is in fortune..either for welfare or euilfare.

†**'evil-'favoured,** *a. Obs.* [f. EVIL + FAVOUR + -ED[2].] Having a repulsive appearance or aspect, ill-looking; = ILL-FAVOURED.

1530 PALSGR. 217/2 Evylfavoured face, *grimace*. 1535 COVERDALE *Lev.* xxi. 18 Blynde, lame, with an euell fauoured nose, with eny myssshappen membre. 1563 *Homilies* II. *Idolatry* III. (1859) 229 Evilfavoured and rude lumpes of clay. 1579 TOMSON *Calvin's Serm. Tim.* 348/2 They seeke for nothing but plaisters to couer the foule euilfauoured matter. 1607–12 BACON *Ess., Custom* (Arb.) 366 Macciauell well noteth (thoughe in an Evill favoured instance), there is [etc.]. 1775 in ASH; hence in mod. Dicts.

Hence †**,evil'favouredly** *adv.*, in an ill-favoured manner; defectively, imperfectly, improperly; maliciously. †**,evil'favouredness,** the quality of being ill-favoured, deformity, ugliness.

*a*1556 CRANMER *Wks.* I. 33 How evil-favouredly you and Smith agree among yourselves. 1568 TURNER *Herbal* III. 60 Selfe heale is called of some of the Germanes, evelfavoredly, *Prunella*. 1577 HARRISON *England* Ded., The curious, and such as can rather euill fauouredlie espie than skilfullie correct an error. 1581 MARBECK *Bk. of Notes* 525 That Painter..had euill fauouredlie proportioned a painted Henne. 1624 CAPT. SMITH *Virginia* (1629) 38 Images.. made evill favouredly according to their best workmanship. 1535 COVERDALE *Deut.* xvii. 1 Thou shalt offre..no oxe or shepe that hath a blemish or eny euell fauouredenesse on it. 1547 *Homilies* I. *Contention* I. (1859) 134 You shall see..the evilfavouredness and deformity of this most detestable vice. 1594 *Mirr. Policy* (1599) 164 Riches make a woman proud.. Euilfauouredenesse maketh her odious. 1775 in ASH; hence in mod. Dicts.

†**'evilful,** *a. Obs.*[−0] [f. EVIL *sb.* + -FUL.] Harmful, malicious. Hence **'evilfully** *adv.*, in a harmful or malicious manner.

*c*1400 *Apol. Loll.* 76 þu schal do no þing ȝeuelfuly to þi neȝbor in his nedis to be releuid.

†**'evilless,** *a. Obs.* In 4 evelles. [f. EVIL + -LESS.] Without evil; free from evil.

*c*1394 *P. Pl. Crede* 242 Syghthen Christ deyed Oure ordre was euelles.

evilly ('iːv(ə)llɪ), *adv.* [f. EVIL *a.* + -LY[2].] In an evil manner.

1. Viciously, wickedly, censurably.

a. 1580 *Apol. Pr. Orange* in *Phenix* (1721) I. 501 Who have ..very evilly, and without any cause, withdrawn themselues from us. 1603 KNOLLES *Hist. Turks* (1638) 96 They haue euilly prosecuted that their pretended right and title. 1624 QUARLES *Job* (1717) 197 His plenty..evilly come..shall soon pass away. 1730–6 BAILEY (folio), *Evilly*, in a bad manner. 1863 J. C. MORISON *St. Bernard* III. iii. 331 No knowledge or power is evil, however evilly it may be employed. 1871 ALABASTER *Wheel of Law* p. xxxvi, He has lived evilly in previous generations.

2. With evil purpose or result; injuriously; maliciously, mischievously; noxiously.

1631 GOUGE *God's Arrows* I. §20. 27 Who more..evilly entreated and persecuted in the world. 1655 FULLER *Ch. Hist.* IV. ii. §14 Others, who publish..evilly and falsly..that Richard late King of England..is still alive. 1670 COTTON *Espernon* II. VII. 320 She would..make known who-ever should be so evilly affected. 1677 *Lond. Gaz.* No. 1239/4 A Spanish Man of War..commanded the Masters on board, very evilly intreated them. 1845 R. CHAMBERS *Vest. Creat., Mental Const. Anim.*, The production of those evilly disposed beings is in this manner. 1872 HOWELLS *Wedd. Journ.* 81 The hot, greasy biscuit, steaming evilly up into the face. 1873 OUIDA *Pascarel* I. 35 They eyed me askance very evilly and munched their chocolate chicchi. 1875 FARRAR *Seekers* II. iii. 215 Two or three evilly-squalling brats. 1879 *Premature Death* 62 It tells evilly on the health-condition of large sections of the population.

3. Unfavourably.

1668 HOWE *Bless. Righteous* (1825) 260 Not to desire heaven..is so evilly thought of, that, etc. 1823 LAMB *Let. B. Barton* in *Life & Lett.* xii. 119 And let 'em talk as evilly as they do of the envy of poets. 1864 DK. MANCHESTER *Court & Soc. Eliz. to Anne* II. 160 This latter, evilly celebrated in his day, was Ferdinando, Marquis de Paleotti. 1883 *Daily News* 20 June 5/6 The evilly reputed spot—the guet-apens where we were all to be massacred.

4. Not well, badly: †**a.** Faultily, insufficiently, defectively (*obs.*). **b.** Unhappily.

1587 FLEMING *Contn. Holinshed* III. 1278/2 Robert Baldocke..a man evillie beloved. 1590 *Disc. Sp. Invas.* in *Harl. Misc.* (Malh.) II. 162 The which embassage..made the gentleman to be evilly entertained by our men. 1655 DIGGES *Compl. Ambass.* 121 How evilly they rest satisfied.. is well known. 1683 SALMON *Doron Med.* III. 643 Restores the whole Skin (though evilly framed as to its Pores) making it well coloured. 1845 J. H. NEWMAN *Ess. Developm.* 223 Superstitious men fare most wretchedly & evilly.

†5. With difficulty; reluctantly, impatiently.

1595 SHAKS. *John* III. iv. 149 This Act so euilly borne shall coole the hearts Of all his people. 1630 *R. Johnson's Kingd. & Commw.* 234 The Provinces of Aragon also..doe evilly brooke this government.

†6. Incorrectly, inappropriately, improperly.

*c*1555 HARPSFIELD *Divorce Hen. VIII.* (1878) 293 How well and godly he..preached..through the place were very evily applied. 1607 TOPSELL *Serpents* (1653) 803 These words of Arstotle, evilly understood by Pliny and other ancient writers. 1607 SHAKS. *Timon* IV. iii. 468 Oh Monument And wonder of good deeds, euilly bestow'd! 1677 GALE *Crt. Gentiles* II. IV. 112 Natural libertie in it self good but evilly applied.

'evilmost, *a. rare*[−1]. [f. EVIL *a.* 5 on the analogy of HINDMOST.] Most evil or unlucky.

1857 COLLINS *Dead Secret* (1861) 258 One day (he said) of all the days in the year the evilmost for Sarah she changed that name.

evilness ('iːv(ə)l-, 'iːvɪlnɪs). [OE. *yfelnyss*, f. as prec. + -NESS.] The quality or condition of being evil.

1. Badness, viciousness; wickedness, depravity.

1000 ÆLFRIC *Hom.* II. 278 þæt we sceoldon wistfullian na on yfelnysse beorman, ac on þeorfnyssum. *c*1175 *Lamb. Hom.* 17 þet he icherre from þan uuelnesse ear his ende dei. *a*1300 *E. E. Psalter* li. 5 [lii. 3] þou loved ivelnes ovre betternes. 1489 CAXTON *Faytes of A.* I. i. 4 That cometh nothyng of the right of warre but by euylnes of the peple. 1553 BP. PONET in Strype *Eccl. Mem.* II. II. xxiii. 445 The evilness of the abuse hath marred the goodness of the word. 1677 HALE *Prim. Orig. Man.* I. ii. 55 The..evilness..and unseasonableness of moral or natural actions, which falls not within the verge of a brutal faculty. 1730–6 in BAILEY (folio).

†2. Evil influence, hurtful character, noxiousness. *Obs.*

1563 HYLL *Art Garden.* (1593) 19 That the euilnes and corruptnes of the grounde, may be washed awaye with the winter showers. 1564–78 BULLEYN *Dial. agst. Pest.* (1888) 31 When as the Sunne and Moone doe enter into any of their circles in those greate bodies, then our little bodies in earth do feele the goodnes or euilnesse of them. 1620 VENNER *Via Recta* Introd. 7 The Inhabitants, by reason of the euilnesse of the aire, haue grosse..spirits.

†3. Ill-health, illness. *Obs.*

1599 HARSNET *Agst. Darell* 315, I oftentimes heard M. Darrell say before my pretended Evilnes that [etc.].

†4. Poor or bad quality, inferiority. *Obs.*

1548 CECIL *Pref. to Q. Catherine's Lament.*, Neither the goodnes of the cause can mooue them to saie more, neither the euilnesse less. 1549 LATIMER *Ploughers* (Arb.) 27 They saye that the euylnes of money hath made all things dearer. 1621 AINSWORTH *Annot. Pentat.* Gen. xli. 20, I have not seen their like, in all the land of Egypt, for evilness.

†**'evilty.** *Obs.* [ME. *evelté*: see EVIL *a.* and -TY, and cf. *everlastingty*. Substituted in a late MS. of the *Cursor Mundi* for *vileté*, the reading of the Cotton MS. in both passages.] Evil, harm.

*c*1330 *Assump. Virg.* 280 in *Cursor M.* App. ii, þerof be þi most þouȝt, When I am parted Iohan, fram þee, That þei do my bodi none euelte [sic MS.; printed *eneste*]. *Ibid.* 439 Men dide me moche euelte..thei token me & bette me sore.

†**evil-willer.** *Obs.* [f. EVIL *sb.* + WILLER.] One who wishes evil to another; an ill-wisher.

1460 EARL MARCHE in Ellis *Orig. Lett.* I. 5. I. 9 Ayenst thentent & malice of your evil willers. 1567 BOND in Keith *Hist. Scot.* 381 Our comoune Enimyis and evill Willeris. 1610 HOLLAND *Camden's Brit.* I. 16, I fear me lest malitious evilwillers would wrest them to the detraction and slander of the said nations.

†**evil-willing,** *a. Obs.* [f. EVIL *adv.* + WILLING *a.* or *pr. pple.*]

1. Unwilling, disinclined. Const. *to* with *inf.*

1525 LD. BERNERS *Froiss.* II. cxl. 151 a, He was euell willinge to shewe the trouthe. 1563 *Homilies* II. *Rogat. Week* III. (1859) 492 This Spirit will never enter into an evil-willing soul.

2. quasi-*sb.* An ill-wisher, enemy.

*c*1340 *Cursor M.* 6829 (Trin.) If þou fynde of þyne euele willonde Vndir birþen his beest liggonde helpe him.

Hence **evil-willingly** *adv.*, grudgingly, unwillingly.

1549 CHALONER tr. *Erasm. Moriæ Enc.* Siv, They doe it evilwillyngly.

†**,evil-'willy,** *a. Obs.* [parasynthetically f. *evil will*: see EVIL *a.* and WILLY.] **a.** Having evil desires. **b.** Malevolent, spiteful.

1382 WYCLIF *Wisd.* i. 4 In to an euell willi soule shal not gon in wisdam. *c*1400 *Apol. Loll.* 25 Prelats mai sore drede, þat her..iuilwilly cursing be in cause whi þe puple drediþ not cursing. 1500–20 DUNBAR '*In secreit place this hyndir nycht*', Be warme hairtit & nocht ewillwillie.

evince (ɪ'vɪns), *v.* [ad. L. *ēvincĕre*, f. *ē* out + *vincĕre* to conquer. (For the Lat. senses see EVICT.)]

†1. *trans.* To overcome, subdue, prevail over.

1620 VENNER *Via Recta* viii. 167 Because it cannot be concocted, and euinced of nature, [it] filleth the body with crude..humours. 1650 HUBBERT *Pill Formality* 100 They will keep their hold until they be evinced and cast out. 1671 MILTON *P.R.* IV. 235 Error by his own arms is best evinc't. 1678 H. VAUGHAN *Thalia Rediv.*, *Day-spring*, My Prince Whose fulness no need could evince.

†2. To convince. Also *absol. Obs.*

1621 I. C. in *T. Bedford's Serm.* sig. I. 6 a, Whether their ..Consciences bee not..euidently euinced of the truth of the Gospell. 1664 POWER *Exp. Philos.* Pref. 7 Such, I am sure our modern Engine [the Microscope] will ocularly evince and unlearn them their opinions. 1668 HALE *Pref. to Rolle's Abridgm.* 2 His arguments were fitted to prove and evince, not for ostentation, plain yet learned. 1670 G. H. *Hist. Cardinals* I. I. 13 The principal drift of his discourse was to evince the people, that the Religious were oblig'd to reprehend the Errors..of all people.

†**b.** To confute, convict of error. *Obs.*

1608–11 BP. HALL *Epist.* VI. §5 Were we euer the true Church of God? Who hath admonished, euinced, excommunicated, us? 1661 COWLEY *Advanc. Exper. Philos.*, The Popular and received Errors in Experimental Philosophy..shall be evinced by tryal. 1672 SIR P. LEYCESTER *Prolegom.* in Ormerod *Cheshire* (1880) I. 29 Not evinced by any solid answer or reason to the contrary.

†3. To constrain, compel (assent), extort (concessions, etc.) by force of argument or persuasive motives. *Obs.*

1631 T. ADAMS in *Lett. Lit. Men* (Camden) 149 His profession of love..of readiness to assist in any thing..all

which evince my most grateful acknowledgment. *a* **1658** CLEVELAND *Gen. Poems, etc.* (1677) 170, I shall wave the Arguments wherewith you endeavour to evince our Consent.

†**4.** To prove by argument or evidence; to establish. Also, *rarely*, To prove the rightness of, vindicate. Const. **a.** with simple *obj.*; **b.** with *obj. clause*; **c.** with *inf.* To prove (a person or thing) to be (so and so); **d.** *absol. Obs.*

a. **1610** BP. HALL *Apol. Brownists* §5 Wee holde, and wish no lesse; your places evince no more. **1621** BURTON *Anat. Mel.* Democr. (1676) 11/1 You shall see by what.. arguments I will evince it, that most men are mad. **1661** BOYLE *Examen* iii. (1682) 20 Having said thus much to evince against Mr. Hobbs the Gravity of the Air. **1709** STRYPE *Ann. Ref.* I. xx. 247 Who did..make it their business in their sermons to prove and evince the present proceedings in religion. **1738** WARBURTON *Div. Legat.* I. 77 We require no more to evince the Falshood of that Assertion.

b. **1611** SPEED *Hist. Gt. Brit.* VI. ix. 80 Our former allegations doe euince that, etc. **1695** WOODWARD *Nat. Hist. Earth* I. (1723) 16 Having detected the Insufficiency of them, by evincing how far they are from being conclusive. **1767** GOOCH *Treat. Wounds* I. 419 We want not instances from lithotomy to evince, that wounds of this part are curable.

c. **1635** JACKSON *Creed* VIII. xx. Wks. VIII. 39 Judicious commentators do clearly evince this form of congratulation Hosanna to be precatory. **1647** LILLY *Chr. Astrol.* clxxvii. 750 ♄—being in ♉ an earthly Signe—will evince the Native to accumulate Wealth by Pastorage, Tillage, etc. **1667** *Naphtali* Postscr. (1761) 276 They will evince him to be the archest traitor that ever Scotland bred. **1709** STRYPE *Ann. Ref.* I. xi. 136 The practice of the lawyers..evinced this and the rest to be good laws.

d. BP. HALL *Cases Consc.* II. v. (1654) 116 The Accuser complaines, the Witnesse evinceth, the Judge sentences.

5. To be an indication or evidence of; to make evident or manifest. Const. **a.** with simple *obj.*; **b.** with *obj. clause* or preceded by *as.*

a. **1772–84** COOK *Voy.* (1790) IV. 1481 Their pacific disposition is thoroughly evinced, from their friendly reception of all strangers. **1802** PALEY *Nat. Theol.* xxvi. (1819) 465 The contrivances of nature decidedly evince intention. **1811** J. PINKERTON *Petral.* I. 597 The presence of ..resin, and fibre, are esteemed to evince the original vegetable character. *a* **1866** GROTE *Eth. Fragm.* iii. (1876) 52 Nothing can more clearly evince the preponderance of this view.

b. **1621** BURTON *Anat. Mel.* II. ii. VI. iii. (1651) 299 Fishes ..which, as common experience evinceth, are much affected with music. **1702** W. J. *Bruyn's Voy. Levant* vii. 22 The Ruins that are round about do sufficiently evince that anciently there were great Buildings in this Place. **1726** LEONI tr. *Alberti's Archit.* I. 40b, A Tower..made its way thro' the ground it stood upon, which, as the fact evinced, was a loose weak soil. **1779** J. MOORE *View Soc. Fr.* (1789) I. vii. 45 What is mentioned in my last letter..evinces how very opposite their sentiments are. **1864** BOWEN *Logic* xi. 359 These considerations appear to me to evince very clearly, that [etc.].

6. To give tokens of possessing; to reveal the presence of (a quality, condition, feeling); to display, exhibit, manifest.

1829 SCOTT *Rob. Roy* Introd. 18 The knees and upper part of the leg..evincing muscular strength. **1853** C. BRONTË *Villette* xxxvii. (1876) 420 His answers..evinced both wisdom and integrity. **1879** HARE *B'ness Bunsen* I. iii. 65 The extreme truthfulness..of both her father and mother is so quaintly evinced in the following letter.

b. *refl.* To show oneself (to be) *so and so.*

1804–8 FOSTER in *Life & Corr.* (1846) I. 267, I evince myself a social man.

evinceable, obs. form of EVINCIBLE.

†**e'vincement.** *Obs.* [f. EVINCE + -MENT.] The action or process of evincing; proof.

1655 EARL ORRERY *Parthen.* (1676) 19 As an evincement of the greatness of my flame. **1686** H. MORE *Real Presence* 20 A plain Evincement that our Saviour meant figuratively, when, etc.

e'vincible, *a.* Also 6 -eable. [f. as prec. + -IBLE.] **a.** That may be evinced; demonstrable. †**b.** Of proofs: Demonstrative, convincing.

1593 BILSON *Govt. Christ's Ch.* 335, I see utterly nothing euinceable by these examples. **1677** HALE *Prim. Orig. Man.* I. ii. 63 Possibly the Immortality of the Soul is evincible by very great reason. **1761** HUME *Hist. Eng.* II. xxxix. 356 *note*, That Bothwell was young, appears, among many other evincible proofs from Mary's instructions to the bishop of Dumblain. **1828** in WEBSTER.

Hence †**e'vincibly** *adv.*, in an evincible manner; so as to prove convincingly.

1736 in BAILEY; hence in ASH, etc.

evincing (ɪ'vɪnsɪŋ), *ppl. a.* [f. as prec. + -ING².] That evinces; †convincing.

1641 MILTON *Animadv.* (1851) 192 The inference is undeniable..from the general to the particular, an evincing argument in Logick. **1673** *Lady's Call.* I. §1. 12 The more evincing attestation they must attend from the unerring tribunal hereafter. **1759** DILWORTH *Pope* 65 He thought the arguments there offered so evincing. **1794** G. ADAMS *Nat. & Exp. Philos.* II. xxi. 423 [He] will feel the evidence of the hereditary evil of man..evincing.

Hence †**e'vincingly** *adv.*, in an evincing manner; convincingly.

1656 H. MORE *Antid. Ath.* II. ii. (1712) 43 That the foregoing Phænomena are not by chance or luck..will be more evincingly confirmed. **1664** POWER *Exp. Philos.* II. 107 By which it most evincingly appears that water does gravitate in its own Sphære.

evincive (ɪ'vɪnsɪv), *a.* [f. EVINCE + -IVE.] Giving indications or proof; indicative. Const. *of.*

1806 FESSENDEN *Democr.* II. 96 A few particulars, which shall be evincive of the kind of talents, which are necessary to qualify a man. **1812** J. J. HENRY *Camp. agst. Quebec* 48 It may be proper to relate the following anecdote as more evincive of the fact. **1870** J. STORY *Equity Jurispr.* xxiv. 167 Any writing sufficiently evincive of a trust..will create a trust by implication.

evin(g), obs. var. *eaving*, q.v. under EAVE.

1651 OGILBY *Æsop* (1665) 187 A little Mouse Streight she presents on th' Evins of the House. **1736** BAILEY *Househ. Dict.* 331 Near unto the evings of the house [Hen House] should be long perches.

†**e'vintegrous,** *a. Obs.*⁻⁰ [f. L. *æv-um* age + *integr-um* whole, entire + -OUS.] (See quot.)

1674–81 BLOUNT *Glossogr.*, *Evintegrous*, that bears age without decay. **1692–1732** in COLES. **1775** in ASH.

Evipan ('ɛvɪpæn). *Pharm.* Also **evipan.** A proprietary name of HEXOBARBITONE.

1932 *Trade Marks Jrnl.* 8 June 719/2 *Evipan*, a medicine for human use as a hypnotic. Bayer Products, Limited.. Manufacturers. **1933** *Lancet* 1 July 18/2 Evipan-sodium is the sodium salt of N-methyl-C-C-cyclo-hexenyl-methyl barbituric acid. **1936** A. CHRISTIE *Cards on Table* xxx. 278 N-methyl-cyclo-hexenyl-methyl-malonyl urea... Known more simply as Evipan. Used as an anaesthetic for short operations. **1940** 'G. SAVA' *Ring at Door* ix. 133, I took out a hypodermic syringe from my bag and filled it with a dose of evipan. **1968** J. H. BURN *Lect. Notes Pharmacol.* (ed. 9) 52 As anaesthetics thiopentone..and hexobarbitone (Evipan) are used.

evir, obs. form of IVORY.

†**'evirate,** *ppl. a. Obs.* [ad. L. *ēvirāt-* ppl. stem of *ēvirāre*: see next.] Castrated, emasculated; deprived of manly strength or vigour.

1606 HOLLAND *Sueton.* Annot. 15 The water..drunken, caused men to be evirate and effeminate. **1609** —— *Amm. Marcel.* XXVII. x. 321 A certaine esquier or targuetier, borne a verie evirate Eunuch. **1650** CHARLETON *Paradoxes* Prol. 11 Nature is not yet evirate, but holds out bravely.

evirate ('iːvɪreɪt, 'ɛvɪreɪt), *v.* [f. L. *ēvirāt-* ppl. stem of *ēvirāre* to deprive of virility, f. *ē* out + *vir* man.] *trans.* To deprive of virility or manhood. **a.** To castrate (a male). **b.** To deprive of manly qualities or attributes; to render unmanly in character or appearance.

a. **1621** BURTON *Anat. Mel.* II. iii. II. (1651) 312 Some Philosophers and Divines have evirated themselves, and put out their eyes voluntarily the better to contemplate. **1640** BP. HALL *Chr. Moder.* I. §4 Origen and some others that have voluntarily evirated themselves. **1846** LANDOR *Exam. Shaks.* Wks. II. 280 The Pope offered a hundred marks in Latin to whoever should eviscerate and evirate him [Doctor Glaston].

b. **1626** W. SCLATER *Exp. 2 Thess.* (1629) 272 How doth it [idleness] euirate, un-man men? **1650** BULWER *Anthropomet.* 131 Without..impiety [we] cannot.. eradicate our Beard..but we must renounce that, and account it for a sport so fondly to Evirate ourselves. **1875** BROWNING *Aristoph. Apol.* 90 On thee whose life work preached 'Raise soul, sink sense! Evirate Hermes!'

Hence **'evirating,** *vbl. sb.*

1657 REEVE *God's Plea* 245 Oh, look with shame..upon this wofull evirating, or dis-humaning yourselves.

eviration (ɛvɪ'reɪʃən). [ad. L. *ēvirātiōn-em*, n. of action f. *ēvirāre*: see EVIRATE *v.*] The action of depriving of virility; the state of being deprived of virility; emasculation. Also *fig.*

1603 HOLLAND *Plutarch's Mor.* 1232 They had saved the children of Greeks from eviration. **1654** USSHER *Ann.* vi. (1658) 122 The wrong which had been done him in his eviration. **1730–6** BAILEY (folio), *Eviration*, a gelding, an unmanning; also making effeminate.

fig. **1829** LANDOR *Imag. Conv.* (1846) II. 51 If he could recover his senses under a worse and more shameful eviration.

‖**evirato** (evi'rato). Pl. **evirati.** [Italian, ad. L. *ēvirātus*, pa. pple. of *ēvirāre*: see EVIRATE *v.*] A male singer castrated in boyhood so as to retain an alto or soprano voice. Cf. CASTRATO.

1796 BURNEY *Metastasio* III. 330 The exquisite voices and refinements in singing of the Evirati. **1879** J. MARSHALL in Grove *Dict. Mus.* I. 514 He [Ferri] seems to have surpassed all the evirati in brilliance and endurance.

†**e'virtuate,** *ppl. a. Obs. rare.* [f. as next + -ATE².] Deprived of virtue, strength, or power; enervated.

1799 S. T. COLERIDGE in Mrs. Sandford *T. Poole & Friends* (1888) I. 304 The most heaven-inspired penmaker that..these superficial, weak, and evirtuate ages have produced to redeem themselves from ignominy.

†**e'virtuate,** *v. Obs.* Also 7 evertuate. [f. Fr. *(s')évertu-er*, f. *é-* (for *es-*):—L. *ex-* out + *vertu* virtue (cf. Pr. *esvertudar*) + -ATE³.]

1. a. *refl.* To put forth virtue from (oneself); to exert oneself (to do something). **b.** *intr.* To put forth virtue, exert influence.

1642 HOWELL *For. Trav.* (Arb.) 72 One should evertuate himselfe to bring something home, that may accrue to the publique benefit. *c* **1645** —— *Lett.* (1650) II. lxi, Thus my noble Lord have I evertuated myself, and strech'd all my sinnews..to satisfy your Lordship's desires touching this subject. **1675** EVELYN *Terra* (1729) 25 The Secret we enquire after, and which does most apparently seem to evirtuate towards this end [manuring land], is some vegetable Salt.

2. *trans.* To take away the virtue of, to deprive of authority, power, or strength.

1640 LD. DIGBY *Sp. Trienn. Parl.* (1641) 24 Where is the legislative Authority?.. In the King circled in, fortified and evirtuated by his Parliament. **1644** H. PARKER *Jus Pop.* 65 The Comitia are totally depraved and evirtuated by being called out of the field into the palace. **1656** BLOUNT *Glossogr.*, *Evertuate.* **1721–1800** BAILEY, *Evertuate.*

eviscerate (ɪ'vɪsərət), *ppl. a.* [ad. L. *ēviscerāt-us*, pa. pple. of *ēviscerāre*: see next.] Drawn from the bowels (of the earth).

1830 W. PHILLIPS *Mt. Sinai* IV. 352 Lay blocks of sapphire shapeless, out of earth As fresh eviscerate.

eviscerate (ɪ'vɪsəreɪt), *v.* [f. L. *ēviscerāt-* ppl. stem of *ēviscerāre* (= sense 1), f. *ē-* out + *viscer-a* (pl. of *viscus*) the internal organs, VISCERA.]

1. *trans.* To take out the internal organs or entrails of; to disembowel; to gut. Also *absol.*

1623 in COCKERAM. **1651** R. WITTIE tr. *Primrose's Pop. Err.* IV. xxxvi. 353 They are taken out of creatures that are slain and eviscerated. **1846** [see EVIRATE *v.*]. **1856** KANE *Arct. Expl.* II. xii. 127 He was first harpooned, then eviscerated. **1862** *Macm. Mag.* Oct. 511 The weird-like gutters eviscerate in desperation, as basketful after basketful is poured into the gutting-trough. **1862** ALCOCK *Capit. Tycoon* II. 6 Declaring that if he did not obtain full justice on the spot, he would eviscerate himself in the Prince's presence. **1882** T. J. PARKER in *Nature* XXV. 352 The fish is eviscerated, the gills removed and placed in strong spirit.

b. *refl.* of the spider. Also *fig.* †*to eviscerate one's brains.*

1621 BURTON *Anat. Mel.* I. ii. III. xiv. (1651) 125 If he be a Scholar so commended for his much reading..he will eviscerate himself like a spider, study to death. **1623** DRUMM. OF HAWTH. *Cypress Grove* Wks. 119 The spider.. for the weaving of a scornful web eviscerateth it self many days. **1633** T. ADAMS *Exp. 2 Peter* ii. 5 A spider eviscerates herself, spends her own bowels in making a web to catch a fly. **1654** TRAPP *Comm. Job* xxxii. 11 Your..most elaborate demonstrations, for the which you had eviscerated your brains.

c. *transf.* To clear out the contents of; to empty, gut.

1834 *Blackw. Mag.* XXXV. 656 In vain did I, as it were, eviscerate..every pocket. **1837** CARLYLE *Fr. Rev.* I. IV. iii, A Paper-Warehouse eviscerated by axe and fire.

2. In various figurative applications.

a. To draw out what is vital or essential in (any thing); to elicit the 'pith' or essence of. *rare.*

1664 EVELYN *Sylva* Pref. to Rdr., They..as it were eviscerating Nature..have collected innumerable Experiments, etc. **1768** BLACKSTONE *Comm.* III. 205 To prevent fraud and chicane, and eviscerate the very truth of the title. **1872** O. W. HOLMES *Poet Breakf.-t.* ix, Some single point I could..eviscerate and leave..settled.

b. To empty *of* vital contents; to deprive (an argument, institution, enactment, etc.) of all that gives it value or importance.

1834 *Blackw. Mag.* XXXVI. 329 France was eviscerated of all the nobler organs which once gave it a European existence. **1845** W. SEWELL *Hawkstone* I. 79 The hymn.. was..one of Watts' which Mr. Priestley had previously eviscerated of all peculiar doctrines. **1881** *Daily News* 15 Feb. 2/1 Amendments intended to eviscerate the clause were moved by Dr. Commins..and others.

†**c.** *transf.* To bring out the inmost secrets of; *refl.* to disclose one's inmost thoughts. Also *fig. Obs. rare.*

1607 J. KING *Serm.* Nov. 32 Yet was..the deep and vnsearchable hell of their harts..eviscerated, ransacked, etc. *c* **1645** HOWELL *Lett.* I. VI. 270 Now that I have thus eviscerated myself and dealt so clearly with you, I desire by way of correspondence that you would tell me, etc.

eviscerated (ɪ'vɪsəreɪtɪd), *ppl. a.* [f. prec. + -ED¹.] **a.** Disembowelled; *fig.* deprived of vital contents. †**b.** Sent forth from the vitals (*obs.*).

1643 *True Informer* 35 The poor penitent peccant soul may be said to breath out herself into the bosome of her Saviour by tender ejaculations..and eviscerated ingeminations. **1858** SEARS *Athan.* III. ii. 266 A question to which our eviscerated Protestantism is incapable of returning a consistent answer. **1884** *Spectator* 5 Apr. 439/2 Eviscerated prophecy of this kind is a mockery.

e'viscerating, *vbl. sb.* [f. as prec. + -ING¹.] The action of the vb. EVISCERATE; *lit.* and *fig.*

1599 NASHE *Lenten Stuffe* 72 Nor liuest thou [O Herring] by the unlyuing or euiscerating of others, as most fishes do. **1692** SIR T. P. BLOUNT *Ess.* 112 The Eviscerating, and disclosing the secrets of nature.

evisceration (iːvɪsə'reɪʃən). [as if ad. L. **ēviscerātiōn-em*, n. of action f. *ēviscerāre*: see EVISCERATE. Cf. F. *éviscération.*]

1. The action or process of eviscerating or taking out the viscera; disembowelling.

1692 EDWARDS *Remarkable Texts* 161 This evisceration is very remarkable, for 'tis emphatically said his bowels, yea all his bowels gushed out. **1845** SYD. SMITH *Irish Rom. Cath. Ch.* Wks. 1859 II. 234/2 The O'Sullivans have a still earlier plea of suspension, evisceration, and division.

transf. **1886** *Boston* (Mass.) *Jrnl.* 3 Sept. 2/2 Another attributes it [earthquake] to volcanic evisceration.

2. *fig.* (cf. EVISCERATE 2.) †**a.** Manifestation of one's inmost thoughts; unbosoming. **b.** The extracting or eliciting of the inner meaning (of

anything). **c.** The depriving (an enactment or statement) of all that gives it value.

1628 Donne *Serm.* (1640) xxiii. 230 Gods laying himself open, his manifestation.. his evisceration and embowelling of him-selfe to us there [in heaven]. **1831** Coleridge *Table-t.* 27 Oct., If a certain latitude in examining witnesses is.. a necessary mean towards the evisceration of the truth of matters of fact. **1874** H. R. Reynolds *John Bapt.* viii. 498 The practical evisceration or modification of the Mosaic legislation by carnal or ceremonial additions. **1880** Stanley *Ess., Subscription* (1884) 179 A form of subscription which, after the evisceration of the old form, contains nothing of a safe-guard and something of an offence. **1880** E. White *Cert. Relig.* 54 The enormous labour of evisceration expended upon their writings by the Unitarian commentators.

evitable ('ɛvɪtəb(ə)l), *a.* [ad. L. *ēvītābilis* avoidable, f. *ēvītāre*: see evite *v.* Cf. F. *évitable.*] That admits of being avoided; avoidable. (Now chiefly in negative contexts.)

1502 *Ord. Crysten Men* (W. de W. 1506) iv. xix. 218 By necessyte euytable or not. *c* **1555** Harpsfield *Hen. VIII* (1878) 110 Wherefore necessity only, though it be evitable, is sufficient to procure a dispensation. **1597** Hooker *Eccl. Pol.* v. (1617) 198 Of two such euils, being not both euitable, the choice of the lesse is not euill. **1665** Boyle *Occas. Refl.* ii. i. (1675) 100 How many evitable Mischiefs our own Appetites or Vices expose us to. **1803** W. Taylor in *Ann. Rev.* I. 31 So much evitable difficulty, so much fruitless expenditure is incurred by every new enterprize. **1836** A. Walker *Beauty in Woman* 36 The scarcely evitable consequence of great fortune.. will ever be the ruin of the rich.

† **'evitate,** *v. Obs. rare.* [f. L. *ēvītāt-* ppl. stem of *ēvītāre*: see evite *v.*] *trans.* To avoid, shun; = evite *v.*

1588 R. Parke tr. *Mendoza's Hist. China* 409 Many other thinges.. left out for to euitate tediousness. **1598** Shaks. *Merry W.* v. v. 241 She doth euitate and shun A thousand irreligious cursed houres. **1603** Florio *Montaigne* (1634) 518 Whereas honest men profit the commonwealth in causing themselves to be imitated, I shall happily benefit the same, in making my selfe to be evitated. **1775** in Ash.

evi'tation (ɛvɪ'teɪʃən). [a. L. *ēvītātiōn-em*, n. of action f. *ēvītāre*: see evite *v.*] The action of avoiding or shunning; avoidance, shirking.

1626 Bacon *Sylva* §293 In all Bodies, there is an Appetite of Union, and Evitation of Solution of Continuity. **1655–60** Stanley *Hist. Philos.* (1701) 479/2 Election of things convenient, and Evitation of their Contraries. **1790** Paley *Horæ Paul.* i. 7 In the first of these [apocryphal epistles] I found, as I expected, a total evitation of circumstances. **1885** R. W. Dixon *Hist. Ch. Eng.* xvii. III. 172 The Englishman Pole.. true to his destiny of evitation, had declined the toils and honours of the Papacy.

'Evite, *sb.* [f. *Eve* the first woman + -ite. Cf. Adamite *sb.*[1]] A name humorously applied to a woman wearing little clothing.

1713 Addison in *Guardian* No. 134 ¶6 There being so many in all Public Places, who show so great an Inclination to be Evites. *Ibid.* No. 142 That the Evites daily increase, and that fig-leaves are shortly coming into fashion.

evite (ɪ'vaɪt), *v. arch.* [ad. F. *éviter*, ad. L. *ēvītāre*, f. *ē-* out + *vītāre* to shun.] *trans.* To avoid, shun. (In 18–19th c. almost peculiar to Scotch writers.)

1503 *Sheph. Kalender* viii, When they would evite and eschue the wonderful blasts of the wind, they plunged into the water. **1599** A. M. tr. *Gabelhouer's Bk. Physicke* 132/2 You must also evite all cibaryes which cause heate, alsoe spices. **1635** Quarles *Embl.* i. viii. (1718) 33 What we ought t' evite As our disease, we hug as our delight. **1697** W. Cleland *Poems* 79 (Jam.) We're obleidg'd in conscience, Evill's appearance to evite. *a* **1746** Maclaurin *Algebra* (ed. 4) 265 In order to know how to evite this absurdity let us suppose [etc.]. **1814** Scott *Wav.* xiv, Balmawhapple could not.. evite giving satisfaction to both. **1834** Wilson in *Blackw. Mag.* XXXV. 1005 The only position in which we could have evited death. **1889** Stevenson *Master of Ballantrae* xii. 314 Others.. were scarce able to support his neighbourhood—Sir William evite to be near him.

Hence **e'viting** *vbl. sb.*, the action of the verb evite; avoiding, avoidance.

1541 *Act 33 Hen. VIII*, c. 21 For euiting of such like hainous and abhominable treasons. **1707** Sir W. Hope *New Meth. Fencing* (1714) 167 Carrying sometimes your sword-hand low.. for the better eviting of your adversary's parade.

† **evi'ternal,** *a. Obs.* Also æviternal. [f. L. *æviternus* (whence by contraction *æternus*), f. *æv-um* age + -al[1]. Cf. Fr. *eviternel* (16th c. in Godef.), which may be the source.

In med.L. *æviternus* (owing to its more obvious connexion with the etymon *ævum*) was sometimes used to express eternity of *duration*, as contrasted with the notion of timelessness expressed by *æternus*.]

= eternal; used *esp.* with reference to future duration (see quot. s.v. æviternal). Johnson's explanation (quot. 1755) is not supported by our examples.

1596 Fitz-Geffray *Sir F. Drake* (1881) 33 Celestiall Goddesse, eviternall Fame, Minerva's daughter by faire Maia's sonne. **1600** Tourneur *Transf. Met.* Prol. 81 What pallid spirit tells of strange euents? Of euiternal night? **1611** T. Farnaby *Panegyr. Verses* in Coryat *Crudities*, Hang monuments of eviternall glory.. to th' honour of Thomas Coryate. **1652** Bp. Hall *Myst. Godl.* §9 The angels are truly existing, spiritual.. powerful, eviternal creatures. **1755** Johnson, *Eviternal*, eternal in a limited sense; of duration not infinitely but indefinitely long.

Hence † **evi'ternally** *adv.* = eternally.

1609 Bp. Hall *Passion Serm.* Wks. (1627) 437 The body hangs on the crosse, the soule is yeelded; the Godhead is euiternally vnited to them both. *a* **1641** Bp. Mountagu *Acts & Mon.* 6 The Soule, is an essence.. eviternally subsisting, and immortall as Angels are.

eviternity (iːvɪ'tɜːnɪtɪ). [ad. late L. *æviternitas*, f. *æviternus*: see eviternal. Cf. OF. *eviternité*.] Eternity of duration; everlastingness. (See also quot. 1755.)

1596–1640 [see æviternity]. **1652** Bp. Hall *Invis. World* (L.), There shall we.. passe our eviternity of blisse in lauding and praising.. our Creator. **1656** [J. Serjeant] tr. *T. White's Peripatet. Instit.* 329 The notion and difference of three Durations is evident: of Time.. of Eternity [explicated] when we treated of God: lastly, of Eviternity in Intelligences. **1755** Johnson, *Eviternity*, duration not infinitely, but indefinitely long. **1828** D'Israeli *Chas I*, I. iii. 33 The questions.. whether his [God's] eternity was only an evi-ternity.

evittate (iː'vɪteɪt), *a. Bot.* [f. e- *pref.*[3] + vitta + -ate[2].] Having no vittæ or oil-canals; said of the fruit of some umbelliferous plants.

1866 in *Treas. Bot.*

evocable ('ɛvəkəb(ə)l), *a.* [a. F. *évocable*, f. *évoquer*, ad. L. *ēvoc-āre*: see evoke.] That may be called forth.

evocate ('ɛvəkeɪt), *v.* [f. L. *ēvocāt-* ppl. stem of *ēvocāre*: see evoke.]

† **1.** *trans.* To call forth. *Obs.* in gen. sense.

1639 Bp. Reynolds *Lord's Supp.* xviii, The seed to be scattered.. the Sun to evocate and excite the seminal virtue. **1665** G. Harvey *Advice agst. Plague* 6 The said Arsenical bodies.. require.. a very dry and warm.. air, to melt and open the surface of the Earth.. to attract and evocate them thence. [Misquoted by Johnson s.v. *Evacate*.]

2. To call up (spirits) from the dead, (events) from past times.

1675 J. Smith *Chr. Relig. Appeal* ii. 10 Thyestes his Ghost groans.. when ere that is evocated to attend the pleasure of the black Artist. **1732** Stackhouse *Hist. Bible* v. iii. iii, [Saul] thinking there was any efficacy in magical operations to evocate the dead. **1817** Byron *Let. Murray* 15 Feb. in Wks. (1846) 175/2 He.. goes.. to evocate a ghost. **1822** T. Taylor *Apuleius* 277 The ancient Egyptians evocated the souls of demons, or angels, and inserted them in sacred images. **1827** Sir H. Taylor *Isaac Comnenus* i. iv, Where memory evocates imperial deeds Such as betray'd Britannicus of old. **1851** G. S. Faber *Many Mansions* (1862) 392 *note*, Here Ulysses evocates the souls of the dead.

3. *nonce-use.* To call out (from a house, etc.).

1834 Beckford *Italy* II. 228 Driving to the palace [I] evocated the archbishop's confessor.

Hence **'evocated,** *ppl. a.*

1816 G. S. Faber *Orig. Pagan Idol.* III. 350 The evocated spirits come up.

evocation (ɛvəʊ'keɪʃən). [ad. L. *ēvocātiōn-em*, n. of action f. *ēvocāre*: see evoke.] The action of evoking; a calling forth or out.

† **1. a.** The calling (of a person) from a specified place or association; (of the spirit) from present surroundings. *Obs.*

1574 Hellowes *Gueuara's Fam. Ep.* (1577) 202 In this euocation of Abraham is taught howe needefull it is to.. Gods people, to be deuided and drawn from vices. **1612–5** Bp. Hall *Contempl. O.T.* xx. ii, The hastie evocation of so noted a person, to such a secrecie. *a* **1631** Donne *Serm.* cxxi. V. 150 His Night-watchings are Ecstatics and Evocations of his Soul into the Presence and Communion of Saints. *a* **1640** Jackson *Creed* xii. vii, The Greek 'Εκκλησία [signifies] a society elected or called out. This evocation or selection is of divers sorts.

transf. **1656** tr. *Hobbes' Elem. Philos.* (1839) 448 Our spirits and blood, and whatsoever is fluid within us, is called out from the internal to the external parts of our bodies.. He that can give a possible cause of this evocation and swelling [etc.].

b. *Rom. Antiq.* The calling upon the gods of a besieged city to forsake it and come over to the besiegers.

1656 Cowley *Davideis* iv. notes 149 Their solemn Evocation of Gods from the Cities which they besieged. **1753** in Chambers *Cycl. Supp.* **1853** De Quincey *Wks.* (1862) XIV. 73 The Pagan practice of evocation applied to the tutelary deities of such a state.

† **2.** = avocation 2, 3.

1769 *Hist. Europe* in *Ann. Reg.* 2/2 If the empress of Russia finds no evocation from disturbances at home.. the Turkish empire may.. fall by the hands of a woman. **1810** Scott *Let. to W. Hayley* 12 July, A number of most unpoetical evocations have made me appear very ungrateful.

3. a. The evoking or calling up a spirit. Const. *of.* **b.** The formula to be used in evoking a spirit.

a. 1633 Ames *Agst. Cerem.* ii. 147 [They] paved the way for invocation of Saints in heaven, and evocation of men out of Hell. **1681** H. More in *Glanvill's Sadducismus* Postscr. 43 She turning her face from Saul, mutters to her self some Magical form of evocation of Spirits. **1843** *Blackw. Mag.* LIV. 675 The rapidity of her evocation was most surprising, as M. de Cagliostro had no idea of the person I should desire him to call up. **1856** R. A. Vaughan *Mystics* (1860) I. 83 Divination and evocations are practised with increasing credulity.

b. 1631 A. B. tr. *Raleigh's Ghost* i. xiii. 208 The like Negromantical euocation to be made by Scipio, is read in Siluius. **1823** D'Israeli *Cur. Lit., Dreams Dawn Philos.*, The abbot.. sent three or four leaves stuffed with the names of devils, and with their evocations.

4. The calling out or removal of a cause or action from an inferior to a superior court; = med.L. *evocatio*, Fr. *évocation*.

[**1611** Cotgr., *Evocation*, an euocation.. also, a calling before one by authoritie; a transferring, or remouing of causes vnto a higher Court by command of the Judges thereof.] **1644** Bp. Maxwell *Prerog. Kings* i. 8 Nor can he be debarred.. by precognition.. or evocation to determine or Judge in any thing that concerneth that his Kingdome. **1682** *News fr. France* 10 The one [Edict] was that no Protestant may have the Relief of an Evocation (or appeal) from any Court of Justice. **1694** Falle *Jersey* vii. 206 We have a Jurisdiction established among our selves, and our Properties secured against vexatious suits and Evocations into England. **1759** Hume *Hist. Eng.* (1818) IV. 90 The evocation which came a few days after from Rome. **1791** *St. Papers* in *Ann. Reg.* 171* The citizens cannot be withdrawn from the judges.. by any other attributions or evocations than those which are determined by the laws. **1832** in Webster. **1862** S. Lucas *Secularia* 363 Other matters.. were from time to time withdrawn from the ordinary tribunals, and by a process of evocation transferred to the Council.

5. a. The action of evoking or calling forth into existence or activity; an instance of the same. Const. *of.* Also *concr.*

1775 Harris *Philos. Arrangem.* (1841) 259 There is no one.. who imagines.. every recent production.. to be an absolutely fresh creation.. an evocation of something out of nothing. **1822** De Quincey *Confess.* (1862) 84 Magical power of evocation which Christianity has put forth. **1845** R. W. Hamilton *Pop. Educ.* iv. (ed. 2) 84 You have caused him who was created a thinking being, to think. You have done reverence to the Father of spirits in the evocation of that spirit. **1861** McCaul *Aids to Faith* v. 215 The evocation of light is the prominent object of the first day's work. **1881** E. Mulford *Republic of God* viii. 173 The faith which is the gift and the evocation of this revelation. **1887** Gladstone in *Times* 6 Sept. 12/3 There is a growing necessity for the cultivation of local resources.. the evocation of which will be a most healthy proceeding.

b. With reference to the Platonic theory of recollection (ἀνάμνησις): A calling up of knowledge acquired in a previous state of existence.

1646 Sir T. Browne *Pseud. Ep.* To Rdr. A iij a, We could be content with Plato, that knowledge were but Remembrance; that Intellectual acquisition were but Reminiscentiall evocation. **1865** Grote *Plato* I. xix. 530 This magical evocation of knowledge from an untaught youth.

† **6.** *Gram.* (See quots.) *Obs.*

1612 Brinsley *Pos. Parts* (1669) 27 Every Vocative case is of the second Person.. by a figure called Evocation.. Because *Tu* or *Vos* are understood in every Voc. case. **1657** J. Smith *Myst. Rhet.* 190 Evocation is an immediate Reduction of the third person either to the first or second. **1678–96** Phillips *Evocation*, in Grammar it is a figure of Construction, being a reducing of the third Person, either to the first or second; as *Ego tuæ deliciæ istuc veniam.*

7. *Biochem.* and *Embryol.* The action of an evocator.

1934 [see evocator b]. **1940** C. H. Waddington *Organisers & Genes* iv. 24 Evocation can be produced by compounds of several radically different kinds. **1963** J. Cohen *Living Embryos* 52 The chemical stimulation [resulting in induction] is called evocation.

evocative (iː'vɒkətɪv, 'ɛvəʊkeɪtɪv), *a.* [ad. L. *ēvocātīv-us*, f. *ēvocāre*: see evocate.] Tending to call or draw forth. Const. *of.*

1657 Tomlinson *Renou's Disp.* 160* Gargarismes.. whose faculty is either levative, or repressive, or evocative. **1855** Bailey *Mystic* 61 At his will-fraught and evocative word, The strange star brightened largelier. **1881** *Brit. Q. Rev.* Jan., The soul of good in things evil which has proved.. so evocative of some of the least natural graces, so productive of spiritual energy.

evocator ('ɛvəkeɪtə(r)). [a. L. *ēvocātor*, agent-n. f. *ēvocāre*: see evocate.] **a.** One who evocates or evokes; *esp.* one who evokes or calls up a spirit.

1794 T. Taylor *Pausanias* I. 305 [He] went to Phigalea, to the Arcadian evocators of souls. **1817** Byron *Manfred* ii. ii. 188 He.. roused The Arcadian Evocators to compel The indignant shadow to depose her wrath. **1835** *Blackw. Mag.* XXXVIII. 647 Imagination.. like an olden Evocator rears The gorgeous phantoms of forgotten years.

b. *Biochem.* and *Embryol.* A chemical substance in part of an embryo that stimulates the development of another part.

1934 J. Needham et al. in *Proc. R. Soc.* B. CXIV. 409 We suggest that the first type of determination be spoken of as Evocation, since it consists in the evoking of an embryonic axis from the competent ectoderm... The organiser, or the evocator, as it might now be called, is soluble in ether and petroleum ether. **1936** *Nature* 15 Feb. 251/2 This stimulus, which the author [*sc.* C. H. Waddington] calls the evocator, is a chemical substance and is not specific for a particular kind of animal. But the tissue acted upon must be in a 'competent state' for the evocator to work. **1958** B. M. Patten *Found. Embryol.* vi. 134 The chemical substance it [*sc.* the tissue] gives off is known as the organizing substance or evocator.

evocatory (iː'vɒkətərɪ), *a.* [ad. late L. *ēvocātōri-us*, f. *ēvocāre*: see evocate and -ory.] Having the function of evoking or calling forth.

a **1711** Ken *Psyche* Poet. Wks. 1721 IV. 266 Satan.. Saw an old Clinick breathing out his last, And his evocatory Fiends enjoin'd Whom he to tare away his Soul assign'd. **1817** tr. *Dubois' People of India* xi, The Mantras.. are of various sorts, invocatory, evocatory, deprecatory, conservatory.

evoˈcatrix. *rare*⁻¹. [a. L. **ēvocātrix*, fem. of *ēvocātor*: see EVOCATOR.] A female evocator; a woman who calls up spirits.

1847 De Quincey *Protestantism* Wks. VIII. 138 She was an Evocatrix, or female necromancer, evoking phantoms that stood in some unknown relation to dead men.

‖**evoe,** *int.* (*sb.*) Also **evohe.** [a. L. *evoe*, more correctly *euœ*, *euhœ*, a. Gr. εὐοῖ.] The Bacchanalian exclamation 'Evoe!'

1586 *Praise of Mus.* 6 Those dronken euohes and howlinges. **1819** Shelley *Prometh. Unb.* II. iii. 9 Like Mænads who cry loud, Evoe! Evoe! **1830** Carlyle *Misc.* (1872) III. 2 The earth is giddy with their clangour, their evohes.

†**eˈvoid,** *v.* *Sc. Obs.* Also 6 **evode.** [ad. OF. *evuider* (mod.F. *évider*), f. *é-* out + *vuider*, f. *vuide* (Fr. *vide*) VOID.] *trans.* To clear out, empty out, remove, get rid of.

1533 Bellenden *Livy* v. (1822) 424 He maid thame [the army] to evode all dredoure, takand na fere of inemyis. **1536** —— *Cron. Scot.* (1821) I. p. lvii, Thay wald nevir evoid the displeseir..out of thair hertis.

evoir, obs. form of IVORY.

evoke (iːˈvəʊk), *v.* [ad. Fr. *évoquer*, ad. L. *ēvocāre*, f. *ē-* out + *vocāre* to call.]

1. *trans.* To call forth; *esp.* to summon up (spirits, etc.) by the use of magic charms.

1623-6 Cockeram, *Euoke*, to call forth. **1774** Warton *Hist. Eng. Poetry* xxxiii. (1840) II. 509 The only..use of this character is..to evoke the Devil, and summon the court. *Ibid.* lxi. (1840) III. 399 To evoke the Queen of the Fairies in the solitude of a gloomy grove. **1812** Landor *Ct. Julian* Wks. 1846 II. 503 If only warlike spirits were evoked By the war-demon. **1871** Tyndall *Fragm. Sc.* (ed. 6) II. ii. 15 It is a monster thus evoked that we see stalking abroad.

2. *transf.* and *fig.* **a.** In various associations, with more or less obvious allusion to magical operations.

1749 Warburton *Lett.* (1809) 13, I had no sooner evoked the name of Shakespear from the..former editions than a crew of strange devils..come chattering..round about me. **1757** Hurd *On Marks of Imitation*, Johnson evokes Fancy out of her *cave of cloud*. **1844** Emerson *Lect. Yng. Amer.* Wks. (Bohn) II. 293 Railroad iron is a magician's rod..to evoke the sleeping energies of land and water. **1868** Stanley *Westm. Ab.* i. 21 On his way he evoked with his staff the two springs of the Island.

b. To call (a feeling, faculty, manifestation, etc.) into being or activity. Also, To call up (a memory) from the past.

1856 Emerson *Eng. Traits, Wealth* Wks. (Bohn) II. 70 The ambition to create value evokes every kind of ability. **1866** Max Müller *Chips* (1880) III. vii. 183 He rather likes now and then to evoke a smile. **1877** Browning *La Saisiaz* (1878) 82 Be this, sad yet sweet, the sole Memory evoked from slumber! **1879** Carpenter *Ment. Phys.* I. i. §16. 18 Unable to evoke a respondent movement from the exhausted Muscles.

3. To summon (a cause) from an inferior to a superior tribunal (cf. AVOKE).

1752 Carte *Hist. Eng.* III. 474 *marg.*, The conference at York evoked to London. **1839** Keightley *Hist. Eng.* II. 10 She protested against the competency of the court, as the cause had been evoked to Rome by the Pope. **1851** Hussey *Papal Power* i. 5 Authority to evoke causes to Rome.

Hence **eˈvoked** ppl. a.; **eˈvoker,** one who or that which evokes; **eˈvoking** *vbl. sb.*, the action of the vb. EVOKE.

1849 S. R. Maitland *Illustr. Mesmerism* I. 49 Where do we read about magic circles, and evoked fiends, black cats, etc.? **1845** Mozley *Ess.* (1878) I. 121 An evoker of all his cleverness and ready wit. **1853** De Quincey *Autobiog. Sk.* Wks. I. 27 The playfulness of the scene is the very evoker of the solemn remembrances that lie hidden below. **1848** W. H. Kelly tr. *L. Blanc's Hist. Ten. Y.* II. 189 The evoking of this famous and terrible name provoked scandal.

†**ˈevolate,** *v.* *Obs.* *rare*⁻¹. [f. L. *ēvolāt-* ppl. stem of *ēvolāre*, f. *ē-* out + *volāre* to fly.] *intr.* To fly forth or away.

1657 Tomlinson *Renou's Disp.* 369 Flowers..at length evolating in dawen.

†**evoˈlatic,** *a.* *Obs.*⁻⁰ [f. L. *ēvolāt-* ppl. stem of *ēvolāre* (see prec.) + -IC.] 'Flying abroad'. Bailey (*folio*, 1730-6).

1775 in Ash; hence in mod. Dicts.

†**evoˈlatical,** *a.* *Obs.*⁻⁰ = prec.

1656-81 in Blount *Glossogr.* **1721-1800** in Bailey; hence in mod. Dicts.

†**evoˈlation.** *Obs.* Also 7 in bad form **evolition.** [ad. late L. *ēvolātiōn-em*, n. of action f. *ēvolāre*: see EVOLATE.] The action of flying out or away.

1644 Bp. Hall *Free Prisoner* §7 (T.) These walls of flesh forbid that evolation [of the soul]. **1645** —— *Remedy Discontents*, How did he triumph over your cruelty? how did he by his happy evolation make all those stones precious? **1664** Evelyn *Sylva* (1776) 31 Forest trees and woods..hinder the necessary evolition of this superfluous moisture. **1669** J. Rose *Eng. Vineyard* (1675) 22 Salts and spirits which a more moderate fire would preserve from evolition and flying away.

†**eˈvoluble,** *a.* *Obs.* *rare*⁻¹. [f. as if ad. L. **ēvolūbilis*, f. *ēvolvĕre*: see EVOLVE. Cf. VOLUBLE.] Rolling swiftly away.

1667 H. More *Div. Dial.* (1713) 558 That Life which is consumed by an evoluble succession.

‖**évolué** (evɔlɥe), *sb.* (and *a.*). [Fr., pa. pple. of *évoluer* to evolve.] An African (from a part of Africa formerly Belgian or French) who has been educated on European principles; an African who has adopted European modes of thought. Hence as *adj.*, designating, pertaining to, or characteristic of such a person; Europeanized.

1953 J. Packer *Apes & Ivory* vii. 80 'Exactly what is an *evolué*?' 'A Native of some education—a clerk or an office worker.' **1956** K. Hulme *Nun's Story* xi. 183 A first generation to work with whites..that queer lonely society of the *évolués* which was neither black nor white. **1958** *Listener* 9 Oct. 549/1 The man of colour, tribal as well as *évolué*, in every French territory had to say 'yes' or 'no' to a continued relationship within the French community. **1961** P. Mason *Common Sense about Race* IV. i. 113 The man who had become entirely 'évolué' or assimilated to Western ways. **1970** D. Caute *Fanon* i. 12 The black French *évolué* (the relatively educated, Europeanized and privileged native).

evolute (ˈɛvəljuːt), *a.* and *sb.* [ad. L. *ēvolūt-us*, pa. pple. of *ēvolvĕre* to roll out: see EVOLVE.]

A. *adj.*

a. ***evolute curve*** = B 1. **b.** (See quot. 1835.)

1796 Hutton *Math. Dict.* I. 453/1 s.v., The values of the absciss and ordinate of the Evolute curve EC. **1828** —— *Course Math.* II. 351 Any radius of curvature..is a tangent to the evolute curve at the point F. **1835** Lindley *Introd. Bot.* (1848) II. 65 Exorhizie evolute, or fully developed.

B. *sb.*

1. *Math.* A curve which is the locus of the centres of curvature of another curve (its *involute*), or the envelope of all its normals. ***radius of the evolute, imperfect evolute*** (see quots. 1751).

The end of a stretched thread unwound from the evolute will trace the involute; hence the names.

1730-6 in Bailey (folio). **1751** Chambers *Cycl.* s.v., The radius of the Evolute is the part of the thread comprised between any point where it is a tangent to the evolute, and the correspondent point where it terminates in the new curve. *Ibid.*, *Imperfect Evolute*..This curve would be a sort of evolute, and would have its radii; but an imperfect evolute, since the radii are not perpendicular to the first curve. **1852** G. Salmon *Higher Plane Curves* 110 If we take a fourth harmonic to the tangent and the lines joining its point of contact to two fixed points, we shall have a line which may be called the quasi-normal, and its envelope will be a quasi-evolute. **1881** W. Spottiswoode in *Nature* No. 624. 571 The phosphorescence takes the form, approximately, of the evolute of an ellipse. **1882** Proctor in *Knowledge* 24 Nov. 423 The evolute of a circle is a point—the circle's centre. The evolute of a straight line is either of the points at infinity in direction perpendicular to the line.

¶**2.** Erroneously used for INVOLUTE. Also *attrib.* in ***evolute-cog***, a cog the two sides of which are involutes of circles.

1812-6 Playfair *Nat. Phil.* (1819) I. 81 One of the curves there proposed [for the teeth of wheels] is the evolute of the circle. **1860** *Merc. Marine Mag.* VII. 140 A wheel, having on its circumference a series of evolute-cogs.

3. The developed surface, 'development', of a cone or cylinder. *rare.*

1793 Smeaton *Edystone L.* §60 *note*, The figure thus formed would become a kind of evolute of the surface of the whole building.

evolute (ˈiːvəljuːt), *v.* orig. *U.S.* [Back-formation from EVOLUTION.]

1. *intr.* To develop by evolution; = EVOLVE *v.* 8.

1884 *Cambridge* (Mass.) *Tribune* 15 Aug., If those miserable vagrants could only evolute into respectable people there would be converts to evolution at once. **1891** *Daily News* 11 Dec. 6/3 No one had started lower than himself, but now he had evoluted. **1907** *Daily Chron.* 21 Oct. 4/4 This movement, which started so promisingly, and ought by now to have evoluted into honourable well-paid work. **1926** W. J. Locke *Old Bridge* IV. xv, You must let me evolute my own way, *carissima*. **1966** *New Statesman* 22 Apr. 575/3 Teenagers who had evoluted in their own style like the fauna of Australia.

2. *trans.* To evolve, develop. *Journalese.*

1885 *Rep. Indian Affairs* (U.S.) 33 The changed mode of life..will eventually 'evolute' 'Poor Lo' to a higher sphere. **1896** *Daily News* 29 Feb. 6/2 It was to be an attempt to 'evolute' Mr. Tom Hughes's 'Tom Brown' in various directions, to glorify him and bring him up to date. **1899** *Ibid.* 28 Dec. 6/2 The book plate of a millionaire who yesterday was a barman..may in the course of a few generations be 'evoluted' into a family emblem fit to take rank with the arms of any aristocratic Briton. **1930** *Publishers' Weekly* 4 Jan., Many more individual factors which are evoluted from knowledge gained by years of experience as well as teaching.

evolutility (iːˌvɒljuːˈtɪlɪtɪ). [f. L. *ēvolūt-* (ppl. stem of *ēvolvĕre*: see EVOLVE. Cf. *contractility*.] 'The faculty possessed by all substances which are capable of self-nourishment to manifest the nutritive acts by changes of form, or of volume, or of structure' (*Syd. Soc. Lex.* 1884).

evolution (ɛvəˈljuːʃən, iːvəˈljuːʃən). [ad. L. *ēvolūtiōn-em* (recorded in the sense 'unrolling of a book'), n. of action f. *ēvolvĕre*: see EVOLVE. Cf. Fr. *évolution.*]

I. The process of unrolling, opening out, or disengaging from an envelope.

1. The opening out or unfolding of what is wrapped up (*e.g.* a roll, a bud, etc.); *fig.* the spreading out before the mental vision (of a series of objects); the appearance in orderly succession of a long train of events. Also *concr.* 'the series of things unfolded or unrolled' (J.).

1647 H. More *Poems* 150 Evolution Of outward forms spread in the worlds vast spright. **1667** —— *Div. Dial.* i. §15 The whole evolution of..ages, from everlasting to everlasting, is..represented to God at once. **1678** Cudworth *Intell. Syst.* 878 The Periods of Divine Providence, here in this World, are commonly Longer, and the Evolutions thereof Slower. **1742** Young *Nt. Th.* IV. 510 Beyond long ages, yet roll'd up in shades..What evolutions of surprising fate! **1762** —— *Resignation* II. xxxvi, Flowers..When ev'ning damps and shades descend, Their evolutions close. **1759** Johnson *Idler* No 70 ¶11 He whose task is to reap and thresh will not be contented without examining the evolution of the seed. **1843** G. S. Faber *Sacred Cal. Proph.* (1844) I. p. xv, The evolution of time has served only to confirm me in..the honest persuasion, that, etc.

2. Emergence or protrusion from the folds of an envelope. Frequent in *Biol.*

1762 Hudson in *Phil. Trans.* LII. 500 Our author asserts, That every Fungus is contained in an entire and perfect state ..in the egg, or as it is called, the seed, and wants nothing but evolution, in order to imbibe the necessary juices. **1800** *Med. Jrnl.* III. 5, I determined to leave Nature undisturbed, to effect the evolution of the child. **1817** T. Say *Hessian Fly*, Entom. Wks. 1859 II. 7 The specious circumstance of its evolution from the pupa itself of the destroying larva. **1887** *Gray's Anat.* (ed. Pike) 85 The first appearance of the eye consists in the protrusion or evolution from the medullary wall of the..interbrain of a vesicle.

3. The process of evolving, disengaging, or giving off (gas, heat, light, sound, etc.); an instance of this process.

1806 *Med. Jrnl.* XV. 289 A powerful evolution of the muriatic acid is painful and dangerous. **1816** J. Smith *Panorama Sc. & Art* II. 278 Two dissimilar metals are not essential to the evolution of galvanism. **1839** G. Bird *Nat. Philos.* 138 The evolution of musical sounds during the cooling of heated metals. **1875** Lyell *Princ. Geol.* II. II. xxxii. 214 There is a constant evolution of heat and light. **1878** Huxley *Physiogr.* 82 Decomposed by the acid with the evolution of carbonic acid gas.

4. *Math.* **a.** *Geom.* The unfolding or opening out of a curve: †(*a*) the straightening it out, through all intermediate degrees of curvature, till it becomes a straight line; (*b*) the production from it of an involute, such as would be traced by the end of a stretched flexible thread unwound from the outside of the curve.

1700 *Phil. Trans.* XXII. 445 By the Equable Evolution of a Circle, I mean such a gradual approach of its Periferie to Rectitude, as that all its parts do together and equally evolve or unbend. **1727-51** Chambers *Cycl.*, *Evolution*, in geometry, the unfolding, or opening of a curve, and making it describe an evolvent. **1828** Hutton *Course Math.* III. 352 To determine the nature of the curve by whose evolution the common parabola AB is described.

b. *Arith.* and *Alg.* The extraction of any root from any given power; the reverse of involution.

1706 in Phillips (ed. Kersey). **1734** *Builder's Dict.*, *Evolution*, The Extraction of Roots out of Powers. **1806** Hutton *Course Math.* I. 200 Evolution is..the method of finding the square root, cube root, etc., of any given quantity. **1859** Barn. Smith *Arith. & Algebra* (ed. 6) 262 Evolution is the inverse of Involution; being the method of finding any root of a given quantity.

5. a. The process of evolving, developing, or working out in detail, what is implicitly or potentially contained in an idea or principle; the development of a design, argument, etc.

1677 Hale *Prim. Orig. Man.* III. ii. 259 It must have potentially at least the whole Systeme of Humane Nature, or at least that Ideal Principle..thereof, in the evolution whereof the complement and formation of the Humane Nature must consist. **1768** Johnson *Pref. to Shaks.* Wks. IX. 247 His plays..in the successive evolutions of the design, sometimes produce seriousness and sorrow, and sometimes levity and laughter. **1774** J. Bryant *Mythol.* I. p. xv, They [certain names] may be again resolved by an easy and fair evolution. **1820** Coleridge *Let. C. A. Tulk* (in *Sotheby's Catal.* May 1890), I had arrived at this conclusion by necessary evolution from the First Principle of my Philosophy. **1870** R. W. Dale *Week-day Serm.* iv. 83 Some slip in the evolution of an argument. **1878** Simpson *Sch. Shaks.* I. 140 A chorus is introduced to make up for the want of dramatic evolution.

b. *concr.* The result of this process.

1820 Coleridge *Let. C. A. Tulk* (in *Sotheby's Catal.* May 1890), The sensible world is but the evolution of the Truth, Love, and Life, or their opposites, in Man. **1856** R. A. Vaughan *Mystics* (1860) I. 19 Philosophers who believe themselves organs of the world-soul, and their systems an evolution of the Deity. **1862** F. Hall *Hindu Phil. Syst.* 55 *note*, In the Sánkhya, happiness, misery, will, and activity.. are evolutions from..the internal organ.

6. *Biol.* **a.** Of animal and vegetable organisms or their parts: The process of developing from a rudimentary to a mature or complete state.

1670 *Phil. Trans.* V. 2078 By the word Change [in Insects] is nothing else to be understood but a gradual and natural Evolution and Growth of the parts. **1745** Needham *Microsc. Disc.* Introd. 1 Nature..ever exerting its Fecundity in a successive Evolution of organised Bodies. **1791** E. Darwin *Bot. Gard.* II. 8 *note*, The gradual evolution of the young animal or plant from its egg or seed. **1801** *Med. Jrnl.* V. 588 A series of experiments on the evolution of the Chick. **1805** *Ibid.* XIV. 336 The formation and evolution of this part of the brain. **1839** Johnston in *Proc. Berw. Nat. Club* I. 201 Masses of eggs, in different stages of their evolution, are met with in the same nest.

b. ***theory of evolution***: the hypothesis (first propounded under that name by Bonnet 1762) that the embryo or germ, instead of being brought into existence by the process of fecundation, is a development or expansion of a pre-existing form, which contains the rudiments of all the parts of the future organism. Also called 'the theory of Preformation'; the latter name is now preferred, to avoid confusion with the following sense.

1831 [see EPIGENESIS]. **1877** HUXLEY *Encycl. Brit.* VIII. 745.

c. The origination of species of animals and plants, as conceived by those who attribute it to a process of development from earlier forms, and not to a process of 'special creation'. Often in phrases ***doctrine, theory of evolution.***

1832 LYELL *Princ. Geol.* II. 11 The testacea of the ocean existed first, until some of them by gradual evolution, were improved into those inhabiting the land. **1852** H. SPENCER *Developement Hypoth.* Ess. (1883) I. 381 Those who cavalierly reject the Theory of Evolution, as not adequately supported by facts, seem quite to forget that their own theory is supported by no facts at all. **1859** DARWIN *Orig. Spec.* vii. (1873) 201 At the present day almost all naturalists admit evolution under some form. **1863** E. V. NEALE *Anal. Th. & Nat.* 185 The diversity of species has arisen by the evolution of one species out of another. **1881** SIR J. HOOKER in *Nature* No. 619. 446 The doctrine of the orderly evolution of species under known laws.

7. The development or growth, according to its inherent tendencies, of anything that may be compared to a living organism (*e.g.* of a political constitution, science, language, etc.); sometimes contrasted with ***revolution***. Also, the rise or origination of anything by natural development, as distinguished from its production by a specific act; 'growing' as opposed to 'being made'.

1807 KNOX & JEBB *Corr.* I. 367 Its [our British constitution's] tardy evolution bespeaks something fitter to endure. **1833** CHALMERS *Const. Man* (1835) II. vii. 39 When commerce is left to its own spontaneous evolutions. **1837** SIR F. PALGRAVE *Merch. & Friar* (1844) 138 Our constitutional form of government has been produced by evolution. **1847** GROTE *Greece* II. xvii. (1862) II. 431 The same great evolution of Scythian power. **1873** H. SPENCER *Study Sociol.* v. 98 Psychology..deals with the evolution of the faculties..by what processes..ideas grow from concrete to abstract and from simple to complex.

8. The formation of the heavenly bodies according to the received theory which supposes it to have taken place by the concentration and consolidation of cosmic matter.

1850 NICHOL *Archit. Heav.* Pt. III. (*title*) Psyche, or Evolution. *Ibid.* 239 (*heading of page*) Universal Evolution. **1851** *Ibid.* (ed. 9) 289 As on Earth, there is [*sic*] also—ruling these high Heavens—vast processes of evolution. **1880** HAUGHTON *Phys. Geog.* i. 2 The idea of the evolution of planets is due to the great astronomer..Laplace.

9. In recent philosophical speculation used in a more comprehensive sense, of which the senses 6a, 6c, 7, 8 are regarded as special applications. ***social evolution***, the development of human societies.

According to Herbert Spencer, whose views have greatly influenced not only the technical but also the popular use of the word, all the changes in the universe, whether material or psychical, are phenomena either of Evolution or of the reverse process of Dissolution; his definition of the former is quoted below.

1853 H. MARTINEAU tr. *Comte's Positive Philos.* II. VI. 156 The elements of our social evolution are connected, and always acting on each other. **1862** H. SPENCER *First Princ.* II. xvii. §145 (1875) 396 The formula finally stands thus:—Evolution is an integration of matter and concomitant dissipation of motion; during which the matter passes from an indefinite, incoherent homogeneity to a definite, coherent heterogeneity; and during which the retained motion undergoes a parallel transformation. **1865** GEO. ELIOT in *Fortn. Rev.* I. 54 The high complexity of the causes at work in social evolution. **1878** J. SULLY in *Encycl. Brit.* VIII. 765 Mental evolution is a progressive composition of units of feeling in more and more complex forms. *Ibid.*, Mr. Spencer's elaboration of the subject of social evolution has not been carried far enough. **1883** A. BARRATT *Phys. Metempiric* 32 The laws of Evolution apply to both universes..a universe of material forces, and a universe of conscious states. **1885** CLODD *Myths & Dr.* II. i. 144 Evolution is advance from the simple to the complex. **1907** J. LONDON *Iron Heel* viii. 113 You fellows have studied business..but you have not studied social evolution at all. **1958** A. R. RADCLIFFE-BROWN *Method in Social Anthropol.* II. v. 179 In social evolution societies with more complex structure or organisation have been progressively developed from less complex forms.

II. A tactical movement (and derived senses).

10. *Mil.* and *Naut.* The unfolding or opening out of a body of troops or squadron of ships; hence *gen.* any movement or change of position, such as counter-marching, wheeling, etc., required in the due disposition of a force, whether for review, or for active operations. Also *fig.*

1622 F. MARKHAM *Bk. War* IV. viii. 151 But if it be to performe any Evolution or alteration of figure..then he shall see that they obserue at least six foote distance.. betweene one Horseman and another. [**1697** P. HOSTE (*title*) L'Art des Armées Navales, ou Traité des Evolutions Navales]. **1704** COCKER App. *Terms of War, Evolutions*, when a Body of Men change their form..This is done by doubling of Ranks or Files, Counter-marches, or Wheelings. **1751** CHAMBERS *Cycl.* s.v., By naval evolutions he [Hoste] means, the motions made by a fleet, squadron, or naval armament, in order to put themselves into a proper disposition for attacking the enemy, or defending themselves with the most advantage. **1796–7** *Instr. & Reg. Cavalry* (1813) 90 This countermarch of each division is an evolution of great utility. **1836** THIRLWALL *Greece* II. xv. 307 The Persian ships were turned by the wind and the waves, their evolutions were thwarted. **1853** STOCQUELER *Mil. Encycl.* s.v., That evolution is best which, with a given number of men, may be executed in the least space. **1878** BOSW. SMITH *Carthage* 253 The surrounding country was level and suitable to the evolutions of cavalry.

fig. **1771** BURKE *Corr.* (1844) I. 296 That versatility, those sudden evolutions..have something derogated from the credit of all public professions. **1841** D'ISRAELI *Amen. Lit.* (1867) 580 Jonson's intense observation was microscopical when turned to the minute evolutions of society. **1847** HELPS *Friends in C.* (1873) I. vii. 90 Evolutions of patience and temper are performed at the fireside.

11. *transf.* **a.** A wheeling about; a movement in dancing, gymnastics, etc. Also, one of the regulated and recurring movements of a portion of a machine.

a **1691** BOYLE (J.), The spontaneous coagulation of the little saline bodies was preceded by almost innumerable evolutions. **1770** LANGHORNE *Plutarch* (1879) I. 79/1 They move in an agreeable manner, performing certain involutions and evolutions in a quick measure. **1823** J. BADCOCK *Dom. Amusem.* 41 Clouds..of a dark brown colour, floating in varied evolutions. **1825** J. NICHOLSON *Operat. Mechanic* 73 The various evolutions and positions to which every revolution of the wheel subjects each paddle. **1833** J. HOLLAND *Manuf. Metals* II. 214 The short evolution which the bar has to traverse, not being more than one fourth of a circle. **1837** *New Monthly Mag.* LI. 471 A perfect artiste of the ballet..going through her admirable evolutions. **1850** MRS. STOWE *Uncle Tom's C.* xi, Haley.. made him..perform various evolutions to show his muscles.

†**b.** A winding about, an intricate form. *Obs.*

1763 JOHNSON 5 July in *Boswell*, It is not in the showy evolutions of buildings..that the wonderful immensity of London consists. **1774** J. BRYANT *Mythol.* I. 270 Roots.. and sprays are often so fantastic in their evolutions as to betray a remote resemblance [to a human fabric].

III. 12. In etymological sense: The action of rolling (anything) out on a spindle. *rare.*

1880 R. OWEN *Sanctorale Cathol.* 271 From the horrible manner of his death by the evolution of his intestines, Italians regard him [St. Elmo] as their advocate against spasmodic pains.

evolutional (ɛvəˈljuːʃənəl), *a.* [f. prec. + -AL¹.] Of or pertaining to evolution; due to or produced by evolution.

1862 F. HALL *Hindu Philos. Syst.* 181 *note*, The Upanishads..describe Brahma..as unchangeable; and this notion would be contravened by that of his being an evolutional material cause. **1874** MORLEY *Compromise* (1886) 209 The evolutional theory of society.

evoˈlutionally, *adv.* [-LY².] In an evolutional way.

1922 O. LODGE *Raymond Revised* 207 They would not be apparent to us now, with our particular evolutionally-derived sense organs. **1969** *Sci. Jrnl.* Jan. 48/2 High fertility is evolutionally profitable only under favourable conditions.

evoˈlutionarily, *adv.* [f. EVOLUTIONARY *a.* + -LY².] In an evolutionary way; from an evolutionary point of view.

1945 *Scrutiny* XIII. III. 163 The development of a balanced, critical prose style is of course a compensating (and evolutionarily necessary) virtue, but one that itself is perhaps evidence of a failing creativity. **1969** R. B. FULLER *Operating Man. Spaceship Earth* viii. 117 We cannot have mass production unless we have mass consumption. This was effected evolutionarily by the great social struggles of labor to increase wages and spread the benefits. **1970** *Nature* 5 Sept. 1006/2 The transport mechanism, probably universal in cells, is primitive and conservative evolutionarily.

evolutionary (ɛvəˈljuːʃənərɪ), *a.* [f. as EVOLUTIONAL *a.* + -ARY.]

1. Of or pertaining to evolution or development; evolutional.

1846 WORCESTER cites *Eclectic Rev.* **1875** *N. Amer. Rev.* CXX. 255 The bond of continuity which makes man the central link between his ancestors and his posterity is evolutionary. **1883** H. DRUMMOND *Nat. Law in Spir. W.* xii. (1884) 407 The development throughout obeys the evolutionary law in being from the general to the special.

b. Of language, opinions, methods, etc.: In accordance with the theory of evolution. Hence qualifying personal designations: Following evolutionary methods.

1864 F. HALL in Wilson tr. *Vishnu Purana* III. 25 The evolutionary doctrine. **1881** G. ALLEN *Vignettes fr. Nat.* x. 93 These self-same..outer flowers..make the guelder rose so interesting a plant in the eyes of the evolutionary biologist. **1876** C. E. APPLETON *Life & Lit. Relics* (1881) 184 Its process, as we should now say in evolutionary language. **1881** ROMANES in *Nature* XXIII. 501 The evolutionary psychologist.

2. Of, pertaining to, or performing the evolutions or manœuvres of troops or ships of war.

1859 in WORCESTER. **1861** J. H. MACDONALD *Evolut. Battalion* 8 The first object of all evolutionary operations in the field..is to move towards the enemy. **1881** *Army & Navy Gaz.* 23 July 570/2 The French Evolutionary squadron will visit Oran..Algiers, etc. **1890** *Daily News* 9 May 5/6 The evolutionary grounds on which the special review is to be held..cover a magnificent area of level steppe.

evolutionism (ɛvəˈljuːʃənɪz(ə)m). [f. as prec. + -ISM.] The theory of evolution or development.

1869 HUXLEY in *Sci. Opin.* 28 Apr. 487/1 The three schools of geological speculation which I have termed Catastrophism, Uniformitarianism, and Evolutionism. **1872** E. FRY in *Spectator* 21 Sept. 1201 Evolutionism does not propose to explain the unfolding of life out of dead matter. **1873** DAWSON *Earth & Man* xiv. 348 Evolutionism ..excluded creation and theism.

evolutionist (ɛvəˈljuːʃənɪst). [as prec. + -IST.]

1. One who upholds the doctrine of evolution; an adherent of evolutionism.

1859 DARWIN *Orig. Spec.* vii. (1873) 189 It is admitted by most evolutionists that mammals are descended from a marsupial form. **1873** DAWSON *Earth & Man* xiv. 349 The evolutionist is really in a position of absolute antagonism to the idea of creation.

b. *attrib.* or *adj.*

1877 DAWSON *Orig. World* xv. 338 The prevalence of the evolutionist philosophy. **1882** *Athenæum* 24 June 789/2 Right conduct on evolutionist principles can only be such conduct as is in accord with the conditions of social vitality.

2. An advocate of the theory of 'Evolution', as opposed to Epigenesis. Cf. EVOLUTION 6 b.

1875 tr. *Schmidt's Desc. & Darw.* 45 The vehement dispute..between Evolutionists and Epigenists.

3. One skilled in evolutions.

1864 in WEBSTER; and in mod. Dicts.

evolutionistic (ˌɛvəljuːʃəˈnɪstɪk), *a.* [f. prec. + -IC.] **a.** Tending to support the doctrine of evolution. ¶**b.** Tending to produce evolution.

1883 *Daily News* 21 Sept. 6/1 The address was a striking array of facts, all evolutionistic in their character. **1885** C. DIXON in *Nature* XXXIII. 128 Nor do I consider it fair..to infer that isolation, etc., do not explain the cause of variation, and therefore that they fail as evolutionistic agents.

evoˈlutionize, *v. rare.* [f. EVOLUTION + -IZE.] *trans.* To develop by evolution.
Hence **evoˈlutionized** *ppl. a.*

1883 *Westm. Rev.* July 273 Our knowledge of evolutionized human nature. **1885** *Brit. & For. Evang. Rev.* July 436 Those who speak of angels do not speak of them as evolutionised men.

evolutive (ˈɛvəljuːtɪv), *a.* [f. L. *ēvolūt-* ppl. stem of *ēvolvĕre*: see EVOLVE.] Pertaining or tending to evolution or development; promoting evolution.

1874 LEWES *Problems Life & Mind* I. 112 The special evolutive conditions, namely, etc. **1883** *Nature* 15 Feb. 367 The life of the sieve tubes may be divided into 2 periods; the evolutive and the passive. **1886** F. MYERS in *Phantasms of the Living* I. Introd. 43 We have induced [by hypnotism] a change of personality which is not *per se* either evolutive or dissolutive.

evolvable (ɪˈvɒlvəb(ə)l), *a.* Also **-ible** (-ɪb(ə)l). [f. next + -ABLE.] That may be evolved; capable of being drawn out or developed.

1869 BROWNING *Ring & Bk., Pope* 231 Truth..lies.. everywhere, in these, Not absolutely in a portion, yet Evolvible from the whole. **1888** J. I. SWANDER in *Microcosm* (N.Y.) Oct., Setting free that substantial form of force— either light or electricity—evolvable by these respective processes.

evolve (ɪˈvɒlv), *v.* [ad. L. *ēvolvĕ-re* to roll out, unroll, f. *ē* out + *volvĕre* to roll.]

1. *trans.* To unfold, unroll (something that is wrapped up); to open out, expand. Almost always *fig.*

a **1641**, **1647** [see EVOLVED *ppl. a.*] **1677** HALE *Prim. Orig. Man.* I. i. 31 This little active Principle as the Body increaseth..evolveth, diffuseth and expandeth if not his Substantial Existence, yet his Energy and Virtue. **1835** I. TAYLOR *Spir. Despot.* ii. 54 If we wish to see..the Voluntary Principle fully evolved and ripened under a summer heat. **1839–40** W. IRVING *Wolfert's R.* (1855) 67 Mr. Glencoe.. would stimulate and evolve the powers of his mind. **1855** H. REED *Lect. Eng. Lit.* vi. (1878) 188 Their condensed wisdom may be evolved for new applications.

†**b.** *lit.* To unwind (a thread, also a curved line). *Obs. rare.*

1730–6 BAILEY (folio), *Evolute*, the first curve supposed to be opened, or evolved, which being opened describes other curves. **1796** HUTTON *Math. Dict.*, *Evolute*..is any curve supposed to be evolved or opened, by..beginning to evolve or unwind the thread from the other end, keeping the part evolved, or wound off, tight stretched. **1811** —— *Course Math.* II. 334 If AE, BF, etc. be any positions of the thread, in evolving or unwinding; it follows, etc.

2. To disengage from wrappings, disclose gradually to view; to disentangle; to set forth in orderly sequence. (Only with reference to immaterial objects, though often consciously *fig.* from the physical sense).

1664 H. MORE *Myst. Iniq.* xvii. 63, I have not yet evolved all the intangling superstitions that may be wrapt up. **1737** THOMSON *To Memory of Ld. Talbot* 144 He thro' the Maze of Falsehood urg'd it [the Truth] on, Till, at the last evolv'd, it full appear'd. **1744** AKENSIDE *Ep. to Curio*, Time.. Evolves their secrets, and their guilt proclaims. **1773** MONBODDO *Lang.* I. I. viii. 101 With so many various forms and substances, that it is difficult to evolve them and shew them by themselves. **1852** LD. COCKBURN *Jeffrey* I. 189 Jeffrey's..whole opinions and tastes were evolved in these articles. **1858** SEARS *Athan.* III. ix. 325 The outlines of Paul's

system of Pneumatology.. have been sufficiently evolved in the preceding pages.

3. *Math.* To extract (the root of a number or quantity). Cf. EVOLUTION 4 b.

1810 HUTTON *Course Math.* I. 202 To Evolve or Extract the Roots of Surd Quantities.

4. To give off, emit, as a product of chemical, vital, or other internal action; to liberate or disengage from a state of chemical combination.

1800 *Med. Jrnl.* III. 125 The expectorated fluid.. may.. evolve fetor. **1806** DAVY in *Phil. Trans.* XCVII. 9 The fixed alkali is not generated, but evolved, either from the solid materials employed, or from saline matter in the water. **1822** IMISON *Sc. & Art* II. 63 The chlorine will be evolved. **1844–57** G. BIRD *Urin. Deposits* (ed. 5) 80 Nitrogen and carbon evolved from the system.. in the form of urea and uric acid. **1869** PHILLIPS *Vesuv.* iii. 69 In September the vapours evolved from Vesuvius grew to be considerable.

5. To bring out (what exists implicitly or potentially): *e.g.* to educe (order from confusion, light from darkness, etc.); to deduce (a conclusion, law, or principle) from the data in which it is involved; to develop (a notion) as the result of reflection or analysis; to work out (a theory or system) out of pre-existing materials.

1831 CARLYLE *Sart. Res.* (1858) 47 An English Editor, endeavouring to evolve printed Creation out of a German printed and written Chaos. **1851** HUSSEY *Papal Power* iii. 172 New claims of authority.. were gradually evolved from the doctrine of the Supremacy. **1859** MILL *Liberty* (1865) 30 Other ethics than any which can be evolved from exclusively Christian sources. **1864** BOWEN *Logic* viii. 262 The particular instances are first stated as facts, and then the law they constitute is evolved. **1874** SAYCE *Compar. Philol.* vii. 296 The idea of a subject-pronoun was evolved last of all. **1883** MRS. PLUNKETT in *Harper's Mag.* Jan. 241/2, I evolved a satin-covered heart-shaped Christmas leaf.

6. Of circumstances, conditions, or processes: To give rise to, produce by way of natural consequence.

1851 LONGF. *Gold. Leg.* I. *Castle Vaultsberg*, The new diseases that human life Evolves in its progress. **1866** HUXLEY *Phys.* x. (1872) 236 The simple sensations which are thus evolved. **1868** HELPS *Realmah* xvii. (1876) 476 New felicities—evolved in each representation. **1879** *Spectator* 7 June 719 That habits of gregariousness tend eventually to evolve a morality.

7. To develop by natural processes from a more rudimentary to a more highly organized condition; to originate (animal or vegetable species) by gradual modification from earlier forms; in wider sense, to produce or modify by 'evolution'. (See EVOLUTION 6–9). Chiefly in *pass.* without reference to an agent.

1832 LYELL *Princ. Geol.* II. i. 14 The orang-outang, having been evolved out of a monad, is made slowly to attain the attributes and dignity of man. **1837** SIR F. PALGRAVE *Merch. & Friar* (1844) 204 Was the first Ichthyosaurus gradually evolved from some embryo substance? **1849** MURCHISON *Siluria* ii. (1867) 23 Lying upon them, and therefore evolved after them, other strata succeed. **1873** H. SPENCER *Study Sociol.* v. 102 Societies are evolved in structure and function as in growth. **1881** SOLLAS in *Science Gossip* No. 202. 217 The organism.. was evolved in the course of ages from some simpler form of life. **1884** E. P. ROE in *Harper's Mag.* Apr. 737/2 If God.. chooses to evolve His universe, why shouldn't He?

8. *intr.* for *refl.* in various of the above senses: To open out, expand; to come gradually into view; to arise by way of natural or logical consequence; to be developed by 'evolution'.

1799 S. TURNER *Anglo-Sax.* (1836) I. IV. iv. 288 When great political exigencies evolve.. they are usually as much distinguished by the rise of sublime characters. **1800** A. CARLYLE *Autobiog.* 488 The excellence of that character which gradually evolved on his admiring countrymen. **1827** G. S. FABER *Sacred Cal. Proph.* (1844) I. 201 Then come the days of blessedness, which both Daniel and John describe as evolving.. in the course of the present visible sub-lunary world. **1849** C. BRONTË *Shirley* v. 57 May feel ripe to evolve in foliage. **1863** W. PHILLIPS *Speeches* ix. 235 Everything else will evolve from it. **1879** H. SPENCER *Data of Ethics* §104. 269 How does mechanical science evolve from these experiences? **1881** *Student* II. 35 A tree evolves in obedience to his [God's] laws.

evolved (ɪ'vɒlvd), *ppl. a.* [f. prec. + -ED¹.] †**a.** Unfolded, opened up, made manifest or clear (*obs.*). **b.** Developed; developed by evolution.

a **1641** BP. MOUNTAGU *Acts & Mon.* (1642) 172 Speaking so plaine and in evolved termes. **1647** H. MORE *Song of Soul* II. iii. IV. xi, Evolved reason cannot stand at one Stoutly to guard thy soul from passion. **1857** H. REED *Lect. Eng. Poets* II. 268 The best efforts of mind are those which are purely self-evolved. **1884** H. SPENCER in *19th Cent.* XV. 12 By future more evolved intelligences, the course of things now apprehensible only in parts may be apprehensible all together. **1887** *Spectator* 29 Oct. 1456 Inorganic matter, like water, which is not an evolved product.

Hence, †**e'volvedly** *adv.*, explicitly, in express terms.

a **1641** BP. MOUNTAGU *Acts & Mon.* (1642) 77 In none of them [the Prophets] was it plainly, directly, evolvedly said and foretold, that, etc.

evolvement (ɪ'vɒlvmənt). [f. EVOLVE *v.* + -MENT.] The action of evolving, the condition of being evolved; evolution.

1845 STOCQUELER *Handbk. Brit. India* (1854) 168 India owes to its exertions.. the evolvement of the products of a soil unrivalled for its richness. **1852** *Blackw. Mag.* LXXI. 596 Eyes, heart, mind, all fixed on the wondrous.. evolvement of the story. **1866** *Eng. Leader* 22 Dec. 352 Jesus.. showed that he aspired at an evolvement, and not.. a revolution, though historically and philosophically it may be proved that the only real revolutions are evolvements. **1883** T. WRIGHT in *19th Cent.* No. 72. 280, I am in a position to speak.. not.. from any process of evolvement from an inner consciousness but from personal knowledge.

b. *concr.* in *pl.* The displayed folds (of a banner).

1849 JANE PORTER *Scot. Chiefs* (1854) 156 As its vast evolvements floated in the air, the cry of triumph.. burst from every heart.

evolvent (ɪ'vɒlvənt), *a.* and *sb.* *Math.* [ad. L. *ēvolvent-em*, pr. pple. f. *ēvolvĕre*: see EVOLVE.]

A. *adj.* That evolves. †*evolvent line*: the right line (the tangent to the evolute), the extremity of which is the locus of the involute. **B.** *sb.* **1.** The involute of a curve. **2.** (See quot. 1862.)

1708 tr. *Gregory's Prop. Catenaria* in *Misc. Cur.* II. 236 The Evoluent Line UF is a third Proportional to AC and CB. **1727–51** CHAMBERS *Cycl.*, *Evolvent*, in geometry.. the curve resulting from the evolution of a curve; in contradistinction to the evolute. **1796** in HUTTON *Math. Dict.* **1862** F. HALL *Hindu Philos. Syst.* Introd. 9 *note*, 'Originant' might answer, or 'evolvent' [for *prakṛiti*]; and 'originate' or 'evolute' for *vikṛiti*. **1882** E. B. COWELL in tr. *Sarva-darśana-saṃgraha* 221 That which is evolvent only [*note*, I borrow this term from Dr. Hall.].

evolver (ɪ'vɒlvə(r)). [f. EVOLVE *v.* + -ER¹.] One who, or that which, evolves.

1803 W. TAYLOR in *Ann. Rev.* I. 398 They may be.. useful as seminaries of instruction, useful as evolvers of merit. **1825** COLERIDGE in *Rem.* (1836) II. 345 The fates, the evolvers of the endless thread. **1883** MONIER-WILLIAMS *Relig. Th. in India* iii. 44 The male god Brahma.. the apparent Evolver of all the inferior forms.

evolvible: see EVOLVABLE.

evolving (ɪ'vɒlvɪŋ), *vbl. sb.* [f. EVOLVE + -ING¹.] The action of the vb. EVOLVE; an instance of the same. Also *attrib.*

1831 FARADAY *Exp. Res.* xlvii. 333 This evolving and involving motion continues. **1890** *Athenæum* 8 Feb. 184/2 He by himself planned everything, and gods, men, and things came into existence from his evolvings.

e'volving, *ppl. a.* [f. as prec. + -ING².]

1. That evolves; in quots. *intr.* **a.** Opening. **b.** issuing forth, emitted.

c **1720** PRIOR *Solomon* III. Poems 1723 I. 187 Ambrosial Odor.. Does round the Air evolving Scents diffuse. **1773** J. ROSS *Fratricide* (MS.) v. 800 Thou shalt quit Thy earthy prison, and evolving Heaven Shall snatch thee.

2. That is in process of evolution.

1862 H. SPENCER *First Princ.* II. xix. §149 (1875) 401 The genesis of the re-arrangement undergone by every evolving aggregate, is in itself one. **1883** H. DRUMMOND *Nat. Law in Spir. W.* (ed. 8) 244 The evolving batrachian. **1888** *Pall Mall G.* 21 Sept. 3/1 This evolving town council was a purely native growth.

‖**Evolvulus** (ɪ'vɒlvjʊləs). [mod.L., f. *ēvolvĕre* (see EVOLVE). Cf. CONVOLVULUS.] *Bot.* A genus of the Nat. Order *Convolvulaceæ*, containing about 60 species, natives chiefly of tropical America.

1847 in CRAIG. **1866** *Treas. Bot.*, *Evolvulus*.. bear entire usually small nearly sessile leaves, and small flowers, etc. **1884** in *Syd. Soc. Lex.*

†**e'vome**, *v.* *Obs.* [ad. L. *ēvomĕ-re*: see next.] = next. *lit.* and *fig.*

c **1450** *Mirour Saluacioun* 3446 On the thredde day therafter on the land hym [Jonas] evomed [*v.r.* kest out]. **1524** *St. Papers Hen. VIII*, VI. 231 He shall at the last, fynding tyme and oportunitie, evome and discouer his pestiferous intent. **1535** STEWART *Cron. Scot.* II. 308 Suddanelie it [stomack] will.. Evome agane all that it tuik befoir.

†**e'vomit**, *v.* *Obs.* Also 5–6 evomette, -et. [f. L. *ēvomit-* ppl. stem of *ēvomĕre*, f. *ē-* out + *vomĕre* to VOMIT.] *trans.* To vomit, throw out, eject (the contents of the stomach). Also *transf.* and *fig.*

1432–50 tr. *Higden* (Rolls) I. 65 That oper.. be seyde to deuoure waters and evomette theyme twyes in a day. **1550** BALE *Image Both Ch.* II. Pref., These hath he not yet all, as vnsauerye morsels evometed for Christ. **1578** BANISTER *Hist. Man* v. 82 If any part free from the same elaboration [in the spleen].. it is euomitted in to the Ventricle to a great purpose and vse. **1714** J. WYETH *Supp. to Ellwood's Autobiog.* (1765) 405 He hath evomitted Floods, not of Reproach only—but of the most malicious Slanders.

evomi'tation, erron. form for EVOMITION, q.v.

It occurs in some edd. of Swift *T. Tub* iv. (see quot. 1704 in next.)

†**evo'mition.** *Obs.* [ad. L. **ēvomitiōn-em*, n. of action f. *ēvomĕre*: see EVOMIT.] The action of vomiting forth. *lit.* and *fig.*

1653 GAUDEN *Hierasp.* Pref. to Rdr. 23 That evomition, or Gods spewing this Church of England out of his mouth. **1661** LOVELL *Hist. Anim. & Min.* 35 [Cows' milk] helps against the ephemeron or cantharides, causing the evomition of the same. **1704** SWIFT *T. Tub* (ed. 1) iv, He was to.. receive immediate Benefit either by Eructation or expiration, or Evomition. **1755** in JOHNSON; whence in mod. Dicts.

b. *concr.*

1674 DURANT in *Phil. Trans.* XLIV. 221 As it was not possible to gather the Evomitions of our Vulcano's.

evonymus: see EUONYMUS.

evorye, evour(e, obs. ff. IVORY.

evulgate (ɪ'vʌlgeɪt), *v.* *Obs.* or *arch.* [f. L. *ēvulgāt-* ppl. stem of *ēvulgāre*, f. *ē-* out + *vulgāre* to spread among the multitude, f. *vulgus* the multitude.] *trans.* To send out among the people, make commonly known or public; to divulge; to circulate, publish (a book).

1563–87 FOXE *A. & M.* (1596) 1085/1 He did euulgate and disperse abroad.. great numbers of bookes. **1804** W. TAYLOR in *Ann. Rev.* II. 689 Anecdotes.. in which many amusing particulars occur that had not before been compiled, or at least not evulgated here. **1822** *Blackw. Mag.* XII. 656 They may permit younger sisters in the craft to evulgate what they may have 'lisped in numbers'. **1831** *Fraser's Mag.* IV. 177 Haller, in 1732, evulgated the first edition of his Swiss poems.

evulgation (iːvʌl'geɪʃən). *Obs.* or *arch.* [f. as if ad. L. **ēvulgātiōn-em*, n. of action f. *ēvulgāre*: see prec.] The action of making commonly known; publishing, publication.

1638 W. SCLATER (Jun.) in *W. Sclater's Serm. Exper.* To Rdr., I was so studious of their Evulgation. **1730–6** in BAILEY (folio). **1786** (*title*) Advice to the Clergy of every Denomination.. with the Evulgation of the Resolutions of a late Congress held in Germany. **1797** W. TAYLOR in *Monthly Rev.* XXIV. 509 A century and half after the evulgation of Roman and Greek literature. **1807** F. WRANGHAM *Serm. on Transl. Script.* 3 Rebellion, as well as heresy, would accompany the evulgation of Scripture.

†**e'vulge**, *v.* *Obs.* [ad. L. *ēvulg-āre*: see EVULGATE.] = EVULGATE.

1611 CORYAT *Crudities* Ep. to Rdr., Being by so much the more doubtfull to evulge the same. **1654** T. KECK in *Sir T. Browne's Relig. Med.* Addr. to Rdr., I made this recueil meerly for mine own entertainment, and not with any intention to evulge it.

evulse (ɪv 'ʌls), *v.* [f. L. *ēvuls-*, *ēvellĕre* to pluck out.] *trans.* To pluck or pull out, tear away. Cf. EVULSED *ppl. a.*

1827 LAMB *Let.* 18 Sept. (1935) III. 131 Twas with some pain we were evuls'd from Colebrook. **1910** *Practitioner* June 786 Polypi (myomatous or mucous) may be evulsed or scraped away. **1926** *Daily Tel.* 6 Aug. 5/7 Until the tooth is loosened and finally evulsed.

†**e'vulsed**, *ppl. a.* *Obs.*⁻⁰ [ad. L. *ēvulsus*, pa. pple. of *ēvellĕre*, f. *ē-* out + *vellĕre* to pluck.] Plucked, pulled off or out by force.

1730–6 in BAILEY (folio). **1775** in ASH.

evulsion (ɪ'vʌlʃən). [ad. L. *ēvulsiōn-em*, n. of action f. *ēvellĕre*, f. *ē-* out + *vellĕre* to pluck. Cf. Fr. *évulsion*.] The action of pulling or plucking out by force; forcible extraction.

c **1611** CHAPMAN *Iliad* xxi. 171 Thrice he pluck'd [to get his lance out], and thrice sure Pelias barr'd His wish'd evulsion. **1661** LOVELL *Hist. Anim. & Min.* 340 The gall with rosin of Cedar hindereth the growing of hairs on the eyeliddes, after evulsion. **1721–1800** in BAILEY. **1865** WOOD *Homes without H.* 27 Its [the fur of the animal] evulsion produces no such disastrous effects. **1879** J. TIMBS in *Cassell's Techn. Educ.* IV. 107/1 Mr. L.... removed by evulsion both sides of the great toe-nail. **1884** in *Syd. Soc. Lex.*

evulsive (ɪ'vʌlsɪv). [f. L. *ēvuls-* ppl. stem of *ēvellĕre* (see prec.) + -IVE. Cf. F. *évulsif, -ive.*] 'An instrument used for evulsion, such as a tooth forceps' (*Syd. Soc. Lex.* 1884).

‖**evviva** (ɛv'viːva). [It., f. *e* (:—L. *et*) used intensively + *viva* (:—L. *vīvat*), optative of *vivere* to live.] The cry of 'Long live (the king)'; hence, a shout of applause.

1887 *Edin. Rev.* July 147 No loud evvivas from applauding Christendom.

Evzone, evzone ('ɛvzəʊn). [ad. mod.Gr. εὔζωνος *sb.*, f. Gr. εὔζωνος dressed for exercise, f. εὐ- EU- + ζώνη girdle (see ZONE *sb.* 3).] A member of a select infantry regiment in the Greek army, originally recruited from the Greek highlands and conspicuous for their uniform which includes a fustanella. Also *attrib.*

1897 W. K. ROSE *With Greeks in Thessaly* iii. 36 The Colonel placed at my disposal a guard of half-a-dozen Evzones. **1927** *Times* (weekly ed.) 10 Mar. 276/3 The massive upturned pompon clogs worn by the Evzone soldiers. **1941** 'R. WEST' *Black Lamb* II. 529 The petticoated Evzones who dealt with Italians were predominantly Albanians.

ew, obs. form of YEW.

†**'ewage**¹. *Obs.* [a. OF. (*jagounce*) *ewage*, (?jacinth) of the colour of water:—L. *aquāticus* in same sense, f. *aqua* water]. A precious stone having the colour of sea water.

1377 LANGL. *P. Pl.* B. II. 14 Hir fyngres were fretted with golde wyre, And þere-on red rubyes.. Orientales and ewages enuenymes to destroye. *c* **1430** LYDG. *Ballad of our Lady* xiv, Blewe ewage Stable as the loupe ewage of pitie.

†**ewage**². *Obs.* [AF., f. *ewe* (mod.F. *eau*) water + *-age* (see -AGE), as if repr. L. type **aquāticum*,

f. *aqua* water.] See quots.; also in med.Lat. form *ewagium.*

1706 in PHILLIPS (ed. Kersey). **1753** CHAMBERS *Cycl. Supp. Ewage,* Ewagium, in our old writers, the same with Aquage, which is toll paid for water-passage.

ewai, obs. form of AWAY.

ewden-drift. *Sc.* Also 7 ewindrift, 8 youden drift, 9 contracted form endrift. 'Snow raised, and driven by the wind' (Jam.).

1630–56 SIR R. GORDON *Hist. Earls Sutherl.* 246 Their fell such ane extream tempest, ewindrift, sharp snow, and wind, full in their faces. **1790** SHIRREFS *Poems* 285 When to my Meg I bend my tour, Thro' Ewden drift, or snawy-show'r. **1790** MORRISON *Poems* 121 (Jam.) The strongest wind.. Tho' mixt wi' hail, wi' rain or youden drift, Brings ay a calm at last. **1813** W. BEATTIE *Tales* 35 The first thing meets him is a dose Of styth endrift and hail.

'ewder. *Sc.* Also yowther. Vapour, smoke, fume.

1755 R. FORBES *Ajax his Speech* 4 Fan Hector try'd Thir barks to burn an' scowder.. He cou'd na bide the ewder. **1755** —— *Jrnl. fr. Lond. to Portsmouth* He was like to smore us i' the coach wi' the very ewder o't [his pipe]. **1814** *Northern Antiq.* 271 The yowther drifted sae high i' the sky, The sun worth a' sae red.

ewe (juː), *sb.*[1] Forms: α. 1 eowu (3 awe, ouwe), 6–8 ew, (6 eawe), 1– ewe. β. 4 yoo, 6 *Sc.* yeowe, ȝow, (ȝown), 6–7 *Sc.* ȝoue, 6–8 yew(e, 4–9 *Sc.* and *north. dial.* yow(e. [Com. Teut. and Aryan: OE. *eowu* (? *éowu*), corresp. to OFris. *ei* (MDu. *oie, eie,* Du. *ooi*), OHG. *ouwi, au, ou* (MHG. *awe, ou,* mod.HG. dial. *au-* in *aulamm* ewe-lamb), ON. *ær*:—OTeut. **awi-z*:—OAryan **owi-s*; cf. L. *ovi-s,* Gr. *ὄ(ϝ)ις,* OIr. *oi,* OSl. *ovĭ-ca,* Lith. *avì-s,* Skr. *avi.*

The OE. represents a type **ewwi*:—WGer. **awwi,* the word having assumed the ending of the short *a-* stems; cf. *dęnu* from OTeut. **dani-z.* It is disputed whether the diphthong is long (*éo*:—*eu* from *ęw*) or short (*eo,* a modification of *ę* due to the influence of the following *w*; cf. *eo* as *u-* umlaut of *e*). The latter view is favoured by the retention of the final *-u,* which is normal only in short stems.]

1. A female sheep.

α. *a* **700** *Laws of Ine* lv, Eowu biþ, mid hire ȝeonge sceape scilling weorþ. *c* **1000** ÆLFRIC Gen. xxxiii. 13 Ic hæbbe.. ȝ eeane eowa and ȝecelfe cy mid me. *a* **1100** in *Cod. Dipl.* IV. 307 To eastran two ewe mid twam lamban. *a* **1240** *Cuckoo Song* in Ritson *Anc. Songs* 3 Sumer is icumen in.. Awe bleteþ after lomb. *a* **1300** *Debate Soul & Body* in *Map's Poems* (Camd.) 335, I scholde have ben dumb as a schep, or as a nouwe. **1393** LANGL. *P. Pl.* C. XVIII. 21 (MS. T.) By meris mylk lyuede & Ewis. **1465** *Mann. & Househ. Exp.* (1841) 296 For a ram and xix ewes, pryse the pece, xx.*d.* **1599** *Broughton's Lett.* ii. 8 It is a poore flocke of sheepe where the Ew must beare the bell. **1667** MILTON *P.L.* XI. 649 Ewes and thir bleating Lambs. **1728** RAMSAY *Gentle Sheph.* II. iv, When.. I to milk the ewes first tried my skill. **1842** BISCHOFF *Woollen Manuf.* II. 293 They seldom mistake the ewe to which each lambkin belongs.

β. *c* **1386** CHAUCER *Sec. Nun's T.* 199 Sche sendeth here As meek as ever was eny lamb to yow. ? *a* **1400** *Chester Pl., Shepherds* I. 120 Be it weither or be it yoo. **1513** DOUGLAS *Aeneis* V. xiii. 22 In wirschip of Erix.. a blak ȝow to god of tempestis fell. **1535** COVERDALE *Ps.* lxxvii. 71 As he was folowinge the yowes greate with yonge. **1560** ROLLAND *Crt. Venus* Prol. 54 The Watter is compart to the ȝowrn. **1562** J. HEYWOOD *Prov. & Epigr.* (1867) 19 She can wynke on the yew, and wery the lam. **1578** LYTE *Dodoens* II. lxxv. 540 The Cheese that they use to make of Yeowes and Goates mylke. **1587** MASCALL *Govt. Cattle, Sheep* (1627) 249 There is also in the teats of.. yeaws a certaine stopping in some of their teats. **1616–61** HOLYDAY *Persius* 305 Bless thou my lambs! And make my tender yews the happy dams Of many young-ones. **1714** *Fr. Bk. of Rates* 51 Sheep, Yews per Head. **1781** BURNS *Death of Mailie,* Warn him.. To stay content wi' yowes at hame.

b. (See quot)

1879 A. GALLETLY *Wool* in *Cassell's Techn. Educ.* IV. 260/1 The term.. 'ewes' is applied in long-stapled wools, to the short, tender, inferior fleeces.

2. *transf.*

1610 B. JONSON *Alch.* v. v, [*To his sister*] *Kas.* Come on, you yew, you haue match'd most sweetly, ha you not? *a* **1700** B. E. *Dict. Cant. Crew, Ewe,* or *the White Ewe,* a Top-woman among the Canting Crew, very Beautiful. *Ibid., Strowling-morts*.. Travel the Countries, making Laces upon Ewes. **1725** *New Cant. Dict.,* Yews. **18..** JAMIESON *Rotten yow,* metaph., Applied to a person.. subjected to much expectoration.

3. *attrib.* and *Comb.,* as ***ewe-mutton, -trade***; also, **ewe-bught,** *Sc.* (see BOUGHT *sb.*[2]); **ewegang** (see quot. and GANG *sb.*); **ewe-hog** (see quot. and HOG); **ewe lamb,** a female lamb; also *fig.* (with spec. reference to *2 Sam.* xii.); **ewe-lease,** a pasture for ewes (see LEASE *sb.*[2]); **ewe-milk,** milk of ewes; also *attrib.*; **ewe-milker,** one who milks ewes; also **ewe-milking,** *vbl. sb.*; **ewe-teg,** a ewe in its second year (see TEG).

1724 RAMSAY *Tea-t. Misc.* (1733) I. 88 Will ye go to the *ew-bughts Marion And wear in the sheep wi' me? **1813** HOGG *Queen's Wake* 252 At ewe-bught, or at evening fold. **1836** HOR. SMITH *Tin Trump.* I. 157 Comes dancing in from the ewe-bughts the bright-eyed Bessie. **1769** BP. WILTON *Inclos. Act* 7 A certain sheep-walk called *ewegang.. the said ewegang shall remain. **1614** MARKHAM *Cheap Husb.* (1623) 106 The first year a male Lambe is called a weather-Hog and a female Lambe an *Ewe-Hog. **1388** WYCLIF *Gen.* xxi. 28 Abraham settide seuene *ewe lambren of the flok asidis. **1611** BIBLE *2 Sam.* xii. 3 Nothing saue one litle ewe lambe. **1828** SCOTT *F.M. Perth* v, I cannot afford the church my only and single ewe-lamb. **1884** TENNYSON *Becket* 81 The black sheep baaed to the miller's ewe-lamb. **1874** T. HARDY *Madding Crowd* I. xiv. 168 Over the snowy down or *ewe-lease on Weatherbury Upper Farm. **1549** *Compl. Scot.* vi. 42 Thai maid grit cheir of euyrie sort of mylk, baytht of ky mylk & *ȝoue mylk. **1818** SCOTT *Hrt. Midl.* xxxviii, Maybe ye may like the ewe-milk.. cheese better. **1815** —— *Guy M.* xxiii, A half-dressed *ewe-milker.. shut it [the door] in their faces. **1728** RAMSAY *Gentle Sheph.* II. iv, When.. I at *ewe-milking first sey'd my young skill. **1602** MARSTON *Ant. & Mel.* v., A good fat legge of *ewe mutton. **1888** *Daily News* 1 Nov. 7/3 (Meat) Ewe mutton.. improved in value. **1696** *Lond. Gaz.* No. 3194/4 There is 2 Rams.. and 7 or 8 *Ewe Tegs among them. **1890** *Daily News* 2 Sept. 2/7 The *ewe trade was extremely dull.

b. in the names of various plants, as **ewe-bramble,** *dial.,* the common bramble, *Rubus fruticosus*; **ewe-daisy,** *Potentilla Tormentilla*; **ewe-flower,** ? the daisy; **ewe-gowan,** *Sc.,* the common daisy, *Bellis perennis.*

1818 HOGG *Brownie of Bodsbeck* I. 215 (Jam.) Eneugh to make the pinks an' the ewe-gowans blush to the very lip. **1825** —— *Queen Hynde* 14 The little ewe-flower starr'd the lea. **1847–78** *Halliwell, Ewe-gowan,* the common daisy. *North.* **1853** G. JOHNSTON *Nat. Hist. E. Bord.,* Ewe Daisy, Potentilla Tormentilla. **1876** in BRITTEN & HOLLAND *Dict. Plant.-n.* **1888** *W. Somerset Word-bk., Ewe-brimble,* the common bramble, *Rubus fruticosus.*

ewe, *sb.*[2] *dial.* (See quot.)

1863 MORTON *Cycl. Agric.* in *Old C. & Farm. Wds.* (E.D.S.) 142 White ewe is a shelly kind of earth in the fens.

ewe, *v.* [f. EWE *sb.*[1]]

†**1.** *trans.* To yean, give birth to (a lamb). *Obs.*

1579 E. K. *Gloss. Spenser's Sheph. Cal.* Feb. 83 *Rather lambes,* that be ewed early. *c* **1660** HEXHAM *Dutch Dict., Spade geboren,* A Lambe Late ewed.

2. *trans.* To give a 'ewe-neck' look to.

1848 G. F. RUXTON in *Blackw. Mag.* LXIII. 730 The severities of a prolonged winter.. had robbed his bones of fat and flesh.. and 'ewed' his neck.

Hence **ewed** *ppl. a.*

c **1611** CHAPMAN *Iliad* IV. 116 The God of Light.. To whom a hundred first-ewed lambs vow thou.

ewe, obs. form of YEW.

Ewe ('eɪweɪ), *a.* and *sb.*[3] [Native name.] **A.** *adj.* Of or pertaining to a Negro people of West Africa or their language. **B.** *sb.* **a.** A member of this people; also *collect.* **b.** The language of this people.

1861 (*title*) Nya nyuie h'akpãle ene le wegbe me. The Four Gospels in the Ewe language. **1884** *Encycl. Brit.* XVII. 319/1 *Ewe Group*: Acra (Ga), Fantee, Ashantee, [etc.]. **1890** A. B. ELLIS *Ewe-speaking Peoples of Slave Coast* p. v, Tshi, Ga, Ewe, and Yoruba are now four distinct languages. **1902** *Encycl. Brit.* XXI. 115/1 *Upper Guinea family*... Ewe (Awuna, Agbosimi, Togo, Dahoman, Krepe, Fra, Appi). **1936** *Discovery* June 168/2 The Twi-, Ewe-, and Yoruba-speaking peoples succeed each other from west to east. **1950** D. JONES *Phoneme* 100 The Ewe word ma (not) is indistinguishable from mã (to divide). **1962** [see ASHANTI].

†**ewe ardaunt.** *Obs.* [a. OF. *ewe ardant* (mod. *eau ardente*), lit. 'burning water'.] Ardent spirit.

c **1315** SHOREHAM 9 So mey me nauȝt in ewe ardaunt That neth no wateris wyse.

ewelinge, ewinlynge, var. ff. EVENLING, *Obs.*

c **1375** *Sc. Leg. Saints, Paulus* 48 Als in-to sum othir thinge he wes to petir as ewelinge. *Ibid., Adrian* 480 Sa he mycht.. be to þame ewinlynge.

ewelle, obs. form of EVIL.

ewen, obs. form of YEWEN *a.*

ewe-neck. A thin hollow neck (in a horse).

1820 W. IRVING *Sketch-bk. Sleepy Hollow* (1887) 410 A broken-down plough-horse.. with a ewe neck, and a head like a hammer. **1856** 'STONEHENGE' *Brit. Sports* (ed. 3) 322 Between the two extremes of the ewe-neck and its opposite there are many degrees.

Hence **ewe-necked** *a.*

1704 *Lond. Gaz.* No. 45 18/4 A grey Mare.. Ewe-Neck'd. **1840** BARHAM *Ingol. Leg., Grey Dolphin,* His dapple-grey steed.. was a little ewe-necked. **1858** O. W. HOLMES *Aut. Breakf.-t.* (1883) 222 Drawn by a rat-tailed, ewe-necked bay. **1878** *Cumberld. Gloss., Yowe neck't,* the arch of the neck bending downwards.

†**'ewer**[1]. *Obs.* Forms: 4–7 ewer(e, 5 ewar(e, euwere, 6 y(ewre. [a. OF. *ewer* (Cotgr. *eauïer*):—L. *aquārius,* f. *aqua* (OF. *ewe,* mod. *eau*) water.] = EWERER.

1361 in Nichols *Royal Wills* 53 Davy, *q'est* Barber *et* Ewer. *c* **1450** *Bk. Curtasye* in *Babees Bk.* 641 An euwere in halle þere nedys to be.. He schalle gef water to gentil-men. **1461–83** *Liber Niger Edw. IV* in *Househ. Ord.* 84 Twoe yomen ewars.. that resceyveth of the sergeaunt all naperyes, basins, ewers, chauffyrs.. for the halle. **1601** F. TATE *Househ. Ord. Edw. II,* §50 (1876) 35 Thei shal carri the flesh, and the fish.. with the helpe of the Ewers from the kitchin to the dresser.

Hence †**'eweress,** a female 'ewerer'.

1509 HAWES *Past. Pleas.* IV. 20 The marshall yclipped was dame Reason, And the yewres also Observaunce.

ewer[2] ('juːə(r)). Forms: 4–5 ewere, 5–6 euer, ewar, (5 ewear, ewyr, hure, yore), 6 eure, (ower, ure, yower), 6–7 ewre, 7 eawer, eawr, 5– ewer. [ad. AF. **ewiere,* parallel with OF. *aiguiere* (mod. *aiguière*), *eviere* (17th c. in Cotgr.), repr. Lat. type **aquāria,* f. *aqua* water; cf. prec.]

1. 'A pitcher with a wide spout, used to bring water for washing the hands' (W.). In mod. use the trade name for a bedroom water-jug.

c **1325** *E.E. Allit. P.* B. 1457 þer wer bassynes ful bryȝt of brende golde clere, Enaumaylde with azer & eweres of sute. **14..** *MS. Cantab.* Ff. i. 6, f. 58 (Halliw.) Yore [= ewer]. **1413** LYDG. *Pilgr. Sowle* v. xi. (1483) 103 This sygne is Aquarius with his ewer. **1494** FABYAN VII. 345 He gaue to yᵉ abbot.. a basyn with an ewyr of syluer. **1513** DOUGLAS *Æneis* XIII. ix. 17 As quhow the crystall eweris [ed. **1710** eueris] to thair handis The watir gave. **1574** *Gifts to Queen* in Nichols *Progr. Q. Eliz.* I. 413 A very smale fountayne of golde with ower in it, enamuled. **1634** SIR T. HERBERT *Trav.* 73 The holding up aloft a silver Ewre, after washing. **1725** POPE *Odyss.* I. 179 The golden ewer a maid obsequious brings. **1815** SCOTT *Guy M.* xxiv, Ailie.. at that instant entered with basin and ewer.

2. *Comb.,* as ***ewer-wise.***

1599 MINSHEU *Dial. in Sp. & Eng.* 11/2 This pot made ewer wise.

ewer[3]. *dial.* Also 8 yewer, 9 ure, yure, yooer, yawer. [a. ON. **júðr* (Icel. *júgr,* Sw. *jur*):—OTeut. **euðr-,* ablaut-variant of **ûðr-,* whence UDDER.] = UDDER.

1787 GROSE *Provinc. Gloss., Ewer,* an udder. N. **1788** W. MARSHALL *E. Yorksh.* (E.D.S.) s.v., *Ewer* and *Yewer.* **1847–78** in HALLIWELL. **1873** *Swaledale Gloss. Yure,* an udder. **1878** *Cumberld. Gloss., Yooer, Yawer,* the udder of an animal.

ewer, ? corrupt form of OYER.

1583 STUBBES *Anat. Abus.* II. 106 Maye Byshops.. bee Iustices of Assises, Ewer, Determiner, and the lyke.

'ewerer. [f. EWER[1] or EWER-Y + -ER[1].] A servant who supplied guests, etc. at table with water to wash their hands.

c **1450** *MS. Sloane* 1986. 40 The ewerer [*v.r.* euwer] schal hele his lordes borde With dowbull napere at on bare worde. **1851** TURNER *Dom. Archit.* III. iii. 79 When the ewerer brought water. **1858** G. GILFILLAN *Mem.* in *Wyatt's Poet. Wks.* p. vii, At Anne Boleyn's marriage in July 1533.. Wyatt officiated as ewerer, in room of his father.

ewery, ewry ('juːərɪ). Forms: (5 ewary, -erye, eawerie, eurey, 6 ewe-, yewrie, 6–7 ewrie, 7 eawrye), 5– ewery, ewry. [f. EWER + -Y[3].]

1. The apartment or office for ewers, *esp.* in former times, in the royal household; a room where ewers of water, table linen, and towels were kept. Also ***groom, sergeant of the ewery.***

[**1392** *Will Earl of Arundel* in Turner *Dom. Archit.* III. iv. 114 Pur l'ewerye un paire basyns d'argent.] *c* **1460** *Plumpton Corr.* 25 John Felton groom of the Chamber, and John Ward groom of the Eurey. *c* **1460** J. RUSSELL *Bk. Nurture* 256 in *Babees Bk.,* Take it [þe surnape] vppe.. and to þe Ewery bere hit youre silf agayne. **1513** *Bk. Keruynge* ibid. 155 So thyn ewery be arayed with basyns & ewers, & water hote & colde. **1541** *Act 33 Hen. VIII,* c. 12. §11 The sergeant of the Ewrie.. shal also be.. redy with clothes sufficient for the surgeon. **1577–87** HOLINSHED *Chron.* III. 920/1 In the butterie two yeomen, two groomes, and two pages: and in the yewrie likewise. **1671** EVELYN *Diary* 1 Mar., The King .. walking along the entries.. as far as the ewry. **1723** *Hist. Reg., Chron. Diary* 36 Master of the Ewry to their Royal Highnesses.

b. *attrib.*

c **1460** J. RUSSELL *Bk. Nurture* 232 in *Babees Bk.,* þan emperialle.. by Ewry borde with basons & lauour. **1502** *Privy Purse Exp. Eliz. York* (1830) 80 Thewry doore at Baynardes Castell.

†**2.** 'The scullery of a religious house'. *Obs.* In mod. Dicts.

'ewest, *adv.* (quasi-*adj.*) *Sc.* Also 6 ewoss, ewous, euous, euuse, ewuse. Comp. *more ewous.* [Perh. evolved by a wrong division of ANEWST (*an ewest* for *a newest*).] Close at hand.

1527 *Burgh. Rec. Aberd.* 3 June (Spald. Club) I. 117 One of your landis liand mair evuse to ws.. interchange the saidis landis with wtheris haiffand landis liand mair ewuse [*printed* evnse] to ws. **1543** *Aberd. Reg.* V. 18 (Jam.) Causing of your folkis that ar maist ewous wss to be in redenes. I haf gewin command & charge to my friendis & folkis maist ewous yow. **1572** *Sc. Acts Jas. VI,* §48 The Manses.. maist ewest to the Kirk. **1637–50** Row *Hist. Kirk* (1842) 153 That a gleeb of four aikers of land be designed off the most ewest and commodious land. *a* **1657** SIR J. BALFOUR *Ann. Scotl.* (1824–5) II. 258 The remanent Lordes of the clergie, being ewest to him. **1814** SCOTT *Wav.* xlii, 'To be sure, they lie maist ewest' said the Bailie.

ewfras, ewft(e, obs. ff. EUPHRASY, EFT.

ewgh, ewghen, obs. ff. YEW, YEWEN.

ewhow ('eːhwaʊ), *int. Sc.* [f. EH + WHOW.] 'An exclamation of regret or pity'.

1816 SCOTT *Old Mort.* v, 'But ewhow! they are puirly armed, and warse fende wi' victual.'

‖**Ewigkeit, ewigkeit** ('eːvɪçkaɪt). [G., = eternity.] Eternity, infinity; *spec.* in jocular phr. ***in(to) the ewigkeit,*** 'into thin air'.

[**1857** C. G. LELAND *Hans Breitmann's Party* (1869) 15 Hans Breitmann gife a barty—Vhere ish dat barty now?... All goned afay mit de lager beer—Afay in de ewigkeit!] **1877** E. S. DALLAS *Kettner's Book of Table* 75 There is more gluttony now in the world.. and none the less because we are quiet over it—and pretend to think a great deal more of the *ewigkeit.* **1900** W. TUCKWELL *Reminisc. Oxford* 255 The old monastic Oxford has evaporated into the *Ewigkeit.* **1924** 'L.

BROCK' *Deductions of Col. Gore* viii, The thumb of one of his hands, which had been rubbing the pad of his second finger thoughtfully, flicked the chances of any other supposition's being the right one into the *ewigkeit*. **1958** *Observer* 18 May 14/2 The sage of Stuttgart [*sc.* Hegel] should have been viewing last week, selectively, from his anti-fireside in the *Ewigkeit*. **1969** 'D. CORY' *Night Hawk* 61 We leaped together parachute-less out into the *Ewigkeit*.

ewin, obs. form of EVEN.

e-wis, variant form of I-WIS, *Obs.*

ewk, var. of YEKU, *Sc.*, to itch.

ewle, obs. form of YULE.

ewlow, ? obs. form of YELLOW.
1541 *Lanc. Wills* I. 80 In yᵉ chapel ij. old ewlow quishens.

†**ewre**, *sb. Obs. rare*$^{-1}$. [? var. of ORE.] ? Rust, oxide.
1597 LOWE *Chirurg.* (1634) 97 By the continuall sorting and telling of this coyne, then did enter of the ewre of that brasse and copper under the nails of her fingers.

ewre, var. of EURE, *Obs.*, destiny.

†**ewrose**. *Obs.* Also 4 eurose, 5 euerose, euerrose. [a. OF. *ewe rose*, mod. *eau (de) rose.*] Rose-water.
c **1350** *Med. MS.* in *Archæol.* XXX. 364 Jows of betonye wᵗ eurose clere Counfortyth yᵉ herynge of yᵉ ere. *a* **1440** *Sir Degrev.* 1391 With.. Watyr of everrose clere, They wesche. *c* **1440** *Anc. Cookery* in *Househ. Ord.* (1790) 455 And a pynte of water of ewrose. **1486** *Bk. St. Albans* B viij a, Wash hir with euerose.

ewse-dreep, obs. form of EAVESDRIP.
1639 *Bury Wills* (1850) 180 The.. edifices.. gardens, waies, water courses, easemᵗˢ, ewse-dreepes, and appurtenances.

ewt(e, obs. form of EFT.
1584 R. SCOT *Discov. Witchcr.* XIII. v. 238 The carcases of snakes, ewts, and other serpents.

ewte, *v. dial.* [repr. OE. *ʒéotan*: see YETE.]
1746 *Exmoor Scolding* (E.D.S.) 65 *Ewte*, to pour in. **1787** in GROSE *Provinc. Gloss.* **1847–78** in HALLIWELL.

†**ewté**, corrupt form of *lewté*, LEWTY, loyalty.
1401 *Pol. Poems* (1859) II. 62 Lust of fleich and lust of iȝe, and pride in oure lyvynge. On this three, Jak, by my ewté, is groundid al ȝour colege.

ewteuth, obs. var. OUTWITH *prep.*, outside of.

ewyn(e, obs. form of EVEN.

ex, obs. form of AXE *sb.*[1]
a **1400** *Sir Degrev.* 325 Wyth scharpe exus of stelle He playtede here basnetus welle. *c* **1440** *Prompt. Parv.* 144 Ex, instrument. *Securis.*

ex (ɛks), *prep.* [a. L. *ex* out of (archaically also *ec*), corresp. to Gr. ἐξ, ἐκ (see EX- *pref.*[2]), Gaulish *ex-* (OWelsh *eh-* in *ehofn* fearless), OIr. *ass*, *ess-*, *e-*, Lith. *isz*, ? OSl. *izŭ* (Russ. *iz*'). Before consonants sometimes reduced to *ē*.]

1. In Lat. phrases (some of which are in Eng. written as single words), as EX ANIMO, EX PARTE, EXTEMPORE, EX-VOTO, etc., q.v. in alphabetical place.

2. *Comm.* **a.** Used for 'out of', 'landed from' (a ship), with reference to goods. Similarly in phrase ***ex warehouse***: (sold directly) from the warehouse. **b.** With sense 'without,' 'exclusive of'; *esp.* in phrase ***ex dividend*** (abbreviated *ex div.* or *x.d.*), used with reference to sales of stocks or shares to indicate that the dividend next to be paid is not included in the sale. So formerly ***ex interest*** (abbreviated *ex int.*, *ex in.*, *x.i.*); also ***ex new*** (*ex n.*, *x.n.*), intimating that the right to an allotment of new shares or stock is not included in the sale.

1845 *Times* July [In the daily lists of prices of railway shares the following frequently occur], ex. div., x.d., ex in., ex int., x.i., ex new, ex n., x.n. **1874** *Porcupine* XV. 775/2 It is no unusual thing for brokers and merchants to sell their goods 'ex quay'. **1877** R. GIFFEN *Stock Exch. Securities* 59 The price quickly rising from 125 cum div early in July to 136 ex div in September. **1878** E. C. MADDISON *Specul. Stock Exch.* ii. 13 After prices have been quoted 'ex dividend'. **1882** R. BITHELL *Counting-house Dict.* 122 *Ex drawing*. Since the prices of stocks and shares quoted in the official list carry with them the right to claim all accruing advantages in respect of those stocks or shares; and since the 'drawings' for the Sinking Fund or amortization are among those advantages, it is usual to state, about the time when drawings take place, whether the prices carry with them the right to the drawing, or whether that right has ceased. This is done by inserting, after the price, the phrase 'ex drawing' or 'cum drawing'. **1884** *Times* 4 July 11 The landing shed.. with its contents, about 100 tons of flax ex the Maria A. Hinde.. was totally destroyed by fire. **1885** [see X, 7]. **1887** *Daily News* 8 July 6/8 During the week a good deal of business, ex-warehouse, has been transacted. **1888** *Ibid.* 5 Oct. 5/3 The.. price.. is said to have been fully fivepence farthing a pound ex ship. *Mod.* The custom-house expenses amount to £5, ex stamps. **1893** R. BITHELL *Counting-house Dict.* (ed. 2) 118 *Ex all* (x all.). When these words are added to the quotation of the price of any stock, they signify that the coupon or dividend just due on such stock, and any preference claim to new stock, bonus, or other privilege arising from the possession of the stock sold, is retained by the seller. **1903** *Pitman's Business Man's Guide*, *Ex coupon*, .. without the interest coupon. **1906** in Poley & Gould *Stock Exch.* (1907) 292 When Securities on which Options are open are quoted 'Ex Rights' an official price will.. be fixed for the Rights. **1928** *Daily Mail* 25 July 19/3 Ex rights. Ex all. Ex bonus. Ex return capital. Ex drawing. Ex cash bonus. **1955** *Times* 28 July 12/2 It was on an ex works basis. **1962** H. O. BEECHENO *Introd. Bus. Stud.* vi. 59 The terms 'xr' (ex rights) or 'xc' (ex capital).. seen against the price. This means that the special rights extended to existing share-holders do not apply. **1962** *Times* 13 Feb. 4/6 The cost, ex yard, is the same as for a boat built in this country. **1965** J. L. HANSON *Dict. Econ.* 164/2 *Ex-quay*, goods sold on this condition must be taken charge of by the purchaser after they have been landed from the ship. **1967** K. GILES *Death in Diamonds* ix. 170 All the billing is done ex London.

ex- *prefix*[1], of Latin origin.

I. repr. L. *ex-*, the prep. *ex* (see prec.) in combination.

1. In Latin the form *ex-* appears before vowels and *h*; also before *c*, *p* (exc. in *ēpotāre*, *ēpōtus*), *q*, *s*, *t*; before *f* it becomes *ef-* (in inscriptions *ec-*: cf. Gr. ἐκ); before other consonants (exc. in *exlex*) it becomes *ē*. All these various forms are represented in many Eng. derivatives; e.g. *ebullient*, *effervesce*, *extend*. An *s* following the prefix was in mediæval spelling commonly omitted, and this practice has been adopted in English orthography, as in *exert*, *extinct*; in some scientific terms, however, the *s* has been retained in order to exhibit the composition more clearly, as in *exsert* to protrude (etymologically = *exert*), *exsanguineous*, *exsiccate*. The euphonic rules affecting the prefix in class. Lat. did not prevail in vulgar Lat., the universal form being *ex-*, represented in Romanic by *es-* (see ES-). In OF. and in ME., words with the prefix *es-* were occasionally written with *ex-*, after the analogy of words adopted from Latin; a few of these refashioned forms remain in mod. Eng., as *exchange*, *expound*.

When it has primary or secondary stress, the prefix is pronounced (ɛks); in unstressed position this remains before a (written) cons., though in southern usage (ɪks) is commonly substituted; before a stressed vowel the pronunciation is usually (ɛgz), becoming (ɪgz) in southern speech; this rule, however, has many exceptions, chiefly in rare words and in words affected by the analogy of cognates differently accented.

2. The Lat. compounds of *ex-* chiefly belong to the following classes, all which are represented by English derivatives. 1. Verbs formed from other verbs; in some of these *ex-* has its primary force of 'out', 'forth', as in *exclūdĕre*, *exīre* (whence Eng. *exclude*, *exit*); in some it means 'upward', as in *extollĕre* (whence Eng. *extol*); in others it has the sense 'thorougly', as in *excruciāre* (whence Eng. *excruciate*). 2. Verbs formed from adjs., with general sense 'to bring into a certain state', as *exacerbāre*, *exasperāre* (whence Eng. *exacerbate*, *exasperate*). 3. Verbs formed from sbs.; some of these are really formed on phrases in which *ex* governs the sb., and have the senses to 'to remove, expel, or relieve from (that which is denoted by the sb.)', as *excūsāre*, *expatriāre*, *exonerāre* (whence Eng. *excuse*, *expatriate*, *exonerate*); others have the sense 'to deprive of (what is denoted by the sb.)', as *excoriāre*, *excorticāre* (whence Eng. *excoriate*, *excorticate*). 4. Adjs. formed from sbs., with the general sense 'deprived of something', as *exsanguis* bloodless (whence Eng. *exsanguineous*); in imitation of these, many terms of mod. science have been formed in which *ex-* has the non-Latin sense 'destitute of', as *exalbuminous*, *exstipulate*; the form *e-* (see E- *pref.*[3]) has however more frequently been employed, even where Lat. euphony would require *ex-*, as in *ecaudate*.

II. *ex-* (with hyphen) prefixed to Eng. words.

3. Prefixed to titles of office or dignity, to form designations for persons who have formerly held the position in question. In more restricted sense these compounds denote the immediate predecessor (when still living) of the present holder of the position. After the analogy of these words, *ex-* is prefixed indiscriminately, with the sense expressed by 'former', 'sometime', 'quondam', to sbs. designating persons with respect to their calling, station, character, or the like, as ***ex-wife***.

[On the analogy of forms of expression like *ex exsule consul*, '(that has become) a consul from an exile', the phrases *ex consule*, *ex magistro equitum*, etc. were in the Latin of the empire added as titles to the names of men who had filled the offices of consul, master of the horse, etc. At a later period these phrases gave rise to the compounds *exconsul*, *exmagister*, in the same manner as the compounds *proconsul*, *proprætor* had been developed from the older *pro consule*, *pro prætore*. In med.Lat. this usage was greatly extended, such forms as *ex-Augustus* ('ex-emperor') being of frequent occurrence. Some words of this formation (e.g. *ex-professor*) passed in adapted forms into It. and Fr., and on the analogy of these *ex-* was prefixed to Romanic words. The Eng. use, imitated from Fr., seems to have first become common towards the end of the 18th c.]

1398 TREVISA *Barth. De P.R.* XIV. xlviii. (1495) 484 Exconsul is he that leuyth the offyce of Consul. **1683** CAVE *Ecclesiastici*, *Athanasius* 80 Sending the Ex-consular Dionysius to be a Witness of their Transactions. **1793** BURKE *Policy of Allies* Wks. VII. 129 The ex-bishop of Autun. **1796** S. PERRY *Argus* 20 Feb. 368 This ex-mayor was brought into Paris.. and conducted.. to the mayoralty. **1805** G. ELLIS *Let.* 9 Jan. in Lockhart *Scott*, This is Frere —our ex-ambassador for Spain. **1806** WOLCOTT (P. Pindar) *Tristia* Wks. 1812 V. 238 The mad ex-courtiers cry Thou old black sheep. **1815** WRAXALL *Hist. Mem.* II. 35 He eulogized Laurens, the American expresident, when a prisoner in the Tower. **1819** *Edin. Rev.* XXXII. 52 The anti-commercial system of the Ex-emperor.. has.. been adopted.. by his.. successors. **1828** STEUART *Planter's G.* 500, I shall beg leave, as a sort of Ex-professor of that art, to offer a few hints. **1839** THIRLWALL *Greece* III. 19 This body, at once a council and a court of justice, was composed.. of the ex-archons. **1849** THACKERAY *Pendennis* xxxiv, An ex-beau about town. **1859** LANG *Wand. India* 192, I was now alone with the ex-Commander of the Seik Cavalry. **1860** L. V. HARCOURT *Diaries G. Rose* II. 1 The ex-secretary for the Treasury. **1875** POSTE *Gaius* II. (ed. 2) 206 The remedy of the ex-proprietor of the accessory is an in factum actio. **1876** *Gentl. Mag.* XVII. 147 His ex-wife.. is dragging out slow years. **1884** A. FORBES *Chinese Gordon* ii. 48 Some were ex-mates of merchant-ships. **1891** *Daily News* 16 Mar. 7/3 A husband or wife who has obtained a divorce has a right after it is granted to sue the ex-spouse for alimony. **1962** *Oxford Mail* 19 Feb. 6/5 His daughter is in his ex-wife's custody.

b. When the designation to which *ex-* is prefixed is a phrase, the hyphened prefix has the appearance of being attached simply to the first word. Hence *ex-* occas. occurs in actual combination with an adj., with sense 'formerly'. ***ex-service(s)*** adj., having formerly belonged to one of the fighting services; of or pertaining to former servicemen.

1826 BENTHAM in *Westm. Rev.* VI. 457 Ex-learned as I am, and, therefore, if ever, no longer learned—in the law in general, never learned at all. **1834** T. MEDWIN *Angler in Wales* II. 184, I have heard him more than once tell of his rencontre with an ex-flogging Secretary at War. **1859** LANG *Wand. India* 413 A score of ex-Thuggee officers. **1887** *Charity Organ. Rev.* June 254 One of our ex-boarded-out boys enlisted some three years ago. **1887** *Pall Mall G.* 21 Sept. 12/1 The 6,000,000 dols... is mainly made up of this ex-Russian capital. **1890** *Ibid.* 14 Jan 2/2 Such nonsense.. is unworthy of an ex-Liberal ex-Lord Chancellor. **1907** *Daily Chron.* 5 Dec. 6/7 March of the unemployed ex-service men through the West-end of London to Hyde Park. **1910** *Vanity Fair* 13 Jan. 55/1 Employment for ex-Service men is always a pressing question. **1940** J. BETJEMAN *Old Lights for New Chancels* 25, I have my ex-Service man and Mamie's done a lino-cut. **1941** *Times Weekly* 23 Apr. 12/3 (Advt.), Please send your donation to.. Ex-Services Welfare Society. **1945** *Ann. Reg. 1944* 156, Maori ex-servicemen and ex-servicewomen can participate fully in all benefits.

c. From some of these combinations sbs. have occas. been formed by the addition of suffixes.

1793 W. TAYLOR in *Monthly Rev.* XII. 82 Among the Prussian clergy, the alarm of ex-Jesuitism has nearly rendered orthodoxy disreputable. **1865** *Morning Star* 29 May, The rage of the priests and ex-dynastists at the spirit, splendour, and immense success of the solemnity.

4. ***ex-party*** (nonce-wd.), the party of the 'outs'.

1809 SYD. SMITH in *Edin. Rev.* XIV. 44 He should recollect that his Methodists are the ex-party.

ex- *prefix*[2], of Greek origin. The Gr. ἐξ out of, etymologically = L. *ex-* (see prec.) occurs only before vowels, as in the words adopted into Eng. in the forms *exanthema*, *exarch*, *exegesis*, *exodus*, *exorcize*, etc. Before consonants it is replaced by the related and synonymous form ἐκ-, which becomes *ec-* in Latin, and hence in the Eng. derivatives, as *ecbasis*, *eccentric*, *eclipse*, *ecstasy*, etc.

ex (ɛks), *a. colloq.* [EX-[1] 3.] Former, quondam; outdated, passé.

1823 BYRON *Age of Bronze* xvii, And the *ex*-empress grows as *ex* a wife. **1892** KIPLING *Lett. of Travel* (1920) 91 Nothing looks so hopelessly 'ex' as a President 'returned to stores'. **1952** WODEHOUSE *Barmy in Wonderland* xiii. 126 'I allude to my fiancée. Or, rather, my ex-fiancée.' 'Is she ex?' 'Ex to the last drop. You never saw anything Ex-er.' **1955** *Times* 16 June 12/2 'Is she a member, or an ex-member, of the Communist Party?'—'She is an ex-member'. 'When did she go 'ex'?'

ex (ɛks), *sb.*[1] *colloq.* Pl. **exes**, **ex's**, **exs.** [EX-[1] 3.] One who formerly occupied the position or office denoted by the context; *spec.* a former husband or wife.

1827 MOORE *Cash, Corn & Catholics* 125 'But *don't* you perceive, dear, the Church have found out That you're one of the people call'd *Ex's* at present?' 'Ah, true—you have hit it.. (his Lordship replies), And, with tears, I confess—God forgive me the pun!—We X's have proved ourselves *not* to be Y's.' **1915** *Boston Pilot* 13 Mar. 4/4 The various kinds of Ex's [*sc.* ex-Catholics] are allowed to advertise their nasty anti-Catholic talks. **1929** E. WILSON *I thought of Daisy* ii. 96 'Phil was your first husband, was he?' 'Yes: he's my ex,' she said. **1930** BYRNE *Golden Goat* ix. 68 Here was an ex-king, one of the first exes. **1944** A. CHRISTIE *Towards Zero* 25 Leonard's new wife and his Ex were the best of friends. **1971** *Ladies' Home Jrnl.* Feb. 30/3 His 'ex' also got away with every stick of furniture and household equipment.

ex (ɛks), *sb.*² Colloq. abbrev. of EXPENSE 3c. Always in pl. forms *exes*, *ex's*, *exs*. (Cf. quot. 1894 s.v. X 7.)

1864 HOTTEN *Slang Dict.* 129 *Exes*, expenses; written thus —EXS. **1874** *Ibid.* 156 Just enough to clear our exes. **1878** *Porcupine* 10 Aug. 295/2 You are.. pretty sure to cover your 'ex's'. **1883** *Referee* 18 Mar. 3/3 The piece was ready, but the 'pieces' were not, and without the exes Morton would not allow.. the curtain to go up. **1908** A. BENNETT *Old Wives' Tale* IV. i. 436 The mater will fork out all my exes. **1915** F. M. HUEFFER *Good Soldier* III. v. 203, I have offered to pay her ex's myself. **1929** J. B. PRIESTLEY *Good Companions* III. i. 482 I'll fix that too—stand all the exes. **1970** K. GILES *Murder Pluperfect* 85 Their ten thousand bucks per year plus exes.

ex (ɛks), *v.* [f. the pronunciation of the letter X.] *trans.* To cross *out*; to delete with an x.

[*a* **1849** POE *Tales* (1896) 109, 'I *shell* have to *x* this ere paragrab,' said he... So *x* it he did, unflinchingly and to press it went *x-ed.*] **1935** R. STOUT *League of Frightened Men* xiii. 157 He wasn't so good at the typewriter; he had exed out a good deal. **1958** D. NILAND *Call Me when Cross turns Over* iv. 126 Ex the lot out and give you the whole blank page to yourself. **1962** A. LEJEUNE *Duel in Shadows* xi. 149 He exed out..'e' and 'a' and substituted 'eye' and 'aye'. **1965** K. GILES *Some Beasts no More* vi. 163 'Was he a good typist?' 'Quite fast, sir, but a lot of exing out, not expert.'

exaccion, -oun, -yon, obs. ff. EXACTION.

† **e'xacerate,** *v. Obs.* [f. EX- *prefix*¹ + L. *acus* (*acer-*) chaff + -ATE³.] *trans.* To clear away the chaff from, winnow.

Hence **e'xacerated** *ppl. a.* **exace'ration,** the action of winnowing.

1656-81 BLOUNT *Glossogr.*, *Exacerate.* **1692-1732** COLES, *Exaceration.* **1736** BAILEY, **1775** ASH, *Exacerated.*

exacerbate (ɛgz-, ɛk'sæsəbeɪt), *v.* [f. L. *exacerbāt-* ppl. stem of *exacerbā-re*, f. *ex-* intensive + *acerb-us* harsh, bitter, grievous.]

1. *trans.* To increase the smart of (a pain), the virulence of (disease), the bitterness of (feeling, speech, etc.); to embitter, aggravate. Also, to embitter or sour the feelings of (a person); to irritate, provoke.

1660 *Hist. Wars Scot. under Montrose* App. 206 The Ministers never ceased to exacerbate his misery. **1755** in JOHNSON. **1818** *Art Preserv. Feet* 11 The radical cause of the complaint is often attributed to that which.. merely exacerbates the pain. **1843** POE *Gold Bug* Wks. 1864 I. 56, I thought it prudent not to exacerbate the growing moodiness of his temper. **1852** MISS YONGE *Cameos* (1877) II. viii. 102 Exacerbated by disappointment.. he had let loose his rage and passion. **1876** J. WEISS *Wit, Hum. & Shaks.* vii. 243 A woman's language becomes exacerbated because she is so inadequate to protest by actions.

2. *intr.* for *refl.*

1837 *Penny Cycl.* VIII. 410/1 The feverish symptoms disappear or remit soon to recur or exacerbate. **1837** CARLYLE *Fr. Rev.* II. IV. v, The sour doubting humour has had leave to accumulate and exacerbate.

Hence **e'xacerbated** *ppl. a.*

1730-6 BAILEY (folio), *Exacerbated*, provoked or vexed, afresh. **1804** *Miniature* No. I. (1806) I. 6 The ponderous dignity of the Rambler would, with 'exacerbated' severity, lament the sad degeneracy of the present day, etc. **1853** KANE *Grinnell Exp.* xxxvi. (1856) 326 The disease had come back with.. exacerbated virulence. **1857** G. GILFILLAN in *Waller & Denham's Poems* 208 Butler, then a disappointed and exacerbated man, was malignant enough to lampoon him for lunacy.

exacerbation (ɛgz-, ɛk,sæsə'beɪʃən). [ad. L. *exacerbātiōn-em*, n. of action f. *exacerbāre* to EXACERBATE.]

1. The action of exacerbating or provoking to anger or hatred; the condition of being exacerbated; embitterment, irritation; an instance of the same.

1582 N. T. (Rhem.) *Heb.* iii. 15 Do not obdurate your hartes as in that exacerbation. **1605** G. POWELL *Answ. Puritan-Papist* 39 It breedeth exacerbation of minde. **1638** BP. REYNOLDS *Peace Ch.* 21 Which course usually tendeth to mutuall exacerbation. **1797** GODWIN *Enquirer* I. x. 86 Fits of peevishness and exacerbation. **1808** T. JEFFERSON *Writ.* (1830) IV. 105 Political controversy, and the exacerbation of spirit into which it degenerates. **1827** CAPT. T. HAMILTON *C. Thornton* (1845) 81 Those exacerbations of temper to which he was habitually liable. **1874** FARRAR *Christ* (ed. 2) II. xliii. 106, *footn.*, The exacerbation between Jews and Samaritans was always at its worst during the anniversaries of the national feasts.

2. Increase in severity (of disease, sufferings, punishments, etc.); an instance of this. Chiefly *Path.*, a paroxysm (of a fever, etc.); also *transf.*

1625 HART *Anat. Ur.* II. iii. 64 Coniectures of I know not what kinde of feauer, the which now and then was not without some exacerbations. **1668** CULPEPPER & COLE *Barthol. Anat.* 366 A Fit or Exacerbation at every Circuit of the blood. **1732** ARBUTHNOT *Rules of Diet* 348 A great Exacerbation of this Pain the Moment after swallowing anything. **1785** PALEY *Mor. Philos.* (1818) II. 297 A vigilant magistracy, an accurate police.. contribute more to the restraint.. of crimes than any violent exacerbations of punishment. **1809** W. IRVING *Knickerb.* (1861) 111 He absolutely trembled with.. the exacerbations of his valour. **1861** J. GRAHAM *Pract. Med.* 608 There are few diseases more painful to witness than is tetanus, especially during the exacerbations of the spasm. **1877** ROBERTS *Handbk. Med.* (ed. 3) I. 80 Hectic fever is of a distinctly intermittent or remittent type, there being exacerbations.

† **exacer'bescence.** *Path. Obs.* [f. as next: see -ENCE.] Increase of violence or severity (in a disease); = EXACERBATION 2.

1794-6 E. DARWIN *Zoon.* (1802) II. 162 Hectic fever.. having the exacerbescence towards evening.

exacerbescent (ɛg,zæsə'bɛsənt), *a.* [ad. L. *exacerbescent-em*, pr. pple. of *exacerbescĕre* to become angry, f. *ex-* (see EX- *pref.*¹) + *acerb-us* harsh, bitter.] Tending to become embittered.

1889 H. F. WOOD *Englishm. of Rue Caïn* xi. 155 That exacerbescent irritability had been partly assumed.

† **e,xacer'vation.** *Obs.* [as if a. L. **exacervātiōn-em*, n. of action f. *exacervāre*, f. *ex-* intensive + *acervāre* to heap, f. *acervus* heap.] The action of heaping up, accumulation.

1730-6 in BAILEY (folio); whence in JOHNSON, ASH, etc.

† **exacinate,** *v. Obs.* [f. med.L. *exacināt-* ppl. stem of *exacināre*, f. *ex-* out + *acinus* grape-stone.] *trans.* To remove kernels or stones from fruit.

1656-1681 in BLOUNT *Glossogr.*

Hence † **,exaci'nation.** *Obs.*

1658-96 in PHILLIPS, **1730-6** in BAILEY (folio), **1775** in ASH.

exacion, obs. form of EXACTION.

exact (ɛg'zækt), *a.* [ad. L. *exact-us*, pa. pple. of *exigĕre*: see EXACT *v.*

The L. adj. has the senses (1) 'highly finished, consummate', from the vb. in the sense 'to complete, bring to perfection', and (2) 'accurate, precise', from the vb. in the sense 'to calculate precisely'. See EXACT *v.*]

I. Perfected, consummate, 'finished'.

† **1.** Of qualities, conditions, attainments, etc.: Consummate, finished, refined, perfect. Rarely in bad sense. *Obs.*

Expressions like 'exact taste' have a mixed notion of sense 5b, to which the later instances should perh. be referred.

1633 G. HERBERT *Temple, Providence* viii, We all acknowledge both thy power and love To be exact, transcendent, and divine. *a* **1659** OSBORN *Queries* Epist. (1673) S s iv b, The imployment of Children in their exactest Innocencie, being to make Houses and raise Pies of Dirt. **1661** LOVELL *Hist. Anim. & Min.* Introd., The hearing is most exact in the hare. **1676** HALE *Contempl.* I. 123 They.. pursued.. their Redeemer with.. exact Bitterness. **1702** C. MATHER *Magn. Chr.* III. III. (1852) 546 Certain Indians, whose exacter education he was desirous of. **1726** W. R. CHETWOOD *Adv. Capt. R. Boyle* 203 Every Feature so exact and uniform.. that I was amaz'd. **1727** SWIFT *To a very yng. Lady*, A man.. of an excellent understanding, and an exact taste.

† **2.** Of persons: Highly skilled, accomplished, (in taste) refined. *Obs.*

1599 HAKLUYT *Voy.* II. I. 28 Baldwine a Deuonshire man.. was a very eloquent man, an exact Philosopher. *c* **1616** FLETCHER *Q. Corinth* I. ii, A Lady of your youth.. a most exact lady, may doe all this Out of a vertuous love. **1656** R. ROBINSON *Christ All* 80 Christ, he is as exact in all spiritual diseases as he is in any disease. **1667** MILTON *P.L.* IX. 1017 Eve, now I see thou art exact of taste. **1725** POPE *Odyss.* XVI. 275 Two Sew'rs.. Exact of taste.

† **3.** Of material objects: Highly wrought, elaborate. Of buildings, etc.: Well-designed. *Obs.*

1667 MILTON *P.L.* VII. 477 Smallest Lineaments exact In all the Liveries dect of Summers pride. *c* **1710** C. FIENNES *Diary* (1888) 89 A very Exact house and gardens.

II. Precise, rigorous, accurate.

4. Of law and its administration, rules, order, procedure, etc.: Admitting of no deviation, precise, rigorous. †Of diet: Strictly regulated.

1538 STARKEY *England* I. ii. 52 Hyt was not possybul sodeynly, by exacte law and pollycy, to bryng such a rude multytude to perfayt cyvylyte. **1594** HOOKER *Eccl. Pol.* I. ii. (1611) 4 Obserueth in working a most exact order or lawe. **1732** ARBUTHNOT *Rules of Diet* 355 The Patient.. may protract a miserable Life with an exact thin Diet of Whey Broths, etc. **1748** HARTLEY *Observ. Man* I. iii. 296 Here there is the exactest Uniformity. **1818** JAS. MILL *Brit. India* II. v. iii. 414 The troops were kept in such exact discipline, that the people.. remained in their houses. **1870** EMERSON *Soc. & Solit.*, *Eloq.* Wks. (Bohn) III. 41 Eloquence.. rests on laws the most exact and determinate.

5. a. Of actions, processes, investigations, knowledge, etc.: Accurate in detail, strict, rigorous.

1533 MORE *Apol.* i. Wks. 845/2 Suche exacte cyrcumspeccion.. to be by me vsed in my wryting. **1561** T. NORTON *Calvin's Inst.* I. 6b, There nedeth.. an exacter diligence. **1603** JAS. I in Ellis *Orig. Lett.* I. 244. III. 81 How waire iudgis should be in trusting accusations withoute an exacte tryall. **1658** *Vestry Bks.* (Surtees) 324 That Tho. Johnson and Robᵗ Chilton doe take an exact veiw of all the leads about the church. **1791** COWPER *Odyss.* I. 549 Folding it with the exactest care. **1794** MRS. RADCLIFFE *Myst. Udolpho* i, He gave an exact acquaintance with every part of elegant literature. **1857** DICKENS *Lett.* (1880) II. 19, I shall act upon it in the most exact manner. **1857** BUCKLE *Civiliz.* I. vii. 337 [Boyle] was the first who instituted exact experiments into the relation between colour and heat.

b. Of persons or their faculties: Characterized by accuracy of knowledge, observation, statement, workmanship, conduct, etc. Of a judge, etc.: Strict, rigorous.

1597 BACON *Ess.*, *Studies* (Arb.) 10 Reading maketh a full man, conference a readye man, and writing an exacte man. **1607** SHAKS. *Timon* II. ii. 165 Call me before th'exactest Auditors And set me on the proofe. **1659** HAMMOND *On Ps.* cxliii. 2 Paraphr. 690 To appear with hope or comfort before thine exact tribunal! **1682** BURNET *Rights Princes* v. 148 Mezeray is the exacter Writer. **1696** WHISTON *Th. Earth* I. (1722) 34, I have followed our most exact Observer Mr. Flamstead. **1725** POPE *Odyss.* XXI. 439 The bow perusing with exactest eye. **1780** COWPER *Table-t.* 646 Then Pope, as harmony itself exact.. Gave Virtue and Morality a grace. **1848** M. ARNOLD *Poems* 1877 I. 26, I.. Am the exacter labourer. **1849** GROTE *Greece* II. xlvii. (1862) IV. 144 The poorer citizens.. were more exact in obedience and discipline.

6. Of ideas, images, representations, expressions, descriptions, resemblances, etc.: Perfectly corresponding, strictly correct, precise, accurate.

1645 MILTON *Tetrach.* (1851) 236 The visible and exactest figure of lonelines it selfe. **1663** COWLEY *Royal Society* iv, Who to the Life an exact Piece would make. **1672** WILKINS *Nat. Relig.* 400 This book contains as the most ancient, so the most exact story of the world. **1753** HOGARTH *Anal. Beauty* iii. 19 The exact similarity of the two halves of the face. **1782** PRIESTLEY *Corrupt. Chr.* I. I. 79 It is not easy to give an exact translation of this passage. **1796** H. HUNTER tr. *St. Pierre's Stud. Nat.* (1799) III. 178 Such a one is able to form in his own mind an exact idea of order. **1816** SCOTT *Antiq.* vii, It was some time before they [shouts] were in exact response to their own. **1881** TYLOR *Anthropol.* v. 133 Man's efforts to get easier, fuller, and exacter expression for his thoughts.

7. a. Of a calculated result, a quantity or quantitative relation, a position, figure, date, etc.: Precise as opposed to approximate. Also with defining word: That is precisely what is designated; = '(the) precise'.

1601 SHAKS. *All's Well* III. vi. 65 The merit of seruice is sildome attributed to the true and exact performer. **1664** EVELYN *Kal. Hort.* (1729) 187 The Cutting and the Pruning were perform'd in such and such an exact Minute of the Moon. **1802** PALEY *Nat. Theol.* iii. §1. 21 The pupil, under all its different dimensions, retains its exact circular shape. **1806** HUTTON *Course Math.* I. 205 When the given surd contains no exact power, it is already in its most simple terms. **1849** MRS. SOMERVILLE *Connex. Phys. Sc.* iv. 32 Not following the exact law of gravity. **1860** TYNDALL *Glac.* I. vii. 50 The exact appearance of a mountain of cast copper. **1861** FLO. NIGHTINGALE *Nursing* 5 The exact value of particular remedies.. is by no means ascertained. **1878** HUXLEY *Physiogr.* 7 At the instant of reaching its greatest height, or in other words at exact noon. *a* **1891** *Mod.* These are his exact words. A is an exact multiple of B.

b. *Calculus.* ***exact differential***, a linear differential function of two or more variables that is equal to the total differential of some function of those variables. Also ***exact (differential) equation*** (see quot. 1959).

1825 D. LARDNER *Elem. Treat. Differential & Integral Calculus* II. xvii. 284 As there are many differentials of two variables which are not exact differentials, so also there are many differential equations which are not the immediate differentials of any primitive equation. **1877** B. WILLIAMSON *Differential Calculus* (ed. 3) vi. 143 Condition that $Pdx + Qdy$ shall be a total Differential.—This implies that $Pdx + Qdy$ should be the exact differential of some function of x and y. **1920** H. T. H. PIAGGIO *Elem. Treat. Differential Equations* ii. 12 The expression $ydx + xdy$ is an exact differential. Thus the equation $ydx + xdy = 0$.. is called an exact equation. **1958** *Van Nostrand's Sci. Encycl.* (ed. 3) 511/1 Suppose that an integrating factor, v exists so that $vL(u)dx$ is an exact differential. **1959** G. & R. C. JAMES *Math. Dict.* (ed. 2) 116/1 *Exact differential equation*, a differential equation which is obtained by setting the total differential of some function equal to zero.

8. Of methods, instruments of research, language, etc.: Characterized by precision, not admitting of vagueness or uncertainty. ***exact sciences***: those which admit of absolute precision in their results; *esp.* the mathematical sciences.

1665 *Phil. Trans.* I. 37 Having no instruments exact enough. **1681** CHETHAM *Angler's Vade-m.* Pref. (1689) 4 Perfect knowledge of the exactest ways of the practical part of the Art. **1762-71** H. WALPOLE *Vertue's Anecd. Paint.* (1786) II. 73 The exactest arts of building ships.. were not unknown to him. **1841** MYERS *Cath. Th.* III. §7. 22 No spoken language has yet been found exact enough to express the highest generalisations. **1863** FAWCETT *Pol. Econ.* I. i. 3 All who have studied an exact science must have experienced the formidable difficulties which elementary chapters invariably present. **1866** J. MARTINEAU *Ess.* I. 3 The exact sciences constituted the preponderant discipline. **1875** JOWETT *Plato* (ed. 2) IV. 26 Of the creative arts.. we may make two classes—the less exact and the more exact.

† **9.** As *adv.* = EXACTLY. *Obs.*

1677 GILPIN *Demonol.* (1867) 407 In seeming exact-suiting scripture suggested. **1692** LOCKE *Educ.* §11 Nature.. works of her self a great deal better and exacter than we can direct her. **1703** MOXON *Mech. Exerc.* 182 Guide his Foot the firmer and exacter. **1737** POPE *Hor. Epist.* II. ii. 97 There's a Rehearsal, Sir, exact at one. **1791** COWPER *Yardley Oak* 36 Two lobes, protruding, paired exact.

† **e'xact,** *pple. Obs. rare*⁻¹. [? ad. L. *exact-us*, pa. pple. of *exigĕre*: see EXACT *v.*] Drawn forth by descent, descended.

1602 WARNER *Alb. Eng.* XI. lxi. (1612) 267 Of noble Parentage and rich was Mandeuil exact.

exact (ɛg'zækt), *v.* [f. L. *exact-* ppl. stem of *exigĕre*, f. *ex* out + *agĕre* to drive. The lit. sense is thus 'to drive or force out'; hence the various derivative senses 'to demand, require'; 'to try, weigh accurately'; 'to complete, bring to

perfection'; with other significations not retained in the English derivative.]

1. *trans.* To demand and enforce the payment of (fees, money, taxes, tolls, penalties, etc.); to extort. Const. *from*, *of*, †*on*, †*upon*.

1529 MORE *Supplic Soulys* Wks. 308/1 The freres quarterage, which he sayd that thei exacte of euery houshold. **1531** in W. H. Turner *Select Rec. Oxford* 102 The Mayre..and Burgesses..exact apon them..tolls. **1548** FORREST *Pleas. Poesy* in *Starkey's England* App. 95 Too reyse his Rent alas it neadethe not or fyne texact for teanure of the same. **1651** HOBBES *Leviath.* II. xxviii. 164 Where a Law exacteth a Pecuniary Mulct. **1661** MARVELL *Corr.* Wks. 1872–5 II. 68 In it [the Patent] none of those fees or summs exacted are specifyd. **1703** MAUNDRELL *Journ. Jerus.* (1732) 4 They take occasion to exact from Passengers..arbitrary.. Sums. **1749** FIELDING *Tom Jones* I. vi, Flatterers..exact the same taxes on all below them which they themselves pay to all above them. **1856** EMERSON *Eng. Traits, Voy. to Eng.* Wks. (Bohn) II. 14 This seafaring people..exacted toll.. from the ships of all other peoples.

†**b.** To require or enforce the surrender of (an object). *Obs.*

1655–60 STANLEY *Hist. Philos.* (1701) 468/2 His Books burnt..After that they had been diligently exacted of all that had any of them.

c. *loosely.* To inflict (vengeance). Const. *against*, *from*.

1858 FROUDE *Hist. Eng.* III. xii. 3 The revenge which he would one day exact against his uncle. **1874** GREEN *Short Hist.* ii. 65 The King angrily bade him exact vengeance from the town.

†**d.** With *personal obj.* To extort money, etc. from; to oppress with exactions. *Obs.*

1534 *Act 26 Hen. VIII*, c. 6. §2 The officers..unlawfully exacted the Kinges subiectes. **1597** DANIEL *Civ. Wares* III. lxxxix, The poor concussed state Shall ever be exacted for supplies.

2. To require by force or with authority the performance of (duty, labour, etc.), the concession of (anything desired); to insist upon. Const. *from*, *of*; in early use sometimes with *clause* or *inf.* as *obj.*

1564 GOLDING tr. *Justin* (1570) 87 The common people.. importunately exacted to haue all dettes clerely released. **1576** FLEMING *Panopl. Epist.* 97 The courtesie which I exact of you. **1602** MARSTON *Antonio's Rev.* I. v, Let my breath exact You strike sad tones unto this dismal act. **1638** R. WEST in *Jonsonus Virb.* 56 Thou exact'st our best houres industrie. **1665** MANLEY *Grotius' Low-C. Warres* 175 All the Wealth is almost in their Hands, whereof an Account is exacted. **1690** NORRIS *Beatitudes* (1694) I. 148 A Precept.. too perfect to be severely exacted in that Infant Age. **1754** SHERLOCK *Disc.* (1759) I. iii. 95 Christ came to exact Obedience from every Creature. **1848** MACAULAY *Hist. Eng.* I. 235 Ever since the reign of Elizabeth the oath of supremacy had been exacted from members of the House of Commons. **1863** FR. A. KEMBLE *Resid. Georgia* 39 Labor exacted with stripes. **1871** FREEMAN *Norm. Conq.* (1876) IV. xvii. 91 William exacted strict attendance at divine service from all his company.

3. Of circumstances, conditions, dignities, etc.: To render becoming, desirable, necessary, or unavoidable; to call for, demand, require. Const. *from*, *of*, rarely with *direct personal obj.* and *inf.*

1592 WEST *Symbol.* §56. Cij b, Then followeth the drawing of such Instruments in forme..as the qualitie of the fact or contract exacteth. **1601** BP. BARLOW *Serm. Paules Crosse* 27 The crowne exacteth of us reuerence. **1602** MARSTON *Antonio's Rev.* II. ii, Our state exactes, Our subjects not alone to beare, but praise our acts. **1672** VILLIERS (Dk. Buckhm.) *Rehearsal* (1714) 47 The place you fill, has more than amply exacted the Tallents of a wary Pilot. **1680** BOYLE *Scept. Chem.* v. 289, I must withhold my Beleef..till their Experiments exact it. **1683** D. A. *Art Converse* 18 Their gray hairs exact of us a particular respect. **1853** C. BRONTË *Villette* xxx. (1876) 344 No form of friendship under the sun had a right to exact such a concession. **1856** KANE *Arct. Expl.* I. xxxi. 423 The scurvy exacts a comfortable temperature and a drying one.

†**4.** *intr.* To practise exactions, impose contributions. Const. *on*, *upon*. Also in *indirect pass.*

c **1591** in *Lett. Lit. Men* (Camden) 78 Gevinge to the nobilitie..vnjuste..libertie to exact on the baser sorte of people. **1611** BIBLE *Ps.* lxxxix. 22 The enemie shall not exact vpon him. *a* **1619** DANIEL *Coll. Hist. Eng.* (1621) 35 He was again informed..how he exacted upon the Normans. **1679** in Gutch *Coll. Cur.* I. 276 Others were exacted upon in what they bought. **1687** BURNET *Trav.* ii. (1750) 86 Innkeepers think they have a right to exact upon Strangers. **1727** SWIFT *Modest Prop.* Wks. 1755 II. II. 67 To cheat and exact upon us in the price, the measure, and the goodness.

5. *trans.* In etymological sense: To force out, extract. *arch.*

1639 FULLER *Holy War* II. xliv. (1647) 103 It passeth my Chymistrie to exact any agreement herein out of the contrariety of writers. **1674** *Govt. Tongue* vi. §23. 130 We do like witches with their magical chymistry, exact all the venom. **1883** R. BRIDGES *Prometheus* (1884) 6 He next withdrew The seeds of fire that else had still lain hid In..the blue flakes of flint For man to exact and use.

6. In various occasional uses: †**a.** To interpret rigorously (*obs.*). †**b.** To render exact, finish, perfect (*obs.*). **c.** *nonce-use* (after L. *exigere*). To produce (a work of art).

1646 J. GREGORY *Notes & Obs.* (1650) 27 This [Matt. ii. 12] is a strange Phrase, if it should be exacted by our manner of expressing. **1669** BARROW in Rigaud *Corr. Sci. Men* (1841) II. 67, I have tore out some leaves..which I shall send you somewhat more exacted. **1870** RUSKIN *Lect. Art* iii. (1875) 70, I think the 'Dunciad' is the most absolutely chiselled and monumental work 'exacted' in our country.

7. *Law.* (See quots.)

1607 COWEL *Interpr.* s.v. *Exigent*, This writ..seemeth to be called an *Exigent* because it exacteth the party, that is, requireth his expearance or forthcomming, to answer the lawe. **1769** BLACKSTONE *Comm.* III. 283 A writ of *exigent* or *exigi facias*..which requires the sheriff to cause the defendant to be proclaimed, required, or exacted, in five county courts successively, to render himself;..if he does not appear, he shall then be outlawed.

transf. **1858** HOGG *Life Shelley* I. 289 Shelley..ought to have been exacted five times..before the outrageous sentence of outlawry was passed against him.

exacta (ɛg'zæktə). *N. Amer.* [f. EXACT *a.*] (See quot. 1964.)

1964 A. WYKES *Gambling* viii. 193 The bettor tries to pick the first and second horse of a race... (With fewer than eight horses, the bettor must predict their order; in New York state, this bet is called an 'exacta'.) **1968** *Globe & Mail* (Toronto) 13 Feb. 29/9 Exacta (7–3) paid $78.80.

exactable (ɛg'zæktəb(ə)l), *a.* [f. EXACT *v.* + -ABLE.] That can be exacted.

1838 *Blackw. Mag.* XLIV. 622 A certain percentage is exactable. **1847** *Tait's Mag.* XIV. 798 The highest rate of interest 'exactable' by law was five per cent.

exacted (ɛg'zæktɪd), *ppl. a.* [f. EXACT *v.* + -ED[1].] In senses of the vb.

1618 *Barnevelt's Apol.* E iv b, The third part of the exacted debts. **1624** CAPT. SMITH *Virginia* v. 183 Finding the Inhabitants..abhorring all exacted labour. **1874** MISS MULOCK *My Mother & I* 138 Beyond exacted lessons I had never cared to study.

exacter (ɛg'zæktə(r)). [f. EXACT *v.* + -ER[1]: see EXACTOR.]

1. One who enforces payment of (dues); also one who demands more than his due, an extortioner. Const. *of*; = EXACTOR 1 and 2.

1598 HAKLUYT *Voy.* I. 55 They [the Tartars] are most intollerable exacters. **1612** BACON *Ess., Judicature* (Arb.) 458 The attendance of Courts is subiect to foure bad instruments..The fourth is the Poler and exacter of fees. **1673** TEMPLE *Observ. United Prov.* Wks. 1731 I. 47 They.. take Advantage of other Mens Ignorance..as great Exacters, where the Law is in their own Hands. **1681** H. MORE *Expos. Daniel* 183 Antiochus Epiphanes shall be a great exacter of Tributes.

transf. **1596** B. GRIFFIN *Fidessa* (1876) 8 Vnkind exacters of their fathers bream.

2. = EXACTOR 3. Const. *of*; also *upon* with *pers. obj.*

1561 T. NORTON *Calvin's Inst.* II. 110 A rigorous exacter that will not be satisfied but with his ful task performed. **1640** BP. HALL *Episc.* I. viii. 31 The rigid exacters of the.. Judaicall observation of the Lords day. **1648** *Eikon Bas.* 81 Prone to be..rigorous exacters upon others. **1702** *Eng. Theophrast.* 185 No men are so strict exacters of modesty in a servant as those that are most prodigal of their own. **1759** *Charac.* in *Ann. Reg.* 317/2 He was so rigid an exacter of perfection. **1788** *Disinterested Love* II. 144 A severe exacter of pensive looks and solemn faces.

exacting (ɛg'zæktɪŋ), *vbl. sb.* [f. EXACT *v.* + -ING[1].] The action of the vb. EXACT.

1603 SHAKS. *Meas. for M.* III. ii. 295 Disguise shall by th'disguised Pay with falshood, false exacting. *a* **1716** SOUTH *Serm.* I. v. (R.), By a vigilant exacting from them [teachers] ..the instruction of their respective flocks.

exacting (ɛg'zæktɪŋ), *ppl. a.* [f. prec. + -ING[2].] That exacts, in senses of the vb.

†**1.** That collects taxes. *Obs.*

a **1618** RALEIGH *Prerog. Parl.* 9 Hee called all his exacting officers to accompt.

2. That demands excessive payment, extortionate.

1583 STUBBES *Anat. Abus.* II. 85 If he for the execution therof should aske me more.. than we agreed for, were not this man a naughtie, exacting, and fraudulent felowe?

3. Of persons, their feelings, temper, etc.: That requires or is disposed to require too great advantages, exertions, or sacrifices.

1634 HABINGTON *Castara* (Arb.) 107 Set at liberty by death thou owest no debt T' exacting Nature. **1848** DICKENS *Dombey* xl, Mrs. Skewton..was in the irresolute, exacting, jealous temper that had developed itself on her recovery. **1873** BLACK *Pr. Thule* ix. 132 You are naturally jealous and exacting. **1882** MISS BRADDON *Mt. Royal* I. i. 4 All the exacting ideas of early youth in relation to love and lovers. *absol.* **1847** BUSHNELL *Chr. Nurt.* II. v. (1861) 328 There is a great difference between..the exact and the exacting. **1868** PEARD *Water-Farm.* xi. 115 The returns shall..satisfy the most exacting.

Hence **e'xactingly** *adv.*, in an exacting manner. **e'xactingness**, the quality of being exacting.

1849 *Lit. World* (N.Y.) No. 127. 4 It [truth] applies to particulars as exactingly as to generals. **1866** *Contemp. Rev.* II. 188 A sensitiveness about his own position..which might have turned to jealous exactingness. **1889** MORLEY *Walpole* 107 The boundless activity and exactingness of a reformed House of Commons.

exaction (ɛg'zækʃən). [a. F. *exaction*, ad. L. *exactiōn-em*, n. of action f. *exigĕre*: see EXACT *v.*] The action of exacting.

1. The action of demanding and enforcing payment (of fees, taxes, penalties, etc.); an instance of the same.

c **1380** WYCLIF *Sel. Wks.* III. 517 Þe þinggus þat ben duwe to prest shulde..be ȝoven frely, wiþouten exaccioun. **1382** —— *2 Macc.* iv. 27 Exactioun of tributis perteynede to hym. **1489** *Sc. Acts Jas. IV* (1597) §18 Of the quhilk tak thair, and exaction thairof, our Souerane Lord..knew na..cause. **1596** SHAKS. *Merch. V.* I. iii. 166 What should I gaine By the exaction of the forfeiture? **1652** NEEDHAM tr. *Selden's Mare Cl.* 6 Assigning of places for the exaction of it [customs]. **1818** JAS. MILL *Brit. India* III. i. 30 He was the proper object of penal exaction. **1832** HT. MARTINEAU *Ireland* 108 He could not allow that its [tithe's] exaction deserved the name of plunder. **1875** JOWETT *Plato* (ed. 2) III. 303 Exactions of market and harbour dues.

b. The action of enforcing the performance of (a task) or the rendering of (respect, service, obedience, etc.).

1674 S. VINCENT *Gallants Acad.* 93 He..is strictly just in the exaction of respect. **1868** M. PATTISON *Academ. Org.* v. 161 The exaction of a written dissertation on a given thesis ..seems likely to be efficacious.

2. The action of demanding or requiring more than is due or customary; an instance of the same; an illegal or exorbitant demand; extortion.

1494 FABYAN *Chron.* IV. lxiv. 43 [Allectus] vsed and exercysyd many Tyrannyes and exaccions. **1578** T. N. tr. *Conq. W. India*, Complaintes against Mutezuma of many wrongs and exactions done by him. **1632** LITHGOW *Trav.* v. 180 The Master..(who as he was an Infidell, vsed me with great exaction). **1655** DIGGES *Compl. Ambass.* 21 Great exactions used by the innkeepers at Gravesend. **1785** BURKE *Sp. Nabob Arcot's Debts* Wks. IV. 286 Tyrannous exaction brings on servile concealment. **1863** MARY HOWITT *F. Bremer's Greece* II. xiv. 108 The Christians of the plain are especially exposed to exactions of the Government. **1873** F. HALL *Mod. Eng.* 348 We may, without being chargeable with exaction, ask of him to remit a little the rigour of his requirements.

3. A sum of money which is exacted; an arbitrary and excessive impost.

1398 TREVISA *Barth. De P.R.* VI. xix. (1495) 205 Lordes.. ouersette..the people wyth exaccyons and talyages. **1460** CAPGRAVE *Chron.* 227 Many cytees in Gyan fel fro the obediens of Prince Edward..for grevous exacciones that were leyde upon hem. **1516** PYNSON *Life St. Birgette* in *Myrr. our Ladye* Introd. 53 The kyng of Swecia wolde haue charged his comons with a great exacion. **1613** SHAKS. *Hen. VIII*, I. ii. 25 They vent reproches Most bitterly on you, as putter on Of these exactions. **1786** BURKE *W. Hastings* Wks. 1842 II. 123 The small balance of fifteen thousand pounds remaining of the unjust exaction aforesaid. **1856** FROUDE *Hist. Eng.* (1858) II. viii. 256 The exactions might have been tolerated if the people had been repaid by protection.

4. *Law.* (See quot.)

1641 *Termes de la Ley* 149 Extortion is where an Officer demaundeth and wresteth a greater summe or reward than his iust fee: And Exaction is where an Officer or other man demaundeth and wresteth a fee..where no fee..is due at all. **1672** in *Cowel's Interpr.*

b. (See quot. and EXACT *v.* 7).

1816 CHITTY *Crim. Law* I. 359 The five exactions or callings of the defendant, and his non-appearance at the five successive county courts.

†**e'xactious**, *a. Obs. rare.* [f. EXACTI-ON + -OUS.] Characterized by exaction; exorbitant.

1630 *R. Johnson's Kingd. & Commw.* 477 An exactious Prince. **1633** *Cal. St. Papers* Dec., The parish clerk..would not suffer a poor parishioner..to be buried without such exactious fees as were unreasonable.

exactitude (ɛg'zæktɪtju:d). [a. F. *exactitude*, f. *exact*: see EXACT *a.* and -TUDE.] The quality of being exact; attention to minutiæ, accuracy of detail, precision. †Also (as in Fr.) = EXACTNESS, perfect correctness (of a statement).

1734 tr. *Rollin's Anc. Hist.* V. 132 There is..in virtue, an exactitude and steadiness or rather a kind of stiffness. **1794** G. ADAMS *Nat. & Exp. Philos.* I. xi. 440 The weight of the balloon determined with the most scrupulous exactitude. **1825** T. JEFFERSON *Writ.* (1830) IV. 419, I have no doubt of the exactitude of the statement in your letter. **1859** GEO. ELIOT *A. Bede* 87 Performing the initial duties to her dead with the awe and exactitude that belong to religious rites. **1870** LOWELL *Among my Bks.* Ser. I. (1873) 153 To occupy himself with the exactitudes of science.

exactive (ɛg'zæktɪv), *a. rare.* [f. L. *exact-us* (see EXACT *v.*) + -IVE.] Disposed to exact or be exacting. Const. *of*. Hence **e'xactiveness**, the quality of being exactive.

1822 [G. GROTE] *Anal. Infl. Nat. Relig.*, Personal affections..almost always frivolous and exactive. **1868** W. HANNA *Ministry in Galilee* 216, I am selfishly exactive of affection.

1628 LE GRYS tr. *Barclay's Argenis* 250 It was..an exactiueness of vertue, that had made him carry himselfe with such modesty.

exactly (ɛg'zæktlɪ), *adv.* [f. EXACT *a.* + -LY[2].]

†**1.** In a perfect manner, perfectly; to a perfect degree, to perfection; completely. *Obs.*

a **1533** FRITH *Disput. Purgat.* (1829) 85 The Scripture is for that intent left with us, that it may be understood of us exactly, and to the uttermost point. **1602** SHAKS. *Ham.* I. ii. 200 A figure like your Father, Arm'd at all points exactly, Cap a Pe, Appeares before them. **1639** FULLER *Holy War* v. xxx. (1647) 283 His Frontier cities..are exactly fortified. **1663** BOYLE *Consid. Exp. & Nat. Phil.* I. 60 In the Life to come, when we shall questionless glorifie God exactliest, we shall have, etc. **1664** POWER *Exp. Philos.* II. 88 Glass-Tubes ..exactly closed; or Hermetically sealed at the one end. **1667** BOYLE *Orig. Formes & Qual.* 32, I could not find it had any in places exactly darkened. **1680** BURNET *Rochester* (1692) 7 He was exactly well bred. *c* **1710** C. FIENNES *Diary* (1888) 108 On the top of wch hill you see a vast prospect Exactly Round it. **1726** W. R. CHETWOOD *Adv. Capt. R. Boyle* 357 They are..exactly proportion'd in their Features.

2. In an exact or accurate manner; with careful attention to detail; with strict conformity to

rule; punctually; with propriety. Now somewhat *rare.*

1612 BRINSLEY *Lud. Lit.* xxi (1627) 249 Learning to construe the Hebrew into the Latine exactly. **1644** EVELYN *Mem.* (1857) I. 66, I went to see more exactly the rooms of the fine Palace of Luxembourg. **1709** STEELE *Tatler* No. 5 ¶1 He remembered he was to sup with a Friend, and went exactly to his Appointment. **1712** TICKELL *Spect.* No. 410 ¶1 A Lady most exactly dressed from Head to Foot. **1756** C. LUCAS *Ess. Waters* I. 87 Let it be quickly dried on the outside, and exactly weighed. **1774** CHESTERF. *Lett.* I. xlii. 135 We must..not pass a word which we do not understand ..without exactly inquiring the meaning of it. **1818** JAS. MILL *Brit. India* II. v. viii. 682 The sixth part [of his revenues] had been exactly paid. **1832** HT. MARTINEAU *Hill & Vall.* iv. 66 He paid for his lodging exactly and regularly.

†**3.** Precisely, as opposed to *vaguely*; in express terms. *Obs.*

1646 SIR T. BROWNE *Pseud. Ep.* I. ix. 36, I adhere unto Archimedes who speaketh exactly, rather than the sacred Text which speaketh largely.

4. Of knowledge or statement: Accurately, with strict correctness.

1776 *Trial Nundocomar* 23/1, I do not know his age exactly, he is a young man. **1866** G. MACDONALD *Ann. Q. Neighb.* xi. (1878) 225, I could not repeat the words exactly to Old Rogers. **1879** LOCKYER *Elem. Astron.* vii. 240 The circumference..more exactly expressed..is 3·14159 times the diameter.

5. a. Of resemblance, agreement, adaptation, correlation: Precisely; without any discrepancy.

1662 STILLINGFL. *Orig. Sacr.* II. vi. §2 Every event is not exactly correspondent to the prediction. **1766** GOLDSM. *Vic. W.* xi, I was of opinion, that two such places would fit our two daughters exactly. **1806** HUTTON *Course Math.* I. 145 Divide the numerators by each other, and the denominators by each other, if they will exactly divide. **1860** TYNDALL *Glaciers* I. x. 65 When this hail was squeezed together, it exactly resembled a mass of oolitic limestone.

b. Qualifying a predication of identity, a specified quantitative relation, position, manner, time, etc.: Precisely, 'just', as opposed to *approximately.*

1658 F. OSBORNE *Hist. Mem. Q. Eliz.* A v, Good Books.. running..so exactly the fate of Acorns. **1776** ADAM SMITH *W.N.* I. I. i. 12 Every other workman being exactly in the same situation. **1809** ROLAND *Fencing* 26 It is not a general rule to recover exactly in the same position of your sword. **1816** J. SMITH *Panorama Sc. & Art* II. 720 The seventh division falls exactly on the bend of the knee. **1823** LAMB *Elia* (1867) 99 Had I twenty girls, they should be brought up exactly in this fashion. **1845** FORD *Handbk. Spain* I. 56 The English will go exactly as if they were in England. **1858** LARDNER *Hand-bk. Nat. Phil., Heat* 329 The difference.. will be found to be exactly equal to the height of a column, etc. *a* **1891** *Mod.* Exactly at one o'clock Her Majesty arrived. You are exactly the man for the post.

c. *ellipt.* expressing entire approval of, or concurrence in, a suggested statement. *colloq.*

1869 W. S. GILBERT *Bab. Ball., 'Nancy Bell'* xvi, 'I'm boiled if I die, my friends', quoth I, And 'exactly so', quoth he. *a* **1891** *Mod.* 'Then you think the letter is a forgery?' 'Exactly'.

d. with expressed or implied negative, often used when the statement denied is to be replaced by another somewhat similar in effect.

a **1891** *Mod.* Without exactly denying it, he led me to believe it was not true. He is not exactly a scholar, but he has read a great deal.

e. ***not exactly***: used ironically for 'not at all; by no means'. *colloq.*

1893 YONGE & COLERIDGE *Strolling Players* xxxii. 292, I wasn't exactly going to send in my checks this time. **1905** A. LANG *Adv. among Books* 222 Though some of our modern novelists think it coarse and degrading, Hawthorne did not think so, and they are not exactly better artists than Hawthorne. **1949** M. MUGGERIDGE *Affairs of Heart* vii. 125 She was not exactly pretty even then. In fact, she was not pretty at all—which is what the use of the word 'exactly' usually signifies. **1964** E. AMBLER *Kind of Anger* vi. 169 'And you're not laughing?' 'I'm not exactly bursting my sides, no.' **1968** *Win* 15 Oct. 16/1 Yeah, I'm scared out of my mind. The thought of prison doesn't exactly excite me.

exactment (ɛg'zæktmənt). *rare.* [f. EXACT *v.* + -MENT.] The action of exacting; exaction.

1808 LAMB *Spec. Eng. Dram. Poets* 527 The hours and half-hours as they expire..bring him nearer and nearer to the exactment of his dire compact.

exactness (ɛg'zæktnɪs). [f. EXACT *a.* + -NESS.] The quality or condition of being exact.

†**1.** Consummate skill; perfection of workmanship, high finish; elaborateness. *Obs.*

1564 HAWARD *Eutropius* To Rdr. 6 That worthy orator apperceived that Tully should in processe of time bereft yᵉ Gretians of theyr exactnesse in all sciences. **1658** USSHER *Ann.* VI. 592 Young men, who gave offence to every body by ..the exactnesse of their hair. **1668** D. SMITH *Voy. Constantinople* in *Misc. Cur.* (1708) III. 19 For curious Painting rich Altars, and exactness of Architecture, incomparable. **1695** LD. PRESTON *Boeth.* III. 121 How fleeting, and of how short Duration is Beauty and Exactness of Feature. **1697** *C'tess D'Aunoy's Trav.* (1706) 123 He went to walk in his Gardens, whose exactness yields in nothing to ours.

†**2.** Of laws, rules, observances: Strictness, rigour. *Obs.*

1631 R. BYFIELD *Doctr. Sabb.* 82 They observed their Festivals with severe exactnesse from all worke. **1633** BP. HALL *Hard Texts, N.T.* 34 If thou knewest the exactnesse of the law and thine owne weakness. **1732** BERKELEY *Alciphr.* IV. §23 Doth any one find fault with the exactness of geometrical rules. **1747** WESLEY *Prim. Physic* (1762) p. xvii, Observe..the greatest Exactness in your Regimen.

3. Of processes, results, methods, statements, etc.: Minute accuracy, precision.

1646 SIR T. BROWNE *Pseud. Ep.* IV. vii. 197 We made triall in Scales of good exactnesse. **1658** A. FOX tr. *Wurtz' Surg.* II. v. 58 Other Wounds..require not such exactness in the dressing. **1667** *Phil. Trans.* II. 435 At Sea..the Meridian is not so easie to be found to any tolerable exactness. **1736** BUTLER *Anal.* Introd. Wks. 1874 I. 4 Persons..who require things to be stated with greater exactness than our faculties appear to admit of. **1747** BERKELEY *Tar-water in Plague* Wks. III. 487 These [medicines] require an exactness in the dose, where a small error may produce a great mischief. **1841** W. SPALDING *Italy & It. Isl.* II. 47 A plan of the old church, representing with sufficient exactness its state at Charlemagne's coronation. **1876** J. H. NEWMAN *Hist. Sk.* I. II. v. 263 This very absence of scientific exactness.. constituted in Roman eyes a principal charm of Cicero's compositions.

4. Minute attention to detail; carefulness, accuracy. In *pl.* Instances of the same.

1645 MILTON *Tetrach.* Ded. (1851) 141 The industry, the exactnesse, the labour in it, confess'd to be more then ordnary. **1662** STILLINGFL. *Orig. Sacr.* III. i. §16 With the same exactness hee goes through all the parts of the body. **1716** LADY M. W. MONTAGUE *Lett.* I. ii. 10, I shall follow your orders with great..exactness. **1754** RICHARDSON *Grandison* (1810) VI. lii. 337 Has Lady G. dated? No, I protest! We women are above such little exactnesses. **1797** MRS. RADCLIFFE *Italian* xxiv, He reviewed, with exactness, the late behaviour of the Marchesa. **1855** MACAULAY *Hist. Eng.* IV. 463 He had..that sort of exactness which would have made him a respectable antiquary. **1875** WHITNEY *Life Lang.* ii. 29 Every writer who aims at exactness has to begin with definitions.

†**b.** Of personal habits: Regularity, punctuality. Of deportment, dress, etc.: Preciseness, formal propriety. *Obs.*

1683 D. A. *Art Converse* 4 A certain exactness in all our words and expressions. **1689** BURNET *Tracts* I. 8 A mixture of a French openness and an Italian exactness. **1712** STEELE *Spect.* No. 423 ¶2 An unaffected Exactness in his Dress and Manner. **1800** MRS. HERVEY *Mourtray Fam.* I. 167 Six o'clock is our hour: you know my exactness.

exactor (ɛg'zæktə(r)). Also 4 **exactoure**, 5–7 **exactour**, 7 **exactore**. [a. L. *exactor*, agent-n. f. *exigĕre*: see EXACT *v.* and -OR. Cf. EXACTER.]

1. One who exacts: (in Lat. senses) **a.** An officer who levies or collects tribute, taxes, or customs; a tax-collector. *arch.*

1563–87 FOXE *A. & M.* (1596) 259/2 The popes exactors went about to extort from the Churchmen the fift part of their goods. **1611** BIBLE *Isa.* lx. 17, I will also make thy officers peace, and thine exactours righteousnesse. **1867** FREEMAN *Norm. Conq.* (ed. 3) I. iii. 99 *note*, The word [Reeve], under the form of *Grieve*, has changed from a public to a private *exactor*.

†**b.** An officer of justice (see quot.). *Obs.*

1388 WYCLIF *Deut.* xvi. 18 *marg.*, Exactours ben thei that enqueren the truthe bi mesurable betingis and turmentis; and performen the sentence of iugis. **1582** *N. T.* (Rhem.) *Luke* xii. 58 Lest..the iudge deliuer thee to the exactour [**1611** officer] and the exactour cast thee into prison.

c. One whose duty it is to enforce the performance of work; a taskmaster.

1609 BIBLE (Douay) *Ex.* v. 6 He commanded in that day the overseers of the workes and the exactores of the people. **1611** —— *Job* xxxix. 7 Neither regardeth he the cry of the driver [*marg.* exactor].

2. One who makes illegal or unjustifiable exactions; an extortioner, oppressor.

1382 WYCLIF *Zech.* ix. 8 The exactoure, or the vniust axer, shal na more passe vpon hem. *c* **1530** H. RHODES *Bk. Nurture* in *Babees Bk.* 106 Bee not an exactour of another man. **1586** T. B. *La Primaud Fr. Acad.* I. (1594) 624 Provided..he become not prodigall, which would soone make him an exactor. **1650** tr. *Caussin's Ang. Peace* 45 No force of treasure is comparable to the greedinesse of the exactours themselves. **1818** JAS. MILL *Brit. India* II. v. vii. 604 Whatever it was the pleasure of the exactor to take. **1833** I. TAYLOR *Fanat.* v. 108 The warfare against ghostly exactors.

3. One who demands, lays claim to, or insists upon (something) as a matter of right; often with the added notion of excess. Const. *of.*

a **1619** FOTHERBY *Atheom.* I. vi. §2 (1622) 42 As they reposed great Religion in an oath, in respect of the Actor: so did they likewise, in respect of the Exactor. **1648** *Eikon Bas.* 146 The will of my Enemies seems to be their onely rule.. their success the exactor of what they please to call justice. **1670** G. H. *Hist. Cardinals* II. III. 197 He was then an exactor of certain punctilioes. **1752** JOHNSON *Rambler* No. 193 ¶6 There are unmerciful exactors of adulation, who withhold the wages of venality. **1828** SOUTHEY in *Q. Rev.* XXXVII. 218 So severe an exactor of accuracy..ought to be more observant of it himself. **1875** A. R. HOPE *My Schoolboy Friends* 10 As the exactor of tasks.

fig. **1642** J. EATON *Honey-c. Free Justific.* 83 Moses his Law is a severe exactor.

exactress (ɛg'zæktrɪs). *rare.* [f. EXACTOR + -ESS¹.] She that exacts, a female exactor.

1611 BIBLE *Isa.* xiv. 4 How hath the oppressor ceased! the golden city [*marg.* exactress of gold] ceesed! **1624** B. JONSON *Neptune's Triumph* Wks. (Rtldg.) 639/2 That were a heavy and hard task, to satisfy expectation, who is so severe an exactress of duties. **1833** J. KENRICK in *Philol. Mus.* II. 351 The name..more probably means 'exactress of justice'.

†**e'xacuate,** *v. Obs.* [irreg. f. L. *exacu-ĕre* (f. *ex-* intensive + *acuĕre* to sharpen) + -ATE³.]

1. *trans.* To make keen or sharp; to sharpen, stimulate, excite.

1632 B. JONSON *Magn. Lady* III. iii, Sense of such an injury received Should so exacuate, and whet your choler. **1684** tr. *Bonet's Merc. Compit.* XIX. 680 Some Cephalicks.. exacuate and strengthen the Inhabitants thereof [the Brain], the animal Spirits. **1721–1800** in BAILEY.

2. To make acrid or pungent.

1674 *Phil. Trans.* IX. 104 The Nitro-aerial Spirit..doth sooner or later exacuate and make fluid the Salino-metallic parts.

Hence †**e'xacuated** *ppl. a.*, †**exacu'ation.**

1627–77 FELTHAM *Resolves* II. xxxiii. 227 The exacuated Tortures of Antiochus. **1623** COCKERAM, *Exacuation*, a whetting. **1692–1732** COLES, *Exacuation.*

†**e'xadverse,** *a. Obs. rare*⁻¹. [f. L. *exadversum*, *-us* adv., over against, opposite, f. *ex* out + *adversum*, *-us* towards, f. *adversus*: see ADVERSE.] Directly opposed.

1647 WARD *Simp. Cobler* 22 If the whole conclave of Hell can..compromise exadverse and diametriall contradictions.

exæcation, obs. form of EXCECATION.

exædify, var. f. EXEDIFY.

†**e'xæstuate,** *v. Obs.* Also 7 exe-. [f. *exæstuāt-* ppl. stem of *exæstuā-re*, f. *ex-* (see EX- *pref.*¹) + *æstuā-re* to boil up. Cf. ÆSTUATE.]

1. *intr.* To boil up; to ferment; (of flames) to flare up.

1642 *Strangling Gt. Turk* in *Harl. Misc.* (Malh.) V. 192 No flames could exestuate more than their fury and ravings. **1730–6** BAILEY (folio), *Exæstuate*, to boil or cast up waves, or as a boiling pot does. **1775** in ASH.

2. *trans.* To overheat.

1657 TOMLINSON *Renou's Disp.* 53 That it may not too much exestuate the liver.

¶(Wrongly explained; see quot.).

1657 *Phys. Dict., Exestuate*, destroy the heat of any part.

Hence †**e'xæstuating** *ppl. a.*, that boils or surges up.

1684 tr. *Bonet's Merc. Compit.* VI. 219 The unloadings or things cast over-board by the exestuating bloud.

†**exæstu'ation.** *Obs.* Also 7–8 **exestuation.** [ad. L. *exæstuātiōn-em*, n. of action f. *exæstuā-re*: see prec.] A boiling up; fermentation.

1666 G. HARVEY *Morb. Angl.* iv. 44 If..the patient is discommoded with a glowing heat under the short ribs, you may suppose it to be an exæstuation. **1710** T. FULLER *Pharm. Extemp.* 296 These Earths mix in with it [the Bile] ..and put a restraint upon its preternatural exestuation. **1730–6** in BAILEY (folio). **1775** in ASH.

†**e'xagger,** *v. Obs.* [ad. L. *exagger-āre*: see EXAGGERATE.] *trans.* (and *absol.*) = EXAGGERATE.

1535 JOYE *Apol. Tindale* 26 Se how this man exaggereth. **1597** T. BEARD *Theatre God's Judgm.* 378 Iulian..exaggered also his sacriledge with scornefull ieasts.

exaggerant (ɛg'zædʒərənt). *rare*⁻¹. [as if ad. L. *exaggerant-em*, pr. pple. of *exaggerāre*: see EXAGGERATE.] One who holds exaggerated or extreme views; an extremist.

1803 W. TAYLOR in *Ann. Rev.* I. 351 The moderate have less courage than the exaggerants, and therefore suit the majority.

exaggerate (ɛg'zædʒəreɪt), *v.* Also 6 **exagerat.** [f. L. *exaggerāt-* ppl. stem of *exaggerā-re*, f. *ex-* intensive + *aggerā-re* to heap up, f. *agger* heap. Cf. F. *exagérer*, 16th c. *exaggerer*.]

†**1.** *trans.* To heap or pile up, accumulate: said with reference to both material and immaterial objects; also to form by accumulation. *Obs.*

1533 MORE *Apol.* Wks. 871/1 Yf hee woulde..take no suche bywayes, he woulde not..accumulate and exaggerate the gryefes. **1553** T. WILSON *Rhet.* 63 b, In praisyng or dispraisyng, we muste exaggerate those places towardes the ende, whiche make menne wonder at the straungenesse of any thyng. **1583** STUBBES *Anat. Abus.* (1877) 58 With their flipping and flapping up and down in the dirte they exaggerate a mountain of mire. **1621** BURTON *Anat. Mel.* II. iii. III. (1651) 330 What a deal of trouble..do we sustain and exaggerate unto ourselves, to get that secure happiness.. which we peradventure shall never have. **1677** HALE *Prim. Orig. Man.* II. vii. 191 Trees of Oak and Firr..covered by.. the Silt and Moorish Earth exaggerated upon them. *Ibid.* IV. ii. 299 The water..exaggerating and raising Islands and Continents in other parts.

†**2.** To 'pile up' (eulogies, accusations); to emphasize (statements); to make much of, dwell on the greatness of (virtues, faults, conditions, etc.).

1564 *Brief. Exam.* Sig.* iij, To exagerat the matter agaynste them..shall..be spared. **1581** MARBECK *Bk. of Notes* 707 This word (Mene) is doubled..to exaggerate the certaintie of the matter. **1603** KNOLLES *Hist. Turks* (1621) 1123 Alledging and exaggerating many his most cruell actions. **1620** SHELTON *Quix.* (1725) III. II. xxv. 175 They told..what had happened in the search for the ass, the one exaggerating the other's cunning in braying. **1650** R. STAPYLTON *Strada's Low-C. Warres* x. 19 Exaggerating, indeed not falsely, the Necessity of the Provinces. **1656** EARL MONM. *Advt. fr. Parnass.* 387 It was..very praiseworthy in Bishop Jovius to exaggerate the praises of the Princes his Benefactors. *a* **1734** NORTH *Lives* I. 401 His lordship..used to exaggerate the monstrous impudence of Counsel that insisted so iniquitably.

3. To magnify beyond the limits of truth; to represent something as greater than it really is.

(The 16th century quots. may belong to 2.)

[**1563–87** FOXE *A. & M.* (1596) 359/2 Thus they aggrauate and exaggerating the fault to the vttermost flie vpon the poore asse and deuour him. **1599** MARSTON *Sco.*

Villanie I. iii. 182 Rufus, Ile terme thee but intemperate, I will not once thy vice exaggerate.] **1613** R. C. *Table Alph.* (ed. 3), *Exaggerate*, to make a thing more then it is. *a* **1631** DONNE *Septuagint* (1633) 105 Men, when they heare anything..to utter and augment the same..and to exaggerate the same by words odious and bitter. **1712** ADDISON *Spect.* No. 399 ¶5 A Friend exaggerates a Man's Virtues, an Enemy inflames his Crimes. **1772** *Junius Lett.* Pref. 10 They..greatly exaggerate the evil they complain of. **1832** WEBSTER, *Exaggerate*, in Painting to heighten in colour or design. **1868** J. H. BLUNT *Ref. Ch. Eng.* I. 401 A modern historian..has done his best to exaggerate everything that would tell against the clergy. **1874** GREEN *Short Hist.* vi. 333 The charges were grossly exaggerated, but there is no ground for believing them to have been wholly untrue.

absol. **1781** GIBBON *Decl. & F.* III. xlviii. 29 Calumny is more prone to exaggerate than to invent. **1840** CARLYLE *Heroes* (1858) 266 In no point does he [Shakspeare] exaggerate but only in laughter. **1878** GLADSTONE *Prim. Homer* 59 Early navigators exaggerate without fear to enhance the interest of their tales.

4. To intensify, aggravate (conditions, etc.), abnormally; to make (physical features, etc.) of abnormal size.

1850 L. HUNT *Autobiog.* I. vii. 276 A nose exaggerated by intemperance. **1868** ROGERS *Pol. Econ.* viii. (ed. 3) 73 The existing distress was exaggerated by this great social change. **1873** MIVART *Elem. Anat.* ii. 51 In the preponderating size of the Lumbar Vertebrae man but exaggerates a character generally present in his class.

exaggerated (ɛgˈzædʒəreɪtɪd), *ppl. a.* [f. prec. + -ED[1].]

†**1.** Heaped up. *Obs. rare*⁻⁰.

1552 HULOET, Exaggerated, *repositus, a, um.*

2. Magnified or inflated beyong the limits of fact, justice, propriety, or truth; excessive.

The ordinary application of the pple. and ppl. adj. now differs from that of the finite verb: we say that a speaker 'exaggerates his *facts*,' but it is his *statements* that are described as 'exaggerated'.

1725 POPE *Pref. to Shaks.*, The most exaggerated thoughts; the most verbose and bombast expression. **1812** SIR H. DAVY *Chem. Philos.* 18 His exaggerated censure of the methods of the ancients..had an effect in diminishing their popularity. **1843** BETHUNE *Sc. Fireside Stor.* 39 Before any exaggerated report could reach them. **1849** COBDEN *Speeches* 37 There has prevailed a most exaggerated idea as to the necessity of that force. *a* **1862** BUCKLE *Misc. Wks.* (1872) I. 308 Gods were exaggerated heroes, and their heroes were exaggerated men.

3. Abnormally enlarged, monstrous, overgrown.

1860 TYNDALL *Glac.* I. x. 65 My route was an exaggerated zigzag. **1885** O. T. MILLER in *Harper's Mag.* Mar. 600 He resembles an exaggerated wren.

e'xaggeratedly (ɛgˈzædʒəreɪtɪdlɪ); *adv.* [f. prec. + -LY[2].] To an exaggerated or excessive degree; unduly.

1854 KINGSLEY *Alexandria* iii. 94 He perceived so deeply, I may say so exaggeratedly, the analogy between, [etc.]. **1870** RUSKIN *Lect. Art* ii. 47 The persons who most clearly estimate their value, exaggeratedly estimate it. **1879** PROCTOR *Pleas. Ways Sc.* x. 210 Turn we..from..the exaggeratedly monstrous cuttle-fish, to the..sea-serpent.

†**e'xaggerately,** *adv. Obs. rare*⁻¹. [f. **exaggerate* ppl. adj., ad. L. *exaggerāt-us* pa. pple. of *exaggerāre* (see EXAGGERATE *v.*) + -LY[2].] = prec.

1646 N. LOCKYER *Serm.* 28 Oct. 3 The action of the Father towards the Sonne is sad, and exprest exaggerately, etc.

exaggerating (ɛgˈzædʒəreɪtɪŋ), *ppl. a.* [f. EXAGGERATE *v.* + -ING[2].] That exaggerates.

1818 JAS. MILL *Brit. India* II. v. viii. 667 The exaggerating language of Mr. Hastings. **1833** THIRLWALL in *Philol. Mus.* II. 576 In this Mr. Ast discovers the hand of an exaggerating rhetorician. **1881** MRS. LYNN LINTON *My Love* I. 77 You always were one of the most exaggerating children possible.

Hence **e'xaggeratingly** *adv.*

1858 *Chamb. Jrnl.* IX. 376 She retailed what Lisa saw.. fluently, unfailingly, and, we regret to add, exaggeratingly. **1876** W. GRAHAM *Mem. J. Macfarlane* iii. 144 Neither heartlessly inappreciative of the past, nor exaggeratingly friendly to the present.

exaggeration (ɛgˌzædʒəˈreɪʃən). [ad. L. *exaggerātiōn-em*, n. of action f. *exaggerā-re*: see EXAGGERATE.]

†**1.** The action of heaping or piling up; *e.g.* of silt by a river or the sea; also *concr.* that which is so piled up. *Obs.*

1677 HALE *Prim. Orig. Man.* II. ix. 221 Lakes grow by the exaggeration of Sand by the Sea. *Ibid.* II. xii. 241 The fruitfullest part of Egypt..is an Exaggeration, or Ground gained by the Inundation of Nilus.

†**2.** The action of emphasizing or dwelling on the greatness of (a good or bad quality or action).

1586 A. DAY *Eng. Secretary* II. (1599) 93 In this exaggeration of vices, so also might there bee the like of Vertues, as if one should exhort a man to Pietie after hee had set forth all the commodities thereof. **1611** BP. ANDREWES *Serm.* II. 277 Of Himself it is said, and by way of exaggeration, He humbled Himself to death, the death of the Cross. *c* **1647** BOYLE *Agst. Swearing* Wks. (1772) VI. 11 They swear not but when they are angry; and then (for all our clamours and exaggerations) they mean no harm at all. *a* **1745** SWIFT (J.), Exaggeration of the prodigious condescensions in the prince to pass good laws, would have an odd sound at Westminster.

3. The action of exaggerating or magnifying unduly in words or representation. Also, an instance of this; an exaggerated statement.

1565 JEWEL *Repl. Harding* 88 Which [smal] companies he [Chrysostome]..by an exaggeration..calleth Nobody. **1685** *Gracian's Courtiers Orac.* 35 Exaggeration is a kind of lying: by Exaggeration one gets himself the reputation of a man of bad discerning. **1776** GIBBON *Decl. & F.* I. xvii. 442 Such exaggerations will be reduced to their just value. **1848** W. H. BARTLETT *Egypt to Pal.* xxiv. (1879) 489 If we were to accept the account of Josephus as not an utterly baseless exaggeration. **1878** HUXLEY *Physiogr.* 177 The exaggeration of the vertical height in the diagram.

b. *transf.* in *Painting* and *Sculpture*: A heightened representation of a subject either in design or by excessive colouring.

1734 in *Builder's Dict.* s.v. **1738** CHAMBERS *Cycl.* s.v., This exaggeration must be conducted in such manner, as not to put the objects out of their natural characters. **1828** in WEBSTER; and in mod. Dicts.

c. *concr.* An exaggerated copy.

1841–4 EMERSON *Ess., Spir. Laws* Wks. (Bohn) I. 63 Hideous dreams are exaggerations of the sins of the day. **1872** BAKER *Nile Tribut.* viii. 131 The eye of this animal is the most beautiful exaggeration of that of the gazelle.

4. Aggravation of a condition, etc.; also *concr.*

1661 COWLEY *O. Cromwell* (1669) 70 The diligence of wicked persons..is only an Emphasis and Exaggeration of their wickedness.

exaggerative (ɛgˈzædʒərətɪv), *a.* [f. EXAGGERATE *v.* + -IVE. Cf. Fr. *exagératif.*]

1. Of a statement, representation, etc.: Marked by exaggeration, hyperbolical.

1797 A. GEDDES *Bible* II. Pref. 8 This exaggerative language warns us not to take words of that kind in a strict theological meaning. **1863** *Sat. Rev.* Jan. 123 The exaggerative character of these drawings. **1880** J. HAWTHORNE *Ellice Quentin* I. 97 Let this confession put the reader on his guard against..exaggerative or prejudicial statements.

2. Of persons: Given to exaggerate; prone to exaggeration.

1837 CARLYLE *Fr. Rev.* III. v. iv, 'Out of doors', continues the exaggerative man, 'were mad multitudes dancing round the bonfire'. **1854** H. MILLER *Sch. & Schm.* xxiii. (1857) 505 The tender passion is always a strangely exaggerative one. **1870** J. H. FRISWELL *Mod. Men Lett.* 32 Dickens was very often exaggerative and pantomimic.

Hence **e'xaggeratively** *adv.*, in an exaggerative manner. **e'xaggerativeness**, the quality of being exaggerative.

1856 *Chamb. Jrnl.* V. 365 Exaggeratively exhibiting the defects of the system. **1867** CARLYLE *Remin.* II. 16 'It were better to perish', as I exaggeratively said to myself, 'than continue schoolmastering'. **1873** *Spectator* 22 Feb. 245/1 A certain exaggerativeness in some of his anecdotes.

exaggerator (ɛgˈzædʒəreɪtə(r)). [a. late L. *exaggerātor*, agent-n. f. *exaggerā-re* to EXAGGERATE.] One who or that which exaggerates.

1822 J. FLINT *Lett. Amer.* 60 This is the hill that a florid exaggerator has described as a solid mass of coal. **1828** *Blackw. Mag.* XXIV. 47 Fear is a great exaggerator. **1856** MRS. BROWNING *Aur. Leigh* I. 858 Those virtuous liars, dreamers after dark, Exaggerators of the sun and moon.

exaggeratory (ɛgˈzædʒərəˌtərɪ), *a.* [f. EXAGGERATE *v.* + -ORY.] Containing or characterized by exaggeration; prone to exaggerate.

1759 JOHNSON *Rasselas* xxviii. 63 You fall into the common errors of exaggeratory acclamation. **1849** *Tait's Mag.* XVI. 539 The peculiar, egotistical, and exaggeratory temperament characteristic of the Americans.

†**e'xagitate,** *v. Obs.* 7 *pa. pple.* exagitat(e. [f. L. *exagitāt-* ppl. stem of *exagitā-re*, f. *ex-* (see EX- *pref.*[1]) + *agitā-re* to put in motion, AGITATE.]

1. *trans.* To stir up (the humours, spirits, etc.); to quicken (the breathing); to set in motion (the blood); to excite.

1621 BURTON *Anat. Mel.* I. ii. II. v, The divell..gets in with the aire, and exagitates our spirits, and vexeth our souls. **1651** BIGGS *New Disp.* 155 The anxiety and powerfullest respiration of the arteries is exagitated. **1655** CULPEPPER, etc. *Riverius* XV. v. 419 Sharp Clysters..which do exagitate the Humor..whereby the Symptomes are wont to become more fiery. **1717** J. KEILL *Anim. Œcon.* (1738) 294 A continual Heat..exagitated by the Temptations of the Town. **1727** FIELDING *Love in Sev. Masq.* Wks. 1775 I. 20 It [business] has exagitated my complexion to that exorbitancy of Vermeile, that, etc. **1732** ARBUTHNOT *Rules of Diet* 328 The warm Air of the Bed exagitates the Blood.

2. a. Of a disease, pain, etc.: To torment, worry. **b.** Of a man's foes: To harass, persecute.

a. 1532 in Burnet *Hist. Ref.* II. 168 Being so long sick and exagitate with this same sore. **1596** FITZ-GEFFRAY *Sir F. Drake* (1881) 15 The paines that now exagitate his soule, Time cannot tame. **1657** TOMLINSON *Renou's Disp.* 198 When..too much waking hath exagitated the mind. **1677** GALE *Crt. Gentiles* II. IV. 32 When it [the soul] shal see and instil the desire of him into it self..it shal cease to be exagitated by pricking dolors.

b. 1602 T. FITZHERBERT *Defence* 7 a, S. Chrisostome..was so exagitat by the calumnious, and contumelious tongues of heretykes..that, etc. **1618** T. GAINSFORD *P. Warbeck* in *Select. Harl. Misc.* (1793) 86 The king..not determining to give them battle, or exagitate them at all till, etc. *a* **1656** HALES *Gold. Rem.* (1688) 485 He was sorry Martinius should be so exagitated for a speech which..was true.

3. To attack violently (a doctrine, error, fault, etc.); to inveigh against, rail at.

1594 HOOKER *Eccl. Pol.* III. (1632) 163 This their defect and imperfection I had rather lament in such case than exagitate. **1656** TRAPP *Comm. Eph.* i. 5 The doctrine of predestination was much misused and exagitated. **1685** BAXTER *Paraphr. N.T.* 1 Pet. iii. 8 Christians..live in concord, not exagitating, but compassionating each others infirmities.

4. To debate, discuss.

1610 DONNE *Pseudo-Martyr* 294 His last Title..we have no reason to exagitate in this place. *a* **1649** DRUMM. OF HAWTH. *Jas. III*, Wks. 43 During his abode at Rome, the old question..began to be exagitated. **1662** S. P. *Acc. Latitude Men* in *Phenix* II. 581 Tho this name of Latitude-Men be daily exagitated amongst us, both in Taverns and Pulpits. **1749** BP. LAVINGTON *Enthus. Methodists & Pap.* III. (1751) 330 Aristophanes in such a free manner exagitates the mysterious solemnities.

5. In etymological sense: To shake out. *rare.*

1642 *Answ. to Observ. agst. King* 11 Traiterously exagitate and tosse the Royall Scepter out of his hand.

Hence †**e'xagitated** *ppl. a.* †**e'xagitating** *ppl. a.*, producing agitation, disturbing.

1655–60 STANLEY *Hist. Philos.* (1701) 578/1 A coacervate and exagitated Wind. **1659** W. CHAMBERLAYNE *Pharonnida* III. ii, Th' ensuing storms exagitated rage. **1662** S. P. *Acc. Latitude-Men in Phenix* (1708) II. 507 Having taken an impartial View of this so much exagitated Company of Men. **1646** SIR T. BROWNE *Pseud. Ep.* IV. ix. 200 In diseases of the chest..Hippocrates condemneth it [sneezing] as too much exagitating.

†**exagi'tation.** *Obs.* [ad. L. *exagitātiōn-em*, n. of action f. *exagitā-re*: see EXAGITATE *v.*] **a.** The action of stirring up (the blood, humours, etc.), setting in motion or exciting; also an instance of the same, an excitement. **b.** Discussion.

1603 HOLLAND *Plutarch's Mor.* 1134 This is but a flatulent exagitation. **1615** CROOKE *Body of Man* 474 Animall spirits are made of the vitall, changed by many exagitations and alterations by the arteries. **1632** tr. *Bruel's Praxis Med.* 401 Neyther is there any danger of the exagitation of the humors. **1684** tr. *Bonet's Merc. Compit.* VI. 216 The exagitation of the more gross particles [of the blood] is.. more languid. **1737** *Common Sense* (1738) I. 139 Exagitations of Choler, which are apt to break out into Rogue and Rascal.

†**e'xagite,** *v. Obs.* [ad. OF. *exagite-r*, f. L. *exagitāre*: see EXAGITATE.] *trans.* = EXAGITATE; in quot. to keep on demanding.

1621 W. SCLATER *Tythes* (1623) 149 It is my liberalitie to affoord answer to the Argument from first fruits; why doe you so punctually exagite, exact it?

exagon, -gonal, obs. ff. HEXAGON, etc.

exalacion, obs. form of EXHALATION.

exalbuminose (ɛksælˈbjuːmɪnəʊs), *a. Bot.* [f. EX- *prefix*[1] + L. *albūmen* (*albūmin-*) + -OSE.] = next.

1866 *Treas., Exalbuminose*, having no albumen.

exalbuminous (ɛksælˈbjuːmɪnəs), *a. Bot.* [f. as prec. + -OUS.] Having no albumen in the seed.

1830 LINDLEY *Nat. Syst. Bot.* 226 They [Lentibulariæ] are known from Primulaceæ by their..exalbuminous embryo. **1880** GRAY *Struct. Bot.* ii. 14 Seeds are distinguished into albuminous and exalbuminous, those supplied with and those destitute of albumen.

exalgin (ɛksˈældʒɪn). *Pharmacy.* Also exalgine. [f. EX- *prefix*[1] + Gr. ἄλγ-ος pain + -IN.] A methyl compound of acetanilide, so called from its use as an anodyne.

1889 *Pharm. Jrnl.* 30 Mar. 781/1 Exalgine occurs in needles or in large white tablets. **1890** *Daily News* 1 Dec. 5/6 A prescription ordering exalgine.

exa'llotriote, *a. nonce-wd.* (bombastic). [as if ad. Gr. *ἐξαλλοτριωτός, f. ἐξαλλοτριό-ειν, f. ἐξ + ἀλλότριος foreign.] Brought from a foreign country.

1849 LYTTON *Caxtons* II. III. lxvi, Is there no mission in thy native land, O planeticose and exallotriote spirit?

exalt (ɛgˈzɒlt, -ɔː-), *v.* Also 5 exsaulte, (8 exhalt). [ad. L. *exaltāre*, f. *ex-* (see EX- *pref.*[1]) + *altus* high. Cf. Fr. *exalter* (16th c. in Littré).

Vulgar Lat. had **exaltiare* of similar formation and meaning, of which the regular phonetic descendant is OF. *essalcier, essaucier*, represented in mod.F. by the two vbs. *exhausser* to lift up, and *exaucer* to listen favourably to (a prayer): with the latter cf. 6.]

1. *trans.* To raise or set up on high; to lift up, elevate. In physical sense now *arch.* or *rhetorical*, or in humorously bombastic use.

1535 COVERDALE *2 Esdras* xv. 53 Thou haddest..slayne my chosen, exaltinge the stroke of thy handes. **1582** N. T. (Rhem.) *Matt.* xi. 23 Thou Capharnaum, shalt thou be exalted vp to heauen? **1601** SHAKS. *Jul. C.* I. iii. 8, I haue seene Th' ambitious Ocean swell..To be exalted with the threatning clouds. **1613** T. MILLES tr. *Mexia's Treas. Anc. & Mod. Times* 954 Exalting his Courtlax to strike the stroke. **1698** LUTTRELL *Brief Rel.* (1857) IV. 401 Yesterday one Hoyle was fined; as also to be exalted in the market place.. instead of a pillory. **1712** POPE *Messiah* 86 Imperial Salem, rise! Exalt thy tow'ry head. **1808** J. BARLOW *Columb.* I. 325 Exalt your heads, ye oaks. **1823** LAMB *Elia* Ser. I. xvii. (1865) 131 Exalting his umbrella over her poor basket of fruit. **1832** *Blackw. Mag.* Feb. 287 Let the rogues swing, And thus be exalted.

b. *transf.* To 'lift up' (the voice, a song). *arch.* Cf. ENHANCE 1 c.

1611 BIBLE *2 Kings* xix. 22 Against whome hast thou exalted thy voyce? **1709** PRIOR *Henry & Emma* 737 Now, Mars, she said, let Fame exalt her voice. **1762** FALCONER *Shipwr.* I. 642 The warbling birds exalt their evening lay. **1795** AGNES MUSGRAVE *Cicely* I. 35 Jane, exalting her voice, cried, etc.

2. In various *fig.* or non-material senses: **a.** To raise in rank, honour, estimation, power, or wealth. †Formerly *occas.* with title as complement. †Also (rarely) with *up*.

? *a* **1400** *Chester Pl.* (Shaks. Soc.) I. 9 The three tryalles in a throne, And trewe Trenitie, Be grounded in my God heade, Exsaulted by my excelencye. **1430** LYDG. *Chron. Troy* II. x, One she [Fortune] can high in riches exalte And an other plonge in pouertye. **1494** FABYAN *Chron.* VII. ccxix. 241 Wyllyam exalted the Normans, and gaue vnto theym the chief possessyons of the lande. **1565** CDL. ALLEN in Fulke *Confut. Doctr. Purgatory* (1577) 377 Proue me that your mother Church prayeth not for her departed..you shall be exalted up for euer. **1568** GRAFTON *Chron.* II. 72 It seemeth likely that you will aspire to take his crowne from him, and to be exalted king yourselfe. **1611** BIBLE *Ezek.* xxi. 26 Exalt him that is low, and abase him that is high. *a* **1658** WALLER *Poems, To my Ld. Protector* xxi, Still as you rise, the state, exalted too, Finds no distemper. **1667** MILTON *P.L.* I. 736 Scepter'd Angels..whom the supreme King Exalted to such power. **1771** *Junius Lett.* lxvii. 330 Society can exalt the meanest and worst of men. **1861** MAY *Const. Hist.* (1863) I. i. 10 He [George III] came to the throne determined to exalt the kingly office.

†**b.** To elate with pride, joy, etc. Also *intr.* for *refl.* *Obs.*

a **1533** LD. BERNERS *Gold. Bk. M. Aurel.* (1546) I v b, With a littell fauour ye wyl exalt, augement, and grow into gret prid. **1568** GRAFTON *Chron.* II. 44 When the Empresse had ..committed the king to warde..she was not therewith a little exalted. **1605** SHAKS. *Lear* v. iii. 67 Not so hot: In his owne grace he doth exalt himselfe, More then in your addition. **1647** CLARENDON *Hist. Reb.* II. (1843) 48/2 The covenanters..were very reasonably exalted with this success. **1708** POPE *Ode St. Cecilia* 27 Music..when the soul is press'd with cares, Exalts her in enlivening airs.

c. *refl.* To assume superiority. *arch.*

1611 BIBLE *1 Kings* i. 5 Then Adoniiah the sonne of Haggith exalted himselfe, saying, I wil be king. **1878** B. TAYLOR *Deukalion* III. i, Exalt thyself past limits of my law, I feed thee still.

transf. **1742** *Lond. & Country Brew.* I. (ed. 4) 73 That the Salt does not exalt itself above the Sulphur.

d. To praise, extol, magnify. Also *absol.*

1430 LYDG. *Chron. Troy.* I. v, He that lyst her name so hyghe exalte. **1526** *Pilgr. Perf.* (W. de W. 1531) 59 b, And exalting it [his holy lyfe] moost hye, meke thyselfe in herte moost lowe. *c* **1532** DEWES *Introd. Fr.* in Palsgr. 1023 In Heven..they may laude and exalte with the saintes. *a* **1545** CROKE *Ps.* (Percy Soc.) 18 My tonge shall both daye and houre, Dewly exalte thy iustice styll. **1611** BIBLE *Ps.* xxxiv. 3 O magnifie the Lord with me, and let vs exalt his name together. **1632** J. HAYWARD tr. *Biondi's Eromena* 132 Taking opportunely hold of an occasion..to exalt the valour of the younger [Prince]. **1719** WATTS *Ps.* xcix. II, Exalt the Lord our God. *a* **1845** HOOD *Tale Trump.* 140 The brandy and salt We now exalt, Had made a noise in the public ear.

e. To raise to a higher class, a higher degree of value or excellence; to dignify, ennoble.

1711 STEELE *Spect.* No. 4 ¶8, I shall not lower but exalt the Subjects I treat upon. **1788** REID *Aristotle's Log.* iv. §3. 80 A negative may be exalted into an affirmative. **1791** BOSWELL *Johnson* 5 Apr. an. 1772 Men less exalted by spiritual habits. **1836** EMERSON *Nat., Lang.* Wks. (Bohn) II. 152 The moment our discourse..is..exalted by thought, it clothes itself in images.

f. To stimulate (powers) to higher activity.

1744 THOMSON *Summer* 307 Each liquid..Inflames, refreshes, or exalts the taste. **1860** GEO. ELIOT *Mill on Fl.* VI. iii, Trivial causes had the effect of rousing and exalting the imagination.

†**3.** In Alchemy and early Chemistry: To raise (a substance or its qualities) to a higher 'degree'; hence, in wider sense, to raise in quality, refine, mature; to intensify, render more powerful (physical agents or effects). Also *fig.*

1471 RIPLEY *Comp. Alch.* x. in Ashm. (1652) 178 Then up to Hevyn they must Exaltyd be..to be intronyzate In Clowds of clerenesse. **1570** DEE *Math. Pref.* 8 A liquid Medicine whose Qualitie of heate is in the 4 degree exalted. **1610** B. JONSON *Alch.* I. i, Have I..Sublimed thee, and exalted thee, and fix'd thee I' the third region? **1691** RAY *Creation* (1714) 92 Other stones being exalted to that degree of Hardness. **1725–6** POPE *Odyss.* XXIV. 400 The hours produce their [vines'] latent buds, and Sol exalts the juice. **1744** BERKELEY *Siris* §44 Oil, purified and exalted by the organical powers of the plant. **1762** *Gentl. Mag.* 269 The sun is known to exalt the poison of the viper. **1790** A. CRAWFORD in *Phil. Trans.* LXXX. 402 A little strong vitriolic acid, by which the smell was exalted, and a slight effervescence was produced. **1795** BURKE *Regic. Peace* iv. Wks. IX. 14 This is Jacobinism sublimed and exalted into most pure..essence. **1813** SIR H. DAVY *Agric. Chem.* (1814) 257 The seeds of plants exalted by cultivation.

†**b.** To volatilize, carry off in vapour. *Obs.*

1686 W. HARRIS tr. *Lemery's Chem.* III. iii. (ed. 3) 735 The fuliginosity which made it black will be exalted and leave the Harts-horn white.

4. To raise in degree, intensify, heighten.

1842 W. GROVE *Corr. Phys. Forces* 92 If this intensity be exalted to a certain point the sulphuret becomes luminous. **1859** GULLICK & TIMBS *Paint.* 202 They [varnishes] enliven or exalt the colours by their colourless transparency. **1870** *Eng. Mech.* 4 Feb. 512/2 To colour gold, or as it is technically called, to exalt the colour of gold.

5. *Astrol.* in *passive* of a heavenly body: To be in the position of greatest influence.

1647 *Almanak for* 1386, 2 The Son is exalted and raised uppe in þe 19 gre of þe Ram, þe Mone is exalted in þe 3 gre of þe Bul. **1652** CULPEPPER *Eng. Physic.* (1656) 48 Saturn being exalted in Libra, in the house of Venus. **1819** JAS. WILSON *Dict. Astrol.* s.v. *Exaltation*, If power may be deemed exaltation, all planets must be exalted when they arrive at their northern nodes, and advance towards our zenith.

¶ **6.** *nonce-use.* Of a deity: To grant (a prayer) [after OF. *essalcier*, F. *exaucer*].

1490 CAXTON *Eneydos* xvi. (1890) 61 The god almyghty Iupyter..wolde exalte his requeste.

† **e'xalt,** *sb.* *Obs.* [f. EXALT *v.*] The action of exalting; in quot. = EXALTATION 2 c.

1617 MARKHAM *Caval.* VI. 2 To the exalt of the most seruiceable Beast that euer was created.

e'xalt, *pple.*, short for EXALTED.

1871 BROWNING *Pr. Hohenstiel* 1835 Bravest of the brave Doers, exalt in Science. **1873** —— *Red Cott. Nt.-cap* 1122 Out I stand Exalt and safe, and bid low earth adieu.

‖**Exaltado** (eksal'tado). [Sp., pa. pple. of *exaltar* to EXALT.] A member of the extreme radical party in Spain. Also *transf.*

1824 *Westm. Rev.* I. 25 An apprehension of being esteemed somewhat of an *exaltado*, may have induced him [T. Moore] to make this little sacrifice. *Ibid.* I. 293 Much has been said in Spain..on the distinction..between the *Moderados* and the *Exaltados.*

†**exaltate,** *v.* *Obs.* [f. L. *exaltāt-* ppl. stem of *exaltāre* to EXALT.] *trans.* = EXALT *v.* 3.

1471 RIPLEY *Comp. Alch.* x. in Ashm. (1652) 179 Yf thou therfore thy Bodys wyll Exaltat.

†**exaltate,** *pple.* *Obs.* [ad. L. *exaltāt-us*, pa. pple. of *exaltāre* to EXALT.] = EXALTED.

c **1386** CHAUCER *Wife's Prol.* 704 In Pisces, wher Venus is exaltat. *a* **1420** HOCCLEVE *De Reg. Princ.* 5227 Every man willethe to ben exaltate. *c* **1430** LYDG. *Bochas* VII. iv. (1554) 167 b, Amid the heauen, was Venus exaltate. *c* **1450** *Mirour Saluacioun* 1161 Salomones throne was with sex graces exaltate [*v.r.* reisid]. *c* **1500** *Lancelot* 2551 Sum in to worschip to be exaltate.

exaltation (ɛgzɔːl'teɪʃən). Forms: 4 **exaltacioun,** 4–7 **exaltacion, -yon,** 6 **exhaltation.** [a. F. *exaltation*, ad. L. *exaltātiōn-em*, f. *exaltāre*: see EXALT.] The action of exalting; the fact or state of being exalted.

1. In physical sense: The action of lifting up or raising on high; the state of being lifted up, or set in a high position.

1616 LANE *Sqr.'s Tale* XI. 278 He comes: whose horse fomed the seas invndation, as th' rider felt him on owne exaltation. **1686** HORNECK *Crucif. Jesus* xvi. 403 Lift me up from the earth, that I may relish the comfort of thy exaltation. **1794** G. ADAMS *Nat. & Exp. Philos.* I. x. 429 When the sun is at its greatest exaltation in summer. **1860** TYNDALL *Glac.* II. viii. 265 [Glacier] tables..a limit is placed to their exaltation by the following circumstance.

b. *Exaltation of the Cross*: a feast observed on Sept. 14th (see quot. 1884).

1389 in *Eng. Gilds* (1870) 54 Yᵉ exaltacion of yᵉ holy crouche. **1480** CAXTON *Chron. Eng.* v. (1520) 60 b/1 Than was the feest of the exaltacyon of the crosse made. **1700** TYRRELL *Hist. Eng.* II. 770 Thursday after the Exaltation of the Cross in September. **1884** *Catholic Dict.* s.v. *Cross*, The 'Exaltation of the Cross' was celebrated from ancient times in memory of the miraculous apparition which Constantine saw in the year 317..The day was afterwards kept with greater solemnity, when after the victory over the Persians in 627, Heraclius recovered the true cross.

†**c.** *concr.* A fanciful name for: A flight (of larks). *Obs.*

c **1430** LYDG. *Hors Shepe & G.* (1822) 30 A exaltacion of larkes. **1824** J. MᶜCULLOCH *Scotland* III. 407, I have never spoken of 'an exaltation of larks'. **1883** *Standard* 26 Sept. 5/1 Every one with any pretence to be gentle-folk spoke of..an exaltation of larks.

2. In non-material sense: **a.** Elevation in authority, dignity, power, station, wealth, etc.; *esp.* the elevation of a sovereign to a throne. †Also *occas.* An exalted position; elevated rank.

1490 CAXTON *Eneydos* vii. 33 The place where hir glorye and exaltacion ought to be..manyfested. **1539** TONSTALL *Serm. Palm Sund.* (1823) 15 Here it is to be noted, that God gaue to Christe his exaltation, as to man, and not as to god. **1568** GRAFTON *Chron.* II. 72 Ye have presumed thus to stande against the exaltation of this oure sovereigne. **1611** BIBLE *Judith* xvi. 8 The exaltation of those that were oppressed. *a* **1631** DONNE in *Selections* (1840) 104 Though faith be of an infinite exaltation above understanding. **1670** G. H. *Hist. Cardinals* III. II. 268 The Exaltation of this Pope happen'd upon Ascension day. **1719** DE FOE *Crusoe* (1840) II. ii. 42 Like that of Joseph's brethren, when he..told them the story of his exaltation in Pharaoh's court. **1791** BOSWELL *Johnson* (1816) II. 188 A master..is in his highest Exaltation when he is *loco parentis.* **1858** FROUDE *Hist. Eng.* III. xiii. 88 The Reformation in their minds was associated with the exaltation of base blood.

b. Elation of feeling; a state of rapturous emotion; an undue degree of pleasurable excitement. Also *Path.* (see quot. 1884).

1494 FABYAN *Chron.* VI. ccvi. 219 In tyme of whiche exaltacion of his mynde, he..charged the water that he shulde flowe no hygher. **1707** *Lond. Gaz.* No. 4351/1 We want Words to express the Exaltation it has rais'd in us, to see Your Majesty's unwearied Endeavours..crown'd with such..Success. **1870** EMERSON *Soc. & Solit.* vii. 144, I knew a man in a certain religious exaltation, who thought it an honor to wash his own face. **1874** MAUDSLEY *Respons. in Ment. Dis.* vii. 234 There was nothing particularly noticeable in him except..a condition of exaltation in the spring. **1884** *Syd. Soc. Lex.*, *Exaltation*, the immoderate increase of the action of an organ.

c. An extolling, a laudation.

1650 HUBBERT *Pill Formality* 190 Your praises, and exaltations of free grace.

d. The raising to a lofty point of excellence; exalted degree; an exalted manifestation.

1656 COWLEY *Pindar. Odes, Brutus* ii, Th' Heroick Exaltations of Good, Are so far from Understood, We count them Vice. **1667** RUST *Fun. Serm. Bp. Taylor* (1672) 67 Those Heavenly Bodies..are fit..instruments for the Soul, in its highest Exaltations. *a* **1694** TILLOTSON *Serm.* i. Wks. (1714) 4 In God all Perfections in their highest degree and exaltation meet together. **1837** HT. MARTINEAU *Soc. Amer.* III. 1 The degree of civilisation of any people corresponds with the exaltation of the idea which is the most prevalent among that people. **1848** MACAULAY *Hist. Eng.* I. 12 That chivalrous spirit..was found in the highest exaltation among the Norman nobles. **1883** *Christian Commw.* 6 Dec. 174/1 Is this exaltation of the ideal of life an evil?

e. Augmentation in degree or intensity.

1732 LAW *Serious C.* v. (ed. 2) 75 The refinement and exaltation of our best faculties. **1842** W. GROVE *Corr. Phys. Forces* 80 We obtain an indefinite exaltation of chemical power. **1855** BAIN *Senses & Int.* II. ii. §1. (1864) 177 The skin is therefore marked by a great exaltation of the common sensibility of the body.

f. Of prices: A rise. *rare.*

1866 ROGERS *Agric. & Prices* I. xxi. 536 The last two years being affected by the exaltation in the price. **1884** —— *Work & Wages* 22 Quite as great is the exaltation in the price of millstones.

3. *Astrol.* The place of a planet in the zodiac in which it was considered to exert its greatest influence. Also *fig.*

c **1386** CHAUCER *Sqr.'s T.* 41 Phebus the sonne..was neigh his exaltacioun. **1398** TREVISA *Barth. De P.R.* VIII. ix. (1495) 307 The sonne hath his vertue and exaltacion in the eyghteenth gree of Aries. *a* **1625** FLETCHER *Rollo* IV. ii, Mars his gaudium rising in the ascendant That joint with Libra too, the house of Venus And Imum Cœli, Mars his exaltation [*printed* exultation] Ith' seaventh house. **1632** MASSINGER *City Madam* II. ii, She in her exaltation, and he in his triplicite trine and face, assure a fortunate combination to Hymen. **1751** CHAMBERS *Cycl.* s.v., The 15th degree of Cancer, is the exaltation of Jupiter, according to Albumazar. **1819** JAS. WILSON *Dict. Astrol.* s.v., The original meaning of the planets' exaltations seems to have been unknown in the time of Ptolemy. **1839** BAILEY *Festus* (1854) 121 Your exaltations and triplicities, Fiery, airy and the rest.

fig. **1607–12** BACON *Ess., Custom & Educ.* (Arb.) 372 In such places the force of Custome is in his exaltacion.

†**4.** In the older chemistry and physiology: The action or process of refining or subliming; the bringing a substance to a higher degree of potency or purity; an instance of the same. *Obs.*

1471 RIPLEY *Comp. Alch.* x. in Ashm. (1652) 178 Exaltacion, Full lyttyl yt ys dyfferent from Sublymacyon. **1576** BAKER *Jewell of Health* 176 a, Let the exhaltation of the vineger be after done on a soft fyre. **1605** TIMME *Quersit.* III. 184 Exaltation is euaporation of the impure humour. **1666** J. SMITH *Old Age* 107 The Chyle it self..receiving yet farther exaltations. **1686** W. HARRIS tr. *Lemery's Chem.* II. v. (ed. 3) 486 Tincture of Cinnamon..is an exaltation of the more oily parts of Cinnamon in Spirit of Wine. **1718** QUINCY *Compl. Disp.* 8 Salts, most capable of Exaltation, wrapped up in a small Portion of Phlegm. **1751** CHAMBERS *Cycl.* s.v., It is this exaltation of the sulphurous part in strawberries, that gives them their agreeable, vinous taste.

†**b.** *concr.* A substance in a highly refined condition. *Obs.*

1686 W. HARRIS tr. *Lemery's Chem.* I. xx. (ed. 3) 437 Flower of Sulphur..is an exaltation of Sulphur.

exaltative (ɛg'zɒltətɪv), *a.* *rare.* [f. L. *exaltāt-* ppl. stem of *exaltāre* (see EXALT) + -IVE.] Tending to exalt.

1810 BENTHAM *Packing* (1821) 23 Of these two branches of the art of deception, the first mentioned may be termed the depressive..the other the self-exaltative.

‖**exalté** (ɛgzalte), *a.* Also fem. **exaltée.** [Fr., pa. pple. of *exalter* to EXALT.] Excited, elated, abnormally happy. Hence as *sb.*, a person in a state of elation; a fanatic.

1831 J. S. MILL *Let.* 20–22 Oct. (1910) I. i. 7 The agricultural people are as determined as the manufacturers. The West is as *exalté* as the North. **1842** *Ibid.* Nov. iii. 123 Capable of almost any degree of *exalté* feeling from poetry. **1922** J. AGATE *Red Let. Nights* (1944) 76 It [*sc.* Ibsen's *Hedda Gabler*] contains nothing of awe or terror, nothing to make us fearful lest our *exaltées* should take to pistol-practice in the garden. **1937** *New Statesman* 30 Oct. 688/1 Costals detests cerebral women, and *exaltées* are not his type at all. **1941** AUDEN *New Year Let.* I. 17 Singing or sighing as they go: Exalté, piano, or in doubt. **1946** M. DICKENS *Happy Prisoner* ix. 200 She was *exaltée*, beside herself. **1967** *Punch* 1 Mar. 321/1 Gerold Frank has enough *exaltés* on his hands to set Dickens and Dostoevsky up in business for a dozen lifetimes.

exalted (ɛg'zɒltɪd, -ɔː-), *ppl. a.* [f. EXALT *v.*]

1. Raised or set up on high; elevated.

1601 SHAKS. *Jul. C.* I. i. 65 Weepe your teares Into the Channell, till the lowest streame Do kisse the most exalted Shores of all. *a* **1631** DRAYTON *Elegies, To W. Brown*, Thoughts..winged to fly To that exalted stand. **1728** POPE *Dunc.* II. 175 Thro' half the heav'ns he pours the exalted urn. **1781** GIBBON *Decl. & F.* II. 108 The Great King..from an exalted throne beheld the misfortunes of his arms.

†**b.** Of the voice: Elevated, raised aloud. *Obs.*

1711 STEELE *Spect.* No. 147 ¶2 These pronounce the first part of a Sentence with a very exalted Voice. **1743** BULKELEY & CUMMINS *Voy. S. Seas* 74 With an exalted Voice, Captain

C——p, says, etc. **1790** 'A LADY' *Norman & Bertha* II. 148 Mrs. Westbrook and Norman heard their exalted voices, but could not distinguish their words.

2. Elevated in rank, station, or public estimation. Usually without implication of any previous lower condition: Highly placed, of high station, etc. ***an exalted personage***: used for someone of high (usually royal or princely) rank, whom it is not desired to designate explicitly.

1623-6 COCKERAM II, *Exalted*, promoted. **1737** POPE *Hor. Epist.* II. ii. 106 Peers give way, exalted as they are, Ev'n to their own S-r-v-nce in a car. **1800** FISHER AMES *Eulogy on Washington* Wks. (1809) 116 Time never fails to bring every exalted reputation to a strict scrutiny. **1828** SCOTT *F.M. Perth* xxii, The physician..hoped he saw his exalted patient merry and happy. **1847** DR. CORRIE in Holroyd *Memorials* (1890) 248 To place over us an exalted personage who has not been educated among us. **1855** MACAULAY *Hist. Eng.* IV. 41 Any man whom a revolution has..hurled down from an exalted position.

3. Of persons: Impassioned, rapturously excited.

1712 STEELE *Spect.* No. 503 ¶2 When the Musick was strong and bold, she look'd exalted, but serious. **1814** SOUTHEY *Roderick* XII, From vale To vale the exalted Adosinda went.

b. Of the pulse: High, rapid.

1742 FIELDING *J. Andrews* I. xiii, His pulse was very exalted.

4. Of feelings, powers, sentiments, states of the mind: †**a.** Carried to a high degree; intense. **b.** Elevated, lofty in character; sublime, noble. Cf. EXALTATION 2 d, e.

1601 SHAKS. *Twel. N.* II. v. 30 Besides she uses me with a more exalted respect, than any one else. **1665** BOYLE *Occas. Refl.* I. vi, He, whose high Reason, and exalted Piety, has.. plac'd him above them. **1704** J. TRAPP *Abra-Mulé* II. i. 381 You cannot boast a more exalted Hatred Against the Visier's Person. **1746-7** HERVEY *Medit.* (1818) 160 The light of God's countenance will irradiate..all their exalted faculties. **1812** SIR H. DAVY *Chem. Philos.* 12 Warm with the ardor of an extending and exalted religion. **1847** EMERSON *Repr. Men, Goethe* Wks. (Bohn) I. 382 Some men are born with exalted powers for this second creation.

c. Of diction: Elevated, 'high-flown'.

1647 CLARENDON *Hist. Reb.* I. (1843) 6/1 After many exalted expressions to that purpose. **1684** EARL ROSCOM. *Ess. Translated Verse* 26 In what exalted streins Sicilian Muses..Proclaim Saturnian Times. **1739** T. SHERIDAN tr. *Persius* Ded. 8 A most exalted Lecture, instructing us in the true Freedom of the Mind.

†**5.** *Chem.* and *Phys.* Refined, sublimed, concentrated. Cf. EXALT *v.* 3. Of flavour, smell, etc.: Intense, strong. *Obs.*

1594 PLAT *Jewell-ho.* III. 85 To make proiection..with a medicine so exalted, as that one shal extend vpon a hundreth. **1712** tr. *Pomet's Hist. Drugs* I. 14 It contains a great deal of exalted Oil. **1746** R. JAMES *Introd. Moufet's Health's Improv.* 18 The Solan Goose..whose Flesh is of a very exalted Taste. **1751** CHAMBERS *Cycl.* s.v. *Exaltation*, Most sulphurous matters, much exalted, are observed to be of a red colour. **1796** PEGGE *Anonym.* (1809) 146 The venom of the Adder, or English Viper, is not so exalted..as that of the Italian.

exaltedly (ɛg'zɒltɪdlɪ), *adv.* [f. prec. + -LY².] In an exalted manner or degree; in a high style; also, with exaltation or excitement.

1790 G. WALKER *Serm.* II. xviii. 51 No one can think exaltedly of God, and think meanly of man, who is the work of God. **1852** *Blackw. Mag.* LXXI. 747 One does not require to dine exaltedly in order to dine well. **1855** DICKENS in J. Forster *Life* (1874) III, Old Lemaître plays his famous character, and never did I see anything, in art, so exaltedly horrible and awful. **1887** T. HARDY *Woodlanders* II. xvii. 323, 'I knew I was right!' said Grace exaltedly.

exaltedness (ɛg'zɒltɪdnɪs). [f. as prec. + -NESS.] The quality or condition of being exalted. **a.** in character, mind, nature, etc.: **b.** in social position, rank, etc.

a. **1659** H. MORE *Immort. Soul* (1662) 171 The Soul of the Mother, in which there is no such measure of..exaltedness. **1742** GRAY *Wks.* (1825) II. 113 The exaltedness of some minds..may make them insensible to these light things. **1816** BYRON *Siege Cor.* xii, The stern exaltedness of zeal. **1881** A. B. BRUCE *Chief End Revelat.* iii. 132 The Divine perfection..is judged of by reference, not to the idea of grace, but rather to that of exaltedness above the world. **b.** **1730-6** BAILEY (folio), *Exaltedness*..height of promotion. **1860** PUSEY *Min. Proph.* 375 Pride doth imitate exaltedness.

exalter (ɛg'zɒltə(r)). [f. EXALT *v.* + -ER¹.] One who, or that which, exalts (in senses of the vb.).

1471 RIPLEY *Comp. Alch.* Pref. in Ashm. (1652), Fro thys envyos valey of vanyte, O our Exalter. **1580** SIDNEY *Arcadia* (1622) 309 O noble sisters..who were the onely exalters of all womankinde. **1678** R. BARCLAY *Apol. Quakers* viii. §6. 250 Our Adversaries are Exalters of the Scriptures in words. **1684** tr. *Bonet's Merc. Compit.* XVIII. 621 Cinnabar..is an useful Exalter, and a..safe Alexiterick. *c* **1732** SWIFT *Answ. to 'A Conclusion'* in Anderson *Poets Gt. Brit.* (1794) IX. 147 Her majesty never shall be my exalter; And yet she would raise me, I know, by a halter! **1731** A. HILL *Adv. Poets*, Epist. 5 A Poet is..an Exalter of what is most dignified, and substantial, in Nature. *a* **1849** J. C. MANGAN *Poems* (1859) 176 The Grave is the only Exalter.

e'xalting, *vbl. sb.* [f. as prec. + -ING¹.] The action of the vb. EXALT; in quot. *concr.* † = EXALTATION I c.

1486 *Bk. St. Albans* F vj a, An Exaltyng of Larkis. **1688** R. HOLME *Armoury*, Exalting of larks.

exalting (ɛg'zɒltɪŋ), *ppl. a.* [f. as prec. + -ING².] That exalts (in various senses of vb.).

1665 BOYLE *Occas. Refl.* I. ii. (1675) 79 The exalting Efficacy of this kind of Distillation. **1844** EMERSON *New Eng. Reformers* Wks. (Bohn) I. 261, I find nothing healthful or exalting in the smooth conventions of society. **1859** GULLICK & TIMBS *Paint.* 202 The peculiar exalting effect of varnishes upon colours.

Hence **e'xaltingly** *adv. rare.*

1855 *Chamb. Jrnl.* IV. 222 The soul's glory..shone through them [her features] so exaltingly.

†**e'xaltive**, *a. Obs.* [f. EXALT *v.* + -IVE.] Tending to exalt or elevate.

1560 ROLLAND *Crt. Venus* I. 257 Me to perswade with wrang enarrative Lufe to abstene, it is so exaltive.

†**e'xaltment.** *Obs.* [f. as prec. + -MENT.] The action of exalting; the state of being exalted; exaltation.

1660 W. SECKER *Nonsuch Prof.* 109 As he was abased for the creatures exaltment, so he was exalted for the creatures abasement. *a* **1677** BARROW *Wks.* (1687) I. 496 Sanctity implying..an exaltment in nature or use of the thing, which is denominated thereby.

†**e'xaltress.** *Obs. rare.* [f. EXALTER + -ESS.] She who exalts.

1650 WEEKES *Truth's Confl.* iii. 81 Yours [your opinion] will be found the great exaltresse of free-will in men.

exam (ɛg'zæm). *colloq.* [Short for EXAMINATION.] An examination (sense 5).

1877 *Driven to Rome* 67 (D.) Things may be altered since the writer of this novelette went through his exam. **1882** J. HAWTHORNE *Fort. Fool* I. xix, He sported his oak once five consecutive days and nights before an exam. **1884** *Athenæum* 15 Mar. Advt., Matriculation and other Exams.

†**e'xame**, *v. Obs. Sc.* Also 6 exem(e. [Shortened var. of EXAMINE; cf. *examne* among the forms of the latter.] = EXAMINE *v.*

1513 DOUGLAS *Æneis* XII. vii. 48 Begouth for till exem, and till assay The wond wyth mony crafty medycyn. **1572** *Sempill Ball.* (1872) 146 Gif thay repent not..Exame thair conscience of particular pactioun. **1588** A. KING tr. *Canisius' Catech.* 209 Befoir judgement exame thy self and thow sal find grace in the sight of God.

examen (ɛg'zeɪmɛn). [a. (through Fr. *examen* or directly) L. *exāmen* means of weighing, tongue of a balance, *fig.* testing, examination, for **exagmen*, f. **exag-*, *exigĕre* to weigh accurately: see EXACT *v.*

The sense 'tongue of a balance' (*ligula*) rests on the authority of the scholiast to Persius; it seems to occur in Virg. *Æn.* XII. 725, where, however, 'scale-beam' would equally suit the context. Servius obscurely explains it as 'filum quo trutina regitur.' (L. *exāmen* 'swarm of bees, flock' is related to *exigĕre* in the sense 'to lead or drive out'.) The Romanic forms, It. *esame*, Sp. *exámen*, Fr. *examen*, are synonymous with Eng. *examination*.]

1. Examination, scrutiny (of a doctrine, system, etc.); investigation (of an affair). Now *rare.*

1618 BOLTON *Florus* To Rdr. 4 The doctrines..are such as thou art to expect from an Heathen..and their examen will elsewhere fall out fitly. **1645** *City Alarum* 17 They allow the Prince of Orange every summer a tun or two of gold without examen, for Intelligence. **1715** LEONI *Palladio's Archit.* (1742) I. 45 Things..which I had learnt by a very laborious Examen and long Study. **1801** FUSELI *Lect. Art* i. (1848) 370 Recalled his pupil to the examen of the great principle. **1890** E. JOHNSON *Rise Christendom* 123 That only [is] wise which..the law of God or the examen of his senior has pointed out.

b. *Eccl.* and *Law.* (*a*) A formal examination (of the conscience or soul). (*b*) The examination (of a candidate for ordination). (*c*) †A legal examination or inquiry (*obs.*).

1651 *Life Father Sarpi* (1676) 99 In all those days he made a most exact examen of his Soul. **1669** WOODHEAD *St. Teresa* II. vii. 59 This Examen shall have a Bell to ring to it..Let every one..at the time of the Examen, kneel down and briefly examine her conscience. **1685** H. CONSETT *Pract. Spirit. Courts* 95 To compel them to..undergo the Examen the Judge imposeth upon them. **1696** PHILLIPS, *Examen*, a Trial, Proof, particularly of one that is to be admitted to Orders or Employment. [So **1721** in BAILEY.] **1853** FABER *All for Jesus* 36 We might ask it..in our examen of conscience. **1885** *Catholic Dict.* s.v. *Examination of Conscience*, St. Ignatius..also recommends a particular examen to be made, at least daily..on that particular sin into which the individual most frequently falls.

†**2.** A critical dissertation or treatise (on any subject); an examination, disquisition. *Obs.*

1606 HOLLAND *Sueton.* To Rdrs, Correct what is amisse according to the Examen and Review annexed to the end of all. **1651** BAXTER *Inf. Bapt.* Apol. 7 Having greedily read over his Exhortation and Examen a little before. **1667** BOYLE (*title*), An Examen of The Origine (and Doctrine) of Substantial Formes. **1738** JOHNSON *Let. to Cave* Sept. in *Boswell*, An Examen of Mr. Pope's Essay, &c.

†**3.** Investigation by experiment; a test, assay.

1661 GLANVILL *Vanity Dogmat.* viii. 73 The only way to know what is sophisticate is to bring all to the Examen of the Touchstone. **1664** EVELYN *Sylva* (1776) 25 Some..might here recommend to us a more accurate Microscopical Examen. **1717** F. SLARE in *Phil. Trans.* XXX. 565, I made a yet more nice and certain Examen of these Waters, by mixing Milk with them. **1765** WILKINSON *ibid.* LV. 103 We proceeded to the more important examen, to discover the precise quantity of cork necessary to sustain a man in the water.

4. The tongue of a balance. *rare.*

[**1832** GELL *Pompeiana* I. iii. 44 Common scales..were found..without that little projecting point above the beam which serves to mark more accurately the absence of equipoise, and which was called by the..Romans..ligula, and examen.] **1833** J. HOLLAND *Manuf. Metals* II. 292 When the beam does, by the position of its examen or vertical spur over the axis, appear to have its two brachia exactly *in equilibrio*. **1850** WEALE *Dict. Terms* s.v.

exameter, -tron, obs. ff. HEXAMETER.

examinability (ɛg,zæmɪnə'bɪlɪtɪ). [f. next: see -ITY.] The quality of being examinable.

1879 *Law Rep.* App. Cases Ho. Lords IV. 801 No question arose as to the validity, or examinability of a foreign judgment.

examinable (ɛg'zæmɪnəb(ə)l), *a.* [f. EXAMINE *v.* + -ABLE.]

1. Capable or admitting of being examined. †Of a body: That is to be tested (*obs.*).

1605 BACON *Adv. Learn.* II. xxv. 122 The Draughts and first lawes of the Game are positiue, but..not examinable by reason. **1651** DAVENANT *Gondibert* Pref. (1673) 8 Great bodies are more examinable by being scatter'd into parcels. **1677** HALE *Prim. Orig. Man.* II. vii. 200 Whatever the truth of this Opinion be, it is not here properly examinable. **1678** R. RUSSELL *Geber* III. II. III. iii. 220 Blow upon the Surface of the Examinable Body until it flows. **1794** G. ADAMS *Nat. & Exp. Philos.* II. xxi. 404 The smallest examinable quantity of matter. **1808** BENTHAM *Sc. Reform* 70 Half a dozen witnesses not examinable but at so many different days. **1853** KANE *Grinnell Exp.* xxxvii. (1856) 340 The horn ..was perfectly examinable.

†**b.** Sc. ***examinable persons***: parishioners eligible to be examined for admission to communion.

1719 R. ERSKINE *Let.* in Fraser *Life* 46 [There are] upwards of 5000 examinable persons in the congregation. **1722** WALKER *Life of Cargill* 30 In which Parish 300 out of 900 examinable Persons wasted away. **1850** *Form of Petit.* in Cook *Styles of Writs Ch. Crts. Sc.* 185 The present examinable population of the parish amounts to—persons.

2. *Law.* Subject to examination or inquiry; competent to be examined or inquired into; cognisable.

1594 WEST *Symbol* II. *Chancery* §71 That it be such as is examinable in this court. **1666** PEPYS *Diary* 21 Feb., The privileges of Parliament..are few to the Commons' house, and those not examinable by them, but only by the House of Lords. **1765** BLACKSTONE *Comm.* I. xviii. 471 His determinations are final, and examinable in no other court whatsoever. **1818** CRUISE *Digest* (ed. 2) V. 300 A fine..is properly examinable in that court only where it is entered. **1884** SIR C. S. C. BOWEN in *Law Rep. Q. Bench* XIII. 87 His intentions are examinable to this extent.

examinant (ɛg'zæmɪnənt). *sb.* and *a.* Also 7 -ante, 8 -ent. [ad. L. *exāminant-em*, pr. pple. of *exāmināre*: see EXAMINE *v.* and -ANT.

The passive sense 2 (in our quots. earlier than 1) is unetymological; app. it was felt that the older EXAMINATE *sb.* etymologically meant rather 'one who *has been* examined' than 'one who *is being* examined,' and the derivative of the pr. pple. was adopted to express the latter notion.]

A. *sb.*

1. One who examines; *esp.* one who conducts a judicial or academic examination; an examiner.

1620 SHELTON *Quix.* III. II. i, Don Quixote..was so discreet, that the two examinants undoubtedly believed he was quite well. **1661** EVELYN *Diary* 13 May, The Examinants or Posers were Dr. Duport, Greek Professor at Cambridge; Dr. Fell, etc. *a* **1797** H. WALPOLE *Mem. Geo. II*, III. 271 The chief examinents were General Cholmondeley and Lord Albemarle. **1818** SCOTT *Hrt. Midl.* xiii, The upper end, where the examinants sate, was thrown into shadow. **1847** DISRAELI *Tancred* VI. xi, The converts..were..older Christians than either of their examinants. **1859** J. C. HOBHOUSE *Italy* I. 288 Objects whose authenticity may be questioned by the first cool examinant.

b. In comb. *self-examinant* (nonce-word).

1825 COLERIDGE *Aids Refl.* (1854) 126 If the self-examinant will abandon this position.

†**2. a.** One who is being examined; one who is being examined as a witness; a deponent. *Obs.*

1588 *Losses Sp. Navy* in *Harl. Misc.* (Malh.) II. 52 The admiral came away with seven and twenty sail, which this examinant did tell. **1621** ELSING *Debates Ho. Lords* (Camden) 29 She slaundered the examinant: being tolld of the daunger of a sclaunder, she is fledd. **1712** ARBUTHNOT *John Bull* viii, He brought a certain powder to his mistress, which the examinant believes to be the same. **1777** T. MᶜKEAN in Sparks *Corr. Amer. Rev.* (1853) I. 446 One of the examinants said that..a great number of..officers were killed. **1812** J. J. HENRY *Camp. agst. Quebec* 161 The questions did not admit of equivocation, if the examinants had been so inclined.

†**b.** One who undergoes an examination as to his fitness for church-membership, ordination, etc.; an examinee. *Obs.*

1633 D. ROGERS *Treat. Sacraments* ii. 14 To instruct all Christian examinants, in their triall to be careful of themselves. **1663** *Flagellum; or O. Cromwell* (1672) 148 The questions these men put to the Examinants, was not of Abilities or Learning, but, etc. **1715** PRIDEAUX *On Ref. Two Univ.* in *Life* 234 The examiners shall examine two at a time ..the examinants shall appear before them, in classes of six at a time.

†**B.** *adj.* That has the function of examining.

1653 MILTON *Hirelings* Wks. (1851) 373 For the Magistrate..by his examinant committies to circumscribe her free election of Ministers.

examinate (ɛg'zæmɪnət), *ppl*. and *sb*. Also 6-7 **examinat**. [ad. L. *exāmināt-us*, pa. pple. of *exāmināre*: see EXAMINE *v*.]

†**A.** *pple*. = Examined. (In first two quots. app.: Tortured. But possibly it may be a misprint for *exanimate*.)

1471 RIPLEY *Comp. Alch*. x. in Ashm. (1652) 178 Whych must be Crusyfyed and examynat: And then contumulate both Man and Wyfe. **1560** ROLLAND *Crt. Venus* II. 364 So vp he rais into ane stakkerand stait, As he had bene fra wit examinat. **1818** SCOTT *Rob Roy* xxxvi, Unless ane were judicially examinate.

B. *sb*.

1. A person under examination, either as a witness or accused person.

1537 in Froude *Hist. Eng*. III. 192 *note*, Sir Francis Bigod .. did read to this examinate a book made by himself. **1587** FLEMING *Contn. Holinshed* III. 1409/1 This examinat called on the earle, telling him the lieutenant was there. **1609** HOLLAND *Amm. Marcel*. XIV. v. 435 *note*, To this the tormentors .. fastened the armes and feet of the poor examinate or condemned person to be tortured. **1709** STRYPE *Ann. Ref*. I. xxv. 290 There appeared to this examinate one in white apparel. **1855** KINGSLEY *Westw. Ho!* (1861) 52 The examinate found it so difficult to answer the question that he suddenly became afflicted with deafness.

2. One who undergoes examination with a view to a certificate, degree, etc.

1599 HAKLUYT *Voy*. II. II. 71 The other examinates founde insufficient to proceed are sent backe to their studie againe. **1868** *Daily News* 20 Oct., A system of inter-collegiate lectures .. open to all the examinats.

†**e'xaminate**, *v*. *Obs*. [f. L. *exāmināt-* ppl. stem of *exāmināre*: see EXAMINE *v*.] = EXAMINE *v*.

1560-78 *Bk. Discipl. Ch. Scot*. (1621) 27 The persons that are to be examinated, must be commanded to appeare before men of soundest judgement.

examination (ɛgˌzæmɪ'neɪʃən). Forms: 4 -cioun, 5 -tyowne, 4-7 -cion, etc. [a. F. *examination*, ad. L. *exāminātiōn-em*, n. of action f. *exāmināre*: see EXAMINE *v*.] The action of examining; the state of being examined.

†**1.** A testing, trial, proof, assay. Also *fig*. *Obs*. exc. as a contextual use of 3.

c **1510** MORE *Picus* Wks. 32 In straite balance .. If thou shouldest our sinne ponder .. Who able were to beare thy punishement .. The whole engine of all this worlde .. With suche examinacion might not stande. **1552** LATIMER *Serm. St. Stephen's Day* Wks. (Parker Soc.) II. 104 Calamities .. be but examinations and proofs to provoke us to call upon God. [**1799** G. SMITH *Laborat*. I. 73 The examination, or *assay*, of the purity of gold or silver.]

2. a. The action of testing or judging by a standard or rule. Now only with some notion of 3 or 6. Cf. EXAMINE *v*. 2 a. Cf. *self-examination*.

c **1386** CHAUCER *Melib*. 301 For as moche as the Examinacioun is necessarie, let us bry ginne at the Surgiens. *c* **1425** WYNTOUN *Cron*. VI. ii. 40 That all examynatyowne Off thai persownys propyrly The kyrk suld hawe in gret party. *c* **1460** tr. *T. à Kempis* 139 Grace .. in euery understondinge submitteþ himself .. to goddis examynacion. **1627** H. MASON (*title*), The Tribunal of Conscience, or a Treatise of Examination; shewing .. how a Christian should examine his Conscience. **1885** *Catholic Dict., Examination of Conscience* should be made at least every evening.

†**b.** Judicial inquiry into the guilt or innocence of an accused person. *Obs*. Cf. 6.

1387 TREVISA *Higden* (Rolls) VII. 165 Sone þe day of examinacioun was sette. **1494** FABYAN *Chron*. VI. ccx. 224 The bysshop he commytted to the examynacion & correccion of the clergy. **1526-34** TINDALE *Acts* xxv. 26, I have brought him vnto you .. that after examinacion had, I myght have sumwhat to wryte. **1557** *Order of Hospitalls* D j, For the Examination of Single Women being gotten with Child. **1662** STILLINGFL. *Orig. Sacr*. II. v. §3 After a particular examination of Jeremiah .. they acquit him. **1685** —— *Orig. Brit*. v. 304 They anointed Kings .. and not long after they without Examination took them off.

3. The action of investigating the nature, qualities, or condition of any object by inspection or experiment; minute inspection, scrutiny. *postmortem examination*: = AUTOPSY *sb*. 2.

1630 *R. Johnson's Kingd. & Commw*. 99 The examination of passengers at .. the frontier Tounes of the Princes of Italie. **1819** J. G. CHILDREN *Chem. Anal*. Introd. 10 The examination of a substance containing few elements. **1836** *Act 6-7 Will. IV*, c. 89 It shall be lawful for the Coroner .. to direct the performance of a post-mortem Examination. **1863** *Royal Charter* §42 in *Lond. Univ. Calendar* 35 Which accounts shall be subject to such examination and audit as the said Commissioners may direct. **1875** URE *Dict. Arts* II. 727 The colour of the stroke made upon the touchstone by the metal under examination. **1884** *Syd. Soc. Lex., Physical Examination*, the investigation of disease by means of the senses, as when the cardiac respiratory sounds and movements are examined with the ear, or by means of instruments devised to render them more conspicuous. **1888** E. EGGLESTON *Graysons* xxiv, Bob made what a surgeon would call a 'digital examination' of the dungeon door.

4. The action or process of searching or inquiring into (facts, opinions, statements, etc.); investigation, scrutiny.

1538 STARKEY *England* I. iii. 74 That was agred at the begynnyng for the bettur examynatyon of every thyng. *c* **1626** WOTTON *Let*. in *Reliq. Wotton*. (1672) 549 After the examination of circumstances, there is a liberty of judgment. *a* **1716** SOUTH *Serm*. (1737) V. vii. 321 Surely nothing that is self-evident, can be the proper subject of examination, or tryal. **1794** MRS. RADCLIFFE *Myst. Udolpho* i, To look with cool examination upon the disappointments he sometimes threw in her way. **1864** J. H. NEWMAN *Apol*. 129 In that very agreement .. would really be found on examination, the elements .. of an essential discordance. **1878** STANFORD *Symb. Christ* i. 4 Such an account now claims our examination.

5. The process of testing, by questions oral or written, the knowledge or ability of pupils, or of candidates for office, degrees, etc. For *honour, local, middle-class, pass, Senate-house examinations*, see those words.

1612 BRINSLEY *Lud. Lit*. v. 48 Which worke of continuall examination, is a notable quickner and nourisher of all good learning. *Ibid*. xxviii. 282 That euery yeere .. there be a solemne examination by the Gouernours of the schoole. **1694** GIBSON in Ellis *Lett. Lit. Men* (Camden) 235 We met him .. just as he was going for Pauls to [*sic*: ? *read* to Pauls for] examinations. **1783** *Lett. Radcliffe & James* (Oxf. Hist. Soc.) 232 To day .. I went through part of my examination for Orders. **1848** DICKENS *Dombey* xiv, A dreadful uncle .. volunteered examinations of him in the holidays on abstruse points. **1866** *Lond. Univ. Calendar* 40 The Examination shall be conducted by means of Printed Papers.

6. Formal interrogation, *esp*. of a witness, or an accused person. ***examination-in-chief***, that made by the party calling the witness. See CROSS-, RE-EXAMINATION. †Also, Interrogation under torture.

The judicial interrogation of accused persons has no place in the criminal process of the common law, but by various statutes from 16th c. justices of the peace were directed to 'take the examination' of prisoners before sending them for trial. This expression has survived, though the practice which it denotes no longer exists; hence the preliminary investigation before justices of the peace or police-magistrates is still called the *examination* of the prisoner, so that the word in this connexion has reverted to the obsolete sense 2 b.

a **1555** LATIMER in Foxe *A. & M*. (1684) III. 383, I was once .. in Examination before five or six Bishops .. every week thrice I came to Examinations. **1592** GREENE *Art Connycatch*. III. 5 What hee spake of either came to him by examinations, or by riding in the circuits. **1728** MORGAN *Algiers* II. iv. 274 The Tormentors examined him .. for several hours they ceased not their Examinations. **1838** *Penny Cycl*. X. 103/1 s.v. *Evidence*, The cross-examination of a witness .. is founded upon what the witness has stated in his examination in chief. **1841** MACAULAY *W. Hastings* Ess. 1854 II. 651/2 There remained examinations and cross-examinations. **1861** W. BELL *Dict. Law Scot*. 234/2 The party is brought before a magistrate for examination.

b. The statements or depositions made by a witness or accused person when examined; the record of such statements. ***to take the examination of***: to interrogate and note down the answers.

1533 *Frith's Answ. More* Title-p., Vnto which boke are added .. the articles of his examinacion before the bishoppes. **1554** *Acts 1-2 Ph. & Mary* c. 13 §4 The said justices .. before any bailment or mainprise, shall take the examination of the said prisoner. **1591** J. HORTOP *Trav*. in Arb. *Garner* V. 329 The Earl of Sussex .. commanded his Secretary to take my name and examination. **1600** *Essex Rebell. Exam*. in *Shaks. C. Praise* 35 The examination of Sr. Gelly merick Knyght taken the xvijth of February, 1600. **1621** ELSING *Debates Ho. Lords* (Camden) 10 The clerke reade the examinacions taken in Courte. **1826** *Act 7 Geo. IV*, c. 64 §3 Every Justice of the Peace before whom any Person shall be taken .. shall take the Examination of the Person charged. **1848** *Act 11-12 Vict*. c. 42 §19 *marg*., Place where Examination taken, not an open Court. **1861** W. BELL *Dict. Law Scot*. 234/2 The examinations of the witnesses at the precognition .. never can be used .. against the witnesses.

7. *attrib*. and *Comb*., as ***examination fever, questions, statute, system***, etc.; **examination-paper**, (*a*) paper specially prepared for use in examinations; (*b*) a written or printed series of questions, etc. to be answered by the examinee; (*c*) a written series of answers by an examinee; **examination-schools**, in Oxford parlance: (*a*) the several branches of the University curriculum in which a formal examination is instituted; (*b*) the building in which University examinations are held.

1884 CRICHTON-BROWNE in *Pall Mall G*. 16 Sept. 11/1 The '*examination fever,' as it has been called, that leaves such unpleasant sequelæ behind it .. is now endemic in the metropolis. **1837** (*title*) *Examination Papers for Theological Students. **1838** (*title*), *Examination Questions and Answers, from 'Butler's Analogy.' **1868** M. PATTISON *Academ. Org*. vi. 244 If he [a professor] wishes for any auditors at all, he must make himself subservient to the *examination schools. **1886** *Oxf. Univ. Calendar* 55 Full information .. will be found .. in the *Examination Statutes. *Mod*. (Oxford) The Examination-schools are beyond University College.

Hence **exami'national** *a*., of or pertaining to examination or examinations; based upon (academical, etc.) examinations. **exami'nationism**, the habit of relying upon or the practice of employing examinations as the test of fitness, knowledge, etc. **exami'nationist**, one who upholds the system of examinations.

1826 BENTHAM in *Westm. Rev. VI*. 492 Tests preferred by Mr. Chancellor of the Exchequer, presumably the financial .. by their humble servant, the examinational. **1859** *Sat. Rev*. 12 Feb. 178/2 The establishment of what .. we may call an examinational franchise. **1884** H. M. JONES *Hints on Senses* 148 For future success in life the test of early examinational proficiency is a most fallacious one. **1884** *Lond. Jrnl. Sc*. XXI. 240 A reaction against that miserable examinationism which earns for us the title of the 'Chinese of Europe.' **1889** *Pall Mall G*. 27 June 3/1 Much emphasis is laid by the theoretical examinationists on the supposed difficulty that the public have in discriminating between a trained and an untrained nurse.

†**e'xaminative**, *a*. *Obs*. [f. EXAMINE *v*. + -ATIVE.] Concerned with examination.

c **1630** JACKSON *Creed* IV. iii. Wks. III. 27 In opposition to such as restrain assent only unto the reflexive or examinative acts of understanding.

examinator (ɛg'zæmɪneɪtə(r)). [a. late L. *exāminātor*, f. *exāmināre*: see EXAMINE *v*.] One who examines.

†**1.** = EXAMINER 1. *Obs*.

1646 SIR T. BROWNE *Pseud. Ep*. VI. vi. 299 An inference somewhat Rabbinicall, and not of power to perswade a serious examinator. **1783** *Town & Country Mag*. 168 John Hewitt, Esq. .. examinator of the hearth money in Dublin. **1830** MOIR in *Blackw. Mag*. XXVIII. 698 That severe and acute examinator of historical truth.

†**2.** *Sc*. = EXAMINER 2. *Obs*.

1752 J. LOUTHIAN *Form of Process* (ed. 2) 109 The Witness .. repeats the Words after the Lord Examinator. **1815** SCOTT *Guy M*. xxxii, Having, like a prudent examinator, suffered his witness to give vent to all her .. indignation.

3. = EXAMINER 3. *rare* exc. *Sc*.

1621 BURTON *Anat. Mel*. Democr. (1676) 38/1 Qualified .. by the strict approbation of deputed examinators. **1706** tr. *Dupin's Eccl. Hist. 16th Cent*. II. IV. xx. 362 These Examinators shall be Masters or Doctors, or Licentiates in Divinity or Canon Law. **1813** J. THOMSON *Lect. Inflam*. Introd. 25 To collect the suffrages of the surgeons who were the examinators. **1835** *Fraser's Mag*. XII. 259 It was not unusual to obtain a private hint from the examinators on what chapter their questions were to be founded. **1852** SIR W. HAMILTON *Discuss*. 485 In no European Faculty of Arts was Theology a subject on which its examinators had a right to question the candidate.

examinatorial (ɛgˌzæmɪnə'tɔərɪəl), *a*. [f. late L. *exāminātōri-us* (see next) + -AL[1].] Of or pertaining to an examiner or an examination.

1866 *Reader* 10 Mar. 247/1 A person who has frequently felt the examinatorial pulse. **1868** DICKENS *Lett*. 21 Mar., Johnnie has my profound sympathy under his examinatorial woes. **1881** *Sat. Rev*. 26 Feb. 270 Examinatorial experience is not without its peculiar bitterness.

examinatory (ɛg'zæmɪnəˌtərɪ), *a*. [ad. L. *exāminātōri-us* belonging to examination, f. *exāminātor*: see EXAMINATOR and -ORY.] = prec.

1887 *Athenæum* 23 July 109/3 It .. will probably be found more useful for examinatory purposes than the latter.

†**e'xamine**, *sb*. *Obs*. exc. *Hist*. [f. next vb. (or ? ad. L. *exāmen, -inis*: cf. *origin*).] = EXAMINATION. Also *attrib*.

1605 *Answ. supposed Discov. Romish Doctr*. 43 Therefore the examine of such things we entreate may be left to God. **1630** I. CRAVEN *Serm*. (1631) 14 Vpon a second examine, it may seeme to be personall. **1662** J. LAMONT *Diary* 21 Sept., Divers persons were excommunicat .. both for ignorance, and being absent from the dyetts of examine. **1885** A. EDGAR *Old Ch. Life Scot*. 124 *note*, It may be presumed that the examine roll was very carefully made up by the minister.

examine (ɛg'zæmɪn), *v*. Forms: 4-6 **examen(e, examyn(e**, (4 **examini**, 5 **examne**, **exammæn**, 6 **examme**, **exemne**), 6-7 **examin**, 4- **examine**. See also EXAME. [ad. F. *examiner*, ad. L. *exāmināre* to weigh accurately, test, try, inquire into, f. *exāmen*: see EXAMEN.]

†**1.** *trans*. To try, test, assay (precious metals, etc.). Said both of personal and material agents. Also *fig*. *Obs*.

a **1340** HAMPOLE *Psalter* xi. 7 Syluyre examynd in fire. *Ibid*. xvi. 4 In fire þou examynd me. **1382** WYCLIF *2 Sam*. xxii. 31 The speche of the Lord examynyd bi fier. **1387** TREVISA *Higden* (Rolls) VI. 11 Þis fuyre schal examyne and serche alle men dedes. *c* **1440** HYLTON *Scala Perf*. (W. de W. 1494) II. xxviii, Suffreth it .. to be well examyned thorugh ghostly trybulacyons.

2. a. To test judicially or critically; to try by a standard or rule. *Obs*. exc. with mixture of sense 3 or 6, to one or other of which phrases like *to examine oneself, one's conscience*, etc. now chiefly belong.

1340 *Ayenb*. 137 He nele naȝt lete ne smal ne grat þet ne ssel by examened .. and y-demd ine þe cort of merci. *Ibid*. 153 He ssel .. wel examini his þoȝtes. *c* **1386** CHAUCER *Melib*. ¶236 In examynyng of youre counseiloures, ye schul considre many thinges. *c* **1400** MAUNDEV. (1839) xxxi. 315 Þei schewed me a boke, þat my boke was examynde by. **1526** TINDALE *1 Cor*. xi. 28 Let a man .. examen him silfe and so let him eate of the breed and drynke of the cup. —— *1 Thess*. v. 21 Examen all thynges and kepe that which is good. **1580** BARET *Alv*. E 398 Doe you not examine or measure such thinges as be done at Lacedemon, according to your lawes and ordinances. **1599** SHAKS. *Much Ado* II. i. 291 Nay mocke not .. examine your conscience. **1611** BIBLE *Ps*. xxvi. 2 Examine me, O Lord, and proue me; try my reines and my heart. **1684** ABP. W. WAKE *Prep. for Death* (1688) 26 We ought .. before it be too late, to examine our Souls, and provide for futurity. **1690** J. HARRINGTON *Def. Rights Univ. Oxford* Pref., Examined by the unequal standard of the immunities of mean corporations.

†**b.** To try, investigate the guilt or innocence of (an accused person). *Obs*. Cf. 6.

c **1400** MAUNDEV. (1839) viii. 91 And there was oure Lord examyned in the nyght and scourged and smyten. *a* **1471** *Chron. Rich. II to Hen. VI* (Camden 1856) 10 Yf thou .. were wel examned, thou hast do more ayens the kyng than I. **1526** TINDALE *Acts* iv. 9 Yf we .. are examined [so **1611**] of the good dede done to the sycke man.

3. To investigate by inspection or manipulation the nature, qualities, or condition of (any object); to inspect in detail, scan, scrutinize. Also in various specific uses: To check, verify in detail (a calculation, an account); to investigate by inspection or experiment the pathological condition of (an organ, a person, or animal); to subject to autopsy; to search, inspect (baggage, etc.) for contraband goods.

c **1330** R. BRUNNE *Chron.* (1810) 248 þei brouht þe cronykles..þe old chartres & titles..Of ilk a bisshop se, & ilk a priourie..Examend þam & cast ilk amountment. **1387** TREVISA *Higden* (Rolls) III. 205 From humeres he [Pictagoras] tornede hym to examyne strenges, and streyned guttes and senewes of schepe. **1476** *Proclam.* 3 Apr. in *York Myst.* Introd. 37 To serche, here, and examen all þe plaiers and plaies and pagentes. **1580** BARET *Alv.* E 397 To discusse and examine diligently the account and reckoning of the souldiers. **1595** SHAKS. *John* I. i. 89 Mine eye hath well examined his parts, And findes them perfect Richard. **1644** MILTON *Areop.* (Arb.) 50 It will ask..the work of twenty licencers to examin all the lutes, the violins, and the ghittarrs in every house. **1699** DAMPIER *Voy.* II. I. 77 The Watch-men..stand in the Street by the Watch-houses, to examin every one that passeth by. **1742** POPE *Dunc.* IV. 234 The critic Eye..Sees hairs and pores, examines bit by bit. **1776** *Trial of Nundocomar* 23 Doss examined the books, and found the following entry. **1781–3** COWPER *Poet, Oyster, etc.* 33 Many a grave and learned clerk, With curious touch examines me, If I can feel as well as he. **1828** SCOTT *F.M. Perth* xix, Let the chirurgeon, Dwining examine that poor piece of clay, that he may tell us how he came by his fatal death. **1860** TYNDALL *Glac.* I. xi. 73 Our guide had examined the glacier for some distance. **1876** GRANT *Burgh Sch. Scotl.* II. iv. 154 The visitors..met to examine the Latin versions. **1879** HARLAN *Eyesight* v. 64 Of a large number of men examined in Europe..four or five per cent. have been found color-blind.

absol. *a* **1822** SHELLEY *Allegory* ii, Many passed it by with careless tread..But others..Pause to examine.

4. To inquire or search into, investigate (a question or subject); to consider or discuss critically; to try the truth or falsehood of (a proposition, statement, etc.).

1382 WYCLIF *2 Macc.* i. 34 The kyng byholdynge and diligently examyninge the thing, made a temple to hym. *c* **1490** *Plumpton Corr.* (Camd. Soc.) 76 The cause wherof..hath bene..shewed unto you; and..I desire and pray you reply to exammæn it. **1538** STARKEY *England* I. ii. 28 Thys thyng of Socrates semyth to me somewhat straunge..let vs a lytyl examyn thys. **1599** SHAKS. *Hen. V*, IV. i. 69 If you would take the paines but to examine the Warres of Pompey the Great. **1678** R. L'ESTRANGE *Seneca's Mor.* (1702) 102 It Examins all the Circumstances of Time. **1704** ADDISON *Italy* Pref., Few Men..have Talents or Opportunities for examining so copious a Subject. **1785** REID *Int. Powers* II. ix. (1803) I. 235 We shall examine this theory afterwards. **1874** MORLEY *Compromise* (1886) 221 The plea which we are examining..would have to be expressed in this way.

absol. **1621** BURTON *Anat. Mel.* Democr. (1676) 43/2 At the first sight all is well, but farther examine, you shall find them wise on the one side, and fools on the other.

b. with indirect question as *obj.*: To inquire, try to ascertain.

1303 R. BRUNNE *Handl. Synne* 9618 Prestes shulde..examyne what she [the midwife] couthe. **1526** *Pilgr. Perf.* (W. de W. 1531) 10 Godproueth vs, what we be, and..examyneth how moche we profyte in grace. **1594** HOOKER *Eccl. Pol.* I. viii. (1611) 22 Men will not bend their wits to examine whether things..be good or euill. **1647** CLARENDON *Hist. Reb.* v. (1843) 204/2 It was time to examin how he had lost those Priviledges. **1785** REID *Int. Powers* II. viii. (1803) I. 195 To examine whether there might not be other first principles.

5. To test (a person) by questioning; *esp.* to interrogate in order to test the capacity or knowledge of (a pupil, a candidate for a certificate, degree, official employment, etc.). Const. *in*, †*of*, *on*, *upon*.

c **1380** WYCLIF Wks. (1880) 40 ȝif ony wille..comen to oure breþeren..late þe mynystris diligently examyne hem of þe comun feiþ and þe sacramentis of holy chirche. **1612** BRINSLEY *Lud. Lit.* iii. 16 Examine them in syllables of three letters, after in moe. **1715** PRIDEAUX *Reform. Univ.* liii. in *Life* 235 Such only, as shall obtain a certificate of approbation from the two Examiners who examined them, shall be qualified for the said Degree. **1730** *Burgh Rec. Dingwall* 30 Nov., in Grant *Burgh Sch. Scotl.* II. vi. (1876) 221 The particular passages upon which he was examined. *a* **1838** LD. ELDON in H. Twiss *Life* I. 57, I was examined in Hebrew and History. **1868** M. PATTISON *Academ. Org.* vi. 251 At the end of the time the poor wretches were examined ..on all these subjects.

absol. **1612** BRINSLEY *Lud. Lit.* xxviii. 283 The Visitours.. who are not satisfied, to examine where, and as they please. **1863** *Royal Charter* §38 in *Lond. Univ. Calendar* (1866) 33 The said Chancellor..shall have power to examine for..the several..Degrees.

†**b.** To put questions on (what has been learned).

1612 BRINSLEY *Lud. Lit.* vii. 79 Especially examine those Verbs often, which haue two Preterperfect tenses. *Ibid.* 80 In examining the Syntax, it is the best to do it in Latine.

6. To interrogate formally, question (*esp.* a witness, an accused person).

c **1380** WYCLIF *Sel. Wks.* III. 438 ȝif alle bisshopis..and freris weren wislyche examyned wheþer þey weren heretikis. *c* **1425** WYNTOUN *Cron.* VIII. xxiv. 54 The dravere he gert and oþir ma Swa be examynyd, þat etc. **1533** EARL DERBY in Ellis *Orig. Lett.* I. 115 II. 43 William Dalton squyer examyned..deposith and saith. **1549** *Compl. Scotl.* xii. 98 Quhen thir ten hyrdis var exemnit..quhar the samnete armye vas campit. *c* **1590** MARLOWE *Faustus* (Bullen) vi. 113 Now, Faustus, examine them of their several names and dispositions. **1673** *Essex Papers* (1890) 90 There were no questions..asked but..what they who were examined knew concerning Mr. Peter Talbott's exercising of Ecclesiasticall Jurisdiction. **1779** J. HARRIS in *Lett. 1st Earl Malmesbury* (1870) I. 410 Sir Guy Carlton was four hours being examined at the Bar of the House. **1818** CRUISE *Digest* (ed. 2) V. 429 The usage had always been, upon a common recovery against husband and wife, to examine the wife. **1838** *Penny Cycl.* X. 101/2 If a plaintiff consents to be examined as a witness his evidence may be admitted.

†**b.** To interrogate under torture. Cf. *question.*

1580 BARET *Alv.* E 395 To take awaie violently, and examine by torments. **1611** BIBLE *Acts* xxii. 24 The chiefe captaine..bad that hee [Paul] should be examined by scourging. **1728** MORGAN *Algiers* II. iv. 274 The Tormentors examined him all the while, and to no Purpose.

7. *intr.* †**a.** To look carefully, 'see to it' *that.* etc. (*rare*). **b.** To make examination, inquire *into.*

1712 STEELE *Spect.* No. 426 ¶2 To examine that no one over-heard them. *a* **1764** LLOYD *Dial. betw. Author & Friend*, Read their works, examine fair—Show me invention, fancy there. **1837** *Penny Cycl.* VIII. 46/1 Authority is given to the court..to examine in a summary manner into any offence. **1839** KEIGHTLEY *Hist. Eng.* II. 90 To examine into the charges. **1869** M. ARNOLD *Cult. & An.* (1882) 223 That is, to examine into the nature of real good.

Hence **e'xamined** *ppl. a.*

1817 SELWYN *Law Nisi Prius* II. 722 To be prepared with an examined copy of the writ. **1861** W. BELL *Dict. Law Scot.* s.v., In..English law, an examined copy of a deed..is a copy ..examined and certified by the proper officer.

examinee (ɛgˌzæmɪ'niː). [f. prec. vb. + -EE.] One examined; a person under examination.

1788 T. TWINING in *Mad. D'Arblay's Diary* 20 Jan., Don't you think..that the Examinee..has a natural right.. to examine the Examiner? **1813** *Examiner* 12 Apr. 228/1 The answers given by examinees. **1840** *New Monthly Mag.* LVIII. 528 'What verb should you like?' inquired the examinee. **1868** M. PATTISON *Academ. Org.* v. 296 What kind of knowledge can they [examination questions] be the test of, in the examinee?

examiner (ɛg'zæmɪnə(r)). [f. as prec. + -ER¹.] **1.** One who looks into the nature or condition of (a person or thing); one who inquires or searches into (facts); an investigator. Also †an official inspector (*obs.*). Const. *of.*

1561 T. NORTON *Calvin's Inst.* III. 202 Sinne is a spirituall leprosie, therfore let vs be also examiners of sinn. **1639** MASSINGER *Vnnat. Combat* v. ii, Be but a just examiner of thyself. **1665** *Orders Ld. Mayor Lond.* in De Foe *Plague* (1840) 39 That these examiners be sworn by the aldermen to ..learn..what persons be sick. **1668** HALE *Pref. Rolle's Abridgm.* 2 He was a strict Searcher and Examiner of businesses. **1799** V. KNOX *Consid. Lord's Supp.* §21 Wks. 1824 VII. 452 The rigid examiners of Christ's pretensions.. seldom take into consideration..the love of God.

b. Hence: a frequent title of newspapers.

1710–14 SWIFT, etc. (*title*) The Examiner. **1808–36** L. HUNT, etc. (*title*) The Examiner.

c. (More fully ***Examiner of India Correspondence.***) Under the East India Company, the title of an official at the India House, who was responsible for the conduct of the Company's correspondence.

1779 *Royal Kalender* 212 Examiner of India correspondence, S. Wilks. **1836** *Gent. Mag.* Aug. 212 The duties of his [J. Mill's] important office, that of Chief Examiner to the East India Company. **1883** *Encycl. Brit.* XVI. 309 The duty of the so-called examiners was to examine the letters of the agents of the Company in India, and to draft instructions in reply. The character of the Company's government was almost entirely dependent upon their abilities as statesmen.

†**2.** One who examines or interrogates (an accused person, a witness, etc.); one who conducts an official jury. *Obs.*

1530–1 *Act 22 Hen. VIII*, c. 14 If the same person so endited..do make suche profe as the saied examiners..shall thynke sufficiente. **1541** R. COPLAND *Maner to Exam. Lazares* Q ij, The examyners ought to enquyre of theym by the prymatyfe causes of lepry. **1557** PAYNELL *Barclay's Jugurth* 44 He was electe to be one of the examinours or commyssioners to make inquisicion of these thre pointes rehersed. *a* **1676** HALE *Com. Law Eng.* xii. §9 A crafty Clerk, Commissioner, or Examiner, will make a Witness speak what he truly never meant. **1681–6** J. SCOTT *Chr. Life* (1747) III. 606 Nor did they [the Apostles]..alter any one of them [Circumstances] upon different Examinations before different Examiners.

b. *spec.* An officer, formerly of the Court of Chancery, now of the High Court of Justice, whose duty it is to take the depositions of witnesses when so directed by the court. Formerly more fully ***Examiner in Chancery.***

3. A person appointed to conduct an examination of pupils, candidates for degrees, etc.

1715 [See EXAMINE 5]. **1861** *Times* 29 Aug., To defeat cramming is the most useful..art of the Examiner. **1886** *Oxf. Univ. Calendar* 56 An Examination..conducted by the Regius Professor of Civil Law..with three or four other Examiners.

Hence **e'xaminership**, the office of examiner.

1880 in WEBSTER *Supp.* **1881** *Athenæum* 14 May 655/2 It ought to make examinerships less the monopoly of resident tutors than they have been. **1885** *Law Times* 25 July 237/1 Solicitors would not like to take paid examinerships on the terms suggested.

examining (ɛg'zæmɪnɪŋ), *vbl. sb.* [f. EXAMINE *v.* + -ING¹.] The action of the vb. EXAMINE, in various senses.

c **1386** CHAUCER *Melib.* ¶236 In the examynyng of ȝoure conseilloures. *c* **1460** *Towneley Myst.* 193, I my self shalle make examynyng. **1590** SIR J. SMYTH *Disc. Weapons* 20, I will now therefore proceed to the consideration and examining of three most important things. **1612** BRINSLEY *Lud. Lit.* xxii. (1627) 257 This strict examining will be a good meanes to make them attentive. **1884** *Pall Mall G.* 2 Apr. 6/1 Unskilled examining is doing serious damage to the cause of education.

attrib. **1793** NELSON 14 Feb. in Nicolas *Disp.* (1845) I 300 He must be in London before the 7th of March as that is the examining day.

¶ Used gerundially with omission of *in.*

1815 MRS. PILKINGTON *Celebrity* I. 222 During the time the wound was examining, Augustus worked himself up to a pitch of agony.

e'xamining, *ppl. a.* [f. as prec. + -ING².] That examines; appointed to examine.

a **1608** DONNE *Sat.* iv. in *Poems* (1633) 338 One, to whom, the examining Justice sure would cry. **1783** *Lett. Radcliffe & James* (Oxf. Hist. Soc.) 232 The Bishop of Lincoln ordains. Bowerbank acts as examining chaplain. **1868** M. PATTISON *Academ. Org.* vi. 244 Oxford is now, with respect to its candidates for honours, little more than an examining body. **1928** A. CHRISTIE *Mystery of Blue Train* xxvii. 218 You will, perhaps, accompany us immediately to the office of the Examining Magistrate. **1937** *Discovery* June 191/2 Higher School Certificate, Open Scholarships and other examining bodies. **1966** *Listener* 9 June 827/1 Their formal title was bestowed on the examining justices by statute as long ago as 1848. Their role is now mainly ceremonial.

Hence **e'xaminingly** *adv.*, in an examining or scrutinizing manner; searchingly.

1876 GEO. ELIOT *Dan. Der.* VII. li, She still kept her hand in his, and looked at him examiningly. **1890** *Chamb. Jrnl.* 4 Jan. 16/1 He looked at her so examiningly that she could not but pause.

examplar (ɛg'zɑːmplə(r), -æ-), *sb.* Now *rare.* Forms: 5 **examplaire, -ayre, -eir, -ire, exawmplere,** 5–7 **exampler,** 6– **examplar.** [a. OF. *examplaire, exemplaire* (see EXEMPLAR), semi-learned form of *essamplaire*:—late L. *exemplārium*, f. *exemplum* EXAMPLE *sb.*

Now almost superseded by *exemplar*; it is possible that some of the recent instances may be merely misprints.]

1. A pattern, model; a perfect specimen (of some quality); a person or thing to be imitated.

c **1430** LYDG. in *Pol. Rel. & L. Poems* 47 Moder of ihesu, myrrour of chastite..Trew examplire of verginite. **1483** CAXTON *G. de la Tour* D iij b, After the exampalyre of his sone. **1561** T. NORTON *Calvin's Inst.* IV. 60 They..toke their examplar out of the dotages of the Gentiles. **1568** E. TILNEY *Flower of Friendship*, A silent person is the exampler of wisedome. **1582** N. T. (Rhem.) *Heb.* ix. 23 It is necessarie therefore that the examplers of the cælestials be cleansed with these. **1603** DANIEL *Panegyr. King* xxiii, There, great examplar! prototype of kings! **1794** PALEY *Evid.* (1825) II. 311 He could no longer have a living examplar to copy from. **1860** THACKERAY *Round. Papers, Nil nisi bonum* 228 An examplar of goodness, probity, and pure life.

†**b.** ? A deterrent example. *Obs.*

[**1560** (see EXAMPLAR *a.*).]

†**2.** A book of (moral) examples. *Obs. rare*⁻¹.

1483 CAXTON *G. de la Tour* A ij, I tolde them that I wolde make a book and an examplayre for my doughters.

3. †A copy, transcript (*obs.*). **b.** An exemplar (of a book), one of the 'copies' of which the edition consists.

1413 LYDG. *Pilgr. Sowle* IV. xxix. (1859) 62 Euery good kynge is preised by the exampler [Fr. *lexemplaire*], figure, or statua of his good condicion, and knowen therby, ryght as a man is known by his visage. *c* **1475** *Partenay* Prol. 131 That I ther take the exampleir wold Off a boke of his which that he had made. **1572** W. MALIM in Hakluyt *Voy.* (1599) II. I. 121 With what paine and diligence, I referre me to them which are skilfull in the Italian tongue, or may the better iudge, if it please them to trie the same, casting aside this exampler. **1880** *Academy* 4 Sept. 163/1 Pamphlets existing in unique examplars.

†**4.** A piece of needlework containing examples of stitches, etc.: see SAMPLER. *Obs.*

1530 PALSGR. 217/2 Exampler for a woman to worke by, *exemple.* **1583** RICH *Phylotus & Emelia* (1835) 13 She might goe seeke out her examplers, and to peruse whiche woorke would doe beste in a Ruffe.

†**e'xamplar,** *a. Obs.* Also 6 **examplair.** [ad. OF. *examplaire*: see EXEMPLAR *a.*] = EXEMPLARY in various senses: **a.** Serving or fitted to serve as an example, pattern, or model; **b.** ? Serving as a deterrent (quot. 1560; but this may be an instance of prec. sb.).

1560 ROLLAND *Crt. Venus* II. 819 To that falt [unchastity in a Vestal] is na grace, Bot eirdit quik, to the laif examplair. **1602** T. FITZHERBERT *Defence* 8 Wee ad therto his religious lyfe, so examplar for all kynd of vertue. *a* **1631** DONNE in *Selections* (1840) 26 Wash thyself in these three examplar baths of Christ's tears.

examplary: see EXEMPLARY.

example (ɛg'zɑːmp(ə)l, -æ-), *sb.* Forms: 4–6 **exemple, exsaumple,** 5–6 **exaumple, -awmple,** (5 **exampil, exsawmple,** 6 **exampul(l),** 5–6 *Sc.* **exaimple, exampill, -empill,** 5– **example.** [a. OF. *example, exemple*, a refashioning (after Lat.) of earlier *essample* (see ASAUMPLE):—L. *exemplum*, f. *exem-*, *eximĕre* to take out: see EXEMPT. The

primary sense is thus 'something taken out, a SAMPLE, specimen'. The main Eng. senses are derived from Lat. through Fr. In the arrangement below the presumed logical order has been adopted in preference to the order in which the senses are recorded in Eng. See also ASAUMPLE, ENSAMPLE, SAMPLE, which are ultimately the same word.]

1. A typical instance; a fact, incident, quotation, etc. that illustrates, or forms a particular case of, a general principle, rule, state of things, etc.; a person or thing that may be taken as an illustration of a certain quality. Phrases, ***for, by way of, example***; formerly also (ellipt.) *example* in same sense.

1447 BOKENHAM *Seyntys* Introd. (Roxb.) 3 And to thys manyfold of nature Exaimplys, acordyth weel scrypture. **1538** STARKEY *England* I. i. 22 They see exampullys of many and dyverse, wych wythout profyt had attemptyd the same. **1548** GEST *Pr. Masse* 123 Example his reporting of the baptisme wordes over himselve.. maketh nether baptisme ne absolution. **1552** ABP. HAMILTON *Catech.* (1884) 12 Foure familiar exempilles drawin fra the haly scripture. **1585** JAS. I. *Ess. Poesie* (Arb.) 61 As for exempill ȝe man not say Then feir nocht Nor heir ocht. **1611** BIBLE *Transl. Pref.* 2 Wee shall finde many the like examples. **1663** GERBIER *Counsel* 52 Eight pence difference, example, There goeth four load of Sand. **1697** DRYDEN *Æneid* Ded. Wks. 1887 XIV. 164 Can we, for example, give the praise of valour to a man who [etc.]. **1752** HUME *Ess. & Treat.* (1777) I. 210 No criticism can be instructive which.. is not full of examples and illustrations. **1842** W. GROVE *Corr. Phys. Forces* 62, I might weary you with examples, showing that, etc. **1860** TYNDALL *Glac.* II. viii. 265 Almost all glaciers present examples of such [glacier] tables. **1875** JOWETT *Plato* (ed. 2) I. 273 A round, for example, is 'a figure' and not simply 'figure'. **1885** F. TEMPLE *Relat. Relig. & Sc.* iii. 69 The will is to Science the first example of power.

b. A problem framed to exemplify a rule in arithmetic, mathematics, etc.; an exercise.

1674 PLAYFORD *Skill Mus.* II. 96 Practice to play this Example of the Notes ascending and descending. **1847** GOODWIN (*title*), A Collection of Problems and Examples adapted to the Elementary Course of Mathematics. **1888** WOLSTENHOLME (*title*), Examples for Practice in the use of Seven-figure Logarithms.

c. A specimen (of workmanship). Also, a 'copy' of a book, etc. (now only with reference to rarities).

1530 PALSGR. 217/2 Example of a boke, *copie*. *a* **1553** ASCHAM in Fleming *Panopl. Epist.* (1576) 437, I have sent examples [of this Epistle] to the Kinges majestie, and the rest of that noble and gallant companie. **1578** LYTE *Dodoens* I. v. 11 Whiche a man shall finde described in some examples of Dioscorides. **1875** FORTNUM *Majolica* v. 48 This Florentine porcelain is especially rare; scarcely thirty examples being known to exist. **1880** *Daily News* 2 Dec. 5/3 A London bookseller lately disposed of an example for four shillings and sixpence. *Mod.* The gallery contains several examples of this master.

2. *Logic.* = Gr. παράδειγμα (Aristotle). The species of argument in which the major premiss of a syllogism is assumed from a particular instance.

a **1679** HOBBES *Rhet.* I. ii. (1681) 3 An Example is a short Induction, and an Enthymeme a short Syllogisme. **1774** REID *Aristotle's Logic* iv. §7 Aristotle gives some observations upon imperfect syllogisms; such as.. example, which is an imperfect induction. **1860** ABP. THOMSON *Laws Th.* 249 The Example is an argument which proves some thing to be true in a particular case from another particular case. **1875** JOWETT *Plato* (ed. 2) IV. 505 Example comes into use when we identify something unknown with that which is known.

3. A signal instance of punishment intended to have a deterrent effect; a warning, caution; a person whose fate serves as a deterrent to others. Chiefly in phrases, ***†for, † in example, to make (a person, etc.) an example, an example of (a person)***; also, ***to take example***.

1382 WYCLIF *Jude* i. 7 Sodom and Gomor.. ben maad ensaumple [*v.r.* exsaumple], sustenynge peyne of euerlastinge fijr. **1548** HALL *Chron.* 204 Caused the lord Welles.. to be behedded there, to the terrible example of other, which shal put their confidence in the promise of a prince. **1568** GRAFTON *Chron.* 1253 Hanged at Greenewiche ..for robberies, in example of all other. *c* **1592** MARLOWE *Massac. Paris* III. iv, All rebels under Heaven Shall take example by his punishment. **1599** SHAKS. *Much Ado* v. i. 332 An arrant knaue.. which I beseech your worship to correct your selfe, for the example of others. **1631** *Star Chamb. Cases* (Camden) 76 Brought to the barre to be punished for example sake. **1665** MANLEY *Grotius' Low C. Warres* 389 Let these mens unhappy examples be a warning to others. **1711** ADDISON *Spect.* 16 ¶3, I.. will not be provoked.. to make an Example of any particular Criminal. **1793** GOUV. MORRIS in Sparks *Life & Writ.* (1832) II. 388 The examples are so striking and terrifying that every individual trembles. **1803** *Pic Nic* No. 4 (1806) I. 140 They must be made an example of. **1827** POLLOK *Course T.* x, Has he not given at times Example fierce of wrath and judgment?

4. A parallel case in the past; also in phrases, ***beyond, without example***.

1530 PALSGR. 217/2 Example a symilitude of a thyng, *exemple*. **1595** SHAKS. *John* III. iv. 13 Such temperate order in so fierce a course, Doth want Example. **1707** FREIND *Peterborow's Cond. Sp.* 50 A Discipline and Generosity without example. **1726** BUTLER *Serm.* iv. 76 He was mild and gentle beyond Example. **1817** *Parl. Deb.* 205 The demand upon gunsmiths for every species of fire-arms has been beyond all former example. **1821** SHELLEY *Hellas* Pref., A spirit and a wisdom which has few examples.

5. A precedent appealed to, to justify or authorize any course of action. *arch.* or *Obs.*

1509-10 *Act. 1 Hen. VIII*, c. 20 §1 That thees grauntz be not take in example to the Kyngez of England in tyme to comme. **1581** SAVILE *Tacitus' Hist.* IV. x. (1591) 188 Hordeonius.. beganne a very ill example, that all letters sent from abroade should be deliuered to the standerdbearers of the Legions. **1647-8** COTTERELL *Davila's Hist. Fr.* (1678) 11 Katherine of Medicis.. according to many Examples of former times, pleaded the right.. to assume.. the regency. **1700** TYRRELL *Hist. Eng.* II. 853 With a Saving Clause, that it should not be drawn into Example.

6. A person's action or conduct regarded as an object of imitation; often qualified by adjs. *good, bad, evil*, etc. Phrases, ***to give, leave, set an example***. Also, a person whose conduct ought to be imitated; a 'pattern' of excellence.

1382 WYCLIF *1 Tim.* iv. 12 Be thou ensaumple [*v.r.* exsaumple] of feithful men in word.. in feith, in chastite. *c* **1460** FORTESCUE *Abs. & Lim. Mon.* (1714) 10 They, by Example of Nembroth, made them Realmys. **1470-85** MALORY *Arthur* II. i, Gyuyng example to alle the Barons. *c* **1500** *Lancelot* 3099 Neuer we.. mycht Have bet axampil than iffith ws ȝone knycht. **1570** ASCHAM *Scholem.* (Arb.) 66 This Court also neuer lacked many faire examples, for yong ientlemen to folow. **1664** EVELYN *Kal. Hort.* (1729) 185 Forc'd either to Imitate, or as I do, to celebrate your Example. **1718** ROWE tr. *Lucan* I, He copies from his master Sylla well, And would the dire example far excell. **1796** H. HUNTER *St. Pierre's Stud. Nat.* (1799) III. 588 Of this our own Country ought to set the example to the Nations. **1853** ROBERTSON *Serm.* Ser. II. 241 You copy the outline of a model: you imitate the spirit of an example. **1870** DICKENS *E. Drood* viii, If you will set me that example, I promise to follow it.

b. In generalized sense: Action or conduct that induces imitation; *hence*, 'influence that disposes to imitation' (J.).

1398 TREVISA *Barth. De P.R.* II. xvi. (1495) C ij a/1 The angels take by yefte and yeue forth by example. **1653** WALTON *Angler* 47 Well, you know what example is able to do. *a* **1680** BUTLER *Rem.* (1759) I. 73 Example, that imperious Dictator Of all that's good, or bad to human Nature. *a* **1729** J. ROGERS *19 Serm.* iv. (1735) 70 Example is a Motive of a very prevailing Force on the Actions of Men. **1796** BURKE *Regic. Peace* i. Wks. VIII. 196 Example is the school of mankind. **1871** SMILES *Charac.* ii. (1876) 35 Example is far more than precept. It is instruction in action.

c. ***to take example***: to learn by, or copy, the example of another. Const. *†at, by, †of*.

c **1386** CHAUCER *Prol.* 568 A gentil Mauncriple was ther of a temple, Of which achatours mighten take exemple. **1477** EARL RIVERS (Caxton) *Dictes* 86 He is right happy that can chastyse himself taking example by other. **1548** UDALL, etc. *Erasm. Par. John* 103 b, Ye shall take exaumple at me. **1587** *Mirr. Mag., Porrex* ix, Example take you Princes of the land. **1611** COTGR., *Exemplairement*, exemplarily; for others to follow, or to take example by. **1632** SHERWOOD, To take example by, *patronner*.

d. ***of (bad) example*** (= L. *mali exempli*, Fr. *de mauvais exemple*). *rare*.

1865 M. ARNOLD *Ess. in Criticism* 66 Some people will say these are little things; they are not, they are of bad example.

¶**e.** A pattern, design to be copied. *Obs.* (A mere Latinism.)

1539 BIBLE (Taverner) *1 Chron.* xxviii. 12 Dauid gaue Salomon his son the paterne of the porch.. and the example of that was in his mynde. **1609** —— (Douay) *Num.* viii. 4 According to the example which our Lord shewed to Moyses, so wrought he the candlesticke.

¶**7.** An alleged designation for a company (of 'masters'). *Obs.*$^{-0}$

1486 *Bk. St. Albans* F vij a, A Example of maisteris.

8. Comb., as ***example-giver***.

1540 COVERDALE *Fruitf. Less.* i. (1593) R iv b, Before vs we haue an high perfect example giuer.

example (ɛg'zɑːmp(ə)l, -æ-), *v.* Also 5 exawmplyn, 5–6 exaumple, 6 exemple. [f. prec. sb. Cf. OF. *exemplier*.]

1. *trans.* To exemplify; to furnish a model or pattern of; to find or give an example or instance of; also with sentence as *obj. Obs.* exc. in *passive*.

c **1440** *Promp. Parv.* 144/2 Exawmplyn, *exemplifico*. *c* **1449** PECOCK *Repr.* 452 For to exaumple bi hise dedis to othere men the seid iiij principal gouernaunce. **1556** J. HEYWOOD *Spider & F.* lxxviii. 128 My meaning.. last exampled by my fleeing with flise. **1598** CHAPMAN *Iliad* IV. 238 He examples this With toiling, like the worst, on foot. **1613** SHERLEY *Trav. Persia* 18 To example to other how much it pleaseth God to fauour good intentions. **1655** E. TERRY *Voy. E. India* 218 Keeping to their old fashions exampled to them by their predecessors. **1795** SOUTHEY *Joan of Arc* VI. 343 Exampling hardiest deeds, Salisbury struck down the foe. **1828** CARLYLE in *Foreign Rev.* II. 116 Of an interest altogether peculiar, and not in this degree exampled in recent literature. **1879** MORLEY *Burke* 89 Burke devoted himself to this duty with a fervid assiduity that has not often been exampled, and has never been surpassed.

b. Of things: to be an example of.

1881 *Athenæum* 25 June 840/1 Mr. Arnold quotes, as exampling Wordsworth at his highest, the single line, Will no one tell me what she sings?

†**2.** To hold forth (a person) as an example. Also with *out. Obs.*

1625 FLETCHER *Lover's Progr.* II. iii, You are the pattern of fair friendship, Exampled for your love. **1639** W. SCLATER (Jun.) *Worthy Communicant* 7 The stroke of God's displeasure; of which Nadab and Abihu.. are exampled out for our warning. **1654** GAYTON *Pleas. Notes* IV. xx. 268 Fortune had an intent to example him.. for his sufferings.

†**3.** To furnish an antecedent example or precedent for; to justify by precedents. *Obs.*

1587 (*title*), A Defence of the honorable Sentence and Execution of the Queene of Scots, exempled with analogies. **1588** SHAKS. *L.L.L.* I. ii. 121 That I may example my digression by some mighty president. **1595** —— *John* IV. iii. 57 [This shall] proue a deadly blood-shed but a iest, Exampled by this heynous spectacle.

4. †**a.** Of things: To serve as an example or warning to (*obs.*). **b.** Of persons: To set an example to, instruct by example. *rare*.

1592 GREENE *Art Conny-catch.* III. 25 Let the poore Cutlers mishap example others. **1631** LAUD *Seven Serm.* (1651) 325 And what a Kings Son may learne, when he is exampled by such a Father. **1772** J. WOOLMAN *Jrnl.* x. (1840) 147 Placing children.. where they may be likely to be exampled and instructed. **1816** COLERIDGE *Statesm. Man.* (1839) 315 Taught by God's word, exampled by God's providence, commanded by God's law. **1881** W. E. HENLEY in *Academy* 27 Aug. 156/1 The pair settle quietly down.. generally exampling their friends and neighbours. **1883** E. BALFOUR in *Mag. Art* Aug. 398 They.. example those whom they are engaged in teaching.

†**5.** *intr.* **a.** To serve as an example or warning. **b.** To quote an example. *Obs.*

1571 HENRYSON *Mor. Fables* 28 This suddaine death.. of this false Tod.. examples exhortand folke to amend. **1599** B. JONSON *Cynthia's Rev.* v. ii, I will example unto you: Your opponent makes entry as you are engaged with your mistress.

Hence **e'xampled** *ppl. a.*, that is made an example. **e'xampling** *ppl. a.*, that sets an example.

a **1637** B. JONSON *Underwoods, Epithal.* x, Search, Sun, and thou wilt find They are th' exampled Paire, and mirrour of their kind. **1715-20** POPE *Iliad* VI. 75 A dreadful lesson of exampled fate. *c* **1611** CHAPMAN *Iliad* IV. 337 Thy brave exampling hand Might double our young Grecian spirits.

†**e'xampleless,** *a. Obs. rare.* Also 7 **examplesse**. [f. EXAMPLE *sb.* + -LESS.] Without an example or precedent; unexampled.

1603 FLORIO *Montaigne* III. xii. (1632) 587 What is become of that.. wonderfull examplelesse example? **1603** B. JONSON *Sejanus* II. iv, So examplêsse [*sic*] and vnblam'd a life, As that of the renown'd Germanicus.

exampleship (ɛg'zɑːmp(ə)lʃɪp). *rare*$^{-1}$. [f. EXAMPLE *sb.* + -SHIP.] The function of setting an example.

1864 *Sat. Rev.* XVIII. 743/2 Exampleship belongs to them [the queen on her throne, the father in his family, etc.] as a sort of heritage.

†**e'xamplify,** *v. Obs. rare*$^{-1}$. [f. EX- *prefix*[1] + AMPLIFY.] *trans.* = AMPLIFY.

1677 WYCHERLEY *Plain Dealer* III i, I will, as I see cause, extenuate, or examplify Matter of Fact.

examplify, obs. form of EXEMPLIFY.

examply, var. of EXEMPLY *v. Obs.*

exan.

1597 GERARD *Herbal, Suppl. to Table Eng. Names*, Exan is Croswort, yet not our *Cruciata*.

†**exange'ration.** *Obs. rare.* [irreg. f. EX- *pref.*[1] + ANGER *v.* + -ATION.] Provocation to anger.

1631 R. H. *Arraignm. Whole Creature* xviii. 306 Instead of hoped Contentation: wee reape vexation, exangeration, distraction. *Ibid.* 307 They subject the Soule to exceeding divisions, distractions, exangerations and vexations.

exanguin, -guious, -guous, etc.: see EXS-.

†**e'xangulous,** *a. Obs.*$^{-0}$. [f. EX- *prefix*[1] + L. *angul-us* ANGLE + -OUS.] Without angles or corners.

1730-6 in BAILEY (folio). **1775** in ASH, etc.

†**e'xanimal,** *a. Obs.*$^{-0}$ [ad. L. *exanimāl-is*, f. *ex-* (see EX-) + *anima* breath. Cf. *animal*.] Lifeless, breathless.

1730-6 in BAILEY (folio).

exanimate (ɛgz-, ɛk'sænɪmət), *ppl. a.* [ad. L. *exanimāt-us*, pa. pple. of *exanimāre*: see next.]

1. Deprived of life, lifeless, dead; rarely of an inorganic substance = INANIMATE.

1552 HULOET, Exanimate or kylled, *confectus*. **1590** SPENSER *F.Q.* II. xii. 7 Ships, which had been wrecked late ..stuck with carcases exanimate. **1635** SWAN *Spec. M.* ix. §1 (1643) 469 Oftentimes by dust and knocks they [bears] are almost exanimate and without life. **1804** J. GRAHAME *Sabbath* (1839) 23/2 The circling halo beam'd.. Upon that face, clothed in a smile benign, Though yet exanimate. **1848** MILLER *First Impr.* ii. (1857) 23 It is a petrifaction—a fossil ..an exanimate stone. **1858** *Chamb. Jrnl.* IX. 338 Thither, almost exanimate from fright.. was he conveyed.

b. Lifeless in appearance; without respiration.

1619 R. JONES *Serm.* in *Phenix* (1708) II. 490 They were exanimate; but whether that Fit held them only by way of Syncope, or [etc.]. **1837** *Old Commodore* I. 219 Exanimate, collapsed, the Commodore.. was.. lifted on board. **1849** LYTTON *Caxtons* XVIII. viii, Squills again closed his eyes, and became exanimate.

2. Deprived or destitute of animation or courage; spiritless.

c **1534** tr. *Pol. Verg. Eng. Hist.* (Camden) I. 185 At whose fall the residew became so hartelesse and exanimate that.. they were all slayne. **1668** WILKINS *Real Char.* 253 Out of heart, crest-faln, exanimate. **1728** THOMSON *Spring* 1049 The grey morn Lifts her pale lustre on the paler wretch Exanimate by love. **1808** J. BARLOW *Columb.* v. 853 Pale, curbed, exanimate, in dull despair. **1841** *Fraser's Mag.* XXV. 217 The comparatively exanimate productions of a hundred moralists.

exanimate (ɛgz-, ɛk'sænɪmeɪt), *v. rare* in mod. use. Also 7 **exanimat**. [f. L. *exanimāt-* ppl. stem of *exanimāre* to deprive of life, f. *ex-* out + *anima* breath of life.]

†**1.** *trans.* **a.** To deprive of life; to kill. **b.** To deprive of the appearance of life; to render breathless or unconscious. *Obs.*

1593 B. BARNES *Parthenophil & P.* Sonn. lvi, Thy love, which doth each part exanimate. **1620** VENNER *Via Recta* (1650) 225 A Charcoal-fire will quickly exanimate you and cast you into a sowne. **1657** TOMLINSON *Renou's Disp.* 24 That they might exanimate..all those whose life..they envy or hate.

c. *fig. humorous.* To knock the breath out of.

1878 *Fraser's Mag.* XVII. 738 Mr. Sayce has furnished enough grammatical details, not only to 'flutter' the Aryans, but to exanimate most believers in a grammar at all.

†**2.** To deprive of courage or spirit; to dishearten, dispirit. *Obs.*

1552 in HULOET. **1567** DRANT *Horace' Epist.* II. i. G vj, These two doth much exanimate And strykes the hart full coulde. **1638** A. READ *Chirurg.* ii. 14 Ustion..is horrible to the..apprehension; for it doth in a manner exanimat cowardly persons. **1667** FLAVEL *Saint Indeed* (1754) 141 If it be attended..with suffering, it will exanimate and sink him.

1721-1800 in BAILEY.

Hence **e'xanimated, e'xanimating** *ppl. adjs.*

1689 T. PLUNKET *Char. Gd. Commander* 3 But our brave Hero, whom I now describe, Is none of that exanimated Tribe. **1607** TOPSELL *Four-f. Beasts* (1673) 341 The old Magicians by reason of this exanimating property, did not a little glory in these beasts.

exanimation (ɛgz-, ɛk,sænɪ'meɪʃən). [ad. L. *exanimātiōn-em*, n. of action f. *exanimāre*: see EXANIMATE *v.*]

†**a.** Deprivation of life (*obs.*). **b.** 'Apparent death from swooning' (*Syd. Soc. Lex.* 1884). **c.** Deprivation of spirits, disheartening, discouragement.

a. 1670 MAYNWARING *Vita Sana* xvi. 148 Fear.. scattering [the spirits] from the Fountain of Life, into the external parts, making a dissolution almost to exanimation. **b. 1731-1800** BAILEY, *Exanimation*..a swooning or such a sinking of the Spirits as is attended with the Loss of Sense for some time. **c. 1604** T. WRIGHT *Passions* v. 175 Euery accent.. exclamation, indignation..exanimation, exultation, fitly deliuered, is, etc. **1635** VALENTINE *Four Sea-Serm.* 55 An examination of the mariners..because of the greatnesse of the danger.

‖**ex animo** (ɛks 'ænɪməʊ). [L. *ex* out of + *animō*, abl. of *animus* soul.] Literally: From the soul; hence, heartily, sincerely.

1612 BRINSLEY *Lud. Lit.* xviii. (1627) 214 To dispute, as if *ex animo* in good earnest, with all contention and vehemencie. **1843** ROBERTSON in *Life* I. 101 As to the Church of England, I am hers, *ex animo*.

†**e'xanimous**, *a. Obs.*⁻⁰ [f. L. *exanim-is* lifeless + -OUS.] (See quot.)

1730-6 BAILEY (folio), *Exanimous*, without spirit or life. Hence in Johnson and in mod. Dicts.

†**e'xannual**, *a. Obs. rare*⁻¹. [App. f. EX- *prefix*¹ + ANNUAL.] In ***Exannual Roll***: a roll kept at the Exchequer to which debts to the Crown presumed to be irrecoverable were transferred, instead of being carried forward in the 'Annual Roll' from year to year.

1650 *Order Ct. of Exchequer* in Hale *Sheriffs Accompts* (1683) 96 So much of the said Firmes as..are become illeviable, shall be..conveyed out of the said annual Roll and Sheriffs Accompts into the exannual Roll of this Court.

exannulate (ɛks'ænjʊlət), *a. Bot.* [f. EX- priv. + ANNUL-US + -ATE².] Having no *annulus* or ring round the sporangium, as certain ferns; opposed to ANNULATE.

1861 BENTLEY *Bot.* 369 Those in which the ring is absent are said to be exannulate. **1880** GRAY *Struct. Bot.* x. §2. 361 Not dehiscent, exannulate.

†**e'xannulose**, *a. Zool. Obs.* [f. EX- privative + ANNUL-US + -OSE.] Of certain invertebrate animals: Having a body not consisting of rings or ring-like segments.

1832 JOHNSTON in *Proc. Berw. Nat. Club.* I. 8 Communications relating to the exannulose invertebrate tribes have been made as yet only by myself.

exanthalose (ɛk'sænθələʊs). *Min.* [f. Gr. ἐξανθ-έειν (see EXANTHEMA) + ἅλ-ς salt + -OSE. (First used in Fr. by Beudant *Minéral.* (1832) II. 475.)] (See quots.)

1837 R. ALLAN *Phillips' Min.* 198 Exantholose. **1844** DANA *Min.* 221. **1868** *Ibid.* 637 *Exanthalose*..is a white efflorescence, such as results from the exposure to the air of glauber salt. **1882** WATTS *Dict. Chem.* II. 613 *Exanthalose*, native sulphate of sodium.

exanthem (ɛk'sænθɪm). *Path.* [Anglicized form of next.] = next.

1656 BLOUNT *Glossogr.*, *Exanthemes*, the Small-Pox, wheals or pushes in a mans skin, Measles. **1861** BUMSTEAD *Ven. Dis.* (1879) 737 The extensive superficial exanthems are peculiar to the first months of the disease. **1876** J. S. BRISTOWE *Th. & Pract. Med.* 290 The term *exanthem*.. should be exclusively applied to the several eruptions which attend and characterise the infectious fevers.

‖**exanthema** (ɛksæn'θiːmə). Pl. **-ata**. [late L., a Gr. ἐξάνθημα eruption, f. ἐξανθέειν, f. ἐξ- out + ἀνθέειν to blossom, f. ἄνθος blossom.]

1. *Path.* An efflorescence, eruption, or rash such as takes place in measles, small-pox, etc. Also a disease characterized by efflorescence; an eruptive disease. Chiefly *pl.*

1657 *Phys. Dict.*, *Exanthemata*, the small pox are pustules, and the measles spots which, etc. **1766** SMOLLETT *Trav.* I. xxiv. 367 Some few persons of gross habits have..been seized with putrid fevers, attended with exanthemata. **1806** *Med. Jrnl.* XV. 383 Frambœsia..resembles variola and the other exanthemata. **1876** tr. *Wagner's Gen. Pathol.* 15 Certain febrile affections, especially the acute exanthemata.

2. *Bot.* Blotches and eruptive excrescences on the surface of leaves.

1866 in *Treas. Bot.* **1884** in *Syd. Soc. Lex.*

exanthematic (ɛk,sænθɪ'mætɪk), *a. Path.* [f. Gr. ἐξανθηματ-, stem of ἐξάνθημα (see prec.) + -IC.] Of or pertaining to, or of the nature of, an exanthema; eruptive.

1860 in MAYNE *Exp. Lex.* **1869** E. A. PARKES *Pract. Hygiene* (ed. 3) 106 Hospital gangrene is a precursor of exanthematic typhus.

exanthematology (,ɛksænθiːmə'tɒlədʒɪ). [f. as prec.: see -LOGY.] The doctrine or study of the exanthemata; a treatise on eruptive fevers.

[**1730-6** BAILEY (folio), *Exanthematologia*, an account or treatise of eruptive fevers, the measles and small pox.] **1860** in MAYNE *Exp. Lex.* **1884** in *Syd. Soc. Lex.*

exanthematous (ɛksæn'θiːmətəs), *a.* [f. as prec. + -OUS.] Of, or pertaining to, or of the nature of an exanthema; efflorescent.

1755 JOHNSON, *Exanthematous*, pustulous; efflorescent; eruptive. **1780** LAYARD *Cattle Distemp.* in *Phil. Trans.* LXX. 543 The contagion was not of the exanthematous sort. **1836** TODD *Cycl. Anat.* I. 429/1 In the exanthematous diseases, the blood partakes of the general disorder of the system. **1838** *Penny Cycl.* X. 108/1 Fever is an essential element in exanthematous disease.

exanthine (ɛk'sænθaɪn). [f. Gr. ἐξανθ-έειν (see EXANTHEMA) + -INE.] The Purree or Indian yellow of India.

1875 in URE *Dict. Arts.*

†**e'xantlate**, *a. Obs. rare*⁻¹. [ad. L. *exantlāt-us*, pa. pple. of *exantlāre*: see EXANTLATE *v.*] Pumped out; drained.

1651 BIGGS *New Disp.* ¶81 Not yet exantlate and exhausted with generating and concocting.

†**e'xantlate**, *v. Obs.* [f. L. *exantlāt-* ppl. stem of *exantlāre* to draw out (a liquid).

The etymology of the L. word is disputed; some, relying on the variant spelling *exanclare* (which seems to be the better attested of the two), consider it to be f. *ex-* out + *anculus* servant, so that the primary sense would be 'to draw (water, etc.) as a servant.' Others regard the word as ad. Gr. ἐξαντλεῖν to pump out, empty (liquids), f. ἐξ out + ἄντλος hold of a ship. In any case the fig. use of *exantlare* or *exanclare* for 'to endure to the uttermost' must have been suggested by the precisely similar use of the Gr. word.]

1. *trans.* To draw out as from a well.

c **1650** CHARLETON cited by BLOUNT *Glossogr.* (1656) [cf. quot. **1650** s.v. EXANTLATION].

2. To waste away, spend, exhaust. Also *refl.*

1660-3 BOYLE *Usef. Nat. Phil.* II. v, Acid or saline liquors, which..soon coagulate, or exantlate themselves by working, and thereby become unfit for future operations. **1680** —— *Scept. Chem.* II. 117 By time those seeds are Weari'd or Exantlated, or unable to Act their Parts..any Longer.

†**exant'lation**. *Obs.* [f. prec.: see -ATION.]

1. The action of drawing out, as water from a well; *fig.* only.

1646 SIR T. BROWNE *Pseud. Ep.* I. v. 18 Truth which wise men say doth lye in a well, is not recoverable but by exantlation. **1650** CHARLETON tr. *Van Helmont's Delir. Catarrhi* Pref. 7 A deplorable remora to the timely exantlation of Truth. **1704** SWIFT *T. Tub* Introd., To draw up by exantlation or display by incision. **1731-1800** in BAILEY; and in mod. Dicts.

2. Exhaustion; exhausted condition.

1651 BIGGS *New Disp.* 42 Most of them have annexed their own cruelties..rottennesse, exantlation of their powers.

exappendiculate (,ɛksæpən'dɪkjʊlət), *a. Bot.* [f. EX- *prefix*¹ + L. *appendicul-a* (APPENDICLE) + -ATE².] Having no appendicles or appendages.

1870 HOOKER *Stud. Flora* 48 Petals exappendiculate.

exarate ('ɛksəreɪt), *a. Entom.* [ad. L. *exarāt-us*, pa. pple. of *exarāre*: see next *v.*] (See quot.)

1870 ROLLESTON *Anim. Life* 76 The chrysalis..differs..in being 'free' or 'exarate'. **1888** —— (ed. Jackson) 152 Of the first kind of pupa two varieties are distinguishable. In one the larval skin is simply thrown off. It is known as incomplete, exarate or *libera*.

†'**exarate**, *v. Obs.* [f. L. *exarāt-* ppl. stem of *exarāre* to plough up; also, to trace characters on a waxen tablet, f. *ex-* out + *arāre* to plough.]

1. *trans.* To dig or plough up.

1656-81 in BLOUNT *Glossogr.*

2. To write or note down.

1656 in BLOUNT *Glossogr.* **1657** REEVE *God's Plea* 230 God hath an observing eye over a Penitent, and doth exarate and can enumerate all his manifestations.

exaration (ɛksə'reɪʃən). [ad. late L. *exarātiōn-em*, n. of action f. *exarāre*: see EXARATE *v.*]

†**1.** The action of ploughing. *Obs.*⁻⁰

1658-96 in PHILLIPS. **1721-1800** in BAILEY.

2. The action of tracing (characters) upon stone, or writing. Also *concr.* a writing; a composition; *rare* in mod. use.

1631 R. BYFIELD *Doctr. Sabb.* 76 This pleadeth the necessitie of..their exaration, or drawing, as it were, with his pencill on the Tables of stone. **1683** E. HOOKER *Pref. Ep. to Pordage's Mystic Div.* 94 These exarations of his Penn. **1716** M. DAVIES *Athen. Brit.* II. 389 The Whimsical Exarations of Socinus, Crellius, etc. **1755** in JOHNSON. **1840** W. H. MORLEY in Lane *Arab. Nts.* (1841) III. 743 The story in the Persian MS...is written in three different hands. The first part..has been apparently added since the exaration of the other two.

†**e'xarceate**, *v. Obs. rare*⁻¹. [irreg. f. EX- *prefix*¹ + L. *arcē-re* to keep off + -ATE³.] *trans.* To hinder, prevent.

1657 TOMLINSON *Renou's Disp.* 256 It [aloes] takes away obstructions, exarceates putretude.

exarch ('ɛksɑːk), *sb.* Also 6 **exarke**. [ad. L. *exarch-us*, a Gr. ἔξαρχος, in class. Gr. a leader, chief, f. ἐξάρχειν to take the lead, f. ἐξ (see EX- *pref.*²) + ἄρχειν to begin, rule. In the post-classical uses represented by the Eng. word, the prefix was perh. taken in the sense 'out, sent out'.]

1. Under the Byzantine emperors, the governor of a distant province, as Africa or Italy; in the latter case with title 'Exarch of Ravenna'. (The title was revived in the Holy Roman Empire: see quot. 1751.)

1588 ALLEN *Admon.* 44 So did S. Gregory the first moue Genadius the Exarke, to make warres against the heritikes. **1601** R. JOHNSON *Kingd. & Commw.* (1603) 107 Ravenna, where some Emperors have kept their courts, and after them their Exarches or lieutenants. **1751** CHAMBERS *Cycl.* s.v., The emperor Frederic created Heraclius..exarch of the whole kingdom of Burgundy. **1788** GIBBON *Decl. & F.* xlix. V. 120 These remote provinces [Italy and Africa] required the presence of a supreme magistrate; he was indifferently styled the exarch or the patrician. **1832** tr. *Sismondi's Ital. Rep.* i. 11 Governed by a lieutenant of the Emperor of Constantinople, under the title of exarch of the five cities of Pentapolis. **1855** MILMAN *Lat. Chr.* (1864) II. III. vii. 132 The Exarch of Ravenna, the representative of the Byzantine Empire. **1872** E. W. ROBERTSON *Hist. Ess.* 205 The Pope.. anointing..Pepin and his two sons..as Patricians of the Romans thus occupying the condition of the Exarch.

2. *Eccl.* In the Eastern Church, a title originally equivalent to 'archbishop', 'metropolitan', or 'patriarch', which in early use were employed almost indiscriminately. Subsequently, 'a bishop having charge of a province, and next in rank to a patriarch' (*Catholic Dict.*); also, a legate or deputy of the patriarch, entrusted with some special charge or mission.

a **1600** HOOKER *Eccl. Pol.* VII. xvi. 421 In the council of Carthage..it was decreed, that the bishop of the chief see should not be entitled the exarch of priests. **1635** PAGITT *Christianogr.* I. ii. (1636) 58 Gregorius Hieromonachus, the Patriarchal Exarch from Trapezunt. **1751** CHAMBERS *Cycl.* s.v., In 493 Sebas was established exarch, or chief, of all the anchorets within the territory of Jerusalem. **1851** HUSSEY *Papal Power* ii. 74 Bishops or clergy should appeal from their metropolitan to the exarch of the Province. **1877** E. VENABLES in *Dict. Chr. Biog.* I. 288/1 He [Basil of Caesareia] was metropolitan of Cappadocia, and exarch of Pontus. **1884** ARNOLD-FORSTER in *Contemp. Rev.* Mar. 412 The constitution of the Bulgarian Exarch by the Porte in 1870.

Hence **e'xarchal** *a.*, of or pertaining to an exarch.

1855 MILMAN *Lat. Chr.* (1864) II. IV. ix. 414 The exarchal government from the first had only been powerful to tyrannise and feeble to protect.

exarch ('ɛksɑːk), *a. Bot.* [f. EX-² + Gr. ἀρχή beginning, origin.] Having the protoxylem adjacent to the pericycle.

1891 H. E. F. GARNSEY tr. *Solms-Laubach's Fossil Bot.* xi. 257 Had he called..the leaf-strand of Cycadeae mesarch, and that of Isoëtes exarch.., we might..have been spared this misconception. **1900** B. D. JACKSON *Gloss. Bot. Terms*, *Exarch*, used of vascular bundles in which the whole primary wood is centripetal, almost the same as perixylic. **1902** *Encycl. Brit.* XXV. 413/1 When the protoxylem strands are situated at the periphery of the stele, abutting on the pericycle, as in all roots, and many of the more primitive Pteridophyte stems, the stele is said to be *exarch*. **1959** FOSTER & GIFFORD *Compar. Morphol. Vascular Plants* iii. 46 Xylem differentiation which occurs *centripetally*..is termed exarch.

exarchate ('ɛksɑːkeɪt, ɛk'sɑːkət). Also 6-7 **exarchat, -cat**. [ad. late L. *exarchāt-us*, f. *exarchus*: see EXARCH *sb.* Cf. Fr. *exarchat*.]

1. The office, dignity, or jurisdiction of an exarch, whether **a.** civil, or **b.** ecclesiastical.

a. 1561 DAUS tr. *Bullinger on Apoc.* (1573) 196 b, Longinus brought in a new name of dignitie, that is to witte, the exarchate of Italie. **1635** PAGITT *Christianogr.* 259* After the overthrow of the Exarchat..the Romans began to be governed by..the Popes. **1678** WANLEY *Wond. Lit. World* v. ii. §16. 469/2 Justinus the second instituted the Exarchate of Ravenna. **1751** CHAMBERS *Cycl.* s.v. *Exarch* The exarchs subsisted about a hundred and eighty-five years, and ended

in Eutychius; under whose exarchate the city of Ravenna was taken by the Lombard king.

b. **1876** *Daily News* 16 Dec. 5/6 A self-governed province, including the territory of the Bulgarian exarchate.

2. The province or territory governed by an exarch, whether **a.** civil, or **b.** ecclesiastical.

a. **1563-87** FOXE *A. & M.* (1596) 117/1 Pipinus..gaue..to the said see of Rome, the exarchat or princedome of Rauenna. **1764** GIBBON *Misc. Wks.* (1814) V. 39 Pepin and Charlemagne..gave the duchy of Rome and the exarchate of Ravenna to the popes. **1861** J. SHEPPARD *Fall Rome* vi. 314 The Byzantines still retained the exarchate.

b. **1877** E. VENABLES in *Dict. Chr. Biog.* I. 290/2 He [Basil] was to be found in every part of his exarchate.

Hence †**e'xarchate,ship**, *Obs.*

1606 G. W[OODCOCKE] tr. *Justin's Hist.* Hh vj a, Iustinivs..instituted the Exarchatship.

Exarchist ('ɛksɑːkɪst, ɛk'sɑːkɪst). [f. EXARCH + -IST.] A supporter of the Exarch of Bulgaria against the Patriarch of Constantinople. Also *attrib.*

1903 *Daily Record & Mail* 10 Apr. 5 The Greeks..declare that they will kill two exarchists in the towns for every patriarchist killed in the country. **1903** *Westm. Gaz.* 28 Sept. 2/2 Although the Christians are divided among themselves, Patriarchists and Exarchists being at daggers drawn, the Turkish soldiers and Bashibazouks are treating all alike. **1907** A. FORTESCUE *Orthod. Eastern Ch.* IV. x. 321 In 1890..the Sultan gave his firman for the erection of two more Exarchist sees (Ochrida and Skopia). **1927** *Contemp. Rev.* Apr. 734 Hostility between Exarchists and Patriarchists..long poisoned the life of Macedonia. **1937** *Times Lit. Suppl.* 3 Apr. 246/3 An Exarchist Bulgarophone Hellene.

†**'exarchy.** *Obs.*$^{-0}$ [f. EXARCH *sb.* + -Y[3].] = EXARCHATE.

1656-81 BLOUNT *Glossogr.*, *Exarchy*, the chief place of dignity under the Emperor, the Lieutenancy of the Empire. **1721-1800** in BAILEY.

exareolate (ɛksə'riːəleɪt), *a. Bot.* [f. EX- *prefix*[1] + AREOLA + -ATE[2].] Unmarked by areolæ; not areolate.

1866 in *Treas. Bot.*

exarillate (ɛks'ærɪleɪt), *a. Bot.* [f. EX- *prefix*[1] + L. *arill-us* ARIL + -ATE[2].] Having no aril; not arillate.

1830 LINDLEY *Nat. Syst. Bot.* 150 Corolla with a twisted æstivation..exarillate seeds.

exaristate (ɛksə'rɪsteɪt), *a. Bot.* [f. EX- *prefix*[1] + ARISTA + -ATE[2].] Having no arista, awn, or beard; not aristate.

1866 in *Treas. Bot.* **1884** in *Syd. Soc. Lex.*

exarticulate (ɛksɑː'tɪkjʊlət), *a. Entom.* [mod. f. EX- *pref.*[1] + L. *articul-us* joint + -ATE[2]. (Late L. had *exarticulātus* in sense 'inarticulate'.)] Not jointed; not consisting of two parts.

1835 KIRBY *Hab. & Inst. Anim.* II. xvi. 78 An elongated exarticulate base, representing the handle of a whip.

exarticulate (ɛksɑː'tɪkjʊleɪt), *v.* [f. as prec. + -ATE[3].] *trans.* †**a.** 'To put out of joint; dislocate' (Blount *Glossogr.* 1656-81). *Obs.* **b.** 'To remove a limb, or a part of a limb, at a joint' (*Syd. Soc. Lex.* 1884).

exarticulation (,ɛksɑːtɪkjʊ'leɪʃən). [f. as prec. + -ATION.]

†**1.** The putting (a limb) out of joint; dislocation, luxation. *Obs.*

1658 in PHILLIPS. **1721** in BAILEY; whence in mod. Dicts.

2. Amputation at a joint; removal of a limb, or a part of a limb, at a joint.

1884 in *Syd. Soc. Lex.*

†**e'xartuate,** *v. Obs.*$^{-0}$ [f. late L. *exartuāt-* ppl. stem of *exartuāre* (Carpentier), f. *ex-* (see EX- *pref.*[1]) + *artus* joint: cf. ARTUATE.]

1656-81 BLOUNT *Glossogr.*, *Exartuate*, to carve as meat is carved, to quarter as the hangman doth.

†**e'xasper,** *v. Obs.* [ad. (directly or through F. *exaspér-er*) L. *exasper-āre*: see EXASPERATE *v.*] = EXASPERATE *v.*

1545 JOYE *Exp. Dan.* vii. 96 b, A lyon is a cruell beast yf he be exaspered. **1637** R. HUMPHREY tr. *St. Ambrose* i. 9 Whosoever hee bee that exaspereth.

exasperate (ɛg'zɑːspəreɪt, -æ-), *pa. pple.* and *ppl. a.* [ad. L. *exasperāt-us*, pa. pple. of *exasperāre*: see EXASPERATE *v.*]

†**A.** *pa. pple.*; in various senses of the vb. *Obs.*

1540-1 ELYOT *Image Gov.* (1549) 160 Wherwith thei beeyng exasperate..wente vnto two gentilmen dwellyng hereby. **1545** RAYNOLD *Byrth Mankynde* 119 Yf it be so that the cough haue exasperat and made rough the tounge. **1585** LLOYD *Treas. Health* H viij, Apply vnto the head beyng shauen: mustarde seed, & the skynne shalbe exasperate and the rewme dryed. **1605** SHAKS. *Macb.* III. vi. 38 This report Hath so exasperate their King, that hee Prepares for some attempt of Warre. **1609** HOLLAND *Amm. Marcel* XIV. v. 8 This rigor of his..was much more exasperate by information given of certain offensive crimes.

B. *ppl. a.*

1. *Bot.* Rough; covered with short stiff points.

1866 in *Treas. Bot.* **1884** in *Syd. Soc. Lex.*

2. = EXASPERATED 2 and 3. *arch.*

1601 HOLLAND *Pliny* (1634) II. 211 Some diseases would be more exasperat and angry. **1606** SHAKS. *Tr. & Cr.* V. i. 34 *Ther.* Do I curse thee? *Patr.* Why no.. *Ther.* No? why art thou then exasperate? **1622** BACON *Hen. VII*, 79 Matters grew more exasperate betweene the two kings of England and France. **1795** SOUTHEY *Joan of Arc* II. 190 To the exasperate patience of the foe [we opposed] Desperate endurance. **1854** *Tait's Mag.* XXI. 167 He pours out the whole full flood, fiery and exasperate, of his emotions. **1856** MRS. BROWNING *Aur. Leigh* IV. 177 Swallows which the exasperate dying year Sets spinning in black circles.

exasperate (ɛg'zɑːspəreɪt, -æ-), *v.* Also 6-7 **exasperat.** [f. L. *exasperāt-* ppl. stem of *exasperāre* to roughen, irritate, f. *ex-* (see EX- *pref.*[1]) + *asper* rough.]

†**1.** To make harsh or rugged; to add harshness to (language, sounds, etc.); to render (laws) more severe. *Obs.*

1597 MORLEY *Introd. Mus.* 177 Cadences bound with the fourth or seuenth..being in long notes will exasperat the harmonie. **1634** H. R. *Salerne Regim.* 155 Nuts..exasperate the voyce and make it like a Cranes voyce. **1643** MILTON *Divorce* II. xvii, Not considering that the Law should be exasperated according to our estimation of the injury. **1651** W. G. tr. *Cowel's Inst.* 264 So great hath been the bloody wickednesse of these times, that this Law hath been somewhat more exasperated. **1692** *Christ Exalted* 99 Our Translators do rather mollifie, than exasperate, the word *timeas*, and say, Thou hast aborred. **1765** BEATTIE *On Churchill* 87 Did hate to vice exasperate thy style, No—Bufo match'd the vilest of the vile.

2. To increase the fierceness or violence of (a disease, pain, appetite, etc.). Now with mixed notion of 3, 4.

1611 COTGR., *Aigrun*, any thing that encreases, or exasperates, a disease, or sore. *a* **1677** BARROW *Serm.* in *Beauties of B.* (1846) 59 Rubbing the sore doth tend to exasperate and inflame it. **1710** T. FULLER *Pharm. Extemp.* 197 All the other Symptoms will be exasperated by the tumult which Evacuations cause. **1783** P. POTT *Chirurg. Wks.* II. 311 Scirrhus or cancer..was exasperated, and made worse by it. **1843** PRESCOTT *Mexico* (1874) II. 347 Two injuries on the head, one of which was so much exasperated by fatigue. **1850** LYNCH *Theoph. Trinal* v. 83 If we do not heed the claim of the different appetites..we exasperate them.

†**b.** To make more grievous or painful; to aggravate. Also, to represent as worse; to exaggerate, magnify. *Obs.*

1561 DAUS tr. *Bullinger on Apoc.* (1573) 36 He speaketh modestly, least by exasperating ouermuch the sinne and errour in the faythfull, he should discourage them vtterly. **1591** SYLVESTER *Du Bartas* I. vi. (1605) 167 Why didst thou..Create These harmefull Beasts, which but exasperate Our thorny life? **1646** SIR T. BROWNE *Pseud. Ep.* VII. xvii. 376 Judas..having sinned beyond aggravation, and committed one villany which cannot bee exasperated by all other. **1651** *Reliq. Wotton.* 33 Not to exasperate the Case of my Lord of Southampton. **1681** *Lond. Gaz.* No. 1625/1 They of Liege do every day more and more exasperate things. **1750** JOHNSON *Rambler* No. 73 ¶5 This visionary opulence..exasperated our necessities.

3. To embitter, intensify (ill-feeling, passion, wickedness.) Now chiefly with mixed notion of 4. Also, in good sense: †To heighten (courage).

1548 UDALL, etc. *Erasm. Par. Matt.* ii. 26 b, That..the vngodlines of Herode..might more and more be exasperated. **1614** RALEIGH *Hist. World* II. IV. vii. §1. 248 The Roman Dictator..to exasperate his souldiers courage, threw their owne ensignes amidst the enemies. **1677** OTWAY *Titus & Berenice* III. i, Why come you thus, t'exasperate my Despair? **1773** JOHNSON in *Boswell* 1 May II. 107 The pride of a common man is very little exasperated by the supposed usurpation of an acknowledged superior. **1794** PALEY *Evid.* II. ix. §3 (1817) 265 These feuds were exasperated by the mutual persecutions of the Jews and Christians. **1855** PRESCOTT *Philip II*, I. IV. vii. 490 His naturally wild and headstrong temper was exasperated by disease.

4. To irritate (a person); to provoke to anger; to enrage, incense. Const. *to*, also *to* with *inf.*

1534 MORE *Let. Marg. Roper* Wks. 1429/2, I should..but further exasperate hys highnes. **1586** JAS. VI, in Ellis *Orig. Lett.* I. 224 III. 19 If I shall persist in that course ye shall rather be exasperattet to passionis in reading the uordis. **1625** SHIRLEY *Traitor* IV. i, I did exasperate you to kill or murder him. **1768** FRANKLIN *Ess.* Wks. 1840 II. 367 The poor are..exasperated against the rich, and excited to insurrections. **1773** GOLDSM. *Stoops to Conq.* IV. Wks. (Globe) 670/1 You know my hasty temper, and should not exasperate it. **1818** SCOTT *Hrt. Midl.* iv, The burghers..were greatly exasperated at the unexpected respite. **1819** SHELLEY *Cenci* II. ii. 37 Thus he is exasperated to ill. **1867** EMERSON *Lett. & Soc. Aims, Progr. Culture* Wks. (Bohn) III. 236 In England..the game laws..exasperated the farmers to carry the Reform Bill.

refl. **1547** BOORDE, *Brev. Health*, Pref. 2 a, Exasperate not yourselfe agaynste me for makynge of this lytle volume of Phisycke. **1871** SMILES *Charac.* vi. (1876) 175 We shall not mend matters by exasperating ourselves against them.

absol. **1606** G. W[OODCOCKE] tr. *Justin's Hist.* 100 a, Phillip exasperated what he could do, to perswade the Etolians to ioyn warre with him. **1614** RALEIGH *Hist. World* II. 254 Not knowing whether such a deniall might satisfie or exasperate. **1645** MILTON *Tetrach.* Ded., Those who ceased not to exasperate without cause.

b. *transf.*

1654 R. CODRINGTON tr. *Justin's Hist.* 67 Injury on this side, and indignitie on the other side did exasperate their swords. **1865** MERIVALE *Rom. Emp.* VIII. lxiii. 30 The stream..foams in a furious torrent, exasperated by the rocky ledges which at some points intercept its course.

†**5.** To irritate physically; to render sore, chafe.

1552 HULOET, Exasperate, *vlcero.* **1610** MARKHAM *Masterp.* II. clxxiii. 494 Though it [myrrh] doth cleanse much, yet it doth not exasperate the arteries. **1621** VENNER *Tobacco* (1650) 411 Not sucking it with a sudden or strong attraction: for then it will exasperate the winde pipe. *a* **1682** SIR T. BROWNE *Tracts* 105 The Mugil, being somewhat rough and hard-skinned, did more exasperate the gutts of such offenders.

†**6.** *intr.* **a.** Of persons: To become enraged or incensed. Cf. 4. **b.** Of things: To become worse or more serious. Cf. 2 b. **c.** Of a disease, etc.: To increase in violence or severity. Cf. 2. *Obs.*

1632 J. HAYWARD tr. *Biondi's Eromena* 94 The more his external wounds healed, the more did his internall exasperate and fret. *c* **1645** HOWELL *Lett.* (1650) II. II. 18 Notwithstanding..that matters began to exasperate more and more..he would abate nothing. **1659** HEYLIN *Animadv.* in Fuller's *Appeal* (1840) 339 The University of Oxford frequently quarrelled and exasperated, upon slight occasions.

a **1734** NORTH *Life Ld. Guildford* 83 The Distemper exasperated, till it was manifest she could not last many Weeks.

exasperated (ɛg'zɑːspəreɪtɪd, -æ-), *ppl. a.* [f. prec. + -ED[1].]

1. In various senses of the vb.

1611 COTGR., *Agacé*..incensed, prouoked, exasperated. **1660** MILTON *Free Commw.* 424 We remain finally secure from the exasperated Regal Power. **1661** LOVELL *Hist. Anim. & Min.* 35 Cows milk..used as a gargarisme, helps the throat straightened by catarrhes, and the exasperated jawes. **1694** PHILLIPS tr. *Milton's Lett. State* 29 July 1655 Such exasperated Cruelties inflicted upon the Professors of the same Religion with our selves. *a* **1714** BURNET *Own Time* (1823) I. 67 That raised the spirits of those that were already but too much exasperated. **1756** LADY M. W. MONTAGU *Lett.* xcv. IV. 73 She eloped one fair morning..leaving her two daughters..to the care of the exasperated marquis. **1875** JOWETT *Plato* (ed. 2) I. 209, I saw that they were getting exasperated with one another.

b. *Her.* (See quot.)

1830 ROBSON *Brit. Her.*, *Exasperated*, depicted in a furious attitude.

†**2.** ? Narrowed gradually to a point, tapered.

1607 TOPSELL *Serpents* (1653) 674 If it were not for these bunches..it would be so exasperated or extenuated toward the end like to the tail of a Rat or great Mouse.

Hence **e'xasperatedly** *adv.*; also †**e'xasperatedness,** *Obs.*$^{-0}$ = EXASPERATION 3.

1872 *Daily News* 26 Aug., The others..raged exasperatedly against him in their clubs. **1886** MRS. E. MOBERLY *Lady Valeria* II. v. 110 Lord Altcar laughed again, but exasperatedly. **1730-6** BAILEY (folio), Exasperatedness, incensedness, the being exasperated. **1775** ASH, *Exasperatedness.*

exasperater: see EXASPERATOR.

e'xasperating, *vbl. sb.* [f. EXASPERATE *v.* + -ING[1].] The action of the verb EXASPERATE.

1611 COTGR., *Exasperation*, an exasperation; prouocation..exasperating, vexing.

exasperating (ɛg'zɑːspəreɪtɪŋ, -æ-), *ppl. a.* [f. as prec. + -ING[2].] That exasperates (in senses of vb.); exceedingly irritating or provoking.

a **1665** J. GOODWIN *Filled w. the Spirit* (1867) 344 A sin of a very exasperating nature. **1674** GREW *Anat. Plants*, Lect. vi. 290 Jalap, Mercury, and Daisy, have all of them that exasperating Tast in the Throat. **1858** FROUDE *Hist. Eng.* III. xvii. 458 An evidence of unmistakeable goodwill in revealing an exasperating secret. **1876** BLACK *Madcap V.* vii. 59 Do you know what an exasperating girl you are?

Hence **e'xasperatingly** *adv.*, in an exasperating manner; provokingly.

1851 DICKENS *Lett.* (ed. 2) I. 262 Stone presents himself with a most exasperatingly mysterious visage. **1884** JUL. WEDGWOOD in *Contemp. Rev.* Mar. 452 The most exasperatingly unreadable stuff ever met with.

exasperation (ɛgzɑːspə'reɪʃən, -æ-). [ad. L. *exasperātiōn-em*, n. of action f. *exasperāre*: see EXASPERATE *v.*]

1. Of a disease, etc.: Increase of violence or malignity; exacerbation; an instance of this.

1633 WOTTON *Let.* in *Reliq. Wott.* (1672) 457 Judging, as of Patients in Feavers, by the exasperation of the fits. **1671** SALMON *Syn. Med.* II. xlvi. 315 Shivering, and Exasperation of the Feaver..are not always to be accounted evil. **1860** EMERSON *Cond. Life, Power* Wks. (Bohn) II. 334 The ecstasies of devotion with the exasperations of debauchery. **1884** in *Syd. Soc. Lex.*

2. The action of exasperating or provoking to anger; embittering; intense provocation; an instance of this. Also, a cause or means of exasperating.

a **1631** DONNE in *Selections* (1840) 38 Forbearing all..exasperations by odious names of subdivision. **1676** OWEN *Worship of God* 172 That he may take no occasion thereby for the exasperation of his own spirit. *a* **1731** ATTERBURY (J.), Their ill usage and exasperations of him..disposed him to take liberty. **1861** GEO. ELIOT *Silas M.* (1868) 26 He had made ties for himself which..were a constant exasperation.

3. The condition of being exasperated or intensely irritated; exasperated feeling, violent passion or anger; †an instance of this.

1547 BOORDE *Introd. Knowl.* xxxii. (1870) 205 Saying..that..I wold set them by the fete..wyth other wordes I had to them of exasperacyon. **1612-5** BP. HALL *Contempl. O.T.* XIX. iv, Neither the furious purposes of Ahaziah, nor the exasperations of a Jezebel can hurt that prophet. **1672** OWEN *Evang. Love* 43 Divisions and Schisms, and mutual Exasperations among themselves. *a* **1716** SOUTH *Serm.* (1774) X. ix. 282 Perhaps..it was a word extorted from him by the exasperation of his spirits. **1817** BENTHAM *Parl. Ref. Catech.* Introd. 56 Should the only remedy be refused [and] oppression continue..then it is not quiet sense that will

speak, but exasperation. **1858** FROUDE *Hist. Eng.* IV. xviii. 13 The exasperation of the people with the English increased the cordiality with which he was received.

†**4.** Exaggeration (in a bad sense); 'malignant representation' (J.). = AGGRAVATION 5. *Obs. rare.*

1648 *Eikon Bas.* §3. 12 An act which My enemies loaded with all the obloquies and exasperations they could. **1755** in JOHNSON; whence **1818** in TODD.

¶**5.** *Punningly*, Misplaced 'aspiration'.

1854 'CUTHB. BEDE' *Verdant Green* II. ix. 80 With a footman's bow, and a footman's *h*exasperation of his h's.

exasperative (ɛgˈzɑːspəreɪtɪv, -æ-), *a.* [f. L. *exasperāt-* ppl. stem of *exasperāre* (see EXASPERATE *v.*) + -IVE.] Of a nature to exasperate or irritate; exasperating.

1837 CARLYLE *Fr. Rev.* I. VII. iv, Maternity..meets there with hunger-stricken Maternity, sympathetic, exasperative.

exasperator, -er (ɛgˈzɑːspəreɪtə(r), -æ-). [f. EXASPERATE *v.* + -OR, -ER¹.] One who exasperates.

1632 SHERWOOD, An exasperater, *agaceur.* **1755** JOHNSON, *Exasperator.* **1837** CARLYLE *Fr. Rev.* I. V. v, Fat are your larders..ye plotting exasperators of the Poor.

exaspidean (ɛksæˈspɪdiːən), *a. Zool.* [f. mod.L. *Exaspideæ* (C. J. Sundevall *Methodi Naturalis Avium Disponendarum Tentamen* (1872) I. 57), f. Gr. ἔξω outside + ἀσπίς shield.] Pertaining to passerine birds that have an anterior series of scutella on the outer side of the tarsus; cf. ENDASPIDEAN *a.*

1889 in *Cent. Dict.* **1907** R. RIDGWAY *Birds N. & Middle Amer.* IV. 328 The several modifications of the tarsal envelope in the present group may be described as follows: 1. *Exaspidean.*—The anterior envelope (acrotarsium) extends entirely across the *outer* side of the tarsus and around the posterior side, sometimes meeting the starting point on the posterior portion of the inner side, the two edges usually separated by a narrow strip or groove of smooth or nonscutellate membrane. **1959** VAN TYNE & BERGER *Fund. Ornith.* ii. 48 Several types of passerine tarsal scutellation have been described... Exaspidean: With anterior, scutellated segment of tarsal sheath extending across the external side of tarsus.

ex-ˈaspirate *v. nonce-wd. trans.* To deprive of an aspirate or *h.*

1832 *Blackw. Mag.* XXXII. 509 Everybody knows her [Medusa's] celebrated head of hair and that she herself was literally the first Wig. Hence the Whigs—for Medusa herself was one, and head of that family ex-aspirated.

exaturate, -ed, -ation: see EXSATURATE, etc.

†**eˈxauctorate**, *pa. pple.* and *ppl. a. Obs.* In 7 exauctorat. [ad. L. *exauctōrāt-us*, pa. pple. of *exauctōrāre*: see next.] Deprived of office; divested of authority.

1680 HICKES *Spir. Popery* 9 Saying, that Jesus Christ is quite exauctorat and unkinged by it. **1718** *Wodrow Corr.* (1843) II. 370 If we refuse to baptize in families, people will go to..the exauctorate Episcopal clergy, and leave our communion. **1818** SCOTT *Hrt. Midl.* iv, 'He [was] then in a point of trust and in point of power..but after Wilson was cut down, it was a' ower—he was clean exauctorate.'

†**eˈxauctorate**, *v. Obs.* Forms: 6–7 exauthorate, 7 exauterate, -orat(e, 7–8 exauctorate. [f. L. *exauctōrāt-* ppl. stem of *exauctōrāre* to dismiss from service, f. *ex-* (see EX- *pref.*¹) + *auctor* AUTHOR *sb.*]

1. *trans.* 'To dismiss from service' (J.); to depose from office, deprive of authority or rank.

1623–6 COCKERAM, *Exauthorate*, to put men of warre out of wages. **1642** JER. TAYLOR *Episc.* Pref., The first Bishop that was exauctorated was..Prince, and Bishop of Geneva. **1660** —— *Duct. Dubit.* II. i. 264 God..can punish and exauthorate whom he please, and substitute others in their room. **1660** WATERHOUSE *Arms & Arm.* 7 Admitting a Plebeian coordinateness which in time ex-auctorated the Senate. **1676** W. ROW *Contn. Blair's Autobiog.* xi. (1848) 336 They did exauctorate and depose the Protector Richard Cromwell. **1726** AYLIFFE *Parerg.* 291 Arius..and other Arch-Hereticks..were by the church treated with no other kind of Punishment than..by exauctorating and depriving them of their Degrees therein. **1731–1800** in BAILEY.

2. To deprive (a law, etc.) of authority; to destroy the authority of.

1593 BILSON *Govt. Christ's Ch.* 311 That men might see them [the new laws] before you exauthorate the olde. **1606** J. HYND *Eliosto Libid.* 51 The yron naturally cleaveth to the forcible Adamant, and nature can not be exauthorated. *a* **1648** LD. HERBERT *Hen. VIII* Ded. (1683) A j a, I hope they [defects] will not be so great or many, as to exauctorate the rest. **1679** S. SMITH in Howell *State Trials* (1816) VII. 587 He [the pope] exautorats, and invalidates their [the Scriptures'] divine original, and superintendency.

Hence **eˈxauctorated** *ppl. a.*, **eˈxauctorating** *vbl. sb.*

1622–62 HEYLYN *Cosmogr.* I. (1682) 239 Conferred on them all the Lands and Possessions of the exauterated Templers. *c* **1661** *Argyle's Will* in *Harl. Misc.* (1746) VIII. 28/1 An alms-house, for the entertaining of all antiquated, exauthorated elders. **1682** EVELYN in *Pepys' Diary* VI. 141 Pharaoh's exauctorated butler. **1785** ARNOT *Trials* (1812) 338 Letters of orders..granted by an exauctorated Bishop. **1648** *Petit. Eastern Assoc.* 3 The exautorating, and well neare the adnulling of our Parliament. **1652** W. SCLATER (Jun.) *Civil Mag.* (1653) 15 Samsons, who would thus..attempt the exauctorating of Civill Magistracy.

†**exauctoˈration.** *Obs.* Also 7 exaut(h)oration. [as if ad. L. **exauctōrātiōn-em*, n. of action f. *exauctōrāre*: see prec. Cf. Fr. *exauthoration* (Cotgr.).] The action of 'exauctorating'.

1. Discharge from military service.

a **1654** BP. J. RICHARDSON *Observ. Old Test.* 327 (T.) No discharge in that war..no dismission from it, no vacation, or exauctoration. **1725** tr. *Dupin's Eccl. Hist. 17th C.* I. II. ii. 30 Degradation..is founded on the Example of Military Exauctoration.

2. a. Deprivation of office or authority; degradation. **b.** Abolition (of an office); annulling (of authority).

1625 DONNE *Serm.* 3 Apr. 17 Exautorations and Excommunications amongst the Bishops. **1641** HEYLIN *Help to Hist.* (1671) 156 On the exauctoration of Bishop Heath, it was assigned..to Master Hooper. **1651** JER. TAYLOR *Serm. for Year* I. xxi. 267 To protect and nourish those that will prove ministers of their [kings'] own exauctoration. *a* **1656** BP. HALL *Rem. Wks.* (1660) 308 Do not you think that those..went somewhat too far..in the exauthoration of Episcopal office and dignity. **1726** AYLIFFE *Parerg.* 206 Deposition, Degradation, or Exauctoration..is ..the removing of a Person from some Degree, Dignity, or Order in the Church. **1822** MRS. E. NATHAN *Langreath* II. 271, I would have used my influence to have averted your exauctoration. [Said by a person fond of pedantic language.] **1834** COLERIDGE *Lit. Rem.* III. 207 Little did Taylor forsee that to indiscreet avowals like these..the exauctorations of the Bishops..would be in no small portion attributable.

†**eˈxaudible**, *a. Obs.* [ad. L. *exaudībilis*, f. *exaudīre*, f. *ex-* (see EX- *pref.*¹) + *audīre* to hear.] In senses of Latin: **a.** Able to be heard easily; distinctly audible. **b.** Hearing readily; giving ear to prayer.

c **1430** tr. *T. à Kempis' Imit.* I. xxiv, Now þy labour is fruytful, þi weping acceptable, þi mornyng exaudible. **1485** CAXTON *St. Wenefr.* 4 Most debonayr fader grante to vs thy sonnes mekely besechyng the benyngne & exaudyble.

†**exauˈdition.** *Obs. rare*⁻¹. [ad. late L. *exaudītiōn-em*, n. of action f. *exaudīre*: see prec.] The action of hearing effectually; hearkening.

1617 COLLINS *Def. Bp. Ely* II. vi. 228 The word inuocation is sometime veryfied vpon them..and so exaudition likewise.

eˈxaugural, *a. rare*⁻¹. [f. EX- + the 2nd element of INAUGURAL in imitation of that word.] Of a discourse: Delivered at the close of a term of office.

1887 *Eng. Hist. Rev.* II. 358 Drawing comparisons between the author of the inaugural and the author of the exaugural address.

†**eˈxaugurate**, *v. Obs.* [f. L. *exaugurāt-* ppl. stem of *exaugurāre* to profane, f. *ex-* (see EX- *pref.*¹) + *augur* AUGUR.] *trans.* **a.** To cancel the inauguration of; to unhallow, make profane. **b.** To augur evil to.

1600 HOLLAND *Livy* I. lv. 38 [Tarquin] determined to exaugurate and unhallow certain churches and chappels. **1652** GAULE *Magastrom.* 240* The presaging Aruspex will exaugurate me with all manner of ill luck. **1695** H. DODWELL *Def. Vind. Deprived Bishops* 47 So far it was from giving him any Power over the High Priesthood itself. He had no Power of Inaugurating, and therefore none of Exaugurating. **1721–1800** in BAILEY.

†**exauguˈration.** *Obs.* [ad. L. *exaugurātiōn-em*, n. of action f. *exaugurāre*: see EXAUGURATE.] The action of unhallowing or making profane.

1600 HOLLAND *Livy* I. lv. 38 The birds by signes..allowed the exauguration and unhallowing of all other cels and chappels. **1651** J. F[REAKE] *Agrippa's Occ. Philos.* 108 To these is added Exauguration, viz. when the rod fell out of the hand of the Augure. **1730** in BAILEY (folio). **1775** in ASH.

exaumple, obs. form of EXAMPLE.

†**eˈxaun.** *Obs. rare*⁻¹. [Meant to represent the pronunciation (ɛgzɑ̃) of Fr. *exempt.* Cf. EXON¹.] = EXEMPT *sb.*

1678 BUTLER *Hud.* III. ii. 600 This comes of Breaking Covenants, And setting up Exauns of Saints.

exausiastick, var. f. EXOUSIASTIC, *Obs.*

†**eˈxauspicate**, *v. Obs.*⁻⁰ [app. f. EX- *pref.*¹ privative + AUSPICATE. (L. had *exauspicāre* to take an augury.)] (See quots.)

1623–6 COCKERAM, *Exauspicate*, to doe a thing vnluckily. **1656–81** in BLOUNT *Glossogr.* **1775** in ASH.

†**exauspiˈcation.** *Obs.*⁻⁰ [f. prec. vb.: see -ATION.] An unlucky beginning of a thing.

1730–6 in BAILEY (folio). **1775** in ASH.

exauthorate, -ation, var. ff. EXAUCTORATE, -ATION, *Obs.*

†**exauthoriˈzation.** *Obs.* [f. next: see -ATION.] The action of depriving of authority.

1640 BP. HALL *Episc.* I. §5. 18 To eject..the knowne instruments of that Papall Tyrannie..without whose perfect exauthorization they could conceive no hope of injoying the Gospel and themselves.

†**eˈxauthorize**, *v. Obs.* In 6 -toryse. [f. EX- + AUTHORIZE.] *trans.*

a. To depose from office. **b.** To deprive of authority; = EXAUCTORATE *v.*

1546 BALE *Eng. Votaries* II. (1550) 93 The kynge made an acte, that men of the church commyttynge offences notable, shulde be exautorysed or dysgraded by the byshop of the dyocese. **1612** SELDEN in Drayton *Poly-olb.* xvii. Notes 272 Sometimes animating the subject by censorious exauthorizing the Prince. **1629** WADSWORTH *Sp. Pilgr.* vi. 52 The Iesuites endeauoring by all possible meanes to exauthorize him vnder hand. **1632** in SHERWOOD.

†**exˈburse**, *v. Obs.*⁻⁰ [f. EX- + BURSE; cf. *disburse.*] *trans.* To disburse, or discharge.

1847–78 in HALLIWELL.

excæcate, -ation, var. ff. EXCECATE, -ATION.

excalate (ˈɛkskəleɪt), *v.* [f. EX-¹ 2 + *-calate* of *intercalate.*] *trans.* To remove from a series: opposed to INTERCALATE.

1900 *Phil. Trans. R. Soc.* B. CXCII. 342 There remains the assumption that vertebræ have been excalated in front of the pelvis. *Ibid.*, Six vertebræ must have been excalated in front of the pelvis.

So **excaˈlation**, the omission, absence, or elimination of a part from the middle of a series; *spec.*, in a race of organisms, the absence of any part, such as one of the middle digits or one of the vertebræ.

1898 *Nature* 22 Dec. 171/2 Kükenthal's discovery of excalation of fingers in the Cetacea. **1900** *Phil. Trans. R. Soc.* B. CXCII. 343 Hence the supposition of excalation of vertebræ in front of the girdle [of *Mustelus vulgaris*] leads also to the necessary corollary that a vast amount of both inter- and excalation must go on at another spot.

excalcarate (ɛksˈkælkəreɪt), *a.* [f. EX- privative + L. *calcar* spur + -ATE².] = ECALCARATE.

1884 in *Syd. Soc. Lex.*

†**exˈcalceate**, *v. Obs.* [f. L. *excalceāt-* ppl. stem of *excalceāre* to take off the shoes, f. *ex-* + *calceus* a shoe.] *trans.* To take off the shoes of.

1623–6 COCKERAM, *Excalceate*, to put off ones shooes. **1751** CHAMBERS *Cycl.* s.v. *Excalceation*, Among the Hebrews..a widow, whom her husband's brother refused to marry..might excalceate him..and spit in his face.

Hence **exˈcalceated** *ppl. a.*

1730–6 in BAILEY (folio). **1751** CHAMBERS *Cycl.* s.v. *Excalceation*, The house of the person..was, thenceforward, called, the house of the excalceated. **1832** in WEBSTER.

†**excalˈceation.** *Obs.* [as if ad. L. **excalceātiōn-em*, n. of action f. *excalceāre*: see prec.] The action of taking or putting off the shoe, or shoes; *spec.* among the Hebrews, the taking off of a shoe by a widow, from her husband's next of kin, upon his refusal to marry her.

1751 in CHAMBERS *Cycl.* **1819** in *Pantologia.* **1876** *Leisure Hour* 155 Excalceation—that is the putting off the shoes as a mark of worship or token of respect.

†**excalˈfaction.** *Obs. rare.* Also 7–8 excalefaction. [ad. L. *excalfactiōn-em*, n. of action f. *excalfacĕre* to warm, heat, f. *ex-* (see EX- *pref.*¹) + *calefacĕre* to heat.] The action or fact of warming; calefaction.

1607 TOPSELL *Four-f. Beasts* (1673) 38 Apply it to a moist body lacking refrigeration, or to a cold body wanting excalfaction. **1656** BLOUNT *Glossogr.*, *Excalfaction.* **1721–1800** BAILEY, *Excalefaction.* **1730–6** —— (folio), *Excalfaction.*

So †**excalˈfactive** *a.*, tending to warm; warming. †**excalˈfactory** *a.* Also 8 excalef-. = prec.

1611 COTGR., *Excalfactif*, excalfactiue; heating, chafing, warming. **1601** HOLLAND *Pliny* (1634) II. 303 The very filth from the wals of their..places of wrestling..(say they) [Greeks] hath a speciall excalfactory vertue. **1730–6** BAILEY (folio), *Excalfactory.* **1775** ASH, *Excalefactory.*

Excalibur (ɛkˈskælɪbə(r)). Also 5 escalibourc, excalaber, excalybur, 7 escalibour, 9 excalibar, -our. [a. OF. *Escalibor* (with many variant spellings), corrupt form of CALIBURN, in Geoffrey of Monmouth (*c* 1140) *Caliburnus.*

The Welsh form in the Mabinogion is *Caledvwlch*, which has a resemblance, that cannot well be accidental, to *Caladbolg*, the name of a famous sword in Irish legend. The Welsh and Irish forms do not correspond phonetically: the one or the other has probably undergone corruption. Prof. Rhys, taking the Irish form as the correct one, suggests the translation 'hard-belly', *i.e.* 'voracious,' and thinks the Welsh form may have come from Breton.]

The name of King Arthur's sword.

[*c* **1300** *Merlin* (Huth MS.) 101 c, Saicies..que l'espee est apielee par son droit non Escalibor.] *a* **1450** *Le Morte Arth.* 3448 Excalaber, my swerd good. *c* **1450** *Merlin* vii. 118 The right name [of the sword] was cleped Escaliboure, whiche is a name in ebrewe, that is to sey in englissh, kyttynge, Iren, tymber, and steill. **1470–85** MALORY *Arthur* v. viii, Kyng Arthur..smote hym ageyne with Excalibur that it clefte his hede. **1598** B. JONSON *Ev. Man in Hum.* III. i, You talk of Morglay, Excalibur, Durindana. **1825** SCOTT *Talism.* xxvii, No sword on earth, were it the Excalibar of King Arthur, can cut that which opposes no steady resistance to the blow. **1842** TENNYSON *Morte d'Arth.* 103 King Arthur's sword, Excalibur, Wrought by the lonely maiden of the Lake.

excamb (ɛk'skæmb), *v. Sc. Law.* [ad. med. L. *excambiāre*: see EXCHANGE *v.*] *trans.* To exchange (land). Also *absol.*

1629 *Charter Chas. I.* in Stair *Instit.* II. xiv. §1 The present Proprietar of the Lands Excambed. **1770** *Act 10 Geo. III*, c. 51 §32 It shall and may be lawful for proprietors of entailed estates to excamb or make exchanges of land. **1847-8** *Act 11-12 Vict.* c. 36 §5 It shall be lawful for any heir of entail ..in possession..to excamb such estate, in whole or in part. **1877** *Encycl. Brit.* VIII. 783 The power to excamb was gradually conferred on entailed proprietors.

Hence **ex'cambed** *ppl. a.*; **ex'camber** [+ -ER¹], one who excambs, a party to excambion.

1836 *Act 6-7 Will. IV*, c. 42 §4 *marg.*, Tenure of excambed lands. **1629** *Charter Chas. I.* in Stair *Instit.* I. xiv. §1 The Excamber and his Heirs should have Regress. **1861** W. BELL *Dict. Law Scot.* s.v. *Excambion*, This right to recur to the original property in case of eviction, is competent to the original excamber and his heirs.

ex'cambie, *v. Sc.* [var. of EXCAMB.]

1808-80 in JAMIESON.

excambion (ɛk'skæmbɪən). *Sc. Law.* [ad. med.L. **excambiōn-em* (= *excambium*), f. *excambiāre*: see EXCAMB.] Exchange or barter, *spec.* of land.

[**1540** *Sc. Acts Jas. V.* 25 Feb. (1814) II. 366 And counsalis þe kingis grace..to geif for his gracis part of þe said excambium als mekle land..as, etc.] **1572** *Sempill Ball.* 147 Sic vane excambion can I not conside As marrow tratours and the trew togidder. *a* **1639** SPOTTISWOOD *Hist. Ch. Scot.* (1655) 100 He gave in excambion the lands of Cambo in the same parish. **1754** ERSKINE *Princ. Sc. Law* (1809) 143 The grant, by which the lands are exchanged, is expressly said to be an excambion. **1861** W. BELL *Dict. Law Scot.* s.v., The land which he has received in excambion.

†**excam'bition**. *Sc. Law. Obs.* [ad. med.L. *excambītiōn-em*, n. of action f. *excambīre*, f. *ex*- out + *cambīre* to exchange: cf. CHANGE *v.*] = EXCAMBION. Const. *with*.

1586 *Contract at Kirkcudbright* 15 Dec., The said Thomas ..dispones to the said Roger Kirkpatrick..in excambition with the said Rogers part of the landis of Auchenflor foirsaid, all and haile the said Thomas tenements, landis, annualls and pertinents underwrytten.

excandescence (ɛkskæn'dɛsəns). [ad. L. *excandēscentia*, recorded in fig. sense, nascent anger, passionateness, f. *excandēsc-ĕre* to grow white-hot, kindle, glow, f. *ex*- (see EX- *pref.*¹) + *candēscĕre*, inceptive of *candēre* to be white, shine: see -ENCE.] Heat, the state of growing hot.

a. The action of bursting into a glow; the condition of giving out a glowing heat; a heated condition. †**b.** A state of violent anger; passion.

a. **1684** tr. *Bonet's Merc. Compit.* VIII. 306 The excandescence of the animal spirits, and the effervescence of the bloud..must be quieted. **1775** in ASH. **1832** in WEBSTER. **1867** T. H. DYER *Pompeii* xi. 45 Not in that state of excandescence in which they would have set fire to any thing.

b. **1730-6** BAILEY (folio), *Excandescence*, great heat or wrath. **1775** in ASH, etc.

†**excan'descency**. *Obs.* [f. as prec.: see -ENCY.] **a.** The quality or state of growing hot; an instance of the same. **b.** Anger, passion.

1604 T. WRIGHT *Passions* I. vi. 26 In passions..I could adde welnie eleven more; as, mercy..excandescencie, envy, etc. **1683** SALMON *Doron Med.* I. 159 Causing a Distraction and Excandescency. **1684** tr. *Bonet's Merc. Compit.* VIII. 306 A Hypercatharsis..drives the animal spirits into excandescencies, not easily appeased. **1721-1800** in BAILEY. **1822** MRS. E. NATHAN *Langreath* II. 271 It raises my excandescency to listen to her. [Said by a lady who uses absurdly pedantic language.]

excan'descent, *a.* [ad. L. *excandēscent-em*, f. *excandēscĕre* to grow hot: see EXCANDESCENCE.] White-hot, glowing hot.

1832 in WEBSTER; and in mod. Dicts.

†**ex'candidate**, *a. Obs. rare*⁻¹. [ad. late L. *excandidāt*- ppl. stem of *excandidā-re* to whiten, f. *ex*- (see EX- *pref.*¹) + *candid-us* white: see CANDID, CANDIDATE.] Whitened, made white.

1560 ROLLAND *Crt. Venus* II. 392 Quhilk Montane [Caucasus] is..all excandidate With snawis fell.

†**excan'tation** (ɛkskæn'teɪʃən). *Obs. rare.* [ad. L. **excantātiōn-em*, n. of action f. *excantāre* to bring out by enchantment, f. *ex*- out + *cantāre* to sing.] The action of removing (anything) by enchantment.

JOHNSON 1755 explains the word as 'disenchantment by a countercharm', which may perh. be the sense in quot. 1580.

1580 LYLY *Euphues* (Arb.) 349 Which imagine that the mynde is eyther by incantation or excantation to bee ruled. **1654** GAYTON *Pleas. Notes* IV. xxiii. 277 The Don.. inchanted in his Cage, out of which there was no possibility of getting, but by the power of a higher excantation. **1863** W. W. STORY *Roba di R.* I. 271 This excantation of fruits was not the same as incantation.

excarnate (ɛks'kɑːnət), *a.* [ad. late L. *excarnāt-us*, f. *excarnāre*: see next.] Divested of flesh, or of a human body: opp. to *incarnate*.

1858 SEARS *Athan.* III. i. 255 The Divine Word..again becoming excarnate, and ascending to a reunion with God.

†**ex'carnate**, *v. Obs.* [f. late L. *excarnāt*- ppl. stem of *excarnāre* to deprive of flesh, f. *ex*- out whence *carn-em* flesh.]

1. *trans.* To strip off or remove the flesh or fleshy parts of.

1648 PETTY *Advice to Hartlib* 14 The Mate [of the Chyrurgeon] shall..excarnate bowels, artificially dry the Muscles, &c. **1693** *Phil. Trans.* XVII. 975 The lateral Fins of it being excarnated, are like the whole Arm. **1709** BLAIR *ibid.* XXVII. 57 The time..was taken up in excarnating, boyling, and taking care of the Bones. **1755** in JOHNSON; whence in mod. Dicts.

b. with reference to plants.

1664 EVELYN *Sylva* (1776) 189 If you sow them [Black Cherry stones] in beds immediately after they are excarnated. **1671** GREW *Anat. Plants* I. i. §25 This Seminal Root..cannot be perfectly excarnated..by the most accurate Hand. **1725** BRADLEY *Fam. Dict.* s.v. *Service*.

2. *intr.* To lose flesh, grow lean.

1740 DYCHE & PARDON *Dict.* (ed. 3), *Excarnate*, to grow lean naturally.

Hence **excarnated** *ppl. a.*, **excarnating** *vbl. sb.*

1730-6 BAILEY (folio), *Excarnated*, become lean, nothing but skin and bone. **1709** BLAIR in *Phil. Trans.* XXVII. 94 A Butcher..assisted at the Excarnating of the Bones.

excarnation (ɛkskɑː'neɪʃən). [n. of action f. prec.: see -ATION.]

1. (See quot.)

1847 CRAIG, *Excarnation*, in Anatomy, a method by which the blood-vessels are isolated after injection from the parts among which they are inserted. The agents are putrefaction or immersion in an acid. **1884** in *Syd. Soc. Lex.*

2. a. Separation (of the soul) from the body at death. **b.** Emergence from corporeal form and conditions: opposed to *incarnation*.

1858 SEARS *Athan.* II. xi. 240 His [Christ's] resurrection is none other than his excarnation, or his emergence out of all natural conditions. *Ibid.* xii. 251 That excarnation of man which..makes him eternally the denizen of a spiritual world.

†**excarnificate** (ɛkskɑː'nɪfɪkeɪt), *v. Obs.* Also *pa. pple.* 6 **excarnificat**. [f. L. *excarnificāt*- ppl. stem of *excarnificā-re* to tear to pieces, f. *ex*- intensive + *carnificāre* to cut in pieces, f. *carnifex* executioner: see CARNIFEX.] *trans.* **a.** To torment, torture, rack. **b.** To do the office of an executioner upon.

1563-87 FOXE *A. & M.* (1596) 89/2 Benjamin the deacon ..was most miserable excarnificat, having twentie sharpe pricks of reeds thrust under his nails. **1611** CORYAT *Crudities* 37 I did euen excarnificate his [my horse's] sides with my often spurring. **1623-6** COCKERAM *Excarnificate*, to hang one. **1664** H. MORE *Myst. Iniq.* xiii. 167 The racking and excarnificating their bodies. **1721-1800** BAILEY *Excarnificate*, to Butcher, to quarter, or cut one to pieces.

Hence **ex,carnifi'cation** [see -ATION], the action of excarnificating or taking away the flesh.

1730-6 in BAILEY (folio). **1755** in JOHNSON; whence in mod. Dicts.

†**ex'carnous**, *a. Obs. rare*⁻¹. [f. EX- priv. + L. *carn-em* (nom. *carō*) flesh + -OUS; cf. CARNOUS.] Without flesh, fleshless.

1686 A. SNAPE *Anat. Horse* II. ix. 89 He affirms them to be excarnous or without flesh.

ex cathedra: see CATHEDRA 2.

excathedral (ɛkskə'θiːdrəl), *a. rare.* [f. the L. phrase *ex cathedra* (see CATHEDRA) + -AL¹.] Official, authoritative.

1880 A. MITCHELL *Past in Present* vi. 143, I say this..with a proper amount of ex-cathedral confidence.

Hence **exca'thedralishly** *adv.*, in an official manner, as if with authority.

1831 *Blackw. Mag.* XXX. 123 Before we can understand any thing of Homer, it has been said ex-cathedralishly, that we must study the manners of the heroic ages.

†**ex'cathedrate**, *v. Obs. rare.* [f. the L. phrase *ex cathedra* (see CATHEDRA) + -ATE³.] *trans.* **a.** To condemn authoritatively or *ex cathedra*. **b.** To remove from the cathedra; to depose.

1644 BP. MAXWELL *Prerog. Chr. Kings* xiv. 135 Ergo in case of male-administration by the Pope..why not excathedrate him too? **1648** HERRICK *Hesper, To Bp. of Exeter*, If I can Stand before you..And never shew..feare To see my lines excathedrated here.

excavate ('ɛkskəveɪt), *ppl. a.* [ad. L. *excavāt-us*, f. *excavāre*: see next.] Hollowed out.

1571 DIGGES *Pantom.* I. xvii. Eiij, Water..contained in these Welles, or in any other Regular excauate body. *Ibid.* III. iv. Qij b, Howe excauate or holowe tymber..is measured. **1848** DANA *Zooph.* 200 Cells excavate, many-rayed.

excavate ('ɛkskəveɪt), *v.* [f. L. *excavāt*- ppl. stem of *excavāre* to hollow out, f. *ex*- out + *cavāre*, f. *cavus* hollow: see CAVE.]

1. *trans.* To make hollow by removing the inside; to make hollow in, to hollow out; to dig out (soil) leaving a hollow. Also, *to excavate* (something) *into*: to form into by hollowing.

Now chiefly with reference to the removal of earth by digging; the wider use tends to be felt as transf. from this.

1599 A. M. tr. *Gabelhouer's Bk. Physicke* 95/2 Take a sweete and fragrant Apple, excavate the same. **1664** EVELYN *Kal. Hort.* (1729) 189 Reserve it [Dung] for Use in some hard-bottom'd shady Place, a little excavated. **1713** DERHAM *Phys.-Theol.* (J.), Flat thecæ, some like hats, some like buttons, excavated in the middle. **1837** WHITTOCK *Bk. Trades* (1842) 197 (Engineer) So much per cubic yard according to the nature of the soil to be excavated. **1853** PHILLIPS *Rivers Yorksh.* viii. 202 The ground is excavated in a circular shape, so as to make a pit. **1866** DICKENS *Repr. Pieces* 117 The foot of the cliff is excavated into a cavern. **1870** HOOKER *Stud. Flora* 45 Viola tricolor..stigma capitate, excavated. Heartsease or Pansy.

2. To form or make (a hole, channel, etc.) by hollowing out.

1839 G. BIRD *Nat. Phil.* 233 If a cavity be excavated at this point. **1850** LYELL *2nd Visit U.S.* II. 329 One of them began to excavate a hole, and soon entirely disappeared under ground. **1873** MIVART *Elem. Anat.* ii. 50 The canal.. excavated inside the neural arches.

3. To uncover or lay bare by digging; to unearth. Also *fig.*

1840 *Penny Cycl.* XVIII. 381/1 About a fourth part of the city [Pompeii] along the western side of the walls has been excavated. **1844** *Mem. Babylonian P'cess* II. 61 In excavating the tomb, a slab has been left about two feet six inches high. **1864** BURTON *Scot Abr.* II. i. 89 A Scotsman.. excavated by the labours of the indefatigable Dr. M Crie.

4. To get out by digging.

1848 W. H. BARLETT *Egypt to Pal.* x. (1879) 220 It seems to be as yet unproved opinion that copper was found and excavated in this place. **1853** KANE *Grinnell Exp.* xl. (1856) 363 Pulpaceous material which he had excavated from the ice.

Hence **'excavated** *ppl. a.*; **'excavating** *vbl. sb.* (also *attrib.*)

1599 A. M. tr. *Gabelhouer's Bk. Physicke* 111/2 An excavatede peece of woode. **1664** EVELYN *Acc. Archit.* 130 Striges..are those excavated Channells by our Workmen call'd Flutings and Groeves. **1691** T. [HALE] *Acc. New Invent.* 124 We come to hollowing or excavating of our Logg. **1712** BLACKMORE *Creation* v. 740 Deep Caves.. Which..wrought with endless Toil, Ran thro' the faithless excavated Soil. **1847** DISRAELI *Tancred* VI. iii, This opened into a covered and excavated way. **1855** H. SPENCER *Princ. Psychol.* 1870) I. v. ii. 516 The..excavating power of the current.

excavation (ɛkskə'veɪʃən). [(? a. F. *excavation*) ad. L. *excavātiōn-em*, n. of action f. *excavāre*: see EXCAVATE.] The action of excavating.

1. The action or process of digging out a hollow or hollows in (the earth, etc.); an instance of the same; the result or extent of the process.

1611 in COTGR. s.v. *Excavation.* **1623-6** in COCKERAM. **1677** HALE *Prim. Orig. Man.* IV. ii. 299 This excavation of the Terrestrial Body, or elevation of other parts thereof whereby the water subsided. **1751** CHAMBERS *Cycl.* s.v., The excavation of the foundations of a building..is settled, by Palladio, at a sixth part of the height of the whole building. **1799** KIRWAN *Geol. Ess.* 89 The utter separation of both continents was most probably the effect of excavations by volcanoes. **1863** LYELL *Antiq. Man* 35 All the remains of organic bodies found during the excavations belonged to living species. **1878** HUXLEY *Physiogr.* 134 The amount of excavation which can be wrought..by means of running water. **1879** *Cassell's Techn. Educ.* I. 38/2 Digging out the hollows for cellars, &c...is called the excavation.

2. *concr.* An excavated space; a cavity or hollow.

1779-81 JOHNSON *L.P.*, *Pope* Wks. IV. 45 Pope's excavation was requisite as an entrance to his garden. **1783** *Phil. Trans.* LXXIII. 145 All spots..which consist of a dark nucleus, and surrounding umbra, are excavations in the luminous matter of the sun. **1848** W. H. BARTLETT *Egypt to Pal.* xxiv. (1879) 489 The wine-press was an oblong excavation in the rock. **1853** KANE *Grinnell Exp.* App. (1856) 550 All great peninsulas..have an excavation or bend inward on their westward side.

3. The process of laying bare by excavating; an unearthing; in quot. *fig.*

1864 BURTON *Scot Abr.* II. i. 73 The excavation of state papers has thrown [light] on the vast designs of, etc.

excavator ('ɛkskəveɪtə(r)). [f. EXCAVATE *v.* + -OR; cf. F. *excavateur.*]

1. One who excavates: **a.** *gen.* (Const. *of*).

b. *spec.* A labourer employed to dig out earth.

1815 [TODD refers to an advertisement of Jan. 2]. **1837** WHITTOCK *Bk. Trades* (1842) 197 (Engineer) To the 'excavators', as they are called, the digging is let. **1848** DICKENS *Dombey* vi, So the Excavator's House of Call had sprung up from a beer shop. **1880** *Echo* 18 Sept. 3/4 A number of excavators were engaged upon the foundations for a block of model dwellings. **1882** *Century* XXV. 303 A more thorough and comprehensive sifting of the Assos ruins by the same able excavator.

c. Said of inanimate agents.

1870 EMERSON *Soc. & Solit.*, *Farming* Wks. (Bohn) III. 59 The railroad dirt-cars are good excavators. **1870** *Echo* 10 Jan., Such is the testimony of Mr. Peach to the power of ocean as an excavator.

2. *spec.* **a.** A machine for digging out earth, etc. **b.** An instrument for removing the carious parts in a tooth previous to filling.

1843 *Niles' Weekly Reg.* 25 Nov. 200/1 With this excavator he is levelling hills. **1848** *Rep. Comm. Patents 1847* (U.S.) 72 Two patents have been granted for excavators. **1874** KNIGHT *Dict. Mech.* I. 814/1 The excavator is mounted on a carriage which traverses on a temporary track. **1884** *Syd. Soc. Lex.*, *Dental Excavator.*

Hence **excavatorial** (ɛkskævə'tɔərɪəl), *a.*, pertaining to excavation, or to the work of the excavator. **excavatory** (ɛks'kævətərɪ), *a.* = prec.

1849 FREEMAN *Archit.* 80 Egyptian and Indian architecture are two separate products of the excavatory process. **1855** *Fraser's Mag.* LI. 271 A long list of brilliant

excavatorial successes. **1887** Ruskin *Præterita* II. x. 358, I got no outlet..for my excavatory fancy.

excave (ɛks'keɪv), *v. rare.* [ad. L. *excavāre*: see excavate. Cf. F. *excaver*.] †**a.** *trans.* To scoop or hollow out (*obs.*). **b.** *absol.* To carry on excavations (*rare*.)

1578 Banister *Hist. Man* I. 2 Some bones are smal, but notably excaued, as of the fingers. **1623-6** in Cockeram. **1884** *Trans. Victoria Inst.* 243 In some of which sites we have been allowed to excave.

exceade, obs. form of exceed.

†**ex'cecate**, *pa. pple.* and *ppl. a. Obs.* [ad. L. *excæcāt-us* blinded: see next.] Blinded, deprived of sight (in quots. *fig.*).

1526 *Pilgr. Perf.* (W. de W. 1531) 249 b, Yf the iewes dyd slee hym, they sholde be excecate & blynded, & so lese the true fayth. **1535** *Goodly Primer* (1834) 93 Lighten our minds excecate, O Lord, our consolation. **1557** Paynel *Barclay's Jugurth* Bj, Man..is excecate by ambicion and desyre of lordship.

†**ex'cecate**, *v. Obs.* Also 6 execate, 7 excæcate. [f. L. *excæcāt-* ppl. stem of *excæcāre* to make blind, f. *ex-* (see ex- *pref.*[1]) + *cæc-us* blind.] *trans.* To make blind, to blind. *lit.* and *fig.*

?**1540** in Hall *Chron.* (1548) 246 a, That the people of Scotlande..is vtterly execated and blinded. **1613** R. C. *Table Alph.* (ed. 3), *Excæcate*, to make blinde. **1665** G. Havers *P. della Valle's Trav. E. India* 29 He caus'd his eyes to be sew'd up..to the end to deprive him of sight without excœcating him. **1721-1800** Bailey, *Excecate.*

Hence **ex'cecated** *ppl. a.*

1550 Bale *Apol.* 19 To make Sathan apere the Aungell of lyghte to the excecated worlde.

excecation (ɛksɪ'keɪʃən) *Obs.* or *arch.* Also 6-7 excœc-, 7-9 excæcation. [f. prec.: see -ation.]

1. The action of putting out the eyes; punishment by blinding; also, an instance of the same; the state or fact of being blinded.

1613 Daniel *Coll. Hist. Eng.* 161 He committed these barbarous examples of cruelty by excæcations and miserable dismembering the people. **1678** Gale *Crt. Gentiles* III. 95 God..punished Elymas, the Sorcerer, with corporal Excecation. **1721-1800** in Bailey. **1827** Sir H. Taylor *I. Comnenus* III. v, Death, Not excaecation, if the thought of that Calls up these looks of horror.

†**2.** *fig.* The action of blinding mentally or spiritually; the condition of being mentally blinded.

1529 Frith *Antithesis* (1829) 317 This excœcation..God hath sent into the world for sin. **1588** Allen *Admon.* 26 The state of kinge Pharao his obduration and excecation in wilfull wickedness. **1622** H. Sydenham *Serm. Jacob & Esau* (1626) 30 God doth concurre to the excæcation and hardening both of the minde and heart. **1640** Bp. Reynolds *Passions* viii. 65 This Deceit and Excecation is a proper worke of Passion.

exced(e, obs form of exceed.

excedandlye, obs. Sc. form of exceedingly.

†**ex'cedent.** *Obs. rare.* [ad. L. *excēdent-em*, pr. pple. of *excēdĕre*: see exceed.] **a.** *adj.* used *absol.* That which exceeds. **b.** *sb.* [after Fr. *excédant*] The portion or quantity in excess; excess.

1655-60 Stanley *Hist. Philos.* III. II. 99 The first excesse and defect is in two, in the excedent and the deficient. **1811** J. Black tr. *Humboldt's Polit. Ess.* I. 108 The population would double in..two hundred and fourteen years, if no war ..were to diminish the annual excedent of the births.

exceed (ɛk'siːd), *v.* Also 4-6 excede, 6 exceade, -ced, 6-7 exceede. [ME. *exceden*, ad. F. *excéder*, ad. L. *excēd-ĕre* to go out, exceed, etc., f. *ex-* out + *cēdĕre* to go.

The trans. use, somewhat rare in Latin, is the only one preserved in the Romanic langs. In Eng. the intr. senses appear to be developed from the transitive.]

1. *trans.* To pass out of (boundaries, etc.); to transcend the limits of; to proceed beyond (a specified point). Also, rarely, to project beyond. *Obs.* or *arch.*

c **1374** Chaucer *Boeth.* v. v. 169 Wit and ymaginacioun ne mowen nat strecchen..hem self to knowynge of vniuersalite for þat þe knowyng of hem ne may exceden..þe bodyly figure. **1413** Lydg. *Pilgr. Sowle* IV. xxiii. (1483) 69 That fyre ..excedeth nought thyne owne subtyle persone ne in dedely bodyes this fyre hath no power. **1655-60** Stanley *Hist. Chald. Philos.* (1701) 1/1 But the Philosophy of the Chaldæans, exceeded the Bounds of their Country, and diffused it self into Persia. **1700** *Pennsylv. Archives* I. 135, I am to Complain of one Capt. Barford, who has exceeded all bounds. **1712** J. James tr. *Le Blond's Gardening* 155 Uncover the Clod, and trim the straggling Roots that exceed it. *Ibid.* 207 Bury them..so that they may a little exceed the Surface of the Wall on both Sides. **1774** J. Bryant *Mythol.* I. p. xii, The Egyptian accounts exceed not only the times of the Deluge, but the æra of the world. **1788** T. Jefferson *Writ.* (1859) II. 370, I..shall pursue the course of the Rhine as far as the roads will permit me, not exceeding Strasburg. **1862** G. C. Lewis *Astron. Ancients* 111 *note*, Cleomedes lays it down that the planets never exceed the zodiac.

†**b.** To transgress (a law). *Obs.*

1393 Gower *Conf.* III. 284 Lust of love excedeth lawe. **1794** S. Williams *Vermont* 360 Laws respecting their increase..which cannot be exceeded.

c. To go beyond, do more than is warranted by (a privilege, right, commission, etc.).

1542 Hen. VIII *Declar. Scots* 195 Liberty was gyuen to the ambassadours to excede their commission. **1606** Shaks. *Ant. & Cl.* III. viii. 4 Do not exceede The Prescript of this Scroule. **1883** *Law Rep.* Q. Bench XI. 595 The defendant by uttering the words complained of exceeded his privilege as an advocate. **1891** *Ibid.* Wkly. Notes 72/2 The arbitrators had exceeded their jurisdiction in awarding that the applicant should pay the costs.

2. To be greater than. Const. *by*.

c **1391** Chaucer *Astrol.* II. §23 Rikne how manye degrees that the first altitude of A excedeth his seconde altitude. *c* **1460** Fortescue *Abs. & Lim. Mon.* (1714) 47 He may esteme what sume thay [charges] be not like to excede. **1637** *Decree Star Chamb.* §27 in Milton *Areop.* (Arb.) 21 Prouided, that they exceede not the number of foure. **1729** Butler *Serm.* Wks. 1874 II. 15 The cares and disappointments of ambition for the most part far exceed the satisfactions of it. **1797** Bewick *Brit. Birds* (1847) I. 15 The male [Merlin] scarcely exceeding the size of a Blackbird. **1821** Shelley *Epipsych.* 181 If you divide pleasure and love and thought, Each part exceeds the whole. **1848** Macaulay *Hist. Eng.* I. 420 Boys and girls..created wealth exceeding what was necessary for their own subsistence by twelve thousand pounds a year.

b. To be too great for; to surpass, overtask.

1596 Spenser *F.Q.* VI. iii. 51 Such chaunces oft exceed all humaine thought. **1635** N. R. tr. *Camden's Hist. Eliz.* I. 2 Such grief..as did exceede all consolation. **1735** Pope *Prol. Sat.* 36 To be grave, exceeds all Pow'r of face. **1765** Bp. Law *Theory of Relig.* I. (ed. 5) 11 *note*, Perhaps it exceeds the power of human understanding to decide where mechanism ends.

3. To surpass, outdo; to be superior to. Now chiefly const. *in*; formerly *for*, *of*.

c **1425** Wyntoun *Cron.* v. ix. 779 A Dochter..Ðat excedyt of Bewte All þe Ladys of þat Cuntre. *c* **1500** *Lancelot* 1173 O knycht..Whois manhed can al otheris to exced. **1553** Eden *Treat. New Ind.* (Arb.) 22 They exceade all other men in bignesse of bodie. **1641** Wilkins *Math. Magick* I. ix. (1648) 60 This latter engine does so far exceed all other contrivances to this purpose. **1653** Walton *Angler* i. 20 In that Psalm..the Prophet David seems even to exceed himself. **1735** Pope *Ep. Lady* 170 She..Observes how much a Chintz exceeds Mohair. *a* **1845** Hood *Stag-eyed Lady* i, There was one [act] in pity might exceed The sack of Troy. **1850** Tennyson *In Mem.* lx, Some poor girl whose heart is set On one whose rank exceeds her own.

†**4.** *intr.* To pass the bounds of propriety; to go too far; to break out. *Obs.*

c **1470** Henry *Wallace* III. 293 Thow excedis to that knycht Fer mayr be treuth than it is ony rycht. **1526** *Pilgr. Perf.* (W. de W. 1531) 303 b, The tyrauntes began more outragyously to excede in all fury and woodnes. **1611** Bible *Job* xxxvi. 9 Then he sheweth them their work, and their transgressions that they have exceeded. **1647** Ward *Simp. Cobler* 48 His Subjects will exceed..in some vitious Liberty, to abate their griefe. **1758** S. Hayward *Serm.* xvii. 543 You cannot possibly exceed in your love to him.

b. To pass the limits of truth; to exaggerate.

1717 Berkeley *Tour Italy* 21 May Wks. IV. 543 Said to contain about 4000 souls. They seem to exceed in the numbers of this town. **1815** J. W. Croker in *C. Papers* (1884) I. iii. 71, I believe I exceed when I say there were 200 persons assembled.

5. To be preëminent, whether in a good or bad sense; to bear the palm; to be greater or better than, surpass others; to preponderate. †*to exceed above*: = sense 3.

1482 *Monk of Evesham* (Arb.) 56 Aboue alle thyng that may be conceyued of any mannys mynde, hyt excedeth of cruelnes and dedly tormenting. **1509** Hawes *Past. Pleas.* XI. iv, Phebus above all sterres in lyght..Dothe exceede. **1593** Shaks. *Lucr.* 229 The guilt being great, the fear doth still exceed. **1599** —— *Much Ado* III. iv. 17 *Marg.* I saw the Dutchesse of Millaines gowne. *Her.* O that exceedes they say. **1651** Hobbes *Leviath.* I. xi. 48 An Emulation of who shall exceed in benefiting. **1654** Ashmole *Chym. Collect.* 21 One of the Contraries exceeding destroies the rest. **1674** Dryden *State of Innocence* v. i, Justice must punish the rebellious deed; Yet punish so, as pity shall exceed. **1875** Jowett *Plato* (ed. 2) V. 76 Men always choose the life which exceeds in pleasure.

b. To abound, teem *with*.

1624 Capt. Smith *Virginia* II. 23 The river exceedeth with abundance of fish.

6. Chiefly in Cambridge use: To have more than usual at a meal; to have extra or holiday fare. Cf. exceeding 2 a. Also of the 'commons' (food): To be in extra quantity.

c **1590** Greene *Fr. Bacon* ix (1630) 39 This day shall be a festiuall day with me: For I shall exceed in the highest degree. *a* **1616** Beaum. & Fl. *Wit at sev. Weapons* I. ii, Sir, these fellows may pray for you; you have made the scholar's commons exceed to-day. **1626** Meade in Ellis *Orig. Lett.* I. 328 III. 231 Dr. Pask made his colledge exceed that night.

¶**7.** To issue, proceed. *Obs. rare*[1].

1607 Topsell *Serpents* (1608) 817 All the hinderance and let [to breeding] is found to exceed of cold.

exceedable (ɛk'siːdəb(ə)l), *a.* [f. prec. + -able.] That may be exceeded.

Todd's explanation, copied into mod. Dicts., is due to a misunderstanding of Fr. *surmontable* in Sherwood.

1611 Cotgr., *Surmontable*..surpassable, exceedable. Hence **1632** in Sherwood. **1819** Todd, *Exceedable*, That may surmount or excel [with reference to Sherwood]. Hence in mod. Dicts.

exceeder (ɛk'siːdə(r)). [f. as prec. + -er[1].] One who exceeds.

1625 Bp. Mountagu *App. Caesar* xxxvi. 317 That abuse doth not evacuate the commission; not in the Exceeders and Transgressors, much lesse in them that exceed not. **1669** Cokaine *Poems* 124 Rich is those vertues..A fair exceeder of the best examples. **1847** in Craig; and in mod. Dicts.

exceeding (ɛk'siːdɪŋ), *vbl. sb.* [f. as prec. + -ing[1].]

1. a. The action of the verb exceed, in various senses. †**b.** An instance of the same; an unusual action, a performance in excess of what is requisite (*obs.*). †**c.** The quality of surpassing others; superiority, excellence (*obs.*).

1480 Caxton *Chron. Eng.* II. (1520) 13/2 Salamon..of the gyfte of our lorde hadde a synguler excedynge above all men. **1593** *Tell-Troth's N.Y. Gift* 29 No more will..a frend crosse her louing exceedinges, in whome his hart delighteth. **1636** Featly *Clavis Myst.* viii. 102 Our defects as well as our exceedings. *a* **1656** Bp. Hall *Occas. Medit.* (1851) 91 But these exceedings should be both rare and moderate. **1711** Addison *Spect.* No. 21 ¶2 There has been a great Exceeding of late Years in the second Division.

2. *concr.* **a.** *pl.* In college language (still used at Cambridge): Extra commons allowed on festival occasions. Also *transf.* Cf. exceed 6. [So L. *excedentia* in *Oxf. Accts. c* 1400.]

1629 Massinger *Picture* v. i, They..hold cheese-parings ..For festival exceedings. **1655** Gurnall *Chr. in Arm.* I. 297 His joys..They are as exceedings, with which he feasts the believer, but the cloth is soon drawn. **1662** J. Strype in *Lett. Lit. Men* (Camden) 178 Sometimes we have Exceedings; then we have two or three dishes..otherwise never but one. *a* **1680** Butler *Rem.* (1759) II. 199 Certain.. Virtuosos..unsatisfied with the Brevity of the Gazette desire to have Exceedings of News, besides their ordinary Commons. **1885** L. Stephen *Life H. Fawcett* iii. 77 The Christmas 'exceedings' as they were called in our official language, had a certain reputation.

†**b.** chiefly *pl.* An amount (of funds, goods, etc.) in excess of calculation, or of what is usual; an excess, a surplus. *Obs.*

1719 W. Wood *Surv. Trade* 54 The Exceedings of the year 1712, which had so prodigious a Ballance in our Favour. **1797** Burke *Regic. Peace* iii. Wks. VIII. 417 Including the fisheries, and making a moderate allowance for the exceedings..beyond his calculations. **1828** Ld. Grenville *Sink. Fund* 5 Without such an exceeding..a sinking fund..can have no solid operation. **1833** Lamb *Elia* (1860) 384 Much ado we used to have every..December to account for our exceedings.

ex'ceeding, *ppl. a.* and *adv.* [f. as prec. + -ing[2].] **A.** *adj.*

†**1.** Of persons, actions, language, etc.: Overstepping the limits of propriety or custom; going to extremes. *Obs.*

1494 Fabyan *Chron.* IV. lxiii. 43 He exercisid Tyranny.. in so excedynge maner, that the Countree waxed wery of hym, & conspyrid his deth. **1529** More *Dyaloge* IV. Wks. 265/1 To shew by that great exceding word [let him be anathema] the vndoubted trouth of the faith. **1585** Abp. Sandys *Serm.* (1841) 315 Why was Anna so exceeding in craving children at the hands of God? **1644** Hunton *Vind. Treat. Monarchy* lv. 27 Exceeding Acts notwithstanding morall limitation are authoritative. **1742** Mrs. Delany *Autobiog. & Corr.* (1861) II. 191 Sir Philip Sydney's famous Romance..is far exceeding the exceedingness of the most exceeding imagination.

2. Surpassing in amount or degree; extremely great, excessive. Now only with sbs. denoting quality, condition, or feeling, or including a notion of magnitude or multitude. Rarely used predicatively.

1547-8 *Order Communion* 10 The excedyng loue of our master and onely sauior Jesus Christ. **1568** Grafton *Chron.* II. 23 In the .vi. yere of his [William II's] reigne were exceedyng floodes. **1596** Spenser *F.Q.* IV. v. 10 Whose beauties beame..daz'd the eyes of all as with exceeding light. **1664** Power *Exp. Philos.* I. 76 The exceeding quantity of Water which at every interval he drinks. *c* **1680** Beveridge *Serm.* (1729) II. 133 It cannot but be an exceeding grief.. to you that you cannot obey..him. **1734** tr. *Rollin's Anc. Hist.* (1827) I. Pref. 41 Attended with a vast concourse of people and exceeding magnificence. **1855** Macaulay *Hist. Eng.* IV. 677 Reports touching the exceeding badness of the beer which he brewed. **1866** Neale *Sequences & Hymns* 112 The exceeding host of priests. **1875** Scrivener *Lect. Grk. Test.* 19 Their exceeding value for illustrating the literary history of these..ages. **1878** G. Macdonald *Phantastes* II. xx. 132 His love for his father was so exceeding.

†**3.** Of surpassing excellence. *Obs.*

1552 Latimer *Serm.* (1571) 166 b, Christ tooke..our nature vpon him..Oh, what an exceeding thing is this? **1599** Jonson *Ev. Man out Hum.* II. ii. Wks. (Rtldg.) 43/1 How long shall I live, ere I be so happy To have a wife of this exceeding form?

B. *adv.* = next. Prefixed to adjs. or advbs. Very common in 17-18th c.; now somewhat *arch.*

1535 Coverdale *1 Chron.* xxii. [xxi.] 13 Yet wyl I rather fall in to yͤ hande of the Lorde, for his mercy is exceadynge greate. **1599** Shaks. *Much Ado* III. iv. 25 My heart is exceeding heauy. **1644** Milton *Educ.* Wks. (1847) 99/2 We Englishmen..are observed by all other nations to speak exceeding close and inward. **1735** Wesley *Wks.* (1872) I. 18 Mr. Delamotte was exceeding sick for several days. **1779** Forrest *Voy. N. Guinea* 96 Our Papua friends..had behaved exceeding civilly. **1814** Wordsw. *Excursion* I. 112 A virtuous household, though exceeding poor. **1857** H. Miller *Test. Rocks.* viii. 321 The controversy is one in which there is exceeding little footing for any party. **1857** Hawthorne *Eng. Note-bks.* 17 Sept., He is of exceeding fluent talk.

exceedingly (ɛk'siːdɪŋlɪ), *adv.* [f. prec. + -ly[2].] In an exceeding manner or degree.

†**1.** Of manner: So as to surpass others. *Obs.*

c **1470** Henry *Wallace* II. 30 Excedandlye he wald lyft mekill mar Than ony twa that thai amang thaim fand.

2. Of degree: Above measure, extremely:

a. with verbs; formerly in extensive use, now chiefly limited to those that indicate emotion, feeling, or the expression of them.

1535 Coverdale *Ps.* civ. [cv.] 24 He increased his people exceadingly. 1591 Spenser *Vis. World's Van.* viii, A gilden towre which shone exceedinglie. 1615 Latham *Falconry* (1633) 124 The wormwood exceedingly shred with a sharp knife. 1665 Boyle *Occas. Refl.* iv. xiii. (1675) 255 The choice of ones Company does exceedingly discover whether a Man be Good, or Bad. 1678 Wanley *Wond. Lit. World* v. i. §93. 467/2 He travelled exceedingly for establishing the Peace of Christendom. 1797 Burke *Corr.* IV. 420, I approve his plan exceedingly. 1841 Lane *Arab. Nts.* I. 53, I praised God..and rejoiced exceedingly. a1845 Hood *Ode to Miss Kelly* ii, I like exceedingly your Parthian dame.

b. with adjs. and advbs. Now only with the positive deg.; formerly occas. prefixed to *more*, *too*.

1535 Coverdale *Jonah* i. 10 Then were ye men exceadingly afrayed. 1588 Shaks. *L.L.L.* iii. i. 145 My good knaue Costard, exceedingly well met. 1660 *Bp. Hall's Rem. Wks.* A ij, That account..of the Life of the Reverend Author..is exceedingly too short. a1677 Barrow *Serm.* (1741) I. i. 2 Exceedingly many needless incumbrances. 1704 Newton *Optics* iii. (1721) 324 Is not this medium exceedingly more rare and subtile than the air? 1772 Priestley *Inst. Relig.* (1782) I. 83 The sole pursuit of sensual pleasure is exceedingly injurious. 1847 James *Convict* ii, She seems to me to be exceedingly pretty. 1881 *Med. Temp. Jrnl.* No. 49. 21 This he found to answer exceedingly well.

†**ex'ceedingness.** *Obs.* [f. as prec. + -ness.] The quality or state of being in excess of usual limits; excessive measure or degree.

1580 Sidney *Arcadia* iv. 439 This complaint..had awaked the spirits of the Arcadians, astonished before with the exceedingnesse of sorrow. 1625 K. Long tr. *Barclay's Argenis* v. ix. 350 Carried away with the exceedingnesse of gladnesse. 1742 [see exceeding *ppl. a.* 1.] 1847 in Craig.

excel (ɛk'sɛl), *v.* Also 5-8 excell(e. [ad. F. *excelle-r*, ad. L. *excellĕre* to rise above others, be eminent, f. *ex-* (see ex- *prefix*¹) + **cellĕre* to rise high, tower, a vb. found only in compds., whose root appears in the adj. *celsus* lofty.]

1. *intr.* To be superior or preëminent in the possession of some quality, or in the performance of some action, usually in a good sense; to surpass others. Const. *in*, sometimes *at*.

14.. *Circumcis.* in *Tundale's Vis.* (1843) 92 And the thyrd he calleth holyness For hit excelleth in perfeccion. c1430 Lydg. *Lyfe St. Albon* (1534) A ij, His goodnes so hyghly doth excell. 1529 More *Comf. agst. Trib.* ii. Wks. 1206/1 Some other vertue..wherein the ryche manne maye..excelle. 1590 Spenser *F.Q.* i. iv. 17 Pecocks, that excell in pride. 1611 Bible *Gen.* xlix. 4 Vnstable as water, thou shalt not excell. 1634 Sir. T. Herbert *Trav.* 185 They are to say truly a warlike..but desperate nation, excell in theeving. 1709 Pope *Ess. Crit.* 15 Let those teach others who themselves excel. 1781 Cowper *Retirement* 793 The Power That..Bids these in elegance or form excel. 1802 Mar. Edgeworth *Moral T.* (1816) I. x. 79 Ambitious of excelling at the game. 1811 Miss Mitford in L'Estrange *Life* I. 132 Scott certainly does not excel in the Spenser stanza.

†b. To be in greater proportion than another thing; to preponderate; = exceed 5. *Obs.*

16.. *Tarquin & Tullia*, It was hard to tell, Whether its [the land's] guilt or losses did excel.

2. *trans.* To be superior to (others) in the possession of some quality, or in the performance of some action; usually in a good sense; to outdo, surpass. Const. *in*, occas. *at*.

1493 *Petronilla* (Pynson) 6 Petronylla..All other maydyns excelled in fairenesse. 1514 Barclay *Egloge* ii. (1570), The wretched lazar..Hath life which doth the courters life excell. 1596 Spenser *F.Q.* v. xii. 35 A wicked hag, and Envy selfe excelling In mischiefe. 1667 Milton *P.L.* iv. 490, I..see How beauty is excelld by manly grace And wisdom. 1675 Hobbes *Odyssey* (1677) 86 We do all other men excel At wrestling..leaping, running well. 1712 Addison *Spect.* No. 273 ⁋2 Homer has excelled all the heroic poets that ever wrote, in the multitude and variety of his characters. 1768 W. Gilpin *Ess. Prints* 167 Goupy very happily caught the manner of Salvator; and in some things excelled him. 1820 Shelley *Hymn to Mercury* ii, She gave to light a babe all babes excelling. 1828 Scott *F.M. Perth* Introd., The Castle may excel us in extent of prospect and natural sublimity of site.

b. To surpass (another's qualities or work). *rare.*

1611 Heywood *Gold. Age* i. Wks. 1874 III. 14 Sibill should produce a sonne, That should his Fathers vertues much excell. 1779-81 Johnson *L.P.*, *Pope* Wks. IV. 18 He has excelled every composition of the same kind.

†3. a. To be greater than, exceed. b. To be too hard or great for, overpower. *Obs.*

1667 Milton *P.L.* ii. 884 She op'nd, but to shut Excel'd her power. *Ibid.* viii. 456 An object that excels the sense. 1703 T. N. *City & C. Purch.* 5 A well proportion'd Ante-chamber, ought..in length..not to excel the breadth.

excellence ('ɛksələns). [a. F. *excellence*, ad. L. *excellentia*, f. *excellent-em* excellent.]

1. The state or fact of excelling; the possession chiefly of good qualities in an eminent or unusual degree; surpassing merit, skill, virtue, worth, etc.; dignity, eminence.

1382 Wyclif *2 Macc.* vi. 23 And he bigan for to thenke the worthi excellence of age. 1413 Lydg. *Pilgr. Sowle* iv. xxviii. (1483) 74 Lucifer and his felaushyp..delytynge them to..wondren vppon theyr owne excellence. 1514 Barclay *Cyt. & Uplondyshm.* (Percy Soc.) 13 All the children..He set in honour, and rowme of excellence. 1526 *Pilgr. Perf.* (W. de W. 1531) 208b, The sublimite or hye excellence of the crosse of Chryst. 1590 Spenser *F.Q.* ii. xii. 87 The mind of beastly man..hath soone forgot the excellence Of his creation. 1599 Shaks. *Hen. V*, ii. ii. 113 Whatsoever cunning fiend it was, That wrought upon thee so preposterously, Hath got the voyce in hell for excellence. 1602 —— *Ham.* v. ii. 143 Sir, you are not ignorant of what excellence Laertes is at his weapon. a1680 Butler *Rem.* (1759) I. 10 One..for his Excellence In height'ning Words and shad'wing Sense..Was magnify'd. 1729 Butler *Serm.* Wks. 1874 II. 178 Superior excellence of any kind..is the object of awe and reverence to all creatures. 1779-81 Johnson *L. P. Pope* Wks. IV. 73 Those..who attain any excellence commonly spend life in one pursuit. 1833 N. Arnott *Physics* (ed. 5) II. 167 The brightest examples have arisen of intellectual and moral excellence. 1856 Froude *Hist. Eng.* (1858) I. i. 49 That..most difficult condition of commercial excellence under which man should deal faithfully with his brother.

b. Phrases: †*in excellence of* = superior to (*obs.*). *by* (*an, way of*) *excellence*; in early use translating L. *per, propter excellentiam*, Gr. κατ' ἐξοχήν, in later use = Fr. *par excellence*: (so called) as being preëminently entitled to the designation given. Now *rare*. Cf. eminence 8c.

c1400 *Sowdone Bab.* 17 While þat Rome was in excellence Of alle Realmes in dignite. 1613 Bp. Hall *Holy Panegyrick* Wks. (1627) 476 Attendance on His [God's] ordinance (which by an excellence is tearmed His seruice). a1704 T. Brown *Sat. Antients* Wks. 1730 I. 18 Lucilius having..embellished it [this poem], ought by way of excellence, to be esteemed the first author. 1822 T. L. Peacock *Maid Marian* ix, Richard the First of England, the arch-crusader and anti-jacobin by excellence. 1838-9 Hallam *Hist. Lit.* II. iii. ii. §5. 102 Cesalpin was denominated, by excellence, the Philosopher. 1846 Grote *Greece* (1854) I. 55 In the mouth of an Athenian, Demeter and Persephone were always the Mother and Daughter, by excellence.

2. That in which a person or thing excels; an excellent feature or quality.

c1391 Chaucer *Astrol.* ii. §26 The excellence of the spere solide..shewyth manifeste the diverse assencions of signes in diverse places. 1601 Shaks. *Twel. N.* i. iii. 127 *To.* What is thy excellence in a galliard, knight? *And.* Faith, I can cut a caper. 1703 Locke in *Four C. Eng. Lett.* 142 The adoration due to your other excellences. 1752 Johnson *Rambler* No. 208 ⁋12 Some [papers] may be found, of which the highest excellence is harmless merriment. 1856 Stanley *Sinai & Pal.* viii. (1858) 325 The great excellence of the eastern table-land was..in pasture and in forest. 1876 J. H. Newman *Hist. Sk.* I. i. iv. 197 Civilized nations allow that foreigners have their specific excellences.

†b. An excellent action; a kindness, favour. *Obs.*

c1385 Chaucer *L.G.W.* 2045 *Ariadne*, Yow that don me this excellence.

†3. a. An excellent personality. *Obs.*

1447 Bokenham *Seyntys* Introd. (Roxb.) 5, I diligence Do to plesyn the wurthy excellence Of thys holy maydyn. 1633 Ford *Broken H.* iv. ii, Y'are to render Account to that faire Excellence, the Princesse. 1722 E. Heywood *British Recluse* 20 Blush not, fair Excellence! 1790 Mrs. A. M. Johnson *Monmouth* II. 95 That sainted excellence fell under the repeated strokes of their bloody swords!

†b. As a title of honour; = excellency 3b. *Obs.*

c1590 Greene *Fr. Bacon* (1630) 51 If it may please the Lady Ellinor, One day shall match your Excellence and her. 1642 Slingsby *Diary* (1836) 91 To treat wth his excellence abt exchange of prisoners. 1670 G. H. *Hist. Cardinals* ii. iii. 184 The accident that happen'd betwixt his Excellences Servants, and the *Corsi*. 1712 Steele *Spect.* No. 497 ⁋2 He told his Excellence, That he [the speaker] had pretended..to be wiser than he really was. 1737 Pope *Hor. Epist.* ii. ii. 44 Next pleas'd his Excellence a town to batter. 1796 Burney *Metastasio* I. 403 Being furnished with a letter from me to your excellence.

Hence **'excellence,ship.** *nonce-wd.*

c1716 *Lett. fr. Mist's Wkly. Jrnl.* (1722) I. 59 To his Excellenceship the Author of the Weekly Journal.

excellency ('ɛksələnsı). Also 5 excelencye. [ad. L. *excellentia*: see prec. and -ency.]

†1. = excellence 1. *Obs.* or *arch.*

?a1400 *Chester Pl.* (Shaks. Soc.) I. 9 Exsaulted by my excelencye. 1526 *Pilgr. Perf.* (W. de W. 1531) 195b, To be had in honour..as theyr vertue or excellency requyreth. 1579 Fulke *Heskins' Parl.* 95 He could not better haue shewed his excellencie aboue Aaron. 1605 Camden *Rem.* (1637) 163 Lady Iane Grey..for her excellency in the Greek tongue was called for Greia, Graia. 1611 Bible *Ps.* lxii. 4 They onely consult to cast him downe from his excellency. 1674 Playford *Skill Mus.* Pref. 1 An high esteem of the Excellency of Musick. 1716-8 Lady M. W. Montague *Lett.* I. xl. 162 Fountains, famous for the excellency of their water. 1783 Hailes *Antiq. Chr. Ch.* iv. 87 There is friendship, says he, between good men and the Divinity, moral excellency uniting them.

b. High degree of skill; proficiency.

a1704 Locke (J.), I have, amongst men of parts and business, seldom heard any one commended for having excellency in musick.

†c. *concr.* Something that excels, or takes the highest place; the 'beauty' or 'flower'. *Obs.*

1611 Bible *Isa.* lx. 15, I will make thee an eternall excellencie, a ioy of many generations. 1660 W. Secker *Non-such Prof.* 8 Man is the excellency of the creature, the Saint is the excellency of the man. 1667 E. Chamberlayne *St. Gt. Brit.* i. iii. (1743) 6 The college of the knights of the garter..is curiously adorned..with the excellency of modern Painting and carving.

†d. In phrases, *by, for, with (an) excellency* = by way of excellence: see excellence 1b. *Obs.*

1574 Hellowes *Gueuara's Fam. Ep.* (1577) 4 For excellencie, it was written of him [Caesar] that he neuer forgot seruice, or euer did remember iniurie. 1631 Gouge *God's Arrows* v. §2. 411 This relative particle..*They*, as here it is used, is to be taken κατ' ἐωξκηυ [*sic*] with an excellency. 1648 N. Estwick *A Treatise* 44 The person here is called, by an excellencie, the Spirit of truth. 1716 M. Davies *Athen. Brit.* III. 3 The fifth advance in Humanity is nam'd Poetry or Humanity it self, by excellency or preference.

2. a. That in which a person or thing excels; an excellent feature or quality; a chief accomplishment, a specialty: = excellence 2.

1601 Shaks. *Twel. N.* ii. iii. 163 Cram'd (as he thinkes) with excellencies. 1640 Fuller *Joseph's Coat* viii. (1867) 195 One's excellency may consist in the unsnarling of a known controversy. 1676 Etheredge *Man of Mode* i. i, That a mans excellency should lie in neatly tying of a Ribbond, or a Crevat! 1712 J. James tr. *Le Blond's Gardening* 143 The Maple has this peculiar Excellency, that it grows in the Shade. 1771 Sir J. Reynolds *Disc.* iv. (1876) 357 Those higher excellencies of which the art is capable. 1839 Ld. Brougham *Statesm. Geo. III, Ld. Grenville* (ed. 2) 144 The faults of his character were akin to some of the excellencies.

†b. With *the*: That which makes (a person or thing) to be excellent; the criterion of excellence.

1643 Burroughes *Exp. Hosea* iii. (1652) 207 What is the excellency of man but Religion? 1703 Moxon *Mech. Exerc.* 98 The Excellency of Sawing is, to keep the Kerf exactly in the Line marked out to be sawn. 1807 T. Thomson *Chem.* (ed. 3) II. 495 The excellency of a good enamel is, that it easily fuses into a kind of paste at the heat which is necessary for baking stoneware.

†3. a. An excellent personality; a 'dignity'. *Obs.*

1688 Collier *Several Disc.* (1725) 278 The Arians..say that Christ is..called God only by way of Participation, as other created Excellencies are.

b. As a title of honour. Cf. eminence 5, excellence 3b.

The quots. show that it was formerly applied to royal personages, to ladies, and others, though in England now limited to ambassadors, ministers plenipotentiary, governors (extended also to their wives) and certain other high officers.

[c1325 *Address to Edw. II.* in Pike *Year-bks. 13 & 14 Edw. III.* 362 Vestra Excellentia.] c1532 Dewes *Introd. Fr.* in Palsgr. 1037 Your excellency [Queen Mary of France] doth styre and move me continually. 1568 Grafton *Chron.* II. 390 Sir John Bushe made request..that it might please the kinges highnesse and excellencie, that, etc. 1632 J. Hayward tr. *Biondi's Eromena* B ij, The Lord grant your Excellencie [Dutchess of Richmond] all increase of felicitie. 1696 Whiston *Th. Earth* iii. (1722) 276 His Excellency the Muscovite Ambassador. 1727 Swift *Gulliver* i. v. 61 Their excellencies, who were privately told how much I had been their friend. 1763 Scrafton *Indostan* iii. (1770) 64 They desired a private conference with the Soubah: but his Excellency, etc. 1821 Shelley *Hellas* Ded., To his Excellency Prince Alexander Mavrocordato, late Secretary for Foreign Affairs. 1848 Macaulay *Hist. Eng.* II. 148 Retaining the guard of honour, the sword of state, and the title of Excellency.

excellent ('ɛksələnt), *pple.*, *adj.*, and *adv.* Forms: 4-5 excelent(e, exellent, -ilent, 5-6 excellente, 6 exelent (*pl.* excellentes), 4- excellent. [a. F. *excellent*, ad. L. *excellent-em*, pr. pple. of *excellĕre* to excel.]

A. as *pr. pple.* [cf. -ent 2]. Excelling.

c1400 *Beryn* 1110 Some fair lusty lady, that of pulcritude Were excellent al othir. c1425 Wyntoun *Cron.* vii. vii. 15 Tat Prynce excellent in vysdwme All Pryncis of þe Crystyndwme. 1513 Douglas *Æneis* xiii. vii. 30 Eneas..excellent all the lave.

B. *adj.*

1. Of a person or thing: That excels or surpasses in any respect; preëminent, superior, supreme. Of qualities: Existing in a greater, or an exceptionally great, degree.

†a. in favourable sense. *Obs.* merged in 3.

1382 Wyclif *1 Cor.* xii. 31 Sue ȝe the bettere gostli ȝyftis. And ȝit I schewe to ȝou a more excellent weye. 1387 Trevisa *Higden* (Rolls) III. 341 Plato was most excellent among Socrates [his] disciples. c1430 *Life St. Kath.* (1884) 17 The excellent beute was so greet that..Adrian..fille doun before hem wyth greet drede. 1539 Tonstall *Serm. Palm Sund.* (1823) 52 John the Euangelist most excellent in innocency. 1555 Eden *Decades* (Arb.) 49 The excellente artificers Ooliab and Beselchel. 1594 Blundevil *Exerc.* iii. i. xxi. (ed. 7) 326 They [the stars] are darkned by the excellent brightnesse of the Sunne. 1604 T. Wright *Passions* iv. i. 115 He that employeth his wit to many sciences, commonly cannot be excellent in any. 1610 A. Cooke *Pope Joan* in *Harl. Misc.* (Malh.) IV. 20 St. Andrew's Church at Bourdeaux, one of the excellentest Churches in all France. 1656 More *Antid. Ath.* (1712) 62 The excellent usefulness of the Horse. 1744 Harris *Three Treat.* (1841) 27 To consider..which, upon the whole, is more excellent than the other two.

†b. in bad or neutral sense. *Obs.* or *arch.*

1588 Shaks. *Tit. A.* ii. iii. 7 A very excellent peece of villany. 1605 —— *Lear* i. ii. 128 This is the excellent foppery of the world. 1606 —— *Ant. & Cl.* i. i. 40 Excellent falshood. 1629 Chapman *Juvenal* v. 282 Nor any excellentest Zany can More then a weeping-gut. [*Lat.* plorante gula] delight a man. 1649 Jer. Taylor *Gt. Exemp.* iii. §15. 160 Crucifixion was an excellent pain, sharp and passionate. 1759 Hume *Hist. Eng.* xlii. (1805) V. 305 Elizabeth..was an excellent hypocrite. 1818 Shelley *Julian* 242 Those absurd deceits..carry through The excellent imposters of this earth.

†2. Excelling in rank or dignity; exalted, highly honourable. In heraldic use, a formal

epithet indicating a rank higher than that denoted by 'noble'. *Obs.*

c **1400** MAUNDEV. (Roxb.) xxiv. 109 He es halden þe maste excellent emperour of þe werld. *c* **1430** *Life St. Kath.* (1884) 17 Than oon þat was more excellent þan anoþer spake first. **1486** *Bk. St. Albans, Her.* A j a, It is shewyd..of rigalities wiche ben noble and wich ben excellent. **1526** TINDALE *Heb.* i. 4 He hath by inheritaunce obteyned an excellenter name than haue they. **1565** HARDING in Jewel *Def. Apol.* (1611) 251 He would..aduance these Creatures [Bread and Wine] to a much excellenter condition. **1611** BIBLE *Ps.* cxlviii. 13 Let them praise the Name of the Lord, for his Name alone is excellent [*marg.* exalted]. *a* **1653** GOUGE *Comm. Heb.* ii. 1 God sent..his Son, more excellent than the excellentest meer creature. **1702** A. DE MOIVRE *Meth. Squaring Curves* in *Misc. Cur.* (1708) II. 158 That Excellent Person thinks this Series not to be General enough.

†**b.** As a title of address. *Obs.*

1611 BIBLE *Luke* i. 3 To write unto thee in order, most excellent Theophilus. **1632** J. HAYWARD tr. *Biondi's Eromena* B ij, To the most Illustrious and right Excellent..The Lord Duke of Richmond. **1634** FORD *P. Warbech* v. i, My commission Extends no further, excellentest lady, Than to a service.

†**c.** Assuming superiority, haughty, 'superior'.

c **1430** A. B. C. in *Babees Bk.* 11 [Don't be] To elenge, ne to excellent, ne to eernesful neiþer.

3. (The current sense; originally a contextual use of 1.) Used as an emphatic expression of praise or approval, whether of persons, things, or actions: Extremely good.

1604 SHAKS. *Oth.* II. iii. 77 'Fore Heauen: an excellent Song. **1606** —— *Tr. & Cr.* I. ii. 197 Here's an excellent place, heere we may see most brauely. **1664** EVELYN *Kal. Hort.* (1729) 186 The..Felicity of an excellent Gard'ner. *Ibid.* 189 The Dung of Pigeons and Poultry..is excellent for the Fig-Tree. **1700** DRYDEN *Fables* Ded., I have enjoy'd the patronage of your family from the time of your excellent grandfather. **1732** ARBUTHNOT *Rules of Diet* Wks. I. 247 A most excellent Drink in bilious Fevers. **1784** COWPER *Task* II. 790 Some minds..taste Of what is excellent in man. **1833** LAMB *Elia* Ser. II. xix. (1865) 371, I rattled off some of my most excellent absurdities. **1849** JAMES *Woodman* vii, Are you sure these excellent friends of yours have gone on? **1855** MACAULAY *Hist. Eng.* III. 325 Colin Macdonald of Keppoch, an excellent specimen of the genuine Highland Jacobite. **1860** TYNDALL *Glac.* I. xviii. 124 The snow was in excellent order.

absol. **1611** BIBLE *Ps.* xvi. 3 My goodnes extendeth..to the Saints..and to the excellent. **1746–7** HERVEY *Medit.* (1818) 220 Hast thou not known, the excellent of the earth, who were living images of their Maker? **1821** *Hist. Geo. Desmond* 85, I did not fail to count myself among the excellent of the earth.

†**b.** as *sb.* in *pl.* Excellencies. *Obs. rare.*

1502 *Ord. Crysten Men* (W. de. W.) II. xvii. N iij, Honour, glorye..and all other excellentes and perfeccyons.

†**C.** *adv.* = EXCELLENTLY. *Obs.*

a. With verbs. **b.** With adjs. and ppl. adjs.; with the latter often hyphened. **c.** With advbs. *well, ill.*

a. 1483 CAXTON *Cato* B j, Alexander..to Socrates made reuerence ryght excellente and publykely. **1607** SHAKS. *Timon* I. i. 29 *Pain*, 'Tis a good Peece. *Poet.* So 'tis, this comes off well, and excellent. **1642** FULLER *Holy & Prof. St.* II. xvi. 109 Here it doth most excellent.

b. 1586 COGAN *Haven Health* xlvi. (1636) 60 It [Blessed Thistle] is excellent good against any kind of Feaver. **1586** A. DAY *Eng. Secretary* I. (1625) 144 A number of excellent penned discourses. **1681** NEVILE *Plato Rediv.* 24 Your excellent-built Vessel. **1719** DE FOE *Crusoe* (1840) II. xvi. 327 Wine.. they have excellent good.

c. 1590 MARLOWE *Edw. II*, v. v. Wks. (Rtldg.) 220/2 *Ligh.* Was it not bravely done? *Gur.* Excellent well. **1604** SHAKS. *Oth.* II. iii. 121 Excellent well. **1612** CHAPMAN *Widowes T.* in Dodsley *O. Pl.* (1780) VI. 202 How excellent ill this humour suits our habit. **1756** W. TOLDERVY *Hist. Two Orphans* II. 116 They..doubted not of doing excellent well.

excellently (ˈɛksələntlɪ), *adv.* [f. prec. + -LY².] In an excellent manner or degree.

†**1.** So as to surpass (others). Const. *of. Obs.*

c **1340** *Gaw. & Gr. Knt.* 2423 þes wer forne þe freest þat folȝed alle þe sele, Ex-ellently of alle þyse oþer.

2. In an unusual degree; exceedingly, superlatively, surpassingly: †**a.** with verbs (*obs.*); **b.** with adjs.: now only in good sense (with mixed notion of sense 3); **c.** with adv. *well* (*arch.*).

a. *c* **1460** tr. *T. à Kempis* 145 Dispute not..why þis is so gretly peyned, & he is so excellently lifte up. **1599** SHAKS. *Much Ado* III. iv. 13, I like the new tire within excellently.

b. 1526 *Pilgr. Perf.* (W. de W. 1531) 2 For it may be ryght well, that some be excellently lerned, and yet, etc. **1548** R. HUTTEN *Sum of Diuinitie* B v a, By the lawe is sin excellently giltye. **1621** FLETCHER *Pilgrim* I. ii, A sorrow shews in his true glory, When the whole heart is excellently sorry. **1651** HOBBES *Leviath.* I. iv. 15 Excellently wise, or excellently foolish. **1677** DRYDEN *State Innocence* Pref., Comedy is both excellently instructive, and extreamly pleasant. **1826** SOUTHEY *Lett.* (1856) IV. 37 Believing that he is an excellently good man.

c. 1529 MORE *Dyaloge* I. Wks. 121/1 Many an holy bishop ..excellently wel lerned in scripture. **1605** BACON *Adv. Learn.* II. xviii. §1 A science excellent, and excellently well laboured. **1712** STEELE *Spect.* No. 270 ¶1 His Part, and that of the Maid..are excellently well performed.

3. Extremely well.

1527 BIBLE *Isa.* xii. 5 in Lewis *Eng. Transl. Bible* (1731) 16 Synge unto the Lorde, for he hath done excellentlye. **1553** EDEN *Treat. New Ind.* Ded., Howe excellently the Poet Homere had set forth his heroical factes. **1603** KNOLLES *Hist. Turks* (1638) 247 A company of braue soldiers excellently furnished. **1653** WALTON *Angler* 51 And so excellently cook'd this fish. **1782** V. KNOX *Ess.* cxxxii. Wks. (1824) II. 68 He [Erasmus] has written so excellently that, etc. **1826** MISS MITFORD *Village* Ser. II. (1863) 272 Our excellently-intentioned governess. **1871** MORLEY *Voltaire* (1886) 65 Excellently constituted as Fontenelle was in a great many ways.

†**'excellentness.** *Obs.* [f. as prec. + -NESS.] = EXCELLENCE.

1569 GOLDING *Heminges Post.* 12 Hee commendeth John for the excellentnesse of his Prophecie. **1576** FLEMING *Panopl. Epist.* 397 Writers of no lesse excellentnesse then ancientnesse. **1730–6** in BAILEY (folio). **1775** in ASH.

excelling (ɛkˈsɛlɪŋ), *vbl. sb.* [f. EXCEL + -ING¹.] The action of the vb. EXCEL; also an instance of the same.

1561 DAUS tr. *Bullinger on Apoc.* (1573) 125 Their excellyng is but in mouth and in boastyng. **1824** SCOTT *Redgauntlet* let. v, They [thy two last letters] excel (though the task was difficult) thy usual excellings.

ex'celling, *ppl. a.* [f. as prec. + -ING².] That excels; superior, surpassing. Now only in good sense. †Of a number: Exceedingly great.

1581 SIDNEY *Apol. Poetrie* (Arb.) 67 They are excelling parts of Poesie. **1604** SHAKS. *Oth.* v. ii. 11 Thou cunning'st Patterne of excelling Nature. **1646** H. LAWRENCE *Comm. Angells* 5 The Divell hath a most excelling malice. **1663** GERBIER *Counsel* D iij b, That may in time make up an excelling number. **1742** RICHARDSON *Pamela* IV. 334 The excelling Youth should be set to read..a little Portion from the best Translations. **1850** MRS. JAMESON *Leg. Monast. Ord.* Introd. 20 These communities produced some of the most excelling of the early artists. **1879** CHR. ROSSETTI *Seek & F.* 34 The Law..was not glorious, as compared with the excelling glory of the Gospel.

Hence **ex'cellingly** *adv.*, **ex'cellingness**, the state or quality of excelling; = EXCELLENCE.

1621 LADY M. WROTH *Urania* 452 Make mee excellingly vnfortunate. **1701** BEVERLEY *Glory of Grace* 31 It is raised to that Excellingness, that, etc.

†**ex'celse,** *a.* and *sb. Obs.* [ad. L. *excels-us* high, lofty, ppl. adj. of *excellĕre*: see EXCEL.]

A. *adj.* Lofty, high; *rare* in lit. sense; *fig.* of high rank, character, or quality.

1568 GRAFTON *Chron.* II. 390 Besechyng his excelse, high, and adorant Majestie, that he would witsafe to graunt him this or that. **1598** YONG *Diana* 48 Any beautie..Though it be neuer so excelse. **1651** HOWELL *Venice* 116 Most excelse and victorious Prince. **1656** EARL MONM. *Advt. fr. Parnass.* 293 They..did chiefly wonder, that the prime Senators of so excelse a Commonwealth did freely exercise marchandising. **1657** TOMLINSON *Renou's Disp.* 458 Those that inhabit excelse plants. **1730–6** in BAILEY (folio). **1775** in ASH.

B. *sb.* [tr. L. *excelsum.*] A 'high place'. *rare*⁻¹.

[**1480** CAXTON *Chron. Eng.* II. (1520) 18/2 Jonathan son to Osyas..toke not away excelsa as other dyde.] **1609** BIBLE (Douay) *Isa.* xvi. 12 Moab hath laboured for his excelses [**1611** the high place].

excelsin (ɛkˈsɛlsɪn). *Biochem.* [f. L. *excels-a* (fem. of *excelsus* high), specific epithet of *Bertholletia excelsa*, Latin name of the Brazil nut + -IN¹.] A crystalline globulin contained in the Brazil nut.

1896 OSBORNE & CAMPBELL in *Jrnl. Amer. Chem. Soc.* XVIII. 621 The globulin of the Brazil-nut... This proteid, being evidently different from all other hitherto examined, deserves a distinct name, and we accordingly propose to designate it *Excelsin.* **1907** *Amer. Jrnl. Physiol.* XIX. 53 The greater part of the protein substance of the Brazil-nut (*Bertholletia excelsa*) consists of the globulin excelsin. **1963** E. G. YOUNG in Florkin & Stotz *Comprehensive Biochem.* VII. i. 6 Some well recognized globulins in plants are.. excelsin of the Brazil nut..and amandin of almonds.

excelsior (ɛkˈsɛlsɪɔː(r)). [L., compar. deg. of *excelsus* high: see EXCELSE.]

‖**1. a.** The Latin motto ('higher') on the seal of the State of New York (adopted by the senate of that state 16 Mar. 1778), the accompanying device being a rising sun. Hence *attrib.* in ***The Excelsior State***, New York. **b.** Used by Longfellow (quasi-*int.* as an expression of incessant aspiration after higher attainment) as the refrain of a popular poem; hence employed with similar sense by many later writers. Also as *sb.* and *attrib.*

The adverbial meaning (= 'upwards') commonly given to the motto cannot be justified by L. grammar. According to S. Longfellow *Life H. W. Longfellow* I. 384, the poet was at first unaware of the solecism in the motto as thus interpreted, and when it was pointed out to him suggested that the word might be taken to stand for *Scopus meus excelsior est*, 'My goal is higher.' It is not clear whether the original use on the seal is a blunder, or whether it was meant as an abbreviation for some grammatically admissible phrase.

1778 *Drawing of Seal* in *N.Y. Senate Rep.* (1881) No. 61 Excelsior. **1841** LONGF. *Excelsior* 30 A voice replied, far up the height, Excelsior! **1858** TROLLOPE *Three Clerks* I. xi. 244 His motto might well have been 'excelsior!' if only he could have taught himself to look to heights that were really high. **1863** *Miss Jemima's Swiss Jrnl.* 30 June (1963) ii. 28 Our guide of Excelsior disposition, who would push on more quickly. **1874** G. M. HOPKINS *Let.* 29 Apr. (1956) 124 The garden is all heights, terraces, Excelsiors, misty mountain tops..flights of steps. **1929** D. H. LAWRENCE *Pansies* 143 Up he goes! Up like a bloomin' little Excelsior In his Sunday clothes!

2. Often used as a 'trade-mark', and *attrib.* in the names given by tradesmen to special articles of manufacture; also in the titles of various periodicals in U.S. and in England.

1851 *Catal. Grt. Exhibition* III. 1467 Excelsior soap [An American exhibit]. **1876** *Furniture Gaz.* 24 June 401/1 The Excelsior spring mattress. **1888** (*title*) The New Excelsior Test Cards in Arithmetic.

3. A trade name for short thin curled shavings of soft wood used for stuffing cushions, mattresses, etc. Also *attrib.* in ***excelsior-machine***. orig. *U.S.*

1868 *Specif. U.S. Patent* No. 75728 A machine for manufacturing that article of commerce technically called 'excelsior' for filling mattresses. **1873** *Furniture Gaz.* 22 May 3/2 'Excelsior' or fine wood shavings used for cheap upholstery purposes. **1874** KNIGHT *Dict. Mech.* I. 815/1 Excelsior-Machine. **1884** *Boston* (Mass.) *Jrnl.* 9 June, Large quantities of poplar-wood, to be used in the manufacture of excelsior. **1928** KIPLING *Limits & Renewals* (1932) 47 Mr. Wilham's fashionable West End pet-shop, where dogs lived in excelsior-floored cubicles. **1934** J. M. CAIN *Postman always rings Twice* xv. 175 She lined it [*sc.* a carton] with excelsior, and on top of that put some woollen clothes.

4. *Printing.* (Usu. with capital initial.) The name of a very small size of type (see quots.). Chiefly *U.S.*

1902 T. L. DE VINNE *Practice Typogr.* ii. 68 Excelsior, or 3-point (the half of nonpareil), is a body used in America for music, piece-fractions, and borders only. It seems to be the same body as the English 'minikin'. **1936** D. THOMAS *Type for Print* II. 83 'News' faces: Ionic..; Excelsior..; Ideal News... Faces such as these, which are designed for the body-matter of newspapers, are rarely cut larger than 9 pt. **1963** KENNEISON & SPILMAN *Dict. Printing* 62 *Excelsior*, the name of a former standard size of type, approximately 4-point.

†**ex'celsitude.** *Obs.* [ad. L. type **excelsitūdo*, f. *excels-us* lofty: see EXCELSE and -TUDE.] Highness, majesty.

c **1470** HARDING *Chron.* CLXXVIII. xvi, Thei..putte their cause to God his hie excelsitude. **1599** NASHE *Lenten Stuffe* 22 To chaunt and carroll forth the Alteza an excelsitude of this monarchall fludy Induperator. **1730–6** in BAILEY (folio). **1775** in ASH.

b. *humorously.* As a title or form of address; = HIGHNESS.

1599 NASHE *Lenten Stuffe* Ep. Ded., Your diminutiue excelsitude and compendiate greatnesse.

†**ex'celsity.** *Obs.*⁻⁰ [ad. L. *excelsitās* loftiness, f. *excels-us* lofty: see EXCELSE.] Height, altitude, loftiness; 'haughtiness' (Bailey *folio* 1730–6).

1623 in COCKERAM. **1656** in BLOUNT *Glossogr.* **1721–1800** in BAILEY. **1775** in ASH.

excentral (ɛkˈsɛntrəl), *a. Bot.* [f. L. *ex-* out of + *centr-um* CENTRE + -AL¹.] Out of the centre; = ECCENTRIC 3.

1847 in CRAIG; and in mod. Dicts.

excentric, *a.* Variant of ECCENTRIC *a.*, q.v.; the preferred spelling for senses 2 and 3 in *Botany*, and in contexts where a writer wishes to avoid the associations of sense 6.

1866 LINDLEY & MOORE *Treas. Bot.* 483/1 *Excentric*, out of the centre. **1895** W. SCHLICH *Man. Forestry* III. I. v. 73 The trees grow generally more or less excentric. **1896** *Ibid.* V. I. i. 11 The pith of a tree is frequently excentric. **1948** L. SPITZER *Linguistics & Lit. Hist.* i. 19 By then he will know whether he is really permanently installed in the center, or whether he finds himself in an 'excentric' or peripheric position. **1962** F. WHITE *Forest Flora N. Rhodesia* 116 B[*rachystegia*] *wangermeeana*..midrib v. excentric. **1965** F. SARGESON *Memoirs of Peon* vii. 231 The individual isolation which I had hitherto always associated with any ex-centric standpoint.

excentrical, etc.: see ECCENTRICAL.

except (ɛkˈsɛpt), *v.* Also 4–6 **excepte**, 6 *Sc.* **excep**, 7 **eccept**, **exept**. [ad. F. *excepte-r*, f. L. *except-* ppl. stem of *excipĕre* to take out, f. *ex-* out + *capĕre* to take. Cf. Pr. *exceptar*; the formally equivalent L. *exceptāre* had only the sense 'to catch, take up'. AF. had *exceper* (Britton II. xvi. §3, IV. iv. §1) app. ad. L. *excipĕre.*]

1. *trans.* To take or leave out (of any aggregate or collective whole); 'to leave out and specify as left out' (J.); to exclude (from an enumeration, the scope of a statement or enactment, a privilege, etc.); to leave out of account or consideration. Const. *from, out of*; also *simply.*

1530 PALSGR. 541/2 He is the best of al his kynne, I excepte none. **1535** COVERDALE *1 Cor.* xv. 27 He is excepted, which put all thinges vnder him. **1594** HOOKER *Eccl. Pol.* II. iii. (1611) 59 All meates indifferent..were it not that God by name excepted some. **1601** SHAKS. *Jul. C.* II. i. 281 Within the Bond of Marriage, tell me Brutus, Is it excepted, I should know no Secrets That appertaine to you. *a* **1656** BP. HALL *Via Media* Rem. Wks. (1660) 376 He hath given his law to all, [he] excepts no man..from salvation. **1680** BAXTER *Answ. Stillingfl.* xii. 20 He that marrieth Persons may not except the Husbands Power of Government. *a* **1714** BURNET *Own Time* II. 302 Another clause in the bill was liable to great objections: all the royal family were excepted out of it. **1776** ADAM SMITH *W.N.* I. xi. I. 227 If you except corn and such other vegetables as are raised by human industry. **1824** SCOTT *St. Ronan's* xxx, I hope you do not except yourself? **1882** J. H. BLUNT *Ref. Ch. Eng.* II. 196 He was excepted from the general pardon.

b. In pa. pple. *excepted* in the *absol.* const., and placed after the sb. Cf. EXCEPT *pa pple.* 2.

1514 EARL WORCESTER in Ellis *Orig. Lett.* II. 69 I. 234 He shall have . . as many [men] more . . to serve his Grace ayenst any Prince leving noon reservid nor exceptid. **1568** GRAFTON *Chron.* II. 72 His father the king excepted there is none whose honor I more tender and love. **1634** SIR T. HERBERT *Trav.* 46 [The Ile] procreates nothing noteworthy, Salt excepted. **1769** ROBERTSON *Chas. V*, III. VII. 18 The whole kingdom, a small corner excepted, was subjected to the Turkish yoke. **1875** BRYCE *Holy Rom. Emp.* xi. (ed. 5) 172 The Church excepted, no agent did so much to keep alive the memory of Roman institutions.

2. *intr.* To make objection; to object or take exception. Const. *against* (exceedingly common in 17th c.), †*at, to*. Also in *indirect passive*.

[From the use of L. *excipere (adversus aliquem)* in Roman Law; the etymological notion being that of limiting the right alleged in an opponent's declaration by setting up a countervailing right in the defendant which excepts his case (see EXCEPTION 4).]

1577 HANMER *Anc. Eccl. Hist.* (1619) 246 He excepteth against Eusebius and his adherents, as open enemies. **1601** SHAKS. *Twel. N.* I. iii. 7 *Mar.* Sir Toby . . your Cosin . . takes a great exceptions to your ill houres. *To.* Why let her except. **1611** BIBLE *Transl. Pref.* 5 Sixtus . . and Alphonsus . . men not to be excepted against by them of Rome. **1620** BACON in Ellis *Orig. Lett.* II. 259 III. 236, I may be allowed to except to the witnesses brought against me. **1647** MAY *Hist. Parl.* II. ii. 33 Parliament consented to all the Propositions; but the King excepted against one of them. **1665** GLANVILL *Sceps. Sci.* 53 He excepts at Gassendus's animadverting on Aristotle's manners. **1713** STEELE *Guardian* No. 34 One . . excepted to the gentility of Sir William Hearty, because he wore a frize coat. **1746** DA COSTA in *Phil. Trans.* XLIV. 406 As for the regular Figure of the Belemnites being excepted against, I believe few Fossilists will argument that. **1850** MERIVALE *Rom. Emp.* (ed. 2) II. 50 The criminals who excepted against Cato were generally condemned. **1885** SIR E. E. KAY in *Law Times Rep.* LII. 84/2 They had got their affidavit, to the sufficiency of which they did not except.

†**b.** *transf.* of a document. *Obs.*

1809 R. LANGFORD *Introd. Trade* 22 If the bill be foreign, a merchant draws two or three of the same . . date, each of which excepts against the rest, that no more than one of them should be paid.

†**3.** *trans.* To offer or allege as an objection; to object. Const. with simple obj. or obj. clause, *against, to*. *Obs.*

a **1592** GREENE *Jas. IV*, v. iv, O lawyer . . Why thrive you by contentions? why devise you Clauses and subtle reasons to except? **1625** BACON *Ess., Marriage* (Arb.) 267 They have heard some talke; Such an one is a great rich Man; And another except to it; Yea, but he hath a great charge of Children. **1639** FULLER *Holy War* II. xxxix. (1840) 102 Others excepted, that this exception was nothing worth. **1680** BURNET *Rochester* (1692) 96, I desired him to . . see what he could except to them. **1753** *Stewart's Trial* 267 The learned gentleman . . has been pleased to except against this part of the evidence; that [etc.].

†**4.** To object to; to take exception to; to protest against. *Obs. rare* exc. in Shaks.

1593 SHAKS. *Rich. II*, I. i. 72 There I throw my gage . . And lay aside my high bloods Royalty, Which feare . . makes thee to except. *c* **1600** —— *Sonn.* cxlvii, I desperate now approve Desire is death, which physic did except.

†**5.** In lit. sense: To take out, extract, excerpt.

1721 STRYPE *Eccl. Mem.* I. xli. 315 The judgments of which two last are excepted out of the rest and printed in the History of the Reformation.

†**6.** To receive, accept. *Obs.* [A frequent sense of L. *excipere*; but in some at least of the examples the word is a mistake for ACCEPT.]

1393 GOWER *Conf.* III. 178 To the pouer and to the riche His [the king's] lawes mighten stonden liche, He shall excepte no persone. **1509** HAWES *Past. Pleas.* XVI. xxxix, Her [fortune's] louring chere she may ryght sone chaunge, And you excepte and cal unto her grace. *c* **1530** LD. BERNERS *Arth. Lyt. Bryt.* (1814) 260 Her grace hath excepted my seruice. **1550** J. COKE *Eng. & Fr. Herald* § 157 (1877) 103 To except them (as they be) very lordes of the narowe sea. **1603** KNOLLES *Hist. Turks* (1638) 149 Which their offer he gladly excepted. **1635** A. STAFFORD *Fem. Glory* (1869) 92 God so willing eccept my ejaculatory Prayrs.

absol. **1597** MONTGOMERIE *Cherrie & Slae* 1002 Quhat wald thou do, I wald we wist: Except, or giue us oure.

except (ɛk'sɛpt), *pple.*, *prep.*, and *conj.* Also 5–6 excepte, 5 *Sc.* excep. [ad. L. *except-us*, pa. pple. of *excipĕre*: see EXCEPT *v.*]

†**A.** *pple.* = *excepted*, pa. pple. of EXCEPT *v.*

†**1.** As predicate (with the vb. *to be*) or as complementary obj.: Not included. Also occas., Exempted. *Obs.*

1482 *Monk of Evesham* (Arb.) 63 He thoughte hym selfe excepte in this worlde fro the comon labur of men. **1523** LD. BERNERS *Froiss.* I. cxlvii. 177 To this truse all parties were agreed, but Bretayne was clerely excepte. **1526** *Pilgr. Perf.* (W. de W. 1531) 62 The greatest synner that is may attayne therto, and none be excepte. **1535** COVERDALE *1 Kings* xv. 22 Kynge Asa caused it be proclamed in all Iuda: Here be no man excepte.

†**2.** ? Accepted. *Obs.* (See EXCEPT *v.* 6.)

(The old edd. read *expert*, which may be correct.)

c **1400** *Rom. Rose* 4291 She was except in his servise.

†**3.** In concord with a sb. in the nominative absolute; = '(being) excepted'. *Obs.* **a.** preceding the sb. (See B. 1.) **b.** following the sb.

1467 in *Eng. Gilds* (1870) 394 Yf eny citezen fforen wolle . . sue eny citezen denesyn for eny matere or cause done wᵗ outforth . . ples of lond only except. **1494** FABYAN *Chron.* v. cx. 84 All other, as well of Brytons as of Saxons, faylyd, or lefte of, that allonly excepte. **1535** COVERDALE *Acts* xxvi. 29, I wolde to God that . . I mighte persuade . . the . . to be soch as I am these bondes excepte. [WYCLIF, out takun thes bondis; Vulg. *exceptis vinculis his.*] **1594** SHAKS. *Rich. III*, v. iii. 243 (Richard except) those whom we fight against, Had rather haue vs win, then him they follow. **1646** E. F[ISHER] *Mod. Divinity* 7 Let all the fruits of Paradise be in thy power, one tree except. **1667** MILTON *P.L.* II 678 God and his Son except, Created thing naught vallu'd he nor shun'd.

B. *prep.*

1. In ME., in the construction A. 3, the pple., like its synonym *out-taken*, might precede the sb. When this collocation of a pple. ceased to be idiomatic, *except* became a prep., with the sense: Excepting, with the exception of, save, but.

Owing to the rarity of instances in which an inflected pron. takes the place of a sb., it is impossible to say definitely how soon the change in the grammatical character of the word took place, but it had prob. begun before 16th c. Cf. Fr. *excepté* and *hormis*, which are now treated as preps. Possibly the word was something taken as the imperative of EXCEPT *v.*; cf. *excipe* in the Eton Latin Syntax.

1377 LANGL. *P. Pl.* B. IX. 140 Alle shal deye . . Excepte one-liche of eche kynde a couple [A. x. 169 out-taken Eihte soules and of vche beest A couple]. *c* **1470** HENRY *Wallace* v. 1026 Thai entryt in, befor thaim fand no ma, Excep wemen. **14..** *Customs of Malton* in *Surtees Misc.* (1890) 58 In yᵉ feyldes and in yᵉ more . . and in all othyr places, exceptt severall of yᵉ lorde. **1560** WHITEHORNE *Arte Warre* (1573) 83 b, No Capitayne will lye neere the enemie except hee that is disposed to fighte the fielde. **1591** SHAKS. *1 Hen. VI*, I. i. 91 France is reuolted from the English quite, Except some petty Townes. **1655** W. F. *Meteors* III. 56 Old Wives are wont to say that no night in the year except one, passeth without Lightning. **1766** GOLDSM. *Vic. W.* xix, The rabble of mankind . . know nothing of liberty except the name. **1860** DICKENS *Uncommn. Trav.* iii, Everybody else in the room had fits, except the wardswoman. **1870** MORRIS *Earthly Par.* I. i. 291 There where we go shall all be new to thee Except the love that thou hast won from me.

†**2.** Leaving out of account; hence, in addition to, besides, as well as. *Obs. rare.*

1578 DALRYMPLE tr. *Leslie's Hist. Scot.* 27 Excepte fleshe, fishe and eldinge . . this Ile hes a pasture . . that may feid sum wethiris. **1756** AMORY *J. Buncle* (1770) I. 101 Except hours of sleep, we were rarely from each other.

†**3.** Without. *Obs. rare*⁻¹.

1588 J. MELLIS *Briefe Instr.* F v b, Neuer enter any parson in your booke . . except the consent of the same person.

C. *conj.*

1. Introducing a predicative clause expressing a fact that forms an exception to the statement made. Now only in full form *except that* (in which *except* looks like a *prep.* with sentence as *obj.*); in 16–17th c. *that* was sometimes omitted. Cf. Fr. *excepté que*.

1568 GRAFTON *Chron.* II. 260 Then there came . . men of estate out of the good Townes of Flaundyrs, except out of Gaunt there came none. **1593** SHAKS. *Rich. II*, I. iv. 6 *Rich.* What store of parting tears were shed? *Aum.* Faith none for me: except the Northeast wind . . Awak'd the sleepie rhewme, and so by chance Did grace our hollow parting with a teare. **1601** —— *All's Well* IV. iii. 300 More of his souldiership I know not, except in that Country, he had the honour to be the Officer . . to instruct for the doubling of files. *Mod.* The cases are quite parallel, except that A. is a younger man than B.

2. Introducing a hypothetical clause expressing a supposed case in which an exception will or may exist; = 'unless', 'if not'.

†**a.** in full form *except that, except that if*. *Obs. rare.*

1513 MORE in *Harding's Chron.* (1543), This is my minde . . excepte that any of you my Lordes anye thinge perceaue to the contrarye [The reading is doubtful; Rastell's text (*More's Wks.* 1557 I. 48) omits *that*]. **1523** LD. BERNERS *Froiss.* I. ccxii. 257 He shall leaue them entierly to us, excepte that if yᵉ Frenche kynges had theym by exchaunge for other landes.

b. as simple *conj.* The use of subjunct. or indic. follows the same rules as with IF.

14.. *Customs of Malton* in *Surtees Misc.* (1890) 59 Exceppvd thay haffe prisoners for to delyver. **1526** *Pilgr. Perf.* (W. de W. 1531) 1 Harde it is for any persone . . to perceyue the . . dryfte of this treatyse . . excepte they rede before . . the two fyrst bokes. **1531** *Act. 23 Hen. VIII*, i. § 4 Every such person . . shall . . abide in perpetuall prison . . Except onely such person . . do fynde two sufficiente suerties. **1641** WINTHROP *New Eng.* (1826) II. 43 He . . said he would not go off the bench except he were commanded. **1678** C. HATTON in *Hatton Corr.* (1878) 163, I desire not to meddle with yᵉ mother, except yʳ Loᵖᵖᵉ will take yᵉ boys. **1703** MOXON *Mech. Exerc.* 252 Except my memory fails me, these are all. **1754** RICHARDSON *Grandison* (1781) IV. xix. 149 Nobody knows of the matter, except he has complained to my Brother. **1850** TENNYSON *In Mem.* xciv, In vain shalt thou . . call The spirits . . Except . . thou too canst say, My spirit is at peace with all. **1872** DASENT *Three to One* I. 219 She never offered any one advice, except it were asked of her.

c. After *except* conj. the phrases *it be, it were*, etc., are often used instead of repeating the principal verb.

1591 SHAKS. *1 Hen. VI*, I. i. 43 Ne're throughout the yeere to Church thou go'st, Except it be to pray against thy foes. *a* **1674** MILTON (Webster 1864), Except it be because her method is so glib and easy. **1812** SOUTHEY *Lett.* (1856) II. 252 No drama . . will be [written] except it be by the same hand.

3. Followed by an adv., phrase, or clause expressing the particular manner, degree, time, place, means, purpose, attendant circumstance, etc., with regard to which the proposition is not applicable: Otherwise (or elsewhere, etc.) than.

This construction may be regarded as an instance of the use of the prep. (see B. 1) with advb phrase as obj., for which cf. expressions like 'The cause was tried in London instead of as York.' It may, however, have arisen from 2 by ellipsis: cf. similar use of *unless*.

1586 A. DAY *Eng. Secretary* i. (1625) 53 The ordering whereof (except in Letters Excusatorie or Defensorie) is wholly exempted the course in those Letters prescribed. **1596** SHAKS. *Merch. V.* II. i. 12, I would not change this hue, Except to steale your thoughts my gentle Queene. **1654** FULLER *Triana* iii, He . . affirms her disease mortal, except one herb procured for her, etc. **1766** GOLDSM. *Vic. W.* xxiv, Nor do I know how to prevent the course of justice, except by paying the money myself. **1816** J. WILSON *City of Plague* I. iii, A lone castaway . . Who hopes no resting-place except in heaven. **1857** BUCKLE *Civiliz.* I. xi. 632 Society can have no hold on any class except through the medium of their interests. **1868** C. CLARKE *Relig. & Duty* 70 The Apostle counted himself weak except as strengthened by the Spirit of God. **1877** F. HALL *Eng. Adj. in -able* 161 Rely, Except metaphorically, has not a personal reference. *Mod.* The city was strongly fortified on all sides, except here.

b. *except for*: exception being made for, were it not for, but for.

†**ex'ceptance** *Obs. rare*⁻¹ [f. EXCEPT *v.* + -ANCE.] = EXCEPTION.

1603 W. WATSON in Dodd *Ch. Hist. of Eng.* (1841) IV. xxxii, None taking, nor imagining how to take, exceptance against the premises.

exceptant (ɛk'sɛptənt), *a.* and *sb.* [ad. L. *exceptant-em*, pr. pple. of *exceptāre*: see EXCEPT *v.*]

A. *adj.* That excepts; taking exception.

1846 WORCESTER cites LD. ELDON. **1846** in WEBSTER; and in mod. Dicts.

B. *sb.* One who excepts; *esp.* in *Law*, one who takes exception to some part of the proceedings in a court, *usually* an accused person who excepts to a judge or juror.

1697 *Exceptions to Decree of Commissioners* in *Cumb. & West. Archæol. Soc. Trans.* VIII. 98 The messuages and lands in the Exceptants possession.

†**excep'tation.** *Obs. rare*⁻¹. [ad. late L. *exceptātiōn-em*, n. of action f. *exceptāre* to take out, receive: see EXCEPT *v.*]

a. = EXCEPTION. **b.** 'An often receiving' (Bailey *folio* 1730–6).

1662 ALLESTREE *Serm.* I. 235 Because David went aside, and was upright with an Exceptation.

excepted (ɛk'sɛptɪd), *ppl. a.* and *prep.* [f. EXCEPT *v.* + -ED¹.]

A. *ppl. a.* **1.** In senses of the vb.

a **1569** KINGESMYLL *Man's Est.* v. (1580) 21 They eate of the excepted tree. **1649** *Nicholas Papers* (Camden) I. 132 Articles contayning nothing in relacion to excepted persons but leave to transport themselves. **1667** MILTON *P.L.* xi. 426 Some . . who never touch'd Th' excepted Tree. **1692** W. LOWTH *Vindication* (1699) 54 The third instance of Excepted Cases. **1853** MAURICE *Proph. & Kings* vii. 107 It is extremely rash . . to deduce the nature . . of prophecy from doubtful and excepted cases.

absol. *a* **1656** BP. HALL *Modest Offer* Rem. Wks. (1660) 338 All the Churches . . (who do all submit themselves to Bishops, or Superintendents, except the fore-excepted).

2. *excepted district* (see quot. 1945).

1944 BEATTIE & TAYLOR *New Law of Education* 13 The council of an excepted district shall then make, after consulting the Local Education Authority, their own scheme of divisional administration. **1945** *Educational System* (H.M.S.O.) 58 *Excepted District*, borough or urban district excepted from the scheme of divisional administration prepared by a county L.E.A. and granted special status as a divisional executive. **1958** *Times* 19 Dec. 2/3 (Advt.), Lancashire Education Committee. Widnes Excepted District. . . Headmaster required.

†**B.** *prep.* = EXCEPT B. I. *Obs.*

1559 BALDWIN in *Mirr. for Mag.* (1563) E i b, The bluddy tyrant brought them all to ende Excepted me.

excepter (ɛk'sɛptə(r)). [f. as prec. + -ER¹.]

a. One who excepts or takes exception (to anything). †**b.** = ACCEPTER (cf. EXCEPT *v.* 6). *Obs.*

1639 AINSWORTH *Annot. Pentat.* Advt. 7 It would be known of this Excepter . . whether he would have men alwaies to follow the word in the line, or in the margin. **1642** ROGERS *Naaman* 9 God is no excepter of persons, grace is free.

excepting (ɛk'sɛptɪŋ), *vbl. sb.* [f. EXCEPT *v.* + -ING¹.] The action of the verb EXCEPT.

a **1626** BACON *Jurisdict. Marches* Wks. 1740 IV. 136 The excepting of that shire by itself doth fortify that, etc. **1634** SANDERSON *Serm.* II. 288 Here is no excepting against any witness: nor refusal of any judge.

excepting (ɛk'sɛptɪŋ), *prep.* and *conj.* Also 6–7 *Sc.* excepand, exceptand. [f. as prec + -ING².]

A. *prep.*

1. quasi-*prep.* The pr. pple. of the vb. used *absol.*: = 'If one excepts'.

1549 *Compl. Scot.* xi. 95 Al the irland men ar sklauis til hym, excepand ane certan that kepis them sel on the strait montanis. **1553** BRENDE *Q. Curtius* 107 b, He commaunded the baggage . . to be brought together in one place excepting only such thinges as were very necessary. **1593** SHAKS. *2 Hen. VI*, I. i. 193 Thy deeds . . Hath wonne the greatest fauour of the Commons, Excepting none but good Duke Humfrey. **1637–50** ROW *Hist. Kirk* (1842) 177 That no meetings be among the pastors without his Majestie's consent, exceptand alwayes their ordinarie Sessions. **1693** DRYDEN *Persius* Sat. v. 129 May I not live without Control or Awe, Excepting still the Letter of the Law? **1796** *Ned Evans* I. 146 His neighbours . . excepting the article of cash, were . . his equals. **1874** MORLEY *Compromise* (1886) 105 Of

all societies..not even excepting the Roman Republic, England has been the most emphatically..political.

2. Hence as simple *prep.*: With the exception of, except.

1618 Hales *Gold. Rem.* (1688) 381 All young Persons, excepting my self. **1697** Collier *Ess. Mor. Subj.* i. iii. (1732) 130 Excepting the Royal Family, they get but little by it. **1766** Goldsm. *Vic. W.* xxxii, This was received with great approbation by all, excepting my wife. **1818** Jas. Mill *Brit. India* II. v. iv. 431 They were in possession of the whole of Mysore, excepting the principal forts. **1863** Mary Howitt *F. Bremer's Greece* II. xvi. 149 Nothing to be seen on the place excepting some blocks of marble.

B. *conj.*

1. With the exception of the fact *that*; = except C. 1.

Mod. The copy is perfectly accurate, excepting that the accents are omitted.

2. Unless; = except C. 2. In early use occas. with *that*.

1652 Gaule *Magastrom.* xxvi, Neither doe any kind of men agree more together then astrologers and poets doe, excepting that they dissent about Lucifer and Vesper. *c* **1714** Lady M. W. Montague *Let. to Mrs. Hewet*, You see what stuff I am forced to write, but to such I am compelled, excepting I should entertain you with York loves and piques. **1804** Wellington in Owen *Disp.* 286 Scindiah certainly could have done nothing excepting he could bring his brigades to Poonah.

3. With adv. or phrase; = except C. 3. Now *rare*.

a **1641** Bp. Mountagu *Acts & Mon.* (1642) 463 Others [fasted], at evening: onely excepting in the weeke before Easter. **1660** Jer. Taylor *Duct. Dubit.* ii. iii. Rule iv, To it self onely it is to be imputed, excepting where the malice of the first agent hath, etc. **1800** Mrs. Hervey *Mourtray Fam.* I. 129 Lady Clannarmon (excepting when she forgot me) provided for my maintenance. **1803** Wellington in Owen *Disp.* 779 The exportation of British manufactures, excepting of military stores, ought to be free. **1849** *Sk. Nat. Hist., Mammalia* IV. 54 Excepting during the rainy season these little animals can never taste fresh water.

exception (ɛkˈsɛpʃən). Forms: 4-7 **excepcion, -cioun,** 5-6 **-cyon,** 6 **-tioun,** 5- **exception.** [a. AF. *excepcioun* (Fr. *exception*), ad. L. *exceptiōn-em*, n. of action f. *excipĕre* to except.]

1. The action of excepting (a person or thing, a particular case) from the scope of a proposition, rule, etc.; the state or fact of being so excepted. Const. *from, to*.

c **1385** Chaucer *L.G.W.* 2653 *Hypermnestra*, Al ȝoure wille..I shal fulfille So it to me be non confusioun. I nele quod he have non excepcioun. *c* **1400** *Rom. Rose* 4087, I shalle defende it..Withouten ony excepcioun Of ech maner condicioun. **1561** tr. *Calvin's 4 Godly Serm.* i. Dj b, Here is no exception or pretence of preuelege. **1709** Steele *Tatler* No. 92 ¶1, I know no Manner of Speaking so offensive as that of giving Praise, and closing it with an Exception. **1832** Lewis *Use & Ab. Pol. Terms* xi. 94 This exception of women and children from the whole community.

¶ The legal maxim, 'Exception proves (or confirms) the rule in the cases not excepted' (*exceptio probat regulam in casibus non exceptis*), which is in its original form an example of sense 1, is commonly quoted as 'The exception proves the rule', the sb. being interpreted in sense 2.

[**1617** Collins *Def. Bp. Ely* 100 Indefinites are equivalent to vniversalls especially where one exception being made, it is plaine that all others are thereby cut off, according to the rule Exceptio figit regulam in non exceptis.] **1640** G. Wats *Bacon's Adv. Learn.* viii. iii. Aph. 17 As exception strengthens the force of a Law in Cases not excepted, so enumeration weakens it in Cases not enumerated. **1662** J. Wilson *The Cheats* Pref., I think I have sufficiently justify'd the Brave man even by this Reason, That the exception proves the rule. **1768** Johnson *Pref. to Shaks.* Wks. (1787) IX. 269 The exception only confirms the rule. **1837** Gen. P. Thompson *Exerc.* (1842) IV. 243 With a view of making (according to another of the expressions which I have heretofore found puzzling) one of those exceptions which confirm the rule. **1855** Jowett *Ess.* 468 We may except one solitary instance (an exception which eminently proves the rule).

2. Something that is excepted; a particular case which comes within the terms of a rule, but to which the rule is not applicable; a person or thing that does not conform to the general rule affecting other individuals of the same class. Const. †*from, to*.

1483 Caxton *Cato* I vj b, This rewle is generalle wythout any excepcion. **1534** Whitinton *Tullyes Offices* i. (1540) 20 Nothynge is more accommodate..to the nature of man, but it hath many cautions and excepcyons. **1590** Swinburne *Testaments* 184 Of which rule, neuerthelesse there be diuers exceptions. **1639** Fuller *Holy War* iii. xxiv. (1840) 162 Egypt was an exception from the rules of all other Countries. **1785** Cowper *Trioc.* 841 Such rare exceptions, shining in the dark, Prove, rather than impeach, the just remark. **1829** A. W. Fonblanque *Eng. under 7 Adm.* (1837) I. 280 Only a little exception from the amiable tenor of their conduct. **1839** G. Bird *Nat. Phil.* 153 The only exceptions to this gradual diminution of the angle of declination, appear to have taken place in 1834. **1856** Stanley *Sinai & Pal.* ii. (1858) 113 The Phenician cities sent forth their fleets. But they were the exception of the world.

b. *the exception* (predicatively): something abnormal or unusual; contrasted with *the rule*.

1862 Stanley *Jew. Ch.* (1877) I. 366 The possession of the gift..was the rule and not the exception. *Mod.* You occasionally get a comfortable bed; but it is quite the exception.

3. Phrases, partaking of senses 1 and 2. *to make (an) exception*; *with (the) exception (of, that)*; *without exception*; †*in exception to*.

c **1391** Chaucer *Astrol.* ii. §34 Of comune, tretis of Astrolabie ne make non excepcioun wheyther the mone haue latitude, or non. *c* **1430** Lydg. *Compl. Bl. Knt.* xxiii, He was..without excepcioun, To speke of manhod, oon the best on lyve. **1529** More *Supplic. Soulys* Wks. 303/2 Excepcion maketh he none, in this worlde. **1626** W. Sclater *Exp. 2 Thess.* (1629) 210 With exception of the crosse. **1651** Hobbes *Leviath.* ii. xxvi. 140 A Law that obliges all the Subjects without exception. **1735** Pope *Ep. Lady* 275 Heav'n..Blends in exception to all gen'ral rules Your Taste of Follies, with our Scorn of Fools. **1777** Priestley *Matt. & Spir.* (1782) I. xiv. 157 Here is no exception made of any part of the man that was not to die. **1778** Bp. Lowth *Isaiah*, Notes 37 With exception..of certain ugly rings. **1780** Burke *Sp. Bristol.* Wks. III. 364 Promises were made..without any exception or reserve. **1817** Coleridge *Biog. Lit.* (1882) 73 With exception of one or two fundamental ideas. **1829** Southey *Sir T. More* II. 300 In exception to the..general course of feeling. **1841** Borrow *Zincali* I. i. 221 All those in Badajoz were very poor, with the exception of one man.

4. *Law.* [after L. *exceptio* in Roman Law; cf. except *v.* 2.] **a.** A plea made by a defendant in bar of the plaintiff's action; in Scots Law = defence. ***peremptory exception***: one tending to the dismissal of the action. ***dilatory exception***: one tending to arrest its progress. ***declinatory exception***: a dilatory exception consisting in a denial of the jurisdiction of the court. **b.** An objection made to the ruling of a court in the course of a trial. **c.** In Courts of Equity (*obs.* in England since 1875): An objection by the plaintiff to the defendant's answer as insufficient.

Bill of Exceptions: a statement of objections to the ruling or direction of a judge drawn up on behalf of the dissatisfied party, and submitted to a higher court. This procedure still exists in Scotland; in England it was abolished by the Judicature Acts of 1873-5.

[*c* **1250** Bracton v. v. i, Sciendum quod exceptio est actionis elisio per quam actio perimitur vel differtur. **1292** Britton ii. xvii. §1 En plusours maneres est ceste assise destourbe que ele ne soit tauntost prise, sicum par excepcioun peremptorie, sicum..et par exceptiouns dilatories.] **1413** Lydg. *Pilgr. Sowle* i. xviii. (1859) 19 Were it so that..by thyn excepcyon I persenelly shold not be herde in thys present Court. **1560** Daus tr. *Sleidane's Comm.* 116a, Hauing no exception, they were caried to Paris. **1560** Rolland *Crt. Venus* i. 800 Charge him compeir ..[With] exceptionis, and causis defensall (Gif he sic hes) that may himself supple. *a* **1599** Spenser *State Irel.* Wks. 1862. V. 323 [A fellon] may have fifty-six exceptions peremptory against the jurors. **1699** Bentley *Phal.* 397 The Defendant makes his exception to the Indictment, because he did not call him 'Ἀνδροφόνον, which was the Word that was penal by Law. *a* **1715** Burnet *Own Time* (1724) I. iv. 676 The first part of it was an exception to the authority of the Court. **1768** Blackstone *Comm.* III. 372 This bill of exceptions is in the nature of an appeal; examinable..in the next immediate superior court, upon a writ of error. **1861** W. Bell *Dict. Law Scot.* s.v., Generally speaking, everything which one alleges for defending himself, and for eliding the action, is called an exception. **1877** C. C. Langdell *Equity Pleading* §82 [If the plaintiff thinks the answer insufficient] he must except to it, *i.e.* specify in writing the parts of the bill which are not sufficiently answered; and thereupon the bill, answer, and exceptions are referred to a master.

†5. *transf.* **a.** A plea tending to evade the force of an opponent's argument. **b.** A formal objection (to a proceeding, a person's status or fitness for office, etc.). *Obs.*

1562 Cooper *Answ. in Def. Truth* (1850) 52 Men that make exception to his possession, and claim the right thereof themselves. **1593** Nashe *Christ's T.* 4 a, That these ill Hus-band-men the Iewes, should haue no credible or trueth-like exception left them (that they tooke him for a counterfeit). **1599** Shaks. *Hen. V*, iv. ii. 25 'Tis positiue against all exceptions..That..our Pesants..were enow To purge this field of such a hilding Foe. **1643** Sir T. Browne *Relig. Med.* i. §25, I cannot but wonder with what exceptions the Samaritans could confine their beliefe to the Pentateuch. **1663** Evelyn *Diary* (1827) II. 212 The chapel dore..was then set open for any to enter and give their exceptions. **1689** *Col. Rec. Pennsylv.* I. 266 More time should have been allowed for their appearing to make their Exceptions.

†6. Objection, demur, faultfinding; an instance of this, an objection, adverse criticism, complaint. *Obs.* or *arch.* exc. in phrases: see 7.

1571 Hanmer *Chron. Irel.* (1633) 17 Many exceptions were made against them. **1611** Bible *Transl. Pref.* 4 To expose themselues to many exceptions and cauillations. **1614** Selden *Titles Hon.* 143 Diogenes presently gaue it to his sweetheart Lysiodos, and shee without exception ware it. **1662** Gunning *Lent Fast* 1 The Pharisees..came to our Saviour, and by way of exception said, 'Why do the disciples of John..fast?' **1667** Pepys *Diary* (1879) IV. 245 Sir C. Sedley's exceptions against both words and pronouncing were very pretty. **1703** *Rules Civility* 31 Fooling..which produces exception and quarrels many times. **1738** Birch *Milton's Wks., Life* I. 18 The Exception to Milton's Piety relates to his being a Protestant. **1767** Blackstone *Comm.* II. 57 It being..unreasonable, that the lord should extend his protection to a person to whom he had exceptions.

†**b.** Dislike, dissatisfaction. *Obs. rare.*

1602 Shaks. *Ham.* v. ii. 242 What I haue done That might your nature, honour, and exception Roughly awake, I heere proclaime was madnesse.

†**c.** A ground of objection; something that is or may be objected to. *Obs.*

1633 Bp. Hall *Hard Texts, N.T.* 110 The disciples neade no open complaint of this their exception and scandall. **1645** *Direct. Lords & Com.* 2 [For the election of Elders], In case no just exception, shall be proued against him. *c* **1665** Mrs. Hutchinson *Mem. Col. Hutchinson* (1846) 247 Having no exceptions against the governor in his own person.

7. Phrases belonging to sense 6. **a.** ***above, beyond,*** †***greater than, without (all) exception***: above, etc., cavil, reproach, or suspicion.

1475 Caxton *Jason* 24 b, She that is veraily withoute ony excepcion. **1641** J. Jackson *True Evang. T.* i. 48 A grand Witnesse of their own, greater than exception. **1661** Bramhall *Just Vind.* vii. 171, I produce two witnesses beyond exception. **1710** Berkeley *Princ. Hum. Knowl.* i. §10 Demonstrate beyond all exception. **1780** Burke *Sp. Bristol* Wks. III. 388 He is a witness without exception.

b. ***liable, open, subject to exception.***

1658 Bramhall *Consecr. Bps.* vii. 156 An Adversaries Testimony..is subject to exception and makes no full proofe. **1765** T. Hutchinson *Hist. Col. Mass.* I. 147 A declaration..which in some parts of it is liable to exception. **1818** Hallam *Mid. Ages* (1872) I. p. v, The treatise of Nathaniel Bacon, itself open to much exception. **1835** I. Taylor *Spir. Despot.* vi. 255 Motion..liable to the most serious exception. **1842** W. Grove *Corr. Phys. Forces* 74 The applications I have made of these terms may be open to some exception.

c. ***to take (an) exception*** (†***exceptions***) ***against, at,*** †***of, to,*** †***unto***: to make objection to, find fault with, disapprove; also (chiefly with *at*), to take offence at. Formerly sometimes without prep., ***to take (an) exception***: to make (an) objection, to object or complain (*that*).

Now only with the obj. an action, statement, quality, etc., not a person or material thing.

1542 Hen. VIII *Declar. Scots* 204 The Scottis wyl take exception to the homages of theyr prynces. **1561** T. Norton *Calvin's Inst.* i. 24 If any man take exception, and say, etc. **1591** Shaks. *Two Gent.* v. ii. 3 *Th.* What saies Siluia to my suit? *Pro.* Oh Sir..she take exceptions at your person. **1597** Hooker *Eccl. Pol.* v. vii. (1611) 196 Not able..to take any strong exception against. **1621** Burton *Anat. Mel.* ii. ii. i. (1651) 232 Galen takes exception at Mutton. **1662** J. Bargrave *Pope Alex. VII* (1867) 15 They took exceptions of the quality of Illustrissimo. *a* **1674** Clarendon *Hist. Reb.* xii. (1704) III. 238 There were not two Persons..who did not take some exception to it. *a* **1703** Burkitt *On N.T.* Mark ii. 12 Observe, the exception which the scribes took against our Saviour. **1715** T. Bennet *Ess. 39 Art.* 215 The animadvertor's stationer taketh exception, that I have printed all his book. **1822** *Edin. Rev.* No. 74. 361 We must, as good Presbyterians take an exception to..the assertion. **1855** Prescott *Philip II*, iv. (1857) 60 Some of the more haughty of the aristocracy did take exception at his neglecting to raise his cap to them. **1868** G. Duff *Pol. Surv.* 190 Exception has..been taken to these figures.

¶8. Erron. for acception. Cf. except *v.* 6.

1382 Wyclif *Ecclus.* xx. 24 Forsothe bi excepcioun of persone he shal leese hymself. **1607** Norden *Surv. Dial.* A iv b, With the sweat of thy face thou shalt eate thy bread ..And this without exception of persons.

†**exˈception**, *v. Obs. rare.* [f. prec. (AF. had *excepcioner* in sense 1).]

1. *intr.* To lodge or state an exception.

1593 Nashe *Christ's T.* (1613) 184 There is no demurring, or exceptioning against his testimony.

2. *trans.* To except (in quot. pr. pple. used *absol.*: cf. excepting *prep.* 1).

1656 Hobbes tr. *Wallis* in *Six Less.* iv. Wks. 1845 VII. 290 He was the worst geometrician of all mortal men, not exceptioning so much as Orontius.

exceptionable (ɛkˈsɛpʃənəb(ə)l), *a.* [f. prec. + -able.]

1. That may be excepted against; open to objection. Now chiefly with negative words.

1691 Ray *Creation* i. (1714) 45 As the theory..is built wholly on a false supposition, so is it all along precarious and exceptionable. **1712** Addison *Spect.* No. 279 ¶5 This Passage I look upon to be the most exceptionable in the whole Poem. **1784** De Lolme *Eng. Const.* i. xii. 123 *note*, The depositions of those witnesses who are adjudged upon trial to be exceptionable, are set aside. **1837** J. D. Lang *New S. Wales* II. 35 The Female Factory at Paramatta has..been under most exceptionable management; insomuch as to have proved an absolute nuisance. **1870** Anderson *Missions Amer. Bd.* III. x. 157 The Greek priest led the way.. chanting the funeral dirge, in which there was nothing exceptionable.

†**b.** of persons. *Obs.*

1754 Richardson *Grandison* (1781) I. xxv. 175 Greville is surely (exceptionable as he is) a better man. **1813** *Examiner* 8 Feb. 88/2 The ladies in that piece, though very exceptionable, are of a stamp far above his *Angelica*.

¶2. Occasionally misused for exceptional.

1801 W. Dupré *Fr. Dict.* in F. Hall *Mod. Eng.* (1873) 201 To add an exceptionable article to a law. **1854** H. Miller *Sch. & Schm.* (1858) 381 A time..in which even fishes.. were so rare and exceptionable, that they occupied a scarce appreciable place in Nature. **1874** Motley *Barneveld* ii. xx. 356 The fact that he had not been stretched upon the rack during his trial was complacently mentioned a proof of exceptionable indulgence.

quasi-*sb.* **1844** Tupper *Twins* xviii, How silly and harmful a thing is secresy (exceptionables excepted).

Hence **exˈceptionableness**; **exˈceptionably** *adv.*

1664 H. More *Myst. Iniq.* 336 The..exceptionableness of his division of the duration of the world into seven Ages. **1820** Hazlitt *Lect. Dram. Lit.* 179, I suspect that the exceptionableness of the subject is that which constitutes the chief merit of the play.

exceptional (ɛkˈsɛpʃənəl), *a.* [f. exception *sb.* + -al[1]: cf. F. *exceptionnel.*] Of the nature of or

forming an exception; out of the ordinary course, unusual, special.

1846 Worcester cites *Q. Rev.* 1852 Disraeli 3 Dec. in *Sel. Sp.* I. 369 As regards its financial condition, Ireland.. has been in a very exceptional state. 1861 Dickens *Gt. Expect.* vi, The subject..ceased to be mentioned saving on exceptional occasions. 1868 M. Pattison *Academ. Org.* v. 121 The founders of the thirteen colleges..were almost all of them exceptional men. 1875 Scrivener *Lect. Grk. Test.* 81 Documents or records of exceptional value.

absol. 1870 Lowell *Study Wind.* 136 The mastery of Shakespeare is shown perhaps more strikingly in his treatment of the ordinary than of the exceptional.

b. Const. *from. rare.*

1883 Sir H. Cotton in *Law Times Rep.* XLIX. 324/1 That, therefore, makes this case exceptional from that of an ordinary case of mortgagor and mortgagee.

Hence **ex'ceptionalness.**

1886 *Spectator* 28 Aug. 1142 It is not the meritoriousness but the exceptionalness of the achievement which makes the few willing to attempt it. 1889 Talbot in *Lux Mundi* (ed. 10) 137 If we still plead that our sense of wonder stipulates for exceptionalness.

exceptionality (ɛkˌsɛpʃə'nælɪtɪ). [f. prec. + -ity.] Exceptional character or quality: *pl.* things exceptional.

1854 Hawthorne *Eng. Note-bks.* (1879) I. 79 The coroner ..had a kind of formality and orderliness..which.. balances the exceptionalities with which he had to deal. 1872 *Contemp. Rev.* XX. 383 The exceptionality of the boon ..helped to deepen the dreariness. 1890 *Harper's Mag.* June 44/2 We remembered the exceptionality of his position.

exceptionally (ɛk'sɛpʃənəlɪ), *adv.* [f. as prec. + -ly².]

1. In an exceptional manner or degree; uncommonly, unusually, unusually well.

1848 T. Sinclair *The Mount* 58 This critic..is exceptionally wise in practical matters. 1879 Wallace *Australas.* x. 212 In its animal life this colony is..not exceptionally rich in species. 1881 *Macm. Mag.* XLIII. 436/2 Music..too shadowy in outline to be grasped by the uninitiated, unless very exceptionally performed.

2. By way of exception; as an exception to rule or custom.

1862 F. Hall *Hindu Philos. Syst.* 144 Such has been, not exceptionally, the history of the Systematists. 1866 Carlyle *E. Irving* 106 The official..invited us exceptionally in for an actual inspection of his theodolite. 1874 Micklethwaite *Mod. Par. Churches* 36 Western galleries should be but exceptionally used in parish churches.

exceptionary (ɛk'sɛpʃənərɪ), *a. rare.* [f. exception + -ary¹.] **a.** Of or pertaining to an exception (see exception 1); indicative of an exception. **b.** = exceptional.

*a*1783 J. Scott *Crit. Ess. Eng. Poets* (1785) 283 The exceptionary 'all but' includes..an aged decrepit matron. 1850 Carlyle *Latter-d. Pamph.* viii. 23 Silent exceptionary individuals.

†**ex'ceptioner.** *Obs. rare*⁻¹. [f. exception *v.* + -er¹.] One who takes exception, or objects (to anything); an objector.

1641 Milton *Animadv.* (1851) 186 For other exceptioners there was no thought taken. Hence 1818 in Todd, etc.

†**ex'ceptionist.** *Obs. rare*⁻¹. [f. exception *sb.* + -ist.] = prec.

1689 *Def. Liberty agst. Tyrants* 53, I..demand of such Exceptionists, whether..magistrates have lost their right.

exceptionless (ɛk'sɛpʃənlɪs), *a.* [f. as prec. + -less.] Without an exception; not admitting of an exception.

1782 Burke *Let. Penal Laws* Wks. VI. 274 The bill..is.. a renewed act of..indispensable, exceptionless disqualification. 1854 *Fraser's Mag.* XLIX. 73 It is only in idea that we can realize..such a moment of universal, indiscriminate..exceptionless deification. 1867 Macfarren *Harmony* vi. (1876) 215 General, uniform and exceptionless.

exceptious (ɛk'sɛpʃəs), *a.* [f. excepti-on + -ous, after the analogy of *captious.*] Disposed to make objections; cavilling, peevish, captious.

1602 W. Bas *Sword & Buckler* Bij, While those things that are done must alwaies lye, As obiects to a nice exceptious eye. 1769 Chesterf. *Lett.* 301 It is the character of Country Ladies to be exceptious, and suspicious of slights. 1822 Hazlitt *Table-t.* (1824) II. vi. 141 He was not exceptious. He gave a cordial welcome to all sorts, provided they were the best in their kind. 1850 W. C. Macready in Pollock *Remin.* II. 353 [Carlyle] was quite in one of his exceptious moods.

Hence **ex'ceptiousness.**

*a*1677 Barrow *Serm.* Wks. (1687) I. 8 It [admonition] becomes unsavory and odious, and..resembles a froward, malitious, exceptiousness. 1688 Collier *Several Disc.* (1725) 316 The blessed Spirits..are too good to have anything of State or Exceptiousness in them. *a*1716 South *Serm.* (1744) X. ix. 282 Alarmed by an experience of the baseness..and the exceptiousness of men. 1818 in Todd, etc.

‖**exceptis excipiendis** (ɛk'sɛptɪs ɛksɪpɪ'ɛndɪs), *advb. phr.* [late Lat., f. L. *exceptis, excipiendis*, ablative pl. respectively of pa. pple. and gerundive of *excipĕre* to except.] Excepting whatever is to be excepted, with proper exceptions. Cf. mutatis mutandis.

1877 Geo. Eliot *Let.* 30 Jan. (1956) VI. 335 The cheap edition of my books—which, exceptis excipiendis, is a beautiful edition. 1887 *Athenæum* 9 July 50/2 Nothing is more notorious..in the spiritual régime of the Republic than the extension of toleration to all *exceptis excipiendis.* 1932 *S.P.E. Tract* xxxvii. 546 He is naturally impatient of the common delusion that we speak (*exceptis excipiendis*) much as we spell.

†ˌ**excep'titious,** *a. Obs.*⁻⁰ [f. L. *exceptīcius, -tius* caught up, intercepted, f. *excipĕre*: see except *v.* and -itious.] 'That is taken or received' (Bailey *folio* 1730–6).

Hence 1775 in Ash.

exceptive (ɛk'sɛptɪv), *a.* and *sb.* [ad. late L. *exceptīv-us*, f. *except-* ppl. stem of *excipĕre*: see except *v.* Cf. OF. *exceptif.*] **A.** *adj.*

1. *Logic*, etc. **a.** Of a word, *esp.* a particle: That introduces an exception.

[*a*1249 W. Shyreswood in Prantl *Gesch. Logik* III. 21 Postquam dictum est de signis et de dictionibus exceptivis.. convenienter dicendum est de hac dictione 'solus'.] 1624 H. Mason *Art of Lying* v. 84 That which this sentence doth deny of the Sonne, it doth by vertue of the exceptiue particle adioyned, affirme of the Father; No man, no nor the Sonne doth know it, but the Father. 1659 *Instruct. Oratory* (1682) 108 (T.) It is to be inferred either by a conjunction, causal, illative, exceptive, etc. 1751 Chambers *Cycl.* s.v. *Conjunction*, Exceptive Conjunctions are, if it be not.. unless that, etc.

b. Of a proposition: That has a specified exception attached to the subject; *e.g.* Nothing on earth *but man* is great.

[*a*1347 W. Occam in Prantl *Gesch. Logik* III. 409 Circa exceptivas est sciendum, quod ex omnibus exceptivis in prima figura non sequitur conclusio exceptiva.] 1563–87 Foxe *A. & M.* (1596) 13/2 The proposition is not exceptiue, excluding other apostles. 1725 Watts *Logic* iii. ii. §4 Exceptive Propositions will make complex Syllogisms. 1870 Jevons *Logic* vii. 68 Exceptive propositions.

c. Of a clause, law, etc.: Making an exception, excepting something from a general rule.

1643 Milton *Divorce* ii. v. (1851) 74 A dispensation..is rather a particular and exceptive law absolving and disobliging from a more general command. 1837 Lockhart *Scott* (1839) VI. 37 *note*, The hostile critic selected for exceptive encomium one 'old Jacobite strain'. 1856 Froude *Hist. Eng.* I. 416 An exceptive clause introduced into the act. 1884 L. Peel in *Law Times* 7 June 104/1 This is again the application of the exceptive distinction.

2. Of persons and their utterances: Disposed or tending to take exception; hypercritical, captious.

1621 W. Sclater *Tythes* (1623) 197 His proceedings, though too too exceptiue, yet such as, being yeilded, inferred nothing against the Diuine ius for Tithing. 1858 *Chamb. Jrnl.* X. 280 Any exceptive persons who are not inclined to rest satisfied with appearances and authorities. 1861 Tulloch *Eng. Purit.* iii. 374 His criticisms..show his singularly exceptive, and over-curious logic.

3. = exceptional.

1849 F. W. Newman *Soul* 168 This is..an exceptive case.

B. *sb.* [The adj. used *absol.*] *Logic.* An exceptive word or proposition. Cf. A. 1 a and b.

1563–87 Foxe *A. & M.* (1596) 20/2 Yet upon his exclusiues and negatiues, this exceptiue must needs be inferred. 1579 Fulke *Heskins' Parl.* 174 The scriptures that say Christ is in heauen speake without exclusiues, or exceptiues. 1633 T. Adams *Exp. 2 Peter* i. 10 All these exceptives, 'but', 'notwithstanding', 'nevertheless', are against us. 1864 Bowen *Logic* v. 145 These [Exponibles] are divided into Exclusives, Exceptives and Restrictives.

Hence **ex'ceptively** *adv.*, in an exceptive manner or sense. **excep'tivity**, *nonce-wd.*, readiness to make exceptions (from rules of conduct).

1609 J. Raynolds *Agst. Bellarmine* (1610) 5 If the worde be taken exceptively, yet may it be an exception negative. 1621 W. Sclater *Tythes* (1623) 39 They are exceptiuely or disiunctiuely only allotted. 1870 *Contemp. Rev.* XV. 447 *Milverton.* They do not know when to make the exceptions. *Ellesmere.* Exceptivity (I like to coin a new word) requires so much moral courage.

†**ex'ceptless,** *a. Obs. rare*⁻¹. [irreg. f. except *v.* + -less.] Making no exception; extending to all.

1607 Shaks. *Timon* iv. iii. 502 Forgiue my generall, and exceptlesse rashness.

exceptor (ɛk'sɛptə(r), -ɔː(r)). *Obs.* exc. *Hist.* (sense 2 b). [a. late L. *exceptor*, agent-n. f. *excipĕre*: see except *v.*]

†**1.** One who objects or takes exception (to anything); an objector. *Obs.* = excepter a.

*a*1641 Bp. Mountagu *Acts & Mon.* (1642) 211 Were such upstart Exceptors to deale with Atheists..how should a man proceed? 1679 Puller *Moder. Ch. Eng.* (1843) 155 Those very exceptors are really like the Romanists. 1690 T. Burnet *Ans. Except. Th. Earth* 1, I shall..follow the learned Exceptor from Chapter to Chapter. 1755 in Johnson; hence in mod. Dicts.

2. †**a.** A reporter, short-hand writer. *Obs.*⁻⁰ **b.** *Hist.* An officer in the Court of Chancery under the later Roman Empire.

1674 Blount *Glossogr.*, *Exceptor*, he that writes ones words as he speaks them; a gatherer. [Hence 1692–1732 in Coles]. 1728 H. Herbert tr. *Fleury's Eccl. Hist.* II. 16 An officer belonging to the Proconsul..who seems to be one of those..called Exceptors or Clerks of the court.

†**excep'torious,** *a. Obs.*⁻⁰ [f. late L. *exceptōri-us* serviceable for receiving (f. *excipĕre*: see except *v.*) + -(i)ous.] 'That receives or contains' (Bailey *folio* 1730–6).

Hence 1775 in Ash.

excercitation, excercite: see exerc-.

†**ex'cerebrate,** *v. Obs.* [f. L. *excerebrāt-*, ppl. stem of *excerebrāre*, f. *ex-* out + *cerebr-um* brain.]

1. *trans.* To clear out from the brain or mind.

1621 S. Ward *Life of Faith* (ed. 2) vii, Hath it [faith] not soueraigne vertue in it to excerebrate all cares, expectorate all feares and griefes?

2. To beat out the brains of.

1623–6 in Cockeram. 1721–1800 in Bailey.

Also **ex'cerebrate,** *a.* [ad. L. *excerebrāt-us*] (see quot.). **ex'cerebrated,** *ppl. a.* [+ -ed¹] (see quot.). **excere'bration** [+ -ation]. (*a*) (see quot. 1721–1800). (*b*) (see quot. 1884).

1884 *Syd. Soc. Lex.*, *Excerebrate*, delirious, out of his mind. 1736 Bailey, *Excerebrated*, having his brains beat out; wanting brains, witless. 1775 in Ash. 1721–1800 Bailey, *Excerebration*, a beating out ones Brains. 1884 *Syd. Soc. Lex.*, *Excerebration*, the removing of the contents of the skull, the brain, and the other structures. Also, a term which has been used to designate abnormal Cerebration.

†**ex'cerebrose,** *a. Obs.*⁻⁰ [f. ex- *pref.*¹ + L. *cerebr-um* brain + -ose.] (See quot.)

1730–6 Bailey (folio), *Excerebrose*, brain-sick, wanting brains. Hence 1775 in Ash, etc.

†**ex'cern,** *v. Obs.* Also 6–7 -cerne. [ad. L. *excern-ĕre*, f. *ex-* out + *cernĕre* to sift.] = excrete.

1. *trans.* Of animals and plants, or their organs: To separate (waste matter) from the blood or sap, preparatory to discharging from the system.

1626 Bacon *Sylva* §542 The Moss of trees is a kind of hair; for it is the juice of the tree that is Excerned. 1691 Ray *Creation* (1714) 294 The Humours excerned by Sweat and Urine are near akin, if not the same. 1737 Bracken *Farriery* (1763) 47 The Serum of the Blood..is excerned or separated by the Glands. 1738 D. Bayne *Gout* 101 The..dissolution of such particles..carries them through the fine strainers in order to be excerned.

absol. 1626 Bacon *Sylva* §299 The Benefits that come of Exercise are..that it helpeth to Excerne by Sweat. 1677 Hale *Prim. Orig. Man.* i. i. 30 That Soul..digests, sanguifies, carnifies, excerns.

2. To discharge, void (an excrement, secretion).

1578 Banister *Hist. Man* v. 72 That the dregges..might be duly excerned or auoyded. 1650 H. Brooke *Conserv. Health* 183 Phlegm that is excerned by the mouth. 1691 Ray *Creation* (1701) 166 Such an unguent or Pap prepared, such an open vessel to excerne it into, to receive it.

excernent (ɛk'sɜːnənt), *a.* [ad. L. *excernent-em*, pr. pple. of *excernĕre*: see excern.] = excretory.

1836 Todd *Cycl. Anat.* I. 798/1 Derangements of the.. excernent organs. 1884 in *Syd. Soc. Lex.*

†**ex'cerp,** *v. Obs.* [ad. L. *excerp-ĕre*: see excerpt *v.*] = excerpt *v.* 1.

1563–87 Foxe *A. & M.* (1596) 45/2 Of this Melito, Eusebius..excerpeth certeine places of his apologie. *a*1640 Jackson *Creed* xi. xliv. Wks. XI. 311 Out of this tractate.. himself had excerpt the two next foreprinted sermons. 1697 Molyneux in *Locke's Lett.* (1708) 241 If their lordships should think fit to excerp anything out of those papers.

†**ex'cerpt,** *pple. Obs.* In 5 excerpte. [ad. L. *excerpt-us*, pa. pple. of *excerpĕre*: see excerpt *v.*] Excerpted, extracted, selected.

1432–50 tr. *Higden* (Rolls) I. 7 Y..intende to compile a tretys of the state of the yle of Breteyne, excerpte of diuerse labores of auctores.

excerpt ('ɛksɜpt, ɛk'sɜːpt), *sb.* Also 8 excerp, 7–8 L. *pl.* excerpta. [ad. L. *excerpt-um*, neut. of pa. pple. of *excerpĕre*: see excerpt *v.*]

1. A passage taken out of a printed book or manuscript; an extract, quotation, selection.

*a*1638 Mede *Par. 2 Pet.* iii. App. Wks. III. 618 Some Excerpta out of the Fathers concerning the Renovation of the World. 1638 Rouse *Heav. Univ.* Advt. (1702) 3 Excerpts out of all the Greek and Latin Fathers. 1704 Hearne *Duct. Hist.* (1714) I. 150 An Epitome of the latter xx Books..is also Extant..And also noble Excerpta by one Theodosius. 1706 Sibbald *Hist. Picts* in *Misc. Scot.* I. 91 The excerpts of the old register of St. Andrew calleth him a bishop, and his companions Clerks. 1817 Southey *Let.* 17 Apr., Papers from the 'Quarterly Review,' together with certain excerpts from the 'Register.' 1876 M. Davies *Unorth. Lond.* 8 Mr. Conway read..an excerpt from one of Mazzini's Orations. 1882 J. T. Fowler *Mem. Ripon* I. i. (*headline*) Excerpts from Chronicles.

2. An article from the 'Transactions' of a learned society or from a periodical, printed off separately for private circulation. Cf. *off-print.*

This sense has long been in use in the official correspondence of learned societies (Royal Society, Society of Antiquaries, etc.), but does not appear to be generally current.

1883 *Proc. Royal Soc.* 369 List Presents, [An author sends several works, of which the titles are quoted.] And fourteen other Excerpts. 1889 *Ibid.* 252 Excerpt. [Added in brackets to the title of a work presented.]

3. In etymological sense: A thing picked out. *rare.*

1837 M. DONOVAN *Dom. Econ.* II. 15 The emperor had a large silver dish, the filling of which..occasioned wholesale slaughter; his excerpts being insignificant parts of various small and rare birds and fishes.

excerpt (ɛkˈsɜːpt), *v.* [f. L. *excerpt-* ppl. stem of *excerpĕre*, f. *ex-* out + *carpĕre* to pluck.]

1. *trans.* To cull out (passages, phrases, etc.); to take out as an extract; to extract, quote. Also *absol.* to make extracts.

c **1536** WOLSEY in Ellis *Orig. Lett.* II. 99 II. 21 A Copy of certain Articles and Clauses excerpted and taken out of the Popes Letters. **1615** CHAPMAN *Odyss.* II. 105 This close note I excerpted. *a* **1662** HEYLIN *Laud* ii. (1671) 301 He had excerpted and laid by many notes and precedents. **1851** CARLYLE *Sterling* II. iii. (1872) 113 An affectionate and eloquent notice of him; which..was excerpted into the newspapers also. **1865** —— *Fredk. Gt.* IX. xx. x. 193 The Book we excerpt from is *Mémoires du Comte de Hordt.* **1874** MAHAFFY *Soc. Life Greece* ix. 281 Athenæus..excerpted largely in this direction.

†**2.** In etymological sense: To pluck out; to abstract, remove; also *fig. Obs.*

1538 LELAND *Itin.* IV. 64 Thinges excerpted out of the East Glasse Window of our Lady Chappell. **1607** TOPSELL *Four-f. Beasts* 429 Which Musk being excerpted before it be ripe, smelleth strongly and unpleasantly. *c* **1612** DONNE *Βιαθανατος* (1644) 23 Every branch which is excerpted from other authors and engrafted here, is not, etc.

¶**b.** To take out, eliminate. *rare.*

1881 J. PAYNE *Villon's Poems* Introd. 22 If one should excerpt from their verse its accidental local colouring.

Hence **exˈcerpted** *ppl. a.*

1818 G. S. FABER *Horæ Mosaicæ* II. 192 Excerpted particles of the pure and ethereal light.

excerptible (ɛkˈsɜːptɪb(ə)l), *a.* [f. prec. + -IBLE.] That admits of being excerpted; suitable to make extracts or selections from.

1880 *Athenæum* 11 Dec. 777/3 What is to be said as to the exclusion of Flaubert, who is easily excerptible? **1883** *Pall M. G.* 1 June 4/2 Such students are never likely to be the majority. For others Goethe is certainly 'excerptible'.

exˈcerpting, *vbl. sb.* [f. as prec. + -ING[1].] The action of the vb. EXCERPT; an instance of it.

1867 CARLYLE *Remin.* II. 55 My time, with little 'Goethe' papers and excerptings..went more prosperously than before.

excerption (ɛkˈsɜːpʃən). [ad. L. *excerptiōn-em*, n. of action f. *excerpĕre*: see EXCERPT *v.*]

1. The action of excerpting, making selections from (a book, manuscript, etc.).

1883 *Pall Mall G.* 13 Nov. 5/1 Mr. Buchanan is a writer exceptionally suited for excerption and revision.

2. *concr.* An extract from a book, document, etc. Also, formerly, a collection of extracts. ***The Excerptions of Egbert***: a work with the title *Excerptiones e dictis et canonibus sanctorum patrum*, erroneously ascribed to Egbert, Abp. of York.

a **1618** RALEIGH (J.), Times have consumed his works, saving some few excerptions. **1635** PRYNNE *Unbish. Tim.* (1661) 73 Egbert Archbishop of York..made a collection or excerption out of the Canons of sundry antient Councils. **1662** MORE *Philos. Writ.* Pref. Gen. (1712) 23 A Book of Excerptions out of Origen's Writings. **1709** J. JOHNSON *Clergym. Vade M.* II. 156 Many of the Excerptions of Egbert were transcribed from it. **1776** G. CAMPBELL *Philos. Rhet.* (1801) I. I. ii. 66 A needless multiplicity of excerptions.

excerptive (ɛkˈsɜːptɪv), *a.* [f. EXCERPT *v.* + -IVE.] Inclined to excerpt; characterized by excerption.

1860 WORCESTER cites MACKENZIE.

exˈcerptor. [a. L. *excerptor*, agent-n. f. *excerpĕre*: see EXCERPT *v.*] One who excerpts or makes extracts (from a book, etc.).

1683 J. BARNARD *Life Heylin* 12, I have not been surreptitious of whole pages together..and appropriated them to myself without any Mark..I am no such Excerptor. **1892** *Graphic* 27 Aug. 254/1 What the monographer does for the classic, that the excerptor does for his works.

excerse, obs. form of EXERCE.

excess (ɛkˈsɛs), *sb.* Also 4–7 **excesse,** 5–6 **exces,** (5 **exesse,** 6 **excysse**). [ad. F. *excès*, ad. L. *excess-us*, n. of action f. *excēdĕre* to EXCEED.]

†**1. a.** In literal sense: The action of going out or forth; adjournment (of Parliament). *Obs. rare.*

c **1450** *Voc.* in Wr.-Wülcker. 581 *Excessus*, excesse, passynge oute. **1621** ELSING *Debates Ho. Lords* App. (Camden) 131 That they be accquainted that Tuesday should be the day of excesse.

†**b.** *fig.* Departure *from* custom, reason, etc. *Obs.*

1709 STEELE *Tatler* No. 51 ⁋2 In all these glorious Excesses from the common Practice, did the happy Orlando live..in an uninterrupted Tranquility. **1738** *Common Sense* (1739) II. 84 Other fashionable Excesses from Reason.

†**c.** ***excess of mind, soul*** (incorrectly *access*; cf. ACCESS *sb.* 9, 10), also simply *excess*: = L. *excessus mentis*, ecstasy, trance, stupefaction. *Obs.*

1382 WYCLIF *Acts* x. 10 An axcess of soule, or rauysching of spirit [*v.r.* mynde] fel on hym. *Ibid.* xi. 5, I was in the citee of Ioppe preiynge, and I sy3 in excess of my soule a visioun. **1526** *Pilgr. Perf.* (W. de W. 1531) 270 b, Saynt Peter was in excesse of mynde in the house of Symon Coryar. *Ibid.* 271, I sayd in myne excesse, euery man is a lyer. **1582** *N.T.* (Rhem.) *Acts* x. 10 There fel vpon him an excesse of minde. **1609** BIBLE (Douay) *2 Esdras* xiii. 30 He shal come in excesse of minde upon them [**1611** to the astonishment of them] that inhabite the earth.

†**2.** 'Violence of passion' (J.); extravagant or rapturous feeling; unrestrained manifestation of grief. *Obs.*

1423 JAS. I *Kingis Q.* cxliv, Off thy distresse and excesse to haue reuth..I will [hir] pray full faire. **1509** HAWES *Past. Pleas.* XXXIII. xxx, La Bell Pucell must love you ever-more, Which for her sake..Doth such actes by chyvalrous exces. **1724** *Wodrow Corr.* (1843) III. 120 The Priests under the Old Testament were, by a particular law, guarded against excesses upon the death of their relations. **1742** COLLINS *Ode* iii. *To Simplicity* 44 Tho' taste, tho' genius, bless To some divine excess. **1775** in ASH. **1818** in TODD.

3. The action of overstepping (a prescribed limit), going beyond (one's authority, rights, etc.); an instance of this. Chiefly in *Law*.

1818 CRUISE *Digest* (ed. 2) IV. 248 She exceeded her power, in appointing to the issue of the son; and there fore the excess was void. **1891** *Daily News* 28 Jan. 3/2 Judges of courts of law..did not notice excess of jurisdiction on the part of the House.

†**4. a.** Extravagant violation of law, decency, or morality; outrageous conduct. *Obs.*

c **1386** CHAUCER *Melib.* ⁋563 Ye shul venge yow..by the lawe and noght by excesse ne by outrage. *c* **1425** WYNTOUN *Cron.* VIII. xxiv. 161 Punysyd exces and trespas. **1480** CAXTON *Chron. Eng.* III. (1520) 20 b/1 Two were chosen that yf ony of theym wolde make ony excesse the other sholde governe hym. **1526** *Pilgr. Perf.* (W. de W. 1531) 140 b, Be sory for your fall, and do due penaunce after the qualite and quantite of your excesse. *c* **1630** MILTON *Ode Circumcision*, The full wrath beside Of vengeful justice bore for our excess. **1682** EVELYN *Diary* (1827) III. 76 This excesse of making churches charnel-houses. **1791** COWPER *Odyss.* III. 262 Ah..that I..the deeds Might punish of our suitors whose excess Enormous..I feel.

b. An instance of this; an outrage. Chiefly *pl.* Now with mixture of sense 5.

14.. *Prose Legends* in *Anglia* VIII. 129 Leste by hir excesses þey schulde scorn þe good name of Cryste. **1677** HALE *Prim. Orig. Man.* II. xi. 240 The great..Governour of the World..brought about ends..to punish their [men's] Excesses and Enormities. **1769** *Junius Lett.* i. 6 They have been driven into excesses little short of rebellion. **1848** MACAULAY *Hist. Eng.* I. 166 The excesses of the Star Chamber..had faded from the minds of men. **1876** J. H. NEWMAN *Hist. Sk.* I. I. iii. 139 Their excesses seem to have been inferior to those which provoked them.

5. The overstepping the limits of moderation; an instance of this: **a.** *gen.*

1552 HULOET s.v., Excesse in aduauncyng or depressyng, as truer then God, falser then the Deuyll. **1594** HOOKER *Eccl. Pol* IV. viii. (1611) 143 To draw men from great excesse, it is not amiss. **1655** DENHAM *Coopers Hill*, One excess Made both, by striving to be greater, less. **1752** HUME *Ess. & Treat.* (1777) I. 193 Excess in love..transports a man beyond himself. **1794** MRS. RADCLIFFE *Myst. Udolpho.* ii, All excess is vicious. **1829** *The Bengallee* 182 The Hookah's monstrous snake..That type of eastern Luxury's excess. **1878** MORLEY *Carlyle* 163 Excess..leads people into emotional transports.

b. *spec.* Intemperance in eating or drinking.

c **1386** CHAUCER *Pard. T.* 514 How manye maladyes ffolwen of excesse and of glotonyes. *c* **1430** LYDG. in *Pol. Rel. & L. Poems* (1866) 25 With holy men speke of holynesse ..With drownkyn men do surfettes by excesse. **1578** *Gude & Godlie Ball.* 17 We pray his godly Maiestie To blys our meit..And saif vs fra exces and drunkinnes. **1662** B. DUPPA *Rules Devot.* (1675) 84 The body, once heavy with Excess and Surfeits, hangs plummets on the nobler part. **1722** WOLLASTON *Relig. Nat.* iv. 64 It is also in his power to forbear excess in eating and drinking. **1840** BARHAM *Ingol. Leg., Spectre Tappington*, Apoplexy, induced by the excesses of the preceding night. **1859** O. W. HOLMES *Punch-bowl* Poems 271 'Tis but the fool that loves excess; hast thou a drunken soul?

6. a. The fact of exceeding something else in amount or degree; preponderance. †Also the fact of surpassing or excelling others (*obs.*). ***in excess of***: to a greater amount or degree than.

a **1618** RALEIGH *Maxims St.* (1651) 64 An excellency or excess above the rest, either in honour, wealth, or virtue. **1704** NEWTON *Optics* II. II. (1721) 127 Rays..retain their colorific qualities, by which those of any sort do by their Excess and Predominance cause their proper Colour to appear. **1756** BURKE *Subl. & B.* Introd. Wks. I. 112 In things whose excess is not judged by greater or smaller, as smoothness and roughness [etc.]. **1838** DE MORGAN *Ess. Probab.* 115 There can be no possible reason for an excess of white, which does not equally..apply in favour of an excess of black. **1860** TYNDALL *Glac.* II. iii. 242 The quantity we receive is in excess of the quantity lost. **1879** HARLAN *Eyesight* ii. 30 When..one or more muscles act in excess of their opponents, a squint is produced.

b. The amount by which one number or quantity exceeds another. ***spherical excess***: (see quot. 1840). ***excess fare*** (on railways): a payment made by a person travelling beyond the place, or in a higher class than that, specified on his ticket. ***excess luggage***: luggage over the weight for which a passenger is allowed free carriage. ***excess profits*** (see quot. 1915[2]); also *attrib.*

1557 RECORDE *Whetst.* M iv, Compare those excesses and wantes well together. **1660** BARROW *Euclid* I. Axiom xv, If to equal things, you add unequal, the excess of the wholes shall be equal to the excess of the additions. **1812** WOODHOUSE *Astron.* xviii. 201 The accumulation of the daily excesses. **1831** BREWSTER *Optics* iv. 36 Divide the index of refraction by its excess above unity. **1840** SNOWBALL *Spherical Trigonom.* §63 (ed. 5) 34 The quantity..by which the sum of the degrees in the angles of the spherical triangles exceeds 180°, is called the Spherical Excess of the triangle. **1882** *Standard* 2 Sept. 6/4 He received a book for the purpose of giving receipts to passengers for 'excess' fares. **1911** A. BENNETT *Card* xi. 261 How much did you pay for the excess luggage? **1915** W. OWEN *Let.* 1 Aug. (1967) 350 The said friend, having no baggage, will lighten my excess-luggage-charge. **1915** *Act 5 & 6 Geo. V* c. 89 §38 Excess Profits Duty. .. There shall be charged, levied, and paid on the amount by which the profits arising from any trade or business to which this Part of this Act applies, in any accounting period which ended after the fourth day of August nineteen hundred and fourteen, and before the first day of July nineteen hundred and fifteen, exceeded, by more than two hundred poundsd, the pre-war standard of profits as defined for the purposes of this Part of this Act, a duty (in this Act referred to as 'excess profits duty') of an amount equal to fifty per cent. of that excess. **1915** *Chemist & Druggist* LXXXVII. 521/1 As regards the excess profits tax, the special appeal tribunal will be competent [etc.]. **1940** G. CROWTHER *Paying for War* 22 It is very right and proper that there should be an Excess Profits Tax and that it should have been imposed in the first month of the war. **1955** *Times* 2 May 20/1 At least we were freed from the ill-conceived Excess Profits Levy.

†**c.** Usury, interest. *Obs.*

1596 SHAKS. *Merch. V.* I. iii. 63 Shylocke..I neither lend nor borrow By taking, nor by giuing of excesse.

7. a. The state of exceeding or being in greater quantity or degree than is usual or necessary; exuberance, superabundance; an instance of this; an extreme degree or amount; an 'extreme', a 'height' (of wickedness, etc.). †***of excess*** = in abundance.

1387 TREVISA *Higden* (Rolls) I. 335 þere is no3t gret passynge and exces..in chele noþer in hete. **1430** LYDG. *Chron. Troy* I. v, The medlynge in conclusion So was ennewed by proportion That fynally excesse was there none. **1503** HAWES *Examp. Virt.* xi. 207 Than I to hym gaue strokes of exces. **1576** FLEMING *Panopl. Epist.* 269 The excesse of vertue worketh no manner of annoyance. **1605** SHAKS. *Lear* IV. i. 73 So distribution should vndoo excesse, And each man haue enough. **1697** DRYDEN *Virg. Georg.* II. 570 Commend the large Excess Of spacious Vineyards; cultivate the less. **1719** YOUNG *Busiris* IV. i, To behold thee In such excess of sorrow, quite destroys me. **1802** PALEY *Nat. Theol.* xxvi. (1819) 406 Their vivacity, their leaps out of the water, their frolics in it, all conduce to show their excess of spirits. **1818** JAS. MILL *Brit. India* II. IV. v. 193 This [he] treated as the highest excess of insolence. **1848** MACAULAY *Hist. Eng.* I. 636 Kirke..was not the last, to whom this excess of wickedness was popularly imputed.

†**b.** *concr.* in *pl.* Resources beyond the 'necessaries' of life; luxuries. *Obs.*

1658 *Whole Duty Man* xiv. §16. 112 That deny relief to their poor parents, that cannot part with their own excesses and superfluities.

c. *Chem.* An amount greater than is needed for a specific purpose, *e.g.* for combination with other elements, or for dissolving a given quantity of a substance. Also ***in (great) excess.***

1807 T. THOMSON *Chem.* (ed. 3) II. 610 It might be called supersulphate of ammonia, as it contains an excess of acid. **1838** —— *Chem. Org. Bodies* 204 At first there was an excess of the former salt, but afterwards xanthate of potash was added till it constituted an excess. **1844–57** G. BIRD *Urin. Deposits* (ed. 5) 383 Liquor potassæ must then be added in great excess; a precipitate of hydrated oxide of copper first falls, which redissolves in excess of alkali.

8. a. The fact or state of being in greater amount or degree than is beneficial or right; 'faulty superfluity' (J.); an excessive amount or degree (of anything). Sometimes in contrast with *defect*.

1393 GOWER *Conf.* II. 276, I bidde never as to my dele But of the hole an halven dele. That is none excess as me thenketh. **1488** CAXTON *Chast. Goddes Chyld.* 72 Excesse of mete feblith and dulleth a mannys wyttes. **1591** SHAKS. *Two Gent.* III. i. 220, I haue fed vpon this woe already, And now excesse of it will make me surfet. **1691** HARTCLIFFE *Virtues* 137 The two Extremes whereof are; on the defect ἀοργησία, to be free from Anger..The other Extreme in the Excess, is ὀργιλότης, a Vice, which..hath not yet found an English Name. **1725** N. ROBINSON *Th. Physick* 314 If the Spirits flag during the Operation from the Excess of the Evacuations. *a* **1731** ATTERBURY *Serm.* (J.), Parsimony..is the more pardonable excess of the two. **1829** I. TAYLOR *Enthus.* i. (1867) 16 If..enthusiasm were only an error in degree or a mere fault by excess. *a* **1871** GROTE *Eth. Fragm.* v. (1876) 165 We ought to choose the middle point and not either the excess or the defect. **1875** JOWETT *Plato* (ed. 2) V. 9 The excess of tyranny in Persia and the excess of liberty at Athens have been the ruin of both.

b. Phrases: ***in, to (an) excess, to carry (something), to drink, eat, go, run to excess.*** †***(object) of excess***, that possesses some quality in excess.

1526–34 TINDALE *1 Pet.* iv. 4 That ye runne not also with them vnto the same excesse of ryote. **1625** BACON *Ess., Goodness* (Arb.) 199 The desire of Power in Excesse, caused the Angels to fall. **1626** —— *Sylva* §261 An Object of surcharge or excess, destroyeth the Sense: As the light of the Sun the eye, a violent sound (near the Ear) the hearing. *c* **1645** HOWELL *Lett.* (1655) II. 71 [Canary wine] leaves less dreggs behind, though one drink it to exces. **1749** FIELDING *Tom Jones* XI. iii, Sophia..was yielding to an excess. **1764** GOLDSM. *Trav.* 97 Till carried to excess..This fav'rite good begets peculiar pain. **1838** W. BEAUMONT *Exper. Digestion* (ed. Combe) 252 Eating voraciously or to excess. **1841** MIALL *Nonconf.* I. 1 At present we have government in excess. **1875** DARWIN *Insectiv. Pl.* vi. 110 Raw meat and other nutritious substances, given in excess, kill the leaves.

¶**9.** = ACCESS *sb.* 10.

1541 R. COPLAND *Galyen's Terap.* 2 D iij, They counceyll them that haue the feuers..to passe the excesse that ought to come the thyrde day or no. **1634** SIR T. HERBERT *Trav.* 168 In twelve dayes I had a thousand bloudy stooles (which excesse kild our Lord Ambassadour Sir Dodmore Cotton at that time).

ex'cess, *a.* Also 4-6 **excesse**, 7 **excysse**. [? attrib. use of EXCESS *sb.*] = EXCESSIVE. **a.** Beyond the usual or specified amount. Cf. EXCESS *sb.* 6 b. †**b.** Beyond what is necessary, proper or right. *Obs.*

?*a* **1400** *Chester Pl.* (Shaks. Soc.) 24 But excesse sleepe behoves me to make one this man heare. **1547-64** BAULDWIN *Mor. Philos.* (Palfr.) VII. v, Excesse bibbing and drinking, pricketh fast forwards to lechery. **1574** HYLL *Conject. Weather* i, And the excesse qualitie..of any of the four quarters is evill and daungerous to the fruites of the earth. **1636** in Picton *L'pool Munic. Rec.* (1883) I. 162 For takeinge excysse fees contrarie to auncient orders. **1902** *Encycl. Brit.* XXV. 646/1 There are also a large number of the 'reserve' who are not required to fill up the vacancies in the battalion going out. These become what are known as 'excess numbers'. **1909** WEBSTER s.v., Excess baggage on a railroad. **1920** A. E. HOUSMAN *Let.* 15 Aug. (1971) 176 A charge for 'Passengers' Excess Baggage'. **1940** *Chambers's Techn. Dict.* 605/1 Damage caused by an excess voltage, i.e. a voltage above normal. **1958** G. BELLAIRS *Corpse at Carnival* iv. 48 The charge for excess baggage was disgusting. I shall complain. **1965** *New Statesman* 29 Oct. 632/3 Only the 'excess demand' (extra long order-books) for construction activity has been snipped away. **1970** *Daily Tel.* 19 Oct. 8/6 Grotowsky's productions strip away all the excess baggage of drama—conventional stage, scenery, make-up, props.

ex'cess, *v.* [f. EXCESS *sb.*] *trans.* To charge with an excess fare.

1888 *Difference of Fare Excess Voucher on N.B. Railway* 16 May, In case of Tickets being excessed before the journey has been accomplished.

†**ex'cessful,** *a. Obs.* [f. EXCESS *sb.* + -FUL.] Characterized by excess; excessive.

1633 BP. HALL *Hard Texts* 475 In a degree above necessity and convenience even to wantonnesse and excessefull curiosity. **1664** H. MORE *Myst. Iniq.* vii. 128 This extreme glory..and excessfull affluency of the World.

†**ex'cession.** *Obs. rare*⁻¹. [ad. late L. *excēssiōn-em*, n. of action f. *excēdĕre* to go out or forth: see EXCEED.] A going out or forth.

1655-60 STANLEY *Hist. Philos.* I. VIII. 112 Motion is a mutation of parts, or an excession out of place.

excessive (ɛk'sɛsɪv), *a.* (*sb.*) and *adv.* Forms: 4 **excessife**, 5 **excessif, excessyfe**, 5-6 **excessyve**, 6 (**accessive**), **excesseve**, 5- **excessive**. [a. F. *excessif, -ive*, as if ad. L. **excēssīv-us*, f. *excēss-* ppl. stem of *excēdĕre*: see EXCEED.]

A. *adj.*

†**1.** Of persons or their actions: Transgressing the bounds of law, decency, or morality; outrageous, lawless, wrongful. *Obs.*

1393 GOWER *Conf.* III. 117 Thinges which are excessife Ayein the lawe, he shal nought do. **1548** HALL *Chron.* 97 Certain ordinaunces, made by the Maire and Aldermen of London, against the excessive takyng of Masons..and other laborers, for their daily jorneis. **1568** GRAFTON *Chron.* II. 164 He made a law also the same time against the excessive takyng of Usurie by the Jewes. **1656** COWLEY *Davideis* IV. 623 Those who before did God's fair Choice with-stand Th' excessive Vulgar now to Death demand.

2. Of qualities, states, actions, magnitudes, etc.

†**a.** In favourable or neutral sense: Exceeding what is usual; 'surpassing'; exceedingly great.

1475 CAXTON *Jason* 20 Wherfore were..ye so haboundantly garnished so well of excessiue ande chief alle beaute. **1526** *Pilgr. Perf.* (W. de W. 1531) 162 They come downe agayn to them selfe from suche excessyue eleuacyon or extasy. **1626** BACON *Sylva* §438 If Panicum be laid below and about the Bottom of a Root, it will cause the Root to grow to an Excessiue Bignesse. **1663** GERBIER *Counsel* B v b, Water, can be easily drawn, an excessive and almost incredible height above its Centre.

b. Exceeding what is right, proportionate, or desirable; immoderate, inordinate, extravagant.

a **1420** HOCCLEVE *De Reg. Princ.* 450 A foule waste of clothe and excessyfe. **1490** CAXTON *Eneydos* xxviii. (1890) 110 A highe colour ouer excessyue and dyshonneste. **1601** SHAKS. *All's Well* I. i. 65 Moderate lamentation is the right of the dead, excessiue greefe [is] the enemie to the liuing. **1651** HOBBES *Leviath.* I. viii. 36 Excessive desire of Revenge, when it becomes habituall, hurteth the organs. **1752** HUME *Pol. Disc.* x. 203 Excessive severity in the laws is apt to beget great relaxation in their execution. **1844-57** G. BIRD *Urin. Deposits* (ed. 5) 84 A man eats an excessive meal of meat, more than he can assimilate into healthy blood. **1875** JOWETT *Plato* (ed. 2) III. 681 A single night of excessive rain ..left the rock of the Acropolis bare.

3. Of persons: Given to excess in anything; intemperate, extravagant. Now only with agent-nouns or predicatively with const. *in.*

1586 T. B. *La Primaud. Fr. Acad.* I. (1594) 190 These excessive fellowes never expect hunger, or thirst..but through intemperance prevent them. **1624** CAPT. SMITH *Virginia* VI. 219 If a man worke but three daies in seuen, hee may get more than hee can spend vnlesse hee will bee exceedingly excessiue. **1663** COWLEY *Verses & Ess., Shortness Life*, A man who is excessive in his pains and diligence. **1670** MILTON *Hist. Eng.* Wks. 1738 II. 118 He is said to be at Table not excessive. **1710** STEELE *Tatler* No. 182 ¶2 Who is not excessive in the Discourse of what he extremely likes? *Mod.* Avoid the company of excessive drinkers.

†**4.** Of expressions: Hyperbolical. *Obs.*

1555 EDEN *Decades* 127 They compare them in bignesse to elephantes..but this..by an excessyue kynde of speache.

5. Of climates: Characterized by extremes.

1830 LYELL *Princ. Geol.* I. 107 There are..excessive climates, as they have been termed, where the temperature of winter and summer is strongly contrasted.

†**6.** as *sb.* Something excessive; an extravagance. *Obs. rare.*

1644 H. PARKER *Jus. Pop.* 49 Great Monarchies are monstrous excessives in Nature.

†**B.** *adv.* = EXCESSIVELY. *Obs.*; very common in 17-18th c.

1569 TURBERV. *Epitaphs & Sonn.* (1837) 366 Ye are excessiue proude. **1634** SIR T. HERBERT *Trav.* 216 The Sea at the brinke of this Ile is excessive deepe. *a* **1720** SHEFFIELD (Dk. Buckhm.) *Wks.* 1753 II. 102 Mr. Lane grew excessive angry. **1768** GOLDSM. *Good-n. Man* II. i, His manner..was excessive harmless. **1774** PENNANT *Tour Scot. in 1772*, 345 The night most excessive dark. **1796** BURNEY *Metastasio* I. 395 This would be an excessive long chapter.

excessively (ɛk'sɛsɪvlɪ), *adv.* [f. prec. + -LY².]

†**1.** Of manner: **a.** Wastefully, lavishly, prodigally. **b.** Greedily. *Obs.*

1552 HULOET, Excessyuely..*profuse.* **1563** GOLDING *Cæsar* 85 The beastes which the Galles do most delight in and whych they pay for excessiuely. **1596** SPENSER *F.Q.* II. xii. 3 Which having swallowd up excessively, He soone in vomit up againe doth lay.

2. In an excessive amount or degree; beyond measure, immoderately. (In mod. use a stronger expression than *exceedingly*.)

c **1460** FORTESCUE *Abs. & Lim. Mon.* (1714) 68 Whan any of his Lords schal happyn to be so excessively grete as [etc.] **1502** *Ord. Crysten Men* (W. de W. 1506) IV. i. 167 He is excessyuely humylyed. **1591** HORSEY *Trav.* (Hakluyt Soc.) 192 He used me but rufflye, by reason I could not drincke excessivlie with him. **1634** H. R. *Salerne Regim.* 2 Anger.. excessiuely chafeth and inflameth the membres. **1646** SIR T. BROWNE *Pseud. Ep.* v. xxi. 271 A conceit..wherein although it seeme excessively ridiculous there may be some-what of truth. **1711** STEELE *Spect.* No. 145 ¶6 The Fellow is rich.. but excessively ill-bred. **1747** WESLEY *Prim. Physic* (1762) 63 It makes them smart and burn excessively. **1841** LANE *Arab. Nts.* I. 80 There came forth from it nothing but smoke ..at which he wondered excessively. **1877** LADY BRASSEY *Voy. Sunbeam* xxii. (1878) 378 The scenery seemed of an excessively rudimentary description.

excessiveness (ɛk'sɛsɪvnɪs). [f. as prec. + -NESS.] The state or quality of being excessive; excessive measure, quantity, or degree.

1494 FABYAN *Chron.* VII. 480 And upon yᵉ ensuyd suche excessyuenes of rayne that corne was therwith drowned in yᵉ erthe. **1600** J. LANE *Tom Tel-troth* 615 A bibbing swilbowle and a bowzing gull, which never drinke but with excessivenesse. **1657** RUMSEY *Org. Salutis* i. (1659) 2 Excessivenesse of heat and cold in several parts of the body; which breeds Agues and Feavers. **1730-6** in BAILEY (folio). **1775** in ASH. **1832** in WEBSTER; and in mod. Dicts.

exchange (ɛks'tʃeɪndʒ), *sb.* Forms: 4-6 **eschaunge**, (6 **eschange**), 5-6 **exchaunge**, (6 **exhaunce**), 6- **exchange**. [ME. *eschaunge*, a. AF. *eschaunge*, OF. *eschange* (F. *échange*):—late L. *excambium*, f. *excambiāre*: see EXCHANGE *v.* In 16th c. the prefix *es-* was, as in some other words, altered to *ex-* after L. analogies.]

I. The action or process of exchanging.

1. The action, or an act, of reciprocal giving and receiving: **a.** of things in general. Proverb, ***exchange is no robbery.***

c **1384** CHAUCER *H. Fame* II. 189 Of loues moo eschaunges Then euer cornes were in graunges. *c* **1400** *Test. Love* I. (1560) 275/2 My moeble is insuffisaunte to countervayle the price of this jewell, or els to make the eschaunge. **1552** *Act 5-6 Edw. VI*, c. 19. §1 To exchange gold for silver..so that no man..did take no profit for making such exchange. **1599** SHAKS. *Much Ado* II. i. 320, I giue away my selfe for you, and doat vpon the exchange. **1655** FULLER *Ch. Hist.* I. v. §11 In lieu of what he left behind him, Exchange is no Robbery, he carried along with him some of St. Alban's Dust. *a* **1719** ADDISON (J.), They lend their Corn, they make Exchanges. **1860** TYNDALL *Glac.* I. xxv. 182 The due exchange of loads having been made, we advanced upon the glacier. **1863** DICKENS *Lett.* (1880) II. 196 Let us make an exchange of child stories.

b. of goods, merchandize; = BARTER; in political economy often with wider sense of 'commerce'.

1553 EDEN *Treat. Newe Ind.* (Arb.) 8 Salomans factours for exchaunge of other marchaundyse. **1767** BLACKSTONE *Comm.* II. 446 If it be a commutation of goods for goods, it is more properly an exchange; but, if it be a transferring of goods for money, it is called a sale: which is a method of exchange introduced, etc. **1863** ROGERS *Pol. Econ.* xvii. (1876) 224 No one questions the natural rights of free exchange.

c. of prisoners of war.

c **1374** CHAUCER *Troylus* IV. 130 Yf þey wolde graunte.. Theschaunge of her. **1494** FABYAN *Chron.* VII. ccxxxiii. 267 Meanys was made..for delyuerie and exchaunge of yᵉ prysoners. **1611** SPEED *Hist. Gt. Brit.* (1632) 479 These two Chief-taines wearied with irksomnesse of Irons made exchange the one for the other. **1698** LUDLOW *Mem.* I. 109 Procuring my exchange for his two Sons. **1780** B. LINCOLN in Sparks *Corr. Amer. Rev.* (1883) III. 96 An exchange, when made a prisoner, is one of the rights of a soldier. **1867** SMYTH *Sailor's Word-bk., Exchange*, a mutual agreement between contending powers for exchange of prisoners.

d. of blows, passes, strokes (in fencing, games, etc.), salutations.

1602 SHAKS. *Ham.* v. ii. 280 If Hamlet give the first or second hit, Or quit in answer of the third exchange. *a* **1687** WALLER *Bat. Summer-Islands* 111, Thus they parted, with exchange of harms. **1862** STANLEY *Jew. Ch.* (1877) I. xiii. 258 We hear the exchange of salutations between the reapers and their master. **1882** *Daily Tel.* 18 July 2 This [game at tennis] fell to E. Renshaw after some good exchanges.

e. of military or naval commissions, etc. (see quot.). Also *attrib.*, as in ***exchange system***.

1823 CRABB *Technol. Dict., Exchange* between officers, who remove from one regiment to another, or from full pay to half pay, for which a consideration is usually given, called the Difference. **1833** MARRYAT *P. Simple* xxxi, Captain Falcon..received his commission that evening, and the next day the exchanges were made. **1867** SMYTH *Sailor's Word-bk., Exchange*, the removal of officers from one ship to another. **1875** *Act 38 Vict.* c. 16 Her Majesty may.. authorise exchanges to be made from one regiment..to another regiment. **1875** D. WOLFF *Sp. Ho. Com.* 22 Feb., In the Artillery, Engineers, and Marines, they had from time immemorial had the Exchange system, yet they had never adopted the Purchase system.

f. in *Chess*, of pieces captured. ***to force the exchange***: to play so as to compel your opponent to take one piece for another. ***to gain, win, lose the exchange***: to take or lose a superior piece in exchange for an inferior.

1823 CRABB *Technol. Dict.* s.v. *Chess*, Exchanges..often give the adversary an advantage. **1848** H. STAUNTON *Chess-Players Handbk.* (ed. 2) 21 When a player gains a Rook for a Bishop or a Knight, it is termed winning the exchange. **1865** *Househ. Chess Mag.* 34 This move loses, at least, the 'exchange'. **1878** H. E. BIRD *Chess Openings* 105 Black gains the exchange, and should win.

g. (*to give, have, take*, etc.) †***by, in exchange*** †***of, for*** (something else).

c **1400** *Destr. Troy* 3182 Priam..may prestly suppose His suster to sese, sent by eschaunge. **1598** SHAKS. *Merry W.* II. ii. 243 There is money..spend all I haue, onely giue me so much of your time in exchange of it. **1611** BIBLE *Matt.* xvi. 26 Or what shall a man giue in exchange for his soule? **1663** GERBIER *Counsel* 109 A very gainfull returne of Amber Greese and vendible commodities in exchange of Iron Tools. **1665** DRYDEN *Ind. Emperor* (J.), O spare her life, and in exchange take mine. **1778** T. JONES *Hoyle's Games Impr.* 147 You can get two Pieces in Exchange for your Queen. **1837** W. IRVING *Capt. Bonneville* III. 193 Giving horses in exchange for the articles of which they stand in need.

2. *Law.* 'A mutual grant of equal interests, the one in consideration of the other' (Blackstone *Comm.* (1767) II. 323).

1574 tr. *Littleton's Tenures* 13 b, In exchange it behoveth, that the estates that bothe parties have in the landes so exchaunged be equal. **1642** PERKINS *Prof. Bk.* iv. §284. 126 Now is to shew in what time the estates of exchanges ought to be executed. **1818** CRUISE *Digest* (ed. 2) V. 203 A husband and wife joined in exchanging lands, which were the estate of the wife, with a stranger, for other lands; and the exchange was executed. **1876** DIGBY *Real Prop.* x. §1. 378 Conveyances by way of exchange.

3. a. The action of giving or receiving coin in return for coin of equivalent value either of the same or a foreign country, for bullion, or for notes or bills; a bargain respecting this; the trade of a money-changer. †***bank of exchange***: the office of a money-changer or banker.

[**1335** *Act 9 Edw. III*, stat. 2 c. 7 Et que table deschange soit a Dovorri & aillours, ou & qᵃnt il semblera a nos & a notre consail per faire eschange.] **1377** LANGL. *P. Pl.* B. v. 249 Eschaunges and cheuesances with suche chaffare I dele. *c* **1386** CHAUCER *Prol.* 278 Wel couthe he in eschaunge scheeldes [*i.e.* Fr. écus] selle. **1526** *Pilgr. Perf.* II. iv. 43 b, He maketh his banke and exchange with some ryche marchaunt. **1552** HULOET, *Exchaunge*, wher as gayne or lucre is gotten at the second hande, *promercium.* **1570-6** LAMBARDE *Peramb. Kent* 127 Not without good cause..hath Douer..beene..assigned by lawes of Parleament as a speciall place for passage and eschaunge. **1580** BARET *Alv.* E 428 The losse and decay for the exchange of some peece of gold or siluer, *collybus.* **1611** COTGR. s.v. *Change*, Banke of Exchange, or place wherein money is exchanged, and commodities bartered for. *Mod.* I lost a good deal by the exchange of some 20-mark pieces that I brought home.

†**b.** The profit obtained by a money-changer or money-lender. *Obs.*

1552 HULOET, *Banqueter* or he that kepeth a banck of mony, of whome people doo borowe money vpon gayne, called exchaunge. **1751** CHAMBERS *Cycl., Exchange* is also used for the profit, which a merchant..or broker makes of a sum of money received..Sometimes also used for the.. profit allowed for the moneys advanced in any one's behalf.

4. a. 'That species of mercantile transactions by which the debts of individuals residing at a distance from their creditors are cancelled without the transmission of money' (McCulloch), by the use of 'bills of exchange'.

The simplest case of such a transaction is when two merchants in one place are respectively debtor and creditor for equal amounts to two merchants in a distant place. The two debts may be settled by the two creditors *exchanging* their claims; the process being that one of the creditors draws a 'bill of exchange' on his distant debtor, and sells it to his neighbour for its value in present money; the latter sends it as payment of his debt to his creditor, who thus obtains a claim upon a neighbour in exchange for his claim on a person at a distance. In practice the matter is much more complicated, and the term *Bill of Exchange* has acquired an extended signification from which the etymological notion has almost disappeared (see BILL *sb.*³ 9). By writers on the theory of finance *exchange* is used for the whole system of transactions effected by 'bills of exchange', and is formally divided into *Inland* and *Foreign Exchange.* But in practice (exc. in the term *bill of exchange* itself) the word now almost exclusively means foreign exchange, and in this use has a mixed notion of sense 3; the price at which

a bill drawn on a foreign country for a given amount may be bought being subject to variations, depending (1) on the varying relation in intrinsic value between the coins of the two countries; (2) on the varying demand for bills; and (3) on the length of time for which the bill has to run.

par of exchange: the recognized standard value of the coinage of one country in terms of the coinage of another; *e.g.* (in 1894) £1 sterling at par = 25.22½ francs French money. ***rate*** or ***course of exchange*** (also simply *exchange*): (*a*) the price at which bills drawn in the currency of a foreign country may be purchased; (*b*) sometimes, the percentage by which this differs from par; *e.g.* 'the (rate of) exchange has risen from 9½ to 10 p.c.' ***arbitration of exchange***: see ARBITRATION.

Economic writers distinguish between the *real* par of exchange, which is the relation in intrinsic value existing between the coins of two nations, and the *nominal* or *conventional* par, which may for convenience be maintained at a fixed level. When the price that must be paid for a foreign bill exceeds par, *the exchange* is said to be *against*, or *unfavourable to*, the country in which the bill is drawn; when the price is below par, *the exchange* is *in favour of* that country.

1485 [see 5]. **1560** in *Harl. Misc.* (Malh.) II. 478 By this reformation of base monies..the accoumpte, which, by merchauntes, is called the Eschaunge, shall..aryse in estimation of the monies of Englande. **1596** SHAKS. *Tam. Shr.* IV. ii. 89, I haue bils for monie by exchange From Florence, and must heere [at Padua] deliuer them. *a* **1627** HAYWARD *Edw. VI* (1630) 9 Hee was skilful in the exchange beyond the seas. **1691** LOCKE *Lower. Interest* Wks. 1727 II. 57 Within a Month a Million must be return'd into Holland, this presently raises the Exchange. *Ibid.* II. 72 Foreign Exchange is the Paying of money in one Country, to receive it in another. **1694** CHILD *Disc. Trade* (ed. 4) 174 The course of the Exchange..being generally above the intrinsick value or par of the coins of foreign Countries, we..lose by such Exchange. **1724** SWIFT *Drapier's Lett.* Wks. 1755 II. II. 44 The difference is almost 25 per cent. which is double to the highest exchange of money. **1776** ADAM SMITH *W.N.* IV. iii. (1869) II. 49 The ordinary course of exchange should be allowed to be a sufficient indication of the ordinary state of debt and credit between any two places. **1788** T. JEFFERSON *Writ.* (1859) II. 468 In this paper, you will see the exchange of yesterday. **1861** GOSCHEN *For. Exch.* 48 The limits within which the exchanges may vary..are on the one extreme, the par value, plus the cost of the transmission of bullion; on the other extreme, the par value, minus this identical sum. *Ibid.* (1864) 75 The natural value of the rouble..would have been ..5 per cent. below the nominal par of exchange. **1868** SEYD *Bullion & For. Exch.* 394 The actual Mintage Par of Exchange between London and Paris is £1 = fcs. 25·2215.. For all practicable purposes, however, we may call the Par of Exchange fcs. 25·22½ centimes.

†**b.** ***dry exchange*** (= It. *cambio secco*, Fr. *change sec*): a method of evading the laws against usury by means of fictitious bills of exchange. *Obs.*

The expression (*trockner Wechsel*) still survives in German in the sense of a promissory note, i.e. a bill drawn by a person upon himself.

1485–6 *Act 3 Hen. VII*, c. 5 Eny bargayne..by the name of drye exchaunge..be utterly voide. **1572** T. WILSON *Disc. Usury* (1584) 117 b, The second kind [of exchange by bills] ..called sicke and drie exchange..is practised when one doth borrowe money by exchange for a strange region, at longer or shorter distance of time, to serue his turne the rather thereby, not minding to make anie reall paiment abroad; but compoundeth with the exchanger to haue it returned backe againe, according as the exchange shall passe from thence to London, for such distance of time as they were agreed vpon. **1682** SCARLETT *Exchanges* 266 Dry Exchanges consist in a giving of Monyes..but the repayment is to be made after a certain time in the same place where the Monyes was given, and such a sum certain over and above, as the giver of Monyes can get and agree for.

c. *Arith.* (See quot.)

1849 FREESE *Comm. Class-bk.* II. 69. **1859** BARN. SMITH *Arith. & Algebra* (ed. 6) 513 Exchange is the Rule by which we find how much money of one country is equivalent to a given sum of another country, according to a given course of Exchange.

5. = Bill of Exchange (see BILL *sb.*³ 9). Still occas. used in commercial correspondence. Also *ellipt.* in ***first, second,*** or ***third of exchange*** (= Fr. *première*, etc. *de change*).

1485 CAXTON *Paris & V.* (1868) 55 He had receued the eschaunge that Vyenne had sent hym. *Ibid.* 57 She sendeth to you an eschaunge of thre thousand floryns. *Mod.* (Form of Foreign Bill.) Sixty days after sight of this Second of Exchange (First and Third unpaid) pay to the order of, etc.

¶**6.** In senses more correctly expressed by CHANGE: **a.** Substitution of one person or thing for another. †**b.** Variation of conduct, etc. †**c.** Transmutation; mutation, alteration.

1393 GOWER *Conf.* III. 351, I se the world stond ever upon eschaunge. *c* **1420** *Pallad. on Husb.* I. 236 Preve eke the unpreved grene afore eschaunge. *c* **1430** LYDG. *Dispraise of Women* xii, These women..Most loue eschaunge and doublenes. **1548** GEST *Pr. Masse* B vij b No more can thee bread be christes body wythoute the exchaunge of the matter therof unto the sayd body. **1572** R. H. tr. *Lauaterus' Ghostes* (1596) 165 The exchange of Empires, and of other things, are in his power. **1588** SHAKS. *L.L.L.* IV. ii. 43 Th' allusion holds in the Exchange. **1589** PUTTENHAM *Eng. Poesie* III. xv. (Arb.) 182 Your figures that worke auricularly by exchange..vsing one case for another, or tense, or person. **1859** REEVE *Brittany* 235 At the only inn.. everything was in comfortless confusion, arising from an exchange of tenants.

II. 7. a. A person or thing that is offered or given in exchange or substitution for another.

1490 *Plumpton Corr.* 100 They will take yt in ferme, or els make yt exchaunce with you of lands lyeing in Yorkshire. **1605** SHAKS. *Lear* IV. vi. 280 A plot vpon her vertuous Husbands life, and the exchange my brother. *Ibid.* V. iii. 97 There's my exchange [a glove]. **1654–66** EARL ORRERY *Parthen.* VI. (1676) 734 Having avowedly in his power a sufficient exchange for him. *a* **1700** DRYDEN (J.), The respect and love which was paid you..was a wise exchange for the honours of the Court.

b. A newspaper sent to the office of another newspaper in exchange for the latter. Also *attrib.*

1798 *Deb. Congress U.S.* 27 Mar. II. 1318/2 The great number of exchange papers which pass between the printers of newspapers. **1837** in *Canadian Hist. Rev.* (1938) XIX. 15 Nineteen-twentieths of our exchanges are printed on a fairer quality [paper]. **1848** *Yale Lit. Mag.* XIV. 47 (Th.), Our exchanges. **1886** *Chr. Life* 23 Jan. 37/3 'The pulpit and the people are rising out of the superstitions into the real religion'—so remarks an exchange.

III. A place of exchange.

8. ***King's*** or ***Queen's Exchange***: see quot.

1601 Q. ELIZ. *Let. base Moneys* in T. Stafford *Pac. Hib.* 149 We require you..to giue all attention of it..[by] bringing in all others according to the course of Our Exchange, which by Our Proclamation you may perceiue that wee haue instituted. [*a* **1623** (see EXCHANGE *v.* 1 b).] **1706** PHILLIPS, *The Queen's Exchange.* **1751** CHAMBERS' *Cycl.* s.v., The King's Exchange or the place appointed by the king for exchange of plate, or bullion for the king's coin.

†**9.** A money-changer's establishment or office.

a **1569** KINGESMYLL *Comf. Afflict.* (1585) A iij, To lay it [a talent] with you in exchange and banke. **1575** FENTON tr. *Gueuara's Gold. Epist.* (1582) 75 Hee whipped out the Usurers, reuersed their exchaunges, and dispearsed their treasures.

10. a. A building in which the merchants of a town assemble for the transaction of business. Cf. BURSE 3 b, CHANGE *sb.* 3.

The 'Burse' or Exchange built in London by Sir T. Gresham in 1566 received from Queen Elizabeth the name of Royal Exchange, which is retained by the present building. Gresham's building is in 17th c. sometimes called the *Old Exchange*, to distinguish it from the *New Exchange*, i.e. 'Britain's Burse'.

1589 NASH *Pasquil's Ret.* 1, I little thought to meete thee so suddainly upon the Exchange. **1593** NORDEN *Spec. Brit., M'sex* I. 35 Sir Thomas Gresham..named it the Burse, whereunto afterward Queene Elizabeth gave the name of Royall Exchange. *a* **1610** HEALEY *Epictetus' Man* (1636) 39 You cannot builde it a schoole, an Exchange, or a bathe. **1611** CORYAT *Crudities* 23 As for their Exchang[e] where they sell many fine and curious things, there are two or three prety walks in it. **1632** MASSINGER *City Madam* I. i, Being forced to fetch these from the Old Exchange, These from the Tower, and these from Westminster. **1710** *Lond. Gaz.* No. 4708/4 Inquire at the..Royal Exchange East Country-Walk in Exchange Time. **1716–8** LADY M. W. MONTAGUE *Lett.* I. xxxviii. 154 Behind the mosque is an exchange, full of shops. **1790** J. WILLOCK *Voy. diverse parts* ix. 298 The exchange [Königsberg] is a beautiful edifice. **1848** DICKENS *Dombey* iv, The Royal Exchange was close at hand.

fig. **1628** EARLE *Microcosm.* liii. (Arb.) 73 It [Pauls Walke] is the great Exchange of all discourse. **1643** DENHAM *Cooper's Hill* 188 His [Thames'] fair bosom is the world's exchange. **1793** BURKE *Corr.* (1844) IV. 196 Sir Gilbert Elliot is not found in a common shop of the diplomatic exchange. **1886** D. C. MURRAY *Cynic Fortune* vi, Fairy banknotes which are only valuable at the Exchange of Fancy.

b. Preceded by some defining word that indicates a special branch of business: as ***coal-, corn-, hop-, stock-, wool-exchange***, for which see those words.

c. = *telephone exchange* (TELEPHONE *sb.* 3).

1887 J. M. W. YERRINGTON *Trial H.K. Goodwin* 11 Mr. Swan..became engaged in the telephone business..having charge of the Lawrence Exchange. **1888** *Encycl. Brit.* XXIII. 133/2 In a large town it is neither practicable nor desirable to connect each subscriber directly with all the other subscribers, hence a system of 'exchanges' has been adopted. **1938** D. DU MAURIER *Rebecca* xxv, Something was buzzing in the telephone. I heard Beatrice shouting, 'Hullo, hullo, don't cut us off, exchange,' and then there was a click, and silence.

11. *U.S.* A dram-shop.

1882 SALA *Amer. Revis.* II. ii. 13 Here [in New Orleans] the dram shops are called 'exchanges'.

12. a. *attrib.* and *Comb.* (sense 6) ***exchange-time***; (senses 3, 4) ***exchange-bank, -broker, -office, -shop***; also **exchange-cap** (see quot.); **exchange clearing** , a method of bilateral payment through central banks; **exchange control**, governmental control of purchases of foreign currency and of transfer of currency to foreign countries; **exchange force** *Physics*, an assumed force between atomic particles responsible for the exchange of charges or other co-ordinates; †**exchange-man**, (*a*) a merchant on Change; (*b*) a shopkeeper at the 'New Exchange'; **exchange paper** (see sense 7 b above); **exchange rate** = RATE *sb.*¹ 5 b (cf. *rate of exchange* under EXCHANGE *sb.* 4 a); **exchange transfusion**, the removal of some of a person's blood with the simultaneous transfusion of other (normal) blood; **exchange-value** = *exchangeable value*; †**exchange-wench, -woman**, a shopwoman at the 'New Exchange'.

1535 COVERDALE *Luke* xix. 23 Wherfore than hast thou not delyuered my money to the *exchaunge banke. **1704** COCKER App., *Exchange Brokers, men that tell how the Exchange of Money goes, and finds those that will Exchange. **1874** KNIGHT *Dict. Mech.* I. 815/1 *Exchange-cap*, a fine quality of paper..used for printing bills of exchange, etc. **1934** P. EINZIG *Exchange Control* xiii. 138 It is difficult even to get an adequate answer to the question as to what *Exchange Clearing really is. Some people simply class it with exchange restrictions. Technically, they are right, for the act of compelling importers to pay the purchase price to the Central Bank instead of..to their creditors undoubtedly interferes with..exchange operations. **1931** *Times* 5 Dec. 16/3 The Financial Committee and the Economic Committee of the League of Nations have placed the question of foreign *exchange control on their agenda. **1932** *Times* 1 Apr. 12/4 Concern is expressed..over the consequences of the exchange control measures and counter-measures in and around Austria. **1934** L. ROBBINS *Gt. Depression* viii. 179 A régime of this sort must necessitate the most extensive measures of exchange control. **1934** *Nature* 30 June 981/1 The possibility of deducing the *exchange forces between neutrons and protons. **1962** *Gloss. Terms Nuclear Sci.* (*B.S.I.*) 44 *Exchange force*, a type of force, acting between two particles, the mathematical expression of which involves an interchange of their coordinates. Such forces are thought to act between nucleons. **1631** DONNE *Polydoron* 108 There are three sorts of honest men: viz. your *Exchangeman for the bearing up of his credit, etc. **1783** AINSWORTH *Lat. Dict.* (Morell) II. *Nūgivendus*..an exchange-man, or milliner. **1863** FAWCETT *Pol. Econ.* III. ix. 416 A person wishing to exchange money for French money goes to an *exchange office in London. **1896** R. BARCLAY *Disturb. Stand. Value* (ed. 2) v. 134 The silver equivalents of the gold prices..would fall in view of the difference in *exchange rates. **1928** *Britain's Industrial Future* (*Lib. Ind. Inq.*) v. xxviii. 413 Stable foreign exchange-rates are not enough. **1631** T. POWELL *Tom All Trades* 48 A pretty way of breeding young Maides in an *Exchange shop, or St. Martins le grand. **1710** *Lond. Gaz.* No. 4708/4 In *Exchange Time. **1946** *Jrnl. Laboratory & Clinical Med.* XXXI. 1017 The main obstacle to the successful performance of an *exchange transfusion in infants is not the injection but the process of withdrawal, which is hampered by the coagulation of the infant's blood. **1963** *Lancet* 12 Jan. 86/1 For some years the umbilical vein in the umbilical cord has been used for exchange transfusions. **1970** *Glasgow Herald* 19 Nov. 1/7 Because of the deterioration of the sugar in the blood it was decided, after consultation, to carry out an exchange blood transfusion. **1863** FAWCETT *Pol. Econ.* I. i. (1876) 7 *Exchange value is the characteristic which stamps a commodity with the attribute of wealth. **1683** *England's Vanity* 32 Every *Exchange-Wench is usher'd in by them [Pearles] into her stalls. **1707** CIBBER *Double Gallant* IV, To treat a Woman of Quality like an Exchange-Wench. **1697** —— *Woman's Wit* III, Your Ladyship's being out of Humour with the *Exchange Woman, for shaping your Ruffles so odiously, made you a little too reserv'd.

b. *spec.* used ***attrib.*** to denote a reciprocal arrangement whereby two teachers, students, etc., occupy each other's position for a limited period of time; also designating one of the two parties in such an arrangement.

1912 *Nation* 6 June 555 The system of 'exchange professors' between France and the United States. **1934** H. MILLER *Tropic of Cancer* 265, I had been offered a trivial post as exchange professor of English, one of those Franco-American amity arrangements. **1936** L. C. DOUGLAS *White Banners* viii. 164 Springer of Cambridge..had just arrived as an exchange lecturer. **1953** D. PARRY *Going Up—Going Down* ii. 51, I might begin with an exchange-fellowship at Yale or Harvard. **1959** *Listener* 26 Feb. 364/1 Nowadays, more emphasis is placed on teaching foreign languages phonetically and on trying to tie lessons in with exchange visits of pupils abroad. **1960** *Encounter* Mar. 77/1 Young exchange students. **1966** J. CAIRD *Perturbing Spirit* xxiii. 253 She'd got an exchange teaching job for a year to the U.S.A. **1967** *Guardian* 29 May 8/5 British exchange teachers in the United States, and vice versa, are tax exempt.

exchange (ɛks'tʃeɪndʒ), *v.* Forms: (? 4 **schange**), 5, 7 **eschange**, 6 **exchaunge**, 6– **exchange**. [a. OF. *eschangier* (mod.F. *échanger*):—late L. *excambiāre*, f. *ex-* (see EX- *pref.*¹) + *cambiāre*: see CHANGE *v.*]

1. *trans.* To change away; to dispose of (commodities, possessions, etc.) by exchange or barter; to give, relinquish, or lose (something) whilst receiving something else in return. Also *absol.*

1484 CAXTON *Curiall* (1888) 13 They selle, bye or exchange somtyme theyr rentes or propre vestementis. **1545** *Act 37 Hen. VIII*, c. 9 §5 The Wares..so bargained, sold, exchanged or shifted. **1611** BIBLE *Ezek.* xlviii. 14 They shall not sell of it, neither exchange, nor alienate the first fruits of the land. **1808** *Hoyle's Game Chess* 19 When you have two pawns on a front line neither should be pushed forward until the adversary proposes to exchange. *Ibid.* Strive to capture or exchange those men which would prevent it [a direct attack]. **1835** I. TAYLOR *Spir. Despot.* ii. 30 Difficulties that may be exchanged sooner than avoided.

b. With *for* (†*with*) before the thing taken in exchange. In mod. use also with *against* (? after Fr. *contre*). Also *absol.*

1611 SHAKS. *Cymb.* I. v. 55 To shift his being, Is to exchange one misery with another. **1621** AINSWORTH *Annot. Pentat.* Gen. xxii. *heading*, Isaak is exchanged with a ram. *a* **1623** CAMDEN (J.), The king called in the old money and erected exchanges where the weight of old money was exchanged for new. **1680** MORDEN *Geog. Rect.*, *Tartary* (1685) 77 The Commodities that the Turks exchange for with the Inhabitants are Slaves. *a* **1704** LOCKE (J.), Exchange his sheep for shells, or wool for a sparkling pebble. **1786** W. THOMSON *Watson's Philip III* (1839) 243 He was impatient to exchange the luxury of a palace for the dangers and hardships of the field. **1833** [see AGAINST 14]. **1868** ROGERS *Pol. Econ.* iii. (ed. 3) 22 Where dealings are transacted on a large scale, it is not difficult for commodities to be exchanged against commodities. **1874** GREEN *Short*

Hist. iii. 123 The vague expressions of the older charters were now exchanged for precise and elaborate provisions.

†**c.** To obtain (something) in exchange *for*.

1588 SHAKS. *L.L.L.* IV. i. 84 What, shalt thou exchange for ragges, roabes. **1596** SPENSER *F.Q.* VII. vi. 6 Ne shee the lawes of Nature onely brake, But eke of Justice..And death for life exchanged foolishlie.

2. To give and receive reciprocally; to make an exchange of; to interchange. *Const.* sing. or pl. obj. *with* (a person).

1602 SHAKS. *Ham.* V. ii. 340 Exchange forgiuenesse with me, Noble Hamlet. **1611** —— *Wint. T.* IV. iv. 284 She wold not exchange flesh with one that lou'd her. **1698** LUDLOW *Mem.* (1721) I. 47 The great Shot was exchanged on both sides for the space of an Hour. **1711** ADDISON *Spect.* No. 12 ¶2, I do not remember that we have exchanged a Word together these five Years. **1797** MRS. RADCLIFFE *Italian* vii, Would we could exchange natures with him for a moment. **1832** HT. MARTINEAU *Each & All* vi. 79 They exchanged smiles, and understood one another immediately. **1844** H. H. WILSON *Brit. India* II. 417 No engagements of allegiance or protection had ever been exchanged. **1855** MACAULAY *Hist. Eng.* III. 5 Blows were exchanged.

3. *Mil.* and *Naval.* **a.** To give up a prisoner to the enemy in return for one taken by them.

1726 TINDAL *Rapin's Hist. Eng.* (ed. 2) I. 207/2 Matilda.. consented he should be exchanged for the King. **1853** STOCQUELER *Mil. Encycl.*, *Prisoners of War* are deprived of their liberty until regularly exchanged. **1860** WOOLSEY *Introd. Internat. Law* §146. 336 Prisoners are generally exchanged within the same rank man for man.

b. *absol.* To pass, by exchange with another officer, *from* or *out of* one regiment or ship *into* another. Cf. EXCHANGE *sb.* 1 e.

1787 NELSON 10 July in Nicolas *Disp.* (1845) I. 243 Lieutenant Hope wished to exchange out of the Pegasus into the Boreas. **1875** GATHORNE HARDY *Sp. Ho. Com.* 22 Feb., A poor man may find himself in positions where he could not exchange. **1875** TREVELYAN *ibid.*, The officer above them who refuses to exchange out of the battalion.

4. *intr.* Chiefly of coin: To be received as an equivalent *for*.

1776 ADAM SMITH *W.N.* I. xi. (1855) 89 In 1695..the value of the silver coin was not kept up by the gold coin; a guinea then commonly exchanging for thirty shillings of the worn and clipt silver. **1848** MILL *Pol. Econ.* III. iii. §2 Demand and supply always rush to an equilibrium, but the condition of stable equilibrium is when things exchange for each other according to their cost of production. **1890** *Sat. Rev.* 3 May 531/2 An English sovereign exchanged a little while ago for thirteen rupees.

5. *trans.* = CHANGE *v.* 6. Also *to exchange into* = CHANGE *v.* 6 b.

The first quot. may belong to CHANGE *v.*; *schaungen* appears among the forms of that word in 14th c.

a **1300** *Cursor M.* 479 (Gött.) Fra þan his [Lucifer's] name schangid was, Now es he cald foule sathanas. **1548** GEST *Pr. Masse* 83 Can it be hys bodye, onles it be exchaunged into it? **1586** A. DAY *Eng. Secretary* I. (1625) 144 But..as it much differeth..from the other, is also alike exchanged by title, that one tearmed..Friendship, and this other..Love. *c* **1600** SHAKS. *Sonn.* cix, I returne againe, Just to the time, not with the time exchang'd.

exchangeability (ɛksˌtʃeɪndʒəˈbɪlɪtɪ). [f. next: see -ITY.] The quality or condition of being exchangeable.

1778 WASHINGTON *Let.* 8 Mar., Wks. 1834 V. 260 To fix their [captured citizens'] exchangeability upon the easiest and most unequivocal foundation. **1833** *New Monthly Mag.* XXXVII. 501 Mr. Bailey seems to mistake exchangeability for value. **1861** GOSCHEN *For. Exch.* 10 To inquire how the rate of interest..the depreciation of the currency in which the bills are payable, affect their exchangeability.

exchangeable (ɛksˈtʃeɪndʒəb(ə)l), *a.* [f. EXCHANGE *v.* + -ABLE.]

1. That may be exchanged. Const. *for.*

1651 HOBBES *Leviath.* II. xxiv. 127 A mans Labour also, is a commodity exchangeable for benefit. **1778** WASHINGTON *Let.* 8 Mar., Wks. 1834 V. 255 On condition of General Lee being declared exchangeable. **1840** *Tait's Mag.* VII. 638 The notes..are..not easily exchangeable. **1869** TYNDALL *Notes on Light* 14 In optics, the position of an object and of its image are always exchangeable.

2. *exchangeable value*: value estimated by that of the goods for which a thing may be exchanged.

1776 ADAM SMITH *W.N.* (1806) I. I. iv. 38 The principles which regulate the exchangeable value of commodities. **1821** TORRENS *Product. Wealth* 10 Nothing but a vague and inaccurate use of language could have led to the notion that exchangeable value constitutes wealth. **1834** HT. MARTINEAU *Moral* III. 86 It is labour which confers exchangeable value. **1862** RUSKIN *Unto this Last* 114 How good must meat be, in order to possess any exchangeable value?

†**3.** = COMMUTATIVE 1 b. *Obs. rare.*

1575 T. ROGERS *Sec. Coming Christ* 34 a, This Arithmetical proportion Aristotle ascribeth the exchaungeable iustice.

Hence **ex'changeably** *adv.*

1598 FLORIO, *Scambiéuole*, by exchange, mutuall, exchangeablie.

exchanger (ɛksˈtʃeɪndʒə(r)). Also 7 (in *Law*) -or. [f. as prec. + -ER¹.]

1. One who exchanges or makes an exchange.

1531-2 *Act 23 Hen. VIII*, c. 16 The same sale, exchaunge or deliuere..shalbe..felony..in the seller, exchaunger or deliuerer. **1613** SIR H. FINCH *Law* (1636) 116 The exchangor or his heire may vouch to warranty by an exchange without deed. **1642** PERKINS *Prof. Bk.* iv. §263 If any of us the Exchangers dye before attornment it is not good.

†**2.** A money-changer, an exchange-broker; a money-dealer, banker. *Obs.* exc. with allusion to the N.T. †*the King's Exchangers*: officers appointed by the king to give coin in exchange for bullion or plate.

1539 BIBLE (Great) *Matt.* xxv. 27 Thou oughtest therfore to haue delyuered my money to the exchaungers. **1552** *Act 5-6 Edw. VI*, c. 19 §1 No man did..take no Profit for making of such Exchange..except the Kings Exchangers. **1584** FENNER *Def. Ministers* (1587) 98 Christ overthrew the exchaungers banckes. **1682** SCARLETT *Exchanges* 103 An Exchanger should know in the places where Banks are kept, the ordinary times when the Banks are shut. *a* **1704** LOCKE (J.), These exchangers generally chuse rather to buy bullion than run the risk of melting down our coin. **1866** CRUMP *Banking* i. 9 They [*mensularii*] were also authorised by the state to act as exchangers, and give Roman coins for foreign ones.

exchanging (ɛksˈtʃeɪndʒɪŋ), *vbl. sb.* [f. as prec. + -ING¹.] The action of the vb. EXCHANGE.

1553 EDEN *Treat. Newe Ind.* (Arb.) 17 At which exchaunging of wyues, one of them speaketh to another after this manner. **1594** HOOKER *Eccl. Pol.* II. i. (1611) 129 This was the ancient manner in Israel concerning redeeming and exchanging. **1671** H. M. tr. *Erasm. Colloq.* 385 Doth God accept of such exchangings of souls? **1819** in Picton *L'pool Munic. Rec.* (1886) II. 339 Renewal of leases and the exchanging of lives thereon.

excheat, -or, altered forms of ESCHEAT, -OR.

exchequer (ɛksˈtʃɛkə(r)). Forms: 3-6 escheker(e, (4 eschekkere, 4-5 ess-, estcheker), 5-7 eschequer, -eer, excheker, -yr, (6 escheaquer, eschequier, -our, 7 exchecker), 6- exchequer. [ME. *escheker*, a. OF. *eschequier* (mod.F. *échiquier*) = It. *scaccario*, med.L. *scaccārium* chess-board, f. *scacc-us* check, *scacchi* chess: see -ARIUM, -ER. The modern *exchequer* is a literary corruption, caused by mistaking *es-* in this word for the OF. *es-*:—L. *ex-*, as in *eschange*, L. *excambium*, now EXCHANGE, *esploit*, L. *explicitum*, now EXPLOIT, etc. When these words were refashioned after L. analogies, *escheker* was ignorantly altered in the same way. For the derivation see CHEQUER, CHECK.]

†**I. 1.** A chess-board; = CHEQUER *sb.*¹ 1. *to play at* (*to*) *the escheker*: to play at chess. *Obs.*

a **1300** *Floriz & Bl.* 344 He wule come þe nier And bidde þe pleie at þe escheker. Whane þescheker is forþ ibroȝt Biþute panes ne plei þu noȝt. *c* **1380** *Sir Ferumb.* 2224 Þo þat willieþ to leue at hame pleyeþ to þe eschekkere. *a* **1420** HOCCLEVE *MS. Soc. Antiq.* 134 fol. 263 (Halliw.) And alle be hit that in that place square Of the listes, I mene the estcheker. **1474** CAXTON *Chesse* 135 Ther ben as many poyntes in the eschequer voyde as fulle.

II. The King's Exchequer.

2. Under the Norman and Angevin kings of England: An office or department of state managed by the Treasurer, the Justiciary and the other judges of the King's Court, and certain Barons appointed by the King. Its functions combined the collection and administration of the royal revenues with the judicial determination of all causes relating to revenue. In the subsequent development of this institution, it was gradually divided into two distinct branches, the one being charged with judicial, the other with administrative functions: see 3, 4.

The name originally referred to the table covered with a cloth divided into squares, on which the accounts of the revenue were kept by means of counters. It is disputed whether the application of the word to the treasury and the tribunal connected with it originated in Normandy, or whether it was imported into Normandy from England. After Normandy became part of France, the supreme court of law in that province continued to bear the name of *eschequier* until the reign of Francis I, when this name was superseded by that of *parlement*.

[**1292** BRITTON I. i. §9 Ausi volums nous, qe a nos Eschekers a Westmoster et aylours eynt nos Thresorers et nos Barouns illuex jurisdiccioun. **1332** *Literæ Cantuarienses* (Rolls) ccclv. I. 480 Noz seriantz..vienent a Canterbire a nostre Eschekier pur loure acounte rendre.] *c* **1330** R. BRUNNE *Chron.* (1810) 280 To Berwik cam þe kynge eschekere, Sir Hugh of Cressyngham he was chancelere, Walter of Admundesham he was tresorere. **1875** STUBBS *Const. Hist.* I. xi. 377 The Exchequer of the Norman kings was the court in which the whole financial business of the country was transacted.

b. *Chancellor of the Exchequer*: an officer originally appointed in the reign of Henry III. as assistant to the treasurer; now the responsible finance minister of the United Kingdom: see CHANCELLOR 3.

c. *Exchequer of the Jews* (L. *scaccarium Judæorum*): in the thirteenth century, a department of the Exchequer which had charge of the collection of the revenues exacted from the Jews. (See C. Gross *Exchequer of the Jews* in *Papers read at the Anglo-Jewish Exhibition*, 1887.)

3. (More fully *Court of Exchequer*, *Exchequer of Pleas*.) A court of law, historically representing the Anglo-Norman exchequer in its judicial capacity. By the Judicature Act of 1873 it was converted into 'The Exchequer Division' of the High Court of Justice, and by Order in Council in 1881 this was merged in the Queen's Bench Division.

The jurisdiction of the court was theoretically confined to matters of revenue, but in practice was gradually extended to all kinds of cases (except 'real actions') by means of the legal fiction that the wrong suffered by the plaintiff had rendered him unable to pay his debts to the king. In addition to its jurisdiction at common law, the court had a jurisdiction in equity, abolished in 1841. In its latest form it consisted of the Chief Baron and five judges, called the Barons of the Exchequer; the Chancellor of the Exchequer was in theory a member of it, and was entitled to a voice in its decisions when it sat in equity.

1489-90 *Plumpton Corr.* 90 Your matter in the Excheker is grevous; there is iij wryttes agaynst you. *a* **1553** UDALL *Royster D.* v. vi. (1847) 85 For sure I will put you up into the Escheker. **1661** J. STEPHENS *Procurations* 34 It is an hundred years since the Certificate upon the Commission of *Melius inquirendum*..was returned into the Exchequer. **1732** POPE *Hor. Sat.* II. ii. 130 The Temple late two brother Serjeants saw..One lull'd th' Exchequer, and one stunn'd the Rolls. **1816** J. MANNING (*title*), The Practice of the Exchequer of Pleas. **1827** [see ESTREAT *v.* 1].

fig. **1814** SCOTT *Wav.* xxiv, I cannot call you into Exchequer, if you do not think proper to read my narrative.

b. As the designation of analogous courts in Scotland and Ireland: see quots. The Exchequer of Scotland was abolished in 1856 (19 and 20 Vict. c. 6), its functions being transferred to the Court of Session.

1816 *Encycl. Perth.* IX. 204/2 The court of exchequer in Scotland has the same privileges and jurisdiction as that of England. **1833** *Act 3 & 4 Will. IV*, c. 13 All the Powers at present exercised by the said Barons of the Court of Exchequer in Scotland shall from and after the passing of this Act cease and determine.

4. The office or department of the public service, which is charged with the receipt and custody of the moneys collected by the several departments of revenue.

In early use not distinguished from TREASURY; but the department of state called the Treasury has not since the 15th century exercised directly the function etymologically indicated by its name. The office charged with the custody of the revenues was in theory a branch of the Court of Exchequer (see 3), and was sometimes called *the Lower Exchequer*, *the Exchequer of Receipt*, or *Receipt of Exchequer*, to distinguish it from the judicial branch (*Exchequer of Pleas*). By the Exchequer and Audit Act 1866, the offices of Comptroller of the Exchequer and Auditor General, and the departments over which they presided, were united.

a **1420** HOCCLEVE *De Reg. Princ.* 68 Syn thou maist not be paied in the escheker. *c* **1460** FORTESCUE *Abs. & Lim. Mon.* (1714) 43 The expensys of which Houshold may sone be estemyd..by the Clerks of the Escheker. **1555** EDEN *Decades* 133 The fyfthe portion dewe to the kynges Exeheker. **1574** tr. *Littleton's Tenures* 33 b, To bee one of his [the kynges] chamberlaines of his receite of his Eschequer. **1601** F. TATE *Househ. Ord. Edw. II*, §4 (1876) 7 The Contrerollour ought to keepe a countre roll against the tresorer of the warderobe..and testefy it in thexcheker upon the thresorers account. **1638** DK. HAMILTON in *H. Papers* (Camden) 54 Itt onlie restheth hou he shall be payed, for in your excheker heire ther is none. **1672** COWEL *Interpr.* s.v., The other [part of the court] is called The Receit of the Exchequer, which is properly employed in the receiving and paying of Money. **1753** CHAMBERS *Cycl. Supp.* s.v., Exchequer is more particularly used for a chamber, or apartment, in Westminster-hall, consisting of two parts.. the lower Exchequer. **1788** PRIESTLEY *Lect. Hist.* v. lxiv. 514 The money is lying in the exchequer to discharge the interest of the old debt. **1876** BANCROFT *Hist. U.S.* III. vi. 370 His [Grenville's] desire was for..a tellership in the exchequer.

b. *the Exchequer*: short for 'the contents of the Exchequer'.

1647 CLARENDON *Hist. Reb.* I. (1843) 2/1 The exchequer being so exhausted with the debts of king James. **1671** C. HATTON in *Hatton Corr.* (1878) 62 Yᵉ exchequer is at soe low an ebbe.

5. In extended sense: A royal or national treasury.

1565-73 COOPER *Thesaurus*, *Ad ærarium rationes has referre*, to bring in his accompt to the escheker. **1600** HOLLAND *Livy* XXIV. xxiv. 525 The souldiours were..dayly mainteined and fed out of the Kings eschequer. **1756-7** tr. *Keysler's Trav.* (1760) IV. 222 The exchequer for Hungary is kept at Presburg. **1783** WATSON *Philip III* (1839) 221 For the benefit of his exchequer, he might sell the rest for slaves to his Christian subjects in Spain and Italy. **1844** H. H. WILSON *Brit. India* II. 471 A surplus revenue and an unembarrassed exchequer. **1855** PRESCOTT *Philip II*, I. ii. (1857) 19 It seemed to his Spanish subjects that he rarely visited them, except when his exchequer required to be replenished.

b. *fig.* (Common in 17th c.; now *rare*.)

1589 NASHE *Greene's Arcadia* Pref. (1616) 6 The Exchequer of eloquence, Sir John Cheeke. **1596** —— *Saffron Walden* 75 He would..bee a more rare Exchequer of the Muses, than rich Gaza for wealth. **1633** HEYWOOD *Eng. Trav.* II. Wks. 1874 IV. 31 Of all the Treasures of my Hopes and Loue, You were th' Exchequer, they were Stor'd in you. **1660** BOYLE *Seraph. Love* xiv. (1700) 91 Love itself (that poor man's Surety and Exchequer). **1737** M. GREEN *Spleen* (R.), School-helps I want, to..commit a theft On wealth in Greek exchequers left. **1881** G. W. CABLE *Mme. Delphine* ii. 10 The soul of honour..frank—the very exchequer of truth.

6. *transf.* The pecuniary possessions, the 'cash-box', 'purse', of a private person, a society, etc.

1618 BOLTON *Florus* (1636) 216 The poore should live upon their own exchequer. **1675** TRAHERNE *Chr. Ethics*

xxviii. 455 A palace and a coach, an exchequer full of gold.. are all the grounds of the respect that they pay us. **1685** SOUTH *Serm.* (1737) I. x. 384 A command, or call to be liberal..shuts up every private man's exchequer. **1823** LAMB *Elia* (1867) 32 These were..feeders of his exchequer ..to whom he had occasionally been beholden for a loan. **1855** THACKERAY *Fatal Boots* iii, The..impoverished state of my exchequer.

7. *attrib.* and *Comb.*, as ***exchequer-book, -bullion, -chancellor*** (rare), ***-standard***. Also **exchequer-bill**, a bill of credit issued by authority of Parliament (first in 1696), bearing interest at the current rate; hence **exchequer-bill-office**, the office where exchequer-bills are issued and received; **exchequer-bond**, a bond (see BOND 10) issued by the Exchequer at a fixed rate of interest and for a fixed period; **exchequer-court** = *Court of Exchequer* (see 3); also, 'the Prerogative Court of the Archbishop of York' (Bailey); **exchequer-man**, an official of the exchequer; **exchequer-note** = ***exchequer-bill***; **exchequer-tallies** (see TALLY), the notched sticks with which the accounts of the Exchequer were formerly kept. Also EXCHEQUER-CHAMBER.

1701 *Lond. Gaz.* No. 3694/4 Lost..3 *Exchequer Bills of 5*l.* each. **1799** *Hist. Europe* in *Ann. Reg.* 191/1 Exchequer-bills to the amount of £3,000,000. **1855** MACAULAY *Hist. Eng.* IV. 698 In the midst of the general distress and confusion appeared the first Exchequer Bills. **1813** *Examiner* 12 Apr. 237/1 A crowd of brokers..beset the *Exchequer-Bill-Office. **1859** MᶜCULLOCH *Dict. Commerce* 611 In 1853 *Exchequer Bonds were issued bearing interest at 2¾ per cent. for ten years. **1824** R. WATT *Bibl. Brit.* 410/1 The *Exchequer Book, entitled Liber Niger Scaccarii. **1805** P. L. D. BONHOTE (*title*) Logarithm Tables, adapted to the calculation of *Exchequer Bullion. **1824** BYRON *Juan* XVI. xcviii, All *Exchequer Chancellors endeavour..to dispense with Cocker's rigours. **1721–1800** BAILEY, **Exchequer Court.* **1853** MARSDEN *Early Purit.* 401 A merchant of London was brought before the exchequer court for not paying tonnage and poundage. **1579** TOMSON *Calvin's Serm. Tim.* 223 1 We shall lack no *Exchequer man to put vs in shute. **1625** in Rushw. *Hist. Coll.* (1659) I. 207 The Exchequer-man making his profit from the Kings wants. **1795** *Hist. Europe* in *Ann. Reg.* 1796, 70/1 The discount given occasionally on *Exchequer notes was equally discreditable and alarming. **1653** R. MASON in Bulwer *Anthropomet.* Let. to Author, And so insolently violate the *Exchequer standard of Heaven without a blush. **1690** CHILD *Disc. Trade* (ed. 4) 21 Such as have disposed of his Majesty's *Exchequer-tallies.

exchequer (ɛks'tʃɛkə(r)), *v.* [f. prec.]

1. *trans.* To place in an exchequer or treasury; to treasure up. *Obs. rare*⁻¹.

1705 HICKERINGILL *Priest-cr.* II. vii. 67 Vast Bulk and Heaps of Treasure exchequer'd in the Lateran Palace.

2. To proceed against (a person) in the Court of Exchequer.

1809 *Chron.* in *Ann. Reg.* 408/2 The lord was exchequered; that is, the attorney-general filed his information against him. **1844** J. T. HEWLETT *Parsons & W.* xl, If ever he heard of Titus..shooting..on his grounds again, he would exchequer him as sure as he was born. **1864** SIR F. PALGRAVE *Norm. & Eng.* IV. 215 Anselm was Exchequered for the imputed fault.

b. (See quot. 1867.)

1828 SOUTHEY in *Q. Rev.* XXXVIII. 93 The vessel was seized by a custom-house officer, brought back and exchequered. **1867** SMYTH *Sailor's Word-bk*, *Exchequered*, seized by government officers as contraband.

exchequer-chamber. Also CHEQUER-CHAMBER.

1. The chamber devoted to the business of the royal exchequer.

[**1494–1611**: see CHEQUER-CHAMBER 1.] **1819** *Pantologia* s.v. *Exchequer*, The court of equity is held in the exchequer chamber before the treasurer, chancellor, and barons.

2. 'A tribunal of error and appeal' (Wharton) abolished in 1875 by the Judicature Acts, which transferred its jurisdiction to the Court of Appeal.

[**1528–1714**: see CHEQUER-CHAMBER 2.] **1640** SAINT-JOHN (*title*), Argument on the case of Ship-money, before the Judges in the Exchequer-Chamber. **1768** BLACKSTONE *Comm.* III. 56 The court of exchequer chamber..then consists of all the judges of the three superior courts. **1827** HALLAM *Const. Hist.* (1876) II. xviii. 18 The cause..was heard..before all the judges in the exchequer-chamber. **1838** *Penny Cycl.* X. 110/2 The Court of Exchequer chamber was first erected in England by stat. 31 Edw. III. **1848** WHARTON *Law Lex.* s.v. *Exchequer*. The 40 Geo. III. c. 39, established a Court of Exchequer Chamber in Ireland.

exchete, -er, -our, obs. f. ESCHEAT, -OR.

exchew(e, -chue, obs. ff. ESCHEW *v.*¹

excide (ɛk'saɪd), *v.*¹ [ad. L. *excīdĕ-re* to cut out, f. *ex-* out + *cædĕre* to cut.] *trans.* To cut out. Also *fig.* Hence **ex'cided** *ppl. a.*

1758 J. S. *Le Dran's Observ. Surg.* (1771) 78 We were obliged to excide..the Bigness of a large Nut. **1819** LAMB *Final Mem., To Wordsw.* 250 The gods..cut off every seed of envy in his bosom. But with envy they excided curiosity also. **1883** *American* VI. 397 The excided parts. **1888** GLADSTONE in *19th Cent.* May 781 Our Lord's divinity draws after it all that Robert Elsmere would excide.

†**ex'cidion.** *Obs. rare*⁻¹. [ad. L. *excidiōnem* destruction, believed to be f. *exscid-*, *exscindĕre* to extirpate, destroy, f. *ex-* out + *scindĕre* to cut.] Extirpation, destruction.

1490 CAXTON *Eneydos* i. (1890) 11 Troye was enuyronned in fourme of siege, and of excidyon, by Agamenon.

excimer ('ɛksɪmə(r)). *Chem.* [f. EXCI(TED *ppl. a.* + DIMER.] **1.** An exciplex; *spec.* one formed from two identical atoms or molecules.

1960 STEVENS & HUTTON in *Nature* 25 June 1046/2 These properties of the collisionally formed excited dimer which has virtually the lifetime of a triplet state and the multiplicity of a singlet state are those of an ideal sensitizer ...We suggest the term 'excimer' be used to distinguish it from the short-lived dimer excited directly in solutions exhibiting an absorption spectrum dependent on concentration. **1962** *Ibid.* 6 Oct. 34/2 The difference by a factor of 2 between the excimer components of the observed mixture spectrum *Z* and (*A*+*B*) is therefore attributed to 'mixed excimers' (*AB*)*. **1972** DEPUY & CHAPMAN *Molec. Reactions & Photochem.* iv. 53 These dimers may be formed via an excimer..derived from the $^3(\pi, \pi^*)$ cyclohexenone and a molecule of ground state cyclohexenone. **1979** MATAGA & OTTOLENGHI in R. Foster *Molecular Assoc.* II. i. 2 Excimer formation has now been observed for a multitude of aromatic hydrocarbons and their derivatives in fluid solutions. Excimers are also known in crystals and in low-temperature rigid solvents.

2. Special Comb.: **excimer laser**, a laser in which an excimer is used as the excited state for stimulated emission.

1973 S. E. HARRIS *Investigation Laser Dynamics* (NASA Rep. CR-136024), Studies of the sodium-xenon excimer laser. **1985** *Time* 11 Mar. 21/2 Excimer lasers..produce beams of short wavelengths that could destroy a missile by focusing on it for only a second. **1986** *New Scientist* 13 Nov. 44/1 The excimer laser..emits ultraviolet light that cuts and marks materials without damaging them with heat...They are gas lasers that emit light when a halogen atom and a rare gas atom combine temporarily.

†**ex'cipient,** *a.* and *sb. Obs.* [ad. L. *excipient-em*, pr. pple. of *excipĕre* to take out, except, take up, receive, f. *ex-* out + *capĕre* to take.]

A. *adj.* That takes exception; objecting.

1726 AYLIFFE *Parerg.* 252 The persons pronouncing it [Excommunication], ought to be set forth in the Pleading by the Party Excipient within eight Days.

B. *sb.* **1.** One who takes up or receives in succession. *rare.*

1852 *Tait's Mag.* XIX. 605 That excipient of avuncular traditions first quotes from the reply made by Napoleon.

2. (See quot. 1753.)

1753 CHAMBERS *Cycl. Supp.*, *Excipient*..a term used to express that ingredient in a compound medicine, the business of which is to receive all the rest; such is the conserve in electuaries, the syrup in bolusses, &c. **1831** J. DAVIES *Manual Mat. Med.* 25 The excipient serves as a vehicle. **1890** *Nation* (N.Y.) 10 Apr. 287/2 Sugar of milk.. as an excipient in such medicines as lacto-peptine, pepsine, etc.

3. The material or surface that receives the pigments in painting.

1855 tr. *Labarte's Arts Mid. Ages* iv. 101 Painting on a metallic excipient.

exciple ('ɛksɪp(ə)l), **excipule** ('ɛksɪpju:l). Anglicized forms of EXCIPULUM.

1866 in *Treas. Bot.*

exciplex ('ɛksɪplɛks). *Chem.* [f. EXCI(TED *ppl. a.* + COM)PLEX *sb.*] A molecule formed by a metastable bond between two atoms or molecules and existing only in an excited state, from which it dissociates into the constituent atoms or molecules. Cf. EXCIMER.

1966 M. WALKER et al. in *Jrnl. Chem. Physics* 3456/1 The results appear to confirm the existence of 1:2 excited complex states, which we have termed exciplex states, for both solutes. **1972** DEPUY & CHAPMAN *Molec. Reactions & Photochem.* iv. 50 It is probable that the reaction involves an exciplex..that collapses to the biradical. **1976** K. DAVIS in R. Foster *Molecular Association* I. iii. 187 For systems in which no ground-state complex formation is detectable, formation of a complex is possible between an excited donor (or acceptor) and a ground-state acceptor (or donor)... Such a complex has been termed..an 'exciplex' or excited state complex and is similar to the complex formed between an excited-state molecule and a ground-state molecule of the same species termed an excimer. **1984** *Science* 23 Nov. 917/1 Electronically excited molecules, being better electron donors and acceptors than their ground states, form charge-transfer complexes (exciplexes) which can lead to radical ions. Ex(iplex emission is widely used to probe polymers and organized media such as membranes and micelles.

‖**excipulum** (ɛk'sɪpjʊləm). *Bot.* [L. *excipulum* a receptacle, found only in pl., f. *excipĕre*: see EXCIPIENT.] A layer of cells lying beneath and partially enclosing, as a cup, the APOTHECIUM (q.v.) in lichens.

1857 BERKELEY *Cryptog. Bot.* §292. 284 The form of the aperture depends upon the form of the apothecium, or excipulum, the margins of which are rounded. **1874** COOKE *Fungi* 37 There is no proper excipulum or peridium. **1882** VINES *Sachs' Bot.* 324 The part of the thallus which surrounds the excipulum rises and grows with it forming a bowl-like rim.

excisable (ɛk'saɪzəb(ə)l), *a.*¹ [f. EXCISE *v.*¹ + -ABLE.] Needing to be excised or expunged.

1855 *Chamb. Jrnl.* IV. 362 There are excisable passages in Shakspeare.

excisable (ɛk'saɪzəb(ə)l), *a.*² Also 7–9 exciseable. [f. EXCISE *v.*² + -ABLE.] Of things: Liable or subject to excise duty. Of persons: Liable to the imposition of excise duty.

1689 *Lond. Gaz.* No. 2416/3 The Brewers and Retailers of Excisable Liquors. **1797** BURKE *Regic. Peace* iii. Wks. VIII. 406 The general licences which the law requires to be taken out by all dealers in exciseable commodities. **1858** BRIGHT *Sp. Reform* 21 Dec., Every man who..consumes any exciseable articles, pays taxes. **1876** BANCROFT *Hist. U.S.* III. xxii. 563 The Americans were henceforward excisable and taxable at the mercy of parliament. *Mod. Advt.*, I, A.B. ..do hereby give notice that it is my intention to apply..for a License to sell Excisable Liquors by Retail.

excise ('ɛksaɪz, ɛk'saɪz), *sb.* Also 5, 7 excyse, 7 accize, 7–8 accise. [app. a. MDu. *excijs, exziis* (1406 in *Keurboeken van de Stad Leiden* 14), also *accijs*, prob. ad. OF. *acceis* tax (12th c., riming with *defeis*:—L. *defēnsum*) or some earlier form:— late L. type **accēnsum*, verbal sb. f. *accēnsāre* to tax (whence OF. *accenser, acenser*), f. *ad* to + *cēnsus* tax: see CENSUS.

OF. had also the learned form *accens*, whence prob. MDu. *excijns, exchijns*, mod.Du. *accijns*. For the treatment of late L. or primitive Romanic *ē(n)s* in early adoptions into Du., cf. Du. *spijs* viand, repr. late L. *expēnsa*, and *cijns* repr. L. *cēnsus*. The mod.F. *accise* occurs only with reference to the Low Countries and England, and is prob. adopted from Du. A med.L. *accisia* is mentioned by Du Cange (who gives no quots.) as occurring in imperial documents as a variant of *assisa* (see ASSIZE *sb.*); this may be a latinization of the MDu. word. In Du. the two words *accijs* 'excise' and *assijs* 'assize' have been to a great extent confused, having both the meaning 'tax'; the Du. etymologists regard the former as a corruption of the latter, and the form *accijns* as a further corruption due to confusion with *cijns*, Lat. *census*. By Lat. writers in the Low Countries (16–17th c.) the word is often rendered by *excensus*. The notion of derivation from L. *excisum* 'something cut out' (cf. EXCISE *v.*¹) may have been the cause of the substitution of *ex-* for *ac-* in the MDu. form.]

1. *gen.* Any toll or tax.

[**1490** *Commercial Treaty Eng. & Florence* in Rymer *Fœd.* XII. 391 Quas excisas, gabellas, et dacias dicti subditi Regis Angliæ in dicta civitate Pisarum solvent et dabunt.] **1494** FABYAN *Chron.* VII. 505 As well by chaungynge of the moneys as other many vnlefull excysys. **1555** BRADFORD in Strype *Eccl. Mem.* III. App. xlv. 135 So wyll they..bringe in excises upon cytie and vyllage. **1622** MALYNES *Anc. Law-Merch.* 193 Whereas Customes, Subsidies, Impositions, Toles, Accizes, Imposts and other duties..are due by the Law of Nations. **1631** MASSINGER *Emperor East* I. ii, No man should dare To..kill a hen Without excise. *a* **1763** SHENSTONE *Levities, Stanzas*, He..Full gladly pays four parts in eight To taxes and excises.

2. *spec.* 'A duty charged on home goods, either in the process of their manufacture or before their sale to the home consumers' (*Encycl. Brit.*). In England this kind of taxation was first adopted in 1643, in acknowledged imitation of the example of Holland. It long continued to be highly unpopular: see Johnson's definition below.

The taxes levied under the name of Excise by the Ordinance of 1643 included certain duties imposed, in addition to the customs, on various foreign products; it was not until the present century that the actual use of the word became strictly conformed to the preceding definition.

a. in Holland.

1596 SPENSER *State Irel.* Wks. (Globe) 669/2 All the townes of the Lowe-Countreyes doe cutt upon themselves an excise of all things towarde the mayntenaunce of the warre. **1613** in *North. N. & Q.* I. 73 The Consergerie is frie of all excyses of wyne and beir. *c* **1645** HOWELL *Lett.* I. I. vii, The monstrous Accises which are impos'd upon all sorts of Commodities [in Amsterdam]. **1665** *Surv. Aff. Netherl.* 193 Their very enemies, though they hate the States, yet love their Liquor, and pay Excise. **1690** CHILD *Disc. Trade* (ed. 4) 5 The lowness of their customs, and the height of their excise, which is certainly the most equal and indifferent tax in the world.

b. in England or the United Kingdom.

1642 *Declar. Ho. Com.* 8 Oct., Aspersions are by malignant persons cast upon this House that they intend to ..lay excizes upon..commodities. **1643** *Ord. Lords & Com.* 22 July §2 An Office..is hereby erected..called or known by the name of the Office of Excise or New Impost. **1647** CLARENDON *Hist. Reb.* VII. (1843) 471/1 This [July 22, 1643] was the first time that ever the name of the payment of excise was heard of, or practised in England. **1667** MARVELL *To a Painter*, Excise..With hundred rows of teeth, the shark exceeds, And on all trades like Cassawar she feeds. **1755** JOHNSON *Excise*, a hateful tax levied upon commodities, and adjudged not by the common judges of property, but wretches hired by those to whom excise is paid. **1776** ADAM SMITH *W.N.* (1869) II. v. ii. 492 Such duties..become properly a sort of inland customs or excises. **1845** MᶜCULLOCH *Taxation* II. vi. §1 (1852) 271 The duty on bricks, the article most recently subjected to the excise, was imposed in 1784.

c. in the United States.

1789 T. JEFFERSON *Writ.* (1859) III. 17 Excise is a duty.. paid in the hands of the consumer or retailer. *Ibid.* But in Massachusetts they have perverted the word excise to mean a tax on all liquors, whether paid in the moment of importation or at a later moment, and on nothing else. **1875** A. DELMAR in *Johnson's New Univ. Encycl.*, Excise..in the U.S...is confined to the tax on the production or sale of spirituous or fermented liquors, or the productive capacity of liquor stills, revenue from liquor stamps, etc.

d. ***Board, Commissioner, Officer, Supervisor of Excise,*** or ***Excise Revenue.***

1695 LUTTRELL *Brief Rel.* 16 Jan., The officers of the excise there [Bristol] will be dismist. **1724** WATTS *Logic* 52 A supervisor of the excise. **1815** SCOTT *Guy M.* iii, I hae a cousin at the board of excise—that's Commissioner Bertram. **1819** *Pantologia* s.v. *Excise laws*, The officers of

excise are to be appointed..by the commissioners. *Ibid.* s.v. *Excise laws*, Commissioners of excise are empowered to make restitution of exciseable goods. **1838** *Penny Cycl.* X. 111/2 The commissioners of excise revenue.

e. *transf.* and *fig.*

1658 F. OSBORNE *Hist. Mem. Q. Eliz.* 36 *Greatnesse, seldome admitted to a cheap Market*: Sellers recompensing their want of honour, by the Excise they put on such as owne it. *a* **1659** CLEVELAND (J.), Ambitious now to take excise Of a more fragrant paradise. *a* **1683** OLDHAM *Poet. Wks.* (1686) 95 And for each pleasurable sin exacts excise.

3. Payment or imposition of excise. *Obs.*

1710 STEELE *Tatler* No. 183 ¶1 The Brewer in his Excise, the Merchant in his Customs..think never the worse of themselves for being guilty of their respective Frauds towards the Publick. **1732** POPE *Ep. Bathurst* 120 Ask you why Phrynè the whole auction buys? Phrynè foresees a general excise. **1733** SWIFT *Advice to Freemen of Dublin* Wks. 1745 VIII. 292 A pamphlet printed in England by authority, to justify the bill for a general excise.

4. The government office or department charged with the collection of excise. Now merged in the Department of Inland Revenue.

1784 COWPER *Task* IV. 504 Th' excise is fatten'd with the rich result Of all this riot. **1838** *Penny Cycl.* X. 111/2 The last named [tea] of these [foreign products] was the last that was withdrawn from the management of the Excise. **1845** MCCULLOCH *Taxation* II. vi. (1852) 249 The vexatious surveillance formerly exercised by the excise. **1884** POE *Eustace* 220 It's not the first time she has baulked the hungry hounds of the Excise.

5. *attrib.*, as ***excise-bill, -commissioners, -dues, -duty, -house, -office, -people, -spies, -system, -yacht***, etc. **excise duties**, those collected by the Board of Inland Revenue, or its officers, comprising many to which the name 'excise' does not properly belong, *e.g.* the tax for armorial bearings..game licenses, etc.; **excise law**, a law relating to excise; *spec. U.S.*, the licensing or liquor law. Also EXCISEMAN.

1733 MAYOR LONDON in *Swift's Lett.* 6 Aug., In the late affair of the *Excise Bill..I acted consistent with..honest principles. **1828** CARLYLE *Misc.* (1857) I. 196 The Honourable *Excise Commissioners. *Ibid.* 201 Computing *excise-dues upon tallow. **1751** *Pref. Arbuthnot's Serm. Union* Wks. II. 174 A Barrel of Beer, or Ale..is never to pay more than two Shillings Sterling *Excise-Duty. **1834** *Brit. Husb.* I. 378 In consequence of the former excise duty..the use of salt, as manure, has been upon too limited a scale. *c* **1645** HOWELL *Lett.* (1650) II. 107 They burnt down to the grownd the *Excise house in Smithfield. **1765** BLACKSTONE *Comm.* I. 318 The rigour and arbitrary proceedings of *excise-laws. **1792** *Steele Papers* I. 82 Repealing the excise law since that vote was taken Seems to be out of the question. **1903** *N.Y. Even. Post* 3 Dec. 3 His proposed amendment of the Excise Law to allow the saloons to keep open during certain hours on Sunday. **1698–9** LUDLOW *Mem.* II. 59 (R.) An order given to the *Excise-office for satisfying an old debt. **1738** [G. SMITH] *Cur. Relat.* II. 190 They go to the Accise Office to pay the Duty. **1820** SHELLEY *Œdipus* II. i. 178 Ladies..Walked..Through rebels..Tithe-proctors, and *excise people, uninjured! **1676** MARVELL *Mr. Smirke* Wks. 1875 IV. 10 They itinerated like *excise-spyes from one house to another. **1873** *Financial Reformer* May 78 *note*, Exactly descriptive of the effects of our *Excise system. **1815** SCOTT *Guy M.* iii, Little curlie Godfrey..he's on board an *excise yacht.

excise (ɛk'saɪz), *v.*[1] [f. L. *excīs-* ppl. stem of *excīdĕre* to cut out, f. *ex-* out + *cædĕre* to cut.]

†**1.** *trans.* To cut off a portion of skin from (a person); = CIRCUMCISE 1. The quots. refer chiefly to an analogous operation upon females.

1634 SIR T. HERBERT *Trav.* 168 Such women or girles of Christians that live in slavery, by price or conquest, are excised forceably. **1650** BULWER *Anthropomet.* Pref., Women are, as an ornament, excis'd. *Ibid.* xx. 209 The Mahometans of Africa do excise themselves.

2. To cut out (a passage or sentence) from the context; to expunge.

1647 J. BIRKENHEAD *Assembly-Man* To Rdr., They Excis'd what they liked not. **1874** H. R. REYNOLDS *John Bapt.* ii. 68 Marcion excised other portions of the Gospel which contradict his views. **1884** *Manch. Exam.* 9 Apr. 5/6 All reference to Ireland shall be excised from the Bill.

3. To cut out (a limb, organ, etc.). Also *fig.*

1836 TODD *Cycl. Anat.* I. 792/2 The heart of a salamander may be excised, and yet the animal will live for several hours. **1875** E. WHITE *Life in Christ* III. xx. (1878) 278 We do not understand how by transgression he [Adam] succeeded in excising one part of his nature.

4. To cut or hollow out; to notch. Chiefly *Bot.* and *Zool.*

1578 BANISTER *Hist. Man* I. 32 The transuerse Processes of Os sacrum..are excised, and engrauen. **1851** DARWIN *Cirripedia* 121 Scutal margin [of *Dichelapsis warwicki*] deeply excised at a point corresponding with the apex of the scuta. **1870** HOOKER *Stud. Flor.* 102 Vicia sativa..leaflets linear-obovate, obtuse truncate or excised at the tip.

Hence **ex'cised** *ppl. a.*: see 3 and 4.

1866 T. WRIGHT in *Intell. Observ.* No. 50. 143 Excised marks and sculptures on stones. **1871** *Daily News* 13 Feb., On either side of the excised joints.

excise (ɛk'saɪz), *v.*[2] [f. EXCISE *sb.*]

†**1.** *trans.* **a.** To impose an excise or tax upon (a thing). Also *transf.* and *fig. Obs.*

1652 BENLOWES *Theoph.* III. xcix. 49 Love, Thou canst..such oregrown Behemoths please As tax the scaly Nation, and excise the Seas. *a* **1659** CLEVELAND *Hue & Cry* iii, When zealous hinting and the yawn Excise our Miniver and Lawn. **1662** PETTY *Taxes* 24 The first way we propose, is, to excise the very land itself in kind. **1761** CHURCHILL *Night* in Chalm. *Poets* XIV. 286 No Statesman e'er will find it worth his pains To tax our labours, and excise our brains. *a* **1764** LLOYD *Charity* Poet. Wks. 1774 II. 155 Worth is excis'd, and Virtue pays A heavy Tax for barren praise. **1765** BLACKSTONE *Comm.* I. 320 Brandies and other spirits are now excised at the distillery.

b. To force (a person) to pay an excise-due; hence, to overcharge; also *fig.*

a **1659** CLEVELAND *London Lady* in Wks. (1687) 238 Thus purely now herself homewards she packs, Excis'd in all the dialects of her knacks: Squeezed to the utmost Thread, and latest Grain. **1687** W. W. in *Cleveland's Wks.* 281 Yet did he ne'er Excise the Natives; nor Made Forreign Mines unto his Mint bring Oar. **1732** POPE *Hor. Sat.* II. ii. 134 In Southsea days not happier, when surmis'd The Lord of Thousands, than if now Excis'd. **1815** SCOTT *Guy M.* xliv, 'We'll no excise you neither, though we live sae near the Custom-house.' *c* **1830** —— *Monast.* Introd. Ep., 'I wadna hae excised Johnnie.'

†**2.** To deduct by way of excise. *Obs. rare*$^{-1}$.

1713 *Guardian* 11 May (1756) 232 Tis impossible to conceive that more than an eighth part can be excised from the expences of your subjects.

Hence **ex'cising** *ppl. a.*

1735 POPE *Donne, Sat.* IV. 147 Shortly no lad shall chuck, or lady vole, But some excising Courtier will have toll.

exciseman ('ɛksaɪz-, ɛk'saɪzmən). [f. EXCISE *sb.* + MAN.]

An officer employed to collect excise duties and prevent infringement of the excise laws.

1647 S. SHEPPARD (*title*), The Committee Man curried..A Comedy..discovering the Corruption of Committee Men and Excisemen. **1681** PRIDEAUX *Lett.* (Camden) 107 The mayor haveing unreasonably taken many licences for ale houses without a legal cause, the excisemen came and complained to the Vice-Chancellor of it. *a* **1704** T. BROWN *Table T.* Poems 133 A broken Shopkeeper, ends in an Exciseman. **1789** J. PILKINGTON *View Derbyshire* I. 405 Mathematical rulers and excisemen's gauging sticks. **1828** CARLYLE *Crit. & Misc. Ess., Burns* Wks. VII. 67 Tomorrow he must go drudge as an exciseman. **1863** FAWCETT *Pol. Econ.* IV. iii. 557 The exciseman can visit the malt-house whenever he pleases.

Hence **ex'cisemanship**, the office of exciseman.

1837 LOCKHART *Life Scott* (F. Hall).

excision (ɛk'sɪʒən). [ad. (either directly or through Fr. *excision*), L. *excisiōn-em*, n. of action f. *excīdĕre*: see EXCISE *v.*[1]]

1. The action or process of cutting off or out (any part of the body).

1541 R. COPLAND *Galyen's Terap.* 2 A ij b, Holowe vlceres..procede of two causes, that is to wete of excysyon and of eroysion. **1641** SYMONDS *Serm. bef. Ho. Com.* D ij b, In a gangræne to endure the excision of a limb. **1758** JOHNSON *Idler* No. 17 ¶5 The excision or laceration of the vital parts. **1836** TODD *Cycl. Anat.* I. 462 1 Excision of the lower jaw. **1864** *Sat. Rev.* 21 May, Slitting of noses and excision of ears had, indeed, gone out of fashion.

b. *fig.*

1791 HAN. MORE *Relig. Fash. World* 133 A christian life seems to consist of two things..the adoption of good habits, and the excision of such as are evil. **1796** MORSE *Amer. Geog.* II. 256 By a manifesto published March 25, 1793..it [Poland] underwent another excision. **1851** ROBERTSON *Serm.* Ser. IV. ix. (1863) I. 60 The manlier and more vigorous feelings and emotions did not undergo excision. **1878** LECKY *Eng. in 18th C.* I. iii. 435 Defoe and the Speaker Onslow both desired the excision of rotten boroughs.

2. The action of cutting off from existence; destruction; extirpation; the condition or state of being cut off. Also *fig.*

1490 CAXTON *Eneydos* xxi. (1890) 76 All the grekes folke swore that troye shold be distroyed. The harde conspyracion of the same grete excysion was made ferre from my lande. **1531** ELYOT *Gov.* II. III. xxiii. 358 O poure and miserable citie! what sondry tourmentes, excisions..and other euill aduentures hathe happed unto the citie. **1626** DONNE *Serm.* xxi. 211 a, It shall not work as a Circumcision, but as an Excision; not as a lopping off, but as a rooting up. **1702** C. MATHER *Magn. Chr.* I. iii. (1852) 58 Lest the inhabitants of Plymouth should revenge that excision of their countrymen. **1846** TRENCH *Mirac.* xxiii. (1862) 343 That accursed race once doomed of God to a total excision, root and branch.

3. The action of cutting off (a person) from a religious society; excommunication.

1647 *Power of Keys* iv. 74 Excommunication..denotes the excision from all or any degree of Communion *in sacris*. **1699** BURNET *39 Art.* xvi. (1700) 143 Among the Jews some sins were punished by a total excision or cutting off. **1834** CAUNTER *Orient. Ann.* ix. 118 Doomed to the penalties of everlasting excision. **1879** FARRAR *St. Paul* II. 92 A wrong..which the Mosaic law had punished with excision from the congregation.

4. The action of cutting out or erasing (a passage from a book, a clause from a bill, etc.); an instance of the same.

1858 GLADSTONE *Homer* I. 42 Shall we..hold the received text provisionally and subject to excision. **1881** —— *Sp. at Leeds* Oct., It would be my imperative duty to make large excisions. **1884** *Manch. Guard.* 3 Oct. 5/5 To throw upon the House of Commons the excision of the proposed clause.

5. The action of cutting or hollowing out: in quot. *concr.* A space hollowed out. *rare.*

1823 J. BADCOCK *Dom. Amusem.* 29 A spade-deep excision for the planks..to rest upon.

excisor (ɛk'saɪzə(r)). *rare.* [f. EXCISE *v.*[2] + -OR.]

An exciseman.

1835 *Blackw. Mag.* XXXVII. 859 No longer excisors and curs'd supervisors Shall vex us.

excitability (ɛkˌsaɪtə'bɪlɪtɪ). [f. next: see -ITY. Cf. Fr. *excitabilité.*]

1. The quality of being excitable, liability or tendency to excitement; in *pl.* excitable feelings.

a **1803** FOSTER in *Life & Corr.* (1846) I. 187 Excitement is excitability too. **1840** CARLYLE *Heroes* (1858) 250, I fancy, the rigorous earnest man, with his keen excitabilities, was not altogether easy to make happy. **1863** GEO. ELIOT *Romola* III. 60 Romola..shrank..from the shrill excitability of those illuminated women.

2. *Phys.* Of an animal or vegetable organ or tissue: The capacity of being excited to its characteristic activity by the action of a specific stimulus. (In the Brunonian physiology *excitability* or *incitability* was regarded as the essential principle of vitality; the earlier quots. refer more or less to this theory.)

1788 J. BROWN *Elem. Med.* §14 The property, by which both sets of powers act, should be named Excitability; and the powers themselves Exciting Powers. **1799** E. DARWIN *Phytol.* XIV. i. i. 316 The buds of vegetables..possess irritability, and sensibility, and voluntarity, and have associations of motion..But..the three latter kinds of excitability are possessed in a much less degree by vegetable buds. **1802** *Med. Jrnl.* VIII. 333 Opium acts primarily on the living principle, or, as he terms it, excitability of the system. **1807** J. E. SMITH *Phys. Bot.* 65 In forced plants the irritability, or..excitability, is exhausted. **1825** COLERIDGE *Aids Refl.* (1848) I. 34 Pleasure..consists in the harmony between the specific excitability of a living creature, and the exciting causes correspondent thereto. **1854** BUSHNAN in *Circ. Sc.* (*c* 1865) II. 3/1 The chemical laws are brought into operation by the agency of an organic excitability. **1866** HUXLEY *Phys.* ix. (1872) 220 The excitability of the retina is readily exhausted.

excitable (ɛk'saɪtəb(ə)l), *a.* [ad. L. *excitābilis*, f. *excitāre*: see EXCITE *v.* Cf. Fr. *excitable.*]

Capable of being excited; prone to, or susceptible of, excitement; easily excited. Const. *to.*

1609 BP. BARLOW *Answ. Nameless Catholic* 305 Their persons are liable to Deposing and killing; and their Subiects excitable to Insurrection. *a* **1677** BARROW *Serm.* xxxii. Wks. 1741 I. 342 His affections were..excitable by their due objects. **1837** LYTTON *E. Maltrav.* 25 His flexile and excitable fancy was conjuring up a thousand shapes. **1863** MISS BRADDON *Eleanor's Vict.* I. ii, One of those excitable natures which cannot endure the influence of strong drinks. *a* **1864** HAWTHORNE *Amer. Note-bks.* (1879) I. 53 He is..wonderfully excitable to mirth.

Hence **ex'citableness**, the condition or quality of being excitable.

1875 JOWETT *Plato* (ed. 2) V. 238 A precaution against the excitableness of youth.

'excitancy. [f. next: see -ANCY.] The property of exciting or calling into activity.

1834 COLERIDGE *Lit. Rem.* IV. 25 The active life or excitancy belongs to the former, the passive life or excitability to the latter.

excitant ('ɛksɪtənt, ɛk'saɪtənt), *a.* and *sb.* [ad. L. *excitant-em*, pr. pple. of *excitāre*: see EXCITE. Cf. Fr. *excitant.*]

A. *adj.* That rouses, excites, or stimulates; exciting, stimulating. Cf. EXCITE, senses 1, 4, 6.

1607 R. CRACKENTHORP *Serm.* (1608) 11 Gods grace, in our conversion, is not onely an excitant but a viuificant grace. **1661** BP. NICHOLSON *Exp. Catech.* (1678) 60 The Donation of Heavenly Grace..excitant, adjuvant, or co-operant. **1773** *Phil. Trans.* LXIII. 337 Cushions..covered with silk..are much more powerfully excitant. **1801** *Med. Jrnl.* V. 471 The excitant powers of the fixed alkali were not at all, or very little known. **1860** MAYNE *Exp. Lex.*, *Excitant*, raising up; exciting; provoking; stimulating.

B. *sb.* An agent which excites (organs or tissues) to increased vital activity; a stimulant. Also, an agent for inducing electrical action.

1833 COLERIDGE *Table-t.* 2 Sept., The English affect stimulant nourishment—beef and beer. The French excitants..alcohol, champagne. **1836** *Blackw. Mag.* XXXIX. 309 Salts are the excitants of the growth of plants. **1875** BEDFORD *Sailor's Pocket-bk.* viii (ed. 2) 300 A warm bath..should only be employed as a momentary excitant. **1885** *Pall Mall G.* 11 Feb. 4/2 A weak solution of potash as the excitant.

†**'excitate,** *v. Obs.* Also 6 **exitat.** *Pa. tense* 6 **excitate.** [f. L. *excitāt-* ppl. stem of *excitāre*: see EXCITE.] = EXCITE.

1548 BP. HOOPER *Declar. 10 Commandm.* iv, To shew what profit followeth the doing of it, that the commodity might excitate the mind. **1560** ROLLAND *Crt. Venus* II. 435 Thir wordis scho said richt sone him excitate. **1591** NASHE *Prognost.* 3 Celestiall bodies, whose influence doth exitat and procure continuall mutability in the lower region. **1646** SIR T. BROWNE *Pseud. Ep.* II. iv. 81 If you touch a piece of wax already excitated with common oyle, it will..attract. **1658** —— *Hydriot.* 58 Their iterated clamations to excitate their dying or dead friends. **1655–60** STANLEY *Hist. Philos.* (1701) 389/2 It was the custom of the Pythagoreans as soon as they waked, to excitate their souls with the Lute.

Hence **'excitating** *ppl. a.*

a **1643** J. SHUTE *Judgem. & Mercy* (1645) 29 The sinnes of other men, they may bee the externall, irritating, exitating cause of Gods judgements.

excitation (ɛksɪ'teɪʃən). Also 5–6 **exce-, excitacion, -ioun, excytacyon.** [a. F. *excitation*,

ad. L. *excitātiōn-em*, n. of action f. *excitāre* to EXCITE.]

1. a. The action of exciting (in various senses of the verb); an instance of this. † *by (a person's) excitation*: at (a person's) instigation. *rare* or *arch.* in general sense.

c **1400** MAUNDEV. (Roxb.) xxxi. 139 Thurgh comforth of þaire wordes and þe excitacioun of þaim, we schrafe vs clene and herd messe. **1462** EDW. IV. in Ellis *Orig. Lett.* II. 41 I. 127 The malicious counseyle and exitacion of Margaret his wife. *c* **1489** CAXTON *Blanchardyn* xx. (1890) 69 The.. impetuous excitacions, that often tymes thy messangers made vnto me. **1548** HALL *Chron.* 99 A man, that.. confessed, that he was there by myne excitacion. **1587** FLEMING *Contn. Holinshed* III. 1413/1 Bookes conteining false, seditious, and slanderous matter.. to the excitation of insurrection. *c* **1630** JACKSON *Creed* IV. iii. Wks. III. 462 The excitation of God's gifts in us, whereby we are united to Christ. **1681–6** J. SCOTT *Chr. Life* (1747) III. 95 His Excitation of the Graces of Prayer in us, is called his making Intercession for us. **1788** V. KNOX *Winter Even.* xlv, The alternate excitation of hope and fear is attended with considerable delight. **1836–7** SIR W. HAMILTON *Metaph.* xxx. (1870) II. 214 The ceaseless excitation of the mind to new knowledge.

b. In various physical senses: †the process of setting in motion; †contagion (of a putrid substance); calling forth (of heat, sound, etc.); the exciting (an organ or tissue) by an external stimulus.

1541 R. COPLAND *Guydon's Form.* T iv, The helpes for woundes composed with corrupte sores are they that requyre excytacyon. **1557** *Sarum Primer* E iv, Rejoyse, bicause he ascended.. into heaven again By his proper excitacion. **1626** BACON *Sylva* §330 The Second [means to induce Putrefaction] is by Inuitation or Excitation; as when a Rotten Apple lieth close to another Apple that is Sound. **1831** BREWSTER *Nat. Magic.* xiii. 331 Highly expansive elements.. called into tremendous action by the excitation of heat. **1862** H. SPENCER *First Princ.* (1867) §79 The order of excitation is from muscles that are small.. to those which are larger. **1866** HUXLEY *Phys.* ix. (1872) 222 The excitation of the retina proper.

2. A means of excitement, an influence that excites; a stimulus, encouragement, instigation. *arch.*

1627–77 FELTHAM *Resolves* I. lxxxviii. 136 Music.. as the Spartans used it.. served still for an excitation to Valor. **1670** *Devout Commun.* (1688) 65 Descend into my heart by the excitations of thy grace. **1755** TAYLOR *Let.* in E. Law *Th. Relig.* 402 The subject yields.. the warmest, and strongest excitations to piety. **1817** MAR. EDGEWORTH *Ormond* xxiii. (1832) 280 Tommy, with this excitation.. soon got to the head of his class. **1819** SOUTHEY *Lett.* (1856) III. 163 Here is a fellow publishing the most direct excitations to assassination and rebellion. **1877** MRS. OLIPHANT *Makers Flor.* viii. 212 His example was a continued.. excitation to his brethren.

3. The state of being excited, excitement; an instance of this. Now somewhat *rare*.

1393 GOWER *Conf.* III. 20 They two [Galba and Vitelle] through her dronkenhede Of witles excitation Oppressed all the nacion Of Spaine. **1638** ROUSE *Heav. Univ.* v. (1702) 49 Kindling them unto a more Incentive Excitation. **1698** tr. *Fenelon's Maxims of Saints* 53 All hasty and unquiet Excitation fore-running Grace. **1830** COLERIDGE *Table-t.* 1 May, It is said that every excitation is followed by a commensurate exhaustion. **1876** GEO. ELIOT *Dan. Der.* III. xxiii, His temperament was still in a state of excitation.

4. *Electricity* and *Magnetism.* The action or process of inducing an electric or magnetic condition; the condition so induced.

1656 tr. *Hobbes' Elem. Philos.* (1839) 526 As for jet, it must first be excited by rubbing.. whereas the loadstone hath sufficient excitation from its own nature. **1709** HAUKSBEE *Phys.-Mech. Exp.* II. (1719) 71 The Easie Excitation of the Electrical Matter. **1822** IMISON *Sc. & Art* I. 322 The simple rubber. will produce a very slight excitation of the cylinder. **1846** J. JOYCE *Sci. Dial.* iii. *Electr.* 359 Electrical machines.. so formed as, by excitation to collect Electricity. **1871** TYNDALL *Fragm. Sc.* (ed. 6) I. xiii. 375 Its polar excitation is at once manifested.

5. *Physics.* **a.** The action or process of causing the emission of a characteristic spectrum of radiation by a substance.

1914 O. W. RICHARDSON *Electron Theory of Matter* xx. 532 When the green mercury line is used for excitation it is found that.. the fluorescent lines are made up of fine lines having a structure similar to the.. absorption lines covered by the exciting spectrum. **1922** A. D. UDDEN tr. *Bohr's Theory of Spectra* II. ii. 34 Experiments on the excitation of spectral lines and production of ionization by electron bombardment. **1963** R. W. DITCHBURN *Light* (ed. 2) xvii. 657 (*heading*) Excitation of spectra by slow electrons.

b. The action or process of raising an atom, etc. to a state of higher energy. Freq. *attrib.*

1921 *Chem. Abstr.* XV. 1854 The excitation of an atom by electron impact consists in the removal of an electron from a stationary orbit to one with a higher quantum number. **1923** *Ibid.* XVII. 683 Their excitation potentials were not accurately det[ermine]d. **1931** *Nature* 30 May 838/1 An accurate experimental determination of excitation energy by electron impact in helium. **1951** L. H. SNYDER in *Frontiers in Medicine* (*N.Y. Acad. Med.*) 52 Excitation is the raising of an electron in a molecule or atom to a state of higher energy. **1958** W. K. MANSFIELD *Elem. Nucl. Physics* i. 7 An excited state is one in which energy is given to the atom, either by collisions, or by absorption of electromagnetic radiant energy, permitting the electron to revolve in an empty outer orbit. The energy required to produce this change is known as the *excitation energy*. **1968** M. S. LIVINGSTON *Particle Physics* x. 170 One type is the excitation function which is a plot of the yeild of products from a particle interaction as a function of bombarding energy.

excitative (ɛk'saɪtətɪv), *a.* [a. F. *excitatif, -ive*, as if ad. L. **excitātīv-us*, f. *excitāre*: see EXCITE *v.*]

Able or tending to excite: in senses of the verb. Const. *of*.

1490 CAXTON *Eneydos* xxii. (1890) 78 Exhortacions & pyetous remonstrances excytatiue of all well wyllyng. *a* **1677** BARROW *Exp. Creed* (T.) Admonitory of duty and excitative of devotion. **1704** HEARNE *Duct. Hist.* (1714) I. 408 The Pythagoreans.. said that Fire is the.. Excitative Power. **1847** R. W. HAMILTON *Disq. Sabbath* iv. (1848) 135 Who can say what shall be the growth of holiness.. where all is auspicious and excitative? **1881** *Nature* XXIV. 208 [Paper read] on the thermal laws of the excitative spark of condensers.

† **exci'tator.** *Obs. rare.* [a. L. *excitātor*, agent-n. f. *excitā-re*: see EXCITATE and -OR. Cf. Fr. *excitateur*.]

1. One who excites; *spec.* one whose business it is to rouse others from sleep.

1688 R. HOLME *Armoury* III. 182/1 The Excitator, who wakeneth the Jesuites in the Morning.

2. (See quot.)

1847 CRAIG, *Excitator*, an instrument employed to discharge a Leyden jar, or other electrical apparatus, without exposing the operator to the consequences of the shock. **1864** in WEBSTER; and in mod. Dicts.

excitatory (ɛk'saɪtətərɪ), *a.* [f. L. *excitāt-* ppl. stem of *excitāre* (see EXCITATE) + -ORY.]

Tending to or productive of excitation; characterized or produced by excitation.

1803 *Med. Jrnl.* IX. 147 Communication was produced between the two armatures by a silver wire or excitatory arc. **1874** COOKE *Fungi* (1875) 58 Excitatory organs for the dehiscence of the asci. **1882** *Nature* No. 637. 258 Changes in the electrical relations of the two surfaces [of a leaf] (called the excitatory variation). *Ibid.* XXVI. 353 The excitatory motions both of plants and of animals.

excite (ɛk'saɪt), *v.* Also 4–5 exite, 4–6 excyte, 5 excit, exyte. [a. Fr. *exciter* (= Pr. and Sp. *excitar*), ad. L. *excitāre*, freq. of *excīere* to set in motion, awaken, call forth, instigate, f. *ex-* out + *ciēre* to set in motion.]

1. *trans.* To set in motion, stir up.

a. *fig.* To move, stir up, instigate, incite. Const. †*til, to, unto*; *to* with *inf.* or *that* (with subord. clause); also *simply*. Now only with mixed notion of 5.

a **1340** HAMPOLE *Psalter* Prol., þe sange of psalmes.. excites aungels til oure help. *Ibid.* ix. 25 Antecrist sall.. excite him [God] in his synn to punysch him. **1398** TREVISA *Barth. De P.R.* v. xxiii. (1495) 131 Oxen ben excited to traueile more by the swete songe of the heerd than by strokes and pryckes. **1494** FABYAN *Chron.* I. v. 12 Gwentolena.. excyted her Fader and frendes to make warre vpon the sayd Lotryne. *a* **1575** ABP. PARKER in Farr *S.P. Eliz.* (1845) I. 2 Of Sabbath day the solemn feast Doth vs excyte by rest, God's mighty workes that we declare. **1655–60** STANLEY *Hist. Philos.* (1701) 185/1 Exciting the Soul of the World and converting it to himself. **1703** MAUNDRELL *Journ. Jerus.* (1732) 135 Excite those People to use a little more fervour in their Prayers. **1722** WOLLASTON *Relig. Nat.* v. 118 We excite children by praising them. **1818** JAS. MILL *Brit. India* II. IV. iv. 129 That veteran intriguer.. excited his attendants to resist. **1839** KEIGHTLEY *Hist. Eng.* II. 54 He was sent to try to excite the emperor to a crusade. **1850** MᶜCOSH *Div. Govt.* II. iii. (1874) 254 The imagination is apt to be still more excited by the stirring incidents of war.

absol. *c* **1380** WYCLIF *Sel. Wks.* III. 516 þe kyng may take awey þes temporaltees from prelatis, whan laweful cause exitiþ. **1590** SPENSER *F.Q.* III. ii. 3 Whose prayse I would endyte.. as dewtie doth excyte. **1683** SOAME & DRYDEN *Art of Poetry* ii. 9 There native beauty pleases and excites.

†**b.** To provoke, challenge. *Obs.*

a **1340** HAMPOLE *Psalter* v. 12 Out pute þaim: for þai excitid þe lord. **1388** WYCLIF *Judith* xiv. 12 Myis ben goon out of her caues, and doren excite us to batel. **1485** CAXTON *Chas. Gt.* 40 Of Fyerabras how he came to excyte thexersyte of Charles.

†**c.** In physical sense: To set in motion, stir up (so L. *excitare harenam*, Sallust.) *Obs. rare*$^{-1}$.

1697 DRYDEN *Virg. Georg.* III. 362 He snuffs the Wind, his Heels the Sand excite.

2. To rouse, awaken.

†**a.** *lit.* To rouse from unconsciousness. *rare.*

c **1440** LOVE *Bonavent. Mirr.* xlv. (Sherard MS.) 101 Than was oure lady excited and roos as it hadde ben fro sleep.

†**b.** To call up (a departed spirit). *Obs. rare.*

1651 WALTON in *Reliq. Wotton.* (1672) 208 Unless.. we could.. excite them again, and confer a while with their naked Ghosts.

c. To call forth or quicken (a faculty, feeling, etc.) from potential into actual existence; to rouse up, awaken (what is dormant, sluggish, or latent).

1393 GOWER *Conf.* III. 18 Venus.. Hath yive him drinke .. Of thilke cuppe., whiche exciteth The lust. **1447** BOKENHAM *Seyntys* Introd. (Roxb.) 4 The fyrst cause is for to excyte Menys affeccyoun. **1641** WILKINS *Math. Magick* I. i. (1648) 3 Such mysticall expressions, as might excite the peoples wonder. **1697** DRYDEN *Virg. Georg.* IV. 98 With Shouts, the Coward's Courage they excite. **1699** BENTLEY *Phal.* xi. 304 'Tis the design of Tragedy to excite Compassion in the Auditory. **1703** MOXON *Mech. Exerc.* 242 The Fire in Lime burnt.. lies hid.. but Water excites it again. **1722** WOLLASTON *Relig. Nat.* iii. 55 A master may, by the exercises he sets, excite the superior capacity of his scholars. **1766** FORDYCE *Serm. Yng. Wom.* (1767) I. iii. 103 Who can describe the detestation it excites? **1875** JOWETT *Plato* (ed. 2) IV. 495 The characters excite little or no interest.

3. To induce, elicit, provoke (actions, manifestations); to bring about, occasion (active conditions).

1398 TREVISA *Barth. De P.R.* VII. lxvii. (1495) 285 It is a generall medycyne to excyte spewynge. *c* **1400** *Three Kings Cologne* (1886) 122 þe deuyll.. excited.. among þe pepil diuers opynyouns of heresy. **1576** NEWTON tr. *Lemnie's Complex.* (1633) 104 It is expedient to excite and cherish native heat with exercise. **1612** *Enchir. Med.* 111 Through a catarrhall distillation the cough is excited. **1704** PENN in *Pa. Hist. Soc. Mem.* IX. 341 Excite his return, or to send for his family to him. **1786** GILPIN *Mount. & Lakes Cumbld.* (1788) II. 60 Brass guns, for the purpose of exciting echoes. **1787** WINTER *Syst. Husb.* 73 Heat.. excites and promotes a motion in the fluids. **1797** BURKE *Regic. Peace* iii. Wks. VIII. 303 They [the English ministry] did not excite the general confederacy in Europe. **1803** *Phil. Trans.* XCIII. 84 The bar.. was melted in the strongest heat which could be excited. **1856** FROUDE *Hist. Eng.* (1858) II. vii. 176 [He] had .. endeavoured to excite an insurrection in the eastern counties. **1860** MOTLEY *Netherl.* (1868) I. v. 192 Fire-ships, intended only to excite a conflagration of the bridge. **1871** BLACKIE *Four Phases* i. 142 It may excite a smile when I say so.

4. To affect by a stimulus (bodily organs or tissues), so as to produce or intensify their characteristic activity.

1831 BREWSTER *Nat. Magic* iii. 37 We observe it [the retina] to be so excited by local pressures.. as to see in total darkness moving and shapeless masses of coloured light. **1855** BAIN *Senses & Int.* I. ii. §18 (1864) 51 Irritation or contact with a surface excites a single group of muscles in one way. **1875** DARWIN *Insectiv. Pl.* i. 4 Changes which take place within the cells of the tentacles when the glands are excited.

5. In modern use: To move to strong emotion, stir to passion; to stir up to eager tumultuous feeling, whether pleasurable or painful. Also *intr.* and *absol.*

1821 P. EGAN *Life in London* I. vi. 85 If some of the plates should appear rather *warm*, the purchasers of 'Life in London' may feel assured, that nothing is added to them tending to excite. **1850** THACKERAY *Pendennis* lxi. (1879) 601 All the events of life, however strongly they may move or eagerly excite him never can remove that sainted image from his heart. **1855–79** [see EXCITED *ppl. a.* 1]. **1886** LESLIE STEPHEN *Life H. Fawcett* viii. 352 The only result of his endeavours to bring it before the House had been to excite the Under-Secretary for India. **1891** *Punch* CI. 121/2 'It excites me—it amuses me to talk to a *cocher*.' **1968** *Listener* 22 Feb. 252/3 Last week's legitimate television drama failed to excite.

6. a. *Electricity* and *Magnetism.* To induce electric or magnetic activity in (a substance); to set (an electric current) in motion; also *absol.* **b.** *Photography.* To render (a plate, etc.) sensitive to light; to sensitize.

1646 SIR T. BROWNE *Pseud. Ep.* II. ii. 60 If an iron or steele not formerly excited, be held perpendicularly or inclinatorily unto the needle, the lower end thereof will attract the cuspis or southerne point. **1827** FARADAY *Chem. Manip.* xxiv. 631 Excite a glass rod by silk. **1839** G. BIRD *Nat. Phil.* 157 The magnets.. are used merely to excite in the manner already explained. *Ibid.* 277 The remarkable fact of magnets exciting electric currents in wires moved near them. **1879** *Cassell's Techn. Educ.* III. 270 For exciting the collodion film a bath should be mixed. J. C. LEAKE *ibid.* IV. 323/2 When excited the plate should be placed in the dark-slide.

7. *Physics.* **a.** To induce a condition in (a substance) in which it emits a characteristic spectrum of radiation; to bring about the emission of (a spectrum). **b.** Hence, to render (an atom, etc.) excited (see EXCITED *ppl. a.* 2 e).

a. **1913** *Proc. R. Soc.* A. LXXXVIII. 24 Elements.. which emit secondary fluorescent X-radiation when excited by a suitable beam of Röntgen rays. **1926** [see EXCITING *ppl. a.* b]. **1959** *Chambers's Encycl.* XIII. 70/1 The electric arc is most suitable for exciting the line spectra of elements. **1966** *McGraw-Hill Encycl. Sci. & Technol.* XII. 581/1 Sources of radiation for spectrography are incandescent or electrically excited.

b. **1921** *Chem. Abstr.* XV. 1854 (*heading*) Observations on atoms excited by electron impact. **1934** H. E. WHITE *Introd. Atomic Spectra* vi. 92 If in collision the energy exchange between.. an electron and atom is all energy of translation, the atom is not excited and the collision is said to be elastic. **1953** P. MORRISON in E. Segrè *Exper. Nucl. Physics* II. vi. xi. 150 One nucleon enters the nucleus.. while four more are excited but 'captured', leaving the residual nucleus excited by 66 Mev. **1969** *Times* 11 July 14/2 Radio signals emitted by helium atoms excited by the high temperatures in the interstellar gas clouds.

excited (ɛk'saɪtɪd), *ppl. a.* [f. prec. + -ED¹.]

1. a. Stirred by strong emotion, disturbed, agitated.

1855 MACAULAY *Hist. Eng.* III. 275 The population of Edinburgh was in an excited state. **1864** MRS. CARLYLE *Lett.* III. 216 The excited people.. rushed out to me. **1879** MᶜCARTHY *Own Times* I. 199 Thiers carried with him much of the excited public feeling of France.

b. Of trade: Abnormally brisk or active.

1878 JEVONS *Prim. Pol. Econ.* 123 Business men must become.. careful during excited trade.

2. a. *Electricity* and *Magnetism.* In which electrical or magnetic action has been induced; electrized, magnetized. **b.** Of bodily organs or tissues: Affected by a stimulus. **c.** Of a seismographic instrument: Agitated.

1660 BOYLE *Seraph. Love* 144 Excited Needles, when they stick fastest to each other, owe their Union to their having both been touched by the Loadstone. **1812** SIR H. DAVY *Chem. Philos.* 129 The different states may be known by

presenting a metallic point to the excited body. **1831** BREWSTER *Newton* (1855) I. x. 235 The visible direction of an object should be a line perpendicular to the curvature of the retina at the excited point. **1863** TYNDALL *Heat* ii. §35 (1870) 37 The excited magnetic field. **1881** *Standard* 12 Aug., The instruments become less excited, and gradually fall back to more normal conditions.

d. *excited radioactivity*: Rutherford's name for artificial or induced radioactivity, as opposed to that which occurs naturally.

1900 RUTHERFORD in *Phil. Mag.* XLIX. 161 Thorium compounds under certain conditions possess the property of producing temporary radioactivity in all solid substances in their neighbourhood... Attention was first drawn to this phenomenon of what may be termed 'excited radioactivity' by the apparent failure of good insulators..to continue to insulate. **1913** —— *Radioactive Substances* x. 391 The activity thus produced on inactive substances was..known as 'induced' or 'excited' radio-activity.

e. *Physics.* Of an atom or an orbiting electron, or a nucleus, molecule, etc.: not in its ground state; able to lose energy by emitting electromagnetic radiation or a particle; ***excited state***, a state of a quantized system having more energy than the ground state.

1921 *Chem. Abstr.* XV. 3931 Recent researches..lead to the establishment of the existence of excited atoms in a metastable state. **1927** T. VERSCHOYLE tr. *Haas's Atomic Theory* 176 His observations..lead to an approximate value of 10^{-8} sec. for the mean duration of the excited state. **1938** R. W. LAWSON tr. *Hevesy & Paneth's Man. Radioactivity* (ed. 2) ix. 99 Excited states have only a limited life, and..the energy surplus of the excited nuclei will gradually be emitted in the form of γ-rays. **1953** P. MORRISON in E. Segrè *Exper. Nucl. Physics* II. vi. v. 63 The outgoing particles will in general take away only a small part of the excitation energy, leaving behind an excited residual nucleus. **1968** M. S. LIVINGSTON *Particle Physics* x. 170 We might expect the mesonic cloud surrounding a nucleon core to be capable of existing in excited states of higher energy..and to 'radiate' mesons.

excitedly (ɛkˈsaɪtɪdlɪ), *adv.* [f. prec. + -LY².] In an excited manner.

1852 J. B. OWEN in Vct. Ingestre *Meliora* I. 137 The children looked excitedly at their father. **1858** MRS. CARLYLE *Lett.* II. 389 He now talks incessantly, and excitedly. **1875** FLO. MARRYAT *Open Sesame* I. vi, 'Let him come', cries the girl excitedly. **1882** J. H. BLUNT *Ref. Ch. Eng.* II. 101 The young king..dashed his pen excitedly through some words of the oath.

†**exˈciteful**, *a. Obs. rare.* [f. EXCITE *v.*; cf. *assistful.*] Tending to excite to action.

1615 CHAPMAN *Odyss.* II. 56 To..Stern Pluto and Persephone, apply Exciteful prayers. **1618** —— *Hesiod* II. 423 Many a fore-studied exercise Was instituted, with exciteful prize.

excitement (ɛkˈsaɪtmənt). [f. EXCITE *v.* + -MENT. First used in sense 3 (= L. *irritamentum*) which is the only sense recognized by Johnson.]

1. The action of exciting; the fact of being excited; = EXCITATION. Somewhat *rare.*

1830 HERSCHEL *Stud. Nat. Phil.* II. ii. (1851) 89 The excitement and propagation of motion. **1840** MILL *Diss. & Disc.* (1859) I. 116 *note*, Experience..must precede the excitement of any ideas in the mind.

2. Excited state or condition.

a. *Path.* A state of abnormal activity in any organ. †Also, in the 'Brunonian' physiology, the effects resulting from the presence of the vital principle in the organism.

1788 J. BROWN tr. *Elem. Med.* §16 The effect of the exciting powers, acting upon the excitability, is to be denominated Excitement [Latin 1780 *Incitatio*]. **1793** BEDDOES *Consumption* 148 Diseases of excitement on the one hand, and debility on the other. **1799** *Med. Jrnl.* II. 452 The greatest degree of excitement, consistent with life, may be communicated by this agent [electric fluid]. **1801** *Ibid.* V. 82 An addition..to that just degree of excitement which constitutes health.

b. Stimulation, titillation (of the senses).

1823 LAMB *Elia* Ser. I. xxii, No possible taste or odour..can convey a delicate excitement comparable to this mixture.

c. In recent use: The condition of being mentally excited, whether by pleasurable or painful emotion. Cf. EXCITE *v.* 5.

1846 TRENCH *Miracles* vi. (1862) 185 Men in their thirst for excitement..have a kind of pleasure in being the bearers even of evil tidings. **1860** TYNDALL *Glac.* I. xxii. 152 He approached me with some excitement of manner. **1864** J. H. NEWMAN *Apol.* 156 The excitement it [Tractarianism] caused in England.

3. Something that excites; a means of exciting.

†**a.** Something that tends to excite (a feeling); a motive or incentive *to* action; an exhortation, encouragement. *Obs.* or *arch.*

1604 SHAKS. *Ham.* IV. iv. 58 (Qq.) A father kill'd, a mother stain'd, Excitements of my reason, and my blood. **1633** MAY *Hen. II*, VII. 79 Excitements every where From Pulpits sounded in the peoples eare, To aid their brother-Christians. **1642** FULLER *Holy & Prof. St.* II. xvi. 112 Rather are diligent lads to be encouraged with all excitements to Learning. **1736** BUTLER *Anal.* I. v. Wks. 1874 I. 89 Perception of danger is a natural excitement of passive fear, and active caution. **1741** WARBURTON *Div. Legat.* IX. ii. (1846) 373 The General encouraging his followers, by all the usual excitements to do their duty. **1817** COLERIDGE *Lay Serm.* 420 In any half dozen sermons of..Jeremy Taylor, there are..more excitements to inquiry..than are presented to the congregations of the present day..during twice as many months. **1858** DE QUINCEY *Autobiog. Sk.* Wks. I. 239 Each..had yet its own separate occasions and excitements.

b. In physical sense.

1862 DARWIN *Fertiliz. Orchids* iv. 153 I suspect that it does explode..without the excitement of a touch.

c. An occasion of mental excitement.

1878 R. W. DALE *Lect. Preach.* vii. 186 Their knowledge brings them some noble excitements and satisfactions.

exciter (ɛkˈsaɪtə(r)). Also 5 **excitour.** Cf. EXCITOR. [f. EXCITE *v.* + -ER¹.]

1. One who, or that which, excites; †an instigator.

1387 TREVISA *Higden* (Rolls) VIII. 267 Lewelynes broþer David..þat was exciter [L. *incentor*] of all þis woo. *c* **1400** *Test. Love* I. (1560) 277/2 Excitours to the matters were so painted and coloured, that etc. **1617** COLLINS *Def. Bp. Ely* II. ix. 360 He would haue relligion to be..an exciter..of our reuerence to Saints. **1795** *Hist.* in *Ann. Reg.* 89 Exciters of the insurrection. **1812** SHELLEY in Hogg *Life* (1858) II. 58 The personal exciter and strengthener of my virtuous habits. **1862** R. H. PATTERSON *Ess. Hist. & Art* 325, I am simply looking upon War as the strongest exciter of the human mind.

2. *Med.* An excitant; a stimulant.

1832 in WEBSTER; whence in mod. Dicts.

3. *Electr.* An apparatus to produce excitation; a machine, as a small auxiliary dynamo, used to energize the field magnets of a dynamo; a device to charge the plates of an electrostatic generator; a sparking device to generate electric waves. Also *attrib.*

1885 W. GARNETT *Physicists* 318 The idea which occurred to Siemens, Varley, and Wheatstone was to use the whole, or a part, of the current produced by the armature to excite its own electro-magnet, and thus to dispense with the magneto-electric machine which served as the separate exciter. **1902** *Encycl. Brit.* XXVII. 592/2 A small auxiliary continuous-current dynamo, called an exciter. **1930** *Engineering* 24 Jan. 97/2 The generator is of the standard vertical-shaft type with direct connected exciter. **1940** *Chambers's Techn. Dict.* 314/1 *Exciter lamp*, the electric lamp for providing the light to be modulated for recording sound photographically on a sound-track, or the light-source for modulation by the sound-track in the sound-head of a projector. **1959** *Times* 16 Oct. 15/5 The exciters are gear-driven from the generator shaft.

exciting (ɛkˈsaɪtɪŋ), *vbl. sb.* [f. EXCITE *v.* + -ING¹.] The action of the verb EXCITE. Also an instance of it. †Phrase, *at* (*of, by*) *exciting of*: by the instigation of.

1387 TREVISA *Higden* (Rolls) II. 133 At excitynge of quarta decimanorum þat helde Esterday þe xiiij^{e} day of þe mone Chedde was i-take. **1413** LYDG. *Pilgr. Sowle* I. ii. (1483) 3 Yf that my pylgrim hath ought done..of thyne excytyng. **1494** FABYAN *Chron.* VI. clxxxix. 192 A company of them, by the exityng of Hurkus..folowed the kynges hoost. **1525** LD. BERNERS *Froiss.* II. xciii. [lxxxix.] 279 The chiefe excytyng of these maters came by the kynges uncles. **1626** BACON *Sylva* §354 It must proceed..from the Quickning and Exciting of the Natural heat. **1652** G. HERBERT *Country Pars.* xxii, Wanting many excitings of grace [when not attending the Communion].

exciting (ɛkˈsaɪtɪŋ), *ppl. a.* [f. as prec. + -ING².]

a. That excites. ***exciting cause***: (chiefly *Path.*) that which immediately causes disease, etc.; opposed to *predisposing cause.*

1811 HOOPER *Med. Dict.*, *Exciting cause.* **1826** DISRAELI *Viv. Grey* V. xiii, Story after story..followed each other with exciting haste. **1834** *Cycl. Pract. Med.* III. 57/1 The exciting causes of hepatitis may be enumerated as follows. **1849** RUSKIN *Sev. Lamps* i. §2. 9 Principles..exciting rather than directing. **1855** MACAULAY *Hist. Eng.* IV. 542 The public attention was occupied by other and far more exciting subjects. *a* **1871** GROTE *Eth. Fragm.* i. (1876) 13 Certain acts and forbearances considered as the exciting cause of disposition on the part of others.

b. That excites an electric current, a magnetic field, an atom, etc., a spectrum, or radioactivity.

1884 F. KROHN tr. *Glaser de Cew's Magn.- & Dyn.-Electr. Mach.* 218 When the thickness of the exciting coil is equal to the diameter of the iron core. **1914** [see EXCITATION 5 a]. **1926** R. W. LAWSON tr. *Hevesy & Paneth's Man. Radioactivity* v. 51 The initial velocity of the β-rays excited in matter by γ-rays is independent of the intensity of the γ-rays... On the other hand, the initial velocity is dependent on the hardness of the exciting γ-radiation. **1964** N. N. HANCOCK *Matrix Analysis of Electr. Machinery* viii. 113 All the exciting functions (i.e. applied voltages and currents). **1967** CONDON & ODISHAW *Handbk. Physics* (ed. 2) VI. vii. 145/1 Absorption of the exciting radiation..produces only excited Hg^{199} atoms.

Hence **exˈcitingly** *adv.*, in an exciting manner.

1860 in WORCESTER; and in mod. Dicts.

excitingness (ɛkˈsaɪtɪŋnɪs). [f. EXCITING *ppl. a.* + -NESS.] Exciting character or quality.

a **1910** W. JAMES *Some Probl. Philos.* (1911) iv. 49 The perceptual flux..shows duration, intensity, complexity or simplicity, interestingness, excitingness, pleasantness or their opposites. **1930** A. HUXLEY *Brief Candles* 7 You must leave the discovery of the excitingness to the artists. **1965** *Listener* 28 Oct. 677/2 A wonderful hybrid of Kafka and Sapper, combining the paranoiac horror of the one with the sheer low-brow excitingness of the other.

excitive (ɛkˈsaɪtɪv), *a.* [f. EXCITE *v.* + -IVE.] Tending to excite. Const. *of.*

1774 N. WRAXALL *Let.* in *Tour North. Europe* (1776) 164 A sight rather excitive of disgust than desire. **1862** BURTON *Bk. Hunter* 51 The least excitive of the bad passions.

excito-motor (ɛkˌsaɪtəʊˈməʊtə(r)), *a.* = next.

1870 ROLLESTON *Anim. Life* Introd. 90 The three typical pairs of excitomotor ganglia are easily recognisable. **1881** POWER *Carpenter's Hum. Physiol.* §404 Such movements are properly distinguished as excito-motor.

excito-motory (ɛkˌsaɪtəʊˈməʊtərɪ), *a. Phys.* [f. EXCIT-OR + MOTORY; formed by Marshall Hall in 1836.] Of or pertaining to the spinal group of nerves, composed of the excitor and the motor nerves. Often applied to the reflex actions which are produced by this division of the nervous system.

1836 M. HALL *Lect. Nervous Syst.* 12, I propose to divide [the Nervous System] into 1. The Cerebral..2. The True Spinal or the Excito-motory; and 3. The Ganglionic. **1847** TODD *Cycl. Anat.* III. 609/2 A distinct series of excito-motory fibres. **1854** WOODWARD *Mollusca* II. 189 Besides this excito-motory system..the Nudibranches possess a 'sympathetic' system. **1861** T. GRAHAM *Pract. Med.* 593 In infancy, when the voluntary power is as yet undeveloped, the excito-motory is in the fullest activity.

exciton (ˈɛksɪtɒn, ɛkˈsaɪtɒn). *Physics.* [f. EXCIT(ATION 5 + -ON.] In a crystalline semi-conductor or insulator, an excited electron and an associated hole which together form a concentration of energy with certain properties characteristic of a particle.

1936 J. FRENKEL in *Phys. Zeitschr. der Sowjetunion* IX. 159 Just as the positive hole can be pictured as a collectivized positron, the excited state can be pictured as a kind of particle which we shall call a (collectivized) exciton. **1938** *Nature* 7 May 839/1 An exciton can move a certain distance through the crystal by transferring its energy from atom to atom, before the energy is all dissipated. **1967** CONDON & ODISHAW *Handbk. Physics* (ed. 2) VI. vii. 155/2 An exciton in a crystal such as KCl is considered to result from the transfer of an electron from Cl^- to K^+, forming an excited and neutral KCl combination... Excitons can migrate through the crystal by exchange of condition with lattice ions. **1968** *New Scientist* 14 Nov. 384/1 Excitons are quasiparticles which arise in semiconductor crystals.

Hence **exciˈtonic** *a.*

1958 *Physical Rev. Lett.* I. 452/1 For these materials the dissociation energies of the 'excitonic ion' + + — and the 'excitonic molecule' + + — — are an appreciable fraction of the binding energy of the exciton itself. **1966** *New Scientist* 27 Oct. 175/1 Known as the excitonic molecule, this stable entity is built up of two electrons and two 'holes'. **1969** *Sci. Jrnl.* Mar. 15/1 Fenton's arguments do not favour a resistanceless flow of electrons in DNA, but rather that the molecule might be what he calls an excitonic insulator.

excitor (ɛkˈsaɪtə(r), -ɔː(r)). Cf. EXCITER. [f. EXCITE *v.*, on the analogy of *motor.*] **a.** = EXCITER. **b.** An afferent nerve belonging to the spinal division of the nervous system. Also *attrib.* or as *adj.*

1816 JANE AUSTEN *Mansfield Park* II. 126 All those fine feelings of which he had hoped to be the excitor, were already given. **1836** M. HALL *Lect. Nervous Syst.* 15 The true Spinal Nerves. I. The Excitors. *Ibid.* 21 The incident excitor nerves, the medulla, and the reflex motor nerves, constitute the system. **1865** *Cornh. Mag.* XI. 592 It is quite credible that the messenger of death operated through..the usual excitors of disease. **1871** NAPHEYS *Prev. & Cure Dis.* III. iii. 674 Another excitor is a brush of fine wires. **1874** CARPENTER *Ment. Phys.* I. ii. §62 (1879) 63 Other excitor fibres..are included in the ordinary nerve-trunks.

excitory (ɛkˈsaɪtərɪ), *a.* [f. as prec. + -ORY.] Fitted to excite; instrumental in exciting.

1818 BOSTOCK *Galvanism* I. i. 18 The excitory arc, or the metallic part of the circle. **1861** HULME tr. *Moquin-Tandon* II. I. 48 The females are provided with a..vagina or sheath for the reception of the excitory organ of the male.

excitress (ɛkˈsaɪtrɪs) *rare.* [f. EXCITER + -ESS.] A female exciter.

a **1860** 'Used somewhere by H. H. WILSON' (F. Hall).

excitron (ˈɛksɪtrɒn). [f. EXCI(TATION 5 + -TRON.] A kind of mercury-arc rectifier having a pool cathode and a single anode, and capable of handling large currents; it differs from an ignitron in having a cathode hot spot maintained continuously and a grid to control the output.

1940 O. K. MARTI in *Trans. A.I.E.E.* LIX. 928/2 Tests encouraged the Allis-Chalmers Manufacturing Company to build a six anode rectifier, consisting of six single tanks using an ignition-excitation system for the main arc with a continuous cathode spot... This type of rectifier has been called the Excitron rectifier. *Ibid.* 929/1 (*caption*) A 600-volt Excitron with control cabinet. **1950** P. G. ANDRES *Survey Mod. Electronics* vi. 248 An important improvement in the field of mercury-arc rectification consisted in the development of a single-anode rectifier..equipped with auxiliary electrodes for establishing and controlling the arc current. A group of such individual tanks are assembled to produce a polyphase rectifier termed an *Excitron.* **1958** *Engineering* 14 Mar. 341/3 The excitron uses the conventional continuous excitation (supplied by an auxiliary d.c. source) throughout every cycle.

exclaim (ɛkˈskleɪm), *v.* Also 6–7 **exclame, -aime.** [ad. F. *exclamer*, ad. L. *exclāmāre* to call out, f. *ex-* out + *clāmāre* to call, shout.]

1. *intr.* To cry out suddenly and vehemently; to cry out from pain, anger, delight, surprise, etc. Rarely with *out.*

1570 LEVINS *Manip.* 18 To Exclame, *exclamare.* **1591** SHAKS. *1 Hen. VI*, IV. i. 83 Say Gentlemen, what makes you thus exclaime? **1667** MILTON *P.L.* x. 416 On either side

Disparted Chaos over built exclaimed. **1768** STERNE *Sent. Journ., The Bidet*, Grant me but decent words to exclaim in. **1845** DARWIN in *Life & Lett.* (1887) I. 342, I assure you the contrast made me exclaim out.

b. with quoted words, either in direct or indirect speech.

1591 SHAKS. *1 Hen. VI*, I. i. 125 The French exclaym'd, the Deuill was in Armes. **1630** *R. Johnson's Kingd. & Commw.* 311 Exclaiming that the tyranny of the Nobilitie had inforced them to this action. **1709** POPE *Ess. Crit.* 279 'What! leave the Combat out?' exclaims the Knight. **1781** COWPER *Hope* 437 'Spoke like an oracle', they all exclaim. **1828** SCOTT *F.M. Perth* xxi, 'By Saint Andrew, Robin!' exclaimed his father, 'thou art like a screech-owl'. **1858** FROUDE *Hist. Eng.* III. xiv. 191 The people exclaimed that they were betrayed by the gentlemen.

2. a. *to exclaim against*: to cry out loudly and suddenly against, accuse loudly, blame (persons, their actions and attributes); to make an outcry against, protest against, rail at (a thing). Also with *indirect passive. arch.*

1593 SHAKS. *Lucr.* 757 Here she exlaims against repose and rest. **1652** NEEDHAM tr. *Selden's Mare Cl.* 338 The Inhabitants did indeed exlaim..against this kind of Jurisdiction. **1658** *Mem. Reign Jas. I*, 25 None ever exclaimed more against that Prince then usually he did. **1724** T. BURNET *Life Bp. Burnet* in *Own Time* I. 59 In his charges to the Clergy he exclaimed against the pluralities. **1726** CHETWOOD *Adv. Capt. R. Boyle* 35, I began to exclaim against him in a friendly manner. **1734** tr. *Rollin's Anc. Hist.* V. XII. 158 Sparta..was already much exclaimed against for the treaty of Antalcidas. **1860** *Sat. Rev.* IX. 9/2 Satisfied with exclaiming against the inconsistencies which he detected in the conduct of remarkable persons.

b. *to exclaim at, on, upon*: in same sense; also, (quots. 1589, 1818), to apostrophize. *arch.*

1583 BABINGTON *Commandm.* x. (1637) 98 So as I may not be..exclaimed upon justly in the world. **1589** PUTTENHAM *Eng. Poesie* III. xix. (Arb.) 245 We do sodainly flye out and either speake or exclaime at some other person or thing..as a louer to his vnkind mistresse. **1633** FORD *Love's Sacr.* III. i, I will exclaim to the world on thee, and beg justice of the duke himself. **1709** STRYPE *Ann. Ref.* I. xxxvii. 424 These men..sometimes he makes sport with..and sometimes declaimes and exclaimes upon them. **1822** LAMB *Elia, Christ's Hospital*, How I would wake weeping, and in the anguish of my heart exclaim upon sweet Calne in Wiltshire! **1823** SOUTHEY *Hist. Penins. War* I. 184 He exclaimed on the horrid treatment they were giving him.

†**c.** *to exclaim of*: to complain loudly *of*.

1578 T. N. tr. *Conq. W. India* 116 They came..exclaiming of the Captains of the power of Tlaxcallan, who had bounde them. **1624** CAPT. SMITH *Virginia* (1629) 39 [Some bad natures] exclaime of all things.

†**3.** *trans.* To express by exclamation. With *compl. obj.* To proclaim loudly. *Obs. rare.*

c **1592** MARLOWE *Massac. Paris* III. ii. Wks. (Rtldg.) 242/1, I curse thee, and exclaim thee, miscreant. **1782** *Fashionable Follies* II. 75 The beautiful creature exclaimed thus her abhorrence of inconstancy.

Hence **ex'claimer**, one who exclaims or cries out with sudden vehemence. **ex'claiming** *vbl. sb.*, the action of the vb. EXCLAIM; an outcry. **ex'claiming** *ppl. a.*, that exclaims.

1689 LOCKE *Toleration* 17 The Opposers of Errors, the Exclaimers against Schism. **1809–10** COLERIDGE *Friend* (ed. 3) III. 225 The exclaimer relates half a dozen similar instances. **1872** DASENT *Three to One* I. 3 Some one exclaims 'regular old fogies'. Let us reason with this exclaimer. **1585** ABP. SANDYS *Serm.* (1841) 226 The exclaiming of the people hath many times as much cause as had the harlot's complaint made unto Solomon. **1688** R. L'ESTRANGE *Brief Hist. Times* III. 292 They both brake out in Violent Exclaymings, Lord! What will become of us! **1741** RICHARDSON *Pamela* III. 188 Our intermingling Exclaimings and Observations. **1877** *Daily News* 1 Nov. 6/1 There was a questioning and exclaiming that I refrain from repeating. **1580** SIDNEY *Arcadia* (1622) 216 The happy dwellers of these vallies Haue prayed me leaue my straung exclaiming musike. **1633** T. STAFFORD *Pac. Hib.* iii. (1821) 259 The exclayming mouths of these discontented people.

exclaim (ɛk'skleɪm), *sb. rare.* 'Now disused' (J.). [f. prec. vb.] Exclamation, outcry.

c **1489** CAXTON *Blanchardyn* 213 With these or the like exclaimes. **1586** J. HOOKER *Girald. Irel.* in *Holinshed* II. 150/1 He thought by waie of exclames to aggrauat his owne case. **1633** *Costlie Whore* I. i, in Bullen *O. Pl.* IV, Intending by exclaimes to raise the Court. **1812** W. TENNANT *Anster F.* v. ii, It needed not that with a third exclaim King James's trumpeter aloud should cry. **1840** BROWNING *Sordello* III. 344 Thus I bring Sordello to the rapturous Exclaim at the crowd's cry.

exclamation (ɛksklə'meɪʃən). Forms: 4–6 **exclamacioun**, 5–6 **-cion, -cyon**, 6 **-tioun, -tyon**, 6– **-tion.** [a. Fr. *exclamation*, ad. L. *exclāmātiōn-em*, n. of action f. *exclāmāre*: see EXCLAIM *v.*]

1. The action of exclaiming or crying out; the loud articulate expression of pain, anger, surprise, etc.; clamour, vociferation. Also, an instance of this, an outcry; an emphatic or vehement speech or sentence.

1382 WYCLIF *Mark* Prol., He ordeynynge in the vois of a prophetis exclamacioun, schewith the ordre of dekenis eleccioun. **1494** FABYAN *Chron.* VI. ccvii. 220 Therfore the mydwyfe made an exclamacyon, and sayde, this childe shall be a kynge. **1533** MORE *Apol.* viii. Wks. 860/1 Tyndall.. aunswereth me wyth an hedious exclamacion, and crieng oute vppon my fleshelynesse and foly. **1568** GRAFTON *Chron.* II. 72 At these wordes one of them burst out in exclamation. **1637** STIRLING *Doomes-day, 10th hour* st. lvi. in Chalmers V. 392 Huge exclamations burst abruptly out. **1719** DE FOE *Crusoe* (1840) I. vi. 106 What my Tongue might express..was rather Exclamation, such as, Lord! what a miserable Creature am I. **1828** SCOTT *F.M. Perth* xix, The..cries and exclamations of a woman..screaming ..'Oh, my husband!—my husband'. **1850** MRS. STOWE *Uncle Tom's C.* vii, Always making these exclamations in some..rough part of the road. **1873** BLACK *Pr. Thule* (1874) 24 They were startled by an exclamation from Ingran.

2. The action of loudly complaining or protesting; a loud complaint or protest; a derogatory outcry; a 'vociferous reproach' (J.). Const. *against*, †*of*, †*on*, and in phrases *to* †*infer, make exclamation against*, †*upon. arch.*

1430 LYDG. *Chron. Troy* III. xxii, Well maye I make an exclamacion Of ignoraunce. **1494** FABYAN *Chron.* VI. clxxxii. 180 Charlys heryngе this exclamacion of his subgettes..was right..heuy in his herte. **1513** DOUGLAS *Æneis, Exclamacion* (1710) 485 Ane Exclamacioun Aganis detractouris. **1530** *Calisto & Melib.* in Hazl. *Dodsley* I. 54 Oh, his lamentations and exclamations on fortune. *a* **1533** LD. BERNERS *Gold. Bk. M. Aurel.* (1546) O ij b, The myserable person..maketh exclamacion vpon the rightwise goddes. **1576** FLEMING *Panopl. Epist.* 425 Inferring an exclamation and outcrie, against the croked..condition of this life. **1613** SHAKS. *Hen. VIII*, I. ii. 52 These exactions..They say..are deuis'd by you, or else you suffer Too hard an exclamation. **1722** DE FOE *Plague* (1840) 34, I might spend a great deal of my time in exclamations against the follies..of those things. **1777** PRIESTLEY *Disc. Philos. Necess.* iii. 24 What exclamation and abuse must he not expect? **1821** SCOTT *Kenilw.* xi, Dame Crank..began a horrible exclamation against Jack Hostler.

†**3.** Formal declaration; proclamation. Const. *of. Obs.* Cf. EXCLAIM *v.* 3.

1602 MARSTON *Antonio's Rev.* II. v, Ile stand amaz'd, And fall in exclamations of thy vertues. **1631** T. POWELL *Tom All Trades* 132 Many Patrons are content to present..upon.. due exclamation of the integrity of the life of such suitors.

4. a. *Rhet.* = ECPHONESIS or EPIPHONEMA. **b.** *Gram.* = INTERJECTION. **c.** *note, point of exclamation*, also (orig. U.S.) *exclamation-mark* or *point*: = *note of admiration*: see ADMIRATION 5. Also *fig.*

a. 1552 HULOET, Exclamation, *epiphonema.* **1589** PUTTENHAM *Eng. Poesie* III. xix. (Arb.) 221 The figure of exclamation [*marg.* Ecphonisis or the Outcry]. **1706** PHILLIPS (ed. Kersey), *Exclamation*..a Figure in Rhetorick; as Now I speak to thee O Africanus.

b. 1862 H. SPENCER *First Princ.* II. xv. §123 (1875) 347 The lowest form of language is the exclamation, by which an entire idea is vaguely conveyed through a single sound.

c. 1657 J. SMITH *Myst. Rhet.* 271 A note of Exclamation or Admiration, thus noted! **1755** JOHNSON, *Exclamation*..a note by which a pathetical sentence is marked thus! **1824** L. MURRAY *Eng. Gram.* (ed. 5) I. 408 A sentence, in which any wonder or admiration is expressed..may be..terminated by a note of exclamation. **1824** [see POINT *sb.*[1] 3 a]. **1841** W. SAVAGE *Dict. Art Printing* 668 The Exclamation point, ! *Ibid.* 669 The Interrogation and exclamation points are indeterminate as to their quantity or time. **1864** WEBSTER, *Exclamation*, A sign by which emphatical utterance or outcry is marked; thus [!];—called also exclamation point. **1896** S. R. CROCKETT *Cleg Kelly* xiii. 93 The egg..made a long yolky mark of exclamation on the ground. **1926** FOWLER *Mod. Eng. Usage* 569/2 Excessive use of exclamation marks is..one of the things that betray the uneducated or unpractised writer. **1959** *Times* 29 May 18/2 Characterization [of a play] is in exclamation points. **1963** V. NABOKOV *Gift* iii. 153 She was slowly mixing a white exclamation mark of sour cream into her borshch.

†**d.** *Music.* (See quot.) *Obs.*

1674 PLAYFORD *Skill Mus.* I. xi. 43 Exclamation properly is no other thing but the slacking of the Voice to re-inforce it somewhat more.

exclamative (ɛk'sklæmətɪv), *a.* and *sb. rare.* [f. L. *exclāmāt-* ppl. stem of *exclāmāre* (see EXCLAIM *v.*) + -IVE. Cf. mod.F. *exclamatif.*] Containing or expressing exclamation; exclamatory. Also as *sb.*

1730–6 BAILEY (folio), *Exclamative*, of or pertaining to exclamation. **1775** in ASH. **1838** *Fraser's Mag.* XVIII. 471 Renowned O! Y? (thou exclamative—interrogation). **1938** in *Language Sciences* (1968) Oct. 10/1 Such exclamative constructions as 'Oh Charley!' 'What a man!' **1964** E. A. NIDA *Toward Sci. Transl.* ix. 209 There are..certain minor types in English, e.g..., exclamatives (*Fire! Police! Ouch!*).

Hence **ex'clamatively** *adv.*, with exclamation, exclamatorily.

1836 in SMART. **1860** in WORCESTER; and in mod. Dicts.

exclamatory (ɛk'sklæmətərɪ), *a.* [f. L. *exclāmāt-* ppl. stem of *exclāmāre* + -ORY.]

1. That exclaims or cries out loudly; that utters exclamations. Of a feeling, etc.: That vents itself in exclamation; noisy, outspoken.

1593 NASHE *Christ's T.* 22 b, Wold God there were no other exclamatory crime then this to be obiected against thee. *a* **1631** DONNE *Serm.* lxiii. (1640) 635 Whom afflictions supple and mollifie no farther but to an intemperate..and exclamatory Sorrow. **1755** JOHNSON, *Exclamatory*, practising exclamation. **1803** W. TAYLOR in *Ann. Rev.* I. 400 The exclamatory vehemence and contagious zeal of his manner. **1883** STEVENSON *Treasure Isl.* I. vi. (1886) 48 You are so..hot-headed and exclamatory that I cannot get a word in.

2. Of or pertaining to exclamation; of the nature of or resembling an exclamation; containing, expressing, or marking an exclamation.

a **1716** SOUTH *Serm.* IV. vii. 346 Those exclamatory words of St. Paul..How unsearchable are his judgements. **1727** *Art Speaking in Public* (ed. 2) 129 To pronounce those exclamatory Expressions without either Grace or Exclamation. **1767** STERNE *Tr. Shandy* (1802) IX. xxxiii. 283 Beginning the sentence with an exclamatory whistle. **1824** L. MURRAY *Eng. Gram.* (ed. 5) I. 408 (*heading of* §) Of the Exclamatory point (!). **1866** GEO. ELIOT *F. Holt* I. Introd. (1866) 2 The tube-journey..is as barren as an exclamatory O!

Hence **ex'clamatorily** *adv.*, in an exclamatory manner.

1836 in SMART *Walker's Dict.* **1863** *Not an Angel* I. 41 'My darling!' exclamatorily. 'What do you want?' 'My darling?' interrogatively.

exclave ('ɛkskleɪv). [f. EX-[1] + EN)CLAVE *sb.*] A portion of territory separated from the country to which it politically belongs and entirely surrounded by alien dominions: seen from the viewpoint of the 'home' country (as opp. to an *enclave*, the same portion of territory as viewed by the surrounding dominions). Also *transf.* and *fig.*

1888 *Encycl. Brit.* XXIII. 331/2 Besides these, the term Thuringia..includes the various 'exclaves' of Prussia, Saxony, Bavaria, and Bohemia which lie embedded among them. **1939** S. VAN VALKENBURG *Elem. Pol. Geogr.* vii. 111 Small disconnected sections in a foreign territory are enclaves of the surrounding area and exclaves of the country to which they politically belong. **1951** E. W. ZIMMERMANN *World Resources* (ed. 2) 129 An economic exclave may be defined as a splinter of one economy lying inside another ecomony. **1956** N. PEVSNER *Englishness of English Art* 179 New Towns, which are towns and not garden suburbs with odd shopping centres as urban exclaves and a trading estate along the railway.

exclosure (ɛks'kləʊʒ(j)ʊə(r)). [f. EX-[1] + CLOSURE *sb.*, after ENCLOSURE.] An area from which unwanted animals, etc., are excluded.

1920 F. E. CLEMENTS *Plant Indicators* 313 Each pasture contains an exclosure termed an isolation transect. **1938** WEAVER & CLEMENTS *Plant Ecology* (ed. 2) ii. 37 Fenced areas of varying size and shape..the exclosure keeping out one or more species of animals and the enclosure restricting them to a definite area. **1968** A. G. HART et al. *Small Animals & Birds* (U.S. Forest Service) 2 Exclosure to exclude birds but admit small mammals.

exclude (ɛk'sklu:d), *v.* Also 5–6 **exclud**, 5 *pa. pple.* **exclud**, 6 *Sc.* **excluid.** [ad. L. *exclūdĕ-re* to shut out, f. *ex-* out + *claudĕre* to shut.]

I. To bar or keep out (what is already outside).

1. *trans.* To shut out (persons, living things), hinder from entering (a place, enclosure, society, etc.). Const. *from*, †*out of*, and †with double obj. by omission of *from.*

c **1440** *York Myst.* xv. 32 The force of the feende to felle in sighte, And all his pouer excluded shulde be. *c* **1465** *Eng. Chron.* (Camden) 10 Thi childryn shall be disheritid. and excludid fro the parlement..for evirmore. **1526** *Pilgr. Perf.* (W. de W. 1531) 7 b, Therby all menkynde was vtterly lost and excluded out of paradyse. **1635** PAGITT *Christianogr.* (1646) I. 132 Far be it from us to believe that all these Christians are excluded heaven. **1670** R. COKE *Disc. Trade* 71 Plato..excluded every one his School who was ignorant in Geometry. **1697** DRYDEN *Virg. Georg.* II. 512 Exclude th' incroaching Cattle from thy Ground. **1708** J. CHAMBERLAYNE *St. Gt. Brit.* II. I. ii. (1743) 329 The first occasion of building the Roman Wall was..to exclude the Scotish Highlanders. **1722** SEWEL *Hist. Quakers* (1795) I. II. 144 Out of God's kingdom you are excluded. **1870** YEATS *Nat. Hist. Comm.* 170 Nobody was excluded who laid down his penny at the bar. **1879** LUBBOCK *Sci. Lect.* iii. 96 We.. find in flowers various modes..of excluding ants.

b. To shut out, prevent the entrance of (noise, air, light, etc.).

1598 BARRET *Theor. Warres* IV. ii. 105 All rumour and lowd noises are to be excluded. **1664** EVELYN *Kal Hort.* (1729) 190 When Branches are so thick..that they..exclude the sun and air. **1704** POPE *Windsor For.* 18 Waving groves ..part admit, and part exclude the day. **1885** *Law Times* LXXIX. 366/2 Hoods will also be fitted over the tops of the doors so as to further exclude the draught.

2. With an immaterial thing as obj.: To shut out, give no place to; to prevent the existence, occurrence, or use of. Const. *from*, and with double obj.

1382 WYCLIF *Rom.* 1st Prol., Lest happili hate of the prelatis name, shulde exclude the profit of the lessoun. **1393** GOWER *Conf.* III. 366 None arte..Through which it mighte ben excluded, That he ne was fully concluded To love. **1450–1530** *Myrr. our Ladye* 59 Iesu cryst wyllyng that all suche songe shulde be excluded from thys order. **1545** JOYE *Exp. Dan.* xii. 220 Wherfore our faithe stayed vpon god.. excludeth al maner a doute. **1604** ROWLANDS *Looke to it* 44 Eate, drinke, be merry..Exclude all Pittie, Conscience, and Remorce. **1729** BUTLER *Serm.* Wks. 1874 II. 50 It is impossible that this subject should be wholly excluded conversation. **1794** MRS. RADCLIFFE *Myst. Udolpho* v, Sometimes the thick foliage excluded all view of the country. **1841–44** EMERSON *Ess., Poet* Wks. (Bohn) I. 160 The vocabulary of an omniscient man would embrace words and images excluded from polite conversation.

b. To shut out or reject from consideration, notice, or use.

1594 HOOKER *Eccl. Pol.* II. v. (1611) 63 And so exclude the rest of the Scripture. **1612** BRINSLEY *Lud. Lit.* Addr. to Rdr. 10 Not..excluding the better way when it is found. **1632** J. HAYWARD tr. *Biondi's Eromena* 148 The world..excludes those things for which it can give no reason.

c. Not to admit of, to leave no room for, be incompatible with, the presence of (a material or immaterial object). Also † *to exclude out.*

1625 BP. MOUNTAGU *App. Caesar.* 104 The freedome of will doth not exclude out God's prerogative royall. **1690** LOCKE *Hum. Und.* II. iv, A solid substance..excludes all other solid substances. **1736** BUTLER *Anal.* I. vi. Wks. 1874 I. 112 This Necessity does not exclude deliberation. **1771**

Junius Lett. lxi. 318 He is fond of introducing any law that contradicts or excludes the common law of England. **1875** JOWETT *Plato* (ed. 2) I. 407 The number three excludes the number four. **1884** H. SPENCER in *19th Cent.* XV. 7 Absolute indifference excludes the conception of will.

3. To shut off, debar *from*; to preclude, prohibit. †Formerly const. *of*; also *to* with *inf.*

1495 *Act 11 Hen. VII*, c. 40. Preamb, The same Erle is excluded to have or enjoye the seid Manoris. *a* **1533** LD. BERNERS *Gold. Bk. M. Aurel.* (1539) Prol. ad fin., Euery wyse man.. wyll not saye that I am the principall auctour of this warke, nor yet.. exclude me clene from it. **1538** STARKEY *England* I. ii. 34 He ys therby excludyd also from the vse and vtward exercyse almost of al vertue. **1574** tr. *Littleton's Tenures* 52 a, Theye bee excluded duringe their lyves to defete the particion. *a* **1626** BACON *Max. & Uses Com. Law* ii. 7 These were to exclude him utterly of his right. **1659** B. HARRIS *Parival's Iron Age* 103 Francis of Vaudemont being next heir by the said [i.e. Salic] Law, which excludes Females. **1667** MILTON *P.L.* III. 202 And none but such from mercy I exclude. **1737** WHISTON *Josephus' Hist.* IV. vii. §4 Placidus's concern was to exclude them.. from getting into the village. **1759** ROBERTSON *Hist. Scot.* I. III. 169 They laboured to exclude the English from the treaty of Chateau en Cambresis. **1856** KANE *Arct. Expl.* II. ii. 29 Here, completely excluded from the knowledge of things without.

†**b.** with double obj. *Obs.*

1692 LOCKE *Toleration* iii. Wks. 1727 II. 333 Excluding them the ordinary and probable Means of Conversion. *a* **1718** PENN *Tracts* Wks. 1726 I. 547 Professors of Christianity, that exclude both such Men, and such Knowledge the Kingdom of God.

4. To leave out, omit purposely, except (from a category, list, the scope of a proposition or enactment, etc.); 'not to comprehend in any grant or privilege' (J.). Const. *from*, †*out of*; also *simply*.

c **1400** *Purif. Marie* in *Tundale's Vis* (1843) 129 Thys meyde.. Excluded was for condycion. **1689** C. HATTON in *Hatton Corr.* (1878) II. 131 Ye author.. is threaten'd by Sr. Robt. to be excluded out of ye Act of indemnity. **1707** *Curios. in Husb. & Gard.* 118 Having excluded them from the Society of Men, he places them among.. Beasts. **1724** [see 5]. **1755** in JOHNSON.

†**b.** To let off, relieve, exempt (a person) *from* (an obligation). *Obs. rare.*

1632 J. HAYWARD tr. *Biondi's Eramena* 83 Excluded and exempted from the debt which others owe by the common law of nature.

c. Of a word, term, proposition, etc.: To shut out of or not to include in its scope, application, or meaning.

1532 MORE *Confut. Tindale* Wks. 384/1 If saint James sayd that god had begotten vs by his goodnes, do these wordes exclude al the meanes that hys goodnesse vsed toward it. **1659** PEARSON *Creed* (1839) 234 When we say the conception of our Saviour was wrought by the operation of the Spirit.. observe, What is excluded by that attribution to the Spirit. **1862** H. SPENCER *First Princ.* I. iv. §26 (1875) 87 Excluding as they [these propositions] do an all-important fact. **1882** J. SEELEY *Nat. Relig.* I. iv. (1891) 85 Nature.. excludes the whole domain of human feeling.

5. The pr. pple. used *absol.*

a. = 'To the exclusion of'. †**b.** = EXCEPTING.

1660 R. COKE *Power & Subj.* 76 Whatsoever the son does acquire, it is his own, excluding his Father. **1724** R. FALCONER *Voy., Adv. & Escapes* (1769) 273 A Court Marshall.. found them guilty of Cowardice, excluding Constable.

II. In pregnant sense; to expel and shut out.

6. To put out (of a room, a society, a possession, etc.), to banish, expel. Const. †*out of*, *from*; also with double object and *simply*.

1388 WYCLIF *Num.* xii. 15 So Marie was excludid [1382 putte] out of the tentis. *a* **1400-50** *Alexander* 2842 In pacience possede at he mi3t [pan] Be excludit [*Dublin MS.* exclud] out of his erd. **1531** ELYOT *Gov.* II. xii. II. 154 They excluded him out of their counsayle. **1604** in *Eng. Gilds* (1870) 435 If any man be lawfully seazed.. of any tenement .. he shall never be excluded.. but by the kings writ. **1667** MARVELL *Corr.* lxxix. Wks. 1872-5 II. 224 They voted that he be excluded the House. **1777** ROBERTSON *Hist. Amer.* I. III. 229 As Las Casas excepted against the members of the council of the Indies, all of them were excluded. **1850** PRESCOTT *Peru* II. 133 They then caused the women to be excluded from the church.

7. a. After L. *excludere ova*. To draw, put or thrust forth from (a receptacle); to hatch (chickens, etc.); also *fig.*; to give birth to (young), to lay (eggs). Also †of the midwife: To extract. Const. *from*, *out of*.

c **1400** *Lanfranc's Cirurg.* 117 If that ony þing of corrumpcioun abide þe place schal be opened wiþ an instrument, & so schal þe quyttur be excludid. **1603** HOLLAND *Plutarch's Mor.* 53 To rid and exclude the winde and aire out of leather bagges or bladders. **1610** GUILLIM *Heraldry* III. xvii. (1660) 208 Spiders.. are no sooner hatched and excluded out of their egs, but forthwith they practise to make webs. **1646** SIR T. BROWNE *Pseud. Ep.* (ed. 2) 151 A Cock will.. fertilitate the whole.. cluster of egges, which are not excluded in many weeks after. **1684** tr. *Bonet's Merc. Compit.* I. 2 The next day she excluded the Fœtus that was four months old. **1713** DERHAM *Phys. Theol.* VII. iv. 393 The Eggs of the Ostrich.. are cherished only by the heat of the Sun till the Young be excluded. **1721** BRADLEY *Wks. Nat.* 59 The.. male [fish] covers it [the egg] with a prolifick Juice as soon as it is excluded from the Body of the Female. **1754-64** SMELLIE *Midwif.* I. Introd. 8 He describes the method of excluding the Fœtus. **1851** DARWIN *Cirripedia* I. 10 In some cases.. the larvæ, when first excluded from the egg, have not an eye.

†**b.** To discharge, void. *Obs.*

1677 PLOT *Oxfordsh.* 196 Who out of the corners of her eyes excluded a sort of congealed matter.

excluded (ɛk'skluːdɪd), *ppl. a.* [f. prec. + -ED[1].] In senses of the verb. Also *absol.*

1672 in *Essex Papers* (1890) I. 27, I lately believd.. that they would of themselves have readmitted their excluded Alderman. **1717** LADY M. W. MONTAGUE *Lett.* II. xliv. 24 It is easy to see in her manner, that she has lived excluded from the world. **1860** MILL *Repr. Govt.* (1865) 22/2 The interest of the excluded is always in danger of being overlooked. **1879** GREEN *Read. Eng. Hist.* xvii. 83 The excluded monks.

b. *excluded middle, third*: (see quots.)

1837-8 SIR W. HAMILTON *Logic* (1860) I. 83 The principle of Excluded Third or Middle—viz. between two contradictories—enounces that condition of thought, which compels us, of two repugnant notions, which cannot both coexist, to think either the one or the other as existing. **1849** ABP. THOMSON *Laws Th.* 295. **1884** tr. *Lotze's Logic* 10 Every physical enquiry employs the logical principles of Identity and Excluded Middle for the attainment of its results.

†**ex'cludent**, *Obs.* [ad. L. *exclūdent-em*, pr. pple. of *exclūdĕre*: see EXCLUDE.] = EXCLUDER b.

1670 *Conclave wherein Clement VIII was elected Pope* 9 It is now in your power.. to make unto yourself and the rest of the Excludents an immortal Friend of Santa Severina. [See also EXCLUDING *ppl. a.*]

excluder (ɛk'skluːdə(r)). [f. EXCLUDE + -ER[1].] One who or that which excludes or shuts out.

b. *spec.* One who attempts to exclude a candidate from office by voting against him; *esp.* one who voted for the Exclusion Bill (EXCLUSION 1 b).

1670 G. H. *Hist. Cardinals* III. II. 276 They left no stone unturned, that might mollifie the excluders, and prevail with them to give their votes for Montalto. **1685** *Addr. Middlesex Just. of Peace* in *Lond. Gaz.* No. 2010/4 The race of Regicides and Excluders (who Murthered the Royal Martyr your Father). **1848** MACAULAY *Hist. Eng.* I. 476 The grand jury of Suffolk expressed a hope that the parliament would proscribe all the excluders.

excluding (ɛk'skluːdɪŋ), *vbl. sb.* [f. as prec. + -ING[1].] The action of the vb. EXCLUDE.

1581 J. BELL *Haddon's Answ. Osor.* 505 b, The life and the health of the body is nothing els, but an excluding of death and Sickenesse. **1657-8** *Burton's Diary* (1828) II. 428 The excluding of the old peerage, which have right and are a considerable party. **1662** STILLINGFL. *Orig. Sacr.* III. ii. §18 We need not fear.. the excluding of a Deity from being the prime efficient cause of the world.

ex'cluding, *ppl. a.* [f. as prec. + -ING[2].] That excludes or shuts out; exclusive.

1670 G. H. *Hist. Cardinals* III. III. 329 If the Head of the including Faction, offers the Head of the Excluding Party, to assist him.. in the Election of one of the Excludents, let him alwayes be suspicious. **1836** E. HOWARD *R. Reefer* vi, A sect of.. Methodists, more dismal and more excluding.

Hence **ex'cludingly** *adv.*

a **1641** BP. MOUNTAGU *Acts & Mon.* (1642) 30 Who out of that respect are all of them, not excludingly, any one of them, styled, The Lords Anointed.

†**ex'cluse**, *v. Obs. rare*[−1]. [f. L. *exclūs-* ppl. stem of *exclūdĕre*.] *trans.* = EXCLUDE.

1513 HEN. VIII in Tytler *Hist. Scot.* (1864) II. 288 *note*, The King of Navarre being exclused from his realme for the assistance given to the French King.

†**ex'cluse**, *pa. pple. Obs. rare*[−1]. [ad. L. *exclūsus*, pa. pple. of *exclūdĕre*: see EXCLUDE.] Excluded; shut out.

c **1420** *Pallad. on Husb.* XII. 278 Thai [chestnut trees] not refuse.. clyves ther humoure is not excluse.

†**ex'clusible**, *a. Obs. rare*[−1]. [f. L. *exclūs-* (see EXCLUSE *v.*) + -IBLE.] That may be or should be excluded.

1650-3 tr. *Hales' Dissert. de Pace* in *Phenix* 1708 II. 371 Neither seem they exclusible from Heaven, who, etc.

exclusion (ɛk'skluːʒən). [ad. L. *exclūsiōn-em*, n. of action f. *exclūdĕre*: see EXCLUDE.] The action of excluding in various senses.

1. a. Shutting from a place, a society, etc., debarring from privilege, omitting from a category, from consideration, etc.; an instance of the same.

1614 RALEIGH *Hist. World* I. 80 The most high God is also an infinite God, not onely by exclusion of place, but by the dignity of nature. **1622** BACON *Hen. VII*, Wks. (1857) 372 To have the disposing of the marriage of Britain with an exception and exclusion, that he should not marry her himself. **1626** —— *Sylva* §318 All exclusion of open Air.. maintaineth the Body in his first freshness. **1667** MILTON *P.L.* III. 525 To dare The Fiend.. or aggravate His sad exclusion from the dores of Bliss. **1670** G. H. *Hist. Cardinals* III. II. 276 There were 32 Cardinals in the Conclave for the Election of that person, and twenty for his Exclusion. **1690** LOCKE *Hum. Und.* II. iv, Solidity consists in repletion, and so an utter exclusion of other bodies out of the space it possesses. **1698** LUDLOW *Mem.* (1751) I. 14 An Act for the exclusion of the Bishops out of the House of Lords. *a* **1731** ATTERBURY *Serm. on Matt.* xxvii. 25 (Seager) Their exclusion from offices and honours. **1791** BURKE *App. Whigs* Wks. VI. 110, I cannot be of opinion, that by his [Burke's] exclusion they have had any loss at all. **1826** SCOTT *Woodst.* viii, Cromwell was wont to invest his meaning.. in such a mist of words, surrounding it with so many exclusions and exceptions. **1832** AUSTIN *Jurispr.* (1879) II. xlix. 832 That [mode of property].. which implies the largest power of user and exclusion. **1863** H. COX *Instit.* III. iii. 619 The.. exclusion of the female line.. from succession to fiefs in England.

b. Phrases, †*in exclusion of, to*; *to the exclusion of.*

1691 T. H[ALE] *Acc. New Invent.* 87 Establishing this Method of sheathing, in Exclusion to all that had been till then used in the Navy. **1716** ADDISON *Freeholder* No. 5 To the Exclusion of all common Humanity to Strangers. **1774** SIR J. REYNOLDS *Disc.* v. (1876) 391, I take this study in aid and not in exclusion of the other. **1865** DICKENS *Mut. Fr.* I. 15 He spoke in the singular number to the express exclusion of Eugene. **1871** B. STEWART *Heat* §116 Two vessels entirely filled with water and vapour of water to the exclusion of air or any other gas.

c. *bill of exclusion, Exclusion Bill*: a bill brought before parliament in the reign of Charles II (1679) for excluding or preventing James, Duke of York, the king's brother, from succeeding to the crown, on the ground of his being a Roman Catholic. So *Exclusion Parliament*.

1700 LUTTRELL *Brief Rel.* (1857) IV. 667 Sir William Williams, speaker of the exclusion parliaments in the reign of King Charles the 2d, is dead. **1729** J. BRAMSTON *Art of Politics* 15 When the Exclusion-Bill was in suspense. **1827** HALLAM *Const. Hist.* (1876) II. xii. 432 The bill of exclusion was drawn with as much regard to the inheritance of the duke of York's daughter as they could reasonably demand. **1872** J. S. BREWER *Stuarts* in *Eng. Stud.* (1881) 197 Halifax had spoken with great energy against the Exclusion Bill.

2. Method or *process* of Exclusion(s): the process of discovering the cause of a phenomenon, or the solution of a problem, by successively disproving all but one of the conceivable hypotheses. In *Mathematics*, applied to a method, now obsolete, devised by Frenicle *c* 1666 for solving problems in the Theory of Numbers.

3. The action of putting or thrusting forth from any receptacle; of laying (eggs), hatching (chickens), bringing forth (a fœtus). †Also *concr.* that which is excluded.

1646 SIR T. BROWNE *Pseud. Ep.* III. vi. 117 That the.. time of the Beares gestation.. lasting but a few dayes.. the exclusion becomes precipitous.. There may.. from this narrow time of gestation ensue a minority or smalnesse in the exclusion. **1692** BENTLEY *Boyle Lect.* 145 The strange sagacity of little insects in choosing fit places for the exclusion of their eggs. **1748** HARTLEY *Observ. Man.* I. ii. 176 The Exclusion of the Fœtus. **1836** TODD *Cycl. Anat.* I. 629/2 The larva of the Newt.. a few days after its exclusion from the egg.

†**4.** The action of discharging (excrement). Also *concr.* matter excluded, excrement. *Obs.*

1646 SIR T. BROWNE *Pseud. Ep.* III. iii 110 The salt and lixiviated serosity.. hath but a single descent, by the guts, with the exclusions of the belly. **1664** POWER *Exp. Philos.* I. 10 The excrements in the Louse, there reposited just before exclusion.

5. exclusion principle *Physics*, the hypothesis that no two particles of the same kind can exist in states designated by the same quantum numbers, found to be true for the particles known as fermions; **exclusion zone**, an area into which entry is restricted or prohibited, *esp.* a maritime zone forbidden to enemy ships.

1926 [see PAULI]. **1928** *Chem. Abstr.* XXII. 4351 (*heading*) The Pauli exclusion principle. **1930** *Physical Rev.* XXXV. 580 Pauli's exclusion principle.. was stated in the form that no two electrons in an atom can have the same set of quantum numbers. **1948** *Mind* LVII. 539 Broadly speaking, the Exclusion Principle comprises two distinct features concerning the individuality of electrons and their occurrence in atomic systems: (a) electrons are regarded as intrinsically indistinguishable, and (b) in a given atom, no two electrons can occupy the same 'energy level'. **1976** *Power at Sea* (Internat. Inst. Strategic Studies) 31/1 The Blue moderates have declared a maritime exclusion zone. **1977** *Federal Register* (U.S.) 21 Apr. 20781/2 'Exclusion zone' means an area surrounding an LNG facility in which the operator has the authority.. to control all activities.. including the exclusion or removal of persons and property. **1982** *Peace News* 9 July 7/2 At an early stage in the conflict, Britain declared a maritime exclusion zone with a radius of 200 miles from the Falklands. **1985** *Financial Times* 30 Sept. 3/5 The Vega, a 34-foot Greenpeace ketch.., is just outside the atoll's 12-mile exclusion zone, shadowed by a French naval vessel.

exclusionary (ɛk'skluːʒənərɪ), *a.* [f. prec. + -ARY[1].] Of or pertaining to exclusion; characterized by exclusion.

1817 BENTHAM *Parl. Ref. Catech.* p. cliv, Note well the persons to whom, in this instance, the exclusionary force is in an immediate way applied. **1849** W. M. BEST *Law Evid.* (1870) 32 Some of these rules are of an exclusionary nature, and reject as legal evidence facts in themselves entitled to consideration.

ex'clusioner. *Obs.* exc. *Hist.* [f. as prec. + -ER[1].] One who upholds exclusion; *spec.* a supporter of the 'Exclusion Bill' (see EXCLUSION 1 b).

1685 *Lond. Gaz.* No. 2019/3 Other Disaffected Exclusioners. *a* **1734** NORTH *Exam.* II. v. (1740) 321 How rampant these Procurators of Power, the Exclusioners, were under such Circumstances. **1771** GOLDSM. *Hist. Eng.* III. 439 The court.. were willing to draw up a libel, which should be imputed to the exclusioners, and thus render them hateful to the people.

exclusionism (ɛk'skluːʒənɪz(ə)m). [f. as prec. + -ISM.] The character, manner, or principles of an exclusionist; exclusivism.
1846 WORCESTER cites *Chr. Observer.* 1864 in WEBSTER; hence in later Dicts.

exclusionist (ɛk'skluːʒənɪst). [f. as prec. + -IST.] One who favours exclusion; one who would exclude another from some privilege.
1822 HAZLITT *Table-t., On Reading New Bks.* (1852) 22 And those who claim it for themselves or others are exclusionists in literature. 1825 *New Monthly Mag.* XVI. 372, I am not.. an exclusionist in matters of society. 1841-4 EMERSON *Ess., Compensation* Wks. (Bohn) I. 47 The exclusionist in religion does not see that he shuts the door of heaven on himself in striving to shut out others.
attrib. 1860 *Sat. Rev.* IX. 7/1 How..could any Minister attempt to remove the relics of the exclusionist system?
b. *Eng. Hist.* A supporter of the *Exclusion Bill*: see EXCLUSION 1 b.
1756 HUME *Hist. Eng.* (1854) VI. lxviii. 329 The reasoning of the exclusionists appeared the more convincing. 1848 MACAULAY *Hist. Eng.* I. 256 Opponents of the court were called Birminghams, petitioners and exclusionists.

exclusive (ɛk'skluːsɪv), *a.* and *sb.* [ad. med.L. *exclūsīv-us*, f. *exclūs-* ppl. stem of *exclūdĕre* to EXCLUDE: see -IVE. Cf. F. *exclusif, -ive.*]
A. *adj.*
I. That excludes.
1. Having the power or the function of excluding. *rare.* ***exclusive voice***: right of veto.
1570 LEVINS *Manip.* 153 Exclusiue, *exclusiuus.* 1667 MILTON *P.L.* VIII. 625 We..obstacle find none Of membrane, joynt, or limb, exclusive barrs. 1682 TATE *Abs. & Archit.* II. 254 Who with exclusive bills must now dispense, Debar the heir, or starve in his defence. 1706 PHILLIPS (ed. Kersey) s.v., Soveraigns have an Exclusive Voice in the Election of Popes. 1754 RICHARDSON *Grandison* V. xxxiv. 217 Your 'tutor'..your friend, your 'BROTHER' (too clearly do I see the *exclusive* force of that last recognition!).
†2. Excluding (some other) from participation. Const. *of, to.* Sometimes quasi-*adv.* = 'to the exclusion *of*'. *Obs.*
1670 R. COKE *Disc. Trade* 66 The Dutch..will drive the Trade of the World exclusive to the English. 1698 LOCKE *Govt.* 125 One that was, by Right of Nature, to Inherit all.. exclusive..of his brethren. 1709 STRYPE *Ann. Ref.* I. xxxii. 370 By this sudden peace exclusive to the English, the Protestants were..weakned.
3. Not admitting of the existence or presence *of* (something); unable to co-exist, incompatible. ***exclusive concepts*** (Logic): (see quot.)
a 1716 BLACKALL *Wks.* (1723) I. 4 The lowest Degree [of eternal Life and Happiness] is exclusive of all Pain and Misery. 1796 BURKE *Regic. Peace* i. Wks. VIII. 201 Various persons may concur in the same measure on various grounds. They may be various, without being contrary to, or exclusive of each other. 1864 BOWEN *Logic* iv. 93 Exclusive Concepts—*animal* and *vegetable*, for instance—do not coincide in any part of their Extension.
4. a. Of a statement, enumeration, measurement, etc.: Excluding, not comprising (something). Const. *of*, †*to.* Of an interval: Not including one or both of the specified terminal points. Opposed to *inclusive.*
1649 SELDEN *Laws Eng.* II. Pref. (1739) 3 Not one instance in all that Book is exclusive to the Commons. 1651 BAXTER *Inf. Bapt.* (1656) 105 The word, 'To such' is ..rather inclusive as to them, then exclusive.
b. quasi-*adv.* (and *adv.*) So as to exclude; according to the exclusive mode of computation. (In the earlier instances the word is perh. the Lat. adv. *exclūsīvē*: cf. *esp.* quot. *a* 1626.)
1515 in Pitcairn *Crim. Trials* I. *261 Fra the xiiij day forsaid inclusiue, to xx day of þe samyn exclusiue. [*a* 1626 BACON *Jurisdict. Marches* Wks. 1740 IV. 133 The distinction of *exclusivè* and *inclusivè* is a distinction both in time and place.] 1679-88 *Secr. Serv. Money Chas. & Jas.* (Camden) 90 From 25th Decemb. last exclusive, to 29th Feb'ry following incl. 1724 SWIFT *Wks.* (1778) III. 384 Nor do I know whether he reckons the dross exclusive or inclusive with his three hundred and sixty tons of copper. 1751 CHAMBERS *Cycl., Exclusive*..is also used adverbially: as..He sent him all the Gazettes, from No. 195 to No. 300 exclusive. 1860 TYNDALL *Glac.* I. iii. 24 The châlet.. contained four men exclusive of myself and my guide.
¶ In 18th and early 19th c. *exclusive of* is often used where we should now say 'irrespective of', 'apart from (the question of)', 'not to speak of'.
1762 MRS. SHERIDAN *Miss S. Bidulph* (1767) V. 35, I.. should (exclusive of any other reasons) have thought myself bound, etc. 1792 *Eliz. Percy* II. 101 He could not, exclusive of his moral character, excape the slur of villany. 1825 R. WARD *Tremaine* II. xii. 118, I think I should like to know her, exclusive of having lost my way. 1827 SOUTHEY *Hist. Penins. War* II. 676.
II. Excluding all but what is specified.
5. *Logic.* Of propositions and particles: (see quots. 1864).
1581 J. BELL *Haddon's Answ. Osor.* 111 Logicians.. framyng a sounde and probable Argument from the proposition Exponent, to the Exclusive. 1725 WATTS *Logic* III. ii. §4 Exclusive Propositions will form a complex Argument; as, pious Men are the only Favourites of Heaven. 1864 BOWEN *Logic* v. 135 The English Exclusive particles are, one, only, alone, exclusively, etc. *Ibid.* v. 145 Exclusive Propositions limit the Predicate to this one Subject, thereby excluding it from every other Subject.
6. a. Of a monopoly or grant: Excluding all other persons from the rights conferred. Hence of a right, privilege, possession, quality, etc.: In which others have no share, esp. of journalistic news or other published matter. *Sc. Law*: (see quot. 1861).
1765 T. HUTCHINSON *Hist. Prov. Mass.* i. 129 The French claim..an exclusive fishery upon the sea-coast. 1790 BURKE *Fr. Rev.* 20 The king's exclusive, legal title. 1810 WELLINGTON in Gurw. *Disp.* V. 488 They must be under the immediate and exclusive command of their own commanding officer. 1841 *Punch* 17 July p. iii, An experienced nobleman..who..is frequently in a position to supply exclusive reports. *Ibid.* 28 Aug. 81/2 (*heading*) Further particulars. (Particularly exclusive.) *Ibid.* 13 Nov. 205/1 Our positive tone on the occasion serves to show the exclusive nature of all our intelligence. 1844 H. H. WILSON *Brit. India* III. 477 The right of exclusive trade with India, had been withdrawn from the Company. 1845 *Douglas Jerrold's Shilling Mag.* I. 262/1 What you get from me will be exclusive—from your 'own' correspondent. 1847 *Sporting Life* 18 Sept. 52/2 It paid for extensive and exclusive reports. 1861 W. BELL *Dict. Law Scot.* 354/1 Exclusive Privilege..is used in a limited acceptation to signify the rights and franchises of the nature of monopolies, formerly enjoyed by the incorporated trades of a royal burgh. 1885 *L'pool Daily Post* 1 June 5/2 The *Daily News*.. has, by the accuracy of its exclusive information, made, etc. 1928 D. L. SAYERS *Unpleasantness at Bellona Club* xix. 247 Hardy, with Fleet Street's delicate reticence towards the man with an exclusive story, did not press the question. 1966 *New Statesman* 13 May 680/3 The rival's story is no longer exclusive—it can now be decently lifted: i.e. hastily rewritten.
b. Exclusively confined *to.*
1804 J. GRAHAME *Sabbath* 450 Nor is regret exclusive to the old. 1959 *Times* 12 Jan. 11/3 Anti-Flam: Permanent flame-resistant finish exclusive to Horrockses Crewdson.
c. Of clothing, furniture, etc.: of a pattern or model exclusively belonging to or claimed by a particular establishment or firm.
1901 *Tatler* 18 Oct. p. iv (Advt.), Some very charming artistic novelties in exclusive and original designs are now ready for inspection. 1919 *Ibid.* 2 July (Advt.), Charming and exclusive designs. 1924 *Queen* 2 July p. xiv (Advt.), The absurdly low prices of the most exclusive gowns in London. *Ibid.* 9 July p. ix (Advt.), Practical designs for golfing, country and travelling wear. Exclusive but inexpensive. 1959 [see sense 6 b].
7. Of actions, sentiments, etc.: Strictly limited to the object or objects designated. ***exclusive dealing***: the practice of confining one's custom to certain special tradesmen, *esp.* on political or ecclesiastical grounds.
1836 DICKENS *Sk. Boz, Election for Beadle* 46 A threat of exclusive dealing was clearly established against the vestry clerk. 1883 H. SPENCER in *Contemp. Rev.* XLIII. 9 Exclusive devotion to work has the result that amusements cease to please.
8. Employed or followed to the exclusion of everything else; single, sole.
1790 BURKE *Fr. Rev.* Wks. V. 355 If he had been made the exclusive channel. 1862 SIR. B. BRODIE *Psychol. Inq.* II. i. 5, I do not see why these should be the exclusive studies of our schools. 1865 TYLOR *Early Hist. Man.* iv. 70 By no means the exclusive medium of thought. 1873 MIVART *Elem. Anat.* ii. 58 The main or exclusive locomotive organ.
III. 9. Of a corporate body, government, class of society, social circle, etc.: Disposed to resist the admission of outsiders to membership or to intimacy of association. Hence of persons as members of such associations, their temper or principles. Now also in general use, high-class, expensive; highbrow.
1822 HAZLITT *Table-t.* Ser. II. xvi. (1869) 312 The same exclusive and narrow-minded spirit [as that of Dissenters]. 1826 DISRAELI *Viv. Grey* II. xiii. 62 Exclusive! pooh! trash! talk to every body. 1847 EMERSON *Repr. Men, Montaigne* Wks. (Bohn) I. 336 The literary class is usually proud and exclusive. 1857 MAX MÜLLER *Chips* (1880) I. x. 256 No religion..was more exclusive than that of the Brahmans. 1870 E. PEACOCK *Ralf Skirl.* I. 162 An oligarchic government, as exclusive as that of the worst days of the Venetian Republic. 1878 BOSW. SMITH *Carthage* 179 The strange animals and rich minerals..which had so enlarged the ideas..of the untravelled and exclusive Israelites. 1942 *London Calling* 15 Jan. 10/1 Claridges, probably the most exclusive hotel in the world. 1942 *John o' London's* 10 Apr. 6/2 The short story of today is roughly one of two kinds—what is called the Magazine Story; and the newer kind which derives from Tchekov and is cultivated by the more exclusive periodicals.
B. *sb.*
1. An exclusive proposition or particle. Cf. A. 5.
1533 MORE *Debell. Salem* Wks. 943/1 This man hath a special insight in inclusiues & exclusiues, when he weneth yᵗ in my words it wer included [etc.]. 1579 FULKE *Heskins' Parl.* 174 The scriptures that say Christ is in heauen, speake without exclusiues, or exceptiues. *a* 1655 VINES *Lord's Supp.* (1677) 285, I will not now stand to prove the exclusive. 1864 BOWEN *Logic* v. 145 These [Exponibles] are divided into Exclusives, Exceptives and Restrictives.
†2. = *exclusive voice* (see A. 1; cf. It. *exclusiva*).
1599 SANDYS *Europæ Spec.* (1632) 147 Whereby having the Exclusive as they terme it; no Pope can be made but with his liking.
3. An exclusive person. Cf. A. 9.
1825 R. WARD *Tremaine* II. ii. 24 She came out..in full maturity of fastidiousness, a finished Exclusive. 1837 LOCKHART *Scott* (1839) VIII. 75 One by one, the other exclusives were seen engaged in a little tête-à-tête with her Ladyship. 1867 LYD. CHILD *Rom. Repub.* xxiii. 283 She used to be the most fastidious of exclusives.
4. An article, news-item, etc., contributed exclusively to, or published exclusively by, a particular newspaper or periodical. Also *transf.*
1901 *Westm. Gaz.* 28 Aug. 2/2 When he goes beyond this to supply his paper's demand for 'exclusives', he has to rely on second-hand versions of events. 1903 *Daily Chron.* 9 Dec. 5/2 [He] had the experience this week of reading his own obituary notice, which the 'Fermanagh Times' had as an 'exclusive'. 1904 F. LYNDE *Grafters* xxviii. 367 You'll have all the exciting details for an 'exclusive', to say nothing of the batch of affidavits in the oil scandal. 1917 C. N. BENNETT *Kinematography* 122 A good exclusive will have a 'life' of six months at least. 1936 [see BREAK *v.* 39 b]. 1959 F. USHER *Death in Error* x. 156 He had a good story and was.. hoping to clean up with a world-wide exclusive when it broke. 1967 *Punch* 8 Feb. 191/1 The *Sun*..has had a number of useful exclusives.

exclusively (ɛk'skluːsɪvlɪ), *adv.* [f. prec. + -LY².]
†1. In an exclusive sense; by an exclusive mode of computation; with exclusion of the extreme points of a series. *Obs.* Cf. EXCLUSIVE A. 4 b.
1597 MORLEY *Introd. Mus.* 70 In reckoning your distances ..you vnderstood mee exclusiuely, and I meant inclusiuely. 1656 COWLEY *Davideis* III. (1669) 119 *note*, Some understand this gift exclusively, as to the Sword, Bow, and Girdle. 1661 BOYLE *Spring of Air* III. ix. (1682) 74 All the Experiments from the 9 to the 17 exclusively our examiner leaving uncensured. 1679-88 *Secr. Serv. Money Chas. & Jas.* (Camden) 146 Com'encing the 20th of September last exclusively, and ending the 14th Dec. instant inclusively. 1726 AYLIFFE *Parerg.* 152 The first Part lasts from the Date of the Citation to the..Contestation of Suit, exclusively. 1805 EAST *Reports* V. 246 The word *until*..is used indifferently either inclusively or exclusively.
†2. To the exclusion of, without the participation of, the persons or things designated. Const. *of, to. Obs.*
1650 BP. TAYLOR *Lib. Proph.* App. to §18 (1817) 409 [In baptism] when water is taken exclusively to the Spirit, it is very true that it is not water that cleanses the soul. *a* 1691 BOYLE (J.), To be esteemed, exclusively to all the rest, its inexistent elementary ingredients. 1725-6 BROOME *Notes to Odyssey* (J.), Ulysses addresses himself to the queen chiefly or primarily, but not exclusively of the king. 1748 HARTLEY *Observ. Man* I. iii. 389 These Criterions might establish the Genuineness of the Prophecies, exclusively of all other Evidences.
3. So as to exclude all except some particular object, subject, etc.; solely.
1650 CROMWELL *Lett.* 12 Sept., Are you troubled that Christ is preached? Is preaching so exclusively your function? 1794 PALEY *Evid.* (1825) II. 294 The power of life and death resided exclusively in the Roman governor. 1825 McCULLOCH *Pol. Econ.* II. ii. 153 We do not owe our fires exclusively to the miner, or exclusively to the coal merchant.
†4. In a spirit of exclusiveness. *Obs. rare.*
1814 JANE AUSTEN *Mansf. Park* (1851) 71 A set of men you condemn so exclusively.

exclusiveness (ɛk'skluːsɪvnɪs). [f. as prec. + -NESS.] The quality or condition of being exclusive; the desire or tendency to exclude others; exclusive character.
1730-6 BAILEY (folio), *Exclusiveness*, exclusive quality. 1827 HARE *Guesses* Ser. II. (1873) 340 Exclusiveness arises from the monopolizing spirit of selfishness. 1845 R. JEBB in *Encycl. Metrop.* II. 715/1 The exclusiveness of property. 1882 MISS BRADDON *Mt. Royal* II. vii. 136 There were others who preferred the exclusiveness of a separate table.

exclusivism (ɛk'skluːsɪvɪz(ə)m). [f. as prec. + -ISM.] The principle or practice of being exclusive; systematic exclusiveness.
1834 *Tait's Mag.* I. 598 *Exclusivism*, —or the principle of keeping others without a certain pale, and boasting of being within ourselves. 1840 *Ibid.* VII. 798 That spirit of gain or exclusivism which has seized those who are called the owners of the streams. 1887 LANG *Myth, Ritual & Relig.* II. 280 We may deprecate the charge of exclusivism.

ex'clusivist. *rare.* [f. as prec. + -IST.] One who maintains the exclusive validity (of a theory).
1885 GLADSTONE in *19th Cent.* Nov. 701 The field of Greek mythology..is the favorite sporting-ground of the exclusivists of the solar theory.

exclusivity (ɛksklu'sɪvɪtɪ). [ad. F. *exclusivité*, f. EXCLUSIVE *a.* + -ITY.] = EXCLUSIVENESS, EXCLUSIVISM.
1926 *Science* 2 July 5 From the reactions of oxidation we deduce the principle of the exclusivity of oxidation. 1930 *Economist* 20 Dec. 1166/2 Inducing his Party not to accompany their acceptance of his request for their cooperation with any declaration of 'exclusivity' against M. Tardieu or anybody else. 1934 E. POUND *ABC of Reading* 183 The plenum of letters is not bounded by primaeval exclusivity. 1960 'M. CAINE' *S Man* 107 There is nothing society clings to so determinedly as the notion of exclusivity. 1967 'LA MERI' *Sp. Dancing* (ed. 2) xi. 130 He took an exclusivity contract and presently got me an engagement in Mexico City.

exclusory (ɛk'skluːsərɪ), *a.* [ad. late L. *exclūsōri-us*, f. *exclūs-* ppl. stem of *exclūdĕre*: see EXCLUDE *v.* and -ORY.] Having the power or the function of excluding; tending to exclude; = EXCLUSIVE A. 1. Const. *of.*
1585 BONNER in Burnet *Hist. Ref.* II. 179 To put out the Term *peremptory*, and other that were exclusory of further disputations. 1654 'PALÆMON' *Friendship* 25 'Twere

extreamly tedious to run over all the Vices and shew how they were particularly exclusory of Friendship. **1721–1800** in BAILEY. **1865** *Daily Tel.* 4 Nov. 4/5 The exclusory laws were the result of the narrowest and most exasperating religious intolerance.

†**ex'coct**, *v. Obs.* [f. L. *excoct-* ppl. stem of *excoquĕre*, f. *ex-* out + *coquĕre* to boil, melt.]

1. *trans.* To produce, extract, or obtain (chiefly, a metal) by heat.

1601 HOLLAND *Pliny* II. 508 There is a stone..out of which..(with burning) they excoct brasse. **1626** BACON *Sylva* §843 Salt and sugar, which are excocted by Heat, are dissolved by Cold, and Moisture. **1671** J. WEBSTER *Metallogr.* iii. 56 A new Iron is excocted forth of them. **1755** in JOHNSON.

b. To drive off by heat. In quot. *fig.*

1563–87 FOXE *A. & M.* (1596) 204/1 If [Becket].. through immoderat violence of zeale, did exceede..the same was excocted agaİne and purged by the fire of his suffring. **1651** H. MORE in *Enthus. Tri.* (1656) 208 Put thy soul into a crysiple..and set it on that fire that will excoct and purge out thy drosse.

2. To drive off the moisture of; to elaborate, refine, mature, ripen.

1572 J. JONES *Bathes of Bath* II. 18 b, Arguinge an earthy dryenes, temperatly excocted, and not parched. **1576** NEWTON tr. *Lemnie's Complex.* (1633) 179 Their head..is not of ability to excoct the nutriment into the use and comlinesse of haires. **1710** T. FULLER *Pharm. Extemp.* 182 The Saliva..so excocted and viscid as to bring hazard of Suffocation. *Ibid.* 297 Bile..too much excocted..makes wild Mischief.

†**ex'coct**, *pa. pple. Obs. rare*$^{-1}$. [ad. L. *excoct-us*, pa. pple. of *excoquĕre*: see prec.] Boiled thoroughly.

1576 NEWTON tr. *Lemnie's Complex.* (1633) 173 An unsavory humour..which being excoct, settled..and fined from the dregges..is brought to the nature of pure and good Wine.

†**ex'coction.** *Obs. rare.* [ad. late L. *excoctiōn-em*, n. of action f. *excoquĕre*: see EXCOCT.] The action of extracting or elaborating by heat.

1640 G. WATS tr. *Bacon's Adv. Learn.* v. ii. 228 In the excoctions and depurations of Metalls it is a familiar error, that to advance excoction, they augment the heate of the Fornace. **1715** tr. *Pancirollus' Rerum Mem.* II vii. 316 There are other Things, which are not as yet found out, as.. Excoction of the thinnest Waters.

†**excodi'cation.** *Obs. rare*$^{-1}$. [ad. late L. *excōdicātiōn-em*, n. of action f. *excōdicā-re* to remove the soil from the roots of a tree, f. *ex-* (see EX- *pref.*[1]) + *cōdex*, *cōdic-em*, later form of *caudex* stem, trunk.] The action of digging up or removing the soil from the roots of a tree.

c **1420** *Pallad. on Husb.* II. 3 Excodicacion..is hem [vines] to desolate Of erthe, and all from every roote abate.

excogitable (ɛks'kɒdʒɪtəb(ə)l) *a.* [as if ad. L. **excōgitābilis* f. *excōgitāre*: see next.] That admits of being excogitated. (In quot. mistake for *inexcogitable*; the It. original has *inescogitabile*.)

1592 R. D. *Hypnerotomachia* 67 They brought mee into a fayre Orchy-ard of excogitable expense, tyme, and subteltie of woorke-manshippe.

excogitate (ɛks'kɒdʒɪteɪt), *v.* [f. L. *excōgitāt-* ppl. stem of *excōgitāre* to find out by thinking, f. *ex-* out + *cōgitāre* to think: see COGITATE.]

1. *trans.* To think out; to construct, frame, or develop in thought; to contrive, devise. Also with *inf.* or *sentence* as *obj.*

c **1530** H. DOWES in Froude *Hist. Eng.* I. 39, I have endeavoured myself..to excogitate how I might most profit him. **1546** LANGLEY *Pol. Verg. De Invent.* I. vi. 12 b, Plinie saieth he euer thought yᵗ the Assirians Excogitated the letters, which Cadmus brought out of Phenice into Grece. **1647** LILLY *Chr. Astrol.* clxxii. 734 The Ancients have excogitated many and sundry wayes for to find out the true time. **1665** EVELYN *Mem.* (1857) III. 167 Dr. Wilkins, Sir Wm. Petty, and Mr. Hooke, with our operator..are excogitating new rigging for ships. **1836–7** SIR W. HAMILTON *Metaph.* xx. (1870) II. 4 We here excogitate no new, no occult principle. **1868** BROWNING *Ring & Bk.* III. 712 He..did at last excogitate How he might keep the good and leave the bad.

absol. **1814** CHALMERS *Evid. Chr. Revel.* viii. 214 He ceases to observe, and begins to presume, or excogitate.

¶ **2.** *intr.* = COGITATE.

1630 J. TAYLOR (Water P.) *Wks.* II. xxxvi. 266/1 When thereon I doe excogitate, Intrinsicall and querimonious paines Doe pulverise the concaue of my braines.

†**ex'cogitate**, *pple. Obs.* [ad. L. *excōgitāt-us*, pa. pple. of *excōgitā-re*: see prec.] Used as pa. pple. of prec.

1531 ELYOT *Gov.* II. vii, What noble statutes, ordinances, and actes of counsaile from time to time haue bene excogitate. **1542** HENRY VIII *Declar. Scots* 196 It appereth a playne deuise only excogitate for a delay. **1689** tr. *Buchanan's De Jure Regni* 30 Honour..can be told or excogitate to be in any Man.

excogitated (ɛks'kɒdʒɪteɪtɪd), *ppl. a.* [f. prec. verb + -ED[1].] Thought out, contrived, devised.

a **1619** FOTHERBY *Atheom.* I. vii. §3 An excogitated and composed tale, to deceiue the world. **1814** CHALMERS *Evid. Chr. Revel.* x. 267 An assumed or excogitated principle of our own. **1869** J. MARTINEAU *Ess.* II. 177 An excogitated system, arising by the evolution of pure thought.

excogitation (ɛks,kɒdʒɪ'teɪʃən). [ad. L. *excōgitātiōn-em*, n. of action f. *excōgitāre* to think out: see EXCOGITATE.]

1. The action of excogitating; thinking out; reflection, mental contrivance. Const. *of.*

1531 ELYOT *Gov.* I. xxiii, To consideration pertaineth excogitation and auisement. **1655** H. VAUGHAN *Silex Scint.* I. Pref. (1858) 3 Many of them cast away all their fair portion of time, in..excogitation of idle words. **1759** JOHNSON *Rasselas* xliii, The labour of excogitation is too violent to last long. **1854** H. ROGERS *Ess.* (1860) II. 12 Patient excogitation must be the metaphysician's great instrument. **1865** DICKENS *Mut. F.* I. ii, To the excogitation of this problem, [he] had devoted many anxious hours.

2. A result of the action; a plan thought out; a contrivance, an invention.

1664 POWER *Exp. Philos.* I. 81 The second Experiment is one of the ingenious Excogitations of M. Gascoign's. *a* **1687** PETTY *Pol. Arith.* i (1691) 21 All these Particulars, said to be the subtile Excogitations of the Hollanders. **1706** PHILLIPS, *Excogitation*, an Invention or Device. **1721–1800** in BAILEY. **1748** SMOLLETT *Rod. Rand.* (1812) I. 292, I will impart my own simple excogitations.

excogitative (ɛks'kɒdʒɪteɪtɪv), *a.* [f. EXCOGITATE *v.* + -IVE.] Adapted for, concerned with, or having the power of excogitating.

1846 H. ROGERS *Ess.* I. iv. 170 In mathematics, where the demands on the excogitative faculties are so great. **1864** SALA in *Daily Tel.* 23 Nov., I had an acute excogitative ability. I could reason out an idea.

excogitator (ɛks'kɒdʒɪteɪtə(r)). [agent-n. f. L. *excōgitāre*: see EXCOGITATE and -OR.] One who excogitates.

1847 SIR W. HAMILTON *Let. De Morgan* 28 An original excogitator of the doctrine.

†**ex'cogitous**, *a. Obs. rare*$^{-1}$. [f. L. *excōgit-āre* + -OUS; after med.L. *cōgitōsus*] Inventive.

1646 N. LOCKYER *Serm.* 15 Impatience is very excogitous.

†**exco'lation.** *Obs. rare*$^{-1}$. [ad. L. *excōlātiōn-em*, n. of action f. *excōlāre* to strain out, f. *ex-* out + *cōlāre* to filter.] The action of filtering or straining out.

1578 BANISTER *Hist. Man* v. 83 A certaine worke made in the reynes to the excretion or excolation of Urine.

†**exco'mmenge**, *v. Obs.* [ad. AF. **excomenger*, OF. *escomenger*, corresp. to Pr. *escomeniar*, *escomengar*:—L. *excommūnicāre* to EXCOMMUNICATE.] *trans.* To excommunicate.

1502 *Ord. Crysten Men* (W. de W. 1506) IV. vii. 186 Yf the synner be fallen into sentence, excommenged or interdyted. **1577** HOLINSHED *Chron.* II. 26/2 The pope excommenged the towne. **1641** *Termes de la Ley* 149 Excommengement.. is where a man by the iudgement in Court Christian is Excommenged.

Hence †**exco'mmengement** [OF. *escomengement*], excommunication.

1495 *Act 11 Hen. VII*, c. 24 §1 Any..excommengement pleded or alleged in the partie playntif. **1531** *St. German's Doctor & Stud.* II. xxxii, Yf the excommengement be of record in the kynges courte. **1628** COKE *On Litt.* 134 a, None can certifie excommengement but only the Bishop. **1641** [see above].

†**ex'common**, *v. nonce-wd.* [f. EX- *pref.*[1] + COMMON: cf. next.] = DISCOMMON (see quot.).

1667 E. CHAMBERLAYNE *St. Gt. Brit.* I. III. x. (1743) 241 For lighter offences they [members of Lincoln's Inn, etc.] are only excommoned, or put out of commons, not to eat with the rest.

†**ex'commune**, *v. Obs.* Also 5–6 excom(m)yne. [ad. F. *excommunier*, ad. L. *excommūnicāre*: see EXCOMMUNICATE.]

1. *trans.* (*Eccl.*) = EXCOMMUNICATE I.

1483 CAXTON *Cato* F ij, Alle those that byleve the sortleges and devynours been excommunyd. **1502** *Ord. Crysten Men* (W. de W. 1506) I. vii. 77 To be excommyned & departed by mortall synne from..the holy chyrche catholyke. **1608** T. MORTON *Preamb. Incounter* 27 He was admonished and excommuned before he was degraded.

2. *transf.* With double obj.: To excommunicate or exclude from.

1650 FULLER *Pisgah* II. IV. i. 15 We cannot recover Paphos proportionably into this Map, behold it therefore peeping in, but excommuned the lines thereof. **1654** GAYTON *Pleas. Notes* I. vi. 21 Poets..were excommun'd Plato's Common Wealth.

†**ex'communement.** *Obs.*$^{-0}$ [ad. OF. *excomuniement.*] = EXCOMMUNICATION.

1530 PALSGR. 218/1 Excomunement, *excommenge.*

excommunicable (ɛkskə'mjuːnɪkəb(ə)l), *a.* [f. EXCOMMUNIC-ATE *v.* + -ABLE.] Liable to be excommunicated; deserving excommunication. Of an offence: Punishable by excommunication.

1594 HOOKER *Eccl. Pol.* III. i. (1617) 84 Altho' they be impious idolaters, wicked Heretikes, persons excommunicable. **1646** *Burd. Issach.* in *Phenix* 1708 II. 281 This Assembly is above the King..to their Orders he must give Obedience: otherwise he is excommunicable. **1680** BAXTER *Cath. Commun.* (1684) 13 To render each other odious, or vile, and excommunicable. **1836** KEBLE in *Hooker's Wks.* (1845) I. Pref. 28 What offences are excommunicable.

excommunicant (ɛkskə'mjuːnɪkənt). [ad. L. *excommūnicant-em*, pr. pple. of *excommūnicāre*: see EXCOMMUNICATE. (With sense 2 cf. EXAMINANT 2.)]

1. One who excommunicates; an excommunicator.

1651 HOBBES *Leviath.* III. xlii. 308 Might be a greater pain to the Excommunicant than to the Excommunicate.

¶ **2.** = EXCOMMUNICATE B.

1586 FERNE *Blaz. Gentrie* 313 Likewise with these, we arraunge all..excommunicants, heretiques, vsurers, pandars, histrions, or stage players. **1641** HEYLIN *Hist. Episcopacy* (1657) II. 365 When as the wickednesse of Felicissimus..was growne unto the height, the Father of his owne authority denounced him excommunicant. **1887** J. MARTINEAU *National Church* in *Contemp. Rev.* LI. 416 Innumerable swarms of excommunicants—Donatists, Arians, Monophysites, Albigenses, Hussites. [In mod. Dicts.]

excommunicate (ɛkskə'mjuːnɪkət), *pa. pple.*, *ppl. a.* and *sb.* Also 6, 8 -icat. [ad. L. *excommūnicāt-us*, pa. pple. of *excommūnicā-re* (see next).]

A. *pa. pple.* and *ppl. adj.*

1. Excommunicated. *arch.*

1526 TINDALE *John* ix. 22 He shulde be excommunicat out of the Sinagoge. **1662** LAMONT *Diary* 21 Sept. 195 Divers persons were excommunicat att this tyme. **1762** HUME *Hist. Eng.* xiv. 129 They..engaged the bishops..to pronounce him [Gavaston] excommunicate if he remained any longer in the kingdom. **1839** BAILEY *Festus* Proem (1848) 5/1 Nor is this An outlawed orb nor excommunicate. **1874** GREEN *Short Hist.* iii. §2. 121 None of his allies..could fight side by side with an excommunicate king.

¶ **2.** *excommunicate things* (tr. Heb. *ḥerem*): objects devoted to destruction.

1551 BIBLE (Matthew) *Josh.* vi. 18 If you take of the excommunicate thynges so shal you make the hooste of Israell excommunicate. **1635** PAGITT *Christianogr.* 213 Achan..took of the excommunicate things of Jerico.

B. *sb.* An excommunicated person.

1562 in Strype *Ann. Ref.* I. xxxi. 349 Those excommunicates, for whom there is a *Significavit* directed. **1670** MILTON *Hist. Eng.* IV. (1851) 159 Thou hast neglected to abstain from the House of that Excommunicate. *a* **1711** KEN *Hymns Evang.* Poet. Wks. 1721 I. 135 Jews you as Excommunicates will treat. **1852** MISS YONGE *Cameos* (1877) III. xxx. 309 They turned the coffin of Gaston de Foix, as an excommunicate, out of the Cathedral.

transf. **1626** SHIRLEY *Brothers* III. i, Poor Fernando, for her sake, must stand An excommunicate from every blessing. **1640** T. CAREW *To my inconstant Mistris* i, Thou, poore excommunicate From all the joyes of love.

excommunicate (ɛkskə'mjuːnɪkeɪt), *v.* Also 6 -icat. [f. late (Eccl.) L. *excommūnicāt-* ppl. stem of *excommūnicāre* lit. 'to put out of the community,' f. *ex-* out + *commūnis* common, on the analogy of *commūnicāre* (see COMMUNICATE).]

1. *trans.* (*Eccl.*) To cut off from communion; to exclude, by an authoritative sentence, from participation in the sacraments and services of the church, or from religious rites in general.

1526–34 TINDALE *John* xvi. 2 They shall excommunicat you. **1579** TOMSON *Calvin's Serm. Tim.* 118/1 To deliuer to Sathan is nothing else, but to excommunicate a man. **1660** R. COKE *Power & Subj.* 10 If a man be excommunicated, he shall have no advantage or relief in any plea by the common law. **1757** BURKE *Abridgm. Eng. Hist.* Wks. X. 189 They [the Druids] were further armed with a power of.. excommunicating any obnoxious persons. **1815** WELLINGTON 19 Jan. in Gurw. *Disp.* XII. 250 The actors of the Théâtre Français having been excommunicated..the curate of St. Roch refused to receive the body into the Church. **1875** BRYCE *Holy Rom. Emp.* xiii. (ed. 5) 209 Excommunicated by Gregory IX for not going to Palestine, he [Frederick II] went, and was excommunicated for going.

†**b.** To forbid (an action) under pain of excommunication. *Obs. rare.*

1644 MILTON *Areop.* Wks. (1847) 106/1 Martin the fifth by his bull..was the first that excommunicated the reading of heretical books.

2. *transf.*

1602 ROWLANDS *Greene's Ghost* 3 To be reiected and excommunicated from the fellowship of all honest men. **1666** J. SMITH *Old Age* (1752) 46 [In assimilation] those [parts of the chyle] that are like to prove unconformable, are excommunicated to the pores. **1823** LAMB *Elia* Ser. I. iii. (1865) 24 He was excommunicated; put out of the pale of the school. **1848** MACAULAY *Hist. Eng.* II. 93 If he were contumacious he might be excommunicated, or, in other words, be deprived of all civil rights and imprisoned for life.

Hence **exco'mmunicated** *ppl. a.*; also *absol.*, **exco'mmunicating** *vbl. sb.* and *ppl. a.*

1580 BARET *Alv.* E 430 Excommunicated. **1648** JENKYN *Blind Guide* i. 4 The faithfull with a holy scorn neglect his excommunicating of you. **1669** GALE *Crt. Gentiles* I. III. ix. 93 That none eat or drink with such an excommunicated person. **1715** M. DAVIES *Athen. Brit.* I. 252 Neither bound to..Obey an Excommunicated Queen. **1814** SCOTT *Ld. of Isles* II. xxiv, Or dream of greeting, peace or truce, With excommunicated Bruce! **1837** CARLYLE *Fr. Rev.* II. v. vi, Plotting Aristocrats, and excommunicating Dissident Priests. **1845** S. AUSTIN *Ranke's Hist. Ref.* II. 487 The right of excommunicating..is inherent in every man. **1862** TRENCH *Mirac.* xviii. 303 In case the excommunicated showed no sign of repentance.

excommunication (ɛkskəmjuːnɪ'keɪʃən). Also 5 excomunycacion. [ad. late L. *excommūnicātiōn-em*, f. *excommūnicāre*: see prec. and -ATION. Cf. F. *excommunication.*] The action of excom-

municating or cutting off from fellowship.

1. *Eccl.* The action of excluding an offending Christian from the communion of the Church; the state or fact of being so excluded. Also in wider sense: The exclusion of an offending member from any religious community, *e.g.* Jewish or heathen.

The Canon Law recognizes two kinds of excommunication: the lesser, by which an offender is deprived of the right to participate in the sacraments; the greater, by which he is cut off from all communication with the church or its members.

1494 FABYAN *Chron.* VI. clxiv. 168 This to be obseruyd vpon payne of excomunycacion. **1555** EDEN *Decades* 172 We furthermore streightly inhibite all maner of persons..vnder the peyne of the sentence of excommunication..to trauayle for marchaundies. **1651** HOBBES *Leviath.* (1839) 502 This part of the power of the keys, by which men were thrust out from the kingdom of God, is that which is called excommunication. *a* **1744** POPE *Love of the World Reproved,* A part in every swine No friend..May taste..On pain of excommunication. **1781** GIBBON *Decl. & F.* III. 34 A sentence of excommunication was pronounced, which enjoined Ambrose to depart from Milan without delay. **1856** FROUDE *Hist. Eng.* (1858) I. iii. 192 Excommunication seems but a light thing when there are many communions.

b. *transf.*

1830 HOOD *Haunted H.* I. iii, A house—but under some prodigious ban Of Excommunication. **1840** —— *Up the Rhine* 16 The yellow flag which indicates that sanitary excommunication [quarantine]. **1873** F. HALL *Mod. Eng.* 34 He calls you a utilitarian. The greater excommunication being thus denounced against you.

2. Short for 'sentence of excommunication'.

1647 CLARENDON *Hist. Reb.* II. (1843) 43/2 To restrain any excommunication from being pronounced..without the approbation of the bishop. **1781** GIBBON *Decl. & F.* III. lvi. 366 By some acts of rapine or sacrilege, he had incurred a papal excommunication. **1866** KINGSLEY *Herew.* vii. 129 The pope fulminated an excommunication against him.

3. (See quot.)

1751 CHAMBERS *Cycl.* s.v., The rule of the Benedictines gives the name Excommunication, to the being excluded from the oratory, and the common table of the house.

excommunicative (ɛkskəˈmjuːnɪkeɪtɪv), *a.* [f. EXCOMMUNICATE *v.* + -IVE.] **a.** Characterized by the refusal of communion. **b.** Containing a sentence of excommunication. **c.** Also of persons: Disposed or eager to excommunicate.

1825 COLERIDGE *Aids Refl.* (1848) I. 166 No other Church acts on so narrow and excommunicative a principle. **1858** CARLYLE *Fredk. Gt.* (1865) I. II. iv. 68 Thomas à Becket.. coming home excommunicative. **1876** *Contemp. Rev.* XXVIII. 65 There was in existence an excommunicative decree against comedians.

excommunicator (ɛkskəˈmjuːnɪkeɪtə(r)). [f. as prec. + -OR.] One who excommunicates.

1643 PRYNNE *Treachery & Disloy.* 8 King John..himselfe was one of the Excommunicators. **1681** BAXTER *Answ. Dodwell* ii. 12 Who will judg, but the Excommunicator, what is unsinful as to his act? **1828** D'ISRAELI *Chas. I,* I. vi. 169 The Pope, who succeeded the excommunicator of Elizabeth. **1855** MILMAN *Lat. Chr.* (1864) IV. VII. ii. 94 He must obtain the absolution from his excommunicator.

excommunicatory (ɛkskəˈmjuːnɪkətərɪ), *a.* [f. as prec. + -ORY.] **a.** Of or pertaining to excommunication. **b.** = EXCOMMUNICATIVE c.

a. **1683** CAVE *Anc. Ch. Govt.* 292 The Excommunicatory letter sent to Acacius himself. **1855** MILMAN *Lat. Chr.* (1864) III. VI. iii. 458 The spiritual death inflicted by the excommunicatory decree of the church at Augsburg. **1884** M. RULE *Pref. to Eadmeri Historia Novorum* III, The excommunicatory sentence which the council of Bari adjudged the Red King to have incurred.

b. **1837** CARLYLE *Fr. Rev.* II. v. vi, The excommunicatory Priests give new trouble in the Maine and Loire.

†**excoˈmmunion.** *Obs.* [? f. EXCOMMUNE *v.*, on the analogy of *communion.* Cf. Pg. *excomunhaõ.*] = EXCOMMUNICATION. (Frequent in Milton.)

1641 MILTON *Ch. Govt.* II. iii. Wks. (1847) 51/1 They.. holding forth the dreadful sponge of excommunion pronounce him wiped out of the list of God's inheritance. **1642** *Remonstr. Ch. Irel.* 32 There was an Excommunion from the chief of their Church, against any of his Religion that would not do the like. **1659** MILTON *Civ. Power Eccl. Causes* Wks. 1738 I. 549 Such are punished by Excommunion only.

†**exˈcommuny.** *Obs.* In 6 excomunye. [a. OF. *excommunie,* f. *excommunier* to excommunicate.] = EXCOMMUNICATION.

1502 *Ord. Crysten Men* (W. de W. 1506) IV. ix. 195 Paynes canonycalles as ben excomunye, suspencyon, interdyte.

exco(m)myne, var. form of EXCOMMUNE *v. Obs.*

†**exˈconcavate,** *v. Obs.* [f. L. *ex-* out + *concavus* CONCAVE + -ATE³.] *trans.* To hollow out.

1599 A. M. tr. *Gabelhouer's Bk. Physicke* 141/2 Exconcavate an onione, replenishe him agayne with saffern, etc.

ex-ˈconjugant. Also ex-conjugate. [f. EX-¹ + L. *conjugānt-em* pr. pple. of *conjugāre* (see CONJUGATE *v.*); *conjugate* f. the vb.] One of a pair of protozoa, bacteria, etc., that have recently been in conjugation. Also *attrib.* or as *adj.*

1902 *Proc. R. Soc. Edin.* XXIII. 420 He succeeded in getting exconjugates to conjugate within that small number of divisions. **1903** *Archiv für Entwicklungsmechanik der Organismen* XV. 174 After separation, the two ex-conjugants have been isolated and their divisions carefully recorded. **1953** R. P. HALL *Protozool.* ii. 95 Exconjugant and non-conjugant lines of *Paramecium caudatum* and *Pleurotricha lanceolata.* **1960** *New Biol.* XXXI. 109 The two paramecia, when they separate after conjugation (they are then known as ex-conjugants) have the same nuclear (genic) material. **1964** W. HAYES *Genetics of Bacteria & their Viruses* xxii. 557 A different approach is to carry out a pedigree analysis of single, exconjugant, recipient bacteria and their progeny with the aid of a micromanipulator.

ex-convict. [EX-¹.] A former convict. Also *attrib.* and in shortened slang form *ex-con.*

1867 *Cassell's Mag.* II. 471/2 The clutches of some vulgar ex-convict mistress. **1887** *Chambers's Jrnl.* 1 Oct. 637/2 An appointment is made with the ex-convict. **1907** J. LONDON *Road* (1914) 146 An 'ex-con' who had done five years in Sing Sing. **1955** *Publ. Amer. Dial. Soc.* XXIV. 34 Better than fifty per cent of Pinkertons are ex-cons. *Ibid.,* This estimated percentage of ex-convicts hired by Pinkerton is much too high. **1965** *Austral. Encycl.* III. 38/1 An ex-convict wanting to return had either to work his passage or pay his fare from his savings.

†**exˈcordiate,** *ppl. a. Obs.* [f. EX- + L. *cord-, cor* heart + -(I)ATE².] Deprived of heart or courage.

1594 *Zepheria* xxxix, If at last, she all, through fear excordiate, Command thee not to peace.

excoriable (ɛksˈkɔərɪəb(ə)l), *a. rare*⁻¹. [f. L. *excoriā-re* (see next) + -BLE.] Capable of being excoriated; that may be rubbed or stripped off.

1658 SIR T. BROWNE *Gard. Cyrus* iii. 147 Such a natural net is the scaly covering of fishes..even in such as are excoriable and consist of smaller scales, as Bretts, Soals.

excoriate (ɛksˈkɔərɪeɪt), *v.* Also pa. pple. 6–9 EXCORIATE. [f. L. *excoriāt-* ppl. stem of *excoriāre* to strip off the hide, f. *ex-* out + *corium* hide.]

†**1.** *trans.* To pull off the skin or hide from (a man or beast); to flay. *Obs.*

1614 RALEIGH *Hist. World* III. 41 Otanes..whom Cambyses had excoriated for false judgement. *a* **1653** GOUGE *Comm. Heb.* iv. 13 Beasts..being excoriated or flayed, were cut down from the neck to the rump. *a* **1681** WHARTON *Fasts & Fest.* Wks. (1683) 26 He [St. Bartholomew] was..Excoriated, or fleaed alive. **1826** DISRAELI *Viv. Grey* II. xv. 77 They compliment them [their victims] upon..the delicacy of their limbs prior to excoriating them.

b. *transf.* To strip off the rind or bark from.

1775 ASH, *Excoriating,* taking off the bark.

2. To remove portions of the skin (or analogous membrane) from. Now chiefly *Path.* of the action of corrosives, of abrasion, etc.

1497 BP. ALCOCK *Mons Perfect.* E ij a, Excoriate and wounde dayly theyr self with sharpe hayr. **1605** TIMME *Quersit.* I. xiii. 60 The intralls being excoriated, death by a lingering consumption ensueth. **1656** RIDGLEY *Pract. Physick* 109 The ends of his Fingers are supposed to be excoriated. **1771** SMOLLETT *Humph. Cl.* (1815) 77 Stuffing my nose with spirit of hartshorn, till the whole inside was excoriated. **1857** C. BRONTË *Professor* II. xx. 104 My lips.. were excoriated as with vinegar and gall. **1867** F. H. LUDLOW *Little Briggs & I.* 201 The grand idea of how to fix it in a boy's memory was to excoriate his palm.

3. *transf.* and *fig.*

1633 J. FISHER *True Trojans* III. viii. in Hazl. *Dodsley* XII. 506 Though wrongs excoriate the heart. **1661** R. W. *Conf. Charac., Colledge Butler* (1860) 67 He can excoriate a loafe. **1708** MOTTEUX *Rabelais* (1737) V. 233 Excoriating the Language Latiale. **1809** *Naval Chron.* XXV. 209 It [lightning] excoriated the lower part of the head post.

4. To strip or peel off (the skin); to remove (the lining membrane) by corrosion.

1547 BOORDE *Brev. Health* cix. 41 b, Excoriat the skyn and maturat the matter. **1615** CROOKE *Body of Man* 71 Because it may bee excoriated or flayed off. *a* **1691** BOYLE *Hist. Air* xix. Wks. 1772 V. 694 The heat of the Island Squauena.. excoriates the skin. **1767** GOOCH *Treat. Wounds* I. 445 To prevent..the matter..from excoriating the skin. **1843** BETHUNE *Sc. Fireside Stor.* 62 Exuding acrid matter, and thereby excoriating the cuticle.

excoriate (ɛksˈkɔərɪeɪt), *pple. arch.* Also 6–7 -at. [ad. L. *excoriāt-us,* pa. pple. of *excoriā-re:* see next.] **A.** Used as pa. pple. of prec. **B.** *ppl. a.* = next.

1544 PHAER *Regim. Lyfe* (1546) Kj, If the bowels be excoriat, ye shal give thys peculiar remedy. **1560** ROLLAND *Crt. Venus* II. 344 Tratour..Thow seruis quick to be excoriate. **1681** COLVIL *Whigs Supplic.* (1751) 109 While hips excoriat, made him swaddle Through all the corners of the saddle. **1791** COWPER *Yardley Oak* 5 A shattered veteran.. with excoriate forks. **1814** CARY *Dante* 55 The pack..came Excoriate from the lash.

†**b.** with allusion to the practice of circumcision.

1611 *Panegyr. Verses* in Coryat *Crudities,* He more prevail'd against the 'xcoriate Iewes Then Broughton could.

excoriated (ɛksˈkɔərɪeɪtɪd), *ppl. a.* [f. EXCORIATE *v.* + -ED¹.] Having the skin or rind rubbed or stripped off. Also *transf.* and *fig.*

1661 LOVELL *Hist. Anim. & Min.* 49 The decoction of a Fox excoriated and embowelled..used as an embrocation. **1676** WISEMAN *Chirurg. Treat.* (J.), An hypersarcosis arises upon the excoriated eyelid. **1708** MOTTEUX *Rabelais* (1737) V. 233 'Tis meer excoriated Latiality. **1819** G. S. FABER *Dispensations* (1823) II. 296 Pointing to his excoriated frame.

excoriation (ɛksˌkɔərɪˈeɪʃən). [f. EXCORIATE *v.*: see -ATION. Cf. F. *excoriation.*]

1. The action of excoriating; the state of being excoriated: †**a.** the action or process of flaying (a man or beast (*obs.*)); **b.** the action of abrading a portion of the cuticle, or of the coating of any organ of the body; an instance of this; **c.** the action of stripping off (the bark of a tree).

a. **1607** BREWER *Lingua* III. v, A little before the excoriation of Marsyas. **1635** AUSTIN *Medit.* 220 Some keep the day of his [Bartholomew's] Excoriation; and some, the day of his Decollation holy. **1669** GALE *Crt. Gentiles* I. II. ix. 141 After the killing of the Holocaust, follows the excoriation, and dissection.

b. **1447** BOKENHAM *Seyntys* (Roxb.) 259 The reed flyx.. wyth of the guttys excoryacyoun Sendyth owte sangweyn agestyoun. **1578** LYTE *Dodoens* IV. lxxx. 544 They drinke it [tragacanth]..against excoriation or knawing of the bladder. **1596** DANETT tr. *Comines* 296 A sharpe sicknes of excoriation and the stone. **1664** H. MORE *Myst. Iniq.* xxii. 84 What Flagellations and Excoriations of the Body. **1751** JOHNSON *Rambler* No. 133 ¶3, I was punished with artificial excoriations in hopes of gaining new graces with a new skin. **1774** GOLDSM. *Nat. Hist.* (1776) VII. 99 The Germans.. complained of a slight excoriation of the lips. **1813** W. HEBERDEN in *Med. Trans.* (1815) V. 39 Stopping the Excoriation..consequent upon continual Pressure in Bed. **1844** TUPPER *Twins* xv, Lash, lash, lash, in furious and fast succession..to the universal excoriation of Mr. Julian Tracy.

c. **1830** J. G. STRUTT *Sylva Brit.* 125 The constant excoriation of the bark also produces a variety of hues.

2. *fig.*

1640 HOWELL *Dodona's Gr.* 207 Hee hath marvailously enhanc'd the revenues..of the Crowne, though with a pitifull excoriation of the poorer sort. **1651** BAXTER *Inf. Bapt.* Apol. 22 It is the excoriation and exulceration of mens spirits that usually causeth the smart.

3. An excoriated place (on the body): a sore.

c **1540** in *Vicary's Anat.* App. ix. (1888) 221 A plastre devised by the kinges Maiestie at Grenewich, and made at Westminstre, to..heale excoriacions. **1751** CHAMBERS *Cycl.* s.v., He had a grievous excoriation behind, with riding post. **1874** tr. *Van Buren's Dis. Genit. Org.* 19 The epithelium comes off in patches, leaving irregular excoriations.

†**exˈcorporate,** *ppl. a. Obs.* [f. L. *ex-* (see EX- *pref.*¹) + *corpor-, corpus* body + -ATE³. Cf. INCORPORATE.] Disembodied.

a **1629** T. GOFF *Bajazet* IV. ix, So Jove I come, excorporate, divine, Immortal as thyself.

excorse: see EXCOURSE *v. Obs.*

excorticate (ɛksˈkɔːtɪkeɪt), *v.* [f. L. *ex-* out + *cortic-* stem of *cortex* bark, shell + -ATE³.] *trans.* To pull or strip off the bark from (a tree), or the shell from (a nut, seed). Also *fig.*

1657 TOMLINSON *Renou's Disp.* 63 The seeds..are excorticated by a knife. **1664** EVELYN *Sylva* 69 Moss is to be rubb'd and scrap'd off with some fit instrument of Wood, which may not excorticate the Tree. **1844** ALB. SMITH *Adv. Mr. Ledbury* v. (1886) 16 Looking about the nails as if he had been excorticating millions of new walnuts.

b. *fig.*

1600 O. E. *Repl. to Libel* III. vi. 31 To make his eloquence seeme more admirable, he doth excorticate certaine Latin words according to his Romish fashion.

Hence **exˈcorticated** *ppl. a.*

1657 *Phys. Dict., Excorticated,* fleyed or pieled. **1693** SIR E. KING in *Phil. Trans.* XVII. 863 (Whole Oatmeal, or) an Excorticated Oat. **1725** BRADLEY *Fam. Dict.* s.v. *Diahexapte,* Take Juniper-Berries unexcorticated, and Bay Berries excorticated.

excortication (ɛksˌkɔːtɪˈkeɪʃən). [f. prec.: see -ATION. Cf. F. *excortication.*] The action of stripping off or peeling the bark (from a tree).

1664 EVELYN *Sylva* (1776) 517 The prejudice accruing thereby as to the Tanner (in regard of the more difficult Excortication). **1725** BRADLEY *Fam. Dict.* s.v. *Infirmities of trees,* Excortication and Bark-Baring.

†**exˈcourse,** *sb. Obs.* [variant of EXCURSE, after the analogy of COURSE.]

1. The action of running forth or out; an excursion or sally; usually a hostile or marauding one.

1523 *St. Papers Hen. VIII,* IV. 35 The rodes and excourses divised, to be made or not made, as ye shal se the cace to requyre. **1557** PAYNEL *Barclay's Jugurth* 20 b, He assailed and inuaded more inwardly..by excourses of his horsemen. **1584** R. SCOT *Discov. Witchcr.* III. ii. 43 During the whole time of the witches excourse, the diuell occupieth the roome and place of the witch.

2. a. The means of sallying forth. **b.** The extent of ground covered, range (of a person's activity, also of a chain of mountains).

c **1534** tr. *Pol. Verg. Eng. Hist.* I. 6 The nation of Britons ..havinge thether excourse owt of Fraunce did occupie the ilonde. *Ibid.,* The mountayne Grampius..from the entree of the ryver Dee..hathe excourse to the Irish seas. **1555** BONNER *Necess. Doctr.* C, The Excourse of hym is even unto the helles.

3. = EXCURSUS 2.

1579 FULKE *Heskins' Parl.* 144 He interlaceth a fond excourse of the authoritie of the later writers.

† **ex'course**, *v.* *Obs.* ? Also excorse. [var. of SCOURSE.] *intr.* To exchange, barter, 'swop'. (It is doubtful whether quot. 1593 belongs here.)

1593 NASHE *Christ's T.* 52 b, So shall you be ready to curse God, and desire to be swallowed quicke, to excorse the agony you are in. **1623** COCKERAM II, To Change.. Excourse, Trucke, Traffique.. Barter.

† **ex'creable**, *a.* *Obs.* *rare*$^{-0}$. [ad. L. *ex(s)creābilis* f. *ex(s)creā-re*: see EXCREATE and -ABLE.] That may be spit out.

1623-6 COCKERAM, *Excreable*, which easily may be spit out. **1656-81** BLOUNT *Glossogr.*, *Excreable*, that may be voided by spitting or retching. *a* **1745** SWIFT (W.). **1832** in WEBSTER; and in mod. Dicts.

excrease, var. of EXCRESCE *v.* *Obs.*

† **excre'ate**, *v.* *Obs.*$^{-0}$ [f. L. *ex(s)creāt-*, ppl. stem of *ex(s)cre-āre* to spit out by coughing (f. *ex-* out + *scre-āre* to hawk, hem) + -ATE^3.]

trans. To cough or hawk up; to spit out.

1623-6 in COCKERAM. **1721-1800** in BAILEY; whence in mod. Dicts.

† **excre'ation.** *Obs.* [ad. L. *ex(s)creātiōn-em*, n. of action f. *ex(s)creā-re*: see prec.] The action of coughing up or spitting out; expectoration.

a **1556** CRANMER *Wks.* II. 320 Extreme coughing and excreations which I cannot eschew. **1607** TOPSELL *Four-f. Beasts* (1673) 204 The rennet.. stayeth bleeding, and refresheth excreations of bloud. **1610** HEALEY *St. Aug. Citie of God* 277 Sweet.. Incrassating Things.. may help Excreation out of the Throat. **1620** VENNER *Via Recta* (1650) 323 The excrements of the braine must daily be avoyded thorow the mouth by spetting and excreation.

excrement^1 ('ɛkskrɪmənt). [a. F. *excrément*, ad. L. *excrēment-um* what is sifted out, f. *excrē-*, *excernĕre* (see EXCERN, EXCRETE), f. *ex-* out + *cernĕre* to sift.]

† **1.** That which remains after a process of sifting or refining; the dregs, lees, refuse. In quots. *pl.* only. *Obs.*

1576 BAKER *Jewell of Health* 161 b, When as in it shall no other be contayned or remaine then the excrementes of the sage. **1610** MARKHAM *Masterp.* II. clxxiii. 501 Tartar is the excrements of wine, which sticke to the vessell. **1698** KEILL *Exam. Th. Earth* (1734) 299 This Earth.. he stiles the very dregs and excrements of nature.

2. *Phys.* **a.** 'That which is cast out of the animal body by any of the natural emunctories' (*Syd. Soc. Lex.*); superfluous matter thrown off by the bodily organs; an excreted substance. Now *rare* in general sense.

1565 COOPER *Thesaurus*, *Excrementum*, the dregges or excrementes of digestion made in the bodie; as fleume, choler, melancholie, urine, sweate, snivell, spittel, milke, ordure. **1570-6** LAMBARDE *Peramb. Kent* (1826) 289 Why doe they not.. offer us their Spittle, and other excrements of the body to be kissed? **1607** TOPSELL *Four-f. Beasts* (1673) 356 This excrement [urine] is meerly proper to four-footed living-beasts. **1658** A. FOX tr. *Wurtz' Surg.* III. iv. 227 Corruption is the excrement of wounds. **1725** BRADLEY *Fam. Dict.* II. S iv b/2 The Nose serves to.. give a Passage to a Sort of Excrement. **1745** BERKELEY *Let.* Wks. 1871 IV. 305 The gout.. throws off a sharp excrement from the blood to the limbs.

transf. **1577** B. GOOGE *Heresbach's Husb.* IV. (1586) 180 b, Whether it [manna] bee the sweate or excrement of the Heavens, or a certaine spittle of the starres. **1751** CHAMBERS *Cycl.* s.v., Some hold ambergrise.. an excrement of the sea.

b. *esp.* 'The alvine fæces or the waste matter discharged from the bowels' (*Syd. Soc. Lex.* 1884). Commonly *pl.* or *collect. sing.*; rarely *sing.* with *an.*

1533 ELYOT *Cast. Helthe* II. (1541) 18 b, Breade haueing moch branne, fylleth the bealy with excrementes. **1555** EDEN *Decades* 213 The excremente which they auoyde is a lyuynge worme. **1678** MARVELL *Growth Popery* Wks. 1875 IV. 413 But.. he is an ill woodman that knows not the size of the beast by the proportion of his excrement. **1704** SWIFT *T. Tub* (1711) 209 A fly, driven from a Hony-pot, will.. finish his Meal on an Excrement. **1843** J. A. SMITH *Product. Farming* (ed. 2) 88 The excrements of all animals contain less nitrogen than their food. **1875** DARWIN *Insectiv. Pl.* xiv. 326 Sausage-shaped masses of excrement.

† **c.** Superfluous matter thrown off by a plant. *Obs.*

1606 BRYSKETT *Civ. Life* 43 Trees and plants.. grow, bloome, and bring forth fruit; which fruit Aristotle sayth, cometh from them instead of excrement. **1664** POWER *Exp. Philos.* I. 29 How should an excrement [Cuckow-spitt] of so many several Plants, still breed one and the same Animal. **1751** CHAMBERS *Cycl.* s.v., Gums, diverse juices, balms, &c. issuing spontaneously from their respective trees, are sometimes called excrements.

3. *fig.* (In 16–17th c. often as an opprobrious designation of persons.)

1561 T. NORTON *Calvin's Inst.* Author's Pref., Abject sillie men we be.. yea and if you will, certaine excrements and outcasts of the world. **1642** ROGERS *Naaman* 17 Ipta was thrown out for a base excrement from the family of Gilead. *a* **1688** VILLIERS (Dk. Buckhm.) *Poems* (1775) 142 Thou common-shore of this poetic town, Where all our excrements of wit are thrown.

† **'excrement**^{2}. *Obs.* [ad. L. *excrēment-um*, f. *excrē-*, *excrescĕre*, f. *ex-* out + *crēscĕre* to grow.]

1. That which grows out or forth; an outgrowth; said *esp.* of hair, nails, feathers.

1588 SHAKS. *L.L.L.* v. i. 109 It will please his Grace.. to dallie with my excrement, with my mustachio. **1609** C. BUTLER *Fem. Mon.* i. (1623) Cj, Men, beasts and fowles.. haue outwardly some offensive excrement, as haire, or feathers. **1615** W. HULL *Mirr. Maj.* A iv a, Siluer and gold, the white and yellow excrements of the earth? **1688** R. HOLME *Armoury* II. 85/2 Agarick, an Excrement or hard Mushroom, growing out of the sides of old Trees. **1705** BOSMAN *Guinea* xiv. 236 That Excrement in the Negroes being more like Wool than hair.

b. A growth, product.

1616 SURFL. & MARKH. *Country Farme* 507 The excrements of the poole.. are the frogge and the creuisse.

2. *fig.* (When the notion is that of 'superfluous outgrowth', this is sometimes not easily distinguished from the fig. use of EXCREMENT^1.)

1549 *Compl. Scot.* vi. 59 The myst, it is the excrement or the superfluite of the cluddis. **1590** NASHE *Pasquil's Apol.* I. A iij b, Our Religion in England is no newe excrement of the braine of man. **1606** WARNER *Alb. Eng.* xv. xciv. (1612) 376 Wit so is wisedomes Excrement. *a* **1677** BARROW *Serm.* Wks. 1716 I. 322 Unwilling to part with the very superfluities and excrements of their fortune.

3. *abstr.* Growth, increase, augmentation.

1607 TOPSELL *Serpents* (1653) 653 Otherwise they [great Worms] would increase after the same sort in all respects, as the common Wasps do. The excrement is only in the small Worms. **1609** DOWLAND *Ornith. Microl.* 47 Augmentation .. is the excrement of some Note. For in it is put a Minime for a Semibreefe.

† **'excrement**, *v.* *Obs.* *rare*$^{-1}$. [f. EXCREMENT *sb.*] *intr.* To void excrement.

1632 LITHGOW *Trav.* VIII. 347 [She] had neyther eate, nor drunke, nor yet excremented for thirteene yeares.

excremental (ɛkskrɪ'mɛntəl), *a.*^{1} [f. EXCREMENT^1 + -AL^1.]

† **1.** Pertaining to, or consisting of, the dregs or baser part of any substance. Cf. EXCREMENT^1 1. Of food: Consisting largely of matter useless for nutrition. *Obs.*

1576 BAKER *Jewell of Health* 193 b, Vitrioll containeth much of the waterie and excrementall moysture in it. **1600** TOURNEUR *Transf. Met.* xxvi. 179 The flesh, the soule's imprisoner, Of excrementale earth is wholy fact. **1607** TOPSELL *Four-f. Beasts* (1673) 525 Swines flesh.. is less excremental then Pigs flesh, and therefore more nutrible. **1620** VENNER *Via Recta* (1650) 85 They have in their flesh much moist and excrementall juyce. **1655** MOUFET & BENN. *Health's Improv.* (1746) 183 A Cuckow, whose much spitting argueth a corrupt and excremental Flesh. **1662** R. MATHEW *Unl. Alch.* § 110. 180 To take a few grains of the excremental parts, out of an ounce of the substantial parts.

2. Of the nature of excrement or evacuated matter.

1574 NEWTON *Health Mag.* 2 The filth and excrementall matter of the bodie is thereby [by exercise] scattered and avoyded. **1658** SIR T. BROWNE *Pseud. Ep.* II. vii. (ed. 4) 115 Whether those little dusty particles upon the lower side of the leaves be seeds and seminal parts, or rather.. excremental separations, we have not been able to determine. **1878** FOSTER *Phys.* II. i. § 1. 183 The nutritious digested material is separated from the indigested or excremental material.

b. *fig.* (cf. EXCREMENT^1 3).

1591 GREENE *Disc. Coosnage* (1859) 40 Vipers of the world, and an excrementall reversion of sin. **1593** NASHE *Christ's T.* (1613) 159 In a damnable state are you, O ye excrementall vessels of lust.

3. Pertaining to or consisting of excrements; concerned with or proceeding from excrements.

1599 A. M. tr. *Gabelhouer's Bk. Physicke* 139/2 When any man his excrementalle intestine issueth out. **1624** DONNE *Serm.* xvii. 164 a, The spitting places and excremental corners of the Streets. **1762** LLOYD *Genius, Envy & Time* 97 Mere excremental maggots, bred In poets topsy-turvy head. **1875** W. HOUGHTON *Sk. Brit. Insects* 115 Besides excremental food they prey on insects. **1884** *Boston* (Mass.) *Jrnl.* 15 Nov. 2/4 In excremental contaminations especially lies the greatest risk [of cholera poison].

† **excre'mental**, *a.*^{2} *Obs.* *rare.* [f. EXCREMENT^2 + -AL^1.] Of the nature of an outgrowth or excrescence.

1644 MILTON *Areop.* (Arb.) 45 Her whitenesse is but an excrementall whitenesse. **1656** *Artif. Handsom.* 46 Art [the polling of the hair, paring the nails, etc.] doth dayly turn.. those things which are but excrementall, to be ornamentall.

excremential (ɛkskrɪ'mɛnʃəl), *a.* *rare*$^{-1}$. [f. EXCREMENT^1 + -(I)AL. Cf. Fr. *excrementiel.*] = EXCREMENTAL^1.

1847 JOHNSTON in *Proc. Berw. Nat. Club* II. 226 Its pores are choked by excremential fluids.

† **excre'mentious**, *a.* *Obs.* *rare.* [f. as prec. + -(I)OUS.] = EXCREMENTITIOUS *a.*^{1}

1636 FEATLY *Clavis Myst.* liii. 740 If nature produceth.. precious stones of excrementious moisture. **1694** WESTMACOTT *Script. Herb.* 22 Green beans are cold and moist and excrementious. **1707** FLOYER *Physic. Pulse-Watch* 24 Excrementious Humours, as Urine, Sweat, and hot Fumes from the Blood.

excrementitial (ɛkskriːmɛn'tɪʃəl), *a.* Also 7 -all. [f. as next + -AL^1. Cf. Fr. *excrémentitiel.*] = EXCREMENTITIOUS.

1620 VENNER *Via Recta* iii. 51 If it [veal] be too young, then it is ouer-moist, crude, and excrementitiall. **1857** BULLOCK tr. *Cazeaux' Midwif.* 230 An excrementitial part, charged with carbon, forms the meconium.

excrementitious (ɛkskriːmɛn'tɪʃəs), *a.*^{1} [f. assumed L. **excrēmentīci-us* (f. *excrēment-um* EXCREMENT^1) + -OUS.]

† **1.** Of the nature of the dregs or worthless part of any substance. Of food: Consisting largely of matter useless for nutrition; = EXCREMENTAL^1 1.

1623 HART *Arraignm Ur.* ii. 8 The.. excrementitious part of the food is voided forth. **1661** LOVELL *Hist. Anim. & Min.* Introd., The flesh of wild beasts is lesse excrementitious and dryer, than that of the tame.

2. Of the nature of excrement or excreted matter.

1586 BRIGHT *Melanch.* xix. 118 The aged.. faile in the execution of externall actions.. by excrementitious humiditie. **1623** ROWLANDSON *God's Bless.* 35 As if mildew were.. an excrementitious humor. **1670** BOYLE in *Phil. Trans.* V. 2013 We kept the same Duckling in the same Receiver very close.. to keep in the excrementitious steams of her body. **1744** BERKELEY *Siris* § 30 Exhaling vessels, for carrying off excrementitious parts, are discovered throughout the whole surface of the vegetable. **1761** *Brit. Mag.* II. 435 The scent of excrementitious animal juices, such as musk, civet, etc. **1826** KIRBY & SP. *Entomol.* (1828) III. xxxii. 297 Almost all insects discharge some drops of an excrementitious fluid. **1875** URE *Dict. Arts* II. 740 s.v. *Guano*, This extraordinary excrementitious deposit of certain sea-fowls.

fig. **1641** *Compl. conc. Corruptions & Grievances* 4 Sweare to all we must, or else be thrust out as.. excrementitious burthens of the Church. **1683** D. A. *Art Converse* 39 The very scum of the world, and.. the very excrementitious part of mankind.

3. Pertaining to or arising from excrement. ¶Also (*nonce-use*), Full of excrement, foul with ordure.

1792 A. YOUNG *Trav. Fr.* 160 When brisk mountain gales do not ventilate these excrementitious lanes. **1887** *Q. Rev.* 7 Jan. 209 There is indeed reason to suspect the existence of such excrementitious pollution of the soil.

Hence † **excremen'titiously** *adv.*, (*a*) so far as the excrementitious portion is concerned; (*b*) (*nonce-use*) nauseatingly, disgustingly. † **excremen'titiousness**, excrementitious quality; in quot. *concr.*

1638 T. WHITAKER *Blood of Grape* 44 Cold and dry in temper, but excrementitiously moist. **1660** FISHER *Rusticks Alarm* Wks. (1679) 374 Men Excrementitiously exact and diligent to very Dotage. **1660** tr. *Paracelsus' Archidoxis* II. 81 On this wise are all the voidings of the excrementitiousness of the body.

† **excrementitious**, *a.*^{2} *Obs.* [f. assumed L. **excrēmentīci-us* (f. *excrēment-um* EXCREMENT^2) + -OUS. Cf. prec.] Consisting of, or of the nature of, an outgrowth.

c **1645** HOWELL *Lett.* I. xxx. 60 Hair is but an excrementitious thing. **1677** HALE *Prim. Orig. Man.* III. iv. 266 These [feathers] are excrementitious, and not really parts of the Bird.

† **excre'mentive**, *a.* *Obs.* *rare*$^{-1}$. [f. EXCREMENT^1 + -IVE.] Fitted to carry off or discharge excrement (from the body).

1627-77 FELTHAM *Resolves* II. lii. 262 It may, indeed, be thought a modesty in nature, to cover those excrementive parts, which, left uncover'd, perhaps might offer offence.

† **excre'mentize**, *v.* *Obs.* *rare*$^{-1}$. [f. EXCREMENT^1 + -IZE.] *intr.* To void excrements.

c **1670** WOOD *Life* (1848) 135 Inflamed with strong liquors, they went into the balcony.. and excrementized in the street.

† **excre'mentous**, *a.*^{1} *Obs.* *rare.* [f. L. *excrēment-um* (see EXCREMENT^1) + -OUS.] Pertaining to, or of the nature of, EXCREMENT^1.

1616 SURFL. & MARKH. *Country Farme* 391 The common Nut hath power to drie.. the excrementous moisture of all things whereunto it is applyed. **1646** SIR T. BROWNE *Pseud. Ep.* II. vi. 95 The corrupt and excrementous humors in man are animated into lyce. **1721-1800** in BAILEY.

† **excre'mentous**, *a.*^{2} *Obs.* *rare*$^{-1}$. [f. L. *excrēment-um* (see EXCREMENT^2) + -OUS.] Pertaining to, or of the nature of, an outgrowth.

1597 LOWE *Chirurg.* (1634) 23 *Pe.* Which are the Members called excrementous? *Jo.* The nailes and the haire.

† **excre'mentuous**, *a.* *Obs.* [f. EXCREMENT^1 + -(U)OUS.] Of the nature of excrement, refuse, or dregs; = EXCREMENTITIOUS *a.*^{1}

1576 BAKER *Jewell of Health* 4 b, When therefore.. the grosser and excrementuous partes abyde in the bottome of the Lymbecke. **1616** SURFL. & MARKH. *Country Farme* 672 Although the heronshew be a royall meate.. his flesh is full of excrementuous parts.

† **ex'cresce**, **ex'crease**, *sb.* *Obs.* [f. next.] A growing out; in quots. *concr.* excess amount, increase.

1707 STEWART *Index to Scots Acts* 14 (Jam.) The excresce of the excise or the inland salt and forraign commodities, etc. **17..** W. FORBES *Suppl.* Dec. 56 (Jam.) There happened in the coining sometimes an excresce on the tale, of five or six shillings or thereby, in one hundred pounds.

† **ex'cresce**, **ex'crease**, *v.* *Obs.* Also 6 *Sc.* excresse. [ad. L. *excrēscĕre*: cf. INCREASE.] *intr.* To grow out or forth; to constitute an excrescence; to increase inordinately; to exceed what is usual.

1570 B. GOOGE *Pop. Kingd.* II. (1880) 236 So hath this wretched kinde of men in little time excreast. **1588** A. KING tr. *Canisius' Catech.* h vij, Quhilk [xi days] addit to yat ȝere quhairin it excresseis makis ye same to exeid the common ȝere of ye sone be 19 dayes. **1691** ED. TAYLOR tr. *Behmen's Theos. Philos.* 71 The Pores..so numerous in the Skin, thro' which the Hairs excresce.

Hence †**ex'creasing** *ppl. a.*

1578 BANISTER *Hist. Man* 2 a, When a bone in any part, stretcheth forth his substance in excreasing maner. **1671** *True Nonconf.* 145 How this excresing power should have crept into the whole Church.

excrescence (ɛk'skrɛsəns). Also 6 excressence. [ad. L. *excrēscentia*, f. *excrēscent-em*: see EXCRESCENT and -ENCE. Cf. Fr. *excrescence*.]

†**1.** The action of growing out or forth. Also, immoderate growth, overflow, abnormal increase.

1533 BELLENDEN *Livy* v. (1822) 409 Thare gudis war multiplyit be excrescence of the proffitt that thay have won. **1615** CROOKE *Body of Man* 83 There is a double limit, beyond which the excrescence of the Haire dooth not proceede. **1649** SELDEN *Laws Eng.* I. xl. (1739) 60 This Island..became a common Sewer to the Excrescence of those Eastern peoples. **1677** HALE *Prim. Orig. Man.* II. ix. 225 Our annual Winters correct the excrescence of Insects. **1752** D. CAMPBELL in *Scots Mag.* (1753) July 347/1 The said excrescence of the rents of that farm would..be accounted for to them.

†**b.** = EFFLORESCENCE 4. *Obs.*

1718 J. CHAMBERLAYNE *Relig. Philos.* III. xxvii. §12 The Excrescence of Salt-Petre from old Walls made of Mortar and Stone.

c. Of a feeling, etc.: Exuberant outburst; exuberance. Now *rare*. In early use: †Overblown pride; swagger.

1629 in *Biblioth. Regia* 28 The insolence and excrescence of the Popish pretended clergy. **1648** MILTON *Observ. Art. Peace* Wks. (1858) 565 Of such like stuff we meet not any where with more excrescence then in his own lavish Pen. *a* **1667** JER. TAYLOR (W.), Excrescences of joy. **1768** JOHNSON *Pref. to Shaks.* in *Wks.* (1787) IX. 281 The exuberant excrescence of his diction I have often lopped. **1867** A. BARRY *Sir C. Barry* vi. 232 The excrescences of that ardent desire for perfection.

2. Something that grows out; a natural outgrowth or appendage. Now somewhat *rare*.

1633 T. ADAMS *Exp. 2 Pet.* ii. 20 Even these excrescences [hairs] are ornaments. **1664** POWER *Exp. Philos.* I. 8 Nature having imp'd her [Butterfly's] wings..with these plumeous excrescences. **1782** W. F. MARTYN *Geog. Mag.* I. 38 Nor ever cutting their hair or nails to whatever length these excrescences may grow. **1849** RUSKIN *Sev. Lamps* vi. §15. 177 Their character of sublimity passes into excrescences; —into mane and beard as in the lion. **1871** DARWIN *Desc. Man* II. xii. 35 These horns consist of an excrescence of bone covered with a smooth sheath.

fig. *a* **1681** GLANVILL *Serm. on 1 Pet.* i. 22 (1681) 122 Shall we lose a Limb for an Excrescence, or..an Essential of Religion for that which is but accessary? **1755** YOUNG *Centaur* Wks. 1757 IV. iv. 191 They are mere excrescences to the good man's happiness; and he has no more feeling in them than in his hair, or his nail. **1768–74** TUCKER *Lt. Nat.* (1852) I. 42 Have we not motives for those excrescences of action? **1868** M. PATTISON *Academ. Org.* v. 253 The professor was an excrescence on the examination system.

3. An abnormal, morbid, or disfiguring outgrowth; a disfiguring protuberance or swelling on an animal or vegetable body.

1578 LYTE *Dodoens* I. xli. 61 Wartes, and such like excressence, or superfluous out growings. **1599** [see ALIENATE *ppl. a.* 2]. **1681** tr. *Willis' Rem. Med. Wks.* Voc., *Excrescences*..warts or pieces of flesh. *a* **1682** SIR T. BROWNE *Tracts* 60 This is no proper Berry, but a kind of Vessicular excrescence. **1713** CHESELDEN *Anat.* I. i. (1726) 7 Bony excrescences upon the bones are frequent. **1752** BERKELEY *Tar-Water* Wks. 1871 III. 500 Tumours, wens, and preternatural excrescences. **1807** J. E. SMITH *Phys. Bot.* 346 Many of our Willows bear round excrescences, as large as peas, on their leaves. **1844** DUFTON *Deafness* 97 Fungous excrescences [of the ear] may be removed either by the forceps or the knife.

b. *transf.* and *fig.*

a **1680** BUTLER *Rem.* (1759) I. 226 Pedantry is but..A stupified Excrescence, like a Wen, Fed by the peccant Humours of learn'd Men. **1796** MORSE *Amer. Geog.* I. 378 A room..from the upper part of which are dependent many excrescences. **1839** MURCHISON *Silur. Syst.* I. xxxvi. 498 An irregular excrescence from the main ridge of trap. **1871** B. TAYLOR *Faust* (1875) I. 318 *note*, The piece [Oberon and Titania's golden wedding] can only be regarded as an excrescence.

excrescency (ɛk'skrɛsənsɪ). Also 6–7 -sy, -sie. [f. as prec.: see -ENCY.]

1. Excrescent state or condition; the quality or fact of growing out or forth; abnormal or excessive development; an instance of the same. †In early use also: An exuberant outburst, an extravagance.

1638 FEATLEY *Strict. Lyndom.* II. 12 The excrescensie and superabundance of Saints satisfactions. **1649** JER. TAYLOR *Gt. Exemp.* Exhort. §7 Some Saints have had excrescencies and eruptions of holiness in the instances of uncommanded duties. *Ibid.* I. ii. §25 Our Fasts..and all exteriour acts of religion are to be guided by our Superiour, if he sees cause to asswage any excrescencie. **1650** BULWER *Anthropomet.* 172 The Deduction and Moderation of their [the Nails'] Excrescencie to a just extendure. *a* **1661** HOLYDAY *Juvenal* 149 An extraordinary excrescency of bones below..the rump bone. **1748** tr. *Vegetius' Distemp. Horses* 202 If there is an Excrescency of Flesh, you shall boil Grass with Oil and put it in it.

†**2.** Something that is excrescent; an outgrowth; = EXCRESCENCE 2. Often applied to fungi. *Obs.*

1545 RAYNOLD *Byrth Mankynde* 146 Warts and suche lyke excrescensys on the face. **1597** GERARD *Herbal* clxii. 1384 The earthie excrescencies, called Mushrums. **1648** *Hunting of Fox* 5 Pruned of their luxuriant excrescencies. **1646** J. HALL *Poems* Pref., A Mushrome though but an excrescency, well drest is no poyson, but a Salad. **1653–5** H. MORE *Antid. Ath.* II. xi. (1712) 73 The red pugger'd attire of the Turky, and the long Excrescency that hangs down over his Bill. **1704** SWIFT *Batt. Bks.* (1711) 246 Excrescencies in form of Teats. **1736** BAILEY, *Excrescency*, that which sticks to or grows upon another thing, as cat's tails upon a nut tree, etc.

†**3.** An abnormal, morbid, or unsightly outgrowth; = EXCRESCENCE 3. *Obs.*

1641 MILTON *Reform.* II. (1851) 43 A huge and monstrous Wen little lesse then the Head it selfe, growing to it by a narrower excrescency. **1691** RAY *Creation* (1701) II. 236 A large Wen upon our Faces..or any the like superfluous Excrescency.

b. *transf.* and *fig.*

1649 MILTON *Eikon.* xi. (1851) 424 Hee..would have onely the excrescencies of evil prun'd away for the present. *a* **1677** BARROW *Serm.* Wks. 1716 I. 158 Oaths as they commonly pass are mere excrescensies of speech. **1713** *Guardian* No. 1 ¶5 Ambition, lust, envy, and revenge are excrescencies of the mind. **1756–82** J. WARTON *Ess. Pope* (1782) I. III. 132 The two last books of the Iliad may be thought not to be excrescencies but essential to the poem.

excrescent (ɛk'skrɛsənt), *a.* Also 6 excressent. [ad. L. *excrēscent-em*, pr. pple. of *excrēscĕre*: see EXCRESCE *v.*]

1. †**a.** *gen.* That grows out. Const. *from* (*obs.*). **b.** *Bot.* of a peduncle (see quot. 1857).

1650 BULWER *Anthropomet.* 172 The excrescent, supercrescent, and ever-crescent parts. **1677** HALE *Prim. Orig. Man.* III. ii. 257 The first spontaneous production of Men..was in certain Folliculi or Bladders, excrescent from the Earth. **1779** *Projects* in *Nat. Hist.* 107/2 They will wash this excrescent substance off. **1834–43** SOUTHEY *Doctor* (1862) 24 Matter will arise contingent to the story..or excrescent from it. **1857** HENFREY *Bot.* §139 Sometimes the peduncles undergo expansion during the ripening of the seeds, so as to form part of the fruit; such an inflorescence or peduncle is called excrescent.

2. †**a.** Growing in excess or beyond normal limits; excessive (*obs.*). **b.** Growing abnormally out of something else; constituting an excrescence; redundant, superfluous.

1633 T. ADAMS *Exp. 2 Peter* ii. 13 We pare off such excrescent blemishes that the body may be perfect. **1657** TOMLINSON *Renou's Disp.* 69 The virtue of chrysocal is..to cohibit excrescent flesh. **1671** *True Nonconf.* 153 Their Immediate successors are against your Prelatick excrescent power. **1697** POTTER *Antiq. Greece* IV. x. (1715) 248 She from the Fore-head of a new foal'd Colt Th' excrescent Lump doth seek. **1732** POPE *Ess. Man* II. 49 Expunge the whole, or lop the excrescent parts [of Science]. **1886** F. FORD in *Mag. Of Art* Nov. 8 There is an excrescent structure of wood stuck on the wall.

3. Constituting an excess over the normal quantity. Formerly, *spec.* in Chronology.

1609 HOLLAND *Amm. Marcel.* XXVI. i. 456 *note*, The odde day which everie fourth yeare arising out of the six excrescent howers in each yeare, maketh the leape yeare. *a* **1654** SELDEN *Fortescue's De Laud. Reg.* (1672) 128 The four excrescent quadrants of a day in the Julian yeare were and are, at the end of every four years space, put into one day. **1832** CHALMERS *Pol. Econ.* vii. 220 The excrescent, or the superinduced population.

b. *Gram.* Of a sound in a word: Having no etymological value, but developed by the influence of euphony.

1868 KEY *Philol. Essays* 204 Excrescent Consonants. I have thought it desirable to ask for one [a new grammatical term]..because the ordinary term 'epenthesis' seems to have been formed on a false theory. **1881** SKEAT *Etym. Dict.* s.v. *Sound, The final d*..is excrescent, just as in the vulgar *gownd* for *gown*.

excrescential (ɛkskrɛ'sɛnʃəl), *a.* [f. L. *excrēscenti-a* (see EXCRESCENCE) + -AL[1].] Of the nature of an excrescence, redundant.

1849 RUSKIN *Sev. Lamps* vi. §15. 177 Mane and beard as in the lion..are..excrescential characters. *a* **1864** HAWTHORNE *Eng. Note-bks.* (1879) II. 183 The vestry.. occupies that excrescential edifice.

excrescen'titious (ɛkskrɛsən'tɪʃəs), *a. rare*[−1]. [badly f. EXCRESCENT + -ITIOUS; after *adventitious*.] Of the nature of an excrescence.

1833 *New Monthly Mag.* XXXVIII. 189 This wart on the 'great wen' is as distinct and excrescentitious as if, etc.

excress, -ence, -ent, obs. ff. EXCRESCE, etc.

†**ex'cression.** *Obs.* Also 7 excrescion, -sion. [A non-etymological formation (for EXCRETION) on L. *excrēscĕre*. Cf. CONCRESSION.] An outgrowth; = EXCRETION[2].

1610 MARKHAM *Masterp.* II. cxxix. 430 Such bones, knobs, or bunches, are called excresions. **1623–6** COCKERAM, *Excrescion*. **1635** MARKHAM *Faithful Farrier* (1638) 102 Any bony excression..upon any member of an Horse; as Splint, Spaven. **1725** BRADLEY *Fam. Dict.* s.v. *Rules*, If there are hard knots on the outside, they are screws or excressions.

fig. **1647** J. LAWNIND *Putney Projects* 39 Those excressions of nature, the great Lawyers.

‖**excreta** (ɛk'skriːtə). [Lat.; neut. pl. of pa. pple. of *excernĕre*: see EXCERN, EXCRETE.] Excreted matters; the waste expelled from the animal body; now often limited to the fæces and urine, or to the former only.

1857 LIVINGSTONE *Trav.* xxx. 614 The excreta had been expelled a full yard from the orifice. **1877** ERICHSEN *Surg.* I. 8 The lungs and skin..are unable to set free their excreta. **1878** HUXLEY *Physiogr.* 227 The smoke and ashes of the animal are..the fæcal and urinary excreta.

excretal (ɛk'skriːtəl), *a.* [f. EXCRET(A + -AL.] Of or pertaining to excreta.

1864 *Jrnl. R. Agric. Soc.* XXV. 496 Human excretal matters. **1964** M. HYNES *Med. Bacteriol.* (ed. 8) xxxi. 478 A lower ratio suggests excretal contamination.

excrete (ɛk'skriːt), *v.* [f. L. *excrēt-* ppl. stem of *excernĕre*, f. *ex-* out + *cernĕre* to separate, sift. See EXCERN.]

1. *trans.* Of animals and plants or their organs: To separate (chiefly waste matters) from the vital fluids preparatory to discharging from the system; to separate and expel from the system through the emunctory organs; often used with reference to the process of expulsion merely.

1668 *Phil. Trans.* III. 890 Nature copiously excretes by the Reins..a liquor..compounded of Aqueous, Saline, Sulphury, and other particles. **1720** W. GIBSON *Diet. Horses* iv. (ed. 3) 58 Things excreted and retained. **1802** PALEY *Nat. Theol.* xix. (1803) 366 Slime excreted by the animal's skin. **1836** TODD *Cycl. Anat.* I. 401/1 A sanguineous fluid is excreted from the bladder. **1859** DARWIN *Orig. Spec.* iv. (1873) 73 Certain plants excrete sweet juice. **1880** HAUGHTON *Phys. Geog.* iii. 79 Animals..live by absorbing oxygen and excreting carbonic acid.

†**b.** *intr.* for *refl.* with *forth*.

1620 VENNER *Via Recta* (1650) 301 Vaporous fumes that excrete forth from the brain.

c. *absol.* (In quot. 1832 humorously for 'spit'.)

1832 *Blackw. Mag.* XXXI. 830 English 'commercial gentlemen' excrete in spit-boxes. **1872** HUXLEY *Phys.* i. 15 The body feeds, and it excretes. **1881** MIVART *Cat* 232 The lungs excrete.

†**2.** Of drugs, etc., and of personal agents: To cause the excretion of. Also with *forth*, *out*. *Obs.*

1620 VENNER *Via Recta* II. 36 It..maketh the body soluble, by excreting forth of yellow cholericke humors. *Ibid.* vii. 119 They loose the belly, and excrete out choler. **1651** BIGGS *New Disp.* ¶187 Adæquate meanes to excrete the catarrhous matter.

Hence **ex'creted** *ppl. a.*, sifted out and discharged. **ex'creter**, that which excretes or discharges. **ex'creting** *vbl. sb.* and *ppl. a.*

1802 PALEY *Nat. Theol.* xiii. Wks. 1825 III. 145 The nature and quality of the excreted substance. **1844–57** G. BIRD *Urin. Deposits* (ed. 5) 449 This remarkable critical increase in the excreted solids of the urine is observed. **1849** J. F. JOHNSTON *Exp. Agric.* 32 Excreting is the final function exercised by the animal in reference to its food. **1852–9** TODD *Cycl. Anat.* IV. 843/2 The skin is..an active excreter of free phosphoric..acids. **1855** H. SPENCER *Princ. Psychol.* (1872) I. I. v. 92 The excreting structures of the skin.

excretes (ɛk'skriːts), *sb. pl. rare*[−1]. Anglicized form of EXCRETA.

1883 B. W. RICHARDSON *Prevent. Med.* vii. 281 The grand outlet for the nitrogenous excretes of the animal body.

†**ex'cretic,** *a. Obs. rare*[−1]. [f. L. *excrēt-* after Gr. analogies: cf. *eccritic*.] Of or pertaining to excretion.

1612 *Enchir. Med.* iii. 74 Panting..of the heart..is caused from the Excreticke facultie, which doth endeavour to exclude that which is hurtfull.

excretin (ɛk'skriːtɪn). *Chem.* Also 9 -ine. [f. L. *excrēt-* (see EXCRETE *v.*) + -IN.] (See quots.)

1854 *Proc. Royal Soc.* VII. 153 This crystalline body the author [W. Marcet] proposes to call Excretine. **1889** MORLEY & MUIR *Watts' Dict. Chem.* II. 530/1 *Excretin* $C_{20}H_{36}O$. Obtained by exhausting fresh excrements with boiling alcohol and leaving the solution to stand for a week ..100 pounds of fresh excrements yielded 8 grams of pure excretin.

excretion[1] (ɛk'skriːʃən). [(? a. Fr. *excrétion*) ad. L. *excrētiōn-em*, n. of action f. *excernĕre* to sift out, separate: see EXCRETE.]

The action or process of excreting.

1. Separation of animal products (chiefly, those useless for nutrition) from the blood.

1605 TIMME *Quersit.* III. 148 Excretion, or separating in bodies of superfluities and excrements. **1691** RAY *Creation* II. (1692) 115 The constant separation and excretion whereof [Urine] is necessary for the preservation of Life. **1731** ARBUTHNOT *Aliments* 14 The common Symptoms of the Excretion of the Bile being vitiated, are a yellowish Colour of the Skin..a loss of Appetite, [etc.] **1859** TODD *Cycl. Anat.* V. 488/2 Calcareous integument formed by excretion.

b. An analogous process in plants.

1862 DARWIN *Fertil. Orchids* vi. 278 The secretion acts also..as an excretion. **1876** —— *Cross-Fertil.* x. 403 The excretion [of a sweet fluid] manifestly depends on changes in the sap.

c. Of the teeth: The (supposed) formation of the teeth by matter 'excreted' from the pulp. Hence *attrib.* in *excretion-theory*.

1812 CUVIER *Les Ossemens Fossiles, Elephans* 65 Les substances dont se composent les dents se forment toutes par excrétion et par couches. *transl.* (ed. 4, 1835) 198 Formed by excretion and by layers. **1839** NASMYTH *Research. Teeth* 28 He [Cuvier] holds that the different substances which constitute the teeth are formed by

excretion and in layers. **1854** Owen *Skel. & Teeth* (1855) 292 The 'excretion theory' of dental development.

2. The action of casting out of the body that which has been separated by any of the organs; *esp.* evacuation of the bowels.

1640 *Erotomania* 51 Excretion, or Retention. **1645** Milton *Tetrach.* (1851) 170 The fleshly act..beeing at best but an animal excretion. **1658** Rowland *Moufet's Theat. Ins.* 1122 Children are continually provoked to excretion. **1732** Arbuthnot *Rules of Diet* 274 What stimulates and promotes the Excretion of the Blood. **1865** *Englishman's Mag.* Oct. 297 A common central aperture, through which the functions of secretion and excretion are carried on.

3. *concr.* That which is separated and ejected from the body.

1630 Brathwait *Eng. Gentl.* (1641) 60 None held it then a grace to have..the very excretions of beasts to sent them. *a* **1682** Sir T. Browne *Tracts* 113 In hawks and cormorants I have sometimes observed bloody excretions. **1802** Paley *Nat. Theol.* xix. (1803) 366 The aptness of this excretion [slime] to the purpose. **1842** Abdy *Water Cure* (1843) 21 A slight yellow excretion, by which morbific matter is eliminated. **1872** Huxley *Phys.* i. 3 Those products which are thrown out of the body, and are called excretions.

†**ex'cretion**². *Obs.* [as if ad. L. **excrētiōn-em*, n. of action f. *excrēscĕre* to grow out or forth, f. *ex-* out + *crēscĕre* to grow.] **a.** The action of growing out or forth. **b.** *concr.* Anything that grows out (whether naturally or abnormally) in animals or plants; = EXCREMENT², EXCRESCENCE. Also *fig.*

1612-5 Bp. Hall *Contempl., O.T.* x. v, [Samson] had ceased to be a Nazarite..not for the want of that excretion [his hair]. **1627-77** Feltham *Resolves* ii. xlv. 247 The excretions of the Body grow but insensibly. **1633** T. Adams *Exp. 2 Peter* i. 16 From her..shave and pare off..those superfluous excretions of sin. **1725** Bradley *Fam. Dict.* s.v. *Splint*, The Cure of all Splints and boney Excretions.

excretionary (ɛk'skriːʃənərɪ), *a.* [f. EXCRETION¹ + -ARY.] Of, pertaining to, or of the nature of excretion.

1872 Huxley *Phys.* i. 16 These excretionary matters are separated from the blood by the excretory organs.

excre'titious, *a.*¹ *rare*⁻¹. [f. L. *excrēt-* ppl. stem of *excernĕre*: see EXCRETION¹ and -ITIOUS.] Of the nature of excreta; = EXCREMENTITIOUS *a.*¹

c **1865** in *Circ. Sc.*, Uric acid, with other excretitious matters.

excre'titious, *a.*² *rare.* [f. L. *excrēt-* ppl. stem of *excrēscĕre*: see EXCRETION² and -ITIOUS.] Of the nature of an outgrowth.

1820-7 Bentham *Wks.* (1843) II. 82 An excretitious suit is a suit which has grown out of a former one. *Ibid.* VI. 379 This excretitious crime.

excretive (ɛk'skriːtɪv), *a.* [f. L. *excrēt-* (see EXCRETE *v.*) + -IVE, repr. L. type **excrētīvus*.]

Having the power or function of excreting or promoting excretion.

1666 G. Harvey *Morb. Angl.* 15 Some..fault in the Excretive faculty of the parts. **1673** Lister in *Phil. Trans.* VIII. 6062 Excretive glanduls. **1707** *Curios. in Husb. & Gard.* 240 It has a nutritive..excretive, expulsive Faculty. **1775** in Ash; and in mod. Dicts.

excretolic (ɛkskriː'tɒlɪk), *a.* *Chem.* Also excreto'leic. [f. EXCRET-IN + -OL (see CARBOLIC) + -IC.] In *excretolic acid*, 'a fatty acid, obtained by Marcet from the alcoholic extract of human excrements' (Watts *Dict. Chem.*).

1867 A. Flint *Physiol. Man* ii. 399 The substance called excretoleic acid is very indefinite in its composition and properties. **1878** Kingzett *Anim. Chem.* 82.

excretory (ɛk'skriːtərɪ, 'ɛkskriːtərɪ), *a.* and *sb.* *Phys.* [f. L. *excrēt-* (see EXCRETE *v.*) + -ORY. Cf. Fr. *excrétoire*.] **A.** *adj.*

1. Having the function of excreting; pertaining to or connected with the process of excretion. *excretory duct, vessel*, etc.: one which either in an animal or plant conveys the excretion to the surface, as the lachrymal duct, or into a prepared cavity, as the bile duct.

1681 tr. *Willis' Rem. Med. Wks.* Voc. **1684** Boyle *Porousn. Anim. & Solid Bod.* iii. 11 The Orifices of small excretory vessels. **1708** Keill *Anim. Secretion* 131 The Water passes off through the Pores or Excretory Ducts of the Plant. **1839-47** Todd *Cycl. Anat.* III. 315/1 The excretory outlet. **1854** Woodward *Mollusca* ii. 167 Respiratory and excretory orifices. **1883** *Fortn. Rev.* Feb. 197 The excretory function was admirably active.

2. Of the nature of excreta.

1878 Bell *Gegenbauer's Comp. Anat.* 46 Gaseous excretory matters are eliminated from the organism for the respiratory organs.

B. *sb.* An excretory vessel or duct.

1715 Cheyne *Philos. Princ. Relig.* i. 134 The other Excretories of the Body. **1741** Monro *Anat.* (ed. 3) 57 One can squeeze out of their Excretories a mucilaginous Liquor. **1805** W. Saunders *Min. Waters* 5 The morbid saline parts [are] carried off by the excretories.

excribe, var. form of EXSCRIBE.

†**ex'criminate,** *v. Obs. rare.* [f. L. *ex-* out (see EX- *pref.*¹) + *crimin-* stem of *crimen* accusation, charge + -ATE³.] *trans.* To clear from an imputation; to shift an imputation from (a person) *upon* (another); in quot. *refl.*

1661 Marvell *Corr.* xxix. Wks. 1872-5 II. 71, I had rather..undergoe any blame then to..excriminate my selfe upon any one of you. **1796** Coleridge *Watchman* 92 To excriminate themselves in the opinion of the public.

excruciable (ɛk'skruːʃɪəb(ə)l), *a.* [ad. L. *excruciābilis*, f. *excruciāre*: see EXCRUCIATE *v.* and -ABLE.] Capable of being tormented; liable, subject to, or deserving of torture.

1731-6 Bailey (folio), *Excruciable*, worthy to be tormented. **1831** Hogg in *Blackw. Mag.* XXIX. 916 The greedy heart On which the gnawing worm of avarice Preyed ..straining every sense To that excruciable and yearning core.

†**ex'cruciament.** *Obs. rare*⁻¹. [as if ad. L. **excruciāment-um*, f. *excruciāre*: see EXCRUCIATE *v.*] = EXCRUCIATION.

1599 Nashe *Lenten Stuffe* 65 To this wild of sorrowes and excruciament she was confined, either to be held a flat thornback, or sharp pricking dog-fish, etc.

†**ex'cruciate,** *ppl. a. Obs.* [ad. L. *excruciātus*, pa. pple. of *excruciāre*: see next.] **a.** = EXCRUCIATED *ppl. a.* ¶ **b.** = EXCRUCIATING *ppl. a.*

a **1615** Beaumont & Fletcher (W.), Would she sit thus then excruciate? **1615** Chapman *Odyss.* vii. 398 My heart, long time excruciate, Amongst the leaves I rested all that night. **1773** J. Ross *Fratricide* (MS.) ii. 620 Excruciate pains Seiz'd on our Father's frame.

excruciate (ɛk'skruːʃɪˌeɪt), *v.* Also 7 excruciat, -tiat(e. [f. L. *excruciāt-* ppl. stem of *excruciāre*, f. *ex-* intensive (see EX- *pref.*¹ 2) + *cruciāre* to torment, f. *cruc-em* cross.]

1. †**a.** *lit.* To subject to torture, put on the rack, etc.; *fig.* to 'rack' (one's brains) (*obs.*). **b.** *transf.* To cause intense pain to, torment acutely (a person's senses). Often *hyperbolical*.

1570 Levins *Manip.* 41 To Excruciate, *excruciare*. **1593** Nashe *Christ's T.* (1613) 154 They..by pining and excruciating their bodies, liue in hell here on earth, to auoid the hell neuer ending. **1593** —— *Four Lett. Confut.* 56 You shall not excruciate your braine to be conceited and haue no wit. **1623** Cockeram iii, *Perillus*..invented a brazen Bull ..made redhot to torment and excruciate malefactors. **1717** Bullock *Wom. a Riddle* i. i. May convulsions seize and excruciate my optick nerves. **1830** Miss Mitford *Village* Ser. iv. (1863) 256 The bassoon, on which George Evans was wont..to excruciate the ears of the whole congregation.

2. *fig.* To torture mentally, inflict extreme mental anguish upon.

1586 Marlowe *1st Pt. Tamburl.* i. i, This..doth excruciate The very substance of my vexed soul. **1611** Markham *Countr. Content.* i. xi. (1668) 61 He must.. neither vex nor excruciate himself with losses or mischances. **1655-60** Stanley *Hist. Philos.* (1701) 617/2 He neither blunts his mind, nor excrutiats it with cares. **1758** Johnson *Idler* No. 47 ⁋ 17 If a customer talks longer than he is willing to hear, he will complain that he has been excruciated with unmeaning verbosity. **1879** Froude *Cæsar* xxvi. 445 He described himself as excruciated with anxiety. *absol.* **1651** Charleton *Ephes. & Cimm. Matrons* ii. (1668) 44 Their joys are infested with such calamities, that they excruciate.

Hence **ex'cruciated** *ppl. a.*, tormented, tortured.

1792 *Minstrel* (1793) I. 80 Oh my excruciated heart!

excruciating (ɛk'skruːʃɪeɪtɪŋ), *ppl. a.* [f. prec. + -ING².] That excruciates or causes extreme pain or anguish, whether bodily or mental; tormenting, torturing, agonizing. Const. *to*.

1664 H. More *Myst. Iniq.* xx. 75 The excruciating fear of a worse then Pagan Purgatory. **1770** Goldsm. *Life Bolingbroke* Wks. (Globe) 467/2 A cancer in his cheek, by which excruciating disease he died. **1791** Boswell *Johnson* an. 1756 (1831) I. 299 That most difficult and excruciating question, the Origin of Evil. **1833** I. Taylor *Fanat.* vi. 179 Excruciating deaths; especially empalement or crucifixion. **1860** Tyndall *Glac.* i. xxiii. 161 The biting of the hydrocarbons was excruciating to the eyes.

b. *hyperbolically*, in humorous use.

1819 Campbell *Spec. Brit. Poets* III. 2 He [Drayton] is a less excruciating hunter of conceits [than Cowley]. **1824** W. Irving *T. Trav.* I. 348 Blunders in sense and sound, that were excruciating to an author's ears. **1865** Miss Braddon *Only a Clod* i. 6 If there's one thing in the world that's more excruciating than another, it's that fellow's cheerfulness. **1876** M. Davies *Unorth. Lond.* 26 An excruciating chorus having been performed.

excruciatingly (ɛk'skruːʃɪeɪtɪŋlɪ), *adv.* [f. prec. + -LY².] To an excruciating degree; in an extremely painful manner. Often *hyperbolically* in humorous use.

1808 *Ann. Reg.* 1806, 878 His sarcasm was.. excruciatingly severe. **1838** Dickens *Nich. Nick.* xxxiv, Why is she so excruciatingly beautiful? **1861** Bumstead *Ven. Dis.* (1879) 182 Emissions..which are excruciatingly painful. **1865** Miss Braddon *Sir Jasper* xxxiii, A negro melody of an excruciatingly lively character.

excruciation (ɛkˌskruːsɪ'eɪʃən). [ad. L. *excruciātiōn-em*, n. of action f. *excruciāre*: see EXCRUCIATE *v.*] The action of causing or the state of suffering extreme pain; an instance of this.

1618 T. Gainsford *Hist. P. Warbeck* in *Select. Harl. Misc.* (1793) 61 After she had lived a while in..excruciation both of soul and body. **1627-77** Feltham *Resolves* ii. lvii. (T.), The thwartings, and the excruciations of life. **1646** Gaule *Cases Consc.* 191 Can his excruciation be a sufficient cause for our execution? **1885** G. Meredith *Diana* II. i. 5 The doom of men to excruciation in endlessness.

excruciator (ɛk'skruːʃɪeɪtə(r)). *rare.* [ad. L. *excruciātor*, agent-n. f. *excruciāre* to EXCRUCIATE.] One who excruciates; a tormentor.

1864 *Realm* 20 Apr. 8 Signor Sivori..turned round upon his excruciators, and stamped most furiously.

excrustation (ɛkskrʌ'steɪʃən), *rare.* [ad. med.L. *excrustātiōn-em* f. *excrustāre*, f. *ex-* (see EX- *pref.*¹) + *crusta* CRUST, covering.] The stripping a book of its covering of precious metal.

1844 Maitland *Dark Ages* Ess. xiii. 218 Charity and need, as well as cupidity were likely to produce what was then termed *excrustation*, and to risk..the destruction of the manuscript. [Maitland refers in footnote to *Vit. Aldhelmi*, Die uno xii textus Evangeliorum..et auro nudata et excrustata sunt.]

excubant ('ɛkskjuːbənt), *a. rare* (*pedantic*). [ad. L. *excubant-em*, pr. pple. of *excubāre* to lie on guard, f. *ex-* out + *cubāre* to lie down.] Keeping watch.

1831 T. L. Peacock *Crotchet Castle* xviii. 186 The enemy may be still excubant; and we had better not disperse till daylight.

†**excu'bation.** *Obs.*⁻⁰ [ad. L. *excubātiōn-em*, n. of action f. *excubāre*: see prec.] The action of watching or of keeping guard.

1623 in Cockeram; **1721-1800** in Bailey.

†**ex'cubitor.** *Obs. rare*⁻¹. [a. L. *excubitor* watchman, agent-n. f. *excubāre*: see EXCUBANT *a.*] A watchman, sentinel.

1775 G. White in *Phil. Trans.* LXV. 261 The swallow.. is the excubitor to the house-martins..announcing the approach of birds of prey.

'**excudate,** *v. rare.* [badly f. L. *excūd-ĕre* (see next) + -ATE³.] *trans.* = next.

1831 *Fraser's Mag.* III. 748 The world would have need of consolation, should a single sentence excudated in such a smiddy peradventure escape record.

†**ex'cude,** *v. Obs.*⁻⁰ [ad. L. *excūd-ĕre*, f. *ex-* out + *cūdĕre* to strike, beat.] *trans.* 'To beat or strike out; to find out with study' (Blount *Glossogr.* 1674).

1775 in Ash.

†**ex'culcate,** *v. Obs.*⁻⁰ [f. L. *exculcāt-* ppl. stem of *exculcā-re*, f. *ex-* (see EX- *pref.*¹) + *calcā-re*: see CALCATE.] *trans.* To tread or trample out.

1656-81 in Blount *Glossogr.* **1721-61** in Bailey.

Hence **excul'cation**, the action of treading out.

1730-6 in Bailey (folio); **1775** in Ash.

exculp, var. of EXSCULP *v. Obs.*

exculpable (ɛks'kʌlpəb(ə)l), *a. rare.* [f. EXCULPATE *v.* + -ABLE.] Capable of being exculpated or freed from blame or accusation.

1646 Buck *Rich. III*, iii. Contents, How the Sonnes of King Edward came by their deaths: King Richard Exculpable thereof. Hence **1827** in Todd; and in mod. Dicts.

exculpate (ɛks'kʌlpət), *ppl. a.* [f. next: see -ATE².] Declared guiltless; free from blame.

1814 Cary *Dante* (Chandos) 227 These spirits stood exculpate. **1830** W. Phillips *Mt. Sinai* iv. 163 Casting on his peers The burden of their mutual sin, Himself exculpate.

exculpate ('ɛkskəlpeɪt, ɛks'kʌlpeɪt), *v.* [f. EX- *pref.*¹ + L. *culp-a* blame + -ATE³. Cf. It. *scolpare*, med.L. **exculpāre* implied in *exculpātio* (Du Cange).]

1. *trans.* To free from blame; to declare free from guilt; to clear *from* an accusation or blame.

1656-81 [see 1 b]. **1721** in Bailey. **1758-9** Lowth *Life Wykeham* v. 156 Men who had been.. punished in the parliament of 1376, and who had gotten themselves exculpated in the succeeding parliament. **1841** James *Brigand* xx, She exculpates me from blame in this matter. **1850** Grote *Greece* ii. lxii, The latter stood exculpated on both charges.

refl. **1748** Richardson *Clarissa* (J.), A good child will not seek to exculpate herself at the expence of the most revered characters. **1809-10** Coleridge *Friend* (1865) 110 From this charge of inconsistency I shall best exculpate myself by the full statement of the third system. **1863** Mrs. Oliphant *Salem Ch.* iv. 63 Poor Vincent made a hasty effort to exculpate himself from the soft impeachment.

†**b.** *intr.* for *refl. Obs. rare.*

1656-81 Blount *Glossogr.*, *Exculpate*, to cleer ones self of a fault. **1780** Burke *Corr.* (1844) II. 315 To be over earnest in endeavours to exculpate, previous to accusation, would imply [etc.]. **1783** —— *Rep. Affairs India* Wks. XI. 326 Doubts whether the refusal to exculpate by oath can be used ..to infer any presumption of guilt.

2. Of things: †**a.** To serve as an excuse for; to justify. *Obs. rare.* **b.** To furnish ground for exculpating. Const. *from*.

1706 Phillips (ed. Kersey) s.v., Good meaning will never exculpate blind and Superstitious Devotion. **1783** Burke *Rep. Affairs India* Wks. XI. 132 Evidence, which may tend to criminate, or exculpate, every person. **1875** Farrar

Seekers I. vi. 83 The tenor of his life has sufficient weight to exculpate him from an unsupported accusation.

exculpation (ɛkskʌl'peɪʃən). [f. prec. vb.: see -ATION.] The action of exculpating or clearing from blame, or from an alleged crime; an instance of this; a ground or means of exculpating; an excuse or a vindication.

a **1715** BURNET *Own Time* an. 1684 (R.) In Scotland the law allows of an exculpation, by which the prisoner is suffered before his trial to prove the thing to be impossible. **1751** SMOLLETT *Per. Pic.* (1779) I. xviii. 159 She maintained a sort of ceremonious distance, which she thought requisite ..for her own exculpation. **1752** J. LOUTHIAN *Form of Process* (ed. 2) 100 To bear..Witnessing.. anent the said Complainer's Innocence and Exculpation of the Crime libelled against him. **1788** REID *Act. Powers* IV. vi. 619 The madness of a short fit of passion..is incapable of proof; and therefore is not admitted in human tribunals as an exculpation. **1828** SCOTT *F. M. Perth* xxx, Ramorny did not attempt an exculpation. **1873** SYMONDS *Grk. Poets* viii. 238 Without seeking to offer any exculpation for what offends us in the moral sensibilities of the Greeks.

b. *letters of exculpation* (in *Sc. Law*): a warrant issued to a defender in a criminal prosecution for citing witnesses in his defence.

1773 ERSKINE *Instit. Law Scotl.* (1838) IV. v. 1123 Letters of exculpation are granted of course, at the suit of a defender in a criminal trial, for citing witnesses, etc. **1861** in W. BELL *Dict. Law Scotl.* 354/2.

exculpative (ɛks'kʌlpətɪv), *a.* *rare*$^{-1}$. [f. EXCULPATE *v.*: see -ATIVE.] Intended to exculpate.

1827 BENTHAM *Ration. Evid.* Wks. (1843) VI. 155 In England, scarcely any crime is so common as that of exculpative perjury.

exculpatory (ɛks'kʌlpətəɪ), *a.* [f. as prec. + -ORY.] Of statements, evidence, etc.: Adapted or intended to clear from blame or a charge of guilt; apologetic, vindicatory. Const. *of.*

1779–81 JOHNSON *L.P.*, *Pope* Wks. IV. 58 He wrote an exculpatory letter to the Duke. **1837** CARLYLE *Fr. Rev.* III. IV. vii, Witnesses..exculpatory, inculpatory. **1846** GROTE *Greece* I. iii. (1862) I. 67 Two exculpatory pleas. **1848** *Blackw. Mag.* LXIII. 594 The statement..is not, however, altogether so exculpatory of the French.

excur (ɛk'skɜː(r)), *v.* *rare.* Also 7 excurre. [ad. L. *excur-rĕre*, f. *ex-* out + *currĕre* to run.]

†**1.** *intr.* To go out of or beyond the ordinary or proper course or path; to digress; to go to an extreme. *Obs.*

1656 M. CASAUBON *Enthus.* iii. 80 Beyond which not to excurre..is my chiefest care. **1669** FLAMSTEED in Rigaud *Corr. Sci. Men* (1841) II. 85 Thus far..this heat for the concerns of science hath caused me to excur. **1672** G. HARVEY *Morb. Angl.* (ed. 2) 47 His Disease was..an Asthma, oft excurring to an Orthopnœa.

2. *U.S.* (See quot.)

c **1850** *Nat. Encycl.* I. 619 [Americanisms:] *Excur*, used as a verb in the sense of to take an excursion.

†**ex'curiate**, *v.* *Obs.*$^{-0}$ [f. L. *excūriāt-* ppl. stem of *excūriāre* to eject from the curia, f. *ex-* out + *cūria* the senate-house.] 'To throw out of the Court' (Blount *Glossogr.* 1656–81).

Hence **excuri'ation**.

1692–1732 COLES, *Excuriate.* **1658** PHILLIPS, *Excuriation.*

ex'currency. *rare*$^{-1}$. [f. L. *excurrent-em*: see next and -ENCY.] A digression.

1650 B. *Discolliminium* 14, I shall make bold to speak a word to them all, though I make a little excurrency.

excurrent (ɛk'skʌrənt), *a.* [ad. L. *excurrent-em*, pr. pple. of *excurrĕre*: see EXCUR.]

1. That runs out or forth. Of arterial blood: That flows from the heart.

1826 KIRBY & SP. *Entomol.* xxxii. (1828) III. 293 The excurrent (or arterial) stream took its course along the inner margin. *Ibid.* xxxix. IV. 92 In the excurrent part of its course. **1887** W. J. SOLLAS in *Encycl. Brit.* XXII. 413/1 s.v. *Sponges*, The insoluble residue..is carried out through the oscule by the excurrent water.

†**2.** Passing beyond bounds or limits; overflowing, superabundant (in quot. *fig.*). *Obs.* *rare*$^{-1}$.

1605 TIMME *Quersit.* I. iv. 12 Restraining a matter excurrent, within bondes and limits.

3. Admitting of or affording an exit.

1854 WOODWARD *Mollusca* (1856) 277 Fig. 185..showing the relative extent of the liver and ovarium..*e*, excurrent orifice. **1887** W. J. SOLLAS in *Encycl. Brit.* XXII. 414/2 s.v. *Sponges*, In higher forms of sponges the chambers cease to open abruptly into the excurrent canals.

4. *Bot.* **a.** (See quot. 1835.) **b.** Projecting beyond the tip or margin, as when the midrib of a leaf is continued beyond the apex.

a. 1835 LINDLEY *Introd. Bot.* (1848) II. 362 Excurrent; in which the axis remains always in the centre, all the other parts being regularly disposed round it; as the stem of abies. **1880** GRAY *Struct. Bot.* iii. §3. 40.

b. 1847 in CRAIG. **1870** HOOKER *Stud. Flora* 375 Horned Pond-weed..Stamen 1..connective excurrent. **1882** *Gard. Chron.* XVIII. 70 Excurrent at the apex.

†**ex'curse**, *sb.* *Obs.* *rare*$^{-1}$. [ad. L. *excurs-us*: see EXCURSUS.] An outrush, raid, hostile sally.

1586 J. HOOKER *Girald. Irel.* in *Holinshed* II. 15/1, I am to require thee that thou doo retire and withdraw these excurses of strangers.

excurse (ɛk'skɜːs), *v.* [f. L. *excurs-* ppl. stem of *excurrĕre*: see EXCUR.]

1. *intr.* To run off, wander, digress. Chiefly *fig.*

1748 RICHARDSON *Clarissa* (1811) III. x. 71 How I excurse! Yet thou usedst to say, thou likedst my excursions. **1887** *Sat. Rev.* 17 Sept. 403 The text excurses in Mr. Carroll's usual style about babies and cakes. **1891** MISS DOWIE *Girl in Karp.* 239 At first I excursed in various directions thinking to light upon a track.

2. To make, or go upon, an excursion.

1775 *Sterne's Sent. Journ. Contd.*, *Tilt of Arms* 177 Who can dispute a Parisian's word, who never has excursed beyond the gates? **1820** KNOX & JEBB *Corr.* II. 440, I..am to excurse ten miles, on the Dover road. **1841** CAR. FOX *Mem. Old Friends* 7 Aug., When the Franklins..were excursing in Ireland, they went through some difficult pass.

3. *trans.* 'To journey or pass through' (Webster 1864).

a **1859** HALLAM is cited by WORCESTER (1860).

excursion (ɛk'skɜːʃən), *sb.* [ad. L. *excursiōn-em*, n. of action f. *excurrĕre* to run out: see EXCUR. Cf. F. *excursion.*]

†**1. a.** The action of running out; escape from confinement; 'progression beyond fixed limits' (J.); running to extremes; an instance thereof.

1579 TWYNE *Phisicke agst. Fortune* II. Ep. Ded. 153 b, What roaring of flooddes, what excursion of riuers. **1654** H. L'ESTRANGE *Chas. I.* (1655) 4 Nor is it any excursion beyond the precincts of verity to say, that [etc.]. **1729** SHELVOCKE *Artillery* IV. 266 These round boards—prevent the Excursion of the least Atom of the Moving Power..till the Projectile is departed. **1732** RAY *Dissol. World* I. iii. (ed. 4) 44 Stop and inhibit their [the winds'] excursions. **1733** ARBUTHNOT *Ess. Air* iv. 87 Those great Excursions of the Seasons into the Extremes of Cold and Heat.

b. *transf.* The fact or state of 'running out' or projecting in any direction (*rare*). Hence formerly †*concr.*: Something that runs out or projects; an extension, projecting addition (of a building); an offshoot, branch, projection (of land, mountains, etc.).

1622–62 HEYLIN *Cosmogr.* I. (1682) 33 Of this large Mountain most of the Hills..are but the excursions. **1655** FULLER *Ch. Hist.* VI. vi. §18 Countrey Churches..wherein such excursions of building as present themselves beyond the old fabrick..were since erected. *a* **1682** SIR T. BROWNE *Tracts* 191 An excursion of land shooting out directly. **1852** SIR W. HAMILTON *Discuss.* App. i. 620 Quantity is marked by the relative length of a terminal line within, or its indefinite excursion before, the limit of comparison.

fig. a **1626** BACON *War Spain* in *Harl. Misc.* (Malh.) IV. 133 The ravishing whereof was a mere excursion of the first wrong, and a superinjustice.

†**2.** *fig.* An outburst (of feeling); a sally (of wit); an overstepping of the bounds of propriety or custom, a freak; vagary, escapade. *Obs.*

1662 H. MORE *Philos. Writ.* Pref. Gen. (1712) 22 Which was no inconsiderate excursion of a juvenile fervour in him, but a permanent faithfulness..of Spirit. **1680** BURNET *Rochester* (1692) 124, I have not enlarged on all the Excursions of his wit. **1701** SWIFT *Contests Nobles & Com.* Wks. 1755 II. I. 21 Alcibiades, having been formerly noted for the like frolicks and excursions, was immediately accused of this. **1711** ADDISON *Spect.* No. 34 ¶4, I think your Raillery has made too great an Excursion, in attacking several Persons of the Inns of Court. **1719** DE FOE *Crusoe* (1840) I. i. 15 This indeed was..an excursion of his spirits. **1785** COWPER *Tiroc.* 228 His wild excursions, window-breaking feats..are made their favourite themes. **1793** BURKE *Cond. Minority* Wks. 1842 I. 612 His friends saw no security..after this excursion of his, but in the re-union of the party.

†**3.** *Mil.* An issuing forth against an enemy; a sally, sortie, raid. *Obs.* exc. in phr. *alar(u)ms and excursions* (see ALARM *sb.* 4 and 11).

1577–87 HOLINSHED *Chron.* I. 43/2 Trenches that you have made for your oune defense, to keepe off their excursions. **1603** KNOLLES *Hist. Turks* (1621) 1230 The Turks..were determined yet to make a great excursion for the spoiling of the countrey. **1665** MANLEY *Grotius' Low C. Warres* 637 Placing Forts and Guards along the River, to..repress any Excursions from Fort Andrew. **1701** *Lond. Gaz.* No. 3756/13 The Germans make Excursions beyond the Adda..to fetch in Forage.

4. a. A journey, expedition, or ramble from one's home, or from any place with the intention of returning to it.

1699 DAMPIER *Voy.* II. II. 42 Many little Excursions that I made..in these parts. **1743** BERKELEY *Let.* 29 Oct. Wks. IV. 289 My health..suffers me to make no excursions farther than a mile or two. *a* **1788** N. COTTON *Fire-side* iv, Giving her vain excursions o'er, The disappointed bird [Noah's dove] once more Explor'd the sacred bark. **1816** J. SMITH *Panorama Sc. & Art.* II. 159 The longest aëronautic excursion ever taken was by Blanchard. **1823** J. D. HUNTER *Captivity N. Amer.* 124, I started..on a hunting and trading excursion. **1860** TYNDALL *Glac.* I. vii. 47, I made a long excursion up the glacier.

b. *fig.*

1665 GLANVILL *Sceps. Sci.* xiv. 81 The excursions of our roving phancies which cannot be kept to a close attendance. **1704** SWIFT *T. Tub* Author's Apol., It is the frequent error of those men..to make Excursions beyond their talent and their office. **1764** REID *Inquiry* vii. 211 Many authors have made excursions into this vast territory. **1888** BRYCE *Amer. Commw.* I. ii. 21 The only excursion into the historical domain which I shall have to ask the reader to make.

c. *transf.* in *Physics*, etc.: One of the individual movements executed by any body or particle in oscillating or alternating motion; the distance traversed in such a movement.

1799 YOUNG in *Phil. Trans.* XC. 136 In the middle of the chord, the excursions on each side the axis are always equal. **1878** HUXLEY *Physiogr.* 171 The particles themselves perform very small excursions, merely vibrating up and down. **1879** G. PRESCOTT *Sp. Telephone* 16 The excursions of the plunger rod vary with the amplitude of the several vibrations made by the diaphragm to which it is attached.

5. *spec.* A journey or 'trip' undertaken for the sake of pleasure or health. In recent use often: a pleasure-trip taken by a number of persons; occas. short for *excursion-party* or *excursion train.*

1779 COWPER *Lett.* July Wks. (1876) 38 It was an excursion of pleasure to go to see Ramsgate. **1832** G. DOWNES *Lett. Cont. Countries* I. 297 We had yesterday a delightful excursion on the lake. **1860** MRS. GASKELL *Let.* ?26 May (1966) 621 Fare *by excursion* to London, is 12-6, second class... Now second class *excursion* to London wd not be agreeable I think. **1911** *Daily Colonist* (Victoria, B.C.) 2 Apr. 14/6 (Railway Advt.), Low excursion rates to eastern points. **1920** GALSWORTHY *Foundations* II. I tuk 'ee therr [*sc.* to Margate] by excursion when yu was six months. **1966** J. BETJEMAN *High & Low* 29 By tramway excursion.. In search of diversion The millworkers come.

6. Deviation from a definite path or course.

a. in physical sense. Now only *Astron.*

1603 HOLLAND *Plutarch's Mor.* 1307 The defect of the Moone and her occultation, be as it were the excursions, deviations out of course. **1727** SWIFT *Desire & Possess.* Wks. 1755 IV. I. 82 He strove to pick up all he found, And by Excursions lost his Ground. **1732** RAY *Dissol. World* III. v. (ed. 4) 374 The Excursions of these last [the Comets] do argue it more than possible that..the Sun..may quite lose his light. **1833** HERSCHEL *Astron.* ix. 288 The excursions of the earth on either side of the ellipse, are so very small as to be hardly appreciable.

†**b.** A deviation from custom, rule, or propriety. Cf. 2. *Obs.*

1615 CROOKE *Body of Man* 299 Monsters Aristotle calleth Excursions and Digressions of Nature. **1627–77** FELTHAM *Resolves* 38 A Watch, to observe thy fails, and thy excursions. *a* **1656** BP. HALL *Life* Rem. Wks. (1660) 11 Finding that..somewhat out of my way, not without a secret blame of my self for so much excursion, I fairly gave up that task. *a* **1711** KEN *Hymnotheo* Poet. Wks. 1721 III. 109 On ev'ry Sense he kept strict jealous Eyes, Ready the least Excursion to chastise. **1769** SIR J. REYNOLDS *Disc.* ii. (1884) 18 A Student..is always apt..to mistake the most trifling excursions for discoveries of moment.

†**c.** A deviation from the direct course in argument or discourse; 'ramble from a subject' (J.); a digression. *Obs.*

1574 WHITGIFT *Def. Answ.* ii. Wks. 1851 I. 208 It is an argument that you lack good matter, when you make such excursions from the purpose. **1670** BAXTER *Cure Ch. Div.* 259 Pardon this long excursion on this subject. **1684** EARL ROSCOM. *Ess. Transl. Verse* 215 Excursions are inexpiably bad, And 'tis much safer to leave out, then add. *c* **1720** W. GIBSON *Farriers Dispens.* vii. (1734) 167 We shall take the liberty of a short Excursion, to put this matter yet into a better light. **1823** LAMB *Elia* Ser. I. xi. (1865) 89 You cannot make excursions with him..for he sets you right [in conversation].

7. *attrib.* (sense 5), as in **excursion-train**, a train intended to convey persons making a pleasure excursion, usually at reduced fares; also *excursion-agent*, *-fare*, *-party*, *-ticket*.

1850 THACKERAY in *Scribn. Mag.* I. 688/2, I should like to come..by the Excursion train. **1866** R. M. BALLANTYNE *Shift. Winds* xxiv, It chanced to be an excursion day, and several..were besieging the ticket-windows. **1870** DICKENS *E. Drood* ii, Tope, Chief Verger and Showman, was accustomed to be high with excursion parties. **1878** F. S. WILLIAMS *Midl. Railw.* 626 The exceptional colours [tickets] are for excursion trains.

Hence **ex'cursion** *v.*, *intr.* to make or go on an excursion. **ex'cursional** *a.*, of or pertaining to an excursion. **ex'cursionary** *a.*, of the nature of an excursion; of a person, going on an excursion. †**ex'cursioner** = EXCURSIONIST. **ex'cursionism**, the custom or practice of making or organizing excursions.

1792 MAD. D'ARBLAY *Diary* Jan. V. 283 You have been excursioning and travelling all the world o'er since I saw you last. **1825** LAMB in Talfourd *Life & Lett.* xv. 142 Yesterday I excursioned twenty miles. **1885** *Daily News* 6 Oct. 5 The members of the Church Congress are not much given to excursioning. **1848** DICKENS *Let.* 22 July, Pray let me divide the little excursional expenses of the journey among the gentlemen. **1769** *Garrick's Vagary* 53, I conclude..my excursionary Trip from London to Stratford. **1858** MAYNE REID in *Chamb. Jrnl.* IX. 77 Was it..the excursionary belles from Saratoga..who came to visit us? **1786** MAD. D'ARBLAY *Diary* III. 111 The Royal excursioners did not return till between six and seven o'clock. **1886** GOLDW. SMITH in *Macm. Mag.* Oct. 406 Excursionism, which began with the Exhibition of 1851, has now assumed immense proportions.

excursionist (ɛk'skɜːʃənɪst). [f. prec. + -IST.]

1. One who goes upon a (pleasure) excursion; one who travels by an excursion-train.

1830 LAMB *Lett.* xvii. 164 The excursionists reached home..a little after four. **1851** W. COLLINS *Rambles beyond Railw.* ix. (1852) 183 A company of excursionists from a remote inland district of the county. **1861** *Times* 10 July, A large party of excursionists left Crewe for Trentham-park.

2. *colloq.* One whose business it is to arrange means for travelling on pleasure excursions; an excursion-agent.

excursionize (ɛkˈskɜːʃənaɪz), *v.* [f. as prec. + -IZE.]

1. *trans.* To make excursions to or about (a district, etc.). *rare.*

1827 *Blackw. Mag.* XXII. 555 Fixing your head-quarters in..Inverleithen, and excursionizing the whole country-side. **1861** *Sat. Rev.* XII. 489/1 This perverse system of excursionizing a building.

2. *intr.* To make, or go on, an excursion or excursions.

1866 *Pall Mall G.* 27 Aug. 5 Most of the British Association people went out excursionizing on Saturday. **1881** MISS BRADDON *Asph.* III. 220 Edgar and Daphne had excursionised a little upon the nearest hillsides.

Hence **exˈcursioˌnizing** *vbl. sb.*

1881 MISS BRADDON *Asph.* xxix. 328 There was more excursionising next day.

excursive (ɛkˈskɜːsɪv), *a.* [f. L. *excurs-* ppl. stem of *excurrĕre* (see EXCUR) + -IVE; very common in 18th c.]

1. a. Of the nature of an excursion; consisting of excursions or sallies (*obs.* in literal sense). **b.** Of reading, etc.: Desultory; varied in direction.

1673 RAY *Journ. Low C., Montpellier* 463 From Montpellier we made an excursive voyage into Provence. **1749** *Power Pros. Numbers* 54 Excursive Flights..natural to those who have dealt much in Verse. **1799** S. TURNER *Anglo-Sax.* I. IV. viii. 321 They made excursive ravages over the adjacent country. **1816** KIRBY & SP. *Entomol.* xxiii. (1828) II. 352 Then resumes its gay excursive flights. **1836** W. IRVING *Astoria* II. 60 We are wandering..into excursive speculations. **1848** SOUTHEY *Comm.-pl. Bk.* Ser. I. (1850), Johnson's excursive reading.

2. a. That makes excursions or sallies in various directions; capable of, or addicted to, varied flights; having a wide range of pursuits or interests. **b.** Apt to diverge from a definite course; prone to stray, erratic; digressive.

1744 THOMSON *Spring* 953 Your eye excursive roams. **1774** WARTON *Hist. Eng. Poetry* lxiii. (1840) III. 425 The first [book of Hall's Satires] is miscellaneous and excursive. **1779–81** JOHNSON *L.P., Pope* Wks. IV. 103 An intelligence perpetually on the wing, excursive, vigorous, and diligent. **1816** KIRBY & SP. *Entomol.* xxxv. (1828) III. 644 The order to which the excursive butterfly belongs is the Lepidoptera. **1823** RUTTER *Fonthill* 81 That brilliant and excursive genius which created the design. **1825** SCOTT *Betrothed* Introd., Keeping in the straight road his excursive black cattle. **1838–9** HALLAM *Hist. Lit.* III. iii. III. §127. 110 Bacon was sometimes too excursive to sift particulars. **1868** HELPS *Realmah* ix. (1876) 256 Do keep to the point, my excursive friends.

excursively (ɛkˈskɜːsɪvlɪ), *adv.* [f. prec. + -LY².] In an excursive or rambling manner; erratically, desultorily, digressively.

1791 BOSWELL *Johnson* an 1728, The flesh of animals who feed excursively is allowed to have a higher flavour than that of those who are cooped up. **1841** HOR. SMITH *Moneyed Man* III. vii. 193 How excursively have I speculated on a lady's glove. **1871** ARNOLD *Lect. Mod. Hist.* i. (1878) 98 He must now break forth excursively to the right and left.

excursiveness (ɛkˈskɜːsɪvnɪs). [f. as prec. + -NESS.] The quality of being excursive; a tendency to depart from the beaten track, or from any fixed course; digressiveness; capacity for mental 'flights' in varied directions.

1754 RICHARDSON *Grandison* (1781) VI. xxxiv. 251 An excursiveness of imagination. *a* **1859** DE QUINCEY *Conversation* Wks. XIV. 177 The natural excursiveness of colloquial intercourse..is one of its advantages. **1866** WHIPPLE *Char. & Charac. Men* 222 The very process which gave depth and excursiveness to his mental vision.

† **exˈcursory.** *Obs. rare*⁻¹. [f. L. *excurs-* ppl. stem of *excurrĕre* (see EXCUR) + -ORY.] A rambling speech.

1590 GREENWOOD *Answ. Def. Read Prayers* 12 To this ignorant excursorie I answered, that all false..worship..was Idolatrye.

excursus (ɛkˈskɜːsəs). *Pl.* excursus, after Lat.; now usually excursuses. [a. L. *excursus*, n. of action f. *excurrĕre* lit. 'to run out': see EXCUR and cf. EXCURSION *sb.*]

1. The Lat. word is used by editors of the classics to signify: A detailed discussion (usually in the form of an appendix at the end of the book, or of a division of it) of some point which it is desired to treat more fully than can be done in a note. Hence occas. applied to a similar appendix in other works.

1803 *Ann. Rev.* I. 527/2 This subject is considered in the first excursus of the 8th book [in Heyne's Homer]. *Ibid.* 535/2 Of those excursus which relate to the historical illustration of the poet. **1858** *Sat. Rev.* V. 536/1 The volume is closed by two carefully-written excursus. **1861** M. PATTISON *Ess.* (1889) I. 30 They..should be read as excursuses to accompany his text. **1878** W. H. SIMCOX in *Academy* 594/3 He adds..a series of excursuses on the leading ideas of the Epistle.

2. A digression in which some incidental point is discussed at length.

1845 *Athenæum* 11 Jan. 48 We shall quite bewilder..our readers by this excursus. **1876** M. DAVIES *Unorth. Lond.* 384 He concluded a most interesting excursus by dwelling on the prospects of Church extension. **1882** A. W. WARD *Dickens* vi. 160 The excellent description of a winter journey ..with an excursus on inns in general.

excurvation (ɛkskɜːˈveɪʃən). [f. EX- *pref.*¹ + CURVATION.] A bending or curving outwards.

1877 ERICHSEN *Surg.* (ed. 7) 299 When excurvation has taken place, there has been loss of substance. **1884** *Syd. Soc. Lex.*, *Spinal excurvation*, posterior curvature of the spine.

excurved (ɛksˈkɜːvd), *ppl. a.* [f. EX- *pref*¹ + CURVED.] Curved outwards (as the antennæ of certain insects).

1884 in *Syd. Soc. Lex.*

exˌcusaˈbility. *rare.* [f. next: see *-bility*, -ITY.] = EXCUSABLENESS.

a **1711** KEN *Lett.* Wks. (1838) 51 Allowing all degrees of excusability to those who are of a different persuasion.

excusable (ɛkˈskjuːzəb(ə)l), *a.* Also 5 excusabil, 6–7 excuseable. [a. Fr. *excusable*, ad. L. *excūsābilis*, f. *excūsāre*: see EXCUSE *v.*]

1. Of a person: Deserving to be excused; that may be excused or acquitted. †Const. *of.*

1393 GOWER *Conf.* I. 76 If any man forswey Through hem, they be nought excusable. *c* **1440** HYLTON *Scala Perf.* (W. de W. 1494) II. xviii, They are somwhat excusable for her astate of lyuynge. **1576** FLEMING *Panopl. Epist.* 336 Daily..remembraunce of your goodnesse..shall pleade me excusable of unthankfulnesse. *c* **1645** HOWELL *Lett.* (1650) I. 340 Those are the excuseablest kind [of pagans] who adore the sun and moon, with the host of heaven. **1743** H. WALPOLE *Lett. H. Mann* (1834) I. lxx. 254, I don't sell you my news and therefore should not be excusable to invent. **1786** BURKE *W. Hastings* Wks. 1842 II. 155 That the said Warren Hastings was the less excusable in this.

2. Of actions, conduct, etc.: Admitting of excuse or palliation. ***excusable homicide*** (see quot. 1769).

c **1374** CHAUCER *Troylus* III. 981 Som manere Ialousye Is excusable more þan som. **1460** CAPGRAVE *Chron.* 281 And that her rebellion schuld be more excusabil. **1561** T. NORTON *Calvin's Inst.* III. xxii. (1634) 460 Dallying by shifts is never excusable. **1646** SIR T. BROWNE *Pseud. Ep.* I. vii. 26 With more excusable reservation may we shrink at their bare testimonies. **1709** ADDISON *Tatler* No. 121 ¶4 The only Extravagance of this Kind which appears to me excusable. **1769** BLACKSTONE *Comm.* IV. xiv. 182 Excusable homicide is of two sorts; either *per infortunium*, by misadventure; or *se defendendo*, upon a principle of self-preservation. *Ibid.* 183 Homicide in self-defence..is also excusable, rather than justifiable, by the English law. **1825** LYTTON *Falkland* 29 Emily felt a strong yet excusable curiosity.

excusableness (ɛkˈskjuːzəb(ə)lnɪs). [f. prec. + -NESS.] The quality of being excusable; capability of palliation.

1657 S. W. *Schism Dispach't* 75 In their excusableness is terminated the controversy in hand. **1684** SHARP *Disc. Conscience* 56 The Innocence or Excuseableness of some Mens mistakes. **1754** EDWARDS *Freed. Will* IV. iii. (ed. 4) 292 Our ideas of excusableness or faultlessness. **1755** in JOHNSON; whence in mod. Dicts.

excusably (ɛkˈskjuːzəblɪ), *adv.* [f. as prec. + -LY²] In a manner admitting of excuse; so as to deserve being excused.

a **1619** DONNE *Βιαθανατος* (1644) 124 Priviledges and exemptions from that Law, he may be excusably ignorant of. **1704** HEARNE *Duct. Hist.* (1714) I. 411 He taught..that no Man could excusably live Idle in the World. **1824** L. MURRAY *Eng. Gram.* (ed. 5) I. 426 His ideas may, very excusably, be on some subjects incomplete. **1884** *Manch. Exam.* 21 Nov. 6/1 On this matter Lord Northbrook was excusably angry.

excusal (ɛkˈskjuːzəl). [f. EXCUSE *v.* + -AL¹.] The action or fact of excusing; an instance of this. Const. *of.* In later use chiefly of local rates.

1584 PEELE *Arraignm. Paris* IV. iv, I must plead For safe excusal of my guiltless thought. **1620** ALLURED in Rushw. *Hist. Coll.* (1659) I. 91 Yea, upon the excusal of some, and refusal of others [who were bade to the marriage]. **1864** R. A. ARNOLD *Cotton Fam.* 286 The deficiency caused by the excusals on account of poverty. **1888** *Whitby Gaz.* 5 Oct. 3/3 The committee had met..to go through the list of excusals and irrecoverables. **1898** *Daily News* 4 Jan. 2/2 The justices had been in the habit of signing excusal lists at the rate collector's office and elsewhere, but not in petty sessions, as the law required. **1899** *Punch* 19 Apr. 190/3 When they press him to tax them excusal he begs. **1906** *Edin. Rev.* Apr. 507 The excusal of rates being one of the most abused forms of out-door relief.

† **excuˈsation.** *Obs.* Also 5 aphetic SCUSATION. [a. Fr. *excusation*, ad. L. *excūsātiōn-em*, f. *excūsāre*: see EXCUSE.]

1. The action of offering an excuse, defence, or apology; also, the condition of being excused, in phrase ***to have in excusation.***

a **1300** *Cursor M.* 9261 (Gott.) He sal find widvten excusacions Sexti alde generacions [from Adam to Christ]. *c* **1380** WYCLIF *Sel. Wks.* III. 440 Worldliche excusacioun shal not þenne assoyne [*printed* assoyre]. *c* **1450** LONELICH *Grail* xxxix. 478, I am a synnere In alle thynge..therfore haueth me now in excusaciown. **1526** *Pilgr. Perf.* (W. de W. 1531) 84 Whiche maner of excusacyon may be many wayes. **1605** BACON *Adv. Learn.* I. iii. §6 It [learning]..needs the less disproof or excusation. **1677** GALE *Crt. Gentiles* II. IV. 6 Ligation or Excusation and Accusation.

2. The action of setting free, or the state of being set free, from a duty, obligation, etc.; release from a duty, etc.

c **1400** *Apol. Loll.* 34 Wiþout excusacoun, but if..Crist despens wiþ hem, & excuse hem, or for bed hem. **1502** *Ord. Crysten Men* (W. de W. 1506) II. i. 87 Yᵉ we sholde not haue excusacyon not doynge them. *a* **1540** COVERDALE *Let. to Crumwell* Wks. II. 491, I was required..to deliver this writing to your mastership mine own self: notwithstanding ..I must desire favour on your behalf for my excusation [etc.]

3. An excuse, a real or alleged ground of excuse; a plea or apology; = EXCUSE *sb.* 2 and 3.

a. for an offence, etc.

c **1380** WYCLIF *Wks.* (1880) 411 Heere ben þre excusaciouns..to excuse prestis synne. *a* **1450** *Knt. de la Tour* (1868) 97 She wost not what she might do nor sey, for there was none excusacion in her folye. **1563** DAVIDSON *Answ. Kennedy* in *Wodr. Soc. Misc.* 192 Men that had fallin in error wald have had ane juste excusation, that the wrang [etc.]. **1650** B. *Discolliminium* 45, I..shall be allowed the full benefit of all the..excusations..that I..can devise.

b. for release from a duty, obligation, etc.

c **1386** CHAUCER *Pars. T.* ¶90 No man may been absent for certes there auailleth noon Essoyne ne excusacion. *c* **1440** *Gesta Rom.* II. xxxvi. (1838) 388 Now is there none excusacione on thi side, but thou shalt take me to thyne husbonde. **1530** *Proper Dyaloge* (1863) 41 Yᵗ it be not lefull to yᵉ by no excusacion to tarye fyue dayes. **1563–87** FOXE *A. & M.* (1596) 281/2 Neither by petition made to the pope, nor yet by his lawfull excusation. **1662** GUNNING *Lent Fast* 157 The 4 Excusations are..bodily infirmity [etc.].

excusative (ɛkˈskjuːzətɪv), *a. rare.* [f. EXCUSE *v.* + -ATIVE. Cf. OF. *excusatif, -ive.*] Tending to excuse.

1865 *Reader* 20 May 571/2 The excusative-censorial style, in which there is neither just praise nor honest blame.

excusator (ɛkskjuːˈzeɪtər). *Obs.* exc. *Hist.* [a. late L. *excūsātor*, agent-n. f. *excūsāre* to EXCUSE.] One who makes an excuse, defence, or apology; *esp.* a person officially authorized to present an excuse.

a **1661** FULLER *Worthies* (1840) III. 543 King Henry.. despatched him thither [to Rome] for his excusator. **1752** CARTE *Hist. Eng.* III. 110 The laws do not oblige an excusator or defender to give any security. **1873** DIXON *Two Queens* IV. XXI. vii. 164 The Council sent out Carue..as an excusator from the English people.

excusatory (ɛkˈskjuːzətərɪ), *a.* [ad. med.L. *excūsātōri-us*, f. late L. *excūsātor*: see prec.] Tending or intended to excuse; making or containing an excuse; apologetic.

1535 BONNER *Let.* in Burnet *Hist. Ref.* II. 175 The matters excusatorie to be admitted by his Holiness. **1642** SIR E. DERING *Sp. on Relig.* To Rdr., Let those who are in a fault ransom themselves with excusatory defences. **1748** RICHARDSON *Clarissa* (1811) VII. lix. 234, I hear the fellow's voice in a humble, excusatory tone. **1818** LAMB *Last Ess. Elia, Pop. Fallacies* 482 It would be a good face if it were not marked by the small-pox—a compliment which is always more admissive than excusatory. **1865** DICKENS *Mut. Fr.* III. vii, Offering these excusatory words as if they reflected great credit on himself.

excuse (ɛkˈskjuːs), *sb.* Also 5–6 escuse, aphetic SCUSE, q.v. [a. OFr. *excuse*, fem., f. *excuser*: see EXCUSE *v.*

The pronunciation with (s), instead of (z) as in the verb, is due to the analogy of pairs of words like *use, abuse* vbs. and sbs., *advise* and *advice*, etc., where the sb. was in OF. masc., and ended in *-s*.]

1. The action of the vb. EXCUSE.

a. The action of offering an apology for a person, or in extenuation of an offence. Const. *of* or *possessive case* of pers. pron. Now *rare* exc. in phrase ***in excuse of.*** Also rarely the action of begging off from a duty or obligation.

c **1374** CHAUCER *Anel. & Arc.* 308 Yf þat I to yowe myne othes beede For myn excuse a scorne shall be my mede. **1460** CAPGRAVE *Chron.* 227 Ser Robert..sent him mech tresoure, and than he cam to his excuse. **1477** EARL RIVERS (Caxton) *Dictes* 149 For excuse of the saide socrates. **1526** *Pilgr. Perf.* (W. de W. 1531) 76b, After that folowed doublenes and excuse of his synne. **1608** SHAKS. *Per.* II. iii. 96 Come, gentlemen..Even in your armours..I will not have excuse. **1632** MASSINGER *Maid of Hon.* II. i, Letters.. in excuse Of these forces sent against her. **1637** MILTON *Lycidas* 18 Hence with denial vain and coy excuse. **1792** *Anecd. W. Pitt* I. iv. 73 In excuse of their conduct it is said [etc.]. **1823** LINGARD *Hist. Eng.* VI. 251 Henry pleaded the scruples of his conscience in excuse of his precipitancy. **1825** LYTTON *Zicci* I. i, The old woman gave me a note of excuse.

b. The action of looking indulgently upon an offender or an offence; consideration, indulgence, pardon.

1655–60 STANLEY *Hist. Philos.* (1701) 24/2, I will.. condemn without excuse those that deserve it. **1675** in *Essex Papers* I. 318 He begs your Ex^cy^ Excuse that you doe not heare from him by this post. **1728** MORGAN *Algiers* I. Pref. 23, I heartily crave the excuse and pardon of every Reader. *a* **1810** TANNAHILL *Poems* (1846) 25, I see my fau'ts..And now I'm come to beg for your excuse. **1814** SCOTT *Ld. of Isles* III. vii, He pray'd excuse for mirth broke short.

†c. The action of releasing (a person) from an obligation; a dispensation, release. *Obs.*

1577 HANMER *Anc. Eccl. Hist.* (1619) 288 Supposing they had got their desired excuse, absented themselves. **1607** SHAKS. *Cor.* I. iii. 114 *Val.* I pray go with vs. *Virg.* Giue me excuse good Madame, I will obey you in euery thing heereafter.

2. That which is offered as a reason for being excused; sometimes in bad sense, a (mere) pretext, a subterfuge. **a.** A plea in extenuation of an offence; **b.** A plea for release from a duty, obligation, etc. Const. *for*, †*from.*

a. *c* **1500** *Melusine* 260 Yf it might plese you to here my lord & husband & his escuse. **1579** GOSSON *Sch. Abuse* (Arb.) 42 A bad excuse is better, they say, then none at all.

1590 Shaks. *Mids. N.* iii. ii. 245 Stay gentle Helena, heare my excuse. **1651** Hobbes *Leviath.* ii. xxvii. 156 Place..for Excuse, by which that which seemed a Crime, is proved to be none at all. **1667** Milton *P.L.* ix. 853 To him she hasted, in her face excuse Came Prologue. *a* **1700** B. E. *Dict. Cant. Crew*, *Lame Excuse*, a sorry Shift or Evasion. **1754** Richardson *Grandison* III. xxii. 202 Excuses are more than tacit confessions. **1761** F. Sheridan *Sidney Bidulph* I. 305, I am weary of inventing excuses from absenting myself. **1858** Doran *Crt. Fools* 70 The excuse was worse than the crime.

Comb. **1850** Mrs. Stowe *Uncle Tom's C.* xviii. 175 Dinah was mistress of the whole art and mystery of excuse-making.

b. *a* **1533** Ld. Berners *Huon* xlvi. 156 None excuse can auayle, for it must be thus. **1576** Fleming *Panopl. Epist.* 405 As for excuse, which peradventure you wil make by reason of the great showers, I meane to admitt none. **1606** Shaks. *Tr. & Cr.* ii. iii. 173 *Vlis.* Achilles will not to the field to morrow. *Ag.* What's his excuse? **1758** Johnson *Idler* No. 19 ¶8 He..has only time to taste the soup, makes a short excuse to the company [etc.].

3. That which serves to excuse, or which tends to extenuate (a fault or offence); a cause, reason, or ground for excuse; *esp.* in phrase ***without excuse***. Also, a ground for release from duty.

1494 in *Eng. Gilds* 188 Noo man then be absent wᵗ-oute a resonable and sufficiaunt excuse. **1533** Frith *Answ. More Let.* 9 Them am I bounde to beleve, and am dampned wythoute excuse yf I beleve them not. **1596** Shaks. *1 Hen. IV*, v. ii. 17 My Nephewes trespasse..hath the excuse of youth. **1632** J. Hayward tr. *Biondi's Eromena* 140 Wondring..why Eromilia would not be seene, for which he beleeved not her vow an excuse sufficient. *a* **1694** Tillotson *Serm.* cciii. (1743) X. 4631 The consideration of our own impotency is no excuse to our sloth and negligence. **1729** Butler *Serm.* Wks. 1874 II. 129 They tell you for an excuse..that they did not think they were so much in debt. **1794** Paley *Evid.* iii. iv. (1817) 304 Seeking out some excuse to themselves for not receiving Jesus. **1814** Chalmers *Evid. Chr. Revel.* Advt. 5 The external testimony of Christianity ..leaves infidelity without excuse. **1887** *Times* 29 Aug. 13/6 Charged with knocking without lawful excuse at the door.

4. At Cards (in the game of Tarocco).

1816 Singer *Hist. Cards* 239 If a king is played, and you have not the queen to form a sequence, you play the fool, and this is called an *excuse*.

excuse (ɛk'skjuːz), *v.* Forms: 3–6 **escuse(n**, (4 **excusi**), 4–5 **ascuse, -kuse, -kewse, -kewese**, 4– **excuse**. Also aphetic scuse, q.v. [ME. *escusen*, *excusen*, ad. OF. *escuser*, *excuser*, ad. L. *excūsāre*, f. *ex-* (see ex- *pref.*[1]) + *causa* cause, accusation.]

I. To offer, or serve as, an exculpation for.

1. *trans.* To offer an apology for.

a. To attempt to clear (a person) wholly or partially from blame, without denying or justifying his imputed action. Chiefly *refl.*

a **1225** *Ancr. R.* 304 Mon schal..nout werien [*v.r.* escusen] him ne siggen, Ich hit dude þuruh oðre. **1340** *Ayenb.* 7 Ne he ne may habbe skele: þ et he him moȝe excusi. **1382** Wyclif *2 Cor.* xii. 19 Ȝe wenen, that we schulen excuse vs anentis ȝou. *a* **1450** *Knt. de la Tour* (1868) 61 Whanne God asked her whi she had broke his comaundement..she beganne to excuse her. **1653** Walton *Angler* Ep. Ded. 6, I should rather excuse myself, then censure others. **1675** Crowne *Country Wit.* v. 84 My Lord has been to seek me in such a rage, that if you do not excuse me, it will be a parting quarrel. **1771** *Junius Lett.* xlix. 257 To excuse yourself, you publicly impeach your accomplice.

b. To seek to extenuate or remove the blame of (an acknowledged fault). †Also *rarely* with sentence as *obj.*

1303 R. Brunne *Handl. Synne* 12357 He [Adam] wulde haue excusede hys fame As who seyþ, 'Gode was to blame'. **1340** *Ayenb.* 61 Þe blondere defendeþ and excuseþ..þe zennes of ham þet he wyle ulateri. *c* **1460** *Towneley Myst.* 77 For shame yit shuld she let, To excuse her velany by me. **1548** Hall *Chron.* 184 b, The Mayre sent the recorder..to excuse the matter. **1590** Shaks. *Com. Err.* iii. i. 92 She will well excuse Why at this time the dores are made against you. **1660** Marvell *Corr.* Wks. 1872–5 II. 17, I had rather expose mine own defects..then excuse thereby a totall neglect of my duty. **1667** Milton *P.L.* iv. 394 So spake the Fiend, and with necessitie..excus'd his devilish deeds. **1751** E. Heywood *Betsy Thoughtless* I. 216 She..excused having made him wait. **1793** Gouv. Morris in Sparks *Life & Writ.* (1832) II. 372 He is driven to..excusing a step, which it is not possible to justify. **1856** Froude *Hist. Eng.* (1858) II. ix. 368 It was a strange proceeding, to be excused only..by the pressure of the times.

c. *absol.*

1590 Shaks. *Mids. N.* v. i. 363 Neuer excuse; for when the plaiers are all dead, there need none to be blamed. **1651** Hobbes *Leviath.* ii. xix. 97 To accuse, requires lesse Eloquence than to excuse.

†**d.** [after L. *excusare se esse*, etc.] ***to excuse*** (a person or thing) ***to be***, etc., ***to excuse oneself that***, etc.: to allege by way of excuse or explanation, that (it is), etc. *Obs.*

a **1340** Hampole *Psalter* xviii. 7 No man may excuse him 'þat he ne is sum tyme stird fra synn to gode'. **1393** Langl. *P. Pl.* C. xxiii. 6 Couþest þou nat excuse þe..þat þow nome no more þan neode þe tauhte? *a* **1532** Ld. Berners *Huon* xcv. 309 The prouost..excusynge hym selfe that he knew nothynge of yᵉ trewes. **1605** Bacon *Adv. Learn.* i. iii. §10 Excusing himselfe that it was reason to yeeld to him, that commaunded thirtie Legions. **1668** Culpepper & Cole *Barthol. Anat.* iii. i. 323 The Father excepts the Nerves of the Privity manifestly hollow, which nevertheless his Son excuses to have been meant of the hollow Ligaments of the Privity.

†**2. a.** To maintain the innocence of (a person); to defend from an accusation (*of*); to maintain the rightness of, seek to justify (an action). *Obs.*

c **1315** Shoreham 40 The thef..escusede Jhesu Cryst, And hym gelty gan ȝelde. *c* **1350** *Will. Palerne* 4045 Sche of þat sclaunder excused hire al-gate. *c* **1384** Chaucer *H. Fame* i. 427 She desired no-thinge ellis But to excusen Eneas. **1481** in *Eng. Gilds* (1870) 323 John Mather askused hymsell ..wᵗ ij men sworyn apon a boke. **1526–34** Tindale *Rom.* ii. 15 Their thoughtes accusynge one another or excusynge. **1531** *St. German's Doctor & Stud.* liv. 148 a, Howe may the playntyfe there be excused of an untruthe? **1577** Holinshed *Chron.* II. 140 To excuse him of the death of the archbishop Thomas. **1696** Stillingfl. *Serm.* ii. 66 To have excused these two commands from a palpable contradiction.

†**b.** with complement, or *to be* (so and so). *Obs.*

1583 Golding *Calvin on Deut.* xlvii. 281 Is there not any of vs all that can excuse himselfe to bee vnsubject to such haughtinesse. **1587** *Mirr. Mag.*, *Porrex* vii, Can I excuse my selfe deuoide of faut.

3. a. To obtain exemption or release for; to allege reasons for the exemption of (a person) from a duty or obligation. Const. †*for*, *from*, in early use with *that ... not*.

1340 *Ayenb.* 33 He him excuseþ þet he hit ne may do. **1389** in *Eng. Gilds* (1870) 4 Al þe oþ er schul comen to þe placebo and dirige..but ȝif he may hym excuse resonabely. **1460** Capgrave *Chron.* 141 He excused him be the werre that he had with Frauns. **1467** *Mann. & Househ. Exp.* (1841) 172, I promessed the Kenge I wolde make in al haste a new schepe..were fore, I pray ȝowe helpe to askewese me fore my komenge. **1593** Shaks. *3 Hen. VI*, v. v. 46 Clarence excuse me to the King my Brother. **1697** Dampier *Voy.* (1698) I. 356 Captain Swan excused himself, and said..he would have nothing to do with it. **1712** Hearne *Collect.* (Oxf. Hist. Soc.) III. 361, I excus'd myself upon account of my being oblig'd to return speedily to Oxford. **1788** Reid *Aristotle's Log.* iv. §5. 96, I am very willing to excuse myself from entering upon this great branch of Logic.

absol. **1382** Wyclif *Luke* xiv. 18 Alle bigunnen togidere to excuse [**1388** excusen hem].

†**b.** To beg off from (doing something); to decline with apologies. *Obs.*

1548 Hall *Chron.* 204 Willing him..with all hast to repayre unto hym, which oftentymes he had excused by syckenes and debilitie of his body. **1588** R. Parke tr. *Mendoza's China* 162 They could not excuse to go vnto them to accomplish their commandement. **1591** Shaks. *Two Gent.* i. iii. 71 To morrow be in readinesse, to goe, Excuse it not: for I am peremptory. **1624** Capt. Smith *Virginia* i. (1629) 14 He did what he could to excuse it, yet their importunities would not cease till he undertooke it. **1709** Strype *Ann. Ref.* I. xiii. (*heading of ch.*), The Bishop of Ely excuseth his ministring in the chapel by reason thereof. **1754** J. Hildrop *Misc. Wks.* II. 123 He pressed me..to dine with him, which I excused.

†**4. a.** To screen, shelter. [Cf. late L. *se a calore excusare* Palladius).] To save from punishment or harm, *esp.* by suffering (in a person's stead); to exempt (a person) from a duty by taking his place. Const. *of*, *from*. *Obs.*

a **1340** Hampole *Psalter* xviii. 7 He suffirs nan to be þat may excuse þaim of the hete of his luf. **1461–83** *Liber Niger* in *Househ. Ord.* 16 Every officer in unitie of love applyed to excuse other by servyce and attendaunce. *Ibid.* 82 Everye yoman to helpe to excuse others for his busyness in his absence. **1543** Sir J. Wallop in Maclean *Carew* 126, I wold wische to God the next kynesman I have..had excused him. **1576** Fleming *Panopl. Epist.* 426, I would her life might have beene excused by my death. **1653** H. More *Antid. Ath.* ii. xi, An Armature..often excuses the more useful parts of his head from harm. **1711** Steele *Spect.* No. 82 ¶3 At School, he was whipped thrice a Week for Faults he took upon him to excuse others.

†**b.** To regard as exempt or safe *from*. *rare.*

1643 Sir T. Browne *Relig. Med.* i. §28, I excuse not Constantine from a fall off his Horse..upon the wearing those nayles on his bridle.

5. a. Of things, circumstances, etc.: To serve as an excuse or exculpation for.

1538 Starkey *England* i. ii. 31 Such ignorance excusyth not errorys in mannys lyfe. **1685** Baxter *Paraphr. N.T.* Matt. iii. 4 Other men's superstition..will not excuse mens superfluity. **1702** Pope *Wife of Bath* 97 Shape excuses the defects of face. **1800** Addison *Amer. Law. Rep.* 13 The wife's presence will not excuse the husband. **1856** Froude *Hist. Eng.* (1858) I. v. 434 There are some acts of injustice which no national interest can excuse.

absol. **1658–9** *Burton's Diary* (1828) IV. 2 Ignorance will not excuse. **1736** Butler *Anal.* ii. i. Wks. I. 163 Ignorance ..will..just as little, excuse in one case as in the other.

b. In *passive*. To have a sufficient excuse; to be freed from blame.

c **1340** Hampole *Prose Tr.* 27 If þou leue nedfull besynes of actyf lyfe..by-cause of desire..to gyffe þe to gastely ocupacyone, wenande þat þou arte thereby excusede..þou dose noghte wysely. **1548** Udall, etc. *Erasm. Par.*, *John* 57 b, The common people and the vnlearned are to be holden excused, and may be forgeuen. *a* **1626** Bacon *Max. & Uses Com. Law* v. 26 If a warrant..come from the King to sell wood upon the ground whereof I am tenant..I am excused in waste. **1787** *Minor* 96 Cupid being blind was partly excused accompanying a counterfeit.

II. To accept an excuse for or from.

6. a. To accept a plea in exculpation of (a person); to judge leniently on the ground of extenuating circumstances. Const. †*of*, *for*.

c **1325** *E.E. Allit. P.* A. 281 To be excused I make requeste. *c* **1386** Chaucer *Knt.'s T.* 908 Although his ire here gylt accused, Yet in his resoun he hem bothe excused. *c* **1450** *Castle Hd. Life St. Cuthb.* (Surtees) 7305 Þai were excused þan, for why þai did wrange vnwitandly.. **1651** Hobbes *Leviath.* ii. xxvii. 157 He is totally Excused, for the reason next before alledged. **1862** Sir B. Brodie *Psychol. Inq.* II. iii. 85 We may excuse altogether those who labour under the illusions of actual insanity. **1875** Jowett *Plato* (ed. 2) V. 179 The people may be excused for following tradition only.

b. Phrase, ***Excuse me***: used parenthetically in conversation as apology for an impropriety in speech, etc., or as a polite way of disputing a statement. Also used as a polite form in addressing a stranger, or in interrupting the speech of another. Hence as *sb.* (in full, ***excuse-me dance***), a dance in which one may 'cut in' (see cut *v.* 55 d).

1606 Shaks. *Tr. & Cr.* i. ii. 87 *Pan.* Hector is not a better man than Troylus. *Cre.* Excuse me. *Pan.* He is elder. **1814** Jane Austen *Mansf. Park* II. vi, Excuse me, your Ladyship must not see your cards. **1831** J. Banim *Smuggler* xii, Excuse me, sir; but though you have been my guest..this is the first time we have met. **1889** A. Lang *Lett. Lit.* iii. (ed. 2) 33 That infernal (excuse me) coward and villain. **1894** *Home Chimes* XVI. 353 'Excuse me, sir.' Mr. Gill stopped, and addressed a passer-by. **1901** R. S. W. Bell *Tales of Greyhouse* 255 Excuse me—you are an old boy? **1902** Kipling *Just So Stories* 66 ''Scuse me,' said the Elephant's Child most politely, 'but have you seen such a thing as a Crocodile in these promiscuous parts?' **1924** W. Deeping *Three Rooms* iii, Excuse me, but would you care to make up a four? **1940** Harrisson & Madge *War begins at Home* ix. 229 Whereas pre-war excuse-me's were almost always quicksteps, now fox-trots and waltzes are frequently included. **1942** A. P. Jephcott *Girls growing Up* v. 121 'Excuse me' and 'Buzz off' dances give the girl an opportunity to go up to any couple and abstract the boy for her partner. **1953** E. Simon *Past Masters* ii. vi. 113 Jonquil..had emerged as mistress of ceremonies, decreeing now an excuse-me-dance, now a Paul Jones. **1965** J. P. Carstairs *Concrete Kimono* xv. 125 'You actually danced with Reba?' 'Is that so crazy?.. It was an *Excuse Me*, anyway.'

c. To admit apology for, overlook, condone (a fault, offence, impropriety, etc.); to regard indulgently, pardon the faults of (a performance). Also with indirect personal object.

c **1391** Chaucer *Astrol.* Prol. 2, I prey..every discret pesone..to have my rewde endytyng for excused. **1553** T. Wilson *Rhet.* 107 Some tymes we excuse a fault and accuse the reporter. **1591** Shaks. *Two Gent.* iv. i. 54 We cite our faults, That they may hold excus'd our lawlesse liues. **1607** —— *Cor.* iv. vii. 11, I must excuse, What cannot be amended. **1702** *Eng. Theophrast.* 125 It is a very dangerous mistake to excuse these vile inclinations upon the tenderness of their age. **1737** Pope *Hor. Epist.* ii. i. 215 (Excuse some courtly stains) No whiter page than Addison's remains. **1775** Sheridan *Rivals* i. i, Excuse my glove, Thomas. **1825** Macaulay *Milton* Ess. (1854) I. 13/2 If ever despondency and asperity could be excused in any man, they might have been excused in Milton. **1857** Robertson *Serm.* Ser. iii. xvii. 217 The boldest heart may be excused a shudder.

7. a. To set free (a person) from a task, duty, obligation; dispense from payment, attendance, etc. Const. †*for*, *from*; also with double obj.

1382 Wyclif *Luke* xiv. 19, I preie thee, haue me excusid. **1839** in *Eng. Gilds* (1870) 7 That they come to þe dirige..but he haue a resonable cause to be excused. **1597** Shaks. *2 Hen. IV*, v. i. 3 *Shal.* You shall not away to night. *Fal*, You must excuse me, M. Robert Shallow. **1647** Clarendon *Hist. Reb.* i. (1843) 33/1 Laud attended..throughout that whole journey, which he..no doubt would have been excused from. **1697** *C'tess D'Aunoy's Trav.* (1706) 85 She sent word to all the Ladies of Brussels and Antwerp, she would excuse them for their Visits. **1725** De Foe *Voy. round World* (1840) 295 He would not be excused..from going back with us. **1777** Sheridan *Sch. Scand.* ii. ii, Your ladyship must excuse me; I'm called away by particular business. **1817** Mar. Edgeworth *Two Guardians* iii. iv, *Beauchamp.* Come, shake hands, and be friends. *St. Albans.* Excuse me, Mr. Courtington. *Mod.* The jury were excused from attendance for the rest of the week. He was excused the extrance-fee.

b. ***to excuse oneself***: to ask permission or apologize before leaving.

1926 T. E. Lawrence *Seven Pillars* (1935) vii. lxxxix. 496 After an hour he excused himself, because he had just married a Shobek wife. **1964** B. Malamud *Idiots First* 69 The waiter brought drinks and when Mary Lou had finished hers she excused herself, went to the ladies' room.

c. ***to be excused***: to be allowed to leave a room, esp. a schoolroom; *spec.* to go to the lavatory. *colloq.* (chiefly in school language).

1954 *Harrap's Stand. Fr. & Eng. Dict.* Suppl. (ed. 2) 55/2 *Sortir... Est-ce que je peux sortir?*, May I be excused? **1963** S. Marshall *Exper. in Education* ii. 60 He could not tie up his own shoe, put on his own coat, or even 'be excused' without help. **1968** 'P. Hobson' *Titty's Dead* xiii. 138 'Please may I be excused? ' she said.

8. 'To remit; not to exact' (J.); to grant excuse for the want or absence of; to dispense with.

1646 Sir T. Browne *Pseud. Ep.* i. ix. 35 If any man shall from hence conclude, the Moone is second in magnitude unto the Sun, he must excuse my beliefe. **1726** Chetwood *Adv. Capt. R. Boyle* 58, I must beg you to excuse my waiting on you for a little while. **1814** Byron *Note in Orig. MS.* Wks. (1846) 90/1 *note*, He will excuse the '*Mr.*'——we do not say *Mr.* Cæsar. **1836** Lytton *Duchess de la Vallière* v. v, From our royal court We do excuse your presence.

†**ex'cusedly**, *adv. Obs. rare.* [f. *excused*, pa. pple. of excuse *v.* + -ly[2].] In a manner admitting of excuse; with (more or less) excuse.

1654 R. Codrington tr. *Justin's Hist. World* 297 More excusedly to perform what he had determined. *Ibid.* 403 He hoped that he more excusedly should commit Sacriledge.

excuseless (ɛk'skjuːslɪs), *a.* [f. prec. + -less.] Without excuse.

1. Of a person: **a.** Having no excuse to offer.

1548 Turner *Names of Herbes* 5 Because..that Poticaries shoulde be excuselesse..I have shewed in what places..the herbes growe. **1608** W. Sclater *Malachy* (1650) 5 Then surely are we utterly excuseless. **1711** *Peace in Divinity* 2

The Reprobate shall have such Grace only procur'd for him, as will render him excuseless.

†**b.** Not offering an excuse. *Obs.*

1640 QUARLES *Enchirid.* II. ii, Charity is a naked child.. Naked, because excuselesse and simple.

2. Of things: Admitting of no excuse; inexcusable.

1611 W. SCLATER *Key* (1629) 96 Such an excuselesse sinne is vnthankefulnesse. **1654** WHITLOCK *Zootomia* 301 Excuselesse is the idle mans *nihil agendo*, sleeping out his Lamp. **1667** *Decay Chr. Piety* xvi. ¶3 The voluntary enslaving my self is more excuseless. **1889** *Eng. Illust. Mag.* Sept. 894/2 An absolutely excuseless egotism.

†**ex'cusement.** *Obs. rare*⁻¹. [a. OF. *escusement*: see EXCUSE *v.* and -MENT.] = EXCUSE *sb.* 2.

1393 GOWER *Conf.* I. 76 Thilke excusement was none.

excuser (ɛk'skjuːzə(r)). [f. EXCUSE *v.* + -ER[1].] One who excuses.

1. One who offers an excuse for or extenuates (a fault).

1580 HOLLYBAND *Treas. Fr. Tong*, *Excuseur*, an excuser. **1643** MILTON *Divorce* II. xi. (1851) 89 Miserable excusers. **1730** SWIFT *Vind. Ld. Carteret* Wks. 1761 III. 189 In vain would his excusers endeavour to palliate his enormities by imputing them to madness. **1824** MISS MITFORD *Village* Ser. I. (1863) 164 She was the excuser-general of the neighbourhood, turned every speech and action the sunny side without. **1871** SMILES *Charac.* iv. 92 To the sophistries of such an excuser, Sir Samuel Romilly once wrote [etc.].

†**2.** One who obtains the release of another from a duty, etc., by taking his place; a substitute, deputy. Cf. EXCUSE *v.* 4. *Obs.*

1461-83 *Liber Niger* in *Househ. Ord.* 65 The Steward and Thesaurers excusers and attorneys.. may take it in absence of the gretter and elder.

excusing (ɛk'skjuːzɪŋ), *vbl. sb.* [f. EXCUSE *v.* + -ING[1].] The action of the verb EXCUSE in various senses; also, an instance of this; a plea or ground of excuse.

a **1340** HAMPOLE *Psalter* cxl. 3 Swa be oure lippis.. sperd til excusynge of syn. *c* **1380** WYCLIF *Sel. Wks.* III. 512 ȝif þis excusinge were soþ. *c* **1400** *Rom. Rose* 6588 Noon excusynges A parfit man ne shulde seke. *c* **1460** *Towneley Myst.*, *Annunc.* 78 They sayde ther helpyd none excusyng, And wed us thus togeder. **1590** SWINBURNE *Testaments* 103 Those lawes concerninge excusinge of tutors and curators are verie seldome.. practised. **1664** SOUTH *Serm. John* xv. 15 (1737) II. ii. 58 Many.. things.. may go a great way towards an excusing of the agent.

ex'cusing, *ppl. a.* [f. as prec. + -ING[2].]

1. That excuses, or makes excuse; containing an excuse.

1657 S. W. *Schism Dispach't* 93 His excusing words, that they, etc. **1688** COLLIER *Several Disc.* (1725) 213 Others.. omit the most.. excusing Circumstances.

2. = EXCEPTING *prep.* and *conj.* *U.S.* (chiefly *dial.*).

1887 T. N. PAGE *In Ole Virginia* 199 Torm.. said 'he was the grettest gent'man in the country skusin him [*sc.* Torm] and the Colonel'. **1938** M. K. RAWLINGS *Yearling* iv. 42, I ain't done much today, excusin' fret and worry, and mess with the sausage. *Ibid.* ix. 85 You kin tame arything, son, excusin' the human tongue. **1964** F. O'ROURKE *Mule for Marquesa* (1967) i. 12 He had not slept in two days, excusing catnaps during the train ride.

Hence **ex'cusingly** *adv.*, in an excusing tone or manner; by way of excuse.

1876 MISS BRADDON *J. Haggard's Dau.* vi. 83 She remembered excusingly that [etc.]. **1883** J. G. BUTLER in *Bible Wks.* II. 35 Peter.. had spoken so gently, and even excusingly, to the crucifiers of Christ.

excusive (ɛk'skjuːsɪv), *a.* [f. EXCUSE *v.* + -IVE.] That tends to excuse; excusing.

1592 *Nobody & Someb.* (1878) 288 Our eares are deafe to all excusive pleas. **1641** *Arminian Nunnery* 4 The Priestlike Prolocutor did not want a premeditated excusive Iustification. **1855** T. T. LYNCH *Lett. to Scattered* (1872) ix. 118 Say whatever may be found excusive on behalf of the very bad. **1903** CRICHTON-BROWNE *New Lett. Jane W. Carlyle* I. p. lxix, Hurried, excusive scribbles. **1929** E. LINKLATER *Poet's Pub* iii. 52 Mr. Wesson smiled all round, an excusive, propitiating smile.

Hence †**ex'cusively** *adv.*

1641 *Disc. Prince Henry* in *Harl. Misc.* (Malh.) III. 522 To the first, he gave answers satisfactorily.—To the other, excusively.

†**ex'cuss,** *v.* *Obs.* [f. L. *excuss-* ppl. stem of *excutĕre*, f. *ex-* out + *quatĕre* to shake; the vb. had also the sense of searching a person by shaking his loose robe. Cf. sense 2.]

1. *trans.* To shake off, cast off, get rid of. Said with reference to things material and immaterial.

1607 TOPSELL *Four-f. Beasts* (1673) 239 To brush over their Horses with a little linnen instrument.. whereby they excusse all dust from the beast. —— *Serpents* (1653) 603 Snakes with tender skin excuss'd their years enlarge. **1657** TOMLINSON *Renou's Disp.* 164* That the exterior shell and all glumosity may be excussed. **1662** STILLINGFL. *Orig. Sacr.* I. i. §12 They could not totally excuss the notions of a deity out of their minds. **1668** HOWE *Bless. Righteous* (1825) 119 The holy soul's release.. will excuss and shake off this drowsy sleep.

2. To shake out the contents of anything; hence, to investigate thoroughly, discuss (a question or document); also, to get (the truth) *from* (a person).

1570 FOXE *A. & M.* (ed. 2) 689 If I should.. take in hand your Popishe portues and.. excusse euery Popishe martyr and sancte there canonised. **1577** tr. *Bullinger's Decades* (1592) 496 Saint Augustine doth more fully excusse and handle this argument. **1579** G. HARVEY *Letter-bk.* (Camden) 59, I then excussid the matter. **1654** JUNIUS (Webster 1864), To take some pains in excussing some old documents. **1726** AYLIFFE *Parerg.* 438 To examine a Delinquent on Oath to excuss the Truth of some Crime from him.

3. *Mod. Civ. Law.* [Cf. OF. *escosser*, *escousser*, 'saisir, dépouiller' (Godef.).] To seize, take in execution (a debtor's goods).

1726 AYLIFFE *Parerg.* 272 The Person of a Man ought not by the Civil Law to be taken for a Debt, unless his Goods and Estate has been first excuss'd. **1755** in JOHNSON; whence in mod. Dicts.

†**ex'cussable,** *a.* *Obs.*⁻⁰ [f. prec. + -ABLE.] That may be shaken off.

1730-6 in BAILEY. **1775** in ASH.

†**ex'cussion.** *Obs.* [ad. L. *excussiōn-em*, n. of action f. *excut-ĕre*: see EXCUSS.]

1. The action of shaking, casting, or putting out or off, material or immaterial things.

1607 TOPSELL *Four-f. Beasts* 125 The new bunches swelling vp.. do thrust off the old horns, being holpe.. by the willing excussion of the beast that beareth them. **1620** BP. HALL *Hon. Mar. Clergy* I. §3 The iust excussion of that seruile yoke. **1649** BULWER *Pathomyot.* II. vi. 183 Extrusion or excussion of the Muscle that moves the Jaw. **1650** CHARLETON *Paradoxes* 73 Fire is, by excussion, kindled from flint. **1698** *Consid. conc. Succession & Alleg.* 33 The late King's Excussion of his Regal Authority. **1721-1800** in BAILEY.

2. 'Diligent inquisition or examination' (Bailey).

RICHARDSON cites an example of this sense from Wats' tr. *Bacon's Adv. Learn.* (1640) vi. ii. 274; but the word is a misprint for *excursion* (the original having *excursio*).

3. *Mod. Civ. Law.* [Cf. OF. *escussion* in same sense.] Seizure of goods for debt, etc.

1622 MALYNES *Anc. Law-Merch.* 453 Debarring.. the exceptions of Prescription, Excussion, etc. **1726** AYLIFFE *Parerg.* 272 If upon such an Excussion there are not Goods found sufficient.. his Body may be attach'd. **1755** in JOHNSON; whence in ASH, etc.

†**ex'cussive,** *a.* *Obs. rare*⁻¹. [f. L. *excuss-* ppl. stem of *excut-ĕre* (see EXCUSS) + -IVE.] Designed for shaking out.

1657 TOMLINSON *Renou's Disp.* 484 Sieves made of Horses-hairs.. called.. sometimes excussive incernicles.

†**ex'cutient,** *a.* *Obs.*⁻⁰ [ad. L. *excutient-em*, pr. pple. of *excutĕre*: see EXCUSS.] 'Shaking off' (Bailey *folio* 1730-6).

1775 in ASH.

excuti'fidian. *nonce-wd.* [f. L. *excut-i*)- stem of *excutĕre* (see EXCUSS) + *fid-es* faith + -IAN.] 'One who believes that saving faith or grace can be wholly lost or shaken off.' (Davies *Suppl. Gloss.*).

a **1656** BP. HALL *Lett. Fall. fr. Grace* Rem. Wks. (1660) 389, I am sorry that any of our new Excuti-fidians should pester your Suffolk.

†**ex'decimate,** *v.* *Obs.*⁻⁰ [f. EX- *pref.*[1] + L. *decim-āre* (f. *decimus* tenth, f. *decem* ten) + -ATE[3]. Cf. EDECIMATION.] *trans.* '*To tithe out*' (Cockeram 1623-6).

ex-di'rectory, *a.* [f. EX *prep.* + DIRECTORY *sb.*] Denoting a telephone-number that is not listed in the directory at the request of the subscriber; also of a person who has such a number.

1936 *P.O. Teleph. Sales Bull.* Mar. 41/2 It was possible.. to allow the separate exchange lines for the house exchange system to be ex-directory... This.. provides.. an isolated example where ex-directory facilities may be used as a selling argument. **1963** 'R. EAST' *Pin Men* ii. 32 Virginia's home number was not ex-directory. **1964** C. E. MAINE *Never let Up* xv. 151 'He's ex-directory.' 'But *you* must know his number.' **1966** 'W. Haggard' *Power House* xi. 116 He'd been woken.. by a call on an ex-directory number.

ex div., abbrev. *ex dividend*: see EX *prep.* 2.

exe, obs. form of AXE *sb.*[1], AX.

exeat ('ɛksiːæt). [L. *exeat* let (him) go out, 3rd pers. sing. pres. subj. of *exīre* to go out: see EXIT *sb.*]

‖**A.** In Lat. use as verb.

In plays of the early 16th c. used as a stage direction, equivalent to the later EXIT *sb.* (So also **'exeant**, 'let (them) go out', for which EXEUNT was afterwards used.)

c **1485** *Digby Myst.* (1882) I. 275 Exeant. *a* **1553** UDALL *Royster D.* I. ii. (Arb.) 19 Exeat.

B. *sb.* A permission to go out. [So used in Fr.]

1. A permission to leave the diocese, granted to a priest by the bishop.

1730-6 in BAILEY (folio). **1855** R. BOYLE *Boyle v. Wiseman* 71 Armed with the above exeat, I immediately applied for employment to the.. Bishop of Southwark.

2. In English public schools and colleges, in monastic houses, etc.: A permission for temporary absence. Also **'exeant**, such a permission granted to more than one person.

1727-51 CHAMBERS *Cycl.* s.v., His master has given him an exeat. **1806** K. WHITE *Let.* 30 June, He would not give me an exeat, without which no man can leave his college for the night. **1852** C. A. BRISTED *Eng. University* I. 193 *note*, Exeats.. were never granted [at King's Coll. Camb.] but in cases of life and death. **1859** FARRAR *J. Home* 259 How shall I get my exeat to go to London.

exec, colloq. abbrev. of EXECUTIVE *sb.*

1896 G. B. SHAW *Let.* 20 Mar. (1965) 614 The Execs will be safe, I should think, to sanction the expenditure. *Ibid.*, We could appeal to the exec. to grant us the price of the report. **1933** B. J. CHIPMAN *Hey Rube!* 194/1 *Execs*, executives. **1958** 'P. BRYANT' *Two Hours to Doom* 16 The exec.. did not enjoy staff work and administration. **1966** *Punch* 30 Mar. 464/1 The execs must have fallen into transports of delight.

execate, -ation, var. ff. EXCECATE, -ATION.

execrable ('ɛksɪkrəb(ə)l), *a.* Also 5 excecrable, 6 *Sc.* execrabill, 7 exsecrable. [ad. L. *execrābil-is* (*exsecrābil-is*), (*a*) execrating, cf. sense 1; (*b*) accursed, detestable, f. *execr-ārī* (*exsecr-ārī*): see EXECRATE. Cf. Fr. *exécrable*.]

†**1.** Expressing or involving a curse; hence, of an imprecation: Awful, fearful. *Obs.*

1382 WYCLIF *2 Pet.* ii. 11 Aungels.. beren not aȝens hem the execrable.. doom. **1580** BARET *Alv.* C 1802 A Cursing and oth execrable. **1622** FLETCHER *Sea Voy.* II. ii, Did we then.. here plant ourselves, With execrable oaths never to look On man? *c* **1630** in Risdon *Surv. Devon* §108 (1810) 100 A fearful and execrable curse on all such as shal deminish.. it.

2. Of persons and things: Deserving to be execrated or cursed; abominable, detestable.

1490 CAXTON *Eneydos* iv. (1890) 19 Full of so execrable cruelte. **1513** MORE *Rich. III*, Wks. 36/2 The execrable desire of soueraynte, prouoked him to theire destruccion. *c* **1590** MARLOWE *Faust* Wks. (Rtldg.) 95/2 Thou execrable dog. **1667** MILTON *P.L.* XII. 64 O execrable Son so to aspire Above his brethren. **1703** MAUNDRELL *Journ. Jerus.* (1721) 68 It was.. shut out of the Walls of the City, as an execrable and polluted place. **1736** BERKELEY *Disc. Magistrates* Wks. III. 427 That execrable Fraternity of Blasphemers, lately set up within this city of Dublin. **1871** MORLEY *Voltaire* (1886) 169 He is either a lover of parasites.. or else the most execrable cynic. **1878** TENNYSON *Q. Mary* II. ii, A knot of ruffians.. With execrating execrable eyes.

†**b.** That is put under a curse; accursed. *Obs.*

1557 N. T. (Genev.) *1 Cor.* xii. 3 No man speaking in the Spirite of God, calleth Iesus execrable. **1597** HOOKER *Eccl. Pol.* v. xvii. (1611) 209 Reserue, as.. Saul did, execrable things, to worship God withall.

†**c.** Calling forth expressions of horror; piteous, horrifying, shocking. *Obs.*

1490 CAXTON *Eneydos* vi. (1890) 22 Y[e] aduentures of fortune harde & dyuersly excecrable. **1596** DRAYTON *Legends* iii. 529 Whereby brake out that execrable Rage. **1610** G. FLETCHER *Christ's Vict.* (1632) 36 The heav'n put out his guilty eye, That durst behold so execrable sight. **1613** R. HILL *Commun. Instruct.* 20 His [the Minister's] breaking of bread.. [doth signifie] the execrable passion of Christ. *a* **1704** T. BROWN *On Dk. Ormond's Recov.* Wks. (1730) I. 49 Bellona me invites To seas of blood, and execrable sights. **1805** FOSTER *Ess.* I. iii. 33 The execrable image of this scene.

3. *hyperbolically.* Calling forth expressions of extreme disgust; of wretched quality, bad beyond description. [So mod.Fr. *exécrable*.]

1738 WARBURTON *Div. Legat.* I. 79 His execrable paradox. **1753** ARMSTRONG *Taste* 15 Blindly we.. good, and bad, and execrable swallow. **1789** LD. AUCKLAND *Corr.* II. 191 Our mule-drivers were wicked enough to carry us to an execrable posada. **1815** MOORE *Lalla R.* (1824) 127 The versification .. was, to say no worse of it, execrable. **1867** MISS BRADDON *Run to Earth* iii, What execrable weather.

Hence **'execrableness.**

1730-6 BAILEY (folio), *Execrableness*, accursedness, impiousness. **1775** in ASH.

execrably ('ɛksɪkrəblɪ), *adv.* [f. EXECRABLE + -LY[2].] In an execrable manner.

†**a.** So as to deserve execration (*obs.*). **b.** Accursedly, abominably, detestably, atrociously.

1633 PRYNNE *Histrio-Mastix* I. VI. ii. 154 These Playes themselves must certainely be execrably odious to all good Christians. **1671** MILTON *Samson* 1362 What act more execrably unclean? **1693** DRYDEN *Persius* I. 14 'Tis Fustian all; 'tis execrably bad. **1697** VANBRUGH *Relapse* I. iii, They [the shoes] pinch me execrably. **1794** V. KNOX *Antipolemus* 27 The object of a battle was.. sordid lucre, or something still more execrably flagitious. **1806-7** J. BERESFORD *Miseries Hum. Life* (1826) II. xxxvii, Bells execrably rung for some hours every evening. **1858** HAWTHORNE *Fr. & It. Jrnls.* (1872) I. 6 Pictures, execrably bad in all cases.

execrate ('ɛksɪkreɪt), *v.* [f. L. *execrāt-* (*exsecrāt-*) ppl. stem of *execrāri* (*essecrāri*) to curse, f. *ex-* (see EX- *pref.*[1]) + *sacrāre* to devote religiously (in good sense, to a deity; in bad sense, to destruction), f. *sacr-um* (masc. nom. *sacer*) devoted, religiously set apart; hence, in good sense, hallowed to a deity, SACRED; and in bad sense, devoted to destruction, accursed. Cf. *consecrate*.]

†**1.** *trans.* To pronounce a curse upon; to declare accursed. ***to execrate out***: to drive out with a curse. *Obs. rare.*

1639 FULLER *Holy War* IV. xxviii. (1840) 229 His own share [of goods] he execrated, and caused it to be burnt. **1691** ED. TAYLOR tr. *Behmen's Theos. Philos.* xv. 272 Became execrated out of Paradise.

absol. **1612** T. TAYLOR *Comm. Titus* i. 13 It is one thing.. to excommunicate, another to curse and excerate.

†**b.** Occasionally used by way of antithesis to *consecrate*: To make unholy. *Obs.*

a **1572** KNOX *Hist. Ref.* Wks. 1846 I. 193 The bastard Bischope, who yit was not execrated (consecrated thei call it). **1647** WARD *Simp. Cobler* 33 Execrating a Protestant Parish Church one day, and consecrating it the next. **1656** *Artif. Handsom.* 156 As if meer plebeian noyse.. were enough to.. execrate anything as.. devilish.

2. To imprecate evil upon (as an expression of hatred); to express or feel intense loathing or abhorrence for; to abhor, detest.

1561 tr. *Calvin's 4 Godly Serm.* i. D j, The Iewes.. of that time.. are commaunded.. to execrate the idolatrie of the Chaldeans. *a* **1698** TEMPLE (J.), Some form contrary to that which they lately execrated and detested. **1765** G. COLMAN *Terence* Pref. 42 Le Fevre wrote a most elegant copy of Latin verses, execrating the Flute. **1782** PRIESTLEY *Corrupt. Chr.* I. I. 58 The name of Arius was execrated. **1857** BUCKLE *Civiliz.* I. viii. 543 Their views.. would have been execrated as impious novelties.

†**3.** To call down (something) *upon* (a person) as a curse; to imprecate. *Obs. rare.*

1602 WARNER *Alb. Eng.* Epit. (1612) 374 In maintenance of a falsehood.. he execrated vpon himselfe a choaking.

4. *intr.* To utter curses.

1786 *Francis, the Philanthropist* III. 3 He received a thousand curses from his master, who continued to execrate, the whole way to Dartford. **1840** BARHAM *Ingol. Leg., The Ghost*, He execrated Ere he crawled into bed. **1858** CARLYLE *Fredk. Gt.* (1865) I. IV. iii. 294 England.. execrates lamentably over its William Conqueror.

Hence **'execrated** *ppl. a.*, accursed, detested. **'execrating** *ppl. a.*, that execrates.

1660 R. COKE *Power & Subj.* 174 If any man who serves at the altar be accused of a crime.. let him eat the execrated bread [mistranslation of OE. *corsnæd*]. **1769** *Oxford Mag.* II. 144/1 This execrated, because culpable child. **1772–84** COOK *Voy.* (1790) IV. 1371 We saw this execrated island at the distance of about four leagues. **1829** *The Bengallee* 61 All these.. spake execrating volumes against the complicated cruelty. **1878** [see EXECRABLE 2].

execration (ɛksɪˈkreɪʃən). [ad. L. *execrātiōn-em* (*exsecrātiōn-em*), n. of action f. *execrā-ri* (*exsecrā-ri*) to EXECRATE. Cf. Fr. *exécration.*]

1. The action of execrating.

†**a.** The action of solemnly laying under a curse; an instance of this. *Obs.* or *arch.*

1382 WYCLIF *2 Chron.* xv. 15 Thei sworen to the Lord with a grete voice.. with execracioun. *c* **1585** R. BROWNE *Answ. to Cartwright* 34 The power of the word.. to rebuke and giue ouer to execration. **1652** BENLOWES *Theoph.* Author's Prayer 21 The execration of the Son of Thy Love. **1729** BUTLER *Serm.* Wks. 1874 II. 84 To assist with the religious ceremony of execration. **1754–62** HUME *Hist. Eng.* II. xxxi. 210 The ecclesiastics.. kept the world in subjection by holy execrations. **1863** J. G. MURPHY *Comm. Gen.* xxvi. 28 An oath of execration on the transgressor.

b. The utterance of curses (as an expression of hatred).

1688 in Ellis *Orig. Lett.* II. 379 IV. 174 The Lord Chancellor was taken and brought amid universal execration of the People before the Lord Mayor. **1769** ROBERTSON *Chas. V*, III. VIII. 104 The name of Maurice was mentioned, with execration. **1840** MACAULAY *Clive* 79 A tempest of execration and derision.. burst on the servants of the Company.

c. Utter detestation; intense abhorrence.

[**1557** N. T. (Genev.) *1 Cor.* xvi. 22 If any man loue not the Lord Iesus Christe, let him be had in execration.] **1563–87** FOXE *A. & M.* (1596) 11/2 It [the title pope] is now worthilie come into contempt and execration. *a* **1699** STILLINGFLEET (J.), The Indians, at naming the devil, did spit on the ground in token of execration. **1748** *Anson's Voy.* II. xiv. 282 The Peruvian Indians held the name.. in execration. **1848** MARIOTTI *Italy* I. i. 91 The Sicilian Vespers have long been made a subject of horror and execration.

2. An uttered curse; an anathema, an imprecation.

1563–87 FOXE *A. & M.* (1684) III. 949 All the Country.. with Execrations detested them. **1603** B. JONSON *Sejanus* v. x, With such black and bitter execrations.. she fills the air. **1650** B. *Discolliminium* 21 The Romane proverbiall execration, *abi in malam Crucem.* **1793** MRS. E. PARSONS *Woman as she should be* II. 207, I could write volumes.. in execrations against the match. **1820** KEATS *Eve St. Agnes* x, Lords, Whose very dogs would execrations howl Against his lineage. **1873** SYMONDS *Grk. Poets* iv. 100 A man who.. would have been hunted from society with execrations.

3. That which is execrated; an object of cursing.

1611 BIBLE *Jer.* xliv. 12 They shall be an execration and a reproach. **1871** R. ELLIS *Catullus* xiv. 22 Clumsy Poet-rabble, an age's execration!

†**exe'cratious,** *a.* *Obs. rare*⁻¹. [f. EXECRATI-ON + -OUS.] Of the nature of an execration.

1748 RICHARDSON *Clarissa* (1811) VIII. 99 A whole volley of.. execratious wishes.

execrative (ˈɛksɪkreɪtɪv), *a.* [f. *execrāt-* ppl. stem of *execrāri* (*exsecrāri*) to EXECRATE + -IVE.] Of or pertaining to execration; prone to execration; characterized by or containing an execration.

1830 JAMES *Darnley* xxvii. 121 Manifold.. opportunities.. for the captain and pilot to exercise their execrative faculties. **1837** CARLYLE *Fr. Rev.* III. I. i, Into the body of the poor Tatars execrative Roman History intercalated an alphabetic letter; and so they continue Tartars of fell Tartarean nature, to this day. **1871** —— in *Mrs. Carlyle's Lett.* II. 99 On which day Nigger Question [in 'Fraser'] had come out with execrative shrieks from several people.

Hence **'execratively** *adv.*

1837 CARLYLE *Fr. Rev.* III. I. i, When.. those Northmen.. came in.. foul old Rome screamed execratively her loudest.

execrator (ˈɛksɪkreɪtə(r)). *rare.* [a. L. *execrātor* (*exsecrātor*), f. *ex(s)ecrāri*: see EXECRATE.] One who execrates or pronounces an execration.

1748 RICHARDSON *Clarissa* (1811) III. 311 O that it had turned.. to a mortal quinsy, and.. had choked the old execrator. **1835** LYTTON *Rienzi* v. vi, The curse worked best in the absence of the execrator.

†**execratory,** *sb.* *Obs.* [as if ad. L. **ex(s)ecrātōrium*, neut. sb. f. *ex(s)ecrāri*: see EXECRATE and -ORY.] 'A formulary of execrations' (Todd).

1675 L. ADDISON *State Jews* xx. 179 The Execratory.. Wherein they profoundly curse the Christians.

execratory (ˈɛksɪkreɪtərɪ), *a.* [as if ad. L. **exsecrātōrius*, f. *exsecrāri*: see prec. Cf. Fr. *exécratoire.*] Of or pertaining to execration; of the nature of or containing an execration.

1611 SPEED *Hist. Gt. Brit* IX. ix. §82 The King.. sware to keepe all Liberties vpon paine of that execratory sentence. **1851** KINGSLEY *Yeast* xiv, Narrating Lancelot's fanatical conduct, without execratory comment.

exect, etc.: see EXSECT, etc.

executable (ɛkˈsɛkjʊtəb(ə)l), *a.* [f. EXECUTE *v.* + -ABLE. Cf. Fr. *exécutable.*] That can be executed, performed, or carried out.

1796 in *Bentham's Wks.* (1842) XI. 114 Without communication with the river.. the Contract not executable. **1841–4** EMERSON *Ess.* Ser. I. x. (1876) 246 Truths profound and executable only in ages. **1856** *Edin. Rev.* Jan. 244 The whole project.. is set down as executable at eight millions. **1871** CARLYLE in *Mrs. Carlyle's Lett.* II. 249 [An intention] not executable either when the time came.

executancy (ɛkˈsɛkjʊtənsɪ). [f. EXECUTANT: see -CY.] The qualification of an executant; power and skill in performing (music).

1858 *Times* 30 Nov. 10/5 Such music lying hardly within the sphere of amateur executancy. **1866** MACFARREN in *Athenæum* No. 2004 Musical progress.. in executancy.

executant (ɛkˈsɛkjʊtənt), *a.* and *sb.* [a. F. *exécutant*, pr. pple. of *exécuter* to EXECUTE.]

A. *adj.* That performs (music). *rare.*

1865 *Reader* No. 123. 523/2 Any living executant musician.

B. *sb.*

1. *gen.* One who executes, performs, or carries out. Const. *of.*

1858 J. MARTINEAU *Studies Chr.* 151 This world may be regarded.. as the stage of divine agency, using the visible actors as the executants of an invisible thought. **1860** *Times* 11 Oct. 10/6 Mr. Philip being the executant of the whole of the work. **1868** BROWNING *Ring & Bk.* v. 2003 Absolve then me law's mere executant.

2. *esp.* A musical performer.

a **1859** DE QUINCY in H. A. Page *Life* (1877) II. xix. 174 All great executants on the organ. **1862** R. H. PATTERSON *Ess. Hist. & Art* 90 The soul, at once composer and executant. **1872** GEO. ELIOT *Middlem.* xvi, Rosamond, with the executant's instinct, had seized his manner of playing.

†**executative,** *a.* *Obs. rare*⁻¹. [f. next: see -ATIVE.] = EXECUTIVE.

1647 *Mercurius Brit., His Spectacles* 4 The derived and executative power in Parliamentary Acts.

execute (ˈɛksɪkjuːt), *v.* Also 5 excecute, 6 exequute, *Sc.* exsecute. [ad. Fr. *exécute-r* = Pr. *executar*, Sp. *ejecutar*, It. *esecutare*, ad. med.L. *execūtāre*, f. L. *ex(s)ecūt-* ppl. stem of *ex(s)equī* lit. 'to follow out', f. *ex-* out + *sequī* to follow.]

I. To follow out into effect, carry out.

1. *trans.* To follow out, carry into effect (an intention, purpose, plan, instruction, or command.)

c **1386** CHAUCER *Knt.'s T.* 806 The destine.. That executeth.. The purveans, that God hath seye byforn. *c* **1430** LYDG. *Thebes* 414 To execute the biddyng of the Kyng. **1477** EARL RIVERS (Caxton) *Dictes* 13 When ye thinke any good thought execute it. **1555** EDEN *Decades W. Ind.* 71 Yet durst they at noo tyme execute theyr lordes commaundemente. **1696** TATE & BRADY *Ps.* civ. 4 To execute his dreadful Will. **1776** ADAM SMITH *W. N.* II. v. I. 371 The capital of all the individuals of a nation.. is capable of executing only certain purposes. **1833** HT. MARTINEAU *Manch. Strike* ix. 97 Large orders, which we have been unable to execute. **1837** DICKENS *Pickw.* vii, The boy departed to execute his commission. **1858** FROUDE *Hist. Eng.* IV. xviii. 16 The regent and his friends imagined measure after measure, which they wanted resolution to execute.

absol. **1606** DANIEL *Fun. Poem Earl Devon.* 211 With courage on he goes; doth exiqute With counsell. **1633** FORD *Broken H.* I. ii, Judgment commands, But resolution executes. **1703** ROWE *Ulyss.* II. i. 797 When I bid 'em execute, 'tis done.

†**b.** To give practical effect to (a passion, sentiment, principle). Also, to bring (a weapon) into operation. *Obs.*

14.. *Circumcis.* in *Tundale's Vis.* (1843) 88 Tyrranitis that the bodye slethe.. To execute hur venym vp by deth. *c* **1477** CAXTON *Jason* 10 b, To execute his dampnable enuye. **1568** GRAFTON *Chron.* II. 83 The people.. refrayned not.. untill they had executed the full of their malice. **1606** SHAKS. *Tr. & Cr.* v. vii. 6 In fellest manner execute your arme. **1608** *Yorksh. Trag.* I. iii, What! may I not look upon my dagger? Speak villain, or I will execute the point on thee. **1681–6** J. SCOTT *Chr. Life* (1747) III. 338 He attempted to execute his Rage and Malice upon him.

c. To carry into effect ministerially (a law, a judicial sentence, etc.). Cf. 6.

1413 LYDG. *Pilgr. Sowle* IV. xxxiv. (1483) 82 The gouernement.. shold be admynystred and executed by suche as were of grettest bounte. **1475** *Bk. Noblesse* (1860) 41 Whan dew diligence have be shewed by us in executing the saide right. **1548** HALL *Chron.* 213 This judgement.. was.. executed before the Castell gate of Bristow. **1647** CLARENDON *Hist. Reb.* I. (1843) 5/1 After his return, he [Villiers] executed the same authority in conferring all favours.. and revenging himself [etc.]. **1752** FIELDING *Amelia* 3 Good laws should execute themselves in a well regulated state. **1769** GOLDSM. *Rom. Hist.* (1786) II. 487 The only reparation.. was the putting Fausta.. to death; which was, accordingly, executed upon her. **1855** PRESCOTT *Philip II*, II. iii. (1857) 225 No choice was left to the civil magistrate but to execute the terrible sentence of the law against heretics. **1861** W. BELL *Dict. Law Scot.* 355/1 The messenger.. has given the citation, or executed the diligence.

d. To perform or carry out the provisions of (a will).

1463 *Bury Wills* (1850) 30 To.. se that my wille be executyd trewly. **1641** *Termes de La Ley* 150 *Executor*.. the person that shall execute his Testament. **1751** CHAMBERS *Cycl.*, *Executor*, a person nominated by a testator.. to see his will, and testament, executed or performed. **1861** W. BELL *Dict. Law Scot.* 360/1 The acknowledgment of the debts by the defunct in his last will, which it is the duty of the executor to execute.

2. To carry out, perform (an action, operation, movement, etc., that has been planned or prescribed, or that requires skill or care).

1477 EARL RIVERS (Caxton) *Dictes* 1 To seke & execute þe werkes.. most acceptable to hym. **1549** *Compl. Scot.* iii. 25 The kyng anchises lamentit the distructione of the superb troy, exsecutit be the princis of greice. **1574** tr. *Marlorat's Apocalips* 28 To make John the redyer too execute the worke enioyned vntoo hym. **1611** BIBLE *2 Kings* x. 30 Thou hast done well in executing that which is right in mine eyes. **1727** SWIFT *Gulliver* III. iii. 198 Always averse from executing so terrible an action. **1809** ROLAND *Fencing* 19 To discover what is necessary to execute, at the instant the adversary exposes his body. **1826** DISRAELI *Viv. Grey* VI. ii, The Prince executed a blast with great skill. **1842** ALISON *Hist. Europe* V. xxxi. 309 Moreau executed a change of front, arranging his army parallel to that of the enemy. **1884** *Punch* 25 Oct. 195/2 They.. execute.. a wild dance.. as Act-drop descends.

†**b.** *spec.* To perform, celebrate (ceremonies, religious service). *Obs.*

1450 *Pol., Rel. & L. Poems* (1866) 6 Who shall execute yᵉ fest of solempnite. **1514** BARCLAY *Cyt. & Uplondyshm.* (Percy Soc.) p. xxxii, To ordeyne ministers to execute service. **1548** GEST *Pr. Masse* 114 Not any real and true sacrifice.. executed by the priest. **1582** N. T. (Rhem.) *John* vi. *annot.*, The Clergie.. when they doe not execute or say Masse themselues. **1737** WATERLAND *Eucharist* 417 Ancient Forms.. properly executed.. by.. venerable Men.

absol. **1546** in Strype *Eccl. Mem.* II. App. A 5 The Bishop of Winchester was appointed to make the sermon: and.. to execute. **1709** —— *Ann. Ref.* I. ix. 127 The Abp of Canterbury.. who did execute, began the service.

c. To perform acts of (justice, cruelty, vengeance, etc.). *arch.*

1530 RASTELL *Bk. Purgat.* III. i, [God] executyth.. good & indyfferent justyce to.. his creatures. **1612** BRINSLEY *Lud. Lit.* xxviii. (1627) 286 Justice cannot be executed, nor any gouvernment or authority maintained. **1685** R. BURTON *Eng. Emp. Amer.* i. 25 Where they executed great severity, as well as in other places. **1821** SOUTHEY in *Q. Rev.* XXV. 332 Lord Clarendon says that all manner of cruelty was executed.

3. *Law.* To go through the formalities necessary to the validity of (a legal act, *e.g.* a bequest, agreement, mortgage, etc.). Hence, to complete and give validity to (the instrument by which such act is effected) by performing what the law requires to be done, as by signing, sealing, etc.

1737 POPE *Hor. Epist.* II. ii. 92 My counsel sends to execute a deed. **1804** WELLINGTON in Owen *Disp.* 434 The proposed treaty of peace.. after being attentively perused, was executed by his Highness without the slightest hesitation. **1855** PRESCOTT *Philip II*, i. (1857) 6 Charles the Fifth executed an instrument by which he ceded to his son the sovereignty of Flanders. **1866** CRUMP *Banking* iii. 85 An undertaking to execute a mortgage if called on to do so.

absol. **1818** CRUISE *Digest* (ed. 2) IV. 33 One who executes a deed for another.. must execute in the name of his principal.

b. *to execute an estate*: to convey or confer an estate in property, etc., *esp.* by some particular operation of law, as under the Statute of Uses. Cf. †*to make an estate* (ESTATE *sb.* 11 b).

1536 *Act 27 Hen. VIII*, c. 10 Any person or persons.. which shall haue any estate to them executed by authority of this Act. *a* **1626** BACON *Max. & Uses Com. Law* 55 A use may be created and the estate of the land thereupon executed. **1642** PERKINS *Prof. Bk.* iv. 123 He hath fee simple executed in the same acre. **1876** DIGBY *Real Prop.* vii. 333 Which estates could not be executed or transferred from the common law grantee to the beneficiary.

4. a. To fulfil, discharge (an office, a function). Also, formerly, †To perform the functions of (an official position). †**b.** *absol.* or *intr.* Of a thing: To perform its functions, 'work' (*obs.*).

1387 TREVISA *Higden* (Rolls) VII. 133 He ordeyned anoþer pope for to execute þe office of holy chirche. *a* **1627** HAYWARD (J.), The cannon against St. Stephen's gate executed so well, that the portcullis and gate were broken. **1659** RUSHW. *Hist. Coll.* I. 78 A Fee belonging to the Place which he then executed. *a* **1672** WOOD *Life* (1848) 172 Dr. Fell would not suffer him to execute the place of architypographer. **1833** J. H. NEWMAN *Lett.* (1891) I. 343 Places which..none but Maltese deputies can execute. **1863** COX *Instit.* III. viii. 718 The question arose how his office was thenceforth to be executed.

5. To carry out the design for (a product of art or skill); to produce as an artist or skilled workman; to perform (a musical composition).

1735 J. PRICE *Stone Br. Thames* 10 The Manner of executing the intended Bridge. **1768** W. GILPIN *Ess. Prints* 146 Etchings..executed in a bold and masterly manner. **1778** *Eliza Warwick* II. 31 She took in plain linen, and executed a good deal of it. **1804** *Ann. Rev.* II. 97/2 The translation is wretchedly executed. **1822** B'NESS BUNSEN in Hare *Life* I. vi. 192, I saw executed in marble the Mercury and the Hope. **1826** *Ibid.* II. vii. 259 An oratorio which he has this winter composed, but which has never yet been executed. **1839** YEOWELL *Anc. Brit. Ch.* vii. (1847) 75 Egbert..executed a Saxon version of the four Gospels.

absol. **1768** W. GILPIN *Ess. Prints* 32 Every artist.. executes in a manner peculiar to himself. **1774** *The Trinket* 46 Charlotte did not execute amiss.

II. To do execution upon.

[It is not quite clear whether these uses, which occur early in Fr. and med.L., were merely developed from 1 c, or whether they partly represent the etymological notion of L. *exsequi* 'to pursue to the end.']

6. To inflict capital punishment upon; to put to death in pursuance of a sentence. More fully, †*to execute to death* [= Fr. †*exécuter à mort*]. †*to execute by the head*: to behead.

1483 CAXTON *Cato* B iij b, To robbe and to stele wherfore they be hanged or otherwyse executed by Justyse. **1523** LD. BERNERS *Froiss.* I. clxxxvii, They were executed by dyuers tourmentes of dethe. **1548** HALL *Chron.* 13 b, Sir Thomas Blonte and all the other prysoners were executed. **1577** HANMER *Anc. Eccl. Hist.* (1619) 182 First of all Theotecnus himselfe..he executed to death. **1579** FENTON *Guicciard.* IV. (1599) 180 He was executed by the head the day following. **1603** FLORIO *Montaigne* (1634) 514 Divers of their chieftains have been executed to death. *a* **1687** PETTY *Pol. Arith.* Pref. (1691) A iij, No more Beggars in the Streets, nor executed for Thieves, than heretofore. **1715** M. DAVIES *Athen. Brit.* I. 133 Prosecuting and Executing those to death, who [etc.]. **1847** JAMES *Gowrie* xlvi, Three of the Earl's faithful servants were executed at Perth.

†**b.** Hence for: To put to death, kill. *rare.*

[**1557** NORTH tr. *Gueuara's Diall Pr.* 68 b/2 When death hathe done his office, executing all earthelye men.] **1593** SHAKS. *Rich. II*, IV. i. 82 Thou Aumerle, didst send two of thy men, To execute the Noble Duke at Callis.

†**7.** To take the body of (a debtor) in execution. (See EXECUTION 7.) *Obs. rare.*

1608 *Yorksh. Trag.* I. iv, Your brother..lies in bond executed for your debt.

†**8.** [after Fr. *exécuter*] To subject (a country) to military execution. (See EXECUTION 9.) *Obs.*

1679 *Lond. Gaz.* No. 1393/3 The French..are resolved to exact the Contributions..from the Mayery of Bolduc, and in case they are not paid, to execute the Countrey.

†**III. 9.** To deal with as an executor; to administer. *Obs. rare*⁻¹.

1483 CAXTON *Gold. Leg.* 352/3 Late euery executour be ware that he execute well the goodes of them that they haue charge of.

†**'execute,** *pa. pple. Obs.* Also 4–7 execut(t, 6 *Sc.* exsecut. [ad. L. *execūt-us*, pa. pple. of *exequī*: see EXECUTE *v.*] = EXECUTED.

c **1374** CHAUCER *Troylus* III. 622 (Camp. MS.) But execut was al byside here leue At the goddes wyl. *c* **1430** LYDG. *Thebes* 255 Wher the domys and plees of the toun weren execut. **1549** *Compl. Scot.* Ep. Ded. 2 The actis that ȝour prudens garris daly be exsecut. **1560** ROLLAND *Crt. Venus* I. 863 Heir we..Be this our letter Execute and Indorsat dewlie. **1642** PERKINS *Prof. Bk.* ii. 75 The estate taile shall bee execute in the Donee. **1682** *Lond. Gaz.* No. 1682/1 The said Archibald Earl of Argile to be Execute to the Death. **1711** *Countrey-M. Let. to Curat* 6 This act..was oftimes severely Execute.

executed ('ɛksɪkjuːtɪd). *ppl. a.* [f. EXECUTE *v.* + -ED¹.] In senses of the verb. **a.** *gen.* Carried out, performed, practised, inflicted.

1643 MILTON *Divorce* II. xiv. (1851) 98 When those worst faults..are committed, by whoso dares under strict and executed penalty. **1678** NORRIS *Coll. Misc.* (1699) 302 The Positiveness of sins of Commission, lies..in the executed Act.

b. *Law.* Of a consideration, contract, estate, etc.: Performed, carried out or into effect, completed, fulfilled; opposed to EXECUTORY, q.v.

1592 WEST *1st Pt. Symbol.* §44 C, Euerie estate is either executed maintenant, or executorie by limitation of vse. **1601–2** FULBECKE *2nd Pt. Parall.* 70 Two sorts of damages ..the one executorie, the other executed. **1751** CHAMBERS *Cycl., Executed fine.* **1767** BLACKSTONE *Comm.* II. 443 A contract may..be either executed..or it may be executory. **1848** WHARTON *Law Lex., Executed Contract*, is where nothing remains to be done by either party. **1861** W. BELL *Dict. Law Scot.* 354/2 s.v.

executer ('ɛksɪkjuːtə(r)), [f. EXECUTE *v.* + -ER¹.] One who executes; = EXECUTOR I.

1532–3 *Act 24 Hen. VIII*, c. 12 §4 Eueryе suche personne ..so doynge, and their fauctours..procurers, executers, and counsaylours. *a* **1677** BARROW *Wks.* (1741) I. 119 The executers of his edicts. *a* **1734** DENNIS (J.), Sophocles and Euripides, in their most beautiful Pieces, are impartial executers of poetick justice. **1837** MARRYAT *Dog-Fiend* iv, An obedient executer of all his tyranny.

†**executi'bility.** *rare*⁻¹. [f. L. *execūt-*; cf. EXECUTE *v.* and *perfectibility*.] Capability of being executed, performed, or carried out.

1801 *Ann. Reg.* 1799, 176 The committee had seen the advantages of that principle, imperfect as its executibility was.

'executing, *vbl. sb.* [f. EXECUTE *v.* + -ING¹.] The action of the vb. EXECUTE.

1480 *Bury Wills* (1850) 60 For the due executyn and performauns of this my testament. **1536** *Act 27 Hen. VIII*, c. 10 The executing of any estate..to any person. *a* **1633** AUSTIN *Medit.* (1635) 239 These Bags (like executing waights) waighed downe his [St. Matthew's] Conscience. **1626** in Rymer *Fœdera* XVIII. 675/2 We doe give..for the executeing of the said Office..the Fee of twelve Pence.

'executing, *ppl. a.* [f. as prec. + -ING².] That executes.

1680 OTWAY *Orphan* II. i, With this bold executing arm I struck The..monster.

execution (ˌɛksɪ'kjuːʃən). Forms: 4 execucoun, 4–6 execucion, -cioun, -cyon, 4–7 -sio(u)n, -syon, 5 excecussyon, 6 executyon, excecucione, (exicucyon), *Sc.* exsecutione, (7 exequition), 6– execution. [ME. *execucion*, a. AF. *execucioun*, F. *exécution*, ad. L. *execūtiōn-em, exsecūtiōn-em*, n. of action f. *ex(s)equī*: see EXECUTE *v.*] The action of executing; the state or fact of being executed.

1. The action of carrying into effect (a plan, design, purpose, command, decree, task, etc.); accomplishment: an instance of this. Also, *to carry*, †*order*, *put in* or *into execution.*

c **1374** CHAUCER *Troylus* III. 472 He..Had every thing.. put in Execucion. **1388** WYCLIF 1 *Esdras* vi. 13 [vii. 1]Therfor Tathannai..and hise counseleris, diden execucioun..bi that that kyng Darius hadde comaundid. **1494** FABYAN *Chron.* I. i. 7 In all olde Storyes..is nat founde ..that any suche Storye..was put in execucion. **1591** SHAKS. *Two Gent.* I. iii. 36, I like thy counsaile..and..how well I like it, The execution of it shall make knowne. **1651** *Nicholas Papers* (Camden) 259 He beggs me to further the execusion of the Kings comission. **1707** FREIND *Peterborow's Cond. Sp.* 208 To such extraordinary Thoughts, and such diligent executions, were owing all our successes in Spain. **1772** JOHNSON *Let. Mrs. Thrale* 29 Oct., His intention and execution are not very near each other. **1810** WELLINGTON in Gurw. *Disp.* V. 507 The mode in which directions given to the Portuguese authorities are carried into execution. **1863** FR. A KEMBLE *Resid. Georgia* 109, I..determined to put into execution a plan I had formed. **1871** MORLEY *Voltaire* (1886) 11 There are..eras of counsel and eras of execution.

†**b.** The giving practical effect to (a passion, sentiment, or principle); exercise (of powers); manifestation in act (*rarely*, in speech). *Obs.*

1581 MARBECK *Bk. of Notes* 780 Workes..are rather the executions and the ministring of righteousnesse. **1586** T. B. *La Primaud. Fr. Acad.* I. (1594) 17 He may..represse them [his wicked inclinations]..that they breake not out into any damnable execution. **1593** SHAKS. *3 Hen. VI*, II. ii. 111 Scarse I can refraine The execution of my big-swolne heart Vpon that Clifford. **1604** —— *Oth.* III. iii. 466. **1606** —— *Tr. & Cr.* I. iii. 210. **1622** R. HAWKINS *Voy. S. Sea* (1847) 208 Griefe and rage..caused me to breake forth into this reprehension and execution following—'Great is the crosse' [etc.]. **1652** BENLOWES *Theoph.* Pref. 21 My redemption from the execution of thy wrath.

c. The executing or carrying into effect (a law, agreement, writ, sentence, etc.). Cf. 7, 8.

c **1380** WYCLIF *Wks.* (1880) 37 Bynde men to here wickid lawis & wrong execucions of hem. **1512** *Act 4 Hen. VIII*, c. 10 Fynes..levyed for the execucion and performaunce of the said Indentures. **1591** LAMBARDE *Archeion* (1635) 209 The Writ came so late to his hands, that he could not..make execution of it. **1651** HOBBES *Leviath.* II. xxi. 109 To cause those laws to be put in execution. **1710** PRIDEAUX *Orig. Tithes* ii. 54 We have God's Precedent in the Execution of that Law to guide us. **1766** GOLDSM. *Vic. W.* xxviii, The coward is determined to put the law in execution against me. **1803** WELLINGTON in Gurw. *Disp.* I. 492 The sentence on this sepoy should be carried into execution. **1845** MCCULLOCH *Taxation* II. iv. (1852) 185 Commissioners have been appointed to carry the act into execution.

2. The effecting or carrying out (a prescribed or designed operation or movement); the production (of a work of art or skill); the vocal or instrumental rendering (of a musical composition); in early use, †the performance (of rites or ceremonies). Hence often, The manner in which an operation, work, piece of music, is 'executed'.

c **1534** tr. *Pol. Verg. Eng. Hist.* (Camden) I. 166 After the execution of divine service. *a* **1700** DRYDEN (J.), The excellency of the subject contributed much to the happiness of the execution. **1713** *Guardian* No. 1 ¶3 This gentleman is, as to the execution of his work, a Mechanick. **1751** LABELYE *Westm. Br.* 16 The two largest Piers were ordered into Execution, of solid Portland Stone. **1751** CHAMBERS *Cycl., Execution* is particularly used in French music, for the manner of singing. **1768** GILPIN *Ess. Prints* 85 His [Rembrandt's] execution is peculiar to himself. It is rough or neat, as he meant a scetch or a finished piece. **1855** PRESCOTT *Philip II*, II. iv. (1857) 243 A new palace.. presenting in the beauty..of its execution one of the noblest monuments of the architecture of the eighteenth century. **1879** *Cassell's Techn. Educ.* IV. 62/1 The execution of the requisite tools and machinery.

†**b.** An instance of the same; a performance.

1581 MULCASTER *Positions* xxxix. (1887) 191 How it may ..be helpt..I will hereafter in my priuate executions declare. *a* **1628** PRESTON *Breastpl. Love* (1631) 125 Look to your actions, to your doings, to your executions and performances. **1728** R. MORRIS *Ess. Anc. Archit.* 89 Those Executions, which are perform'd conformable to the Practice of the Ancients. *Ibid.* 94 Our Moderns, whose Executions are generally standing Monuments to their Shame.

c. Excellence of execution; *esp.* in the performance of music, mastery of the processes by which the required artistic effect must be produced.

1795 MASON *Ch. Mus.* ii. 137 The term Execution is generally applied to that volubility of throat which expresses accurately such divisions. **1807** JAS. JOHNSON *Orient. Voy.* 54 Most of them are taught music..and some have acquired a tolerable degree of execution. **1824** BYRON *Juan* XVI. xli, The circle..applauds..The lines, the feeling, and the execution. **1842–76** GWILT *Archit.* 176 They [statues] were not equal in execution to those of France. **1854** E. BRADLEY (C. Bede) *Verd. Green* II. ix, A firework piece of Music, in which execution takes the place of melody.

3. The performance or fulfilment (of an office or function). *to put in execution*: to execute.

1576 FLEMING *Panopl. Epist.* Q iv, Before, the sense of seeing was delighted..now the sense of feeling beginnes to put in execution his office. **1605** SHAKS. *Lear* I. i. 139 The Sway, Reuennew..Execution of the rest..be yours. **1631** GOUGE *God's Arrows* IV. §15. 401 Papists..are by law interdicted the execution of ministeriall functions. **1836** MARRYAT *Midsh. Easy* xli, You will have no obstruction from us in the execution of your duty. **1876** J. H. NEWMAN *Hist. Sk.* I. IV. i. 344 He gave himself up to..the due execution of his high duties.

†**b.** Action, operation. *Obs.*

1526 *Pilgr. Perf.* (W. de W. 1531) 49 b, Whiche yf he had not tasted and put in execucyon, he sholde neuer haue dyed. **1634** SIR T. HERBERT *Trav.* 212 Like the Dodoes wings, more to looke at, then for execution. **1684** *Scanderbeg Rediv.* v. 116 The King had not with him above 4000 men..and of those scarce 1500 came up to Execution. **1729** SHELVOCKE *Artillery* IV. 295 The best Opportunity you can have for putting these [Poisonous] Balls in Execution, is when the Heavens are clouded over.

†**4.** Efficiency in action, executive ability. *Obs.*

1549 *Compl. Scot.* Ded. 4 Be his magnanyme proues ande martial exsecutione, he delyurit the holy land. **1600** HOLLAND *Livy* XXXVIII. xli. 1008 He was a man of much valour and execution. **1601** —— *Pliny* II. 213 Lucullus..a captain of great execution lost his life by such a loue potion.

5. Effective action (*esp.* of weapons); destructive effect, infliction of damage or slaughter. Now almost exclusively in phr. *to do execution.*

1588 SHAKS. *Tit. A.* II. iii. 36 An Adder when she doth vnrowle To do some fatall execution. *Ibid.* IV. ii. 84. **1605** —— *Macb.* I. ii. 18 His brandisht Steele, Which smoak'd with bloody execution. **1590** SIR J. SMYTH *Disc. Weapons* 4 b, Short..daggers are..of greater execution amongst al sorts of armed men. **1649** SELDEN *Laws Eng.* I. xiv. (1739) 26 Though the Canons roar loud, yet the execution is not mortal. *a* **1672** WOOD *Life* (1848) 26 The two gallant majors charged the rebells up thro the street, doing execution al the way. **1828** G. W. BRIDGES *Ann. Jamaica* II. xviii. 342 The most cruel execution is usually inflicted..on the backs of a ..flying enemy. **1855** PRESCOTT *Philip II*, I. viii. (1857) 137 The shot, probably from the distance of the ships, did no great execution.

concr. **1581** STYWARD *Mart. Discipl.* I. 45 The heart of the battaile, vsuallie called the slaughter of the field, or execution of the same.

b. *fig.* of the effect of arguments, personal charms, etc.

1678 CUDWORTH *Intell. Syst.* 683 Certain metaphysical arguments for a Deity..can do but little execution upon the minds of the generality. **1707** FARQUHAR *Beaux Strat.* II. ii, You are so well dress'd..that I fancy you may do Execution in a Country church. **1766** GOLDSM. *Vic. W.* i, Sophia's features were not so striking at first, but often did more certain execution. **1840** THACKERAY *Paris Sk.-bk., Beatrice Merger* 1 Black eyes, which might have done some execution had they been placed in a smoother face.

6. *Law.* The due performance of all formalities, as signing, sealing, etc., necessary to give validity to a deed or other legal document.

1776 *Trial Nundocomar* 17/1 Is the name..at the bottom of the paper, written as a witness to the execution? **1848** WHARTON *Law Lex., Execution of Deeds*, the signing, sealing, and delivery of them by the parties, as their own acts and deeds. **1891** *Law Times* XC. 462/2 One of Wayman's clerks attested Mrs. Headley's execution of the deed.

7. The enforcement by the sheriff, or other officer, of the judgement of a court; 'the obtaining of actual possession of anything acquired by judgement of law' (Coke *On Litt.* (1628) 154 a); chiefly, the seizure of the goods or person of a debtor in default of payment. Also in phrases, *(to have) for execution*, *(to be, take) in execution*, *to sue, take (forth) execution.*

writ of execution, or simply *execution*: the process under which the sheriff or other officer is commanded to execute a judgement. *to return an execution*: to report the service of the writ. So *return of execution.*

[**1292** BRITTON I. i. §5 A fere nos commaundementz..et les execucions de nos jugementz.] **1503–4** *Act 19 Hen. VII*, c. 36 §1 It [shall] be lawefull..to sue execucion..ayenst the seid sir Edward..by write or wryttes of Elegit. **1523** FITZHERB. *Husb.* §157, I doo..haue theyr bodyes in prisone for execution, tylle they haue made me payment. **1586** J. HOOKER *Girald. Irel.* in *Holinshed* II. 128/1 No action or sute taking effect..except also executions in law, awarded.. before the beginning of the parlement. **1592** WEST *1st Pt. Symbol.* §104 B, When he shall thinke it most to him conuenient to sue forth execution upon the said statute

marchant. **1597** WARNER *Alb. Eng.* x. lvi, The Writ of Execution, that her Heading did purport. **1632** MASSINGER & FIELD *Fatal Dowry* I. ii, Let our executions That lie upon the father be returned Upon the son. **1632** *Star Chamb. Cases* (Camden) 128 Did afterwardes take forth execution against the defendant..and the partie was in execution. **1670** *Moral State Eng.* 30 By the next Term is presented with an Execution, from his Taylor, or Landlord. **1697** LUTTRELL *Brief Rel.* (1857) IV. 315 Two bailifs endeavouring to enter a house..upon an execution. **1725** *Lond. Gaz.* No. 6404/7 A Prisoner in Execution at Ruthyn Gaol. **1767** BLACKSTONE *Comm.* II. 447 Unless..the writ of execution is actually delivered to the sheriff. **1807** J. MARSHALL *Const. Opin.* (1839) 37 One court never awards execution on the judgment of another. **1817** SELWYN *Law Nisi Prius* II. 722 It may be prudent..to be prepared with an examined copy of the writ of possession and return of execution. **1827** HALLAM *Const. Hist.* (1876) I. vi. 302 A member having been taken in execution on a private debt before their [Parliament's] meeting. **1875** POSTE *Gaius* III. (ed. 2) 342 The English process in an ordinary execution is, etc.

b. Hence, in popular language: The actual levy or seizure of goods by a sheriff's officer.

1777 SHERIDAN *Sch. Scand.* I. i, I am told he has had another execution in the house yesterday. **1840** HOOD *Up the Rhine* 233 A..squalid, comfortless room, hardly furnished enough to invite an execution. **1849** THACKERAY *Pendennis* xix, Coming..with a piteous tale that..there was an execution in their house.

c. *Scots Law* (see quot.).

1752 J. LOUTHIAN *Form of Process* 93 The Letters, with the Executions against the Prisoner. *Ibid.* 130 The Executor returns his Executions against the Criminals in the following manner. **1861** W. BELL *Dict. Law Scot.*, *Execution* by a Messenger-at-Arms or other officer of the Law..is an attestation under the hand of the messenger [etc.] that he has given the citation, or executed the diligence, in terms of his warrant for so doing.

¶**d.** An alleged designation for a company of officers. *Obs.*$^{-0}$

1486 *Bk. St. Albans* F vij a, An Execution of Officerys.

8. The infliction of punishment in pursuance of a judicial sentence; an instance of this. (In legal use also more fully ***criminal execution.***)

a. *gen.* (but chiefly with reference to corporal penalties).

c **1430** *Hymns Virg.* (1867) 20 Medele þou merci with execusioun. **1563** *Homilies* II. *Wilful Rebel.* III. (1859) 575 Let us..fear the dreadful execution of God. **1640** W. PRYNNE *Petit.* in Rushw. *Hist. Coll.* III. I. 76 The small Remainder of his Ears, left after his first Execution. *a* **1656** BP. HALL *Occas. Medit.* (1851) 105 Let others rejoice, in these public executions. **1827** A. FONBLANQUE *Eng. under 7 Administr.* (1837) I. 81 In..military executions, a medical man stands by and sees what the sufferer under the scourge can bear. **1848** MACAULAY *Hist. Eng.* (ed. 3) I. 489 After the execution Dangerfield..was taken back to prison.

b. *spec.* The infliction of capital punishment; the putting (a person) to death in pursuance of a judicial or authoritative sentence. Also called †*execution of death.*

c **1360** *Song of Mercy* 37 in *E.E.P.* (1862) 119 Riht wolde sle vs. for vr sunne. Miht wol don execucion. **1471** DK. CLARENCE in *12th Rep. Comm. Hist. MSS.* App. IV. I. 4 Edmund late Duc of Somerset taken and put to execucion. *c* **1489** CAXTON *Sonnes of Aymon* xvi. 366 Maye ye doo execusion vpon hym. **1494** FABYAN *Chron.* II. xxxvii. 27 To be put to dethe..by heddyng, fleyng, brennynge, and other Cruel Execucions. **1517** TORKINGTON *Pilgr.* (1884) 69 To be put to execucion of Dethe by and bye. **1536** SIR W. KINGSTON in Ellis *Orig. Lett.* I. 122 II. 63, I have told my lord of Rocheford that he be in aredynes to morow to suffur execusyon. **1556** *Chron. Gr. Friars* (Camden) 25 Thys yere the commons of Cornwall arose..The captayns tane and put to excecucione. **1605** SHAKS. *Macb.* I. iv. 1 Is execution done on Cawdor? **1631** GOUGE *God's Arrows* IV. viii. 385 Disgrace, Torture, Execution of death..and other externall crosses like unto these. **1680** H. DODWELL *2 Lett. of Advice* (1691) 39 The stakes and gridirons, and other the most terrible executions. **1727** SWIFT *Gulliver* II. v. 137 To see an execution..of a man who had murdered. **1880** MCCARTHY *Own Times* IV. liii. 147 The execution of these men did not even tend to prevent crime.

9. 'The ravaging and destroying of a country that refuses to pay contribution' (Smyth *Sailor's Word-bk.* 1867). Also ***military execution.*** [After Fr. *exécution.*]

1618 FLETCHER *Loyal Subj.* V. vi, You know his marches, You have seen his executions. Is it yet peace? **1689** *Lond. Gaz.* No. 2423/3 To put the Dutchies.. under Military Execution, in case they do not pay, etc.

10. *attrib.* and *Comb.* (chiefly in sense 8), as ***execution man, Monday, part, place,*** etc.; **execution-day** (see quot.); **Execution-Dock**, the dock (at Wapping) where criminal sailors were executed.

a **1700** B. E. *Dict. Cant. Crew*, **Execution-day*, Washing-day. **1694** LUTTRELL *Brief Rel.* 1 Mar. (1857) III. 277 Some of the persons convicted lately for pyracy will be hanged at *Execution Dock on Saturday next. **1883** STEVENSON *Treasure Isl.* xxix. (1886) 211 It..looks mighty like a hornpipe in a rope's end at Execution Dock by London town. *c* **1575** *Cambyses* in Hazl. *Dodsley* IV. 200 Good *execution-man, for need Help me with him away. **1891** W. J. LOFTIE *Lond. City* 125 A Sunday always elapsed between 'Trial Friday' and '*Execution Monday'. **1710** NORRIS *Chr. Prud.* ii. 96 Policy agrees with Prudence, as to the *Execution part, the use of fit or effectual means. **1594** NASHE *Unfort. Trav.* Wks. 1883–4 V. 168 To the *execution place was he brought.

Hence **exe'cution** *v. Obs.*, = EXECUTE *v.* 6.

1565 T. STAPLETON tr. *Bede's Hist. Ch. Eng.* 18 The executioner..desired..that he might be executioned, ether for him or with him.

exe'cutional, *a. rare.* [f. prec. + -AL[1].] Of or pertaining to the execution of a plan or design.

1652 URQUHART *Jewel* Wks. (1834) 275 Employments, whether preparatory to or executional in war.

executionary (ɛksɪ'kjuːʃənərɪ), *a.* [f. EXECUTION + -ARY[1].] Of or pertaining to execution.

1909 *New Schaff-Herzog Encycl. Relig. Knowl.* III. 313/1 The executionary order caused the *titulus* to be fastened at the upper end of the cross. **1920** *Chambers's Jrnl.* Dec. 849/2 The Prince..was considerably relieved to find that he was not on the visitor's executionary list. **1928** *Observer* 8 Jan. 11/5 Dr. Guillotin, who persuaded the Assembly to accept the principle of executionary equality.

exe,cutio'neering, *ppl. a. nonce-wd.* That is employed in executions (of criminals).

a **1834** LAMB *Inconven. fr. being Hanged* Wks. 563 The cimetar of an executioneering slave in Turkey.

executioner (ɛksɪ'kjuːʃənə(r)). Also 6 exequutioner. [f. EXECUTION *sb.* + -ER[1].]

1. One who executes or carries into effect (a command, design, instructions, law, justice, etc.); a perpetrator (of an evil deed). *Rare* in mod. use.

1598 BARRET *Theor. Warres* III. i. 37 To haue a souldier to be very perfect, and a good executioner indeede. **1619** HALES *Golden Rem.* (1688) 455 With them God the Father alone is the Author of our Election, and Christ only the Executioner. **1673** BAXTER *Let.* in *Answ. Dodwell* 83 The People are Executioners of Excommunications while they withdraw from the Excommunicate. **1683** *Apol. Prot. France* ii. 27 The soldiers are employed as Executioners of these Outrages. **1719** DE FOE *Crusoe* (1840) I. xvi. 277 To take upon me to be..an executioner of his [God's] justice. **1827** SCOTT *Napoleon* Introd., The people had a right..to act as the executioners of their own will. **1879** BARING GOULD *Germany* II. 245 German right..trusted to the moral sense as its executioner.

†**b.** One who performs the duties of a place or office. *Obs. rare.*

1587 FLEMING *Contn. Holinshed* III. 1491/2 The verie situation of the place ministreth incouragement to the executioners. *a* **1626** BACON (J.), The executioners of this office..cannot be guilty of oppression.

c. *transf.* said of things. *rare.*

1647 CRASHAW *Poems, Sospetto d' Herode* xli, All along The walls..Are tooles of Wrath, anvills of torments hung; Fell executioners of foul intents. **1755** in JOHNSON; whence **1818** in TODD; and in mod. Dicts.

2. *gen.* One who carries a sentence or judgement into effect: a punisher.

1578 TIMME *Calvin on Gen.* 222 Howsoever Magistrates do wink, God raiseth up elsewhere exequutioners which repay to bloodshedders their reward. **1678** tr. *L. de Gaya's Art War* I. 34 The Provost Mareschal..hath a Troop of Officers on Horseback, with an Executioner to punish those that offend against the Orders of the..General. *a* **1703** BURKITT *On N.T.* Matt. xxvii. 5 Conscience is a powerful, though invisible executioner. **1798** MALTHUS *Popul.* IV. vii, When nature will govern and punish for us, it is a very miserable ambition to wish to..draw upon ourselves the odium of executioner.

3. The official who carries out a sentence of death; a headsman, hangman, etc.

1561 BRENDE *Q. Curtius* VIII. 153 He being a kynge had vsed the detestable office of an execucyoner. **1603** SHAKS. *Meas. for M.* IV. ii. 222 Call your executioner, and off with Barnardines head. **1698** LUDLOW *Mem.* I. 245 The King.. kneeled down at the block, and the executioner performed his office. **1776** GIBBON *Decl. & F.* I. 320 The executioners ..were fatigued. **1859** L. OLIPHANT *China & Japan* II. ix. 194 Criminals who have committed crimes worthy of death, forestall the public executioner.

4. *transf.* and *fig.* **a.** One who puts another to death. **b.** One who or that which tortures like an executioner or hangman.

1594 SHAKS. *Rich. III*, I. ii. 186 Though I wish thy death, I will not be thy Executioner. **1621** BURTON *Anat. Mel.* I. ii. III. iv, A poysoned worme..gnawing the very heart, a perpetuall executioner. **1658–9** *Burton's Diary* (1828) IV. 48 It is likely they will not be their own executioners. **1755** in JOHNSON. **1840** HOOD *Up the Rhine* 322 What is war..but a great wholesale executioner.

Hence **exe'cutioneress**, a female executioner.

1656 S. HOLLAND *Zara* (1719) 92 Your name should be hang'd, drawn, and quartered by the common Executioneress Fame. **1864** R. F. BURTON *Dahome* II. 40 The Mingan had a billhook in her left hand, as executioneress of the inside.

executive (ɛk'sɛkjʊtɪv, ɛg'z-), *a.* and *sb.* [ad. L. type **ex(s)ecūtīv-us*, f. *ex(s)ecūt-* ppl. stem of *exsequī*: see EXECUTE *v.* and -IVE. Cf. F. *exécutif.*]

A. *adj.* †**1. a.** Capable of performance; operative. *Obs.*

1646 SIR T. BROWNE *Pseud. Ep.* III. xvii. 148 They [some Laws] enjoyned perpetuall chastity; for [Hermaphrodites] being executive in both parts, male and female, and confined by some Laws unto one, they restrained a naturall power.

¶**b.** That executes sentence of death. (Stressed '*executive.*) *Obs. rare*$^{-1}$.

1773 J. ROSS *Fratricide* (MS.) I. 268 First whirl'd aloft the executive blade.

2. †**a.** Active in execution, energetic (*obs. rare*). **b.** Apt or skilful in execution. (Chiefly *U.S.*)

1708 PENN in *Pa. Hist. Soc. Mem.* X. 291 Rouse up, and be vigorous and executive. **1825** *New Monthly Mag.* XIV. 178 He is tolerably executive in converting his wishes into acts. **1888** BRYCE *Amer. Commw.* II. III. lix. 412 The Americans are, to use their favourite expression, a highly executive people.

3. a. Pertaining to execution; having the function of executing or carrying into practical effect.

1677 HALE *Prim. Orig. Man* I. i. 29 They are the.. strongest Instruments, fittest to be executive of the commands of the Soul. **1685** R. BAXTER *Paraphr. N.T.* 2 Tim. i. 7 The three great faculties of the Soul, the Executive Faculty..the Will..and the Intellect. **1691** NORRIS *Pract. Disc.* 19 The Ship indeed has good Sails, there is nothing wanting to the Executive part. **1753** N. TORRIANO *Gangr. Sore Throat* 105 The Method of Treatment is always founded on the general Indications, but the executive Part is subordinated to Circumstances. **1867** SMYTH *Sailor's Word-bk.*, *Executive branch*, the commissioned and working officers of the ship, as distinguished from the civilian branch. **1875** HAMERTON *Intell. Life* IV. ii. 149 A most experienced artist, a man of the very rarest executive ability. **1879** LUBBOCK *Addr. Pol. & Educ.* iii. 47 Two executive Commissions were subsequently constituted.

b. *esp.* as the distinctive epithet of that branch of the government which is concerned or charged with carrying out the laws, decrees, and judicial sentences; opposed to 'judicial' and 'legislative'.

1649 SELDEN *Laws Eng.* I. xvi. (1739) 29 The executive power of the Law rested much in the Nobility. **1689** LOCKE *Govt.* II. xii, The legislative and executive power come often to be separated. **1742** HUME *Ess.* vi. *Indep. Parl.*, The executive power in every government is altogether subordinate to the legislative. **1790** BURKE *Fr. Rev.* 288 This their first executive officer is to be a machine. **1848** MACAULAY *Hist. Eng.* I. 469 The executive government could undertake nothing great without the support of the Commons. **1863** COX *Instit.* III. iii. 631 The king has absolute power to retain executive ministers against the declared wish of the nation.

c. ***executive privilege*** (U.S.), the privilege claimed by the President for the executive branch of the U.S. government to withhold information if it is deemed to be in the public interest to do so.

1940 *Federal Rep.* (2nd. Ser.) CXVII. 277/2 We have previously held a communication, released generally to the press, within this executive privilege. **1964** J. R. WIGGINS *Freedom or Secrecy* (rev. ed.) xi. 228 Subordinate executive personnel invoked executive privilege as authority for withholding information from Congress on forty-four separate occasions. **1974** *Black Panther* 9 Feb. 13/3 As the time of impeachment approaches, additional claims of executive privilege can be expected. **1987** *Washington Post* 6 Mar. A3/5 The Justice Department, citing executive privilege, refused to give Congress internal EPA documents on the 'Superfund' cleanup program.

4. Of or pertaining to the Executive (see B. 1). ***executive session***, U.S. (see quot. 1888).

1811 J. QUINCY *Speech* 30 Jan. (1874) 235 Those.. desirous of places in the executive gift. **1837** H. MARTINEAU *Soc. Amer.* II. 289 The fear and complaint are..of the increase of executive patronage. **1865** LINCOLN *Message to Congress* 6 Jan., If the people should..make it an Executive duty to re-enslave such persons. **1888** BRYCE *Amer. Commw.* II. II. xl. 97 A State Senate..has..the power of confirming or rejecting appointments to office made by the governor. When it considers these it is said to 'go into executive Session'.

B. *sb.*

1. a. That branch of the government which is charged with the execution of the laws.

1790 BURKE *Fr. Rev.* Wks. V. 99 A Council..holds a sort of middle place between the supreme power exercised by the people..and the mere executive. **1847** MRS. A. KERR *Hist. Servia* 298 This force constituted a sort of armed executive. **1866** BRIGHT *Sp. Irel.* 30 Oct., By the forbearance and permission of the Irish executive.

fig. **1842** MRS. BROWNING *Grk. Chr. Poets* (1863) 146 The drama is the executive of literature.

b. The person or persons in whom the supreme executive magistracy of a country or state is vested. Chiefly U.S., applied to the President (also called ***chief executive***), and to the governors of states.

1787 *Resolution* 1 June in *Jrnl. Fed. Conv.* (1819) 89 Resolved, That a national executive to consist of a single person be instituted. **1787** RANDOLPH in Bancroft *Hist. U.S.* (1885) VI. 213 A national executive chosen by the national legislature and ineligible a second time. **1811** J. QUINCY *Speech* 30 Jan. (1874) 242 It may be admitted that all executives for the time being are virtuous. **1855** A. BARNES *Way Salvation* xi. 138 It might contribute much.. to dispose an executive to pardon an offender if he was satisfied that he was truly penitent. **1876** GARFIELD *Sp. Policy Pacif.* in Kirke *Life* 30/2 Our great military chieftain [Grant]..had command as chief executive during eight years of..eventful administration. **1876** BANCROFT *Hist. U.S.* VI. 294 The executive was henceforward [from 6 Aug. 1787] known as the 'President'. **1891** *Nation* (N.Y.) 5 Nov. 345/1 A Governor who had shown himself one of the best executives the State has ever had.

2. *transf.* Any administrative body.

1868 PEARD *Water-farm.* ix. 100 Sixteen shillings per week to each water-keeper, would..secure a grateful, and honest executive. **1884** SIR J. BACON in *Law Rep.* 26 Chanc. Div. 133 Directors, who were to form the executive of the association.

3. A person holding an executive position in a business organization; a person skilled in executive or administrative work; a business man. Also *attrib.* orig. *U.S.*

1902 G. H. LORIMER *Lett. Merchant* 22 They will never climb over the railing that separates the clerks from the executives. **1927** HUNTINGTON & WHITNEY *Builders Amer.* 15 All over the United States business men deplore the scarcity of good executives. **1930** B. COLBY *Close of Wilson's Admin.* 17 Decisions were..reached..with a rapid ease that

marked the born executive. **1930** *Monotype Recorder* Special No. Mar.–Apr. 5 Chosen as the chief executive of one of our most important industries. **1936** J. B. PRIESTLEY *They Walk in City* i. 6 Mr. Welkinghurst, who knew his business, spotted it at once. So did all the executives, of course. **1951** M. MCLUHAN *Mech. Bride* 35/1 Do you have a personality? Our executive clinic will get rid of it for you. **1958** *Spectator* 7 Feb. 173/1 The type of men who used to go into union politics..are now becoming technicians, administrators and executives. **1958** *Manch. Guardian* 20 Mar. 10/3 In New York..over two thousand business banquets were held last year, involving three to four million executive man-hours. **1959** *Times Lit. Suppl.* 6 Feb. 74/3 He is away from the sophisticated anxieties of his executive suite, and back in Aunt Mabel's brown-stone house on 62nd Street. **1962** *Guardian* 5 Oct. 15/2 The comforts of executive-class prosperity. **1968** 'R. SIMONS' *Death on Display* xv. 77 Most of the cars parked in the driveways were large, new and expensive, and it was the kind of area that estate agents describe gladly as 'executive class'. **1971** *Times* 8 Jan. 8/2 An executive toy can mean—and has meant—anything from worry beads to a laughing box.

executively (ɛkˈsɛkjʊtɪvlɪ). *adv.* [f. prec. + -LY².] In an executive manner; in execution; by the action of the Executive.

1661 *Papers on Alter. Prayer-bk.* 124 In absolving the excommunicate..the Church both judiciously, and executively remitteth the penalty of excommunication. *a* **1677** BARROW *Serm.* Wks. (1716) I. 345 God the Holy Ghost..did executively by miraculous operation conduct our Saviour into his fleshly tabernacle. **1716** M. DAVIES *Athen. Brit.* III. 4 Protestant Countries where Jesuitism and Papism are Legislatively Tolerated or Executively Permitted.

executor (ɛkˈs-, ɛgˈzɛkjʊtə(r) in sense 3; ˈɛksəkjʊtə(r) in sense 1). Forms: 3–4 executur(e, esecutor, (4 exceketour), 4–5 excecuto(u)r, 4–6 exequitour, -quutor, 4–7 executour, 6 exectour, 4– executor. See also SECUTOR. [a. AF. *executour*, a. L. *ex(s)ecūtōr-em*, agent-n. from *exsequī* to EXECUTE.]

1. One who executes or carries out (a purpose, design, command, work, etc.); one who carries into action, or puts into practice (some quality); a conductor or manager (of affairs); an administrator or enforcer of (a law, vengeance, etc.); an agent, doer, performer, executer; *in Scots Law*, one who serves a writ or executes a warrant. Now *rare* exc. in legal uses: see EXECUTER.

1388 WYCLIF *1 Esdras* v. 58 Executours [**1382** foleweris out], or folewers, of the lawe. **1483** *Cath. Angl.* 119 An Executor, *executor*. **1563** FOXE *A. & M.* (1596) 113/2 Ioseph an excellent doctor and executor of chastitie..and other vertues. **1567** THROGMORTON in Robertson *Hist. Scot.* (1759) II. App. 45 The said Earl [Bothwell] was one of the principal executors of the murder [of Darnley]. **1610** SHAKS. *Temp.* III. i. 13 Such basenes Had neuer like Executor. **1662** PETTY *Taxes* 63 When the executors of them [penal laws] keep them hid until a fault be done. **1720** DE FOE *Capt. Singleton* xiv. (1840) 242 The executor of his own vengeance. **1726** LEONI tr. *Alberti's Archit.*, *Life* 5 His Assistant and the faithful Executor of his designs. **1752** J. LOUTHIAN *Form of Process* 83 So soon as the Letters are execute against the Criminal..the Executor is to apprehend and imprison him. **1864** *Realm* 11 May 1 Ordinary exhibitions result only in the advantage of the shopkeeper; the designer and executor being studiously ignored. **1875** STUBBS *Const. Hist.* §811 (ed. 2) III. 588 His [the mayor's] functions as receiver and executor of writs devolved on the sheriffs of the newly constituted shire.

b. One who performs the duties, etc. (of an office, service, ceremony, etc.).

c **1450** *Pol., Rel. & L. Poems* 7 Executor of this office, dirge for to synge, Shall begynne yᵉ bisshope of seynt as [Asaph]. **1548** GEST *Pr. Masse* 106 Bee not also the ful Executors of the same justly named sacryfycers? **1558** FORREST *Grysilde Sec.* 96 He was, emonges other thynges all, The Executor of her Funerall. **1560** in Strype *Ann. Ref.* I. xvii. 214 The ministers receiving the Communion at the hands of the executor. **1841** MYERS *Cath. Th.* IV. §26. 304 The Priests were simply sacrificers and executors of ceremonial.

†**2.** = EXECUTIONER. *Obs.*

1494 FABYAN *Chron.* VI. clxxxvi. 186 After whiche sentence..Hebert was by the executours..moste shamefully hanged. **1599** SHAKS. *Hen. V*, I. ii. 203 The sad-ey'd Iustice..Deliuering ore to Executors pale The lazie yawning Drone. **1614** BP. HALL *Contempl. O.T.* IV. iv, How much rather had they [the Egyptians] to send them [the Israelites] away wealthy, than to have them stay to be their executors.

†**b.** One who or that which gives effect to (a passion). *Obs.*

c **1386** CHAUCER *Sompn. T.* 302 Ire engendrith homiside; Ire is in soth executour of pride.

3. A person appointed by a testator to execute or carry into effect his will after his decease. ***literary executor***: one who is entrusted with the care of the papers and unpublished works of a literary man.

c **1280** *E.E.P.* 19 Þe deuil is his executur, of is gold an is tresure. **1340** *Ayenb.* 38 Kueade exequitours of bekuydes. *c* **1440** *Gesta Rom.* II. liii. 372 (Add. MS.) Lordes, or othere rauenours that ben Eyres ande excecutores. **1558** in *Vicary's Anat.* App. v. (1888) 185 The said Thomas Dunkyn, his heyrs, executors, admynystrators or assignes. **1647** CLARENDON *Hist. Reb.* I. (1843) 22/2 His grandfather had been..left by King Harry the Eighth one of the executours of his last will. **1771** BROWN in *Gray's Corr.* (1843) 163 No discharge..against any claims which his executors might make. **1858** LD. ST. LEONARDS *Handy Bk. Prop. Law* xviii. 141 Creditors or executors may prove a will to which they are attesting witnesses. **1868** G. DUFF *Pol. Surv.* 105 Mr. Senior's conversations..which we trust his literary executor will soon publish.

b. in various legal phrases (see quots.).

1670 BLOUNT *Law Dict.*, *Executor de son tort*, Or of his own wrong, is he that takes upon him the Office of an Executor by intrusion, not being so constituted by the Testator. **1767** BLACKSTONE *Comm.* II. 507 If a stranger takes upon him to act as executor, without any just authority ..he is called in law an executor of his own wrong, *de son tort*, and is liable to all the trouble of an executorship, without any of the profits or advantages. **1861** W. BELL *Dict. Law Scot.* 214/2 *Confirmation of Executor*, is the form in which a title is conferred on the executor of a person deceased, to..administer the defunct's moveable effects [etc.]. *Ibid.* 358/1 The office of executor is conferred either by the written nomination of the defunct, or, failing that, by decree of the commissary; the executor, in the former case, being called an executor-*nominate*, and, in the latter, an executor-*dative*. *Ibid.* 362/1 Any creditor of the deceased holding a liquid ground of debt may obtain himself confirmed executor-creditor.

c. *transf.* and *fig.*

1580 SIDNEY *Sidera* xiii. in *Arcadia* (1622) 501 His death-bed peacocks folly..His sole exectour blame. *c* **1600** SHAKS. *Sonn.* iv, Thy unused beauty must be tomb'd with thee, Which, used, lives th' executor to be. **1607** TOPSELL *Four-f. Beasts* (1673) 177 He destroyeth them..and so maketh himself executor to their heaps of hony. **1645** BP. HALL *Remed. Discontents* 23 His greatnesse..is dead..before him, and leaves him the surviving executour of his own shame.

executorial (ɛkˌsɛkjuːˈtɔərɪəl), *a.* and *sb.* Also 6–7 executoriall, -ell. [ad. med.L. *execūtoriālis*, f. L. *ex(s)ecūtōri-us*: see EXECUTORY.]

A. *adj.* Of or pertaining to an executor. **b.** *Scots Law.* Pertaining to the execution of a warrant, etc. **c.** Canon Law. ***executorial letters*** (med.L. *litteræ executoriæ* or *executoriales*): a mandate issued by the Pope requiring the collation of a specified clergyman to a benefice.

1748 RICHARDSON *Clarissa* (1811) VIII. 275 Excuse me, Sir, for the sake of my executorial duty and promise. **1754** ERSKINE *Princ. Sc. Law* (1809) 35 In this office are sealed.. letters of executorial diligence. **1767** BLACKSTONE *Comm.* II. 508 Letters of administration..whereby an executorial power to collect and administer..is vested in him. **1796** BURNEY *Metastasio* I. 68, I received..the executorial letters against Cardinal Coscia. **1850** JAMES *Old Oak Chest* I. 49 Two lawyers were also there, arranging the executorial affairs. **1865** MRS. WHITNEY *Gayworthys* lx, His legal and executorial bag.

†**B.** *sb. Scots Law.* 'Any legal authority employed for executing a decree or sentence of court' (Jamieson). *Obs.*

1525 Q. MARGT. (Scotl.) in Miss M. A. E. Wood *Lett. R. & Illust. Ladies* (1852) I. 371 In like manner we have superseded executorials and sharp process which we have on him. **1640** *Act 34 Chas. I* (1870) V. 287 The estates of parliament..ordeanes þe lordis of Sessione to grant lettiris and other executoriellis against the excommunicat prelates. **1728** in *Mem. Domestica* (1889) 12 Letters of horning and all other executorials may pass hereupon.

executorship (ɛkˈsɛkjʊtəʃɪp). [f. EXECUTOR + -SHIP.] The office or duty of an executor.

1530 in W. H. Turner *Select Rec. Oxford* 90 Thomas Johns ought no peny to Falowfyld..but by way of executorshyp. **1661** PEPYS *Diary* 15 Sept., If she will not be ruled, I shall fling up my executorship. **1754** RICHARDSON *Grandison* (1781) II. xxx. 288 He went to town this morning on the affairs of his executorship. **1823** LAMB *Elia*, *South Sea House* (1867) 7 He made the best executor in the world: he was plagued with incessant executorships accordingly.

executory (ɛkˈsɛkjʊtərɪ), *a.* and *sb.* [ad. L. *ex(s)ecūtōri-us*, f. *ex(s)ecūtor*: see EXECUTOR and -ORY. Cf. F. *exécutoire.*]

A. *adj.*

1. Of or pertaining to the execution or carrying out of a command, decree, law, instructions, etc.

1658–9 *Burton's Diary* (1828) III. 158 The question is only executory, not declarative; only as a direction to your Committee. **1706** BP. OF LINCOLN *Charge* 19 This Constitution..was..only an Executory Declaration of the Ancient Ecclesiastical Law. *a* **1734** NORTH *Exam.* III. vii. §30 (1740) 524 The Contrivance at last came out of a Gray's Inn Cabal, as the Persons, active in the executory Part, make plain. **1790** BURKE *Fr. Rev.* Wks. V. 357 What sort of person is a king to command executory service, who has no means whatsoever to reward it? **1851** GLADSTONE *Glean.* VI. xl. 27 The machinery for applying our principles to executory details is..very imperfect.

b. Of a law, etc.: In execution or operation; in force, of force, operative.

1483 *Act 1 Richard III*, c. 6 §4 The aforesaid Ordinance [shall]..be executory from the Feast of the Annunciation.. perpetually after to endure. **1649** SELDEN *Laws Eng.* II. xxviii. (1739) 131 A Law, that was executory all the days of Henry Eighth. **1791** *St. Papers in Ann. Reg.* 139* Their decrees are rendered executory without requiring sanction. **1882** *Manch. Guard.* 21 July, The Canal Convention..as far as France is concerned is only executory after the Chamber has ratified it. **1885** *Pall Mall G.* 13 May 7/2 An action on the judgment..if the court sees in it nothing contrary to French law..may be declared executory without going into the merits.

2. Concerned or charged with the execution of a command, decree, law, etc.; = EXECUTIVE A. 3.

1649 SELDEN *Laws Eng.* I. liv. (1739) 95 The power of Militia is either the Legislative or Executory power. **1796** BURKE *Corr.* (1844) IV. 414 As far as I know anything of Mr. Dundas's office, it is merely executory. **1829** *Blackw. Mag.* XXV. 43 The Lord Lieutenant and the Secretary were cut down..into mere executory agents of the British Government. **1858** GLADSTONE *Homer* II. 128 The lower and executory parts of each of these functions..are taken up ..by deities far inferior to her.

3. *Law.* Of acts or dispositions: Designed to take or capable of taking full effect only at a future time. Opposed to *executed.*

1592 WEST *1st Pt. Symbol.* §44 C, Euerie estate is either executed maintenant, or executorie by limitation of vse. **1670** BLOUNT *Law Dict.* s.v. *Agreement*, The third is.. Executory, in regard the thing is to be done afterwards. **1767** BLACKSTONE *Comm.* II. xxx. 443 A contract..may be executory, as if they agree to change [horses] next week. **1818** COLEBROOKE *Treat. Obligations & Contracts* I. 16 An executory contract..is one which is to be subsequently fulfilled. **1827** J. POWELL *Devises* II. 203 The terms of the executory trust seemed to import that no conveyance was to be made to J. until the death of the wife. **1876** DIGBY *Real Prop.* vii. 328 Devises of future interests in land, or, as they were called, executory devises.

†**4.** Of or pertaining to an executor or to his duties: = EXECUTORIAL. *Obs. rare*⁻¹.

1560 in Spottiswood *Hist. Ch. Scot.* (1677) III. 164 The Rector..of the University must be exempted from all.. burdens that may abstract them from attending the youth, such as Tutory, Curatory, Executory, and the like.

B. *sb.*

†**1.** = EXECUTORSHIP, EXECUTRY. *Obs. rare*⁻¹.

1496 *Dives & Paup.* (W. de W.) IX. vi. 355/2 Them that have mysgoten them by myspurchace, or by withholdynge of dette, or by false executorye.

2. An executive body (see EXECUTIVE B. 2.)

1868 W. T. THORNTON in *Fortn. Rev.* May 521 Unionist executories have all the requisite capacity for practising the compulsion with which current belief charges them.

executress (ɛkˈsɛkjʊtrɪs). ? *Obs.* Also 6 exequetresse. [a. OF. *executeresse*, fem. of *executeur*: see EXECUTOR.] = EXECUTRIX.

1591 *Troub. Raigne K. John* (1611) 27 A will indeed.. Wherein the diuell is an ouerseer, And prowd dame Elianor sole Executresse. *c* **1600** *Distracted Emp.* II. i. in Bullen *O. Pl.* (1884) III. 187 But how fares The Empresse now, my dear exequetresse? **1818** in TODD; hence in mod. Dicts.

†**eˈxecutrice.** *Obs.* Also 5 executorice, -tryse. [(? a. AF. *executrice) ad. L. *execūtrice-m* (nom. *execūtrix*): see next. Cf. It. *esecutrice.*] = next.

c **1374** CHAUCER *Troylus* III. 568 O Fortune, executrice of werdis! **1410** *E.E. Wills* (1882) 17 Y be-queþe..my godys to Ione my wyff..myn Executorice Cheff. *c* **1450** *Mirour Saluacioun* 1197 Oure ladie..wold be purified to be of the lawe Executrice. **1526** in *Eng. Gilds* (1870) 254 Agnes Lenche my wife, Whom I ordeigne..my soole Executrice. **1594** CAREW *Tasso* (1881) 79 Weaue thou the web begun by my deuice, Of warie age as bold executrice.

executrix (ɛkˈsɛkjʊtrɪks). *Pl.* -trices. [a. med.L. *execūtrix*, fem. of *ex(s)ecūtor*: see EXECUTOR.] A female executor; *esp.* a woman appointed by a testator to execute his will.

1502 *Bury Wills* (1850) 95 Of this my testament and last will I make myn executrix the seid Anne my wyff. *a* **1577** SIR T. SMITH *Commw. Eng.* (1609) 120 [Wives] bee..made at the death of their husbands eyther sole or chiefe executrices of his last will and Testament. **1650** BULWER *Anthropomet.* xxii. 249 Unlesse the intelligences the executrices of Gods providence have used this Art in some Region. **1765** BLACKSTONE *Comm.* I. xvii, A female..at seventeen may be executrix. **1827** J. POWELL *Devises* II. 33 A testator.. appointing his wife S. sole executrix of his will.

Hence †**eˈxecutrixship.** *Obs. rare*⁻¹, the office of executrix.

1654 GAYTON *Pleas. Notes* IV. viii. 229 The executrixship of all is thine.

executry (ɛkˈsɛkjʊtrɪ). *Sc.* [f. EXECUT(O)R + -Y³.] **a.** = EXECUTORSHIP. **b.** 'The general name given to the moveable estate and effects of a defunct' (W. Bell *Dict. Law Scot.* 1861).

1655 in *Z. Boyd's Zion's Flowers* (1855) App. 28/2 Accompt of Mr. Zachary Boid's Executry and Movable Goods. **1754** ERSKINE *Princ. Sc. Law* (1809) 428 Executry, though it be sometimes said to carry a certain degree of representation of the deceased, is properly an office. **1843** *Tait's Mag.* X. 314 Having performed the last sad offices of friendship..we shared their executry among the survivors. **1885** *Law Rep.* 10 App. Cases 457 Our said Lords..should remove the defenders from their said office of trust and executry.

†**eˈxede,** *v. Obs.* [f. L. *exedĕre*, f. *ex-* out + *edĕre* to eat.] *trans.* To eat out, corrode.

1669 EVELYN *Sylva* (1776) 342 A bar of iron..exeded and consumed with Rust. **1752** *Monthly Rev.* Jan. 69 The antient piece of money..is not the least blurred or exeded. **1754** LEWIS in *Phil. Trans.* XLVIII. 688 All metallic substances, except gold, are exeded from platina by the simple acids.

exedent (ˈɛksɪdənt), *a.* [ad. L. *exedent-em*, pr. pple. of *exedĕre*: see EXEDE.] 'Eating up; consuming; ulcerating' (*Syd. Soc. Lex.* 1884).

†**eˈxedify,** *v. Obs. rare.* In 7 exædifie. [ad. L. *exædificā-re* to build up, construct. f. *ex-* + *ædificā-re*: see EDIFY.] *trans.* To build up; to complete, finish.

a **1617** P. BAYNE *Diocesan's Tryall* (1621) 76 The.. exædifying of the body of Christ. **1641** 'SMECTYMNUUS' *Vind. Answ.* §13 Bishops are given..not to lay foundations, or to exædifie some imperfect beginnings.

‖**exedra, exhedra** ('ɛksɪdrə, ɛk'siːdrə). *Pl.* 8–9 exedræ, -hedræ. [a. L. *exedra*, f. Gr. ἐξ- (see EX- *pref.*²) + ἕδρα a sitting place. Cf. F. *exèdre*.]

1. *Ancient Arch.* **a.** 'The portico of the palæstra or gymnasium in which disputations of the learned were held among the ancients; also, in private houses, the pastas or vestibule, used for conversation' (Parker *Gloss. Archit.* 1874).

1706 PHILLIPS (ed. Kersey), *Exedræ*. **1832** GELL *Pompeiana* I. vi. 90 The vestibulum and the exedra. **1841** W. SPALDING *Italy & It. Isl.* I. 189 Exedræ, the usual scenes of the afternoon slumber. **1858** R. A. VAUGHAN *Ess. & Rev.* I. 5 He sees them..sitting in the shady retirement of the exhedra, discussing their theories.

b. = APSIS 3 b *a*: cf. CATHEDRA.

1725 tr. *Dupin's Eccl. Hist. 17th c.* I. v. 69 The Preacher was plac'd in a Chair lifted up, which the ancients called.. Exedra. **1842–76** GWILT *Archit.* Gloss. s.v. *Apsis*, The bishop's throne..was sometimes called exhedra. **1875** PARKER *Gloss. Archit.*, *Exedra*, used as synonymous with Cathedra, for a throne or seat of any kind.

2. (See quots.)

1850 WEALE *Dict. Terms*, *Exedra*..a by-place, or jutty. **1875** PARKER *Gloss. Archit.*, *Exedra* or *Exhedra*, a recess or large niche in a wall..sometimes applied to a porch or chapel which projects from a larger building.

exeem, var. form of EXEME *Sc.*

†**exege'matic**, *a.* *Obs. rare*⁻¹. [as if f. Gr. *ἐξηγηματ- stem of *ἐξήγημα explanation (f. ἐξηγέεσθαι: see EXEGESIS) + -IC.] Explanatory.

1683 E. HOOKER *Pref. Ep. to Pordage's Mystic Div.* 102 By waie of an Exegematic Character.

exegence, -ency, -ent, obs. ff. EXIGENCE, etc.

exegesis (ɛksɪ'dʒiːsɪs). [a. Gr. ἐξήγησις, f. ἐξηγέεσθαι to interpret, f. ἐξ- (see EX- *pref.*²) + ἡγέεσθαι to guide, lead. Cf. F. *exégèse*.]

1. Explanation, exposition (of a sentence, word, etc.); *esp.* the interpretation of Scripture or a Scriptural passage.

1823 in CRABB *Technol. Dict.*, Exegesis, an explication of words or an elucidation of sentences. *a* **1848** R. W. HAMILTON *Rew. & Punishm.* Notes (1853) 423 The exegesis of Scripture is conducted by instituting inquiry into what certain parties understood. **1857** GLADSTONE *Glean.* VI. xix. 59 That most wretched consummation, which reduces all exegesis to a profane and deluding art. **1876** M. ARNOLD *Lit. & Dogma* 161 A very small experience of Jewish exegesis will convince us.

b. An explanatory note, a gloss.

1619 *Sacrilege Handl.* App. 33 The Septuagint makes the 23. vers. but as an Exegesis of the former verse. *a* **1638** MEDE *Chr. Sacrif.* v. Wks. II. (1672) 364 Κλάσις τοῦ ἄρτου and προσευχαί, Breaking of Bread and Prayers, are to be referred to κοινωνίᾳ Communion, as the Exegesis thereof. **1653** W. SCLATER (Jun.) *Fun. Serm.* (1654) 5 The exegesis and exposition of the former [expression]. **1751** CHAMBERS *Cycl.* s.v., The second [word] is only an exegesis, or explanation of the first.

c. An expository discourse.

1727–51 in CHAMBERS *Cycl.* Hence **1832** in WEBSTER; and in some mod. Dicts.

†**2.** *Algebra.* (See quot.) *Obs.*

1706 PHILLIPS (ed. Kersey), *Exegesis* Numerosa..the Numeral, or Lineal Solution, or Extraction of Roots, out of Adfected Equations. **1796** HUTTON *Math. Dict.* s.v.

exegete ('ɛksɪdʒiːt). [ad. Gr. ἐξηγητής an expounder, interpreter, f. ἐξηγέεσθαι (see EXEGESIS): cf. F. *exégète*.] An expounder, interpreter.

1. *Greek Antiq.* At Athens, one of those three members of the Eumolpidæ, whose province it was to interpret the religious and ceremonial law, the signs in the heavens, and oracles.

1730–6 in BAILEY (folio), *Exegetes*, persons among the Athenians learned in the laws of the juris consulti; whom the judges used to concult in capital cases. **1869** A. W. WARD tr. *Curtius' Greece* II. II. iv. 19 Apollo himself was the supreme Exegete, the ultimate source of legality.

2. One who explains or interprets difficult passages; one skilled in exegesis; an expounder.

1859 ELLICOTT *Comm. Gal.* Pref. (ed. 2) 25 For the former [Chrysostom]..as an exegete, I entertain the greatest respect. **1872** *Contemp. Rev.* XXI. 74 Goodwin, an exegete ..hardly second to Chillingworth. **1885** PLUMPTRE *Spir. in Prison* 364 Unrivalled as an exegete of Scripture.

‖**exegetes** (ɛksɪ'dʒiːtiːz). [a. Gr. ἐξηγητής: see prec.] (See quots.)

1846 GROTE *Greece* I. i. I. 83 The exegetes or local guide and interpreter belonging to each temple..recounted to curious strangers these traditional narratives. *Ibid.* (1854) I. 381 The Theban exegetes assured Pausanias of this fact.

exegetic (ɛksɪ'dʒɛtɪk), *a.* and *sb.* [ad. Gr. ἐξηγητικός, f. ἐξηγέεσθαι: see EXEGESIS. Cf. Fr. *exégétique*.] **A.** *adj.*

1. = EXEGETICAL. Const. *of*.

1655–60 STANLEY *Hist. Philos.* (1701) 175/1 Of Platonick discourse there are two kinds Hyphegetick, and Exegetick. **1677** GALE *Crt. Gentiles* II. IV. 187 Plato oft..joins them [Law and Order] together as exegetic each of other. **1801** W. TAYLOR in *Monthly Mag.* XII. 577 It is..behind the present state of exegetic knowledge. **1837** CARLYLE *Fr. Rev.* II IV. iv, This strange autograph Letter the National Assembly decides..on transmitting to the Eighty-three Departments, with exegetic commentary. **1841** G. S. FABER *Provinc. Lett.* (1844) I. 206 *note*, The *etiam* is exegetic and explanatory of what Reinerius had said just before.

2. *Alg.* [after mod.L. *exegeticus*, so used by Vieta in 1600.] The distinctive epithet of Vieta's process (see EXEGESIS 2) for the solution of equations.

1843 DE MORGAN in *Penny Cycl.* XXV. 317 His [Vieta's] extension of the antient rules for division and extraction of the square and cube roots to the exegetic process for the solution of all equations.

B. *sb.* **1.** = Gr. ἐξηγητική (τέχνη) (see quot.).

1838 SIR W. HAMILTON *Logic* xxxiv. (1866) II. 199 The Art of Interpretation, called..technically Hermeneutic or Exegetic.

2. *pl.* (after Gr. τά ἐξηγητικά) = *exegetical theology*: see EXEGETICAL.

1852 J. H. NEWMAN *Scope Univ. Educ.* 17 Aquila, Symmachus..have supplied materials for primitive exegetics. **1864** CARLYLE *Fredk. Gr.* IV. 310 An uncommonly frugal rate of board, for a man skilled in Hermeneutics, Hebraics..Exegetics, etc.

exegetical (ɛksɪ'dʒɛtɪkəl), *a.* [f. as prec. + -AL¹.]

†**1.** Of the nature of a gloss; explanatory. Const. *of*, *to*. *Obs.*

a **1623** W. PEMBLE *Exp. Zachary* (1629) 115 This Exegeticall interpretation of this place sounds harshly. **1642** W. PRICE *Serm.* 32 The one verse is exegeticall to the other. **1666** J. SMITH *Old Age* (ed. 2) 135 Life, and soul, and spirit, are..often made exegetical one of another. **1721** *Wodrow Corr.* (1843) II. 533, I take this proposition to be exegetical.

2. Of, pertaining to, or of the nature of exegesis, exposition or interpretation; *esp.* of the Scriptures; expository. ***exegetical theology***: that branch of theological learning which deals with the interpretation of the Scriptures and the subjects therewith connected; = *exegetics*.

1838–9 HALLAM *Hist. Lit.* (1864) IV. ii. IV. 57 In the.. exegetical theology, the English divines had already taken a conspicuous station. **1844** STANLEY *Arnold* (1858) I. iii. 148 Dogmatical instruction..conveyed..in a practical or exegetical shape. **1862** H. J. ROSE in *Replies to Ess. & Rev.* 120 He has attributed to Jerome exegetical absurdities.

3. Of or pertaining to exegetics.

1884 *Nonconf. & Indep.* 14 Feb. 157/1 Exegetical study is not new to him.

exegetically (ɛksɪ'dʒɛtɪkəlɪ), *adv.* [f. prec. + -LY².] In an exegetical manner: †**a.** By way of gloss or explanation. *Obs.* **b.** In an expository manner.

a **1638** MEDE *Chr. Sacrif.* iv. Wks. II. 361 Here you see Oblations and Eucharists exegetically joined together. **1659** PEARSON *Creed* I. 201 The 'form of a servant' exegetically continued 'in the likeness of man'. *a* **1710** BP. BULL *Wks.* (1713) I. 200 This is not added exegetically, or by way of Exposition. **1845** R. JEBB in *Encycl. Metrop.* (1847) II. 675/1 The science of jurisprudence properly admits of being treated in four different ways, philosophically, didactically or dogmatically, and exegetically.

exe'getist (ɛksɪ'dʒiːtɪst). [f. Gr. ἐξηγητ-ής (see EXEGETE) + -IST.] = EXEGETE 3.

1848 GEO. ELIOT in *Life* iii. (1887) 101, I speak to an experienced exegetist. **1882–3** SCHAFF *Encycl. Relig. Knowl.* I. 640 Diodorus..was, as an exegetist, one of the masters of the Antiochian school.

exeime, obs. form of EXEME *v.* *Sc.*

exelent, obs. form of EXCELLENT.

exeleuthe'rostomize, *v.* *nonce-wd.* [as if ad. Gr. *ἐξελευθεροστομίζ-ειν, f. ἐξ out + ἐλεύθερος free + στόμα mouth.] *trans.* To speak out freely.

1854 BADHAM *Halieut.* 181 The heroes of the Iliad—shall we hide it to live, or exeleutherostomize it and die?—are for the most part boors.

exeltree, obs. form of AXLE-TREE.

exembryonate (ɛk'sɛmbrɪəneɪt), *a.* *Bot.* [f. EX- *pref.*¹ + med.L. *embryōn-em* + -ATE.]

1866 *Treas. Bot.*, *Exembryonate*, a name given to cryptogams in consequence of their spores not containing an embryo.

†**e'xeme**, *v.* Chiefly *Sc.* *Obs.* Also 6–9 exeem(e, 7 exeime, exime. [ad. L. *exim-ĕre*, f. *ex-* out + *emĕre* to take. For the phonology cf. *redeem*.]

1. *trans.* To set free, release: **a.** *from* a payment, an obligation, *from* obedience to (a law, rule, etc.); = EXEMPT *v.* 4 a and b.

1563 DAVIDSON *Answ. Kennedy* in *Wodr. Soc. Misc.* (1844) 251 The Gentiles that belevis is exemit fra the Law of Moyses. **1639** *Procl. Chas. I. Scotl.* 2 [We] eximed all ministers at their entry from giving any other oath than, etc. *a* **1657** SIR J. BALFOUR *Ann. Scot.* (1824–5) II. 28 All knowen merchants..wer exeimed from taking this othe. **1733** P. LINDSAY *Interest Scot.* 174 So many of them [foreign Materials] as are used at publick Bleach-fields, should be exeemed from the Payment of Duty. **1814** SCOTT *Wav.* xii, He hath no title to exeemed from the obligations of the code of politeness.

b. *from* pain, a penalty, etc; also *simply*; = EXEMPT *v.* 4 c.

1578 in Spottiswood *Hist. Ch. Scot.* VI. (1677) 299 Nor doth it agree with the Scripture that they should be exeemed from the correction of their brethren. **1585** *Commend. Verses* in *Jas. I's Ess. Poesie* (Arb.) 10 My minde exemed was from caire. **1637** GILLESPIE *Eng.-Pop. Cerem.* II. vii. 29 His Majesties Auctority, did..exeeme the affirmers from the paines of probation. **1647** H. MORE *Song of Soul* II. III. IV. ii, It no man can exeem from miseries. **1716** J. Row in *Wodrow Corr.* (1843) II. 135 He had paid his cess; yet this exeemed him not.

2. To take away, remove; also, to select, except *from*; = EXEMPT *v.* 1, 2.

a **1605** MONTGOMERIE *Misc. Poems* xvii. 59 Beuties freshest florish, fair, Exemed clene from Loves lair. **1640** *Canterb. Self-Convict.* 63 They exeeme all tenets controverted this day among any Christians from being the Subject of heresie. *a* **1651** CALDERWOOD *Hist. Kirk* (1843) II. 342 She did what she could to exeme all feare and doubts out of his minde. **1688** *Ess. on Magistracy* in *Harl. Misc.* (1808) I. 5 Express liberty is a stipulation, whereby some things are by express paction eximed from the power of the Sovereign.

†**'exemie**, *a.* *Obs. rare.* [ad. L. *eximi-us* distinguished, f. *eximĕre*: see prec. Cf. OF. *exemme*.] Excellent, illustrious.

1497 BP. ALCOCK *Mons Perfect.* Aij 4 The exemie prophete Ysay exhorteth al mankynde.

exempill, obs. form of EXAMPLE.

†**e'xemplable**, *a.* *Obs.* [ad. med.L. *exemplābilis*, f. *exemplar* EXEMPLAR *sb.*] 'That may be imitated' (Bailey 1721–61).

1775 in ASH.

exemplar (ɛg'zɛmplə(r)), *sb.* Forms: 4–5 exemplaire, -ayre, 5–6 exemplare, 5– exemplar. [ME. *exemplaire*, a. OF. *exemplaire*: see EXAMPLAR. The mod. form is partly a descendant of this, partly an adoption of L. *exemplar*, *-āre*, sb., orig. neut. of *exemplāris* adj.: see next.]

1. A person or thing which serves as a model for imitation; an example. Formerly also, †a pattern for work: cf. SAMPLER.

1432–50 tr. *Higden* (Rolls) I. 5 In this tyme.. thexemplares of acciones spectable scholde not be patent. **1490** CAXTON *Eneydos* xi. (1890) 41 [Nature] hathe produced hym [Aeneas] for to make one fayer chief werke to thexemplayre of alle other. **1530** PALSGR. 157 *Vne exemple*, an exemplar for a woman to worke by. **1549** LATIMER *Serm. bef. Edw. VI* (Arb.) 109 Christ is the..patrone and the exemplar, that all preachers oughte to folowe. **1694** POMFRET *Poems, Death Q. Mary* 128 Him for her high exemplar she design'd. **1744** *Epitaph* in Brand *Hist. Newcastle* (1789) I. 676 His Master's presence will reward.. his virtues by a more intimate converse with the great Exemplar. **1793** T. MAURICE *Ind. Antiq.* (1806) I. 105 It is impossible for the artist to deviate from the exemplar before him. **1875** JOWETT *Plato* (ed. 2) V. 25 The Republic is..the pattern of all other states and the exemplar of human life.

†**b.** = EXAMPLE 3 b. *Obs. rare*⁻¹.

1393 GOWER *Conf.* II. 31 Fulfilled of slouthes exemplaire There is yet one his secretaire, And he is cleped negligence.

2. The model, pattern, or original after which something is made; an archetype whether real or ideal.

a **1618** RALEIGH (J.), The idea and exemplar of the world was first in God. **1651** *Raleigh's Ghost* 158 Christ was like to Moses, as..the Exemplar, or Sample [is] to the image. **1725** WATTS *Logic* I. iii. §3 Real ideas are such as..have real objects or exemplars, which did, or do..actually exist. **1829** JAS. MILL *Hum. Mind* (1869) I. viii. 251 The external exemplars according to which individual things were made. **1882** FARRAR *Early Chr.* I. 269 A spiritual world, which was the archetype and exemplar of the visible.

3. An instance, example; a parallel instance, a parallel.

1677 HALE *Prim. Orig. Man.* I. i. 26 It doth give me not only an undeniable evidence, but an exemplar in analogy and explication. **1863** GEO. ELIOT *Romola* I. vi, Those frivolous productions of which Luigi Pulci has furnished the most peccant exemplar. **1866** H. PHILLIPS *Amer. Paper Curr.* II. 11 Modern history is not wanting in exemplars.

4. A typical instance; a type, specimen (of a class); a typical embodiment or personification (of a quality, system, etc.).

1656 SANDERSON *Serm.* (1689) 131 There is scarce to be found such another complete Exemplar of a wicked Magistrate [as Caius Verres]. *c* **1676** SOUTH *Serm. Worldly Wisd.* (1715) I. 340 Cromwell..the..grand Exemplar of Hypocrisy. **1744** HARRIS *Three Treat.* III. II. (1765) 216 An Offer to paint them a Helen, as a Model and Exemplar of the most exquisite Beauty. **1812** WOODHOUSE *Astron.* xxiv. 258 A kind of sample and exemplar of almost all Astronomical processes. **1837** THIRLWALL *Greece* IV. xxxv. 361 Sisyphus, the legendary exemplar of cunning. **1862** STANLEY *Jew. Ch.* (1877) I. xvii. 323 They are the true exemplars of the grasping and worldly clergy of all ages. **1868** HELPS *Realmah* xii. (1876) 309 The friendship between a dog and a man is the highest form and exemplar of friendship.

5. A 'copy' of a book, etc.

1539 TAVERNER *Bible* Pref., To amend the same [default] according to the true exemplars. **1570** BILLINGSLEY *Euclid* XV. Introd. 431 In the Greke exemplars are found in this 15. booke only 5 propositions. **1665** *Phil. Trans.* I. 102 His second Tome, whereof he lately presented some Exemplars to his Friends. **1864** HAZLITT *E.P. Poetry* IV. 1 Many pamphlets..remain to us only in a single exemplar. **1875** SCRIVENER *Lect. Grk. Test.* i 4 All exemplars of the same edition resemble each other.

†**e'xemplar**, *a.* *Obs.* Also 5 exemplair(e, 7 exemplare. [ad. (either through F. *exemplaire* or directly) L. *exemplār-is* (see -AR¹), f. *exemplum*.]

1. Typical; = EXEMPLARY *a.* 2.

1570 DEE *Math. Pref.* 3 The Exemplar Number of all thinges Numerable. *a* **1668** DAVENANT *To the Queen* Poems (1673) 246 That Sand's th'exemplar Seed, by which we know How th' Hour's of the ensuing Year will grow.

2. Of a penalty; = EXEMPLARY *a.* 3.

1588 R. PARKE tr. *Mendoza's China* 92 Coockoldes..are punished with exemplar punishments. **1626** T. H. *Caussin's*

Holy Crt. 414 If he were found culpable of such a villany, he would inflict an exemplar punishment vpon him. **1639** G. DANIEL *Ecclus.* xix. 10 He shall be worne with ranke Infirmities, Corrupt, and made Exemplar to the Eyes Of other Men. **1656** COWLEY *Davideis* IV. 120 Ely's curs'd House th' exemplar Vengeance bears Of all their Blood.

3. Likely to become an example or precedent; extraordinary, flagrant; = EXEMPLARY *a.* 4.

1605 BACON *Adv. Learn.* II. xxiii. §6 One judicial and exemplar iniquity in the face of the world doth trouble the fountains of justice more than [etc.]. *a* **1634** CHAPMAN *Rev. Honour* Wks. (1873) III. 331 That which on others would be fitting justice, On..your..son wil be exemplar crueltie.

4. = EXEMPLARY 6.

c **1475** *Partenay* 6377 Thys lady full swete and ryght debonair, To all other lades exemplair. *a* **1500** *Flower & Leaf* lxxii, The nine crowned be very exemplaire, Of all honour longing to chivalry. **1603** FLORIO *Montaigne* (1634) 3 Having with an unmatched countenance and exemplar constancie endured these two affronts. **1621** DONNE *Serm.* xxi. 205 Exemplar men that might be our patterns for sobriety. **1683** *Lond. Gaz.* No. 1864/1 Your Exemplar and happy Government in Church and State. **1706** DE FOE *Jure Div.* XII. 273 Exemplar Vertue took the Reins in Hand. **1739** 'R. BULL' tr. *Grobianus* 39 Like his thy Life, like his thy Manners be; And shine exemplar to Posterity.

b. Having the force of an example.

1642 CHAS. I. *Answ. Petit. Lds. & Com.* 17 *June* 6 The Fidelity..of His good Subjects of this County, which He hopes will prove exemplar over His whole Kingdom.

Hence †**e'xemplarly** *adv.*, by means of example; in an exemplary or signal manner.

1626 T. H. *Caussin's Holy Crt.* (1634) Aijb, A Pious Queene, who exemplarly maketh good, what diffusedly is heere handled. **1676** W. ROW *Contn. Blair's Autobiog.* xii. (1848) 413 Duty which lieth..more eminently and exemplarly on the Ministers of the Gospel.

ˌexem'plaric, *a. rare.* [f. EXEMPLAR *sb.* + -IC.] Serving as an exemplar.

1836 G. S. FABER *Election* (1842) 311 The typical or exemplaric Election of the Israelites under the Law.

exemplarily (for pronunc. cf. EXEMPLARY), *adv.* Also 7 **-aryly**. [f. EXEMPLARY *a.* + -LY².] In an exemplary manner.

†**1.** In various obs. senses: As an example, pattern, or archetype; by way of example or illustration; signally, conspicuously. Cf. EXEMPLARY 2, 4, 5.

1634 SIR T. HERBERT *Trav.* (1677) 114 These wild dogs.. vary their species; as exemplarily we see in the Indian Ounce, which is the product of an Europæan cat. *a* **1677** BARROW *Wks.* 1686 II. 341 Hence..he could..describe an exact copy of righteousness for us to transcribe; shewing us exemplarily how as men we should behave our selves. **1678** CUDWORTH *Intell. Syst.* 503 Considerations of the Deity as vertually and exemplarily conteining all things. **1683** E. HOOKER *Pref. Ep. to Pordage's Mystic Div.* 21 Sin is not only ..in private, connived at..but autoritativly, exemplarily and Diabolicly, in public, countenanced. *a* **1703** BURKITT *On N.T.* Luke vi. 19 How rare it is to find those who are eminently great, exemplarily good?

2. By way of deterrent example or warning.

1627 HAKEWILL *Apol.* IV. xiv. 1 (1630) 503 Some he punisheth exemplarily in the world. **1684** *Lond. Gaz.* No. 1952/3 His Excellency..being resolved to have the promoters of these Tumults exemplarily punished. **1774** WILKES *Corr.* (1805) IV. 180 The perfidy of the French, and the treachery of the Dutch, were exemplarily chastised. **1880** SALA in *Illust. Lond. News* 18 Dec. 587 Their leaders.. were exemplarily hanged.

3. So as to deserve imitation.

1611 COTGR., *Exemplairement*, exemplarily; for others to follow, or to take example by. **1625** DONNE *Serm.* iii. 20 Such as were noted to be exemplarily religious and sanctified men. **1754** RICHARDSON *Grandison* (1781) III. ix. 62 Mrs. Oldham..lived now very happily and very exemplarily. **1858** HOLLAND *Titcomb's Lett.* i. 173 The cast iron husband..provides for his family exemplarily. **1876** BANCROFT *Hist. U.S.* I. viii. 226 Exemplarily faithful to his country and to its prince.

exemplariness (for pronunc. cf. EXEMPLARY). Also 7–8 **examplariness**. [f. as prec. + -NESS.] The quality of being exemplary.

1. The quality of being worthy of imitation; fitness to serve as a model for imitation.

1650 DAVENANT *Gondibert* Pref., Wit..is, in Divines, Humility, Examplariness [*edd.* **1651**, **1673** Exemplariness], and Moderation. **1698** ATTERBURY *Disc. Lady Cutts* 10 The Exemplariness of her Behaviour call'd off the Eyes of several to observe it. **1752** CARTE *Hist. Eng.* III. 619 The examplariness of her conduct. *Ibid.* IV. 337 The exemplariness of their lives. **1883** SCHAFF *Encycl. Relig. Knowl.* II. 973/2 [P. Henry] is remembered for the purity and exemplariness of his life.

†**2.** The quality of being likely to be taken as an example; prominence. *Obs.*

1665 BOYLE *Occas. Refl.* IV. xii, The exemplariness and influence as well of their [kings'] vices as of their virtues.

exemplarism (ɛg'zɛmplərɪz(ə)m). [f. EXEMPLAR *sb.* + -ISM.] **1.** The doctrine that divine ideas are the source of finite realities.

1893 in *Funk's Stand. Dict.* **1908** *Cath. Encycl.* IV. 271 Exemplarism, or the doctrine of archetypic ideas and the supposed knowledge of things in these divine ideas. **1958** G. LEFF *Medieval Thought* vii. 200 Now the whole of St Bonaventure's outlook is governed by what has been called exemplarism. That is to say, all creation was a sign of God ..a creature was to be regarded only insofar as it provided a trace of God.

2. The doctrine that Christ became incarnate as an exemplar to mankind.

1926 K. E. KIRK in E. G. Selwyn *Ess. Cath. & Crit.* viii. 275 One final criticism of exemplarism may be mentioned. The theory fails to show any grounds for belief in the *necessity* of the death of Christ.

exemplarist (ɛg'zɛmplərɪst), *sb.* (and *a.*) [f. prec. + -IST.] One who believes in or advocates exemplarism. Also as *adj.*

1926 K. E. KIRK in E. G. Selwyn *Ess. Cath. & Crit.* viii. 256 If we must have a name for theories of this type, let us ..call them 'exemplarist'—because their emphasis is upon the moral value of Christ's example. *Ibid.* 275 A somewhat confused criticism of the appeal to gratitude in Exemplarist theories, based on the fact that *some* Exemplarists had forgotten to emphasise the objective value of an example of loyalty. **1936** *Times Lit. Suppl.* 22 Feb. 166/3 But his book shows him to be very far from the 'exemplarist' type of thought about the Atonement which dominated the nineteenth century. **1958** *Times* 19 Apr. 8/4 To help the 'exemplarists' to enter into the necessity of Christ being a sacrifice as well as an example.

exemplarity (ɛgzɛm'plærɪtɪ). [f. L. *exemplār-is* + -ITY. Cf. Fr. *exemplarité*.] The quality of being exemplary. Cf. EXEMPLARY *a.* 3 and 6.

1. The quality of being fit to serve as a model or pattern for imitation; exemplary conduct; exemplariness; also, an instance of such conduct.

1619 BRENT tr. *Sarpi's Counc. Trent* (1676) 134 His Holiness should send ten or twelve Prelates..men rare, of exemplarity and learning. **1644** J. GOODWIN *Fighting agst. God* 39 Such exemplarities of life and conversation, which are sanctified and appointed by God. **1681** H. MORE *Exp. Dan.* iv. 127 *note.* John..having by the exemplarity of his Life..drawn the eyes of all so upon him. **1789** BENTHAM *Princ. Legisl.* xvii. §13 The properties of exemplarity and frugality seem to pursue the same immediate end though by different courses. **1868** BROWNING *Ring & Bk.* XII. 271 Defunct in faith and exemplarity.

†**2.** The quality or fact of acting as an example or pattern. *Obs.*

a **1677** BARROW *Wks.* 1686 III. 33 Some performances [of our Lord]..were done for exemplarity.

†**3.** The quality or fact of acting as an example or warning. *Obs.*

1648 CROMWELL *Let.* 21 Sept. (Carlyle), I hope the exemplarity of justice will testify for us our great detestation of the fact. **1660** JER. TAYLOR *Duct. Dubit.* IV. iv. §11 Not upon any direct account of justice, but..for terror and exemplarity.

†**e'xemplarize,** *v. Obs. rare*⁻¹. [f. EXEMPLAR + -IZE.] To illustrate by example.

Hence **e'xemplarizing** *ppl. a.*

1652 GAULE *Magastrom.* 103 The historizing or exemplarizing [*misprinted* exemplanizing] Astrologers.

exemplary (ɛg'zɛmplərɪ, 'ɛgzɛmplərɪ), *a.* and *adv.* Also 6–7 **exemplarie**, 6–9 **examplary**, 7 **exempleary**. [f. late L. *exemplār-is* (see EXEMPLAR *a.* and -ARY²), f. *exemplum*.] **A.** *adj.*

†**1.** Of or pertaining to an example; furnishing examples. *Obs.*

1623 COCKERAM, *Exemplarie*, of or belonging to an example. **1640** J. MABBE (*title*) Cervantes' Exemplarie Novells. *a* **1649** R. HOLDSWORTH in Spurgeon *Treas. Dav.* Ps. cxxiii. 2 It is an exemplary particle, to stir them [men] up to do the like. **1692–1732** in COLES. **1822** (*title*) The Exemplary Novels of M. de Cervantes Saavedra.

2. That may serve as a specimen or type; in a typical form; typical.

1614 SELDEN *Titles Hon.* 5, I allow, that a Family..was as an exemplary Monarchie. **1670** MILTON *Hist. Eng.* III. (1851) 94 This third Book having to tell of accidents various and exemplary. **1683** tr. *Erasmus' Moriæ Enc.* 31 The two Cato's are exemplary instances. **1878** RUSKIN *Notes on Turner* 72 Four exemplary drawings he..[Turner] made for specimens.

b. Serving for an illustration; illustrative.

1639 FULLER *Holy War* v. xxiv. (1647) 271 Exemplary is the Coat of George Villiers Duke of Buckingham; five Scallop-shells on a plain Crosse, speaking his predecessours valour in the Holy warre. **1817** W. TAYLOR in *Monthly Rev.* LXXXII. 82 Collecting exemplary passages which can only assist a reader to infer the meaning of a word by induction.

3. Of a penalty, damages, etc.: Such as may serve for a warning, or act as a deterrent.

1603 KNOLLES *Hist. Turks* (1638) 196 The Christians sent by Lazarus..suffered many of them exemplary punishment. *a* **1661** FULLER *Worthies* (1840) III. 99 His justice was exemplary on thieves and robbers. **1734** tr. *Rollin's Anc. Hist.* (1827) III. VII. 298 He took an exemplary vengeance. **1809** *Observer* 7 May, From the frequency of this offence, it became necessary to punish it with exemplary severity. **1888** BRYCE *Amer. Commw.* II. App. 672 The plaintiff, in addition to the actual damage, may..recover exemplary damages.

†**b.** Phrases: *to be exemplary*: to become a warning. *to make* (*a person*, also *a thing*) *exemplary*: to make an example of. *Obs.*

1591 LAMBARDE *Archeion* (1635) 181 These offences might be made exemplary and forewarning to other men. **1658–9** *Burton's Diary* (1828) III. 251 Let him be exemplary in his punishment. Send him to the Tower, and fine him 1000*l.* **1669** *Lond. Gaz.* No. 411/4 The Ring-leaders in the late Tumult, whom he intends to make exemplary. **1692** R. L'ESTRANGE *Josephus' Antiq.* IV. ii. (1733) 79 That dark Way of Proceeding ought to be made exemplary in time.

4. Of a kind to become an example, liable to be turned into a precedent. Hence in weaker sense: Such as to attract notice; remarkable, extraordinary, signal. *arch.*

1589 PUTTENHAM *Eng. Poesie* I. xx. (Arb.) 58 The good and bad of Princes is more exemplarie..then the priuate persons. **1629** CHAPMAN *Juvenal* 185 A lamprey of an exemplary size, That for dimension bears the prize from all. **1649** SELDEN *Laws Eng.* II. iii. (1739) 18 Such crimes as are contrary to..the publick profit or peace, in a more exemplary way than ordinary. **1718** PRIOR *Solomon* II. 986 From this abyss of exemplary vice Resolv'd..to rise. **1829** GEN. P. THOMPSON *Exerc.* (1842) I. 137 There was nobody that made a more exemplary bawling for the constable.

5. Of things: Serving as a model or pattern, after which something may be made; archetypal.

1594 HOOKER *Eccl. Pol.* I. iii. 8 We are not of opinion.. that nature in working hath before her certaine exemplary draughts or patternes. **1659** H. L'ESTRANGE *Alliance Div. Off.* 40 So that what Osmund intended peculiarly for his own use became exemplary to others. **1702** *Lond. Gaz.* No. 3809/8 An exemplary Invoice, proper for those at Sea and Land. **1816** W. TAYLOR in *Monthly Rev.* LXXXI. 525 Manuscript books..sufficiently popular to be exemplary. **1854** TRENCH *Synon. N.T.* Ser. I. (1860) 83 The first edition of 1611..should have been considered authoritative and exemplary for all that followed.

6. Of persons and personal attributes: Fit to serve as an example or pattern for imitation.

1589 PUTTENHAM *Eng. Poesie* I. xix. (Arb.) 55 The good and exemplarie things and actions of the former ages. **1612** T. TAYLOR *Comm. Titus* ii. 7 In..good doctrine, and good life..exemplarie to his [a minister's] people in publike and priuate. **1640** T. HEYWOOD (*title*), The exemplary Lives and memorable Acts of nine the most worthy Women of the World. **1663** GERBIER *Counsel* Aj a, Your Lordship hath been exemplary to better Building. **1709** STEELE *Tatler* No. 104 ¶3 This Lady lived several Years an Exemplary Pattern of Conjugal Love. **1848** MACAULAY *Hist. Eng.* II. 92 He was a man of learning and fervent piety..and an exemplary parish priest. **1883** W. R. S. RALSTON in *19th Cent.* XIII. 88 Popular tales are, as a general rule, provided with exemplary morals.

Hence †**b.** Excellent, perfect. *Obs.*

1644 BULWER *Chirol.* 11 The most faithfull guide to the exemplary knowledge of any matter of Fact.

†**B.** *adv.* In an exemplary manner; to an exemplary degree; so as to be exemplary. *Obs.*

1626 G. SANDYS *Ovid's Met., Life* 3 Continuing to the end exemplarie faithfull. **1658** A. FOX tr. *Wurtz' Surg.* I. iii. 8 Such Surgeons..deserve to be punished severely and exemplary. **1729** MORGAN *Algiers* I. iv. 74 That good Pastor [S. Augustine] persuaded him to live exemplary in his Station. **1772** WILKES *Corr.* (1805) IV. 139 Our captain.. had been exemplary humane and good.

†**exemplary,** *sb. Obs.* [ad. late L. *exemplārium* (whence Fr. *exemplaire*: see EXEMPLER), f. *exemplum* EXAMPLE.]

1. a. A type or figure. **b.** A typical instance, an example. **c.** An example, pattern of conduct.

c **1430** LYDG. *Bochas* I. viii. 118 (1558) 15 a/1 Let Zisara be your examplary. *Ibid.* II. xxii. 7. 56 b/1 An examplary of porte & maner. **1579** FULKE *Heskins' Parl.* 374 Basill calleth breade & wine ἀντίτυπα, or *exemplaria*, exemplaries of the bodie and bloud of Christ. **1583** STUBBES *Anat. Abus.* B vj, The pride of apparel remaining in sight, as an exemplary of evill.

2. a. A 'copy' of a book; = EXEMPLAR *sb.* 5. **b.** A copy or transcript (of a writing).

1538 LELAND *Itin.* I. p. xix, Parte of the examplaries.. hath beene imprinted yn Germany. **1548** UDALL *Erasm. Par., Luke* Pref. 5 b, The Latine exemplaries..do vary and not well agree. **1633** J. DONE *Hist. Septuagint* 29 The exemplary of Demetrius his request to the King was this: Great sir, Since [etc.]. **1706** A. BEDFORD *Temple Mus.* vii. 143 Moses had ordered the Kings a Copy of the Law. The Exemplary of the Temple was taken away.

†**e'xemplate.** *Obs. rare*⁻¹. [ad. late L. *exemplāt-um*, neut. pa. pple. of *exemplāre*: see next.] Something made after an exemplar or pattern. Contrasted with *exemplar*.

1677 GALE *Crt. Gentiles* II. IV. 321 The Divine Essence, which representes al things; as an Exemplar directes the operation of God in producing the Exemplates or things formed according thereunto.

†**exemplate,** *v. Obs. rare.* [f. late L. *exemplāt-*, ppl. stem of *exemplāre* 'to example' (in various senses), f. *exemplum* EXAMPLE.] *trans.* To show by examples.

c **1601** W. WATSON *Decacordon* 193 Might it be without offence to exemplate out of Parsons Philopater by what meanes the change of religion came, I could, etc.

†**e'xemplative,** *a. Obs. rare*⁻¹. [f. L. *exempl-um* EXAMPLE *sb.*; cf. *figurative*.] Furnishing an example.

c **1450** HENRYSON *Mor. Fab.* 84 The sentence was fructuous and agreable, In Moralitie exemplatiue prudent.

exemple, -er, obs. ff. EXAMPLE, -ER.

exemplifiable (ɛg,zɛmplɪ'faɪəb(ə)l), *a. rare.* [f. EXEMPLIFY + -ABLE.] That may be exemplified.

1807 COLERIDGE *Lit. Rem.* (1836) I. 263 The psychological cause is easily stated, and copiously exemplifiable. **1864** in WEBSTER; and in mod. Dicts.

†**e'xemplificate,** *v. Obs. rare*⁻¹. [f. med.L. *exemplificāt-* ppl. stem of *exemplificāre*: see EXEMPLIFY.] *trans.* = EXEMPLIFY 8.

1577–87 HOLINSHED *Chron.* III. 1124/1 The words whereof for the more euidence, I thought here to exemplificat.

†**e'xemplificate,** *sb. Obs. rare*⁻¹. [ad. med.L. **exemplificātum*, neut. of pa. pple. of *exemplificāre*: see prec.] A copy, transcript.

1577 HARRISON *England* II. xxv. (1877) I. 365 Sundrie exemplificats of the grants are yet to be seene in writing.

exemplification (ɛg,zɛmplɪfɪ'keɪʃən). [a. AF. *exemplification*, ad. med.L. *exemplificātiōn-em*, n. of action f. *exemplificāre*: see EXEMPLIFY.]

1. The action of exemplifying; showing or illustrating by example; an instance of this. *in exemplification of*: so as to exemplify.

1548 HALL *Chron.* Hen. VIII. an. 22 For the more exemplification of the same, he sent the Lorde de Roche with letters of credence. **1631** GOUGE *God's Arrows* III. §1. 179 Before the particular exemplification of the foresaid promise, the Issue thereof is inserted. **1779–81** JOHNSON *L.P.*, *Addison* Wks. III. 87 The mention of another like consequence from a like cause..is not a simile, but an exemplification. **1809** COLERIDGE *Friend* (1865) 20 So much in proof and exemplification of the probable expediency of pious deception. **1864** BURTON *Scot. Abr.* II. i. 60 In exemplification of some of the recondite principles laid down.

2. That which exemplifies, or serves as an illustration of a law, general principle, statement, etc.

1582 G. MARTIN in *Fulke's Defence* (1843) 490 As is plain by the exemplification immediately following, of king, and dukes, and other sent or appointed by him. **1650** ELDERFIELD *Tythes* 310 Let thy life be..a counterpart or exemplification of thy book of religion. **1798** MALTHUS *Popul.* (1817) I. 52 An exemplification of the obvious truth, that population cannot increase without the food to support it. **1865** GROTE *Plato* I. ii. 379 Particular exemplifications of the Beautiful, substituted in place of the general concept.

3. An attested copy or transcript of a record, deed, etc.

[**1382** *Act 1 Rich. II*, c. 4 Quodque exemplificaciones illæ ..ejusdem sint vigoris..sicut..munimenta illa forent. **1429** *Act 8 Hen. VI*, c. 12 Saunz ascun rasure en une mesme lieu en mesme lexemplification & lenrollement.] **1542–3** *Act 34–5 Hen. VIII*, c. 27 §39 Euery exemplificacion vpon any recorde..shall be sealed with the Kinges iudiciall seale. **1653** in Somers *Tracts* (1795) II. 538 To the Masters of the Chancery for examining every Skin of an Exemplification of a Record. **1767** T. HUTCHINSON *Hist. Coll. Mass.* II. 212 An exemplification of Burgess's commission was obtained. **1884** *Roscoe's Law of Evidence* (ed. 15) 91 An exemplification produced from the proper custody..is evidence.

†**4.** ? A setting forth at length. *Obs.*

1588 J. H[ARVEY] *Disc. Probleme* 54 But which of them were the originall record of the maker, or phantastical exemplification of the writer..it is to little purpose to know.

Hence **e,xemplifi'cational** *a.*, of or pertaining to exemplification.

1826 BENTHAM in *Westm. Rev.* V. 498 Case to which the exemplificational [shape of a code] more particularly applies, that of an as yet only proposed code.

exemplificative (ɛg'zɛmplɪfɪkətɪv), *a.* Tending to exemplify; furnishing an example. Const. *of*.

1826 BENTHAM in *Westm. Rev.* VI. 498 Distinguishable shapes..the ratiocinative, the instructional, the exemplificative. **1889** F. HALL in *Nation* (N.Y.) XLVIII. 96/2 Of this truism..the still frequent onslaughts on reliable are noticeably exemplificative.

exemplificator (ɛg'zɛmplɪfɪ,keɪtə(r)). *rare*⁻¹. [a. med.L. *exemplificātor*, agent-n. f. *exemplificāre* (see EXEMPLIFY).] An exemplifier, exemplar.

1832 *Fraser's Mag.* VI. 604 Byron is the least exemplificator of this.

exemplified (ɛg'zɛmplɪfaɪd), *ppl. a.* [f. EXEMPLIFY + -ED¹.] In the senses of the verb. **a.** That has been copied out; of which an attested copy has been made. **b.** Made into an example; notorious.

1586 A. DAY *Eng. Secretary* II. (1625) 45 Your exemplified discourse. **1638** in Harwood *Lichfield* (1806) 482 As appeareth by the old exemplified lease. **1660** BOYLE *Seraphic Love* 72 Wonders wrought for a generation that.. ascrib'd them to the Devil, and return'd them with so exemplifi'd an Ingratitude. **1730–6** BAILEY (folio), *Exemplified*, cleared, proved or confirmed by an example or instance; also, copied out from a deed or writing.

exemplifier (ɛg'zɛmplɪfaɪə(r)). [f. as prec. + -ER¹.] One who exemplifies.

1552 HULOET, Exemplifier, or he that foloweth the example of others, *ascriptor*. *a* **1677** BARROW *Serm.* III. xlv. 374 Jesus (the Author, Master, and Exemplifyer of these doctrines). **1775** in ASH. **1832** in WEBSTER; and in mod. Dicts.

exemplify (ɛg'zɛmplɪfaɪ), *v.* Also 5–6 **examplify**. [ad. med.L. *exemplifi-cāre* f. *exemplum* EXAMPLE + *-ficāre*: see -FY.]

†**1.** *trans.* To instruct by example, set a (good) example to. Also *absol. Obs.*

1430 LYDG. *Chron. Troy* IV. xxxv, Priestes..should the worlde exemplefye With good doctryne of perfection. **1513** BRADSHAW *St. Werburge* I. 2299 To instructe and informe and to exemplyfy.

†**2.** *trans.* To make an example of (a person).

1632 B. JONSON *Magn. Lady* III. iv, Your exemplified malefactors, That have survived their infamy and punishment. **1642** D. ROGERS *Matrim. Honour* 337 A just and jealous God, not sparing to exemplifie..his best servants.

†**3.** To set an example of, exhibit a model of.

1649 SELDEN *Laws Eng.* II. xiii. (1739) 69 A thing that none of his Predecessors ever exemplified to him. **1673** *Lady's Call.* I. iii. 21 If the poor happen not to have more charity then they exemplify to them.

†**4.** To fashion after an example or model. *Obs.*

1579 FULKE *Heskins' Parl.* 475 They make the body of Christ, both the exemplar, and the thing exemplified. **1681–6** J. SCOTT *Chr. Life* (1747) III. 576 Those outward Images, which they exemplified from the Similitudes which they fram'd of him in their own Fancies.

†**5.** To adduce, allege, quote, use as an example. *to exemplify to*: to compare *to* by way of example or specimen. *to exemplify to be*: to quote by way of example as being. *Obs.*

1509 HAWES *Past. Pleas.* XI. xiii, For whych poetes hym so exemplyfied. **1592** DANIEL *Compl. Ros.* Wks. (1717) 39 Exemplify my Frailty. **1593** NASHE *4 Lett. Confut.* 54 Canst thou exemplifie vnto mee..one minnum of the particular deuice of his play that I purloind? *a* **1618** RALEIGH in Gutch *Coll. Cur.* I. 83 The emphyteusis or feudum..for understanding sake may be exemplified to an estate at this day allowed. **1641** MILTON *Ch. Govt.* II. (1851) 63 Not to exemplifie the malapert insolence of our owne Bishops. **1649** SELDEN *Laws Eng.* I. lxii. (1739) 121 Glanvil.. exemplifies Sedition and destruction of the Kingdom, to be in equal degree a Wound of Majesty. **1794** G. WAKEFIELD *Exam. Paine's Age of Reason* 24 To exemplify their morality in contradistinction to that of the gospel.

†**b.** *absol.* To find precedents, excuse oneself by example. *Obs.*

1597 DANIEL *Civ. Wares* I. xcvii, That our times might not have t' exemplifie with aged staines.

6. (The current sense.) **a.** To illustrate by examples; to find or furnish an example or instance of. Occas. with sentence as *obj.*

c **1430** LYDG. in *Pol., Rel. & L. Poems* (1866) 46, I exemplifye by kyndly prouidence Bewte wyll shew thow hornys be away. **1588** FRAUNCE (*title*), Lawiers Logike, exemplifying the præcepts of Logike by the practice of the Common Lawe. **1610** HEALEY *St. Aug. Citie of God* 214 His desire of..armes and war wherby to exemplifie his valour. **1637** GILLESPIE *Eng. Pop. Cerem.* II. iii. 18, I will really examplify that which I say. **1646** SIR T. BROWNE *Pseud. Ep.* II. vi. 22 How far they exceeded, may be exemplified from Palæphatus, in his book of fabulous narrations. **1668** BARROW in Rigaud *Corr. Sci. Men* (1841) II. 48 The rules I sent you concerning the hyperbola, I cannot well exemplify. **1752** JOHNSON *Rambler* No. 208 ¶3, I have rarely exemplified my assertions by living characters. **1818** JAS. MILL *Brit. India* II. v. viii. 683 A completeness never before exemplified. **1864** BP. OF LINCOLN *Charge* 8 Its Principal.. has exemplified to its pupils how labor best prospers when it is the labor of love. **1869** PHILLIPS *Vesuv.* ii. 31 Nor is it the earliest style of wall..exemplified in Mycenæ.

b. To be or serve as an example of.

1793 BEDDOES *Math. Evid.* 147 The mode of expression of children and Africans frequently exemplifies this remark. **1845** MCCULLOCH *Taxation* II. vi. (1852) 277 The roads in the Highlands exemplify the correctness of this statement. **1860** TYNDALL *Glac.* II. xxx. 406 The third action is exemplified by the state of the rails near a station, etc. **1878** C. STANFORD *Symb. Christ* i. 31 The principle which the ancient payment of tithes exemplified.

c. *intr.* To quote examples or instances by way of illustration. †*to exemplify in, of*: = 'to instance in', i.e. to cite (something) as an instance.

1582 G. MARTIN in Fulke *Def.* (1843) 213 Suppose he had exemplified of the two condemned heretics, Jovinian and Vigilantius also. **1587** HARRISON *England* II. v. (1877) I. 136, I could exemplifie also in manie other. **1598** R. HAYDOCKE tr. *Lomazzo on Painting* II. 157 And thus, if I woulde inlarge my discourse, I might exemplifie in the light passing through a glasse ful of red wine. **1619** BRENT tr. *Sarpi's Hist. Counc. Trent.* (1676) 590 He exemplified in Darius, who, etc. **1641** BP. HALL *Misch. Faction* Rem. Wks. (1660) 66 It were to no purpose to exemplifie, where the instances are numberlesse.

7. To make an official copy of; *esp.* to make an attested copy of (a legal document) under an official seal.

1523 FITZHERB. *Surv.* 20b, Any partie..may..haue a copye..exemplyfied vnder the seale of offyce of the same place. **1581** *Act 23 Eliz.* c. 3 §3 Fines..shall be exemplified under the Great Seal of England. **1603** HOLLAND *Plutarch's Mor.* 928 He proposed..that their tragœdies should be exemplified and engrossed faire. **1687** *Lond. Gaz.* No. 2277/4 The Laws for the preservation of the Spawn and Spatt of Oysters..were Signed and Exemplified under the Seal of the High Court of Admiralty. **1710** *Ibid.* No. 4735/4 Which Recovery was exemplified under the Great Seal. **1884** *Roscoe's Law of Evidence* (ed. 15) 91 An exemplification produced from the proper custody and purporting to exemplify a commission from the crown is evidence though the seal has been lost.

†**8.** To copy (a document); to quote in writing.

1570–6 LAMBARDE *Peramb. Kent* (1826) 221 The storie of King Vortigers Wassailing..I have already exemplified. **1581** —— *Eiren.* II. iv. (1588) 149 This last Statute I have exemplified the more at large. **1629** A. HAMILTON in *Ussher's Lett.* (1686) 405 If your Grace..hath a mind to exemplify, write out, or collect any thing out of any of the said Books. **1665** J. WEBB *Stone-Heng* (1725) 85 That Inscription..mentioned by Camden..and by him exemplified. **1709** STRYPE *Ann. Ref.* I. ii. 58 Because it is a private act, and unprinted, I exemplify it in the Appendix.

‖**exempli gratia** (ɛg'zɛmplɪ 'greɪʃɪə), *phr.* Also **exempli causa.** [L.] For the sake of example; for instance. Freq. abbreviated to *e.g.* (see E III), occas. *ex. gr.*

1569 ABP. PARKER *Let.* 1 July (1853) 352 *Exempli causa*, I urge the Injunction upon all ministers. **1654** GAYTON *Pleas. Notes* 102 The intrinsecall radicall moysture must be supplied, recruited, and replenished with the extrinsecall liquids, that is, *exempli gratia*, in the morning with a sphericall Tost in a pot of Ale of good capacity. **1765** GIBBON *Let.* 31 Oct. in *Misc. Wks.* (1796) I. 437 *Exempli gratiâ*, your letter is dated Vienna, October 12th, 1765; it made its appearance at Beriton,..October 29th. **1798** COLERIDGE *Lett.* (1884) 61 There are some ludicrous blunders—exemp. gratiâ—this erudite philosopher mistakes Moses's autograph for the publication of the law. **1802** *Ibid.* 85 In English now, *exem. causâ*, we might say, [etc.]. **1868** G. V. COX *Recoll. Oxford* iv. 45 His subtle and ingenious narration of Aesop's Fable of the Dog and the Wolf, and his running comments on it, Ex. gr. 'Just see how fat and sleek I am,' said the Dog. **1933** *Nature* 7 Oct. 533/1 The concept and the word are freely scattered through Wheatstone's Bakerian lecture of 1843, where we find, *ex gr.*, 'in two circuits..when the same resistance is introduced, the strength of the two currents may be weakened'.

‖**exemplum** (ɛg'zɛmpləm). Pl. **exempla.** [L., see EXAMPLE *sb.*] An example; *spec.* a moralizing tale or parable; an illustrative story.

1890 T. F. CRANE *J. de Vitry's Exempla* p. lxxx, The *exempla* which we have thus far examined have been illustrative stories intended for insertion in sermons. The moral lesson to be drawn from them was left..to..the preacher. In other words, the *exemplum* was a story which had no independent value, and..was..to be expanded at the preacher's will. **1910** *Encycl. Brit.* IX. 610/2 Homilies.. abounding in *exempla* or illustrative stories. **1954** B. WHITE in *Year's Work Eng. Studies 1952* 63 Considered as a piece of 'practical advice for comfortable living in a world not operated altogether under reason and justice', an exemplum told to illustrate and enforce a thesis, the tale is artistically and dramatically satisfying. **1956** *Essays & Studies* New Ser. IX. 57 Shakespeare, Blake and Dante: all three offering ..*exempla* of the energy to be derived from sexual experience. **1968** *Neophilologus* 171 In order to make the sermon more convincing, the preacher..here introduces an *exemplum*—that of the thief on the cross who, by sincere penitence, entered through the Gates of Paradise with his Lord.

†**e'xemply,** *v. Obs.* Also **examply.** [ad. OF. *exemplier*, f. *exemple*: see EXAMPLE *sb.*] *trans.* = EXEMPLIFY 6 and 7.

1561 EDEN (*title*) Martin Cortes' Art of Navigation.. examplied [Sp. *exemplificado*] by many Demonstrations. **1656** *Burton's Diary* (1828) I. 184 They produced an Act of Parliament..exemplied [? *mispr. for* exemplified] under seal, and offered it to a clerk to read it.

e'xempt (ɛg'zɛm(p)t), *ppl. a.* and *sb.* [a. Fr. *exempt* = Pr. *exempt*, ad. L. *exempt-us*, pa. pple. of *eximĕre* to take out, f. *ex-* out + *emĕre* to take.]

A. *pple.* and *adj.*

1. With distinctly ppl. sense: = *exempted* pa. pple. and ppl. adj.

a. Taken away, removed *from*; abolished. *Obs.* exc. *arch.* †**b.** = EXCEPTED; also *exempt case*; cf. EXEMPTED. *Obs.* †**c.** Cut off, debarred, excluded. *Obs.* †**d.** Removed *from* (*out of*) allegiance, liability, or obligation to. *Obs.*

The pple. may have been referred variously to the Eng. vbs. *exeme*, *exempt*, or have been employed in direct imitation of the use of L. *exemptus*.

a. *c* **1374** CHAUCER *Boeth.* II. vii. 60 Þe soule..beynge in heuene reioiseþ þat it is exempt from alle erþely þinges. **1551** ROBINSON tr. *More's Utop.* I. (Arb.) 46 They..be cleane quite and exempte out of the bondes and daunger to Gods commaundement. *a* **1631** DONNE *6 Serm.* i. (1634) 18 Men appropriated to God, men exempt out of the world. **1697** DRYDEN *Æneid* VII. 287 When exempt from Mortal Earth. **1874** HOLLAND *Mistr. Manse* 125 Blessed Sleep! in which exempt From our tired Selves long hours we lie.

b. **1426** *Pol. Poems* (1859) II. 137 The cours suyng in alle is hole entent, And in no wise list not be exempte. **1679** DRYDEN & LEE *Œdipus* 15 Hear then this dreadful imprecation; hear it: 'Tis lay'd on all; not any one exempt. **1705** STANHOPE *Paraphr.* IV. 572 These are very rare and exempt cases. **1788** WESLEY *Wks.* (1872) VI. 281 With regard even to these exempt cases.

c. *c* **1450** *Castle Hd. Life St. Cuthb.* (Surtees) 3712 My teching eftir my dissese Sall' noȝt be had in contempt, Na all' oute of doyng all exempt. *c* **1450** LONELICH *Grail* I. 562 In Wanhope weren they falle, and exempt from graces alle. *c* **1500** *Melusine* 8 Whens may be suche a fayr..lady..so exempt & vnpurveyed of felawship. **1580** LUPTON *Sivqila* 111 Judges that favour falshood shall be exempt from Gods presence. **1598–9** E. FORDE *Parismus* I. (1661) 49 Being exempt from the clear light of the sun.

d. *c* **1380** WYCLIF *Sel. Wks.* III. 351 Þei [priests] ben exempt fro Goddis lawe by privylegies þat þei han getun. *a* **1400** *Cov. Myst.* (Shaks. Soc.) 209 Alle thynge must obeye to Goddys look, Out of his myght is non exempt. **1482** *Monk of Evesham* (Arb.) 101 Y saw hym..exempte and delyueryd frome al peynys. **1513–4** *Act 5 Hen. VIII*, c. 6 [They] haue been exempt and discharged from all offices and businesse. **1538** STARKEY *England* II. iii. 205, I wold haue no offycer of cyte nor towne to be exempt from theyr authoryte. **1651** DAVENANT *Gondibert* I. IV. ii, Lands exempt from Nature's law.

†**2.** Picked out, choice, select. *Obs.*

c **1611** CHAPMAN *Iliad* IX. 604 Of whose faire sexe, we come to offer seauen, The most exempt for excellence.

†**3.** Not subject to a superior authority; independent. *Obs.*

1552 HULOET, Exempt or privileged by the kinges charter, *exemptus*. **1583** STUBBES *Anat. Abus.* II. 8 Is the lande diuided into shires, counties, precincts, and seuerall exempt liberties? **1601** HOLLAND *Pliny* I. 73 The Locri, surnamed Ozolæ, free states and exempt. **1628** COKE *On Litt.* 133 The wife of the King of England is an exempt person from the King, and is capable of lands. **1738** *Common Sense* (1739) II. 113 The Tea-Table is a Place which seems to prescribe for an exempt Jurisdiction from Common Sense.

b. *esp.* of a monastery or other religious foundation. *Obs.* exc. *Hist.*

1460 CAPGRAVE *Chron.* 261 William bischop of Canntirbury..gat..bulles fro the Court to have IIIId. of the pound, both of exempt [cherchis] and not exempt. **1525** (*title*), The Boke of Comfort..Enprented in the Exempt Monastery of Tavestok in Denshyre. **1621** ABP. ABBOT in *Fortesc. Papers* 165 The Churche of Westminster being an exempt and privileged place. **1726** AYLIFFE *Parerg.* 13 An Abbot cannot without the Knowledge and Advice of his Convent, subject an Exempt Monastery to any Person. **1868** STANLEY *Westm. Ab.* vi. 516 The Primate..preferred to avoid the question of the exempt jurisdiction of Westminster.

4. Freed *from* allegiance or liability to; not subject to the control or influence of.

1667 MILTON *P.L.* II. 318 To live exempt From Heav'ns high jurisdiction. **1716** LADY M. W. MONTAGUE *Lett.* xli. II. 11 There were some people exempt from their [enchantments'] power. **1850** GLADSTONE *Glean.* (1879) V. lxiii. 211 There is no European country in which ecclesiastical societies are exempt from civic control. **1874** MICKLETHWAITE *Mod. Par. Churches* 117 The old builders neither were infallible, nor are exempt from criticism.

5. Not liable to suffering, hardship, or inconvenience †*of, from*; not exposed or subject to: **a.** danger, disease, or evil of any kind.

a **1420** HOCCLEVE *De Reg. Princ.* 1116 This worldes power and riche abundaunce Of drede of perile never ben exempte. **1490** CAXTON *Eneydos* viii. (1890) 35 To kepe hir cyte and the cytezeyns vnhurt and exempt from oppressyons. *a* **1637** B. JONSON (J.), To..live exempt From all the nets that thou canst spread. **1658** EVELYN *Fr. Gard.* (1675) 199 Where they may be exempt from the frost. **1711** STEELE *Spect.* No. 4 ¶2 Exempt from the Passions with which others are tormented. **1759** J. MILLS *Duhamel's Husb.* II. ii. (1762) 241, I did not see any one field exempt from this distemper. **1846** TRENCH *Mirac.* xxix. (1862) 393 They whom Christ loves are no more exempt than others from their share of earthly trouble and anguish.

b. a charge, duty, payment, tax, etc.

1471 RIPLEY *Comp. Alch.* in Ashm. (1652) 108 Exempt from Claustrall observance. **1517** in *Vicary's Anat.* (1888) App. viii. 212 Those Surgeons which be exempt from Almaner offices, enquestes & wacches. **1555** *Fardle Facions* I. v. 62 This sorte of menne is priuileged, and exempte from all maner of charges. **1794** SULLIVAN *View Nat.* II. 432 These..lived exempt from all public concerns and duties. **1853** STOCQUELER *Mil. Encycl.* s.v., Men of a certain age are exempt from serving in the militia. **1871** MORLEY *Voltaire* (1886) 75 A man because he is a noble or a priest was not exempt from paying certain taxes.

6. Unsullied, unaffected by; clear, free *from* (a defect, flaw, stain, weakness).

1586 A. DAY *Eng. Secretary* I. (1625) 8 These..being utterly exempt from any waight or gravity at all, are rightly termed..familiar letters. *c* **1611** CHAPMAN *Iliad* VIII. 435 Hector..led to a place, pure and exempt from blood, The Trojan forces. *a* **1704** T. BROWN *Sat. agst. Woman* Wks. 1730 I. 57 Celia alone's exempt from all these crimes. **1821** SHELLEY *Prometh. Unb.* III. iv. 156 From custom's evil taint exempt and pure. **1875** SCRIVENER *Lect. Grk. Test.* 6 Not exempt from the common failings of humanity.

B. *sb.*

1. *gen.* An exempted person; *esp.* one relieved from performance of a duty, payment of a tax, etc.

1846 PRESCOTT *Ferd. & Is.* II. II. iii. 315 The only legal exempts [from this military service] were the clergy, hidalgos, and paupers. **1860** EMERSON *Cond. Life* ix. 184 To point at one or another fine madman, as if there were any exempts. **1876** BANCROFT *Hist. U.S.* IV. xxvii. 518 Old men ..who were exempts, except in case of immediate danger to the town.

2. *Eccl.* A person or religious establishment not subject to the jurisdiction of the bishop. Cf. A. 3 b. *Obs.* exc. *Hist.*

1532 R. BOWYER in Strype *Eccl. Mem.* I. xvii. 134 Reformators of divers orders of religion..as well exempts as not exempts. **1577** HARRISON *England* II. ii. (1877) I. 42 Though it [the archdeaconrie of S. Albons] be under the Bishop of London for visitations & synods, yet is it otherwise reputed as member of the see of Lincolne, and therefore worthily called an exempt. **1706** tr. *Dupin's Eccl. Hist. 16th C.* II. IV. xxi. 377 The Holidays..shall also be observed by all Regulars, even Exempts.

†**3.** In the French army: **a.** An inferior cavalry officer who commanded in the absence of the captain and lieutenant, and was exempt from ordinary military duty. *Obs.* exc. *Hist.*

1670 COTTON *Espernon* II. VIII. 347 Mazure, and du Lion Exempts of her Guards. **1702** *Lond. Gaz.* No. 3822/3 Our Men took an Exempt of the Life-Guard. **1751** SMOLLETT *Per. Pic.* (1779) II. xlv. 83 A file of musqueteers commanded by an Exempt [in Paris]. **1753** *Scots Mag.* XV. 64/1 Three exempts of the guards. **1823** in CRABB *Technol. Dict.*

†**b.** A French police officer. *Obs.* exc. *Hist.*

Originally, a sub-officer of the mounted police (*maréchaussée*) corresponding in rank and function to the 'exempts' of the cavalry.

1678 tr. *Gaya's Art of War* I. 34 The Provost Mareschal ..hath a Troop of Officers on Horseback, with a Lieutenant, Exempts, etc. **1772** *Birmingham Counterf.* I. 240 In the midst of this scene, an exempt of the police arrives. **1840** THACKERAY *Paris Sk. Bk.* (1867) 115 He slipped through the exempts, quite unsuspected.

4. In the English army †**a.** after Fr. usage: A sub-officer of cavalry. *Obs.*

1706 PHILLIPS (ed. Kersey), *An Exempt*, a Life-Guard.. free from Duty. **1721–1800** in BAILEY. **1739** LADY HARTFORD *Corr.* (1806) I. 116 An exempt in my Lord's Troop.

b. One of the four officers who in turn command the Yeomen of the Guard in the absence of their superior officers. Now more commonly EXON^{1}, q.v.

1700 LUTTRELL *Brief Rel.* (1857) IV. 711 Mr. Dormer is made exempt of the yeomen of the guards in the room of Mr. Uphill. **1717** *Hist. Reg., Chron. Diary* 5 One of the Exempts of his Majesty's Yeomen of the Guards. **1844** W. J. THOMS *Bk. of Court* (ed. 2) 370 The Exempt of the Yeomen of the Guard is a resident officer who sleeps at St. James's, as Commandant of the Yeomen on duty.

exempt (ɛg'zɛm(p)t), *v.* Pa. pple. 5–6 **exempt.** [ad. Fr. *exempter*, f. *exempt* adj.: see *prec.*]

†**1.** *trans.* To take out or away; to put far away, remove, cut off. Const. *from, out of. Obs.*

1553 T. WILSON *Rhet.* 39 Exempted from Sathan, to lyve for ever with Christe our Savioure. **1563** *Homilies* II. *Right Use Church* II. (1859) 165 They..were exempted and banished (as it were) from the house of the Lord. **1565** GOLDING *Ovid's Met.* IV. (1593) 97 He hist: for nature now had cleane exempt All other speach. **1589** GREENE *Arcadia* (1616) 40 Ile exempt them [flowers] all from my smell. **1595** R. JOHNSON *7 Champions* II. v. (1608) 4 The Emperours onely daughter..exempted herselfe from all company. **1599** A. M. tr. *Gabelhouer's Bk. Physicke* 4/1 The payne will totallye be exemptede, and abolishede. **1635** *Tom a Lincolne* in Thoms *Prose Rom.* (1858) II. 267 Being once exempted from my sight.

†**b.** To single out, select. *Obs.*

1538 STARKEY *England* I. iv. 139 For theyr vertue they schold be..from the commyn pepul, as hyt were, exemptyd. **1548** UDALL, etc. *Erasm. Par. Matt.* i. 22 She exempted out of the sorte and order of common women, was chosen. **1648** MILTON *Sonn.* xiii. *To H. Lawes*, Thy worth and skill exempts thee from the throng.

†**2.** To take away or omit (from a category or enumeration); to except. Const. *from, out of*; rarely with double *obj.* Also in the pa. pple. in concord with a sb. in the nominative absolute; = EXCEPT 3 b; and in the pr. pple. used absol. as quasi-*prep.*; = EXCEPTING *prep.* A. 1. *Obs.*

1548 GEST *Pr. Masse* 120 Praying to Christ at the masse, hys supper or els where, heaven exempted. **1571** FORTESCUE *Forest Hist.* 5 A small matter is it in niene hundred or a thousande yeeres to exempte twentie or thirtie. **1581** J. BELL *Haddon's Answ. Osor.* 129 S. John..doth not exempt himselfe out of the same number. **1586** A. DAY *Eng. Secretary* I. (1625) 53 The ordering whereof (except in Letters *Excusatorie*, or *Defensorie*) is wholly exempted the course in those Letters prescribed. **1604** HOOKER *Eccl. Pol.* Pref. viii. §9 Their error exempted [*ed.* **1594** excepted] they seemed otherwise right good men. **1665** GLANVILL *Sceps. Sci.* ix. 47 While all complain of Ignorance and Error, every one exempts himself. **1731** *Lett. from Fog's Jrnl.* (1732) II. 286 Invited..by all Ranks..not exempting even a Branch of the Royal Family.

†**3.** To debar, exclude *from* the enjoyment of or participation in something. *Obs.*

1553 T. WILSON *Rhet.* 101 b, They..exempted brybers frome bearynge rule in the commune weale. **1579** NORTH *Plutarch, Agesilaus* 670 Them selues [the Thebans] onely exempted from treatie of peace. **1667** H. MORE *Div. Dial.* I. xxxv. (1713) 78 Cogitation is..exempted or prescinded from all Extension. **1689** EVELYN *Mem.* (1857) II. 311 The Convention..exempt the Duke of Hanover from the succession to the Crown.

4. To grant to (a person, etc.) immunity or freedom *from* a liability to which others are subject:

a. from (the payment of) a fine, tax, etc. Also const. *of, simply,* and *absol.*

1467 in *Eng. Gilds* (1870) 393 Euery citezen and Burgeys w^toutforth shal pay at euery taske, vigille, lones..except certeyn persones that..be exemted. **1496–7** *Act 12 Hen. VII*, c. 13 § 1 Tounes and places..exempted or discharged of payment to suche xv^{mes}. **1573** COOPER *Thesaur., Eximere de vectigalibus*, to exempt from paying tribute. **1705** ARBUTHNOT *Coins* 279 Valentinian..exempted them [Mariners] from all Taxes. **1855** THACKERAY *Newcomes* I. 149 When did..his bailiff exempt from the rent? **1872** YEATS *Growth Comm.* 163 Other towns were exempted.. from..customs dues.

b. from (the control of) laws, (obedience to) an authority.

1401 *Pol. Poems* (1859) II. 28 Why have ye exempt you from our kings lawes. **1530** PALSGR. 541/2 Many abbayes be exempted from their bysshoppe. **1655** FULLER *Ch. Hist.* II. iii. §25 King Kenulphus..had power to exempt this Abbot from the Iurisdiction of the Bishop. **1761** HUME *Hist. Eng.* III. liv. 160 Those high churchmen..were desirous of exempting the mitre from all subjection to the crown. **1829** I. TAYLOR *Enthus.* ii. (1867) 33 The religious emotions are exempted from this general law.

c. from pain, penalty, suffering, or inconvenience; also, from a defect, weakness, etc.

1484 CAXTON *Curiall* 1 Fortune hath exempte the fro the anguysshes that I suffre. **1561** T. NORTON *Calvin's Inst.* III. 195 Y^{e} cursednesse of old Adam, from which we are exempted by Christ. **1647** CLARENDON *Hist. Reb.* I. (1843) 4/1 The course of exempting men from prosecution, by dissolving of parliaments. **1692** BENTLEY *Boyle Lect.* ix. 330 Our Saviour's own Disciples were not exempted from the common Error. **1707** *Curios. in Husb. & Gard.* 218 A Delay from which we are exempted by our new Method. **1856** FROUDE *Hist. Eng.* (1858) I. v. 443 Clergy who committed felony were no longer exempted from the penalties of their crimes.

d. from a burden, duty, or obligation, a burdensome state or condition.

1479 in *Eng. Gilds* (1870) 414 King Edwarde the thirdde ..by his honourable chartres exemptid the saide maires, to ..feche their saide charges at the castell Yate. **1571** GOLDING *Calvin on Ps.* xxxiii. 16 Kings and Tyrants..being exempted from the comon lot, seeme to themselves to be out of danger of gunshot. **1603** KNOLLES *Hist. Turks* (J.), The religious were not exempted, but fought among the other soldiers. *c* **1665** MRS. HUTCHINSON *Mem. Col. Hutchinson* (1846) 39 Living constantly in the country he could not be exempted from administering justice among them. **1703** MAUNDRELL *Journ. Jerus.* (1732) 128 The Beast..has the privilege to be exempted from all other Burdens ever after. **1718** LADY M. W. MONTAGUE *Lett.* I. II. 70 The quarantine, from which nobody is exempted. **1836** LANE *Mod. Egypt.* II. 345 The Copts..are exempted from military service. **1845** McCULLOCH *Taxation* Introd. (1852) 36 A conscription..pressing with its utmost severity on certain classes of the population, and exempting others.

exempted (ɛg'zɛm(p)tɪd), *ppl. a.* [f. prec. + -ED^{1}.] †**a.** Withdrawn from care; unburdened. Of a soul: Withdrawn from the body; separate. †**b.** = EXCEPTED. **c.** To whom immunity (from punishment, burdens, or obligations) has been granted.

1598 YONG *Diana* 76 In braue loue and fortunes art, There is not anything lesse sure Then such a free exempted hart. **1603** R. NICCOLS *Fun. Orat. Q. Eliz.*, If exempted soules may be subject to passions. **1712** BERKELEY *Pass. Obed.* §17 Whether obedience to the supreme power be not one of those exempted cases. **1725–6** POPE *Odyss.* XXII. 418 With tim'rous awe From the dire scene th' exempted two withdraw. **1775** BURKE *Sp. Conc. Amer.* Wks. 1842 I. 199 The abuses have been full as great..in the exempted as in the punished.

†**e'xemptible.** *Obs.* [f. EXEMPT *v.* + -IBLE.] **a.** Capable of being exempted. **b.** That may be easily removed; = next.

1611 COTGR., *Exemptible*, Exemptible; loosse, free, quit, priuiledged. **1623–6** COCKERAM, *Exemptible*, which may be easily taken away.

exemptile (ɛg'zɛm(p)tɪl), *a.* [ad. late L. *exemptil-is*, f. *eximĕre*: see EXEMPT *a.*] That may be taken out, removable.

1607 TOPSELL *Four-f. Beasts* (1673) 352 Jupiter..gave her [Lamia] exemptile eyes that might be taken in and out at her own pleasure. **1657** TOMLINSON *Renou's Disp.* 488 A Money-Counter..should have many exemptile boxes in its antick part. **1832** LEWIS in *Philol. Mus.* I. 137 He withheld the pay and provisions of his mercenaries on the exemptile days (ἐξαιρέσιμοι ἡμέραι).

exemption (ɛg'zɛm(p)ʃən). Forms: 4–5 **exempcion, -coun,** (6 **-tioun**), 6– **exemption.** [a. Fr. *exemption*, ad. L. *exemptiōn-em*, n. of action f. *eximĕre* to EXEMPT.] The action of exempting; the state of being exempted.

†**1. a.** The action of taking out or away; the state of being taken out or away. **b.** Exception, exclusion from an enumeration, etc. *Obs.*

a. 1598 ROWLANDS *Betraying of Christ* 44 By death of Christ, the Law was in exemption. **1610** GUILLIM *Heraldry* II. iii. (1611) 42 Adumbration or Transparency is a cleere exemption of the substance of the charge.

b. 1538 STARKEY *England* I. iv. 139 Thys exemptyon..ys to be gyven to the dygnyte of presthod. **1670** G. H. *Hist. Cardinals* I. III. 70 The Cardinals should be chosen out of all the Provinces..without exemption of any.

2. a. The action of exempting, or the state of being exempted (see EXEMPT *v.* 4) from a liability, obligation, penalty, law, or authority; freeing, freedom; an instance of the same, an immunity.

c **1380** WYCLIF *Wks.* (1880) 93 He schal geten a priueilege or exempcion..for his gold sent & spendid at rome. **1488–9** *Act 4 Hen. VII*, c. 5 This acte of adnullacion..of exempcions of payment or colleccion of dismes. **1578** *Gude & Godl. Ball.* 77 Our tungis hes ane exemptioun. **1651** HOBBES *Leviath.* II. xxi. 109 We take Liberty, for an exemption from Lawes. **1656** BRAMHALL *Replic.* iv. 189 King Henries exemption of himself from all spirituall jurisdiction. **1671** MILTON *P.R.* III. 115 Thy great Father.. requires Glory from all men..no exemption. **1705** BURNET *Own Time* v. (1734) II. 158 An exemption for twenty one years from all Taxes and Customs. **1742** YOUNG *Nt. Th.* v. 262 Genius..pleads exemption from the laws of sense. **1809** TOMLINS *Law Dict.* s.v., A writ of exemption, or of ease, to be quit of serving on juries, and all public service. **1825** BENTHAM *Ration. Rew.* 14 An exemption from punishment already incurred, is a pardon. **1874** GREEN *Short Hist.* iv. 172 Some [boroughs] bought charters of exemption from the troublesome privilege [of sending burgesses to parliament].

b. *spec.* 'A privilege by which persons or places are withdrawn from the jurisdiction of the ordinary and immediately subjected to the Holy See' (*Catholic Dict.* 1885).

1460 CAPGRAVE *Chron.* 167 There was the Provincial of the ordre alegging for him here exempcion. **1661** BRAMHALL *Just Vind.* 145 He complains..of the exemption of Abbats from their Bishops. **1751** CHAMBERS *Cycl.* s.v., The first exemptions granted to monks were only for the liberty of electing their abbot, independently on the bishop. **1868** J. H. BLUNT *Ref. Ch. Eng.* I. 7 He protests especially against exemptions.

3. Freedom, immunity *from* a defect, disadvantage, or weakness.

a **1662** HEYLIN *Laud* I. (1671) 53 Humane frailty from which the holiest and most Learned men cannot plead Exemption. **1711** ADDISON *Spect.* No. 105 ¶ 5 The Men who value themselves most on their Exemption from the Pedantry of Colleges. **1784** COWPER *Task* I. 404 Even age itself seems privileged in them With clear exemption from its own defects. **1842** H. ROGERS *Introd. Burke's Wks.* I. 7 A tolerable exemption from faults..will generally be their highest merit. **1853** KANE *Grinnell Exped.* xxiv. (1856) 199 Water free from ice; the exemption being due to the island ..acting as a barrier. **1884** *Q. Rev.* Apr. 350 A singular exemption from the ferocious forms of life.

†**4.** *concr.* (see quot.) *Obs. rare*$^{-1}$.

a **1610** HEALEY *Theophrastus* To Rdr., Pomœrium is a certaine space about the walls of the City or Towne.. where 'tis not lawfull to plough, build houses, or inhabite.. termed the territorie, or exemption.

5. *attrib.* (sense 2).

1898 *Daily News* 5 July 2/5 Under the exemption clauses of the Acts. **1902** *Westm. Gaz.* 16 Aug. 2/3 Exemption certificates. **1909** *Englishwoman* Apr. 286 The Home Secretary's withdrawal of the Exemption Order.

† **exemp'titious**, *a. Obs.* [f. L. *exempt-* (see EXEMPT *v.*) + -ITIOUS.] Capable of being taken out; separable.

1667 H. MORE *Div. Dial.* I. xxv. (1713) 50 If Motion were a thing that was loose or exemptitious from Matter.

exemptive (ɛg'zɛm(p)tɪv), *a. rare.* [f. as prec. + -IVE.] Tending to procure exemption (from guilt or punishment).

1827 BENTHAM *Ration. Evid.* Wks. 1843 VII. 15 To disprove the commission of the crime.. by proving the existence of some.. exemptive circumstance.

exen, obs. form of *oxen*: see OX.

‖ **exencephalus** (ɛksɛn'sɛfələs). Pl. exencephali. [mod.L. *exencephalus*, f. Gr. ἐξ out + ἐγκέφαλος brain.] 'I. G. St. Hilaire's term for a monstrosity in which the brain lies wholly or chiefly outside the cranial cavity at the back of a very flattened head' (*Syd. Soc. Lex.* 1884).

exenterate (ɛk'sɛntərət), *ppl. a.* [ad. L. *exenterāt-us*, pa. pple. of *exenterāre*: see next.] = EXENTERATED.

1835 SOUTHEY in C. C. Southey *Life* VI. 280 The pig.. which.. was not yet bacon.. scalded, exenterate and hardly yet cold. **1868** BROWNING *Ring & Bk.* v. 2010 A soldier bee That yields his life exenterate with the stroke O' the sting that saves the hive.

exenterate (ɛk'sɛntəreɪt), *v.* Also 7 exenterat. [f. L. *exenterāt-* (*exinterāt-*) ppl. stem of *exenterāre* (*exinterāre*, f. *ex-* out + Gr. ἔντερ-ον intestine. Cf. Gr. ἐξεντερίζειν.]

1. *trans.* To take out the entrails of; to eviscerate, disembowel. *Obs.* in literal sense.

1613 PURCHAS *Pilgrimage* v. xv. §3 (R.) In this beastly caruing of humane bodies.. sometimes exenterating women. **1630** DONNE *Serm.* xxv. 246 Such bodies as were exenterated and embowelled and then.. plastered about with spices and gums. **1646** SIR T. BROWNE *Pseud. Ep.* III. xiii. 136 Nor doe they [toads] containe.. urinary parts.. as may appeare unto any that exenterats or dissects them. *a* **1697** AUBREY *Life Bacon* in *Lett. Emin. Persons* (1813) II. 227 They went into a poore woman's house.. and bought a hen, and made the woman exenterate it. **1721–1800** in BAILEY.

fig. **1636** W. AMBROSE in *Ann. Dubrensia* 37 Summon the world, exenterate old stories. **1641** *Frogs of Egypt* 5 Great God!.. Who justly dost exenterate with shame All Enemies to Thee. **1822** SOUTHEY *Lett.* (1856) III. 337 A boxful of papers.. which I have to read and exenterate. **1886** BLACKIE in *19th Cent.* Apr. 535 Exenterating itself of its own better soul.

† **2.** To take out (the bowels or internal parts).

1607 TOPSELL *Four-f. Beasts* (1673) 21 The reins [of an Ape] exenterated, bruised and put into new pure wine. **1609** BP. BARLOW *Answ. Nameless Catholic* 68 A Carrionly Curre, entring her Tombe, and exenterating her very bowels to staunch his rage.

trans. **1612** J. COTTON *Dang. Pract. Physic* II. i. 88 They unlawfully exenterate and eate out the bowels of poore mens purses. **1623** MABBE tr. *Aleman's Guzman d'Alf.* II. 212 It [riches] exenterates and pulls out the very bowells from the profoundest parts of the earth.

Hence **e'xenterated** *ppl. a.*, deprived of entrails, disembowelled: also *fig.* **e'xenterating** *vbl. sb.*

1657 TOMLINSON *Renou's Disp.* 88 Exenterated animals.. are stuffed with medicamental things. **1663** *Flagellum or O. Cromwell* (1672) 17 The Kingdom had one Viper more fostered, to the exenterating of her bowels. **1827** HARE *Guesses* (1859) 141 Exenterated rulemongers and eviscerated logicians. **1857** KINGSLEY *Two Y. Ago* I. 60 Fragments of exenterated maids (belonging to the order Pisces).

exenteration (ɛksɛntə'reɪʃən). [as if ad. L. **exenterātiōn-em*, n. of action f. *exenterāre*: see EXENTERATE.]

1. The action or process of exenterating or taking out the entrails.

1646 SIR T. BROWNE *Pseud. Ep.* III. xxi. 157 Upon exenteration he found these animals in their bellies. **1705** T. GREENHILL *Embalming* 121 If we can arrive at this Perfection, without Exenteration or Incision. **1823** MOORE *Rhymes on Road* Introd. 59 A hero.. wrote..'mid all the pains And horrors of exenteration, Nine charming odes. **1884** *Cornh. Mag.* July 69 There is no exenteration, no steeping in palm-wine.

fig. **1808** LAMB *Charac. Dram. Writers* Wks. 531 A faint bodily image of this.. exenteration of the inmost mind. **1850** KINGSLEY *Alt. Locke* xix, There is self-exenteration enough and to spare in my story.

2. The condition of being devoid of entrails.

1831 *Fraser's Mag.* IV. 633 A lankness of figure that denoted almost utter exenteration.

exenteritis (ɛksɛntə'raɪtɪs). *Path.* [f. EX- *pref.*² + ENTERITIS.] 'Inflammation of the outer or peritoneal coat of the intestines' (*Syd. Soc. Lex.*).

1847 in CRAIG.

exept, obs. form of EXCEPT.

† **exe'quation.** *Obs. rare*⁻¹. [ad. L. *exæquātiōn-em*, f. *exæquāre* to make equal, f. *ex-* (see EX- *pref.*¹) + *æqu-us* EQUAL.] The state of being exactly equal.

1656 JEANES *Fuln. Christ* 138 The union is not by way of exequation, or equipatency.

exequatur (ɛksɪ'kweɪtə(r)). [a. L. *exequātur* he may perform, 3rd pers. sing. pres. subj. of *exequī* (see EXECUTE).]

1. An official recognition of a consul or commercial agent by the government of the country to which he is accredited, authorizing him to exercise his power.

1788 T. JEFFERSON *Writ.* (1859) II. 498 There shall be delivered to them.. the Exequatur necessary for the exercise of their functions. **1826** KENT *Comm.* 43 If any consul be guilty of illegal or improper conduct, he is liable to have his exequatur.. revoked. **1879** *Daily News* 26 May, The Spanish Foreign Office objects to granting the Exequatur for the Chinese Consuls.

2. An authorization granted by a temporal sovereign for the exercise of episcopal functions under Papal authority, or for the publication of Papal bulls. Hence, the right of insisting on the necessity of such authorization.

1859 PRESCOTT *Philip II*, III. 365 The councils in those states.. refused to allow the publication of his bulls without the royal exequatur. **1885** *Catholic Dict.* s.v., The Roman Pontiff.. allows Italian bishops.. to apply for the exequatur to the sovereign.. as the *de facto* occupant of power.

† **'exequent**, *a. Obs.* [ad. L. *exequent-em*, pr. pple. of *exequi* to EXECUTE.] That executes.

1617 COLLINS *Def. Bp. Ely* II. ix. 359 Dirigent, not exequent, as your School-men loue to speak.

exequial (ɛk'siːkwɪəl), *a.* [ad. L. *exequiāl-is* (*exsequiāl-is*), f. *ex(s)equiæ*: see EXEQUY.] Of or pertaining to a funeral.

1613 J. DUNSTER in Spurgeon *Treas. Dav.* Ps. lxxix. 2 The manner of our burial, the exequial pomp, etc. **1725–6** POPE *Odyss.* XXIV. 108 Thetis herself to all our peers proclaims Heroic prizes and exequial games. **1751** CAMBRIDGE *Scribleriad* IV. 16 Rites exequial [must] grace his honour'd tomb. **1820** *Blackw. Mag.* VII. 194 The last book of the Iliad.. has supplied a great part of the exequial diction. **1866** F. HALL in Wilson *Vishńu Puráńa* III. 120 *note*, The former term imports undeserving of exequial offerings.

† **e'xequious**, *a. Obs. rare*⁻¹. [f. L. *exequi-æ* + -OUS.] = prec.

1603 DRAYTON *Bar. Wars.* II. lxiii, Build the funeral-pile, Lay your pale hands to this exequious fire.

exequy ('ɛksɪkwɪ), now always in pl. **exequies** ('ɛksɪkwɪz). Forms: *α. sing.* 5–7 exequie, -y, 7, exquie. *β. pl.* (4 exequises, exeqwyis, exquies) 6 exequeis, 4– exequies. [a. OF. *exequies, exeques* = Pr. *ex(s)equias*, a. L. *ex(s)equiās*, acc. of *exsequiæ* pl., lit. 'train of followers', f. *exsequī* to follow out, follow to the grave (see EXECUTE). The OF. word, on adoption into English, was treated partly as a sing. (cf. pl. form *exequises*), and partly as a pl.; from the latter of which the sing. *exequy* was afterwards developed.]

Funeral rites; funeral ceremony; occas. in sense of 'funeral train' or 'bier'.

† **a.** *sing.*; with *pl.* in sense 'funerals'. *Obs.*

1389 in *Eng. Gilds* (1870) 74 Þay shul fynden iiij torches, ffor to brenne.. at exequies of euery brothir and sistir þat dies. *c* **1400** *Apol. Loll.* 50 For sepulturis, or exequies, diriges of þe dead.. or oþer sacraments. **1474** CAXTON *Chesse* 130 He was borne to chirche and his exequye doon. **1560** DAUS tr. *Sleidane's Comm.* 210 At this Obite or Exequie was his wyfe. **1602** *Return fr. Parnass.* I. ii. (Arb.) 11 Carelesse care to preuent his exequy, Scarce deigning to shut vp his dying eye. **1691** WOOD *Ath. Oxon.* I. 179 Sermon at the Exequy of Joan Queen of Spayne.

b. *pl.*

1382 WYCLIF *2 Sam.* iii. 31 Kittith ȝoure clothis, and beth gird with sackis, and weileth before the exequies [**1388** heersis, ether dirige] of Abner. *c* **1425** WYNTOUN *Cron.* VII. viii. 469 Eftyre þ a exeqwyis als fast Til Lwndyn þis ilk Rychard past. **1482** *Paston Lett.* No. 861 III. 282 Xij pore meen.. to holde xij torches abowte myn herse.. during the exequies and masse of my berying. **1538** LELAND *Itin.* IV. 64 The which Body.. was layed with solemne Exequies in a fayre Chest made of Stone. **1615** G. SANDYS *Trav.* 83 A father following the exequies of his sonne. **1639** G. DANIEL *Ecclus.* xxii. 37 Exequies to the Dead will but require Seaven daies. **1700** DRYDEN *Fables, Sigismonda & G.* 661 There yet remained thy funeral exequies. **1771** *Antiq. Sarisb.* 182 If [the Choral Bishop] died within the month, his exequies were solemnized with great pomp. **1832** MOTHERWELL *Poems, Midn. Lamp*, Thou wilt not die until the morrow bright Has seen thy exequies. **1837** THIRLWALL *Greece* IV. xxxii. 272 The festival of Adonis.. was celebrated.. with the representation of funeral exequies.

¶ An alleged sense, 'a funeral ode', has been wrongly inferred from the title of a poem 'The Exequy' in Bp. H. King *Poems* (1657) 52.

† **e'xerce**, *sb. Obs. Sc.* In 6 excerse. [f. next.] Exercise.

1549 *Compl. Scot.* Prol. 9 Throucht sic excerse, ther membris mycht be purgit fra corruppit humours.

† **exerce**, *v.* Chiefly *Sc. Obs.* Forms: 4 exercen, 5–6 excers(e, 6 exers, 5– exerce. [a. OF. *exercer*, ad. L. *exercēre*: see EXERCISE *sb.*]

1. *trans.* To set in motion; to give play to (anger); to display (wisdom); = EXERCISE *v.* 1 b.

1535 STEWART *Cron. Scot.* (1858) I. 84 Amang the Britis for till exers thair ire; Tha enterit in baith with blude and fyre. **1578** *Gude & Godl. Ball.* (1868) 85 The just mannis mouth exercis sapience.

2. To give employment to (a person); to employ with a view to improvement; to discipline, train. Const. *in*. Also *absol.* of a thing: To keep employed or busy; = EXERCISE *v.* 2 and 4.

c **1374** CHAUCER *Boeth.* IV. vii. (1561) 234 a, Certes all thyng that exerceth or corrigeth it profiteth. **1548** *Compl. Scot.* Prol. 9 He statut ane ordinance til exerce his propir childir ande the ȝong princis. **1584** T. HUDSON *Du Bartas' Judith* (1608) 696 The honie bees Exerce themselfes on buddes of sweetest trees. **1585** JAS. I *Ess. Poesie* (Arb.) 29 The bookes of Troy.. Exerce but cease thy toung and eke thy pen. **1596** DALRYMPLE tr. *Leslie's Hist. Scot.* (1885) 92 In handling of waiponis exerce thame.

3. To carry on, carry out, perform (deeds, trades, etc.); to put in force, wield (power, right, etc.); to fulfil (a duty), fulfil the duties of (an office). Cf. EXERCISE *v.* 5. Also *intr.* to serve (as a soldier).

c **1374** CHAUCER *Boeth.* II. vi. 52 But wher shal men fynden any man þat may exercen or haunten any ryȝt vpon an oþer man but oonly vpon hys body. *a* **1450** *Knt. de la Tour* (1868) 118 For to use and excerse the werkys of thaire sauement. **1483** CAXTON *Gold. Leg.* 427/1 He had.. excerced.. the fayte of aduocacye in the bysshoppes courte of Tryguyer. **1513** DOUGLAS *Æneis* VIII. viii. 141 To excers vnder the, And lerne the fate of knychtlie cheulrye. **1528** LYNDESAY *Dream* 1074 Be exampyll to thy peple all, Exersing vertewous deidis honorabyll. **1588** A. KING tr. *Canisius' Catech.* 9 Our lord Iesus thairfor sittis one the rycht hand of the power of god, exerceing æqual pouer with yᵉ father. *a* **1639** SPOTTISWOOD *Hist. Ch. Scot.* v. (1851) 196 The Iustice Aires.. were exerced with much rigour. **1681** *Lond. Gaz.* No. 1670/1 The Intrinsick Spiritual Power of the Church.. as it was exerced by the Apostles. **1707** DK. ATHOL in *Vulpone* 21 To retain, enjoy or bruik and exerce all their Rights.

Hence **e'xerced** *ppl. a.*, in scholastic phrase *exerced act* (= 'exercised act': see EXERCISED *ppl. a.*)

1652 URQUHART *Jewel* Wks. (1834) 293 Figures and tropes .. in their *actu signato*.. somewhat harsh and scabrous, yet in their exerced act, etc.

† **e'xercent**, *a.* and *sb. Obs.* [ad. L. *exercent-em*, pr. pple. of *exercēre* to EXERCISE.]

A. *adj.* That is actively exercising the duties of his calling or profession, or the characteristic functions of his office. Said *esp.* of an advocate: That is practising his profession, in practice.

1643 OWEN *Puritan turned Jesuit* 45 The Tyrant exercent .. a Prince, that doth wilfully dissolve all, or the chiefest compacts of the Common-wealth. **1720** STRYPE *Stow's Surv.* (1754) I. I. xxiv. 173/1 The Doctors Exercent in these courts in the year 1694 being forty four. **1721–1800** in BAILEY. **1726** AYLIFFE *Parerg.* 56 The Judge may oblige every exercent Advocate to give his Patronage and Assistance unto a Litigant in Distress for want of an Advocat. [**1857** *Act 20 & 21 Vict.* c. 77. §116 'The College of Doctors of Law exercent in the Ecclesiastical and Admiralty Courts', incorporated under that style.. 22nd June 8 Geo. III.]

B. *sb.* One who exercises or follows a profession.

1720 STRYPE *Stow's Surv.* I. I. xxiv. 155/2 Anno 1585 the doctors then inhabiting the Commons and Exercents in these courts were.. but sixteen or seventeen in all.

exercisable ('ɛksə,saɪzəb(ə)l), *a.* Also 8–9 exerciseable, 8 -ible. [f. next + -ABLE.] Of an office, power, right, etc.: Capable of being exercised, employed, or enforced.

1741 T. ROBINSON *Gavelkind* II. ii. 170 Not only Lands, and other corporeal Inheritances.. but also all Inheritances .. annexed to or exerciseable within the same. **1767** BLACKSTONE *Comm.* II. iii. 20 Exercisible within the same. **1818** CRUISE *Digest* (ed. 2) III. 127 Judicial offices.. are only exerciseable by persons of skill and capacity. **1882** J. H. BLUNT *Ref. Ch. Eng.* II. 38 Spiritual powers which are exercisable in all parts of the world.

exercise ('ɛksəsaɪz), *sb.* Forms: 4–6 excercise, -cyse, -sise, -sice, 5–6 exercyse, 6 *Sc.* exerceis(s, -cyiss, exercice, 4– exercise. [ME. *exercise*, a. OF. *exercice* = Pr. *exercici, exercisi*:—L. *exercitium*, f. *exercēre* to keep at work, busy, employ, practise, train (cf. EXERCISE *v.*), f. *ex-* (see EX- *pref.*¹) + *arcēre* to shut up, restrain.

The etymological notion of *exercēre* is obscure: it is often regarded as having meant primarily 'to drive forth (tillage beasts),' and hence 'to employ, set to work'.]

1. a. The action of employing in its appropriate activity, (an organ, a faculty, or power) of giving practical effect to (a right), of exerting (influence or authority); the state or condition of being in active operation.

c **1340** HAMPOLE *Psalter* iii. 5, I rase fra ded til lyf, fra ydelnes til excercise in godis seruys. **1608** SHAKS. *Per.* I. iv. 38 These mouths.. are now starv'd for want of exercise. **1659** PEARSON *Creed* (1839) 331 Thou shalt not suffer me.. to continue without exercise, or power of exercising my vital faculty. **1698–9** LUDLOW *Mem.* (1751) I. 246 Whether the House of Commons should take advice of the House of

Lords in the exercise of the legislative power? 1729 BUTLER *Serm.* iv. Wks. 1874 II. 46 Their conversation is merely an exercise of the tongue. 1792 *Anecd. W. Pitt* II. xxix. 129 The exercise of this, their constitutional right, of giving.. their own money. 1820 SCOTT *Ivanhoe* xxii, A large mouthful, which required the exercise of both jaws at once. 1820 KEATS *Hyperion* I. 107 Godlike exercise Of influence benign. 1836–7 SIR W. HAMILTON *Metaph.* i. (1877) I. 7 The one condition under which all powers.. are developed is exercise. 1879 GEO. ELIOT *Coll. Breakf. P.* 164 That exercise of soul Which lies in full obedience. 1890 SIR C. S. C. BOWEN in *Law Times Rep.* LXIII. 735/1 Such a matter as this is not one for the exercise of the judge's discretion.

b. The use *of* or method of using (a weapon).

1490 CAXTON *Eneydos* xiv. 50 The excercyse of armes is dyscontynued. 1632 J. HAYWARD tr. *Biondi's Eromena* 161 Nerves hardened with the continuall exercise of the sling. 1678 tr. *Gaya's Art of War* II. 57 The Exercise of the Pike. 1685 *Abridgm. Eng. Mil. Discipl.* 3 The Officer must first command silence, and then proceed to the Exercise of the Musquet.

†**2.** Habitual occupation or employment; customary practice. ***to make it one's exercise***: to make it one's employment. *Obs.*

1551 ROBINSON tr. *More's Utop.* II. (Arb.) 149 Thinking felicitie after this life to be gotten by.. good exercises. 1593 SHAKS. *3 Hen. VI*, IV. vi. 85 Hunting was his dayly Exercise. 1614 RALEIGH *Hist. World* v. ii. 581 So he makes it his exercise to torment and murther all whom he suspecteth. 1668 in T. W. Marsh *Early Friends Surrey & Sus.* vii. 57 This is none of the Quakers exercise. 1738 WESLEY *Psalms* I. ii, His Exercise by Day and Night To search his Soul-converting Word.

3. The practice (of virtues or vices); the habitual carrying out (of any particular kind of conduct); the practice or fulfilment of the duties of (a profession, office, etc.); the execution of (functions).

1393 GOWER *Conf.* III. 19 Upon the nature of this vice, Of custume and of exercise.. A tale.. I shall reherecn. 1432 *Paston Lett.* No. 18 I. 32 He may putte hem from excercise and occupacion of the Kinges service. 1538 STARKEY *England* II. ii. 187 Abbeys and monasterys for the exercyse of a monastycal lyfe. 1552 HULOET, Exercise of marchandise, *negotiatio*. 1594 HOOKER *Eccl. Pol.* IV. xiv. (1611) 167 Suspence of iudgement and exercise of charity were safer. 1651 HOBBES *Leviath.* II. xxx. 181 To defend private men in the exercise of severall Trades. 1677 HALE *Prim. Orig. Man.* I. i. 6 The Rules and Exercise of Architecture. 1773 *Observ. State Poor* 42 The exercise of cruelty is too frequently a concomitant of the acquisition of power. 1850 MRS. JAMESON *Leg. Monast. Ord.* (1863) 332 After some years spent in the exercise of every virtue. 1871 FREEMAN *Norm. Conq.* (1876) IV. xvii. 55 A.. larger exercise both of concert and secrecy.

4. The practice and performance of rites and ceremonies, worship, etc.; the right or permission to celebrate the observances (of a religion). †Formerly also *ellipt.* = 'exercise of worship'. Cf. 10.

1658 B. HARRIS *Parival's Iron Age* 49 The Emperours brother Mathias.. granted the Exercise of the Confession of Auxbourgh, throughout all Austria. *Ibid.* 64 He.. re-established the Exercise of the Roman Catholick Religion. *Ibid.* 222 The King hath lost seven Provinces, and the said Church, her exercise. 1704 ADDISON *Italy* 508 [Lewis] refus'd even those of the Church of England.. the publick Exercise of their Religion. 1781 GIBBON *Decl. & F.* III. 92 The exercise of public worship appears to be the only solid foundation of the religious sentiments of the people.

†**5. a.** The action or process of training or drilling scholars, troops, etc.; an instance of this. Const. *of*. ***camp of exercise***: a camp established for the purpose of training troops. *Obs.*

*a*1533 LD. BERNERS *Gold. Bk. M. Aurel.* (1546) H, Now wil we speake of his laudable exercises of them that came to hym. 1538 STARKEY *England* II. i. 161 A commyn place appoyntyd to the exercyse of vthe. 1685 *Abridgm. Eng. Mil. Discipl.* 25 The Exercise of Horse consists in fewer Words of Command, then that of Foot. 1819 REES *Cycl.* s.v. *Camp*, A Camp of peace and exercise.

¶**b.** The action of working the ground (after L.).

1697 DRYDEN *Virg. Georg.* I. 143 He with frequent Exercise Commands Th' unwilling Soil [tr. *exercet tellurem*].

6. a. Practice for the sake of training or improvement, either bodily, mental, or spiritual.

*c*1340 HAMPOLE *Prose Tr.* 14 A saule þat haues.. by gastely excercyse ouercomene and dystroyede concupyscens and passiouns. 1483 CAXTON *Cato* B iij, For by the same playe one may doo his excersise. 1509 FISHER *Fun. Serm. C'tess Richmond* Wks. 292 For her exercyse.. she dyde translate dyuers maters of deuocyon out of the Frensshe into Englysshe. 1557 RECORDE *Whetst.* F ij b, Exercise is the beste instrument in learnyng. *c*1570 *Short Sum 1st Bk. Discipl. Ch. Scot.* §5 Reiders fvnd unabill, efter tua ȝeiris exerceis, for the ministrie. 1663 GERBIER *Counsel* 8 b, In the drawing of a line.. he meant a continual exercise to perfection. 1725–6 POPE *Odyss.* VIII. 201 Skill'd in heroic exercise, I claim A post of honour. 1845 STOCQUELER *Handbk. Brit. India* (1854) 12 An army of exercise was assembled on the Gwalior frontier. 1853 —— *Mil. Encycl.*, *Exercise*, the practice of all those motions and actions, together with the whole management of arms, which are essential to the perfection of a soldier, and the rendering him fit for service.

†**b.** Acquired skill. *Obs.*

1602 SHAKS. *Ham.* IV. vii. 98 Hee.. gaue you such a Masterly report, For Art and exercise in your defence.

c. Disciplinary suffering, 'trial'; an instance of this. Also, a state of distress or anxiety, a painful mental struggle. Now *rare*.

*c*1386 CHAUCER *Clerk's T.* 1100 For our exercise, With sharpe scourges of adversitee.. to be bete. 1526 *Pilgr. Perf.* (W. de W. 1531) 1 b, Goostly exercyse, or mortifycacyon of the senses. 1657 CROMWELL *Sp.* 20 Apr. (Carlyle), The exercise that hath been upon me these three or four days. *a*1662 D. DICKSON in Spurgeon *Treas. Dav.* Ps. lxxxviii. (*title*), The heaviest exercise we can imagine possible for a saint. *a*1713 ELLWOOD *Autobiog.* (1714) 31 For I presently saw, it would bring a very great exercise upon me. 1861 MRS. STOWE *Pearl Orr's Isl.* 26 These 'ere forty years that I've been round.. tendin' funerals I've watched people's exercises.

7. Exertion of the muscles, limbs, and bodily powers, regarded with reference to its effect on the subject; *esp.* such exertion undertaken with a view to the maintenance or improvement of health. Often with modifying words, as ***carriage-***, ***horse-***, ***open air***, ***walking***, etc., ***exercise***.

*c*1386 CHAUCER *Nun's Pr. T.* 19 Attempre dyete was al hir phisik, And exercise and hertes suffisaunce. 1531 ELYOT *Gov.* I. xvi, By exercise.. the health of man is preserued. 1626 BACON *Sylva* §299 Use not Exercise and a Spare Diet.. if much Exercise, then a Plentifull Diet. *a*1700 DRYDEN (J.), The wise for cure on exercise depend. 1732 ARBUTHNOT *Rules of Diet* 261 Violent Exercise or Labour produceth this Effect. 1779 JOHNSON *Let. to Mr. Thrale* 23 June, Exercise is labour used only while it produces pleasure. 1806–7 J. BERESFORD *Miseries Hum. Life* (1826) II. xvi, To work in your garden for the sake of exercise. 1865 *Handy Horse Bk.* 32 Two hours' daily exercise at a fast walk will be enough to keep a hack fit for his work.

8. A task prescribed or performed for the sake of attaining proficiency, for training either body or mind, or as an exhibition or test of proficiency or skill.

a. *gen.*

1576 FLEMING *Panopl. Ep.* 356 As well in bodilie exercises as in the also that beelong unto the minde. 1655 WALTON *Angler* (ed. 2) 23 What more manly exercise then hunting the Wild-Boare? 1662 STILLINGFL. *Orig. Sacr.* II. iv. §5 The exercises of those who were educated in these Schools of the Prophets, were instructions in the Law. 1817 CHALMERS *Astron. Disc.* i. (1852) 18 It is truly a most Christian exercise to extract a sentiment of piety from the works and the appearances of nature. 1860 RUSKIN *Mod. Paint.* V. IX. iv. §6. 238 Of these the mason's exercises are in the worst possible taste. *Mod.* The use of the sloping ladder is an improving exercise.

b. In *pl.* Military drill, athletics, field sports, dancing, etc. Also in *sing.* as a collective term, or in sense of 'a drill or parade'. Often with modifying words, as ***bayonet-***, ***cutlass-***, ***small arm-***, ***sword-***, etc., ***exercise***; also ***manual exercise*** (see MANUAL).

*a*1533 LD. BERNERS *Gold. Bk. M. Aurel.* (1546) B viij b, The father of Marke Aurelee themperour, had bene pretour in exercyses [mistranslating *de los exercitos*]. 1600 SHAKS. *A.Y.L.* I. i. 76 Allow me such exercises as may become a gentleman. 1647 CLARENDON *Hist. Reb.* I. (1843) 4/2 [George Villiers] spent two or three years in.. learning the exercises of riding and dancing. 1704 *Lond. Gaz.* No. 3104 Let them [able Bodied Men] repair to Captain Silver.. at his House.. or at the Exercise on Black-Heath. *a*1719 ADDISON (J.), The French apply themselves more universally to their exercises than any nation. 1728 POPE *Dunc.* II. *Argt.*, Then follow the exercises for the Poets, for tickling, vociferating, diving. 1776 GIBBON *Decl. & F.* I. xviii. 483 The exercises of the body prepared them for the fatigues of war. 1788 FRANKLIN *Autobiog.* Wks. 1840 I. 197 The several companies were forming and learning their exercise. 1796–7 *Instr. & Reg. Cavalry* (1813) 199 As steady in the ranks, as if he was at a common exercise.

c. As a University term: An academical declamation or disputation; a *vivâ voce* examination; a dissertation, musical composition, etc., required from candidates for degrees.

1563 FOXE in *Latimer's Serm. & Rem.* (1845) p. x, After some continuance of exercises in other things, he gave himself to the study of divinity. *a*1656 BP. HALL *Life* Rem. Wks. (1660) 10 Never durst I appear in any of those Exercises of Scholarship [public Disputations]. 1701 W. WOOTON *Hist. Rome, Marcus* i. 3 He.. obliged him to frequent the Lectures and Exercises of the Rhetoricians. 1705 *Addr. Univ. Oxf.* in *Lond. Gaz.* No. 4086/1 The Exercise performed in our Theater on New-year's-Day. 1726 AMHERST *Terræ Fil.* xlii. (1754) 219 They have [at Oxford] long, tedious forms, which they call exercises, through which every candidate for a degree must pass. 1856 EMERSON *Eng. Traits, Aristocr.* Wks. (Bohn) II. 87 Noblemen are exempted from the public exercises for the degree. 1886 *Oxf. Univ. Calendar* 56 The exercise [a piece of Vocal Music] is to be performed in public, and a copy of it to be deposited in the Music School. *Ibid.* 58 Doing the Exercises [Dissertations or exegetical Lectures] for one of the two [degrees] only.

d. A composition or translation written by pupils at school; a piece of music, a problem, etc., designed to afford practice to learners.

1612 BRINSLEY *Lud. Lit.* iv. (1627) 32 Now those that write exercises, may take the opportunitie of that time, to write them so faire as they can. 1712 BUDGELL *Spect.* No. 337 ¶8 A theme or copy of verses are the usual exercices. 1740 J. CLARKE *Educ. Youth* (ed. 3) 34 The Scribling a few lines of Latin Exercise every Night. 1751 JOHNSON *Rambler* No. 141 ¶4, I.. was furnished with exercises and instructed in my lessons by some kind patron. 1841 J. T. HEWLETT *Parish Clerk* II. 235 To prepare their exercises and lessons for the following day. 1853 MISS SHEPPARD *C. Auchester* I. xvii. 168 She began to sing her florid exercises.

e. A written composition; an essay, sermon, treatise.

1703 MOXON *Mech. Exerc.* 95 In my former Exercises, I did not teach you how to chuse the Tools a Smith was to use. *a*1716 SOUTH *Serm.* (1744) XI. 103 Would the time and measure of this exercise permit. *a*1742 BENTLEY *Serm.* viii. (R.), Having abundantly proved in our last exercise that, etc. 1880 T. FOWLER *Locke* i. 8 These compositions do not rise much above, or sink much below, the ordinary level of such exercises.

†**f.** *concr.* The object of exercises; 'the sport'.

1628 FORD *Love's Mel.* I. i, To be man, my lord, Is to be but the exercise of cares In several shapes.

g. *pl.* Formal acts or ceremonies on some special occasion. *U.S.*

1841 J. S. BUCKINGHAM *America* II. 47 The First Reformed Dutch Church, where the 'exercises', as all proceedings of public meetings are here called, were to take place. 1863 'E. KIRKE' *Southern Friends* xxvi. 262 A few minutes before the 'exercises' [*sc.* an auction sale] commenced, the negroes were marched upon the lawn. 1891 in M. A. Jackson *Memoirs* (1895) 640 The exercises [*sc.* unveiling of a monument] were held upon the campus of Washington and Lee University. 1911 *Springfield Weekly Republ.* 16 Nov. 9 The chief feature of the inauguration exercises [of the Lord Mayor of London] was a pageant and tableaux. 1926 *Publishers' Weekly* 1 May 1474 Dedicatory exercises.

h. ***the object of the exercise***: the (whole) point or purpose of (something stated in the context).

1958 *Spectator* 24 Jan. 103/1 Its report is a living document which.. will gradually influence public opinion. That was the object of the exercise. 1959 *Times* 20 June 4/4 The main object of the exercise is to merge Theatre Tickets and Messengers' turnover with ours. 1970 J. SANGSTER *Touchfeather* i. 2 If we knew what it looked like.. we would simply bribe a member of the crew.. to take it from his cabin. But that is not the object of the exercise.

†**9.** A recreative employment, pastime. *rare.*

1622 BACON *Hen. VII.* 17 Thinking.. to performe all things now, rather as an Exercise then as a Labour.

10. A religious observance. Cf. 4.

a. *gen.* (*sing.* and *pl.*) Also ***religious exercise***(***s***, ***exercises of devotion***, ***religion***, or ***worship***.

1560–1 *1st Bk. Discipl. Ch. Scot.* (1621) 60 That exercise which St. Paul calls prophecying. 1604 SHAKS. *Oth.* III. iv. 41 Fasting, and Prayer, much Castigation, Exercise deuout. 1641 HINDE *J. Bruen* xxvii. 85 Constancy in maintaining all good exercises of Religion. 1644 *Direct. Publ. Worship* Ordinance 2 In all exercises of the publique worship. 1771 SMOLLETT *Humph. Cl.* (1815) 167 He had assisted in Lady Griskin's, and several private houses, at exercises of devotion. 1848 MACAULAY *Hist. Eng.* I. 606 His followers.. passed a great part of the day in religious exercises. 1868 FREEMAN *Norm. Conq.* (1876) II. viii. 168 Punctual in every exercise of devotion. 1869 PHILLIPS *Vesuv.* iii. 49 Producing great terror and much religious exercise. 1880 T. FOWLER *Locke* i. 5 Locke.. must have occasionally found these tedious, and doubtless lengthy, exercises [religious services at college] somewhat irksome.

b. An act of public worship.

1574 WHITGIFT *Def. Answ.* ii. Wks. (1851) I. 197 The exercises of 'praying, singing of psalms, interpreting, and prophesying'. 1628 EARLE *Microcosm.*, *Shee precise Hypocrite* (Arb.) 63 She.. thinkes the Weeke-dayes Exercise farre more edifying then the Sundaies. 1636 DAVENANT *Witts* in Dodsley *O. Pl.* (1780) VIII. 413 And squire thy untooth'd Aunt to an exercise. 1674 *Consid. Peace & Goodw. Prot.* 22 The main upholder of two famous Exercises. 1888 E. EGGLESTON *Graysons* x. 117 The 'exercises' lasted a full hour longer, and it was half-past 10 before the presiding elder gave the benediction.

c. An act of preaching or prophesying; a discourse.

1594 SHAKS. *Rich. III*, III. ii. 112, I am in your debt, for your last Exercise. 1604 *Const. & Canons Eccl.* lxxii, Sermons, commonly tearmed by some Prophesies or Exercises, in market-towns, or other places. 1650 EVELYN *Mem.* (1857) I. 272 Having a mind to see what was doing among the Rebels.. I went.. and found one at exercise in the chapel. 1799 C. WINTER in W. Jay *Mem.* 30 When he closed his exercise, the people.. seemed to say, etc. 1868 J. G. MIALL *Congreg. Yorksh.* 22 Prophesyings, or, as they were now [in 1603] called, 'Exercises'.

d. An act of private worship.

1592 GREENE *Art Conny-catch.* III. 11 They had said praiers, their euening exercise. 1663 *Flagellum; or O. Cromwell* (1672) 21 The Family was called together to prayers, at which Exercise.. they continued long. 1822 GALT *Steam-Boat* 299, I went down stairs again to the parlour to make exercise. 1824 SCOTT *St. Ronan* xxviii, That honest person was, according to his own account.. engaged in the exercise of the evening. 1825 J. NEAL *Bro. Jonathan* I. 34 On a Saturday evening.. after the 'exercises' have been finished.. they fall into serious conversation.

e. *Sc.* The discussion of a passage of Scripture; a meeting of the Presbytery for holding such a discussion. ***Exercise and Addition***: see quot. 1709.

1572 *Lament. Lady Scot.* in *Scot. Poems 16th C.* II. 246 The word of God is.. in the schuills exercise trewlie teichit. 1598 *Sc. Acts. Jas. VI* (1814) 189 Exemit.. fra all teiching in kirkis and congregatiounis, except in exerceissis and censuring of doctrine in exerceissis. 1709 W. STEUART *Collect. & Observ.* 30 The Presbyterial Exercise and Addition; The Exercise gives the Coherence of the Text and Context, the Logical Division, etc. The Addition gives the Doctrinal Propositions or Truths. 1884 C. ROGERS *Soc. Life Scot.* II. xi. 89 In 1638 the Presbytery of St. Andrews at their weekly meetings were proceeding through St. John's Gospel with an exercise and addition on every verse.

f. Hence the Presbytery itself.

1578 *Act Presb. Edin.* in *Wodr. Soc. Misc.* (1844) 407 The Brethren of the Exercyiss of Edinburgh beand convenit. 1612 *Sc. Acts Jas. VI* (1814) 499/1 The Ministers of the exercise of Dalkeith fand the best meane for reparing of the Kirk.. to be, etc. 1884 C. ROGERS *Soc. Life Scot.* II. xi. 89 Members of each presbytery, then styled 'the Exerceis'.

11. *attrib.* in (sense 7) ***exercise-ground, -time, -yard; exercise-loving*** adj.; **exercise bone** (see quot.); **exercise book**, a blank book of the kind used in schools for the writing of exercises; also, a book containing set exercises.

1890 BILLINGS *Med. Dict., Exercise bone,* bony deposit produced in or over a tendon by continued and repeated use or pressure. **1813** M. EDGEWORTH *Let.* 1 May (1971) 33 Saw Edward 6th's famous little manuscript exercise book. **1838** MRS. GASKELL *Let.* 17 July (1966) 17 We are 'here today, & gone tomorrow', as the fat scullion maid said in some extract in Holland's Exercise book. **1873** *Young Englishwoman* Apr. 207/3 Can the Editor mention a good musical exercise book? I believe the German books are the best. **1932** L. GOLDING *Magnolia St.* II. xiv. 461 The little shiny blue-backed exercise-book he used as a diary. **1788** W. DYOTT *Diary* Sept. (1907) I. 54 His Royal Highness went on shore to see a most extensive display of fireworks on the exercise ground. **1906** J. JOYCE *Let.* 4 Oct. (1966) II. 171 The interspaces being used as military exercise-grounds. **1930** BLUNDEN *Leigh Hunt* viii. 103 It became an exercise-ground in which, edition by edition, its author tried fresh evolutions. **1897** *Daily News* 30 Aug. 5/7 Exercise-loving England. **1897** P. WARUNG *Tales Old Régime* 209 To be deprived of their exercise-time added fresh pangs to the punishment of the virtuous. **1901** *Wide World Mag.* VIII. 170/1 He was to put up a solid palisade round the outer edge of my exercise-yard. **1966** *Listener* 18 Aug. 237/1 There was no bath..and there was no big exercise yard as there had been in Pretoria.

exercise ('ɛksəsaɪz), *v.* Forms: see the sb. [f. prec. sb.

The vb. has taken the place of the obsolete EXERCE, and is thus the representative in sense of L. *exercēre*, Fr. *exercer*, from which many of its uses are directly taken.]

1. *trans.* To put in action or motion.

†a. To put in operation, employ, use (an instrument, remedy, or any agency); to work (an animal). *Obs.*

1526 *Pilgr. Perf.* (W. de W. 1531) 299 Vpon the asse, whiche of no man before had ben vsed ne exercised. **1590** SPENSER *F.Q.* III. iii. 53 Let us..our weake hands..teach The dreadful speare and shield to exercize. **1612** DRAYTON *Poly-olb.* A, Some exercising their pipes, some singing roundelaies. **1691** T. H[ALE] *Acc. New Invent.* 18 Without the least other Preparation or Mixture exercised upon the Metal it self. **1697** DRYDEN *Virg. Georg.* II. 489 Then exercise thy sturdy Steers to plough Betwixt thy Vines. **1726** SWIFT *Gulliver* II. ii. 37 My Nurse gave me part of a Straw, which I exercised as a Pike. **1753** *Stewart's Trial* 153 The King's factor should venture to exercise his Majesty's property freely. **1792** *Munchhausen's Trav.* xx. 66 When they quarrel they exercise a strait horn.

b. To employ, bring to bear, apply (power, skill); to make practical use of (a right or privilege).

c **1386** CHAUCER *Knt.'s T.* 578 Ther as he might his vertu excersise. **1535** COVERDALE *1 Kings* xvi. 27 Amri, & all that he dyd, and his power that he exercysed. **1594** HOOKER *Eccl. Pol.* I. x. (1611) 25 The life is led most happily, wherin all vertue is exercised without impediment. **1622** MASSINGER *Virg. Mart.* I. i, To..exercise that power Heaven has conferr'd upon me. **1651** HOBBES *Leviath.* II. xxviii. 162 That right of Punishing, which is exercised in every Common-wealth. **1690** LOCKE *Hum. Und.* IV. xiv. §4 This faculty of the mind, when it is exercised immediately about things, is called judgement. **1711** E. FENTON *Ep. to Southerne* 11 Sculpture exercis'd her Skill..to make the Marble breathe. **1836** J. GILBERT *Chr. Atonem.* viii. (1852) 224 The Divine Being..exercises the right to forgive without any compensation. **1874** GREEN *Short Hist.* vii. 394 An arbitrary power of imprisonment was still exercised by the Council. **1891** *Law Reports, Weekly Notes* 77/1 The co-heiresses could have exercised the trust for sale.

2. a. To employ habitually, practise (a person); to busy. Const. *in.* (Now only *refl.* and *pass.*, with some notion of gaining skill by practice: cf. 3).

1382 WYCLIF *2 Macc.* xv. 12 Onye..was exercised, or haunted, in vertues fro a chijld. *c* **1460** FORTESCUE *Abs. & Lim. Mon.* (1714) 90 Thay [Archers] nedyn to be mich exercysyd in schotyng. **1526** *Pilgr. Perf.* (W. de W. 1531) 2 Some..be..moche exercysed in goostly conuersacyon. **1553** EDEN *Treat. Newe Ind.* (Arb.) 10 He had been wel exercised in Astronomy. *Ibid.* 24 They are exercysed in fyshing. **1583** STUBBES *Anat. Abus.* II. 51 Cut off the haire..in such comelie and decent maner as these barbers exercised therein can doe. **1613** SIR. H. FINCH *Law* (1636) 162 A Clarke of the Crowne..which was neuer exercised in the Office. **1647** CLARENDON *Hist. Reb.* IV. (1702) I. 298 Untainted with any of those vices, which the Officers of that Army were exercised in. **1751** JORTIN *Serm.* (1771) I. iv. 78 They exhort us to exercise ourselves in godliness. **1781** GIBBON *Decl. & F.* III. 223 To give battle to an innumerable people, exercised in arms. **1794** MRS RADCLIFFE *Myst. Udolpho* i, She usually exercised herself in elegant arts. **1835** WORDSW. *C. Lamb,* The hermit, exercised in prayer and praise..Is happy. **1874** MAHAFFY *Soc. Life Greece* viii. 241 He and his fellows were all exercised as jurymen in deciding political and social disputes.

†b. *transf.* To employ, occupy (time). *Obs.*

1711 ADDISON *Spect.* No. 94 ¶3 Those Parts of Life which are exercised in Study, Reading, and the Pursuits of Knowledge.

†c. To till (the ground); = L. *exercēre terram.*

1382 WYCLIF *Gen.* ix. 20 Noe, a man erthe tylyer, began to excercise [**1388** tile] the erthe. **1654** R. CODRINGTON tr. *Justin's Hist.* 507 To exercise and mitigate the fields with ploughs. **1697** DRYDEN *Virg. Georg.* I. 232 Unless the Land with daily Care Is exercis'd.

3. a. To train by practice; to employ, put into action or movement, for the sake of acquiring skill or strength; to drill (soldiers, etc.), to put through evolutions for practice or display; to put (the limbs, the body) through a course of movements for the sake of strength or health. Also, to subject to ascetic discipline.

1388 WYCLIF *1 Sam.* xx. 20 Y schal caste as excercisynge [**1382** hauntynge] ether pleiynge me at a signe. **1533** FRITH *Another Bk. agst. Rastell* 336 God..left the Philistines to exercise and nurture the children of Israel. **1549** LATIMER *6th Serm. bef. Edw. VI* (Arb.) 161 Menne of Englande..when they woulde exercyse theym selues..were wonte to goo a brode in the fyeldes a shootynge. **1557** BIBLE (Genev.) *Heb.* v. 14 Them..which through custome haue their wittes exercised, to iudge both good and euyl. **1557** in *Babees Bk.* (1868) 247 Moderatly exercise your body with some labour. **1684** R. H. *School Recreat.* 84 Here [in tennis] the Body is briskly exercised more than ordinary. *a* **1695** WOOD *Life* (1848) 266 A company of scholars..exercised themselves in feats of arms privately in All Souls coll. quadrangle. **1743** R. POCOCKE *Descr. East* I. 57 The Arabs who came out to meet the cashif exercised themselves all the way on horseback. **1825** CARLYLE *Schiller* II. (1845) 116 The objects..to which I had been exercising all my powers. **1838** PRESCOTT *Ferd. & Is.* II. v. 478 [Ximenes] exercised himself with fasts, vigils, and stripes. **1842** MISS MITFORD in L'Estrange *Life* III. ix. 142 He exercised the horses at Newmarket.

b. *transf.* To practise soldiers in the use of (weapons); to put (a gun) through its evolutions.

1713 ADDISON *Cato* II. vi, I'll draw up my Numidian troops..to exercise their arms. **1836** MARRYAT *Midsh. Easy* xviii, Exercising the great guns on board ship.

†c. To accustom, inure. *Obs.*

1558 in Strype *Ann. Ref.* I. App. iv. 6 To exercise the queen's majesty's subjects to obedience. **1607** TOPSELL *Four-f. Beasts* (1673) 110 In the mean time exercise them to meat.

4. a. To give employment to; to engage the attention or feelings of; to tax the powers of.

1538 STARKEY *England* II. i. 176 Such poverty, exercysyth wel the pytuose myndys of them wych have enough. **1614** RALEIGH *Hist. World* III. 71 The continuall Warres which exercised King Darius. **1780** HARRIS *Philol. Enq.* Wks. (1841) 394 The authors of our own country..having exercised many critics of learning. **1818** JAS. MILL *Brit. India* II. IV. v. 170 The situation was calculated to exercise Hindu duplicity and address. **1879** *Cassell's Techn. Educ.* IV. 66/1 Various breeds had great celebrity—a celebrity which exercised the pens of their most famous writers.

b. *esp.* To harass, vex, worry; to afflict, make anxious, 'prove'.

Originally in religious use with some notion of disciplinary exercise (see 3); the wider use was prob. at first *transf.* from this. Cf. EXERCISE *sb.* 6 c.

a **1555** LATIMER *Serm. & Rem.* (1845) 323 Exercised with my old disease in my head. **1596** BP. BARLOW *3 Serm.* ii. 87 There is also another cause why God thus exerciseth his children. *c* **1665** MRS. HUTCHINSON *Mem. Col. Hutchinson* (1848) 159 Injurious prosecutions, wherewith the governor was afterwards much exercised. *a* **1715** BURNET *Own Time* (1823) I. 78 God..thought fit to exercise him with calumny. **1722** SEWEL *Hist. Quakers* (1795) I. 24 At times his mind was much exercised. **1758** S. HAYWARD *Serm.* xvii. 520 The melancholy disorder he [Job] was exercised with. *a* **1847** MRS. SHERWOOD *Lady of Manor* I. iii. 68 The..dispensation with which it had pleased the Almighty to exercise her. **1861** HUGHES *Tom Brown at Oxf.* v. (1889) 42 Tom..[was] much exercised in his mind as to what manner of man he had fallen upon. **1878** SIMPSON *Sch. Shaks.* I. 113 The minds of people at Rome were exercised concerning the division of the expected spoil. **1888** *N. & Q.* Ser. VII. V. 418 My own housemaid was very much exercised..by an inexplicable tinkling..of her door-bell.

5. To carry on, carry out, perform.

†a. To perform (*esp.* habitually), practise, take part in (an action, feat, game, etc.); to play (a part). ***to exercise the great horse*** (see HORSE).

c **1430** tr. *T. à Kempis* 37 Breþern..þat exercisen not þo þinges as þei are called to! **1531** ELYOT *Gov.* I. xxvii, He neuer exercised any other play or game. **1538** STARKEY *England* I. ii. 41 Frely hyt exercysyth vertues actys. **1541** R. COPLAND *Guydon's Quest. Chirurg.* A iij a, What dyuers operacions exerciseth the Cyrurgyen? **1547** *Homilies* I. *Short Declar. Faith* I. (1859) 38 The living body of a man ever exerciseth such things as belong to a naturall and living body. **1548** HALL *Chron.* 197 b, The Poleaxe the whiche feate he had greatly exercysed. **1552** HULOET, *Tragœdus,* he that dothe exercise some parte in a tragedie. **1580** STOW *Ann.* (1605) 481 Henry Hotespurre..maketh inuasion vpon them..exercising laudable factes. **1592** CHETTLE *Kindeharts Dr.* (1841) 19 But now, I heare, my blinde brother, that exercisde the base. **1644** EVELYN *Mem.* (1857) I. 70 Here I ..went to see them ride and exercise the great horse. **1667** MILTON *P.L.* IV. 551 About him exercis'd Heroic Games Th' unarmed youth of Heav'n. **1760** C. JOHNSTON *Chrysal* (1822) I. 201 The matron..immediately began to exercise her donations to public charities.

†b. To carry on, ply, pursue (an occupation, trade, etc.); to discharge the functions of (an official post); to practise oneself in (an art, language, etc.). *Obs.*

1467 in *Eng. Gilds* (1870) 407 The craft that he canne or exercisith. **1511-2** *Act 3 Hen. VIII,* c. 23 §9 They..may occupie and excercise their roomes and offices of foreyn Auditours. **1555** EDEN *Decades W. Ind.* 35 They had graneges & exercised tyllage. **1598** HAKLUYT *Voy.* I. 61 It..is a kinde of porte towne, hauing a great marte exercised therein. **1601** R. JOHNSON *Kingd. & Commw.* (1603) 13 Many good townes and riche places where clothing is exercised. **1603** JAS. I in Ellis *Orig. Lett.* I. 239 III. 66 We have thought good to appoint..the lord Thomas Howard de Walden to exercise that place. **1611** CORYAT *Crudities* 396 Which hunting of wilde boares is more exercised by the Germans then by any other Christian nations. **1651** *Life Father Sarpi* (1676) 5 In Venice he exercised Merchandise, though with no great prosperity. **1683** DRYDEN *Life Plutarch* 17 He had neither the leisure to study, nor so much as to exercise the Roman language. **1771** GOLDSM. *Hist. Eng.* I. 249 The inhabitants exercised pasture in the open country.

†c. To celebrate, perform (a ceremony, religious service, etc.); to perform the observances of (a religion). *Obs.*

a **1400** *Cov. Myst.* 71 This we clepe festum Encenniorum, The new ffest of whiche iij in the ȝere we exercyse. **1483** CAXTON *Gold. Leg.* 78/3 With the drede of God they excersised the feste of theyr weddynges. **1486** in *Lichfield Gild Ord.*, Owr ordinary visitacion had and exercysed in the chapell of owr lady beside the market place of Lichfield. **1612** BREREWOOD *Lang. & Relig.* xxvi. 228 The Gregorians ..exercise notwithstanding their liturgies in the Greek tongue. **1698** LASSELS *Voy. Italy* II. 94 In this place was exercised the first publick profession of Christian religion. *a* **1732** ATTERBURY *Serm. Matt.* xxvii. 25 (Seager) They were permitted by their conquerors freely and publickly to exercise their religion. **1807** J. JOHNSON *Orient. Voy.* 357 They have a regular form of government, and exercise the Mahometan religion.

d. To perform or practise acts of (justice, cruelty, oppression, duplicity, etc.). Cf. 1 b.

1494 FABYAN *Chron.* II. xxxii. 25 Gurguncius..exercisyd Iustyce to his subiects. **1548** HALL *Chron.* 223 Thei exercised their crueltie, against their awne selfes. **1611** SHAKS. *Cymb.* v. iv. 82 No longer exercise, Upon a valiant Race, thy harsh..iniuries. *a* **1703** BURKITT *On N.T.* Matt. vii. 5 To exercise severity in judging of ourselves. **1791** BURKE *Corr.* (1844) III. 356 So much perfidy, pride, cruelty, and tyranny, never was exercised in a like case. **1818** JAS. MILL *Brit. India* II. v. viii. 679 The greatest oppression was evidently exercised upon the unhappy cultivators.

e. To discharge, fulfil (functions); to exert, wield, possess (dominion, jurisdiction, etc.).

1590 MARLOWE *2nd Pt. Tamburl.* IV. i, I exercise a greater name, The scourge of God. **1658** *Whole Duty Man* xiv. §8. 108 Those..who dare presume to exercise the offices of it, without being lawfully called to it. *a* **1704** LOCKE (J.), That dominion which their governours had a right to exercise over them. **1736** BUTLER *Anal.* I. iii. Wks. 1874 I. 47 Government of the..same kind with that, which a master exercises over his servants. **1790** GOUV. MORRIS *Life & Writ.* (1832) II. 117 It engrosses all functions though incapable of exercising any. **1828** D'ISRAELI *Chas. I,* I. vi. 150 The late exiles..attempted to exercise their ministry. **1880** L. STEPHEN *Pope* v. 111 Swift did not exercise either so gentle or so imperial a sway as Addison.

f. Of things: To 'exert', possess efficiently (force, influence, effect).

1862 H. SPENCER *First Princ.* II. iv. §54 (1875) 178 The force which a given quantity of matter exercises, remains always the same. **1867** SMILES *Huguenots Eng.* xi. (1880) 179 The Exodus of the French Protestants exercised a highly important influence on European politics.

6. *absol.* or *intr.* for *refl.* in various senses.

†a. To ply one's calling, to 'practise'. *Obs.*

1511-2 *Act 3 Hen. VIII,* c. 11 That noo person..take upon hym to excercise and occupie as a Phisicion. **1565** *Act 8 Eliz.* c. 13 §5 Sea-faring Men..may freely and quietly exercise and row in their own Wherries.

†b. To perform one's office, practise, *upon.* Also, To treat *upon* a subject. *Obs.*

1610 SHAKS. *Temp.* I. ii. 328 Vrchins Shall for that vast of night, that they may worke, All exercise on thee. **1616** LANE *Sqr.'s Tale* 120 Wheare such surgeons on flesh exercise. **1703** MOXON *Mech. Exerc.* Pref. 6 And lastly, as a close to Smithing, I shall Exercise upon Steel, and its several Sorts.

c. To go through exercises or evolutions; *esp.* of soldiers, 'to drill'.

1606 SHAKS. *Ant. & Cl.* III. vi. 12 I'th' common shew place where they exercise. **1678** tr. *Gaya's Art of War* II. 53 Exercise. *Ibid.* 57 Whilst the Pikes are exercising, the Musketteers are made to order, or rest upon their Arms. **1697** POTTER *Antiq. Greece* I. viii. (1715) 38 For Wrestlers, Dancers, and all others that would, to Exercise at the same Time. **1782** COWPER *Gilpin* 64 In which I bear my trusty sword When I do exercise.

d. To take exercise.

1655 MOUFET & BENNET *Health's Improv.* (1746) 211 Thirdly, Exercise not presently upon it [milk]. *a* **1698** TEMPLE *Health & Long Life* Wks. 1720 I. 279 In the course of common Life, a Man must either often Exercise, or Fast, or take Physic, or be sick. **1734** J. ROGERS *Ess. Epid. Dis.* 257 A spare Diet is necessary, when we can't Exercise. **1877** H. JAMES *Amer.* i, If it was necessary to walk to a remote spot, he walked, but he had never known himself to exercise. **1897** *Daily News* 1 Dec. 5/3 The other prisoners exercised as usual yesterday.

†7. *intr.* To conduct or engage in a religious exercise or service; to expound or interpret Scripture. *Obs.* exc. *Hist.* Cf. EXERCISE *sb.* 10.

1561 T. NORTON *Calvin's Inst.* Contents, Leaving the inferiour manner of exercising which hee used among the Israelites. **1635** WINTHROP *New Eng.* (1853) I. 214 Mr. Shepherd prayed with deep confession of sin, etc., and exercised out of Eph. v. **1649** EVELYN *Mem.* (1857) III. 38 Lieutenant-Gen. Cromwell..exercised yesterday at Whitehall, to inquire of the Lord, etc. **1663** P. HENRY *Diaries & Lett.* (1882) 130 In yᵉ morning I exercis'd at home, I hope to edification.

exercised ('ɛksəsaɪzd), *ppl. a.* [f. prec. + -ED¹.] In senses of the vb.

exercised act: tr. med.L. *actus exercitus,* a scholastic term used in various senses opposed to *actus signatus*; in Duns Scotus it means specific being viewed in itself, not as an object of predication. See EXERCED, EXERCITE *a.*

1552 HULOET, Exercised, *Exercitatus.* **1590** C. S. *Right Relig.* 19 He..disclaimeth..such exercised lordship ouer the Cleargie. **1597** J. PAYNE *Royal Exch.* 37 We must be all exercised soldiers. **1607-12** BACON *Ess. Fortune* (Arb.) 379 The exercised fortune maketh the Able man. **1628** T. SPENCER *Logick* 53 Therfore the end hath an actiue, and an exercised act, in the producing of the effect. **1631** T. MAY tr. *Barclay's Mirr. Mindes* II. 33 The strongest and most exercised head in Contemplation. **1690** PENN *Rise & Progr. Quakers* (1834) 63 We were an exercised people. **1791** BOSWELL *Johnson* an. 1756 We..venerate in Johnson one of the most exercised minds that our holy religion hath ever

formed. **1841** MYERS *Cath. Th.* III. §40. 147 Questions.. decided..by the exercised faculties of each spiritual mind.

exerciser ('ɛksəsaɪzə(r)). [f. EXERCISE *v.* + -ER¹.] One who or that which exercises.

1. In senses of the vb. Const. *of*.

1552 HULOET s.v., Exerciser of anye of these fiue games. **1604** *Const. & Canons Eccl.* cxxvi, Possessours & Exercisers of peculiar Iurisdiction. *c* **1619** HIERON *Wks.* I. 16 Crosses.. are trialls of faith, exercisers of patience. **1686** J. SERGEANT *Monast. Conventions* 11 They [the monks of St. Basil] became so industrious, that their Monastery was called the place of Exercise, and they the Exercisers. **1805** W. TAYLOR in *Ann. Rev.* III. 240 Excellent sharp-shooters and exercisers. **1831** *Blackw. Mag.* XXIX. 146 The..virtual exercisers of the elective privilege. **1864** DICKENS in *Daily Tel.* 12 May, [The player's] is not a vocation the exerciser of which can profit by the labours of others.

2. An apparatus for exercising the limbs, etc.

1889 *The Voice* (N.Y.) 3 Oct. Advt., The best health exerciser on the market. *Mod.* A.B. and Co's Home-exerciser.

exercising ('ɛksəsaɪzɪŋ), *vbl. sb.* [f. EXERCISE *v.* + -ING¹.] The action of the verb EXERCISE; an exercise. Also *attrib.*

1509 FISHER 7 *Penit. Ps.* li. Wks. 100 The excercysynge and doynge of many good werkes. **1548** R. HUTTEN *Sum Diuinity* 266 They be exercisynges of faythe. **1616** BINGHAM tr. *Ælian's Tacticks* 156 In exercising you must onely use these three termes of direction. Make ready. Present. Give fire. **1631** GOUGE *God's Arrows* III. xi. 206 All sorts of trainings and exercising of armes. **1709** W. BISHOP in *Ballard MSS.* (Bodleian) XXXI. 54 The Free Exerciseing of Their Religion. **1874** KNIGHT *Dict. Mech.*, *Exercising-apparatus*, an apparatus for the use of gymnasts, or for the training of special muscles.

¶ Used gerundially with the omission of *in*.

1736 CHANDLER *Hist. Persec.* 358 Whilst these severities were exercising against Protestants.

exercising ('ɛksəsaɪzɪŋ), *ppl. a.* [f. as prec. + -ING².] That exercises.

1711 SHAFTESB. *Charac.* (1737) I. 343 The exercising-authors of this kind have been above describ'd, in the beginning of this treatise.

†**e'xercist**, *Obs. rare*⁻¹. [f. EXERCE *v.* + -IST.] One who practises (religious) exercises.

1715 M. DAVIES *Athen. Brit.* I. 245 Mr. Ignatius's Rules for his meditating Exercists.

exercitant (ɛg'zɜːsɪtənt). [a. F. *exercitant*, ad. L. *exercitant-em*, pr. pple. of *exercitāre*, frequentative of *exercēre* to exercise: see EXERCE.] One who is engaged in spiritual exercises.

1858 FABER *Life Xavier* 465 He gave the spiritual exercises of his blessed father Ignatius; though generally speaking the exercitants were chiefly confined to the first week. **1890** *Tablet* 30 Aug. 356 The exercises were to lead the exercitant, to saintliness.

†**e'xercitate**, *pa. pple. Obs.* [ad. L. *exercitāt-us*, pa. pple. of *exercitāre*: see prec.] Exercised; *e.g.* with spiritual discipline.

c **1425** tr. *T. à Kempis' Consol.* II. ix, He is not hye yn contemplacion of god, yet [*read* þat] is not exercitate for god in som tribulacion. *Ibid.* III. xxi, So mi3 tily temptid, so greuously troublid, so manifolde preued and exercitate.

exercitation (ɛg,zɜːsɪ'teɪʃən). Forms: 4–5 exercitacion, -cioun, 6 exercetation, -cytacyon, 5– exercitation. [ad. L. *exercitātiōn-em*, n. of action f. *exercitā-re*: see EXERCITANT.]

1. The exercising, putting in operation, or exerting (of faculties, powers, etc.); an instance of this.

c **1374** CHAUCER *Boeth.* IV. vi. 140 þei sholden conferme þe vertues of corage by þe vsage and exercitacioun of pacience. **1603** FLORIO *Montaigne* II. xii. (1632) 304 Asclepiades [held the soul to be] an exercitation of the senses. **1743** FIELDING *J. Wild* I. iii, He was..never detected in such furtive compositions, nor indeed in any other exercitations of his great talents. **1829** SOUTHEY *Sir T. More* II. 109 They have an ambitious propensity for intellectual exercitation. **1880** J. B. CROZIER *Relig. Future* ii. 123 Emerson's religion requires no..exercitations of the imagination to vivify it.

†**2.** The practising (of a trade), habitual performance (of actions). *Obs.*

1579 *Burgh Rec. Aberd.* in Grant *Burgh Sch. Scotl.* II. xiv. (1876) 480 The exercetation of all crafts. **1633** J. DONE *Hist. Septuagint* 180 You use to Whet and sharpen your understanding in the exercitation of high deedes and gests.

b. An accustomed employment, a duty belonging to one's office.

1737 *Common Sense* (1738) I. 20 Not to mention what a fatal Hinderance a prominent Abdomen would prove to his royal Exercitations in the Seraglio. **1760** GOLDSM. *Cit. W.* v, His health..is still pretty well; nor is he in the least unfit.. for any kind of royal exercitation. *Ibid.* cix.

3. The training (of a person or his faculties) by practice; practice (of an art, etc.) for the sake of improvement; an instance or a mode of this.

1475 *Bk. Noblesse* 21 The second was exercitacion and usage in dedis of armes. **1586** FERNE *Blaz. Gentrie* Ded., From industrious exercitations many vtillities..do flowe and source. **1655–60** STANLEY *Hist. Philos.* (1701) 283/2 Nothing in Life can be rightly done without exercitation. **1713** STEELE *Englishm.* No. 38. 244 Let us for our own Exercitation..turn to the Description of it. **1748** CHESTERF. *Lett.* II. clxiv. 97 Consider them [systems] only as exercitations for the mind. **1831** SOUTHEY in *Q. Rev.* XLIV. 99 The practice had become so much an exercitation of subtlety, on the part of its professors. **1864** LOWELL *Biglow P.* Wks. (1879) 313 The writing of verses is a good rhetorical exercitation.

†**b.** Spiritual discipline. *Obs.*

1398 TREVISA *Barth. De P.R.* XVIII. i. (1495) 748 Some beestes ben made for exercitacion of man..and therfore ben made flyes and lyce. *c* **1425** tr. *T. à Kempis' Consol.* II. ix, Whan spiritual exercitation is 3oven of god, receiue it with gret þankinges.

†**4.** Exercise of the body; a mode of exercise.

1382 WYCLIF *1 Tim.* iv. 8 Bodili excercitacioun, or traueling, or abstinence, to litil thing is profytable. *a* **1500** *Prose Legends* in *Anglia* VIII. 154 Exercitacyone of body she sette litil by. **1541** R. COPLAND *Galyen's Terap.* 2 C ij, Ye ought to haue cure of all the body, in strengthyng it with dyuers exercytacyons. **1640** G. WATTS tr. *Bacon's Adv. Learn* IV. ii. 191 Walking [is good] against the crudities of the stomack, and for other diseases other exercitations. **1658** ROWLAND *Moufet's Theat. Ins.* 898 To the Conservation or keeping of Bees, many things are required, to wit, orderly, diet..air, exercitation.

5. Devotional exercise; an act of public or private worship.

1655–60 STANLEY *Hist. Philos.* III. I. 31 He had morning exercitations at his own house. **1673** PENN *The Chr. a Quaker* x. Wks. 558 Spiritual Exercitation. **1792** G. WAKEFIELD *Enquiry* 14 Diurnal exercitations for spiritual improvement. **1828** CARLYLE *Misc.* (1857) I. 101 Werner appears to have assisted at certain 'Spiritual Exercitations'.

6. An exercise or display of skill, *esp.* literary or oratorical; a written or spoken disquisition, essay, discourse.

1632 J. WEEMSE (*title*) Divine Exercitations, containing divers Questions and Solutions for the right understanding of the Scriptures. **1689** *Dial. Tim. & Titus* 39 (*heading*) A Friendly and Cordial Exercitation to my Brethren in the Ministry. **17..** in Somers *Tracts* II. 240 Scaliger, in his 323d Exercitation against Cardan. **1736** NEAL *Hist. Purit.* III. 162 He..published a Latin exercitation upon the same subject. **1816** SCOTT *Old Mort.* Introd., Indulging..a flowing..diction in his prose exercitations. **1876** C. M. DAVIES *Unorth. Lond.* 352 A very wild campanological exercitation. **1877** M. ARNOLD *Last Ess. on Ch.* 22 The superb exercitations of Bossuet or the reasoning and rhetoric of Pascal.

†**exerci'tator.** *Obs. rare.* [a. L. *exercitātor*, agent-n. f. *exercitā-re*: see prec.] One who writes an 'exercitation'.

1649 NEEDHAM *Case Commw.* 21 The Exercitator objects, that the present Governours have usurped over the Majority of the House. **1650** A. A. *Reply Sanderson* 10 The Exercitator..confesses..That such an Oath may be.. suspended.

†**exerci'tatory**, *a.* *Obs. rare*⁻¹. [ad. L. *exercitātōri-us*, f. *exercitāre*: see EXERCITATION.] Of the nature of an exercitation or dissertation.

1672 *Life & Death of Arminius & Episc.* II. 4 Diligent and industrious in disputations, and exercitatory Sermons.

†**exercite**, *sb.*¹ *Obs.* Also 5 excercyte, -syte, exeercyte. [a. OF. *exercite*, ad. L. *exercitus* army (*u* stem), action of exercising, hence *concr.*, f. *exercēre*: see EXERCE *v.*] An army, host.

1485 CAXTON *Chas. Gt.* 21 In that tyme were baptysed.. thre thousand men of hys excersyte. **1490** —— *Eneydos* xxii. 83 He sawe the felawes of the Emmendes and alle their excercyte. *c* **1490** *Blanchardyn* (1890) 9 He arryued wyth alle his Exeercyte nyghe to the oost of Subyon. **1550** J. COKE *Eng. & Fr. Herald* §72 (1877) 81 Wyllyam Conquerour.. passed, with his exercite of the noble Englyshemen, into Fraunce.

†**e'xercite**, *sb.*² *Obs.* Forms: 5 excersite, -yte, 5–6 exercite, -citie, -cyte. [a. OF. *exercite*, of obscure formation; perh. f. *exerciter* (see EXERCITE *v.*); possibly ad. L. *exercitus* (see prec.).] In various senses of EXERCISE *sb.* Drilling (of soldiers); practice (of virtue, etc.); occupation (of time); discharge (of the duties of an office); also, ***exercite of*** = practices preparatory to.

1485 CAXTON *Chas. Gt.* 20 It is tyme..to forsake the false goddes..whyche..do no thynge but excersite of dampnacyon. **1489** —— *Faytes of A.* I. vii. 15 The excercyte of their offyce. **1502** *Ord. Crysten Men* (W. DE W. 1506) III. iii. 148 Excellente in contemplacyon, & in the exercyte or usynge of lyfe spyrytuall. *a* **1533** LD. BERNERS *Gold. Bk. M. Aurel.* (1546) R iij a, The kepyng of hyr selfe [Lucrece] close in her house, the exercytie of her tyme.

†**exercite**, *ppl. a.* *Obs. rare*⁻¹. [ad. L. *exercitus*, pa. pple. of *exercēre*: see EXERCE.] In ***exercite act*** = 'exercised act'; see EXERCISED *ppl. a.*

1711 tr. *Werenfelsius' Disc. Logomachys* 101 Then [follow] Acts..divided, signate, exercite.

†**exercite**, *v.* *Obs.* Also 5 excercyte. [a. OF. *exerciter* to exercise, ad. L. *exercitāre*: see EXERCITANT.] *trans.* To exercise, practise; to discipline, drill; to wield, bring into play (a weapon).

1475 *Bk. Noblesse* 27 Good men of armes well lerned and exercited. **1483** CAXTON *Gold. Leg.* 427/4 He excercytyng and ocupyeng hym in thys holy operacion or werke. *c* **1500** *Melusine* 224 In many other appertyse of armes they exercyted them self. **1541** R. COPLAND *Galyen's Terap.* 2 B iij b, The boke of medycamentes, wherin it behoueth to be exercyted who soeuer wyll take any fruyte of these present comentaries. **1556** J. O[LDE] tr. *Walther's Antichrist* 161 But the material sweord must be exercited for the churche, and the spiritual sweorde of the churche.

†**exer'cition.** *Sc. Obs. rare.* In 6 -tioun(e. [ad. L. *exercitiōn-em*, n. of action f. *exercēre*: see EXERCE.]

a. Exercise, whether bodily or mental. **b.** Military exercise, drill. **c.** Enforcement (of law).

1525 *Sc. Acts Jas. V* (1816) 295 þe hail lordis referris the exercitioune of the Kingis maist noble persoune to the discrecioune of the Lordis being with him for þe tyme. **1528** LYNDESAY *Dream* 874 Quhy want we lawis Exersitioun? **1536** BELLENDEN *Cron. Scot.* (1821) I. p. xxiv, Corporall exercitioun of the handis. **1540** *Sc. Acts. Jas. V* (1814) 363 That exercitioune may be had throwout all þe realme amangis all our souirane lordis liegis for exercing of þare personis in ordoure. **1552** ABP. HAMILTON *Catech.* (1884) 16 Tha war ordanit also for our..spiritual exercitioun.

‖**exercitor** (ɛg'zɜːsɪtɔː(r)). *Roman Law.* [Lat. *exercitor*, agent-n. f. *exercēre.*] (See quot.)

1850 BURRELL *Law Dict.* s.v., The exercitor was bound for the acts of the master. **1880** MUIRHEAD tr. *Instit. Gaius* IV. §71 *Exercitor* is the name given to the individual who is drawing the daily profits of the ship.

exerci'torian, *a.* [f. L. *exercitōri-us* (f. EXERCITOR: see prec.) + -AN.] Of or pertaining to an exercitor. ***exercitorian action*** (see quots.).

1880 MUIRHEAD tr. *Instit. Gaius* 494 Exercitorian action, a prætorian action *in solidum* granted to a creditor against a *paterfamilias* or owner, who, as *exercitor* of a ship, had placed his *filius familias* or slave in charge of it.

‖**exer'gasia.** *Rhet. Obs.* Also 6 erron. **exargasia.** [a. Gr. ἐξεργασία lit. 'working out,' f. ἐξεργάζεσθαι to work out, perfect, f. ἐξ out + ἐργάζεσθαι to work, f. ἔργον work.] (See quots.)

1589 PUTTENHAM *Eng. Poesie* III. xx. (Arb.) 254 *Exargasia* ..a terme transferred from these polishers of marble. **1657** J. SMITH *Myst. Rhet.* 221 *Exergasia*..a figure when we abide still in one place, and yet seem to speak divers things, many times repeating one sentence, but yet with other words, sentences and exornations. **1721–1800** in BAILEY.

†**exer'gastic** *a.* *Obs.* In 7 erron. **exargastic.** [ad. Gr. ἐξεργαστικ-ός able to accomplish, f. ἐξεργάζεσθαι, f. ἐξ out + ἐργαζέσθαι to work.] Tending to work out.

1652 URQUHART *Jewel* Wks. (1834) 292, I could have introduced, in case of obscurity, synonymal, exargastick, and palilogetick elucidations.

†**e'xergasy.** *Obs.*⁻⁰ Anglicized form of EXERGASIA.

1730–6 in BAILEY (folio). **1775** in ASH.

exergual (ɛg'zɜːgəl), *a.* [f. next + -AL¹.] Pertaining to the exergue.

1856 SMYTH *Rom. Fam. Coins* 233 The exergual letters are cut clearer than those in the field. **1864** EVANS *Coins Anc. Britons* 299 There is an exergual line.

exergue ('ɛksɜːg, ɛg'zɜːg). *Numism.* Also 7 **exerge, -urg.** [a. F. *exergue* (used freq. by De Bie 1634), app. f. Gr. ἐξ out + ἔργον work; prob. intended as a quasi-Gr. rendering of Fr. *hors-d'œuvre*, something lying outside the work.] A small space usually on the reverse of a coin or medal, below the principal device, for any minor inscription, the date, engraver's initials, etc. Also, the inscription there inserted.

1697 EVELYN *Numism.* v. 188 Position of the Legenda.. some on the Exerge only. *Ibid.* 98 Exurg. **1761** *Phil. Trans.* LII. 29 The inscription in the exergue is formed of the Etruscan characters. **1842** BRANDE *Dict. Sc. Lit. & Art* 833/1 When occupying the lower extremity of the pieces, and separated from the rest by a horizontal line, they [the words] are termed the exergue. **1864** C. W. KING *Gnostics* 54 In the exergue is set out a table supporting a loaf.

transf. **1851** LANDOR *Popery* 49 Never tear a hole in the exergue of the pantaloon because they have been sitting in a dirty place.

e'xergum. [Latinized form of prec., as if ad. Gr. *ἐξεργον.] = prec.

1730–6 in BAILEY (folio). **1856** W. H. SMYTH *Catal. Northumberland's Rom. Family Coins* 232 On the exergum P(ublius) Galb(a).

†**e'xert**, *pple.* and *ppl. a.* *Obs.* [ad. L. *ex(s)ert-us* pa. pple. of *exserĕre* to EXERT.] Used as pa. pple. of next. Also as *ppl. a.* EXSERT, EXSERTED.

1647 H. MORE *Song of Soul* I. I. xxxix, The self-same power (Which is exert upon each mortall wight). *Ibid.* II. ii. I. i, To view the various frie from their dark wombs exert. **1661** LOVELL *Hist. Anim. & Min.* Introd., They [the teeth] are not exert or serrate in any [animals] that are horned: but concavous in all.

exert (ɛg'zɜːt), *v.* [f. L. *exert-*, better *exsert-*, ppl. stem of *exserĕre* to put forth, bring out, f. *ex-* out + *serĕre* to bind, entwine. The formation is prob. due to antithesis with *inserĕre* to INSERT. See EXSERT *v.*]

†**1.** *trans.* To thrust forth; to push out or up; to discharge (a seed); to emit (light, etc.). *Obs.* Cf. EXSERT.

1660 tr. *Amyraldus' Treat. Relig.* II. v. 231 The seeds of venome..will infallibly be exerted to our mischief. *a* **1688** CUDWORTH *Immut. Mor.* IV. i. §11 He that should say the Sun had a Power of exerting Light out of his own Body. **1690** J. BANISTER in *Phil. Trans.* XVII. 671 The Film, the Nautilus..exerts, may be analogous to this. **1697** DRYDEN *Virg. Georg.* II. 596 Apple Trees, whose Trunks are strong to bear Their spreading Boughs, exert themselves in Air.

1708 J. PHILIPS *Cyder* II. 60 The Orchart loves to wave With Winter Winds, before the Gems exert Their feeble Heads.

†**b.** To bring to light (something previously hidden); to exhibit, reveal. Also, to put forth in action (one's latent character). *Obs.* [Cf. L. *paulatim exseruit principem*, Suet. *Tib.*]

a 1700 DRYDEN (J.), The several parts lay hidden in the piece, Th' occasion but exerted that or this. 1711 ADDISON *Spect.* No. 130 ¶1 My Friend was in some doubt whether he should not exert the Justice of the Peace upon such a Band of Lawless Vagrants. 1743 FIELDING *Wedding-day* II. i, They lead us into ruin with the face of angels, and when the door is shut on us, exert the devil.

2. To manifest in action, bring into active operation (force, a quality, etc.); to exercise, bring to bear. † *to exert every nerve* = to strain every nerve.

1681 FLAVEL *Right. Man's Ref.* 210 God's Faithfulness.. is actuated, and exerted in his Providences. 1693 SOUTH *Serm.* 582 The fore mentioned faith..will..recover and exert itself. 1711 ADDISON *Spect.* No. 112 ¶1 And exerting all such qualities as are apt to give them a figure in the eye of the Village. 1766 GOLDSM. *Vic. W.* xii, Deborah exerted much sagacity in conjecturing. 1781 BURKE *Corr.* (1844) II. 453, I should have exerted every nerve for Mr. Laurens. 1804 *Med. Jrnl.* XII. 298 To exert a power truly consistent with their constitutional prerogative. 1816 J. SMITH *Panorama Sc. & Art* II. 303 All bodies are capable of exerting electrical attraction. 1860 TYNDALL *Glac.* II. xxi. 344 Supposing..the unimpeded thrust of the whole glacier ..to be exerted on the ice at the Montanvert, etc. *a* 1862 BUCKLE *Misc. Wks.* (1872) I. 133 In the middle ages the influence of the church was almost invariably exerted on the side of order and peace.

3. *to exert oneself*: to put forth one's latent powers; to use efforts or endeavours; to strive.

1736 BUTLER *Anal.* I. ii. Wks. 1874 I. 35 By thus exerting ourselves, we obtain and enjoy these objects. 1796 H. HUNTER tr. *St. Pierre's Stud. Nat.* (1799) I. 62 Every individual..is under obligation to exert himself for the general good. 1861 TROLLOPE *Barchester T.* xiii, Every one must now exert himself who would not choose to go to the wall.

†**b.** *intr.* for *refl.* *Obs.*

a 1749 PHILIPS *Pastorals* v, To try How art exerting, might with nature vie. 1799 MACKINTOSH *Law Nat. & Nations* Wks. 1846 I. 363 Other men..have exerted to disguise the most miserable common-places in the shape of paradox.

†**4.** To perform, practise. *Obs.*

1662 GLANVILL *Lux Orient.* iii. 29 An occasioning him to exert an operation of his mind which he did not before. 1667 SYDENHAM in J. Brown *Horæ Subsec.* Ser. I. (1882) 125 If it shall happen yt the Mercury shall..exert its operation by stooles. *a* 1716 SOUTH (J.), When the will has exerted an act of command upon any faculty of the soul. 1757 BURKE *Abridgm. Eng. Hist.* III. iv, The youth..after exerting many useless acts of unfortunate bravery, fell in battle.

exerted (ɛg'zɜːtɪd), *ppl. a.* [f. prec. + -ED¹.]

†**1.** Thrust out; projecting; EXSERTED. *Obs.*

1697 DRYDEN *Æneid* XI. 944 Resistless, through the War, Camilla rode..One side was bare for her exerted Brest. 1698 TYSON in *Phil. Trans.* XX. 113 Eyes Black, small, vivid and exerted. 1756 T. AMORY *J. Buncle* (1770) I. xiii. 51 Its exerted clavicle has several volutions. 1816 KIRBY & SP. *Entomol.* iv. (1828) I. 121 With a very long exerted sting. 1823 W. SCORESBY *Jrnl. North Whale Fishery* 418 The front teeth of both jaws would appear to be exerted during the life of the animal.

2. Roused to effort; brought into vigorous action; strained.

1675 M. CLIFFORD *Hum. Reason* in *Phenix* (1708) II. 550 Men often move their Bodies, without any particular exerted Thought of doing so. 1701 ROWE *Amb. Step-moth.* I. i, The utmost Power of my exerted Soul Preserves a being only for your service. 1715–20 POPE *Iliad* XVII. 767 His exerted sight Pass'd this and that way, through the ranks of fight. *Ibid.* XVII. 833 Two mules..with exerted strength, Drag some vast beam.

Hence **e'xertedness**, *rare*⁻¹, the quality of being exerted or brought into vigorous action.

1681 H. MORE *Exp. Dan.* iii. 74 The ethereal purity, exertedness, and activity of their [Angels'] nature.

exerting (ɛg'zɜːtɪŋ), *vbl. sb.* [f. as prec. + -ING¹.] The action of the vb. EXERT; †an instance of this, an exertion.

1676 HALE *Contempl.* I. (1689) 260 This habit of piety in your soul..will put forth actual exertings of it self in applications of short occasional prayers. 1677 —— *Prim. Orig. Man.* I. i. 31 This analogical Providence..though it accomodate not it self to the finger in those exertings of those Senses of Seeing or hearing, yet, etc. 1695 PEPYS *Let. Tanner* in *Academy* 23 Aug. (1890) 152/2 Inviteing our learned Professor to ye exerting of his Strength.

exertion (ɛg'zɜːʃən). [as if ad. L. **exertiōn-em* (*exsertiōn-em*): see EXERT *v.* and EXSERTION.]

†**1.** The action of putting forth; manifestation, display. Const. *of*. *Obs.*

1668 HOWE *Bless. Righteous* (1825) 252 O my Soul take thy allowed pleasure in such exertions of God, as thou dost now experience in thyself. 1682 SIR T. BROWNE *Chr. Mor.* 33 Could we..apprehend the ideated man, and as he stood in the intellect of God upon the first exertion by creation. *a* 1768 SECKER *Serm.* I. x, A proper exertion of that chearfulness, which God hath plainly designed us to shew. 1796 JANE AUSTEN *Sense & Sens.* (1849) 99 An exertion of spirits, which increased with her increase of emotion.

2. The action or habit of exerting or putting into active operation (an organ, the faculties, or habit of the body or mind); the action of exercising or putting in force (power, a principle). Also an instance of this. Const. *of*.

1677 HALE *Prim. Orig. Man.* I. i. 21 The several exertions of the several organs relating to their several functions. 1736 BUTLER *Anal.* I. v. Wks. 1874 I. 88 Habits of the mind are produced by the exertion of inward practical principles. 1756 BURKE *Vind. Nat. Soc.* Wks. 1842 I. 15 A timidity which hinders the full exertion of his faculties. 1761–2 HUME *Hist. Eng.* (1806) III. App. iii. 600 [Elizabeth's] imperious temper..rendered her exertions of power violent and frequent. 1818 JAS. MILL *Brit. India* II. v. vi. 568 Carrying the exertion of their powers to a height more extraordinary than they had before attempted. 1828 SCOTT *F.M. Perth* xxiv, By a skilful exertion of strength and address, the body of Bonthron was placed safely on the ground.

attrib. 1889 *Pall Mall G.* 2 Dec. 6/2 Exertion money, that is, the girls are set to work against one another by the promise that those who work hardest shall be paid..extra.

3. The action of exerting oneself; vigorous action; effort; an instance or mode of exerting oneself.

1777 ROBERTSON *Hist. Amer.* I. II. 125 The constitution of their bodies [was] naturally..unaccustomed to the laborious exertions of industry. 1806–7 J. BERESFORD *Miseries Hum. Life* (1826) II. xxxvi, Working the dumb-bells and other irrational exertions. 1810 WELLINGTON in Gurw. *Disp.* VI. 327 To stimulate others to similar exertions. 1844 THIRLWALL *Greece* VIII. lxi. 100 The fire was soon extinguished by the exertions of the soldiers. 1855 SIR H. DOUGLAS *Mil. Bridges* vi. 289 Every exertion should be made..to restore a passage. 1860 TYNDALL *Glac.* I. xxii. 152 To keep up the proper supply of heat by increased exertion. 1876 J. H. NEWMAN *Hist. Sk.* I. II. i. 247 His health..was as yet unequal to the exertion of pleading.

exertive (ɛg'zɜːtɪv), *a.* [f. EXERT *v.* + -IVE.]

1. Tending to exert or rouse to action.

1836–7 SIR W. HAMILTON *Metaph.* xi. (1877) I. 186 Exertive faculties, the best expression to denote the faculties —of will and desire. 1881 J. C. DOLAN in *Pennsylv. Sch. Jrnl.* XXX. 82 The will is universally conceded to be the conative or exertive faculty.

2. (Meaning obscure: perh. some error in text.)

1560 ROLLAND *Crt. Venus* I. 24 Be Fische in flude swowming so exertiue.

†**e'xertment.** *Obs. rare*⁻¹. [f. EXERT *v.* + -MENT.] The action of exerting; display, exertion.

1696 EDWARDS *Exist. & Provid. God* I. 153 This unusual exertment of divine providence we of this nation..have lately felt with surprise. 1860 WORCESTER cites CLARKE.

exes: see EX *sb.*¹ and *sb.*²

†**e'xesion.** *Obs.* [as if ad. L. **exesiōn-em*, n. of action f. *exedĕre* (see EXEDE), f. *ex-* out + *edĕre* to eat.] The action of eating out.

1646 SIR T. BROWNE *Pseud. Ep.* III. xvi. 145 Theophrastus ..denieth the exesion or forcing through the belly [of the viper]. 1684 tr. *Bonet's Merc. Compit.* 87 Exesion is made by tarrying for Concoction. 1775 in ASH.

exestuate, -ating, -ation: see EXÆSTUATE.

Exeter ('ɛksɪtə(r)).

1. The name of an English city, used *attrib.* in ***Exeter-elm*** (see quot.). Also, as the name of a bait for salmon.

1882 *Garden* 11 Nov. 419/3 The Exeter Elm..is simply a fastigiate variety. 1883 *Fisheries Exhib. Catal.* 54 Phantoms, Exeters..and various other Baits for Salmon.

2. Exeter Hall, a building in the Strand, London, erected in 1830–31, used chiefly for religious and philanthropic assemblies till 1907; often used *allusively* to denote a type of evangelicalism.

1835 MOORE *Fudge Fam. England* i. 78 'Tis rumour'd our Manager means to bespeak The Church tumblers from Exeter Hall for next week. 1849 CARLYLE *Latter-d. Pamph., Nigger Q.* (1858) 3 Exeter Hall, my philanthropic friends, has had its way in this matter. *Ibid.*, A state of matters.. which has earned us not only the praise of Exeter Hall,..but lasting favour (it is hoped) from the Heavenly Powers themselves. *Ibid.* 5 Exeter-Hall Philanthropy. *Ibid.* 15 We must be patient, and let the Exeter-Hallery and other tragic Tomfoolery rave itself out. 1860 W. H. RUSSELL *Diary India* I. 356 Our Christian character in Europe, our Christian zeal in Exeter Hall, will not atone for usurpation and annexation in Hindostan. 1888 *Contemp. Rev.* Apr. 531 Thither [*sc.* Africa] Manchester turns her longing eyes, thither the heart of Exeter Hall is yearning. 1907 *Daily Chron.* 4 Mar. 6/6 The vanishing of Exeter Hall from the world of Evangelicalism.

‖**exeunt** ('ɛksiːʌnt), *v.* [L. *exeunt* they go out, 3rd. pers. pl. pres. indic. of *exīre* to go out: see EXIT *sb.*] A stage direction (*orig.* **exeant**: see EXEAT) signifying that at this point two or more actors leave the stage. So in ***exeunt omnes*** 'all go out', a direction for all to retire.

c 1485 *Digby Myst.* (1882) IV. 832 We shall gife hire attendance..Exeunt. 1613 SHAKS. *Hen. VIII*, I. ii. 214 *Kin.* By day and night Hee's Traytor to th' height. *Exeunt.* 1673 DRYDEN *State Innoc.* III. i, [Stage direction]..the two Angels exeunt severally. 1779 SHERIDAN *Critic* II. ii, Exeunt praying..would vary the established mode of springing off with a glance at the pit.

‖**ex facie** (ɛks 'feɪʃiː). *Sc. Law.* [L. *ex* out of + *faciē*, abl. of *facies* face.] On (*lit.* from) the face (of a document); so far as appears from the document itself. Also *attrib.*

1861 W. BELL *Dict. Law Scot.* 348/2 A deed *ex facie* valid and regular, but..reducible on the head of deathbed, etc. *Ibid.*, *Ex facie* nullities, whether at common law or founded on statute, are pleadable by way of exception.

exfamiliation (ˌɛksfəˌmɪlɪ'eɪʃən). *rare*⁻¹. [n. of action f. EX- + L. *familia* family, on analogy of *expatriation.*] Exclusion from a family.

1879 HEARN *Aryan Household* 131 This power of admission on the one side, and on the other side of expatriation, or, perhaps, I should rather say of exfamiliation.

exfetation (ɛksfiː'teɪʃən). *Med. rare*⁻⁰. Also **exfœtation.** [f. EX- *pref.*¹ + L. *fētā-re* to impregnate: see -ATION.] 'Imperfect fetation in some organ exterior to the uterus' (Hoblyn 1858).

exfiltration (ˌɛksfɪl'treɪʃən). *rare*⁻¹. [n. of action f. EX- *pref.*¹ + FILT(E)R: see -ATION.] The action or process of filtering out.

1878 LAWRENCE tr. *Cotta's Rocks Class.* 25 Zeolites 'are products of exfiltration or of the internal decomposition and transmutation of the mother rock.'

exflagellation (ˌɛksflædʒə'leɪʃən). *Zool.* [f. EX-¹ + FLAGELLATION 2.] The formation or shedding of flagella; the development of microgametes resembling flagella. So **ex'flagellate** *v. intr.*

1909 in WEBSTER. 1912 E. A. MINCHIN *Introd. Study Protozoa* xv. 357 The male sporonts..form filamentous male gametes resembling flagella, and are consequently said to 'exflagellate'. *Ibid.* 364 The 'exflagellation', or formation of microgametes, which takes place, under normal circumstances, in the stomach of the mosquito, can be seen also in blood freshly drawn and examined on a slide, if ripe sporonts are present. 1926 C. M. WENYON *Protozool.* I. I. 85 The microgametocyte gives rise in the course of a few minutes to six or ten microgametes by a violent process known as exflagellation. 1964 M. HYNES *Med. Bacteriol.* (ed. 8) xxviii. 441 From the male cell, flagella-like gametes develop, a process known as ex-flagellation.

exflect (ɛks'flɛkt), *v. rare*⁻¹. [f. EX- + L. *flectĕre* to bend, turn.] *trans.* To bend out or outwards.

1877 COUES *Fur Anim.* vii. 204 The lower border is.. emarginate, and the angle itself is scarcely..exflected.

ex-focal (ɛks'fəʊkəl), *a. rare*⁻¹. [f. EX- *pref.*¹ + FOCAL.] Not passing through the focus.

1881 T. STEVENSON in *Nature* XXIII. 560 The ex-focal rays proceeding from the outer edges of the flame.

†**ex'fodiate.** *v. Obs. rare*⁻¹. [f. L. *exfodi-* stem of *exfodĕre* (*effodĕre*) to dig out or up (f. *ex-* out + *fodĕre* to dig) + -ATE³.] *trans.* To dig out.

a 1860 'Used somewhere by H. H. Wilson' (F. Hall).

Hence **ex'fodiated** *ppl. a.* **exfodi'ation**, the action or process of digging out: in quot. *fig.*

1795 *Hull Advertiser* 24 Oct. 4/3 The women carefully wash the..exfodiated clay. 1823 *New Monthly Mag.* VII. 124 It was necessary that he should attain the light by a long process of exfodiation [*printed* exfodation].

exfœtation, var. form of EXFETATION.

exfoliate (ɛks'fəʊlɪeɪt), *v.* [f. late L. *exfoliāt-* ppl. stem of *exfoliāre* to strip of leaves, f. *ex-* (see EX- *pref.*¹) + *folium* leaf: see -ATE³. (In Fr. *exfolier.*) Cf. EFFOLIATE.]

1. *trans.* **a.** *Pathol.* To cast off, shed (the cuticle, the surface of a bone) in the form of 'leaves' or scales. **b.** *Surg.* To remove the surface of (a bone, etc.) by exfoliation.

1612 WOODALL *Surg. Mate* Wks. (1653) 391 Nature doth of her self exfoliate, and cast off the part putrid. 1671 SHADWELL *Humorist* v, I have hurt myself just upon the shin-bone that was exfoliated. 1683 SALMON *Doron Med.* II. 588 It is an excellent thing to scale and exfoliate Bones. 1799 *Med. Jrnl.* II. 446 The other [wound] continued..to exfoliate a little bone. 1810 *Charac.* in *Ann. Reg.* 1808 116 Animals that exfoliate their cuticle annually.

2. *intr.* Of a bone, horny substance, a scar, the skin, etc.: To separate or come off in thin leaf-like layers or scales; to desquamate, scale off.

1676 WISEMAN *Chirurg. Treat.* II. vii. 184 The Heel-bone ..rarely exfoliates by rough handling. 1774 GOLDSM. *Nat. Hist.* (1862) II. I. vi. 26 [The horny helmet of the cassowary] exfoliates slowly like the beak. 1807 *Med. Jrnl.* XVII. 278 The eschar produced by the caustic exfoliated very kindly. 1818 *Art Preserv. Feet* 177 The nails..are subject..to exfoliate. 1844–57 G. BIRD *Urin. Deposits* (ed. 5) 359 The warm bath was daily used as soon as the skin began to exfoliate. 1856 KANE *Arct. Expl.* II. xi. 34 Down with a frozen heel; the bone exfoliating.

3. *transf.* **a.** Of the cellular tissue of trees: To peel off. Of the trunk: To throw off layers of bark. **b.** Of minerals, metals, rocks, etc.: To split into laminæ, come off in layers or scales.

1807 J. E. SMITH *Phys. Bot.* 23 The Cellular Integument exfoliates..in trees. 1811 PINKERTON *Petral.* I. 591 Trunks of trees, lying one on the other..easily exfoliate, by drying in the open air. 1831 J. HOLLAND *Manuf. Metals* I. 152 The wrought iron exfoliates, or separates in laminæ. 1839 MURCHISON *Silur. Syst.* I. xxxvi. 501 The columnar green-stone exfoliates at the angles of the prisms. 1862 DANA *Man. Geol.* 64 Before the blowpipe it [anhydrite] does not exfoliate like gypsum. 1879 *Cassell's Techn. Educ.* IV. 145/1 The fire is only moderate at first, lest the cupel should crack and exfoliate by being too suddenly heated.

4. *trans.* In etymological sense: To unfold the leaves of; to open out, develop. In quot. *fig.*

1808 KNOX & JEBB *Corr.* I. 447 To make a sermon out of one of his discourses..partly, by exfoliating ideas, that are

like rosebuds. **1877** WRAXALL tr. *Hugo's Miserables* v. xxxix. 26 Questions exfoliated themselves.

Hence **ex'foliated, ex'foliating** *ppl. adjs.*

1676 WISEMAN *Chirurg. Treat.* v. ix. 398 The exfoliated edges of the bone. **1859** REEVE *Brittany* 236 The columns were getting rusty and exfoliated. **1882** *Times* 23 Mar. 9/5 The dust of their exfoliating skin.

exfoliation (ɛksˌfəʊlɪˈeɪʃən). [a. F. *exfoliation*, f. as prec.: see -ATION.]

1. *Surg.* and *Path.* The action or process of exfoliating.

1676 WISEMAN *Chirurg. Treat.* IV. iv. 264 The bone laid bare in order to Exfoliation. *c* **1720** W. GIBSON *Farrier's Dispens.* I. i. (1734) 25 Euphorbium.. It's Tincture is often applied to Bones that are laid bare, to hasten an Exfoliation. **1741** MONRO *Anat.* (ed. 3) 51 The Exfoliation which Cartilages are subject to. **1797** M. BAILLIE *Morb. Anat.* (1807) 89 The cricoid cartilage, being converted into bone, was separated by exfoliation. **1851** CARPENTER *Man. Phys.* (ed. 2) 173 This moulting is precisely analogous to the exfoliation and new formation of the Epidermis, in Man.

b. *transf.* Cf. EXFOLIATE 3.

1802 PLAYFAIR *Illustr. Hutton. Th.* 31 This stone is.. subject to perpetual exfoliation. **1816** R. JAMESON *Char. Min.* (1817) 294 Exfoliation, or the separation of the folia of a mineral from each other. **1848–53** LAYARD *Nineveh* ix. 223 A kind of exfoliation had taken place on the surface of the glass vase. **1860** TYNDALL *Glac.* I. i. 6 The exfoliation of rails, the fibres of iron, etc. **1884** BOWER & SCOTT *De Bary's Phaner. & Ferns* 413 In old age they [parenchymatous cells] die off.. after breaking up into layers or rows (exfoliation).

2. That which is exfoliated; an exfoliated portion; a 'coat' or layer in the stem of a tree.

1750 G. HUGHES *Barbadoes* 110 The several exfoliations of its [a tree's] green part were equal in number to its branches. **1835** LINDLEY *Introd. Bot.* (1848) I. 238 The spongelets of the aerial roots consist of.. exfoliations of the epiphlœum. **1876** GROSS *Dis. Bladder* 27 Such casts.. are mistaken for exfoliations of the lining membrane.

exfoliative (ɛksˈfəʊlɪətɪv), *a.* and *sb.* [a. F. *exfoliatif, -ive*, f. *exfolier*, ad. L. *exfoliāre*: see EXFOLIATE *v.* + -IVE.]

A. *adj.* 'Capable of causing, or favourable to, exfoliation' (*Syd. Soc. Lex.* 1884).

1730–6 BAILEY (folio), *Exfoliative Trepan*, one proper to scrape, and at the same time to pierce a bone, and so to exfoliate or raise several leaves or flakes one after another. **1746** AMYAND in *Phil. Trans.* XLIV. 196 With the exfoliative Trepan, to make a fair Opening into the medullary Cavity of the Bone. **1875** H. WALTON *Dis. Eye* 494 Occasionally an exfoliative effort is seen on the surface of the eye.

B. *sb.* Something which produces exfoliation.

1676 WISEMAN *Chirurg. Treat.* II. vii. 185 Dress the Bone with the milder Exfoliatives, and keep the Ulcer open, till the burnt Bone cast off.

exforcipate (ɛksˈfɔːsɪpeɪt) *nonce wd.* [f. EX- *pref.*[1] + L. *forcip-em* forceps + -ATE[3].] *trans.* To extract with a forceps. In quot. *fig.*

1838 COLERIDGE *Lit. Rem.* III. 383 Wrapped up in the womb of this or that text of Scripture to be exforcipated by the logico-obstetric skill of High Church doctors.

†**ex'fuse,** *v. Obs. rare*⁻¹. = EFFUSE *v.*

1612 W. PARKES *Curtaine-Dr.* (1876) 16 View with what delight and greedinesse of appetite he [the drunkard] infuseth and exfuseth, powres out and powres in.

†**ex'generate,** *v. Obs. rare.* [f. EX- *pref.*[1] + GENERATE *v.*] *trans.* To generate or produce out of something else. Hence **ex'generated** *ppl. a.*

1662 J. SPARROW tr. *Behme's Rem. Wks., Apol. Perfect.* 9 The Divine Love is an Exgenerated Substance. *Ibid., 2nd Apol. Tylcken* 47 How is the New Birth performed in Us? is it entering in or exgenerating? is it not performed in us in our Souls?

ex. gr.: see EXEMPLI GRATIA.

‖**ex gratia** (ɛks ˈgreɪʃɪə), *adj.* and *advb. phr.* [L.] Of or by favour; done or given as a favour and not under compulsion; *spec.* implying the absence of any legal obligation.

1769 W. BLACKSTONE *Commentaries Laws Eng.* IV. xxx. 385 Writs of error to reverse attainders in capital cases are only allowed *ex gratia*; and not without express warrant under the king's sign manual. **1920** *Act 10 & 11 Geo. V.* c. 32 Sch. B. xvi, Ex gratia grants in respect of losses and injuries. **1928** *Daily Chron.* 9 Aug. 5/6 An ex-gratia payment in consequence of his wrongful.. imprisonment for nearly 19 years. **1955** *Times* 30 May 11/5 In addition to our existing ex-gratia pensioners there is a sizable body of employees who by reason of their age are not eligible to join the scheme.

exgurgitate, obs. var. of EGURGITATE. Hence **exgurgi'tation,** *Obs.* (see quot.).

1623–6 COCKERAM, *Exgurgitate*, to vomit. **1730–6** BAILEY (folio), *Exgurgitation*, a casting or voiding up.

exh-. In the more common of the words beginning with these letters, such as *exhaust, exhibit*, the *h* is usually silent; many persons, however, sound it (esp. in deliberate or public utterance) when the word has the stress on the second syllable. To avoid inconvenient repetition the more frequent of the two alternative pronunciations will alone be indicated. In words of little colloquial currency the *h* is ordinarily sounded when it begins a stressed syllable.

exhæredate, -ation, obs. ff. EXHEREDATE, -ATION.

exhalable (ɛgz-, ɛksˈheɪləb(ə)l), *a.* Also 7 **-ible.** [f. EXHALE *v.* + -ABLE.] That can be exhaled; capable of being evaporated.

1675 GREW *Anat. Plants, Lect.* vi. (1682) 291 Plants, whose Virtue lieth in their exhalible Parts. *a* **1691** BOYLE *Hist. Air* viii. (1692) 29 The Body by Exsiccation is deprived of those liquid and exhalable Parts. **1748** *Phil. Trans.* XLV. 544 These exhalable Parts. **1775** in ASH. **1847** in CRAIG; and in mod. Dicts.

exhalant (ˈɛgz-, ɛksˈheɪlənt), *a.* and *sb.* Also 8–9 **-ent.** [a. Fr. *exhalant*, ad. L. *exhālant-em*, f. *exhālāre* to EXHALE.]

A. *adj.*

1. That exhales, exhaling.

1811 *Edin. Rev.* XIX. 52 Carbonic acid.. is.. given out directly by the exhalent vessels of the lungs. **1854** WOODWARD *Mollusca* II. 243 The exhalent siphon [in Bivalves] has but a single row of tentacles. **1883** C. F. HOLDER in *Harper's Mag.* Jan. 187/2 Their orifices so arranged that the inhalent are upon the outside of the cylinder, and the exhalent upon the inner side.

2. *exhalant (artery, vessel*, etc.): that transfuses or conveys (blood, etc.) in minute quantities.

1771 T. PERCIVAL *Ess. Med. & Experim.* (1777) I. 253 The lymph which is thrown out, from the exhalant arteries, into the intestines. **1782** A. MONRO *Anat.* 35 These exhalent arteries must have corresponding absorbent veins. **1830** R. KNOX *Béclard's Anat.* 181 Exhalent arterioles opening at the surface of the peritoneum. **1847** YOUATT *Horse* xii. 252 Increased action of the exhalent vessels.

B. *sb.* An exhalant vessel or organ. *Obs.*

1796 MITCHELL in Morse *Amer. Geog.* I. 200 *note*, Its odour resides in the cuticular exhalants. **1805** W. SAUNDERS *Min. Waters* 463 In fever.. the exhalents on the surface of the body will not admit of a free passage to the perspirable fluid. **1820** E. P. LUSCOMBE *Health of Soldiers* 46 The Sun's rays, by which the exhalants on the surface of the body are kept in a state of high excitement. *a* **1841** SIR A. COOPER in T. Graham *Dom. Med.* (1844) 407 Dropsy.. arises from an increased action of the exhalents.

attrib. **1836** TODD *Cycl. Anat.* I. 605/1 The important exhalent function of the skin is annihilated.

†**exhalate,** *v. Obs.* Also 7 **exhallate.** [f. L. *exhālāt-* ppl. stem of *exhālāre* to EXHALE.]

1. *trans.* **a.** To send off as vapour; to evaporate. **b.** To produce by evaporation.

1598 SYLVESTER *Du Bartas* II. ii. (1608) 282 The flitting Clouds it [the sea] cease-les exhalates. **1599** A. M. tr. *Gabelhouer's Bk. Physicke* 70/1 Let it seeth till it be sodden, and exhalatede awaye the depth of thre fingers. **1600** W. WATSON *Decacordon* (1602) 334 Dewes of cold.. deuotions .. mixt with exhalated smokes of.. sublimed aspires. **1643** I. STEER tr. *Fabricius' Exp. Chirurg.* xii. 47 Those sharpe.. humours may be exhallated.. by the pores of the skin.

2. *intr.* **a.** = EXHALE 2. **b.** (See quot. 1623.)

1599 A. M. tr. *Gabelhouer's Bk. Physicke* 125/1 Cover the same least the vigor therof exhalate. **1623** COCKERAM II, To Breath on something, *Exhalate, Euaporate.*

exhalation (ɛkshəˈleɪʃən). Forms: 4–6 **exalacion,** (4 **-tion,** 5 **-cyon,** 6 **-tione),** 5 **exalacioun, -cyoun,** 6– **exhalation.** [ad. L. *exhālātiōn-em*, n. of action f. *exhālāre* to EXHALE.]

1. The action or process of exhaling, breathing forth or throwing off in the form of vapour; evaporation. Const. *of.*

1398 TREVISA *Barth. De P.R.* III. xv. (Tollem. MS.), To hot sunne.. makeþ to greet exalacion and wastynge of þe kynde hete. *c* **1400** *Lanfranc's Cirurg.* II. iii. 152 It is drede of sodeyn deeþ, for sodeyn exalacioun of þe spiritis. **1582** HESTER *Secr. Phiorav.* I. xxxii. 39 The Feuer is dissolued with.. exhalation and exsication. **1603** HOLLAND *Plutarch's Mor.* 41 The aire.. by exhalation is elevated, and doth rise from the earth. **1676** GREW *Anat. Plants, Lect.* ii. (1682) 240 Exhalation; when not only fumes, but visible steams are produced. **1836** TODD *Cycl. Anat.* I. 135/2 The skin and pulmonary surface are the great implements of exhalation among animals.

fig. **1670** G. H. *Hist. Cardinals* I. II. 60 A Pinnacle of Grandeur above all exhalation of scandal.

b. The action of emitting the breath; expiration; an instance of this; a puff. Also *fig.* the blowing off or getting rid of (anger, excitement, etc.).

a **1734** NORTH *Lives* I. 416 After these exhalations.. his mind became more composed. **1834** T. MEDWIN *Angler in Wales* I. 249 There are some who.. shorten the brief span of our [a cigar's] being, making it only a few volcanic exhalations. **1854** EMERSON *Lett. & Soc. Aims, Poet. & Imag.* Wks. (Bohn) III. 159 The length of lines in songs.. is determined by the inhalation and exhalation of the lungs. **1878** H. JAMES *Europeans* I. ii. 73 Gertrude gave a little long, soft exhalation.

2. *concr.* That which is exhaled; a mist, vapour, etc.; an emanation or effluvium, a scent. Also *collect.*

1393 GOWER *Conf.* III. 95 Through divers exalations.. Men sene diverse forme appere Of fire. **1398** TREVISA *Barth. De P.R.* XIV. iii. (1495) 469 Hylles gendre exalatcyon, smokes and vapours. **1447** BOKENHAM *Seyntys* (Roxb.) 287 She ouery stynking exalacyoun Of þe eyr bare alwey ful heuyly. **1540–1** ELYOT *Image Gov.* 64 Sickenesses, whiche undoubtedly dooe growe of corrupt exhalacions ventynge out of mens bodies. **1562** BULLEYN *Bk. Simples* 1 b, Abstain from soche meates, as.. make exalacion, or smoke up into the braine. **1610** ROWLANDS *Martin Markall* 32 So noysome an exhalation, that birds.. are poysoned with the very breath and ayre thereof. **1750** JOHNSON *Rambler* No. 78 ¶ 2 The Indian wanderers among his native spices without any sense of their exhalations. **1862** MERIVALE *Rom. Emp.* (1865) VII. lx. 282 Nero's golden house had risen like an exhalation, and like an exhalation it disappeared. **1869** E. A. PARKES *Pract. Hygiene* (ed. 3) 117 Pulmonary and cutaneous exhalations of men.

fig. **1592** NASHE *P. Penilesse* 11 a, Exhalations, drawen vp to the heauen of honor, from the dunghil of obiect fortune. **1871** R. H. HUTTON *Ess.* II. 342 The turbid malarious exhalations of visionary excitement.

3. A body or portion of vapour, usually enkindled vapour; a meteor. *arch.*

1561 EDEN *Arte Nauig.* II. xx. 51 b, Shining exhalations.. appeare in tempestes. **1601** SHAKS. *Jul. C.* II. i. 44 The exhalations, whizzing in the ayre, Giue so much light, that I may reade by them. **1660** GLANVILL *Vanity Dogm.* xviii. 174 The Galaxy is no exhalation from the Earth, but an heap of smaller Luminaries. **1720** OZELL tr. *Vertot's Rom. Rep.* I. IV. 201 This Year.. fiery Exhalations were seen in the Air. **1871** FARRAR *Witn. Hist.* ii. 58 The star of the shepherds was a meteoric exhalation.

†**exhalative,** *a. Obs. rare*⁻¹. [f. L. *exhālāt-* ppl. stem of *exhālāre* (see EXHALE) + -IVE.] Of a nature to be exhaled; exhalable.

1594 PLAT *New Sorts of Soil* 25 When they [corne and other seedes] are ripe.. the exhalative water flyeth away, and the generative remaineth.

exhalatory (ɛgz-, ɛksˈhælətərɪ). [as if ad. L. **exhālātōrium*, f. *exhālāre* to EXHALE + -ORY.] A passage or vent for exhalation (of gas).

1813 *Monthly Mag.* XXXVI. 138 In Persia, there are several natural exhalatories of hydrogen gas.

exhale (ɛgz-, ɛksˈheɪl), *v.*[1] Forms: 5 **exale,** 6 **exhall,** 7 **exhael,** 8 **exhal,** 7– **exhale.** [ad. F. *exhaler*, ad. L. *exhālā-re* to breathe out, evaporate, f. *ex-* out + *hālāre* to breathe.]

I. To give, pass, or draw off in vapour.

1. *trans.* To breathe, give forth, or disengage from the surface; to send up (fumes, gas, vapour, etc.): to give off in vapour. Also *fig.*

a **1628** SIR J. BEAUMONT *Epiph.* in Farr *S.P. Jas. I* (1848) 144 We shall exhale our vapours vp direct. **1664** POWER *Exp. Philos.* I. 29 It had lost near two drams of its former weight, which was exhaled by insensible Transpiration. **1667** MILTON *P.L.* V. 421 Nor doth the Moon no nourishment exhale, From her moist Continent to higher Orbes. **1727** DE FOE *Syst. Magic* I. iv. (1840) 103 The vapours which by their acquired heat they have exhaled. **1772** SIR W. JONES *Laura* Poems (1777) 80 Every bower exhal'd the sweets of May. **1805** W. SAUNDERS *Min. Waters* 248 This mineral water.. exhales no perceptible smell. **1849** MRS. SOMERVILLE *Connex. Phys. Sc.* xxvii. 301 They [plants] exhale oxygen. **1870** EMERSON *Soc. & Solit., Civiliz.* Wks. (Bohn) III. 38 Eloquence.. may warm itself until it exhales symbols of every kind and colour. **1878** HUXLEY *Physiogr.* 67 Water.. exhaled from the leaves of plants and from the lungs and skin of animals.

2. *intr.* Of vapour, perfume, †heat, etc.: To pass off into the air. Of a liquid, etc.: To pass off as vapour; to evaporate. Const. *from, out of.*

c **1400** *Lanfranc's Cirurg.* II. iii. 149 (MS. B) Spirites exaleþ ƿat buþ frendys, boþe to þe body & eke to þe soule. *c* **1420** *Pallad. on Husb.* I. 303 Se the floode be goode ther thou wil duelle: For ofte of it exaleth myst impure. **1626** BACON *Sylva* §399 Fire doth lick up the Spirits and Blood of the Body, so as they exhale. **1641** FRENCH *Distill.* iii. (1651) 66 Let it be melted.. with a soft fire, that all the moisture may exhale. **1707** *Curios. in Husb. & Gard.* 257 Cover the Earth with good Straw-Mats, that the Heat may not exhale. **1718** J. CHAMBERLAYNE *Relig. Philos.* (1730) II. xviii. §6 The same has been observed as to Acid Liquors, by the sowre Smell that exhales from them. **1799** G. SMITH *Laborat.* I. 329 When the matrass is made red hot, sulphurous matters will exhale. **1860** EMERSON *Cond. Life, Worship* Wks. (Bohn) II. 407 When flowers reach their ripeness, incense exhales from them.

b. *transf.* and *fig.*

1621 BURTON *Anat. Mel.* I. ii. IV. vii, As if all our dearest friends lives had exhaled with his. **1667** MILTON *P.L.* VII. 255 When Orient Light Exhaling first from Darkness they beheld. **1697** DRYDEN *Virg. Georg.* IV. 710 His Hopes exhal'd in empty Smoke. **1849–50** ALISON *Hist. Europe* III. xviii. §35. 561 His indignation exhaled in a letter to the Count d'Artois. **1858** HAWTHORNE *Fr. & It. Jrnls.* I. 174 The illusion and lifelikeness.. exhales out of a picture as it grows old.

3. *Phys.* and *Path.* Of animal fluids: To pass off in minute quantities through a membrane or blood-vessel. Also in *passive.*

c **1400** *Lanfranc's Cirurg.* 126 (MS. A) Þei loken if ony þing exale out bi þilke rimelle—as blod or ony other mater. **1830** R. KNOX *Béclard's Anat.* 79 The fluid which the ultimate ramifications of the arteries exhale in it [the cellular tissue]. **1834** MCMURTRIE *Cuvier's Anim. Kingd.* 19 The extremities of the vessels simply spread themselves over large surfaces, whence the produced fluid exhales. **1836** TODD *Cycl. Anat.* I. 401/1 Blood is.. rarely exhaled at the internal surface of the bladder. **1865** *Morn. Star* 23 Feb., The blood merely oozes through the coats of the relaxed vessels—in medical phrase we say it is exhaled.

4. *trans.* To draw up or drive off in the form of vapour; to evaporate; *rarely*, †to draw up (a vapour); to draw out the perfume of (*e.g.* a rose).

1589 NASHE in *Greene's Menaphon* Pref. (Arb.) 9 The Sea exhaled by drops, will in continuance be drie. **1592** SHAKS. *Rom. & Jul.* III. v. 13 Yon Light.. is some Meteor that the Sun exhales. **1622** T. SCOTT *Belg. Pismire* 53 The Sunne exhales vapours from the Sea. **1626** BACON *Sylva* §413 The November Rose is the sweetest, having been less exhaled by the Sun. **1641** FRENCH *Distill.* iii. (1651) 65 These Salts must.. be calcined, which is done by exhaling their flegme. **1707** *Curios. in Husb. & Gard.* 235 A prodigious Quantity of

clear Water must be exhal'd, to get an Ounce of dry Sediments. **1825** SCOTT *Talism.* i, Bitumen and sulphur, which the burning sun exhaled from the waters of the lake. **1836** EMERSON *Nature, Prospects* Wks. (Bohn) II. 173 The.. filths of nature, the sun shall dry up, and the wind exhale.

b. *transf.* and *fig.*

1588 SHAKS. *L.L.L.* IV. iii. 70 Thou, faire Sun, which on my earth doest shine, Exhalest this vapor-vow. **1632** J. HAYWARD tr. *Biondi's Eromena* 105 Teares.. not sufficient to exhale and evaporate the heavinesse of her heart. **1725-6** POPE *Odyss.* XXII. 431 The warm sun exhales their soul away.

II. To breathe or blow forth from within.

5. To breathe out (life, soul, words, a prayer, etc.).

1589 GREENE *Menaphon* (Arb.) 57 Hee exhaled into his eyes such deepe impression of his perfection, as that, etc. *c* **1611** CHAPMAN *Iliad* XVIII. 196 Twelue men, of greatest strength in Troy, left with their liues exhald. *a* **1619** FOTHERBY *Atheom.* I. xiii. §3 (1622) 140 In these miserable torments, they both.. exhaled their execrable soules. *a* **1638** MEDE *Chr. Sacrif.* v. Wks. II. (1672) 362 An Oration exhaled .. from sanctified Souls. **1816** J. WILSON *City of Plague* I. i. 355 And silent words Of mercy breathed from heaven will be exhaled.. into thy wither'd heart. **1885** CLODD *Myths & Dr.* II. ix. 203 The Romans, conceived the soul.. as exhaled with the dying breath.

6. To blow off (as steam); chiefly *fig.* to get rid of (enthusiasm, wrath, etc.) as if by blowing. Also, *to exhale oneself.* Cf. BLOW *v.* 10.

1745 *Fortunate Orphan* 237, I exhaled my Grief in the bitterest Exclamations. **1802** MAR. EDGEWORTH *Moral T.* (1816) I. xi. 92 A... suffered him to exhale his passion in.. oaths. **1831** T. L. PEACOCK *Crotchet Castle* viii. 104 To narrate his misadventures, and exhale his budget of grievances. **1845** DARWIN in *Life & Lett.* (1887) I. 341, I have exhaled myself with a paragraph or two in my journal on the sin of Brazilian slavery. **1860** PIESSE *Lab. Chem. Wonders* 9 Sulphur is exhaled from the volcanoes at the time of their activity. **1860** W. COLLINS *Wom. White* II. narr. viii. 245, I.. exhale the rest of my enthusiasm in the open air. **1867** *Month* 512, I could not exhale my wrath before his grace.

7. *intr.* To make an expiration; opposed to INHALE.

1863 TYNDALL *Heat* iii. 54 When we exhale, we pour out from the lungs carbonic acid.

Hence **ex'haled** *ppl. a.* (in senses 1 and 4).

1593 SHAKS. *Lucr.* 779 Let their exhaled unwholesome breaths make sick The life of purity. **1596** —— *1 Hen. IV*, v. i. 19 Will you.. be no more an exhall'd Meteor. **1635** SWAN *Spec. M.* v. §2 (1643) 180 That which we call a fired whirl-wind, being an exhaled blast set on fire.

†**ex'hale,** *v.*[2] *Obs.* Also 6 exhall. [f. EX- *pref.* + HALE *v.*] To drag out or draw forth.

1. *trans.* To drag (a person) away; to draw (a thing) out of. Also *absol.* to draw (a sword) from the scabbard.

1599 SHAKS. *Hen. V*, II. i 66 O Braggard vile.. The Graue doth gape, and doting death is neere, Therefore exhale. **1601** B. JONSON *Poetaster* III. i. Wks. (Rtldg.) 116/1 Nay, I beseech you, gentlemen, do not exhale me thus. **1607** TOPSELL *Four-f. Beasts* (1673) 400 A mouse being flead.. and put unto a wound.. will presently.. exhale and draw them [the head of a dart, etc.] out of the same. **1615** T. ADAMS *Spir. Navigators* 34 Couetous wretches, that would dig to the Center to exhale riches.

b. To cause (blood, tears) to flow. Const. *from.* (Prob. influenced by EXHALE *v.* 4.)

1594 SHAKS. *Rich. III*, I. ii. 58 'Tis thy presence that exhales this blood From cold and empty Veines. **1611** SPEED *Hist. Gt. Brit.* IX. ix. (1632) 633 These words exhaled ioyfull teares from many of the hearers. **1613** W. BROWNE *Brit. Past.* I. v, That did from Fida's eyes salt teares exhale.

2. To draw up; raise (a person) to a higher position. *rare.* Cf. EXALT *v.* 2.

1595 MARKHAM *Sir R. Grinvile* B vij b, Thou.. Whom men adore, and all the gods exhall [*rime* call] Into the books of endlesse memorie. **1604** DRAYTON *Owle* 689 They whose Minds should be exhal'd and hie. **1647** WARD *Simp. Cobler* 48 When Kings rise higher than they should, they exhale Subjects higher than they would.

exhalement (ɛgz-, ɛks'heɪlmənt). [f. EXHALE *v.*[1] + -MENT.] = EXHALATION.

1646 SIR T. BROWNE *Pseud. Ep.* II. v. 86 Nor will polished amber although it send forth a grosse and corporall exhalement be found a long time defective upon the exactest scales. **1816** MOORE *Go, let me Weep* i, While tears, that from repentance flow, In bright exhalement reach the skies. **1839** G. DARLEY *Introd. Beaum. & Fl. Wks.* I. 26 Our present poet.. speaks.. to no end save exhalement of superfluous animal spirits.

†**ex'halence.** *Obs.*[−0] [f. as prec. + -ENCE.] 'The action of exhaling, or matter exhaled'. **1850** in OGILVIE.

exhalible: see EXHALABLE.

exhaling (ɛgz-, ɛks'heɪlɪŋ), *vbl. sb.* [f. EXHALE *v.*[1] + -ING[1].] The action of the vb. EXHALE; an instance of this.

1616 SYLVESTER *Tobacco Battered* Wks. (1621) 1146 Those that.. Offend the Nose, with filthy Fumes exhalings. **1626** BACON *Sylva* §333 The fifth [means to induce Putrefaction] is.. by the Exhaling.. of the Principal Spirits.

ex'haling, *ppl. a.* [f. as prec. + -ING[2].] That exhales; in senses of the verb. *lit.* and *fig.*

1660 BOYLE *New Exp. Phys. Mech.* xxii. 178 The exhaling and imprison'd steams. **1765** HAMILTON in *Phil. Trans.* LV. 154 Evaporation is vastly promoted by a current of fresh air passing over the exhaling surface. **1767** GOOCH *Treat. Wounds* I. 289 Moisture, by the exhaling vessels, may be conveyed to the extravasated fluids. **1811** PINKERTON *Petral.* II. 357 Exhaling fumes prevented him from approaching the upper crater. **1890** *Spectator* 15 Mar., An ever-dwindling and exhaling experience of the conscience.

exhall, obs. var. EXHALE *v.*

exhaltation, obs. form of EXALTATION.

†**ex'hance,** *v. Obs.* Also 5-7 -ha(u)nse, 6 exhaunce. [alteration of ENHANCE, after words beginning with EX-.] = ENHANCE 2 b, 4, 5.

a **1450** *Knt. de la Tour* lxix. (1868) 91 The iugementis of God are merueilous, for.. he exhaunsithe the meke, that besechithe his grace and mercy. *c* **1590** *Secret Mem. Earl Leicester* (1706) 73 He that may.. return the same [lands].. into Her Majesties Hands by a fresh Exchange, Rent for Rent, for other Lands never exhaunced before. **1656** SANDERSON *Serm.* (1689) 427 Exhaunsing of Fees, trucking for Expedition, racking of Rents. **1667** WATERHOUSE *Fire Lond.* 104 The.. pretended Labourers.. exhansed the rates of their own portage.

†**ex'hauriate,** *v. Obs. rare*[−1]. [irreg. f. L. *exhaurī-re* (f. *ex-* out + *haurīre* to draw) + -ATE[3].] *trans.* To draw out or forth (a humour).

1683 SALMON *Doron Med.* II. 423 Powerfully exhauriates Serous Humors.

†**ex'hause,** *v. Obs. rare.* [ad. F. *exhaus-ser* (mod.F. in this sense *exaucer*), earlier *essaucier, essalcier:*—popular L. **exaltiāre*, f. as *exaltāre*: see EXALT *v.* ¶6.] *trans.* To hearken to, hear (a prayer, etc.).

1599 A. HUME *Hymns* (Bannatyne Club) 7 Exhause my prayer and thy praise. *Ibid.* 29, I.. to the Lord did.. call, Quhilk ever did exhause my voice & healed me with speede.

exhaust (ɛg'zɔːst), *sb.* [f. EXHAUST *v.*] The process or means of exhausting.

1. a. (*a*) *Steam-engine.* The exit of steam from the cylinder after having done its work in propelling the piston; the passage through which this takes place; = EDUCTION 5. (Also in similar sense with reference to water-power and gas engines.)

Etymologically, this is appropriate only to the case of a low-pressure engine, in which the steam is literally 'exhausted' from the cylinder by opening communication with the condenser; but when high-pressure engines were introduced, the word continued to be used as a synonym of EDUCTION, which it has almost superseded.

1848 *Pract. Mech. Jrnl.* I. 44, I have before seen double valves with the duplex steam passages, but in all of them the exhaust was single. **1865** BURGH *Slide Valve* 71 In some instances an increase is deemed necessary to allow a more free exhaust. **1875** MARTIN *Winding Mach.* 76 Back-pressure in the exhaust, owing to the large masses of steam which are suddenly let out through contracted.. passages. **1887** J. A. EWING in *Encycl. Brit.* XXII. 487 If during the back stroke the process of exhaust is discontinued before the end. **1889** *Blackw. Mag.* Sept. 322 The rapid pulse-like beats of the exhaust [in a locomotive]. **1890** *Engineer* 30 May 441 No choking of the exhaust can prevent an increase of speed.

(*b*) The expulsion of combustion products from the cylinder of an internal-combustion engine, the products so expelled, or the valve or pipe by which they escape.

1896 B. DONKIN *Text-bk. Gas, Oil, & Air Engines* (ed. 2) II. xxvii. 391 The engine, oil tanks, and exhaust are arranged in the same way as in the Capitaine launches. **1902** *Daily Chron.* 4 Sept. 7/4 The exhausts crackling like quick firers. **1904** A. B. F. YOUNG *Compl. Motorist* iii. 53 The problem of silencing has been to reduce the sound of the exhaust to a minimum and to retain the maximum of power given off by the engine. **1906** *Macm. Mag.* Nov. 60 Offensive exhaust is the Committee's polite name for what.. we must dignify with its proper title, an intolerable stink. **1912** *Motor Man.* (ed. 14) 235 There is no mistaking the somewhat pungent odour of an over-rich mixture exhaust, whilst an excessively over-rich mixture produces a 'black' exhaust. **1915** D. O. BARNETT *Lett.* 176 Suddenly he blew a cloud of smoke out of his exhaust, and up went his tail, and he began going down in spirals. **1957** *Encycl. Brit.* VII. 348/2 The four-stroke cycle engine operates as follows: (1) intake..; (2) compression..; (3) power..; (4) exhaust. **1961** L. MUMFORD *City in History* x. 296 The reek of gasoline exhaust.

b. The process of exhausting (a vessel) of air; the degree to which exhaustion is carried.

1880 DE LA RUE in *Nature* XX. 33 The greatest exhaust that we have produced, 0·000055 millim. *Ibid.* As the exhaust is carried further it becomes a pale milky white.

2. a. The production of an outward current of air by creating a partial vacuum. **b.** Any apparatus for effecting this. Cf. *exhaust-fan.*

1852 *Pract. Mech. Jrnl.* V. 54 A free and copious exhaust is secured on both sides of the cylinder [fan]. **1884** *Bath Herald* 27 Dec. 6/4 An exhaust [in a flour mill] carries away the lightest particles. **1887** *Pall Mall G.* 11 Oct. 11/1 There are two great exhausts to draw off smoke and heat from the stage. **1889** *Daily News* 2 Jan. 2/4 A steam exhaust, which produces an artificial air current.

3. *attrib.* and *Comb.*, chiefly in sense 1 a, as ***exhaust-box, -cylinder, -gas, -lap, -manifold, -passage, -pipe, -stroke, -valve***; also **exhaust-fan** (= earlier *exhausting fan*), a fan for producing a current by creating a vacuum; **exhaust fumes** orig. *U.S.*, the gases emitted through the exhaust system of a motor vehicle; **exhaust injector**, an injector for feeding a steam-boiler with water, worked by exhaust steam; **exhaust-port**, the opening in the slide-valve of a steam-engine for the escape of exhaust-steam (= *exhaust-passage*); **exhaust-steam**, the waste steam discharged from the cylinder of a steam-engine.

1903 *Motoring Ann.* 141 Few things are more annoying than an intermittent, loud report from the *exhaust box of a petrol motor. **1912** *Motor Man.* (ed. 14) 235 A car that is addicted to exhaust-box explosions. **1892** *Daily News* 4 Oct. 3/3 The proceeds of combustion pass from an *exhaust cylinder in form of a gas that cannot be seen. **1874** KNIGHT *Dict. Mech.* I. 815/2 **Exhaust-fan.* **1882** *Birmingham Wkly. Post* 24 June 3/7 An exhaust fan for drying hay and corn in the stack. **1937** *Amer. Jrnl. Public Health* XXVII. 322/1 The *exhaust fumes of internal combustion engines introduce gases, both malodorous and otherwise, capable of producing nausea, headache, and, in extreme concentrations, death. **1975** B. BAINBRIDGE *Sweet William* ii. 62 The absurd man climbed back into his car and drove away in a cloud of exhaust fumes. **1902** A. C. HARMSWORTH et al. *Motors* vii. 118 The exhaust pipe from the engine which conducts off the *exhaust gases after they have done their work in the cylinder. **1904** GOODCHILD & TWENEY *Technol. & Sci. Dict.* 212/1 In gas and oil engines the exhaust gases consist of the products of combustion, together with any unburnt gases remaining after the explosion. *a* **1930** D. H. LAWRENCE *Last Poems* (1932) 32 The weather in town is always benzine, or else petrol fumes Lubricating oil, exhaust gas. **1890** *Engineer* LXX. 473 We have for years made *exhaust injectors that.. utilise waste steam. **1888** LOCKWOOD *Dict. Mech. Engin.* 130 **Exhaust lap*, the reduction or narrowing of the inner faces of a slide valve to less than that distance which would correspond with a length measured between the inner edges of the steam ports, by which difference the ports are closed earlier than they would be if their edges coincided exactly with those of the arch of the valve. **1848** *Specif. Varley's Patent* No. 12,238. 2 *Exhaust-passage. **1854** *Pract. Mech. Jrnl.* VI. 115 As the exhaust passage [in a water pressure engine] is open to the pipe, the waste water passes off through this pipe. **1889** *Cent. Dict.*, **Exhaust-pipe*, in a steam-engine, the pipe that conveys waste steam from the cylinder to the condenser, or through which it escapes to the atmosphere. **1902** Exhaust pipe [see *exhaust-gas* above]. **1919** *Gloss. Aeronaut. Terms* (*R. Aeronaut. Soc.*) 48 The exhaust pipe extends from the exhaust manifold to the silencer. **1848** *Pract. Mech. Jrnl.* I. 44 The central *exhaust port of the slide valve. *Ibid.* 80 The *exhaust steam from the cylinders. **1890** *Engineer* 7 Nov. 386 (*title of paper*) Treatment and Utilisation of exhaust steam. **1894** B. DONKIN *Text-bk. Gas, Oil, & Air Engines* I. i. 16 There are always two strokes, the forward or motor stroke, and the return or *exhaust stroke. **1913** W. E. DOMMETT *Motor Car Mech.* 8 On the next up stroke, and the exhaust valve being open, the burnt gases are forced out of the cylinder, the piston performing the exhaust stroke. **1848** *Specif. Varley's Patent* No. 12,238. 2 The two *exhaust valves. **1899** *Motor-Car World* I. 54/2 To the casual observer the greatest failing of the Bollée is the noise, but to the owner the exhaust valve will probably be the most troublesome part. **1919** H. SHAW *Text-bk. Aeronaut.* x. 118 When the piston is nearing its lowest position, the exhaust valve is opened by a cam.

†**e'xhaust,** *pa. pple.* and *ppl. a. Obs.* Also 7 exhauste, *erron.* exhaused. [ad. L. *exhaust-us*, pa. pple. of *exhaurīre*: see next.]

A. *pa. pple.* (in various senses of the vb.).

1523 WOLSEY in Fiddes *Life* II. 114 The enemy exhaust of money. **1540-1** ELYOT *Image Gov.* (1549) 123 Charges enforced, haue exhaust.. the more parte of your substaunce. **1627** MAY *Lucan* VIII, They.. when their quivers are exhaust, must flee. **1649** *Lanc. Tracts* (Chetham Soc.) 278 Most men's estates being.. now almost quite exhauste by the present scarsity. **1654** R. CODRINGTON tr. *Justin's Hist.* 121 The Kingdom exhaused of souldiers did much distract him. **1708** PHILIPS *Cider* I. 124 When the alien compost is exhaust, Its Native Poverty again prevails.

B. *ppl. a.* = EXHAUSTED *ppl. a.* in various senses.

1621 BURTON *Anat. Mel.* I. ii. I. vi. (1676) 39/1 Intemperate, dissolute, exhaust through riot. **1624** F. WHITE *Repl. Fisher* 555 Contemning the merits of Christ, accounting the same drie and exhaust. **1627** tr. *Bacon's Life & Death* (1651) 28 The eager flames, do dry Bodies and render them exhaust and saplesse. **1647** H. MORE *Song of Soul* III. II. xliii, His brain In time would be exhaust and void of wit. **1708** J. PHILIPS *Cyder* II. 55 Reject the apple-cheese tho quite exhaust.

exhaust (ɛg'zɔːst), *v.* [f. L. *exhaust-* ppl. stem of *exhaurīre*; see EXHAURIATE.]

1. *trans.* To draw off or out (now only, air); *lit.* and *fig.*

1540 *Act 32 Hen. VIII*, c. 24 Innumerable summes of monei, crafteli exhausted out of this realme. **1607** SHAKS. *Timon* IV. iii 119 The Babe, Whose dimpled smiles from Fooles exhaust their mercy. **1632** MASSINGER & FIELD *Fatal Dowry* II. i, Your thankless Cruelty, and Savage Manners.. Exhaust these Floods [of tears]. **1665** G. HARVEY *Advice agst. Plague* 23 Exhaust a convenient proportion of blood. **1705** DERHAM in *Lett. Lit. Men* (Camden) 319 Those.. with double Barrells.. exhaust the air with greater ease and quickness. **1728** EARBERY tr. *Burnet's St. Dead* I. 157 These things we have exhausted from the sacred Scriptures. **1839** G. BIRD *Nat. Phil.* 101 Exhaust the air from beneath the bladder. **1858** O. W. HOLMES *Aut. Breakf. T.* xii, Putting an animal under the bell of an air-pump and exhausting the air from it.

†**b.** To take a draught of; to drink or suck up. Cf. L. *exhaurire vinum. Obs.*

1599 HAKLUYT *Voy.* II. II. 331 The Dragon thrusteth his head into his [the Elephant's] tronke and exhausteth his breath. **1626** BACON *Sylva* §360 Some that have kept Chamelions.. might observe their Bellies to swell after they had exhausted the air. **1679** JANE *Fast. Serm.* 8 Salmanasser .. like an insatiable gulph devoured and exhausted all.

2. To use up completely (either a material or immaterial thing); to expend the whole of; to consume entirely.

1533 ELYOT *Cast. Helthe* II. vii. (1541) 18b, The fyre hathe not exhausted the moysture of them. *a* **1704** LOCKE (J.), Though the knowledge they have left us be worth our study, yet they exhausted not all its treasures. **1709** POPE *Ess. Crit.* 555 Here point your thunder, and exhaust your rage! **1751** JOHNSON *Rambler* No. 87 ⁋14 A student may easily exhaust his life in comparing divines and moralists. **1786** BURKE *W. Hastings* Wks. 1842 II. 125 Whatever relief was given..the same was soon exhausted. **1853** H. ROGERS *Ecl. Faith* 223 How do they almost exhaust the resources of language to express their sentiments.

†**b.** in weaker sense: To expend, spend. *Obs.*

1616 BULLOKAR, *Exhaust* to consume, spend, or waste. **1659** HAMMOND *On Ps.* xvii. 14 Paraphr. 87 To leave abundantly to their children..having no care of charity or mercy to others, on which to exhaust anything.

c. To account for or utilize the whole number or quantity of (anything).

1748 HARTLEY *Observ. Man* II. i. 23 In the same manner as Mathematical Quantities are exhausted by the Terms of an infinite Series. **1816** BENTHAM *Chrestom.* 241 The parts ..exhaust the contents of the whole. **1846** MILL *Logic* III. xxv. §6 There have taken place a sufficient number of drawings to exhaust all the possible combinations. **1874** MORLEY *Compromise* (1886) 227 Good ideas are not all exhausted by the ancient forms.

3. To empty by drawing the contents off or out; to drain; to empty *of* (specified contents).

1614 EARL STIRLING *Dooms-day* 3rd Hour lxxvi, The litle Brookes exhausted in their Springs. **1660** BOYLE *New Exp. Phys. Mech.* Proem 19 We never were able totally to exhaust the Receiver. **1697** DRYDEN *Virg. Georg.* III. 484 The.. Udders never fail; But when they seem exhausted, swell the Pail. **1784** *Specif. Watt's Patent* No. 1432 Which vessel [a condenser] by cooling and condensing part of the steam does partly exhaust the steam vessel [i.e. the cylinder]. **1807** T. THOMSON *Chem.* (ed. 3) II. 138 Having..closed my nostrils and exhausted my lungs. **1860** TYNDALL *Glac.* II. iii. 245 A tube which could be exhausted of air. **1871** —— *Fragm. Sc.* (ed. 6) I. ii. 38 Let us suppose the glass tube..to be exhausted by an air-pump.

b. *refl.* Of a river: To empty itself. *rare.*

1833 LYTTON *Eng. & English* III. i, The waters of Terek exhaust themselves in the Caspian Sea.

c. *intr.* Of steam: To escape from the cylinder after doing its work; cf. EXHAUST *sb.* 1 a.

1851 *Pract. Mech. Jrnl.* IV. 146 The steam exhausts through the centre opening. **1865** BURGH *Slide Valve* 52 Before the steam can exhaust, the valve must open the same port.

4. To draw out all that is essential or interesting in (an object of investigation or exposition); to treat or study (a subject) so as to leave nothing further to be explained or discovered.

1704 ADDISON *Italy* Pref., There are still several of these topics that are far from being exhausted. **1751** JOHNSON *Rambler* No. 150 ⁋6 He who..soon exhausts any single subject, is always eager for new enquiries. **1845** M. PATTISON *Ess.* (1889) I. 2 Hooke was considered to have exhausted the history of the Roman Republic. **1860** TRENCH *Serm. Westm. Ab.* ix. 92 It is not easy to exhaust them [words of Scripture] so to draw out all their meaning. **1875** HAMERTON *Intell. Life* IX. i. 301 We do not easily exhaust the mind of another.

5. To drain (a person, kingdom, etc.) of strength or resources, or (a soil) of nutritive ingredients; hence, to weary out, enfeeble extremely.

1631 GOUGE *God's Arrows* III. xcv. 364 The Kingdome was much exhausted of men and mony. *c* **1676** WISEMAN *Surgery* (J.), Spermatick matter of a vitious sort..exhausts it [the blood] of its best spirits. **1707** ADDISON *Pres. St. War* Wks. 1746 III. 253 The French monarchy is already exhausted of its best and bravest subjects. **1711** EARL OXFORD in Ellis *Orig. Lett.* II. 409 IV. 266 This the Queen has done..notwithstanding the great need we have of peace, and that the nation is exhausted. *a* **1714** J. SHARP *Serm.* (1754) III. iii. 44 There is no man that thinks warmly.. upon a thing, but mightily exhausts his spirits. **1787** WINTER *Syst. Husb.* 31 Lime..exhausts the earth by absorbing its oily particles. **1798** FERRIAR *Eng. Histor.* in *Illustr. Sterne* 233 Great exertions seem to exhaust the moral, as well as the physical world. **1860** TYNDALL *Glac.* I. xi. 79 The thought of being absolutely exhausted had never occurred to me. **1862** MERIVALE *Rom. Emp.* V. xlii. 163 The inhospitable wilderness was exhausted of its scanty resources. **1887** STUBBS *Med. & Mod. Hist.* 230 The Thirty Years' War exhausted Germany.

¶ Incorrectly used for EXHANCE.

1622 F. MARKHAM *Bk. War* II. iii. 50 The priuiledge whereof doth..exhaust and raise up his entertainment.

exhausted (ɛg'zɔːstɪd), *ppl. a.* [f. EXHAUST *v.* + -ED¹.] In senses of vb.

1. Consumed, used up, expended.

1656-81 BLOUNT *Glossogr.*, *Exhausted*, drawn out, emptyed, consumed. **1701** ROWE *Amb. Step-moth.* III. i, Fresh Supplies renew th' exhausted Stores.

2. Emptied of contents; chiefly said of a vessel or receiver: Emptied of air.

1667 BOYLE in *Phil. Trans.* II. 583 In one exhausted Receiver, I had observed [etc.]. *c* **1790** IMISON *Sch. Art* I. 69 To prevent any air from getting into the exhausted glass. **1801** SOUTHEY *Thalaba* I. xxi, Exhausted mines Supplied their golden store. **1869** MRS. SOMERVILLE *Molec. Sc.* I. I. ii. 39 The whole amount of radiant heat that passed thro' the exhausted tube.

3. Of air, soil, etc.: Deprived of essential properties; effete, 'spent', worn out. Also, deprived of resources, completely impoverished.

1664 EVELYN *Kal. Hort.* (1729) 230 The Funnel..which carries up..the..exhausted Air of the Green-house. **1719** LONDON & WISE *Compl. Gard.* Advt. 9 Take out all the old, worn out, or exhausted Earth. **1781** GIBBON *Decl. & F.* III. 177 The revenue of exhausted provinces. **1832** HT. MARTINEAU *Ireland* i. 14 He had grown potatoes: but the soil became exhausted. **1858** GREENER *Gunnery* 17 We still fruitlessly fall back on exhausted principles.

4. Of persons or living things: Having one's strength, energy, etc. used up; tired out.

1667 MILTON *P.L.* VI. 852 Fire..that..of thir wonted vigour left them draind, Exhausted. **1796** BURNEY *Metastasio* II. 296 A tired and exhausted individual, loaded with years. **18..** *Parl. Deb.*, Lord Holland did not mean to discuss the subject at any length in the present exhausted state of the House. **1846** PEEL *Sp.* 28 June in McCarthy *Own Times* (1879) I. 412 When [working men] shall recreate their exhausted strength with abundant and untaxed food. **1881** LADY HERBERT *Edith* 1 The exhausted cart and cab horses staggered under their loads.

Hence **e'xhaustedly** *adv.*, in an exhausted manner. **e'xhaustedness**, exhausted state or condition, worn out condition.

1835 *New Monthly Mag.* XLIII. 161 The poor beasts.. toiled exhaustedly on. **1883** CABLE *Dr. Sevier* vi, Her..skirt dropping between her knees, and her hands pressed on them exhaustedly. **1840** *Fraser's Mag.* XXI. 713 The disquietude of utter prostration and exhaustedness produced by the application of violent remedies.

exhauster (ɛg'zɔːstə(r)). [f. as prec. + -ER¹.] One who, or that which, exhausts.

1743 J. ELLIS *Knowl. Div. Things* iv. 346 Now which of the Ancients was this Exhauster of Nature. **1792** A. YOUNG *Trav. France* 389 Would it be no advantage to strike out one of these exhausters [wheat, rye, barley, and oats], and substitute an improver. **1853** JOHNSTON in *Jrnl. R. Agric. Soc.* XIV. I. 10 The wind..is probably a still more rapid and widely-acting exhauster of these forest lands. **1884** *Health Exhibit. Catal.* 60/1 Apparatus for manufacturing.. concentrated manure, comprising Concentrator, Condenser, Exhauster, and Agitator.

b. In *Gas-making*: (see quot. 1859).

1841 *Specif. Grafton's Patent* No. 9062. 3 The gas from this end of the retort is thereafter drawn through the pipe *h* directly into the exhauster. **1859** CLEGG *Coal Gas* 186 Various kinds of machines have been contrived for pumping the gas in a continuous flow out of the retorts—for that is in fact the principle of the action of exhausters. **1889** *Jrnl. Gas Lighting* 19 Nov. 964 The engine and exhauster are connected by a..flexible coupling.

exhaustibility (ɛg,zɔːstɪ'bɪlɪtɪ). [f. next: see -ITY.] The quality of being exhaustible; capability of being exhausted.

1836 *Fraser's Mag.* XIII. 349 His extractive power was such, that it never admitted the exhaustibility of a subject. **1872** W. S. SYMONDS *Rec. Rocks* x. 367 The question of the exhaustibility of our coal-fields is highly complicated. **1884** *Syd. Soc. Lex.*, *Exhaustibility*, Benedict's term for the condition where the electro-muscular contractility diminishes greatly after a short application. **1889** COURTNEY *Mill* i. 25 The possible exhaustibility of musical combinations.

exhaustible (ɛg'zɔːstɪb(ə)l), *a.* [f. EXHAUST *v.* + -IBLE.] That admits of being exhausted.

1667 BOYLE in *Phil. Trans.* II. 587 A very small Receiver, exhaustible at a Suck or two. **1779-81** JOHNSON *L.P.*, *Collins*, His uncle..left him about two thousand pounds; a sum which Collins could scarcely think exhaustible. **1848** MILL *Pol. Econ.* I. 35 Coal..and other useful substances.. are not only strictly local, but exhaustible.

exhausting (ɛg'zɔːstɪŋ), *vbl. sb.* [f. as prec. + -ING¹.] The action of the vb. EXHAUST in its various senses; an instance of this. Also *attrib.*

1539 TONSTALL *Serm. Palm. Sund.* (1823) 66 Sucke out of this realme..innumerable sommes of money yerelye, to the great exhausting of the same. **1764** BURN *Poor Laws* 153 The populousness of the kingdom still increaseth, notwithstanding its great exhaustings by wars, and plagues. **1827** FAREY *Steam Engine* 448 The steam..must be evacuated from it, through one or other of the two exhausting valves. **1831** LARDNER *Pneumat.* v. 280 The most simple form of instrument for producing the rarefaction of air is that which is called the exhausting syringe. **1853** *Pract. Mech. Jrnl.* VI. 209 (*title of article*) Blowing and exhausting fans. **1887** *Daily News* 11 Nov. 3/6 Exhausting nozzles are used as well as injecting ones, so that while fresh air is supplied foul air can be removed.

e'xhausting, *ppl. a.* [f. as prec. + -ING².] That exhausts; *chiefly*, that exhausts the strength; wearying, tiring, enfeebling.

18.. MASON GOOD *System Med.* (L.), A series of exhausting paroxysms succeeds. **1847** EMERSON *Repr. Men, Plato* Wks. (Bohn) I. 289 The misfortune..of coming after this exhausting generalizer. **1855** MACAULAY *Hist. Eng.* IV. 297 A mighty effort..it was but too exhausting to be repeated. **1858** O. W. HOLMES *Aut. Breakf.-t.* i, There are men of *esprit* who are excessively exhausting to some people. **1860** TYNDALL *Glac.* I. xi. 71 The exhausting journey over the boulders and debris.

Hence **e'xhaustingly** *adv.*, in an exhausting manner, so as to exhaust or tire out.

1882 BUXTON in *19th Cent.* Nov. 791 The matter..was exhaustively (some might say exhaustingly) discussed.

exhaustion (ɛg'zɔːstʃən). [as if ad. L. **exhaustiōn-em*, n. of action f. *exhaurīre*: see EXHAUST *v.* Cf. F. *exhaustion.*] The action of exhausting; the state of being exhausted.

1. The action or process: **a.** of drawing out or forth, *esp.* air; **b.** of emptying of contents; the condition of being emptied.

1661 BOYLE *Spring of Air* III. xx. (1682) 80 Upon the exhaustion of the air incumbent on the water [etc.]. **1800** VINCE *Hydrostat.* viii. (1806) 82 You make a more perfect exhaustion by the other method. **1881** SPOTTISWOODE in *Nature* No. 623. 550 In the next tube the exhaustion has been carried further.

c. *spec.* (*Steam-Engine*) The discharge of waste steam from the cylinder; cf. EXHAUST *sb.* 1 a. Also *attrib.*

1782 *Specif. Watt's Patent* No. 1321. 5 The regulating valve is then to be shut and the exhaustion regulating valve is opened. **1824** R. STUART *Hist. Steam Engine* 107 The exhaustion-cock was shut, the steam was readmitted into the cylinder, and the operation was repeated. **1848** E. ALBAN *Steam Engine* 57 The exhaustion openings are usually made much too small. **1849** *Specif. Unwin's Patent* No. 12,410. 2 This improved method of clearance or exhaustion is applied to an engine suitable for locomotive purposes.

2. The action or process of consuming or using up completely.

1831 KNOX *Cloquet's Anat.* p. v, The rapid sale and exhaustion of that work. **1881** SIR W. THOMSON in *Nature* No. 619. 449 This exhaustion [of heat] would not be complete until the absolute zero of temperature was reached.

3. The state of being exhausted of strength, energy, etc.; extreme loss of strength.

1646 SIR T. BROWNE *Pseud. Ep.* III. xxi. 163 There ensueth no destructive exhaustion. **1651** *Reliq. Wotton.* (1672) 334 Great exhaustions cannot be cured with sudden remedies. **1793** BEDDOES *Calcul., etc.* 175 In the state of temporary exhaustion the fibre loses its tone. **1854** H. MILLER *Sch. & Schm.* (1858) 253 Lacking in their utter exhaustion strength for fighting and breath for scolding. **1877** ERICHSEN *Surg.* I. 11 Exhaustion.. is an occasional cause of death after severe operations.

b. The draining (anything) of valuable properties; the condition of being so drained.

1813 SIR H. DAVY *Agric. Chem.* viii. (1814) 359 When cattle are fed upon land not benefited by their manure, the effect is always an exhaustion of the soil.

c. *Chem.* (See quots.)

1874 W. CROOKES *Dyeing & Calico-print.* 32 The precipitate from the alkaline extract of cotton, after exhaustion with boiling alcohol, was, without being previously dried, dissolved in dilute caustic soda-lye. **1884** *Syd. Soc. Lex.*, *Exhaustion*, In Pharmacy, the term is applied to any process, such as percolation, whereby the active constituents of a drug are removed in solution, leaving it exhausted.

4. Exhaustive enumeration or treatment; cf. EXHAUST *v.* 2 c, 4.

1868 GLADSTONE *Juv. Mundi* iii. (1869) 96 The..lists are presented, by way, not of exhaustion, but of example.

5. a. *gen.* The process of establishing the correctness of a hypothesis by 'exhausting' all the other conceivable hypotheses relating to the question; the process of arriving at a conclusion by the successive elimination of unsuitable alternatives.

fig. **1877** OWEN in *Wellesley's Disp.* p. xxxvi, By a process of exhaustion, the specific gravity of the inefficient would gradually deposit them below their betters.

b. *Math.* *method of exhaustions*: (see quot. 1730-6).

1685 J. WALLIS *Treat. Algebra* lxxiii. 280 It will be necessary to premise somewhat concerning (what is wont to be called) the Method of Exhaustions. **1730-6** BAILEY (folio), *Exhaustions* (in Mathematics) a way of proving the equality of two magnitudes by a *reductio ad absurdum*; shewing that if one be supposed either greater or less than the other, there will arise a contradiction. **1881** ROUTLEDGE *Science* ii. 37 The method of exhaustions..is only an application of the general principle of limits. **1884** MERZ *Leibniz* iii. 49 The method of exhaustions..in which the area of a surface enclosed by a curve is found by inscribing polygons of an increasing number of sides.

exhaustive (ɛg'zɔːstɪv), *a.* [f. L. *exhaust-* ppl. stem of *exhaurīre* (see EXHAUST *v.*) + -IVE.]

1. Tending to exhaust or drain of strength, resources, etc.

1818 JAS. MILL *Brit. India* II. IV. viii. 278 The fierce and exhaustive contentions which the rival strangers in Carnatic were waging against one another. **1868** J. H. BLUNT *Ref. Ch. Eng.* I. 98 In what imminent peril the revenues..were from the exhaustive squandering..of the Court. **1874** MOTLEY *Barneveld* II. xii. 70 The parasites who fed on the Queen Regent were exhaustive of the French exchequer.

2. Characterized by exhausting a subject, etc.; leaving no part unexamined or unconsidered; complete, comprehensive.

1786-9 BENTHAM *Wks.* (1843) II. 540 Proceeding..upon the exhaustive plan. **1798** W. TAYLOR in *Monthly Rev.* XXV. 585 His transcendental deduction of the categories of criticism [is] neither discretive nor exhaustive. **1813** *Edin. Rev.* XXII. 23 His method of handling the subject..has been termed exhaustive. **1853** TRENCH *Proverbs* 125 *The things of friends are in common.* Where does this find its exhaustive fulfilment, but in the Communion of Saints? **1878** GLADSTONE *Prim. Homer* 127, I shall attempt in this limited work no exhaustive survey.

b. (Cf. EXHAUSTION 5 a.)

1879 FARRAR *St. Paul* I. 405 *note*, By the exhaustive method, therefore, we see that the visit dwelt on in Gal. ii. must have been the third.

exhaustively (ɛg'zɔːstɪvlɪ), *adv.* [f. prec. + -LY².] In an exhaustive manner; so as to treat of every point; fully.

1816 BENTHAM *Chrestom.* 319 A system of logical division in the exhaustively bifurcate mode. **1862** F. HALL *Hindu Philos. Syst.* 175 It is neither my desire, nor is it my intention to treat the subject exhaustively.

exhaustiveness (ɛg'zɔːstɪvnɪs). [f. as prec. + -NESS.] The quality of being exhaustive.
1816 BENTHAM *Chrestom.* 280 The idea of exhaustiveness as applied to logical division. **1872** MINTO *Eng. Lit.* II. v. 386 The exhaustiveness and subtlety of the thought. **1885** FARRAR in *Libr. Mag.* Dec. 500 The exhaustiveness of the curriculum of your University.

exhaustless (ɛg'zɔːstlɪs), *a. poet.* and *rhetorical.* [f. EXHAUST *v.* + -LESS.] Incapable of being exhausted; inexhaustible.
1712 BLACKMORE *Creation* III, When we..Nature's..exhaustless energy respect. **1746** HERVEY *Flower Garden Medit.* (1818) I. 135 The fields are our exhaustless granary. **1845** STOCQUELER *Handbk. Brit. India* (1854) 396 An exhaustless supply of clear water. **1863** MRS. C. CLARKE *Shaks. Char.* xvi. 403 Delicate lights thrown into his characters that render them exhaustless as studies.
Hence **e'xhaustlessly** *adv.*, in an exhaustless manner, so as to be inexhaustible. **e'xhaustlessness**, the quality of being inexhaustible.
1766 G. CANNING *Anti-Lucretius* III. 187 Exhaustlessly prolifick, shall they ne'er In shapes by Fancy unconceiv'd appear? **1886** W. M. CONWAY *Flemish Artists* 20 The exhaustlessness of the miniaturist's fancy.

†**e'xhaustment.** *Obs. rare.* [f. EXHAUST *v.* + -MENT.] The action or means of exhausting; the state of being exhausted; an instance of the same, a 'drain' of money.
1621 BP. G. WILLIAMS in *Cabala* (1654) 55 This Bishoprick being..meanly endowed in regard of the continual charge, and exhaustments of the place. **1648** *Petit. Eastern Assoc.* 22 We can see no possible end of our exhaustments.

†**e'xhausture.** *Obs.* [f. as prec. + -URE.] The action of exhausting; the state of being exhausted; also, an instance of this.
1611 SPEED *Hist. Gt. Brit.* IX. xx. (1632) 970 Yet was he the feebler..by reason of so fresh exhaustures. **1687** N. JOHNSTON *Assur. Abbey Lands* 54 Alledging the exhausture of the Exchequer by the late War. **1778** *Hist. Eur.* in *Ann. Reg.* 105/2 So great an exhausture of blood and treasure. *Ibid.*, The state of debility and exhausture brought on by our civil contest. **1786** *Ibid.* 174/1 Religious prejudices are..wearing away in France, and..it will not require a very long succession of years for their entire exhausture.

exhedra, var. of EXEDRA.

†**ex'herb**, *v. Obs.*$^{-0}$ [ad. L. *exherb-āre*, f. *ex-* (see EX- *pref.*[1]) + *herba* grass.] 'To take herbs from any place' (Cockeram 1623–6).

exheredate (ɛks'hɛrɪdeɪt), *v.* Now *rare.* Also 7 exhæredate, 9 *Sc.* -heridate. [f. L. *exhērēdāt-* ppl. stem of *exhērēdāre* to disinherit, f. *ex-* (see EX- *pref.*[1]) + *hērēd-em* heir.] *trans.* To disinherit. Also *fig.*
In recent use only in Sc. writers (misspelt). It was never a term of Common Law.
1552 HULOET, Exheredate, *abominor.* [Cf. Augustine *in Ps.* v, Solent enim abominati dici exheredati.] **1623–6** COCKERAM, *Exheredate*, to disherite. **1660** WATERHOUSE *Arms & Arm.* 207 Other virtues of equal merit, must not be exheeredated, or become spurious, to advance its legitimation. **1721–1800** in BAILEY. **1820** SCOTT *Abbot* xxxvi, 'Madam,' replied the youth, 'though exheridated and disowned, I am yet a Douglas'. **1834** M. NAPIER *Mem. Napier of Merchistoun* i. 32 The anxiety of Duke Arnold was to exheridate his only son.
Hence **ex'heredated** *ppl. a.*
1828–40 TYTLER *Hist. Scot.* (1864) II. 192 Henry [VI.] the exheridated monarch.

exheredation (ɛkshɛrɪ'deɪʃən). Also 7 exhæredation. [ad. L. *exhērēdātiōn-em*, n. of action f. *exhērēdāre* to EXHEREDATE.] The action of exheredating or disinheriting; disinheritance; an instance of this.
1515 in W. H. Turner *Select. Rec. Oxford* 12 Ye same ground [they] have..inclosed to their owne use in exheredation and gret p'iudice..unto ye Mayr. **1609** SKENE *Reg. Maj.* 41 The trespas of the sonne or of the heire, sall not be ane cause of exheredation of the father. **1651** W. G. tr. *Cowel's Inst.* 47 For the many Exheredations that hapned: Their Guardianshipp was conferred..upon the King. **1751** CHAMBERS *Cycl.* s.v., By the ancient Roman law, the father might pronounce exheredation without any cause. **1875** STUBBS *Const. Hist.* II. xiv. 95 A general sentence of forfeiture or 'exheredation' was issued.

†**exheredi'tation.** *Obs. rare.* = prec.
1583 STOCKER *Civ. Warres Lowe C.* II. 6 a, All Grauntes, Exhereditations, and other disposed goodes.

†**ex'hibe**, *v. Obs. rare*$^{-1}$. In 5 exhybe. [a F. *exhibe-r*, ad. L. *exhibēre* to EXHIBIT.] *trans.* To exhibit, produce.
1491 CAXTON *Vitas Patr.* (W. de W. 1495) II. 245 a/2 Yf he hadde not conne exhybe and shewe that same ayen..he sholde haue lost his hede.

†**'exhibent.** *Obs. rare*$^{-1}$. [ad. L. *exhibentem*, pr. pple. of *exhibēre*: see EXHIBIT.] One who administers (a rite). Cf. EXHIBIT *v.* I.
1658 J. ROBINSON *Eudoxa* iii. 25 Baptism received unworthily, that is, either on the exhibents or receivers part.

†**e'xhibit**, *pple. Obs.* Forms: 6 exhibet, -yte, exhybet, exibite, 6–7 exhibit(e. [ad. L. *exhibit-us*, pa. pple. of *exhibēre*: see EXHIBIT *v.*] = *exhibited*, pa. pple. of EXHIBIT *v.*
1526 *Pilgr. Perf.* (W. de W. 1531) 192 b, Worshyp exhibyte and done to the payntes of God. **1529** WOLSEY in Ellis *Orig. Lett.* I. 104 II. 8 Thys kyndnes exibite from the Kyngs Hyghnes shall prolong my lyff. **1534** WHITINTON *Tullyes Offices* II. (1540) 103 Who is he..that wyll not prefer in his dyligence exhybet the fauour of a ryche man. **1552** ABP. HAMILTON *Catech.* (1884) 4 We have exhibet to you this present Catechisme. **1639** CHAS. I *Proclam. Scot.* 4 Some whereof were produced and exhibit by our Commissioner.

exhibit (ɛg'zɪbɪt), *sb.* [ad. L. *exhibit-um* pa. pple. neut. of *exhibēre*: see EXHIBIT *v.*]
1. *Law.* **a.** (See quot. 1672.) **b.** Any document (or, more recently, any material object) produced in court and referred to and identified in written evidence.
1626 *Impeachm. Dk. Buckhm.* (Camden) 40 The exhibite ..shewed unto him..is the true..bill of ladeinge. **1636** *Divine Trag.* 43 Suppressing the Gentlemans exhibits and defence. **1662** *Act. 14 Chas. II*, c. 14 All the Processes, Exhibites, Writings..and Orders were had, taken, made and done in the said Court of Admiralty. **1667** E. CHAMBERLAYNE *St. Gt. Brit.* I. II. viii. (1743) 73 The office of the Register is to attend the court, to receive all libels, or bills, allegations and exhibits of witnesses. **1672** COWEL *Interpr.*, *Exhibit*, Exhibitum, When a Deed, Acquittance, or other writing is in a Chancery-suit exhibited to be proved by Witnesse, and the Examiner writes on the back that it was shewed to such a one at the time of his Examination; this is there called an Exhibit. **1776** *Trial of Nundocomar* 46/2 Nagree paper fixed and marked exhibit M. **1798** *St. Papers* in *Ann. Reg.* 288 Eight pages of ciphered exhibits. **1888** CHITTY 5 *Rep. Pat., etc. Cases* 673, I have also an exhibit of goods which the Applicants manufacture or sell.
c. *exhibit A*: the first document or object produced in court as evidence; hence *transf.* and *fig.*, an object or person considered as a piece of evidence, esp. the most important evidence.
[**1902** J. M. LELY *Wharton's Law-lex.* (ed. 10) 303 *Exhibit*, a document..referred to in, but not annexed to, an affidavit. .. Usually the deponent merely refers to it in the affidavit as 'the exhibit hereto annexed marked A', or as the case may be.] **1906** E. DYSON *Fact'ry 'Ands* iv. 49 John was..so limp that the policeman had to hold him up, like exhibit A. **1932** W. FAULKNER *Light in August* (1933) xv. 325 To preach to them [*sc.* Negroes] humility before all skins lighter than theirs, preaching the superiority of the white race, himself his own exhibit A. **1948** C. DAY LEWIS *Otterbury Incident* iv. 47 The button—let us call it Exhibit A—was found by me. **1963** K. EBLE *F. Scott Fitzgerald* x. 158 His short stories will be the supporting evidence—*The Great Gatsby* is Exhibit A —of his lasting claim to attention. **1970** J. PORTER *Rather Common Sort of Crime* xiv. 163 Pimp..tossed a crumpled looking paper bag over to the Hon. Con. 'Exhibit A,' said Jack the John.
2. A detailed and formal statement of particulars (as debts, liabilities, etc.); *orig.* one intended for production in court; hence *gen.*
1702 *Lond. Gaz.* No. 3778/4 They are desired..to bring or send such their Exhibits of Book Debts, Bonds, etc. **1864** D. A. WELLS *Our Burden & Str.* 6 Having thus presented an exhibit of our present and prospective national liabilities.
3. *Eccl.* in *pl.* The documents (letters of orders, institution and induction, etc.) which a beneficed or licensed clergyman may be required to produce at the first visitation after his admission. Hence, the fees payable on presenting these documents.
1629–30 BP. BEDELL in *Ussher's Lett.* (1686) 422 By Fees, he..seeks to take..for Exhibits at Visitations. **1767** BURN *Eccl. Law.* (1824) IV. 19 None but the bishop, or [his representative] hath right *de jure communi* to require these exhibits of the clergy. **1863** BLYTH *Hist. Notices Fincham* 72 At the Bishop's primary visitation in 1858 the synodals were 5*s.* and the exhibits 13*s.* 4*d.*
4. Something exhibited or presented to view.
†**a.** *gen.* A spectacle, sight. *Obs.*
1676 HALE *Contempl.* I. 449 In the study of a poor Fly, there would be such a confluence of so many wonderful and difficult Exhibits in it.
b. One of the objects composing an 'exhibition'.
1862 *Leader* (Melbourne) 5 July, Exhibits for the Geelong and Western District Agricultural and Horticultural Society's Show. **1876** *Fam. Herald* 2 Dec. 79/2 An exhibit.. in the Peruvian section..attracted an unusual share of attention. **1884** *Graphic* 16 Aug. 166/2 The horses were a grand show of 390 exhibits.
c. The collection of articles sent by any one person, firm, country, etc. to an 'exhibition'.
1871 *Daily News* 7 Dec., There is not much the matter.. with his exhibit [of cattle]. **1881** *Harper's Mag.* June 50 The Portuguese exhibit at the last Universal Exposition at Paris. **1887** F. E. CHADWICK in *Scribn. Mag.* I. 517/1 The only French exhibit was that of the Bureau Veritas.
5. A showing, producing in evidence, display.
1654 GAYTON *Pleas. Notes* III. v. 95 The Play was to be presented to some few friends before the publick exhibit. **1864** FESSENDEN in *Times* 24 Dec., The power to compel an exhibit of books of account. **1886** B. W. RICHARDSON in *Pall Mall G.* 27 Sept. 6/2 There was no exhibit in these workers of any deficiency of muscular perception or skill.

exhibit (ɛg'zɪbɪt), *v.* Forms: 5 exhibete, 6–7 exhibite, (6 exhybet, exibyte), 6– exhibit. [f. L. *exhibit-* ppl. stem of *exhibēre*, f. *ex-* out + *habēre* to hold.]
I. To offer, furnish, administer.
†**1.** *trans.* To offer, present (sacrifice, etc.); to administer (an oath). *Obs.*
1490 CAXTON *Eneydos* v. (1890) 21 His felaushyppe chosen by hym for to make and exhibete the sayd sacrefyce. **1532** MORE *Confut. Barnes* VIII. Wks. 805/2 We..exhibite our bodies a liuely host. **1589** PUTTENHAM *Eng. Poesie* I. xii. (Arb.) 44 To him [God] we can not exhibit ouermuch praise. **1651** HOBBES *Leviath.* I. xii. 54 The worship which naturally men exhibite to Powers invisible. **1657** HOWELL *Londinop.* 37 That the said Commissioners should have power to exhibit an Oath.
†**2.** To grant, provide, furnish; const. *to*, *unto*; hence, to defray (expense). *Obs.*
1548 HALL *Chron.* 195 b, Frendes..will not..remember a great gratuitie and benefite in time of necessitie, to them shewed and exhibited. **1563–83** FOXE *A. & M.* II. 997/1 To D. Royston..he [Humfrey Mummuth] exhibited fortie or fiftie pounds. **1577** VAUTROULLIER *Luther on Ep. Gal.* 178 The blessing promised to Abraham and exhibited by Christ. **1577** HANMER *Anc. Eccl. Hist.* (1619) 107 Whose necessary expences and charges Ambrose exhibited. **1597** HOOKER *Eccl. Pol.* v. lx. (1611) 319 Wee defraude them of such outward helps as wee ought to exhibit. **1623** BINGHAM *Xenophon* 32 We will exhibite you a market. **1654** *Triana* in Fuller *Cause & Cure* (1867) 162 He kept Feliciano..as a gentle almsman, exhibiting diet and some slender accommodations unto him.
†**b.** *intr.* To provide maintenance; to give an 'exhibition'; to minister (to a person's wants). Const. *to*, *unto*. *Obs.* Rarely *trans.*: To give an exhibition to (a student).
1601 F. GODWIN *Bps. of Eng.* 312 [The] Deane of York.. sent him to Oxford, and so long as he liued..exhibited vnto him there. *a* **1695** WOOD (cited by Webster) He was a special friend to the university..exhibiting to the wants of certain scholars. **1709** STRYPE *Ann. Ref.* I. xlviii. 520 Well disposed people..used to exhibit to poor students. **1868** M. PATTISON *Academ. Org.* IV. 107 The sum paid out of endowments to students exhibited.
3. *trans.* (*Med.*) To administer (a remedy, etc.).
1601 HOLLAND *Pliny* II. 251 They were wont to exhibit it [Scammony] for a purgation. **1620** VENNER *Via Recta* viii. 168 If the meat desired be of a very naughty and ill property, then it is not to be exhibited. **1650** BULWER *Anthropomet.* 233 As if they would exhibit a medicine to the Head. **1725** N. ROBINSON *Th. Physick* 295 Let a Vomit be exhibited in the first Place. **1821** T. SANDWITH *Observ. Med. & Surg.* 16 A tea-spoonful of the antimonial wine was exhibited every hour. **1874** A. B. GARROD *Mat. Med.* (ed. 4) 166 The patient should fast for four or five hours before chloroform is exhibited.
II. To submit or expose to view; to show, display.
4. To hold out, or submit (a document) for inspection; *esp.* to produce, lodge, put in (a document) in a court of law, to append as an 'exhibit' *to* written evidence. Const. *to*; also †*into* (a court).
1529 *Act 21 Hen. VIII*, c. 5 So that the said testament be exhibited to him..in wrytyng. *c* **1538** STARKEY *Lett.* p. lxxv, I haue not fayned to exibyte to your grace this rude commentary. **1591** SHAKS. *1 Hen. VI*, III. i. 151 Accept this Scrowle..Which..We doe exhibite to your Maiestie. *a* **1626** BACON *Max. & Uses Com. Law* 67 They are to exhibite the will into the Bishops court. **1848** MACAULAY *Hist. Eng.* II. 44 One of the persons to whom the manuscripts were exhibited was Archbishop Sancroft. **1884** *Law Rep.* 14 Q. Bench Div. 205 The records..exhibited to the affidavits filed in the cause.
absol. **1880** MUIRHEAD tr. *Instit. Gaius* IV. §163 His application for an arbiter involved an admission that he was bound to restore or exhibit.
†**b.** To give up (oneself to justice). *Obs. rare*$^{-1}$.
1628 HOBBES *Thucyd.* (1822) 64 Pausanias..came forth and exhibited himself to justice.
5. a. To submit for consideration; to present, prefer (a petition, an accusation, etc.). Cf. I.
1529 *Act 21 Hen. VIII*, c. 16 §11 Our true and faithful Subjects..exhibited unto us a lamentable Bill of Complaint. **1598** SHAKS. *Merry W.* II. i. 29 Why Ile Exhibit a Bill in the Parliament for the putting downe of men. **1634** W. TIRWHYT tr. *Balzac's Lett.* 66 May easily impetrate at Gods hands any supplication you shall exhibite. **1647** CLARENDON *Hist. Reb.* I. (1843) 10/1 He..exhibited another charge of high treason against the duke. **1709** STRYPE *Ann. Ref.* I. iii. 75 A discourse exhibited to the Queen's Council. **1747** *Col. Rec. Pennsylv.* V. 99 The several Charges exhibited by the Complainants against Mr. Ruston were frivolous and malicious. **1805** *East's Rep.* V. 353 Where two libels are exhibited against two inhabitants of a parish for tithes. **1829** I. TAYLOR *Enthus.* iv. (1867) 79 Our part is merely to exhibit against the system the charge of delusion or enthusiasm. **1883** *Rules Supreme Court* xxxi. §7 Any interrogatories may be set aside on the ground that they have been exhibited unreasonably.
†**b.** To promulgate, publish (a decree or order).
1693 *Mem. Ct. Teckely* III. 2 Orders should be exhibited for maintaining Officers and Souldiers.
6. To set forth (in words or figures); to detail.
1534 WHITINTON *Tullyes Offices* I. (1540) 27 In exhybetynge these offyces and dutyes, we must, etc. *a* **1656** HALES *Gold. Rem.* (1688) 420 Leave to exhibit their Mind in writing. *a* **1687** PETTY *Pol. Arith.* viii. (1691) 109 Mr. Samuel Fortry..exhibits the particulars. **1774** WARTON *Hist. Eng. Poetry* ii. (1840) I. 82 Which [entries] I choose to exhibit in the words of the original. **1807** T. THOMSON *Chem.* (ed. 3) II. 381 The following Table exhibits the result of these experiments. **1846** MILL *Logic.* I. iii. §1 To exhibit an enumeration of all kinds of things which are capable of being made predicates.
7. To manifest to the senses, *esp.* to the sight; to present (a material object) to view.
1573 (*title*), The Whole Works of W. Tyndall, etc...now in print here exhibited to the Church. **1659** HAMMOND *On Ps.* xxiv. 6 Annot. 138 Where God hath promised to exhibite

himself to those that worthily approach him. **1774** GOLDSM. *Nat. Hist.* (1776) VII. 318 Out of this opening they exhibit their real head and eyes. **1796** MORSE *Amer. Geog.* I. 128 The coasts.. sometimes exhibit extensive beaches. **1805** W. SAUNDERS *Min. Waters* 9 Water is..made up of two substances, neither of which can be exhibited separately, except in the gaseous form. **1837** GORING & PRITCHARD *Microgr.* 187 For a solar intended to exhibit large objects. **1860** TYNDALL *Glac.* I. iv. 33 It may be that the lake simply exhibits the colour of pure water.

b. To present to mental view.

1577 tr. *Bullinger's Decades* (1592) 590 We haue of this, very many examples exhibited vnto vs. **1607** C. LEVER in Farr *S.P.Q. Eliz.* (1845) II. 522 Exhibite, Lord, my pardon in thy prayer. **1780** JOHNSON *Let. Mrs. Thrale* 18 Apr., She and her husband exhibited two very different appearances of human nature. **1781** GIBBON *Decl. & F.* II. xli. 506 The general exhibited a memorable lesson of firmness and severity. **1802** *Med. Jrnl.* VIII. 532 Oxydated muriatic gas ..exhibits..the surest means of checking contagion. **1821** J. Q. ADAMS in C. Davies *Metr. Syst.* III. (1871) 84 In both, the phenomenon is still exhibited.

†**c.** *intr.* for *refl. Obs.*

1656-81 BLOUNT *Glossogr.*, *Exhibite*..to shew it self. **1768-74** TUCKER *Lt. Nat.* (1852) I. 119 It is in the nature of the mind to assent to whatever appearances that exhibit when all other evidence that might correct them is removed out of her reach.

8. To represent by a figure, drawing, etc.: said also of the drawing itself.

1799 *Med. Jrnl.* I. 210 Embellished only with 34 plates, but they exhibit mostly new, rare, and valuable plants. **1825** J. NICHOLSON *Operat. Mechanic* 279 One of these branches is exhibited in the figure. **1831** BREWSTER *Optics* vi. 63 The following method..of exhibiting caustic curves I have found exceedingly convenient.

b. To present a delineation or an embodiment of in words or in action.

1848 MACAULAY *Hist. Eng.* I. 404 In the power of exhibiting character by means of dialogue he was deficient. **1875** JOWETT *Plato* (ed. 2) V. 12 [They] are to exhibit in their lives that virtue which is the basis of the state.

9. To manifest by signs, indicate the existence of, display.

1799 *Med. Jrnl.* II. 251 Countenance exhibits more distress. **1832** HT. MARTINEAU *Ireland* 113 More exhibited their uncomplaining poverty in their looks and dress. **1845** M. PATTISON *Ess.* (1889) I. 15 Gregory exhibits..a union of prudence..and unshrinking principle. **1854** BREWSTER *More Worlds* ix. 147 The power, and wisdom, and goodness of the Creator, are exhibited to us every day and every hour.

10. To show publicly for the purpose of amusement or instruction, or in a competition; to make a show of; *rarely*, to perform in public.

1797 BEWICK *Brit. Birds* (1847) I. 65 A living bird exhibited in a show. **1832** G. DOWNES *Lett. Cont. Countries* I. 31 This celebrated musician, whose laurel also is exhibited. **1845** *Florist's Jrnl.* 201 Mr. Eyles exhibited the best six. **1845** E. HOLMES *Mozart* 19 One of them.. happening to exhibit a solo on the violin. **1871** MORLEY *Voltaire* (1886) 112 After supper Voltaire would exhibit a magic lantern. **1878** JEVONS *Prim. Pol. Econ.* 57 Except to exhibit as curiosities.

absol. **1766** GOLDSM. *Vic. W.* xviii, Carrying their scenes ..to the next village where they were to exhibit. **1806** *Gazetteer Scotl.* (ed. 2) 145 A theatre, where a party of strolling comedians occasionally exhibit. **1818** JAS. MILL *Brit. Ind.* II. v. v. 493 With as much..regularity, as if they had been exhibiting on a parade.

b. *U.S.* To present or declaim (a speech or an essay) in public. Also *absol.*

1817 *Laws Yale Coll.* iv. §11 If any student..shall exhibit anything not allowed by the Faculty. *Ibid.* viii. §28 No Student who shall receive any appointment to exhibit before the class..shall give any treat of wine.

c. *intr.* for *refl.*

1863 MRS. C. CLARKE *Shaks. Char.* vi. 152 He there exhibits in rampant folly.

Hence **e'xhibited** *ppl. a.*

1730-6 BAILEY (folio), *Exhibitea*, presented or offered. **1775** ASH, *Exhibited*, brought forth to view, presented, displayed. **1861** THORNBURY *Turner* I. 258 The 'Moonlight at Millbank'..was his first exhibited oil-picture.

exhibitable (ɛg'zɪbɪtəb(ə)l), *a.* [f. EXHIBIT *v.* + -ABLE.] That admits of being exhibited.

1838 COLERIDGE *Lit. Rem.* III. 388 They are all δυνάμεις, exhibitable powers. **1860** CHAMBERS *Encycl.* s.v. *Balance of Trade*, Both actually gain, though the gain may not be exhibitable in the form of a money-balance.

exhibitant (ɛg'zɪbɪtənt). *rare.* [f. EXHIBIT *v.* + -ANT.] **a.** One who exhibits or displays (qualities). †**b.** One who prefers or presents (an accusation).

1818 *Morn. Chron.* 9 Feb., Articles of peace exhibited by the Right Honourable Henry Viscount Sidmouth..against Arthur Thistlewood..First this exhibitant saith, that in the month of April last, Arthur Thistlewood was committed to the Tower of London on charges of high treason, etc. **1846** *Blackw. Mag.* LIX. 16 Liberality, and generosity..secure for the memory of their exhibitant gratitude and reverence.

exhibiter (ɛg'zɪbɪtə(r)). [f. as prec. + -ER[1].] One who exhibits (in various senses of the vb.). Now *rare*; = EXHIBITOR.

1599 SHAKS. *Hen. V*, I. i. 74 He seemes..rather swaying more vpon our part, Then cherishing th'exhibiters against vs. **1613** T. GODWIN *Rom. Antiq.* (1658) 99 The master or exhibiter thereof, did..give notice unto the people, what day the prize should be performed. **1836** HOR. SMITH *Tin Trump.* (1876) 267 The pig exhibiter remonstrated with the author of the mischief.

e'xhibiting, *vbl. sb.* [f. as prec. + -ING[1].] The action of the vb. EXHIBIT in various senses.

1620 VENNER *Via Recta* ii. 30 How many precepts ought there to be obserued in the exhibiting of pure wine in respect of the age. **1643** in *Select. Harl. Misc.* (1793) 311 The giving and the exhibiting of the poison. **1721** STRYPE *Eccl. Mem.* III. xi. 106 Wealthy and well-disposed citizens deposited their charitable monies, for the exhibiting to ingenious men at the universities.

exhibition (ɛksɪ'bɪʃən). Forms: 5-6 **exibicion, -ycion,** 5 (**exebucion, -hebicion**), **exhibicion, -hibycion, -hybycyon,** 7 (**exhibicon**), 6- **exhibition.** [a. OF. *exhibicion*, Fr. *exhibition*, ad. late L. *exhibitiōn-em*, n. of action f. *exhibēre* to EXHIBIT.]

I. The action of providing or furnishing.

†**1. a.** Maintenance, support. *Obs.* [Cf. late L. *exhibitio et tegumentum* = 'food and raiment' (Forcellini).]

1432-50 tr. *Higden* (Rolls) VII. 259 Havynge..a litelle summe assignede to his exhibicion. **1480** *Bury Wills* (1850) 65, I will that..oon parte therof to be applied and conuerted to thexibicion and sustentacion of a perpetuall chapleyn. **1567** R. MULCASTER *Fortescue's De Laud. Leg.* (1572) 113 Charges for the exhibition [L. *exhibitione*] of their Children. *a* **1625** FLETCHER *Nice Valour* III. i, My maintenance, rascals; my Bulk, my exhibition! **1711** STRYPE *Parker* (1821) I. 503 To bestow £8 of the said £10..towards the use and exhibition of three grammar scholars.

†**b.** The 'foundation' of a grammar-school.

15.. in Whiston *Cathedral Trusts* 12 That no childe be admitted to thexhibicion of the said churche, whose father is knowne to be worthe in goodes above ccc^{li}.

†**2. a.** *sing.* and *pl.* An allowance of money for a person's support; a pension, salary. *Obs.*

1498 *Patent Roll 13 Hen. VII*, On reasonable wages or exebucion. **1501** *Plumpton Corr.* 163 He sendeth you but x^{li} towards the exibicions of my nese his wyfe. **1635** SIR R. BOYLE *Diary in Lismore Papers* Ser I. (1884) IV. 138 50^{li} was lent to my son..which I am to abate owt of his next Easter exhibicon. **1676** WYCHERLEY *Pl. Dealer* v. i, He must have a setled Exhibition of forty pounds a Year. **1741** SWIFT *Pres. St. Affairs* Wks. 1755 II. I. 215 He..is driven to live in exile upon a small exhibition.

†**b.** A gift, present. *Obs.*

1579 FULKE *Confut. Sanders* 553 His owne bondslaues, whom he hyreth with a little exhibition, to blase his charitie. **1604** SHAKS. *Oth.* IV. iii. 75, I would not doe such a thing for a joynt Ring..nor any petty exhibition.

3. †**a.** Pecuniary assistance given to a university student (*obs.* in general sense). **b.** Now only *spec.* A fixed sum given for a term of years from the funds of a school, college, or university, generally upon the result of a competitive examination. Cf. BURSARY 3 and SCHOLARSHIP.

a. *c* **1525** SKELTON *Replyc.* 143 To gyve you exhybycion To mainteyne with your skolls. **1581** MULCASTER *Positions* xxxix. (1887) 194 They will giue a scholer some petie poore exhibition to seeme to be religious. **1598** E. GILPIN *Skial.* (1878) 11, I have sized in Cambridge, and my friends a season Some exhibition for me there disburst.

b. **1631** T. ADAMS in *Lett. Lit. Men* (Camden) 146 An exhibition of £40 per annum for two or three years. **1692** SIR R. BULKELEY in *Evelyn's Mem.* (1857) III. 323 At St. Paul's school he was chosen (with a small exhibition of £10 a year ..) to go off to Cambridge. **1772** *Hist. Rochester* 91 A yearly exhibition was to be paid to four scholars. **1806** K. WHITE *Let.* 30 June, My last term bill amounts only to £4 5*s.* 3*d.*, after my exhibitions are deducted. **1886** *Oxf. Univ. Calendar* 37 Candidates for the [Junior Mathematical] Exhibition must be Members of the University who have not exceeded eight Terms from their matriculation inclusively.

II. 4. *Med.* The administration of a remedy.

1785 J. PEARSON in *Med. Commun.* II. 77 The most proper remedy against such a diarrhœa, is the exhibition of a cathartic. **1806** *Med. Jrnl.* XV. 101 During the exhibition of all these medicines, purgative glysters also..were used. **1875** B. MEADOWS *Clin. Observ.* 28 As the result of the exhibition of arsenical treatment.

III. 5. a. The action of exhibiting, submitting for inspection, displaying or holding up to view; manifestation; visible show or display (of a feeling, quality, etc.); an instance of this. Const. *of.*

1663 BARROW *Serm.* (1683) I. xii. 162 The ancient exhibition of a gracious promise. **1692** RAY *Dissol. World* III. ix. (1732) 400 The Exhibition of the Messiah. **1701** GREW *Cosm. Sacra* II. v. §17 What are all mechanick works, but the sensible exhibition of mathematick demonstrations? **1755** MAGENS *Insurances* I. 453 The Exhibition of the usual Clearances and Certificates. **1780** HARRIS *Philol. Enq.* Wks. (1841) 427 A dramatic piece, or play, is the exhibition of an action. **1833** CHALMERS *Const. Man* (1835) I. v. 208 Anger, if we but study its history and actual exhibitions. **1850** MRS. JAMESON *Leg. Monast. Ord.* (1863) 94 Dunstan never would have dared such an exhibition of presumption.

b. The action of producing (an object of litigation) in court.

1880 MUIRHEAD tr. *Instit. Gaius* IV. §157 He is pursuer who desires exhibition or restitution.

c. *Sc. Law.* An action for compelling production or delivery of writings.

1861 in W. BELL *Dict. Law Scotl.*

d. *concr.* Something that is exhibited; a display, sight, spectacle.

1786 GILPIN *Observ. Mts. & Lakes* I. p. xxvii, The windings of a noble river—or some other exhibition. *c* **1790** IMISON *Sch. Art* II. 51 Some excellent prints..held in great esteem among the admirers of exhibitions of this kind. **1848** MACAULAY *Hist. Eng.* I. 665 Exhibitions which humane men generally avoid.

e. *to make an exhibition of oneself*: to behave in such an ostentatious or conspicuous manner as to appear contemptible or laughable. *colloq.*

1853 DICKENS *Child's Hist. Eng.* (1854) III. xxxii. 162 His Sowship was making such an exhibition of himself..as is not often seen in any sty. **1914** G. B. SHAW *Misalliance* 83, I know Ive made a silly exhibition of myself here. **1935** I. COMPTON-BURNETT *House & its Head* i. 10 Am I to believe it was you, who chose to make an exhibition of yourself with a maid-servant behind the house?

6. a. A public display (of works of art, manufactured articles, natural productions, etc.); also, the place where the display is made. In early quots. often *spec.* the exhibition of pictures of the Royal Academy; now applied *esp.* to those exhibitions on a large scale of which the 'Great Exhibition' held in London in 1851 was the first and typical example.

1761 JOHNSON *Let. Baretti* 10 June in *Boswell*, The artists have instituted a yearly exhibition of pictures and statues.. This year was the second exhibition. **1818** BYRON *Beppo* lxxviii, No exhibition glares with annual pictures. **1824** MISS MITFORD in L'Estrange *Life* (1870) II. ix. 183 Is it possible that the Exhibition has closed and 'Silenus' not been sold? **1851** *Expositor* 11 Jan. 163/3 The Exhibition is to be no mere fancy fair or amateur show-room. **1890** (*title*), Catalogue of the Royal Military Exhibition.

b. *attrib.* and *Comb.*

1840 DICKENS *Old C. Shop* xxvii, It was too late to repair to the exhibition-room. **1861** THORNBURY *Turner* I. 91 The lad's own productions at Somerset House would have been quite enough to attract an exhibition-haunting amateur.

7. A public examination or display of the attainments of students. *U.S.*

1786 P. FRENEAU *Poems* 352 Lines, intended for Mr. Peele's Exhibition, Philadelphia, May 10, 1784. **1829** *Regul. Boston School Comm.* 11 There shall be two general visitations of the schools annually, for the purpose of exhibition. *Ibid.*, These exhibitions. **1887** J. KIRKLAND *Zury* 186 It was customary to have on February 22nd a school 'Exhibition' with speeches, dialogues, and so forth. **1899** E. E. HALE *Lowell* 29 They were within the number of twenty-four students [at Harvard] who had had honors at the several exhibitions. **1943** A. G. POWELL *I can go Home Again* 51 At the close of the school next spring, we had the 'Exhibition', with charades, dialogues, recitations, and so forth.

Hence **exhi'bitional** *a.*, of or pertaining to an exhibition. **exhi'bitionize** *v.*, *nonce-wd.*, *intr.* to frequent exhibitions.

1834 *New Monthly Mag.* XLI. 245 Hackneyed as we are in exhibitionizing, we did not contemplate this scene without the liveliest pleasure. **1882** J. PARKER *Apost. Life* (1884) III. 294 There is no touch of merely exhibitional genius. **1886** *New Princeton Rev.* I. 121 Madame and her suite had gone to partake of their yearly exhibitional refreshments.

exhibitioner (ɛksɪ'bɪʃənə(r)). [f. prec. + -ER[1].]

†**1.** One who pays for (a person's) maintenance. *Obs.*

c **1575** FULKE *Confut. Doctr. Purgatory* (1577) 438 To make a fond florish a farre of in wordes of common wrangling, to please your patrones and exhibitioners.

2. One who holds an exhibition at a university.

1679 BURNET *Hist. Ref.* I. III. 227 (an. 1536) Yet severe Impositions and heavy Taxes were laid on them; a fifth part for Repairs, a tenth at least for an Exhibitioner. **1707** HEARNE *Collect.* 24 Jan. (Oxf. Hist. Soc.) I. 319 10 Exhibitioners who are to study the Hebrew and Greek Tongues. **1843** COLERIDGE in Arnold *Stanley's Life & Corr.* (1844) I. i. 9 Corpus is a very small establishment..with four exhibitioners. **1886** *Oxf. Univ. Calendar* 117 There is a power of renewal..if the College are satisfied with the Scholar or Exhibitioner.

3. = EXHIBITOR 1, 2.

1791 G. WAKEFIELD *Enquiry Publ. Worship* 30 The effect is not so correspondent to the nature of the expected visitant, as to the faculties of the exhibitioner. **1792** —— *Ibid.* (ed. 2) 42 *note*, The indefensible mode of our dissenting exhibitioners. **1840** *Fraser's Mag.* XXI. 730 There is among the present exhibitioners [at the Royal Academy] no lack of this kind of talent.

exhibitionism (ɛksɪ'bɪʃənɪz(ə)m). [f. EXHIBITION + -ISM.]

1. Indecent exposure of the sexual organs, esp. as a manifestation of sexual perversion. Also *fig.* and *gen.*, a tendency towards display; indulgence in extravagant behaviour.

1893 C. G. CHADDOCK tr. *Krafft-Ebing's Psychopathia Sexualis* v. 394 In his dreams he exhibited himself to young, voluptuous women... In this hereditary and degenerate impulsive exhibitionism, it is interesting to note how the perverse sexual impulse is awakened from its latency by.. alcohol. **1908** *Practitioner* Jan. 10 A hyperaesthesia sexualis, with an insufficient power to satisfy his impulses, will lead to strained marital relations, immorality, and promiscuous intercourse, exhibitionism, and even sexual perversions. **1919** M. K. BRADBY *Psychoanalysis* 136 An expression of sexuality on a level with childish 'exhibitionism'. **1921** *19th Cent.* Mar. 476 Its [*sc.* love's] regression and narcissism, exhibitionism, masochism, [etc.]. **1924** C. GRAY *Surv. Contemp. Music* 15 Others for whom art is an opportunity for spiritual exhibitionism and literature a confessional. **1926** T. BEER *Mauve Decade* v. 180 A species of exhibitionism that makes one grin. **1928** *Sunday Dispatch* 5 Aug. 11/2 Heroin is a drug that promotes exhibitionism. The user..is prompted to false bravery, extravagant behaviour, showiness. **1964** A. STORR *Sexual Deviation* ix. 91 Of these deviations, by far the commonest is exhibitionism, or, as the law terms it, indecent exposure.

2. The mania for exhibitions (sense 6). *rare.*

1920 W. R. Lethaby *Form in Civiliz.* (1922) 182 This exhibitionism is one of the many symptoms of 'the sickness of acquisitive society'.

exhibitionist (ɛksɪˈbɪʃənɪst). [f. EXHIBITION + -IST.] **1.** One who takes part in an exhibition or public performance; a performer. *rare*$^{-1}$.

1821 *Blackw. Mag.* IX. 571 The whole of the service is to devolve upon the clergyman and the precentor, with a few hired or trained exhibitionists.

2. One who indulges in exhibitionism. Also *attrib.*

1893 C. G. Chaddock tr. *Krafft-Ebing's Psychopathia Sexualis* v. 383 There are various categories of exhibitionists. **1928** *Daily Express* 15 Aug. 15 Two 'exhibitionist' bathers at Deauville. **1949** M. Mead *Male & Female* vii. 156 Some societies do not..forbid his playing sexual games, exhibitionist games with other boys. **1958** *Times* 18 Feb. 5/2 A 'hard core of exhibitionists' wanting to get on television. **1963** A. Heron *Towards Quaker View of Sex* 67 Male exhibitionists in particular are seeking through their sexually aggressive act to assert their impoverished sexuality. **1965** F. Sargeson *Memoirs of Peon* vii. 206 Apart from my exhibitionist drive, I had some warrant for my desire.

exhibitionistic (ɛksɪˌbɪʃəˈnɪstɪk), *a.* [f. prec. + -IC.] Pertaining or given to exhibitionism. So **exhibitioˈnistically** *adv.*

1928 A. Huxley *Let.* 23 May (1969) 297 I'd do a little lying out with my belly exhibitionistically exposed to the natural sun. **1930** *Psychol. Abstr.* Dec. 539/1 Descriptions of exhibitionistic acts which manifest atypical phases are here presented. **1931** *Nation* (N.Y.) 23 Dec. 702 Harris, the exhibitionistic satyr, finally worried the prudish Shaw into giving him a statement concerning the latter's sex life. **1932** S. Zuckerman *Soc. Life Monkeys & Apes* xix. 310 It is difficult to say what is the significance of such behaviour. There is no obvious justification for the view expressed by Tinklepaugh that it is exhibitionistic. **1937** *Scrutiny* Mar. 439 The 'good student', whose fountain-pen slides and skates exhibitionistically over the page. **1949** M. Mead *Male & Female* vii. 156 The lusty, exhibitionistic self-confidence of the five-year-old. *Ibid.* xviii. 369 He is proudly, exhibitionistically sure of his masculinity. **1970** *Daily Tel.* 15 Jan. 16/2 Technically testing yet not unduly exhibitionistic, both cadenzas avoided..excessive length and complexity.

exhibitive (ɛgˈzɪbɪtɪv), *a.* [ad. mod.L. *exhibitīvus*, f. *exhibit-*: see EXHIBIT *v.* and -IVE.] †**1.** Having the function of imparting or communicating. Cf. EXHIBIT *v.* 1. Const. *of*. *Obs.*

[**1550** Bucer *Conf. de Euch.* §54 Malo dicere..pane & vino dari corpus & sanguinem Domini, quam significari, et panem hic signum esse corporis exhibitivum quam signum simpliciter.] **1607** *Schol. Disc. agst. Antichr.* I. ii. 98 The signes of the old Testament be not in his iudgment exhibitiue of any grace, but significatiue only. **1681** R. L'Estrange *Apol. Prot.* IV. i. 112 That the Species of Bread and Wine are not only Signs..but that they are also Exhibitive and Communicative..of the very things that they represent.

2. Having the property or function of exhibiting or showing forth. Const. *of*.

1596 H. Clapham *Briefe Bible* I. 32 Togither with his Covenant, the Lord adioyneth a Seale, or exhibitiue Signe. **1708** *Brit. Apollo* No. 45. 1/2 Words exhibitive of a double figure. **1737** Waterland *Eucharist* 168 The Sacramental Bread..representative and exhibitive of the natural Body.

†**3.** Used for: Self-manifesting. (Of the Divine mind: by Norris opposed to *conceptive*.) *Obs. rare.*

1678 Norris *Coll. Misc.* (1699) 159 The Simple Essences of Things..are the same with that [*sc.* the Divine] Understanding it self, consider'd as variously exhibitive or representative. *Ibid.* 352 By the mind of God Exhibitive, is meant the essence of God, as thus or thus imitable, or participable by any Creature.

Hence **eˈxhibitively** *adv.*

1610 T. Higgons *Serm. Pauls Crosse 3 Mar.* (1611) 21 This grace is, equally, in all the persons, but originally in the Father, exhibitiuely in the Son. **1739** Waterland *Sacram. Part Eucharist* 12 The Trope lies in the Verb *was*, put for signify, or exhibitively signifie.

exhibitor (ɛgˈzɪbɪtə(r)). [a. L. *exhibitor*, agent-n. f. *exhibēre* to EXHIBIT.]

1. One who shows (something) as a curiosity; a showman, one who produces in public a show or spectacle. Cf. EXHIBITER b.

1654 Gayton *Pleas. Notes* IV. xi. 245 The exhibitors of that shew politiquely had plac'd Whiflers arm'd and link'd through the Hall. **1814** Wordsw. *Excursion* VIII. 29 The spectator, who a while was pleased More than th' exhibitor himself. *a***1845** Hood *Ode to J. Ireland* i, Oh, very reverend Dean and Chapter, Exhibitors of giant men. **1875** Buckland *Log-bk.* 19 The exhibitor told us a wonderful story.

2. One who contributes an article for public exhibition.

1845 *Florist's Jrnl.* 205 The only exhibitor in the class for 12 species. **1851** *Expositor* 11 Jan. 163/3 The hosts of exhibitors [at the Exhibition of 1851].

Hence **eˈxhibitorship.**

1862 *Sat. Rev.* XIV. 72/1 Medal and Honourable Mention become little more than a certificate of exhibitorship.

exhibitory (ɛgˈzɪbɪtərɪ), *a.* and *sb.* [ad. L. *exhibitōri-us*, f. *exhibēre*: see EXHIBIT and -ORY.]

A. *adj.*

1. a. Intended to exhibit, set forth, or display. **b.** Of or pertaining to display or exhibition.

1772 Warton *Life Sir T. Pope* (1780) 379 *note*, An exhibitory bill..of expences for their removal this year. **1849** Ruskin *Sev. Lamps* i. §8. 18 The treatment of the Papists' temple is eminently exhibitory; it is surface work throughout. **1879** H. N. Hudson *Hamlet* Pref. 15 Knowledge..less available for..exhibitory purposes. **1882** *Century Mag.* XXV. 101 The gay, storm-beleaguered camp, in the words of its exhibitory press, began to 'boom'.

2. Intended to cause the exhibition or production of an article in dispute.

1886 Muirhead in *Encycl. Brit.* XX. 709/1 If the respondent obeyed the order in a restitutory or exhibitory decree, there was an end of the matter.

†**B.** *sb.* A procedure with regard to the 'exhibition' of remedies. *Obs.*

1607 Walkington *Opt. Glass* 14 Physicians..(whose exhibitories to themselues do not parallele their prescripts..to others).

exhilarant (ɛgˈzɪlərənt), *a.* and *sb.* [a. F. *exhilarant*, ad. L. *exhilarant-em*, pr. pple. of *exhilarāre* to EXHILARATE.]

A. *adj.* That exhilarates; exhilarating.

1866 Mrs. Whitney *L. Goldthwaite* xii. 294 The exhilarant draught in which they drank the mountain-joy. **1872** Blackie *Lays Highl.* Introd. 49 The breeze..and the tide..impart a healthy and an exhilarant stimulus.

B. *sb.* An exhilarating medicine.

1803 Pilkington *View Derbysh.* I. 329 It has been holden in high repute as a cordial and exhilerant [*sic*]. **1839** *New Monthly Mag.* LVII. 371 The use of this drug as an exhilerant [*sic*] is not confined to the poor. *a***1843** Southey *Doctor* (1849) 164 An exhilarant and a cordial which rejoiced and strengthened him. **1868** Garrod *Mat. Med.* (ed. 3) 390 Exhilarants are medicines whose primary effect is to cause an exaltation of the spirits.

exhilarate (ɛgˈzɪləreɪt), *v.* Forms: 7-8 exhilerate, (6 -arite), 6- exhilarate. [ad. L. *exhilarāt-* ppl. stem of *exhilarāre*, f. *ex-* (see EX- *pref.*[1]) + *hilar-is* cheerful: see HILARITY.]

1. *trans.* To make cheerful or merry; to cheer, enliven, gladden (a person, his spirits, etc.).

1540 Morysine *Vives' Introd. Wysd.* E vj b, A cleane and a pure conscience maye exhilarate the mynde. **1621** Burton *Anat. Mel.* II. ii. VI. iii, Sundry are the meanes..to exhilerate a sorrowfull heart. **1751** Smollett *Per. Pic.* (1779) II. xxxviii. 22 Peregrine..advised him to exhilarate his spirits with a glass of wine. *a***1763** Shenstone *Ess.* 36 He would be exhilarated at the sight of the first beggar that he saw. **1796** C. Marshall *Garden.* xx. (1813) 426 Frost..exhilarates our spirits. **1848** Dickens *Dombey* xxxvi, It seemed greatly to delight and exhilarate him to say so.

b. To impart cheerfulness to, enliven (a thing or pursuit).

1751 Johnson *Rambler* No. 177 ¶5 A select company of curious men, who met once a week to exhilarate their studies. **1795** Anderson *Embassy China* 274 A joyous dinner, exhilarated by plenty of spirits.

†**2.** *intr.* To become cheerful. *Obs. rare*$^{-1}$.

1620 Bacon *Sp. in Parl.* in *Lett. & Life* (1874) VII. 177 The shining of the sun, whereby all things exhilarate, is hindered by clouds.

exhilarating (ɛgˈzɪləreɪtɪŋ), *ppl. a.* [f. as prec. + -ING[2].] That exhilarates; cheering, enlivening, inspiriting.

1643 Milton *Divorce* II. ix. (1851) 87 Marriage..was especially giv'n as a cordiall and exhilarating cup of solace. **1708** J. Philips *Cyder* II. 66 A Continual Tide Flows from th' exhilerating Fount. **1779-81** Johnson *L.P., Denham*, Nothing is less exhilarating than the ludicrousness of Denham. **1845** Darwin *Voy. Nat.* iv. (1879) 76 We..started for another exhilarating gallop. **1865** Livingstone *Zambesi* xxv. 519 The air which was exhilarating to Europeans.

Hence **eˈxhilaratingly** *adv.*

1850 in Ogilvie.

exhilaration (ɛgˌzɪləˈreɪʃən). Also 7-8 exhileration. [ad. late L. *exhilarātiōn-em*, n. of action f. *exhilarāre* to EXHILARATE.]

1. The action or means of exhilarating; a cheering or enlivening influence.

1623-6 Cockeram, *Exhileration.* **1629** J. Maxwell tr. *Herodian* (1635) 301 To use all..exhilarations for joy of the gods wedding. **1792** V. Knox *Serm.* xi. 247 This remedy..enlivens..by an unnatural exhilaration. **1864** Longf. *Falc. Ser. Feder.* 139 There was..that wild exhilaration in the air.

2. The condition or feeling of being exhilarated.

1626 Bacon *Sylva* §721 Exhilaration hath some Affinity with Joy. **1802** Cogan *Philos. Treat. Passions* I. ii. (ed. 2) 63 Every species of torpor is subdued; an exhilaration succeeds. **1838** Dickens *Nich. Nick.* xxiv, A bill of fare that might kindle exhilaration in the breast of a misanthrope. **1875** Hamerton *Intell. Life* x. v. 388 The feeling of..exhilaration will last for several hours.

exhilarative (ɛgˈzɪlərətɪv), *a.* [f. L. *exhilarāt-* ppl. stem of *exhilarāre* to EXHILARATE + -IVE.] Tending to produce exhilaration.

1864 Carlyle *Fredk. Gt.* IV. 356 Pamphlets..sapid, exhilarative. **1873** *St. Paul's Mag.* Feb. 133 It was a morning most exhilarative. **1875** H. C. Wood *Therap.* (1879) 200 A feeling of lassitude..preceded..by a short period of exhilarative excitement.

exhilarator (ɛgˈzɪləreɪtə(r)). [f. EXHILARATE *v.* + -OR.] One who, or that which, exhilarates.

1807 *Edin. Rev.* X. 88 We certainly do not approve of cards and wagers as the best exhilarators of the spirits. **1822** *Blackw. Mag.* XII. 279 Where Erskine parted his mantle of puns among the..aspiring exhilarators of the Bar.

eˈxhilaratory, *a. rare.* [f. EXHILARATE *v.* + -ORY.] Having the effect of exhilarating.

1871 L. Stephen *Playground of Europe* 284 The danger is trifling enough to be merely exhila[ra]tory.

exhilient, bad form of EXILIENT, *Obs.*

exhort (ɛgzˈhɔːt, ɛgˈzɔːrt), *v.* Forms: 4-6 exort(e, -horte, 4- exhort. [ad. L. *exhort-āri*, f. *ex-* intensive + *hortāri* to encourage: see HORTATORY. Cf. F. *exhorter* and ENHORT. Not now in colloquial use.]

1. *trans.* To admonish earnestly; to urge by stimulating words to conduct regarded as laudable. Said also of circumstances, etc.: To serve as an incitement. **a.** *simply.*

*c***1400** *Apol. Loll.* 30 If prestis ouerwile exort or monest þe peple. *a***1533** Ld. Berners *Huon* lxxxi. 247 He soo exorted me that at the houre of mydnyghte he made me to aryse hastely. **1538** Starkey *England* I. i. 25 To the wych purpos ..the tyme exhortyth us. **1548-9** (Mar.) *Bk. Com. Prayer, Offices* 19 Then shall the minister exhort the sicke person after this fourme. **1604** Shaks. *Ham.* IV. iv. 46 (Qq.) Examples, gross as earth, exhort me. **1825** Lytton *Falkland* 40 Write to me..exhort me, admonish me.

absol. *c***1400** *Apol. Loll.* 31 þe prest be mi3ti to exort in al doctrin. **1526-34** Tindale *2 Tim.* iv. 2 Exhorte with all longe sufferinge and doctryne. **1651** Hobbes *Leviath.* II. xxv. 131 The words..of him that Exhorteth. *a***1845** Barham *Ingol. Leg., Jerry Jarvis*, Whether the Rev. Mr. Hyandry exhorted or made way for the Rev. Mr. Tearbrain. **1881** Bible (R.V.) *Rom.* xii. 8 He that exhorteth, to his exhorting.

b. Const. *to* with *inf.* or *subord. clause.*

1490 Caxton *Eneydos* iv. (1890) 19, I the exhorte and counceylle that thou ne defoylle nomore thyn hondes wyth my bloode. **1532** *Thynne's ed. of Chaucer's L.G.W. Hyps. & Medea* 73 That he in his neuewe Iason wolde exhorte To saylen to that londe. **1535** Coverdale *Neh.* ix. 26 Thy prophetes (which exhorted them so earnestly, that they shulde conuerte vnto the). **1611** Bible *Tit.* ii. 6 Yong men likewise exhort, to bee sober minded. **1735** Berkeley *Def. Free-think. in Math.* §37, I have long ago done what you so often exhort me to do. **1860** Hook *Lives Abps.* (1869) I. v. 226 The bishops were exhorted not to engage in secular affairs more than was necessary.

c. Const. *to* an action or course, a condition.

1529 More *Dyaloge* I. Wks. 162/2 To call and exorte the worlde from all pleasure of the fleshe to the puritie and clennes of the body and soule. **1594** Hooker *Eccl. Pol.* I. x. (1611) 25 The Apostle, in exhorting men to contentment. **1747** Johnson *Plan Eng. Dict.* Wks. IX. 185 Commonly..we exhort to good actions, we instigate to ill. *a***1785** Glover *Athenaid* II. 45, I through each city..Have pass'd, exhorting ..Greece To bold defence. **1848** Macaulay *Hist. Eng.* II. 79 The people would be exhorted to liberality.

2. With *obj.* a thing: To recommend earnestly; to insist upon.

*c***1500** *New Not-br. Mayd* in *Poet. Tracts* (Percy Soc.) 47 What I exhorte Not herde is. **1526-34** Tindale *1 Tim.* vi. 2 These thynges teache and exhorte. **1667** Milton *P.L.* II. 179 While we..Designing or exhorting glorious Warr. **1771** Franklin *Autobiog.* Wks. 1840 I. 8 Exhorting the repeal of those laws, so contrary to charity. **1856** Froude *Hist. Eng.* (1858) I. ii. 96 He..again exhorted a reform.

†**exˈhort**, *sb. Obs.* [f. prec. vb.] = EXHORTATION.

*c***1475** *Partenay* 3972 By the exort of vntrew man. **1525** Ld. Berners *Froiss.* II. Pref., The princely exhorte, whiche ..our foresaid gracyous soueraygne gaue me. **1590** Lodge *Euphues Gold. Leg.*, Did he make a large exhort unto concord? *c***1611** Chapman *Iliad* XI. 183 Everywhere he breathed exhorts. **1715-20** Pope *Iliad* XII. 324 Drown Hector's Vaunts in loud Exhorts of Fight. **1829** A. W. Fonblanque *Engl. under 7 Administr.* (1837) I. 238 Perpetual exhorts to a new birth unto Toryism.

†**exˈhortance.** *Obs.* In 7 *Sc.* exhortans. [f. as prec. + -ANCE.] = EXHORTATION.

(But possibly *exhortans* may be an abbreviation in the MS. for *exhortations.*)

*c***1646** T. Craufurd *Hist. Univ. Edinb.* (1808) 45 He [Mr. Robert Rollock]..with most pithy exhortans setting them on to vertue and pietie.

†**exˈhortary.** *Obs. rare*$^{-1}$. In 6 -arie. [f. EXHORT *sb.* + -ARY.] = EXHORTATION.

1584 Lodge *Alarum* 54 The father..having ended this exhortarie is answered..of his dissembling sonne thus.

exhortation (ɛksɔːˈteɪʃən). Forms: 4-5 exhort-, exhortacioun, 5-6 exhortacion, -yon, exortacion, (6 exhortatyoun, exortation) 5- exhortation. [ad. L. *exhortātiōn-em*, n. of action f. *exhortārī* to EXHORT. Cf. Fr. *exhortation.*]

1. The action or process of exhorting, of earnestly admonishing or urging to what is deemed laudable conduct; an instance of this.

1382 Wyclif *1 Tim.* iv. 13 Til I come take tent to redynge, to exortacioun and techynge. *c***1425** Wyntoun *Cron.* VII. viii. 720 Eftyr..syndry exhortatyownys. **1477** Earl Rivers (Caxton) *Dictes* 6 To gadre money or tresor by subtyl exortation. **1505** Fisher *Penit. Ps.* Wks. 1 This treatyse..was made..at the exortacion and sterynge of..princesse Margarete. **1552** Abp. Hamilton *Catech.* (1884) 30 Thair mother gaf exhortacion to ilkane of thame. *a***1656** Hales *Tracts* (1677) 11 Exhortations from all sin. *a***1732** Atterbury *Serm.* (1723) II. vi. 224 There is no Room for any Exhortations to charity. **1828** Whately *Rhet.* III. Introd., A great part of the Preacher's business consists of Exhortation. **1841** D'Israeli *Amen. Lit.* (1867) 177 An exhortation to the youthful monarch to check his own self-indulgence.

2. A set speech delivered for the purpose of exhorting; a discourse; *esp.* a formal address in the course of a religious observance, liturgical formulary or rite. Also in phrase, ***to make an exhortation***.

c **1450** *Why I can't be a Nun* 373 in *E.E.P.* (1862) 148 Now, ladyes, taketh gode hede to thys exhortacion That I haue tawȝt yow in thys lore. **1547** Boorde *Introd. Knowl.* xxxvii. 215 All the people war gathered about him, to heare him make an exortation. **1614** Raleigh *Hist. World* II. 326 The place..where Moses made those divine exhortations some say was Bethabara. **1704** Nelson *Fest. & Fasts* II. ix. (1739) 582 As the Exhortation before the Communion suggests to us. **1848** Dickens *Dombey* v, The clergyman..delivering (very unaffectedly and simply) the closing exhortation. **1875** Stubbs *Const. Hist.* III. xviii. 28 The result of this exhortation was a long and..important session.

3. *attrib.*

1872 Shipley *Glossary* 190 *Exhortation Week*, The week before Septuagesima Sunday; so called in the Eastern Church because the faithful are then exhorted to prepare for the Great Fast. Also called *Exhortatory Week*.

exhortative (ɛg'zɔːtətɪv), *a.* [ad. L. *exhortātīv-us*, f. *exhortārī*: see EXHORT and -IVE. Cf. F. *exhortatif, -ive.*] Of, pertaining to, or containing exhortation; intended to exhort.

1564 J. White (*title*), Agapetus, An Exposition of Chapters Exhortative. **1583** [see CONSULTATIVE]. **1631** Weever *Anc. Fun. Mon.* 246 Laurence writ..exhortatiue Epistles to the Bishops. **1687** T. Tramallier in *Magd. Coll. & Jas. II* (Oxf. Hist. Soc.) 213 The exhortative part of his Speech. *c* **1810** Coleridge *Notes on Jer. Taylor, Lit. Rem.* III. 301 The words of the Apostle are exhortative and dehortative. **1836** *Blackw. Mag.* XXXIX. 231 The dictatorial exhortative style of the leading journal. **1836** Lane *Mod. Egypt.* I. x. 317 A few words..exhortative to charity.

Hence **ex'hortatively** *adv.*

1693 Leighton *Comm. 1 Pet.* (1850) I. 146 Some read these words exhortatively.

exhortator (ɛksɔː'teɪtər). *rare*⁻⁰. [a. late L. *exhortātor*, agent-n. f. *exhortārī* to EXHORT.] One who exhorts or encourages; = EXHORTER.

1846 Worcester cites *Penny Cycl.* In mod. Dicts.

exhortatory (ɛg'zɔːtətərɪ), *a.* and *sb.* [ad. late L. *exhortātōri-us*, f. *exhortārī* : see EXHORT *v.* and -ORY.]

A. *adj.* Of, pertaining to, or containing exhortation, intended to exhort.

1544 'H. Stalbrydge' (*title*), Epistel exhortatorye.. agaynst the pompous popysh Bischops. **1616** N. Brent tr. *Sarpi's Hist. Counc. Trent* (1676) 314 They used..an exhortatory remedy to the Prelates. **1640** Bp. Hall *Episc.* III. ix. 269 An exhortatory conclusion to our brethren at home. **1780** Arnot *Hist. Edin.* i. (1816) 38 The minister preached an exhortatory discourse. **1818** T. Jefferson *Writ.* (1830) IV. 448, I could take no part in it [the discussion] but an exhortatory one. **1870** tr. *Lange's Comm. Eccl.* 76 The entire contents..are of an exhortatory character.

†**B.** *sb.* An exhortatory discourse. *Obs.*

1656 H. Hammond (*title*), A Parænesis or Exhortatory to all True Sons of the Church. **1675** J. Smith *Chr. Relig. Appeal* i. 37 Justin Martyr..in his Exhortatory to the Gentiles.

exhorter (ɛg'zɔːtə(r)). Also 6 **exhortoure**, *Sc.* **exhortar.** [f. EXHORT *v.* + -ER¹.]

1. One who exhorts or urges on to action. *Obs.*

1552 Huloet, Exhortoure, *suasor.* **1554** T. Martin *Marr. Priests* A a iv, A moste deuoute exhorter, & a most earnest perswader. **1655-60** Stanley *Hist. Philos.* (1701) 85/2 Socrates as being a Man Absolute and Perfect..never needed any exhorter. **1875** C. F. Wingate in *N. Amer. Rev.* CXX. 146 He took a lively interest in prayer-meetings..and was an earnest exhorter.

2. *spec.* In various Christian Churches, a person appointed to give religious exhortation under the direction of a superior minister. Cf. EVANGELIST 3 c.

1513-75 *Diurn. Occurr.* (Bannatyne Club) 88 It was ordanit be the Ministeris, exhortaris and reidaris of this realme. **1564** *Act Edin. Gen. Assembly* 25 Dec., An Act ..'Ordaining every Minister, Exhorter and Reader to have one of the Psalm Books'. **1637-50** Row *Hist. Kirk* (1842) 40 The Generall Assemblie [to] appoynt the proportion how much shall a Superintendent have..how much ane Exhorter, how much a Reader. **1772** Wesley *Jrnl.* 5 June, One of these exhorters was Jacob Rowell. **1845** A. Wiley in *Indiana Mag. Hist.* (1927) XXIII. 202 He joined the church ..and was made class-leader, then exhorter, and then local preacher. **1901** W. N. Harben *Westerfelt* 253, I got hugged by a whole string of exhorters.

exhorting (ɛg'zɔːtɪŋ), *vbl. sb.* [f. as prec. + -ING¹.] The action of the vb. EXHORT; encouragement, instigation; an exhortation, address.

c **1489** Caxton *Blanchardyn* xx. 65 The proude mayden in amours, after this exhortyng..sayde that she sholde noo more speke therof vnto her. **1490** —— *Eneydos* xl. 132 Euander slewe his fader by exhortynge of his moder that vyceta was called. **1591** Harington *Orl. Fur.* xxviii. xcvi, The godly Frier..With new exhortings bad her to beware.

exhumate ('ɛkshjuːmeɪt), *v.* Also 6 *pa. pple.* **exhumate.** [f. med.L. *exhumāt-* ppl. stem of *exhumā-re* to EXHUME.] = EXHUME *v. lit.* and *fig.*

1548 Hall *Chron.* (1809) 796 The Kyng hearyng his subject to be exhumate and brent without his knowledge. **1619** 'R. Jones' [Lushington] in *Phenix* (1708) II. 480 The Women gave the Watch-word to the Disciples, who immediately do exhumate his Body. **1715** M. Davies *Athen. Brit.* I. 175 His [Wiclif's] Body was Exhumated and Burnt. *Ibid.* I. 272 The present Sermon-maker would needs exhumate poor Fryar John. **1846** Worcester cites Dr. Hitchcock. **1881** *Gd. Words* XXII. 45/1 The writer whose hands are cramped with the pen will draw his legs from under the desk, and..exhumating his knapsack, dry with a winter's dust, [will] make straight for the mountain.

exhumation (ɛkshjuː'meɪʃən). [a. Fr. *exhumation*, ad. med.L. *exhumātiōn-em*, n. of action f. *exhumā-re* to EXHUME.] The action or process of digging up or removing (a body, etc.) from beneath the ground. Also, an instance of this.

1797 W. Seward *Suppl. to Anecd.* 288 Tracts relative to the exhumation in the great church at Dunkirk. **1819** Southey in *Q. Rev.* XXI. 373 The details of this barbarous exhumation are curious. **1831** Brewster *Newton* (1855) II. xxiv. 344 The dead body of Arsenius was, after exhumation, produced before the council of Tyre. **1851** D. Wilson *Preh. Ann.* II. III. vi. 163 The exhumation of two oaken cists. **1869** E. A. Parkes *Pract. Hygiene* (ed. 3) 114 Febrile affections produced by exhumations..of bodies.

exhumator ('ɛkshjuːmeɪtə(r)). [agent-n. f. L. *exhumāre* to EXHUME.] One who exhumes.

1820 *Blackw. Mag.* VII. 321 The fraternal embrace of the exhumator of Tom Paine's bones. **1831** *Fraser's Mag.* III. 271 The exhumators of the remains of Adam Smith. **1832** Maginn in *Blackw. Mag.* XXXII. 417 If the reformers of our day have no Hampden, they have his exhumator and biographer, Lord Nugent.

exhume (ɛks'hjuːm), *v.* [ad. F. *exhume-r*, ad. med.L. *exhum-āre* (13th c. in Du Cange), f. *ex-* out + *hum-us* ground.]

1. *trans.* To dig out or remove (something buried) from beneath the ground.

1783 Watson *Philip III* (L.), More than a dozen bodies were thus unnecessarily exhumed. **1848** Mrs. Jameson *Sacr. & Leg. Art* (1850) 101 It was not the manner of those days to exhume..the bodies of holy men. **1862** Dana *Man. Geol.* 643 Bones that have been exhumed by the waves. **1863** Lyell *Antiq. Man* 48 No less than 17 canoes had been.. exhumed. **1872** Baker *Nile Tribut.* viii. 112 The wild animals might have exhumed the body.

b. *transf.* and *fig.* To unearth, bring to light.

1819 Scott *Let.* 3 Oct. in *Lockhart*, I..go a day sooner to exhume certain old monuments of the Rutherfords at Jedburgh. **1865** Lecky *Ration.* I. i. 104 The industry of modern antiquarians has exhumed two or three obscure works. **1866** Motley *Dutch Rep.* III. iii. 403 The letters of the royal assassin..were exhumed.

2. To remove the overlying soil from. *rare.*

1872 Nicholson *Palæont.* 31 When we exhume an old land-surface the remains of Mammals may be found in tolerable plenty.

Hence **ex'humed** *ppl. a.* (in quots. *fig.*).

1840 Gladstone *Ch. Princ.* 19 They will give to those, as it were, exhumed verities a degree of weight and prominence. **1878** H. M. Stanley *Dark Cont.* II. xii. 356 The aborigines of these new and exhumed regions.

exhumer (ɛks'hjuːmə(r)). [f. as prec. + -ER¹.] One who exhumes.

1872 Mark Twain *Innoc. Abr.* xxxi. 243 The exhumers of Pompeii. **1886** *Pall Mall G.* 24 Apr. 5/2 The work of the exhumer is amply repaid.

exhybe: see EXHIBE, *Obs.*

‖**ex hypothesi** (ɛks haɪ'pɒθɪsaɪ), *advb. phr.* [mod.L.] From or according to the hypothesis; as a result of the assumptions made; supposedly, hypothetically.

1603 C. Heydon *Jud. Astrol.* 211 The Spring and neape tides, the foure seasons of the yere, with infinite like, they are phisically necessarie, they are ineuitable *ex hypothesi.* **1694** J. Howe *Enq. conc. Trinity* 49 Yet that necessity not being absolute, but *ex hypothesi* only. *a* **1734** North *Exam.* (1740) I. iii. 215 The Jury, *ex Hypothesi*..inclined on the Plot Side. **1829** *Edin. Rev.* Oct. 219 The universe, *ex hypothesi*, is only an effect. **1887** *Athenæum* 1 Oct. 430/2 A people to whom it was *ex hypothesi* unknown. **1941** W. Temple *Citizen & Churchman* ii. 33 Inasmuch as *ex hypothesi* there is no God for the State to serve, the State becomes an absolute. **1945** R. Knox *God & Atom* vi. 82 To give priority to Something which, *ex hypothesi*, claims absolute priority.

exibilate, exiccate, etc.: see EXSIBILATE, etc.

†**e'xiconize**, *v. Obs. rare*⁻¹. [ad. Gr. ἐξεικονίζ-ειν, f. ἐξ- (see EX- *pref.*²) + εἰκών image.] *trans.* To portray, depict.

1641 Earl Manchester in *Mountague's Let., etc.* 12 Our faith..is no other but what is exiconized in the Apostles' creed.

[**exidemic, -al.** Errors for EPIDEMIC, -ICAL, due to the similarity of *x* and *p* in 16th and 17th cent. hands.

1608 Topsell *Serpents* 76 A certaine token..that some exidemicall [ed. 1658 epidemicall], generall pestilence or plague rageth amongst them. **1847-78** Halliwell, Exidemic (citing Hall).]

†**'exient.** *Chronol. Obs. rare.* [ad. L. *exiens*, pr. pple. of *exīre*: see EXIT *sb.* Cf. *transient.*] Preceded by a numeral: The (first, second, etc.) year reckoned from any epoch.

1677 Cary *Chronol.* 67 The fourth Exient of the sixth Olympiad. *Ibid.* 223 The 3rd exient of Asa.

exies ('ɛksiːz), *sb. pl. Sc.* [? corruption of ACCESS *sb.*] ? Hysterics.

1816 Scott *Antiq.* xxxv, 'Jenny Rintherout has ta'en the exies, and done naething but laugh and greet'. **1818** —— *Br. Lamm.* xi, 'The cook-maid in the trembling exies'.

‖**exigeant** (ɛksiʒɑ̃), *a.* [Fr. pr. pple. of *exiger*, ad. L. *exigĕre*: see EXIGENT.] = EXACTING *ppl. a.* 3. Also used (with sbs. denoting women) in fem. form **exigeante** (ɛksiʒɑ̃t).

1803 Mar. Edgeworth *Belinda* viii, Clarence Hervey had been used to the brilliant and exigeante lady Delacour. **1837** C'tess Blessington in C. Heath *Bk. of Beauty* 190 It scarcely satisfied the jealous and exigeant lover. **1871** R. H. Hutton *Ess.* I. 22 Falling into the jealous, exigeant, selfish type of affection.

exigence ('ɛksɪdʒəns). Also 7 **exegence.** [a. F. *exigence*, ad. L. *exigentia*, f. *exigent-em*, pr. pple. of *exigĕre*: see EXIGENT.]

1. The state or fact of being exigent; urgent want; need, necessity.

1589 Puttenham *Eng. Poesie* I. xx. (Arb.) 58 A priuat person, whose manner of life and calling hath no such exigence. **1633** P. Fletcher *Purple Isl.* VIII. xvi, Their violence..Was none, or weak in time of greatest exigence. **1691** T. H[ale] *New Invent.* 130 So many..as will suffice in time of Exigence. **1849** C. Brontë *Shirley* xxi, A churchwarden who feels the exigence of whitewash.

†**b.** What is needed or required; demands, exigency, need, requirement; = EXIGENCY 2. *Obs.*

1594 Hooker *Eccl. Pol.* I. xiv. (1611) 43 According to the exigence of that speciall end whereunto they are intended. **1642** Jer. Taylor *Episc.* (1647) 92 The nature of his offices ..and the whole exigence of the Epistle proclaime him Bishop. **1676** Hale *Contempl.* I. 443 For the convenient support of the Exigences of my nature and condition. **1710** *Tatler* No. 252 ⁋2 If we drink the least Proportion beyond the Exigence of Thirst. **1784** Cowper *Task* II. 557 Ghostly counsel, if it..fall Below the exigence. **1818** Jas. Mill *Brit. India* II. IV. ix. 287 Supervisors, with powers adapted to the exigence of the case.

2. A pressing state of circumstances, or one demanding immediate action or remedy; a sudden or pressing necessity; an emergency; a difficulty, extremity, strait.

1643 *True Informer* 15 His Majesty..summoned all his Nobles to appeare, to advise with them in this exigence. **1671** Crowne *Juliana* IV, A warlike Fantome By heaven created for this exigence. **1702** C. Mather *Magn. Chr.* II. iv. (1852) 124 Mr. Winthrop..being..in this exigence chosen the governour. **1726** De Foe *Hist. Devil* I. xi. (1840) 160 God himself relieved the Israelites in every exigence. **1824** Scott *Redgauntlet* xxiii, Escape..as unexpected as the exigence was threatening. **1863** Mrs. C. Clarke *Shaks. Char.* xvii. 434 Falstaff is equal to any exigence.

¶**3.** As a personal quality: Exactingness. *rare.* [After Fr. use; cf. EXIGEANT.]

[**1839** Lady Lytton *Cheveley* (ed. 2) I. ii. 35 Mortgaging my time and patience by her *exigence* every hour in the day]. **1859** Helps *Friends in C.* Ser. II. II. 102 The habit of exigence. That last is not a common English word.

exigency ('ɛksɪdʒənsɪ). [ad. L. *exigentia*: see prec. and -ENCY.] The quality of being exigent.

1. a. Exigent character, pressing state (of circumstances, etc.), stringency (of requirements). **b.** Urgent want; pressing necessity; an instance of this; in *pl.* pressing needs, straits.

a. 1769 Robertson *Chas. V*, III. x. 224 Such immediate ..assistance as the exigency of her affairs required. **1794** Paley *Evid.* I. iv. (1817) 66 To inspire them with fortitude proportioned to the increasing exigency of the service. **1836** J. Gilbert *Chr. Atonem.* ix. (1852) 289 Nor whatever the exigency of our circumstances, can we rationally doubt of needful assistance. **1848** Macaulay *Hist. Eng.* I. 577 The exigency of the case warranted him in borrowing..a fine horse belonging to Dare.

b. 1630 Wadsworth *Pilgr.* vii. 70 [He] was driuen to such an exigency that he was constrained [etc.]. **1659** *Gentl. Calling* (1696) 88 The amazing Exigencies of a sinking Man ..excuse the folly of catching at Reeds. **1697** Dryden *Virg. Past.* Pref. (1721) I. 79 The Romans in great Exigency, sent for their Dictator from the Plow. **1707** Addison *Pres. St. War* Wks. 1746 III. 245 We already complain of our want of bullion and must at last be reduced to the greatest exigencies. **1761** Sterne *Tr. Shandy* (1802) III. ii. 260 The natural exigency my father was under of rubbing his head. **1833** I. Taylor *Fanat.* ii. 37 The extreme exigency of the moment. **1863** Froude *Hist. Eng.* VIII. 61 Yet the Exigencies of England required peace.

2. That which is needed or required; demands, needs, requirements: **a.** *sing.*; now *rare* exc. in *Law* (see quot. 1883). **b.** *pl.*

a. 1581 Lambarde *Eiren.* III. i. (1588) 329 The residue were fined..according to the exigencie and temper of their fault. **1662** *Bk. Com. Prayer* Pref., The various exigency of times and occasions. **1818** Jas. Mill *Brit. India* III. VI. i. 37 In his demands upon the Rajah..Mr. Hastings had exceeded the exigency. **1850** W. Irving *Mahomet* xxxii. (1853) 164 The talents of Mahomet rose to the exigency of the moment. **1883** Sir F. Pollock in *Law Rep. 11 Q. Bench* 433 When the sheriff has seized the debtor's goods, it is his duty to go on selling until he shall have realized enough to satisfy the exigency of the writ.

b. 1674 Brevint *Saul at Endor* iv. 73 Devout persons are directed to several saints, for their several exigencies. **1724** Swift *Drapier's Lett.* iii, I intreat you will never suffer Mr. Wood to be a judge of your exigencies. **1857-8** Sears *Athan.* iv. 28 Those who think God will..work miracles..to meet the exigencies of theology.

exigend(e: see EXIGENT *sb.*²

†**exi'gendary.** *Law. Obs.* [ad. med.L. *exigendārius*, f. *exigenda*: see EXIGENT *sb.*² and -ARY¹.] = EXIGENTER.

1607 COWEL *Interpr.* Exigendarie of the common bank..is otherwise called Exigenter. **1721** in BAILEY. **1848** in WHARTON *Law Lex.*

exigent ('ɛksɪdʒənt), *a.* and *sb.*¹ Also 5 -ente, 6-7 exegent(t, 7 exiggent. [ad. L. *exigent-em*, pr. pple. of *exigĕre*, f. *ex-* out + *agĕre* to drive: see EXACT *v.* Cf. OF. *exigent.*] **A.** *adj.*

1. Requiring immediate action or aid; pressing, urgent.

1670 CLARENDON *Contempl. on Ps.* Tracts (1727) 617 That exigent cry for help. **1796** BURKE *Lett. Noble Ld.* Wks. VIII. 46 At this exigent moment the loss of a finished man is not easily supplied. **1856** EMERSON *Eng. Traits, Univ.* Wks. (Bohn) II. 94 A fop..in exigent circumstances, will play the manly part. **1882** T. MOZLEY *Remin.* II. lxxxiii. 98 There were other and more exigent demands [upon Denison's means].

2. Requiring a great deal; demanding more than is reasonable; exacting, pressing.

1828 A. W. FONBLANQUE *Engl. under 7 Administr.* (1837) I. 144 It was said of some exigent man, that, etc. **1842** SIR H. TAYLOR *Edwin the Fair* II. ii, A love that clings not, nor is exigent, Encumbers not the active purposes, Nor drains their source. **1870** EMERSON *Soc. & Solit., Clubs* Wks. (Bohn) III. 92 Varied foods, climates, beautiful objects.. are the necessity of this exigent system of ours. **1871** MORLEY *Voltaire* (1878) 76 His restlessness..was never tyrannical and exigent.

b. Const. *of*.

1834 SIR H. TAYLOR *Artevelde* II. I. ii, But now this body, exigent of rest, Will needs put in a claim. **1871** MORLEY *Vauvenargues* Crit. Misc. 20 An age when the intellect is usually most exigent of supremacy.

B. *sb.*¹

†**1.** A state of pressing need; a time of extreme necessity; a critical occasion, or one that requires immediate action or remedy; an emergency, extremity, strait. ***to bring, drive, put,*** etc. ***to, to take (an) exigent.*** *Obs.*

c **1430** LYDG. *Ord. Fools* 4 Bacus and Iuno hath set abroche a tonne, [And] Brouthe the[r] braynys vn-to exigente. *a* **1548** *Hye way to Spyttel Hous* 1011 in Hazl. *E.P.P.* IV. 67 In theyr fury they be so vyolent, That they wyll bryng one to an exegent. **1577** HOLINSHED *Chron.* II. 3 The duke seeing himselfe to be driuen to such an exigent. **1580** SIDNEY *Arcadia* IV. (1622) 413 In steed of doing any thing as the exigent required, he began to make circles. *a* **1639** W. WHATELEY *Prototypes* I. xvi. (1640) 162 God will have a well in store, and shew it us at the exigent. **1729** SHELVOCKE *Artillery* IV. 300 In such Exigents this Manipulus may be recurred to. **1755** in JOHNSON. **1818** in TODD.

b. Last pinch; end, extremity.

1586 A. DAY *Eng. Secretary* II. (1625) 92 Here by degrees is passed to the last exigent. **1591** SHAKS. *1 Hen. VI*, II. v. 9 These Eyes..Waxe dimme, as drawing to their Exigent. **1600** *Dr. Dodypoll* IV. iii. in Bullen *O. Pl.* III. 146, I feare my barbarous rudenesse to her Hath driven her to some desperate exigent. **1631** HEYWOOD *Eng. Eliz.* (1641) 141 What a dangerous exigent must she needs come to, whose life was thus assaulted?

†**2.** *pl.* Needs, requirements. *Obs.*

1609 BIBLE (Douay) *2 Esdras* vii. 65 He is bountiful, because he wil geve according to exigentes. **1641** CHAS. I in Rushw. *Hist. Coll.* III. (1692) I. 536 Most effectual and proper for the present exigents of the Kingdom. **1677** HALE *Contempl.* II. 11 Because it is not accommodate to all Uses and Exigents.

b. A required amount; a needed quantity.

1840 BROWNING *Sordello* III. 337 His enterprise Marked out anew, its exigent of wit Apportioned.

Hence '**exigently** *adv.*, in an exigent manner.

1889 W. SHARP in *Academy* 30 Nov. 352/3, I..cannot but hope that he will not pursue too exigently his latest method.

†'**exigent,** *sb.*² *Law. Obs.* Also 5-6 exigend. [In 15th c. *exigend*, a. AF. *exigende*, ad. med.L. *exigenda*, gerundial pple. of *exigĕre*: see prec.] A writ commanding the sheriff to summon the defendant to appear and deliver up himself upon pain of outlawry; also called ***writ of exigent.***

[**1292** BRITTON I. ii. §8 Et si le pleyntif face defaute a nuli Counté, adunc cessent les exigendes jekes a nostre venue en le pays.] **1464** *Paston Lett.* No. 491. II. 161 He hath taken suerte that ye schall appere in the crastino animarum upon the exigents returnable. **1491** *Act 7 Hen. VII*, c. 24 By reason of eny processe or exigend made within the same Countie. **1502-3** *Plumpton Corr.* 173 On tewsday last was the court..and then was ther none exegent called agaynst you. *c* **1508** *Ibid.* 204 If I wold suffer the exigend, which I had agaynst you, not to goe out agaynst you. **1670** VAUGHAN *Bushell's Case in Phenix* (1721) I. 429 The Party came into Court and demanded Oyer of the Exigent. **1678** BUTLER *Hudibras* III. i. 1036 What Charms [must that Lady have], that can..null Decree and Exigent. **1768** BLACKSTONE *Comm.* III. 283 If a *non est inventus* is returned upon all of them, then a writ of *exigent* or *exigi facias* may be sued out. **1848** in WHARTON *Law Lex.*

b. Phrases: ***Clerk of the Exigents; to put in exigent; to sue to (an) exigent.***

a **1577** SIR T. SMITH *Commw. Eng.* II. xiv. (1609) 61 The Clarke of the Exigent is to frame all manner of Processes of *Exigi facias.* **1628** COKE *On Litt.* 114 a, Goods and chattels of those that be put in exigent. **1657** *Burton's Diary* (1828) II. 146 This Beavor, in Michaelmas term, had caused him to be sued to exigent. **1677** *Lond. Gaz.* No. 1209/4 Benjamin Hill, late Clerk of the Exigents. **1690** in Picton *L'pool. Munic. Rec.* (1883) I. 300 John Hodgson is sued to an Exgent by one John Brier..in Trespasse.

'**exigent** ('ɛksɪdʒənt), *v.* [f. EXIGENT *sb.*¹ and ².] *trans.* †**a.** To subject (a person or thing) *to*. **b.** To carry out a writ of exigent against.

1656 S. H. *Gold. Law* 4 [They] forfeit their faith..to their Lord, the Publike Welfare, by exigenting it to intolerable sufferings and dangers. **1837** PALGRAVE *Merch. & Friar* iv. 241 Were you by the Coroner in County Court duly exigented and proclaimed?

†'**exigenter.** *Law. Obs.* Also 7 exigentor, -egenter. [a. AF. *exigenter*, f. *exigente, exigende*: see EXIGENT *sb.*²] An officer of the Court of Common Pleas who made out all exigents and proclamations in cases pertaining to outlawry. Also, in 18-19th c., a similar officer of the Court of King's Bench.

[**1432** *Act 10 Hen. VI*, c. 4 Null Filicer Exigenter ne autre Officer.] **1512** *Act 4 Hen. VIII*, c. 4 §1 The Felyssour or exigenter in whose offyce suche sute is taken. **1654** *View Regulation of Chancery* 20 The Filacers and Exigentors..in the Court of Common Pleas. **1672** E. CHAMBERLAYNE *Angliae Notitia* (ed. 6) 218 [In the Court of Common Pleas] There are also four Exigenters, whose Office is to make all Exigents and Proclamations in all Actions where Process of Outlawry doth lye. **1691** WOOD *Ath. Oxon.* I. 317 He..had given to him the Exegenters Office of the Common Pleas. **1784** *Town & Country Mag.* 7 Jan. 56 Ackland, esq. deputy filazer and exigenter to the court of King's bench. **1837** *Act 7 Will. IV & 1 Vict.* c. 30 sched. A, Offices abolished by this Act..On the Plea Side of the Court of Queen's Bench.. Filacer, Exigenter, and Clerk of the Outlawries..In the Court of Common Pleas..Exigenter and Clerk of the Supersedeas.

exigible ('ɛksɪdʒɪb(ə)l), *a.* [as if ad. L. **exigibilis*, f. *exigĕre*: see EXACT *v.* Cf. F. *exigible.*] That may be exacted; demandable, requirable, chargeable. Const. *against, from* (a person).

1610 W. FOLKINGHAM *Art of Survey* III. v. 72 This [service] is not now exigible. **1792** T. JEFFERSON *Writ.* (1859) III. 339 There is no part of our debt exigible at this time. **1834** *Tait's Mag.* I. 543 They were all charged the full sum exigible on their rent. **1883** LD. BLACKBURN in *Law Rep.* 9 App. Cases 65 Whether the duty on post-horses was exigible in respect of post-horses carrying an express, etc.

‖**exigi facias** ('ɛksɪdʒaɪ 'feɪʃɪæs). *Law.* [L. phrase, lit. 'that you cause to be demanded', f. *exigĕre* to demand, exact, and *facĕre* to make, cause.] = EXIGENT *sb.*²

a **1577** SIR T. SMITH *Commw. Eng.* II. xiv. (1609) 61 The Clarke of the Exigents is to frame all manner of Processes of Exigi facias. **1848** in WHARTON *Law Lex.*

exiguity (ɛksɪ'gjuːɪtɪ). [ad. L. *exiguitās*, f. *exiguus*: see EXIGUOUS.] The quality or condition of being exiguous; scantiness in measure; smallness in size or quantity, littleness.

1623-6 in COCKERAM. **1658** J. ROBINSON *Eudoxa* I. 116 Sense is..puzled at the exiguity of particular moats. **1664** POWER *Exp. Philos.* I. 34 Their exceeding exiguity; for certainly of all Animals they are the least. **1846** *Blackw. Mag.* LX. 589 Astonished at the exiguity of the *plats* placed before him. **1873** WHITNEY *Orient. Stud.* 242 We are disappointed at the exiguity of the results.

concr. **1664** POWER *Exp. Philos.* Pref. 8 The Insectile automata (those living exiguities).

exiguous (ɛg'zɪgjuːəs), *a.* [f. L. *exigu-us* scanty in measure or number (f. *exigĕre* to weigh strictly: see EXACT *v.*) + -OUS.] Scanty in measure or number; extremely small, diminutive, minute.

1651 BIGGS *New Disp.* ¶ 141 Of great vertue, yet of an exiguous quantity. **1654** tr. *Scudery's Curia Pol.* 39 If they have any being, it is so exiguous, that it is scarce visible. *a* **1708** J. PHILIPS *Fall of Chloe's Jordan* 100 Protected mice, The race exiguous..Their mansions quit. **1858** CARLYLE *Fredk. Gt.* V. v, The soldier's pay is in the highest degree exiguous; not above three half-pence a day. **1882** *Pall Mall G.* 23 May 3 The judgment of the House of Lords on the exiguous point raised by the Bordesley appeal.

Hence **e'xiguousness** = EXIGUITY.

1730-6 BAILEY (folio), *Exiguousness*, littleness, smallness. **1755** in ASH. **1888** *Sat. Rev.* 22 Sept. 352/1, No. 1, though its apparent exiguousness might suggest a different conclusion, is a number of the highest importance.

Exilarch ('ɛksɪlɑːk). *Jewish Hist.* [f. EXILE *sb.*² + Gr. ἀρχός ruler, translating Aramaic *rêš galûta* 'chief of the captives'.] One of a line of Jewish princes or rulers in Babylon who exercised authority over, and received tribute from, Jews in all countries from about the third century to the tenth century A.D. Hence **Exi'larchate**, the period during which there were exilarchs; also, the people over whom the exilarch had power.

1893 *Q. Rev.* Jan. 111 Under a succession of Exilarchs,.. they found themselves in another Holy Land.

exile ('ɛksaɪl, 'ɛgzaɪl), *sb.*¹ Also 4 exil, 5-6 exyl(e, exyll(e. [a. OF. *exil*, refashioned form of *essil*, state of banishment, also (cf. sense 2) devastation, destruction = Pr. *essilh*, semi-popular ad. L. *exsilium* state of banishment, f. *ex-* out + *sal-* (= Skr. *sar-* to go), root of *salīre* to leap (whence also *exsul*: see EXUL); cf. *consilium* COUNSEL. In sense 2, OF. *essil* is a vbl. sb. f. *essiller*: see EXILE *v.* 4. (Formerly accented *e'xile.*)]

1. Enforced removal from one's native land according to an edict or sentence; penal expatriation or banishment; the state or condition of being penally banished; enforced residence in some foreign land. Phrases, ***† to go, put in*** or ***to exile; to drive, go, send into exile.***

In Israelitish history *spec.* the captivity of the Jews in the 5th century B.C.

a **1300** *Cursor M.* 1154 (Cott.) Wit all þou sal bi halden vile, Quar-sa þou wendes in exile. *c* **1330** R. BRUNNE *Chron.* (1810) 131 How alle his kynde exile was on þam laid. *c* **1374** CHAUCER *Boeth.* I. iii. 10 Whi art þou comen in to þis solitarie place of myn exil. *c* **1425** WYNTOUN *Cron.* VII. viii. 44 Saynt Thomas In Frawns, as in-til Exile, was. **1529** RASTELL *Pastyme* (1811) 41 He was put to exyle in to yᵉ yle of Sardeyn. **1592** SHAKS. *Rom. & Jul.* V. iii. 211 Griefe of my Sonnes exile hath stopt her breath. **1667** MILTON *P.L.* I. 632 These puissant Legions, whose exile Hath emptied Heav'n. **1709** STRYPE *Ann. Ref.* I. xiii. 177 The first bishops..newly returned out of their exiles, as Cox, Grindal [etc.]. **1732** LEDIARD *Sethos* II. x. 365 He had taken the advantage of his exile to travel. **1838** LYTTON *Leila* II. i, I accept them: provided, first, that thou obtainest the exile or death of Muza. **1845** S. AUSTIN *Ranke's Hist. Ref.* III. 35 Zapolya neglected no means by which he could, from his exile at Tarnow, keep Hungary in a state of agitation. **1868** E. EDWARDS *Raleigh* I. xxi. 460 Exile was made the condition of his pardon.

b. *gen.* Expatriation, prolonged absence from one's native land, endured by compulsion of circumstances or voluntarily undergone for any purpose.

1393 GOWER *Conf.* III. 187 To do profite to the comune He toke of exile the fortune. *c* **1400** *Destr. Troy* 724 Soche a maiden..þat forsec hir fader & hir fre londe..Auntrede hir to Exile euer for þi [Jason's] sake. **1526** *Pilgr. Perf.* (W. de W. 1531) 298 For thy exile and fleynge in to Egypte. **1548** HALL *Chron.* 242 b, He so..greved his nobilitie..that some of their voluntarie will, went into Exile. **1848** MACAULAY *Hist. Eng.* I. 519 After an exile of many years, Dudley North returned to England with a large fortune.

c. *transf.* and *fig.*

c **1315** SHOREHAM 19 Godes flesche and eke hys blode.. frevereth ous in oure exil. **1340** HAMPOLE *Pr. Consc.* 1165 Þe world es na thyng elles Bot en hard exil, in qwilk men duelles. **1340** *Ayenb.* 131 Huan he..y-ziȝþ þise wordle þet ne is bote an exil and a dezert uol of lyons. *c* **1450** *Castle Hd. Life St. Cuthb.* (Surtees) 7994 Þe same bischope..Fra his kirke was putt in exile. **1547** *Act 37 Hen. VIII*, c. 2 The couersion therof [Hounsloo Heathe] into tillage..by mennes labour..shall be an exile of idlenesse in those parties. **1592** SHAKS. *Rom. & Jul.* III. iii. 20 Banished is banisht from the world, And worlds exile is death. **1606** SYLVESTER *Du Bartas* II. iii. *Vocation*, All our life and Age Is but an exile and a Pilgrimage. **1878** B. TAYLOR *Deukalion* I. i. 20 And out of its exile The passion return.

d. *attrib.*

1720 WELTON *Suffer. Son of God* I. viii. 202 Thou Deigned to Come down..to dwell with Me in this Exile-World. *Ibid.* I. ix. 207 Man, a Pilgrim upon Earth..should sanctify his Exile-state, by these Trials.

†**2.** Waste or devastation of property; ruin, utter impoverishment. ***to put in exile*** [OF. *metre a essil*]: to ravage (a country), ruin (a person). *Obs.*

[**1267** *Act 52 Hen. III*, c. 23 Item firmarii tempore firmarum suarum vastum, vendicionem, seu exilium non faciant, in domibus, boscis, hominibus, neque, &c.] *c* **1386** CHAUCER *Melib.* ¶ 869, I..purpose me..to putte hem in exil for ever-more. *c* **1450** LONELICH *Grail* liii. 96 Ȝif oure rem withowten kyng be ony while, It myhte sone thanne fallen into exylle. **1483** CAXTON *G. de la Tour* E vj b, He began werre to his neyghbours..in so much that the reame was put in exyl. **1490** —— *Eneydos* xxii. (1890) 81 Her cyte and landes of Cartage are all dystroied and tourned in exyll. **1548** UDALL, etc. *Erasm. Par. John* 74 a, The temple was.. repayred after the exile that was made at Hierusalem by the Persians. **1618** PULTON *Stat. 52 Hen. III*, c. 23 Fermors, during their termes, shall not make wast, sale, nor exile of House, Woods, and Men..without speciall licence. [So **1700** in J. Tyrell *Hist. Eng.* II. 1114.]

exile ('ɛksaɪl), *sb.*² [Of obscure formation; perh. merely a concrete use of EXILE *sb.*¹ 1 (cf. OF. and ME. *prison* = prisoner); the development of sense may have been produced by direct association with L. *exsul*. It may however be f. EXILE *v.*]

1. A banished person; one compelled to reside away from his native land.

c **1330** *Arth. & Merl.* (Kölbing) 8922 To lese his londes & ben exil. *c* **1450** *Castle Hd. Life St. Cuthb.* (Surtees) 5308 Of þair bischop, þat lange whyle had bene fra his kirk exile. **1588** SHAKS. *Tit. A.* III. i. 285 Get thee from my sight, Thou art an Exile, and thou must not stay. **1611** BIBLE *Isa.* li. 14 The captiue exile hasteneth that he may be loosed. **1697** DRYDEN *Virg. Ecl.* I. 91 O must the wretched Exiles ever mourn, Nor after length of rowling Years return? **1759** ROBERTSON *Hist. Scot.* I. II. 85 This unhappy exile..was destined to be the father of a race of kings. **1824** W. IRVING *T. Trav.* II. 105 Had been found guilty of the crime of patriotism, and was..an exile from his country. **1874** GREEN *Short Hist.* vii. 399 Thousands of Flemish exiles found a refuge in the Cinque Ports.

attrib. and *Comb.* **1790** *Norman & Bertha* I. 2 Thither froward fate pursued this amiable exile pair. **1856** GROTE *Greece* II. xcv. XII. 439 The officers of Antipater, called in the language of the time exile-hunters, were..on the look-out to seize these proscribed men. **1888** *Century Mag.* May 3 A careful study of the exile system [of Russia.] *Ibid.* 4 Officers of the Exile Administration.

b. *transf.* and *fig.*

1770 GOLDSM. *Des. Vill.* 365 The poor exiles..Hung round the bowers, and fondly looked their last. **1820** W. IRVING *Sketch Bk.* I. 144 An exile from the paternal roof. **1843** NEALE *Hymns for Sick* 58 Thy grace in us, poor exiles yet, implant. **1852** EARP *Gold. Col. Australia* 100 The convict system ceased in New South Wales in 1839; but 'exiles' as they were termed, *i.e.* men who had passed their probation at home, were forwarded till 1843.

2. *attrib.* in *exile-tree, exile-oil-plant*, a name applied in India to the *Thevetia neriifolia* (N.O. *Apocynaceæ*), a plant introduced into that country from the West-Indies or tropical America.

It has large saffron-coloured flowers, and the bark is used in medicine as an antiperiodic.

1865 *Madras Quart. Jrnl. Med. Science* VIII. 195, I met with a large solitary tree..and from its situation, it occurred to me..that the popular English name of 'Exile' seemed very appropriate. **1868** WARING *Pharmacopœia of India* 138 A West Indian shrub, domesticated in India, and cultivated under the name of *The Exile* or *Yellow Oleander*. **1884** *Syd. Soc. Lex.*, Exile-tree. **1884** MILLER *Plant-n.* s.v. *Oil-plant*, Exile. *Ibid.* s.v. *Thevetia*, Exile-oil-plant.

exile ('ɛksaɪl, 'ɛgzaɪl), *a. Obs.* or *arch.* [ad. L. *exīlis* thin, lank. Cf. F. *exile* (Cotgr.).

The ultimate etymology is disputed; some regard it as contracted from **exigilis*, f. *exigĕre* (cf. EXIGUOUS); others as f. *ex-* privative + *ilia* entrails, the primary sense being assumed to have been 'disembowelled'.]

1. Slender, shrunken, thin; diminutive.

c **1420** *Pallad. on Husb.* XI. 387 Ache seede..Wherof the flaume hath lefte a core exile. **1611** COTGR. s.v. *Champ*, Excellent spirits are often lodged in exile, or small, bodies. **1671** FLAMSTEED in Rigaud *Corr. Sci. Men* (1841) II. 124, I saw the Anses of Saturn very exile. **1687** H. MORE *App. Antid.* (1712) 225 This actual division of the whole into so many subtile, exile, invisible particles.

2. Attenuated, thin. Of theories: Fine-spun.

1610 W. FOLKINGHAM *Art of Survey* I. viii. 18 That ground which..breathes..forth exile and fumie vapours quickly vanishing..is..plyant for the plowe. **1626** BACON *Sylva* §75 Meanes..to draw forth the Exile heat which is in the Air. *Ibid.* §155 His Voice plainly..made extreame sharp and exile, like the Voice of Puppets. **1647** H. MORE *Song of Soul* I. Pref., These exile Theories. **1797** *Hist.* in *Ann. Reg.* 178/1 It is not..the paper that is, in fact, the substitute for money but something still more exile; the promise..stamped upon it.

†**b.** *Gr. Gram.* Unaspirated. *Obs.*

1671 H. M. tr. *Erasm. Colloq.* 202 If οὐ be acuted and exile, etc.

3. Meagre, scanty; 'lean', poorly endowed. Also of soils: Poor, barren.

c **1420** *Pallad. on Husb.* XI. 30 In lande ther ayer is hoot and drie, And erthe exile or hilly drie or lene, Vynes beth best ysette. **1525** WOLSEY in Ellis *Orig. Lett.* II. 99 II. 18 The Suppression of certain exile and small Monasteries. **1535** CRANMER in Strype *Eccl. Mem.* I. xxvi. 189 Their benefices were so exile..that no learned man would take them. **1565** W. ALLEY *Poor Man's Libr.* I. Ded. A iij, The little talent of my exile and sclender learnyng. **1654** FULLER *Comm. Ruth* (1868) 123 Is it not a petty, a small, exile courtesy. **1685** H. MORE *Paralip. Proph.* 451 A more magnificent expression of what is, Chap. II, said in more exile phrase. **1863** J. R. WALBRAN *Mem. Fountains Ab.* (Surtees) I. 50 The convent was in the most exile condition.

b. quasi-*adv.*

1654 GAYTON *Pleas. Notes* I. iii. 8 The ingeniousest Wits in the world have been such who feed exilest, or most slenderly.

exile ('ɛksaɪl, 'ɛgzaɪl), *v.* Forms: 4–6 exil(l, excile, 4 exile-n, 5 exyl(e, 4– exile. [ad. OF. *exilier* (12th c.), learned form of *essillier, esseillier*, etc.:— late L. *exiliāre*, f. *ex(s)ilium* EXILE *sb.*[1] In OF. the vb. has chiefly the sense to ravage, devastate (cf. sense 4 below); for the development of meaning cf. *exterminate*. (Formerly accented *e'xile*; so always in Shaks. and Milton.)]

1. *trans.* To compel (a person) by a decree or enactment to leave his country; to banish, expatriate: **a.** with *from*, †*out of*; also †*into, to*.

a **1330** *Roland & V.* 39 Þe king ebrahim Out of lond exiled him. **1393** GOWER *Conf.* II. 156 Afterwarde into an ile This Jupiter him didde exile. *c* **1450** *Merlin* x. 145 [They should] go vpon the kynge Arthur..and so exile hym fro all the contree. **1493** *Festivall* (W. de W. 1515) 73 The emperour exyled Iohan..into the yle of Pathmose. **1592** SHAKS. *Rom. & Jul.* III. i. 192 For that offence, Immediately we doe exile him hence. **1664** H. MORE *Myst. Iniq.* xi. 35 Whom assuredly they could not think exiled from Heaven. **1756–7** tr. *Keysler's Trav.* (1760) III. 242 Ravenna..very kindly received Dante, when he was exiled from Florence.

b. with *double obj.* (Cf. BANISH.)

1570–6 LAMBARDE *Peramb. Kent* (1862) 179 Godwine..and his Sonnes were exiled the Realme. **1606** EARL NORTHAMPTON in *True & Perfect Relat.* E e iij a, For Conspiracy..was the Archb. Cant. exiled the Kingdom. **1608** J. KING *Serm.* 24 Mar. 3 He..was exiled the world. **1812** S. ROGERS *Columbus* III. 21 All, exiled the realms of rest, In vain the sadness of their souls suppressed.

c. *simply.* Also † *to exile forth.*

c **1330** R. BRUNNE *Chron.* (1810) 58 Þerfor was þe dome gyuen..To exile þe erle Godwyn. **1393** GOWER *Conf.* III. 263 The fader..Forth with the sone they exile. *c* **1400** *Destr. Troy* 13070 Orestes..shuld render his londes, And be exilede for euermore. *c* **1470** HENRY *Wallace* IV. 182 Sum part off thaim..That Makfadȝan had exilde furth beforne. *a* **1471** *Chron. Rich. II, etc.* (Camden 1856) 13 The kyng [Rich. II]..exilid the duke of Hereforde for terme of x. yeer. **1579** LYLY *Euphues* (Arb.) 186 Thou takest it heavily that thou shouldest be..exiled without cause. **1697** DRYDEN *Æneid* I. 3 The man..who forc'd by fate..Expell'd and exil'd. **1840** MRS. BROWNING *Drama of Exile* Poems 1850 I. 91 Hear us sing above you 'Exiled is not lost'.

†**d.** *intr.* To be in exile; = L. *exsulare. rare.*

a **1300** *Cursor M.* 2582 (Cott.) A uoice..said..In egipte suld his sede exile In tharldon four hundret ȝere. *a* **1618** SYLVESTER *Du Bartas* (1621) 1041 The more the Body dures, Soul more indures; Never too soon can Shee from thence exile.

2. *transf.* and *fig.* To banish or separate *from* (one's home, a pleasant or endeared place or association). Const. as in 1 a, b, c.

1340 HAMPOLE *Pr. Consc.* 2974 Þe saules here..Er exild fra þis lyf til payn, With-outen any turnyng agayn. **1500–20** DUNBAR *In Prays of Woman*, Exylit he suld be of all gud company. **1526** TINDALE *Acts* iii. 23 Every soule which shall not heare that same prophet shal be exyled [ed. **1534** destroyed; so in WYCLIF (1382–8), BIBLE (1611), etc.] from the people. **1578** *Gude & Godl. Ball.* 118 That will [free will] thy presence hes me exilit. **1590** SHAKS. *Mids. N.* III. ii. 386 They wilfully themselves exile from light. **1601** B. JONSON *Poetaster* IV. vii, Exiled the circle of the court. **1749** G. WEST tr. *Pindar, 1st Pythian Ode* (R.), Exil'd from Praise, from Virtue, and the Muse. **1781** COWPER *Charity* 243, I am free; At my best home, if not exiled from thee. **1814** JANE AUSTEN *Watsons* xxvi, You are fitted for society and it is shameful you should be exiled from it. **1856** EMERSON *Eng. Traits, Aristocr.* Wks. (Bohn) II. 80 The French live at court, and exile themselves to their estates for economy.

†**3.** To banish, expel, get rid of. *Obs.*

c **1380** WYCLIF *Sel. Wks.* II. 385 Þis oonhede þat Crist made is wel nyȝe excilid. **1393** GOWER *Conf.* I. 13 Þe pestilence, Which haþ exiled pacience Fro þe clergie in special. *c* **1430** LYDG. *Compl. Bl. Knt.* lxxiii, For to exile Trouthe..Out of her Court. **1483** CAXTON *G. de la Tour* Q iv, Her lord exyled and put her fro hym. *c* **1534** tr. *Pol. Verg. Eng. Hist.* (Camden) I. 27 Gildas..exilinge all fables, most ernestlie embraceth truth. **1563–87** FOXE *A. & M.* (1684) III. 431 None, that had not clean exiled all humanity. **1593** SHAKS. *2 Hen. VI*, III. i. 46 Equitie [is] exil'd your Highnesse Land. *a* **1649** DRUMM. OF HAWTH. *Poems* Wks. 27 That place..Where black-brow'd night doth not exile the day. **1700** DRYDEN *Fables, Cymon & Iphig.* 218 His brutal manners from his breast exiled.

†**II. 4.** To devastate, ravage, bring to ruin. *Obs.* Cf. EXILE *sb.*[1] 3.

c **1430** *Pilgr. Lyf Manhode* I. xv. (1869) 12 Þilke þat wolen exile þe hous of grace dieu and dispoile it of hire goodes. *a* **1470** TIPTOFT *Cæsar* xiii. (1530) 18 Hys cuntry so robbed, pylled & exyled [*vastatis*]. **1481** CAXTON *Myrr.* I. vi. 32 Yf ne were theyre..good prechynge..Cristente shold be exyled by errour and euyl byleue. **1523** LD. BERNERS *Froiss.* I. xxvi. 38 He wasted..all the playn countrey of Scotland, and exiled diuerse townes. *a* **1533** —— *Huon* clxii. 633 They exyle your countre, they sle men, women and chyldren.

[exiled, *a.* Explained as: Slender, weak. Error for EXILE *a.*, meagre, scanty.

1577 NORTHBROOKE *Dicing* Ded. 4 My exiled and slender learning. [So in the undated edition, supposed to be of 1577; but the much better edition of 1579 has 'exile'.] Hence in **1859** NARES (quoting the above), and in *Century Dict.*]

exiled ('ɛksaɪld), *ppl. a.* [f. EXILE *v.* + -ED[1].] In various senses of the verb.

c **1375** *Lay Folks Mass-bk.* (MS. B.) 379 Hom þat are in ille lyue..seke or prisonde..pore, exilde, deserit. *c* **1430** tr. *T. à Kempis' Imit.* 125 Þe exiled sones of Eue weilen. *c* **1500** *Melusine* 112, I..forbede you that ye byleue not the Counseill of none exilled and flemed fro his land. **1605** SHAKS. *Macb.* v. viii. 66 Our exil'd Friends. **1632** J. HAYWARD tr. *Biondi's Eromena* 108 The sicke woman..recovered together with her strength, her before exiled beauty. **1718** ROWE tr. *Lucan* I. 505 To thee, behold, an Exil'd Band we come. **1794** SOUTHEY *Bot. Bay Eclog.* I, Still wilt thou..present The fields of England to my exiled eyes. **1874** GREEN *Short Hist.* vi. 298 The exiled Greek scholars were welcomed in Italy.

absol. **1839** E. D. CLARKE *Trav.* vi. 24/2 Tobolski, from the number..of the exiled, is become a..populous city.

exilement ('ɛksaɪlmənt). *rare* in mod. use. Also 7 exilment. [f. as prec. + -MENT.] The action of exiling; the state or fact of being exiled; banishment, exile.

1548 GEST *Pr. Masse* 117 The godlye fathers in theyr exilement wandering in forren contreis. **1651** GATAKER *Life Bale* in *Fuller's Abel Rediv.* 504 An inseparable..companion ..with him in all his troubles and exilments. **1738** NEAL *Hist. Purit.* IV. 233 He [Charles II] abjured the Protestant religion soon after the exilement of the Royal family. **1803** W. TAYLOR in *Ann. Rev.* I. 435 Their exilements..have increased the number of foreign scholars among them.

exilent, obs. form of EXCELLENT.

†**exiler.** *Obs.* [f. as prec. + -ER[1].] One who, or that which, exiles (in senses of vb.). Also *fig.*

1382 WYCLIF *Judith* viii. 25 Thei..that temptaciouns resseyueden not with the drede of God..ben exilid of the exilere [**1388** distried of a distriere; Vulg. *exterminati sunt ab exterminatore*] and of serpentis pershiden. *c* **1450** *Crt. of Love* 598 Love is exiler aye of vice and sin. **1645** J. BOND *Occasus Occid.* 25, I find that sin notoriously branded as an Exiler, not only of Persons, but of whole Churches.

exilian (ɛg'z-, ɛk'sɪlɪən), *a.* [f. L. *ex(s)ili-um* (see EXILE *sb.*[1]) + -AN.] = next.

1882–3 SCHAFF *Encycl. Relig. Knowl.* III. 2106 Wellhausen considers the second account as..of exilian or post-exilian origin. **1888** CAVE *Inspir. O. Test.* v. 277 The prophetical writers prior to the exilian period.

exilic (ɛg'z-, ɛk'sɪlɪk), *a.* [f. EXILE *sb.* + -IC.] Of or pertaining to exile; *esp.* the exile, or period of the exile, of the Jews in Babylon.

[**1871** F. BOLTON *Delitzsch's Comm. Ps.* cxviii. III. 223 It is without any doubt a post-exilic song.] **1888** S. R. DRIVER *Isaiah* v. 188 Whether..it be Isaiah or an exilic prophet who speaks. **1890** G. A. SMITH *Isaiah* II. p. xvii, Almost every metaphor..may be referred to the book of Isaiah, and mostly to its exilic half.

†**e'xilience.** *Obs. rare.* [f. EXILIENT: see -ENCE.] The state of being 'exilient'; exultation, rapture; also *fig.*

1623 HOLYDAY *Serm.* (1626) 1 His iust exilience is so great. **1655** tr. *Francion* xi. 15 This News did so ravish him with an exilience of joy. *a* **1711** KEN *Anodynes* Poet. Wks. 1721 III. 473 You may..my full Exilience hit. —— *Preparatives* ibid. IV. 126 Heav'n-born Perfume will..raise Exilience.

†**e'xiliency.** *Obs.* [f. EXILIENT: see -ENCY.] = prec. Also *concr.* an outburst, outcome.

1640 BP. REYNOLDS *Passions* xi. 100 In embracings, kisses, in the exiliency and egresse of the spirits in the expansion of the heart. *a* **1662** HEYLIN *Laud* II. 294 Which..ought to be rather attributed to some exiliency of humane frailty.

†**e'xilient,** *a. Obs.* Also 7 exh-. [ad. L. *ex(s)ilientem*, pr. pple. of *ex(s)ilīre* to spring out or forth, f. *ex-* out + *salīre* to spring.] That leaps forth or springs up; exulting, bounding; active, alert.

1669 *Addr. to Yng. Gentry Eng.* 77 He might have the high spring-tides of exhilient joy enlarging their channels. *a* **1711** KEN *Christophil* Poet. Wks. 1721 I. 478 Th' exilient Strings ..leap up into Chords. —— *Edmund* ibid. II. 20 God's Will ..you all live exilient to fulfil. —— *Hymnotheo* ibid. III. 84 The Saints exilient Dust from Tombs uncas'd, Shall into Limbs be mutually embrac'd.

†**exilila.** *Obs.* Also 6 exeleres, exilya, exulila.

1526 *Will Ric. Hanchett* (Somerset Ho.), A pair of beades of exilila gauded with silver. **1528** *MS. List of Jewelry* (Pub. Rec. Office), A pair of bedys of exulila, with the v woundes. **1537** *Will C'tess Oxford* (Somerset Ho.), Exeleres bedes. **1538** *Will Paxforde* (Somerset Ho.), Bedes of exilya.

exiling ('ɛksaɪlɪŋ), *vbl. sb.* [f. EXILE *v.* + -ING[1].] The action of the vb. EXILE; an instance of the same; the state of being exiled, banishment, exile. Now only gerundial.

c **1374** CHAUCER *Boeth.* I. iii. 11 Yif þou hast not knowen þe exilynge of anaxogore. *c* **1380** *Antecrist* in Todd 3 *Treat. Wyclif* 116 Whenne cristen men weren compellid bi exilyngis, betyngis & deþis to make sacrifice to ydols. **1387** TREVISA *Higden* (Rolls) II. 343 Cadmus chees his exilynge in Grecia. **1398** —— *Barth. De. P.R.* XVIII. xxv. (1495) 784 The kynge came oute of exilynge. *c* **1430** LYDG. *Bochas* I. vii, [He] Humble of his cheare toke his exilinge. **1516** PYNSON *Life St. Birgette* in *Myrr. our Ladye* p. lv, In the exilynge of a certeyn man I was ouermoche rygorouse. **1635** SIBBES *Soul's Confl.* (1638) 3 His exiling from Gods house.

†**exi'lition.** *Obs.* [f. L. *ex(s)ilī-re* (see EXILIENT) + -TION.] A leaping or springing up or forth.

1646 SIR T. BROWNE *Pseud. Ep.* II. v. 88 Sulphur and small-coale mixed will not take fire with noise, or exilition. **1656–81** in BLOUNT *Glossogr.* **1711** J. GREENWOOD *Eng. Gram.* 194 This *ing*..is used..to denote a single but not manifold exilition or leaping up. **1755** in JOHNSON.

exility (ɛk'sɪlɪtɪ). [ad. L. *exīlitāt-em*, n. of quality f. *exīlis* EXILE *a.*]

1. Shrunken or attenuated condition, smallness in number or size; thinness, slenderness, meagreness.

1528 *St. Papers Hen. VIII*, II. 130 The Kingis revenues be brought to suche exilitie, that they suffice nat to ordinarie charges. *c* **1534** tr. *Pol. Verg. Eng. Hist.* (Camden) I. 72 The place wherin thei foughte was verie streyght, and therfor commodius to the exilitee of the Romains. **1641** PRYNNE *Antip.* 270 The exilitie and smalenesse of his learning. **1750** G. HUGHES *Barbadoes* 41 They [Guinea worms] are exceeding long in respect to their great exility and thinness. **1779–81** JOHNSON *L.P., Cowley* Wks. II. 24 Subtlety..in its original import means exility of particles. **1813** J. FORSYTH *Remarks on Antiq., etc. during an Excursion Italy* 382 The apparent height and the exility admired in a Gothic pillar. **1819** H. BUSK *Vestriad* IV. 313 His exility of snout. **1847** in CRAIG.

†**b.** Smallness or slenderness of income or revenue; poorness, poverty. *Obs.*

1559 ABP. PARKER, etc. in *Parker's Corresp.* (1853) 100 In consideration of the exility of the bishopricks. **1562** GRINDAL *Let. to Abp. Parker* Wks. (1843) 252 If by exility or decay of benefices..any arrearages be. **1651** *Fuller's Abel Rediv., Andrewes* (1867) II. 161 His majesty..(because of the exility of that bishopric) soon after added the parsonage of Cheyham. **1774** HUTCHINS *Hist. Dorset* I. 63 The bishop of Sarum sets forth the exility of the two churches..which were not sufficient to maintain a priest each.

2. Of a sound, spirit, a woven substance, etc.: Tenuity, thinness, fine texture. Hence of immaterial things: Refinement, subtlety.

1626 BACON *Sylva* §154 The Voice or other Sound is reduced, by such passage to a great Weakness or Exility. **1647** H. MORE *Song of Soul* II. ii. II. xxi, This souls thin spread exility. **1751** HARRIS *Hermes* III. vi. Wks. (1841) 232 Bodies so exceedingly fine, that their very exility makes them susceptible of sensation. **1802** PALEY *Nat. Theol.* xxi. §4 (1819) 334 This extreme exility [of light] though difficult to conceive, is easy to prove. **1802** *Ann. Reg.* 11 The Act of Faith..is expressed..on the thinnest paper, the exility of which [etc.]. **1841** D'ISRAELI *Amen. Lit.* (1859) I. 286 [They] could not appreciate such exility of elegance, and such sublimated refinement. **1866** J. MARTINEAU *Ess.* I. 144 The extreme exility of the evidence.

b. *concr.* A refinement, subtlety.

1647 H. MORE *Poems* 111 The soul..contemns as nought unseen exilities.

† **eximiety.** *Obs.*⁻⁰ [ad. late L. *eximietātem*, f. *eximius*: see EXIMIOUS.] Excellency.
1656–81 in BLOUNT *Glossogr.* **1692** in COLES. **1730–6** in BAILEY (folio). **1775** ASH, *Eximity*.

eximious (ɛgˈzɪmɪəs), *a.* Now *rare.* [f. L. *eximi-us* excepted, select, choice (f. *eximĕre*: see EXEMPT *v.*) + -OUS.]
Common in 17th c. literature: the few examples in 19th c. are humorously bombastic or pedantic.
Excellent, distinguished, eminent.
1547 BOORDE *Brev. Health* ccxxxvi, Kynges, and kynges sones, and other noble men hath ben eximious Phisicions. **1619** W. SCLATER *Expos. 1 Thess.* (1630) 236 Things.. eximious and eminent in loue aboue many other Graces. **1657** TOMLINSON *Renou's Disp.* 502 This syrupe is eximious against many affections. **1678** CUDWORTH *Intell. Syst.* I. v. 709 Our Saviour Christ, was unquestionably, that One Eximious Prophet, which God..promised to send. **1681** GLANVILL *Sadducismus* II. 187 There is in this Relation an eximious example of the Magical venome of Witches. **1710** R. WARD *Life H. More* 22 This Eximious Person. **1829** T. L. PEACOCK *Misfort. Elphin.* 103 All [were] the most eximious and transcendent persons of the earth. **1865** CARLYLE *Fredk. Gt.* XIII. ii, Oh ye wigs, and eximious wig-blocks, called right-honourable. **1868** BROWNING *Ring & Bk.* IX. 109 The picture be for our eximious Rome.
Hence † **eˈximiously**, in an 'eximious' manner; excellently, notably, singularly. Also † **eˈximiousness**, the quality of being 'eximious'.
1650 W. SCLATER (Jun.) in *W. Sclater's Exp. Rom.* iv. Ep. Ded., It being so eximiously beautified. **1657** TOMLINSON *Renou's Disp.* 505 It is most eximiously medicinal. **1681** H. MORE *Exp. Dan.* ii. 42 Is not this part of the Prophecy also eximiously fulfilled? **1730–6** BAILEY (folio), *Eximiousness*. Hence **1775** ASH, *Eximiousness*.

† **eˈxinanite**, *v. Obs.* [f. L. *exinānīt-* ppl. stem of *exinānīre* to make empty, f. *ex-* (see EX- *pref.*¹) + *inānis* empty.]
1. *trans.* To make void or of none effect; to deprive of force, virtue, etc.
c **1555** HARPSFIELD *Divorce Hen. VIII* (Camden) 216 It doth utterly frustrate, exinanyte and annul the..validity of the said brief. **1646** EVANCE *Noble Ord.* 10 Sinne will (ἐξουθενεῖν) Exininate honour. **1661** BRAMHALL *Just. Vind.* vi. 151 The coming..of the Popes infamous messenger..by which oathes..rights, priviledges, were not only weakned, but exinanited.
2. To reduce (a person) to emptiness; to empty (of dignity, power, etc); to abase, humble; chiefly *refl.* said of Christ with reference to *Phil.* ii. 7.
1577 BULL *Luther's Comm. Ps. Grad.* cxxv. 1 Gods power taketh no place in vs vntill we be vtterly..exinanited. **1582** N. T. (Rhem.) *Phil.* ii. 7 He exinanited him self [**1611** made himselfe of no reputation], taking the forme of a servant. **1624** GATAKER *Transubst.* 195 They thinke hee..was not throughly enough exinanited..here on Earth.

† **exinaˈnitiate**, *v. Obs. rare. trans.* = prec.
1698 *Christ Exalted* §61. 48 For the Sin it self they utterly deny it, though by it they evacuate or exinanitiate many Texts of Scripture. *Ibid.* §67. 53 He wholly evacuates and exinanitiates the Gospel.

exinanition (ɛkˌsɪnəˈnɪʃən). Now *rare.* Also 8 **exhinanition.** [ad. L. *exinānītiōn-em*, n. of action f. *exinānīre*: see EXINANITE.]
1. The action or process of emptying or exhausting, whether in a material or immaterial sense; emptied or exhausted condition.
1603 FLORIO *Montaigne* III. viii. (1632) 522 It [learning] doth..purifie..and subtilize them [minds] even unto exinanition or evacuation. *a* **1631** DONNE *Ess.* (1651) 118 Replenishing the World after the great Exinanition by the generall Deluge. **1633** EARL MANCH. *Al Mondo* (1636) 201 Some..cared not to afford common assistance to nature, and so have dyed through exinanition and want of strength. **1649** JER. TAYLOR *Gt. Exemp.* I. 6 A life whose stories tell of..fastings to the exinanition of spirits. **1720** GIBSON *Diet. Horses* v. (ed. 3) 81 Whether the signs be Repletion and fulness, or Exhinanition and Lowness of his Flesh. **1819** COLERIDGE in *Athenæum* 7 Jan. 1888, 17/3 Dante..asks for an evacuation and exinanition of Marsyas, that so he [Dante] might become a mere vessel..of the Deity. **1862** A. H. CLOUGH in *Macm. Mag.* Aug. 323 Life at very birth destroyed, Atrophy, exinanition! **1884** *Syd. Soc. Lex.*, *Exinanition*, a thorough and complete emptying.
2. The action or process of emptying of pride, self-will, or dignity; abasement, humiliation; an instance of this; also, a state of humiliation.
1627 DONNE *Serm.* v. 45 This exinanition of ourselves is acceptable in the sight of God. **1649** JER. TAYLOR *Gt. Exemp.* III. xv. 129 He was to take upon him all the affronts, miseries and exinanitions of the most miserable. **1652** BENLOWES *Theoph.* IV. lviii, I'l press still Th' Exinanition of my o'regrown will. **1686** H. MORE in Norris *Theory Love* (1688) 187 The scope they aym at..is a perfect exinanition of ourselves, that we may be filled with the sense of God.
b. *esp.* of Christ; with reference to *Phil.* ii. 8.
a **1612** DONNE *Βιαθανατος* (1644) 188 Christ said this now, because his Passion was begun; for all his conversations here were degrees of exinanition. **1659** PEARSON *Creed.* I. 200 His exinanition consisted in..the assumption of the form of a servant. **1855** W. H. MILL *Applic. Panth. Princ.* (1861) 26 The death of the God-man is only the throwing off of his exinanition or humiliation. **1882–3** SCHAFF *Encycl. Relig. Knowl.* I. 463 [The Kenotic theory] teaches a temporary self-exinanition..of the pre-existent Logos.

exindusiate (ɛksɪnˈdjuːsɪət), *a. Bot.* [f. EX- *pref.*¹ + L. *indūsi-um* (see INDUSIUM) + -ATE².] 'Not having an indusium' (*Treas. Bot.* 1866).

ˈ**exine.** *rare.* [f. L. *ex-* out + -INE.] = EXTINE.
1884 *Syd. Soc. Lex.*, *Exine*, Fritzche's name for the *Exhymenine*, or outer layer of a pollen grain.

† **eˈxinfluence**, *v. Obs. rare*⁻¹. [f. EX- *pref.*¹ + INFLUENCE *sb.*] *trans.* To deprive of influence.
1667 WATERHOUSE *Fire Lond.* 59 These repulsives shall be exinfluenced, and their vigour..be abated.

exinguinal (ɛkˈsɪŋgwɪnəl), *a.* and *sb. Entom.* [f. EX- *pref.*¹ + L. *inguin-*, *inguen* groin + -AL¹.]
A. *adj.* Situated outside the groin. **B.** *sb.* 'The second segment or trochanter of the limbs of the Arachnida' (*Syd. Soc. Lex.* 1884).

extine (ɛkˈsɪntɪn, -taɪn). [f. L. *ex-* (see EX- *pref.*¹) + *int-us* within + -INE¹.] 'The membrane of the pollen grain which lies between the *Extine* and the *Intine*' (*Syd. Soc. Lex.* 1884).
1852 in BRANDE (Supplement). **1866** in *Treas. Bot.*

† **ex-ˈintricate**, *v. Obs. rare*⁻¹. [f. EX- *pref.*¹ 2 + L. *intrīcāt-* ppl. stem of *intrīcāre* to entangle: see INTRICATE *v.*] *trans.* To disentangle, extricate. Const. *from.* (In quot. *refl.*)
1661 FELTHAM *Resolves* II. lx, A disadvantage, from which he hath no way to ex-intricate himself, but by the dextrousness of his ingenuity.

exion. Blunder of Mrs. Quickly for 'action'.
1597 SHAKS. *2 Hen. IV*, II. i. 32, I pra' ye, since my Exion is enter'd..let him be brought in to his answer.

† **exiˈpotic**, *a. Med. Obs.* [ad. Gr. ἐξιπωτικ-ός fit for squeezing out, purgative, f. ἐξιπόειν to squeeze out, f. ἐξ out + ἰπόειν to press down.] (See quots.)
[**1823** CRABB *Technol. Dict.*, *Exipoticos*..an epithet for digesting or detersive medicines.] **1860** MAYNE *Exipoticos*, *Exipoticus*, *Pharm.*, Formerly applied to medicines.. esteemed digestive, detergent; exipotic. **1884** in *Syd. Soc. Lex.*

exist (ɛgˈzɪst), *v.* [ad. Fr. *exist-er*, ad. L. *ex(s)istĕre* to stand out, be perceptible, hence to exist, f. *ex-* out + *sistĕre* reduplicated form of *stă-* to stand. (The late appearance of the word is remarkable: it is not in Cooper's Lat.-Eng. Dict. 1565, either under *existo* or *exto*.)]
1. To have place in the domain of reality, have objective being.
1605 SHAKS. *Lear* I. i. 114 The orbs From whom we do exist. *a* **1716** SOUTH *Serm.* (1737)) I. ii. 45 To conceive the world..to have existed from eternity. **1793** BLACKSTONE *Comm.* (ed. 12) 593 Corporations which exist by force of the common law. **1797** GODWIN *Enquirer* I. vi. 41 The Roman historians are the best that ever existed. **1846** MILL *Logic* I. iii. §6 The man called father might still exist though there were no child. **1871** MORLEY *Voltaire* (1886) 14 The conception of justice towards heretics did not exist (in unscientific ages).
2. To have being in a specified place or under specified conditions. With advb. phrase or *as*; formerly with simple complement. Of relations, circumstances, etc.: To subsist, be found, occur.
1602 MARSTON *Antonio's Rev.* IV. i, Most things that morally adhere to soules, Wholly exist in drunke opinion. *a* **1704** LOCKE (J.), That combination does not always exist together in nature. **1786** H. TOOKE *Purley* (1860) 201 A quality which..would make me rather chuse..to exist a mastiff or a mule. **1807** CRABBE *Par. Reg.* I. 609 But though no weed exists his garden round. **1823** H. J. BROOKE *Introd. Crystallogr.* 165 The character of the modifying planes.. may..be considered to exist in all the prisms belonging to this class. **1833** N. ARNOTT *Physics* (ed. 5) II. I. 122 Which substances..usually exist as airs. **1860** TYNDALL *Glac.* I. xv. 102 A space of a foot existed between ice and water.
3. To have life or animation; to live.
1828 SCOTT *F.M. Perth* xxxii, The Prince of Scotland was not to be murdered..he was only to cease to exist.
4. To continue in being, maintain an existence.
1790 BURNS *Let. to P. Hill* 2 Mar., We are under a cursed necessity of studying selfishness, in order that we may exist. **1791** BURKE *Corr.* (1844) III. 359 That government is strong indeed which can exist under contempt. **1797** MRS. RADCLIFFE *Italian* Prol., How does he contrive to exist here?

existability: see EXISTIBILITY.

existence (ɛgˈzɪstəns). Also 6 *Sc.* existens. [a. OF. *existence*, ad. med.L. *existentia*, n. of state f. *ex(s)istent-em* (see EXISTENT), pr. pple. of *ex(s)istĕre*: see EXIST and -ENCE.] The state of being existent.
† **1.** Actuality, reality. *Obs.*
(Opposed to *apparence*: the Fr. words often so occur in the *Roman de la Rose*.)
c **1384** CHAUCER *H. Fame* I. 266 Allas what harme dothe Apparence Whan hit is fals in existence. *c* **1400** *Rom. Rose* 5552 To se Hym that is freend in existence From hym that is by apparence. **1430** LYDG. *Chron. Troy* I. v, A deceyte is couertly yment..As it were sothe in very existence.
2. a. Being; the fact or state of existing; 'actual possession of being' (J.). ***in existence***: as predicate = 'extant'.
c **1430** LYDG. *Pol. Rel. & L. Poems* (1866) 45 Thyng counterfetyd hath non existence. **1432–50** tr. *Higden* (Rolls) I. 267 The coloures of faces, quantites of bodies, qualites of sawles, haue theire existence in man after the diuersite of heuyn. **1552** ABP. HAMILTON *Catech.* (1884) 38 God allone is be himself; of his awin natural existens. **1665** GLANVILL *Sceps. Sci.* 20 Matter is not necessary to the Soul's existence. **1725** WATTS *Logic* III. ii. §8 An Argument taken from the Nature or Existence of Things. **1768–74** TUCKER *Lt. Nat.* (1852) II. 462 Existence belongs solely to substances, and essence solely to qualities. **1816** J. SMITH *Panorama Sc. & Art* I. 585 The earth was the most consequential aggregate of matter in existence. **1818** JAS. MILL *Brit. India* III. IV. ix. 298 It created some evils of the greatest magnitude which previously had no existence. **1856** SIR B. BRODIE *Psychol. Inq.* I. ii. 56 These facts sufficiently proved the existence of some actual disease. **1871** ALABASTER *Wheel of Law* p. xxxvii, Buddhists..see more reason to lament existence than to be grateful for it.
b. Continued being; continuance in being.
1736 BUTLER *Anal.* I. i. Wks. 1874 I. 17 We know not at all upon what the existence of our living powers depends. **1811** WELLINGTON in Gurw. *Disp.* VIII. 274 People who absolutely depend for their existence upon the continuance of His Royal Highness' protection. **1874** GREEN *Short Hist.* viii. 492 The colony was now firmly established and the struggle for mere existence was over.
c. Continuance of being as a living creature; life. (Sometimes in disparaging sense: 'a mere existence not worthy the name of life'.)
1634 SIR T. HERBERT *Trav.* 169 Their famous Æscalapius, seeing no more money, limited my life to five dayes more existence. **1825** LANDOR in *Four C. Eng. Lett.* 441, I shall remember his [friendship] to the last hour of my existence. **1838** DE MORGAN *Ess. Probab.* 223 [An annuity] to be paid at the end of the year in which the joint existence fails. **1860** B'NESS BUNSEN in Hare *Life* II. v. 276 His existence of bodily ease and freshness. **1870** DICKENS *E. Drood* vii, We have had a wretched existence.
3. A mode or kind of existing.
a **1763** SHENSTONE *Ess.* (1765) 52 Such appears to me to be the true existence of apparitions. **1867** M. ARNOLD *Empedocles on Etna* I. ii, Other existences there are, that clash with ours. **1878** BROWNING *La Saisiaz* 28 New existence led by men and women new.
4. *concr.* **a.** All that exists; the aggregate of being.
1751 HARRIS *Hermes* Wks. (1841) 142 Existence may be considered as an universal genus. **1868** GEO. ELIOT *Sp. Gipsy* 51 All beauteous existence rests, yet wakes.
b. Something that exists; a being, an entity.
1605 TIMME *Quersit.* I. iii. 10 Things naturall are called properly naturall existences or beings. **1624** MASSINGER *Renegado* v. ii, Prosper, thou Great Existence, my endeavours! *a* **1754** FIELDING *True Patriot* Wks. 1775 IX. 329, I have heard of a man who believed there was no real existence in the world but himself. **1820** KEATS *Hyperion* II. 337 When all the fair existences of heaven Came. **1846** MILL *Logic* I. iii. §1 An enumeration of Existences, as the basis of Logic, did not escape the attention of the schoolmen. **1891** C. R. FRANCIS in *Indian Mag.* Sept. 459 There is no limit to the ever-increasing number of deified existences.
5. *attrib.*, as **existence-proposition**, a proposition asserting existence, an existential proposition; **existence-theorem** (see quot. 1903).
1937 *Mind* XLVI. 53 This is certainly intended to be or to contain an empirical existence-proposition. **1939** *Ibid.* XLVIII. 144 Plato was at this time deeply concerned with the logic of existence-propositions. **1944** M. WEITZ in P. A. Schilpp *Philos. B. Russell* 86 An existence proposition is the traditional 'I' or 'O' proposition. For Russell it is a proposition which asserts the truth of at least one value of a propositional function; e.g., 'Some men are brutal'. **1900** J. ROYCE *World & Indiv.* I. v. 213 Modern Analysis, and the Theory of Functions, contain very many propositions of the class that are sometimes called 'Existence-Theorems'. **1903** B. RUSSELL *Princ. Math.* lix. 497 The existence-theorems of mathematics—*i.e.* the proofs that the various classes defined are not null—are almost all obtained from Arithmetic.

† **eˈxistency.** *Obs.* [ad. med.L. *existentia*: see prec. and -ENCY.]
1. The fact or state of existing; continuance of being; = EXISTENCE 2.
1646 SIR T. BROWNE *Pseud. Ep.* III. xiii. 137 It..may be doubted whether it be of existency, or really any such stone in the head of a Toad at all. **1654** S. ASHE *Fun. Serm.* 10 Mar. 25 The existency of Christ in Believers giveth existence to their hopes of glory. **1677** HALE *Prim. Orig. Man.* I. v. 113 It is impossible that any Being can be eternal with..variety of states or manner of existency. **1683** PORDAGE *Myst. Div.* 1 Before the Globe of Eternity was in existency. **1708** H. DODWELL *Nat. Mortal. Human Souls* 5 Existency depending on the arbitrary Divine Pleasure.
b. A state or mode of being.
1710 *Tatler* No. 246 ⁋1 We stand in the middle of existencies [*i.e.* between angels and brutes].
2. Something which exists; a being, an entity; = EXISTENCE 4.
1628 T. SPENCER *Logick* 202 A whole, sayth he, is twofold, viz. Vniversall; or a totall existency. **1631** *Celestina* I. 5 See what difference there is betwixt apparencies and existencies. **1691** ED. TAYLOR tr. *Behmen's Theos. Philos.* 338 Where lye innumerable multiplicity of Existencies or Beings. **1824** *Westm. Rev.* I. 480 By the greater intensity of sensations.. we judge of real existencies.
b. A concrete form; a substance.
1651 W. G. tr. *Cowel's Inst.* 235 And bodies Politick have not visible Existencies whereby they may be taken.

existent (ɛg'zɪstənt), *a.* and *sb.* [ad. L. *ex(s)istent-em*, pr. pple. of *ex(s)istĕre*: see EXIST.]

A. *adj.*

1. That exists, existing; having being or existence. Often emphasized by *actually, really, truly*, etc.

1561 EDEN *Arte Nauig.* Pref., One common sence existent in them all. **1594** *Mirr. Policy* (1599) Qiij, Some bad Societie aimeth at an apparent but not existent good. **1656** tr. *Hobbes' Elem. Philos.* (1839) 18 Whether that thing be truly existent, or be only feigned. **1734** JACKSON *Existence of God* 46 There is but one necessarily existent Being. **1793** GOUV. MORRIS in Sparks *Life & Writ.* (1832) II. 302 Forty five thousand men were about the existent force. **1818** BYRON *Ch. Har.* IV. lxxxvii, And thou, dread statue! yet existent in The austerest form of naked majesty. **1860** BRIGHT *Sp. Ch. Rates* 27 Apr., A power which is found to be greatly less existent in a congregation of the Established Church. **1868** ROGERS *Pol. Econ.* iii. (ed. 3) 27 The quantity [of gold] existent and in circulation.

absol. **1603** HOLLAND *Plutarch's Mor.* 1352 Usurping the name of the true Jehovah or alwaies Existent. **1653** H. MORE *Antid. Ath.* I. viii. (1712) 146 He declares why the Existent should exist. **1875** *Encycl. Brit.* II. 522/2 Pure unconditioned actuality, the ever existent, or God.

2. Now existing; present-day.

1791 BURKE *Th. Fr. Affairs* Wks. VII. 72 To govern the existent body with as sovereign a sway as they had done the last. **1874** RUSKIN *Fors Clav.* IV. xliii. 153 It gives you types of existent Frenchmen..of a very different class.

B. *sb.* An existent person or thing.

1644 BP. MAXWELL *Prerog. Chr. Kings* ii. 31 Frequently expressions in the abstract expresse existents in the concrete. **1655** H. MORE *App. Antid.* (1662) 146 If there be any necessary Existent, it is plain that it is Matter. **1722** WOLLASTON *Relig. Nat.* v. 69 For He is a necessary existent. *a* **1878** LEWES *Study Psychol.* (1879) 51 These same phenomena viewed..no longer as modes or existences, but as subjects or existents.

Hence **e'xistently** *adv.*

1694 R. BURTHOGGE *Reason* 67 Sentiments (as such) are, in their own formalities, but apparently only, not existently, without the faculties that so conceive them.

existential (ɛgzɪ'stɛnʃəl), *a.* [ad. late L. *existentiāl-is*, f. *existentia* EXISTENCE.]

1. Of or pertaining to existence.

1693 tr. *Barlow's Exercit.* i. Rem. 483 Enjoying the good of existence..and..the being deprived of that existential good. **1809–10** COLERIDGE *Friend* (1818) III. 96 *note*, The essential cause of fiendish guilt, when it makes itself existential and peripheric. **1878** S. HODGSON *Philos. Refl.* II. III. vii. §1. 12 There is a certain parallelism between the logical and existential analyses.

2. *Logic.* **a.** Of a proposition, etc.: Expressing the fact of existence; predicating existence.

1819 COLERIDGE *Philos. Lect.* (1949) ix. 276 This necessarily led men..to doubt whether a logical truth was necessarily an existencial one, i.e. whether because a thing was logically consistent it must be necessarily existent. **1837–8** SIR W. HAMILTON *Logic* xiii. (1866) II. 229 Existential propositions, that is, those in which mere existence is predicated. **1846** —— *Diss.* in *Reid's Wks.* 811 The character of the existential Judgments they involve. **1888** J. VENN in *Mind* July 415 Convention does not allow us to say 'It executes'..But we can just as conveniently adopt the existential form, 'There was an execution'.

b. *existential import*: significance concerning the existence of something, usually of items denoted by the subject-term of a propostion; the implication that something exists.

1887 J. N. KEYNES *Formal Logic* (ed. 2) II. viii. 138. §101 (*title*) Formal logic and the existential import of propositions. **1898** A. N. WHITEHEAD *Treat. Univ. Algebra* p. vii, A conventional mathematical definition has no existential import. **1946** *Mind* LV. 109 The *Ethics* [of Spinoza] is a prolonged effort to deduce truths of existential import out of a combination of definitions. **1962** W. & M. KNEALE *Devel. Logic* 412 Those Aristotelian inferences which depend on existential import.

3. *Philos.* Concerned with or relating to existence (freq. as distinct from 'essence'), esp. human existence as seen from the point of view of existentialism; ***existential philosophy*** = EXISTENTIALISM.

[**1846** KIERKEGAARD *Afsluttende Uvidenskabelig Efterskrift* in *Wks.* (1902) VII. II. iv. 374 Den existentielle Pathos er Handling, eller Existentsens Omdannelse.] *a* **1937** M. GEIGER in *Philos. & Phenomenol. Res.* (1943) III. 256 'Existential Philosophy' is a collective term for many problems, many methods of thinking, many points of view. *Ibid.* 257 The distinguishing feature of all existential philosophy is the fact that its basic category is *existential significance*. **1939** V. A. DEMANT *Religious Prospect* vii. 186 The '*existential* theology' declares that human life can gain religious meaning only by a bare act of faith which has no relation to and is even falsified by attempts to give the object of faith, God, any content in man's consciousness. **1940** H. READ *Annals of Innocence* II. vii. 182 That philosophy is an existential one: it is the expression of all my faculties, of the whole consciousness of a living organism. **1941** *Philosophy* XVI. 267 Its influence permeates the whole school both of existential philosophy and dialectical theology. **1941** SWENSON & LOWRIE tr. *Kierkegaard's Concl. Unscientific Postscript* II. ii. 74 The existing subjective thinker is in his existential relation to the truth as negative as he is positive. *Ibid.* iv. 386 Existential pathos is action, the reconstruction of the individual's mode of existence. **1944** [see EXISTENTIALISM]. **1956** C. WILSON *Outsider* ix. 273 Kierkegaard's attitude is so Existential that his Christianity is a religion that regards God as the intermediary between himself and his fellow human beings, and cannot even accept their existence without first accepting the existence of God. **1962** R. G. OLSON *Introd. Existentialism* iv. 129 Existential psychoanalysis, the method for discovering an individual's fundamental project of being. **1964** *Amer. Philos. Q.* I. 122/1 Existential psychiatrists seem to be publishing much more.

Hence **exi'stentially** *adv.*, by virtue of existence; also, in an existential manner; according to existentialism.

a **1834** COLERIDGE (Webster 1864) Whether God was existentially as well as essentially intelligent. **1895** W. JAMES *Coll. Ess. & Rev.* (1920) 400 The various [mental] 'contents'..are integers, existentially, and their parts only live as long as *they* live. **1938** M. R. ADAMSON tr. *Maritain's True Humanism* i. 13 A *perfect natural wisdom*, of which man considered existentially was supposed to be in fact capable. **1941** *Philos. & Phenomenol. Res.* I. 349 According to the fundamental principle of the philosophy of existence..even the fundamental analysis is in the last analysis 'existentially rooted' and is in agreement with the system's phenomenological claims. **1948** E. WAUGH *Loved One* 7 Sir Ambrose had a more adventurous past but he lived existentially. He thought of himself as he was at that moment, brooded fondly on each several excellence and rejoiced. **1959** *Times Lit. Suppl.* 20 Mar. p. x/5 Interpreting myth 'existentially', which is what the New Testament is trying to do.

existentialism (ɛgzɪ'stɛnʃəlɪz(ə)m). *Philos.* [ad. G. *existentialismus* (see below), f. EXISTENTIAL *a.* + -ISM.] A doctrine that concentrates on the existence of the individual, who, being free and responsible, is held to be what he makes himself by the self-development of his essence through acts of the will (which, in the Christian form of the theory, leads to God).

The existentialist movement was mainly originated by the Danish writer Søren Kierkegaard (1813–55), who frequently used the term *Existents-forhold* 'condition of existence, existential relation'. It was developed in the 20th c. chiefly in continental Europe by Jaspers, Sartre, and others, and the Eng. word *existentialism* answers to G. *existentialismus*, which is first recorded in 1919 (see below).

[**1846** KIERKEGAARD *Afsluttende Uvidenskabelig Efterskrift* in *Wks.* (1902) VII. II. ii. 62 Den existerende subjective Tænker er i sit Existents-Forhold til Sandheden ligesaa negativ som positiv. **1849** R. NIELSEN *J. Climacus og H. Martensens Christelige Dogmatik* 126 Thi det skal vist Ingen negte, at der i denne Dogmatik forefindes en Mængde Grundsætninger 'Speculationen' og det religiøse 'Existentialforhold' betræffende. **1919** W. MOOG *Logik, Psychologie und Psychologismus* II. 195 Der Relativismus..ist in der Regel auch ein Existentialismus, das heisst, er behauptet die Abhängigkeit des Logischen vom Existierenden. *Ibid.* 231 Die Fiktion ist nach Husserl..'das Lebenselement der Phänomenologie'..des Existentialismus. *Ibid.* 195 Wie der Fiktionalismus auf existentialistischen Voraussetzungen beruht.] **1941** J. KRAFT in *Philos. & Phenomenol. Res.* I. 345 Kierkegaard, Nietzsche, and pragmatism are examples of real or possible starting points of existentialism, capable of being multiplied by further examples. *Ibid.* 357 The philosophy of existence is philosophizing only what the practice of the time realizes: the frenzy connected with the conjuring up of highest meanings. The authoritarian thoughts of existentialism are only a dissonant accompanying music to the authoritarian acts under which man in the twentieth century groans. **1944** *Ibid.* V. 127 Existentialism or existential philosophy..is the extreme attempt to find a meaning in the existence of modern man whose philosophy and science *originated* in the will to make himself, through knowledge, the master of the world and whose philosophy and science have ended in a complete nihilism. **1945** *Harper's Mag.* Sept. 270/2 Sartre's *existentialism* is profoundly pessimistic, but in the colloquial sense that the human lot is an absurd and unhappy one, rather than in the formal sense that man is 'by nature' evil. .. In his view..no 'Human Nature' transcends the actual, which is composed of infinitely diverse existences. **1948** *Mind* LVII. 258 What is Existentialism? Historically speaking it is a philosophy of will that stems from that unhappy Danish genius, Soren Kirkegaard. **1957** H. READ *Tenth Muse* xix. 168 That is existentialist dogma, but it is also the romantic dogma, and existentialism is nowadays the philosophical aspect of romanticism. **1957** *Observer* 8 Sept. 6/4 We asked Miss Greco what Existentialism implied. Apparently its essence is summed up by 'whatever you do, you become'. **1958** W. BARRETT *Irrational Man* i. 7 Existentialism was a literary movement as well. **1961** N. MAILER *Advts. for Myself* 91 Willy-nilly I had had existentialism forced upon me. **1965** *Eng. Studies* XLVI. 390 If we define Existentialism as the belief that man is born into an alien..universe..then..Melville must be recognized as America's first existentialist writer. **1967** A. MACINTYRE in *Encycl. Philos.* III. 147/2 Existentialism may perhaps be considered most fruitfully as a historical movement in which connections of dependence and influence can be traced from one writer to another... The key themes are the individual and systems; intentionality; being and absurdity; the nature and significance of choice; the role of extreme experiences; and the nature of communication.

existentialist (ɛgzɪ'stɛnʃəlɪst), *sb.* and *a.* [f. as prec. + -IST.] **A.** *sb.* An exponent or adherent of existentialism.

1945 A. J. AYER in *Horizon* July 12 Philosophically, he [*sc.* Sartre] is usually described as an Existentialist. The use of this label is justified in so far as he clearly owes much to Husserl, from whom the group of contemporary German philosophers who are commonly known as Existentialists has chiefly drawn its inspiration. **1950** A. HUXLEY *Themes & Variations* 115 Biran was an existentialist, who insisted that man must always be considered as he really is, an incarnate spirit or mindbody. **1952** M. MCCARTHY *Groves of Academe* (1953) vii. 142 He wore a long dark back-belted coat of a cheap shaggy material much affected by priests and young existentialists. **1961** *Daily Tel.* 24 Feb. 19/5 The long, greasy hair, the scraggy beards, the short tight jeans and grubby fingernails now dubbed 'Beat-nik' were immediately after the war the uniform in Paris of young people who called themselves Existentialists.

B. *adj.* Of or pertaining to existentialism or existentialists.

1946 *Time* 23 Dec. 40/2 Jean-Paul Sartre, the leader of the French Existentialist movement, vigorously, often brilliantly, drags a shady topic into the light. **1948** *Mind* LVII. 370 Existentialist reaction against the abstract ideas of personality characteristic of Kantian and post-Kantian idealism. **1956** A. J. AYER *Probl. Knowl.* i. 23 Existentialist philosophers have gone so far as to deny the law of identity. **1957** *Times* 28 Dec. 7/6 The decline of the existentialist movement has left French intellectual life dispersed and fluid. **1957**, **1965** [see prec.].

exister (ɛg'zɪstə(r)). *rare.* [f. EXIST + -ER[1].] One who or that which exists.

1887 *Atlantic Mag.* Apr. 572/1 Given a somewhat humdrum and monotonous existence; the exister finding 'Denmark a prison'.

existibility (ɛg,zɪstɪ'bɪlɪtɪ). Also **-ability**. [f. next: see -ITY.] The quality of being existible; capability of existing.

1888 *Nature* 1 Mar. 417/2 The inquiry into the existability of perfect numbers.

existible (ɛg'zɪstɪb(ə)l), *a. rare.* [f. EXIST + -IBLE.] That can exist; capable of existing.

1701 GREW *Cosm. Sacra* III. iv. 119 It is evident, That all Corporeal and Sensible Perfections, are in some Analogous way, Existible, in the Human Mind. **1730–6** in BAILEY (folio). **1775** in ASH; hence in some mod. Dicts.

†**e'xistimate**, *v. Obs.* [f. L. *existimāt-* ppl. stem of *existimāre*, f. *ex-* (see EX- *pref.*[1]) + *æstimāre*: see ESTEEM *v.*] = ESTEEM *v.* 5.

1656–81 BLOUNT *Glossogr.*, *Existimate*, to suppose, to judge, to think or deem. **1721–1800** in BAILEY.

†**existi'mation**. *Obs.* [ad. L. *existimātiōnem*, f. *existimāre*: see prec.] = ESTIMATION.

1. Valuation in respect of excellence or merit; appreciation; worth in the opinion of others, repute, credit; = ESTIMATION 2 a, b.

1538 STARKEY *England*, II. i. 151 Such honowre and exystymatyon as ys gyven to maryed men. **1551** ROBINSON tr. *More's Utop.* II. (Arb.) 82 One rather willing the harme ..of the weale publike then any..diminution of his owne existimation. **1670** *Moral State Eng.* Pref., He who striveth to wound his Brother's Existimation, at the same time stabbeth his own. **1712** STEELE *Spect.* No. 456 ¶6 Mens Existimation [*ed. Morley* Estimation] follows us according to the Company we keep.

2. Opinion based on reasoning; judgement.

1655–60 STANLEY *Hist. Philos.* VIII. (1701) 324/1 Faith is proper to a wise man, for it is a firm existimation. **1658** PHILLIPS, *Existimation*, a thinking or judging. **1721–1800** in BAILEY.

existing (ɛg'zɪstɪŋ), *ppl. a.* [f. EXIST + -ING[2].] That exists or has existence; that exists at any implied or specified time.

1762 FOOTE *Orator* I. Wks. 1799 I. 204 They are not at present existing in this kingdom. **1801** SOUTHEY *Thalaba* IX. xiv, In Nature are two hostile Gods, Makers and Masters of existing things. **1827** JARMAN *Powell's Devises* II. 343 All the expressions applied to females, shewing that he meant existing daughters, not future issue. **1848** MACAULAY *Hist. Eng.* I. 98 He bound himself not to..dissolve the existing Parliament without its own consent. **1871** MORLEY *Voltaire* (1886) 5 His sympathy with existing sources of comfort.

Hence †**e'xistingly** *adv.*, actually, as a matter of fact, in reality.

1601 DEACON & WALKER *Spirits & Divels* 147 They were not existingly, but appearingly, turned into serpents.

exit ('ɛksɪt), *sb.* [Two formations: (1) a. L. *exit*, 3rd pers. sing. ind. of L. *exīre* to go out, f. *ex-* out + *īre* to go; (2) ad. L. *exitus* (*u-* stem) going out, departure, n. of action f. *exīre*.

In the subst. use the two formations often do not admit of being distinguished; senses B. 1–3 appear to belong chiefly to the first, while B. 4 (at least chiefly) and B. 5 belong to the second.]

A. *Lat. phr.* **1.** Used as a Latin word in stage directions; formerly EXEAT was also used. Also *transf.*

[*c* **1485** *Digby Myst.* II. 244 Et exiat Deus. *Ibid.* IV. 1423 Tunc exit Iohannes; et dicit Petrus.] **1538** BALE *Thre Lawes* 743 Awaye now wyll I rounde. *Exit.* **1593** SHAKS. *Rich. II.* I. iii. 248 Six yeares we banish him, and he shall go. *Exit.* *a* **1652** BROME *Love-sick Court* III. i, And kill'd the Patient was but sick before. *Exit.* **1747** SMOLLETT *Regicide* IV. vi, I hope to see thee bloom With vernal freshness, and again unfold Thy beauties to the sun! [*Exit* Dunbar]. **1817** COLERIDGE *Biog. Lit.* II. 282 So exit Clotilda, and enter Bertram. **1826** DISRAELI *Viv. Grey* IV. iv, Come, a bon-mot, or a Calembourg, or exit Mr. Vivian Grey.

B. *sb.*

1. a. The departure of a player from the stage.

1588 SHAKS. *L.L.L.* v. ii. 598 Keepe some state in thy *exit*, and vanish. **1600** —— *A.Y.L.* II. vii. 141 They haue their Exits and their Entrances. **1648** C. WALKER *Relat. & Observ.* 18 My Exit shall be accompanied with an applauze. **1711** STEELE *Spect.* No. 51 ¶6 When the Actors made their Exit. **1802** MAR. EDGEWORTH *Moral T.* (1816) I. xx. 192 The eyes of all..were upon her, as she made her exit.

b. *transf.* and *fig.*

a **1652** J. SMITH *Sel. Disc.* vi. 231 This sleep was upon the exit of his vision. **1685** *Gracian's Courtiers Orac.* 58 The difficult matter is to have the same applause at ones exit. **1843** CARLYLE *Past & Pr.* (1858) 234 The last exit of us all is in a Fire-Chariot of Pain. **1874** MORLEY *Compromise* (1886) 126 Progress would mean something more than mere entrances and exits on the theatre of office.

c. *esp.* Departure from the scene of life; death.

1661 FELTHAM *Lusoria* xxiii. *On Sir R. Cotton*, He scorn'd an Exit by the common means. **1684–5** in Ellis *Orig. Lett.* I.

382 III. 338 He made as very glorious christian exit..as ere was known. **1768–74** TUCKER *Lt. Nat.* (1852) II. 448 Such of our malefactors as make a penitent exit. **1794** SCOTT in Lockhart *Life* I. vii. 222, I stayed..in town to witness the exit of the cidevant Jacobin, Mr. Watt.

2. a. A going out or forth, a departure from any place or situation; an emergence; also, liberty or opportunity to go out, passage out of any place.

1659 T. PECKE *Parnassi Puerp.* 4 Sowre is the Exit..Of the salacious Cyprian Emperess. **1665** GLANVILL *Sceps. Sci.* vi. 26 They might finde an easie..exit almost everywhere. **1713** DERHAM *Phys. Theol.* VII. iv. 390 There should be one part provided for the Formation of the Body before it's Exit into the World. **1816** J. SMITH *Panorama Sc. & Art* II. 320 The cover should contain two holes, one for the exit of the steam, etc. **1829** LYTTON *Devereux* IV. i, No one had perceived their entrance or exit. **1849** JAMES *Woodman* xxxv, The man had just given admission or exit to some one. **1860** MAURY *Phys. Geog. Sea* viii. §393 There is sometimes, if not always, another exit of warm water from the Indian Ocean. **1884** BOWER & SCOTT *De Bary's Phaner. & Ferns* 271 A leaf-trace consisting of a single bundle, which does not divide into three bundles till its exit at the node into the leaf.

fig. **1791** PAINE *Rts. Man* (ed. 4) 72 This species of imaginary consequence..hastens to its exit. **1862** MERIVALE *Rom. Emp.* (1865) VI. l. 175 Life, she urged, is over; nought remains to look for but a decent exit from it. **1875** JOWETT *Plato* (ed. 2) IV. 76 Forgetfulness is the exit of memory.

b. *Cards* (esp. *Bridge*). A means of deliberately relinquishing the lead; also, the action of doing this. Freq. *attrib.*

1935 *Bridge Mag.* Oct. 231/1 Possibly the term 'exit play' is not the best name for the manœuvre of which I speak. It is called an end play, or an elimination, or a throw-in. **1959** *Listener* 24 Sept. 506/2 If South has a doubleton club he will have the safe exit which was denied him. **1960** T. REESE *Play Bridge with Reese* iii. 20, I have got to eliminate their cards of exit.

†**3.** The last portion or end of anything. *Obs.*

1627–77 FELTHAM *Resolves* I. xlviii. 76 The exit of the Verse will tell him. **1664** EVELYN *Sylva* (1776) 125 Towards the exit of January, or early in February.

4. A channel of egress; an outlet. Esp. a door affording exit from a public building. Also *attrib.*

1695 WOODWARD *Nat. Hist. Earth* III. i. §4 The rest [of the rain]..cannot make its Way to Wells, the perpendicular Fissures, or the like Exits. **1786** GILPIN *Observ. Mts. & Lakes* I. 165 At the conclusion of this..amphitheatre..we found an exit. **1881** JOWETT *Thucyd.* I. 66 An enclosure..which was surrounded by a great ditch and had no exit. **1881** D'OYLY CARTE in W. Hamilton *Aesthetic Movement* (1882) 39 There are exits and entrances on all four sides, giving two exits from every part of the house. **1890** A. LANSDOWNE *Life's Remin. Scotland Yard* xiii, To leave the Monument Station by the exit staircase. **1911** *Encycl. Brit.* XXV. 766/1 Exit doors must open outwards. **1939** JOYCE *Finnegans Wake* (1964) 127 Endurses his doom at chapel exit.

5. = L. *exitus terræ.*

[**1597** SKENE *De Verb. Sign.* s.v., *Exitus Terræ*, the rentes, fruites, and profites of the land.] **1866** ROGERS *Agric. & Prices* I. xxviii. 674 The exits of the manor are little more than a fourth of the amount recorded in 1332.

6. *attrib.* and *Comb.* *exit-pipe, speech*; **exit cue**, the cue for an actor to make his exit; **exit line**, the line spoken by an actor before making his exit; also *transf.*; **exit permit, visa**, a permit or visa authorizing a person to leave a particular country; **exit poll** *Pol.* (orig. *U.S.*), an unofficial poll in which people leaving a polling station are asked how they have voted, used in predicting the result of an election.

1860 G. VANDENHOFF *Dramatic Rem.* xiii. 200 If he perceived any eggs or harder missiles flying, not to wait, but to take the first shot for his *exit-cue*. **1919** A. PLATT *Pract. Hints Playwriting* viii. 108 An exit line should be so written that it can be spoken at the door. **1933** F. BALDWIN *Innocent Bystander* xvi. 306 That's always a good exit line. **1941** KOESTLER *Scum of Earth* 232 Both Breitscheid and Hilferding had *visas* for the United States, but their French exit permits had been refused. **1955** G. GREENE *Quiet American* I. i. 9 The police..could..refuse me an exit permit. **1852–9** TODD *Cycl. Anat.* IV. 464/1 Their usual exit-pipe is no longer open. **1980** *Washington Post* 2 Apr. A12 Exit polls showed Reagan picking up as many Democratic crossover votes as Anderson was. **1984** *Gainesville* (Florida) *Sun* 31 Mar. 5A/2 Time and resources are spent on 'exit polls' to predict results before voting has even ended. **1987** *Oxf. Diocesan Mag.* Aug. 10/1 The polls remained..stable (except for that curiously errant 'exit poll' put out by the BBC which accepted the possibility of a hung parliament). **1859** GEO. ELIOT *A. Bede* 7 With this exit speech..Wiry Ben shouldered his basket and left the workshop. **1949** H. READ *Gauguin 1848–1903* 3/1 A world where innocence and *naïveté* no longer exist, where currency restrictions and exit visas effectively deprive us of even Gauguin's illusion of liberty. **1968** *Listener* 23 May 657/1 An exit visa from Vietnam now costs a fortune in bribes.

exit ('ɛksɪt), *v.* [f. prec. sb.]

1. a. *intr.* To make one's exit, depart, disappear; *fig.* to decease, die.

1607 *Barley-Breake* (1877) 10 Much like vnto a Player on a stage..As one distract doth exit in a rage. *a* **1652** BROME *Love-sick Court* II. i, My souls better part exited, left The other languishing. **1806** SURR *Winter in Lond.* I. 201 [She would become] duchess of Delaware, if old Pomposo would exit. **1844** W. H. MAXWELL *Fort. O'Halloran* vii, She exited from the chamber. **1890** *Temple Bar* Aug. 579, I desire to exit with the fiddlers playing, the foot-lights ablaze, the house looking on.

b. *Cards* (esp. *Bridge*). To lose the lead deliberately; to use an exit (EXIT *sb.* 2 b).

1958 *Listener* 2 Oct. 541/2 East..exited with a further Club, defeating the contract. **1959** *Ibid.* 12 Nov. 850/2 South won with the King and exited with the three.

2. *trans.* To leave (a building, road, etc.); to get out of (a vehicle, etc.). Also *transf.* orig. *U.S.*

1976 N. THORNBURG *Cutter & Bone* v. 115 At the first Union 76 sign he saw, he exited the freeway. **1976** *National Observer* (U.S.) 29 May 10/2 Once having dispensed with her clothes at the pool at dawn, our titian-haired employee began exiting her clothes at later hours. **1979** *Vassar Q.* Summer 17/1 A policeman..relates that the 'alleged perpetrator exited the vehicle'. **1979** D. R. HOFSTADTER *Gödel, Escher, Bach* (1980) i. 37 Person A may think he understands the problem, and try to remedy it by exiting the present system. **1985** M. TRUMAN *Murder at FBI* xi. 80 The .22 shell never exited his body.

exitacion, -ation, obs. ff. EXCITATION.

exitat, var. form of EXCITATE *v.*, *Obs.*

exite ('ɛksaɪt). *Zool.* [f. Gr. ἔξω outside + -ITE[1] 3.] In Crustacea, a process on the outer side of the phyllopodium.

1881 [see ENDITE *sb.*]. **1893** A. E. SHIPLEY *Zool. Invert.* 260 The abdominal appendages [of *Astacus*]..present an unjointed axis which bears on its inner edge six processes termed endites, which bear numerous setae. The axis ends in a sub-apical lobe, and carries on its outer sides two exites. **1967** G. A. KERKUT *Borradaile & Potts's Invertebrata* (ed. 4) xi. 351 There is in this limb [*sc.* the phyllopodium] an axial portion or corm which bears..on the outer side one or more lobes known as exites.

exite, obs. form of EXCITE.

† **e'xitelite.** *Min. Obs.* [f. Gr. ἐξίτηλ-ος evanescent (f. ἐξιέναι, f. ἐξ out + ἰέναι to go) + -ITE.] A synonym of VALENTINITE.

1841 CHAPMAN *Min.* 39 *Exitelite*, Oxide of Antimony. **1868** DANA *Min.* 184.

† **e'xitiable**, *a.* *Obs. rare.* [ad. L. *exitiābilis* destructive, f. *exitium* a going out, destruction, f. *exīre*: see EXIT *sb.*] Destructive, ruinous.

1607 TOPSELL *Four-f. Beasts* (1673) 189 Their [goats'] teeth are exitiable to all tender plants. **1730–6** in BAILEY (folio).

exitial (ɛg'zɪʃəl), *a.* *Obs.* or *arch.* [ad. L. *exitiāl-is* destructive, f. *exitium*: see prec.] Hurtful; destructive to life, deadly, fatal.

c **1534** tr. *Pol. Verg. Eng. Hist.* (Camden) I. 123 These menn..had ynoughe to doe to..defer the exitiall fall of their contrie. *Ibid.* I. 177 The charge of regalitie..had benne hurtfull and exitiall to so manie his predecessors. **1607** TOPSELL *Serpents* (1653) 749 The biting of it is very exitial and deadly. **1633** T. ADAMS *Exp. 2 Peter* ii. 1 They [heresies]..are exitial and pestilent to the kingdoms..where they are admitted. **1699** EVELYN *Acetaria* (1729) 177 [Mushrooms are] malignant, exitial, mortal and deleterious. **1721–1800** in BAILEY. **1884** in *Syd. Soc. Lex.*

exition (ɛk'sɪʃən). ? *Obs.* [ad. L. *exitiōn-em*, n. of action f. *exīre*: see EXIT *sb.*] The action of going out or forth; departure, exit; also, place or point of exit.

1670 *Conclave wherein Clement VIII. was Elected Pope* 17 That..his exition might not be prevalent with any other, the door was presently shut. **1676** WORLIDGE *Cyder* (1691) 143 Which so condenseth its spirits, that they seek not any exition. **1816** KEATINGE *Trav.* II. 65 The building..has but one gate or outlet, where the search upon exition is as close as in the diamond-mines.

† **exiti'ose**, *a.* *Obs.*⁻⁰ = next.

1730–6 in BAILEY (folio). **1775** ASH [*mispr.*] Exitose.

† **e'xitious**, *a.* *Obs.* [ad. L. *exitiōs-us* destructive, f. *exitium*: see EXITIABLE.] = EXITIAL.

1563 *Homilies* II. *Idolatry* III. (1859) 242 Setting up of images in churches..proved not only harmful, but exitious and pestilent. **1651** BIGGS *New Disp.* ¶241 Exitious humours are forced out of the body. **1657** TOMLINSON *Renou's Disp.* 378 In Persia they found this tree [Peach] to be exitious. **1709** *Brit. Apollo* II. No. 74. 3/1 Blind to Events, however they might prove, Or Proditorious or Exitious. **1730–6** in BAILEY (folio). **1775** in ASH. **1884** in *Syd. Soc. Lex.*

† **'exiture.** *Obs.* In 5 exitour. [ad. med.L. *exitūr-a*, f. *exīre*: see EXIT *sb.* Cf. OF. *exiture.*]

1. Passage out or forth.

1578 BANISTER *Hist. Man* I. 13 Children..hauing in the vtmost part of the chinne a lineall ascense..for the exiture of Ligamentes. **1615** CROOKE *Body of Man* 154 The Sphincter..a round muscle..compassing about the end of the right gut to hinder the exiture of the excrements.

2. A running abscess. [So in OF.]

c **1400** *Lanfranc's Cirurg.* 52 (MS. A) His cure schal be seid in þe chapitle of apostymes & of exitours [*MS.* B exitures]. **1543** TRAHERON *Vigo's Chirurg.* II. xxi. 33 An exiture is everye kynde of an aposteme. **1657** TOMLINSON *Renou's Disp.* 722 It cures green wounds..and exitures. [**1811** HOOPER *Med. Dict.*, *Exitura*, a running abscess. **1860** MAYNE *Exp. Lex.*, *Exitura*. **1884** *Syd. Soc. Lex.*, *Exitura.*]

Hence † **exi'tural** *a.*, of or pertaining to an 'exiture' or abscess.

1758 J. S. *Le Dran's Observ. Surg.* (1771) 312 Accidents, that accompany exitural Tumours. *Ibid.* 321 A small exitural Tumour appeared in the Ham.

exitus ('ɛksɪtəs). [L. *exit-us* (*u* stem) a going out or forth, f. *exīre*: see EXIT *sb.*]

† **1.** A going out or forth; a departure, exodus (see also quot. 1706). *Obs.*

1664 H. MORE *Exp. 7 Epist.* 5 The Exitus of the Ephesine Church. **1677** HALE *Prim. Orig. Man.* II. vii. 178 The Period between the Flood and the Exitus of the People out of Egypt was about 800 Years. **1706** PHILLIPS (ed. Kersey), *Exitus*.. a going forth, the end of a Business, Death.

2. *Path.* (See quots. 1811 and 1884.)

1811 HOOPER *Med. Dict.*, *Exitus*, a prolapsus, or falling down of the womb or anus. **1884** *Syd. Soc. Lex.*, *Exitus*.. the termination of a disease, especially when well marked.

† **ex'legal**, *a.* *Obs. rare.* [f. L. *exlēg-em* lawless (f. *ex-* EX- *pref.*[1] + *lēg-em* law) + -AL[1].] Lawless.

1602 W. WATSON *Decacordon* 306 But the best..course to be taken..is by this exlegall legifers lawes set downe. *Ibid.* 300 The exlegall legifer Fa. Parsons.

exlex ('ɛkslɛks), *a.* Also ex-lex. [f. L. *ex* outside + *lex* law.] Beyond the law, outside the law. Also as *sb.*

1909 G. DRAGE *Austria-Hungary* 560 The *ex lex* years had shown that the relations between the two partners in the monarchy rested upon shifting sand. **1909** *Westm. Gaz.* 21 Aug. 4/3 The correct date for the beginning of *ex-lex* in Hungary. **1917** DENNEY *Chr. Doctr. Reconcil.* 7 The only alternative is to pronounce God *exlex*—without law—which is as good as to abandon thinking altogether.

‖ **ex-libris** (ɛks 'laɪbrɪs). Used also as *pl.* [f. L. *ex librīs*, lit. 'out of the books', *i.e.* 'from the library' (of the person whose name follows); mod. Lat. phrase often used in inscriptions indicating the ownership of books.]

An inscription, label, or stamp indicating the owner of a book; *esp.* a label or stamp of this kind artistically designed, bearing, *e.g.* the person's arms or crest, or some emblematic device; a book-plate or the like.

1880 WARREN *Book-plates* i. 1 In England we call such a ticket as this, William Downing's book-plate, as abroad it would be called his ex-libris. *Ibid.* xii. 124 In Germany, ex-libris have undoubtedly existed for more than three centuries and a half. **1884** *N. & Q.* 21 June 486/1 A curious ex-libris..stamped on the paper lining the cover of the book, front and back.

attrib. **1891** (*title*), The Journal of the Ex-Libris Society.

ex-librist (ɛks'laɪbrɪst). [f. EX-LIBR-IS + -IST.] One who collects specimens of 'ex-libris'.

1880 WARREN *Book-plates* i. 4 The ex-librist is but a humbler class of bibliophile. **1892** E. CASTLE *Eng. Book-Plates* 12 The ex-librist of advancing centuries. **1893** *Sat. Rev.* 11 Feb. 157/2 The modern American can be a very keen Ex librist.

So **ex-librism** (ɛks'laɪbrɪz(ə)m), the collecting and study of ex-libris.

1893 *Sat. Rev.* 11 Feb. 158/1 Among the public that is curious of ex-librism Mr. Hamilton is widely known.

† **exlineal**, *a.* *Obs. rare.* [f. EX- *pref.*[1] + L. *linea* LINE + -AL[1].] Out of the direct line of descent.

1716 M. DAVIES *Athen. Brit.* III. 40 Melampus and Chiron..seem to be of an exlineal Race and perchance of a mystical Offspring.

ex-meridian (ɛksmə'rɪdɪən), *a.* *Navigation.* [f. L. *ex* outside + MERIDIAN.] Of an observation of the sun or other heavenly body: not taken on the meridian, but sufficiently close to it to be reducible to a meridian altitude. Also, of, pertaining to, or calculated from such an observation.

1849 J. T. TOWSON *Tables Reduct. Ex-Meridian Altitudes* 3 Where cloudy weather prevails, the reduction of ex-meridian observations, for the determination of the latitude, is only second in importance to the observed meridian altitude. **1881** S. T. S. LECKY '*Wrinkles*' *in Pract. Navig.* iv. 147 If the sun's meridian altitude be about 80°, the time from noon of an Ex-meridian observation should be less than ten minutes. **1904** J. GILL *Text-bk. Navig.* (new ed.) xiv. 145 On account of the proximity of the Pole Star to the North Pole..it is..a very suitable object for determining latitude by ex-meridian method at any time when visible. **1953** C. H. COTTER *Elem. Navig.* xxxvi. 397 The ex-meridian tables in Norie seem to be the most popular with officers of the Merchant Navy. **1961** C. H. MCDOWELL *Dict. Math.* (new ed.) 48 *Ex-meridian altitude*, observations of the sun a few minutes before or after noon (when the sun is obscured at noon).

Exmoor ('ɛksmʊə(r), -mɔə(r)). The name of a district in Somerset and Devon used *attrib.* or *absol.* to designate the particular breeds of ponies and sheep which it produces.

1808 C. VANCOUVER *Gen. View Agric. Devon* 338 A cross was some years since made at Chittlehampton, of the old Leicester upon the Exmoor. *Ibid.* 345 A Dartmoor or Exmoor ewe..which in November would cost about 18s. will by the June following produce a lamb worth 20s. **1831**, **1902** [see DARTMOOR]. **1831** W. YOUATT *Horse* iv. 58 The Exmoor Ponies, although generally ugly enough, are hardy and useful. **1837** —— *Sheep* vii. 255 The sheep..bore considerable resemblance to the Exmoor sheep, and to the Dorsets. **1862** *Chambers's Encycl.* IV. 195/1 Throughout this tract there is a native breed of ponies, known as Exmoor ponies. **1902** *Encycl. Brit.* XXV. 194/2 The Exmoors are delicately formed about the head and neck, and they have a close, fine fleece of short wool. **1937** HULL & WHITLOCK *Far-Distant Oxus* i. 24 A dark-brown Exmoor with a trailing tail and a shaggy mane. **1960** *Farmer & Stockbreeder* 8 Mar. 15/1 *Sheep*... Hill types include..Rough Fell,..Welsh Mountain and Exmoor Horn. **1969** *Times* 13 Jan. 11/3 A Suffolk..ewe would not be regarded as outstanding unless she produced four lambs at a time, but three would be remarkable for an Exmoor Horn.

‖**ex nihilo** (ɛks ˈnaɪhɪləʊ), *phr.* [L. *ex* out of + *nihilō*, ablative of *nihil* nothing.] Out of nothing.

1573–80 G. HARVEY *Letter-Bk.* (1884) 132 And then, in a fantasticall fitt, I cried owte, Ex nihilo nihil fitt. **1656** T. RECK *Annotations upon Relig. Med.* in T. Browne *Relig. Med.* (ed. 4) 209 They had defined creation to be the production of a thing *ex nihilo*. **1681** T. GOODWIN *Wks.* I. I. xxvi. 341 The work of Grace is a work of *Creation*; and why a Creation? Because 'tis *ex nihilo*. **1855** *Punch* 17 Feb. 69/2 (*heading*) Ex Nihilo nihil fit—or unfit. **1920** M. BEER *Hist. Brit. Socialism* II. IV. xiv. 277 No man creates *ex nihilo*, but out of the materials supplied to him by his predecessors, his contemporaries, and his own experience. **1963** AUDEN *Dyer's Hand* I. 23 Even the language of *Finnegans Wake* was not created by Joyce *ex nihilo*. **1965** J. D. NORTH *Meas. of Universe* xviii. 399 The difficulty of accepting the idea of a creation *ex nihilo* was the source of much medieval casuistry.

exo- (ˈɛksəʊ; before two unstressed syllables ɛkˈsɒ), *prefix*[1] (before a vowel sometimes reduced to *ex-*), repr. Gr. ἔξω, without, in many compounds of modern formation, as **ˌexarteˈritis, ˌexo-arteˈritis** [see ARTERITIS], *Path.*, inflammation of the outer coat of an artery; **exoatmosˈpheric** *a.*, occurring or working outside the atmosphere; **exobiˈology** (see quot. 1960); hence **exobiˈologist**; **exoˈcannibalism**, the custom of eating the flesh of persons belonging to another tribe; exophagy; **exoˈcardial** *a. Phys.* [cf. CARDIAL], pertaining to the exterior of the heart; **ˈexocarp** [Gr. καρπ-ός fruit], (in fruits) the outermost layer of the pericarp; = EPICARP; **exoˈcellular** *a.*, outside the cell; **exoˈchorion**, *Anat.* [see CHORION], the outer layer of the chorion or membrane that encloses the fœtus; **exoˈcœlar** *a.* [CŒL-OM + -AR], pertaining to the outer side of the cœlom or body-cavity; **exocœle** (ˈɛksəʊsiːl) *Zool.*, the space which lies between different pairs of mesenteries of a zoantharian polyp; also **exocœl**; so **exoˈcœlic** *a.*; **exoˈclinal** *a. Geol.*, characteristic of or pertaining to an exocline; **ˈexocline**, an inverted fan-fold (see quot.); **exoˈcyclic** *adj.*, (*a*) *Zool.*, of an irregular sea-urchin, having the anus displaced from the apical position in which it is found in the regular forms; (*b*) *Chem.*, situated outside the ring; **exocyˈtosis** *Biol.*, the expulsion of matter by a living cell; **ˈexoderm** [Gr. δέρμα skin], the outer layer of the blastoderm; = ECTODERM; also, the external crust of the body of an insect; **exo-erythroˈcytic** *a.*, existing outside the red blood-corpuscles; **ˌexogaˈstritis**, *Path.* [see GASTRITIS], inflammation of the outer coat of the stomach; **eˈxogynous** *a.* [Gr. γυνή woman + -OUS], having the style projecting prominently out of the flower; **exoˈmorphic** *a. Geol.*, designating contact metamorphic changes in the surrounding rocks by the intrusion of igneous matter; so **exoˈmorphism**, the process of causing or undergoing exomorphic changes; **exoˈnarthex** [see NARTHEX], the outer vestibule of a Greek church (cf. ESONARTHEX); **exoˈneural** *a.* [see NEURAL], operating outside the nerves; hence **exoˈneurally** *adv.*; **exoˈnormative** *a. Linguistics*, of language standardization: drawing on foreign models of usage as a basis for the standard language; contr. with *endonormative* s.v. ENDO-; **exoˈpathic** *a.* [Gr. πάθ-ος suffering + -IC], (of disease) originating outside the body (cf. AUTOPATHIC); **exoˈpeptidase** *Biochem.*, any of a group of proteolytic enzymes which split terminal peptide bonds only; **eˈxophagous** *a.* [Gr. φαγ-εῖν to eat + -OUS], (see quot.); **eˈxophagy** [as prec. + -Y], the habit of being exophagous; **exoˈphoria** *Med.*, a tendency of the visual axes to diverge laterally from parallelism; latent divergent squint; hence **exoˈphoric** *a.* and *sb.*; **exoˈphyllous** *a.* [Gr. φύλλ-ον leaf + -OUS], (see quot.); **ˈexoplasm** [Gr. πλάσμα something moulded or formed], the outermost layer of the cuticular protoplasm of some Protozoa (cf. ECTOPLASM, ENDOPLASM, s.v. ECTO-, ENDO-); **exopod** (ˈɛksəʊpɒd) *Zool.*, = exopodite; **eˈxopodite** [Gr. ποδ- πούς foot + -ITE], 'the outermost of the two processes appended to the basal process of the hinder limbs of some of the Crustacea' (*Syd. Soc. Lex.*); hence **exopoˈditic** *a.*; **eˈxoptile** *a. Bot.* [Gr. πτίλον feather], having a naked plumule; **exoˈr(h)eic** *a. Geogr.*, characterized by exoreism; **exoˈr(h)eism** *Geogr.* [ad. F. *exorrhéisme*, 'ou, si l'on admet une orthographe simplifiée', *exoréisme* (E. de Martonne 1926, in *Compt. Rend.* CLXXXII. 1396)], land drainage reaching the sea; **exoˈ(r)rhizal** *a. Bot.* [Gr. ῥίζ-α root + -AL[1]], (of plants) having the radicle naked, *i.e.* not enclosed in a sheath; also **exoˈrrhizous** *a.*; **exoˈscopic** *a.* [Gr. -σκοπ-ος watching], viewing from the outside; having regard to external appearances or relations; hence **exoˈscopically** *adv.*; **exoˈseptum** *Zool.*, each of the calcareous septa appearing in the exocœle of a coral polyp; **exoˈskeletal** *a. Anat.*, of or pertaining to the **exoˈskeleton**, the external integument, whether bony or calcified, as in some animals, or leathery as in others; also *fig.*; **exosoˈmatic** *a. Biol.*, designating or pertaining to a device that an animal uses which is not one of its own organs; **ˈexosperm**, *Bot.* [Gr. σπέρμα seed]; **ˈexosphere**, the layer of the atmosphere farthest from the earth; hence **exoˈspheric** *a.*; **ˈexospore**, *Bot.* [see SPORE], the outer coat of a spore or oosphere in fungi or lichens; hence **exoˈsporal** *a.*, pertaining to an exospore; **exoˈsporous** *a.*, a term applied to fungi whose spores are on the outer surface of the sporangium; **ˈexostome**, *Bot.* [Gr. στόμα mouth], the aperture in the outer integument of the ovule; **exoˈtentacle** *Zool.*, a tentacle arising from an exocœle in certain polyps; **exoˈtheca**, *Zool.* [Gr. θήκη case], the hard exterior wall of the gonosome of the Hydrozoa; hence **exoˈthecal** *a.*, pertaining to the exotheca; **exoˈthecium**, *Bot.* [mod.Lat., f. Gr. θήκ-η case], 'the cuticular or outer layer of the anther' (*Syd. Soc. Lex.*); **exoˈtoxin**, a toxin liberated by a living bacterium or other micro-organism into the medium in which it grows; **exoˈtropia**, divergent strabismus; hence **exoˈtropic** *a.*; **eˈxotropism** (see quot.).

1966 *Economist* 5 Mar. 898/1 A 'new, long-range *exoatmospheric interceptor' to which the short-range Sprint missile would be a supplement. **1967** *Listener* 9 Feb. 185/2 The resulting pulse of radiation should make almost everything in range boil; this would happen beyond the atmosphere and the principle is called exoatmospheric interception. **1964** *New Scientist* 26 Nov. 573/2 One of the greatest difficulties the *exobiologists are up against is that of making sure that their equipment does not carry any extraneous terrestrial bacteria. **1969** *New Yorker* 12 Apr. 85/1 Exobiologists will be looking for traces of life on the moon. **1960** *Daily Tel.* 14 Jan. 11/1 Dr. Lederberg is building up a team for work on *exobiology, as this branch of the study of life on other planets is called. **1960** *Space Research* I. 1153 The problems of exobiology have important applications for the development of theoretical biology and the understanding of the mechanism of the evolution of life. **1969** *Times* 11 Jan. 15/6 The novel feature of the research carried out by staff of the exobiology division of the Nasa Ames Research Centre in California is that the amino-acids discovered in these ancient rocks have the asymmetry characteristic of living things. **1900** tr. *Deniker's Races of Man* 148 '*Exocannibalism', that is to say the habit of eating the flesh of strangers. **1866** A. FLINT *Prince. Med.* (1880) 315 The sign is called..sometimes, in contradistinction from the murmur produced by blood-currents within the heart, an *exocardial murmur. **1845** GRAY *Bot. Text-bk.* I. x. 252 **Exocarp*. **1870** HOOKER *Stud. Flora* 326 Euphorbia..valves with a coriaceous exocarp. **1946** *Nature* 23 Nov. 745/1 The *exocellular enzymes previously elaborated by the growing myxococci. **1857** BULLOCK *Cazeaux' Midwif.* 195 The external..also called the *exochorion, is wholly destitute of vessels. **1901** *Exoclinal [see *endoclinal* s.v. ENDO-]. **1889** *Exocline [see *endocline* s.v. ENDO-]. **1940** L. H. HYMAN *Invertebrates* I. vii. 568 In the case of paired septa, the space between the members is named endocoel, between pairs, *exocoel. **1967** P. A. MEGLITSCH *Invertebrate Zool.* vi. 159 (*caption*) The retractor muscles face the exocoel in directive septa. **1879** tr. *Haeckel's Evol. Man* I. ix. 271 The *exocœlar, that is, the outer, or parietal cœlom—epithelium. **1885, 1963** *Exocœle [see *entocœle* s.v. ENTO-]. **1902** *Exocœlic [see *entocœlic* s.v. ENTO-]. **1888** ROLLESTON & JACKSON *Forms Anim. Life* 562 Anus *exocyclic. **1913** J. B. COHEN *Org. Chem. Adv. Stud.* II. iv. 298 Dispersivity..is increased by the double bond in the side-chain (exocyclic) as compared with that in the nucleus (endocyclic). **1965** PHILLIPS & WILLIAMS *Inorg. Chem.* I. xvi. 594 The exocyclic atoms are markedly electronegative. **1966** *Treat. Invertebrate Palaeontol.* (Amer. Geol. Soc.) U.I.U 289/2 This exocyclic tendency was not very successful in the Diademataces. **1963** C. DE DUVE in De Rueck & Cameron *CIBA Symp. Lysosomes* 126 The process sometimes referred to as reverse pinocytosis and believed to be involved in secretory mechanisms could be called **exocytosis*. **1970** *Nature* 8 Aug. 620/2 He proposed that chromaffin cells released their contents after attaching to the cell membrane, through 'exocytosis'. **1879** tr. *Haeckel's Evol. Man* I. viii. 197 The protoplasm of the *exoderm cells. **1884** *Syd. Soc. Lex.*, Exoderm. **1946** *Nature* 16 Nov. 707/2 Therapeutic potency is..apparent not only against the erythrocytic but also against the *exo-erythrocytic forms of the malaria parasite. **1968** J. H. BURN *Lect. Notes Pharmacol.* (ed. 9) 115 The exo-erythrocytic parasites are very important in the chemotherapy of malaria because they are much more resistant to treatment than the red cell forms. **1888** F. H. HATCH in J. J. H. Teall *Brit. Petrogr.* 430 **Exomorphic*, applied by Fournet to contact-metamorphism when produced in the rock through which the molten mass is erupted. Used in contradistinction to endomorphic. Syn. Exogenous. **1903** *Amer. Jrnl. Sci.* CLXV. 280 The density increment due to exomorphic changes. **1931** F. H. LAHEE *Field Geol.* (ed. 3) vi. 133 The contact metamorphic zone (exomorphic zone)..varies in thickness from a fraction of an inch to many hundred yards. **1909** *Cent. Dict.* Suppl., **Exomorphism*, that variety of contact-metamorphism which is developed, in the surrounding walls, by an intruded mass of eruptive rock. **1966** *McGraw-Hill Encycl. Sci. & Technol.* X. 84/1 The crystallization of the larger intrusives may result in profound alterations in the adjacent wall rocks (exomorphism). **1850** NEALE *Hist. East. Ch.* I. 245 The esonarthex opens on to the church by nine doors, to the *exonarthex by five. **1851** H. MAYO *Pop. Superst.* (ed. 2) 73 To denote mental phenomena of the kind I am supposing, I propose the term *exoneural (ἔξω νεῦρον). **1881** W. F. BARRETT in *Nature* XXIV. 212 There seemed to be a veritable exoneural action of the mind. **1968, 1980** *Exonormative [see *endonormative* s.v. ENDO-]. **1984** *English World-Wide* V. I. 145 The well-known problem of stylistic invariability in EFL speakers may well be aggravated in ESL countries such as Singapore..where exonormative standards may well be supplied from different sources. **1881** J. SIMON *ibid.* 372 We see the various causes of death as under two great heads, respectively autopathic and *exopathic. **1936** *Exopeptidase [see *endopeptidase* s.v. ENDO-]. **1962** A. SPECTOR in A. Pirie *Lens Metabolism Rel. Cataract* 334 In neither investigation were sufficient substrates studied to indicate that the activity..was associated with a true exopeptidase. **1883** *Pall Mall G.* 30 Nov. 5/1 The Indians are '*exophagous', that is, do not eat members of their own tribe. **1886** G. T. STEVENS in *N.Y. Med. Jrnl.* 4 Dec. 626/2 The different relations of the visual lines..may be defined and arranged as follows..I. *Generic Terms.—Orthophoria*: A tending of the visual lines in parallelism. *Heterophoria*: A tending of these lines in some other way. II. *Specific Terms.*—Heterophoria may be divided into: 1. *Esophoria*: A tending of the visual lines inward. 2. **Exophoria*: A tending of the lines outward. 3. *Hyperphoria*: A tending of the right or left visual line in a direction above its fellow. **1964** Exophoria [see ESOPHORIA]. **1906** *Jrnl. Amer. Med. Assoc.* 1 Sept. 674/1 Practically two-thirds of the whole number of *exophorics were what might be called near workers. **1909** *Cent. Dict.* Suppl., Exophoric, adj. **1962** H. C. WESTON *Sight, Light & Work* (ed. 2) ii. 41 People who are exophoric for distance are usually progressively more so as the point of fixation approaches the eyes. **1839** LINDLEY *Introd. Bot.* I. ii. 252 *Exophyllous; because the young leaves of..dicotyledons are always naked. **1888** *Athenæum* 4 Feb. 151/1 The granulated structure of its *exoplasm..was described. **1893, 1959** *Exopod [see *endopod* s.v. ENDO-]. **1927** *Geogr. Rev.* XVII. 399 The boundary between the endoreic and the exoreic regions can be drawn without hesitation. **1870** ROLLESTON *Anim. Life* 92 The anterior extremities of the palpiform *exopodites. **1877** HUXLEY *Anat. Inv. Anim.* vi. 281 The exopodite, metamorphosed into another such bowl shuts down over the endopodite. **1957** G. E. HUTCHINSON *Treat. Limnol.* I. iv. 226 The *exorheic regions contain the main lake districts of the world. **1927** *Exorheism [see *endoreism* s.v. ENDO-]. **1963** D. W. & E. E. HUMPHRIES tr. *Termier's Erosion & Sedimentation* 404 *Exorheism*, drainage towards the oceans surrounding a land mass. **1870** BENTLEY *Bot.* 120 Such a mode of root-development has been called *exorhizal. **1884** *Syd. Soc. Lex.*, *Exorrhizous. **1816** BENTHAM *Chrestom.* Wks. 1843 VIII. 94 Division of Politics and Government into Esoscopic..and *Exoscopic, i.e. external-concerns-regarding, viz. International Government and Politics. **1853** SYLVESTER in *Phil. Trans.* CXLIII. I. 409 The method becoming as it may be said endoscopic instead of being exoscopic as in the first section. *Ibid.*, The subject is treated..*exoscopically in the first and last sections. **1885, 1903** *Exoseptum [see *entoseptum* s.v. ENTO-]. **1904** *Biol. Bulletin* July 82 The dorsal and middle pairs of exosepta arose bilaterally in advance of the two ventral pairs. **1870** ROLLESTON *Anim. Life* Introd. 57 *Exoskeletal ossifications. **1877** HUXLEY *Anat. Inv. Anim.* i. 55 From the epidermis, all cuticular and cellular exoskeletal parts..are developed. **1847** TODD *Cycl. Anat.* III. 846/2 *Exoskeleton. **1864** H. SPENCER *Illustr. Univ. Progr.* 409 In the highest Annulosa, the exo-skeleton and the muscular system, never lose all traces of their segmentation. **1872** NICHOLSON *Palæont.* 187 The Mollusca..commonly possessing an exoskeleton or shell. **1888** J. JACOBS *Bidpai* lii, These are the facts that form the exoskeleton of his life. **1945** A. J. LOTKA in *Human Biol.* Sept. 188 In place of slow adaptation of anatomical structure and physiological function in successive generations by selective survival, increased adaptation has been achieved by the incomparably more rapid development of 'artificial' aids to our native receptor-effector apparatus, in a process that might be termed **exosomatic* evolution. **1951** *New Biol.* XI. 21 Exosomatic adaptations. *Ibid.*, Most exosomatic organs are instruments or tools..like spectacles, radio sets,.. hammers, scalpels, motor cars and guns. **1951** *Jrnl. Brit. Interplan. Soc.* X. 18 The atmosphere can conveniently be divided into four parts, the troposphere, the stratosphere, the ionosphere and the *exosphere. **1955** E. BURGESS *Frontier to Space* 150 The density and extent of the exosphere. **1969** *Sci. Jrnl.* May 67/1 The lunar atmosphere is a true exosphere in direct communication with space, to which its molecules can escape freely unless inhibited by gravity. **1951** *Jrnl. Brit. Interplan. Soc.* X. 18 The exospheric gases. **1859** TODD *Cycl. Anat.* V. 246/2 The *exosporal membrane dehisces in three valves. *Ibid.* V. 246/1 The sporangium..burst by the swelling of the *exospore. **1882** VINES *Sachs' Bot.* 325 The exospore is usually smooth and often variously coloured. **1884** *Syd. Soc. Lex.*, *Exosporous. **1845** GRAY *Bot. Text-bk.* I. ix. 241 The orifice of the primine is called the *Exostome, that of the secundine of the inner Endostome; literally the outer and the inner orifice. **1870** HOOKER *Stud. Flora* 81 The arillus being produced from the exostome. **1904** *Biol. Bulletin* July 88 The *exotentacles in *Siderastrea radians* have been found to appear throughout in advance of the entotentacles. **1877** NICHOLSON in *Encycl. Brit.* VI. 374 They [the costæ of the coral]..may be united by transverse plates ('*exothecal dissepiments') which run horizontally across the intercostal spaces. **1870** BENTLEY *Bot.* 239 An outer which..is called the *exothecium. **1920** H. ZINSSER in *Jrnl. Immunology* V. 286 There was much unclearness..regarding the so-called *exotoxins of bacteria. **1964** M. HYNES *Med. Bacteriol.* (ed. 8) vi. 67 The reaction between endotoxins and their antibodies does not follow the law of multiple proportions which is so characteristic of exotoxin-antitoxin reactions. **1897** G. T. STEVENS in Norris & Oliver *Syst. Dis. Eye* II. viii. 172 The class Heterotropia..may be divided into two sub-classes... The specific divisions of the sub-class *a* are—1. Esotropia, a deviation of the visual lines inward. 2. *Exotropia, a deviation of the visual lines outward. 3. Hypertropia (right or left), a deviation of one visual line above the other. 4. Hyperesotropia and Hyperexotropia are the compound deviations. **1961** *Lancet* 7 Oct. 812/1 Increase of the interpupillary distance with exotropia. **1906** G. T. STEVENS *Motor Apparatus of Eyes* III. xlviii. 384

*Exotropic persons are, much more than esophoric subjects, accustomed to close one eye when reading or working. **1898** H. C. PORTER tr. *Strasburger's Text-bk. Bot.* 258 A torsion must..occur when a geotropic organ, which has become curved over toward its parent axis, turns itself about so as to face outwards (*exotropism).

exoccipital (ɛksɒk'sɪpɪtəl), *a.* and *sb.* [f. Gr. ἔξω (see EXO-) + L. *occipit-, occiput* the back of the head + -AL¹.]

A. *adj.* That is outside the occipital bone.

1847 TODD *Cycl. Anat.* III. 308/1 The groove between the occipital condyle and the exoccipital process. **1869** *Proc. Amer. Phil. Soc.* XI. 577 The great extent of the exoccipital element.

B. *sb. pl.* Those parts of the occipital bone which form the sides of the foramen magnum and support the condyles. Cf. CONDYLE 2.

1854 OWEN in *Circ. Sc.* (c. 1865) II. 59/1 The exoccipitals ..are very irregular subtrianglar bones. **1855** —— *Skel. & Teeth* 26 The two condyles being developed from the two exoccipitals. **1881** MIVART *Cat* 61 Each ex-occipital supports one of the condyles before noticed.

exocentric (ɛksəʊ'sɛntrɪk), *a. Linguistics.* [f. EXO- + CENTRIC *a.*] Of compounds or constructions: having a different grammatical function from that of the constituent parts (see quots.). Opp. ENDOCENTRIC *a.*

1914 BLOOMFIELD *Introd. Study. Lang.* v. 161 The so-called 'exocentric' compounds..denote an object *having* the thing named in the compound, as *long-nose, short-horn, swallow-tail.* **1933** —— *Lang.* xii. 194 *John ran* is neither a nominative expression (like *John*) nor a finite verb expression (like *ran*). Therefore we say that the English actor-action construction is exocentric: the resultant phrase belongs to the form-class of no immediate constituent. **1968** J. LYONS *Introd. Theoret. Ling.* vi. 232 *In Vancouver* is exocentric, since its distribution is different from that of either the preposition *in* or the noun *Vancouver.*

Exocet ('ɛksəsɛt). *Mil.* [a. F. *exocet* flying fish, ad. L. *exōcœt-us*, ad. Gr. ἐξώκοιτος sleeping out, a fish that comes up on to the beach, f. ἔξω (see EXO-) + κοῖτος bed.] A proprietary name for a kind of rocket-propelled short-range guided missile used esp. in tactical sea warfare. Freq. *attrib.* in ***Exocet missile.***

1970 *Trade Marks Jrnl.* 25 Nov. 1990/1 *Exocet*... Surface-to-surface, sea-to-sea, or submarine-to-surface self guided rocket-propelled missiles; rocket launching apparatus for use therewith. Société Nationale Industrielle Aerospatiale.., France. **1972** *Official Gaz.* (U.S. Patent Office) 14 Nov. TM85/1 Societe Nationale Industrielle Aerospatiale,..France... *Exocet*... For surface-surface, sea-sea, or submarine-surface missiles with autonomous fore and self-guiding systems and launching equipment. **1976** *Facts on File Yearbk.* XXXVI. 714/1 French MM38 Exocet missiles, which had a 25-mile range at near supersonic speed. **1979** *Jrnl. R. Soc. Arts* CXXVII. 566/1 To sink the enemy's ships we must now rely on..ships equipped with Exocet, a weapon which we bought off the shelf from the French. **1982** *Daily Tel.* 26 Nov. 5/1 Britain's forces in the South Atlantic take into account the presence in Argentina of Exocet-carrying Super Etendards. **1983** *Ann. Reg. 1982* 13 On 4 May HMS *Sheffield*, a type 42 destroyer, was sunk by a French-made Exocet air-to-sea missile.

exocrine ('ɛksəʊkraɪn, -ɪn), *a. Physiol.* [f. Gr. ἔξω outside + κρίνειν to separate, cf. ENDOCRINE *a.* and *sb.*] Having external secretion; designating or pertaining to the discharge of a secretion through a duct or the secretion itself.

Quot. 1911 is an erroneous definition.

1911 STEDMAN *Med. Dict.* 296/2 *Exocrin*, external secretion of a gland. **1937** *Ann. Internal Med.* X. 1848 (*heading*) The exocrine functions of the pancreas. **1946** *Nature* 21 Sept. 419/1 Spaces..permit the passage of small quantities of the exocrine secretion of the gland into contact with special thin-walled capillaries. **1964** A. R. MUIR in G. H. Haggis *Introd. Molecular Biol.* v. 138 The exocrine cells of the guinea-pig pancreas fulfil these criteria, for they commence secretion if a meal follows a period of starvation. **1967** *New Scientist* 2 Nov. 295/1 The exocrine pancreas cell, which secretes an enzyme that digests protein. **1970** T. S. & C. R. LEESON *Histol.* (ed. 2) v. 87/1 A gland of the exocrine type passes its secretion to a duct system and thus to a body surface.

exoctohedron: see HEXOCTAHEDRON.

exoculation (ɛksɒkjuː'leɪʃən). [as if ad. L. **exoculātiōn-em*, n. of action f. *exoculāre* to put out the eyes, f. *ex-* out + *oculus* eye.] The action of putting out the eyes, *e.g.* in execution of a judicial sentence; blinding.

1630 *R. Johnson's Kingd. & Commw.* 13 From these Nations..have tortures..taken their originals: as exoculations..and impalements on stakes. **1814** SOUTHEY *Roderick* II. *note*, The history of Europe during the dark ages abounds with examples of exoculation.

exocuticle ('ɛksəʊkjuːtɪk(ə)l). Also exocu'ticula. [f. EXO- + CUTICLE.] The middle layer of a cuticle. **a.** The hard, chitinous outer part of the procuticle of an insect or other arthropod.

1929 [see ENDOCUTICLE a]. **1951** A. G. RICHARDS *Integument of Arthropods* xvi. 149 In calcified cuticles, at least of decapod crustacea, the exocuticle and outer portion of the endocuticle become calcified. **1967** P. A. MEGLITSCH *Invert. Zool.* xvi. 676 Beneath it [*sc.* the epicuticle] is the procuticle, made up of two layers, an outer exocuticle, often pigmented and impregnated with the substances found in the epicuticle, and an inner endocuticle. It is the exocuticle that is thickened to form the skeletal plates or sclerites.

b. The middle part of the cuticle that surrounds animal fibres or hairs, etc.

1949 [see EPICUTICLE b]. **1962** W. J. ONIONS *Wool* ii. 16 The exocuticle, which constitutes about half of the scale, is a protein resistant to digestion by trypsin.

exode ('ɛksəʊd), *sb.*¹ Also 9 exod. [anglicized form of EXODUS. Cf. Fr. *exode.*]

†**1.** The Book of Exodus; = EXODUS 1. *Obs.*

a **1225** *Ancr. R.* 196, I þisse wildernesse wende ure Louerdes folc, ase Exode telleð.

2. = EXODUS 2 a. Somewhat *rare.*

a **1751** BOLINGBROKE *Minutes Ess.* Wks. 1754 V. 141 They [the Israelites] could bring, at the time of the Exode, six hundred thousand fighting men into the field. **1826** G. HIGGINS *Horæ Sabbat.* (1833) 41 The Sabbath was first.. instituted, on their exod from Egypt. **1853** G. S. FABER *Downf. of Turkey* 47 The circumstances of the exode.

3. *transf.* = EXODUS 2 c.

1882 T. M. POST in *Chicago Advance* 22 June, The Exode [of colored people from the South about 1880].

exode ('ɛksəʊd), *sb.*² [a. Fr. *exode*, ad. late L. *exodium*: see EXODIUM.] **a.** in the Gr. drama = EXODIUM 1; hence *gen.* the ending, catastrophe of a play; **b.** in the Roman drama = EXODIUM 2.

a **1684** EARL ROSCOM. *Wks.* (1753) 176 The Romans had.. three plays acted, one after another, on the same subject; the first a real Tragedy; the second the Attellane; the third a Satyr or Exode, a kind of Farce of one act. **1759** W. MASON *Caractacus* Argt. in *Poems* (1805), The Exode, or Catastrophe, is prepared by the coming of Arviragus the King's son. **1833** *Blackw. Mag.* XXXIV. 721 Hindu writers are in general successful in maintaining the character of their exode.

exoderm: see EXO- *pref.*

†**e'xodiary.** *Obs.* [ad. L. *exodiāri-us*, f. *exodium*: see EXODIUM.] A player in the exodium.

1793 J. WILLIAMS *Calm Exam.* 100 Britons will admit of no Exodiary, like the Romans, to divert them with unappropriate merriment, when the business of the Tragedy has ceased.

exodic (ɛk'sɒdɪk), *a.* [f. Gr. ἔξοδ-ος way out, issue, EXODUS + -IC.]

1. Of or pertaining to an exodus.

In some mod. Dicts.

2. *Phys.* 'Proceeding out of or from the spinal marrow' (*Syd. Soc. Lex.*).

1850 [see ESODIC].

exodist ('ɛksədɪst). *rare.* [f. EXODE *sb.* + -IST.]

1. One who makes an exodus. In quot. applied to the Israelites.

1883 R. F. BURTON in *Academy* 5 May 311/2 The Exodists would naturally travel by the present Háj highway from Suez to El-'Akabah.

2. One who departs or goes out from one place to settle in another; an emigrant.

1849 LOWELL *Biglow P.* Wks. (1879) 179 Want was the prime foe these hardy exodists had to fortress themselves against.

‖**e'xodium.** Also 6 *pl.* exodia. [a. L. *exodium*, ad. Gr. ἐξόδιον, f. ἐξόδιος of or belonging to an exit, f. ἔξοδος: see EXODUS.]

1. *Gr. Drama.* The concluding part of a play; the catastrophe.

1842 in BRANDE. In mod. Dicts.

2. *Rom. Drama.* A comic interlude originally attached to the Atellanæ, but afterwards given as a separate performance after tragedies.

1600 HOLLAND *Livy* 251 Merrie scoffes and jestes..which thereupon were afterwards called Exodia, and were inserted commonly in the Atellane Comedies. **1751** CHAMBERS *Cycl.* s.v., Among the Romans, the exodium..was pretty nearly what farces are with us.

exodontia (ɛksəʊ'dɒnʃɪə). [mod.L., f. EX-¹ + Gr. ὀδούς, ὀδοντ- tooth.] The extraction of teeth. Hence **exo'dontist**, a specialist in exodontia.

1913 G. B. WINTER (*title*) Exodontia; a practical treatise on the technic of extraction of teeth. *Ibid.* iv. 69 Dental anatomy, from the standpoint of the exodontist, should be studied in the light of mechanics. **1927** M. H. FELDMAN *Man. Exodontia* i. 17 The development of skill in inducing anesthesia..has made it possible to perform the ofttimes intricate phases of exodontia in such a manner as to grant the patient..freedom from the sensation of pain. **1936** DUNNING & DAVENPORT *Dict. Dental Sci. & Art* 203/1 Exodontist. **1960** *Times* 30 Mar. 3/5 (Advt.), Oral surgery including exodontia.

Exodus ('ɛksədəs). [a. L. *exodus*, a. Gr. ἔξοδος going out, f. ἐξ out + ὁδός way.]

1. The title of the book of the Old Testament which relates the departure of the Israelites out of Egypt.

(In 14–16th c. sometimes 'Book of Exodi', retaining the Lat. genitive.)

c **1000** *Ælfric On O.T.* (Sweet) 63 Seo oðer boc is Exodus ȝehaten. **1388** WYCLIF *Ex.* Prol., This book of Exodi, that is to seie, of going out, makith mencioun, that, etc. **1549** COVERDALE *Erasm. Par. Rom.* ix. 15 That, whiche in the boke of Exodi is by God spoken, I wyl shewe mercy, to whom soeuer I shewe mercy. **1579** FULKE *Heskins' Parl.* 8 In Exodus and Leuiticus..are many thinges..very easie and plaine. **1611** BIBLE (*heading*), The Second Booke of Moses, called Exodus. [So **1885** —— (Revised).]

2. A going out or forth.

a. *spec.* The departure of the Israelites from Egypt.

a **1646** J. GREGORY *Posthuma* (1649) 107 The Men of Hamel date all their publick Matters especially, from this Exodus, or going forth of the Children. **1740** WARBURTON *Div. Legat.* IV. §6 (1755) IV. 85 The two generations, between the exodus from Egypt and the entrance into Canaan. **1882** FARRAR *Early Chr.* I. 460 *note*, Pharaoh consented to the Exodus, but it was only in wrath and fear.

b. *gen.* (more or less consciously *transf.* from 2 a). *lit.* and *fig.*

1623–6 COCKERAM, *Exodus*, a going out. **1721–1800** in BAILEY. **1830** GALT *Laurie T.* III. i. (1849) 81 Our Exodus from New York..commenced under the happiest auspices. **1847** LYTTON *Lucretia* (1853) 228 To trace that son's exodus from the paternal mansion. **1858** MAURY *Phys. Geog. Sea* vi. §306 The air..at its exodus, is dry. **1862** R. VAUGHAN *Nonconformity* 383 The exodus from the established church which dates from the 17th August, 1662. **1881** MAHAFFY *Old Grk. Educ.* xi. 140 A formal exodus of philosophic students, who only returned with Theophrastus.

c. *esp.* The departure or going out, usually of a body of persons from a country for the purpose of settling elsewhere. Also *fig.* Cf. EMIGRATION 2.

1831 CARLYLE *Sart. Res.* (1858) 49 This Genesis of his can properly be nothing but an Exodus (or transit out of Invisibility into Visibility). **1856** EMERSON *Eng. Traits, Wealth* Wks. (Bohn) II. 75 The poor-rate was..forcing an exodus of farmers and mechanics. **1862** T. C. GRATTAN *Beaten Paths* I. 132 The rushing exodus, as it was the fashion to call this continuous transatlantic movement. **1879** FROUDE *Cæsar* xiv. 202 A complete exodus of the entire tribe.

Exody ('ɛksədɪ). *rare.* [ad. Gr. ἐξοδία going out, f. ἐξ out + ὁδός way.]

1. The Book of Exodus; = EXODUS 1.

1832 in WEBSTER; **1847** in CRAIG.

2. = EXODUS 2 a.

1677 HALE *Prim. Orig. Man.* II. iii. 146 Ever since the time of the Jewish Exody. **1832** in WEBSTER.

3. = EXODUS 2 b.

1775 ASH, *Exody*, a departure, a journey from any place. **1832** in WEBSTER. **1882** G. MACDONALD *Castle Warlock* I. xx. 332 The plomp of the cork's exody, and the gurgle of the wine..speedily consoled him.

‖**ex officio, ex-officio,** *advb. phr.*, (*a.*, and *sb.*) [L. *ex* out of, according to + *officiō*, abl. of *officium* duty, office.] **A.** *advb. phr.* In discharge of one's duty, in virtue of one's office; *spec.* designating a particular type of oath or legal suit (see quots.); hence, as quasi-*adj.* = OFFICIAL.

Discussed further in *N. & Q.* (1960) Oct. 365 f.

1532 *Division betw. Spiritualtie & Temporaltie* fol. 16ᵛ Diuers sutes..haue ben taken in the spiritual courtes of office, that is called in latyn, ex officio: so that the partyes haue not knowen who hath accused them. **1533** MORE *Apol.* xl. Wks. 907/2 The conuenting of heretikes *ex officio.* **1607** COWEL *Interpr.* s.v. *Office*, A thing found by Inquisition made *ex officio.* **1610** BP. HALL *Apol. Brownists* §40 No Enquiry *Ex officio* may be thus made. **1637** E. ROSSINGHAM *Let.* 4 Jan. in *Court & Times Chas. I* (1848) II. 260 In one of my last letters I wrote, that Mr. Burton had refused to take the oath *ex officio.* I hear since that he hath..been suspended from..his ministry. **1661** *Act 13 Car. II* st. 1, c. 12 The oath usually called the oath *ex officio*, or any other oath whereby such person..may be charged or compelled to confess or accuse, or to purge him or herself of any criminal matter or thing, whereby he or she may be liable to any censure or punishment. **1712** PRIDEAUX *Direct. Ch.-wardens* (ed. 4) 94 He may call them *ex Officio* to Account. **1729** G. JACOB *Law Dict.* s.v. *Information*, When the Attorney General exhibits an *Information*, he does it *ex Officio.* **1769** BLACKSTONE *Commentaries Laws Eng.* IV. xxiii. 304 Informations, that are exhibited in the name of the king alone, are..of two kinds: first those which are truly and properly his own suits, and filed *ex officio* by his own immediate officer, the attorney general. *Ibid.* [Index], *Ex officio* informations. **1797** JACOB & TOMLINS *Law-Dict.* I, *Ex Officio Informations*, informations at the suit of the King, filed by the Attorney-General, as by *virtue of his office.* **1812** *Examiner* 24 Aug. 529/1 He does not strike at the Ex-officio Information itself. **1886** *Oxf. Univ. Calendar* 18 The Proctors are *ex-officio* members of each of the under-mentioned Committees. **1886** *Athenæum* 24 July 111/2 It was enacted that any one in Great Britain or Wales 'who is or shall be a Popish Recusant or Papist, or is or shall be educated in the Popish Religion, or whose parent or parents shall be a Papist or Papists', shall on or before January 20th, 1716, take the usual *ex officio* oath. **1936** M. H. MAGUIRE in *Essays in Hist. & Pol. Theory in Honor of C. H. McIlwain* 200 Otho's emphasis fell on the point of answering truly every question that might be asked... It is this specialized form of the oath of calumny which becomes practically equivalent to the oath *ex officio.* **1938** *Act 1 & 2 Geo. VI.* c. xliii. §12 Criminal informations, other than informations filed ex officio by His Majesty's Attorney-General, are hereby abolished. **1970** M. STOCKS *My Commonplace Book* 106 A Proctor has ex-officio the right to move resolutions in the Hebdomadal Council. *Ibid.* 203 And as Principal of a constituent college of London University I was *ex-officio* a member of its Senate and of its Collegiate Council, as well as of many *ad hoc* appointments committees.

B. As *sb.*, a person serving *ex officio*; an *ex-officio* officer.

1817 *Black Dwarf* I. 329 Their cabinet deliberations On soldiers' caps, or wars of nations, On ex-officios, new suspensions. **1886** *Lett. from Donegal* 13 The ex-officios go for laying out most on the great..arterial roads. **1893** *Westm. Gaz.* 22 Dec. 2/2 The first [principle] is that the Local Government shall appoint ex-officios, the second is that the Guardians themselves shall co-opt ex-officios.

Hence **ex-o'fficial** *a.*, proceeding from office or authority.
1847 in CRAIG; hence in some mod. Dicts.

exogamous (ɛk'sɒgəməs), *a.* [f. Gr. ἔξω (see EXO-) + γάμ-ος marriage + -OUS.] Characterized by, of the nature of, or pertaining to, exogamy.
1865 McLENNAN *Prim. Marriage* iii. 56 Various circumstances common to exogamous tribes. **1883** A. LANG in *Contemp. Rev.* Sept. 411 The exogamous prohibition in Rome was as complete as among the Hindoos.

exogamy (ɛk'sɒgəmɪ). [f. as prec.: cf. ENDOGAMY.] The custom by which a man is bound to take a wife outside his own clan or group. Hence **exo'gamic** *a.* [see: -IC], pertaining to exogamy.
1865 McLENNAN *Prim. Marriage* iii. 48 The words 'endogamy' and ' exogamy' are new. **1870** LUBBOCK *Orig. Civiliz.* iii. (1875) 132 A strict system of exogamy prevails. **1873** *Contemp. Rev.* XXII. 423 The transition which sometimes takes place from the exogamic to the endogamic system. **1885** TYLOR in *Academy* 1 Aug. 67/2 A social development late in comparison with the really early stages—female descent and exogamic totemism.

exogastritis: see EXO- *pref.*

exogen ('ɛksəʊdʒɪn). *Bot.* [in Fr. *exogène* (De Candolle 1813), mod.L. *exōgena, -us* (imitating L. *indigena, -us*) adj., growing on the outside, used in fem. as sb., f. Gr. ἔξω (see EXO-) + γενής born, produced.] A plant whose stem grows by deposit on its outside; opposed to ENDOGEN.
The class of Exogens is identical with that of the Dicotyledons, one of the two main divisions of phanerogamous plants. (But see: quot. 1889, and cf. BALFOUR in *Encycl. Brit.* IV. 99).
[**1830** LINDLEY *Nat. Syst. Bot.* 1 Exogenæ have a distinct deposition of pith, wood, and bark.] **1838** *Penny Cycl.* X. 128/1 Exogens have an embryo so robust as to be able to spring at once into existence. **1873** DAWSON *Earth & Man.* vi. 121 Those higher plants which start in life with two seed-leaves, and have stems with distinct bark, wood, and pith—the Exogens. **1889** *Chambers' Cycl., Exogenous Plants*, or *Exogens*, a term applied to dicotyledons by Lindley to express an erroneous view of the mode of stem-thickening from that of monocotyledons, and now wholly disused by botanists.

exogenesis (ɛksəʊ'dʒɛnɪsɪs). *Med.* [mod.L., f. Gr. ἔξω EXO- + γένεσις GENESIS.] Origin (of a disease) from external causes.
1903 *Jrnl. Trop. Med.* VI. 227, I am satisfied that the exogensis of cancer is clinically and logically proved.

exogenetic (ˌɛksəʊdʒɪ'nɛtɪk), *a.* [f. as EXOGENESIS: see -GENETIC.] Having an external cause or origin. **1.** *Med.* Of a disease: having a cause outside the body.
1874 DUNGLISON *Dict. Med. Sci.* (new ed.) 385/2 *Exogenetic*, having an origin from external causes, as exogenetic diseases.
2. *Geol.* **a.** Of rock: produced by the action of forces external to the material from which it was formed.
1904 A. W. GRABAU in *Amer. Geologist* Apr. 229 Contrasted with this group is that of the clastic rocks... These owe their origin chiefly to agents acting from without, and hence may be termed exogenetic. **1957** F. J. PETTIJOHN *Sedimentary Rocks* (ed. 2) i. 4 It is desirable to discuss the textures of the exogenetic (clastic) rocks, the endogenetic (chemical) rocks, and the epigenetic (diagenetic) rocks separately.
b. Of rock or processes affecting rocks and landforms: formed or ocurring at the surface of the earth.
1914 T. CROOK in *Mineral. Mag.* XVII. 72 The terms 'endogene' and 'exogene' have long been used by German and French geologists, chiefly as the equivalents of 'eruptive' and 'sedimentary'... It seems permissible to use them as here required, in the forms *endogenetic* and *exogenetic*. *Ibid.* 73 Exogenetic processes are best subdivided ..with reference to..weathering and denudation... Exogenetic rocks..are formed at ordinary or comparatively low tempertures. **1937** WOOLDRIDGE & MORGAN *Physical Basis Geogr.* v. 54 Exogenetic forces co-operate in all cases with the forces of upheaval. **1961** L. D. STAMP *Gloss. Geogr. Terms* 184/1 Exogenetic is the usual English form, Exogenic ..the American. **1970** H. H. READ *Rutley's Elem. Mineral.* (ed. 26) I. v. 212 Exogenetic deposits are due to surface-processes such as deposition in a salt-lake or sorting by river-action.

exogenic (ɛksəʊ'dʒɛnɪk), *a.*, [f. EXO- + -GENIC.] Exogenetic.
1. *Med.* Of a disease.
1900 GOULD *Pocket Med. Dict.* (ed. 4) 246 *Exogenic, exogenous.* See Exogenetic. **1961** *Lancet* 23 Sept. 706/1 During the epidemic stage the study of an exogenic factor would be complicated by various confusing factors—social and immunological as well as virological.
2. *Geol.* = EXOGENETIC *a.* 2 b. Chiefly *U.S.*
1942 O. D. VON ENGELN *Geomorphology* iv. 56 Some of the relief features..result from external, that is, exogenic, forces and processes. **1954** W. D. THORNBURY *Princ. Geomorphol.* ii. 19 In general, the endogenic processes tend to build up or restore areas which have been worn down by the exogenic processes. **1961** [see EXOGENETIC *a.* 2 b]. **1968** R. W. FAIRBRIDGE *Encycl. Geomorphol.* 309/1 In geomorphology, one may distinguish structural land forms (endogenic) from denudational land forms (exogenic).

exogenous (ɛk'sɒdʒɪnəs), *a.* [f. mod.L. *exōgen-a, -us* (see EXOGEN) + -OUS.] **a.** *Bot.* Growing by additions on the outside; of the nature of an exogen; pertaining to or characteristic of the exogens. **b.** *Path.* and *Psychiatry*. = EXOGENETIC. **c.** *Anat.* Of a portion of bone (see quot. 1854); opposed to *autogenous*.
a. 1830 LINDLEY *Nat. Syst. Bot.* Introd. 19 A section of the trunk of an Exogenous plant exhibits bark on the outside. **1833** LYELL *Princ. Geol.* III. 98 There is a considerable analogy between the mode of increase of a volcanic cone and that of trees of exogenous growth. **1872** M. MACMILLAN *True Vine* iii. 76 As examples of exogenous plants may be mentioned the oak..the apple..and the rose. *fig.* **1874** MRS. WHITNEY *We Girls* ix. 191, I am going to try if one little bit of social life cannot be exogenous. **1885** MRS. LYNN LINTON *Stabbed in Dark* iv. 40 [He had] a more exogenous nature than had the other; a nature which lived more on, and adopted more from, externals.
b. 1883 *Fortn. Rev.* 1 Aug. 177 An exogenous contagion is one that depends for its potency upon favouring conditions outside the body. **1925**, **1962** [see ENDOGENOUS *a.* e].
c. 1854 OWEN in *Circ. Sc.* (c. 1865) II. 48/2 Parts that grow out from previously ossified parts are called 'exogenous'.
d. *Geol.* Formed or occurring outside some structure or mass of rock (specified or understood); *spec.* = EXOGENETIC *a.* 2 b.
1845, **1890** [see ENDOGENOUS *a.* d]. **1888** [see *exomorphic* s.v. EXO-]. **1905** J. GEIKIE *Struct. & Field Geol.* xiv. 204 Exogenous or intrusive veins.—These are simply protrusions proceeding from a mass of granite into the contiguous rocks. **1933** R. A. DALY *Igneous Rocks & Depths of Earth* viii. 150 Originating within the crater, all of these young bodies may be described as endogenous domes and are thus distinguished from the vastly bigger exogenous domes of the Mauna Loa or Icelandic type. **1954** W. D. THORNBURY *Princ. Geomorphol.* iii. 34 The agencies thus far mentioned and the processes performed by them originate outside the earth's crust, and..have been designated by Lawson as epigene and by Penck as exogenous. **1968** R. W. FAIRBRIDGE *Encycl. Geomorphol.* 209/1 Rittmann (1962) refers to the volcanoes that build up from simple surface flows and cinders as exogenous cones and those that freeze over readily (the viscous ones) and push up from the inside as endogenous domes.
Hence **e'xogenously** *adv.*
1879 *Spectator* 6 Sept. 1125/1 Why should it [the Temple] not grow exogenously, building not towards the inside, but the outside? **1890** WILLIAMSON in *Nature* 17 Apr. 573 The former of these plants possessed a highly organized, exogenously developed xylem zone.

exogynous: see EXO- *pref.*

† **'exolete**, *a. Obs.* [ad. L. *exolēt-us*, pa. pple. of *exolēscĕre* to grow up, grow out of use, f. *ex-* (see EX- *pref.*[1]) + *ol-* to grow; cf. *adolēscĕre*.] **a.** That has gone out of use; disused, obsolete. **b.** That has lost its virtue; effete, insipid. **c.** Of flowers: Faded.
a. 1611 CORYAT *Crudities* 178 A Greeke inscription which I could not understand by reason of the antiquity of those exolete letters. **1621** BURTON *Anat. Mel.* II. iv. I. v, In which [apothecaries' shops] many..exolete, things out of date are to be had. **1651** LD. DIGBY, etc. *Lett. conc. Relig.* iv. 125 Paganism is ridiculous, Judaism exolete. **1652** URQUHART *Jewel* Wks. (1834) 211 Plautus exolet phrases have been [exploded] from the eloquent orations of Cicero. **1705** tr. *Cowley's Hist. Plants* Pref. (1795) 20, I declaimed..against the use of exolete and interpolated repetitions of old fables.
b. 1657 TOMLINSON *Renou's Disp.* 283 The vulgar carpo-balsame being..faint, rancid, exolet. **1676** *Phil. Trans.* XI. 708 How exolete Blood falls asunder. **1684** tr. *Bonet's Merc. Compit.* x. 358 These Exoticks..are now and then deprived partly of their virtues and exolete.
c. 1730–6 BAILEY (folio), *Exolete*, faded, or withered, as flowers.

† **exo'lution.** *Obs.* Also 7 exolusion, exsolution. [ad. L. *ex(s)olūtiōn-em*, n. of action f. *exsolvĕre*: see next.]
1. The action of loosening or setting free; the state of being loosened or set free; *esp.* the emission or escape of 'animal spirits' formerly assumed as the cause of swooning.
1615 CROOKE *Body of Man* 41 There is an exolusion, and so a defect of vitall spirits. **1634** T. JOHNSON tr. *Parey's Chirurg.* 805 An..exolution of the spirits like sowning. **1652** FRENCH *Yorksh. Spa* iv. 46 A canine appetite, & other ill symptomes caused by the exolution of the skin. **1657** TOMLINSON *Renou's Disp.* 591 Honey..boyled to the exolution of the aqueous humidity. **1662** STUBBE *Ind. Nectar* i. 4 At that time of the year, our bodies suffer a greater exolution of Spirit.
¶ Used for: Dissolution, end.
1846 DR. S. BROWN *Hist. Sci.* in *Lectures* (1858) I. 339 The evening..twilight of an era is always the time when the poets who are to..sing its..approaching exolution come abroad.
b. Relaxation (of the bodily powers); faintness.
1634 T. JOHNSON tr. *Parey's Chirurg.* XXII. xx. (1678) 504 By this kind of disease [Plague] there cometh..exsolution of the faculties. **1650** SIR T. BROWNE *Pseud. Ep.* (ed. 2) III. ix. 101 The exolution and languor ensuing that act [of spermaticall emission]. **1651** BIGGS *New Disp.* ¶ 198 The exolution of the powers thence depending, would not bear those swift motions. **1674–81** in BLOUNT *Glossogr.*; whence **1692–1732** in COLES.
c. In mystical sense.
1658 SIR T. BROWNE *Hydriot.* v. 83 If any have been so happy as truely to understand Christian annihilation, extasis, exolution.

2. 'A full and perfect payment' (Blount *Glossogr.* 1674).
Hence **1692–1732** in COLES.

† **e'xolve**, *v. Obs.* [ad. L. *ex(s)olvĕre*, f. *ex-* out + *solvĕre* to loosen.] **a.** *trans.* To slacken, diminish. **b.** *intr.* for *refl.* To dissolve. **c.** 'To pay clear off' (Bailey 1730–6 *folio*).
1578 BANISTER *Hist. Man* v. 68 By lightly receiuing them, do gently exolue the violence of euery motion. **1657** TOMLINSON *Renou's Disp.* 41 Their virtue cannot so easily exolve and perish.

‖ **exomion** (ɛk'səʊmɪən). [as if a. Gr. *ἐξωμίον, dim. of ἐξωμίς: see next.] = next.
1875 BROWNING *Aristoph. Apol.* 140 Describe the new exomion, sleeveless coat He..robbed me of.

‖ **exomis** (ɛk'səʊmɪs). [Gr. ἐξωμίς, f. ἐξ out + ὦμος shoulder.] A vest without sleeves, leaving the shoulders bare; worn by artisans and slaves.
1850 LEITCH tr. *Müller's Anc. Art* 400 The exomis, worn by artisans, while it supplied at the same time the place of the himation..left the right shoulder with the arm free.

‖ **exomologesis** (ɛkˌsɒmɒlə'giːsɪs). Also 6 exh-. [Gr. ἐξομολόγησις f. ἐξομολογέειν, f. ἐξ intensive + ὁμολογέειν to confess: see HOMOLOGATE.] A full confession, a public confession.
1592 tr. *Bullinger's Decades* 575 Exhomologesis is the discipline of prostrating and humbling men in habite, in liuing, to lie in sacke and ashes. **1655** JER. TAYLOR *Unum Necess.* ix. §4. 613 All publick criminals were tied to a publick Exomologesis or Repentance in the Church. **1679** PULLER *Moder. Ch. Eng.* (1843) 276 Doctor Cressy may be thought to owe a penance for his Exomologesis. **1868** *Q. Rev.* Jan. 59 Auricular confession put in place of the old exomologesis.

‖ **exomphalos** (ɛk'sɒmfəlɒs). Also in mod.L. form **exomphalus**. [Gr. ἐξόμφαλος, f. ἐξ out + ὀμφαλός navel.] (See quots.)
1754–64 SMELLIE *Midwif.* I. 423 This compression must be continued for some time in order to prevent an Exomphalus, or rupture at the navel. **1842** DUNGLISON *Med. Lex.* (ed. 3) *Exomphalus.* **1878** T. BRYANT *Pract. Surg.* I. 647 An umbilical hernia or exomphalos is a protrusion at the navel.

exomphalous (ɛk'sɒmfələs), *a.* [f. prec. + -OUS.] Having a ruptured or protuberant navel.
1863 R. F. BURTON *Abeokuta* I. 43 The children..are all more or less exomphalous.

exon[1] ('ɛksɒn). [app. intended to express the pronunciation (ɛgzɑ̃) of Fr. *exempt*.
Cf. EXAUN, occurring as a spelling of *exempt* in 1678; also *exant* (quot. 1655 below), used in the sense of EXEMPT *sb.* 4 a. The 'exempts' or 'exons' of the Yeomen of the Guard, according to Thoms *Bk. of the Court*, were first appointed in 1668.]
The ordinary title of the four officers of the Yeomen of the Royal Guard, 'styled *corporals* in their commissions' (Thoms) and ranking below the 'Ensign'; = EXEMPT *sb.* 4 b.
[**1655** in *Nicholas Papers* (1892) II. 354 The Court gaue Moreland (Cromwells express) two Exants of yᵉ guards to conduct him in safety.] **1767** *Royal Calendar* 83 Yeomen of the Guards..Exons [4 names follow]. **1843** MACAULAY *Ess., Mad. d'Arblay*, It never occurred..to the Exons, and Keepers of the Robes, that, etc. **1873** *Daily News* 19 June 6/5 Colonel Bourke (the Exon in Waiting). **1891** *New Army List* 132 Yeomen of the Guard..Exons [4 names].

exon[2] ('ɛksɒn). *Genetics.* [f. EX(PRESSED *ppl. a.* + -ON[1]: see quot. 1978.] A section of a DNA or RNA molecule that codes for a protein, in cases where such sections are separated by non-coding ones. Cf. INTRON.
1978 W. GILBERT in *Nature* 9 Feb. 501/1 The notion of the cistron..must be replaced by that of a transcription unit containing regions which will be lost from the mature messenger—which I suggest we call introns (for intragenic regions)—alternating with regions which will be expressed — exons. **1982** P. N. GRAY in T. M. Devlin *Textbk. Biochem.* xviii. 909 The introns are removed by endonucleolytic enzymes, and the exons are joined or spliced together forming a continuous informational sequence. **1983** *Nature* 21 July 215/3 The residues forming the active site are encoded in three different exons, similar to other serine proteases. **1985** *Sci. Amer.* Oct. 57/1 (*caption*) In eukaryotes the protein-coding sequences of DNA (exons) are often separated by intervening sequences (introns) that must be excised from a primary transcript to make messenger RNA (mRNA).
Hence **e'xonic** *a.*
1978 *Nature* 9 Feb. 501/3 Middle repetitious sequences within introns may create hot spots for recombination to rearrange the exonic sequences. **1979** *Ibid.* 6 Dec. 571 (*caption*) The length of the exonic sequence 4″ is 119 ± 29 base pairs. **1981** *Sci. Amer.* May 55/1 Protein-coding exonic sequences evolve slowly, mainly by point mutations in which one base replaces another, whereas such noncoding sequences as introns evolve much faster by insertion and deletion events of variable extent.

exonarthex: see EXO- *pref.*

exoner (ɛg'zəʊnə(r)), *v. Sc.* [ad. Fr. *exonér-er*, ad. L. *exonerāre*: see EXONERATE *v.*] = EXONERATE in various senses: To relieve from a

burden; to free from responsibility, liability, or blame. Now only in *Sc. Law.*

1533 BELLENDEN *Livy* II. (1822) 149 Commanding the saidis consulis to exoner thaimself of all auctorite. **1582** in Spottiswood *Hist. Ch. Scot.* VI. (1677) 323 They..should be exonered of all Action, civil or criminal. **1637** GILLESPIE *Eng. Pop. Cerem.* Epist. C, You shall neither convince your Adversaries, nor yet exoner your owne consciences. **1753** *Scots Mag.* XV. 86/1 She hath exonered herself. **1866** *Times* 6 Aug. Advt., For the purpose of having the Trust Funds.. divided..and the pursuers exonered of the said trust. **1881** *Daily Tel.* 16 Feb., Thereafter to exoner and discharge him of his office and management as judicial factor.

e'xonerate, *pple. Obs.* exc. *arch.* Also 6 exoneratt. [ad. L. *exonerāt-us*, pa. pple. of *exonerāre*: see next.] Used as pa. pple. of next.

1528 in Burnet *Hist. Ref.* II. 83 How may his Holiness find his Conscience towards God exonerate. **1546** in *Vicary's Anat.* (1888) App. viii. 219 [They] shalbe clerely exoneratt & dyscharged of beryng eny maner of Armour. **1621** BOLTON *Stat. Irel.* 275 (an. 2 Eliz.) To be cleerly exonerate, acquited, and discharged. **1868** LOWELL *Willows* in *Amer. Poems* (Routl.) 372 By right of birth exonerate from toil.

exonerate (ɛg'zɒnəreɪt), *v.* Also 6–7 -at. [f. L. *exonerāt-* ppl. stem of *exonerā-re*, f. *ex-* (see EX- *pref.*[1]) + *oner-*, *onus* burden. Cf. Fr. *exonérer*.]

1. *trans.* To take off a burden from; to relieve *of* (a burden, material or immaterial); to unload, lighten (a ship); also *humorously*, to 'relieve' (a person) of his money. Now *rare*.

1524 HEN. VIII. in Strype *Eccl. Mem.* I. App. xiii. 30 Discharging or exonerating their galeis. **1566** PAINTER *Pal. Pleas.* I. 46 [They] haue prayed to God to be exonerated of loue, aboue all other diseases. **1615** T. ADAMS *Spir. Navigator* 34 He strives to exonerate his shoulders. *a* **1634** CHAPMAN *Bacchus* 110 Exonerate Our sinking vessel of his deified lode. **1637** BASTWICK *Litany* III. 13 They would quickly exonerate their families of them. **1640** BP. REYNOLDS *Passions* xxi. 218 It exonerateth the mind of all those dulling Indispositions. **1785** BURKE *Sp. Nabob Arcot's Debts* Wks. IV. 308 The debt thus exonerated of so great a weight of its odium. **1798** WELLINGTON in Owen *Disp.* 29 Success would certainly exonerate our finances. **1807–8** SYD. SMITH *Plymley's Lett.* x, Be exonerated of his ready money and his constitution.

†**2.** To discharge the contents of (the body, an organ), *esp.* by evacuation. ***to exonerate nature, oneself***: to relieve the bowels. *Obs.*

1542 BOORDE *Dyetary* viii. (1870) 248 And exonerate your selfe at all tymes that nature wold expell. *Ibid.* xxx. 293 To exonerat the blader and the bely whan nede shall requyre. **1615** G. SANDYS *Trav.* 65 They sit all the day long, vnlesse they rise to exonerate nature. **1634** SIR T. HERBERT *Trav.* 149 [They] over-load their mouthes..and by a sudden laughter exonerate their chaps. **1710** T. FULLER *Pharm. Extemp.* 322 Cachectic Pills..exonerate the Habit of the Body. **1829** *Health & Longevity* 269 The bowels..ought to be exonerated at least once in two days.

†**b.** *intr.* for *refl. Obs.*

1631 R. H. *Arraignm. Whole Creature* xiii. §1. 178 Over-charged..till they..exonerate as a Wolfe or Dog, too full gorged, with Carion. **1704** J. PITTS *Relig. & Mann. Mahometans* iv. 25 These Moors..accounting it a great piece of Rudeness to exonerate in the sight of another. **1762** B. STILLINGFL. *Econ. Nat.* Misc. Tracts 123 Care is taken that these animals should exonerate upon stones, etc.

†**3.** *refl.* Of a lake, river, sea, etc., also of a blood-vessel: To empty itself, its waters, or contents; to disembogue, discharge. *Obs.*

1598 HAKLUYT *Voy.* I. 113 Neither did this riuer exonerate itself into any sea. **1635** JACKSON *Creed* VIII. xx. Wks. VIII. 43 We all meet in the main or ocean whereinto this psalm and others do exonerate themselves. **1659** MACALLO *Can. Physick* 25 The great Veines..do exonerate themselves into the little. **1715** HALLEY in *Phil. Trans.* XXIX. 298 That [gulf] of Paria, into which the Lake of Titicaca does in part exonerate it self.

†**4.** *trans.* **a.** To discharge, pour off (a fluid product, a body of water). **b.** To cast off, get rid of (persons, population). *Obs. rare.*

a. 1615 CROOKE *Body of Man* 429 It [the bile] is.. exonerated into that which is called the Caua or hollow veine. **1635** N. CARPENTER *Geog. Del.* II. vi. 96 The streitnesse of the channell, wherein a great..sea is to bee exonerated. **1672** *Phil. Trans.* VII. 5009 The Lympha does wholly exonerate itself into the sub-clavial and jugular veins.

b. 1614 RALEIGH *Hist. World* I. viii. §4 These borderers.. might exonerate their swelling multitudes. **1657** HAWKE *Killing is M.* 23 Whereby such nefarious and facinerous persons may be exonerated.

5. To relieve *from*, †*of* (anything burdensome, a duty, obligation, payment, task, etc.).

1548 HALL *Chron.* 227 That he might..exonerate them of the great charges, travayles & labors, that they now were in. *c* **1555** HARPSFIELD *Divorce Hen. VIII.* (1878) 25 Would God Sir Thomas Moore..had exonerated and discharged me of this my pains & labour. **1692** *Lond. Gaz.* No. 2786/3 To exonerate and discharge them from all Arrears of Heath-money. **1783** BURKE *Rep. Affairs India* Wks. 1842 II. 62 Mr. Hastings..offered to exonerate the company from that 'charge'. **1835** I. TAYLOR *Spir. Despot.* ii. 75 A body of clergy exonerated of all solicitude. **1851** *Ord. & Regul. R. Engineers* ii. 2 Commanding Royal Engineers will not exonerate any Officers..from the performance of such Duties.

6. To free from blame; to exculpate; also, to relieve from the blame or burden *of*; to relieve or set free *from* (blame, reproach).

1575 CHURCHYARD *Chippes* (1817) 40 That lord Oxford might be induced..to exonerate Churchyard. **1654** H. L'ESTRANGE *Chas. I.* (1655) 21 Nothing would prevail, nor would the Duke be exonerated. **1678** R. BARCLAY *Apol. Quakers* v. §12. 136 Such a season..sufficiently exonerateth God of every Man's Condemnation. **1824** W. IRVING *T. Trav.* I. 334 To exonerate myself of a greater crime. **1825** MAD. D'ARBLAY *Diary* I. 561 To exonerate her from the banal reproach of yielding unresisting to her passions. *a* **1848** R. W. HAMILTON *Rew. & Punishm.* viii. 489 Do we seek to exonerate His justice..by the denial of His faithfulness? **1884** PAE *Eustace* 187, I won't exonerate the Government.

exoneration (ɛg,zɒnə'reɪʃən). [ad. L. *exonerā-tiōn-em*, n. of action f. *exonerāre*: see prec.] The action of exonerating.

†**1.** The action of discharging or relieving the contents of the bowels, etc.; evacuation; the action of disburdening nature. Const. *of*. *Obs.*

1651 HOBBES *Leviath.* I. vi. 24 Some [appetites] are born with men; as..Appetite of excretion and exoneration. **1701** GREW *Cosm. Sacra* III. iv. 116 The body is adapted unto Eating, Drinking, Nutrition, Coition, and other ways of Repletion and Exoneration. **1727** A. HAMILTON *New Acc. E. Ind.* I. xi. 123 In each Cabbin, is a Kitchin and a Place for Exoneration. **1784** HENLEY in *Beckford's Vathek* (1868) 137 *note*, The ablution and prayer indispensably required on the exoneration of nature.

2. The action of disburdening or relieving, or the state of being relieved from a duty, office, obligation, payment, etc.; also, from blame or reproach; an instance of this, a formal discharge. Const. *of*. In *Sc. Law*: see EXONER.

1640–1 *Kirkcudbr. War-Comm. Min. Bk.* (1855) 90 And the coppie thairof delyverit to thame for thair exoneratione. **1641** in Rushw. *Hist. Coll.* III. (1692) I. 372 To receive account of all Commissions granted..and grant Exonerations thereupon. **1660** R. COKE *Power & Subj.* 211 An act concerning the exoneration of the Kings subjects from exactions and impositions. **1676** W. ROW *Contn. Blair's Autobiog.* x. (1848) 229 Papers had been prepared by the Commissioners of Estate and Kirk for their exoneration. **1866** *Times* 6 Aug. Advt., A Process of Multiplepoinding and Exoneration has been instituted.

exonerative (ɛg'zɒnərətɪv), *a.* [f. L. *exonerāt-* ppl. stem of *exonerāre* (see EXONERATE) + -IVE.] Tending to give relief (from an obligation).

1819 in TODD. **1875** POSTE *Gaius* I. Introd. (ed. 2) 3 Title ..is any fact Collative or Privative of a Right and Impositive or Exonerative of an Obligation.

exonerator (ɛg'zɒnəreɪtə(r)). [a. late L. *exonerātor*, agent-n f. *exonerāre*: see EXONERATE.] One who exonerates.

a **1834** DANE cited by WORCESTER **1846**.

‖**exoneretur** (ɛg,zɒnə'riːtə(r)). *Law. Obs.* [f. L. *exonerētur* let him be discharged, 3rd pers. sing. pres. subj. passive of *exonerāre*: see EXONERATE *v.*] 'An entry made upon the bail-piece upon render of a defendant to prison in discharge of his bail' (Wharton *Law Lex.* 1848).

1824 BINGHAM *Reports* I. 206 The Court..refused to enter an exoneretur on the bail-piece.

exoneural, -pathic, -phagous: see EXO- *pref.*

Exonian (ɛk'səʊnɪən). [f. L. *Exonia* Exeter: see -IAN.] A native or inhabitant of Exeter.

1871 The English Boy Himself Again or the 'Dame's' Wigging Denied, by An Exonian. **1891** *Where to buy at Exeter* 7/2 In the wars between Stephen and Matilda the Exonians upheld the interests of the Queen, and were subject to a severe siege. **1903** *Daily Chron.* 16 July 5/1 In Durham, the Cathedral is affectionately called 'The Abbey' while that of Exeter is named 'St. Peter's', perhaps more often still shortened by Exonians to 'Peter'. **1913** F. B. ROSE-TROUP *Western Reb.* xviii. 282 Reference to the 'entrie' and other events occur in certain depositions of Exonians a few years later.

exoph'thalmia. [mod.L. f. EXOPHTHALMUS.] = EXOPHTHALMUS.

1721–1800 in BAILEY; whence in mod. Dicts.

exophthalmic (ɛksɒf'θælmɪk), *a. Path.* [f. EXOPHTHALM-US + -IC.] Of, pertaining to, or characterized by exophthalmus.

1878 T. BRYANT *Pract. Surg.* I. 191 The exophthalmic goitre..or Basedow's disease. **1889** *Med. Jrnl.* 28 Sept. 720/2 Rapid action of the heart—in exophthalmic goitre.

exophthalmus, -os (ɛksɒf'θælməs, -ɒs). *Path.* [mod.L., a. Gr. ἐξόφθαλμος, f. ἐξ out + ὀφθαλμός eye.] Protrusion of the eye-ball.

1872 DARWIN *Emotions* vi. 162 Dr. Gunning has lately recorded a case of exophthalmos in consequence of whooping-cough. **1876** tr. *Wagner's Gen. Pathol.* 565 Exophthalmus is constantly present in suffocation.

exoph'thalmy. Anglicized f. EXOPHTHALMIA.

1706 in PHILLIPS (ed. Kersey); whence in mod. Dicts.

exophyllous, -plasm, -podite: see EXO- *pref.*

†**e'xopt**, *v. Obs. rare*$^{-1}$. [ad. L. *exopt-āre*, f. *ex-* (see EX- *pref.*[1]) + *optāre* to wish.] *trans.* To wish or desire greatly.

1548 FORREST *Pleas. Poesye* 66 a, ['The goods of the world' induce] the soone withe the father also to mache, By vttre diffiaunce his deathe to exopte.

†**e'xoptable**, *a. Obs.*$^{-0}$ [ad. L. *exoptābilis*, f. *exoptāre*: see EXOPT.] To be desired or wished.

1656 in BLOUNT *Glossogr.* **1721–1800** in BAILEY. **1818** in TODD; whence in mod. Dicts.

†**e'xoptate**, *v. Obs.*$^{-0}$ [f. L. *exoptāt-* ppl. stem of *exoptā-re*.] *trans.* To desire earnestly.

1692 in COLES. **1721–1800** in BAILEY.

†**exop'tation**. *Obs.* [as if ad. L. **exoptātiōn-em*, n. of action f. *exoptāre* to long: see EXOPT.] The fact or state of earnestly desiring.

1633 T. ADAMS *Exp. 2 Peter* iii. 18 The former is by way of gratulation, the other by way of exoptation. **1721–1800** in BAILEY; **1847** in CRAIG.

exoptile: see EXO- *pref.*

,exora'bility. [f. next + -ITY.] The quality or condition of being exorable.

1871 R. ELLIS *Catullus* ciii. 2 The sesterces all, give back ..Silo, Then be a bully beyond exorability, you.

exorable ('ɛksərəb(ə)l), *a.* Now *rare*. [ad. L. *exōrābilis*, f. *exōrāre*: see next. Cf. Fr. *exorable*.]

1. Capable of being moved by entreaty, accessible to entreaty.

1563–87 FOXE *A. & M.* (1684) III. 259 For he is exorable, and hath no pleasure in the death of a Sinner. **1641** W. CARTWRIGHT *Ordinary* II. i, A Usurer is somewhat exorable When he is full. *a* **1694** TILLOTSON *Serm.* xxxi. (1742) II. 356 They shall address themselves to the mountains and rocks, as being more pitiful and exorable than he. **1788** V. KNOX *Winter Even.* III. VII. i. 8 Death, whom no arts can render exorable, disappointed his ambition. **1867** *Contemp. Rev.* VI. 371 Entreaty was for the exorable, and it failed; action for the inexorable, and it succeeded.

†**2.** In active sense: Effectual in entreaty. *Obs.* [Cf. L. *exorabile carmen*.]

1574 HELLOWES *Gueuara's Fam. Ep.* (1577) 361 Good workes be more exorable vnto God than holy desires.

Hence **'exorableness**, the condition or quality of being accessible to entreaty.

1642 ROGERS *Naaman* 55 A spirit of mildnesse, mercie, exorablenesse and easinesse to be intreated. **1679** J. GOODMAN *Penit. Pardon.* I. i. (1713) 2 The exorableness of a Father upon his Son's submission. **1730–6** in BAILEY (folio).

†**'exorate**, *v. Obs.* [f. L. *exōrāt-* ppl. stem of *exōrāre*, f. *ex-* (see EX- *pref.*[1]) + *ōrāre* to pray.]

1. *trans.* **a.** To request earnestly, implore. **b.** To prevail upon (a person) by entreaty.

1599 PORTER *Angry Wom. Abingd.* Prol., Let a poore scholler implore and exerate [*sic*] that you would make him riche in the possession of a mite of your favours. *c* **1600** *Timon* II. iv. (1842) 32 Let it, O lett it bee lawfull for mee.. to orate and exorate. **1654** H. L'ESTRANGE *Chas. I.* (1655) 21 Nothing could prevail, nor would the duke be exorated.

2. To obtain by request.

1623–6 in COCKERAM.

†**exo'ration**, *Obs.* [ad. L. *exōrātiōn-em*, n. of action f. *exōrāre*: see EXORATE.] The action of beseeching or entreating; an entreaty.

1609 BIBLE (Douay) *Ecclus.* xvi. 12 Mightie [is] exoration, and powring out wrath. **1616** R. C. *Times' Whistle* VI. 2511, I leave thee with my best exoration For thy most speedy.. reformation. *a* **1625** FLETCHER *Love's Cure* v. iii, Deafe to your cries: and Marble To all impulsive exorations.

†**e'xorb**, *v. Obs.* [ad. L. *ex(s)orb-ēre* to suck up, f. *ex-* (see EX- *pref.*[1]) + *sorbēre* to suck.] *trans.* To suck up or out.

1657 TOMLINSON *Renou's Disp.* 720 Alwayes agitating them till the whole humour be exorbed.

†**e'xorbeate**, *v. Obs.* [f. L. *ex(s)orbē-re* (see EXORB) + -ATE[3].] *trans.* To swallow up, engulph.

1623 in COCKERAM II.

e'xorbital, *a.* [f. EX- *perf.*[1] + ORBIT *sb.* + -AL[1].] Outside the orbit.

1876 *Catal. Sci. App. S. Kens.* 553 For the determination of the exorbital protrusion of the eye-ball.

exorbitance (ɛg'zɔːbɪtəns). Also 7–8 exh-. [f. EXORBITANT: see -ANCE. Cf. Fr. *exorbitance*.] The quality or condition of being exorbitant.

†**1.** Divergence or aberration from the prescribed or ordinary track; eccentricity, irregularity, anomaly, or an instance of these. Also, aberration of mind; an attack of insanity. *Obs.* or *arch.*

1631 PRESTON *Life Eternal* (1634) 26 Now, whence comes this uneven walking, this exorbitance of the wheeles. **1663** J. SPENCER *Prodigies* 133 All these exorbitances in Nature serve to foil and set off the general beauty..of its Works. **1684** tr *Bonet's Merc. Compit.* XI. 373 The first exorbitance [in a case of mania] was very violent and lasted for ten months. **1685** BOYLE *Enq. Notion Nat.* 149, I shall not.. mention those Grand Anomalies, or Exorbitances. **1707** FLOYER *Physic. Pulse-Watch* 186 By the Pulse we find by what Method we must regulate all Exorbitances. **1842** DE QUINCEY *Philos. Herodotus* Wks. IX. 208 Our growing exorbitance from our limits warns us to desist.

2. Divergence from the right path; transgression of law or morality; misconduct, lawlessness, criminality; an instance of the same. *arch.*

1611 SPEED *Hist. Gt. Brit.* IX. viii. §58 A project..so execrable, as well may justifie King Johns exorbitances. *a* **1618** SYLVESTER *St. Lewis* 324 Eyes deep-vail'd with Ignorance Or Knowledge stained with Sinnes Exorbitance. **1632** MASSINGER *City Madam* I. i, 'Tis strange my master.. can Give the reins to such exorbitance. **1663** GERBIER *Counsel* D v b, Beware of ill Builders..since by their exorbitances, happen many irreparable accidents. **1769** *Hist. Europe* in *Ann. Reg.* 32/2 A picture..sullied with the most dreadful exhorbitances. **1810** SCOTT *Lady of L.* II. xxviii. *foot-n.*, The Border robbers..had committed many exorbitances. **1850** GROTE *Greece* II. lv. (1862) V. 30 Such unprincipled exorbitances of behaviour.

3. Excessiveness, extravagance; an instance of this. Now chiefly, outrageous excessiveness, of demands, charges, prices, estimates, etc.

1646 MRQ. ORMOND in Carte *Life* (1735) III. 470 To heighten the exhorbitance of their expectations and demands. **1706** GARTH *Dispens.* (ed. 6) II. 19 They riot still, Unbounded in Exorbitance of Ill. **1793** BP. HORSLEY *Serm.* (1824) I. 198 The barriers..against..the exorbitance of licentiousness..will soon be borne down. **1845** MCCULLOCH *Taxation* II. v. (1852) 212 The exorbitance of the duties on tea and tobacco. **1868** BROWNING *Ring & Bk.* x. 186 The exorbitance Of sin in this one sinner. **1884** *Law Rep. 26 Chanc. Div.* 240 The exorbitance of Hobson's charge for collecting the debts.

exorbitancy (ɛg'zɔːbɪtənsɪ). [f. EXORBITANT: see -ANCY.] The quality of being exorbitant.

1. = EXORBITANCE 1. Now *rare*. Also, †an irrational opinion.

1621 W. SCLATER *Tythes* (1623) 103 Exorbitancie enough from the primary rule of assignement to Parish Churches. **1649** MILTON *Eikon.* xxvi. 468 That planetary motion, that unblamable exorbitancy. **1672** *Phil. Trans.* VII. 5126 To suppose..an infinite profundity of the Stellar Sphere: an Exorbitancy not to be admitted. **1677** HALE *Prim. Orig. Man.* III. iii. 265 This witty Man..hath somewhat rectified the exorbitancy of Epicurus. **1879** H. N. HUDSON *Hamlet* 13 Frequent displays of mental exorbitancy.

†**2.** = EXORBITANCE 2. *Obs.*

1619 W. SCLATER *Exp. 1 Thess.* (1627) II. Ep. Ded. 4 Information of exorbitancy in some particulars of the Church. **1647** CLARENDON *Hist. Reb.* I. (1843) 29/1 The exorbitancy of the house of commons..proceeded principally from their contempt of the laws. **1658** BP. L. WOMOCK *Exam. Tilenus* 40 There are sins..as in blasphemie..wherein the act is not to be distinguished from the exorbitancie. **1670** G. H. *Hist. Cardinals* I. II. 58 Any Treatise that..rebukes the Exorbitancy of their Lives. **1702** *Lond. Gaz.* No. 3795/3 His..zealous Endeavour to curb the Exorbitancy of France.

3. (Cf. EXORBITANT A. 4). **a.** = EXORBITANCE 3. †**b.** Disposition to exceed one's rights; excessive greed or rapacity; an instance of this (*obs.*).

a **1638** MEDE *Wks.* (1672) Gen. Pref., I..am..far from interpreting your Love Exorbitancy. **1653** A. WILSON *Jas. I* 102 The exorbitancy of the new buildings about the City.. being a shelter for them. **1669** W. SIMPSON *Hydrol. Chym.* 81 Gout..roused up from the exorbitancy of a spurious acid ferment in the ultimate digestion. **1674** *Govt. Tongue* vii. (1684) 168 This monstrous exorbitancy of discourse. **1722** SEWEL *Hist. Quakers* Pref. (1795) I. 14 The exorbitancies to which some launched out. **1749** *Numbers in Poet. Comp.* 26 One can hardly imagine the Antients could have run into.. Exorbitancies in protracting their Rhythms. **1768–74** TUCKER *Lt. Nat.* (1852) II. 363 The exorbitancy of the Romans swallowing up their neighbouring nations one after another. **1783** BURKE *Rep. Affairs India* Wks. 1842 II. 23 A system of restraint on the exorbitancies of their servants. **1791** W. MAXWELL in Boswell *Johnson* (1831) I. 381 Who knows any real sufferings [from love] more than from the exorbitancy of any other passion? **1803** WELLINGTON in Gurw. *Disp.* II. 386 From the exorbitancy of that [duty] in particular levied at Collun. **1877** MORLEY *Crit. Misc.* Ser. II. 375 Divested of all the exorbitancies of his spirit and his style.

exorbitant (ɛg'zɔːbɪtənt), *a.* and *sb.* Also 6 exorbytant, 6–8 exhorbitant, -ent. [ad. late L. *exorbitant-em*, pr. pple. of *exorbitāre* to go out of the track, f. *ex-* out + *orbita* wheel-track: see ORBIT *sb.* Cf. Fr. *exorbitant*.] **A.** *adj.*

†**1.** Leaving a specified track; deviating *from* a specified rule or principle. Of remarks, discussions, etc.: Wandering from the subject, irrelevant. *Obs.*

1534 WHITINTON *Tullyes Offices* I. (1540) 46 Suche play as is not exorbytant fro the exercyse of honesty. **1599** *Broughton's Lett.* ix. 30 A..government, exorbitant from the milde course of law and iustice. **1607** TOPSELL *Four-f. Beasts* (1673) 369 Having..mentioned such a story, it is not exorbitant to add in one word other fictions. **1644** JESSOP *Angel of Eph.* 50 How exorbitant from this rule the practices of our Prelates have been. **1674** OWEN *Holy Spirit* (1693) 45 Exorbitant from the Principles of Nature.

†**b.** Projecting, salient. *Obs.*

1714 DERHAM *Astro-theol.* v. v. (1769) 144 [Had the earth been square] they must have been..retarded..by the exorbitant angles.

2. Deviating from the normal, prescribed, or customary track. †**a.** Of movements, conduct, etc.: Eccentric, erratic, irregular (*obs.*).

1613 DANIEL *Coll. Hist. Eng.* (1626) 67 Strong raines to hold him in, from all exorbitant courses. **1654** H. L'ESTRANGE *Chas. I* (1655) 35 The Commons when they see such a Blazing-star in course so exorbitant..cannot but look upon it. **1673** *Lady's Call.* I. §1. 5 The vanity of wit..has no where a more free and exorbitant range than in censuring and deriding.

b. [After use of *exorbitans* in Roman Law.] Of cases, offences, etc.: Anomalous, not coming within the intended scope of a law. Of powers, privileges, enactments: Abnormal, not in accordance with general principle.

c **1460** FORTESCUE *Abs. & Lim. Mon.* (1714) 47 What sume thay [the king's charges] be not like to excede, but if..ther fal a Case over much exorbitant. **1594** HOOKER *Eccl. Pol.* III. xi. (1611) 114 Causes exorbitant, and such as their lawes had not provided for. **1675** [cf. 4 a]. *a* **1754** FIELDING *Charge to Grand Jury* Wks. 1784 X. 161 The punishment..is fine or imprisonment; and if the case be exorbitant, by pillory and loss of ears. **1756** NUGENT *Montesquieu's Spir. Laws* (1758) I. II. iii. 19 A magistrate invested with an exorbitant power. **1832** AUSTIN *Jurispr.* (1879) II. 909 Though the law and the right are 'exorbitant' or 'eccentric'. *Ibid.* II. 981 They are mere anomalies: exorbitant or irregular commands.

†**c.** Aberrant from the common type, monstrous, abnormal. *Obs.*

1607 TOPSELL *Four-f. Beasts* (1673) 358 The colour of Lions is generally yellow, for these before spoken of, black, white and red, are exorbitant. **1662** GERBIER *Princ.* 23 Those passions become the original causes of exorbitant Features and Forms.

†**d.** Of an insane person or his condition: Extravagant, frantic, wild. *Obs.*

1667 *Phil. Trans.* II. 620 We found him [a madman] somewhat less exorbitant. **1702** C. MATHER *Magn. Chr.* III. II. i. (1852) 358 The wretch continued in an exorbitant frame for a few days.

†**3.** Forsaking, or apt to forsake, the right path; erring, faulty, transgressing, trespassing. *Obs.*

1556 LAUDER *Tractate* 195 Raisand gret derth, exhorbitent Aganis ȝour actis of Parliament. **15..** SIR H. SIDNEY in *Ussher's Lett.* (1686) App. 25 That thou, entring into this exorbitant Age, mayest be..prepared to shun those courses. **1605** B. JONSON *Volpone* IV. vi, I haue..transgrest Against the dignitie of the court..And beene exorbitant. *a* **1638** MEDE *Disc. Prov.* iv. 23 Wks. I. 203 We must resist and crush every exorbitant thought which draws to sin. **1640** BP. HALL *Chr. Moder.* 8/2 The very patriarchs and princes of God's peculiar people were palpably exorbitant in this kind. **1649** MILTON *Eikon.* Pref., The people exorbitant and excessive in all thir motions. *a* **1716** BLACKALL *Wks.* (1723) I. 98 Over-rule their exorbitant Passions.

4. Exceeding ordinary or proper bounds.

a. Going to excess in any action or quality. Of actions, appetites, desire, etc.: Excessive, immoderate. *arch.* Now with stronger sense: Grossly or flagrantly excessive.

1621 BURTON *Anat. Mel.* I. ii. III. xi, Appetites both good ..if they be moderate, both pernitious if they be exorbitant. **1622–62** HEYLIN *Cosmogr.* III. (1673) 58/2 They had formerly been exorbitant in the worship of Idols. **1659** WHARTON *Disc. Astrol.* Wks. (1683) 185 The exorbitant Practice of frequent Blood-letting. **1675** tr. *Machiavelli's Prince* xvii. (Rtldg. 1883) 104 Exorbitant mercy has an ill effect. **1719** J. RICHARDSON *Science Connoisseur* 147 Some are Exorbitant in the Praises of what Themselves Possess. **1802** PALEY *Nat. Theol.* xxvi. (1826) 389 The exorbitant multiplication of some troublesome insects. **1853** HERSCHEL *Pop. Lect. Sc.* ii. §21 (1873) 63 The excessive, exorbitant prodigality of diffusion of the sun's light and heat. **1871** BROWNING *Balaust.* 282 They wondered strangers were exorbitant In estimation of Euripides.

†**b.** Exceeding one's rights, encroaching. *Obs.*

1631 WEEVER *Anc. Fun. Mon.* 790 By the exorbitant authoritie of the Pope, this election was disanulled. *a* **1635** NAUTON *Fragm. Reg.* (Arb.) 45 My Lord of Essex..was so exorbitant in the limitation of the Soveraign aspect.

c. Of a price, rate, stipulation, demand, claim, etc.: Grossly excessive.

1670 R. COKE *Disc. Trade* 24 The Exorbitant Impositions of the King of Denmark. **1722** DE FOE *Moll Flanders* (1840) 845 Nor were his conditions exorbitant. **1729** FRANKLIN *Ess.* Wks. 1840 II. 255 To restrain men from giving and receiving exorbitant interest. **1781** GIBBON *Decl. & F.* II. xlvi. 721 He exhausted their wealth by exorbitant tributes. **1836** W. IRVING *Astoria* III. 159 The Indians..raised the price of horses to an exorbitant rate. **1860** KINGSLEY *Misc.* II. 205 The landlord can obtain an exorbitant rent. **1875** JOWETT *Plato* (ed. 2) I. 385 The informers..are far from being exorbitant in their demands. **1879** M. ARNOLD *Irish Catholicism* Mixed Ess. 126 To advance pretensions the most exorbitant.

d. Of power, wealth, etc.: Overgrown, enormous, excessive. *arch.*

1648 *Nicholas Papers* (Camden) I. 116, I hold Lord Jermins..power as vast and exorbitant. **1693** LOCKE *Educ.* §7 An exorbitant fortune. *c* **1771** J. FLETCHER *Check* iv. Wks. 1795 III. 12 Your favourite doctrines..would lose their exorbitant influence. **1816** F. H. NAYLOR *Hist. Germany* I. I. ix. 362 Prescribing bounds to the exhorbitant power of Austria.

e. Of a material object, an outline, or surface: Disproportionately large, excessive in any dimension; in mod. use, outrageously or extravagantly large. Also *fig.* *arch.*

1662 GERBIER *Princ.* 9 Those exorbitant Chimney-Shafts. **1667** E. CHAMBERLAYNE *St. Gt. Brit.* I. III. x. (1743) 228 The exorbitant extent and compass of Parishes. **1688** R. HOLME *Armoury* III. 382/1 The exorbitant and over-burnt Wick in a candle. **1709** SACHEVERELL *Serm.* 15 Aug. 15 This Overgrown, this Exorbitant Sinner. **1711** SHAFTESB. *Charac.* II. iv. (1737) II. 303 Its chief Bulk being compos'd of two exorbitant Muscles. **1843** CARLYLE *Past. & Pr.* (1858) 169 With exorbitant breast-pin. **1863** GEO. ELIOT *Romola* (1880) I. 5 The exorbitant line of the Pitti [palace] roof [at Florence] is hidden from San Miniato.

†**B.** *sb.* One who or something which exceeds proper limits. *Obs. rare.*

1626 W. SCLATER *Exp. 2 Thess.* (1629) 277 Howsoeuer exorbitants behaued themselues, they [Brethren] yet should continue in weldoing. **1654** H. L'ESTRANGE *Chas. I* (1655) 25 His Majesty..demanded justice against those exorbitants. *a* **1714** M. HENRY *Wks.* I. 135 The most.. daring exorbitants of an ungoverned tongue.

exorbitantly (ɛg'zɔːbɪtəntlɪ), *adv.* [f. prec. + -LY².] In an exorbitant manner or degree; at an exorbitant rate.

a **1635** SIBBES *Serm. John* xiv. 11 Affections are..raised up irregularly and exorbitantly. **1668** CLARENDON *Contempl. Ps.* Tracts (1727) 604 Using the power..so exorbitantly. **1693** CONGREVE *Double Dealer* III. x, The old fat fool that paints so exorbitantly. **1711** *Vind. Sacheverell* 20, I know you to be exorbitantly wicked. **1837** SYD. SMITH *Let. Singleton* Wks. 1859 II. 257/1 Incomes..exorbitantly and absurdly great. **1864** MRS. CARLYLE *Lett.* III. 220, I get plenty of cream, quite good, paying for it exorbitantly.

exorbitate (ɛg'zɔːbɪteɪt), *v.* *Obs.* or *arch.* [f. L. *exorbitāt-* ppl. stem of *exorbitāre*: see EXORBITANT.] *intr.* To deviate from the usual course; to stray.

1600 ABP. ABBOT *Exp. Jonah* 116 We are ready to exorbitate. **1643** PRYNNE *Sov. Power Parl.* I. (ed. 2) 5 The Law..ought to bridle him [the King] when he exorbitates from the Law. **1643** HUNTON *Treat. Monarchy* I. iv. (1689) 28 If one exorbitate, the power of restraint..should be in the rest. **1651** SMITH in *Fuller's Abel Rediv.* 572 Such as least exorbitate [*printed* exoribitate] from the Doctrine..of the Church of Rome. **1671** H. STUBBE *Reply* 31 When other Mens Flatteries did thus Exorbitate, etc.

b. Of heavenly bodies: To deviate from the usual orbit; to follow an erratic course.

1693 BENTLEY *Atheism* viii. 12 They would..sometimes have exorbitated beyond the distance of Saturn. **1747** HERVEY *Medit.* II. 231 The heavenly bodies would exorbitate into wild confusion. **1817** COLERIDGE *Biog. Lit.* 22 To describe the earth as in imminent danger of exorbitating.

Hence † e'xorbitating *ppl. a.*

1632 LITHGOW *Trav.* x. 487 No inference can prye, nor strange illation prooue, In your exorbitating [*printed* exorbitanting] braines, my period I did mooue. **1644** HUNTON *Vind. Treat. Monarchy* vii. 55 Parliament [is].. bound to resist..the destruction of liberties, by exorbitating Princes. **1659** H. MORE *Immort. Soul* (1662) 175 Rather the work of Art then of exorbitating Nature.

exorbitation (ɛgzɔːbɪ'teɪʃən). [ad. L. *exorbitātiōn-em*, n. of action f. *exorbitāre*: see EXORBITATE.] Deviation from the usual path or track; an instance of the same.

a **1628** PRESTON *New Covt.* (1634) 200 If there be an exorbitation of the line..it is not straight. **1631** R. BYFIELD *Doctr. Sabb.* 172 The exorbitation of discipline. **1635** HEYWOOD *Hierarch* I. 12 They are..an Exorbitation and bringing out of Square. **1847** DE QUINCEY *Wks.* (1862) VII. 76 No deliberative body would less have tolerated such philosophic exorbitations from public business.

exorcise: see EXORCIZE.

†**exorcision.** *Obs. rare.* [f. *exorcise*, EXORCIZE *v.* + -ION¹.] = EXORCISM.

1502 *Ord. Crysten Men* (W. de W. 1506) I. ii. 13 And that is as now of the exorcysyon.

exorcism ('ɛksɔsɪz(ə)m, 'ɛksɔː-, ɛg'zɔːsɪz(ə)m). Forms: 5–7 exorcisme, (4–5 exorsism, 6 exorcysme, -cyme), 5– exorcism. [ad. late L. *exorcism-us*, a. Eccl. Gr. ἐξορκισμός, f. ἐξορκίζειν: see EXORCIZE. Cf. Fr. *exorcisme*.

In this and the related words Johnson and nearly all later Dicts. mark the stress on the first syllable; but the second pronunciation is often heard, esp. in *exorcize*, which otherwise is liable to confusion with *exercise*.]

1. The action of exorcizing or expelling an evil spirit by adjuration or the performance of certain rites; an instance of this.

¶ In first quot. misused for *exorcist*.

13.. *E.E. Allit. P.* B. 1579 Sorsers & exorsismus & fele such clerkes. *c* **1450** *Castle Hd. Life St. Cuthb.* (Surtees) 3815 Be þe vertu of exorcisme. **1502** *Ord. Crysten Men* (W. de W. 1506) I. ii. 14 And that suffyseth as now of the exorcysme & cathecysme. **1550** VERON *Godly Saiyngs* (1846) 44 Ye did give your names, & began to be ground with fastinges & exorcymes. **1641** MILTON *Reform.* I. (1851) 3 Then was Baptisme chang'd into a kind of exorcisme. **1750** WARBURTON *Doctr. Grace* II. v. Wks. (1811) VIII. 336 To evince these great Truths, seems to have been the end both of Possessions and of the Exorcisms. **1818** BYRON *Ch. Har.* IV. xxiv, The spectres whom no exorcism can bind. **1856** MRS. BROWNING *Aur. Leigh* II. 872 An exorcism against the devildom Which plainly held me. **1879** FARRAR *St. Paul* I. 492 The calm authoritative exorcism restored the broken harmony of her being.

†**b.** *improperly.* The action of calling up spirits; the ceremonies observed for that purpose; conjuration. *Obs.*

1430 LYDG. *Chron. Troy* I. v, But moste she wrought by nycromancye With exorsismes and conjuracions. **1593** SHAKS. *2 Hen. VI*, I. iv. 5 Will her Ladyship behold and heare our Exorcismes? **1602** DEKKER *Satiromastix* 183 This ghost of Tucca..was raised up (in print) by new Exorcismes. *a* **1652** J. SMITH *Sel. Disc.* ii. 37 This root of superstition..branched forth..into magic and exorcisms.

2. A formula employed in exorcizing.

1550 BALE *Apol.* 23 b, I found an olde bishoppes ordynary or boke of their exorcismes for church halowinges, etc. **1651** HOBBES *Leviath.* IV. xliv. 339 The same Exorcisme is repeated once more. **1751** SMOLLETT *Per. Pic.* (1779) I. xxxiv. 306 Morgan..began to utter exorcisms with great devotion. **1755** YOUNG *Centaur* (1757) IV. vi. 251 Here, then, I shall begin my exorcism. Its words must be strange and barbarous, suited to the occasion. **1816** SCOTT *Antiq.* xxv, Fortified with..as many exorcisms as his memory could recover, he advanced.

†**b.** An imprecatory oath. *Obs.*

1601 HOLLAND *Pliny* II. 225 That prescript forme of exorcisme, whereby the two Decij, both the father and sonne, betooke themselues to all the hellish furies.

Hence **exor'cismal** *a.*, pertaining to, or of the nature of, exorcism.

1887 *Fortn. Rev.* May 740 The exorcismal practices of the clergy.

'exor,cisory, *a.* [f. *exorcise*, EXORCIZE + -ORY.] Serving to exorcize.

1836 E. HOWARD *R. Reefer* xliv, The exorcisory cantation of the previous night.

exorcist ('ɛksɔːsɪst, 'ɛksɔː-, ɛg'zɔːsɪst). Forms: 4-6 exorciste, (6 exerciste), 6- exorcist. [ad. late L. *exorcista*, ad. Gr. ἐξορκιστής, f. ἐξορκίζειν: see EXORCIZE. Cf. Fr. *exorciste*.] One who exorcizes.

1. One who drives out evil spirits by solemn adjuration, etc.

1382 WYCLIF *Acts* xix. 13 Summe of the Iewis exorcistis, or coniureris. 1649 SELDEN *Laws Eng.* I. x. (1739) 18 Exorcists, that served to dispossess such as were possessed by the Devil. 1774 PENNANT *Tour Scot. in* 1772. 344 The exorcist was called in to drive away these evil Genii. 1853 H. ROGERS *Ecl. Faith* 86 A dumb demon, awaits to find a voice..at the summons of an exorcist.

transf. 1877 'RITA' *Vivienne* III. viii, Hard work is the best exorcist for dark hours and painful memories.

b. *spec.* The third of the four lesser orders in the Roman Catholic Church. Cf. BENET.

1560 BECON *Catech.* Wks. (1564) 462 a The exorciste must cast out devils, & say unto the people, that all suche as wyll not communicate, must departe & go awaye. 1579 FULKE *Heskins' Parl.* 245 Acolytes, exercistes, readers, etc. 1642 JER. TAYLOR *Episc.* (1647) 174 The office..of an exorcist ..[is] no way dependent on the office of a deacon. 1844 LINGARD *Anglo Sax. Ch.* (1858) I. iv. 133 We soon meet.. with..exorcists..these were ordained.

†**2.** One who calls or pretends to call up spirits by magical rites. *Obs.*

1601 SHAKS. *Jul. C.* II. i. 323 Thou like an Exorcist, hast conjur'd vp My mortified Spirit. 1621 BURTON *Anat. Mel.* I. iii. III. (1651) 211 The knavish impostures of Juglers, Exorcists, Mass-Priests and Mountebanks.

3. *Comb.*

1606 SYLVESTER *Du Bartas* II. iv. I. 454 David's sacred Ditty..Exorcist-like chac't Nature's cruel Foe.

Hence **exor'cistical** *a.*, of or pertaining to an exorcist or to an exorcism.

1664 H. MORE *Myst. Iniq.* xviii, And uses an Exorcistical form for the ejecting. 1749-51 BP. LAVINGTON *Enthus. Method. & Papists* III. (1754) 185 A rare Instance of Exorcistical Virtue. 1827 W. G. S. *Excursion of Village Curate* 128 Exorcistical, necromantical and demonological charms.

exorcization (ɛksɔːsaɪ'zeɪʃən). Forms: 4 **exorcisacioun, -zacion, exorsisacion, -cyon, -tion,** 6 **exorcysacyon,** 6- **exorcisation.** [f. next + -ATION.] The action of exorcizing; *i.e.* **a.** of driving out evil spirits by adjuration, etc.; †**b.** of calling up spirits by magic.

1375 BARBOUR *Bruce* IV. 750 Throu exorcizaciones, To ger spiritis to thame apeir. c1384 CHAUCER *H. Fame* III. 173 Old witches, sorceresses, That usen exorsisations. 1502 *Ord. Crysten Men* (W. de W. 1506) I. ii. 13 And do that solempnyte of exorcysacyon. 1563-87 FOXE *A. & M.* (1596) 467/2 The booke of exorcisation..which is sprinkled in the church. 1664 H. MORE *Myst. Iniq.* xviii, The Priest's Exorcization in the Names of God..does not excuse him from the guilt of Enchantment. 1684 I. MATHER *Remark. Provid.* (1856) 183 To cure diseases, and drive away evil spirits by..exorcizations, etc. 1749-51 BP. LAVINGTON *Enthus. Method. & Papists* III. (1754) 115 His better Friends ..have inserted a Prayer in the Office of Exorcization. 1856 KANE *Arct. Expl.* II. xxv. 252 My promised exorcisation of the demon in his stomach.

exorcize, -ise ('ɛksɔːsaɪz, 'ɛksɔː-, ɛg'zɔːsaɪz), *v.* Also 6 exorsize. [(? ad. Fr. *exorcise-r*,) ad. late L. *exorcizāre*, ad. Gr. ἐξορκίζειν, f. ἐξ out + ὅρκος oath.

'Owing perh. to association with *exercise*, the spelling *-ise* is now almost universal; the better form *exorcize* is marked in most Dicts. as obsolete' (N.E.D., 1894).]

1. *trans.* To drive away (an evil spirit) by the invocation or use of some holy name; to call forth, expel. Const. *from, out of.*

1546 BALE *Eng. Votaries* 35 All vayne & craftye scyences, ..exorcysynge, incautynge & coniurynge. 1711 STEELE *Spect.* No. 141 ⁋6 Something..in this Comedy..wants to be exorcised more than the Witches. 1850 MRS. JAMESON *Leg. Monast. Ord.* (1863) 21 Touched him on the shoulder with his staff and exorcised the demon. 1870 GLADSTONE *Glean.* IV. vi. 202 The spirit which devised it, is not exorcised, either from the priesthood or the rural population.

2. To clear (a person or place) *of* evil spirits; to purify or set free from malignant influences.

1645 EVELYN *Mem.* (1857) I. 178 They were..exorcised at their entering the church with abundance of ceremonies. 1711 ADDISON *Spect.* No. 110 ⁋5 The Knight..ordered all the Apartments to be flung open, and exorcised by his Chaplain. 1742 YOUNG *Nt. Th.* IX. 1362 Exorcise his heart So long possest. 1826 W. JAY *Christian Contemplated* ix. 292 This joy exorcises a man, of carnal affection. 1848 LYTTON *Harold* XI. ix. 291 Muttering hymns, monks huddled together..as if to exorcise the land of a demon.

3. To call upon (an evil spirit) with a solemn asseveration; to adjure. Also, to conjure up. Now *rare.*

1584 R. SCOT *Discov. Witchcr.* XV. xii. 412, I doo conjure and I doo exorcise you, by the father, by the sonne, and by the Holy-ghost..that..you doo come unto me. 1649 R. HODGES *Plain. Direct.* 8 His daily exercise is to exorcise or adjure. 1732 NEAL *Hist. Purit.* (1822) I. 44 The devil was exorcised to go out, and enter no more into him. 1848 MRS. JAMESON *Sacr. & Leg. Art* (1850) 406 Having exorcised the dragon in the name of Him who was born of a virgin.

transf. 18.. DE QUINCEY *Wks.* (1871) XVI. 16 Secrets of ages remote from each other have been exorcized from the accumulated shadows of centuries.

Hence **exorcized** *ppl. a.* **exorcizement**, the action of exorcizing; exorcizing influence. **exorcizer** (also 6-7 **exorcisor**), one who exorcizes. **exorcizing** *vbl. sb.* and *ppl. a.*

1664 H. MORE *Myst. Iniq.* xviii, The derivation or distribution of these Exorcized Elements into several Superstitious uses. 1679 PULLER *Moder. Ch. Eng.* (1843) 205 Never..aneling any with exorcised oil..till, etc. 1782 *Fashionable Follies* I. 102 He..was become sensible to the exorcisement of holy water. 1873 L. WALLACE *Fair God* VII. ii. 452, I am not an evil spirit, to fly the exorcisement of thy bell. 1502 *Ord. Crysten Men* (W. de W. 1506) I. ii. 12 But for the good understanding the which is exorciser that is to be noted. a1806 HORSLEY *Serm.* (1810) I. x. 230 Things that they had seen done..by professed exorcisers. 1610 BP. HALL *Apol. Brownists* §45 Their anoylings, their exorcizings. 1664 MORE *Myst. Iniq.* xviii, Of the Enchanting or Exorcizing of Water [etc.]. 1817 T. L. PEACOCK *Melincourt* i, The invariable exorcising apparatus of a large venison pasty.

exorcize, *sb. rare.* [f. prec. vb.] The action of the vb. EXORCIZE.

1863 THORNBURY *True as Steel* II. 107 Let us drink to the exorcise of the evil spirit of treachery.

†**e'xord**, *v. Obs.*$^{-0}$ [ad. L. *exord-īrī*: see EXORDIUM.] *intr.* To begin.

1613 in R. C. *Table Alph.* (ed. 3).

exordial (ɛg'zɔːdɪəl), *a.* [f. L. *exordi-um* + -AL^{1}.] Of, pertaining to, or of the nature of, an exordium; introductory.

1682 SIR T. BROWNE *Chr. Mor.* (1756) 127 To undervalue that, unto which this is but exordial. 1751 JOHNSON *Rambler* No. 158 ⁋11 If the exordial verses of Homer be compared with the rest of the poem. 1846 SIR W. HAMILTON *Diss.* in *Reid's Wks.* 905 But it would seem in general, that the exordial movement..is also the central movement.

†**e'xordiate**, *v. Obs.* [f. L. *exordi-um* + -ATE^{3}.] *intr.* To utter an exordium, begin.

1594 *Zepheria* xxxix. in Arb. *Garner* V. 85 If..she.. Command thee not to peace, ere thou exordiate!

†**e'xordinary**, *a. Obs.* [f. EX- *pref.*^{1} + ORDINARY.] = EXTRAORDINARY.

1601 DEACON & WALKER *Spirits & Divels* 233 The approoued priuiledge of any exordinarie power from the Lord.

‖**exordium** (ɛg'zɔːdɪəm). *Pl.* **exordiums, exordia.** [L. *exordium*, f. *exordīrī* to begin, f. *ex-* + *ordīrī* to begin.] The beginning of anything; *esp.* the introductory part of a discourse, treatise, etc.; 'the proemial part of a composition' (J.).

[1531 ELYOT *Gov.* I. xiv, Onely they lacke pleasaunt fourme of begynnyng, called in latin Exordium.] 1581 MARBECK *Bk. of Notes* 515 Saint Paule..doeth with a godly *Exordium* touch the arrogancie of the false Apostles. 1594 DRAYTON *Idea* 533 Some..With Flames and Lightnings their Exordiums paint. 1649 SELDEN *Laws Eng.* II. Pref. (1739) 2, I shall consider them jointly, as in way of Exordium to the rest. 1736 WEST *Let.* in *Gray's Poems* (1775) 11 My poor little Eclogue..has been condemned.. an exordium of about sixteen lines absolutely cut off. 1838 DICKENS *Nich. Nick.* iii, With this exordium..Nickleby took a newspaper from his pocket. 1850 GROTE *Greece* II. lvii. (1862) V. 133 Alkibiades started up forthwith—his impatience breaking loose from the formalities of an exordium.

exordize ('ɛksɔdaɪz), *v. rare.* [f. EXORDI-UM + -IZE.] *intr.* To make an exordium; to begin.

1887 *Sat. Rev.* 23 Apr. 596 Mr. Symons..exordizes with the words 'I have ever held' etc.

†**exordy.** *Obs.* Anglicized f. EXORDIUM.

c1430 LYDG. *Bochas* VII. (1554) 167 a, With an exordye her to diffame. —— *Hors, Shepe, & G.* (Roxb.) 14 With an exordye of latyn he dide thus expresse, Veste purpurea, etc.

†**e'xore**, *v. Obs.* [ad. L. *exōr-āre*, f. *ex-* (see EX- *pref.*^{1}) + *ōrāre* to entreat.] *trans.* To beseech, prevail upon by entreaty; = EXORATE.

1598 TOFTE *Alba* (1880) 54 Exorde, desirde, intreated, they'le not be.

†**e'xorn**, *v. Obs.* Also 5 exourn. [ad. L. *exornāre*, f. *ex-* (see EX- *pref.*^{1}) + *ornāre* to adorn.] *trans.* To adorn, embellish; = EXORNATE *v.*

c1450 *Mirour Saluacioun* 1167 Twelve leonnceux oure sex greces Salomones throne exourned. 1509 HAWES *Past. Pleas.* 37 Yet Elocusion..The mater exorneth right well. c1555 HARPSFIELD *Divorce Hen. VIII* (1878) 115 With long painted supervacaneall words exorned. 1609 T. HIGGONS in T. Morton *Answ.* 1 Iames Gretzer..hath exorned it with a speciall encomion.

†**e'xornate**, *pple. Obs.* [ad. L. *exornāt-us*, pa. pple. of *exornāre*: see prec.] Adorned.

1509 HAWES *Past. Pleas.* XII. i, Whan the matter is founde by invencyon..And by elocucyons famous clerenes Exornate well.

†**e'xornate**, *v. Obs.* [f. ppl. stem of L. *exornāre*: see EXORN.] *trans.* To adorn, embellish.

1539 TAVERNER *Gard. Wysed.* II. 17 b, Gods propertye is, to garnyshe and exornate the offyce of the magistrat and rulers. 1572 L. LLOYD *Pilgr. Pr.* (1607) 30 Nature was alwayes desirous..to exornate and beautifie her selfe with knowledge. 1589 PUTTENHAM *Eng. Poesie* II. (Arb.) 142 Their *hemimeris* or halfe foote serued..to bewtifie and exornate the verse. 1656-81 in BLOUNT *Glossogr.*

†**exor'nation.** *Obs.* [ad. L. *exornātiōn-em* (used *Rhet.* by Cicero and Cornificius), n. of action f. *exornāre*: see EXORN.]

The action of adorning, the condition of being adorned; decoration, embellishment. Also, an instance, method, or means of embellishment; an adornment. Chiefly *Rhet.*

1548 UDALL *Erasm. Par. Luke* Pref. 3 a, The painted colours, and exornacions of Rethorike. 1553 T. WILSON *Rhet.* 90 Exornacion is a gorgiousse beautifiynge of the tongue with borowed wordes. 1589 WARNER *Alb. Eng.* (1612) 331 For the greater reuerence and exornation of the present solemnity. 1624 *Gag for Pope* 14 In the Orchards.. amongst other exornations and furnitures of comelines, they haue whole trees of Sauine. a1640 JACKSON *Creed* XI. xlvi. Wks. XI. 364 Artificial exornations, or words more choice than such as spring out of the matters handled. 1657 J. SMITH *Myst. Rhet.* 221 Many times repeating..but yet with other words..and exornations.

†**e'xornatory**, *a. Obs.* [f. L. *exornāre*: see EXORNATE *v.* and -ORY.] Concerned with adornment.

1657 TOMLINSON *Renou's Disp.* 707 The Exornatory Art.

†**e'xornify**, *v. Obs.*$^{-0}$ [f. EXORN + -(I)FY.] *trans.* To deck or garnish.

1613 in R. C. *Table Alph.* (ed. 3).

exorrhizal, -ous: see EXO- *pref.*

†**e'xort**, *v. Obs.* [f. L. *exort-* ppl. stem of *exorīrī*, f. *ex-* (see EX- *pref.*^{1}) + *orīrī* to arise.] *intr.* To spring up, issue forth.

a1400 *Cov. Myst.* (1841) 107 Alle myn Aungellys..crye that grace to man myghte exorte.

exort(e, obs. form of EXHORT.

exortacion, -ation, obs. ff. EXHORTATION.

†**e'xortion.** *Obs.* [f. as if ad. L. **exortiōn-em*, n. of action f. *exorīrī*: see EXORT.] The action of arising or (of a leaf) emerging; the point of emergence.

1657 TOMLINSON *Renou's Disp.* 382 Its fruits..erupt about the exortion of its leafes.

†**e'xortive**, *a. Obs.*$^{-0}$ [ad. L. *exortīv-us*, f. *exorīrī*: see EXORT.] Pertaining to the rising of the sun or to the east.

1656-81 in BLOUNT *Glossogr.* 1730-6 in BAILEY (folio).

†**e'xorture.** *Obs. rare.* [f. L. type **exortūra* f. *exorīrī* (see EXORT).] Rise, origin.

1578 BANISTER *Hist. Man* I. 21 Whiche [processes] rising also from the sides of the Vertebres, do erect their exorture upwardes. *Ibid.* I. 32 From [the ridge of Ilium]..flow Ligamentes, and the exorture of these Muscles, that constitute the buttockes.

exoscopic: see EXO- *pref.*

†**e'xosculate**, *v. Obs.*$^{-0}$ [f. ppl. stem of L. *exosculārī*, f. *ex-* (see EX- *pref.*^{1}) + *osculārī* to kiss, f. *oscul-um* a kiss.] *trans.* To kiss heartily.

1570 in LEVINS *Manip.* 1623-6 in COCKERAM. 1721-1800 in BAILEY.

†**exoscu'lation.** *Obs.* [ad. L. *exosculātiōn-em*, n. of action f. *exosculārī*: see prec.]

1. The action of 'exosculating'; a hearty kiss.

a1560 BECON *Displ. Pop. Mass* (1637) 298, I passe over your..genuflexions..and exosculations. 1652 SPARKE *Prim. Devot.* (1663) 522 Asking him forgiveness..which St. James expressed by prayer for him, and exosculation.

2. *Anat.* Anastomosis.

1634 T. JOHNSON tr. *Parey's Chirurg.* III. xi. (1678) 64 Pressing the blood on both sides..until you shall find the exosculation of these vessels.

exoskeletal, -on: see EXO- *pref.*

exosmic (ɛk'sɒzmɪk), *a.* [f. Gr. ἔξω (see EXO-) + ὠσμό-ς (see EXOSMOSIS) + -IC.] 'Of or belonging to EXOSMOSE' (*Syd. Soc. Lex.* 1884).

exosmose ('ɛksɒzməʊs). *Physics* and *Phys.* [a. Fr. *exosmose*, formed by Dutrochet as if ad. mod.L. *exōsmōsis*: see next. Cf. ENDOSMOSE, OSMOSE.] = next.

1828 *Edin. Jrnl. Science* IX. 104 This action M. Dutrochet calls exosmose or impulse *outwards*, from the Greek words ἐξ out and ωσμος, an impulse. 1875 DARWIN *Insectiv. Pl.* v. 82 The impairment of the leaves may be attributed to injury from exosmose.

fig. 1888 J. JACOBS *Bidpai* xxxvi, There was an exosmose of ideas and tales between the literate and illiterate.

exosmosis (ɛksɒz'məʊsɪs). *Physics* and *Phys.* [mod.L. (quasi-Gr.), f. Gr. ἐξ-ω (see EXO-) + ὠσμός pushing; = EXOSMOSE. Cf. ENDOSMOSIS.] The passage of a fluid 'outwards' through a porous septum, to mix with external fluid.

1839 TODD *Cycl. Anat.* II. 98/2 There is then a current of ..exosmosis which enters it [the bladder]. **1874** JONES & SIEV. *Pathol. Anat.* 406 The menstrual, and hæmorrhoidal discharge, is rather analogous to the process of exosmosis.

exosmotic (ɛksɒz'mɒtɪk). [f. as prec. on Gr. analogies; cf. *anastomosis, anastomotic.*] 'Relating to exosmose' (*Syd. Soc. Lex.* 1884).

exosperm, -spore, -sporous: see EXO- *pref.*

exossate (ɛk'sɒseɪt), *v.* [f. L. *exossāt-* ppl. stem of *exossāre* to deprive of the bones, f. *ex-* (see EX- *pref.*¹) + *oss-*, *os* bone.] *trans.* To deprive of bones; †to cause (fruits) to grow without stones. Hence **e'xossated** *ppl. a.* **exo'ssation** (of fruits) (see quots.).

1721–1800 BAILEY, *Exossate.* **1828** LANDOR *Imag. Conv.* (1846) II. 8 Signor Flavio..reaches Florence, eviscerated, exossated. **1626** BACON *Sylva* §854 *Marg. note*, Experiment Solitary touching Exossation of Fruits. **1660** SHARROCK *Vegetables* 138 Another experiment is the exossation of fruit, or causing it to grow without stones or core. **1703** *Art's Improv.* p. xxiii, Exossation of Fruit.

†**e'xosseous**, *a. Obs. rare*⁻¹. [f. L. *exoss-is* boneless (f. *ex-* (see EX- *pref.*¹) + *oss-*, *os* bone) + -EOUS; after *osseous.*] Boneless.

1646 SIR T. BROWNE *Pseud. Ep.* III. xiii. 137 Snailes, a soft and exosseous animal.

†**e'xoster.** *Antiq. Obs.* [ad. L. *exōstra*, a. Gr. ἐξωστρα (f. ἐξ (see EX- *pref.*²) + ὠθέειν to thrust).] A hanging bridge anciently used by besiegers; also (see quot. from Blount).

1569 J. SANFORD tr. *Agrippa's Van. Artes* 33 b, Ye engins called..Exosters. **1656–81** BLOUNT *Glossogr.*, *Exoster*, an ancient Engine for war; now used for a Petard to blow open a Port or Gate. **1692–1732** in COLES.

exostome: see EXO- *pref.*

†**e'xostosated**, *ppl. a. Obs.* In 8 **exhostosated.** [f. as next + -ATE + -ED¹.] Affected with exostosis; = EXOSTOSED.

1758 J. S. *Le Dran's Observ. Surg.* (1771) L iij b, It was carious, and exhostosated.

exostosed (ɛk'sɒstəʊzd), *ppl. a.* [ad. Fr. *exostosé*, f. *exostose* EXOSTOSIS: see -ED¹.]

1. Affected with exostosis.

1758 J. S. *Le Dran's Observ. Surg.* (1771) 96, I..found the ..sixth of the true Ribs..exostosed. *Ibid.* 320 You may see ..an exostosed Ridge. **1766** JUSTAMOND in *Phil. Trans.* LVI. 270 An entire tibia, exostosed and carious.

¶**2.** Having an external bony covering; = EXOSKELETAL. *rare.*

1887 E. D. COPE *Origin of the Fittest* 46 The cartilaginous, osseous, and exostosed..characters distinguish otherwise nearly allied genera.

‖**exostosis** (ɛksɒ'stəʊsɪs). [mod.L., a. Gr. ἐξόστωσις (Galen) outgrowth of bone, f. ἐξ (see EX- *pref.*²) + ὀστέον bone.]

1. *Path.* **a.** The formation of bone on another bone, or on some other structure in the body. **b.** *concr.* A bony tumour found upon a bone or cartilage.

a. 1804 ABERNETHY *Surg. Observ.* 32 Tumours growing near, and compressing the surface of bones, frequently occasion a degree of exostosis.

b. 1736 FREKE in *Phil. Trans.* XLI. 369 It may be said to come under the Denomination of an Exostosis. **1782** W. HEBERDEN *Comm. Hist. & Cure Dis.* xi, Except some exostoses of the vertebræ of the thorax. **1839** TODD *Cycl. Anat.* II. 220/2 Exostosis appears most frequently on the upper jaw. **1868** DARWIN *Anim. & Pl.* II. xii. 23 Bony exostoses on the legs [of a horse] caused by too much travelling on hard roads.

2. *Bot.* 'A diseased condition in plants, in which hard masses of wood are produced, projecting like warts or tumours from the main stem or roots' (*Treas. Bot.* 1866).

exostotic (ɛksɒ'stɒtɪk), *a.* [f. as prec.: see -OTIC.] Of or pertaining to exostosis; of the nature of an exostosis.

1836 TODD *Cycl. Anat.* I. 460/1 We distinguish a node from a truly exostotic growth by the rapidity of its formation. **1875** H. WALTON *Dis. Eyes* 35 Exostotic spiculæ.

†**exostracism** (ɛk'sɒstrəsɪz(ə)m). *Obs.* [ad. Gr. ἐξοστρακισμός, f. ἐξοστρακίζειν: see next.] = OSTRACISM.

[**1580** NORTH *Plutarch* (1676) 275 Ostracismon, or Exostracismon, was no ordinary punishment for any fault committed.] **1617** T. LYDYAT in *Ussher's Lett.* (1686) 58 Themistocles's expulsion or exostracism from Athens. **1697** BENTLEY *Ep. Themistocles* (1836) 183 The Letters had a worse exostracism than their author. **1699** —— *Phal.* 89 Banish'd..by way of Exostracism.

exostracize (ɛk'sɒstrəsaɪz), *v.* [ad. Gr. ἐξοστρακίζειν, f. ἐξ (see EX- *pref.*²) + ὀστρακίζειν to OSTRACIZE.] *trans.* To banish by ostracism; also *fig.* Hence **e'xostracized** *ppl. a.*

1838 F. LIEBER *Man. Pol. Ethics* I. 429 The exostracised citizen was not punished. **1872** F. HALL *False Philol.* 70 This word [bountiful] which Mr. White exostracizes.

exoteric (ɛksəʊ'tɛrɪk), *a.* and *sb.* [ad. late L. *exōteric-us*, a. Gr. ἐξωτερικ-ός, f. ἐξωτέρω, compar. of ἔξω outside.] **A.** *adj.*

1. Pertaining to the outside; external. Now only with some allusion to sense 2.

1662 H. MORE *Philos. Writ.* Pref. (1662) p. vi, An Exoterick Fence or exteriour Fortification about Theologie. **1790** PALEY *Horæ Paul.* Wks. 1825 III. 127 This motive appears to have been always exoteric, viz. a love of order and tranquillity. **1808** SCOTT *Autobiog.* in *Lockhart* (1839) I. 50 All the knights and ladies and dragons and giants in their outward and exoteric sense. **1858** GLADSTONE *Homer* II. 60 Charged with the exoteric and material parts of several.. functions.

b. *Phys.* 'Applied to those periodic, vital phenomena, which result from causes external to, and independent of, the organism.' (*Syd. Soc. Lex.* 1884).

1860 in MAYNE *Exp. Lex.*

2. Of philosophical doctrines, treatises, modes of speech, etc.: Designed for or suitable to the generality of disciples; communicated to outsiders, intelligible to the public. Hence of disciples, etc.: Belonging to the outer circle; not admitted to the esoteric teaching. Of an author: Dealing with ordinary topics; commonplace, simple. Opposed to ESOTERIC, q.v. for the history of the words.

1655–60 STANLEY *Hist. Philos.* (1701) 232/1 The Discourse and Doctrine which he [Aristotle] delivered to his Disciples was of two kinds. One he called Exoterick. **1738** WARBURTON *Div. Legat.* III. iii. Wks. (1811) III. 58 He divided his disciples into two classes; the one he called the Esoteric, the other, the Exoteric. *a* **1754**, **1768** [see ESOTERIC A. 1]. **1791** BOSWELL *Johnson* 1 July an. 1763, With an air of superiority, like that of an esoterick over an exoterick disciple of a sage of antiquity. **1847** LEWES *Hist. Philos.* (1867) I. 210 Plato like Pythagoras had exoteric and esoteric opinions. **1870** R. C. JEBB *Sophocles' Electra* (ed. 2) 44/2 As if Apollo were an exoteric name for the Sun. **1870** LOWELL *Among my Bks.* Ser. I. (1873) 153 In mind and temperament too exoteric for a mystic.

3. *transf.* **a.** Current among the outside public; popular, ordinary, prevailing. **b.** Qualifying a personal epithet: That is such exoterically, or with regard to his popular utterances.

1813 MAR. EDGEWORTH *Patron.* xxxvi, This exoteric practice goes on to this hour among literary performers. **1850** CARLYLE *Latter-d. Pamph.* iii. 6 Such..is the exoteric public conviction about these sublime establishments in Downing Street. **1876** [see ESOTERIC A. 2].

B. *sb.*

1. *pl.* (after Gr. τὰ ἐξωτερικά) Exoteric doctrines; exoteric treatises.

1738 WARBURTON *Div. Legat.* iii. *note* Wks. (1811) III. 359 In his exoterics, he gave the world both a beginning and an end. **1768–74** TUCKER *Lt. Nat.* (1852) II. 31 Our exoterics will run directly contrary to our esoterics.

2. An uninitiated person, an outsider.

1697 *State Philadelph. Soc.* 19 The Philadelphians have many things to say that cannot be declared among the Exotericks. **1824** MACAULAY *Crit. Ital. Writers* Misc. Writ. & Sp. (1889) 51, I am an exoteric—utterly unable to explain the mysteries of this new poetical faith.

exoterical (ɛksəʊ'tɛrɪkəl), *a.* [f. as prec. + -AL¹.] = prec. adj.

1637 R. HUMPHREY tr. *S. Ambrose* Pref., Two sorts, one exotericall, which is in common and civill use. *a* **1656** HALES *Gold. Rem.* (1688) 189 Aristotle was wont to divide his Lectures..into Acroamatical and Exoterical. *a* **1751** BOLINGBROKE *Ess., Monotheism* §11 in Wks. 1754 IV. 235 Exoterical, or publick doctrines. **1827** WHATELY *Logic* Introd. p.v, A loose, vague, and popular kind of language; such as would be the best suited indeed to an exoterical discourse. **1858** R. A. VAUGHAN *Ess. & Rev.* I. 32 His partisans have resorted in his defence to his exoterical writings.

exoterically (ɛksəʊ'tɛrɪkəlɪ), *adv.* [f. prec. + -LY².] In an exoteric manner; in a style suited to the uninitiated.

1738 WARBURTON *Div. Legat.* III. iii. Wks. (1811) III. 90 The subject..must needs be handled exoterically. **1831** CARLYLE *Sart. Res.* (1858) 43 [The] Dingy Priest..preaches forth (exoterically enough) one little textlet from the Gospel of Freedom. **1864** MAX MÜLLER *Sc. Lang.* Ser. II. vii. (1868) 304 He may have represented him exoterically as a human being.

exotericism (ɛksəʊ'tɛrɪsɪz(ə)m). [f. EXOTERIC *a.* and *sb.* + -ISM.] Exoteric doctrines, or belief in these. Hence **exo'tericist**, one who holds such doctrines.

1886 WEBSTER Exotericism. **1954** P. TOWNSEND tr. *Schuon's Transcendent Unity Religions* iii. 53 We must now answer more explicitly the question as to the truths that exotericism must of necessity ignore. **1954** EXOTERICIST [see ESOTERICISM]. **1955** *Jrnl. Theol. Stud.* VI. 339 Exotericism as such is according to Schuon not blameworthy, but necessary.

e'xotery. [? f. Gr. ἐξωτέρω + -Y³. (But prob. a misprint.)] Exoteric doctrine or instruction.

1763 [see ESOTERY].

exotheca, -thecal, -thecium: see EXO- *pref.*

exotherm ('ɛksəʊθɜːm). *Chem.* [f. Gr. ἔξω EXO- + θέρμη heat; cf. next.] A compound which liberates heat during its formation and which absorbs heat or energy during its decomposition. So **exo'thermal** *a.* = EXOTHERMIC *a.*; **exo'thermally** *adv.*

1895 C. S. PALMER tr. *Nernst's Theoret. Chem.* IV. v. 584 The direction of the chemical change does not necessarily coincide with the direction in which the reaction progresses exothermally. **1906** A. SMITH *Introd. Gen. Inorg. Chem.* ii. 27 Exothermal actions, as those which produce heat are called, are usually of the spontaneous order. **1909** *Cent. Dict.* Suppl., Exotherm. **1954** *Electronic Engin.* XXVI. 139 It is possible to control the exotherm by maintaining the resin and the hardener at a low temperature. **1959** *Jrnl. Iron & Steel Inst.* CXCII. 389/3 Compositions and physical properties of insulating firebricks and fireclay bricks are compared, and compositions and exothermal qualities..are given. **1965** PHILLIPS & WILLIAMS *Inorg. Chem.* I. xiii. 506 Water reacts exothermally with very many oxides.

exothermic (ɛksəʊ'θɜːmɪk), *a. Chem.* [ad. F. *exothermique* (M. Berthelot *Essai de mécanique chimique* (1879) II. IV. ii. 18), f. as prec. + -IC.] Characterized by, or attended by, the development of heat; *spec.* designating an exotherm. Cf. ENDOTHERMIC *a.* Hence **exo'thermically** *adv.*

1884, 1945 [see ENDOTHERMIC *a.*]. **1958** *Engineering* 4 Apr. 431/2 The neutral hydrogen mesic atoms drift around and can exchange their muons with deuterium atoms. The exothermic nature of this exchange makes it highly probable. **1962** W. B. THOMPSON *Introd. Plasma Physics* iv. 58 It is known that many exothermic nuclear reactions with high intrinsic cross sections are inhibited at low energies by the Coulomb repulsion between the like charges on the nuclei. **1964** N. G. CLARK *Mod. Org. Chem.* vi. 108 Ammonia and amines react readily and exothermically with ethylene oxide. **1966** PHILLIPS & WILLIAMS *Inorg. Chem.* II. xxii. 142 They are formed exothermically from the elements. *Ibid.*, It is a refractory substance, strongly exothermic.

exotic (ɛg'zɒtɪk), *a.* and *sb.* [ad. L. *exōtic-us*, a. Gr. ἐξωτικός, f. ἔξω outside. Cf. Fr. *exotique.*]

A. *adj.*

1. †**a.** Belonging to another country, foreign, alien (*obs.*). **b.** In narrowed sense: Introduced from abroad, not indigenous. Now chiefly of plants (in popular language with added sense of 'not naturalized or acclimatized'); also, of words, forms of speech or writing, fashions, etc.

1599 B. JONSON *Ev. Man out of Hum.* IV. iii, Magick, Witchcraft, or other such exotick arts. **1646** SIR T. BROWNE *Pseud. Ep.* II. vi. §3. 98 As Exotick observers deliver, it groweth upon Almond trees. **1650** FULLER *Pisgah* I. xii. 38 It was an exotick and forain territory. **1660** SHARROCK *Vegetables* 34 [The] Mulbery is..an exotique plant. **1680** MORDEN *Geog. Rect., Wales* (1685) 27 [Welsh] hath the least mixture of Exotick words of any now used in Europe. **1756** FOOTE *Engl. ret. fr. Paris* Wks. 1799 I. 123 I'll have these exotic attendants..sent post to the place from whence they came. **1779–81** JOHNSON *L.P., Hughes*, The Italian Opera, an exotick and irrational entertainment. **1793** MURPHY *Tacitus* (1805) I. 235 And invited to reign over them an exotic king. **1839** DE QUINCEY *Recoll. Lakes* Wks. 1862 II. 78 Rome had cast much of her literature in her own moulds before these exotic models had begun to domineer. **1845** *Florist's Jrnl.* 23 The exotic class of the order.

†**c.** Drawn from outside; extrinsic. Also, Foreign in character, alien *to*. *Obs.*

1671 R. BOHUN *Disc. conc. Wind* 56 They run streaming between two Mountains..and are guarded on all sides from the inroads of other Exotique Winds and Air. *a* **1718** PENN *Tracts* Wks. 1726 I. 473 These and the like Practices, strange and exotick to the Primitive and Christian Faith and Worship. **1727** DE FOE *Syst. Magic* I. iii. (1840) 79 An absolute necessity of some exotic helps.

2. a. Of or pertaining to, or characteristic of a foreigner, or what is foreign (now *rare*); hence **b.** Outlandish, barbarous, strange, uncouth. Also, having the attraction of the strange or foreign, glamorous.

a. *a* **1659** BP. MORTON *Episc. Justified* (1670) 51 Mr. Selden, the Ornament of our Nation for Exotick Learning. **1720** SWIFT *Mod. Educ.* Wks. 1755 II. II. 34 An exotick habit and demeanor, added to other foreign accomplishments. **1833** I. TAYLOR *Fanat.* vi. 167 When shall the European families drive the exotic tyranny for ever from their shores! **1875** MAINE *Hist. Inst.* viii. 230 The exotic extraction of one of the Original Tribes.

b. 1629 MAXWELL tr. *Herodian* (1635) 295 Entring the City..in that exoticke and barbarous garbe. **1630** BRATHWAIT *Eng. Gentlem.* (1641) 149 The boarish and exoticke speech of Diogenes. **1634** SIR T. HERBERT *Trav.* 224 Lest your entreated patience turne into exoticke passion. **1720** WELTON *Suffer. Son of God* I. x. 252 A Man, who would make this the Rule of his Conduct, Passes for an Extraordinary, Singular..and Exotick spirit. **1739** CIBBER *Apol.* xi. 312 In his dealing with so exotick a Partner. **1815** SCOTT *Guy M.* xxix, I have not the poor satisfaction of interesting a human being—not even the exotic monster of a parson. **1919** F. HURST *Humoresque* 85 She was about as exotic as a flowering weed which can spring so strongly and so fibrously from slack. **1933** F. BALDWIN *Innocent Bystander* (1935) ix. 172 She hadn't bothered to be exotic and provocative with him. **1933** *Punch* 15 Nov. 546, I want a perfume thuitable to an ecthotic blonde with innothent green eythe and a lithp. **1958** *Listener* 7 Aug. 202/3 An enormous hangar fitted with exotic devices.

c. *spec.* Of or pertaining to strip-tease or a strip-teaser. orig. *U.S.*

1954 *Newsweek* 8 Nov. 96/2 One mushrooming by-product of burlesque,..is what the 1954 billboards call the

exotic dancer. *Ibid.* 97/1 Night-club owners who want to bolster attendance hire an exotic dancer. **1955** *Evening Sun* (Baltimore) 19 July 1 The League of Exotic Dancers.. a group within the American Guild of Variety Artists, through which all the girl entertainers are booked. **1965** R. Hardwick *Plotters* (1966) xiii. 114 'Exotic dancer—' 'A euphemism for stripper.' **1967** E. Ambler *Dirty Story* I. ii. 20 My wife.. is an exotic dancer.

d. Designating any of various high-energy fuels, esp. non-hydrocarbon ones, developed orig. for rocket engines; also applied to certain metals not previously used to a significant extent in technology. orig. *U.S.*

1957 in *Amer. Speech* (1960) XXXV. 285 Fuels that combine hydrogen with boron or lithium are considered to be exotic fuels. **1958** [see BEEF *v.* 2 b]. **1958** C. C. Adams et al. *Space Flight* iii. 83 During recent months the terms 'exotic propellants', 'Zip-fuels', and 'Hi-Cals' have come into the pages of the trade and technical literature of rocketry. These generally embrace efforts outside strictly conventional lines to develop high-energy power sources but do, on occasion, include merely high-energy types of liquids and solids. **1961** *Technology* Nov. 282 Alloys of columbium (niobium), one of the new 'exotic' metals noted for its strength and corrosion resistance. **1963** *Machinery* 20 Mar. 631/2 Quite recently it has become increasingly fashionable to describe certain metals as exotic. **1970** M. Smith *Aviation Fuels* lv. 414 In the early stages of the development programme on these exotic fuels they were prohibitively expensive.

B. *sb.*

1. a. A plant, formerly also an animal, of foreign extraction; in popular language, a foreign plant not acclimatized or naturalized.

c **1645** C. Morton *An Enquiry* 2 The crane is an exotick. **1672** Grew *Anat. Plants, Idea Philos. Hist.* §8 All Exoticks .. may probably be reduced to some such Domesticks. **1762–71** H. Walpole *Vertue's Anecd. Paint.* (1786) IV. 294 In the bishop of London's garden at Fulham are many exotics of very ancient date. **1796** C. Marshall *Garden.* xix. (1815) 387 What has been said of Geraniums, applies to all .. Exotics. **1812** *Rees's Cycl.* s.v., The generality of exotics .. do not thrive in England without some peculiar care and culture. **1846** J. Baxter *Libr. Pract. Agric.* (ed. 4) II. Introd. 4 Potatoes were first.. cultivated as a rare exotic.

b. *transf.* and *fig.*

1795 W. Taylor in *Monthly Rev.* XVII. 410 The Welsh is wholly self-derived, and free from exotics. **1823** Lamb *Elia* Ser. I. iii. (1865) 19 Roast veal, or.. griskin (exotics unknown to our palates). **1849** H. Rogers *Ess.* II. vi. 303 Other systems of religion are usually delicate exotics, and will not bear transplanting. **1858** Buckle *Civiliz.* (1869) II. viii. 543 In a country like Spain, a great bank was an exotic which might live with art but could never thrive by nature.

c. An exotic dancer (see sense A. 2 c, above), a stripper. orig. *U.S.*

1954 *Daily Oklahoman* 24 Jan. 29 (*heading*) New exotics at the Derby [Club]. **1965** L. Whitten *Progeny of Adder* (1966) 30 A still-famous tenor shared billing with the immense breasts of an 'exotic' named Telly Stahr.

2. A person of foreign origin; a foreigner. *rare.*

1651 *Fuller's Abel Rediv.* 516 Proclamations were every where set up against exotics. **1763** Wilkes *Corr.* (1805) I. 80 One other exotic, too, I must not forget: Arthur Murphy, gent. **1841** Catlin *N. Amer. Ind.* (1844) II. lviii. 230 An exotic, with a pale face, and from across the ocean. **1863** Mrs. C. Clarke *Shaks. Char.* vi. 159 These same exotics are received by our easy, gullible brethren with 'outstretched arms'.

Hence † **e'xoticness**, exotic or foreign quality.

1631 Weever *Anc. Fun. Mon.* 697 The very exoticknesse of the workemanship.

‖**exotica** (ɛg'zɒtɪkə), *sb. pl.* [L., neut. pl. of *exōticus* EXOTIC *a.*] Exotic objects or items.

1876 W. E. A. Axon (*title*) Exotica... Translations in verse. **1957** A. Graf (*title*) Exotica. Pictorial cyclopedia of indoor plants. **1958** Blesh & Janis *They all played Ragtime* iv. 73 The brasses included exotica like flügelhorn, euphonium, French horn, and Sousaphone. **1959** *Listener* 2 Apr. 592/2 Glass-sided office buildings, banks, cafeterias, department stores—all have become filled with *exotica*. **1970** *Sunday Times* 6 Dec. 43/5 Mrs. Boston, whose small shop.. will contain a wide spectrum of exotica.

†**e'xotical**, *a. Obs.* [f. EXOTIC *a.* + -AL[1].]

1. Of foreign origin or growth; imported from abroad; = EXOTIC *a.* 1.

1601 Holland *Pliny* XXII. xxiv, We may both preserve and recover our health.. without these exoticall and forraine drugs. **1672** H. Dodwell *2 Lett. of Advice* (1691) 204 Most of them [certain canonized Heroes] are exotical (which is the reason of their strangeness in the Greek). **1678** Cudworth *Intell. Syst.* 309 This word 'Αθηνᾶ.. was not originally Greekish, but exotical.

2. Of or pertaining to foreigners, or a foreign country; foreign; hence barbarous, outlandish, strange; = EXOTIC *a.* 2.

1608 Bp. Hall *Epist.* I. viii, Many.. have brought nothing from forraine countries, but mishapen cloathes, or exoticall gestures. **1641** 'Smectymnuus' *Vind. Answ.* xvi. 207 Nor did we ever intend to affixe those exoticall positions of unsound teachers.. upon her. **1716** M. Davies *Athen. Brit.* III. 51 Of the same Colour and Complexion with some Sectary exotical Tenets.

Hence **e'xotically** *adv.*, in an exotic, foreign, or outlandish manner. †**e'xoticalness**, the quality or state of being exotic.

1670–98 Lassels *Voy. Italy* II. 116 A great train of horsemen and trumpeters clad exotically. **1730–6** Bailey (folio), *Exoticalness*; whence in mod. Dicts. **1947** 'W. Targ' *Carrousel for Bibliophiles* 398 Arthur Morrison's exotically titled *The Green Eye of Goona*.. was transmuted by the American publisher—and one wonders why—into *The Green Diamond*.

exoticism (ɛg'zɒtɪsɪz(ə)m). [f. EXOTIC *a.* + -ISM.] **a.** Tendency to adopt what is exotic or foreign. **b.** Exotic character; an instance of this, anything exotic; *esp.* a foreign idiom or expression.

1827 Hare *Guesses* (1859) 503 The Greek original.. is tainted with many exoticisms and other defects. **1837** *Fraser's Mag.* XVI. 641 Academic forcing houses for the promotion of exoticism. **1887** F. Robinson *New Relig. Med.* 31 An opposite extreme, tending to exoticism.

exotism ('ɛksətɪz(ə)m). [ad. Fr. *exotisme*, f. *exotique*: see EXOTIC and -ISM.] Resemblance to what is foreign; a foreign 'air'.

1811 E. Jerningham in Robberds *Mem. W. Taylor* II. 328 A kind of energetic Exotism that tells me that the portrait is very like.

exotospore (ɛk'səʊtəʊspɔə(r)). *Zool.* [f. Gr. ἐξωτικός EXOTIC + -O- + SPORE.] = *sporozoite* (s.v. SPORO-).

1902 E. R. Lankester in *Nature* 27 Mar. 500/1 The malaria-germ which is brought by the stab of the Anopheles into the human blood-vessels.. is needle-like in shape,.. but the most important fact about it for description and comparison is that it has been formed outside the human body, and is introduced as a strange element into the human blood by the agency of the mosquito. I.. call it the Exotospore.

Exoucontian: see EXUCONTIAN.

†**exousi'astic**, *a. Obs. rare.* [ad. Gr. ἐξουσιαστικός, f. ἐξουσιάζειν to exercise authority, f. ἐξουσία authority.] Of or pertaining to authority; authoritative.

1688 Renwick *Serm.* (1776) 539 The exousiastick power of trying, sending and authorising office-bearers in the church is made void. *Ibid.* 568.

†**expalpate**, *v. Obs.*—[0] [f. L. *expalpāt-* ppl. stem of *expalp-āre*, f. *ex-* (see EX- *pref.*[1]) + *palpāre* to pat + -ATE[3].] *trans.* To get by flattery.

1623–6 in Cockeram.

expand (ɛk'spænd), *v.* Pa. pple. 5 **expande**. [ad. L. *expandĕre*, f. *ex-* (see EX- *pref.*[1]) + *pandĕre* to spread. Cf. OF. *espandre*, mod.F. *épandre* to diffuse, scatter.]

1. *trans.* To spread out; to spread out flat or smooth; to open out, unfold; †to remove the folds or wrinkles from, to smooth (the forehead); also, to spread out to view, display. *lit.* and *fig.*

1432–50 [see EXPANDED]. *a* **1667** Cowley *Ess. Avarice* 130 You laugh now, and expand your careful Brow. **1695** Woodward *Nat. Hist. Earth* v. (1723) 264 The upper.. Stratum that was expanded over those Valleys and Plains. **1706** J. Logan in *Pa. Hist. Soc. Mem.* X. 145 Money, like a mistress coming in view, expanded its charms. **1725** Pope *Odyss.* XII. 105 Expand thy sails, Ply the strong oar, and catch the nimble gales. **1768** Beattie *Minstr.* II. xxvii. Where yon oak expands her arms. **1770** Gibbon *Autobiog.* (1796) 136 The descent of Eneas.. to the world of spirits, expands an awful and boundless prospect. **1801** Southey *Thalaba* VI. xx, Here the rose expands Her paradise of leaves. **1848** L. Hunt *Jar Honey* x. 132 Sicily then lay expanded like a map beneath our eyes. **1877** J. D. Chambers *Div. Worship* 52 Stoles as a rule should not be expanded at the extremities.

b. To develop what is implicit in (a statement); to write out in full what is expressed by (a graphical contraction). Also in *Alg.* to work out the processes indicated by the terms of a contracted expression and state the result in full; to express at length in a series.

1802 Woodhouse in *Phil. Trans.* XCII. 88 $x\cdot(1 + x)^{-1}$ must be expanded, and the integrals of the several terms taken. **1858** Todhunter *Algebra* 296 Expand each of the following expressions to four terms. **1860** Maury *Phys. Geog. Sea* xx. §824 Let us examine, expand, and explain this fact. *Mod.* The editor has expanded the contractions in the MS.

†**c.** To give ample utterance to, 'pour out' (one's feelings); *refl.* to manifest unrestrainedly one's feelings; to overflow. *Obs.* Cf. Fr. *épancher*.

1656–81 Blount *Glossogr.*, *Expand*, to declare or utter. **1660** tr. *Amyraldus' Treat. Relig.* I. ii. 19 He takes pleasure to expand himself in acts of goodness towards his creatures. **1801** Fuseli *Lect. Art.* i. (1848) 357 The adoring figure of a priest.. expanding his gratitude at the shrine of the god whose arrows avenged his wrongs.

2. *intr.* for *refl.* To spread itself out; to unfold, open out; to develop. Const. *into*, *to*.

1560 Rolland *Crt. Venus* II. 859 Expand on hie, ga far about the wall. **1680** Dryden *Epit. Sir P. Fairborne's Tomb*, Like rising flames expanding in their height. **1684** R. H. *Sch. Recreat.* 32 Stars that will expand in flame, and appear like natural Stars. **1764** Goldsm. *Trav.* 6 A weary waste expanding to the skies. **1776** Withering *Brit. Plants* (1796) III. 675 Flowers.. expand at 6 or 7, and close at 2 in the afternoon. **1856** Kane *Arct. Expl.* I. v. 53 Hailed its folds with three cheers as they expanded in the cold midnight breeze. **1860** Tyndall *Glac.* I. viii. 59 Streams.. expanding here and there to deep green lakes. **1882** J. H. Blunt *Ref. Ch. Eng.* II. 391 The Wickliffity 'Known-men'.. of Henry VIII.'s day, expanded into the 'Gospellers' of Edward VI.'s reign.

b. To 'open out'; to grow communicative.

1823 Lamb *Elia* Ser. I. i. (1865) 5 How would he chirp, and expand over a muffin.

3. *trans.* 'To spread out every way' (J.); to cause to fill a larger space; to widen the boundaries, increase the area of capacity of; to dilate, enlarge: **a.** a material object. Also *refl.*

1665 *Phil. Trans.* I. 49 What Bodies are expanded by being frozen. **1707** Floyer *Physic. Pulse-watch* 217 All the hot Passions of Anger, Joy, expand the Spirits, and give them a more vehement Motion. **1796** Hutton *Math. Dict.* I. 456/1 Air compressed.. as soon as the compressing.. force is removed, expands itself.. to its former dimensions. **1835** Macaulay *Sir J. Mackintosh* Ess. (1854) I. 315/1 [The editor] has thus succeeded in expanding the volume into one of the thickest.. that we ever saw. *Mod.* The object of this gymnastic exercise is to expand the chest.

b. an immaterial object. Also *refl.*

c **1645** Howell *Lett.* IV. xxix, Let Christianity expand her self still by a passive fortitude. **1838** Prescott *Ferd. & Is.* II. xviii, The grand object to which he [Columbus] dedicated himself seemed to expand his whole soul. **1862** Stanley *Jew. Ch.* (1877) I. xviii. 333 Would these.. changes.. diminish or expand the faith.. of the Chosen People? **1867** Freeman *Norm. Conq.* (1876) I. App. 626 The longer version only expands, and in no way contradicts, the shorter one.

4. *intr.* for *refl.* To increase in bulk, swell; to become dilated or enlarged.

1807–26 S. Cooper *First Lines Surg.* (ed. 5) 403 To wet the sponge and make it expand. **1816** J. Smith *Panorama Sc. & Art* I. 2 Cast iron expands in passing from the fluid to the solid state. **1854** Ronalds & Richardson *Chem. Technol.* (ed. 2) I. 202 When air is warmed it expands and becomes lighter. **1882** Vines *Sachs' Bot.* 789 The pith very soon begins to become turgid and to expand.

fig.

1791 Mrs. Radcliffe *Rom. Forest* i, Her heart expanded in momentary joy. **1836** W. Irving *Astoria* I. 47 Such is a brief outline of the enterprise.. which continually expanded in his mind. **1865** Tylor *Early Hist. Man.* ii. 18 As his knowledge and power of reasoning expand under instruction. **1885** *Manch. Exam.* 28 Sept. 4/7 Our trade with China is steadily expanding.

expandable (ɛk'spændəb(ə)l), *a.* [f. EXPAND *v.* + -ABLE.] That can be expanded; expansible.

1926 H. W. Fowler *Mod. Eng. Usage* 3/1 For the italicized words.. it is recommended to substitute the accompanying form in *-able*.. *expansible*, expandable. **1965** *Language* XLI. 239 P (preposition) and C (conjunction) are expandable only to the extent that PP.. and CC sometimes functions as P and C respectively. **1969** *Jane's Freight Containers 1968–69* 113/3 Pole trailers (expandable to 55 ft).

expanded (ɛk'spændɪd), *ppl. a.* Also 5 **expande**. [f. EXPAND *v.* + -ED[1].] In the senses of the verb.

1. a. Spread open, outspread, outstretched, extended; †covering an extensive area.

1432–50 tr. *Higden* (Rolls) I. 81 There is a figge tre soe expande, that mony multitudes of peple may sytte vnder the latitude of oon figge tre. **1667** Milton *P.L.* I. 225 Then with expanded wings he stears his flight Aloft. **1795** Southey *Vis. Maid Orleans* II. 34 A wide expanded den. **1854** Woodward *Mollusca* (1856) 316 The animal holds fast by the expanded end of its foot. **1864** Boutell *Heraldry Hist. & Pop.* xix. §5 (ed. 3) 310 A wyvern, its tail nowed and wings expanded or. **1875** Ure *Dict. Arts* III. 641 s.v. *Printing*, Roman and Italic types.. *expanded* or letters widened horizontally.

b. *expanded metal*, *steel*, sheet metal slit and stretched into a lattice, used for making screens and lockers, and for reinforcing concrete, etc.

1890 *Builder* 28 June 477/3 A strip of steel.. is fed into a powerful automatic machine, which.. produces a sheet of expanded metal. **1891** [see LATHING *vbl. sb.*[1] 2]. **1913** *Lockwood's Dict. Mech. Engin.* (ed. 4) 434 *Expanded steel*, steel sheet which is pierced and opened out in a machine, yielding lozenge-shaped spaces, which are filled, and the whole embedded in concrete. **1937** *Discovery* January 20/2 A concrete jacket reinforced by expanded metal and pieces of scrap iron. **1958** *Observer* 3 Aug. 7/3 The first expanded metal.. was to replace timber laths in plaster work. **1968** *Gloss. Terms Mechanized & Hand Sheet Metal Work* (*B.S.I.*) 10 *Expanded metal*, a mesh consisting of a lattice-work of undulating strands.

2. a. Increased in area or bulk; enlarged. Also *fig.*

a **1734** North *Lives* I. 272 The husbandmen.. were.. provided for in his large expanded house. **1807** T. Thomson *Chem.* (ed. 3) II. 409 If one part in bulk of this expanded oxygen be mixed with three parts of pure oxygen gas. **1881** Westcott & Hort *Grk. N.T.* App. 9 The embolism, or expanded last double petition.

b. *Gram.* Designating the tense in which a form of the verb *to be* is used with a present participle (see quots.).

1931 O. Jespersen in *S.P.E. Tract* XXXVI. 524 By the side of the simple tenses we have in English expanded tenses, e.g.: *simple*: he works, he worked, he has worked; *expanded*: he is working, he was working, he has been working. *Ibid.* 527 The expanded infinitive often serves to emphasize the present moment, as in *What can he be doing?* as against the more general *What can he do?* **1932** *Jrnl. Eng. & Germanic Philol.* XXXI. 469 The expanded form must always be employed where the simple form, if used, might be construed as having general force. **1963** F. T. Visser *Hist. Syntax* I. iii. 189 When.. *to be* occurs in the 'expanded' or 'progressive' form, as in 'You are being naughty'.

Hence **ex'pandedness**.

1829 Bentham *Wks.* (1843) XI. 18 What you say.. shows the expandedness and expansiveness of your mind.

expander (ɛk'spændə(r)). [f. as prec. + -ER.] One who, or that which, expands (in senses of

the verb). *chest expander*: a calisthenic appliance for 'expanding' the chest.

1862 *Lit. Churchm.* VIII. 338/2 Nor can the animus of our 'expanders' [*i.e.* advocates of 'Church Expansion'] be at all doubtful. **1867** EMERSON *Lett. & Soc. Aims* vii. 183 Great love is the inventor and expander of the frozen powers. **1886** FREEMAN *Greater Greece, etc.* (*title of Lect.*), George Washington, the Expander of England. **1887** *Scientific Amer.* 18 June 394 A tube expander has been patented for expanding the ends of boiler tubes.

expanding (ɛk'spændɪŋ), *vbl. sb.* [f. as prec. + -ING¹.] The action of the vb. EXPAND in its various senses. Also *attrib.*

1844 UPTON *Physioglyphics* 9 Putting *g*, then, first, and attaching to it its expanding sense. **1866** G. MACDONALD *Ann. Q. Neighb.* xxx. (1878) 517 Expanding of umbrellas.

ex'panding, *ppl. a.* [f. as prec. + -ING².] That expands (in senses of the verb).

1. a. That opens out, or is opening out.

1776 WITHERING *Brit. Plants* (1796) I. 239 Cup with 4 or 5 divisions, expanding, coloured, permanent. **1793** BEDDOES *Math. Evid.* p. ix, An unseasonable frost upon the tender petals of an expanding blossom.

b. *expanding universe*, the universe regarded as continually expanding, so that the galaxies are steadily receding from one another.

1931 *Times* 7 Nov. 7/1 'The Expanding Universe' was the subject of Sir Arthur Eddington's presidential address to the Physical Society at their meeting.. last evening. **1932** A. S. EDDINGTON (*title*) The expanding universe. **1942** *Time* 1 June 62/2 Chandrasekhar's inspiration was the 'expanding universe' theory of Belgium's Canon Georges Lemaître, who eleven years ago suggested that all the matter in the universe was once condensed into a single primordial atom. **1958** *Listener* 4 Dec. 934/1 The modern concept of the expanding universe.

2. That increases in bulk, or becomes enlarged. ***expanding bullet*** = ***dum-dum bullet***.

1859 *National Mag.* VI. 56/1 Rifles employing expanding or upsetting bullets. **1873** J. WHITWORTH *Guns & Steel* 21 With all expanding bullets, a quick burning powder must be employed. The expansion depends on the sudden action of the powder upon a bullet possessing inertia. **1874** KNIGHT *Dict. Mech.*, *Expanding-alloy*, such as expands in cooling. *Ibid.*, *Expanding-bit*, a boring-tool whose diameter is adjustable. **1887** *Spectator* 2 Apr. 458/2 Prosperity of many kinds, continuous and expanding, has been the characteristic of the period. **1909** *Westm. Gaz.* 29 Dec. 7/4 The ammunition from Europe consists of expanding bullets.

†ex'panse, *a. Obs.* Also 4 **expans**, 5 **expance**. [ad. L. *expans-us*, pa. pple. of *expandĕre* to EXPAND.] = EXPANDED.

1. *Bot.* (See quot.)

1819 *Pantalogia*, *Expanse*, in botany, expanded, spread out: as the calyx in helianthus. **1823** in CRABB *Techn. Dict.*

2. ***expanse years***: 'When a table contains quantities denoting the amount of a planet's motion during only a few years, viz. from 1 to 20 years, such changes are entered separately under the headings 1, 2, 3, etc. years, which are designated the expanse (or separate) years' (Skeat in *Chaucer's Astrolabe* (1872) Gloss.). Opposed to COLLECT.

c **1386** CHAUCER *Frankl. T.* 547 Neither his collect, nor his Expans yeeres. *c* **1391** —— *Astrol.* II. §45. *c* **1430** LYDG. *Thebes* 380 The yeeres collecte and expance also.

expanse (ɛk'spæns), *sb.* [ad. L. *expans-um*, neut. sb. f. *expansus*: see EXPANSE *a.*]

1. That which is expanded or spread out; a widely extended space or area; a wide extent of anything; 'the length and breadth'.

1667 MILTON *P.L.* VII. 340 Th' Almightie spake: Let there be Lights High in th' expanse of Heaven. **1711** POPE *Temp. Fame* 436 The smooth expanse of crystal lakes. **1742** GRAY *Ode on Eton* 6 Th' expanse.. Of grove, of lawn, of mead survey. **1781** COWPER *Expostulation* 9 Her fields a rich expanse of wavy corn. **1828** SCOTT *F.M. Perth* ix, The.. blue eyes, with the broad expanse of brow. **1858** HAWTHORNE *Fr. & It. Jrnls.* (1872) I. 18 Hung with broad expanses of black cloth. **1869** FREEMAN *Norm. Conq.* (1876) III. xii. 235 The army crossed over that vast expanse of sand.

fig. **1758** JOHNSON *Idler* No. 2 ¶7 Those who wander at large through the expanse of life.

b. *esp.* in ***the expanse***: the 'firmament'. Cf. EXPANSUM.

1667 MILTON *P.L.* II. 1014 Satan.. Springs upward.. Into the wild expanse. *a* **1711** KEN *Hymnotheo* Poet. Wks. 1721 III. 304 All the Expanse.. Was straw'd with Rays of ante-solar Light. **1765** SMART *Ps.* cxlviii. (1791) 219 Moon and Stars.. Silv'ring in the blue expanse. **1863** R. YOUNG *Lit. Tr. Bible, Gen.* i. 8 And God calleth the expanse Heaven.

2. The action of expanding; the state of being expanded; enlargement, expansion. Also, the amount or distance of expansion; = EXPANSION 3.

1860 MOTLEY *Netherl.* (1867) IV. lii. 532 To shut off the mighty movement of the great revolt from its destined expanse. **1874** COUES *Birds N.W.* 544 Audubon mentions one nearly ten feet in alar expanse.

†ex'panse, *v. Obs.* [f. L. *expans-* ppl. stem of *expandĕre* to EXPAND. The pa. pple. prob. originated before the vb. as ad. L. *expans-us*: see -ED¹.] *trans.* = EXPAND *v.* 1, 3.

1477 NORTON *Ord. Alch.* v. in Ashm. (1652) 62 In Winter men eaten more meate Than in Summer, when expansed in their heate. **1600** FAIRFAX *Tasso* III. lv. 50 A gentle valley.. Expansed faire and wide. **1610** GUILLIM *Heraldry* III. xx. (1611) 156 A swan with her wings expansed. **1615** G. SANDYS *Trav.* 121 After they had.. clozed their iawes; which they expanse against the rays of the Sun. **1642** SIR T. BROWNE *Relig. Med.* I. §16. 32 Nature.. that lies expans'd unto the Eyes of all. **1642** J. JACKSON *Bk. Conscience* 140 God enlargeth and expanseth the hearts of his Saints. **1661** MORGAN *Sph. Gentry* I. ii. 17, I shall refer Books born in arms, if open blazoned expansed, if shut clasped. **1705** HEARNE *Collect.* 12 Dec., A Book Expansed in Fesse. **1706** PHILLIPS (ed. Kersey), *Expansed* (in Heraldry), displayed, or set out. **1721–1800** in BAILEY.

†ex'pansed, *ppl. a. Obs.* [f. prec. + -ED¹.] Outspread; having a wide expanse or stretch. (See ppl. uses in prec.)

1627–77 FELTHAM *Resolves* I. xv. 26 Let him view th' expansed skies. **1664** POWER *Exp. Philos.* I. 7 The.. diversity of colours in her expansed wings. **1675** COCKER *Morals* 20 God Essence gave to Heav'ns Expansed Frame.

expansibility (ɛkˌspænsɪ'bɪlɪtɪ). [f. next: see -ITY. Cf. F. *expansibilité*.] The quality of being expansible: **a.** superficially; **b.** in volume; **c.** in non-material senses.

a. 1755 in JOHNSON. **1890** *Nature* 2 Jan. 205 The extreme expansibility of oil when floating upon the water.

b. 1701 GREW *Cosm. Sacra* I. iii. §19 [In] atoms of all Fluids, there is some difference in Bulk.. else all Fluids would be alike in.. expansibility. **1778** *Phil. Trans.* LXVIII. 462 A greater expansibility in the air enclosed in their Manometers. **1873** W. LEES *Acoustics* III. i. 81 The expansibility of platinum and glass is nearly the same. **1884** *Syd. Soc. Lex.*, *Expansibility*, applied to the condition of an organ which allows of erection.

c. 1857 *National Mag.* II. 277 Proofs.. of the expansibility of human nature. **1882** *Spectator* 8 Apr. 455 The infinite expansibility of House of Commons loquacity.

expansible (ɛk'spænsɪb(ə)l), *a.* [as if ad. L. **expansibil-is*, f. *expans-* ppl. stem of *expandĕre*: see EXPAND and -IBLE. Cf. Fr. *expansible*.] That can be expanded.

1. That can be opened or spread out.

1730–6 in BAILEY (folio). **1876** BARTHOLOW *Mat. Med.* (1879) 89 An intra-uterine speculum with expansible blades.

2. That can be made to occupy or contain a larger space; *esp.* of material substances, capable of expansion by heat, etc.

a **1691** BOYLE *Hist. Air* ii. (1692) 5 Readily expansible.. by Heat. **1792** *Phil. Trans.* LXXXII. 401 Whenever water is in a state of evaporation, an expansible fluid, composed of water and fire, is produced. **1812** SIR H. DAVY *Chem. Philos.* 70 Glass is less expansible than any of the metals. **1871** B. STEWART *Heat* §80 The most expansible metal will form the outside or convex surface of the curve, and the least expansible the concave.

b. Of an immaterial object: Capable of being enlarged in scope or operation.

1850 DE QUINCEY in H. A. Page *Life* (1877) II. xvii. 73 The great moving and expansible system of theology. **1884** SIR N. LINDLEY in *Law Times Rep.* 9 Feb. 727/2 A market.. limited by metes and bounds, so as not to be expansible.

Hence **ex'pansibleness**, the quality of being expansible; expansibility. **ex'pansibly** *adv.*, in an expansible manner; so as to be expanded.

1847 in CRAIG; and in mod. Dicts.

expansile (ɛk'spænsɪl, -aɪl), *a.* [f. L. *expans-* ppl. stem of *expandĕre* to EXPAND + -ILE.]

1. Having the property of being expanded; capable of expansion, dilatable.

1776 T. PERCIVAL *Philos. Med. & Exp. Ess.* III. 265 This effect it [heat] produces.. by its expansile power. **1783** POTT *Chirurg. Wks.* II. 63 Its natural soft.. expansile state. **1793** FORDYCE in *Phil. Trans.* LXXXIV. 5 Expansile and contractile by heat and cold. **1869** GILLMORE *Reptiles & Birds* iii. 117 Others have.. an expansile gular pouch. **1884** W. C. WILKINSON *E. Arnold* II. vii. 166 The illimitably expansile cloud-land of Hindu philosophy.

2. Of or pertaining to expansion; of the nature of or tending to or capable of producing expansion.

1730–6 in BAILEY (folio). **1873** ROBERTS *Handbk. Med.* 465 Expansile movements are greatly deficient or absent.

expansion (ɛk'spænʃən). [ad. late L. *expansiōn-em*, n. of action f. *expandĕre* to EXPAND.] The action of expanding, the fact or state of being expanded.

I. Spreading out, unfolding, opening out.

1. a. The action or process of spreading out or unfolding; the state of being spread out or unfolded; the opening of a bud, flower, etc. Also, †a spreading out to view, a display.

1646 SIR T. BROWNE *Pseud. Ep.* IV. v. 191 The.. distance betwixt the extremity of the fingers of either hand upon expansion. **1656** tr. *Hobbes' Elem. Philos.* (1839) 458 Whereupon there will follow a great expansion of light, with vehement flame. **1664** POWER *Exp. Philos.* II. 101 The Spring of a Watch.. if the String be broke.. flyes out into its fullest expansion. **1701** GREW *Cosm. Sacra* I. v. 28 The easie expansion of the wing of a bird. **1731** POPE *Ep. Burlington* 145 The gilded clouds in fair expansion lie. **1847** DE QUINCEY *Sp. Mil. Nun* §8 (1853) 18 A mob orator, whose brawling mouth open to its widest expansion, [etc.]. **1867** JEAN INGELOW *Laurance*, She.. knew.. The pleasure of the leaf in exquisite Expansion.

b. The detailed expression of what is implicitly contained in a statement; the writing out in full the meaning of graphical contractions. Also in *Alg.* the process of working out a contracted expression (cf. EXPAND 1 b.) and stating the result in full; the result or statement thus obtained.

1858 TODHUNTER *Algebra* xxxvi. §519 The subject of the expansion of expressions is.. properly a portion of the Differential Calculus. *Ibid.* xxxvi. §524 To find the number of terms in the expansion of any multinomial. **1886** J. EDWARDS *Diff. Calc.* 96 Now assuming the possiblility of such an expansion, let, etc.

c. *Naval Arch.* The mathematical enlargement of a ship's lines from a drawing or model to the full size of building. Also *attrib.*

1869 E. J. REED *Shipbuilding* 186 Either a model of one side of the ship or an expansion drawing is prepared, on which to set off the edges and butts of the plates. *Ibid.* 439 An expansion batten is applied to the line on the floor representing the moulding edge of the frame. **1877** THEARLE *Theor. Naval Archit.* I. 163 When an expansion drawing is made, the several strakes of plating can be shown upon it, also their thicknesses... It is obviously impossible to calculate the position of the centre of gravity from an expansion.

2. *concr.* Anything that is spread out; an expanse; *esp.* the expanse of heaven, the firmament.

1611 BIBLE *Gen.* i. 6 Let there be a firmament [*marg.* expansion] in the midst of the waters. **1659** PEARSON *Creed* (1839) 70 This house of God.. is not all of the same materials.. there is a vast difference between the heavenly expansions. **1760** BEATTIE *Lucretius* I. 6 All that lies Beneath the starr'd expansion of the skies. **1823** LAMB *Elia* Ser. I. xxvi. (1865) 211 Less time.. than it took to cover the expansion of his broad moony face.. with expression. *a* **1845** HOOD *Kilmansegg* cxl, Venus and Mars Are rolling along in their golden cars Through the sky's serene expansion. **1862** ANSTED *Channel Isl.* I. iv. (ed. 2) 64 Some.. flat expansions of hard.. rock, afford a kind of irregular pavement.

fig. **1662** R. MATHEW *Unl. Alch.* §57. 61 That ocean or expansion of wrath.

†3. a. Extent; space to which anything is extended. **b.** Pure space (see quot. from Locke).

1690 LOCKE *Hum. Und.* II. vii. §10 The capacious Mind of Man.. extends its thoughts often, even beyond the utmost expansion of Matter. *Ibid.* II. xv. §1 Distance or Space, in its simple abstract conception.. I call Expansion to distinguish it from Extension, which by some is used to express this distance only as it is in the solid parts of Matter. **1712** BLACKMORE *Creation* IV. (1718) 121 Lost in expansion, void and infinite. **1755** in JOHNSON.

4. a. The action or process of causing something to occupy or contain a larger space, or of acquiring greater volume or capacity; dilatation; an instance of this.

1664 *Phil. Trans.* I. 29 To prove the expansion of glass by heat. **1665** *Ibid.* I. 49 What Bodies are expanded by being frozen, and how that expansion is evinced. **1692** BENTLEY *Boyle Lect.* viii. (1693) 27 The condensation and expansion of any portion of the Air is always proportional to the weight and pressure incumbent upon it. **1782** *Specif. Watt's Patent* No. 1321. 5 The piston continues to descend by virtue of the expansion of the steam. **1830** R. KNOX *Béclard's Anat.* 235 They are furnished with tensor muscles, whether proper, or simply by expansion of their tendons. **1875** URE *Dict. Arts* II. 319 s.v., Some remarkable examples of expansion are furnished by the influence of sunshine on the Britannia Tubular Bridge. **1882** VINES *Sachs' Bot.* 874 These movements depend not upon alternate expansion and contraction of the tissue.. but, etc.

fig. **1634** HABINGTON *Castara* (Arb.) 103 My heart Expanssion wants, to thinke what now thou art.

b. of immaterial things.

1682 SIR T. BROWNE *Chr. Mor.* 19 Spread not into boundless expansions either of designs or desires. **1856** SIR B. BRODIE *Psychol. Inq.* I. i. 31 A high education.. may.. have the effect of preventing the full expansion of genius. **1864** D. G. MITCHELL *Sev. Stor.* 69, I felt.. an unusual expansion. **1879** M. ARNOLD *Mixed Ess.* Pref. 7 The love of liberty is simply the instinct in man for expansion.

c. *Comm.* and *Finance.* (*a*) An extension (of business transactions). (*b*) An increase in the amount of the circulating medium. More fully ***expansion of the currency***.

1847 CRAIG, *Expansion*, in commerce, an increase of issues of bank notes. **1864** in WEBSTER. **1891** *Pall Mall G.* 10 Nov. 7/1 In some directions there has been expansion, so that the losses have been partially neutralized.

d. Extension of the territorial rule or sway of a country.

1882 J. R. SEELEY in *Macm. Mag.* XLVI. 456 (*title*) The Expansion of England in the Eighteenth Century. **1903** *Sun* (N.Y.) 1 Dec. 2 When he indorsed the doctrine of expansion the cheers were pronounced.

5. The amount or degree of dilatation.

1790 BLAGDEN in *Phil. Trans.* LXXX. 322 The whole expansion of pure spirit from 30° to 100° of Fahrenheit's thermometer, is not less than $\frac{1}{25}$th of its whole bulk at 30°. **1816** J. SMITH *Panorama Sc. & Art* II. 32 Taking a proportional part of the difference of the two expansions. **1875** URE *Dict. Arts* II. 391 s.v., The expansion of the solid corresponding to two degrees of the thermometer, is twice the expansion which corresponds to one degree.

6. *concr.* **a.** An expanded or dilated portion. **b.** A product of expansion; what (a thing) is expanded into.

1860 TYNDALL *Glac.* II. vii. 261 This lake [Geneva] is simply an expansion of the river Rhone. **1865** RUSKIN *Sesame* 178 A man has a personal work.. and a public work.. which is the expansion of the other. **1866** HUXLEY *Phys.*

ix. (1869) 239 The structure..of the sensory expansion in which the optic nerve terminates. **1882** VINES *Sachs' Bot.* 544 The membranous expansions or appendages.

7. *Steam-engine.* The increase in bulk of the steam which takes place in a partially filled cylinder after communication with the boiler is cut off.

The improvement introduced by Watt's patent of 1782 consisted in the economizing of steam by allowing the piston to be propelled, during the latter portion of its excursion, by the 'expansion' of the steam first introduced. An engine in which this is done is said to work 'by expansion'. A *double* (or *triple*) *expansion* engine is one in which the steam passes from one cylinder into another, so that the expansive force is used twice (or thrice).

1782 [see 4]. **1819** *Rees's Cyclop.* XXXIV. sig. M. 2 b (art. *Steam-Engine*), Mr. Watt's principle of expansion. **1874** KNIGHT *Dict. Mech.* I. 817/1 An automatic expansion is one which is regulated by the governor, and varies with the amount of power required. **1875** R. F. MARTIN tr. *Havrez' Winding Mach.* 80 The engineman must be able to work his engine with a variable expansion with as great ease as an ordinary high-pressure engine. *Ibid.*, MM. Scohy and Crespin..took out a patent for applying a system of expansion to winding engines.

8. *attrib.* and *Comb.*, as *expansion theory*; **expansion apparatus, chamber** = *cloud chamber* (see CLOUD *sb.* 12); see also quot. 1968; **expansion board** *Computing*, a circuit board that may be connected to or inserted in a computer in order to provide extra facilities or memory; **expansion box**, a chamber fitted to a pipe to allow for the expansion of the liquid, gas, etc., which flows through the pipe; **expansion card** *Computing* = *expansion board* above; **expansion-coupling, -curb, -drum** (see quots.); **expansion-engine** (see 7); **expansion-gear**, an apparatus for cutting off steam from the cylinder at a given point of the stroke; **expansion-joint** (see quots.); **expansion-slide**, a slide belonging to the **expansion-valve**, a valve which shuts off the steam in its passage to the cylinder.

1897 C. T. R. WILSON in *Phil. Trans. R. Soc.* CLXXXIX. A. 267 (*heading*) Conditions to be satisfied by the *expansion apparatus. **1978** *Pract. Computing* July–Aug. 4 The chassis houses the computer, power supply, fans, and has three additional slots for *expansion boards. **1985** *Acorn User* Feb. 11/4 Watford Electronics' 32k RAM expansion board gives your Beeb 27k of program space plus 20k for graphics. **1838** *Civil Eng. & Arch. Jrnl.* I. 237/2 As the water warms, it rises through the pipe into the *expansion box... To guard against the danger of exceeding the proper degree of heat, the expansion box is furnished with a pipe. **1939** *Jrnl. R. Aeronaut. Soc.* XLIII. 748 The exhaust gases from a group of cylinders are discharged through a number of expansion boxes, the expansion boxes being shaped as a flattened streamline member lying in the airstream. **1982** *Pract. Computing* Nov. 66 Very reasonably priced for those who already have an Apple II and *expansion card. **1986** *Managem. Accounting* Aug. 56 If all the sockets on the Mother Board are filled..you will have to install an 'expansion card' to increase its memory. **1933** *Discovery* Apr. 107/2 This recoiling nucleus..is an efficient ionizer and so can be detected either by its electrical effect or its track can be photographed in an *expansion chamber. **1968** *Practical Motorist* Nov. 333/1 *Expansion tank* (*chamber*), a small tank connected to the overflow of the radiator on some modern cars which collects water and steam forced through the overflow pipe. The water is drawn back into the main system when the engine cools. **1874** KNIGHT *Dict. Mech.* I. 816/2 **Expansion-coupling.* The coupling represented consists of an expansion-drum of thin copper *x* between the extremities of two pipes *a i*, Fig. 1901, which, in elongating, press the sides of the drum in, and draw them out in cooling. **1847** CRAIG, **Expansion curb*, in Horology, a contrivance for counteracting expansion or contraction. **1874** KNIGHT *Dict. Mech.* I. 816/2 **Expansion-drum*, an arrangement by which an occasional change of speed may be effected. **1847** CRAIG, **Expansion engine.* **1886** *Pall Mall G.* 21 Sept. 13/2 These steamers..are provided with triple expansion engines. **1850** *Pract. Mech. Jrnl.* III. 28 (*heading*) Whitelaw's steam-engine *expansion gear. **1875** R. F. MARTIN tr. *Havrez' Winding Mach.* 80 MM. Scohy and Crespin add to the regular form of cylinder the expansion gear of M. Meyer. **1849–50** WEALE *Dict. Terms*, **Expansion-joint*, a stuffing-box joint connecting the steam pipes, so as to allow one of them to slide within the enlarged end of the other when the length increases by expansion. **1864** WEBSTER, *Expansion-joint*, an attachment of the framing to the boiler, which allows the boiler to expand without bending the framing. **1882** *Worc. Exhib. Catal.* iii. 5 Samples of improved expansion joints. **1848** E. ALBAN *Steam Engine* 261 The *expansion slide is made to act through the motion of the principal slide below. **1886** F. B. JEVONS in *Jrnl. Hellenic Studies* VII. 292 Every form of the *expansion theory [*i.e.* the theory that the Iliad is an 'expansion' of a smaller poem]. **1849** FAIRBAIRN in *Mech. Mag.* LI. 255 A new construction of *expansion valves for condensing steam engines.

expansional (ɛk'spænʃənəl), *a.* [f. EXPANSION + -AL.] Of or pertaining to expansion.

1925 J. JOLY *Surface-Hist. Earth* vii. 115 The sum of the fluctuating changes of volume of the one sign (either expansional or contractional).

expansionary (ɛk'spænʃən(ə)rɪ), *a.* [f. EXPANSION + -ARY^1.] Of, tending to, or directed towards expansion.

1936 *Yale Rev.* Sept. 25 Labor..insisted..on an expansionary policy. **1958** *Listener* 31 July 151/2, I imagine the British Government, at any rate, will soon start to turn towards positively expansionary policies. **1960** *Times* 22 Jan. 18/2 Are we so certain that the economy will run into bottlenecks, heavy over-stocking, and all the signs of overstrain quite so early in an expansionary phase? **1966** *New Statesman* 30 Sept. 468/2 The central agency can only function in an expansionary situation. **1969** *Daily Tel.* 30 Aug. 18/5 This will tend to mitigate the inflationary and expansionary effect of the increase in bank lending.

expansionism (ɛk'spænʃənɪz(ə)m). [f. EXPANSION + -ISM.] Advocacy of, or furtherance of, a policy of expansion, esp. of territorial expansion.

1900 *Daily News* 2 May 3/5 By Imperialism British Liberals ought not to understand militarism or even expansionism. **1959** *Economist* 28 Feb. 761/1 The expansionism which marks the common market's view of the future. **1960** *Spectator* 7 Oct. 512 We are afraid of Russian expansionism.

expansionist (ɛk'spænʃənɪst) *sb.* (and *a.*) [f. EXPANSION + -IST.] One who advocates a policy or a theory of expansion, *esp.* an advocate of expansion of the currency, or of territorial expansion (see EXPANSION 4 d). Also *attrib.*

1862 *Lit. Churchm.* VIII. 339/1 'We look for the time' (says the Expansionist) 'and doubt not it will come', etc. **1881** *Nation* (N.Y.) XXXII. 160 Whether the new Secretary ..would be an expansionist or a contractionist. **1884** GOLDW. SMITH *Expansion of Eng.* in *Contemp. Rev.* Apr. 531 Standing on his historical island, the British Expansionist sees all the other communities of the race revolving round him. **1886** F. B. JEVONS in *Jrnl. Hellenic Studies* VII. 292 The expansionists [i.e. those who maintain that the Iliad was 'expanded' from an original shorter poem] therefore have set to work to remove these incrustations. *Ibid.* VII. 295 Fick himself supports the expansionist theory. **1898** *Daily News* 3 Jan. 6/4 Truly a tempting country for an Expansionist son of Japhet to fix eye upon. *Ibid.* 14 Mar. 4/5 The editor of 'The Free Press' has been expelled from Siam for..advocating a French expansionist policy. **1898** *Westm. Gaz.* 11 Nov. 1/2 Expansionist Republicans. **1909** *Ibid.* 17 Apr. 2/1 It seems..doubtful if those reasons will commend themselves either to 'Irredentists' or to 'Expansionists'. **1940** *Economist* 10 Aug. 190/1 The banks, much more than the insurance companies, have the compensatory advantage that expansionist war finance means a progressive increase in earning assets. **1961** *Daily Tel.* 29 Nov. 20/4 The Ethiopians are traditionally wary of a Somalia 'expansionist' policy.

expansive (ɛk'spænsɪv), *a.* [f. L. *expāns-* ppl. stem of *expandĕre* to EXPAND + -IVE.]

1. Tending or adapted to expand in volume, to spread over a larger surface, or fill a larger space; having the capacity to expand or develop to larger dimensions; dilatable. Said both of material and immaterial objects.

1651 DAVENANT *Gondibert* II. i. 3 By increase of swift expansive light The lost Horizon was apparent growne. **1728** THOMSON *Spring* 28 No more Th' expansive atmosphere is cramp'd with cold. **1805** W. SAUNDERS *Min. Waters* 4 Water is composed..of a fluid expansive ether. **1879** ATCHERLEY *Boërland* 148, I changed my cartridge for another with an expansive ball. **1884** tr. *Lotze's Metaph.* 96 The heightened temperature..bringing about in the expansive materials the movement of dilatation.

b. Of persons, their affections, utterances, etc.: Freely going out, effusive, open.

1658–9 *Burton's Diary* (1828) IV. 137 It is said our affections..to France have been more expansive. **1858** O. W. HOLMES *Aut. Breakf.-t.* x. 98 That ripe and discreet age which invites confidence and expansive utterance. **1884** F. CHANCE in *N. & Q.* Serv. VI. X. 397/1 We English are not an expansive people.

2. Of a force, a movement or tendency: Acting in the direction of expansion; directed towards expansion: **a.** within the object or substance itself; **b.** in some other object.

a. 1656 tr. *Hobbes' Elem. Philos.* (1839) 471 This expansive motion of the air. **1685** BOYLE *Effects of Mot.* viii. 103 These stones being lodged in a Cement extremely hard, their expansive endeavour was rendered ineffectual. **1775** JOHNSON *Tax. no Tyr.* 20 The intumescence of nations would have found its vent like all other expansive violence. **1824** R. STUART *Hist. Steam Engine* 143 The steam..from its expansive power, will press [etc.]. **1828** CARLYLE *Misc.* (1857) I. 199 Impelled by the expansive movement of his own irrepressible soul. **1833** N. ARNOTT *Physics* (ed. 5) II. I. 95 The liquid..may force a column of mercury to an elevation marking the expansive tendency. **1846** GROTE *Greece* I. xvi. (1862) I. 300 The expansive force of Grecian intellect.

b. 1744 BERKELEY *Siris* §170 Such is the rarefying and expansive force of this element [fire]. **1874** BLACKIE *Self-cult.* 85 The direct genial expansive virtue of some great moral sun. **1886** CROLL *Climate & Cosmol.* 253 This internal pressure..acts on the mass of ice as an expansive force.

3. Of or pertaining to expansion. Of an engine, process, etc.: Involving or depending upon the principle of expansion.

1782 *Specif. of Watt's Patent* No. 1321. 4 The said new or expansive engine. **1858** GREENER *Gunnery* 33 In the expansive principle of rifles. *Ibid.* 353 The principles of the expansive rifle. **1888** *Pall Mall G.* 6 Nov. 8/1 These messages were printed exactly as he sent them, and did not undergo any 'expansive' process.

4. a. Of material things: Expanding over or occupying a large surface or space; having wide bounds, broad, extensive. **b.** Of immaterial things (*e.g.* thoughts, designs, sympathies): Having a wide range; comprehensive.

1806 T. SURR *Winter in Lond.* I. iv. 64 It was situated..on the borders of an expansive lake. **1813** EUSTACE *Tour Italy* ix. 204 A more expansive and generous compassion for the fate of cities and states. **1818** JAS. MILL *Brit. India* Pref. 16 If an observer were to take an expansive view of India. **1830** D'ISRAELI *Chas. I*, III. v. 72 The intellect of Laud was neither expansive nor elevated. **1834** T. MEDWIN *Angler in Wales* II. 175 He had the character..of being remarkably handsome..his forehead expansive. **1835** I. TAYLOR *Spir. Despot.* i. 12 That enlightened and expansive charity.. which should recommend the Christian profession. **1870** EMERSON *Soc. & Solit.* vii. 137 Czar Alexander was more expansive, and wished to call the Pacific *my ocean*. **1890** *Standard* 10 Mar., We doubt..whether expansive skirts of the old style will 'catch on' in America.

expansively (ɛk'spænsɪvlɪ), *adv.* [f. prec. + -LY^2.] In an expansive manner; at large, extensively. With respect to the steam-engine: On the principle of expansion.

1839 R. S. ROBINSON *Naut. Steam Eng.* 160 Very little power is lost by working the steam expansively. **1865** CARLYLE *Fredk. Gt.* XI. iii, Voltaire, at his leisure in Brussels ..writes much more expansively. **1865** MASSON *Rec. Brit. Philos.* 100 The Absolute going forth expansively..is Nature. **1875** R. F. MARTIN tr. *Havrez' Winding Mach.* 93 For throttling of the steam through the regulator will be substituted working expansively.

expansiveness (ɛk'spænsɪvnɪs). [f. as prec. + -NESS.] The quality of being expansive.

1. a. Tendency to expand. **b.** Wide-spreading character or nature.

1829 BENTHAM *Wks.* (1843) XI. 18 What you say on this subject shows the expandedness and expansiveness of your mind. *a* **1853** ROBERTSON *Serm.* Ser. III. xiv. 172 The.. affections of the Apostle Paul..tending to expansiveness rather than concentration. **1854** H. MILLER *Sch. & Schm.* xii. (1860) 122/2 The scenery..was imposing..from its bare and lonely expansiveness. **1857** TOULM. SMITH *The Parish* 11 While the..expansiveness of the Common Law will be thus shown. **1879** GEO. ELIOT *Theo. Such* ix, That would restrict the expansiveness of trade. **1884** tr. *Lotze's Metaph.* 96 The..expansiveness of the gaseous elements.

2. Absence of reserve in feeling or speech; genial frankness, freedom, openness; unrestrained flow of sympathy or conversation.

1856 EMERSON *Eng. Traits, Lit.* Wks. (Bohn) II. 115 That expansiveness which is the essence of the poetic element. **1862** MRS. GORDON in H. A. Page *De Quincey* (1877) I. viii. 160 In the expansiveness of his own heart. **1864** *Sat. Rev.* 9 July 45 Gifted female friends..can praise with a large, ungrudging expansiveness. **1867** LEWES *Hist. Philos.* II. 520 In the expansiveness of private conversation. **1883** G. A. BOUGHTON in *Harper's Mag.* Dec. 95/1 Who greeted Miles with..noisy familiarity and expansiveness.

expansivity (ɛkspæn'sɪvɪtɪ). *rare.* [f. as prec. + -ITY.] = EXPANSIVENESS.

1837 CARLYLE *Mirabeau* Misc. Ess. (1888) V. 231 Offences (of elasticity or expansivity) have accumulated. **1838** *Blackw. Mag.* XLIV. 612 The expansivity and soaring heavenwardness of the gases have full play.

expansometer (ɛkspæn'sɒmɪtə(r)). [f. EXPANSION + -(O)METER, after *electrometer*, etc.] (See quot.)

1883 NASMYTH *Autobiog.* vi. 119 One of my earliest attempts at original contrivance was an Expansometer—an instrument for measuring in bulk all metals and solid substances.

‖**ex'pansum.** *Obs.* [L., neut. of *expansus*, pa. pple. of *expandĕre* to EXPAND. Adopted by scholars of 16–17th c. as lit. rendering of Heb. *rāqīaʿ* (Vulg. *firmamentum*, AV. *firmament*).] = EXPANSE *sb.*

1635 SWAN *Spec. M.* iv. §1 (1643) 54 The Expansum, or stretching out of the Heavens. **1640** WILKINS *New Planet* II. (1684) 39 The common People usually think the Rain to proceed from some Waters in the Expansum. **1651** JER. TAYLOR *Serm. for Year* I. xxv. 314 The mercy of God [is] a vast expansum and a huge Ocean. **1794** SULLIVAN *View Nat.* II. 403 Till the whole expansum was cleared of these gross and opaque parts of matter.

†**ex'pansure.** *Obs.* [f. L. *expans-* ppl. stem of *expandĕre* to EXPAND + -URE.] **a.** The process of expanding; expansion. **b.** = EXPANSE *sb.* I.

1606 CHAPMAN *Hero & Leander* v, All your parts employ, And suit Night's rich expansure with your joy. **1606** *Sir G. Goosecappe* IV. iii. in Bullen *O. Pl.* III. 70 My immortall part admits expansure. *c* **1611** CHAPMAN *Iliad* XVII. 317 Such expansure of his beams he [the sun] thrust out of his throne.

†**ex'papillate,** *v. Obs.*$^{-0}$ [f. L. *expapillāt-us* bared to the breast, f. *ex-* out + *papilla* nipple.] 'To lay the breasts open to the paps' (Cockeram 1623–6).

‖**ex parte, ex-parte** (ˌɛks'pɑːtiː), *adv.*, chiefly *attrib.* as quasi-*adj.* [L. phrase *ex* out of + *parte*, abl. of *pars* part, side.]

1. *Law.* On one side only: said respecting an affidavit, application, commission, evidence, testimony, etc. (See quots.)

1672 COWEL *Interpr.* s.v., A Commission *ex parte*, is that which is taken out and executed by one side onely. **1779** J. REED in Sparks *Corr. Amer. Rev.* (1853) II. 277 No ex parte testimony ought to be received by the Court. **1839** HOLTHOUSE *New Law Dict.* s.v., An Ex-parte application to the court is an application made by one party only. **1853** WHARTON *Pa. Digest* 854 An exparte affidavit may be admitted to prove pedigree.

2. *transf.* Of statements, etc.: Made with respect to, or in the interest of, one side only.

1812 LD. PALMERSTON *Parl. Deb.* 21 Dec., *Ex-parte* statements like the present. **1823** LINGARD *Hist. Eng.* VI. 346 Ex parte statements, to which the accused had no

opportunity of replying. 1856 READE *Never too late* xxiv, I object to an *ex parte* statement from a personal enemy.

expat, colloq. abbrev. of EXPATRIATE *sb.*

1962 D. J. ENRIGHT in *Times Lit. Suppl.* 10 Aug. 582 (*title of poem*) Expat. 1968 *Listener* 25 Jan. 102/3 The 'expats', as the expatriate British refer to themselves, are understandably fond of Ghana.

†**ex'patiate**, *ppl. a. Obs.* or *arch.* [ad. L. *ex(s)patiāt-us*, pa. pple. of *ex(s)patiārī*: see next.] Equivalent to the later EXPATIATED. In quots. Widespread; laid at full length.

1702 DE FOE *Reform. Manners* 30 There lye the Seeds of high expatiate Sin. 1854 SYD. DOBELL *Balder* xxvii. 186 Stretch him out, like the prophet on the dead.. Bound and prone, expatiate with nice art To the invenient horror.

expatiate (ɛk'speɪʃɪeɪt), *v.* Also 7 exp-, exspaciate, 6-8 exspatiate. [f. L. *ex(s)patiāt-* ppl. stem of *ex(s)patiārī*, f. *ex-* (see EX- *pref.*[1]) + *spatiārī* to walk about, f. *spatium* space.]

1. *intr.* To walk about at large, to roam without restraint; to move about freely in space, wander at will. Now somewhat *rare* in lit. sense.

1538 LELAND *Itin.* I. p. xxi, I have more exspatiated yn this Campe then they did. 1615 CROOKE *Body of Man* 429 Wherein this ætheriall body might expatiate and disport it selfe. 1657 S. PURCHAS *Pol. Flying-Ins.* 16 They will expatiate and dance the Hay in circling motions. *a* 1760 J. H. BROWNE *Design & Beauty* Poems (1768) 102 He not content the shallow shore to keep Dauntless expatiates in the boundless deep. 1765 GRAY *Let.* in *Poems* (1775) 308 You will.. catch the breezes on the coast of Taranto.. expatiate to the very toe of the continent. 1796 MORSE *Amer. Geol.* I. 258 Workmen.. by expatiating from Europe, have improved their condition. 1849 *Blackw. Mag.* LXV. 236 He ..has it in his power to expatiate where he will. 1864 LOWELL *Biglow P.* Poet. Wks. (1879) 275/2 Winter-flies.. crawl out.. to expatiate in the sun. 1875 HAMERTON *Intell. Life* XII. i. (1876) 435 Points upon which the cattle expatiate.

b. Said of the eye, or hand.

1650 BULWER *Anthropomet.* 20 In this Cephalical compression to the sides, the Eyes more freely expatiate to the back-parts. 1712 ADDISON *Spect.* No. 412 ¶2 Where the Eye has Room to range abroad, to expatiate at large on the Immensity of its Views. 1836–7 SIR W. HAMILTON *Metaph.* xxxii. (1859) II. 252 The hand of a skilful musician expatiates over the keys of the most complex organ.

c. *fig.*

1612 DRAYTON *Poly-olb.* II. Notes 37 So farre haue the indigested reports of.. Monkish inuention expatiated out of the lists of Truth. 1650–3 tr. *Hales' Dissert. de Pace* in *Phenix* (1708) II. 373 Ambition finds not room enough for her swelling to expatiate in. 1697 J. SERGEANT *Solid Philos.* 321 But I expatiate too much into the Subject of Predication. 1704 SWIFT *T. Tub* vii, Without farther expatiating from the subject. 1787 BONNYCASTLE *Astron.* vi. 84 The flighty imagination of those who.. expatiate in the wilds of fiction. 1849 ROBERTSON *Serm.* Ser. I. ii. (1866) 35 We.. expatiate into that which is infinite.

†**d.** *trans.* (Cf. *to walk the road.*) *Obs. rare.*

1627 J. CARTER *Exposition* 109 The ungodly.. enter in.. at the broad gates, and expatiate all the fields and countrie.

2. To speak or write at some length; to enlarge; to be copious in description or discussion. Const. *on*, *upon*. Also in *indirect passive*.

1612 DRAYTON *Poly-olb.* I. Notes 18 But you blame me thus expatiating. 1655 CROMWELL *Sp.* 22 Jan. (Carlyle), I could not say more upon this subject if I listed to expatiate thereupon. 1721 BERKELEY *Prevent. Ruin Gt. Brit.* Wks. III. 207 Ancient orators used to expatiate in praise of their country. 1793 BEDDOES *Math. Evid.* 14 Frequently as the topic is expatiated upon. 1817 CHALMERS *Astron. Disc.* i. (1852) 17 Those who expatiate with delight on the wonders and the sublimities of creation. 1850 MERIVALE *Rom. Emp.* (1865) I. Pref. 7 The remarkable deficiency of our recent literature.. has constantly tempted me to expatiate.

†**3.** *trans.* To enlarge, extend, expand (territory, etc.); to spread abroad (glory, shame); to exalt, magnify; to spread wide (the arms). *Obs.*

1603 *Patient Grissil* (Shaks. Soc.) 22 Sir Owen, and signors both, do not expatiate my obloquy. 1633 T. ADAMS *Exp. 2 Peter* ii. 4 Princes expatiate their dominions. 1660 WATERHOUSE *Arms & Arm.* 6 The symmetry and exact order of which.. expatiated the glory of their valor almost thorowout the Continent. *Ibid.* 125 A benign umbrage expatiates little spires of grass into the magnitude of Lawrels. 1668 *The Rivals* 17, I would expatiate my Wanton arms. 1677 SIR T. HERBERT *Trav.* 189 Where after a little space the channel is well-nigh expatiated so broad as the Thames at London.

†**b.** *refl.* and *intr.* for *refl. Obs.*

1620–55 J. JONES *Stone-Heng* (1725) 34 Salisbury Plain.. expatiates it self through the Middle of Wiltshire. 1650 FULLER *Pisgah* II. iv. 107 The Jordan.. expatiateth itself into the waters of Merom. 1668 CULPEPPER & COLE *Barthol. Anat.* II. vi. 98 The Crown-vein.. Expatiates in a large tract from the right Eare. 1681 H. MORE *Exp. Dan.* App. ii. 287 This dead condition.. is not to expatiate unto 1260 days. 1738 *Common Sense* (1739) II. 48 The Stock of Wealth a Nation possesses must expatiate, or it is of no Benefit to the Publick.

†**c.** 'To let loose, to allow to range' (J.). *refl.* only; = 1 b and 2. *Obs.*

1659 *Instruct. Oratory* 10 The best way therefore is, to give it [the Wit] leave to expatiate itself in its work. 1665 BOYLE *Occas. Refl.* (1675) 21 The thoughts being licens'd to expatiate themselves. 1683 CAVE *Ecclesiastici, Greg. Naz.* 296 Nazianzen.. welcom'd his Arrival with an Oration, wherein he expatiated himself in his praises for the Nobility of his birth. 1695 DRYDEN tr. *Du Fresnoy's Painting* §70 A Subject which shall.. afford.. Art an ample field of matter wherein to expatiate it self.

d. *nonce-use.* To develop (views).

1859 C. BARKER *Assoc. Princ.* i. 8 Mr. Carlyle expatiating from its text his peculiar views of.. political economy.

Hence †**ex'patiated** *ppl. a.*, widespread; cf. sense 3 of vb. **ex'patiater** (also **ex'patiator**), one who expatiates. **ex'patiating** *vbl. sb.*, the action of the vb. EXPATIATE; in quot. expansion; cf. sense 3 b of vb. **ex'patiating** *ppl. a.*, that expatiates; whence **ex'patiatingly** *adv.*

1681 tr. *Willis' Rem. Med. Wks.* Vocab., *Expatiated*, enlarged. 1713 C'TESS WINCHELSEA *Misc. Poems* 62 Th' expatiated Downs Shall wider Scenes display of rural Glee. *a* 1766 PEGGE *Anonym.* v. (1809) 201 The person, intended ..as an Expatiator on the word Endovellicus. 1839 *New Monthly Mag.* LVII. 160 Such is the mind of our expatiater upon flowers. 1717 J. KEILL *Anim. Œcon.* (1738) 131 There was no.. room for the division and expatiating of the Vessels. 1789 *Trifler* xxxv. 456 An expatiating and florid diffusion would.. weaken and dissolve their close and well-compacted strength. 1692 BEVERLEY *Disc. Dr. Crisp* 16 Why may not the most expatiating Expressions be used in so good a Sense? 1887 *Pall Mall G.* 29 Dec. 11/1 A pleasant space into which to turn loose some.. expatiating gossiper to talk of what so seemeth him best. 1748 RICHARDSON *Clarissa* (1811) III. xxi. 131 What a folly.. to be so expatiatingly sincere.

expatiation (ɛkˌspeɪʃɪ'eɪʃən). [f. prec. vb.: see -ATION.] The action of expatiating.

1. The action of walking abroad, or wandering at large; also, an instance of the same. *lit.* and *fig.* Also, opportunity or room for expatiating. *rare.*

1640 G. WATTS tr. *Bacon's Adv. Learn.* II. xiii. 115 There are no other Errors, or manifest Expatiations in Heaven, save those of the seaven Planets. 1647 FARINGDON *Serm. Jas.* i. 27. 2 Take them from the Devil's latitudes and expatiations. 1666 G. HARVEY *Morb. Angl.* iv. 35 Gladness ..is an expansion, or an expatiation of the said sensitive spirits out of their cells into some larger Meatus. *a* 1848 R. W. HAMILTON *Rew. & Punishm.* iv. (1853) 159 A proper self-love finds in religion a perfect expatiation.

†**2.** The action of extending, expanding, or developing; expansion, development. Cf. sense 3 of vb. Also *concr.* an extended portion, a projection. *Obs.*

1612 J. COTTA *Discov. Pract. Physic* II. ii. 94 The unlimited expatiation of so foule wrongs. 1652 BP. HALL *Height Eloquence* p. lii, A periphrasis very often winds up it self in its own expatiation. *a* 1661 FULLER *Worthies, Surrey* III. 76 Surrey.. may be allowed to be a Square (besides its Angular Expatiation in the South-west) of two and twenty miles.

3. The action of discussing at large; extended talk or description.

1816 KEATINGE *Trav.* I. 277 The tact of the person who has thus had the discretion to turn away the bolt, is the theme of expatiation. 1831 T. L. PEACOCK *Crotchet Castle* xv. (1887) 154 This tempting field of interesting expatiation. 1878 *N. Amer. Rev.* CXXVII. 423 The reason is too apparent to need any expatiation. 1885 *Manch. Exam.* 28 Jan. 3/4 The whole article is an example.. of tamely edifying expatiation.

expatiative (ɛk'speɪʃɪətɪv), *a.* [f. EXPATIATE *v.* + -IVE.] Tending to spread itself out, expansive.

1820 SHELLEY *Œdipus Tyr.* I, A leech.. with lubricous round rings Capaciously expatiative, which make His little body like a red balloon.

expatiatory (ɛk'speɪʃɪətərɪ), *a.* [f. EXPATIATE *v.* + -ORY.] Characterized by or indulging in expatiation.

1816 W. TAYLOR in *Monthly Rev.* LXXXI. 468 The method adopted.. is more expatiatory. 1860 J. P. KENNEDY *Swallow B.* vii. 73 Everybody seems to understand the advantage of silence when M. is inclined to be expatiatory.

expatriate (ɛks'peɪtrɪət), *ppl. a.* and *sb.* [f. as next, on the analogy of ppl. adjs. from Lat. pa. pples.: see -ATE[2].] **A.** *adj.* = EXPATRIATED. **B.** *sb.* An expatriated person. In modern usage, a person who lives in a foreign country.

1812 SHELLEY *Let. to Hitchener* in Hogg *Life* II. 94 An Irishman has been torn from his wife and family.. because he was expatriate. 1818 *Q. Rev.* XIX. 55 Patriots and expatriates are alike the children of circumstances. 1829 I. TAYLOR *Enthus.* x. 284 These expatriate millions [of Chinese] are accessible to instruction. 1871 B. TAYLOR *Faust* (1875) II. III. 168 But a God took hold of her, The Expatriate. 1902 *Daily Chron.* 26 Feb. 3/5 'The Expatriates' is a novel by Miss Lilian Bell... Its principal characters are rich Americans and titled Parisians, and the action takes place largely in Paris. 1961 *Economist* 25 Mar. 1193/1 In Dar-es-Salaam all the talk is about 'expatriates', the technical name for the Europeans who run the country alongside or behind the African ministers. 1969 *Age* (Melbourne) 24 May 2/4 Mr. Barnes said the Gordon estate sub-division would be one of several new area developments which would enable closer integration of Papuans and New Guineans and expatriates.

expatriate (ɛks'peɪtrɪeɪt), *v.* [f. ppl. stem of late L. *expatriāre*, f. *ex-* (see EX- *pref.*[1]) + *patri-a* native land + -ATE[3]. Cf. Fr. *expatrier.*]

1. *trans.* To drive (a person) away from (his) native country; to banish.

1817 G. CHALMERS in *Churchyard's Chippes* 163 Morton was thus expatriated. 1828 D'ISRAELI *Chas. I*, I. v. 113 This minister, after having been expatriated, outlived his great enemy. 1856 OLMSTED *Slave States* 261 He apologizes at length for proposing to expatriate the negroes.

2. *refl.* (rarely *intr.* for *refl.*) To withdraw from one's native country; in the *Law of Nations*, to renounce one's citizenship or allegiance.

1784 BERINGTON *Hist. Abeillard* (1787) IV. 187 He [Abeillard] indulged the romantick wish of expatriating himself for ever. 1804 COLEBROOKE *Husb. & Comm. Bengal* (1806) 61 *note*, Another person.. who has expatriated, or who has removed to other land. 1846 GROTE *Greece* I. v. (1862) I. 89 Ætôlus.. having been forced to expatriate from Peloponnêsus. 1856 EMERSON *Eng. Traits, Ability* Wks. (Bohn) II. 40 Sir John Herschel.. expatriated himself for years at the Cape of Good Hope. 1889 PHILLIMORE *Internat. Law* (ed. 3) IV. 30 The *status* of aliens, and the capacity of subjects to expatriate themselves under the present English law.

Hence **ex'patriated** *ppl. a.* **ex'patriating** *ppl. a.*, that expatriates (in sense 2 of vb.).

1768 STERNE *Sent. Journ., Pref. in Desobligeant*, The balance of sentimental commerce is always against the expatriated adventurer. 1793 BURKE *Rem. Policy Allies* Wks. VII. 147 The expatriated landed interest of France. 1855 MACAULAY *Hist. Eng.* IV. 384 The ruined and expatriated Protestant Lord. 1846 GROTE *Greece* I. xvii. (1862) II. 420 The œkist and some of the expatriating chiefs.

expatriation (ɛksˌpeɪtrɪ'eɪʃən). [f. EXPATRIATE *v.*: see -ATION.]

1. The banishing of a person from his own country; the state of being banished; banishment, exile.

1816 KEATINGE *Trav.* I. 31 This part of France appears never to have recovered the effects of.. an expatriation. 1848 MACAULAY *Hist. Eng.* I. 524 The longer his expatriation, the greater does this hallucination become. 1860 MOTLEY *Netherl.* (1868) I. iii. 92 The expatriation of wealthy merchants.

2. The action of leaving one's country for another; emigration. Also, in the *Law of Nations*, renunciation of one's country.

1825 T. JEFFERSON *Autobiog.* Wks. 1859 I. 8 Expatriation being a natural right. 1839 YEOWELL *Anc. Brit. Ch.* x. (1847) 107 The bishops and clergy.. sought refuge in expatriation. 1868 ROGERS *Pol. Econ.* xix, The voluntary expatriation of those who have the energy or enterprise to leave the home of their birth. 1889 PHILLIMORE *Internat. Law* (ed. 3) IV. 274 *Expatriation*, Any British subject.. who may.. after the passing of this Act.. voluntarily become naturalized in such state.. shall.. be deemed to have ceased to be a British subject.

†**expe'ccation.** *nonce-wd.* [f. EX- *pref.*[1] + L. *peccāre* to sin: see -ATION.] (See quot.)

a 1631 DONNE *Serm.* lxiv. 645 It is.. this Expeccation.. this taking away of Sins formerly committed that restores me.

expect (ɛk'spɛkt), *v.* Also 7-8 exspect. [ad. L. *ex(s)pect-āre* to look out for, await, f. *ex-* (see EX- *pref.*[1]) + *spect-āre* to look, freq. of *spec-ĕre* to see. Cf. OF. *especter* (14th c.) to await.]

I. To wait.

†**1. a.** *intr.* To wait; to defer action until some contingency arises. *to expect of*: = sense 2. *Obs.*

1560 DAUS tr. *Sleidane's Comm.* 408 a, He desireth.. that Duke Maurice woulde be content to expect so long as he may goe and come. 1600 HOLLAND *Livy* XXI. xlviii. 420 Scipio.. thinking it good to expect of the other Consull his Colleague. 1611 BIBLE *Heb.* x. 13 From henceforth expecting till his enemies be made his footstoole. 1653 H. MORE *Antid. Ath.* II. xii. (1712) 82 A Dog expects till his Master has done picking of the bone. 1703 *Rules of Civility* 15 We must not knock, but expect patiently. 1765 G. COLMAN *Terence's Comedies* 388 To sit at home, expecting till a kinsman Came.. to marry her.

†**b.** quasi-*trans.* with *out. Obs. rare.*

a 1664 M. FRANK *Serm.* (1672) 497 Men having.. diligently made use of the opportunity, and expected it out.

†**2. a.** *trans.* To wait for, await. *Obs.*

1585 ABP. SANDYS *Serm.* xiv. §19. 239 Note in Cornelius with what humanitie.. he receiued Peter.. he called to him his kinsmen and friends, and expected him. 1609 BIBLE (Douay) *Ecclus.* xi. *Comm.*, Expect the end of an other mans speach, before you beginne to answer. 1633 BP. HALL *Hard Texts N.T.* 223 Yee.. eate your owne good cheere not expecting your poorer brethren. 1710 STEELE *Tatler* No. 202 ¶5 There was a great crowd in my Antichamber, who expected Audience. 1781 GIBBON *Decl. & F.* II. 92 The.. king of the Goths, instead of expecting the attack of the Legions, boldly passed the Danube. 1801 SOUTHEY *Thalaba* IX. xviii, With.. talons sheathed The ounce expects his liberty. 1822 SHELLEY in R. Garnett *Relics* (1862) 189 With what anxiety I expect your news of her health!

b. With indirect question as obj.: To wait to see or know. ? *Obs.* or *arch.*

1572 G. BUCHANAN *Detect. Q. Mary* N j, Do you now expect quhat sentence men chosen agaynst law.. haue pronounced? 1603 KNOLLES *Hist. Turks* (1621) 79 All this great fight the Constantinopolitanes beheld.. expecting what should bee the event thereof. 1687 T. BROWN *Saints in Uproar* Wks. 1730 I. 72, I expected every minute when it would come to downright kick and cuff between 'em. 1741 MIDDLETON *Cicero* (ed. 3) II. VII. 191 While he [Cicero] lay encamped.. expecting what way the Parthians would move. 1794 GODWIN *Cal. Williams* 20 Mr. Tyrrel.. expected every moment when he would withdraw to another part of the room.

†**c.** Of a destiny, etc.: To be in reserve for, be in store for. Cf. AWAIT 8. *Obs.*

c 1611 CHAPMAN *Iliad* XVIII. 113 If such fate expect my life, where death strikes I will lie. 1659 HAMMOND *On Ps.* lxxxii. 7 Paraphr. 409 That severe account.. of their actions, which after death expects all such. 1741 MIDDLETON *Cicero* (ed. 3) III. x. 166 If any other fate expects me, I tast a joy beforehand, in the sure foresight of your punishment. 1781 COWPER *Charity* 280 Prisons expect the wicked.

II. To look for mentally.

†**3.** To look forward to as one's goal or motive.

1578 T. N. tr. *Conq. W. India* 24 Good men doe rather expect renowne, then treasure.

4. To look forward to (an event), regard (it) as about to happen; to anticipate the occurrence of (something whether good or evil). Also, to 'look for', anticipate the coming of (a person or thing), the receipt of (anything).

Often with advbs. or phrases indicating time, which by a sort of ellipsis relate to the event 'expected'; e.g. 'I expect him next week'; 'When do you expect payment'?

a. with simple *obj*. When the obj. denotes an action, manifestation, etc., often const. *of, from*. In colloq. phr. ***expect me when you see me***: implying that the speaker is uncertain as to when he will return.

1601 SHAKS. *Jul. C.* I. ii. 297 *Cassi.* Will you Dine with me to morrow? *Cask.* I. *Cassi.* Good, I will expect you. **1605** BP. HALL *Medit. & Vows* I. viii. 14, I will expect the woorst, because it may come; the best, because I know it will come. **1651** HOBBES *Leviath.* III. xli. 263 They that bare rule..and they that were governed, did all expect the Messiah. **1701** DE FOE *True-born Eng.* Pref., I expect a Storm of Ill Language. **1724** R. FALCONER *Adv. & Esc.* (1769) 83 Finding we could not expect his Life, we prayed for a speedy and painless Release from it. **1802** MAR. EDGEWORTH *Moral T.* (1816) I. xiii. 104 They expected a visit in a few hours. **1866** GEO. ELIOT *F. Holt* (1868) 24, I am afraid of ever expecting anything good again. **1876** R. D. BLACKMORE *Cripps* II. xi. 179 If I do not ring then, send everybody to bed. And do not expect me until you see me. **1882** J. H. BLUNT *Ref. Ch. Eng.* II. 18 If he did similar things, he should expect similar punishment. **1891** *Speaker* 2 May 533/1 The book is very much what might have been expected from the author. *a* **1894** *Mod.* I expect my mother to dinner. **1923** J. BUCHAN *Midwinter* xii. 191, I..may be absent for days. Expect me back when you see me. **1963** 'B. GRAEME' *Almost without Murder* xi. 124 Sometimes I travel at an hour's notice. My brothers expect me when they see me. **1967** B. WHITAKER *Of Mice & Murder* vi. 73, I might go off for the day somewhere. All right if you expect me when you see me? **1968** 'P. HOBSON' *Titty's Dead* v. 54, I must be off. Expect me when you see me.

b. with *obj*. and *inf*.; when the action or condition anticipated is that of the subject, with *inf*. alone.

1659 B. HARRIS *Parival's Iron Age* 142 The Imperial Garrisons, who were not expected to be ever seen again in those parts. **1660** WILLSFORD *Scales Comm.* 182 A Captain of a Castle expecting to be beleagured, makes good his outworks. **1710** HEARNE *Collect.* (Oxf. Hist. Soc.) III. 6, I expect to receive them this week. **1724** DE FOE *Mem. Cavalier* (1840) 172 They expected us, and we expected to come. **1818** JAS. MILL *Brit. India* I. II. vi. 226 He expected to perform to him one of the most agreeable of all possible services. **1876** JEVONS *Logic Primer* 9 Seeing a bright flash of lightning, I expect thunder to follow. **1891** *Law Times* XC. 473/2 We are now daily expecting the question to come again before the Divisional Court.

c. with *clause* as obj.; also with ellipsis of subordinate clause.

1603 SIR D. CARLETON in Ellis *Orig. Lett.* I. 245 III. 82 It is expected the two courts being joyned will produce somewhat extraordinary. **1726** CHETWOOD *Adv. Capt. R. Boyle* 74 They did not expect she could ever recover. **1749** FIELDING *Tom Jones* II. ix, This lady was..as well as could be expected for one in her condition. **1860** TYNDALL *Glac.* I. xi. 79 The Mur..was by no means so bad as we had expected.

d. *absol*.

1779 JOHNSON *L.P.* Wks. 1816 IX. 170 We love to expect; and when expectation is disappointed or gratified we want to be again expecting. **1847** TENNYSON *Princ.* III. 191 Our King expects—was there no precontract?

¶**e.** *ellipt*. (*a*) *Anglo-Irish* (see quot. 1813); (*b*) to be pregnant; usu. in phr. *to be expecting*. *colloq*.

1813 MAR. EDGEWORTH *Patron.* (1815) II. 22 'Sure I tould you he was not expicted, that is if you don't know in England, not expicted to live.' **1817** JANE AUSTEN *Let.* 23 Mar. (1952) 489 She *expects* much about this day three weeks, & is generally very exact. **1845** MRS. S. C. HALL *Whiteboy* v. 48 Poor Mrs. M.... *isn't expected*—indeed I must ride hard to overtake her. **1890** FARMER *Slang Dict.*, *Expecting*, with child. **1906** GALSWORTHY *Man of Property* I. vi. 82 Whether young Roger's wife was really—expecting. **1939** M. SPRING RICE *Working-class Wives* iv. 71 She is 32 and has three children, very well spaced and is 'expecting again'. **1957** R. LONGRIGG *Switchboard* 208 'Make him do a Charleston.' 'Have a heart,' said Sue. 'I'm expecting.'

†**f.** *intr. to expect for* = to look for. *Obs.*

1591 HARINGTON *Orl. Fur.* Pref., A Sophister..made a long..Oration..expecting at the end thereof for some great thankes. **1630** *R. Johnson's Kingd. & Commw.* 98 Travellers ..expecting in an Almanacke for a yeare of Jubile, flie over Sea by flocks towards Rome. **1659** B. HARRIS *Parival's Iron Age* 277 A peace, for which so many people long, and earnestly expect.

5. In sense 4 with various additional notions.

a. In combination with *can*, with expressed or implied negation, this vb. often = ' to look for with reason or likelihood, or without great risk of disappointment'. Cf. *count on, rely on*, in similar connexion.

1650 R. STAPYLTON *Strada's Low-C. Warres* Strada to Rdr., A History..which I cannot expect should be either praised or pardoned. **1759** [see ERRONEOUS 3]. **1848** MACAULAY *Hist. Eng.* I. 538 The despotic viceroy soon found that he could not expect entire support from Argyle. **1871** MORLEY *Voltaire* (1886) 135 Nor can we be expected to be deeply moved by a form of art that is so unfamiliar to us.

b. To look for as due from another. In stronger sense: To look for (something) with an implied injunction or requisition.

1634 SIR T. HERBERT *Trav.* 184 These Negroes..impart freely of what they have to any civill Traveller, expecting some small retribution for their curtesie. **1650** CROMWELL *Lett. & Sp.* (1871) III. 104, I expect it be encouraged. **1690** DRYDEN *Amphitryon* Pref., There is a Pride of doing more than is expected from us. **1711** ADDISON *Spect.* No. 115 ¶5 Providence furnishes Materials, but expects that we should work them up ourselves. **1729** BUTLER *Serm.* Wks. 1874 II. 72 The unhappy, from whom can be expected no returns either of present entertainment or future service. **1805** NELSON in Southey *Life* ix, [Nelson's last signal] England expects every man to do his duty! **1818** WHATELY *Commpl. Bk.* (1864) 97 Thus I may fairly expect that one who has received great kindness from me should protect me in distress. **1884** *Punch* 6 Dec. 276/1 What do you expect me to do? **1890** BESANT *Demoniac* v. 55 The crew won't expect any drink.

†**c.** Hence of things, conditions, etc.: To call for, need, require. *Obs.*

1664 J. STRYPE in *Lett. Lit. Men* (Camden) 181, I am sensible of the charges that a College life doth expect. **1687** J. BOYSE in *Thoresby's Corr.* (ed. Hunter) I. 93 One assertion in it I could not but think expected greater evidence. **1691** T. H[ALE] *Acc. New Invent.* 29 To order the doing of that now, which the Practice of the Navy..would have expected their having done long since.

6. To anticipate that it will turn out to be the case *that*; hence, to suspect, suppose, surmise.

Now *rare* in literary use. The misuse of the word as a synonym of *suppose*, without any notion of 'anticipating' or 'looking for', is often cited as an Americanism, but is very common in dialectal, vulgar or carelessly colloquial speech in England.

1592 UNTON *Corr.* (Roxb.) 382 It is expected that the Duke of Guiese's horse was shott under him. **1607** TOURNEUR *Rev. Trag.* v. i, The Duchesse is expected fowly bent. **1645** in *Select. Harl. Misc.* (1793) 346, I..expect they [the forces] are much stronger than I am made believe. **1763** T. JEFFERSON *Corr.* Wks. 1859 I. 186, I say *has been*, because I expect there is one [an opening] no longer. **1785** *Ibid.* I. 384. **1812** —— *Writ.* (1830) IV. 177. **1821** WHEWELL in Todhunter *Acc. W.'s Wks.* (1876) II. 43, I expect they are of a character which will not set you upon making comparisons. **1856** *Sebastopol* II. xiv. 385, I expect my friend was a paragon of sanctity. **1861** SIR G. W. DASENT *Burnt Njal* I. Pref. viii, It is an old saying, that a story never loses in telling, and so we may expect it must have been with this story. **1877** W. H. MALLOCK *New Republic* (1878) 184 Now, I expect, Lady Ambrose, that, in its true sense, you know a good deal more history than you are aware of.

†**ex'pect**, *sb. Obs. rare.* [f. prec. vb.] = EXPECTATION 3.

1597 J. PAYNE *Royal Exch.* 4 Not for the expect of any vayne glorye. **1606** SHAKS. *Tr. & Cr.* I. iii. 70 Speak Prince of Ithaca, and be 't of lesse expect, That matter needless.. Divide thy lips, than, etc.

expectable (ɛk'spɛktəb(ə)l), *a.* Also 7 *erron.* **expectible.** [ad. L. *exspectābilis*, f. *exspectāre*: see EXPECT *v.* and -ABLE.] To be expected.

1646 SIR T. BROWNE *Pseud. Ep.* II. v. §3. 85 Nor is its substantiall conversion expectible in any composition or aliment wherein it is taken. **1653** GAUDEN *Hierasp.* 18 It is not expectable, that ministers should increase in favor with God and man, unless, etc. *a* **1677** BARROW *Serm.* Wks. 1686 II. xviii. 261 In that measure which is expectable from the natural infirmity..of man. **1886** TUPPER *My Life as Author* 230 It is expectable they [telescopes] would show us only our own composites in those of other worlds.

¶[Erron. after Sp. *espectable*, ad. L. *spectābile-m*: see SPECTABLE.] Distinguished, illustrious.

1574 HELLOWES *Gueuara's Fam. Ep.* 175 Expectable gentleman, and magnificent knight. *Ibid.* 197 Right expectable and noble knight. I haue receaued your letter.

†**expectaltee.** *Obs. rare.* [? Corruption of Sp. *espectante*, one who is on the look-out.]

1654 WHITTOCK *Zootomia* A, Peeces compiled..out of Plutarchs fulness..would undoubtedly fill the mouth of the most gaping Expectaltee among Readers. *Ibid.* A vij, To all gaping Expectaltees (that look for more than here they are like to finde) my Book replyeth [etc.].

expectance (ɛk'spɛktəns). [f. L. *expectantia*, n. of state f. *expectant-em*: see EXPECTANT.]

1. The action or state of waiting for anything. In later use only with mixture of sense 2 in phrase ***after long expectance***. Somewhat *arch.*

1603 KNOLLES *Hist. Turks* (1621) 1092 At length after long expectance..they were..brought forth into the field. **1628** DIGBY *Voy. Medit.* (1868) 4 In expectance of the others companie. **1682** WHELER *Journ. Greece* I. 20 After a long and fruitless expectance of Succours. *a* **1717** PARNELL *Gift of Poetry* (1758) 149 Long expectance of a bliss delay'd Breeds anxious doubt. **1724** SWIFT *Drapier's Lett.* iv, The addresses of both houses after long expectance produced nothing but a report in favour of Wood. **1818** R. SOUTHEY in *Q. Rev.* XVIII. 8 The slow season of expectance past, True Love ..[might] Requite the sorrows of this hard delay. **1863** KINGLAKE *Crimea* II. 249 Now at length, and after long expectance, they indeed would go into action.

†**b.** With indirect question: The state of waiting to know. *Obs.*

1606 SHAKS. *Tr. & Cr.* IV. v. 46 There is expectance here from both the sides, What further you will doe?

2. The action of mentally looking forward to the occurrence of anything, or to the coming of any one; anticipation; = EXPECTATION 2 and 3. *Obs.* or *arch.*

1640 SLINGSBY *Diary* (1836) 64 Great expectance their is of a happy Parliament. *a* **1641** BP. R. MOUNTAGU *Acts & Mon.* (1642) 427 They..make him stay, and stand without in expectance a whole yeere. **1691** T. H[ALE] *Acc. New Invent.* p. xc, Their expectance of being better used abroad. **1768–74** TUCKER *Lt. Nat.* (1852) II. 330 Some particular person in whom that general expectance might centre. **1814** CARY *Dante* (Chandos) 173 The thirst did feel abatement of its edge E'en from expectance.

b. In phrases ***against, beyond expectance, to answer expectance***. ? *Obs.*

1631 R. H. *Arraignm. Whole Creature* x. §1. 74 They answere not expectance. **1659** *Lady Alimony* v. vi. in Hazl. *Dodsley* XIV. 365 Who..rais'd their ruin'd fortunes Above expectance! **1756** BURKE *Subl. & B.* IV. xvii, When any thing happens against the expectance of the mind.

†**c.** The state or condition of being expected. In phrase, ***in expectance***. *Obs.*

1611 COTGR. s.v. *Expectative..Benefices conferez en expectative*, in reversion, or expectance. **1640** FULLER *Joseph's Coat* iii. (1867) 127 In hope and expectance he hath the reversion of heaven and happiness.

†**d.** A resource from which results are expected. Cf. *hope*. *Obs.*

a **1668** DAVENANT *Siege of Rhodes* Wks. (1673) 33 Being to their last expectance driven, Ianthe, now they cry!

†**3.** Ground, reason, or warrant for expecting; prospect of attaining to something. Cf. EXPECTANCY 2 b, 4, EXPECTATION 4, 4 b. *Obs.*

1602 WARNER *Alb. Eng.* Epit. (1612) 373 The expectance of the Crowne in Right..rested in this Edgar. **1603** KNOLLES *Hist. Turks* (1621) 1385 Being a man of small fortune, and little expectance in his owne countrey. **1650** R. STAPYLTON *Strada's Low-C. Warres* IX. 36 There could be no expectance of a forrein expedition. **1701** N. WILSON in Keble *Life Bp. Wilson* (1863) I. 158 Wishing that they may live so as to have a just expectance of that blessed immortality. **1754** RICHARDSON *Grandison* I. ii. 7 Having a good estate in possession; fine expectances besides. **1793** MRS. E. PARSONS *Woman as she should be* I. 153 An aunt.. from whom he has great expectances.

†**4.** That which is expected. *Obs.*

1684 Z. CAWDREY *Cert. Salvation* 30 Towards his servants he was so just, that he..gave them all their due Expectances, and, etc.

expectancy (ɛk'spɛktənsɪ). Also 7 **expectansie.** [ad. L. *expectantia*: see prec. and -ANCY.]

†**1.** = EXPECTANCE 1. *Obs. rare*$^{-1}$.

1649 G. DANIEL *Trinarch., Hen. IV*, cxxi, Only this is worth The King's Expectancie.

2. The quality or state of being expectant; often, the action or fact of expecting (= EXPECTANCE 2); also, an instance of this; a counting on; a forecast, calculation.

1600 HOLLAND *Livy* 1187 The Macedonians, who depended upon the hope and expectancie of their aid. **1656** JEANES *Mixt. Schol. Div.* 131 It gives therefore an assured expectancy of a better life after death. *a* **1714** SHARP *Serm.* (1754) I. ii. 34 How often doth a man do that in the fury and expectancies of lust, for which [etc.]. **1807** COGAN *Eth. Treat. Passions* I. i. 38 According to the degrees of our expectancy of success. **1823** SCOTT *Peveril* xxv, Fortune.. loves to confound the calculations and expectancies of humanity. **1876** GEO. ELIOT *Dan. Der.* v. xl, The first-prompted suspicion..gave way to a more submissive expectancy.

b. *esp.* The position of being entitled to any possession at some future time, either as a remainder, or reversion, or on the death of some one.

1811 L. M. HAWKINS *C'tess & Gertr.* I. 37 Miss Toms, the great heiress in expectancy. *a* **1832** MACKINTOSH *France in* 1815, Wks. 1846 III. 191 Persons..interested..in the sale of confiscated property..by mortgage, or by expectancy. **1867** MISS BROUGHTON *As a Flower* xi. 105 Happy partly in present fruition, far more in expectancy.

c. That from which expectations are entertained. *arch.* Cf. *hope* and EXPECTANCE 2 d.

1602 SHAKS. *Ham.* III. i. 160 Th' expectansie and Rose of the faire State. **1805** WORDSW. *Prelude* VI. Wks. (ed. Morley) 280/2 The Nation hailed Their great expectancy.

3. The state or condition of being expected, or looked forward to; *esp.* in *Law* (see 2 b).

1598 KITCHIN *Courts Leet* (1675) 305 The Fee was but in expectancy. **1767** BLACKSTONE *Comm.* II. 482 The bankrupt..is bound..to make a full discovery of all his estate and effects, as well in expectancy as possession. **1777** BURKE *Corr.* (1844) II. 200 A practical reputation, to do any good, must be in possession, not in expectancy. **1838** DICKENS *Nich. Nick.* xxii, The whole capital which Nicholas found himself entitled to either in possession, reversion, remainder, or expectancy. **1848** WHARTON *Law Lex.* 241/1 s.v. *Expectation*, A sum of money in expectancy..has a determinate value.

b. Anything in expectancy; anything which a person is entitled to expect.

[**1767** BLACKSTONE *Comm.* II. 163 Of expectancies there are two sorts; one..called a remainder; the other..called a reversion.] **1858** LD. ST. LEONARDS *Handy Bk. Prop. Law* xx. 152 You may devise and bequeath any of your expectancies. **1883** *Stubbs' Mercantile Circ.* 8 Nov. 1000/2 Taking an assignment of her expectancy for what it is worth.

4. The extent to which expectation may be reasonably cherished; prospective chance of possession, or of the occurrence of an event.

1620 *Horæ Subsec.* 454 From meane fortunes expectancies cannot be great. **1793** BURKE *Rem. Policy Allies* Wks. 1842 I. 594, I..have been taught..to moderate my calculation of the expectancy of human abilities. **1879** GEO. ELIOT *Theo. Such* xv, Calculating expectancy concerning parishoners' turkeys.

expectant (ɛk'spɛktənt), *ppl. a.* and *sb.* [a. Fr. *expectant*, or perh. ad. its original L. *ex(s)pectant-em*, pr. pple. of *exspectāre*: see EXPECT.]

A. *adj.*

1. a. That is in an attitude or state of expectation; waiting, looking out. Const. †*for*, *of*, †*on*.

c **1400** *Rom. Rose* 4571 Abide in hope.. Expectant ay tille I may mete. **14..** *Purific. Mary* in *Tundale's Vis.* (1843) 131 Symeon.. That was expectaunt.. On the comfort and consolacion of Isrel. **1641** Sir E. Dering *Sp. on Relig.* 22 Nov. xv. 65 The people are expectant for a Declaration. **1730–6** in Bailey (folio). **1801** Southey *Thalaba* iii. xvii, His dog.. Now lifts an anxious and expectant eye, Courting the wonted caress. **1856** Mrs. Browning *Aur. Leigh* iv. 899 Romney at the porch Looked out expectant of the bride. **1862** Trench *Mirac.* xv. (ed. 3) 253 From among this suffering expectant multitude Christ singles out one. **1872** A. W. Hutton *Posit. Catholics in Ch. Eng.* 33 The Church Militant, the Church Expectant.

b. *esp.* That has the prospect, in ordinary course, of succeeding to a possession, office, etc., or of occupying a certain position; 'that is to be' (so-and-so). Also, that expects, thinks himself likely, to be appointed to an office, etc. ***expectant mother***, a pregnant woman; also *transf.*; so ***expectant father***.

1393 Gower *Conf.* I. 216 As he that tho was apparant Upon the regne expectant. **1640–1** *Kirkcudbr. War-Comm. Min. Bk.* (1855) 57 The supplicatioun presentit by Johne Somervaill, expectant minister. *a* **1691** Bp. Barlow *Rem.* (1693) 276 The Supernumerary expectant Clergy. **1714** Swift *Pres. State Affairs* Wks. 1755 II. i. 220 Scruples artificially raised in the mind of the expectant heir. **1838** Lytton *Calderon*, A pious Catholic, expectant of the cardinal's hat. **1861** M. Reid *Hero in spite of Himself* I. 12 Whenever a Zapoteque woman is about to add one to the number of their community, the expectant father of the child assembles all his relations in his cabin. **1878** Trollope *Is he Popenjoy?* III. v. 56 There was a brutality about this which for a time made the expectant father almost mad. **1882** R. K. Douglas *China* iv. 87 The expectant mother's next desire is to discover of what sex her child will be. **1886** *Law Times* LXXXII. 94/2 An expectant occupier has a *locus standi* to apply for the renewal of a public-house licence. **1918** *Act 8 & 9 Geo. V* c. 29 §1 Arrangements.. for attending to the health of expectant mothers and nursing mothers. **1960** M. Burton *Wild Animals Brit. Isles* 97 In fox-hunting countries artificial burrows are constructed.. of which the expectant-mother vixen will avail herself. **1963** 'G. Bagby' *Murder's Little Helper* (1964) ii. 14 'What kind of a burglar is it that swipes maternity clothes?' 'Expectant father?'

c. *Eng. Law* (see quot.).

1875 Sir G. Jessel *Law Rep.* 10 Chanc. Appeals 391 That peculiar position of reversioner or remaindersman which is oddly enough described as an expectant heir. This phrase is used, not in its literal meaning, but as including.. every one who has the hope of succession to the property of an ancestor.

2. Characterized by expectation or waiting for the course of events; *esp.* in *Medicine*, in ***expectant method***, etc. (see quot. 1866).

1816 Southey in *Q. Rev.* XVI. 513 Like the continental physicians, such statesmen would pursue the expectant system. **1860** Motley *Netherl.* (1868) I. iii. 80 The policy of England continued to be expectant and dilatory. **1866** A. Flint *Princ. Med.* (1880) 112 The treatment of a disease is expectant whenever the physician does not attempt to abridge or arrest it, but strives to aid in conducting it to a favorable termination.

3. *Law.* Existing in expectancy, or belonging to one in reversion or remainder; reversionary. Hence, in ordinary lang.: To be expected or anticipated.

1628 Coke *On Litt.* 21 He hath.. a fee simple expectant. **1670** Sir T. Culpeper *Necess. Abating Usury* 13 Upon the Encouragement of a long.. lease, he.. will be enabled to venture on Improvements chargeable and expectant. **1765** Blackstone *Comm.* I. 217 On her.. the remainder of the crown, expectant on the death of king William.. without issue, was settled by statute. **1768–74** Tucker *Lt. Nat.* (1852) II. 660 We encourage ourselves to any.. disagreeable task by prospect of the profit expectant therefrom. **1818** Cruise *Digest* (ed. 2) V. 25 The right of the remainder-man, expectant on the determination of the estate tail. **1827** Jarman *Powell's Devises* II. 111 The fee expectant on his wife's life estate. **1858–9** *Act 21–2 Vict.* c. 44 §11 in *Oxf. & Camb. Enactm.* 264 The reversion immediately expectant on the determination thereof.

B. *sb.*

1. One who expects an arrival, occurrence, etc.; one who looks to receive something.

a **1661** Fuller *Worthies, Middlesex*, [Sir Julius Cæsar] though heaved at by some Expectants, sate still in his place. **1664** H. More *Myst. Iniq. Apol.* 539 Eager Expectants of this great happiness. **1706** Collier *Refl. Ridic.* 235 They'll submit all their inferiours and expectants to all their whims and fancies. **1725** Pope *Odyss.* i. 323 Vain expectants of the bridal hour. **1866** J. G. Murphy *Comm. Ex.* xxxii. 1 Moses delayed, literally, put the expectants to shame by his non-appearance. **1877** Kinglake *Crimea* (ed. 6) V. i 235 From moment to moment he was an expectant of death.

2. a. One entitled to expect something to which he will succeed or come in due course, as an owner in reversion, the next heir, etc. In Eng. Law = *expectant heir*: see A. 1 c.

1625–8 tr. *Camden's Hist. Eliz.* iv. 564 Those that are Expectants of the Crown. **1654** Gayton *Pleas. Notes* III. ix. 127 This puts.. the Expectant, to fresh charge. **1686** Kettlewell *Serm. Death Ld. Digby* 3 Those who are now no longer.. Expectants, but inherit the Promises. **1751** Ld. Hardwicke *2 Ves. Sr.* 157 [The species of fraud] which infects catching bargains with heirs, reversioners, or expectants, in the life of the father, etc. **1788** H Walpole *Remin.* iii. 27 Some devoting themselves to the wearer of the crown, and others to the expectant. **1817** Canning in *Parl. Deb.* 330 The impatient expectants of a dilapidated inheritance. **1853** Marsden *Early Purit.* 186 James, King of Scotland, the eager expectant of their throne.

b. A candidate for, or one who expects, any office or employment. In Scotland, formerly, 'a candidate for the ministry who has not yet received a license to preach the gospel' (Jam.).

1641 *Act Assembly Glasgow* 7 Aug. (Jam.), No expectant shall be permitted to preach in publike before a congregation til first he be tryed after the same manner. **1646** *Burd. Issach.* in *Phenix* (1708) II. 264 Students in Divinity.. are enrol'd Expectants of such or such a Presbytery. **1647** N. Bacon *Disc. Govt. Eng.* i. vi. (1739) 28 This may give some liking to the present Incumbents, but not to the Expectants. **1692** in *J. Fisher's Life* i. 10 [They would be pleased] to desire Mr. Thomas Fisher expectant.. to come and preach to them. **1802** *Ann. Reg.* 2 The spirit of violence.. manifested.. by.. the expectants of government. **1852** Sir W. Hamilton *Discuss.* 401 A clerical expectant, whose hopes are bounded by a College living. **1855** Macaulay *Hist. Eng.* III. 295 Name whom he might, he could not fail to disappoint.. a multitude of expectants.

Hence **ex'pectantly** *adv.*, in an expectant manner; in the attitude of expectation.

1857 W. Collins *Dead Secret* (1861) 238 His head turned expectantly in the direction in which he had last heard.. his wife's voice. **1876** Geo. Eliot *Dan. Der.* iv. xxx, The children.. stood in front of her with their sweet faces up-turned expectantly.

expectation (ɛkspɛk'teɪʃən). [ad. L. *expectātiōn-em*, n. of action f. *exspectāre* to expect.]

1. The action of waiting; the action or state of waiting for or awaiting (something). Now only with mixture of sense 2: Expectant waiting.

1550 Bale *Image Both Ch.* B iiij, Dilygent Expectacion in the faith of Gods promyses. **1601** Shaks. *Jul. C.* i. i. 46 [You] haue sate The liue-long day, with patient expectation, To see great Pompey. **1605** —— *Lear* iv. iv. 23 Our preparation stands In expectation of them. *c* **1667** South *Serm. Consecration* (1715) 282 A daily Expectation at the Gate, is the readiest Way to gain Admittance into the House. **1675** Bentley *Pref. to Dryden's Mistaken Husband* 250 This Play was left in Mr. Dryden's hands many years since.. After Twelve years expectation, Mr. Dryden gave it to the Players. **1721–1800** in Bailey. **1853** Kane *Grinnell Exp.* xxvii. 221 After another hour of cold expectation they came again.

b. = *expectant method*: see expectant A. 2.

1689 G. Harvey (*title*), The Art of Curing Diseases by Expectation. **1866** A. Flint *Princ. Med.* (1880) 112 The treatment of a disease by expectation consists in watching carefully its progress, and meeting with appropriate measures unfavorable events as they arise. **1884** in *Syd. Soc. Lex.*

c. *attrib.*, as in ***expectation-week*** (see quot.).

1622 Sparrow *Bk. Com. Prayer* (1661) 196 Sunday after Ascens. This is called Expectation-week for now the Apostles were.. expecting the fulfilling of that promise of our Lord.

2. The action of mentally looking for some one to come, forecasting something to happen, or anticipating something to be received; anticipation; a preconceived idea or opinion with regard to what will take place. Phrases. ***against, beyond, contrary to,*** †***out of***, etc. ***expectation.***

1552 Abp. Hamilton *Catech.* (1884) 42 Expectatioun or loking for the blys of hevin. **1553** Eden *Treat. Newe Ind.* (Arb.) 6 If dew successe.. shoulde not chaunce according vnto theyr hope & expectation. **1563** Fulke *Meteors* (1640) 70 b, Some perchance, would looke that wee.. should entreat of.. precious stones, which matter though it be out of our purpose.. yet seeing it is not out of the expectation. **1563** Golding *Cæsar* 149 When contrarye to theyr expectacion, our enemyes saw vs.. return. **1599** Shaks. *Much Ado* ii. iii. 220 If he do not doat on her vpon this, I wil neuer trust my expectation. **1603** Daniel *Panegyr. King* lxi, Where mens expectations intertaine Hopes of more good. **1736** Butler *Anal.* Introd. Wks. 1874 I. 2 Our expectations that others will act so and so in such circumstances. **1767** Gooch *Treat. Wounds* I. 404 Nature, assisted by art, perfected a cure beyond expectation. **1792** *Anecd. W. Pitt* III. xliv. 205 Is it.. within the utmost stretch of the most sanguine expectation, that [etc.]. **1851** Robertson *Serm.* Ser. iv. iii. (1863) I. 22 Their attitude of Expectation—they were waiting for the coming of the Lord. **1874** Green *Short Hist.* vi. 301 No accession ever excited higher expectations among a people than that of Henry the Eighth.

b. The looking for something as one's due (cf. expect 5 b); in *pl.* what one looks for or requires one's (mental) demands.

1655 in *Nicholas Pap.* (1892) II. 225 Though those princes be punctuall in their expectations of compliments of that nature.

c. Supposition with regard to what is present or past. Cf. expect *v.* 6.

1793 T. Jefferson *Writ.* (1859) III. 548 The expectation that you are always from home prevents my writing to you. **1822** Mrs. E. Nathan *Langreath* III. 88 A fond expectation that the Duke had come in search of her.

3. The state or condition of expecting or mentally looking for something; the mental attitude of one who expects; expectancy. Formerly occas. in *pl.*

1538 Starkey *England* i. i. 24 In such expectatyon they spend theyr lyfe. **1653** Walton *Angler* i. 11, I am now become so full of expectation, that, etc. **1659** B. Harris *Parival's Iron Age* 189 And yet was he degraded before his death, and in hourly expectation of the Hangman. **1667** Milton *P.L.* x. 782 No fear of worse.. would torment me With cruel expectation. **1745** *Fortunate Orphan* 235 She is in the highest Expectations. **1772** Priestley *Inst. Relig.* (1782) II. 99 Expectation begins to awake in the infant mind. **1827** Pollok *Course T.* ix, Upon the tiptoe raised of expectation. **1864** *Spectator* 454 Influences.. that substitute the flutter of expectation for hope.

4. Ground or warrant for expecting; the condition of being likely, or entitled, to receive or experience something in the future.

1611 Bible *Ps.* lxii. 5 My soule wait thou onely vpon God; for my expectation is from him. **1708** Atterbury *Serm. on Job* xxii. (1723) II. 198 To whom can we betake our selves with greater Expectations to succeed in our Addresses?

b. *pl.* Prospects of inheritance or of profiting by testament.

1669 Lady Chaworth in *12th Rep. Hist. MSS. Comm.* App. v. 11 Lord Huntingtons marriage is as good as concluded with Sir James Langhams daughter, who gives 20,000*l.* downe, besides expectations. **1777** Sheridan *Sch. Scandal* iii. iii, I have a rich old uncle.. from whom I have the greatest expectations. **1837** Lytton *E. Maltrav.* 45 O yes; I have what are called expectations. **1861** Dickens (*title*), Great Expectations.

†**c.** = expectative B. 2. *Obs. rare*$^{-1}$.

1536 Latimer in *27 Serm.* (1562) 9 b, Some brought forth Canonizations, some Expectations, some pluralities and vnions.

5. The state or condition of being expected; only in phrase ***in expectation.***

1657 J. Smith *Myst. Rhet.* 252 Desire.. is a strange countrey.. where corn is still in grass.. and birds alwayes in the shell.. all is there only in expectation. **1785** Reid *Int. Powers* ii. xx. 271 Belief of good or ill either present or in expectation. **1832** Webster s.v., A sum of money in expectation, when an event happens, has a determinate value before that event happens.

†**6.** ***of*** (***great***, etc.) ***expectation***: affording ground for favourable anticipations; promising. *Obs.*

a **1586** Sidney *Arcadia* i. xii. (1590) 51 b You, borne so great a Prince, and of so rare, not onely expectation, but proofe. **1605** Verstegan *Dec. Intell.* viii. (1628) 246 The worthiest names, were to bee giuen to such as were of worthiest expectation. **1788** *Lond. Mag.* 423 He was so bred.. and was of such expectation, that he looked like a miracle of a man.

7. That which is expected; the object of expectance; a thing expected or looked forward to.

1596 Shaks. *1 Hen. IV*, iii. ii. 36 The hope and expectation of thy time Is ruin'd. **1667** Milton *P.L.* xii. 379, I understand Why our great expectation should be call'd The seed of Woman.

8. The degree of probability of the occurrence of any contingent event.

1832 Webster s.v., If the chances of receiving or not receiving a hundred dollars.. are equal; then.. the expectation is worth half the money. **1838** De Morgan *Ess. Probab.* v. (1841) 97 The balance is the average required, and is known by the name of the mathematical expectation. **1848** Wharton *Law Lex.*, *Expectation*, in the doctrine of chances, is applied to any contingent event, upon the happening of which some benefit is expected. *Ibid.*, The value of the expectation is.. £5.

b. ***expectation of life***: (see quots.)

1725 De Moivre *Ess. Annuities*, The expectation of life is that duration which may be justly expected from a life of a given age. **1796** Hutton *Math. Dict.*, *Expectation of Life* is the.. number of years of life, which a person of a given age may, upon an equality of chance, expect to enjoy. **1846** McCulloch *Acc. Brit. Empire* (1854) I. 420 The expectation of life among the government annuitants.

expectative (ɛk'spɛktətɪv), *a.* and *sb.* [ad. late L. *ex(s)pectātīvus*, f. *ex(s)pectāre* to expect.]

1. Of or pertaining to expectation.

a. *Canon law.* Reversionary; of or pertaining to the reversion of benefices, etc. ***expectative grace***: a mandate given by the pope or king conferring the expectation or right of succession to a benefice.

1488 *Sc. Acts Jas. IV* (1814) 210 Quhat tym it be declarit that ony persone or personis be gracis expectativis [*printed* expectavis] acceptis or purchessis ony beneficez [etc.]. **1560** Daus tr. *Sleidane's Comm.* 366 a, Bishops of Rome.. by reseruations and graces expectatiue.. haue deriued all the gaine to Rome. **1619** T. Mason *Christ's Vict.* 148 Expectatiue Aduousons are graunted without number. **1751** Chambers *Cycl.*, *Expectative Canons* were such as did not officiate in the Canonries to which they belonged. *Ibid.*, In France.. the right of conferring expectative graces, is looked on as one of the regalia. **1769** Robertson *Chas. V*, II. ii. 112 Expectative graces.. were brought into use.

†**b.** *gen.* Of prospective effect. *Obs.*

1630 S. Ward in *Ussher's Lett.* (1686) 440 Ablution of infants from original sin is only conditional and expectative. **1653** H. Whistler *Upshot Inf. Baptism* 17 The Covenant of baptism holding out such expectative grace of Repentance.

2. Characterized by waiting for events; = expectant A. 1, 1 b.

1611 Cotgr., *Expectatif, -ive*, expectative. **1689** G. Harvey *Curing Dis. by Expect.* xxiii. 206 To give you an instance of its expectative mode of curing. **1847** in Craig. **1870** *Daily News* 11 Oct., 'We are preserving', they say, 'a dignified expectative attitude'.

B. *sb.*

†**1.** Something in expectation; an expectancy; = expectation 6. *Obs.*

a **1528** Skelton *Image Hypocr.* Wks. II. 343 His expectatives Many a man unthrives. **1618** Wotton *Let.* in *Reliq. Wotton.* (1672) 486, I am abundantly satisfied in some Expectatives. *a* **1631** Donne *Serm.* xii. 119 Though Blessednesse seem to be but an Expectative, a reversion reserved to the next Life. **1758** Chesterf. *Lett.* IV. 137 He is young enough to forgive and to be forgiven the possession and the expectative at least for some years.

2. = *expectative grace* (see A. 1).

1563-87 FOXE *A. & M.* (1596) 4/1 The.. reservations, expectatives, and such other proceedings of the popes pretended jurisdiction. **1616** N. BRENT tr. *Sarpi's Hist. Counc. Trent* (1676) 714 Expectatives..did make the incumbents death to be desired. **1725** tr. *Dupin's Eccl. Hist. 17th C.* I. II. iii. 47 The Council of Basle..abolish'd the Expectatives..and all the other exactions of the Court of Rome. **1818** HALLAM *Mid. Ages* (1872) II. 213 Gregory IX pretended to act generously in limiting himself to a single expectative. **1838** PRESCOTT *Ferd. & Is.* II. 475 Ximenes obtained a papal bull, or expectative, preferring him to the first benefice..which should become vacant.

expected (ɛk'spɛktɪd), *ppl. a.* [f. EXPECT *v.* + -ED[1].] Looked for, anticipated.

1586 A. DAY *Eng. Secretary* II. (1625) 28 You would according to your honourable promises have done me an expected good. **1664** H. MORE *Myst. Iniq.* 109 That expected eminent false prophet who does antichristianly oppose himself against the Spirit of truth. **1712** POPE *Messiah* 21 Swift fly the years, and rise th' expected morn! **1828** SCOTT *F.M. Perth* xix, Busied with things about the expected combat. **1875** JOWETT *Plato* (ed. 2) I. 101 Fear is not of the present..but is of future and expected evil. *Mod.* The mod. English *give* is irregular; the expected form would be *yeve*.

Hence **ex'pectedly** *adv.*, in the manner expected, according to expectation; cf. *unexpectedly*.

1758 H. WALPOLE *Let. H. Mann* 31 May, Lord Mansfield ..unexpectedly is supported by the late Chancellor..and very expectedly by Mr. Fox.

expecter (ɛk'spɛktə(r)). Also 6-8 **expector**. [f. as prec. + -ER[1].]

1. One who expects (in senses of vb.); one who looks for a person or thing to arrive.

1584 R. PARSONS *Copy of Letter* 107 Wher she is like by nature to out-liue the expector. **1610** HEALEY *St. Aug. Citie of God* 723 Hee [Christ] must..be desired of the expecters. **1670** EACHARD *Cont. Clergy* Pref., I am not..any expecter of a reign of nothing but saints and worthies. **1725** SWIFT *Corr.* Wks. 1841 II. 575 These are not likely to be great expecters [*Wks. ed.* **1745** expectors] under your excellency's administration. **1775** in ASH; whence in mod. Dicts.

2. Name of a religious sect (see quot.).

1645 PAGITT *Heresiogr.* (ed. 4) 145 Many have wrangled so long about the Church, that at last they have quite lost it, and go under the name of *Expecters* and *Seekers*.

expectible, incorrect f. EXPECTABLE.

expecting (ɛk'spɛktɪŋ), *vbl. sb.* [f. EXPECT *v.* + -ING[1].] The action of the vb. EXPECT; expectation. Now only gerundial.

1606 DRUMM. OF HAWTH. *Let.* Wks. 232 After many reports and long expecting, the king of Denmark is coming hither. **1617** HIERON *Wks.* II. 296 Sometimes, some vnseasonablenesse of the yeere frustrates his expecting.

ex'pecting, *ppl. a.* [f. as prec. + -ING[2].]

1. That expects; expectant.

1714 SWIFT *Pres. St. Affairs* Wks. 1755 II. I. 219 That impatience which the frailty of human nature gives to expecting heirs. **1726** CHETWOOD *Adv. Capt. R. Boyle* 80 The Captain came in with an expecting Face. **1804** JANE AUSTEN *Watsons* (1879) 319 Her little expecting partner. **1842** G. S. FABER *Provinc. Lett.* (1844) II. 95 To reside and labour in his own expecting Greek Diocese.

¶**2.** *catachr.* = EXPECTED. *Obs. rare*[−1].

1621 LADY M. WROTH *Urania* 496 The Campe they gained the night before the expecting time of Combat.

Hence **ex'pectingly** *adv.*, in an expecting manner or attitude; expectantly.

1693 DRYDEN *Juvenal* VI, Prepar'd for fight, expectingly she lies. **1833** *Blackw. Mag.* XXXIII. 112 The waiter was standing expectingly. **1838** *New Monthly Mag.* LII. 195 Firmly, yet expectingly, sat the last woman. **1871** *Lit. World* 6 Jan. 1 We thought well enough of Napoleon III. to listen expectingly for some word [etc.].

†**ex'pection.** *Obs.* Also 6 **expeccion**. [erron. f. EXPECT, after apparent analogy of *inspect, inspection.*] = EXPECTATION.

1532 MORE *Confut. Tindale* Wks. 520/1 There is..nowe lefte vs..a terryble expeccion and lookyng for of iudgement. **1568** C. WATSON *Polyb.* 856 Acquiting himself very well of the expection which the people conceived of him. **1640** NABBES *Bride* B ij/2 Shee makes my patience tyre With so much expection. **1658** W. BURTON *Itin. Anton.* 136 So impatient was his expection.

ex'pective *a. rare.* [erroneously f. EXPECT, after apparent analogy of *respect, respective*: cf. prec.] = EXPECTATIVE.

1660 R. COKE *Power & Subj.* 221 Provisions, Reservations Expective graces, etc. have no place in France. **1882-3** SCHAFF *Encycl. Relig. Knowl.* III. 2559/1 [Ximenes] visited Rome, and returned..with an expective letter from the Pope on the archpriestship of Uzeda.

†**ex'pectless,** *a. Obs. rare*[−1]. [f. EXPECT *v.* or *sb.* + -LESS.] Unexpected, unlooked for.

1607 CHAPMAN *Rev. Bussy D'Ambois* II. Dij b, 124 When hee saw mee enter so expectlesse.

expector: see EXPECTER.

expectorant (ɛk'spɛktərənt), *a.* and *sb.* [ad. L. *expectorant-em*, pr. pple. of *expectorāre*: see next. Cf. Fr. *expectorant.*]

A. *adj.* That promotes expectoration.

1811 A. T. THOMSON *Lond. Disp.* (1818) 387 Storax is stimulant, and in some degree expectorant. **1884** *Standard* 7 Jan. 2/6 He prescribed an expectorant medicine.

B. *sb.* An expectorant medicine.

1782 E. GRAY in *Med. Commun.* I. 36 Expectorants seem to have been very seldom given. **1834** J. FORBES *Laennec's Dis. Chest* 229 Expectorants, such as squills, and especially antimony. **1875** H. C. WOOD *Therap.* (1879) 522 Expectorants may be arranged under two heads; the nauseant or sedative expectorants, and the stimulating expectorants.

expectorate (ɛk'spɛktəreɪt), *v.* Also 7 **-at.** [f. L. *expectorāt-* ppl. stem of *expectorāre*, f. *ex-* (see EX- *pref.*[1]) + *pector-, pectus* the breast; in class. L. only in sense 3. Cf. Fr. *expectorer.*]

†**1.** *trans.* Of a drug or its action: To clear, drive out (phlegm, etc.) from the chest or lungs.

1601 HOLLAND *Pliny* XXIV. xvi, As well the one as the other, doth expectorat the fleame gathered in the chest. **1656** CULPEPPER *Eng. Physic. Enl.* 80 The Decoction of the Herb [crosswort] in Wine helpeth to expectorate flegm out of the chest. **1678** SALMON *Lond. Dispens.* 769/1 Green Oyntment ..is given..to..expectorate flegm.

absol. **1710** T. FULLER *Pharm. Extemp.* 121 It [the Electuary]..powerfully expectorates.

2. To eject, discharge (phlegm, etc.) from the chest or lungs by coughing, hawking, or spitting.

1666 G. HARVEY *Morb. Angl.* (1672) xxiii, Excrementitious humours such as are expectorated by a Cough. **1732** ARBUTHNOT *Rules of Diet* 334 Morbifick Matter is..expectorated by Coughing. **1846** G. E. DAY tr. *Simon's Anim. Chem.* II. 71 Thick clots of mucus are expectorated in the morning. **1861** F. H. RAMADGE *Curab. Consumption* 30 He expectorated blood. **1877** ROBERTS *Handbk. Med.* (ed. 3) I. 360 Laryngeal tissues may be expectorated.

fig. **1782** V. KNOX *Ess.* vi, All the venom which a virulent party could expectorate upon them. **1831** CARLYLE *Sart. Res.* (1858) 67 Teufelsdröckh had not already expectorated his antipedagogic spleen.

b. *absol.*; often = to spit.

1827 LYTTON *Pelham* ii, The men [at Cambridge].. expectorated on the floor. **1882** QUAIN *Dict. Med.* s.v. *Expectoration*, By teaching the patient 'how to expectorate' life may be prolonged.

3. †**a.** To expel from the 'breast' or mind (*obs.*). **b.** *refl.* and *intr.* for *refl.* To ease or relieve one's mind.

1621 S. WARD *Life of Faith* (ed. 2) vii, Hath it [faith] not soueraigne vertue in it to.. expectorate all feares? **1656** TRAPP *Comm. Matt.* xxiii. 17 The dust of covetousness had put out the eyes of these buzzards, and expectorated their understandings. **1667** WATERHOUSE *Fire Lond.* 185, I could enlarge in this Subject which is so pleasing to me, to expectorate my self by. **1754** H. WALPOLE *Corr.* (1837) I. 246 Sir George came..to expectorate with me as he called it. **1865** CARLYLE *Fredk. Gt.* XVIII. vii, Friedrich..took to verses, by way of expectorating himself.

Hence **ex'pectorated** *ppl. a.* **ex'pectorating** *vbl. sb.* **ex'pectorating** *ppl a.* = EXPECTORANT *a.*

1656 RIDGLEY *Pract. Physick* 212 Give expectorating means. **1732** ARBUTHNOT *Rules of Diet* 266 Substances expectorating are such as cleanse and open. **1783** S. CHAPMAN in *Med. Commun.* I. 285 From the expectorating mixture, he never seemed to receive any benefit. **1809** PEARSON in *Phil. Trans.* XCIX. 319 This expectorated substance swims on water. **1845** G. E. DAY tr. *Simon's Anim. Chem.* I. 335 Dr. Chiaje..found the polystoma sanguiculum in the expectorated blood of two phthisical patients.

expectoration (ɛkˌspɛktə'reɪʃən). [f. prec. vb.: see -ATION.]

1. The action or process of expectorating; discharge of phlegm from the chest by coughing, etc.

1672 SIR T. BROWNE *Lett. Friend* xv. (1881) 138 Expectoration and spitting out. **1793** BEDDOES *Consumpt.* 134 Even when the expectoration..goes on favourably. **1826** SCOTT *Woodst.* v, A slight expectoration, just like what one makes before beginning a long speech. **1834** J. FORBES *Laennec's Dis. Chest* 84 The varying secretion and expectoration of the pearly sputa. **1860** EMERSON *Cond. Life, Behav.* Wks. (Bohn) II. 382 In the pews of the churches [are] little placards..against..expectoration.

fig. **1816** SCOTT *Antiq.* xxii, This expectoration of spleen was suddenly interrupted.

2. *concr.* Expectorated matter; a quantity of it.

1817 *Med. Jrnl.* XVII. 557 A considerable expectoration mixed with blood. **1843** ABDY *Water Cure* 31 Slimy glutinous expectoration frequently. **1879** KHORZ *Princ. Med.* 40 Expectoration may contain mucus, pus, or blood.

expectorative (ɛk'spɛktərətɪv), *a.* and *sb.* [f. EXPECTORATE *v.*: see -ATIVE.]

A. *adj.* Of or pertaining to expectoration.

1883 GRANT WHITE *Adams in Eng.* 125 Leaning against the stone, he began an expectorative demonstration.

B. *sb.* = EXPECTORANT *sb.*

1666 G. HARVEY *Morb. Angl.* (1672) xxvi. 64 Syrups or other expectoratives.

expectorator (ɛk'spɛktəreɪtə(r)). [agent-n. f. L. *expectorāre*: see EXPECTORATE.]

†**1.** A medicine which promotes expectoration; = EXPECTORANT *sb. Obs.*

1671 SALMON *Syn. Med.* III. xxii. 415 Bitter Vetch..is an Expectorator. **1710** T. FULLER *Pharm. Extemp.* 278 There are no such Things as Expectorators..except Volatiles and Balsamics.

2. One who expectorates or spits; in quot. *fig.*

1835 *Blackw. Mag.* XXXVII. 112 Volumes of the slaver [= spittle]..lettered with the name of the expectorator on the outside.

ex'pectoratory. *nonce-wd.* A place for expectorating; a spitting-place.

1836 *Blackw. Mag.* XXXIX. 357 The expectoratory (we mean the principal cabin) of a handsome American packet.

expede (ɛk'spiːd), *v. Sc.* Also 7 **expeed**. *Pa. pple.* 6 **expeid**, 7 **exped**, 7-8 **expede**. [ad. L. *expedīre*: see EXPEDITE *v.*]

†**1.** *refl.* To get (oneself) out of a difficulty; to extricate; = EXPEDITE 1 b. *Obs.*

1645 RUTHERFORD *Tryal & Tri. Faith* (1845) 243 They shall never expede themselves.

†**2.** *trans.* To get out of hand; to accomplish, complete, dispatch. Cf. EXPEDITE 2 and 3. *Obs.*

1513-75 *Diurn. Occurr.* (Bannatyne Club) 281 Lord Sanct-johne..obtenit litill or nathing of his errands expeid. **1560-1** *Bk. Discipl. Ch. Scot.* (1621) 10 That the matter may be the better & sooner exped. *a* **1657** SIR J. BALFOUR *Ann. Scot.* (1824-5) II. 148 The assessor to expeed all bussines the second weeke. **1716** *Wodrow Corr.* (1843) II. 145, I shall omit other things of my..studies till I get that expede.

3. To send out, issue officially (a document); = EXPEDITE 4. *to expede letters* (Scots Law): 'to write out the principal writ, and get it signeted, sealed, or otherwise completed' (W. Bell *Dict. Law Scot.* 1861).

1600 *Sc. Acts. Jas. VI* (1816) 219 That the said Infeftment be expede in dew forme. *a* **1651** CALDERWOOD *Hist. Kirk* (1843) II. 495 Als sufficient as if the samine were expede by the General Assemblie of the kirk. **1679** BURNET *Hist. Ref.* I. ii, His Bulls were expeded at Rome. **1687** A. LOVELL tr. *Bergerac's Comical Hist.* II. 136 My Pass-ports then were expeded. **1752** J. LOUTHIAN *Form of Process* (ed. 2) 218 After the Letters are expede, the private Party employs a Macer or Messenger to execute the same. **1827** in *Law Times Rep.* L. 708/2 Executors..with power..to..expede confirmations. **1884** *Law Times* 8 Mar. 345/2 A Scotch notary public will expede a notarial instrument.

†**4.** To hasten (a person); to dispatch with all speed. *Obs. rare.*

1600 in Pitcairn *Crim. Trials Scot.* II. 286, I man intreit yowr lo[rdship] to expede Bowr.

Hence **ex'peding** *vbl. sb.*

1595 in Spottiswood *Hist. Ch. Scot.* VI. (1677) 413 The expeding of Signatures. **1678** *Trans. Crt. Spain* II. 9 The expeeding of Penaltas Commissions.

‖**ex pede Herculem** (ɛks pɛdiː 'hɜːrkjʊlɛm), *phr.* [L., 'Hercules from his foot'.] Inferring the whole of something from some small or insignificant part of it, as Pythagoras is said to have calculated the height of Hercules from an estimate of the size of his foot.

1665 R. HEAD *Eng. Rogue* sig. Aaa 6r°, I perceived she was endued with ingenuity, by the quaintness of her expressions, *Ex pede Herculem.* *a* **1734** R. NORTH *Examen* (1740) I. ii. 102 But *ex pede Herculem.* They, that let so much be seen, had notable Reserves however couched. **1881** W. D. HAY *300 Years Hence* p. vii, From it he may glean some knowledge of Professor Meister's character: *ex pede Herculem.* **1936** *Times Lit. Suppl.* 10 Oct. 805/2 Ex pede Herculem; these changes may not seem serious except to connoisseurs of English prose rhythm. **1953** W. V. QUINE *From Logical Point of View* iii. 63 The finished lexicon is a case..of *ex pede Herculem*... In projecting Hercules from the foot we risk error.

†**ex'pediate,** *a. Obs.* [f. Fr. *expedié*, pa. pple. of *expédier*, ad. med.L. *expediāre* (= L. *expedīre*): see EXPEDE and -ATE[2].] Expeditious.

1658 EVELYN *Fr. Gard.* (1672) 62 This way..is more prompt and expediate.

[**expediate,** *v.* Error for EXPEDITE in an imperfect and unauthorized edition of Sandys' *Relation of the State of Religion*, reproduced by Cockeram, copied by Todd, 1818; hence in later Dicts.

1605 SANDYS *Rel. State Relig.* K 3, Some great alterations in some kinde of marchandise..which may serve for that present instant to expediate [*MS. correction by author and ed.* 1629 expedite] their businesse. **1623** COCKERAM, *Expediate*, to dispatch, or make ready.]

expedience (ɛk'spiːdɪəns). [a. Fr. *expédience*, f. *expédient*: see EXPEDIENT.]

†**1. a.** Haste, speed, dispatch. **b.** That which requires speed; an enterprise, expedition. *Obs.*

a. **1593** SHAKS. *Rich. II*, II. i. 287 Eight tall ships, three thousand men of warre Are making hither with all due expedience. **1599** —— *Hen. V*, IV. iii. 70 The French.. will with all expedience charge on vs.

b. **1596** SHAKS. *1 Hen. IV*, I. i. 33 In forwarding this deere expedience. **1606** —— *Ant. & Cl.* I. ii 185, I shall breake The cause of our Expedience to the Queene.

2. = EXPEDIENCY 1. ? *Obs.*

1619 W. SCLATER *Exp. 1 Thess.* (1630) 577 Those expediences, which the Lord hath reuealed himselfe willing to make knowne. **1638** CHILLINGW. *Relig. Prot.* I vi. §50 The lawfulnesse and expedience of Latine Service. *a* **1714** SHARP *Serm.* vii. (1754) I. 184 The expedience of actions; that is to say, whether it be best and fittest for a man to do them or no. **1781** COWPER *Let. Johnson* 27 Nov., I have doubts about the expedience of mentioning the subject on which that paragraph is written. **1804** WELLINGTON in Owen *Disp.* 432 The expedience of admitting the Peishwa to a participation in our late conquests.

3. = EXPEDIENCY 2. *pl.* Interested motives or considerations.

1608 BP. HALL *Char. Virtues & V.* I. 13 Justice is his [the honest man's] first guide, the second law of his actions is expedience. **1796** MORSE *Amer. Geog.* I. 253 Expedience may operate to continue the privilege. **1834** J. H. NEWMAN

Par. Serm. (1837) I. xxiv. 365 They have sacrificed Truth to expedience. **1848** LYTTON *Harold* VI. v, Expediences began to dim to his conscience the healthful loveliness of truth.

expediency (ɛk'spiːdɪənsɪ). Also 7 **expedency**. [f. EXPEDIENT: see -ENCY.]

1. The quality or state of being expedient; suitability to the circumstances or conditions of the case; fitness, advantage; †an advantage.

1612 BRINSLEY *Lud. Lit.* xxviii. (1627) 281 Though some good Schoolemasters doe doubt of the expediency. **1661** *Grand Debate* 10 Those who are unsatisfied concerning their lawfulness, or expedency. *a* **1677** BARROW *Serm.* xxxii. (1741) II. 333 From a wise consideration of humane affairs ..we may collect the..expediency, the..necessity of a future judgment. **1680** H. DODWELL *2 Lett.* (1691) C j b, Many other expediencies hereof [of this Compendium] might have been mentioned. **1741** MIDDLETON *Cicero* II. IX. 309 In some perplexity..about the expediency of the voyage. **1879** *Cassell's Techn. Educ.* III. 194/2 It is not a question of expediency, it is a question of sheer necessity.

†**b.** *concr.* = EXPEDIENT B. 2. *Obs.*

1683 BARNARD *Life Heylin* 117 He proposed a most excellent expediency..for the satisfaction of some scrupulous members.

2. The consideration of what is expedient, as a motive or rule of action; 'policy', prudential considerations as distinguished from those of morality or justice. In mod. use often in a bad sense, the consideration of what is merely politic (esp. with regard to self-interest) to the neglect of what is just or right.

1612-5 BP. HALL *Contempl. N.T.* I. i, Matters of good order in holy affairs may be ruled..according to reason and expediency. **1754** CHATHAM *Lett. Nephew* vi. 43 Matters of mere expediency, that affect neither honor, morality, or religion. **1786** BURKE *W. Hastings* Wks. 1842 II. 168 Warren Hastings did act..contrary to his own declared sense of expediency, consistency, and justice. **1815** JANE AUSTEN *Emma* I. xviii. 126 Following his duty instead of consulting expediency. **1828** D'ISRAELI *Chas. I*, II. ix. 230 Where political expediency seems to violate all moral right. **1862** RUSKIN *Unto this Last* 8 For no human actions ever were intended..to be guided by balances of expediency. **1875** JOWETT *Plato* (ed. 2) III. 156 The right of private property is based on expediency.

b. occas. in *pl.* Motives of expediency; the requirements of expediency.

1843 CARLYLE *Past & Pr.* (1858) 139 Looming with shapes of expediencies. **1859** MILL *Liberty* i. 25 These reasons must arise from the special expediencies of the case.

3. *Comb.*

1853 G. S. FABER *Revival Fr. Emp.* 54 Even those wise men of this world, our liberalising Expediency-Mongers, have been constrained to admit, etc.

expedient (ɛk'spiːdɪənt), *a.* and *sb.* Forms: 5 **exspedyent**, 5-6 **expedyent(e**, 6 **expediente**, (**expedien**), 4- **expedient**. [a. Fr. *expédient*, ad. L. *expedient-em*, pr. pple. of *expedīre*: see EXPEDITE *v.* In sense 2 the modern adjective follows the sense of the L. verb 'to forward matters, be helpful or serviceable', a development from the sense represented by EXPEDITE *v.* 2.]

A. *adj.*

I. †**1.** Hasty, 'expeditious', speedy. Also, of a march: Direct. *Obs.* Cf. EXPEDITE *a.* 4.

c **1485** *Digby Myst.* (1882) III. 817 In ower weyys we be expedyent. **1593** SHAKS. *Rich. II*, I. iv. 39 Expedient manage must be made my Liege. **1594** —— *Rich. III*, I. ii. 217, I will with all expedient duty see you. **1595** —— *John* II. i. 60 His marches are expedient to this towne.

†**b.** quasi-*adv.* Nimbly, skilfully. *Obs.*

1509 HAWES *Past. Pleas.* XVI. ii, Musyke, the lady excellent, Played on base organs expedient.

II. 2. Conducive to advantage in general, or to a definite purpose; fit, proper, or suitable to the circumstances of the case. Const. *for*, †*to*.

a. as *pred.* or *complement*, often with subj. *it*, and followed by infinitive phrase or noun-sentence.

1398 TREVISA *Barth. De P.R.* XIX. xxi. (1495) 876 It is not expedient..to reherse alle the causes of wanne colour. *c* **1430** LYDG. *Bochas* III. xii. (1554) 85 a, To their noblesse.. Nothing in earth was more expedient. **1519** *Interl. Four Elem.* in Hazl. *Dodsley* I. 17 Those things to know for me be full expedient. **1548-9** (Mar.) *Bk. Com. Prayer, Offices* 1 It is expediente that Baptisme be ministred in the Englishe tounge. **1586** COGAN *Haven Health* cxiii. (1636) 114 [Pomegranates] that are soure bee more expedient and wholesome. **1651** HOBBES *Leviath.* II. xvii. 86 What he thinks expedient for the common benefit. **1659** B. HARRIS *Parival's Iron Age* 217 That nothing could be more expedient to the safety of the common-wealth, than to bring him to the Bar of Justice. **1793** T. JEFFERSON *Writ.* (1859) IV. 29 The President thought it expedient..to remind our fellow-citizens that we were in a state of peace. **1799** BEDDOES *Contrib. Phys. & Med. Knowl.* 277 These, if not necessary to the existence of vegetables, may be expedient to their flourishing state. **1841** MYERS *Cath. Th.* III. xlii. 160 Alterations..become expedient from time to time. **1845** MCCULLOCH *Taxation* II. vi. (1852) 277 It may..be expedient..that roads should be constructed.

b. qualifying a sb.

1643 MILTON *Divorce* Pref. (1851) 18 An expedient liberty and truth. **1676-7** MARVELL *Corr.* Wks. 1872-5 II. 531 To propound some expedient proposalls. **1806** W. TAYLOR in *Ann. Rev.* IV. 885 The most expedient settlements for a trading country. **1841** CATLIN *N. Amer. Ind.* (1844) I. xviii. 127 The most expedient measures. **1891** F. HALL in *Nation* (N.Y.) LIII. 447/3 Its [the word gotten] expedient disappearance from Matthew xi.

3. In depreciative sense, 'useful' or 'politic' as opposed to 'just' or 'right'. Often *absol.*

1774 GOLDSM. *Retal.* 40 Too fond of the right to pursue the expedient. **1861** MILL *Utilit.* ii. 32 The expedient, in the sense in which it is opposed to the Right, generally means that which is expedient for the particular interest of the agent himself.

4. Studious of 'expediency'.

1828 L. HUNT *Byron & Contemp.* I. 304 Triflers with their hourly word for gain; expedient statesmen.

B. *sb.*

†**1.** Something that helps forward, or that conduces to an object; a means to an end. *Obs. rare.*

1665 BOYLE *Occas. Refl.* IV. viii. (1675) 218 Employing the Methods and Expedients afforded us by Reason. **1667** *Decay Chr. Piety* vii. 150 God..does not project for our sorrow, but our innocence; and would never have invited us to the one, but as an expedient to the other.

†**b.** A medium or means of reconciliation. *Obs.*

a **1661** FULLER *Worthies* (1840) I. 340, I know not how to reconcile this rhyme with another which I meet with in the same author..But, in order of an expedient betwixt them, etc. *Ibid.* II. 1 The earth..may pass for an expedient betwixt pleasure and profit.

2. A contrivance or device adopted for attaining an end; a resource, 'shift'.

1653 H. COGAN tr. *Pinto's Trav.* iv. 9 As for us seven Portugals..we could find out no better expedient to save our lives, then to return. **1674** BREVINT *Saul at Endor* xi. 240 Finding out expedients..for shifting from one to another all personal Punishments. **1719** LONDON & WISE *Compl. Gard.* iv. 325 By the same expedient of Hotbeds we may also raise in..cold Weather, little Sallads. **1782** PRIESTLEY *Corrupt. Chr.* I. I. 37 The wretched expedients to which the orthodox ..had recourse. **1874** GREEN *Short Hist.* vi. 328 When every expedient had been exhausted by Norfolk..Cromwell came again to the front.

3. Comb. *expedient-monger*.

1656 HARRINGTON *Oceana* (1700) 134 Their Counsillors ..are expedientmongers. *a* **1745** SWIFT (Jod.), Expedient-mongers shake their heads.

Hence **ex'pedientness**, fitness, convenientness.

1730-6 in BAILEY (folio). **1775** in ASH.

expediential (ɛkˌspɛdɪ'ɛnʃəl), *a.* [f. as if L. **expedientia* EXPEDIENCY + -AL[1].] Of, pertaining to, or having regard to what is expedient.

1850 KINGSLEY *Raleigh* Misc. I. 65 A worldly expediential letter, appealing to low motives. *a* **1855** HARE in F. Hall *Mod. Eng.* viii. 316 *note*, An expediential policy. **1890** *Sat. Rev.* 12 Apr. 434/1 The expediential issues involved in the Home Rule question.

Hence **expedi'entially** *adv.*, in an expediential manner, as a matter of expediency.

1873 F. HALL *Mod. Eng.* 39 We should never deviate, save expedientially, from established usage.

ex'pediently, *adv.* [f. EXPEDIENT + -LY.]

1. As is expedient; suitably, conveniently.

1398 TREVISA *Barth. De P.R.* XIX. xlvi. (1495) 948 Exspedyently to adde and put more therto. **1526** *Pilgr. Perf.* (W. de W. 1531) 123 This gyfte of goostly scyence may do the same..more expedyently for mannes soule. **1804** W. TAYLOR in *Ann. Rev.* II 258 The office of the philosopher may expediently be separated from that of the historian.

†**2.** Expeditiously, promptly; out of hand. *Obs.*

1600 SHAKS. *A.Y.L.* III. i. 18 Do this expediently.

expediment (ɛk'spɛdɪmənt). [ad. med.L. *expedīment-um* (sense 2), f. *expedīre*: see EXPEDITE.]

†**1.** A means of getting out of a difficulty; an expedient. *Obs.*

1547-64 BAULDWIN *Mor. Philos.* (Palfr.) III. iii, When they be chafed in reasoning..solutions..similitudes, and expediments, doe..flow vnto their remembrance. *a* **1677** BARROW *Serm.* (1686) III. ix. 106 A like expediment to remove discontent is good company.

2. 'The whole of a person's goods and chattels, bag and baggage' (Wharton *Law Lex.* 1848).

†**ex'pedit.** *Obs.* [ad. late L. *expedītus* (*u* stem), f. *expedīre*: see EXPEDITE *v.*] An expedition.

1613 DANIEL *Coll. Hist. Eng.* 167 [The King's Coffers] must bee emptied in Scotland, whither agayne..he makes his third expedit.

expeditable (ɛk'spɛdɪtəb(ə)l), *a. rare.* [f. EXPEDITE *v.* + -ABLE.] (See quot.)

1820-7 BENTHAM *Wks.* (1843) II. 84 By expeditable understand capable of being terminated, etc.

†**ex'peditate**, *pple. Obs.*[-1] [ad. med.L. *expeditātus.*] In early use as pa. pple. of next.

expeditate (ɛk'spɛdɪteɪt), *v. Hist.* [f. med.L. *expeditāt-* ppl. stem of *expeditāre*, f. *ex-* (see EX- *pref.*[1]) + *ped-em* foot: on analogy of med.L. *excapitāre.*] *trans.* To cut off from (a dog) three claws or the ball of the forefoot; to law.

1502 *Chart. Forests* in Arnolde *Chron.* (1811) 209 He of whom the hounde were not expeditate. **1594** CROMPTON *Jurisdiction* 152 *Expeditate*, that is to saye, haue the balles of their feete cutt out. **1679** BLOUNT *Anc. Tenures* 91 The Amerciaments for expeditating Dogs. **1866** *Chamb. Jrnl.* XXVIII. 261 The Court of Regards was held..for the purpose of lawing or expeditating mastiffs.

Hence **ex'peditated** *ppl. a.*; **ex'peditating** *vbl sb.*

1598 MANWOOD *Lawes Forest* xvi. §8 (1615) 115/1 Such expeditating of mastiues shal be done according to the Assises. **1610** W. FOLKINGHAM *Art of Survey* III. iv. 71 Foote-geld implies a Priuiledge to keepe Dogges within the Forrest not expeditated. **1751** CHAMBERS *Cycl.* s.v. *Expeditation*, Every one that keeps a great dog not expeditated, forfeits three shillings and four pence to the king.

expedi'tation. *Hist.* Also 6 **expeditacion.** [ad. med.L. *expeditātiōn-em*, n. of action f. *expeditāre*: see EXPEDITATE.] The action of 'expeditating' or 'lawing' a dog.

1502 *Chart. Forests* in Arnolde *Chron.* (1811) 209 Fro hens-forth be ther noo one taken for expeditacion of houndis. *a* **1693** ASHMOLE *Antiq. Berks.* (1719) II. 425 The king granted to him..Freedom from Expedition of Dogs. **1768** BLACKSTONE *Comm.* III. 72 The Court of regard.. holden..for the lawing or expeditation of mastiffs. **1885** M. COLLINS in *Eng. Illust. Mag.* 586/1 These permitted dogs had to suffer expeditation.

†**'expedite**, *a. Obs.* Also 5 **-dyte**, 7 **-dit**. [ad. L. *expedīt-us*, pa. pple. of *expedīre*: see next.]

1. Of a place, road, way: Clear of obstacles or impediments, unimpeded; free from difficulties.

1581 STYWARD *Mart. Discipl.* II. 118 Descending from high and hillie places..to places expedite and open. **1581** SAVILE *Tacitus' Agric.* (1622) 197 All things to follow in an easie and expedite course. *a* **1677** BARROW *Serm.* (1686) III. xix. 216 To the one the way is rough and thorny, to the other beaten and expedite. *a* **1694** TILLOTSON *Serm.* xi. (1743) I. 260 It being so short and expedite a way for the ending of controversies.

fig. **1654** JER. TAYLOR *Real Pres.* 174 Is there in the world any thing more certain and expedite then that what you see ..should be judged to be that which you see.

b. Of an action or motion: Unrestricted, unembarrassed; easy, free.

1578 BANISTER *Hist. Man* II. 40 The expedite mouyng of the armes procured thereby. **1677** CARY *Chronology* II. II. I. ii. 190 The Exposition of that place being to me easie, expedite, and literal. **1691** RAY *Creation* II. (1704) 327 The Provision that is made for the easie and expedite Motion of them [the bones].

2. Of soldiers, etc. (after L. use): Lightly equipped, prepared for moving quickly.

1609 HOLLAND *Amm. Marcell* XXI. ii. 169 The most expedite and lightest appointed companies of his auxiliarie forces. **1622** BACON *Hen. VII*, 182 Hee sent the Lord Chamberlain with expedite Forces to speed to Execester. **1628** HOBBES *Thucyd.* (1822) 126 Eleven days journey for an expedite footman. **1737** WHISTON *Josephus' Antiq.* Dissert. III. xi, With them cohorts that were expedite and nimble. **1792** BURKE *Pres. State Affairs* Wks. 1842 I. 584 To support the expedite body in case of misadventure.

b. Unencumbered, free to move, active, nimble.

1612 T. TAYLOR *Comm. Titus* i. 6 The Iewes..tuck up their long garments to make them more expedite and free to a journey or busines. **1748** HARTLEY *Observ. Man* I. i. §2. 84 Death may..render us more expedite in the Pursuit of our true End. **1794** BURKE *Petit. Unit.* Wks. 1842 II. 478 A smaller number more expedite, awakened..courageous.

3. a. Of persons: Ready for action; prompt, alert, ready.

1603 BP. BARLOW *Conf. Hampton Crt.* in *Phenix* I 148 The king..in points of Divinity shewed himself so expedite and perfect. **1641** 'SMECTYMNUUS' *Answ.* xii. (1653) 47 The Arians were very expedite in worldly affaires. **1692** SOUTH *Serm.* (1697) I. 59 His faculties were quick and expedite.

b. Of contrivances, instruments, etc.: Ready for immediate use, conveniently serviceable, handy.

1609 HOLLAND *Amm. Marcell.* XVII. iv. 84 Now adaies a certaine set and expedite number of letters..declareth what-soever mans mind is able to conceive. **1638** CHILLINGW. *Relig. Prot.* I. Pref. §11 If she once had this power..expedite and ready for use. **1662** STILLINGFL. *Orig. Sacr.* I. vi. §8 The square letters are less operose, more expedite and facile. **1702** C. MATHER *Magn. Chr.* III. II. xv. (1852) 429 Several other contrivances made the whole more expedite for the use of them that consulted it. **1792** W. ROBERTS *Looker-on* (1794) I. 115 Their dress..he wishes to be rendered as expedite as possible.

4. Of an action or process, a means, remedy, etc.: Prompt, speedy, expeditious.

1545 RAYNOLD *Byrth Mankynde* (1564) 56 Tokens of an expedite and easye deliuerance. **1609** HOLLAND *Amm. Marcell.* XXXI. xvii. 431 Remarkable above the rest, was the profitable and expedite service of Julius. **1635** BRATHWAIT *Arcad. Pr.* 142 A distemper..requisite to have the expeditest cure. **1664** EVELYN *Pomona* Advts. (1729) 81 The vast Store of Cherries..and their expedite Growth. *a* **1734** NORTH *Exam.* III. viii. §13 This [the writ de nomine replegiando]..is..more effectual and expedite than an Habeas Corpus. —— *Lives* II. 392 A wrong determination, expedite, is better than a right one, after ten years vexation.

Hence †**'expeditely** *adv.*, †**'expediteness.**

1560 BECON *Jewel of Joy* Wks. (Parker Soc.) II. 418, I fear lest my servant doeth not his message expeditely. **1681** GREW *Musæum* i. 19 Nature..left his..ears naked, that he may turn them more expeditely for the reception of sounds from every quarter. **1623** in Rushw. *Hist. Coll.* (1659) I. 134 With what alacrity, with what expediteness and uniformity of heart. **1635** BRATHWAIT *Arcad. Pr.* II. 89 The expeditenesse of his cure expressed the infinitenesse of his care. **1684** H. MORE *Answ. Remarks Exp. Apocal., etc.* 240 The readiness and expediteness of their Ministry.

expedite ('ɛkspɪdaɪt), *v. Pa. pple.* 5 expedyte. [f. L. *expedīt-* ppl. stem of *expedīre*, f. *ex-* (see EX- *pref.*[1]) + *ped-em* foot.

The L. word etymologically means 'to free (a person's) feet from fetters' (the contrary of *impedīre*: see IMPEDE), hence, to free from difficulties, to help forward, to get (a work) out of hand, to dispatch, send off, etc.]

†**1.** *trans.* To clear of difficulties; to clear up (confusion); to facilitate (action or movement); to disentangle, untie (a knot). *Obs.*

1614 LODGE *Seneca* 1 The Bookes are..confused in order ..which a man though circumspect shall hardly expedite. **1643** MILTON *Divorce* Introd. (1851) 10 To expedite these knots were worthy a learned and memorable Synod. **1655** FULLER *Ch. Hist.* II. i. §9 His [Ethelbert's] power had influence even to Humber..which afterward much expedited the passage of the Gospel in England. **1667** MILTON *P.L.* x. 474 A broad way now is pav'd To expedite your glorious march.

†**b.** *refl.* To get (oneself) out of difficulties; to extricate, set free. Const. *from*. *Obs.*

1626 W. SCLATER *Exp. 2 Thess.* (1629) 172 Two things I commend to euery one desirous herein to expedite himselfe. *a* **1661** FULLER *Worthies, Exeter* I. 272 This active Gentleman had much adoe to expedite himself, and save his life. **1681** GLANVILL *Sadducismus* I. (1726) 85 She knows not how to expedite herself from gross corporeal Phantasms.

†**c.** To get (a person) out of the way; to get rid of, dispatch. *Obs.*

1678 *Trial Coleman* 25 Ashby brought..Treasonable Instructions..to expedite the King by Poison.

2. To help forward, hasten the progress of.

a **1618** RALEIGH *Mahomet* (1637) 62 Which hee doubted not would expedite his desires. **1655** FULLER *Ch. Hist.* IV. iii. §33 When a Royal Family is once falling, all things conduce to expedite their destruction. **1791** COWPER *Odyss.* VII. 275 But expedite ye at the dawn of day My safe return. **1828** J. H. MOORE *Pract. Navig.* (ed. 20) 40 It will greatly expedite the working the proportions..if..all the statings be first made. **1855** MACAULAY *Hist. Eng.* IV. 550 The Speaker.. received from the City a thousand guineas for expediting a local bill. **1872** H. MACMILLAN *True Vine* iii. 122 Nature.. expedites the process of flowering and seeding.

b. *intr.* To push on with speed (in travelling).

1602 WARNER *Alb. Eng.* XI. lxvi. (1612) 281 And thence, to expedite for Ob, his Labours did reuiue.

3. To perform quickly; to 'get out of hand', dispatch, accomplish.

1471 RIPLEY *Comp. Alch.* VII. in Ashm. (1652) 169 In few words yt wylbe expedyte. **1618** SIR L. CRANFIELD in *Fortesc. Papers* 61, I have signified his Majesties pleasure..which wee will expedite. **1655** FULLER *Ch. Hist.* II. iii. §9 The Virgin Mary..is pretended to have shewed her self..to Egwin, Bishop of Worcester, prompting him to expedite a Structure therein. **1698-9** LUDLOW *Mem.* (1751) I. 139 The Earl of Ormond..being willing..to expedite that service, accepted their invitation. **1793** SMEATON *Edystone L.* §116 A place..less capable of expediting my orders. *c* **1850** LANE *Arab. Nts.* (ed. Rtldg.) 550 We will..expedite her business. **1871** B. TAYLOR *Faust* (1875) II. IV. i. 235 Such is my wish: dare thou to expedite it.

4. To send out, issue officially (a document, etc.); to dispatch (a message). Now *rare*.

a **1626** BACON *New Atl.* iii. (1635) 149 Though such charters be expedited of course. **1648** EVELYN *Mem.* (1857) III. 10 A positive answer to be expedited within fifteen days. **1753** tr. *Voltaire's Micromegas* 232 All the public acts were expedited in that [Norman] language. **1815** MAD. D'ARBLAY *Diary* (1876) IV. 303 Thither, also, I expedited a letter, under cover to the Duke. **1818** JAS. MILL *Brit. India* I. III. iii. 527 The instruments of government to be expedited. **1852** MRS. JAMESON *Leg. Madonna* (1857) 47 When the Bull of Paul V was formally expedited.

b. *transf.* To send out (†an army, munitions of war); to dispatch (a courier). *rare*.

1606 WARNER *Alb. Eng.* XVI. ci. 398 Hee To expedite against Prince Rees an armie did decree. **1694** LUTTRELL *Brief Rel.* (1857) III. 347 Orders are sent to the Tower to expedite 10,000 bombs and 10,000 carcasses to the lord Berkly. **1876** BANCROFT *Hist. U.S.* VI. xli. 246 A Russian courier was expedited to Stockholm.

Hence '**expediter**, '**expediting** *vbl. sb.*

1643 T. CASE *Quarrell of Covenant* (1644) 99 Thou hast not grace enough..for the expediting thy self out of the next difficulty. **1678** *Trans. Crt. Spain* 169 For the more diligent expediting of this, it would be convenient [etc.]. **1891** *Pall Mall G.* 20 Oct. 1/3 Expediter of the business of the House.

expedition (ɛkspɪ'dɪʃən). Forms: 5 expediccione, expedision, 5-6 expedicion, -icyon, -ycion, -ycyon, -itioun, 6- -ition. [ad. L. *expeditiōn-em*, n. of action f. *expedīre*: see EXPEDITE *v.* Cf. F. *expédition*.]

†**1.** The action of expediting, helping forward or accomplishing; speedy performance or prompt execution (of justice, a journey); prompt supply (of anything), dispatch. *Obs.*

1464 *Paston Lett.* No. 493 II. 166 The Kyng shall..shewe his good grace and favour in the expedision therof. *c* **1477** CAXTON *Jason* 13 If hit plese you ye shal gyue me audience and goode expedicion. *c* **1489** —— *Blanchardyn* xxxiv. (1890) 127 They retourned wyth-out expedicyon of that wherfore they were goon thyder. **1528** in Strype *Eccl. Mem.* I. xiv. 108 Any..thing that might conduce to the furtherance and expedition of the cause. **1536** BELLENDEN *Cron. Scot.* (1821) I. 92 The ambassatouris..returnit but ony expeditioun of thair message. **1543-4** *Act 35 Hen. VIII*, c. 6 §2 For reformation whereof, and for the more expedition of iustice hereafter. **1543** W. CLEBE *MS. Addit.* 4609 f. 409 in Turner *Dom. Archit.* III. 79 For puryance and hasty expedition of the necessities aforsaide. **1606** G. W[OODCOCKE] tr. *Justin's Hist.* 65 b, Alexander..prepared for reuengfull warre..and for expedition thereof he desired of Demetryus, etc. **1649** *Answ. Petit. City Oxf.* in J. Harrington *Def. Rights Univ. Oxford* (1690) 19 There is as quick expedition in our courts as in any other courts.

†**b.** The condition of being expedited or set in motion; only in phr. ***in expedition***. *Obs.*

1599 SHAKS. *Hen. V*, II. ii. 191 Let us deliuer our Puissance into the hand of God Putting it straight in expedition. **1667** MARVELL *Corr.* Wks. 1872-5 II. 223 A Bill against Pluralityes is committed. Several other things in expedition.

2. A sending or setting forth with martial intentions; a warlike enterprise.

1430 LYDG. *Chron. Troy* I. viii. *heading*, In this expedicion towardes Colchos. **1598** HAKLUYT *Voy.* I. 59 Notwithstanding, he conquered not in that expedition. **1662** STILLINGFL. *Orig. Sacr.* I. iv. §11 Strabo confesseth as much [ignorance] of the Western parts of Europe till the Roman expeditions thither. **1724** DE FOE *Mem. Cavalier* (1840) 269 This was the best and most successful expedition I was in during this war. **1839** THIRLWALL *Greece* VII. lviii. 311 Ptolemy, having suppressed an insurrection in Cyrene, made an expedition in person to Cyprus.

b. A journey, voyage, or excursion made for some definite purpose.

1591 SHAKS. *Two Gent.* I. iii. 77 You shall be imployd, To hasten on his Expedition. **1667** MILTON *P.L.* VII. 193 Mean while the Son On his great Expedition now appeer'd. *a* **1716** SOUTH *Serm.* iii. (1737) I. 81 A hard expedition..to go amongst wolves. **1840** DICKENS *Barn. Rudge* viii, It was not a very choice spot for midnight expeditions. **1868** FREEMAN *Norm. Conq.* II. App. 536 This was not the last begging expedition of Gervinus to our shore.

3. *concr.* A body of persons, also a fleet, etc., sent out for a warlike or other definite purpose.

1693 LUTTRELL *Brief Rel.* III. 192 A draught is made out of the several regiments..to goe on board the expedition. **1837** W. IRVING *Capt. Bonneville* I. 11 Mr...Seton..had accompanied one of the expeditions sent out by Mr. Astor. **1863** LYELL *Antiq. Man* 37 M. Girard, of the French expedition to Egypt. **1880** W. CORY *Mod. Eng. Hist.* I. 194 *note*, An expedition may consist of a single ship.

†**4.** The action of issuing or sending out official documents. Hence *concr.* the documents sent out. *Obs.*

1513 BRADSHAW *St. Werburge* I. 2423 Whan they had optayned perfyte expedycyon Of all theyr bulles. **1533-4** *Act 25 Hen. VIII*, c. 20 §3 No person..shall pay any sommes of money..for expedicion of any..bulles, breues, or palles. **1685** F. SPENCE *House Medici* 431 Leo did often.. examine the expeditions..presented him to sign. **1706** tr. *Dupin's Eccl. Hist. 16th C.* II. v. 81 The Seals..of the Expeditions which he [the Nuncio] had made during his Legation.

b. *gen.* after Fr. *expédition*. The sending forth, dispatch (of articles of any kind).

1796 M. PERREGAUX in *Ld. Auckland's Corr.* (1862) III. 350 The expedition of the 'Moniteurs' to the 8th of May.

5. The quality of being 'expedite'; quick movement; promptness, haste, speed. Also in phr. ***with expedition; to †make, use, expedition***.

1529 WOLSEY in *Four C. Eng. Lett.* 10 That expedicion be usyd in my persuts. **1590** MARLOWE *2nd Pt. Tamburl.* IV. iii, To Babylon, Whither we next make expedition. **1591** SHAKS. *Two Gent.* I. iii. 37 Even with the speediest expedition I will despatch him to the Emperors Court. **1671** MILTON *Samson* 1283 With winged expedition, Swift as the lightning glance. **1701** PENN in *Pa. Hist. Soc. Mem.* IX. 54 With all possible vigilance and expedition. **1747** *Col. Rec. Pennsylv.* V. 77 He was told to use all the Expedition Possible. **1815** T. JEFFERSON *Writ.* (1830) IV. 265 How can expedition be expected from a body which we have saddled with an hundred lawyers.

b. Readiness.

1579 FENTON *Guicciard.* (1618) 4 In Alexander..was a subtiltie, sharpnesse and expedition of wit most singular.

6. *Rhet.* (See quots.)

[**1586** A. DAY *Eng. Secretary* II. (1625) 98 Expeditio.. when many reasons of averment being numbred together, we make a confutation of them, each one in particular. **1589** PUTTENHAM *Eng. Poesie* III. xix. (Arb.) 241 Expeditio, or the speedie dispatcher.] **1657** J. SMITH *Myst. Rhet.* 250 Expedition is a figure when many parts or reasons of an argument being enumerated and touched, all are destroyed, save that only upon which the speaker intends to conclude, stand to, and rest upon.

7. *Comb.* **expedition-fee, -money**, a fee or money paid for hastening the performance of any work; ***expedition-squadron***.

1672 WYCHERLEY *Love in Wood* IV. ii, If you will not let me have an end on't, I shall lose my expedition-fee. **1694** LUTTRELL *Brief Rel.* (1857) III. 366 Sir Clowdesly Shovell, with the expedition squadron, sailed out of the Downs. **1725** BERKELEY *Let.* 12 June Wks. IV. 112 The Charter..hath cost me 130 pounds..besides expedition-money to men in office. **1794** BURKE *Sp. agst. W. Hastings* Wks. XV. 41, I next inquired what expedition-money might have been given. **1866** *Daily Tel.* 20 Jan. 4/1 He claimed a sum of about £26,000 for expedition money.

†**expe'ditional**, *a. Obs. rare*⁻¹. [f. prec. + -AL[1].] Of or pertaining to an expedition.

c **1601** W. WATSON *Decacordon* (1602) 234 In that exploit expeditionall against England intended.

expe'ditionary, *a.* (*sb.*) [f. as prec. + -ARY.]

A. *adj.* Of or pertaining to an expedition; sent on an expedition.

1817 *Blackw. Mag.* I. 201 The expeditionary troops destined to act against South America were reviewed. **1859** THACKERAY *Virgin.* xii. 96 The northward track which the expeditionary army had hewed out for itself. **1871** PROCTOR *Light Sc.* 104 Inviting them, in the name of the American expeditionary parties, to accept this much needed assistance.

†**B.** *sb.* An officer who took care of dispatches at the Pope's court. *Obs.*

1706 in PHILLIPS (ed. Kersey). **1721-1800** in BAILEY.

†**expe'ditioner**. *Obs. rare*⁻¹. [f. as prec. + -ER[1].] One engaged in an expedition.

1758 BP. WARBURTON *Lett.* (1809) 266 The Cherbourg expeditioners being twice drove in hither by contrary winds.

expe'ditionist. [f. as prec. + -IST.] One who goes on an expedition; an excursionist.

1841 *Blackw. Mag.* L. 449 Her travellers and expeditionists are exploring the frozen regions of either pole. **1861** *Temple Bar* III. 393 Puffing expeditionists.. hurry helter-skelter through so many given cities. **1871** PROCTOR *Light Sc.* 103 The zeal of the expeditionists averted the risk.

expeditious (ɛkspɪ'dɪʃəs), *a.* [f. EXPEDITION: see -TIOUS.] Characterized by expedition.

1. Of action, a voyage, etc.: Speedily performed. Of a method: Leading to speedy performance. Of an answer: Quickly given, ready.

1610 SHAKS. *Temp.* V. i. 315, I..promise you..auspicious gales And saile, so expeditious, that shall catch Your Royall fleete farre off. **1664** EVELYN *Kal. Hort.* (1729) 201 Turning up of the Earth..is to be preferr'd to Hand weeding, and more expeditious. **1692** WAGSTAFFE *Vind. Carol.* xiv. 96 A most expeditious Answer. **1709** SHARP *Serm.* VII. iv. 63 The..short expeditious way of appealing to the Bishop of Rome. **1748** *Anson's Voy.* II. xiii. 278 Capable of making an expeditious passage. *a* **1832** BENTHAM *Wks.* (1843) I. 182 Obviating a dissatisfaction, which expeditious measures would excite. **1866** J. G. MURPHY *Comm. Ex.* xii. 10 Equipped for expeditious travelling.

2. Of an implement or weapon: Fitted for quick movements; handy. *rare*.

1747 SMOLLETT *Regicide* II. ii, With the broad targe and expeditious sword.

3. Of persons: Acting or moving with expedition; speedy.

1599 MASSINGER, etc. *Old Law* I, Let us be all most expeditious. **1726** CHETWOOD *Adv. Capt. R. Boyle* 3 He.. desir'd I would be expeditious in going. **1771** GOLDSM. *Hist. Eng.* III. 242 An expeditious set of workmen. **1858** FROUDE *Hist. Eng.* III. xvii. 439 The German commission was as expeditious as the Spanish had been dilatory. **1881** JOWETT *Thucyd.* I. 162 An expeditious traveller..will accomplish the journey in eleven days.

expe'ditiously, *adv.* [f. prec. + -LY[2].] In an expeditious manner; speedily, with expedition.

1603 DRAYTON *Bar. Wars* I. li, He expeditiously prouided That part of land into his power to get. **1663** BOYLE *Wks.* (1772) II. 11, I once made a menstruum to draw it [the tincture of the glass of antimony] more expeditiously. **1749** FIELDING *Tom Jones* VIII. xiii, The surgeon having very expeditiously..finished his business. **1863** P. BARRY *Dockyard Econ.* 51 [Russia's] ships will be built cheaper and more expeditiously.

expe'ditiousness. [f. as prec. + -NESS.] The quality of being expeditious; celerity; handiness.

1708 *Lond. Gaz.* No. 4426/12 Whose audacious Attempts ..are..by the Expeditiousness of your Fleet, totally.. defeated. **1715** M. DAVIES *Athen. Brit.* I. 86 He was thought to have surpass'd..Ovid for Expeditiousness in Versifying. **1861** SMILES *Engineers* II. 222 The simplicity, economy, and expeditiousness of the plan.

†**ex'peditive**, *a. Obs.* [f. EXPEDITE + -IVE.] Performing with expedition, expeditious.

1617 BACON in Spedding *Life & Lett.* (1872) VI. 191, I mean not to purchase the praise of expeditive in that kind. **1847** in CRAIG; and in mod. Dicts.

†**ex'peditory**, *a. Obs. rare*⁻⁰. [f. L. *expedīt-* ppl. stem of *expedīre* (see EXPEDITE) + -ORY.] Making haste; expeditious.

a **1790** FRANKLIN (cited in Worcester 1846).

expel (ɛk'spɛl), *v.* Forms: 4-5 expelle, 6-7 expell, 6- expel. [ad. L. *expell-ĕre*, f. *ex-* out + *pellĕre* to drive, thrust: cf. COMPEL. OF. had *espellir*, and in 15th c. *expeller*.]

1. *trans.* To drive or thrust out; to eject by force. Const. *from* (rarely *out of*) also with double obj. (by omission of *from*).

a. With obj. a person, etc.: To eject, dislodge by force from a position; to banish from, compel to quit, a place or country.

c **1489** CAXTON *Sonnes of Aymon* xx. 446 Reynawde and his brethern were thus expelled out of it [mountalban]. **1532** MORE *Confut. Tindale* Wks. 819/2 God..expelled those heretikes and scismatikes out of heauen. **1577** tr. *Bullinger's Decades* (1592) 838 The Apostles receiued power from the Lord..that they should expell and cast them [the devils] out. **1628** HOBBES *Thucyd.* (1822) 8 The Bœotians..expelld Arne by the Thessalians seated themselues in that Country [Bœotia]. *c* **1710** C. FIENNES *Diary* (1888) 266 Such a State takes Care..to Expel him their Dominions by proclamation. **1749** WEST tr. *Pindar's Olympic Odes* xii. 36 Sedition's Civil Broils Expell'd thee from thy native Crete. **1754** HUME *Hist. Eng.* I. xi. 229 He sent..two knights..to expel them the convent. **1863** FR. A. KEMBLE *Resid. Georgia* 31 Bidding the elder boys..expel the poultry.

b. With a material thing as obj.: To drive out from a receptacle, etc. by mechanical force; to discharge, send off (*e.g.* a bullet from a gun, †an arrow from a bow); to drive off or dislodge (a substance) from a chemical compound, mixture, solution, etc. Also, † ***to expel forth***.

1669 STURMY *Mariner's Mag.* v. xii. 80 The Shot is.. expelled with no other thing, than by the Air's exaltation. **1695** WOODWARD *Nat. Hist. Earth* III. (1723) 151 It [water] is usualy expelled forth in vast Quantities. *a* **1700** DRYDEN (J.), The virgin huntress was not slow T'expel the shaft from her contracted bow. *c* **1790** IMISON *Sch. Art* I. 74 Expelling the water into the bason. **1807** T. THOMSON *Chem.* (ed. 3) II. 394 Alcohol.. absorbs about its own weight of nitrous gas, which cannot afterwards be expelled by heat. **1838** —— *Chem. Org. Bodies* 168 Not capable of being expelled by a stronger base. **1860** MAURY *Phys. Geog. Sea* xi. §512 If still more heat be applied.. the air will be entirely expelled. **1878** HUXLEY *Physiogr.* 77 The matter.. thus expelled from the powder by heat.

c. Of the body or its organs: To cast out, eject (the contents, any foreign substance, excrements, etc.); = EXCLUDE *v.* 7. Also said of the action of drugs, etc.

c **1386** CHAUCER *Knt.'s T.* 1893 The vertu expulsif, or animal.. Ne may the venym voyden ne expelle. **1542** BORDE *Dyetary* iv. (1870) 237 To expell.. all corrupt and contagyous ayre. **1547** —— *Brev. Health* §356 Vnto the tyme the matter be expelled.. out of the throte. **1671** SALMON *Syn. Med.* III. xxii. 395 Chervil expells wind. **1767** GOOCH *Treat. Wounds* (ed. 2) II. 216 Some months after, a piece of cloth was expelled, till which time the wound kept open. **1809** *Med. Jrnl.* XXI. 338 The child had been very recently expelled from the womb. **1836** TODD *Cycl. Anat.* I. 519/2 There is an organ for.. expelling an inky fluid.

absol. **1626** BACON *Sylva* §36 Other parts of the Body.. are moued to expell by Consent.

d. With immaterial object. In *Math.* formerly = ELIMINATE.

c **1500** *Lancelot* 1271 Hir cusynace hath don al at she mycht.. to expel that thing out of hir thocht. **1540** COVERDALE *Fruitf. Less.* i. Wks. I. 259 To expel from us all pride and presumptuousness. **1610** SHAKS. *Temp.* v. i. 76 You, brother mine, that.. Expelld remorse, and nature. **1611** DONNE *Ignat. Conclave* (1635) 7 He gloried of having expelled an old Religion. **1697** DAMPIER *Voy.* I. ii. 14 These hardships quite expell'd the thoughts of an Enemy. **1828** HUTTON *Course Math.* II. 49 *note*, The quantity *c*.. must be expelled from this formula. **1862** H. SPENCER *First Princ.* II. iii. §46 (1875) 160 Our ability to expel the idea from consciousness.

2. To turn out, eject (a person) from a society, community, etc. Const. as in 1.

1534 ANNE BOLEYN in Ellis *Orig. Lett.* I. 116 II. 46 Richard Herman.. was.. put and expelled from his fredome and felowshipe in the Englishe house there. **1648** *Hunting of Fox* 11 Yet were they.. expell'd the University. *a* **1680** BUTLER *Rem.* (1759) I. 215 His Scholar striving to expel all Poets his poetic Commonweal. **1769** *Junius Lett.* xvi. 69 The house of Commons have a right to expel one of their own members. **1820** SOUTHEY *Life Wesley* II. 497 Whoever acted contrary.. should be expelled the Society. **1884** PAE *Eustace* 57 You are expelled from the house which you have indelibly disgraced.

†**3.** To reject from attention or consideration; to refuse. *Obs.*

1575 in W. H. Turner *Select. Rec. Oxford* 365 The common welth are.. utterly expeld and let goe for lacke of loking to. **1591** SPENSER *M. Hubberd* 95 Would you not poor fellowship expel, Myself would offer you t'accompany. **1640–1** *Kirkcudbr. War-Comm. Min. Bk.* (1855) 5 The said day the Committie expelles the resounes preponit be Borge and Johne Gordoun. **1742** POPE *Dunc.* IV. 196 Each fierce Logician, still expelling Locke.

†**4.** 'To keep off, exclude, keep out' (J.). *Obs.*

1602 SHAKS. *Ham.* v. i. 239 Oh, that that earth [Cæsar's dead body], which kept the world in awe, Should patch a Wall, t'expell the winters flaw.

Hence **ex'pelled** *ppl. a.*, **ex'pelling** *vbl. sb.* and *ppl. a.*

1532 MORE *Confut. Tindale* Wks. 1557 819/2 Receiuing of synne is expelling of grace. **1545** RAYNOLD *Byrth Mankynde* (1564) 69 b, The expellyng of the second byrth. **1552** HULOET, Expelled, *expulsus*. **1632** tr. *Bruel's Praxis M.* 376 These stirre vp the expelling faculty. **1744** BERKELEY *Siris* §84 This expelling diuretic virtue consisted rather in the salts than the resin. **1774** GOLDSM. *Grecian Hist.* I. 105 Hippias, the expelled tyrant of Athens. **1846** GREENER *Sc. Gunnery* 293 How get you an equal pressure of the expelling force?

expellable (ɛk'spɛləb(ə)l), *a.* [f. prec. + -ABLE.] Capable of being, or liable to be, expelled.

1665 WITHER *Lord's Prayer* 177 All other Kings, Kingdoms and States, are.. expellable at his pleasure. **1802** KIRWAN in *Phil. Trans.* LXXX. 225 The nitrous acid.. expellable even by the vegetable acids. **1839** BAILEY *Festus* xix. 62/2 And that [soul] Infernal, but expellable by prayer.

expellee (ɛkspɛ'liː). [f. EXPEL + -EE.] One who has been expelled, esp. from his own country.

1888 *Sat. Rev.* 29 Dec. 758/1 The expellee would only be sure of a triumphant re-election. **1947** *Current History* Apr. 323/1 The Trades Union Congress finally agreed.. that 500,000 D.P.'s and expellees in Germany might be admitted. **1961** R. KEE *Refugee World* iii. 21 For the Germans, left to deal with the expellees almost entirely by themselves.. there was no sense in complaining. **1967** *Guardian* 15 Feb. 6/2 The neo-Nazi NPD party has probably rendered a service in drawing off the hard-core expellees.

expellent (ɛk'spɛlənt), *a.* and *sb.* Also **-ant**. [ad. L. *expellent-em*, pr. pple. of *expellĕre* to EXPEL.]

A. *adj.* That expels or tends to expel.

1858 GREENER *Gunnery* 33 The construction of the gun being perfect.. can the expellant force be brought to an equal state of perfection. **1885** J. STRONG *Own Country* iv. 32 The expellent influences of Europe.. send new waves of immigration to our shores.

B. *sb.* An expellent medicine.

1823 CRABB *Technol. Dict.*, *Expellents*, medicines supposed to expel morbid humours from the body.

expeller (ɛk'spɛlə(r)). Also 8 expellor. [f. EXPEL *v.* + -ER[1].]

1. One who, or that which, expels. Const. *of.*

1577 HOLINSHED *Chron.* (1807) I. v. xvii. 585 The expeller of manie tyrants. **1647** FANSHAW tr. *Guarini's Pastor Fido* II. *Chorus*, Unspotted faith, expeller of all vice. **1725** BRADLEY *Fam. Dict.* II. s.v. *Wind Cholick*, The most effectual expeller of Wind. **1741** WARBURTON *Div. Legat.* II. 288 Their mistake was only about the Expellor. **1794** T. TAYLOR *Pausanias' Descr. Greece* II. 39 Jupiter Apomyius, or the expeller of flies. **1846** ELLIS *Elgin Marb.* I. 109 The Expeller of the Bacchidæ from Corinth.

†**2.** = EXPELLENT B. *sb. Obs.*

1683 SALMON *Doron Med.* II. 443 A powerful expeller.

expend (ɛk'spɛnd), *v.* Forms: 5–6 expende, exspende, 6– expend. *Pa. pple.* 5 expent, 6 expend. [ad. L. *expend-ĕre*, f. *ex-* out + *pend-ĕre* to weigh, pay. Cf. also DISPEND, SPEND.]

I. To pay out, spend. It differs from *spend* in being less colloquial, and (in mod. use) in implying some determinate direction or object of outlay.

1. *trans.* To pay away, lay out, spend (money).

†**a.** To spend, make away with, consume in outlay. *Obs.*

1477 EARL RIVERS (Caxton) *Dictes* 106 By expending more than his lyuelode cometh to. **1483** CAXTON *Cato* A vij, Zeno expended bothe hys goodes and the goodes of his fader and played hit at the dyse. **1608** SHAKS. *Per.* III. ii. 29 Riches careless heirs May.. expend. *a* **1627** HAYWARD *Edw. VI* (1630) 111 The King of England wasted the French Kings country, and thereby caused him to expend such summes of mony as exceeded the debt.

b. To lay out (money) for determinate objects. Const. *in, upon.*

1484 *Churchw. Acc. Wigtoft Lincolnsh.* (Nichols 1797) 79 For hiryng of 2 wrightes to mend ye belles.. expent 4*d.* **1552** HULOET, *Expend* or laye out money. **1698–9** LUDLOW *Mem.* I. 71 Part of this sum I expended upon the garison. **1763** LD. BARRINGTON in Ellis *Orig. Lett.* II. 505 IV. 474 If £50,000 had been given for that Speech, it would have been well expended. **1839** THIRLWALL *Greece* VII. 323 They began to doubt whether they were not about to expend their resources less for their own defence, than, etc. **1867** MRS. H. WOOD *Life's Secret* II. 152 Too fond of beer, to expend in much else the trifle allowed them.

absol. **1605** BP. HALL *Medit. & Vows* II. §54 The eare and the eye are the minds receivers; but the tongue is onely busied in expending. **1720** in Picton *L'pool Munic. Rec.* (1886) II. 64 To expend and lay out very extravagantly in repairing the highways, &c. **1848** MACAULAY *Hist. Eng.* I. 352 They go elsewhere to enjoy and to expend.

2. *transf.* and *fig.* To lay out, spend (blood, care, labour, time, etc.); to employ for a given purpose.

c **1440** *Gesta Rom.* xv. 53 (Harl. MS.) The first doughter.. is þe worlde, whom a man loveth so well, that he expendith alle his lif aboute hit. **1550** BALE *Image Both Ch.* I. x. §5 More God desireth not of the christian minister, than to expend his whole study, labour, and time for the lightening of others. **1602** SHAKS. *Ham.* II. ii. 23 To expend your time with vs a-while. **1728** YOUNG *Love Fame* ii. (1757) 97 These all their care expend on outward show For wealth and fame. **1841–4** EMERSON *Ess. Prudence* Wks. (Bohn) I. 98 As much wisdom may be expended on a private economy as on an empire. **1854** J. S. C. ABBOTT *Napoleon* (1855) I. vii. 142 The blood that must be expended in the attempt. **1864** SKEAT *Uhland's Poems* 42 Thyself hast thou expended As every poet should. **1874** L. MORRIS *To Unknown Poet* ix, A humble healer thro' a life obscure, Thou didst expend thy homely days.

3. To use up (material or force) in any operation; also *refl.* Formerly, †to consume (provisions); cf. EXPENSE I c.

1745 P. THOMAS *Jrnl. Anson's Voy.* 9 To procure what fresh Provisions we could expend during our Stay. **1825** J. NICHOLSON *Operat. Mechanic* 80 The quantity of water expended in a minute was 96⅔ pounds. **1859** JEPHSON *Brittany* xii. 193 The English archers.. having expended their arrows, drew their swords. **1860** TYNDALL *Glac.* II. xix. 329 Gravity in this case has expended a certain amount of force. **1869** PHILLIPS *Vesuv.* iii. 51 After the currents had expended themselves. **1871** MORLEY *Voltaire* (1886) 15 All the social feeling and intellectual effort.. seemed to have expended themselves.

b. *Naut.* To lose (spars, masts, etc.) either in action or by storms, etc. Also, to use up (a quantity of rope, etc.) in winding it round a spar or a rope.

1801 NELSON 23 May in Nicolas *Disp.* (1845) IV. 384 An account.. of the spars expended in consequence of the Action of April 2nd. **1830** MARRYAT *King's Own* xli, Have you expended any boat's masts? *c* **1860** H. STUART *Seaman's Catech.* 34 Expend the spunyarn round both parts of the lanyard. **1882** NARES *Seamanship* (ed. 6) 137 The heel rope is.. expended round the jackstay and boom.

†**II.** **4.** To weigh mentally; to consider, determine accurately. Often, *to expend with oneself* [after L. *expendere secum*]. *Obs.*

1531 ELYOT *Gov.* III. ix, Where fortitude expendeth euery thinge and acte diligently. **1533** TINDALE *Lord's Supper* Wks. (Parker Soc.) III. 266 Exhort every man deeply to consider and expend with himself, the signification of this sacrament. **1563** *Homilies* II. *Rogat. Week* III. (1859) 491 To expend the gracious good will of God to usward. **1625** HART *Anat. Ur.* I. ii. 21 It behooueth the Physitian to.. expend with himselfe.. the strength of euery accident apart. **1677** HALE *Prim. Orig. Man.* To Rdr., Moral Evidences.. are herein particularly expended and examined.

Hence **ex'pended** *ppl. a.*

1742 YOUNG *Nt. Th.* IV. 196 What can awake thee unawak'd by this, 'Expended Deity on human weal'?

expendable (ɛk'spɛndəb(ə)l), *a.* (and *sb.*) Also expendible. [f. prec. + -ABLE.] That may be expended; considered as not worth preserving or salvaging; normally consumed in use; *spec.* of military personnel: that may be allowed to be sacrificed to achieve a military objective. Hence as *sb.*, an expendable person or object.

1805 W. TAYLOR in *Ann. Rev.* III. 240 That property should be dividable, transferrable, and expendable. **1942** W. L. WHITE *They were Expendable* 7 In a war anything can be expendable—money or gasoline or equipment or most usually men. **1942** *Reader's Digest* Oct. 40/1 They would be considered in part as expendable ammunition much as the Navy considers its PT boats. **1942** *Topeka Jrnl.* 9 Nov. 4/4 When an army is retreating, a small force is left behind to cover the retreat and be sacrificed to the enemy. They are 'expendables'. **1956** A. TOYNBEE *Historian's Approach to Religion* xix. 266 The true purpose of an institution is simply to serve as a means for promoting the welfare of human beings. In truth it is not sacrosanct but is 'expendible'. **1966** D. HOLBROOK *Flesh Wounds* 81 We're expendable, see, so you want to watch out. **1966** *Aviation Week & Space Technol.* 5 Dec. 22/2 With five years of supplies and all the expendables, including a crew.

expender (ɛk'spɛndə(r)). [f. as prec. + -ER[1].] One who, or that which, expends. Const. *of.*

1804 W. TAYLOR in *Ann. Rev.* II. 352 The expenders of rents are the most unproductive.. class of citizens. **1863** H. SPENCER *Princ. Biol.* I. II. i. §49 Organisms which are large expenders of force. **1882** G. ALLEN *C. Clout's Garden* vii. (1883) 40 Flowers are mere expenders of food.

expending (ɛk'spɛndɪŋ), *vbl. sb.* [f. as prec. + -ING[1].] The action of the vb. EXPEND: now only gerundial (const. *of*). Formerly occas.: Expenditure; consideration; consumption.

1545 JOYE *Exp. Dan.* xi. Z ij b, This moch haue I learned by the expending and waying of the text. **1561** T. NORTON *Calvin's Inst.* IV. xx. (1634) 745 Money, which they waste upon mad prodigall expendings. **1605** BP. HALL *Medit. & Vows* II. §27 If my money were another mans, I could but keepe it; onely the expending showes it my own. **1610** —— *Apol. Brownists* §11 The holy expending of Sabbath daies appointed. **1745** P. THOMAS *Jrnl. Anson's Voy.* 11 We likewise had fresh Beef for present expending plenty enough.

expenditor (ɛk'spɛndɪtər). *Law.* Also 7 -our. [a. med.L. *expenditor*, agent-n. incorrectly (on the analogy of *venditor*, etc.) f. *expendĕre*: see EXPEND.] One who has charge of expenditure; *spec.* an officer formerly appointed by the Commissioners of Sewers to expend or disburse the money collected by tax for the repair of sewers; also an officer of the British Museum (see quot. 1847).

1499 in *Hist. Co. Lincoln* I. 69 Expenditors.. shall have by the day 1*s.* 8*d.* *Ibid.*, The said expenditors shall have a clerk of sewers for the work. **1531–2** *Act 23 Hen. VIII*, c. 5. §3 Expenditours and other ministers and officers for.. the making of the premisses. **1587** FLEMING *Contn. Holinshed* III. 1547/1 The charge of these two wals.. as appeareth in the expenditors books. **1622** CALLIS *Stat. Sewers* (1647) 134 A Collector, or Expenditor, or other Officer of Sewers. **1726** *Laws of Sewers* 87 The Expenditor is the Person appointed by the Commissioners, to.. expend the Money collected by the Tax. **1847** *Evidence Royal Comm. Brit. Mus.* 1 You [Sir H. Ellis] were also the expenditor?—That was an office.. always given to the principal librarian. *Ibid.* 9 What is the nature of his duties as expenditor?—He receives the moneys. **1899** *Westm. Gaz.* 25 Sept. 4/2 Expenditor of the level of Romney Marsh. **1901** *N. & Q.* 9th Ser. III. 303/1 General Expenditor to East Kent Sewers.

transf. **1646** J. BENBRIGGE *Vsura Acc.* 19 We are but his [God's] Expenditours.

†**ex'penditrix.** *Obs. rare*[−1]. [f. EXPENDITOR, after Lat. analogy: see -TRIX.] A woman who has charge of expenditure.

a **1734** NORTH *Exam.* II. iv. §51 (1740) 257 Mrs. Celier was the Go-between and Expenditrix in Affairs, which lay much in relieving of Catholics.

expenditure (ɛk'spɛndɪtjʊə(r)). [f. med.L. *expendit-us*, pa. pple. (irregularly formed after *venditus*) of *expendĕre* (see EXPEND) + -URE.]

1. The action or practice of laying out, paying away, or spending (money). Const. *of.* ***at his own expenditure*** (nonce-use): at his own expense.

1769 BURKE *On late State Nation* 15 Our expenditure purchased commerce and conquest. **1776** ADAM SMITH *W.N.* IV. ix, The collection and expenditure of the public revenue. **1873** BROWNING *Red Cott. Nt.-cap* 317 His shop.. turned out the masterpiece.. at his own expenditure. **1874** GREEN *Short Hist.* vii. 364 Her [Elizabeth's] expenditure was.. ever miserly.

b. *transf.* The expending or laying out (of energy, labour, time): often with notion of waste.

1823 LAMB *Elia* Ser. I. v. (1865) 45 To grudge at the expenditure of moments. **1866** GEO. ELIOT *F. Holt* (1868) 30 He disliked all quarrelling as an unpleasant expenditure of energy. **1878** BROWNING *Poets Croisic* 54 After a vast expenditure of pains. **1890** *Spectator* 16 Aug., The Nationalist laity disobey with much expenditure of speech.

c. The action or process of using up or consuming; consumption.

1812 WELLINGTON in Gurw. *Disp.* IX. 141 We have made such an expenditure of engineers, that I can hardly wish for any body. **1855** BAIN *Senses & Int.* II. i. §11 A peculiar expenditure of the substance of the muscular mass. **1863** H.

SPENCER *Princ. Biol.* I. II. v. §69 A mature animal, or one which has reached a balance between nutrition and expenditure. **1871** TYNDALL *Fragm. Sc.* (ed. 6) I. xvi. 427 Its [the sun's] combustion would only cover 4600 years of expenditure. **1879** *Cassell's Techn. Educ.* II. 194/2 The economical expenditure of ammunition.

2. The amount expended from time to time.

1791 R. RAYMENT (*title*), The Income and Expenditure of Great Britain of the last 7 years. *a* **1800** COWPER *Sparrows self-domesticated*, A single doit would overpay The expenditure of every day. **1844** H. H. WILSON *Brit. India* III. 331 A loss of life and waste of expenditure. **1863** P. BARRY *Dockyard Econ.* 99 During the year 1860–61 the expenditure in these [mast-houses] amounted to [etc.].

expense (ɛk'spɛns). Forms: 4–9 **expence**, 5 **expens, exspense**, 6 **exspence**, 4– **expense**. See also SPENCE. [a. AF. *expense* (OF. *espense*), ad. late L. *expēnsa*, orig. pa. pple. fem. of *expendĕre*: see EXPEND. Cf. Sp. *expensas* pl., also It. *spesa*, which is the only popular representative of the word in Romanic, the Fr. and Sp. forms being of learned origin.

Ger. *speise* 'viand' is an early adoption of the L. word.]

†**1.** The action of expending; the state of being expended. *Obs.* Cf. EXPENDITURE 1.

†**a.** Disbursement, spending, laying out (of money); an instance of this. Also *occas.* wasteful expenditure, extravagance. ***person of expense***: one who spends largely; so also, ***person of great, little expense***. *Obs.*

1393 GOWER *Conf.* III. 153 That he mesure in his expence So kepe, that of indigence He may be sauf. *c* **1430** *Compl. Christ* 169 in *Pol. Rel. & L. Poems* (1866) 179 My waast expensis y wole with-drawe. **1597** BACON *Ess., Expense* (Arb.) 50 Extraordinarie Expence must bee limited by the worth of the occasion. **1633** FORD *'Tis Pity* v, This suddaine solemne Feast Was not ordayn'd to riott in expence. **1644** QUARLES *Barnabas & B.* (1851) 18 God is not honored in the expense of that money which is bedewed with the tears of the oppressed. *a* **1715** BURNET *Own Time* (1766) I. 130 A man of great expence. **1750** JOHNSON *Rambler* No. 26 ⁋3 This exuberance of money displayed itself in wantonness of expence. **1766** FORDYCE *Serm. Yng. Wom.* (1767) I. iv. 141 All of them..dread a woman of expence. **1794** GODWIN *Cal. Williams* 267 An obscure house of entertainment for persons of small expence.

†**b.** The expending or using up (of material or immaterial resources); the state of being expended or used up; expenditure (of substance, strength, labour, time, etc.); loss (of blood, etc., of men in battle, etc.). *Obs.*

1588 SHAKS. *L.L.L.* v. II. 523, I implore so much expence of thy royall sweet breath, as will vtter a brace of words. **1594** HOOKER *Eccl. Pol.* I. xi. (1611) 36 With bootlesse expense of trauell. **1608** *Yorksh. Trag.* I. x. 218 My body.. is yet faint With much expense of blood. **1626** BACON *Sylva* §352 Fire and Flame are in continual expence. **1647** SPRIGGE *Anglia Rediv.* I. ii. (1854) 14 After the expense of about fourteen men upon it, the design was given over. **1669** WORLIDGE *Syst. Agric.* (1681) 293 They..move as other Meteors do, from a certain expence of their own substance the one way, which inforceth their motion another. **1749** *Power Pros. Numbers* 70 The former require too great Expense of Breath to pronounce them. **1752** FRANKLIN *Wks.* 1840 V. 286 The sun is not wasted by expense of light. **1797** NELSON 23 June in Nicolas *Disp.* (1846) XII. p. cxliv, No service that could have made an expense [of stores].

†**c.** Consumption (of produce, provisions). *Obs.*

1587 HARRISON *England* II. vi. (1877) I. 156 The gentlemen commonlie make sufficient malt for their owne expenses onelie. **1594** in Arb. *Garner* I. 299 Proclamations for the expense and observation of Fish Days. **1668** *Markham's Way to Wealth* IX. III. i. 96 To gather [Pears] for expence, for transportation, or to sell.

†**d.** Loss (of a possession). *Obs.*

1600 SHAKS. *Sonn.* xxx. 8 Then can I..mone th' expence of many a vanished sight. **1607** TOURNEUR *Rev. Trag.* I. iii, Enter upon..Her honour, which she calls her chastity, And bring it into expence.

†**2.** Money expended (cf. EXPENDITURE 2); a sum expended. *Obs.*

(The apparent instances in recent use belong to 3 or 3 c.)

1382 WYCLIF *Ex.* xxi. 19 That he restore..the expensis into leches. *c* **1460** FORTESCUE *Abs. & Lim. Mon.* (1714) 32 If a Kyng be powre, he schal by necessite make his Expences ..by Creaunce of borrowyng. **1673** TEMPLE *Ess. Irel.* Wks. 1731 I. 111 The Country loses the Expence of many of the richest Persons. *a* **1687** PETTY *Pol. Arith.* vii. (1691) 103 Where a People thrive, there the income is greater than the expence. **1737** WHISTON *Josephus' Antiq.* XI. iv. §9 You..do not supply them with the expences..for their sacrifices. **1765** A. DICKSON *Treat. Agric.* III. (ed. 2) 402 The difference betwixt these, is the expense which the farmer may lay out.

transf. **1692** RAY *Dissol. World* II. ii. (1732) 78 The Receipts from the Rivers fall short of the Expence in Vapour. **1693** *Phil. Trans.* XVII. 616 As to the Expence of the Sea-Water by Vapour, he concludes the Receipts of the Mediterranean to fall short of its expence.

3. a. Burden of expenditure; the pecuniary charge, cost, or sacrifice involved in any course of action, mode of living, etc., or requisite for the attainment of any object. Also *transf.* [Originally a contextual use of 1.]

1632 J. HAYWARD tr. *Biondi's Eromena* 27 Many companies of souldiers to be levied..without a penny of expence, of either his, or his complices. **1711** ADDISON *Spect.* No. 102 ⁋11, I have several little plain Fans made for this Use, to avoid expence. **1799** T. JEFFERSON *Writ.* (1859) IV. 277 The direct tax and stamp tax will add two millions clear of expence. **1808** A. PARSONS *Trav.* iii. 65 Those who can afford the expence, usually go to some part of the sea coast. **1851** C. APPERLEY *Chase, Turf, etc.* 62 All got up 'regardless of expense'. **1856** EMERSON *Eng. Traits, Char.* Wks. (Bohn) II. 62 The scale of expense on which people live. **1872** RAYMOND *Statist. Mines & Mining* 135 A long list of legal expenses.

fig. **1839** DE QUINCEY *Recollect. Lakes* Wks. (1862) II. 214 Who took upon herself the whole expenses of the flying colloquies exchanged with stragglers on the road.

b. Phrases. †*to lie at expense*: (of a prisoner) to be a cause of outlay. ***at an expense of***: at a cost or loss amounting to. ***at the expense of***: at the cost of (a certain sum), by the sacrifice of (something); so ***at (a) great, little***, etc. ***expense***. ***to be at expense***: to incur expenditure; so, ***to put (a person) to expense***. ***to be at the expense, expenses (of)***: to defray the costs (of); also const. *to* with *inf.*

a **1610** HEALEY *Theophrastus* (1636) 41 Now what expence soever he is at, he proclaimeth. **1658–9** *Burton's Diary* (1828) IV. 6 He lies at expense. I move therefore, to call him in. **1710** STEELE *Tatler* No. 262 ⁋3 The new Pair of Gloves and Coach-hire that he was at the Expence of in her Service. *c* **1710** C. FIENNES *Diary* (1888) 153 Some part of that mer one Mr. Fleetewood has been at the Expence to draine. **1712** ADDISON *Spect.* No. 418 ⁋7 He is at no more Expence in a long Vista, than a short one. **1713** *Guardian* No. 9 ⁋4 Where, at the expence of 4 or 5000*l*...he built a new one. **1765** H. WALPOLE *Otranto* iii. (1798) 62 Vowing to guard the princess at the expence of his life. **1774** GOLDSM. *Nat. Hist.* (1862) I. I. i. 254 We have been at such expence and trouble. **1793** BURKE *Corr.* (1844) IV. 160 All operations between the tropics are at an immense expense of human lives. **1859** *Musketry Instruct.* 52 At a considerable expense, to erect marker's butts. **1882** *Daily Tel.* 12 June, The home eleven had got 52 at an expense of two wickets.

c. In *pl.* esp.: The charges, costs, items of outlay, incurred by a person in the execution of any commission or duty; 'money out of pocket'; also, money paid to a person in reimbursement of these.

1382 WYCLIF *1 Macc.* x. 44 Expensis shuln be ȝouen of the kyngies resoun..to bilde out the wallis of Jerusalem. **1460** CAPGRAVE *Chron.* 198 The old Edward had every month to his expensis a hundred mark. **1535** COVERDALE *Jer.* xl. 5 The chefe captayne gaue him his expenses with a rewarde. **1601** SHAKS. *Twel. N.* III. i. 49 There's expences for thee. **1656** BEN ISRAEL *Vind. Judæorum* in *Phenix* (1708) II. 410 Of the Tribute, Expences should be forthwith given unto the Elders. *Mod.* You will allow me my expenses.

d. A cause or occasion of expense. Also *transf.*

1873 H. SPENCER *Study Sociol.* iii. 51 Exertion is a physiological expense. *Mod.* His sons have been a great expense to him.

4. a. ***at (†on) the expense (†expenses) of a person***, etc.: so that he defrays the cost; 'at the charges of'.

c **1400** MAUNDEV. (1839) xx. 221 The grete Chane haþ euery day folk at His costages & expense. *c* **1477** CAXTON *Jason* 69 Appollo dide do make the arke..at the expensis of the king. **1549** *Compl. Scot.* xi. 89 He furnest..tua hundreth lycht horse, on his auen expensis. **1609** SHAKS. *Per.* IV. iii. 46 Us, At whose expense 'tis done. **1678** BUTLER *Hud.* III. iii. 456 Lawyers have more sober sense Than to argue at their own expence. **1697** POTTER *Antiq. Greece* III. ii. (1715) 7 The Soldiers were all maintain'd at their own Expences. **1834** MEDWIN *Angler in Wales* I. 67 Our piscator ..declined dining at our expense. **1873** *Act 36–7 Vict.* c. 71 §59 The Secretary of State may..cause any water-course to be widened at the expense of such board.

b. *transf.* ***at the expense of a person (or thing)***: so that he (or it) suffers consequent loss, injury, or diminution.

1695 LD. PRESTON *Boeth.* Pref. 6 And so, at his Expence, advance a little Trophy of Reputations to themselves. **1754** SHERLOCK *Disc.* (1759) I. xiii. 344 Gratify our Envy at the Expence of our Neighbour's Reputation. **1807** T. THOMSON *Chem.* (ed. 3) II. 189 The copper wires..were oxidized at the expence of the acid. **1818** JAS. MILL *Brit. Ind.* II. v. ix. 711 The interest of the subordinates..is..pursued at the expense of the service. **1849** ROBERTSON *Serm.* Ser. I. vii. (1866) 120 There was obedience at the expense of..feeling. **1879** M. ARNOLD *Mixed Ess.* 234 But the lovers of Hampden cannot forbear to extol him at Falkland's expense.

5. *attrib.* and *Comb.* ***expense-reforming, -saving*** adjs.; **expense account, sheet**, an account of expenses or expenditure; *spec.* an account of the expenses incurred by an employee in the course of his work and payable by his employer(s); also, the money so paid; freq. *attrib.*; **expense-book**, *Naut.* (see quot. 1867); **expense magazine**, a magazine in which a small portion of ammunition is kept for immediate use.

1872 RAYMOND *Mines* 284 The item of roads is a big one in the expense account. **1922** S. LEWIS *Babbitt* x. 141 It went down on my expense-account—gosh, if I'd been paying it instead of the firm, I'd 'a' tramped the streets all night. **1933** J. B. PRIESTLEY *Wonder Hero* iii. 68 What about a quick drink and then some lunch?..It'll all go down on my expense account to the paper. **1937** W. S. MAUGHAM *Theatre* ix. 75 When he directed a play he put down on the expense account the fee that a director of the second rank would have received. **1953** 'S. RANSOME' *Drag Dark* (1954) xi. 119 They went off together...To lunch. Nice, expense-account place. **1959** R. POSTGATE *Good Food Guide 1959–1960* 87 Offering a good, soigné, 'expense-account' type menu. *Ibid.* 222 Designed in menu and price for business executives with expense accounts. *Ibid.* 387 The eaters were given precisely the same attentive service as the expense-account-wallahs. **1970** *New Yorker* 15 Aug. 66/2 Pills for expense-account indigestion. **1828** J. M. SPEARMAN *Brit. Gunner* (ed. 2) 80 Expence Books. **1867** SMYTH *Sailor's Word-bk, Expense books*, accounts of the expenditure of the warrant officer's stores, attested by the signing officers. **1839** W. F. NAPIER *Penins. War* XIII. v, The explosion of an expense magazine. **1845** STOCQUELER *Handbk. Brit. India* (1854) 174 There are, also, branch or expense magazines in the outworks. **1880** *Fortn. Rev.* Feb. 267 Any expense-reforming proposal meets with scant courtesy from the House. **1942** G. GREENE *Brit. Dramatists* 18 The scenes of *Tamburlaine*, unlimited by pasteboard sets and an expense-sheet, shifted boldly all over Asia. **1945** J. B. PRIESTLEY *Three Men in New Suits* v. 91 We'll pay you thirty-five pounds a week and give you a reasonable expense sheet.

†**ex'penseful**, *a. Obs.* [f. prec. + -FUL.] Attended with or characterized by expense; costly, expensive. Also, Given to expense, extravagant.

1605 CHAPMAN *All Fools* in Dodsley *O.P.* (1780) IV. 144 To stay him yet from more expenceful courses. **1624** WOTTON *Archit.* in *Reliq. Wotton.* (1672) 35 There is no part of Structure more expencefull then Windows. **1667** PEPYS *Diary* (1879) IV. 389 The Duchess is not only the proudest woman in the world, but the most expensefull. **1688** *Lett. Present State Italy* 162 The expencefull humour that their late Marriages with France has spred among them. *a* **1716** SOUTH *Serm.* (1717) V. 147 An expenseful and laborious Education. **1775** in ASH.

Hence †**ex'pensefully** *adv.*, in a manner involving much expense. †**ex'pensefulness**, costliness; *rarely* (of persons) extravagance.

1631 WEEVER *Anc. Fun. Mon.* 316 Sir William Sidley, a learned Knight, painefully and expensfully studious of the common good of his countrey. *a* **1613** OVERBURY *Archduke's Country* Wks. (1856) 232 The cause of the expensefulnes of it [the war]..is the remotenesse of those provinces from Spaine. **1688** LD. DELAMER *Let. to daughter* Wks. (1694) 34 She will..by her expencefulness leave her husband no better than she found him.

†**ex'penseless**, *a. Obs.* [f. EXPENSE + -LESS.] Without expense. Of things: Inexpensive. Of persons: Free from expense, frugal(ly.

1644 MILTON *Educ.* 5 He..may at some time or other, save an Army by this frugall and expencelesse meanes. **1703** PENN in *Pa. Hist. Soc. Mem.* IX. 241 Keep my son as expenseless as may be. **1712** BLACKMORE *Creation* (1786) 108 What health promotes..Is all expenseless, and procur'd with ease. **1786** *Francis the Philanthropist* III. 152, I gave him my time for expenceless promises.

expensilation (ɛkˌspɛnsɪ'leɪʃən). *Rom. Law.* [ad. L. *expensilātiōn-em*, properly *expensilātiō* a setting down of expenditures. Cf. ACCEPTILATION.] A process by which an existing cause of debt was merged in a new formal obligation (compare the English 'account stated', and the contract of exchange in the law merchant).

1875 POSTE *Gaius* III Comm. (ed. 2) 363 Expensilation or Literal contract. *Ibid.* 408 One species of Literal obligation, namely Expensilation,..was effected by an entry in these domestic registers.

expensive (ɛk'spɛnsɪv), *a.* [f. L. type **expensīvus* f. *expendĕre* (see EXPEND and -IVE); but early associated with EXPENSE.]

†**1. a.** Of a person: Given to profuse expenditure (of money, time, health, etc.); lavish. Of an employment: Tending to consume (time, health, etc.). Const. *of*. *Obs.*

1628 EARLE *Microcosm., Universal Dun* (Arb.) 74 Hee is now very expensiue of his time. **1655** JER. TAYLOR *Golden Grove* (1659) 55 Use what innocent refreshment you please ..[but] let it not be too expensive of time. *a* **1656** BP. HALL *Episc. & Liturg.* Rem. Wks. (1660) 421 See whether any have been more expensive either of their ink, or their blood. **1704** STEELE *Lying Lover* II. (1747) 36 Young Men of this Age are..so expensive both of their Health and Fortune. **1817** J. GILCHRIST *Intell. Patrimony* 112 A regular arrangement of extracts..is..more expensive of time.

b. Fond of expense; extravagant. Now *rare.*

1650 JER. TAYLOR *Holy Living* (1727) 99 What is it to me ..whether his wife be expensive. *a* **1698** TEMPLE (J.), Frugal and industrious men are friendly to the established government, as the idle and expensive are dangerous. **1782** MISS BURNEY *Cecilia* IX. v, She was far other than expensive. **1845** CARLYLE *Cromwell* (1873) I. 19 Sir Oliver, likewise an expensive man.

†**c.** 'Liberal, generous, distributive' (J.). *rare.*

1678 SPRAT *Serm.* (1722) 103 An active, expensive, indefatigable goodness..such as our Apostle calls..a Labour of Love.

2. a. Of a thing: Attended with expense; costly, dear. ***to come expensive***: see COME 24 b. Also *fig.*

1634 BRERETON *Trav.* (Chetham Soc.) 70 The two late expensive and chargeable sieges of Buss. **1664** EVELYN tr. *Freart's Archit.* 119 Till..the remedy [be] impossible or expensive. *a* **1715** BURNET *Own Time* (1734) II. 658 The Law of England is..very expensive and dilatory. **1726–31** TINDAL *Rapin's Hist. Eng.* (1743) II. XVII. 109 He..lived at so expensive a rate. **1776** ADAM SMITH *W.N.* I. xi. (1869) I. 232 To collect the produce of unimproved lands..would be too expensive. **1838** DICKENS *Nich. Nick.* iv, It's expensive keeping boys at home. **1865** BUSHNELL *Vicar. Sacr.* II. i. 192 God..will bend Himself to any most expensive, lowest burden of sympathy. **1883** FROUDE *Short Stud.* IV. I. ii. 16 The father..was unable to give the child as expensive an educaton as he had desired.

b. *transf.* At cricket, of bowling or a bowler.

1882 *Daily Tel.* 27 May, Barrett's bowling was getting rather expensive. **1891** *Daily News* 30 June 3/7 Mr. Ferris, the Australian, proving very expensive.

c. *Comb.*, as ***expensive-looking*** adj.

1925 T. DREISER *Amer. Trag.* I. II. v. 184 Such expensive-looking and apparently smart displays. **1965** F. SARGESON *Memoirs of Peon* vi. 147 A fancy and somewhat expensive-looking purse.

† **3.** quasi-*adv.* = EXPENSIVELY. *Obs.*
1796 E. PARSONS *Mysterious Warning* iv. 236 They lived very expensive.

Hence **ex'pensively** *adv.*, in an expensive manner, with (great) expense.
a **1631** DONNE *Let. to Sir H.G.* in *Poems* 279 Our court tooke the resolution..to receive him [the French Prince] solemnly, ceremoniously; and expensively. *a* **1745** SWIFT (J.), I never knew him live so great and expensively. **1809–10** COLERIDGE *Friend* (1865) 146 Our immense military force is better and more expensively clothed. **1886** *Law Times Rep.* LIII. 611/1 The liquidators could collect the outstanding calls..less expensively than the plaintiffs.

expensiveness (ɛk'spɛnsɪvnɪs). [f. prec. + -NESS.]
1. The quality of being expensive or costly, or of requiring large outlay; costliness.
1655 FULLER *Hist. Camb.* (1840) 224 Considering the expensiveness of the place [Cambridge]. **1656** PRYNNE *Rights Eng. Freemen* 21 The expensivenesse..of their Law sutes. **1705** ARBUTHNOT *Coins* viii. (1727) 75 Their Highways, for their extent, solidity or expensiveness, are some of the greatest monuments of the grandeur of their Empire. **1876** GEO. ELIOT *Dan. Der.* I. x, That..celebrity which makes an artist great to the most ordinary people by their knowledge of his great expensiveness. **1882** SEELEY in *Macm. Mag.* XLVI. 457 The expensiveness of the wars.
2. Disposition to lavish expenditure, extravagance. Now *rare.*
1642 FULLER *Holy & Prof. St.* I. xiv. 45 Ulrick Fugger.. was disinherited of a great patrimony onely for his studiousnesse, and expensivenesse in buying costly manuscripts. **1796** JANE AUSTEN *Sense & Sens.* III. xi. 304 His expensiveness is acknowledged even by himself. **1819** L. HUNT *Indicator* No. 1 (1822) I. 7 An improved knowledge which does not confound good taste with expensiveness.

expergefacient (ɛkˌspɜːdʒɪ'feɪʃɪənt), *a. rare.* [ad. L. *expergēfacient-em*, pr. pple. of *expergēfacĕre*: see next.] Awakening; of a nature to rouse or wake up.
1821 *Blackw. Mag.* X. 117 Which..would prove as expergifacient [sic] as a sternutatory to the parties addressed.

expergefaction (ɛkˌspɜːdʒɪ'fækʃən). Now *rare.* [ad. late L. *expergēfaction-em*, n. of action f. *expergēfacĕre*, f. *experg-ĕre* to awake, rouse + *facĕre* to make, cause.] The action of awaking or rousing; the state, condition or fact of being awakened or aroused.
1638 O. SEDGWICKE *Serm.* (1639) 15 An heavenly expergefaction. **1651** BIGGS *New Disp.* ⁋ 204 The dilatory expergefaction from a disease. **1660** HOWELL *Parly of Beasts* 45 Having, after such a long noctivagation..return'd to my perfect expergefaction. **1824** *Blackw. Mag.* XV. 94 Another propitious recollection; namely, my first expergefaction at Farsa. **1827** G. S. FABER, *Sacr. Calendar Prophecy* (1844) III. 118 The first Head, after a long reign of more than 1800 years subsequent to its expergefaction by Augustus, etc.

expergefactor (ɛksˌpɜːdʒɪ'fæktə(r)). [agent-n. f. L. *expergēfacĕre* (see prec.).] One who, or that which, awakens; an awakener.
1823 *Mechanic's Mag.* No. 7. 108 The newly invented Hydraulic Expergefactor rings a bell at the time when a person wishes to rise.

† **ex'pergefy**, *v. Obs.*$^{-0}$ [ad. L. *expergēfacĕre*: see prec. and -FY.] *trans.* To awaken.
1623–6 in COCKERAM.

† **exper'giscence.** *Obs. rare*$^{-1}$. [f. L. *expergiscent-em*, pr. pple. of *expergiscī* to awake, be awakened: see -ENCE.] An awaking from sleep.
a **1734** NORTH *Lives* (1890) III. 144 If it will save him I should perceive a plain expergiscence though I had no sense of drowsiness.

experience (ɛk'spɪərɪəns), *sb.* Also 4–6 experiens, -ians, -yens, 5–6 experyence. [a. Fr. *expérience*, ad. L. *experientia*, f. *experient-em*, pr. pple. of *experīrī* to try, put to the test.]
† **1. a.** The action of putting to the test; trial. *to make experience of*: to make trial of. *Obs.*
1388 WYCLIF *Gen.* xlii. 15 Now y schal take experience [**1382** experyment] of ȝou. **1393** GOWER *Conf.* I. 14 At Avynon thexperience Therof haþ ȝoue an euidence. **1596** SPENSER *F.Q.* v. i. 7 Of all the which..She [Astræa] caused him [Artegall] to make experience Vpon wild beasts. **1631** SHIRLEY *School of Complement* I. i, Make Experience of my loyalty, by some service. **1668** WILKINS *Real Char.* Ep. Ded. A ij b, The Art of Shorthand..much wondered at by Travailers, that have seen the experience of it in England.
† **b.** A tentative procedure; an operation performed in order to ascertain or illustrate some truth; an experiment. *Obs.*
c **1384** CHAUCER *H. Fame* II. 280, I prove it..Be experience, for if that thou Threw in a water now, a stone [etc.]. *c* **1420** *Pallad. on Husb.* VIII. 47 Nowe have I made inoculacion Of pere and appultree: the experience Hath preved wel. **1576** BAKER *Jewell of Health* 112 a, The Aucthour..hath both seene, and done many experiences worthy memorie. **1649** BLITHE *Eng. Improv. Impr.* (1653) 60 They will tell you a story of I know not what experiences they have made, when alas they never knew that an Experiment must hold in all its parts. **1678** R. R[USSELL] *Geber* II. I. IV. i. 86 All which..we shall..declare, with their Causes and with easie Experiences. **1763** ELIZ. CARTER in Pennington *Mem.* (1816) I. 301, I was..assured, by people who have made the experience, that [etc.].

† **2.** Proof by actual trial; practical demonstration. *to put in experience*: to fulfil in practice. *Obs.*; passing into 3.
c **1391** CHAUCER *Astrol.* II. §1, I..found the point of my rewle..a lite with-in the degree & than haddy of this conclusioun the ful experience. **1393** GOWER *Conf.* II. 138 Thus hath this king experience, How fooles done the reverence To gold. **1447** BOKENHAM *Seyntys* (Roxb.) 5, I had hereof good experyence. *c* **1489** CAXTON *Sonnes of Aymon* xxii. 469 Ye maye well perceyve the experyence of it every day. **1494** FABYAN *Chron.* v. cxix. 96 Augustyne.. warnyd them..that..they shuld..receyue warre and wreche; the whiche was after put in experience by Ethelfridus Kynge of Northumberland. **1594** MARLOWE & NASHE *Dido* IV. iv, And now to make experience of my love, Fair sister Anna, lead my lover forth. **1614** RALEIGH *Hist. World* II. v. i. §1. 261 The experience that Pyrrhus hath giuen, of the Roman power, in his dayes. **1715** DE FOE *Fam. Instruct.* I. iii. (1841) I. 58, I have a full experience of that, and thought my happiness always complete in it.
3. The actual observation of facts or events, considered as a source of knowledge.
1377 LANGLAND *P. Pl.* B. XVIII. 151 Thorw experience.. I hope þei shal be saued. **1563** FULKE *Meteors* (1640) 13 Therefore the Mariners by experience trying, that one flame ..signified tempest at hand, supposed the same flame to be the goddess *Helena*. **1577** B. GOOGE *Heresbach's Husb.* III. (1586) 121 b, To poure into his mouth wine and oyle..we finde by experience, is verye good. **1651** WITTIE tr. *Primrose's Pop. Err.* I. xiv. 51 Experience teacheth that Agarick purges fleame. **1736** BUTLER *Anal.* I. ii. 35 It is not so much a Deduction of Reason, as a Matter of Experience. **1764** GOLDSM. *Trav.* 371 Just experience tells..That those that think must govern those that toil. **1785** REID *Int. Powers* 627 Experience informs us only of what has been, but never of what must be. **1830** HERSCHEL *Stud. Nat. Phil.* II. i. (1851) 76 The..only ultimate source of our knowledge of nature and its laws, experience; by which we mean..the accumulated experience of all mankind in all ages, registered in books or recorded by tradition. **1851** HELPS *Friends in C.* I. 19 By making men as gods, enabling them to understand without experience. **1862** [SIR J. F. STEPHEN] *Ess. by a Barrister* 329 Daily experience informs us of the consequences.
4. a. The fact of being consciously the subject of a state or condition, or of being consciously affected by an event. Also an instance of this; a state or condition viewed subjectively; an event by which one is affected.
1382 WYCLIF *Gen.* xxx. 27 Laban seide to him..thurȝ experyens Y haue lernyd for God hath blissid to me for thee. *c* **1386** CHAUCER *Wife's Prol.* 1 Experiens..were ynough for me To speke of wo that is in mariage. **14..** *Purific. Marie* in *Tundale's Vis.* 129 To have experiens Only of chyldyng. *c* **1532** DEWES *Introd. Fr.* in Palsgrave 1049 Please God that ye understande it by experiens. **1615** J. STEPHENS *Satir. Ess.* (ed. 2) 172 A complete man..knowes what experience can teach, but is not taught by experience. **1693** C. MATHER *Wond. Invis. World*, Churches, whose Communicants have been seriously examined about their Experience of Regeneration. **1846** HAWTHORNE *Mosses* (1883) 47 A man of science who..had made experience of a spiritual affinity more attractive than any chemical one. **1848** MACAULAY *Hist. Eng.* II. 254 Both..had learned by experience how soon James forgot obligations. **1874** MISS MULOCK *My Mother & I* 8 Many another girl has gone thro' a similar experience. **1878** HOOKER & BALL *Marocco* 269 Another unlooked-for experience was in store for us.
b. In religious use: A state of mind or feeling forming part of the inner religious life; the mental history (of a person) with regard to religious emotion. Also *attrib.*, esp. in *experience-meeting*, a meeting (*e.g.* a Methodist class meeting or love-feast) held for the recital of religious experiences.
1674 OWEN *Holy Spirit* (1693) 49 Testified unto by the Experience of them that truely believe. **1684** BUNYAN *Pilgr.* II. 47 *marg.*, A Repetition of Christiana's Experience. *a* **1758** J. EDWARDS *Wks.* III. 32 Those experiences which are agreeable to the word of God are right. **1841–4** EMERSON *Ess.* Ser. I. 256 The rapture of the Moravian and Quietist.. the experiences of the Methodists, are varying forms [etc.]. **1854** H. MILLER *Footpr. Creat.* xiii. (1874) 235 Ought the Christian controversialist to avail himself, in this question, of the experience argument? **1857** GOODRICH *Recoll.* I. 214 [At these meetings] there was praying, and exhorting, and telling experiences, and singing..sentimental religious hymns.
5. In senses 3, 4 often personified; *esp.* in various proverbial phrases.
c **1450** *Nun* 150 in *E.E.P.* 142 'What ys yowr name, dame empryse?' Sche seyde 'my name ys experience.' **1578** TIMME *Calvin on Gen.* 249 Experience..is the schoolmaistresse of fooles. **1590** SIR J. SMYTH *Disc. Weapons* Sig. *2 b, Experience is the mother of Science. **1611** SHAKS. *Cymb.* IV. ii. 34 Experience, oh thou disproou'st Report. **1650** BP. HALL *Balm Gil.* 301 If experience be the mistresse of fools, I am sure it is the mother of wisdome. **1667** *Decay Chr. Piety* 104 Experience is the daughter of Time. **1826** DISRAELI *Viv. Grey* v. i, Experience is the child of Thought.
6. What has been experienced; the events that have taken place within the knowledge of an individual, a community, mankind at large, either during a particular period or generally.
1607 NORDEN *Surv. Dial.* 31, I can finde nothing in mine experience to contradict your speech. **1759** ROBERTSON *Hist. Scot.* I. VI. 423 Her animosity against the queen of Scots was greatly augmented by recent experience. **1860** MILL *Repr. Govt.* (1865) 141/2 Profound study of Indian experience.
7. a. Knowledge resulting from actual observation or from what one has undergone.
1553 EDEN *Treat. Newe Ind.* (Arb.) 7 It hardelye agreeth with the principles of Philosophie & common experience. **1600** SHAKS. *A.Y.L.* IV. i. 26 *Jaq.* Yes, I haue gain'd my experience. *Ros.* And your experience makes you sad. **1607** NORDEN *Surv. Dial.* 39, I have no further experience of you then the bare report of my Tenant. **1658** SIR T. BROWNE *Hydriot.* Ep. Ded., Having no old experience of the Duration of their Relics. **1791** GOUV. MORRIS in Sparks *Life & Writ.* (1832) III. 20 Most men have the generosity to pay for their own experience. **1860** TYNDALL *Glac.* I. ii. 22, I had had but little experience of alpine phenomena.
† **b.** A piece of experimental knowledge; a fact, maxim, rule, or device drawn from or approved by experience; *concr.* something expertly fashioned. *Obs.*
1570 DEE *Math. Pref.* 24 This Arte [Astrology] is furnished with many other great Artes and experiences. **1577** B. GOOGE *Heresbach's Husb.* IV. (1586) 170 Some have an other experience for this purpose, and that is Potshardes beaten small..and given unto them [Doves]. **1588** SHAKS. *L.L.L.* III. i. 27 How hast thou purchased this experience? **1621** BOLTON *Stat. Irel.* 330 Sir Percy Sidney..hath.. found amongst other experiences the great abuse of the clergie there. **1657** T. BARKER *Art of Angling* (1659) 51, I have found an experience [i.e. salmon roe as bait] of late which you may angle with, and take great store of this kind of fish. **1669** STURMY *Mariner's Mag.* I. ii. 14, I will add one old approved Experience for the Mariners use..that is, to cut Hair, the Moon in [Taurus, etc.]. **1670–98** LASSELS *Voy. Italy* II. 128 Here I saw the schools..full of pretty curiosities and experiences, Mechanical, Mathematical, and Hydraulical.
8. The state of having been occupied in any department of study or practice, in affairs generally, or in the intercourse of life; the extent to which, or the length of time during which, one has been so occupied; the aptitudes, skill, judgement, etc. thereby acquired.
1483 CAXTON *Cato* A viij, He ought to haue thexperience ..to knowe what thynge right is. **1494** FABYAN *Chron.* 3 To theym that..haue in Cronycles full experyence. **1509** FISHER *Fun. Serm. C'tess Richmond* Wks. 292 The duke of suthfolke..was a man of grete experyence. **1511–2** *Act 3 Hen. VIII*, c. 11 To the perfecte knowlege wherof bee requisite bothe grete lernyng and ripe experience. **1586** J. HOOKER *Girald. Irel.* II. xl. in Holinshed, By reason of their continuall wars they are very valient, bold, and of great experiences. **1591** SHAKS. *Two Gent.* II. iv. 69 His yeares but yong, but his experience old. **1647** CLARENDON *Hist. Reb.* I. (1702) I. 38 Observations, and Reflections; out of which, that, which is commonly call'd Experience, is constituted. **1709** STEELE *Tatler* No. 98 ⁋ 2 You are stricken in Years, and have had great Experience in the World. **1735–8** BOLINGBROKE *On Parties* 2 There is need of..those Habits in Business called Experience. **1770** BURKE *Corr.* (1844) I. 240 His experience in the world is but moderate. **1828** WHATELY *Rhet.* II. §7 The authority derived from Experience.
transf. **1880** MISS BIRD *Japan* I. 124 Making a difficult meal from a fowl of much experience.
9. *attrib.*, as **experience philosophy**, experiential philosophy; **experience school**, the school of empiricism; **experience table**, a table of mortality computed from the experience of one or more life-assurance companies.
1859 J. S. MILL *Lett.* (1910) I. 225 The experience philosophy and the association psychology are getting up again. **1909** W. JAMES *Pluralistic Universe* 390 This *is* effectuation in the only shape in which, by a pure experience-philosophy, the whereabouts of it anywhere can be discussed. **1882** A. BAIN *J. S. Mill* iii. 69 Mr. Ward has continued to uphold his peculiar tenets against the Experience-school. **1936** *Mind* XLV. 242 He holds (as some members of the 'experience-school' do) that feeling..is also a cognitive function. **1879** W. S. CHAMPNESS *Insur. Dict.* (1883) 106 The Experience Table is based on that of seventeen British Life Offices.

experience (ɛk'spɪərɪəns), *v.* [f. prec. sb.]
I. † **1. a.** *trans.* To make trial or experiment of; to put to the test; to test, try. *Obs.*
1533 ELYOT *Cast. Helthe* III. vi. (1541) 62 b, In extreme necessitie it were better experience some remedy, than to do nothynge. **1670** G. H. *Hist. Cardinals* II. III. 195 Alexander ..experienc'd him in some intricate business, and found him a person of worth. **1681** CHETHAM *Angler's Vade-m.* iv. §14 (1689) 46 Having never experienced them for these Fish, I dare not be positive. **1774** PENNANT *Tour Scot. in* 1772, 368 Persuade their governess to experience their zeal. **1780** in Picton *L'pool Munic. Rec.* (1886) II. 200 That the expences of the Sessions dinners..be experienced for a few Sessions.
† **b.** To ascertain or prove by experiment or observation; chiefly with sentence as *obj.* Also rarely, To prove or reveal (a thing) *to* (a person) by experience. *Obs.*
1533 ELYOT *Cast. Helthe* (1541) G iij b, I my selfe have often experienced, the best remedy is [etc.]. **1656–7** *Burton's Diary* (1828) I. 333 This Quartermaster..had one hundred good horses in town..for what purpose time will experience. **1690** LADY RUSSELL *Lett.* cxvi. II. 80 This trial has..experienced to me my sad weakness. **1750** tr. *Leonardus' Mirr. Stones* 82 It has been experienced, that if it be hung about the neck, it will cure the epilepsy.
2. a. To have experience of; to meet with; to feel, suffer, undergo.
1588 PARKE tr. *Mendoza's Hist. China* 349 [He] declared unto them, as one that had experienced the same, the rewarde of that good deede. **1645** SALTMARSH *Open. Prynne's New Bk.* 3 We experience in part some remainders of Prelacy. **1646** —— *Smoke in Temple* 56 [The author defends his use of the verb (see prec. quot.) on the ground that useful neologisms are permissible]. **1736** BUTLER *Anal.* I. ii. Wks. 1874 I. 45 The whole passage is..applicable to what we experience in the present world. **1773** J. ALLEN *Serm. St. Mary's Oxf.* 25 They who experience his loving kindness. **1847** MRS. A. KERR *Hist. Servia* 334 He was himself soon to experience a similar fate. **1860** TYNDALL

Glac. I. xviii. 129, I experienced no trace of mountain sickness.

b. To learn (a fact) by experience; to find. With direct obj. and compl. inf., or with sentence as *obj.* Now *rare.*

1580 SIR P. SIDNEY *Arcadia* (1613) 207 Pamela..had now experienced how much care doth sollicite a lovers heart. **1736** BUTLER *Anal.* I. iii. 65 The divine government, which we experience ourselves under the present state. **1739** LABELYE *Short Acc. Piers Westm. Bridge* 63 That River is experienced not rapid enough to occasion any Damage to the Piers of those Bridges. **1796** H. HUNTER tr. *St.-Pierre's Stud. Nat.* (1799) III. 621, I then experienced what I knew before hand, that there are [etc.]. **1858** HAWTHORNE *Fr. & It. Jrnls.* I. 88, I have experienced that a landscape and the sky unfold the deepest beauty.

c. *transf.* Of a thing: To meet with, undergo.

1786 T. JEFFERSON *Writ.* (1859) II. 24 The treaties..have experienced greater delay than was expected. **1794** SULLIVAN *View Nat.* I. 217 Holland often experiences a degree of cold greater than countries placed under higher latitudes. **1828** J. M. SPEARMAN *Brit. Gunner* (ed. 2) 198 The resistance experienced by the base of the cone. **1888** BURGON *Lives 12 Gd. Men* II. XII. 420 His bodily strength was..visibly experiencing decay.

d. *to experience religion*: to be converted. *U.S.*

1837 *Knickerbocker* IX. 356, I have 'experienced religion', as well as thousands of others, and in the same way. *a* **1852** MRS. WHITCHER *Widow Bedott Papers* (1883) xx. 80 He was a wonderful pious pedlar..had jest experienced religion. **1868** O. W. HOLMES *Guard. Angel* xii, Some went so far as to doubt if she had ever experienced religion, for all she was a professor. **1891** MRS. K. D. WIGGIN *Timothy's Quest.* 136 You'd think nobody ever experienced religion afore, he's so set up 'bout it.

†**II. 3. a.** To give experience to; to make experienced; to train (soldiers). Also, in *passive*: To be informed or taught by experience (Const. *of*, or with *subord. clause*). *Obs.*

c **1534** tr. *Pol. Verg. Eng. Hist.* (Camden) I. 64 Well experienced that mistruste or confidence depended on the first casualltie of the battaile. **1607** TOPSELL *Four-f. Beasts* (1673) 249 The Foot-men..being experienced to run suddenly with the Horse men, leaped into the battail. **1612** W. PARKES *Curtaine-Dr.* (1876) 33 Whom no tryall can experience, whom no de[s]truction can forewarne. **1621** LADY M. WROTH *Urania* 509 Able to heare of Cupid, though not..experienced by wound of his force. **1627** SIR R. COTTON *Short View* in *Phenix* I. 70 The King, by this experienced of the intents of his rebellious lords, and finding, etc. **1654** WHITLOCK *Zootomia* 567 Experience thy Soule in the comforts of Christs dying.

†**b.** To gain experience in, practise the use of (arms). *Obs. rare.*

1727 W. HARTE *Statius' 6th Thebaid* 24 The youthful sailors..Their arms experience, and for sea prepare.

experienceable (ɛk'spɪərɪənsəb(ə)l), *a.* [f. EXPERIENCE *v.* + -ABLE.] Capable of being experienced.

1907 W. JAMES *Pragmatism* vi. 224 So far as reality means experienceable reality, both it and the truths men gain about it are everlastingly in process of mutation. **1927** J. W. DUNNE *Experiment with Time* xxiii. 170 Like all other sensations, its [*sc.* pain's] range of experienceable intensity must be limited. **1963** *Times Lit. Suppl.* 4 Jan. 3/4 The former is experienceable, can be lived from within as a style of life; the latter are stereotypes used or abused from without.

experienced (ɛk'spɪərɪənst), *ppl. a.* Also 6–7 -enc't, -enst. [f. EXPERIENCE *sb.* and *v.* + -ED¹.]

1. Of persons, their faculties and powers; occas. of animals, and humorously of inanimate things: Having experience; wise or skilful through experience. Const. *in*, †*of*.

1576 J. KNEWSTUB *Confut.* (1579) Qijb, Men not experienced of his goodness particularly must needs think, etc. **1592** CHETTLE *Kind-harts Dr.* (1841) 28 The worshipfull company of experienst chirurgions. **1606** SHAKS. *Tr. & Cr.* I. iii. 68 To his experienc'd tongue. **1654** CROMWELL *Sp.* 4 Sept. (Carlyle), It will be the wisdom of all knowing and experienced Christians to do as Jude saith. **1667** MILTON *P.L.* I. 568 He through the armed Files Darts his experienc't eye. **1725** DE FOE *Voy. round World* (1840) 328 A crew of fifty men, all able and experienced sailors. **1727** SWIFT *Vanbrugh's House*, Th' experienc'd bricks that knew their trade. **1832** HT. MARTINEAU *Hill & Valley* ii. 29 The stray sheep may come back experienced in pasturage. **1849** THOREAU *Week Concord Riv.* Saturday 27 His old experienced coat hanging..straight and brown as the yellow pine back. **1855** MACAULAY *Hist. Eng.* IV. 325 At that Board sate Godolphin the most prudent and experienced..of financiers.

absol. **1612** BRINSLEY *Lud. Lit.* 176 Graue testimonies..of the..wisest, and most experienced. **1838** LYTTON *Alice* 13 The young ever wonder why the experienced should be sad.

†**2.** Of remedies, etc.: Tested, tried, approved.

1569 R. ANDROSE (*title*), Alexis' Secrets..containing 680 and odd experienced medecines. **1641** BEST *Farm. Bks.* (Surtees) 1 The experienced adage '*omne animal generat sibi simile*'. **1676** HALE *Contempl.* I. 2 It is the most certain, known, experienced truth in the World that all men must die. **1780** JOHNSON *Let. Mrs. Thrale* 24 Aug., To..counteract by experienced remedies every new tendency.

3. Met with in the course of experience; felt, suffered, undergone.

1604 STIRLING *Aurora* Song II. 8 For long experienc'd wo well witnesse beares, That teares cannot quench sighes. **1633** P. FLETCHER *Purple Isl.* XII. xxxvii, Too well we know his power by long experienc't harms. **1686** R. DUNNING *Overseer of Poor* 7 The experienced effects of our Method. **1849–50** ALISON *Hist. Europe* VIII. li. §11. 235 A cautious and guiltless reformation of experienced grievances.

Hence †**ex'periencedly** *adv.*, by experience.

1617 STRAFFORD in Browning *Life* 289, I having felt [him] experiencedly to be very little friendly towards me.

experienceless (ɛk'spɪərɪənslɪs), *a.* [f. EXPERIENCE *sb.* + -LESS.] Having no experience.

1875 BROWNING *Aristoph. Apol.* 167 Unobservant or experienceless. **1881** *Amer. Missionary* (N.Y.) July 189 They started out homeless..and experienceless.

experiencer (ɛk'spɪərɪənsə(r)). [f. EXPERIENCE *v.* + -ER¹.]

1. One who experiences something.

1862 F. HALL *Hindu Philos. Syst.* 214 Neither doer, nor experiencer. **1889** WRIGHT *Chalice of Carden* xiii. 92 A fine enthusiasm, of such potency..that..the experiencer of it has already in imagination attained unto the end.

†**2.** One who makes experiments. *Obs.*

1644 DIGBY *Nat. Bodies* viii. 4 A curious experiencer did affirme, that the likenesse of any obiect [etc.]. Hence **1755** in JOHNSON, **1775** in ASH, and in mod. Dicts.

†**ex'periency.** *Obs. rare.* In 6 experiensie, -ensy. [ad. L. *experientia*: see EXPERIENCE *sb.* and -ENCY.] = EXPERIENCE *sb.* 6, 7.

1556 J. HEYWOOD *Spider & F.* liii. 33 Unknowne to all that haue not felinglie Felt of the same, in their experiensie. *Ibid.* lvii. 101 Hauing in all times had experiensy, Of rashe beginning of war.

ex'perient, *a.* and *sb.* [ad. L. *experient-em*: see EXPERIENCE *sb.*]

A. *adj.* Having experience; = EXPERIENCED 1. *experient of*: acquainted with.

c **1420** *Pallad. on Husb.* II. 96 The wardeyne with his rodde experient May be therof thourgh putting every went [i.e. space dug]. *c* **1523** BARCLAY tr. *Mancini's Mirr. Gd. Manners* Hiiij b, The manner..Of a wyse Phesician or Leche experient. **1605** CHAPMAN *All Fooles* Plays 1873 I. 121 Which wisedome sure he learn'd Of his experient father. **1630** LORD *Persees* 29 The knowledge of the latter in these experient times seemeth unnecessary. **1926** A. N. WHITEHEAD *Sci. & Mod. World* ix. 211 The ego-object, as consciousness here-now, is conscious of its experient essence as constituted by its internal relatedness to the world of realities, and to the world of ideas. **1933** —— *Adventures of Ideas* xiv. 216 In this transmutation the experient occasion in question belongs to the personal succession of occasions which is the soul of the animal.

absol. **1642** HERLE *Fuller Answ. to Ferne* To Rdr. 1 No man can write well of it, but he must..eate the Roll..the experient herein are only eloquent.

B. *sb.* †**1.** Something experienced, tested, or tried. *Obs.*

1605 TIMME *Quersit.* III. 156 This noble experient.

2. One who experiences something; one who undergoes an experience.

1899 J. WARD *Natural. & Agnost.* II. 181 His [*sc.* Descartes's] doctrine reduces the individual experient to a mere automaton. **1917** *Mod. Churchman* VII. 79 Experience implies an experient. **1918** E. GRUBB *Relig. Experience* iii. 37 Religious Experience..is..personal and incommunicable; however abundant the assurance of Reality it brings to the experient, he cannot share that certainty with others as he can the normal experience of the senses. **1925** J. E. TURNER *Theory of Direct Realism* 16 Sense-contents..depend in part for their own existence and character directly upon the existence and activity of the percipient observer or experient. **1938** R. G. COLLINGWOOD *Princ. Art* 252 The emotions it expresses are not only the emotions of a merely conscious experient, they include the emotions of a thinker.

experiential (ɛkˌspɪərɪ'ɛnʃəl), *a.* [f. L. *experienti-a* (see EXPERIENCE *sb.*) + -AL¹.] Of or pertaining to experience or observation; based on or derived from experience. ***experiential philosophy***: the system which regards all knowledge as derived from experience. So ***experiential philosopher, doctrine***, etc.

1816 COLERIDGE *Statesm. Man.* App. p. xi, The understanding or experiential faculty, unirradiated by the reason..has no appropriate object but the material world. **1836–7** SIR W. HAMILTON *Metaph.* (1877) I. iii. 54 It is called empirical or experiential..because it is given us by experience or observation. **1871** MORLEY *Voltaire* (1886) 67 The same method..presided over the birth of the experiential psychology. **1874** CARPENTER *Ment. Phys.* I. ii. §58 The experiential acquirement of knowledge. **1882–3** H. D. CALDERWOOD in Schaff *Encycl. Relig. Knowl.* 1224. The sceptical assault of Hume on the experiential philosophy.

Hence **experi'entialism**, the theory or doctrine that all knowledge is derived from experience. **experi'entialist**, a supporter of, or a believer in, experientialism. **experi'entially** *adv.*, with regard to experience, in experience.

1865 MASSON *Rec. Brit. Philos.* 37 As Mr. Mill has used the adjective 'Experiential'..perhaps the substantive Experientialism..might be brought into use. **1870** *Contemp. Rev.* XIV. 286 The Experientialists are always saying to the Axiomatic moralists, 'You do not understand—we believe in Conscience just as much as you do.' **1876** FOX BOURNE *Locke* II. x. 114 Locke's piety..did not make him less of an experientialist or utilitarian.

1647 H. MORE *Song of Soul* I. Introd. 12/1 This trinall effect or spirituall influence on the Soul is experientially true. **1697** J. SERGEANT *Solid Philos.* 124 The Reflex Act is experientially known by the very Act it self. **1887** MRS. C. READE *Maid o' the Mill* I. xvii. 246 He is, socially, as well as experientially, vastly her superior.

†**ex'periently**, *adv. Obs.* [f. EXPERIENT + -LY².] By or in experience; experimentally.

1413 LYDG. *Pilgr. Sowle* v. xiv. (1483) 107 Bodely thynges ye men knowen experyently. **1504** tr. *T. à Kempis* 278 That I may experyently haue the heuenly manna.

experiment (ɛk'spɛrɪmənt), *sb.* Also 4–5 -yment, 6 -imente. [a. OF. *experiment*, ad. L. *experiment-um*, n. of action f. *experiri* to try.]

1. a. The action of trying anything, or putting it to proof; a test, trial; *esp.* in phrases, *to make*, †*take* (*an*) *experiment*. Const. *of*. Now somewhat *arch.*, and conveying some notion of sense 3.

1382 [see EXPERIENCE *sb.* 1 quot. 1388]. **1542** UDALL in *Lett. Lit. Men* (Camden) 7 Oons again to take experimente of me. **1598** SHAKS. *Merry W.* IV. ii. 36 To make another experiment of his suspition. **1618** WITHER *Motto*, '*Nec Careo*' (1633) 533, I want not much experiment to show That all is good God pleaseth to bestow. **1691** T. H[ALE] *Acc. New Invent.* 6 The making the first Experiment thereof at Portsmouth. **1758** JOHNSON *Idler* No. 2 ¶10 He may..make a cheap experiment of his abilities. **1778** BURKE *Corr.* (1844) II. 241 The thing was worth the experiment. **1818** JAS. MILL *Brit. India* II. IV. iii. 99 A short experiment of resistance. **1847** EMERSON *Repr. Men, Napoleon* Wks. (Bohn) I. 381 Here was an experiment..of the powers of intellect without conscience.

†**b.** An expedient or remedy to be tried. *Obs.*

1586 COGAN *Haven Health* (1636) 120 The water..is given to drinke..as a certaine experiment. **1657** W. COLES *Adam in Eden* lxxviii, You will find it a sure Experiment for the Quinsey. **1676** LISTER in *Ray's Corr.* (1848) 124 The vinegar..from Gallium luteum, which I have tried, and is a rare experiment. **1719** DE FOE *Crusoe* (1840) I. 146 At length I found out an experiment for that, also, which was this, etc.

2. A tentative procedure; a method, system of things, or course of action, adopted in uncertainty whether it will answer the purpose.

1594 CAREW *Huarte's Exam. Wits* (1616) 307 Let him..cause some shepheards to try this experiment. **1625** BACON *Ess., Innovations* (Arb.) 527 It is good..not to try Experiments in States. **1664** EVELYN *Kal. Hort.* (1729) 194 Begin again in ten or twelve Days..to make Experiments. **1874** GREEN *Short Hist.* viii. 582 Puritanism..as a political experiment..had ended in utter failure. **1875** JOWETT *Plato* (ed. 2) V. 72 The experiment had never been tried of reasoning with mankind.

3. An action or operation undertaken in order to discover something unknown, to test a hypothesis, or establish or illustrate some known truth.

a. in science.

1362 LANGL. *P. Pl.* A. XI. 157 Experimentis of Alconomye Of Alberdes makynge, Nigromancye and perimancie. *c* **1400** *Lanfranc's Cirurg.* 7 (MS. A.) Confermynge my wordis..wiþ experiment þat I have longe tyme used. **1471** RIPLEY *Comp. Alch.* in Ashm. (1652) 189 Many Experyments I have had in hond. **1594** PLAT (*title*), Diverse new and conceited Experiments from which there may be sundrie both pleasing and profitable uses drawne. **1690** LOCKE *Hum. Und.* IV. xii. §10 A Man accustomed to rational and regular Experiments, shall be able [etc.]. **1717** J. KEILL *Anim. Œcon.* (1738) 417 An Observation or Experiment carefully made..leads us with greater Certainty to the Solution. **1842** W. GROVE *Corr. Phys. Forces* (1850) 50 If the experiment be performed in an exhausted receiver..the substance forming the electrodes is condensed.

b. *gen.* (*transf.*)

1597 HOOKER *Eccl. Pol.* v. 12 The gathering of principles out of their owne particular experiments. **1750** HUME *Lib. & Necess.* 134 These records of wars [etc.] are so many collections of experiments, by which the politician..fixes the principles of his science.

†**c.** The object experimented on; the subject of an experiment. *Obs. rare.*

a **1678** MARVELL *Let. Sir J. Trott* Wks. I. 431 Where you yourselves are the experiment.

4. a. The process or practice of conducting such operations; experimentation.

1678 R. R[USSELL] *Geber* III. II. I. viii. 161 This is proved by Experiment. **1751** WATTS *Improv. Mind* i. §4 (1801) 17 This sort of observation is called experiment. **1794** J. HUTTON *Philos. Light, etc.* 117 Experiment is the wise design of a scientific mind, inquiring after the order of events. **1830** HERSCHEL *Stud. Nat. Phil.* 76 By putting in action causes and agents over which we have control, and purposely varying their combinations, and noticing what effect takes place; this is experiment. *a* **1862** BUCKLE *Civiliz.* (1869) III. v. 462 Experiment..is merely experience artificially modified.

b. *concr.* Experimental apparatus.

1962 F. I. ORDWAY et al. *Basic Astronautics* iv. 128 The solar particle experiment includes six solid-state, semiconductor devices. **1967** *Lebende Sprachen* XII. 161/1 *Experiment* wissen-schaftliche Apparatur(en), Messgerät(e). The experiment will measure the distribution of oxygen in the atmosphere. **1969** *New Yorker* 12 Apr. 104/3 The three pots are the passive seismic experiment, the solar-wind experiment, and the suprathermal-ion-detector. *Ibid.* 110/3 A small stool..for the experiment to sit on.

†**5.** Practical acquaintance with a person or thing; experience; an instance of this. Const. *of*.

1560 ROLLAND *Crt. Venus* II. 662 He thairof had na experiment. **1586** A. DAY *Eng. Secretary* I. (1625) 101 Of his..good behaviour [I] have had sound and large experiment. *c* **1645** HOWELL *Lett.* (1650) II. 113, I know by som experiments which I have had of you. **1699** BENTLEY *Phal.* Pref. 4, I speak from Experiment. **1741** MIDDLETON *Cicero* (ed. 3) II. VII. 255 This first experiment of Caesar's clemency.

†**6.** Practical proof; a specimen, an example.

1526 *Pilgr. Perf.* (W. de W. 1531) 209b, By apparicyons and many argumentes and experymentes..he appered to his discyples. **1578** TIMME *Calvin on Gen.* 264 This is a true experiment of our obedience. *a* **1628** PRESTON *New Covt.* (1634) 302, I will give you an experiment of it; you shall see two notable examples of it. **1684** tr. *Eutropius* VII. 177[He] could not shew any experiment of himself..for..when he was beat in a skirmish..He kill'd him self.

7. *attrib.*, as **experiment farm, station**, an institution provided with means for carrying out scientific research into methods of agriculture, etc.

1893 J. AULD *Picturesque Burlington* 128 State Experiment Farm, including farm house, barn, creamery, [etc.]. **1905** *Daily Chron.* 28 Aug. 4/4, I have seen a crop of 100 bushels of oats growing on one of the experiment farms in Canada. **1874** *Connecticut Bd. Agric. Rep.* 66 The establishment of experiment stations. **1892** *Pall Mall Gaz.* 4 Apr. 3/1 The most careful investigations at many of the experiment stations show that not only are all traces of the poisons removed before the fruit ripens, but [etc.]. **1964** *Economist* 19 Dec. 1352/1 Their [*sc.* the Americans'] research departments or 'experiment stations'.

experiment (ɛk'spɛrɪmənt), *v.* [f. prec. sb.]

† **1.** *trans.* To have experience of; to experience; to feel, suffer. *Obs.*

1483 CAXTON *Æsop* 3 And these thynges sene and experymented Esope retourned to his labour. **1503** *Sheph. Kalender* lii, He shall .. experyment evill fortunes. *a* **1577** GASCOIGNE *Wks.* (1587) Ep., But a man of middle yeares who hath to his cost experimented the vanities of youth. **1627-77** FELTHAM *Resolves* I. xxv. 44 Having so often experimented his juggling. **1659** HAMMOND *On Ps.* iii. 7 Paraphr. 23 Thy fatherly mercy .. so often experimented by me. **1727** A. HAMILTON *New Acc. E. Ind.* I. viii. 86 Having experimented the Turkish wholesom Chastisements of plundring and bastonading.

† **2.** To ascertain or establish by trial (a fact, the existence of anything, etc.). Also with *obj.* and compl. inf., and with sentence as *obj. Obs.*

1481 CAXTON *Myrr.* I. v. 22 Til they had experimented whiche was trewe, and who knewe most. **1561** HOLLYBUSH *Hom. Apoth.* 27 a, Thys helpeth very well and is experimented. **1564** HAWARD *Eutropius* II. 19 They had .. experimented that they wer of great force upon the sea. **1581** J. BELL *Haddon's Answ. Osor.* A iv, The greater part .. we have allready experimented to be accomplished in these our dayes. **1699** DAMPIER *Voy.* II. III. 50 This I .. experimented by exposing a couple of Goats to the Asperity thereof. **1755** B. MARTIN *Mag. Arts & Sc.* III. xi. 381 That may be easily experimented in a small Bird. **1812** SOUTHEY *Omniana* I. 258 What is more wonderful, and .. may be experimented every day.

3. To make an experiment upon, make trial of, test, try (? a gallicism).

1524 WOLSEY in Strype *Eccl. Mem.* I. App. xii. 24 The said viceroy [of Naples] wolde .. experiment batail with the .. French king. **1558** WARDE tr. *Alexis' Secr.* (1568) 42 a, The pouder that was experimented in England. **1594** CAREW tr. *Huarte's Exam. Wits* (1616) 181 In experimenting of medicines, hee should kill an infinit number of persons. **1692** LUTTRELL *Brief Rel.* (1857) II. 559 Yesterday the duke of Leinster's engine for working of wrecks was experimented on the Thames. **1703** T. N. *City & C. Purchaser* 91, I could very well experiment the strength of Mortar. **1776** ENTICK *London* I. 309 Several articles were proposed to be experimented, and if found good .. to be confirmed. **1899** *Westm. Gaz.* 18 May 1/3 They are about to experiment another system, on a six months' probation. **1900** *Ibid.* 5 Jan. 10/1 It was he who first experimented the new battle formation of the French Army at the famous manœuvres of 1881-2.

4. *intr.* To make an experiment or experiments. Const. *on*; also in indirect passive.

1787 W. MARSHALL *Norfolk* I. 366 The laudable spirit of experimenting. **1837** GORING & PRITCHARD *Microgr.* 193 A person who has experimented with a reflector. **1857** KINGSLEY *Th. in Gravel-pit* Misc. II. 388 The more I experiment .. the more unexpected puzzles and wonders I find. **1880** RICHARDSON in *Med. Temp. Jrnl.* 72 To compel those experimented on to abide by the definition.

experimental (ɛk.spɛrɪ'mɛntəl), *a.* and *sb.* [f. as prec. + -AL¹.] **A.** *adj.*

I. Relating to experience.

† **1. a.** Of a witness: Having actual or personal experience of anything. **b.** Of things: Coming within the range of experience; observed. *Obs.*

c **1449** PECOCK *Repr.* IV. iv. 448 The same hool noumbre of homeli and experimental witnessers of Cristis deedis. **1620** MELTON *Astrolog.* 29 It is vncerteine whether the experimentall effect is to be ascribed to this or that planet. **1704** NEWTON *Optics* III. (1721) 364 We have no other evidence of universal impenetrability, besides a large experience, without an experimental exception. **1749-51** BP. LAVINGTON *Enthus. Meth. & Papists* (1754) II. 218 Of this he himself is an experimental witness.

2. a. Based on or derived from experience as opposed to mere testimony or conjecture. †Of a remedy: Discovered by experience. **b.** Founded on experience only; empirical.

1526 *Pilgr. Perf.* (W. de W. 1531) 46 b, Experymentall knowlege of the heuenly lyfe to come. **1599** SHAKS. *Much Ado* IV. i. 168 Trust not my reading, nor my obseruations, Which with experimental seal dothe warrant The tenure of my booke. **1608** TOPSELL *Serpents* 594 A certain experimental unguent known to be practised in this sport, made of the oyl pressed out of wilde radish. **1635** W. WOOD (*title*) Nevv Englands Prospect. A true, lively, and experimentall description of that part of America, commonly called Nevv England. **1668** *Excellency of Pen & Pencil* 46 An experimental Rule practised by the best Etcher in England. **1709** BERKELEY *Th. Vision* §72 Not a necessary but only an experimental connexion. **1869** GOULBURN *Purs. Holiness* Pref. 10 To bring myself and others to an experimental knowledge of God. **1879** KEANE tr. *Lefèvre's Philos.* ii. 141 Aristotle never ceases to oppose science to experimental knowledge.

c. *experimental religion*: practical experience of the influence of religion on the powers and operations of the soul. † *experimental divinity*:

the method of dealing with the conscience and religious feelings; so † *experimental divine*.

1614 BP. HALL *Epist.* I. vii, The one excelled in experimentall divinity; and knewe well how to stay a weake conscience, how to raise a fallen. **1658** L. WOMOCK *Exam. Tilenus* 85, I was never much taken with those Obadiahs .. give me your experimentall Divines.

II. Relating to experiment.

3. a. Based on, derived from, or ascertained by experiment.

1570 DEE *Math. Pref.* 30 That, was rather a kinde of Experimentall demonstration. **1674** C. GOODALL *College Phys. Vind.* (1676) 89 Their experimental demonstrations of the circulation of the Chyle. **1830** HERSCHEL *Stud. Nat. Phil.* 73 Legislation and politics become gradually regarded as experimental sciences. **1881** CARPENTER in *19th Cent.* 615 Experimental evidence has not yet .. been obtained of the direct penetration of the solar rays to more than 100 fathoms.

b. *experimental philosophy*: (*a*) the philosophy which insists on experiment as the necessary foundation and test of all reasoned conclusions; (*b*) physics or 'natural philosophy' as studied or demonstrated by means of experiments (now *rare*). So also, *experimental chemistry, physics, psychology, science.* Hence *experimental philosopher, physicist, psychologist, chemist*, etc.

1651 G. THOMSON (*title*), A vindication of Lord Bacon, the Auctor of Experimental Philosophy. **1665** GLANVILL *Sceps. Sci.* 68 All experimental philosophers have been needlessly imployed. **1706** S. CLARKE *On the Evidences* Pref. A iij, Robert Boyle was .. diligent and successful in improving experimental philosophy. **1809** *Med. Jrnl.* XXI. 175 Lectures .. at Guy's Hospital .. [on] Experimental Philosophy. **1819** *Pantologia, Experimental Philosophy* is an investigation of the wisdom of God in the works and laws of nature. **1833** J. S. MILL *Lett.* (1910) I. 59 Detrosier .. has some prospect of picking up a living as a lecturer on experimental physics. **1871-2** *Cassell's Techn. Educ.* II. 303 A physician and experimental chemist. **1878** S. H. HODGSON *Philos. Reflection* I. 227 Fortunately we possess a genuine *a posteriori* experimental psychology, a true science. **1887** J. THOMAS *Dict. Biog.* I. 421 Boyle .. a celebrated chemist and experimental philosopher. **1935** *Discovery* June 183/2 The *gestalt*-theorists, the behaviourists, and the experimental psychologists. **1952** J. A. PASSMORE in Stout *God & Nature* p. xxxvii, To Stout .. experimental psychology was a source of information, not a substitute for thinking. **1957** G. RYLE in C. A. Mace *Brit. Philos. in Mid-Century* 258 A not very ancient Oxford Chair of Physics still retains its old label, the Chair of Experimental Philosophy. **1958** J. CLEUGH tr. *Jungk's Brighter than Thousand Suns* i. 17 It was the theoretical, not the experimental, physicists who were to blame for the confusion.

transf. **1796** BURKE *Let. Noble Ld.* Wks. VIII. 55 As speculatists he [the Duke of Bedford] is a glorious subject for their experimental philosophy.

4. Of persons: Skilled in experiment. *rare.*

1811 PINKERTON *Petral.* II. 421 A more candid and equitable judge cannot be invoked than the patient and experimental Saussure.

5. Of the nature of an experiment; tentative.

1818 JAS. MILL *Brit. India* I. I. i. 16 A first and experimental attempt. **1857** RUSKIN *Pol. Econ. Art* 35 A young man's work .. may be more or less experimental.

6. a. Of or pertaining to experiments; used in or for making experiments. Freq. as *experimental farm.*

1792 A. YOUNG *Trav. France* 213 Signore Arduino .. shewed me the experimental farm. **1812** SIR H. DAVY *Chem. Philos.* Introd. 9, I have .. received much useful experimental aid from Mr. E. Davy. **1869** TYNDALL in *Fortn. Rev.* 1 Feb. 236 The experimental tube now before you. **1881** N. LOCKYER in *Nature* No. 617. 398 The spectrum of potassium .. varies very much under different experimental conditions. **1894** *Trans. R. Soc. Canada* XII. iv. 143 Six years ago the testing of trees and shrubs .. was begun at the experimental farms at Brandon, Manitoba. **1906** *Daily Colonist* (Victoria, B.C.) 14 Jan. 10/3 The Cigarmakers' union .. urged that the experimental farms for the growth of tobacco be established in Canada. **1911** C. E. W. BEAN *'Dreadnought' of Darling* xxv. 319 When Australian subeditors want to make the open page of their papers especially attractive, they cast on to it the great plans that are immediately ahead .. about new experimental farms to be planted in every district.

b. *spec.* of a theatre, play, etc.

1929 S. W. CHENEY *Theatre* xxiii. 520 Jacques Copeau .. administered one of the .. most fruitful of twentieth century experimental theatres. **1931** W. ROTHENSTEIN *Men & Memories* II. xxiv. 205 Experimental theatres are expensive things. **1961** BOWMAN & BALL *Theatre Lang.* 127 *Experimental*, said of drama, staging, a type of theatre, etc., which seeks freshness in the writing and production of plays rather than the traditional formulas for commercial or conventional success. **1969** GISH & PINCHOT *Lillian Gish* xiv. 194 An experimental theater was also hit.

† **B.** *sb.* [The *adj.* used *absol.*]

a. A trial, an experiment. **b.** An experimental proof. **c.** A fact or datum of experience. **d.** *pl.* Things learned by experience; experimental or practical knowledge.

a. 1659 C. NOBLE *Moderate Answ. to Immod. Queries* 1 Experimentals that have been made .. what kind of Government would best go down. **b. 1664** POWER *Exp. Philos.* II. 130 Pre-demonstrate them, by calculation, before the Senses give an Experimental thereof. **c. 1628** T. SPENCER *Logic* 5 Art is made, when as one vniversall thing, is framed out of many experimentalls. **1651** N. BACON *Disc. Govt. Eng.* II. xl. (1739) 176 Whose Counsels

are .. Notionary, and grounded .. not upon experimentals of most publick concernment. **d. 1748** RICHARDSON *Clarissa* (1811) III. 361 As to experimentals .. a mere novice.

experimentalism (ɛk.spɛrɪ'mɛntəlɪz(ə)m). [f. prec. + -ISM.]

1. a. The principles of the experimental school in philosophy or science; adherence to empirical doctrines. **b.** Empiricism in practice.

a **1834** COLERIDGE in *Rem.* (1836) III. 159 A scheme of physics and physiology compounded of Cartesian Mechanics and empiricism (for it was the credulous childhood of experimentalism). **1855** *Ess. Intuitive Mor.* 157 If this principle of general rules cannot be logically grafted on experimentalism. **1860** J. P. KENNEDY *Rob of Bowl* xvi. 183 A ready votary of that credulous experimentalism which has filled the world with victims to medical imposture.

2. Experimental research; the conducting of experiments. Cf. EXPERIMENTALIST 1. *rare.*

1842 *Fraser's Mag.* XXVI. 562 He has not the genius of experimentalism.

experimentalist (ɛk.spɛrɪ'mɛntəlɪst). [f. as prec. + -IST.]

1. One who devotes himself to experimental research in some branch of science; one who is skilled in performing experiments.

1762 W. JONES (of Nayland) *Ess. Nat. Phil.* I. iii. 26 There is hardly a motion in nature, which this fluid, when applied by a diligent experimentalist, is not capable of producing. **1787** W. MARSHALL *Norfolk* I. 366 Praise is due to every experimentalist in agriculture. **1794** G. ADAMS *Nat. & Exp. Philos.* I. v. 175 The qualities that distinguish an observer of nature from a mere experimentalist. **1812** SIR H. DAVY *Chem. Philos.* 20 This person .. was the last active experimentalist who believed that transmutation has actually been performed. **1881** LUBBOCK in *Nature* No. 618. 411 Faraday, the prince of pure experimentalists.

2. One who is fond of trying experiments, or who advocates new schemes.

1828 WHATELY *Rhet.* I. iii. §2 Being regarded as a dangerous experimentalist. **1857** TOULM. SMITH *The Parish* 363 Making 'districts' .. seems .. the favourite scheme of the experimentalists.

3. *nonce use.* One who has an experimental sense of religion.

1806 A. KNOX *Serm.* I. 34 The .. disagreement between the merely moral Christian and the experimentalist.

experimentalize (ɛk.spɛrɪ'mɛntəlaɪz), *v.* [f. as prec. + -IZE.] *intr.* To make or try experiments. Const. *on, upon*; also, in indirect passive.

1800 SOUTHEY *Life* (1850) II. 38 You may experimentalise, if you like. **1831** FR. A. KEMBLE *Let. in Rec. Girlhood* (1878) II. ix. 249 Though a poet should have a strongly passionate nature, he should .. be able to .. experimentalize with it. **1862** THORNBURY *Turner* I. 64 A few old masters that have been experimentalized on. **1873** SYMONDS *Grk. Poet* I. 2 We cannot experimentalize upon the process of ethnical development.

Hence **experi'mentalizer, experi'mentalizing** *vbl. sb.*

1857 TOULM. SMITH *The Parish* 1 A great saving of time and trouble to the experimentalizer. **1882** F. G. KERR in *Macm. Mag.* XLVI. 448 The device .. left the experimentaliser with a virtual mute on his hands. **1865** *Pall Mall G.* 17 Oct. 10 They continue their guessings and experimentalizings, and wisely continue them.

experimentally (ɛk.spɛrɪ'mɛntəlɪ), *adv.* [f. EXPERIMENTAL *a.* + -LY².]

1. By experience; as the result of experience.

1593 R. HARVEY *Philad.* 106 Trusting none, but which they find certainly, and experimentally true. **1644** BP. HALL *Serm. Rem. Wks.* (1660) 110 Those solid divines that experimentally know what belongs to the healing of a sinful soul. **1674** R. GODFREY *Inj. & Ab. Physic* 25, I speak experimentally: for I .. took several .. such poysonous Medicines. *a* **1716** SOUTH *Serm.* (1744) VII. vii. 135 A king .. experimentally acquainted with the ways .. of flatterers. **1833** LAMB *Elia* (1860) 367, I do not understand these matters experimentally. **1836** W. BURGH (*title*), The Divinity of Christ experimentally Considered.

2. By means of experiment.

1646 SIR T. BROWNE *Pseud. Ep.* III. iv. 112 Thus was it .. experimentally refuted by one Sestius a Physitian. **1684-5** BOYLE *Min. Waters* Advt., The way of experimentally exploring portions of a Mineral Water. **1762** FOOTE *Orator* I. Wks. 1799 I. 205 Several churches and chapels .. where the sleep-compelling power will be experimentally demonstrated to exist. **1793** BEDDOES *Math. Evid.* Ded. 7 For who ever heard of .. Geometry .. being proved experimentally? **1856** KANE *Arct. Expl.* I. x. 110 The curvature of the runners was determined experimentally.

3. By way of experiment.

1862 *Rep. Dir. E. Ind. Railw. Co.* 15, I proposed a road entirely of wrought iron, experimentally, of a mile in length.

† **ex.perimen'tarian**, *a.* and *sb. Obs.* [f. EXPERIMENT *sb.* + -ARIAN.]

A. *adj.* Relying on experiment; = EXPERIMENTAL. **B.** *sb.* One who relies on experiment, an experimental philosopher.

1661 BOYLE *Examen* v. (1682) 46 Mr. Hobbs is pleased to call us Experimentarian Philosophers. **1690** —— *Chr. Virtuoso* I. Wks. 1772 V. 536 Another thing that qualifies an experimentarian for the reception of a revealed religion .. is that [etc.]. **1816** D. STEWART in *Encycl. Brit.* Supp. I. 62 Hobbes .. treating the experimentarian philosophers as objects only of contempt.

† **experi'mentate**, *ppl. a. Obs. rare*⁻¹. [ad. Fr. *expérimenté*, pa. pple. of *expérimenter* f.

*expérimen*t EXPERIMENT *sb.* See -ATE².] Arising in the course of experience; experimental.

1651 BIGGS *New Disp.* Pref. 2 And having had an experimentate opportunity to know.

†**experi'mentate,** *v. Obs. rare*⁻¹. [f. Fr. *expérimenter* to EXPERIMENT *sb.*: see -ATE³.] *trans.* To make an experiment of, to try as an experiment.

1670 G. H. *Hist. Cardinals* III. III. 325 This advertisement was experimentated by the Heads of the Factions.

experimentation (ɛkˌspɛrɪmən'teɪʃən). [f. EXPERIMENT *v.* + -ATION. Cf. Fr. *expérimentation.*] The action or process of experimenting or making experiments; a series of experiments.

1675 PETTY *Disc. Dupl. Proportion* 67 If the just length of any one Gun hath been well found by good Experimentation, then may also be known the length of every Gun. *a* **1734** NORTH *Lives* III. 230 He was..resolved not to be a subject of the artist's experimentations. **1862** R. H. PATTERSON *Ess. Hist. & Art* 78 Many things in science were deduced which only modern experimentation could establish. **1875** H. C. WOOD *Therap.* (1879) 47 This method of experimentation can throw but little light upon, etc.

experimentative (ɛkˌspɛrɪ'mɛntətɪv), *a.* [f. EXPERIMENT *v.* + -ATIVE.] Inclined to make or venturing upon an experiment; of the nature of an experiment.

1825 COLERIDGE *Aids Refl.* Pref. (1848) I. 19 Without a certain portion of gratuitous and..experimentative faith in the writer. **1885** G. W. CABLE in *Century Mag.* XXIX. 412 Any experimentative truce.

†**ex'perimenˌtator.** *Obs. rare.* [f. EXPERIMENTATE *v.* + -OR.] **a.** An experimenter. **b.** One who relies on experiment; an empiric.

a. 1651 BIGGS *New Disp.* ¶72 As that mechanick experimentator hath it in his Sylva Sylvarum. *a* **1691** BOYLE *Contn. New Exp.* Wks. 1772 IV. 507 The experiments themselves, and also the design of the experimentators requiring [etc.]. **1748** *Lond. Mag.* 209 The Lead..would depart in a rectilinear Direction from the Hands of the Experimentator.

b. 1684 tr. *Bonet's Merc. Compit.* Pref. 2 He..may be called..an Experimentator, if he practise Physick upon Experiments, not true Experience.

experimented (ɛk'spɛrɪməntɪd), *ppl. a.* Also 6 experiment. [f. EXPERIMENT *v.* + -ED¹.]

1. Of persons: Experienced; practised or versed *in* (an art). Now *rare.* Cf. Fr. *expérimenté.*

c **1477** CAXTON *Jason* 120 b, Ye are right wise and well experimented in plente of hye sciences. *c* **1520** PACE in Strype *Eccl. Mem.* I. App. xi. 21 Spanyardys, in that facultie wonderfullie experimentid or learnid. **1549** *Compl. Scot.* Prol. 14 He estemeis vs to be litil experementit in the veyris. **1582–8** *Hist. James VI* (1804) 110 Learnit men, weill experiment in physick. **1662** GERBIER *Princ.* 16 Divers experimented Architects. **1883** *Gd. Words* 144 No mere writer, but a man thoroughly experimented in the world.

†**2.** Of a remedy: Proved or tried by experiment or experience; approved. Of a fact, etc.: Known by experience or experiment; ascertained, authenticated. *Obs.*

1545 RAYNOLD *Byrth Mankynde* Prol. (1634) 2 Diuers..more experimented and more familiar medicines. **1584** R. SCOT *Discov. Witchcr.* XIV. viii. 312 So manie experimented examples. **1608** TOPSELL *Serpents* 622 A late physitian, prescribeth an experimented..oyl against any poyson taken into the body. **1677** HALE *Prim. Orig. Man.* I. i. 8 For want of a clear, and sensible, and experimented observation. **1710** T. FULLER *Pharm. Extemp.* 103 A Noble, Experimented..Remedy. **1807** HUTTON *Course Math.* (1811) II. 376 The experimented resistance..is nearly ¼ part more than that which is assigned by the theory.

†**3.** Met with in the course of experience; = EXPERIENCED 2. *Obs.*

1682 *Lond. Gaz.* No. 1707/5 Disorder, Slavery, and the worst of Experimented Mischiefs. **1715** D'ANOIS *Wks.* 105 The experimented Vexations of my first Marriage made me afraid to venture. **1812** HENRY *Camp. agst. Quebec* 199 This is said from experimented woe and extreme calamity.

exˌperimen'tee. *rare.* [f. EXPERIMENT *v.* + -EE¹.] One on whom an experiment is made.

1890 *Lippincott's Mag.* Feb. 241 A second trial is made to test the length of time during which the experimentee can maintain his previous grip. **1904** *Daily Chron.* 14 May 4/6 After a year of this 'starvation diet' the 'experimentees' were stronger.

experimenter (ɛk'spɛrɪməntə(r)). Also 7, 9 (*erron.*) -or. [f. EXPERIMENT *v.* + -ER¹.] One who experiments; one who makes or tries experiments.

1570 DEE *Math. Pref.* 28 You see, how the Mechanicien and Experimenter..are..tought. **1660** BOYLE *New Exp. Phys. Mech.* i. (1682) 17 That noble experimenter—Monsieur Pascal. **1694** SLARE in *Phil. Trans.* XVIII. 203 The Experimentors of this Age. *a* **1774** GOLDSM. *Exper. Philos.* (1776) I. 293 A work of this kind would require assiduity in the experimenter. **1816** J. SMITH *Panorama Sc. & Art* II. 87 The experimentor should have the weights of his globe in air and in water. **1830** HERSCHEL *Stud. Nat. Phil.* 319 Dilatation of solids has been made a subject of repeated and careful measurement by several experimenters.

experimentist (ɛk'spɛrɪməntɪst). [f. EXPERIMENT *sb.* + -IST.] A systematic experimenter.

1667 EVELYN *Mem.* (1857) III. 195 Our registers have outdone..all the Experimentists, nay, the great Verulam himself.

experimentize (ɛk'spɛrɪmənˌtaɪz), *v. rare.* [f. as prec. + -IZE.]

1. *intr.* To make an experiment or experiments.

1847 DARWIN in *Life & Lett.* (1887) I. 359, I thought I would experimentise on Falconer and Bunbury. **1860** *Chamb. Jrnl.* XIV. 313 Sir Thomas Browne..experimentised unsuccessfully in spontaneous generation.

2. *trans.* To make the subject of an experiment.

Hence **ex'perimentized, -izing** *ppl. adjs.*

1779 T. TWINING *Recreat. & Stud.* (1882) 74 He is a searching, experimentizing, active-minded man. **1832** *Fraser's Mag.* IV. 721 Shameful experiments..which threatened destruction to the experimentised.

†**ex'perimently,** *adv. Obs.* [f. EXPERIMENT *sb.* + -LY².] By experience; as a matter of experience; only in phrase ***to know experimently.***

1546 BALE *Eng. Votaries* I. (1550) 21 Se what our auncient Englysh writers had sayth in thys matter, whych more experimently knewe it. **1658** A. FOX tr. *Wurtz' Surg.* II. xiv. 105 Which I know experimently. **1805** SOUTHEY *Lett.* (1856) I. 318 If you did but know as experimently as I do.

experimentor: see EXPERIMENTER.

‖**experimentum crucis** (ɛkspɛrɪˌmɛntəm 'kruːsɪs). [mod.L., 'crucial experiment': see CRUCIAL *a.* 2.] A decisive test that shows which one of several hypotheses is correct; a crucial experiment.

1672 [see CRUCIAL *a.* 2]. **1751** HUME *Eng. Princ. Mor.* v. ii. 84 The *Experimentum crucis,* or that Experiment, which points out the Way we should follow, in any Doubt or Ambiguity. **1814** *Phil. Trans. R. Soc.* CIV. 212 We may therefore consider the preceding result as an *experimentum crucis,* which establishes the opinion respecting the structure of the agate. **1856** *Spiritual Herald* Mar. 37 The injustice of our opponents in imposing any conditions of their own at an *experimentum crucis* of this kind. **1880** W. JAMES *Coll. Ess. & Rev.* (1920) 169 The partizans of feelings of efferent innervation regard them [*sc.* illusions of a certain kind] as *experimenta crucis.* **1949** W. KNEALE *Probability* §22. 110 If..they..cannot devise an *experimentum crucis,* they begin to suspect that the two rival hypotheses differ only in their symbolic formulation.

†**expe'rrection.** *Obs.* [n. of action f. L. *expergisci* (ppl. stem *experrect-*) to wake up.] The action of waking up.

1603 HOLLAND *Plutarch's Mor.* 1314 The Phrygians..celebrate in the one season, the feast of lying in bed and sleeping: in the other of experrection or waking.

expert ('ɛkspɜːt, ɛk'spɜːt), *a.*¹ Also 4–6 experte. [a. OF. *expert, espert,* ad. L. *expert-us,* pa. pple. (act. and pass.) of *experīrī* to try: see EXPERIENCE *sb.* Cf. APERT, ASPERT.]

I. In active sense.

†**1.** Experienced (*in*), having experience (*of*). *Obs.*

c **1374** CHAUCER *Troylus* II. 1318 Tho that bene expert in love. *c* **1386** —— *Can. Yeom. Prol. & T.* 698 That ye mow taken heede, And ben expert of this..This dicipline, and this crafty science. **14..** *Prose Legends* in *Anglia* VIII. 133 Þe þridde tyme [she] was experte of dethe. **1432–50** tr. *Higden* (Rolls) I. 67 The testimonies of men experte whiche haue writen theyme to haue seen that place. *a* **1556** LD. MORLEY tr. *Boccaccio's De Preclaris Mulieribus* i, [Eve] beynge after experte of the paynes of berynge of children. **1630** *R. Johnson's Kingd. & Commw.* 52 Frequent the company of the expert, that by noting their observations..you may [etc.]. **1672** PETTY *Pol. Anat.* (1691) 27 A Protestant Militia of 25,000, the most whereof are expert in War.

¶As pa. pple. act. with verbal regimen: Having tested, having had experience of. *Obs.* (a mere Latinism).

1382 WYCLIF *Eccl.* viii. 5 Who kepeth the hest, shal not ben expert any thing of euel. *c* **1400** *Lanfranc's Cirurg.* 33 (MS. A) Galion and Auicen and I þat am expert here seiynge, we seie þat [etc.]. **1513** DOUGLAS *Æneis* I. iv. 77 The craigis quhar monstrous Ciclopes dwell ȝe ar expert.

2. Trained by experience or practice, skilled, skilful. Const. *at, in,* †*intil,* †*of,* to with *inf.*

c **1374** CHAUCER *Troylus* I. 67 Calcas..in science so experte. *c* **1386** —— *Prol.* 577 Maystres..That were of lawe expert and curious. **14..** *Prose Legends* in *Anglia* VIII. 143 Men were often expert to socour. *c* **1425** WYNTOUN *Cron.* VIII. xxxv. 36 He expart wes in-tyl swilk thyng. **1549** *Compl. Scot.* Prol. 12 Clerkis..ar mair expert in latyne tong nor i am. **1570** DEE *Math. Pref.* 12 Many places, in the Ciuile law, require an expert Arithmeticien. **1632** LITHGOW *Trav.* v. 188 Neither are they [Turks] expert Mariners. **1697** DAMPIER *Voy.* (1729) I. v. 116 Thick woods, where the Spaniards might easily lay in ambush..at which they are very expert. **1777** WATSON *Philip II* (1793) III. XIX. 23 Expert both in the arts of peace and war. **1870** BRYANT *Iliad* I. II. 67 Idomeneus expert to wield the spear. **1873** HALE *In His Name* viii. 69 The Florentine was not expert in ecclesiastical matters.

b. Hence of personal qualities or acquirements.

1542 UDALL tr. *Erasm. Apoph.* 269 a, In the experte knowelage of warre kepyng. **1563** SHUTE *Archit.* B ij b, To haue experte knowladg in drawing. **1665** MANLEY *Grotius' Low C. Warres* 176 The War..grew very hot, not so much by the greatness of the Forces as the expert Valour of the Captains.

c. ***expert system*** (*Computing*): a program or group of programs designed to store and apply the knowledge of experts in a given field, so that others can use it for deciding, evaluating, or inferring in that field.

1977 *Proc. 5th Internat. Joint Conf. Artificial Intelligence* 994/1 The development of expert systems in the context of formal task environments such as mathematics. **1983** *Austral. Microcomputer Mag.* Nov. 18/2 A market exists for expert systems because in certain decision-making situations, the systems are better than the human experts in the field. **1983** *Internat. Managem.* Dec. 5/3 ICOT is concentrating for now on the development of two 'expert systems' — intelligent computer programs that can solve problems or reach conclusions usually requiring the knowledge of human experts. **1986** *McGraw-Hill Yearbk. Sci. & Technol.* 1987 75/2 Attempts to use this technology began in 1976 with the development of an expert system to diagnose diseased soybean plants.

†**II. 3.** In passive sense: Tried, proved by experience. In early use often (after Lat.) as mere pple. *Obs.*

1387 TREVISA *Higden* (Rolls) I. 119 Whiche thynge was experte..of ii. men. *c* **1430** LYDG. *Bochas* III. xiii. 112 a, This same thyng was wel expert and preued. *c* **1450** *St. Cuthbert* (Surtees) 6030 For his [St. Cuthbert's] help in othir case..þis true monk had expert. **1494** FABYAN *Chron.* VII. 463 That as well was experte in Fraunce as in the ile of Englande. **1523** LD. BERNERS *Froiss.* Pref. 1 He that hath the perfyte knowledge of others joye..hath thexpert doctryne of all parylles. **1586** COGAN *Haven Health* xiv. (1636) 39 A perfect water, and expert against melancholy. **1604** SHAKS. *Oth.* II. i. 49 His Pylot [is] Of verie expert, and approu'd Allowance. **1612** *Enchirid. Med.* 156 It is an expert medicine.

†**ex'pert,** *a.*² *Obs.* [ad. L. *expert-em,* lit. 'having no part (in)', f. *ex-* (see EX- *pref.*¹) + *part-, pars* PART.] Destitute or devoid of, free from.

1432–50 tr. *Higden* (Rolls) I. 337 Thouȝhe..Bede..seye that londe not to be experte of vynes. **1608** CHAPMAN *Byron's Conspiracy* Plays 1873 II. 197 Into purest ayre Expert of humor. **1616** —— *Homer's Hymns, To Venus* 358 He..should immortality breathe, Expert of age and woe as well as death. **1655–60** STANLEY *Hist. Philos.* (1701) 190/2 A principle is expert of generation and corruption.

expert ('ɛkspɜːt), *sb.* [a. mod. F. *expert* (the adj. used subst.); see EXPERT *a.*¹]

1. One who is expert or has gained skill from experience. Const. *at, in, with.*

1853 KANE *Grinnell Exp.* xxxiii. (1856) 283 Every man arranged his knapsack and blanket-bag..with the practiced discretion of an expert. **1856** —— *Arct. Expl.* I. xi. 24 Hans Christian..an expert with the kayak and javelin. **1866** ROGERS *Agric. & Prices* I. xxi. 523 Such manors as possessed wood generally containing an expert at hurdle-making. **1882** A. W. WARD *Dickens* iv. 100 He was frank and explicit with experts, in the writer's art.

2. One whose special knowledge or skill causes him to be regarded as an authority; a specialist. Also *attrib.*, as in ***expert evidence, witness,*** etc.

1825 *Act 6 Geo. IV*, c. 59 §4 The nomination of experts to ascertain and fix the price. **1858** *Sat. Rev.* VI. 645/1 Experts in insanity. **1869** ROGERS *Adam Smith's W.N.* Pref. I. 11 Misled by the selfish misrepresentations of reputed experts. **1873** BROWNING *Red Cott. Nt.-cap* 184 Purchase at the price adjudged By experts. **1884** *Pall Mall G.* 22 Sept. 6/1 An expert court of first instance..might be of use. **1890** *Law Times' Rep.* LXIII. 684/2 A mining engineer and expert of well-known reputation.

b. In recent use *esp.* one skilled in the study of handwritings.

1858 *Sat. Rev.* V. 656/1 Professional experts swear to their belief in the peeress's authorship. **1868** E. EDWARDS *Raleigh* I. xix. 385 The obliterated names can scarcely..be read by the most painstaking expert. **1882** *Standard* 21 Oct. 2/5 To him [Netherclift] the term 'Expert' was first applied. **1886** BESANT *Childr. Gibeon.* II. xiii, My writing was well known; experts swore that the forgery was by me.

†**ex'pert,** *v.*¹ *Obs.* [f. L. *expert-* ppl. stem of *experīrī* to try: see EXPERIENCE *sb.*, EXPERT *a.*¹] *trans.* To experience; to know by experience. Hence **ex'perted** *ppl. a.*, experienced.

1432–50 tr. *Higden* (Rolls) I. 183 The women experte the knowledge of diverse men. **1475** *Bk. Noblesse* (1860) 60 They have no sufficient bookis..and be not expertid. **1553** S. CABOT *Ordinances* in Hakluyt *Voy.* (1589) 262 For declaration of the trueth which you shall haue experted. **1579** SPENSER *Sheph. Cal.* Nov. 183 Knewe wee..what it [death] us bringes untill, Dye would we daylie, once it to expert. **1587** FLEMING *Contn. Holinshed* III. 1. 306/1 This Thomas was a man..experted..in ecclesiasticall matters.

'**expert,** *v.*² Chiefly *N. Amer. colloq.* [f. EXPERT *sb.*] *trans.* To examine as an expert; to have (books, etc.) examined by an expert. So **ex'perting** *vbl. sb.*, expert examination or its results.

1889 in *Cent. Dict.* **1901** *Daily Colonist* (Victoria, B.C.) 26 Oct. 6/6 Colonel Linsley with a party of men has been in the coal region for the past couple of weeks experting the fields for the company. **1948** G. H. JOHNSTON *Death takes Small Bites* i. 13 'But what about Japan or the Philippines? Wouldn't you find more there to write about?' 'No. Both played out. They've been experted all the way from page one to the obituaries.' **1956** G. BOWEN *Wool Away!* (ed. 2) vi. 74 The next phase of experting a new comb is to scrape

or rub the tips on wood. *Ibid.* 75, I trust that the experting as set out in this text will be a practical guide and help to all, as good gear is the foundation of all good shearing. **1969** 'H. PENTECOST' *Girl Watcher's Funeral* (1970) III. ii. 148 We've done some experting on the trajectory of the body's fall.

expertise (ɛkspəˈtiːz). [Fr.] **a.** Expert opinion or knowledge, often obtained through the action of submitting a matter to, and its consideration by, experts; an expert's appraisal, valuation, or report. **b.** The quality or state of being expert; skill or expertness in a particular branch of study or sport.

1868 READE *Foul Play* III. x. 120, I have distanced my competitors in expertise. **1897** *Daily News* 19 Nov. 5/1 This looks as though Mr. Sellar has been uniformly unfortunate in his expertise. **1898** *Ibid.* 10 Feb. 5/4 He was suffered to attack the 'expertise', which the first court-martial accepted. **1898** *2nd Rep. Sci. & Art Mus.* 28 in *Parl. Papers* XI. 9 Sir Edward Maunde Thompson.. pointed out that expertise is not necessarily gained by having a large staff. **1907** A. BENNETT *Grim Smile of Five Towns* 283 How could I be expected..to judge delicate points of expertise in earthenware? **1922** J. D. BERESFORD *Prisoners of Hartling* ii. 17 Arthur [a doctor] would have liked to give a ready diagnosis of this abnormal condition, but his expertise was not equal to the task. **1924** R. H. MOTTRAM *Spanish Farm* 50 He was measuring fields for an 'expertise', a professional assessment. **1934** *Discovery* June 175/2 The expert is only capable of giving opinions within the special field of his own *expertise*. **1950** B. WOOTTON *Testament Social Sci.* p. v, Unfortunately, those who have sufficient *expertise* are few, and greatly occupied with their own specialisms. **1953** 'M. INNES' *Christmas at Candleshoe* ix. 104 '*Why* does he get a fee?' 'For making an expertise... That, it seems, is the technical term.' **1955** W. GIRVAN *Flying Saucers* v. 63 One might just as reasonably deny the existence of the stars in which he claims such expertise. **1970** *Insight* Nov. 1/2 A team of people with highly specialised expertise: buyers, economists, journalists, researchers with the knowledge and training to deal with consumer problems.

expertism (ˈɛkspətɪz(ə)m). [f. EXPERT *sb.* + -ISM.] The quality of being an expert.

1886 *Sat. Rev.* 30 Jan. 150 Mr. Arch..could claim..the right of expertism. **1890** *Cape Law Jrnl.* VII. 109 Medical Expertism considered from its legal standpoint.

ˈexpertize, *v.* [f. as prec. + -IZE.] **1.** *intr.* To act as an expert. Freq. **ˈexpertizing** *vbl. sb.*

1889 *Harper's Mag.* Feb. 336/2 So complex and difficult are the questions involved in expertizing. **1900** *Spectator* LXXXV. 521/1 (*title*) The morality of 'expertizing'. **1922** *Readers' Guide to Periodical Lit. 1919–21* V. 525/1 Expertising in art. **1956** R. STOUT *Before Midnight* 158 A mob of experts was expertizing in every direction, and Fritz was seated on Wolfe's chair behind his desk, watching them.

2. *trans.* (Also **expertise.**) To give an expert opinion on; to evaluate, assess.

1930 *Times Lit. Suppl.* 24 July 613/4 By applying the methods he used in 'expertising' old paintings and furniture John Ballinger, art expert, discovered the murderer. **1932** *Brooklyn Mus. Q.* XIX. 74/1 Professor Jean Capart..has been..expertizing the Wilbour collections.

expertly (ˈɛkspɜːtlɪ, ɛkˈspɜːtlɪ), *adv.* [f. EXPERT *a.*[1] + -LY[2].] In an expert manner. †**a.** As one who has had experience; by actual experiment. †**b.** As one who has been proved or tried. **c.** Skilfully.

a. *c* **1420** *Pallad. on Husb.* VII. 110 Unbynde it thenne, and there expertly se How oon tree is in til an other ronne.
b. **1548** VICARY *Anat.* (1888) 11 Not for them that be expertly seene in the Anatomie. **1652** GAULE *Magastrom.* 114 Their..counselling..that an astrologer be a man both expertly ethicall and physicall?
c. **1798** EDGEWORTH *Pract. Educ.* (1811) I. 457 Children may answer expertly to the questions, What is attention? What is memory?

expertness (ˈɛkspɜːtnɪs, ɛkˈspɜːtnɪs). [f. as prec. + -NESS.]

The quality or condition of being expert.

†**a.** Experience, thorough knowledge. Const. *of.*

1659 B. HARRIS *Parival's Iron Age* 302 Their enemies expertnesse of the Countrie troubling their marches.

b. Skill derived from practice; readiness, dexterity. Const. *in.*

1601 SHAKS. *All's Well* IV. iii. 202 You shall demaund.. what his valour, honestie, and expertnesse in warres. **1682** NORRIS *Hierocles* 17 Great knowledge and expertness in the laws of God. **1797** BEWICK *Brit. Birds* (1847) I. 286 From it's expertness in cracking them [it] has obtained it's name [nuthatch]. *a* **1859** MACAULAY *Hist. Eng.* V. 84 Portland, with..great expertness in business, was no scholar. **1884** SEELEY in *Contemp. Rev.* Nov. 656 He might pass for a prodigy of literary expertness.

‖**experto crede** (ɛkˌspɜːtəʊ ˈkriːdɪ), *phr.* [ad. L. *experto credite* (Virgil *Aeneid* xi. 283), f. *experto* dat. sing. of *expertus*, pa. pple. of *experiri* to experience + *crede*, *credite* imp. sing. and pl. of *credere* to believe.] Believe one who has experienced or tried; believe me, I know.

1579 GOSSON *Sch. Abuse* f. 17ʳ, *Experto crede*, I have seene somewhat, and therefore I thinke I may say the more. **1732** SWIFT *Let.* 4 May (1965) IV. 14 You may beckon a blackguard boy under a gate, near your visiting place (*experto crede*) Save eleven pence; and get half a crown's worth of health. **1872** GEO. ELIOT *Middlem.* III. v. xlv. 49 Take care—*experto crede*—take care not to get hampered about money matters. **1906** 'Q' *Mayor of Troy* ix. 124 Sir Felix, whose temper—*experto crede*—is seldom at its best in the small hours. *a* **1936** KIPLING *Something of Myself* (1937) viii. 208 The magic lies in the Brush and the Ink...*Experto crede.* **1937** J. M. MURRY *Necessity of Pacifism* 131 Such a discipline.. I have come to believe is necessary to the spiritual health of such a community as I here envisage. *Experto crede.*

expertship (ˈɛkspɜːtʃɪp). [f. EXPERT *sb.* + -SHIP.] The condition or dignity of an expert.

1880 *Daily News* 9 Sept. 5/1 Persons who would be.. affronted if their expertship in cricketing matters were denied.

†**exˈpetible**, *a. Obs.* [ad. L. *expetibil-is*, f. *expetĕre* to desire, f. *ex-* (see EX- *pref.*[1]) + *petĕre* to seek.] To be wished for or desired; desirable.

1569 NEWTON *Cicero's Old Age* 30 a, Somethinge.. excellente, and for itself onely expetible. **1655–60** STANLEY *Hist. Philos.* I. IV. 4 Particular pleasure is expetible in it selfe. **1679** PULLER *Moder. Ch. Eng.* xiv. 410 An establishment, somewhat less perfect with [uniformity]..is more expetible than an appointment in some Circumstances more perfect, without [uniformity]. **1721–1800** in BAILEY.

Hence †**exˈpetibleness**, the quality of being desirable.

1775 in ASH.

expiable (ˈɛkspɪəb(ə)l), *a.* [a. F. *expiable*, ad. L. *expiābilis*, f. *expiāre*: see EXPIATE.] Capable of being expiated; admitting of expiation.

1570 LEVINS *Manip.* 3 Expiable, *expiabilis*. **1575** FULKE *Conf. Purg.* (1577) 225 The popish purgatory, where none but veniall and light sinners are expiable. **1614** BP. HALL *Epist.* III. vii, Gothes..have thought this wrong [adultery] not expiable, but by blood. **1838** LYTTON *Leila* III. i, Any connexion between a Christian knight and a Jewess was deemed a sin, scarce expiable.

†**ˈexpiament.** *Obs.*$^{-0}$ [as if ad. L. **expiāmentum* f. *expiāre*: see EXPIATE.] An expiation.

1727 in BAILEY vol. II.

†**ˈexpiate**, *ppl. a. Obs. rare*$^{-1}$. [ad. L. *expiāt-us*, pa. pple. of *expiāre*: see next.] Of an appointed time: Fully come. Cf. EXPIATE *v.* 7.

1594 SHAKS. *Rich. III*, III. iii. 23 Make haste, the houre of death is expiate [*later folios*, now expir'd].

expiate (ˈɛkspɪeɪt), *v.* Also 7 expiat. [f. L. *expiāt-* ppl. stem of *expiāre* to make satisfaction, f. *ex-* (see EX- *pref.*[1]) + *piāre* to seek to appease (by sacrifice), f. *pius* devout.]

†**1.** *trans.* To avert (evil) by religious ceremonies; to avert the evil portended by (a prodigy or prophecy). *Obs.* exc. *Antiq.*

1611 BIBLE *Isa.* xlvii. 11 Mischiefe shall fall vpon thee, thou shalt not be able to put it off [*marg.* expiate]. **1652** BROME *Joviall Crew* II. Wks. 1873 III. 381 You bring him a perpetual Peace and Joy By expiating the Prophecy that torments him. **1865** DYER *Hist. City Rome* II. (1883) 114 Frequent showers of stones..could..be expiated only by bringing to Rome Cybele, or the Idæan mother.

†**2.** To cleanse, purify (a person, a city) from guilt or pollution by religious ceremonies. Occas. Const. *of. Obs.*

1603 FLORIO *Montaigne* (1634) 292 Iphigenia..should by her death..expiate, towards God, the Grecians armie of the offences which they had committed. **1618** BOLTON *Florus* I. xiii. (1636) 41 That the city..might..seeme to have been.. hallowed and expiated. **1652** GAULE *Magastrom.* 262 The Elæans condemned the Oxe for the murder, and..were admonished by the Delphick Oracle to expiate the oxe. **1655–60** STANLEY *Hist. Philos.* (1701) 57/2 He Lustrated and Expiated the City.

3. To do away or extinguish the guilt of (one's sin); to offer or serve as a propitiation for. †*to expiate oneself* (*rare*): to do penance.

1608 BP. HALL *Char. Virtues & V.* II. 89 No repentance can expiate that [sin]. **1634** HABINGTON *Castara* (Arb.) 134 Once dead, his sin Man cannot expiate with teares. **1673** MARVELL *Reh. Transp.* II. 379 J. M...has ever since expiated himself in a retired silence. **1711** ADDISON *Spect.* No. 99 ¶7 An Affront that nothing but Blood can expiate. **1736** BUTLER *Anal.* II. v. Wks. 1874 I. 213 Repentance alone being sufficient to expiate guilt, appears to be contrary to the general sense of mankind. **1847** GROTE *Greece* II. xxxii. (1849) IV. 279 The Agyllæans were still expiating the sin by a periodical solemnity. **1867** SMILES *Huguenots Eng.* ix. (1880) 154 By punishing them, he flattered himself that he was expiating his own sins.

4. To pay the penalty of.

1665 MANLEY *Grotius' Low C. Warres* 691 These Pirats.. expiated their inhumane Villanies with their heads. **1823** LAMB *Elia* Ser. I. xxiii. (1865) 179 The child and parent.. expiating their fallen condition upon..[a] shopboard. **1848** MACAULAY *Hist. Eng.* I. 655 Some of the girls who had presented the standard to Monmouth at Taunton had cruelly expiated their offence. **1875** STUBBS *Const. Hist.* I. iii. 43 He has to expiate the act with his life.

5. To make amends or reparation for.

a **1626** BACON *Speech* in *Rem.* (1679) 132 Such..Felons, who..shall implore His Majesty's..Permission to expiate their Offences by their Assiduous Labours. **1774** PENNANT *Tour Scot.* in 1772, 209 [They] expiated their crime by restoring the plunder. **1856** EMERSON *Eng. Traits, Result* Wks. (Bohn) II. 135 They are expiating the wrongs of India by benefits.

†**6.** *intr.* To make expiation *for. Obs.*

1600 HOLLAND *Livy* I. I. xiv. 10 To expiate for the injuries of the Embassadours. **1681–6** J. SCOTT *Chr. Life* (1747) III. 590 My Mediation, which was..to expiate for you as a Priest. **1710** PRIDEAUX *Orig. Tithes* iv. 165 He gave..Tithes ..to expiate for the Death of Ethelbert. **1778** *Eliza Warwick* II. 131, I trust this will expiate for all my offences towards her. **1827** SOUTHEY *Hist. Persian War* II. 692 His success in sieges did not expiate..for the loss in men.

†**7.** To extinguish (a person's rage) by suffering it to the full; to end (one's sorrows, a suffering life) by death. *Obs.*

1594 MARLOWE & NASHE *Dido* v. ii, Cursed Iarbas, die to expiate The grief that tires upon thine inward soul! **1594** [see EXPIATE *ppl. a.*]. *c* **1600** SHAKS. *Sonn.* xxii, Then look I death my daies should expiate. **1610** TOFTE *Honour's Acad.* 39 Nothing could appease and expiat his cankred rage. **1615** T. ADAMS *Lycanthropy* 29 Somewhat to expiate their savage fury.

Hence **ˈexpiated**, **ˈexpiating** *ppl. adjs.*, **ˈexpiatist** = EXPIATOR.

1840 G. S. FABER *Regeneration* 38 A light from above had infused itself into my expiated..bosom. **1793** PENNANT *London* (1813) 270 Lying within their [friaries'] expiating walls. *a* **1848** R. W. HAMILTON (Ogilvie) *Expiatist.*

expiation (ɛkspɪˈeɪʃən). [ad. L. *expiātiōn-em*, n. of action f. *expiāre* to EXPIATE.]

1. The action of expiating or making atonement for (crime, etc.). *in expiation* (*of*): for the purpose of expiating. *to make expiation*: to atone. Also, the condition or state of being expiated.

1482 *Monk of Evesham* (Arb.) 68 The recompensacyon and expyacyon of the grete and longe schrewdenes and cursydnes. **1561** T. NORTON *Calvin's Inst.* IV. 146 The sacrifice of expiation is that which tendeth to appease the wrath of God. **1611** SPEED *Theat. Gt. Brit.* (1614) 141/2 The Abbey..at Dublin, builded..in expiation of the murther of Thomas Archbishop of Canterbury. **1681–6** J. SCOTT *Chr. Life* (1747) III. 101 He made Expiation for our Sins on the Cross. **1796** BURKE *Regic. Peace* iii. Wks. VIII. 297 Modes of expiation..devised by anxious, restless guilt. **1828** SCOTT *F.M. Perth* xx, I will found masses for his soul, in expiation of my guilt. **1883** FROUDE *Short Stud.* IV. I. xii. 156 A more complete expiation..might be necessary before the avenging spirit..could be pacified.

b. *Fast* (or *Feast*) *of Expiation* : a ceremony observed by the Jews on the 10th day of Tisri, at which the High Priest made expiation for his own sins and the sins of the people. *Day of Expiation*: the day set apart for this observance; = 'Day of Atonement'. Also *Expiation-Day.*

1674 BLOUNT *Glossogr.*, The Feast of Expiation. *a* **1711** KEN *Hymns Festiv.* Poet. Wks. 1721 I. 317 God no Command for Fasts wou'd lay, But on their [Jews'] Expiation-Day. *a* **1713** SHARP *Serm. Matt.* xii. Wks. 1754 III. xi. 201 The solemn day of expiation, which came once a year. **1886** *Whitaker's Almanack* 9 [*Jewish Calendar*], Oct. 9 Fast of Expiation 5647 Tisri 10.

c. The action of ceremonially purifying from guilt or pollution.

1532 MORE *Confut. Tindale* Wks. 376/1 The ceremonies of the expiacion or purgyng of the tabernacle. **1651** BAXTER *Inf. Bapt.* 264 The Gentiles had Rites for the expiation of Infants.

d. The action of averting portended evil by religious means.

1734 tr. *Rollin's Anc. Hist.* (1827) IX. xx. i. 6 By expiation of prodigies and various sacrifices offered to the gods.

†**e.** Propitiation (of a deity). *Obs. rare*$^{-1}$.

1675 R. BURTHOGGE *Causa Dei* 383 That conformity of Customs that the Gauls had with them [the Phœnicians] in sacrificing men for expiation of God.

2. The means by which atonement (for a crime or offence) is made; something done, or a rite observed, for the purpose of expiating.

1538 BALE *Thre Lawes* 832 Offerynges & expiacyons. **1646** SIR T. BROWNE *Pseud. Ep.* VII. i. 339 Some have conceived it [Forbidden fruit] a Vine, in the mystery of whose fruit lay the expiation of the Transgression. **1777** ROBERTSON *Hist. Amer.* II. v. 30 To demand a certain number of human victims as an expiation for their guilt. **1828** SCOTT *F.M. Perth* vi, The only expiation would be that thou shouldst come a mile into the Low Country. **1856** FROUDE *Hist. Eng.* (1858) I. iv. 348 The payment of money was ever welcomed as the ready expiation of crime.

b. A rite intended to avert portended evil.

a **1627** SIR J. HAYWARD *K. Edw. VI* (1630) 167 Vpon birth of such monsters, the Grecians..did vse diuerse sorts of expiations.

Hence **expiˈational** *a.*, pertaining to expiation.

1874 BUSHNELL *Forgiveness & Law* 91 The most intensely expiational form of christianity.

expiative (ˈɛkspɪeɪtɪv), *a. rare.* [f. *expiāt-* ppl. stem of *expiāre* to EXPIATE + -IVE.] Tending or adapted to expiate.

1641 R. BAILLIE *Parallel of Lit. with Mass-bk.* 92 An expiative Purgatorie wherein by the prayers of the living the sinnes of the dead are put away.

expiator (ˈɛkspɪeɪtə(r)). [a. L. *expiātor*, f. *expiāre*: see EXPIATE.] One who expiates or makes satisfaction (for sin).

1847 in CRAIG. **1872** J. G. MURPHY *Comm. Lev.* iii. 17 To ..foreshadow the death of the great Expiator. **1878** B. TAYLOR *Deukalion* II. iii, They..made me your Expiator.

†**expiaˈtorious**, *a. Obs. rare*$^{-1}$. [f. L. *expiātōri-us* (see next) + -OUS.] = next.

1651 JER. TAYLOR *Clerus Dom.* 48 The first grace, which in the Schools is understood onely to be expiatorious.

expiatory (ˈɛkspɪəˌtərɪ), *a.* [ad. L. *expiātōrius*, f. *expiātor*: see EXPIATOR and -ORY.] Having the attribute of expiating or making satisfaction for an offence; serving to expiate. Const. *of.*

1548 LATIMER *Serm. Plough* Wks. I. 68 Expiatory..is nothing else but a thing whereby to obtain remission of sins. **1603** HOLLAND *Plutarch's Mor.* 62 He hath patiently

endured a while the first expiatorie purifications and troubles. *a* **1677** Barrow *Serm. Matt.* i. 20 The sacrifice expiatory for our offences was to be a lamb without blemish. **1793** Gouv. Morris in Sparks *Life & Writ.* (1832) II. 355 The first great misfortune will call them from their dungeons as expiatory victims. **1812** Cogan *Theol. Disquisitions* II. 183 Human sacrifices..being the most valuable..were considered as the most expiatory. **1869** Goulburn *Purs. Holiness* xi. 105 That bloody and shameful death was..expiatory of sin.

Hence **'expia,toriness.**

1730-6 Bailey (folio), *Expiatoriness*, expiating quality.

† **'expilate**, *v. Obs. rare*⁻¹. [f. L. *expīlāt-* ppl. stem of *expīlāre*, f. *ex-* (see EX- *pref.*¹) + *pīlāre* to plunder.] *trans.* To pillage, plunder.

1627 Bp. Hall *Serm. Chapel Earl Exeter* Wks. 526 What peace was vnder the Herodian temple?.. Pilate would expilate the treasures of it for *aquæ ductæ*.

expilation (ɛkspɪˈleɪʃən). Now *rare*. [ad. L. *expīlātiōn-em*, n. of action f. *expīlāre*: see prec.]

1. The action of pillaging; spoliation, plunder.

1563 Grindal *Let. Sir W. Cecil* Wks. (1843) 257 Take order..not to leave the poor tenants subject to the expilation of these country gentlemen. **1597** Daniel *Civ. Wares* II. cxiv, Whence..proceeds This rav'nous expilation of the state. *a* **1661** Fuller *Worthies, Sussex* III. 104 He was loth to go back to Bath, having formerly consented to the expilation of that Bishoprick. **1675** tr. *Machiavelli's Prince* xxvi. (Rtldg. 1883) 159 Taxes and expilations in the kingdom of Naples. **1885** R. W. Dixon *Hist. Ch. Eng.* xxi. III. 536 This final expilation..avenged upon the son the sacrilege of the father.

b. *concr.* A collection made by plundering.

1715 M. Davies *Athen. Brit.* I. Pref. 51 A compleat Collection or Expilation of all the tart Reparties..out of all the Play-Books that ever were printed in England.

†**2.** *Civil Law.* (See quot.) *Obs.*

1730-6 in Bailey (folio). **1751** Chambers *Cycl.*, *Expilation*, in the civil law, the act of withdrawing, or diverting, something belonging to an inheritance, before any body had declared himself heir thereof. **1848** in Wharton *Law Lex.*

† **'expilator.** *Obs. rare.* [a. L. *expīlātor*, f. *expīlāre*: see EXPILATE.]

1. A pillager, plunderer.

1658 Sir T. Browne *Hydriot. & Gard. Cyrus* 15 For which the most barbarous Expilators found the most civil Rhetorick.

2. *Civil Law.* One who commits an act of expilation (see EXPILATION 2).

1753 Chambers *Cycl. Supp.* s.v., An expilator was looked upon as a greater criminal than a common thief.

expirable (ɛkˈspaɪərəb(ə)l), *a. rare*⁻⁰. [f. EXPIRE *v.* + -ABLE.] That may expire or come to an end.

1832 in Webster; and in mod. Dicts.

expirant (ɛkˈspaɪərənt). *rare.* In 9 *erron.* expirent. [ad. L. *ex(s)pīrant-em*, pr. pple. of *ex(s)pīrāre*: see EXPIRE.] **a.** (See quot. 1846.) **b.** *nonce-wd.* A name for a supposed vessel in plants, which assists in evaporation or perspiration.

1836 I. Taylor *Phys. Th. Another Life* (1858) 156 The Mechanical adjustment of parts, as seen..in the vessels, the absorbents, the expirents, the flower..the seed. **1846** Worcester, *Expirant*, one who expires [citing I. Taylor: but see prec. quot.]. So **1864** in Webster, and in later Dicts.

† **'expirate**, *v. Obs. rare.* [f. ppl. stem of L. *ex(s)pīrāre*: see EXPIRE *v.*] *trans.* = EXPIRE *v.* 1.

1615 Crooke *Body of Man* 421 It is better expirated or breathed out then water. **1620** Venner *Via Recta* (1650) 7 Aire breathed in is not again expirated or breathed out.

expiration (ɛkspɪˈreɪʃən). Also 7 exsp-. [ad. L. *ex(s)pīrātiōn-em*, n. of action f. *ex(s)pīrāre* to EXPIRE.] The action of expiring.

1. The action of breathing out (air, etc.); emission (of air, wind, etc.); an instance of this. Const. *of.*

1642 *Preparative for Fast* 4 This tends to the very expiration of the animall and vitall spirits. **1796** Morse *Amer. Geog.* I. 613 Regular inspirations and expirations of air, by caverns and fissures. **1874** T. Hardy *Madding Crowd* II. vi. 80 There came finally an utter expiration of air from the whole heaven in the form of a slow breeze.

fig. **1839** Bailey *Festus* xxix. (1848) 340 Prayer is..The expiration of the thing inspired.

†**b.** = RESPIRATION. *Obs.*

1638 Wilkins *New World* I. xiv. (1684) 180 The extream thinness of it [air]..may make it unfit for Expiration.

2. The action, or an act, of breathing out air from the lungs; also applied to a supposed analogous action in plants.

1603 Holland *Plutarch's Mor.* 689 (R.) It [the breast] transmitteth back againe the superfluity thereof into the lungs, whereby it [the wind] is sent forth by way of exspiration. **1624** Heywood *Gunaik.* IV. 189 In her last expiration expressing the invincible spirit of her son Alexander. **1793** Beddoes *Let. to Darwin* 44 Having by a strong expiration expelled from his lungs as much atmospheric air as possible. **1807** J. E. Smith *Phys. Bot.* 202 He is recorded as the discoverer of the expiration of plants. **1861** Ramadge *Curab. Consumption* 36 The impeded expiration..caused..the lower lobes of the lungs to be exceedingly enlarged.

†**3.** The action of exhaling or evaporating; exhalation. *Obs.*

1626 Bacon *Sylva* §866 The true Cause of Cold, is an Expiration from the Globe of the Earth. **1643** J. Steer tr. *Fabricius' Exp. Chyrurg.* xvi. 66 They doe hinder the expiration of the venome. *c* **1645** Howell *Lett.* IV. l, By the expiration of such Atomes, the dogg finds the sent as he hunts. **1755** in Johnson. **1847** in Craig.

†**b.** *concr.* That which is expired or exhaled; an exhalation. *Obs.*

1576 Newton tr. *Lemnie's Complex.* (1633) 13 The spirit is a certaine vapour..or expiration proceeding out of the humours. **1664** Power *Exp. Philos.* III. 154 The Magnetical Exspirations of the Loadstone may..be seen in the form of a mist. **1667** *Phil. Trans.* II. 579 The moist steams and exspirations of the Heart. **1755** in Johnson.

†**4.** The action of breathing one's last; death, decease. *Obs.*

1526 *Pilgr. Perf.* (W. de W. 1531) 210 Yf [he] had taken his body to lyfe agayn, streyght after his expiracyon. **1607** Topsell *Four-f. Beasts* (1673) 450 She lyeth down as though she were dead..shutting her eyes, and shewing all other tokens of expiration. **1647** Clarendon *Hist. Reb.* I. (1702) I. 41 The Lord Treasurer..had notice of the Clark's expiration. **1779-81** Johnson *L.P., Pope* Wks. IV. 87 The attendants did not discern the exact time of his expiration. **1807** G. Chalmers *Caledonia* I. III. vii. 383 He died, by a quiet expiration, at his castle of Dunadeer. **1847** in Craig; and in mod. Dicts.

†**b.** *transf.* and *fig.* Of a flame, a sentiment, etc.: The fact or process of dying out; the state of being extinct. *Obs.*

1649 Jer. Taylor *Gt. Exemp.* iii. §1 A very great cause of the dryness and expiration of men's devotion. **1660** Boyle *New Exp. Phys. Mech.* xiii. 85 To satisfie our selves of its expiration, we had darken'd the Room, and in vain endeavored to discover any spark of Fire.

5. The fact of coming to an end; termination, end, close: **a.** of a period of time, or of something made to last a certain time, as a law, truce, etc.

1562 *Act 5 Eliz.* c. 15 §1 Sithence the Expiration and Ending of the Statute. **1593** Shaks. *Rich. II*, II. iii. 111 Thou..art come Before th'expiration of thy time. **1647** Clarendon *Hist. Reb.* VIII. (1843) 538/1 A fortnight after the expiration of the treaty at Uxbridge. **1664** Evelyn *Kal. Hort.* (1729) 197 About the Expiration of this Month carry into the Shade..Auriculas's. **1790** Paley *Horæ Paul.* Rom. ii. 19 The shaving of the head denoted the expiration of the Nazaritic vow. **1841** Lane *Arab. Nts.* I. 110 And thus she continued to do..until the expiration of the second year. **1862** Merivale *Rom. Emp.* (1871) V. xlii. 148 The government of the Gaulish provinces..followed on the expiration of his functions in the city.

†**b.** of a race, the world. *Obs.*

1677 Plot *Oxfordsh.* 181 After the expiration of which ancient Race, there came..another Colony [of bees]. **1684** T. Burnet *Th. Earth* II. 32 What hath appear'd..relating to the chronology of the world: giving..certain marks of its expiration.

expirator (ˈɛkspɪreɪtə(r)). [agent-n. f. L. *ex(s)pīrāre* to EXPIRE.] An instrument for forcing out air.

1875 Ure *Dict. Arts* s.v. *Aspirator*, The following form of spirator..may be employed either as aspirator in drawing, or as expirator in forcing air through an apparatus.

expiratory (ɛkˈspaɪərətərɪ), *a.* [f. Lat. type **ex(s)pīrātōrius*, f. *ex(s)pīrāre*: see EXPIRE *v.* and -ORY.] Of or pertaining to the process of expiration.

1847 in Craig. **1861** T. Graham *Pract. Med.* 294 The expiratory [murmur] is..distinctly audible under the clavicles. **1866** Huxley *Phys.* iv. (1872) 90 Whenever a violent expiratory effort is made, the walls of the abdomen are obviously flattened. **1878** Foster *Phys.* II. ii. §1. 263 They are in fact the chief expiratory muscles.

b. *Gram.* (Often spelt *exspiratory*.) In ***expiratory accent***, a kind of accent consisting in variation of stress, as distinguished from that which consists in variation of pitch.

expire (ɛkˈspaɪə(r)), *v.* Also 5 expyre, -spyre, 5-7 exspire, (6 expiere, -perie, 7 expayer). [ad. Fr. *expirer*, ad. L. *ex(s)pīrāre* to breathe out, f. *ex-* out + *spīrāre* to breathe.]

I. To breathe out.

1. *trans.* To breathe out (air, etc.) from the lungs; also with *forth.*

1590 Spenser *F.Q.* I. xi. 45 The scorching fire, Which he from hellish entrailes did expire. **1649** G. Daniel *Trinarch., Rich. II*, ccxcviii, Wee yawne..the same Ayre which wee expired erst. **1695** Woodward *Nat. Hist. Earth* IV. (1723) 236 The Fluid, which is..expired forth along with the Air, goes off in insensible Parcels. **1715-20** Pope *Iliad* VI. 223 Her pitchy nostrils flaky flames expire. **1859** Lewes *Sea-side Stud.* 234 In the daytime we expire more carbonic acid than during the night. **1866** Huxley *Phys.* iv. (1872) 82 The breath..afterwards is driven out or expired.

b. *absol.* To breathe out air from the lungs.

1633 P. Fletcher *Purple Isl.* IV. xi, Loose when he sucks in aire, contract when he expires. **1653** [see EXPIRING *vbl. sb.*]. **1851** Gosse *Nat. in Jamaica* 4 [The Whales] expired with a rushing sound, the instant the blow-hole was exposed.

†**2.** To give off (a perfume, vapour, etc.); to exhale, emit. Of a volcano: To emit, eject (flames, rarely solid substances). Also, To give out under pressure. *Obs.*

1603 Drayton *Odes* II. 4 Where Altars..Doe od'rous Fumes expire. **1665** G. Harvey *Advice agst. Plague* 29 It [the Earth] purges it self by expiring those Arsenical fumes. **1697** Dryden *Virg. Georg.* I. 205 And force the Veins of clashing Flints t'expire The lurking Seeds of their Cœlestial Fire. **1727** C. Pitt *Paraphr. Ps.* cxliv, The lab'ring hills expire Thick clouds of smoke and deluges of fire. *Ibid.* I. 636 What Rocks did Ætna's bellowing Mouth expire from his torn entrails. **1762** Churchill *Ghost* II. Poems I. 205 Ev'ry shrub expires perfume. **1808** J. Barlow *Columb.* v. 484 Lighted bombs that fusing trails exspire.

absol. **1626** Bacon *Sylva* §294 Heat drieth Bodies that do easily expire; as Parchment, Leaves [etc.].

†**3.** *intr.* To pass out in, or like, breath; to be breathed forth or exhaled; hence of the winds, flame, a projectile: To rush forth. Cf. L. *expirent ignes*, Lucr. VI. 640. *Obs.*

1626 G. Sandys *Ovid's Met.* xv. 312 Furious winds..Pent in blind cauernes, strugling to expire. **1654** Earl Orrery *Parthen.* (1676) 563 Tell my Princess..my breath expir'd in repeating the fair name of her [etc.]. **1666** Dryden *Ann. Mirab.* clxxxviii, The linstocks touch, the ponderous ball expires. **1684** R. H. *Sch. Recreat.* 32 When the Rocket expires, they take Fire and spread into a Flame, hovering in the Air like Stars. **1697** Dryden *Virg. Georg.* I. 129 Redundant Humours thro' the Pores expire. *Ibid.* IV. 254 Huge Flakes of Flames expire. **1729** Savage *Wanderer* I. 234 Thro' the bor'd rock above, the smoke expires.

II. To breathe one's last breath, die.

†**4.** *trans.* To breathe out (the soul, etc.) in the article of death; also, ***to expire one's last.*** *Obs.*

[Only a special use of sense 1; but the starting-point of a distinct series of senses.]

c **1450** *Mirour Saluacioun* 3287 On gude ffriday when crist his sawle on crosse expired. *c* **1477** Caxton *Jason* 84 b, Syn recommanded him to the Goddes and that don expired his lyf. **1509** Barclay *Shyp of Folys* 58 b, Medas..With paynfull hunger his lyfe breth dyd expyre. *a* **1612** Donne *Βιαθανατος* (1644) 122 A youth..ready to expire his soule by sickenesse. **1642** Jer. Taylor *Episc.* (1647) 128 As soon as their Apostle had expired his last breath. *a* **1671** Ld. Fairfax *Mem.* (1699) 56 My daughter..in appearance was ready to expire her last. **1715-20** Pope *Iliad* XVI. 1000 Patroclus thus..So many lives effused, expires his own.

5. *intr.* Of a person or animal: To breathe one's last; to die.

a **1400** *Cov. Myst., Assump.* (Shaks. Soc.) 387 The thrydde day hens ye schul ben expirand. **1485** Caxton *St. Wenefr.* 3 The yong man forthwith fyll down to therthe and exspyred. **1651** Hobbes *Leviath.* IV. xliv. 344 God onely knows..what becomes of a mans spirit, when he expireth. **1724** R. Falconer *Adv. & Escapes* 83 When he found himself just upon the Point of expiring, he made this short Prayer. **1741** tr. *D'Argens' Chinese Lett.* 209 They..stand round making respectful Bows to them [Goats and Sheep] till they are expired. **1839** Keightley *Hist. Eng.* II. 74 The King pressed his hand and expired. **1843** Mrs. Carlyle *Lett.* I. 275 Leaving my two gentlemen ready to expire of laughter.

b. *transf.* in various nonce-uses. Also of a fire: To die out.

c **1593** Spenser *Sonn.* xxvii. 11 (1611) Dj, This verse, that neuer shall expire. **1595** Shaks. *John* v. iv. 36 Euen this ill night your breathing shall expire. **1634** Sir T. Herbert *Trav.* 209 Palmeto..is a soft pith in which consists the soule and vegetative vertue of that tree, which cut out the tree expires. **1660** Jer. Taylor *Duct. Dubit.* 139 The Jews religion..was to expire into the Christian. **1666** Dryden *Ann. Mirab.* ccxii, London..By an high fate thou greatly didst expire. **1769** O. Goldsmith *Hist. Rom.* II. 49 Brutus was..reading by a lamp that was just expiring. **1847** Longf. *Ev.* I. i. 113 The sparks expired in the ashes.

6. To come to an end: **a.** Of a period of time: To reach its close; to terminate, end: *rarely*, to elapse, pass. Sometimes conjugated with *be.*

1455 Richard Dk. of York in Ellis *Orig. Lett.* II. 40 I. 126 And that yere expired to geve my said servaunt.. your licence to retourne. **1494** Fabyan *Chron.* VI. cci. 210 From the firste yere of Pepyn..to the first yere of Hughe Capet expyred or passed cc.xxxix. yeres. *c* **1500** *Melusine* 317 After your lyf naturel expired, no man shal..hold your land. *c* **1550** Cheke *Mark* I. 15 Jesus..said yᵉ time is now expired ..repent and belev yᵉ gospel. **1608** Shaks. *Per.* III. iv. 14 Until your date expire. **1653** H. Cogan tr. *Pinto's Trav.* xxix. 115 The three dayes abstinence being expired, lots were cast. **1812** Southey *Lett.* (1856) II. 278 Lord Sunderlin..has it for three years, one of which is expired. **1818** Cruise *Digest* (ed. 2) VI. 560 Till all the lives, during which it was directed to accumulate, should expire. **1865** Trollope *Belton Est.* xi. 118 Till the next session of Parliament should have nearly expired.

¶ Spenser's use in the following quot. seems to be a forced extension of this sense.

1590 Spenser *F.Q.* I. vii. 9 She..Trebling the dew time In which the wombes of women doe expire Brought forth this monstrous masse.

b. Of a condition (in a bond or the like), a law, patent, truce, etc. appointed for a limited time: To become void through lapse of time; to reach its term; to determine.

c **1477** Caxton *Jason* 95 b, The triews faylled at time sette and exspired. **1596** Shaks. *Merch. V.* I. iii. 160 A month before This bond expires. **1659** B. Harris *Parival's Iron Age* 171 There was a truce for six yeares, which expired in that of 1635. **1790** Paley *Horæ Paul.* Rom. ii. 43 St. Paul's vow was expired before he set forward upon his voyage. **1804** Earl Lauderd. *Publ. Wealth* (1819) 162 When the patent expires. **1817** W. Selwyn *Law Nisi Prius* (ed. 4) II. 668 A notice expiring that day of the year. **1855** Macaulay *Hist. Eng.* IV. 540 To ascertain what temporary statutes were about to expire.

c. Of an action, state, legal title, etc.: To cease, come to an end, die out, become extinct.

c **1450** *St. Cuthbert* (Surtees) 4479 þe paynyms pride it sall' expire. *c* **1600** Shaks. *Sonn.* xxvii, To worke my mind, when boddies work's expired. **1610** Holland *Camden's Brit.* I. 353 When this dignity was expired in this family. **1659** B. Harris *Parival's Iron Age* 221 This War, which had lasted almost ninety years..expired in the Spring time, 1648. **1671** Marvell *Corr.* Wks. 1872-5 II. 388 Dover Peere was not able to get in its report; so that matter is expired. **1712-4** Pope *Rape Lock* III. 15 Amazed, confused, he found his power expired. **1783** Burke *Rep. Affairs India* Wks. 1842 II. 28 This trade..was now itself expiring in the hands of the company. **1818** Cruise *Digest* (ed. 2) II. 266 An

estate tail..expires whenever there is a failure of issue inheritable to it. *Ibid.* III. 373 The title of the daughters expired on the birth of the son. **1833** Bp. Thirlwall in *Philol. Mus.* II. 522 The death of Ajax, with which, according to modern notions, the interest expires. **1844** Lingard *Anglo-Sax. Ch.* (1858) I. ii. 77 *note*, The extensive authority..was meant to expire.

†**d.** Of food: To be consumed, exhausted, or spent. *Obs. rare*⁻¹.

a **1533** Ld. Berners *Huon* cix. 375 Or xv. dayes were passyd, all theyr vytayles were expyred.

†**7.** *trans.* To cause to expire or cease; to bring to an end, conclude; to put an end to. *Obs.*

1579 Lyly *Euphues* (Arb.) 77 To swill the drinke that will expyre thy date. **1592** Shaks. *Rom. & Jul.* I. iv. 109 Some consequence..Shall..expire the tearme Of a despised life. **1594** Nashe *Unfort. Trav.* 6 If I woulde expire the miserie of his vnspeakable tormenting vncertaintie. **1610** Selden *Duello* iv. 15 Death was vmpire by expiring the best spirit of the one. **1612** T. Taylor *Comm. Titus* i. 10 These seducers ..will not haue it [circumcision] dated, when the Lord hath expired it.

†**b.** To cause (time) to pass; to spend. *rare*⁻¹.

1589 Nashe in Greene *Menaphon* Ded. (Arb.) 11 Those yeares, which shoulde bee employed in Aristotle, are expired in Epitomes.

†**ex'pire**, *sb. Obs. rare.* [f. prec. vb.] = expiration, expiry.

1612 Sylvester *Lacrymae Lacrym.* 168 But, day by day, vntill our last expire..Prostrate our Soules..Before the Footstool of th' Empyreall Chaire. **1646** Sir T. Browne *Pseud. Ep.* vii. ix. 357 Having seen the expire of Daniels prediction..he [John] accomplished his Revelation.

expired (ɛk'spaɪəd), *ppl. a.* [f. expire *v.* + -ed¹.] In senses of the verb.

1. Breathed out, emitted from the lungs, etc.

1794 J. Hutton *Philos. Light, etc.* 301 Heat..expended.. for..heating the expired atmosphere. **1833** Sir C. Bell *Hand* (ed. 3) 237 In speaking there is..required a certain force of expired air. **1876** Foster *Phys.* ii. ii. (1879) 307 The temperature of expired air is variable.

2. Of a person or animal: That has breathed the last breath, dead. Of a fire: Extinct. Of a law: That has reached its term; obsolete. Of a date or period: Completed.

1622 Callis *Stat. Sewers* (1647) 71 A Law expired in time, though it hath lost his vigor and force, yet it is like a vertuous man deceased. **1631** Heywood *Eng. Eliz.* (1641) 184 The bones of those which had been long since expired. **1647** *Beaum. & Fletcher's Wks.* Ded. Ep., The then expired sweet Swan of Avon Shakespeare. **1648** H. G. tr. *Balzac's Prince* 104 The Greatnesse and Majestie of the expired Common-Wealth. **1671** H. M. tr. *Erasm. Colloq.* 246 The expired period of ages hath not yet brought that fatal day. **1674** J. B[rian] *Harv. Home* ii. 5 Soon or late, We clasp our Earth in Lifes expired date. **1823** Lamb *Elia* Ser. i. xxii. (1865) 171 The expired..kitchen fires. **1875** Lyell *Princ. Geol.* II. iii. xliv. 515 In recently expired animals.

expiree (ɛk,spaɪə'riː). Chiefly *Austral.* [f. expire *v.* + -ee; after Fr. *expiré* in same sense.] One whose term of punishment has expired; an ex-convict. Also *attrib.*

1802 Bentham *Wks.* (1843) xi. 123 As to returns to England, the idea of preventing them on the part of expirees ..is now disclaimed. **1838** *Tait's Mag.* V. 781 The free emigrants of South Australia, and the emancipists and expirees of Van Dieman's Land. **1847** J. D. Lang *Cooksland* ix. 271 Very many of their servants, being old hands or Expiree convicts from New South Wales and Van Diemen's Land, are thoroughly unprincipled men. **1863** *Lond. Rev.* 3 Jan. 4/2 Sir Walter Crofton..traces every expiree where he can. **1883** E. M. Curr *Recoll. Squatting in Victoria* v. 40 Wages were high, and labourers (almost all old gaol-birds and expiree convicts) exceedingly independent and rowdy. **1884** *Pall Mall G.* 21 Oct. 1/9 Convicts in New Caledonia, who may be expected to overflow into Victoria either as fugitives or expirees.

†**ex'pirement.** *Obs. rare.* [a. OF. *expirement*, f. *expirer* to expire.] = expiration 5 a.

1526 in *Househ. Ord.* (1790) 212 The two Masters of the household..shall not depart from thence after the expirement of the said time. *Ibid.* 220 Within three dayes of th' expirement of every Moneth.

expirent: see expirant.

expirer (ɛk'spaɪərə(r)). [f. expire *v.* + -er¹.] **a.** One who expires. **b.** = expiree.

1793 J. Beresford in *Looker-on* (1794) III. No. 79. 257 The personal property of the abrupt expirer. **1862** *Lond. Rev.* 30 Aug. 179 The atrocities of this year would be committed by a different batch of ruffians, by the expirers of 1862 instead of by the ticket-of-leave men of 1861.

expiring (ɛk'spaɪərɪŋ), *vbl. sb.* [f. as prec. + -ing¹.] The action of the vb. expire in its various senses.

1612 R. Sheldon *Serm. St. Martin's* 26 From the day of his circumcision..vntill the apertion of his side, after his expiring. **1626** Bacon *Sylva* §69 The Expiring of cold out of the Inward Parts of the Earth in Winter. **1639** Dk. Hamilton in *H. Papers* (Camden) 80 The day befor the expayering of the 8 gevene in your Ma^tis last proclamatione. **1662** Stillingfl. *Orig. Sacr.* ii. vi. §5 At the expiring of the LXX. years.

b. *attrib.*

1661 Walton *Angler* (ed. 3) i. i. 9 If the inspiring and expiring Organ of any animal be stopt, it suddenly dies. **1665** Boyle *Occas. Refl.*, The opportunity 'tis hop'd an expiring State may give Men for Repentance.

expiring (ɛk'spaɪərɪŋ), *ppl. a.* [f. as prec. + -ing².] That expires (in senses of verb).

1. That breathes out air from the lungs, etc.

2. Of a person or animal: That is in the act of breathing his or its last; dying; often applied metonymically (like 'dying') to the breath, words, etc. of a person expiring. Of a flame, etc.: That is dying out, becoming extinguished.

1634 Habington *Castara* (Arb.) 104 My name..even thy expiring breath Did call upon. **1683** T. Hoy *Agathocles* 3 Left in danger of th' expireing Light. **1746–7** Hervey *Medit.* (1818) 194 The last accents which quiver on your pale, expiring lips. **1822** Bp. Heber in *Bp. Taylor's Wks.* (1839) I. cxxxv, A few expiring lamentations..were to expiate for many years of obstinate transgression. **1838** Dickens *Nich. Nick.* viii, An expiring candle shone before his eyes. **1870** Disraeli *Lothair* xxviii. 121 It frantically moved its expiring wings.

fig. **1660** Milton *Free Commw.* 453 The last words of our expiring liberty. **1696** Tate & Brady *Ps.* cxiii. 9 To rescue their exspiring Fame. **1776** Gibbon *Decl. & F.* I. 328 The expiring senate..blazed for a moment, and was extinguished for ever. **1849** Ruskin *Sev. Lamps* iii. §20. 87 Like bubbles in expiring foam. **1862** Stanley *Jew. Ch.* (1877) I. viii. 154 It was the last expiring effort of the old traditions.

3. Of a period of time: That comes to an end; that is in the act of coming to an end.

1609 Tourneur *Fun. Poem* 14 Nor can Death or Fate Confine his fame to an expiring date. **1665** J. Spencer *Prophecies* 112 The *last daies*, being the expiring times of the Jewish Oeconomie. **1705** J. Logan in *Pa. Hist. Soc. Mem.* X. 46 The expiring year will by that time show what has been done. **1823** Byron *Age of Bronze* xiv, The impatient hope of the expiring lease.

Hence **ex'piringly** *adv.*, like a thing expiring; as if dying away.

1835 *New Monthly Mag.* XLIII. 167 The tones were so expiringly soft and low.

expiry (ɛk'spaɪərɪ). [f. expire *v.* + -y.]

1. Dying, death; = expiration 4. Also *fig.* of an immaterial thing: Destruction, extinction. *rare.*

c **1790** Burns *Let. to Grose* Wks. 1856 III. 152 About the time nature puts on her sables to mourn the expiry of the cheerful day. **1803** W. Taylor in *Ann. Rev.* I. 260 Ancient history ought..not to cease with the expiry of the Roman empire. **1855** Bailey *Mystic* 131 But, on expiry, the rebellious soul Shall other bodies enter. **1864** Pusey *Daniel* ii. 62 Men had witnessed..the inherent vitality of the Gospel. They predicted the date of its expiry.

2. Close, termination, end; = expiration 5.

a. of a period of time.

1752 J. Louthian *Form of Process* (ed. 2) 272 No Decreet shall be extracted till after the Expiry of six free Days. **1862** Smiles *Engineers* II. 108 A lease..renewable at the expiry of that term. **1878** Black *Green Past.* xxxii. 254 At the expiry of her year of banishment.

b. of anything that lasts a certain time, as a contract, truce, etc. ***expiry of the legal*** (see quot. 1861).

1807 W. Taylor in *Ann. Rev.* V. 562 [He] left the situation..before the expiry of his indentures. **1828–40** Tytler *Hist. Scot.* (1864) I. 227 The truce was now within a single year of its expiry. *a* **1847** Chalmers *Posth. Wks.* I. 100 Previous to the expiry of the famine. **1861** W. Bell *Dict. Law Scot.* s.v., *Expiry of the Legal*: is the expiration of the period within which the subject of an adjudication may be redeemed, on payment of the debt adjudged for. **1863** Smiles *Indust. Biog.* 218 On the expiry of this contract the Government determined to establish works of their own. **1868** Rogers in *Adam Smith's W.N.* Pref. I. 9 He returned [to Scotland] at the expiry of his exhibition [at Oxford].

expiscate (ɛk'spɪskeɪt), *v.* [f. L. *expiscāt-*, ppl. stem of *expiscārī*, f. *ex-* out + *piscārī* to fish, f. *piscis* fish.] *trans.* To 'fish out'; hence, to find out by scrutiny. Occas. with sentence as object.

Chiefly in Sc. writers; elsewhere usually humorously, with distinct reference to the etymology.

c **1611** Chapman *Iliad* x. 181 O friends, remains not one That will..mix..With their outguards, expiscating if the renown'd extreme They force on us will serve their turns? **1721** Wodrow *Hist. Suff. Ch. Scot.* iii. vii. §3 This Method was fallen upon to expiscate Matter of Criminal Process. **1830** Galt *Lawrie T.* iii. xii, I just propounded the project that I might expiscate some kind of satisfaction to my curiosity. **1831** Wilson in *Blackw. Mag.* No. 180 To Corresp., Should we observe any farther impertinence on his part, we shall expiscate it. **1848** H. Miller *First Impr.* xvii. (1857) 285 The evidence already expiscated on this point. **1864** D'Arcy W. Thompson *Day Dreams* iv. (ed. 2) 38 Have they ever expiscated one intelligible reason?

¶ *nonce-use.* To exhaust of fish.

1858 *Sat. Rev.* V. 569/1 Norway is nearly expiscated.

expiscation (ɛkspɪ'skeɪʃən). [as if ad. L. **expiscātiōn-em*, n. of action f. *expiscārī*: see prec.] The action of expiscating or fishing out; the investigation or examination *of* or *into* (a matter).

1605 Chapman *Commend. Verses on B. Jonson's Sejanus*, The Castalian Head; In expiscation of whose Mysteries, Our Netts must still be clog'd with heauy Lead. **1753** *Scots Mag.* July 364/2 There should be the fullest expiscation into the truth or falsity of these deeds. **1874** R. H. Story *W. Carstares* 183 Busied in the expiscation of the various machinations.

expiscator (ɛk'spɪskeɪtə(r)). *rare*⁻¹. [f. expiscate *v.* + -or.] One who expiscates; an investigator. Const. *of.*

1882 J. Brown *John Leech* 320 These mighty expiscators and exploders of myths.

expiscatory (ɛk'spɪskətərɪ), *a. rare.* [as if ad. L. *expiscātōri-us*, f. *expiscārī*: see expiscate and -ory.] Tending to expiscate or 'fish out'.

1829 *Blackw. Mag.* XXVI. 586, I was moved thereunto by an expiscatory curiosity. **1837** Carlyle *Diam. Neckl.* Misc. (1888) V. 190 By..expiscatory questions..this most involute of Lies is finally winded off.

explain (ɛk'spleɪn), *v.* Forms: 6 explaine, 6–7 explayne, 6–8 explane, 7– explain. [ad. L. *explānāre*, f. *ex-* (see ex- *pref.*¹) + *plān-us* flat, plain. Cf. OF. *ex-*, *esplaner*.]

†**1.** To smooth out, make smooth, take out roughness from. *Obs.*

1549 Chaloner tr. *Erasm. Moriæ Enc.* Bj, He must caulme and explane his forehead. **1650** Bulwer *Anthropomet.* 9 Their faces are explained or flatted by art.

†**2. a.** To open out, unfold, spread out flat (a material object). Also *refl.* and *intr.* for *refl.* ***to explain (itself) into***: to develop. *Obs.*

1607 Deloney *Strange Hist.* i. (Percy Soc.) 10 Her wit.. like a ship her selfe explaines. **1644** Bulwer *Chiron.* 53 The left hand explained into a Palme. **1664** Evelyn *Sylva* (1776) 231 Before they [buds] explain into leaves. **1684** —— in *Phil. Trans.* XIV. 560 The Horse-Chesnut is..ready to explain its leaf. **1721** R. Bradley *Wks. Nat.* 46 In the Gourd..a Seed..coming to explain itself into a Plant of full Perfection, will spread its Vine in six months. *Ibid.* 144 Beetles..have..Wings..so disposed as to fold up or explain themselves at the Will of the Insect.

†**b.** To make plainly visible; to display; also, ***to explain itself to be*** (something). *Obs.*

1607 Rowlands *Famous Hist.* 71 That life she entertains ..And such severity therein explains. **1608** R. Johnson *7 Champions* ii. P iv b, The darke night began..to give Aurora libertie to explayne her purple brightnesse. **1647** N. Bacon *Disc. Govt. Eng.* i. lvii. 105 England would..explain itself unto the World to be a regular Government.

3. a. To unfold (a matter); to give details of, enter into details respecting. Occas. with indirect question as obj. Also *absol.*

(In some examples, sense 3a is indistinguishable from 3b.)

1513 More *Rich. III.* Wks. 63/2 Other thinges, which the ..doctor rather signified then fully explaned. **1571** Digges *Pantom.* iv. xxv. Ff iv b, To explane the composition, fourme, nature, and proportion. **1729** Butler *Serm.* Pref. Wks. II. 9 The following Discourses..were intended to explain what is meant by the nature of man. **1756** C. Lucas *Ess. Waters* I. Pref., I thought it just to explane the Medicinal Qualities. **1856** Reade *Never too Late* II. v. 83 'Then what were you in the black hole for?' 'For obeying orders.' 'Nonsense! hum! Explain.' **1866** J. Martineau *Ess.* I. 71 Does he explain the business of Ethics? *Mod.*, You have not explained how your results are obtained. **1886** 'M. Gray' *Silence of Dean Maitland* iii. xi, He took a card from his pocket... 'That will explain to Dr. Everard,' he said. **1899** Skeel & Brearley *King Washington* 122, I cannot explain about the robbery in your father's garden without disloyalty to my duty. **1922** Joyce *Ulysses* 449 Gentlemen of the jury, let me explain. **1968** Wodehouse *Do Butlers burgle Banks?* (1970) 28 Horace..lost no time in going on to explain.

absol. **1671** Milton *Samson* 1583 Wearied with slaughter then, or how? explain. **1741** Middleton *Cicero* I. iii. 169 A tongue that could explane.

b. To make plain or intelligible; to clear of obscurity or difficulty.

1552 Huloet, Explayne, *explico.* **1579** Fulke *Heskins' Parl.* 345 He hath not explaned the manner of the mysterie. **1651** Hobbes *Leviath.* iv. xlvi. 378 The Power of Explaining them [Laws] when there is need. **1676** Glanvill *Ess., Confidence in Philos.* 6 How the pure Mind can receive information from things that are not like it self..is..not to be explain'd. *a* **1732** Gay (J.), You will have variety of commentators to explain the difficult passages to you. **1875** Manning *Mission H. Ghost* ii. 44 What the child cannot understand you explain. **1875** Jowett *Plato* (ed. 2) III. 131 Allow me to explain my meaning.

4. a. To assign a meaning to, state the meaning or import of; to interpret.

1608 Shaks. *Per.* ii. ii. 14 'Tis now your honour, daughter, to explain The labour of each knight, in his device. **1667** Milton *P.L.* ii. 518 The sounding Alchymie By Harald's voice explain'd. **1692** Dryden *St. Euremont's Ess.* 109 An innocent word maliciously explained. **1726** Chetwood *Adv. Capt. R. Boyle* 48 This he told Mirza in the Moorish Tongue, but explain'd it to me in English. **1744** Berkeley *Siris* §221 To define fire by heat would be to explain a thing by itself. **1878** Browning *La Saisiaz* 30 Hindrance is the fact acknowledged, howso'er explained as Fate, Fortune, Providence.

b. ***to explain away***: to modify or do away with (a meaning, etc.) by explanation; to explain so as to deprive of force or significance, *esp.* an offensive one. †***to explain oneself away***: to explain away one's meaning.

1709 Pope *Ess. Crit.* 117 Those explained the meaning quite away. **1729** Butler *Serm.* Pref. Wks. II. 22 There is a strange affectation in many people of explaining away all particular affections. **1786** H. Tooke *Purley* Introd. (1798) 11 You shall not be permitted to explain yourself away. **1855** Macaulay *Hist. Eng.* IV. 741 His words were taken down; and, though he tried to explain them away, he was sent to the Tower. **1877** Mozley *Univ. Serm.* vii. 154 To explain away the natural meaning of this part of Scripture language. **1885** Hemming in *Law Rep.* 29 Chanc. Div. 293 He seeks to explain away the authorities we rely on.

5. To make clear the cause, origin, or reason of; to account for.
1736 BUTLER *Anal.* I. v. Wks. I. 90 It may be hard to explain the faculty, by which we are capable of habits. **1777** SHERIDAN *Sch. Scand.* IV. iii, I make no doubt—but I shall explain everything to your satisfaction. **1860** TYNDALL *Glac.* II. viii. 267 The principles we have laid down enable us to explain the difference. **1863** MARY HOWITT *F. Bremer's Greece* II. xiv. 91 It has been known from the most ancient times, but has never yet been explained in a satisfactory manner.

6. *refl.* To make one's meaning clear and intelligible, speak plainly. Also, to give an account of one's intentions or motives. Formerly with *subord. clause*: To state in explanation of one's conduct *that*, etc.
1624 GATAKER *Transubst.* (1626) 86 More particularly explaining himselfe he saith. **1647** N. BACON *Disc. Govt. Eng.* I. xliv. (1739) 71 The Duke must now explain himself, that it was the value of the English Crown, and not the Title, that brought him over. **1660** FULLER *Mixt Contempl.* (1841) 216 Being desired farther to explain himself; I mean, said he, [etc.]. **1791** MRS. RADCLIFFE *Rom. Forest* ix, Explain yourself, lovely Adeline.

7. *intr.* **a.** With *subord. clause.* To say in explanation *that.*
1867 BAKER *Albert N'yanza* II. 162 Explaining that I was quite out of stores and presents. **1875** JOWETT *Plato* (ed. 2) IV. 132 He..explains to Socrates that he has attained the conception of ideas by a process of generalization.

†**b.** To speak one's mind *against, upon.* (Somewhat common in 18th c.)
1709 STEELE *Tatler* No. 45 ¶9 My intended Purpose.. was to explain upon the Order of Merry Fellows. **1718** HICKES & NELSON *J. Kettlewell* II. xxxiv. 141 The Designs.. which they had..so loudly explained against. **1764** CHESTERF. *Lett.* IV. 202 The Public..begins to explain upon him.

c. With a direct statement as obj.: to utter in explanation.
1856 READE *Never too Late* II. v. 94 'Yes sir clammed and no mistake.' 'North-country word for starved' explained Mr. Eden. **1903** R. LANGBRIDGE *Flame & Flood* x, Tears came into Susette's eyes... 'I have bitten my tongue,' Susette explained. **1908** *Smart Set* June 93/1 He slapped down a yellow envelope upon the desk. 'Telegram,' he explained tersely.

Hence **ex'plained** *ppl. a.*; in quot. as compar.
1685 *Col. Rec. Pennsylv.* I. 140 Ye Assembly requested.. that a further Explainter Sence might be admitted.

explainable (ɛk'spleɪnəb(ə)l), *a.* Also 7 explanable. [f. prec. + -ABLE.] That may or can be explained, made clear, or accounted for; capable of interpretation.
1610 HEALEY *St. Aug. Citie of God* 842 Many of these examples..are..but explanable by weake conjectures. **1646** SIR T. BROWNE *Pseud. Ep.* v. xxi. §13. 268 Thus is it symbollically explainable and implieth purification. **1768–74** TUCKER *Lt. Nat.* (1852) II. 657 Virtues which have a worth of their own explainable to his understanding. **1842** DICKENS *Lett.* (1880) I. 77, I have an idea not easily explainable in writing. **1875** H. C. WOOD *Therap.* (1879) 176 Phenomena..explainable by the action of the drug upon the sensitive nerves.

explainer (ɛk'spleɪnə(r)). [f. EXPLAIN + -ER[1].] One who or that which explains.
1589 PUTTENHAM *Eng. Poesie* III. xii. (Arb.) 179 The Greekes call him [a maner of speach] Prolepsis, we the Propounder, or the Explaner. **1643** MILTON *Divorce* II. iii. (1851) 68 According to our common explainers. **1695** MOTTEUX *St. Olon's Morocco* 41 Their Prophet, whom they call God's great Favorite, and the Explainer of his Will. **1860** BAGEHOT *Unref. Parl.* 37 He must be, if not a great orator, a great explainer. **1881** *Daily News* 29 Dec. 5/2 He was the expounder and explainer of the reforms.

ex'plaining, *vbl. sb.* [f. EXPLAIN + -ING[1].] The action of the vb. EXPLAIN; †an explanation.
1580 SIDNEY *Arcadia* (1622) 383 This Sonnet, which might serue as an explaining to the other. **1656** H. PHILLIPS *Purch. Patt.* (1676) 175 The Table is so plain it needs no explaining. **1721** R. BRADLEY *Wks. Nat.* 110 No more than the unfolding and explaining of their Parts one after another. **1740** WATTS *Remnants of Time* §21, I am quite tired ..of these human explainings, so various and uncertain.

explaining (ɛk'spleɪnɪŋ), *ppl. a.* [f. EXPLAIN + -ING[2].] That explains or makes clear.
1850 MRS. BROWNING *Poems* I. 261 Ere her last Explaining words were said.

Hence **ex'plainingly** *adv.*
1889 *Sat. Rev.* 14 Dec. 684/2 'Black Prince—the name of my horse,' she added explainingly.

†**ex'plait,** *v. Obs. rare*[−1]. In 7 explat(e?). [? f. EX- + PLAIT *v.*] *trans.* To remove the plaits from; to unravel. In quot. *fig.*
c **1613** B. JONSON *Underwoods*, lxiv, Thou..Like Solon's self, explat'st the knotty laws.

explanandum (ɛksplə'nændəm). *Philos.* Pl. **explananda.** [L., neut. of gerundive of *explānāre*: see EXPLAIN *v.*] The thing to be explained. Cf. EXPLICANDUM.
1892 *Academy* 6 Aug. 114/2 Whenever a psychical explanandum is run to earth in some feature of nerve structure or function, the pursuit is over. **1948, 1962** [see EXPLANANS]. **1964** I. SCHEFFLER *Anat. Inquiry* 29 This account construes every explanation as consisting of an explanandum..and an explanans.

explanans (ɛksplə'nænz). *Philos.* [L., pres. pple. of *explānāre*: see EXPLAIN *v.*] The explaining element in an explanation; the explanatory premisses. (Opp. EXPLANANDUM.)
1948 HEMPEL & OPPENHEIM in *Philos. of Sci.* XV. 136 We divide an explanation into two major constituents, the explanandum and the explanans. **1962** L. J. COHEN *Diversity of Meaning* iv. 133 An explanation of naming that is futile and circular because the explanans cannot be conceived except through the explanandum.

explanate ('ɛkspləneɪt), *a. Ent.* and *Zool.* [ad. L. *explānāt-us*, pa. pple. of *explānāre* to flatten out (see EXPLAIN).] Spread out flat.
1846 DANA *Zooph.* iv. (1848) 67 Such forms have been called explanate or foliaceous. **1848** MAUNDER *Treas. Nat. Hist.* App., *Explanate*, when the sides of the prothorax are so depressed and dilated as to form a broad margin.

explanation (ɛksplə'neɪʃən). Also 4 explanacioun. [ad. L. *explānātiōn-em*, n. of action f. *explānāre*: see EXPLAIN.]
1. The action or process of explaining; an instance of the same. ***in explanation of***: for the purpose of explaining. †***Act of Explanation*** = *Explanatory Act.*
1382 WYCLIF *Josh.* Prol., We han demed..to sitten to the explanacioun of the prophetis. **1532** MORE *Confut. Tindale* Wks. 478/2 By which explanacions by mouth the people came into ye vndouted trouth. **1664** EVELYN *Kal. Hort.* (1729) 229, I pass to the Explanation of the following Table. **1689** LUTTRELL *Brief Rel.* (1857) I. 555 The..parliament.. have repealed..the acts of settlement and explanation. **1729** BUTLER *Serm.* Wks. II. 153, I proceed to the particular explanation of the precept before us. **1767** *Junius Lett.* xxi. 99 A few lines in explanation of some passages in my last letter. **1848** MACAULAY *Hist. Eng.* I. 666 The malignity.. seemed to require explanation.

2. That which explains, makes clear, or accounts for; a method of explaining or accounting for; a statement that makes things intelligible. Also (as title), a treatise composed for the purpose of explaining.
a **1610** HEALEY *Cebes* F 7 b, This explanation resembleth the riddle of Sphynx. **1664** H. MORE *Myst. Iniq.* i. 3, I have more at large discoursed in my Explanation of the Mystery of Godliness. *a* **1715** BURNET *Own Time* (1734) II. 214 The ill effects that were like to follow on those different Explanations [of the Trinity]. **1791** MRS. RADCLIFFE *Rom. Forest* i, La Motte now asked for an explanation of the scene. **1856** SIR B. BRODIE *Psychol. Inq.* I. vi. 233 Facts are not to be rejected merely because the explanation offered of them proves to be erroneous. **1883** FROUDE *Short Stud.* IV. I. iv. 44 Vast sums were found to have been received..of which no explanation had been given.
Comb. **1716** M. DAVIES *Athen. Brit.* III. 46 It passes through his own Explanation-strainer.

3. A mutual declaration of the sense of spoken words, motives of actions, etc., with a view to adjust a misunderstanding and reconcile differences; hence, a mutual understanding or reconciliation of parties who have been at variance.
1840 BARHAM *Ingol. Leg., Spectre of Tapp.*, I shall come to an immediate explanation with your father on the subject.

explanative (ɛk'splænətɪv), *a.* [f. L. type **explānātīv-us*, f. *explānāre*: see EXPLAIN.] Tending to explain, containing an explanation.
1750 WARBURTON *Julian* II. 181 What follows..is explanative of what went before. **1837** *New Monthly Mag.* LI. 117 He grows more explicit and explanative.

expla'nato-, combining form of L. *explānātus* EXPLANATE, in sense 'spread, or spreading out in a plane, or flat surface'.
1846 DANA *Zooph.* (1848) 253 The species which grow from a central attachment (explanato-glomerate). *Ibid.* 279 Explanato-foliaceous, suborbiculate, unifacial. *Ibid.* 602 Carnose, explanato-gemmate Alcyonidæ.

explanator ('ɛkspləneɪtə(r)). *rare.* [f. as prec. + -OR.] An explainer.
1816 KEATINGE *Trav.* I. 285 Time, the grand explanator. **1858** MISS MULOCK *Th. ab. Wom.* 50 We are acute and accurate historians; clear explanators of science.

explanatory (ɛk'splænətərɪ), *a.* and *sb.* [f. as prec. + -ORY.] **A.** *adj.*
1. Serving or adapted to explain (something), containing or helping to an explanation. Const. *of.* ***Explanatory Act***: an Act of Parliament passed to explain the meaning, drift, or application of a previous Act.
1618 BOLTON *Florus* To Rdr. 2 The words..here and there inserted in a different letter..are for the most part explanatory of the Authors meaning. **1672** *Essex Papers* (Camden) I. 1 Ye seaven yeers granted for it, in ye Explanatory Act, are neere Expired. **1753** HOGARTH *Anal. Beauty* 1 A short essay, accompanied with two explanatory prints. **1856** FROUDE *Hist. Eng.* (1858) II. ix. 326 To guard against misconception, an explanatory document was drawn up by the government. **1883** PROCTOR in *Knowledge* 7 Sept. 156/1, I feel tempted to lay down in despair the explanatory pen.

2. Of persons, their qualities, etc.: Having the function of explaining, disposed or ready to give explanation.
1743 WALPOLE *Lett. H. Mann* (1834) I. lxxxix. 313, I find you still overwhelmed with Richcourt's folly and the Admiral's explanatory ignorance. **1756** FOOTE *Eng. fr. Paris* I. Wks. 1799 I. 96 The law is an oracular idol, you are explanatory ministers. **1848** DICKENS *Dombey* vi. 59 He rendered himself as explanatory as he could.

†**B.** *sb.* = EXPLANATION 2. *Obs.*
1650 R. HOLLINGWORTH *Exerc. conc. Usurped Powers* 49 This may be the best explanatorie of that.

Hence **ex'planatorily** *adv.* **ex'planatoriness,** the quality of being explanatory.
1865 DICKENS *Mut. Fr.* I. xii, The city which Mr. Podsnap so explanatorily called 'London, Londres.' **1870** MISS BROUGHTON *Red as Rose* I. 208 Miss Craven has had a fall.. he remarks explanatorily.
1730–6 BAILEY (folio), *Explanatoriness.* **1885** *Voices crying in Wilderness* iv. 119 A sort of general explanatoriness that seemed intended to check further questions.

ex'plant, *v.* [ad: mod.L. *explant-āre*, f. *ex-* (see EX- *pref.*[1]) + *plantāre* to plant, f. *planta* plant, on the analogy of *implantāre.*] †**1.** *trans.* To send forth as an offshoot. *Obs.*
1578 BANISTER *Hist. Man* v. 84 These [fibres] are explanted from the second cauitie or cell in the kidneys.
2. *Biol.* To transfer (living tissue) from its site in the body to some other place, usu. a nutrient medium in which a culture of the tissue is initiated. Hence **ex'planted** *ppl. a.*
1915 *Amer. Jrnl. Anat.* XVII. 342 Around the piece of explanted tissue the new growth forms a more or less radiating reticulum. **1922** *Jrnl. Exper. Med.* XXXVI. 393 If part of an organ, for instance a toe of a chick embryo, was explanted, an uncontrolled proliferation of cells began from the injured parts. **1937** *Nature* 6 Mar. 413/1 A typical maturation division figure was observed in an explanted ovary from a four-day (post-embryonic) rat after 9 days' cultivation. **1968** *Sci. Jrnl.* Nov. 55/2 If the embryos are explanted during these three days, cell multiplication may continue.

explant ('ɛksplɑːnt, -plænt), *sb. Biol.* [f. the vb.] A piece of tissue, an organ, etc., that has been explanted.
1917 *Amer. Jrnl. Anat.* XXII. 171 The explants consist of small pieces of muscle..taken from the muscles of the back, wing or leg of chick embryos. **1926** *Proc. R. Soc.* B. XCIX. 352 During the first few days of life *in vitro* most of the explants showed 'uncontrolled' growth from the cut surface. **1957** *New Biol.* XXIII. 115 Transplanting pieces to abnormal positions on the embryo, or..growing such pieces in isolation as 'explants', away from any influence of other tissues. **1970** PASSMORE & ROBSON *Compan. Med. Stud.* II. xviii. 100/2 It is sometimes advantageous to use a tissue explant to study the growth of a virus.

explan'tation. [f. EXPLANT *v.* + -ATION.]
†**1.** The action of sending forth as an offshoot; *concr.* an offshoot, outgrowth. *Obs. rare.*
1578 BANISTER *Hist. Man* v. 84 [The bladder] goeth into a necke, for the emplantation and explantation of certaine passages. **1615** CROOKE *Body of Man* 378 Thredy strings.. to which more fleshy explantations or risings do accrew.
2. *Biol.* The action of explanting tissue.
1915 *Amer. Jrnl. Anat.* XVII. 341 The trouble lies either in..poor chick material, or some manipulation during the process of explantation. **1937** *Nature* 6 Mar. 413/1 Only spermatogonia were present at the time of explantation. **1970** tr. E. Wolff in *J. A. Thomas's Organ Culture* i. 3 Explantation *in vivo* consists of grafting a fragment of tissue or organ into the body of an adult or embryonic host.

†**ex'play,** *v. Obs. rare.* [ad. L. *explicāre*, after the analogy of *display.* Cf. Fr. *esploier.*] *trans.* To unfold, display.
a **1619** FOTHERBY *Atheom.* II. viii. §3 (1622) 285 Mans minde doth dayly such it selfe explay, As Gods great Will doth frame it euery day. **1639** H. VINTENER in Fuller *Holy War* (1647) A vij a, As light embroiderie explayes its glorie.

†**explees,** obs. form of ESPLEES, *Law.*
1628 COKE *On Litt.* 17 b, The patron shall not allege the explees or taking of the profits in himself. **1642** PERKINS *Prof. Bk.* v. §334. 148 The issue of the donee shall..alledge the Explees in his Father. **1775** in ASH.

expleite(n, obs. form of EXPLOIT *v.*

†**'explement.** *Obs.* [f. L. *explēment-um* that which fills up, f. *explēre* to fill up: see EXPLETE and -MENT.] That which fills up; fulfilment.
1593 NASHE *Christ's T.* 38 a, Thou wert blinded, & wantedst the sence, in Vespasian to picke out his [a prophecy's] explement [ed. **1613** expletement]. **1658–78** in PHILLIPS.

†**ex'plendency.** *Obs. rare*[−1]. [f. L. *ex-* out + *splendent-em*, pr. pple. of *splendēre* to shine: see -ENCY.] Brightness. Cf. RESPLENDENCY.
1647 H. MORE *Song of Soul* II. III. II. xiv, They have close clapt up all his [Phœbus'] explendency.

†**ex'plenish,** *v. Obs. rare*[−1]. [f. EX- *pref.*[1] + PLENISH.] *trans.* To appease, satisfy.
1612 SHELTON *Quix.* I. III. iv. 137 He had his Fantasy ever explenished with these Battels, Enchantments..Loves and Challenges.

†**ex'plete,** *ppl. a. Obs.* Also 6 expleat. [ad. L. *explēt-us*, pa. pple. of *explēre*: see next.] Filled up, completed; complete, perfect.
1534 *Hildebrand* (W. de W.) A vj, The yere explete, the wydowe..tyed an haulter aboute her sonnes necke and [etc.]. **1570** in LEVINS *Manip.* **1608** MIDDLETON *Mad World* v. ii, A very explete justice!

†**ex'plete,** *v. Obs.* Also 7 expleat. [f. L. *explēt-* ppl. stem of *explēre*, f. *ex-* (see EX- *pref.*[1]) + *plēre*

to fill. In some examples perh. a var. of EXPLOIT.]

1. *trans.* To fill out; to satiate, satisfy; to complete (a period of time).

c **1430** LYDG. *Bochas* v. vii. (1554) 128 a, Texplete their lust certaine. **1635** HEYWOOD *Hierarch.* III. 167 The Great Yeare..some hold to be expleted in 36000 Solarie yeres. **1650** FULLER *Pisgah* IV. vii. 123 Nothing under an Infinite, can expleat..the immortall minde of man. **1657** TOMLINSON *Renou's Disp.* 293* Wax..moderately expletes the body.

2. To do fully; to complete, accomplish.

1430 LYDG. *Chron. Troy* Prol., This worke texplete that ye not refuse. **1529** in Fiddes *Wolsey* II. 171 Of such yers as was mete & hable to explete that act. **1611** SPEED *Hist. Gt. Brit.* IX. xxi. §71 Being of yeeres able to explete the act.

expletement: see EXPLEMENT.

†**ex'pletion.** *Obs.* [ad. L. *explētiōn-em*, n. of action f. *explēre*: see EXPLETE *v.*] The action of filling, the state of being filled to the full; satisfaction.

1629 GAULE *Holy Madn.* 400 Expletion but increases the Malady. **1677** HALE *Prim. Orig. Man.* IV. viii. 377 The expletion of the Faculties of the Sensible Nature. **1717** KILLINGBECK *Serm.* xviii. 374 The Expletion of their Desires.

expletive ('ɛksplɪtɪv, ɛk'spliːtɪv), *a.* and *sb.* [ad. L. *explētīv-us* serving to fill out, f. *explēre*: see EXPLETE. Cf. Fr. *explétif.*] **A.** *adj.*

1. Serving to fill out; introduced merely to occupy space, or to make up a required quantity or number: **a.** *gen.*

1656–81 in BLOUNT *Glossogr.* **1666** TILLOTSON *Rule of Faith* I. §3 Those expletive topicks which popish writers..do generally make use of to help out a book. **1761** CHURCHILL *Rosciad* Poems 1763 I. 16 Expletive Kings, and Queens without a name. *a* **1833** HAN. MORE in Leslie & Taylor *Sir J. Reynolds* (1865) II. vii. 209 Scarce an expletive man or woman of the party. **1874** KNIGHT *Dict. Mech.*, *Expletive-stone* (Masonry), one used for filling a vacuity.

b. *esp.* Of words and phrases: Serving merely to fill out a sentence, help out a metrical line, etc. Also occas. of a mode of expression: Redundant, wordy.

a **1677** BARROW *Wks.* (1741) I. xv. 10 He useth them [oaths] as expletive phrases..to plump his speech. *a* **1771** R. WOOD *Genius of Homer* (1775) 288 Homer's particles were [not] altogether condemned to this mere expletive duty. **1779–81** JOHNSON *L.P.*, *Addison* Wks. III. 89 The lines, which there is little temptation to load with expletive epithets. **1804** SOUTHEY in Robberds *Mem. W. Taylor* I. 494 'The Key my loose, powerless fingers forsook', a lame and expletive way of saying 'I dropt the key'. **1874** SAYCE *Compar. Philol.* i. 29 The influence of Emphasis will..show itself..in the introduction of expletive ones [sounds].

¶**c.** *nonce-use.* Given to using expletives.

1857 MAYNE REID in *Chamb. Jrnl.* VII. 329 The old trapper had grown expletive.

†**2.** Having the attribute of supplying a deficiency. *Obs.*

1816 KEATINGE *Trav.* I. 38 Reymond..supplies this deficiency: but he is not sufficiently expletive in regard to this eastern part of the chain.

3. Tending or seeking to supply a loss; compensative. *rare.* (Cf. quot. 1853 s.v. EXPLETORY.)

1838–9 HALLAM *Hist. Lit.* III. iv. III. §117. 202 Punishment..is not a part of attributive, and hardly of expletive justice.

B. *sb.*

1. An expletive word or phrase, one used for filling up a sentence, eking out a metrical line, etc. without adding anything to the sense.

1612 BRINSLEY *Lud. Lit.* viii. (1627) 97 As also Conjunctions, Copulatives [etc.]..so expletives, and certaine others. **1668** WILKINS *Real Char.* I. iv. §6. 18 Words that are mere Expletives, not adding any thing to the Sense. **1779–81** JOHNSON *L.P.*, *Pope* Wks. IV. 136 Expletives he very early ejected from his verses. **1816** J. GILCHRIST *Philos. Etym.* 185 Must insignificant particles be consecrated into elegant expletives? **1838–9** HALLAM *Hist. Lit.* III. v. III. §71. 277 Articles and expletives..are..employed for the sake of the metre, not of the sense.

b. Often applied to a profane oath or other meaningless exclamation.

1815 SCOTT *Guy M.* xxviii, Retaining only such of their expletives as are least offensive. **1840** BARHAM *Ingol. Leg.*, *Spectre of Tapp.*, Tom..replied..with an expletive. **1891** E. PEACOCK *N. Brenton* I. 63 'Confound him!' or some stronger expletive exploded from the Earl's lips.

2. An 'expletive' person or thing; one that merely serves to fill up space.

1688 R. L'ESTRANGE *Brief Hist. Times* II. 69 This Article [of an Impeachment] is an Expletive; and Signifies just nothing. **1755** YOUNG *Centaur* ii. Wks. 1757 IV. 110 Was man made only to flutter, sing, and expire? A mere expletive in the mighty work..of the Almighty? **1772** GRAVES *Spir. Quixote* IX. xv. (1783) III. 52 A gooseberry tart; with other ornamental expletives of the same kind. **1872** O. W. HOLMES *Poet Breakf.-t.* i. 9 He is a sort of expletive at the table, serving to stop gaps.

b. Something that supplies deficiencies; a supplement. *rare.*

1879 SIR G. G. SCOTT *Lect. Archit.* I. 207 They may..be studied [in Italy]..as an aid and expletive to what we learn elsewhere.

Hence **expletively** *adv.*, in an expletive manner, with redundancy of expression. **expletiveness**, the quality of being expletive.

1607 HIERON *Defence* I. 160 To be put in expletiuely and by way of explication. **1860** J. YOUNG *Prov. Reason* 171 Loosely, expletively, rhetorically, we speak of the Infinite Life. **1730–6** BAILEY (folio), *Expletiveness*, expletive or filling up quality.

expletory ('ɛksplɪtərɪ), *a.* [as if ad. L. type **explētōrius*, f. *explēre*: see EXPLETE *v.*] Serving to fill up; = EXPLETIVE A.

1679 BURNET *Hist. Ref.* I. III. 243 An expletory word. **1797** *Brit. Critic* Feb. 171 Dr. Garden is so fond of this expletory embellishment. **1823** LAMB *Elia* (1860) 31 With the expletory yell, 'and I will, too.' **1853** WHEWELL tr. *Grotius de Jure Belli et Pacis* II. II. §3 In punishment the justice which is exercised is expletory justice [L. *justitia expletrix*].

explicable ('ɛksplɪkəb(ə)l), *a.* [ad. L. *explicābilis*, f. *explicāre* to EXPLICATE.] That may be explicated or explained; that admits of being cleared of difficulty, or of being accounted for.

1556 J. HEYWOOD *Spider & F.* lxiv. 82 All parts of best wit had bene vnable To catch, kepe, and make, thacount explicable. **1578** BANISTER *Hist. Man* VIII. 102 How the sight is made..is not with facilitie explicable. **1624** FISHER in F. White *Reply Fisher* 266 This Text being thus cleerely explicable. **1660** BOYLE *New Exp. Phys. Mech.* i. (1682) 12 That notion by which it seems likely that most if not all of them [experiments] will prove explicable. **1783** BURKE *Rep. Affairs India* Wks. XI. 300 It is not explicable..why the Nabob..could not have equally given them [bills] in discharge of the debt. **1804** W. TAYLOR in *Ann. Rev.* II. 229 The word Coning or king, and the word Tascio, purse or scrip, are as explicable in Gothic as in Welsh. **1877** OWEN in *Wellesley's Disp.* p. xxxi, His apparently harsh conduct..is ..mainly explicable on this ground.

†**b.** Of an equation: Solvable. *Obs.*

1694 E. HALLEY *Roots Equat.* in *Misc. Cur.* (1708) II. 84 The Equation proposed, is not explicable by any other Root.

Hence **'explicableness**, the quality of being explicable.

1727 in BAILEY vol. II; and in mod. Dicts.

explicand (ɛksplɪ'kænd). *Philos.* [ad. L. *explicandus*, gerundive of *explicāre* to EXPLICATE.] = next.

1882 W. JAMES in *Mind* VII. 195 Such a system of explaining *notum per ignotum*, of making the *explicans* borrow credentials from the *explicand*,..is a strange candidate for the honour of being a complete rationaliser of the world.

explicandum (ɛksplɪ'kændəm). *Philos.* Pl. **explicanda.** [L., neut. of gerundive of *explicāre*: see EXPLICATE *v.*] The fact, thing, or expression to be explained or explicated. Cf. EXPLANANDUM.

1867 J. S. MILL *Lett.* (1910) II. 92 In the higher departments he leaves everything unexplained, or smuggles the explicandum into its own explanation. **1948** H. H. JOACHIM *Log. Stud.* i. 30 The *explicandum*..since it is a whole must in some sense consist of parts. **1953** C. S. BAZELL *Linguistic Form* 106 The explanation is not based on any facts known independently of the explicandum. **1953** R. B. BRAITHWAITE *Sci. Explan.* x. 319 The primary explicanda for science are particular empirical facts. **1966** J. J. KATZ *Philos. Lang.* iii. 54 Pragmatical concepts which could serve as explicanda.

explicans (ɛksplɪ'kænz). *Philos.* [L., pres. pple. of *explicāre*: see EXPLICATE *v.*] The explanatory part of an explanation; in the analysis or explication of a concept or expression, the part that gives the meaning. (Opp. EXPLICANDUM.)

1882 [see EXPLICAND]. **1953** R. B. BRAITHWAITE *Sci. Explan.* x. 321 The explicans in such an explanation is an event.

†**explicate** ('ɛksplɪkeɪt), *ppl. a. Obs.* [ad. L. *explicāt-us*, pa. pple. of *explicāre*: see EXPLICATE *v.*] **a.** Unfolded, expanded. **b.** Unfolded in words, fully stated; *esp.* of a syllogism. **c.** Made clear; plain, intelligible.

a. **1661** LOVELL *Hist. Anim. & Min.* Introd., The intestine in some is small..The appendices are explicate.

b. **1532** HEN. VIII in Burnet *Hist. Ref.* II. 169 When our cause was proponed to your holiness, when it was explicate and declared afore the same. **1605** A. WOTTON *Answ. Pop. Articles* 4 A simple syllogisme is either contract or explicate. *Ibid.* 5 In an explicate syllogisme the proposition is generall. **1628** T. SPENCER *Logick* 270 A sufficient reason why we should call a Syllogisme explicate: for thereby it is vnfolded to the full. **1648** N. ESTWICK *Treat. Holy Ghost* 53 The Proposition..is unwarrantable in the second explicate, or first figure.

c. **1647** JER. TAYLOR *Lib. Proph.* i. 7 Whatsoever is expressed..is made articulate and explicate. **1686** GOAD *Celest. Bodies* I. ix. 33 How explicate is the Solution of this great Question. **1698** R. FERGUSON *View Eccles.* 61 Thought them hardly either vindicable or explicate without it.

Hence †**'explicately** *adv.* = EXPLICITLY I.

a **1617** BAYNE *Dioc. Tryall* (1621) 19 People, who though explicately they did not beleeve in Christ, yet had in them the faith of the Messiah.

explicate ('ɛksplɪkeɪt), *v.* [f. L. *explicāt-* ppl. stem of *explicā-re*, f. *ex-* out + *plicāre* to fold, PLY.]

†**1. a.** *trans.* To unfold, unroll; to smooth out (wrinkles); to open out (what is wrapped up); to expand (buds, leaves, etc.). *Obs.*

1620 BP. KING *Serm.* 8 When he intendeth his business to purpose, then hee standeth vpon his feet, explicateth and displayeth his limbes. **1646** SIR T. BROWNE *Pseud. Ep.* II. vi. §4. 99 The Rose of Jericho will..explicate its flowers contracted. **1651** BEDELL *Life Erasmus* in *Fuller's Abel Rediv.* 69 A gold Ring, which explicated, became an exact celestiall sphere. **1660** SHARROCK *Vegetables* 37 The leaves ..explicate themselves. **1710** T. FULLER *Pharm. Extemp.* 193 It [the Glyster]..explicates Corrugations of the Fibres. **1712** BLACKMORE *Creation* 66 They explicate the leaves.

fig. **1536** LATIMER *1st Serm. bef. Convoc.* Wks. I. 32 If ye diligently roll them in your minds, and after explicate and open them. *a* **1652** J. SMITH *Sel. Disc.* v. 140 Our love is wont to explicate and unfold its affection.

†**b.** To spread out, expand in area or volume.

1578 BANISTER *Hist. Man* VIII. 103 The Muscles..explicatyng their owne substaunce, do constitute a tendinous Membran. **1666** G. HARVEY *Morb. Angl.* iv. 31 The blood being thus expanded and explicated into a turgency.

†**c.** To spread out to view, display. *Obs.*

1647 H. MORE *Poems* 235 From her centre Her pregnant mind she [the soul] fairly explicates In actuall forms. **1678** WANLEY *Wond. Lit. World* III. xliv. §30. 227/2 There the Zodiack did explicate its Signs.

†**2. a.** To disentangle, unravel; *fig.* (cf. 6). **b.** To disentangle, extricate *from*, *out of* difficulties.

a. **1663** SIR G. MACKENZIE *Relig. Stoic* xiii. (1685) 124 Apter to beget than to explicate difficulties. *a* **1713** ELLWOOD *Autobiog.* Supp. (1714) 438, I might cite a great deal more, to explicate this Controversie.

b. **1614** RALEIGH *Hist. World* II. v. v. §6. 582 Hee did neuer meet with any difficultie, whence hee could not explicate himselfe. **1668** CLARENDON *Vind.* Tracts (1727) 53 No way to explicate the kingdom out of those intricacies.

3. To develop, bring out what is implicitly contained in (a notion, principle, proposition).

1628 T. SPENCER *Logick* 260 A simple Syllogisme hath the parts contracted, or explicated. *a* **1716** SOUTH *Serm.* (1717) VI. 427 To explicate and draw forth this General into the several Particulars wrapt up and included in it. **1837–8** SIR W. HAMILTON *Logic* xix. (1866) I. 383, I do not think it necessary to explicate these two reasonings. **1864** BOWEN *Logic* iii. 48 By logicians generally..this principle has been explicated into three general Axioms.

4. To unfold in words; to give a detailed account of. Sometimes with indirect question as *obj.* Now *rare*; = EXPLAIN 3 a.

1531 ELYOT *Gov.* I. xv, I name him a gramarien..that can expounde good autours explicating the figures as well of sentences as wordes. **1553** POLE in Strype *Cranmer* II. 173 Ye have explicated how the whole matter..may be concluded. **1657** TOMLINSON *Renou's Disp.* 145 We might dilucidly explicate the..composition of medicaments. *a* **1734** NORTH *Exam.* III. vii. §52 (1740) 541 The Terms good and bad..being beforehand well explicated to the People. **1831** *Crayons from Commons* 48 In dismal doleful ploratory strain He explicates the amount of loss and gain. *a* **1834** LAMB *Misc. Wks.* (1871) 504 An unfairness..which this would not be quite the proper place for explicating.

absol. **1596** DALRYMPLE tr. *Leslie's Hist. Scot.* (1885) 8 Bot will explicat mair at large. **1651–3** JER. TAYLOR *Serm. for Year* i. (1850) 17 As Christ related, and His Apostles recorded and explicated.

†**5.** To disclose the cause or origin of (a phenomenon); to account for. *Obs.*; = EXPLAIN *v.* 5.

1605 TIMME *Quersit.* I. vii. 29 To explicate the sowernes of the vineagar. **1660** BOYLE *New Exp. Phys. Mech.* i. (1682) 13 There is yet another way to explicate the Spring of the Air. **1729** BUTLER *Serm.* Pref. Wks. 1874 II. 10 Perceptions ..which..it may not be very easy at first view to explicate.

6. a. To make clear the meaning of (anything); to remove difficulties or obscurities from; to clear up, explain; = EXPLAIN *v.* 3 b.

1622–62 HEYLIN *Cosmogr.* Introd. (1674) 18/1 Geography we will first define..And after explicate such terms..as are not obvious. **1650** S. CLARKE *Eccl. Hist.* I. (1654) 45 He was wondrous quick to explicate obscure passages. **1693** DRYDEN *Juvenal* Ded. liii, The last Verse of his last Satire.. is not yet sufficiently explicated. **1814** W. VAN MILDERT *Bampton Lect.* iii. (ed. 2) 82 Vain attempts to explicate points which..must ever remain enveloped in..mystery. **1865** BUSHNELL *Vicar. Sacr.* IV. i. (1868) 450 Terms by which they [the lustral figures] must be explicated. **1959** *Times Lit. Suppl.* 20 Mar. p. x/5 The *kerygma*..attempts to explicate it by saying that it only happens 'existentially' in human experience. **1966** J. J. KATZ *Philos. Lang.* iii. 17 Ordinary language philosophers tried to explicate the standards of usage underlying the linguistic behavior of those who do not abuse this freedom. **1967** C. L. WRENN *Word & Symbol* 2 Literary texts..are now being explicated in terms of 'symbolic realism', cultural anthropology, folk-myth and allegory.

†**b.** *refl.* To explain oneself; to make clear one's meaning. *Obs.*

1563 NOWEL *Serm. bef. Queen* (1853) 225 To explicate myself, I say, etc. **1631** BP. HALL *Rem. Wks.* (1660) 295 The Church of England having plainly explicated herself. **1638** FEATLY *Transub.* 253 Once more explicate your selfe.

†**c.** *intr.* To enter into explanations. *Obs. rare.*

1781 MAD. D'ARBLAY *Diary & Lett.* II. 77 We explicated about the letters and the coach and so forth.

Hence **'explicated** *ppl. a.*, unfolded, expanded; explained. **'explicating** *vbl. sb.*, the action of the verb EXPLICATE. **'explicating** *ppl. a.*, that unfolds; in quot. *intr.* for *refl.* expansive.

1884 FAIRBAIRN in *Contemp. Rev.* Mar. 362 A religion always is as its deity is..as it were the explicated idea of Him. **1531** ELYOT *Gov.* I. xiii, To him belongeth the explicating or unfoldinge of sentence. **1692** RAY *Dissol. World* III. v. (1732) 376 For the better explicating of Natural Things. **1616** BEAUM. & FL. *Faithful Friends* IV. i, Surcease a while this explicating joy.

explication (ɛksplɪˈkeɪʃən). [a. F. *explication*, ad. L. *explicātiōn-em*, n. of action f. *explicāre*: see EXPLICATE *v.*] The action of explicating.

†**1.** The action or process of unfolding (flowers, leaves, etc.). *Obs.*

1658 SIR T. BROWNE *Gard. Cyrus* II. 514 In the flowers of Sycamore..before explication. **1660** SHARROCK *Vegetables* 24 The moones being in the full at the first explication of the two dissimilar leaves.

2. The process of developing or bringing out what is implicitly contained in a notion, proposition, principle, etc.; the result of this process.

1656 tr. *Hobbes' Elem. Philos.* (1839) 70 Definitions..are nothing but the explication of our simple conceptions. **1837–8** SIR W. HAMILTON *Logic* xxiv. (1866) II. 12 A declaration is called an Explication, when the predicate or defining member indeterminately evolves only some of the characters belonging to the subject. **1864** BOWEN *Logic* iii. 48 The ground of this explication may be thus set forth.

3. The action or process of stating or describing in detail; a detailed statement or description.

1528 ROY *Sat.*, Of wholy Roodes there is soche a sight That bitwene this and mydnyght I coulde not make explication. **1588** FRAUNCE *Lawiers Log.* Ded., The more orderly explication of the Lawe. **1660** SHARROCK *Vegetables* 51 Explication of the manner of propagation by stems cut off from the Mother-plant. **1674** tr. *Scheffer's Lapland* i. 1 Olaus Magnus in the explication of his map of Scandinavia. **1674** GREW *Anat. Plants* III. II. (1682) 123 The Explication therefore of all those Particulars..will be my present Task. **1759** JOHNSON *Idler* No. 70 ¶4 Diffusion and explication are necessary to the instruction of those who..can only learn what is expressly taught.

†**4.** The action or process of unfolding the cause or origin of a phenomenon; a statement made for this purpose. *Obs.*

1692 BENTLEY *Boyle Lect.* 226 Those common attempts toward the explication of gravity. **1717** J. KEILL *Anim. Œcon.* Pref. (1738) 24 The Explications of the Animal Œconomy are equally certain..with the Propositions of Geometry. **1752** HUME *Ess. & Treat.* (1777) II. 114 No other explication can be given of this operation. **1764** REID *Inquiry* I. i. §2. 99 An explication..of the various phænomena of human nature.

5. The action or process of removing difficulty or obscurity from, or making clear the meaning of (a word, statement, symbol, etc.). Also, that which effects this; an explanation, interpretation.

1548–9 (Mar.) *Bk. Com. Prayer, Offices* 37 Certayne notes for the more playne explicacion..of things. **1578** TIMME *Calvin on Gen.* 43 The second word was added instead of an explication. **1651** C. CARTWRIGHT *Cert. Relig.* I. 235 Now take any of all these foure Explications of the Apostles words. **1660** BARROW *Euclid* Introd., The explication of the Signs or Characters. **1709** SWIFT *Merlin's Proph.*, I have not forced the words by my explication into any other sense. **1751** JOHNSON *Rambler* No. 99 ¶13 A better explication of a controverted line. *c* **1760** IBBOTS in *Times* 18 Apr. (1884) 4/2 Ten plates of Anglo-Saxon coins with explications. **1838–9** HALLAM *Hist. Lit.* II. ii. III. §20. 419 Such explication of contrarieties as might make them appear less incompatible with outward unity. **1872** BLACK *Adv. Phaeton* xix. 274 A mystery beyond explication.

†**b.** An exposition; a paraphrase. *Obs.*

1651 *Fuller's Abel Rediv., Life Luther* (1867) I. 59 In the year 1544, th 17th of November, he finished his explication of Genesis. *a* **1789** BURNEY *Hist. Mus.* (ed. 2) II. iv. 252 Two choristers sung the explication or paraphrase.

†**6.** = EXPLANATION 3.

1707 COLLIER *Refl. Ridic.* 70 If the Person they are address'd to is affronted, and demands an Explication. **1745** *Fortunate Orphan* 128 He told him, he desir'd to have an Explication with him.

‖**explication de texte** (ɛksplikasjɔ̃ də tɛkst). [Fr.] A detailed examination of the text of a literary work.

1935 G. N. HENNING *Representative Fr. Lyrics* (rev. ed.) p. vii, Following the Notes is a new feature in American textbooks, *Explications de textes*, whose minute analyses of *l'Expiation* and *Midi* may serve for a more improved appreciation of these and other poems. **1950** W. STEVENS *Let.* 13 Oct. (1967) 694 It is not only a skillful example of explication de texte, but it reveals yourself. **1962** N. NOWOTTNY *Lang. Poets Use* i. 19 The tradition of *explication de texte* offers methods of examining verifiable features of poems. **1962** R. QUIRK *Use of English* xiv. 244 It requires no pedestrian *explication de texte* to see here the tie between 'a passive bucket' and the grammatical passive 'be pumped into'.

explicative (ˈɛksplɪkeɪtɪv), *a.* and *sb.* [ad. L. *explicātīv-us*, f. *explicāre*: see EXPLICATE *v.*]

A. *adj.*

†**1.** Tending to unfold, or to unfold itself; expansive. In quot. *fig. Obs.*

1627–77 FELTHAM *Resolves* I. xxiv. 43 How contrary it is to Christianity, and the Nature of explicative Love.

2. a. Having the function of explaining; explanatory, interpretative. †Of a person: Explicit, affording explanation. **b.** *Logic.* Of a proposition or judgement: That merely explains what is implied in the subject; = ESSENTIAL. †**c.** *Gram.* (See quot. 1824).

1649 JER. TAYLOR *Gt. Exemp.* II. ix. 123 Here is forbidden ..an anger with deliberation, and purpose of revenge, this being explicative and additionall to the precept forbidding murder. **1725** WATTS *Logic* II. ii. §5 The term..is called explicative; for it only explains the subject. **1757** *Herald* (1758) I. No. 4. 62, I shall be particularly explicative in the course of these publications. **1824** L. MURRAY *Eng. Gram.* (ed. 5) I. 216 An explicative sentence is, when a thing is said to be or not to be.. in a direct manner. **1852** SIR W. HAMILTON *Discuss.* 273 In Mathematics the whole Science ..is only the evolution of a potential knowledge into an actual, and its procedure is thus merely explicative. **1877** E. CAIRD *Philos. Kant* II. i. 207 The new judgments..are all explicative or analytic. **1878** BAYNE *Purit. Rev.* x. 393 These are for Mr. Carlyle, the vital, the explicative facts in Cromwell's career and character.

B. *sb.* An explicative term.

1775 ADAIR *Amer. Ind.* 77 By the first name [green ear of corn], the Indians, as an explicative, term their passover. **1864** BOWEN *Logic* v. 144 With regard to Explicatives.

Hence **'explicatively** *adv.*, in an explanatory manner.

1775 ADAIR *Amer. Ind.* 22 They often call the bleak north-wind, explicatively, very evil, and accursed.

†**'explicator.** *Obs. rare.* Also 7 **explicater.** [a. L. *explicātor*, f. *explicāre*: see EXPLICATE *v.*] An expounder, explainer.

1677 HALE *Prim. Orig. Man.* I. i. 10 The Supposition of Epicurus, and his Explicator, Lucretius. **1697** J. SERGEANT *Solid Philos.* 36 The Explicaters of Ideas by Resemblances must be forced.

explicatory (ˈɛksplɪkətərɪ), *a.* [f. L. type **explicātōrius*, f. *explicātor*: see prec. and -ORY.] Having the function of explaining. Const. *of.*

1625 USSHER *Answ. Jesuit* 304 The like explicatorie repetition is noted..to haue been vsed by the Prophet. *a* **1677** BARROW *Serm.* I. xxv, Those evangelical commands, explicatory of this law. **1716** T. VINCENT (*title*), Explicatory Catechism, or an Explanation of the Assembly's Shorter Catechism. **1870** DISRAELI *Lothair* lxxi. 377 Making every allowance..for explicatory circumstances. **1889** *Spectator* 9 Nov., They were compelled to wait for the correspondents' full and explicatory accounts.

†**'explicature.** *Obs. rare*⁻¹. [f. *explicāt-* ppl. stem of *explicāre* (see EXPLICATE) + -URE.] ? The action of unfolding or displaying.

1592 R. D. *Hypnerotomachia* 85 b, Which stones [table diamonds] were wonderfully cut of a Cataglyphic explicature.

‖**'explicit,** *sb.* **a.** A med.L. word, used by scribes in indicating the end of a book, or of one of the separate pieces contained in a MS. It was regarded as a vb. in 3rd pers. sing., 'Here ends' (such a book, piece, etc.), the form *expliciunt* being used as pl. It seems, however, to have been originally an abbreviation of *explicitus* pa. pple., in *explicitus est liber*, lit. 'the book is unrolled'; cf. quot. 949. *Obs.*

[*a* **420** HIERONYMUS *Ep.* XXVIII. iv, Solemus completis opusculis..interponere Explicit aut Feliciter aut aliquid istius modi. **949** in Yepez *Chron. Ord. S. Benedicti* I. 92 (Du Cange) Explicitus est liber iste à Notario Sebastiano Diacono, notum perfectionis diem 4. Kalend. Februarii æræ 987.] *c* **1250** *Gen. & Ex.* (end), Explicit liber Exodus. *c* **1374** CHAUCER *Troylus* (end), Explicit liber Troili et Criseide. *c* **1450–60** in *Babees Bk.* (1868) 331 Expliciunt Statuta Familie bone Memorie. **1485** CAXTON *Chas. Gt.* (end), Explicit per William Caxton. **15..** *Piers of Fullham* 287 in Hazl. *E.P.P.* II. 12 Explysyth peers of fulham. **1595** G. M. *Gentleman's Acad.* 54 Explicit prima pars. [**1663–76** BULLOKAR, *Explicite*..ended or finished. **1866** KINGSLEY *Herew.* II. 402 Explicit.]

b. An instance of the use of this indication; hence, the last words or lines of a volume or section of a book; also *fig.*, conclusion, finis. (Cf. INCIPIT.)

a **1658** CLEVELAND *Poems, Agst. Sleep* 11 Sleep..Reasons Assassine, Fancies Bail; The Senses Curfew..Joys Explicite, unfathom'd Gulf of time. **1885** H. A. DOBSON *At Sign of Lyre* 45 Tired the hand and tired the wit Ere the final *Explicit!* **1897** [see INCIPIT]. **1932** BLUNDEN *Face of England* 81 The last man..came..to provide the *explicit.* **1963** *Times Lit. Suppl.* 22 Feb. 143/4 Appendices listing all the *explicits* and *incipits.*

†**ex'plicit,** *v. Obs.* [f. L. *explicit-* ppl. stem of *explicāre* to unfold: see EXPLICATE.] *intr.* Of a leaf: To unfold, open out.

1657 TOMLINSON *Renou's Disp.* 650 Leaves of red Roses perfectly explicited.

explicit (ɛkˈsplɪsɪt), *a.* Also 7 **explicite.** [a. Fr. *explicite*, ad. L. *explicit-us*, pa. pple. of *explicāre* to unfold: see EXPLICATE.]

†**1.** Of the brow: Free from folds or wrinkles; smooth. Of a plot: Free from intricacies; simple.

1671 MILTON *Samson* Introd., That commonly called the plot, whether intricate or explicit. **1697** EVELYN *Numism.* ix. 296 The chearful Forehead is Explicit and smooth.

2. Of knowledge, a notion, etc.: Developed in detail; hence, clear, definite. ***explicit faith, belief*** (*Theol.*): the acceptance of a doctrine with distinct apprehension of all that is logically involved in it; opposed to *implicit faith.*

1651 BAXTER *Inf. Bapt.* 119 Every man is bound to have a personall explicite Faith of his own. **1656** BRAMHALL *Replic.* ii. 85 The explicite beliefe of them is no necessary part of Christian communion. **1690** LOCKE *Hum. Und.* I. ii. (1695) 11 The Understanding hath an implicit Knowledge of these Principles, but not an explicit, before this first hearing. *a* **1716** SOUTH *Serm.* (J.), How impossible it is for us to have a clear and explicit notion of that which is infinite. **1880** LITTLEDALE *Plain Reas.* xxv. 73 Implicit belief in the Pope is not sufficient; that must be explicit.

3. a. Of declarations, indications, utterances: Distinctly expressing all that is meant; leaving nothing merely implied or suggested; express.

1613 R. C. *Table Alph.* (ed. 3), *Explicite*, made manifest, vnfolded. **1642** MILTON *Argt. conc. Militia* 26 An Oath ought to be explicite, I mean, without implications or etcetera's. **1654** CROMWELL *Sp.* 12 Sept., There was an explicit consent and an implicit consent. **1726** DE FOE *Hist. Devil* I. v. (1840) 66 What their [the angels'] sin was is not explicit. **1769** ROBERTSON *Chas. V*, III. VII. 62 The Landgrave..wrote to Granvelle..begging an explicit declaration of what they had to fear or hope. **1789** BENTHAM *Princ. Legisl.* xi. §42 If a poor man who is ready to die with hunger steal a loaf of bread, it is a less explicit sign of depravity than etc.]. **1856** FROUDE *Hist. Eng.* (1858) II. vii. 201 Promises more explicit had been held out to him of forgiveness.

b. Of a magazine, film, etc.: sexually explicit, that describes or portrays nudity or sexual activity.

1971 *Hansard Lords* 21 Apr. 643 There are, my expert friend said, still some prohibitions..in the cinema—including what he calls 'explicit penetration'. **1972** R. MICHAEL et al. *ABZ of Pornography* 39 His films are not explicit—no genitals for instance—and they are often intentionally droll and whimsical. **1977** *Washington Post* 21 Sept. B6/3 Juveniles are not mature enough to cope with the often provocative and explicit material of sex magazines. **1985** *Times* 4 Dec. 1/2 The aim..would be to prevent newsagents and other shops from selling explicit magazines or other publications. **1986** *Daily Tel.* 3 Jan. 12/4 Michael O'Connor of Marine City, Michigan, complained that the connotation of 'explicit' is getting lost, especially when it is linked to certains [*sic*] nouns, such as 'lyrics'. 'Will this rich and expressive word have its meaning narrowed and inextricably entwined with sex, violence and drugs?' he asked.

4. Hence of persons, their qualities, etc.: Speaking out fully all that is meant; definite and unreserved in expression; outspoken.

1726 BUTLER *Serm.* vii. 134 How explicit they are with themselves, is another Question. **1756** POTT *Chirurg. Wks.* (1790) II. 10 To express myself in as plain, explicit and intelligible manner as I am able. **1770** *Junius Lett.* xxxvi. 172 The explicit firmness and decision of a king. *a* **1859** MACAULAY *Biog.* (1867) 180 No man who is at the head of affairs always wishes to be explicit.

5. *Math.* Of a function: having the dependent variable defined directly in terms of the independent variable or variables. Cf. *implicit function* (IMPLICIT *a.* 2).

1814 P. BARLOW *New Math. & Philos. Dict.* sig. X7 (recto) Having given the methods..of obtaining the derived functions, of functions of one or more quantities, whether those functions be explicit or implicit,..we will now show how this theory may be applied. **1830** *Encycl. Metrop.* (1845) I. 796 If z were expressed by an explicit function of x and y, to determine dz/dx we should consider y as a constant in that function, and then differentiate it as a function of x alone. **1886** J. EDWARDS *Diff. Calc.* i. 4 If the equation connecting the variables be solved for the dependent variable, that variable is reduced from being an implicit to being an explicit function of the remaining variable or variables. **1955** D. A. QUADLING *Math. Analysis* xiii. 223 There is no hard and fast distinction between implicit and explicit functions. Any function defined explicitly by an equation $y = f(x)$ could equally well be defined implicitly by the equation $g(x, y) = 0$, where $g(x, y) \equiv y - f(x)$.

explicitly (ɛkˈsplɪsɪtlɪ), *adv.* [f. as prec. + -LY².] In an explicit manner.

1. As a matter of 'explicit' knowledge, belief, or statement; expressly and not merely by implication. Opposed to *implicitly.* Now only (exc. *Theol.*) with reference to statements, in which use it approaches sense 2.

a **1638** MEDE *Wks.* IV. lxxvii. 863 That the Roman Church ..erreth not *in..Fundamentalibus Fidei Articulis*, because explicitely they profess them, howsoever..implicitely and by consequent they subvert them. **1651** HOBBES *Govt. & Soc.* xiv. §8. 217 Every civill Law hath a penalty annexed to it, either explicitly or implicitly. **1791** BURKE *App. Whigs* Wks. 1842 I. 511 He explicitly limits his ideas of resistance. **1875** MANNING *Mission H. Ghost* xvi. 437 Faith believes the whole revelation of God explicitly so far as it knows it; implicitly so far as it is not known as yet. **1879** *Cassell's Techn. Educ.* I. 323 Passages of various dates speak explicitly of the use of the compass for land purposes.

2. In a definite and unambiguous manner; unequivocally.

1756 BP. LOWTH *Let. to Bp. Warburton* 129, I thought it incumbent upon me to tell you explicitly..that I was not to be frightened. **1797** MRS. RADCLIFFE *Italian* iii, Speak explicitly and to the point. **1841** MIALL *Nonconf.* I. 1 We.. avow most explicitly that [etc.].

3. With detailed exposition.

1729 BUTLER *Serm.* Wks. 1874 II. 24 This part of the office of conscience is beyond my present design explicitly to consider. **1875** JOWETT *Plato* (ed. 2) V. 195 Will you tell me a little more explicitly what [etc.]?

explicitness (ɛkˈsplɪsɪtnɪs). [f. as prec. + -NESS.] The quality of being explicit; distinctness of statement or (formerly) of apprehension; freedom from ambiguity or obscurity of meaning; outspokenness.

1647 JER. TAYLOR *Lib. Proph.* xii. 187 Whose judgement (of speculative doctrine) is..with lesse curiosity and explicitenesse declared in Scripture. *a* **1716** SOUTH *Serm.* (1737) IV. vii. 284 The knowledge of this article..was by no means received with..explicitness in the ancient Jewish Church. **1748** RICHARDSON *Clarissa* (1811) I. xxxii. 236 An explicitness that can admit of no mistake. **1826** DISRAELI *Viv. Grey* IV. iv, Explicitness is not the language of such as

I am. **1873** EARLE *Philol. Eng. Tongue* §581 That explicitness of syntax.

†ex'plike, *v. Obs. rare*⁻¹. [ad. F. *explique-r* to explain, ad. L. *explicāre*: see EXPLICATE.] *trans.* To unfold in words; to narrate at length.

1491 CAXTON *Vitas Patr.* (W. de W. 1495) I. Prol. 1 a/1 The feruente charytee of the freres..haue ofte tymes requyred vs to..explyke the lyues of holy Heremytes.

explodable (ɛkˈspləʊdəb(ə)l), *a.* [f. EXPLODE *v.* + -ABLE.] That may be exploded.

1871 LE FANU *Ten. Malory* lix. 343 As I have seen people at a chemical lecture eye the explodable compounds on the professor's table.

explode (ɛkˈspləʊd), *v.* [ad. L. *explōdĕre*, *explaudĕre* to drive out by clapping, hiss (a player) off the stage, f. *ex-* out + *plaudĕre* to clap: cf. APPLAUD, PLAUDIT. Cotgr. 1611 has Fr. *exploder* in sense 1.

With the non-Lat. senses 4–6 cf. late L. *displōdĕre* (see DISPLODE) used of the bursting of a bladder. Senses 5 and 6, now the prevailing senses, are not recognized by Johnson.]

†**1. a.** *trans.* To clap and hoot (a player, play, etc.) off the stage; hence *gen.* to drive away with expressions of disapprobation; to cry down; to banish ignominiously. Also *fig.* Const. *from*, *out of*, and with double obj. *Obs.*

1621 BURTON *Anat. Mel.* Democr. to Rdr. (1651) 19 Vertue and Wisdom..were hissed out, and exploded by the common people. **1663** COWLEY *Verses & Ess.* (1669) 69 Why they did not hiss, and explode him off the Stage. **1670** *Moral State Eng.* 12 Religion is a thing they explode conversation. **1749** FIELDING *Tom Jones* IV. vi, In the playhouse..when he doth wrong, no critic is so apt to hiss and explode him. *a* **1785** GLOVER *Athenaid* xxx. 94 Of justice and religion..He [Enoch] spake exploded. **1823** LAMB *Elia*, *Artif. Comedy* Wks. 402 Congreve and Farquhar show their heads once in seven years only, to be exploded and put down. [**1849** W. FITZGERALD tr. *Whitaker's Disput.* 21 Who would not cry out against and explode the patrons of Cerinthus.]

†**b.** To mock at, deride. *Obs. rare.*

1618 CHAPMAN *Hesiod* II. 570 When thou hast once begun to build a house, Leav't not unfinish'd, lest the..Ill-spoken crow..from her bough thy means outgone explode.

†**c.** Of a thing: To cause to be hooted (off the stage). *nonce-use.*

1768 TUCKER *Lt. Nat.* (1852) I. 335 The absurdity..was so glaring, that it has quite exploded that notion off the stage.

2. To reject with scorn (an opinion, proposal, custom). Also in weaker sense: To reject, discard. *Obs.* exc. in *passive*, which is still occas. used with the sense: To be disused, to be rejected as obsolete (cf. 3).

1538 LELAND *Itin.* V. 56 When Glan is set with a worde præceding G is exploded. **1609** BACON *Case of Post-nati* Wks. 1803 IV. 343 But the court *una voce* exploded this reason, and said [etc.]. **1696** TRYON *Misc.* xliv. 99 Not that I wholly Explode Astrology; I believe there is something in it. **1739** LABELYE *Short Acc. Piers Westm. Bridge* 46 This Method of building..having been exploded by the Hon. Board as insufficient. **1790** BEWICK *Quadrupeds* (1807) 55 This breed is now nearly exploded, being considered..as unprofitable. **1822** IMISON *Sc. & Art* I. 132 These effects..were formerly attributed to suction; a word which ought to be exploded. **1850** DAUBENY *Atom. Th.* iii. (ed. 2) 94 As new views came into vogue, or old errors became exploded. **1861** ELSIE GARRETT in *Gd. Words* 410 The old airs..are exploded for Italian bravuras.

3. To cause to be rejected; to bring into disrepute; to expose the hollowness of; to discredit; †to bring into disuse.

Now often associated with sense 6; hence it tends to be restricted to cases in which the fig. use of that sense would be applicable.

a **1635** NAUNTON *Fragm. Reg.* (Arb.) 43 The Priests forged Letter..was soon after exploded by the Priests own confession. **1764** *Mem. G. Psalmanazar* 203, I was farther hired to explode their doctrine of predestination. **1762–71** H. WALPOLE *Vertue's Anecd. Paint.* (1786) III. 173 The famous crown-piece..did not explode the others. **1808** *Med. Jrnl.* XIX. 266 Cullen..laboured to explode the humoral pathology. **1846** WRIGHT *Ess. Mid. Ages* I. iii. 97 Their existence has entirely exploded the old notion that England never possessed any native romances. **1872** LIDDON *Elem. Relig.* i. 30 When the idol has been pulverized and the lie is exploded. **1881** WILLIAMSON in *Nature* No. 626. 607, I thought that I had thoroughly exploded that fallacy.

†**4. a.** To drive forth (air); to emit. **b.** To drive out with violence and sudden noise. *Obs.*

a. *a* **1660** BOYLE *New. Exp. Phys. Mech.* 352 The inspired Air..when 'tis exploded, carrys them away with it self. **1676** H. MORE *Remarks* 174 The smallest charge of Gun-powder will..explode the Bullet with equal force. **1731** E. BAYNARD *Health* (1740) 28 That air again the lungs explode When robbed of its nitrous load.

b. **1671** R. BOHUN *Wind* 300 These Raging Minerals..are exploded with the greatest violence. **1679** PLOT *Staffordsh.* (1686) 15 The effects of Lightning, exploded from the Clouds. **1712** BLACKMORE *Creation* v. (ed. 2) 257 The kindled Powder did explode The massy Ball. **1755** in JOHNSON. **1807** SOUTHEY *Espriella's Lett.* III. 324 Pieces of this [earth-coal] are frequently exploded into the room. **1813** SOUTHEY *Nelson* (1844) 154 The vast height to which they [masts] had been exploded. **1826** [see EXPLODED *ppl. a.* 3].

5. a. *intr.* To 'go off' with a loud noise. Of gas, gunpowder, etc.: To expand violently with a loud report under the influence of suddenly developed internal energy; hence, of a charged jar, mine, etc. Of a boiler, gun, etc.: To fly in pieces, burst, from a similar cause.

1790 GOUV. MORRIS in Sparks *Life & Writ.* (1832) II. 96 All Europe is like a mine ready to explode. **1816** J. SMITH *Panorama Sc. & Art* II. 232 Let one ball..touch the ball of the charged jar..the jar will then of course explode. **1858** GREENER *Gunnery* 281 Place upon a plate a few grains of powder..As the plate becomes heated..the whole explodes. **1879** TYNDALL *Fragm. Sc.* I. x. 319 They [rockets] exploded with a very loud report in the air.

b. *transf.* and *fig.*

1817 LD. CASTLEREAGH in *Parl. Deb.* 279 A desperate conspiracy..which had..exploded already. **1840** DE QUINCEY *Wks.* (1862) X. 179 We..rushed down forty-five stairs, and exploded from the house with a fury, etc. **1867** BAKER *Albert N'yanza* II. 280 The effect produced made the crowd..explode with laughter. **1888** BURGON *12 Gd. Men* II. v. 63 Conscious that I must certainly explode if he kept me for another half-minute. **1891** E. PEACOCK *N. Brendon* I. 63 'Confound him!' or some stronger expletive exploded from the Earl's lips.

c. *Phys.* To break out or burst forth *into*.

1882 E. G. LORING in *Alien. & Neurol.* (1887) VIII. 130 The irritation..may..develop gradually, or explode suddenly, into an actual inflammation.

d. Of population: to increase suddenly or rapidly. Cf. EXPLOSION 4 b.

1959 *N.Y. Times* 15 Nov. 25/2 The population of the Bandung area has exploded from 167,000 in 1930 to 1,200,000 this year. **1962** *Listener* 15 Nov. 795/2 The relentlessly exploding population. **1965** *New Statesman* 30 Apr. 672/2 Population has 'exploded' only in the last three centuries because of our new-found science, technology and humanity.

6. a. *trans.* To cause (a gas, gunpowder, also a magazine, mine, etc.) to 'go off' with a loud noise; to 'blow up'.

1794 SULLIVAN *View Nat.* I. 192 In an exhausted receiver ..neither can a bell be heard..nor gun-powder be exploded. **1807** T. THOMSON *Chem.* (ed. 3) II. 110 When oxygen and hydrogen gas are exploded. **1875** URE *Dict. Arts* II. 762 The gun-cotton was exploded under the pressure of a confined space. **1890** *Spectator* 15 May, On Tuesday night, Lord Randolph Churchill exploded his little mine.

b. *transf.* and *fig.*

1822, **1832** [see CATAMARAN 2]. **1842** S. R. MAITLAND *Notes Foxe's Martyrs* II. Mr. Cattley..exploded all this conceit and insolence upon a matter which, etc. **1850** REDDING *Yesterday & To-day* (1863) III. 42 So he took out his snuff-box, once more at his ease, Inhaled a full pinch, and exploded a sneeze. **1864** LOWELL *Fireside Trav.* 256 They [Italians] explode each other on mere contact..like two hostile gases. **1878** SIMPSON *Sch. Shaks.* I. 11 The plot was exploded by the committal of Somerset..to the Tower.

exploded (ɛkˈspləʊdɛd), *ppl. a.* [f. prec. + -ED¹.] In senses of the verb.

†**1.** That has been hissed off the stage. *Obs.*

1713 SWIFT *Cadenus & V.* Wks. 1755 III. II. 13 Fustian from exploded plays. **1779–81** JOHNSON *L.P.*, *Pope* Wks. IV. 81 After the *Three Hours after Marriage* had been driven off the stage..while the exploded scene was yet fresh in memory.

2. a. Held in contempt; rejected, scouted. Also in weaker sense, disused, out of fashion. (Said of customs, opinions, etc.; rarely of persons.)

1626 MASSINGER *Rom. Actor* IV. ii, To put in an exploded plea In the court of Venus. **1710** STEELE *Tatler* No. 58 ⁋2 A Thing so exploded as speaking hard Words. **1790** BURKE *Fr. Rev.* 36 A conflict with some of those exploded fanatics of slavery. **1793** BEDDOES *Catarrh* 160 The exploded theories of Boerhaave or Cullen. **1868** MILMAN *St. Paul's* xix. 486 When mercy was on all sides an exploded virtue, he dared to be merciful. **1879** MCCARTHY *Own Times* II. xxiii. 185 The time..had gone by when such exploded politics could even interest the people.

†**b.** Of a material object: Discarded, disused; out of fashion. *Obs.*

1823 LAMB *Elia* Ser. I. xviii. 194 The little cool playful streams those exploded cherubs uttered. **1829** *The Bengallee* 169 An old Dowager's now exploded pair of pockets.

†**3.** Driven forth with violence and sudden noise.

1826 DISRAELI *Viv. Grey* VI. i, The exploded cork whizzed through the air.

4. a. In sense 6 of the verb.

1858 GREENER *Gunnery* 209 Conical form being best suited..to the action of the exploded fluid.

fig. **1876** HOLLAND *Sev. Oaks* viii. 109 It had been.. occupied for a year or two by an exploded millionaire.

b. Of a model or illustrated technical drawing: showing all the separate components as if 'exploded' from the complete unit but retaining their relative positions.

1947 H. C. ELLIOTT *Textbk. Nerv. Syst.* p. xi/2 New features are encountered..; among these is a simplified form of the 'exploded diagram'. **1949** *Jrnl. R. Aeronaut. Soc.* LIII. 60/2 They had to study the exploded drawing of the components. **1951** *Engineering* 13 July 33/2 An 'exploded' model shows the layout of a pit head. **1962** CORSON & LORRAIN *Introd. Electromagn. Fields* ii. 42 The exploded view shows one of the volume elements in detail.

explodent (ɛkˈspləʊdənt). *Phonetics.* [ad. L. *explōdent-em*, pr. pple. of *explōdĕre* to EXPLODE.] A consonant-sound produced by the sudden escape of breath after the closure of the oral passage (as *p*, *b*, *t*, *d*, *k*, *g*); a 'check', 'mute', or 'stop'; = EXPLOSIVE B. 1.

1861 *Proc. Amer. Phil. Soc.* VIII. 371 The combination of two explodents. **1865** *Pall Mall G.* 11 Feb. 6 The two adjectives horrible and abominable—three explodents and one aspirate in three words. **1885** *Athenæum* 14 Mar. 349/2 Mr. Cayley held that all explodents suggested impact.

exploder (ɛkˈspləʊdə(r)). [f. EXPLODE + -ER¹.] One who, or that which, explodes.

†**1.** One who rejects (a doctrine, etc.); one who denies the existence of (something). *Obs.*

1659 H. MORE *Immort. Soul* (1662) 39 Mr. Hobbs, that confident Exploder of Immaterial Substances out of the world. **1678** CUDWORTH *Intell. Syst.* Pref. 17 [Some affirm that atheists do not exist, but] these so confident exploders of them are both unskilled in..antiquity, and unacquainted with the present age. **1681** HALLYWELL *Melampr.* 3 This age hath produced too many confident Exploders of Immaterial Substances. *a* **1716** SOUTH *Serm.* (1737) VI. vii. 276 Scandalous exploders of the doctrine of passive obedience.

2. One who refutes a theory, etc.

1863 J. BROWN *Horæ Subs.* (1882) 320 Mighty expiscators and exploders of myths.

3. Something which bursts with a loud noise.

1858 GREENER *Gunnery* 238 Things..called guns. Pocket volcanoes would be a fitter title, or portable exploders.

4. That which causes explosion; a contrivance for exploding gunpowder, etc.

1874 KNIGHT *Dict. Mech.* I. 853/2 The gun..has..the needle-exploder and bolt breech. **1880** *Libr. Univ. Knowl.* VI. 359 For mining, electric fuses are used, called also exploders. **1884** A. G. HAKE *Chinese Gordon* x. 254 Firing a gun 150 yards off with a magnetic exploder.

exploding (ɛkˈspləʊdɪŋ), *vbl. sb.* [f. as prec. + -ING¹.] The action of the verb EXPLODE in various senses.

1665 GLANVILL *Sceps. Sci.* Addr. 13 The confident exploding of all immaterial Substances. *Ibid.* 71 Our Author's Metaphysical argument against a Vacuum (the exploding of which he thinks so necessary).

b. *attrib.*

1822 IMISON *Sc. & Art* II. 15 These instruments are called exploding tubes. **1881** GREENER *Gun* 336 The tumbler strikes an exploding-pin screwed into the false breech.

ex'ploding, *ppl. a.* [f. as prec. + -ING².] That explodes. †**a.** That drives away with scorn. **b.** That causes a loud and sudden noise. **c.** That flies into pieces with loud report. ***exploding wire***, a wire subjected to a sudden and very high current so that it explodes violently; also *attrib.*

1667 MILTON *P.L.* x. 546 Thus with th'applause they meant, Turnd to exploding hiss. **1853** KANE *Grinnell Exp.* xxxvii. (1856) 337 The howling, the clattering, the exploding din. **1883** *Academy* 23 June 444/1 That tree..has the air of an exploding shell. **1920** *Astrophysical Jrnl.* LI. 40 The larger part of the energy of the condenser is expended in the exploding wire. **1961** *Aeroplane* 3 Feb. 110/2 U.S. Air Force is investigating the use of 'exploding wires' made of magnetic materials which can be accelerated and controlled by magnetic fields for the electrical propulsion of space vehicles. **1963** *New Scientist* 16 May 386/1 The term 'exploding wire' has..been applied to almost any situation where a conductor..disintegrated with a loud report. *Ibid.* 386/2 The objective in an exploding wire experiment is to bring a large amount of energy into the wire very quickly.

exploit (ˈɛksplɔɪt, ɛkˈsplɔɪt), *sb.* Forms: 4 esploit(e, 5 explait, expleyte, 5–7 exployt(e, (6 exploicte), 6– exploit. [a. OFr. *esplait*, *esploit* m., *esploite* fem., and their refashioned forms *exploit*, *exploite*, etc. = Pr. *espleit* m., *esplecha* fem.:—vulgar L. **explic'tum*, *explic'ta* (med.L. *esplectum*, *expletum* n., *explecta* fem.), L. *explicitum*, *explicita*, neut. and fem. pples. of *explicāre*: see EXPLICATE. The etymological sense is thus 'something unfolded, brought out, or put forth'; the action of unfolding or developing.]

†**1.** Advantage, progress, speed, success; furtherance. Const. *of*. ***to make exploit***: to make speed, to meet with success. *Obs.*

1393 GOWER *Conf.* II. 258 The sail goth up, and forth they straught, But none esploit therof they caught. *c* **1400** *Destr. Troy* 3661 For explait of þere spede, þai spekyn in fere To chese hom a cheftayn. **1430** LYDG. *Chron. Troy* I. vi, For he full sory was withouten dread, Of the expleyte and of the happye spede Of this Iason. **1494** FABYAN *Chron.* VI. clxxvi. 173 Of whose exployt or spede myne auctour maketh no mensyon. **1525** LD. BERNERS *Froiss.* II. xci. [lxxxvii.] 272 His ambassadours hadde made no better exployte.

†**2.** The endeavour to gain advantage or mastery over (a person or place); an attempt to capture or subdue; hence, a military or naval expedition or enterprise. † ***in exploit***: in action or combat. *Obs.*

1483 CAXTON *Gold. Leg.* 87/4 He began to helpe them in theyr exployte of the see and anon the tempest cessed. **1555** *Fardle Facions* II. iii. 133 Thei prophecied..vnto Alexandre victory, when he made his exploicte towarde Darius. **1601** SHAKS. *All's Well* IV. i. 41, I must giue my selfe some hurts, and say I got them in exploit. *a* **1627** J. HAYWARD *Annals Four Y. Eliz.* (1840) 55 The Captaines drewe to consideration all the meanes for the exploit of the towne. **1692** LUTTRELL *Brief Rel.* (1857) II. 495 Captain Mees..has undertaken the exploit of St. Maloes. **1755** SMOLLETT *Quix.* (1803) II. 24 The glory of having undertaken such an exploit no malice..can impair.

b. An enterprise, project. *rare* (after mod.F.).

1879 TROLLOPE *Thackeray* 50 Thackeray had become big enough to give a special éclat to any literary exploit to which he attached himself.

3. An act or deed; a feat; in modern use, an achievement displaying a brilliant degree of bravery or skill.

c1538 R. COWLEY in Ellis *Orig. Lett.* II. 126 II. 96 They doo noo exployte not so moche as to shote oon gone. **1594** SHAKS. *Rich. III*, IV. ii. 35 Whom corrupting Gold Will tempt vnto a close exploit of Death. **1610** HEALEY *St. Aug. Citie of God* 845 Magicians can doe such exployetes by the devills meanes. **1725** DE FOE *Voy. round World* (1840) 15 For many years it was counted a great exploit to pass this strait. **1868** E. EDWARDS *Raleigh* I. vii. 110 Drake's exploits strung the patriotism..of the sailors to a lofty pitch. **1879** FROUDE *Cæsar* xix. 308 The conquest of Gaul had been an exploit of extraordinary military difficulty.

†**4.** Carrying out, execution, performance. ***to put in exploit***: to put in practice. *Obs.*

1581 J. BELL *Haddon's Answ. Osor.* 213 If..the whole exployt of thinges be governed by hym. **1599** SANDYS *Europæ Spec.* (1632) 75 A..Captaine, who scornes to imitate any stratageme..used by the enemy, though the putting it in exploit might give him assured victory.

†**5.** *Law.* A citation or summons; a writ. Cf. Fr. *exploit*. *Obs.*

[**1611** COTGR., *Exploict*..an adiournement or citation.] **1622** MALYNES *Anc. Law-Merch.* 457 Any summons or arrest, exploit or assignement. **1682** WARBURTON *Hist. Guernsey* (1822) 82 Exploits, which is the adjourning or citing of such persons, against whom any action is brought.

exploit (ɛk'splɔɪt), *v.* Forms: 4 **expleiten**, 5 **expleyt**, **explite**, 5–7 **exploite**, **-yte**, 6– **exploit**. [ad. Fr. *exploit-er* = Pr. *expleitar*, *explectar*:—L. **explicitāre*, freq. of *explicāre*: see EXPLICATE. Sense 4 is a recent adoption of the mod. vb.]

†**1.** *trans.* To accomplish, achieve, execute, perform; to fight (a battle). *Obs.*

c**1400** *Rom. Rose* 6177, I dwelle with hem..That worship of this world coveiten, And grete nede kunnen expleiten. c**1430** LYDG. *Min. Poems* (Percy Soc.) 218 Massageres.. T'expleyte the journe al tymes of the yeere. **1483** CAXTON *Gold. Leg.* 362/2 They knewe wel that they sholde no thyng exployte of their entente. c**1500** *Melusine* 81, I ordeyne the bataill to be to morow exploited. **1531** ELYOT *Gov.* I. xxvi, They departed without exploytinge their message. **1577–87** HOLINSHED *Chron.* (1806) I. 502 P. Turpilianus..sat still without exploiting anie notable enterprise. **1611** SPEED *Hist. Gt. Brit.* IX. xi. §47 It is euident, that these tragedies against the Lords were exployted by others. **1674** *Lond. Gaz.* No. 882/4 We doubt not..but something considerable will be exploited by them. **1687** A. LOVELL tr. *Bergerac's Com. Hist.* I. 127 The first thing they exploited, was to distribute my Body among them into several Provinces. **1775** in ASH.

†**b.** ***to exploit out***: to achieve the expulsion of.

c**1525** SKELTON *Sp. Parrot* 307 To exployte the man owte of the mone.

2. †**a.** *refl.* To apply, exert oneself. Cf. OFr. *s'exploiter*. *Obs.*

1490 CAXTON *Eneydos* xxvi. 95 Why consumest thy self slepynge without exploityng the in thy vyage. **1530** PALSGR. 542/1 They exployted them so faste that within shorte space they came to their journayes ende.

†**b.** *intr.* To act with effect; to get on, prosper, speed. Also in *impers. pass. Obs.*

c**1477** CAXTON *Jason* 10 b, Peleus..not knowing how he might exploite for to attayne to execute his dampnable enuye. *Ibid.* 66 If I abode here I should not exployte but lose my tyme. c**1500** *Melusine* 188 The knight..rehereed to them how he had exployted. **1592** WYRLEY *Armorie* 154 Some did to me vnfold..how at Arde Gomigines did hold, Exploiting well. **1602** WARNER *Alb. Eng.* Epit. (1612) 384 During the minoritie of this King Richard..brauely was it exployted in Fraunce by his Agents.

†**3.** *trans.* ? To cause to succeed, prosper. *Obs.*

c**1430** LYDG. *Lyfe our Ladye* (Caxton) C v a, Let thy grace to me descende..My rude tunge to explite and spede.

4. To 'work' (a mine, etc.); to turn to industrial account (natural resources). **b.** *transf.* To utilize for one's own ends, treat selfishly as mere workable material (persons, etc.); to 'make capital out of'.

1838 *New Monthly Mag.* LIII. 306 The Humbughausens ..have exploited the obscure (to use a French phrase where we have no proper equivalent) with..profit. **1847** MRS. CARLYLE *Lett.* II. 25 Exploiting that poor girl for their idle purposes of curiosity. **1865** E. ARNOLD in *Reader* No. 115. 282/1 In exploiting mineral resources. **1878** *Print. Trades Jrnl.* XXIII. 7 The great German naturalist..finds himself coolly exploited by a Paris publisher. **1888** *Westm. Rev.* July 58 An association of capitalist shareholders, exploiting their wage-paid labourers. **1890** *Nature* 6 Feb. 313 European exiles..were then..exploiting the riches of the East.

5. *intr.* To conduct mining operations *for*.

1887 *Pop. Sci. Monthly*, Apr. XXX. 857 Some two years ago a Belgian engineer proposed to exploit for petroleum.

Hence **ex'ploited**, **ex'ploiting** *ppl. a.* and *vbl. sb.*

1883 *Pall Mall G.* 28 Aug. 1/1 The Jews..attracting to themselves alone the animosity which is deserved by the whole 'exploiting' class. **1887** *Ibid.* 20 Aug. 4/2 There is no such exploited class as trained nurses in fashionable 'institutions'. **1887** T. KIRKUP *Inq. Socialism* iii. 87 The domineering and exploiting spirit.

exploita'bility. [f. EXPLOITABLE *a.*: see -ILITY.] Capability of being exploited.

1960 *Commentary* June 469/2 Enemies of capitalism.. never predicted..its bounteous exploitability. **1969** *New Scientist* 20 Feb. 395/2 The 'exploitability' criterion means in effect that the sea-bed and subsoil underneath all the oceans of the world have already been partitioned between the coastal states.

ex'ploitable, *a.* [f. EXPLOIT *v.* + -ABLE.]

†**a.** Capable of being accomplished. *Obs.* **b.** Capable of being exploited (in sense 4 b).

1611 COTGR., *Exploitable*..readie to be performed, easie to be done. **1887** tr. *Marx' Capital* II. xxv. 633 This excess of capital..makes exploitable labour-power sufficient.

ex'ploitage. [f. as prec. + -AGE.] = next.

1884 *My Ducats & Daughter* III. xxiii. 35 He would not lend himself to exploitage. **1884** W. MORRIS in *Century Mag.* July (1886) 397 It [profit-sharing] would do nothing toward the extinction of exploitage.

exploitation (ɛksplɔɪ'teɪʃən). [a. Fr. *exploitation*, f. *exploiter*: see EXPLOIT *v.*]

1. The action of exploiting or turning to account; productive working or profitable management (of mines, cattle, etc.). Also, an instance of this.

1803 W. TAYLOR in *Ann. Rev.* I. 362 Similar proofs of the deficient commercial exploitation of these colonies perpetually occur. **1825** *New Monthly Mag.* XIII. 588 Clear evidence of success, wanting to all other 'exploitations' (excuse the gallicism). **1836** *Blackw. Mag.* XL. 766 What is to be the next exploitation of genius? Travels? **1881** P. GEDDES in *Nature* No. 622. 534 The second..inquires whether the exploitation of plants or animals be more profitable in the given society. **1885** A. J. EVANS in *Archaeol.* XLIX. 8 Cities..owed their rise..to the exploitation of the mineral wealth of the province.

b. The action of turning to account for selfish purposes, using for one's own profit.

[**1844** M. HENNELL *Social Syst.* 108 Slavery, the use of man by man (*exploitation*) was the reigning principle of society in its first stages.] **1857** O. BROWNSON *Convert* Wks. V. 116 A poor man..becoming rich by trade, speculation, or the successful exploitation of labour. **1868** *Pall Mall G.* No. 1017. 1827/2 The exploitation of the credulous public. **1877** MRS. OLIPHANT *Makers Flor.* ix. 225 Their whole existence [was] an exploitation of the helpless people they reigned over. **1887** L. OLIPHANT *Fashionable Philos.* 33 The exploitation and subjugation of Eastern countries.

2. The action of reconnoitring.

1871 *Daily News* 18 Sept., It surely indicated lax exploitation that the advance column should have blindly butted its head against this broken bridge.

exploitative (ɛk'splɔɪtətɪv), *a.* [f. EXPLOIT *v.* + -ATIVE] Concerned with exploiting or turning to account natural resources. Also, of or pertaining to the exploitation of people.

1885 *Century Mag.* XXIX. 363 'Industries', divided into 'Exploitative' and 'Elaborative' groups. **1908** *Westm. Gaz.* 11 Jan. 1/3 The Tariff Reformers now attack Lord Cromer for what is called his 'exploitative Imperialism'. **1947** E. FROMM *Man for Himself* 64 The exploitative orientation, like the receptive, has as its basic premise the feeling that the source of all good is outside, that whatever one wants to get must be sought there, and that one cannot produce anything oneself. **1949** M. MEAD *Male & Female* ix. 200 Protections for all the young..against any exploitative or inhuman treatment. **1951** *Mind* LX. 287 The receptive, exploitative, hoarding, and marketing orientations.

exploitee (ɛksplɔɪ'tiː). [f. EXPLOIT *v.* 4 b + -EE[1].] One who is exploited.

1941 *New Republic* 17 Feb. 216, I should feel easier in my mind..if I knew and liked my exploitees. **1951** S. SPENDER *World within World* 118 This meant I was a potential exploitee, because I could never feel within myself the rightness of a social situation which would rebuke the wrongness of others. **1960** *Spectator* 29 July 192 Exploiters and exploitees were gathered together.

exploiter (ɛk'splɔɪtə(r)), *sb.* [f. EXPLOIT *v.* + -ER[1].] One who exploits. **a.** One who turns to account. **b.** One who turns to account for selfish purposes.

a. 1870 *Nation* (N.Y.) 10 Mar. X. 152/2 Happy mining company..these fortunate exploiters. **1890** *Montreal Weekly Gaz.* 11 Sept. 4/1 The coal seam opened lay on the north side of Cow Bay, and a considerable trade was carried on between the French exploiters, and..the West Indies. **b. 1870** *Nation* (N.Y.) 17 Feb. X. 101/2 The pockets of all the railroad exploiters..have..been crammed with public money. **1883** *Athenæum* 24 Feb. 245 That shrewd and often not ungentle character whom his 'exploiters' malign as Hodge. **1887** T. KIRKUP *Inq. Socialism* iii. 86 The capitalists and exploiters of the new industrial era.

ex'ploiter, *v.* [a. Fr. *exploiter*: see EXPLOIT *v.* (the inf. being irregularly adopted instead of the stem).] *trans.* To make use of, develop, turn to account. Hence **ex'ploiterer**.

1853 T. PARKER *Theism, etc.* Introd. 41 It is sad to see.. disciples of this church..exploitered by a twofold jesuitry. **1864** *Fraser's Mag.* Apr. 406 It..[the idea of the Book of Snobs] was repeated, diversified, and—to use an American adaptation of a French word..—'exploitered', till it became rather wearisome. **1864** G. DYCE *Bella Donna* I. 48 Every proprietress of a 'banner screen' invariably determined to exploiter her work by the agency of the lottery-ticket. **1868** YATES *Rock Ahead* II. ii, The probable profits which would accrue were he to exploiter her musical talent. **1853** T. PARKER *Theism, etc.* (1863) 67 The God of the popular theology is the exploiterer of the human race.

exploiting (ɛk'splɔɪtɪŋ), *vbl. sb.* [f. EXPLOIT *v.* + -ING[1].] The action of the vb. EXPLOIT.

a. in senses of the vb. **b.** see quot. 1867.

1603 HOLLAND *Plutarch's Mor.* 922 Having contributed (for the exploiting of this service) two thousand dragmes weight in silver. **1605** CAMDEN *Rem.* 18 And left more of glory to vs by their exploiting of great actes. **1615** W. HULL *Mirr. Maiestie* 23 The..exployting of any thing tending to the promoting of the Romish brethren. **1867** SMYTH *Sailor's Word-bk.*, *Exploiting*, transporting trees or timber by a river. **1890** *Nature* 18 Sept., They..think too much of competition as the exploiting of labour by capital.

exploitive (ɛk'splɔɪtɪv), *a.* [f. EXPLOIT *v.* + -IVE.] Tending to exploit; exploitative.

1921 J. R. COMMONS *Trade Unionism* 574 The ownership of homes, free from the grasp of exploitive and speculative interests. **1937** *Geogr. Jrnl.* XC. 368 An exploitive and wasteful system of agriculture has ruined the soil. **1959** M. MEAD *Male & Female* xvii. 354 Affairs that do not lead to marriage are seen as exploitive.

exploiture (ɛk'splɔɪtjʊə(r)). [f. EXPLOIT *v.* + -URE.] The action of the vb. EXPLOIT.

†**1.** The action of achieving or accomplishing. Const. *of*. Also, a performance; and *collect.* what has been accomplished. *Obs.*

1531 ELYOT *Gov.* I. xi, The Commentaries of Julius Cesar whiche he made of his exploiture in Fraunce and Brytayne. *Ibid.* III. x, In his counsayles, affaires, and exploytures, he omitted no tyme. c**1534** tr. *Pol. Verg. Eng. Hist.* (Camden) I. 18 Paulinus finished not there his exploitures with such facilitie. **1548** UDALL. etc. *Erasm. Par. Mark* ix. 67 Whose seruice thou canst not lacke for thexploiture of such affaires.

2. In mod. use: The action of exploiting or developing.

1883 *Harper's Mag.* Sept. 554/2 A plot..was never so old but that it rewarded some further exploiture by Marion.

ex'plorable, *a. rare*$^{-1}$. [a. F. *explorable*, f. *explorer*: see EXPLORE *v.* + -ABLE.] Capable of being explored.

1768–74 TUCKER *Lt. Nat.* (1852) II. 677 The intricate ways of Providence explorable only by the all-seeing eye.

†**ex'plorate,** *ppl. a. Obs. rare*$^{-1}$. [a. L. *explōrāt-us* pa. pple. of *explōrāre*: see EXPLORE.]

Thoroughly examined, carefully prepared.

1655 W. HOW in *Sir T. Browne's Wks.* (1852) III. 517 Any of your mature explorate additions.

†**'explorate,** *v. Obs.* [f. L. *explōrāt-* ppl. stem of *explōrāre*: see EXPLORE.] = EXPLORE.

1549 HOOPER *Declar. 10 Commandm.* iii, The twelve princes that were sent to explorate and search the privities and condition of the land of Canaan. **1646** SIR T. BROWNE *Pseud. Ep.* III. xx. 155 Snails..exclude their hornes, and therewith explorate their way. **1721–1800** in BAILEY.

exploration (ɛksplə'reɪʃən). [ad. L. *explōrātiōn-em*, n. of action f. *explōrāre* to EXPLORE.]

†**1.** The action of examining; investigation, scrutiny. *Obs.*

1543–4 *Act 35 Hen. VIII*, c. 10 Sir William Bowyer..by diligente searche and exploration founde out dyuers greatte and plentyfull sprynges, at Hampsted heath. **1602** FULBECKE *1st Pt. Parall.* Introd. 5 Men..who might by exploration seuer the dross from the gold. **1646** SIR T. BROWNE *Pseud. Ep.* v. xxi. §20. 271 [The use of the divining rod] is a fruitlesse exploration, strongly senting of Pagan derivation. a**1655** VINES *Lord's Supp.* (1677) 413 The exploration..of their competency. **1690** BOYLE *Med. Hydrostat.* Wks. 1772 V. 463 Our hydrostatical way of exploration.

b. *Med.* and *Surg.* The examination of an organ, a wound, etc. by the use of the finger, probe, or other physical appliance.

1860 in MAYNE *Exp. Lex.* **1880** W. BODENHAMER (*title*) The Physical Exploration of the Rectum. **1884** in *Syd. Soc. Lex.*

2. The action of exploring (a country, district, place, etc.); an instance of this. Also *transf.*

1823 LAMB *Elia*, *Praise Chimney-sweepers* 257 A lost chimney sweeper..tired with his tedious explorations..laid his black head upon the pillow. **1872** JENKINSON *Guide Eng. Lakes* (1879) 299 This side of the Scawfell Pikes is deserving exploration. **1880** HAUGHTON *Phys. Geog.* v. 222 The exploration of the sources of the Blue Nile.

attrib. **1891** *Pall Mall G.* 11 Nov. 5/2 Mr. H. M. Stanley ..would resume exploration work in Africa.

explorational (ɛksplə'reɪʃənəl), *a.* [f. EXPLORATION + -AL.] Pertaining to, connected with, or involving exploration.

1923 E. F. WYATT *Invis. Gods* II. iii. 57 The explorational tokens of the past in the Government Building. **1927** *Daily Tel.* 31 May 9/5 A blue-book which has had no superior as a contribution to explorational geography.

explorative (ɛk'splɒrətɪv, -splɔər-), *a.* [f. L. *explōrāt-* (see EXPLORATE) + -IVE. Cf. F. *exploratif*, *-ive*.] Concerned with, or having the object of, exploration or investigation; inclined to make explorations.

1738 WARBURTON *Div. Legat.* App. 63 Albinus..divides Plato's Dialogues into Classes..explorative, obstetric and subversive. **1852** *Fraser's Mag.* XLV. 664 Should the visitor be of a very inquisitive turn, he may satisfy his explorative disposition. **1875** MASSON *Wordsworth, etc.* 172 A Wordsworth, he admits, might have a genius of the explorative or mystery-piercing kind. **1887** *Daily News* 16 Nov. 5/6 An explorative operation in May would have enabled the physicians to recognise the existence of cancer. **1890** *Pall Mall G.* 8 Aug. 4/2 Few men of his age have done so much explorative tramping.

Hence **ex'ploratively** *adv.* **ex'plorativeness.**

1837 CARLYLE *Fr. Rev.* III. II. i, Behoves us, not to enter exploratively its dim embroiled deeps. **1841** *Blackw. Mag.* L. 155 To prevent your snout, in a fit of explorativeness, from being snubbed by the impudent claws of a..rock.

explorator ('ɛksplə,reɪtə(r)). Also 5-6 -our. [a. L. *explōrātor* f. *explōrāre*: see EXPLORE. Cf. F. *explorateur*.] One who or that which explores.

†**1.** One who is employed to collect information, *esp*. with regard to an enemy, or an enemy's country; a scout, a spy. *Obs.*

c **1450** BURGH *Secrees* 2452 Expert in language have explo[ra]tourys..to knowe alle ther labourys. *c* **1450** *Mirour Saluacioun* 2483 Two exploratours..that broght the grape clustre to desert fro the lande of promissionne. **1536** BELLENDEN *Cron. Scot.* (1821) I. 104 Vespasian..was advertist by his exploratouris, that Caratak..had renewit his army. **1616** *Rich Cabinet* 68 b, Thus did the explorators of the land of Canaan terrifie the Jewes. **1685** COTTON *Montaigne* III. 370 Thou art the explorator without knowledge, the magistrate without jurisdiction. **1721-1800** in BAILEY.

†**b.** *transf.* One who searches diligently. *Obs.*

1583 *Exec. for Treason* 38 These Seminaries, secrete wanderers, and explorators in the darke. **1681** H. HALLYWELL *Melampr.* 92 This envious Explorator or searcher for faults [Satan].

2. One who explores (a country) for the purpose of discovery.

1844 *N. Brit. Rev.* I. 145 America has sent forth to the Holy Land its best explorators.

3. †**a.** An apparatus invented by Beccaria for ascertaining the electrical condition of the atmosphere (Craig 1847). **b.** (See quot.) **c.** ***electric explorator*** = 'electrical explorer'.

b. 1884 *Syd. Soc. Lex.*, *Chest explorator*, an exploring needle or trochar used for introduction between the ribs to diagnose the presence of empyema.

exploratory (ɛk'splɒrətərɪ), *a.* [ad. L. *explōrātōri-us*, f. *explōrāre*: see EXPLORE.]

1. Of or pertaining to exploration; connected with investigation or searching.

1651 *Reliq. Wotton.* (1685) 507 This is but an exploratory, and pretentative purpose between us. **1655** GURNALL *Chr. in Arm.* II. 183/1 When God seems to delay..before he comes with the mercy he promiseth, and we pray for; 'tis exploratory to faith. *a* **1711** KEN *Div. Love* Wks. (1838) 275, I renounce..all abuse of thy name..in..exploratory lots. **1828** *Edin. Rev.* XLVIII. 429 Early in this century.. remarkable exploratory zeal arose. **1862** MERIVALE *Rom. Emp.* (1865) VI. xlviii. 80 A new kind of military chaplet.. to which he gave the name of *the crown exploratory*.

2. a. Constructed or selected for exploration or observation (of the surrounding country).

1732 *Hist. Litt.* III. 500 At some distance were also exploratory Forts. **1774** PENNANT *Tour Scot. in 1772*, 91 On the very summit of the hill is a small intrenchment, intended as exploratory. **1807** G. CHALMERS *Caledonia* I. I. iv. 167 The Romans placed several posts, as exploratory forts, along the banks of the Forth.

b. Undertaken for the sake of exploration, examination, or discovery.

1620 JAS. I in *Reliq. Wotton.* (1685) 495 Your imployment is, for the present, meerly exploratory and provisional. **1692** BP. HOPKINS *Exp. Lord's Pr.* 123 There is an Exploratory Temptation, to search out and discover what is in Man. **1825** SOUTHEY in *Q. Rev.* XXXII. 25 Herefordshire..a favourite scene of their exploratory travels. **1887** SIR S. FERGUSON *Ogham Inscriptions* 17 At present the study is exploratory rather than demonstrative. **1891** *Spectator* 11 July, An exploratory operation..to find out whether or not it would be possible to remove a tumour.

c. Charged with the duty of exploration. Also (*nonce-use*), bent on exploration.

1837 CARLYLE *Fr. Rev.* II. IV. v, Chalons sends forth exploratory pickets of National Volunteers. **1848** DICKENS *Dombey* xxiii, An exploratory blackbeetle now and then was found immovable upon the stairs.

†**exploratress.** *Obs. rare*$^{-1}$. [f. EXPLORATOR + -ESS.] A female explorer.

1616 CHAPMAN *Homer's Hymns, To Apollo* (1858) 22 All Heaven's most supreme and worthy Goddesses, Dione, Rhæa, and th' Exploratress Themis.

explore (ɛk'splɔə(r)), *v.* [ad. F. *explore-r*, ad. L. *explōrā-re* to search out.

Usually explained as f. *ex-* out + *plōrāre* to make to flow, f. *pluĕre* to flow.]

1. a. *trans.* To investigate, seek to ascertain or find out (a fact, the condition of anything). Also with indirect question as obj.

1585 Q. ELIZ. in *Four C. Eng. Lett.* 29 Stratagems..by.. sondry meanes to be explored. **1624** MASSINGER *Renegado* V. iii, A cunning spy, sent to explore The city's strength or weakness. **1697** DRYDEN *Virg. Georg.* II. 47 Let the Learned Gard'ner..Explore the Nature of each sev'ral Tree. **1715-20** POPE *Iliad* I. 84 Let some prophet..Explore the cause of great Apollo's rage. **1823** LAMB *Elia* Ser. I. xv. (1865) 120 Who or what sort of persons inherited Mackery End..we..determined some day to explore. **1862** MERIVALE *Rom. Emp.* (1871) V. xlii. 165 The imperator resolved to explore, disguised..the real temper of his soldiers.

†**b.** To search for; to find by searching; to search out. *Obs.*

1615 CHAPMAN *Odyss.* II. 328, I now am bound..to explore My long-lack'd father. **1700** DRYDEN *Fables, Meleager & A.* 201 With his pointed dart Explores the nearest passage to his heart. **1712** POPE *Messiah* 51 The good shepherd..Explores the lost, the wandering sheep directs. **1769** GOLDSM. *Hist. Rome* (1786) I. 255 The Alps, over which he was to explore a new passage into Italy. **1822** T. TAYLOR *Apuleius* 59 Exploring..a fit opportunity.

¶ To try, make proof of. (A Latinism.)

1667 MILTON *P.L.* II. 632 Satan..toward the Gates of Hell Explores his solitary flight.

2. a. To look into closely, examine into, scrutinize; to pry into (either a material or immaterial object). In later use coloured by association with 3.

1592 DAVIES *Immort. Soul* (1869) I. 152 Her selfe in instants doth all things explore; For each thing's present. **1729** T. COOKE *Tales, Proposals, etc.* 92 Some unexperienc'd Fool her Eyes explore. **1747** WESLEY *Prim. Physic* (1762) p. ix, They explored the several Kinds of..vegetable Substances. *a* **1800** COWPER *Mischievous Bull*, Woodpeckers explore the sides Of rugged oaks for worms. **1818** JAS. MILL *Brit. India* II. v. viii. 683 Of no man..was the public conduct so completely explored. **1833** LAMB *Elia* Ser. II. xi. (1865) 308, I digress into Soho to explore a bookstall. **1847** EMERSON *Poems* (1857) 179 He looketh seldom in their face, His eyes explore the ground. **1848** MACAULAY *Hist. Eng.* I. 440 *note*, The Dutch archives have been too little explored.

b. To examine by touch; to probe (a wound). Cf. EXPLORATION 1 b.

1767 GOOCH *Treat. Wounds* I. 66 The finger is better than any instrument to explore some kinds of wounds. **1784** COWPER *Task* IV. 361 The learned finger never need explore Thy vig'rous pulse. **1870** BRYANT *Iliad* I. IV. 114 The physician must explore thy wound.

3. a. *esp.* To search into or examine (a country, a place, etc.) by going through it; to go into or range over for the purpose of discovery. Fig. phr. ***to explore every avenue*** (or ***to explore avenues***), to investigate every possibility.

a **1616** BEAUMONT *Loving at First Sight* Poems (1653), Not caring to observe the wind Or the new sea to explore. **1697** DRYDEN *Virg. Past.* IV. 41 Another Typhis shall new Seas explore. **1733** POPE *Ess. Man* III. 105 Who bid the stork, Columbus like, explore Heav'ns not his own? **1781** COWPER *Retirement* 151 The busy race..explore Each creek. **1791** BOSWELL *Johnson* 12 Apr. an. 1783, He..recommended us to explore Wapping. **1845** M. PATTISON *Ess.* (1889) I. 10 It is the old historical lands of Europe that the lover of history longs to explore. **1867** LADY HERBERT *Cradle L.* vii. 194 We spent a couple of hours..exploring the ruins.

fig. **1869** J. MARTINEAU *Ess.* II. 235 The Scotch School.. entered the mind to explore it. **1868** MAX MÜLLER *Chips* III. v. 118 He had explored the modern languages of Europe. **1922** G. EDWARDS *From Crow-scaring to Westminster* xii. 142, I intended to explore every avenue during the next few days before the final crash came to secure peace. **1926**, **1927** [see AVENUE *sb.* 2]. **1940** N. MITFORD *Pigeon Pie* xv. 232 In war-time we are bound to explore every avenue, whether it is likely to be productive of results, or not.

b. *intr.* To conduct operations in search *for*.

1872 R. B. SMYTH *Mining Statist.* 27 A large expenditure of public money in exploring for coal. **1919** M. K. BRADBY *Psycho-analysis* 165 Those striking characteristics are on the surface. We do not explore for others less obvious, because these that we see satisfy systems of repressed or under-expressed emotion.

c. To make an excursion; to go on an exploration (*to*).

1816 JANE AUSTEN *Emma* II. xiv. 263 While they are with us, we shall explore a great deal. *Ibid.* 264 We explored to King's-Weston twice last summer. **1924** R. MACAULAY *Orphan Island* ii. 29 Wouldn't the Royal Geographical Society finance the expedition? It ought to, as it's to explore to an undiscovered island.

Hence **ex'plored** *ppl. a.*

1823 LAMB *Elia* (1860) 15 Some rotten archive, rummaged out of some seldom-explored press.

explorement (ɛk'splɔəmənt). *rare.* [f. EXPLORE *v.* + -MENT.] The action of exploring; = EXPLORATION.

1646 SIR T. BROWNE *Pseud. Ep.* III. xiii. 137 The frustrated search of Porta, who upon the explorement of many, could never finde one. **1692-1732** in COLES. **1839** G. DARLEY *Introd. Beaum. & Fletcher's Wks.* I. 15 An author's ..explorements and excursions are those in the world of.. Imagination.

explorer (ɛk'splɔərə(r)). [f. as prec. + -ER[1].]

1. One who explores (a country or place).

1740 WARBURTON *Div. Legat.* IV. vi. II. 288 The report of the cowardly Explorers of the land. **1812** SIR R. WILSON *Diary* I. 375 The explorers enter, and immediately find themselves in a marble cave. **1848** W. H. BARTLETT *Egypt to Pal.* xxvii. (1879) 537 A rich harvest may be awaiting the antiquarian explorer [at Ephesus]. **1856** E. A. BOND *Russia at Close 16th C.* (Hakluyt Soc.) Introd. 19 Anthony Jenkinson, the enterprising explorer of the Persian route to India. **1860** TYNDALL *Glac.* I. i. 8 An explorer of the Alps.

fig. **1872** SPURGEON *Treas. Dav.* Ps. lxiv. 6 These are.. explorers in iniquity.

†**2.** One who or that which examines or tests.

1684-5 BOYLE *Min. Waters* 40 The extent of this explorer of Waters [a Powder] is not very great.

3. An apparatus for exploring or examining; *spec.* **a.** (see quot. 1874); **b.** an apparatus for exploring a wound or a cavity in a tooth.

1874 KNIGHT *Dict. Mech.* I. 817/2 *Explorer*, an apparatus by which the bottom of a body of water is examined, when not beyond a certain depth. **1884** *Syd. Soc. Lex.*, *Electrical explorer*, an apparatus for detecting a bullet or other metallic substance in the tissues.

exploring (ɛk'splɔərɪŋ), *vbl. sb.* [f. as prec. + -ING[1].] **1.** The action of the vb. EXPLORE.

1841-4 EMERSON *Ess.*, *Manners* Wks. (Bohn) I. 203 Our Exploring Expedition saw the Feejee Islanders getting their dinner off human bones. **1863** FR. A. KEMBLE *Resid. Georgia* 261, I went on an exploring expedition round some distant fields. **1872** JENKINSON *Guide Eng. Lakes* (1879) 326 Deepdale is wild and beautiful..and will repay exploring. **1883** STEVENSON *Treasure Isl.* II. xii. (1886) 96 When you want to go a bit of exploring, you just ask old John [etc.].

2. *Comb.* **exploring coil** *Electr.*, a small flat coil of insulated wire connected with a galvanometer, used for determining the strength of a magnetic field from the current induced in the coil when it is quickly turned over or withdrawn from the field; a search coil; **exploring conductor** (see quot.); **exploring needle, trochar**, surgical instruments for 'exploring' tumours, etc.; **exploring wire** (see quots.).

1884 S. P. THOMPSON *Dynamo-Electric Machinery* iv. 60 At 0° a certain number of lines of force would thread themselves through the exploring coil. **1913** *Year-bk. Wireless Telegr. & Telephony* 316 The moveable exploring coil is attached to a handle and index. **1879** *Noad's Text-bk. Electr.* 75 The Exploring Conductor at Kew Observatory. —This is a conical tube of thin copper raised 16 feet above the dome of the building, carrying at the top a small lantern or collecting lamp, provided with a little cowl. **1884** *Syd. Soc. Lex.*, *Exploring needle, trochar*. **1879** *Noad's Text-bk. Electr.* 83 The late Mr. Crosse and the late Mr. Weekes examined the electrical condition of the lower regions of the atmosphere..by means of exploring wires insulated on appropriate supports. **1892** MRS. A. CROSSE *Redlet. Days* I. 178, I have an apparatus arranged for testing the electricity of the atmosphere. It is connected with exploring wires carried on high poles for more than a mile round the woods.

ex'ploring, *ppl. a.* [f. as prec. + -ING[2].] That explores.

1680 BOYLE *Produc. Chem. Princ.* Pref., To doubt whether they be agreeable, to..the exploring Experiments of the fire. **1771** FLETCHER *Wks.* (1795) II. 43 This life begins by an exploring desire.

Hence **ex'ploringly** *adv.*

1866 ALGER *Solit. Nat. & Man* II. 79 To go exploringly forward into the obscure future. **1889** L. KEITH *Hurricane in Petticoats* I. viii. 167 Teddy looked at him exploringly, as if to test the sincerity of the apology.

†**ex'plose**, *v. Obs.* [f. L. *explōs-* ppl. stem of *explōdĕre* to EXPLODE.] = EXPLODE 1, 2.

c **1534** tr. *Pol. Verg. Eng. Hist.* (Camden) I. 134 Our relligion..being eche where explosed and contemned. **1563-87** FOXE *A. & M.* (1596) 25/2 Their doctrine..most worthie to be explosed out of all Christian Churches. *Ibid.* 32/1 Some also reade the Epistle written to Laodicia, but that is explosed of all men.

explosibility (ɛkspləʊzɪ'bɪlɪtɪ). [f. EXPLOSIBLE: see -ITY.] Liability to explode.

1879 *Mind* IV. 335 All the other peculiarities both of choke-damp and of suffocation, such as convulsions and agony on the one hand, density and explosibility on the other. **1909** C. A. KEANE *Mod. Org. Chem.* 315 This condition of strain in acetylene and its derivatives is a factor of importance in regard to their explosibility. **1922** *Daily News* 28 Jan. 5/6 The range of explosibility of water-gas-air mixtures is considerably wider than that of coal-gas-air mixtures.

explosible (ɛk'spləʊzɪb(ə)l), *a.* [f. L. *explōs-* ppl. stem of *explōdĕre* to EXPLODE + -IBLE. Cf. F. *explosible*.] Capable of being exploded.

1799 *Med. Jrnl.* II. 361 The air..was found so much mixed with atmospheric air, as to be rendered explosible. **1888** *Athenæum* 14 Apr. 473 It proved itself to be by no means so readily explosible as has usually been supposed.

explosion (ɛk'spləʊʒən). [ad. L. *explōsiōn-em*, n. of action f. *explōdĕre* to EXPLODE. Cf. Fr. *explosion*.] The action of exploding.

†**1.** The action of treating with scorn, rejecting or scouting (a notion, system, etc.); rejection.

1656-81 BLOUNT *Glossogr.*, *Explosion*, a casting off or rejecting, a hissing a thing out. **1783** POTT *Chirurg. Wks.* II. 8 The explosion of the long continued notion that such wounds were poisonous. **1796** MORSE *Amer. Geog.* I. 27 Observation and reason long ago triumphed in its [Ptolemaic System's] explosion, and universal rejection by the learned.

2. a. The action of driving out, or of issuing forth, with violence and noise; an instance of the same; †*spec.* a volcanic eruption.

[**1623-6** COCKERAM, *Explosion*, a driuing out.] **1667** *Phil. Trans.* II. 601 Producing them [animal Motions] by a kind of Explosion or Shooting. **1695** WOODWARD *Nat. Hist. Earth* III. (1723) 157 Those Parts of the Earth which abound with Strata of Stone..are the most furiously shatter'd..an Event observable not only in this but all other Explosions whatever. **1704** NEWTON *Optics* III. i. (1721) 317 In gunpowder..the Spirit of the Nitre being..rarified into Vapour, rushes out with Explosion..The Sulphur also.. augments the Explosion. **1772** *Ann. Reg.* 71/2, I am.. convinced that the whole of it [the soil] has been formed by explosion. **1796** MORSE *Amer. Geog.* I. 363 The garrison.. was alarmed with frequent explosions of fire and smoke, emitted from the mountain. **1855** BAIN *Senses & Int.* I. ii. §18 (1864) 52 A momentary increase of the expiratory force ..so as to amount to an explosion, or a shot, which propels the material out of the tube. **1862** DARWIN *Fertil. Orchids* iv. 130 The sudden explosion of viscid matter.

fig. **1670** EACHARD *Cont. Clergy* 35 The right one [word].. that at the explosion made such a goodly report. **1804** J. GRAHAME *Sabbath* 835 Ten thousand times ten thousand voices rise In slow explosion.

b. Explosive utterance (of a sound).

1879 H. SWEET in *Philol. Soc. Trans.* 471 The initial voiceless stops have a stronger explosion than in English.

3. a. Of a gas, gunpowder, etc.: The action of 'going off' with a loud noise under the influence of suddenly developed internal energy; an instance of this; also used of electric discharges. Of a boiler, bomb, gun, etc.: The action of

suddenly bursting or flying in pieces from a similar cause.

1744 THOMSON *Summer* 1120 Following slower, in Explosion vast, The Thunder raises his tremendous voice. **1762** SYMMER in Ellis *Orig. Lett.* II. 495 IV. 453 The explosion of this bomb proved to be but the bursting of a bubble. *c* **1790** IMISON *Sch. Arts* I. 94 When the discharge [of a glass jar, battery, etc.] is considerable, it is often called an explosion. **1807** T. THOMSON *Chem.* (ed. 3) II. 15 When electric explosions are made to pass through this gas. **1816** J. SMITH *Panorama Sc. & Art* II. 232 The discharge will fire the powder, and the explosion of the latter will throw off the roof. **1864** WEBSTER, *Explosion* (*Steam-eng.*), the shattering of a boiler by a sudden and immense pressure, in distinction from rupture. **1867** W. W. SMYTH *Coal & Coal-mining* 134 The tendency..of the results of explosion to spread through the entire colliery.

attrib. **1828** J. M. SPEARMAN *Brit. Gunner* (ed. 2) 81 The explosion bulk-head, of three-inch plank.

b. The resulting noise; a detonation.

1775 in ASH. **1855** *Encycl. Brit.* (ed. 8) IX. 456 The explosion resembled the discharge of hundreds of cannon fired at once. *Mod.* Didn't you hear the explosion? Explosions are still heard at intervals.

c. *transf.* (*Phys.*)

1706 PHILLIPS (ed. Kersey), *Explosion*, an Action of the Animal spirits, whereby the Nerves are suddenly drawn together, when some Particles of a different kind are mixed with the Spirits, by which they are violently expanded, or spread forth and driven into confusion, like the parts of fired Gun-powder. **1878** HOLBROOK *Hyg. Brain* 37 Life is a continual explosion of nerve material. **1883** MAUDSLEY *Body & Will* III. iii. 261 The..complex organisation of nerve-structure is damaged by the intense molecular commotion which is the condition of the epileptic explosion.

d. *Golf.* An explosive (sense 3 b) shot. Also *attrib.*

1924 C. J. H. TOLLEY *Mod. Golfer* x. 149 If the ball is lying well, you can either play an 'explosion' or take the ball cleanly. **1926** WODEHOUSE *Heart of Goof* viii. 259 An explosion-shot out of the bunker on the fourteenth. **1957** L. T. STANLEY *Fontana Golf Bk.* 106 *Explosion Shot.* The most reliable recovery shot of all if played firmly.

4. a. A breaking or bursting forth into sudden activity; an outbreak, outburst (of anger, indignation, laughter, etc.).

1817 COLERIDGE *Lit. Rem.* I. 51 When novelties explode around us in all directions [etc.]. But alas! explosion has followed explosion so rapidly that novelty itself ceases to appear new. **1817** LD. CASTLEREAGH in *Parl. Deb.* 279 A desperate conspiracy which threatened an explosion, and which had, in point of fact, exploded already. **1827** SCOTT *Highl. Widow* v, Elspat was prepared for the first explosion of her son's passion. **1844** H. ROGERS *Ess.* I. ii. 90 If there was any explosion at all, it was an explosion of merriment. **1848** MACAULAY *Hist. Eng.* I. 146 This step was the signal for a general explosion. The people..refused to pay taxes.

b. A rapid or sudden marked increase or development; esp. in ***population explosion***.

1953 *Time* 19 Oct. 28/1 Latin America is in the midst of a 'population explosion'. Its people are multiplying 2½ times as fast as the populations in the rest of the world. **1961** 'R. MACDONALD' *Wycherly Woman* (1962) ii. 20 Those sudden institutions of learning that had been springing up..to handle the products of the wartime copulation explosion. **1961** *New Yorker* 28 Oct. 43/2 After the population explosion came the home-run explosion, the rental explosion,..a piety explosion, a culture explosion, [etc.]. **1962** *P.M.L.A.* LXXVII. II. 4/2 We have all heard of 'explosions', of which the 'population explosion' is only one. Well, here is yet another type of explosion.., 'the sky-rocketing volume of knowledge'. **1965** *Listener* 4 Nov. 714/2 We must achieve..the contraception explosion before the population explosion. **1970** *Daily Tel.* 17 Mar. 7/8 British Rail is being forced to join the current 'wages explosion' and concede new substantial pay increases.

5. *attrib.*, as ***explosion point***; **explosion chamber**, a chamber at the end of the cylinder of an internal combustion engine in which the charge is exploded; **explosion machine** (see quot.); **explosion pipette**, a pipette in which an explosive mixture of gases may be fired by an electric spark; so ***explosion-tube***.

1888 *Lockwood's Dict. Mech. Engin.*, *Explosion chamber*, the hinder extension of a cylinder of a gas engine in which the charge is exploded. **1903** *Motoring Ann.* 282 It reduces the space of the explosion chamber. *a* **1884** KNIGHT *Dict. Mech.* Suppl., *Explosion machine*, a motor which depends for its force upon the explosion of substances generating a gas which is used under pressure in an engine or apparatus. **1901** M. W. TRAVERS *Exper. Study Gases* 136 In the earlier experiments the tap of the explosion pipette was lubricated with a hydrocarbon grease. **1890** W. JAMES *Princ. Psychol.* II. xviii. 75 The level of tension in the cells does not rise to the higher explosion-point. **1938** W. S. CHURCHILL *Into Battle* (1941) 17 The war-lust of Dictator Powers had reached its culminating explosion point. **1893** *Phil. Trans. R. Soc.* A. CLXXXIV. 550 By opening tap 8 quantities of the mixed gases are drawn over into the explosion-tube.

Hence **ex'plosionist**, one who is addicted to planning explosions.

1880 *Daily Tel.* 13 Nov., In some respects the Nihilist explosionists are guiltier than the Gunpowder Plot conspirators. **1883** *Birm. Weekly Post* 14 Apr. 4/6 The explosionists are quite as well acquainted with the imbecility of our laws as with the potency of dynamite.

explosive (ɛk'spləʊsɪv), *a.* and *sb.* [f. L. type **explōsīv-us*, f. *explōdĕre* to EXPLODE: see -IVE. Cf. F. *explosif, -ive.*]

A. *adj.*

1. Tending to drive something forth with violence and noise.

1667 *Phil. Trans.* II. 601 Upon which Elastick, or Explosive power he establish's his whole Doctrine of Convulsions. **1695** WOODWARD *Nat. Hist. Earth* III. i. (1723) 157 A kind of Natural Gunpowder, which taking fire ..occasions..that subterranean Thunder..and by the Assistance of its Explosive Power, renders the Shock much greater. **1755** in JOHNSON. **1860** C. G. WILLIAMS in Ure *Dict. Arts* (ed. 5) s.v. *Gunpowder*, The explosive force will be less than it should be. **1869** PHILLIPS *Vesuv.* viii. 219 The opening once made, the subsequent efforts are explosive. **1874** CARPENTER *Ment. Phys.* I. i. §15 (1879) 17 An expulsion of the offending particle by an explosive cough.

2. a. Driven forth or produced by explosion.

1735 THOMSON *Liberty* I. 312 From the red Abyss New Hills, explosive, thrown.

b. Of a consonant-sound: Produced by an explosion of breath; stopped.

1854 BUSHNAN in *Circ. Sc.* (*c* 1865) I. 289/1 The explosive consonants, *b, d, g, p, t,* and *k.* **1878** W. H. STONE in Grove *Dict. Mus.* I. 459 Alternating the linguo-dental explosive T with another explosive consonant produced differently.

c. ***explosive bolt***, a bolt that can be released by being blown out of position by an explosive charge; ***explosive rivet***, a rivet containing an explosive charge by means of which it is fixed in place.

1948 *Aeroplane* 3 Sept. 288/1 The four launching rockets ..were then jettisoned, by the shearing of explosive bolts. Such components—a development of the explosive rivets of Heinkel—were frequently applied to German guided missiles. **1962** S. CARPENTER in *Into Orbit* 54 The escape tower..is attached to the capsule by explosive bolts which blow apart and separate the two components when the tower is no longer needed. **1966** *Times* 4 June 1/1 The shroud [of an unmanned satellite] is in two sections..and explosive bolts and built-in springs were supposed to thrust it off.

3. a. Tending to explode or 'go off' with a loud noise; tending to cause explosion.

1796 BURKE *Lett. Noble Ld.* Wks. VIII. 60 Democratick, explosive, insurrectionary nitre. **1802** *Med. Jrnl.* VIII. 307 Towards the end it [air] approached to the explosive kind. **1850** MRS. STOWE *Uncle Tom's C.* xxix. 273 Miss Ophelia sat ..as if she had swallowed some explosive mixture, and was ready to burst. **1884** SIR E. J. REED in *Contemp. Rev.* Nov. 617 A limited use of explosive-shell-fire from mortars had been made.

fig. **1865** MERIVALE *Rom. Emp.* VIII. lxiv. 101 The nobles ..might have nursed an explosive spirit of discontent.

b. *Golf.* Causing a ball to jump out of a bunker as if an explosion had taken place beneath it.

1924 C. J. H. TOLLEY *Mod. Golfer* x. 149 If you are lying badly..the ball must be dug out, and the method employed is called an explosive shot.

4. Of or pertaining to an explosion; of the nature of an explosion.

1844 DICKENS *Mart. Chuzz.* liii, He entertained them.. with some comic passage or other..so that explosive laughs were constantly issuing from the side-board. **1856** KANE *Arct. Expl.* I. xxx. 411 Breaking it [the ice] up with an explosive puff. **1875** URE *Dict. Arts* II. 761 Gun-cotton has about three times the explosive rapidity of gunpowder. **1878** HUXLEY *Physiogr.* 109 They combine with explosive violence, if exposed to sunshine.

B. *sb.*

1. An explosive letter or consonant (see A. 2 b); = EXPLODENT.

1878 [see A. 2. b]. **1883** I. TAYLOR *Alphabet* II. viii. §2. 144 *note*, The law of least effort requires that the vowel should precede continuants and follow the explosives.

2. An explosive agent or compound. (See A. 3.) ***high explosive***, an explosive compound, such as dynamite, guncotton, etc., which is more rapid and powerful than gunpowder. Also *attrib.*

1874 KNIGHT *Dict. Mech.* I. 818/1 s.v., M. Berthelot gives ..a table showing the relative force of explosives. **1877** *Van Nostrand's Eclectic Engin. Mag.* XVII. 300 (*heading*) Transportation of high explosives. *Ibid.* 300/2 Nitroglycerin, the basis of what are generally known as the high explosive powders, is a light colored, oily liquid. **1881** RAYMOND *Mining Gloss.* s.v., The principal explosives used in mining are gunpowder..nitroglycerin [etc.]. **1890** G. S. CLARKE *Fortification* ix. 113 High explosives produce great local destructive effect against masonry. **1892** HAKE & MACNAB tr. *Berthelot's Explosives* 2 Generally speaking, we mean by 'high' explosives, those in which the chemical transformation is very rapid, and which exert a crushing or shattering effect. *Ibid.*, The more common 'high' explosives are bodies containing a large amount of oxygen, and possessing a definite chemical composition. **1899** J. W. MACKAIL *Morris* II. 237 High-explosive bombs. **1917** *Nature* C. 101/2 High-explosive and armour-piercing shell. **1941** *Ann. Reg. 1940* 95 The bulk of the damage had been caused not by high explosive..bombs. **1941** KOESTLER *Scum of Earth* 284 A man might be happier amongst a shower of high-explosives and incendiaries than under the *Pax Swasticana.*

attrib. **1883** *Pall Mall G.* 7 Apr. 7/1 The Explosives Bill.

explosively (ɛk'spləʊsɪvlɪ), *adv.* [f. prec. + -LY².] In an explosive manner; in the manner of an explosion; from or with explosion.

1805 HATCHETT in *Phil. Trans.* XCV. 292 So great a portion of gas was almost explosively produced, as to overset the jar. **1822** *Blackw. Mag.* XI. 190 Our hero..was..in danger of bursting explosively like an overcharged musket. **1859** R. F. BURTON *Centr. Afr.* in *Jrnl. Geog. Soc.* XXIX. 271 Every word seems to be articulated so explosively that a stranger would imagine the offended speaker to be spitting at him.

explosiveness (ɛk'spləʊsɪvnɪs). [f. as prec. + -NESS.] The quality of being explosive; tendency to explode.

1826 HENRY *Elem. Chem.* I. 236 The explosiveness of a mixture of hydrogen and oxygen gases. **1859** SMILES *Stephenson* 98 The wire-gauze of the Davy lamp becomes red-hot from the high explosiveness of the gas. **1879** *Cassell's Techn. Educ.* I. 154/2 Sift out the glass, when the powder would resume its natural explosiveness.

†**ex'ploy**, *v. Obs.*⁻⁰ In 6 **exploye**. [var. of EXPLAY.] (See quots.)

1552 HULOET, Exploye or do a thynge, *administro.* Exploye studye, *conferre studium.*

Expo ('ɛkspəʊ). [Abbrev. of EXPOSITION 3 b.] A large international exhibition; *spec.* the world fair held at Montreal in 1967.

1963 *Montreal Star* 31 Dec. 3/2 The request of the Expo to study the selection of a new symbol. *Ibid.*, They have been asked by the Expo authorities to meet. **1965** *Economist* 10 July p. xxxviii/1 On April 28, 1967, the world will know whether the Montreal Expo is a work of creative imagination or an overblown exercise. **1968** *Guardian* 16 July 11/1 Ever since the first World Exposition was held in London in 1851, every Expo has been held in the Western Hemisphere. **1969** *N.Z. News* 11 June 3/4 Executive chef for the New Zealand restaurants at Expo 70 in Japan. **1970** *Daily Tel.* (Colour Suppl.) 13 Mar. 17/2 International power-game politics are never far away from the realities of an Expo.

expoliate, -ation: see EXSPOLIATE, -ATION.

†**ex'polish**, *v. Obs.* [ad. L. *expolīre* (see next); assimilated to *polish.*] *trans.* To polish exquisitely or thoroughly. In quot. *absol.*

1624 HEYWOOD *Gunaik.* 269 To polish and expolish, paint and staine, Unguents to daube and then wipe out againe.

†**expo'lite**, *a. Obs.* [ad. L. *expolīt-us*, pa. pple. of *expolīre*, f. *ex-* (see EX- *pref.*¹) + *polīre* to POLISH.] Thoroughly polished, highly finished.

1592 R. D. *Hypnerotomachia* 88 b, All the rest of the Charyot..was of..Carbuncle..of an expolite cutting.

‖**expolitio** (ɛkspəʊ'lɪʃɪəʊ). [a. L. *expolītio* adorning, embellishing.] = EXPOLITION b.

[*c* **82** B.C. *Rhetorica ad Herennium* IV. xlii. §54 Expolitio est cum in eodem loco manemus et aliud atque aliud dicere videmur.] **1589** PUTTENHAM *Eng. Poesie* III. xx. 206 For the glorious lustre it setteth vpon our speech and language, the Greeks call it (*Exargasia*) the Latine (*Expolitio*). **1943** J. W. H. ATKINS *Eng. Lit. Crit., Mediaeval Phase* 203 *Expolitio*, enlarging on a topic in different ways. **1964** C. S. LEWIS *Discarded Image* vii. 192 One kind of *mora* is *Expolitio*. Its formula is 'Let the same thing be disguised by a variety of form; be different, yet the same.'

†**expo'lition.** *Obs.* [ad. L. *expolītiōn-em*, n. of action f. *expolīre*: see EXPOLITE *a.*] **a.** The action of polishing. **b.** *Rhet.* (See quots.)

[**1589** PUTTENHAM *Eng. Poesie* III. xx. (Arb.) 254 [Expolitio] doth..polish our speech and as it were attire it with copious and pleasant amplifications and much varietie of sentences, all running vpon one point and one intent]. **1656-81** BLOUNT *Glossogr.*, *Expolition* a trimming, polishing or burnishing. **1730-6** BAILEY (folio), *Expolition* (in Rhetorick), a figure whereby the same thing is explained in different phrases, in order to shew it more fully. **1751** in CHAMBERS *Cycl.*

†**ex'pone**, *v. Obs.* [ad. L. *expōn-ĕre* to put forth, set forth, display, declare, publish, f. *ex-* out + *pōnere* to put, place. Cf. the cognate EXPOUND, also EXPOSE *sb.*¹ (Since 16th c. chiefly *Sc.*; in earlier use perh. sometimes only a graphic variant of *expowne* EXPOUND.)]

1. *trans.* To set forth in words, declare.

c **1375** *Sc. Leg. Saints, Machor* 1302 (in Horstmann *Alt. Leg.* 202) þat þai..þe priwete mare opynly Wald expone þaime. *c* **1380** WYCLIF *Sel. Wks.* III. 433 Ensaumple of siche deds exponeþ best Cristis lawe. **1552** ABP. HAMILTON *Catech.* (1884) 28 Christ..has ratifeit & exponit thame in the new law. **1632** in *Row's Hist. Kirk* (1842) p. xl, Whilk day the ministers of Perth expone and shew to the brethren that the town..had made..agreement with a schoolmaster. [**1860** J. PATERSON *Life & Poems Dunbar* 306 We have him exponing the salutary change which age had effected].

b. To set forth the character of; to represent, characterize.

1663 SPALDING *Troub. Chas. I* (1792) II. 200 Taking them [the people of Aberdeen] to be worse exponed than they were indeed.

2. To expound, explain, interpret.

c **1440** *Gesta Rom.* lxiii. 272 (Harl. MS.) They..praide him that he wolde declare and expone the versys to hem. **1549** *Compl. Scot.* x. 83 The inglismen exponis the prophesye of merlyne to there auen affectione, as the ieuis exponit the prophesie of cayphas. **1640** *Canterb. Self-Convict.* 120 His oath and promise at his coronation to keep the laws, is to be exponed of his resolution to make his laws to be keeped by others. **1676** W. ROW *Contn. Blair's Autobiog.* xii. (1848) 464 They exponed Scripture and prayed.

3. To put forth (effort); lay out, expend (money).

1527 *Burgh Rec. Aberd.* (Spalding Club 1844) I. 118 The mony and proffeit of the said land..nocht to be exponit in vothir vssis. **1563-87** FOXE *A. & M.* (1684) II. 299 The King..hath been always contented..to expone all his study, labour..treasure [etc.]..for the Pope's aid.

4. To expose (a person or thing *to* danger, etc.).

1564 HAWARD *Eutropius* To Rdr. 1 They exponed themselves..to no smal daungers. *a* **1572** KNOX *Hist. Ref.* (1586) 98 They lying without trench or gabion, were exponed to the force of the whole ordinaunce of the sayd castle. *a* **1651** CALDERWOOD *Hist. Kirk* (1843) II. 48 If he so did, he sould.. expone religioun to the uttermost danger.

exponence (ɛk'spəʊnəns). *rare.* [f. next: see -ENCE.] The function of an exponent of something. So also **ex'ponency**.

1880 *Daily Tel.* 19 Feb., For the vocal exponence of [sacred music]..she is exceptionally gifted. 1880 *Harper's Mag.* LX. 908 Streets and avenues, squares and rows, enough to require the exponency of a good-sized directory.

exponent (ɛk'spəʊnənt), *a.* and *sb.* [ad. L. *expōnent-em*, pr. pple. of *expōnĕre*: see EXPONE *v.*]

A. *adj.* That sets forth or interprets. In *Logic*, of a proposition.

1581 J. BELL *Haddon's Answ. Osor.* 111 The..same rule.. framyng a sounde and probable Argument from the proposition Exponent, to the Exclusive. 1847 SIR W. HAMILTON *Let. De Morgan* 6 The doctrine of which the requirements were exponent.

B. *sb.* One who or that which sets forth.

1. One who sets forth in words, expounds, or interprets; in recent use occas. one who 'interprets' music, an executant. Also, that which serves to explain or interpret.

1812 COLERIDGE in *Southey's Omniana* II. 12 Whatever is common to all languages..must be the Exponent and Consequent of the common consciousness of man. 1834 H. N. COLERIDGE *Grk. Poets* (ed. 2) 28 One of those tongues may be an imperfect exponent of the other. 1841 MYERS *Cath. Th.* IV. xxxi. 322 Jesus Christ is the clearest exponent of His own purposes. 1856 FROUDE *Hist. Eng.* (1858) II. vi. 13 This form of discontent found its exponent in John Wycliffe. 1875 OUSELEY *Mus. Form* ii. 27 Vocal music is very dependant on the words to which it is set, and of which it should be the exponent.

2. *Math.* **a.** *Algebra.* A symbol denoting the number of times a particular quantity is to be taken as a factor to produce the power indicated; an index. It is now written as a small letter or figure at the right hand of and above the symbol of the quantity affected by it. †**b.** ***exponent of the ratio*** (see quot. 1706). **c.** *Physics.* ***exponent of refraction***: = 'index' or 'coefficient' of refraction (? *obs.*).

1706 PHILIPS (ed. Kersey), *Exponent of the Ratio* or Proportion between two Numbers or Quantities, is the Quotient arising, when the Antecedent is divided by the Consequent. Thus 6 is the Exponent of the Ratio that 30 has to 5. 1734 BERKELEY *Analyst* §45 We may often observe that the Exponents of Fluxions..are confounded with the Fluxions themselves. 1807 HUTTON *Course Math.* II. 283 Whether the exponent be positive or negative, integral or fractional. 1859 BARN. SMITH *Arith. & Algebra* (ed. 6) 198 The figures 2, 3..m..are called Exponents.

3. He who or that which sets forth as a representative or type, as a symbol or index.

1825 COLERIDGE *Aids Refl.* (1848) I. 260 To one or other of these four heads all the numerous forms and exponents of Christ's mediation in St. Paul's writings may be referred. 1833 HT. MARTINEAU *Fr. Wines & Pol.* ix. 145 Price is the exponent of exchangeable value. 1842 W. GROVE *Corr. Phys. Forces* 25 The motion of the mass becomes the exponent of the amount of heat of the molecules. 1880 L. STEPHEN *Pope* v. 135 Theobald..as a plodding antiquarian, was an excellent exponent of dullness.

exponential (ɛkspəʊ'nɛnʃəl), *a.* and *sb.* [f. prec. + -(I)AL.] **A.** *adj.*

1. That has the function of setting forth or exhibiting. *rare.*

1730–6 in BAILEY (folio). 1809–10 COLERIDGE *Friend* (1818) III. 185 Where the hypothesis is an exponential image..of an idea.

2. a. *Math.* Involving the unknown quantity or variable as an exponent, or as part of an exponent. So ***exponential equation, function, quantity***, etc.

exponential curve, one expressed by an exponential equation. † ***e. calculus***: see quot. 1796. ***e. series***, the infinite series $1 + x + \frac{1}{2}x^2 + \frac{1}{6}x^3$ etc. ***e. theorem***, the theorem that the value of e^x (the 'exponential', or Napierian antilogarithm, of x) is expressed by this series.

1704 J. HARRIS *Lex. Techn.* II. *s.v.*, Exponential curves are such as partake both of the nature of Algebraick and Transcendent ones. 1715 *Phil. Trans.* XXIX. 212 These Equations he now calls Exponential. 1739 ANDERSON in Rigaud *Corr. Sci. Men* (1841) I. 342 The exponential equation $x^x = d$. 1784 *Phil. Trans.* LXXIV. 401 *P* is either an algebraical, exponential, or fluential fluxion of *X*. 1796 HUTTON *Math. Dict.*, Exponential Calculus the method of differencing or finding the fluxions of Exponential quantities, and of summing up those differences or finding their fluents. 1881 MAXWELL *Electr. & Magn.* I. 221 We call the exponential quantity..the hyperbolic cosine of β.

b. ***exponential horn***, a loudspeaker horn in which the diameter and the transverse cross-sectional area increase exponentially with the distance from the diaphragm. Hence ***exponential-horned*** adj.

1927 *Wireless World* 16 Nov. 664 Whereas a conical horn increases in diameter by a constant additive factor per unit of length, the exponential horn increases its diameter by a *constant multiple* per unit of length. 1954 K. AMIS *Lucky Jim* viii. 87 The rondo of some boring piano concerto Welch had once insisted on playing him on his complicated exponential-horned gramophone. 1962 A. NISBETT *Technique Sound Studio* 269 A flared (exponential) horn is provided to improve coupling.

c. ***exponential pile*** or ***reactor***, a small, subcritical section of a reactor lattice with a neutron source at one end, used to obtain information about the full-sized critical reactor.

1945 H. D. SMYTH *Gen. Acct. Devel. Atomic Energy Mil. Purposes* vi. 58 By this time [*sc.* 1942] it was known that the neutron density decreased exponentially with increasing distance from the neutron source (hence the name often used for experiments of this type, 'exponential pile'). 1963 F. A. VALENTE *Man. Exper. Reactor Physics* viii. 262 In principle, exponential piles have the same structure and composition as the potential or proposed reactor of which they are supposed to be a copy and for which they are supposed to obtain design information by experiment.

B. *sb. Math.* An exponential quantity or function; *spec.* the Napierian base *e* raised to the power denoted by the variable; the Napierian antilogarithm of the variable.

1784 WARING in *Phil. Trans.* LXXIV. 395 When the terms are exponentials of superior orders. 1833 SIR W. R. HAMILTON in R. P. Graves *Life* II. 58 My extension of Herschel's theorem for the development of functions of exponentials. 1885 *Athenæum* 11 July 52/1 The discussion of logarithms and exponentials by means of the properties of the logarithmic spiral.

exponentially (ɛkspəʊ'nɛnʃəlɪ), *adv.* [f. EXPONENTIAL *a.* + -LY².] By exponentials; in an exponential manner.

1909 in *Cent. Dict.* Suppl. 1938 R. W. LAWSON tr. *Hevesy & Paneth's Man. Radioactivity* (ed. 2) xi. 127 The β-radiation of the iron salt does not remain constant, but decreases exponentially. 1949 G. BATESON in M. Fortes *Social Structure* 49 A vista of unknowable factors whose number increases (probably exponentially) into the future. 1968 H. HARRIS *Nucleus & Cytoplasm* iii. 54 In cells growing exponentially, ribosomal RNA appears to be essentially stable. 1970 *Nature* 22 Aug. 865/2 Population genetics, like any other branch of science, is growing exponentially.

exponentiation (,ɛkspənɛnʃɪ'eɪʃən). [irreg. f. EXPONENT *sb.* + -ATION.] The mathematical operation of raising one quantity (the base) to the power of another (the exponent).

1903 B. RUSSELL *Princ. Math.* xii. 120 Moreover exponentiation unavoidably introduces ordinal notions, since a^b is not in general equal to b^a. 1940 *Mind* XLIX. 246 Positive integers compounded by successive exponentiation. 1953 BIRKHOFF & MACLANE *Surv. Mod. Algebra* (ed. 2) xii. 367 For arbitrary cardinal numbers α, β, and γ the following laws on exponentiation hold: (i) $\alpha^{\beta}\alpha^{\gamma} = \alpha^{\beta+\gamma}$; [etc.]. 1968 CORLETT & TINSLEY *Pract. Programming* ii. 15 The operator ↑ is the sign of exponentiation.

†**ex'poner.** *Obs.* [f. EXPONE + -ER¹.] One who sets forth; an expounder.

1588 A. KING tr. *Canisius' Catech.* 50 Ane keipar, and ane exponer of the veritie.

exponible (ɛk'spəʊnɪb(ə)l), *a.* and *sb.* [ad. med.L. *expōnibilis*, f. *expōnĕre*: see EXPONE and -BLE.]

A. *adj.* That admits of or requires explanation; *spec.* in *Logic*, of a proposition, that requires restatement in order to be employed in a syllogism.

[*a* 1276 PETRUS HISPANUS vii. 6. 1 in Prantl *Geschichte der Logik* (1861) III. 67 *n*, Propositio exponibilis est propositio habens sensum obscurum expositione indigentem]. 1788 REID *Aristotle's Log.* iv. §7. 101 Such propositions are by some called exponible, by others imperfectly modal.

B. *sb.* An exponible proposition.

1569 J. SANFORD tr. *Agrippa's Van. Artes* 22 b, Of Consequences, of Indissolubles, of Exponibles. 1653 URQUHART *Rabelais* I. viii, The exponibles of Master Hautechaussade. 1864 BOWEN *Logic* v. 145 The latter [Compound Propositions in which the plurality of Judgments is concealed] are called Exponibles, because they need to be analyzed and explained.

†**expo'rrect,** *ppl. a. Obs.* [ad. L. *exporrect-us*, pa. pple. of *exporrigĕre*, f. *ex-* out + *porrigĕre* to stretch out, f. *por-* = *pro-* forth + *regĕre* to keep straight.] Stretched out; (of the forehead) unwrinkled.

1649 BULWER *Pathomyot.* II. ii. 109 The forehead seemes exporrect and unfolded.

†**expo'rrected,** *ppl. a. Obs.* = prec.

1650 BULWER *Anthropomet.* i. 19 The Brain is..a little exporrected in length. *Ibid.* iii. 62 The people..use great care to have exporrected foreheads. *Ibid.* vii. 129 The Face ..is more exporrected according to latitude then longitude.

†**expo'rrection.** *Obs. rare*⁻¹. [n. of action f. L. *exporrigĕre*; see EXPORRECT.] (See quot.)

1697 J. SERGEANT *Solid Philos.* 104 Let them take Extension, Stretching out, or Exporrection how they will.

export (ɛk'spɔət, 'ɛkspɔət), *v.* [ad. (either directly or through Fr. *exporter*) L. *export-āre*, f. *ex-* out + *portāre* to carry: see PORT *v.*]

†**1.** *trans.* (*gen.*) To carry (things or persons) out of a place; to take away, carry off. Also *fig. Obs.*

(The sense of the two first quots. is obscure.)

c 1485 *Digby Myst.* (1882) III. 458 Swych desepcyouns, potyt peynes to exsport, prynt yow in sportes whych best doth yow plese. 1548 GEST *Pr. Masse* 81 Thensuyng saying ..Gracian exporteth and fathereth upon Austyne. *a* 1612 DONNE *Βιαθανατος* (1644) 133 Paulinus..delivered himselfe as a slave to the Vandals, and was exported from Italy to Afrique. 1612 BACON *Ess., Followers & Fr.* (Arb.) 35 They export honour from a man and make him a returne in Enuy. 1641 *Nicholas Papers* (Camden) I. 29 Fowr thousand men to bee exported hence for the service of..forreine Princes. 1691 RAY *Creation* II. (1704) 319 The Arteries are known to export the Blood.

2. *Comm.* To send out (commodities of any kind) from one country to another.

1665 MANLEY *Grotius' Low C. Warres* 179 They might export any thing, but Materials for War and Corn. 1672 PETTY *Pol. Anat.* (1691) 57 There are 60 M. [black cattle] exported alive, and 30 M. dead in Barrels. 1745 *De Foe's Eng. Tradesman* Introd. (1841) I. 2 Exporting the growth and manufacture of England to other countries. 1841 W. SPALDING *Italy & It. Isl.* III. 399 Olives..could always be exported without duty. 1845 McCULLOCH *Taxation* II. v. (1852) 209 Customs duties were charged..on all sorts of commodities, whether exported or imported.

absol. 1776 ADAM SMITH *W.N.* IV. i. 28 By exporting to a greater value than it imported. 1873 C. ROBINSON *N.S. Wales* 75 We exported to Great Britain to the value of £30,208,485.

b. *transf.* and *fig.*

1760 STERNE *Trist. Shandy* 290 Susannah was sufficient by herself..in exporting a family secret. 1781 COWPER *Expostulation* 365 Hast thou..Exported slavery to the conquered East?

Hence **exported** *ppl. a.*, **exporting** *vbl. sb.* and *ppl. a.*

1716 ADDISON *Freeholder* No. 41 The Exported commodities amounted to Two Hundred Ninety Four Thousand Pounds. 1727 W. MATHER *Yng. Man's Comp.* 409 The Exporting and Importing so many and great Quantities of rich Commodities. 1812 G. CHALMERS *Dom. Econ. Gt. Brit.* 171 The value of exported cargoes in 1766. 1845 McCULLOCH *Taxation* II. iv. (1852) 197 Poland and other exporting countries.

export ('ɛkspɔət), *sb. Comm.* [f. prec.]

1. That which is exported; an exported article. Also, the amount exported.

1690 CHILD *Disc. Trade* (ed. 4) 167 The Exports were more in value than the Imports. 1735 BERKELEY *Querist* §179 Schedules of our Trade, containing an Account of the Imports and Exports of the foregoing Year. 1796 BURKE *Regic. Peace* i. Wks. VIII. 155 Our commerce, the imports and exports of the nation. 1821 J. Q. ADAMS in C. Davies *Metr. Syst.* III. (1871) 113 In the year 1354 the balance of exports above the imports was of more than 250,000 pounds.

2. The action of exporting, exportation; an instance of this. (Not in Johnson or Todd. First in Webster 1864.)

1804 COLEBROOKE *Husb. & Comm. Bengal* (1806) 192 Buffalo's horns might..become an article of export. 1824 LD. HAREWOOD in Bischoff *Woollen Manuf.* II. 48 Allowing the free export of British wool. 1874 GREEN *Short Hist.* viii. 476 He gave license for the export of arms to Spain.

3. a. *attrib.* In senses: Of, pertaining to, concerned with or adapted for, exportation; as ***export-capacity, -demand, -goods*** (specified, as e.g. ***export-yarns***), ***-direction, -merchant,*** (***-book-seller, -clothier***, etc.), ***-trade***; **export bill**, a bill drawn against or for the value of exported goods; **export drive** (see DRIVE *sb.* 1 g); **export duty**, a duty paid on exported goods; **export reject**, an imperfect article withdrawn from export and sold on the home market; also *transf.* and *fig.*; **export surplus**, the amount by which exports exceed imports (see also quot. 1965).

1861 GOSCHEN *For. Exch.* 39 Buying-up and remitting the *export-bills as soon as the goods have been shipped. 1885 *Bookseller* 5 Mar. Advt., Wholesale and *export booksellers. 1888 *Daily News* 19 Nov. 2/7 The *export demand is well maintained for furs, skins, and hairs. 1817 F. ROBINSON in *Parl. Deb.* 565 The bill..to diminish the *export duty on the smaller sorts of coal. 1845 McCULLOCH *Taxation* II. v. (1852) 204 Great caution is usually required in imposing export duties. 1952 O. LANCASTER in *Daily Express* 2 Feb. 1/3 The Americans regard Paul Robeson as an *export reject. 1962 M. URQUHART *Frail on North Circular* xxiii. 126, I got a new suit... Off the peg. Export reject. 1967 J. PORTER *Chinks in Curtain* xii. 121 Don't you start bandying words with me, laddie, or you'll finish up with a mouthful of export reject teeth. 1931 *Economist* 24 Jan. 165/1 It will be noticed that two of our rivals have maintained an *export surplus during the past year. 1964 *Ann. Reg. 1963* 75 The world boom in sugar prices enabled Queensland to sell its record export surplus. 1965 J. L. HANSON *Dict. Econ. & Comm.* 163/1 *Export surplus*, a rather ambiguous term, it may be taken to mean an overall surplus in the balance of payments, the doctrine of the mercantilist system, or a surplus of visible exports over visible imports. *Ibid.* 163/2 The aim has been to secure an export surplus in order to build up investment abroad... Immature economic systems tend to have export surpluses of goods in order to pay the interest on foreign loans. 1795 LD. AUCKLAND *Corr.* III, 295 The naval preparations oblige us to suspend the *export trade which is a check to manufactures. 1831 SIR J. SINCLAIR *Corr.* II. 307 The Emperor and his Ministers were ignorant that there existed any advantageous export trade. 1889 *Daily News* 11 Dec. 2/7 *Export yarns were a shade better.

b. *attrib.* or quasi-*adj.* Designating an article of a quality suitable for exporting, usually of a better quality than that made for home consumption. Also *ellipt.*, beer of export quality; a glass of this beer.

c 1898 in A. Davis *Package & Print* (1967) Plate 40, Export pilsener beer. 1936 BENTLEY & ALLEN *Trent's Own Case* ix. 105 M. Dupont proceeded..to order two glasses of export-cassis. 1951 A. CHRISTIE *They came to Baghdad* iii. 29 The materials for a suit were considered. 'Fortunately, I can give you our own export quality...' 1959 'H. CARMICHAEL' *Stranglehold* i. 11 I'll have a small whisky.. followed by a bottle of your export special. 1962 *Economist* 5 May 465/2 The..beers..are mainly *Pils*..and *Export* (with a greater proportion of malt). 1964 W. J. GASTON *Drifting Death* ii. 18 Cluny ordered a round of exports. 1969 *Guardian* 16 July 18/2 The work that was specially prepared for the Western market which is now either known as Export

Porcelain or *Chine de commande*. **1970** G. LORD *Marshmallow Pie* iv. 32 Get in a couple of crates of Export.

exportable (ɛk'spɔətəb(ə)l), *a.* and *sb.* [f. prec. + -ABLE.]

A. *adj.* Capable of being exported.

1717 NEWTON in Rigaud *Corr. Sci. Men* (1841) II. 425 Silver in bullion exportable is usually worth 2*d.* or 3*d.* per oz. more than in coin. **1803** SYD. SMITH *Wks.* (1867) I. 41 The..exportable articles..which Ceylon produces are pearls, cinnamon, and elephants. **1877** *Fraser's Mag.* XV. 85 The principal staples of her exportable wealth.

transf. **1807** *Med. Jrnl.* XVII. 118 What transmutation.. renders it [yellow fever] exportable to Europe from us?

B. *sb. pl.* Articles of exportation. *rare.*

1873 A. L. PERRY *Pol. Econ.* 522 The greatest loss falls on the exportables of a country.

†**ex'portance.** *Obs. rare*⁻¹. [f. EXPORT *v.* + -ANCE.] = next.

1630 J. LEVETT *Ordering of Bees* (1634) 16 The exportance of increase and profit by them [bees].

exportation (ɛkspɔə'teɪʃən). [a. F. *exportation*, ad. L. *exportātiōn-em*, n. of action f. *exportāre*: see EXPORT.] The action of exporting.

†**1. a.** *gen.* Carrying out from a place. **b.** The conveying or sending (persons) out of the country.

a **1610** HEALEY *Theophrastus, Ostentation* (1636) 80 He [Antipater], when there was granted a free exportation [from Macedonia], when the courtesie was offered him, refused it. **1666** J. SMITH *Old Age* 239 The Instruments of the vital Faculty, which serve for..exportation and rejection of the same [bloud and spirits]. **1725** H. BOURNE *Antiq. Com. People* ii. 15 They were wont to sit by it [the corpse], from the Time of its Death till its Exportation to the Grave. **1774** PENNANT *Tour Scot. in 1772*, 47 The melancholy exportation of..natives of Great Britain. **1789** *Hist.* in *Ann. Reg.* 142 It [Stanhope's bill] also repealed the laws..prohibiting the exportation of women.

2. *Comm.* The sending out (of commodities) from one country to another.

1641 *Nicholas Papers* (Camden) I. 20 Statutes restrayning the exportacion of yᵉ native commodities of that kingdome. **1678** MARVELL *Corr.* Wks. I. 362 The Committee against Exportation of Wooll sate yesternight. **1797–8** WELLINGTON in Owen *Disp.* 779 The exportation of British manufactures, excepting of military stores, ought to be free. **1870** ANDERSON *Missions Amer. Bd.* II. xxxi. 271 Wheat, and other products for exportation.

transf. **1807** *Med. Jrnl.* XVII. 119 An indigenous and local disease..capable of exportation to distant countries.

3. quasi-*concr.* **a.** Something carried out. †**b.** That which is exported; *pl.* commodities exported, exports (*obs.*).

a. 1817 COLERIDGE *Biog. Lit.* 238 Feverishness and want of appetite which..was certainly not decreased by the exportations from the cabin.

b. 1664–5 PEPYS *Diary* (1879) III. 109 If the exportations exceed the importations. **1673** TEMPLE *Ess. Ireland* Wks. 1731 I. 112 The Native Commodities or common easie Manufactures..make up the Exportation of this Kingdom. **1691** T. H[ALE] *Acc. New Invent.* 131 As much..as they now receive in Exchange for their said Exportations.

4. *Logic.* The inference that if two propositions together imply a third, then the first of them on its own implies that the second implies the third.

1903 B. RUSSELL *Princ. Math.* ii. 16 If *pq* implies *r*, then *p* implies that *q* implies *r*. This is the converse of the preceding principle, and is called exportation. **1954** I. M. COPI *Symbolic Logic* iii. 43 Exportation (Exp.): $[(p.q) \supset r] \equiv [p \supset (q \supset r)]$. **1965** HUGHES & LONDEY *Elem. of Formal Logic* xviii. 125 This is known as the Law of Exportation.. since its effect is to 'export' one proposition from the antecedent to the consequent.

exporter (ɛk'spɔətə(r)). [f. as prec. + -ER¹.] One who exports; an export trader.

1691 LOCKE *Lower. Interest* 174 'Twill be the Interest of every Exporter, to buy Plate to send out before Money. **1720** *Lond. Gaz.* No. 5833/2 The Duty..payable by the Exporter. **1796** MORSE *Amer. Geog.* I. 296 The company.. became their own exporters. **1861** GOSCHEN *For. Exch.* 40 The exporters sell to the same bankers.

exposal (ɛk'spəʊzəl). [f. next + -AL¹.]

1. The fact of exposing or of being exposed.

1651 H. MORE in *Enthus. Tri.* (1656) 254 It is no exposall or hardship at all to be exposed to mercy. **1656** JEANES *Fuln. Christ* 199 Gods exposall of him unto death for his members. **1666** G. HARVEY *Morb. Angl.* vi. 66 Their exposal to those injuries, we have just now instanced. **1721** SWIFT *Let. of Advice to yng. Poet* 26, I believe our corrupted air, and frequent thick Fogs, are in a great measure owing to the common exposal of our Wit. **1839** S. DAVIDSON *Biblical Crit.* 62 The version itself manifests its exposal to Jewish influences.

2. A setting forth, an exposition, 'exposé'.

1885 *Sat. Rev.* 15 Aug. 220 An eloquent and able exposal of the financial..aspect of Indian affairs.

expose (ɛk'spəʊz), *v.* [a. Fr. *exposer* (14th c.), formed as an adaptation of L. *expōnĕre* to put out, expose (see EXPONE, EXPOUND); the vb. *poser* (:—L. *pausāre* to rest, lay down) having been associated by erroneous etymology with L. *pōnĕre* (pa. pple. *positus*), and employed as its regular representative in compounds. See COMPOSE, POSE.]

I. To put out; to deprive of shelter.

†**1.** *trans.* To put out; to put (a person) ashore; to expel from a country, etc. Also *refl.* of a river: To empty itself *into*. *Obs. rare.*

1632 LITHGOW *Trav.* I. 43 The Genueses have abandoned the society of Iewes, and exposed them from their iurisdiction. *Ibid.* II. 46 There the Carmoesaloe [a vessel] stayed, and I was exposed to seek passage for Ragusa. **1658** W. BURTON *Itin. Anton.* 134 Where the river Tearn exposeth it self into it [the Severn]. **1726** SHELVOCKE *Voy. round World* 151 In short, I would expose no hostages.

2. To turn out of doors; 'to cast out to chance' (J.); *esp.* to abandon (an infant), often in *Antiq.* as the rendering of L. *exponere*, Gr. ἐκτιθέναι.

1611 SHAKS. *Wint. T.* v. ii. 78 All the Instruments which ayded to expose the Child, were euen then lost. **1697** POTTER *Antiq. Greece* II. xx. (1715) 371 The latter [Ariadne] being the same that was expos'd big with Child upon that Coast by Theseus. **1752** HUME *Ess., Populousness Anc. Nations* (1779) I. 416 The only country where this practice of exposing children prevails. *a* **1859** MACAULAY *Hist. Eng.* (1861) V. 102 In old time he would have been exposed as soon as he came into the world.

3. To place in an unsheltered or unprotected position; to leave without shelter or defence; to remove the covering of; to put (plants) out in the open air. In early use also, To risk, imperil.

c **1477** CAXTON *Jason* 78 b, And semblably ben alle peple bounden to expose body and goodes for their kyng. **1590** SPENSER *F.Q.* III. i. 46 He that hath espyde a vermeill rose, To which sharpe thornes..the way forestall, Dare not for dread his hardy hand expose. **1664** EVELYN *Kal. Hort.* (1729) 201 Set out and expose *Flos Cardinalis*. *Ibid.* 212 Be careful not to expose the Fruit without Leaves sufficient to skreen it from the Sun. **1667** MILTON *P.L.* II. 828, I go This uncouth errand sole, and one for all My self expose. **1704** *Lond. Gaz.* No. 4020/2 He exposed his Person very much in the Action. **1796** C. MARSHALL *Garden.* (1813) 309 An awning..will continue them in perfection of blow much longer than if always exposed. **1885** *Blackw. Mag.* 584/1 The gunners are never exposed as is the case with all embrasure..batteries. *Mod.* This costume is injurious to health because it unduly exposes the chest.

4. To lay open (to danger, ridicule, censure, etc.); to place in the way of something that would be better avoided; to render accessible or liable. Const. *to*, †*unto*; also *to* with inf. clause.

1474 CAXTON *Chesse* 144 He exposith hym vnto the parilles of batayelle. **1601** SHAKS. *All's Well* III. ii. 106 Expose Those tender limbes of thine, to the euent Of the none-sparing warre. **1605** —— *Lear* III. iv. 34 Expose thy selfe to feele what wretches feele. **1611** BIBLE *Transl. Pref.* 4 Rather then..to expose themselues to many exceptions and cauillations. **1667** MILTON *P.L.* II. 27 Whom the highest place exposes Formost to stand against the Thunderers aime. **1697** DRYDEN *Virg. Georg.* III. 646 [The Snake] leaves expos'd to Blows, his Back and batter'd Sides. **1725** DE FOE *Voy. round World* (1840) 336 Not so low as to be exposed to the overflowing of the river. **1789** BENTHAM *Princ. Legisl.* xviii. §44 Offences to which the condition of a Guardian is exposed. **1865** R. W. DALE *Jew. Temp.* ix. (1877) 89 The faith of the Hebrew Christians..was..exposed to severe trials. **1874** MICKLETHWAITE *Mod. Par. Churches* 226 In positions little exposed to be walked over.

5. a. To lay open *to* (†*into*) the action or influence of.

1594 PLAT *Jewel Ho., Divers New Exper.* 33 The greene timber which you doe expose into the ayre. **1697** DRYDEN *Virg. Georg.* II. 448 While the balmy Western Spirit blows, Earth to the Breath her Bosom dares expose. *a* **1704** LOCKE (J.), Those who seek truth only, freely expose their principles to the test. **1744** BERKELEY *Siris* §28 Trees that grow on mountains, exposed to the sun or the north wind. **1751** JOHNSON *Rambler* No. 112 ⁋4 Exposed to a microscope, the smoothest polish..discovers cavities. **1807** T. THOMSON *Chem.* (ed. 3) II. 176 When liquid sulphurous acid is exposed to atmospheric air. **1866** J. MARTINEAU *Ess.* I. 3 He was exposed to two singularly inharmonious influences. **1879** HARLAN *Eyesight* ii. 22 The way in which they [the eyebrows] are instantly drawn down when we are suddenly exposed to a dazzling light.

b. *pass.* To be open *to* a certain quarter of the heavens, situated in a certain aspect.

1710 LONDON & WISE *Compl. Gard.* (1719) 76 It's an admirable Peach when planted in a good Soil, and well expos'd. **1765** A. DICKSON *Treat. Agric.* (ed. 2) 307 The richest lands in Scotland..are exposed to the north.

c. *Photogr.* To submit (a sensitized surface) to the action of actinic rays. Often *absol.*

1839 *Visitor* Dec. 479/1 In one specimen which had been exposed only thirty seconds, the plate was still intensely black, excepting in the sky. **1848** *Chambers's Jrnl.* 24 June 403/2 On another plate, exposed for twenty minutes, a long black stripe was produced. **1878** W. ABNEY *Treat. Photogr.* xxxi. 246 As regards the exposure to be given to a picture there is one golden rule to follow: 'Expose for the shadows and let the lights take care of themselves'. **1903** A. WATKINS *Photogr.* (ed. 2) 9 In the all-important question, 'how long to expose?'..the size of the stop has a most important influence. **1905** *Westm. Gaz.* 2 Sept. 14/2 A simple lesson in exposing a plate. **1959** F. LUTHER *Microfilm* xii. 116 Dagron exposed his microfilms in the camera as conventional glass plates.

II. To present to view, put forth.

6. a. To exhibit openly; to display to the public gaze.

1623–6 COCKERAM, *Expose*, to set to view. **1712** STEELE *Spect.* No. 280 ⁋3 The Beggar, who exposes his Sores. **1727** DE FOE *Syst. Magic* I. iv. (1840) 95 By persuading him [Noah] to drink himself drunk..had..made him expose himself in a beastly manner. **1801** SOUTHEY *Thalaba* VI. xxvi, Transparent garments to the greedy eye Exposed their harlot limbs. **1855** MACAULAY *Hist. Eng.* III. 250 He was then carried to the market place, and exposed..as a malefactor. **1875** JOWETT *Plato* (ed. 2) V. 176 The dead are only to be exposed for three days.

b. *Eccl.* To exhibit (the Host, relics) for adoration.

1644 EVELYN *Diary* 18 Mar., Neere Easter..many images were expos'd. **1850** J. H. NEWMAN *Diffic. Anglic.* 213 The Blessed Sacrament is exposed in all the churches all over the city.

c. To disclose, display, allow to be seen.

1851 CARPENTER *Man. Phys.* 401 The amount of surface exposed by the walls of these minute cavities. **1853** KANE *Grinnell Exp.* xxxvi. (1856) 324 A pit was sunk in the ice around her..so as to expose her stern. **1870** HARDY & WARE *Mod. Hoyle, Whist* 7 A card by accident being exposed during the deal. **1872** RAYMOND *Statist. Mines & Mining* 248 An open cut 30 feet long exposes a vein of rather solid-looking quartz.

7. a. To offer publicly, 'put up' *for* (or *to*) *sale*. (The ordinary phrase in Scotland: in England now somewhat formal).

a **1610** HEALEY *Theophrastus, Ostentation* (1636) 82 Those which expose their wares to sale. **1653** H. COGAN tr. *Pinto's Trav.* x. 30 [They] exposed me to sale three several times, and yet could meet with nobody that would buy me. **1704** SWIFT *T. Tub* Concl. 221 To expose the talents I have acquired. **1762–71** H. WALPOLE *Vertue's Anecd. Paint.* (1786) II. 103 It was again exposed at Mr. Scawen's sale. **1771** *Phil. Trans.* LXI. 324 *note*, A fishmonger..in the winter, exposes for sale a bushel..of carp and tench. **1848** MACAULAY *Hist. Eng.* I. 409 The first barometers ever exposed to sale. **1868** *Perthshire Jrnl.* 18 June, There will be exposed for Sale..on Saturday..about 2,000 Trees.

†**b.** To put forth, publish (a discourse). Also (after Fr. *exposer*) to put (coin) in circulation. *Obs.*

1644 *Vindex Angl.* in *Harl. Misc.* (Malh.) V. 431 Did ever nation expose choicer..discourses, than ours hath done? **1686** tr. *Chardin's Trav.* Pref., The last things which I shall expose to the Publick. **1751** CHAMBERS *Cycl.* s.v. *Exposing*, It is prohibited to expose false and clipped money.

8. a. To make known, disclose (secrets, one's intentions or projects, etc.). Formerly in wider sense: To explain, set forth or describe in detail.

1483 CAXTON *Cato* I vj b, His fyrste frend..to whom he ex-posed his caas and nede. *c* **1489** —— *Blanchardyn* lii. 199 The prouost..exposed vnto the..comynalte the charge that he had of blanchardyn. **1541** R. COPLAND *Galyen's Terap.* 2 G iv, In the boke..we haue exposed all the differences of vlceres. **1586** A. DAY *Eng. Secretary* II. (1625) 126 Which as an action most singular, I have judged fit to be exposed in this place unto him. **1701** tr. *Le Clerc's Prim. Fathers* (1702) 103 They exposed..their Reasons. **1779** in *Athenæum* 16 Aug. (1884) 213/1 He..exposes his intention of returning during winter to Sandwich Island. **1791** BOSWELL *Johnson* Ded., The whole truth is not always to be exposed. **1855** PRESCOTT *Philip II*, I. II. viii. 237 Egmont..exposed to the monarch the evils that beset the country. **1873** HOLLAND *A. Bonnic.* xxiii. 346, I exposed my project, which..met with his hearty approval.

†**b.** To set forth the meaning of; to explain, expound. *Obs.*

1483 CAXTON *Gold. Leg.* 436/3 Saynt Jherome exposeth hit thus. —— *Cato* D v b, Or otherwyse hyt may be exposed that [etc.].

9. a. To unmask, show up (an error or misrepresentation, an impostor); to hold up to ridicule or reprobation (faults, follies, or those who are guilty of them).

1693 DRYDEN *Juv.* Ded. (1697) 4 Like Horace, you only expose the Follies of Men, without arraigning their Vices. **1711** ADDISON *Spect.* No. 23 ⁋7, I have in this Paper endeavoured to expose that particular Breach of Charity. **1777** SHERIDAN *Sch. Scand.* II. ii, It has led me into so many cursed rogueries, that I doubt I shall be exposed at last. **1826** HALLAM in *Edin. Rev.* XLIV. 9 It would be idle to expose the spuriousness of what no one appeared to think authentic. **1876** MOZLEY *Univ. Serm.* ii. (1877) 33 He..saw the imposture and exposed it. **1885** *Manch. Exam.* 6 Nov. 5/2 It will serve to expose the hollowness of the hopes.

†**b.** Hence in 17–18th c.: To hold up to ridicule (what is not a fault). *Obs.* (Stigmatized by Johnson as 'an improper colloquial abuse'.)

1685 STILLINGFL. *Orig. Brit.* i. 14 But lest I should seem to expose so ancient a Tradition..I now proceed [etc.]. **1705** STANHOPE *Paraphr.* I. 73 The most Sacred Things, exposed by insolent Buffoonry. **1712** ADDISON *Spect.* No. 291 ⁋7 A little Wit is equally capable of exposing a Beauty, and of aggravating a Fault. **1772** FLETCHER *Logica Genev.* 29 The round attires of the head exposed by Isaiah.

exposé (‖ɛkspoze, ɛk'spəʊzeɪ), *sb.* Also (chiefly *U.S.*) expose. [Fr.; pa. pple. of *exposer*: see EXPOSE *v.* There is some 19th c. evidence for a disyllabic pronunc. corresponding to the spelling *expose*.]

1. A statement put forth; a recital of facts or particulars.

1715 J. CHAPPELOW *Right Way to be Rich* (1717) 137 Mercy..should, with such an Acclamation of exulting Joy, make a visible and glorious Expose of the Blessed Jesus, to Divine Justice. **1803** PITT in *G. Rose's Diaries* (1860) II. 11 The Consul's *exposé* speaks pretty plain. **1812** *Examiner* 28 Dec. 822/1 This is the result of the Exposé which has just been made. **1813** *Ibid.* 13 Mar. 168/2 The French Exposé states, that France will have..150 sail of the line. **1846** WORCESTER cites MACKINTOSH ? 1765–1832.

2. A showing up of something discreditable. Also *attrib.*

1809 P. COXE (*title*) The Exposé; or, Napoleone Buonaparte unmasked, in a condensed statement of his career and atrocities. **1813** *Niles' Reg.* IV. 185/1 (*title*) Expose of the French Empire. **1818** *Massachusetts Spy* 14 May (Th.), The expose of the situation of the interior [of the French empire] exceeds the style of modern romance. **1828** LYTTON *Pelham* I. xxii. 171 Such an *exposé* might be attended with a loss the good woman valued more than

reputation, viz., lodgers. 1830 *Massachusetts Spy* 12 May, Chilton's expose. [Heading of an article on the shortcomings of the Jackson administration.] 1831 Disraeli *Yng. Duke* v. xiii, She has been negotiating..for some time ..and the late exposé will not favour her interests. 1841 *Congress. Globe* 25 Jan. App. 152/3 And how was this honest expose met? 1845 W. H. Maxwell *Hints to a Soldier* I. 163 This wretched exposé of Blake's incompetency. 1888 *St. Louis Globe Democrat* 30 Mar. (Farmer), The expose of the Coal Hill convict camp horror. 1902 E. Banks *Newspaper Girl* 106 'Don't go into it with the idea of an "expose",' said the editor. 1965 *Times Lit. Suppl.* 25 Nov. 1061/2 A startling series of exposé articles. 1966 *Listener* 17 Nov. 749/1 This talk..dealt mainly with exposé journalism. *Ibid.*, No newspaper embarked on an exposé without giving really serious thought to the matter. 1967 *Boston Sunday Herald* 2–8 Apr. 67/1, I am..all for more exposes of the calibre of a recent one on British TV, 'Cathy Come Home'. 1968 *Globe & Mail* (Toronto) 5 Feb. 13/4 Some expose likely in the political arena.

exposed (ɛk'spəʊzd), *ppl. a.* [f. expose *v.* + -ed[1].] In the senses of the vb. **a.** Displayed, disclosed to view. *exposed card* (see quot. 1870). **b.** Unsheltered or unprotected from the elements, or from hostile attack. **c.** *esp.* Of children: Cast out or abandoned to chance.

a. 1630 Brathwait *Eng. Gentl.* 28 When that Sex..gives way to foments of exposed loosenesse. 1656 tr. *Hobbes' Elem. Philos.* (1839) 139 Quantity is determined two ways; one by the sense..the other by memory, that is, by comparison with some exposed quantity. 1870 Hardy & Ware *Mod. Hoyle, Whist* 3 If a player plays a card from his hand..without waiting to know if a card under the penalty of being called for is demanded, this card..is an exposed card. 1890 *Pall Mall G.* 20 Oct. 7/1 D..placed the detached card on the table..and the 'detached' card then became an 'exposed' card.

b. 1664 Evelyn *Kal. Hort.* (1729) 197 Cover with dry Straw..your young exposed Ever-greens. 1837 Ht. Martineau *Soc. Amer.* III. 153 A passage..too exposed to be endurable in a hot sun. 1867 Smyth *Sailor's Word-bk.*, *Exposed anchorage*, an open and dangerous place, by reason of the elements or the enemy. 1878 Huxley *Physiogr.* 40 Vapour is drawn up..from every exposed piece of water.

c. 1662 Petty *Taxes* 4 The maintenance of..found and exposed children. 1772 *Ann. Reg.* 223 The hospital for the maintenance of exposed and deserted young children.

exposedness (ɛk'spəʊzɪdnɪs). [f. prec. + -ness.] The state or condition of being exposed.

1620 Bp. Hall *Hon. Mar. Clergy* I. §23 The exposednesse of the city to sale. *a*1665 J. Goodwin *Filled w. the Spirit* (1867) 191 An exposedness unto trouble. *c*1741 Brainerd in Edwards *Life* i. (1851) 5 Showed me so plainly my exposedness to damnation. 1863 J. G. Murphy *Comm. Gen.* xi. 25 Shame implies..an exposedness to the searching eye of a condemning judge.

†**ex'posement.** *Obs. rare*[−1]. [f. expose *v.* + -ment. Cf. OFr. *exposement*.] The action of exposing.

1632 Lithgow *Trav.* viii. 353 Measuring largely their owne infranchized fortune, with the voluntary exposement of many vnnecessary Viadants.

exposer (ɛk'spəʊzə(r)). [f. as prec. + -er[1].] One who exposes (in senses of vb.).

1611 in Cotgr. s.v. *Exposeur*. 1676 Marvell *Mr. Smirke* Wks. 1875 IV. 34, I shall henceforth take notice of him as the Church of England's Exposer. 1772 *Hist. Europe* in *Ann. Reg.* 99*/2 The overthrower of Bolingbroke, and the exposer and detector of his dangerous fallacies. 1870 Hardy & Ware *Mod. Hoylc, Whist* 3 If the exposer denies that he has shown the card. 1885 *Law Times* LXXX. 115/1 Their..exposure for sale in England..rendered the..exposer liable to conviction.

exposing (ɛk'spəʊzɪŋ), *vbl. sb.* [f. as prec. + -ing[1].] The action of the vb. expose *sb.*[1] (in its various senses); an instance of this.

*a*1612 Donne Βιαθανατος (1644) 124 These Omissions, and Desertions, and Exposings of our selves. 1627 tr. *Bacon's Life & Death* (1651) 8 In wild Creatures, their Exposing to all weathers, often intercepteth them. 1721 *Wodrow Corr.* (1843) II. 593, I have nothing but..the exposing of tyranny, persecution, and arbitrary power, in my view. 1726 Leoni tr. *Alberti's Archit.* I. 76 a, The exposing of merchandizes to sale. 1732 Berkeley *Alciphr.* v. §12 Their unnatural exposing of their own children.

exposit (ɛk'spɒzɪt), *v.* [f. L. *expositus*, pa. pple. of *expōnere* to set forth.] *trans.* To reveal, exhibit, show clearly; to expound.

1882 C. Van Norden *Outermost Rim* viii. 104 The law of retribution is fully exposited only in the history of a great nation. 1949 Wellek & Warren *Theory Lit.* (1961) ix. 99 Examples could be multiplied indefinitely. One can assemble and exposit the 'world' of each, the part each gives to love and marriage, to business, to the professions. *Ibid.* xvii. 244 That case we have partly put in expositing the principle of aesthetic purity.

exposita (ɛk'spɒzɪtə), *sb. Logic.* [L., fem. sing. (cf. maxim) of pa. pple. *exposit-us* of *expōn-ēre*: see expone.] = convertend.

1827 [see converse *sb.*[2] 3]. 1851 H. L. Mansel *Proleg. Logica* 202 Either the converted proposition is a new judgment distinct from the *exposita*, or it is merely the same judgment expressed in different language. 1857 W. Spalding in *Encycl. Brit.* XIII. 605/1 The antecedent is called the Convertend, or Exposita (the proposition set forth to be converted).

exposition (ɛkspəʊ'zɪʃən). Forms: 4–5 exposicioun, 4–6 exposicion, -yon, (4 expossission), 5 expositioun, -ycion, -yon, (6 exposytion), 6- exposition. [a. F. *exposition*, ad. L. *expositiōn-em*, n. of action f. *expōnĕre* (pa. pple. *exposit-us*): see expone.]

†**1. a.** The action of putting, or the condition of being put, out of a place; expulsion. Cf. expose *v.* 1. *Obs. rare.*

1530 Palsgr. 218/1 Exposytion, *exposition*. 1532 More *Confut. Tindale* Wks. 819/2 No time of taryenge betwene their [angels'] synne and their exposicion.

b. *esp.* The action of putting (a child) out in the open; abandonment to chance; = exposure 1 b.

1581 Mulcaster *Positions* xxxvi. (1887) 136 To disburden a common weale of vnnecessary number..by exposition..of enfantes. 1654 R. Codrington tr. *Justin's Hist.* 8 Hearing of the exposition of this royall Infant. 1747 *Orig. Hum. Appetites* i. ¶5 in Parr *Metaph. Tracts 18th C.* (1837), The exposition of children without distinction.. either of family or sex. 1869 Lecky *Europ. Mor.* I. i. 47 The murder or exposition of the children of poor parents. 1875 Poste *Gaius* i. Comm. (ed. 2) 65.

†**2.** Situation with respect to the quarter of the heavens; 'aspect'. *Obs.* = exposure 3.

1688 *Lett. Pres. State Italy* 145 The water within them is in a full exposition to the Sun. 1693 Evelyn *De la Quint. Compl. Gard.* I. 128 An Easterly Exposition. 1710 London & Wise *Compl. Gard.* (1719) 268 Those sorts which blow only in good Expositions. 1758 Jortin *Erasm.* I. 76 Erasmus ..ascribes the plague..partly to the..bad exposition of the houses. 1775 Johnson *Journ. W. Isl.* Wks. X. 413 By choosing an advantageous exposition, they can raise all the more hardy esculent plants. 1834 Beckford *Italy* II. 107 The exposition..is singularly happy; skreened by sloping hills.

3. a. The action of putting out to public view; an instance of this; a display, show, exposure. †Also (*rarely*) = exposure 1 c, d.

1649 Jer. Taylor *Gt. Exemp.* xvi. §2 The Synagogue had been thrown out to an inglorious Exposition and Contempt. 1788 *Trifler* xviii. 245 The country 'squires dreaded the exposition of their rustic conversation to the ordeal of her criticism. *Ibid.* xxiv. 318 The exposition of these absurdities ..should be forwarded by every man of sense. 1834 Beckford *Italy* I. 4 There happened to be an exposition of the holy wafer. 1835 Browning *Paracelsus* 128 Grown Grey in the exposition of such antics. 1836 *New Monthly Mag.* XLVI. 3 The practice of exposition on the pillory. 1844 Pugin *Gloss.* 182 The Exposition of any Relic without an authentication has been strictly prohibited. 1884 *Catholic Dict.* 331 The Host after High Mass (the Mass of Exposition) is placed on a throne above the altar..Relics and images must be removed from the Altar of Exposition.

b. After mod.French use; = exhibition 6.

1851 *Illustr. London News* 29 Mar. 259/1 This Exposition usually takes place annually in the Louvre. 1851 Geo. Eliot *Let.* 5 Aug. (1954) I. 358 She seems to prefer London... A glance or two at the Exposition she thinks would do her no harm. 1868 Sala *Notes & Sk. Paris Exhibition* ii. 15 The Universal Exposition of 1867; that, you know..is the official designation. 1873 Browning *Red Cott. Nt.-cap* 270 Paint! The last Exposition warrants me Plenty of people must ply brush with toes. 1879 Howells *L. Aroostook* (1883) II. 126 Typical villages of the different civilisations at the international expositions. 1891 *Soc. of Arts, Title of Paper* 11 Dec. 9 The World's Columbian Exposition at Chicago in 1893.

4. a. The action or process of setting forth, declaring, or describing, either in speech or writing.

1460 Earl Marche in Ellis *Orig. Lett.* i. 5 I. 10 We have charged your servant..for to declare..certayne things.. Wherefore we beseche your graciouse lordeschip..to here him in exposicion of the same, and to his relacion to yeve ful feith and credence. 1783 H. Blair *Lect. Rhet.* II. 78 In the conduct and exposition of his arguments, he [Cicero] may and ought to be imitated. 1871 Morley *Voltaire* (1886) 66 Clear exposition was the only thing needed to convert him to the new theory.

b. A statement in which any matter is set forth in detail.

1388 Wyclif *2 Macc.* ii. 13 These same thingis weren put in discripcions and exposicions [Vulg. *commentariis*] of Neemye. 1494 Fabyan *Chron.* vii. ccxx. 241 For the which dede, after the exposycion of some auctours the sayd erle was punysshed. 1552 Huloet, Exposition, *commentarium.* 1842 A. Combe *Physiol. Digestion* (ed. 4) 189 If we look to the exposition of the objects of eating already given. 1860 Tyndall *Glac.* ii. xvi. 311 The author of the theory has at various times published expositions of his views. 1875 Stubbs *Const. Hist.* I. i. 10 Of the great expositions of feudal custom, most are from Northern France. 1884 Bower & Scott *De Bary's Phaner. & Ferns* 504 A question..that does not belong to the present anatomical exposition.

c. *Music.* (See quots.)

1869 Ouseley *Counterp.* xxiii. 178 Every fugue must commence with what is called 'the exposition' of the subject and answer. By this is simply meant the first entry of the subject, answer, and countersubject. 1880 —— in Grove *Dict. Mus.* I. 568/2 After the exposition is completed by the successive and regular entry of every part. 1889 Grove *Dict. Mus.* IV. 630/2 In forms of the harmonic order the term Exposition is commonly used of the first half of a movement in Binary form, because that part contains the statement of the two principal subjects. 1947 A. Einstein *Mus. in Romantic Era* vii. 67 The exposition of the first is a perfect example of demoniac explosion, while, in the first movement of the C-major Symphony the exposition is a piece of inexorable consummation. 1959 Westrup & Harrison *Collins Mus. Encycl.* 230/1 *Exposition*, the statement of the musical material on which a movement is based... In a movement in sonata form it..consists in the presentation of the principal thematic material partly in the tonic key and partly in a subsidiary key or keys.

5. a. The action of expounding or explaining; interpretation, explanation. Also an instance or mode of this; an explanation, interpretation.

*a*1340 Hampole *Psalter* Comm. 19 Hit nedeth exposicyon. 1340 —— *Pr. Consc.* 3856 An exposicion Of þe haly godspelle in a lesson. *c*1386 Chaucer *Pars. T.* ¶969 The exposicioun of this holy praier..I bitake to these maystres of theology. *c*1440 *Gesta Rom.* lxiii. 271 (Harl. MS.) The exposicion of theise vers is this. 1596 Shaks. *Merch. V.* iv. i. 237 You know the Law, your exposition Hath beene most sound. 1672 Sir T. Browne *Lett. Friend* xix. (1881) 140 Some dreams I confess may admit of easie and feminine exposition. 1699 Bentley *Phal.* 302 The other Exposition, that makes Μοσχος the name of an Harper. 1729 Franklin *Ess.* Wks. 1840 II. 39 The unaccountable expositions that are put upon some of my works. 1741–3 Wesley *Jrnl.* (1749) 69 Attending the expositions of the persons commonly called Methodists. 1795 Wythe *Decis. Virginia* 8 This exposition of the testament fulfilleth the intention of him who made it. 1868 E. Edwards *Raleigh* I. xxvii. 690 It was..suggested..that Bacon's exposition of the law was unsound. 1877 Sparrow *Serm.* ix. 122 The exposition of the Bible.

Comb. 1826 Bentham in *Westm. Rev.* VI. 500 Exposition-requiring terms.

b. An expository article or treatise; a commentary.

1460 Capgrave *Chron.* Ded. 1 Specialy to gader eld exposiciones upon Scripture into o colleccion. 1532 More *Confut. Tindale* Wks. 553/1 In his exposicion vpon the first pistle of saint John. 1664 H. More *Myst. Iniq.* 107 The reading of such expositions of Scriptures as are writ by.. sincere followers of Christ. 1685 A. Lovell tr. *Simon's Relig. & Cust. East. Nations* 149 They have..Expositions on those Books. 1773 Mrs. Chapone *Improv. Mind* (1774) I. 66 The Prophecies..you had better..read..with a good exposition.

c. *Logic.* (In various senses: see quots.)

1588 Fraunce *Lawiers Log.* i. ii. 4 b, There be two parts of Logike, Exposition of the nature of argumentes, and Disposition of the same. *Ibid.* i. ii. 6 Exposition, the first part of Logike, declareth the particular affection and nature of every severall argument. 1656 tr. *Hobbes' Elem. Philos.* (1839) 139 Quantity is determined two ways; one by the sense, when some sensible object is set before it..which way of determining is called exposition. 1837–8 Sir W. Hamilton *Logic* xxiv. (1866) II. 12 It [a declaration] is called an Exposition, when the evolution of a notion is continued through several explications. 1860 Veitch & Mansel *Hamilton's Logic* I. 263 *note*, The term Exposition (ἔκθεσις) is employed by Aristotle and most subsequent logicians to denote the selection of an individual instance whose qualities may be perceived by sense, in order to prove a general relation apprehended by the intellect.

Hence **expo'sitional** *a.*, of the nature of an exposition; explanatory. **expo'sitionary** *a.*, inclined to exposition or setting forth in detail.

1845 Mozley *Blanco White*, Ess. 1884 II. 138 All those creeds..the simply expositional and interpretative form of the original revealed truth..—all this is thrown aside. 1867 J. Garfield in *Century Mag.* Jan. 1884, 413/2 Spurgeon.. accompanied his reading with sensible..expositional comments. 1882 J. Hawthorne *Fort. Fool* i. xviii, He was of an argumentative and expositionary turn of mind.

†**exposi'titious,** *a. Obs. rare*[−1]. [f. L. *expositīcius* (f. *exposit-*: see next and -itious).] Of a child: That has been 'exposed'.

1622 Donne *Serm.* cliv. VI. 150 An expositious Child laid out in the streets..of unknown parents.

expositive (ɛk'spɒzɪtɪv), *a.* and *sb.* [ad. L. *expositīv-us*, f. *exposit-* ppl. stem of *expōnĕre*: see expone and -ive.]

A. *adj.* **a.** Tending to set forth or describe in detail; descriptive. **b.** Serving to explain; explanatory, expository. Const. *of*.

1535 Joye *Apol. Tindale* 38 Usyng thys particle *Et* in englyssh as myche to saye *And* expositiue. 1571 Golding *Calvin on Ps.* xxiv. 4 A man may gather it by the percell expositiue whiche is added streight after. 1655–60 Stanley *Hist. Philos.* (1701) 378/2 Expositive terms. 1659 Pearson *Creed* (1683) 230 The opinion..is to be rejected, as not expositive of the Creed's confession. 1846 Worcester, *Expositive*, explanatory. 1884 *Christian World* 24 Apr. 304/2 The book..may be briefly described as..hortatory and expositive.

†**B.** *sb.* An explanation, 'argument'. *Obs.*

1687 Burnet *Contn. Reply to Varillas* 43 He cites on the Margin the expositive or Preamble of it.

Hence †**ex'positively** *adv.*, in an expositive manner or sense; by way of exposition or gloss.

1571 Golding *Calvin on Ps.* xxxiv. 9 The particle [*Chi*] is taken expositiuely. 1631 J. Burges *Answ. Rejoined* 82 Unless wee may take..*and*, the copulatiue, expositiuely, as if it signified *that is to say*. 1656 Jeanes *Fuln. Christ* 170 Interpreters thinke this clause to be added *appositivè*, or expositively, to explaine what is meant by Philosophy.

expositor (ɛk'spɒzɪtə(r)). Forms: 4 expositur, -pocitour, 4–6 -posytour, 4–7 -itour, 7 expositer, 6- expositor. [a. AF. *expositour = OF. *expositur*, Fr. *expositeur*, ad. L. *expositōr-em*, agent-n. from *expōnĕre*: see expone, expose *sb.*[1]]

1. One who sets forth in detail, expounds, or lays open; a declarer, narrator. Const. *of*.

1398 Trevisa *Barth. De P.R.* xviii. lxxxviii. (1495) 89 Expositours say that some lyce gendre of sangweyn humour and been red and grete. *c*1430 Lydg. *Thebes* i. 122 Some expositours Groundyng hem, vpon old aucthours, Sain that Cadmus [etc.]. 1533 Elyot *Cast. Helthe* iii. (1541) 52 b, The tongue, whiche is raysons exposytour. 1588 Shaks. *L.L.L.* ii. i. 72 A mirth-mouing iest Which his faire tongue (conceits expositor) Deliuers in..apt..words. 1807 G. Chalmers *Caledonia* I. iii. viii. 440 The clergy acquiesced in the dictates of a learned queen, as delivered by the royal expositor. 1876 Bancroft *Hist. U.S.* VI. xxix. 73 Reid.. and Rousseau were..expositors of the active powers of man.

2. One who sets forth the meaning (of a passage, word, etc.); one who explains; an interpreter (of dreams, etc.); an expounder. Const. *of*.

*a*1340 HAMPOLE *Psalter* cxlvi. 8 Thorgh expositurs ha redyis rayne of soft lare. *c*1380 WYCLIF *Wks.* (1880) 145 Good expositours on þe Gospellis. *c*1440 *Gesta Rom.* xxvii. 348 (Add. MS.) Trew expositours, that is, discrete confessours or prelates. 1584 R. SCOT *Discov. Witchcr.* x. i. 143 To..hearken to the expositors of dreames. 1634 SIR T. HERBERT *Trav.* (1677) 330 The Hodgei, Emeri, and Mulai, the first are Expositors, the other Mendicants. 1658 T. WALL *Comm. Times* 29 The word..signifies both a company and a Beast, say Expositors upon the text. 1778 R. LOWTH *Isaiah* Notes (ed. 12) 362 Difficulties in which expositors are frequently engaged. 1833 S. HOOLE *Discourses* ix. 109 By some learned expositors the Grecian philosophy has been blended with Christian Theology. 1850 GLADSTONE *Glean.* V. xci. 227 If such be the view of the expositors of the law.

fig. *a*1716 SOUTH *Serm.* (J.), The sinner's conscience is the best expositor of the Mind of God, under any judgement or affliction. 1853 LEWES *Hist. Philos.* 280 Reason is the expositor of Faith.

b. *transf.* That which explains or interprets. (Sometimes used as title of a book.)

1530 PALSGR., Ep. 5, I have..added..a thirde boke, whiche is a..comment and exposytour unto my seconde. 1604 HIERON *Wks.* I. 526 The scripture speaketh by the voyce of man, and so it is fitted and applied to be the expositer of it selfe by the industry of man. 1616 BULLOKAR (*title*), An English Expositor Or Compleat Dictionary: Teaching The Interpretation of the hardest words. *a*1754 FIELDING *Charac. Man* Wks. 1784 IX. 414 Actions are their own best expositors. 1760–2 DODDRIDGE (*title*), The Family Expositor. 1818 CRUISE *Digest* (ed. 2) VI. 497 The intention of the devisor expressed in his will was the best expositor.. and disposer of his words.

expositorial (ɛkspɒzɪ'tɔːrɪəl), *a.* [f. prec. + -(I)AL] Of or pertaining to, or characteristic of an expositor.

1833 G. S. FABER *Recapitulated Apostasy* 38 The common expositorial practice of pitching upon this title or upon that title. *Ibid.* 40 The wantonness of expositorial licence.

expository (ɛk'spɒzɪtərɪ), *a.* and *sb.* [ad. med.L. *expositōri-us* (Boethius), f. *expositor*: see EXPOSITOR. Cf. OF. *expositoire*.]

A. *adj.*

1. Of, pertaining to, or of the nature of, exposition; serving to set forth the meaning (of something); containing an exposition; explanatory. ***expository syllogism***, etc.: (see quots. 1628, 1860).

1628 T. SPENCER *Logick* 262 First they call this forme an Expository Syllogisme..because the third argument is as it were an exposition. 1651 BAXTER *Inf. Bapt.* 251 Name me one place..that more evidently speaks in an Expository way of any Text. 1756 JOHNSON *Pref. Abridged Dict.*, This book may serve as a glossary or expository index to the poetical writers. 1850 GROTE *Greece* II. lxxiii. (1862) VI. 402 To be able to elude inconvenient texts..by expository ingenuity. 1860 VEITCH & MANSEL *Hamilton's Logic* I. 263 *note*, The instance selected is called the expositum (τὸ ἐκτεθέν); and hence singular propositions are called expository. 1867 MILL *Inaug. Addr.* 38, I could wish that it [instruction] were more expository, less polemical, and above all less dogmatic. 1884 LD. SELBORNE in *Law Rep.* 25 Chanc. Div. 493 Are the words 'or in contemplation' simply expository of the word 'upon'?

2. *Comb.* † **expository-wise**, after the manner of an exposition; = EXPOSITORILY *adv.*

1600 ABP. ABBOT *Exp. Jonah* 422 Whereas exegetically or expositorie-wise it is now more largely amplified.

B. *sb.* = EXPOSITOR 2 b.

1751 in CHAMBERS *Cycl.*

Hence **ex'positorily** *adv.*, in an expository manner; by way of exposition, explanatorily.

*a*1631 DONNE *Ess.* (1651) 66 Of these words..I will expositorily say nothing.

expositress (ɛk'spɒzɪtrɪs). *rare.* [f. EXPOSIT(O)R + -ESS.] A female expositor.

1840 GLADSTONE *Ch. Princ.* 12 A faithful expositress of the truths of Catholic Christianity. 1869 *Pall Mall G.* 29 June 5 Her right to be his expositress was never more conclusively proved than on this occasion.

†**ex'positure.** *Obs. rare.* [f. L. type **expositūra*, f. *exposit-*: see above and -URE.] The state of being exposed; = EXPOSURE 3.

1798 W. MAVOR *Brit. Tourists* V. 41 According to the expositure, and the prevalence of the winds.

†**'expost.** *Obs. rare*$^{-1}$. [f. IMPOST by substitution of EX- *pref.* for IM-.] A tax or duty on goods exported.

1643 PRYNNE *Sov. Power Parl.* App. 166 Under which names Portages, Imposts, Exposts..and such like are comprehended.

‖**ex post facto** (ɛks pəʊst 'fæktəʊ). [med.L. phrase, lit. 'from what is done afterwards' (*ex* from, out of, *postfacto*, abl. of *postfactum*, neut. pa. pple. of **postfacĕre*, f. *post* after + *facĕre* to do). The separation of *postfacto* in current spelling is erroneous.] **a.** From an after act or deed; = 'after the fact'.

1632 *Reply to Remonstrance of Netherlands E. India Co. in Justification of Proceedings at Amboyna* (E. India Co.) 11 For first for the notoriousnesse of the pretended conspiracie; although now *ex post facto*, they cry it out for notorious. 1649 BP. HALL *Cases Consc.* I. x. 89 To buy those goods wᶜʰ you know..to be stoln..for what doe you else herein, but ex-post-facto partake with that theefe, who stole them? 1679 J. GOODMAN *Penit. Pard.* I. iii. 77 Whatsoever sin..is not repented of when it is come to our knowledge, is by that means become a voluntary transgression, increasing its guilt *ex post facto*. 1835 *Tomlins's Law-dict.* (ed. 4) *s.v.*, An act done..may be made good by matter *ex post facto*, that was not so at first. 1966 *Listener* 10 Nov. 705/2 A piano suite by Cornelius Cardew eccentrically titled (one supposes *ex postfacto*) *Three Winter Potatoes*.

b. quasi-*adj.* Done after another thing, and operating retrospectively, *esp.* in ***ex post facto law***.

1789 BENTHAM *Princ. Legisl.* xv. §3 Cases in which punishment must be inefficacious..Such are the cases of an ex-post facto law. 1812 R. CUMBERLAND in T. Mitchell *Aristoph.* II. 148 May not I Take up the cause of youth.. Remitting and consigning to oblivion All ex post facto beating? 1823 LINGARD *Hist. Eng.* VI. 486 By an ex post facto law, those who had taken the first oath against the papal authority, were reputed to have taken..a second and much more comprehensive oath, which was afterwards enacted. 1845 MᶜCULLOCH *Taxation* II. vi. §2 They might have objected to the tax had it been *ex post facto*.

expostulant (ɛk'spɒstjʊlənt), *a.* [ad. L. *expostulant-em*, pr. pple. of *expostulāre* to EXPOSTULATE.] Expostulating.

1880 RUSKIN *Elem. Eng. Prosody* 23 The weighty and appellant or expostulant use of the Iambic monometre. 1898 I. ZANGWILL *Dreamers of Ghetto* vii. 295 He would wander tipsily through the sleeping streets..arguing metaphysics with expostulant watchmen. 1922 L. HOUSMAN *Dethronements* 78 Ex-Pres. [Wilson]. You can't reproach me with it, Tumulty. Tumulty (*expostulant*). I'm not doing that, Governor!

expostulate (ɛk'spɒstjʊleɪt), *v.* [f. L. *expostulāt-* ppl. stem of *expostulāre*, f. *ex-* (see EX- *pref.*[1]) + *postulāre*, to demand: see POSTULATE.

The L. senses were 1. to demand; 2. to demand the reason for (a person's conduct); 3. to complain of injury; to remonstrate.]

†**1.** *trans.* To ask for, demand, claim. *Obs.*

*c*1534 tr. *Pol. Verg. Eng. Hist.* (Camden) I. 108 Thei weare constrained to expostulat succors of the Romains. 1548 HALL *Chron.* (1809) 484 He hasted..with as much hast as the gravitie of the cause did require and expostulate. 1604 T. WRIGHT *Passions* 112 To expostulat a certeine fauour. 1645 MILTON *Tetrach.* Introd., If men want manlinesse to expostulate the right of their due ransom. 1670 SIR T. CULPEPPER *Necess. Abating Usury* To Rdr. 3 To such as yet further expostulate my meaning, I answer.

†**b.** With indirect question as obj.: To demand *how* or *why*. *Obs.*

*c*1645 HOWELL *Lett.* (1650) I. 471 They expostulate how a man that was born blind..should presently know the shapes of trees. 1650 COL. ANDREWE in F. Buckley *Relat. Trial* (1660) 71 Some may be so forward as to expostulate, why this great judgment is fallen upon me. 1688–9 LADY RUSSELL *Lett.* II. lxxxiv. 11, I cannot..stay to expostulate why I would do so.

†**2.** To complain of (grievances); to plead or remonstrate *with* a person about (conduct). *Obs.*

1586 A. DAY *Eng. Secretary* II. (1625) 18 They sometime mildely..expostulate the injury. 1602 MARSTON *Ant. & Mel.* IV. Wks. 1856 I. 48 Doe not expostulate the heavens will. 1603 KNOLLES *Hist. Turks* (1621) 314 Some..seemed to expostulate their grife with God. 1678 WANLEY *Wond. Lit. World* v. i. §82. 466/2 The Emperour did expostulate the unseemliness of the deed with him. *a*1716 SOUTH *serm.* (1744) X. 192 Being smote upon the face, they expostulated the injury of the blow.

†**b.** To argue or debate (a matter) as an aggrieved person. Also in wider sense, to debate, argue out, discourse upon. *Obs.*

1573 G. HARVEY *Letter-bk.* (Camden) 31 M. Osburn.. must needs..expostulate the matter with your wurship. 1586 A. DAY *Eng. Secretary* II. (1625) 76 Having at large expostulated my true meaning. 1624 CAPT. SMITH *Virginia* 75 Powhatan began to expostulate the difference of Peace and warre after this manner. [Followed by a speech.] 1665 R. B. *Comm. on 2 Tales* 48 While he thus expostulated the case..she..clapt the window to. 1765 COLMAN *Terence* 326 Let us expostulate the matter with her. 1789 WESLEY *Wks.* (1872) XIII. 123 Do not fail mildly to expostulate the case.

†**c.** To say or utter in expostulation. *Obs.*

1577 FENTON *Gold. Epist.* 245 We neede not feare the quareller, if we expostulate no words with him. 1741 RICHARDSON *Pamela* I. 75 Let me but expostulate a Word or two with you, Pamela.

†**3.** *intr.* **a.** To complain, set forth one's grievances. **b.** To discourse, discuss, dilate. *Obs.*

1561 T. NORTON *Calvin's Inst.* III. 213 The complaintes.. wherein the lord oftentimes doth expostulate of the vnkindenesse of the people. 1593 SHAKS. *3 Hen. VI*, II. v. 135 Nay, stay not to expostulate, make speed. 1605 *Tryall Chev.* IV. i. in Bullen *O. Pl.* (1884) III. 332 But for my haste, I would expostulate of other things. *a*1644 HEYWOOD *Fortune by Land* II. Wks. 1874 VI. 389, I cannot now stand to expostulate. 1772–84 COOK *Voy.* (1790) V. 1639 They often expostulate, in a kind of stanza, or recitative. 1773 J. ROSS *Fratricide* (MS.) VI. 467 Thou who..hast.. Expostulated hours on Virtue's charms!

4. To make friendly remonstrances or representations for the purpose or reprehension or dissuasion; to reason or remonstrate in a friendly manner *with* (a person), *about*, *for*, *on*, or *upon* (a thing).

1574 WHITGIFT *Def. Answ.* 704, I haue great cause to expostulate with you for this your vnchristian..and most vniust handling of me. 1611 BEAUM. & FL. *King & No King* I. i, I have..Expostulated with my wandring thoughts. *a*1674 CLARENDON *Hist. Reb.* (1704) III. XIV. 411 The Keeper expostulated with him in vain upon the dishonour. 1699 BENTLEY *Phal.* 253 He'll give me leave to expostulate ..about his Conduct. 1726 CAVALLIER *Mem.* IV. 290, I expostulated for the Non-performance of the late Conditions. 1794 MRS. RADCLIFFE *Myst. Udolpho* xvi, The Count followed to expostulate and entreat. 1833 J. H. NEWMAN *Lett.* (1891) II. 8 An article from the Editor.. expostulating with the imprudence of his 'friends at Oxford'. 1865 LIVINGSTONE *Zambesi* vii. 161 He expostulated with him on the impropriety of such conduct to strangers.

Hence **ex'postulating** *vbl. sb.*, the action of the vb. EXPOSTULATE. **ex'postulating** *ppl. a.*, that expostulates. **ex'postulatingly** *adv.*

1586 A. DAY *Eng. Secretary* II. (1625) 18 This kinde of expostulating falleth most with persons of equality. 1614 EARL STIRLING *Doomsday* x. lxxvii, The reprobate.. Expostulating blasphemy doe use. 1885 *Pall Mall G.* 19 Feb. 6/4 Men, women, and children rushed past the excited and expostulating officers. 1883 *Harper's Mag.* Oct. 697/1 She..laid her hand on one of his expostulatingly.

expostulation (ɛkˌspɒstjuː'leɪʃən). [ad. L. *expostulātiōn-em*, n. of action f. *expostulāre*: see EXPOSTULATE.]

1. The action of expostulating or remonstrating in a friendly manner; earnest and kindly protest. An instance of the same.

1586 A. DAY *Eng. Secretary* I. (1625) 144 Request, complaint, expostulation. 1646 SIR T. BROWNE *Pseud. Ep.* I. ii. 4 Adam..upon the expostulation of God..replyed, I heard thy voice, etc. 1726 AYLIFFE *Parerg.* 25 Private Accusation of one Friend touching another, is nothing else but a friendly Expostulation with him. 1838 LYTTON *Calderon* vii, All my expostulations have been in vain. 1852 MRS. JAMESON *Leg. Madonna* (1857) 274 Mary stands before her Son in an attitude of expostulation.

2. An expostulatory exclamation or address; an uttered remonstrance, protest, or reproof.

1597 HOOKER *Eccl. Pol.* v. lxv. (1611) 341 Those gracious expostulations; Simon seest thou this woman? 1628 WITHER *Brit. Rememb.* II. 935 Some who need this tart expostulation. 1748 J. MASON *Elocut.* 26 That pathetick Expostulation..of Ezekiel. Why will ye die! 1797 MRS. RADCLIFFE *Italian* vi, Vivaldi delivered this expostulation with rapidity. 1840 MACAULAY *Clive* 80 That lofty expostulation..glows with the very spirit of the Hebrew poets.

expostulative (ɛk'spɒstjʊlətɪv), *a.* [f. EXPOSTULATE + -IVE.] Aiming at or tending to expostulation.

1837 CARLYLE *Fr. Rev.* I. VII. vi, Maillard..repressive with the one hand, expostulative with the other, does his best.

Hence **ex'postulatively** *adv.*, in an expostulative manner.

1888 *Longm. Mag.* Apr. 635 'What's the harm?' responded the young gentleman expostulatively.

expostulator (ɛk'spɒstjʊleɪtə(r)). [f. as prec. + -OR.] One who expostulates; †one who rebukes or complains of.

1727 in BAILEY vol. II. 1795 G. WAKEFIELD *Reply to Part II of 'Age of Reason'* 37 An open and warm expostulator of arrogance. *a*1834 LAMB *Let. to Coleridge* (L.), He is no opponent; only an expostulator.

expostulatory (ɛk'spɒstjʊləˌtərɪ), *a.* [f. as prec. + -ORY.] Characterized by, or of the nature of, expostulation.

1586 A. DAY *Eng. Secretary* II. (1625) 26 An example of an Epistle expostulatorie touching unkindnesse received. 1660 S. FISHER (*title*), The Rustick's Alarm to the Rabbies..In four Apologeticall and Expostulatory Exercitations. 1758 BP. WARBURTON *Lett.* (1809) 275 Mr. Jane..wrote me an expostulatory letter. 1849 STOVEL in *Canne's Necess.* Introd. 63 Expostulatory defences in the ecclesiastical courts.

†**2.** *Comb.*

1600 ABP. ABBOT *Exp. Jonah* 526 He prayed indeed, but it was tumultuously, and expostulatory-wise.

†**ex'posture.** *Obs. rare*$^{-1}$. [f. EXPOSE *sb.*[1] or L. *exposit-* (see EXPOSITION), on the analogy of *posture*, *composture*, etc.] = EXPOSURE.

1607 SHAKS. *Cor.* IV. i. 36 A wilde exposture, to each chance That start's i' th' way before thee.

exposure (ɛk'spəʊʒjʊə(r)). [Appeared with *composure*, *disposure*, *c*1600; app. of English formation, from EXPOSE *sb.*[1], by form-assoc. with *enclose*, *enclosure*, or other words in which the formation was etymological, repr. L. *-sūra*: see -URE.]

1. The action of exposing; the fact or state of being exposed.

a. The action of uncovering or leaving without shelter or defence; unsheltered or undefended condition. Also, the action of subjecting, the state or fact of being subjected, *to* any external influence.

1606 SHAKS. *Tr. & Cr.* I. iii. 195 To weaken and discredit our exposure, How ranke soeuer rounded in with danger. **1793** SMEATON *Edystone L.* §324 The ball..notwithstanding its exposure..appears as bright as it did the first day it was screwed on. **1796** BURKE *Let. Noble Ld.* Wks. VIII. 44 Whatever in his pedigree has been dulcified by an exposure to the influence of heaven. **1802** PALEY *Nat. Theol.* xvi. (ed. 2) 304 So unusual an exposure of the globe of the eye. **1807** *Med. Jrnl.* XVII. 233 The eruption..appeared in consequence of her exposure to the variolous infection. **1844** T. J. GRAHAM *Mod. Dom. Med.* 579 Free exposure to cold is highly serviceable in small pox. **1856** KANE *Arct. Expl.* II. xv. 165 Days and nights of adventurous exposure and recurring disaster. **1878** HUXLEY *Physiogr.* 66 After exposure, the acid is found to be weaker. **1879** *Cassell's Techn. Educ.* III. 1 The exposure of the plate to light is continued for the requisite time.

b. The action of abandoning (an infant).

1863 DRAPER *Intell. Devel. Europe* v. (1865) 117 He recommends the exposure of deformed and sickly infants.

c. Presentation or disclosure to view; public exhibition, *esp.* of goods for sale.

1605 SHAKS. *Macb.* II. iii. 133 When we haue our naked Frailties hid, That suffer in exposure. **1853** *Chamb. Jrnl.* Oct., The exposure of ordinary goods in a store is not more open to the public than are the sales of slaves in Richmond. **1874** GREEN *Short Hist.* viii. 514 Prynne and his fellow pamphleteers..listened with defiance to their sentence of exposure in the pillory. **1885** *Law Rep.* 14 Q. Bench Div. 251 Those Acts expressly prohibit the exposure for sale of goods in those streets.

d. The action of bringing to light (something discreditable); the unmasking or 'showing up' of an error, fraud, or evil, of an impostor or secret offender.

1826 DISRAELI *Viv. Grey* II. v, By this unfortunate exposure..Lorraine was obliged to give in a match..with.. Miss Mexico. **1871** MORLEY *Voltaire* (1886) 127 The exposure of Mahomet would have been counted a glorification of the rival creed. **1873** BURTON *Hist. Scot.* VI. lxxii. 298 The exposure of the forgery makes a dramatic scene.

e. *Photogr.* The exposing of a sensitized surface to the action of actinic rays (see EXPOSE *v.* 5 c); also, the time occupied by this action. Also *attrib.*, as **exposure meter**, a device that indicates the correct time to allow a film, etc., to be exposed.

1839 *Visitor* 479/1 Living objects, if they remain motionless during the short periods of exposure, are given with perfect fidelity. **1847** *Phil. Trans. R. Soc.* CXXXVII. 256 After ten seconds of exposure I put the prepared plate in the mercury box. **1878** W. ABNEY *Treat. Photogr.* xxxi. 246 As regards the exposure to be given to a picture. **1891** *Anthony's Photogr. Bull.* XXII. 285/2 He would like to know whether these exposure meters would give the correct exposures. **1892** [see BACKGROUND *sb.* 1 b]. **1905** *Westm. Gaz.* 2 Sept. 14/2 It is little use for the amateur to use exposure tables to guide him as to the correct exposures to be given under certain conditions. **1918** *Photo-Miniature* Mar. (Glossary), *Exposure indicator*, a device attached to plate-holders to show that the shutter has been withdrawn and re-inserted, i.e., exposure of plate. **1919** *Brit. Jrnl. Photogr. Alm.* 244 The taking of a photograph is known as an exposure, *e.g.*, 'I made 6 exposures'; and the term is also used for the time occupied, *e.g.*, '6 seconds exposure'. **1926** [see ACTINOMETER 2]. **1940** A. L. M. SOWERBY *Wall's Dict. Photogr.* (ed. 15) 281 Exposure calculators are identical in principle with exposure tables... The calculator-mechanism is simply a substitute for the more usual addition of a series of numbers. **1958** *Oxf. Mail* 19 May 6/4 An exposure meter..shows how much light is falling on the subject you want to photograph, and the exposure required.

f. ***indecent exposure***, the action of publicly exposing one's body in an indecent manner. Also *fig.*

1851 *Act 14 & 15 Vict.* c. 100 §29 Any public and indecent Exposure of the Person... It shall be lawful for the Court to sentence the Offender to be imprisoned. **1872** WHARTON *Law Lex.* (ed. 5) 470/2 *Indecent exposure*, an indictable offence at common law. **1928** G. B. SHAW *Platform & Pulpit* (1962) 188 Disgraceful conduct in the parks, indecent exposure. **1958** J. CANNAN *And be a Villain* iii. 49 He took himself off to deal with a case of indecent exposure on the tow-path. **1959** N. MARSH *Singing in Shrouds* iv. 67 Have you witnessed his weekly exhibitions of indecent exposure on the television? **1970** *Sunday Times* (Colour Suppl.) 6 Dec. 24/2 One hard-working executive would have become the only male in an office containing 100 women, if Ian Withers had not discovered that the man had convictions for indecent exposure.

g. *Mountaineering.* (See quots.)

1935 D. PILLEY *Climbing Days* i. 17 You really do feel suspended over the valley with nothing but air below. 'Exposure', in other words, to use the climbing technicality, is continuous. **1940** F. SMYTHE *Adv. Mountaineer* vii. 102 Exposure..is simply the height and nature of the drop beneath the climber. **1957** R. G. COLLOMB *Dict. Mountaineering* 66 *Exposure*, a climber's awareness or feeling of height; his appreciation of the open position on a steep cliff or mountain... The effect of exposure is a temporary set-back or nervousness.

h. The action of bringing to public notice; the condition of being exposed to the attention of the general public, publicity. Now used esp. of publicity achieved through broadcasting or advertising. orig. *U.S.*

1956 *Post-Dispatch* (St. Louis) 23 Aug. 2F/1 Years ago a performer was hired for a performance... Now it's exposure. **1957** *Variety* 5 June 1/4 Nikita Krushchev's.. interview on CBS-TV's 'Face the Nation' will get wide exposure. **1966** *Wall St. Jrnl.* 25 July 1 All..are designed to get broadcast 'exposure' for records that otherwise might be drowned in the unending torrent of new releases. **1971** *Radio Times* 19 Aug. 47/2 People who're doing something worthwhile but aren't getting any exposure for it. **1979** D. HALBERSTAM *Powers that Be* (1980) II. vii. 320 Television was giving him the access and exposure that the party machinery would have loved to deny him. **1980** *Oxford Star* 23 Oct. 22/1 Zanussi..have until now not attained full exposure in this country because they've concentrated mainly on manufacturing goods to be sold under such labels as Tricity, Hotpoint and Hoover. **1986** *Times* 2 Oct. 7/1 By the time California voters go to the polls..the issue will have received a remarkable amount of exposure.

2. *concr.* †**a.** An exposed or unprotected point (*obs.*). **b.** A surface laid open to view, or to the operation of any agency.

c **1611** CHAPMAN *Iliad* VII. 62 If he with home-thrust iron can reach the exposure of my life. **1878** HUXLEY *Physiogr.* 73 The sea..offers a vast exposure of salt water to the heat of the sun. *Ibid.* xvii. 289 Below these come the Thanet beds of which good exposures may be seen at Herne Bay. **1888** DAWSON *Geol. Hist. Plants* 65 Specimens obtained from the rich exposures at Gaspé Bay.

3. The manner or degree in which anything is exposed; *esp.* situation with respect to sun and wind; 'aspect' with regard to the quarter of the heavens.

1664 EVELYN *Kal. Hort.* (1729) 202 Transplant Sampier to some very warm Exposure, as under a South-Wall. *Ibid.* 229 [The Green-house] being plac'd at the most advantageous Exposure to the Sun. **1710** LONDON & WISE *Compl. Gard.* (1719) 175 The Fruits of the Northern Exposure ripen last of all. **1793** SMEATON *Edystone L.* §55 This Lighthouse proves the practicability of a similar erection in any like exposure in the known world. **1827** STEUART *Planter's G.* (1828) 514 The shoots might measure more than two and a half feet, in similar exposures. **1873** TRISTRAM *Moab* xiii. 237 Scarped rocks..far down the southern exposure.

expound (ɛk'spaʊnd), *v.* Forms *α.* 4–5 expounen, -pown-en, 4–6 expoun(e, -pown(e (5 exponne); *β.* 3–6 expounde, expownd(e (5 exspound), 4– expound. *Pa. t.* and *pa. pple.* 5–6 expouned, -powne(d, -pownd(e, -pound(e. [ME. *expoune-n*, *expounde*, ad. OF. *espondre*, *espundre*, *ex-* (3 pl. *esponent*, derivs. *espon-*, *espond-*) = Pr., Sp. *esponer*, Pg. *espōr*, It. *esporre*:—L. *expōnĕre*, to put out, set forth, explain: see EXPONE. The *d* of the Fr. inf. *-pondre* was mechanically developed in the transition from the *n* to the *r* of *-ponre* the regular contraction of L. *-pōnĕre*; a pa. pple. *-pondu* and various derivatives were formed on the inf. stem.

In ME. the prevailing form was *expoune*, adopted according to the usual practice from the finite parts of the Fr. vb.; but the form *expound(e*, from the inf., appeared equally early in northern writers (Hampole and the *Cursor Mundi*). In the course of the 16th c. *expoune* became obsolete, the general adoption of *expound* being favoured by the phonetic tendency exhibited in *sound* for the earlier *soun*, and also by the frequent occurrence of *expound* as pa. pple. In accordance with the analogy of *expound* = L. *exponere*, the earlier *compoune*, *compone* were in 16th c. replaced by *compound*, and *propone* by *propound*; in the former case the substitution may have been partly due to other causes; see COMPOUND *v.*]

1. *trans.* To set forth, declare, state in detail (doctrines, ideas, principles; formerly, with wider application).

c **1325** *E.E. Allit. P.* A. 37 To þat spot þat I in speche expoun I entred in þat erber grene. *Ibid.* B. 1058 Clopyngnel expounez..a speche, to hym þat spede wolde Of a lady to be loued. **1382** WYCLIF *Isa.* xliv. 7 The ordre expoune to me. **1519** *Interl. Four Elements* in Hazl. *Dodsley* I. 37 He hath expound cunningly Divers points of cosmography. **1526** TINDALE *Acts* xxviii. 23 There cam many vnto hym..to whom he expounded and testifyed the kyngdom off God. **1736** SHENSTONE *School-mistress* x, She..quaintly cou'd expound The Chicken-feeding Pow'r of ev'ry Crumb she found. **1748** HARTLEY *Observ. Man* I. iii. 344 Ideas, or the Motions by which they are expounded. **1812** WOODHOUSE *Astron.* xvi. 171 Formulæ expounding its quantity and law. **1845** S. AUSTIN *Ranke's Hist. Ref.* I. 455 The doctrines expounded by St. Augustine. **1875** JOWETT *Plato* (ed. 2) I. 162, I have..an excellent interpretation..which I will expound to you.

absol. **1502** ARNOLDE *Chron.* (1811) 70 We will and ordeigne that all curattz..iiij tymes in the yere in the masse tyme publish and expowne. **16..** DRYDEN *Poems* (1822) I. 242 The carrier's not commission'd to expound.

b. To set forth, represent (a mathematical function or quantity) by figures, symbols, etc.

1708 E. HALLEY in *Misc. Cur.* II. 102 The roots may be expounded by Perpendiculars let fall, upon the Axis or given Diameter of the given Parabola, from the Intersections of that Curve with a Circle. **1812** WOODHOUSE *Astron.* xxvi. 268 These perturbations, when numerically expounded, are so insignificant, etc.

2. To explain, interpret.

a. *gen.* To explain (what is difficult or obscure); to state the signification of; to comment on (a passage or an author).

c **1325** *E.E. Allit. P.* B. 1727 Now expowne þe þis speche spedly I þenk. **1436** *Pol. Poems* (1859) II. 182 Expoune me this, and ye shall sothe it fynde. **1483** *Cath. Angl.* 119 To Expo(w)nde, *commentari*. **1511–2** *Act 3 Hen. VIII*, c. 23 §12 The same Ambiguyte..[shall] be declared, expownned..by the Chaunceller. **1628** T. SPENCER *Logick* 113 This definition hath nothing in it to be expounded. **1826** SCOTT *Woodst.* viii, One who was expounding some religious Mystery to them. **1869** J. MARTINEAU *Ess.* II. 100 Our author proceeds to expound his own analysis.

b. *esp.* To interpret, comment upon (Scripture, religious formularies, etc.). Now chiefly with reference to homiletic exposition. Also *absol.*

a **1300** *Cursor M.* 17288 + 383 (Cott.) And þus he.. expounded þe prophesyes. **1340** HAMPOLE *Pr. Consc.* 4272 His ministres sal swa lette yhit þat na man sal expound haly writ. *c* **1449** PECOCK *Repr.* I. ix. 47 To expowne or interprete or glose dewli and treuly Holi Scripture. **1526** *Pilgr. Perf.* (W. de W. 1531) 3 Saynt Gregory expoundynge the same place of Scripture sayth. **1545** UDALL, etc. *Erasm. Paraph.* (1548) *Luke* viii. 90 b, Many other parables..all which..he expounded severally unto his disciples. **1656** BRAMHALL *Replic.* i. 5 The primitive Fathers expounded it [the Creed] where it did stand in need of clearer explication. **1715** DE FOE *Fam. Instruct.* I. i. (1841) I. 17 The Spirit of God expounds the word of God to us. **1867** LADY HERBERT *Cradle L.* viii. 220 Our..Lord, having read..the words regarding Himself..expounded them to the people.

absol. *a* **1340** HAMPOLE *Psalter* Prol., In expounynge i fologh haly doctours. **1733** NEAL *Hist. Purit.* II. 272 He was suspended..for expounding upon the Catechism. **1778** FLETCHER *Lett.* Wks. 1795 VII. 222, I have ventured..to expound once in the church. **1854** MACAULAY *Bunyan* Misc. Writ. 1860 II. 230 Those martial saints who fought and expounded in Fairfax's army.

†**c.** To interpret the motives or reasons of a person. *Obs.*

1605 BACON *Adv. Learn.* I. iii. §5 Cicero doth excuse and expound the Philosophers for going too far. *a* **1680** BUTLER *Rem.* (1759) II. 25 He, that says what he thinks, lays him-self open to be expounded by the most ignorant.

†**d.** To give the meaning of (a word or name); also, to give a version of in another language; to translate. *Obs.*

1377 LANGL. *P. Pl.* B. XIV. 277 In englisch..it is wel harde wel to expounen. *c* **1386** CHAUCER *Sec. Nun's T.* 86 First wol I yow the name of seint Cecilie Expoune..It is to say on Englisch, hevenes lilie. *c* **1400** *Lanfranc's Cirurg.* 7 (MS. A) We moun knowe surgerie bi expownynge of his name: for siurge comeþ of siros..& in englisch siros is an hand. *c* **1450** *St. Cuthbert* (Surtees) 6691 Þe kyng his preching walde expound, And telle it in englyssh tonge. **1549** LATIMER *Serm. Ploughers* (Arb.) 33 For them yat be vnlearned I wyll expounde it. **1653** H. COGAN tr. *Pinto's Trav.* xxii. 79 As soon as the Interpreter had read the Letter, and expounded the contents thereof.

e. To interpret, explain the significance of (a dream, vision, symbol, etc.); to interpret, solve (a riddle); *rarely*, to explain, account for (a phenomenon). *arch.*

1375 *Cantic. de Creatione* 773 in *Anglia* I, Þe angel anon gan it expoun and tolde him what it [a tree] was. *c* **1386** CHAUCER *Monk's T.* 166 Daniel..the dremes of the kyng expowned. *c* **1400** *Rom. Rose* 7176, I wole bigynne, To expowne you the pith withynne. *c* **1450** *St. Cuthbert* (Surtees) 728 His mayster on þis wyse had Expounde his visyoun. **1535** COVERDALE *Judges* xiv. 14 They coulde not expounde the ryddle. **1596** SHAKS. *Tam. Shr.* IV. iv. 79 My Master..has left mee here behinde to expound the meaning or morrall of his signes and tokens. *a* **1680** BUTLER *Rem.* (1759) I. 215 The Stagyrite, unable to expound The Euripus, leapt into 't, and was drown'd. **1814** WORDSW. *White Doe* I. 223 Studious to expound The spectacle.

f. To infer from indications. *rare*$^{-1}$.

1821–56 DE QUINCEY *Confess.* (1862) 269 The clouds by which chiefly the eye expounds the distance of the blue pavilion stretched over our heads.

g. *refl.* †To explain one's meaning (*obs.*). Also, to be one's own expositor.

1601 CORNWALLYES *Ess.* II. xlviii. (1631) 307 An abilitie to behold things ambiguous with the true sight gives.. circumstances, leave to expound themselves. **1661** BRAMHALL *Just Vind.* vii. 163 The Pope was forced to expound him-self. **1859** TENNYSON *Vivien* 316 The people call you prophet: let it be: But not of those that can expound them-selves.

3. To give a particular interpretation to; to construe in a specified manner. With *adv.* or *phrase.* Now chiefly in *Law.*

1533–4 *Act 25 Hen. VIII*, c. 21 §19 Prouided alwaies, that this act nor anythinge..therein conteined, shalbe.. interpreted or expounded, that, etc. **1534** MORE *On the Passion* Wks. 1314 Some expowne also those woordes..to sygnifye that [etc.]. **1590** SPENSER *F.Q.* III. iv. 28 That deadly wownd..The which his mother vainely did expownd to be hart-wownding love. **1685** BAXTER *Paraphr. N.T.* Matt. x. 23 This hard Text is variously expounded. **1767** BLACKSTONE *Comm.* II. 381 That a devise be most favourably expounded. **1818** CRUISE *Digest* (ed. 2) VI. 191 The courts..expound the will in such a manner as to carry the testator's intention into effect. **1839** THIRLWALL *Greece* IV. 445 Sparta..was constituted the interpreter of the treaty; she expounded it by the rule, not of reason, but of might.

†**b.** ***to expound*** (a statement, etc.) ***concerning*** or ***of***: to explain as referring to. *Obs.*

c **1380** WYCLIF *Serm.* Sel. Wks. II. 241 Men expownen comounly þis prophecie of oure Jesus. *c* **1450** *Mirour Saluacioun* 3767 This may be wele expovned of the blissed virgyne marie. **1574** tr. *Marlorat's Apocalips* 14 They..that go about to expound this place concerning Christ, according to the letter; do wrest it too violently. **1645** USSHER *Body Div.* (1647) 85 Which place Paul expoundeth of the Holy Ghost. **1724** A. COLLINS *Gr. Chr. Relig.* 236 Those of whom they are ordinarily expounded.

†**c.** To render by a specified term. With *complement*, or const. *for*. *Obs.*

1530–1 *Act 22 Hen. VIII*, c. 13 No person..being a comon Baker, Brewer..shall be interpreted or expounded handicrafts men. **1531** ELYOT *Gov.* I. i, *Chaos*..of some is expounde a confuse mixture. **1533** MORE *Answ. Poisoned Bk.* Wks. 1087/2 Men..that expounde those wordes of Christ..to be spoke and ment of the very eating of hys blessed body. **1599** THYNNE *Animadv.* (1875) 33 'Orfrayes' you expounde 'Goldsmythes Worke'. **1607** TOPSELL *Four-f. Beasts* (1658) 69 Rabbi Solomon, and Abraham Ezra, expound Egel, for a Calf of one year old.

†**d.** To interpret as a prognostic of something. Const. *to*. *Obs.*

c **1430** LYDG. *Bochas* I. iv. (1544) 7 a, Worthy Ninus.. expouned his laughter to great felicitye.

†**4.** In etymol. sense of L. *expōnere* (cf. EXPOSE *sb.*¹). To expose to view. *Obs. rare*

1651 *Life Father Sarpi* (1676) 38 He celebrated the Mass, and every Wednesday expounded upon his Altar the holy Sacrament. **1664** BUTLER *Hud.* II. iii. 1087 First, he expounded both his Pockets, And found a Watch, with Rings and Lockets.

Hence **ex'pounded** *ppl. a.*, **ex'pounding** *vbl. sb.*, the action of the vb. EXPOUND; *concr.* an exposition or interpretation. **ex'pounding** *ppl. a.*

c **1380** WYCLIF *Sel. Wks.* III. 272 False expounyng of holy writt. *c* **1440** HYLTON *Scala Perf.* (W. de W. 1494) II. xli, I fele wel of thy Name þe true expownynge that thou art Jhesu hele. **1483** *Cath. Angl.* 119 An Expow(n)dynge; *commentum.* **1571** GOLDING *Calvin on Ps.* viii. 2 A fullfilling or expownding part of speache. **1642** J. EATON *Honey-c. Free Justific.* b ij a, Expounded texts and verses. **1643** MILTON *Divorce* xiii. (1851) 55 A yoke.. which.. nothing but unwary expounding hath brought upon us. **1745** WESLEY *Answ. Ch.* 3 One of our English Brethren.. said in his Publick Expounding, 'As many go to Hell by praying as by thieving. **1881** MAHAFFY *Old Grk. Educ.* xi. 137 The repeating and expounding of the founder's view.

expoundable (ɛk'spaʊndəb(ə)l), *a.* [f. prec. + -ABLE.] That may be expounded or explained; capable of being expounded.

1887 *Twin Soul* II. i. 2 To expound their views, as far as they were expoundable.

expounder (ɛk'spaʊndə(r)). Also 4–5 **expowner**, 5 **expownder**. [f. as prec. + -ER¹.] One who expounds; an expositor. Occasionally *transf.* of a thing: That which serves to expound.

1388 WYCLIF *Gen.* xli. 7 He [Farao] sente to alle the expowneris of Egipt.. and.. he telde the dreem. *c* **1449** PECOCK *Repr.* I. xii. 65 Alle expowners and glose ȝeuers to Holi Scripture. **1535** COVERDALE *1 Sam.* xxviii. 3 Saul had dryuen the soythsayers and expounders of tokens out of yᵉ londe. **1565** JEWEL *Repl. Harding* 120 The Custome and practise of the people, is the best expounder of the Lawe. **1786** BURKE *W. Hastings* Wks. 1842 II. 115 Magistrates and expounders of the Mahomedan law. **1869** tr. *Pouchet's Universe* (1871) 3 Bonnet, one of the most zealous expounders of natural history. **1875** JOWETT *Plato* (ed. 2) V. 6 The argument of which the Athenian is the expounder.

Hence †**ex'poundress**, *Obs. rare*, a female expounder.

1604 *Supplic. Masse Priests* §37 The Romish Church, whom they make chiefe expoundresse of Scriptures.

†**ex'pounitour**. *Obs. rare*⁻¹. [f. *expoune*, EXPOUND *v.*, on the analogy of *expositor*.] An expounder, expositor.

c **1380** WYCLIF *Sel. Wks.* III. 202 Expounitouris on þe gospellis and pistelis.

expouse, obs. form of ESPOUSE *v.*

expoyl, var. of EXSPOIL *obs.*

†**ex'preme**, *v. Obs.* Chiefly *Sc.* Forms: 5–7 **expreme**, 6 **exprime**, 7 **expreeme**, **-eime**. [ad. (directly or through F. *exprimer*), L. *exprimĕre* to EXPRESS. For the phonology cf. *redeem*.] *trans.* = EXPRESS *v.*¹ 6–8.

c **1470** HARDING *Chron.* XXXI. iii, The first he was, as chronicles expreme, That in this isle of Brytein had croune of golde. **1524** *St. Papers Hen. VIII*, VI. 222, I cannot with my tong or penne exprime the inwarde joye which I haue taken. **1588** A. KING tr. *Canisius' Catech.* 15 That sinne bringes sua greate skaithe to the saule, as na tonge is abil to expreme. **1609** SKENE *Reg. Maj.*, *Stat. Robt. I*, 23 In pleyes of debt, sould be named and expreimed, the zeare, day, the quantitie of the debt. *a* **1651** CALDERWOOD *Hist. Kirk* (1843) II. 353 He hath offered to doe his devoire, by the law of armes, in maner before expreemed.

express (ɛk'sprɛs), *a.*, *adv.*, and *sb.*¹ Forms: 4–6 **expres**, 4–7 **expresse**, 6– **express**, 7 *compar.* **expresser**. [ad. Fr. *exprès* (fem. *expresse*) = Pr. *expres*, Sp. *espreso*, Pg. *espresso*, It. *espresso*, ad. L. *express-us*, pa. pple. of *exprimĕre*: see EXPRESS *v.*¹]

A. *adj.*

I. 1. a. Of an image or likeness: Truly depicted, exactly resembling, exact. Now chiefly with reminiscence of *Heb.* i. 3. Cf. EXPRESS *v.*¹ 5.

1513 MORE *Rich. III.* Wks. 61/2 This is yᵉ fathers own figure.. yᵉ playne expresse lykenes of yᵉ noble Duke. **1579** LYLY *Euphues* (Arb.) 36 Thy byrth doth shewe the expresse and liuely Image of gentle bloud. **1611** BIBLE *Heb.* i. 3 The expresse image of his person. **1612** T. TAYLOR *Comm. Titus* ii. 7 Shew thy selfe a patterne, and expresse type wherein [etc.]. **1667** MILTON *P.L.* VII. 528 Hee Created thee, in the Image of God Express. **1764** REID *Inquiry* I. ii. 69 Language is the express image and picture of human thoughts. **1774** J. BRYANT *Mythol.* II. 431 The Deity is here described sitting .. in the express form of the Minotaur. *a* **1853** ROBERTSON *Serm.* Ser. III. x. 125 The universe is the express image and direct counterpart of the souls that dwell in it.

b. Well framed or modelled. *nonce-use.*

1602 SHAKS. *Ham.* II. ii. 317 What a piece of worke is a man!.. In forme, and mouing, how expresse and admirable!

II. (Cf. EXPRESS *v.*¹ 6–10).

†**2.** Of a fact, condition, etc.: Stated, explicitly recorded. In early use as *pa. pple. Obs.*

c **1386** CHAUCER *Wife's Prol.* 719 Lo here expresse of wommen may ye fynde, That woman was the losse of al mankynde. *c* **1386** —— *Wife's T.* 313 Ther shull ye seen expresse.. That he is gentil that doth gentil dedis. **1686** GOAD *Celest. Bodies* II. v. 225 There is not above 30 days but are windy, and rainy, or of express heat [cf. *ibid.* I. xii. 56 We must distinguish of warm Days, Days of Expressed Notation for Warmth or Heat].

3. a. Of a meaning, purpose, stipulation, law, etc.: Expressed and not merely implied; definitely formulated; definite, explicit. Of language, statements, indications: Definite, unmistakable in import.

When used of a law, stipulation, grant, etc., the adj. may have either this sense or sense 4, and often appears to have a mixed notion of the two.

c **1386** CHAUCER *Wife's Prol.* 61 Wher can ye seen.. That highe God defended mariage By expresse word? *c* **1425** WYNTOUN *Cron.* IX. xxvii. 151 Agane þe Lauch expres.. chosyn wes Þis Knychtis son. **1550** BALE *Apol.* 117 b, Neyther.. is ther any expresse doctryne of vowes in all the whole wurke. **1578** T. N. tr. *Conq. W. India* 75 [He] commaundid that none of his men shoulde goe out.. without his expresse licence upon paine of death. **1594** HOOKER *Eccl. Pol.* I. xvi. (1611) 49 We have no expresse purpoce to make that our end. **1605** BP. MORTON (*title*), Exact Discoverie of Romish Doctrine.. collected out of the expresse dogmatical principles of Popish Priests and Doctors. **1616** B. JONSON *Epigr.* xl, All the gazers on the skies Read not in fair heaven's story Expresser truth.. Than they might in her bright eyes. **1659** HAMMOND *On Ps.* cxviii. 27 Annot. 594 The insuing verse is express. **1662** STILLINGFL. *Orig. Sacr.* III. iv. §13 We have the express testimony of Epiphanius. **1767** BLACKSTONE *Comm.* II. 443 Express contracts are where the terms of the agreement are openly uttered and avowed at the time of the making. **1851** HT. MARTINEAU *Hist. Peace* (1877) III. IV. ix. 22 Mr. Stanley's answer was express and clear. **1888** BRYCE *Amer. Commw.* II. li. 285 Sometimes by express, more often by a tacit understanding.

†**b.** Hence of persons or an authority: Distinct in making a statement, outspoken, explicit. Of a state of mind: Fixed, free from vacillation. *Obs.*

a **1593** H. SMITH *Wks.* (1867) II. 425 Theodoret.. is most express against transubstantiation. **1665** GLANVILL *Sceps. Sci.* 17 Trismegistus is express in the assertion of the same Doctrine. **1667** H. MORE *Div. Dial.* I. iii. (1743) 14, I love to feel myself of an express and settled judgment. *a* **1704** LOCKE (J.), Where reason or Scripture is express for any opinion, or action, we may receive it as of divine authority. **1704** *Lond. Gaz.* No. 4037/5 Her Majesty is very express in what She proposes. **1778** N. LAURENS in Sparks *Corr. Amer. Rev.* (1853) II. 117 Our Commissioners.. are not so express .. as they might have been.

†**c.** Of a voice: Distinctly uttered. *Obs.*

c **1450** *St. Cuthbert* (Surtees) 5667 Þe childe foloude and sayde þan, with' a voyce expresse. **1700** DRYDEN *Fables, Ovid's Met.* XII. 71 Nor silence is within, nor voice express, But a deaf noise of sounds that never cease.

d. ***express malice*** (*Law*): malice of which there is actual evidence; opposed to *implied malice*, that which is inferred merely from the nature of the unlawful act committed. †***express witchcraft***: ? manifest, open witchcraft.

1567 *Scot. Poems 16th C.* II. 260 O faithles flock!.. Mantenaris of murther, witchcraft expres, Tresoun amang ȝow does daylie incres. **1769** BLACKSTONE *Comm.* IV. xiv. 199 Malice may be either express, or implied in law. Express malice is.. when one, with a sedate.. deliberate mind and formed design, doth kill another. **1808** LE BLANC in East *Rep.* IX. 363 Without proof of malice, either express or implied.

e. Specifically designated or considered; special.

1848 MILL *Pol. Econ.* III. xiv. §4 When we treat of that express subject. **1855** BAIN *Senses & Int.* III. ii. §23 Natural History makes a more express business of the classifying operation.

4. a. Specially designed or intended for a particular object; done, made, or sent 'on purpose.' Of a messenger: Specially dispatched. Also *absol.* in phrase †*in express*: ? for a purpose (unless this be an early instance of EXPRESS *sb.*²).

a **1400** *Cov. Myst.* 115 Ffarewel, Gabryel.. Goddys masangere expresse. *c* **1420** *Pallad. on Husb.* II. 403 Rapes make wele to smelle In condyment is nowe the tyme expresse. *c* **1460** *Towneley Myst.* 209 *Pilatus.* I am sakles of this bloode.. Both my handes in express weshen shalle be. **1524** WOLSEY in *St. Papers Hen. VIII.* (1849) VI. 317, I receyvid new letters from you, sent by an expresse curror. **1619** VCT. DONCASTER in *Eng. & Germ.* (Camden) 137 Send.. with all possible speede by an expresse messenger. **1782** PRIESTLEY *Corrupt. Chr.* II. x. 260 Express laws were made to prevent [it]. **1845** CARLYLE *Cromwell* (1871) I. 16 In these two little offhand bits of writing.. there is more in-sight obtainable, than in any of the express Biographies. **1874** MORLEY *Compromise* (1886) 123 The social union is the express creation.. of the Deity.

b. ***express train***. Originally = 'special train'; but about 1845 applied to a train running 'expressly' for the conveyance of passengers to one particular place, and not stopping at the intermediate stations; now, a train running at a high rate of speed, and stopping only at a few important stations. Hence ***express speed***.

1841 SAUNDERS *Rep. Committee Railw.* Q. 2051 It was probable that an express train would come up. **1842** W. F. COOKE *Telegr. Railw.* 19, I will now follow an Express, and therefore unexpected train in its course from Derby to Leicester. **1845** *Bradshaw's Rail. Guide* May 14 The accommodation by the Express Trains being limited, Passengers who arrive first will have the preference. **1845** C. B. VIGNOLES in *Life* (1889) 269 Went down to Birmingham by the 'express' train. **1849** MACAULAY *Jrnl.* 16 Aug., The express train reached Holyhead. **1862** *Gifts & Graces* xii. 127 We must step into an express train.

c. ***express rifle***: a rifle constructed to discharge a bullet with a high initial velocity and a low trajectory. ***express bullet***: an expanding bullet for use with an express rifle. ***express shooting***: shooting with an express rifle.

1884 METFORD in Walsh *Mod. Sportsman's Gun* II. 12 This being a sort of 'rough and tumble' gauge of Express shooting at 100 yards. **1884** SIR H. HALFORD *ibid.* II. 14 These rifles [made by Purdey in 1859] must be considered as the first of the class now known as Express—a term believed to have been first used either by the late Lord Henry Bentinck or by Lord Leconfield. **1888** *Pall Mall G.* 10 July 7/1 It has been proved that 'express' bullets are used by the Zulus or their allies.

d. ***express delivery***: (in the Postal service) immediate delivery by special messenger, on a system introduced in 1891; so ***express fee***, ***messenger***, ***packet***, etc. [Here it is difficult to separate the *adj.* from attrib. uses of the *sb.*]

1891 *Post Office Guide* Oct. 227 There is no Express delivery.. on Sunday, Good Friday, or Christmas Day. **1892** *Ibid.* Apr. 17 On the delivery of an Express Packet, the delivering Messenger may take a reply.. The Express fee must be prepaid. *Ibid.* 18 Letters and Parcels are accepted for conveyance by Express Messenger to the General Post Office.

e. = HIGH-SPEED *a.*; ***express boiler***, a boiler capable of getting steam up with great rapidity; ***express highway***, etc.: see EXPRESSWAY; ***express lift***, a lift which does not stop at every floor. Cf. 4 b.

1897 KIPLING *Day's Work* (1898) 217 Express freight's what pays. **1902** *Encycl. Brit.* XXVI. 285/2 The types, sometimes called 'Express' boilers, which are largely used in torpedo-boats,.. where the most important requirement is very high power with a very small weight of boiler. **1909** *Cent. Dict.* Suppl., *Express-pump*, a high-speed pump; one that makes a high number of strokes per minute. **1909** *Westm. Gaz.* 9 June 11/4 Six electric passenger lifts, two of which are known as 'express' lifts. **1938** E. BOWEN *Death of Heart* I. ix. 160 Matchett is sending Anna's white velvet dress to the express cleaners. **1967** W. PINE *Protectors* xi. 91 The two men rode up from the basement to the twenty-first floor by express lift. **1971** *Daily Tel.* 4 Jan. 7/2 Those express lifts (sorry elevators) which serve New York's highest buildings.

B. *adv.* [Cf. EXPRESSLY.]

†**1.** Clearly, plainly, unmistakably. With verbs of speaking: In distinct terms, positively. *Obs.*

c **1325** *E.E. Allit. P.* B. 1158 Danyel.. devysed sum tyme, As.. is proued expresse in his profecies. **14..** *Purif. Mary* in *Tundale's Vis.* 130 To the law sche mekely wold obey From poynt to poynte the gospel seyth expresse. *c* **1450** *St. Cuthbert* (Surtees) 3389 Þis chapiter it schewes expresse What fandyng he tholed in sekenes. **1556** LAUDER *Tractate* 255 Haue ȝe thare herts, I say expresse, Than all is ȝours that thay possesse. **1712** BERKELEY *Pass. Obed.* §23 Such a contract is an express known part of the fundamental constitution of a nation.

†**2. a.** Followed by *against*: Directly. **b.** With respect to dimension or number: Exactly. **c.** Completely. *Obs.*

a. *c* **1386** CHAUCER *Doctor's T.* 182 Virginius.. holdeth expresse aȝeinst þe wille of me My seruaunt. **1578** *Gude & Godly Ball* 158 The Leuittis.. reft thair teind and mekill mair, Expres aganis Goddis command.

b. *c* **1475** *Partenay* 3004 Fiftene fote long this Geaunt was expresse. **1513** BRADSHAW *St. Werburge* I. 142 Also the yeres of our blessed sauyoure Syxe hundreth foure score and nyne expresse The Brytons were expulsed.. From Englande to walles.

c. *c* **1475** *Partenay* 4357 Hys hauberke dismailled all expresse. **1513** DOUGLAS *Æneis* XIII. ii. 52 To mak end of our harmis and distres! Our panefull labour passit is expres.

3. a. Specially, on purpose, for a particular end; hence (to go, send, etc.) with speed. In mod. use also, by express messenger or train.

1386 CHAUCER *Doctor's T.* 105 This mayde, of which I telle my tale expresse. **1667** PEPYS *Diary* (1879) IV. 368, I sent Mr. C. express thither to see how matters go. **1708** *Lond. Gaz.* No. 4490/3 M. Osten.. came Express.. to make his Compliments to his Prussian Majesty. **1760** T. HUTCHINSON *Hist. Coll. Mass.* iii. 398 A small vessel had been sent to England express.. with a representation of the exposed state of the colony. **1844** DISRAELI *Coningsby* IV. ix, As if the grand furniture and the grand servants had all come down express from town. **1870** LOWELL *Study Wind.* 2 A piece of news worth sending express.

Comb. **1870** EMERSON *Soc. & Solit.* xi. 278 No expressrider, no attorney, no magistrate.

b. Without a stop.

1892 *Harper's Mag.* Feb. 426/1 The managers of certain tall buildings now arrange them [*sc.* elevators] so that some run 'express' to the seventh story.

C. *sb.*¹

1. a. = *express messenger*: see A. 4. Now *Hist.* or *arch.* exc. in sense of an express messenger of the Postal Department.

1619 VCT. DONCASTER in *Eng. & Germ.* (Camden) 177, I will spedily advertise his Maᵗʸ by an expresse. **1680** *Lond. Gaz.* No. 1536/4 An Express is arrived in 14 days from Madrid, but we know not what he brings. **1780** R. R. LIVINGSTON in Sparks *Corr. Amer. Rev.* (1853) III. 2 This hasty letter is written while the express waits. **1816** KEATINGE *Trav.* I. 34 Faster than an express could travel: at least in these regions. **1856** EMERSON *Eng. Traits, The Times* Wks. (Bohn) II. 118 Its expresses outrun the despatches of

the government. **1891** *Daily News* 4 Apr. 6/7 We expect the Post Office to convey the necessary orders—either by post, by telegraph, by telephone, or by 'express.'

b. *transf.* The message sent by an 'express'; a dispatch.

1642 MILTON (*title*) Observations upon some of his Majestie's [Charles I.] late Answers and Expresses. **1659** PEARSON *Creed* (1839) 282 By an express written to Tiberius, and by him presented to the senate. **1676** DRYDEN *Aurengz.* I. i, A new Express all Agra does afright. **1741** MIDDLETON *Cicero* I. v. 356 Cicero..received two expresses from his Brother Quintus. **1807** *Beverley & Kexby Road Act* 6 Conveying the mails of letters and expresses under the authority of His Majesty's Post-Master General. **18..** WELLINGTON in *Daily News* 20 Nov. (1891) 5/1 Blucher picked the fattest man in his army to ride with an express home. **1854** DICKENS *Hard T.* II. ix, Bitzer had come..with an express from Stone-Lodge.

c. ? A special errand.

c **1817** HOGG *Tales & Sk.* III. 215 Tam's wife had occasion to cross the wild heights on some express.

2. Short for **a.** *express-train*; **b.** *express rifle.*

a. **1848** DICKENS *Dombey* lv, Express comes through at four, Sir. **1867** TROLLOPE *He Knew* xxiii, [He] went down.. by the early express to Exeter.

b. **1884** *Pall Mall G.* 19 Aug. 5/1 A wealthy 'potter'.. blazed away with a double express at the deer compelled to pass him. **1888** RIDER HAGGARD *Maiwa's Revenge* 127 I, handing him the carbine, took from him my express.

3. a. Chiefly *U.S.* An institution (conducted by private enterprise) for the transmission of parcels, etc. Also, goods or other articles conveyed by this method. Cf. EXPRESS. *a.* 4 d and *pony-express* (PONY *sb.* 7 b).

The carrying of goods by 'express,' first introduced in 1839 (see quot. 1858) has had an enormous development in the United States. In Great Britain the system exists, but the name is little used, though it has been adopted in the distinctive designations of one or two of the 'forwarding agencies,' as they are usually called.

1794 D. M'GILLIVRAY *Jrnl.* (1929) 40 No goods are sent him by this express. *Ibid.*, We expect an express from him very soon. *Ibid.*, The Canoe containing the express. **1839** *Boston Transcript* 21 Mar. 2/2 Harnden's Express, between Boston and New York, has been running since the 4th of March. **1840** *Boston Daily Advertiser* 7 Feb. 4/3 Mr. Harnden will for the present send his Express via Worcester. **1869** *Trans. Ill. Agric. Soc.* VII. 522 They can be handled as roughly, almost, as these express agents handle boxes. **1858** HOMANS *Cycl. Comm.* 644 s.v. *Express*, William F. Harnden..started the express business in the spring of 1839. **1839** *Boston Transcript* 27 Feb. 4/1 Boston and New York Express Car. **1879** F. R. STOCKTON *Rudder Grange* vii. 76 My package was wheeled to the express-car. **1882** W. D. HAY *Brighter Britain* I. ii. 32 Omnibuses.. express-carts, waggons. **1922** O. JESPERSEN *Lang.* v. 108 Hilary M...called an express-cart a *press-cart.* **1880** *Daily News* 20 Nov. 5/4 An express clerk walks through the train, takes the checks of passengers who want their baggage delivered, and gives written receipts for them. **1858** HOMANS *Cycl. Comm.* 645 The express companies.. transmit nearly all the specie and bullion, etc. **1860** BARTLETT *Dict. Amer.*, *Express Office*, an establishment which rapidly transmits parcels and goods. *Ibid.*, *Express Wagon*, the wagon in which packages, boxes, etc., are taken to and from an express office. **1862** C. R. THATCHER *Dunedin Songster* No. 1, 9 There was a little express waggon waiting to convey these Melbourne notables to Dunedin. **1863** *Stamped Envelope Inscr.*, Paid, Wells, Fargo, & Co. Through our California and Atlantic Express. **186..** *Postage Stamp Inscr.*, Pony Express.

b. The goods carried by an 'express'.

1858 HOMANS *Cycl. Comm.* 644 Harnden himself acted in that capacity [as 'messenger'] carrying his entire express in an ordinary valise.

Hence **ex'pressage**, the sending of a parcel by express; the charge or cost of this.

1857 C. E. DE LONG *Jrnl.* 12 May in *Q. Calif. Hist. Soc.* (1930) IX. 143 Paid Farley $5 for expressage. **1864** WEBSTER *Expressage*, the charge for carrying a parcel by express. **1883** *Amer. Newspaper Advt.*, The books will be sent by express C.O.D., the receiver paying expressage or freight. **1888** *Harper's Mag.* Dec. 161/1 The expressage or postage has not been prepaid. **1936** M. H. BRADLEY *Five Minute Girl* x. 197 The expressage will entail some expense.

†**express** (ɛk'sprɛs), *sb.*² *Obs.* [f. the vb. Cf. late L. *expressus* (*u* stem).]

1. The action of expressing or representing by words, signs, or actions; an instance of this. Const. *of.*

1644 BULWER *Chirol.* 8 The Hand seems to..vie expresses with the Tongue. **1648** *Eikon Bas.* 94 With expresses of my desires. **1654** R. BOREMAN *Serm.* Ep. Ded., So they might give to the world a Cleare Expresse of their gratitude to your Lordship. **1672** J. HOWARD *All Mistaken* I. in Hazl. *Dodsley* XV. 332 My grief, alas! is far beyond express. *a* **1716** SOUTH *Serm.* (1744) XI. 156 Allow of no other expresses of our honour to him [God] but distance and amazement.

b. A condition or product in which something is expressed; a manifestation. (Revived by Kingsley with stress *'express*, after *'impress.*)

1644 JER. TAYLOR *Psalter* cxxxvi, Making all Thy creatures to be expresses of Thy power. **1663** J. SPENCER *Prodigies* (1665) 349 It seems to have been the common maxim..that all afflictions were the expresses of displeasure. **1848** KINGSLEY *Saint's Trag.* IV. iii. 232 Grace brings no merit When 'tis the express of our own self-will.

2. A mode of speech, phrase; an utterance.

1644 HUNTON *Vind. Treat. Monarchy* v. 42 He compares these serious expresses to Trajans sudden and excessive speech. **1647** JER. TAYLOR *Lib. Proph.* v. 84, I have shewed Scripture in its plain expresses to be an abundant rule of Faith. *a* **1677** BARROW *Serm.* Wks. 1687 I. 361 Surely those expresses are used in condescension to signify the.. charitable benignity of God.

b. A specific mention, statement, or injunction.

1646 SIR. T. BROWNE *Pseud. Ep.* II. v. §6. 91 This Gentleman..caused a man to goe downe..into the Sea.. with expresse to take notice..where it [Coral] groweth. **1660** FULLER *Mixt Contempl.* (1841) 206 They had no express in scripture that they should be freed from the particular miseries relating to this war. **1687** TOWERSON *Baptism* 343 Some express to signifie such a thing to be its purpose. *a* **1711** J. NORRIS *Misc.* (1687) 215 They.. contradict the general design and particular expresses of the Gospel.

3. A graphic representation, image; *fig.* a type, model (of virtues).

1513 DOUGLAS *Æneis* XI. vi. 161 This Ene was first, all out, expres Of reuth, compassioun, and of gentilnes. **1646** SIR T. BROWNE *Pseud. Ep.* v. xx. 262 They discoursed in silence, and were intuitively understood from the theory of their Expresses. **1646** J GREGORY *Notes & Observ* (1684) 51 Some ancient Coyns have been called by the name of their Expresses, as..(saith Pollux) καὶ ἐκαλεῖτο βοῦς, ὅτι βοῦν εἶχεν ἐμτετυπωμένον, from the figure of an ox imprinted.

b. A 'stamp,' impressed character.

1667 WATERHOUSE *Fire Lond.* 2 This fatal accident had a more than ordinary express of fury.

express (ɛk'sprɛs), *v.*¹ Also 4–6 **expresse**. [ME. *expresse*, a. OF. *espresser*, *expresser* = Pr. *espressar*, Sp. *espresar*, Pg. *expressar*, med.L. *expressāre* (15th c. in Du Cange), f. L. *ex-* out + *pressāre* to press, frequentative of *premĕre*, to press. Taken as Eng. repr. of L. *exprimĕre* of which the chief senses were 1. to press out; 2. to form (an image) by pressure, to represent in sculpture or painting 3. to represent or set forth in words or actions.] **I.** To press out.

1. a. *trans.* To press, squeeze, or wring out; to press (juice, air, etc.) *from, out of* (anything). *spec.* to press or squeeze out (milk or other secretion) from the breast.

c **1400** *Lanfranc's Cirurg.* 127 (MS A.) & þei fulfillen þe wounde..as I have seid, with þe cloop expressid of þe white of an ey. **1430** LYDG. *Chron. Troy* I. vi, When men of malice ..his venym vtterly expresse. **1569** R. ANDROSE tr. *Alexis' Secr.* IV. II. 37 Put them all into an Orenge..and boyle them in hote embers, then expresse it. **1594** PLAT *Jewell-ho., Chem. Concl.* 16 Expresse their oile according to the manner herafter set down. **1638** T. WHITAKER *Blood of Grape* 18 Newly exprest from the grape. **1757** A. COOPER *Distiller* III. iii. (1760) 226 Express the Juice and Spirit. **1804** ABERNETHY *Surg. Observ.* 94 To puncture the upper tumour, to express the contents. **1880** *Daily News* 26 Feb. 5/2 The oil or oleomargarine is expressed from the fat. **1932** R. C. JEWESBURY *Mothercraft* III. 37 Milk can be expressed manually, but this often causes pain. **1953** CARTER & DODDS *Dict. Midwifery* 82/1 The patient should be taught how to express secretion from the nipple so that the milk may be able to flow freely later on. **1955** B. SPOCK *Baby & Child Care* 33 If you can learn the knack of expressing a little milk at the same time, it will lure him on.

b. *fig.* (*a*) To extort or elicit by pressure. †(*b*) To expel, get rid of, by force (*obs.*).

(*a*) **1547** J. HARRISON *Exhort. Scottes* 232 Youre countrey weepinge to you with bloody teares, which your selfes do expresse, and wring out of her, and enforce her to shed. **1609** HOLLAND *Amm. Marcell.* XXIX. iv. 365 The truth was by torture expressed. **1612** WEBSTER *White Devil* I. i, Perfumes ..chaf'd..render Their pleasing scents; and so affliction Expresseth virtue fully. **1818** HALLAM *Mid. Ages* (1872) I. 209 To employ them [Jews] as a spunge to suck their subjects' money, which they might afterwards express.

(*b*) **1565** GOLDING *Ovid's Met.* Ep. (1593) 6 Temperance which doth all fowle concupiscence expresse. **1583** K. JAMES VI in Holinshed *Hist. Scotl.* (1585) 442 That..the veritie may be tried and all heresie and schisme..expressed.

2. To emit or exude, as if by pressure.

1621 BURTON *Anat. Mel.* I. i. II. ii. 21 Spirit is a most subtile vapor, which is expressed from the Blood. **1634** SIR T. HERBERT *Trav.* 46 Ormus is an ile. of which..the Silver-shining Sand expresseth Sulphur. **1657** S. PURCHAS *Pol. Flying-Ins.* 158 Waxe..expressing in some sort a scent of honie. **1855** THACKERAY *Newcomes* I. 110 Essences into which a thousand flowers have expressed their sweetest breath. **1882** *Pall Mall G.* 28 June 5/1 Their honey-dew, which the aphides express when caressed by the antennæ of their masters.

3. To press or squeeze out the contents of. Now *rare.*

1633 BP. HALL *Hard Texts* 289 To expresse and make use of that sweet fruit. **1646** SIR T. BROWNE *Pseud. Ep.* IV. vii. 197 A bladder blowne is weightier then one empty, and if it containe a quart, expressed and emptied it will abate about halfe a graine. **1725** BRADLEY *Fam. Dict.* s.v. *Nutmeg*, Heat the Nutmegs in a Kettle, and then to express them strongly. **1882** *Med. Temp. Jrnl.* LI. 141 After the grapes have been expressed.

†**4.** To press hard (in battle). *Obs. rare*$^{-1}$.

c **1489** CAXTON *Blanchardyn* xli. (1890) 152 Seeng herself so sore expressyd, her knyghtes and her men slayne.

II. To portray, represent.

5. a. To represent by sculpture, drawing, or painting; to portray, delineate, depict. In general sense *obs.* or *arch.*; but surviving as a transferred use of sense 8: To render, set forth, convey a notion of (facts, characteristics, details) by plastic or graphic representation.

1382 WYCLIF *Ezek.* xxiii. 14 The ymagis of Caldeis expressid..in colours. **1588** FRAUNCE *Lawiers Log.* I. i. 2 b, That paynter is most cunning who can most lively expresse his face whose counterfaite he is to drawe. **1611** CORYAT *Crudities* 311 Whereof [Amphitheatre at Verona] I have expressed a picture in this place. **1720** STRYPE *Stow's Surv.* (1754) II. VI. ii. 598/2 In every part of this tomb are all the sons and daughters of this King expressed in solid brass. **1762–71** H. WALPOLE *Vertue's Anecd. Paint.* (1786) V. 155 Loggan used long strokes in expressing flesh. **1839** MURCHISON *Silur. Syst.* I. xx. 265 Quarried down below the ordinary surface of the adjacent ground, as rudely expressed in this woodcut.

†**b.** To be an image or likeness of; to resemble [After L. *exprimere*]. *Obs.*

1483 CAXTON *Gold. Leg.* 45/1 His handes expressyd the lyknes and symylitude of the more brother. **1548** UDALL, etc. *Erasm. Par. Acts* xvii. 64 Man expresseth God..as the childe doeth resemble hys father or mother. **1635** A. STAFFORD *Fem. Glory* (1869) 147 Her arms express the Crosse on which Hee dide. **1697** DRYDEN *Virg. Past.* I. 32 Kids and Whelps their Sires and Dams express.

6. To represent symbolically. Said both of the agent and the symbol employed. In *Math.* to represent by a figure, symbol, or formula. Phrase, *to express* (a quantity) *in terms of* (another).

1649 BP. REYNOLDS *Hosea* ii. 83 They should the better expres the condition of strangers. **1662** STILLINGFL. *Orig. Sacr.* II. ii. §6 A Child to express coming into the world, an old man for going out of it. **1684** R. H. *Sch. Recreat.* 115 The Characters placed on the five Lines, express the Notes themselves. *a* **1749** BOYSE *Triumphs Nat.* 199 The dim twilight of the arch above Seems to express the queen's disastrous love. **1751** CHAMBERS *Cycl.* s.v. *Fluxion*, To express the fluxions of simple variable quantities..you need only put the..letters which express them with a dot over them. **1811** HUTTON *Course Math.* III. 372 The fluxional equa. expressing the relation between *x* and *z.* **1816** J. SMITH *Panorama Sc. & Art* I. 38 Instruments have even been described, which express upon paper..the several winds that have blown. **1838** T. THOMSON *Chem. Org. Bodies* 34 If we express the composition of camphoric acid by the formula $5(C^2H^1_2) + O^5$. **1857** MAURICE *Ep. St. John* xvii. 275 The divine, holy, self-sacrificing life which it [the blood sign] would appear to express.

7. a. To manifest or reveal by external tokens. Of actions, appearances, etc.: To betoken. Now almost exclusively with reference to feelings or personal qualities, the wider use being *arch.* or *poet.*

1549 COVERDALE *Erasm. Par. 1 Pet.* 1 He admonisheth them, that..they expresse a life worthie of their profession. **1612** BEAUM. & FL. *Cupid's Rev.* I. i, If he be A god, he will express it upon thee my child. **1665** SIR T. HERBERT *Trav.* (1677) 276 Such was the singular personal valour Ismael expressed. *c* **1720** PRIOR *Henry & Emma* 429 No longer shall thy bodice aptly lac'd..That air and harmony of shape express. *a* **1763** SHENSTONE *Elegies* xi. 31, I pray'd..To see the trees express their planter's care. **1814** JANE AUSTEN *Mansf. Park* (1851) 177 Never did tone express indifference plainer. *c* **1850** NEALE *Hymns East. Ch.* 80 The excellence of beauty In Jesus was expressed. **1859** TENNYSON *Vivien* 220 A robe..that more exprest Than hid her, clung about her lissome limbs. **1877** E. R. CONDER *Bas. Faith* i. 10 Worship ..directly expresses sentiment and emotion.

b. *refl.*

1549 COVERDALE *Erasm. Par. 1 Pet.* II. 10 The inheritance is ready..the possession whereof he hath..entered for your sakes, so that you expresse yourselves worthy of it. **1655–60** STANLEY *Hist. Philos.* (1701) 275/2 They have expressed themselves faithful in the performance of such things as were committed to their Charge. **1858** HAWTHORNE *Fr. & It. Jrnls.* I. 262 God expressed himself in the landscape to mankind. **1859** KINGSLEY *Misc.* I. 357 The inward beauty seldom fails to express itself in the outward.

8. a. To represent in language; to put into words, set forth (a meaning, thought, state of things); to give utterance to (an intention, a feeling).

Now the prevailing use; sense 5–7, so far as they survive, are often felt as transferred from this.

1386 CHAUCER *Prioress' T.* 24 Lady..Thy vertu and thy grete humylitee, Ther may no tonge expresse. **14..** *Epiph.* in *Tundale's Vis.* 108 With hys mowthe who con the myrthe expresse? *c* **1425** WYNTOUN *Cron.* VIII. iv. 236 Til hawe of þame knawlage Expressyd..in oure Langage. **1535** COVERDALE *Prov.* i. 23 Lo, I wil expresse my mynde vnto you. **1633** EARL MANCH. *Al Mondo* (1636) 190 As griefes concealed, so joyes expressed grow greater. **1672** VILLIERS (Dk. Buckhm.) *Rehearsal* I. i. (Arb.) 27 A phrase they have got among them, to express their no-meaning by. *a* **1684** EARL ROSCOM. *Ess. Verse* 42 Harmonious Horace flows With Sweetness not to be exprest in Prose. **1768** STERNE, *Sent. Journ.*, *The Rose*, I could not have expressed it half so well. **1832** A. FONBLANQUE *Eng. under 7 Administ.* (1837) II. 257 The Princess expressed her surprise that the people in a famine did not eat buns. **1860** TYNDALL *Glac.* II. xxviii. 397 My chief difficulty..may be expressed in a very few words. **1885** *Law Rep.* 29 Chanc. Div. 448 The lease correctly expressed the bargain between the parties.

b. *refl.* To put one's thoughts into words; to utter what one thinks; to state one's opinion. †Also *intr.* for *refl.*

1601 SHAKS. *Twel. N.* II. i. 16 It charges me in manners, the rather to expresse myselfe. **1609** B. JONSON *Silent Wom.* III. ii, What an excellent choice Phrase this Lady expresses in. **1659** *Burton's Diary* (1828) IV. 325 Every man has not the gift of expressing himself so in short as others. **1711** ADDISON *Spect.* No. 5 ¶5 English Writers in their way of thinking and expressing themselves. **1884** A. R. PENNINGTON *Wiclif* viii. 247 He expresses himself still more strongly in his unprinted writings.

¶ *confused use.*

1744 E. HEYWOOD *Female Spectator* (1748) I. 182 The admiration he expresses to have for her.

c. Of a word, phrase, or statement: To represent (a thought, sentiment, state of facts); to denote, import, signify. Also with sentence as *obj.*

1526 *Pilgr. Perf.* (W. de W. 1531) 4 b, The ordynary glose vpon the fyrst epystle of Saynt Paule to yᵉ Corinthes doth

expresse that..&c. **1588** SHAKS. *L.L.L.* IV. iii. 124 Something..That shall expresse my true-loues fasting paine. **1729** BUTLER *Serm.* Wks. 1874 II. 51 No words can express too strongly the caution which should be used. **1870** JEVONS *Elem. Logic* iii. 16 Every assertion or statement expresses the agreement or difference of two things.

†**9. a.** To mention, specify. *Obs.*

*c*1400 MAUNDEV. (Roxb.) xxiv. 112 Þe messangere of Godd expressed þat nowmer [nyne] so specially. **1447** BOKENHAM *Seyntys* Introd. (Roxb.) 2 An austyn frere Whos name as now I ne wyl expresse. **1463** *Bury Wills* (1850) 17 My frendys..as many as ben expressyd be name in this my seid wille. **1611** BIBLE *Num.* i. 17 These men, which are expressed by their names. **1640** YORKE *Union Hon.* 84 M. Milles in his Catalogue never expresseth him. **1668** CULPEPPER & COLE *Barthol. Anat.* I. iii. 5 In this Table are expressed the common Coverings of the Belly. **1772–84** COOK *Voy.* (1790) IV. 1204 The respective crews of both ships, remained as expressed in the two underwritten lists.

†**b.** To give an account of, describe. *Obs.*

*c*1386 CHAUCER *Can. Yeom. Prol. & T.* 752 It werieth me to telle of his falsnesse; And natheles yit wol I it expresse. **1548** TINDALE (*title*) A Briefe declaration of the Sacraments, expressing the fyrst oryginall how they came up. **1573** ABP. PARKER *Corr.* (1852) 425, I thought it not against my profession to express my times, and give some testimony of my fellow-brothers. **1613** HEYWOOD *Silver Age* III. Wks. 1874 III. 129 Heardsman, thou hast exprest a monstrous beast. **1697** DRYDEN *Virg. Georg.* III. 12 Pelops' Iv'ry Shoulder..with all the rest Of Grecian Tales, by Poets are exprest. **1798** MALTHUS *Popul.* (1878) p. v, The Essay..was suggested as is expressed in the preface.

†**c.** To state or describe (an object) as, or *to be* (so and so). Also with *for*. *Obs.*

1523 FITZHERB. *Surv.* xx. 41 Homage, fealte, and ii.*s.* by the yere..And this he maye expresse the seruyce of the rent. **1579** FENTON *Guicciard.* (1618) 7 The Pope..was not ashamed..to call them his children, and expressed them to the world for such. **1662** STILLINGFL. *Orig. Sacr.* I. vi. §3 He expresseth Adrastus to be the first King of Sicyon. **1784** COWPER *Task* II. 399, I would express him simple, grave, sincere. **1798** DALLAS *Amer. Law Rep.* I. 3 The bills of lading express this rum to be shipped on the risk of C.

†**d.** To designate, mention by a certain title.

1659 PEARSON *Creed* (1839) 122 So Isaiah, Ezekiel, and Hosea, have expressed him, as we shall hereafter have farther occasion to show. **1677** HALE *Contempl.* II. 45 The Wise man chuseth to express him by that Title of Creator.

†**e.** *intr.* To make mention, give an account *of*. *Obs.*

1430–50 tr. *Higden* (Rolls) I. 79 Mony prouinces, of whom hit schalle be expressede by ordre. **1509** HAWES *Past. Pleas.* XI. i, Fame gan to expresse Of jeoperdous way to the toure peryllous.

10. a. To state or mention explicitly; opposed to *imply*.

1596 SHAKS. *Merch. V.* IV. i. 260 Is it so nominated in the bond? It is not so expressed; But what of that? **1651** HOBBES *Leviath.* II. xxii. 121 To other intent, than is in the Writing ..expressed. **1724** WATTS *Logic* III. i, Wheresoever any of these words are used, there is a perfect syllogism expressed or implied. **1732** BERKELEY *Alciphr.* I. §4 Hints and allusions, expressing little, insinuating much. **1817** W. SELWYN *Law Nisi Prius* (ed. 4) II. 751 The promise must be expressed in the written memorandum or note.

†**b.** To draw up (a commission) in express terms; to make out expressly. *Obs. rare*$^{-1}$.

1462 *Paston Lett.* No. 453 II. 104 Debenham hathe a comyscion of the Kyng expressed oonly for that schip named in hes comyscion.

11. *Genetics.* To display or make manifest in a phenotype (a character or effect attributed to a particular gene); to cause (a gene) to produce its associated character in a phenotype. Chiefly *pass.* or (occas.) *refl.*

1918 BABCOCK & CLAUSEN *Genetics* v. 69 The condition of dominance..is determined by the fact that in the hybrid that character is expressed to the exclusion of its contrasted character. **1927** *Genetics* XII. 153 In these cultures the radius incompletus character is usually expressed more strongly in those flies which show the character Alae divergentes. **1946** R. R. GATES *Human Genetics* I. ii. 15 Many cases are now known in which the same abnormality is strictly dominant in some pedigrees and sometimes skips a generation in others... The gene is present in the germplasm, as shown by its transmission to the next generation, but for some reason it has completely failed to express itself. **1965** H. E. SUTTON *Introd. Human Genetics* ix. 109 A dominant gene may be defined as one that is expressed when present in a single copy. **1968** *New Scientist* 7 Nov. 313/1 As every cell in a multi-cellular organism contains an identical set of genes directing the synthesis of its proteins, the problem of development comes down to a question of controlling the expression of genes (a gene is said to be 'expressed' when the protein for which it codes is actually being made in the cell). Thus in a liver cell, different genes are expressed than in, say, a brain cell. **1970** *Sci. Jrnl.* June 42/3 In parthenogenesis..the lethal gene is dominant and consequently its lethal effect is expressed.

express (ɛk'sprɛs), *v.*^{2} orig. *U.S.* [f. EXPRESS *a.*, *adv.*, and *sb.*^{1}] *trans.* To send by express messenger; to send (letters, goods, etc.) by a special delivery or by express (EXPRESS *sb.*^{1} 3 a); to send by express delivery.

1716 *Jrnls. Ho. Repr. Mass.* I. 81 Isaac Winslow Esq., brought down..several letters that had been expressed to his Honour the Lieut. Governour from the Eastward. **1847** J. S. ROBB *Streaks of Squatter Life* 112 News, now-a-days, ..is not news unless expressed, and..the President's message, received in the old fashioned wait-till-you-get-it manner, would not be read with interest. *a* **1860** *Washington Republic* Bartlett *Dict. Amer.* The President's message will be expressed through to Boston, by order of the Postmaster-General. **1880** *Daily News* 20 Nov. 5/4 There is a saving in going by the horse-cars and 'expressing' the luggage at a shilling a trunk. **1892** STEVENSON & OSBOURNE *Wrecker* x. 161 Did he express his baggage, ma'am? **1898** L. MERRICK *Actor-Manager* xv. 210 Perhaps if the news were 'expressed' to the office at once. **1899** *Post Office Guide* Jan. 18 A Letter may be posted in any Letter Box, from which it will be collected by a Postman and be expressed on reaching the proper office. **1930** *Daily Express* 6 Nov. 1/1, I telephoned to my mother to express my passport to me at Croydon. **1936** J. G. COZZENS *Men & Brethren* I. 128 After expressing their luggage, they had come over the mountains from Bologna on foot.

Hence **ex'pressed** *ppl. a.*^{2}, sent by express.

1902 A. BENNETT *Grand Babylon Hotel* vi. 72 It was ..'expressed' luggage despatched in advance. **1909** [see CURLY *a.* 3].

expressed (ɛk'sprɛst), *ppl. a.*^{1} Also 6–8 **exprest**. [f. EXPRESS *v.*^{1} + -ED^1.]

1. Pressed out; extracted or forced out by mechanical pressure. ***expressed oil*** (see quot. 1859).

1599 A. M. tr. *Gabelhouer's Bk. Physicke* 116/1 The best expressed oyle of Nutmegges. **1660** BOYLE *New Exp. Phys. Mech.* xxiv. 188 After this express'd Oyl, we made tryal of a distill'd one. **1732** ARBUTHNOT *Rules of Diet* 269 The express'd Juices of several Vegetables. **1859** GULLICK & TIMBS *Paint.* 206 They [the fixed oils] are termed 'expressed' oils because they are not extracted by distillation, like the essential oils. **1875** URE *Dict. Arts* III. 432 s.v. *Oils*, Recently-expressed or very fresh oils.

†**b.** That has had the juice, etc., pressed out of it; squeezed or wrung dry. *Obs.*

a **1682** SIR T. BROWNE *Tracts* 13 They might after give the expressed and less usefull part unto their swine. **1705** T. GREENHILL in *Phil. Trans.* XXV. 2010 Like an expressed Sponge. **1743** *Lond. & Country Brew.* II. (ed. 2) 101 As is.. plain in all expressed Vegetables.

2. Uttered or made known in words.

1548 UDALL, etc. *Erasm. Par. John* 122 a, By the expressed voyce of this man. **1892** *Daily News* 6 Feb. 6/1 In accordance with the expressed wish of the deceased. *Mod.*, Inconsistent with his own expressed opinions.

†**b.** Express, explicit. Also of a functionary: Stated, recognized. *Obs.*

1534 WHITINTON *Tullyes Offices* I. (1540) 15 The vttermost of right is expressed wronge. **1553** EDEN *Treat. Newe Ind.* (Arb.) 8 It is not written by expressed wordes that, etc. **1554** KNOX *Godly Let.* C viij, No such promese haue we..but rather the exprest contrarie. **1658** USSHER *Ann.* VI. 440 Gorgias their exprest Commander was from them. **1736** BUTLER *Anal.* I. vi. 159 The..perception of good and ill desert..makes [the sanction] appear, as one may say expressed.

3. ***expressed species*** (transl. L. *species expressa*): in Scholastic Philosophy, a 'species' or essential form imposed on outward objects by the activity of the mind itself. The term was revived by Le Clerc in his pseudo-scientific Optics: see quot.

1751 CHAMBERS *Cycl.* s.v. *Species*, Expressed Species are those..which proceed from within..Le Clerc, in his system of vision..has called upon the stage again the *species expressæ* of the ancient philosophers. For according to him, it is not by species or images impressed on the optic nerve, that the soul sees objects, but by rays which she herself directs to them. [**1857** MAURICE *Mor. & Met. Philos.* III. v. §90. 232 The mind knows itself..not by a species impressed upon it, but by a species expressed from it.]

expressed, *ppl. a.*^{2}: see EXPRESS *v.*^{2}

†**ex'pressedly**, *adv. Obs.* [f. EXPRESSED *ppl. a.*^{1} + -LY^2.]

Statedly, avowedly; explicitly, expressly.

a **1555** RIDLEY *Wks.* 137 Other words, which the same writer hath expressedly in other places. **1558** KNOX *First Blast* (Arb.) 33 Here expressedly is a man apointed to be chosen king. **1609** J. RAYNOLDS *Agst. Bellarmine* (1610) 46 Whether expressedly, or implyedly. **1646** SIR T. BROWNE *Pseud. Ep.* I. v. 17 This is..detractory unto the intellect, and sense of man expressedly disposed for that inquisition.

expresser, -or (ɛk'sprɛsə(r)). [f. EXPRESS *v.*^{1} + -ER^1, -OR.] One who or that which expresses.

1581 MULCASTER *Positions* v. (1887) 32 Reading being but the expresser of the written characters. **1587** GOLDING *De Mornay* vi. 73 And the Second [Worker] is the liuely expresser of the First. **1623** *Shakspere's Wks.* To Rdr., Who, as he was a happie imitator of Nature, was a most gentle expresser of it. **1642** LD. DIGBY *Elvira* (1667) 5 Ready..To make his Sword th' expresser of his mind. **1872** CONINGTON *Aeneid* v. 340 *note*, Expressers of a favourable or adverse opinion.

b. One who possesses expressive power; a master of the art of expression.

c **1611** CHAPMAN *Iliad* I. Comm. (1865) 26 Our most accomplished expressor helps the illustration in a simile of his fervour. **1615** —— *Odyss.* VIII. 708 The divine expressor did so give Both act and passion, that he made it live. **1856** MASSON *Ess., Shaks. & Goethe* 23 He [Shakespeare] was the greatest expresser that ever lived.

†**ex'pressful**, *a. Obs. rare*$^{-1}$. [f. as prec. + -FUL.] = EXPRESSIVE.

1621 LADY M. WROTH *Urania* 395 True confession of that you then seemed with expressefull joy..to entertaine. **1629** H. BURTON *Babel no Bethel* 17 A question..set downe in most cleare and expresseful termes.

expressible (ɛk'sprɛsɪb(ə)l), *a.* Also 7 **-able**. [f. as prec. + -IBLE.]

1. Capable of being expressed.

1605 R. CAREW in *Lett. Lit. Men* (Camden) 100 In some [words] we buylde others not expressable in their mother tongue. *a* **1628** PRESTON *Serm.* (1630) 43 As farre as it is expressable, we will explaine unto you. **1677** GILPIN *Dæmonol.* II. ix. 403 They are under an expressible sense of Divine Wrath. **1794** SIR W. JONES *Orthogr. Asiatic Words* Wks. 1799 I. 192 A diphthong composed of our first and third vowels, and expressible, therefore, by them. **1851** RUSKIN *Mod. Paint.* II. III. II. iii. §26 Michael Angelo held the imagination to be entirely expressible in rock. **1875** JEVONS *Money* 70 Easily expressible in terms of the unit.

†**2.** Able to express oneself. *Obs.*

1627–77 FELTHAM *Resolves* II. xli. 240 In Loue and Thanks..tis in a Mans own power to be expressible.

expressing (ɛk'sprɛsɪŋ), *vbl. sb.* [f. as prec. + -ING^1.] The action of the vb. EXPRESS; the action **a.** of pressing out, pressing out the contents of; **b.** of representing, uttering, or manifesting (thoughts, meanings, etc.). Now gerundial.

1530 PALSGR. Introd. 17 No parte of the vowell, at his expressyng, shulde passe forth by the mowth. **1627** *Lisander & Cal.* I. 4 Pleasant beyond expressing. *a* **1631** DONNE *Lett.* (1651) 260, I cannot hope for better expressings (in Poems) than I have given of them. **1668** WILKINS *Real Char.* 355 The expressing of any one syllable in a word, with a little higher tune, and longer time then others. **1889** *Pall Mall G.* 6 May 2/1 The..expressing of seed for oils.

expression (ɛk'sprɛʃən). [a. F. *expression*, ad. L. *expressiōn-em*, n. of action f. *exprimĕre*: see EXPRESS *v.*^{1}]

I. 1. a. The action of pressing or squeezing out.

1594 PLAT *Jewell-ho.* 59 After..the Coast-men have by expression..gotten that kind of traine oyle..from the fish. **1626** BACON *Sylva* §633 Their Juyces..are so fleshy..they cannot make Drink by expression. **1725** BRADLEY *Fam. Dict.* s.v. *Plague*, Separate the Vinegar from the Herbs by way of strong Expression. **1822** IMISON *Sc. & Art* II. 129 Many vegetables afford essential oil by expression or by distillation. **1859** TENNENT *Ceylon* II. IX. vi. 542 The crushing of the coco-nut for the expression of the oil.

†**b.** *concr.* Something pressed or squeezed out; an expressed drink, juice, liquor, etc. *Obs.*

1612 *Enchirid. Med.* 158 Let it bee againe boyled. Then make a strong expression. **1616** SURFL. & MARKH. *Country Farme* 435 Mixe together both these expressions, letting them coole. **1686** W. HARRIS tr. *Lemery's Chym.* (ed. 3) 504 Express through a Linen Cloth..and let the expression settle.

II. Representation, manifestation. Cf. EXPRESS *v.*^{1} II.

2. a. The action of expressing or representing (a meaning, thought, state of things) in words or symbols; the utterance (of feelings, intentions, etc.). Also, in early use: †Explicit mention; description (*obs.*). **b.** The action or process of manifesting (qualities or feelings) by action, appearance or other evidences or tokens.

1460 CAPGRAVE *Chron.* Ded. 2 Elde bokes..make more expression of thoo stories..than I have. **1634** W. TIRWHYT *Balzac's Lett.* 48 You have now no further use of Cyphers, for the expression of your minde to my Lorde the Cardinall. **1647** CRASHAW *Sosp. d'Her.* xxv, The forehead's shade, in grief's expression there, Is what in sign of joy..a smile is here. **1659** PEARSON *Creed* (1839) 282 It behoved us to take notice of the Roman governor in the expression of our Saviour's passion. **1856** FROUDE *Hist. Eng.* (1858) I. iii. 207 To encourage the fullest expression of public feeling.

c. phr. ***beyond, past expression***, †***within the compass of expression to seek, find expression.***

1624 MASSINGER *Parl. Love* v. i, This is cruelty Beyond expression. **1665** SIR T. HERBERT *Trav.* (1677) 17 The greatest peace of barbarity within the compas of expression. **1667** MILTON *P.L.* III. 591 The place he found beyond expression bright. **1700** DRYDEN *Theodore & H.* 384 The unhappy man..who past expression loved. **1830** TENNYSON *Adeline* i, Faintly smiling Adeline..beyond expression fair. **1870** MAX MÜLLER *Sc. Relig.* (1873) 218 Some of the fundamental ideas that found expression in the ancient systems of faith and worship. **1878** M. A. BROWN *Nadeschda* 44 Born in love's own heaven Was all that sought expression.

3. quasi-*concr.* **a.** An utterance, declaration, representation. **b.** An action, state, or fact whereby some quality, feeling, etc., is manifested; a sign, token. (Now only const. *of.*)

a. 1634 HABINGTON *Castara* (Arb.) 134 You'le..hate th' expressions of your heart. *a* **1649** CHAS. I. *Wks.* 206 Who have..made most real expressions to prevent the present Distractions. **1665** MANLEY *Grotius' Low C. Warres* 898 King Philips expressions were not written in Latine or French, but in the Spanish Tongue. **1714** OCKLEY in *Lett. Lit. Men* (Camden) 350 Upon the account of an unguarded expression. **1875** JOWETT *Plato* (ed. 2) III. 256 Your words ..are the very expression of my own feelings.

b. *a* **1628** PRESTON *New Covt.* (1634) 385 That fearfullnesse at Mount Sinai, was but only an expression of the feare which [etc.]. **1669** W. HOLDER *Speech* 5 Common life is full of this kind of significant Expressions, by Knocking, Beckoning, Frowning..and the like. **1734** *Grub St. Jrnl.* 2 May 4/3 A Conference on their [the Passions'] general and particular Expressions. **1816** MACKINTOSH *Bacon & Locke* Wks. 1846 I. 336 To render theory the simple expression of facts. **1836** J. GILBERT *Chr. Atonem.* viii. 308 The death of Christ was the expression of Divine love. **1878** HUXLEY *Physiogr.* 222 Every change in the form and size of the growing plant is simply the expression of the mode of growth.

†**c.** *nonce-use.* *to become expression*: to become a byword, or proverbial type of something.

c 1634 W. CARTWRIGHT *Ordinary* III. iii. in Hazl. *Dodsley* XII. 262 *Mean.* Let me be More miserable than Littleworth. *Jane.* Is he become expression?

4. a. Manner or means of representation in language; wording, diction, phraseology.

1628 WITHER *Brit. Rememb.* II. 18 Such a plaine Expression, to acquire, That ev'ry one my meaning may discerne. **1669** W. HOLDER *Speech* 5 The variety of instructive Expressions by speech, wherewith Man..is endowed..for the communication of his thoughts. **1709** POPE *Ess. Crit.* 317 Expression is the dress of thought. **1738** BIRCH *Milton* I. 78 Stuffed with gawdy Metaphors and Fancy, far more Expression than Matter. **1757** GRAY *Let.* Poems (1775) 252, I..mean by expression..the whole dress, fashion, and arrangement of a thought. **1859** GEO. ELIOT *A. Bede* 7 Gyp..gave a short bark..he had not a great range of expression. **1887** *Pall Mall G.* 28 Feb. 12/1 It is not merely the authors of books who should study right expression.

b. A word, phrase, or form of speech.

1646 SIR T. BROWNE *Pseud. Ep.* III. xviii. 153 His eyes were dimme..*caligarunt oculi*, saith Jerom..which are expressions of diminution, and not of absolute privation. *a* **1661** FULLER *Worthies* (1840) II. 542 The Scripture expression, 'From Dan to Beersheba'. **1749** FIELDING *Tom Jones* XVIII. iii, Having left Mr. Miller a little while *to chew the cud* (if I may use that expression). **1886** FROUDE *Oceana* i. 7 Ambiguous expressions were explained away when challenged.

†**c.** A designation, descriptive title. *Obs.*

a **1631** DONNE *On Transl. Ps.* Wks. 1839 VI. 562 Eternal God, for whom whoever dare Seek new expressions, do the circle square.

d. *Alg.* A collection of symbols together expressing an algebraical quantity.

1796 HUTTON *Math. Dict.* I. 460/2 The expression..2 *ab.* **1807** —— *Course Math.* II. 294 When the given Fluxional Expression is in this Form..namely, a Fraction. **1841** J. R. YOUNG *Math. Dissert.* Pref. 3 The analytical expression for the radius of curvature. **1871** B. STEWART *Heat* §51 We have obtained an expression for the difference in pressure.

5. a. Of the countenance, voice, or (occas.) attitude, etc.: Capacity or fact of expressing feeling or character; expressive quality. **b.** The aspect (of the countenance), intonation (of the voice) as indicating a state of feeling.

a. 1774 GOLDSM. *Nat. Hist.* (1776) II. 95 The parts of the head which give the least expression to the face, are the ears. **1779** J. MOORE *View Soc. Fr.* II. li. 23 There is more expression in the countenances of French women. **1834** MEDWIN *Angler in Wales* II. 175 His eyes possessing wonderful fire and expression. **1842** MISS MITFORD in L'Estrange *Life* III. ix. 156 A want..of shifting shadow—of that transition which is as expression to a lovely face. **1847** L. HUNT *Jar Honey* x. 132 Infusing a soul into the features of nature, as expression lights up a beautiful countenance.

b. 1830 E. PORTER *Analysis* (ed. 3) Introd., The nameless and ever varying shades of expression which real pathos gives to the voice. **1830** D'ISRAELI *Chas. I*, III. vi. 111 The countenance whose peculiar expression afterwards was so faithfully..transmitted to us. **1834** PRINGLE *Afr. Sk.* iii. 158 The peculiar expression of the sound..instantly undeceived me. **1860** TYNDALL *Glac.* I. xi. 7 An expression of fatigue stamped upon his countenance. **1865** DICKENS *Mut. Fr.* I. vi, 'Can't I!' said Abbey, with infinite expression.

6. *Fine Arts.* **a.** In Painting and Sculpture: The fact or way of expressing character, sentiment, action, etc. Also (rarely) a feature intended for expression.

1715 J. RICHARDSON *Th. Paint.* 86 Passerotto has drawn a Christ's Head as going to be Crucified, the Expression of which is marvellously fine. *Ibid.* 99 Robes, or other Marks of..a Profession..are Historical Expressions common in Portraits. **1768** W. GILPIN *Ess. Prints* 79 There is more expression both in action and feature, than was ever perhaps shewn in so small a compass. **1816** J. SCOTT *Vis. Paris* 253 Raphael's feeling for expression was probably the most intense feeling ever bestowed on a human being. **1856** RUSKIN *Mod. Paint.* III. IV. iii. §19 The chief masterpieces of expression which the world possesses are small pictures by Angelico.

b. In *Music.* The manner of performance (with respect, *e.g.* to degrees of loudness or softness) suited to bring out the feeling of a musical passage.

1773 BARRINGTON in *Phil. Trans.* LXIII. 288 Expression is wanting, without which music is so languid and inanimate. **1797** MRS. RADCLIFFE *Italian* i, Which she touched with most affecting and delicate expression. **1864** MISS BRADDON *H. Dunbar* xxi, She played with brilliancy, and, what is much rarer, with expression.

7. *Genetics.* The appearance in a phenotype of a character or effect attributed to a particular gene; also, the process by which possession of a gene leads to the appearance in the phenotype of the corresponding character. Cf. EXPRESS *v.*[1] 11. (In quot. 1927[1] = EXPRESSIVITY b.)

1927 N. W. TIMOFÉEFF-RESSOVSKY in *Genetics* XII. 131, I use the word 'manifestation' to signify the presence of the given character in the phenotype of the fly, and the word 'expression' to signify the degree and form of the character. *Ibid.* 157 Some cases of strong hereditary variations of the expression of radius incompletus..enable us to suppose that a great hereditary variability of the phenotypic expression of this gene could be obtained with the aid of a more precise accounting. **1946** R. R. GATES *Human Genetics* I. xi. 422 Just as families can differ greatly in the degree of expression of polydactyly, so they can differ in the degree of dominance of the character. **1957** C. H. WADDINGTON *Strategy of Genes* iii. 91 Geneticists commonly use the word 'expressivity' to indicate the degree of expression of some phenotypic character. **1957** *Jrnl. General Microbiol.* XVI. 115 Expression of the character Az[r] begins at the time of dilution ..of the zygotes and then rises exponentially to become complete just before the recombinants which inherit start to divide. **1968** [see EXPRESS *v.*[1] 11]. **1969** *Nature* 10 May 541/1 The expression of certain genes is controlled by the products of specific regulator genes which act as repressors.

8. *attrib.* in **expression-mark** (*Music*), a sign or word indicative of the desired kind of expression; **expression-stop,** in the Harmonium, a stop by which the performer is enabled to vary the pressure of the air and thus produce expression.

1880 GROVE *Dict. Music* s.v. *Harmonium*, The Expression stop is used, by which the air reservoir is cut off and the pressure made to depend entirely upon the management of the bellows.

expressionable (ɛkˈsprɛʃənəb(ə)l), *a.* [f. EXPRESSION + -ABLE.] Capable of showing expression.

1892 *Blackw. Mag.* CLI. 43/2 Mozart..discovered the soul-reaching and expressionable capacity of instrumental music. **1908** *Daily Chron.* 15 Jan. 8/4 The mouth is an orator's mouth; clear cut, expressionable.

expressional (ɛkˈsprɛʃənəl), *a.* [f. EXPRESSION + -AL[1].] Of or pertaining to expression: **a.** in language; **b.** with reference to the countenance; **c.** in the fine arts, *esp.* painting, etc.

a. 1803 W. TAYLOR in *Monthly Mag.* XVI. 221 The conscious display of expressional skill and the anxious elaboration of a style freaked with allusions. **1873** F. HALL *Mod. Eng.* 36 The verbal and expressional solecisms which disfigure our literature.

b. 1867 BUSHNELL *Mor. Uses Dark Th.* 285 Bearing the expressional stamp of man.

c. 1856 RUSKIN *Mod. Paint.* III. IV. iii. §9 Hunt's Light of the World, is..the most perfect instance of expressional purpose with technical power. **1861** *Sat. Rev.* XI. 584/2 There is some expressional force here.

expressionism (ɛkˈsprɛʃənɪz(ə)m). Freq. with capital initial. [f. EXPRESSION + -ISM; cf. next.] The methods, style, or attitude of expressionists; *spec.* a style of painting in which the artist seeks to express emotional experience rather than impressions of the physical world; hence, a similar style or movement in literature, drama, music, etc. Cf. *abstract expressionism* (ABSTRACT *a.* 6).

1908 *Edin. Rev.* Oct. 466 The appearance of these later and more extreme forms of expressionism..has aided the understanding of beauty partly through a deeper probing of the sensuous elements in æsthetic experience. **1920** *Arts & Decoration* XIII. 88 (*title*) Mid-European Expressionism. *Ibid.*, The sole aim of impressionism was to reflect the impression of nature upon the artist's eye; expressionism, on the contrary, proceeds from the subjectivity of the artist and seeks to form a picture according to the laws of an arbitrary, inner world. **1921** GALSWORTHY *To Let* I. i. 13 Expression! Ah, they were all Expressionists now, he had heard, on the Continent... He wondered where this—this Expressionism —had been hatched. The thing was a regular disease! **1923** MACGOWAN & JONES *Continental Stagecraft* iii. 27 A Symbolism that is far on the way towards Expressionism. *Ibid.* 31 Expressionism..is a violent storm of emotion beating up from the unconscious mind. **1924** A. DUKES *Youngest Drama* 136 Realism and expressionism represent attitudes of mind and not uses of theatrical machinery. **1924** A. D. SEDGWICK *Little French Girl* II. iv. 132 Giles..felt that he could not adequately defend his theories, which rested upon an objection to the use of the body as a means of primitive expressionism. **1925** H. CARTER *New Spirit European Theatre* 220 Expressionism is simply expression taking the form of a new technique for the purpose of giving the most intense effect..to the species of drama that expressed pre-war and war time insurrectionary tendencies. **1926** [see ABSTRACTIONISM 2]. **1926** F. V. P. RUTTER *Evol. Mod. Art* v. 112 The kaleidoscopic paintings of the Italian Futurists were matched at Munich by the Expressionism of the Russo-Polish artist Wassily Kandinsky. **1929** P. SCHOLES *Listener's Hist. Mus.* III. 142 Critics writing of plays (but it applies all round) have spoken of Expressionism as 'the objectivization of the subjective'. *Ibid.* 144 The Schönbergians and their Expressionism in music. **1937** *English Studies* XIX. 241 (*title*) The birth of expressionism in the work of D. H. Lawrence. *Ibid.*, Expressionism, a term used here in its widest sense to cover all anti-realist as well as anti-idealist movements..reaching from Strindberg in the north to Marinetti in the south. **1938** *Oxf. Compan. Mus.* 303/2 Expressionism in music, judged by its products, is just an advanced phase of Romanticism in music. **1958** *Listener* 27 Nov. 897/3 Expressionism implies an uncompromisingly violent utterance, coupled too often with a self-pitying sensibility. **1970** *Oxf. Compan. Art* 396/1 The most important forerunner of Expressionism in its specific sense was van Gogh.

‖**expressionismus** (ɛkˌsprɛʃəˈnɪzməs). [G.] = prec.

1925 A. HUXLEY *Those Barren Leaves* IV. v. 307 German romanticism, a little *détraqué*, turns..into expressionismus. **1926** [see ABSTRACTIONISM 2].

expressionist (ɛkˈsprɛʃənɪst) *sb.* (and *a.*) [f. as EXPRESSIONAL *a.* + -IST.] An artist whose work aims chiefly at 'expression'; *spec.* (freq. with capital initial) an artist, composer, writer, etc., who exhibits the style or technique of EXPRESSIONISM. Also *attrib.* or as *adj.* Cf. *abstract expressionist* (ABSTRACT *a.* 6).

1850 *Tait's Mag.* XVII. 394/2 The expressionist school of modern painters. **1880** *Papers Manch. Lit. Club* VI. 184 The expressionists..who undertake to express special emotions, or passions. **1914** W. LEWIS in *Blast* June 143 Of all the tags going, 'Futurist'..serves as well as any for the active painters of to-day... We may hope before long to find a new word. If Kandinsky had found a better word than 'Expressionist' he might have supplied a useful alternative. *Ibid.* 144 Balla..is a rather violent and geometric sort of Expressionist. His paintings are purely abstract. **1915** *Ibid.* July 39/1 There have grown up three distinct groups of artists in Europe... The third group is formed by the *expressionist* movement, that is Kandinsky. **1915** *Observer* 1 Aug. 5/6 The reviled Post-Impressionists,..Cubists, Futurists, Expressionists, Vorticists of to-day may be the honoured masters of to-morrow. **1920** *Arts & Decoration* XIII. 88/3 Arnold Schönberg, the musical expressionist—who also painted. **1921** [see EXPRESSIONISM]. **1924** *New Statesman* 2 Aug. 494/2 Elmer Rice's play, *The Adding Machine*..has two or three expressionist scenes, but is for the most part not in the expressionist manner. **1927** *Observer* 11 Sept. 6 A cocaine romance written by one of the most gifted of those men who joined the band of expressionists early in the movement. **1938** *Oxf. Compan. Mus.* 303/2 The music of the composers who call themselves Expressionists..is..simply 'ultra-emotional'. **1962** *Listener* 20 Sept. 453/1 The peculiar tension of the characteristic Expressionist instrumental form lies in the aphoristic compression of a dreamlike state.

expressionistic (ɛksprɛʃəˈnɪstɪk), *a.* [f. EXPRESSIONIST + -IC.] Of, pertaining to, or produced by expressionists; characterized by expressionism. Hence **expressioˈnistically** *adv.*

1921 GALSWORTHY *To Let* III. x, She had begun to exchange her Empire for her Expressionistic furniture. **1924** *Sunday Times* 23 Mar. 6/3 The fourth scene shows his feelings expressionistically. **1924** *Glasgow Herald* 17 July 4 An example of the expressionistic type of drama. **1927** *Ibid.* 6 Oct. 6 Careless, expressionistic young men. **1928** *Observer* 29 Jan. 15/4 His expressionistic ingenuity achieved many stimulating effects. **1966** *Listener* 6 Oct. 513/2 Jakov Lind's *Landscape In Concrete* is a German miasma-novel, expressionistic, nightmarish, and confusedly allegorical. **1970** *Daily Tel.* 17 June 16/5 A Bach chorale (expressionistically anticipated at the beginning of the second movement).

expressionless (ɛkˈsprɛʃənlɪs), *a.* [f. EXPRESSION + -LESS.]

1. Of the features, voice, etc. Destitute of expression; giving no indication of character, feeling, etc.; inexpressive. Const. *of.*

1831 WILSON *Blackw. Mag.* XXIX. 301 An image as expressionless as the block on which his own buzz-wig was trimmed. **1859** H. KINGSLEY *G. Hamlyn* I. xiii. 184 He was a small man, with an impenetrable, expressionless face. **1864** CROWDY *Ch. Choirmaster* 53 Monotonic recitation is more expressionless than reading in the ordinary voice. **1870** DICKENS *E. Drood* ix, So expressionless of any approach to spontaneity were his face and manner.

b. Expressing nothing, conveying no meaning.

1871 TYLOR *Prim. Cult.* I. 215 But it may..become by wear of sound and shift of sense an expressionless symbol.

2. That finds no expression.

1819 SHELLEY *Cenci* III. i. 214 A wrong, Which, though it be expressionless, is such As asks atonement.

Hence **exˈpressionlessly** *adv.* **exˈpressionlessness,** the state or condition of being destitute of expression, want of expression.

1865 *Cornh. Mag.* Aug. 225 Faces..expressive of 'expressionlessness'. **1876** G. MEREDITH *Beauch. Career* III. xii. 227 Rosamund eyed her husband expressionlessly. **1888** W. C. RUSSELL *Death Ship* III. 3 Faces whose expressionlessness forbade your comparing them to sleeping dreamers.

expressive (ɛkˈsprɛsɪv), *a.* Also 5 expressif. [a. F. *expressif, -ive*, ad. L. type **expressiv-us*, f. *exprimĕre*: see EXPRESS *v.*[1] and -IVE.]

†**1.** Tending to press out or expel. *Obs.*

c **1400** *Lanfranc's Cirurg.* 137 (MS. A.) Þat oile haþ a vertu expressif..bi þe whiche..akþis ben swagid.

2. Of or pertaining to, or concerned with, expression; having the function of expressing.

1747 COLLINS *Passions* 16 Each, for Madness ruled the Hour, Would prove his own expressive Pow'r. **1764** REID *Inquiry* iv. §2 118 The best judge in all the expressive arts. **1891** J. JASTROW in *Educational Rev.* I. 262 The receptive powers are in advance of the expressive ones.

3. Serving to express, indicate, or represent.

1711 SHAFTESB. *Charac.* VI. i. (1737) III. 355 A situation expressive of Suspence and Doubt. **1794** S. WILLIAMS *Vermont* 378 Tables expressive of this diurnal variation. **1802** MAR. EDGEWORTH *Moral T.* (1816) I. 222 An air of dignity, which seemed expressive of conscious innocence. **1873** EARLE *Philol. Eng. Tongue* §490 This has a rhetorical use expressive of contempt.

4. Full of expression. **a.** Of a word, phrase, or symbol: Expressing its meaning with striking accuracy or force. Formerly also of a statement: Explicit. **b.** Of the countenance, voice, actions, works of art: Characterized by expression.

a. *a* **1690** J. HARRINGTON *Def. Rights Univ. Oxf.* Pref., The Priviledges of this University have been in so..expressive words granted to our Predecessours. **1711** P. H. *View two last Parlts.* 141 This Clause they would have had more expressive. **1712–4** POPE *Rape Lock* III. 40 Four fair Queens whose hands sustain a flow'r, Th' expressive emblem of their softer pow'r. **1859** *Athenæum* 23 July 113 The expressive term of Bung, as signifying a public-house landlord. **1884** CHURCH *Bacon* ix. 223 His Latin..is singularly forcible and expressive.

b. 1718 LADY M. W. MONTAGUE *Lett.* II. l. 69 The expressive beauty of that face and bosom gives all the passion of pity and admiration. **1747** LD. G. LYTTELTON *Monody to Lady* xi, Through her expressive eyes her soul distinctly spoke. **1768** W. GILPIN *Ess. Prints* 70 He engraves with a noble, firm, expressive line. **1832** HT. MARTINEAU *Ireland* ii. 29 The Italian gentleman..used an expressive gesture. **1847** JAMES *J. Marston Hall* vii, His countenance was a very expressive one. **1851** D. WILSON *Preh. Ann.* II.

IV. viii. 452 The most expressive features of every style of Gothic architecture. **1864** PR. ALICE *Let.* 22 Jan. in *Biog. Sk. & Lett.* (1884) 66 Baby is so expressive, she makes such a face when she is not pleased.

5. Of a person: Open or emphatic in expressing (sentiments). Const. *of*. *rare.*

1601 SHAKS. *All's Well* II. i. 54 Vse a more spacious ceremonie to the Noble Lords..be more expressiue to them. **1658** JER. TAYLOR *Let.* in 12th *Rep. Hist. MSS. Comm.* App. v. 5 Her..love and veneration to your Ladiship; in which she is so..expressive. **1815** LAMB *Let. to Wordsw.* 95 We felt as we had been not enough expressive of our pleasure.

†**6.** Expressing itself in action; tending to outward manifestation. *Obs.*

1627-77 FELTHAM *Resolves* I. lxxxvi. 134 Solomon's good man, is merciful to his Beast, nor take I this to be only intentional; but expressive. **1639** F. ROBARTS *God's Holy Ho.* viii. 58 Expressive holinesse is the outward manifestation of the former, by the words of our mouthes. **1747** GOULD *Eng. Ants* 30 There is such a strong expressive Affection imprinted on them towards the Eggs.

†**7.** quasi-*adv.* So as to be plainly exhibited; manifestly, visibly. *Obs.*

1718 PRIOR *Solomon* II. 745 Golden sayings..On large phylacteries expressive writ.

expressively (ɛk'sprɛsɪvlɪ), *adv.* [f. prec. + -LY[2].] In an expressive manner; with expressive significance. †Formerly also, In respect of (practical) expression (*obs.*).

1627-47 FELTHAM *Resolves* II. lxxxii. 424 We seldom find the ignorant man honest; if he be mentally, yet he failes expressively. **1640** G. WATTS tr. *Bacon's Adv. Learn.* II. xiii. 114 Nature..is most expressively set forth with a biformed body. **1762** STERNE *Let.* 19 Mar., A gentleman..has taken it [portrait] most expressively. **1800** MRS. HERVEY *Mourtray Fam.* III. 114 Emma fixed her eyes expressively on her father. **1858** FROUDE *Hist. Eng.* IV. 148 The clerk of the prison [was sent] to a place expressively called 'Little Ease.'

expressiveness (ɛk'sprɛsɪvnɪs). [f. as prec. + -NESS.] The quality of being expressive.

1655 FULLER *Ch. Hist.* v. iv. §39 Our English tongue was not improved to that expressivenesse whereat at this day it is arrived. **1697** DRYDEN *Virg. Georg.* (1721) I. 209 The Murrain at the end [of the third Georgic] has all the Expressiveness that Words can give. **1711** J. GREENWOOD *Eng. Gram.* 282 This praxis is to show the peculiar force or expressiveness of a great many single words. **1751** BUTLER *Serm.* Wks. 1874 II. 324 We should study what St. James, with wonderful..expressiveness, calls meekness of wisdom. **1812** *Examiner* 11 May 301/2 A song..composed..in a style of great expressiveness and insinuation. **1883** A. ROBERTS *Old Test. Revis.* vi. 134 Passages of rich expressiveness occur.

expressivity (ɛksprɛ'sɪvɪtɪ). [f. EXPRESSIV(E *a.* + -ITY.] **a.** The quality of being expressive.

1944 *N.Y. Herald Tribune* 28 Mar. 16/2 This equalized expressivity ends by making Beethoven sound sometimes a little meretricious as a composer. **1948** L. SPITZER *Linguistics & Lit. Hist.* iv. 155 The self-destruction brought about by excessive expressivity was seen by Diderot as a danger to which any artistic nature is exposed. **1961** L. F. BROSNAHAN *Sounds of Language* i. 16 It is not at all clear why the relative infrequency of the latter in French should have led to its selection on the grounds of expressivity.

b. spec. *Genetics* [ad. G. *expressivität* (N. W. Timoféeff-Ressovsky 1925)]. The kind or degree of phenotypic expression of a gene.

1934 N. W. TIMOFÉEFF-RESSOVSKY in *Biol. Reviews & Biol. Proc. Cambr. Phil. Soc.* IX. 433 The phenotypic manifestation of the mutant allelomorphs may be full and constant, or it can be variable and even dependent upon other factors (low penetrance, variable expressivity and specificity of the genes). **1946** R. R. GATES *Human Genetics* I. ii. 15 Related to penetrance is *expressivity*, which means the degree to which a particular gene expresses itself. **1957** [see EXPRESSION 7]. **1962** HENDERSON & GILLESPIE *Text-bk. Psychiatry* (ed. 9) iv. 36 The genes have a range of variability in their manifestation which is called their expressivity.

expressivo, bad form of ESPRESSIVO.

1823 in CRABB *Technol. Dict.*; and in mod. Dicts.

expressless (ɛk'sprɛslɪs), *a. arch.* [f. EXPRESS *a.* + -LESS.] That cannot be expressed; inexpressible.

1586 MARLOWE *1st Pt. Tamburl.* v. ii, Of our expressless bann'd inflictions. **1704** D'URFEY *Abradatus & Panthia* i. 23 Whilst..my verse you read Reflect on joys expressless that proceed. **1860** LD. LYTTON *Lucile* II. I. xi, Thou art An expressless and imageless truth in the heart.

expressly (ɛk'sprɛslɪ), *adv.* [f. EXPRESS *a.* + -LY[2].] In an express manner.

1. †**a.** In an early use: In full detail (*obs.*). **b.** In direct or plain terms; clearly, explicitly, definitely. †**c.** With distinct enunciation (*obs.*).

*c***1380** WYCLIF *Serm.* Sel. Wks. II. 225 Treuþis þat ben more nedeful ben writun þere more expresly. **1447** BOKENHAM *Seyntys* (Roxb.) 13, I wolde compyle A clere descrypcyoun ful expressely Of alle hyr feturys. **1509** HAWES *Past. Pleas.* XIV. ix, The pamflete shewith it expressely. **1551** ROBINSON tr. *More's Utop.* II. (Arb.) 156 The people..rehearse solempne prayers in woordes expresslye pronounced. **1613** SHAKS. *Hen. VIII*, III. ii. 235 Who dare crosse 'em, Bearing the Kings will from his mouth expressely? **1671** MILTON *P.R.* II. 3 Him whom they heard so late expressly call'd Jesus. **1755** YOUNG *Centaur* i. Wks. 1757 IV. 116 All which the Scriptures have expressly delivered as catholic truths. **1848** C. BRONTË *J. Eyre* xvii, She must not..think of venturing..unless expressly sent for. **1848** MILL *Pol. Econ.* Prelim. Rem. 2 It was assumed, either expressly or tacitly, that wealth consisted solely of money. **1892** *Law Times* XCII. 158/1 If the backer intends to retain the power of revoking the authority..he must expressly say so.

†**2.** Avowedly, directly. *Obs.*

1393 GOWER *Conf.* I. 357 For this may every man well wite, That bothe kinde and lawe write Expressely stonden there ayein. **1656** BRAMHALL *Replic.* v. 205 Whom doe the Conclave chuse? An uniuersall Pastor? No, but expressely a Bishop of Rome. *a* **1699** STILLINGFL. (J.), The beginning of the worship of images in these western parts, was..expressly against the will of their own bishop.

†**3.** Of resemblance: Exactly. Cf. EXPRESS *a.* I. *Obs.*

1642 MILTON *Apol. Smect.* (1851) 285 The child doth..expresly refigure the visage of his Father.

4. Distinctly, positively.

1526 *Pilgr. Perf.* (W. de W. 1531) 75, I rede not that whan the serpent came to tempte her [Eue] she was doynge ony thynge expresly good. **1586** A. DAY *Eng. Secretary* I. (1625) 68 There be some things that are expresly good in themselves or expresly evill. **1768** W. GILPIN *Ess. Prints* 174 Some of his [Hogarth's] other pieces, are expressly of this humourous kind.

5. For the express purpose; 'on purpose'.

1607 SHAKS. *Timon* II. ii. 32, I Am sent expressely. **1659** B. HARRIS *Parival's Iron Age* 98 Felton, who went expresly out of Holland, to sacrifice him [Buckingham] to the hatred of the People. **1774** PENNANT *Tour Scot. in 1772*, 77 Went..expressly to free the country from moroders. **1879** M. ARNOLD *Irish Cathol.* Mixed Ess. 102 The Queen's Colleges invented expressly for Ireland.

expressman (ɛk'sprɛsmən). [f. EXPRESS *sb.*[1] 3 + MAN.] A man employed in receiving and delivering parcels, etc.; *esp.* an employee of one of the U.S. express companies.

1847 H. D. THOREAU *Let.* in *Atlantic Monthly* (1892) LXIX. 744 Munroe..tells the expressman that all is right. **1858** HOMANS *Cycl. Comm.* 644 The 'expressman' is only an improvement upon the 'common carrier'. **1884** A. WAINWRIGHT in *Harper's Mag.* July 270/1 We stand in a crowd of..hack-drivers and expressmen on the New York side. **1889** FARMER *Americanisms* 229/2 William F. Harnden was the first expressman, and he began his business in 1837.

†**ex'pressment.** *Obs. rare*$^{-1}$. [f. EXPRESS *v.*[1] + -MENT.] The action or fact of expressing.

1494 FABYAN *Chron.* v. cxxxvii. 123 As shall appere..whan the tyme conuenyent of the expressement of them shall come.

expressness (ɛk'sprɛsnɪs). [f. EXPRESS *a.* + -NESS.] The quality or state of being express; clearness, definiteness, exactness.

1645 J. GOODWIN *Innoc. Triumph.* 21 It was nothing but what in expressness and plainness of words was required of them. *a* **1680** GLANVILL *Serm.* ix. (1681) 361 Heathens..had not the knowledge of God's law..in the fulness and expressness of it. **1877** H. A. PAGE *De Quincey* I. i. 3 What he said of Lamb may with far greater expressness be applied to himself.

expresso (ɛks'prɛsəʊ), var. ESPRESSO.

†**ex'pressure.** *Obs.* [f. L. *express-* ppl. stem of *exprimĕre* + -URE: cf. *pressure*.] The action of expressing; = EXPRESSION in various senses.

a. = EXPRESSION I: also the operation of a force pressing outwards; outward pressure. **b.** Expression by words or signs; manifestation, description. **c.** An image, picture; cf. EXPRESS *sb.* 2.

a. 1656 tr. *Hobbes' Elem. Philos.* (1839) 334 And this expressure, when the forces are equal, is in a line perpendicular to the bodies pressing. **1713** DERHAM *Phys. Theol.* IV. viii. 163 A good Contrivance..to afford a due expressure of it [mucilage] at all times. **1850** H. H. WILSON tr. *Rigveda* I. 6 *note*, The acid Asclipias..yields to expressure a copious milky juice.

b. 1601 SHAKS. *Twel. N.* II. iii. 171 By ..the expressure of his eye..he shall finde himselfe most feelingly personated. **1606** — *Tr. & Cr.* III. iii. 204 There is a mysterie..in the soule of State; Which hath an operation more diuine, Than breath or pen can giue expressure to. **1671** FLAVEL *Fount. Life* v. 14 These high expressures of His Love. **1681** *Right. Man's Ref.* 246 The..more comprehensive Promises are found in the general expressures of the Covenant.

c. 1598 SHAKS. *Merry W.* v. v. 71 Th' expressure that it beares: Greene let it be.

expressway (ɛk'sprɛsweɪ). orig. *U.S.* Also **express way.** [f. EXPRESS *a.* + WAY *sb.*[1]] A wide road for fast motor-traffic (see quots.); an urban motorway. Also ***express highway, road, route.***

*c***1938** L. MUMFORD *Report on Honolulu* in *City Development* (1946) vi. 94 The municipality..withholding assent from ill-advised express highways. **1945** *Public Roads* XXIV. VI. 178/1 An analysis was made to determine the traffic which would use an expressway in Tulsa, Okla. **1945** *Britannica Bk. Year 1944* 607/1 A significant event of..1944 was submission of the report of the President's National Interregional Highway committee recommending postwar construction... An important feature of the plan is the construction of express routes through cities. **1952** *Newsweek* 15 Dec. 84/3 Another 'solution' is the expressway —the free, dual-lane, high-speed thoroughfare which either by-passes or cuts through cities. Entrances and exits are at selected places; ramps and overpasses are arranged so that vehicles do not cross in front of each other. **1956** *Planning* XXII. 178 The average estimated cost for the 213 miles of new expressways (urban motorways)..proposed for the Detroit region..is more than £2,500,000 a mile. **1959** *Mod. Lang. Notes* LXXIV. 364 'Express ways' is the general term including both toll roads and free roads, for cars and trucks. **1961** L. MUMFORD *City in History* viii. 215 Just as our expressways are not articulated with the local street system, so the great sewers of Rome were not connected with water-closets above the first floor. **1966** *Guardian* 23 Dec. 4/5 The Right Bank express road through the city. **1967** *Listener* 6 July 10/2 Old people's homes, urban expressways, nuclear power stations.

exprime, var. form of EXPREME. *Sc.*

†**'exprobrate**, *v. Obs.* Also 6-9 **exprobate.** [f. L. *exprobrāt-* ppl. stem of *exprobrāre* to make a matter of reproach, f. *ex-* (see EX- *pref.*[1]) + *probrum* shameful deed. The variant *exprobate* appears to arise from association with *reprobate*; cf. It. *esprobare*.]

†**1.** To make (a thing) a subject of reproach; to 'cast in one's teeth.' Of a thing: To manifest to a person's shame. Const. *to*, *unto*, or dat. *Obs.*

1543 GRAFTON *Contn. Harding* 438 He myght..exprobrate vnto hym the pleasures y[t] he had done for hym. **1580** SIDNEY *Arcadia* III. (1590) 248 His service..did exprobate..unto her, her unworthy estate. **1583** FULKE *Defence* xvii. 510 You exprobrate to us our knowledge in the tongues. **1604** PARSONS *3rd Pt. Three Convers. Eng.* 136 Exprobratinge vnto them that they did honour the Crosse. *a* **1643** W. CARTWRIGHT *Siege* II. vi, He Shall..avoid Thy sight, as somthing that doth exprobrate His sins unto him. *a* **1670** HACKET *Cent. Serm.* (1675) 149 Hermolaus..exprobrates him that he was violently made away.

b. with the personal object unexpressed.

1582 N. T. (Rhem.) *Mark* xvi. 14 He exprobrated their incredulity and hardness of hart. *c* **1610** *Women Saints* (1886) 149 Which he reputing and exprobating to be impotencie of spirite. **1646** SIR T. BROWNE *Pseud. Ep.* III. xxv. §3. 173 To exprobrate their Stupiditie, he induceth the providence of Storkes. **1665** MANLEY *Grotius' Low-C. Warres* 738 There were some that stuck not to exprobrate the divulsions of Ireland.

¶**c.** = REPROBATE. *nonce-use.*

1867 MUSGRAVE *Nooks & Corners* I. 333 One can hardly sufficiently exprobate the..officiousness of Carreaux.

2. To reproach (a person). Const. *with.*

1630 *R. Johnson's Kingd. & Commw.* 102 The Venetians ..have not spared to exprobrate us with the nick-name of Cursore Englese. **1638** *Penit. Conf.* vii. (1657) 159 Many a railing Doeg began to exprobrate and deride the Penitents.

Hence †**'exprobrating** *ppl. a.*, that reproaches, reproachful.

1673 *Lady's Call.* I. §3. 22 Least hereafter they fall under the same exprobrating remembrance with the rich man in the Gospel. **1675** *Art Contentm.* III. §18. 191 That exprobrating complaint we find in the Prophet.

exprobration (ɛksprəʊ'breɪʃən), *arch.* Also 6 exprobracion, -cyon, 6-8 exprobation. [ad. L. *exprobrātiōn-em*, n. of action f. *exprobrāre*: see EXPROBRATE.]

†**1.** The action of 'exprobrating', upbraiding, or speaking reproachfully; an instance of this. *Obs.*

1526 *Pilgr. Perf.* (W. de W. 1531) 17 Remembrynge..to the exprobracyon and reproue of god, the potage potte..in Egypte. **1577** FENTON *Gold. Epist.* 337 To exacte recompence, is a manifest exprobation of benefits receiued. **1635** PAGITT *Christianogr.* 203 His [St. Paul's] commemoration is an exprobration to the Corinthians of their neglect of him. **1705** J. PHILIPS *Blenheim* 121 Exprobrations false Of cowardice. *a* **1843** SOUTHEY *Doctor* (1849) 380 Uttering the words exultantly, not in exprobration.

b. *Rhet.* (See quot.)

1753 CHAMBERS *Cycl. Supp.*, Exprobration..in rhetoric, is the reproaching a person with ingratitude, and unmindfulness of some particular benefit conferred upon him.

c. That which acts as a reproach, or serves the purpose of reproaching.

1680 SIR W. WALLER *Div. Medit.* (1839) 150 This sun-set ..is to me an exprobration. **1682** NORRIS *Hierocles* 66 If any throw him something by way of alms, that aggravates his discontent as an exprobation of his poverty.

2. A reproachful or upbraiding utterance; reproachful language.

1549 LATIMER *6th Serm. bef. Edw. VI* (Arb.) 167 He hath stirred vp the people to persecute it wyth exprobacions and slaunderous wordes. *a* **1600** HOOKER *Eccl. Pol.* VI. 320 The ears of the accused [are] not always subject to glowing with contumely and exprobration. **1692** SOUTH *Serm.* (1697) I. 127 A denial with scorn, with taunting exprobrations. **1877** R. W. DIXON *Hist. Ch. Eng.* I. ii. 143 This weak exprobration [protest against the Anti-Papal statutes] itself was the last instrument of an English primate [Warham] who died legate of the Apostolic See.

†**ex'probrative**, *a. Obs.* [f. EXPROBRATE + -IVE.] Expressing reproach, reproachful.

1613 SHERLEY *Trav. Persia* 132 All benefites loosing much of their splendor..that doe beare with them an exprobrative terme of necessitie.

†**ex'probratory**, *a. Obs.* [f. as prec. + -ORY.] Serving to upbraid or reproach.

1586 A. DAY *Eng. Secretary* II. (1625) 31 To use this exprobratory manner of writing..shall not be amisse. **1860** WORCESTER cites MACKENZIE.

‖**ex professo** (ɛks prəʊ'fɛsəʊ), *phr.* [L. *ex* out of + *profess-ō*, abl. of *profess-us* professed, pa. pple. of *profitēri* to avow publicly, f. *pro* before + *fatēri* to avow.] Professedly, by profession.

1823 in CRABB *Technol. Dict.*

expromission (ɛksprəʊ'mɪʃən). *Civil Law.* [ad. mod.L. *exprōmissiōn-em*, n. of action f.

exprōmittĕre: see next. Cf. Fr. *expromission*.] (See quot.; and cf. next).

1818 COLEBROOKE *Treat. Oblig. & Contracts* I. 208 The intervention of a new debtor, substituted for the former one, who is, in consequence, discharged by the creditor.. has been termed expromission. **1875** POSTE *Gatius* III. Comm. 399.

expromissor (ɛksprəʊˈmɪsə(r)). *Civil Law.* Also 8 expromissar. [a. L. *exprōmissor*, agent-n. f. *exprōmittĕre* to promise to pay, f. *ex-* (see EX- *pref.*¹) + *prōmittĕre* to PROMISE.] One who promises to pay; *spec.* one who unconditionally undertakes the debt of another, so as to become the principal debtor in his stead; distinguished from a 'surety' or 'bail'.

1695 S. LOBB *Let. Dr. Bates* 12 You distinguish between the Covenant of Grace, and the Covenant of Redemption, and grant Christ to be a Surety in the One and an Expromissor in the other. **1775** ASH, *Expromissar*. **1818** COLEBROOKE *Treat. Oblig. & Contracts* I. 211 The expromissor, who is to undertake the debt. **1875** POSTE *Gaius* III. Comm. (ed. 2) 406 A woman does not, like an Expromissor, discharge a pre-existing obligation.

†**exˈpropriate**, *ppl. a. Obs. rare*⁻¹. In 5 expropriat. [ad. late L. *expropriāt-us*, pa. pple. of *expropriāre*: see next.] = EXPROPRIATED. In quot.: Debarred from owning property.

c **1449** PECOCK *Repr.* 478 Religiouns.. in which is vow of wilful and expropriat poverte.

expropriate (ɛkˈsprəʊprɪeɪt), *v.* [f. late L. *expropriāt-* ppl. stem of *expropriāre* to deprive of property, f. *ex-* + *proprium* property, neut. of *proprius* own: see PROPER. Cf. Fr. *exproprier*.]

1. *trans.* To dispossess (a person) of ownership; to deprive of property. Const. *from*.

Now chiefly to deprive of property either wholly or in part, for the public use, usually with provision of compensation.

1611 COTGR., *Exproprié*, expropriated. **1852** GROTE *Greece* II. lxxix. X. 406 All those proprietors had been.. expropriated. **1875** J. H. BENNET *Winter Medit.* II. xiii. 480 The Government gives.. a power to expropriate the owner of the land required. **1881** *Macm. Mag.* XLIV. 132 To expropriate the owners from their estates must be a very bitter pill.

2. † **a.** To put (a thing) out of one's own control (*obs.*). **b.** To take out of the owner's hands.

1660 BOYLE [see EXPROPRIATED *ppl. a.*]. **1775** in ASH. **1881** *Daily Tel.* 14 Feb., A corner of the garden.. was 'expropriated' by Baron Haussman for the purpose of widening the Rue Lafayette. **1884** *Contemp. Rev.* Oct. 518 The State.. expropriates private property for public utility.

Hence **exˈpropriated** *ppl. a.*

1660 BOYLE *Seraph. Love* iii. (1700) 29 When you have Resign'd, or rather Consign'd your expropriated Will to God. **1889** *Pall Mall G.* 4 June 2/3 The wrath of the expropriated exploiteurs is extreme.

expropriating (ɛkˈsprəʊprɪeɪtɪŋ), *ppl. a.* [See -ING².] Dispossessing, depriving of property.

1908 H. G. WELLS *First & Last Things* 104 A class conflict between the expropriated Many and the expropriating Few. **1910** *Daily Chron.* 24 Mar. 4/3 The expropriating authority is in justice bound to appropriate such land for all time.

expropriation (ɛkˌsprəʊprɪˈeɪʃən). [n. of action f. late L. *expropriāre*: see EXPROPRIATE. Cf. Fr. *expropriation*.] The action of expropriating.

†**a.** The action of giving up one's whole property. Also the action of giving up control *of*. †**b.** Removal *from* the ownership or dominion of. **c.** The action of depriving (a person) of property; deprivation; an instance of this. **d.** The action of taking (property) out of the owner's hands (*esp.* by public authority); an instance of this.

a. *c* **1449** PECOCK *Repr.* v. v. 505 Ech religioun.. in which is vow of expropriacioun. **1648** W. MOUNTAGUE *Devout Ess.* I. xix. §2. 342 The expropriation of our Reason.

b. **1626** T. H. tr. *Caussin's Holy Crt.* 353 Poverty of affection, is an expropriation from the inordinate loue of terrene goods.

c. **1848** MILL *Pol. Econ.* II. x. §1 A complete expropriation of the higher classes in Ireland. **1877** WALLACE *Russia* ix. 142 The expropriation of the peasantry or small landholders.

d. **1878** LADY HERBERT tr. *Hübner's Ramble* III. i. 460 The construction of public buildings, or expropriations, or sanitary improvements. **1880** *19th Cent.* Nov. 774 Compulsory expropriation of property in towns. **1889** *Times* 20 Nov. 5/5 The expropriation of the railways.

expropriator (ɛksˈprəʊprɪˌeɪtə(r)). [agent-n. f. *expropriāre*: see EXPROPRIATE.] One who expropriates. Const. *of*.

1869 *Daily News* 28 Apr., The expropriators of the national will. **1879** S. B. GOULD *Germany* II. 268 The expropriator will be himself expropriated.

expuate, var. of EXSPUATE, *Obs.*

†**exˈpugn**, *v. Obs.* Also 5-7 expugne. [ad. OF. *expugn-er*, ad. L. *expugn-āre* to take by storm, f. *ex-* out + *pugnāre* to fight, f. *pugna* a fight.]

1. *trans.* To capture by fighting; to take by storm.

1432-50 tr. *Higden* (Rolls) I. 187 Kynge Alexander gedrede his hoste, intendinge to expugne alle the worlde. **1555** EDEN *Decades* 316 The sayde Admirall attempted to expugne the Iland. **1599** HAYWARD *1st Pt. Hen. IV*, 103 Nabuchadnezzar.. oppugned Hierusalem a long time, and at the last expugned it. **1635** N. R. tr. *Camden's Hist. Eliz.* II. xii. 107 Dunbritton should be expugned. *a* **1640** JACKSON *Creed* XI. xxxv. Wks. XI. 101 They.. use it as a fort.. till they can watch an opportunity for expugning a better.

fig. **1569** CROWLEY *Soph. Dr. Watson* ii. 84 Which.. many have assaulted and oppugned with such direct scriptures.. that it is by them expugned, and can not be by you propugned. **1579** TWYNE *Phisicke agst. Fortune* II. xiii. 184 a, By a golden showre of rayne Danaes virginitie was expugned. **1612-5** BP. HALL *Contempl. N.T.* IV. x, That their conjoined forces might expugn that gracious ear.

b. In weaker sense: To assault, attack, storm.

1407 *Exam. W. Thorpe* in Arb. *Garner* VI. 91 They enforce them to expugn the freedom of Holy Church. **1554** BRADFORD in Strype *Cranmer* II. 196 Matters expugned by the Papists. **1582** N. T. (Rhem.) *Gal.* i. 23 He.. doth now evangelize the faith which sometime he expugned. **1657** EARL MONM. tr. *Paruta's Pol. Disc.* 159 Solyman.. wasted so much time in expugning the strong Hold of Buda as it proved the safety of that Country.

2. To overcome or expel by force of arms; to vanquish, overpower.

1563-87 FOXE *A. & M.* (1596) 244 The pope.. stirred up .. the young French king.. to expugne and extinguish these Albigenses his enimies. *Ibid.* (1641) III. 666 They could not expugne him by arguments or disputation. **1610** BARROUGH *Meth. Physick.* VIII. (1639) 439 Cancre, and Elephantiasis, which diseases do expugne gentle medicines. **1628** HOBBES *Thucyd.* (1822) 41 Lest making them desperate we make them also harder to expugne. **1674** JOSSELYN *Voy. New Eng.* 48 This assertion is not expugned by Geocentricks. **1699** EVELYN *Acetaria* 90 The Nasturtia are.. the most effectual .. agents in conquering and expugning that cruel Enemy.

Hence †**exˈpugned** *ppl. a.* †**exˈpugner**, one who takes by storm. †**exˈpugning** *vbl. sb.*

1598 MARLOWE *Hero & L.* III. Wks. (Rtldg.) 292/1 So far'd fair Hero in th' expugned fort Of her chaste bosom. **1608** CHAPMAN *Byron's Conspir.* Plays 1873 II. 190 He will prooue Of the yet taintlesse fortresse of Byron A quick Expugner. **1589** WARNER *Alb. Eng.* (1612) 330 The reuengeful flames of Troy.. had perfected the more than Ten yeares Siege of the Græcians expugning of the same. **1657** TOMLINSON *Renou's Disp.* 128 The expugning of several affections.

†**exˈpugnable**, *a. Obs.* [a. OF. *expugnable*, ad. L. *expugnābilis*, f. *expugnāre*: see EXPUGN.] That may be taken by force, conquered, or overcome.

1570 in LEVINS *Manip.* **1586** A. DAY *Eng. Secretary* II. (1625) 37 An expugnable wickednesse. **1625** PURCHAS *Pilgrims* II. 1213 Syracon tooke an expugnable Fort. **1765** *Hist. Europe* in *Ann. Reg.* 12/2 A place which no art was requisite to defend, though a great deal to take in if at all expugnable.

†**exˈpugnance.** *Obs. rare*⁻¹. [f. EXPUGN + -ANCE.] Storming (of a city), conquest.

c **1611** CHAPMAN *Iliad* VIII. 247 Grant to me Th' expugnance of well-builded Troy.

†**exˈpugnancy.** *Obs. rare*⁻¹. [f. EXPUGN + -ANCY.] Opposition, conflict.

1620 J. WILKINSON *Treat. Coroners & Sherifes* 32 b, In the new bookes before they have expugnancy of opinion in the case where purgation is to be done.

†**exˈpugnat**, *pple. Obs. rare*⁻¹. [ad. L. *expugnāt-us*, pa. pple. of *expugnāre*: see EXPUGN.] Taken by storm; conquered.

1536 BELLENDEN *Cron. Scot.* (1821) I. 253 Thus wes Rome finalie expugnat [*printed* expugnant].

†**exˈpugnate**, *v. Obs.* [f. L. *expugnāt-* ppl. stem of *expugnāre*.] *trans.* = EXPUGN.

1568 C. WATSON *Polyb.* 67 a, There began a wonderful tempest to arise, which the Carthaginian maryners espying .. counsayled Carthalon to expugnate [mistransl. κάμψαι, 'to double'] the promontarie Pachynus. **1625** PURCHAS *Pilgrims* II. 1266 Dominicke.. had helpers with the sword to expugnate those which his word could not.

†**expugˈnation.** *Obs.* Also 6 expugnacion. [a. OF. *expugnation*, ad. L. *expugnātiōn-em*, n. of action f. *expugnāre*: see EXPUGN.]

1. The action of taking by storm; conquest.

1524 MORE in Ellis *Orig. Lett.* I. 88 I. 255 At Pavia by th' expugnation wherof he thought to put all the remanant in fere and drede. **1555** EDEN *Decades* 171 The expugnation and recouerie of the kyngedome of Granata. *a* **1639** SPOTTISWOOD *Hist. Ch. Scot.* v. (1677) 270 The Regent intreateth.. help for the expugnation of the Castle. **1680** MORDEN *Geog. Rect.* Spain 176 The Phocensis.. a little before their Expugnation by Cyrus.

b. Storming, assault.

1536 BELLENDEN *Cron. Scot.* (1821) I. 254 Fergus.. went with him to the expugnation of sindry othir townis in Italie. **1579** FENTON *Guicciard.* IV. (1599) 165 To preuent that succour by the expugnation of Bybienna. **1618** T. GAINSFORD *P. Warbeck* in *Select. Harl. Misc.* (1793) 88 The worthy general.. cast up a strong.. battery, for the expugnation.

2. Subduing or expelling by force of arms.

1429 in Rymer *Fœdera* (1710) X. 424 The Reduction and Expugnation of th' Eretikes. **1604** T. WRIGHT *Passions* I. i. 5 The life of a spirituall man ought to bee imployed in the expugnation of these molestfull Jebusites. **1624** GEE *Foot out of Snare* 76 He fought a good fight.. in expugnation of Heresies. **1657** TOMLINSON, *Renou's Disp.* 497 Medicaments for the expugnation of all diseases.

†**exˈpugnative**, *a. Obs. rare*⁻¹. [f. L. *expugnāt-*, ppl. stem of *expugnāre*: see EXPUGN and -IVE. Cf. OF. *expugnatif, -ive*.] Tending to take by storm; tending to drive out.

c **1630** JACKSON *Creed* IV. III. ix. Wks. III. 466 The expugnative or expulsive force.

†**exˈpugnatory**, *a. Obs.* [ad. L. *expugnātōrius* conquering, f. *expugnāre*: see EXPUGN.]

a. Of weapons: Adapted for attack, offensive. **b.** Adapted for breaking down (an argument).

a. **1601** BP. BARLOW *Def. Prot. Relig.* 63 Weapons, both defensive and expugnatorie. **1693** URQUHART *Rabelais* III. Prol., Warlike Engines, expugnatorie and destructive. **1737** OZELL *Rabelais* III. 211 He calls 'em *Repugnatory* Weapons, not *Expugnatory*.

b. **1652** GAULE *Magastrom.* 180 Not with an invitatory operation, but an expugnatory refutation.

expuition, var. of EXSPUITION.

†**expulˈsation.** *Obs. rare*⁻¹. [f. L. *expuls-* ppl. stem of *expellĕre* (see EXPULSE) + -ATION. Cf. PULSATION.] = EXPULSION.

1615 CROOKE *Body of Man* 407 As attractions and expulsations are in other parts, so it is likely they are in the heart.

†**exˈpulsative**, *a. Obs.* [f. as prec. + -ATIVE.] Tending to expel or drive out; in quot. quasi-*sb.*

1659 FULLER *App. Inj. Innoc.* I. 20 A Defensative against, or expulsative of, Poyson.

expulsatory (ɛkˈspʌlsətərɪ), *a.* [f. L. *expulsāt-, -āre* (see EXPULSE *v.*) + -ORY².] Of or pertaining to expulsion; that expels.

1594 CHAPMAN *Shadow of Night* sig. C iv *verso*, Expulsatorie Balme that serues To quench lusts fire. **1768** LD. MANSFIELD in J. Wesley *Let.* Dec. (1931) V. 378 The expulsatory power of the House. **1910** *Practitioner* Mar. 406 When its [*sc.* the uterus'] muscular fabric is engaged in expulsatory efforts.. pain of extreme intensity is endured.

†**exˈpulse**, *sb. Obs. rare*⁻¹. [f. EXPULSE *v.*; after *repulse*.] An act of expelling or driving out.

1565 GOLDING *Ovid's Met.* IX. (1593) 229 Unhappie wench she takes from daie to daie Repulse upon expulse.

†**expulse** (ɛkˈspʌls), *v. Obs.* Also 6 expoulse, -pulce, -puls. [ad. L. *expulsāre*, frequentative of *expellĕre*: see EXPEL. Cf. F. *expulser*.] *trans.* A synonym of EXPEL; sometimes expressing more strongly the notion of violence. Very common in the 16-17th c.; now *Obs.*, though casual examples occur in 19th c. Const. *from, out of*; also with double obj. by omission of *from*.

a. with obj. a person, etc.: To drive or thrust out from a place; to eject, evict from a possession or holding; to turn out of an office, community, etc. Cf. EXPEL 1 a, 2.

1432-50 tr. *Higden* (Rolls) I. 209 Saturnus, expulsede of Iupiter his son, commenge to the realme of Ianus, made a cite. *c* **1500** *New Not-br. Mayd* in 5 *Poet. Tracts* (Percy Soc.) 37 From his thought, I that hym bought, Shall be espoulsed playne. **1581** LAMBARDE *Eiren.* II. iv. (1588) 164 A lessee for yeeres of lande, that is expulsed by force. **1583** STUBBES *Anat. Abus.* II. 49 Adam our first parent was expulsed paradise. **1604** *Eng. Gilds* (1870) 436 He shall never be.. expullsed [from a tenement] but by the kings writ. **1640** YORKE *Union Hon.* 40 King Edward the fourth.. being.. expulsed the realme by the powerfull Earle of Warwicke. **1660** R. MOSSOM *Apol. Sequest. Clergy* 7 Other Pastours were displac't and expulst. **1725** BROOME *Odyssey* III. XI. 159 *note*, Peleus was expuls'd from his kingdom by Acastus. **1842** *Tait's Mag.* IX. 438 Unless you wish to be expulsed for ever from your mother's house.

b. with a material thing as obj.: To drive out by mechanical force. Of the body, its parts or organs: To eject, expel (the contents, any foreign substance, excrements, etc.). Also said of the action of drugs, etc. Cf. EXPEL 1 b, c.

1542 BOORDE *Dyetary* iv. (1870) 237 To.. expulse all corrupt and contagyous ayre. **1605** BACON *Adv. Learn.* II. xvii. §9 The Kernel being.. expulsed with the torture and presse of the methode. **1660** tr. *Paracelsus' Archidoxis* II. 81 The Phlegm is expulsed by the Nostrils. **1758** *Monthly Rev.* 197 Sand, gravel and ashes only were expulsed. **1823** J. BADCOCK *Dom. Amusem.* 78 To expulse all atmospheric air.

c. with immaterial obj.

1505 FISHER 7 *Penit. Ps.* Wks. 115 Almyghty god expulsed synne. **1596** *Edw. III.* III. ii. 38 Sweet-flowering peace.. Is quite abandon'd and expuls'd the land. **1605** BACON *Adv. Learn.* I. ii. §7 No man need doubt that learning will expulse business. **1767** A. CAMPBELL *Lexiph.* (1774) 6 Expulse hereditary aggregates.. which may obumbrate your intellectual luminaries. [Intended as a caricature of 'Johnsonese'.]

Hence **exˈpulsed** *ppl. a.* **exˈpulsement** = EXPULSION. **exˈpulsing** *vbl. sb.*

1603 B. JONSON *Sejanus* V. x. Wks. (Rtldg.) 171/2 The expulsed Apicata, finds them there. **1691** ED. TAYLOR tr. *Behmen's Theos. Phil.* 46 The Expulsed Dragon.

1537 *Irish Acts, 28 Hen. VIII*, c. 1 §9 Such manors.. or other hereditaments so had by disseisin or expulsement.

1548 UDALL *Erasm. Par.* Pref. 5 The expulsyng of the Romishe Antichriste. **1574** tr. *Littleton's Tenures* 87 b, No expulsing of the franke tenemente of the heyre.

1578 BANISTER *Hist. Man* v. 73 The expulcing of flegme. **1640** *Jrnl. Ho. Com.* II. 73 The Expulsing of the Priests and Jesuits.

expulser (ɛkˈspʌlsə(r)). *Obs.* [f. prec. + -ER¹.] One who or that which expels or drives out; in senses of the vb. Const. *of*.

1540 HYRDE tr. *Vives' Instr. Chr. Wom.* (1592) Aa vj, The man standeth as it were in the middest betweene his mother and his wife: and so either of them hateth other, as an expulser of her selfe. **1546** LANGLEY *Pol. Verg. De Invent.* I. xiii. (1560) 24 b, The Science of Philosophy which Tully calleth the.. expulser of vyce. **1605** TIMME *Quersit.* III. 148 Nature.. stirreth up the expulser, and prouoketh it to send forth the excrements. **1823** D'ISRAELI *Cur. Lit.* (1858) III. 424 The expulser of the Tarquins.

expulsion (ɛk'spʌlʃən). [ad. L. *expulsiōn-em*, n. of action f. *expellĕre*: see EXPEL. Cf. Fr. *expulsion*.] **a.** The action of expelling, or driving out by force (a person or thing); the turning out (of a person) from an office, a society, etc. Also the fact or condition of being expelled. Also *attrib.*, as ***expulsion order***.

1494 FABYAN *Chron.* II. xxx. 22 Brenne.. takyng sore to mynde his expulsion from his naturall countre. **1526** *Pilgr. Perf.* (W. de W. 1531) 93 b, Somtyme foloweth thexpulsyon of yᵉ holy goost and his grace. **1557** PAYNEL *Barclay's Jugurth* 90 Neyther to acquisicion of vertue nor expulsion of vyce. **1659** B. HARRIS *Parival's Iron Age* 221 The total expulsion of the Spaniards. **1661** COWLEY *Adv. Exper. Philos.* Wks. 48 The perseverance in any enmity shall be punish'd by the Governors with expulsion. **1698** LUDLOW *Mem.* I. 292 Such extraordinary Expulsions as had been lately used. **1796** BURKE *Corr.* IV. 336 He forgets.. his kind behaviour to me, at the time of my expulsion from the party. **1816** SINGER *Hist. Cards* 258 *note*, It.. affords the first precedent of the expulsion of a member from the House of Commons. **1860** TYNDALL *Glac.* II. v. 250 The change.. consists in the gradual expulsion of the air. **1905** *Act 5 Edw. VII* c. 13 §3 The Secretary of State may.. make an order (in this Act referred to as an expulsion order) requiring an alien to leave the United Kingdom within a time fixed by the order, and thereafter to remain out of the United Kingdom.

b. In physiological use. Formerly *spec.*; now contextual. †*virtue of expulsion* = *expulsive virtue* (EXPULSIVE 1).

c **1400** *Lanfranc's Cirurg.* 168 (MS. A) In þe cloop þat is wiþoutforþ þere ben longe villis and þat makiþ expulcioun. *Ibid.* 194 In morphea þe vertu of expulcion is strong. *c* **1532** DEWES *Introd. Fr.* in Palsgr. 1054 A body.. may nat grow by the vertue of such degestion without expulsion. **1626** BACON *Sylva* §353 The Bringing forth of Living Creatures may be Accelerated.. if there be some cause from the Mothers Body of Expulsion or putting it down. **1732** ARBUTHNOT *Rules of Diet* 359 Soft Liquors drank plentifully.. promote the Expulsion of the Stone Gravel. **1851** CARPENTER *Man. Phys.* (ed. 2) 392 The alternate admission and expulsion of air.. in Insects.

Hence **ex'pulsionist**, one who favours the expulsion of any person or persons.

1885 *Athenæum* 20 June 791/3 The 'expulsionists' were 'nowhere'! **1886** *Pall Mall G.* 11 June 3/2 All the Prince's arguments are better than those of the expulsionists.

†**ex'pulsitive**, *a. Obs. rare.* Erroneous form of next.

a **1592** GREENE & LODGE *Looking Glass* Dram. Wks. I 68 Of the nature of ginger, 'tis expulsitive in two degrees.

expulsive (ɛk'spʌlsɪv), *a.* and *sb.* Also 4 **expulsif**, 5 **-syfe**, 6 **-cive**. [a. F. *expulsif, -ive*, ad. med.L. *expulsīv-us*, f. *expellĕre* to EXPEL: see EXPULSE and -IVE.] **A.** *adj.*

1. Tending or having the power to expel. Chiefly with reference to the action of drugs and medical appliances for the expulsion of morbid influences or deleterious substances from the system. Very frequent in phr. †***expulsive faculty, virtue***.

c **1386** CHAUCER *Knt.'s T.* 1891 The vertu expulsif.. Ne may the venym voyde, ne expelle. **1471** RIPLEY *Comp. Alch.* III. in Ashm. (1652) 141 Of poysons most expulsyfe. **1541** R. COPLAND *Guydon's Quest. Chirurg.*, Other maner of byndynge is called expulsiue.. to expell and put out the mater from the botome. **1547** BOORDE *Brev. Health* Pref. 4 Chierurgyons must knowe.. what sygnes [of the moon] be expulcive. **1658** A. FOX tr. *Wurtz' Surg.* II. viii. 70 An expulsive vulnerary potion. **1686** GOAD *Celest. Bodies* I. ix. 30 Cold is.. Expulsive of its Contrary. **1758** J. S. *Le Dran's Observ. Surg.* (1771) 52 In the Application of expulsive Compresses. **1803** J. KENNY *Society* 29 Duties congenial to thy gentle heart Her lessons teach, expulsive of despair. **1885** *Manch. Exam.* 26 Oct. 5/2 The enormous expulsive force of the steam in its endeavour to escape.

†**2.** Subject to expulsion; hence, driven out. *rare.*

1509 HAWES *Past. Pleas.* XVI. viii, Her goodly fygure I graved in my thought; Except her selfe all were expulcyfe.

†**3.** Tending to repel; = REPELLENT. *Obs.*

1618 CHAPMAN *Hesiod* II. 225 Even ox-hides also want expulsive stuff. **1662** R. MATHEW *Unl. Alch.* §24 This little World hangeth upon the two Poles, Attractive and Expulsive.

†**B.** *sb.* An expulsive drug. *Obs.*

1576 BAKER *Jewell of Health* 235 b, The lyke neyther in the laxatives, purgatives, and expulsives is to be found.

Hence **ex'pulsiveness**.

1727 in BAILEY vol. II.

†**ex'pulsor**. *Obs. rare*⁻¹. [a. L. *expulsor*, agent-n. f. *expellĕre* to EXPULSE.] = EXPULSER.

1432-50 tr. *Higden* (Rolls) I. 405 If a peple expulsede be abowte to expelle the expulsores of hit.

expulsory (ɛk'spʌlsərɪ), *a. rare*⁻¹. [f. L. type **expulsōri-us*, f. *expulsor*: see prec. and -ORY.] Of or pertaining to expulsion; of the nature of expulsion.

1866 HUXLEY *Phys.* v. (1869) 123 The far longer intervals between the expulsory acts.

†**ex'pulsure**. *Obs. rare.* [f. L. *expuls-* ppl. stem of *expellĕre* (see EXPEL) + -URE.] The action of expelling.

c **1611** CHAPMAN *Iliad* II. 339 To have infix'd it in thy breast, Ev'n to the expulsure of thy soul. **1669** COKAINE *Poems* 23 'Tis he.. that sternly should advance (To the expulsure of a Soul) a Lance.

†**ex'pumicate**, *v. Obs.* [f. ppl. stem of *expūmicāre*, f. *ex-* out + *pūmic-*, *pūmex* PUMICE.] *trans.* To clean with pumice-stone; 'to purge or make clean' (Blount). Hence †**expumi'cation**, the action of cleaning with pumice.

1656-81 BLOUNT *Glossogr.*, *Expumicate*. **1658** PHILLIPS, *Expumication*. So **1775** in ASH.

ex'punct, *v.* [f. L. *expunct-* ppl. stem of *expungĕre*: see EXPUNGE.] *trans.* = EXPUNGE. Cf. next.

1610 BARROUGH *Meth. Physick.* VIII. (1639) 452 These simples be withdrawne and expuncted out of that Electuary. **1847** MADDEN *Laȝamons Brut* I. 127 Written at first *ældade*, and the *a* subsequently expuncted. *Ibid.* III. 460 The ancient scribes, who often in such cases expunct the superfluous letter. **1868** SKEAT *Havelok* 21 *note*, The MS. has 'ig', but the *g* is expuncted. **1908** —— in *N. & Q.* 10th Ser. IX. 116/1 The scribe first of all copied 'Ætheredes' as 'Atheredys',.. and after that he.. divided it as 'At heredys', and then, by expuncting *h*, produced 'At eredys'.

expunction (ɛk'spʌŋkʃən). [ad. L. *expunctiōn-em*, n. of action f. *expungĕre*: see EXPUNGE *v.*]

1. a. The action of expunging; an erasure.

1606 W. CRASHAW *Rom. Forgeries & Falsific.* G iij b, That which is to be corrected, may be done with some small addition or expunction. *c* **1611** CHAPMAN *Iliad* II. Comm. (1857) 59 Of which verse his interpreters cry out for the expunction. **1768** SWINTON in *Phil. Trans.* LVIII. 249 The expunction of the L.. and the substitution of the V in its stead. **1810** BENTHAM *Packing* (1821) 188 The omission—and.. the expunction—of names. **1823** W. ROSCOE tr. *Sismondi's Lit. Eur.* xxxvi. (1846) II. 448 *note*, The consonant in the middle of the words being.. fixed upon for expunction.

b. *Palæogr.* The indication of an erasure to be made in a manuscript by means of dots placed beneath the relevant letter or letters.

1954 N. DENHOLM-YOUNG *Handwriting in Eng. & Wales* viii. 78 The point in the Middle Ages was used.. beneath letters to denote *expunction*, i.e. they are to be regarded as not written. **1960** N. R. KER *Eng. MSS. after Norman Conquest* 51 Small errors were repaired by expunction or erasure, the correct reading being added above the line.

†**2.** A wiping out, removal. *Obs.*

1615 T. ADAMS *Leaven* 120 The Gospell intends the expunction of the old Image. **1660** Z. CROFTON *Fasten. St. Peter's Fetters* 64 Total expunction of such Doctrine.

expunctuation (ɛkspʌŋktju:'eɪʃən). *Palæogr.* [Blend of EXPUNCTION and PUNCTUATION.] = EXPUNCTION 1 b.

1957 N. R. KER *Catal. MSS. containing Anglo-Saxon* 325 Letters are cancelled by expunctuation. **1968** *Medium Ævum* XXXVII. 31 Corrections made by a later corrector.. with expunctuation or heavy deletion. **1969** M. B. PARKES *Eng. Cursive Bk. Hands 1250-1500* p. xxviii, [] enclose words and letters which have been deleted by the scribe by means of crossing out, erasure, or expunctuation.

expunge (ɛk'spʌndʒ), *v.* [ad. L. *expung-ĕre* to mark for deletion (a name in a list) by points set above or below, f. *ex-* out + *pungĕre* to prick: see PUNCTURE, POINT.

The L. word was by the earlier Lat.-Eng. lexicographers taken to denote actual obliteration by pricking. The Eng. use is prob. influenced by phonetic association with *sponge*.]

1. *trans.* To strike out, blot out, erase, omit (a name or word from a list, a phrase or passage from a book or record).

1602 FULBECKE *1st. Pt. Parall.* 68 These words.. were ordered by the Court to be expunged or blotted out. **1655** FULLER *Ch. Hist.* II. ii. §25 Some of after-Ages.. purposely expunged the Year (..the Date of this Epitaph). **1711** ADDISON *Spect.* No. 23 ¶3 Having expunged the Passages which had given him offence. **1839** KEIGHTLEY *Hist. Eng.* II. 47 His office was expunged from the breviary. **1879** M. ARNOLD *Guide Eng. Lit.* Mixed Ess. 184 It is a gain to shorten it by expunging anything superfluous.

2. *fig.* To wipe out, efface, annihilate, annul, destroy, put an end to.

1628 HOBBES *Thucyd.* (1882) 13 Neither had there ever been so many cities expunged and made desolate. **1638** G. SANDYS *Job* 11 Wilt thou not.. expunge th' offence? **1712** STEELE *Spect.* No. 432 ¶9 Reflexions of this nature have expunged all Prejudice out of my Heart. **1817** CHALMERS *Astron. Disc.* v. (1852) 113 The infidel argument of astronomers goes to expunge a natural perfection from the character of God. **1871** C. DAVIES *Metr. Syst.* II. 42 We have expunged the yard, used in connection with the arm, more or less in every family.

3. †**a.** To strike out the name of (a person) from a book or list. *Obs.* Hence **b.** To get rid of, remove.

1616-61 HOLYDAY *Persius* 303 Would I might expunge this young rich ward. **1655** FULLER *Ch. Hist.* XI. ii. §89 The Court was moved to expunge those Witnesses, which made most against the King. **1875** MANNING *Mission H. Ghost* vii. 192 To expunge God from Science.

Hence **ex'punger**, one who expunges, or seeks to expunge. **ex'punging** *vbl. sb.* and *ppl. a.*

c **1611** CHAPMAN *Iliad* XVI. Comm. (1857) II. 104 Which is as poorly conceited of the expungers as the rest of the places in Homer that have groaned or laughed under their castigations. **1875** N. SARGENT *Public Men* I. 339 The expungers had the numbers. **1719** SWIFT *To Yng. Clergym.*, The many alterations, additions, and expungings made by great authors. **1834** H. N. COLERIDGE *Grk. Poets* (ed. 2) 38 The.. Iliad, amounting, after all curtailments and expungings, to upwards of 15,000 hexameter lines. **1846** WORCESTER, *Expunging*, blotting out, effacing.

expungement (ɛk'spʌndʒmənt). *rare.* [f. prec. + -MENT.] The action of expunging.

1891 *Scott. Leader* 28 Jan. 4 Yesterday's act of expungement [of resolution from House of Commons Journals].

expurgate ('ɛkspɜ:geɪt), *ppl. a. rare.* [ad. L. *expurgāt-us*, pa. pple. of *expurgāre*: see next.] = EXPURGATED.

1833 H. COLERIDGE *North. Worthies* I. 19 An expurgate liturgy.

expurgate ('ɛkspɜ:geɪt, ɛk'spɜ:geɪt), *v.* [f. L. *expurgāt-* ppl. stem of *expurgāre*, f. *ex-* (see EX- *pref.*¹) + *purgāre* to make clean.]

†**1.** *trans.* To purge or clear out (something excremental). Also *absol. Obs.*

1621 BURTON *Anat. Mel.* I. i. II. iv, That watery matter the two kidnies expurgate. **1652** WORDSWORTH *Chocolate* Introd. Verses, For though that water Expurgate 'Tis but the dregs of Chocolate.

2. a. To purify or amend (a book, etc.) by removing what is thought objectionable. **b.** To purge, make pure (*rare*). Also *absol.*

a. **1678** T. JONES *Rome no Mother Ch.* 64 The Church of Rome.. hath.. cracked her credit by.. forgeing, expurgating, etc. **1819** BYRON *Juan* I. xliv, Juan was taught from out the best edition Expurgated by learned men. **1846** HAWTHORNE *Mosses* II. vii. 117 Carefully corrected, expurgated and amended. **1871** TYLOR *Prim. Cult.* i. 209 The collection [of Sound-Words] would afford the practical means of expurgating itself. **1873** SYMONDS *Grk. Poets* xi. 344 His principal object was to expurgate it from impurities. b. **1845-6** TRENCH *Huls. Lect.* Ser. II. viii. 285 *note*, It is Christianity.. which has really expurgated.. literature.

3. To expurgate as objectionable.

1853 KANE *Grinnell Exp.* xxx. (1856) 257, I copy them from my scrap-book, expurgating only a little.

Hence **'expurgated** *ppl. a.*

1831 MACAULAY *Johnson* Ess. (1851) I. 174 What man of taste.. can endure.. abridgements, expurgated editions? **1872** O. W. HOLMES *Poet Breakf.-t.* i. 17 A kind of expurgated.. copy of Voltaire.

expurgation (ɛkspɜ:'geɪʃən). Also 5 **-acion**. [ad L. *expurgātiōn-em*, n. of action f. *expurgāre*; see EXPURGATE. Cf. Fr. *expurgation*.]

†**1.** The action of expurgating or cleansing from impurity (*lit.* and *fig.*); an instance of this. *Obs.*

c **1420** *Pallad. on Husb.* IV. 942 Thaire [bees'] dwellyng places expu[r]gacion Of every filthe aboute Aprill Calende Wol have of right. **1615** CROOKE *Body of Man* 31 Sorts ordained onely for the expurgation or cleansing of the principall. **1646** SIR T. BROWNE *Pseud. Ep.* Pref. a vj a, Arts and Learning want this expurgation. **1669** GALE *Crt. Gentiles* I. ii. ix. 138 A pure bodie; which puritie was attained by Expurgations, Washings, etc.

2. The removal from a book, etc., of that which is deemed objectionable; an instance of this.

1614 BP. HALL *Epist.* II. iii, Nothing can argue guiltines so much, as unjust expurgations. **1644** MILTON *Areop.* (Arb.) 53 This work will ask as many more officials, to make expurgations. **1694** PEPYS *Lett.* in *Academy* 9 Aug. (1890) 110/3 Yʳ politicall as well as philologicall Expurgations. **1820** SOUTHEY *Lett.* (1856) III. 199 Sewell's History of the Quakers.. has undergone a like expurgation. **1858** GLADSTONE *Homer* I. 70 It seems to invite expurgation in order to establish the consistency of its contents.

3. The action of purging from imputed guilt; clearing; exculpation; after L. *expurgatio. arch.*

1828 SCOTT *F.M. Perth* xxiii, The evidence of the Duke of Rothsay in expurgation, as it was termed, of Sir John.

4. The action of purging away (impurities, etc.); *transf.* the clearing out, removal (of objectionable members of a community).

1615 CROOKE *Body of Man* 183 The melancholly iuyce.. needes the more forcible expurgation. **1648** BP. HALL *Serm.* Rem. Wks. (1660) 190 The severe censure and expurgation of those whom the Psalmist.. calls leavened persons. **1651** BIGGS *New Disp.* ¶244 A Cautery or Fontanell is not set to the expurgation of a malignant humour. **1839** JAMES *Louis XIV*, I. 448 The expurgation of all those members opposed to the Fronde, was advised. **1864** *Sat. Rev.* 31 Dec. 797/2 The later months of the year have ended in the expurgation of weak speculators.

†**5.** *Astr.* The re-appearance of the sun after an eclipse; emersion. *Obs.*

1730-6 in BAILEY (folio). **1751** in CHAMBERS *Cycl.* **1862** *Chambers' Encycl.* s.v. *Eclipse*, Emersion or expurgation is the time when the luminary begins to reappear.

expurgator ('ɛkspɜ:geɪtə(r), ɛk'spɜ:gətə(r)). [as if a. L. **expurgātor*, agent-n. f. *expurgāre*: see EXPURGATE.] One who expurgates or purifies; *esp.* one who strikes out objectionable passages from books.

1638 LD. G. DIGBY *Let. conc. Religion* (1651) 3 Eusebius.. and St. Augustine.. may well be by both sides allowed an Expurgator. **1688** R. JENKINS *Hist. Exam. Councils* I. §3 Boschornius.. was one of the principal Expurgators. **1760** JORTIN *Erasm.* II. 283 The inoffensive book of Grotius.. was put amongst the Libri Prohibiti, by those Expurgators. **1811** SOUTHEY in *Q. Rev.* VI. 333 The expurgator of the book. **1861** *Life & Corr. Bacon* xix. 387 He has not merely

procured Coke's dismissal..but has had himself appointed expurgator to his Reports.

expurgatorial (ɛkˌspɜːgəˈtɔərɪəl), *a.* [f. mod.L. *expurgātōri-us* (f. *expurgātor*: see prec.) + -AL¹.]
a. Of or pertaining to an expurgator (of books). **b.** Tending to expurgate or clear of guilt.

1807 SOUTHEY *Lett.* (1856) I. 416 Drawing his expurgatorial pen through it. **1838** DE QUINCEY *Mod. Greece* Wks. (1863) XII. 292 Many excellent works.. intercepted in their rudiments by these expurgatorial ruffians. **1854** MILMAN *Lat. Chr.* II. v. ii. 323 Himself he exculpated by a solemn expurgatorial oath..from all participation in the deed.

†**expurgaˈtorious,** *a. Obs.* [f. as prec. + -OUS.] = next.

1641 MILTON *Animadv.* Wks. 1738 II. 78 Your Monkish Prohibitions, and expurgatorious Indexes.

expurgatory (ɛkˈspɜːgətərɪ), *a.* [ad. mod.L. *expurgātōrius*: see EXPURGATE and -ORY.] Of or pertaining to expurgation; disposed or tending to expurgate or clear of impurity, guilt, etc.

1646 SIR T. BROWNE *Pseud. Ep.* II. vi. §10. 103 Expurgatory animadversions, whereby wee might strike out great numbers of hidden qualities. **1675** MARVELL *Divine in Mode* Wks. III. 22 We seem to have got an expurgatory press, though not an index. *a* **1797** BURKE *Tracts Popery Laws* ii. Wks. IX. 339 The party has failed in his expurgatory proof. **1821** J. BOSWELL *Shaks. Wks.* Advt. I. 8 There are some annotations..I should gladly have omitted, but..such an expurgatory liberty seemed to me to be going beyond the bounds of my 'limited service'.

b. ***Expurgatory Index***: the list of authors and writings forbidden by the Church of Rome to be read unless they shall have been expurgated. (The Lat. *Index expurgatorius* is now commonly used.)

1625 USSHER *Answ. Jesuit* 513 Their Old Expurgatory Index..set out by Cardinall Quiroga. **1667** POOLE *Dial. Protest. & Papist* (1735) 139 [The Church of Rome's] expurgatory Indices. **1826** E. IRVING *Babylon* I. ii. 125 No other book..hath been permitted to escape..their.. Expurgatory Indices.

transf. **1794** MATHIAS *Purs. Lit.* (1798) 87 There..should be an expurgatory index to..Shakspeare.

expurge (ɛkˈspɜːdʒ), *v.* Rare in mod. use. [a. Fr. *expurge-r*, refashioned from *espurger* = Pr. *espurgar*:— L. *expurgāre*: see EXPURGATE.]

1. *trans.* **a.** To cleanse, purify *from*, *of* (anything unclean or objectionable). **b.** To purge away (anything offensive). Const. *from*, *out of*.

a. 1483 CAXTON *Gold. Leg.* 178/2 Desyre..expurged fro the dust of al worldely affeccion. **1853** MISS SHEPPARD *C. Auchester* II. 179 [It did] expurge [me] of all earthly.

b. 1542 BECON *Potation for Lent* Wks. (Parker Soc. 1843) 118 It is not enough..to expurge and put sin out of you. **1578** BANISTER *Hist. Man.* I. 12 The pituitous excrements expurged from the head vnto the eyes. **1620** VENNER *Via Recta* v. 86 [It]..expurgeth the sharpe and cholericke humors. **1657** TOMLINSON *Renou's Disp.* 505 Melancholical humour easie to be expurged.

2. a. To EXPURGATE (a book, etc.). **b.** To expunge as objectionable from a book.

a. 1635 PAGITT *Christianogr.* I. iii. (1636) 170 In these.. Liturgies..some..seeme to be corrupted and expurged. **1662** J. CHANDLER *Van Helmont's Oriat.* Pref., Take all my Writings, as well those crude and uncorrected, as those that are thorowly expurged.

b. 1638 T. WHITAKER *Blood of Grape* 62 We may therfore expurge this pernicious and intolerable mistake. *a* **1672** WOOD *Life* (1848) 168 To have that passage expurg'd. **1832** H. MELVILL in *Preacher* III. 100/2 If a few portions of the Bible were expurged, it would be hard..to prove the doctrine from the remainder.

Hence **exˈpurging** *vbl. sb.* ***Expurging Index*** = *Expurgatory Index*.

1635 PAGITT *Christianogr.* (1646) I. 105 They plainly confesse the expurging of the Indian Liturgie. **1644** MILTON *Areop.* (Arb.) 39 The council of Trent, and the Spanish Inquisition..perfeted those Catalogues and expurging Indexes. **1645** BP. HALL *Peace Maker* §20 The expurging of those [authors] of their own, whom they dare not deface.

exputation, -pute, var. ff. EXSPUTATION, -PUTE. *Obs.*

†**exˈquire,** *v. Obs.* [ad. L. *exquīrĕ-re* to search out diligently, f. *ex-* out + *quærĕre* to seek.]
trans. To search out, seek for; to find out by searching.

1607 CHAPMAN *Bussy D'Ambois* v. i, Make her name her conceald messenger..That passeth all our studies to exquire. **1615** —— *Odyss.* IV. 520 Who can the deeps of all the seas exquire. *c* **1618** FLETCHER *Q. Corinth* IV. iii. (1st fol.), How she came by it, is not yet exquired. **1652** BENLOWES *Theoph.* XI. lxxi, The soul, that beauteousnesse of Grace exquires.

†**exˈquised,** *a. Obs. rare.* [? f. Fr. *exquis*, pa. pple. of OF. *exquerre, esquerre*:— L. *exquīrĕre* (see prec.) + -ED¹; or var. of *exquisite*.] = next.

1521 *Balade* in *Bradshaw's St. Werburge* (1887) 201 With termes exquised and sence retoriall.

exquisite (ˈɛkskwɪzɪt, ɪkˈskwɪzɪt), *a.* and *sb.* Also 5–6 exquisyt(e, 6–8 -it. [ad L. *exquīsīt-us*, pa. pple. of *exquīrĕre* to search out, f. *ex-* out + *quærĕre* to search, seek.]

A. *adj.*

1. Sought out, 'recherché'. †**a.** Of an expedient, explanation, reason: Sought out, ingeniously devised, far-fetched. Of studies: Abstruse.

c **1460** FORTESCUE *Abs. & Lim. Mon.* (1714) 36 He schal by necessite be artid, to fynd exquisyte [*Laud MS.* requisite] meanys of getting of goods. **1565** JEWEL *Repl. Harding* (1611) 299 If this exposition seeme to M. Harding ouer exquisite, or curious. **1601** SHAKS. *Twel. N.* II. iii. 155, I haue no exquisite reason for't, but I haue reason good enough. **1665** G. HAVERS *P. della Valle's Trav. E. India* 8 The English..well understand all the most exquisite points of Navigation.

†**b.** Of language, expression, terms: Carefully selected; aptly chosen, choice. Hence, out of the way, uncommon; in unfavourable sense, affected, over-laboured. *Obs.*

c **1430** HENRYSON *Test. Creseide* xxxix, To here His faconde tonge, and termes exquisite. **1521** in *Bradshaw's St. Werburge* (1887) 201 Fragrant and facunde of englisshe exquisite. **1549** *Compl. Scot.* Prol. 16, I thocht it nocht necessair til hef fardit..this tracteit vitht exquisyte termis, quhilkis ar nocht daly vsit. **1593** R. HARVEY *Philad.* 70 If the phrase be not exquisit, or the observation not singular. **1650** R. STAPYLTON *Strada's Low C. Warres* III. 54 Which benefit Granvel ascribed to the Dutchess, with exquisite thanks. **1698–9** MAUNDRELL *Let.* in *Journ. Jerus.* end, The most hideous Execrations: in which way these Eastern Nations have certainly the most exquisite Rhetorick of any People upon Earth.

c. Of meat, drink, etc.: Carefully chosen; choice, dainty, delicious (passing into sense 5).

1561 T. NORTON *Calvin's Inst.* IV. 86 The filthy desire of exquisite meates. **1585** LLOYD *Treas. Health* Ciij, In al diseases of long continuance the pacyent most vse lytle meate & exquisite. **1671** MILTON *P.R.* II. 346 All Fish from Sea or Shore..of Shell or fin, And exquisitest name. **1715** NELSON *Addr. Pers. Qual.* 66 The Devil..nourishes himself with the most exquisite morsels. **1716** LADY M. W. MONTAGUE *Lett.* I. vii. 22 Eighteen different sorts [of wine] all exquisite in their kinds. **1781** GIBBON *Decl. & F.* II. 10 The Propontis..renowned for..the most exquisite fish.

†**2. a.** Carefully ascertained or adjusted; accurate, exact. Of an action, investigation, etc.; whence of persons or agents: Careful, curious, minute. *Obs.*

1533 ELYOT *Cast. Helthe* (1541) 52 a, The meate that shall make syckenes, must not a lyttell excede the exquisite measure. **1571** CAMPION *Hist. Irel.* vii. (1633) 22 It will be no hard matter to discry the falshood, wherein I would be more exquisite, were it worth my labour. **1581** MULCASTER *Positions* xli. (1887) 249 The framing of the minde..craueth exquisite consideration. **1602** FULBECKE *2nd Pt. Parall.* 2. In the due performance of his Tithe, he was alwaies diligent and exquisite. **1605** BACON *Adv. Learn* I. iv. §2 A necessitie of a more exquisite trauaile in the languages originall, wherein those Authors did write. **1624** WOTTON *Archit.* (1672) 26 There must be an exquisite care to place the Columnes precisely one over another. **1634** MILTON *Comus* 359 Be not over exquisite To cast the fashion of uncertain evils. **1715** J. RICHARDSON *Th. Paint.* 28 A curious Mechanick's Hand must be exquisite, but his Thoughts are ..pretty much at Liberty. **1757** BURKE *Abridgm. Eng. Hist.* II. vii, Accuracy or exquisite digestion of their laws.

†**b.** of knowledge. *Obs.*

1564 GOLDING *Justine* 94 Takyng his iourney first into Egipt, and afterward to Babilo..he [Pythagoras] attained to meruelous exquisite knowledge. **1651** CULPEPPER *Astrol. Judgem. Dis.* Ep. (1658) 2 To make judgement sound, is required an exquisite knowledg.

†**c.** *Path.* [transl. Gr. ἀκριβής, rendered *exquisitus* in the Lat. versions of Galen.] Of a specified disease: Accurately so named; typical, genuine, as opposed to *spurious*. Cf. F. (*fièvre*) *exquise*.

1610 BARROUGH *Meth. Physick* v. xvi. (1639) 307 In an exquisite Erysipelas make no detraction of bloud. **1656** RIDGLEY *Pract. Physick* 136 An exquisite differs from a bastard Tertian. **1684** tr. *Bonet's Merc. Compit.* IV. 120 An exquisite Diabetes caused by attraction of urine.

3. Carefully elaborated; brought to a high degree of perfection.

†**a.** Of art, workmanship, a product of art or nature: Elaborate, highly finished, excellent. Of an action or process, a state or condition: Carried to a high degree of perfection or completeness. *Obs.*; merged in 4.

1561 T. NORTON *Calvin's Inst.* I. 5 They se that exquisite workmanship in al their members. **1589** NASHE *Greene's Menaphon* Ded. (Arb.) 13 Manie other exquisite editions of Divinitie, turned by him [Golding] out of the French tongue. **1607** TOPSELL *Four-f. Beasts* (1673) 264 Forum Trajani, the most exquisite building of all the world. **1616** SURFL. & MARKH. *Country Farme* 144 The hearbe called Rose-baie, or Oleander..is an exquisite remedie for this disease. **1633** BP. HALL *Hard Texts* 379 They shall make an exquisite dispatch of the inhabitants. **1709** STRYPE *Ann. Ref.* I. xxi. 250 Wherein he hath done such exquisite service to the Protestant cause. *a* **1711** KEN *Hymns Evang.* Poet. Wks. 1721 I. 52 All things which exquisitest Poysons breed. **1752** HUME *Ess. & Treat.* (1777) II. 193 Everything, belonging to a vain man, is the best that is any where to be found..his cookery is more exquisite. **1802** PALEY *Nat. Theol.* viii. §3 (1819) 87 Small pipes which..might.. distribute this exquisite supply to every part of the body.

b. Of torture: Elaborately devised; hence, excruciating, intensely painful. Cf. 6.

1603 KNOLLES *Hist. Turks* (1621) 475 He caused [them] to be put to death with most exquisite torments. **1630** *R. Johnson's Kingd. & Commw.* 13 Tortures of more exquisite device. **1672** CAVE *Prim. Chr.* I. i. (1673) 2 Put to death with the most exquisite arts of torture.

c. Of qualities, dispositions, habits, whether good or bad: Cultivated to a high degree of intensity; consummate, extreme. Now with some notion (in the case of bad qualities, ironical) of sense 4.

1552 HULOET, Exquisite or immoderate clenlines. **1648** *Eikon Bas.* xii, With exquisite malice they have mixed the gall and vinegar of falsitie and contempt with the cup of My Affliction. **1774** WESLEY *Wks.* (1830) IV. 18 His exquisite want of judgement. **1818** JAS. MILL *Brit. India* I. II. x. 465 *note*, The exquisite ignorance and stupidity of the Mysoreans in the art of war. **1848** MACAULAY *Hist. Eng.* II. 54 A new religious order..animated by intense enthusiasm and organised with exquisite skill.

†**4.** Of a person, etc.: Accomplished either in good or bad things; consummate, excellent, perfect. Const. *at*, *of*, *in*, also *to* with *inf*. *Obs.*

1530 PALSGR. Introd. 44 If any..be desyrous to be exquisyt in the frenche tong. **1581** J. BELL *Haddon's Answ. Osor.* 59 A bishop, so exquisite in divinity, as you are. **1607** TOPSELL *Four-f. Beasts* (1673) 393 It is a creature very diligent and exquisite, both to compass, seek out and chuse the same. **1634** SIR T. HERBERT *Trav.* 236 Regia Bander, an exquisite vilaine, murders the olde and young Moguls. **1650** R. STAPYLTON *Strada's Low C. Warres* VI. 21 Captaine Campin an exquisite Enginere. **1719** DE FOE *Crusoe* (1840) II. xiii. 277 His honour must..be a most exquisite sloven. **1771** FRANKLIN *Autobiog.* Wks. 1840 I. 82 A most exquisite mechanic, and a solid, sensible man. **1806–7** J. BERESFORD *Miseries Hum. Life* (1826) xv. Introd., I made her write..to an exquisite gentleman. **1823** SCOTT *Quentin D.* xxvi, 'I guessed he had some exquisite instructer', said Louis.

5. Of such consummate excellence, beauty, or perfection, as to excite intense delight or admiration. (Now the prevailing sense; in early examples a contextual use of 3, sometimes of 1 or 2.)

1579 LYLY *Euphues* (Arb.) 38 A woman so exquisite that in some mens judgement Pigmalions image was not halfe so excellent. **1611** SHAKS. *Cymb.* I. vi. 190 Jewels, Of rich, and exquisite forme. **1632** J. HAYWARD tr. *Biondi's Eromena* 1 The youngest among them was a babe of exquisite beauty. *Ibid.* 51 Caused the March or Levata to be sounded..with such exquisite melodie [etc.]. **1845** L. HUNT *Stories Ital. Poets* I. 168 A lovely spot..enamelled with flowers that surpassed the exquisitest dyes. **1860** TYNDALL *Glac.* I. x. 67 The weather was so exquisite. **1876** HUMPHREYS *Coin-Coll. Man.* xxvi. 387 The Greeks found means to invest with exquisite symmetry even a..vine leaf. **1879** HARLAN *Eyesight* ii. 12 An exquisite adaptation of every part to the great object of the whole. **1884** Q. VICTORIA *More Leaves* 292 As we drove, the setting sun bathed the hills in crimson ..the effect was exquisite.

6. Of pain, pleasure, etc.: Intense, acute, keen.

1644 BP. HALL *Serm.* Rem. Wks. (1660) 105 The Spirit feels more exquisite pain without the Body..then it could feel in the former conjunction with it. **1745** FIELDING *Tom Jones* II. vi, The distresses of the vicious..became too exquisite. **1836** SPARKS *Biog., Mather* VI. iv. 262 She was thrown into exquisite misery. **1860** MOTLEY *Netherl.* (1868) I. v. 198 It was a moment of exquisite triumph. **1865** LECKY *Ration.* (1878) I. iii, 320 Surgeons..have derived the most exquisite pleasure from the operations of their profession.

7. Of the power of feeling, bodily or mental, the senses, etc.: Keenly sensitive to impressions; acutely susceptible of pain, pleasure, etc.; delicate, finely-strung.

1643 PRYNNE *Sov. Power Parl.* Ded. A ijb, One person of the exquisitest judgement. **1668** CULPEPPER & COLE *Barthol. Anat.* I. xix. 51 They have an exquisite sense, and are pained when stones pass through them. **1712** STEELE *Spect.* No. 508 ⁋3 We thought him a Person of an exquisite Palate. **1796** MORSE *Amer. Geog.* II. 19 The serpent's olfactory nerves being remarkably exquisite. **1842** MACAULAY *Fredk. Gt.* Ess. (1877) I. 660 He had an exquisite ear, and performed skilfully on the flute. **1852–9** TODD *Cycl. Anat.* IV. 219/1 The sensibility of the eye to light is very exquisite.

8. quasi-*adv.* = EXQUISITELY.

1529 MORE *Supplic. Soulys* Wks. 289/2 In perill of exquisite payneful punyshemente. **1743** BULKELEY & CUMMINS *Voy. S. Seas* 145 They [Guanacoes] are exceeding nimble, of an exquisite quick Sight..and difficult to be shot.

B. *sb.* A person (usually a man) who is over-nice in dress, etc.; a coxcomb, dandy, fop.

1819 'R. RABELAIS' *Abeillard & H.* 34 Like modern dashing Exquisites. **1830** ARNOLD in Stanley Life & Corr. (1844) II. App. 388 Our exquisites imitate the outside of foreign customs without discrimination. **1849** SIR J. STEPHEN *Eccl. Biog.* (1850) I. 147 The unlucky Exquisite was degraded on the spot. **1868** M. PATTISON *Academ. Org.* v. 241 The foppish exquisite of the drawing-room.

†**exquisited,** *a. Obs. rare*⁻¹. [f. L. *exquīsītus*: see prec. and -ED¹.] Made exquisite; refined.

1581 J. BELL *Haddon's Answ. Osor.* 367 To declare unto us ..where thys exquisited eloquence of writyng, and speaking ..was fourty yeares agoe?

exquisitely (ˈɛkskwɪzɪtlɪ), *adv.* [f. prec + -LY².] In an exquisite manner or degree.

†**1.** With delicate accuracy, exactly; carefully, minutely, thoroughly. *Obs.*

1526 *Pilgr. Perf.* (W. de W. 1531) 163 That he.. pronounce every lettre..curyously & exquisytly. **1599** A. M. tr. *Gabelhouer's Bk. Physicke* 23/1 Pionye kernelles.. exquisitelye pouldrede. **1647** LILLY *Chr. Astrol.* xliv. 270 If the certaine hour.. cannot exquisitely be knowne. **1658** EVELYN *Fr. Gard.* (1675) 276 Reserve them in great round boxes exquisitely shut. **1759** *Duhamel's Husb.* I. ix. (1762) 52 Till the whole mass is exquisitely mingled.

2. In a highly finished manner; with perfection of detail; elaborately, beautifully, excellently.

Now with emotional sense (cf. EXQUISITE 5): With such delicate beauty or subtle perfection as to excite intense pleasure or admiration.

1535 JOYE *Apol. Tindale* 29 He hath so exquysitly translated the testament. **1593** *Rites & Mon. Ch. Durh.* (Surtees) 43 The picture of Bushop Cedda..with..his crosier staffe in his lefte hand exquistelie shewed. *a* **1639** WOTTON *Life Dk. Buckhm.* (1642) 16 A Collection of certain rare Manuscripts, exquisitly written in Arabique. **1791** COWPER *Iliad* XVI. 272 A goblet exquisitely wrought. **1871** H. AINSWORTH *Tower Hill* I. xv, The tender melancholy was exquisitely expressed by her voice and looks. **1877** LADY BRASSEY *Voy. Sunbeam* ix. (1878) 145 A vast chain of exquisitely tinted snow-peaks.

3. In the highest degree; exceedingly. Now with emotional sense; cf. 2 and EXQUISITE 3 c, 4.

1603 FLORIO *Montaigne* I. xxv. (1632) 84 Exquisitely readie and skilfull in the Latine. **1647** WARD *Simp. Cobler* (1843) 35 When the coards of a State are exquisitely tight. **1683** tr. *Erasmus' Moriæ Enc.* 92 They are exquisitely dexterous in unfolding the most intricate mysteries. **1712** STEELE *Spect.* No. 497 ¶3 This fellow, in a dress the most exquisitely ridiculous. **1746** HERVEY *Medit.* (1818) I. 151 As exquisitely fine as the rainbow. **1794** G. ADAMS *Nat. & Exp. Philos.* II. xv. 139 Exquisitely minute they must be. **1838** DICKENS *Nich. Nick.* xxix, There was something so exquisitely absurd in such a cartel of defiance. **1855** MACAULAY *Hist. Eng.* IV. 369 Humour of the most austere flavour, yet exquisitely delicious. **1882** E. O'DONOVAN *Merv Oasis* I. i. 22 The roads were in such exquisitely bad condition.

4. With reference to perception or sensation: †**a.** With nicety or delicacy (*obs.*).

1626 BACON *Sylva* §868 We see more exquisitely with One Eye Shut than with Both Open. **1684** R. H. *Sch. Recreat.* 19 It is a very sagacious and exquisitely Smelling Creature. **1748** HARTLEY *Observ. Man* I. ii. 116 It is customary, in endeavouring to feel exquisitely, to rub the Ends of the Fingers against the tangible Object.

b. In an exquisite degree; intensely, acutely, keenly.

1678 CUDWORTH *Intell. Syst.* 891 Shoud..a Son not only murder his own Parents..but also Exquisitely torture them. **1737** WHISTON *Josephus' Antiq.* Diss. i, These he punished exquisitely. **1802** *Med. Jrnl.* VIII. 431 A swelling..becoming exquisitely painful. **1851** HELPS *Friends in C.* I. 14 To see ten human beings..making each other exquisitely uncomfortable. **1855** MACAULAY *Hist. Eng.* III. 284 A people exquisitely sensitive on points of national honour.

exquisiteness ('ɛkskwɪzɪtnɪs). [f. as prec. + -NESS.] The quality of being exquisite.

a. Elaborateness, high degree of finish, perfectness of detail; now usually, delicate perfection, refined and perfect beauty. †**b.** Scrupulous care; nicety, fastidiousness. †**c.** Consummate skill. **d.** Of pleasure or pain: Refined degree, acuteness, intensity. **e.** Of the senses, taste, judgement, etc.: Delicate sensibility.

a. 1599 SANDYS *Europæ Spec.* (1632) 18 The exquisitenesse [of their Religion consisting most] in an infinity of intricate dumb Ceremonies. *a* **1691** BOYLE *Fluidity & Firmness* II. Wks. 1744 I. 258/1 It is..difficult to procure..either glasses or marbles so much as approaching such an exquisiteness. **1823** LAMB *Elia* Ser. I. xxii. (1860) 172 The exquisiteness of the fun. **1884** *Spectator* 4 Oct. 1304/2 That dainty exquisiteness of utterance.

b. *c* **1534** tr. *Pol. Verg. Eng. Hist.*, (Camden) I. 78 The same exquisitenes in banquitinge did from thence discend unto our time. **1673** MARVELL *Reh. Transp.* II. 370 Suetonius describes..Augustus his heriditary exquisiteness in that particular [propriety of language]. **1772** BURKE *Corr.* (1844) I. 377 In public life, it will be necessary to avoid the exquisiteness of an over-attention to small parts.

c. 1622 MARKHAM *Bk. War* II. v. 59 The [drummer's] exquisitenesse and skilfulnesse in his Art and Instrument.

d. 1650 FULLER *Pisgah* III. xii. 345 The exquisiteness of his bodily temper, increasing the exquisiteness of his torment. **1750** CARTE *Hist. Eng.* II. 775 This man unable to bear the exquisiteness of the pain, accused..Sir Gervase Clyfton. **1832** in WEBSTER; and in mod. Dicts.

e. 1650 [see d]. **1664** POWER *Exp. Philos.* I. 26 Which will try the exquisiteness both of your Glass and Eye to behold. **1748** HARTLEY *Observ. Man.* I. ii. 115 The different Degrees of Exquisiteness in the Sense of Feeling. **1790** BEWICK *Quadrupeds* (1807) 346 The Beagle..follows by the exquisiteness of its scent.

†**exqui'sition.** *Obs.* [ad. L. *exquīsītiōn-em*, n. of action. f. *exquīrĕre*: see EXQUIRE.] The action of searching out. *proper exquisition*: self-seeking.

c **1430** tr. *T. à Kempis' Wks.* 108 Seldom is eny founde fre fro þe venym of propre exquisicion. —— *Imit.* I. iii, He..labouriþ to be ydel in him from al maner exquisicion of propre witte.

exquisitism ('ɛkskwɪzɪˌtɪz(ə)m). [f. EXQUISITE *sb.* + -ISM.] The quality or character of an exquisite; dandyism, foppishness.

1831 LYTTON *Godolphin* viii, The..prim, hedge-clipped indolence of..national exquisitism. **1843** *Fraser's Mag.* XXVIII. 133 No well-trained husband will ever dare to ask a friend to..take pot-luck with him in these days of universal exquisitism.

†**exquisi'titious,** *a. Obs.*$^{-0}$ [f. L. *exquīsīt-* ppl. stem of *exquīrĕre* (see EXQUISITE) + -ITIOUS.] (See quot.)

1727 BAILEY vol. II, *Exquisititious*, not natural, but procured by art. **1775** in ASH.

†**ex'quisitive,** *a. Obs.*$^{-0}$ [f. as EXQUISITITIOUS *a.* + -IVE.] Tending to search out; bent on searching out; curious.

1818 in TODD.

exquisitively (ɛk'skwɪzɪtɪvlɪ), *adv. rare.* [f. prec. + -LY².] = EXQUISITELY.

1660 BOYLE *Seraph. Love* xxiv. (1700) 145 How exquisitively the several Parts of Scripture are fitted to the several Times..and Occurrences. **1662** EVELYN *Chalcogr.* iv, Leonardo..cut exquisitively in wood. **1836** E. HOWARD *R. Reefer* lxvi, The white, exquisitively-shaped..arm of the lady. **1878** BAYNE *Purit. Rev.* iv. 103 She had an organisation exquisitively sensitive to beauty in painting.

†**ex'quisitiveness.** *Obs. rare*$^{-1}$. [f. as prec. + -NESS.] = EXQUISITENESS.

1761 STERNE *Tr. Shandy* IV. i. 75 If this specimen of Slawkenbergius's tales, and the exquisitiveness of his moral, should please the world.

†**exsangui'nality.** *Obs. rare*$^{-1}$. [f. EXSANGUINE + -ALITY.] Bloodlessness.

1651 BIGGS *New Disp.* ¶192 Appear'd as a pale statue of exanguinality.

exsanguinate (ɛks'sæŋgwɪneɪt), *v.* [f. L. *exsanguināt-* ppl. stem of *exsanguināre*, f. *ex-* (see EX- *pref.*¹) + *sanguin-em*, *sanguis* blood.]

trans. To drain of blood.

1849 W. S. MAYO *Kaloolah* (1887) 37 He had been so nearly exsanguinated that his recovery was necessarily slow. **1863** KITTO & ALEXANDER *Cycl. Biblical Lit.* I. 31/2 They should be..duly exsanguinated.

Hence **ex'sanguinated** *ppl. a.*

1800 *Med. Jrnl.* IV. 550 She appeared exsanguinated, and very feeble. **1861** HULME tr. *Moquin-Tandon* II. III. 161 The exsanguinated animals..revived.

exsanguine (ɛks'sæŋgwɪn), *a.* Also 7 exan-. [f. EX- *pref.*¹ + L. *sanguin-*, *sanguis* blood: cf. SANGUINE.] Bloodless, wanting blood; anæmic.

1661 LOVELL *Hist. Anim. & Min.* Introd., Exanguine aquaticks. **1805** W. SAUNDERS *Min. Waters* 301 Very delicate exsanguine chlorotic habits. **1836** TODD *Cycl. Anat.* I. 422/2 Those who have suffered large losses of blood remain exsanguine for many months. **1876** BRISTOWE *Th. & Pract. Med.* (ed. 2) 102 Blood is admitted freely to the comparatively exsanguine parts.

fig. **1647** WARD *Simp. Cobler* 88 Nothing but exsanguine feeble exility of Spirit. *a* **1834** LAMB *Let. to Barton* (L.), Such versicles exsanguine and pithless, yield neither pleasure nor profit. **1872** DASENT *Three to One* II. 259 A poor exsanguine ghost of its former self.

exsanguineous (ˌɛksæŋ'gwɪniːəs), *a. Obs.* exc. *Hist.* Also 7 **exanguinious.** [f. as prec. + -EOUS.] Bloodless.

1664 POWER *Exp. Philos.* I. 58 These puny automata, and exsanguineous pieces of Nature. **1672** SIR T. BROWNE *Pseud. Ep.* III. xx, Those inferior and exsanguineous animals. **1861** HULME tr. *Moquin-Tandon* II. II. 53 The Ancients divided animals into those with blood and..those without..These latter..were named..exsanguineous.

exsanguinity (ɛkssæŋ'gwɪnɪtɪ). [f. as prec. + -ITY.] The state of being without blood or the proper amount of it; bloodlessness; anæmia.

1844 in HOBLYN *Dict. Med. Terms.* **1884** in *Syd. Soc. Lex.*

exsanguinous (ɛks'sæŋgwɪnəs), *a.* Also 7–8 exanguinous. [f. as prec. + -OUS.] = next.

1692–1732 COLES, *Exanguinous.* **1721–1800** BAILEY, *Exsanguinous.* **1889** H. F. WOOD *Eng. Rue Caïn* vii. 104 The exsanguinous visage of M. Renaud.

Hence **ex'sanguinousness,** the quality of being without blood.

1727 in BAILEY vol. II. **1775** in ASH.

exsanguious, -eous (ɛks'sæŋgwɪəs), *a.* Also 7–9 exan-. [f. L. *exsangu-is* bloodless (f. *ex-* out + *sanguis* blood) + -IOUS, -EOUS.] Bloodless.

1646 SIR T. BROWNE *Pseud. Ep.* III. xxi. 162 The ayre was a sufficient maintenance for these exanguious [*printed* exauguious] parts. **1776** COSTA *Conchology* 3 All shell animals are exanguious. **1841** T. R. JONES *Anim. Kingd.* i. 1 The lowest embracing animals which in his view were..exsangueous or provided with a colourless fluid instead of blood.

†**ex'sanguous,** *a. Obs.* In 7–8 exanguous. [f. L. *exsangu-is* bloodless + -OUS.] = prec.

1684 tr. *Bonet's Merc. Compit.* XVI. 560 Worms, as also Snails, Sows, and other exanguous Animals. **1721–1800** BAILEY, *Exanguous.*

†**ex'satiate,** *v. Obs. rare*$^{-1}$. [f. L. *exsatiāt-* ppl. stem of *exsatiāre*, f. *ex-* (see EX- *pref.*¹) + *satiāre* to satisfy, SATIATE.] *trans.* to satiate or satisfy thoroughly.

1599 SANDYS *Europæ Spec.* (1632) 159 Whose prides and pleasures, thirteene millions of yeerely revenew..is not able to exsatiate.

†**ex'saturate,** *v. Obs.*$^{-0}$ In 7–8 **exaturate.** [f. L. *exsaturāt-* ppl. stem of *exsaturāre*, f. *ex-* (see EX- *pref.*¹) + *saturāre* to fill: see SATURATE.] *trans.* To fill completely (with food); to satiate. Also *fig.* Hence †**exsatu'ration.**

1623–6 in COCKERAM. **1656–81** BLOUNT *Glossogr.*, *Exaturate*, to fill an hungry stomach, to satisfie a greedy mind. **1721–1800** in BAILEY. **1658–78** PHILLIPS, *Exaturation*, a satiating. **1721–1800** BAILEY, *Exaturation.*

exschew, obs. form of ESCHEW *v.*

exscind (ɛk'sɪnd), *v.* Also 7, 9 *erron.* excind. [f. L. *exscind-ĕre*, f. *ex-* out + *scindĕre* to cut.]

trans. To cut out, excise. *lit.* and *fig.* In early use: †To cut off, destroy (a nation, etc.).

1662 PETTY *Taxes* 21 If an aliquot part of every landlord's rent were excinded or retrenched. **1785** D. LOW *Chiropodologia* 133 He exscinded the remainder with a pair of scissors. **1831** *Fraser's Mag.* IV. 184 From whose proofs the said phrases were fraudulently exscinded. **1860** I. TAYLOR *Spir. Hebrew Poetry* (1873) 288 The Christian man will not attempt to exscind the irascible emotions, but he will strive to master them.

Hence **ex'scinded** *ppl. a.* **ex'scinding** *vbl. sb.* and *ppl. a.*

a **1677** BARROW *Serm.* (1686) III. 405 The exscinding..of the Amorites. *a* **1711** KEN *Hymns Evang.* Poet. Wks. 1721 I. 63 God with his exscinding Sword in Hand. **1877** SHIELDS *Final Philos.* 488 We are not now inquiring into the legitimacy..of any of the exscinded sciences. **1884** *Syd. Soc. Lex.*, *Exscinded*, term applied to a part from the extremity of which an angular notch has been cut out.

exscreation, var. of EXCREATION.

†**ex'scribe,** *v. Obs.* Also 7 excribe. [ad. L. *exscrīb-ĕre*, f. *ex-* out + *scrībĕre* to write.]

trans. To copy or write out; to transcribe.

1607 TOPSELL *Serpents* (1653) 661 As Aelianus in his ninth Book and thirty nine Chapter, word for word hath exscribed out of Aristotle. **1658** USSHER *Ann.* 351 Demetrius caused it to be fairely exscribed. **1716** M. DAVIES *Athen. Brit.* II. 19 Clerks or Secretaries..exscribing..Particulars of or for it. **1727** in BAILEY vol. II.

Hence **ex'scribed** *ppl. a.* = ESCRIBED. †**ex'scriber,** one who writes out, a copyist. †**ex'scribing** *vbl. sb.*

a **1612** DONNE *Βιαθανατος* (1644) 20 A Councell in France..punished with Excommunication the excribing, reading, or having that booke. *a* **1631** —— *Ess.* (1651) 128 Some other exscriber..reformed it deformly since his [St. Luke's] writing. **1677** CARY *Chronology* II. I. I. iii. 99 This Canon hath gone abroad..very imperfect, occasioned at first by Heedless Exscribers. **1879** SALMON *Conic Sect.* 127 The equation of one of the exscribed circles.

†**exscript.** *Obs.* [ad. L. *exscrīpt-um*, neut. pa. pple. of *exscrībĕre*: see prec.] A copy, written extract.

1609 DAVIES *Holy Rood* (Grosart 1876) 13 Ah, might it please Thy dread exuperance To write th' excript thereof in humble hearts. **1677** CARY *Chronology* II. I. I. 90 The Variety of Copies or Exscripts. **1775** in ASH.

†**ex'scription.** *Obs. rare*$^{-1}$. [f. as if ad. L. **exscrīptiōn-em*, n. of action f. *exscrībĕre*: see EXSCRIBE.] The action of transcribing; in quot. *concr.* = prec.

1637 ABP. WILLIAMS *Holy Table* 211 The poore man is abused by some wag that fits him with these Exscriptions.

†**ex'sculp,** *v. Obs. rare.* Also 6, 8 exculp. [ad. L. *exsculp-ĕre* to dig or cut out, f. *ex-* out + *sculpĕre* to cut, carve: see SCULPTOR.] *trans.* To cut out, hollow out by cutting.

1578 BANISTER *Hist. Man* I. 20 In all others [of the Vertebræ] exculped out one ech side round. **1767** BRYAN FAUSSETT *Invent. Sepulchr.* App. 214 On one side is exculpt a word which we cannot yet make out.

†**ex'sculption.** *Obs. rare*$^{-1}$. [ad. L. *exsculptiōn-em*, n. of action f. *exsculpĕre*: see prec.] A carving or chiselling out.

1659 PEARSON *Creed* (1839) 315 That excavation was performed, by incision or exsculption.

exscutellate (ɛks'skjuːtəleɪt), *a. Ent.* [f. EX- 2 (4) + SCUTELLUM + -ATE².] Without, or apparently without, a scutellum: said of certain insects.

1848 in MAUNDER *Treas. Nat. Hist.* Gloss. App.

exsect (ɛk'sɛkt), *v.* Also 7 exect. [f. L. *exsect-* ppl. stem of *exsecāre*, f. *ex-* out + *secāre* to cut.]

trans. To cut out. Also *fig.*

1641 J. JOHNSON *Acad. Love* 96 Our courtly Dames study onely to exect or cut off their thread bare curtesans. **1672** G. HARVEY *Morb. Angl.* vii. (ed. 2) 18 Were it not for the effusion of blood..which would necessarily follow an exection, the Liver might..be exected. **1758** J. S. *Le Dran's Observ. Surg.* (1771) 51 Part of which [Tumour] had been exsected. **1800** E. DARWIN *Phytologia* xv. §5. 430 Exsect the exuberant growth. **1823** *Blackw. Mag.* XIII. 691 The ham, exsected from Westphalian hog.

Hence **ex'sected** *ppl. a.*

1667 BOYLE in *Phil. Trans.* II. 595, I caused the..exsected piece to be put into a..Receiver. **1880** BLACKIE in *Contemp. Rev.* 289 The exsected books of the Iliad.

exsectile (ɛk'sɛktɪl, -aɪl). [f. L. *exsect-* ppl. stem of *exsecāre* (see prec.) + -ILE.] Capable of being cut out.

1861 HULME tr. *Moquin-Tandon* II. III. ii. 88 The [Coral] polyps..consist of a globular portion which is fixed, and of a free exsectile cylindrical portion terminated by a mouth.

exsection (ɛk'sɛkʃən). Chiefly *Surg.* Also 8 exection. [ad. L. *exsectiōn-em*, n. of action f. *exsecāre*: see EXSECT.] The action of cutting out or away; an instance of this.

1607 *Schol. Disc. agst. Antichr.* I. iv. 174 Instrumentes of exsection. **1609** C. BUTLER *Fem. Mon.* (1634) 155 Exsection..is the cutting out of part of the Combs. **1671** BOYLE

Usefulness Nat. Philos. (1772) II. v. xii, The exsection of the spleen. **1794** E. DARWIN *Zoon.* I. 151 The heart of a viper or frog will renew its contractions..for many minutes of time after its exsection from the body. **1889** *Syd. Soc. Lex.*, *Exsection*, a cutting out.

b. *concr.* A 'cutting'.

1812 COLERIDGE in Southey *Omniana* I. 316 An exsection, from the Kingston Mercantile Advertiser.

exsene: see EYE-SENE.

†**ex'sensed**, *ppl. a. Obs. rare*$^{-1}$. [f. EX- + SENSE + -ED^1.] Out of his senses.

1654 GAYTON *Pleas. Notes* III. ii. 74 Exsensed..and only a man of Phantasie.

exsert (ɛks'sɜːt), *ppl. a.* [ad. L. *exsert-us*, pa. pple. of *exserĕre* to EXSERT.] = EXSERTED.

1846 DANA *Zooph.* vii. (1848) 115 Lamellæ even and not exsert. **1856-8** W. CLARK *Van der Hoeven's Zool.* I. 231 Sænuris Hoffmeister. Upper lip exsert, spoon-shaped.

exsert (ɛks'sɜːt), *v.* [f. L. *exsert-*: see the variant EXERT.] *trans.* †**a.** = EXERT *v.* 2. **b.** (Chiefly *Biol.*) To thrust forth or out, protrude.

1665 *Phil. Trans.* I. 111. Their Poyson..exserts not its noxiousness, till after some time. **1836** TODD *Cycl. Anat.* I. 692/1 The body is exserted through the brachial slit. **1876** DARWIN in *Life & Lett.* (1887) I. 53 Whilst examining some pollen-grains on a damp surface, I saw the tubes exserted.

exserted (ɛks'sɜːtɪd), *ppl. a. Biol.* [f. prec. + -ED^1.] Stretched forth or out; thrust out from (or as from) a sheath, projecting beyond the surrounding parts. ***exserted sting***, etc.: one that cannot be drawn within the body.

1816 KIRBY & SP. *Entomol.* (1843) I. 95 One with a concealed sting and..another..with a very long exserted one. **1826** *Ibid.* (1828) IV. xliv. 223 One of those Ichneumons that have an exserted ovipositor. **1830** LINDLEY *Nat. Syst. Bot.* 67 Stamens long, exserted.

exsertile (ɛks'sɜːtɪl), *a. Biol.* [a. F. *exsertile*, f. L. type **exsertilis*, f. *exserĕre*: see EXSERT and -ILE.] Capable of being exserted.

1828 STARK *Elem. Nat. Hist.* II. 340 Ovipositor articulated, interior, exsertile, and terminated in a sharp point. **1839** TODD *Cycl. Anat.* II. 990/1 In some instances we find long, exsertile..organs. **1869** GILLMORE *Reptiles & Birds* iii. 99 The tongue is elongate, forked, and exsertile.

exsertion (ɛks'sɜːʃən). [as if ad. L. **exsertiōn-em*, n. of action f. *exserĕre* to EXSERT. Cf. EXERTION.] The action of exserting or protruding; the state or fact of being exserted.

ex'sibilate, *v. rare.* In 7 exib-, pa. pple. exsibilat. [f. L. *exsībilāt-* ppl. stem of *exsībilāre*, f. *ex-* out + *sībilāre* to hiss: see SIBILANT.] *trans.* To hiss off the stage.

1601 BP. BARLOW *Defence* 6 Cardinal Allen hath long since exibilated this rash illation. **1637** GILLESPIE *Eng. Pop. Cerem.* III. iv. 58 He is to be ignominiously exsibilat. **1721-1800** in BAILEY.

exsibilation (ɛkssɪbɪ'leɪʃən). *rare.* [n. of action f. L. *exsībilāre*: see prec.] The action of hissing off the stage; ignominious rejection. Also *fig.*

1640 BP. HALL *Episc.* II. xix, So many ages of exsibilation. **1727** in BAILEY vol. II. **1842** DE QUINCEY *Pagan Orac.* Wks. VIII. 184 *note*, The brief exsibilation from the stage by the stern Roman of all Greek testimony.

exsiccant (ɛk'sɪkənt), *a.* and *sb.* ? *Obs.* [ad. L. *exsiccānt-em*, pr. pple. of *exsiccāre*: see EXSICCATE *v.*]

A. *adj.* Drying, having the power or quality of drying up.

1657 RUMSEY *Org. Salutis* Ep. Ded. (1659) 18 The exsiccant quality it hath to dry up the crudities of the stomach. **1676** WISEMAN *Chirurg. Treat.* VI. v. 422 Some dry or exsiccant Medicine. **1755** in JOHNSON. **1832** in WEBSTER.

B. *sb.* An exsiccant drug or medicine.

1676 WISEMAN *Chirurg. Treat.* IV. iv. 296, I caused his knee to be fomented with Discutients and Exsiccants.

†**exsiccate**, *ppl. a. Obs.* Also 6 exiccat, 7 exc-, exsiccat, 8 exiccate. [ad. L. *exsiccāt-* pa. pple. of *exsiccāre*: see next.] Dried, dried up.

1545 RAYNOLD *Byrth Mankynde* 61 So that the preuy passage be left exiccat and Drye. **1613** T. GODWIN *Rom. Antiq.* (1658) 53 They were not ulcerous, exsiccate or impostumated. **1663** J. SPENCER *Prodigies* (1665) 42 The heated and exsiccate Air. **1773** J. ROSS *Fratricide* (MS.) II. 747 O let me..think The fountains of thy eyes are exiccate. *fig.* **1622** J. ABERNETHY *Chr. Treat. Phys. Soul* vi. 81 So in the spirituall hardnesse, the liquor of grace, of light, and of reason is exciccat.

exsiccate ('ɛksɪkeɪt, ɛk'sɪkeɪt), *v.* Also 6 exc-, exiccate, 7-8 exiccate. [f. ppl. stem of L. *ex(s)iccāre*, f. *ex-* (see EX- *pref.*^{1}) + *siccus* dry.]

1. *trans.* To dry, make dry, absorb or remove all moisture from; to drain (a spring) dry; to dry up (moisture).

1545 RAYNOLD *Byrth Mankynde* 56 Let her auoyde such thynges the which shold exiccat..her. **1563** T. GALE *Antidot.* II. 11 These ij vnguentes are excellent in exciccating ericipelas. **1677** HALE *Prim. Orig. Man.* II. vi. 171 Bodies..that have been exsiccated into Mummy. **1679** PLOT *Staffordsh.* (1686) 87 The Spring near the Church..has been sometimes exsiccated. **1707** J. MORTIMER *Husb.* VII. i. (1708) 228 Heats and Droughts..exsiccate and waste the moisture and vegetative Nature of the Earth. **1809** PEARSON in *Phil. Trans.* XCIX. 327 This dissolution being exsiccated grew liquid on exposure to air.

absol. **1612** WOODALL *Surg. Mate* Wks. (1653) 67 Cortex Guaiaci hath the same vertue..but exsiccateth much more. **1627-47** FELTHAM *Resolves* 209 Ayre exsiccates & drawes to itself.

2. *intr.* for *refl.* To dry up, lose all moisture.

1686 GOAD *Celest. Bodies* II. xii. 321 'Tis a question worth while, adds he, how they can exsiccate.

Hence **exsiccated** *ppl. a.*, **exsiccating** *vbl. sb.* and *ppl. a.*

1620 VENNER *Via Recta* vi. 106 They are of a more exiccating nature. **1646** SIR T. BROWNE *Pseud. Ep.* II. iii. 68 The exsiccated powder..ascends not unto the Loadstone. **1669** WORLIDGE *Syst. Agric.* (1681) 3 By the heat of the Sun, or exsiccating power of the Air. **1799** G. SMITH *Labor.* I. 427 Throw common exsiccated salt in it. **1872** O. W. HOLMES *Poet Breakf.-t.* ix, That exsiccated..organism.

exsiccation (ɛksɪ'keɪʃən). Forms: 6 exsiccatione, 7 exiccation, exsiccasion, 7- exsiccation. [ad. L. *exsiccātiōn-em*, n. of action f. *exsiccāre*: see EXSICCATE *v.* Cf. Fr. *exsiccation.*] The action of drying what is moist; complete removal or absorption of moisture; thoroughly dried condition, absolute dryness.

1599 A. M. tr. *Gabelhouer's Bk. Physicke* 10/2 Exsiccatione of the Rheumes. **1614** SYLVESTER *Tobacco Battered* 478 Som also think it causeth exsiccation (As of the Bloud) of Seed of generation. **1620** VENNER *Via Recta* ii. 23 Let wine be moderately vsed, that neither..exiccation, or drunkennesse follow. **1677** PLOT *Oxfordsh.* 95 For exsiccation of wounds. **1794** SULLIVAN *View Nat.* I. 467 Neither is an absolute degree of exsiccation in any wise necessary. **1826** *Blackw. Mag.* XX. 324 The exsiccation of the pond in St. James's Park. **1832** LYELL *Princ. Geol.* II. 202 The aërial current..arrives in a state of complete exsiccation at Peru.

exsiccative ('ɛksɪkeɪtɪv, ɛks'sɪkətɪv), *a.* and *sb.* Forms: 5 exsiccatif, 6-7 exiccative, (6 excicatiue), 7-8 exs- (exss-)iccative. [ad. med.L. *exsiccatīvus*, f. L. *exsiccāre*: see EXSICCATE. Cf. Fr. *exsiccatif* (Cotgr.).]

A. *adj.* Tending to make dry or to produce dryness, having the power or quality of drying up.

c **1400** *Lanfranc's Cirurg.* (MS.B.) 87 A medycine mundyficatyff & exsiccatif. **1563** T. GALE *Antidot.* II. 55 Vertue, alteratiue, resoluative, and excicatiue. **1657** TOMLINSON *Renou's Disp.* 378* Zopissa..is more efficaciously exsiccative. **1755** in JOHNSON. **1884** in *Syd. Soc. Lex.*

B. *sb.* An exsiccative medicine or substance.

1562 BULLEYN *Dial. Soarnes & Chir.* 28 a, I will giue you the difference of exiccatiues, or drying Simples. **1675** EVELYN *Terra* (1729) 24 If too moist, apply Exssiccatives. **1765** *Univ. Mag.* XXXVII. 355/2 Incrustatives and exsiccatives, as myrrh, aloes.

exsiccator ('ɛksɪkeɪtə(r)). [agent-n. f. L. *exsiccāre*: see EXSICCATE.] (See quots.)

1873 WATTS *Fownes' Chem.* 47 Such an apparatus..is called an Exsiccator. **1882** — *Dict. Chem.*, *Exsiccator*, a drying apparatus, consisting of an enclosed space containing substances which rapidly absorb moisture, such as oil of vitriol, dry chloride of calcium, etc.

†**ex'sicce**, *v. Obs. rare*$^{-1}$. [ad. L. *exsicc-āre.*] = EXSICCATE.

1657 TOMLINSON *Renou's Disp.* 264 The juice..is exsicced, formed into lumps, and preserved.

‖**ex silentio** (ˌɛks sɪ'lɛnʃɪəʊ), *advb. phr.* [L.] 'From silence': a phrase used to designate an argument or conclusion based on lack of contrary evidence. Freq. in phr. ***argumentum ex*** (or *e*) ***silentio*** (see ARGUMENT 3 c).

1909 L. R. FARNELL *Cults Gk. States* V. iv. 88 On this point the argument is not merely *ex silentio*. **1945** *Scrutiny* XIII. II. 93 Electra..shows them that the dead have no objection to her dancing and argues *ex silentio* that they approve. **1953** W. R. TRASK tr. *Curtius's Europ. Lit.* iii. 50 The discussion is very summary, and hence forbids conclusions *ex silentio*. **1961** *Times* 2 Oct. 13/2 The only supportable concentrations of power or wealth are those that are at the direct disposal of the state (an exception in the case of trade unions being implied *ex silentio*).

exsolution: see EXOLUTION.

exspect, obs. form of EXPECT.

exspiration, obs. form of EXPIRATION.

†**ex'spoil**, *v. Obs. rare*$^{-1}$. In 6 expoyl. [ad. L. *exspoliāre* (see next) after SPOIL *v.*] *trans.* To despoil.

1526 *Pilgr. Perf.* (W. de W. 1531) 208 b, Spoylynge hym of his pray..expoylyng the princes and potestates of hell.

†**exspoli'ation.** *Obs.* In 7 expoliation. [ad. L. *ex(s)poliātiōn-em*, n. of action f. *ex(s)poliāre* to spoil, f. *ex-* (see EX- *pref.*^{1}) + *spoliāre* to strip, f. *spolium* spoil.] The action of spoiling; the stripping (a person) of his clothes or of his spoil; a stripping off or removal.

1612-15 BP. HALL *Contempl. N.T.* IV. xxxii, A cruel expoliation begins that violence..merciless soldiers..strip thee naked. **1651** BIGGS *New Disp.* ¶205 A subitaneous expoliation of the powers. **1678** R. R[USSELL] *Geber* I. ii. 6 The Expoliation of Accidents.

†**exspuate**, *a. Obs. rare*$^{-1}$. In 7 exp-. [f. L. *exspu-ĕre* to spit out + -ATE^2.] Spit out, ejected.

1604 CHAPMAN *Byron's Conspir.* II. Plays 1873 II. 204 A poor and expuate humour of the Court.

exspuition (ɛkspjuː'ɪʃən). Also 7-9 expuition. [ad. L. *exspuitiōn-em*, n. of action f. *exspuĕre*, f. *ex-* out + *spuĕre* to spit. Cf. F. *exspuition.*] The action of spitting out from the mouth. Const. *of.* Also *transf.* and *concr.*

1650 BULWER *Anthropomet.* 122 Whose office was..the potation of the same aliment, expuition, and locution. **1759** DARWIN in *Phil. Trans.* LI. 527 That these hæmorrhages were from the pulmonary artery..appears from the sudden exspuition. **1852-9** TODD *Cycl. Anat.* IV. 1147/2 A sort of expuition.

†**exspu'tation.** *Obs. rare*$^{-1}$. In 7 exputation. [f. L. *ex(s)pūt-* ppl. stem of *ex(s)puĕre* (see prec.) + -ATION.] The action of spitting out.

1657 TOMLINSON *Renou's Disp.* 710 It cures..the exputation of virulent humours through the mouth.

†**ex'spute**, *v. Obs. rare*$^{-1}$. In 8 expute. [f. L. *exspūt-* ppl. stem of *exspuĕre*: see EXSPUITION.] *trans.* To spit out.

1704 F. FULLER *Med. Gymn.* (1705) 198, I spit Blood, and exputed a viscous tough Matter.

exsputory (ɛk'spjuːtərɪ), *a. rare*$^{-1}$. [f. L. *exspūt-* (see prec.) + -ORY.] *lit.* and *fig.* That is spit out or ejected.

1784 COWPER *Let. to Unwin* 20 Nov., I cannot immediately recollect the exsputory lines.

†**exsquamate**, *v. Obs. rare*$^{-1}$. In 7-8 exsquammate. [f. EX- *pref.*^{1} + L. *squām-a* scale + -ATE^3.] *intr.* Of a bone, etc.: To scale off or come off in scales; to desquamate, exfoliate.

1684 tr. *Bonet's Merc. Compit.* XIII. 394 Bones must exsquammate and be taken out, when they are corrupt.

exstancy, var. of EXTANCY, *Obs.*

exstant, obs. form of EXTANT.

exstatic, -al, obs. ff. ECSTATIC, -AL.

exsteme, obs. form of ESTEEM.

1507 *May & June* 201 in Hazl. *E.P.P.* II. 128, I exsteme verely Euery man of them was the more redy.

†**ex'stercorate**, *v. Obs. rare*$^{-1}$. In 7-8 extercorate. [f. ppl. stem of late L. *exstercorāre*, f. *ex-* out + *stercor-*, *stercus* dung.]

a. *trans.* To eject as dung. **b.** *intr.* To carry out dung. Hence **exsterco'ration**.

1609 DAVIES *Holy Rood* (Grosart 1876) 20 Shall euer Flesh Extercorate her filth Thee to annoy? **1656-81** BLOUNT *Glossogr.*, Extercorate, to carry forth dung. **1692-1732** COLES, *Exstercorate.* **1727** BAILEY vol. II, *Extercoration.*

†**ex'still**, *v. Obs.* In 7-9 extill. [ad. L. *exstillāre*, f. *ex-* out + *stillāre* to drop, f. *stilla* a drop.]

a. *intr.* To drop or trickle out; to come out in drops. **b.** *trans.* To send out in drops; to exude.

1651 CHARLETON *Ephes. & Cimm. Matrons* (1668) 30 Sweat, extilling from the pores of her snow-white skin. **1657** TOMLINSON *Renou's Disp.* 379* That which extills first, is more fluid and humid. **1664** EVELYN *Sylva* (1776) 233 Out of this aperture will extill a limpid and clear water. **1804** *Med. Jrnl.* XII. 40 A yellowish..juice extilled. **1819** H. BUSK *Vestr.* IV. 145 Myrtle and balsam rich extilling gum.

†**exsti'llation.** *Obs.* Also 7 extillation. [n. of action f. L. *exstillāre*: see prec.] The action of dropping out or falling down in drops.

1605 TIMME *Quersit.* I. xiii. 57 Sundry cohobations and extillations. **1713** DERHAM *Phys. Theol.* III. i. 64 They seemed..to be made by an..Exstillation of some petrifying juices out of the rocky Earth.

†**exstilla'titious**, *a. Obs. rare*$^{-1}$. [f. L. *exstillāt-* ppl. stem of *exstillāre* (see EXSTILL) + -ITIOUS.] That drops or trickles out.

1657 TOMLINSON *Renou's Disp.* 680 Extillatitious liquor.

†**ex'stimulate**, *v. Obs.* Also 7 extimulate. [f. L. *exstimulāt-* ppl. stem of *exstimulāre*, f. *ex-* + *stimulāre*: see STIMULATE.] *trans.* To stimulate to activity (organs or faculties); to provoke (appetites or desires); to spur on, incite (persons). Const. *to.*

1603 SIR C. HEYDON *Jud. Astrol.* xx. 425 The Sunne..extimulateth all creatures to the acte of propagation. **1672** H. STUBBE *Justif. Dutch War* 33 The King..extimulated by Ambition. **1683** A. SNAPE *Anat. Horse* I. xv. (1686) 32 It serves..to extimulate the Guts.

absol. **1646** SIR T. BROWNE *Pseud. Ep.* VII. vii. 353 Opium..is conceived to extimulate unto venery.

†**exstimu'lation.** *Obs.* Also 7 extim-. [n. of action f. *exstimulāre* (see prec. and -ATION).] Stimulation, incitement; stimulating property.

1626 BACON *Sylva* §842 The Aire..maketh Things insipid, and without any Extimulation. **1654** H. L'ESTRANGE *Chas. I.* (1655) 118 To allay the boiling extimulations of their own, rarely of others lusts. **1657** REEVE *God's Plea* 229 Repentance doth exhibit..all the..instigations, extimulations, that should make God propense to favour. **1721-1800** in BAILEY.

†**ex'stimulatory**, *a.* *Obs.* *rare*⁻¹. In 7 extimulatory. [f. L. *exstimulāt-* ppl. stem of *exstimulāre* (see EXSTIMULATE) + -ORY.] Tending to stimulate; of stimulating nature.
1657 REEVE *God's Plea* 120 God's messages..are not..extimulatory, instigatory, and impulsory.

exstipulate (ɛk'stɪpjʊlət), *a.* *Bot.* [f. EX- *pref.*[1] + L. *stipul-a* stalk (see STIPULE) + -ATE[2].] Having no stipules.
[**1793** MARTYN *Lang. Bot.*, *Exstipulatus.*] **1830** LINDLEY *Nat. Syst. Bot.* 53 Shrubs with alternate..exstipulate leaves. **1870** BENTLEY *Bot.* 128 When the stipules are absent, it is exstipulate.

exstirpation, obs. form of EXTIRPATION.

exstraught, var. of EXTRAUGHT, *Obs.*

exstrophy ('ɛkstrəfɪ). *Path.* Also **extrophy**. [mod. ad. assumed Gr. *ἐκστροφία, f. ἐκ-, ἐξ- out (see EX- *pref.*[2]) + στροφ- ablaut-form of the root of στρέφ-ειν to turn. Cf. Fr. *exstrophie*. The proper spelling according to the analogy of Gr. derivatives would be *ecstrophy*.] A turning inside out of a part; *esp.* a congenital malformation in which the bladder appears to be turned inside out.
1836 TODD *Cycl. Anat.* I. 391/1 Extrophy of the bladder. **1875** H. C. WOOD *Therap.* (1879) 642 A case of exstrophy of the bladder.

†**ex'struct**, *v.* *Obs.* Also 7-8 **extruct**. [f. L. *ex(s)truct-* ppl. stem of *ex(s)truĕre*, f. *ex-* + *struĕre* to pile up, build.] *trans.* To build or pile up.
c **1534** tr. *Pol. Verg. Eng. Hist.* (Camden) I. 122 In the abbey of Glastonburie was extructed for Arthur a magnificent sepulchre. **1657** TOMLINSON *Renou's Disp.* 216 It is expedient that we extruct a Shop for the student in the Pharmaceutical Art. **1755** in JOHNSON.
Hence †**ex'structed** *ppl. a.*
1647 H. MORE *Poems* 161 Those fair extructed loads Of carved stone. *a* **1763** BYROM *Remarks Horace* II. III. xvii, These high extructed spires.

†**ex'struction**. *Obs.* In 7 extruction. [ad. L. *ex(s)tructiōn-em*, n. of action f. *ex(s)truĕre*: see prec.] The action of building up.
1652 GAULE *Magastrom.* xxvi, The order of extruction. **1663** CHARLETON *Chor. Gigant.* 57 The honour of it's Extruction. **1665** J. WEBB *Stone-Heng* (1725) 228 We meet ..not so much as with the least pieces of broken Crags, of the Extruction of the Danes. **1721-1800** in BAILEY.

†**ex'structive**, *a.* *Obs.* *rare*⁻¹. In 6 **extructive**. [f. L. *ex(s)truct-* ppl. stem of *ex(s)truĕre* (see EXSTRUCT) + -IVE.] Tending to build up.
1580 FULKE *Answ. Frarine's Declar.* 41 Papistry is both affirmative and extructive of al wickednes. **1818** in TODD. **1832** in WEBSTER.

†**ex'structor**. *Obs.*⁻⁰ In 8 extructor. [a. L. *ex(s)tructor*, agent-n. f. *ex(s)truĕre*: see EXSTRUCT.] One who builds up, a builder.
1727 in BAILEY vol. II. **1775** in ASH.

†**exsuccate**, *v.* *Obs.* *rare*⁻¹. [f. L. *exsuccāt-* ppl. stem of *exsuccāre* (*ex(s)ūcāre*) to deprive of juice, f. *exsuccus*: see EXSUCCOUS.] *trans.* To deprive of juice; to suck dry.
1657 REEVE *God's Plea* 207 Your distemper, your exsiccating, and your exsuccating yourselves.

†**exsu'ccation**. *Obs.* *rare*⁻¹. [n. of action f. L. *exsuccāre*: see prec.] The action of driving off juice.
1697 *Phil. Trans.* XIX. 416 The Cassava Root..by Exsuccation and Baking alone, proves..wholesome.

exsuccous (ɛks'sʌkəs), *a.* Also in 7 **exuccous**. [f. L. *exsucc-us* without juice, f. *ex-* (see EX- *pref.*[1]) + *succus* (*sūcus*) juice + -OUS.] Without juice, sapless. Also *fig.*
1646 SIR T. BROWNE *Pseud. Ep.* II. vi. 99 That which is brought exuccous and dry unto us. **1672** —— *Lett. Friend* xv. (1881) 138 Most Men expected to find a consumed Kell ..in this exuccous corps. **1818** *Q. Rev.* XVIII. 235 A hard, dry, 'exsuccous' style of writing. **1821** *Blackw. Mag.* X. 561 The clouds hung like exsuccous sponges in the sky.

exsuction (ɛk'sʌkʃən). Also 7 **exuction**. [n. of action f. L. *exsūgĕre*, f. *ex-* out + *sūgĕre* to suck. Cf. SUCTION.] The action of sucking out, *esp.* the drawing out (air) by an air-pump.
1660 BOYLE *New Exp. Phys. Mech.* Proem 5 The exsuction of Air. **1713** DERHAM *Phys. Theol.* 8 *footn.*, In the Air-pump..[some] Animals..die in less than half a Minute, counting from the very first Exsuction. **1832** in WEBSTER; and in mod. Dicts.

exsudate, obs. form of EXUDATE.

exsufflate, *v.* *Obs.* exc. *Hist.* [f. L. *exsufflāt-* ppl. stem of *exsufflāre*, f. *ex-* out + *sufflāre* to blow up, f. *sub-* up + *flāre* to blow.] *trans.* To blow out, blow away, also *spec.*: see EXSUFFLATION 2.
1666 G. HARVEY *Morb. Angl.* iv. 44 Volatil salts..being exsufflated to the heart produce syncopees. **1884** E. B. TYLOR in *Science* IV. 547 The exorcising such a demon is practised by white men as a religious rite, even including the act of exsufflating it, or blowing it away.

†**exsu'fflation**. *Obs.* exc. *Hist.* [ad. mod.L. *exsufflātiōn-em*, n. of action f. *exsufflāre*: see prec. Cf. Fr. *exsufflation*.]
1. The action of blowing out; an instance of it.
1620 VENNER *Via Recta* (1650) 310 Let not with lesse diligence the superfluities of the nose by exsufflation. *a* **1626** BACON *Physiol. Rem.* Wks. 1727 VII. 209 It will fly upwards over the helm, by a kind of exsufflation, without vapouring. **1689** G. HARVEY *Curing Dis. by Expect.* xvi. 124 Such offensive Ebullitions and Exufflations. **1775** in ASH.
b. *concr.* That which is snuffled up.
1666 G. HARVEY *Morb. Angl.* iv. 45 Those..exufflations crowding into the sphere of the cranium do create most dreadful Head-akes.
2. *Eccl.* The action of blowing, performed by the priest upon a child or grown person at baptism, by way of exorcising the devil, or by the person baptized in token of renouncing the devil.
1502 *Ord. Crysten Men* (W. de W. 1506) I. iii. 17 By yᵉ exsuflacyon yᵉ the preest doth upon yᵉ chylde. **1584** R. SCOT *Discov. Witchcr.* XV. xxiv. 371 The right order of exorcisme ..requireth that exsufflation..be doone toward the west. **1709** J. JOHNSON *Clergym. Vade M.* II. 267 The exorcisms and exsufflations made by the priest on persons to be baptized. **1858** *Sat. Rev.* 31 July 103 The old Mumbo Jumbo of 'unchristianizing the Legislature' must not be consigned to the eternal limbo..without a parting exsufflation.

†**ex'suffle**, *v.* *Obs.* [ad. L. *exsufflāre*: see EXSUFFLATE.] *trans.* To breathe upon (see prec. 2).
1610 HOLLAND tr. *Camden's Brit.* I. 768 They..were.. exorcised, and exsuffled with sundry ceremonies.

†**ex'sufflicate**, *a.* *Obs.* *rare*⁻¹. In 7 **exufflicate**. [app. an arbitrary formation on EXSUFFLATE. Hanmer 1744 proposed to read *exsuffolate*, from It. *suffolare* 'to whistle, to bizze, to whizze' (Florio); this was adopted by some later editors.] ? Puffed up, inflated, 'windy'.
1604 SHAKS. *Oth.* III. iii. 182 Such exsufflicate, and blow'd Surmises.

†**ex'suffolate**, *a.* *Obs.* (See prec.)
1744 HANMER *Shaks. Othello* III. iii. [see EXSUFFLICATE]. **1773** J. ROSS *Fratricide* (MS.) II. 301 Solacing his Joy..with proud speech exsuffolate and fell.

†**ex'superable**, *a.* *Obs.*⁻⁰ Also **exuperable**. [ad. L. *ex(s)uperābilis*, f. *ex(s)uperāre*: see EXSUPERATE and -ABLE.] That may be surpassed, excelled, or conquered.
1656-81 in BLOUNT *Glossogr.* **1721-1800** in BAILEY.
Hence †**ex'superableness**.
1727 BAILEY vol. II, *Exuperableness.*

†**ex'superance**. *Obs.* Also 7-8 **exuperance**. [a. F. *exsuperance* (Montaigne), ad. L. *ex(s)uperantia*, n. of state f. *ex(s)uperant-em*, pr. pple. of *ex(s)uperāre*: see EXSUPERATE.] The condition or fact of exceeding; superabundance, excess.
1603 HOLLAND *Plutarch's Mor.* 1256 The excesse of Nete and Mese by arithmeticall proportion, sheweth the exuperances in equall partie. **1607** TOPSELL *Four-f. Beasts* 428 Until the like exsuperance of bloud come unto the same place again. **1644** DIGBY *Nat. Bodies* x. §8. 83 The exuperance of the density of A to water is 10 degrees. **1682** SIR T. BROWNE *Chr. Mor.* (1756) 85 Nor will his attributes admit of expressions above their own exuperances.
†**b.** As a title of honour. *Obs.*
1609 [see EXSCRIPT].
c. *concr.* That which is in excess; that which towers above other things. Const. *of.*
1635 HEYWOOD *Hierarch.* II. Comm. 86 Simplicitie is sole ..Prince and Ex-Superance of all things that have being.

†**exsuperancy**. *Obs.* In 7 **exup-**. [ad. L. *ex(s)uperantia*: see prec. and -ANCY.] = prec.
1638 WILKINS *New World* I. (1684) 117 The Exuperancy of the Light in the other parts. **1647** M. HUDSON *Div. Right Govt.* I. iv. 19 That over-plus and exuperancie of Manna.

†**ex'superant**, *a.* *Obs.* In 7-8 **exuperant**. [ad. L. *ex(s)uperant-em*, pr. pple. of *exsuperāre*: see next.] Excessive, superabundant.
1604 T. WRIGHT *Passions* v. 285 Exuperant ill wil. **1610** BARROUGH *Meth. Physick* VIII. (1639) 455 The great exuperant heat. **1727-31** BAILEY vol. II, *Exuperant.*

†**ex'superate**, *v.* *Obs.* Also 8 **exuperate**. [f. L. *ex(s)uperāt-* ppl. stem of *ex(s)uperāre*, f. *ex-* + *superāre* to rise above, f. *super* above.]
1. *trans.* To overtop, surpass, excel; to overcome.
1559 W. E[LDERTON] *Pangs of Love* (Percy Soc.) I. 28 Good lady, let no wilfulnesse Exuperate your bewtie, then, To slaye the hertes, that yeld and crave. **1568** C. WATSON *Polyb.* 56 Yet hath she [Fortune] wrought nothing which exsuperateth..these in our dayes. **1610** BARROUGH *Meth. Physick* IV. v. (1639) 228 It may exuperate and overcome the rottennesse. **1708** MOTTEUX *Rabelais* (1737) V. 230 Nectar ..exuperates all your Wines. **1721-1800** in BAILEY.
2. *intr.* (See quot.)
1623 COCKERAM II, To abound, *exuperate.*

†**exsupe'ration**. *Obs.* *rare*⁻¹. In 7-8 exuperation. [ad. L. *ex(s)uperātiōn-em*, n. of action f. *ex(s)uperāre*: see prec.] The action of surpassing or exceeding (due limits); exaggeration.
1623 in COCKERAM. **1657** J. SMITH *Myst. Rhet.* Aiij b, *Hyperbole*, Exuperation. **1721-1800** in BAILEY.

exsurge (ɛks'sɜːdʒ). Also 6 **exurge**. [ad. L. *ex(s)urg-ĕre*, f. *ex-* + *surgĕre* (*surrigĕre*) to rise.] *intr.* To rise up, start out.
1578 BANISTER *Hist. Man* I. 25 A certaine roughnes, whence springeth and exurgeth a valiaunt long Muscle. **1868** WHITMAN *Chants Democratic* Poems 109 All doctrines ..exsurge from you.

†**ex'surgence**. *Obs.*⁻⁰ In 7 exurg-. [f. L. *ex(s)urgentem*: see the next and -ENCE.] The action of rising or coming into view.
a **1691** BAXTER cited by WORCESTER 1846, *Exurgence.*

exsurgent (ɛks'sɜːdʒənt), *a.* In 7 **exurgent**. [ad. L. *ex(s)urgent-em*, pr. pple. of *ex(s)urgĕre*: see EXSURGE.] †**a.** Arising, emerging. **b.** Rising up above the rest.
a. **1619** FAVOUR *Antiquit. Triumphing* 536 Determining exurgent controuersies in a Synod.
b. **1846** DANA *Zooph.* (1848) 404 The centre of the cells exsurgent.

†**ex'suscitate**, *v.* *Obs.* *rare*⁻¹. In 6-8 **exuscitate**. [f. L. *ex(s)uscitāt-* ppl. stem of *ex(s)uscitāre*, f. *ex-* + *suscitāre* to raise, rouse, awaken.] *trans.* To rouse up, awaken.
1574 NEWTON *Health Mag.* 65 Slepe after meate..is thought..to stir up and exuscitate the powers. **1623** COCKERAM, *Exuscitate*, to wake up out of sleep. **1721-1800** in BAILEY.

†**ex,susci'tation**. *Obs.* *rare*⁻¹. Also 8 **exus-**. [ad. L. *ex(s)uscitātiōn-em*, n. of action f. *ex(s)usitāre*: see prec.] The action of rousing up.
1692 H. HALLYWELL *Excell. Mor. Virtue* 54 Virtue is..an exuscitation and raising up of..Intellectual Principles. **1721-1800** in BAILEY.

‖**exta** ('ɛkstə). [L. *exta* in same sense.] See quot. 1884; *spec.* (*Antiq.*) the entrails of a victim from which auguries were taken by soothsayers.
1663 J. SPENCER *Prophecies* (1665) 23 Diviners by the Smoke, the Exta, the Incense on the Altar. **1730-6** in BAILEY (folio). **1855** SMEDLEY *Occult Sciences* 152 None of the 'exta', however favourable they might have been, were of the slightest avail. **1884** *Syd. Soc. Lex.*, *Exta*, the viscera of the chest, originally. Also, occasionally used for the abdominal viscera, especially the bowels.

†**extable**. = *acceptable* (Hal.). (?)
1545 LISLE *to Hen. VIII* in *St. Papers* (1830) I. 815 Suche news..as shalbe extable unto the same.

extacie, -cy, obs. ff. ECSTASY.

†**ex'taint**, *v.* *Obs.* *rare*⁻¹. [f. OF. *extaint*, pa. pple. of *ex-*, *estaindre* (Fr. *éteindre*):— L. *exstinguĕre*: see EXTINGUISH.] *trans.* To extinguish.
c **1400** *Destr. Troy* XII. 4927 Pes, þat we proffer our pouer to extaint.

†'**extance**. *Obs.* *rare*⁻¹. [ad. L. *ex(s)tantia*, n. of state f. *ex(s)tant-em*, pr. pple. of *ex(s)tāre*: see EXTANT.] Emergence.
1682 SIR T. BROWNE *Chr. Mor.* (1756) 127 He..who hath in his intellect the ideal existences of things, and entities before their extances.

†'**extancy**. *Obs.* [f. as prec.: see -ANCY.] The fact, quality, or state of standing out or being protuberant; also *concr.* a protuberance.
1644 DIGBY *Nat. Bodies* xxv. (1658) 284 When water falleth out of the skie, it hath all the little corners or extancies of its body grated off by the air. **1662** EVELYN *Chalcogr.* (1769) 107 One may express to the eye..the relievo or extancie of objects. **1667** BOYLE *Orig. Formes & Qual.* 36 The little Exstancies by their Figure resisted a little the Motion of our Finger. **1689** EVELYN *Let.* 12 Aug. in *Mem.* (1889) III. 441 The filing, sharpnes, and due extancie [*printed* extancie], varnish, & other markes necessary to be critically skill'd in.

extant ('ɛkstənt, ɛk'stænt), *a.* and *sb.* Forms: 6 **extaunt**, (7 **extent**), 7-8 **exstant**, 5- **extant**. [ad. L. *ex(s)tant-em*, pr. pple. of *ex(s)tāre* to stand forth, be prominent, be visible, exist, f. *ex-* out + *stāre* to stand. Cf. Fr. *extant*.]
A. *adj.*
1. Standing out or above any surface; projecting, protruding, protuberant. *arch.*
1545 RAYNOLD *Byrth Mankynd* 110 After that the parte extante or the knot of the nauyll is fallen, etc. **1660** JER. TAYLOR *Duct. Dubit.* II. ii. rule vi. §30 An image..contains ..all sorts of representations, flat or extant. **1669** BOYLE *Contn. New Exp.* I. (1682) 166 The Plug was extant above the orifice of the vessel. **1766** ENTICK *London* IV. 205 In St. Paul's it is extant out of the wall. **1791** COWPER *Iliad* IV. 174 Neck and barb observing from the flesh Extant. **1814** CARY *Dante* XII. 116. **1841** BORROW *Zincali* (1843) I. I. vii. 126 Its naked body half extant from the coarse blanket.
2. Standing forth to view; in early use, with phrase *extant to the sight, to be seen*: prominent, conspicuous, manifest. Now *arch.* *rare*.

1557 *Order of Hospitalls* F v The same booke is ordered, extant to be seene. **1570–6** LAMBARDE *Peramb. Kent* (1826) 155 There are yet extant to the eie, the ruined walles of an auncient fortification. **1627** F. E. *Hist. Edw. II* (1680) 21 Old Quarrels are ript up, to make his spleen more extant. **1677** HALE *Prim. Orig. Man.* I. iii. 95. **1863** KINGLAKE *Crimea* (1877) IV. xii. 278 The truth should be visibly extant.

†**3.** Existing so as to be publicly seen, found, or got at; accessible, get-at-able. *Obs.*

1555 *Lydgate's Chron. Troy* To Rdr., Whose bokes..were not of long extant, yet at the last beyng found at Athenes, have [etc]. **1638** PENKETHMAN *Artach.* C iv, He..may with the assistance of the Constable seise all the Bread extant at the Bakers house.

4. In existence; existing. †Of time: Present. *arch.* †Of a fashion, etc.: In vogue, current.

1561 T. NORTON *Calvin's Inst.* I. 18 b, Among so manifold miserable afflictions of the Jewes..they [the tables of God's covenant] remained still safe and extant. **1581** LAMBARDE *Eiren.* II. v. (1588) 191 Other matters not extant in the booke of the Termes. **1590** SWINBURN *Testaments* 280 The alienation made before the condition were extant or accomplished. *a* **1593** H. SMITH *Wks.* (1867) II. 106 Looke how many heresies are extant in the church. **1606** SHAKS. *Tr. & Cr.* IV. v. 168 In this extant moment. **1618** WITHER *Motto,* 'Nec Curo' (1633) 545 The fashions that last extant be. **1630** PRYNNE *Anti-Armin.* 126 There is not an Arminian, a Pelagian this day extant. **1709** STEELE & SWIFT *Tatler* No. 66 ¶ 1 The most proper Form of Words that were ever extant in any..Language. **1822** MISS MITFORD in L'Estrange *Life* II. vii. 152 If routes and reviews had been extant in Shakespeare's time. **1835** I. TAYLOR *Spir. Despot.* v. 229 A religious community..everywhere extant. **1849** STOVEL *Canne's Necess.* Introd. 10 Cromwell, Vane, and their companions were extant.

b. Continuing to exist; that has escaped the ravages of time, still existing.

1581 J. BELL *Haddon's Answ. Osor.* 462 b, In the same Church is extaunt the Altar whereupon he prayd. **1610** A. COOKE *Pope Joan* in *Harl. Misc.* (Malh.) IV. 57, I say, there are few of his works extant; and in those which are extant, he shews no gall against the popes. **1634** SIR T. HERBERT *Trav.* 191 She leapes into..fire, which leaves nothing extant save fame and ashes. **1791** BOSWELL *Johnson* an. 1745–6, None of his letters during those years are extant. **1848** LYTTON *Harold* I. iv, The Roman temple, extant in the time of Geoffry of Monmouth. **1864** BOWEN *Logic* xii. 384 These fossils do not differ more from the extant types. **1874** GREEN *Short Hist.* i. 7 The only extant British account is that of the monk Gildas.

†**B.** *sb.* **a.** An extant copy (cf. EXTAT). **b.** *pl.* Remains. *Obs.*

1592 tr. *Julius on Rev.* xi. 7 There is an extant of that matter written by the same Boniface. *a* **1659** CLEVELAND *Poor Cavalier* 40 Now Peace be with thy Dust..For the next motion to a Calm..Will thy poor Extants into peices tear.

extascie, -ase, -asie, -asy, obs. ff. ECSTASY.

†**'extat.** *Obs. rare*⁻¹. [subst. use of L. *ex(s)tat* it stands forth, 3rd pers. sing. pres. t. of *exstāre* (see EXTANT).] ? A recorded example.

1625 BP. MOUNTAGU *App. Cæsar* 124 There is no such Extat of any Generall Councell.

extatic, -al, obs. ff. ECSTATIC, -AL.

exteame, obs. form of ESTEEM.

extemporal (ɛk'stɛmpərəl), *a.* Now *rare.* [ad. L. *extemporāl-is* arising out of the moment, f. *ex tempore*: see EXTEMPORE. Cf. TEMPORAL.]

1. Done, said, or conceived on the spur of the moment; not premeditated or studied beforehand; impromptu; off-hand.

1570 LEVINS *Manip.* 14 Extemporall *extemporalis.* **1577** HOLINSHED *Chron.* IV. 225 Hir maiesties extemporall oration. **1607** TOURNEUR *Rev. Trag.* III. vi, Aduizing you to ..extemporall execution. **1649** MILTON *Eikon.* xxiv. 492 He ..makes a difficulty how the people can joyne thir hearts to extemporal prayers. **1753** *Adventurer* No. 81 An extemporal poem in praise of the city. **1836** J. KEBLE *Sermons* viii. Postscript (1848), The light extemporal way in which many reject it. **1857** DE QUINCEY *R. Bentley* Wks. VII. 114 Bentley sat down and wrote extemporal emendations on three hundred and twenty-three passages in the Fragments.

†**b.** Of a person: Speaking, able or given to speak, extempore. *Obs.*

1588 FRAUNCE *Lawiers Log.* I. v. 31 b, An affect of an extemporall Rhetor. **1588** SHAKS. *L.L.L.* I. ii. 189 Assist me some extemporall god of Rime. **1596** *Edw. III*, IV. iv. 60 He cannot pray without the book; I think him no divine extemporal. **1622** DONNE *Serm.* 15 Sept. 67 Those Preachers..are not ignorant, vnlearned, extemporall men. **1636** B. JONSON *Discov.* Wks. (Rtldg.) 742/1 Many foolish things fall from wise men, if they speak in haste, or be extemporal.

†**c.** Of faculty or habit: Pertaining to, or concerned with, extempore speech or action. *Obs.*

1573 G. HARVEY *Letter-bk.* (Camden) 7 M. Lewins extemporal faculti is better then M. Becons is. *a* **1605** STOW in D'Israeli *Cur. Lit.* (1866) 228 He had a wondrous, plentiful, pleasant, extemporal wit. **1624** WOTTON *Archit.* in *Reliq. Wotton.* (1685) 67 The Judging must flow from an extemporal Habit. **1642** BP. DURHAM *Presentment of Schismatic* 24 Their extemporall faculty wᶜʰ they bragge of.

†**2.** Made for the occasion. *Obs.*

1612–5 BP. HALL *Contempl. O.T.* xx. ii, Having now erected an extemporall throne.

Hence †**ex'temporally** *adv.*, in an extemporal manner; impromptu. †**ex'temporalness**, the quality of being extemporal; the faculty of speaking extempore.

1577 G. HARVEY *Letter-bk.* (Camden) 55 A fewe delicate poeticall devises of Mr. G. H. extemporally written by him. **1592** SHAKS. *Ven. & Ad.* 836 She..sings extemporally a wofull dittie. **1656** W. D. tr. *Comenius' Gate Lat. Unl.* §694 Hee..[is called] Eloquent..especially if hee bee ready even to extemporalness. **1674** A. G. *Quest. conc. Oath of Alleg.* 31 Any other remedy than what true Reason..will extemporally dictate in such an occasion.

†**ex'temporality.** *Obs.*⁻⁰ [f. L. *extemporāl-itas*: see -ITY.] Extemporariness; the faculty of extemporaneous speaking.

1656–81 in BLOUNT *Glossogr.* **1775** in ASH.

†**extempo'ranean,** *a. Obs.* [f. as next + -AN.] = next.

1621 BURTON *Anat. Mel.* Democr. 9 Those other faults of Barbarisme, Doricke dialecte, extemporanean stile. **1691** WOOD *Ath. Oxon.* II. 184 He was accounted..a ready or extemporanean speaker.

extemporaneous (ɛkˌstɛmpə'reɪnɪəs), *a.* [f. late L. *extemporāne-us* (in some texts of Quintilian for *extemporālis*; f. *ex tempore*: see EXTEMPORE) + -OUS. Cf. F. *extemporané.*]

1. Not premeditated or studied, off-hand, extempore; *esp.* of discourse, prayer, etc. Rarely of a person: Speaking extempore; also, inclined to promptness of action.

1656–81 in BLOUNT *Glossogr.* **1673** BOYLE *Excell. Theol.* Wks. IV. 54 If it happen (as it often will in extemporaneous discourse) that a philosopher be not rightly understood. **1722** WOLLASTON *Relig. Nat.* v. 124 This cannot be done in extemporaneous effusions; and therefore there must be forms premeditated. **1812** *Religionism* 60 Extemporaneous pulpiteers, your text Prepare. **1825** LD. COCKBURN *Mem.* 418 He seldom utters an extemporaneous word. His habit is to have every thing written, to the very letter. **1847** L. HUNT *Men, Women, & B.* II. x. 230 Ladies of an extemporaneous turn of mind. **1848** MACAULAY *Hist. Eng.* I. 159 There might be a revised liturgy which should not exclude extemporaneous prayer. **1863** ROBINSON in *Macm. Mag.* Mar. 416 Extemporaneous preaching is..best adapted to interest and amuse the hearers.

2. Made for the occasion, hastily erected or prepared. Of a medicine: Needing to be prepared at the time of prescription; opposed to *officinal*. So ***extemporaneous practice.***

1725 BRADLEY *Fam. Dict.* s.v. *Water Germander*, [It is] somewhat strange, that it is not oftner met with in extemporaneous Practise. **1727** *Ibid.* s.v. *Cup Moss*, Mosses ..have never obtain'd officinal or extemporaneous prescription. **1754** WARBURTON *Ld. Bolingbroke's Philos.* ii. (1756) 72 His famous book..taken as an extemporaneous cordial,..to support himself under his frequent paroxysms. **1830** SOUTHEY in *Q. Rev.* XLII. 99 This extemporaneous architecture was soon completed. **1872** YEATS *Growth Comm.* 61 He directed his servants to furnish an extemporaneous supper.

Hence **extempo'raneously** *adv.*, in an extemporaneous manner; **extempo'raneousness**, the quality of being extemporaneous.

1764 HARMER *Observ.* IV. v. 212 The extemporaneousness of them [Eastern songs]. **1791** *Edin. New Disp.* 525 Any proper tincture..may be extemporaneously joined. **1794** G. ADAMS *Nat. & Exp. Philos.* IV. li. 415 The barometer thus extemporaneously made, will be nearly as perfect..as before. **1836** H. COLERIDGE *North. Worthies* (1852) I. 66 Questions which it were worse than folly to treat extemporaneously. **1891** *Spectator* 28 Feb. 308/1 Insufficient preparation, and all the other evils which are briefly comprehended in the description of extemporaneousness.

†**ex'temporany,** *a. Obs. rare*⁻¹. [ad. late L. *extemporāne-us*: see prec.] = prec.

1673 RAY *Journ. Low C.* 397 Sometimes extemporany, sometimes premeditated.

extemporary (ɛk'stɛmpərərɪ), *a.* and *sb.* [f. EXTEMPORE *a.* + -ARY.] **A.** *adj.*

1. Unpremeditated; *esp.* of prayer, discourse, composition, etc.; = EXTEMPORE *a.* 2. Occas. of a speaker; †formerly also of the ability to speak.

1610 BP. HALL *Apol. Brownists* §42 The seruice said in our parish-churches is as good a seruice to God as the extemporary deuotions in your parlours. **1648–9** *Eikon. Bas.* 78 Those men who gloried in their extemporary vein and fluency. **1684** WINSTANLEY in *Shaks. C. Praise* 400 Queen Elizabeth coming into a Grammar-School made this extemporary Verse. **1849** LD. COCKBURN *Jrnl.* II. 244, I have never known a truly extemporary preacher. **1875** EMERSON *Lett. & Soc. Aims* vi. 157 Cardinal de Retz.. described himself in an extemporary Latin sentence. **1880** VERN. LEE *Stud. Italy* II. ii. 27 Italy appears at all times to have produced extemporary poets.

quasi-*adv.* **1629** N. C[ARPENTER] *Achitophel* 38 David's prayer..proceeded from him extemporary.

†**b.** *nonce-use.*

1642 SIR T. BROWNE *Relig. Med.* I. §33. 78, I believe they [the Angels] have an extemporary knowledge.

†**2.** Arising at the moment, occasional, casual; sudden, unexpected. *Obs.*

1639 FULLER *Holy War* I. xxiv. (1840) 46 Being no slip of an extemporary passion, but a studied and premeditated act. *a* **1660** HAMMOND *Serm. on Matt.* xi. 30 Wks. IV. 480 The most extemporary view of the commands of the decalogue. **1672** SHADWELL *Miser* IV, Extemporary love is most commonly as hypocritical as extemporary prayer. **1758** JOHNSON *Idler* No. 94 ¶ 4 A calm delight, such as..is yet easily quitted for some extemporary joy.

3. Made for, or suggested by the occasion; hastily built, framed, prepared, or provided; makeshift; = EXTEMPORE *a.* 3.

1631 T. MAY tr. *Barclay's Mirr. of Mindes* I. 199 They.. constitute one common and extemporary home. **1655–60** STANLEY *Hist. Philos.* (1701) 349/2 As soon as he landed, they..rear'd an extemporary Altar before him. **1699** EVELYN *Acetaria* (1729) 153 Such Plants..are easily prepar'd for an Extemporary Collation. **1779–81** JOHNSON *L.P., Milton* Wks. II. 117 The system of extemporary government..fell into fragments. **1841** D'ISRAELI *Amen. Lit.* (1867) 581 Such elaborate dramatic personages were not extemporary creations thrown off in the heat of the pen. *a* **1864** HAWTHORNE *Amer. Note-bks.* (1879) II. 146 A sty even more extemporary than the shanties.

†**B.** *sb.* An extemporary speech or action; an impromptu. *Obs.*

a **1661** FULLER *Worthies* III. 9 His extemporaries were often better than his præmeditations. **1685** *Gracian's Courtiers Orac.* 52 Extemporaries are the gentile feats of a good discerning.

Hence †**extempo'rarian**, one who speaks extempore; one who maintains the propriety of speaking extempore. **ex'temporarily** *adv.*, in an extemporary manner; without premeditation. **ex'temporariness**, extemporary quality.

1680 G. HICKES *Spirit Popery* 45 Either the Church of England, or the People called Quakers are in the right, and Extemporarians, not Inspired, certainly in the Wrong. **1667** H. MORE *Div. Dial.* II. vi. (1713) 108, I have answered as well as I could thus extemporarily. *a* **1754** FIELDING *Demosth. 1st Olynthiac* Wks. 1775 IX. 238 Extemporarily, and without premeditation. **1840** MILL *Diss. & Disc.* (1875) I. 400 Extemporarily adapting means to ends. **1671** *True Nonconf.* 245 You endeavour thereby, to impugne extemporariness, multiplicity, and variety of words, in Prayer.

†**ex'temporate,** *a. Obs.* [f. EXTEMPORE *adv.* + -ATE².] **a.** Done or produced extempore; **b.** = EXTEMPORAL.

1590 GREENE *Never too late* (1600) 104 In an extemporate humor he made this sonnet. **1651** BAXTER *Inf. Bapt.* Apol. 4 To my first Paper I could never have answer (save to the extemporate writing before at our meeting). **1661** *Papers on Alter. Prayer-bk.* 37 Prayers, both prepared and extemporate have been ordinarily used. **1685** BAXTER *Paraphr. N.T.* Ephes. v. 19 It would be mad Work for a Congregation to sing extemporate Songs.

extempore (ɛks'tɛmpərɪ:), *adv.*, *a.*, and *sb.* [a. L. phrase *ex tempore* lit. 'out of the time'.]

A. *adv.*

1. At the moment, without premeditation or preparation; at first sight; off-hand. Now usually with reference to speech, composition, or musical performance. ***to speak extempore*** in present use often merely means to speak without notes, or without reading from manuscript. ***to pray extempore*** is opposed to using a set form of prayer.

a **1553** UDALL *Royster D.* (Arb.) 32 Yea and extempore will he dities compose. **1588** BABINGTON *Exp. Lord's Pr.* 175 Afterward..he..began to preach *extempore.* **1594** PLAT *Jewell-ho.* III. 29 A speedie..drinke which trauailers may make for themselves (ex tempore) when they are distressed for want of good Beer. **1642** P. RUPERT *Declaration* 2 Noblemen..could then fight so valiantly ex tempore. *a* **1688** BUNYAN *Wks.* II. 677 It is at this day wonderful common, for men to pray Ex-tempore..To pray by a Book..is now out of fashion. **1697** COLLIER *Ess. Mor. Subj.* I. (1709) 140, I don't like a Man that can hate at first Sight, and kill Ex-tempore. **1752** *Phil. Trans.* 11 June, [The tackle and pullies] ..being easily..applied ex tempore as occasion requires. **1756** LADY M. W. MONTAGUE *Lett.* xcviii. IV. 81, I wrote, extempore, on the back of the song, some stanzas, that went perfectly well to the tune. **1837** MRS. CARLYLE *Lett.* I. 72 He proposes to speak these lectures extempore. *a* **1845** HOOD *Open Question* ix, He played extempore as well As certain wild Itinerants on Sunday. **1847** GROTE *Greece* (1862) III. xxxvi. 289 The right expedient seemed to flash upon his mind extempore. **1866** G. MACDONALD *Ann. Q. Neighb.* xi. (1878) 209, I always preach extempore.

†**2.** On the instant; at once; immediately. *Obs.*

1593 NASHE *Four Lett. Confut.* 65 You shall see me cast a figure for him extempore. **1604** *Meeting Gallants at Ordinarie* 22 The body must be removed..extempore: it would affect all the Ayre round about else. **1663** J. SPENCER *Prodigies* Pref., I'd yeeld extempore my breath.

†**3.** ***to live extempore***: to live 'from hand to mouth'. *Obs.*

1679 J. GOODMAN *Penit. Pardoned* II. i. (1713) 146 When a man lives not ex tempore, but premeditates. **1728** T. SHERIDAN *Persius* iii. (1739) 47 To live extempore without any Regard to the future. **1794** SULLIVAN *View Nat.* IV. 58 There are too many in the world..who seem to live extempore..being immersed only in present matters.

B. *adj.*

1. Arising out of the moment; casual, occasional; sudden, unprepared for. Now only of personal actions (cf. 2).

1639 FULLER *Holy War* v. xiv. (1840) 267 It was..an extempore water, flowing from the snow which melted on hills. **1679** J. GOODMAN *Penit. Pardoned* II. ii. (1713) 174 It was but a flash, an extempore motion. *a* **1716** SOUTH *Wks.* IV. 50 To make the salvation of an immortal soul, such a slight, extempore business. **1755** YOUNG *Centaur* v. Wks. 1757 IV. 240 Shall we..leap plumb into the jaws of extempore death? **1809** W. IRVING *Knickerb.* (1861) 150 He was somewhat subject to extempore bursts of passion. **1840** HOOD *Up the Rhine* 228 Markham's extempore championship of the twelve tribes.

2. Of a discourse, etc.: Composed, spoken, performed, or acted at the moment, without premeditation or preparation. Now usually understood to mean: Without the assistance of notes, or without reading.

a 1637 B. JONSON *Leges Convivales* Wks. (Rtldg.) 727 Let no poetaster command Another extempore verses to make. 1665 WITHER *Lord's Prayer* Preamb., There is in many, an excellent gift of extempore vocal Prayer. a 1704 LOCKE *Paraphr. 1 Cor. xiv. note* Wks. 1714 III. 199 Their singing ..was of extempore hymns by the impulse of the Spirit. 1756 CIBBER *Apol.* (ed. 4) II. 112 Extempore farces or dialogues continued till they were displaced by the exhibition of the mysteries. 1795 MASON *Ch. Mus.* i. 54 Voluntaries..continue to be always extempore productions. 1837 J. H. NEWMAN *Par. Serm.* (1839) I. xx. 301 To be present at extempore prayer, is to hear prayers. 1841 D'ISRAELI *Amen. Lit.* (1867) 292 The boy..acted an extempore part of his own invention. 1844 STANLEY *Arnold* I. iii. 141 His [Dr. Arnold's] power of extempore translation into English.

b. Of speakers, performers.

1791–1823 D'ISRAELI *Cur. Lit.* (1866) 226/2 This accomplished extempore actor. 1886 *Beeton's Complete Orator* II. 122 Tillotson failed altogether as an extempore preacher.

3. Contrived for the occasion, makeshift.

1694 F. BRAGGE *Disc. on Parables* I. 7 To..have an extempore superficial religion. 1806–7 J. BERESFORD *Miseries Hum. Life* (1826) x. xxi, Dinner dressed by the housemaid with extempore spits, saucepans etc. 1823 BENTHAM *Not Paul* 347 A sort of mixed and extempore judicatory. 1856 MISS MULOCK *J. Halifax* (ed. 17) 176 John lay on an extempore sofa.

†C. *sb.* Extempore composition, speech, or performance; an impromptu, improvisation. *Obs.*

1598 B. JONSON *Ev. Man in Hum.* v. A poet! I will challenge him my selfe presently, at ex tempore. 1610 *Histrio-m.* I. 127 *Post.* We can all sing and say, And so (with practise) soone may learn to play. *Inc.* True, could our action answer your extempore. 1660 PEPYS *Diary* 6 July, W. H. and I did sing extempores. 1737 *Common Sense* (1738) I. 312 Anagrams..and ex Tempores are all their own. 1798 WOLCOTT (P. Pindar) *Tales of Hoy* Wks. 1812 IV. 410 The extempore, the extempore on the Flys, or you shan't have your Passage for nothing. 1813 SCOTT *Trierm.* II. Interl. at end, ii, Such may hither secret stray, To labour an extempore. 1815 W. H. IRELAND *Scribbleomania* 49 A specimen of Mr. Pratt's extempore.

†ex'tempore, *v. Obs. rare*⁻¹. [f. prec.] *trans.* = EXTEMPORIZE.

1771 SMOLLETT *Humph. Cl.* III. 3 Oct., A loud laugh..he could at all times extempore.

†extemporean, *a. Obs. rare*⁻¹. [? f. EXTEMPORE + -AN; but perh. mispr. for *extemporanean*, which Burton uses elsewhere.] Extemporaneous.

1621 BURTON *Anat. Mel.* Democr. (1651) 12 It was first written..in an extemporean stile.

extemporist (ɛk'stɛmpərɪst). *rare*⁻¹. [f. EXTEMPOR-E *adv.* + -IST.] One who is given to extemporize.

1812 *Religionism* 60 Extemporists.

extemporization (ɛkˌstɛmpəraɪ'zeɪʃən). [f. next + -ATION.] The action of speaking, or of composing and executing music, extempore; improvisation; an extempore performance.

1860 WORCESTER cites *Athenæum*. 1865 *Pall Mall G.* 19 June 4 For three-quarters of an hour last Sunday, I was obliged to listen to Mr. Y.'s extemporization. 1879 O. W. HOLMES *Motley* xxi. 164 A conversation must necessarily imply a certain amount of extemporization on the part of both.

extemporize (ɛk'stɛmpəraɪz), *v.* [f. EXTEMPORE *adv.* + -IZE.]

1. *intr.* To speak extempore. Also, to compose and perform music off-hand; to improvise.

a 1717 [see EXTEMPORIZING *vbl. sb.*]. 1775 in ASH. 1883 A. PHELPS *Eng. Style* vii. 109 Preachers are prone either to extemporize always or to write always. 1887 *Pall Mall G.* 30 Dec. 13/2, I resolved on a certain Sunday night to extemporize.

2. *trans.* To compose on the spur of the moment; to compose and utter off-hand.

1817 BYRON *Beppo* xxxiii, He..could himself extemporise some stanzas. 1841 MIALL *Nonconf.* I. 12 The plain, simple Scottish writer, who..ex-temporised the contents of this book. 1880 VERN. LEE *Stud. Italy* v. 238 Their successors were obliged to leave half of the dialogue to be extemporised.

3. To produce or get up on the spur of the moment; to invent for the occasion.

1858 *Times* 9 Nov., Gunners..cannot be extemporized. 1864 *Ibid.* 24 Dec., The Federals..extemporized a Budget exactly as they extemporized an army. 1874 CARPENTER *Ment. Phys.* I. ii. §43 The Amœba..when it has met with a nutritive particle, extemporises a stomach for its reception. 1878 BOSW. SMITH *Carthage* 197 The canoes which he had extemporised. 1880 L. STEPHEN *Pope* vii. 159 It was his [Bolingbroke's] special glory to extemporize statesmanship without sacrificing pleasure.

Hence **ex'temporized** *ppl. a.*, in senses of the verb. **ex'temporizer**, one who speaks or composes extempore. **ex'temporizing** *vbl. sb.*, also *attrib.* and *ppl. a.*

1856 FROUDE *Hist. Eng.* I. 61 It was an extemporized allegory. 1868 FREEMAN *Norm. Conq.* (1876) II. viii. 211 The extemporized jurisprudence of a later age. 1812 *Religionism* 62 Th' extemporizer's art who knows, Than pray had rather hear him blow his nose. 1852 *Meanderings of Mem.* I. 47 Matter to sustain The staggering extemporizer's pain. 1692 SOUTH *Serm.* (1697) II. 159 The Extemporizing faculty is never more out of its Element, than in the Pulpit. 1644 MILTON *Areop.* (Arb.) 56 The cursory eyes of a temporizing and extemporizing licenser. 1880 GROVE *Dict. Mus.* I. 499/2 Extemporizing machine, an invention for printing the notes of an extemporaneous performance, by means of mechanism connected with the keyboard of a pianoforte or organ.

†ex'tempory, *adv.* and *a. Obs.* [Anglicized form of EXTEMPORE.] = EXTEMPORE.

1623 COCKERAM II, Out of Hand, *Extempory*. 1655 FULLER *Ch. Hist.* VIII. i. §30 Some being for extempory prayers, but none to my knowledge for extempory pollicy. 1658 USSHER *Ann.* 351 Whereunto they extempory made him very prudent and well advised answers. 1679 *Hist. Jetzer* 27 His Knife (which for a piece of extempory Service he always wore about him). 1775 M. GUTHRIE in *G. Colman's Posth. Lett.* (1820) 118 Celebrating our activity.. with extempory Song.

Hence **†ex'temporiness.**

1727 in BAILEY vol. II. 1775 in ASH.

extend (ɛk'stɛnd), *v.* Also 5 estend. [ME. *extenden*, ad. L. *extendĕre*, f. *ex-* out + *tendĕre* to stretch. The form *estend* is through Fr. *estendre*.]

I. To stretch out.

1. *trans.* To stretch forcibly, strain.

†a. To stretch or pull out (anything) to its full size; to strain (nerves); to hold or maintain in a stretched condition. Also, to train (a vine); after L. *extendere vitem*. *Obs.*

c 1420 *Pallad. on Husb.* I. 140 In landes drie and hoote noo vyne extende. 1526 *Pilgr. Perf.* (W. de W. 1531) 255 b, He was extended & strayned on yᵉ crosse. 1541 BARNES *Wks.* (1573) 246/1 Her wrinckles bee extended and stretched out. 1661 LOVELL *Hist. Anim. & Min.* 6 It [Asse's milk] extending the skinn, making it tender and removing wrinkles. 1725 POPE *Odyssey* v. 438 To reach Phæacia all thy nerves extend. 1794 *Rigging & Seamanship* I. 83 Quadrilateral sails are extended by yards.

b. *Manege.* (See quot. 1727). Esp. *pass.* and *refl.* of a horse: to exert itself to the full; to go 'all out'; so, of a runner, oarsman, etc.; hence *gen.*, to use all one's efforts; to try one's utmost; to be at full stretch.

1727 BAILEY vol. II, *To extend* (a Horse) signifies to make him go large. 1753 in CHAMBERS *Cycl. Supp.* 1856 'STONEHENGE' *Man. Brit. Sports* 332/1 The horse is made to extend himself. 1886 *Sat. Rev.* 6 Mar. 327/1 Considering.. what his [the horse's] stride is when really extended. 1915 WODEHOUSE *Something Fresh* v, The Blandings *chef* had extended himself in honour of the house-party, and had produced a succession of dishes which, in happier days, Mr. Peters would have devoured eagerly. 1921 *Baily's Mag.* Jan. 3/2 The flying Pharmacie, who has not only won all the eight races in which she has taken part, but has never been really extended for a single stride. 1923 WODEHOUSE *Inimitable Jeeves* xiii, He delivered an address of twenty-six minutes by Claude's stop-watch. At a village wedding, mark you! What'll he do when he really extends himself! 1931 *Morn. Post* 25 Feb. 16/3 Corpus held their place at the Head of the River without being extended. 1955 *Times* 11 May 5/1 The main interest will be to see how he extends himself on the race-course. 1964 E. WAUGH *Little Learning* v. 137 An indolent, humorous clergyman, who we did not think was extending himself fully in coaching us.

†c. To strain the capacity of, distend (a vessel, etc.). Also *fig. Obs.*

1481 CAXTON *Mirr.* I. iv. Biij b, Of alle goodes they extende them & discorde fro god. 1533 ELYOT *Cast. Helthe* II. xxxv. 53 Men and women..muste reade oftentimes lowde..extendyng out the wyndepype. a 1642 JOS. SHUTE *Judgem. & Mercy* (1645) 99 No man should extend himself beyond the latitude of his own calling. 1704 SWIFT *Mech. Operat. Spirit* Misc. (1711) 299 The Saint felt his Vessel full extended in every Part. c 1720 PRIOR *Turtle & Sparrow* 19 Fair swans, extend your dying throats.

d. *intr.* for *refl.* To expand; to become distended.

1753 N. TORRIANO *Midwifry* 18 Some Authors alledge, that the Womb grows thinner, others that it grows thicker in uterine Gestation, as it extends.

2. a. In weaker sense: To straighten out, place at full length; to lay out (the body, limbs, etc.) in a horizontal position. †Also *intr.* for *refl.*

c 1386 CHAUCER *Man of Law's T.* 363 Flemer of feendes, out of him and here On which thy lymes feithfully extenden, Me kepe. 1624 DONNE *Devotions* 61 If those pieces were extended and stretched out in Man. a 1729 CONGREVE *Lament. Hecuba* in Chalmers X. 276 Hector's Corps extended on a Bier. 1872 HUXLEY *Phys.* vii. 174 A limb is flexed, when it is bent; extended, when it is straightened out. 1888 HATCH *Hibbert Lect.* (1890) III. 74 When it was said 'The government shall be upon his shoulder,' it was meant that Christ should be extended on the cross.

b. To write out at full length; *esp.* to transcribe (shorthand notes) in longhand; to expand (graphical contractions). Also, to write out (a legal instrument) in proper form (now chiefly *Sc.*).

a 1639 WOTTON *Reliquiæ* (1672) 89 The contracting and extending the lines and sense of others..would appear a thankless office. a 1693 URQUHART *Rabelais* III. xxiii, We will take Instrument formally and authentically extended. 1826 J. WILSON *Noct. Ambr.* Wks. 1855 I. 334 'Takin down the conversation in heeroglyphics, and at hame, extendin your notes.' 1874 in *Ripon Ch. Acts* Pref. 8 The Surtees Society has always adhered to the plan of 'extending' contractions. 1882 OLGIVIE, *To extend a deed*, to make a fair copy of a deed on paper, parchment, or the like, for signature; to engross a deed. [Scotch.]

c. *Comm. to extend an invoice*, etc.: to calculate and 'carry out' the amount of each line contained in it. (Cf. branch III.)

3. a. To stretch, draw (*e.g.* a cord, a line of troops) in a specified direction, or so as to reach to a certain point. In Practical Geometry, etc.: To open out (a pair of compasses); also *absol.*

1624 GUNTER *Descr. Crosse-staffe* I. vi. 20 Extend the compasses from the diuisor to 1, the same extent shall reach from the diuidend to the quotient. 1697 DRYDEN *Eneid* I. 587 Some extend the Wall, some build the Citadel. 1703 MOXON *Mech. Exerc.* 343 Then removing the string the space of 15 degrees in the Quadrant, and extending it to the Equator on the Cieling. 1709 STEELE *Tatler* No. 55 ¶5 His Troops are extended from Exilles to Mount Genevre. 1724 DE FOE *Mem. Cavalier* (1840) 170 Colonel Sandys..extends himself to the left..and began to form his men. 1794 J. H. MOORE *Pract. Navig.* 64 Extend from radius or 90° to the course 5 points on the line of sines.

b. *refl.* and *intr.* for *refl.* To stretch or continue for a specified distance; to reach, be continuous, to or towards a certain point of space or time.

1481 CAXTON *Godfrey* 73 Thens departeth an arme like a fresshe water, And estendeth it toward the eest. 1514 BARCLAY *Cyt. & Uplondsyshm.* (Percy Soc.) 9 An hepe of snowe So hye extendynge our steple is more lowe. 1553 BRENDE *Q. Curtius* VII. (1570) 193 So much ground as his campe did conteyne, extendyng in compasse lx. furlonges. 1607 SHAKS. *Timon* II. ii. 160 To Lacedemon did my Land extend. 1662 GRAUNT *Observ. Bills Mortal.* (1665) 116 No greater than that unto which the voice of a Preacher of a middling Lungs can easily extend. 1711 POPE *Temp. Fame* 265 Arches widen, and long iles extend. 1769 *De Foe's Tour Gt. Brit.* I. 183 The Shore extends itself a great Way into the Sea. 1796–7 *Instr. & Reg. Cavalry* (1813) 169 The point and division on which the whole are to form will be named; the whole will extend from it. 1845 M. PATTISON *Ess.* (1889) I. 16 Neustria..extended from the Meuse almost to the present southern limits of France. 1872 E. SPAULDING in Raymond *Statist. Mines & Mining* 90 The Blue Lead.. extends through the county parallel to the main range. 1886 *Manch. Exam.* 9 Feb. 5/2 The strike has extended over 22 weeks.

fig. 1552 HULOET, Extende to, or be as much worth as his word, *suppeto*.

†c. To be directed *to* an object; to tend. Also, to belong, pertain. *Obs.*

a 1533 LD. BERNERS *Gold. Bk. M. Aurel.* (1546) C v, He trauayled..too..serche what extended to the arte of Nygromanycye. 1580 BARET *Alv.* E 492 To Extend to: to touch a thing, *pertineo*. 1581 MARBECK *Bk. of Notes* 49 Anger is no sinne, so that..the ende whether it extendeth be vertuous. 1605 BACON *Adv. Learn.* II. vi. §1 No light of nature extendeth to declare the will and true worship of God.

4. a. *trans.* To lengthen, prolong; to continue to a greater distance; to push forward in space.

1569 ABP. PARKER *Corr.* (Parker Soc.) 351, I take some heed not to extend my sleeve beyond my arm. 1765 A. DICKSON *Treat. Agric.* (ed. 2) 18 Let the earth be extracted, and plants cannot extend themselves. 1854 *Act 17–8 Vict.* c. clxxxvi. (*title*), An Act to enable the Portsmouth Railway Company..to extend their..Line from Godalming to Shalford.

b. To prolong in duration.

1580 BARET *Alv.* E 492 Is extended to this time. 1605 SHAKS. *Macb.* III. iv. 57 If much you note him You shall offend him, and extend his Passion; Feed, and regard him not. a 1631 DONNE *Serm.* vii. (1640) 62 If I extend this Sermon, if you extend your Devotion, or your Patience, beyond the ordinary time. 1725 POPE *Odyss.* IV. 18 To Helen's bed the Gods alone assign Hermione t' extend the regal line. 1796 C. MARSHALL *Garden.* xix. (1813) 349 The season may be extended. 1882 CUSSANS *Handbk. Heraldry* Introd. 14 It is the labour..of vanity to extend the term of this ideal longevity.

c. To carry to a further point of completeness.

1727 SWIFT *Gulliver* III. iii. 196 This advantage hath enabled them to extend their discoveries much farther. 1832 HT. MARTINEAU *Life in Wilds* ix. 118 Machinery might be extended to the utmost perfection.

5. a. To spread out in area; to make to cover a certain space; †to open out (something furled up).

1675 EVELYN *Terra* (1676) 148 You may..extend a Tent over it, to keep out Rain. 1730 A. GORDON tr. *Maffei's Amphith.* 349 An Awning was extended over the Amphitheatre. 1767 FRANKLIN *Lett.* (1833) 107 Men.. carry umbrellas in their hands, which they extend in case of rain.

b. *Metaph.* Used in *passive* with generalized sense: To possess 'extension' or spatial magnitude.

1666 [see EXTENDED *ppl. a.* 4]. 1690 LOCKE *Hum. Und.* II. i. (1695) 48 'Tis..as intelligible to say, that a body is extended without parts, as that any thing thinks without being conscious of it. 1717 PRIOR *Alma* I. 96 The mind, say they, while you sustain To hold her station in the brain; You grant, at least she is extended. 1759 JOHNSON *Rasselas* xlvii, 'I know not'..'how to conceive anything without extension; what is extended must have parts'. 1796 HUTTON *Math. Dict.* I. 460/2 It is usual to consider it [a body] as extended only in length, breadth, and thickness. 1862 [see EXTENDED *ppl. a.* 4].

c. *intr.* To cover an area; to stretch out in various directions. Of immaterial things: To have a certain range or scope.

1481 CAXTON *Myrr.* III. xxi. 181 This [heaven] is that gyueth to vs his colour blew, the whiche estendeth aboue thayer. 1559 in Strype *Ann. Ref.* I. App. x. 28 The parliament, which I knowledge to be of great strengthe in matters whereunto it extendethe. 1597 DANIEL *Civ. Wares* VI. 97 All the purple plains that wide extend. 1605 BACON

Adv. Learn. I. viii. §3 The commandment extendeth more over the wills of men, and not only over their deeds and services. **1697** DRYDEN *Virg. Georg.* III. 514 Some ancient Oak, whose Arms extend In ample Breadth. **1722** DE FOE *Plague* (1884 Rtldg.) 113 These Robberies extended chiefly to Wearing-Cloths. **1729** BUTLER *Serm.* Wks. 1874 II. 162 Moral obligations can extend no further than to natural possibilities. **1841** LANE *Arab. Nts.* I. 88 Thou art he whose goodness extendeth to all men. **1876** J. H. NEWMAN *Hist. Sk.* I. I. ii. 70 Its commerce extended from China to Europe.

6. a. *trans.* To widen, enlarge (boundaries); to enlarge the area of. Also *intr.* for *refl.*

1580 BARET *Alv.* E 492 To extend the bounds. **1697** DRYDEN *Virg. Georg.* IV. 177 My Song to flow'ry Gardens might extend. **1869** FARRAR *Fam. Speech* ii. 40 First westward and northward..the Aryans extended. **1876** E. JENKINS *Blot on Queen's Head* 3 The way in which this inn had gone on extending.

b. To widen the range, scope, area of application of (a law, operation, dominion, state of things, etc.); to enlarge the scope or meaning of (a word).

1584 R. SCOT *Discov. Witchcr.* x. i. 177 *Onen*..is extended to the interpretation of dreames. **1594** HOOKER *Eccl. Pol.* I. viii. (1611) 21 Yet do we not so far extend the law of reason. **1606** SHAKS. *Ant. & Cl.* v. ii. 62 You do extend These thoughts of horror further than you shall Finde cause in Cæsar. **1655–60** STANLEY *Hist. Philos.* (1701) 40/1 Crœsus wondered to see their Plenty extended to the very Beasts. **1709** STEELE & ADDISON *Tatler* No. 103 ⁋3 To strengthen and extend his Sight by a Glass. **1751** JORTIN *Serm.* (1771) IV. xv. 302 We are taught to extend our prayers beyond our own private necessities. **1853** O. GORDON in *Report, etc. on Recomm. Oxf. Univ. Comm.* 196, I have nothing to say about the fourth mode suggested of extending the University. **1854** H. SPENCER *Genesis of Science* Ess. (1858) 162 The invention of the barometer enabled men to extend the principles of mechanics to the atmosphere.

refl. **1798** FERRIAR *Illustr. Sterne* i. 11 The fashion extended itself among the courtiers. **1855** BREWSTER *Newton* II. xix. 207 The reputation of Newton had been gradually extending itself on the continent.

†**c.** *refl.* To give oneself space; to dilate, enlarge on a subject. *Obs.*

a **1635** NAUNTON *Fragm. Reg.* (Arb.) 41, I forbear to extend myself in any further relation upon this subject. **1655** EARL ORRERY *Parthen.* (1676) 242 He extended himself eloquently and largely upon this subject.

†**7.** To magnify in representation; to exaggerate. *Obs.*

1509 HAWES *Past. Pleas.* XXIX. (Percy Soc.) 143, I can nothing extende the goodlines Of her temple. **1611** SHAKS. *Cymb.* I. i. 25, *Second Gent.* You speake him farre. *First Gent.* I do extend him (Sir) within himselfe.

II. To stretch forth, hold out.

8. To stretch forth (the arm or hand). Cf. 2. Also, to hold out, put forward (a staff, etc.).

1601 SHAKS. *Twel. N.* II. v. 72, I extend my hand to him thus. **1611** CORYAT *Crudities* 87 That they [vines] may the more extend their branches in length. **1697** DRYDEN *Æneid* I. 683 See..his old Sire his helpless Hand extend. **1788** COWPER *Dog & Water Lily* v, With cane extended far. **1809** ROLAND *Fencing* 56 It is necessary to parry with the arm a little extended. **1822** M. A. KELTY *Osmond* I. 51 Extending his hand, he took her's. **1841** CATLIN *N. Amer. Ind.* (1844) II. lviii. 244 The strong arm of the Government could be extended out to protect them.

9. a. To hold out, accord, grant (kindness, indulgence) *to, towards* a person; to offer (advice). †Formerly also, to display (malice), inflict (vengeance), issue (a legal process) *against, upon.*

1540–1 ELYOT *Image Gou.* (1544) 59 a, He..extended a more stately facion than purteyned to his degree. **1547** *Act 1 Edw. VI*, c. 3 §16 Such as are in unfained miserie..to whom charitie ought to be extended. **1561** T. NORTON *Calvin's Inst.* I. 3 He extendeth vengeance vpon the wicked. **1597** J. KING *On Jonas* 256 Since thou hast malice to bestowe, extende it vpon Ahab. **1611** SHAKS. *Cymb.* II. iii. 65 Towards himselfe..We must extend our notice. **1611** BIBLE *Ps.* cix. 12 Let there be none to extend mercy unto him. **1712–4** POPE *Rape Lock* II. 11 To all she smiles extends. **1802** MAR. EDGEWORTH *Moral T.* (1816) I. ix. 68 You should extend to me the same..indulgence. **1875** JOWETT *Plato* (ed. 2) III. 687 You..begged that some allowance might be extended to you.

b. *U.S.* *to extend a call* (to a pastorate). Cf. CALL *sb.* 6 g.

1887 *Troy Daily Times* 5 Nov., Plymouth Church has decided to extend a call to the Rev. Charles A. Berry.

c. *Law.* To present (a protest).

1889 [see EXTENDED 5]. *Mod.* 'A captain of a merchant vessel, in case of loss or average, *extends* his protest. So does a notary when he has to protest a bill of exchange.' (H. H. Gibbs.)

III. To value, assess. [Of somewhat obscure origin; perh. derived inversely from EXTENT, and thus etymologically = 'to ascertain the extent of'; perh. with notion of setting down at length; cf. 2 b, c.]

10. To assess, value; *esp.* in *Law*: To value (lands, etc.).

[**1292** BRITTON III. vii. §4 Maunderoms al viscounte..qe par chevalers et autres bones gentz..face estendre totes les terres.] *c* **1330** R. BRUNNE *Chron.* (1810) 202 Now wille kyng R. alle his lond extende, Merschalle & stiward þerfor about dos sende. **1523** FITZHERB. *Surv.* Prol., It is necessarye to be knowen, howe all these maners..shulde be extended, surueyed..and valued in euery parte. **1602** FULBECKE *2nd Pt. Parall.* 41 That which was within the bayliwicke..himselfe caused to be extended by parcels, and at the end he put the summe of the value. **1848** WHARTON *Law Lex.* 242/1 *Extend*, to value the lands, etc., of one bound by a statute, who has forfeited his bond, at such an indifferent rate, as by the yearly rent, the creditor may in time be paid his debt.

11. a. *Law.* To take possession of by a writ of extent; to seize upon (land, etc.) in satisfaction for a debt; to levy upon.

1585 ABP. SANDYS *Serm.* (1841) 82 Our goods are not spoiled..our lands extended, our bodies imprisoned. **1625** MASSINGER *New Way* v. i, When This manor is extended to my use, You'll speak in an humbler key. *a* **1626** BACON *Max. & Uses Com. Law* (1635) 45 The land is to be extended for a yearely value, to satisfie the debt. **1767** BLACKSTONE *Comm.* II. 331 A use could not be extended by writ of *elegit*, or other legal process, for the debts of *cestuy que use.* **1798** Dallas *Amer. Law Rep.* II. 76 Whether a life estate could be extended. **1818** CRUISE *Digest* (ed. 2) II. 56 If he releases all his right to the land, yet he may extend it afterwards. **1823** in CRABB *Technol. Dict.*

b. *transf.* To seize upon, take possession of, by force.

1606 SHAKS. *Ant. & Cl.* I. ii. 105 Labienus..Hath with his Parthian Force Extended Asia. **1610** TOFTE *Honour's Acad.* 31 For where the publique good is extended, not any man there should seeke his owne particular quiet. **1678** BUTLER *Hud.* III. iii. 436 The law..Will soon extend her for your bride.

†**c.** *intr.* with *upon*: To levy upon. *Obs. rare.*

1564–78 BULLEYN *Dial. agst. Pest.* (1888) 11, I haue extended vpon aunciente landes in the Countrie for the breach of couenauntes.

¶ Erron. used for ATTEND.

1483 CAXTON *Gold. Leg.* 239/1 Prayeng god..that he wold gyue hym grace that he myght estende to the helthe of his neyghbours.

Hence **ex'tending** *vbl. sb.*, the action of the vb. EXTEND; also an instance of this. **ex'tending** *ppl. a.*, that extends; that is expanding, spreading out, or becoming larger.

1541 R. COPLAND *Guydon's Quest. Chirurg.*, The whiche [veins] after the braunches..and the extending by the arme are diuersified. *a* **1649** DRUMM. OF HAWTH. *Hist. Jas. V* Wks. (1711) 107 For the amplifying and extending of the Christian religion. **1760** J. WOOLMAN *Jrnl.* vii. 95 Through the gracious extendings of Divine help. **1812** SIR H. DAVY *Chem. Philos.* 12 Warm with the ardor of an extending and exalted religion. **1887** *Pall Mall G.* 28 Feb. 1/1 A profitable and extending business in these goods. *Mod. Furnisher's Price-list*, An extending Dining Table.

extendable, obs. form of EXTENDIBLE.

†**ex'tendant**, *a. Obs.* [f. EXTEND + -ANT[2].]

a. *Sc.* Amounting *to.* **b.** *Her.* Having the wings expanded; = DISPLAYED.

1549 *Compl. Scot.* xiii. 111 He sende ane riche present extendant til thre scoir of thousandis peces of gold. **1825** BERRY *Encycl. Herald.*, *Extendant*, or Displayed, laid open in full aspect. **1851** in OGILVIE; and in later Dicts.

extended (ɛk'stɛndɪd), *ppl. a.* [f. as prec. + -ED[1].]

1. a. Stretched out to the full. Of troops, etc.: Spread out. Of a horse's gait (see quots.); opp. *collected.* Cf. EXTEND *v.* 1 b.

1552 HULOET, Extended in breadth or length, *porrectus.* **1625** MARKHAM *Souldiers Accid.* 14 Marching in an extended Battayle. **1629** CHAPMAN *Juvenal* 251 The length of his extended limbs. **1778** EARL PEMBROKE *Mil. Equit.* 62, I mean by the extended that trot in which the horse trots out without retaining himself, being quite straight. **1841** LANE *Arab. Nts.* I. 127 We rode along in an extended line. **1864** COL. McMURDO in *Daily Tel.* 12 Sept., Extended order simply means skirmishing order. **1938** H. WYNMALEN *Equitation* xi. 52, I start teaching him the extended trot... I begin by varying the pace of his trot a little... I gradually increase the margin between the slowest and the fastest pace. **1952** R. S. SUMMERHAYS *Elem. Riding* xxvi. 148 *Extended walk*, The horse should cover as much ground as quickly as possible without haste or breaking the regularity of the beats. **1953** G. BROOKE *Introd. Riding* vii. 77 To change from an extended to a collected pace.

b. Of an arm, spear, etc.: Outstretched. Of a corpse: buried at full length; ***extended burial***, burial in which the corpse is laid at full length. (Some of the examples are participial rather than adjectival.)

1703 POPE *Thebais* 723 The youth surround her with extended spears. **1875** *Encycl. Brit.* III. 398/2 At the chief's head lay the skeleton of a female..extended upon a sheet of pure gold. **1939** V. G. CHILDE *Dawn Europ. Civilization* (ed. 3) xvi. 277 The dead were generally buried, contracted or extended, in the settlements. **1952** —— *New Light on Most Anc. East* (ed. 4) ix. 187 At Harappa these are represented only by extended and flexed burials in Cemetery H. **1960** K. M. KENYON *Archæol. in Holy Land* ix. 227 The burials appear to have been extended, lying on their backs.

†**c.** Of a passion: Strained, intensified. Of the voice: Strained. *Obs.*

1711 SHAFTESB. *Charac.* (1737) II. II. 164 Anger..and other extended Self-Passions. **1727** DE FOE *Syst. Magic* I. iv. (1840) 109 And as loud as his utmost extended voice would admit.

2. a. Drawn out in length in space or time; continued, prolonged.

c **1450** BURGH *Secrees* (E.E.T.S.) 2591 Eeyen longe, and extendid visage, Signe be of malice and Envye. **1737** POPE *Imit. Hor.* IV. i. 42 Thee, drest in Fancy's airy beam, Absent I follow thro' th' extended Dream. **1786** GILPIN *Mts. & Lakes* II. 8 The vale of Lorton is of the extended kind, running a considerable way between mountains. **1832** MARRYAT *N. Forster* iii, The coast was one extended sheepwalk. **1874** KNIGHT *Dict. Mech.* I. 818/2 *Extended-letter* (*Printing*), one having a face broader than usual with a letter of its height.

†**b.** ***extended proportionality***: = *continued proportional*: see CONTINUED 4 a. *Obs.*

1570 BILLINGSLEY *Euclid* v. def. xx. 136.

c. In *Insurance* (see quots.).

1889 C. E. WILLARD *ABC of Life Insurance* 42 If the death of the insured occurs during the term of the 'extended' insurance, the full amount of the policy is paid. **1909** WEBSTER, *Extended insurance*, insurance for the full face of a policy on which payments are stopped, granted for an additional period in consideration of retaining part or all of the cash surrender value of the policy. **1913** *Jrnl. Chartered Insurance Inst.* XVI. 146 He can discontinue premiums as before, and remain assured for the full amount for a limited period. This, you will perceive, is a Paid-up Term policy, and is known as Extended Assurance. **1925** *Act 15 & 16 Geo. V* c. 69 §4 A further period thereafter ending on such date as the Minister may by order prescribe, not being a date later than the first day of the insurance year commencing next after the end of the aforesaid deficiency period (the aggregate of which two periods is in this section referred to as 'the extended period'). **1928** *Britain's Industrial Future* (*Lib. Ind. Inq.*) IV. xx. 278 Claimants to 'extended' benefit.

d. *Bibliography.* (See quots.)

1952 J. CARTER *ABC for Book-collectors* 78 *Extended.* When used of individual leaves, this means that the inner margin has been renewed... Occasionally, however, if a book has had to be made-up from a narrower copy, the alien leaves may be extended so that their outer margins range with those of their neighbours. **1960** H. HAYWARD *Antique Coll.* 236/2 When one or more of the three outer margins of the leaf of a book has been restored, it is said to be re-margined. If it is the inner margin only, the proper term is extended.

e. ***extended-play*** adj., used of a gramophone record, tape, etc., which contains a longer recording than a record, tape, etc., of a designated 'normal' capacity; *spec.* denoting a record seven inches in diameter, each side playing for about six minutes at 45 revolutions per minute. Abbrev. *E.P.* (E III.).

1954 *Gramophone* Apr. p. ix (Advt.), Extended play records. *Ibid.* May 491/2 (*heading*) Extended play. **1960** *Times Lit. Suppl.* 2 Sept. 553/4 The sentimental Extended Play record. **1962** A. NISBETT *Technique Sound Studio* iv. 83 The thinner backing of extended and double-play tape produce a higher print level.

3. a. Enlarged in area; wide-spread, extensive.

1710 POPE *Windsor For.* 315 Here..Edward sleeps: Whom not th' extended Albion could contain. **1779** FORREST *Voy. N. Guinea* 196 The river Curuan, boasting much gold and clear extended plains of grass.

b. Enlarged in comprehension or scope; having a large scope, extensive.

1700 DRYDEN *Fables* Ded., That your power of doing generous..actions may be as extended as your will. **1863** LYELL *Antiq. Man* 6 The introduction of such a fourth name ..must render the use of Pliocene in its original extended sense impossible. **1882** CUSSANS *Handbk. Heraldry* Introd. 15 Its scope and influence are far more extended.

c. *Sociology.* Of a family, etc.: that comprises not only parents and children but also consanguine and conjugal relatives living in proximity.

a **1942** B. MALINOWSKI *Sci. Theory of Culture* (1944) 168 The function of the extended family I would define in terms of a more effective exploitation of communal resources. **1951** R. FIRTH *Elem. Social Organiz.* iv. 142 The help is given as part of the reciprocities of kinship relations—to a second cousin, or uncle, or other member of an extended kin group. **1960** *New Left Rev.* Jan./Feb. 27/2 Among working-people you had extended families, often overlapping. **1966** D. JENKINS *Educated Society* iii. 98 The extended, as distinct from the nuclear family.

4. Having or possessing the quality of extension. See EXTENSION 7 b.

1666 BOYLE *Orig. Formes & Qual.* 3 A Substance extended, divisible and impenetrable. **1710** J. CLARKE *Rohault's Nat. Phil.* I. vii. (1729) 25 A Surveyor of Land conceives at first Sight, that a Field is extended. **1785** REID *Int. Powers* III. v. (1803) I. 483 From the contemplation of finite extended things. **1862** H. SPENCER *First Princ.* I. iii. §16 The idea of resistance cannot be separated in thought from the idea of an extended body which offers resistance.

5. *Law.* **a.** Valued; seized upon and held in satisfaction for a debt, etc.; levied upon. **b.** Of a protest: (see EXTEND *v.* 9 c.).

a **1625** COPE in Gutch *Coll. Cur.* I. 124 For the extended lands, where ill officers became indebted to the crown, and made an art to have their lands extended at easy rates. **1768** BLACKSTONE *Comm.* III. xxvi. 420 The process is usually called an extent..because the sheriff is to cause the lands, etc. to be appraised to their full extended value. **1889** *Case Bp. of Lincoln* (1891) 53 The costs of the Promoters occasioned by..the said Extended Protest.

Hence **ex'tendedly** *adv.*, in an extended manner; at length, fully; to a great extent, continuously, extensively; so as to possess extension. **ex'tendedness**, the quality or condition of being extended.

1660 EARL BRISTOL *Sp.* in *Parl. Hist.* (1763) XXII. 388 To speak unto your Lordships somewhat more extendedly than what is my Use. **1678** CUDWORTH *Intell. Syst.* 779 Reason dictates, that Here and There, is so to be understood of the Deity, not as if it were Extendedly Here and There. **1791** *Gilbert's Law Evid.* I. 147 We must consider the Nature of Bills of Exchange a little more extendedly from their original. **1806** HERSCHEL in *Phil. Trans.* XCVI. 406 The polar regions are more extendedly flat than..they would have been if [etc.]. **1873** MASSON *Drumm. of Hawth.* xxi. 477 'The Midden-Fecht', or, more extendedly, 'The Midden-Fecht between Vitarva and Neberna'. **1674** N. FAIRFAX *Bulk & Selv.* 173 Neither is extendednes the measure of God's immensity. **1727** BRADLEY *Fam. Dict.* s.v. *Fever*, A Redness in the Face..Strength, Quickness and Extendedness of the Pulse.

extender (ɛkˈstɛndə(r)). Also **extendor**. [f. EXTEND + -ER[1]. In sense 3 a. AF. *estendour*, f. *estendre* to EXTEND.] One who, or that which, extends, in senses of the vb.

1. a. *gen.*

1611 COTGR., *Extenseur*, an extender..stretcher out at length. **1612** WOODALL *Surg. Mate* Wks. (1653) 154 The extenders raising their hands too high, or putting them down too low, etc. **1676** WISEMAN *Chirurg. Treat.* VII. i. 467 The Extension made, the Extenders are to be loosened gently. *a* **1677** BARROW *Pope's Suprem.* v. (1687) 176 The extenders of Empire are admired and commended. **1706** A. BEDFORD *Temple Mus.* viii. 158 *Pashta* signifies an Extender of the Voice.

b. A substance added to paint or ink to increase its quantity or bulk, or to dilute its colour; also, a similar substance added to glue, etc.

1920 F. H. JENNISON *Manuf. Lake Pigments* (ed. 2) 53 There is a considerable difference between the base of a lake, and the filler or extender that is used in the paint trade to let down strong colours. **1957** *Brit. Commonw. Forest Terminol.* II. 67 *Extender*, a substance added by the user to synthetic resin glue to provide body... Some extenders, such as grain, clay or wood flours, may be relatively inert. Others, such as soluble dried blood can be used..both as an extender and as a supplementary glue. **1960** *World's Press News* 16 Dec. 40 The relative ratio of pigment to extender in the solid portion of the ink is governed by several considerations. **1967** *Gloss. Paper/Ink Terms Letterpress Printing* (*B.S.I.*) 9 *Extenders*, materials used by the ink maker or printer to adjust the colour strength and working properties of an ink.

†**2.** Of a muscle; = EXTENSOR. *Obs.*

1615 CROOKE *Body of Man* 782 The fourth muscle or the second extender..occupieth the outward part of the backside of the arme. **1666** J. SMITH *Old Age* (ed. 2) 65 Their origination may be..from the back..outwardly as the first extendor. **1771** J. S. *Le Dran's Observ. Surg.* Gloss., *Crureus Musculus*, an Extender of the Tibia.

†**3.** A surveyor or valuer; *esp.* in *Law*, one who values land, etc., under a writ of extent. *Obs.*

[**1292** BRITTON III. vii. §6 Et cele estente..soit enroullé et enselé desuth les seaus des estendours jurez. *transl.* This extent..shall be enrolled and sealed under the seals of the sworn extendors.] *c* **1330** R. BRUNNE *Chron.* (1810) 83 In his auhtend ȝere..Extendours he [William] sette forto extend þe land. **15..** *Skelton's Wks.*, *Vox Populi* 366 Framyng fynes for fermes..Withe inclosyers and extenders.

4. *University Extender*, a University Extension lecturer (see EXTENSION 9 g).

1893 *National Observer* 11 Nov. 652/1 The University Extender is a familiar type. **1894** *19th Cent.* XXXVI. 207 The University Extender exults in the hapless ones who attend his ministrations.

extendibility (ɛkˌstɛndɪˈbɪlɪtɪ). [f. next: see -ITY.] Capability of being extended; extensibility.

1477 NORTON *Ord. Alch.* v. in Ashm. (1652) 58 Fier is cause of extendibility, And causeth matters permiscible to be. **1820** L. HUNT *Indicator* No. 32 (1822) I. 249 The extendibility of this judicious imprecation to deeds.

extendible (ɛkˈstɛndɪb(ə)l), *a.* In 7 **extendable**. [f. EXTEND + -IBLE.]

1. Capable of being extended or stretched out; capable of being enlarged in length, area, or duration, or in range or scope of meaning or operation; = EXTENSIBLE.

1477 NORTON *Ord. Alch.* v. in Ashm. (1652) 69 [Sweet smell] is in Aier more penetrative, And is more extendible. **1643** *Answ. Ld. Digby's Apol.* 58 The meaning of some words of great latitude, and very extendible in the said Protestation. **1654** GAYTON *Pleas. Notes* IV. xviii. 263 Warrants for Vagrants are not extendable to Knight Errants. **1693** J. BEAUMONT *On Burnet's Th. Earth* II. 121 The most ductile and extendible of all Bodies. **1731** ARBUTHNOT *Aliments* (1732) 42 Such Tubes as have often suffered this Force grow rigid, and hardly more extendible therefore. **1816** *Q. Rev.* XVI. 49 The elastic and extendible nature of those links in the moral chain. **1832** in WEBSTER; and in mod. Dicts.

2. *Law.* Subject to seizure under a writ of extent; liable to be levied upon for debt, etc.

1622 CALLIS *Stat. Sewers* (1647) 165 The Lands Intailed were not extendable. *a* **1626** BACON *Max. & Uses Com. Law* (1635) 47 Not extendable for the debts of the party after his death. **1755** in JOHNSON. **1818** CRUISE *Digest* (ed. 2) II. 139 An equity of redemption is..not extendible by a judgement creditor. **1832** in WEBSTER; and in mod. Dicts.

†**exˈtendlessness.** *Obs. rare*[−1]. App. intended to mean 'boundlessness'.

1677 HALE *Prim. Orig. Man.* I. i. 10 Certain Moleculæ Seminales must be supposed..to keep the World and its Integrals from an Infinitude and Extendlessness of excursions every moment into new Figures and Animals.

†**exˈtendment.** *Obs. rare*[−1]. [f. EXTEND + -MENT. Cf. OF. *estendement*.] The action of extending; extension.

1612 BREREWOOD *Lang. & Relig.* xv. 153 Which great extendment of the Greek patriarch's jurisdiction.

†**exˈtendure.** *Obs.* [f. EXTEND + -URE. Cf. OFr. *estendure*.]

1. = EXTENSION.

1610 *Hellish Councell by Iesuites* 15 It hath beene a deplorable..property of sinne, which was committed by the first man, to have his extendure ouer others. **1634** SIR T. HERBERT *Trav.* 4 This Ile..by reason of its extendure, towards the Tropicke of Cancer..becomes exceeding hot. **1650** BULWER *Anthropomet.* vii. 81 They..labour to prohibite the natural extendure of the Nose. **1690** D'URFEY *Collin's Walk Lond.* i. 7 His person..tall and slim; With parts of large extendure born, To look o're hedges.

2. = EXTENT.

1613 T. MILLES *Treas. Anc. & Mod. Times* 15/2 The Fire which is large in extendure, and burning brightly. **1620** tr. *Boccaccio's Decameron* I. 60 b, The night ensuing and the next daies full extendure are not sufficient. **1634** SIR T. HERBERT *Trav.* 217 Plato..supposing the extendure, comparable to Afrique and Asia, joyned together.

exˈtense, *a.* and *sb. Obs.* or *arch.* [ad. (directly, or through OF. *extense*) L. *extens-us*, pa. pple. of *extendĕre* to EXTEND.]

A. *adj.* **a.** Possessing the quality of 'extension'. **b.** Widely extended; extensive.

a. 1647 H. MORE *Song of Soul* II. ii. II. xxvi, Common sense, that's not extense But like a centre that around doth shoot Its rayes. *Ibid.* II. ii. III. xx, Is that Idea extense? or indivisible?

b. 1644 HUNTON *Vind. Treat. Monarchy* iv. 26 An *Absolute* Monarch who hath a power of doing, as extense as his Reasonable Will. **1652** BENLOWES *Theoph.* Author's Prayer 17 Their [our Transgressions'] guilt more extense than any thing but Thy mercie. **1847** EMERSON *Poems, Alphonso of Castile* 63 Men and gods are too extense;—Could you slacken and condense?

†**B.** *sb.* **a.** What is extended, an expanse. **b.** ? = EXTENSION (quot. 1630). *Obs.*

1614 SYLVESTER *Litt. Bartas* 583 Wee may not match the heav'n's extense Unto Thy Circle, infinite, immense. **1630** LANE *Sqr.'s Tale* 187 Meeke love and stern iustice so convert as each, in each, own scopes have to insert, as reason seeth cause to make extense.

Hence **exˈtensely** *adv.*

1626 W. SCLATER *Expos. 2 Thess.* (1629) 144 This comming of the Lord is not to bee taken in atoms, but extensely.

extensibility (ɛkˌstɛnsɪˈbɪlɪtɪ). [f. next: see -ITY. Cf. F. *extensibilité*.] The quality of being extensible; capability of being extended.

a. Capacity of being stretched out to greater length or area.

a **1640** J. BALL *Power Godl.* II. v. (1657) 145 Water..is a..moist body, greater then the earth if we respect naturall extensibility. **1662** BOYLE *Acc. Freezing* Wks. 1772 II. 706 A copper box..which did bear three several freezings, by reason of the great extensibility of that metal. **1711** GREW *Cosm. Sacra* II. v. 54 In what precise manner they are Mixed, so as to give a Fiber Extensibility..who can say? **1871** B. STEWART *Heat* §173 An increase of temperature affects also the extensibility of bodies.

b. in immaterial sense.

1826 *Blackw. Mag.* XIX. 448 An extensibility of power, all but boundless. **1881** WHITNEY *Mixt. Lang.* 9 A pure scientific induction..dependent for..its extensibility to further cases..upon the number..of the cases already observed.

extensible (ɛkˈstɛnsɪb(ə)l), *a.* [a. Fr. *extensible*, ad. L. **extensibil-is*, f. *extens-* ppl. stem of *extendĕre* to EXTEND.]

1. Of a material object: **a.** Capable of being extended in any dimension or direction. **b.** Capable of being protruded; = EXTENSILE 2.

1611 COTGR., *Extensible*, extensible; which may be extended, or drawne out in length. **1656** in BLOUNT *Glossogr.* **1669** HOLDER *Speech* 163 The Malleus, being fixed to an extensible Membrane, follows the Traction of the Muscle, and is drawn inwards. **1671** J. WEBSTER *Metallogr.* xiii. 200 This perfect Metal..extensible like unto Gold. **1767** GOOCH *Treat. Wounds* I. 161 An artery is an extensible, elastic tube. **1828** STARK *Elem. Nat. Hist.* I. 87 Lips extremely long and extensible. **1836** TODD *Cycl. Anat.* I. 148/1 The skin is more pliant and extensible. **1882** VINES *Sachs' Bot.* 796 A layer of tissue..so extremely extensible. *fig.* **1871** tr. *Lange's Comm. Jerem.* 138 Our patience and steadfastness are as elastic and extensible as our faith is firm.

2. Of an immaterial object: Capable of being enlarged in scope or meaning.

1654 HAMMOND *Answ. Animadv. Ignat.* iii. §4. 76 If Lombard's words should..be thought farther extensible. **1665** GLANVILL *Sceps. Sci.* xiv. 87 And that Love is blind, is extensible beyond the object of Poetry. **1755** in JOHNSON. **1775** in ASH. **1875** WHITNEY *Life Lang.* ii. 20 A system which is extensible to everything short of infinity. **1890** *Spectator* 18 Jan., Italy..has acquired..an indefinite but extensible protectorate over Abyssinia.

Hence **exˈtensibleness**, the quality of being extensible; extensibility.

1727 in BAILEY vol. II. **1755** in JOHNSON. **1877** E. CAIRD *Philos. Kant* II. xvii. 601 There is no contradiction between finite extent, and infinite extensibleness.

extensile (ɛkˈstɛnsaɪl, -ɪl), *a.* [f. L. *extens-* ppl. stem of *extendĕre* to EXTEND + -ILE.]

1. Capable of being stretched out; extensible.

1744 ARMSTRONG *Preserv. Health* II. 55 *note*, As these small vessels become solid, the larger must of course grow less extensile. **1831** R. KNOX *Cloquet's Anat.* 603 It is connected with the neighbouring parts by an extensile cellular tissue. **1883** *Chamb. Jrnl.* 131 The capsules of its [a child's] joints [are] more extensile than ours.

2. Of the tongue, a tentacle, etc.: Capable of being protruded.

1802 BINGLEY *Anim. Biog.* (1813) I. 125 The tongue [is] cylindrical and extensile. **1858** T. R. JONES *Aquar. Nat.* 69 The Hydratuba..with thirty or more very extensile, flexible, slender tentacula. **1879** WALLACE *Australas.* iii. 56 A true honeysucker with an extensile tongue.

extension (ɛkˈstɛnʃən). Also 4–5 **extencioun**, 6 **extencion**, 6–7 **extention**. [The two forms *extention* (ME. *extencioun*) and *extension* are ad. L. *extentiōn-em*, *extensiōn-em*, n. of action f. *extendĕre* (pa. pples. *extentus*, *-tensus*) to EXTEND.]

1. The action of forcibly stretching or straining; strained state or condition.

†**a.** Stretching or pulling out to greater length. *Obs.*

1526 *Pilgr. Perf.* (W. de W. 1531) 114 b, Thynke on his extension or paynfull straynyng on the crosse. **1599** A. M. tr. *Gabelhouer's Bk. Physicke* 207/2 The Paralisis..and extention of the Synnues. **1646** SIR T. BROWNE *Pseud. Ep.* III. i. 105 That is an extension of the muscles and organs of motion maintaining the body at length. **1656** tr. *Hobbes' Elem. Philos.* (1839) 344 Removed from their places by forcible compression or extension. **1824** TREDGOLD *Ess. Strength Cast Iron* p. x, Experiments on the extension of bodies..when the strain exceeds the elastic force.

b. *Surg.* (See quot. 1860.)

1612 WOODALL *Surg. Mate* Wks. (1653) 154 You must use extention almost to every Dislocation. **1676** WISEMAN *Chirurg. Treat.* VII. i. 467 The extension made, the extenders are to be loosened gently. **1753** CHAMBERS *Cycl. Supp.* s.v., When the fractured parts recede from one another, some degree of Extension is necessary. **1860** MAYNE *Exp. Lex.*, *Extension*, the pulling of a fractured limb in a direction away from the trunk, in order to obviate retraction of the lower fragments; also applied to similar treatment in dislocations. **1884** *Syd. Soc. Lex.*, *Extension apparatus*, In case of hip-joint disease extension is employed ..to prevent the contact of the two diseased surfaces.

†**c.** The action of straining the capacity of a vessel, etc.; distension, swelling. *Obs.*

c **1400** *Lanfranc's Cirurg.* 98 Þat may be knowen..bi reednesse & extencioun of þe face. **1533** ELYOT *Cast. Helthe* IV. iv. (1572) 78 b, An heuinesse with extencion or thrustinge out of the body. **1626** BACON *Sylva* (1627) vii. 171 Fulnesse of Meat..causeth an Extension of the Stomacke. **1662** R. MATHEW *Unl. Alch.* §106. 173 This Powder you may use in all Diseases where Humors do offend..or extention above Nature.

†**d.** Straining (of the voice). *Obs.*

a **1653** GOUGE *Comm. Hebr.* v. 7 We take 'crying' for extension of voice.

e. The utmost lengthening of a horse's stride at a particular pace.

1951 G. A. BENNETT *Let's All enjoy Horse Show* xii. 107 These exercises are primarily intended to test the horse's extensions. **1953** G. BROOKE *Introd. Riding* vii. 72 Extension signifies that a horse is taking its fullest stride at whatever pace it may be moving.

2. a. The action of straightening out, or of placing at full length.

1615 CROOKE *Body of Man* 741 The second motion of the Muscle is Extention, which is not proper but aduentitious or accidentall: for when the contracted Muscle is extended it is loosened by another and not by it selfe. **1667** E. KING in *Phil. Trans.* II. 426 You may perceive a feeble motion of flexion and extension. **1872** HUXLEY *Phys.* vii. 174 The levers..are capable of performing..flexion and extension; a limb is extended, when it is straightened out.

b. The action of adding up a horizontal line of figures or computing a sub-total, as on an invoice; the figure thus obtained. Cf. EXTEND *v.* 2 c.

1861 F. H. CARTER *Book-keeping* iii. 40 The book..should be ruled with the debtor and creditor columns on the same page,..no necessity existing for an extension of periodical balances. **1891** G. VAN DE LINDE *Bookkeeping* iii. 88 An extension money column for the total Interest charged.

c. *Ballet.* The stretching of the leg at an angle from the body.

1934 WEBSTER, *Extension*, in fancy dancing, a posture with one leg extended. **1952** KERSLEY & SINCLAIR *Dict. Ballet Terms* 64 An 'extended' position can look beautiful with dancers of the *jarreté* type who are loose enough to sustain such a position without straining too noticeably and are therefore said to have a good 'extension'. **1957** *Ballet Ann.* XI. 130/1 She has some lovely high, sustained extensions.

3. The reaching or stretching (the arm, hand) out or forth; protrusion (of the tongue, etc.).

1741 BETTERTON *Eng. Stage* v. 67 This Extension of the Hand [upwards] sometimes signifies Pacification.

4. *Law.* The 'extending' of a protest: see EXTEND 9 c.

1889 *Case Bp. Lincoln* (1891) 51 On which day Brooks and Jenkins..in extension of such their Protest alleged, etc.

5. The fact or condition of extending or reaching to a certain distance or in a certain direction.

1790 JAS. BRUCE *Source Nile* I. I. iii. 52 We entered a large and thick wood of palm-trees, whose greatest extension seemed to be south by east. **1856** KANE *Arct. Expl.* I. xxiii. 309 Showing..the former extension of the Esquimaux race to the higher north.

6. a. The action or process of spreading out in area; the condition of being so spread out. †Also *concr.* A 'stretch', expanse (of country).

1684 T. BURNET *Th. Earth* I. I. vii. 86 This Foundation of the Earth upon the Waters, or extension of it above the Waters, doth agree to the antediluvian earth. **1786** GILPIN *Mts. & Lakes* (1788) II. 76 This extension of wild country we looked at with regret.

†**b.** Mode of extending superficially. *Obs.*

1570 BILLINGSLEY *Euclid* I. def. vii. 2 A plaine superficies, is the shortest extension..from one lyne to an other.

†**c.** Extensibility; capability of being extended (by dilution). *Obs.*

1594 PLAT *Jewell-ho., Chem. Concl.* 45 That infinite extention of the glasse of Antimonie.

†**7. a.** The amount of space throughout which anything extends; size, extent. *Obs.*

1614 SELDEN *Titles Hon.* 14 There were..some Monarchique States, but not of any large extension perhaps. **1677** HALE *Prim. Orig. Man.* II. vii. 187 The quantity or extension of the Body of the Air..commonly called the Atmosphere. *a* **1693** R. HOOKE in Sir T. P. Blount *Nat. Hist.* (1693) 202 Though I kept it..red-hot..yet it seem'd not at all to have diminish'd its extention. **1708** J. CHAMBERLAYNE *St. Gt. Brit.* I. III. x. (1743) 204 The City of London is of a vast extention.

b. *Physics* and *Metaph.* The property of being extended or of occupying space; spatial magnitude.

1624 GATAKER *Transubst.* 162 As if locall extension..and other..sensible properties could not..be severed from his owne bodie. **1647** H. MORE *Immort. Soul* II. iii. IV. 35 Extension That's infinite implies a contradiction. **1690** LOCKE *Hum. Und.* II. iv. §5 The Extension of Body, being nothing but the cohesion or continuity of solid, separable, moveable Parts; and the Extension of Space, the continuity of unsolid, unseparable and immoveable Parts. **1816** J. SMITH *Panorama Sc. & Art.* I. 270 Extension is another property of matter inseparable from its existence. **1855** H. SPENCER *Princ. Psychol.* II. VI. xi. 147 Our perceptions of the specific extension of the body—its size and shape.

c. An extended body or space.

1739 HUME *Hum. Nat.* II. ii. (1874) I. 337 If..any finite extension be infinitely divisible..a finite extension contains an infinite number of parts. **1813** SHELLEY *Q. Mab* VI. 231 A shrine is raised to thee..The sensitive extension of the world. **1836-7** SIR W. HAMILTON *Metaph.* xxvii. (1859) II. 160 The whole primary objects of sight, then, are colours and extensions, and forms or figures of extension.

8. a. Of immaterial things: The range over which anything extends; degree of extensiveness.

1604 T. WRIGHT *Passions* v. 293 The extension or varietie [of the obiects of delight] taketh away a certaine distastfull loathsomenesse which one kind of vniforme pleasure draweth with it. **1605** CAMDEN *Rem.* (1637) 21 This tongue is of that extension at this present, that it reacheth from Suiserland..over all ancient Germany. **1651** HOBBES *Govt. & Soc.* xvii. §26. 330 A Christian City cannot be excommunicated, for a Christian City is a Christian Church ..and of the same extension. **1761** JENYNS *Immort. Soul* I. 123 Rate not th' extension of the human mind By the Plebeian standard of mankind. **1782** SIR J. REYNOLDS *Disc.* xi. (1876) 36 The same extension of mind which gives the excellence of genius. **1846** MILL *Logic* Introd. §7 The extension of Logic as a Science is determined by its necessities as an Art.

b. *esp.* in *Logic.* Of a term or concept: Its range as measured by the number of objects which it denotes or contains under it. Opposed to *intension* or *comprehension.*

[**1677** HALE *Primitive Origination of Mankind* IV. iii. 311 God's Perfections are infinite both in extention and intention.] **1725** WATTS *Logic* I. iii. §3 The Extension of an universal Idea regards all the particular Kinds and single Beings that are contained under it..So a Bowl, in its Extension, includes a wooden Bowl, a brass Bowl, etc. *Ibid.* III. ii. §2 In all affirmative propositions, the predicate has no greater extension than the subject; for its extension is restrained by the subject. **1864** BOWEN *Logic* iv. 66 It denotes a number of objects..This is its Quantity of Extension. **1876** JEVONS *Logic Prim.* 22 War-screw-steam-ship is a still narrower term, that is, has much less extension.

9. Enlargement. **a.** Increase in length; prolongation, lengthening; *spec.* in a camera, the distance by which the front part carrying the lens can be drawn away from the back part carrying the photo-sensitive surface. Also *attrib.*

1796-7 *Instr. & Reg. Cavalry* (1813) 216 Some small increase of distances between squadrons may be permitted ..and whatever extension is thereby occasioned, will be immediately corrected. **1839** MURCHISON *Silur. Syst.* I. xxxiv. 452 A considerable extension is given to the limestone. **1880** HIPKINS in Grove *Dict. Mus.* II. 719/1 Broadwood..having carried the compass of the grand piano up to F, found that the wrestplank was so much weakened by this extension that [etc.]. **1893** *Jrnl. Soc. Arts* XLI. 3 Mar. 381/1 With this form of lens system there can be only one definite extension of camera..in which the entire system is aplanatic. **1958** M. L. HALL *Newnes' Compl. Amat. Photogr.* xxiii. 199 Miniature cameras..use extension tubes ..between the lens and the camera body.

b. *concr.* An extended portion; *esp.* an additional section, a prolongation (of a railway, or the like). Also (orig. *U.S.*), an addition to (esp. the rear of) a house or other building, usually not so high as the main building; an annex.

1852 *Congress. Globe* 24 Mar. 845/2 A statement of the materials to be used in the construction..of the proposed extension [of the Capitol]. **1854** *Act 17-8 Vict.* c. cxxxiii, An Act to alter the Line of the London, Tilbury, and Southend Extension Railway. **1863** *Bradshaw's Railway Man.* §288. 271 By subsequent acts, an extension from Chepstow to Grange Court was authorised. **1867** [see *extension-room* in 10]. **1880** HAUGHTON *Phys. Geog.* vi. 300 The Alpine Flora occupies the extension southwards of the Arctic regions. **1889** *Century Mag.* Mar. 781/1 They were making beds together in the extension. **1889** *Century Dict.* s.v., A dining-room extension. **1891** *Bradshaw's Railway Man.* §179. 231 The extension was opened for traffic on the 1st of March 1880. **1903** R. HALL *Pine Grove House* 12 The tin roof blew off the extension one windy night.

c. *Gram.* A word or words serving to amplify a subject or predicate; also an extended form (of a word) produced by the addition of a suffix.

d. Enlargement in duration. *spec.* Permission for the sale of alcoholic drinks until a later time than is usual at a particular place. Also *attrib.*, as ***extension night***.

extension of time: (*Comm.*) the concession by a creditor of a later date than that stipulated for the payment of a debt. Also in *Law*, a grant of additional time for the fulfilment of legal formalities.

a **1631** DONNE in *Select.* (1840) 30 This better resurrection is..an extension even of that eternity of happiness. **1880** HIPKINS in Grove *Dict. Mus.* II. 722/1 In 1835 Pierre Erard obtained an extension of his patent. **1923** WODEHOUSE *Inimitable Jeeves* xvi. 213 We will toddle along to Ciro's after dinner. It's an extension night, isn't it? **1930** A. BENNETT *Imperial Palace* lxiv. 522 I've seen enough alcohol drunk to-night to float a company. And I hear this is what you call your extension night, and you keep it up till two o'clock. **1936** 'G. ORWELL' *Diary* 15 Mar. in *Coll. Ess.* (1968) I. 200 About 200 people there, all busily tucking into beer and sandwiches, though it was only 4.30 pm—they had got an extension for the day. **1965** *New Statesman* 14 May 753/1 To mark the sense of public joy.., the nightclubs in Bonn have got a late extension until 11 p.m. **1967** *Listener* 7 Sept. 297/2 At Bath,..where the pubs normally shut at 10.30, they all have an extension till 11.

e. Enlargement in area.

1841-71 T. R. JONES *Anim. Kingd.* (ed. 4) 563 The extension of the shell is entirely effected by the margin of the mantle. **1854** *Act 17-8 Vict.* c. cxxv. (*title*), An Act for..the Extension of the Boundaries of the said Borough. **1884** BOWER & SCOTT *De Bary's Phaner. & Ferns* 581 When the normal cambium has begun its growth at the outer side of the ring of wood, radial extension..begins in a middle layer.

f. Enlargement in scope or operation.

1590 SWINBURNE *Testaments* 181 b, Which conclusion is diuersly..extended..The first extension is, that [etc.]. **1660** R. COKE *Power & Subj.* 222 The Sacriledge and extention of the civil Jurisdiction in giving the civil Magistrate licence to take cognizance of the publique Liturgy. **1791** BOSWELL *Johnson* an. 1712, What no child..could produce, without an extension of its faculties. **1844** H. H. WILSON *Brit. India* III. 164 The great extension of agriculture that followed the re-establishment of peace. **1853** O. GORDON in *Report Recomm. Oxf. Univ. Comm.* 198, I look for the extension of the University to the poor. **1862** SIR B. BRODIE *Psychol. Inq.* II. I. 7 A question whether..the extension of human knowledge really leads to an extension of human happiness.

g. ***University Extension***: the extending of the scope and work of the universities, *esp.* by affording some of the advantages of university teaching and examination to non-resident students. Also *attrib.* (freq. *ellipt.*), as (***university***) ***extension course, lecture, lecturer, student***. Also *transf.* and *fig.*

1850 MANSEL *Evid. Oxf. Univ. Comm.* 19, I do not think that any great scheme of University extension is practicable in the present day. **1867** *N. Brit. Rev.* Mar. XLVI. 224 The various schemes of University extension which have been suggested. **1871** J. STUART (*title*), A letter on University Extension. **1885** MOULTON *Univ. Extension Movement* 4 University Extension is mainly occupied with carrying, by itinerant teachers, University teaching to the doors of the people who cannot come up to the Universities. *Ibid.* 45 Chesterfield University Extension Association.. Northampton University Extension Society. *Ibid.* 27 To assign one-half of a winter's session to a University Extension Course..University Extension Certificates in Science subjects. **1890** MACKINDER & SADLER *University Extension* i. 37 Cambridge Extension Lecturers do much of the work at University College, Nottingham. *Ibid.* ii. 77 Patience to wait until the public mind had caught the desire for University Extension courses. *Ibid.* 79 Four Extension students. *Ibid.* iii. 92 The towns which find it most difficult to raise funds for Extension Lectures are generally those for which an experienced lecturer is most needed. **1892** E. J. JAMES in *Proc. First Ann. Mtg. Nat. Conf. on Univ. Extension* (Philad.) 29-31 Dec. 101 The University Extension Lecturer... There is no greater opportunity of showing his skill open to the Extension lecturer than is open to him in the conducting of a class [etc.]. **1934** C. DAY LEWIS *Hope for Poetry* vi. 29 Life for the average child of the twentieth century becomes an endless series of extension-lectures on everything under the sun. **1936** C. S. LEWIS *Allegory of Love* III. v. 142 It was the tendency of the age to make every lengthy poem something of an encyclopedia... It may be thought that this extension-lecture function of the medieval poets has nothing to do with their poethood. *Ibid.* 144 The roles of poet and extension lecturer are no longer habitually doubled. **1959** H. NIELSEN *Fifth Caller* xii. 178 His name was on the roster of an extension course in anthropology.

h. A subsidiary telephone, loudspeaker, etc., connected to, but placed at a distance from, the main instrument; also, the number of such a telephone. Freq. *attrib.*

1906 *Ann. Rep. Amer. Teleph. & Telegr. Co.* 14 There have been developed to a substantial extent new classes of service..such as..extension sets. **1908** *Sears, Roebuck Catal.* 204/1 Telephone Parts...80-ohm Extension Bell. **1914** A. B. SMITH & W. L. CAMPBELL *Automatic Telephony* iii. 82 Arrangements for connecting up a wall telephone with an extension. **1924** S. R. ROGET *Dict. Electr. Terms* 85 *Extension bell*, an additional bell arranged to ring at the same time as the ordinary telephone or other bell. *Ibid.*, *Extension lines*, lines radiating over a telephone installation from a private switchboard to the various extension instruments. **1928** *Delineator* July 78 Extension telephones are important in many other ways. **1959** A. LEJEUNE *Crowded & Dangerous* v. 56 You ring the War Office and ask for this extension. **1959** G. FREEMAN *Jack would be a Gentleman* iv. 66 She enjoyed owning the extension more than the actual telephone. **1966** N. FREELING *Dresden Green* I. 16 There was a record-player with an extension speaker. **1970** A. PRICE *Labyrinth Makers* ix. 125 Audley..[made] a reversed call to the department... Extension 28 eventually brought him Stocker.

10. *attrib.* **a.** (sense 1 b) as ***extension-apparatus, -splint***. **b.** (sense 2) as ***extension-motion***. **c.** (sense 9 a) as ***extension-ladder, -pedal, -table***, etc. **extension bag** *U.S.*, a bag that can be extended; **extension lens**, a lens that may be used in a combination to increase its focal length (see quot.). **d.** (sense 9 b) as ***extension-room***.

1874 KNIGHT *Dict. Mech.* I. 818/2 **Extension-apparatus*, an instrument designed to counteract the natural tendency of the muscles to shorten when a limb has been fractured or dislocated. **1897** *Outing* (U.S.) XXX. 386/1 Utensils and food for two days in an *extension bag. **1904** *Delineator* Oct. 547 With the genial season arrived every kind of drummer. They came with extension bags filled with samples. **1874** KNIGHT *Dict. Mech.* I. 818/2 **Extension-ladder*, a ladder having a movable section, which is projected in prolongation of the main section. **1902** *Nature* 17 July 280/1 The replacement of the back component by a lens of greater focal length, increasing the focal length of the objective by about 50 per cent. we referred to some time ago, the alternative back lens being known as an '*extension lens'. **1859** *Field Exerc. Infantry* I. §4. 7 In order to supple the soldier..the following *extension motions will be practised. **1867** F. H. LUDLOW *Brace of Boys* 288 He heard an earnest, boyish voice in the *extension-room. **1884** *Syd. Soc. Lex.*, **Extension splint*. **1864** WEBSTER **Extension table*, a table that can readily be extended or contracted in length. **1884** *N.Y. Herald* 27 Oct. 1/2 *Extension Top Phaetons.

extensional (ɛkˈstɛnʃənəl), *a.* [f. prec. + -AL[1].]

1. Of, pertaining to, or possessed of extension.

1647 H. MORE *Song of Soul* II. ii. III. xx, But that some virtue's not extentionall May thus be proved. **1667** —— *Div. Dial.* II. xxxiv. (1668) 149 You run always into these extensional Phantasms. **1773** in JOHNSON; whence in mod. Dicts.

2. *Logic.* Of, or relating to, logical extension (cf. EXTENSION 8 b); *esp.*, concerned with the objects denoted rather than with the predicates applied.

1852 H. L. MANSEL *Aldrich* (ed. 2) App. 221 In this respect it [*sc.* Aristotelian Induction] is synthetical, the parts and whole being viewed in their logical or extensional relation. **1903** B. RUSSELL *Princ. Math.* §68 Thus Brown and Jones are a class, and Brown singly is a class. This is the extensional genesis of classes. **1926** F. P. RAMSEY in *Proc. London Math. Soc.* XXV. 348 In calling mathematics extensional we mean that it deals not with predicates but with classes, not with relations in the ordinary sense but with possible correlations, or 'relations in extension'.

extensionality (ɛkstɛnʃəˈnælɪtɪ). *Philos.* [f. EXTENSIONAL *a.* + -ITY.] The state or fact of being extensional (see prec.). So ***thesis of extensionality*** (see quot. 1956).

1926 F. P. RAMSEY in *Proc. London Math. Soc.* XXV. 348 The difficulties of the tautology theory..spring from a fundamental characteristic of modern analysis which..may be called *extensionality*, and the difficulties may be explained as those which confront us if we try to reduce a calculus of extensions to a calculus of truth-functions. **1937** A. SMEATON tr. *Carnap's Logical Syntax Lang.* IV. §67. 245 The Thesis of Extensionality. Wittgenstein..put forward the thesis that every sentence is 'a truth-function of the elementary sentences' and therefore (in our terminology) extensional in relation to partial sentences. **1944** K. GÖDEL in P. A. Schilpp *Philos. B. Russell* 137 The axiom of extensionality (i.e., that no two different properties belong to exactly the same things). **1956** J. O. URMSON *Philos. Analysis* I. ii. 12 This thesis that language is throughout truth-functional was often called the thesis of extensionality. Every statement anyone ever makes must, according to this thesis.., be either a logically simple statement or else a truth-function of such statements.

extensionally (ɛkˈstɛnʃənəlɪ), *adv.* [See -LY[2].] By way of extension.

1903 *Nature* 3 Sept. 411/1 A class may be defined either extensionally, by an enumeration of its terms, or intensionally, by the concept which denotes its terms. **1935** *Mind* XLIV. 152 An abstract deductive structure capable of interpretation not only extensionally, for example as the traditional two-valued calculus of truth-values, but also intensionally, as a calculus of unasserted propositional meanings. **1951** Z. S. HARRIS *Methods in Struct. Ling.* 17 The element *X* is thus associated with an extensionally defined class consisting of so many features in so many of the speech occurrences in his [*sc.* the linguist's] corpus. **1964** E. BACH *Introd. Transformational Gram.* vii. 155 Like classes, relations can be considered intensionally or extensionally.

extensionist (ɛkˈstɛnʃənɪst). [f. as EXTENSIONAL *a.* + -IST.] **a.** One who advocates the extension of anything. **b.** A member of the Association for the Extension of University Teaching. *colloq.* A University Extension student, *esp.* one attending the 'Summer Meeting' begun in Oxford in 1888.

1864 in WEBSTER. **1879** H. RICHARD in *Daily News* 11 Dec. 3/1 County suffrage extensionists.

extensionless (ɛkˈstɛnʃənlɪs), *a.* [-LESS.] Without extension.

1919 A. N. WHITEHEAD *Enq. Princ. Nat. Knowledge* 112 An extensionless moment of time. **1922** tr. *Wittgenstein's Tractatus* 153 The I in solipsism shrinks to an extensionless point.

extensity (ɛkˈstɛnsɪtɪ). [f. L. *extens-us* (see EXTENSE) + -ITY.] The quality of having (a certain) extension; in *Psychol.* of the breadth of sensation, as opposed to intensity (see quot. 1886).

a **1834** COLERIDGE in *Blackw. Mag.* (1882) CXXXI. 125/2 Intensity and extensity combinable only by blessed spirits. **1874** CARPENTER *Ment. Phys.* I. i. §25 Its intensity is in a precisely inverse ratio to its extensity. **1886** J. WARD in *Encycl. Brit.* XX. 46 In our organic sensations, we can distinguish..variations of quality, of intensity, and of what Dr. Bain has called massiveness, or, as we will say, extensity.

This last characteristic..is..an essential element in our perception of space.

extensive (ɛk'stɛnsɪv), *a.* [ad. late L. *extensīvus*, f. *extendĕre* (pa. pple. *extensus*): see EXTEND and -IVE. Cf. F. *extensif.*]

†**1.** Capable of being extended; extensible. *Obs.*

1610 B. JONSON *Alch.* II. iii, These two [sulphur and mercury] Make the rest ductile, malleable, extensiue. **1656** in BLOUNT *Glossogr.* *a* **1691** BOYLE (J.), Silver beaters chuse the finest coin, as..most extensive under the hammer.

†**2. a.** Tending to cause extension or stretching out. *Obs. rare*$^{-1}$.

1646 SIR T. BROWNE *Pseud. Ep.* III. i. 105 Station is..one kinde of motion..which Physitians..doe name extensive or tonicall.

b. That has the effect of extending or enlarging in scope.

1832 AUSTIN *Jurispr.* (1879) II. xxxiii. 597 This bastard extensive interpretation *ex ratione juris* is frequently styled 'analogical'.

3. a. Of material things: Extending over or occupying a large surface or space; having a wide extent, widely extended. Of capital, purchases, etc.: Large in amount.

1706 PHILLIPS (ed. Kersey), *Extensive*..that Extends, or Reaches far. **1774** PENNANT *Tour Scot. in 1772*, 357 The extensive plantations..round his lands. **1776** ADAM SMITH *W.N.* I. iii. I. 19 By means of water-carriage a more extensive market is opened. **1845** BUDD *Dis. Liver* 28 Along the extensive mucous tract..absorption is constantly going on. **1849–50** ALISON *Hist. Europe* VII. xlii. §53. 134 Extensive capital had..been sunk in the traffic. *a* **1859** MACAULAY *Hist. Eng.* V. xxiii. 71 That empire..was the most extensive that had ever obeyed a single chief. **1872** RAYMOND *Statist. Mines & Mining* 283 Extensive silver veins and deposits.

b. Of immaterial things: Far-reaching, large in comprehension or scope; wide in application or operation; comprehensive; also, lengthy, full of detail. † *extensive to*: that extends to, applicable to, comprehensive of.

1605 BACON *Adv. Learn.* I. iv. §5 The reprehension of Saint Paul was..extensive to all knowledge. **1651** BAXTER *Inf. Bapt.* 105, I am bound to take scripture in the most extensive sence. *a* **1748** WATTS *Improv. Mind* II. i, An extensive survey of the branches of any science. **1754** EDWARDS *Freed. Will* III. iv. 165 Inability..may be more general and extensive to all Acts of that Kind. **1756** BURKE *Vind. Nat. Soc.* Wks. 1842 I. 14 A piece of flagrant and extensive wickedness. **1846** J. BAXTER *Libr. Pract. Agric.* (ed. 4) I. p. ix, Our limits will not permit us to indulge in extensive quotation. **1863** H. COX *Instit.* III. viii. 705 The Mutiny Act constitutes an extensive code of martial law.

c. So of persons, their faculties, etc. *Obs.* or *rare.*

a **1631** DONNE 6 *Serm.* i. (1634) 2 A Livie or a Guicciardine or such extensive and voluminous authours. **1719** DE FOE *Crusoe* (1840) II. vi. 128 He was extensive in his charity. **1725** POPE *Odyss.* XI. 138 The God of day, Who all surveys with his extensive eye. **1749** BERKELEY *Word to Wise* Wks. III. 448 Idleness, that extensive parent of many miseries and many sins. **1768** GILPIN *Ess. Prints* 67 In a word, he was..a Man of a very extensive genius.

d. *Econ.* Applied to methods of cultivation in which a relatively small crop is obtained from a large area with a minimum of attention and expense; opp. INTENSIVE *a.* 5.

1832 [see INTENSIVE *a.* 5]. **1949** P. E. JAMES *Geogr. of Man* 60 Where the expenditure of labor and capital per unit of land is relatively small, the economy is said to be *extensive.*

4. Of or pertaining to extension (in sense 7 b); characterized by, or possessed of, extension; occupying space.

1624 GATAKER *Transubst.* 114 Unlesse his bodie had therein a corporall, extensive and sensible manner of existing. **1877** E. CAIRD *Philos. Kant* II. xi. 442 Space and time are necessarily represented as extensive quanta. **1886** J. WARD in *Encycl. Brit.* XX. 53 We do not first experience a succession of touches..by means of movements, and then, when these impressions are simultaneously presented, regard them as extensive because they are associated with..the original series of movements.

5. Of or pertaining to extension (in sense 8 b); denoting a large number of objects. Opposed to *intensive.*

1686 GOAD *Celest. Bodies* II. xiii. 333 This haps mostly when there wants of Assistance, Extensive or Intensive. **1725** WATTS *Logic* I. vi. §13 This Art teaches us to distribute any extensive Idea into its different Kinds or Species. **1837–8** SIR W. HAMILTON *Logic* xv. (1866) I. 272 Every notion has not only an Extensive, but likewise an Intensive quantity.

extensively (ɛk'stɛnsɪvlɪ), *adv.* [f. prec. + -LY².] In an extensive manner.

1. Widely, largely; to a great extent; on a large scale; with a wide range.

1730–6 in BAILEY (folio). **1741** WATTS *Improv. Mind* I. xvi. §3 'Tis impossible for any to pass a right judgement concerning them, without..surveying them extensively. **1804** L. MURRAY *Eng. Grammar* Advt., He may..indulge a hope, that the book will be still more extensively approved and circulated. **1841–71** T. R. JONES *Anim. Kingd.* (ed. 4) 298 Numerous arterial canals..ramify extensively in the surrounding structures. **1879** LUBBOCK *Sci. Lect.* v. 158 A period when bronze was extensively used for..implements.

2. In extent or scope; with respect to range of application. Often opposed to *intensively.* † *extensively with*: so as to be co-extensive with.

1645 E. CALAMY *Indictm. agst. Eng.* 3 Christ here sets out the greatnesse of the ruine..and that both Intensively, and Extensively. *a* **1661** FULLER *Worthies, Westminster* (1811) II. 103 Let it [Westminster] be taken..extensively with the Liberty of Lancaster from Temple Bar, and it filleth as much ground [etc.]. **1713** *Lond. Gaz.* No. 5119/2 A Peace so extensively great in all its Circumstances. **1794** MATHIAS *Purs. Lit.* (1798) 380 The most extensively learned book I ever saw. **1836** J. GILBERT *Chr. Atonem.* iii. (1852) 64 As *truly* we say, not as extensively; but in considering the *justice* of such substitution, the extent is of no moment. **1855** BAIN *Senses & Int.* III. iii. §7 Increase of resemblance extensively ..has the same power as increase of resemblance intensively, in rendering the restoration of the past more certain.

b. In extension (in Logic); with respect to extension. See EXTENSION 8 b.

1837 SIR W. HAMILTON *Logic* viii. (1866) I. 146 A notion is extensively great in proportion to the greater number..of determinations or attributes it contains under it. **1864** BOWEN *Logic* viii. 237 Reasoning Extensively, we say, men are a part or class of responsible agents, and are, therefore, also a part of free agents.

3. With respect to extension (or the quality of occupying space). See EXTENSION 7 b.

1888 G. C. ROBERTSON in *Mind* July 423 By more complex efforts..we distinguish this and that extensively within such body.

ex'tensiveness. [f. as prec. + -NESS.] The quality or fact of being extensive.

1. Extensive character or nature; widespread range; comprehensiveness, breadth; also, the dimensions to which a thing is extended; extent.

1639 SIR R. BAKER in Spurgeon *Treas. Dav.* Ps. cxxx. 6 Of the extensiveness [of our watching] there can be none [question]. **1666** J. SERJEANT *Let. of Thanks* 99 Tradition, when a Heresy arises, gains more of Intensitiveness and vigor than it loses in it's Extensiveness. **1726** LEONI tr. *Alberti's Archit.* II. 28 b, A sufficient number of Columns for the extensiveness of their area. **1796** MORSE *Amer. Geog.* I. 260 The extensiveness of the uses to which the article can be applied. **1880** T. HARDY *Trumpet-Major* III. xxxv. 127 Her interests had grandly developed..to an extensiveness truly European.

†**2.** The fact of being extended; wide diffusion.

1656 JEANES *Fuln. Christ* 215 The bounty and liberality of men may be disinabled, by extensivenesse unto too many. **1768** HEWSON *Lymph. System* in *Phil. Trans.* LVIII. 223 The extensiveness of this system through so many classes of animals.

†**3.** Capability of being extended or dilated.

1691 RAY *Creation* I. (1704) 30 We take notice of the wonderful dilatability or extensiveness of the Throats..of Serpents. **1708** W. KING *Cookery* i, What extensiveness can there be in their souls. **1755** in JOHNSON. **1818** in TODD.

4. = EXTENSITY.

1887 W. JAMES in *Mind* Jan. 2 Extensiveness, being an entirely peculiar kind of feeling..can itself receive no other name than that of sensational element.

extensometer (ɛkstɛn'sɒmɪtə(r)). [f. L. *extensus*, pa. pple. of *extendere* to EXTEND + -OMETER.] An instrument for measuring the deformation of metal under stress, or an instrument in which such deformation is used to register the elastic strains borne by other materials (*e.g.* concrete); (see also quot. 1958).

1887 *Proc. Physical Soc.* VIII. 183 Screw-Micrometer Extensometer. **1902** *Encycl. Brit.* XXXIII. 10/1 Extensometers, or apparatus for observing the small deformation which a test-piece in tension or compression undergoes before its limit of elasticity is reached. **1925** E. S. ANDREWS *Strength of Materials* (ed. 2) 371 Extensometers are instruments for measuring the elastic strains of materials in tension or compression. **1950** *Engineering* 25 Aug. 172/3 Twin extensometers were mounted in a manner similar to that employed in tests on reinforced-concrete beams using the Lamb extensometer. **1958** *New Scientist* 15 May 38/3 Earth strains in the Andes are to be studied by.. seismologists working with 'extensometers'... The extensometer or strain-seismograph measures the differential motion between two nearby points, those at the ends of the instrument. The change of length between the two ends—which may either stretch or squeeze—divided by the original length gives the change in strain. **1966** *Ibid.* 23 June 796/2 A hydraulic extensometer sensitive to dimensional changes in the order of one part in 10 000.

extensor (ɛk'stɛnsə(r)), *sb.* [a. late L. *extensor*, agent-n. f. *extendĕre* to EXTEND.]

1. A muscle which serves to extend or straighten out any part of the body. Opposed to *flexor.*

[**1706** PHILLIPS (ed. Kersey), *Extensor Digitorum Communis*..a Muscle of the Fingers.] **1713** DERHAM *Phys.-Theol.* v. ii. (1747) 286 *note*, The *peronæus Longus* helps to.. direct the Power of the other Extensors towards the Ball of the great Toe. **1748** HARTLEY *Observ. Man* I. ii. 245 The Limbs have both long and short Flexors and Extensors. **1870** ROLLESTON *Anim. Life* 14 The long radial extensor of the metacarpus.

2. *attrib.* in ***extensor-muscle***; also **extensor-surface**, the surface of a bone to which the extensor muscles are attached.

1830 R. KNOX *Béclard's Anat.* 317 The contrary takes place with respect to the extensor muscles. **1859** DARWIN *Orig. Spec.* vi. (1878) 139 This flank membrane is furnished with an extensor muscle. **1881** MIVART *Cat* 94 Its anterior or extensor surface is grooved for the passage of tendons.

extensory (ɛk'stɛnsərɪ), *a. rare.* [f. L. type **extensōrius*, f. *extendĕre*: see EXTEND and -ORY.] Of the nature of or tending to extension.

1885 G. CLEVELAND in *Ann. Messenger* Dec., Following out the intimation given by me when the extensory arrangement above described was negotiated.

‖**ex'tensum.** *rare*$^{-1}$. [L.; neut. of *extensus*, pa. pple. of *extendĕre* to EXTEND.] An extended body; a body possessed of extension.

1678 CUDWORTH *Intell. Syst.* v. 825 To suppose every Soul to be but one Physical Minimum, or Smallest Extensum, is to imply..an Essential Difference in Matter or Extension.

†**ex'tensure.** *Obs.* [f. L. *extens-* ppl. stem of *extendĕre* to EXTEND + -URE. Cf. EXTENDURE.]

a. The condition of being extended or strained. **b.** The action of stretching or spreading out; in quot. *concr.* **c.** Extent.

1594 *Zepheria* xxxvi. in Arb. *Garner* V. 84 Mistrust.. Hath my crime racked, yet to more high extensure. **1604** DRAYTON *Owle* 36 A goodly Tree; Under th' extensure of whose Lordly Armes, The small Birds warbled their harmonious Charmes. **1631** WEEVER *Anc. Fun. Mon.* 866 A smooth plaine..some two miles in extensure.

extent (ɛk'stɛnt), *sb.* Also 5 **astent**. [ME. *extente*, a. AF. *extente, estente* (= med.L. *extenta*), fem. pa. pple. of *estendre* to EXTEND used subst. (cf. mod.Fr. *étendue*) in various senses; (1) extent in space, (2) superficial area, (3) valuation; f. *estendre* (F. *étendre*):—L. *extendĕre*: see EXTEND.]

I. 1. *Hist.* **a.** The valuation of land or other property; *esp.* such a valuation made for the purpose of taxation; assessment; an instance of this. **b.** The value assigned to such land or property; assessed value; = STENT. ***old extent, new extent*** (see quots.).

[**1292** BRITTON III. vii. §5 La estente soit fete en ceste manere. En primes soit enquis par serment des jurours, cum bien les edifices et chief maner..vaillent par an de cleer.] *c* **1330** R. BRUNNE *Chron.* (1810) 83 William wist of alle what it suld amounte, Of lordyng & of thralle þe extente þorgh acounte. **1424** *Sc. Acts Jas. I*, §10 That all schirefis be sworne..that thai sall lelely and treuly ger this extent be fulfillit of all the landis and gudis. **1479** *Acta Audit.* 89 (Jam.) That Dauid Halyday..sal bruk and joyse the xs worth of land of ald astent of Dalruskel. **1540** *Act 32 Hen. VIII*, c. 5 Such Lands..have been by reasonable Extent to them delivered in execution for the satisfaction of their said debts. **1597** SKENE *De Verb. Sign.*, Extent of landes, signifies the rents, profites, and issues of the samin, quhair of there is twa kindes, the auld extent, and the new extent. *Ibid.* s.v. *Extent*, Ane vther taxation and extent was maid in the time of peace..quhilk therefore is called the new or second extent. **1682** WARBURTON *Hist. Guernsey* (1822) 75 The extent of the King's revenue in the island, taken 5 Edw. III. 1331, gives an account..of all the lands, rents, and duties belonging to the King. **1778** PENNANT *Tour Wales* (1883) I. 23 [Coals] were discovered in the township..as early as the time of Edward I, as appears by an extent of that place, in.. his reign. **1872** E. W. ROBERTSON *Hist. Ess.* 140 The valuation of Bagimont..became the standard..of ecclesiastical assessment..lay lands remaining at the earlier standard known..as the Old Extent.

†**c.** A tax levied on such a valuation. *Obs.*

1597 SKENE *De Verb. Sign.* s.v. *Extent*, They suld baith make personall service, and also pay extent or taxation. **1746–7** *Act 20 Geo. II*, c. 50 §2 Lands..liable to the annual payment of the new extent or retour duty.

2. *Law.* **a.** (In full ***writ of extent***): A writ to recover debts of record due to the Crown, under which the body, lands, and goods of the debtor may be all seized at once to compel payment of the debt. ***extent in aid, in chief*** (see quots.).

1630 J. TAYLOR (Water P.) *Wks.* I. 911 Her small shot are Arrests and Actions, her great Ordnance are Extents, outlawries and Executions. **1754** FIELDING *Voy. Lisbon* Wks. 1784 X. 256 He..was by extents from the Court of Exchequer, soon reduced below his original state. **1817** *Parl. Deb.* 761 Extents of the Crown were formidable to persons who became debtors of the Crown. **1848** WHARTON *Law Lex.* 242/1 Extent in chief..issues from the Court of Exchequer..It directs the sheriff to take an inquisition or inquest of office, on the oaths of lawful men, to ascertain the lands, etc. of the debtor, and seize the same into the Queen's hands. **1866** CRUMP *Banking* v. 111 A bill seized under an extent, for instance.

b. Seizure of lands, etc., in execution of a writ; the condition of being seized and held in satisfaction for debt, sequestration; also, the right of seizure; also = EXECUTION 7 b. In *U.S.* 'A levy of an execution upon real estate by metes and bounds' (Webster 1864).

1592 WEST *1st Pt. Symbol.* §104 c, By force of the said statute and extent. **1600** SHAKS. *A.Y.L.* III. i. 17 *Duke.* Push him out of dores And let my officers of such a nature Make an extente vpon his house and Lands. **1632** MASSINGER *City Madam* v. ii, An under-sheriff, who..will serve An extent on lords or lowns' land. **1768** [see EXTENDED 5]. **1776** FOOTE *Bankrupt* III. Wks. 1799 II. 134 They say an extent is brought into the house. *Ibid.* 138 Only an extent, to seize on all his effects. **1818** CRUISE *Digest* (ed. 2) II. 75 All such remedies to recover a moiety of the rent, as the cognizor himself might have had..before the extent. **1867** KNIGHT *Begg'd at Court* iv. 66 And is it come to this! An extent in my house. I must get a bed and a supper at the Bolt-in-Tun.

†**c.** *transf.* A predatory attack; an assault.

1594 ? GREENE *Selimus* Wks. (Grosart) XIV. 196 On all the world we make extent. **1601** SHAKS. *Twel. N.* IV. i. 57 In this vnciuill, and vniust extent Against thy peace.

†**3.** Rents, etc., arising from extended lands.
1303 R. BRUNNE *Handl. Synne* 6076 Persones, prestes, þan han here rente And ouþer þat han grete extente. *a***1626** BACON *Max. & Uses Com. Law* (1630) 78 All the propertie of their Goods..Wardships and Extents.

II. 4. 'Space or degree to which anything is extended' (J.). **a.** Of a material thing: The amount of space over which it extends; dimensions, compass, size; †a space or distance 'taken' with a pair of compasses.
1624 [see EXTEND *v.* 3]. **1634** SIR T. HERBERT *Trav.* 60 The greatest extent [of this Citie] from the South-east to North-west [is] neere three miles. **1667** MILTON *P.L.* VII. 496 The Serpent..Of huge extent. **1680** MORDEN *Geog. Rect.* Introd. (1685) 6 No Country doth in all parts of its Territories make use of the same extent in measuring. **1720** OZELL *Vertot's Rom. Rep.* I. I. 6 The Power of a State consists not so much in its Extent, as in the Number of its Inhabitants. **1794** J. H. MOORE *Pract. Navig.* (ed. 10) 60 That extent will reach from the departure 406 to the distance 449 miles. **1797–1804** BEWICK *Brit. Birds* (1847) I. 37 The Extent of its [the Kite's] wings is more than five feet. **1863** LYELL *Antiq. Man* 17 Such platforms must have been of considerable extent. **1881** JOWETT *Thucyd.* I. 235 The place..was in danger of having to capitulate owing to the extent of the wall.

b. Breadth of comprehension; width of application, operation, etc.; scope.
1594 HOOKER *Eccl. Pol.* I. viii. (1611) 21 In goodnesse..there is a latitude or extent. **1604** SHAKS. *Oth.* I. iii. 81 True, I haue married her; The verie head, and front of my offending, Hath this extent, no more. **1652** NEEDHAM tr. *Selden's Mare Cl.* 108 This Law, in the extent of it, reached as well to forraigners, as to the King's subjects. *a***1715** BURNET *Own Time* I. 285 He [Leighton] gave his vote for it, not having sufficiently considered the extent of the words. **1752** JOHNSON *Rambler* No. 208 ¶11 Whoever knows the English tongue in its present extent, will be able to express his thoughts. **1855** MACAULAY *Hist. Eng.* IV. 376 The Act..had not defined the extent of the power which was to be exercised by the Sovereign.

c. Phrases: *to a certain, great,* etc., *extent, to the (full) extent of.* Hence: the limit to which anything extends; *e.g.* in phr. *to reach the extent.*
1671 MILTON *P.R.* III. 406 If I..David's..full Scepter sway..To just extent over all Israel's sons. **1724** R. FALCONER *Adv. & Escapes* (1769) 2 You know..that my Fortune is but small, and I living to the Extent of it. **1754–64** SMELLIE *Midwif.* I. 174 The patient ought..to be blooded to the extent of eight or twelve ounces. **1844** *Mem. Babylonian P'cess* II. 90 Having reached the extent of our intended pilgrimage. **1850** MRS. STOWE *Uncle Tom's C.* xviii. 175 Hidden things of darkness were brought to light to an extent that alarmed all the..powers of kitchen and chamber. **1866** CRUMP *Banking* viii. 165 It [silver] is a legal tender only to the extent of 40*s.* **1875** JOWETT *Plato* (ed. 2) III. 236 He immediately becomes unjust to the full extent of his power.

d. *Logic.* = EXTENSION 8 b.
1656 tr. *Hobbes' Elem. Philos.* (1839) 20 For the understanding of the extent of an universal name, we need no other faculty but [etc.]. *a***1718** PENN *Tracts* Wks. 1726 I. 620 It [λογος] is a Word of the same Extent with Conversation. **1864** BOWEN *Logic* vii. 192 Not only is the Predicate of the Minor the Subject of the Conclusion and of less Extent than its own Subject.

5. *concr.* **a.** An extended space; the 'length and breadth'.
1627 DRAYTON *Battle Agincourt* xxviii, Those Territories, of whose large extent The English Kings were owners of before. **1690** LOCKE *Hum. Und.* II. i. §24 In all that great Extent wherein the Mind wanders. **1697** DRYDEN *Virg. Georg.* III. 531 Such an extent of Plains..Allures their Eyes. **1725** DE FOE *Voy. round World* (1840) 282 Let them see..what a vast extent of land we possess. **1737** GLOVER *Leonidas* v. 44 Th' imperial race That rul'd th' extent of Asia. **1825** WATERTON *Wand. S. Amer.* I. i. 88 Here you may see a sloping extent of noble trees. **1862** MARSH *Eng. Lang.* i. 11 They occupied only a small extent of England.

b. Something possessed of extension: see EXTENSION 7 b.
1871 FRASER *Life Berkeley* x. 371 I am..independent of the changing tastes..and coloured or resistant extents, which form my transitory sense-given phenomena.

†**6.** The action of extending. **a.** The showing or exercising (justice, kindness, etc.). *Obs.*
1588 SHAKS. *Tit. A.* IV. iv. 3 Was euer seene An Emperour in Rome thus ouerborne..and for the extent Of egall iustice, vs'd in such contempt? **1602** —— *Ham.* II. ii. 390 Gentlemen, you are welcom..The appurtenance of Welcome, is Fashion and Ceremony. Let me comply with you in the Garbe, lest my extent to the Players..should more appeare like entertainment then yours. **1635** SHIRLEY *Royal Master* I. i, My extent in all things Is but to bid you welcome.

†**b.** Enlargement in scope or operation. *Obs.*
1657 S. W. *Schism Dispach't* 502 To disacknowledge such extents of his Authority. **1668** HOWE *Bless. Righteous* (1825) 58 How pleasant to think, not only of the extents, but of the restraints of this power. **1719** W. WOOD *Surv. Trade* 77 Our Wealth [will] encrease in proportion..to the new Extents or Encouragements it [our trade] shall receive.

7. *Campanology.* (See quot. 1901.)
1901 H. E. BULWER *Gloss. Techn. Terms Bells* 14 *Extent.* (*a*) The full number of distinct 'changes', of which a 'method' admits, is the 'extent' of the 'method'. (*b*) The full number of times a bell, or some definite combination of bells, can occupy a given position, without repetition of any one of the 'changes' containing such bell, or bells, in that position. **1928** *Daily Tel.* 27 Nov. 10/7 Three 'extents' (i.e. 720 changes each) upon the six large bells there, in three different methods, 2,160 changes in all.

†**ex'tent,** *a. Obs.* [ad. L. *extent-us*, pa. pple. of *extendĕre* to EXTEND.]
1. Of the hand, etc.: Stretched out; held out. Of strength: Strained, exerted to the full.
1436 *Pol. Poems* (1859) II. 193 Oure kynge..Wyth swerde drawe, bryght and extente. **1590** SPENSER *F.Q.* II. vi. 61 Both his hands..Above the water were on high extent. **1664** *Flodden F.* viii. 78 The Admiral with strength extent, Then in the field fierce fighting was.

2. a. Continued or prolonged in length. **b.** Spread out in area. **c.** Possessed of extension.
1432–50 tr. *Higden* (Rolls) I. 297 Burguyn is a parte of Fraunce Cenonense to Alpes Pirene extente allemoste. *Ibid.* 321 Where trees be extente in altitude by a c. and xl^ti foote. **1633** P. FLETCHER *Purple Isl.* II. v, Whose matter..Thro' all the isle, and every part extent. **1641** *Songs Costume* (Percy Soc.) 171 Tell me no more that roarers waire Their hair extent below their ear. **1647** H. MORE *Song of Soul* II. i. II. lvi, Some be extended, others not extent.

†**ex'tent,** *v. Obs.* [f. L. *extent-* ppl. stem of *extendĕre* to EXTEND.]
1. *trans.* To assess, make an assessment of, for the purpose of taxation. *Sc.* = STENT.
1424 *Sc. Acts Jas. I*, §10 He sall cheiss lele men and discret ..gif thai haif doune thair deuoir at the end of the taxacione; and that alsa mony personys as may sufficiently extent þe cuntre.
b. *intr.* To be assessed.
1583 in Maitland *Hist. Edin.* III. (1753) 234 The Merchand, Prenteis, and sic Kynd of People as wer wont to extent with them..to pay at his Entrie..Threttie Shillings.
2. *trans.* To seize in satisfaction for debt.
1664 in *Rec. Soc. Lanc. & Cheshire* XI. 41 Plaintiffs estate in Lowton and Newton 'extented' upon judgments at the suit of defendant.

extention, obs. form of EXTENSION.

†**ex'tentionable,** *a. Obs.*^–0 [f. *extention* (see EXTENSION) + -ABLE.] = EXTENSIBLE.
1727 BAILEY vol. II, *Extentionable*, that may be stretched out large and wide.

†**ex'tentive,** *a. Obs. rare*^–1. [f. L. *extent-* ppl. stem of *extendĕre* to EXTEND + -IVE. Cf. EXTENSIVE.] = EXTENSIVE.
1658 J. HARRINGTON *Prerog. Pop. Govt.* II. v. (1700) 371 These had the whole extentive Power.

†**ex'tentor.** *Sc. Obs.* In 5 -our. [agent-n. f. *extendĕre* to EXTEND. Cf. late L. *extensor.*] 'An assessor; one who apportions a general tax' (Jam.); = STENT-MASTER.
1424 *Sc. Acts Jas. I*, §11 That the extentour salbe sworne befor the baronys of the srefdome that thai sall do thar full power to þe saide extent.

†**ex'tenuable,** *a. Obs. rare*^–1. [f. as if ad. L. **extenuābilis*, f. *extenuāre*: see EXTENUATE.] Capable of being extenuated or made less dense.
1662 J. CHANDLER *Van Helmont's Oriat.* 343 Water..is a Body..extenuable into a vapour.

†**ex'tenuant,** *a. Obs. rare*^–1. In 8 extenuent. [f. L. *extenuant-em*, pr. pple. of *extenuāre*: see next.] Extenuating.
1756 C. LUCAS *Ess. Waters* II. 65 All salts of this class are ..resolvent, extenuent, and, in some measure, septic.

†**ex'tenuate,** *ppl. a.* and *a. Obs.* [ad. L. *extenuāt-us*, pa. pple. of *extenuāre*: see next.]
a. Of the body or its parts: Shrunken, attenuated; whence, prostrated. **b.** Impoverished. **c.** Of a sound: Thin. Of a quality: Diminished; weakened. Of a number: Thinned out, reduced.
1528 GARDINER in Pocock *Rec. Ref.* I. l. 117 He is greatly extenuate therewith when it [gout] cometh. **1533** in Strype *Eccl. Mem.* I. App. xli. 107 By the same exaction of annates, bps. have been so extenuate that they have not been able..to repair their Churches. **1555** EDEN *Decades* 132 The number of the poore wretches is woonderfully extenuate. **1605** SYLVESTER *Du Bartas* II. III. iv. 1153 That same Majesty..Is not extinguisht nor extenuate. *a***1626** BACON *New Atl.* (1650) 31 Great sounds, Extenuate and sharpe. **1689** tr. *Buchanan's De Jure Regni apud Scotos* 9 The..Body is Cured..by nourishing that which is extenuate.

extenuate (ɛk'stɛnjuːeɪt), *v.* [f. L. *extenuāt-* ppl. stem of *extenuāre*, f. *ex-* (see EX- *pref.*^1) + *tenuis* thin. Cf. F. *exténuer.*]
I. To make thin, slender, or weak.
1. *trans.* To make (the body, flesh, a person) thin or lean; to render emaciated or shrunken. Somewhat *arch.*
1533 ELYOT *Cast. Helthe* III. xii. (1541) 66 Sorowe..dothe extenuate or make the body leane. **1650** H. BROOKE *Conserv. Health* 160 They that are fat may exercise *ad Sudorem*..and that will extenuate them. **1669** WOODHEAD *St. Teresa* II. 282 The flesh is extenuated every day more and more. **1717** J. KEILL *Anim. Oecon.* (1738) 292 Bodies..which are extenuated by Hunger. **1824** SOUTHEY *Bk. of Ch.* (1841) 182 It was deemed meritorious..to extenuate it [the body] by fasting. **1862** CARLYLE *Fred. Gt.* IX. vii, Extenuated with fatigues. **1887** LECKY *Eng. in 18th C.* V. xx. 385 Peasants were so extenuated by hunger that they could scarcely hold the spade.
†**2.** To draw out to thinness; to beat (metal) into thin plates. *Obs.*
1599 HAKLUYT *Voy.* II. II. 90 The Chinians can very cunningly beate and extenuate gold into plates and leaues. **1603** KNOLLES *Hist. Turks* (1621) 537 The straightnesse of the waies enforced the Turks to extenuat their rankes. **1655** W. F. *Meteors* 164 Gold..extenuated as fine as the threds in the Spiders web. **1681** GREW *Musæum* I. v. 85 His [the Sawfish's] body behind his head becomes..broad..from whence it is again extenuated all the way to the end of his Tail.
¶ To stretch out; also *intr.* ? Confused with *extend.*
1583 STUBBES *Anat. Abus.* (1877) 54 Rather abbreuiat oure dayes by manye yeres, than extenuate our liues one minut of an houre. **1601** CHESTER *Love's Mart.* vi. (1878) 81 The plaines..Whose fertill bounds farre doth extenuate.
3. To thin out in consistency, render less dense.
1559 MORWYNG *Evonym.*, Moist thinges put into a body by the force of heate are extenuated into a vapour. **1601** HOLLAND *Pliny* (1634) I. 431 To extenuate that grosse substance into which the Oliue had turned the..iuice and humor. **1638** G. SANDYS *Job* 46 He the congealed vapors melts againe Extenuated into drops of Raine. **1686** GOAD *Celest. Bodies* II. xii. 322 A misle of Vapour or Fume may be extenuated into some hundreds [of miles]. **1800** VINCE *Hydrostat.* vii. 81 Accumulating and extenuating the air.
†**b.** *spec.* in *Med.* To render thinner (the humours or concretions of the body, etc.); = ATTENUATE 2 b. *Obs.*
1563 HYLL *Art Garden.* (1593) 71 The seeds doe extenuate and diminishe the clammy and grosse humours. **1610** MARKHAM *Masterp.* II. clxxiii. 487 It extenuateth humors.
absol. **1533** ELYOT *Cast. Helthe* (1541) 27 a, Almondes do extenuate and clense. **1607** TOPSELL *Serpents* (1608) 624 Those medicines..which do extenuate.
†**c.** To thin out (the hair, eyebrows, etc.). *Obs.*
1585 LLOYD *Treas. Health* Bj, Want of theyr humours doth extenuat the same [hair]. **1661** LOVELL *Hist. Anim. & Min.* 39 The fat..extenuateth the eyebrows.
4. †**a.** To diminish in size, number, or amount; to reduce to meagre dimensions. *Obs.*
1555 EDEN *Decades* 273 By forcible extenuatinge the gooddes and poure of them whom they desired to kepe in subiection. **1630** *R. Johnson's Kingd. & Commw.* 22 Small numbers are soon..extenuated by a long warre. **1634** SIR T. HERBERT *Trav.* 205 In which Citie is a great Colossus..To extenuate the bulke of this their Pagod, they place him sitting. **1647** SPRIGGE *Anglia Rediv.* III. v. (1854) 164 [They] were reduced to so much lesser number; and were yet further extenuated.
†**b.** To lessen (a quality, etc.) in degree; to weaken the force of (a blow), mitigate (a law). *Obs.*
1561 T. NORTON *Calvin's Inst.* II. 90 We do obscure and extenuate it [God's grace] with our vnthankfulnesse. **1590** SHAKS. *Mids. N.* I. i. 120 Else the Law of Athens yeelds you vp (Which by no meanes we may extenuate) To death. **1598** E. GILPIN *Skial.* (1878) 45 Some great sicknes..doth..extenuate Thy fraile remembrance. **1643** PRYNNE *Sov. Power Parl.* App. 162 Kings cannot by Law change or extenuate Laws. **1672** SIR T. BROWNE *Lett. Friend* vi. (1881) 130 The incurable state of his disease might somewhat extenuate your Sorrow. **1744** SHENSTONE *Wks. & Lett.* (1777) III. 100 No time shall extenuate our mutual friendship. **1773** J. ROSS *Fratricide* (MS.) IV. 53 A heaviness ..Extenuates my strength.
II. To lessen in representation.
†**5.** 'To diminish in honour' (J.), depreciate, disparage (a person, his actions, or attributes). *Obs.*
1601 WEEVER *Mirr. Mart.* C iij b, Extenuate no more worth's matchlesse deedes. **1605** BACON *Adv. Learn.* I. ii. §3 It hath beene ordinarie..to extenuate and disable learned men by the names of Pedantes. **1667** MILTON *P.L.* x. 645 Just are thy ways..Who can extenuate thee? **1705** STANHOPE *Paraphr.* II. 380 The Reply he made, extenuates the One, when put into the Ballance with the Other.
6. To estimate or state at a low figure; to disparage the magnitude or importance of; to underrate, make light of. Somewhat *arch.*
1529 MORE *Dyaloge* III. Wks. 1218/1 With wordes and reasoning, to extenuate and minysh the vygour and asperite of the paynes. **1553** T. WILSON *Rhet.* 58 b, In accusyng any persone it is best..whereas anythyng semeth to make for hym to extenuate the same to the outermoste. **1607** NORDEN *Sun. Dial.* 34 The feare of this maketh the Tenants to extenuate the values. **1625–8** tr. *Camden's Hist. Eliz.* IV. (1688) 626 Cuffe extenuated both the Danger and Difficulty. **1658** SIR T. BROWNE *Hydriot.* iv, Nor can we extenuate the valour of ancient Martyrs. **1749** FIELDING *Tom Jones* VII. xi, Every man seemed wholly bent to extenuate the sum which fell to his share. **1832** LYELL *Princ. Geol.* II. 288 Extenuating the comparative magnitude of coral limestones. **1882** SEELEY *Nat. Relig.* II. i. 128 Christianity has never altogether denied, but only extenuated the claims of Art and Science.
7. *esp.* To underrate, treat as of trifling magnitude (guilt, faults, crimes). Hence, in later use: To lessen, or seek to lessen, the seeming magnitude of (guilt or offence) by partial excuses. Also of circumstances: To serve as an extenuation of.
1570 T. NORTON tr. *Nowel's Catech.* (1853) 149 Let no man extenuate the most heinous offence of man as a small trespass. **1651** HOBBES *Leviath.* II. xxvii. 154 None that can Excuse (though some of them may Extenuate) a Crime. **1693** CONGREVE *Juv.* xi. 295 Fortune, there, extenuates the Crime. What's Vice in me, is only Mirth in him. **1840** MACAULAY *Clive* 93 The same sense of justice..forbids us to conceal or extenuate the faults of his earlier days. **1871** MORLEY *Voltaire* (1886) 160 A baseness that we ought never to pardon and never to extenuate.
¶**b.** Improperly used for: To extenuate the guilt of; to plead partial excuses for.

1741 MIDDLETON *Cicero* II. VIII. 141 Pompey's fate would extenuate the omission of that step. **1791** MRS. RADCLIFFE *Rom. Forest* x, She..endeavoured to extenuate the conduct of Madame La Motte. **1811** LAMB *Immod. Indulg. Palate* Wks. (1889) 635 He thought it necessary to extenuate the length of time he kept the dinner on the table. **1860** *All Y. Round* No. 67. 404 The purser's steward..extenuated himself calmly enough.

extenuated (ɛk'stɛnjuːeɪtɪd), *ppl. a.* [f. prec. + -ED.] In senses of the vb. **a.** Made slender; shrunken, emaciated. **b.** Attenuated, rarefied.

a. 1620 VENNER *Via Recta* ii. 36 It is..more profitable for loose and extenuated bodies. **1726** LEONI tr. *Alberti's Archit.* I. 5b, Their Faces become thin and extenuated. **1781** *Char.* in *Ann. Reg.* 19/1 The person of Dr. Fothergill was of a delicate, rather of an extenuated make. **1863** HAWTHORNE *Our Old Home* (1879) 76 We..are getting too nervous, haggard, dyspeptic, extenuated.

b. 1661 BOYLE *Spring of Air* II. ii. (1662) 33 Calling this extenuated substance a Funiculus.

ex'tenuating, *vbl. sb.* [f. as prec. + -ING¹.] The action of the vb. EXTENUATE. (For quot. cf. sense 6 of vb.)

1671 H. M. tr. *Erasm. Colloq.* 397 A too sollicitous extenuating thy provision is all one as if thou should boast of it.

ex'tenuating, *ppl. a.* [f. as prec. + -ING².] That extenuates in senses of the vb. Now chiefly in phrase ***extenuating circumstances***: circumstances that tend to diminish culpability.

1607 TOPSELL *Four-f. Beasts* (1673) 525 A thin extenuating diet. *a* **1653** GOUGE *Comm. Heb.* i. 2 These words..are extenuating words. **1655** CULPEPPER *Riverius* II. i. 63 Let him use things extenuating, as Hysop, Fennel.. and especially Nutmeg. **1679** J. GOODMAN *Penit. Pardoned* II. ii. (1713) 198 It was not an extenuating but a just reflection which the Historian makes upon..Alexander. **1694** R. BURTHOGGE *Reason* 139 Its Emanation..is from a Center into an Orb or Sphere, in Extenuating Lines. **1750** tr. *Leonardus' Mirr. Stones* 98 Galen holds that it is warming and extenuating. **1840** MACAULAY *Clive* 55 In Clive's case, there were many extenuating circumstances. **1875** JOWETT *Plato* (ed. 2) I. 494 [Those] who have taken the life of another under the like extenuating circumstances.

Hence **ex'tenuatingly** *adv.*, in an extenuating manner.

1884 MRS. HOUSTOUN *Caught in Snare* II. xv. 171 'Perhaps,' said Helen, extenuatingly, 'she suffers.'

extenuation (ɛkˌstɛnjuː'eɪʃən). [ad. L. *extenuātiōn-em*, n. of action f. *extenuāre* to EXTENUATE. Cf. F. *exténuation*.] The action of extenuating; extenuated condition.

1. The action or process of making or becoming thin; an instance of this; a shrunken condition; leanness, emaciation.

1576 BAKER *Jewell of Health* 171 a, This mightily helpeth the extenuation of members. **1655** CULPEPPER *Riverius* I. v. 19 A yong man..had an extenuation for want of nourishment in his Limbs. **1707** FLOYER *Physic. Pulse-Watch* 183 Galen commends tepid Baths for..curing all Extenuations. **1781** JOHNSON *Let. Mrs. Thrale* 27 Oct., The extenuation is her only bad symptom. **1825** SCOTT *Betrothed* xxx, The female..exhibited..some symptoms of extenuation. **1828** *Biog.* in *Ann. Reg.* 474/2 Some pallid from extenuation.

†**2.** Making less dense; rarefaction (of air).

1655–60 STANLEY *Hist. Philos.* (1701) 64/2 Winds proceed from extenuation of the Air, by the Sun.

†**3.** The action or process of making slender or diminishing in bulk; an instance of this. *Obs.*

1619 DONNE *Serm.* xiv. 140 All Dilatation is some degree of Extenuation. **1665** SIR T. HERBERT *Trav.* (1677) 186 The Sea is the same at all seasons; what it gets by Rivers and showers, losing by exhalations and extenuations through the excessive heats..within the Torrid Zone. **1777** PRIESTLEY *Matt. & Spir.* (1782) I. xix. 229 Gregory the Great..says that God penetrates everything without extenuation.

fig. **1627** BP. HALL *Holy Observ.* 63 No lesse well doth God take these submisse extenuations of our selues.

†**4.** The action of making less or weak; an instance of this; a weakening, impoverishment. Also mitigation (of blame or punishment). *Obs.*

1542–3 *Act 34–5 Hen. VIII*, c. 18 The saide citie is much decaid..not a little to the extenuacion of that part of this realme. **1596** SHAKS. *1 Hen. IV*, III. ii. 22 Such extenuation let me begge, As in reproofe of many Tales deuis'd..I may ..Finde pardon on my true submission. **1654** H. L'ESTRANGE *Chas. I* (1655) 1 The gallantry of Henry's heroique spirit tended somewhat to the..extenuation of Charles his glory. **1707** ATTERBURY *Serm.* v. (1723) II. 159 What Deeds of Charity we have to alledge in Extenuation of our Punishment.

5. The action of representing (something) as slight and trifling; underrating; an instance of this, a plea to this end; a modification in terms.

1614 BP. HALL *Recoll. Treat.* 209 Sometimes..wee humble ourselves lower than there is cause..And no lesse well doth God take these submisse extenuations of our selves. **1621** BURTON *Anat. Mel.* I. i. IV. ii. 228 Through their..extenuation [of their grievance], wretchedness and peevishness they undo themselves. **1722** DE FOE *Plague* (1840) 6 Many died of it every day, so that now all our extenuations abated. **1859** MILL *Liberty* ii. (1865) 13/2 The utmost they allow is an extenuation of its absolute necessity.

†**b.** *Rhet.*

1589 PUTTENHAM *Eng. Poesie* III. xix. (Arb.) 227 We call him the Disabler or figure of Extenuation. **1657** J. SMITH *Myst. Rhet.* 56 When for extenuation sake we use a lighter and more easie word or terme then the matter requires. **1706** in PHILLIPS. **1823** in CRABB *Technol. Dict.*

6. The action of lessening, or seeking to lessen, the guilt of (an offence or fault) by alleging partial excuses; an instance or means of doing this; a plea in mitigation of censure. Also ***in extenuation of***.

1651 HOBBES *Leviath.* II. xxvii. 156 Extenuation, by which the Crime, that seemed great, is made lesse. *a* **1674** CLARENDON *Surv. Leviath.* (1676) 180 He..was to find excuses and extenuations for sins. **1712** ADDISON *Spect.* No. 297 ¶1 Whatever may be said for the Extenuation of such Defects. **1750** JOHNSON *Rambler* No. 39 ¶7 It may be urged, in extenuation of this crime..that [etc.]. **1839** MACKINTOSH *Eth. Philos.* Wks. 1846 I. 28 In extenuation of a noble error. *a* **1832** BENTHAM *Wks.* (1843) I. 174 The differences of castes..furnish a copious stock of extenuations..to different classes of offences.

7. *U.S.* Used humorously in *pl.* for: Thin garments.

1881 G. W. CABLE in *Scribner's Mag.* May 23 They were clad in silken extenuations from the throat to the feet. **1883** *Pall Mall G.* 12 Sept. 2/2 One side wore..extenuations of a ..green colour.

ex'tenuative, *a.* and *sb.* [f. EXTENUATE *v.* + -IVE.]

A. *adj.* **a.** Tending to make lean. **b.** Tending to extenuate (guilt).

1610 BARROUGH *Meth. Physick* II. ix. (1639) 85 They have more need of extenuative meates then those that have the Pleurisie. **1827** BENTHAM *Ration. Evid.* Wks. 1843 VII. 15 Proving the existence of some justificative, or extenuative, or exemptive, circumstance.

B. *sb.* **a.** Something serving to extenuate guilt. **b.** A medicine producing 'extenuation' or emaciation.

a **1734** NORTH *Exam.* II. v. §90 Another Extenuative of the intended Rebellion. **1818** *Blackw. Mag.* III. 524 Be a little more sparing of extenuatives and soporifics.

extenuator (ɛk'stɛnjuːeɪtə(r)). [agent-n. f. L. *extenuāre*: see EXTENUATE *v.*] One who extenuates. †**a.** One who depreciates or makes light of. **b.** One who alleges extenuating or excusatory considerations; an apologist.

1748 RICHARDSON *Clarissa* (1811) VIII. 57 Not..classed among such extenuators. **1799** V. KNOX *Lord's Supp.* iv, The extenuators of the Sacrament..suggest a hint that the command to perform this slight service..might have been confined to the Apostles. **1869** MOZLEY *Univ. Serm.* i. (1876) 15 The extenuators of the Council.

extenuatory (ɛk'stɛnjuːətərɪ), *a.* [ad. L. *extenuātōri-us*, f. *extenuāre*: see EXTENUATE and -ORY.] Characterized by extenuation; having the function or effect of extenuating.

1807 W. TAYLOR in *Ann. Rev.* V. 172 The translation adopts an extenuatory turn. **1831** CROKER in *Boswell's Johnson* an. 1744 I. 142 *note*, The veil, of stately diction and extenuatory phrases. **1870** *Contemp. Rev.* XIV. 618 The sweeping verdict..on Martial's palpable faults, without any extenuatory mention of his tenderer touches.

†**ex'tenue,** *v. Obs. rare*⁻¹. [(? ad. F. *extenue-r*), ad. L. *extenu-āre*: see EXTENUATE.] *trans.* To make thinner.

1574 NEWTON *Health Mag.* 8 The matter..which remained in the fleshe might be extenued.

†**exte'nuity.** *Obs. rare*⁻¹. [f. EXTENU-ATE *v.* after TENUITY.] Extreme fineness or subtility; *concr.* in *pl.*

1601 HOLLAND *Pliny* (1634) II. 535 Making up the pourfils and extenuities of his lineaments [*argutias voltus*].

exter (ɛk'stɜː(r)), *v. rare*⁻¹. [f. L. *ex-* out + *ter-ra* earth; on the analogy of INTER.] *trans.* To dig out of the earth.

1835 *Blackw. Mag.* XXXVIII. 149 From gold mines that precious metal..is exterred.

extercorate, var. of EXSTERCORATE. *Obs.*

†**ex'terebrate,** *v. Obs.*⁻⁰ [f. L. *exterebrāt-* ppl. stem of *exterebrāre*, f. *ex-* out + *terebrāre* to bore, f. *terebra* boring tool, f. *terĕre* to rub.]

trans. To bore out; *fig.* 'to search curiously'.

1623–6 in COCKERAM. **1727** in BAILEY vol. II.

†**ex'terge,** *v. Obs.* [f. L. *extergēre*. f. *ex-* out + *tergēre* to wipe off.] *trans.* To wipe out, cleanse. In quots. *absol.*

1657 TOMLINSON *Renou's Disp.* 38 It [sour sapour] corrodes, bites..and exterges. **1684** tr. *Bonet's Merc. Compit.* XVIII. 666 Manna..and things that exterge without biting.

†**ex'tergent,** *a. rare*⁻⁰. [ad. L. *extergent-em*, pr. pple. of *extergēre*: see prec.] = ABSTERGENT.

1706 in PHILLIPS. **1727–31** in BAILEY vol. II.

†**ex'terial,** *a. Obs.* [a. obs. F. *exterial*, f. L. *exter-us* outward.] Outside, external.

1528 ROY *Rede me* (Arb.) 123 Beware..Of the outwarde man exteriall. **1547** BOORDE *Brev. Health* Pref. 4 Sickenes in the exteriall partes.

exterior (ɛk'stɪərɪə(r)), *a.* and *sb.* Also 6 exteryor, 6–7 exteriour. [a. L. *exterior*, compar. of *exter-us* outside. Cf. F. *extérieur*.]

A. *adj.*

1. a. Outer; pertaining to or connected with the outer portion or outside of anything; visible or perceptible on the outside; external. (In many uses not clearly distinguishable from the sb. used *attrib.*)

exterior angle (*Geom.*): the angle included between any side of a triangle or polygon and the production of the adjacent side; also, an angle included between a straight line falling upon two parallel lines and either of the latter on the outside. ***exterior †polygon, screw, side, slope*** (see quots.). †***exterior epicycloid***: see EPICYCLOID.

1570 DEE *Math. Pref.* 2 Things Naturall, of the sense exterior, ar hable to be perceiued. **1583** STUBBES *Anat. Abus.* (1877) 30 The sinne of the heart..bursteth not foorth into exteriour action. **1602** MARSTON *Ant. & Mel.* Induct., Frame your exterior shape To hautie forme of elate majestie. **1602** SHAKS. *Ham.* II. ii. 6 Not th' exterior, nor the inward man Resembles that it was. **1706** PHILLIPS (ed. Kersey), *Exterior Polygon*, the Out-lines of all the Works drawn from one outmost Angle to another. **1761** HUME *Hist. Eng.* II. xxxii. 219 His exterior concurrence with..the prosecutions. **1823** LAMB *Elia, Diss. Roast Pig* (1867) 160 What a sacrifice of the exterior tegument! **1858** HAWTHORNE *Fr. & It. Jrnls.* (1872) I. 47 Whose exterior front is covered. **1863** MRS. C. CLARKE *Shaks. Char.* xii. 300 Beatrice possesses a fund of hidden tenderness beneath her exterior gaiety. **1867** SMYTH *Sailor's Word-bk.*, *Exterior side*, the side of an imaginary polygon, upon which the plan of a fortification is constructed. *Exterior slope*, in fortification, that slope of a work towards the country which is next outward beyond its superior slope. **1874** KNIGHT *Dict. Mech.* I. 819/1 *Exterior-screw*, one cut upon the outside of a stem or mandrel.

†**b.** Concerned with externals. *rare.*

1541 BARNES *Wks.* (1573) 341/2 What more exteriour honour can you diuise then this is? and yet you doe say yᵗ you honour no stockes nor stones. **1797–1803** FOSTER in *Life & Corr.* (1846) I. 164 Why was the Jewish dispensation so strange, so exterior, so inadequate?

2. a. Situated outside or without (an object); coming from without; concerned with what is without; external, extrinsic. Const. *to*.

1533 ELYOT *Cast. Helthe* II. xxiv. (1572) 38b, The exteriour ayre which compasseth the body. **1538** STARKEY *England* I. ii. 50 Exteryor thyngys—fryndys, ryches, and abundance of necessarys..are..requyryd. **1667** MILTON *P.L.* IX. 336 Without exterior help sustaind. **1780** COWPER *Table T.* 247 Happiness depends..less on exterior things than most suppose. **1815** JANE AUSTEN *Emma* II. xiii. 226 Giving particulars of his journey and feelings..and describing everything exterior and local. **1834** MRS. SOMERVILLE *Connex. Phys. Sc.* iv. (1849) 32 The attraction of a sphere on any exterior body. **1885** LEUDESDORF *Cremona's Proj. Geom.* 219 If the conic is a hyperbola..the centre is a point exterior to the curve.

†**b.** Foreign. *Obs. rare.*

1540 *Act 32 Hen. VIII*, c. 14 This realme of England and any other exteriour potentates.

B. *sb.* (Not in Johnson.)

1. a. The adj. used *absol.*: An exterior thing. *rare* in *sing.* In *pl.* Outside parts, features, habits, manners, trappings, etc.; externals.

1591 *Troub. Raigne K. John* (1611) 58, I speake not onely for eies priuilege, The chief exterior that I would enioy. **1598** SHAKS. *Merry W.* I. iii. 72 She did course o're my exteriors with..a greedy intention. **1646** SIR T. BROWNE *Pseud. Ep.* To Rdr., Discoursers, who look beyond the shell and obvious exteriours of things. **1712** J. HENLEY *Let.* in *Spect.* No. 518 Without producing a suitable Revolution in his Exteriors. **1784** J. BARRY *Lect. Art* i. (1848) 76 Riches, dignities, and all..showy pompous exteriors.

b. An outdoor scene represented on the stage or in a film or television programme; a film, or sequence of a film, photographed outdoors.

1872 *Daily Tel.* 11 Mar. 3/4 The cottage garden exteriors, by Mr. Hawes Craven..are as pretty and effective stage pictures as have ever been seen. **1918** H. CROY *How Motion Pictures are Made* 74 The few pictures that had been made were made outdoors in the open—'exteriors', as they are called. **1949** *Here & Now* (N.Z.) Nov. 27/2 The exteriors, shot unglamorously in a dead daylight, have a harsh gritty quality.

2. a. The outward surface, the outside. **b.** That which appears outside; outward aspect or demeanour.

a. 1695 WOODWARD *Nat. Hist. Earth* i. 3 Nor..did I neglect the exteriour or Surface. **1853** SIR H. DOUGLAS *Mil. Bridges* (ed. 3) 28 Wooden frames, covered on the exterior with sheet copper.

b. 1801 HAN. MORE *Wks.* VIII. 99 The engaging exterior of urbanity. **1874** GREEN *Short Hist.* viii. 464 Under this ridiculous exterior however lay a man of much natural ability. **1876** MOZLEY *Univ. Serm.* xiv. (1877) 247 These were covered by the most pious exterior.

ex'teriorate, *v. rare*⁻¹. [f. prec. + -ATE³.] *trans.* To make (something) a matter of externals.

1871–2 H. MACMILLAN *True Vine* iv. 149 How different is this from the notion of those who exteriorate religion.

exˌterio'ration. [f. as prec. + -ATION.]

1. The action of making more outward. *nonce-use*, after *deterioration*.

a **1831** A. KNOX *Rem.* (1834) I. 66 To a person..much occupied in inward converse with God, there is something felt of comparative exterioration in..the more public means.

2. 'The physiological cerebral act by which the sensation produced by an impression on any part of the course of a nerve is referred to its terminal extremity' (*Syd. Soc. Lex.* 1884).

exteriority (ɛkˌstɪərɪˈɒrɪtɪ). [f. as prec. + -ITY. Cf. F. *extériorité*.]

1. The state or fact of being outward or outside, or of having an external existence; outwardness.

1611 COTGR., *Exterieureté*, exterioritie, outwardness. **1664** H. MORE *Myst. Iniq.* xvi. 56 The exteriority and palpability of the exercise of their affections. **1803** *Edin. Rev.* I. 261 Interiority and exteriority, by which is meant the distinction of the attributes of an object as originally existing in itself or as acquired from without. **1836-7** SIR W. HAMILTON *Metaph.* xxviii. (1859) II. 174 The sense of touch by itself.. is not even cognizant of local exteriority [*örtliches auseinanderseyn*]. **1864** WEBSTER, *Exteriority*, surface, superficies.

2. In religious sense occas.: Devotion to the external instead of to the inward and spiritual.

a **1875** BP. FORBES, (O.) And this leads on to a third point which hinders progress, and that is what for want of a better word may be termed exteriority. **1885** BISSELL *Pentateuch* 311 These men of God.. in the midst of a tendency to pure exteriority.

3. 'The psychical act by which sensations are referred to the external world, as when an impression on the retina is referred to an object outside and not to the place of sensation' (*Syd. Soc. Lex.*).

exteriorization (ɛkˌstɪərɪəraɪˈzeɪʃən). In quot. exteriorisation. [f. next + -ATION.] The action of exteriorizing (see next).

1886 F. W. H. MYERS in *Proc. Soc. Psych. Research* Oct. 169 It was like the awakening and exteriorisation of sensations already stored up in the organism. **1917** C. R. PAYNE tr. *Pfister's Psychoanalytical Method* xi. 264 The exteriorization by which the patient thinks he can perceive his separate organs in the reality. **1961** R. CROOKALL *Supreme Adventure* II. i. 58 The latter also applies to exteriorisations (of both mediumistic and non-mediumistic men) that are enforced by anaesthetics, etc. **1962** *Listener* 17 May 854/2 The final exteriorization of a work was frequently difficult for him [*sc.* Debussy].

exteriorize (ɛkˈstɪərɪəraɪz), v. [f. EXTERIOR + -IZE.] *trans.* To make exterior; to realize (a conception) in outward form; to attribute an external existence to (states of consciousness). Also *absol.* Hence **ex'teriorized** *ppl. a.*

1879 MAUDSLEY *Pathol. Mind* 449 It is the unfailing tendency of the mind to project its affections outwards and to transfer them to objects as qualities—to exteriorize its states as qualities. **1890** *Harper's Mag.* May 821/1 His painting is a means of exteriorizing his conceptions. **1892** *Pall Mall Gaz.* 15 Dec. 2/1 A woman went off into hypnotic sleep close by, and on the girl's exteriorized sensitiveness coming in contact with her she drew away. **1959** *Times Lit. Suppl.* 9 Oct. 576/4 A poem must be set at a distance from its reader.. but to exteriorize too soon is to refuse to suffer. **1961** R. CROOKALL *Supreme Adventure* II. i. 59 His exteriorised double is often seen by mortals at about this time. *Ibid.* 61 The vehicle of vitality takes longer to exteriorise than the Soul Body. **1962** *Lancet* 19 May 1055/1 Outside the forearm the cannulas are connected by a shunt .. which forms an exteriorised semipermanent arteriovenous fistula.

exteriorly (ɛkˈstɪərɪəlɪ), *adv.* [f. as prec. + -LY².]

1. On the outside or surface; as regards the outside; superficially.

1595 SHAKS. *John* IV. ii. 257 My forme, Which howsoeuer rude exteriorly, Is yet the couer of a fayrer minde. **1669** WOODHEAD *St. Teresa* II. xxvi. 162 It scorched her exteriorly. **1707** *Curios. in Husb. & Gard.* 49 New Parts uniting themselves exteriorly to the former. **1791** MACIE in *Phil. Trans.* LXXXI. 372 It was still white, both exteriorly and interiorly. **1879** *Glasgow Herald* 8 Oct., Viewed as a whole, whether exteriorly or interiorly the.. room is a remarkably fine architectural production.

2. With outward act; as regards externals.

1550 THOMAS *Ital. Gram.*, *Cofto*, is the worshippe or honour that is exteriorly vsed towardes God. **1626** T. H. tr. *Caussin's Holy Crt.* 269 Exteriously applying your selfe to ordinary seruices. **1685** tr. *Bossuet's Doctr. Cath. Ch. Advt.* 15 The Holy Ghost.. establishes Pastors and Teachers to act exteriorly. **1751** CHESTERF. *Lett.* III. ccliv. 167 Endeavour to please every body, I mean exteriorly. **1872** BORROW *Gypsies of Spain* (ed. 2) 101 They exteriorly accommodate themselves to the religion of the country.

3. In an exterior position or direction; as being outside something.

1877 E. CAIRD *Philos. Kant* II. xvii. 609 We have again to regard the cause, not as exteriorly related to the effect, but as identical with it. **1880** C. & F. DARWIN *Movem. Pl.* 513 Producing only 3 or 4 perfect flowers, which are situated exteriorly. **1882** *Q. Rev.* Jan. 190 Each leaf is drawn in exteriorly to the first one.

ex'terminable, *a.* rare. [f. L. *exterminābil-is*, f. *extermināre*: see EXTERMINATE and -ABLE.] That may be exterminated.

1667 H. MORE *Div. Dial.* I. xxvii. (1713) 57 No Essence that is exterminable can be the Essence of God.

¶ Used by Shelley for 'illimitable'.

1813 SHELLEY *Q. Mab.* VII. 23 The exterminable spirit it contains Is nature's only God.

exterminate (ɛkˈstɜːmɪneɪt), v. Also 6-7 *pa. pple.* exterminate. [f. L. *extermināt-* ppl. stem of *extermināre* to drive beyond the boundaries, f.

ex- out + *terminus* boundary-line. Cf. F. *exterminer*.

Only sense 1 is found in class. Lat.; the developed sense 2 appears in the Vulgate, and in Fr.]

†**1.** *trans.* To drive (a person or thing) *from*, *of*, *out of* the boundaries or limits of (a place, region, community, state, etc.); to drive away, banish, put to flight. Also with double *obj.* by omission of *from*. *Obs.*

1541 ELYOT *Image Gov.* (1549) 146 Oppression, extorcion .. were out of the citee of Rome.. vtterly exterminate. **1560** ROLLAND *Crt. Venus* III. 621 It hes.. mony of life extirminate. **1597** BACON *Coulers Good & Evil* vii. (Arb.) 148 Most thinges do.. chase and exterminate their contraries. **1653** BAXTER *Meth. Peace Consc.* 50 Do not those men deserve to be exterminated the Churches. *a* **1677** BARROW *Pope's Suprem.* Wks. 1741 I. 609 They deposed, exterminated, and deprived him of communion. **1677** HALE *Prim. Orig. Man.* II. iv. 165 Their [the Britons'] Language was wholly exterminated from hence with them. **1692** BENTLEY *Serm.* 6 June 27 A discovery.. which alone is sufficient to.. exterminate rank Atheism out of the World.

2. To destroy utterly, put an end to (persons or animals; now only, to root out, extirpate (species, races, populations, sects, hence opinions, etc.).

1649 *Alcoran* 65 Who can hinder God to exterminate the Messiah.. with whatsoever is in the Earth, when it shall seeme good to him? **1651** HOBBES *Leviath.* II. xxiv. 128 A People comming into possession of a Land by warre, do not alwaies exterminate the antient Inhabitants. **1705** ARBUTHNOT *Coins* (1727) 229 Alexander had left Grecian Governors and Colonies in the Indies; but they were almost exterminated by Sandro-cottus. **1788** PRIESTLEY *Lect. Hist.* v. xl. 290 Clovis.. exterminated all his family, lest any of them should be chosen king. **1860** MOTLEY *Netherl.* (1868) I. i. 5 The Holy League.. was to exterminate heresy. **1868** PEARD *Water-farm.* xvi. 164 In the dawn of domestic agriculture, beasts of prey.. were exterminated.

†**3.** To get rid of (a thing); to abolish, put an end to, destroy. *Obs.*

1591 SYLVESTER *Du Bartas* I. vii. (1641) 63/1 Th' one [Sabbath] but a Day endures; th' others Date Eternity shall not Exterminate. **1650** BULWER *Anthropomet.* 158 Exterminating or out-lawing their own Face, to put on another. **1691** RAY *Creation* (1714) 38 Who endeavour to.. evacuate and exterminate this Argument. **1794** GODWIN *Cal. Williams* 92 A remorse that stung his conscience and exterminated his peace.

†**b.** *Math.* To get rid of (an unknown quantity, etc.); = ELIMINATE. *Obs.*

1743 W. EMERSON *Fluxions* II. iii. 139 By help of the Equation of the Curve, exterminate $\dot{x}$ or $\dot{y}$ out of the Quantity $\frac{\dot{y}\dot{x}}{\dot{y}}$. **1756** SAUNDERSON *Meth. Fluxions* 159 To exterminate the impossible Quantity in the Denominator. **1827** HUTTON *Course Math.* I. 246 By adding or subtracting them [equations].. one of the letters may be exterminated.

Hence **ex'terminated** *ppl. a.* **ex'terminating** *vbl. sb.* and *ppl. a.*

1694 tr. *Milton's Lett. State* 19 May an. 1655, We believe it to be the general Interest of us all.. to relieve our exterminated and indigent Brethren. **1813** *Q. Rev.* IX. 341 The exterminated nations.. deserved the vengeance of a moral governor by their idolatry and depravity. **1664** H. MORE *Myst. Iniq.* 274 The exterminating of Idolatry out of the empire. **1667** *Decay Chr. Piety* vi. 120 Unlucky vices, on whom the exterminating lot hapned to fall. **1796** COLERIDGE *Ode Departing Year*, The exterminating fiend is fled. **1867** FREEMAN *Norm. Conq.* (1876) I. ii. 33 The last exterminating conquest waged.. against the Britons.

extermination (ɛkˌstɜːmɪˈneɪʃən). Also 5 -mynacion, 6 -minatione. [ad. L. *exterminātiōn-em*, n. of action f. *extermināre*: see EXTERMINATE.] The action of exterminating.

†**1.** Expulsion from the bounds or limits of a country, state, or community; an instance of this; banishment, excommunication. *Obs.*

1577 DEE *Relat. Spirits* I. (1659) 430 The Lord Rosenberg .. did.. advise the Emperour of his error committed in our extermination. *a* **1626** BACON *Holy War* Wks. 1740 III. 542 Displanting and extermination of people. **1641** *Vind. Smectymnuus* ix. 104 All the important businesse of the Church, whether censures or exterminations. **1660** BLOUNT *Boscobel* II. (1680) 33 His Majesties sufferings and forced extermination. **1664** H. MORE *Myst. Iniq.* 272 The slaughter of the Beast, or extermination of him out of Being.

2. a. Putting an end to, total extirpation; utter destruction.

1549 *Compl. Scot.* vii. 68 To succumb hyr haistylye, in the maist extreme exterminatione. **1681** in Somers *Tracts* II. 152 Forcible pursuit against such persons, to the utter extermination of them. **1790** HAN. MORE *Relig. Fash. World* (1791) 140 The almost total extermination of religion. **1794** S. WILLIAMS *Vermont* 160 The savage aims at the utter extermination of his enemy. **1803** *Med. Jrnl.* IX. 540 The Jennerian Society for the Extermination of the Small-pox. **1862** SIR B. BRODIE *Psychol. Inq.* II. iv. 141 One species prospers and multiplies by the extermination of another. **1867** DEUTSCH *Rem.* (1874) 8 A new decree for the extermination of the Talmud.

b. *attrib.,* as **extermination camp,** a concentration camp for the mass murder of human beings, applied esp. to the camps set up by Nazi Germany in the war of 1939-45.

1945 *Atlantic Monthly* July 55 Among the workers a threat of being sent to an extermination camp has its uses. **1952** C. P. BLACKER *Eugenics* 146 We have witnessed the inhumanities of concentration and extermination camps. **1957** H. ROOSENBURG *Walls came tumbling Down* 10 The Jews.. were sent to the extermination camps.

3. *Math.* = ELIMINATION 4.

1753 in CHAMBERS *Cycl. Supp.* **1784** WARING in *Phil. Trans.* LXXIV. 411 The extermination of all the terms. **1827** HUTTON *Course Math.* I. 256 *note*, Cubic equations.. may usually be reduced to quadratics, by extermination.

¶ **4.** Used as = TERMINATION; ending; decay.

1490 CAXTON *Eneydos* xxii. (1890) 80 The owle['s].. song termyneth in pyetous extermynacion. **1549** *Compl. Scot.* i. 20 Siklyik lordschips ande digniteis hes incressing, declinatione, ande exterminatione.

exterminative (ɛkˈstɜːmɪneɪtɪv), *a.* [f. EXTERMINATE + -IVE.] Tending to exterminate.

1884 *Pall Mall G.* 2 Apr. 5/1 [She] writes inflammatory odes about 'hunting the savage'.. we scarcely seem to appreciate either her exterminative or her literary 'gifts'.

exterminator (ɛkˈstɜːmɪneɪtə(r)). [a. L. *exterminātor*, agent-n. f. *extermināre*: see EXTERMINATE.] One who or that which exterminates, destroys, or puts an end to.

1611 COTGR., *Exterminateur*, an exterminator, banisher; destroyer. **1732** *Hist. Litt.* III. 289 He made such a dreadful havoc of the Spaniards, that he was very justly surnamed the Exterminator. **1858** BUCKLE *Civiliz.* (L.), Simon de Montfort, the exterminator of the Albigenses.

exterminatory (ɛkˈstɜːmɪnəˌtərɪ), *a.* [f. EXTERMINATE + -ORY.] Tending to extermination; characterized by attempts at extermination.

1790 BURKE *Fr. Rev.* 207 This exterminatory war. *c* **1795** — *Let. to R. Burke* Wks. IX. 444 Those terrible, confiscatory, and exterminatory periods. **1863** MRS. C. CLARKE *Shaks. Char.* xvi. 393 That exterminatory code which hitherto had kept them in abeyance.

exterminatress (ɛkˈstɜːmɪˌneɪtrɪs). [f. EXTERMINATOR + -ESS.] A female exterminator.

1891 *Sat. Rev.* 12 Sept. 289/2 Miss Ormerod, the exterminatress of insects.

exterminatrix (ɛkˈstɜːmɪˈneɪtrɪks). [a. L. *exterminātrix*, fem. of EXTERMINATOR.] = prec.

1880 *Daily News* 3 Nov. 5/7 She is.. less of an exterminatrix than the exasperated people represent her to be.

†**ex'termine,** v. *Obs.* [ad. F. *exterminer*, f. L. *extermināre*: see EXTERMINATE.]

1. = EXTERMINATE 1. Const. *from*, *out of*.

1634 HEYWOOD *Witches of Lanc.* IV. Wks. 1874 IV. 228 Thou had'st extermin'd Thy selfe out of the blest society Of Saints and Angels. **1637** — *Royal Ship* 42 This word.. was absolutely extermin'd and excommunicated from all grammaticall construction.

2. = EXTERMINATE 2, 3.

1539 in *Vicary's Anat.* (1888) App. iii. 172 By fyer & sworde to extermyn & vtterly to destroy the hole nacion. **1563-87** FOXE *A. & M.* (1596) 181/2 Roger bishop of Salisburie.. was.. miserablie, but iustlie, extermined. **1600** SHAKS. *A.Y.L.* III. v. 89 Your sorrow, and my griefe Were both extermin'd. **1632** LITHGOW *Trav.* VII. 331 To extermine their power.

†**exterminion.** Chiefly *Sc. Obs.* Also 6 extermynion, 6-7 exterminioun. [after L. type *exterminiōn-em*, f. *extermin-āre*: see EXTERMINATE. Cf. *opiniōn-em*, f. *opīnāri*. Late L. had *exterminium* in same sense.] Extermination.

1528 GARDINER in Pocock *Rec. Ref.* I. l. 105 The extermynion of the emperors army. **1582-8** *Hist. James VI* (1804) 207 For punishment and utter exterminion of these. **1629** SYMMER *Spir. Posie* I. iii. 12 The bleare eye of carnall reason could not see any issue, or way to escape that imminent exterminion. **16..** *Sc. Acts Chas. I* (1814) V. 309 (Jam.), Thair is nothing les intendit againes this.. kingdome nor ane uttir exterminioun and totall destructioun.

extern (ɛkˈstɜːn), *a.* and *sb.* Forms: 5-7, 9 externe, 6- extern. [ad. L. *extern-us* outward, f. *exter* outside. Cf. F. *externe*.]

A. *adj.*

1. Pertaining to or connected with the outside; outwardly perceptible; consisting in outward acts; pertaining to the outward form; = EXTERNAL A. 1 and 2. Now only *poet.* (*rare*).

1537 in Strype *Eccl. Mem.* I. App. lxxxviii. 240 At that time it was necessary to have extern gifts. **1640** HOWELL *Dodona's Gr.* (1645) 68 If the Almightie would assume a visible extern shape. **1666** G. HARVEY *Morb. Angl.* vi. 63 The Lungs.. [are] very much exposed to extern and intern injuries. **1678** GALE *Crt. Gentiles* III. 145 The extern act. **1683** E. HOOKER *Pref. Ep. Pordage's Mystic Div.* 78 The.. extern exertions of the.. visibl form of som Persons. **1882** M. ARNOLD in *19th Cent.* Jan. 8 Pullulating rites externe and vain.

� quasi-*adv. a* **1845** HOOD *Lamia* iv. 90 Women—fair externe, But viperous within.

2. Situated outside, not included within the limits of, the object under consideration; = EXTERNAL A. 3. Const. *to.* Now chiefly *poet.*

1598 BARCKLEY *Felic. Man* I. (1603) 59 O man.. that troublest thy selfe with externe things. **1642** HOWELL *For. Trav.* (Arb.) 70 Nor are the observations of the Eye any thing profitable, unless the Mind draw something from the Extern object to enrich the Soul withall. **1649** J. ECCLESTON tr. *Behmen's Epist.* ii. (1886) 8 The visible world being a procreation or extern birth. **1854** *Jrnl. Roy. Agric. Soc.* XV. 276 Materials altogether extern to an animal.. are made to contribute to the maintenance of its life. **1868** BROWNING *Ring & Bk.* IX. 88 Your artist.. broods.. away from aught vulgar and extern On the inner spectrum.

absol. **1850** MRS. BROWNING *Poems* II. 290, I feel the externe and insensate creep in On my organized clay.

†**b.** Situated in or belonging to foreign countries; = EXTERNAL 3 b. *Obs.*

1543 GRAFTON *Contn. Harding* 573, I shuld desire the helpe of externe nacions and countrees. *a* **1577** SIR T. SMITH *Commw. Eng.* (1633) 225 Souldiers..when they have no externe service..to occupie their busie heads and hands. **1605** *Answ. Discov. Romish Doctrine* 48 Any externe Prelate. **1656** *Artif. Handsom.* vii. 83 Those things of extern mode and fashion.

c. Not belonging to a specified community; that is a non-member. Cf. B. 2 a.

1866 *Clerical Jrnl.* 7 June 548/1 The matter..affecting the congregation alone, he put it to the good sense of extern visitors who might be present, not to claim a hearing.

3. Coming from without, having an outside origin; = EXTERNAL A. 4. Now *rare.*

1533 BELLENDEN *Livy* I. (1822) 30 The faderis began to haif grete fere..traisting sum extern and uncouth violence of divers cieteis. *a* **1617** P. BAYNE *On Eph.* (1658) 116 No extern help can make us bring forth good fruit. *c* **1645** HOWELL *Lett.* II. (1650) 103 It consisted in extern mechanicall artifice only. **1799** LAMB *John Woodvil* III, Having a law within..He cannot..be bound by any Positive laws or ordinances extern.

†**b.** *Law.* Not essential, accidental; in phr. ***extern adjunct.*** *Obs.*

1592 WEST *1st Pt. Symbol.* §36 G, Externe Adiuncts be those..in the contract, that may also be absent from it, but in it only when it so Couenanted. **1605** BACON *Adv. Learn.* II. xxii. §5 Which are inherent and not externe.

B. *sb.*

†**1.** Outward appearance, exterior. *Obs. rare.*

c **1600** SHAKS. *Sonn.* cxxv, Wer't ought to me I bore the canopy, With my extern the outward honoring?

2. An outsider; one who does not belong to or does not reside in an establishment or institution: **a.** *gen.* Also a foreigner; formerly, †one of collateral descent. **b.** A day-pupil in a school (Fr. *externe*); also *attrib.* **c.** In hospitals (see quot. 1860). **d.** In monastic use.

a. *c* **1610** *Women Saints* 30 Being no Romane, but an externe and a Barbarian. **1666** J. SERJEANT *Let. Thanks* 97 Not by Lineall Descendents..but a few Externs. **1823** G. DARLEY *Lett. Dramatists* in *Lond. Mag.* Dec., Joanna Baillie and young Beddoes, a female extern and a freshman. **1834** H. O'BRIEN *Round Towers Irel.* 52 The bungling of natives and the claims of externs. **1839** *Fraser's Mag.* XIX. 170 It would be worth gold..to any unlucky extern this pinching night.

b. **1848** THACKERAY *Van. Fair* lii, An extern school grew round the old..foundation. **1853** C. BRONTE *Villette* viii, The externes or day-pupils exceeded one hundred in number. **1890** *Q. Rev.* July 86 At the collège Mazarin..he followed [the courses] as an extern.

c. **1860** MAYNE *Exp. Lex.*, *Extern*, applied to patients, of hospitals, dispensaries, etc. who are not inmates; to out-patients; also to the assistants, dressers, etc. who attend such or who do not dwell in the institution.

attrib. **1881** *Encycl. Brit.* XII. 302 s.v. *Hospital*, The 'extern maternity' charities.

d. *c* **1610** *Women Saints* 169 Greate companies of kinsfolkes, friends, and externes compassed her all-aboute. **1870** *Contemp. Rev.* XV. 590 If there were not some person representing the outer world, some extern, as the Catholics would say. **1887** *Law Rep.* Weekly Notes 32/2 No sister should seek advice of any extern without..leave.

Hence †**ex'ternly** *adv.*, outwardly, on the outside.

1568 ABP. PARKER *Corr.* (1852) 325 Nothing hath chanced externly to her Majesty wherein her prudence shall be more marked. **1591** SYLVESTER *Du Bartas* I. iii. (1641) 28/1 Or stately Toombs, externly gilt and garnisht With dust and bones inwardly fill'd and furnisht.

external (ɛk'stɜːnəl), *a.* and *sb.* Also 6–7 **externall.** [f. L. *extern-us* outward (see EXTERN *a.*) + -AL[1].]

A. *adj.* (Opposed to *internal.*)

1. a. Situated or lying outside; pertaining to, or connected with, the outside or outer portion of anything. ***external angle***: one made by producing outwardly a side of a figure. ***external contact***: (see quot. 1867).

1591 SHAKS. *1 Hen. VI*, v. v. 3 Her vertues graced with externall gifts. **1606** —— *Ant. & Cl.* v. ii. 349 If they had swallow'd poyson, 'twould appeare By externall swelling. **1635** N. CARPENTER *Geog. Del.* I. vii. 163 Externall I call those parts which are without the Spheare it selfe. **1706** PHILLIPS (ed. Kersey), *External angles.* **1796** HUTTON *Math. Dict.* s.v. *Angle*, The external angle of a triangle is equal to both the internal opposite ones taken together. **1834** McMURRIE *Cuvier's Anim. Kingd.* 227 Having those organs free on the external edge. **1840** LARDNER *Geom.* 83 All the external angles of the polygon must also be equal to four right angles. **1842** E. WILSON *Anat. Vade-m.* 335 The External or Cellular coat is dense and resisting. **1867** SMYTH *Sailor's Word-bk.*, *External contact*, in a transit of Mercury or Venus over the sun's disc, this expression means the first touch of the planet's and sun's edges, before any part of the former is projected on the disc of the luminary. **1870** BENTLEY *Bot.* 58 External Glands may be..divided into stalked..or not stalked.

b. *Anat.* Of veins, nerves, etc.: Lying towards the outer surface of the body.

1831 R. KNOX *Cloquet's Anat.* 489 External descending branches..are four or five in number..furnishing to the same parts an equal quantity of twigs. **1842** E. WILSON *Anat. Vade-m.* 342 The External Jugular Vein. *Ibid.* 418 The External Cutaneous Nerve. **1878** T. BRYANT *Pract. Surg.* I. 389 The external meatus.

c. Of remedies, treatment, etc.: Outward, applied to the exterior of the body.

1706 in PHILLIPS (ed. Kersey), *External Digestives* are such as ripen a Swelling or breed good and laudable Matter in a Wound, and prepare it for Mundification or cleansing. **1799** *Med. Jrnl.* II. 300 He recommends external warmth..but not internal stimulants. **1841** LANE *Arab. Nts.* I. 87 This man hath cured me by an external process. **1851** CARPENTER *Man. Phys.* 72 The application of external heat.

2. Pertaining to the outward or bodily form as opposed to the inner nature or spirit; outwardly visible or perceptible; consisting in outward acts or appearances.

1556 *Calvin's Bk. Com. Prayer* in *Phenix* (1708) II. 233 The external Face of the same is polluted. **1564** *Brief Exam.* C ij, The externall partes of the sacramentes. **1647** H. MORE *Song of Soul* II. I. III. xxviii, They..Appear in thickned Aire with shape externall. *a* **1699** STILLINGFL. (J.), He that commits only the external act of idolatry is as guilty as [etc.]. **1736** BUTLER *Anal.* II. i. Wks. 1874 I. 167 The external worship of God. **1779–81** JOHNSON *L.P.*, *Milton* Wks. II. 142 Religion..will glide..out of the mind, unless it be invigorated..by external ordinances, by stated calls to worship. **1871** MORLEY *Voltaire* (1886) 120 The external qualities of this striking style.

3. a. Situated outside, not included within the limits of, the object under consideration. Const. *to.*

1595 SHAKS. *John* II. i. 571 Maids..having no externall thing to loose But the word Maid. **1801** *Med. Jrnl.* XXI. 84 The external air. **1865** LECKY *Ration.* (1878) I. 359 All who were external to Christianity were doomed to eternal damnation. **1885** LEUDESDORF *Cremona's Proj. Geom.* 209 F and G are both external to the conic.

†**b.** Situated in or belonging to foreign countries; foreign. *Obs.*

1577–87 HOLINSHED *Scot. Chron.* (1805) II. 54 Singular prowesse shewed by him (in external battell). **1599** *Life Sir T. More* in Wordsw. *Eccl. Biog.* (1853) II. 96 His external friends were these: Budæus a learned Frenchman, etc.

c. *Metaph.* Belonging or pertaining to the world of things or phenomena, considered as outside of the perceiving mind. ***external world***: the totality of objects existing outside the conscious subject; the objective world; the 'non-ego'.

1667 MILTON *P.L.* v. 103 All External things Which the five..senses represent. **1762** KAMES *Elem. Crit.* (1855) 11 Nothing external is perceived till it first makes an impression. **1779–81** JOHNSON *L.P.*, *Milton* Wks. II. 95 The knowledge of external nature. **1884** tr. *Lotze's Metaph.* 445 Our mental life is aroused anew at every moment by sensations which the external world excites.

4. Arising or acting from without, originating from something outside. ***external evidence***: evidence derived from circumstances or considerations outside or independent of the thing discussed.

1651 HOBBES *Leviath.* II. xxix. 167 Not by externall violence, but intestine disorder. **1695** WOODWARD *Nat. Hist. Earth* v. §5 (1723) 255 These Shells..being..exposed..to many external Accidents are..worn, fretted, and broken to Pieces. **1747** WESLEY *Prim. Physic* (1762) p. iv, Without the Aid of external Violence. **1812–6** PLAYFAIR *Nat. Phil.* (1819) I. 43 The motion of a body..must be ascribed to the action of an external cause or force. **1814** CHALMERS *Evid. Chr. Revel.* Advt. 5 The external testimony of Christianity..leaves infidelity without excuse. **1836** J. GILBERT *Chr. Atonem.* v. (1852) 124 The idea that the punishment of sin is solely some external evil brought upon us. **1868** GLADSTONE *Juv. Mundi* i. (1870) 20 The external evidence to a contrary effect..is considerable.

5. a. Connected with, or having reference to, what is outside; having an outside object or sphere of operation. ***external perception***: the perception of external objects, as opposed to ***internal perception***, the perception of what takes place within the mind. So ***external senses.***

1836–7 SIR W. HAMILTON *Metaph.* xxii. (1859) II. 43 As this [the Acquisitive] faculty is again subdivided into two, according as it is conversant either about the phænomena of matter or about the phænomena of mind, the non-ego or the ego, I gave precedence to the former of these,—the faculty known under the name of External Perception. *Mod.*, It is necessary to consider the subject in its external relations. The external affairs of the society were managed by the secretary.

b. *spec.* Having reference to dealings with foreign countries.

1770 BURKE *Pres. Discont.* Wks. 1842 I. 139 The persons now in the external administration. **1891** *Law Rep.* Weekly Notes 138/2 The external debt of the Republic of Chili.

6. In education, of a student: that does not attend a university but takes its examinations; of an examiner: that tests students of a college, school, etc., of which he is not himself a member; hence of such an examination or the degree so obtained.

1888 *Cal. Univ. Coll., Bristol, 1888–9* 21 An Honour Certificate shall be granted, after examination by an External Examiner, in conjunction with the Professor or Lecturer of the subject. **1898** [see INTERNAL *a.* 2 c]. **1900** *Univ. Birmingham Cal. 1900–1901* 65 The Examiners of the University shall be the Professors of the University with such Lecturers of the University as the Council from time to time appoint and such External Examiners not being Professors Lecturers or Teachers in the University as may be from time to time appointed by the Council. **1912** *University of London Regs. for External Students* 23 An External B.A. Pass Examination... The External Final Examination. **1959** *Listener* 19 Mar. 515/1 What is the real effectiveness of the device of 'external' marking of papers?

B. *sb.*

1. *sing.* The outside; the exterior.

1792 *Munchausen's Trav.* xxii. 95 The external of the chariot. **1814** SOUTHEY *Roderick* x. 202 Deformity and hollowness beneath The rich external.

2. That which is external. In *pl.* **a.** Outward features or aspect; bodily qualifications; outward ceremonies or observances. **b.** Things lying outside or distinct from a person or object; external or outward circumstances or conditions; also, non-essentials.

a. *a* **1635** NAUNTON *Fragm. Reg.* (Arb.) 15 A time in which (as for externals) she was full blown. *a* **1662** GAUDEN *Let. to Chas. II*, 6 The externals of decent forms. *a* **1716** SOUTH *Serm.* (1737) I. ii. 67 Adam was..glorious in his externals; he had a beautiful body. **1751** JORTIN *Serm.* (1771) I. i. 15 The Externals of religion. *a* **1764** LLOYD *The Puff* Wks. (1774) I. 171 Externals have the gift of striking, And lure the fancy into liking. **1853** MARSDEN *Early Purit.* 24 An agreement in externals ought to prevail amongst all the reformed. **1857** BUCKLE *Hist. Civiliz.* I. xiv. 793 He [Condillac] found it utterly impossible to escape from those tendencies towards the external which governed his own age. **1868** G. DUFF *Pol. Surv.* 188 The system has all the externals and much of the reality of constitutional government.

b. **1652** GAULE *Magastrom.* 80 Why should the planets have such influences upon externals and accidentalls, that had none upon the internalls and essentialls? **1661** LOVELL *Hist. Anim. & Min.* 431 Fractures..are divisions of bones, caused by externals violently forced on them. **1676** HALE *Contempl.* I. 280 Such a state of externals as might be suitable to the exigence and nature of my condition in this life. **1734** POPE *Ess. Man* IV. 66 God in Externals could not place Content. **1883** *Athenæum* 10 Feb. 178/3 The concluding remarks on..the subordination of externals to essentials.

ex'ternalism. [f. prec. + -ISM.]

1. Excessive regard for what is external, to the neglect of what is essential, *esp.* in religion; an instance of this.

1856 R. A. VAUGHAN *Mystics* (1860) I. VI. ii. 158 The despotic externalism of the time. **1875** MRS. CHARLES in *Sunday Mag.* May 506 Pharisaic formalities and externalisms. **1879** FARRAR *St. Paul* II. 265 Christianity might be frittered away into a troublesome and censorious externalism.

2. The worship of the external world.

1874 BLACKIE *Self-cult.* 11 This is the very madness of externalism.

ex'ternalist. [f. as prec. + -IST.] One who has undue regard for externals.

1879 FARRAR *St. Paul* (1883) 770 The Pharisaic conceit of the externalist.

externality (ɛkstə'nælɪtɪ). [f. as prec. + -ITY.] The quality of being external.

1. a. The quality of displaying itself in external forms. **b.** The quality of being 'all on the outside'; superficiality, hollowness. **c.** The condition or fact of being outside another object, or of being an outsider. **d.** The quality of operating or striving to operate from without.

a. **1673** H. MORE *App. Antid.* 23 Worship, in the natural externality thereof. **1836** HARE *Guesses* (1859) 72 [In France] the externality of the classical spirit has worn away into mere superficiality.

b. **1684** H. MORE *Answ. Remarks Exp. Apocal.* 243 If that Externality or Superficiality were aimed at. **1856** EMERSON *Eng. Traits* vi. 115 There is a prose in certain Englishmen..a knell in the..externality of their voice.

c. **1877** HUXLEY *Anat. Inv. Anim.* viii. 473 In relation to the body of the animal, all ligaments are external, and their internality or externality is in respect of the hinge line..along which the edges of the valves meet. **1881** *Echo* 1 July 1/6 The pleas of ignorance or of externality..cannot possibly be urged against one who has been the very foremost and most trusted champion of the system.

d. **1857** M. PATTISON *Ess.* (1889) II. 255 Its [the New Lutheran Orthodoxy's] whole principle is that of the externality of the Christian Institute.

2. *Metaph.* The quality or fact of being external to a perceiving subject; the fact of belonging to the external world, or having an existence in space.

a **1790** ADAM SMITH *Ess. Philos. Subjects* (1795) 198 Pressure or resistance necessarily supposes externality in the thing which presses or resists. **1846** MILL *Logic* II. vii. §3 While looking at a solid object they cannot help having the conception, and..the momentary belief of its externality. **1871** FRASER *Life Berkeley* iii. 62 The scientific world was preparing for that reconstruction of its conception of what sensible things and externality mean.

3. a. An external object; an outward feature or characteristic. **b.** *collect.* Outward things in general; an outward environment or observance.

1839 J. ROGERS *Antipopopr.* xviii. §3. 346 A huge bulk of trifling ceremonial and idle externality. *a* **1853** ROBERTSON *Serm.* Ser. IV. xxvi. (1876) 288 The externalities of it may seem to be joy and brightness, but in the deep beneath there is a stern aspect. **1867** J. H. STIRLING in *Fortn. Rev.* Oct. 385 So uneasy an externality, of which he is himself the powerless and apprehensive centre. **1871** MISS MULOCK *Fair France* 13 All these are sensuous externalities. **1874** CARPENTER *Ment. Phys.* I. i. §10 (1879) 11 Force being that externality of which we have the most direct..cognizance.

4. Absorption in externals.

1833 LAMB *Elia* Ser. II. *Product Mod. Art*, Deeply corporealized, and enchained hopelessly in the grovelling fetters of externality, must be the mind, to which [etc.]. **1860** EMERSON *Cond. Life, Worship* Wks. (Bohn) II. 397 What proof of infidelity like..the externality of churches that once sucked the roots of right and wrong?

externalization (ɛkˌstɜːnəlaɪˈzeɪʃən). [f. next + -ATION.] The action or process of externalizing; an instance of this; also *concr.* an embodiment.
1803 W. TAYLOR in *Monthly Mag.* XIV. 491 As a telescope is a copy or externalization of the process of vision; so written language may be a copy or externalization of the process of thinking. **1855** *Fraser's Mag.* LI. 379 The externalisation of the will. **1877** MALLOCK *New Republic* IV. i. II. 127 Such a city..would be the externalisation of the human spirit in the highest state of development.

externalize (ɛkˈstɜːnəlaɪz), *v.* Also 9 **externalise.** [f. EXTERNAL + -IZE.] *trans.* To make external; to embody in outward form; to give or attribute external existence to; to treat as consisting in externals.
1852 MORELL tr. *Tennemann's Hist. Philos.* 29 His fancy externalizing the divinations of his reason. **1875** SYMONDS *Renaiss. Italy* I. i. 30 This high political abstraction, latent in Christianity..was externalised in the French Revolution. **1877** E. CAIRD *Philos. Kant* II. x. 427 The universe is the process whereby spirit externalises itself. **1884** *Chicago Advance* 14 Feb., The more ancient mistake has been to externalize religion too much.

Hence **exˈternalized** *ppl. a.* **exˈternalizing** *vbl. sb.*, the action of the vb. EXTERNALIZE.
1865 MASSON *Rec. Brit. Philos.* 98 The externalizing of one's own thoughts. **1876** FAIRBAIRN in *Contemp. Rev.* June 135 Creation is the evolution of deity, man externalized God. **1886** GURNEY *Phantasms of Living* I. 186 Divides the cases [of telepathy] into two great families—those (A) where the impression is sensory or externalised, and those (B) where it is not sensory or externalised.

externally (ɛkˈstɜːnəlɪ), *adv.* [f. as prec. + -LY².] In an external manner.
1. On or with regard to the outside or outer surface; outwardly; by external application.
1767 GOOCH *Treat. Wounds* I. 185 There is not yet any appearance of swelling externally. **1802** PALEY *Nat. Theol.* xi. (ed. 2) 202 The cavities of the body are so configurated as externally to exhibit the most exact correspondency of the opposite sides. **1812** FOSTER in *Life & Corr.* (1846) I. lxxxviii. 432 Distinguished externally by wig and gown. **1838** T. THOMSON *Chem. Org. Bodies* 442 This butter is employed on the continent in medicine, and always externally. **1875** BRYCE *Holy Rom. Emp.* x. (ed. 5) 157 The attitude of the Roman Church to the imperial power..was externally respectful.
2. In an outside position, outside; with regard to what is outside; by external agency; so as to produce external effects. *to operate externally*: to produce effects outside of oneself. *to marry externally*: to marry out of the family or community (*rare*).
1594 HOOKER *Eccl. Pol.* I. xi. (1611) 33 All things..receive externally some perfection from other things. **1649** JER. TAYLOR *Apol. Liturgy* §126. 81 Those holy incitements to vertue and good life, which God's spirit ministers to us externally, or internally. **1718** FIDDES *Theol. Spec.* I. I. II. vi. 98 If he had never proceeded to make anything or to operate externally. **1844** M. HENNELL *Soc. Systems* 51 When they marry externally..the community portions them in ready money.

†**exˈternalness.** *Obs.* [f. as prec. + -NESS.] The fact, condition, or quality of being external; outwardness or formality (of religious observances).
1667 H. MORE *Div. Dial.* v. xi. (1713) 442 But Carnality and Externalness, especially after the Reign of Constantine, quickly over-ran all. **1727** in BAILEY vol. II. **1775** in ASH.

‖**externat** (ɛkstɛrna). [F. *externat*, f. *externe* day-scholar: see EXTERN *sb.* 2 b.] A day-school.
1853 C. BRONTE *Villette* viii, The establishment was both a pensionat and an externat.

externate (ˈɛkstəneɪt), *v. rare.* [f. EXTERN + -ATE³.] *trans.* To embody in outward form.
1890 tr. *Pfleiderer's Devel. Theol.* 73 The idea externates itself.
Hence **exterˈnation**, outward embodiment.
1845 CDL. WISEMAN *Fabiola* (1855) 347 The externation of His Wisdom. **1862** F. HALL *Hindu Can. of Dramaturgy* (1865) 6 Pantomime, grounded on externation of the feelings. **1876** M. DAVIES *Unorth. Lond.* 250 The externation of religion was especially necessary.

†**externe**, *v. Obs. rare*⁻¹. [f. med.L. *externāre* to make external, f. *extern-us* outward: see prec.] *trans.* (in quot.) To alienate.
c **1420** *Pallad. on Husb.* x. Epil. 215 Yf synne in oure entente hem nolde externe.

externity (ɛkˈstɜːnɪtɪ). Also 8 **externeity.** [f. as prec. + -ITY.] The quality or state of being external or outward, outwardness; also quasi-*concr.* the external part or characteristics.
1713 A. COLLIER *Clavis Univ.* i. 10 The seeming externeity of a visible object, is no argument of its real externeity. **1767** H. BROOKE *Fool of Qual.* (1770) V. 216 The Internity of his ever-living light kindled up an Externity of corporeal irradiation. **1836** *Blackw. Mag.* XXXIX. 359 For what a man may do or suffer..so far as his externity is concerned, I care not.

externization (ɛkˌstɜːnaɪˈzeɪʃən). [f. next + -ATION.] The action of externizing; in quot. *concr.* the outward or objective manifestation.
1841–4 EMERSON *Ess., Poet* Wks. (Bohn) I. 159 The Universe is the externization of the soul.

externize (ɛkˈstɜːnaɪz), *v.* [f. EXTERN + -IZE.] *trans.* To embody in an outward shape or form; = EXTERNALIZE.
1836 EMERSON *Nat., Prospects* Wks. (Bohn) II. 170 The laws of his [man's] mind..externized themselves into day and night. **1875** WHITNEY *Life Lang.* xiv. 304 Our inner consciousness is externized.

exteroceptor (ˌɛkstərəʊˈsɛptə(r)). *Physiol.* [irreg. f. L. *externus* exterior + *-ceptor* of RECEPTOR.] A sense organ which receives external stimuli, as those of touch, etc. Hence **exteroˈceptive** *a.* Cf. INTEROCEPTOR, PROPRIOCEPTOR.
1906 C. S. SHERRINGTON *Integr. Action Nerv. Syst.* 130 There exist..two primary distributions of the receptor organs, each a field in certain respects fundamentally different from the other. The surface field lies freely open to the numberless vicissitudes of the environment... This field, extero-ceptive as it may be called, is rich in the number and variety of receptors which adaptation has evolved in it. *Ibid.*, The reaction of the animal to stimulation of one of its extero-ceptors excites certain tissues, and the activity thus produced in these latter tissues excites in them their receptors, which are proprioceptors. **1927** HALDANE & HUXLEY *Animal Biol.* i. 24 The exteroceptor organs are the windows of the animal into the outside world. *Ibid.* v. 123 Receptors and nerves with this function are called proprioceptive, whilst those whose stimuli come from outside are called exteroceptive. **1932** S. ZUCKERMAN *Soc. Life Monkeys & Apes* xvii. 268 The multitude of exteroceptive stimuli presented by the social activities of its fellows. **1964** J. Z. YOUNG *Model of Brain* xiv. 232 The same circuits also serve to maintain the cells that were stimulated by the exteroceptor in a suitably receptive state to receive the signals that indicate results. **1968** *New Scientist* 7 Nov. 315/1 Exteroceptive feedback yields information about events on the surface of the skin through the skin senses such as touch and heat.

†**ˈexterous**, *a. Obs. rare.* [f. L. *exter* outward + -OUS.] Outward, outside; far removed.
1570 LEVINS *Manip.* 225 Exterouse, *exterus.* **1647** H. MORE *Song of Soul* II. iii. III. lxiii, When in her full, She seemeth least; which proves she's exterous Beyond the Sunne, and further off doth roll.

exterraneous (ɛkstəˈreɪnɪəs), *a.* [f. late L. *exterrāne-us* (f. *ex-* out + *terra* land) + -OUS.] Of or pertaining to a foreign country.
1656–81 in BLOUNT *Glossogr.* **1730–6** in BAILEY (folio). **1832** in WEBSTER; and in later Dicts.

exterrestrial (ɛkstəˈrɛstrɪəl), *a.* [f. EX- *pref.*¹ + TERRESTRIAL.] Originating or located outside the earth. Cf. *extra-terrestrial*: see EXTRA- *pref.*
1870 PROCTOR *Other Worlds* xii. 279 The light of this nebula, unlike any other ex-terrestrial light. **1871** —— *Light Sc.* (1879) 110 Ex-terrestrial observers, such as these, may know much more.

exterritorial (ɛkstɛrɪˈtɔərɪəl), *a.* [f. EX- *pref.*¹ + TERRITORIAL; after next.] Of or pertaining to exterritoriality.
1880 in OGILVIE. **1892** *Law Times* XCII. 392/1 To those who..administer exterritorial laws, this book will be of great use.
Hence **exterriˈtorially** *adv.*, beyond the limits of 'one's' own territory.
1853 *Fraser's Mag.* XLVIII. 124 The moment she [France] proceeds exterritorially..that moment she throws down the gauntlet of defiance to all Europe.

exterritoriality (ɛkstɛrɪˌtɔərɪˈælɪtɪ). [ad. F. *exterritorialité* (in Littré): see prec. and -ITY.] The condition of being considered outside the territory of the state in which (a person) resides, and therefore of not being amenable to its laws. Also EXTRATERRITORIALITY.
The privilege of exterritoriality belongs by international law to ambassadors and their families; stipulations according it to various other classes of persons have been granted by certain Asiatic powers in treaties with European nations.
[**1756** RUTHERFORD *Institutes* II. II. ix. §20. 603 That as by one fiction of positive law an ambassador is considered as the representative of the nation which sends him, so by another like fiction of the same law he is considered as if he was out of the territory, though he is in it.] **1836** WHEATON *Internat. Law* I. 273 The fiction of exterritoriality has been invented, by which the minister though actually in a foreign country, is supposed still to remain within the territories of his own sovereign. **1859** *Times* 17 Mar. 5/2 The system of exterritoriality which Christian nations have deemed it necessary for the interests and protection of their subjects to establish in China. **1878** W. B. LAWRENCE *N. Amer. Rev.* CXXVII. 40 The United States courts have always been scrupulous in recognizing the exterritoriality of public ships.
attrib. **1887** H. KNOLLYS *Life in Japan* 317 That everlastingly sore point, the ex-territoriality question.

exterritorialize (ˌɛkstɛrɪˈtɔərɪəlaɪz), *v. rare*⁻¹. [f. EXTERRITORIAL + -IZE.] *trans.* To secure the privileges of exterritoriality for; to withdraw (a person) from liability to the laws of the country in which he resides.
1870 *Pall Mall G.* 5 Nov. 11 The Roman Catholic missionaries..in their ill-judged and indefensible attempts to exterritorialize their Chinese converts.

†**exˈterse**, *v. Obs.*⁻⁰ [f. L. *extērs-* ppl. stem of *extergĕre*, f. *ex-* out + *tergĕre* to wipe.] *trans.* To wipe off or out. Hence **exˈtersed** *ppl. a.*
1727 in BAILEY vol. II.

†**exˈtersion.** *Obs.*⁻⁰ [as if ad. L. **extersiōn-em*, n. of action f. *extergĕre*: see prec.] The action of rubbing or wiping off or out.
1656–81 in BLOUNT *Glossogr.* **1721** in BAILEY.

†**exˈtersive**, *a. Obs. rare.* [f. L. type **extersīvus*: see EXTERSE and -IVE.] Having the property of wiping off or out; cleansing.
1657 TOMLINSON *Renou's Disp.* 700 We have..concinnated this..extersive Medicament. **1661** LOVELL *Hist. Anim. & Min.* 73 The ashes..are extersive and digesting.

†**exˈtersory**, *a. Obs.*⁻⁰ [f. as prec. + -ORY.] = prec.
1727–36 in BAILEY; whence **1775** in ASH.

extesticulate (ɛksteˈstɪkjʊlət), *a. rare*⁻⁰. [f. EX- *pref.*¹ + L. *testicul-us* testicle + -ATE².] 'Castrated' (*Syd. Soc. Lex.* 1884).

extill, -ation, -atious, var. ff. of EXSTILL, etc.

†**ˈextimate**, *a. Obs. rare.* [f. L. *extim-us*, superl. of *exter* outside: on the analogy of *ultimate.*] Outmost, uttermost.
1659 H. MORE *Immort. Soul* (1662) 178 Personal figuration in the extimate parts..that represent the Body, Face, and Vestments, etc. **1672** *Brief Reply* 119 The supreme or extimate Heaven is in no place.

extime, obs. form of ESTEEM.

extimulate, -ation, -atory, obs. ff. EXSTIMULATE, etc.

extinct (ɛkˈstɪŋkt), *pa. pple.* and *a.* Also 5 **extincte.** [ad. L. *ex(s)tinct-us*, pa. pple. of *ex(s)tinguĕre*: see EXTINGUISH. As used by Caxton and writers of the 16th c. it may be regarded as pa. pple. of EXTINCT *v.*]
A. *pple.* Extinguished (see senses of EXTINCT, EXTINGUISH, *vbs.*). Now *rare.*
1432–50 tr. *Higden* (Rolls) I. 219 That fyre was extincte. *Ibid.* I. 347 This duke Turgesius was perischede and extincte. **1483** CAXTON *Gold. Leg.* 176/4 The more they lyght them [candellys] the more were they extyncte. **1548–9** (Mar.) *Bk. Com. Prayer, Offices* 8 Graunt that al sinne and vice here maie be so extinct. **1598** ROWLANDS *Betraying of Christ* 30 They blind his sight, whose soules more blind Had quite extinct the light of grace. **1612** BREREWOOD *Lang. & Relig.* iv. 33 The Spanish and Pannonian tongues not extinct by the Romans. **1631** R. BYFIELD *Doctr. Sabb.* 99 It tooke fire..but was quickly extinct. **1734** LAW *Enquiry Space* 26 Take away the Things and their respective Order and Distance..may cease and be extinct. **1887** *Pall Mall G.* 30 Dec. 13/2 As I uttered the last word of my manuscript, the lights were suddenly extinct.
B. *adj.* (In early use with distinctly ppl. sense; in mod. use it usually denotes a state without reference to the action from which this results.)
1. a. Of a fire, flame, light: Extinguished, quenched, put out; no longer burning. *extinct volcano*: a volcano that has ceased eruption; also *fig.*, *spec.* a person who has lost the considerable energy, etc., he once possessed.
1432–50 tr. *Higden* (Rolls) I. 119 A lawnterne..extincte is drownede in to hit. **1526** *Pilgr. Perf.* (W. de W. 1531) 197 b, The lampe of grace in thy soule wyll soone be extinct. **1652** GAULE *Magastrom.* 355 Neither the husband nor any of the family could be awaked till that torch was extinct. **1784** COWPER *Task* VI. 684 A spark or two not yet extinct. **1834** MEDWIN *Angler in Wales* I. 249 There are some who..when we [cigars] are not half extinct throw us contemptuously away. **1843** *Penny Cycl.* XXVI. 427/2 Active or extinct volcanoes. **1865** H. C. ROBINSON *Diary* 21 Jan. (1967) 314 Allsop, whose name has been long forgotten... An extinct volcano. **1865** J. A. SYMONDS *Let.* 20 Aug. (1967) I. 566 My illusions & conceits are Extinct volcanoes. **1878** HUXLEY *Physiogr.* 193 A group of small extinct volcanoes. **1914** F. M. FORD *Let.* Jan. (1965) 59 Your list of extinct and semi-extinct volcanoes..is..only window dressing.
†**b.** *quicksilver extinct* [= Fr. *mercure éteint*]: mercury triturated with fats or chalk, and therefore no longer lustrous. *Obs.*
1610 MARKHAM *Masterp.* II. cxxx. 432 Quicke-siluer extinct, and verdigrease, of each an ounce.
2. Of things comparable to a fire or light (*e.g.* life, hope, passion, disease, etc.): Quenched; that has ceased to burn or shine.
1494 FABYAN *Chron.* v. cxviii. 94 The feythe..was well nere extyncte thoroughe all the lande. **1591** *Troub. Raigne K. John* (1611) 67 Young Arthurs eies are blinded and extinct. **1777** PRIESTLEY *Matt. & Spir.* (1782) I. v. 56 Every faculty of the mind..is liable..to become wholly extinct before death. **1826** DISRAELI *Viv. Grey* v. xii, Conversation seemed nearly extinct. **1828** SCOTT *F.M. Perth* xxiv, He was cut down..before life was extinct. **1857** BUCKLE *Civiliz.* I. vi. 294 The last hope of the Mohammedans was extinct.
†**3.** Of a person: Cut off; dead; blotted out of existence. Also, passed away, vanished. *Obs.*
1483 CAXTON *Gold. Leg.* 5/2 All were..deed and extynct. **1530** HEYWOOD *Four P.P.* in Hazl. *Dodsley* I. 375 He may at liberty Pass safe..Till that he be from us extinct. **1611** BIBLE *Job* xvii. 1 My dayes are extinct. **1654** H. L'ESTRANGE *Chas. I* (1655) 4 The usuall ceremony ordained to the bodies of extinct princes. **1665** G. HAVERS *P. della Valle's Trav. E.*

India 93 Nagar..lost together with his life a great part of his Dominions, and became in a manner extinct. **1675** tr. *Machiavelli's Prince* xi. (Rtldg. 1883) 75 The Pope being dead and Valentine extinct.

4. That has died out or come to an end. **a.** Of a family, a class of persons, a race or species of animals or plants: Having no living representative; 'without progressive succession' (J.).

1683 *Brit. Spec.* 156 The Line of Henry VIIIth..being extinct. **1719** DE FOE *Crusoe* I. 331 My Father was dead, and my Mother, and all the Family extinct. **1748** JENYNS *Imit. Hor. Epist.* II. i. 48 Let's try and fix some æra, if we can, When good ones [ministers] were extinct, and bad began. **1868** FREEMAN *Norm. Conq.* (1876) II. ix. 434 The royal house..was not yet extinct. **1874** HELPS *Soc. Press.* iii. 35 The great book collectors (except in America) seem to be an extinct race.

b. Of an institution, dignity, office, etc.: Obsolete. Of a title of nobility: Having no qualified claimant.

1581 J. BELL *Haddon's Answ. Osor.* 51 Y^e Supper of the Lord..you have so defiled..that the true use thereof is almost utterly extinct. **1651** HOBBES *Leviath.* II. xxix. 174 The Assembly it selfe is extinct. **1818** CRUISE *Digest* (ed. 2) III. 244 The dignities limited to the heirs male of Sir Robert Sydney became extinct. **1836** J. GILBERT *Chr. Atonem.* iv. (1852) 103 They imagine the office of moral rule in another state to become extinct. **1841** W. SPALDING *Italy & It. Isl.* III. 181 The three extinct republics, Florence, Pisa, and Siena. **1848** MACAULAY *Hist. Eng.* I. 537 His marquisate became extinct.

c. *Law* in phr. ***possibility of issue extinct.***

1574 tr. *Littleton's Tenures* 7 b, He..is tenaunt in the tayle after possibilitie of issue extinct. **1818** CRUISE *Digest* (ed. 2) I. 154 A person may be tenant in tail, after possibility of issue extinct.

d. Of a law, legal power or right, etc.

1628 COKE *On Litt.* 147 All the Rent charge is extinct. **1726** AYLIFFE *Parerg.* 156 A Censure inflicted *à Jure* continues, tho' such Law be extinct. **1818** CRUISE *Digest* (ed. 2) VI. 457 Such a power, though extinct at law, would certainly be enforced in equity.

†**ex'tinct,** *sb. Obs.* [? ad. L. *ex(s)tinct-us* (*u*-stem), f. *ex(s)tinguĕre* (see EXTINGUISH); or f. EXTINCT *v.*] = EXTINCTION.

1606 FORD *Honor Tri.* iii. *To Earl Pembroke*, To the vttermost extinct of life. **1611** SPEED *Hist. Gt. Brit.* VII. xliv. 364 The extinct of the English Nations renowne. *Ibid.* IX. xvii. (1632) 877 The vtter extinct of the House of Yorke.

†**ex'tinct,** *v. Obs.* Forms: 5–6 **extynct(e,** (5 **estyncte),** 6 **extincte, (extinkt),** 6– **extinct.** Pa. t. 5–6 **extyncte.** [f. L. *ex(s)tinct-* ppl. stem of *ex(s)tinguĕre* to EXTINGUISH.]

1. *trans.* = EXTINGUISH *v.* 1.

1483 CAXTON *Gold. Leg.* 250/1 The blessid laurence had fyue brennynges withoute forthe whiche he al ouercam manly and extyncte them. **1513** BRADSHAW *St. Werburge* II. 166 The feruent great fire extincted was in-dede. **1563–87** FOXE *A. & M.* (1596) 66/2 Eugenia was..put into hot baths, which were extincted, and she preserued.

2. = EXTINGUISH *v.* 2.

1542 BOORDE *Dyetary* 280 Purslane dothe extynct the ardor of lassyuyousnes. **1556** J. HEYWOOD *Spider & F.* vii. 39 It is more hard, loue to our selues to extinkt. *a* **1568** COVERDALE *Hope Faithf.* Pref. (1574) A iij b, Not to stirre vp Gods grace in vs..were to..extincte the spirite.

3. = EXTINGUISH *v.* 3 a.

1483 CAXTON *G. de la Tour* A vij b, The grete good dedes and abstynence that I dyde quenchyd and estyncted al my synnes. **1538** LELAND *Itin.* IV. 16 The name of the Barony of Say is extinctid. **1547** in Cardwell *Documentary Ann.* (1839) I. 42 They have..utterly extincted and destroyed..all images. **1598** F. MERES in Arb. *Garner* II. 105 One strain of musick extincte the pleasure of another. **1603** H. CROSSE *Vertues Commw.* (1878) 35 Two contraries, cannot ioyntly hold possession, but one will vtterly extinct the other.

b. To put an end to, make void (a law, legal right, status, ordinance). Also, to cancel (a licence, the claim of a creditor). Cf. EXTINGUISH 3 b.

1527 in Fiddes *Wolsey* II. 142 The jurisdiction of the Prerogative should be extinctyd. **1531** *Dial. on Laws Eng.* II. xiv. (1638) 84 He..would extinct former rights by such a fine with proclamation. **1541** BARNES *Wks.* (1573) 311/2 Gods blessed ordinaunce were rather to bee extincted and abhorred. **15..** R. MORICE in Strype *Eccl. Mem.* III. xxviii. 236 Divers report that Mr. Latimers licence was extincted. **1588** J. MELLIS *Briefe Instr.* G ij, Yee shall extinct the Creditors of the olde book by the contrary of his opposite. *a* **1626** BACON *Max. & Uses Com. Law* ix. (1635) 39 If I had purchased the land myselfe, then I had extincted mine owne condition.

c. To abolish, suppress (a state of things, custom, institution).

1531–2 *Act 23 Hen. VIII*, c. 20 To extinct and make frustrate the paymentys of the said Annates or first fruytes. **1540** *Act 32 Hen. VIII*, c. 22 §3 Many chanteries..ben sins y^t time vtterly dissolued and extincted. *c* **1555** HARPSFIELD *Divorce Hen. VIII* (1878) 283 Julius Cæsar..extincted the ancient liberty..of the people of Rome.

d. = EXTINGUISH *v.* 3 e.

1545 JOYE *Exp. Dan.* Argt. A vj, Nether the regale famylye nor thee stok of Juda to be extyncted. **1553** BRENDE *Q. Curtius* VIII. 36 Theyr latter kynges..whose lynage the power of the Romans longe after dyd extinct.

e. = EXTINGUISH *v.* 3 f.

1548 HALL *Chron.* 38 a, Scater kyng of Scottes..was by Dunwallo..slayn and extincted. **1587** *Mirr. Mag., Albanact* l, The Britains..Were ready still to fighte at euery call, Till time they had extynct, the monsters all.

Hence **ex'tincted** *ppl. a.* **ex'tincting** *vbl. sb.*

1513 HEN. VIII *Let.* in Strype *Eccl. Mem.* I. App. i. 3 Wee ..have, for the extincting of the detestable Schisme..entred actual war. **1604** SHAKS. *Oth.* II. i. 81 He may..Giue renew'd fire to our extincted Spirits. **1631** WEEVER *Anc. Fun. Mon.* 113 For the..vtter extincting of..power and authoritie.

‖**extincteur** (ɛkstɛ̃tœr, ɛkstɪŋk'tɜː(r)). [F., ad. L. *ex(s)tinctor*, agent-n. f. *ex(s)tinguĕre*: see EXTINGUISH.] An apparatus for extinguishing fire, patented 1862.

[**1865** *Jrnl. Soc. Arts* 27 Oct. 749 A curious apparatus called *l'Extincteur* was tested a short time since..in Paris.] **1878** LADY BRASSEY *Voy. Sunbeam* xxi, The extincteur was used freely. **1885** J. J. MANLEY *Brit. Almanac Comp.* 24 Extincteurs..and domestic fire-escapes.

extinction (ɛk'stɪŋkʃən). Also 5 **extinccion.** [ad. L. *ex(s)tinctiōn-em*, n. of action f. *ex(s)tinguĕre*: see EXTINGUISH. Cf. F. *extinction.*] The action of extinguishing; the fact or state of being extinguished.

1. a. The quenching, putting out (of fire, light, anything burning or shining; *fig.* hopes, passions, life, etc.); the fact of being quenched; the process of becoming, or the condition of being, extinct.

In *Optics* occas. used for the stoppage of light by absorption, interference, etc.

1494 FABYAN *Chron.* VII. 589 He ordeyned at Westminster to brenne perpetuelly w'out extinccion .iiii. tapers of waxe. **1646** SIR T. BROWNE *Pseud. Ep.* II. iii. 68 Red hot needles or wires extinguished in quicksilver, do yet acquire a verticity according to the Laws of position in extinction. **1669** BOYLE *Contn. New Exp.* I. Notes (1682) 191 Several Ignitions and Extinctions. **1672** G. HARVEY *Morb. Angl.* v. 14 The parts are consumed through extinction of their native heat. **1838** PRESCOTT *Ferd. & Is.* (1846) I. iii. 186 The sudden extinction of those hopes which she had so long..cherished. **1843** *Penny Cycl.* XXVI. 424/1 The birth..and extinction of volcanoes are phenomena seen in separate parts of the earth's surface. **1860** TYNDALL *Glac.* I. xxvii. 204 The alternate appearance and extinction of the light. **1866** CARLYLE *Remin.* (1881) II. 275 A bright lamp flickering out into extinction.

b. The slaking (of lime); †'the quenching of red-hot minerals in some liquor, to abate their sharpness, or to impart their virtue to the liquor' (Phillips 1706); †*concr.* a tincture made by this process. ***extinction of mercury***: (see quot. 1842).

1646 SIR T. BROWNE *Pseud. Ep.* II. v. §3. 85 Gold inwardly taken..either in substance, infusion, decoction or extinction. *Ibid.* II. v. §3. 86 [Alloyed gold] is actually dequantitated by fire, and possibly by frequent extinction. *Ibid.* III. xxii. 165 For speedier operation we make extinctions, infusions, and the like. **1842** DUNGLISON *Med. Lex.* (ed. 3), *Extinction of mercury*, trituration of mercury with lard or other substance, until the mercury disappears. **1848** CRAIG, *Extinction* of lime.

c. *Physics.* Reduction in the intensity of radiation. (i) Reduction in the intensity of a beam of light as a result of absorption and scattering as it passes through a medium.

1794 G. ADAMS *Nat. & Exp. Philos.* II. xxi. 406 Reflexion, refraction, and extinction, are affections of light by transparent bodies. **1827–8** J. F. W. HERSCHEL in *Encycl. Metrop.* (1845) IV. 431 The extinction of a beam of homogeneous light in passing through a homogeneous medium. **1957** H. C. VAN DE HULST *Light Scattering by Small Particles* xviii. 388 Extinction can be measured by observing the intensity..of a light source as seen through a container with scattering particles. **1963** J. M. STONE *Radiation & Optics* xiv. 335 Extinction is accounted for partly as scattering and partly as absorption. Extinction may ..consist entirely of absorption (for example, in an opaque screen of negligible reflectance) or almost entirely of scattering (for example, from..a very thick cloud in the sky).

(ii) The state or condition of darkness in a crystal placed in polarized light between crossed nicols. Hence ***angle of extinction***, the angle formed, on rotation, between the position of extinction of a ray of light and a principal crystallographic direction. Also *attrib.*

1873 J. TYNDALL *Six Lectures on Light* iv. 133 This brings us at once to the part played by the analyzer, the sole function of which is to recompound the two vibrations emergent from the gypsum. It reduces them to a single plane, where, if one of them be retarded by the proper amount, extinction will occur. **1912** R. W. CLARK tr. *Weinschenk's Petrogr. Meth.* 67 Maximum brightness is obtained when the vibration directions of the crystal are at 45° to those of the nicols. It diminishes upon further rotation and passes gradually over into complete darkness when these directions are respectively parallel. This latter position is also called the position of extinction, and the vibration directions in the crystal, the extinction directions. *Ibid.* 70 Extinction Curve for Diopside. *Ibid.*, In triclinic minerals the determination of the extinction angles is of value only when the orientation of the face upon which they are observed is accurately known. **1921** A. HOLMES *Petrogr. Meth.* 126 When a transparent mineral fragment is rotated between crossed nicols various phenomena may be observed... If the object remains dark, and is therefore isotropic, the total extinction indicates an amorphous or cubic (isometric) mineral in an unstrained condition, or a basal section of a uniaxial mineral (tetragonal, hexagonal, or trigonal). **1937** *Discovery* Sept. 283/2 A complete record of the colour variation and the angles of extinction can be permanently obtained.

(iii) A reduction in the intensity of X-rays diffracted by a crystal owing to interference between the incident beam and beams multiply diffracted by the lattice planes (***primary extinction***) and to the progressive weakening of the incident beam in its passage through the crystal as energy is diverted into the diffracted beams (***secondary extinction***).

1914 C. G. DARWIN in *Phil. Mag.* 6th Ser. XXVII. 681 The extinction is complete long before the [X-]rays going in a slightly different direction are appreciably absorbed. This fact is important in explaining the reflexion from an ordinary imperfect crystal. **1922** —— in *Ibid.* XLIII. 804 The extinction itself..exerts two effects, which may be called primary and secondary. **1934** W. P. DAVEY *Study Crystal Struct.* x. 308 The cleavage faces of all actual single crystals are perfect enough to show a little primary extinction and are imperfect enough to show a great deal of secondary extinction. **1948** K. LONSDALE *Crystals & X-Rays* vi. 140 The effect of this primary extinction..is an enormous apparent increase in absorption, over a very restricted range of angle. **1966** D. G. BRANDON *Mod. Techniques Metallogr.* 83 Crystal imperfections will prevent double diffraction and hence prevent extinction, leading to an increased diffracted intensity in regions of lattice strain.

2. Suppression, abolition (of an institution, etc.); the complete wiping out (of a debt).

1651 HOBBES *Leviath.* II. xxix. 168 The Extinction of their Democracy. **1748** ANSON *Voy.* II. xiv. 282 The extinction of their religion, and the slaughter of their ancestors. **1751** JOHNSON *Rambler* No. 145 ¶1 The public would suffer..inconvenience..from the extinction of any common trade. **1839** THIRLWALL *Greece* VIII. 469 After the extinction of the national independence. **1845** McCULLOCH *Taxation* (1852) 462 The plan for the gradual extinction of the national debt.

3. a. The action of blotting (a living being, a soul) out of existence; destruction, annihilation.

1615 CROOKE *Body of Man* 333 We therefore define an abortment to be Either the issuing of an imperfect Infant or his extinction and death in the wombe. **1646** BP. HALL *Balm Gil.* 188 The utter extinction of those we loved. **1676** GLANVILL *Ess.* v. 19 Doctrines, such as..utter extinction, and annihilation of the Wicked after the Day of Judgment. **1796** MORSE *Amer. Geog.* I. 135 Which destruction they call the second death, and describe it as a perfect extinction. **1878** BROWNING *La Saisiaz* 32, I..declare the soul's eclipse Not the soul's extinction.

†**b.** Effacement, utter disgrace or ruin (of a person). *Obs.*

1542 UDALL in *Lett. Lit. Men* (Camden) 5 To recover a man from present extinction.

4. Of a race, family, species, etc.: The fact or process of becoming extinct; a coming to an end or dying out; the condition of being extinct.

1602 FULBECKE *2nd Pt. Parall.* 63 If a man deuise to his daughter his lands..vntill she marie..it onely signifieth an extinction of the legacie when the mariage is accomplished. **1659** C. NOBLE *Mod. Answ. to Immod. Q.* 15 By..extinction of the male blood it received an alteration. *a* **1729** J. ROGERS *19 Serm.* (1735) 135 The Extinction of Nations, and the Desolation of Kingdoms. **1818** CRUISE *Digest* (ed. 2) VI. 569 Any number of lives, the extinction of which could be proved without difficulty. **1875** BRYCE *Holy Rom. Emp.* xix. (ed. 5) 354 The extinction of the male line of Hapsburg in the person of Charles the Sixth. **1880** A. R. WALLACE *Isl. Life* 61 The most effective agent in the extinction of species is the pressure of other species.

5. *attrib.*, as **extinction coefficient**, any coefficient that gives a measure of the total degree of extinction of radiation by a medium; **extinction frequency** (see quot.); **extinction meter**, a photographic exposure meter which gives readings in terms of visual comparisons.

1902 *Encycl. Brit.* XXX. 237/1 After traversing thickness x the intensity I is reduced to $I' = Ie^{-ax}$ where e is the number 2·71828..and a is known as the extinction-coefficient. **1912** P. G. NUTTING *Outl. Appl. Optics* 12 In theoretical work the most useful specification of absorption is the absorption per wave length called the *extinction coefficient* or absorptive index. **1959** H. BARNES *Oceanogr. & Marine Biol.* 162 The clarity of the water, that is, its ability to transmit light (as measured by the so-called extinction coefficient), depends upon the wavelength of the light. **1953** AMOS & BIRKINSHAW *Television Engin.* I. 277 The frequency ..at which zero output occurs is known as the first critical or extinction frequency. **1931** J. H. REYNER *Cine-Photogr. for Amateurs* v. 58 These meters are often known as extinction meters, because the light coming through them is gradually reduced to or worked up from an extinction point. **1951** G. H. SEWELL *Amateur Film-Making* (ed. 2) ii. 19 An early type [of exposure meter] used for cinematography was the extinction meter, in which the subject was observed through a small telescope in which was a density wedge that was used in assessing the correct exposure for the subject.

extinctive (ɛk'stɪŋktɪv), *a.* [f. L. type **exstinctiv-us*, f. *ex(s)tinguĕre* (see EXTINGUISH). Cf. Fr. *exstinctif.*] Tending, or having the power, to extinguish; causing annihilation. Const. *of.*

1600 SWINBURNE *Spousals* (1686) 138 This Condition is..resolutive or extinctive that is to say..threatening a death or destruction to that which is born. **1837** CARLYLE *Fr. Rev.* IV. i, O ye hapless Two, mutually extinctive, the Beautiful and the Squalid, sleep ye well. **1871** *Contemp. Rev.* XVI. 543 The third class of extinctive agencies..seems..to threaten many of the Malayan and Polynesian races. **1883** *Athenæum* 10 Mar. 1/1 The Extinctive Effect of Free Water on the Rolling of Ships.

Hence †**ex'tinctively** *adv.*, so as to be extinguished.

1633 T. ADAMS *Exp. 2 Peter* iii. 4 If they [i.e. souls] die not extinctively, what becomes of them?

ex'tinctness. ? *Obs.*$^{-0}$ [f. EXTINCT *a.* + -NESS.] The quality of being extinct.
1727-36 in BAILEY; whence **1775** in ASH.

†**ex'tincture.** *Obs. rare*$^{-1}$. [f. EXTINCT *v.* + -URE.] = EXTINCTION.
1597 SHAKS. *Lover's Compl.* 294 Cold modesty, hot wrath, Both fire from hence and chill extincture hath.

extine ('ɛkstɪn, -taɪn). *Bot.* [f. L. *ext-* (in *extimus* most outward, f. *ex-*) + -INE^1.] The outer membrane of the pollen grain. Also EXINE.
1835 LINDLEY *Introd. Bot.* (1848) I. 358 The shell of the pollen-grain..has been ascertained to consist..of two or even three membranes, of which the outer (extine) is thicker than the inner (intine). **1882** VINES *Sachs' Bot.* 505 The contents [of pollen grains] enclosed by an extine and intine, divide into two cells.

†**ex'tinguible,** *a. Obs. rare*$^{-1}$. [ad. late L. *extinguibilis* (Lactantius), f. *ex(s)tinguĕre*: see EXTINGUISH.] = EXTINGUISHABLE.
1605 TIMME *Quersit.* I. xii. 50 The most pure and extinguible substance of sulphur.

extinguish (ɛk'stɪŋgwɪʃ), *v.* [ad. L. *ex(s)tinguĕre* (f. *ex-* intensive + *stinguĕre* to quench): see -ISH.]

1. *trans.* To put out, quench (fire, light, anything burning or shining). †In early medical use: To reduce (an inflammation).
1551 BALE *Eng. Votaries* II. 89 b, Ethelredus..by it [cold water]..extynguyshed..the flames of all..vices. **1563** T. GALE *Antidot.* II. 16 It [vnguent] doeth extinguishe..all inflammations of the lyuer. **1596** DRAYTON *Legends* ii. 545 A little sparke extinguish'd to the Eye. **1656** BRAMHALL *Replic.* ii. 110 The light is under a Bushell, but it is not extinguished. **1691** DRYDEN *Lady of May* 10 The soft god of pleasure..Has broken his bow, and extinguish'd his fires. **1710** J. CLARKE *Rohault's Nat. Phil.* (1729) II. 165 Cold extinguishes..Heat. **1732** BERKELEY *Alciphr.* I. §3 They would extinguish the very light of nature. **1825** J. NICHOLSON *Operat. Mechanic* 271 The water is..thrown in a jet through a hose-pipe with great force, to extinguish fire. **1869** TYNDALL *Light* ii. (1873) 65 Natural bodies..extinguish certain constituents of the white solar light.

2. *transf.* and *fig.* **a.** To quench (hopes, passions, strife, life, mental faculties, etc.); to silence (sound).
1545 RAYNOLD *Byrth Mankynde* IV. iii. (1564) 121 b, Suche as haue.. wateryshe Matrixes can not conceyue, for the power of the seede is extinguished in it. **1561** T. NORTON *Calvin's Inst.* I. 21 b, Paule..exhorteth the Thessalonians not to extinguish the spirite. **1626** BACON *Sylva* §212 It deadeth and extinguisheth the Sound utterly. *a* **1627** HAYWARD *Edw. VI* 89 To extinguish the loue of the people to the young King. **1651** BAXTER *Inf. Bapt.* 143 God will not suffer it [truth] to be extinguished. **1667** MILTON *P.L.* IV. 666 Least total darkness should..extinguish life in Nature. **1711** ADDISON *Spect.* No. 126 ¶3 We should soon see that furious Party-Spirit extinguished. **1732** LAW *Serious C.* x. (ed. 2) 143 Extinguishing his reason, instead of putting out his eyes. **1780** HARRIS *Philol. Enq.* (1841) 512 War between great men seldom extinguishes humanity. **1848** MACAULAY *Hist. Eng.* I. 603 Neither his years nor his profession had wholly entinguished his martial ardour.

b. To 'quench' or totally obscure by superior brilliancy; to 'eclipse', put completely into the shade.
1551 GARDINER *Explic. Cath. Faith* 142 In the Sacrament the visible element is not extinguished by the presence of Christes most precious body. **1591** SHAKS. *1 Hen. VI*, v. iii. 192 Naturall Graces that extinguish Art. **1863** MRS. OLIPHANT *Salem Ch.* i. 11 The men..were quite transcended and extinguished by their wives and daughters.

c. In mod. use: To reduce (an adversary) to silence. Chiefly *colloq.*
1878 GLADSTONE *Prim. Homer* 130 The stinging and compressed oration of Odusseus in Scheriè..utterly extinguishes his adversary.

3. To put a total end to, do away with completely, blot out of existence.
1555 EDEN *Decades* 249 By theyr inuasions were extinguyshed all artes and sciences. **1594** HOOKER *Eccl. Pol.* I. viii. (1611) 22 It extinguisheth all heinous crimes. **1615** G. SANDYS *Trav.* I. 44 This late mightie Empire [of the Turks] extinguisht in Ægypt by the Mamalucks. **1669-70** MARVELL *Corr.* cxxxvi. Wks. 1872-5 II. 302 That all memory thereof might be extinguisht. **1711** ADDISON *Spect.* No. 169 ¶2 Half the Misery of human Life might be extinguished. **1783** BURKE *Sp. Fox's E. India Bill* Wks. 1842 I. 285 The authority of the regular and lawful government is every where..extinguished. **1868** J. H. BLUNT *Ref. Ch. Eng.* I. 70 But the confiscation of Wolsey's possessions extinguished the grandeur of these plans.

b. To render void (a bill, claim, right, etc.). In *Law* sometimes *spec.* (see EXTINGUISHMENT 3 b).
1548 LD. SOMERSET *Epist. Scots* 242 That cannot extynguish the title which we haue to the Croune of Scotlande. *a* **1626** BACON *Max. & Uses Com. Law* iii. 13 The warren is not by implication reserued vnto mee either to bee inioyed or extinguished. **1651** W. G. tr. *Cowel's Inst.* 207 The action for the residue is utterly extinguished. **1784** COWPER *Task* VI. 583 Man's..rights and claims Are paramount, and must extinguish theirs [creeping vermin's]. **1866** CRUMP *Banking* v. 132 Cancellation..is considered to extinguish the instrument. **1891** *Law Rep.* Weekly Notes 136/2 The right of way..was extinguished by the mortgage.

c. To discharge, obtain total acquittance of, 'wipe out' by full payment or composition.
1630 *R. Johnson's Kingd. & Commw.* 357 All which so inestimable summes..they have re-imbursed or extinguished. **1777** WATSON *Philip II* (1793) II. XIV. 187 They will ere long extinguish the debt which they owe you, in your blood. **1836** THIRLWALL *Greece* II. xi. 35 The debt itself..was..held to be extinguished. **1845** McCULLOCH *Taxation* III. i. (1852) 429 The only instance of a national debt having been extinguished.

d. To suppress (†books, †customs, offices or corporate institutions).
1590 SIR J. SMYTH *Disc. Weapons* Sig. *ij b, Procuring also ..to suppresse and extinguish the exercise and serviceable use of Long-bowes. **1590** —— in *Lett. Lit. Men* (Camden) 56 A booke conteyninge so disordered matter, that yt should be extinguished. **1611** BIBLE *Transl. Pref.* 2 One that extinguished worthy whole volumes, to bring his abridgements into request. **1656** BRAMHALL *Replic.* ii. 109 The Baronies of the Bishops, and their votes in Parliament were taken away, but the Order was not extinguished. **1722** *Lond. Gaz.* No. 6092/1 It is our Pleasure that the said Sort [of boat] be extinguished, and no longer used. **1839** YEOWELL *Anc. Brit. Ch.* xi. (1847) 117 Though the bishopric..merged into the archbishopric..it was not extinguished. **1868** J. H. BLUNT *Ref. Ch. Eng.* I. ii. 68 It had long been foreseen that..a large number of them [monasteries] must be extinguished.

e. To annihilate, bring to an end, cut off (a family, race, etc.).
1593 R. HARVEY *Philad.* 100 The nation of the Hunnes was almost vtterly extinguished in Greece, by the Emperor. **1641** BAKER *Chron.* (1660) 19 The Danish Line clean extinguished, Edward the Confessour..was..admitted King of England. **1659** B. HARRIS *Parival's Iron Age* 36 The Royal race of the Valois being extinguished by the death of Henry the third. **1837** SIR F. PALGRAVE *Merch. & Friar* (1844) 135 'Extinguishing' the Red man by the progress of civilisation.

†**f.** To make away with, kill (an individual).
1598 GRENEWEY *Tacitus' Ann.* XII. iii. (1622) 158 His [Gotarses'] brothers are extinguished by murder. **1630** *R. Johnson's Kingd. & Commw.* 558 They extinguish the great ones, especially those of royall bloud. **1670** MILTON *Hist. Eng.* Wks. 1738 II. 108 He had first relinquish'd, then extinguish'd Edmund.

†**4.** *intr.* for *refl.* in various senses: To die out. (Quot. 1837 is not strictly an example of this use, but of the idiomatic occas. use of a trans. vb. in passive sense.)
1599 A. M. tr. *Gabelhouer's Bk. Physicke* 52/1 Inscende the same, and let it combure, till of it selfe it extinguishe. *c* **1645** HOWELL *Lett.* II. lxxiii, They..both extinguish like a snuff. **1650** MILTON *Tenure Kings* 53 These..through all stormes and persecutions kept Religion from extinguishing. **1670** G. H. *Hist. Cardinals* II. II. 159 His Family being like to extinguish for want of Heirs. **1723** *Pres. State Russia* I. 220 If a Fire..finds Iron and Stone in its Way, it extinguishes of itself. **1742** HUME *Ess., Stoic* (1779) I. 161 His alacrity suddenly extinguishes. *a* **1797** H. WALPOLE *Mem. Geo. II*, I. 375 He paints that phantom of Royalty the present King extinguishing at Metz. [**1837** CARLYLE *Fr. Rev.* I. VI. iii, This conflagration of the South-East will abate ..extinguish it will not, till the fuel be all done.]

Hence **ex'tinguished** *ppl. a.* **ex'tinguishedly** *adv.* **ex'tinguishing** *vbl. sb.* and *ppl. a.*
1552 HULOET, Extinguished, *extinctus.* **1616** CHAPMAN *Musæus* 471 She..round about the sea's broad shoulders throws Her eye, to second the extinguish'd light. *a* **1641** BP. MONTAGU *Acts & Mon.* (1642) 60 Adam lost the measure, and manner, not utterly and extinguishedly, the thing [i.e. virtue]. **1677** HALE *Prim. Orig. Man* III. vii. 285 Some vast devastation..may endanger..the extinguishing of the species of things. **1784** COWPER *Task* I. 442 His eye relumines its extinguished fires. **1837** in O'Connor *Ld. Beaconsfield* (1879) 174 The laughter, shouts, etc., which accompanied the honourable and extinguished Member's first attempt in Parliamentary oratory. *a* **1863** THACKERAY *Mr. & Mrs. Berry* ii, A strong smell of an extinguished lamp.

extinguishable (ɛk'stɪŋgwɪʃəb(ə)l), *a.* Also 6 **extinguyssible.** [f. prec. + -ABLE.] Able to be extinguished (in senses of the vb.).
1509 HAWES *Past. Pleas.* VI. iii, Who that walketh the waye of derkenes..shall haue payne nothyng extinguyssible. **1667** in *Phil. Trans.* II. 609 The light of the former is readily extinguishable by Compression. **1730-6** in BAILEY (folio). **1832** LEWIS *Use & Ab. Pol. Terms* iii. 31 Not extinguishable by any law. **1886** *Law Times* LXXX. 213/2 Insect life is not extinguishable by scrubbing.

extinguisher (ɛk'stɪŋgwɪʃə(r)). [f. as prec. + -ER^1.]

1. One who or that which extinguishes; *spec.* = *fire-extinguisher* (FIRE *sb.* B. 2).
1560 WHITEHORNE *Arte Warre* (1588) 18 b, Heads [Captains]..extinguishers of discention. **1601** WEEVER *Mirr. Mart.* A vij, This heat extinguisher. **1630** J. TAYLOR (Water P.) *Wks.* II. 257/1 The Glorious Great Extinguisher of Night. **1654** WHITLOCK *Zootomia* 303 Quarrells and Distempers..prove Extinguishers. **1814** SIR R. WILSON *Diary* II. 341 The fat is blazing in the fire, and no extinguisher can be found. **1817** BYRON *Let. to Murray* 4 June, The name of their extinguisher was Gifford. **1887** *Daily News* 7 Mar. 7/1 The Lewis Hand Fire Extinguisher. **1908** *Westm. Gaz.* 14 May 12/2 The extinguishers..have..taps which give the operator absolute control of the instrument. **1930** *Engineering* 10 Oct. 458/2 It was necessary to have a sufficient supply of chemical extinguishers on board.

2. a. *spec.* A hollow conical cap for extinguishing the light of a candle or lamp; also a similar object of large size formerly affixed to the railings of a house to enable the link-boys to extinguish their links.
1641 W. CARTWRIGHT *Ordinary* I. v, In putting of 'm [candles] out..by The extinguisher. **1685** *Lond. Gaz.* No. 2068/4 One Closet Candlestick, with Snuffers and Extinguisher. **1739-40** MRS. DELANY *Life & Corr.* (1861) II. 88 Put out their flambeaux with great silver extinguishers. **1840** DICKENS *Barn. Rudge* xvi, Extinguishers are yet suspended before the doors of a few houses of the better sort. **1857** W. COLLINS *Dead Secret* I. i, She held the candlestick, so that the extinguisher lying loose in it rattled.

b. *transf.* and *fig.*
1697 COLLIER *Ess. Mor. Subj.* II. (1709) 30 Cover it [the vital Flame] with an Extinguisher of Honour. **1774** *Westm. Mag.* II. 96 Put not one grand extinguisher on Plays; But with kind snuffers gently mend their blaze. **1884** *Pall Mall G.* 1 May 4/1 'Eigg Island,' with its singular Scuir or peak hidden under a thick extinguisher of cloud.

3. *attrib.* and *Comb.* ***extinguisher-shaped*** adj.; ***extinguisher-moss***, a moss whose peristome closes inwards when touched by water.
1885 *Daily News* 30 Apr. 4/8 The immeasurable height of the extinguisher hats of women when Richard II. was King. **1881** A. G. C. LIDDELL in *Macm. Mag.* XLIV. 473/2 Sharp extinguisher-like spires..shot into the sky. **1821** S. F. GRAY *Nat. Arr. Brit. Plants* I. 725 *Encalypta.., Extinguisher-moss.* **1876** *Encycl. Brit.* IV. 161/2 The Extinguisher-Moss (*Encalypta*). **1840** BARHAM *Ingol. Leg.* 23 A shocking bad hat, Extinguisher-shaped. **1903** R. GOWER *Rec. & Remin.* 16 The towers with their extinguisher-shaped roofs. **1909** A. MORRISON *Green Ginger* 27 The wide fireplace and its blazing embers, stuck with black extinguisher-shaped beer-warmers. **1859** DICKENS *T. Two Cities* II. ix, Extinguisher-topped towers.

Hence **ex'tinguishership.** *nonce-wd.*
1825 *New Monthly Mag.* XIII. 193 God give his imperial extinguishership 'a good deliverance.'

extinguishment (ɛk'stɪŋgwɪʃmənt). [f. EXTINGUISH *v.* + -MENT.] The action of extinguishing; the fact of being extinguished; = EXTINCTION.

1. The quenching (of fire, light, anything burning or shining). Cf. EXTINGUISH *v.* 1.
1509 HAWES *Past. Pleas.* XLIII. iv, Evermore, without extinguyshment, In burnyng tongues he shall be permanent. **1665** *Sir T. Roe's Voy. E. India* 443 Lamps.. which have burned without extinguishment from many foregoing generations. **1724** T. RICHERS *Hist. R. Geneal. Spain* 326 To endeavour the Extinguishment of those Flames. **1870** *Daily News* 19 Aug. 6 The men skilled in extinguishment far away.

†**b.** A means of extinguishing. *Obs.*
1667 WATERHOUSE *Fire Lond.* 58 Application of remora's and extinguishments, to both wind and fire.

2. *transf.* and *fig.* Cf. EXTINGUISH *v.* 2.
1503 HAWES *Examp. Virt.* xiii. 275 Theyr payne haue none extinguysshement. **1546** in *Vicary's Anat.* (1888) App. viii. 218 The..vtter extingguysshement of the seyd grugge and dyspleasure. **1607** TOPSELL *Serpents* (1653) 636 When once the wound beginneth to be purple, green, or black, it is a sign..of the extinguishment of the venom. *a* **1639** W. WHATELEY *Prototypes* II. xxvi. (1640) 70 An extinguishment of love. **1850** L. HUNT *Autobiog.* x. (1860) 179 The final extinguishment of the king's reason.

3. The putting a total end to (something), blotting out of existence; suppression (of an institution).
1537 *Acts Irel. 28 Hen. VIII*, c. xiii, Statutes..made for the..extinguishment out of this land of the pretended power of the Bishop of Rome. **1586** FERNE *Blaz. Gentrie* 32 The extinguishment of anye one of them [foure complexions] is the destruction of the bodye. *a* **1648** LD. HERBERT *Hen. VIII* (1649) 397 That for extinguishments of all Ambiguities and doubts, it may be enacted, etc. **1741** T. ROBINSON *Gavelkind* v. 66 A Total Extinguishment of the Custom. **1865** *Reader* 2 Sept. 253/2 Munitions of war, which not only influenced banefully..the fortunes of Prince Charlie, but led..to their final extinguishment.

b. The putting an end to (a contract, right, etc.); abolition (of a law, custom, †tax). In *Law* also *spec.* 'the annihilation of a collateral interest, or the supersedure of one interest by another and greater interest' (Wharton *Law Lex.*).
1535 *Act 27 Hen. VIII*, c. 10 §1 The..extinguishment of all suche subtill practised feoffementes. **1554** in *Depositions, etc.* (Surtees Soc. No. 21) 57 For the..extinguishment of a mariage solempnized betwixt them in their infancies. **1574** tr. *Littleton's Tenures* 64 a, A release shall enure by waye of extinguishemente. **1683** T. HUNT *Def. Charter* 36 Charged with the extinguishment of many excellent Laws. **1818** HALLAM *Mid. Ages* (1872) I. 428 A suspension, but not extinguishment of rights. **1886** *Law Rep.* Weekly Notes 35/2 The accounts were limited to the period before Michaelmas, 1881, the time from which the extinguishment took effect.

c. The full discharge, 'wiping out' (of a debt or obligation).
1796 MORSE *Amer. Geog.* I. 266 To provide for the extinguishment of the existing debt. **1847** C. G. ADDISON *On Contracts* II. iv §i. (1883) 664 The extinguishment of the principal obligation necessarily involving in it the discharge of the surety. **1868** ROGERS *Pol. Econ.* iv. (1876) 7 Reciprocal extinguishment of obligations.

†**d.** The cutting off, putting an end to (a family, race, etc.); the fact of becoming extinct. *Obs.*
1539 TAVERNER *Gard. Wysed.* I. 13 b, Syngle lyfe hathe these incommodyties..extinguyshment of bloud, a straunger to be thyne heyre. **1612** DAVIES *Why Ireland, etc.* 210 Rebellion, wherein he perished himselfe, and made a final extinguishment of his house and honour. **1630** *R. Johnson's Kingd. & Commw.* 114 By the extinguishment of the Picts, it reached also unto Tweed.

†**e.** Annihilation (of the soul). *Obs.*
1592 DAVIES *Immort. Soul* xxx. §4 When Death's Form appears, she [the soul] feareth not An utter Quenching, or Extinguishment. **1625** USSHER *Answ. Jesuit* 327 A most absolute extinguishment as well of the soule as of the body.

†**extirp** (ɛk'stɜːp), *v. Obs.* or *arch.* Also 5-6 extyrpe, 5-7 ex(s)tirpe, (7 exsterpe). [ad. F.

extirp-er = Pr. *extirpar*, ad. L. *ex(s)tirpāre*: see EXTIRPATE.]

1. *trans.* To root up (plants); = EXTIRPATE 2.
1490 CAXTON *Eneydos* xix. 73 To extirpe and waste alle the goodes comyng oute of the erth. **1563–87** FOXE *A. & M.* (1641) I. 563 To extirpe and pluck the same [wild cockle] up by the roots. **1601** HOLLAND *Pliny* I. 525 These reeds do multiplie.. after the old plants be extirped & destroied.
absol. *a* **1643** G. SANDYS *Paraphr. Div. Poems, Eccl.* iii. 4 A time to plant, t'extirpe: to Kill, to Cure.

b. *transf.* = EXTIRPATE 2 b.
1622 CALLIS *Stat. Sewers* (1647) 54 These banks.. may be extirped if they be.. a hinderance to the common good.

c. = EXTIRPATE 2 c.
1541 R. COPLAND *Guydon's Quest. Chirurg.* A iv, Tyll that.. which is the causer of the other be totally extyrped the healynge can nat be. **1590** SPENSER *F.Q.* I. x. 25 Festring sore did rankle yett within.. Which to extirpe, he laid him privily Downe. **1621** G. SANDYS *Ovid's Met.* VI. (1626) 123, I.. am fit.. His eyes, his tongue, or what did thee inforce, T'extirp. **1650** BULWER *Anthropomet., Pref. Verse*, [The teeth] filed down, or else extirped quite.

2. To root out, exterminate (a family, sect, or nation); = EXTIRPATE 3.
1547 J. HARRISON *Exhort. Scottes* 216 The race of them is.. not.. extirped. **1598** SYLVESTER *Du Bartas* II iv. I. *Tropheis* 887 He.. Wholly extirps the down-trod Jebusite. **1635** HEYWOOD *Hierarch.* VIII. 501 A large Patent.. T'extirp the Witches thence. *a* **1672** ANNE BRADSTREET *Poems* (1678) 166 His seed to be extirpt, was destined. **1682** R. BURTHOGGE *An Argument* (1684) 122 Antipædobaptisme.. doth put it [the Church] in no small hazard of being utterly extirped.

b. *intr.* To die out, root and all.
1606 G. W[OODCOCKE] tr. *Justin's Hist.* 116 a, They should be vtterly rooted out, and the posteritye of their name extirp.

3. With immaterial obj.; = EXTIRPATE 4.
(Austin's attempted revival of the word has not been imitated so far as our quots. show.)
1483 CAXTON *Gold. Leg.* 430/1 This.. fader.. foughte ageynst the heretykes.. and extyrped their heresye. **1552** LATIMER *Serm. Lord's Prayer* vi. 47 God hath done greater thinges in.. extirping out all popery. **1603** SHAKS. *Meas. for M.* III. ii. 110. **1605** B. JONSON *Volpone* IV. ii, To extirpe the memory Of such an act. **1623** PENKETHMAN *Handf. Hon.* Pref., Wee may extirpe or root out vices. **1721** STRYPE *Eccl. Mem.* I. xxxiv. 250 These monasteries should be extirped. **1832** AUSTIN *Jurispr.* (1873) I. 132. *Ibid.* (1879) I. xxiv. 483. *Ibid.* (1879) II. 986 Errors or defects in the details are readily extirped or supplied.

¶ *erron.* To speak abusively *against*. [Perh. arising from an ignorant misunderstanding of the phrase 'the extirping of the Bishop of Rome', common in controversial literature.]
1605 ROWLEY *When you see me* H, She did exsterp [*ed.* **1613** exstirpe, **1621**, **1632** extirpe] against his Holinesse. *Ibid.* F ij b, Exstirpe.

Hence **ex'tirped** *ppl. a.* **ex'tirper**, one who roots out or destroys. **ex'tirping** *vbl. sb.*
1502 ARNOLDE *Chron.* 159 Encresar off all goodnes, Extirper of synners and.. interpiter of dew lauwe. **1535** *Act 27 Hen. VIII*, c. 10 §1 The extirping and extinguishment of all suche subtill practised feoffementes. **1543** GRAFTON *Contn. Harding* 606 The extirpying and abholyshyng of the vsurped authoritee of the b[ishop] of Rome. **1605** BACON *Adv. Learn.* I. vii. §1 Extirpers of tyrants.. were honoured but with the titles of worthies or demi-gods. *c* **1640** J. SMYTH *Lives Berkeleys* (1883) I. 172 A great journey into Wales for the extirpinge of that nation.

†**ex'tirpable**, *a.* *Obs.* [f. L. *ex(s)tirpāre*: see next and -ABLE.] That may be extirpated.
1676 EVELYN *Phil. Dis. Earth* 131 Lest it infect the Ground with a Plant not easily extirpable.

†**'extirpate,** *pple.* *Obs.* [ad. L. *ex(s)tirpātus*, pa. pple. of *ex(s)tirpāre*: used as pa. pple. of next.] Rooted out, destroyed utterly, rendered extinct.
1541 ELYOT *Image Gov.* (1549) 116 It is profitable.. to haue all occasions of sedicion.. to be extirpate. *a* **1649** DRUMM. OF HAWTH. *Hist. Jas. V.* Wks. (1711) 107 When a vice cannot be extirpate and taken away. **1706** DE FOE *Jure Div.* VII. 146 *note*, The Race of Sinners was extirpate.

extirpate ('ɛkstəpeɪt, ɛk'stɜːpeɪt), *v.* Also 7 extirpat. [f. L. *ex(s)tirpāt-* ppl. stem of *ex(s)tirpāre*, f. *ex-* (see EX- *pref.*[1]) + *stirp-s* stem or stock of a tree. Cf. EXTIRP *v.*]

†**1.** *trans.* To clear of stumps. In quot. *fig.* *Obs.*
1548 HALL *Chron.* (1809) 426 He might wede, extirpate, and purdge the myndes of men.

2. To pull or pluck up by the roots; to root up, destroy, or remove root and branch (a tree, plant).
1651 W. G. tr. *Cowel's Inst.* 278 All such Offenders should have.. their Woods extirpated and grub'd up. **1664** EVELYN *Kal. Hort.* (1729) 213 Pluck up Strawberry Runners, extirpate the tall Stalks. **1691** RAY *Creation* I. (1704) 189 Extirpate noxious and unprofitable Herbs. **1776** GIBBON *Decl. & F.* I. xxv. 746 The vines and fruit-trees.. were extirpated. **1796** C. MARSHALL *Garden.* iii. (1813) 31 The better way.. is.. to extirpate the intermediate trees. **1848** MILL *Pol. Econ.* I. xi. §2 The wood seems to have been.. extirpated.
fig. **1836** J. H. NEWMAN *Par. Serm.* (ed. 2) II. vi. 71 Regeneration.. does not extirpate the root of evil.

†**b.** *transf.*
c **1666** in Murray's *Lincolnshire* (1890) 24 The old Church.. having been 'extirpated by a hurricane' in 1666.

c. *esp.* in *Surg.* To root out, remove (anything spoken of as having roots).
1650 BULWER *Anthropomet.* 131 For men.. to labour to extirpate.. the Beard.. is a practical blasphemy. **1767** GOOCH *Treat. Wounds* I. 167 Extirpating several breasts, and large tumors. **1774** PENNANT *Tour Scot. in 1772*, 74 Small pincers for the purpose of extirpating hairs. **1836** TODD *Cycl. Anat.* I. 242/1 When a nævus is extirpated, it seems to consist of a mass of cellular tissue.

3. To root out, exterminate, or totally destroy (a class, sect, or nation); to kill off, and render extinct (a species of animals or plants). Const. *out of, from.*
1586 J. HOOKER *Girald. Irel.* II. xvi. 41 in *Holinshed*, Yet was their nobilitie so honourable and great; that by no meanes.. was the same to be extirpated or rooted out. **1649** *Alcoran* 41 God.. forgiveth sins to those that believe, and extirpate Infidels. *a* **1704** LOCKE (J.), The breed ought to be extirpated out of the island. **1798** FERRIAR *Illustr. Sterne, Varieties of Man* 206 The Pygmies were extirpated by their wars. **1882** MRS. PITMAN *Mission L. Greece & Pal.* 310 The founder of Islam.. believing in the mission of the sword to extirpate all Christians and Jews.

b. In weaker sense: To do away with, render extinct as such (a specified class of persons); to root out utterly, break up (a gang of thieves). Formerly also, †to drive out, clear away (persons) *from* a locality, etc.
1566 PAINTER *Pal. Pleas.* I. 10, I will driue and extirpate oute of this Citie both L. Tarquinius Superbus, and his wicked wife, with all the race of his children and progenie. **1610** SHAKS. *Temp.* I. ii. 125 He.. Should presently extirpate me and mine Out of the Dukedom. **1713** STEELE *Englishman* No. 4. 23 The Comedies, you see, have extirpated the whole Species of Beaux. **1737** *Common Sense* (1738) I. 186 The Honour of extirpating such a notorious Robber from the Society. **1855** MACAULAY *Hist. Eng.* IV. 205 It is.. one of the first duties of every government to extirpate gangs of thieves.

4. To root out, eradicate (an immaterial thing, *e.g.* heresy, vice, etc.) Const. †*out of, from.*
1539 J. HUSEE in *Lisle Papers* V. 75, I hope it shall please your Lordship to extirpate this sudden desperate sorrow.. out of the bottom of your stomach. **1549** LATIMER *Serm. Ploughers* (Arb.) 37 He destroied al Idolatrie, and clearly dyd extirpate all superstition. **1660** R. COKE *Justice Vind.* Pref. 19 Until monarchy or regal power should be extirpated in all the world. **1789** BENTHAM *Princ. Legisl.* xix. §15 With what chance of success.. would a legislator go about to extirpate drunkenness.. by dint of legal punishment? **1828** SCOTT *F.M. Perth* xxv, The holy Church is awakened.. to extirpate heresy by fire and steel. **1838** EMERSON *Nat., Lit. Ethics* Wks. (Bohn) II. 205 Neither years nor books have yet availed to extirpate a prejudice then rooted in me.

Hence **'extirpated** *ppl. a.* **'extirpating** *vbl. sb.* and *ppl. a.*
1670 MILTON *Hist. Eng.* II. (1851) 65 The final extirpating of that whole Nation. **1674** tr. *Scheffer's Lapland* ix. 34 All possible means were used.. for the extirpating of superstition. **1827** SOUTHEY *Penins. War* II. 25 The Spaniards had to atone for extirpated nations. **1865** BUSHNELL *Vicar. Sacr.* III. v. 279 Sin.. a desolating, extirpating power in souls.

extirpation (ɛkstə'peɪʃən). Also 6 **exterpatione**, **extirpacion**, **-tion**, **exturpacion**. [ad. L. *ex(s)tirpātiōn-em*, n. of action f. *ex(s)tirpāre*: see EXTIRPATE *v.* Cf. F. *extirpation.*] The action of extirpating.

†**1.** The clearing (ground) of trees, etc. Cf. EXTIRPATE *v.* 1. *Obs.*
1607 NORDEN *Surv. Dial.* 217 The generall extirpation.. of coppise grounds in Middlesex.

2. The action of rooting up trees or weeds; total destruction.
1675 M. CLIFFORD *Hum. Reason* in *Phenix* (1708) II. 532 The Extirpation of those Weeds. **1725** BRADLEY *Fam. Dict.* s.v. *Oak*, Grubbing is only to be done where final extirpation is designed. **1796** MORSE *Amer. Geog.* II. 180 The joint extirpation of woods and men. **1837** *Penny Cycl.* VIII. 103/2 The.. extirpation of couch grass is one of the first things which an experienced farmer sets himself to.

b. *Surg.* The operation of removing, by excision or the application of caustics, anything having an inward growth.
1706 in PHILLIPS (ed. Kersey). **1732** ARBUTHNOT *Rules of Diet* 330 The difficulty of.. Breathing, occasioned by Schirrosities of the Glands is not to be cur'd any other-wise than by Extirpation. **1818** *Art Preserv. Feet* 52 A black corn.. on extirpation.. is found to have a black clot of blood at the lower extremity of the stem. **1875** H. WALTON *Dis. Eye* 110 Operations on the eyeball, abscission, and extirpation.

3. The action of extirpating or rooting out; extermination: **a.** of a nation, family, sect, species, etc. **b.** of an immaterial thing, *e.g.* heresy, a religion, vice, etc.
1526 *Pilgr. Perf.* (W. de W. 1531) 56 Extirpation, that is, the pluckyng out of all maner of vyces by the rotes. **1602** T. FITZHERBERT *Apol.* 4 a, The extirpation of heresy. **1699** BURNET *39 Art.* vii. (1700) 95 The Jews were to fall under.. an utter Extirpation. **1708** SWIFT *Abolit. Chr.* Wks. 1755 II. I. 95 The extirpation of the gospel. **1794** GOUV. MORRIS in Sparks *Life & Writ.* (1832) II. 411 It will become on both sides a war of extirpation. **1846** MCCULLOCH *Acc. Brit. Empire* (1854) I. 421 Extirpation of the smallpox. **1877** J. A. ALLEN *Amer. Bison* 559 The extirpation of the buffalo.

Hence **extir'pationist**, one who maintains a theory of extirpation.
1881 *Cornh. Mag.* Sept. 340 The Teutonic extirpationists.

extirpative ('ɛkstəpeɪtɪv), *a.* [f. EXTIRPATE *v.* + -IVE.] Tending to extirpate.
1733 CHEYNE *Eng. Malady* III. Introd. (1734) 266 Of the Medicines, I have mention'd only the.. extirpative ones.

extirpator ('ɛkstəpeɪtə(r), -'tɜːpətə(r)). Also 8 -er. [ad. L. *ex(s)tirpātor*, agent-n. f. *ex(s)tirpāre*: see EXTIRPATE *v.*] One who, or that which, extirpates.
1706 in PHILLIPS (ed. Kersey), *Extirpator* one that Extirpates or Destroys, as an Extirpater of Heresies. **1776–83** JUSTAMOND *Raynal's Indies* (ed. 2) I. 283 These extirpators with all their industry can only execute their commission upon the coast. **1805** R. W. DICKSON *Pract. Agric.* (1807) I. 35 The extirpator is a machine of this sort.. for detroying weeds. **1830** D'ISRAELI *Chas. I*, III. xii. 264 The great extirpator of episcopacy. **1870** ANDERSON *Missions Amer. Bd.* III. viii. 115 Three men.. extirpators of heresy.

‖**extispex** (ɛk'stɪspɛks). *Rom. Antiq.* Pl. **ex'tispices**. [L.; f. *exta* (see EXTA) + *-spex* f. *specĕre* to look at.] One whose duty it was to inspect the entrails of sacrificial victims for the purpose of divination; a haruspex.
1727 BAILEY vol. II, *Extispices*, the same as *aruspices*. **1751** CHAMBERS *Cycl.* s.v. *Extispex*, In Italy, the first extispices were the Hetrurians. **1855** SMEDLEY *Occult Sciences* 332 The officers were extispices or aruspices.

†**extispicine.** *Obs.* [a. Fr. *extispicine*, f. L. *extispicium*: see EXTISPICY.] = EXTISPICY.
a **1693** URQUHART *Rabelais* III. xxv, Will you have a trial of your fortune by the art of aruspiciny? By augury? or by extispicine?

†**exti'spicious,** *a.* *Obs.* *rare*[−1]. Also 7–8 **extispitious**. [f. L. *extispici-um* the function of an EXTISPEX + -OUS.] Of or pertaining to inspection of entrails for the purpose of divination.
1646 SIR T. BROWNE *Pseud. Ep.* I. xi. 44 Thus hath he [Satan] deluded many Nations in his Auguriall and Extispicious inventions. **1755** in JOHNSON.

extispicy (ɛk'stɪspɪsɪ). *Rom. Antiq.* Also 8 **extispice**. [ad. L. *extispicium*: see EXTISPICIOUS.] Inspection of the entrails of sacrificial victims for the purpose of divination; haruspicy.
1681 BLOUNT *Glossogr.*, *Extispacy*. **1721–1800** BAILEY, *Extispice*. **1751** CHAMBERS *Cycl.* s.v. *Medicine*, Extispicy or inspecting the entrails of beasts. **1855** SMEDLEY *Occult Sciences* 292 Extispicy, the observation of entrails.

extol (ɛk'stɒl, ɛk'stəʊl), *v.* Also 5–7 **extoll(e**. [ad. L. *extoll-ĕre*, f. *ex-* (see EX- *pref.*[1]) + *tollĕre* to raise.]

†**1.** *trans.* To lift up, raise, elevate. *Obs.*
1549–62 STERNHOLD & H. *Ps.* lxxxvi. 4 Unto thee Lord I extoll, And lift my soule and minde. **1572** BOSSEWELL *Armorie* II. 96 He cannot.. extol him selfe higher then the earth. **1601** WEEVER *Mirr. Mart.* B iv b, A begger from the dunghill once extold, Forgets him selfe. *a* **1625** BEAUM. & FL. (Webster 1864), Who extolled you in the half-crown boxes. **1650** T. BAYLY *Herba Parietis* To Rdr., A fiery Charriot, able to extoll an Elias up to Heaven.
absol. **1618** CHAPMAN *Hesiod* I. 9 Great Jove's will orders all; For he with ease extols, with ease lets fall. **1646** SIR T. BROWNE *Pseud. Ep.* II. iii. 72 The newtrall point wherein its [the iron's] gravity just equalls the magneticall quality, the one exactly extolling as much as the other depresseth.
fig. **1587** *Mirr. Mag., Bladud* xiv, Our actes extoll our prayse aboue the skie. **1601** ? MARSTON *Pasquil & Kath.* I. 233 Thy praise extold him to the skies.

†**b.** = SUBLIME *v.*
1657 TOMLINSON *Renou's Disp.* 90 Such as are not easily sublevated.. are to be extolled [L. *sublimantur*] in a Retort of very thick glass.

†**2. a.** To lift up in dignity or authority; to uphold the authority of. *Obs.*
1545 JOYE *Exp. Dan.* xii. 209 This kinge.. shall extoll and preferre himself aboue all the goddis. **1552** LYNDESAY *Monarche* 5244 Cardinall, Kyng, or Empriour, Extolland thare Traditionis Abufe Christis Institutionis. **1570** *Act 13 Eliz.* c. 2 §1 That no Person.. shall.. maintain, defend or extol the same usurped Power [of the see of Rome]. **1581** LAMBARDE *Eiren.* II. vii. (1588) 228 The Treason of extolling forein power.

†**b.** To 'lift up' with pride, joy, etc. *Obs.*
1526 *Pilgr. Perf.* (W. de W. 1531) 88 b, Lest the multytude of reuelacyons sholde extoll hym, and make hym proude. **1609** BIBLE (Douay) *Ecclus.* xxxii. 1 Have they made thee Ruler? be not extolled. **1664** *Flodden F.* vi. 54 Because he vex'd our Land of late, Perchance his stomack is extold.

†**c.** To raise too high, make too much of; to exaggerate, boast of. *Obs.*
1494 FABYAN *Chron.* V. cxl. 127 Walshemen extolle so hugely theyr blood & allyaunce.. & regardyd so lytle the.. lynyall dissent of the Saxons. **1503** HAWES *Examp. Virt.* v. 48 No persone can extoll the souerente Of her worthy and royall dygnyte. **1551** GARDINER *Explic. Cath. Faith* 32 b, If man should then waxe proude and.. extolle his owne deuotion in these ministeries. **1652** NEEDHAM tr. *Selden's Mare Cl.* 209 The Hors and Foot and the Sea-Souldiers.. extoll'd every one their own hazards. **1796** C. MARSHALL *Garden.* i. (1813) 1 The praise of gardening it is presumed can hardly be too much extolled.

3. To raise high with praise; to praise highly; to magnify.
1509 FISHER *Fun. Serm. C'tess Richmond* Wks. (1876) 293 Whome my purpose is not vaynly to extol, or to magnifye aboue her merytes. **1582** BENTLEY *Mon. Matrones* 47 S. John extolleth charitie in his Epistle. **1601** B. JONSON *Poetaster* II. Wks. (Rtldg.) 112/1 They.. extoll'd your perfections to the heavens. **1683** *Brit. Spec.* 18 Thou art a glorious Isle extolled and renowned among all Nations. **1712** ADDISON *Spect.* No. 469 ¶6 To find Virtue extolled, and Vice stigmatized. **1762** J. BROWN *Poetry & Mus.* v. (1763) 59 Strabo.. highly extolls this Practice. **1879** FROUDE *Cæsar* xxvi. 450 Some will extol you to the skies, others will find something wanting.

† exto'llation. *Obs. rare*⁻¹. [f. EXTOL + -ATION: cf. med.L. *extollātiōn-em*, OF. *extollation*.] The action of extolling; laudation, praise.

a **1654** WEBSTER *Thracian Wonder* I. i, With extollation of a thing so vile.

extolled (ɛk'stɒld, ɛk'stəʊld), *ppl. a.* [f. EXTOL + -ED¹.]

†**a.** Upraised, upreared; elevated (*obs.*). **b.** Praised, magnified, celebrated.

a. 1607 TOPSELL *Serpents* (1653) 613 Discouraged by the extolled head of the serpent to his breast.

b. 1632 J. HAYWARD tr. *Biondi's Eromena* 44 The Prince.. enamoured of her extolled beautie. **1644** MILTON *Educ.*, Those extolled remains of Grecian lawgivers.

extoller (ɛk'stɒlə(r), ɛk'stəʊlə(r)). [f. EXTOL + -ER¹.] One who extols (see EXTOL 2 a, 3).

a **1626** BACON *Charge Sess. Verge* (1662) 8 Extollers of the Pope's Supremacy. **1684** tr. *Agrippa's Van. Artes* xviii. 60 The worst.. things never want their extollers. **1755** in JOHNSON. Hence in mod. Dicts.

extolling (ɛk'stɒlɪŋ, ɛk'stəʊlɪŋ), *vbl. sb.* [f. as prec. + -ING¹.] The action of the vb. EXTOL.

1558 *Act 1 Eliz.* c. I. §27 If any Person.. shall.. execute any Thing for the Extolling.. or Defence of any such.. usurped Jurisdiction. **1560** *Declar. Faith* in Neal *Hist. Purit.* (1732) I. 161, I do utterly disallow the extolling of Images. **1620** SHELTON *Quix.* II. xxv. 164 These praises and extollings doe more properly belong to you then mee. **1709** STRYPE *Ann. Ref.* I. xxvi. 306 The extolling of the Bishop of Rome made præmunire for the second offence. **1858** FROUDE *Hist. Eng.* III. xii. 75 A third [injunction] forbade the extolling the special virtues of images and relics.

ex'tolling, *ppl. a.* [f. as prec. + -ING².] That extols or praises. Hence **ex'tollingly** *adv.*, in an extolling manner, in commendation or praise.

1886 *Argosy* July 70 A celebrated physician spoke to me extollingly of Bath.

extolment (ɛk'stɒlmənt). ? *Obs.* [f. as prec. + -MENT. Cf. F. *extollement* (Godefr. 1571).] The action of extolling or praising; eulogy.

1602 SHAKS. *Ham.* v. ii. 121 In the verity of extolment, I take him to be a soul of great article. **1640** SIR E. DERING *Prop. Sacr.* (1644) 17 If.. two Fathers.. for honour to the.. sacrament, should in the extollment of it passe an earnest word. **1813** W. TAYLOR in *Monthly Rev.* LXX. 500 Cicero's extolments of Cato and others.

† ex'tonious, *a. Obs. rare*⁻¹. In 6 -youse. [f. OF. *eston-er* to ASTONISH + -IOUS.] Astonishing.

1548 GEST *Pr. Masse* 78 Which graunt [= admission].. is extonyouse and unbeleavable.

† ex'torque, *v. Obs.*⁻⁰ [ad. L. *extorqu-ēre*: see EXTORT.] = EXTORT.

1623-6 in COCKERAM.

† ex'torse, *v. Obs. Sc.* Also 6 extorss, 7 extorce. [f. L. *extors-* rare form of ppl. stem of *extorquēre*: see EXTORT.] *trans.* To practise extortion upon; hence, to oppress.

1567 *Sc. Acts Jas. VI* (1814) III. 42 Neyther the saidis customaris be sufferit to extorss the people as thai haue done in tymes past. **1604** EARL STIRLING *Avrora* Sonn. lxiv. 13 Too many grieuous plagues my state extorse. **1614** —— *Doomes-day, 4th Houre* lxxxix, By men even dead (as oft alive) extorc'd, To avarice, else cruelty, still slave.

absol. **1728** RAMSAY *Gen. Mistake* Wks. 1851 II. 339 A penman.. lends, extorses, cheats.

extorsion (ɛk'stɔːʃən). [f. L. *extorsiōn-em* (see EXTORTION *sb.*).] Outward rotation of a part of the body, esp. of the eye.

1899 A. DUANE tr. *Fuchs's Text-bk. Ophthalmol.* (ed. 2) xiv. 578 The *inferior rectus*.. rotates the eye in such a way that the upper extremity of the vertical meridian is depressed to the outside (extorsion). **1964** S. DUKE-ELDER *Parsons' Dis. Eye* (ed. 14) xxviii. 446 An involuntary movement of torsion: intorsion when the upper pole of the cornea rotates nasally, extorsion when temporally.

extorsion, -er, obs. ff. of EXTORTION *sb.*, -ER.

extorsive (ɛkstɔːsɪv), *a. rare.* [f. L. *extors-* (see EXTORSE *v.*) + -IVE.] **a.** Serving or tending to extort; of the nature of extortion. **b.** Obtained by extortion.

1669 W. SIMPSON *Hydrol. Chym.* 253 If they make any confession.. it's onely extorsive. **1775** A. HAMILTON *Farmer Refuted* Wks. 1851 II. 50 A complication of extorsive measures.

Hence †**ex'torsively** *adv. rare*⁻⁰.

1755 in JOHNSON; whence in mod. Dicts.

† ex'tort, *ppl. a. Obs.* Also 5-6 extorte. [ad. L. *extort-us*, pa. pple. of *extorquēre*: see next.]

a. Extorted, wrongfully obtained (rarely as *pa. pple.*). **b.** *esp.* in *extort power*; whence a sense = 'extortionate' (in *extort exactions*).

1430 LYDG. *Chron. Troy* v. xxxvi, By extorte tytle false successyon. **1492** *Plumpton Corr.* 264 Intendinge.. to keepe the same [land] by extort power contrary to the law. **1540** *Act 32 Hen. VIII*, c. 24 The extorte exactions of innumerable summes of monei. **1596** SPENSER *F.Q.* v. ii. 5 Hauing great Lordships got and goodly farmes, Through strong oppression of his powre extort. *Ibid.* v. x. 25 A Citie .. by force extort out of her hand By her strong foe.

extort (ɛk'stɔːt), *v.* Also 6 extorte. [f. L. *extort-* ppl. stem of *extorquēre*, f. *ex-* out + *torquēre* to twist.] *literally*, To wrest or wring (something) from a person; to extract by torture.

1. *trans.* To obtain from a reluctant person by violence, torture, intimidation, or abuse of legal or official authority, or (in weaker sense) by importunity, overwhelming arguments, or any powerful influence. Const. *of, from, out of,* †*upon.*

a. with obj. money, payments, etc. Also *absol.* to practise extortion.

1529 in Fiddes *Wolsey* II. 175 Not for good order of the diocess but to extort treasure. *c* **1555** *Fisher's Wks., Life* 141 Lykwise for diuers bribes extorted vpon manie of his subiects. **1585** ABP. SANDYS *Serm.* (1841) 287 He went.. not to poll and pill, to extort and wring out of the people what he could; but.. to do good. **1611** SHAKS. *Cymb.* III. i. 48 The .. Romans, did extort This Tribute from vs. **1624** CAPT. SMITH *Virginia* (1629) 120 They would hold it worse than sacrilege to.. extort upon the common souldier a penny. **1716-8** LADY M. W. MONTAGUE *Lett.* I. xxx. 98 The villages are so poor, that only force could extort from them necessary provisions. **1820** MISS MITFORD in L'Estrange *Life* II. iv. 87 Taxes.. are only extorted by threatening notices. **1883** *Law Rep. 11 Q. Bench Div.* 577 That the lord of a manor may ask for as much as he thinks that he can extort from the copyhold tenant.

absol. *c* **1592** MARLOWE *Jew of Malta* II. ii, With extorting, cozening [etc.].. I fill'd the jails with bankrouts in a year. **1598** BARCKLEY *Felic. Man* II. (1603) 125 Bribing and extorting upon his subjects. **1764** GOLDSM. *Lett. Hist. Eng.* (1772) I. 104 He extorted from the Jews.. without any remorse. **1826** HOOD *Death's Ramble* ix, He knew that sort of man would extort, Though summon'd to all eternity. **1855** MACAULAY *Hist. Eng.* IV. 363 The rapacious governor had daily opportunities of embezzling and extorting.

b. with immaterial obj., actions, utterances, manifestation of feeling, concessions, acknowledgements, promises, etc. Said both of persons and of circumstances or influences.

1550 BALE *Image Both Ch.* II. xvii, Confession in the eare was cruellye extorted of Christian people vnder.. payne of death. **1563-87** FOXE *A. & M.* (1596) 5/2 They haue extorted into their own hands the plenarie fulness of power. **1659** HAMMOND *On Ps.* vi. 6 Paraphr. 36 My agonies extort .. tears from me. **1662** STILLINGFL. *Orig. Sacr.* III. i. §15 Neither can hee deserve the name of a man, from whom the observation of the courses of the stars.. does not extort gratitude. **1665** GLANVILL *Sceps. Sci.* i. 12 The extorting a Confession of that Ignorance. **1732** BERKELEY *Alciphr.* I. §14 Concessions, which the force of truth seems to have extorted from you. *c* **1750** SHENSTONE *Ruin'd Abbey* 175 No solemn bell extort a neighbour's tear. **1771** *Junius Lett.* liv. 286 These praises are extorted from me. **1818** JAS. MILL *Brit. India* II. v. iv. 443 A situation which extorted the compassion of Englishmen. **1863** H. COX *Instit.* I. vii. 80 The barons extorted from the King power to elect twelve ordainers.

c. In literal sense: To wrest (a material object) *from. rare.*

1784 COWPER *Task* v. 189 Nations would do well To extort their truncheons from the puny hands Of heroes.

2. To extract forcibly, 'wring' (a sense or conclusion) *from* (a passage, premises, etc.).

1601 SHAKS. *Twel. N.* III. i. 165 Do not extort thy reasons from this clause. **1653** MILTON *Hirelings* (1659) 31 From this example they never will be able to extort that the people in those days paid tithes to priests. *Mod.* How can you extort any other meaning from the passage?

†**3. a.** To practise extortion on (a person); in quot. 1561 with allusion to literal sense 'to rack'. **b.** To 'torture', strain (a law). *Obs.*

1561 *Godly Q. Hester* (1873) 44 The commons he extorteth tyll they bee lame. **1612** DAVIES *Why Ireland, etc.* 276 They did extort and oppresse the people. **1616** J. LANE *Sqr.'s Tale* xi. 360 Captives.. to Greece transported, sold, and by these badd mistresses extorted. **1681** CROWNE *Hen. VI*, II. 14 We may extort the law.. to punish beyond bounds of law.

Hence **ex'torting** *vbl. sb.* and *ppl. a.*

1599 MARSTON *Sco. Villanie* II. v. 196 Though he laid forth all his stock and store Vpon some office.. he will trebble it.. by his extorting wit. **1641** *Tapsters Downfall* 7 Not branded with the extorting seale of avarice. *a* **1711** KEN *Hymns Festiv.* Poet. Wks. 1721 I. 379 Mammon.. set in his extorting stall. **1715** NELSON *Addr. Pers. Qual.* 195 The many extorting Acts, which are practised in those Houses of Bondage. **1771** GOLDSM. *Hist. Eng.* III. 64 She took several very extorting methods by loans.

† ex'tort, *sb. Obs.* [f. the vb.] The action of the vb. EXTORT; extortion, torture.

1556 J. HEYWOOD *Spider & F.* lxxxviii. 165 Ye are sure.. to get ought by your extort, Or get or kepe ought. **1541** *Sch.-house Women* 556 in Hazl. *E.P.P.* IV. 126 They meane it a nother way, And say, she is mans vtter extort. **1599** BP. HALL *Sat.* IV. v. 103 Albee such mayne extort scorns to be pent, in the clay walles of thatched Tenement. [But possibly 'mayne extort' = *extort power*: see EXTORT *ppl. a.*]

extorted (ɛk'stɔːtɪd), *ppl. a.* [f. EXTORT *v.* + -ED¹.] In senses of the vb. Cf. EXTORT *ppl. a.*

1552 HULOET, Extorted, *compilatus.* **1590** SPENSER *F.Q.* I. vii. 18 With extorted powre and borrow'd strength. **1593** SHAKS. *2 Hen. VI*, IV. vii. 105 Are my Chests filled vp with extorted Gold? **1632** LITHGOW *Trav.* V. 206 Weary and extorted Trauellers. **1667** FLAVEL *Saint Indeed* (1754) 136 These extorted complaints. **1784** COWPER *Task* IV. 403 Live without extorted alms From grudging hands. **1826** SCOTT *Woodst.* xv, An extorted promise of silence. **1865** HOOK *Lives Abps.* III. vii. 449 The rack-extorted admissions of the persecuted Templars.

†**b.** Strained, forced. *Obs.*

1622-62 HEYLIN *Cosmogr.* Introd. (1666) 10 How extorted and unnatural are the derivations of the Allumæotæ from Almodad, of the Manitæ from Abimail, etc.

Hence †**ex'tortedly** *adv.*, by extortion.

1640 LD. DIGBY *Sp. Trienn. Parl.* (1641) 14 A King that had.. given all the Rights and Liberties of his Subjects a more cleare and ample confirmation freely and gratiously, then all his Predecessors.. extortedly.

extorter (ɛk'stɔːtə(r)). See also **extortor.** [f. as prec. + -ER¹.]

One who extorts. Const. *of.*

1591 SYLVESTER *Du Bartas* I. iii. (1641) 25/1 You strict Extorters, that the poor oppress. **1605** CAMDEN *Rem.* 186 Edric the extorter. **1794** SIR W. JONES *Instit. Hindu Law* ix. §258 Extorters of money by threats. **1846** TRENCH *Mirac.* xxix. (1862) 424 God, the extorter of those unwilling.. prophecies from wicked men.

extortion (ɛk'stɔːʃən), *sb.* Forms: 4-6 extorcion, -cioun(e, 4 -cyoune, 5 -cyon, 4-7 extorsion, 4 -scion, -siun, 5 -sioun, -syoun, 6 -syon, 4- extortion. [ad. L. *extortiōn-em*, also *extorsiōn-em*, n. of action f. *extorquēre* (see EXTORT). Cf. F. *extorsion.*]

1. The action or practice of extorting or wresting anything, *esp.* money, from a person by force or by undue exercise of authority or power; an instance of this; an act of illegal exaction.

a **1300** *Cursor M.* 27825 (Cott.) O couaitise.. cums.. reuelaic, theft, extorsiun. *c* **1340** HAMPOLE *Prose Tr.* v. (1866) 11 Thurghe extorcyone, as lordes duse. *c* **1386** CHAUCER *Friar's T.* 131 My wages ben ful streyt.. by extorciouns I lyve. **1429** *Pol. Poems* (1859) II. 142 Cherisshe thy lordes, hate extorcioun. **1593** SHAKS. *2 Hen. VI*, I. iii. 132 The Clergies Bags Are lanke and leane with thy Extortions. **1651** HOBBES *Leviath.* II. xxviii. 166 The continuance, and increasing of.. extortion. *a* **1715** BURNET *Own Time* (1724) I. 306 To bring them [the Bankers] to an account for their usury, and extortions. **1858** FROUDE *Hist. Eng.* III. xvii. 494 By bribery and extortion he had obtained vast sums of money.

b. *Law* (see quot. 1769).

1607 COWEL *Interpr.*, *Extortion*.. signifieth.. an unlawful or violent wringing of mony or mony worth from any man. **1674** *Essex Papers* (Camden) I. 229 This Country hath long layn under great Oppressions by yᵉ Extortion of yᵉ Clerks of yᵉ Crowne. **1769** BLACKSTONE *Comm.* IV. 141 Extortion.. consists in any officer's unlawfully taking, by colour of his office, from any man, any money or thing of value, that is not due to him, or more than is due, or before it is due. **1789** BENTHAM *Princ. Legisl.* xiii. §1 An act of extortion on the part of an officer of police. **1848** in WHARTON *Law Lex.* **1861** in W. BELL *Dict. Law Scot.*

†**c.** An extortionate claim or impost. *Obs.*

1745 *De Foe's Eng. Tradesman* I. xxx. 303 Paying an intolerable extortion of fifteen to twenty per cent premium.

†**2.** In etymological sense: **a.** A wresting of the sense of a word or phrase. **b.** A straining (of the nerves). *Obs.*

1652 NEEDHAM tr. *Selden's Mare Cl.* 27 The Italian Lawyers.. do force themselves with all extortion to verifie upon the Western Emperor that saying. **1725** BRADLEY *Fam. Dict.* s.v. *Nerves*, The same will also cure the Extorsions of the Nerves, if apply'd moderately hot.

ex'tortion, *v.* [f. prec. sb.] **a.** *intr.* To practise extortion. Const. *upon.* **b.** *trans.* To charge extortionate prices to; to overcharge.

1494 FABYAN *Chron.* VII. ccxxxiii. 267 The soldyours stale and extorcioned vpon both partyes. **1502** *Ord. Crysten Men* (W. de W. 1506) IV. xxi. 251 Yf he extorcyon or dystresse or gyueth ayde or consentynge that to do. **1663** SPALDING *Troub. Chas. I* (1792) I. 124 For such [meat] as they got they were extortioned. **1833** MARRYAT *P. Simple* viii, A bed and a breakfast.. for which they extortioned me three shillings and sax-pence. [Still in dialectal use (Chesh.).]

Hence †**ex'tortioning** *ppl. a.*

1655 HEYWOOD *Fort. by Land* IV. Wks. 1874 VI. 423 My poor usuring, extortioning Master.

ex'tortionable, *a. rare.* [f. as prec. + -ABLE.] = EXTORTIONATE.

1632 LITHGOW *Trav.* VI. 246 Two extortionable flatterers, Auarice and Ignorance. *Ibid.* IX. 403 Finding the fellow.. somewhat extortionable. **1775** DUCHESS KINGSTON in *Cooke's Mem. S. Foote* (1805) I. 205 An extortionable assassin of private reputation.

ex'tortionary, *a.* [f. as prec. + -ARY.] Given to or characterized by extortion.

1805 W. TAYLOR in *Ann. Rev.* III. 60 The fixed shopkeeper is not only less extortionary to his customer, but is more taxable to the state. **1831** CAPT. TRELAWNEY *Adv. Younger Son* I. 41 The extortionary Jew, chuckling with ecstacy at the usury he was about to realize. **1844** H. H. WILSON *Brit. India* I. 365 The overbearing and extortionary spirit of that military rule.

extortionate (ɛk'stɔːʃənət), *a.* [f. as prec. + -ATE².] **a.** Of persons, their qualities or actions: Characterized by extortion. **b.** Of prices, money demands: Grossly excessive, exorbitant.

1789 MRS. PIOZZI *Journ. France* I. 119 The inns are very extortionate. **1844** H. H. WILSON *Brit. India* I. 457 The amount is not extortionate. *a* **1845** HOOD *Knt. & Dragon* ii, He pounced down like a vulture, And.. Out of every man's meal Took a very extortionate multure. **1853** C. BRONTE *Villette* xli. (1876) 472 You are in good hands. M. Miret will not be extortionate. **1885** *Manch. Exam.* 8 May 5/3 The interest was extortionate and excessive.

extortioner (ɛk'stɔːʃənə(r)). [f. as prec. + -ER¹.] One who practises or is given to extortion.

c **1375** *Pains of Hell* 37 in *O.E. Misc.* App. ii. 211 þese were .. Extorcioners. **1413** LYDG. *Pilgr. Sowle* IV. xxix. (1859) 61 They done none execucion vpon extorcioners, ne tyrauntes.

1484 RICH. III in Ellis *Orig. Lett.* II. 54 I. 162 Many been knowen for open murdrers, advowters, and extortioners. **1526** *Pilgr. Perf.* (W. de W. 1531) 174 b, The vsurer, the thefe, & the extorcioner. **1649** BP. HALL *Cases Consc.* I. v. 46 Some covetous extortioner..buyes up the whole lading of the ship. **1789** BENTHAM *Princ. Legisl.* xiii. §1 The most determined extortioner in office has some bridle and some restraint. **1839** THIRLWALL *Greece* IV. 207 To purge the city of the vile informers and extortioners.

extortionist (ɛkˈstɔːʃənɪst). [f. as prec. + -IST.] One who extorts something from another; an extortioner.

1885 in OGILVIE.

†**exˈtortionize**, *v. Obs. rare.* [f. as prec. + -IZE.] *intr.* To practise extortion. Hence †**exˈtortionizing** *ppl. a.*

1630 J. TAYLOR (Water P.) *Wks.* 6/1 Extortionizing Curr.

†**exˈtortionous**, *a. Obs.* [f. as prec. + -OUS.] Characterized by extortion, oppressive.

1602 *Life T. Cromwell* II. ii. 89, I know this place to be extortionous.

†**exˈtortious**, *a. Obs.* Also 6 **-sious**, 7 **-cious**. [f. EXTORTI-ON + -OUS, after the analogy of *captious*.] **a.** Characterized by extortion, oppressive in exactions. **b.** Gained by extortion; demanded in an extortionate manner.

1602 FULBECKE *2nd Pt. Parall.* 26 The extorcious and tyrannous spoiles of Cleon. **1607** NORDEN *Surv. Dial.* 34 The..overburdening the Tenants..may be extortious. **1615** J. STEPHENS *Satyr. Ess.* (ed. 2) 13 Who threatens..If Clyents..Be slacke in payment of extortious coine. *a* **1656** BP. HALL *Rem. Wks.* (1660) 77 We do well..to curb the extortious cruelties of some. *a* **1734** NORTH *Lives* II. 420 Divers false and extortious demands which they call Avanias. **1776** BENTHAM *Wks.* (1843) I. 239 The lying and extortious jargon of Recoveries.

Hence †**exˈtortiously** *adv. Obs.*

1529 MORE *Comf. agst. Trib.* Wks. 1207 He was growen to substance in that office, that was commonly misseused extorsiously.

extortive (ɛkˈstɔːtɪv), *a.* [f. *extort-* ppl. stem of *extorquēre* (see EXTORT) + -IVE.] Of extortion; disposed to extort, prone to extortion.

1646 EARL MONM. tr. *Biondi's Hist. Civ. Warres Eng.* II. 210 Ambition had made use of cruell means; Avarice..of..extortive means. **1805** *Ann. Reg.* 1803, 292 A compromise between their ability and his extortive capacity. **1879** H. GEORGE *Progr. & Pov.* VII. ii, The extortive power of land ownership.

†**exˈtortor**. *Obs.* Also 7 **extortour**. [a. L. *extortor*, agent-n. f. *extorquēre*: see EXTORT.]

a. One who extorts; = EXTORTER. **b.** One who strains (a law); cf. EXTORT *v.* 3 b.

1590 SWINBURNE *Testaments* 243 An importunate begger is compared to an extortor. **1611** SPEED *Hist. Gt. Brit.* VI. xiii. §7 A great Enemie he was to Promoters, Pettifoggers, and Extortours of penall lawes. **1614** W. B. *Philosopher's Banquet* (ed. 2) 128 The Extortor thereof dyed by Famine.

†**exˈtoxicate**, *a. Obs.* $rare^{-1}$. In 5 **-ycat**. [f. L. *ex-* + *toxic-um* poison + -ATE^2.] Poisoned.

1430 LYDG. *Chron. Troy* IV. xxxiii, An arowe Extoxycat sharpe and venymous.

extra (ˈɛkstrə), *a.*, *adv.*, and *sb.* [prob. originally short for EXTRAORDINARY, which in 17th c. was commonly used as adj., adv., and sb. in the senses now belonging to *extra*. In Fr. *extra* is similarly used, and is explained by Littré as 'a popular abbreviation of *extraordinaire*'; it is uncertain whether the Eng. or the Fr. use is the earlier. Presumably from Fr. the word has been adopted into Ger. (*extra*), Sp. and It. (*estra*). A Ger. quot. for *extra dumm* (= 'extra stupid') in Grimm is dated 1775.]

A. *adj.* **a.** Beyond or more than the usual, stipulated, or specified amount or number; additional.

1776 G. CAMPBELL *Philos. Rhet.* (1801) I. 361 Instances [of barbarisms] are hyp for hypochondriac..penult for penultimate..extra for extraordinary. **1780** T. JEFFERSON *Corr.* Wks. 1859 I. 245 Money..for any extra wants of our own troops. **1782** MISS BURNEY *Cecilia* II. 34 The extra interest I must pay one of those extortioners is absolutely so much money thrown away. **1818** *Art Preserv. Feet* 19 The extra exercise which the person may have been taking. **1846** GREENER *Sc. Gunnery* 217 Cost is a matter of very minor consideration, when contrasted with the extra safety obtained. **1878** LECKY *Eng. in 18th C.* II. v. 66 Soldiers were employed on extra pay to make the roads. **1888** MISS BRADDON *Fatal Three* I. ii, She will have to put up with an extra bed in the housemaid's room.

b. *Electr.*

1834 FARADAY in *Phil. Trans.* (1835) CXXV. 47 The whole of this extra current might be made to pass at that place. **1883** J. E. H. GORDON *Electricity* I. xxx. 330 The transient currents in a coil are produced by the induction of each portion of the current on the neighbouring wires..these..are called the 'Extra Currents'.

c. Prefixed to trade designations of sizes (*esp.* of paper), to denote a size somewhat larger than that indicated by the name.

1811 L. M. HAWKINS *C'tess & Gertr.* I. 134 These 'extra-elephant folios' had not always the most erudite compilers. **1892** *Printer's Catalogue*, Sizes of Cards..Extra Thirds, 3 × $1\frac{7}{8}$ in. Thirds, 3 × $1\frac{1}{2}$ in. **1892** *Publisher's Catalogue*, Extra foolscap octavo.

d. Of superior or unusual quality; in *extra binding*, etc. Hence *extra binder*.

1850 MRS. STOWE *Uncle Tom's C.* iv, Her corn-cakes isn't extra, not extra now, Jinny's corn-cakes isn't. **1875** URE *Dict. Arts* I. 424 The cover of the book in extra binding is generally fitted on piecemeal. *Ibid.* I. 425 The implement generally used by the extra binder for cutting the edges of single books is the plough.

e. *extra cover* (*point*), a fieldsman in cricket whose position is between cover-point and mid-off, but more distant than either from the batsman's wicket; also, his position in the field. Also *ellipt.*

1867 G. H. SELKIRK *Guide Cricket Ground* ii. 26 Extra cover. When the batsman hits much to cover-point an extra man is placed near to aid in fielding the balls. **1888** A. G. STEEL in Steel & Lyttelton *Cricket* iii. 112 If the ground is inclined to be slow, he [*sc.* third man] may be brought forward to extra cover-point, between cover-point and mid-off. **1897** K. S. RANJITSINHJI *Jubilee Bk. Cricket* ii. 50 There is no need to treat extra-cover separately. The position is a cross between cover and mid-off, and its duties are a mixture of the duties required in those two places. **1921** P. F. WARNER *My Cricketing Life* xiv. 268 Skeet..is very quick on his feet at cover or extra cover. **1955** I. PEEBLES *Ashes* xv. 149 May hit the next ball splendidly past extra.

B. *adv.* **a.** With adjs. or advbs.: Beyond the ordinary degree, unusually. Sometimes hyphened as *Comb.*; upon the resulting adj. a parasynthetic sb. is occas. formed, as *extra-moral*, *extra-moralist*.

In recent years, the latest edition of several London evening papers has been called the *extra-special* edition, the latest but one being called 'special'. (*N.E.D.*, 1894). *extra sec* (or *extra dry*), of champagne: very slightly sweetened; also *ellipt.* as *sb.*

1823 SYD. SMITH *Botany B.* Wks. 1859 II. 15/2 Those extra-moralists..refuse to associate with a convict legally pardoned. **1863** KINGSLEY *Water-bab.*, He must be an extra good boy that day. **1868** DARWIN in *Life & Lett.* (1887) III. 80 Any such extra-sterile individuals..if they should here-after breed with other individuals. *Mod.* Extra-superfine cloth. Extra fine tallow. Extra refined petroleum. Extra strong binding. **1891** in C. Ray *Compleat Imbiber* (1967) IX. 122 Champagnes. Cuvée de Réserve. Extra Sec, Sec, and Brut 84/- per Doz. Bottles. **1907** *Yesterday's Shopping* (1969) 98 *Champagne*...Ayala, extra quality, extra dry. **1916** A. BENNETT *Lion's Share* xxxix. 303 He would always command a half-bottle of the extra dry for himself. **1930** —— *Imperial Palace* xxxvi. 247 Their mania for *extra sec*. **1951** R. POSTGATE *Plain Man's Guide to Wine* v. 95 'Brut'..should be really dry..'Extra Sec', 'Extra Dry'..moderately dry. **1965** A. SICHEL *Penguin Bk. Wines* III. 151 The words 'Brut' or 'Extra Dry' or 'Extra Sec' represent the driest of all—a dosage of 1 per cent or 2 per cent of liqueur.

b. In excess of the usual or specified amount.

Mod. The larger edition contains three maps extra. Attendance is charged for extra.

C. *sb.* **a.** What is extra or additional; an item beyond the school curriculum; one not included in a tradesman's contract, or a table d'hôte bill of fare; an additional piece of work; anything given in addition or for which an extra charge is made; the extra charge itself; an extra fee; an additional issue of a newspaper; *spec.* at cricket, a run scored otherwise than off the bat.

1793 *Kentucky Gazette Extra* 23 Mar. **1796** *Herald Extra* II. 30 Mar. **1803** R. PERING in *Naval Chron.* XV. 154 The extra was divided into nights and tides. **1832** *Amer. Railroad Jrnl.* I. 409/1 A newsboy thrust a 'Cholera extra' between us. **1838** DICKENS *Nickleby* I. iii. 19 Tell your uncle, my dear, how far you went in French and extras. **1840** —— *Old C. Shop* xxxiv. 287 'What's the rent?'..'One pound per week. ..The boots and clothes are extras.' **1858** *Bell's Life* 20 June 8/4 They..accomplished an innings of 161... It will be seen there were 26 extras! **1861** THACKERAY *Round Papers, 100 Years hence* 137 We supplied him with little comforts and extras. **1866** L. CARROLL *Alice in Wonderland* ix. 143 'With extras?'..'Yes..we learned French and music.' **1870** DICKENS *E. Drood* iii, They are neither of Miss Twinkleton's inclusive regulars, nor of her extras. **1876** MOZLEY *Univ. Serm.* vi. (1877) 126 A confounding and baffling extra, which was not even formally provided for in his scheme. **1884** *Lillywhite's Cricket Ann.* 55, 332 [runs] including 30 extras. **1888** *Harper's Mag.* LXXVII. 690/1 Hourly extras were issued, and the circulation..reached upon one day of the riot..70,000 copies. **1889** *Daily News* 5 Aug. 7/6 The association figure for this class of iron becomes £7 5*s.*, and hoops and strips are raised 10*s.*..with 'extras' for special gauges. *a* **1894** *Mod.* The builder took the contract very low, hoping to recoup himself by extras. **1895** KIPLING *Day's Work* (1898) 171 The newspaper extra—a slip printed on one side only, and damp from the press. **1912** A. BRAZIL *New Girl at St. Chad's* v. 86 The riding course was a special feature of the summer term... It was an 'extra', not part of the ordinary school curriculum. **1955** *Times* 26 May 9/7 It is just the important 'extra' given to the listener by this new two-sound track system which gives true relaxation and ease of listening.

b. A person engaged for a minor part, or to be present during a crowd scene, in a play, film, etc.; = SUPERNUMERARY *sb.* e. In full †*extra lady*, *gentleman*. Also *transf.*

c **1777–8** in Hodgkinson & Pogson *Early Manch. Theatre* (1960) 82 Or more Extras [to be employed] than cannot be avoided—the Bill for them to be signed by the Prompter. **1880** D. K. RANOUS *Diary of Daly Débutante* 16 May (1910) 185 Who should come to call on the Daly young ladies but one of the Philadelphia 'extras' at the theatre. **1888** G. GROSSMITH *Society Clown* vi. 114 The Marines [in 'H.M.S. Pinafore'] were what is theatrically known as 'extra-gentlemen'. They are not engaged to sing, and therefore do not hold such a good position as the chorus. **1890** BARRÈRE & LELAND *Dict. Slang* II. 206/2 *Scene rats* (theatrical), extras engaged in ballets or pantomimes. **1895** G. B. SHAW *Our Theatres in Nineties* (1932) I. 284 He..marched off..leaving the Republic and its army looking like the merest crowd of 'extras'. **1896** *Ibid.* II. 179 'Extra' Ladies and gentlemen (formerly called 'supers'). **1916** 'R. M. BOWER' *Phantom Herd* 125 Extras may be depended upon for carrying gossip from one studio to another. **1916** R. E. WELSH *A-B-C of Motion Pictures* iv. 42 If the story has scenes calling for the use of hundreds of characters,..he will call for 'extras', who are engaged by the day. **1938** WODEHOUSE *Summer Moonshine* xx. 176 After that [I was] a movie extra. **1958** *Times Lit. Suppl.* 12 Dec. 723/2 Is it that Mr. Crossman is so charmed by the performance of politics that he ignores the subject of the play, so busy in this particular book with the stars that he forgets the extras? **1964** C. CHAPLIN *Autobiogr.* xvi. 272 One can..march twenty thousand extras into the Red Sea. *Ibid.* xviii. 317 I'd do anything—get a job—do extra work in films.

c. (See quot. 1838.) Chiefly *U.S.*

1827 MRS. B. HALL *Let.* 23 Oct. in *Aristocratic Journey* (1931) 106 We wished to get an 'Extra'..but..the Stage Proprietor had the want of conscience to ask thirty-six for an 'Extra'. **1838** J. F. COOPER *Home as Found* ii. 35 Mr. Howel informed him that an extra in America meant a supernumerary coach, to carry any excess of the ordinary number of passengers. **1842** DICKENS *Amer. Notes* II. vi. 161 There being no stage-coach next day..I hired 'an extra', at a reasonable charge. **1846** R. M. BALLANTYNE in E. Quayle *Ballantyne the Brave* (1967) iv. 67 The stage..was full..but..an 'extra' (or separate sleigh of smaller dimensions than the stage) had been provided for us. **1944** E. M. KAHN *Cable Car Days* 103 After six hours of waiting an 'extra' arrived and we resumed our journey.

d. At a ball, a dance additional to those on the dance-programmes.

1885 C. M. YONGE *Nuttie's Father* I. xiii. 151 'Oh dear! I'm engaged all through [*i.e.* for all the dances].'..'Give him one of the extras!' **1900** E. GLYN *Visits Eliz.* 276 When we got to the ball-room an extra was on. **1913** J. VAIZEY *College Girl* xxvii. 369 Not until the three programmes were filled to the last extra did he..think of his own pleasure.

‖**extra** (ˈɛkstrə), *prep. rare.* [L. *extrā* (earlier *extrād*) outside (*adv.* and *prep.*), contracted form of *exterā(d)*, abl. fem. of *exter* (see EXTERIOR) in phrase *exterā parte* on the outer side.] Outside, externally to.

1852 W. GROVE in *Phil. Trans.* CXLII. 87 There was some effect exhibited *extra* the voltaic circuit.

extra- (ˈɛkstrə), *prefix*. The L. adv. and prep. *extrā* (see prec.) does not, strictly speaking, occur in composition during the classical period, though post-classically it formed a few vbs. like *extrāclūdere* to shut out, *extrāvagārī* to wander outside (whence *extravagant*). Classical L. had however the adj. *extraordinārius* EXTRAORDINARY, f. phrase *extrā ordinem* outside the regular order, and late L. also *extrāmundānus* EXTRAMUNDANE, f. phrase *extrā mundum*, *extrāmūrānus* (cf. EXTRAMURAL) f. *extrā mūrum* (or *mūrōs*), *extrānātūrālis* 'extra-natural', f. *extrā nātūrām*. Many similar adjs. were formed in med.L. on phrases in which *extrā* is a prep., and some of these are adopted in Eng., as *extra-provincial*. As the suffix employed in such formations was nearly always identical with that used to form an adj. from the sb. governed by *extra*, the words have the appearance of being f. *extra-* + adj. (the actual formation, on *extra* prep. + sb. + suffix, being obscured); thus *extraordinary* is felt as meaning 'outside of what is *ordinary*'. In recent times an enormous number of adjs. of this type have been formed. The most important compounds of *extra-*, and those requiring etymological explanation, are given in their alphabetical place; of the remainder only a selection can be given in the following lists, many nonce-words of obvious meaning being omitted.

1. Adjs. with general sense 'situated outside something' (*e.g.* in *Anat.* a specified organ or member), 'lying outside the province or scope of' (a specified branch of science, department of speculation or practice).

extra-acaˈdemic, without or external to a university. **extra-ˈacinous** *Anat.*, outside the acinus or racemose gland; see ACINUS 4. **extra-aliˈmentary**, situated outside the alimentary canal. **extra-anaˈlogical**, out of the range of, not in accordance with, analogy. **extra-arˈtistic**, out of the range of, having nothing to do with, art. **extra-atmosˈpheric**, of or pertaining to space beyond the atmosphere. **extra-ˈaxillar** *Bot.* = next. **extra-ˈaxillary** *Bot.*, growing from above or below the axils. **extraˈbranchial**, outside the branchial arches; also as *sb.*, an extrabranchial cartilage. **extra-briˈtannic**, not existing in Britain. **extra-ˈburghal**, beyond the boundary of the burgh. **extra-caˈnonical**, not classed among the canonical books. **extra-ˈcapsular**, 'outside a capsule, having special reference to the articular capsules' (*Syd. Soc. Lex.* 1884). **extra-caˈthedral** [L. *cathedra* chair], outside the pulpit. **extra-ˈcellular** *Biol.*,

situated or taking place outside the walls of a cell. **extra-'Christian**, outside the range of Christian thought; not to be discussed from a Christian point of view. **extra-'civical**, beyond the province or privileges of a citizen; hence **extra-'civically** *adv.* **extra-'claustral**, living out of a cloister; secular. **extra'conscious**, outside or above what is conscious; hence **extra-'consciousness**; **extra-'constellary** *Astron.*, situated outside, hence, not classed under, any constellation. **extra-'constellated** *ppl. a.* = prec. **extra-conti'nental**, beyond or outside a continent; *U.S.*, outside the western hemisphere. **extra-'corial** [L. *cori-um* hide + -AL], pertaining to the outside skin or epidermis. **extra-cor'poreal**, outside the body. **extra-'cosmical**, acting outside the cosmos or universe. **extra-'cranial** *Anat.*, lying or situated outside the skull. **extra-'curial** [f. L. *cūria* court of justice], arranged or made outside a court of law. **extra-cu'rricular**, outside the normal curriculum; also *transf.* and *fig.*. **extra-cu'taneous**, outside the skin, outside the true skin as opposed to the epidermis. **extra-de'cretal**, not included in the 'Decretals'. **extra-di'ocesan**, outside the diocese. **extra'dural**, outside the dura mater. **extra-embry'onic**, outside the embryo. **extra-e'ssential**, not included in the essence of some thing; hence **extra-e'ssentially** *adv.* **extra-Euro'pean**, not found in Europe; also, beyond the boundaries of Europe. **extra-experi'ential**, outside experience. **extra-fa'milial**, outside the family. **extra-foli'aceous** *Bot.*, without or external to the leaf. **extra-'formal**, beyond or away from the strict form; informal. **extra-'foveal**, lying or occurring outside the fovea of the retina. **extra-ga'lactic** *Astron.*, outside the galaxy or Milky-way. **extra-govern'mental**, beyond the province or proper course of government. **extra-gra'mmatical** (see quot.). **extrahe'patic**, outside the liver. **extra-hi'storic**, situated outside or beyond the sphere of history; also **extra-hi'storical**. **extra-'human**, outside the human race, or the conditions of human life. **extra-'hundredal**, not included in any hundred. **extra-in'ductive**, beyond the province of, or unattainable by, induction. **extra-inte'llectual**, beyond the reach of, or imperceptible by, the intellect. **extra-ju'daical**, outside the conditions of the Jewish dispensation. **extra-'jugal**, beyond, or not harnessed to, the yoke. **extra-'jural** [f. L. *jūr-*, *jūs* law + -AL] (see quot.). **extra-'legal**, beyond the province of law; not regulated by law. **extra-'limital** [L. *limit-em*, *limes* + -AL], beyond the limits of a country or district. **extra-'limitary**, situated beyond the limit or bounds. †**extra-'lineal**, beyond or off the line of rectitude. **extra-'lingual**, outside the bounds of language. **extra-lin'guistic**, outside the field of linguistics; = *extra-lingual*. **extra-'logical**, lying beyond the legitimate domain of logic; hence **extra-'logically** *adv.* **extra-'marginal**, outside the field of consciousness. †**extra-ma'rine**, of or pertaining to what is beyond the sea; from beyond the sea. **extra-'marital**, of sexual relationships outside marriage; hence **extra-'maritally** *adv.* **extra-'matrical** [L. *mātrīc-em*, *mātrix* (see MATRIX *sb.*) + -AL], situated outside the matrix or receptacle of a parasitical plant. **extra-matri'monial**, outside of matrimonial relations. **extra-'medial**, lying outside or beyond the middle line. **extra-'mental**, beyond the mind; independent of mental apprehension. **extra-me'ridional** *Astron.*, of or pertaining to deviation from the meridian. **extra-meta'physical**, outside the sphere of metaphysical enquiry. **extra-'metrical**, exceeding the number of feet or syllables proper to a metre; = HYPERMETRICAL. **extra-metro'politan**, situated outside the metropolitan boundary. **extramo'rainic**, situated beyond, or not associated with, a moraine. **extra-'musical**, outside the field of music; not an intrinsic part of music. **extra-'national**, outside the limits of a nation. **extra-'natural** [L. *extrānātūrālis* unnatural], outside the operation of natural laws. **extra-'nuclear**, placed outside the nucleus of a cell. **extra-'ocular**, situated or occurring outside the eyes. **extra-o'fficial**, outside the legitimate duties or emoluments of an office. **extra-'orbital** *Zool.*, situated outside the orbit or eye-cavity (of a crustacean); hence, **extra-'orbitally** *adv.* **extra-or'ganic**, **-orga'nismal**, **-orga'nismic**, outside the organism. **extra-pa'rental**, occurring outside the body of the parent. **extra-patri'archal**, outside the conditions of the patriarchal dispensation. **extra-perito'neal**, 'outside the peritoneum' (*Syd. Soc. Lex.* 1884). **extra-'personal**, situated or coming from outside a person. **extra-'physical**, not subject to physical laws or methods. **extra-'planetary**, beyond the region of the planets' movements. **extra-'popular**, outside or independent of the people; not drawn from the ranks of the people. **extra-pro'fessional**, (*a*) of persons: out of the ranks of a profession; (*b*) of things: outside the course of professional duties. **extra-py'ramidal**, outside the pyramidal tracts (see PYRAMIDAL *a.* 3 a). **extra-red**, said of rays outside the visible spectrum at its red extremity; also *ultra-red*. **extra-'regular**, outside of, or transgressing the rule; in addition to what is regular; hence, **extra-'regularly** *adv.* **extra'renal**, outside the kidneys. **extra-sacer'dotal**, outside or forming no part of the priesthood. **extra-scien'tific**, beyond the scope of science, incapable of scientific investigation. **extra-'scriptural**, drawn from sources outside the Scriptures; hence **extra-scriptu'rality**. **extra-'sensible** *a.* and *sb.*, (something that is) beyond the reach of sensuous perception. **extra-'sensuous** = prec. adj. **extra-'social**, outside society. **extra'solar**, outside the solar system. **extra-'spatial**, not in, or not forming part of, space. **extra-'spectral**, lying outside the visible spectrum. **extra-'stomachal**, taking place outside the stomach. **extra-syllo'gistic**, beyond the scope of, or irreducible to, a syllogism. **extra-sy'stemic**, outside the system; not according to a system. **extra-'tabular**, not contained in a table or list of weights, etc. **extra-te'llurian**, beyond or away from the earth. **extra-te'lluric**, outside or not found among the constituent elements of the earth. **extra-'temporal**, outside of, or forming no part of, the sequence of time. **extra-terrene**, **extra-te'rrestrial** = existing or originating outside the earth or its atmosphere; hence as *sb.*, a being living or originating beyond the earth. **extra-'thecal** *Zool.* and *Bot.*, situated outside the theca. **extra-the'istic**, beyond the range of theism; independent of theistic inquiry. **extra-'torrid**, existing outside the torrid zone. **extra-'tropical**, existing, situated, or taking place outside the tropics. **extra-uni'versity**, of or pertaining to matters outside the university. **extra-'urban**, beyond or outside the walls of a city. **extra-'uterine**, existing, formed, or taking place outside the uterus. **extra-ve'hicular**, outside a vehicle; *spec.* denoting activity outside a space-vehicle while it is in flight. **extra-'verbal**, not employing or describable in words. **extra-violet** *Optics*, said of rays outside the visible spectrum at its violet extremity. **extra-'visual**, not employing or connected with the faculty of sight; outside the normal range of sight. **extra-zo'diacal** *Astron.*, situated outside the zodiac. Also EXTRA-JUDICIAL, EXTRA-MURAL, etc.

1932 T. S. ELIOT *Sel. Ess.* 452 Not aspiring..to academic or *extra-academic honours. **1878** T. BRYANT *Pract. Surg.* (1879) II. 245 The *extra-acinous infiltrations of the same cells. **1877** HUXLEY *Anat. Inv. Anim.* xi. 644 The *extra-alimentary tissues. **1846** GROTE *Greece* (1862) I. xvi. 342 The *extra-analogical features of the stories. **1880** VERN. LEE *Belcaro* i. 12 Those foreign, *extra-artistic, irrelevant interests. **1871** HERSCHEL in *Month. Nat.* XXXI. 169 Evidence not to be refused of its *extra-atmospheric origin. **1851** OGILVIE, **Extra-axillar*. **1829** LOUDON *Encycl. Plants* 433 Flowers solitary, axillary, or *extra-axillary, but more frequently terminating. **1882** VINES *Sachs' Bot.* 490 A few cases of..extra-axillary branching. **1877** PARKER & BETTANY *Morphol. Skull* 39 Four *extrabranchial cartilages.., parallel to the ceratobranchials. *Ibid.* 343 The extrabranchials of the Dogfish are..superficial cartilages related to the branchial arches. **1912** J. S. KINGSLEY *Compar. Anat. Vertebr.* 65 In the branchial region of the elasmobranchs a variable number of extrabranchial cartilages may occur. **1770** PENNANT *Zool.* IV. 87 Catalogue of the European Quadrupeds, Birds, and Reptiles *Extra-Britannic. **1866** CARLYLE *E. Irving* 122 At the southern *extra-burghal park of Kirkcaldy. **1831** W. H. MILL *Christa-sangítá* (1842) Pref. p. xxvii, The *extra-canonical books of Tobit and Judith. **1877** C. GEIKIE *Christ* xlix. (1879) 585 He was intimately familiar..with the honored extra-canonical writings. **1885** E. R. LANKESTER in *Encycl. Brit.* XIX. 849/2 *Extra-capsular protoplasm. **1862** *Athenæum* 1 Nov. 553 Those who would muzzle the clergyman in his literary inquiries and his *extra-cathedral life. **1867** J. HOGG *Microsc.* II. i. 258 This process of a new formation begins in the *extracellular fluid. **1876** tr. *Wagner's Gen. Pathol.* 154 Coloring matter..passes out of the capillaries free or extra-cellular. **1870** HUXLEY *Lay Serm.* xiv. 375 Science and philosophy..are neither Christian, or Unchristian, but are *Extrachristian..I attempted to give you some vision of this Extrachristian world. **1801** W. TAYLOR in *Monthly Rev.* XII. 590 Those men..were proceeding *extra-civically perhaps, but surely with sound patriotism. **1889** R. L. POOLE *Wyclif's De Off. Reg.* 112 *marg.*, The status of the *extraclaustral clergy instituted by Christ is the most perfect. **1865** A. C. FRASER in *N. Brit. Rev.* XLIII. 29 We have no practical need for the *extra-conscious existence of anything that we apply language to. **1900** A. T. ORMOND *Found. Knowledge* iii. 90 An extra-conscious sphere which exists as yet only as implicate or postulate. **1949** KOESTLER *Insight & Outlook* xxiv. 334 Biologists..are..apt to find the solutions of their problems in sleep and extraconscious processes. **1897** W. JAMES *Will to Believe* 311 The '*extra-consciousness', as one may call it, can be kept on tap, as it were, by the method of automatic writing. **1823** CRABB *Technol. Dict.* I, **Extra-constellary stars*. **1860** in WORCESTER, and in mod. Dicts. **1730-6** BAILEY, **Extra-constellated*. **1938** *Tablet* 8 Oct. 469/1 England being an *extra-continental Power, it is to France that the small nations would most readily turn. **1960** *Organization of American States, Declaration* 28 June in *Ann. Reg. 1960* (1961) 532 The Seventh Meeting.. Condemns emphatically intervention..from an extra-continental Power in the affairs of the American republics. **1842** PRICHARD *Nat. Hist. Man* 80 All these varieties have their seat [in] the *extracorial or exodermal structure. **1865** GROTE *Plato* II. xxiv. 218 Its prior *extra-corporeal existence. *Ibid.* I. i. 158 He did not proclaim his Nous to be a powerful *extra-cosmical Architect. **1884** *Syd. Soc. Lex.*, **Extra-cranial*. **1887** S. SEXTON in *Amer. Ann. Deaf* July 153 The hearing organ in man has both an intracranial and an extracranial origin. **1882** B. LEECH in *Contemp. Rev.* Mar. 473 Those *extra-curial settlements, without which the Act will prove a complete legislative failure. **1925** H. CUSHING *Life Osler* I. 491 Lest one lose track of Osler in his daily rounds in the hospital wards during the recital of all these *extracurricular matters. **1930** *Times Educ. Suppl.* 30 July 329/3 Is it not possible to incorporate our extra-curricular activities in our curriculum? **1949** L. CHARTERIS in *Queen's Awards* (1951) IV. 294 He's dumb enough to think that Lucy won't catch on to the extracurricular functions of that busty secretary. **1967** N. FREELING *Strike Out* 140 Covert rendezvous, flirtations, extracurricular carryings on. **1842** PRICHARD *Nat. Hist. Man* 77 The varieties in the colour of the body, and the texture of the inner and outer integuments, depend on the organisation of parts, which are in one sense *extra-cutaneous. **1563-87** FOXE *A. & M.* (1596) 5/1 *Extradecretal & extravagant constitutions. **1789** W. SCOTT in J. Haggard *Rep. Consist. Cases* (1822) I. 34 Supposing the jury..had been of opinion it was extra-parochial,—that the place may be so, and not *extra-diocesan, is not to be denied. **1897** WESTM. GAZ. 14 July 1/3 The island [*sc.* Lundy] is extra-diocesan and extra-parochial. **1900** DORLAND *Med. Dict.* 249/2 Extradural. **1907** *Practitioner* Nov. 731 The causes of exophthalmos.. are..tumours of the optic nerve, which are either intra-dural or *extra-dural. **1962** *Lancet* 27 Jan. 172/1 The 'lucid interval' syndrome, classically associated with extra-dural hæmorrhage. **1913** DORLAND *Med. Dict.* (ed. 7), **Extra-embryonic*, not a part of the embryo proper: applied to that portion of the embryo outside of the umbilical stalk. **1958** *New Biol.* XXVI. 24 The extra-embryonic part of the blastoderm soon becomes divided into chorion and yolk sac. **1666** BOYLE *Orig. Formes & Qual.*, Tis *extra-essential to the Form that is said to be previous. **1676** GLANVILL *Ess.* vii. 25 They perswaded modestly in all extraessential doctrines. **1823** DE QUINCEY *Wks.* (1863) XIII. 50 *note*, Something extra-essential in the philosophy. *a* **1652** J. SMITH *Sel. Disc.* iv. 112 They ought to judge of things as they are in their own naked essences, and not with respect to that which *extra-essentially adheres to them. **1826** KIRBY & SP. *Entomol.* III. 42 Neither can it be affirmed of *extra-European species. **1905** *Westm. Gaz.* 4 May 9/3 The Morocco incident shows that arrangements ought to be made by France and Germany with regard to their extra-European interests. **1942** L. B. NAMIER *Conflicts* 1 European interests and entanglements have defeated the extra-European expansion of the Continental nations. **1904-5** W. JAMES *Meaning of Truth* (1909) iii. 69 There may or may not be an *extra-experiential 'ding an sich' that keeps the ball rolling. **1951** *Mind* LX. 18 Extra-experiential knowledge. **1952** C. P. BLACKER *Eugenics* xi. 312 Their nutrition is surprisingly average—doubtless due to *extra-familial feeding in schools. **1793** MARTYN *Lang. Bot.*, *Extrafoliaceæ stipulæ*. *Extrafoliaceous stipules. **1829** LOUDON *Encycl. Plants* 147 Prickles two, extra-foliaceous. **1884** in *Syd. Soc. Lex.* **1833** SIR W. HAMILTON *Discuss.* (1852) 140 The distinction of the enthymeme through the *extraformal character of its premises. **1904** *Westm. Gaz.* 15 June 1/3 A plate of platinum heated until it is dull and glowing is first seen by the *extra-foveal portions of the retina. **1947** *Nature* 4 Jan. 25 Measurements were also attempted for extra-foveal vision. **1851** NICHOL *Archit. Heav.* 110 An *extra-galactic phenomenon. **1870** PROCTOR *Other Worlds* xi. 264 The scattered stars of very low magnitudes in the extragalactic heavens. **1866** A. L. PERRY *Elem. Pol. Econ.* (1873) 515 [It] is as pitiful on the one side as it is *extra-governmental on the other. **1873** EARLE *Philol. Eng. Tongue* §203 A group ..*extra-grammatical..in the sense that they do not enter into the grammatical construction. **1961** *Lancet* 12 Aug. 341/2 *Extrahepatic biliary exploration had shown no abnormality, but cholecystectomy was performed. **1846** GROTE *Greece* I. iv. I. 111 They included elements human and historical as well as elements divine and *extra-historical. *Ibid.* I. i. I. 1 Various monstrous natures, ultra-human and *extra-human, who cannot with propriety be called gods. **1864** MAINE *Anc. Law* i. (1876) 12 Supposing an extra-human interposition. **1877** MORLEY *Crit. Misc.* Ser. II. 332 His conditions are wholly extra-human. **1875** STUBBS *Const. Hist.* I. xi. 402 *note*, A manor of ancient demesne was *extra-hundredal. **1856** DOVE *Logic Chr. Faith* v. i. §1. 246 The idea of mind is *extra-inductive. **1885** *Life J. Hinton* vi. 118 It is *extra-intellectual as the 'line' is extra-sensuous. **1858** GLADSTONE *Homer* II. 6 The vestiges of extra-patriarchal and *extra-judaical relations between God and man are undeniable. **1782** POWNALL *Antiquities* 259 We read in Homer, in the case of Achilles' chariot, of an additional *extrajugal horse. **1875** POSTE *Gaius* IV. Comm. (ed. 2) 516 *Extra-jural or outside the court. **1644** HUNTON *Vind. Treat. Monarchy* ix. 65 It concernes only..their Absolute, *extra-legall Will; not their Authority. **1806** W. TAYLOR in *Ann. Rev.* IV. 239 The extra-legal perpetuation

of authority. **1871** FREEMAN *Hist. Ess.* Ser. I. xii. 384 The word 'Government'..has come to be applied to this extra-legal body. **1889** *Spectator* 12 Oct. 465/2 The legal and extra-legal expenditure..for election purposes. **1874** COUES *Birds N.-W.* 45 The *extralimital quotations to the southward are very numerous. **1883** *Nature* XXVII. 221 Other species..and hybrids, which are extra-limital, or may sooner or later be found straying into Switzerland. **1820** T. MITCHELL *Aristoph.* I. 73 *note*, The Megarians..had cultivated some sacred *extralimitary land. **1847** in CRAIG. **1691** NORRIS *Pract. Disc.* 254 He [the sinner] chooses by *extra-lineal motions to violate the Sacred interest of Society. **1961** Y. OLSSON *Syntax Eng. Verb* ii. 16 The problem of dealing with language as related to extra-lingual phenomena. **1963** J. LYONS *Structural Semantics* iv. 56 Extralingual features (e.g. situations). **1927** *Mod. Philol.* Nov. 212 *Extra-linguistic group habits. **1935** *Mind* XLIV. 505 The danger of using the material mode is that it misleads us into thinking that pseudo-object sentences are concerned with extra-linguistic objects such as numbers, things, properties, experiences, space, time, and so on. **1964** Extra-linguistic [see EXTRASOMATIC *a.*]. **1833** SIR W. HAMILTON *Discuss.* (1852) 139 The two books of the Prior Analytics [Aristotle's]..are swelled with *extralogical discussions. **1864** BOWEN *Logic* ix. 269 The consideration of Fallacies is extralogical. *a* **1856** SIR W. HAMILTON (Ogilv.), A universal quantification of the predicate in affirmatives has been frequently recognized..*extralogically. **1898** W. JAMES *Coll. Ess. & Rev.* (1920) 440 The humbugging and masquerading *extra-marginal self is as great a paradox for psychology as the comatose spirits are for pneumatology. **1902** —— *Var. Rel. Exper.* 233 Feelings which are extra-marginal and outside of the primary consciousness altogether. **1612** WOODALL *Surg. Mate* Wks. (1653) 20* Medicinall subject, of heathen production, and *extramarine importation. **1929** B. RUSSELL *Marriage & Morals* v. 51 We, however, wish to appeal to reason, and we must therefore employ dull neutral phrases, such as '*extra-marital sexual relations'. **1963** in A. Heron *Towards Quaker View of Sex* i. 6 The incidence of extra-marital intercourse is great. **1967** J. POTTER *Foul Play* vii. 91 Sandwiched between the pair of them: one said to be queer and the other extra-maritally active. **1884** BOWER & SCOTT *De Bary's Phaner. & Ferns* 383 In Cuscuta the *extramatrical portion is very little developed. **1811** W. TAYLOR in *Monthly Mag.* XXXII. 118 Does not Christianity expressly declare against all *extra-matrimonial gratification? **1852** DANA *Crust.* 247 The præmedial and *extramedial [areolets] are usually coalescent. **1853** H. L. MANSEL *Lett.* (1873) 84 This is a criterion..of the mental conceivability, not of the *extra-mental existence of an object. **1886** J. MCCOSH *Psychol., Cognitive Powers* i. 27 All knowledge obtained through the senses is discerned as extra-mental, that is, as out of and beyond the perceiving mind. **1903** C. A. STRONG *Why Mind has Body* 214 Extra-mental realities. **1958** W. STARK *Sociology of Knowledge* 140 But it is *not* claimed by the sociology of knowledge that ideas are the intra-mental *effects* of extra-mental *causes*. **1833** HERSCHEL *Astron.* ii. 90 If it [the pole star] pass from one to the other apparent culmination in unequal intervals of time, it is equally certain that an *extra-meridional error must exist. **1856** DOVE *Logic Chr. Faith* v. i. §1. 244 The hypothesis itself..is *extra-metaphysical. **1863** CLARKE & GLOVER *Shaks. Wks.* I. xviii, Of another practice..making a line end with two unaccented *'extrametrical' syllables. **1885** *Law Times* LXXIX. 253/1 This Act.. only concerned *extra-metropolitan local boards. **1891** *Amer. Geol.* VIII. 239 The thickness of this *extra-morainic till ranges from 30 to 70 feet. **1968** R. W. FAIRBRIDGE *Encycl. Geomorphol.* 460/2 These features are best termed 'proglacial lakes', though the term 'extra-morainic lakes' has also been used. **1925** I. A. RICHARDS *Princ. Lit. Crit.* xviii. 156 These physical laws are, as it were, an *extra-musical piece of knowledge. **1968** *Daily Tel.* 12 Nov. 19/1 It would be difficult..to say just how much of the impact which the work made on the large audience was due to extra-musical reasons. **1864** KINGSLEY *Rom. & Teut.* viii. (1875) 201 Out of a political fact, arose the *extra-national..position. **1794** J. WILLIAMS *Crying Ep.* 55 *note*, This..*extra-natural Statesman. **1876** HUXLEY *Lect. Evolut.* in *Cycl. Sc.* (1883) I. 607 There may have been a time when..extra-natural agencies interfered with the general course of Nature. **1887** *Q. Jrnl. Microsc. Sc.* XXVIII. 96 The *extranuclear network (intracellular) is apparently of the same nature as the intranuclear, since the two have been shown to be continuous in many cells. **1826** KIRBY & SP. *Entom.* (1828) III. xxxiv. 513 In Nepa the antennæ may be called *extraocular. **1875** H. WALTON *Dis. Eye* 768 Complications of cataract with extra-ocular disease. **1797** *Monthly Rev.* XXII. 240 Mr. Robinson..must excuse us from attention to *extra-official matters. **1826** MISS MITFORD *Village* Ser. II. (1863) 332 Many a job, extra-official, hath he turned his hand to. **1852** DANA *Crust.* 373 The arm projects..beyond the *extra-orbital spine. **1870** ROLLESTON *Anim. Life* 3 The duct of the *extraorbitally-placed portion. **1866** J. MCCOSH *Exam. of J. S. Mill's Philos.* 121 The world beyond the body..I call the *extra-organic world. **1935** *Mind* XLIV. 549 It will be necessary, no doubt, 'to recognise that bodily factors, and not only extra-organic things, may, in certain situations, function as objects'. **1923** *Glasgow Herald* 16 Nov. 4/2 There is obviously considerable change from generation to generation, but most of this is *extra-organismal and only repercusses indirectly, if at all, on the flesh and blood constitution. **1955** F. LOUNSBURY in *Georgetown Univ. Inst. Lang. & Linguistics Monogr. Ser.* VIII. 162 The 'meanings' dichotomized by this criterion may be referred to as *intraorganismic* and **extraorganismic* meanings respectively. **1864** *Athenæum* No. 1920. 215/3 The individuality of the butterfly is..perfect through all these visible and *extra-parental metamorphoses. **1858** GLADSTONE *Homer* II. 6 In..*extra-patriarchal..relations. **1836** TODD *Cycl. Anat.* I. 19/2 The viscera intra-peritoneal and *extra-peritoneal. **1909** H. ZIMMERN tr. *Nietzsche's Human, All-Too-Human* I. 48 Everything *extra-personal is imperceptible to them [*sc.* most people]. **1923** J. S. HUXLEY *Ess. Biologist* iv. 152 Some great extra-personal flood of soul, into the meagre stream of everyday life. **1964** M. CRITCHLEY *Developmental Dyslexia* ix. 60 The result of a failure of lateral orientation with reference to corporeal awareness, and the organisation of self within extra-personal space. **1822** [G. GROTE] *Anal. Infl. Nat. Relig.* 109 Applications for *extra-physical guidance. **1869** PHIPSON tr. *Guillemin's Sun* 77 The aphelion distance of the comet of 1844..is lost in *extra-planetary space. **1847** GROTE *Greece* I. xxxi. IV. 211 An *extra-popular or privileged few. **1856** *Ibid.* II. xciv. XII. 358 A greater and a less measure of extra-popular authority. **1799** BEDDOES *Contrib. Phys. & Med. Knowl.* Introd. 10 The leisure of the *extra-professional members. **1849** GROTE *Greece* II. lxviii. (1862) VI. 129 No extra-professional person thinks of contesting the decision of a surgeon. **18..** *Med. Repos.* (Ogilv.), These studies were extraprofessional. **1912** *Brain* XXXIV. 296 This affection, where it occurs in an uncomplicated form, is an *extra-pyramidal motor disease. **1965** *Nursing Times* 5 Feb. 188/1 Parkinsonism may be seen fairly frequently in patients who have had chlorpromazine for a considerable period, owing to its effect on the extra-pyramidal system. **1860** TYNDALL *Glac.* II. vi. 254 Water then absorbs all the *extra red rays of the sun. **1649** JER. TAYLOR *Gt. Exemp.* Pref. ¶24 An *extraregular..punishment. **1678** *Lively Orac.* ii. §53. 258 Men..set up new extraregular Courts of Justice. **1739** J. TRAPP *Right. over-much* (1758) 34 These extra-regular novelists. **1649** JER. TAYLOR *Gt. Exemp.* III. xiv. 21 *Extraregularly..holy persons have miscarried in battle. **1885** C. H. RALFE *Pract. Treat. Dis. Kidneys* iii. 159 *Extra-Renal [albuminuria] in which the albumin is mainly derived from the pus formed in the genito-urinary tract. **1964** O. KINNE in *Oceanogr. & Marine Biol.* II. 302 Both renal and extrarenal active ion transport require oxidative energy. **1835** I. TAYLOR *Spir. Despot.* iii. 95 An *extra-sacerdotal class, namely that of the prophets. **1874** H. R. REYNOLDS *John Bapt.* v. §2. 325 It may be pronounced transcendental, or *extra-scientific. **1825** COLERIDGE *Aids Refl.* (1848) I. 144 Each of these *extra-scriptural articles of faith. **1875** E. WHITE *Life in Christ* IV. xxvi. (1878) 416 We should bring forward some extra-scriptural evidence of the recognition of the doctrine. **1842** G. S. FABER *Provinc. Lett.* (1844) II. 48 That congeries of *Extra-scripturalities and Unscripturalities which characterised the fourth century. **1874** LEWES *Prob. Life & Mind* II. iv. §85 The distinction.. between the conception of atoms as *extrasensibles and the conception of them as convenient fictions. **1885** *Life J. Hinton* vi. 118 *Extra-sensuous. **1934** WEBSTER, *Extra-social. **1958** *Times Lit. Suppl.* 17 Jan. 26/4 The extra-social, inner-directed group-life as practised by Epicurus and his friends. **1889** *Cent. Dict.*, *Extrasolar. **1953** J. BLISH *Case of Conscience* (1958) I. i. 13 Don't forget that Lithia is my first extrasolar planet. **1962** F. I. ORDWAY et al. *Basic Astronautics* vi. 285 The existence of extrasolar planets would have to be proved by astronomical means. **1931** S. BECKETT *Proust* 72 Swann who..spatialises what is *extraspatial. **1943** *Mind* LII. 343 The individual consciousness..does not and cannot regard itself as being literally timeless and extra-spatial. **1849** MRS. SOMERVILLE *Connex. Phys. Sc.* xxiv. 236 There are three *extra-spectral lines beyond the red. **1881** DARWIN *Earthworms* 4, I am not aware of any other case of *extra-stomachal digestion. **1855** H. SPENCER *Princ. Psychol.* (1872) II. VI. viii. 99 Simple deliverances of reason..having the highest degree of certainty, which are entirely *extra-syllogistic. **1935** *Mind* XLIV. 509 We are forced to ask whether these purposes can themselves lie wholly within the system constructed, or whether they are *extra-systemic and thus extra-linguistic. **1964** *Language* XL. 20 An extrasystemic abbreviating device. **1780** KIRWAN in *Phil. Trans.* LXXXI. 29 The *extra-tabular proportions are to be sought in the manner already shewn. **1881** *19th Cent.* 455 Divine beings and *extra-tellurian life. **1868** LOCKYER *Heavens* (ed. 3) 197 The *extra-telluric matters of which the meteor was composed. **1865** GROTE *Plato* I. i. 22 *note*, In the Platonic Parmenides we find τὸ ἐξαίφνης..an *extra-temporal moment. **1863** DE QUINCEY *Ceylon* Wks. XI. 10 A local..upon our earth, and not in some *extra-terrene orb. **1868** LOCKYER *Heavens* (ed. 3) 188 Bodies situated in the *extra-terrestrial regions. **1882** *Nature* XXVII. 173 The oblique direction of the meteor.. is another evidence of its extra-terrestrial origin. **1945** *Wireless World* Oct. 305 (*title*) Extra-terrestrial relays. Can rocket stations give world-wide radio coverage? **1963** M. CAIDIN *Man-in-Space Dict.* 81/1 *Extraterrestrial*, anything or any being beyond the earth, or from some place other than the earth. **1966** *New Statesman* 8 July 58/3 Contact with extra-terrestrials will..come suddenly. **1967** *New Scientist* 5 Oct. 9/1 MacDonald himself, having started to study UFOs 18 months ago, feels that the idea that the UFOs are extraterrestrial must be given serious attention. **1969** *Times* 28 Apr. 10/8 Scientists have looked for signs of extraterrestrial life in meteorites. **1856** LINDSAY *Brit. Lichens* 70 The spores..sometimes appear naked, or *extrathecal. **1887** G. H. FOWLER in *Q. Jrnl. Microsc. Sc.* XXVIII. 7 By far the greatest thickness of the coral is laid down..by the calicoblasts of the extra-thecal part of the polyp. **1881** G. J. ROMANES in *Nature* XXIV. 429 It is neither theistic nor atheistic; it is simply *extra-theistic. **1852** DANA *Crust.* II. 1510 The *extra-torrid species belong almost exclusively to the Mediterranean. **1783** BLAGDEN in *Phil. Trans.* LXXIII. 368 The cold..abated 20 or 30 degrees..no greater alteration than frequently takes place in most *extratropical climates. **1830** LINDLEY *Nat. Syst. Bot.* 232 Verbascum is wholly extratropical. **1862** DANA *Man. Geol.* 615 The cold extratropical currents that flow towards the equator. **1887** *Pall Mall G.* 30 Nov. 4/1 *Extra university experience. **1773** *Gentl. Mag.* XLIII. 634 *Extra-urban cemeteries. **1709** J. YONGE in *Phil. Trans.* XXVI. 428 *Extra-uterine Embryo's have been sometimes found. **1803** *Edin. Rev.* I. 498 An extra-uterine gestation had there taken place. **1965** *New Scientist* 18 Mar. 700/3 This '*extravehicular activity', as it is termed, will be the first exposure of man in this hostile environment without the protection of a heavy metal coat. **1966** *Ibid.* 16 June 703/2 Cernan..had to take repeated rests during his extravehicular activities. **1932** A. GARDINER *Theory Speech & Lang.* I. i. 24 'Things' to be spoken about are not simply illusory and..are *extra-verbal (i.e. outside the words). **1961** *Lancet* 5 Aug. 308/2 The recording also serves to illustrate the various levels of verbal and 'extraverbal' communication. **1863** TYNDALL *Heat* xii. (1870) 409 The pile was caused to pass successively through positions corresponding to the various colours of the spectrum, and to its *extra-violet rays. **1900** DORLAND *Med. Dict.* 769/1 The *extravisual zone just outside of it is practically incapable of accurately focussing light. **1959** H. READ *Conc. Hist. Mod. Painting* i. 14 Before Cézanne..the artist brought in extra-visual faculties—it might be his imagination, which enabled him to transform the objects of the visible world..or it might be his intellect. **1686** GOAD *Celest. Bodies* II. xiv. 344 ♃'s Opposition kindles it in the Asterism *Extrazodiacal. **1869** J. MARTINEAU *Ess.* II. 359 Stellar spheres, seen from an extrazodiacal position.

†**2.** Comb. of L. *extra* adv., with sense 'in an external condition'. *Obs.*

1713 A. COLLIER *Clavis Univ* Introd. (1836) 6 My enquiry is not concerning the Existence, but altogether of the Extra-existence of certain things.

extract (ɛk'strækt), *ppl. a.* [ad. L. *extract-us*, pa. pple. of *extrahĕre* to EXTRACT.] Extracted; in various senses of the vb.

†**1.** *pa. pple.* **a.** Taken out, obtained out of something. **b.** Derived (from a source), descended (from an ancestry). **c.** Distracted, taken out of one's wits; cf. EXTRAUGHT 2, EXTRACTING *ppl. a.*

a. **1515** BARCLAY *Egloges* iv. (1570) C vj/2 To sing one ballade extract of sapience. **1610** MARKHAM *Masterp.* I. civ. 206 Oyles extract out of wood or mettals will last long. *a* **1626** BACON *Max. & Uses Com. Law* iii. (1630) 13 The leasee by implication shall have the warren discharged and extract during his lease.

b. **1483** CAXTON *Gold. Leg.* 425/3 Saynt rigoberte..was extract or come out of the moste excellent lygnage. **1525** LD. BERNERS *Froiss.* II. clxxxi. [clxxvii]. 551 He was extracte by his mother syde of a duke of Bretayne. **1603** HOLLAND *Plutarch's Mor.* 1024 The Sun..is the very issue extract from that Good. *a* **1641** BP. MOUNTAGU *Acts & Mon.* (1642) 233 Herod was..originally a Jew, extract from them who, upon the Edict of Cyrus, returned at the first time..to Jerusalem.

c. **1608** *Hist. Hamblet* ii. C iijb, To try if men of great account bee extract out of their wits.

2. *ppl. a.* Drawn or taken out. Now only in ***extract decree*** (*Scots Law*: cf. EXTRACT *v.* 2 c).

1643 T. GOODWIN *Child of Light* 195 The originall..is more authenticall then extract copies. **1708** J. PHILIPS *Cyder* II. 65 Stor'd with Streams Egregious, Rum and Rice's Spirit extract. **1856** *Act 19-20 Vict.* c. 56 §35 *marg.*, Sheriff may seize Books of Crown Debtor under Extract Decree. **1861** W. BELL *Dict. Law Scot.* 373/2 The form and execution of extract decrees.

extract ('ɛkstrækt), *sb.* [In senses 1–3 ad. L. *extract-um*, neut. pa. pple. of *extrahĕre* to EXTRACT. In sense 5 repr. L. *extracta*, fem. pa. pple., used subst. in Eng. Law (= AF. *estrete*: see ESTREAT). In sense 6 perh. formed in Eng. on EXTRACT *v.*; cf. however OF. *estraite* in same sense.]

I. †**1.** *gen.* Something drawn or taken out of a thing; also *fig.* the 'pith' of a matter. *Obs.*

1570 LEVINS *Manip.* 6/20 An Extracte, *extractum.* **1597** HOOKER *Eccl. Pol.* v. lvi. (1611) 307 The words of Adam ..'flesh of my flesh, and bone of my bones,' a true native extract out of mine owne bodie. **1605** CAMDEN *Rem.* 140 *heading* (Allusions), I will now present vnto you a few extracts out of names. **1651** N. BACON *Disc. Govt. Eng.* II. xiii. 116 The extract of all is, that he [Duke of Hertford] was chosen by the People and Parliament then sitting.

2. a. 'The substance extracted; the chief parts drawn from anything' (J.); in mod. use 'a pharmaceutical term applied to the tough or viscid matter obtained by treating any substance with solvents and then evaporating the solvent' (Watts). Also loosely used for any preparation containing the active principle of a substance in a concentrated form.

1590 MARLOWE *2nd Pt. Tamburl.* IV. ii, An ointment.. Distilled from the..simplest extracts of all minerals. **1605** TIMME *Quersit.* III. 182 One scruple of the extract of betonie. **1656** H. MORE *Enthus. Tri.* 9 This intoxicating Potion is made of the extract of certain hearbs. **1712** tr. *Pomet's Hist. Drugs* I. 28 Schroder makes an Extract of it with..Water. **1811** A. T. THOMSON *Lond. Disp.* (1818) 617 In preparing all kinds of extracts, evaporate the fluid as quickly as possible. **1875** H. C. WOOD *Therap.* (1879) 18 Fluid extracts are very concentrated fluid preparations. **1884** *Syd. Soc. Lex.*, Extract of beef. *Mod. Advt.*, With Malt or Meat Extract an Ideal Diet for Infants.

fig. **1645** QUARLES *Sol. Recant.* vii. 34 Wisdom's th' extract of knowledge. **1677** GILPIN *Dæmonol.* (1867) 12 Not only is he [Satan] wicked, but the spirit and extract of wickedness. **1818** JAS. MILL *Brit. India* II. IV. ix. 299 Englishmen consider English law as the pure extract of reason. **1847** L. HUNT *Men, Women, & B.* II. iii. 45 A specimen of the volatile extract of Steele.

†**b.** = EXTRACTIVE B *sb.* 2. *Obs.*

1807 T. THOMSON *Chem.* (ed. 3) II. 354 Besides tannin, extract must be present in this precipitate. **1810** HENRY *Elem. Chem.* (1840) II. 188 Vegetable Extract or Extractive ..is..of a brownish colour, and generally of a bitterish taste. **1813** SIR H. DAVY *Agric. Chem.* iii. (1814) 85 Extract or the extractive principle exists in almost all plants..it seems to be composed principally of hydrogene, oxygene, carbon and a little azote.

c. *transf.* (See quot. 1879). Also in fuller form ***extract wool.***

1879 *Cassell's Techn. Educ.* IV. 261/1 The latter [cotton in worn-out fabrics] is destroyed by a chemical process, leaving the wool intact, which is then called 'extract'. **1888** *Encycl. Brit.* XXIV. 661/1 Extract wool is that which is recovered from rags of various cloths in which cotton and wool are variously woven together. **1963** A. J. HALL *Textile Sci.* ii. 38 The recovered wool passes under various names such as mungo, shoddy, alpaca and extract (this latter contains cotton fibres also since it is obtained from waste mixture goods).

†**3.** A summary; an outline. *Obs.* Cf. Fr. *extrait*, It. *estratto.*

1549 CHALONER *Erasmus on Folly* G iij b, Let us draw on the other side..the extract of a man of wisedome. **1605** BACON *Adv. Learn.* II. vi. §1 They supposed the world to bee

the Image of God, and man to be an extract or compendious Image of the World. **1625** —— *Ess., Studies* (Arb.) 11 Some Bookes..may be read by Deputy, and Extracts made of them by Others. **1656–81** BLOUNT *Glossogr., Extract*..a breviate or abridgement.

4. A passage copied out of a book, manuscript, etc.; an excerpt, quotation.

1666 PEPYS *Diary* 31 July, [He] brought me up this extract out of the Flanders letters to day come. **1707** FLOYER *Physic. Pulse-Watch* 337 To gratifie the Curiosity of Ingenious Inquirers, I made the following Extract. **1803** *Med. Jrnl.* X. 142 These extracts are long. **1872** RAYMOND *Statist. Mines & Mining* 192 These extracts.. might be still further multiplied.

transf. **1827** LYTTON *Pelham* xii, There was, indeed, a motley congregation; country esquires; extracts from the universities; half-pay officers, etc.

5. *Law.* †**a.** = ESTREAT *sb.* (*obs.*). **b.** *Sc. Law* (see quot. 1861).

a. **1670** BLOUNT *Law Dict., Extracts.* See *Estreats.*

b. **1606** *Act of Council* in *Sc. Acts 23 Jas. VI*, c. 19 Common and ordinarie Extracts, for every sheet extracted, xiii. sh. iiii. d. **1861** W. BELL *Dict. Law Scot.* 374/1 *Extract.* The term extract, in the law of Scotland, signifies either the proper written evidence, or warrant on which diligence or execution on a judicial decree may issue; or it signifies a copy, authenticated by the proper officer, of a deed, writing, or other entry, the principal of which, either is in a public record, or a transcript of which, taken from the principal, has been preserved in a public record. **1868** *Act 31-2 Vict.* c. 100 §68 If no Appeal shall have been taken, the Clerk of the Court may give out the Extract.

†**II. 6.** = EXTRACTION 5. *Obs.* Cf. OF. *extraite.*

1630 B. JONSON *New Inn* I. v, She shews her extract, and I honour her for it. **1691** WOOD *Ath. Oxon.* II. 722 He was a Scot born, or at least of Scotch extract. *a* **1734** NORTH *Exam.* I. iii. (1740) 223 Every Soul, who gets to be rich, immediately enquires into his Extract. **1796** MORSE *Amer. Geog.* I. 344 *note*, The first child of European extract, born in New England.

extract (ɛkˈstrækt), *v.* [f. L. *extract-* ppl. stem of *extrahĕre*, f. *ex-* out + *trahĕre* to draw. Cf. Fr. *extraire.*] To draw out.

1. *trans.* In general sense: 'To draw out of any containing body or cavity' (J.).

Now only with some notion of one or other of the more specific senses.

1570 LEVINS *Manip.* 6/25 To Extract, *extrahere.* **1603** SHAKS. *Meas. for M.* III. ii. 50 Is there none of Pigmalions Images..to bee had now, for putting the hand in the pocket, and extracting [it] clutch'd? **1684** T. BURNET *Th. Earth* I. vii. 83 If these waters were any way extracted and laid upon the surface of the ground, nothing would be gain'd as to the Deluge by that.

2. 'To take from something of which the thing taken was a part' (J.).

1634 SIR T. HERBERT *Trav.* 56 They had whole mountaines of excellent blacke marble..out of which the Imperiall Palace was extracted and cut out. **1667** MILTON *P.L.* VIII. 497 I now see..my self Before me; Woman is her Name, of Man Extracted. **1818** CRUISE *Digest* (ed. 2) III. 258 Freeholders; whose estates were afterwards extracted out of the demesnes of the manor.

b. *esp.* To copy out (a passage in a book, etc.); also, to make extracts from (a book).

1607 TOPSELL *Four-f. Beasts* (1673) 266 Finding nothing of substance in him [Gesner] which is not..extracted..by them. **1724** SWIFT *Drapier's Lett.* iv, I have thought it proper to extract out of that Pamphlet a few of these notorious Falsehoods. **1798** FERRIAR *Illustr. Sterne* ii. 43, I extract the following passages as specimens. **1838–9** HALLAM *Hist. Lit.* I. iii. i. §8. 149 The treatise was..abridged, extracted and even turned into verse. **1855** BAIN *Senses & Int.* II. iv. §13 It will be convenient to extract entire the section devoted to this subject.

c. *Sc. Law.* To take out a copy of (a recorded judgement) with a view to execution. Also †*to extract forth.* Cf. ESTREAT *v.*

1597 *Sc. Acts Jas. VI*, 177b, Collected..and extracted foorth of the Bukes and Register of the Actes of Parliament. **1606** [see EXTRACT *sb.* 5b]. **1681** COLVIL *Whigs Supplic.* (1751) 94 He forg'd records, and them enacted To bear false witness, when extracted. **1752** J. LOUTHIAN *Form of Process* App. (ed. 2) 266 The Expence of extracting the Protestation. **1837** LOCKHART *Scott* xx, The subalterns, who..recorded and extracted the decrees of the Supreme Court. **1868** *Act 31-32 Vict.* c. 100 §57 Notwithstanding that the Interlocutor of the Lord Ordinary may have been extracted and put to Execution.

absol. **1751** *Act Sederunt* 4 Jan. *heading*, Prohibition by the Lords against Agents to extract, or Extractors to agent.

3. To get out (the contents of anything) by force, effort, or contrivance; to take out (anything embedded or firmly fixed). Often with reference to surgical operations, dentistry, and the like.

1628 WITHER *Brit. Rememb.* 219 Upon Argeir we had a faire designe That much extracted from our silver mine. **1695** WOODWARD *Nat. Hist. Earth* IV. (1723) 215 The..mineral Matter..is..so diffused..amongst the crasser matter..that 'twould never be possible to separate and extract it. **1732** ARBUTHNOT *Rules of Diet* 428 The Stone in the Bladder is..a mortal Disease, if not extracted. **1767** GOOCH *Treat. Wounds* I. 210 After many fruitless attempts to extract an arrow. **1794** S. WILLIAMS *Vermont* 190 One of these customs, was that of extracting their beards by the roots. **1807–26** S. COOPER *First Lines Surgery* (ed. 5) 158 Army surgeons..always..extract the ball as soon as possible. **1834** MEDWIN *Angler in Wales* II. 112 One of the best..anglers in England..had only been able to extract three of its inhabitants. **1841** LANE *Arab. Nts.* I. 80 He took out a knife, and picked at the lead until he extracted it from the bottle. **1878** L. P. MEREDITH *Teeth* 127 Fractures in attempts to extract teeth, often expose the pulp.

b. *fig.*; *esp.* to draw forth (a confession, money, etc.) against a person's will.

1599 NASHE *Lenten Stuffe* Wks. 1883–4 V. 297 And there [by torture] eyther tear him limbe from limbe, but hee will extract some capitall confession from him. **1670** MARVELL *Corr.* cl. Wks. 1872–5 II. 328, I had writ sooner could I have extracted out of Sir Philip..anything which I thought materiall. **1765** H. WALPOLE *Otranto* v. (1798) 78 He used every insinuating..argument to extract her consent. **1825** HONE *Every-day Bk.* I. 1116 He had extracted the last extractable halfpenny. **1833** HT. MARTINEAU *Three Ages* iii. 93 Nothing could be extracted from him relative to his former associates. **1860** TYNDALL *Glac.* I. xvi. 108, I..tried to extract some direct encouragement from him.

4. To obtain (constituent elements, juices, etc.) from a thing or substance by suction, pressure, distillation, or any chemical or mechanical operation. Said both of personal and material agents. †Also *intr.* for *refl.* (*obs. rare*).

1594 PLAT *Jewell-ho., Chem. Concl.* 3 The maner of drawing, or extracting of the oiles out of hearbes. **1626** BACON *Sylva* §645 Out of the Ashes of all Plants they extract a Salt, which they vse in Medicines. **1641** FRENCH *Distill.* i. (1651) 33 Let the Spirit extract in digestion till no more feces fall to the bottom. **1667** MILTON *P.L.* v. 25 How the Bee Sits on the Bloom extracting liquid sweet. **1799** G. SMITH *Laborat.* I. 97 Distil them with water..till all the spirits are extracted. **1816** J. SMITH *Panorama Sc. & Art* II. 444 Filter the liquor, wash the sediment with water, till it ceases to extract any thing. **1853** SOYER *Pantroph.* 131 When the cook wanted to extract the salt, he first boiled the meat well in milk. **1875** *Ure's Dict. Arts* III. 1146 The skins being present, the wine which is in process of formation extracts tannic acid from the skins.

absol. **1651** BIGGS *New Disp.* ⁋79 You labour..in extracting after the manner introduc'd by Neotericks.

b. *fig.*; *esp.* to obtain (comfort, pleasure, happiness) from a specified source; also, to draw out (the sense of anything); to deduce (a doctrine, principle, right, etc.).

1596 DAVIES *Orchestra* ciii, He [Love] first extracted from th' earth-mingled mind That heau'nly fire, or quint-essence diuine. **1599** SHAKS. *Hen. V*, II. ii. 101 May it be possible, that forraigne hyer Could out of thee extract one sparke of euill? **1719** YOUNG *Busiris* IV. i, To see us act like prudent men, And out of ills extract our happiness. **1775** JOHNSON *Tax. no Tyr.* 44 No general right can be extracted from them [the charters]. **1796** MORSE *Amer. Geog.* I. 317 *note*, In whatever situation he was placed he [Franklin] extracted something useful for himself or others. **1863** GEO. ELIOT *Romola* I. iii, [He] means to extract the utmost possible amount of pleasure..out of this life. **1890** LD. ESHER in *Law Times Rep.* LXIII. 693/2 It is sought by this defendant to extract from that case this doctrine, that, etc.

5. *Math.* ***to extract the root of a number or quantity***: to obtain the root by a mathematical process. Also †***to extract*** (***a quantity***): to find the root of.

1571 DIGGES *Pantom.* II. xxii. Pij, From the quotient thereof..extracte the quadrate roote. **1676** GLANVILL *Ess.* iii. 13 The Method of Extracting Roots in the most numerous Æquations. **1751** CHAMBERS *Cycl.* s.v. *Extraction*, To extract the root out of a given power, is the same thing as, etc. **1827** HUTTON *Course Math.* I. 86 Mixed numbers may be..extracted by the first or second rule. *Ibid.* I. 89 Extract the cube root of 571482·19.

6. Occasional uses after Lat. or Fr.

†**a.** To take away, withdraw. *Obs.*

a **1572** KNOX *Hist. Ref.* Wks. 1846 I. 60 O Lorde, I have bene wicked, and justlie may thow extract thy grace from me. *Ibid.* 333 By your faynting, and by extracting of your support, the enimeis ar incoraged.

†**b.** Only in *passive*: To be derived or descended. Const. *from, of. Obs.* Cf. EXTRACTION 5.

c **1489** CAXTON *Blanchardyn* xxi. 71 He is a man come of a grete house and extracted of hyghe parentage. **1577–87** HOLINSHED *Chron.* I. 95/1 Of the first, the kings of Kent were lineallie extracted. **1605** CAMDEN *Rem.* 13 This English tongue extracted out of the olde German..is mixed. **1647** CLARENDON *Hist. Reb.* I. (1843) 5/1 The enriching a private family (how well soever originally extracted). **1678** WANLEY *Wond. Lit. World* v. ii. §70. 471/2 Michael the eighth..extracted from the Comnenian Emperours.

†**c.** To 'derive', affirm to be derived from a specified origin. *Obs.*

1634 W. TIRWHYT tr. *Balzac's Lett.* 341 It..angers me, that out of the poorest part of Rhetoricke received among the ancients, they will needes extract all ours.

extractable (ɛkˈstræktəb(ə)l), *a.* Also 8–9 -ible. [f. prec. + -ABLE.]

That may be extracted: **a.** *gen.* (cf. esp. senses 3, 4 of the vb.). **b.** Of a passage in a book, etc.: Suitable for extraction; quotable. **c.** *Sc. Law.* Of a judgement, etc.: Ready to be copied out for execution.

1675 GREW *Anat. Plants* Lect. vi. ii. §2 Their tastable parts [are] less easily extractable by the Tongue. **1776** BENTHAM *Ch. Eng.* (1818) 302 The profit extractible out of the expense. **1825** [see EXTRACT *v.* 3b]. **1835** *Blackw. Mag.* XXXVIII. 380 We will now seek a humorous extractable passage. **1868** *Act 31-32 Vict.* c. 100 §63 The Court..shall ..pronounce Judgment..and such Judgment shall be extractible in common Form. *Ibid.* c. 101 §51 The decree for such expenses shall be extractable by the extractor of the Court of Session. **1891** *Times* 13 July 11/3 The quantity of sugar extractable from the root [of beet].

extracted (ɛkˈstræktɪd), *ppl. a.* [f. EXTRACT *v.* + -ED^1.] Derived, drawn out, in senses of the vb.; *spec.* in *Biol.*, derived by controlled breeding, selected.

1694 W. SALMON tr. *Bate's Dispens.* 237/2 An extracted and digested Tincture of Mars. **1903** *Proc. Zool. Soc. Lond.* II. 76 It is not stated that the 'extracted' albinos were tested, but there is little doubt that..they would have produced nothing but albinos. **1909** W. BATESON *Mendel's Princ. Heredity* v. 92 It was possible and indeed more usual to find whites exclusively produced by the cross of two extracted F_2 whites. **1910** L. DONCASTER *Heredity* vii. 86 The 'extracted' pure individuals in the F_2 generation do not differ recognisably from the original parents in the characters considered. *Ibid.* 136 When two heterozygous individuals are mated together, their homozygous offspring are spoken of as 'extracted' homozygotes.

b. ***extracted honey***: honey separated from the uncrushed comb by centrifugal force or by gravity; so ***extracted comb.***

1881 T. W. COWAN *Brit. Bee-Keeper's Guide Bk.* 88 Pure extracted honey will usually granulate if kept at a low temperature. **1897** BARTRUM & MCCLELLAND *Bees in Bar-Frame Hive* 11 Extract at a distance..from the hives, in a room into which the bees cannot penetrate; return extracted comb at night. **1905** P. N. HASLUCK *Beehives & Bee Keepers' Appliances* 116 A number of hives are worked for extracted honey.

†**exˈtractedly**, *adv. Obs. rare*$^{-1}$. [f. *extracted*, pa. pple. of EXTRACT *v.* + -LY^2.] By extraction or descent.

a **1641** BP. MOUNTAGU *Acts & Mon.* (1642) 236 He was a Romane, though an Israelite extractedly.

extracter: see EXTRACTOR.

extractiform (ɛkˈstræktɪfɔːrm), *a.* [f. mod.L. *extract-um* EXTRACT + -(I)FORM.] Having the nature or appearance of an extract.

1860 in WORCESTER; and in later Dicts.

extracting (ɛkˈstræktɪŋ), *vbl. sb.* [f. EXTRACT *v.* + -ING^1.] The action of the vb. EXTRACT; extraction.

a **1626** BACON *Phys. Rem.* Wks. 1740 I. 217 The drawing one metal or mineral out of another which we call extracting. **1874** MAHAFFY *Soc. Life Greece* x. 315 An extracting of thought from the dormant intellect of a pupil.

attrib. **1635** SIBBES *Soul's Confl.* (1638) 13 Vapours drawne up by the Sun..(when the extracting force of the Sun leaves them) fall downe again to the earth. **1883** *Daily News* 27 July 2/1 The extracting levers [of these guns] have enormous power.

exˈtracting, *ppl. a.* [f. as prec. + -ING^2.]

1. That extracts (in senses of the vb.).

1654 GAYTON *Pleas. Notes* IV. ii. 181 Such an hirudinous and extracting Lady as Dulcinea.

†**2.** ? Used for 'distracting'. *Obs. rare*$^{-1}$.

1601 SHAKS. *Twel. N.* v. i. 288 They say poore Gentleman, he's much distract. A most extracting frensie of mine owne From my remembrance, clearly banisht his.

extraction (ɛkˈstrækʃən). [a. Fr. *extraction* (OF. also in semi-popular form *estracion*), ad. med.L. *extractiōn-em*, n. of action f. L. *extrahĕre*: see EXTRACT *v.*]

1. The action or process of drawing (something) out of a receptacle; the pulling or taking out (of anything) by mechanical means; †withdrawal or removal (of a person); an instance of this.

1530–1 *Act 22 Hen. VIII*, c. 14 He..shal be suffred to remayne..in the same sayntuary, without any extraction from the same. **1626** BACON *Sylva* §481 Rew doth prosper much..if it be set by a Fig-tree: which..is caused..by Extraction of a contrary Juyce. **1794** MORSE *Amer. Geog.* 592 The extraction of gold [from mines] is neither very laborious nor dangerous in Brazil. **1799** NELSON in Nicolas *Disp.* (1845) III. 255, I will not permit the extraction of corn from Sicily. **1799** *Med. Jrnl.* II. 233 The extraction of a fœtus already dead. **1829** S. COOPER *Good's Study Med.* (ed. 3) IV. 238 Extraction [of a cataract] consists in making an incision through the cornea..and letting the lens escape through the pupil. **1863** LYELL *Antiq. Man* 14 The long bones..broken..to allow of the extraction of the marrow. **1878** L. P. MEREDITH *Teeth* 181 The extraction of a tooth might not really be the cause of the trouble.

fig. **1874** MORLEY *Compromise* (1886) 152 The extraction of the first and more permanent elements of the old faith, to make the purified material of the new.

†**b.** The drawing of an inference; a deduction. *Obs.*

1622 T. SCOTT *Belg. Pismire* 12 Here wee finde..advised ..A Conclusion, or profitable extraction from the consultation; *and be wise.*

2. a. The action of extracting or copying out (a passage) from a book, etc.; †**b.** *concr.* An extracted passage, quotation (*obs.*); = EXTRACT *sb.* 4.

1656 JER. TAYLOR in *Evelyn's Mem.* (1857) III. 77, I had occasion to use those extractions out of it [Lucretius]. **1656–81** BLOUNT *Glossogr., Extraction*..a breviate or abridgement, also a Draught or Copy. *Mod.* Much pains has been taken in the extraction of illustrative passages.

3. The action or process of obtaining (the constituent elements, juices, etc.) from any substance by heat, pressure, etc. Cf. EXTRACT *v.* 4. ***spirit of the first extraction***: that which comes off at the first distillation.

1605 TIMME *Quersit.* III. 183 Distillation is an extraction of a liquor from a body by heate. **1627** HAKEWILL *Apol.* III. vii. §5. 231 Their artificiall extractions, seperations, and preparations of their medicines. **1701** LUTTRELL *Brief Rel.*

(1857) V. 54 The duty on low wines and spirits of the first extraction. **1837** M. DONOVAN *Dom. Econ.* II. 265 The extraction of the soluble matter of bone. **1868** ROGERS *Pol. Econ.* iii. (1876) 19 Greater pains and more labour were devoted to the extraction of gold from its ores. **1880** *Act 43–44 Vict.* c. 24 §3 'Low wines' means spirits of the first extraction conveyed into a low wines receiver. **1891** THORPE *Dict. Applied Chem., Extraction apparatus.* The object of extraction is to dissolve out some constituent or constituents from a solid, by heating it with a solvent.

†**b.** *concr.* = EXTRACT *sb.* 2. *Obs.*

1594 PLAT *Jewell-ho., Chem. Concl.* 22 A stiffe and drie substance, which our Chimistes do call the extraction of the hearbe. **1605** B. JONSON *Volpone* II. Wks. (Rtldg.) 183/1 This rare extraction..hath..power to disperse all malignant humours. **1670–98** LASSELS *Voy. Italy* I. 129, I saw their still-house where they make excellent extractions and cordial waters.

c. *transf.* and *fig.*

1587 GOLDING *De Mornay* x. 140 As thou hast taken so great paines in..bringing things backe againe into their first matter; whence commeth it that thy extractions..haue so.. contrarie operations. **1605** *Tryall Chev.* II. iii. in Bullen *O. Pl.* (1884) III. 296 The pure extraction of all beauty Flowes in abundance to my love-sick eye. **1644** MILTON *Areop.* (Arb.) 35 They do preserve..the purest efficacie and extraction of that living intellect that bred them.

4. *Math.* The process or method of extracting (the root of a number or quantity).

1557 RECORDE *Whetst.* C ij, The extraction of rootes [of numbers] should go orderly before the arte of Proportions. **1676** GLANVILL *Ess.* iii. 14 Extraction of Roots (which is a species of Division). **1827** HUTTON *Course Math.* I. 86 Two extractions for the 4th root, three for the 8th root, and so on. **1867** TODHUNTER *Algebra for Beginners* xxxii. §287 We shall then consider.. the extraction of the cube root of compound expressions.

5. a. Of persons: Origin, lineage, descent.

c **1477** CAXTON *Jason* 90 Ye be comen of so noble extraction of ryal lignage. *a* **1533** LD. BERNERS *Huon* lv. 186, I am com of a noble extraccyon. **1630** SIR S. D'EWES *Jrnl.* (1783) 69 Herself and my lord's daughter-in-law doe respect my wife according to her several noble extractions. **1776** GIBBON *Decl. & F.* I. 261 The memory of their common extraction was perpetuated by barbaric rites. **1878** GLADSTONE *Prim. Homer* 98 Dark hair is a note of the foreigner, and of southern extraction.

†**b.** Of things: Origin, source. *Obs.*

1648 BOYLE *Seraph. Love* i. (1700) 2, I could wish..that the extraction of your freedom may no ways blemish it. **1655** FULLER *Ch. Hist.* v. iii. §31 Well therefore may the English ..be ashamed of their Reformation, considering the vitious Extraction thereof.

Hence †**ex'tractionable** *a.*, fit or adapted for extraction.

1797 DOWNING *Disord. Horned Cattle* 113 A calf..cannot be extracted..until replaced..in an extractionable position.

extractive (ɛk'stræktɪv), *a.* and *sb.* [f. L. type *extractīv-us*, f. *extrahĕre* (see EXTRACT *v.*). Cf. F. *extractif, -ive.*]

A. *adj.*

†**1.** Tending to draw out; *esp.* of a plaster or drug having the power of drawing out (anything noxious). Const. *of. Obs.*

1599 A. M. tr. *Gabelhouer's Bk. Physicke* 363/2 Then make an extractive Playster spreade with Copperrooste. **1601** HOLLAND *Pliny* II. 191 The common and ordinary Reeds haue an extractiue or drawing faculty. **1750** *Leonardus' Mirr. Stones* 23 Of which instruments, the one is hot, digestive, and extractive or drying of the humid.

2. Concerned with extraction; tending to extract or remove resources or products; *spec.* ***extractive industry***, an industry concerned with obtaining natural products, esp. non-replaceable raw materials such as coal, metallic ore, etc.

1848 MILL *Pol. Econ.* I. ii. §3 Labour employed in producing materials, on which industry is to be afterwards employed..is, in many cases, a labour of mere appropriation; extractive industry, as it has been aptly termed by M. Dunoyer. **1888** *Scot. Leader* 9 Apr. 5 Land used for the purposes of extractive industry. **1890** *Harper's Mag.* Nov. 921/1 They too abound..in what the French call the extractive industries. **1907** H. W. MACROSTY *Trust Movement* iv. 106 The extractive industries dealing with stone and similar products. **1942** *Rep. Comm. Land Utilization* ix. 61 in *Parl. Papers 1941–42* (Cmd. 6378) IV. 421 *Extractive Industries.* These comprise all the mining and quarrying industries. **1962** *Listener* 1 Feb. 205/2 The interest the West has shown towards Latin America has been a commercial, essentially an extractive, interest.

3. Capable of being extracted; of the nature of an extract. Cf. EXTRACT *sb.* 2. ***extractive principle***: see quot. 1875.

1789 J. KEIR *Dict. Chem.* 27/1 Distillation frees the acid from much of this extractive substance. **1796** KIRWAN *Manures* (1802) 53 He found 1 lb. of it [a soil] to contain from 20 to 30 grains of extractive matter. **1816** ACCUM *Chem. Tests* (1818) 186 Separating the extractive acid, and colouring matter from wine. **1875** *Ure's Dict. Arts* II. 323 Fourcroy..supposed that they [extracts] had all a common basis; which he called the extractive principle.

B. *sb.*

1. An extractive substance: see A. 3.

1844–57 G. BIRD *Urin. Deposits* (ed. 5) 117 The physiological origin of sulphur extractive. **1847** TODD *Cycl. Anat.* III. 483 The separation [of the viscous liquor] into.. albumen, aqueous extractive, and alcoholic extractive. **1854** BUSHNAN in *Circ. Sc.* (*c*1865) II. 21/1 It is..nothing more than a species of animal extractive. **1884** *Health Exhib. Catal.* 19/1 A food..containing, in addition to other meat extractives, the whole of the soluble albumen of the meat.

2. 'The brown insoluble mass of doubtful composition, left after the preparation of vegetable extracts' (Wagstaffe).

1807 T. THOMSON *Chem.* (ed. 3) II. 367 The solution.. approached nearer to the vegetable matter called extractive than tannin. **1838** T. THOMSON *Chem. Org. Bodies* 637 The substances held in solution are chiefly sugar, syrup, gluten, gum, and extractive. **1860** *All Y. Round* No. 45. 442 There are in a hundred parts of wheaten flour about seventy-two of starch and extractive.

extractor (ɛk'stræktə(r)). Also 7–9 **extracter.** [f. as prec. + -OR.]

1. One who extracts.

1611 COTGR., *Spargirique*..an Alchymist, or extractor of quintessences. **1651** BIGGS *New Disp.* ¶79 The juice..is drawn out by the Extractors, who..resolve the dreggs..of the Parenchyma. **1755** JOHNSON, *Extractor*, the person or instrument by which any thing is extracted. **1828** *Blackw. Mag.* XXIV. 198 Healer of diseases, and extractor of money. **1868** *Morn. Star* 16 June, Mr. Abrams..begged to say that his client was not a corn-cutter, but a corn-extractor.

2. a. One who selects and copies out quotations.

1813 *Edin. Rev.* XXI. 267 A judicious extractor..might accommodate both classes of readers. **1884** *Blackw. Mag.* June 824/1 The extractor who looks for a fitting pause in the spate of Mr. Ruskin's eloquence.

b. *spec.* in *Sc. Law.* (See quot. 1861.)

1687 *Act Sederunt* 23 Feb., The Lords do extend the priviledges..to..four extracters in each of the three clarks offices of the Session. **1751** *Ibid.* 4 Jan., The Lords..do.. prohibit..all agents from being extractors, and all extractors from agenting. **1810** in Hansard *Parl. Deb.* June, [Mr. Thomas Scott] was appointed to the office of an Extractor. **1861** W. BELL *Dict. Law Scot.* 374/2 *Extractor*.. the official person by whom the extract of a decree or other judicial proceeding is prepared and authenticated. **1868** [see EXTRACTABLE].

3. An instrument for drawing or pulling out anything; *esp.* that part of a breech-loading gun which removes the cartridge. Also, an instrument for extracting honey from the combs. Cf. *honey-extractor* s.v. HONEY *sb.* 7.

1753 N. TORRIANO *Midwifry* 18 They never turned children..their only Resource was to Knives, Extractors, etc. **1859** F. A. GRIFFITHS *Artil. Man.* (ed. 9) 168, 1 setter. 2 needles. 1 extractor. **1871** *Daily News* 11 Apr. 6 The loaded man opens the breech of his rifle, uses the extracter, takes out the cartridge. **1875** *Encycl. Brit.* III. 501/1 To a German apiarian we are indebted for the invention of a machine called the honey-extractor... There are various patterns of the machine, but the principle of all may be said to be the same, that of centrifugal force. **1885** J. J. MANLEY *Brit. Almanac Comp.* 19 Extractors, comb foundations and other appliances used in bee-keeping. **1886** F. G. JENYNS *Bk. about Bees* 150 When the bee-keeper wishes to obtain the greatest possible quantity of honey he..uses to a great extent the machine called an extractor. **1938–9** *Army & Navy Stores Catal.* 991 All types of Hives, Extractors, etc.

†**4.** A solvent used to extract (juices, etc.). *Obs.*

1678 SALMON *Lond. Disp.* 852/1 The strength of the Extracter or dissolvent.

5. *attrib.*, as **extractor fan**, a ventilation fan in a window, outside wall, etc., which replaces stale air indoors with fresh air.

c **1945** *Design at Home* (C.E.M.A.) 13/1 Extractor fan to remove cooking odours and steam. **1958** *Listener* 23 Oct. 671/1 You can fit extractor fans in your windows. **1967** 'M. HUNTER' *Cambridgeshire Disaster* iv. 26 He..noted the meal half prepared and the whir of the extractor fan.

Hence **ex'tractorship**, the office of an extractor (in sense 2 b).

1837 LOCKHART *Scott* xx, Mr. Thomas Scott's appointment to this Extractorship. **1877** *Geneal. Mem. Family Sir W. Scott* 61 Sir Walter secured for him an extractorship in the General Register House.

ex'tractory, *a.* [ad. L. *extractōrius*, f. *extrahĕre*: see EXTRACT *v.* and -ORY.] Of or pertaining to an extractor; or to extraction.

1727 BAILEY vol. II, *Extractory*, that hath the nature or power to draw out. **1775** in ASH. **1891** *Punch* CI. 179/1 Reviewed it in this..extractory and arbitrary fashion.

†**ex'tracture.** *Obs.* [f. L. *extract-* (see EXTRACT *v.*) + -URE.] Something extracted; an extract; = EXTRACT *sb.* 2, 4.

1602 MARSTON *Ant. & Mel.* IV. Wks. 1856 I. 48 Let each note breath the heart of passion, The sad extracture of extreamest griefe. **1621** ELSING *Debates Ho. Lords* App. (Camden) 134 That they might see the extractures sent up from the Lower House.

extra-curial, etc.: see EXTRA- 1.

†**extra'dictionary**, *a. Obs. rare*⁻¹. [f. L. phrase *extrā dictiōn-em* outside of the mode of expression (see EXTRA *prep.* and DICTION) + -ARY.] Of fallacies: Not consisting in expression; real, not verbal.

1646 SIR T. BROWNE *Pseud. Ep.* I. iv. 15 Of these extra-dictionary and reall fallacies, Aristotle and Logicians make in number six.

‖**extra dictionem** (ɛkstrə dɪktɪ'əʊnɛm), *phr. Logic.* [see EXTRADICTIONARY *a.*; L. tr. of *ἔξω τῆς λέξεως* (Aristotle, *Sophistical Refutations*, ch. 4).] Of fallacies: unconnected with the linguistic expression used; not due to ambiguity, etc.; EXTRADICTIONARY. (Opp. IN DICTIONE.)

1826, 1847 [see IN DICTIONE]. **1852** H. L. MANSEL *Aldrich* (ed. 2) 136 Purely logical fallacies belong, not to the *in dictione*, but to the *extra dictionem*. **1906** H. W. B. JOSEPH *Introd. Logic* xxvii. 534 Later writers..called the fallacies *extra dictionem* fallacies *in re*, or material fallacies. **1970** C. L. HAMBLIN *Fallacies* i. 13 The traditional Latin terms are *in dictione* and *extra dictionem.*

extraditable (ɛkstrə'daɪtəb(ə)l), *a.* [f. next + -ABLE.] **a.** Of a person: That may be extradited, liable to extradition. **b.** Of a crime, etc.: Rendering the perpetrator liable to extradition.

a. 1881 *Philadelphia Press* 12 Aug. 4 Hartmann is extraditable under the law of nations. **1890** *Times* 13 Jan. 5/5 A person..convicted of these crimes is extraditable.

b. 1887 *Pall Mall G.* 19 Mar. 4/2 In the American treaty procuration will also find a place among extraditable offences.

extradite ('ɛkstrədaɪt), *v.* [Back-formation from next.]

1. a. To surrender to another country, state, or power a person accused or convicted of a crime committed there.

1864 SALA in *Daily Tel.* 29 July, Nothing is said about the Emperor of the French being summoned to extradite the men brought into Cherbourg by the French pilot-boats. **1885** *Law Times* LXXX. 116/1 The power of criminal courts of this country to extradite prisoners charged with the commission of offences in foreign countries. **1967** *Listener* 6 July 6/3 Congolese Government asks Algeria to extradite Mr Moise Tshombe.

b. *transf.*

1883 J. PAYN *Thicker than Water* III. 240 She was extradited in a vehicle by herself to the great relief of her fellow culprits.

c. To obtain the extradition of.

1883 *Chicago Advance* 8 Mar., The effort of England to extradite Sheridan, of the Irish World, New York. **1889** *North. Star* 28 Feb. 3/1 The Home Office are taking measures for extraditing 'Pigott'.

2. *Psychol.* To localize (a sensation) at a distance from the centre of sensation. *rare.*

1887 W. JAMES in *Mind* Apr. 207 The next factor is the particular kind of sensation to be extradited.

Hence **'extradited** *ppl. a.*

1889 CHILD *Eng. & Sc. Ball.* III. VI. clxxvi. 410/2 They land Lord Percy at Berwick, a deported, 'extradited' man!

extradition (ɛkstrə'dɪʃən), *sb.* [a. F. *extradition*, f. L. *ex-* out + *trādition-em*, n. of action f. *trādĕre* to deliver up: see TRADITION.]

1. The action of giving up (a person) to the authorities of a foreign state; *esp.* the delivery of a fugitive criminal to the authorities of the state in which the crime was committed. Hence in *gen.* sense: Surrender (of a prisoner) by one authority to another.

1839 DE QUINCEY *Casuistry* Wks. VIII. 308 If the law of extradition should remain unchanged. **1857** *Fraser's Mag.* LVI. 161 A demand for (we must use a foreign and un-English word to express an un-English thing) the extradition of Mazzini. **1870** *Act 33–4 Vict.* c. 52 (*title*) An Act for amending the Law relating to the Extradition of Criminals. **1879** FARRAR *St. Paul* II. 336 They wished to make sure of the extradition of their victim.

2. The process of localizing a sensation at a distance from the centre of sensation.

1874 CARPENTER *Ment. Phys.* I. v. (1879) 186 A kind of extradition of the visual sensation. **1887** W. JAMES in *Mind* Apr. 205 Extradition obtains..even of such sensations as we locate on the exact sensory surfaces where the nerves terminate.

3. *attrib.* (sense 1), as ***extradition act, clause, crime***; **extradition treaty**, a treaty by which two nations mutually bind themselves to surrender any fugitive criminal who has committed in the other's territory any of certain specified offences.

1852 ABBOTT LAWRENCE *Dispatch to D. Webster*, The proposition..to conclude an extradition treaty with the United States. **1870** *Act 33–4 Vict.* c. 52 § 1 This Act may be cited as 'The Extradition Act 1870'. *Ibid.* §26 An extradition crime. **1875** RENOUF *Egyptian Gram.* 35 These words occur in the extradition clause of the Treaty between Rameses II and the king of Cheta.

Hence **extra'dition** *v. trans.*, to bring (a criminal) under the operation of an extradition treaty.

1889 *Scot. Leader* 18 Apr. 5 Barton..obstructed extradition process until quite recently, when he was successfully extraditioned.

extra-domi'ciliate, *v. rare*⁻¹. [f. L. *extrā* + *domicili-um* DOMICILE + -ATE³.] *trans.* To send out of the domicile or house.

1823 LAMB *Elia* (1860) 194 It is..ingratitude..to extra-domiciliate..a blessing.

extrados (ɛk'streɪdəs). *Arch.* [a. F. *extrados*, f. L. *extrā* outside + F. *dos* the back.] The upper or exterior curve of an arch; *esp.* the upper curve of the voussoirs or stones which immediately form the arch. Cf. INTRADOS.

1772 HUTTON *Bridges* p. iii, The relations between their intrados and extrados. **1823** P. NICHOLSON *Pract. Build.* 338 Extrados of a Bridge—The curve of the road-way. **1828** HUTTON *Course Math.* II. 172 So that the extrados is a parabola equal to the intrados, and everywhere vertically

equidistant from it. **1879** Sir G. Scott *Lect. Archit.* II. 141 We have..supposed our arches to be of moderate depth from extrados, or outer line, to intrados or inner line.

extradosed (ɛk'streɪdəst), *a.* [f. prec. + -ED². Cf. F. *extradossé*.] Having an extrados (of a certain kind): a term applied to an arch in which the curves of the intrados and extrados are concentric and parallel.

In mod. Dicts.

extradotal (ɛkstrə'dəʊtəl), *a. Law.* [as if ad. L. **extrādōtāl-is* (cf. It. *estradotale*, 18th c.), f. *extrā* outside + *dōt-em* (nom. *dōs*) dowry: see -AL¹.] (See quot.)

1827 Kent *Comm.* II. 154 *note*, [By the code of Louisiana] the separate property of the wife is divided into dotal, being that which she brings to the husband..and extradotal..being that which forms no part of the dowry.

† **extraduce**, *a. Obs. rare.* [L. *ex trāduce*, *ex* out of + *trāduce*, abl. of *trādux* vine-layer, f. *trā-* (*trans*) across + *dūc-ĕre* to lead.] *lit.* From or after the fashion of a layer; hence, derived as from a parent stock.

[**1641** Clarendon *Ess.* Tracts (1727) 225 That it [the soul] is *ex traduce*, and begotten with the body by the father. **1632** Howell *Lett.* (1655) II. 31 Ther cannot be a more pregnant instance to prove that human souls com not *ex traduce* [**1688** extraduce].] **1720** W. Stukeley in *Mem.* (1882) I. 15 Either an *extraduce* Inclination or Imitation at least of my Father.

† **extra'duction.** *Obs.* Also 6 extraduccion. [f. L. *extrā* + *ductiōn-em* a leading, n. of action f. *dūcĕre* to lead.]

a. A conclusion (to a book); opposed to *introduction.* **b.** *Mil.* The bringing a line of musketeers to the front from the rear of a body of pikemen.

1533 More *Debell. Salem* i. Wks. 932/2 So shoulde he haue called those three chapiters after hys matter, an extraduccion. **1635** Barriffe *Mil. Discip.* lxxx. (1643) 228 The next Firing..to demonstrate shall be by way of Extraduction: which is also a firing in front. *Ibid.* lxxxii. 236 The body standing in this forme, the Musquetiers may sleeve up by way of Extraduction.

extra-essential, etc.: see EXTRA- 1.

extra-foraneous (ˌɛkstrəfə'reɪnɪəs), *a.* [f. EXTRA- *pref.* + med.L. *forāne-us* (f. *foris* door) + -OUS. After the analogy of L. *circumforāneus*, f. *circum* around + *forum* the forum.] Out-door.

1781 Cowper *Let.* 2 Apr., A variety of extra-foraneous occupations..make it difficult for me to find opportunities of writing. **1788** —— *Wks.* (1876) 288 We live near to each other and while the Hall is empty are each other's only extraforaneous comfort. **1830** Macgillivray *Withering's Brit. Plants* Pref., A compendious description of our native plants..neither too bulky for extra-foraneous use, nor too expensive. **1891** J. P. Sheldon in *Times* 17 Mar., All extraforaneous animals took no harm whatever.

extra-formal, -galactic, etc.: see EXTRA- 1.

† **extra'geneous, -genous**, *a. Obs.*$^{-0}$ [incorrectly f. EXTRA- + L. *gen-us* kind, on supposed analogy of *homogeneous*, *-genous*.] (See quot.) Also **extrage'neity**, 'the being of a foreign kind' (Bailey 1727–36).

1706 Phillips (ed. Kersey), *Extra-genous* (in Anatomy and Surgery) that is of a foreign kind; as an Extragenous Body. **1884** *Syd. Soc. Lex.*, *Extrageneous.*

extraght, var. form of EXTRAUGHT *ppl. a. Obs.*

extra-historic, -inductive, etc.: see EXTRA- 1.

extra-'illustrated, *a.* [f. EXTRA- + ILLUSTRATED *ppl. a.*] = GRANGERIZED *ppl. a.* So **extra-illu'stration**, Grangerizing; also **extra-'illustrator**, a Grangerizer.

1889 [see GRANGERIZE *v.*]. **1910** *Encycl. Brit.* XII. 351/2 'Grangerizing' became a term for such an extra-illustration of any work, especially with cuts taken from other books. **1952** J. Carter *ABC for Book-Collectors* 79 Grangerised, or extra-illustrated books as they are now more commonly called, are copies which have had added to them..engraved portraits, prints, etc. **1960** *Times* 1 Mar. 12/5 £180 for an extra-illustrated copy of the first edition of Boswell's Johnson.

† **extrait**, *pa. pple. Obs.* [a. Fr. *extrait*, pa. pple. of *extraire*, earlier *estraire*:—L. *extrahĕre*: see EXTRACT *v.* See EXTRACT, EXTRAUGHT *ppl. adjs.*]

a. Drawn out, extracted. **b.** Derived, descended.

1480 Caxton *Ovid's Met.* XIII. ii, Ulixes..wyl compare with me, that am extrait of suche lygnage. **1481** —— *Myrr.* I. ix. 35 Of this science [Rethoryque] were extrayt and drawen the lawes and decrees whiche by nede serue [etc.]. **1483** —— *Gold. Leg.* 93/1 Saynt Lucye..was..extrayt..of a noble lygnage.

extrajudicial (ˌɛkstrədʒuː'dɪʃəl), *a.* Also 7 extra-iuditiall. [f. L. *extrā* outside + *jūdici-um* judgement + -AL¹.]

1. Lying outside the proceedings in court; forming no part of the case before the court. Of an opinion, confession, etc.: Not delivered from the bench, not made in court, informal.

1630 in Rushw. *Hist. Coll.* (1659) I. 47 The accusation was extra-judicial, and out of Court. **1651** W. G. tr. *Cowel's Inst.* 237 The Plaintiff..requires him [Defendant] to come to make an extrajudiciall satisfaction. *a* **1715** Burnet *Own Time* (1766) II. 20 No extrajudicial confession could be allowed in a Court. **1871** Markby *Elem. Law* §60 The opinion of the judge..is considered as extra-judicial.

2. Outside the ordinary course of law or justice; not legally authorized; unwarranted.

1641 in Clarendon *Hist. Reb.* III. (1843) 87/2 Some rigorous and extrajudicial determinations in cases of plantations. **1706** Rushw. in *Burton's Diary* (1828) III. 47 By an extra-judicial order..the Lieutenant-general was commanded to suffer none but the keepers to speak to him. **1785** Paley *Mor. Philos.* (1818) I. 267 That extrajudicial discipline, which supplies the defects..of law. **1849** J. Grant *Mem. Kirkaldy* xxiv. 273 The extra-judicial murder of his comrade.

extrajudicially (ˌɛkstrədʒuː'dɪʃəlɪ), *adv.* [f. prec. + -LY².] In an extrajudicial manner.

1. Outside the proceedings of the court, informally, privately, out of court.

1590 Swinburne *Testaments* 9 The opinion of a Iudge..deliuered priuatly, or extraiudicially. **1681** Baxter *Acc. Sherlocke* iv. 186 What they do extrajudicially and *extra proprium forum*, is Null. **1752** J. Louthian *Forms of Process* (ed. 2) 273 The Custody of Processes borrowed up from the Clerk extrajudicially, shall be fixed by a Receipt-book. **1845** Ld. Campbell *Chancellors* (1857) I. xvi. 254 He had extrajudicially pronounced opinions, which, etc.

2. In a manner outside or contrary to the usual course of law, without legal justification, unwarrantably.

a **1612** Donne *Βιαθανατος* (1644) 138 A Bishop, being..callumniated by the people extrajudicially. **1660** R. Coke *Power & Subj.* 257 He was never noted to punish any man rashly, or extrajudicially. **1786** Burke *W. Hastings* IV. §10 Sir Elijah Impey, His Majesty's Chief Justice, acting extrajudicially, and not within the limits of his jurisdiction. **1822** J. Flint *Lett. Amer.* 172 Where the squire is supposed to be remiss in the execution of his duty, the people sometimes interfere extrajudicially.

extra-jugal, -jural: see EXTRA- 1.

† **extra-'lath**, *v. Obs. rare.* [f. EXTRA *a.* + LATH *sb.*] *trans.* To furnish with additional laths. Hence **extra-'lathing** *vbl. sb.*

1778 Mahon in *Phil. Trans.* LXVIII. 893 The underside of the stair-case was extra-lathed. *Ibid.* 890 The method of extra-lathing may be applied to cieling joists.

extra-legal, -marine, etc.: see EXTRA- 1.

extrality (ɛk'strælɪtɪ). Syncopated form of EXTRATERRITORIALITY.

1925 *Springfield Republican* 29 June, The question of extraterritoriality—or 'extrality', as some writers are beginning to spell a long word that may fill a good deal of space from now on. **1926** *Spectator* 9 Jan. 38/1 The connecting link between the anti-British campaign and the question of abolishing 'Extrality'—otherwise extraterritoriality—is the Russian policy. **1927** *Glasgow Herald* 5 Mar. 11 Such questions as 'extral[i]ty' and 'concessions' were not strange words in Japanese ears. **1929** *N.Y. Times* 6 Sept. 24/3 That China has suffered grievously as a result of 'extrality' (as it is now commonly called).

† **extra'mission.** *Obs.* [n. of action f. L. phrase *extrā mittĕre* to send outwards: see EXTRA and MISSION.] Sending outwards; emission.

c **1630** Jackson *Creed* IV. II. iv. Wks. III. 244 Nor do faith and love truly Christian arise from every..extra-mission of our faculties unto Christ. **1646** Sir T. Browne *Pseud. Ep.* III. vii. 120 Sight is made by Reception, and not by Extramission. **1673–4** Grew *Anat. Plants* III. II. ii. §1 The Reception, as well as Extramission whereof [the Aer].

† **extra'mit**, *v. Obs. rare*$^{-1}$. [f. L. *extrā* outwards + *mitt-ĕre* to send.] *trans.* To send forth or outward: in quot. *refl.* and *fig.*

1651 Charleton *Eph. & Cimm. Matrons* II. (1668) 67 To Lovers it is the same thing..to see, and to extramit themselves by the eye.

† **extra'mund**, *v. Obs. rare*$^{-1}$. [f. L. *extrā mund-um*: see next.] *trans.* To put out of the universe.

1654 Gayton *Pleas. Notes* III. viii. 117 He would..extramund him, more than Materia Prima it self was at the Chaos.

extramundane (ɛkstrə'mʌndeɪn), *a.* [ad. late L. *extramundān-us*, f. phrase *extrā mund-um* outside the world or universe: see EXTRA- *pref.* and MUNDANE.]

1. Situated outside of, or pertaining to a region outside of, our world.

1665 Glanvill *Sceps. Sci.* xviii. 116 'Tis a philosophy that..gives the exactest Topography of the Extramundane spaces. **1684** T. Burnet *Th. Earth* I. 175 One [opinion] placeth paradise in the extra-mundane regions. **1742** Young *Nt. Th.* IX. 1525 Where, rears His terminating Pillar high Its extra-mundane Head? **1879** Newcomb & Holden *Astron.* 376 Aerolites..were proved to be of extramundane origin.

b. *fig.* (*nonce-uses*). 'Out of the world', remote; pertaining to things not of this world.

1829 Southey *Sir T. More* II. 325 What may be called an extramundane zeal. **1834** *Fraser's Mag.* X. 652 Babbling of poetry in this extra-mundane island. **1837** *Ibid.* XVI. 310 The asseverations in the book are so preposterous..and the dreams so extramundane.

2. Situated outside or beyond the universe; pertaining to what is beyond the universe.

1706 Phillips (ed. Kersey), *Extramundane space*, i.e. the infinite empty void Space, which is supposed by some to reach beyond the Bounds of the Universe. **1715–6** Clarke tr. *Leibnitz's 4th Paper* §7 The same Reason, which shews that extramundane Space [Fr. *l'Espace hors du monde*] is imaginary, proves, etc. **1825** Coleridge *Aids Refl.* (1848) I. 126 The independent (extra-mundane) existence..of the Supreme One.

extramural (ɛkstrə'mjʊərəl), *a.* [f. L. *extrā mūr-ōs* outside the walls + -AL¹: see EXTRA- *pref.* and MURAL. Cf. late L. *extrāmūrānus* in same sense.] **a.** Outside the walls or boundaries of a city or town; *esp.* in *extra-mural interment.* *spec.* in *Education*, of institutions or teaching organized by a university or college for persons other than its resident students.

1854 Cdl. Wiseman *Fabiola* (1855) 155 The extramural basilicas of St. Paul on the Ostian way. **1861** Pearson *Early & Mid. Ages Eng.* 27 Large sewers, large aqueducts, and extramural interment, are common features. **1884** *Science* Mar. 371 The..arrangements by which medical men not connected with the university give..'Extra-mural' instruction. **1901** *Daily Chron.* 1 June 3/4 All extra-mural colleges, high-grade schools, art and technical institutions. **1962** *Lancet* 15 Dec. 1261/1 In the middle 'forties the end of extramural teaching in Glasgow..left the Faculty at a low ebb. **1969** I. & P. Opie *Children's Games* p. xv, The Department of Extramural Studies, Keele University.

b. *transf.* and *fig.*

1955 *Times* 10 June 6/2 The opening of Parliament yesterday was shorn of all such extramural spectacle as the Queen's drive in state. **1964** G. L. Cohen *What's Wrong with Hospitals?* iii. 57 Let the almoner deal with him—a consultant has no time for extra-mural comforting. **1966** J. Wainwright *Crystallised Carbon Pig* xiii. 59 The nightly rendezvous for the city's sugar daddies, extra-mural secretaries, bald-headed Lochinvars.

Hence **extra'muralism**, the practice of giving extramural instruction. **extra'muralist** *nonce-wd.*, one who lives outside the walls of a city. **extra'murally** *adv.*, in an extramural way.

1868 *Imperial Rev.* 7 Mar. 228 All the city..all except the outcast extramuralists..are soon reduced to ashes. **1892** *Sat. Rev.* 14 May 571/1 There remained only the principle of..'Extramuralism' to be reckoned with. **1927** *Observer* 5 June 7/2 The University College of the South-West is the youngest of our University institutions; but during the short period of its career it has developed considerably both intra- and extra-murally.

extranate ('ɛkstrəneɪt), *a. rare*$^{-1}$. [f. L. *extrā* without + *nāt-us* born.] Arising from without; opposed to *innate.*

1856 Ferrier *Inst. Metaph.* IX. xxi. 497 One [element]..is said to be innate, the other which is contributed from without..may be said to be extra-nate.

extra-national, etc.: see EXTRA- 1.

† **ex'traneal**, *a. Obs. rare.* [f. L. *extrāne-us* (see EXTRANEOUS) + -AL¹.] = EXTRANEOUS. So also † **ex'tranean** [+ -AN], † **ex'tranear** [+ -AR].

1565 *Aberdeen Reg.* 23 Jan. (Spalding Club 1844) 358 That the magistrattis tak sic substantious ordour anent the expelling of extranear beggaris. *Ibid.* V. 26 (Jam.) Extraneane cordanaris. **1618** T. Gainsford *Hist. P. Warbeck* in *Select. Harl. Misc.* (1793) 66, I desist from all extraneal and superfluous discourses.

extraneity (ɛkstrə'niːɪtɪ). *rare.* [f. as prec. + -ITY.] The quality of being extraneous.

1849 Abp. Thomson *Laws Th.* Introd. (1860) 19 Extraneity—outness—objective existence.

† **ex'traneize**, *v. Obs. rare.* [f. as prec. + -IZE.] *trans* To make extraneous, remove.

1653 Urquhart *Rabelais* I. xix, To extraneize the blasting mists and whirlwinds upon our Vines. **1788** H. Clarke *School Candidates* (1877) 19 To extraneize the blasting mists and whirlwind of immorality upon the minds of youth.

extraneous (ɛk'streɪnɪəs), *a.* [f. L. *extrāne-us* external (f. *extrā* outside) + -OUS. (Cf. *strange*, ad. OF. *estrange*:—L. *extrāneus*.)]

1. a. Of external origin; introduced or added from without; foreign *to* the object in which it is contained, or to which it is attached.

1638 A. Read *Chirurg.* ix. 67 Such medicaments ought not onely to consume the extraneous humidity, but the natural also. **1690** Locke *Hum. Und.* II. xxv. §8 Relation..though it be not contained in the real existence of Things, but something extraneous, and superinduced. **1774** Goldsm. *Nat. Hist.* (1862) II. IV. iv. 358 Fossil, or, as they are called, extraneous shells. **1797** M. Baillie *Morb. Anat.* (1807) 306 An extraneous body can be..easily introduced into their bladder. **1827** Hare *Guesses* Ser. I. (1873) 183 Many objects are made venerable by extraneous circumstances. **1833** Lyell *Princ. Geol.* III. 187, I sought in vain..for a single fragment of any extraneous rock. **1879** Stainer *Music of Bible* 159 A slight melodic framework, almost hidden beneath a load of extraneous graces.

b. Of an action, etc.: Proceeding from without.

1786 Burke *W. Hastings* Wks. 1842 II. 184 Hastings did for a long time..attribute the weakness of his government to an extraneous interference. **1834** J. Forbes *Laennec's Dis. Chest* (ed. 4) 26 The..application of the naked ear..gives rise to extraneous sounds. **1862** Marsh *Eng. Lang* ii. 40 The Low-German dialects were..exposed to extraneous disturbing forces. **1867** J. Hogg *Microsc.* I. ii. 120 Excluding extraneous light.

c. *nonce-use.* Brought from abroad, 'exotic'.

c **1750** Shenstone *Elegies* xviii. 58 Rob'd in the Gallic loom's extraneous twine.

2. a. External *to*, not comprised in or forming part of, the object under consideration.

1662 BATES in Pepys *Diary* 17 Aug., It is not my manner to speak anything in the pulpit that is extraneous to my text and business. **1690** LOCKE *Hum. Und.* II. xxxi. §4 When ever the Mind refers any of its Ideas to any thing extraneous to them, they are then capable to be called true or false. **1794** PALEY *Evid.* Wks. 1825 II. 377 Of points clearly extraneous to the religion, nothing need be said. **1865** MAFFEI *Brigand Life* II. 121 The question of brigandage being extraneous to all political controversies.

b. Of a person: Not belonging to a specified community, country, or family.

a **1655** VINES *Lord's Supp.* (1677) 212 Heathens and Infidels are excluded from this Table, because they are extraneous and without. **1655–60** STANLEY *Hist. Philos.* (1701) 376/1 If at any time there were any extraneous.. persons amongst them, the Men..signify'd their meaning to one another by Symbols. **1842** ARNOLD *Lect. Mod. Hist.* iii. 187 It has..to feed one or more extraneous persons besides. *a* **1853** ROBERTSON *Serm.* Ser. III. ii. (1872) 20 Nearly all who are of the world are extraneous to it [the church].

†**c.** Foreign in nature, having nothing in common. *Obs. rare.*

1671 J. WEBSTER *Metallogr.* iv. 74 Mercury one thing, and Sulpher another, as extraneous bodies one to another.

d. *Mus.* (See quots.)

1801 T. BUSBY *Dict. Mus.*, *Extraneous*, an epithet applied to those sharps and flats, and those chords and modulations, which, forsaking the natural course of the diatonic intervals, digress into abstruse and chromatic evolutions of melody and harmony. **1839** [see MODULATION 4 c]. **1876** STAINER & BARRETT *Dict. Mus. Terms* 162/1 *Extraneous modulation*, a modulation to an extreme or unrelated key. *Ibid.* 295/1 When a remote key is reached by relative keys, the modulation is by some said to be *extraneous*. **1938** *Oxf. Compan. Mus.* 590/1 Beethoven.., on occasion, leapt, with little notice to the listener, into unrelated keys (*Extraneous Modulation*).

Hence **ex'traneously** *adv.*; **ex'traneousness**, the quality or state of being extraneous.

1755 E. LAW *Th. Relig.* III. 237 *note*, By their being extraneously overruled. **1881** WESTCOTT & HORT *Grk. N.T.* II. Notes 44 Without giving any sign of extraneousness.

extra-nuclear, -ocular, etc.: see EXTRA- 1.

‖**extraordinaire** (ɛkstrɔːdɪ'nɛə(r), ‖ɛkstra ɔrdinɛr), *a.* [a. F *extraordinaire* extraordinary, outstanding; used in colloq. Fr. as a superlative: cf. EXTRAORDINARY *a.*] Remarkable, outstanding; of a person: unusually active or successful in a particular field. Used postpositively.

1940 S. RIDER *Misplaced Corpse* i. 5 It certainly sounds like the binge *extraordinaire*. **1960** *Publisher's note* in J. Webb *Delicate Darling* 1, Juan Alfredo Delicado, poet, adventurer, and lover *extraordinaire*, was a very wanted man. **1975** *Economist* 25 Jan. 45/2 Mr. John Mitchell, who was Mr. Nixon's campaign manager and a law-and-order man extraordinaire, has now been convicted of playing a key role in the Watergate cover-up. **1981** *Washington Post* 12 Jan. B7/3 It is not any crazier than Richard Nixon, in the 1950s communist fighter extraordinaire, turning about to be the man who brought about..detente. **1984** *Observer* 30 Sept. 24/3, I dropped in on fund-raiser extraordinaire, Dr Jerry Nims.

extraordinarily (ɛk'strɔːdɪnərɪlɪ), *adv.* [f. EXTRAORDINARY *a.* + -LY².]

†**1.** 'In a manner out of the common method and order' (J.); often opposed to *ordinarily*. *Obs.*

1564 GOLDING *Justine* (1570) 143 b, The Romaynes.. created Æmilius Paulus consull and made him extraordinarily Lieuetenaunt of the warres of Macedone. *a* **1687** PETTY *Pol. Arith.* vi. (1691) 97 The People..which have extraordinarily perished..above what have died in the ordinary way. *a* **1779** WARBURTON *Alliance Ch. & State* I. notes Wks. 1788 IV. 69 An ordinance, immediately and extraordinarily revealed from God.

†**b.** Otherwise than in ordinary course; on an exceptional occasion. *Obs.*

1579 FULKE *Heskins' Parl.* 31 Luther..by no meanes would haue women to teache, except it were extraordinarily. **1677** *Govt. Venice* 135 When the Council is to be called extraordinarily. **1703** *Lond. Gaz.* No. 3922/2 The Senate has been extraordinarily assembled.

c. *Optics.* (see EXTRAORDINARY A. 1 d).

1831 BREWSTER *Optics* xviii. 161 The ray CF extraordinarily refracted by the first rhomb will be ordinarily refracted by the second. **1875** LOMMEL *Light* xxi. 283 This ray is..said to be extraordinarily refracted.

†**2.** In excess of the usual complement; = EXTRA. *Obs. rare*⁻¹.

1719 DEFOE *Crusoe* 204 The two Quarter-Deck guns that my Nephew took extraordinarily.

3. In an extraordinary degree; very unusually, remarkably, excessively, uncommonly.

1593 NASHE *Christ's T.* Ded., You recompence learning extraordinarilie. **1597** SHAKS. *2 Hen. IV*, I. ii. 235, I meane not to sweat extraordinarily. **1610** BEAUM. & FL. *Maid's Trag.* IV. ii, I..take 't unkindly that mine enemy Should use me so extraordinarily scurvily. **1721** DE FOE *Mem. Cavalier* (1840) 163 The power of the gentry is extraordinarily visible. **1885** *Manch. Guardian* 20 July 5/2 The extraordinarily good score of 98 points out of a possible 100.

extraordinariness (ɛk'strɔːdɪnərɪnɪs). [f. next + -NESS.] The quality or fact of being extraordinary.

1628 DIGBY *Jrnl.* (Camden) 56 The extraordinarinesse of the action. **1675** BAXTER *Cath. Theol.* II. VIII. 189 Wherein the extraordinariness of it consisteth..I think it past mans reach to know. *a* **1703** BURKITT *On N.T.* Luke iii. 17 The extraordinariness of John the Baptist's person. **1881** *Spectator* 19 Feb. 247 Some vital point, which may result quite as easily from ordinariness..as from extraordinariness.

b. *humorously* as a title of address.

1677–81 MRS. BEHN *Rover* III. i, As for that matter, your extraordinariness may do what you please.

extraordinary (ɛk'strɔːdɪnərɪ, ɛkstrə'ɔːdɪnərɪ), *a.*, *adv.*, and *sb.* Also (5 **extraordynary**, 6 **-ordinair**), 6–7 **-ordinarie**. [ad. L. *extraordinārius*, f. phrase *extrā ordin-em* outside (the usual) order: see EXTRA- *pref.* and ORDER, ORDINARY. Cf. F. *extraordinaire.*] **A.** *adj.*

1. Out of the usual or regular course or order; often in expressed opposition to *ordinary*. †Also, acting in an unusual manner; partial. *extraordinary tithe*: (see quot. 1888).

c **1460** FORTESCUE *Abs. & Lim. Mon.* (1714) 39 The Kyngs yerly expencs stondyn in chargs Ordynarye, and in chargs Extraordynary. **1553** GARDINER *True Obedience* 43 b, Do we not se..the chief iudge, when he is required to bee present in extraordinary judgements. **1592** BABINGTON *Genesis* xxxvii. 145 b, If God be extraordinarie to Moses, euen Aaron..will be offended. **1607** TOPSELL *Serpents* (1653) 728 Thus much may suffice for the ordinary and extraordinary generation of Toads. **1642** FULLER *Holy & Prof. St.* II. ix. 84 His Sermons are of an ordinary length except on an extraordinary occasion. **1745** *De Foe's Eng. Tradesman* (1841) I. vii. 49 Let him..take some extraordinary measures to get in his debts. **1888** J. WILLIAMS in *Encycl. Brit.* XXIII. 412 These [tithes] are..divided..into ordinary and extraordinary, the latter being a tithe at a heavier rate charged upon hop and market gardens.

†**b.** Not according to rule, 'out of order'. *Obs.*

a **1647** CLARENDON *Hist. Reb.* VIII. (1843) 519/1 If they proceeded in a martial, or any other extraordinary way, without any form of law. **1709** STRYPE *Ann. Ref.* I. lvii. 627 The order of calling and making of ministers now used in the Church of England, is extraordinary.

†**c.** *Mus.* = ACCIDENTAL *a.* 5. *Obs.*

1597 MORLEY *Introd. Mus.* 157 They..set one ♭ at the beginning of the verses of euerie part, and if there happen anie extraordinary flat they..set the signe before it. **1731** G. KELLER *Rules for Playing Thorow-Bass* in W. Holder *Harmony* 192 If the extream sharp or an extraordinary sharp Note requires a natural Flat 6th, you [etc.].

d. *Optics.* ***extraordinary refraction***: that not following the general law. ***extraordinary ray***: one influenced by extraordinary refraction. ***extraordinary wave***: (see quot.).

1830 HERSCHEL *Stud. Nat. Phil.* I. ii. (1831) 31 The other ray..is..said to have undergone extraordinary refraction. **1872–3** TYNDALL *Light* iii. (1885) 111 The other [beam]..is ..called the extraordinary ray. **1883** GLAZEBROOK *Phys. Optics* xi. 291 An extraordinary wave [consists] of light which is plane polarised in a plane at right angles to the principal plane.

2. Of officials, persons employed, etc.: Outside of or additional to the regular staff; not belonging to the 'ordinary' or fully recognized class of such persons; supernumerary. Often with the notion of being specially employed for a temporary purpose. Now chiefly in official titles, where the sb. usually precedes.

envoy extraordinary: formerly a minister sent on some special diplomatic business; now, merely the designation of the second class of diplomatic ministers, ranking next to the 'ambassadors'; the term no longer practically implying a temporary or special mission. The ***physicians*** (or ***surgeons***, etc.) *extraordinary*, in royal households, rank below those styled 'in ordinary'; similarly an ***extraordinary professor*** (L. *professor extraordinarius*) in a German university is inferior in status to the 'ordinary' professor.

1585 J. HIGGINS tr. *Junius' Nomenclator* 484/2 Milites adventitii..Souldiers of another country that come to serue for paye; extraordinarie souldiers. **1653** MILTON *Hirelings* (1659) 79. **1665** BOYLE *Occas. Refl.* (1675) 354 The first Audience of the Russian Extraordinary Embassadour, at which he made his Emperour's Presents. **1712** STEELE *Spect.* No. 472 ¶9 Her Majesty's Oculist Extraordinary. **1720** SWIFT *Mod. Educ.* Wks. 1755 II. II. 33 His brother Horace is ambassador extraordinary to France. **1768** BLACKSTONE *Comm.* III. xxiii. III. 351 Another species of extraordinary juries, is the jury to try an attaint. **1890** *Dict. Nat. Biog.* XXIII. 334 [Sir W. Gull] was created..in Jan. 1872..physician extraordinary to the queen, and in 1887 physician in ordinary.

3. Of a kind not usually met with; exceptional; unusual; singular. Now with emotional sense, expressing astonishment, strong admiration or the contrary.

1580 SIDNEY *Arcadia* I. ii. (1590) 8 The house..was built of faire and strong stone, not affecting..any extraordinarie kinde of finenes. **1596** SHAKS. *1 Hen. IV*, III. i. 41 These signes haue markt me extraordinarie. **1665** SIR T. HERBERT *Trav.* (1677) 40 During the Night..we saw a perfect Rainbow, which was extraordinary. **1703** DAMPIER *Voy.* III. 81 Our English count the Green Turtle very extraordinary Food. *a* **1704** T. BROWN *Sat. Antients* Wks. 1730 I. 14 Those extraordinary men, who have..gone before us. **1794** S. WILLIAMS *Vermont* 126 Several instances equally extraordinary. **1858** LYTTON *What will he do* I. v, She is an extraordinary child. **1875** HAMERTON *Intell. Life* II. i. 49 The extraordinary power of representation..of Meissonier.

4. Exceeding what is usual in amount, degree, extent, or size. Now with emotional sense as in 3.

1572 *Lament. Lady Scot.* in *Scot. Poems 16th C.* II. 251 Zour drinking extraordinair Make oft zour wyfis and bairns euill to fair. **1588** FRAUNCE *Lawiers Log.* Ded. ¶b, Their extraordinary skill in making of obligations. **1634** BRERETON *Trav.* (1844) 8 No charge in housekeeping extraordinary, nor no entertainment extraordinary. **1656** BRAMHALL *Replic.* i. 6 The extraordinary influence of divine Grace. **1725** DE FOE *Voy. round World* (1840) 7 We took in a very extraordinary store of provisions. **1798** FERRIAR *Illustr. Sterne* iv. 111 An extraordinary nose always carries with it extraordinary greatness. **1860** TYNDALL *Glac.* I. xi. 84 The sun met us here with extraordinary power.

†**5.** Additional to, over and above what is usual; = EXTRA. Often following the sb.; in which case the adj. cannot always be distinguished from the adv. *Obs.*

1649 BLITHE *Eng. Improv. Impr.* (1653) 182 To lay out a five shillings or a noble extraordinary in every Acre. **1658** *Whole Duty Man* x. §20. 85 He must..support him, yea, though it be by his own extraordinary labour. **1664** PEPYS *Diary* (1879) III. 22, I am in good hopes to get two or £300 per annum extraordinary. *c* **1710** C. FIENNES *Diary* (1888) 110 You pay a penny Extra-ordinary for being brought from tunbridge town. **1767** A. YOUNG *Farmer's Lett.* 67 They may hire a labourer extraordinary. **1777** HOWARD *Prisons Eng.* (1780) 99 They have an extraordinary allowance of near a penny a day. **1802–16** MRS. SHERWOOD *Susan Gray* 54 Spending a few extraordinary shillings. **1812** *Examiner* 31 Aug. 546/2 By the help of a glass extraordinary after dinner.

†**B.** *adv.* **a.** = EXTRAORDINARILY in various senses. **b.** = EXTRA *adv.*; cf. A. 5. *Obs.*

a. **1632** J. HAYWARD tr. *Biondi's Eromena* 72 Which Countrey..being extraordinarie hilly. **1642** FULLER *Holy & Prof. St.* II. xiv. 102 Sometimes ordinary scholars make extraordinary good Masters. **1652** COTTERELL *Cassandra* III. (1676) 521 Who..rose extraordinary early. **1709** STRYPE *Ann. Ref.* I. liii. 575 [He] had Mary Queen of Scots in custody, which..was extraordinary expensive to him. **1778** *Eliza Warwick* I. 241 My jewels were extraordinary fine.

b. **1679** PLOT *Staffordsh.* (1686) 376 The Master turning his Key in any of the Servants locks but once extraordinary, the Servants themselves cannot come at their charge.

C. *sb.*

1. Something extraordinary; an extraordinary quality or bearing; an extraordinary action, incident, etc. †**a.** *sing.* (*obs.*)

1589 PUTTENHAM *Eng. Poesie* I. xx. (Arb.) 58 Princes, whose high estates do require in their countenance, speech and expence, a certaine extraordinary. **1654** JER. TAYLOR *Real Pres.* xi. ¶8. 205 That..every day..the same thing should be done, and yet..be called a miracle, that is, a daily extraordinary. **1754** RICHARDSON *Grandison* VI. l. 304 She ..made it [her behaviour] look like an extraordinary.

b. *pl.* Now *rare.*

1650 SIR T. BROWNE *Pseud. Ep.* (ed. 2) I. vi. 17 The greater part [of their Adages] will..be esteemed no extraordinaries. **1739** J. TRAPP *Right. over-much* (1758) 11 To place much religion..in extraordinaries. **1809** WELLINGTON in Gurw. *Disp.* IV. 530 Send two squadrons of hussars to Cevolla, and desire them to report all extraordinaries to you. **1844** R. WARDLAW *Lect. Proverbs* (1869) II. 13 His little stock of common-places, and of such extraordinaries as he has chanced to pick up. **1844** *Regul. & Ord. Army* 299 The blank lines are left for any extraordinaries that may occur.

c. *pl.* Extraordinary receipts or payments. The *pl.* of the *sb.* occurs where we should expect the adj. simply. *Obs.* exc. *arch.*

1599 *Life Sir T. More* in Wordsw. *Eccl. Biog.* (1853) II. 121 His ordinarie alms..amounted yearlie to one thousand pounds; his extraordinaries were as much. **1630** *R. Johnson's Kingd. & Commw.* 367 His ordinary Revenues are thus collected..What his extraordinaries may amount unto, cannot be knowne. **1865** CARLYLE *Fredk. Gt.* XIX. viii, Not only the king's ordinary revenues, but the extraordinaries.

2. = EXTRA *sb.* †**a.** An extra dish, a delicacy; an extra fee or expense. Chiefly *pl.* *Obs.*

1660 BLOUNT *Boscobel* I. (1680) 49 As an Extraordinary.. Penderel's wife made..a Posset. **1664** PEPYS *Diary* 30 Sept., A few extraordinaries for the house. **1664** EVELYN *Mem.* (1857) I. 408 A salary of £1200 a year..besides Extraordinaries. **1732** *Acc. Workhouses* 47 All tradesmen's bills, and extraordinaries paid by the overseers. **1776** WESLEY *Let.* 12 Aug., Desire none of those extraordinaries.

b. *Mil.* (see quot. 1853).

a **1797** H. WALPOLE *Geo. II* (1847) III. vi. 156 Munchausen..presented an ample bill of extraordinaries for forage, etc. **1816** *Gentl. Mag.* LXXXVI. I. 257 This estimate was..exclusive of the extraordinaries. **1853** STOCQUELER *Mil. Encycl.*, *Extraordinaries* (of the army), the allowances to troops beyond the gross pay in the pay-office. Extraordinaries comprehend the expenses for barracks, marches, encampments, staff, &c.

†**3. a.** An extraordinary envoy. **b.** A supernumerary official. *Obs.*

1616 N. BRENT tr. *Sarpi's Hist. Counc. Trent* (1676) 585 Whensoever any extraordinaries came to Trent..the Prelates took occasion to talk. **1622** DONNE *To Sir T. Lucy* 16 Aug. Lett. (1651) 188 There arrived an Extraordinary from Spain..& he brings the title of Count, to Rodrigo de Calderon. **1671** F. PHILLIPS *Reg. Necess.* 139 Besides not a few extraordinaries and such as have no pay or quarter.. attending upon the King.

extra-parental, etc.: see EXTRA- 1.

extra-pa'rochial, *a.* [f. EXTRA- *pref.* + Eccl. Lat. *parochi-a* (see PARISH) + -AL¹.] Not included in any parish; outside the parish; exempt from liability to parish obligations. Also *fig.* (*nonce-use*), outside one's legitimate province.

1674–81 BLOUNT *Glossogr.*, *Extra-parochial*. **1721** *Act Parl.* in *Lond. Gaz.* No. 5927/5 Townships, Vills, or Extraparochial Places. **1765** BLACKSTONE *Comm.* I. 284 The king ..is entitled to all the tithes arising in extraparochial places. **1789** [see *extra-diocesan* s.v. EXTRA- *pref.*]. **1853** DICKENS *Bleak Ho.* xxxviii, Thavies Inn, within the city of London, but extra-parochial. **1897** [see *extra-diocesan* s.v. EXTRA-*pref.*].

fig. **1868** M. PATTISON *Academ. Org.* v. 290 All such enquiries are looked upon by the student with contempt as extra-parochial.

Hence **extra-pa'rochially** *adv.*, in an extra-parochial manner. **extra-pa'rochialness**, the condition of being extra-parochial.

a **1806** S. HORSLEY *Charges* (1813) 207 A chapel extra-parochially situate. **1727–36** BAILEY, *Extraparochialness*.

extrapolate (ɛk'stræpəleɪt, 'ɛkstrəpəleɪt), *v.* [f. EXTRA- + *-polate* of INTERPOLATE *v.*, or 'back-formation f. EXTRAPOLATION.] †**1.** *trans.* To remove (a passage) from written matter. (*Nonce-use* by analogy with INTERPOLATE *v.* 3.)

1831 GLADSTONE *Let.* in C. Wordsworth *Ann. Early Life* (1891) 91 They inserted the letter.., but *extrapolated* or *metabolised* a part where I had mentioned Canning.

2. a. In mathematical or scientific calculations, to estimate the values of (a function or series) outside a range in which some of its values are known, on the assumption that the trends followed inside the range continue outside it; to continue (a curve) on the basis of points already plotted on the graph; freq. *absol.* Also *intr.* (const. *to*), to reach (a specified value) when extrapolated.

1874 W. S. JEVONS *Princ. Sci.* II. xxii. 120 If we wish to assign by reasoning results lying beyond the limits of experiment, we may be said, using an expression of Sir George Airy, to *extrapolate.* **1904** *Biometrika* III. 99 The proportionality of stress and strain is only true within narrow limits, yet the early investigators extrapolated from this linearity all across the mysteries of set, yield-point, and stricture, up to rupture! **1925** *Proc. Nat. Acad. Sci.* XI. 735 This scheme extrapolates to H simply by reducing the shielding to zero. **1933** J. K. ROBERTS *Heat & Thermodynamics* (ed. 2) iv. 100 The liquid and vapour densities..are determined as near to the critical point as is practicable, and..the results are extrapolated to the point itself. **1955** J. A. WHEELER in W. Pauli *Niels Bohr* 183 For the same energy the electron concentration factor, *a*, extrapolates to a value between $\log_{10} a = 1$ and $\log_{10} a = 2$, depending on the value of *Z*. **1957** G. E. HUTCHINSON *Treat. Limnol.* I. ix. 579 This series of observations was extrapolated to 0°C. by Whipple and Parker.

b. *transf.* To apply (a theory, etc.) to unknown situations on the basis of its relevance to known situations; to infer (conclusions) from known facts or observed tendencies. Also *absol.* or *intr.*

1905 W. JAMES *Meaning of Truth* (1909) v. 129 The philosopher here stands for the stage of thought that goes beyond the stage of common sense; and the difference is simply that he 'interpolates' and 'extrapolates', where common sense does not. **1907** *Outlook* 17 Aug. 206/1 History, geology, astronomy, are merely these extrapolated, and only demonstrate their relationship with the whole. **1935** *Mind* XLIV. 393 Most scientific theories..are 'extrapolated beyond the possibility of verification'. **1953** *Times Lit. Suppl.* 28 Aug. 542/4 His documents..are..comments on a particular colony at a particular time; and it is hard work to extrapolate from them any general view about all the colonies. **1956** A. J. AYER *Probl. Knowl.* 153 It may very well be that one does not first form a concept of the relation of temporal precedence, and then extrapolate it to events which are beyond the range of this immediate experience.

Hence **ex'trapolated** *ppl. a.*, that has been extrapolated; obtained by extrapolation.

1931 RUTHERFORD *Coll. Papers* (1965) III. 255 The effective straggling coefficient for any range was calculated from this extrapolated curve. **1938** R. W. LAWSON tr. *Hevesy & Paneth's Man. Radioactivity* (ed. 2) ii. 22 The ranges given in the table are the 'practical' or extrapolated ranges. **1967** J. R. WOLBERG *Prediction Anal.* v. 147 The uncertainty for the extrapolated value of *y* is obtained by analysis of all the experimental data (i.e., 62 separate data points).

extrapolation (,ɛkstrəpəʊ'leɪʃən). [f. INTERPOLATION by the substitution of EXTRA for the first member of the word.] *Math.* The action or method of finding by a calculation based on the known terms of a series, other terms outside of them, whether preceding or following. Hence *transf.*, the drawing of a conclusion about some future or hypothetical situation based on observed tendencies; the inference resulting from such a process. (Cf. prec., sense 2 b.)

1872 W. M. WATTS *Index of Spectra* p. ix, If the line..lies near to the two reference lines, but not between them, the interpolation formula..must be replaced by one of the two following extrapolation formulæ. **1874** W. S. JEVONS *Princ. Sci.* II. xxii. 120 It is a matter of great scientific importance to apprehend precisely how far we can interpolate or extend experimental results by extrapolation. **1878** C. A. YOUNG in Newcomb *Pop. Astron.* III. ii. 279 The process is an unsafe extrapolation. **1889** *Cent. Dict.* s.v., The calculation of the population of the United States in 1900, from the population in 1870, 1880, and 1890, would be an *extrapolation.* **1903** A. M. CLERKE *Probl. Astrophysics* 9 The necessity for having recourse to the risky expedient of 'extrapolation'—that is, of applying unrestrictedly to the unknown, rules gathered from observation over a comparatively narrow area. **1922** J. Y. SIMPSON *Man & Attainm. Immortality* i. 16 By extrapolation of the curve of our knowledge we can reconstruct within the range of conceivability, if not of probability, the course of process. **1926** H. C. MACPHERSON *Mod. Astr.* 135 Dr. Hubble strongly combats the contention that all non-galactic nebulae are spirals, which he characterizes as a 'daring extrapolation', 'not justified by our present knowledge of nebular forms'. **1965** J. D. NORTH *Measure of Universe* xiv. 297 One of the chief concerns of all scientific theories..is to sanction extrapolation..and the expression of the distant and unknown in terms of what is familiar.

Hence **ex'trapolative** *a.*, characterized by or employing extrapolation.

1929 *Physical Rev.* 2nd Ser. XXXIV. 34 The fact that levels of the same name are approaching the same grouping ..might naturally have been expected from our extrapolative way of choosing the names. **1940** *Mind* XLIX. 168 The extrapolative inference from the same set of data to an enormous number of independent propositions. **1968** *Sci. Jrnl.* Nov. 87/1 Extrapolative planning.

extra-popular, etc.: see EXTRA- 1.

,extrapo'sition. *Gram.* [f. EXTRA- + POSITION *sb.*] (See quot. 1933.) Hence **,extrapo'sitional** *a.*

1927 O. JESPERSEN *Mod. Eng. Gram.* III. i. 12 In many cases the *to*-infinitive as a primary is placed in extraposition while *it* represents it in the ordinary position. **1933** —— *Ess. Eng. Gram.* (1939) ix. 95 A word or group of words is often placed by itself, outside the sentence proper, in which it is represented by a pronoun; we then speak of 'extraposition': For the raine, it raineth every day. **1961** Y. OLSSON *Syntax Eng. Verb* v. 88 The extra-positional, but intra-sectional, units.

extraprovincial (,ɛkstrəprəʊ'vɪnʃəl), *a.* [ad. med.L. *extrāprovinciāl-is*, f. *extrā provinciam* outside the province: see EXTRA- and PROVINCIAL.] Outside the limits of a province.

1685 STILLINGFL. *Orig. Brit.* xi. 52 These.. Extraprovincial Britains..were distinct both from the Picts and the Scots. **1726** AYLIFFE *Parergon* 181 An Extra-Provincial Citation is not valid..above two days Journey. **1807** G. CHALMERS *Caledonia* I. II. i. 220 The extraprovincial Britons of Caledonia.

extrapunitive (ɛkstrə'pju:nɪtɪv), *a. Psychol.* Also **extropunitive.** [f. EXTRA- + PUNITIVE *a.*] Reacting aggressively to frustration; characterized by blaming other people or events unreasonably. Contrasted with IMPUNITIVE *a.* and INTROPUNITIVE *a.*

1938 S. ROSENZWEIG in H. A. Murray *Explorations in Personality* vi. 587 He may manifest the emotion of anger and condemn the outer world..for his frustration, adopting an attitude of hostility toward his environment. This type of reaction may be termed 'extrapunitive'. **1945** *Brit. Jrnl. Psychol.* XXXVI. I. 29 *Extrapunitive*, when the individual tends to blame the external world, reacts with anger and hostility, and psychologically defends himself. **1954** G. W. ALLPORT *Nature of Prejudice* xxiv. 383 There is something exhilarating about extropunitive indignation. To be good and angry at someone else, or even at fate, is like being on a spree. **1969** *Daily Tel.* 2 Oct. 25/5 Is his attitude to life 'intropunitive' (tending to blame himself) or is it 'extrapunitive'—i.e. does he attempt to blame others?

,extra-'sensory, *a.* Also **extrasensory.** [f. EXTRA- + SENSORY *a.*] Of perception: made by other means than those of the known sense-organs, *e.g.* by telepathy, clairvoyance, etc.; hence, received by such means; of or pertaining to the study of such perception. (***extra-sensory perception*** is often abbreviated to *E.S.P.*, *ESP.*)

1934 J. B. RHINE *Extra-Sensory Perception* (1935) p. xxx, Let us merely say..'perception by means that are outside of the recognized senses', and indicate this meaning by 'Extra-Sensory Perception' or E.S.P. **1937** A. WOOLLCOTT *Let.* 31 Oct. (1946) 157 It looks like an instance of clairvoyance which might be filed for reference with the extrasensory boys at Duke University. **1941** J. S. HUXLEY *Uniqueness of Man* i. 30 Extra-sensory guessing. **1944** J. F. HENDRY in H. Treece *Herbert Read* 114 He ignores such phenomena as extra-sensory perception or telesthaesia. **1946** A. HUXLEY *Perennial Philos.* ii. 36 When tests for ESP can be repeated under standardized conditions, the subject..achieves..a measure of scientific respectability. **1946** J. S. HUXLEY *Unesco* ii. 37 Extra-sensory knowledge. **1947** J. B. RHINE *Reach of Mind* (1948) iv. 53 Distance..has not shown any effect upon ESP performance. **1958** *Times Lit. Suppl.* 6 June 317/1 Examples of telepathy, of clairvoyance, of precognition (all three grouped together under the heading of extra-sensory perception or ESP). **1968** *Times* 4 Oct. 9/1 A double-blind guessing experiment..is interpreted by its authors to provide evidence for extra-sensory perception (E.S.P.). E.S.P., which covers such terms as telepathy and precognition, is the alleged faculty of perception by means which do not depend on the known sense organs.

extrasomatic (,ɛkstrəsəʊ'mætɪk), *a.* [f. EXTRA- + SOMATIC *a.*] Deriving from or referring to events external to a person considered as an individual or as a member of society.

1938 C. D. BROAD *Exam. McTaggart's Philos.* II. I. xxvii. 59, I begin by dividing ostensible sense-perception into 'extra-somatic' and 'intra-somatic'. In the former the percipient seems to himself to be perceiving foreign bodies or events. *Ibid.*, There are at least three important forms of extra-somatic sense-perception, viz., hearing, sight, and touch. **1947** *Amer. Sociological Rev.* XII. 687/2 Human behavior is, therefore, always and everywhere, made up of these two ingredients: the dynamic organization of nerves, glands, muscles and sense organs that is man, and the extra-somatic cultural tradition. *Ibid.* 693/2 Language has an extra-somatic, non-biological, non-psychological character. It had an existence prior to the birth of any individual speaking it; it comes to each person from the outside. **1964** E. A. NIDA *Toward Sci. Transl.* v. 70 While referential meanings are extralinguistic, extrasomatic, and situational .., emotive meanings are extralinguistic, somatic and behavioral.

,extra-'special, *a.* (and *sb.*) [See EXTRA B. a. note and SPECIAL *a.* 3 c]. Applied to a special extra edition of a newspaper, etc.; also as *sb.*, such an edition. Hence *transf.* and *fig.*, very special; exceptionally good or fine.

1889 E. DOWSON *Let.* 24 Mar. (1967) 54 Special Sunday Edition... This [*sc.* letter] appears to be an *extra* special: it is overunning [*sic*] all limits. **1891** *Literary World* 2 Jan. 11/3 An extra-special edition is to appear on the date named in honour of the birthday of the Proprietor-Editor. **1896** G. B. SHAW *Let.* 8 Sept. in *Shaw on Shakes.* (1962) 44 It is this that makes her pay him the extra special compliment of offering to take the chest into her own bedroom. **1897** *Truth* (Christmas Number) 25 Dec. 13/2 Strange forms came out upon her,..And offered 'Hextry speshuls'. **1901** *Punch* 31 July 86/1 The magazines, the newspapers, the extra-specials of the twentieth century. **1902** *Captain* VII. 8/1 I'm playing owl.., for one or two extra-special reasons. **1960** *Times* 19 Feb. 5/6 An even shorter centenary study of Mahler—it is not intended to be much more than an extra-special programme note to a recital.

extra'spection. *rare*$^{-1}$. [f. L. *extrā* outside + *spectiōn-em*, n. of action f. *specĕre* to see.] Outward observation.

1887 *Westm. Rev.* CXXVIII. 629 This knowledge is obtained through science by extra-spection and by religion through intro-spection.

extraspective (ɛkstrə'spɛktɪv), *a.* [f. EXTRA- + *-spective* of INTROSPECTIVE *a.*]

†**1.** Facing or turning outwards. *Obs. rare*$^{-1}$.

1819 J. G. LOCKHART *Peter's Lett.* (ed. 2) III. lvi. 25 [Hats without] those lawless curves and twists, prospective, retrospective, introspective and extraspective, from under which the unkempt tresses..may at times be seen 'streaming like meteors to the troubled air'.

2. = EXTROSPECTIVE *a.*

1925 C. D. BROAD *Mind & its Place* vii. 328 Those situations in which we seem to be in direct cognitive contact with other minds and their states... For want of a better word, let us call them 'extraspective situations'. **1926** *Public Opinion* 6 Aug. 132/2 He is of the intro-spective rather than the extra-spective order.

extra-spectral, -tabular, etc.: see EXTRA- 1.

extrasystole (ɛkstrə'sɪstəli:). *Path.* [a. G. *extrasystole* (K. F. Wenckebach 1899, in *Zeitschr. f. klin. Med.* XXXVI. 183), f. EXTRA- + SYSTOLE.] A heart-beat outside the normal rhythm.

1900 in DORLAND *Med. Dict.* **1907** *Practitioner* Apr. 454 Experimentally, an extra-systole can be easily produced by mechanical, thermal, chemical, or electrical stimulation. **1958** *Spectator* 11 July 60/2 Then the heart 'thumps'. This is a common effect of stress: in medical terms, extra-systoles.

,extraterri'torial, *a.* [f. mod.L. phrase *extrā territōri-um* outside the territory + -AL[1].] Pertaining to, or possessed of, extraterritoriality.

[**1625** GROTIUS *De Jure Belli et Pacis* II. xviii. §5 [Ut legati] fictione simili constituerentur quasi extra territorium.] **1869** *Echo* 6 Apr., Extra-territorial privileges.

,extraterri,tori'ality. [f. prec. + -ITY.] The privilege accorded by the *Law of Nations* to ambassadors of being regarded as outside the territory of the power to which they are sent, and therefore of being free from its jurisdiction. Also EXTERRITORIALITY. Extended later to denote the right of jurisdiction of a country over its nationals abroad, or the status of persons living in a foreign country but not subject to its laws. Cf. EXTRALITY.

1836 WHEATON *Internat. Law* III. i. §15 The fiction of extra-territoriality..by which the minister, though actually in a foreign country, is supposed still to remain within the territory of his own sovereign. **1869** *Daily News* 8 Jan., In Rome, at one time, this extra-territoriality was made to extend to the inhabitants of the quarter in which the residence of an Ambassador was situated. **1888** *Morn. Post* 24 Sept., By starting from the German embassy instead of from the Quirinal the Emperor will come to the Pope with all the prestige of extra-territoriality upon him. **1901** *Westm. Gaz.* 28 Jan. 1/2 To do in China what we have just done in Japan and are anxious that others should do in Egypt—abolish the principle of extra-territoriality, and submit outselves one and all..to the laws and institutions of China. **1925, 1926** [see EXTRALITY]. **1928** G. W. KEETON (*title*) The development of extraterritoriality in China. **1954** *Ann. Reg.* *1953* 299 The form of extraterritoriality represented by the U.S. bases in Japan. **1957** K. A. WITTFOGEL *Oriental Despotism* 434 The Capitulations, which gave privileged foreigners judicial and economic extraterritoriality, were particularly apparent in Constantinople.

†**ex'traught,** *pa. pple. Obs.* Also 6 **extraght, -aucte, -aughte, -aute.** [var. of EXTRACT *pple.*; cf. *distraught.*]

1. In senses of EXTRACT *v.* **a.** Taken out (from books). **b.** Derived, descended.

1523 LD. BERNERS *Froiss.* I. i. 1 All sciences are extraught and compiled of diuerse clerkes. *a* **1533** —— *Huon* clxi. 625 None that semeth more to be extraute of a hye lynage. **1593** SHAKS. *3 Hen. VI*, II. ii. 142 Sham'st thou not, knowing whence thou art extraught, To let thy tongue detect thy base-borne heart?

2. = DISTRAUGHT. Const. *from*, *of.*

1553 BRENDE *Q. Curtius* Y iij, A woman..being extraught of her minde. **1575** LANEHAM *Let.* (1871) 93 He that.. occupyeth hymself by excessive studye is in daunger for to be extraught from hymself.

extra-urban, etc.: see EXTRA- 1.

extravagance (ɛk'strævəgəns). [a. Fr. *extravagance*, f. late L. *extravagant-em*: see EXTRAVAGANT and -ANCE.]

†**1.** A going out of the usual path; an excursion, digression. Also, the position or fact of erring *from* (a prescribed path). *lit.* and *fig.* *Obs.*

1643 MILTON *Divorce* II. vii. (1851) 80 A doctrine of that extravagance from the sage principles of piety. **1645** HAMMOND *Pract. Catech.* 11, I have troubled you too farre by this extravagance: I shall make no delay to recall my selfe into the rode againe. *a* **1656** BP. HALL *Rem. Wks., Life* (1660) 15 Sollicited me for my Company in a Journey..to the Spa..laying before me..the Benefit of that small Extravagance.

2. The quality of being extravagant or of exceeding just or prescribed limits, *esp.* those of decorum, probability, or truth; unrestrained excess; fantastic absurdity (of opinions, conduct, etc.); outrageous exaggeration or violence (of language).

1676 ETHEREDGE *Man of Mode* III. ii, *L. Town.* Here's the freshest Fool in Town..*Dor.* Sooth him up in his extravagance! **1681** DRYDEN *Sp. Fryar* Ep. Ded. 2 Some Verses of my own, Maximin and Almanzor, cry Vengeance upon me for their Extravagance. **1716–8** LADY M. W. MONTAGUE *Lett.* I. xxxvii. 144 You will accuse me of extravagance in this description. **1841** ELPHINSTONE *Hist. Ind.* I. II. iv. 207 The extravagance of the Braminical chronology and geography. **1864** J. H. NEWMAN *Apol.* 392 Not to enfeeble the freedom or vigour of human thought in religious speculation, but to resist and control its extravagance.

3. An instance or kind of extravagance; an extravagant notion, statement, piece of conduct, etc.; an irrational excess, an absurdity.

1650 FULLER *Pisgah* V. i. 143 Many maps are full of affected extravagances. *a* **1680** BUTLER *Rem.* (1759) I. 71 So Men, who one Extravagance would shun, Into the contrary Extreme have run. **1719** DE FOE *Crusoe* (1840) II. i. 18 An excess of joy..has a thousand extravagances in it. **1782** PRIESTLEY *Corrupt. Chr.* I. I. 69 Later writers..did not follow Hilary in this extravagance. **1809–10** COLERIDGE *Friend* (ed. 3) I. 80 The extravagances of ignorance and credulity. **1857** KEBLE *Eucharist. Adorat.* 1 Had there been no abuse, error or extravagance connected with the practice. **1875** JOWETT *Plato* (ed. 2) V. 181 Impatient of the extravagances to which the love of truth almost necessarily leads.

4. Excessive prodigality or wastefulness in expenditure, household management, etc.

1727 ARBUTHNOT *Coins* II. v. 133 They [the Romans] arrived by degrees to an incredible extravagance. **1805** FOSTER *Ess.* I. iii. 35 Extravagance of ostentatious wealth. **1817** MAR. EDGEWORTH *Rose, Thistle, etc.* II. ii, Such extravagance, to give a penny, and a silver penny, for what you may have for nothing. **1838** DICKENS *Nich. Nick.* iii, I can't support them in their extravagances. **1873** BLACK *Pr. Thule* (1874) 16 Do you think I would take the child to London to show her its extravagance. *Mod.* The cook's extravagance was too much for me.

extravagancy (ɛk'strævəgənsɪ). [f. EXTRAVAGANT: see -ANCY.]

†**1.** A wandering beyond bounds or out of one's course; vagrancy; an instance of this. *Obs.*

1601 SHAKS. *Twel. N.* II. i. 12 My determinate voyage is meere extrauagancie. **1634** SIR T. HERBERT *Trav.* 224, I will lead you through no more extravagancies. **1669** WOODHEAD *St. Teresa* I. Pref. 16 For recollecting of the Thoughts, and hindering them from extravagancy.

2. The quality or fact of being EXTRAVAGANT (in senses 5, 6): †**a.** Abnormal or unusual character, eccentricity; impropriety, unbecomingness (*obs.*). **b.** The quality of exceeding the bounds of decorum, taste, or probability; in later use, flagrant excess, outrageousness. Now somewhat *rare*; cf. EXTRAVAGANCE 2.

1651 HOBBES *Leviath.* I. viii. 33 In Sonnets, Epigrams..the Fancy must be more eminent; because they please for the Extravagancy. **1653** H. COGAN tr. *Pinto's Trav.* xviii. (1663) 62 With the like extravagancy he answered to many other questions. **1690** CHILD *Disc. Trade* (ed. 4) 76 For the bettering of trade, and pareing off the extravagancy of the Law. **1698** VANBRUGH *Prov. Wife* III. i, Were it not for the extravagancy of the example, I should e'en tear out these wicked eyes. **1720** WELTON *Suffer. Son of God* II. xiv. 362 Touch'd with the Extravagancy..of the Jewish Nation.

3. = EXTRAVAGANCE 3.

1625 BP. MOUNTAGU *App. Cæsar* II. xxxiv. 248 Popish extravagancies. **1662** GERBIER *Princ.* 17 The causes of many Deformities and Extravagancies in Buildings. **1671** R. BOHUN *Disc. Wind* 64 The Peruvian [mountains], and some others which may be reckon'd as the Extravagancys of Nature..overlook the Clouds. **1761** HUME *Hist. Eng.* III. lx. 295 Numberless were the extravagancies which broke out among the people. **1834** SIR W. HAMILTON *Discuss.* 491 Luther was betrayed into..extravagancies by an assurance of his personal inspiration. **1838** WHEWELL in Todhunter *Whewell's Writings* (1876) II. 273 Landor's extravagancies of expression.

†**4.** = EXTRAVAGANCE 4. *Obs.*

1666 G. ALSOP *Charac. Maryland* (1866) 36 Natures extravagancy of a superabounding plenty. **1748** RICHARDSON *Clarissa* (1811) I. xlii. 324 All your extravagancies have been supported gratis. **1750** G. HUGHES *Barbadoes* 110, I have always thought it the height of extravagancy and luxury to fell so stately a tree. **1822** MRS. E. NATHAN *Langreath* I. 19 He wanted money to pursue his extravagancies.

extravagant (ɛk'strævəgənt), *a.* and *sb.* Also 6, 7 *aphet.* STRAVAGANT. [In the special use A. 2, B. 1, directly ad. med.L. *extrāvagant-em*, pr. pple. of *extrāvagārī* (or *extrā vagārī*): see EXTRAVAGATE. The wider use came late in 16th c. from Fr. *extravagant*, which appears first in 14th c. The form STRAVAGANT, from It., is somewhat earlier in our quots. Cf. It. *estravagante*, *stravagante* (15th c.), Sp. *estravagante.*]

A. *adj.*

†**1.** That wanders out of bounds; straying, roaming, vagrant. *Obs.* exc. after Shaks.

1602 SHAKS. *Ham.* I. i. 154 At his [the cock's] warning..Th' extrauagant, and erring Spirit hyes to his Confine. **1604** —— *Oth.* I. i. 137 An extrauagant, and wheeling Stranger, Of here, and euerywhere. **1615** G. SANDYS *Trav.* 93 Now dispersed into ample lakes, and againe recollecting his extrauagant waters. **1841–4** EMERSON *Ess., Hist.* Wks. (Bohn) I. 12 Rare, extravagant spirits come by us at intervals.

†**b.** *Mil.* Of an officer: Keeping no fixed place; having a roving function. *Obs.*

1622 MARKHAM *Bk. War* II. viii. 69 He [the Serjeant] hath in the body of the Company, no Raunge at all, but is extravagant, and going vp and downe to oversee all Raunges. **1672** T. VENN *Mil. & Marit. Discipl.* v. 13 The two other Corporals to be extravagant, that is to view and see each Soldier keep his place.

2. *Canon Law.* The distinctive epithet of certain papal constitutions.

[The L. adj. seems originally to have been applied casually to denote 'stray' decrees not codified or collected in the decretals. They were afterwards added to the decretals, but retained their customary designation, to distinguish them from the older portions of the collection.]

1387 TREVISA *Higden* (Rolls) VIII. 285 A constituciouп þat is not i-putte in þe course of lawes is i-cleped a constituciouп extravagant. **1608** T. MORTON *Preamb. Incounter* 109 He citeth the Constitution extrauagant of Pope Bonifacius. **1885** *Catholic Dict.* s.v., Each title being devoted to one or more 'extravagant' Constitutions.

†**3.** Spreading or projecting beyond bounds; straggling. *Obs.*

1605 B. JONSON *Masque Blackness* Wks. (1616) 894 They [the Masquers] were all seene, but in an extrauagant order. **1650** FULLER *Pisgah* III. iv. 323 The prominency of this extravagant Tower. **1664** EVELYN *Kal. Hort.* (1729) 204 Cutting the too thick and extravagant Roots a little. **1669** WORLIDGE *Syst. Agric.* (1681) 111 Trimming up such as you spare for Standards..from their extravagant Branches.

†**4.** Widely divergent or discrepant (*from, to*); remote *from*, irrelevant or foreign *to* a purpose or subject. *Obs.*

1601 BP. BARLOW *Defence Prot. Relig.* 115 A position extrauagant from all learning. **1605** VERSTEGAN *Dec. Intell.* x. (1628) 337 Other languages, such as vnto ours are altogether strange and extrauagant. **1650** S. CLARKE *Eccl. Hist.* I. (1654) 108 He never brake forth into reproaches extravagant from the cause. **1654** H. L'ESTRANGE *Chas. I* (1655) 166 They were indeed the more knowing men, but their learning was extravagant to their Office. **1660** HICKERINGILL *Jamaica* (1661) 55 Whose Character..I deem not much extravagant here to insert. **1665** BOYLE *Occas. Refl.* VI. iii. 200 Wondring to find our Customs so extravagant and differing from those of his Country.

†**5.** Varying widely from what is usual or proper; unusual, abnormal, strange; unbecoming, unsuitable. *Obs.*

1650 FULLER *Pisgah* V. viii. 157 Persons..treacherously slain, which occasioned their hasty, tumultuary, and extravagant interment. **1664** POWER *Exp. Philos.* II. vii. 109 Those extravagant Phænomena, which we observed in the first Experiment of Torricellius. *a* **1668** DAVENANT *Masque* Wks. (1673) 383 In an extravagant posture stood a Tyger. **1689** LUTTRELL *Brief. Rel.* (1857) I. 586 Some..officers, are taken into custody for drinking extravagant healths, and speaking reflectingly of his majestie. **1689** BURNET *Tracts* I. 12 Lausanne is situated on three Hills..This extravagant situation of the Town. **1701** tr. *Le Clerc's Prim. Fathers* (1702) 56 A Garment which is not commonly seen, seems Extravagant, though it was Fashionable in former Times.

6. 'Roving beyond just limits or prescribed methods' (J.); exceeding the bounds of reason or propriety; excessive, irregular, fantastically absurd. Now with stronger sense: Astonishingly or flagrantly excessive or extreme.

a. of persons. Now rare exc. with agent-noun or const. *in*.

1599 B. JONSON *Ev. Man out of Hum.* Induct., Shall I be so extrauagant to thinke, That [etc.]. **1633** DURIE in *Presbyt. Rev.* (1887) 305 Those yᵗ were so extravagant as to maintaine it unlawfull [etc.]. **1662** STILLINGFL. *Orig. Sacr.* I. iii. §1 For them to have been so extravagant in their accounts of themselves. **1704** HEARNE *Duct. Hist.* (1714) I. 211 Zedekiah had..no regard..for Virtue; and his companions were altogether as impious and extravagant as himself. **1815** W. H. IRELAND *Scribbleomania* 73 The extravagant panegyrist of various living characters. **1840** MACAULAY *Ranke* Ess. 1854 II. 556/1 He [the enthusiast] may be vulgar, ignorant, visionary, extravagant.

b. of dispositions, passions, actions, opinions, conditions, demands, etc.

1588 SHAKS *L.L.L.* IV. ii. 68 This is a gift that I haue..a foolish extrauagant spirit, full of formes, figures, shapes [etc.]. **1676** D'URFEY *Mad. Fickle* III. i, Your Father's in an extravagant rage. **1711** ADDISON *Spect.* No. 160 ⁋3 There appears something nobly wild and extravagant in great natural Genius's. **1769** ROBERTSON *Chas. V*, V. IV. 372 It was impossible..that the emperor would listen to these extravagant demands. **1809** *Med. Jrnl.* XXI. 123 A mind poisoned by extravagant opinions. **1821** CRAIG *Lect. Drawing* iv. 204 The extravagant praise bestowed on the best pictures of the Greeks. **1848** MACAULAY *Hist. Eng.* I. 164 Both had..extravagant whimsies about dress. **1868** J. H. BLUNT *Ref. Ch. Eng.* I. 300 It is not extravagant to suppose..that they had secret instructions.

7. Exceeding the bounds of economy or necessity in expenditure, mode of living, etc.; profuse, prodigal, wasteful. **a.** Of persons. (Const. *of.*)

1711 ADDISON *Spect.* No. 243 ⁋8 An extravagant Man..has nothing else to recommend him but a false Generosity. **1739** R. BULL tr. *Dedekindus' Grobianus* 55 What need we prove extravagant of Time. **1814** JANE AUSTEN *Mansf. Park* (1851) 16 His eldest son was careless and extravagant. **1879** FROUDE *Cæsar* i. 6 The rich were extravagant, for life had ceased to have practical interest, except for its material pleasures.

b. Of expense, interest, price, etc.: Exorbitant.

1707 FREIND *Peterborow's Cond. Sp.* 165 His Lordship gave an extravagant interest of 20 per cent. **1725** DE FOE *Voy. round World* (1840) 99 The price..was to us indeed extravagant though to them moderate. **1868** M. PATTISON *Academ. Org.* iv. 106 An extravagant price to pay for the encouragement of sacred learning.

B. *sb.*

1. *Canon Law.* An 'extravagant' constitution: see A. 2.

1502 *Ord. Crysten Men* (W. de W.) IV. viii. 189 Those yᵗ cut..yᵉ body of ony deed persone..ben acursed..by the extrauagant of Bonyface. *a* **1612** DONNE *Βιαθανατος* (1644) 85 The Canon law, to which the Canonist will stand..are the Decretall letters, and all the extravagants. **1765** BLACKSTONE *Comm.* I. 82 Gratian's decree, Gregory's decretals, the sixth decretal, the Clementine constitutions, and the extravagants of John and his successors, form the..body of the Roman canon law. **1882** STUBBS *Hist. Lect.* (1886) 306 The Extravagants as they were called, that is the authoritative sentences of the Popes which were not yet codified.

†**2.** One who strays or wanders from a place; a vagrant, wanderer. *Obs.*

1583 STUBBES *Anat. Abus.* I. (1877–9) 172 May you as rogues, extrauagantes, and straglers from the Heauenlye Country, be arrested of..Christ Iesus. **1615** T. ADAMS *White Devile* 27 I speak to you settled Citizens not Extravagants. **1630–50** BRADFORD *Plymouth Plantation* II. (1856) 187 Ordinarie officers are bound cheefly to their flocks..and are not to be extravagants.

fig. 1654 H. L'ESTRANGE *Chas. I* (1655) 97 [They] are censurable for extravagants from their Commission.

†**3.** One who does not keep within ordinary or reasonable limits; an exceptional or eccentric person; a fanatic. *Obs.*

1626 W. SCLATER *Exp. 2 Thess.* (1629) 242 Haters of God..the stile of some extravagants in nature. **1676** GLANVILL *Ess.* iv. §4. 20 The Extravagants among us may be really distracted in the Affairs of Religion, though their Brains are untouch'd in other Matters. **1678** *Trans. Crt. Spain* II. 147 Whereby it may be seen what the rage of these extravagants was against the Vice-Roy. **1768** RICHARDSON *Clarissa* VII. ii. 60 The dear Extravagant takes a delight in oddnesses.

†**b.** One who exceeds the bounds of moderation in expenditure, expensive living, etc.; a wasteful person, a spendthrift. *Obs.*

1745 DODSLEY *Poems, Pain & Patience* vi, The wild extravagant, whose thoughtless hand, With lavish tasteless pride, commits expence. **1777** SHERIDAN *Sch. Scand.* I. i, Charles..that extravagant, that bankrupt in fortune and reputation. *a* **1797** WALPOLE *Mem. Geo. III* (1859) II. 39 A new club which by the excess of play should draw all the young extravagants thither. **1825** C. M. WESTMACOTT *Eng. Spy* I. 42 A good humoured sporting extravagant.

†**4.** An extravagant act, statement, etc.; = EXTRAVAGANCY 3. *Obs.*

1644 LAUD *Wks.* (1854) IV. 55 He fell foul upon me again..as that I was the author of all the extravagants in the Government. **1652** GAULE *Magastrom.* 107 Figments of mens brain, monsters of nature, devious extravagants, etc. **1700** T. BROWN tr. *Fresny's Amusem. Ser. & Comic* 148 Examine well this serious Extravagant..The Fools Bawble he makes such a pother with, is his Probity.

†**b.** (See quots.). *Obs.*

[Boorde's use may be transf. from 1.]

1547 BOORDE *Brev. Health* II. Pref., By cause I dyd..leaue out many thynges in the fyrste boke..in this boke named 'the Extrauagantes' I haue supplied those matters. **1634** J. BATE *Myst. Nat. & Art* IV. To Rdr., As there were divers experiments that I could not conveniently..dispose in..order..I thought it would not bee amisse to call them by the names of Extravagants.

†**c.** (See quot.). *Obs.*

1622 MALYNES *Anc. Law-Merch.* 129 Certaine Merchants contracts..are called Extrauagants, because the manner either of buying or selling of commodities..is rare and but vsed in some places.

†**ex'travagant**, *v.* *Obs. rare*⁻¹. [f. prec. adj.] *intr.* = EXTRAVAGATE.

1656 S. H. *Gold. Law* 21 To keep the so chosen within their said bounds, that they extravagant not.

†**extrava'gantine.** *Obs.* [f. EXTRAVAGANT + -INE after *Clementine.*] = EXTRAVAGANT B. 1.

1549 LATIMER *6th Serm. bef. Edw. VI* (Arb.) 177 Luther..disputed agaynst the decretales, the Clementines, Alexandrines, Estrauagantines.

extravagantly (ɛk'strævəgəntlɪ), *adv.* [f. as prec. + -LY².] In an extravagant manner; to an extravagant degree.

†**1.** In an irregular position or manner; in no fixed order. *Obs.*

1623 MARKHAM *Country Content.* ii. 126 Setting the Sallets extravagantly about the table. **1625** *Souldiers Accid.* 45 The Corporalls..office is..to ride extravagantly vp and downe on either side the Troope.

2. In a manner transgressing the bounds of reason or propriety; †usurpingly, encroach-

ingly; in later use, with extravagance or undue violence of feeling or expression.

1647 CLARENDON *Hist. Reb.* VI. (1703) II. 53 The two Houses having..extravagantly nominated their own Divines. 1660 R. COKE *Power & Subj.* 13 Who have so extravagantly attributed both powers to be in the King. *a* 1700 DRYDEN (J.), Her passion was extravagantly new; But mine is much the madder of the two. 1710 STEELE *Tatler* No. 246 ¶8 They so extravagantly aim at what they are unfit for. 1796 MORSE *Amer. Geog.* I. 369 The famous fall..is..extravagantly and ludicrously described. 1809–10 COLERIDGE *Friend* (1865) 136 Their antagonists flew off as extravagantly from the sober good sense of our forefathers. 1858 HOLLAND *Titcomb's Lett.* iii. 35 Everybody now dresses extravagantly.

3. In an excessive degree; to an excess.

a 1715 BURNET *Own Time* II. (1724) I. 292 This Act..being extravagantly severe. 1743 WALPOLE *Lett. H. Mann* (1834) I. lxxv. 271 Sold..for £300,000 a year, and that was reckoned extravagantly dear. 1748 HARTLEY *Observ. Man* II. ii. 88 Idolatry, to which all mankind were then extravagantly prone. 1890 *Spectator* 15 Feb., Extravagantly fertile regions.

4. In a too expensive manner; with wasteful profusion or prodigality.

Mod. The house was extravagantly furnished.

ex'travagantness. *rare.* [f. as prec. + -NESS.] The quality or fact of being extravagant.

1727 in BAILEY vol. II.; and in mod. Dicts.

extravaganza (ɛkˌstrævəˈgænzə). [ad. It. *estravaganza* (an) extravagance (more commonly *stravaganza*), refashioned after L. *extra-*.]

1. A composition, literary, musical or dramatic, of an extravagant or fantastic character.

1794 MATHIAS *Purs. Lit.* (1798) 343 Author of the pleasant Extravaganza on the Courage of Sir John Falstaff. 1815 W. H. IRELAND *Scribbleomania 20 note*, A portion of the extravaganza of that writer's Curse of Kehama. 1833 PLANCHÉ *Extravaganzas* (1879) I. 115 High, Low, Jack, and the Game..a most extravagant Extravaganza. 1873 M. ARNOLD *Lit. & Dogma* xii. §3. 372 The difference between the grandeur of an extravaganza and the grandeur of the sea or the sky. 1879 HULLAH in Grove *Dict. Mus.* I. 499/2 A musical extravaganza must be the work of a musician familiar with the forms he caricatures.

2. What resembles an extravaganza; bombastic extravagance of language or behaviour.

1754 *Connoisseur* 7 Mar. 31 Thalia..was..with difficulty restrained from falling into ridiculous drolleries, and what our author calls *extravaganzas* in her manner. 1789 BELSHAM *Ess.* II. xxxvi. 289 The inchantment of Tasso borders upon the extravaganza. 1831 SCOTT *Nigel* Introd., Bardolph, Nym, Pistol..men who had their humours, or their particular turn of extravaganza.

3. *nonce-use.* An 'extravagance' in dress.

1860 *Heads & Hats* 31 Send hoops, crinoline, and all extravaganzas to those bonfires in which we are wont to consume our Guys of every description.

Hence **extrava'ganzist**, an extravaganza writer.

a 1849 POE *Marginalia* Wks. 1864 III. 538 That..school of extravaganzists who sprang from the ruins of Lamb.

extravagate (ɛkˈstrævəgeɪt), *v.* [f. med.L. *extrāvagāt-* ppl. stem of *extrāvagārī* (or *extrā vagārī*) to wander, stray outside limits, f. *extrā* outside + *vagārī* to wander. Cf. Fr. *extravaguer.*] To wander; only in *fig.* sense.

1. *intr.* To wander away, stray, *from*, *into*. Also, † *to extravagate it.*

1600 ABP. ABBOT *Exp. Jonah* 219, I love not to extravagate from my text. 1611 COTGR., *Sortir hors de propos*, To..extrauagate it, fall from the matter. 1643 PRYNNE *Sov. Power Parl.* III. 108 A Maior..extravagating from the common course of Law and Justice. 1684 tr. *Agrippa's Van. Artes* v. 30 Who..when they cannot compass their ends in the right line, extravagate into forreign Pedigrees. 1867 F. OAKELEY in Manning *Ess. Relig. & Lit.* II. 159 Extravagating into ten thousand forms of religious error.

2. To wander at large; to roam at will.

1766 WARBURTON *Serm.* Wks. 1787 V. 326 When the body plunges into the luxury of Sense, the mind will extravagate through all the regions of a viciated Imagination. 1805 WORDSW. *Prelude* v. Wks. (1888) 269/2 Schemes In which his youth did first extravagate. 1833 J. H. NEWMAN *Ch. of Fathers* (1842) 301 Extravagating beyond the beaten paths of orthodoxy.

3. To go beyond bounds; to exceed what is proper or reasonable.

1829 SOUTHEY *Sir T. More* II. 323 A Quakeress does not extravagate when she engages in such an enterprize. 1845 GLADSTONE *Let.* 10 Dec. in S. Wilberforce *Life & Lett.* (1880) I. 328 The Church of England has effectually confined this power from extravagating by the terms of the sixth Article. 1869 F. W. NEWMAN *Misc.* 105 This [scenery] is a topic on which the moderns extravagate.

4. *nonce-use.* To go to extravagance *in*.

1871 M. COLLINS *Mrq. & Merch.* I. vi. 204, I extravagate in magnesium. It is not much dearer than wax candles.

extrava'gation. [f. prec. vb.: see -ATION. Cf. Fr. *extravagation.*] Wandering beyond due or prescribed limits; an extravagance.

1611 COTGR., *Extravagation*, an extrauagation, or extrauagating. 1669 WOODHEAD *St. Teresa* I. Pref. (1671) 16 The thinking of them is apt to cause some extravagation of our thoughts in Prayer. 17.. SMOLLETT (T.), I do not pretend to justify the extravagations of the mob. 1849 A. D. FILLAN *Stories of Rebellions* 39 To check all froward desire of extravagation on the part of Major Drummond. 1899 C. K. PAUL *Mem.* 304 M. Renan never could understand how it was people were so little tolerant of his own extravagations.

†**ex'travage**, *v. Obs. rare.* Also *aphet.* STRAVAIG. [ad. med.L. *extrāvagārī*: see EXTRAVAGATE.] *intr.* **a.** To go beyond the sphere of duty; to digress. **b.** To talk wildly, to ramble.

c 1690 TARBAT in Story *W. Carstares* xi. 198 Churchmen kept to the ministerial function, without extravaging on their fanciful jurisdiction. 1759 FOUNTAINHALL *Decisions* I. 137 The Duke of Albany..extravaged so that, etc.

†**extra'vasal**, *a. Obs.*$^{-0}$ [f. L. *extrā* outside + *vās* vessel + -AL[1].] Outside its proper vessel.

1674–81 in BLOUNT *Glossogr.* 1692–1732 in COLES.

†**ex'travasate**, *a. Obs.* exc. *poet.* [f. next after ppl. adjs. in -ATE[2] from Lat.]

1. **a.** Outside of or not contained in any vessel. **b.** = EXTRAVASATED.

a. 1663–76 in BULLOKAR. 1671 *Phil. Trans.* VI. 2122 All the Juyce of a Plant is not extravasate and loose, and like Water in a Spunge.

b. 1764 WATSON in *Phil. Trans.* LIV. 241 This air was extravasate, had burst through the extremities of the bronchia and vesicular substance. 1868 BROWNING *Ring & Bk.* XI. 303 I'm told one clot of blood extravasate Ends one as certainly as Roland's sword.

2. Formed by extravasation.

1728 NICHOLLS in *Phil. Trans.* XXXV. 443 The Aneurysm..I find to be round like other extravasate Tumors.

extravasate (ɛkˈstrævəseɪt), *v.* [f. L. *extrā* outside + *vās* vessel + -ATE[3]. Cf. F. *extravaser.*]

1. *trans.* To let or force out (a fluid, *esp.* blood) from its proper vessel.

1669 W. SIMPSON *Hydrol. Chym.* 31 The exorbitant latex, which before was extravasated. 1684 BOYLE *Porousn. Anim. & Solid Bod.* iii. 17 Small portions of blood..being extravasated are obliged to stagnate there. 1748 HARTLEY *Observ. Man* I. i. 44 Blood and Serum extravasated, and lying in the Ventricles, suffocate Sensations. 1764 WATSON in *Phil. Trans.* LIV. 244 As..injuries to the lungs are not easily removed, when once a rupture is made, every fit of coughing extravasates more air. 1797 M. BAILLIE *Morb. Anat.* (1807) 349 The matter which had been extravasated during the inflammation. 1880 MAC CORMAC *Antisept. Surg.* 103 Blood is extravasated into the tissues.

2. *intr.* for *refl.* Of a fluid: To flow out; to force its way out, to escape.

1686 W. HARRIS tr. *Lemery's Chym.* II. xiv. (ed. 3) 345 The keen Salts which..raised great effervescencies in the blood so as to make it extravasate. 1774 GOLDSM. *Nat. Hist.* VIII. 82 The juice or sap, turn'd back from its natural course extravasates. 1847 TODD *Cycl. Anat.* III. 641/2 Blood sometimes extravasates into the arachnoid sac.

ex'travasated, *ppl. a.* [f. prec. + -ED[1].]

†1. Placed outside a vessel. *Obs. rare.*

1664 POWER *Exp. Philos.* II. 108 The flux in the extravasated leg of the Syphon, is at first most strong. *fig.* 1726 DE FOE *Hist. Devil* (1840) 259 If he be not in the inside..I have so mean an opinion of all his extravasated powers that [etc.]

2. Of a fluid, *esp.* blood: Let or forced out of its proper vessel; effused.

1681 tr. *Willis' Rem. Med. Wks.* Vocab., *Extravasated*, put or let forth of the vessels as blood out of the veins. 1684 tr. *Bonet's Merc. Compit.* v. 138 The extravasated blood. 1759 tr. *Duhamel's Husb.* I. xv. (1762) 76 The extravasated juice of..ash. 1835 LINDLEY *Introd. Bot.* (1848) II. 343 The coagulation of the extravasated latex.

b. Caused by extravasation of blood.

1853 KANE *Grinnell Exp.* xxxiv. (1856) 304, I have two cases of swelled limbs and extravasated blotches.

3. *Geol.* Poured forth from a subterranean reservoir. Cf. EXTRAVASATION 2.

1875 *N. Amer. Rev.* CXX. 205 Here too we find the germs of his [T. S. Hunt's] theory of 'extravasated' rocks.

extravasation (ɛkˌstrævəˈseɪʃən). [f. EXTRAVASATE *v.*: see -ATION. Cf. F. *extravasation.*]

1. *Path.* The escape of an organic fluid (*e.g.* blood, sap) from its proper vessels into the surrounding tissues; an instance of this.

1676 WISEMAN *Surgery* 2 The Plenitude of Vessels..causeth an Extravasation of bloud. 1796 MORSE *Amer. Geog.* I. 338 A stagnation and extravasation of the juices of the stalk. 1836 TODD *Cycl. Anat.* I. 400/1 The extravasation of urine. 1877 ROBERTS *Handbk. Med.* I. 28 Points of redness..due to minute extravasations of blood.

fig. 1685 BURNET *Lett.* (1687) 143 Such an extravasation..of silver, occasions a great deadness in Trade. 1691 BEVERLEY *Mem. Kingd. Christ* 9 God having suffer'd..so dangerous an Extravasation of the French Power.

b. A mass or spot of extravasated blood.

1836 TODD *Cycl. Anat.* I. 52/2 On the substance of the extravasation there were a..number of spots of red blood. 1878 A. HAMILTON *Nerv. Dis.* 19 The crura and pons are to be examined carefully for softening extravasations.

2. *Geol.* Effusion (of molten rock) from a subterranean reservoir; also, a deposit so formed.

1842 G. P. SCROPE *Volcanos* 9 To permit an extravasation of some of the heated and liquefied and gaseous matters. 1864 C. P. SMYTH *Our Inheritance* II. viii. (1880) 144 Amongst the veins and extravasations of granite and basalt.

extravascular (ɛkstrəˈvæskjʊlə(r)), *a. Anat.* [f. EXTRA- *pref.* + VASCULAR.] Outside the vascular system; not vascular.

1804 CARLISLE in *Phil. Trans.* XCV. 12 The horns..and cuticular coverings, are all of them..extra-vascular. 1854 WOODWARD *Mollusca* (1856) 42 The shell..being extravascular..has no inherent power of repair. 1869 HUXLEY *Phys.* ii. 26 There are certain parts which..are..said to be extra-vascular or non-vascular.

†**'extravase**, *v. Obs.* [ad. F. *extravas-er*, f. L. *extrā* outside + *vās* vessel.] = EXTRAVASATE.

Hence **'extravased** *ppl. a.*

1703 W. COWPER in *Phil. Trans.* XXIII. 1389 The Wax past from the Veins to the Arteries without coming into the Bronchеæ, or being extravas'd. 1852 TH. ROSS tr. *Humboldt's Trav.* II. xx. 276 Extravased and coagulated blood.

†**extra'venate**, *a. Obs.* [f. L. *extrā* + *vēn-a* vein + -ATE[2].] Let out of the veins.

1661 GLANVILL *Van. Dogm.* xxi. 207 The wound is affected in like manner as is the extravenate bloud by the Sympathetick medicine. 1755 in JOHNSON; and in mod. Dicts.

†**extra'venate**, *v. Obs. rare.* [f. as prec. + -ATE[3].] *trans.* To let (blood) out of the veins; to extravasate. Hence **extrave'nated** *ppl. a.* **extrave'nation**, the action of letting blood out of the veins; an instance of this.

1650 CHARLETON *Paradoxes* 36 The blood once extravenated, or effluxed out of its proper conservatory..looseth its..vitality. 1668 CULPEPPER & COLE *Barthol. Anat.* 302 Extravenated Blood, or Blood out of its natural place.

extra'version. [ad. mod.L. *extrāversiōn-em*, f. L. *extrā* outwards + *versiōn-em*, n. of action f. *vertĕre* to turn: see EXTROVERSION.]

†1. A turning out; a rendering manifest. *Obs. rare.*

a 1691 BOYLE *Imperfect. Doctr. Qual.* vii, The supposed extraversion or intraversion of sulphur. 1692–1732 COLES, *Extraversion*, a turning ones thoughts upon outward objects. [1753 CHAMBERS *Cycl. Supp.*, *Extraversio* in chemistry, a term used to express the rendering manifest any thing saline, alcaline, or acid, concealed in mixed bodies.]

2. *Psychol.* = EXTROVERSION 3. (Cf. quot. 1692–1732 in sense 1.)

1915 JUNG in *Jrnl. Abnormal Psychol.* IX. 396, I called the hysterical type the *extraversion* type and the psychasthénic type the *introversion* type. 1916 C. E. LONG tr. *Jung's Coll. Papers Anal. Psychol.* 288, I propose to use the terms 'Extraversion' and 'Introversion' to describe these two opposite directions of the libido. *Ibid.*, I will call 'regressive extraversion' the phenomenon which Freud calls 'transference' (Übertragung), by which the hysteric projects into the objective world the illusions, or subjective values of his feelings. 1924 A. G. IKIN in *Brit. Jrnl. Med. Psychol.* IV. 207 In altroversion psychic energy is not consistently directed inwards or outwards as in introversion and extraversion, but can flow freely either way. 1934 W. BROWN *Psychol. & Psychotherapy* (ed. 3) ix. 112 Re-education must include stimulation of their emotional, ethical, and intellectual powers, particularly in the direction of extraversion.

So **extra'versive** *a.* = EXTROVERSIVE *a.*; **'extravert** *sb.* = EXTROVERT *sb.*; **'extraverted** *ppl. a.* = EXTROVERTED *ppl. a.*

1915 JUNG in *Jrnl. Abnormal Psychol.* IX. 397 An extraverted individual can hardly understand the necessity that forces the introverted to accomplish his adaptation by first formulating a general conception. 1916 C. E. LONG tr. *Jung's Coll. Papers Anal. Psychol.* 288, We say that he is extraverted when he gives his fundamental interest to the outer or objective world, and attributes an all-important and essential value to it. *Ibid.* 348 The extraverted type has his libido to a certain extent externally. *Ibid.* 349 An Extravert can hardly conceive the necessity which compels the Introvert to conquer the world by means of a system. 1924 A. G. IKIN in *Brit. Jrnl. Med. Psychol.* IV. 214, I have suggested the use of the term altroversion for the socialisation of either the introverted or the extraverted types..with balance between the self and the environment. *Ibid.*, The personality which thus combines introvert and extravert reactions..can be..called an 'altrovert'..[as that] resulting from a one-sided synthesis of interest and libido, with over emphasis on ego and object respectively, is called an introvert or an extravert. 1926 G. COSTER *Psycho-Analysis* 38 The extravert goes out to people and things, enjoying contacts and shrinking from solitude and meditation. 1937 *Scrutiny* Dec. 288 They [*sc.* Wiéner's melodies] have a typically French sexual exuberance, are completely extraversive. 1944 *Mind* LIII. 286 Hoernlé's social conscience was persistent, active and extraversive. 1966 *Illustr. London News* 30 July 34/2 Civilisations as advanced as the ones they had left behind—though less aggressive and extraverted.

†**extra'vert**, *v. Obs.* [f. L. *extrā* outwards + *vert-ĕre* to turn: see EXTROVERT.] *trans.* To turn outwards so as to be visible. Chiefly in early Chemistry, to render visible or sensible (the latent constituents of a substance).

1669 W. SIMPSON *Hydrol. Chym.* II. iii. 52 It is not the moist air that extraverts any preexistent nitrous parts from the body of the minerals. *a* 1691 BOYLE *Imperfect. Doctr. Qual.* vii, The sulphur, or other hypostatical principle, is intraverted or extraverted, or as others speak, inverted. — *High Veneration* (1835) 50 All things are naked, and..extraverted to his eyes.

extra-violet: see EXTRA- I.

extravo'lution. *nonce-wd.* [f. L. *extrā* outwards + *volvĕre* to roll; cf. *revolution.*] A rolling outwards; opposed to *intravolution.*

1829 LAMB *Final Mem.* viii. 265 To show the intravolutions, extravolutions of which the animal frame is capable.

†**ex'tray**, *v.* In 5 extraie. [ad. Fr. *extraire*, refashioned form of *estraire*:—L. *extrahĕre*: see EXTRACT.] = EXTRACT *v.*

a **1450** *Knt. de la Tour* Prol. (1868) 3 Ther that y fonde a good ensaumple, y made extraie it out.

extra-zodiacal: see EXTRA- 1.

extre, var. of AX-TREE, *Obs.*

†**ex'treat**, *sb. Obs.* Forms: 5–7 extret(e, (5 exstreit, -treyt), 7– **extreat**. [var. of ESTREAT, *ex-* for *es-* after Lat.: for sense 2 cf. OF. *estraite*:—L. *extracta*.]

1. = ESTREAT *sb.*

1489 in *Ld. Treas. Acc. Scot.* 113 Item, to Thomson to pass in Galway for the exstreitis of the ayris, xij s. **1497** *Ibid.* 316 The extret of the ald air of Fiffe. **1622** CALLIS *Stat. Sewers* (1647) 227 But..though I have omitted them in my extreats, you will allow me them in *Summa totalis.* **1631** WEEVER *Anc. Fun. Mon.* 525 Extreats of fines. **1706** in PHILLIPS (ed. Kersey).

2. Extraction.

1596 SPENSER *F.Q.* v. x. 1 Drawne forth from her by divine extreate.

†**ex'treat**, *v. Obs.* [f. prec. sb.]

1. *trans.* = ESTREAT *v.* 1.

1523 FITZHERB. *Surv.* xv. (1539) 33 The issues and profytes thereof..are nat extreted in to the escheker. **1622** CALLIS *Stat. Sewers* (1647) 137 To extreat the Fines into the Kings Exchequer.

2. To eliminate, get rid of.

1628 VENNER *Baths of Bathe* 23 The..last thing to be considered in the vse of this Water, is, that it be not giuen to such, as..cannot extreate and passe it away by vrine.

extrema, pl. of EXTREMUM.

extremal (ɛk'striːməl), *a.* [f. EXTREME *sb.* + -AL; in sense 2 re-formed on EXTREM(UM, perh. influenced by next.] †**1.** Farthest from the middle of a line or area; outermost. *Obs.*

1432–50 tr. *Higden* (Rolls) III. 211 And if the wire be distreynede in to thre equalites, and the seide instrumente be putte under the oon extremalle diuision other departenge, the longer parte of the wyre ytowchede yeldethe diapente. **1447** BOKENHAM *Hooly Wummen* (1938) l. 6903 The extremal marchys of hys regyoun.

2. *Math.* Of or pertaining to extreme qualities or configurations, or highest or lowest values.

1939 *Nature* 4 Mar. 358/1 There seems to be no objection to extremal laws of the local type; but those of the integral type make our modern mind uneasy. **1957** KENDALL & BUCKLAND *Dict. Statistical Terms* 104 *Extremal quotient*, the ratio of the absolute value of the largest observation to the smallest observation in a sample. **1966** *Mathematical Rev.* XXXI. 17/1 Turán's original theorem on extremal problems in graph theory.

extremal (ɛk'striːməl), *sb. Math.* [ad. G. *extremale* (A. Kneser *Lehrb. der Variationsrechnung* (1900) ii. 24), prob. f. G. *extremum* EXTREMUM.] A function $y(x)$ or its graphical representation that is a solution of the Euler–Lagrange equation and so makes an integral $\int f(x, y, dy/dx)dx$ along an arc of the curve a maximum or a minimum; also applied to a surface the integral over which is a maximum or a minimum. Also *attrib.* or as *adj.*

1901 *Ann. Mathematics* 2nd Ser. II. 108 Any function *y* of *x*..which, at all interior points of an interval (x', x'') throughout which it is considered satisfies Lagrange's equation..is called an *extremal.* **1904** O. BOLZA *Lect. Calculus Variations* i. 27 Every solution of Euler's equation (curve as well as function) is called, according to Kneser, an *extremal.* **1950** C. FOX *Introd. Calculus Variations* iii. 69 Surfaces for which I is stationary will be referred to as extremals. *Ibid.*, An extremal surface. **1962** L. A. PARS *Introd. Calculus Variations* i. 18 In the early history of the subject it was often assumed that if there is a unique extremal through A and B the problem is solved. *Ibid.* ii. 43 An extremal arc.

extreme (ɛk'striːm), *a.*, *adv.*, and *sb.* Forms: 5–7 extream(e, (6 extreeme), 5– **extreme**. [a. OF. *extreme* (F. *extrême*), ad. L. *extrēmus*, superl. of *exterus* outward (see EXTERIOR).

The L. *extrēmus*, like Eng. *utmost*, is scarcely to be found used in its strictly literal sense of 'outermost'; the ordinary senses are 'endmost', 'farthest', 'last'; and, with loss of the distinctively superlative signification, 'very far advanced', 'excessive in degree'. In late L. the adj. was treated as a positive, with compar. and superl. degrees *extrēmior*, *extrēmissimus*. In Eng. *extremer*, *extremest*, and more freq. *more*, *most extreme*, are occasionally used, and (although condemned by Johnson) are justifiable on the ground that the adj. is not always equivalent to a superlative. In some instances the superlative form may be really pleonastic as in *chiefest*.]

1. Outermost, farthest from the centre (of any area); endmost, situated at either of the ends (of a line, series, or scale: opposed to *mean*). ***extreme parts*** (of the body): the 'extremities', hands, feet, fingers, toes, etc. (*obs.* or *arch.*).

1503 *Act 19 Hen. VII*, c. 24 Chichester is in the extream Part of the..Shire. **1557** RECORDE *Whetst.* D iij, Beginnyng with the two extremeste [nombers] that is .2. and .30. thei will by multiplicacion make .60. **1683** SALMON *Doron Med.* I. 32 [Hermodacts] purges Flegm by stool from the extream parts. **1725** POPE *Odyss.* XIII. 281 The fruitful continent's extreamest bound. **1748** F. SMITH *Voy. Disc. N.-W. Pass.* I. 165 The principal Care required being as to the extreme Parts, as to the Feet and Legs, Arms and Hands. **1831** BREWSTER *Optics* x. 89 The refrangibility of the extreme invisible ray which possessed the power of heating. **1871** FREEMAN *Norm. Conq.* IV. xvii. 72 These two extreme points of his province..Hereford on the West and Norwich on the East.

b. *Math.* ***extreme and mean ratio*** (or †*proportion*): = Gr. ἀκρὸς καὶ μέσος λόγος (see quots.).

1570 BILLINGSLEY *Euclid* 153 b, A right line is sayd to be deuided by an extreme and meane proportion, when the whole is to the greater part, as the greater part is to the lesse. **1827** HUTTON *Course Math.* I. 370 Let A B be the given line to be divided in extreme and mean ratio.

c. *Bellringing.* ***extreme bells, change***: (see quots.).

1671 *Tintinnalogia* 8 On four Bells, there are Twenty four several Changes, in Ringing of which, there is one Bell called the Hunt and the other three are Extream Bells. **1677** F. S[TEADMAN] *Campanalogia* 55 The extream changes may be made two ways, viz. either betwixt the two farthest extream bells from the hunt, or else betwixt the two nearest extream bells to it.

2. Farthest, or very far advanced in any direction; utmost, uttermost.

1600 SHAKS. *A.Y.L.* II. i. 42 The hairie foole..Stood on th' extremest verge of the swift brooke. **1705** ADDISON *Italy* 250 Miseno's Cape and Bauli last he view'd, That on the Sea's extreamest Borders stood. **1774** J. BRYANT *Mythol.* I. p. vi, Colonies..are to be found in the most extream parts of the east. **1784** COWPER *Task* II. 92 From th' extremest point, Of elevation down into th' abyss. **1860** B'NESS BUNSEN in Hare *Life* II. v. 273 The extreme point supposed to have been reached. **1882** PROCTOR *Fam. Sc. Stud.* 2, The extremest possible range of Telescopic vision.

3. Last, latest. *Obs.* or *arch.*, exc. in ***extreme unction***, in the Roman Catholic Church, 'a sacrament in which the sick in danger of death are anointed by a priest for the health of soul and body, the anointing being accompanied by a set form of words' (*Catholic Dict.*).

c **1477** CAXTON *Jason* 83 b, The extreme draughtes of deth. **1513** BRADSHAW *St. Werburge* I. 3010 The extreme day. **1552** ABP. HAMILTON *Catech.* (1884) 34 The daie of extreme jugement. **1579** FULKE *Refut. Rastel* 795 Other writers, ascribe the institution of this extreame unction to Felix the fourth. **1669** PENN *No Cross* viii. §8 The extream Moments of Life. **1821** SHELLEY *Adonais* vi, Thy extreme hope, the loveliest and the last. **1875** MANNING *Mission H. Ghost* i. 17 Those who upon a dying bed receive the Sacrament of Extreme Unction.

4. Going to great lengths; opposed to *moderate*.

a. Of a quality, condition, or feeling: Existing in the utmost possible degree, or in an exceedingly high degree; exceedingly great or intense.

The phrase ***extreme old age*** is apprehended as belonging to this sense, though in the original L. *extrema senectus* the adj. has the sense 3.

c **1460** FORTESCUE *Abs. & Lim. Mon.* (1714) 22 Lyvyn in the most extreme Povertie. **1526** *Pilgr. Perf.* (W. de W. 1531) 205 b, The moost extreme paynes. **1550** COVERDALE *Spir. Perle* xii, He himself lieth not in any such extreme necessity. **1634** SIR T. HERBERT *Trav.* 95 Winter colds, and ..the parching Sunne..which in their seasons are there extreame. **1675** TRAHERNE *Chr. Ethics* ix. 125 It is the extremest madness in the world. **1710** HEARNE *Collect.* (Oxf. Hist. Soc.) II. 348 Having an extream desire to be a Bp. **1726** CHETWOOD *Adv. Capt. R. Boyle* 345 With the Day Reflection return'd, sharpen'd with the extreamest Hunger. **1828** SCOTT *F.M. Perth* xxiii, Their surprise at his escape was therefore extreme. **1868** GLADSTONE *Juv. Mundi* x. §1. (1869) 388 The extremest degree of guilt. **1891** E. PEACOCK *N. Brendon* II. 66 He knew that he was in extreme peril.

b. Of a case, circumstance, supposition: Presenting in the utmost degree some particular characteristic.

1597 HOOKER *Eccl. Pol.* v. §9. 16 Cases of necessitie being some but vrgent, sometime extreme. **1875** JOWETT *Plato* (ed. 2) IV. 24 The nature of anything is best known from the examination of extreme cases. **1888** BRYCE *Amer. Commw.* II. lx. 427 Party loyalty [is] strong enough..in all but extreme cases.

c. Of actions, measures, etc.: Severe or violent in the utmost degree, or in an exceedingly great degree; stringent.

1512 *Act 4 Hen. VIII*, c. 20 Pream., Theire adherentes made extreme resistens. *a* **1533** LD. BERNERS *Huon* lxxxii. 256 The doloures wepynges & teeres that they made were so extreme. **1538** BALE *God's Promises* III. in Hazl. *Dodsley* I. 297 Neither kindness nor extreme handling can Make him to know me. **1607** SHAKS. *Timon* III. v. 54 To kill, I grant, is sinnes extreemest Gust. **1614** BP. HALL *Recoll. Treat.* 975 Moderate exercise strengthens, extreame destroys nature. **1685** DRYDEN *Thren. August.* v. 9 Th' extreamest ways they first ordain. **1856** FROUDE *Hist. Eng.* (1858) II. vii. 130 Having been driven to so extreme a measure against his will. **1888** A. K. GREEN *Behind Closed Doors* ii, We never anticipated her taking any such extreme action as this.

d. Of opinions, fashions, etc.: Going to the utmost extent; exceeding the limits of moderation.

1876 J. SAUNDERS *Lion in Path* xi, A lady, dressed in the extremest fashion of the time. **1878** MORLEY *Carlyle* Crit. Misc. Ser. I. 200 Holding one or other of the rival creeds in its most extreme, exclusive and intolerant form.

e. Of persons: Going to great lengths in any action, habit, disposition, or opinion; very 'pronounced'. In early use often: †Strict, severe, harsh. Now chiefly with reference to opinions.

a **1533** FRITH *Disput. Purgat.* (1829) 154 The extreme enemies of God. *a* **1533** LD. BERNERS *Gold. Bk. M. Aurel.* (1546) N vj, He shewed hymselfe as bolde in wordes, as extreme and base in his array. **1535** COVERDALE *Ps.* cxxix. 3 Yf thou (Lorde) wilt be extreme to marcke what is done amysse. **1594** WEST *Symbol.* II. *Chancerie* §139 A. B. accompted of him as of a verie extreame man. **1598** SHAKS. *Merry W.* IV. iv. 11 Be not as extreme in submission, as in offence. **1602** *Life T. Cromwell* v. v. 127 Gardiner's the cause makes Cromwell so extreme. **1634** SIR T. HERBERT *Trav.* 197 The greatest part are Heathens and extreme Idolaters. **1784** COWPER *Task* II. 380 In conversation frivolous, in dress Extreme. **1860** HOOK *Lives Abps.* (1869) I. i. 2 A Master who is not extreme to mark what is done amiss. **1889** *Spectator* 28 Dec., There will be a natural tendency in men who have this note of distinction to be.. what is called 'extreme' men.

†**f.** Of material agents, influences, etc.: Effective in the utmost degree; exceedingly intense or powerful in operation. *Obs.*

c **1489** CAXTON *Blanchardyn* liv. (1890) 212 Extreame contagion of dangerous sicknes. **1612** DRAYTON *Poly-olb.* xvi. 253 Those two extreamer Winds from hurting it to let. **1634** SIR T. HERBERT *Trav.* 104 Supping a delighted Cup of extreme poyson. **1748** F. SMITH *Voy. Disc. N.-W. Pass.* I. 158 The Wind..began to be extreme, or very intense.

5. *Music.* **a.** In sense 1, as ***extreme parts***, the highest and lowest parts in part music. **b.** ***extreme interval***: = 'augmented interval'; see AUGMENTED 2 b. **c.** ***extreme key***: a key other than those related keys into which it is usual to modulate. †**d.** Formerly said of a key having more than three sharps or flats (*obs.*).

1731 G. KELLER *Rules for Playing Thorow-Bass* in W. Holder *Harmony* 164 The extream Sharp second is the same distance as the Flat third. *Ibid.* 191 The extream Sharp 2d. and 4th. generally prepares a Cadence. The 5th. and 7th. and the Flat 5th. and extream Flat 7th. are generally the fore runners of a Cadence. **1876** STAINER & BARRETT *Mus. Terms*, *Chord of the extreme sixth*, a chord of modern growth so called because the interval of an extreme or augmented sixth is contained in it, either directly or by inversion. **1880** PARRY in Grove *Dict. Mus.* s.v. *Interval*, The interval of the augmented sixth is indifferently called 'superfluous' or 'extreme sharp' sixth; and the same terms are applied to the fifth.

†**B.** *adv.* In an extreme degree; = EXTREMELY 2; formerly frequent with adjs., occasional with advbs., rare with vbs. *Obs.*

1593 H. SMITH *God's Arrowe* B iij, Except they be extreame vnthankeful and dissolute. **1594** H. WILLOBIE in *Shaks. C. Praise* 9 The smothered flame, too closely pent Burnes more extreame for want of vent. **1636** EARL STRAFFORDE *Lett. & Disp.* (1739) II. 22 My Lord Marshal writes extream doubtfully of his Success with the Emperor. **1710** HEARNE *Collect.* (Oxf. Hist. Soc.) III. 53 You have done extreme well in speaking to the Vice-Chancellor. **1796** BURNEY *Metastasio* II. 5 In the empty and extreme cold theatre. **1816** KEATINGE *Trav.* (1817) I. 270 Articles..of an extreme costly description.

C. *sb.*

1. quasi-*sb.* The *adj.* used *absol.*; only in phrases, ***in (the) extreme***: in an extreme degree, extremely. †***to be in extreme***: to be at the extreme stage of some state or condition.

1604 SHAKS. *Oth.* v. ii. 347 Of one..Perplex'd in the extreme. *a* **1711** KEN *Sion* Poet. Wks. 1721 IV. 390 Fond Love..Is ever in Extreme. **1780** COWPER *Lett.* 8 May, I am delighted..in the extreme. **1790** *Norman & Bertha* I. 67 Elevated, but not in extreme, by their bacchanalian offering [etc.]. **1823** in Cobbett *Rur. Rides* (1885) I. 321 The labourers' houses..beggarly in the extreme. **1847** GROTE *Greece* II. xlv. (1862) IV. 69 This dismissal, ungracious in the extreme..excited..exasperation.

†**2.** *sb.* The utmost point or verge; that which terminates a body; an end, extremity. *Obs.*

1570 BILLINGSLEY *Euclid* I. Def. iv. 2 A right lyne is that, whose extremes abiding, cannot be altered. **1626** BACON *Sylva* §749 Most of the hard substances fly to the extreams of the Body. **1660** BOYLE *New Exp. Phys. Mech.* vi. 58 The open extream [of the pipe]. **1748** F. SMITH *Voy. Disc. N.-W. Pass.* I. 28 Their Paddle being double bladed..and the Blades one at each Extreme. **1802** PLAYFAIR *Illustr. Hutton. Th.* 304 Plumbago is the extreme of a gradation of which fossil coal is the beginning. **1808** J. BARLOW *Columb.* I. 573 Far in his vast extremes he swells and thaws.

†**b.** ***in (the, his) extremes***: in the last moments or stage of life. *Obs.*; = L. *in extremis* (which is now often used).

1546 BALE *Eng. Votaries* II. (1551) C viij b, As he laye in extremes. **1558** BP. WATSON *Sev. Sacram.* xxx. 193 Sendynge for theym [Priestes] in the extremes when they can doo them least good. **1613** PURCHAS *Pilgr.* IX. iii. (1614) 833 In his extremes he vttered these things to his Confessor. [**1767** GOOCH *Treat. Wounds* I. 286 A person apparently *in extremis*, under a fit of the apoplexy. **1830** SCOTT *Monast.* Answ. Introd. Ep. *note*, Having sent for a Cameronian clergyman when he was *in extremis*.]

3. That which occupies a place at either end of anything; one of two things removed as far as possible from each other, in position, nature, or condition. Also in proverb: ***Extremes meet.***

1555 EDEN *Decades* 175 Not accomptynge the extremes. **1605** SHAKS. *Lear* v. iii. 198 Two extremes of passion, ioy and greefe. **1699** BURNET 39 *Art.* xxv. (1700) 268 The other Extream that we likewise avoid, is [etc.]. **1721** DE FOE *Mem. Cavalier* (1840) 17 As the English were very much out of favour..so the Scots were on the other extreme with the French. **1800** *Med. Jrnl.* III. 251 The intermediate space between those extremes. **1816** BYRON *Parisina* xiv, Now in laughter, now in tears, But madly still in each extreme. **1822** HAZLITT *Table-t.* I. xv. 360 Extremes meet..the most furious anarchists have since become the most barefaced apostates.

b. *Logic.* Each of the extreme terms in a proposition or a syllogism; in a proposition the subject or predicate, as distinguished from the

copula; in a syllogism, the major or minor term as distinguished from the middle.

1628 T. Spencer *Logick* 258 If the last extreame be affirmed of the middle terme, and the middle terme of the first extreame. **1655-60** Stanley *Hist. Philos.* (1701) 182/1 Extreams are the parts of a Proposition. **1837-8** Sir W. Hamilton *Logic* xvi. (1866) I. 295 The Major and Minor Terms [of a syllogism] are called Extremes. **1849** Hoblyn *Dict. Sci. Terms, Extremes.* In Logic, the subject and predicate of a proposition are called its extremes or terms.

c. *Math.* The first or last term of a ratio, series, or set of numbers. †***extremes conjunct*** and ***extremes disjunct***, terms formerly in use in Spherical Trigonometry (see quot. 1796), for which *adjacent parts* and *opposite parts* are now employed.

1571 Digges *Pantom.* iv. Def. iv. Tjb, When foure magnitudes are..in continual proportion, the first & the fourth are the extremes. **1616** Wright tr. *Napier's Descr. Logarithmes* i. iii. 8 Of the Logarithmes of three proportionals, the double of the second, or middle one, is equall to the summe of the extremes. **1753** Chambers *Cycl. Supp.*, Extremes conjunct. **1796** Hutton *Math. Dict.* I. 463 Extremes Conjunct and Extremes Disjunct in Spherical Trigonometry, are the former the two circular parts that lie next the assumed middle part, and the latter the two that lie remote from the middle part. **1806** —— *Course Math.* I. 115 Subtract the less extreme from the greater. **1859** Barn. Smith *Arith. & Algebra* (ed. 6) 432 The terms *a* and *d* are called the Extremes.

d. *Music.* ***the extremes of an interval***: the two sounds most distant from each other.

e. *Bell-ringing*: = 'extreme change': see A. 1 c.

1684 R. H. *Sch. Recreat.* 96 You may make your extream at the first, second, or third single Bob. **1702** J. D. & C. M. *Campanalogia Impr.* 20 An Extream is a distinct Change from the rest, and made by the two farthest Extream Bells from the Half-hunt.

4. The utmost imaginable or tolerable degree of anything; a very high degree. Also in phrases ***in, to an, the extreme; in extremes*** (cf. 1).

1593 Shaks. *3 Hen. VI*, iii. ii. 115 By so much is the Wonder in extremes. *a* **1631** Capt. Smith *True Trav.* ii. 47 Here the Proverbe is true that no extreame long continueth. **1709** Pope *Ess. Crit.* 386 Avoid extreams; and shun the fault of such Who still are pleas'd too little, or too much. **1715** —— *Iliad* I. *Ess. Homer* i. ii, Nor do they [men] equally.. bear that human Nature..Should be prais'd in an Extream without opposition. **1777** Burke *Let. Sheriffs Bristol* Wks. III. 185 The extreme of liberty..obtains no where. **1791** J. Lackington *Mem.* (1792) 228 She was enthusiastical to an extreme. **1846** *Pope's Jrnl. Trade* 109 A climate subject to great extremes. **1846** Greener *Sc. Gunnery* 117 Twisted.. to such an extreme as to resemble the threads of a very fine screw. **1858** Emerson *Lett. & Soc. Aims, Pers. Poetry* Wks. (Bohn) III. 237 Life in the East is fierce, short, hazardous, and in extremes. **1883** F. M. Crawford *Dr. Claudius* ii, He was..dressed in the extreme of the English fashion.

†**b.** *pl.* Extremities, straits, hardships. *Obs.*

1546-7 Paget *Let.* 2 Mar. in Tytler *Edw. VI* (1839) I. 24, I neuer loued extreams. **1594** Marlowe & Nashe *Dido* i. i. 196 Lighten our Extremes with this one boon. **1634** Sir T. Herbert *Trav.* 25 The Sea-men fell into great extreames. **1667** Dryden *Ind. Emperor* iv. ii, What now remains in these Extreams?

5. An excessive degree; a 'very great length', in phrases *to* †***break, carry, run to an extreme***; also, something carried to excess, an extreme measure, a desperate step.

1588 Shaks. *Tit. A.* iii. i. 216 Do not breake into these deepe extreames. **1592** Nashe *P. Penilesse* (ed. 2) 26 b, If I prooue Playes to be no extreame. **1611** Shaks. *Wint. T.* iv. iv. 6 My gracious Lord, To chide at your extreames, it not becomes me. **1752** Young *Brothers* iv. i, On what Extremes extreme distress impels me? **1789** Belsham *Ess.* I. xii. 217 This would be running into a very absurd extreme. **1804** *Med. Jrnl.* XII. 329 The antiphlogistic regimen, carried into extremes..have been the causes. **1867** Mrs. H. Wood *Life's Secret* II. 11, I never thought the masters would go to the extreme of a lock-out.

extremeless (ɛkˈstriːmlɪs), *a. rare.* [f. extreme *sb.* + -less.] Having no extremes or extremities: infinite.

1847 in Craig; and in mod. Dicts.

extremely (ɛkˈstriːmlɪ), *adv.* [f. extreme *a.* + -ly².]

†**1.** To the uttermost degree: in or with a very great degree of some quality, *esp.* severity. *Obs.*

1532 Frith *Mirror* iii. (1626) 43 That thy negligence..be not..extremely imputed unto thee. **1563-87** Foxe *A. & M.* (1684) III. 832 He was extreamly racked, within half a finger breadth as far as Anne Askew. **1661** Pepys *Diary* 2 Nov., I did extremely beat him. **1703** Moxon *Mech. Exerc.* 250 It must be extreamly beaten, which will break all the knots of Lime. **1709** Swift in *Lett. Lit. Men* (Camden) 340 A sinecure..which..would fitt me extremely. **1819** Byron *Juan* i. lxxvi, She..look'd extremely at the opening door.

†**b.** ***to be extremely in*** (superfluity, etc.): to be in state of extreme (superfluity, etc.). *Obs.*

1562 Bulleyn *Def. agst. Sickness* 51 a, Twoo humours, equall aboundyng together, extremely in superfluite. **1655-60** Stanley *Hist. Philos.* (1701) 98/1 A Widow.. extreamly in want.

2. In an extreme degree; exceedingly, very much.

a. with vbs. Now somewhat rare.

1577 B. Googe *Heresbach's Husb.* iii. (1586) 122 You must not suffer your horse to drinke after his journey, till he be colde: howbeit, if he sweate not to extremely..it is not so daungerous. **1607** Shaks. *Timon* iii. ii. 14 One of his men.. vrg'd extreamly for't..and yet was deny'de. **1634** Sir T. Herbert *Trav.* 19 The Seas sweld extremely. **1711** Wallis in J. Greenwood *Eng. Gram.* Pref. 31 Many who stuttered extreamly. **1794** Sullivan *View Nat.* I. 121 The cause of the cohesion of matter has extremely perplexed philosophers. **1841** Lane *Arab. Nts.* I. 85 The king was extremely astonished.

b. with adjs., pples., or advbs.

1540-54 Croke xiii. *Ps.* (Percy Soc.) 11, I am made feble like a wretch, Extremely croked, backe and bone. **1638** Rouse *Heav. Univ.* Advt. (1702) 3 It was so extreamly dangerous. **1644** Milton *Educ.*, If wise Men and Prophets be not extreamly out. **1776** Adam Smith *W. N.* i. iii. (1869) I. 21 The Mediterranean was extremely favourable to the infant navigation of the world. **1808** Han. More *Cœlebs* v. (1809) 55 They used the strongest terms..They were extremely glad and extremely sorry. **1889** *Sat. Rev.* 23 Mar. 335/1 Only an extremely strong and an extremely cool man could make the beating adequate to the offence.

extremeness (ɛkˈstriːmnɪs). [f. as prec. + -ness.] The quality or fact of being extreme.

1530 in Palsgr. 218/1. **1609** Tourneur *Sir F. Vere* 481 By extreamnes in another kind. **1727** in Bailey vol. II. **1839** Poe *Fall House Usher* Wks. 1864 I. 306 The extremeness of the folly. **1891** *Pall Mall G.* 28 Dec. 3/2 The extremeness of its critical position may be judged, etc.

extremism (ɛkˈstriːmɪz(ə)m). [f. extreme + -ism.] Tendency to be extreme; disposition to go to extremes.

1865 *Daily Tel.* 29 Dec. 2/1 These days of extravagance and extremeism. **1887** *The American* XIII. 276 It is..this extremism which makes any effective control of the traffic in liquors so nearly hopeless.

extremist (ɛkˈstriːmɪst), *sb.* (and *a.*) [f. as prec. + -ist.] One who is disposed to go to the extreme, or who holds extreme opinions; a member of a party advocating extreme measures. Also *attrib.* or as *adj.* Hence **exˈtremism**, the views or actions of extremists; **extreˈmistic** *a.*, of or pertaining to extremists or extremism.

1846 in Worcester (citing *Ec. Rev.*). **1850** D. Webster *Sp.* 7 Mar. 53 The extremists of both parts of the country are violent. **1856** Olmsted *Slave States* 177 The extremists of the South esteem their opponents as madmen, or robbers. **1873** Whitney *Orient. Stud.* 122 The extremists of the German school. **1907** *Daily Chron.* 28 Aug. 5/2 Bepin Pal, the Extremist leader. **1920** H. V. Lovett *Hist. Ind. Nationalist Movem.* 69 The reception committee was broken up by a gang of Extremists. *Ibid.* 240 This doctrine is ever the result of Extremism. **1921** *Moplah Reb.* 50 in *Parl. Papers* (Cmd. 1552) XXVI. 237 Certain Extremist Muhammadan agitators..have been..working up the people over the Khilafat. **1921** *19th Cent.* July 148 The Fascismo was born in the provinces, where the extremistic menace was stronger.

†**exˈtremite.** *Obs. rare*⁻¹. [f. as prec. + -ite.] = extremist *sb.*

1546 Gardiner *Decl. Art. Joye* p. xx, Folowynge the newe scoole of extremites, he denied all degrees of grace.

extremity (ɛkˈstrɛmɪtɪ). Forms: 4-6 extremite(e, ex(s)tremyte(e, 6-7 extreamitie, -ty, -extremity. [ad. F. *extrémité*, ad. L. *extrēmitāt-em*, f. *extrēmus* (see extreme *a.*).]

1. The extreme or terminal point or portion of anything; the very end.

c **1400** *Lanfranc's Cirurg.* 155 þe round extremite of þis boon. **1578** Lyte *Dodoens* iii. lxxi. 413 Branches..hauing at their extremities or endes certayne whites. **1607** Shaks. *Timon* iv. iii. 301 The middle of Humanity thou neuer knewest, but the extremitie of both ends. **1657** S. Purchas *Pol. Flying-Ins.* 204 The extremities of their wings are blunt. **1661** Boyle *Style of Script.* 75 In the Mariner's Compasse, the Needle's extremity, though [etc.]. **1726** tr. *Gregory's Astron.* I. 47 From these Extremities *F, D*, draw the very small right Lines *FE, DC*. **1828** Stark *Elem. Nat. Hist.* II. 296 Antennæ thickening towards their extremity. **1867** Smyth *Sailor's Word-bk., Extremities*, the stem and stern posts of a ship. **1870** F. R. Wilson *Ch. Lindisf.* 81 At the extremity of the east end is a mausoleum.

b. *pl.* The uttermost parts of the body; the hands and feet.

1460-70 *Bk. Quintessence* 17 He schal waische al his body and his extremytees wiþ brennynge watir ofte tymes. **1707** Floyer *Physic. Pulse-Watch* 438 Cold in the Extremities. **1768** W. Gilpin *Ess. Prints* 112 His heads are ill-set on; his extremities incorrectly touched. **1804** Abernethy *Surg. Observ.* 185 His extremities were cold. His feet were put into hot water. **1870** Emerson *Soc. & Solit., Courage* Wks. (Bohn) III. 109 Bodily pain is..seated usually in the skin and the extremities.

†**2.** The two things which are at the extreme ends of a scale; the 'extremes' as opposed to the 'mean'. *Obs.*

1375 Barbour *Bruce* vi. 336 Vorschip Extremyteis has twa; Fule-hardyment..And..cowardiss. *c* **1400** *Rom. Rose* 6528 Richesse and mendicitees Ben clepid two extremytees. **1483** Caxton *Gold. Leg.* 179/3 Thextremytees of Justyce ben cruelte and defaulte. **1598** Barckley *Felic. Man* (1631) 620 The extremities of estates, specially the highest, are more subject to those things..than the meane estates.

3. The extreme or utmost degree, that which reaches the utmost point. †Also in phrases ***in, to (an, the, that) extremity***. *Obs.* = extreme *sb.* 4.

1543-4 *Act 35 Hen. VIII*, c. 12 The kynge..is forced..to prosecute his saide ennemies, with the sworde to the extremitie of his power. **1552** Huloet, Extremitye of the lawe. *Summum Ins.* **1590** Shaks. *Com. Err.* i. i. 142 Haplesse Egeon whom the fates haue markt To beare the extremitie of dire mishap. —— *Mids. N.* iii. ii. 3 Which she must dote on, in extremitie. **1638** Rouse *Heav. Univ.* iii. (1702) 23 Having none of them to suffer extremities of Penury and Want. **1653** Walton *Angler* i. xvii. §5 In Derbyshire..the waters.. clear to an extremity. **1692** Dryden *Cleomenes* Pref., Farce, the Extremitie of bad Poetry. **1719** De Foe *Crusoe* (Reprint) 41 The weather was hot to the Extremity. **1722** —— *Plague* (1756) 173 It was encreased to such a frightful extremity. **1776** Gibbon *Decl. & F.* I. xxiv. 708 The last extremities of thirst and hunger. **1882** Farrar *Early Chr.* I. 449 *note*, No more violent extremity of sin..can be described.

†**b.** The utmost penalty. *Obs.*

1591 R. Turnbull *St. James* 103 Before the iudgement seates..they will haue the extremitie of them.

†**4.** Extreme or inordinate intensity or violence (of passion, action, suffering, labour, etc.); an instance of this; a violent outburst. *Obs.*

1509 Hawes *Past. Pleas.* xvi. li, Great extremyte Of fervent love. **1590** Spenser *F.Q.* ii. ii. 38 With equall measure she did moderate The strong extremities of their outrage. **1596** *Edward III*, iii. i. 35 When the exhalations of the air Break in extremity of lightning flash. **1621** Bp. Hall *Heaven upon Earth* §4 An vnwonted extremitie of the blow shall fetch blood. **1632** J. Hayward tr. *Biondi's Eromena* 20 The Admirall..burst..into an extremitie of weeping. **1669** Marvell *Corr.* cxxix. Wks. 1872-5 II. 293 Having the favor to sit by reason of his extremity of the gout.

b. Extreme stress or severity (of weather).

1664 Evelyn *Kal. Hort.* (1729) 197 All such Extremities of Weather. **1692** Luttrell *Brief. Rel.* (1857) II. 348 The extremity of the weather..prevented it. **1716-8** Lady M. W. Montague *Lett.* I. xxi. 65 It is now the very extremity of the winter here. **1797** Bewick *Brit. Birds* (1847) I. 75 The extremity of the weather.

†**5.** Extravagance in opinion, behaviour, or expenditure; an instance of this. *Obs.*

a **1533** Ld. Berners *Gold. Bk. M. Aurel.* (1546) I v b, Ye women are so extreme in all headlong extremitees. **1598** Shaks. *Merry W.* iv. ii. 169 If I..shew no colour for my extremity: Let me..be your Table-sport. **1642** Fuller *Holy & Prof. St.* ii. ix. 86 Many notorious for extremities may find favourers to preferre them. **1709** Strype *Ann. Ref.* I xlvi. 505 This extremity in apparel..tended to the confusion of the degrees of all estates. **1712** Steele *Spect.* No. 426 ¶4 All the Extremities of Houshold Expence.

†**6.** Extreme severity or rigour. *Obs.*

15.. *Hours of Virgin* 100 Entreating me wᵗʰ like extremitie As if I were Thy mortall enemie. **1580** Baret *Alv.* E 505 To vse extreamitie..*Iure summo agere.* **1590** Shaks. *Com. Err.* v. i. 307 Oh times extremity! Hast thou so crack'd and splitted my poore tongue [etc.]. **1639** Massinger *Unnat. Combat.* i. i. B iv b, We sit ingag'd to censure him with all Extremitie and rigour.

7. A condition of extreme urgency or need; the utmost point of adversity, embarrassment, or suffering. Phrases, ***to*** †***bring, drive,*** †***put, reduce to (the last) extremity*** or ***extremities***. †***upon an extremity***: on an emergency.

c **1425** Hoccleve *Minor P.* i. (1892) 208 In swich an houres extremitee. *c* **1542** Udall in Ellis *Orig. Lett.* (1843) 3 Considre in what extremitee and distresse I am constitute. **1560** A. L. tr. *Calvin's Foure Serm. Songe Ezech.* iv, Sometimes thei are brought to such extremitie that onles they digge the earth..they haue not a droppe of water to drinke. **1597** Morley *Introd. Mus.* 21 He vsed it vpon an extremity. **1607** Topsell *Serpents* (1658) 597 A Serpent was the first original of all his extremities. **1681** Dryden *Abs. & Achit.* 159 A daring Pilot in Extremity. *a* **1691** Flavel *Sea-Deliverances* Wks. 1731 II. 608 We knew that man's extremity is God's opportunity. **1719** De Foe *Crusoe* I. viii. 130, I was not driven to any extremities for food. **1781** Gibbon *Decl. & F.* III. 165 Florence was reduced to the last extremity. **1848** Macaulay *Hist. Eng.* II. 95 Driven to extremity.

b. (***to resist***, etc.) ***to the last extremity***: to the death. †***to expect the extremity***: to be prepared for the worst or for death.

1684 *Lond. Gaz.* No. 1969/2 The Besieged..seem resolved to expect the Extremity. **1856** Emerson *Eng. Traits, Aristocracy* Wks. (Bohn) II. 80 The English tenant would defend his lord to the last extremity.

8. A person's last moments; the 'article of death'. *arch.*

1602 Warner *Alb. Eng.* xiii. lxxvi. (1612) 315 Yea..in extremities, thou touchest on his name. *a* **1628** Preston *New Covt.* (1634) 109 At the day of death, at the time of extremity. **1753** N. Torriano *Gangr. Sore Throat* 51 Many Children sick of this Disease, to whom I could give no Help, being not called till the very Extremity. **1838** James *Louis XIV*, III. i. 14 Letters from Mazarin announcing that the King was at extremity. **1863** Sala *Last Crusader* 218 Saint Louis..being in extremities..receives extreme unction.

9. An extreme measure; the utmost point of severity or desperation. Chiefly in *pl.*

1639 Massinger *Unnat. Combat.* ii. i, Look, therefore, for extremities..I will..kill thee As a serpent swollen with poison. **1734** tr. *Rollin's Anc. Hist.* (1827) VIII. xix. ix. 250 Urge me to extremities. **1862** Ld. Brougham *Brit. Const.* xii. 165 In case matters were pushed to the extremity of a civil war. *Ibid.* xv. 234 The extremities to which the leaders went against the King. **1890** *Sat. Rev.* 19 Apr. 483/1 Putting him up as if to be shot, knowing all the while that he could not legally proceed to extremity.

10. The quality of being extreme (in the current senses of the adj.); extremeness. Somewhat *rare.*

1848 Macaulay *Hist. Eng.* II. 555 The extremity of the danger drew Sancroft forth from his palace. **1861** Tulloch *Eng. Purit.* 99 The very extremity of their views gave them strength. **1862** Stanley *Jew. Ch.* (1877) I. xvii. 328 This exact description..required by the very extremity of its destruction.

extremum (ɛkˈstriːməm). *Math.* Pl. **extrema, extremums.** [a. L. *extrēmum*, neut. of *extrēmus* (see extreme *a., adv.*, and *sb.*). First used as a mathematical term (in German) by P. du Bois-Reymond 1879, in *Math. Ann.* XV. 564.] A

value of a function that is a maximum or a minimum (either relative or absolute).

1904 O. BOLZA *Lect. Calculus Variations* i. 10 The word 'extremum' will be used for maximum and minimum alike, when it is not necessary to distinguish between them. **1947** COURANT & ROBBINS *What is Math.?* (ed. 4) vii. 343 A point where the derivative vanishes, whether it is an extremum or not, is called a stationary point. **1962** A. H. FRINK tr. *Akhiezer's Calculus of Variations* i. 5 An extremum in the whole collection M is called an absolute extremum. We shall also consider relative extrema; to define them we must introduce the notion of neighbourhood. **1968** M. J. FORRAY *Variational Calculus in Sci. & Engin.* i. 6 Are $f(\frac{4}{5}) = 4^4/5^5$ and $f(0) = 0$ the absolute maximum and minimum for $f(x)$ [$= x^4 - x^5$] in $-2 \leqslant x \leqslant 2$? We know that these extremums exist for a continuous function defined over a closed interval.

extricable ('ɛkstrɪkəb(ə)l), *a.* [f. L. *extricā-re*: see next and -ABLE.] That may or can be extricated. †**a.** That may be unravelled or solved (*obs.*). **b.** That may be set free or got out.

a. **1623-6** in COCKERAM. **1678** CUDWORTH *Intell. Syst.* 863 Some Difficulty, not easily Extricable by us. *a* **1711** KEN *Hymnotheo* Wks. 1721 III. 274 With Diabolic Eden them [the Labyrinth, Catacombs, etc.] compare, They regular, and extricable are.

b. *a* **1794** SIR W. JONES *Select Ind. Plants* §28 Germ.. scarce extricable from the calyx enclosing and grasping it. **1853** MISS E. S. SHEPPARD *Ch. Auchester* I. 11 When deftly handled, [it] had still some delights extricable.

extricate ('ɛkstrɪkeɪt), *v.* [f. L. *extrīcāt-* ppl. stem of *extrīcāre* to disentangle, f. *ex-* (see EX- *pref.*[1]) + *trīcæ* perplexities.]

1. *trans.* To unravel (what is tangled); *fig.* to clear of intricacies or perplexities. Now *rare*.

1614 SELDEN *Titles Hon.* 384 Neither do I see any Ciuilian able to extricat it enough cleanly. **1677** HALE *Prim. Orig. Man.* I. i. 40 This..extricateth that Question which hath so troubled the World. **1678** CUDWORTH *Intell. Syst.* 350 Thou extricatest the involved threds of Fate. **1684** RAY *Corr.* (1848) 139 Extricating what is perplex and entangled. **1849-50** ALISON *Hist. Europe* III. xvii. §14. 496 Some method of extricating public affairs.

2. To disentangle (a person or thing); to disengage, set free *from, out of* (anything that entangles, a state of confinement, difficulty, or entanglement).

a **1631** DONNE in *Select.* (1840) 181 If we search farther into these points than the Scripture hath opened us a way, how shall we hope to..extricate ourselues? **1654** *True State Commw.* 24 The sense of law could neuer have been extricated out of endless intanglements. **1665** R. HOOKE *Micrographia* 37 All the Springs of the several parts.. immediately extricate themselves and fly asunder every way. *a* **1732** T. BOSTON *Crook in Lot* (1805) 12 A thicket, out of which he knows not how to extricate himself. **1794** SULLIVAN *View Nat.* V. 388 Extricate yourselves from prejudice. **1863** FR. A. KEMBLE *Resid. Georgia* 46 Having at length extricated myself from the group. **1866** OWEN *Anat. Vertebrates* I. xii. §120. 635 The rest [of the development of the embryo] is completed and the young extricated in..two months. **1870** DISRAELI *Lothair* vii, Lothair had promised to extricate his friend from his overwhelming difficulties.

b. *Chem.* To liberate, disengage (gas, etc.) from a state of combination.

1790 KEIR in *Phil. Trans.* LXXX. 365 The quantity of nitrous gas extricated during this action on the tin. **1838** T. THOMSON *Chem. Org. Bodies* 19 The atom of water may be extricated from the acid. **1875** *Ure's Dict. Arts* III. 557 The carbonic acid and other offensive gases..extricated.

Hence '**extricated** *ppl. a.*

1657 REEVE *God's Plea* 29 If man which is but an implicated and mixt Agent, how much more God [may lord it], who is an extricated and free Agent?

extrication (ɛkstrɪ'keɪʃən). [n. of action f. L. *extrīcāre*: see prec. and -ATION.]

1. The action of extricating or disentangling; disentanglement from an involved situation, from difficulty or perplexity.

1650 B. *Discolliminium* 45, I shall be allowed the full benefit of all the..extrications..that I..can devise. **1750** JOHNSON *Rambler* No. 62 ¶3 Too..embarrassed to think much on any thing but the means of extrication. **1854** BRIGHT *Sp.* (1876) 275 A people whose extrication from ignorance and poverty can only be hoped for from the continuance of peace. **1854** H. ROGERS *Ess.* (1860) II. 27 Immense is the difficulty attending the clear extrication and expression of truth in intellectual philosophy. **1856** KANE *Arct. Expl.* I. xxvii. 361, I owed my extrication..to a team-dog.

b. Escape from the egg; hatching.

1797 BEWICK *Brit. Birds* (1847) I. 331 Young Turkies, after their Extrication from the shell, are very tender. **1866** OWEN *Anat. Vertebrates* I. xii. §119. 623 After extrication, the tadpole rapidly grows.

2. *Chem.* The action or process of setting free (an element, gas, etc.) from something containing it; = EVOLUTION 3. Now *rare*.

a **1691** BOYLE *Producibleness Spirits* II. iii, We may suppose it [acid spirit] to have been made rather by transmutation than extrication. **1790** KEIR in *Phil. Trans.* LXXX. 365 No extrication of gas appeared until [etc.]. **1800** HENRY *Epit. Chem.* (1808) 144 Heat and vapour.. accompanied..with an extrication of light. **1811** ABERNETHY *Surg. Wks.* I. 39 The extrication of inflammable air. **1856** W. A. MILLER *Elem. Chem.* II. ii. §286 Chemical action attended with extrication of light and heat.

extrinsic (ɛk'strɪnsɪk), *a.* Forms: 6 **extrynsyke**, 7 **extrinsique**, 7-8 **extrinsick(e**, 7- **extrinsic**. [ad. F. *extrinsèque*, ad. late L. *extrinsec-us*, adj. f. L. *extrinsecus* adv. 'outwardly', f. *exter* outside + *-in* suffix of locality + *secus* prep. 'beside', used as a suffix = Eng. *-side*, f. root of *sequ-ī* to follow; cf. *altrinsecus*, *intrinsecus*, *utrinsecus*. The ending has been assimilated to the suffix -IC.] Outward; opposed to *intrinsic*.

†**1. a.** Situated on the outside; exterior. *Obs. rare*.

1541 R. COPLAND *Guydon's Quest. Chirurg.*, One [skin] is extrynsyke or outforth.

b. Pertaining to the outside; external.

1750 JOHNSON *Rambler* No. 58 ¶6 She disguises life in extrinsic ornaments. **1805** WORDSW. *Prelude* XIII. Wks. (1888) 327 Extrinsic differences, the outward marks Whereby society has parted man From man. **1824** DIBDIN *Libr. Comp.* 765 The notes are worthy of its extrinsic splendour.

†**c.** *absol.* (quasi-*sb.*). The external signs. *Obs.*

a **1797** H. WALPOLE *Mem. Geo. II* (1847) III. iii. 49 He missed that affection..which his virtues..deserved; for he wanted the extrinsic of merit.

2. a. Pertaining to an object in its external relations. Now *rare*.

a **1617** BAYNE *On Eph.* (1658) 19 Christ in regard of his extrinsick nature is the Son of God. **1640** G. WATTS tr. *Bacon's Adv. Learn.* III. iv. 145 Astronomy exhibiteth the extrinsique Parts of Celestial Bodies, (namely the Number, Situation, Motion, and Periods of the starres). **1801** KNOX in *Knox & Jebb's Corr.* (1834) I. 18 To explain these, and similar passages, as if they referred, rather to a relative and extrinsic, than..a real and internal change. **1867** DRAPER *Amer. Civ. War* III. 487 The Confederates suggested.. entering conjointly on some scheme of extrinsic policy.

b. *Anat.*

1871 DARWIN *Desc. Man* I. i. 20 The extrinsic muscles which serve to move the whole external ear. **1884** *Syd. Soc. Lex.*, *Extrinsic limb-muscles*, those muscles which are attached in part to the trunk and in part to the limbs.

3. a. Lying outside, not included in, or forming part of, the object under consideration. Const. *to*, rarely †*from*.

1666 SOUTH *Serm. Tit.* ii. 15 (1715) I. 181 Any.. Discourse extrinsick to the Subject Matter and Design of the Text. **1678** R. BARCLAY *Apol. Quakers* xiii. §4. 456 Things extrinsick from, and unnecessary to, the main matter. **1715** CHEYNE *Philos. Princ. Relig.* I. 144 A Principle quite extrinsick to Matter. **1818** HALLAM *Mid. Ages* (1872) III. 428 The reality of universal ideas, considered as extrinsic to the human mind. **1861** W. BELL *Dict. Law Scot.* 376/1 *Extrinsic*... Applied to evidence..beyond that afforded by the deed or document under consideration. *a* **1866** J. GROTE *Eth. Fragm.* ii. (1876) 36 Authority emanating from the public and extrinsic to the individual.

b. Of a cause or influence: Operating from without, external, extraneous.

1613 SHERLEY *Trav. Persia* 52 The King began to thinke himselfe..established..both from intrinsicke and extrinsicke dangers. **1699** BURNET *39 Art.* i. (1700) 26 God is..just..not by an extrinsick Necessity..but by an Intrinsick Necessity. **1819** W. LAWRENCE *Comp. Anat.* (1822) 73 Some extrinsic aid. **1878** FOSTER *Phys.* III. i 394 A superficial cell which alone is subject to extrinsic stimuli.

c. ***extrinsic factor*** (or ***element***), vitamin B_{12}: so called because, before its identity with vitamin B_{12} was established, an anti-anæmia factor was known which could be supplied extrinsically, i.e. in the diet, but which was ineffective in the absence of an 'intrinsic factor' secreted by the stomach.

1930 *Amer. Jrnl. Med. Sci.* CLXXX. 306 The process freely permits an interaction between a factor present in the normal gastric juice, which may thus be termed intrinsic, and a factor contained in the beef muscle, which is thus an extrinsic element. **1944** *Science* 28 July 82/1 Extrinsic factor can be partially or completely removed from crude casein by repeated precipitation or by extraction with dilute acid or with alcohol. **1970** W. S. HOFFMAN *Biochem. Clin. Med.* (ed. 4) xi. 508 The extrinsic factor..is now regarded as identical with vitamin B_{12}.

4. a. Due to external circumstances; not inherent or essential; accessory, adventitious.

1622 MALYNES *Anc. Law-Merch.* 415 The true value of moneys, according to their intrinsicke weight and finenesse, and their extrinsicke valuation. **1675** WILKINS *Nat. Relig.* II. vi. 364 The Royal stamp upon any..Metal may be sufficient to give it an extrinsick value..but it cannot give an intrinsick value. **1725** WATTS *Logic* I. ii. §4 Extrinsic modes are such as arise from something that is not the subject or substance itself. **1750** JOHNSON *Rambler* No. 60 ¶12 Not to be known from one another but by extrinsic and casual circumstances. **1822** HAZLITT *Table-t.* II. v. 105 Without any extrinsic advantages of birth. **1875** STUBBS *Const. Hist.* III. xxi. 612 The ages in which they would work..with fewer extrinsic incumbrances.

†**b.** Pertaining to what is adventitious. *Obs.*

1680 MORDEN *Geog. Rect.* (1685) 261 The outward Form or Character of the Prince or State [is observable] for the extrinsick Knowledg of Money.

extrinsical (ɛk'strɪnsɪkəl), *a.* and *sb.* Now *rare*. Forms: 6-9 **extrinsecal(l**, 6-7 **extrinsicall**, 7-9 **extrinsical**. [f. as prec. + -AL[1].]

A. *adj.*

1. = EXTRINSIC 1.

1594 BLUNDEVIL *Exerc.* III. I. ix. 292 These two circles having respect to a materiall Spheare, are said to be extrinsicall or outward. **1609** DOULAND *Ornith. Microl.* 44 Extrinsicall [signes] are those..which doe outwardly present themselues. **1645** RUTHERFORD *Tryal & Tri. Faith* (1845) 63 There is carnosity on the ear-drum. This is extrinsical.

b. = EXTRINSIC 1 b.

1580 G. HARVEY *3 Proper Lett.* 14 That..skill I have in extrinsicall & Intrinsecall physiognomie.

2. = EXTRINSIC 2.

1608 D. T. *Ess. Pol. & Mor.* 55 Due consideration must be had of those things..though of themselves, and without extrinsecall relation, they be never so laudable. **1693** LEIGHTON *Comm. 1 Pet.* (1850) I. 24 This our adoption is not a mere extrinsical denomination, as is adoption amongst men.

3. = EXTRINSIC 3.

1641 WILKINS *Math. Magick* II. i (1648) 146 Something which is extrinsecall unto their own frame. **1651** W. G. tr. *Cowel's Inst.* 193 The condition..that the Rent shall be paid in any extrinsecall place. *a* **1797** BURKE *Hints Ess. Drama* Wks. 1812 V. 425 The other [the order of things] is as it were foreign and extrinsecal. **1870** LOWELL *Among my Bks.* Ser. I. 84 Shakespeare..projected himself in his own creations; but those creations never became..so objective, or, as they used to say, extrinsical, to him, so as [etc.].

b. = EXTRINSIC 3 b.

1578 BANISTER *Hist. Man* I. 24 Safetie..from outward, and extrinsecall anoyaunce. **1604** T. WRIGHT *Passions* I. i. 4 Diverse other extrinsecall causes of diseases. **1644** DIGBY *Nat. Bodies* x. (1658) 94 The motion of every body followeth the percussion of extrinsecal Agents. **1718** J. CHAMBERLAYNE *Relig. Philos.* (1730) II. xxii. §36 Some other extrinsical Impediment. **1754** EDWARDS *Freed. Will* III. i. 138 One of our Fellow Creatures who did us Good.. from meer Compulsion, or extrinsecal Necessity.

4. = EXTRINSIC 4.

1593 NASHE *Four Lett. Confut.* 62 Of such extrinsecall things..would I not willingly vaunt. **1649** JER. TAYLOR *Gt. Exemp.* II. xi. 154 All else that is to be considered concerning prayer is extrinsecall, and accidentall to it. **1690** BOYLE *Chr. Virtuoso* I. 94 One Circumstance..may seem more Extrinsecal than those hitherto mentioned.

†**B.** *sb.* Something that is extrinsic.

1622-62 HEYLIN *Cosmogr.* I. (1682) 257 These extrinsecals of Religion. **1659** —— *Animadv.* in *Fuller's Appeal* (1840) 319 The first..is a mere extrinsecal.

extrinsicality (ɛkstrɪnsɪ'kælɪtɪ). [f. prec. + -ITY.] The state of being extrinsical.

1852 in ROGET *Thesaurus* 6. **1860** in WORCESTER; and in later Dicts.

extrinsically (ɛk'strɪnsɪkəlɪ), *adv.* [f. as prec. + -LY[2].] In an extrinsic manner; †on the exterior; †in outward behaviour; with respect to outward qualities or external relations; so as to be outside or distinct from the object under consideration; from an external source, by external influence; unessentially, adventitiously.

1584 R. SCOT *Disc. Witchcr.* IV. iv. 61 They [witches] hurt extrinsecallie with images, hearbs, &c. **1613** J. SALKELD *Treat. Angels* 39 An Angell is said to assume a body, because hee is onely extrinsecally united unto it. **1647** H. MORE *Song of Soul* I. Pref., He will extrinsecally shape..his actions according to that outward Rule. **1659** B. HARRIS *Parival's Iron Age* 148 The Princes..lamented him extrinsecally; but were..glad enough, to be rid of such a Conquerour. **1668** CULPEPPER & COLE *Barthol. Anat.* I. xi. 26 According to the Longitude of the Colon, there are extrinsecally observed certain fat Appendices. **1675** M. CLIFFORD *Hum. Reason* in *Phenix* (1708) II. 545 A Vision or Revelation extrinsecally coming into their Souls. **1855** H. SPENCER *Princ. Psychol.* (1872) II. VII. iii. 320 Time..is extrinsically connoted. **1858** GLADSTONE *Homer* II. ii. 167 The idea of spiritual danger to man through guile tempting him extrinsically but inwardly, entirely disappears.

extrinsicalness (ɛk'strɪnsɪkəlnɪs). [f. as prec. + -NESS.] The state of being extrinsical.

1727-36 in BAILEY; and in modern Dicts.

†**ex'trinsicate**, *a. Obs. rare*[−1]. In 6 -secate. [f. L. *extrinsec-us* (see EXTRINSIC) + -ATE[4].] = EXTRINSIC 2.

1600 *Dr. Dodypoll* II. iii. in Bullen *O. Pl.* (1884) III. 122 Dreames..Which nature doth not forme of her owne power But are extrinsecate.

extrinsicate (ɛk'strɪnsɪkeɪt), *v. rare.* Also 7 **extrinsecate**. [f. as prec. + -ATE[3].] *trans.* To exhibit outwardly; to express.

1645 *City Alarum* 19 To extrinsecate my selfe more plainely, this opinion is spawned by ignorance of our condition. **1887** WORKMAN tr. *Bianchi's Disord. Lang.* in *Alien. & Neurol.* VIII. 219 The idea cannot be extrinsicated either in spoken words or in writing.

extrinsicism (ɛk'strɪnsɪsɪz(ə)m). Also **extrinsecism**. [f. EXTRINSIC *a.* + -ISM.] A state or embodiment of extrinsicality. So **ex'trinsicist** *a.*

1934 *Downside Rev.* LII. 189 To defend the traditional conception of theological science against the accusations of 'extrinsecism' and 'theologism'. **1935** O. F. CLARKE tr. *Berdyaev's Freedom & Spirit* i. 29 The empirical personality ..finds itself condemned to a divided existence. Thus spirit is always in such circumstances an 'extrinsicism'. **1967** C. DAVIS *Question of Conscience* III. iv. 210 The modern historical approach to truth can best be seen in contrast to its opposite extreme. This is extrinsicism. *Ibid.*, The extrinsicist view of truth holds that objective truth..exists already out there, outside history in some unchanging realm.

extro-, a quasi-Lat. prefix, with the sense 'outwards', an alteration of L. *extrā* outside, after the analogy of L. *intrō* inwards, compared with *intrā* inside; cf. also L. *contrō-* (see CONTROVERT). It occurs only in words formed after the model of, and by way of antithesis to, similar compounds of *intro-*.

extroduction (ɛkstrəʊ'dʌkʃən). [f. EXTRO- *pref.* + L. *ductiōn-em* drawing, leading; cf.

introduction.] 'A drawing out or extraction' (*Syd. Soc. Lex.* 1884).

extroitive (ɛk'strəʊɪtɪv), *a. rare.* [f. EXTRO- *pref.* + L. *it-* ppl. stem of *īre* to go + -IVE; cf. *introitive.*] Directed to external objects.

1834 COLERIDGE *Lit. Rem.* (1836) II. 111 Women..feel less proportionate abhorrence of moral evil in and for itself, and more of its outward consequences..their natures being al-most wholly extroitive.

† **extro'mission.** *Obs. rare*⁻¹. [n. of action f. as next; cf. *intromission.*] The action of sending out or forth.

1622 STILLINGFL. *Orig. Sacr.* III. ii. §2 (ed. 3) 424 Not by an extromission of rays of Knowledge but by an intromission of [etc.].

† **extro'mit,** *v. Obs.* [f. EXTRO- + L. *mitt-ĕre* to send.] *trans.* To send or throw out.

*a***1711** KEN *Hymnotheo* Poet. Wks. 1721 III. 36 Satan with Looks, which extromitted Spite. *Ibid.* 267 Eyes.. extromitting lustful Flame.

extrophy, var. of EXSTROPHY.

extropical (ɛk'strɒpɪkəl), *a.* [f. EX- *pref.* + TROPIC + -AL¹.] = *extra-tropical*: see EXTRA-.

1860 MAURY *Phys. Geog. Sea* iii. §169 In the ex-tropical regions of the South.

extrorsal (ɛk'strɔːsəl), *a. Bot.* [f. next + -AL¹.] = next.

1842 in BRANDE, **1846** in WORCESTER.

extrorse (ɛk'strɔːs), *a. Bot.* [a. F. *extrorse*, f. L. *extrors-us* in an outward direction, f. *extrā* adv. (see EXTRA) + *versus* towards.] (See quots.)

1858 GRAY *Bot. Text-bk.* v. §6. 282 When the anther looks away from the pistils and towards the petals..it is said to be extrorse, or turned outwards. **1870** BENTLEY *Bot.* 239 The anther is said to be extrorse. **1882** VINES *Sachs' Bot.* 557 The anthers open inwards towards the gynæceum (introrse), or outwards (extrorse).

extrorsely (ɛk'strɔːslɪ), *adv. Bot. rare*⁻¹. [f. prec. + -LY².] In an extrorse manner.

1870 HOOKER *Stud. Flora* 241 Gentiana..anthers dehiscing extrorsely.

extrospective (ɛkstrə'spɛktɪv), *a.* [f. EXTRO- + *-spective* as in INTROSPECTIVE *a.*] Not introspective; regarding external objects rather than one's own thoughts and feelings. Cf. EXTRASPECTIVE *a.* 2.

1909 *Mind* XVIII. 317 Description or appreciation is based upon..external indications (extrospective psychology). **1925** J. E. TURNER *Theory Direct Realism* v. 51 It [*sc.* the inherence of existence] is offered as an accurate description of consciousness, confirmed both by psychological observation, intro- and extro-spective, and the logical exclusion of any alternative.

extroversion (ɛkstrəʊ'vɜːʃən). [n. of action f. as next; cf. *introversion*. Mod.F. has *extroversion* in sense 2: see EXTRAVERSION.] The action of turning, or the condition of being turned, outwards.

† **1.** In the language of mysticism (see quots.).

1656–81 BLOUNT *Glossogr.*, *Extroversion*..in mystical Divinity..a scattering or distracting one's thoughts upon exterior objects. **1788** WESLEY *Wks.* (1872) VI. 451 The turning of the eye of the mind from him [Christ] to outward things they [the Mystics] call Extroversion.

2. *Path.* The condition of being turned inside out; *esp.* applied to a malformation of the bladder; = EXSTROPHY.

1836 TODD *Cycl. Anat.* I. 391/1 In extroversion of the bladder the anterior part of this organ is more or less completely wanting.

3. *Psychol.* The fact or tendency of having one's interests directed exclusively or predominantly towards things outside the self; the turning outwards of the libido; opp. INTROVERSION. Cf. EXTRAVERSION 2. Hence **extro'versive** *a.*, characterized by or given to extroversion.

1920 A. G. TANSLEY *New Psychol.* IV. viii. 88 Extroversion is the thrusting out of the mind on to life, the use of the mind in practical affairs, the pouring out of the libido on external objects. **1923** *Westm. Gaz.* 21 Mar. 12/3 Every individual possesses both introversive and extroversive mechanisms. **1932** *Brit. Jrnl. Psychol.* Apr. 300 Rorschach..distinguishes two types, the 'introversive' and the 'extroversive'. They are to all intents and purposes the same as Jung's types. **1951** M. MCLUHAN *Mech. Bride* 90/1 Mussolini..was all for this Marinetti extroversion of the self and fusion with the activity of the machine. **1959** *Times Lit. Suppl.* 16 Jan. 29/2 A dissatisfaction with life which is notable in some other panoramas of the time which maintain the virtues of extroversion.

extrovert (ɛkstrəʊ'vɜːt), *v. rare.* [f. EXTRO- *pref.* + L. *vert-ĕre* to turn. Cf. *introvert*: see EXTRAVERT.] *trans.* To turn or thrust outwards (a material object); to give an outward direction to (thought).

1671 J. WEBSTER *Metallogr.* xii. 197 The external and combustible Sulphur..is..protruded and extroverted. **1804** KNOX & JEBB *Corr.* I. 102 Every idea that could, even by possibility, extrovert the thought.

extrovert ('ɛkstrəvɜːt), *sb.* (and *a.*) *Psychol.* [var. EXTRAVERT *sb.* after INTROVERT: see EXTRO-.] A person given to or characterized by extroversion; a sociable or unreserved person; also *transf.* Also *attrib.* or as *adj.* So **'extroverted** *ppl. a.*, **'extrovertish** *a.* = EXTROVERSIVE *a.*

1918 P. BLANCHARD in *Amer. Jrnl. Psychol.* Apr. 163 Jung's hypothesis of the two psychological types, the introvert and extrovert,—the thinking type and the feeling type. **1920** *Times Lit. Suppl.* 1 Apr. 205/4 The external always throws him [*sc.* George Herbert] back into himself, and then his thoughts turn outwards for confirmation... He is, in the language of modern psychology, both introvert and extrovert, yet never an egotist. **1920** *Challenge* 21 May 44/2 An extrovert soldier faced with the problem of escape from war conditions. **1923** *Westm. Gaz.* 21 Mar., Any one of these will display either the introverted or the extroverted attitude. **1925** C. FOX *Educat. Psychol.* 254 The first is called the extroverted type, because in the main he goes outside himself to the object. **1926** W. MCDOUGALL *Outl. Abnormal Psychol.* 440 The characteristic neurosis of the extrovert is hysteria, while that of the introvert is neurasthenia or psychasthenia. **1946** W. S. KNICKERBOCKER *20th Cent. Eng.* 388 Prufrock is the antithetical brother of Eliot's Sweeney, whose extrovertish animalism functions equally without benefit of an ethic. **1957** *Times Lit. Suppl.* 20 Dec. 774/1 Practical and shrewd, irascible and extrovert, he dominated the college from 1792 to 1834. **1958** P. TANNER in P. Gammond *Decca Bk. Jazz* xi. 138 It is also a happy extroverted music, making up in warmth what it may often lack in subtlety. **1968** *Autocar* 25 Jan. 8/1 Certainly not a budget car, this..is already gaining a name as a noisy, successful little extrovert.

extruct, -ion, -ive, -or: see EXSTRUCT, etc.

extrude (ɛk'struːd), *v.* [ad. L. *extrūd-ĕre*, f. *ex-* out + *trūdĕre* to thrust.]

1. *trans.* To thrust (a person) out or forth; to urge or force out; to expel. Const. *from*, †*out of*, and †with double obj. by omission of *from*.

a. with obj. a person.

1570 LEVINS *Manip.* 183 To Extrude, *extrudere*. **1586** WARNER *Alb. Eng.* IV. xxiii. (1612) 110 Let not a Traytors periured Sonne extrude us from our right. **1601** B. JONSON *Poetaster* III. i, Say he should extrude me his house to-day. **1621** G. SANDYS *Ovid's Met.* IV. (1626) 72 Others, that all is possible, conclude, To true-styl'd Gods: but, Bacchus they extrude. **1795** WYTHE *Decis. Virginia* 49 From which any man with a military warrant might extrude the proprietor. **1837** CARLYLE *Fr. Rev.* v. ii, Your Third Estate shall suddenly see itself extruded from its Hall.

b. with obj. a material thing; in mod. use *esp.* to exclude (an embryo, ova, etc.). Also occas. with sense 'to protrude out'.

1566 PAINTER *Pal. Pleas.* I. 78 The like also some do attempt by deuises and subtile secretes to extrude theyr conceptions. **1615** G. SANDYS *Trav.* 120 The Riuer.. bringing down earth with his deluges, and extruding the sea by little and little. **1676** *Phil. Trans.* XI. 770 The bloud from the heart..is again extruded. **1726** *Ibid.* LXXVI. 161 The animal..easily contrives to extrude itself. **1836** TODD *Cycl. Anat.* I. 700/2 The number of eggs extruded by each individual is very great. **1848** CLOUGH *Amours de Voy.* III. 91 Ye..extrude from the ocean your helpless faces. **1870** ROLLESTON *Anim. Life* Introd. 47 The embryos are extruded from the uterine cavities.

c. with an immaterial thing as obj.

1598 YONG *Diana* 137 All hate shall be extruded. **1629** T. HAWKINS *Elegy* in *Sir J. Beaumont's Bosworth F.* 7 Loose Humous vent, and Ballad-Line extrude. *a***1745** SWIFT *Char. P—te M—h*, Wit..was extruded from his head to make room for other men's thoughts. **1856** FABER *Creator & Creature* I. i. (1886) 8 The idea of God..is..extruded..by the press of matter. **1869** M. ARNOLD *Cult. & An.* (1882) p. xxxii, Presbyterianism was only extruded gradually.

d. To shape (metals, plastics, etc.) by forcing them through dies.

1913 *Lockwood's Dict. Mech. Engin.* (ed. 4) 435 *Extruded metal*, malleable alloys of copper and other metals which, when heated are forced through dies into various sectional forms. **1923** GLAZEBROOK *Dict. Appl. Physics* V. 427/1 It is ..possible to extrude alloys which it is extremely difficult.. to roll. **1958** *Engineering* 31 Jan. 133/1 It is made of five-ply with an extruded aluminium framework.

2. *intr.* for *refl.* To protrude out. *rare.*

1852 DANA *Crust.* I. 670 It may be made to extrude by a little pressure. **1865** 'UMBRA' *Trav.* 18 The great fount, the basin of which..extrudes like a large boil from the plain.

Hence **ex'truded** *ppl. a.*, **ex'truding** *vbl. sb.*

1687 *Assur. Abb. Lands* 43 The Canons of the Church.. were no ways questioned by the extruded. *a***1761** LAW tr. *Behmen's Myst. Magnum* xvii. (1772) 71 In the Stead and Place of extruded Lucifer. **1875** BUCKLAND *Log-bk.* 110 With open mouth and extruded tongue. **1881** BLACKIE *Lay Serm.* i. 55 An extruded cat moans woefully. **1930** *Engineering* 21 Feb. 252/2 In such operations as embossing, extruding. **1957** *Encycl. Brit.* XIX. 610/1 Tubing machines, or extruding machines, are devices for forcing continuous strips of rubber from a die.

extruder (ɛk'struːdə(r)). [f. EXTRUDE *v.* + -ER¹.]

1. A machine that extrudes (see prec.).

1959 *Times* (Suppl. Rubber Industry) 27 Apr. p. iv/6 Extruders can be of all sizes up to 15 in. in diameter. **1960** H. POWELL *Beginner's Bk. Pottery* II. 63 *Extruder*, a pressing machine for making clay coils. These may be made also by fitting an extruder on to a pug-mill. **1965** *New Scientist* 12 Aug. 385/1 The engineer has improved his extruders (the machines which make the pipe).

2. *Typogr.* (See quot. 1960.)

1938 D. MEGAW in *Typography* VII. 28/2 Normal stem projection (*i.e.*, the 'extrusion' of ascender and descenders) is a little more than half the body... Recognizability is aided by the slight differentiation caused by the recurrent shapes of a narrower set (this is where 'extruders' come in). **1960** G. A. GLAISTER *Gloss. Bk.* 128/2 *Extruders*, the collective term for ascenders and descenders. **1964** P. A. D. MACCARTHY in D. Abercrombie et al. *Daniel Jones* 169 English in present roman has a proportion..of about 40% extruders.

ex'trumpery, *adv.* Also 6 **extrumpere.** [A humorous perversion of EXTEMPORE *adv.*] = EXTEMPORE *adv.*, with allusion to TRUMPERY.

1583 STANYHURST *Æneis* Ded. (Arb.) 8 Certeyn pild verses clowted vp extrumpere. **1589** NASHE *M.'s Months minde* 14 Such praiers only as themselues make Ex trumperie.

extrusile (ɛk'struːsɪl), *a. rare.* [f. L. *extrūs-* ppl. stem of *extrūdĕre* (see EXTRUDE) + -ILE.] Capable of being thrust forth.

1849 JOHNSTON in *Proc. Berw. Nat. Club* II. 364 The apex is..furnished with a very long extrusile..stylette.

extrusion (ɛk'struːʒən). Also 6 **extrution.** [f. as if ad. L. **extrūsiōn-em*, n. of action f. *extrūdĕre*: see EXTRUDE.] The action of extruding or thrusting out; the fact of being extruded.

1. In physical sense: **a.** The action of pushing out; expulsion by mechanical force. **b.** Protrusion from within an envelope; the putting forth (*e.g.* of a bud or branch, an eruption, etc.).

1638 W. R[AWLEY] tr. *Bacon's Life & Death* 84 In all Alimentation, or Nourishment, there is a two-fold Action; Extrusion, and Attraction. **1684** T. BURNET *Th. Earth* I. 30 A violent depression of some parts of the earth, and an extrusion and elevation of others. **1839** MURCHISON *Silur. Syst.* I. xxxii. 436 This extrusion had been brought about by a succession of small upcasts. **1875** H. C. WOOD *Therap.* (1879) 66 The extrusion of white blood-cells in the frog's mesentery.

c. The pressing of metals, plastics, etc., into the required shape by extruding them through dies; also, the article so extruded (see EXTRUDE *v.* 1 d). Also *attrib.*, esp. in ***extrusion press.***

1921 *Chem. Abstr.* 3967 Details as to the app. used and the method of extrusion are given. In complete extrusions the rod produced was sound from end to end. **1937** *Archit. Rev.* LXXXI. 267/3 Aluminium alloy extrusions are used for casement sections, door frames, etc. **1940** *New Statesman* 16 Mar. 360/1 Extrusion of metal is the same, in principle, as squirting tooth-paste or spaghetti, or, better still, macaroni. *Ibid.*, An extrusion press can make bars with curved cross-sections and bars containing longitudinal holes. **1962** M. G. SAY *Newnes Conc. Encycl. Electr. Engin.* 104/1 The sheath is applied [to an electric cable] through a point and die by means of a ram or continuous extrusion lead-sheathing press. **1964** M. GOWING *Britain & Atomic Energy 1939–1945* xii. 338 New premises..must be provided for the extrusion work on the rods.

2. Expulsion by violent or rigorous measures from an abode, place, position of privilege, etc.

1540 WYATT *Let. to Cromwell* Wks. 1816 II. 394 The treaties shall be followed to the extrusion from all their dominions. **1593** *Tell-Trothe's N.Y. Gift* 37 An vnkind extrution..of her out of dores. **1650** R. HOLLINGWORTH *Exerc. conc. Usurped Powers* 11 Meer forcible extrusion deprives not any lawfull Magistrate of his right. **1736** S. SLEECH in *Lett. Lit. Men* (Camden) 365 An unjust.. Extrusion from his College. **1780** JOHNSON *L.P.*, *Congreve* Wks. III. 163 Upon the extrusion of the Whigs, some intercession was used lest Congreve should be displaced. **1875** MERIVALE *Gen. Hist. Rome* lxxix. (1877) 675 The extrusion of the people from the interior of the city. **1885** *Manch. Exam.* 10 Mar. 5/2 The extrusion of the hereditary principle.

extrusive (ɛk'struːsɪv), *a.* [f. L. *extrūs-* ppl. stem of *extrūdĕre* to EXTRUDE + -IVE.]

a. Tending to extrude or thrust outwards. **b.** Resulting from or characterized by extrusion. **c.** Capable of being protruded.

1816 KEATINGE *Trav.* (1817) II. 24 These hills are not.. the extrusive edges of strata, but rather elevated table land. **1848** JOHNSTON in *Proc. Berw. Nat. Club* II. 307 The shafts are extrusive, being pushed out like a telescope. **1886** PROCTOR in *19th Cent.* May 693 The immense extrusive power of the volcanoes of the tertiary era.

extrusory (ɛk'struːsərɪ), *a.* [f. as prec. + -ORY.] That extrudes or thrusts out.

In some mod. Dicts.

extry, colloq. and dial. (chiefly *U.S.*) var. EXTRA *a.*, *adv.*, and *sb.* (Cf. quot. 1897 s.v. EXTRA-SPECIAL *a.*)

1861 O. W. HOLMES *Elsie V.* viii. 100 When we git crowded jest at the end of a term, or when there is an extry number of p'oopils. **1894** J. W. RILEY *Armazindy* 10 Extry waste o' sympathy. **1895** H. W. NEVINSON *Neighbours of Ours* iii. 51, I was sailin' for a good firm and was makin' from thirty shillin' to two pound reg'lar, and at whiles five bob extry. **1911** W. OWEN *Let.* 12 Dec. (1967) 102 Take something 'extry' (as Mrs. Lott would say) in the way of nourishment. **1934** C. CARMER *Stars fell on Alabama* i. 45 On account of havin' had a *little* more experience and playin' *extry* good, Old Man Ventress gets the five-dollar gold piece.

† **extuberance** (ɛk'stjuːbərəns). ? *Obs.* [f. EXTUBERANT: see -ANCE.] **a.** The quality or condition of being extuberant. **b.** *concr.* Something that swells out or up; a swelling, projection, protuberance. *lit.* and *fig.* Also *collect.* in *sing.*

1607 WALKINGTON *Opt. Glass* 122 The internall hollowes of the extuberances of our artery. **1616** CHAPMAN *Homer's Hymns* Epil., All is extuberance and excretion all, That you your ornaments and glories call. **1786** *Phil. Trans.* LXXVI. 9 The least degree of extuberance in the surface of the metal. **1802** PALEY *Nat. Theol.* viii. §2 (1819) 104 The concave recess of the bone formed by the extuberances on each side.

†**ex'tuberancy.** *Obs.* [f. EXTUBERANT: see -ANCY.] = prec.

1634 T. JOHNSON tr. *Parey's Chirurg.* v. vii. (1678) 111 On each side they have an extuberancy. **1646** J. GREGORY *Notes & Obs.* (1650) 114 [The dry land appeared] not..so precisely globous as before, But recompenced with an extuberancy of Hils and Mountaines. **1703** MOXON *Mech. Exerc.* 183 Take off the Irregularities or Extuberancies.

extuberant (ɛk'stju:bərənt), *a.* Now *rare.* [ad. L. *extūberant-em*, pr. pple. of *extūberāre* to swell out, f. *ex-* out + *tūber* a swelling.] Swelling or standing out, protuberant.

1578 BANISTER *Hist. Man* v. 70 The Orifices [of the ventricle] towardes the interiour partes, obtaine a swelled, or more extuberant part like a circle. **1654** GAYTON *Pleas. Notes* IV. viii. 223 Shaking her extuberant and reverst lips. **1703** MOXON *Mech. Exerc.* 216 Scrapes off the extuberant Mettle. **1793** SMEATON *Edystone L.* §197 A substance.. which..in time becomes so extuberant as to deform the face of the walls. **1819** in TODD; and in mod. Dicts.

†**ex'tuberate,** *v. Obs. rare.* [f. L. *extūberāt-* ppl. stem of *extūberāre* (see prec.).] **a.** *intr.* To swell out or up. **b.** *trans.* 'To make to swell' (Blount *Glossogr.*).

1623-6 COCKERAM, *Extuberate*, to swell like the sea. **1658** ROWLAND *Moufet's Theat. Ins.* 976 Two cornicles..near which the forepart of the head doth a little extuberate. **1692-1732** in COLES. **1721-1800** in BAILEY.

Hence †**ex'tuberated** *ppl. a.* Also *fig.* †**ex'tuberating** *ppl. a.*, protuberant.

1727-36 BAILEY, *Extuberated*, swelling into knobs or knots. **1634** T. JOHNSON tr. *Parey's Chirurg.* III. xi. (1678) 63 [The abdominal muscles] are situate in the eminentest or extuberating region of the belly. **1737** G. SMITH *Cur. Relat.* X. iv. 547 Rising here and there with extuberating Hills and Montains. **1768** *Life & Advent. of Sir Barth. Sapskull* II. 51 An extuberated proof of her singular affection for young Romeo.

†**extube'ration.** *Obs.* [ad. L. *extūberātiōn-em*, n. of action f. *extūberāre* (see prec.).] *concr.* Something that swells out, or up; protuberance.

1615 CROOKE *Body of Man* 752 The..same Teate-like extuberation or Mamillary processe. **1663** FARINGDON *Serm.* (1672) II. 632 Excrescences and extuberations to be lopped off and abated. **1721-1800** in BAILEY.

†**ex'tuberic,** *a. Obs.* [f. EXTUBER-ANT + -IC.] Swelling out, projecting.

1703 MOXON *Mech. Exerc.* 230 The Iron Pin..will resist the extuberick parts of the Edge of the Guide.

†**ex'tuberous,** *a. Obs.*$^{-0}$ [f. EXTUBER-ANT + -OUS.] Swelling out, protuberant. Hence †**ex'tuberousness.**

1706 PHILLIPS (ed. Kersey) *Extuberous*, swelling forth or bunching out. **1721-1800** in BAILEY. **1727-36** BAILEY, *Extuberousness*, the swelling or bunching out in the body. **1775** in ASH.

extue, obs. form of ESCHEW *v.*[1]

extu'mescence. [a. F. *extumescence*, f. L. *extumēscent-em*, pr. pple. of *extumēscĕre* to begin to swell out, f. *extumēre*, f. *ex-* out + *tumēre* to swell.] A swelling out or up.

1611 COTGR., *Extumescence*, an extumescence, a swelling, a rising vp. **1656-81** in BLOUNT *Glossogr.* **1721-1800** in BAILEY. **1884** in *Syd. Soc. Lex.*

†**extu'mescency.** *Obs. rare*$^{-1}$. [f. as prec.: see -ENCY.] = prec.

1684 tr. *Bonet's Merc. Compit.* VIII. 294 Lest..these Bowels should be incited to tetaneous extumescencies.

extund (ɛk'stʌnd), *v.* [f. L. *extund-ĕre*, f. *ex-* out + *tundĕre* to beat.] *trans.* To beat or hammer out; only *fig.*

1610 W. FOLKINGHAM *Art of Survey* To Rdr. 3 To extunde and beat-out this true Proportion, I obserue the Circumstances proiected. *Ibid.* II. iv. 52 Mensuration is conuersant in extunding the lineall extentions of longitudes. **1727** in BAILEY vol. II. **1890** *Pall Mall G.* 16 May 4/2 Leaders..have to be extunded sometimes in..haste.

†**ex'turb,** *v. Obs.* [ad. L. *exturb-āre*, f. *ex-* out + *turbāre* to disturb, f. *turba* tumult.] *trans.* To hustle out, get rid of.

1615 SIR G. BUCK *3rd Univ. of Eng.* xii. in Stow's *Chron.* 971/2 All these noble Tenantes and occupants were thus exturbed, dead, and gon. **1603** SIR C. HEYDON *Jud. Astrol.* xi. 241 That one point of exturbing Esau, and of his inheritance set aside.

†**ex'typal,** *a. Obs.* Variant of ECTYPAL.

1678 CUDWORTH *Intell. Syst.* I. iii. 152 Two worlds—the one archetypal, the other extypal.

exuberance (ɛg'zju:bərəns). [a. F. *exubérance*, ad. L. *exūberantia*, n. of state f. *exūberāre*: see EXUBERANT and -ANCE.]

1. The quality or condition of being exuberant; abundant productiveness; luxuriance of growth; overflowing fullness (of joy, health, etc.).

1664 EVELYN *Kal. Hort.* (1729) 192 Repress the common Exuberance of the leading and middle shoots. **1695** WOODWARD *Nat. Hist. Earth* II. (1723) 118 The primitive Exuberance of the Earth was lessen'd. **1823** SCOTT *Quentin D.* ii, A happy exuberance of animal spirits. **1827** HARE *Guesses* Ser. II. (1873) 557 A sweet guileless child, playing in the exuberance of its happiness. **1882** A. W. WARD *Dickens* iii. 58 Nothing is wanting..to attest the exuberance of its author's genius.

b. Copiousness or redundance of expression.

1717 GARTH tr. *Ovid's Met.* Pref., In his similes that exuberance is avoided. **1758** JOHNSON *Idler* No. 36 ¶6 The man of exuberance and copiousness. **1847** GROTE *Greece* (1862) III. xxix. 69 His exuberance astonishes us.

†**c.** A fault or error of excess. *Obs.*

1749 FIELDING *Tom Jones* III. v, That the different exuberances of these gentlemen, would correct their different imperfections. **1756** BURKE *Vind. Nat. Soc.* Wks. I. 30 Allowing me in my exuberance one way, for my deficiencies in the other.

d. An extravagance, excessive outburst.

1841 D'ISRAELI *Amen. Lit.* (1867) 619 His generous impulses burst into the wild exuberances of the reveries of astrology. **1875** JOWETT *Plato* (ed. 2) IV. 121 The criticism on his own doctrine..has..been considered..an exuberance of the metaphysical imagination.

2. An overflowing amount or quantity; a superabundance.

1638 W. R[AWLEY] tr. *Bacon's Life & Death* 373 Fatnesse is..an Exuberance of Nourishment, above that which is voyded by Excrement. **1768** W. GILPIN *Ess. Prints* 90 There is an exuberance of fancy in him. **1786** —— *Mts. & Lakes* I. 137 An exuberance of water. **1868** E. P. WRIGHT *Ocean World* iii. 65 An exuberance of life of which no other portion of the globe could give us any idea.

†**b.** *ellipt.* An abundance of good things, plenty. *Obs.*

1675 COCKER *Morals* 37 Exuberance is turn'd to Indigence. **1751** JOHNSON *Rambler* No. 105 ¶11 Many had great exuberance, and few confessed any want.

†**3.** *concr.* An overflow; a luxuriant outgrowth; an excrescence, protuberance. *Obs.*

1665 SIR T. HERBERT *Trav.* (1677) 120 Sulphur, or other like exuberances of Nature. **1687** J. CLAYTON *Virginia* in *Phil. Trans.* XLI. 149 Punk..the inward Part of the Excrescence or Exuberance of an Oak. **1781** JOHNSON *Lett. Mrs. Thrale* 14 Apr., Kindness must be commonly the exuberance of content. **1825** WATERTON *Wand. S. Amer.* I. i. 89 They [the rocks] appear..smooth, and their exuberances rounded off.

exuberancy (ɛg'zju:bərənsɪ). [ad. L. *exūberantia*: see prec. and -ANCY.]

1. = EXUBERANCE 1, 1 b.

1649 E. MARBURY in Spurgeon *Treas. Dav.* Ps. xviii. 1-2 Which [praise] he expresseth in this exuberancy and redundancy of holy oratory. **1650** BULWER *Anthropomet.* 179 Cosmetiques..contrived..to restrain the exuberancy of over-grown Breasts. *a* **1722** LISLE *Husb.* (1752) 277 The exuberancy of its juice will make it knotty and sticky. **1843** MARRYAT *M. Violet* xvii, The exuberancy of spirit..had deserted me.

†**2.** = EXUBERANCE 2. *Obs.*

1611 CORYAT *Crudities* 256 The marvellous affluence and exuberancy of all things tending to the sustentation of man's life. **1762** tr. *Busching's Syst. Geog.* III. 611 The levels yield an exuberancy of grain.

†**3.** *concr.* = EXUBERANCE 3. *Obs.*

a **1633** AUSTIN *Medit.* (1635) 61 It was no Meteor; no fire-drake..(Things which wise-men..know to be Exuberancies of Nature). **1655** FULLER *Ch. Hist.* II. vi. §38 And some will censure this Digression for a Struma, or tedious Exuberancy.

exuberant (ɛg'zju:bərənt), *a.* [ad. L. *exūberant-em*, pr. pple. of *exūberāre*, f. *ex-* (see EX- *pref.*[1]) + *ūberāre* to be fruitful, f. *über* fertile, connected with *ūber* udder. Cf. F. *exubérant.*]

1. Luxuriantly fertile or prolific; abundantly productive. Also *fig.*

1645 EVELYN *Diary* 29 Jan., Vines..so exuberant that.. one vine will loade 5 mules with its grapes. **1728** MORGAN *Algiers* II. v. 313 A paltry Recompense for the exuberant Rhodes. **1759** B. MARTIN *Nat. Hist. Eng.* I. 12 The Earth has been so exuberant in the Production of this Metal. **1788** W. GILPIN *Ess. Prints* 163 His fancy is exceedingly fruitful ..It is indeed too exuberant. **1854** EMERSON *Lett. & Soc. Aims, Poet. & Imag.* Wks. (Bohn) III. 168 We know Nature, and figure her exuberant..in her fertility. **1871** ROSSETTI *Jenny* Poems 109 Love's exuberant hotbed.

2. Growing luxuriantly; produced in superabundance or excess.

1513 BRADSHAW *St. Werburge* I. 607 A pure perfyte plante ..Merveylous by growynge..with dyuers proprytes, of grace exuberaunt. **1664** EVELYN *Kal. Hort., August* (1679) 22 Cleanse your vines from exuberant branches. **1796** H. HUNTER tr. *St. Pierre's Stud. Nat.* (1799) III. 583 Both.. may perish with hunger in the midst of our exuberant crops. **1848** PRICHARD *Nat. Hist. Man* 99 Races bearing an exuberant growth of hair. *a* **1862** BUCKLE *Civiliz.* (1869) III. i. 9 An exuberant and therefore a restless population.

¶ Misused for 'superfluous'.

1667 WATERHOUSE *Fire Lond.* 157 An Exuberant Servant ..is better spared, than a Charity to one of these.

3. Of a fountain, stream, etc.: Overflowing. [Cf. Virg. *Æn.* VII. 465 *exuberat amnis.*]

1678 CUDWORTH *Intell. Syst.* 595 He as it were an Exuberant Fountain, this as a Stream derived from him. **1686** GOAD *Celest. Bodies* I. xvi. 105 Even the Sextile..is found at times to usher in exuberant Flouds. **1876** BLACKIE *Songs Relig. & Life* 18 Life's exuberant sea.

4. *fig.* **a.** Of affections, joyous emotions, beneficence, vitality, health, or their manifestations: Overflowing, abounding.

1648 BOYLE *Seraph. Love* xi, Such exuberant goodness as may justly ravish us to an amazement. **1711** ADDISON *Spect.* No. 169 ¶8 Such an exuberant Love to Mankind. **1768-74** TUCKER *Lt. Nat.* (1852) II. 616 An exuberant health without any judgment to guide it, will never make either a happy or a useful man. **1828** MACAULAY *Hallam* Ess. 1854 I. 59 An age of exuberant zeal. **1863** KINGLAKE *Crimea* (1876) I. vi. 85 The English in their exuberant strength.

b. Of persons, their actions or expressions: Effusive in display of feeling. Now more usually, Abounding in health and spirits, overflowing with delight.

1503 HAWES *Examp. Virt.* vii. 131, I vnto you must be well exuberaunt. **1753** JOHNSON *Adventurer* No. 58 ¶3 Exuberant praise bestowed by others. **1815** W. H. IRELAND *Scribbleomania* 48 He has been..exuberant in his encomiums upon individuals. **1863** MISS BRADDON *Eleanor's Vict.* i, She seemed an animated..exuberant creature. **1866** MRS. CARLYLE *Lett.* III. 323 An exuberant letter from Charles Kingsley. **1874** HELPS *Soc. Press.* xxv. 395 After exuberant demonstrations to me.

c. Of diction or composition: Copious, diffuse, lavish in ornament.

1654 FULLER *Ephemeris* Pref. 6 Here may they observe the variety of eloquence in severall persons, some large, copious and exuberant. **1715** POPE *Iliad* Pref. D ij b, His Similes have been thought too exuberant, and full of Circumstances. **1863** GEO. ELIOT *Romola* III. xxxviii, Exclamations of joy and wailing, mingled with exuberant narrative.

d. Of wealth or stores: Overflowing, abundant. Of expenditure or display: Lavish, profuse.

1686 GOAD *Celest. Bodies* III. iv. 499 Our Collections are more exuberant than Stow's. **1751** JOHNSON *Rambler* No. 101 ¶4 My fortune being by no means exuberant. **1796** BURKE *Regic. Peace* Wks. 1842 II. 349 The exuberant display of wealth in our shops. **1869** LECKY *Europ. Mor.* II. i. 99 The exuberant charities of the church.

exuberantly (ɛg'zju:bərəntlɪ), *adv.* [f. prec. + -LY[2].] In an exuberant manner or degree; over-plentifully; with exuberance of growth, feeling, or language; with exuberant delight.

1650 BULWER *Anthropomet.* 181 It..sprouted out exuberantly. **1695** WOODWARD *Nat. Hist. Earth* VI. (1723) 271 The Earth was very exuberantly beset with Trees. **1781** J. MOORE *View Soc. It.* (1790) I. xxxv. 373 The valley from this town to Terni is exuberantly fertile. **1782** V. KNOX *Ess.* I. vii. 32 Those simple delights..which the poets have..no less justly than exuberantly described! **1822** BYRON *Let. to Moore* 8 Mar., It will make the man..exuberantly happy. *a* **1853** ROBERTSON *Serm.* Ser. IV. xxii. (1876) 265 Joy seems to be felt more exuberantly by men who have sinned much. **1883** *Scotsman* 12 May 8/5 The alliance..into which he and Principal Cairns entered so exuberantly.

exuberantness (ɛg'zju:bərəntnɪs). [f. as prec. + -NESS.] The state of being exuberant.

1727-36 in BAILEY. **1775** in ASH.

†**e'xuberate,** *a. Obs.* [ad. L. *exūberāt-us*, pa. pple. of *exūberāre*: see EXUBERANT.] Overflowing, superabundant.

1638 T. WHITAKER *Blood of Grape* 17 The exuberate singularity in Merchants of all nations.

exuberate (ɛg'zju:bəreɪt), *v.* 5 pa. pple. exuberate. [f. L. *exūberāt-* ppl. stem of *exūberāre*: see EXUBERANT.]

1. *intr.* To be exuberant; to abound, overflow.

1623 COCKERAM, *Exuberate*, to abound. **1648** BOYLE *Seraph. Love* (1660) 59 That vast confluence and immensity that exuberates in God. **1656** [J. SERJEANT] tr. *T. White's Peripatet. Instit.* 420 Trees are thrown by Timber-men into water, least their native moisture should exuberate into rottennesse. *a* **1672** WOOD *Life* (1848) 36 Such tow'ring ebullitions do not exuberate in my Aganippe. **1838-9** HALLAM *Hist. Lit.* IV. vii. IV. §51. 328 Scarron was endowed with vast gaiety, which generally exuberated in buffoon jests. **1851** THACKERAY *Eng. Hum.* (1853) 159 One whose.. breast exuberated with human kindness.

b. *to exuberate into*: to pass by exuberance of growth, develop *into*. *to exuberate in*: to indulge in with exuberant feeling.

1716 M. DAVIES *Athen. Brit.* III. *Dissert. Drama* 2 Two of its [*sc.* Ch. of England's] considerable Members exuberating into that of Comprehenders. **1781** JOHNSON 20 Apr. in *Boswell*, He might have exuberated into an atheist. **1887** M. B. EDWARDS *Next of Kin* I. v, She exuberated in the delicious..sense of romance.

†**2.** *trans.* In Alchemy: ? To render fruitful (mercury, the alkahest). [Cf. class. L. *exūberāre* to make fruitful.]

1471 RIPLEY *Comp. Alch.* Pref. in Ashm. (1652) 126 Our Menstrue by labour exuberate. **1654** ASHMOLE *Chym. Collect.* 77 That Earth so mingled with Menstruous Matter, is called Argent vive, Exuberated, which gather speedily, and while it is new. **1671** J. WEBSTER *Metallogr.* xii. 196 Those that know this will dismiss common Mercury from creating the Stone, or exuberating its humidity.

exuberation (ɛg,zju:bə'reɪʃən). *rare*$^{-1}$. [ad. L. *exūberātiōn-em*, n. of state f. *exūberāre*: see EXUBERANT.] Exuberance of spirits; excitement.

1889 B. WHITBY *Awak. M. Fenwick* II. x. 240 The men's exuberation escaped them in shouts..and peals of laughter.

†**e'xuberous,** *a. Obs. rare.* [f. EXUBER-ANT + -OUS.] = EXUBERANT.

1651 *Fuller's Abel Rediv., Gilpin* 361 To set forth Th' exuberous praises of brave Gilpin's worth?

exuccous, -ction, obs. ff. EXSUCCOUS, -SUCTION.

Exucontian (ɛksju:'kɒntɪən). *Eccl.* Also 9 exouc-, exukontian. [f. Eccl. Gr. ἐξουκόντι-ος (f. ἐξ out of + οὐκ not + ὄντ-ων, gen. pl. of pr. pple. of εἶναι to be) + -AN.] (See quots.)

1844 tr. *Socrates' Eccl. Hist.* II. xlv. 230 They [Arians] were also termed..Exucontians by those at Antioch who embraced the orthodox faith. **1875** *Encycl. Brit.* II. 537 [Arius said] 'He is of a substance that once was not (ἐξ οὐκ ὄντων)'—hence the name of Exoucontians sometimes given

to his followers. **1877** P. SMITH in *Dict. Chr. Biog.* s.v. *Arianism*, The Arians were also called Exukontians.

exudate ('ɛksjʊdeɪt), *sb.* [ad. L. *ex(s)ūdāt-um* (that which is) exudated; neut. pa. pple. (see next).] An exuded substance.

1876 BARTHOLOW *Mat. Med.* (1879) 61 Covered with lymph, or some exudate of a whitish color. **1903** [see AUTOLYSIS]. **1907** M. H. GORDON tr. *Abel's Labor. Handbk. Bacteriol.* 164 Pus and various pathological exudates. **1965** V. J. CHAPMAN *Coastal Veget.* iii. 68 Found mainly in coastal waters and derived from algal exudates. **1964** M. HYNES *Med. Bacteriol.* (ed. 8) xxviii. 430 The 'bacillary exudate' consists largely of polymorphs, with a few large endothelial cells... The 'amœbic exudate', on the other hand, contains few pus or tissue cells.

† '**exudate**, *v. Obs.* [f. L. *ex(s)ūdāt-* ppl. stem of *ex(s)ūdāre* to EXUDE.]

1. *intr.* = EXUDE 1.

1646 SIR T. BROWNE *Pseud. Ep.* III. iv. 113 Perforations.. through which the humor..doth exudate. **1757** A. COOPER *Distiller* III. lxiv. (1760) 261 A vegetable Juice, which.. exudated from their Roots.

2. *trans.* = EXUDE 2.

1671 *Phil. Trans.* VI. 2125 A Pole of Ivy did of it self exudate and shew a liquid and yellowish rosin from the bark. **1796** MORSE *Amer. Geog.* I. 524 A soft rock, through the pores of which, the moisture is slowly exudated.

exudation (ɛksju:'deɪʃən). Also 7-8 exsudation. [ad. late L. *ex(s)ūdātiōn-em*, n. of action f. *ex(s)ūdāre* to EXUDE.]

1. a. The process of exuding; the giving off or oozing out (of moisture) in the manner of sweat.

1612 WOODALL *Surg. Mate* Wks. (1653) 95 In these wounds..appear exudations of clammy humours. **1668** *Phil. Trans.* III. 855 A purer sort of Opium, taken from the Husks of Poppy-seed, being prickt, after some time of exsudation and insolation. **1713** DERHAM *Phys. Theol.* 64 *foot-n.*, An Exsudation..of some petrifying Juices out of the rocky Earth. **1794** G. ADAMS *Nat. & Exp. Philos.* II. xiii. 15 Any exudation of the wine through the pores of the bottles. **1862** G. P. SCROPE *Volcanos* (ed. 2) 37 The vapour it once contained escaped..by exudation through extremely minute pores. **1866** TATE *Brit. Mollusks* iv. 88 The Testacella form a kind of cocoon in the ground by the exudation of mucus.

attrib. **1845-6** G. E. DAY tr. *Simon's Anim. Chem.* II. 499 Exudation-corpuscles. **1852-9** TODD *Cycl. Anat.* IV. 119/2 Exudation-Products exhibit themselves in the form of Compound-granule corpuscles. **1882** GEIKIE *Text-bk. Geol.* II. II. §3. 90 'Segregation' or 'exudation' veins.

¶ **b.** Incorrectly: Percolation, trickling through; ? slow and gradual overflow. Cf. EXUDE 1 b.

1793 SMEATON *Edystone L.* §302 The least exudation of moisture down into the rooms. **1856** KANE *Arct. Expl.* I. Notes 460 Looking upon the glaciers of Greenland as canals of exudation.

c. *Metallurgy.* (See quot. 1958). Also *attrib.*

1945 *Jrnl. Iron & Steel Inst.* CLI. 283 A reliable method of determining the extent of lead segregation in a sample of leaded steel is by means of the 'exudation test'. *Ibid.*, If segregated lead is present, this treatment results in the exudation of the lead on the surface in the form of globules. **1958** A. D. MERRIMAN *Dict. Metallurgy* 87/2 *Exudation*, the phenomenon in which the liquid produced by partial or complete melting of a solid is liberated and escapes. It is commonly applied to the liberation of liquid metal from the solid, as in the case of the production of molten lead from a leaded brass on heating at temperatures in excess of the melting point of lead.

2. *concr.* Something which is exuded.

1626 BACON *Sylva* §4 Rock Rubies are the fine Exudations of Stone. **1744** BERKELEY *Siris* §11 Resinous exsudations of pines and firs. **1875** H. C. WOOD *Therap.* (1879) 391 Calomel should not be used..where the exudation is serous.

fig. **1883** *Fortn. Rev.* Feb. 197 Malice is a natural exudation in every mind.

exudative (ɛk'sju:dətɪv), *a.* and *sb.* [f. L. type **ex(s)ūdātīv-us*, f. *exsūdā-re*: see EXUDE and -IVE.]

A. *adj.* Of, pertaining to, or characterized by exudation.

1859 TODD *Cycl. Anat.* V. 617/2 The exudative process having extended from the uterus to the [Fallopian] tube. **1869** J. S. WELLS *Dis. Eye* viii. §6. 348 There are generally no exudative or degenerative changes of the retina. **1876** DUHRING *Dis. Skin* 140 Exudative diseases.

B. *sb.* 'That which is the product of exudation or which has been exuded' (*Syd. Soc. Lex.* 1884).

1889 in WAGSTAFFE *Med. Voc.*

† **e'xudatory**, *a.* and *sb. Obs. rare.* Also 8 **exsudatory**. [f. L. type *ex(s)ūdātōri-us*, f. *ex(s)ūdāre*: see EXUDE and -ORY.]

A. *adj.* Characterized by exudation.

1782 MARSHALL in *Phil. Trans.* LXXIII. 221 While they were in the exsudatory state above described.

B. *sb.* A means of exuding.

1654 GAYTON *Pleas. Notes* I. v. 16 Urine and teares are the great exudatories of sorrow.

exude (ɛk'sju:d), *v.* [ad. L. *ex(s)ūd-āre*, f. *ex-* out + *sūdāre* to sweat.]

1. *intr.* To ooze out like sweat; to pass off in bead-like drops through the pores, an incision, or orifice.

1574 NEWTON *Health Mag.* 8 The matter, which did exude and come out..from the skin. **1731** ARBUTHNOT *Aliments* v. (1735) 145 The green Leaves of Tea contain a narcotick Juice, which exudes by Roasting. **1774** PENNANT *Tour Scot. in* 1772, 263 A yellow Stalagmitic Matter has exuded. **1849** MURCHISON *Siluria* xii. 305 Stone-oil which exudes from the crust of the earth. **1882** VINES *Sachs' Bot.* 532 Gum, which exudes from incisions in thick viscid drops.

¶ **b.** Occas. misused for: To escape as vapour; ? to overflow slowly.

1837 DISRAELI *Venetia* I. xiv. (1871) 69 A savoury steam exuded from the flesh-pot. **1853** KANE *Grinnell Exp.* xxxvii. (1856) 344 The crushed fragments exuding and..rolling down toward the level ice.

2. *trans.* To sweat out or give off like sweat; to discharge through the pores or an incision.

17.. in JOHNSON. **1822** IMISON *Sc. & Art* II. 345 It.. is like milk when exuded from the tree. **1830** J. G. STRUTT *Sylva Brit.* 97 The Poplar..exudes the moisture which it imbibes. **1869** tr. *Pouchet's Universe* (1871) 92 The bee exudes the softening wax from one region of its body.

absol. **1881** BLACKMORE *Christowell* iii, The cool bowl [of a pipe] shines without exuding.

fig. **1874** LISLE CARR *Jud. Gwynne* I. i. 33 The stolid farmer fairly exuded pleasure at every pore. **1882** B. HARTE *Flip* ii, He moved onward silently exuding admiration.

Hence **e'xuded** *ppl. a.* **e'xuding** *vbl. sb.* and *ppl. a.*

1849 CLARIDGE *Cold Water Cure* 97 The exuding of this ointment lasted about eight days. **1875** B. W. RICHARDSON *Dis. Mod. Life* 16 The exuded fluid is..a product of the blood. **1882** VINES *Sachs' Bot.* 513 The pollen-grains..are retained by an exuding drop of fluid.

exudence (ɛk'sju:dəns). *rare*⁻¹. [Incorrectly for **exudance*, f. EXUDE + -ANCE.] The process of exuding.

1874 *Man. Gunnery H.M. Fleet* 196 There is much greater tendency to the exudence of nitro-glycerine from it.

exufflate, -ation, var. ff. EXSUFFLATE, -ATION.

† '**exul**, *sb. Obs.* [a. L. *ex(s)ul*, f. *ex-* out + root *sal-* to go (cf. *salīre* to leap).] A banished person; = EXILE *sb.*²

1566 GASCOIGNE & KINWELMARSH *Iocasta* in *Child's Four Old Plays* (1848) 140 Eteocles should sway the kingly mace, And Polynice as exul should departe. **1595** SPENSER *Col. Clout* 806 They shall..as Exuls out of his court be thrust. **1600** HOLLAND *Livy* II. xix. 56 The regiment of Romane exuls. **1640** G. SANDYS *Christ's Passion* III. (1649) 29 You Legions of Heavens Exuls.

† '**exul**, *v. Obs. rare*⁻¹. [ad. L. *ex(s)ul-āre*: see EXULATE *v.*] *trans.* = EXILE *v.*

1500-20 DUNBAR *None may Assure* viii, Treuth stands barrit at the dure, And exulit is of the toun.

† '**exulant**, *a. Obs. rare*⁻¹. [ad. L. *ex(s)ulantem*, pr. pple. of *ex(s)ulāre*: see EXULATE *v.*] Living in exile.

1636 BRATHWAIT *Lives Rom. Emp.* 260 Iustinian..who was now exulant in Cersonia.

† '**exulate**, *sb. Obs.* [ad. L. *ex(s)ulāt-us*, pa. pple. of *ex(s)ul-āre*: see next.] = EXILE *sb.*²

c **1470** HARDING *Chron.* clxxxviii. iv, The lordes fled..as exulates. **1557** PAYNEL *Barclay's Jugurth* 12 Wo is me miserable exulate. **1647-9** G. DANIEL *Poems* Wks. (Grosart) II. 127 His Maister, (long an Exulate) come in, To claime his proper Right.

† '**exulate**, *v. Obs. rare.* With *pa. pple.* 6 exulat. [f. L. *ex(s)ulāt-* ppl. stem of *ex(s)ul-āre* to be in exile, in late L. also transitive.] **a.** *trans.* To banish, exile. **b.** *intr.* To go into exile; to be in exile.

1535 STEWART *Cron. Scot.* II. 18 Mony Scot..That exulat wer out of Albione. **1640** HOWELL *Dodona's Gr.* 203 Both exulating from their owne patrimoniall Territories.

† **exu'lation**. *Obs. rare*⁻¹. Also 6 -oun. [ad. L. *ex(s)ulātiōn-em*, n. of action f. *ex(s)ulāre*: see EXULATE *v.*] Banishment, exile.

1535 STEWART *Cron. Scot.* (1858) I. 91 In the tyme of his exulatioun The lordis maid gude reparatioun.

† **e'xulcer**, *v. Obs. rare*⁻¹. In 6 exulcere. [ad. F. *exculcére-r*, ad. L. *exulcerā-re* to EXULCERATE.] *trans.* = EXULCERATE *v.* 1.

1541 R. COPLAND *Galyen's Terap.* 2 A iij b, Corrupte blode..maketh erosion and exulcere[th] the body.

† **e'xulcerate**, *a. Obs.* [ad. L. *exulcerāt-us*, pa. pple. of *exulcerā-re*: see next.]

1. = EXULCERATED 1.

1545 RAYNOLD *Byrth Mankynde* p. 1 As yf intestinum rectum be exulcerat. **1601** HOLLAND *Pliny* II. 168 The said green figs..doe cure the wens or exulcerat bunches. **1683** SALMON *Doron Med.* I. 310 The cure of exulcerate Erysipelas.

2. *fig.* Fretted as by an ulcer; vexed; also diseased, disordered. Cf. EXULCERATED 2.

c **1592** BACON *Observ. Libel* Wks. 1862 VIII. 192 Finding the king's mind so exulcerate, as he rejected all counsel. **1609** HOLLAND *Amm. Marceil.* xv. v. 38 Vrsicinus, alreadie exulcerate and carrying rancour in his heart. **1659** RUSHW. *Hist. Coll.* I. 56 In this exulcerate business, so much moderation..hath shined forth in the King of Great Britain. **1684** H. MORE *Answ. Remarks Exp. Apocal.* 125 Their exulcerate rage at the Rising of the Witnesses.

exulcerate (ɛg'zʌlsəreɪt), *v. arch.* [f. L. *exulcerāt-* ppl. stem of *exulcerāre*, f. *ex-* intensive + *ulcerāre* to ULCERATE.]

† **1.** *trans.* To cause ulcers in; to ulcerate.

1533 ELYOT *Cast. Helthe* IV. ii. (1541) 78 b, Yf the reume be sharp..it doth exulcerate the lunges. **1650** HUBBERT *Pill Formality* 13 Wounds and sores..will secretly exulcerate the flesh. **1732** ARBUTHNOT *Rules of Diet* 392 The stagnating Serum..exulcerates and putrifies the Bowels.

absol. **1607** WALKINGTON *Opt. Glass* 63 Bitter and salt phleume..doth exulcerate. **1683** SALMON *Doron Med.* I. 37 They exulcerate, cause Fevers.

2. *fig.* To fret as with an ulcer; to exasperate, irritate; to aggravate (a disease, sorrow).

1594 HOOKER *Eccl. Pol.* III. 90 It is not easie to speake to the contentation of mindes exulcerated in themselues. **1638** CHILLINGW. *Relig. Prot.* I. v. §64. 280 Professe this I cannot, but I must lye perpetually and exulcerate my conscience. **1653** MANTON *Exp. James* i. 16 [This] doth but prejudice men's minds, and exulcerate them against our testimony.

absol. **1671** MILTON *Samson* 633 Thoughts my tormentors ..Exasperate, exulcerate, and raise Dire inflammation. **1842** SIR H. TAYLOR *Edwin the Fair* I. ii, Detraction that exulcerates.

† **3.** *intr.* To break out into ulcers or sores. *Obs.*

1597 LOWE *Chirurg.* (1634) 101 The cholericke humor.. exulcerateth. **1599** A. M. tr. *Gabelhouer's Bk. Physicke* 49/1 The Eyes exulcerate, or are inflamed. **1659** *Lady Alimony* v. vi. in Hazl. *Dodsley* XIV. 362 With balms to close the skin, And leave the wound t' exulcerate within.

exulcerated (ɛg'zʌlsəreɪtɪd), *ppl. a.* [f. as prec. + -ED¹.]

† **1.** Affected with an ulcer, blistered, ulcerated.

1576 BAKER *Jewell of Health* 58 b, This water..healeth the bowels exulcerated and hurt. **1642** FULLER *Holy & Prof. St.* II. iv. 60 Purulent spittle argues exulcerated lungs. **1663** BOYLE *Nat. Phil.* II. iv. i. 121 The exulcerated tumours of one sick of the king's-evil.

2. *fig.* Fretted as by an ulcer; festered, irritated, embittered, exasperated.

1640 BP. REYNOLDS *Passions* xxvi. 273 Exulcerated, and seditious spirits. **1667** H. MORE *Div. Dial.* IV. xxxvii. (1713) 394 That exulcerated Malice..of those marked Servants of the Beast. *a* **1703** BURKITT *On N.T.* Rom. ix. Pref., An exulcerated prejudice against them.

† **e'xulcerating**, *ppl. a.* [f. as prec. + -ING².] That exulcerates: *lit.* and *fig.*

1599 *Broughton's Lett.* v. 16 He..may pleade for him-selfe ..as Iob against his exulcerating comforters. **1611** COTGR., *Mielanacardin*, a venomous and exulcerating oyle. **1702** SIR J. FLOYER in *Phil. Trans.* XXIII. 1172 The Medulla is hot and exulcerating.

exulceration (ɛg,zʌlsə'reɪʃən). [ad. L. *exulcerātiōn-em*, n. of action f. *exulcerāre*: see EXULCERATE. Cf. F. *exulcération*.]

1. Ulceration. Also, 'the early stage or commencement of ulceration' (Mayne *Exp. Lex.*).

1533 ELYOT *Cast. Helthe* (1541) 56 b, Inflamation or exulceration in the guttes or bladder. **1671** SALMON *Syn. Med.* I. xlviii. 113 A Disease which causeth scratching without Exulceration of the Skin. **1748** tr. *Vegetius' Distemp. Horses* 17 The Sharpness of the Exulceration is mitigated. **1889** in WAGSTAFFE *Med. Voc.*

b. *fig.* Embittered condition; exasperation.

1594 HOOKER *Eccl. Pol.* II. v. (1611) 65 Which exulceration of minde made him apt to take all occasions of contradiction. **1680** H. MORE *Apocal. Apoc.* 110 Rage and exulceration of spirit against the risen witnesses.

2. *concr.* An ulcerated place; a sore.

1551 TURNER *Herbal* (1568) K iij a, The whyche pulse.. hurte the sores and exulcerations. **1678** SALMON *Lond. Disp.* 167 It..heals exulcerations, cools the heat of burning Ulcers. **1861** BUMSTEAD *Ven. Dis.* (1879) 355 Herpetic exulcerations, or other solutions of continuity.

† **e'xulcerative**, *a. Obs. rare*⁻¹. [a. F. *exulcératif, -ive*, f. L. *exulcerāt-* ppl. stem of *exulcerāre*: see EXULCERATE and -IVE.] Tending or of a nature to produce ulcers.

1601 HOLLAND *Pliny* II. 149 The leaues and branches be exulceratiue, and wil raise blisters vpon the body.

exulceratory (ɛg'zʌlsərə,tərɪ), *a.* [f. L. type *exulcerātōrius*, f. *exulcerāre*: see EXULCERATE and -ORY.] Tending to produce ulcers.

1727-36 in BAILEY; and in mod. Dicts.

exult (ɛg'zʌlt), *v.* Also 6 exulte. [ad. F. *exulte-r*, ad. L. *ex(s)ultā-re*, freq. of *exsilīre* to leap up, f. *ex-* out + *salīre* to leap.]

† **1.** *intr.* To spring or leap up; to leap for joy. *Obs.*

1570 in LEVINS *Manip.* 187 To Exulte, *exultare*. *c* **1611** CHAPMAN *Iliad* XIII. 28 The whales exulted under him. **1652** FRENCH *Yorksh. Spa* iii. 36 A Fountain..doth at the sound of a pipe rejoycingly exult and leap up. **1715-20** POPE *Iliad* XIII. 47 The sea..Exults, and owns the monarch of the main. **1727** BAILEY vol. II, *Exulted*, leaped and skipped for Joy.

2. To rejoice exceedingly, be elated or glad; to triumph. Const. *in* (*at*, *on*, *over*), and *inf.*

1594 HOOKER *Eccl. Pol.* I. ix. (1611) 24 Nature exulting.. in certaine hope of reward. **1601** SHAKS. *Twel. N.* II. v. 8 *To.* Wouldst thou not be glad?..*Fab.* I would exult man. **1756** C. LUCAS *Ess. Waters* I. Ded., Who can..not exult in being born a Briton? **1801** SOUTHEY *Thalaba* II. xviii, Her soul Exulted. **1828** D'ISRAELI *Chas. I*, II. v. 126 Every one seemed to exult at the happy change which a few days had effected. **1856** KANE *Arct. Expl.* II. viii. 90 We..exult to think we need no catering for the morrow. **1865** SWINBURNE *Poems & Ballads, Satire to C.* 50 As plague in a poisonous city Insults and exults on her dead.

exultance (ɛg'zʌltəns). [ad. late L. *ex(s)ultantia*, f. *ex(s)ultant-em*: see -ANCE.] = next.

1650 HOWELL *Masaniello* I. 137 He was received with extreme exultances of joy by all the people. **1674** *Govt. Tongue* ix. §7 (1684) 151 We have great cause of exultance

and joy. **1755** in JOHNSON. **1830** W. PHILLIPS *Mt. Sinai* III. 446 Again arose Exultance many-voiced.

exultancy (ɛg'zʌltənsɪ). [ad. L. *ex(s)ultantia*: see prec. and -ANCY.] Exultant state or condition; an instance of the same; exultation, gladness, transport, triumph.

1621 BURTON *Anat. Mel.* III. ii. 111, Joys, comforts, exultancies. *a* **1660** HAMMOND *Serm.* viii. Wks. 1684 IV. 614 Always upon terms of Spiritual exultancy. **1721–1800** in BAILEY. **1847** LD. LINDSAY *Chr. Art.* I. 109 Fiery and almost fierce in their exultancy. **1864** CARLYLE *Fredk. Gt.* IV. XI. i. 3 A trace of airy exuberance, of natural exultancy.

†**exultand.** *Obs. rare*$^{-1}$. App. = EXULTET.

1519 *Churchw. Acc. St. Giles, Reading* 6 A Pryk-song boke..wherein is conteyned iiij masses, iij kyries, iii allohuies, and ij exultands.

exultant (ɛg'zʌltənt), *a.* [ad. L. *ex(s)ultant-em*, pr. pple. of *ex(s)ultāre*: see EXULT.] Exulting, triumphantly joyful.

1653 H. MORE *Conject. Cabbal.* ii. 42 With such exultant sympathy and joy. *a* **1745** BROOME *On Death* 156 The Sun..starts exultant, and renews the day. **1844** *Cath. Weekly Instruct.* 127 The wild exultant cry. **1863** GEO. ELIOT *Romola* II. xxiv, The fierce exultant delight to which he was moved by the idea of perpetual vengeance.

Hence **e'xultantly** *adv.*

1883 K. W. HAMILTON in *Harper's Mag.* 846/2 Margaret's heart swelled exultantly. **1885** *Manch. Exam.* 7 Aug. 5/2 It was exultantly proclaimed that the war with Afghanistan would only cost six millions.

exultation (ɛgzʌl'teɪʃən). Also 5 **-cion, -cioune.** [ad. L. *ex(s)ultātiōn-em*, f. *ex(s)ultāre*: see EXULT. Cf. F. *exultation* (from 14th c.).]

†**1.** The action of leaping or springing up. *Obs.*

1599 SANDYS *Europæ Spec.* (1632) 225 With continuall great wagging of their bodies and exultation..sometimes all springing up lightly from the ground.

2. The action or state of exulting or rejoicing greatly; triumph, joyousness, rapturous delight; an instance of the same. Also *concr.* an object exulted over.

c **1425** tr. *T. à Kempis' Consol.* II. xii, Hov gret exultacion to all þe seintes of heven. **1594** HOOKER *Eccl. Pol.* I. xi. (1611) 36 With hidden exultation. **1716** ADDISON *Free-holder* No. 49 ¶1 To swell their Hearts with inward Transports of Joy and Exultation. **1771** *Ess. from Batchelor* (1773) i, O F—d, thou genius of the age, Hibernia's exultation! **1874** GREEN *Short Hist.* viii. 515 Amidst the exultation of the Court over the decision of the judges.

b. *pl.* Shouts of joy, joyful utterances.

1597 HOOKER *Eccl. Pol.* v. §39 (1662) 191 Heavenly Acclamations, Exultations. **1774** J. BRYANT *Mythol.* I. 225 Hymns, and exultations and other uncommon noises.

†**e'xultative,** *a. Obs. rare.* [f. EXULT + -ATIVE.] Inclined or ready to exult; exultant.

? *a* **1500** *Clariodus* (1830) 103 Sad hevie myndis to make exultative.

‖**Exultet** (ɛg'zʌltɛt). [L.] The ancient hymn beginning *Exultet jam angelica turba cælorum*, sung in the Roman Church at the benediction of the paschal candle on Easter-eve; a musical setting of this hymn. ***Exultet Roll*** (see quot. 1957).

[**1519**: see EXULTAND.] **1869** ROCK *Ch. Our Fathers* I. 212 [An illumination representing] the deacon singing the *Exultet* in the 'ambo'. **1882** *Catal. Add. MSS. Brit. Mus. 1876–1881* 70 Exultet-Roll... Written in Lombardic or Beneventine characters of the XIIth century, with pneums. **1884** *Cath. Dict.* 406, s.v. *Holy Week*, The use of the paschal candle goes back..as far at least as the time of Zosimus, who was made Pope in 417, and the sublime words of the 'Exultet'..can scarcely be less ancient. **1937** *Burlington Mag.* Nov. 241/2 Perhaps the strangest of all liturgical MSS. are the rolls containing the text of the formulary for the blessing of the Paschal Candle on the evening of Holy Saturday, and usually known from the first words 'Exultet joui [*sic*] angelica turba', as Exultet Rolls. **1957** *Oxf. Dict. Chr. Ch.* 486/2 In S. Italy, from the early 10th cent. to the 13th cent., it was customary to write out this prose [*sc.* the Paschal Proclamation], with appropriate musical directions, on rolls known as 'Exultet Rolls'.

exulting (ɛg'zʌltɪŋ), *vbl. sb.* [f. EXULT + -ING^1.] The action of the vb. EXULT; exultation.

1744 SARAH FIELDING *David Simple* (ed. 2) I. 85 Dinner pass'd..in Exultings in the Happiness of possessing such a Creature. *a* **1859** L. HUNT *Fancy Concert*, The gong..with exultings that clanged like disasters. **1875** BROWNING *Aristoph. Apol.* 363 Hideous exultings.

e'xulting, *ppl. a.* [f. as prec. + -ING^2.]

1. That exults; exultant, triumphantly joyful.

1757 DYER *Fleece* IV. 689 Th' exulting muse shall then..her flight renew. **1856** FROUDE *Hist. Eng.* (1858) I. ii. 166 An exulting expectation of a dissolution of the church establishment. **1876** J. H. NEWMAN *Hist. Sk.* I. I. i. 42 Solon..was asked by the exulting monarch who was the happiest of men.

2. *nonce-use.* Upspringing, towering, lofty. Cf. EXULT 1.

1798 BLOOMFIELD *Farmer's Boy, Autumn* 318 To climb the woodland hill's exulting brow.

Hence **e'xultingly** *adv.*, in an exulting manner.

1661 BOYLE *Style of Script.* (1675) 244 They exultingly told the woman, Now we believe, etc. **1775** ADAIR *Amer. Ind.* 296 The savage..returned exultingly to his country-men. **1837** HOOD *Drinking Song* ii, Let topers of grape-juice exultingly vapour. **1855** MACAULAY *Hist. Eng.* IV. 203 In London it was announced exultingly that [etc.].

†**e'xultive,** *a. Obs.* [f. EXULT *v.* + -IVE.] Inclined to exult; given up to exultation.

? *a* **1500** *Clariodus* (1830) 192 He than was in joy sa exultive, That of him self almaist he wist no thing.

exultre, obs. form of AXLE-TREE.

1475 in Child *Eng. & Sc. Ball.* v. cxvii. (1888) 90/2 Late vs cast the exultre.

exululate (ɛk'sju:ljʊleɪt), *v. rare.* [f. L. *exululāt-* ppl. stem of *exululāre*, f. *ex-* out + *ululāre* to howl (cf. *ulula* screech-owl).] *intr.* To howl or cry out.

1623–6 in COCKERAM. **1866** J. B. ROSE tr. *Ovid's Fasti* IV. 205 With noisiest clamour they exululate.

Hence **exulu'lation.**

1727 BAILEY vol. II, *Exululation* a Shrieking or crying out. **1864** *N. & Q.* Ser. III. VI. 178 The fiendish exultation (exululation?) wherewith the Dublin demagogues wolved it about the city.

†**exumbili'cation.** *Obs. rare.* [f. L. *ex-* out + *umbilic-us* the navel + -ATION.] The starting out of the navel.

1706 in PHILLIPS (ed. Kersey). **1721–1800** in BAILEY. **1823** in CRABB *Technol. Dict.*

exumbrella (ɛksʌm'brɛlə). *Zool.* [mod.L., f. L. *ex-* out + UMBRELLA 7b.] The aboral or outer surface of the umbrella of a jellyfish. Hence **exum'brellar** *a.*, of or pertaining to the exumbrella.

1886 A. W. GREELY *Arctic Service* II. 400 The genus *Nauphanta* is a characteristic one, and is remarkable in the peculiar sculpturing of the exumbrella, the division of the umbrella on the exumbral side into a central and coronal or peripheral zone. **1888** ROLLESTON & JACKSON *Forms Anim. Life* 745 The mesogalea of the aboral aspect of the bell is much thickened to form the umbrella *s.* exumbrella. *Ibid.* 783 If the *Ephyra* be regarded from the dorsal, i.e. exumbrellar aspect. *Ibid.* 784 The sense-bodies are usually protected by a dorsal, i.e. exumbrellar covering-piece or hood. **1897** PARKER & HASWELL *Text-bk. Zool.* I. 124 The convex outer surface of the bell or umbrella..by which the zooid was originally attached to the blastostyle is distinguished as the ex-umbrella, the concave inner surface as the sub-umbrella. **1907** *Gentl. Mag.* July 97/2 The tentacles..imbedded in ridges of jelly of the exumbrella. **1940** L. H. HYMAN *Invertebrates* I. vii. 373 The medusa form resembles a deep to shallow bowl of gelatin, termed the bell or umbrella; the convex aboral surface is called the exumbrella, the concave oral surface, the subumbrella. **1967** P. A. MEGLITSCH *Invertebrate Zool.* vi. 151/1 Small particles and plankton are caught in slime secreted on the exumbrella.

†**e'xundance.** *Obs.* [ad. L. *exundantia*, f. *exundant-em*: see EXUNDANT and -ANCE.] The fact of flowing forth in waves; an overflow.

a **1654** H. BINNING *Com. Prin. Chr. Relig.* Wks. 1839 I. 156 The infinite excess of perfection and exundance of self-being. **1660** H. MORE *Myst. Godl.* VII. x. 323 Those parenthetical exundances of weighty sense and matter.

†**e'xundancy.** *Obs.* [ad. L. *exundantia*: see prec. and -ANCY.] An overflowing; = prec.

1686 GOAD *Celest. Bodies* II. vii. 249 Which doth ferment, rarifie, and raise the Waters to an Exundancy. **1692** BEVERLEY *Disc. Dr. Crisp* 10 How great Exundancies of Expression are found.

exundant (ɛk'sʌndənt), *a.* [ad. L. *exundant-em*, pr. pple. of *exundāre*, f. *ex-* out + *undāre* to rise in waves, f. *unda* wave.] That flows forth in waves; overflowing, superabundant.

a **1661** HOLYDAY *Juvenal* 187 From their exundant wit their ruine sprung. **1856** SMYTH *Rom. Fam. Coins* 96 Exundant fertility of resource.

†**b.** *Path.* Said of the pulse; in mod.L. *exundans.*

1707 FLOYER *Physic. Pulse-Watch* I. 357 The intense Pulse is..exundant like a torrent.

exundate (ɛk'sʌndeɪt), *v. rare.* [f. L. *exundāt-* ppl. stem of *exundāre*: see prec.] *intr.* To overflow.

1721–1800 in BAILEY. **1844** *Blackw. Mag.* LVI. 210 The stream exundated on every side.

exundation (ɛksʌn'deɪʃən). Now *rare.* [ad. L. *exundātiōn-em*, n. of action f. *exundāre*: see EXUNDANT.] Overflow (of a body of water).

1577 HOLINSHED *Chron.* II. 58 Great part of Flanders being drowned by an exundation or breaking in of the sea. **1679** PLOT *Staffordsh.* (1686) 46 The rising of the former [pool], and exundation of the latter. **1792** A. GEDDES *Bible, Gen.* xlv. 6 *note*, The fertility of Egypt depends on the regular exundations of the Nile. **1853** *Fraser's Mag.* XLVIII. 708 The issue of the waters, or exundation from the pond.

†**e'xungulate,** *v. Obs.* [f. late L. *exungulāt-* ppl. stem of *exungulāre* to lose the hoof, f. *ex-* out + *ungula*, dim. of *unguis* claw, nail.] *trans.* (See quots.)

1623–6 COCKERAM, *Exungulate*, to pare ones nailes. **1727–36** BAILEY, *Exungulate*, to pull off the hoofs, also to cut off the white part from roseleaves. **1775** in ASH, and later Dicts.

Hence †**e'xungulated** *ppl. a.* †**exungu'lation.**

1657 TOMLINSON *Renou's Disp.* 530 It is made of two parts of the succe of exungated [*sic*] Roses. *Ibid.* 652 Roses..reddish, and not exungulated. **1730–6** BAILEY (fol.), *Exungulation*, a pulling off the hoofs. **1742–1800** *Ibid.*, *Exungulation* (among Chymists), the cutting off the white Part from the Leaves of Roses.

exuperable, -ate, etc.: see EXSU-.

exurb ('ɛksɜ:b). orig. *U.S.* [f. L. *ex* out of + *urbs* city, or back-formation f. next.] A district outside a city or town; *spec.* a prosperous area situated beyond the suburbs of a city.

1955 [see EXURBIA]. **1957** *Economist* 16 Nov. 596/2 They have scattered to the four corners of the country and into the suburbs and 'exurbs'. **1966** L. J. BRAUN *Cat who could read Backwards* (1967) ii. 16 To reach the fashionable exurb fifteen miles beyond the city limits, Qwilleran drove through complacent suburbs. **1967** *Observer* 1 Oct. 27/6 Levittown..is not any arcadian upper middle-class exurb.

exurban (ɛk'sɜ:bən), *a.* and *sb.* [f. EX-^{1} + URBAN *a.* after SUBURBAN *a.*] **A.** *adj.* Of or belonging to a district outside a city or town; suburban; *spec.* pertaining to, or characteristic of, an exurb.

1901 *Westm. Gaz.* 18 Dec. 4/2 Pilgrimages of an exurban character, visits to King's Langley.., to Berkhampstead. **1955** *Archit. Rev.* CXVIII. 351/1 The most important architectural consequence of motorized America's post-war flight from the cities has been the emergence of the exurban shopping centre as a differentiated building-type. **1955** [see EXURBIA]. **1961** L. MUMFORD *City in History* xvi. 485 It..anticipates the present 'exurban' emphasis on informal clothing. **1963** *New Statesman* 8 Feb. 188/1 The arc of educated, prosperous suburbia running from near-urban Brookline..to ex-urban Weston and Wayland.

B. *sb.* A resident in an exurban district (see quot.). *rare.*

1957 *Britannica Bk. of Year* 512/1 An exurbanite—or exurban—was one who kept up his city ways and habits in the country [in the U.S.A.].

Hence **e'xurbanite** *sb.*, a resident in an exurban district or in exurbia; *adj.* = EXURBAN *a.* orig. *U.S.*

1955 A. C. SPECTORSKY (*title*) Exurbanites. **1957** [see EXURBAN *sb.*]. **1959** *Encounter* Sept. 50/2 A suburbanite corner..which..dispenses exurbanite pabulum. **1960** *Spectator* 8 Jan. 47/3 The stock types who go through the moves in this upper exurbanite gavotte. **1960** *Observer* 13 Nov. 3/2 The day-old chicks are farmed out to growers, mostly City exurbanites with a place in Sussex.

exurbia (ɛk'sɜ:bɪə). orig. *U.S.* [f. EX-^{1} + *-urbia* after SUBURBIA.] (A quasi-proper name for) the region outside the suburbs of a city; exurbs collectively. Hence **e'xurbian** *a.*

1955 A. C. SPECTORSKY *Exurbanites* ii. 14 Spreading outward from New York City, roughly the first twenty-five miles is solid Suburbia; thereafter, for a belt extending another twenty-five miles, come the exurbs. Exurbia being a recent phenomenon, and a unique one, it may be interesting to explore..how the exurban way of life came to be..superimposed on..earlier cultural patterns in certain areas. **1956** *Archit. Rev.* CXIX. 81/3 (*heading*) Exurbia not necessarily subtopia. *Ibid.*, Some of the brightest American designers are entangled with Exurbian development, and particularly its most characteristic building type, the super-market. **1957** *Technology* Oct. 287/1 First-rate teachers, who are not unduly hard to attract to a new school in a prosperous and pleasant area even in the distant fringes of exurbia. **1968** D. E. ALLEN *Brit. Tastes* ii. 43 That wide belt of smaller towns and villages ('exurbia') to which so many of those who work in the Metropolis return to sleep.

exurge, -ence, -ent: see EXSU-.

†**e'xurgency.** *Obs. rare.* [f. L. *exurgent-em*, pr. pple. of *exurgĕre*, f. *ex-* out + *urgēre* to press, URGE: see -ENCY.] The quality of urging strongly; urgent force.

1659 OWEN *Serm.* xii. Wks. 1851 VIII. 462 The..exurgency of their number and wisdom. **1668–84** —— *Exp. Heb.* (1790) I. 55 This authority..consists partly, in an exurgency, or forcible influence of the holy matter.

exuscitate, -ation, var. of EXSUSCITATE, etc.

†**e'xust,** *a. Obs.* [ad. L. *exust-us*, pa. pple. of *exūrĕre*: see next.] Burnt or dried up.

1657 TOMLINSON *Renou's Disp.* 205 This Rusma is..lighter, blacker, and seemingly exust. **1684** tr. *Bonet's Merc. Compit.* III. 61 Hot, exust and melancholick Bloud.

†**e'xust,** *v. Obs. rare.* [f. L. *exust-* ppl. stem of *exūrĕre*, f. *ex-* out + *ūrĕre* to burn.] *trans.* To burn up. Hence **e'xusted** *ppl. a.*

1623–6 in COCKERAM. **1823** *New Monthly Mag.* VII. 144 The exusted vampyre Arnold Paul had strangled..a number of cattle.

†**e'xustible,** *a. Obs. rare.* [f. prec. + -IBLE.] Capable of being burnt up.

1633 T. ADAMS *Exp. 2 Peter* iii. 7 Do they say, the heavens are not exustible?

†**e'xustion.** *Obs.* [ad. L. *exustiōn-em*, n. of action f. *exūrĕre* (see EXUST). Cf. OF. *exustion.*]

a. The action or process of burning or burning up (something). **b.** Heat attendant upon disease.

a. 1610 BARROUGH *Meth. Physick* v. xiii. (1634) 299 You must use some hote burning instrument..After exustion, minister the juyce of Leekes and other such things as do drie. **1651** *Raleigh's Ghost* 353 The generall exustion and burning of the world. **1720** S. PARKER *Bibl. Biblica* (Gen. xix. 25) I. 424 The frightful Effects which this Exustion [of Sodom and Gomorrah] left are still remaining.

b. 1657 TOMLINSON *Renou's Disp.* 712 It allayes inflammations, exustions and hot distempers.

†**e'xute,** *pa. pple. Obs.* [ad. L. *exūt-us*, pa. pple. of *exuĕre*: see next.] Stripped.

c **1430** tr. *T. à Kempis' Imit.* II. iv, A man conuertyng him holy to god, is exute & taken fro þe body & chaunged into a newe man.

exute (ɛg'zjuːt), *v. Obs.* exc. *Hist.* [f. L. *exūt-* ppl. stem of *exuĕre* to draw or pull off.] *trans.* To strip (a person) *of*; to divest or deprive *of*.

1535 STEWART *Cron. Scot.* III. 182 The governing..In thair handis he did agane resing, And him exutet of office and cuir. **1669** R. B. *Life T. Morton* 98 Exuted of his secretarie's place. **1829** SOUTHEY in *Q. Rev.* XXXIX. 391 [He] was degraded, exuted of all his preferments.

exuviability (ɛg,zjuːvɪə'bɪlɪtɪ). [ad. F. *exuviabilité*, f. *exuviable*: see next and -ITY.] The property of being exuviable. In Dicts. explained as the power of casting off exuviæ.

1841 FLEMING & TIBBINS *Dict. Franc.-Angl.* II. 441 *Exuviabilité*..exuviability, the faculty of sloughing. **1847** in CRAIG.

exuviable (ɛg'zjuːvɪəb(ə)l), *a.* [a. F. *exuviable*, f. L. *exuviæ*: see next and -ABLE.] Capable of being exuviated or sloughed off.

1839 TODD *Cycl. Anat.* II. 882/2 Odier..found chitine in the exuviable skeleton of Crustacea.

‖**exuviæ** (ɛg'zjuːvɪiː). [a. L. *exuviæ* garments stripped off, skins of animals, the spoils of an enemy, f. *exuĕre* to divest oneself of.] Cast skins, shells, or coverings of animals; any parts of animals which are shed or cast off, whether recent or fossil.

1670 BOYLE *Contn. New Exp.* iv. Wks. 1772 III. 378 They [insects] divested the habit they had..and appeared with their exuviæ or cast coats under their feet. *a* **1728** WOODWARD *Catal. For. Fossils* II. (1729) 21 in *Nat. Hist. Fossils*, They appear to be only the Skins or Exuviæ [*printed* Exuvia], rather than entire Bodies of Fishes. **1796** MORSE *Amer. Geog.* I. 184 Fossils and other marine exuviæ which are found imbedded on the tops of mountains. **1826** KIRBY & SP. *Entomol.* (1828) III. xxxii. 290 The insect has quitted the exuviæ of the pupa. **1830** LYELL *Princ. Geol.* I. 23 Living animals..had formerly lived..where their exuviæ are now found. **1851** RICHARDSON *Geol.* (1855) 393 Sea-weeds, sponges, corals, shells, and the other marine exuviæ found in the chalk.

b. *transf.* and *fig.*

1653 H. MORE *Antid. Ath.* III. xvi. (1712) 138 The Exuviæ of Fiddles, it seems, fly up into the air. **1811** LAMB *Burial Societies* Wks. (1876) 629 The departed Spirit is gone. His care is only about the exuviæ. **1821** KNOX *Spir. Despot.* xxix. 66 Lest the despotism of influence should destroy the vitals of a free constitution, and leave nothing behind but the form, the exuviæ, the name. **1851** D. WILSON *Preh. Ann.* (1863) I. II. vi. 439 Curious exuviæ of early art.

exuvial (ɛg'zjuːvɪəl), *a.* and *sb.* [f. prec. + -AL¹.]

A. *adj.* Pertaining to, or of the nature of, exuviæ. In quots. *transf.* and *fig.* †**B.** *sb. pl.* Things stripped off; spoils.

1632 LITHGOW *Trav.* II. 72 Being cled with the exuvials and Trophees of enemies. **1839** THACKERAY *Catharine* i, The load of exuvial coats and breeches under which he [the old clothes man] staggers. **1847** EMERSON *Repr. Men, Shaks.* Wks. (Bohn) I. 364 In the poet's mind, the fact has..lost all that is exuvial.

exuviate (ɛg'zjuːvɪeɪt), *v.* [f. as prec. + -ATE.] **a.** *intr.* To cast off or shed exuviæ. **b.** *trans.* To shed or cast off as exuviæ.

1855 *Fraser's Mag.* LI. 542 Crabs of mature age and full size cease to exuviate. **1880** HUXLEY *Crayfish* i. 37 The young crayfish exuviate two or three times in the course of the first year.

b. **1856** CARPENTER *Microsc. & Rev.* (1891) 889 Even when the Entomostraca have attained their full growth, they continue to exuviate their shell. **1871** HUXLEY *Anat. Vert. Anim.* 9 So much of the allantois as lies outside the walls of the body is..exuviated.

exuviation (ɛg,zjuːvɪ'eɪʃən). [f. prec.: see -ATION.] The action or process of exuviating; shedding (of antlers, skin, etc.).

1839 TODD *Cycl. Anat.* II. 882/2 The exuviation of the skeleton of Crustacea..is similar to that of insects. *a* **1852** MACGILLIVRAY *Nat. Hist. Dee Side* (1855) 463 The exuviation..of the antlers..seems to connect these organs with those parts of the skin..which are subject to this process. **1852** DANA *Crust.* I. 3 Numerous exuviæ of Cirripeds were collected, proving that these animals undergo exuviation.

fig. **1864** H. SPENCER *Illust. Univ. Progress* 114 Society, in all its developements, undergoes the process of exuviation. **1874** DRAPER *Relig. & Sc.* (ed. 3) 328 The most serious trial through which society can pass, is encountered in the exuviation of its religious restraints.

†**e'xuvious**, *a. Obs.* [f. as prec. + -OUS.] Pertaining to, or of the nature of, exuviæ; effluent.

1653 H. MORE *Antid. Ath.* III. xvi. (1712) 137 The Skirmishings in the Air are from the exuvious Effluxes of things. **1678** CUDWORTH *Intell. Syst.* 15 Insinuations of simulachra, or exuvious images of bodies.

ex-vaccine, *a. nonce-wd.* [f. EX- *pref.*¹ + L. *vacca* cow + -INE.] Obtained from a cow.

1804 *Edin. Rev.* III. 340 Six of them [mice] embark upon a bit of dry cow dung, their provision in the middle of this ex-vaccine vessel.

ex-votive, *a.* [f. next + -IVE.] Pertaining to, or performed by, ex-voto offerings.

1863 MARY HOWITT *F. Bremer's Greece* I. i. 14 Nitches in the rocks..indicate the former places of ex-votive worship.

‖**ex-voto** (ɛks'vəʊtəʊ). [f. L. phrase *ex vōtō*, *ex* out of, *vōtō* abl. sing. of *vōt-um* vow.] An offering made in pursuance of a vow. Also *attrib.*

1823 R. BAKEWELL *Trav. Tarentaise* I. 354 *Ex voto* inscriptions. **1834** MEDWIN *Angler in Wales* I. 213, I..perceived that they were ex voto's made by the pious..devotees of the rod in commemoration of their triumphs. **1880** MISS BIRD *Japan* I. 67 Ex votos of all kinds hang on the wall. **1904** CONRAD *Nostromo* II. iii. 131 Anzani's great emporium of boots,..hearts (for ex-voto offerings), rosaries.

exzodiacal (ɛkszəʊ'daɪəkəl), *a.* [f. EX- *pref.*¹ + ZODIAC + -AL¹.] Of the minor planets: Having an orbit that passes out of the zodiac.

1803 SIR W. HERSCHEL in *Phil. Trans.* XCIII. 340 They should be called very small, and exzodiacal.

ey, obs. form of AY.

ey, obs. form of EGG.

†**'eya**, *int. Obs. rare*⁻¹. [a. med.L. *eya* (L. *ēia*) in same sense.] Indeed, surely.

c **1430** tr. *T. a Kempis' Imit.* III. vi, Eya, my lorde god, my holy louer, whan þou shalt come in to myn herte, all myn inwardes shal joy.

eyah, obs. spelling of AYAH, Indian nurse.

‖**eyalet** (ɛ'jɑːleɪt). [Turk. *èyālet*, a. Arab. *iyālah (-at)*, noun of action f. *āl* to preside.] An administrative division of the Turkish empire; now more commonly called VILAYET, q.v.

1853 W. MᶜLEOD *Atlas Scripture Geog.* 52 This province is divided into four eyalets or pashalicks. **1889** *Daily News* 16 Oct. 5/6 Mossoul, in the eyalet of Bagdad.

eyas ('aɪəs). Forms: 5 eyes, 6–7 yas, 6–9 eyess(e, 7 eyasse, (eyeass, iiaes), 7– eyas. [Altered form of NYAS, a. Fr. *niais* (= Pr. *nizaic*, It. *nidiace*):—L. **nīd(i)āc-em*, f. *nīdus* nest. The dropping of initial *n* was due to an erroneous division of *a nyas* (cf. *a nadder* s.v. ADDER); the spelling *eyas* was suggested by popular association with ME. *ey* = EGG and *eyry*; also with *eye* (see quots.).]

1. A young hawk taken from the nest for the purpose of training, or one whose training is incomplete.

1486 *Bk. St. Albans* B ij a, An hawke is calde an eyes of hir eyghen. **1575** TURBERV. *Bk. Falconrie* 31 The firste name and terme that they bestowe on a falcon is an eyasse and this name dothe laste as long as she is in the eyrie. **1629** MASSINGER *Picture* v. i, So ho, birds, how the eyasses scratch and scramble! **1688** R. HOLME *Armoury* II. 236/2 An eyesse is..a young Hawk as long as she is in the Eyrie. **1820** SCOTT *Abbot* iv, Is it thus you feed the eyas with unwashed meat? **1869** LOWELL *Cathedr.* Wks. (1879) 443 As when, an eyas, he followed his high heart To swim on sunshine. **1875** 'STONEHENGE' *Brit. Sports* I. IV. i. §6. 296 This is very easy with the eyess or brancher.

fig. **1602** SHAKS. *Ham.* II. ii. 355 An ayrie of Children, little Yases, that crye out on the top of question. *a* **1625** FLETCHER *Woman's Prize* I. ii, Hang these tame-hearted Eyasses. **1890** SAINTSBURY *Hist. Elizabeth. Lit.* xi. 426 One of the little eyasses who competed with regular actors.

2. *attrib.*, as ***eyas-falcon***, ***-hawk***; in sense 'unfledged, youthful' as ***eyas-thoughts***, ***-wings***. Also **eyas-musket** (see MUSKET), used jocularly for a sprightly child.

1596 SPENSER *Hymns, Heavenly Love* 24 Ere flitting Time could wag his eyas wings. **1598** SHAKS. *Merry W.* III. iii. 22 How now my eyas-Musket what newes with you? **1606** CHAPMAN *Marlowe's Hero & Leander* IV, To still their eyas thoughts with industry. **1616** SURFL. & MARKH. *Countrie Farme* 708 The care of holding..your hawke..may intice you to esteeme the Iiaes hawke. *a* **1653** G. DANIEL *Idyll* iv. 28 Our Eyeass Life Complaines vnpittied. **1826** SEBRIGHT *Observ. Hawking* (1828) 26 Magpies may be flown with eyess slight falcons.

eydent, obs. var. of EIDENT.

eye (aɪ), *sb.*¹ Forms: 1 éaȝe, ēȝe, (éȝo, éȝu, ǽȝe), 2–4 eȝe, 2–3 eȝhe, 2–5 eiȝe (3 ehe), 3–5 eghe, 3–7 eie, 4 egȝe, ei, hei(e, he (*north.*), 4–5 eyȝe, eyghe, eighe, yȝe, iȝe, 4–7 ey, 5 egh, yghe, ighe, eyhe, ehe, yhe, ye, ie, (hyghe, hye, iey, ȝee, hee, iȝee, ieae), 5–6 e (*north.*), (eae, iee), 5– *north.* (and 9 *Poet.*) ee, 6 iye, yie (yey, ye, yae, eey, i,) 4– eye. *Pl.* α. 1 éaȝan, ǽȝan (*north.* éȝo, éȝu), 1–2 éȝan, 2 eaȝen, 2–4 eȝen, 2–5 eiȝen, 3 eihen, æȝen, ehȝen, 3–5 eghen, eien, 3–5 (7 *arch.*) eyn, 4 eyiȝen, eiȝyen, ȝeȝen, hegehen, eye, 4–5 eyȝen, yȝen, eyghen, eighen, iȝen, yen(e, ein, 4–6 (9 *arch.*) eyen, 4–7 (9 *arch.*) eyne, 5 ighen, yeghen, yhen (eene, eyon, ygne), 5– *north.* and *Sc.* een, 6 iyen, ien, yien, (ain) *Sc.* ene, (6–7 eine, 7 aine, 8–9 *Sc.* e'en). β. 3 eȝenen, eȝene, eȝhne, 3–5 ehnen, ehne, 4 egghnen, iȝene, ine, ewine, eiine, 5 eghene, enyn (hynon, enghne). γ. 4 eiȝes, 5 yȝes, 6 iyes, yes, ies, yees, ayes, ees, 6–7 eies, (7 eys) 6– eyes. Also with prosthetic *n*, 5 neghe, ney, 4–6 nie, nye, *Pl.* 5 nyen, -on, -non. [OE. *éage*, wk. neut., corresponding to OFris. *âge*, OS. *ôga* (MDu. *ôghe*, Du. *oog*), OHG. *ouga* (MHG. *ouge*, Ger. *auge*), ON. *auga* (Da. *öie*, Sw. *öga*), Goth. *augo*:—OTeut. **augon-*.

By most scholars referred to the OAryan root **oq-* to see, to which belong the synonymous words in all the other branches of the Aryan family exc. Celtic; but the anomalous representation of OAryan *o* by *au* instead of *a* presents difficulties; for various hypotheses intended to account for it see Brugmann *Grundriss* I. 333, Kluge *Etym. Wb.* (ed. 5) s.v., Fick *Vergl. Wb.* (ed. 4) I. 371. Otherwise, no plausible affinities have been found for the Teutonic word.]

The original plural was in *-an*, in ME *-en*, whence north. dial. *een*, and archaic *eyne*. In some forms of ME. a second inflexional *-en* (reducible to *-e*) was added, making *eȝenen*, *eȝene*, whence in 15th c. *enyn*. Our first instance of the modern *-s* plural is *a* 1375 *eiȝes*.

I. 1. The organ of sight.

a. in man and vertebrate animals.

a **700** *Epinal Gloss.* 1093 Vitiato oculo: unþyotoȝi eȝan [*a* **800** *Erfurt Gloss.* undyctȝi æȝan]. *c* **825** *Vesp. Psalter* xciii. 9 Se ðe hiowede eȝe ne scewað. *c* **950** *Lindisf. Gosp.* Luke xi. 34 Gif eȝo ðin bið milde. *c* **1000** *Ags. Gosp.* Matt. v. 29 Gyf þin swyðre eaȝe þe æ swicie ahola hit ut. *c* **1175** *Lamb. Hom.* 23 þes monnes eȝan, and his fet, and his hondan. *c* **1200** ORMIN 9393 ȝif þatt tin eȝhe iss all unnhal. *a* **1300** *Cursor M.* 9361 (Cott.), Als douues eie hir lok es suete. *c* **1300** *K. Alis.* 1106 His egghnen out of his hed sterte. *c* **1340** *Cursor M.* 3780 (Fairf.), In slepe a ladder him þoȝt he seyghe fra þe firmament riȝt to his eyghe. *c* **1375** *Sc. Leg. Saints, Paulus* 557 With fleshy ewine he na se mocht. *c* **1380** CHAUCER *Min. Poems, Merciles Beaute* I Youre two eyn will sle me sodenly, I may the beaute of them not sustene. *c* **1400** *Rom. Rose* 1023 Hir nose, hir mouth, and eyhe..Wel wrought. *c* **1430** *Bk. Hawking* in *Rel. Ant.* I. 299 Take a tame heron and drawe out the both eyon of her. **1486** *Bk. St. Albans* B jb, The yolow be twene y Beeke & yᵉ yeghen. **1513–75** *Diurn. Occurrents* (Bannatyne Club) 179 Ane monstrous fische..havand greit ene in the head thairof. *a* **1529** SKELTON *Poems agst. Garnesche* 37 Your ien glyster as glasse, Rowlynge in your holow hede. **1586–7** Q. ELIZ. in *Four C. Eng. Lett.* 31 Paine in one of my yees was only the cause. **1605** CAMDEN *Rem.* 125 Piercing the King of Scots through the eie, as Hector Boetius fableth. **1674** BREVINT *Saul at Endor* 116 To set new Eies..instead of those that were bored out. **1725** WATTS *Logic* II. v. i. §7 The Distance at which these Glasses are placed from the Eye. **1774** GOLDSM. *Nat. Hist.* (1776) IV. 192 The orbits of the eyes were deeper. **1797** COLERIDGE *Sibyl. Leaves* (1862) 226 A little sun, no bigger than your ee. **1831** BREWSTER *Optics* xxxv. §166. 286 The human eye is of a spherical form with a slight projection in front. **1856** SIR B. BRODIE *Psychol. Inq.* I. v. 182 The eye of an eagle is nearly as large as that of an elephant. **1858** KINGSLEY *Red King* 37 His eyne were shotten, red as blood.

b. *Poet.* attributed to heaven, the sun, etc. ***the eye of day***, ***of heaven*** = the sun; ***the eyes of heaven***, ***of night*** = the stars.

1590 SPENSER *F.Q.* I. iii. 4 Her angels face, As the great eye of heaven, shyned bright. **1595** SHAKS. *John* III. i. 79 The glorious sunne..Turning with splendor of his precious eye The meager cloddy earth to glittering gold. *c* **1600** —— *Sonn.* xviii, Sometime too hot the eye of heaven shines. **1603** —— *Ham.* II. ii. 540 Would haue made milche the Burning eyes of Heauen. **1738** WESLEY *Psalms* cxlvii. 2 All ye sparkling Eyes of Night. **1820** SCOTT *Monast.* xx, The eye of day hath opened its lids.

c. with adjs. denoting the colour of the iris.

c **1300** *Poem* vi. in *Retrospective Rev.* (1853) I. 307 His hegehen war..grai. *c* **1314** *Guy Warw.* (Abbotsf. ed.) 7806 He loked on þe wiþ wrake Sternliche wiþ his eyȝen blake. **1432–50** tr. *Higden* (Rolls) I. 145 That region hath peple with whyte heire, peyntede eien and ȝelowe. **1500–20** DUNBAR *None may Assure* x, Ene of amiable blyth asure. **1587** MASCALL *Govt. Cattle, Horses* (1627) 167 The Fleabitten, with a thinne crest, hauing blacke eyne. **1704** POPE *Windsor For.* 351 He turn'd his azure eyes Where Windsor-domes and pompous turrets rise. **1815** SCOTT *Guy. M.* xxxii, This young man..was upwards of six feet high, had..blue eyes. *a* **1852** MOORE *Fire Worshippers*, I never nurs'd a dear gazelle, To glad me with its soft black eye.

transf. **1843** JAMES *Forest Days* (1847) 64 The blue eye of heaven had seldom been altogether withdrawn.

d. taken as including the eyelids, or the surrounding parts; the region of the eyes. See BLACK EYE 2.

c **975** *Rushw. Gosp.* John ix. 6, & ahof ðæt lam ofer eȝu his. *c* **1000** *Sax. Leechd.* I. 108 Wiþ eaȝena sar..ȝenim þysse ylcan wyrte seaw, & smyre ða eaȝan þærmid. *c* **1175** *Lamb. Hom.* 121 Summe þer weren þet his eȝan bunden. *a* **1250** *Owl & Night.* 426 He wolde þat he iseȝe Teres in evrich monnes eȝe. **1375** BARBOUR *Bruce* I. 547 Hys Eyn with his hand closit he. *c* **1386** CHAUCER *Prol.* 10 Smale fowles maken melodie, That slepen al the night with open yhe. **1486** *Bk. St. Albans* B ij a, An hauke that is broght vp vnder a Bussard ..hath wateri Eyghen. *a* **1533** LD. BERNERS *Huon* xlvii. 157 The pyrates..bounde his handes..and iyen. **1675** HOBBES *Odyssey* XVI. 11 Kisses his head and hands, and both his eyne. **1751** SMOLLETT *Per. Pic.* II. lxxvi. 306 These gummy eyes, lantern jaws, and toothless chaps. **1840** E. HOWARD *Jack Ashore* III. ix, That kindly looking gentleman, that's blushing up to the eyes.

e. in invertebrate animals. ***compound eye***: see quot. and COMPOUND *a.* 2 d.

1665 R. HOOKE *Micrographia* 178 Each of these Pearls..is a perfect eye. **1700** T. BROWN tr. *Fresny's Amusem. Ser. & Com.* 87 Their Collections of Rarities exceeds that of John Tradusken for here are..the Eyes of Oysters. **1841–71** T. R. JONES *Anim. Kingd.* (ed. 4) 353 The individual eyes, or *ocelli*, as we shall term them. **1878** *Encycl. Brit.* VIII. 816/1 The compound eye..consists essentially of a series of transparent cone-like bodies, arranged in a radiate manner against the inner surface of the cornea. *Ibid.*, The eyes of many insects have a field of about half a sphere. **1881** *Ibid.* XIII. 143/2 In the larval state the eyes [of insects] are ordinarily simple, and each eye is usually a congregation of separate eye-spots.

2. Phrases. (For those relating to the function of the eyes, etc. see 3–6). **a.** ***mind*** (†***beware***) ***your eye*** (now *vulgar*): look to the safety of your eye; *fig.* be careful. ***one might put a thing in one's eye*** (***and see never the worse***): indicating the insignificance or non-existence of the thing. ***for, by reason of the fair eyes of***: for the sake of; cf. Fr. *pour les beaux yeux de*.

1509 *Payne Evyll Marr.* 146 As moche as a man may put in his eye. **1562** J. HEYWOOD *Prov. & Epigr.* (1867) 34, I might put my winnyng in mine eye, And see neuer the woorse. *a* **1572** KNOX *Hist. Ref.* Wks. 1846 I. 119, I shall lodge all the men-of-ware with my Eae, that shall land in Scotland. **1579** TOMSON *Calvin's Serm. Tim.* 222/1 They rule not by reason of their faire eyes. **1583** GOLDING *Calvin on Deut.* clxxxiv. 1145 It is not for their faire Eyes (as they say). *a* **1663** *Robin Hood* xxxi. in Child *Ballads* 1888 III. v. cxlv. 201/2 The ladies gave a shout, 'Woodcock, beware thyn ee!' *a* **1700** B. E. *Dict. Cant. Crew*, All that you get you may put in your Eye and see ne'er the worse. **1851** MAYHEW *Lond. Labour* (1861) II. 224 You must mind your eye, if you are shovelling slop into a cart.

b. Biblical allusions. ***a beam, a mote in one's eye*** (*Matt.* vii. 3). See also MOTE *sb.*[1] 1 a. ***eye for eye*** (*Exod.* xxi. 24).

c **1000** [see BEAM *sb.*[1] 3 a]. *a* **1300** *Cursor M.* 6701 (Cott.) Ei for ei, and toth for toht. **1570** G. HARVEY *Letter-bk.* (Camden) 5 To pluck out the beame out of his own i. **1910** GALSWORTHY *Sheaf* (1916) 120 The old theory, 'an eye for an eye' condemned to death over nineteen hundred years ago, but still dying very hard in this Christian country. **1938** G. GREENE *Brighton Rock* I. iii. 58 That's what I always say—an eye for an eye and a tooth for a tooth. **1942** E. PAUL *Narrow St.* iii. 27 Thérèse's code was 'an eye for an eye', and the result of her interference was salutary in the extreme.

c. Colloq. ***to pipe the eye, to put the finger in the eye***: derisively used for to weep. ***to cry one's eyes out***: to weep excessively. ***eyes out*** = ALL OUT *advb. phr.* 4; esp. in phr. ***to go eyes out*** (*Austral.* and *N.Z. colloq.*).

1590 SHAKS. *Com. Err.* II. ii. 206 No longer will I be a foole, To put the finger in the eie and weepe. *c* **1626** *Dick of Devon* III. iv. in Bullen *O. Pl.* (1883) II. 58 Would one have thought the foolish ape would putt The finger in the eye and tell it daddy! **1655** FULLER *Ch. Hist.* I. v. §22 So blubber'd with teares, that she may seem almost to have wept her eyes out. **1738** SWIFT *Pol. Conversat.* 27, I can't help it, if I would cry my Eyes out. **1863** E. R. CHUDLEIGH *Diary* 8 Jan. (1950) iii. 63 My horse turning to quickly while I was going eyes out, fell and rowled oaver. **1883** STEVENSON *Treasure Isl.* IV. xix, The smoke..kept us coughing and piping the eye. *a* **1894** *Mod. ditty*, Cry, baby, cry; put your finger in your eye. **1895** J. ROBERTS *Diary* 28/1 You weren't travelling 'eyes out' were you? **1907** MRS. HAWDON *N.Z.ers & Boer War* ix. 185 We went 'eyes out' to catch up. **1945** J. PASCOE in *N.Z. Geographer* Apr. 24 Musterers go 'eyes out' to keep the sheds fed with sheep.

d. *colloq.* or *slang*. Referring to drinking or drunkenness. (See also WET *v.* 7 d.)

1601 SHAKS. *Twel. N.* v. i. 205 O he's drunke..his eyes were set at eight i'th morning. **1610** —— *Temp.* III. ii. 10 Drinke seruant Monster..thy eies are almost set in thy head. **1738** SWIFT *Pol. Conversat.* 15 You must own you had a Drop in your Eye..you were half Seas over. **1789** BURNS *O Willie brewed a peck o' maut*, We're nae that fou, But just a drappie in our e'e. **1840** BARHAM *Ingol. Leg.*, *Bagman's Dog* xix, She ask'd him to 'wet t'other eye'.

e. ***up to the*** (also ***one's***) ***eyes***: *fig.* deeply immersed or occupied; also, very much; completely, to the limit; ***painted*** (***up***) ***to the eyes***: heavily made-up with cosmetics; (***mortgaged***) ***up to the eyes***: to the utmost limit.

1778 A. MURPHY *Know your own Mind* I. 10 Up to his eyes Sir Richard was in love with her. **1786** E. SHERIDAN *Let.* 2 July (1960) 91 Miss or Mrs McCartney who was sitting with her poor palsied head dress'd with flowers and painted up to the eyes. **1848** E. RUSKIN *Let.* in W. James *Order of Release* (1948) v. 114 Lady Morgan who is..painted up to the eyes. **1866** TROLLOPE *Claverings* (1867) I. viii. 97 All the Burtons are full up to their eyes with good sense. **1884** READE *Gd. Stories, Born to Gd. Luck*, A neighbour's estate, mortgaged up to the eyes, was sold under the hammer. **1885** A. DOBSON *At Sign of Lyre* 4 The ladies of St. James's! They're painted to the eyes. **1889** GORDON STABLES in *Boy's Own Paper* 16 Nov. 103/3 The stewards were up to their eyes packing baskets and making preparations. **1949** A. WILSON *Wrong Set* 89 Daisy's up to her eyes at the minute trying to jog the local party into action.

f. ***to*** (***make a person***) ***open*** (***his***) ***eyes***: to (make him) stare with astonishment. ***to close an eye*** (negatively), ***to*** †***lay, put one's eyes together***: to go to sleep. †***my eyes draws straws*** (vulgar): I am sleepy. ***to close one's eyes to*** (something): to ignore, refuse to recognize or consider; ***to shut one's eyes to, against, on***: see SHUT *v.* 4 a.

1633 T. JAMES *Voy.* 36 Not one of them put his eyes together all the night long. **1707** J. STEVENS tr. *Quevedo's Com. Wks.* (1709) 350 He could not lay his Eyes together. **1738** SWIFT *Pol. Conversat.* 214 I'm sure 'tis time for honest Folks to be a-bed—Indeed my Eyes draws straws. **1814** D. H. O'BRIAN *Narrative Escape* 132, I never closed an eye. The night at length elapsed. **1889** JESSOPP *Coming of Friars* ii. 72 The new fashions made his neighbours open their eyes. **1923** J. S. HUXLEY *Ess. Biologist* p. x, Most of man-kind..close their eyes to this possibility.

g. *Sporting.* ***to wipe the eye of another shooter***: to kill game that he has missed. (See also WIPE *v.* 9 d.)

1886 WALSINGHAM & PAYNE-GALLWEY *Shooting* I. 128 If you do perchance wipe the eye..of another shooter.. apologize.

h. *slang* or *vulgar*. ***all my eye***: all humbug, 'stuff and nonsense'; also, in same sense, †***all in the eye***. ***my eye(s!*** used as an expression of astonishment or asseveration. ***my eye*** also used as an expression of emphatic denial; hence as *sb.*, nonsense. See also BETTY MARTIN.

1768 GOLDSM. *Good-n. Man* II, That's all my eye—the king only can pardon. **1782** *George Bateman* II. 113 That's all my eye, and my elbow, as the saying is. **1785** GROSE *Class. Dict. Vulg. Tongue* s.v. *Betty Martin*, That's my eye betty martin. **1819** MOORE *Tom Crib's Mem. Congress* 2 All my eye, Betty. **1824** MISS FERRIER *Inher.* I. xxxi. 344 [A bride] sobbed aloud..although, as Bob and Davy afterwards declared, that was all in the eye. **1811** POOLE *Hamlet Travestied* I. i., As for black clothes,—that's all my eye and Tommy. **1826** T. CREEVEY *Let.* 11 Aug. in J. Gore *Creevey's Life* (1902) x. 226 My eye, what a spot for a '*walky, walky*'. **1838** DICKENS *O. Twist* viii, 'My eyes, how green!' exclaimed the young gentle-man. **1842** S. LOVER *Handy Andy* xvi, Church, my eye, woman! church indeed. **1842** HOOD *Spring* xi, The tenderness of Spring is all my eye. **1871** *Punch* 30 Dec. 271 1 'Nothing in the papers!' Isn't there, though. My eye! **1920** D. H. LAWRENCE *Let.* 25 Jan. (1962) I. 617 One becomes indifferent to all political fates—Fiumes, Jugo-Slavakias and such like my-eye. **1929** W. FAULKNER *Sound & Fury* 138 'How about Bigelow's Mill.. that's a factory.' 'Factory my eye.'

i. ***damn one's eyes***: see DAMN *v.* 5.

j. ***to give one's eyes***: (hyperbolically) to make a great sacrifice; to be willing to give up anything (***to*** be able to do a specified thing). Cf. GIVE *v.* 9 c.

1857 TROLLOPE *Barchester T.* II. xiv. 273 Bertie would give his eyes to go with you. **1875** L. TROUBRIDGE *Life amongst Troubridges* (1966) 120, I gave up directly with a very good grace, considering that I would have given my eyes to go.

k. ***to do*** (someone) ***in the eye***: to defraud, injure, humiliate.

1891 J. M. DIXON *Dict. Idiomatic Phrases* 92 The jockey did your friend in the eye over that horse. **1908** *Punch* 20 May 367/1 Done in the eye again. What on earth do you expect? **1922** F. M. FORD *Let.* 12 Feb. (1965) 138, I have just caught a publisher out, doing me in the eye flagrantly over concealed profits. **1922** F. HAMILTON *P. J.: Secret Service Boy* i. 38 That woman means to do you in the eye, and to score off you. **1930** J. B. PRIESTLEY *Angel Pavement* v. 218 He'd invented the job five minutes before, just to do mother in the eye.

3. a. With reference to its function: The eye as possessing the power of vision. Often pleonastically for emphasis in ***to see with one's own eyes***, †***with*** (or ***at***) ***eye***.

In Eng. as in other langs. *to lose an eye* often means merely to become blind of one eye; similarly ***to put out the eyes*** = to deprive of sight.

c **1290** *S. Eng. Leg.* I. 53/215 Huy i-seien alle with eiȝe. **1297** R. GLOUC. (1724) 376 Me ssolde pulte oute boþe hys eye, & make hym pur blynd. *a* **1300** *Cursor M.* 11324 (Cott.) Symeon..he o ded suld neuer die, Till he suld se crist self wit ei. *c* **1385** CHAUCER *L.G.W.* Prol. 100 Men mosten more thyng beleve Then they may seen at eighe. *c* **1450** *Bk. Curtasye* 323 in *Babees Bk.* (1868) 308 Gase not on walles with þy neghe. **1513** DOUGLAS *Æneis* III. x. 12 All his solace for tinsale of his E. **1539** TAVERNER *Erasm. Prov.* (1552) 13 That the eye seeth not, yͤ herte rueth not. **1584** POWEL *Lloyd's Cambria* 31 Let them belieue no more but what they see with their Eies. **1651** HOBBES *Leviath.* II. xxv. 136 Many eys see more then one. **1707** J. STEVENS tr. *Quevedo's Com. Wks.* (1709) 350, I have seen it with my own Eyes. **1738** SWIFT *Pol. Conversat.* 199 They say, Hedges have Eyes, and Walls have Ears. **1776** *Trial of Nundocomar* 24/2, I have seen him..with my own eyes take off his seal. **1820** KEATS *St. Agnes* xxxix, There are no ears to hear or eyes to see. **1846** GREENER *Sc. Gunnery* 300 We..have a friend who lost an eye and blew down a house side. **1871** ROSSETTI *Poems, Dante at Verona* xxxiii, Thou hast beheld, past sight of eyne. **1878** *Encycl. Brit.* VIII. 822/2 If we wish to see each word distinctly, we 'run the eye' along the line.

b. Phrases. (***to have but***) ***half an eye***: even the smallest power of vision. (***to see***) ***with half an eye***: at a glance, without effort. †***at the eye's end***: close at hand. ***to open any one's eyes***: to restore his sight. †***to put out one's eyes with gifts***: *fig.* to bribe. ***where are your eyes?*** said to a person who fails to observe what he ought to see. ***with all one's eyes, with all the eyes in one's head***: with eager gaze. ***eagle eye***: see EAGLE 10. ***the naked eye***: see NAKED. ***eyes and no eyes***: used to express the difference between an observant and an unobservant person; so, said of or to a person who fails to observe; hence used as the title of a book or series of books dealing with the observation of natural objects. ***to keep one's eye(s) peeled*** or ***skinned***: see the pples. ***to have eyes to see***: to be observant or discerning. ***to keep one's eyes open***: to be watchful or observant.

c **1380** WYCLIF *Serm.* Sel. Wks. II. 94 He [Jesus] openede my yȝen. *a* **1547** UDALL, etc. *Erasm. Par. Mark* Pref. 4 Ought with all the iyen in theyr heades to watche. **1579** FULKE *Heskins' Parl.* 348 Euery man that hath but halfe an eye, seeth these grosse inconueniences. **1598** PELEGROMIUS *Synonym. Sylva* 35/2 To Bribe; *vide* to put out ones eyes with giftes. **1598** W. PHILLIPS *Linschoten* (1864) 190 These Haraffos..can discerne it [counterfeit money] with half an eye. **1611** BIBLE *Ps.* cxlvi. 8 The Lord openeth the eyes of the blinde. **1627–77** FELTHAM *Resolves* I. x. 15 We judg them near, at the eyes end. **1743** BULKELEY & CUMMINS *Voy. S. Seas* 10 The Captain..seeing the Light, ask'd the Master, Where his Eyes were? **1794** AIKEN & BARBAULD *Evenings at Home* IV. 93 (*heading*) Eyes, and no eyes; or, The Art of seeing. **1860** RUSSELL *Diary India* II. xiii, I looked with all my eyes, but they failed to detect any difference. **1865** C. M. YONGE *Clever Woman Fam.* iii, 'There is a wonderful charm in a circumscribed view, because one is obliged to look well into it all.' 'Yes; eyes and no eyes apply there,' said Rachel. **1867** (*title*) Eyes and no eyes. A magazine of meteorology and natural history. **1873** GEO. ELIOT *Let.* 17 Nov. (1955) V. 461 Now we are keeping eyes and ears open for any hint of another little country place. **1883** STEVENSON *Treasure Isl.* IV. xviii, I saw with half an eye that all was over. **1901** (*title*) Cassell's 'Eyes and No Eyes' series. **1912** G. L. STRACHEY *Landmarks Fr. Lit.* vi. 228 To him who had eyes to see, there might be significance in a ready-made suit of clothes, and passion in the furniture of a boarding-house. **1939** E. M. FORSTER *What I Believe* 18 With this type of person knocking about, and constantly crossing one's path if one has eyes to see or hands to feel, the experiment of earthly life cannot be dismised as a failure. **1965** *Listener* 22 July 113/1 During the three weeks I stayed in Dar-es-Salaam, keeping my eyes open and renewing contacts, I was hard put to find evidence of Chinese influence.

c. *fig.*; esp. as attributed to the heart, mind, or to quasi-personified objects.

c **1040** *Rule St. Benet* (Logeman) 2 Geopenedum eaȝum urum. *c* **1175** *Lamb. Hom.* 157 [He] mid þe eȝene of his heorte bihalt in to houene and sicð þe muchele blisse þet he is to ilected. *c* **1230** *Hali Meid.* 3 Opene to understonde þe ehne of þin heorte. **1460** in *Pol. Rel. & L. Poems* (1866) 187 Mi goostli iȝen ben ful of dust. **1590** SHAKS. *Mids. N.* III. ii. 435 Sleepe..sometimes shuts vp sorrowes eie. **1687** T. BROWN *Saints in Uproar* Wks. 1730 I. 82 This it is to want the eye of faith. *a* **1703** BURKITT *On N.T.* Mark vi. 6 A spiritual eye can discern beauty in an humbled and abased Saviour. **1837** NEWMAN *Par. Serm.* (ed. 2) III. xxiii. 372 Excitement, which has power to fascinate the eye of our minds. **1851** HERSCHEL *Stud. Nat. Phil.* II. vi. 166 To witness facts with the eyes of reason. **1856** GRINDON *Life* i. (1875) 5 Science needs all its eyes..to discern it.

d. Applied to a person who uses his eyes on behalf, or instead, of another. *spec.* a detective agency or a detective, esp. a private one (see ***private eye***); a lookout man; see also quot. 1914 (*slang* orig. *U.S.*).

1382 WYCLIF *Job* xxix. 15 An eȝe I was to blinde. **1588** A. KING tr. *Canisius' Catech.* 173, I haue been ane Ee to yͤ blind. **1667** MILTON *P.L.* III. 650 The seav'n Who..are his Eyes That..Bear his swift errands. **1689** HICKERINGILL *Ceremony-monger, Wks.* (1716) II. 503 The Bishop's great Eye (Mr. Arch-deacon) is getting himself a Stomach to his Dinner. **1806** WORDSW. *Ode Intim. Immort.* 112 Thou best Philosopher..thou Eye among the blind. **1836–48** B. D. WALSH *Aristoph.* 17 *note*, The Kings of Persia had certain officers who were called 'his Eyes'. **1914** JACKSON & HELLYER *Vocab. Criminal Slang* 31 *Eye* (*the*),..The Pinkerton Detective Agency; an operative of the Pinkerton Detective Agency. Example: 'Blow this joint; it's protected by the Eye.' **1936** J. G. BRANDON *Pawnshop Murder* x. 90 As the existence of this watcher had been known for some considerable time to Inspector McCarthy..that astute young gentleman gave the 'eye' no chance to weigh upon him. **1955** *Publ. Amer. Dial. Soc.* XXIV. 141 The [Pinkerton Detective] agency is called *the eye*, from its trademark, the all-seeing eye.

e. *fig.* Applied to a city, country, province, etc.: The seat of intelligence or light.

1599 HAKLUYT *Voy.* II. 118 The eyes of the realme, Cambridge, and Oxford. **1671** MILTON *P.R.* IV. 240 Athens, the eye of Greece. **1680** MORDEN *Geog. Rect., England* (1685) 25 In the beautiful Body of the Kingdom of England, the two Eyes are the two Universities. **1845** R. W. HAMILTON *Pop. Educ.* vii. (ed. 2) 165 Massachusetts..is the eye of the States. **1878** BOSW. SMITH *Carthage* 355 Corinth the eye of Greece.

f. Applied in local names to a prominent natural object, such as a hill or island.

1837 *Penny Cycl.* IX. 165/2 Ireland's Eye, a rocky picturesque island of thirty acres. **1891** DIXON *Dict. Idiomatic Eng. Phrases* s.v. *Eye*, The eye of the Baltic—Gothland, or Gottland, an island in the Baltic. **1904** *Daily Chron.* 14 Sept. 5/1 A low rugged hill, nicknamed 'Kuropatkin's eye'.

g. A mechanical or electrical device resembling an eye in its function or appearance; cf. *electric eye, magic eye*.

1955 *Sci. News Let.* 15 Oct. 243/1 Humans are still needed to direct the plane until the 15-mile limit, when its radar 'eyes' spot the attacking bomber. **1959** *Listener* 19 Feb. 327/1 The instrument used is called a proton magnetometer. It consists of two parts: the sensing element, or 'eye', which is a half-pint bottle of water with a 1,000-turn coil of wire wound tightly around it [etc.]. **1962** *Daily Tel.* 24 Apr. 20/6 The Ranger's 'eyes', or light-sensitive diodes, were to.. keep the space-craft on course.

4. a. Used in *sing.* and *pl.* for: The action or function of the eyes; the sense of seeing; 'ocular knowledge' (J.), sight. Chiefly in phrases: (***to have***) ***before one's eyes***: *lit.* and *fig.* ***to believe one's*** (***own***) ***eyes. to catch***, †***fix, strike, take the eye.*** †***at*** (***first***) ***eye***: at first sight. ***to meet the eye***: see MEET *v.* 2 e and f. ***to look*** (someone) ***in*** (occas. ***at***) ***the eye(s)***: to look directly at; to look in the face (see FACE *sb.* 2 b). ***to collect eyes***: see COLLECT *v.* 1 g.

a **1200** *Vices & Virtues* 49 He litlede him seluen to-foren mannes eiȝen. *c* **1400** *Apol. Loll.* 50 Þat for a tym desceyuiþ & iapiþ þe ȝee, but þis biggiþ þe vnderstonding perpetual. **1440** *Test. Ebor.* (Surtees) II. 76 Þai, havand Gode before þer eyghen, do trewe execution of þis my presentt testament. **1471** *Arriv. Edw. IV* (Camden) 38 It appered to every mann at eye the sayde partie was extincte. **1509** FISHER *Wks.* I. (1876) 68 Al thynges be naked and open to his [God's] eyen. *a* **1541** WYATT *Poet. Wks.* (1861) 22 With false favour..you deceive th'ayes. **1587** FLEMING *Contn. Holinshed* III. 1986/1 The English capteines..perceiuing at eie that..they were not able to anie aduantage to mainteine this onset. **1599** SHAKS. *Much Ado* IV. i. 72 Is this face Heroes? are our eies our owne? **1605** —— *Macb.* III. i. 125 Masking the Businesse from the common Eye. **1653** MARVELL *Corr.* I. Wks. 1872–5 II. 4 Demonstrating to the ey which way we ought to travell. **1672** SIR T. BROWNE *Lett. Friend* x. (1881) 134 A weak physiognomist might say at first eye, this was a face of earth. **1715** J. RICHARDSON *Th. Painting* 62 The Death of Ananias ..immediately takes the Eye. **1717** POPE *Ep. Jervas* 33 Thy well-study'd marbles fix our eye. **1784** COWPER *Task* II. 818 Every plague that can infest Society..meets the eye. **1848** MACAULAY *Hist. Eng.* II. 207 The conflict in the royal mind did not escape the eye of Barillon. **1870** CONINGTON *Æneid*

VI. (1873) 201 Banquets smile before their eyne. **1880, 1896** [see LOOK *v.* 1 e]. **1931** E. A. GUEST *Friendly Way* 23, I want to be able as days go by Always to look myself straight in the eye. **1933** H. L. ICKES *Secret Diary* (1953) I. 97, I looked those mayors in the eye and I told them what the exact truth was. **1965** *Listener* 1 July 4/1 To be modern enough to look the great industrial powers in the eye on a basis of full equality.

†**b.** *in (the) eye*: in appearance. *by the eye*: ? in unlimited quantity. *Obs.*

c **1394** *P. Pl. Crede* 84 Grete-hedede quenes wiþ gold by þe eiȝen. *c* **1592** MARLOWE *Jew of Malta* III. iv, Thou shalt have broth by the eye. **1613** BEAUM. & FL. *Kn. Burn. Pestle* II. ii, Here's mony and gold bith' eie my boy. **1684** R. H. *Sch. Recreat.* 117 Mark out the Head of your Pond, and make it the highest part of the Ground in the eye, tho' it be the lowest in the true Level.

†**c.** Range of vision, view, sight. Only in phrases: *in eye*; *in, into, out of (a person's) eye*. *Obs.* in lit. sense.

1599 *Warn. Faire Wom.* II. 770 A very bloudy act.. committed in eye of court. **1602** SHAKS. *Ham.* IV. iv. 6 We shall express our dutie in his eye. **1644** BP. HALL *Rem. Wks.* (1660) 125 He fights in the eye of his Prince. **1665** BOYLE *Occas. Refl.* v. ii. (1675) 301 Ill manag'd Persecutions of Doctrine.. bring them into every body's Eye. **1670** COTTON *Espernon* I. II. 82 He was no sooner remov'd out of his Eye, than that confidence began to stagger. **1673** CHAS. II in *Lauderdale Papers* (1885) III. ii. 2 Your sone Yester (who comes but seldome in my eye). **1677** YARRANTON *Eng. Improv.* 38 A Harbour.. in the very Eye of France. **1711** STEELE *Spect.* No. 113 ¶4 She helped me to some Tansy in the Eye of all the Gentlemen in the Country. **1900** J. K. JEROME *Three Men on Bummel* I. 17 Mr. Pertwee asked me if I had a skipper in my eye.

d. *fig.* *in one's (mind's) eye*: in one's mental view, in contemplation. (See also MIND *sb.*[1] 17 d.)

1602 SHAKS. *Ham.* I. ii. 185, I see my father.. In my minds eye. *c* **1680** BEVERIDGE *Serm.* (1729) I. 411 He must always have it in his eye. **1713** BERKELEY *Ess. in Guardian* vi. Wks. 1871 III. 163 The sages whom I have in my eye speak of virtue as the most amiable thing in the world. **1726** LEONI tr. *Alberti's Archit.* II. 55 b, Some had nothing in their eye, but adorning that which was to contain the body. **1791** 'G. GAMBADO' *Ann. Horsem.* Pref. (1809) 54 Having the safety of man's neck in my eye. **1818** COBBETT *Pol. Reg.* XXXIII. 414, I have.. the little thatched cottages of Waltham Chase .. in my mind's eye.

e. (See quots.)

1933 L. G. D. ACLAND in *Press* (Christchurch, N.Z.) 21 Oct. 15/7 *Force*.. is different from *eye*, the dog's control of sheep by staring them in the face. **1938** J. H. MCCULLOCH *Sheep Dogs* ii. 11 The most striking characteristic of the Border Collie is the one which shepherds refer to as 'The Eye', or the power of the dog to control sheep with its eyes.

5. a. With reference to the direction of the eye; hence often equivalent to: Look, glance, gaze. Often with verbs like *cast, lift, turn*, etc. † *to change, mingle eyes (with)*: to exchange amorous glances (with). *to make eyes at*; *to throw the eye at*: to throw amorous or covetous glances at. † *to throw out one's eyes for*: to look out for. *to see eye to eye* (orig. a misapplication of *Isa.* lii. 8): to be of one mind, think alike (usu. in negative contexts). *to cut eyes* or *one's eye*: to cast a glance or glances (*U.S. slang*) (see also quot. 1961). *eyes on stalks*: eyes protruding with amazement, fear, inquisitiveness, etc.

c **975** *Rushw. Gosp.* Matt. xvii. 8 Ða hiȝ hyra eaȝan upphofon, ne ȝesawon hiȝ nænne. *a* **1225** *Ancr. R.* 54 Eue, þi moder, leop efter hire eien; urom hire eien to þe eppel, vrom þe eppel i parais adun to þes eorðe. *c* **1320** R. BRUNNE *Medit.* 643 To hyr fadyr he kast hys yen. *c* **1485** *Digby Myst.* (1882) II. 572 The Iey ys euer the messenger of foly. **1535** COVERDALE *Ecclus.* xxvii. 1 He that seketh to be riche turneth his eyes asyde. **1596** SHAKS. *1 Hen. IV*, I. iii. 143 On my face he turn'd an eye of death. **1604** —— *Oth.* II. i. 39 As well to see the Vessel that's come in As to throw-out our eyes for braue Othello. **1606** —— *Ant. & Cl.* III. xiii. 156 Would you mingle eyes With one that tyes his points. **1610** —— *Temp.* I. ii. 441 At the first sight They haue chang'd eyes. **1781** COWPER *Conversation* 485 Modestly let fall your eyes. **1798** COLERIDGE *Anc. Mar.* III. xv, Each.. curs'd me with his ee. **1827** L. DOW *Jrnl.* (1850) 177/2 Went to New York, took steamboat to New Brunswick thence stage No. 7, strangers crossed words and cut eyes. **1837** *Southern Lit. Messenger* III. 233 'Why, we thought about here' said he ' that you were cutting your eye at Miss Gatty.' **1842** S. LOVER *Handy Andy* viii, Is it one of my colleens you've been throwing the eye at, Sir? **1852** THACKERAY *Esmond* III. i, She used to make eyes at the Duke of Marlborough. **1879** *Print. Trades Jrnl.* XXVI. 4 Unable to see eye to eye with the subscribers. **1885** 'C. E. CRADDOCK' *Prophet Gt. Smoky Mts.* xv. 288 Ter see him cut his blazin' eye aroun' at ye, ye'd low ez he'd never hearn o' grace. **1935** C. ISHERWOOD *Mr. Norris changes Trains* v. 84 I'm afraid Schmidt and I don't quite see eye to eye on the subject just at present. **1935** LADY FORTESCUE *Perfume from Provence* 178, I found myself hugging the edge of a positive precipice... With eyes on stalks I drove on. **1938** M. K. RAWLINGS *Yearling* xi. 102 Look at him cut his eyes. **1955** *Times* 10 May 9/4 The two Governments do not see eye to eye. **1958** M. STEWART *Nine Coaches Waiting* ix. 130 What *they* call a small private party'd make your eyes stand out on stalks, as the saying is. **1961** F. G. CASSIDY *Jamaica Talk* vii. 137 A *cut-eye* is the action of 'cutting' the eye at someone by way of insult—that is, catching the person's eye, then deliberately turning one's own away.

b. In words of command. *Mil.* (see quots.); so in *Boating, Eyes in the Boat.*

1832 *Prop. Regul. Instr. Cavalry* II. 35 Its Leader gives the word '*Eyes Centre*'. **1833** *Regul. Instr. Cavalry* I. 13 On the word *Eyes Right*, glance the eyes to the right with the slightest turn possible of the head. At the word *Eyes Left*, cast the eyes in like manner to the left. On the word *Eyes Front*, the look and head are to be directly to the front, the habitual position of the soldier. **1837** DICKENS *Pickw.* iv, The command 'eyes front' had been given. **1859** F. A. GRIFFITHS *Artill. Man.* (1862) 152 Captains will give the word 'Eyes right', or 'left', as the inspecting officer comes to their batteries, 'Eyes front' when he has passed. **1887** *Times* (weekly ed.) 18 Nov. 2/5 The words of command were ..'Eyes front; by your right; quick march'.

c. with adjs. expressing the disposition or feeling of the person looking, as *angry, contemptuous, friendly, jealous, loving, wondering.*

a **1300** *Cursor M.* (4078) Cott. Ne wald þai apon him sei Fra þis dai forth wit blithful ei. *Ibid.* 17837 (Cott.) Til heuen þai lifted þair eien brade. *c* **1400** *Rom. Rose* 4264 If oon be fulle of vylanye, Another hath a likerous ighe. **1556** *Aurelio & Isab.* (1608) E iv, Chaste and shame-faste ees. **1611** BIBLE *Prov.* xxii. 9 Hee that hath a bounti-full eye, shall bee blessed. **1735** POPE *Prol. Sat.* 199 View him with.. jealous eyes. **1848** MACAULAY *Hist. Eng.* I. 161 Bowls, horseracing, were regarded with no friendly eye.

d. *the glad eye*: see GLAD *a.* 4 d.

e. *to turn a blind eye*: to refuse to take any notice of a situation, state of affairs, etc.

[**1809** CLARKE & M'ARTHUR *Life of Nelson* II. III. iii. 270 Putting the glass to this blind eye, he [*sc.* Nelson] exclaimed, *I really do not see the signal.*] **1823** M. WILMOT *Let.* 1 Oct. (1935) 197, I turn a blind eye and a deaf ear every now and then, and we get on marvellously well. **1923** J. M. MURRY *Pencillings* 92 We turn a blind eye to the signals which a writer hoists against our expectation. **1925** B. N. ODELL in E. F. Norton *Fight for Everest, 1924* 290 The Tibetans appear to turn a blind eye to the wholesale slaughter involved in the collection.. of over 10,000 specimens by our ardent Natural Historian. **1927** G. K. CHESTERTON *Coll. Poems* 108 Nelson turned his blindest eye On Naples and on liberty. **1963** *Times* 7 Mar. 16/6 The police turn a blind eye to this problem because they are only too glad to get lorries from parking on the main roads.

f. *eyes down*: with one's eyes looking down, *spec.* of bingo-players (see BINGO[2]) looking at their cards; hence as *sb.*, the start of a game of bingo.

1962 *Daily Tel.* 25 June 11 The players kept their 'eyes down' for nearly three hours competing for 10 prizes. **1966** P. MOLONEY *Plea for Mersey* 50 And into the Bingo hall I flew. Eyes down—click click—the game is on. **1969** *Oxf. Mail* 17 Jan. 2 (Advt.), Plaza Bingo Club... Eyes Down 7.45. Doors Open 6.0 p.m.

g. *a gleam (glint, twinkle) in one's eye*, a barely formed idea; *spec.* a child who has not yet been conceived.

1964 C. DRIVER *Disarmers* x. 242 As for mass revolutionary civil disobedience, this was never really much more than a gleam in Ralph Schoenman's eye. **1965** E. LACY *Double Trouble* x. 134 You were on the force when I was a gleam in my pop's sexy eye. **1965** B. SWEET-ESCOTT *Baker Street Irregular* ii. 50 At the time of his arrival.., all this was hardly more than a glint in Colin's eyes. **1966** *Guardian* 10 Nov. 3/7 The proposal remains but a twinkle in the Home Secretary's eye. **1967** *Ibid.* 2 Jan. 8/1 This 'walkers' route is now no more than a gleam in the eye—but so was the Pennine Way when Tom Stephenson first thought of it.

6. a. An attentive or observing look, *lit.* and *fig.*; observation, supervision; attention, regard. Chiefly in phrases: *(to be) all eyes*: all attention. †*to bear, give, good eyes upon*: to pay close attention to, watch attentively. *to give an eye to*: to give a share of one's attention to. *to keep, have an (one's) eye †after, upon*: to keep watch upon. *under the eye of*: under the observation or attention of. *to keep, have an* (or *one's*) *eye on*: to keep watch upon; to observe carefully or be wary of; hence, to desire or intend to obtain; to approve of.

c **1430** *Syr Gener.* (Roxb.) 3934 Segryne had euer on him his eye. *c* **1460** J. RUSSELL *Bk. Nurture* 527 Looke ye bere good yȝes vppon oþur connynge kervers. *c* **1475** *Rauf Coilȝear* 695, I mon.. eirnestly efter him haue myne Eay. **1586** J. HOOKER *Girald. Irel.* in *Holinshed* II. 26/2 Maurice Fitzgerald.. gaue good eie and watched the matter verie narowlie. **1605** CHAPMAN *All Fooles* III. i. sig. F 1 *Rin.* What would he be, If you should not restrayne him by good connsell? *Gost.* Ile haue an eye on him, I warrant thee. **1610** SHAKS. *Temp.* IV. i. 59 No tongue: all eyes: be silent. **1641** MILTON *Animadv.* Wks. (1851) 219 He.. hath yet ever had this Island under the special indulgent eye of his Providence. **1659** B. HARRIS *Parival's Iron Age* 211 It was supposed the Earle of Essex had an eie upon Oxford. **1818** COBBETT *Pol. Reg.* XXXIII. 64, I shall keep my eye upon them. **1824** MEDWIN *Convers. Byron* (1832) I. 53, I had.. fallen under the eye of the Government. **1851** W. CLARK in W. Bolland *Cricket Notes* 141 There he was sure to be with his eye on every one to see if all was right. **1874** *N. & Q.* 5th Ser. I. 361/2 *Have one's eye on*; *i.e.*, to approve of. **1877** *Independent* 23 Aug. 20/2 The Devil already controls Chicago, and we have heard it intimated that he has his eye on New York. **1895** W. S. GILBERT *Foggerty's Fairy in Original Plays* 3rd Ser. 29 I'll keep my eye on that young man. **1900** H. JAMES *Notebooks* (1947) 398 Chad has meanwhile continued to deny.. that he has his eye on Mlle de Vionnet, that her mother has.. hers on him. **1945** E. BOWEN *Demon Lover* 92, I needn't exactly hurry. I just ought to keep an eye on the time. **1956** A. WILSON *Anglo-Saxon Att.* I. iv. 156 'And now you are going to leave us, Mr Middleton, we shall miss you very much.' It was usually said by the mothers who had their eye on rich young bachelors. *Ibid.* II. ii. 319 You asked me to keep an eye on that Larrie Rourke.

b. *to have an eye to*: to look to, pay attention to; to have as one's object, have regard for; to have reference to. *with an eye to*: with a view to; with a design upon.

1375 BARBOUR *Bruce* VI. 523 The Kyng.. Till thame, and nouthir ellis-quhar Had ey. *Ibid.* XII. 306, I pray ȝhow That nane of ȝow for gredynes Haf E till tak of thair Richess. **1526** *Pilgr. Perf.* (W. de W. 1531) 73 b, Some feareth synne & payne bothe, hauynge an eye and respecte to bothe in maner indifferently. **1535** COVERDALE *2 Macc.* viii. 2 They called vpon the Lorde, yᵗ he wolde haue an eye vnto his people. **1593** NASHE *Four Lett. Confut.* 67 Haue an eie to the maine-chaunce. **1607** BACON *Ess., Counsel* (Arb.) 322 Men will Councell with an eye to them-selves. **1641** *Jrnl. Ho. Comm.* II. 183 An especial eye may be had over all Counties, where Papists are most residing. **1664** EVELYN *Kal. Hort.* (1729) 210 Have still an Eye to the weeding and cleansing Part. **1713** STEELE *Englishman* No. 11. 74 A Man will have an Eye to his first Appearance in Publick. **1756** C. LUCAS *Ess. Waters* III. 285 The gentlemen of the corporation.. have.. no small eye to gain. **1838** LYTTON *Alice* 171 Maltravers has an eye to the county, one of these days. **1861** THORNBURY *Turner* I. 358 He collects analytical diagrams of Dutch boats, with an eye to get nearer to Vandervelde. **1875** JOWETT *Plato* (ed. 2) V. 58 What I said about the Cretan laws .. had an eye to war only. **1888** FROUDE *Eng. in W. Indies* 40 Gold and silver plate, he observed with an eye to business was.. abundant.

c. *to have eyes for*: to pay attention to; to be interested in or attracted to (freq. in contexts excluding all but one person or thing); to desire. (Hence *eyes* is used in *U.S. slang* to mean 'a desire or inclination'.)

1810 J. PORTER *Scottish Chiefs* IV. xii. 357 Helen had eyes for none but Wallace. **1923** J. S. HUXLEY *Ess. Biologist* i. 56 To be so horrifiedly fascinated by it as not to have eyes for anything else. **1934** A. DUBIN (*song title*) I only have eyes for you. **1948** *New Yorker* 3 July 28 Have you eyes for a sandwich? **1951** W. SANSOM *Face of Innocence* xiii. 189 There's a gaz-and-pneu baron from Bormes has only eyes for her. **1955** L. FEATHER *Encycl. Jazz* x. 346 *Eyes*, desire, ambition. ('No eyes'—'I'm not interested'.)

d. *to keep, have an eye* (or *a sharp eye*) *out*: to be very alert or watchful.

1889 'MARK TWAIN' *Yankee* ii. 17, I moved away,.. keeping an eye out for any chance passenger in his right mind. **1942** *Horizon* July 57 She's got a sharp eye out, Mrs Pike has.

7. (in *sing.* only). The faculty of perception or discrimination of visual objects, either in general or in some special connexion. Often in phrases: *to have, with, the eye of* (a painter, etc.). *to have an eye for (proportion*, etc.). (*to estimate*, etc.) *by (the) eye*: as opposed to measurement, etc. Also, *Sport*: *to have, get, one's eye (well) in*: to be or become able to judge accurately of distance and direction, as in Billiards, Shooting, etc. *a straight eye*: see STRAIGHT *a.* 7.

1657 AUSTEN *Fruit Trees* II. 93 Shew clearly (to a discerning eie). **1715** J. RICHARDSON *Th. Painting* 150 He has a Good Eye on the Sense, as one is said to have a Good Ear for Musick. **1719** —— *Art Crit.* 188 It does not appear to have been done by any other help than the Correctness of the Eye. **1774** M. MACKENZIE *Maritime Surv.* 88 Estimate by the Eye the Distance of C from A. **1796** *Instr. & Reg. Cavalry* (1813) 67 The leader of the column will march by his eye. **1847** L. HUNT *Jar Honey* Pref. (1848) 9 Who saw their colours with the eye of a painter. **1855** MACAULAY *Hist. Eng.* IV. 433 He had not.. the eye of a great captain for all the turns of a battle. **1865** J. PYCROFT *Cricketana* xi. 216 As to his guess hits.. we can only suppose.. that he reserves them till his 'eye is well in', and he has observed the uniform break or rise of the ball. **1875** JOWETT *Plato* (ed. 2) II. 271 An eye for proportion is needed. **1882** *Bell's Life in London* 1 July 4/6 Bannerman.. though he must have fairly 'got his eye in', scarcely ever attempted to hit. **1884** *Q. Rev.* No. 316. 482 Their eyes were well in. **1912** A. BRAZIL *New Girl at St. Chad's* vii. 115 When you're in doubt, watch each ball carefully, till you get your eye in.

8. *fig.* Point of view, manner or way of looking at a thing; estimation, opinion, judgement. In phrases: *in, with the eye(s of (a person)*. *in the public eye*. Also, *in the eye of (the) law, logic*, etc.: according to the terms or rules of. *to look with another eye upon*: to take a different view of.

a **1340** HAMPOLE *Psalter* Prol., Faire & lufly in cristes eghen. **1594** SHAKS. *Rich. III*, III. vii. 112 Some offence, That seemes disgracious in the Cities eye. *a* **1617** BAYNE *On Eph.* (1658) 48 God doth give us love in the eies of some good man. **1628** COKE *On Litt.* fol. 58 *Court baron*.. in the eye of Law it hath relation to the Freeholders, who are Judges of the Court. **1635** A. STAFFORD *Fem. Glory* (1869) 56 Sinnes more odious even in our own eies. **1643** UDALL *Serm.* (1645) 37 To his sad disconsolate wife, mourning too two much, in his eye [etc.]. **1659** B. HARRIS *Parival's Iron Age* 206 The King.. became more considerable in the eyes of the World, then any of his predecessors. **1683** *Lond. Gaz.* No. 1835/3 If the City should Look upon it with another Eye. **1742** POPE *Dunc.* IV. 534 Self-conceit to some her glass applies, Which no one looks in with another's eyes. **1761** HUME *Hist. Eng.* II. xxxvi. 286 Persons not lying under.. attainder were innocent in the eye of the law. **1766** GOLDSM. *Vic. W.* xxviii, No other marriage of his shall ever be legal in my eye. **1818** BYRON *Juan* I. lxviii, I can't tell whether Julia saw the affair With other people's eyes, or if her own Discoveries made. **1869** FREEMAN *Norm. Conq.* (1876) III. xiii. 281 In the eye of logic or of sound morals. **1882** SERJT. BALLANTINE *Experiences* xix. 185 He was a man of mark in the eyes of my family.

†**II. 9. a.** Slight shade, tinge. (Cf. F. *œil*). *Obs.*

1610 SHAKS. *Temp.* II. i. 55 *Ant.* The ground indeed is tawny. *Seb.* With an eye of greene in't. *a* **1641** SUCKLING *Goblins* III. (ed. 2) 25 None of these Beards will serve, There's not an eye of white in them. *a* **1661** FULLER *Worthies* (1840) III. 499 This.. name seemeth to have in it an eye or cast of Greek and Latin. **1664** EVELYN *Kal. Hort.* (1972) 204 A natural Earth with an Eye of Loam in it. **1677** PLOT *Oxfordsh.* 279 A true blue dye, having an eye of red. **1699** EVELYN *Acetaria* 98 Oyl.. with an Eye.. of.. Olive green.

b. (See quot.)

1736 Bailey (folio), *Eye*, the lustre and brilliant of pearls and precious stones, more usually call'd the water.

III. An object resembling the eye in appearance, shape, or relative position.

10. On plants: **a.** the axillary bud; the leaf-bud of a potato; **b.** the remains of the calyx on fruit; **c.** the centre of a flower.

1615 W. Lawson *Orch. & Gard.* III. x. (1668) 26 Let your graff have three or four eyes for readiness to put forth. **1672-3** Grew *Anat. Plants* II. I. i. §7 Potato's [root] where the Eyes or Buds of the future Trunks lie inward. **1710** London & Wise *Compl. Gard.* (1719) 167 Apples..may be plac'd either upon the Eye or Stalk. **1772** Foote *Nabob* II. Wks. 1799 II. 303 For pip, colour, and eye, I defy the whole parish..to match 'em [polyanthuses]. **1787** Winter *Syst. Husb.* 157 Six scotch potatoes, cut into thirty-three sets, with two eyes each. **1858** Carpenter *Veg. Phys.* §121 The points commonly known as the eyes of the Potato. *Ibid.* §586 By the remains of the calyx..the eye of the gooseberry is formed. *Ibid.* §605 The smaller the eye..of the dahlia, the better it is considered to be. **1870** Hooker *Stud. Flora* 268 Corolla minute, pale blue with a white eye. **1882** *Garden* 18 Mar. 183/2 Vine eyes from Spain..make better and stronger Vines than those propagated from eyes produced in this country.

11. ***eye of a crab, a crawfish*** = crab's-eye.

1661 Lovell *Hist. Anim. & Min.* 190 The eyes or stones [of the crab] coole, dry, cleanse, discusse, breake the stone. **1753** Hanway *Trav.* I. I. xv. 98 These eyes [of crawfish] are sent into turkey..to be used in medicines.

12. A spot resembling an eye; *esp.* **a.** One of the spots near the end of the tail-feathers of a peacock. **b.** One of the three spots at one end of a coconut. **c.** A small dark spot in the eggs of fish and insects while hatching. **d.** An eye-like spot in the wing of an insect; an ocellus. (Cf. eyelet *sb.* 3 a.)

1387 Trevisa *Higden* (Rolls) IV. 7 A litel stone wiþ yene. **1398** —— *Barth. De P.R.* XII. xxxii. (1495) 432 The pecok hath..a taylle full of eyen. **1556** *Aurelio & Isab.* (1608) G ij, Delectabler..then seamethe unto the pecocke his tale chargede with ees. **1601** Holland *Pliny* I. 396 They make a shew of the eyes appearing in Peacockes tailes. **1622** Peacham *Compl. Gentl.* (1661) 163 A mantle wrought with gold and Peacocks eyes. **1658** J. Rowland tr. *Moufet's Theat. Ins.* I. xiv. 959 She hath four great wings, every one of them having eyes of divers colours. **1720** E. Albin *Nat. Hist. Eng. Insects* Tab. IV, On the 6th of July came Forth a beautiful Butter-fly with Eyes in his Wings. **1736** Bailey (folio), *Eye of a Bean*, a black speck..in the cavity of the corner-teeth of a horse. **1788** Cowper *On Mrs. Montague's Feather Hangings* 4 The Peacock sends his..starry eyes. **1840** *Penny Cycl.* XL. 334/1 In this last [variety] the eyes or circlets of the train [of the peacock] are shadowed out. **1860** W. S. Coleman *Brit. Butterflies* vi. 72 The 'eyes' are velvety black. *Ibid.* 73 Especially to be admired are the double-ringed 'eyes'. **1863** F. Buckland in G. C. Bompas *Life* vii. (1885) 125 No eyes yet in the [trout's] eggs. **1865** Tylor *Early Hist. Man.* vi. 131 The diviner..will spin a cocoa-nut, and decide a question according to where the eye of the nut looks towards when at rest again. **1876** *Encycl. Brit.* IV. 595/2 The Peacock Butterfly..conspicuous from the 'eyes' on the upper surface of its wings. *Ibid.* 596/2 *Tropæa luna*, ..with wings of a lemon colour, each with a 'transparent eye'. **1885** H. O. Forbes *Nat. Wanderings* ii. 27 Having pierced the proper eye with one of its spindle ambulatory legs, it [the Birgus] rotates the nut round it. **1959** L. H. Newman *Looking at Butterflies* 78 The centre of the eye is black and wine-red... The hind-wings also carry large eye-spots.

e. Also applied to the dark spot in hens' eggs.

1895 *Pearson's Weekly* 18 May 712 The yolk of one average-sized hen's egg (from which the 'eye' has been removed).

f. *Geol.* [tr. G. *auge* eye: cf. augen.] A lens-shaped inclusion in a rock, esp. gneiss, of a different texture from the groundmass of the rock.

1898 *Summary Progr. Geol. Surv. U.K. 1897* 37 Besides the bands and streaks of pegmatite there are many 'eyes' of felspar. **1906** E. H. Adye *Cent. Atlas Microsc. Petrogr.* 52 Sporadic crystals of iron pyrite also occur and often take on the so-called 'eye-structure'. **1920** A. Holmes *Nomencl. Petrol.* 39 *Augen-gneiss*, a general term for gneissose rocks, independently of their origin, containing 'eyes', i.e. phacoidal or lenticular crystals, or aggregates, which simulate the porphyritic crystals of igneous rocks. **1930** Peach & Horne *Geol. Scotl.* iv. 117 The pegmatites show fluxion structure with felspar 'eyes'. **1959** W. W. Moorhouse *Study Rocks in Thin Section* xxv. 409 Augen gneiss is a sheared granulated gneiss containing porphyroclasts or 'eyes' (augen), usually of feldspar.

†**13.** ***eye of the world***: = ***hydrophane***. *Obs.* [transl. of mod.L. ***oculus mundi***: cf. the Arab. name *ʿain aššams* 'eye of the sun'.]

[**1672** Boyle *Origin Gems* 107 Though the Oculus Mundi be reckoned by Classic Authors among the rare Gems.] **1772** *Cronstedt's Min.* App. 6, I have seen the Eye of the World..in Sir Hans Sloane's Collection.

14. *Naut.* '***eyes of her***' (see quot. 1867). Also ***eyes of the ship***, and (simply) ***eyes***.

1840 Marryat *Poor Jack* xxii, Being right in the eyes of her..we could [etc.]. **1867** Smyth *Sailor's Word-bk.* 284 *Eyes of her*, the foremost part of the bay, or in the bows of a ship. In olden times, and now in Spanish and Italian boats ..an eye is painted on each bow. **1880** *Times* 25 Dec. 7/4 A heavy forecastle in the eyes of her. **1890** W. C. Russell *Ocean Trag.* II. xix. 134 Sleeping as he did, right in the 'eyes', he got the very full of the motion. **1908** *Westm. Gaz.* 29 Apr. 4/1 There was also a man in the look-out—at what was called the eyes of the ship.

15. †**a.** A fountain or spring; = Heb. *'ʿayin*, Arab. *ʿain*. **b.** The opening through which the water wells up. Cf. well-eye.

1609 Bible (Douay) *Deut.* xxxiii. 28 The eie of Jacob in the land of corne and wine. **1842** *Penny Cycl.* XXII. 290/2 The place where the river re-appears is called *Los Ojos de Guadiana* (the eyes of the Guadiana). **1857** Livingstone *Trav.* vi. 111 A hollow, which anciently must have been the eye of a fountain. **1883** J. Mackenzie *Day-dawn in Dark Places* 70 There are three separate wells or 'eyes' to this fountain.

16. a. A central mass; the brightest spot or centre (of light).

1864 *Intell. Observ.* V. 371 The net being drawn through a 'scull' or shoal of the fish, breaks what is called the eye of the fish. **1867** Smyth *Sailor's Word-bk.* 284 *Eyght*, the thickest part of a scule of herrings; when this is scattered by the fishermen, it is termed 'breaking the ey'. **1870** J. Roskell in *Eng. Mech.* 18 Mar. 647/2 When the button of melted copper..assumes a bright colour, and the centre, which the essayer calls the *eye*, being dark, the front brick is ..drawn aside.

b. A mass of ore left in a mine to be worked when other ore is becoming scarce or inaccessible; hence *fig.*, a 'plum', a tit-bit left to the last; (*Austral.* and *N.Z.*) the choicest portion of a piece of land; esp. in phr. ***to pick*** (or ***take***) ***the eyes out of*** (or ***from***).

1839 De la Beche *Rep. Geol. Cornwall* 561 The ores thus left in various places are often termed the eyes of the mine; and when it may be necessary, in abandoning the mine,..to remove them, it is termed, picking out the eyes of the mine. **1865** *Ararat Advertiser* (Vict.) 13 June, Sections were taken up and the 'eye picked from the area'. **1865** *Australasian* 23 June, The great prizes—the allotments which were the eyes of the runs. **1891** R. Wallace *Rural Econ. Austral. & N.Z.* i. 24 The original settlers..had in colonial phraseology 'picked the eyes out of the country' in making their selection. **1895** G. Chamier *South-Sea Siren* xi. 165, I took 'the eyes out of it', as we say—spotted all the best patches, secured all the waterholes. **1905** *Westm. Gaz.* 9 Mar. 9/2 We do not want anybody to come in and 'pick the eyes' out of our districts—to take away the profitable load and leave the unprofitable one. **1945** Baker *Austral. Lang.* iii. 56 The word *eye* became the epitome of all that was choice in land.

c. The centre of a target; = bull's-eye 7.

a **1877** in Knight *Dict. Mech.*

d. The bright red spot observed through the mica- or glass-covered sight hole of a blast furnace.

1884 W. H. Greenwood *Steel & Iron* vii. 126 A small slide containing a glass or mica plate, through which the state of the furnace may be observed; the bright spot thus seen is known as the 'eye of the furnace'. **1888** *Lockwood's Dict. Mech. Engin.* s.v., The eye of a furnace is that spot or area embraced or commanded by the sight holes.

e. The main mass of lean meat in a rasher of bacon, cutlet, etc.

1934 in Webster. **1951** S. Bull *Meat for Table* vii. 77 The eye is more tender than the remainder of the bottom round and may be fried. **1959** *Times* 30 Mar. 10/7 The eye of lean on the all important..back rasher was good in both breeds. **1960** *Farmer & Stockbreeder* Suppl. 16 Feb. 14 Judges assess the number of marks to award for 'size and shape of the eye of lean'. **1966** *Guardian* 22 July 10/5-6 The noisettes of lamb are..the small circular eye of meat in the cutlet.

17. *Painting.* (See quot.)

1859 Gullick & Timbs *Paint.* 201 'Eyes', as the abrupt terminations of the longitudinal divisions of folds are named.

18. *Naut.* ***in the wind's eye***: in the direction of the wind. ***into the wind's eye***: to windward. ***to be a sheet in the wind's eye***: *fig.* to be slightly intoxicated.

1562 J. Heywood *Prov. & Epigr.* (1867) 114 The weather-cockis beke is..in the windis eie. **1628** Digby *Jrnl.* (Camden) 50 The 4 galliottes..rowed into the windes eye. **1743** Bulkeley & Cummins *Voy. S. Seas* 135 The Sound.. is not above a League in the Wind's Eye. **1823** Byron *Juan* x. iv, In the wind's eye I have sail'd. **1834** Medwin *Angler in Wales* II. 145 A better sea-boat..but she could not walk in the wind's eye. **1853** Kane *Grinnell Exp.* xxiv. (1856) 179 To see our pack-bound neighbors..steam ahead dead in the wind's eye. **1883** Stevenson *Treasure Isl.* IV. xx, Maybe you think we were all a sheet in the wind's eye. But I'll tell you I was sober.

19. The centre of revolution. Also in phrase ***to open its eye***.

1760-72 tr. *Juan & Ulloa's Voy.* (ed. 3) II. VIII. iii. 210 The cloud..begins, according to the sailor's phrase, to open its eye, i.e. the cloud breaks, and the part of the horizon where it was formed becomes clear. **1867** F. Francis *Angling* v. 144 The eye of the stream..is always the most favourable spot for fish. By the eye I mean the first good eddy on the inside of any stream after it commences its shoot. **1884** *Science* Jan. 63 The..dreadful calm within the whirl, to which sailors have given the name of 'the eye of the storm'.

20. A hole or aperture.

a. In a needle: The hole or aperture formed to receive the thread.

c **950** *Lindisf. Gosp.* Luke xxiii. 25 Ðerh ðyrl *or* eȝnedles. *c* **1000** *Ags. Gosp.* ibid., Eaðelicor mæȝ se olfend ȝan þurh.. nædle eaȝe. **1382** Wyclif *Matt.* xix. 24 It is liȝter, or eysier a camel for to passe thorwȝ a nedelis eiȝe. *c* **1400** *Lanfranc's Cirurg.* 36 A nedle þre cornerid whos iȝe schal be holid on boþe sidis. **1606** Shaks. *Tr. & Cr.* II. i. 87 So much wit.. As will stop the eye of Helens needle. **1712-4** Pope *Rape Lock* II. 128 Wedg'd whole ages in a bodkin's eye. **1740** Cheyne *Regimen* 313 The Rays of Millions of different Flambeaux may pass..through the Eye of a Needle. **1831-4** J. Holland *Manuf. Metal* II. 358 The formation of the gutters and the piercing of the eye.

b. A hole pierced in a tool or implement, for the insertion of some other object.

1554 *Ludlow Churchw. Acc.* (Camden) 57 For makynge the iee of the clapper [of a bell]..xiiijd. **1703** Moxon *Mech. Exerc.* 155 Put the Eyes of the Hindges over the Pins of the Hooks. **1747** Hooson *Miner's Dict.* E j b, When the Miner haums a Pick, there is always Some of the Haum comes through the Eye. **1796** Pearson in *Phil. Trans.* LXXXVI. 445 Its [the axe's] length from eye to edge was seven inches. **1827** J. F. Cooper *Prairie* I. ii. 26 He buried his axe to the eye, in the soft body of a cotton-wood tree. **1867** Smyth *Sailor's Word-bk.* 284 *Eye of an anchor*, the hole in the shank wherein the ring is fixed. **1881** F. J. Britten *Watch & Clockm.* 33 The eye should be made close to the end of the spring which should be rounded.

c. An opening or passage for the introduction or withdrawal of material, as in the 'runner' or upper stone of a mill, in a kiln, etc.; also for exit or ingress, as in a fox's earth, a mine, etc.

1686 Burnet *Trav.* v. (1750) 277 He comes out at the Eye of the Mill all in Wafers. **1741** *Compl. Fam. Piece* II. i. 295 Having found a Fox's Earth, cause all his Holes you can find to be stopt, except the main Hole or Eye that is most beaten. **1747** Hooson *Miner's Dict.* G iv, *Eye of the Shaft*..is the very beginning of the Surface or Grass Clod, sometimes called the Mouth in old Works. **1776** Young *Tour in Irel.* (1780) 301 He burns it in arched kilns, with several eyes. **1812** *Chron.* in *Ann. Reg.* 1811, 5 When the men employed at the lime-kiln..went to their work, they found a man and a woman lying dead on the edge of its eye. ? **1842** E. J. Lance *Cottage Farmer* 19, 4½ bushels of flour from the eye of the mill. **1843** *Jrnl. R. Agric. Soc.* IV. I. 27 The main drain opens into the ditch at a spot called the 'eye'. **1843** Portlock *Geol.* 682 In each quadrant of the kiln, there is an opening, called an eye, or fire-hole. **1884** Knight *Dict. Mech.* IV. 605 A damsel on the spindle..agitates the show beneath the hopper and causes the grain to dribble into the eye of the runner.

d. A small hole or hollow in bread or cheese, etc. (Cf. bull's-eye 12). [Cf. Fr. *œil* in same sense.]

1528 Paynell *Salerne Regim.* E ij, Chese..not to tough.. nor to full of eies. **1607** Topsell *Four-f. Beasts* (1673) 483 Cheeses made of their [Sheep's] milk is..full of eyes and holes. **1649** Blithe *Eng. Improv. Impr.* (1653) 143 A Mud, or Sludg..which is very soft, full of Eyes and Wrinckles. **1688** R. Holme *Armory* III. v. 244 Bad cheese..full of Eyes, not well prest. **1710** J. Clarke *Rohault's Nat. Phil.* (1729) I. 29 Those large Spaces which we call the Eyes of the Bread. **1879** Miss Jackson *Shropsh. Word-bk.* s.v., I like bread full of eyes, cheese without any. **1955** J. G. Davis *Dict. Dairying* (ed. 2) 192 The holes or 'eyes'..are the result of the propionic acid fermentation in the cheese. **1961** *Which?* Sept. 234/2 At times the so-called eyes do not form in Swiss cheese, and the resulting cheese is known as blind cheese.

21. a. A loop of metal or thread in a 'hook and eye', *esp.* that used as a fastening in dresses. Also a metal ring for holding a rod or bolt, or for a rope, etc., to pass through.

1599 Minsheu *Sp. Dict.* (1623), *Hevilla*..hooks and eies of siluer. **1611** Cotgr., *Piton*..an Eye for a curtaine rod [etc.]. *a* **1658** Cleveland *Pet. Poem* 23 My Eyes are out, and all my Button-moulds Drop. **1697** Derham in *Phil. Trans.* XX. 2 On the Top I left an Eye in the Wire. **1715** Desaguliers *Fires Impr.* 130 Two Iron Eyes for the ends of the Axis to play in. **1763** Del Pino *Sp. Dict.*, *Máchos y hémbras*, hooks and eyes. **1831** Brewster *Nat. Magic* x. (1833) 247 Having..made it [the rope] pass through a fixed iron eye. **1865** J. C. Wilcocks *Sea Fisherman* (1875) 35 A piece of brass wire (having eyes turned at the ends). **1880** W. C. Russell *Sailor's Sweetheart* (1881) II. iv. 201 A couple of scuttlebutts lashed..to eyes in the bulwarks. *Mod.* The stair-rods are too large for the eyes.

b. A loop of cord or rope; *esp.* 'the circular loop of a shroud or stay, where it goes over the mast' (Adm. Smyth); and in other nautical applications. Also the loop at one end of a bowstring.

1584 R. Scot *Discov. Witchcr.* XIII. xxix. 277 Put the eie of the one [cord] into the eie or bowt of the other. *a* **1642** Sir W. Monson *Naval Tracts* III. (1704) 345/2 An Eye or two, and a Wall-knot. **1769** Falconer *Dict. Marine* (1789), *Collet d'étai*, the eye of a stay placed over a mast-head. **1797** Nelson in Nicolas *Disp.* II. 324 Two pair of main-shrouds cut in the eyes. **1867** Smyth *Sailor's Word-bk.* 275 *Elliot-eye* ..is an eye worked over an iron thimble in the end of a hempen bower-cable, to facilitate its being shackled to the chain for riding in very deep water. *Ibid.* 283 *Flemish eye*, particularly applied to the eye of a stay, which is either formed at the making of the rope; or by dividing the yarns into two equal parts, knotting each pair separately and pointing the whole over after parcelling. **1882** Nares *Seamanship* (ed. 6) 9 The eyes of the rigging.

22. a. *Arch.* (see quot. 1888).

1727-51 Chambers *Cycl.*, *Eye of the Volute.* **1888** Gwilt *Archit.* Gloss. 1277 *Eye*, a general term signifying the centre of any part: thus the eye of a pediment is a circular window in its centre. The eye of a dome is the horizontal aperture on its summit. The eye of a volute is the circle at the centre, from whose circumference the spiral line commences.

b. *transf.* in *Conchology*.

1755 *Gentl. Mag.* XXV. 32 Volute, is that twist of spirals which winds round the axis or columella, diminishing by degrees, and ending in a point called the eye. *Ibid.* 34 The eye [of the shell] is perfectly white, and shaped like a nipple.

†**23.** *Anat.* ***eye of the knee***: the knee-cap.

c **1400** *Lanfranc's Cirurg.* 177 To kepe þis ioynture from harm, is ioyned þeron a round boon &..of summen it is clepid þe yȝe of þe knee.

24. *Typog.* †**a.** = the face of a type. [Fr. *œil*]

b. The enclosed space in the letters *d*, *e*, *o*, etc.

1676 Moxon *Reg. Trium Ord. Lit. Typo.* 22 In the Parallel of 23 draw a line for the Eye, from the inside of e to the outside on the right hand. **1736** Bailey (folio), *Eye* (with Printers) is sometimes used for the thickness of the types or characters used in Printing; or more strictly the graving in relievo on the top or face of a letter. *Mod.* The eyes of the type are filled up.

c. *Advertising.* (See quot.)

1924 J. McKechnie *Rational Book-Keeping* viii. 111 In advertising, the line at the top is called the 'eye' of an advertisement.

25. ***artificial eye.*** Also simply 'eye'. A glass imitation of the natural eye.

1832 BABBAGE *Econ. Manuf.* §235, I.. determined to think of the dolls' eyes.. I satisfied myself that the eyes alone would produce a circulation of a great many thousand pounds. **1884** *Syd. Soc. Lex.* s.v. *Eye*, Artificial eye, a thin shell or concavo-convex piece of glass or enamel, coloured in imitation of a natural eye, which is introduced beneath the lid when the eye has been enucleated. **1888** *Encycl. Brit.* XXIII. 90/2 Artificial eyes are inserted.. and the specimen is then placed.. to dry.

26. ***glass eye.*** **a.** = prec. **b.** also simply 'eyes': A pair of spectacles. **c.** = BULL'S EYE.

15.. KENNEDY *Agst. Mouth-Thankless* v. (in *Evergreen*), In thy Bag thou beirs thyne Een. **1710** *Acc. Death Tom Whigg* II. 39 A Glass Eye, the Workmanship.. of the Famous Gualtero. **1719** D'URFEY *Pills* III. 18 A pair of Glass Eyes to clap on my Nose. **1785** MRS. A. M. BENNETT *Juvenile Indiscretions* (1786) I. 62, I must put on my eyes.. yes, I see I was mistaken. **1886** *Pall Mall G.* 22 Dec. 5 I The pale rays of the sun show through the glass eyes on deck. **1890** COUES *Handbk. Ornithology* 66 Glass eyes, of all sizes and colours, may be purchased at a moderate cost.

IV. *attrib.* and *Comb.*

27. General relations: **a.** attributive, (portions or natural appendages of the eye) as ***eye-brim, -orbit, -place, -root, -slit, -socket, -stripe***; (actions, properties, qualities, sensations of or pertaining to the eye) as ***eye-colour, -craft, -encounter, -glance, -level, -love, -movement, -pleasure, -range, -reach, -search, -sparkle, -tear, -trouble, -wrinkle***; (surgical appliances for examining or operating on the eye) as ***eye-cup, -douche, -forceps, -instrument, -speculum, -syringe, -wear; eye-like*** adj.; **b.** objective, as ***eye-clearer, -doctor, -guard, -irrigator, -protector; eye-bedewing, -beguiling, -bewildering, -bewitching, -brightening, -dazzling, -delighting, -distracting, -filling, -glutting, -offending, -overflowing, -pleasing, -rejoicing, -retorting, -scaring, -trying***, etc., adjs.; also with indirect obj. ***eye-sweet***, adj.; ***eyeward*** adv.; ***eye-casting, -devouring, -gouging, -watering*** vbl. sbs. **c.** locative as ***eye-blurred, -bold, -starting*** adjs.; ***eye-earnestly*** adv.; instrumental as ***eye-charmed, -checkt, -reasoning, -seen*** adjs.; parasynthetic and similative as ***eye-blue, -headed, -tipped.***

1612 J. TAYLOR (Water P.) *To Sir R. Douglas*, This kingdom weeps.. With.. *eye-bedewing verse. **1645** QUARLES *Sol. Recant.* i. 4 Heart-corrupting, *eye-beguiling Gold. **1637** GILLESPIE *Eng. Pop. Cerem.* IV. ix. 46 The.. *eye-bewitching farding, of fleshly shew. **1831** CARLYLE *Sart. Res.* II. ix, *Eye-bewildering chiaroscuro. **1839** BAILEY *Festus* xix. (1848) 225 Within, the dome Was *eyeblue sapphire. **1592** WARNER *Alb. Eng.* VII. xxxvii. 168 She *eie-blur'd, and adiudged Praies the dastard'st. **1606** SYLVESTER *Du Bartas* II. IV. II. *Magnificence* 424 Th' *eye-bold Eagle never fears the flash.. of Lightning. **1641** MILTON *Ch. Govt.* Wks. 1738 I. 58 Some *eye-brightning Electuary of Knowledge and Foresight. **1729** T. COOKE *Tales, Proposals, &c.* 185 The Caitiff trembles, and his *Eyebrims flow. **1553** T. WILSON *Rhet.* (1580) 88 By suche.. good *eye castyng: thei shall alwaies bee able.. to speake what thei ought. **1649** G. DANIEL *Trinarch., Hen. V*, ccclxii, Amazement but Enthralls *Eye-Charm'd Spectators. **1654** GAYTON *Pleas. Notes* II. iv. 47 He forgot his Table, till *eye-checkt to his duty. **1883** R. TURNER in *Gd. Words* Dec. 790/2 The pretty little Eyebright.. had at one time a great reputation as an *eye-clearer. **1889** F. GALTON *Nat. Inheritance* viii. 138 Stature and *Eye-colour.. are more contrasted in hereditary behaviour than perhaps any other common qualities. **1922** R. C. PUNNETT *Mendelism* (ed. 6) 204 It was natural that eye-colour should be early selected as a subject of investigation. **1925** C. FOX *Educat. Psychol.* 26 The physical characters were such things as stature, length of arm, cephalic index, eye-colour, etc. **1639** HORN & ROBOTHAM *Gate Lang. Unl.* lxxvi. *heading*, Of opticks (*eye-craft) and painting. **1874** KNIGHT *Dict. Mech.*, *Eye-cup, a cup for washing the eye-ball. **1601** CHESTER *Love's Mart. Cantoes* xlv. (1878) 147 *Eye-dazling mistries. **1757** DYER *Fleece* II. 574 The tribe of salts.. *eyedelighting hues Produce. **1887** HISSEY *Holiday on Road* 87 Windmills.. always charming features in the prospect, life-giving and eye-delighting. **1873** BROWNING *Red Cott. Nt.-cap* 1473 Monsieur Léonce Miranda ate her up With *eye-devouring. **1885** E. D. HALE in *Harper's Mag.* Mar. 558/2 They are as good as any *eye-doctor. **1884** *Syd. Soc. Lex.*, **Eye douche*, an instrument by means of which a stream of water or medicated fluid can be applied to the surface of the eye. **1818** KEATS *Endymion* I. 360 Sweeping, *eye-earnestly, through almond vales. **1833** LAMB *Elia* Ser. II. i. (1865) 241 A momentary *eye-encounter with those stern bright visages. **1900** *Daily News* 11 June 10/3 Mr. Panmure Gordon's *eye-filling bay gelding Forrester was third. **1961** *Guardian* 16 Nov. 8/3 'Ben Hur' is both eye-filling and a serious work. **1590** SPENSER *F.Q.* II. iv. 37 His fomeing.. scornefull *ey-glaunce at him shot. **1827** KEBLE *Chr. Y.* Visit. Sick, Your keen eye glances are too bright. **1590** SPENSER *F.Q.* II. vii. 9 To them that covet such *eye-glutting gaine Proffer thy giftes. **1950** J. DEMPSEY *Championship Fighting* v. 20 There's no one to prevent low blows, butting, kicking, *eye-gouging, biting and strangling. **1884** *Health Exhib. Catal.* 128/1 Gauze Wire *Eye-Guards. **1874** KNIGHT *Dict. Mech.*, **Eye-headed Bolt*, a form of bolt having an eye at the head-end. **1884** *Syd. Soc. Lex.*, **Eye-irrigator*, a coil of narrow lead tubing.. readily bent to fit the orbit and the surface of the lids.. through which a constant current of warm or cold fluid is maintained. **1611** COTGR., *Miraillet*, a Thorne-backe which hath on either of her sides.. a great *eye-like spot. **1879** LUBBOCK *Sci. Lect.* ii. 51 Many of the hawk-moth caterpillars have eye-like spots. **1863** OUIDA *Held in Bondage* (1870) 92 And *eye-love expires. **1924** R. M. OGDEN tr. *Koffka's Growth of Mind* iii. 71 Do *eye-movements.. belong among the inherited reflexes, or are they acquired? **1806** J. GRAHAME *Birds of Scot.* 77 A melancholy, *eye-o'erflowing look. **1595** SHAKS. *John* III. i. 47 Patch'd with foule Moles, and *eye-offending markes. **1858** H. MILLER *Rambl. Geol.* II. xii. 434 The snout of the Dipterus was less round; it bore no marks of the *eye-orbits. **1869** BLACKMORE *Lorna D.* ii. (ed. 12) 10 A light came through my *eye-places. **1580** SIDNEY *Arcadia* (1622) 6 Medowes, enamelled with all sorts of *eie-pleasing flowers. **1677** GALE *Crt. Gentiles* II. IV. 446 His spirit hath garnished.. the Heavens, i.e. decked them with those eye-pleasing gloriose lights. **1617** MARKHAM *Caval.* I. 53 If you preserue your Mare for beautie, and *eye-pleasure. **1884** *Syd. Soc. Lex.*, **Eye-protectors.* **1880** MISS BROUGHTON *Sec. Th.* I. xii, The very instant he is out of *eye-range. **1622–62** HEYLIN *Cosmogr.* III. (1682) 12 They had so long together lain in *eye-reach. **1839** BAILEY *Festus* xx. (1848) 234 *Eye-reasoning man. **1645** QUARLES *Sol. Recant.* v. 23 Full heaps of *eye-rejoicing gold. **1818** L. HUNT *Foliage, Orig. Poems* 28 As on the *eye-retorting dolphin's back That let Arion ride him. **1791** COWPER *Odyss.* IX. 458 All his *eye-roots crackled in the flames. **1657** REEVE *God's Plea for Nineveh* 153 All our lip reverence, *eye-search, feet-lackyng, ear-bibbing.. scarce bring forth a conspicuous Penitent. **1871** PALGRAVE *Lyr. Poems* 116 The keen torrents of *eye-searing light. **1853** KANE *Grinnell Exp.* xlii. (1856) 382 *Eye-seen growth. **1922** JOYCE *Ulysses* 55 He watched the dark *eyeslits narrowing with greed. **1841–44** EMERSON *Ess., Hist.* Wks. (Bohn) I. 10 Whose *eye-sockets are so formed that it would be impossible for such eyes to squint. **1854** OWEN *Skel. & Teeth* (1855) 13 The eye-sockets.. are.. large, and usually with a free and wide intercommunication in the skeleton. **1870** EMERSON *Soc. & Solit., Bks.* Wks. (Bohn) III. 90 Laughter and blushes and *eye-sparkles of men and women. **1794** COLERIDGE *Relig. Musings* iv, Fear, the wild-visaged, pale, *eye-starting wretch. **1933** *Brit. Birds* XXVII. 134 The cock bird had the head and ear coverts slate blue, and the *eye-stripe is described.. as pale and less conspicuous than might have been expected. **1938** *Ibid.* XXXI. 380 It had a whitish eyestripe and the legs were dark grey. **1598** J. DICKENSON *Greene in Conc.* (1878) 124 Which spoyle their stommacks with vnsauory myxtures, thereby to seeme *eye-sweete. **1645** RUTHERFORD *Tryal & Tri. Faith* (1845) 187 Not only God, but all his instruments.. must be eye-sweet to us. **1863** *Manch. Exam.* 22 May, The effect of this arrangement is peculiarly 'eye-sweet'. **1616** W. FORDE *Serm.* 42 The hearts griefe and the *eie-teares must goe together. **1791** E. DARWIN *Bot. Gard.* II. 142 The Cherub train.. with wonder touch the sliding snail, Admire his *eye-tip'd horns. **1896** *Westm. Gaz.* 24 Sept. 1/3 Mr. Gladstone's *eye-trouble. *a* **1963** J. LUSBY in B. James *Austral. Short Stories* (1963) 233 Affecting eye-trouble, Rafe jumped in. **1887** *Sat. Rev.* 14 May 703/1 Colours worked on highly glazed *eye-trying paper. **1891** *Daily News* 3 Nov. 5/3 Placidly sharp fat face, puckered *eyeward (as if all gravitating towards the eyes). **1840** HOOD *Up the Rhine* 61 This gaping, and *eye-watering. **1926** *Glasgow Herald* 13 Apr. 11/2 Cameras, telescopes,.. *eyewear, and lenses. **1936** R. CAMPBELL *Mithraic Emblems* 161 You buy dark specs to stare at castles, But I collect such eye-wear free. **1851** H. MELVILLE *Whale* I. xvi. 113 Such *eye-wrinkles are very effectual in a scowl.

28. Special comb.: **eye appeal** orig. *U.S.*, visual appeal or attractiveness; †**eye-apple**, the apple of the eye; **eye-area** (see quot.); **eye-baby**, the image of the spectator seen in another's eye; **eye bank** orig. *U.S.*, a reserve store of human corneas kept for treatment of the blind; **eye-bar**, a steel or iron bar having an eye or hole at either end, used in bridges; **eye-bath**, a cup-shaped vessel designed to fit the orbit of the eye, used to apply a lotion to the eye; **eye-black**, black eye-shadow; mascara; **eye-blight**, something that blights or dims the eye; **eye-blink**, the twinkling of an eye (cf. BLINK *sb.*² 3); **eye-blinking** *vbl. sb.* (cf. BLINK *v.* 6), a half-closing of the eye (to what is indecorous); **eye-bone**, the bony circle round the eye, the orbit; †**eye-brine**, tears; **eye-bugging** *a.* (*U.S.*), having or characterized by bulging eyes (cf. BUG *v.*²); †**eye-cast**, an act of casting the eye, a glance or look; **eye-catcher**, a person or object that draws the eye; so **eye-catching** *a.*, attractive to the eye; striking; prominent; **eye-clip** *v. trans. N.Z.* (see quot. 1933); so **eye-clipping** *vbl. sb.*; **eye contact**, the state or practice of meeting the gaze of a person or animal; an instance of this; **eye-copy**, a copy made by the hand, with the aid of the eye only; **eye-dawn**, the dawn or first appearance (of a feeling) in the eye; **eye-dialect**, unusual spelling intended to represent dialectal or colloquial idiosyncrasies of speech (see quots.); **eye dog** *N.Z.* (see quot. 1951); †**eye-dolp** = *eye-socket*; **eye-dot** = *eye-speck*; **eye-dotter**, a small brush used in graining wood in imitation of bird's-eye maple; **eye-drop**, (*a*) a tear; (*b*) *pl.*, a liquid administered to the eye in drops; **eye-dropper**, a device for administering eye-drops; **eye-end**, that end of a telescope to which the eye is applied; †**eye-flap** = BLINKER 2 b; **eye-fly**, a minute fly which in summer-time in the East is troublesome to the eyes of men and beasts; †**eye-form** (see quot.); **eye-ground**, the fundus or back of the eye; **eye-handle** (of a spade, etc.), a handle having an eye or hole; †**eye-hope**, hope arising from the appearance of a thing; †**eye-lamp**, lamp or light of the eye; **eye-lens**, the lens nearest the eye in an optical instrument; **eye-level**, the level of the eyes; also *attrib.*; **eye-light**, (*a*) the light of the eye, (*b*) a light (candle or lamp) for the eye; **eye-limpet** (see quot.); **eye-line**, (*a*) the field or range of vision, (*b*) in *pl.* the lines above and below the eye of a bird; **eye-liner, eyeliner**, a cosmetic applied in a line around the eye; a brush or pencil for applying this; also *attrib.*; hence ***eye-lining*** vbl. sb.; **eye-loop** = EYE-HOLE, a loop-hole; **eye lotion**, (*a*) lotion for the eyes; (*b*) *slang* (see quot. 1943); **eye-memory** (see quot.); **eye-minded** *a. Psychol.*, tending to a frequent use of visual imagery; having a mental constitution chiefly or exclusively visual, so that thoughts and memories take the form of visual images; thinking in terms of the printed or written word rather than of the spoken word; so **eye-mindedness**, the condition of being eye-minded; **eye muscle**, (*a*) a muscle that moves the eye or one of its components; (*b*) a muscle, the longissimus thoracis, which runs alongside the spine and in an animal gives rise to an eye in a piece of meat (EYE *sb.*¹ 16 e); **eye-observation**, an observation taken by the eye alone; **eye and ear-observation** (see quot.); **eye-opener**, (*a*) *U.S.*, a draught of strong liquor, *esp.* one taken in the morning; (*b*) something that throws sudden light on a subject or that makes clear what was dark and ambiguous; (*c*) something which causes keen surprise; (*d*) an attractive woman; (*e*) a person who reveals facts or clarifies a situation to others; **eye-parley**, communication by interchange of looks; †**eye-pearl**, a facet in a compound eye; **eye-pedicel, eye-peduncle**, *Zool.* a pedicel or peduncle supporting an eye; **eye-peeper** = EYE-LID; **eye-pencil**, a pencil (PENCIL *sb.* 2 c) for drawing cosmetic lines around the eyes; **eye-plate**, (*a*) a chitinous sclerite in which the eyes of *Acarina* are placed; (*b*) (see quot. 1948); **eye-point** = EYE-SPOT; **eye-probe** (see quot.); **eye-purple** (see quot.); **eye-rhyme, -rime** (see quot. 1936); **eye-rim** (see quot.); **eye-ring**, a circular space within which the eye of the user of an optical instrument must be placed in order to obtain the full field of view; **eye-scope** = EYE-SHOT; **eye-seed**, in *pl.* seeds which, when blown into the eye, are said to remove foreign substances; †**eye (3en)-seke** [see SEKE], eyesickness; yearning; †**eye-set** *a.*, set down by eye-witnesses, trustworthy; **eye-shade**, a shade for the eyes, (*a*) one worn or used as a protection from the light; (*b*) a hood attached to a microscope to prevent the entrance of lateral rays to the eye; (*c*) = *eye-shadow*; **eye-shadow** *Cosmetics*, colouring applied to the eyelids or around the eyes; hence *eye-shadowed* adj.; †**eye-sick** *a.*, affected by things one sees; **eye-siren** (see quot.); **eye-sketch** = EYE-DRAUGHT; **eye-sorrow**, (*a*) suffering through the eye; (*b*) = EYE-SORE; **eye-speck**, an eye consisting of a single speck, a rudimentary eye; **eye-stalk**, the stalk or peduncle supporting the eye; = *eye-penduncle*; **eye-star** (see quot.); **eye stitch** (see quots.); **eye-stone**, (*a*) a stone resembling an eye; (*b*) (see quot. 1828); **eye-strain**, weariness or strained condition of the eyes resulting from excessive or improper use of the eyes, or uncorrected defects of vision; so *eye-straining* sb. and adj.; †**eye-streams**, tears; **eye-structure** (see quot.); **eye-sucker** (see quot.); **eye-sweep**, a survey with the eye; **eye-taking** *a.*, that attracts attention; **eye-trap**, something to catch or deceive the eye, a specious appearance; **eye-trick**, a trick of the eye, a covert glance; **eye-tube**, the tube of the eye-piece in a telescope; **eye-veil**, a veil which reaches down as far as the eyes; †**eye-vein**, a branch-vein; **eye-verdict**, the evidence of the eyes; **eye-wages**, such wages as eye-service deserves; **eye-waiter**, one who waits for a look from his master as indicative of his will; = EYE-SERVANT; **eye-ward**, a ward for eye patients in a hospital; **eye-wattle**, a wattle or excrescence near the eye of a bird; **eye-web**, membrane covering the eye (e.g. of a mole); **eye-wig** *v. trans.* (*N.Z.*) = *eye-clip* vb.; **eye-wire**, wire forming the metal frames of spectacles; **eye-wise** *a.*, wise in appearance; **eye-worker**, one whose work needs special use of the eyes; †**eye-worm**, a worm in the eye, in quot. *fig.*; **eye-worship**, adoration performed by the eye; **eye-wright**, one who cures eyes. Also EYE-BALL *sb.*, -BEAM, -BITE, etc.

1926 *National Provisioner* 19 June 25 Through improved wraps, a manufacturer may give his product '*eye appeal'. **1951** M. MCLUHAN *Mech. Bride* 63/1 Color tempted him to accept the appetizing eye appeal of the food ads. **1960** *Guardian* 29 Nov. 5/1 Prewar cars lacked the eye appeal of

modern cars. **1658** A. Fox tr. *Wurtz' Surg.* II. ix. 81 If a party hath received a Wound in the *Eye Apple..then ..[etc.] **1895** A. C. Haddon *Evol. Art* 36 The six rays are but a symmetrical coalescence of two pairs of *eye-areas. *Note*, I have adopted the term 'eye-area' to denote the eye device which includes the eye, the eye-lashes, and often the cheek-fold of that side. **1890** Coues *Field & Gen. Ornith.* II. iv. 271 Our own reflection, diminished to the size of the *'eye-baby'. **1944** *Amer. N. & Q.* IV. 24/2 *Eye Bank: founded at the New York Hospital..May 8; for collecting and preserving 'healthy human corneas'. **1959** Eye bank [bank sb.^{3} 7 f]. **1890** *Daily News* 16 Apr. 6/6 Such important pieces as the *eye-bars of suspension bridges. **1830** *J. & S. Maw's Catal.*, *Eye Baths. **1935, 1943** Eye bath [see *eye lotion* below]. **1927** *Sunday Express* 20 Mar. 1 The police found little besides some lip-stick and *eyeblack. **1963** I. Fleming *On H.M. Secret Service* xvi. 273 Now you've ruined my eye-black. **1800** Coleridge *Piccolom.* v. iii, Therefore are they *eye-blights, Thorns in your foot-path. **1867** Dixon *New Amer.* I. xii. 143 And in an *eye-blink, Carter fell to the ground dead. **1891** *Pall Mall G.* 29 Oct. 2/1 It is a pity that in these days of sham prudery and *eye-blinking such conversations cannot be reproduced. **1793** Holcroft *Lavater's Physiog.* vii. 47 *Eyebones with defined ..firm arches. **1606** Davies *Sir T. Overbury* Wks. (Grosart) 13 The Judge..Powders his words in *Eye-brine. **1672** J. Howard *Mad Couple* II. in Hazl. *Dodsley* XV. 346 There's two of them that make their love together, By languishing *eye-casts. **1927** E. Hemingway *Men without Women* (1928) 102 On the walls of the houses were stencilled *eye-bugging portraits of Mussolini. **1937** L. C. Douglas *Forgive our Trespasses* xi. 218 With many long, cheek-distending, eye-bugging exhalations. **1923** K. G. Karsten *Charts & Graphs* 689 The best kind of *eye-catcher for calling attention to numerical data. **1946** *Vogue* Aug. 31 Let his wife..try..to emulate the appearance of those eye-catchers, and she's pretty soon put in her place. **1969** B. Turner *Circle of Squares* viii. 55 She was wearing lacy black stockings, the sort of eye-catchers that used to be considered very sexy. **1933** *Aeroplane* 6 Sept. 418/2 Another worth-while dodge is the provision of labels of a most *eye-catching design. **1952** D. Dodge *To catch Thief* (1953) ii. 40 She might be really eye-catching if she would make an effort to be. **1930** L. G. D. Acland *Early Canterbury Runs* 1st Ser. vi. 128 Merino sheep..were not handled so often for *eye-clipping and so on. **1933** —— in *Press* (Christchurch, N.Z.) 14 Oct. 15/7 *Eye-clip*, to cut the wool away from round a sheep's eyes. If this is not done, the wool, especially on merinos, is apt to grow over the eyes and make the sheep wool-blind. Some people speak of eye-clipping as *Winking*. **1953** B. Stronach *Musterer on Molesworth* viii. 54 Our next job was to eye clip the lambs, for many of them were wool-blind. **1965** Argyle & Dean in *Sociometry* XXVIII. 289 Without *eye-contact .., people do not feel they are fully in communication. **1977** C. McFadden *Serial* (1978) xx. 46/2 She turned around to make eye contact. **1984** W. Boyd *Stars & Bars* I. iv. 45 The girl came to recognise him, and they would make a long and direct eye-contact throughout their transaction. **1883** I. Taylor *Alphabet* iv. §2 I. 207 An early *eye-copy of a portion of the inscription. **1820** Keats *Ode to Psyche* 20 Tender *eye-dawn of aurorean love. **1925** G. P. Krapp *Eng. Lang. in Amer.* I. iv. 228 The impression of popular speech ..is often assisted by what may be termed '*eye dialect', in which the convention violated is one of the eye, not of the ear. Thus a dialect writer often spells a word like *front* as *frunt*, or *face* as *fase*, or *picture* as *pictsher*, not because he intends to indicate here a genuine difference of pronunciation, but the spelling is merely a friendly nudge to the reader. **1965** *Amer. Speech* XL. 230 Which of the most fastidious elocutionists could object to the vocalized result of *enuff*, probably the oftenest repeated of Capp's eye-dialect usages? **1951** L. G. D. Acland *Early Canterbury Runs* 376 **Eye dog*, dog that commands sheep by his eye. **1963** R. Casey *As Short Spring* 196 What's more, he keeps all eye dogs—hardly ever bark in their lives. They could work sheep with barely a sound on a clear night. **1513** Douglas *Æneis* III. x. 15 Off his *E dolp thæ flowand blude and attir He wische away. **1878** M'Kendrick in *Encycl. Brit.* VIII. 816/1 Eye-specks or *eye-dots met with in Medusæ, Annelidæ, etc. **1873** Spon *Workshop Rec.* Ser. I. 422 Some grainers use small brushes called maple *eye-dotters..for forming the eyes. **1597** Shaks. *2 Hen. IV*, IV. v. 88 That Tyranny..Would..haue wash'd his Knife With gentle *eye-drops. **1938–9** *Army & Navy Stores Catal.* 393/2 Eye Drop Bottle... Eye Drop Tubes. **1961** *Harper's Bazaar* May 95 Improve the whites [of eyes] with..French eye drops, deep blue in colour. **1938** J. Steinbeck *Long Valley* 75 He took an *eyedropper from a drawer. **1962** J. Braine *Life at Top* ii. 33, I..poured her out her usual medicinal dose of brandy... Sometimes I made jokes about using an eye-dropper next time. **1790** Roy in *Phil. Trans.* LXXX. 154 This piece of mechanism in the *eye-end of the telescope. **1878** Lockyer *Stargazing* 311 The eye-end changes its position rapidly. **1611** Cotgr. s.v. *Oeilleres*, A bridle with *eye-flaps for a fore-horse. **1775** Ash, *Eye-flap*. **1815** Kirby & Spence *Ent.* I. App. 8 A very minute black fly ..which, because it flies in swarms into the eyes..is called the *eye-fly. **1951** E. A. Mittelholzer *Shadows move among Them* I. ix. 68 A tickling on his eye-lashes..it was an eye-fly. **1551** Recorde *Pathw. Knowl.* I. Def. B ij b, A figure moche like to a tunne fourme, saue that it is sharp couered [**1574** cornered] at both the endes..and that figure is named an *yey [**1574** eye] fourme. **1900** *Jrnl. Exper. Med.* 25 Oct. 196 The *eye grounds..were normal. **1910** *Practitioner* July 97 Mental and moral deterioration in the one.., normal eye-grounds and active pupils in the other. **1880** *Catal. Tool Wks. Sheffield* 24 The spades above No. 4 have *Eye Handles. **1580** Sidney *Arcadia* (1622) 351 *Eye-hopes deceitfull proue. **1600** J. Lane *Tom Tel-troth* 110 Daigne with your *eye-lamps to behold this booke. **1871** Lockyer *Elem. Astron.* §468 We get an inverted image at..the focus of the *eye-lens. **1879** Newcomb & Holden *Astron.* 63 The eye-lens E receives the pencil of rays, and deviates it to the observer's eye. **1909** *Westm. Gaz.* 16 Oct. 14/2 The *eye-level is the true position for the hand-camera. **1926** *Army & Navy Stores Catal.* 291/2 The 'New-World' eye-level cooker. **1932** E. Bowen *To North* xxiv. 256 Then she discovered them just at eye-level, ranged in a row. **1951** *Good Housek. Home Encycl.* 75/2 *'Eye-level' cookers*.., electric cookers in which the oven is raised to eye-level and the..grill chamber situated alongside. **1956** *Ibid.* 76/1 Eye-level grills. **1958** M. L. Hall *Newnes Complete Amat. Photogr.* 61 Slower in action than an eye-level camera. *Ibid.*, Many cameras do include eye-level viewfinding arrangements. **1961** *Radio Times* 18 May 6/1 This up-to-the-minute Jackson 'extra' fits all the Highline eye-level grills. **1824** J. Bowring *Batavian Anthol.* 59 The brightest of stars is but twilight Compared with that beautiful *eye-light. **1869** J. Martineau *Ess.* II. 378 Eyelight comes out to mingle with the daylight that comes in. **1891** Farmer *Slang*, **Eye-limpet* an artificial eye. **1839** Bailey *Festus* (1854) 532 One unlimited *eye-line of pure space. **1885** *Pall Mall G.* 7 Nov. 4/1 A flycatcher sits lengthwise upon a branch. How beautiful..its white eye-lines and barred forehead. **1960** *Harper's Bazaar* July 67/1 Slim *eye-liner brush for detailed shading. *Ibid.*, A liquid eyeliner complete with brush. *Ibid.*, A soft eye-liner pencil. **1968** *New Scientist* 24 Oct. 178/2 On being sent out by his daughter to buy her a 5s 5d tube of eye-liner, he was amazed at the minute quantity she got for that sum. **1960** *Sunday Express* 6 Nov. 14/4 Gold *eye-lining pencils. **1866** *Cornh. Mag.* Nov. 543 On its walls [may still be traced] the *eye-loops for arrows. **1886** in L. de Vries *Vict. Advertisements* (1968) 34/2 Away with eye-glasses and *eye lotions. **1935** R. Macaulay *Personal Pleasures* 154 But you have..left behind you..a toothbrush, and a bottle of eye lotion with eye bath. **1943** Hunt & Pringle *Service Slang* 30 *Eye lotion*, wines (only enough of them to provide an eye bath). **1880** *Pall Mall G.* 20 Mar. 3/2 Closely akin to quickness of perception is *eye-memory, or 'the impressing by will on memory things which we have seen'. **1888** J. Jastrow in *Pop. Sci. Monthly* XXXIII. 597 (*title*) *Eye-mindedness and ear-mindedness. *Ibid.* 603 An eye-minded person should read, should reduce everything to visual terms. **1897** *Psychol. Rev.* (Monogr. Suppl.) II i. 18 Some persons are ear-minded—they think most readily in auditory ('phonographic') images; others are eye-minded, thinking in visual ('photographic') images. *Ibid.* 21 Eye-mindedness is of course quite different from quickness of visual perception. **1925** Eye-minded [see ear-minded *a.*]. **1881** *Index Med.* III. 183/2 (*title*) Spasm of the intra-ocular *eye muscles. **1924** R. M. Ogden tr. *Koffka's Growth of Mind* iii. 77 The innervations which the eye-muscles undergo in movements of fixation are determined.. by the pre-existing position of the eyes. **1959** *Times* 30 Mar. 10/6 Points for quality..are given for..size and shape of the eye muscle in the back [of a pig]. **1879** Newcomb & Holden *Astron.* 79 *Eye-and-ear observation..is..the part which both the eye and the ear play in the appreciation of intervals of time. The ear catches the beat of the clock, the eye fixes the star. **1889** *Daily News* 3 Jan. 5/3 The camera..gives more reliable results than mere *eye observations. **1818** H. B. Fearon *Sk. Amer.* 252 At table there is neither conversation nor yet drinking; the latter is effected by individuals taking their solitary '*eye openers', 'toddy', and 'phlegm dispersers'. **1846** D. Corcoran *Pickings* 75 A 'pig and whistle' is the only reg'lar eye opener. **1863** *Rio Abajo Press* (Albuquerque, N.M.) 3 Feb. 2 Quite a catalogue of similar examples of injustice and meanness..might be made ..but we merely allude to them as an 'eye-opener' to the public. **1865** Dickens *Mut. Fr.* IV. xvi. (C.D. ed.) 513 That transatlantic dram which is poetically named an eye-opener. **1870** Mark Twain *Innoc. Abr.* xv. 110 The uneducated foreigner could not even furnish..an Eye-Opener. **1879** *N. & Q.* 15 Feb. 140 His lecture must have been a lively..eye-opener for the somnolence of a cathedral town. **1884** E. T. Hooker in *Amer. Missionary* (N.Y.) April, The ability manifested in the discussion..would have been an eye-opener to Dr. Tucker. **1919** F. Hurst *Humoresque* 72 He 'ain't seen her since a child, and all of a sudden he comes West and finds in front of him an eye-opener. **1928** *Manch. Guardian Weekly* 31 Aug. 174/4 He felt his mission to be that of an agitator, of an eye-opener, of a merciless yet undogmatic critic. **1948** E. N. Dick *Dixie Frontier* 189 Ministers regularly took their morning eye-opener and their nightcap in the evening. **1651** Charleton *Eph. & Cimm. Matrons* II. (1668) 33 The *Eye-parly between Leander and Hero. **1665** R. Hooke *Micrographia* 179 There may be by each of these *eye-pearls, a representation to the Animal.. as in a man's eye there is a Picture or sensation in the Retina. **1854** Woodward *Mollusca* (1856) 24 The *eye-pedicels of the snail. **1852** Dana *Crust.* I. 440 The acicle of the outer antennæ is..seldom shorter than the *eye-peduncle. **1786** Mad. D'Arblay *Diary* 25 Dec., When my poor *eye-peepers are not quite closed, I look to the music-books. **1902** *Westm. Gaz.* 20 Nov. 6/3 Sticks of grease-paint, *eye-pencils, lip salve. **1903** *Ann. & Mag. Nat. Hist.* Nov. 505 The comparative structure of the hard chitinous parts of the body, especially of the *eye-plates, mouth-organs, and palps. **1923** *Man. Seamanship* II. iv. 93 On its [*sc.* the planing shoe's] upper surface are three eye-plates, to which are shackled the three legs of a chain sling. **1932** *Times Lit. Suppl.* 14 Jan. 30/1 Thrice Bill hung head-downwards over the eyeplate below the shackles of the mizzen rigging. **1948** R. de Kerchove *Internat. Maritime Dict.* 248/2 *Eye plate*, a plate or casting with an eye normal to its surface and formed solid with the plate. **1856–8** W. Clark *Van der Hoeven's Zool.* I. 51 Animals without *eye-point and tail. **1868** Browning *Ring & Bk.* I. 633 The scrutinizing eye-point of some star. **1860** Mayne *Exp. Lex.*, **Eye-probe*, *Surg.*, name for a probe having an eye or small hole at one end. **1886** *Daily News* 24 Sept. 5/1 A substance termed the visual purple of the eye. Now, this *eye-purple is eminently sensitive to the action of light. **1871** Ellis *E.E. Pronunc.* III. viii. 864/2 The spelling seems to have been changed to make an *eye-rhyme. **1873–4** G. M. Hopkins *Note-bks.* (1937) 246 Unlawful rhymes—We may notice (i) mere eye-rhymes; [etc.]. **1909** O. Jespersen *Mod. Eng. Gram.* I. 5 But eye-rimes are of comparatively recent growth, many of them owing their origin to words of formerly identical or similar sound having now become differentiated, thus *war* and *far*. **1913** Ogilvie & Albert *Pract. Course Secondary Eng.* II. 186 Some poets, particularly Spenser in his *Faerie Queene*, resort to what is called eye-rhyme, that is, rhyme between words of similar spelling, though of different sound. **1936** Treble & Vallins *A.B.C. of Eng. Usage* 157 Especially to be noted are 'eye rhymes', i.e. those which exist only to the eye and not the ear, like *quay—day*. **1874** Knight *Dict. Mech.*, **Eye-rim*, a circular single eye-glass, adapted to be held to its place by the contraction of the orbital muscles. **1902** Mann & Millikan tr. *Drude's Theory of Optics* 77 The exit-pupil is often called the *eye-ring, and its centre is called the position of the eye. **1891** R. Kipling *City Dreadf. Nt.* iv. 24 They can declare truthfully the name of every ship within *eye-scope. **1886** Britten & Holland *Plant-n.* 172 *Eye-seeds..Probably *Salvia Verbenaca*. *c* **1485** *Digby Myst., Mary Magd.* 1577, I am so wexyd with *ȝen sueke, þat [etc.]. **1632** Lithgow *Trav.* x. 507 So may some Stoicall Reader mis-conster..this *eye-set History. **1845** J. T. Smith *Bk. for Rainy Day* 11 The ladies this year [*sc.* 1768] wore half a flat hat as an *eye-shade. **1866** K. R. C. in *N. & Q.* 10 Mar. 196 An eye-shade of card-board..is more useful than ornamental. **1937** L. MacNeice in Auden & MacNeice *Lett. from Iceland* x. 133 Compacts, lipstick, eyeshade, and coiffures. **1930** H. Rubinstein *Art of Feminine Beauty* iv. 67 The most successful way of lending depth and mystery to the eyes is with the *eye shadow. **1950** J. Emerald *Photographic Make-Up* i. 27 Eye-shadow is applied to the eyelids with a flat-top sable brush. **1959** *Daily Sketch* 7 Jan. 9 False eyelashes..give the effect of eye-shadowed lids. **1650** Bp. Hall *Balm Gil.* 299, I have long since left to be *eyesick. **1594** J. Dickenson *Arisbas* (1878) 62 That *eye-Syren, alluring not with the sound, but at the sight. **1774** M. Mackenzie *Maritime Surv.* 84 He may..sound the Depths of the Water, and mark them on an *Eye-sketch of the Coast. **1793** Smeaton *Edystone L.* §317 Of this column, I made an eye-sketch at the time. **1828** Carlyle *Misc.* (1857) I. 132 The law of Destiny which dooms them to such unspeakable '*eye-sorrow'. **1837** —— *Fr. Rev.* II. vi. vi, So many Courtiers..are an eyesorrow to the National Guards. **1839** Todd *Cycl. Anat.* II. 130/2 The *eye-specks are situated a little way behind the head. **1880** Bastian *Brain* iii. 61 The simple 'eye-specks' of some of the lower Worms. **1854** Woodward *Mollusca* (1856) 25 The snail affords a remarkable, though familiar instance, when it draws in its *eye-stalks. **1880** Huxley *Crayfish* i. 24 At the ends of the eye-stalks are the organs of vision. **1834** Southey *Doctor* Pref. I. 41 So many featherlets leading up to..the gem or *eye-star, for which the whole was formed. **1932** D. C. Minter *Mod. Needlecraft* 53/1 *Eye stitch..is formed by sixteen stitches going into a single hole..but spread into a square on the outside edge. *Ibid.* 53/2 Algerian eye stitch.. is worked over a square having four threads on each side. **1934** M. Thomas *Dict. Embroidery Stitches* 84 *Eye stitch*, the stitch consists of 16 Satin Stitches all taken into the same central hole but with their outer ends arranged over a square of eight threads, with two threads between each stitch. **1677** Plot *Oxfordsh.* 129 An Ophthalmites, or some sort of *Eye stone. **1828** S. F. Gray *Suppl. to Pharmacopœia* 143 Guernsey eye-stone being put into the inner corner of the eye works its way out at the outward corner and brings out any strange substance with it. **1865** Emanuel *Diamonds, etc.* 163 These stones [onyx] are also termed by jewellers 'eye-stones'. **1874** *Med. & Surg. Reporter* (Philad.) XXXI. 67 (*heading*) Headaches..from *eye strain. **1909** *Practitioner* Dec. 779 Of all the causes of eyestrain the most frequent is the presence of an error of refraction. **1949** H. C. Weston *Sight, Light & Efficiency* iii. 57 The eye-strain-risk associated with occupations. **1871** *English Mechanic* 380/3 *Eye-straining. **1923** Kipling *Land & Sea Tales* 185 Cold, nose-running, eye-straining work. **1594** Southwell *M. Magd. Fun. Teares* 85 Would our eyes be so dry, if such *eie-streams were behovefull? **1888** F. H. Hatch *Gloss. Terms for Rocks* 11 **Eye-structure*. In this structure..the foliated and secondary minerals are arranged in layers round the larger original constituents, producing lenticular forms which often bear a striking resemblance to eyes. **1744** Baker in *Phil. Trans.* XLIII. 35, I shall..distinguish it by the Name of *Eye-Sucker, as that Name conveys an Idea of the Manner how it lives. **1753** Chambers *Cycl. Supp.*, *Eye-sucker*, a small sea insect, which is sometimes found fixed by the snout to the Eyes of sprats. **1865** E. Burritt *Walk to Land's End* 440 When you have taken your first *eye-sweep, you cannot say which goddess is the fairest. **1868** G. M. Hopkins *Jrnls. & Papers* 18 July (1959) 177 An ash rose with *eye-taking sky-clusters. **1960** *Harper's Bazaar* July 38 She likes..eye-taking colours. **1785** Mrs. A. M. Bennett *Juvenile Indiscr.* (1786) I. 4 The *eye-trap of a good house. **1825** *Blackw. Mag.* XVIII. 152 A got-up thing—a mere eye-trap. **1603** Florio *Montaigne* III. v. (1632) 487 Galba.. perceiving him and his wife beginne to bandy *eye-trickes and signes. **1779** Dollond in *Phil. Trans.* LXIX. 332 The *eye-tube which contains the wires of the telescope. **1837** Goring & Pritchard *Microgr.* 6 The elongation or contraction of the length of the body, by means of the eye-tube. **1928** *Daily Express* 4 June 5/3 The *eye-veil fashion.. is good for the races. **1545** Raynold *Byrth Mankynde* 43 They sende into each of the caules innumerable small *eye veynes. **1657** S. W. *Schism Dispach't* 198 Dr. H. would persuade us to beleeve against our *eye-verdict. **1620** Sanderson *Serm.* I. 150 They do Him but eye-service, and He giveth them but *eye-wages. *a* **1734** North *Lives* II. 249 Most of them were but *eye-waiters. **1879** *St. George's Hosp. Rep.* IX. 465 The average stay of a patient in the *eye-wards..was 25·84 days. **1868** Darwin *Anim. & Pl.* I. vi. 188 A long-beaked carrier, having large *eye-wattles. **1883** W. S. Dugdale tr. *Dante's Purgatorio* XVII. 188 Through which thou couldst see no better than a mole does through his *eyeweb. **1950** *N.Z. Jrnl. Agric.* Apr. 387/3 Each ewe.. is *eye-wigged if necessary. **1881** *Instr. Census Clerks* (1885) 96 *Eye Wire Maker. **1962** L. S. Sasieni *Optical Dispensing* i. 25 This pattern is..produced..by stamping or rolling the eye-wire through dies. **1876** Lowell *Poet. Wks.* (1879) 472 When those *eye-wise..shall be lost In the great light. **1898** G. M. Gould *Biogr. Clinics* (1905) III. 500 A seamstress or ..any hard-pushed *eye-worker. **1591** Lyly *Endym.* III. iv. 45 Love is but an *eye worme, which onely tickleth the head with hopes. *a* **1674** Milton *Prose Wks.* (Jod.), **Eye-worship*. **1656** Heylin *Surv. France* 28 My hostess.. persuaded me to this holy *eye-wright.

†**eye**, *sb.*^{2} *Obs.* [Used erroneously for nye, *neye*; *a neye = an eye*. Cf. adder, eyas, etc.] A brood (of pheasants).

c **1430** *Bk. Hawkyng* in *Rel. Ant.* I. 296, I have founde a covey of pertrich..and eye of fesaunts. **1579** E. K. *Gloss. Spenser's Sheph. Cal.* Apr. 118. **1669** Worlidge *Syst. Agric.* (1681) 252 When you have found an Eye of Pheasants.. place your Nets hollow, loose, and circular-wise. **1725** in Bradley *Fam. Dict.* s.v. *Pheasant*.

†**eye**, *sb.*^{3} *Obs. rare*$^{-1}$. In 5 pl. eyen. (Of doubtful meaning: perh. some error.)

c **1440** *Bone Flor.* 845 Syr Garcy went crowlande for fayne As rampande eyen do in the rayne.

eye (aɪ), *v.* [f. eye *sb.*^{1}]

I. †**1.** *trans.* To perceive with the eyes; to see. *lit.* and *fig.* *Obs.*

1583 STANYHURST *Aeneis* IV. (Arb.) 102 Eyest thou this filthood? **1632** J. HAYWARD tr. *Biondi's Eromena* 77 Never in her life-time ever eyed the Princesse a more pleasing spectacle. **1655** GURNALL *Chr. in Arm.* I. 64 They..who in the performing of divine duties, eye not God through them. **1725** POPE *Odyss.* x. 690 The paths of gods what mortal can survey? Who eyes their motion? **1779** J. NEWTON in *Olney Hymns* III. No. 58 His heart revives, if cross the plains He eyes his home.

2. a. To direct the eyes to, fix the eyes upon, look at or upon, behold, observe. Often with a word or phrase indicative of some feeling (*e.g.* anger, suspicion, wonder, etc.). ***to eye askance, askant***: see ASKANCE, ASKANT.

1566 T. STAPLETON *Ret. Untr. Jewel* IV. 148 Gentle Reader! Eye M. Jewel wel. **1610** SHAKS. *Temp.* III. i. 40 Full many a Lady I haue ey'd with best regard. **1682** SIR T. BROWNE *Chr. Mor.* 12 Eye well those heroes who have held their heads above water. **1725** POPE *Odyss.* XVII. 443 They.. eye the man, majestic in distress. **1797** MRS. RADCLIFFE *Italian* xvii, They eyed the prisoners with curiosity. **1838** DICKENS *Nich. Nick.* ii, The public..were eyeing..the empty platform. **1848** M. ARNOLD *Tristram & Iseult* Poems (1877) 215 The knights eyed her in surprise. **1883** W. C. RUSSELL *Sea Queen* III. xii. 271 My father eyed her askant.

fig. **1689** HICKERINGILL *The Ceremony-Monger* Wks. (1716) II. 437 Eying nothing of..the Beauties of the Mind.

†**b.** To look upon, regard *as* (so and so). *Obs.*

1659 W. BROUGH *Sacr. Princ.* 240 Eying men as mortal and mutable. **1673** JANEWAY *Heaven on E.* (1847) 67 We do not sufficiently eye God as the fountain..of all our excellency.

3. To keep an eye on; to observe narrowly.

1586 A. DAY *Eng. Secretary* II. (1625) 101 At one time or other I have..eyed the demeanours, issues and dispositions of sundry humors. **1611** BIBLE *1 Sam.* xviii. 9 And Saul eyed Dauid from that day. **1639** FULLER *Holy War* IV. xxvi. (1647) 215 It being good to eye a suspicious person. **1667** PEPYS *Diary* (1877) V. 385, I observed my wife to eye my eyes whether I did ever look upon Deb. **1672** SIR T. BROWNE *Lett. Friend* (1712) 33 In consumptive Diseases some eye the Complexion of Moles. **1725** POPE *Odyss.* XIII. 36 He sat, and ey'd the sun, and wished the night; Slow seemed the sun to move. **1797–1804** BEWICK *Brit. Birds* (1847) I. 139 He..succeeded in eyeing the bird to the distant passage..by which it entered and left its nest. **1812** H. & J. SMITH *Rej. Addr.* xiii. (1873) 120, I've stood and eyed the builders. **1877** H. A. PAGE *De Quincy* I. iv. 81 Had eyed the lad hovering about the house.

†**4.** To have or keep in view; to aim at (a mark). Of an expression, text, etc.: To refer to. *Obs.*

1590 SPENSER *F.Q.* II. iv. 7 The aymed marke, which he had eide. **1594** WEST *2nd Pt. Symbol.* §219 In which are chiefly to be eyed the matter and forme. **1621–31** LAUD *Sev. Serm.* (1847) 34 The letter of the psalm reads David..the spirit of the psalm eyes Christ. **1625–8** tr. *Camden's Hist. Eliz.* III. (1688) 367 God, whom alone I eyed and respected. **1659** FULLER *App. Inj. Innoc.* (1840) 563 This my expression did eye another person. **1669** PENN *No Cross* xxii. §3 Let the Glories of another World be ey'd. **1771** WESLEY *Wks.* (1872) V. 201 Therefore, eye him in all.

†**5.** *intr.* **a.** To look or appear to the eye. **b.** To have an eye *to*, look *to*. *Obs.*

1606 SHAKS. *Ant. & Cl.* I. iii. 97 My becommings kill me, when they do not Eye well to you. **1627–77** FELTHAM *Resolves* I. xiv. 22 As if one were, for the contentment of this life; and the other, eying to that of the life to come.

II. 6. *trans.* To furnish with eyes, in senses 20 and 21 of the sb.

1854 T. MORRALL *Needle-making* 30 In that [stage] of eying..4,000 [needles] per hour are..easily produced. **1867** F. FRANCIS *Angling* i. (1880) 48 On the tails eye hang a triangle also eyed. **1883** *Harper's Mag.* 933/1 The ends of the strands are 'eyed'.

7. *intr.* Of eggs: to form eyes (see EYE *sb.*[1] 12 c).

1904 *Daily Chron.* 25 Mar. 8/3 The eggs take from six weeks to three months to 'eye', as it is called.

Hence **ˈeyeing** *vbl. sb.*, the action of the vb. EYE.

a **1732** T. BOSTON *Crook in Lot* (1805) 3 A wise eying of the hand of God in all we find to bear hard upon us.

eye, obs. form of AWE, EGG.

eyeable (ˈaɪəb(ə)l), *a.* [f. EYE *v.* + -ABLE.] That may be seen by the eye; also, that may be looked upon with pleasure; sightly.

1839 BAILEY *Festus* (1852) 458 The furthest things on all sides eyeable Are village temples tapering to the skies. **1887** *Times* (weekly ed.) 19 Aug. 12/1 They take very good care to make their goods 'eyeable' and attractive to purchasers. **1890** *Sat. Rev.* 13 Sept. 327/2 Dr. Hime has spared no pains in making the pages eyeable.

eyeass, obs. form of EYAS.

eye-ball (ˈaɪbɔːl), *sb.* Also eyeball. [f. EYE *sb.*[1] + -BALL.] **1.** = *ball of the eye.* **a.** The apple or pupil. **b.** The eye itself within the lids and socket.

a. 1592 SHAKS. *Ven. & Ad.* 119 Hold up thy head: Look in mine eye balls. **1607** HEYWOOD *Wom. Kilde* Wks. 1874 II. 101 Your companie is as my eie-ball deere. **1614** BEAUM. & FL. *Wit at Sev. Weapons* I. i, The brow of a Military face may not be offensive to your generous eyeballs. *a* **1839** PRAED *Poems* (1864) II. 397 A fitful light in his eyeball glistened. **1871** R. ELLIS *Catullus* lxiv. 219 Ere..these dimly lit eye-balls Feed to the full on thee.

b. 1590 SHAKS. *Mids. N.* III. ii. 369 Crush this hearbe into Lysanders eie, Whose liquor hath this vertuous propertie, To..make his eie-bals role with wonted sight. **1668** DRYDEN *Ind. Emp.* II. i, I feel..my eyeballs rowl. **1798** COLERIDGE *Anc. Mar.* VI. xx, Their stony eye-balls glitter'd on In the red and smoky light. **1802** HOME in *Phil. Trans.* XCII. 354 The eye-lid is very loose upon the eye-ball. **1866** KINGSLEY *Herew.* xv. 214 An arrow was in his eyeball. **1876** FOSTER *Phys.* III. ii. 503 The eyeball is moved by six muscles.

2. Advb. and attrib. phr. ***eye-ball to eye-ball***, confronting closely; with neither party yielding. *colloq.* (orig. *U.S.*).

1962 D. RUSK in *Sat. Even. Post* 8 Dec. 16/1 We're eyeball to eyeball, and I think the other fellow just blinked. **1965** H. KAHN *On Escalation* ii. 43 If there is a direct ('eyeball to eyeball') confrontation.., all participants and observers will take an intense interest in the proceedings. **1966** *Guardian* 16 June 1/3 Mr Wilson said we ought not to 'contract out and leave it to the Americans and Chinese eyeball to eyeball'. **1969** 'E. LATHEN' *When in Greece* vii. 68 Ken had not bargained for an eyeball-to-eyeball confrontation. **1970** M. KELLY *Spinifex* iii. 65 Two extremely ambitious dogs are eyeball to eyeball over the same bone.

eye-ball, eyeball (ˈaɪbɔːl), *v. U.S. slang.* [f. the sb.] *trans.* and *intr.* To look or stare (at).

1901 *Harper's Monthly* Feb. 443/1 'God!' burst from the lips of the man as he eyeballed his attendant. **1942** *Amer. Mercury* July 85 He would eye-ball the idol-breaker. **1968** *Listener* 22 Aug. 229/2 This movie is so richly risible that I advise all, in John Wayne's phrase, to go down to the Warner and eyeball it. **1970** A. CAMERON et al. *Computers & O.E. Concordances* 60 Errors..will be exposed very quickly because you simply 'eyeball' down the centre of the page.

eye-beam (ˈaɪbiːm). [f. EYE *sb.*[1] + BEAM.] A beam or glance of the eye.

1588 SHAKS. *L.L.L.* IV. iii. 28 So sweete a Kisse the golden Sun giues not..As thy eye beames. *a* **1639** T. CAREW *To a Lady*, Through those Crystalls our soules flitting, Shall a pure wreathe of eye-beames twine. **1785** MRS. A. M. BENNETT *Juvenile Indiscr.* (1786) II. 212 Her eye beams shoot through my soul. **1841–4** EMERSON *Ess.* Ser. I. vi. (1876) 155 Read the language of these wandering eye-beams.

†**eye-bite**, *v. Obs. rare.* [f. EYE *sb.*[1] + BITE *v.*] *trans.* To bewitch with the eye.

1584 R. SCOT *Discov. Witchcr.* III. xv. 50 The Irishmen.. affirme, that not onelie their children, but their cattell are.. eyebitten, when they fall suddenlie sicke. **1658** PHILLIPS, *Eyebite*, to fascinate or bewitch by a certain evil influence from the eye. **1721–1800** in BAILEY.

Hence †**eye-biter**, one who 'eye-bites'. †**eye-biting** *vbl. sb.* and *ppl. a.*

1584 R. SCOT *Discov. Witchcr.* III. xv. 50 The Irishmen.. terme one sort of their witches eybiters. **1585** J. HIGGINS tr. *Junius' Nomenclator* 427 *Fascinus*, a bewitching or eye-biting. **1656** T. ADY *Candle in Dark* II. 104 Calling them eye-biting witches.

eye-bolt (ˈaɪbəʊlt). [f. EYE *sb.*[1] + BOLT *sb.*] A bolt or bar having an eye at one end, to receive a hook, ring, etc.

1769 SMEATON in Brand *Newcastle* (1789) II. App. 586 The stones may be laid hold of by eye-bolts fixed in holes bored with a jumper. **1794** *Rigging & Seamanship* I. 35 They are mostly fitted with a..sprig-eye-bolt driven in the middle of their ends. **1859** F. A. GRIFFITHS *Artill. Man.* (1862) 116 They hook the fixed blocks to the eye-bolts.

ˈeye-bree. [f. EYE *sb.*[1] + BREE *sb.*[1]]

†**a.** = EYE-LID. *Obs.* **b.** = EYE-LASH. *Obs.* **c.** = EYE-BROW. *Obs.* exc. *Sc.* and *dial.*

a. *c* **1000** *Sax. Leechd.* I. 352 Niwe ȝate cyse oferȝeseted mid þa eaȝbræwas. *c* **1300** *Song agst. Retinues* in *Pol. Songs* (Camden) 239 Sene is on is browe Ant on is eȝe-brewe, That [etc.]. **1562** TURNER *Herbal* II. 137 b, The juice of it [mustarde]..is good..for the roughnes of the ey-brees. **1604** T. WRIGHT *Passions* I. vii. 29 The fornication of a woman shall be knowen by the lifting vp of her eyes, and in her eye-bries. **1617** MARKHAM *Caval.* v. 17 All those long and stiffe haires which growe close aboue his vpper eye-brees. **1787** in GROSE *Provinc. Gloss., Suppl.*

b. *c* **1577** B. GOOGE *Heresbach's Husb.* (1586) 117 A horse when he beginnes to be olde, his temples waxe hollowe, his eye bries gray. **1615** G. SANDYS *Trav.* 67 Into the same hue do they dy their eie-breis, and eye-browes.

c. *c* **1776** HERD *Scot. Songs* I. 210 And the sweat it dropt down Frae my very eye-brie. *a* **1803** JAMIESON *Water-Kelpie* 43 (in Scott *Minstr.*), Of filthy gar his ee-brees war. **1862** *Dialect of Leeds* 257 'Ee-brees', eyebrows. *Mod. Sc.* He is dirt up to the very ee-brees.

eyebright (ˈaɪbraɪt), *a.* and *sb.* [f. EYE *sb.*[1] + BRIGHT.]

†**A.** *adj.* Bright to the eye, clear. *Obs. rare*$^{-1}$.

1607 *Lingua* II. v. in Hazl. *Dodsley* IX. 381 The shooting stars, Which in an eye-bright evening seem to fall.

B. *sb.* **1.** The popular name of the plant *Euphrasia officinalis*, formerly in repute as a remedy for weak eyes: = EUPHRASY.

1533 ELYOT *Cast. Helthe* (1541) 11 b, Thynges good for the eyes: Eyebryght: Fenell. **1585** LLOYD *Treas. Health* xii. E vij, Take of the wood of Aloes, of eybright [etc.]. **1612** DRAYTON *Poly-olb.* xiii. 202 He Fumitorie gets, and Eye-bright for the eye. **1671** SALMON *Syn. Med.* III. xxii. 399 Eye bright..strengthens the head, eyes and memory, clears the sight. **1718** QUINCY *Compl. Disp.* 79 Eyebright flowers in June. **1758** MRS. DELANY *Life & Corr.* III. 507 The purple vetch and eyebright soften the golden furs and glowing heath. **1848** C. A. JOHNS *Week at Lizard* 271 We find..eye-bright with thick fleshy leaves. **1883** R. TURNER in *Gd. Words* Dec. 790/2 The pretty little Eyebright..had at one time a great reputation as an eye-clearer.

b. *attrib.* Prepared from euphrasy. Also in names of other plants or medicaments used as remedies for weak sight.

1597 GERARD *Herbal* I. lxii. §3. 85 Eiebright Cow wheate. **1616** SURFL. & MARKH. *Country Farme* 43 Drinke euerie morning a small draught of Eye-bright wine. **1648** *Hunting of Fox* 39 The Eye-bright water of Repentance. **1656** RIDGLEY *Pract. Physick* 118 Ey-bright oyl made of the flowers of Succory. **1747** WESLEY *Prim. Physic* (1762) 60 Use Eye bright Tea daily. **1884** MILLER *Plant-n.*, *Eye-bright Cow-wheat.* The genus Bartsia.

†**2.** ? 'A kind of ale in Elizabeth's time' (Latham). *Obs.*

1610 B. JONSON *Alch.* V. i, Men and women..[have] been seen to flock here..In days of Pimlico and Eye-bright.

eyebrow (ˈaɪbraʊ). [f. EYE *sb.*[1] + BROW. Not in OE., which had only *éaȝbrǽw* EYE-BREE.]

1. a. The fringe of hair along the upper orbit of the eye, more or less arched in appearance.

1585 J. HIGGINS tr. *Junius' Nomenclator* 27 *Supercilium*, the ridge of haire aboue the eye lids or the eye browes. **1600** SHAKS. *A.Y.L.* II. vii. 149 The Louer, with a wofull ballad Made to his Mistresse eye-brow. **1691** RAY *Creation* II. (1692) 32 Above stand the Eye-Brows to keep any thing from running down upon the eyes. **1741** MONRO *Anat. Nerves* (ed. 3) 79 An arched Ridge is extended, on which the Eye-brows are placed. **1813** SCOTT *Triermain* III. xxvi, Shade thine eyebrows with thine hand. **1860** FROUDE *Hist. Eng.* VI. 276 He had the arched eyebrow..of the beautiful Plantagenet face.

b. *pl.* Artificial imitations of the same, app. made of mouse-skin.

1703 STEELE *Tend. Husb.* III. i, Pr'y thee, wench, bring me my black eyebrows out of the next room. **1718** PRIOR *Another Reas. Affliction* Poems 270 The Slattern had left in the Hurry..Her Lady's Complexion and Eyebrows at Calais. —— *On the same* Poems 271 If we don't catch a Mouse To-night, Alas! no Eye-brows for To-morrow.

c. ***to raise one's eyebrow(s)*** (or ***an eyebrow***): to show surprise or dubiousness (*at* something).

1918 L. STRACHEY *Emin. Victorians* 28 The most steady-going churchman hardly raises an eyebrow at it now. **1956** G. H. VALLINS *Pattern of Eng.* v. 132 Brown, though he raises his eyebrows a little at the usage, by no means condemns it outright. **1956** A. WILSON *Anglo-Saxon Att.* 407 They will perhaps raise their eyebrows at the old reiterated parrot-cry that the triumph of Roman Christianity brought 'civilization' to our island.

d. ***up to the*** (or ***one's***) ***eyebrows***, up to the eyes (see EYE *sb.*[1] 2 e).

1925 WODEHOUSE *Carry On, Jeeves!* ii. 53 There was a fellow, one would have said, clear up to the eyebrows in the soup. To all appearances he had got it right in the neck. **1954** N. COWARD *Future Indefinite* II. iii. 92 To many of my acquaintances..it was a foregone conclusion that I was involved in espionage up to the eyebrows. **1961** B. FERGUSSON *Watery Maze* x. 252 The commanders concerned were up to their eyebrows in the Sicilian campaign. **1968** A. DIMENT *Gt. Spy Race* iii. 36 He's.. tanked up to the eyebrows with Acid.

2. *Anat.* (see quot. 1840).

1806 *Med. Jrnl.* XV. 208 The organ of finding and recollecting places manifested itself strongly in the corners of his eye-brows. **1840** G. ELLIS *Anat.* 74 The eyebrows.. are two curved prominences formed by the orbicularis and occipito-frontalis muscles.

3. *Arch.* **a.** A moulding over a window. **b.** (See quot. 1842).

1703 T. N. *City & C. Purchaser* 5 Annulet..in Architecture..a..Tince, Eye-brow. **1832** tr. *Tour Germ. Prince* IV. iv. 162 Hatfield is built of brick; only the eyebrows of the windows..&c. are of stone. **1842** GWILT *Archit.* Gloss. 971 *Eyebrow*, a name sometimes given to the fillet.

4. *attrib.* and *Comb.* **eyebrow pencil** (see PENCIL *sb.* 2 c); **eyebrow tweezers**, tweezers for extracting unwanted hairs from the eyebrows.

1718 PRIOR *Another Reas. Affliction* Poems 270 Her Eye-brow-Box one Morning lost. **1881** [see BLANC DE PERLE]. **1936** D. POWELL *Turn, Magic Wheel* II. 135 His wife's eyebrow pencil. **1938** [see EYE-LASH c]. **1760** GOLDSM. *Cit. W.* (1840) 9 Your nose-borers..eyebrow-pluckers, would all want bread. **1854** HOOKER *Himal. Jrnls.* I. iii. 66 Prominence of eyebrow region. **1933** D. L. SAYERS *Hangman's Holiday* 123 A pair of eyebrow tweezers. **1966** P. V. PRICE *France* 113 Eyebrow tweezers (can be invaluable for far more first-aid operations than just plucking eyebrows).

Hence **ˈeyebrowed** *a.*, furnished with eyebrows; *transf.* (of a hill), having a growth of trees resembling an eyebrow. **ˈeyebrowless** *a.*, without eyebrows.

1833 J. HODGSON in J. Raine *Mem.* (1858) II. 314 Steep scars, fringed and eye-browed with wild natural wood. **1859** JEPHSON *Brittany* i. 2 Flock of white-eyebrowed goats. **1868** DICKENS *Uncomm. Trav.* xxv, Those four male personages ..complexionless and eyebrowless. **1884** *Miss. Herald* Sept. 375 They never yet had heard of such a thing as an eyebrowless child.

ˈeyebrow, *v.* [f. prec. sb.] *trans.* **a.** To frown (a person) *out of*: in quot. with *indirect pass.* **b.** To provide with (distinct) eyebrows.

1837 T. HOOK *Jack Brag* xix, Rougeing, powdering..eye-browing, and all concomitant stage tricks. **1876** MRS. WHITNEY *Sights & Ins.* iii. 15, I find it is only the unusual things..that you are eyebrowed out of.

eyed (aɪd), *ppl. a.* [f. EYE *sb.*[1] + -ED[2].]

1. Furnished with eyes.

c **1374** CHAUCER *Troylus* IV. 1459 Youre father is in sleighte as Argus eyed. *c* **1430** LYDG. *Bochas* Prol. (1544) 54 A prince..Eyed as a tigre with reason and foresight. **1553** EDEN *Treat. Newe Ind.* (Arb.) 15 An Elephant..is..eyed lyke a swine. **1579** SPENSER *Sheph. Cal.* Sept. 203 For Roffy is wise, and as Argus eyed. **1643** PRYNNE *Sov. Power Parl.* App. 154 He who even now seemed eyed, eared, strong and flourishing; will suddenly wax blind, deafe, and fall to nothing. **1832** TENNYSON *Œnone* 196 A wild and wanton pard, Eyed like the evening star.

fig. **1869** R. LYTTON *Orval* 117 The eyed air Sees not.

b. With *adj.* prefix, as ***Argus-***, ***blue-***, ***fierce-***, ***hollow-***, ***two-***, ***wet-eyed***: see the adjs.

†**c.** Gifted with sight, clear-sighted, sharp-sighted. Also *fig.* Wide awake *to. Obs.*

1584 T. BASTARD *Chrestoleros* (1880) 82 Men..Eyde to their profit, but blinde to their paine. **1596** SPENSER *F.Q.* IV. iii. 7 They were both so watchfull and well eyde, That [etc.]. **1618** ROWLANDS *Sacred Mem.* 45 Borne blind they knew.. And most miraculous, now perfect ey'd. **1632** J. HAYWARD tr. *Biondi's Eromena* 87 A god, though blinde, yet eyed sufficiently to spie out two spirits.

2. Furnished with an eye. Cf. EYE 20, 21.

1804 ABERNETHY *Surg. Observ.* 215 By means of an eyed probe. **1886** *Academy* 22 May 358/2 Mr. Hall invented eyed-hooks [in fly-fishing].

3. Marked or ornamented as with eyes: dappled, spotted. ***eyed hawk-moth*** (*Smerinthus Ocellatus*): a moth of the family *Sphingidæ*.

1815 SHELLEY *Alastor* 450 Soft mossy lawns..eyed with blooms. **1821** KEATS *Lamia* 50 Eyed like a peacock. **1825** BERRY *Encycl. Herald.* I., *Eyed*..a term used in speaking of the variegated spots in the peacock's tail. **1843** WESTWOOD *Brit. Moths* I. 7 *Smerinthus Ocellatus.* The Eyed Hawk-Moth. **1878** BROWNING *Poets Croisic* 53 That which perks and preens The eyed wing. **1889** in ELVIN *Dict. Heraldry.*

'eye-draught. [f. EYE *sb.*¹ + DRAUGHT.] A drawing or plan made by the eye, not by actual measurement.

1773 *Gentl. Mag.* 265 Eye Draught of the Solway Moss. **1793** SMEATON *Edystone L.* §20 *note*, The print..appears to be made from an Eye Draught. **1823** P. NICHOLSON *Pract. Build.* 170 To take the dimensions of a place..make an eye-draught. **1875** PROCTOR *Expanse Heav.* 273 The stars.. being copied by eye-draughts from the charts.

'eyeful, *sb.* [f. EYE *sb.*¹ + -FUL.] **a.** As much as the eye can take in at once. **b.** A minute quantity; a wink (of sleep).

1832 J. WILSON in *Blackw. Mag.* XXXI. 865 We prefer a miniature picture of the Swiss Giantess to the giantess herself—an eyeful for one to an armful for ten. **1860** READE *Cloister & H.* II. 37 You drop off again, and get about an eyeful of sleep: lo, it is tinkle, tinkle, for matins. **1876** D. STEVENSON in *Gd. Words* 687 [We] with large eye-fuls took the landscape in.

c. Also **eye-full.** A 'good look' at something; an exhilarating or remarkable sight; *spec.* a strikingly attractive woman; esp. in phr. ***to get an eyeful (of)***, to have a good look (at); to see something remarkable, beautiful, etc. (See also quots.) *colloq.*

1899 S. MACMANUS *In Chimney Corners* 248 She took an eyeful out of Jack, an' right well plaised she was with his appearance. **1914** JACKSON & HELLYER *Vocab. Criminal Slang* 31 *Eye full*, the object of scrutiny or of attentive observation... 'Nix crackin'. The mark on your left is getting an eye full.' **1919** W. H. DOWNING *Digger Dial.* 22 *Eye-full*, a complete view. *Ibid.* 26 *Get an eye-full*, see. **1922** JOYCE *Ulysses* 765 Ill put on my shift and drawers let him have a good eyeful out of that. **1929** H. V. MORTON *In Search of Scotland* ii. 46 'You have seen the Crown Jewels in London?' 'I'll say so! They're an eyeful.' **1933** E. CALDWELL *God's Little Acre* XII. 172 When you've got an eyeful of Griselda, there, you know durn well you've been missing a heap thinking such foolishness all your life. **1934** WODEHOUSE *Thank You, Jeeves* iv. 47 Unquestionably an eyeful, Pauline Stoker had the grave defect of being one of those girls who want you to come and swim a mile before breakfast. **1947** N. BALCHIN *Lord, I was Afraid* 52 He thought to himself this is a bit of all right and started right in to get an eye-full, see? **1960** 'A. GARVE' *Golden Deed* vi. 39 You're both quite an eyeful.

'eyeful, *a. Obs.* exc. *dial.* [f. EYE *sb.*¹ + -FUL.] †**a.** Plainly to be seen. **b.** Careful; observant.

c **1611** CHAPMAN *Iliad* x. 396 He hung them up aloft upon a tamarisk bough As eyeful trophies. **1855** ROBINSON *Whitby Gloss.* s.v., 'He's varry eeful over his brass', he is careful in laying out his money. 'Be eeful', mind what you are about.

eye-glass ('aɪglɑːs, -glæs), *sb.* [f. EYE *sb.*¹ + GLASS.]

†**1.** The crystalline lens of the eye. *Obs.*

1611 SHAKS. *Wint. T.* I. ii. 268 Your eye-glasse Is thicker then a Cuckolds Horne.

2. A glass to shield or protect the eye.

1823 J. BADCOCK *Dom. Amusem.* 65 Wearing a visor with eye-glasses in it.

3. †**a.** A magnifying glass, a microscope (*obs.*). **b.** In mod. use, a lens of glass or crystal for assisting defective sight. ***double eye-glass***, (***pair of***) ***eyeglasses***: two such lenses mounted side by side so as to assist the sight of both eyes; the name is by usage restricted to a pair of lenses to be held in the hand or kept in position by a spring on the nose; those which are secured by pieces of metal placed over the ears being called *spectacles.*

1767 HARMER in *Phil. Trans.* LVII. 283, I have often found, by the help of an eye-glass, that..I passed over great multitudes of eggs. **1807** *Director* I. 233 He uses his eye-glass more than his prayer-book. **1859** G. MEREDITH *R. Feverel* xxix, Eyes are bearable, but eye-glasses an abomination. **1863** MISS BRADDON *Eleanor's Vict.* (1878) I. ii. 17 The old man put a double gold eyeglass over his nose, and began to read. **1883** F. M. PEARD *Contrad.* xxvii, She fancied there had been something of the eye-glass manner about him. **1883** F. M. CRAWFORD *Dr. Claudius* iii, She wore gold-rimmed eyeglasses.

4. The lens at that end of any optical instrument to which the eye is applied.

1664 *Phil. Trans.* I. 2 He useth three Eye-Glasses for his great Telescopes. **1672** GREGORY in Rigaud *Corr. Sci. Men* (1841) II. 242 The..plano-convex eyeglass. **1704** NEWTON *Opticks* I. I. viii. (1721) 92 A pretty good Perspective..made with a concave Eyeglass. **1782** RAMSDEN in *Phil. Trans.* (1783) LXXIII. 99 Thus we have a system of eye-glasses which may be taken out of the telescope. **1816** J. SMITH *Panorama Sc. & Art* I. 484 The focal distance of the eye-glass. **1837** GORING & PRITCHARD *Microgr.* 56 The solar focus of its eye-glass. **1867** J. HOGG *Microsc.* I. ii. 31 The other to magnify this image, and from being next the eye of the observer, called the eye-glass.

5. A glass adapted for the application of remedies to the eye.

1842 DUNGLISON *Med. Lex.*, Eye Glass, *Scaphium oculare.* **1884** in *Syd. Soc. Lex.*, *Eye-glass*, a hollow cup-shaped glass for applying lotions to the eye.

Hence **eyeglassed** *a.*, furnished with an eye-glass or eyeglasses.

1848 CLOUGH *Bothie* I. 9 Noble ladies..Bowing their eye-glassed brows. **1891** M. E. MANN *Winter's Tale* II. II. iv. 181 The eyeglassed young man.

'eyeglass, *v. rare.* [f. prec. sb.] *trans.* To look at through an eyeglass; to see through an eye-glass; *intr.*, to use an eye-glass. Also *fig.*

1828 J. BANION *Anglo-Irish* II. 221 Miss Gore.. employed herself..in eye-glassing Gerald. **1841** S. BAMFORD *Passages in Life of Radical* (ed. 2) I. v. 26 Some of the members..were eye-glassing across the house [of Commons]. **1893** *Daily News* 23 Feb. 6/4 That fever heat, insurrection, and great emergency which..Mr. Chamberlain eye-glassed in a not distant future.

eye-glassy, eyeglassy ('aɪglɑːsɪ, -glæs-), *a. colloq.* [f. EYE-GLASS *sb.* + -Y¹.] Pertaining to or characteristic of one who wears an eye-glass; *allusively*, haughtily superior or contemptuous.

1871 G. MEREDITH *H. Richmond* xxi, The interior of the Casino seemed more hostile. I remarked it to him. 'A trifle more eyeglassy' he murmured. **1906** *Cassell's Mag.* Apr. 553/1 Mr. Rodder only laughed—the pleasant laugh that wasn't eye-glassy.

eyehole ('aɪhəʊl). [f. EYE *sb.*¹ + HOLE.] **a.** The cavity or socket containing the orbit of the eye. **b.** A hole to look through. **c.** *dial.* (See quot.)

a. 1637 RUTHERFORD *Lett.* lxxxviii. (1862) I. 227 Let their eyes rot in their eye-holes, who will not receive Him home again. **1855** ROBINSON *Whitby Gloss.*, *Een-holes*, the eye-sockets. **1888** J. SHALLOW *Templars Trials* 68 Wheat grows through the eyeholes of the skull.

b. 1856 KANE *Arct. Expl.* I. xxx. 406 A small eye-hole.. enabled the in-dwellers to peep out. **1863** SALA *Breakfast in Bed* (1864) 286 A crumpled bit of pasteboard covered with black silk, with two eyeholes and a fringe of sham lace. **1878** LOCKYER *Stargazing* 47 The stars were observed..through an eyehole, sliding on a fixed arc.

c. 1884 HOLLAND *Gloss. Chester* (E.D.S.), *Eye-hole*, the depressions in a potato from which the buds spring. **1887** in DARLINGTON *Folk-speech S. Cheshire* (E.D.S.).

eye-lash ('aɪlæʃ). [f. EYE *sb.*¹ + LASH.] **a.** The row or line of hairs fringing the edge of the eye-lid. **b.** A single hair from the same.

1752 SIR J. HILL *Hist. Anim.* 535 Even the eyelashes [of the Simia] are like ours. **1777** ROBERTSON *Hist. Amer.* II. 68 Their..eye-lashes are of the same hue. **1813** SCOTT *Rokeby* IV. v, The eye-lash dark, and downcast eye. **1836** TODD *Cycl. Anat.* I. 306/2 Few birds..possess eye-lashes. **1860** TYNDALL *Glac.* II. i. 235 Looking through their fingers or their eyelashes. **1883** *Harper's Mag.* Sept. 646/2 She fought him [Sleep] to the last eye-lash.

c. *attrib.* and *Comb.*

1907 *Yesterday's Shopping* (1969) 538/3 Eyelash Cream —box 1/5. **1926–7** *Army & Navy Stores Catal.* 494/2 Eyelash brushes. **1938** *Eve's Jrnl.* Jan., Make-up... Eyebrow pencil, eyelash brushes, eyelash comb. **1960** *Harper's Bazaar* July 67/1 Eyelash curlers in simulated gold.

Hence **eye-lashed** *ppl. a.*, provided with eye-lashes; in quot. *transf.*

1854 SYD. DOBELL *Balder* i. 5 Little window in the wall, Eye-lashed with balmy sprays of honeysuckle.

†**'eyelast, 'eyelist.** *Sc. Obs.* [? f. EYE *sb.*¹ + ME. *lest*, *last* fault.]

1. A flaw, deformity, defect.

1591 R. BRUCE *Serm.* Bviij, The last eyelast that appeareth in this denunciatioun is this. **1606** *Sc. Acts Jas. VI* (1816) 357 Ony defaulte or Eilest, be þe quhilk the richt or possessioun of the saidis landis may be challangeit. **1610** J. MELVILL *Diary* (1842) 761 They fand thrie or four dangerous eyelistis that they could not digest. **1624** CALDERWOOD *Ep. Chr. Brother* 12 The uncomely eye-lasts required to be introduced upon the sound work of this Sacrament. **1768** ROSS *Helenore* 142 From any ee-list I'm free.

2. A grievance, grudge; ill-will, malice.

1584 J. CARMICHAEL in *Wodr. Soc. Misc.* (1844) 415 To repare all bygane elistis. **1595** in Pitcairn *Crim. Trials* I. 349 All and sindrie personis amangis quhome deidlie feid and eleist is presentlie standing. **1644** D. HUME *Hist. Douglas* 87 These two lived after..without suspition, grudge, or eye-list on either partie.

eyeless ('aɪlɪs), *a.* [f. EYE *sb.*¹ + -LESS.]

1. Without eyes. **a.** Of certain animals: Having no eyes. **b.** Of a needle: Made without an eye. **c.** Of a plant, etc.: Without buds.

1570 in LEVINS *Manip.* 91. *a* **1822** SHELLEY *Assassins* ii. in *Ess. & Lett.* (Camelot) 171 The eyeless worms of earth. **1848** CARPENTER *Anim. Phys.* 12 In..the great cave of Kentucky are found numerous small eyeless fishes. **1871** *Athenæum* 26 Aug. 275 Paris has sewers, and strange, eye-less..beings swarm through them.

2. Deprived of the eyes, having the eyes removed.

1592 SHAKS. *Rom. & Jul.* v. iii. 126 What Torch is yond that vainely lends his light To grubs, and eyelesse Sculles? **1605** —— *Lear* III. vii. 96 Turne out that eyelesse Villaine. **1671** MILTON *Samson* 38 Ask for this great deliverer now, and find him Eyeless in Gaza. **1725** POPE *Odyss.* XIII. 145 The vengeance vowed for eyeless Polypheme. **1812** BYRON *Ch. Har.* II. vi, Through each lack-lustre, eyeless hole. **1857** WHITTIER *Poems, Wife of Manoah* 15 An eyeless captive. **1866** KINGSLEY *Herew.* xv. 194, I am haunted with spectres eyeless and handless.

3. Blind, sightless. **a.** Without eyes or eyesight, *lit.* and *fig.* **b.** Not using the eyes, undiscriminating; without aid from the eyes.

1627–47 FELTHAM *Resolves* 164 The eye-lesse night. **1717** ADDISON tr. *Ovid's Met.* III. 625 Pentheus only durst deride The Cheated People, and their Eyeless Guide. **1766** G. CANNING *Anti-Lucretius* III. 227 [He] for a pilot eyeless Chance employ'd. **1814** CARY *Dante, Purgatory* XIII. 61 As never beam Of noonday visiteth the eyeless man, E'en so [etc.]. **1859** TENNYSON *Idylls, Vivien* 106, I saw the little elf-god eyeless once. **1867** J. MARTINEAU *Chr. Life* (ed. 4) 464 Sunshine is of no use in an eyeless world. **1871** MORLEY *Condorcet* Crit. Misc. (1878) 73 The fortuitous vagaries of an eyeless destiny. **1877** MORRIS *Sigurd* III. 278 The hungry eyeless sword.

4. Not to be reached by the eye. *rare.*

1839 BAILEY *Festus* (1848) 17/2 Like stars..They shall ever pass at all but eyeless distance.

†**'eyelest.** *Obs.* Also 3 æielest. [:—OE. **eȝelíest*, f. *eȝeleás* AWELESS.] Fearlessness.

c **1275** LAY. 19291 Hii dude ofte onwreste al for heye-leste [*c* **1205** æie-leste].

eyelet ('aɪlɪt), *sb.* Forms: 4 oilet, 5 oylette, olyet, -tte, 7 eielet, eylet, 7– eyelet. [ME. *oilet*, a. Fr. *œillet*, dim. of *œil* eye: the mod. form is influenced by association with EYE and -LET.]

1. a. A small round hole in cloth, sail-cloth, etc., worked like a button-hole for the passage of a lace, ring, or rope; also EYELET-HOLE. **b.** A short metal tube, having its ends flattened for the same purpose.

1382 WYCLIF *Ex.* xxvi. 5 The curtyn shal haue fifti oiletis in either parti. **1611** SPEED *Hist. Gt. Brit.* IX. xv. §9 At euery Eylet the Needle left hanging by the silke. **1627** CAPT. SMITH *Seaman's Gram.* v. 23 Drawing a rope thorow a blocke or oylet to runne vp and down. *a* **1764** LLOYD *To G. Colman*, Peeping the curtains eyelet through.

transf. **1805** WORDSW. *Prelude* VII. Wks. (1888) 288/1 Winding up his mouth..into an orifice..a lurking eyelet, small and only not invisible.

2. An aperture or loophole for observation; *rarely* for the discharge of missiles.

c **1440** *Promp. Parv.*, Olyet, hole yn a walle. *c* **1450** LONELICH *Grail* xiv. 630 Forto han smeten him..Thorwh the oylettes of his helm. **1848** THACKERAY *Van. Fair* lxiii, A woman..with a black mask on, through the eyelets of which her eyes twinkled strangely. **1851** TURNER *Dom. Archit.* I. vii. 336 In which there are loop-holes or eylets for arrows. **1858** BUSHNELL *Nat. & Supernat.* iii. (1864) 65 Eyelet of observation.

3. a. A small eye (*lit.* and *fig.*) *spec.* in a butterfly's wing: an ocellus; = EYE *sb.*¹ 12 d.

1799 W. TAYLOR in *Monthly Mag.* VII. 139 With eyelets, by the fat flesh squeez'd together. **1832** J. RENNIE *Butterfl. & M.* 23 The Eyed Hawk Wings..; second pair rosy at the base, the tips much paler, with a large blue eyelet near the posterior angle. **1832** T. BROWN *Bk. Butterfl. & M.* (1834) I. 120 The wings are angular,..with large compound eyelets, reddish in the centre. **1835** *Tait's Mag.* II. 379 Wicked eyelets, wicked mouth, Face me fairly, tell me truth! **1848** HARDY in *Proc. Berw. Nat. Club* II. 335 Eyelets (*ocelli*) two, small, black. **1876** HARDY *Hand Ethelb.* II. xlvi. 233 They could discern eyelets of light.

†**b.** A small eye or bud of a plant or tree. *Obs.*

1600 SURFLET *Countrie Farme* VI. vi. 737 If it [the vine stock] haue put forth any eielet, you may rub it off with your finger. **1616** SURFL. & MARKH. *Country Farme* 348 Shoots.. full of sappe, hauing grosse and thicke-set eyelets.

4. *attrib.* and *Comb.*, as ***eyelet-punch***, ***-ring***, etc.; *spec.* designating stitching or embroidery composed of eyelets giving an open-work effect (see also quot. 1909).

1864 WEBSTER, *Eyelet-ring*, a small ring of metal, ivory, &c. inserted in an eyelet to prevent wearing. **1874** KNIGHT *Dict. Mech.*, *Eyelet-punch*, a device used at the desk for attaching papers together by eyeleting. **1880** *Catal. Tool Wks. Sheffield* 80 Best bright Eyelet Closing Pliers. **1883** *Harper's Mag.* 813/2 It is a mere eyelet slit of a strait. **1909** *Cent. Dict.* Suppl., *Eyelet-stitch*, in sewing-machine work, the method of placing the stitches in radial lines round an eyelet-hole or over a metal reinforcing ring or eyelet. **1911** *Daily Colonist* (Victoria, B.C.) 30 Apr. 3/4 (Advt.), Eyelet embroidery is an effective feature. **1932** D. C. MINTER *Mod. Needlecraft* 52/1 Eyelet stitch..may be used as a background stitch. *Ibid.* 253/1 Eyelet or English embroidery as decoration. **1960** B. SNOOK *English Hist. Embroidery* 53 Other shirts..have four-sided stitch and eyelet stitch on the front opening.

eyelet ('aɪlɪt), *v.* [f. prec. sb.] *trans.* To make eyelets in: *lit.* and *fig.*

1832 GEN. P. THOMPSON *Exerc.* (1842) II. 323 The cockneys..eyeleted the royalists at Brentford in 1642.

Hence **'eyeleted** *ppl. a.* **'eyeleting** *vbl. sb.*

1874 KNIGHT *Dict. Mech.*, *Eyeleting-machine*, a machine for attaching eyelets to garments and other objects. **1885** NEWHALL in *Harper's Mag.* Jan. 286/2 Self-feeding eyeleting machine, foot-power. **1891** *Ch. Times* 27 Feb. 209/3 Advt., [A card]..eyeleted for hanging up. *Mod.* Eyeleted luggage-labels.

eyeleteer (aɪlɪˈtɪə(r)). [f. prec. sb. + -EER[1].] (See quot.)

1874 KNIGHT *Dict. Mech.*, *Eyeleteer*, a stabbing instrument of the work-table, to pierce eyelet-holes.

eyelet-hole (ˈaɪlɪtˌhəʊl), *sb.* Forms: 6 ilet-, 6–7 oylet-, 6–9 eylet-, 7 eylot-, ilot-, oilet-, 7–8 ey(e)lid-, 8 eilet-, 9 oilete-, 7- eyelet-. [f. EYELET *sb.* + HOLE.]

1. = EYELET 1 a; also a hole for inserting a metal eyelet (see EYELET 1 b).

1497 *Naval Accts. Hen. VII* (1896) 334 Makyng of olyett-hooles with other necessaries for the seid sayles. **1580** NORTH *Plutarch* (1676) 573 A Brigandine made of many folds of Canvas with Oylet-holes. **1599** A. M. tr. *Gabelhouer's Bk. Physicke* 184/2 The thong must lye..on the rupture, which must on both his sydes have 2 eyletholes. **1627** CAPT. SMITH *Seaman's Gram.* vii. 31 The eylot holes of the saile. **1658** A. FOX tr. *Wurtz' Surg.* II. xxiv. 144 Splinters made..with fitting fillets and bands, on which there are small eylid holes. **1743** ZOLLMAN in *Phil. Trans.* XLII. 365 A sort of Boat of Turkey Leather..with..Eilet-holes for receiving Hooks. **1762** FALCONER *Shipwr.* II. 335 The reef-lines next..Through eyelet-holes..were reeved. **1850** CARLYLE *Latter-d. Pamph.*, *Downing Street* 45 This poor tailor's-bodkin, hardly adequate to bore an eyelet-hole. **1861** PEARSON *Early & Mid. Ages Eng.* 206 Wool and flax, with silk for the lappets and the eyelet holes, were the common materials.

transf. **1599** PORTER *Angry Wom. Abingd.* (Percy Soc.) 132 Twill be a good while ere you wish your skin full of ilet holes. **1634** FORD *P. Warbeck* II. iii, Or let my skin be punch'd full of oylet-holes with the bodkin of derision.

2. a. A small hole for the purpose of observation. **b.** A hole or slit for the discharge of missiles.

a. **1797–1803** FOSTER in *Life & Corr.* 1846 I. 178 An eyelet-hole, through which I fancied visions of entrancing beauty. **1848** W. H. AINSWORTH *Lanc. Witches* I. x, Nor was she long in discovering a small eyelet-hole in the carving which commanded the room. **1869** *Latest News* 3 Oct. 15 Scarcely any of the helmets have eyeletholes, but the viser was in general left partly open.

b. **1858** HAWTHORNE *Fr. & It. Jrnls.* I. 606 Embrasures for guns and eyelet holes for musketry. **1879** SIR G. SCOTT *Lect. Archit.* I. 260 In a fortification external windows must be wholly avoided or reduced to mere eyelet-holes.

3. *nonce-use* = EYEHOLE a.

a **1845** HOOD *Jack Hall* xix, Death..gave a wink, As well as eyelet holes can blink.

Hence **ˈeyelet-hole** *v.*, (*a*) *intr.* to make eyelet-holes; (*b*) *trans.*, to make eyelet-holes in; to pierce through and through; to riddle. **ˈeyelet-holed** *ppl. a.*, furnished with eyelet-holes. **ˈeyelet-ˌholing** *vbl. sb.*

1747 *Gentl. Mag.* Feb. 71 These lovers are to eylet-hole one another in Miss Biddy's presence. **1590** BARWICK *Disc. Manuall Weapons* 21 Ilet holed dublets very easie. **1845** DICKENS *Chimes* 63, I introduced pinking and eyelet-holeing among the men.

eyeliad, obs. var. of OEILLADE.

eyelid (ˈaɪlɪd). [f. EYE *sb.*[1] + LID.] One of the lids or covers of the eye, distinguished as *upper* and *lower*; one of the movable folds of skin with which an animal covers or uncovers the eye at pleasure.

a **1240** *Sawles Warde* in *Cott. Hom.* 265 Swifte as þe sunne gleam þe sc[heot from est into west, ase þin] ehe-lid tuneð ant openeð. *a* **1300** *Cursor M.* 19788 (Cott.) Wit þis sco lifted hir eien lidd. **1398** TREVISA *Barth. De P.R.* v. viii. (1495) 114 A foure foted beeste wythout eye lyddes is feble of syghte. *c* **1400** *Apol. Loll.* 74 His ee ledis asken reson of men. **1486** *Bk. St. Albans* A ij b, Put it thorow the ouer igh lid and so of that other. **1597** SHAKS. *2 Hen. IV*, III. i. 7 O Sleepe, O gentle Sleepe, how haue I frighted thee That thou no more wilt weigh mine eye-lids downe. **1626** BACON *Sylva* §870 Those that are Pore-blinde..doe much gather the Eye-lids together. **1690** LOCKE *Hum. Und.* II. ix. (1695) 68 How frequently do we..cover our Eyes with our Eye-lids, without perceiving that we are at all in the dark? **1752** SIR J. HILL *Hist. Anim.* 535 The eyes [of the Simia]..have an upper and under eye-lid, exactly as in our own species. **1814** SCOTT *Ld. of Isles* VI. xv, The eyelid scarce had time to wink. **1855** BAIN *Senses & Int.* I. ii. §18 Touching the edge or inner surface of the upper eye-lid.

Comb. **1870** ROLLESTON *Anim. Life* 31 The eyelid-like valve which guards the entrance of the great veins.

fig. **1382** WYCLIF *Job* xli. 9 His eȝen as eȝelidis of the morntid. **1637** MILTON *Lycidas* 25 Under the opening eye-lids of the Morn We drove afield. **1647** H. MORE *Song of Soul* II. iii. I. xxv, Gilded clouds Arching an eyelid for the glowing Morn. **1862** B. TAYLOR *Poets Jrnl.*, *Mystic Summer*, And sweeter eyelids has the Day.

b. *Phrases.* †*to hang (a thing) by the eyelids*: to keep in suspense. *to hang by the eyelids*: to have a very slight hold, be in a dangerous position.

1659 *Burton's Diary* (1828) IV. 354, I would fain have things at an end, and not hang them by the eyelids thus. **1778** GOUV. MORRIS in Sparks *Life & Writ.* (1832) I. 177 General Lee's affair hangs by the eyelids. **1877** J. T. FIELDS *Underbrush* (1881) 11 A magic quarto..with one of the covers hanging by the eyelids.

†**ˈeyely**, *a.* *Obs.* *rare*[−1]. [f. EYE *sb.*[1] + -LY.] Visible to the eye.

1561 DAUS tr. *Bullinger on Apoc.* (1573) 252 b, A certeine eyely and euident demonstration.

ˈeyemark. [f. EYE *sb.*[1] + MARK.] **a.** Something marked, or to be marked by the eye; an object to look at; a spectacle. Cf. FOOTMARK. †**b.** The action of looking upon, marking with the eye; observation.

1595 SOUTHWELL *Tri. Death* (1596) 24 There are..better eie-markes in youre fortune than a sisters losse. **1654** tr. *Behmen's Myst. Magnum* xl. §29. 272 Where the limit or Eye marck stood. **1840** DE QUINCEY *Mod. Superstit.* Wks. III. 327 Not..the want..of eyemarks, where all is one blank ocean of sand.

eyepiece (ˈaɪpiːs). [f. EYE *sb.*[1] + PIECE.]

1. *Optics.* The lens or combination of lenses, usually two in number, known respectively as the *field-glass* and *eye-glass*, at the eye-end of a telescope, or other optical instrument, by which the image, formed by the mirror or object-glass, is viewed and magnified.

The principal kinds of eye-pieces are (*a*) the *Huyghenian*, or so-called *negative* from the fact of its forming the image between the lenses; (*b*) the *Ramsden*, or common astronomical, called *positive* because the image is formed outside the field-glass; (*c*) the *erecting* or *terrestrial* for ordinary telescopes, which presents the object in an erect position.

1790 ROY in *Phil. Trans.* LXXX. 155 The common eye-piece with two convex glasses. **1831** BREWSTER *Optics* xliii. 360 Achromatic eyepieces..may be composed of two or three lenses. **1867** J. HOGG *Microsc.* I. ii. 40 The two [eye-glass and field-glass] when combined are termed the eye-piece. **1878** LOCKYER *Stargazing* 111 The Achromaticity of the Huyghenian Eyepiece.

b. *attrib.* as *eyepiece micrometer*. (See quot.)

1874 KNIGHT *Dict. Mech.*, *Eye-piece Micrometer*, a graduated slip of glass introduced through slits in the eye-piece tube, so as to occupy the center of the field.

2. *Australian.*

1880 *Leeds Mercury* 16 Nov. 7 The power of a lazy free-selector to pick out the eye-piece of a squatter's run.

eye-pit. [f. EYE *sb.*[1] + PIT.] **a.** The pit or socket of the eye. **b.** The depression between the eye and the orbit.

c **1275** *Death* 241 (Cotton) in *O.E. Misc.* 182 Also beoð his eȝe-puttes ase a bruþen led. **1774** GOLDSM. *Nat. Hist.* III. iii. 78 This animal [Antelope]..has deeper eyepits than the former. **1846** J. BAXTER *Libr. Pract. Agric.* I. 412 By the depth of the eye-pit we are enabled to form some idea of the age of the horse. **1879** E. ARNOLD *Lt. Asia* 58 His eye-pits red with rust of ancient tears.

eyer (ˈaɪə(r)), *sb.* *rare.* [f. EYE *v.* + -ER[1].] **a.** One who eyes; one who looks at; an observer.

1399 LANGL. *Rich. Redeles* 13 The hende Egle the eyere of hem all. **1611** COTGR., *Regardeur*, a looker..eyer, beholder. **1654** GAYTON *Pleas. Notes* II. iv. 47 The sutor was as diligent an eyer of her. **1830** tr. *Aristophanes' Knights* 69 That aged eyer of the bread.

b. A maker of eyes in needles.

1881 *Instr. Census Clerks* (1885) 45 Needle Maker... Eyer.

eyer, var. of AIRE *v.*

eyer, obs. form of HEIR.

eyer(e, obs. f. AIR *sb.*[1]

†**ˈey(e)rer.** *Obs.* Also 5 ayrer. [f. *eyre*, var. of AIRE *sb.*[2] or *v.* + -ER[1].] A brood falcon. Also *attrib.*

1399 in *Archæol.* XXI. 89 Hit was a eyrer good & able, to his lord ryȝt profitable. **1486** *Bk. St. Albans* B vij a, How a man shall take an hawke fro the Eyrer. Who so takys an hawke from the Eyerer: hym behoueth to doo wisely. **1494** *Act 11 Hen. VII*, c. 17 That no Man take any Ayrer Faulcon ..nor purposely drive them out of their Coverts..to cause them to go to other Coverts to breed.

eyerie, -y, obs. ff. of AERIE.

eyes, obs. f. of EYAS.

ˈeyesalve. *Obs.* exc. *fig.* [f. EYE *sb.*[1] + SALVE.] Ointment for the eyes.

c **1000** ÆLFRIC *Gloss.* in Wr.-Wülcker 114 *Colliria*, eaȝ-sealfe. *c* **1200** *Ormin* 1852 Hallȝhe læchedom And sawless eȝhesallfe. **1526** BIBLE (Tindale) *Rev.* iii. 18 Anoynt thyne eyes with eye salve, that thou mayste se. **1616** SURFL. & MARKH. *Country Farme* 137 An Eye-salue made of the iuice of ground Iuie. **1784** COWPER *Task* II. 203 Go, dress thine eye with eyesalve.

fig. **1550** BALE *Image Both Ch.* G iv, Anoynt thyne eyes.. with the eye salve of clerenes which is Jesus Christe. **1641** MILTON *Reform.* I. (1851) 30 If we will but purge with sovrain eyesalve that intellectual ray which God hath planted in us. **1677** GILPIN *Demonol.* (1867) 69 Where grace, as the only eye-salve, doth not restore the sight.

†**ˈeyesene.** *Obs.* Also 2 ec-, 3 æh-, eæh-, ex-, 4 eiȝe-sene, -seon. [f. EYE *sb.*[1] + ME. SENE sight.] Eyesight, presence.

c **1175** *Lamb. Hom.* 143 Ech eorþe scal hwakien on his ecsene. *c* **1205** LAY. 8229 Ut of min æh senen [**1275** hehseht]. *c* **1275** *Prayer to Virgin* 36 in *O.E. Misc.* (1872) 196 Þat ich nocht at dai of dome beo flemed of þin exsene. *c* **1320** *Sir Tristr.* 2222 Anon of lond he ches, Out of markes eiȝe sene.

eye-servant (ˈaɪˌsɜːvənt). *arch.* [f. EYE *sb.*[1] + SERVANT.] One who serves the eye; one who does his duty only when under the eye of his master or employer.

1552 LATIMER *Serm. Lord's Prayer* v. Wks. (Parker Soc.) 394 The most part of servants are but eye-servants. **1613** *Answ. Uncasing Machivils Instr.* F iij b, Keepe not an eye seruant within thy doore. **1682** FLAVEL *Fear* 19 'Tis the reproach of the servants of men to be eye-servants. **1832** CARLYLE *Remin.* I. (1881) 6 No one..will ever say, Here was the finger of a hollow eye-servant.

ˈeye-serve, *v.* [f. EYE *sb.*[1] + SERVE *v.*] *trans.* To wait upon with the eyes; to watch.

1800 HURDIS *Fav. Village* 181 They [sparrows]..Eye-serve the goose for its superfluous down.

ˈeye-ˌserver. [f. EYE *sb.*[1] + SERVER.] = EYE-SERVANT.

1835 MARRYAT *Jac. Faithf.* xviii, I will have no eye-servers under me. **1870** SPURGEON *J. Ploughm. Talk* i. 16 The man who loiters when the master is away is an eye-server.

ˈeye-ˌservice. [f. EYE *sb.*[1] + SERVICE.] **a.** The action or conduct of an eye-servant; service performed only under inspection or under the master's eye. †**b.** Service seen by the eye; outward or formal worship. **c.** The homage of the eye; respectful and admiring looks. *rare.*

1526–34 TINDALE *Col.* iii. 22 Not with eye service as men pleasers. **1550** CROWLEY *Last Trump.* 163 Se thou serue him ..not wyth eye-seruice fainedly. **1688** DELAMER *Wks.* (1694) 26 All their duty will be turned into eye-service. **1736** BERKELEY *Disc.* Wks. (1871) III. 417 This [religion] makes men obey, not with eye-service, but in sincerity of heart. **1884** J. HALL *Chr. Home* 55 Servants that can be trusted to give something better than eye-service.

b. **1641** MILTON *Reform.* I. 2 [To] bring the inward acts of the Spirit to the outward..ey-Service of the body.

c. **1869** BLACKMORE *Lorna D.* lxvi, They [ladies] were worth looking at..but none so well worth eye-service as my own beloved Lorna.

ˈeye-ˌserving, *a.* [f. EYE *sb.*[1] + SERVING.] That serves only under the master's eye; requiring the master's eye.

1615 J. STEPHENS *Satyr. Ess.* (ed. 2) 15 This eye-serving age is quickly gone to all deceit, if we lacke lookers on.

eyeship (ˈaɪʃɪp). [f. EYE *sb.*[1] + -SHIP.] The dignity of being an eye.

1822 T. MITCHELL *Aristoph.* I. 29 The senate bids his eye-ship welcome; And asks his presence to the hall.

ˈeyeshot. [f. EYE *sb.*[1] + SHOT.]

1. The range of the eye, seeing distance, view. Only in phrases (*to come*, etc.) ***beyond, in, out of, within eyeshot of.***

1599 B. JONSON *Ev. Man out of Hum.* v. i, When we come in eye-shot, or presence of this lady. **1690** DRYDEN *Don Sebastian* II. ii, I am..out of eye-shot from the other windows. **1853** KANE *Grinnell Exp.* xli. (1856) 375, I have.. crawled within fair eye-shot, and..watched their movements. **1865** SWINBURNE *Atalanta* 876 Here in your sight and eyeshot of these men. **1867** LOWELL *Biglow P.* Ser. II. 54 Boys beyond eyeshot of the tithing-man.

fig. **1858** HAWTHORNE *Fr. & It. Jrnls.* II. 4 The instant he comes within eye-shot of the fulfilment of his hopes.

2. A 'shot' from the eye; a glance, prospect.

1615 SYLVESTER *Tobacco battered* 291, The Pest..Or deadly Eye-shot of a Basilisk. **1704** STEELE *Lying Lover* v. i, How shall I bear the Eye-Shot of the Crowd in Court? **1709** —— *Tatler* No. 52 ⁋3 The Sexes seem to separate themselves, and draw up to attack each other with Eye-shot. **1860** HAWTHORNE *Marb. Faun* xxviii, The windows.. afforded..extensive eye-shots over hill and valley. **1879** G. MEREDITH *Egoist* III. x. 210 Vernon sent one of his vivid eyeshots from one to the other.

eyesight (ˈaɪsaɪt). [f. EYE *sb.*[1] + SIGHT.]

1. The power or faculty of seeing; sight: attributed also to the heart, soul, etc.

c **1200** *Ormin* 1867 Þatt Drihhtin shollde ȝifenn uss God sawless eȝhesihhþe. *a* **1300** *Cursor M.* 25470 (Cott.) Ert clene and eien sight. *a* **1400** *Cov. Myst.* (Shaks. Soc.) 44 Whantynge of eyesight in peyn doth me bynde. **1401** *Pol. Poems* (1859) II. 98 But him was ȝovun iȝe-siȝt, for al his grete noise. **1587** GOLDING *De Mornay* xiv. 207 The eysight is still good. **1615** J. STEPHENS *Satyr. Ess.* (ed. 2) 420 The Basilisk and Eagle cannot match his eye-sight. **1725** BRADLEY *Fam. Dict.* s.v. *Juice*, It..strengthens the Eye-sight. **1805** *Med. Jrnl.* XIV. 330 These organs..manifest themselves to..the eye-sight. **1873** BAIN in B. Stewart *Conserv. Force* viii. 231 A miser has to pay a high fee to the surgeon that saves his eye-sight.

fig. **1784** COWPER *Task* v. 452 [It] blinds The eyesight of Discov'ry. **1849** ROBERTSON *Sermons* Ser. I. x. 167 To our blinded eyesight it seems a cruel will. **1857** WILLMOTT *Pleas. Lit.* xx. 111 The only eye-sight employed is the critical.

†**2.** The action or fact of seeing or looking; the use of the eyes, look, gaze, observation, view; an instance of this, a look. ***to set good eyesight on***: to look hard at. *Obs.* exc. in ***by, from, in (a person's) eyesight.***

a **1240** *Lofsong* in *Cott. Hom.* 209 Mine sunnen..beoð.. grisliche in þine eih sihðe. *a* **1300** *Signs bef. Judgem.* 143 in *E.E.P.* (1862) 11 For sinful man-is ein siȝt ne let us neuer ben ischend. *a* **1300** *Cursor M.* 4300 (Cott.) Quilum allan wit an ei sight. **1526** TINDALE *Luke* xxii. 56 Won off the wenches ..sett goode eyesight on hym. **1535** COVERDALE *2 Sam.* xxii. 25 So shal yᵉ Lorde rewarde me..acordinge to the clenes of my handes in his eye sighte. **1573** GOLDING *Calvin on Job* 76 Then must we consider euen by eye sight, that our lyfe.. slydeth away from us. **1641** WILKINS *Math. Magick* I. xix. (1648) 135 That in Josephus which he sets down from his own eye-sight. **1839** CARLYLE *Chartism* iv. (1858) 20 Things ..known to us by the best evidence, by eye-sight. **1873** LOWELL *Among my Bks.* Ser. II. 6 His comparisons..are drawn from actual eye-observation.

3. The range of the eye, sight, view.

a **1225** *Juliana* 30 And het swiðe don hire ut of his ehsihðe. *a* **1240** *Ureisun* in *Cott. Hom.* 187 Ich ne mai ne ne dear cum lufsum god in þin ehsihþe. *c* **1400** *Rom. Rose* 7236 He wole not..have God in his iye sight. ? *c* **1475** *Sqr. lowe Degre* 608 That profered you golde and fe, Out of myne eye-syght for to be. **1588** SHAKS. *L.L.L.* II. i. 239 His tongue all impatient to speake and not see Did stumble with haste in his eie-sight

to be. **1633** EARL MANCH. *Al Mondo* (1636) 86 The minde contemplating heaven, walkes beyond eye-sight.

Hence †**eye-sighted** *a.*, gifted with eye-sight.

1651 *Fuller's Abel Rediv., Bucer* (1867) 154 The most judicious and best eye-sighted fryers.

ˈ**eyesome**, *a. Obs.* exc. *poet.* In 6 eysome. [f. EYE *sb.*^{1} + -SOME.] Pleasant to the eyes.

1584 SOUTHWELL *Ep. Comfort* xiv. 191 b, Our syghte shall feede on the most glorious and eysome maiestye of the place. **1922** T. HARDY *Late Lyrics & Earlier* 266, I thought not I should meet an eyesome maiden.

eyesore (ˈaɪsɔə(r)). [f. EYE *sb.*^{1} + SORE *sb.*]

†**1.** A soreness of the eyes. *Obs.*

(In quot. *a*1300 perh. an adj.)

? *a* **1300** *Salomon & Sat.* (1848) 272 Betere is eyesor þen al blynd, quoþ Hendyng. **1562** TURNER *Herbal* II. 76 a, Dates ..are hurtfull for them that haue..the eysore and..the tooth ache. **1562** J. HEYWOOD *Prov. & Epigr.* (1867) 94 Muche lookyng so, breedth much eie sore.

2. Something permanently offensive to the sight; an ugly mark or feature.

1530 RASTELL *Bk. Purgat.* III. viii. 2 The spottes..be a great deformyte and eye sore. **1597** HOOKER *Eccl. Pol.* v. 222 These eyesores and blemishes in continual attendants about the service of Gods sanctuary. **1617** MARKHAM *Caval.* III. 51 To bee..sickle hought behinde..is not amisse, though it be a little eye-sore. **1726** LEONI tr. *Alberti's Archit.* I. 19 b, He is continually repenting and fretting at the Eye-sore. **1827** STEUART *Planter's G.* (1828) 136 This, in parks much exposed, is found a very serious eye-sore. **1867** A. BARRY *Sir C. Barry* viii. 288 All the eyesores on the Surrey bank of the river.

†**b.** On a horse: A scar; also a flaw, defect. *Obs.*

1678 *Lond. Gaz.* No. 1346/4 A dapple grey Gelding..an eye sore above his hoof upon one of his hinder legs. **1690** DRYDEN *Don Sebast.* I. i, He's the best peice of Man's flesh in the Market; not an Eyesore.in his whole body. **1711** *Lond. Gaz.* No. 4795/4 An Eye-sore on the near hind Foot caused in Pacing.

3. A cause of annoyance, offence, or vexation; an object of dislike or disgust.

1548 UDALL, etc. *Erasm. Par. Luke* xvi. 137 He might haue been an iyesore to all. **1586** J. HOOKER *Girald. Irel.* in *Holinshed* II. 63/2, I wote well how great an eiesore I am in your sight. *a* **1618** RALEIGH *Rem.* (1644) 98 Thou shalt be a burthen, and an Eye sore to thy friends. **1759** B. MARTIN *Nat. Hist. Eng.* I. *Hants* 125 The French..to whom they have always been an Eye-sore. **1809** W. IRVING *Knickerb.* (1861) 119 The onion patches of Pyquag were an eyesore to Jacobus Van Curlet and his garrison. **1876** MOZLEY *Univ. Serm.* x. (1877) 206 Many of their neighbours are eyesores to them, and the very sight of them interrupts their repose.

attrib. **1875** W. MCILWRAITH *Guide Wigtownshire* 59 Antiquated and eyesore erections.

ˈ**eyesore**, *a.* [f. EYE *sb.*^{1} + SORE *a.*] That has sore eyes. Hence ˈ**eyesoreness**, soreness of the eyes; in quot. *fig.* Offensive ugliness.

1883 *Harper's Mag.* Feb. 333/1 A bower of charm to the æsthetic sense in the midst of a dirty money-grubbing eye-soreness.

ˈ**eye-splice.** [f. EYE *sb.*^{1} + SPLICE *sb.*] A splice made by turning up the end of a rope, and interlacing its strands with those of the upper part.

1769 FALCONER *Dict. Marine* (1789) N n, The eye-splice being intended to make a sort of eye..at the end of a rope. **1851** H. MELVILLE *Whale* lx. 312 Both ends of the line are exposed; the lower end terminating in an eye-splice, or loop. **1867** in SMYTH *Sailor's Word-bk.* 284.

ˈ**eyespot.** [f. EYE *sb.*^{1} + SPOT *sb.*]

1. a. A spot resembling an eye. **b.** A rudimentary eye. **c.** In a coco-nut: = EYE 12 b.

a. 1879 LUBBOCK *Sci. Lect.* ii. 57 In Chœrocampa tersa, there is an eye-spot on each segment. **1882** *Gard. Chron.* XVII. 10 Calanthe Sandhurstiana..with an eye-spot at the base of the lip. **1890** J. P. BALLARD *Among the Moths* 32 His ..wings..showing two large and elegant eye-spots.

b. 1877 HUXLEY *Anat. Inv. Anim.* iv. 188 One or more eyespots are sometimes seated on the ganglion. **1880** BASTIAN *Brain* viii. 116 In the young Lamprey two pigment spots replace the single 'eye spot' of the Lancelot.

c. 1885 H. O. FORBES *Nat. Wanderings* I. ii. 27 The three eye-spots seen at the end of a cocoa-nut.

2. A kind of lily of a violet or black colour, having a red spot in the middle of each leaf.

1801 SOUTHEY *Thalaba* VI. xx, Here amid her sable cup Shines the red eye-spot..The solitary twinkler of the night.

3. A name given to two fungal diseases: **a.** A disease caused by *Helminthosporium sacchari* that affects sugar-cane. **b.** A disease caused by *Cercosporella herpotrichoides* that affects wheat, other cereals, and some grasses.

1906 *Mem. Dept. Agric. India, Bot. Ser.* I. III. 43 Several other leaf spotting fungi..are known to occur on the sugar-cane... The following are the chief known:—(1.) The 'Eye-spot' of Java canes, produced by *Cercospora Sacchari*. **1929** *Rev. Appl. Mycol.* VIII. 467 The control of eye spot disease of sugar-cane. **1930** *Ibid.* IX. 639 On Bon Fermier wheat affected by foot rot the author noted eye spot lesions of the type usually attributed to *Leptosphaeria herpotrichoides* but associated with an undetermined fungus whose cultural characteristics were quite different. **1942** *Ann. Appl. Biol.* XXIX. 259 Wheat and barley are susceptible to eyespot but oats show considerable resistance. **1968** *Times* 16 Dec. 7/2 The soil-borne diseases, take-all and eyespot. **1970** LIEBSCHER & KOEHLER tr. *Frölich & Rodewald's Pests & Dis. Tropical Crops* 235 Sugar yield losses due to eye spot disease can be very high.

Hence ˈ**eyespotted** *ppl. a.*, having spots resembling eyes.

1590 SPENSER *Muiopotmos* 95 Iunoes Bird in her ey-spotted traine. **1883** *Times* 11 June 4/5 A splendid peacock with a luxuriant train of eye-spotted feathers.

eyess(e, obs. f. of EYAS.

ˈ**eyestring.** [f. EYE *sb.*^{1} + STRING *sb.*] In *pl.* The strings (i.e. muscles, nerves, or tendons) of the eye. (The 'eyestrings' were formerly supposed to break or crack at death or loss of sight.)

1601 B. JONSON *Poetaster* Induct., Crack, eye-strings..let me be ever blind. **1607** BEAUM. & FL. *Woman-hater* II. i, The last words that my dying father spake, Before his eye-strings brake. **1611** SHAKS. *Cymb.* I. iii. 17, I would haue broke mine eye-strings; crack'd them, but To looke vpon him. **1639** FULLER *Holy War* II. xxxix. (1647) 96 When once those eye-strings begin to break, the heart-strings hold not out long after. **1675** HOBBES *Odyssey* (1677) 108 All his eye-strings with the fire did strut. **1682** OTWAY *Venice Preserved* II. i, Gaze on thee 'till my Eye-strings crackt with Love. **1707** MORTIMER *Husb.* 178 See..that their [sheep's] Gums be red ..the Eye-strings ruddy. **1776** TOPLADY *Bk. Praise* 159 When my eyestrings break in death. **1778** *Arminian Mag.* I. 268 His Eye-strings were broke, his Speech entirely gone.

eyet, obs. f. AIT.

Eyetalian (aɪˈtæljən), *a.* and *sb.* Also **Eye-talian.** Spelling used to represent a non-standard or jocular pronunciation of ITALIAN *a.* and *sb.* with initial (aɪ) sound.

1840 *Spirit of Times* 21 Nov. 447/3 Boston galls may boast of their spinetts, and their gytars, and their eye-talian airs, and their *ears for music.* **1919** F. HURST *Humoresque* 189 The Eyetalians maybe didn't know no better. **1930** E. WALLACE *Lady of Ascot* i. 14 It's foreign—Eye-talian. **1930** E. RAYMOND *Jesting Army* I. vii. 102 The Eye-talians'll have landed at Smyrna. **1953** A. BARON *Human Kind* xxiii. 171 You know what I seen them Eyetalians do? **1961** P. WHITE *Riders in Chariot* xi. 402 An Eyetalian boy called Fiddle Paganini was finishing singing a number.

†ˈ**eyethurl.** *Obs.* [f. EYE *sb.*^{1} + THURL.] An eye-hole, a window; also *pl.* the eye-windows.

c **890** K. ÆLFRED *Bæda* IV. iii. ⁊ 3 Ða ontynde se bisceop ðæt eagh-þyrl ðære cyricean. *c* **1175** *Lamb. Hom.* 83 þe sunne scineð þurh þe glesne ehþurl. *a* **1225** *St. Marher.* 8 Heo þa.. biheolden þurh an eyþurl as heo bed hire beoden. *a* **1225** *Ancr. R.* 62 þurh eie þurles deað haueð hire inȝong into þe soule. *Ibid.* 70 Nout one our earen, auh ower eie þurles tuneð aȝein idel speche.

Eyetie (ˈaɪtaɪ), *sb.* and *a.* Also **Eyeto, Eyety, Eyetye, Eytie.** [f. EYETALIAN *a.* and *sb.*] = EYETALIAN *a.* and *sb.*, used with disparaging overtones.

1925 FRASER & GIBBONS *Soldier & Sailor Words* 90 *Eyeties*, Italians. **1941** BAKER *Dict. Austral. Slang* 27 *Eyeto* (pronounced 'eye-toe'), an Italian. **1943** B. J. HURREN *Eastern Med* viii. 100 Such tricks..made our troops utterly despise the Eyeties (as the soldiers called them). **1943** C. S. FORESTER *Ship* iv. 30 There was a buzz that the Eyety navy was out. **1958** E. H. CLEMENTS *Uncommon Cold* i. 16 The Yugoslavians, the two Eyetyes, some West Germans. **1967** K. GILES *Death in Diamonds* vii. 127 They speak Eyetie?

ˈ**eye-tooth.** [f. EYE *sb.*^{1} + TOOTH; cf. Ger. *augenzahn*, Du. *oogtand.*] **a.** A tooth immediately under or next to the eye, orig. one of the upper canine teeth (see CANINE *tooth*), but now extended to the lower also.

1580 HOLLYBAND *Treas. Fr. Tong, Den Macheliére*, the eye tooth. **1607** TOPSELL *Four-f. Beasts* (1673) 379 The eye teeth of a Lion. **1629** CHAPMAN *Juvenal.* 255 Live still gnashing of thy great eye-teeth. **1691** RAY *Creation* II. (1692) 41 The next [teeth] one on each side..called *Canini*, in English Eye Teeth. **1700** T. BROWN tr. *Fresny's Amusem. Ser. & Com.* 87 The Eye-teeth of Flying Toads. **1741** MONRO *Anat. Nerves* (ed. 3) 159 The two superior..are called Eye-teeth, from the Communication of Nerves which is betwixt them and the Eyes. **1831** R. KNOX *Cloquet's Anat.* 77 The Upper Canine Teeth are the longest in the jaws, and for this reason, are vulgarly denominated Eye-teeth. **1863** HUXLEY *Man's Place Nat.* II. 81 Milk-teeth..consist of four incisors..two canines, or eye-teeth; and four molars..in each jaw.

fig. **1740** PARDON *Dyche's Dict.* (ed. 3), *Eye-teeth*.. Quickness or sharpness of understanding and parts.

b. *Phrases.* Chiefly *fig. to cut one's eye-teeth*: to get out of babyhood. *to draw any one's eye-teeth*: to take the conceit out of him. †*to have one's eye-teeth*: to be wide-awake. *(one) would give one's eye-teeth*: (one) is very eager, or ready to make the greatest sacrifices (*to* do something). Cf. EYE *sb.*^{1} 2 j.

1730 MORIER in Atterbury *Misc. Wks.* V. 147 There is no dealing with him without having one's eye teeth. **1837** HALIBURTON *Clockm.* Ser. I. xvi. 147 Them are fellers cut their eye-teeth afore they ever sot foot in this country. **1867** DIXON *New Amer.* I. i. 1 Guess these Yanks must look alive ..unless they should happen to enjoy having their eye-teeth drawn. **1870** EMERSON *Soc. & Solit., Civiliz.* Wks. (Bohn) III. 7 Like progress that is made by a boy 'when he cuts his eye-teeth'. **1930** W. S. MAUGHAM *Cakes & Ale* i. 13 He'd give his eye-teeth to have written a book half as good. **1965** F. SARGESON *Memoirs of Peon* iv. 55, I would give away my eye-teeth to take that girl into the park.

eye view, eye-view. [f. the phr. *bird's-eye view* (BIRD'S-EYE 3).] A view; usu. suffixed to a possessive substantive to denote what is seen from the view-point of the person or thing specified; freq. in phrases *bird's eye view, worm's eye view.*

1762–71, etc. [see BIRD'S-EYE 3]. **1908** *Punch* 10 June 429/2 We fear the population will develop balloon-necks through trying to get a worm's-eye view of the gas-bags in the haze. **1920** A. HUXLEY *Limbo* 137 He prided himself on being able to see the thing as a whole, on taking an historical, God's-eye view of it all. **1952** H. W. TILMAN *Nepal Himalaya* xi. 131 A man looking at a big mountain from a valley has naturally only a worm's-eye view. **1959** *Sunday Times* 4 Oct. 17/3 Here is a bookworm's-eye view of a hazardous trade. **1962** A. HUXLEY *Island* xiii. 218 How should one look at other people?.. Should one take the Freud's-eye view or the Cézanne's-eye view? The Proust's-eye view or the Buddha's-eye view? **1962** J. ROBERTSON *(title)* Hospitals and children: a parent's-eye view. A review of letters from parents to the *Observer* and the BBC. **1963** *Listener* 17 Jan. 129/2 From his own eye-view Sir Compton has no lack of items to add to the history of his time.

eye-wash, eyewash (ˈaɪwɒʃ). [f. EYE *sb.*^{1} + WASH *sb.* 3.] **1.** A wash or lotion for the eye.

1866 *Cornh. Mag.* Sept. 361 Not all the hair-pins, and eye-washes, and affectations can equal it.

2. *colloq.* Something that is intended to obscure or conceal actual facts or motives; humbug, blarney; nonsense; something said or done merely for appearance or effect; *spec.* in *Mil. slang* = BULL *sb.*^{4} 4.

1884 C. T. BUCKLAND *Sk. Soc. Life India* ii. 45 Most officers of any tact understand the meaning of eye-wash. **1889** F. A. GUTHRIE *Pariah* I. i, He came up to me with some eyewash or other about our being neighbours at Gorsecombe now. **1913** *Aeroplane* 20 Mar. 327/2 Well as this may do as 'eye wash', it is not the real thing. **1916** C. E. W. BEAN *Lett. from France* (1917) 197 The ignorance which ..flies to the conclusion that everything written and spoken about the horrors of this war is humbug, and what the Army calls 'eyewash'. **1919** 'I. HAY' *Last Million* ii. 24 The greater the fuss a regiment made about its appearance—'eye-wash', we called it—the better its work in the field. **1919** *War Slang* in *Athenæum* 8 Aug. 728/1 Anything complimentary is termed 'eyewash'. **1920** *Blackw. Mag.* July 91/2 Kemp went ashore to pay a polite visit to the local Sheikh, as 'eye-wash' against our real activities. **1930** W. S. MAUGHAM *Cakes & Ale* xi. 124 What the critics wrote about Edward Driffield was eye-wash. **1939** J. CARY *Mr. Johnson* 208 'More eyewash about sanitation,' he says to Celia, throwing a blue circular on the breakfast table. **1957** *Economist* 28 Sept. 1001/1 This does not mean that the proposals..are so much eyewash.

Hence ˈ**eyewasher**, one who uses 'eye-wash'; ˈ**eye-washing** *vbl. sb.* and *ppl. a.*

1920 *Nat. Rev.* Apr. 142 The President..refused to..be humbugged by 'eyewashers' who besought him to accept amendments that destroyed his handiwork. **1937** L. HOUSMAN *Unexpected Years* 159 The professions of those who offered them, with 'art for art's sake' as an eye-washing accompaniment. **1939** J. CARY *Mr. Johnson* 177 Nobody.. calls Tring an eyewasher, because he is in fact a highly competent officer... But he..can always catch the right eye at the right time.

eyewater (ˈaɪwɔːtə(r)). [f. EYE *sb.* + WATER *sb.*] **a.** Water, i.e. either natural tears, or an abnormal overflow (*stillicidium*), 'tear in the eye', flowing from the eye. Rare in *pl.* **b.** A lotion for the eye. **c.** The humours (aqueous or vitreous) of the eye. **d.** *slang.* = Gin.

a. 1590 SOUTHWELL *M. Magd. Fun. Teares* 125 What anger so fiery that may not be quenched with eye-water, sith a weeping supplyant rebateth the edge of more than a lyon's fury. **1845** G. MURRAY *Islaford* 169 To roll Sorrow's eye-waters from their dark abode. **1849** THACKERAY *Lett.* 50, I can hardly see as I write for the eye-water, but it isn't with grief.

b. 1679 PLOT *Staffordsh.* (1686) 106 All sorts of Eye-waters, such as that of Elder well. **1747** WESLEY *Prim. Physic* (1762) 61 An excellent Eye Water. **1818** S. F. GRAY *Supp. to Pharmacopœias* 237 Common eye water. *Ibid.* 235 Blue eye water. **1841–4** EMERSON *Ess.* Ser. I. vii. (1876) 190 Love is not a hood, but an eye-water.

c. 1874 COUES *Field Ornith.* I. vii. (1890) 57 Eye-water.. is often a great annoyance [in taxidermy].

d. 1869 WHYTE MELVILLE *M. or N.* I. vi. 118 Two bob an' a bender, and a three of eye-water, in? **1886** *Judy* 4 Aug. 58 Jiggered gin, dog's nose and Paddy's eye-water.

ˈ**eye-wink.** [f. EYE *sb.*^{1} + WINK *sb.*] **a.** A wink or motion of the eye, a look or glance. **b.** The time it takes to wink the eye: an instant.

a. 1598 SHAKS. *Merry W.* II. ii. 72 They could neuer get an eye-winke of her. **1818** KEATS *Endym.* IV. 267 Before young Bacchus' eye-wink turning pale. **1868** BROWNING *Ring & Bk.* x. 921 'Twixt her placid eyewinks.

b. 1879 CHR. ROSSETTI *Seek & F.* 88 Until all time dwindle to a mere eye-wink. **1890** *Daily News* 27 Jan. 3/1 You touch a tiny switch..and in an eye-wink your glass button-hole becomes an incandescent lamp.

Similarly ˈ**eye-winker**, eyelash or eyelid.

1808 JAMIESON, *Ee-winkers* the eye-lashes. *a* **1833** A. PICKEN *Changeable Charlie*, The burley scoundrel lifted up his eye-winkers. **1881** *Pennsylv. School Jrnl.* XXX. 57 Every ..hair and eye-winker, revolving 'on its own hook'.

ˈ**eye-witness.** [f. EYE *sb.*^{1} + WITNESS.]

†**1.** One who gives testimony to what he has seen with his own eyes. *Obs.*

1539 TAVERNER *Erasm. Prov.* (1552) 43 One Eye wytnesse, is of more value, than tenne eare wytnesses. **1591** SPENSER *M. Hubberd* 1278 Which yet to prove more true, he meant to see, And an ey-witnes of each thing to bee.

2. One who can give testimony from personal observation; one who has seen a thing done or happen. Also *attrib.*

1590 SIR J. SMYTH in *Lett. Lit. Men* (Camden) 57, I do not write the same of mine owne certaine knowledge, as a eye wittnesse. **1611** BIBLE *2 Pet.* i. 16 Wee..were eye witnesses of his Maiestie. **1615** W. HULL *Mirrour of Maiestie* 89 The death of such a sonne..whereof shee was an eyed witnesse. **1694** LD. MOLESWORTH *Acc. Denmark* 44 Received not only

from eye-witnesses, but also from some of the principal.. Actors. **1744** BERKELEY *Siris* §17 Leo Africanus.. describes, as an eye-witness, the making of tar in Mount Atlas. **1798** FERRIAR *Illustr. Sterne* i. 17 Brantome, an eye-witness.. informs us. **1855** MACAULAY *Hist. Eng.* IV. 93 Different estimates were formed even by eyewitnesses. **1878** *N. Amer. Rev.* CXXVI. 180 It is the narration, by an eye-witness, of the memorable *coup d'etat* of 1851. **1921** *Times Lit. Suppl.* 10 Nov. 722/3 The aim of these volumes is to present eyewitness accounts of some of the most important incidents. **1922** C. E. MONTAGUE *Disenchantment* vii. 95 Eked out with 'Eye-Witness' stuff—official 'word-painting' by some Regular Officer. **1945** W. S. CHURCHILL *Victory* (1946) 13 The following is an eye-witness report by another British officer.

†**3.** The result of actual observation; a report made by one who was present. *Obs.*

1627 HAKEWILL *Apol.* I. i. §5. 9 By the eye-witnesse of Ioachimus Rheticus, and others, it hath been proved. **1671** MILTON *Samson* 1594 Give us.. Eye-witness of what first or last was done.

Hence **'eye-witness** *v. trans.*, to be an eye-witness of (an event); **'eye-witnessed, 'eye-witnessing** *ppl. adjs.* **eye'witnessing** *vbl. sb.*

1844 KINGLAKE *Eothen* viii. 145 Lamartine's eye-witnessing account of the horse saddled by the hands of his Maker. **1857** H. MILLER *Test. Rocks* iv. 154 Had they been revealed by vision as a piece of eye-witnessing. **1905** 'MARK TWAIN' *King Leopold's Soliloquy* (1907) 17 They seemed to be always.. eye-witnessing the happenings. **1912** W. OWEN *Let.* 7 Nov. (1967) 167, I was so glad to hear your own eyewitnessing account of a Flight. **1923** *Glasgow Herald* 25 Oct. 8 An eye-witnessed incident which took place recently in this neighbourhood. **1963** 'N. BLAKE' *Deadly Joker* xiii. 215 A hundred people had eye-witnessed a murder.

eyey (aɪɪ), *a.* [f. EYE *sb.*[1] (sense 20 d) + -Y.] Full of eyes or holes.

1884 HOLLAND *Gloss. Chester* (E.D.S.) 116 Cheese is said to be eyey when it contains holes full of rancid whey.

eyger, obs. f. of EAGER.

eyghe, obs. f. of AWE.

eyght(e, obs. f. of AIT, EIGHT.

eyghte, obs. f. of AUGHT *sb.*[1]

eyȝtyndele: see EIGHTIN.

eygre, var. of EAGRE; obs. f. of EAGER.

eyir, obs. f. of AIR *sb.*[1].

eykorn, obs. f. of ACORN.

eyl(e, var. of AIL *sb.*[2] *Obs.*; obs. f. AIL *v.*

eylace, obs. f. of ALAS.

1556 *Aurelio & Isab.* (1608) C ij, Eylace how lightlye maie one perceave, when the wemen love.

eylde, obs. form of YIELD.

eyldyng, obs. form of ELDING[1].

eyle, obs. form of AISLE, ILL.

'eylebourn. *dial.* Also **nailbourne.** [Of obscure origin; quot. 1480 would suggest that it is f. AIL *sb.* trouble, affliction + BOURN; but this may be popular etymology.] (See quots.)

c **1480** WARKWORTH *Chron.* 24 [mentions an intermittent stream near St. Albans, called Wemere (interpreted 'woo watere'), the flowing of which was 'a tokene of derthe, or of pestylence, or of grete batayle'; and adds:] Also there has ronne dyverse suche other wateres, that betokenethe lykewyse; one at Lavesham in Kent, and another byside Canturbury called Naylborne. **1677** PLOT *Nat. Hist. Oxfordsh.* 30 Of these [springs] there are many in the County of Kent, which.. they call Nailbournes there. **1719** HARRIS *Hist. Kent* 174 Such.. as in this County they call an Eylebourn; (or vulgarly a Nailbourn) which is a Spring that rises all of a sudden out of the Ground, runs a while like a Torrent and then disappears. *Ibid.* 240 There is a famous Eylebourn which rises in this Parish and some-times runs but a little way.. now and then it goes with a very strong Stream. **1727** LEWIS *Faversham* 4 The brakish Creek, into which a spring or Nail-bourne from Ospringe falls. **1736** in PEGGE *Kenticisms* (E.D.S.) 38 **1887** PARISH & SHAW *Kent. Dialect* (E.D.S.), *Eylebourne, Nailbourn*, an intermittent spring.

'eyling. *Obs.* exc. *dial.* Forms: 5-7 elyng, 6-7 eling(e, 7 eyling, 9 *dial.* ealin. [perh. f. *ele* 'wing', AISLE + -ING[2].]

†**1.** ? An aisle or wing of a church. See AISLE I. *Obs.*

1400 *Acct. Roll Vicars Choral, York*, In emendatione i elyng'. **1528** *Test. Ebor.* IX. 464 To be bur' [in the church of Skipton] in the north elyng.

2. A 'lean-to' or shed attached to a house. *dial.*

1625 *Court Roll, Wakefield*, Partem i domus vocatam elinge. **1875** *Lanc. Gloss., Ealin'*, a shed set against another building.. From the verb to heel or lean over.

†**3.** ? A 'bay' of a barn. *Obs.*

1662 in *N. Riding Rec.* VI. 51 An eyling of a barn.

eylod, prob. error for *lyflod*, LIVELIHOOD.

c **1500** *Melusine* 108 He that shuld enheryte the chyef eylod shuld not be able to kepe no grete houshold.

eylsum, obs. ff. of HALESOME, WHOLESOME.

eym(e, *Sc.* var. EME, *Obs.*, uncle.

eymbre, -bery, eymery, obs. ff. of EMBER[1].

eyme, obs. f. of AIM.

eynd (aɪnd). *dial.* [app. a var. of ANDE 2.] (See quot.)

1865 W. WHITE *E. Eng.* II. 176 The Eynd, or watersmoke, as it is called in Norfolk, is a remarkable phenomenon, occurring mostly between spring and autumn, and with peculiar suddenness.

†**'eyndill**, *v. Sc. Obs. rare.* [? connected with *aynd*, ANDE *sb.*] *intr.* To be jealous. Const. *on.*

1576 MAITLAND *Old Age* in Pinkerton *Anc. Scot. Poems* II. 310 Scho will not eyndill on me now And I sa ald.

Hence †**'eyndland, -ing** *ppl. a.* jealous.

1552 ABP. HAMILTON *Catech.* (1884) 57, I am the Lord thi God, stark and jolious or eyndland. **1568** *Sempill Ball.* 235, I wald ze sowld forbid hir Hir eyndling toyis.

eyne, var. of EAN, *Obs.*

eynes, -ez, -is, erroneous ff. EYVES, -EZ, -IS.

eynke, obs. f. of INK.

eyot, more usual var. of AIT, small island. Hence **'eyoty** *a.* [+ -Y], like an eyot or island.

1883 COPE *Hampshire Words* s.v., 'That eyoty piece near the ford.'

eyr, obs. f. of AIR *sb.*[1], and of EAR *v.*[1]

eyra ('aɪrə). [ad. Tupi *eirara, irara.*] In full *eyra cat.* A wild cat, *Felis yagouaroundi*, in its red phase, found in an area from Argentina and Paraguay to southern Texas.

1860 *Proc. Zool Soc.* XXVIII. 415 Eyra Cat, *Felis eyra.* **1873** *Ibid.* XLI. 2 A specimen of the Eyra Cat.. brought from Maranham, Brazil. **1906** E. INGERSOLL *Life Anim.: Mammals* 105 It is a question whether the eyra and yaguarundi are not varieties of the same species. **1955** *Sci. News Let.* 30 July 78/2 The southwestern states, bordering on Mexico, have four exotic big cats—ocelots, jaguars, margays, and jaguarundis or eyras. **1965** D. MORRIS *Mammals* 315 It [*sc.* the Jaguarondi] exists in two colour phases: red and grey. The red phase used to be thought of as a distinct species and was then called the Eyra Cat (*Felis eyra*), but this is no longer accepted.

eyrant ('ɛərənt). *Her.* [f. *eire*, var. of AIRE *v. Obs.* + -ANT.]

1889 ELVIN *Dict. Heraldry* 57 *Eyrant*, Applied to birds in their nests.

†**'eyrar.** *Obs.* Also 6 eyriar. [deriv. of *eyrie* = AERIE: see AERIE 2.] A brood (of swans).

1551 *Will C. Ferrers* (Somerset Ho.), Eyriars of Swannes. **1715** KERSEY, *Eyrar* (O.R.) an Eyrie or Nest of young Birds. **1721-1800** in BAILEY. **1847-78** HALLIWELL, *Eyrar*, a brood of swans. Sometimes the bird itself.

eyre (ɛə(r)). *Obs.* exc. *Hist.* Forms: 3, 6-8 eire, 4 eyr, 5-6, 9 air, 6 oire, 6-7 aire, 7 eier, eyer, 5, 7- eyre. [a. OF. *eire, erre, oirre* masc. and fem. f. *errer* (see ERR *v.*):—late L. *iterāre* to journey.]

1. Itineration, circuit: in the phrase *justices in eyre* (= L. *in itinere* on a journey), also L. *justitiæ itinerantes*, AF. *justisis errauntz*: itinerant judges who rode the circuit to hold courts in the different counties. Also *sessions in eyre.*

These justices were usually members of the superior courts, though the sheriffs sometimes performed this duty. In the year 1176, under Henry II, eighteen justices were appointed to six circuits; the practice continued with considerable irregularity as to number, period, and the matters dealt with, until the judges of ASSIZE *sb.* (q.v. 12) and Nisi Prius were appointed in the year 1285 under Edw. I.

[**1278** *Act 6 Edw. I*, Stat. Glouc. cc. 1-3 (1810) 46 E le Justices en Eire facent de ceo, etc. **1292** BRITTON I. i. §3 Qe Justices errauntz soint assignetz.] **1297** R. GLOUC. (1724) 517 The eire of justize wende aboute in the londe. **1483** *Act 1 Rich. III*, c. 6 §1 Divers Fairs have been holden.. by Prescription allowed afore Justices in Eyre. **1523** FITZHERB. *Surv.* vi. (1539) 11 Alowed before justice in Eire. **1570-6** LAMBARDE *Peramb. Kent* (1826) 485 An especiall sessions in Eire. **1598** HAKLUYT *Voy.* I. 17 The Iustices in Eire, (or Itinerent, as we called them, because they vsed to ride from place to place throughout the Realme, for administration of iustice). **1768** BLACKSTONE *Comm.* III. 57 These judges of assise came into use in the room of the antient justices in eyre. **1866** ROGERS *Agric. & Prices* I. iv. 71 An action before the county court, or the judges in Eyre. **1875** STUBBS *Const. Hist.* I. xi. 441 A regular system of judicial eyres.

2. The circuit court held by these officers. Also *eyre of justice, justice eyre, Commission of Eyre.*

[**1275** *Act 3 Edw. I*, Stat. Westm. c. 18 (1810) 31 Le amerciement de tut le Conte en Eyr de Iustices. **1292** BRITTON I. v. §7 Si le article ne fut mie presenté en le autre heyre. **1300** *Act 28 Edw. I*, c. 5 Presentementz en Eire.] *c* **1350** in *Eng. Gilds* (1870) 362 At þe nexte Eyr and at þe nexte court. **1440** *Sc. Acts Jas. II*, §5 That the Iustices.. set their Iustice aires, and hald them twise in the ȝeir. *c* **1450** HENRYSON *Tale of Dog* 129 Quhilk.. passis furth befoir the Justice Air. **1513-75** *Diurn. Occurr.* (Bannatyne Club) 51 The Governour proclaimit ane generall air throw all Scotland. **1609** SKENE *Reg. Maj.* 1 [They] sould be present and compeire at the Justitiars aire. **1642** MILTON *Argt. conc. Militia* 36 If a Commission of Eier sit in a County, and the Kings Bench cometh thither the Eier ceaseth. **1750** CARTE *Hist. Eng.* II. 122 This new chief justiciary, holding an eyre .. in South-wark. **1779** *Lloyd's Even. Post* 20- 2 Sept. 287/3 The Circuit Court of Justiciary finished the Eyre at Aberdeen. **1805** SCOTT *Last Minstr.* IV. xxxv, Maidens.. wrung their hands for love of him, Who died at Jedwood Air.

†**b.** *Eyre of the Forest*: a circuit court held periodically by the Justices of the Forest, hence called *Justices in Eyre. Obs.*

1622 J. RAWLINS *Recov. Ship of Bristol* Ded. in Arb. *Garner* IV. 583 The.. Marquis of Buckingham.. Justice in Eyre of all His Majesty's Forests. **1702** *Lond. Gaz.* No. 3828/3 Lord Wharton was constituted Warden and Chief Justice and Justice in Eyre of all His Majesty's Forests. **1727-51** CHAMBERS *Cycl.*, *Eyre of the forest* is otherwise called justice seat: which by the ancient customs was to be held every three years, by the justices of the forest journeying up and down for that purpose. **1796** MORSE *Amer. Geog.* II. 103.

c. The record of such a court.

[*a* **1481** LITTLETON *Tenures* §514 Come appiert per l'Report dun plee en le Eire de Nottingham.] **1614** SELDEN *Titles Hon.* 262 That so should the right meaning of Sake bee, is iustified out of an old Eire.

3. *attrib.*

1641 *Termes de la Ley* 131 Eire Justices, or Itinerant.

eyre, var. of AIRE *sb.*[2] and *v. Obs.*

eyre, obs. f. of AIR *sb.*[1]

eyren, -ron(e, -roun, obs. pl. forms of EGG.

eyren, obs. form of IRON.

eyrer: see EYERER.

eyrie. Now the commonest spelling of AERIE.

1667, 1861 [see AERIE 1]. **1902** W. DE LA MARE *Songs of Childhood* 14 A hawk from his eyrie Swooped down like an arrow. **1922** JOYCE *Ulysses* 582 Birds of prey.. swooping from eyries. **1937** J. R. R. TOLKIEN *Hobbit* vi. 115 You ought not to be rude to an eagle, when you are only the size of a hobbit, and are up in his eyrie at night! **1955** W. G. HOSKINS *Making Eng. Landsc.* iii. 62 The limestone crags above Littondale provided eyries for these noble birds. **1965** E. GOWERS *Fowler's Mod. Eng. Usage* 13/1 *Aery, aerie, eyry, eyrie.* The victory of the last form over the other three seems to have been undeserved.

eyryssh(e, obs. form of AIRISH.

eyse, obs. form of EASE, EASY.

eysel, var. of EISELL, *Obs.*, vinegar.

eyst, eyster, obs. ff. of YEAST, OYSTER *sb.*

eyt, obs. form of AIT[1].

eyt, eytand, north. ff. of EAT, EATING.

eyth, obs. form of EATH.

†**eythe.** *Obs. rare.* [OE. *eȝðe, eȝeþe*, corresponding to OHG. *egida*:—WGer. **agiþôn-* f. **agjan* EDGE *v.*[2]] A harrow.

a **800** *Corpus Gloss., Erpica, eȝðe.* **1393** LANGL. *P. Pl.* C. XXII. 273 And harowede.. holy scripture, With to eythes þat thei hadden, an olde and a newe.

eyther(e, -thir, obs. forms of EITHER.

eythyn, Sc. var. of ETEN, *Obs.*

eytike, obs. form of ETHIC.

eyves, eyues, -ez, -is, obs. ff. EAVES.

a **1400** *Morte Arth.* 1283 Thise hende houez on a hille by þe holte eyues [*printed* eynes]. *Ibid.* 2516 Baytand one a wattire banke by þe wodde eyuis [*pr.* eynis].

eyyr, obs. form of HEIR.

‖**ezan.** [Arab. *aðān.*] The formula chanted by the Muezzin at the hour of prayer.

1753 HANWAY *Trav.* (1762) II. VI. i. 144 *note*, I made him this compliment in the tone in which we sing the ezan. **1842** FABER *Styrian Lake* 84, I hear the countless Turkish Ezans swell.

ezlar, obs. Sc. form of ASHLAR *sb.*

†**'ezod.** *Obs.* A variant of IZZARD, the letter Z.

1597 MORLEY *Introd. Mus.* 36 X with y. ezod. & per se.

F

F (ɛf), the sixth letter of the Roman alphabet, represents historically the 6th letter (*waw*) of the Semitic alphabet, which expressed the sounds of *w* (approximately) and the related vowel *u*. In early Greek writing the letter had at first the same twofold power; but subsequently its accidental varieties of form came to be differentiated in function, the form **F** (retaining the 6th place in the alphabet) being appropriated to the consonantal use, while **V** or **Y** served for the vowel, and is the source of the Roman U, V, Y, as explained under those letters. As the sound *w* was lost in the chief literary Greek dialects of the classical period, its sign F (called by the grammarians from its form the DIGAMMA) is not included in the later Gr. alphabet. In the Roman adoption of the Gr. alphabet the sound given to the 6th letter was the voiceless labiodental spirant (f). In OE. the letter retained the sound (f) unless it stood between two vowels, when it was pronounced as the corresponding voiced spirant (v). In the S.W., according to some scholars, the voiced sound was used also initially. In mod. Eng. F is always sounded (f), exc. in the word *of*, where it is voiced to (v) through absence of stress.

In MSS. a capital F was often written as ff. A misunderstanding of this practice has caused the writing of Ff or ff at the beginning of certain family names, *e.g.* Ffiennes, Ffoulkes.

c **1000** ÆLFRIC *Gram.* iii. (*Z.*) 6 Semivocales syndon seofan: f, l, m, n, r, s, x. **1580** BARET *Alv.* F., If ye drawe in length and therewithall put your under lippe to your ouer teeth, ye shall heare the verie sound of EF.

b. *attrib.* (see quots.).

1836 DUBOURG *Violin* (1878) 274 The parallel holes on each side .. were .. straighter than what are called the *f* holes. **1880** GROVE *Dict. Mus.* I. 500 The holes in the belly of the violin are called the *f* holes from their shape.

II. Used as a symbol, with reference to its place (6th) in the alphabet.

1. F, f, *f* is used to denote anything occupying the sixth place in a series. (Cf. A, B, C, etc.)

2. In Music F is the name of the 4th note of the diatonic scale of C major; called F in Germany, *fa* in France and Italy. Also the scale or key which has that note for its tonic. *f. clef*: the bass clef (see CLEF[1]), placed on the line in the stave appropriated to the note F; its form is said to be a corruption of that of the letter.

1848 RIMBAULT *First Bk. Piano* 53 Place the first finger on every black key except F-sharp. **1856** MRS. BROWNING *Aur. Leigh* v. 214 Boldinacci when her F in alt Had touched the silver tops of Heaven itself. **1880** GROVE *Dict. Mus.* I. 184 The Sonata in C .. contained when completed a long Andante in F.

3. ***F-layer, -region***: the highest and most strongly ionized layer in the ionosphere; the Appleton layer.

1928 E. V. APPLETON in *Papers Internat. Union Sci. Radio Telegr. 1927* I. 2/1 'Reflection' .. takes place at an upper layer (F layer) which is richer in ionization. **1930** —— in *Proc. R. Soc.* A. CXXVI. 550 The normally polarised components of primary, secondary and tertiary downcoming rays from F region would be F_1, F_2 and F_3, etc. **1930** APPLETON & GREEN *Ibid.* CXXVII. 170 During the (*a*) series [of day-time tests] .. out of eight runs there were three on which E layer only was recorded, three on which F layer only was recorded, and two days on which both were recorded simultaneously. **1942** *Electronic Engin.* XIV. 632 The F layer .. is composed of two parts .. the lower part, at about 130 miles' height .. and the upper, at 200 miles. **1968** G. M. B. DOBSON *Explor. Atmos.* (ed. 2) viii. 153 During the night .. the ionization of the *E* region is much reduced, and that of the F_1 region is reduced enough to make it indistinguishable from the F_2 region and the two become a single *F* region.

III. Abbreviations.

1. F. = various proper names, as Frederick, Fanny; = Fellow in F.G.S., etc.; = FATHER as a title of Roman Catholic priests. **b.** *Physics.* F. = Fahrenheit (temperature). **c.** *Comm.* F stands for *free* as in F.A.A. or f.a.a. = *free of all average*, *F.O.B.*, etc. **d.** In a ship's log F stands for *fog*; FF for *thick fog*. **e.** In Music *f* stands for *forte* (loud), *ff* for *fortissimo* (very loud), but sometimes *ff* stands for *piu forte* (louder), and *fortissimo* is indicated by *fff*. **f.** F formerly used in criminal procedure (see quots.). **g.** F (orig. standing for 'fine') is the distinctive mark of a particular description of black-lead pencil; also *attrib.* **h.** As a chemical symbol, F = Fluorine.

(f) **1551** *Act 5-6 Edw. VI*, c. 4 To be .. burned in the cheeke with an hot yron, hauing the letter F. whereby .. they may be knowne .. for fraymakers and fighters. **1809** TOMLINS *Law Dict.*, F. is a letter wherewith felons &c. are branded and marked with a hot iron, on their being admitted to the benefit of clergy.

i. *Biol.* F_1, F_2, etc. = first, second, etc., filial generation (see quot. 1949).

1902 W. BATESON et al. *Rep. Evol. Comm. R. Soc.* I. 160 The offspring of the first cross are the first filial generation F. Subsequent filial generations may be denoted by F_2, F_3, &c. **1949** DARLINGTON & MATHER *Elem. Genetics* 391 F_1, the first generation of the cross between two individuals homozygous for the particular genes which distinguished them. F_2, the second filial generation obtained by self-fertilizing or crossing *inter se* individuals of an F_1. F_3, progeny obtained by self-fertilization of an F_2 individual. **1968** M. W. STRICKBERGER *Genetics* vi. 99 The smooth F_1 seeds .. produced upon self-fertilization an F_2 of 5474 smooth seeds and 1850 wrinkled.

j. f or F (*Physics* and *Chem.*): originally used to designate one of the four main series of lines in atomic spectra, but now more frequently applied to electronic orbitals, states, etc., possessing three units of angular momentum.

1910 W. M. HICKS in *Phil. Trans. R. Soc.* CCX. 97 We recognise four typical sequences, the P, S, D and the new F type .., the fundamental or primitive type. **1965** PHILLIPS & WILLIAMS *Inorg. Chem.* I. ii. 46 There occurs a group of 14 elements, the lanthanides or rare-earths, in which the *4f* sub-shell is filled.

k. In *Physics* F is the symbol of the hyperfine quantum number, expressing the resultant of the nuclear spin I and the electronic angular momentum J.

1925 RUARK & CHENAULT in *Phil. Mag.* 6th Ser. L. 947 We call these integers fine quantum numbers, and shall designate them by the letter *f*. **1937** J. W. T. SPINKS tr. *Herzberg's Atomic Spectra & Atomic Structure* v. 187 The total angular momentum *F* of the whole atom, including nuclear spin. **1967** CONDON & ODISHAW *Handbk. Physics* (ed. 2) VII. iv. 68/1 At low magnetic fields *I* and *J* are tightly coupled to form a resultant angular momentum $F = I + J$, whose quantum number *F* at low fields is a good quantum number.

l. *Bacteriol.* [abbrev. of *fertility*.] ***F, F agent, F factor***, etc., a particulate factor which determines the mating type of certain bacteria (esp. *Escherichia coli*); hence F^+, designating cells possessing the factor but not having it integrated into the chromosome; F^-, designating cells lacking the factor; *F′* (or ***F prime***), designating cells in which a chromosomal fragment is attached to the factor. Also ***F duction***, the conveyance of genes from F′ cells into F^- cells.

1952 J. LEDERBERG et al. in *Genetics* XXXVII. 721 At the time, W-1607 was not analyzed further, but in view of later work will be labelled F^-, in contrast to the type F^+. **1953** *Jrnl. Gen. Microbiol.* VIII. 92 The majority .. of F agents must remain bound to the cells. **1959** ADELBERG & BURNS in *Rec. Genetic Soc. Amer.* XXVIII. 57 The wild type sex factor (*F*) of strain K-12 is characterized by its low affinity for the chromosome. **1960** F. JACOB et al. in *Symp. Soc. Gen. Microbiol.* X. 77 The similarities observed between this process, which might be called *F*-duction or sex-duction, and transduction with phage are extremely striking. **1967** F. E. SWATEK *Textbk. Microbiol.* x. 291 In $F^+ \times F^-$ matings the F factor is transferred to F^- bacteria.

2. ***the three F's*** (see quot.).

1881 *Daily News* 19 Jan. 5/4 Fair rents, fixity of tenure, and free sale, popularly known as the three F's. **1891** *Ibid.* 8 Sept. 3/3 Why not go in at once for the three F's—fair rent, fixity of tenure, and free sale.

3. a. (Abbreviations given here with the full stop are frequently found without it.) **F.A.**, = FANNY ADAMS 2; **F.A.**, Football Association; **F.A.F.**, Fresh Air Fund; **F.A.N.Y.**, (a member of the) First Aid Nursing Yeomanry; also ***Fany***; **F.A.O.**, Food and Agriculture Organization (of the United Nations); **f.a.q.**, fair average quality; **F.A.Q. (f.a.q.)**, free alongside quay; **F.A.S. (f.a.s.)**, free alongside ship; **F.B.A.**, Fellow of the British Academy; **F.B.I.**, Federal Bureau of Investigation (*U.S.*); **F.B.I.**, Federation of British Industries; **F.C.**, football club; **F.C.C.**, Federal Communications Commission (*U.S.*); **F.D.C.**, *fleur de coin*; **F.F.(V.)**. the first family or families (of Virginia); a member or descendant of one of these (*U.S.*); **F.G.**, fine grain; **F.H.B.**, family hold back (a colloq. intimation to the members of a family that their guests have first claim on the course or helping about to be served); **F.I.D.O.** (see FIDO); **F.I.T.**, **f.i.t.**, free in truck; **F.L.N.**, (Fr.) Front de la Libération Nationale, an Algerian nationalist organization; **F.M.**, field-magnet; **F.M.**, **f.m.**, frequency modulation; **F.O.**, Foreign Office; **F.O.B.**, **f.o.b.**, free on board; **F.O.B.S.**, fractional orbital bombardment system; **F.O.C.**, Father of the Chapel (see CHAPEL *sb.* 10); **F.O.R.**, **f.o.r.**, free on rail; **F.O.T.**, **f.o.t.**, free on truck; **F.P.A.**, Family Planning Association; **F.P.S.**, **f.p.s.**, feet per second; **F.P.S.**, **f.p.s.**, foot-pound-second; (cf. FOOT *sb.* 35); **F.R.C.S.**, Fellow of the Royal College of Surgeons; **F.R.G.**, Federal Republic of Germany; **F.R.S.**, Fellow of the Royal Society; **F.S.**, **f.s.**, feet per second; **F.W.D.**, **f.w.d.**, front- (or four-) wheel drive.

1919, **1930** *F.A. [see FANNY ADAMS 2]. **1944** *Penguin New Writing* XX. 128 Bread—that's about what we got as kids. Bread, and sweet F.A. **1967** J. GARDNER *Madrigal* ix. 251 The small industrial organisation whose own security officers know sweet FA. **1892** in Gibson & Pickford *Assoc. Football* (1905) I. 112 The meetings of the *F.A. are carried out under rules of procedure. **1930** *Morning Post* 18 Nov. 15/4 The first round proper of the F.A. Cup. **1907** *Westm. Gaz.* 22 July 3/2 Without distinction of creed or race, the *F.A.F. takes away the children of the slums from the festering alleys .. of London. **1918** E. S. FARROW *Dict. Mil. Terms* 218 *Fanny*, in the parlance of the British soldier, the name given to the women of the *F.A.N.Y., or First Aid Nursing Yeomanry. **1940** *War Illustr.* 12 Jan. 599 Two volunteers of the First Aid Nursing Yeomanry, known as 'Fanys', are cleaning their ambulance. **1958** P. KEMP *No Colours or Crest* xi. 243 The Major-General had a suite of offices managed by four or five very tall, very beautiful F.A.N.Y.s known as the Potsdam Grenadiers. **1966** M. R. D. FOOT *SOE in France* viii. 200 Mary Herbert a FANY courier reached the Riviera by felucca. **1946** *New Statesman* 14 Sept. 183 (*heading*) *F.A.O. at work. **1963** *Listener* 21 Mar. 508/3 The F.A.O. has estimated that about half the population of the world suffers from hunger or malnutrition. **1957** *N.Z. Timber Jrnl.* Feb. 45 **f.a.q.*, abbreviation for fair average quality. **1959** *Times* 3 Jan. 10/2 No doubt Sir Allen Brown would be inclined (in the fashion of his countrymen) to dub himself an 'f.a.q. Australian', but in fact 'fair, average quality' hardly does justice to the man. **1928** *Daily Mail* 25 July 19/3 Oats: Plate *f.a.q. afloat 27s. 3d. **1888** *Lockwood's Dict. Mech. Engin.*, **F.A.S.*, free alongside ship. Engages to deliver goods on the wharf without extra charge. **1911** *Jrnl. Roman Stud.* I. p. vi, J. E. Sandys, Litt.D. *F.B.A. **1980** *Who's Who* 201/2 *Berlin*, Sir Isaiah .. FBA 1957. **1936** *Lit. Digest* 21 Nov. 36 The outlaws shot their way out killing one *FBI man. **1952** *Manch. Guardian Weekly* 30 Oct. 3 The FBI and the Central Intelligence Agency. **1921** *Times* 22 Nov. 14/3 (*heading*) Meeting of the *F.B.I. to-morrow. **1958** *Spectator* 4 July 33/2 The FBI has just published the results of its second industrial survey. **1908** A. BENNETT *Old Wives' Tale* II. vii. 254 The Bursley *F.C. had 'tied' with the Knype F.C. on the Knype ground. **1937** *Printers' Ink Monthly* Apr. 53/1 **FCC*, Federal Communications Commission. **1955** *Times* 27 July 9/7 The F.C.C. rules require that if it is extended to one political candidate his opponents must be accorded equal accommodation. **1892** *Spink's Numismatic Circ.* Dec. 14/2 *F.D.C. = Fleur de coin. **1966** P. A. RAYNER *Coin Collecting for Amateurs* i. 5 The following are the main degrees of condition used in this country: F.D.C. (*Fleur-de-Coin*): literally—flower of the coin, a French term used to denote perfect mint state with absolutely no wear or damage, [etc.]. **1813** M. L. WEEMS *Drunkard's Looking-Glass* (ed. 2) 11 With hearts full charged with *F.F. Slings, they came upon the ground. **1850** 'M. TENSAS' *Louisiana Swamp Doctor* 178 Major Smith .. [was] the first one of the race [of Virginians] to acknowledge that he was not an F.F. **1917** *Birds of Amer.* III. 64/2 Better yet, he [*sc.* the cardinal] is an FF of America. **1847** *Knickerbocker* XXIX. 495 We could make out .. a set of letters that looked like a disorderly *F.F.V. ... A Virginia scion insisted that they were an abbreviation he had seen used in the navy to represent 'First Family in Virginia'. **1861** R. H. NEWELL *Orpheus C. Kerr* (1863) I. 253 That piece of American intelleck .. worthy of an F.F.V. **1931** W. FAULKNER *Sanctuary* iii. 22 An F.F.V., or just an unfortunate sojourner there? **1871** *English Mechanic* 17 Mar. 615/3 Medium rifle powder .. is still used .. under the name of 'powder shell *F.G.' (fine grain). **1911** 'I. HAY' *Safety Match* v. 82 She murmured to such of the family as were within earshot the mystic formula, '*F.H.B.!' **1888** *Lockwood's Dict. Mech. Engin.*, **F.I.T.*, free in truck. Engages to load goods in railway trucks without extra charge. **1956** *Times* 7 Apr. 6/4 An office belonging to the other Algerian Nationalist Movement, the National Liberation Front (*F.L.N.), was also raided today. **1958** *Times Lit. Suppl.* 14 Feb. 82/5 The French will inevitably have to negotiate with the F.L.N. **1893** W. P. MAYCOCK *Electr. Lighting* II. viii. §134 The *F.M.s of an alternator must be separately excited. **1942** *Electronic Engin.* XIV. 640 A special f.m. amplifier. **1962** FM [see AMPLITUDE 6d.]. **1859** QUEEN VICTORIA *Let.* 14 June in R. Fulford *Dearest Child* (1964) 194 Lord Palmerston .. could not insist on Lord John's not having the *F.O. if he insisted on having it! **1959** E. POUND *Thrones* civ. 90 Resigned from the F.O. and 'went into the City'. **1890** *Economist* 22 Feb. (Suppl.) 12/1 Bleach opened firm in January at £7 16s per ton for hard wood, *f.o.b., and £7 5s per ton for soft wood f.o.r. **1959** *Ann. Reg. 1958* 490 A total value of about $20 million f.o.b. for the year. **1967** *Economist* 11 Nov. 622/2 *FOBS puts a vehicle into orbit round the earth, in either direction, about a hundred miles up; it then launches a missile, when told to do so, probably before completing a full circuit. **1969** *U.S. News & World Rep.* 10 Mar. 31/3 *FOBS*, fractional-orbit bombardment system. A missile that orbits the earth and can deliver its warheads from space. A Soviet development that has no U.S. counterpart. **1929** *Printing Federation Bull.* Nov. 6/1 Many *F.O.C.'s will agree there are circumstances in many printing firms which militate against the formation of works committees. **1955** R. J. SCHWARTZ *Compl. Dict.*

Abbrev. 73/2 *FOC*, Father of the Chapel. **1986** *Times* 11 Mar. 2/8, I appreciate the FOCs' concern for those who went on strike and were sacked. **1888** *Lockwood's Dict. Mech. Engin.*, **F.O.R.*, free on rail. Signifies the placing of goods on the railway without extra charge. **1890** f.o.r. [see *f.o.b.* above]. **1888** *Lockwoods's Dict. Mech. Engin.*, **F.O.T.*, free on truck. The same as F.I.T. *a* **1940** *9th Ann. Rep. Family Planning Assoc.* 2 The Report on the Committee before which the *F.P.A. presented evidence in December, 1937. **1966** *New Statesman* 17 June 870/1 When Mr Robinson, the Minister of Health, opened the Family Planning Association's recent conference in London he gave the final pat to the..mantle of respectability resting on the FPA's shoulders. **1986** *Roundabout* (Brisbane) 19 June 14/1 The 30 second commercial features Brisbane Bullets captain Larry Sengstock, as part of the FPA's campaign. **1945** T. A. Dickinson *Aeronaut. Dict.* 433/2 **F.P.S.*, feet per second. **1962** J. Glenn in *Into Orbit* 200 It was 25,730 fps instead of 25,738 fps. **1892** G. F. Barker *Physics* I. ii. 10 In applied physics another absolute system is sometimes used, based upon the foot, the pound, and the second... This system is called the foot-pound-second system, or more briefly the *F.P.S. system. **1962** A. R. W. Hayes *Revision Physics* § 1. 4. The *foot-poundal* is the f.p.s. unit of *energy* or *work*. **1829** *Edin. Med. & Surg. Jrnl.* XXXII. p.iv, Observations on painful subcutaneous tubercle, with histories and cases of the disease. By William Wood, *F.R.C.S. **1936** Mencken *Amer. Lang.* (ed. 4) 272 A surgeon is usually plain *Mr.*, and prefers to be so called, though he may have *M.D.* on his card, along with *F.R.C.S.* (fellow of the Royal College of Surgeons). **1984** *Whitaker's Almanack 1985* 221/2 Serjeant Surgeon, W. Slack, M. ch., F.R.C.S. **1960** *Internat. Affairs* (Moscow) Dec. 69/1 The greatest concentration of American armed forces in Europe is in the *F.R.G. **1978** *Europa Year Bk.* I. 712/1 Saarland, under French occupation, was rejoined with the FRG administratively in January 1957. **1731** *Gentleman's Mag.* I. 181/1 The Gardeners Dictionary: By Phillip Miller, *F.R.S. **1969** *Listener* 22 May 728/2 It is heartening these days to find John Sparrow reaffirming his faith in that civilisation.. whose key emblems he takes to be an FRS and a Chancery Judge. **1880** *Encycl. Brit.* XI. 304/2 The bullets themselves should retain a velocity of about 500 *f.s. on striking. **1905** *Kynoch Jrnl.* July-Sept. 156 Accuracy does not demand a muzzle velocity higher than 2,300 f.s. **1958** *News Chron.* 25 Nov. 7/5 (Advt.), The Austin commercial range includes all-purpose vehicles..and the *FWD Gipsy with rubber torsion suspension. **1959** *Motor* 11 Feb. 62/1 Nowadays f.w.d. is invariably combined with independent front wheel springing.

b. *Photogr.* F, f = Focal length. Used in combination with numbers to indicate the ratio between the focal length of the lens and the diameter of the stop.

1892 C. H. Bothamley *Ilford Man. Photogr.* v. 34 For example, *f*/8 and *f*/16 mean that the diameter of the stop is, in the first case, one-eighth, and, in the second case, one-sixteenth of the focal length of the lens. **1903** A. Watkins *Photogr.* (ed. 2) 42 Instead of having to work out afresh the value of the diaphragm, it is much more convenient to regard the lengthening of the camera as a separate influence which I have named the F factor. *Ibid.* 43 The F factor to allow for the lengthened focus of the lens, and S the value of the subject. *Ibid.* 45 The F figure (distance of image to lens in terms of focus of lens) is always the same as the degree of enlargement plus 1. **1918** *Photo-Miniature* XV. Mar. (Gloss.), *F*(*f*/·) Numbers—denote the 'speed' of a lens. About the most rapid lens is *f*/3 to *f*/4·5... The *f*/ number is the number of times the diameter of the stop will divide into the focal length of the lens. **1959** *News Chron.* 20 June 6/7 The apertures or stops, as they are sometimes called, are marked in f/numbers. If a lens is described as an f/4 lens, it means that is its maximum or widest aperture. **1968** A. Diment *Gt. Spy Race* vii. 107, I started photographing right then, the light meter said I was okay on F2·8 at a thirtieth. **1970** *Amateur Photographer* 13 May 66/1 The actual diameter of the hole was marked on it, so that f/11 showed that the hole was one eleventh of the focal length.

fa (fɑː), *sb.* [Originally the first syllable of the L. *famuli*: see gamut.] The name given by Guido to the fourth note in his hexachords, and since retained in solmization as the 4th note of the octave.

c **1325** in *Rel. Ant.* I. 292 Sol and ut and la, And that froward file that men clepis fa. **1597** Morley *Introd. Mus.* (1771) 4 There be in Musicke but vi. Notes, which are called vt, re, mi, fa, sol, la. **1660** Howell *Lexicon*, Fa, one of the highest Notes in Musique. **1890** W. H. Cummings *Rudim. Music* ¶ 202 In France it is customary to call the sounds by fixed syllables instead of letters, as follows:

Do or Ut, Re, Mi, Fa, Sol, La, Si, Do or Ut.
C. D. E. F. G. A. B. C.

Hence as *vb.* (see quot.).

1592 Shaks. *Rom. & Jul.* iv. v. 120, I will carie no Crotchets: Ile Re you, Ile Fa you; do you note me?

fa, obs. f. of few.

fa, faa, obs. ff. of foe.

fa', faa, Sc. ff. of fall.

faam, var. faham.

fa'ard, Sc. pronunc. of *favoured*; only in compounds, as *ill-*, *well-fa'ard*.

fab, colloq. abbrev. of fabulous *a.* 5 b. Also as *sb.*

1961 in Partridge *Dict. Slang* Suppl. 1082/1. **1963** *Times* 26 Jan. 10/6 She stretched her stockinged toes towards the blazing logs. 'Daddy, this fire's simply fab.' **1963** *New Statesman* 18 Oct. 536/1 Those girls in leather gear—the height of fab. **1963** *Meet the Beatles* 22 Most of the Merseyside groups produce sounds which are pretty fab. **1971** *It* 2–16 June 11/4 Seale called the fab philosopher 'a moral coward'.

fab, obs. and Sc. var. of fob.

fabaceous (fəˈbeɪʃəs), *a.* [f. late L. *fabāce-us* (f. *faba* bean) + -ous: see -aceous.] Having the nature of a bean, like a bean.

1727–36 in Bailey. **1775** in Ash; and in later Dicts.

† **ˈfabal**, *a. Obs.*⁻⁰ [ad. L. *fabāl-is*, f. *faba* bean.] 'Of or belonging to a bean' (Blount).

1656–81 in Blount *Glossogr.* **1692–1732** in Coles.

fabel(l, var. of favel.

‖ **fabella** (fəˈbɛlə). Pl. **-æ**. [mod.L. *fabella*, dim. of *faba* bean.] (See quot. 1884.)

1854 Owen *Skel. & Teeth* (1855) 89 A fabella is preserved behind the outer condyle. **1884** *Syd. Soc. Lex.*, *Fabellæ*, a name for the sesamoid bones in the tendon of the gastrocnemius muscle of the dog and other animals.

† **fabellator**. *Obs.*⁻⁰ [as if a. L. **fābellātor*, f. *fābella*, dim. of *fābula* story.]

1656–81 in Blount *Glossogr.* **1775** in Ash.

Fabergé (fabɛrʒe). The name of Peter Carl *Fabergé* (1846–1920), a Russian jeweller famed for his small, intricate ornaments, used *attrib.* to designate pieces of his workmanship. Also *transf.* and *fig.*

[**1902** *Encycl. Brit.* XXIX. 748/1 As a representative of Russia, Fabergé of St. Petersburg deserves to be mentioned.] **1930** V. Sackville-West *Edwardians* iv. 191 The jade ash-trays, the Fabergé cigarette-boxes. **1936** G. Greene *Journey without Maps* II. iii. 162 A beautiful little green snake..poisonous with gentility, a Fabergé jewel. **1952** 'J. Tey' *Singing Sands* xiii. 216 It [*sc.* France seen from an aeroplane] was a small jewelled pattern set in a lapis-lazuli sea; a Fabergé creation. **1959** *Encounter* Oct. 8/1 A sort of Fabergé Russianism clings around parts of Nice.

fabes: see feaberry *dial.*, gooseberry.

Fabian (ˈfeɪbɪən), *a.* and *sb.* [ad. L. *Fabiānus* of or belonging to a Fabius or to the Fabian gens.]

A. *adj.*

1. Of or pertaining to the Roman gens Fabia.

1740 J. Dyer *Ruins of Rome* 23 Who has not heard the Fabian Heroes sung? **1842** Macaulay *Battle Lake Regillus* xvii, Tall Caeso was the bravest man Of the brave Fabian race.

2. a. Pertaining to, or after the manner of, Q. Fabius Maximus, surnamed Cunctator ('Delayer') from the tactics which he employed against Hannibal in the Second Punic War, and which consisted in avoiding a battle, and weakening the enemy by cutting off supplies and by continual skirmishing.

1777 *Publ. Colonial Soc. Mass.* (1906) VIII. 277, I know the comments that some people will make on our Fabian conduct. **1808** J. Barlow *Columb.* v. 826 In vain sage Washington..Plays round his foes with more than Fabian skill. **1843** *Tait's Mag.* Oct. 615/2 The Fabian policy to which Sir Robert Peel has tied himself up. **1849** Ld. Houghton in *Life* (1891) I. x. 433 The Fabian Duke succeeded in checking his zeal. **1965** *New Statesman* 9 Apr. 579/1 His [*sc.* Lincoln's] fabian tactics.

b. ***Fabian Society***: a society founded in 1884, consisting of Socialists who advocate a 'Fabian' policy as opposed to immediate attempts at revolutionary action. Hence ***Fabian principles***, etc.

1884 E. Nesbit *Let.* Mar. (1933) v. 63 The Fabian Society takes up a good deal of my thoughts just now. **1908** G. B. Shaw *Fabian Essays in Socialism* p. iii, Since 1889 The Socialist movement has been completely transformed..and the result..may fairly be described as Fabian Socialism. **1915** A. Huxley *Let.* Oct. (1969) 79 A sort of magnified Fabian society state, organised even further than at present. **1959** B. & R. North tr. *Duverger's Pol. Parties* (ed. 2) p. xxxi, The activity of the Fabian Society in the creation of the Labour party illustrates the influence of philosophical societies.

B. *sb.*

† **1.** ***flaunting Fabian***: see quot. 1598.

[Perh. originally a transl. of L. *licens Fabius*, used by Propertius with reference to the Fabian priests of Pan, and the licence permitted them at the Lupercalia.]

1598 Florio, *Brauazzo*, a swashbuckler, a swaggrer, a cutter, a quareller, a roister, a flaunting fabian. *Ibid.*, *Sfoggiatore*, a riotous, lauish, flauting fabian, a carelesse fellow, an vnthrift. **1599** Nashe *Lenten Stuffe* 46 Of all fishes the flanting Fabian or Palmerin of England..is Cadwallader Herring.

2. A member of the 'Fabian Society', or one who sympathizes with its opinions.

1884 E. Nesbit *Let.* ?Feb. (1933) v. 63, I do think the Fabians are quite the nicest set of people I ever knew. **1891** *Athenæum* 21 Feb. 242/3 The first essay..on 'The Impracticability of Socialism,' will hardly win souls away from the Fabians.

Fabianism (ˈfeɪbɪənɪz(ə)m). [f. Fabian *a.* + -ism.] The doctrines and principles of the Fabian Society. Hence **ˈFabianist** *sb.* and *a.*; **ˈFabianistic** *a.*

1890 G. B. Shaw *Let.* 28 Feb. (1965) 244 A blasphemy against the Fabianism which made it famous. **1909** *Cent. Dict.* Suppl. 457/1 Fabianist, n. **1918** H. Dalton in E. Marsh *R. Brooke* 26 During our years at Cambridge, Fabianism was at its high tide. **1924** *Blackw. Mag.* Sept. 393/1 Fabianism touched her during her last year at school. **1955** Koestler *Trail of Dinosaur* 188 British Socialism which is Christian, non-Marxist, Fabianist, and heaven knows what. **1960** *New Left Rev.* Sept.–Oct. 60/1 An intensified Fabianistic process.

fabiform (ˈfeɪbɪfɔːm), *a.* [f. L. *faba* bean + -(i)form: see -form.] Bean-shaped.

1852 Dana *Crust.* II. 1287 Short; in a side view, very broad fabiform. **1855** Ramsbotham *Obstetr. Med.* 44 Corpus Luteum is somewhat fabiform, of a dull yellow tint.

fable (ˈfeɪb(ə)l), *sb.* Forms: 4, 6 fabel(l, 4–5 fabil(l, fabul(le, 4– fable. [a. F. *fable* (OF. also *flabe*, *fauble*, Pr. *faula*) ad. L. *fābula* discourse, narrative, story, dramatic composition, the plot of a play, a fable, f. *fārī* to speak: see fate.]

1. a. A fictitious narrative or statement; a story not founded on fact.

a **1300** *Cursor M.* 23857 (Cott.), Bot war a ribaude us tald, of a fantime or of a fabel. *a* **1340** Hampole *Psalter* xxxiii. 11, I sall lere ȝow noght þe fabils of poetis, na the storis of tyraunts. **1483** Caxton *Cato* G vj b, The poetes..sayen and rehercen many fables and thynges meruayllous. **1577** Rhodes *Bk. Nurture* in *Babees Bk.* 64 Keepe them [children] from reading of fayned fables..and wanton stories. **1642** Milton *Apol. Smect.* Wks. (Bohn) III. 118 Those lofty fables and romances, which recount in solemn cantos the deeds of knighthood. **1700** Dryden tr. *Ovid's Met.* xii. in *Fables* 441 It seems a Fable, tho' the Fact I saw. **1726** De Foe *Hist. Devil* I. x. (1840) 142 If we may take the story of Job for a history, not a fable. **1840** Dickens *Barn. Rudge* xxi, Some say he kissed her, but that's a fable. **1860** Hawthorne *Transform.* II. i. 3 It is a most enchanting fable..that is, if it be not a fact.

b. *esp.* A fictitious story relating to supernatural or extraordinary persons or incidents, and more or less current in popular belief; a myth or legend. (Now *rare.*) Also, legendary or mythical stories in general; mythological fiction.

a **1300** *Cursor M.* 6995 (Cott.), In his [Saleph's] time war þe fabuls written..Saturnus and sir iubiter. **1494** Fabyan *Chron.* v. cvi. 81 Of this last ende and buriyng of Arthur.. are tolde many fables. **1520** Skelton *Bk. P. Sparow*, I remember the fable Of Penelope. **1592** Davies *Immort. Soul* iv. (1714) 40 Minerva is in Fables said, From Jove, without a Mother, to proceed. **1667** Milton *P.L.* I. 197 [Satan] in bulk as huge As whom the Fables name of monstrous size. **1756–7** tr. *Keysler's Trav.* (1760) II. 288 The old fable of Seth's pillars. **1774** Goldsm. *Nat. Hist.* (1776) II. 251 The existence..of a pigmy race of mankind, being founded in error, or in fable. **1837** Landor *Pentameron* Wks. 1846 II. 215 Scythia was a land of fable..to the Romans. **1855** Milman *Lat. Chr.* (1864) II. iv. i. 170 Mohammedan fable had none of the inventive originality of fiction.

c. A foolish or ridiculous story; idle talk, nonsense; *esp.* in phr. ***old wives'*** (***women's***) ***fables*** (***arch.***). Also † ***to take*** (something) ***for fable, to hold at fable*** (transl. OF. *tenir a fable*).

1382 Wyclif *1 Tim.* iv. 7 Schonye thou vncouenable fablis and veyn [**1388** vncouenable fablis and elde wymmenus fablis]. *c* **1430** *Pilgr. Lyf Manhode* II. xxi. (1869) 83 Wolt þou holde þe gospel at fable? **1508** Fisher *Wks.* (1876) 85 In the whiche confessyon we may not tell fables and other mennes fautes. **1523** Ld. Berners *Froiss.* I. cclxxxviii. 430 Sylvester toke it for no fable. **1605** Bacon *Adv. Learn.* I. iv. §9 After a..time.. they [narrations of miracles] grew to be esteemed but as old wives' fables. **1721** Strype *Eccl. Mem.* III. App. xx. 56 [We] distorted them into old wives fables.

d. A fiction invented to deceive; a fabrication, falsehood. †Phrase, ***without*** (***but, sans***) ***fable***.

a **1300** *Cursor M.* 2349 (Cott.) Bot for þis hight moght be no fabul. *c* **1300** *K. Alis.* 134 Of gold he made a table Al ful of steorren, saun fable. *c* **1330** R. Brunne *Chron.* (1810) 146 Men..þat neuer lufed fable bot mayntend pes & right. *c* **1350** *Will. Palerne* 4608 þis ȝe witeþ wel alle with-oute any fabul. *a* **1500** *Childe of Bristowe* 227 in Hazl. *E.P.P.* (1864) 119 Al thynges..he gaf aboute, withouten fable, to pore men. **1535** Stewart *Cron. Scot.* I. 534 Rycht fair he wes and fecefull als but fabill. **1548** Hall *Chron.* 87 b, The writers of Frenche fables to deface the glorye of the Englishmen, write [etc.]. **1590** Shaks. *Com. Err.* iv. iv. 76 Sans Fable, she her selfe reuil'd you there. **1635** Swan *Spec. M.* i. §1 (1643) 2 The fables of the Egyptians. **1700** Dryden tr. *Ovid's Met.* xiii. in *Fables* 457 This is not a Fable forg'd by me, Like one of his, an Ulyssean lie. **1786** T. Jefferson *Writ.* (1859) II. 52 What is said..on this subject in the Courier d'Europe is entirely fable. **1848** Macaulay *Hist. Eng.* II. 8 The extraordinary success of the fables of Oates.

e. A creation of fable; something falsely affirmed to exist; a 'myth'.

c **1590** Marlowe *Faust.* v. 125 Come I think hell's a fable. **1611** Tourneur *Ath. Trag.* iv. iii, Their walking Spirits are mere imaginary fables. **1691** Hartcliffe *Virtues* p. xxiii, If a Man cannot believe..that the Immortality of the Soul is a Fable; then [etc.]. **1836** J. Gilbert *Chr. Atonem.* v. (1852) 126 Some substitute there plainly must be..or moral administration is a fable.

2. A short story devised to convey some useful lesson; *esp.* one in which animals or inanimate things are the speakers or actors; an apologue. Now the most prominent sense.

1340 *Ayenb.* 155 Herof ȝet ysopes þe fable of þe little hounde and of þe asse. **1483** Caxton *Esope* 3 She gaf to hym the yefte of speche for to speke dyuerse fables and Inuencions. **1576** Fleming *Panopl. Epist.* 227 A fable of the grasshopper and the Ant. **1605** Bacon *Adv. Learn.* I. iv. §11 The husbandman whereof Æsop makes the fable. **1711** Addison *Spect.* No. 183 ¶1 Jotham's fable of the Trees is the oldest that is extant. **1796** H. Hunter tr. *St. Pierre's Stud. Nat.* (1799) III. 496 His Fable of the Belly and the Members. **1841–4** Emerson *Ess. Hist.* Wks. (Bohn) I. 6 A poet makes twenty fables with one moral. **1865** Wright *Hist. Caricature* v. (1875) 75 We find no traces of fables among the original literature of the German race.

3. [After Latin *fabula*.] The plot or story of a play or poem. †Also (*rarely*), a dramatic composition, play.

1678 RYMER *Trag. of Last Age* Ded. 4, I have chiefly consider'd the Fable or Plot, which all conclude to be the Soul of a Tragedy. *Ibid.* 87 This Fable [of *Othello*] is drawn from a Novel..by Giraldi Cinthio. **1711** ADDISON *Spect.* No. 39 ¶3 The modern Tragedy excels that of Greece and Rome, in the Intricacy and Disposition of the Fable. **1767** B. THORNTON tr. *Plautus* II. 112 *note*, The part which Lysimachus afterwards takes in the fable. **1779–81** JOHNSON *L.P.*, *Cowley* Wks. II. 60 The fable [of the Davideis] is plainly implex. **1847** EMERSON *Repr. Men, Shaks.* Wks. (Bohn) I. 355 Shakespeare knew that tradition supplies a better fable than any invention can.

†**4. a.** Talk, in phrase *to hold* (a person) *in fable*; discourse, narration. *Obs. rare.*

c **1400** *Rom. Rose* 1439, I wole nat longe holde you in fable Of alle this gardyn delectable. **1530** BUCKMASTER *Let.* in *Corpus Christi Documents* (1838) 24 Here shalbe an ende for this tyme of this fable. **1598** B. JONSON *Ev. Man in Hum.* II. i, Whilst they, Sir, to relieve him in the fable, Make their loose comments, upon every word, Gesture, or look, I use.

b. The subject of common talk; a person or thing who has become proverbial; a 'byword'. *arch.* [After L. *fabula*: see Hor. *Ep.* I. xiii. 9.]

1535 COVERDALE *1 Kings* ix. 7 Israel shall be come a byworde and fabell [**1382** WYCLIF, schal be into a proverbe and into a fable] amonge all nacions. **1591** SPENSER *Ruines of Rome* vii, Ye sacred ruines..Alas! by little ye to nothing flie, The people's fable, and the spoyle of all. **1605** B. JONSON *Volpone* I. v, Knew you not that Sir? 'Tis the common fable. **1670** COTTON *Espernon* II. VII. 316 He..became..the Fable of the Court. **1766** C. ANSTEY *Bath Guide* xv. 14 I'm a Fable! ..and serve to dispense An Example to all Men of Spirit and Sense. **1842** TENNYSON *Gard. Dau.* 6 We grew The fable of the city where we dwelt. **1849** THACKERAY *Pendennis* lxxv, He..broke the bank several nights, and was the fable of the place.

¶**5.** ? A trifle, toy. *Obs. rare*$^{-1}$.

1552 HULOET, Seller of fables, haberdash wares, or trifles.

6. *attrib.* and *Comb.* **a.** attributive, as ***fable-book***, ***-forge***, †***-lesynge***, ***-poem***, ***-poetry***, ***-tale***, ***-type***; **b.** objective, as ***fable-forger***, ***-maker***, ***-monger***, ***-teller***, ***-weaver***, ***-writer***; ***fable-framing***, ***-making***, ***-mongering***, ***-weaving*** vbl. sbs. and adjs.

1387 TREVISA *Higden* (Rolls) II. 421 Varro telleþ nouȝt a fable lesynge. **1552** HULOET, Fabler, or fable teller, or full of fables, *fabulosus*. **1591** SYLVESTER *Du Bartas* I. IV. 114 And therefore smile I at those Fable-Forges. **1610** HEALEY *St. Aug. Citie of God* 679 How mischievous the presumption of those fable-forgers was. **1647** R. STAPYLTON *Juvenal* 173 Rhodope..(fellow bondwoman to Æsope the fable-maker). **1652** C. B. STAPYLTON *Herodian* VII. 55 Niger..who tells us a fabile tale. *a* **1661** HOLYDAY *Juvenal* Pref., 'The famous Italian fable-weaver, Ariosto. **1677** GALE *Crt. Gentiles* II. III. 72 The Pythagorising Jewish humor of Fable-framing Philosophie. **1678** CUDWORTH *Intell. Syst.* I. iv. Contents 190 The licentious figments of Poets and Fable-mongers. *a* **1700** DRYDEN *Epist.* vii. 32 All these fable-makers. **1734** WATERLAND *Scripture Vindicated* Pref. xxii, The attentive Readers may perceive how to distinguish the true and proper Allegorists from the Fable-mongers or Mythics. **1788** V. KNOX *Winter Even.* I. II. xv. 208 Fable books used for the initiation of children in reading. **1833** H. A. in *Philol. Mus.* II. 442 Men who were not fable-makers or compilers of marvellous stories. **1851** H. MELVILLE *Whale* xxxiv. 168 His credulous, fable-mongering ears. **1905** *Westm. Gaz.* 25 Feb. 10/3 A fable-writer and dramatic poet. **1911** S. S. COLVIN *Learning Process* viii. 117 The tendency to fable-making causes him [*sc.* a child] to make statements..at variance with the truth. **1941** L. MACNEICE *Poetry of Yeats* vi. 111 A new kind of fable-poetry which avoids becoming allegory. *Ibid.*, The fable-poems..are dry, unromantic pieces. *Ibid.* ix. 192 In the plays..fable-types, who correspond to the beggars and fools and hermits of the lyrics. **1946** BLUNDEN *Shelley* 24 In these fable-weavings something of the desire to be an author is seen.

fable ('feɪb(ə)l), *v.* Also 4 fabule. [a. OF. *fabler*:— L. *fābulārī* to talk, discourse, f. *fābula*: see FABLE. The Eng. senses are directly derived from those of the sb.]

†**1.** *intr.* To speak, talk, converse. *Obs. rare*$^{-1}$. [A Latinism.]

1382 WYCLIF *Luke* xxiv. 15 While they talkiden (or fableden) [Vulg. *fabularentur*]..Ihesu him self neiȝynge went with hem. **1570** LEVINS *Manip.* 2 To fable, talke, *confabulari*.

†**2. a.** To tell fictitious tales, speak fiction, romance. **b.** To talk idly. *Obs.*

a. *c* **1380** WYCLIF *Serm.* Sel. Wks. II. 133 Whanne men speken fables þei fablen in þer speche. **1401** *Pol. Poems* (1859) II. 41 Daw, thou fablest of foxes. **1571** GOLDING *Calvin on Ps.* xviii. 16 David..doth not fable like a Poet. **1593** SHAKS. *3 Hen. VI*, v. v. 25 Let Æsop fable in a Winters Night. *a* **1721** PRIOR *1st Hymn Callimachus* 69 Saturn's sons ..Old poets mention, fabling. **1814** SOUTHEY *Roderick* VI. 115, I do not dream nor fable.

b. **1579** J. JONES *Preserv. Bodie & Soule* I. xviii. 31 Let Paracelsus..neuer so foolishly fable to the contrarie. **1653** FISHER *Baby Baptism* 7 Fabling about moods and figures. **1870** *Daily News* 15 Oct., Superstition is at last resolvable into the claim of ignorance..to fable of the ineffable.

3. To speak falsely, talk falsehoods, lie. Const. *with*. *Obs.* exc. *arch.*

1530 *Calisto & Melib.* in Hazl. *Dodsley* I. 68, I wonder where she gets The things that she hath with folks for to fable. **1535** BOORDE *Let.* in *Introd. Knowl.* Introd. (1870) 57 In wytness þat I do not fable with yow. **1612** *Two Noble Kinsmen* III. v, To say verity, and not to fable We are a merry rout, or else a rabble. **1634** SIR T. HERBERT *Trav.* 158 [Those who have made a pilgrimage to Mecca] are euer after accounted Syets or Holy men, and cannot fable from that time forward. **1801** SOUTHEY *Thalaba* x. xiii, Thou hast fabled with me! **1814** MRS. J. WEST *Alicia de Lacy* III. 268 Mother, I do not fable.

4. *trans.* To say or talk about fictitiously; to relate as in a fable, fiction, or myth; to fabricate, invent (an incident, a personage, story, etc.). With simple and complementary object, *to* with *inf.*, with sentence as *obj.*; also *absol.* †***to fable up***: to work up by fiction *into*.

1553 EDEN *Treat. Newe Ind.* (Arb.) 42 What foles do fable, take thou no hede at all. **1567** MAPLET *Gr. Forest* 96 It is fabled with the Poets, that Ixion, Junoes Secretary, prouoked hir to Venery. **1583** STANYHURST *Aeneis* II. (Arb.) 46 Hee fabled sundrye reportes. **1598** STOW *Surv.* vii. (1603) 34 Aldersgate..called not of..Eldarne trees..as some haue fabuled. **1611** SPEED *Hist. Gt. Brit.* I. xi. 21/2 The Hurlers..fabuled to bee men metamorphosed into stones. **1638** FORD *Fancies* III. iii, That is a truth much fabled, never found. **1667** MILTON *P.L.* VI. 292 Turn this Heav'n itself into the Hell Thou fablest. **1726** DE FOE *Hist. Devil* I. x. (1840) 139 Men soon fabled up their histories.. into miracle and wonder. **1741** WATTS *Improv. Mind* (1801) 4 The most learned of mortals will never..act over again what is fabled of Alexander. **1750** WARBURTON *Julian* v, Of these [cannon] the Chinese were at liberty to fable what they pleased. **1774** PENNANT *Tour Scot. in 1772*. 354 This castle is fabled to have been founded by Ewin. **1794** COLERIDGE *Relig. Musings* viii, Armed Deities Such as the blind Ionian fabled erst. **1814** WORDSW. *Wh. Doe* IV. 110 More clear Than ghosts are fabled to appear. **1847** TENNYSON *Princ.* III. 120, I fabled nothing fair But, your example pilot, told her all. **1869** PHILLIPS *Vesuv.* viii. 207 The inhabitants fabled that the birds which attempted to fly over it fell down into the water. **1877** L. MORRIS *Epic Hades* III. 242 And so men fabled me, a huntress.

fabled ('feɪb(ə)ld), *ppl. a.* [f. prec. + -ED¹.] In senses of the verb.

1. Described or mentioned in fable, celebrated in fable; mythical, legendary.

a **1740** T. TICKELL *To a lady, with descr. Phœnix*, Each fabled charm in matchless Cælia meets. **1780** COWPER *Progr. Err.* 231 Like fabled Tantalus. **1813** SHELLEY *Q. Mab* IV. 89 A garden shall arise, in loveliness Surpassing fabled Eden. *a* **1853** ROBERTSON *Serm.* Ser. III. v. Introd. (1872) 61 Like the fabled monsters of old.

2. Having no real existence, fictitious, invented.

1606 WARNER *Alb. Eng.* XIV. lxxxiv. (1612) 350 This for no fabled Caution was obserued, but too trew. **1725** POPE *Odyss.* XVI. 100 Do..priests in fabled oracles advise? **1870** MORRIS *Earthly Par.* III. IV. 188 Men by fabled woes were stirred.

fabledom ('feɪb(ə)ldəm). *rare.* [f. FABLE *sb.* + -DOM.] The 'realm' or 'world' of fable.

1852 (*title*), Freaks and Follies of Fabledom, a little 'Comic' Lempriere. **1891** E. PEACOCK *N. Brendon* II. 334 The literature of fabledom.

fabler ('feɪblə(r)). Also 4, 7 fabuler. [f. FABLE *v.* + -ER¹: perh. after OF. *fableor*:—L. *fābulātōrem*: see FABULATOR.] One who fables. †**a.** A writer of fables or apologues (*obs. rare*$^{-2}$: a literalism of translation). **b.** One who invents fictitious stories; chiefly in contemptuous use, a fiction-monger, fabulous historian. †**c.** One who speaks falsely, a liar (*obs.*).

a. **1382** WYCLIF *Baruch* iii. 23 The fablers, or janglers. **1609** BIBLE (Douay) *ibid.* iii. 23 Marchants of Merrhe, and of Theman, and fablers..searchers of prudence and understanding.

b. **1614** RALEIGH *Hist. World* IV. ii. §21. 485 Our great traveller Mandivile..we account the greatest fabler of the world. **1644** BP. HALL *Rem. Wks.* (1660) 130 The bold legends of lying fablers. **1728** W. SMITH *Ann. Univ. College* 153 Little Credit is to be given to these Fablers. **1821** T. CAMPBELL in *New Monthly Mag.* II. 228 The romantic fablers have generally aggravated the horrors of Circe. **1869** J. D. BALDWIN *Preh. Nations* ii. (1877) 24 That ready fabler, the Carian physician Ctesias. **1878** T. SINCLAIR *Mount* 28 Rather was he [Swedenborg] a mechanical fabler of facts.

c. **1362** LANGL. *P. Pl.* A. II. 157 Alle þis opure Fabulers and Faytours, þat on Fote rennen. **1548** HALL *Chron.* 88b, The inhabitantes of Vernoyle gevyng to light credit to the Frenche fablers, received the duke. **1579** E. K. *Gloss. Spenser's Sheph. Cal.* Apr. 120 Certain fine fablers, and loude lyers. **1607** TOURNEUR *Rev. Trag.* II. i. in Hazl. *Dodsley* X. 46 Y' are villains, fablers!..you lie. **1624** F. WHITE *Repl. Fisher* 86 Some..censure the reporters of Miracles, as..Fabulers and Lyars.

‖**fabliau** (fablio). Pl. fabliaux. [F. *fabliau*, assumed sing. to OF. *fabliaux*, pl. of *fablel*, dim. of *fable*: see FABLE.] A metrical tale, belonging to the early period of French poetry.

1804 SCOTT *Introd. Sir Tristr.* 48 The interesting *fabliaux* of the Anglo-Norman *trouveurs*. **1823** ROSCOE tr. *Sismondi's Lit. Eur.* (1846) I. viii. 221 Some of the Fabliaux very nearly approach the romances of chivalry. **1874** GREEN *Short Hist.* v. (1876) 215 The broad humour of the fabliau.

fabling ('feɪblɪŋ), *vbl. sb.* [f. FABLE *v.* + -ING¹.] The action of the vb. FABLE; the telling of fictitious stories, fabulous narration, romancing, †lying; an instance of the same.

a **1300** *E.E. Psalter* cxviii [cxix.]. 85 Wicked fablinges talde to me. **1530** *Calisto & Melib.* in Hazl. *Dodsley* I. 78 With thy fabling and thy reasoning, i-wis I am beguiled. **1610** HOLLAND *Camden's Brit.* I. 24 In the same veine..of fabling they called this Iland Albion. **1671** MILTON *P.R.* IV. 295 The next to fabling fell and smooth conceits. **1774** WARTON *Hist. Eng. Poetry* (1775) I. 22, I have considered the Saracens..the first authors of romantic fabling among the Europeans. **1821** LAMB *Elia, Old Benchers*, Extinct be the fairies and fairy trumpery of legendary fabling.

b. *attrib.*

1545 ASCHAM *Toxoph.* (Arb.) 45 They wolde thinke you made it but a triflyng and fabling matter. **1565** GOLDING *Ovid's Met.* Ep. (1593) 11 The Poet..in fabling-wise dooth make It happen in Deucalions time.

fabling ('feɪblɪŋ), *ppl. a.* [f. FABLE *v.* + -ING².] That fables, in senses of the vb.; that invents or relates fables; addicted to fable, romancing; in bad sense, mendacious.

1548 HALL *Chron.* (1809) 51 Crafty imaginers of you fablyng French menne. **1570–6** LAMBARDE *Peramb. Kent* (1826) 9 The fonde dreames of doting monkes and fabling friars. **1613** PURCHAS *Pilgrimage* I. x. (1614) 52 As for Noah, the fabling heathen..deified him. **1704** POPE *Windsor For.* 227 The fabling Poets' lays. **1822** B. CORNWALL *Ludovico Sforza* i. 4 She stood Like one of those bright shapes of fabling Greece. **1861** *Sat. Rev.* 21 Dec. 643 Fabling hatred was busy with the name of the fallen usurper.

b. occas. said of utterances, etc.

1620 T. PEYTON *Paradise* in Farr *S.P. Jas. I* (1848) 178 The fabling prayses of Elizium fields. **1755** *Gentl. Mag.* XXV. 420 Confus'd mythology, and fabling song. **1814** SOUTHEY *Roderick* xx. 208 False records, fabling creeds, and juggling priests.

†'**fabor**, '**fabour**. *Obs.* [a. OF. *fauxbourg*: see FAUBOURG.] A suburb.

c **1470** HENRY *Wallace* VIII. 527 On to the ȝettis and faboris off the toun Braithly thai brynt. **1489** K. HEN. VII. in *Paston Lett.* (1874) III. 357 Thei drewe down the fabours of Gyngham, and made theyme mete to defende a siege.

†**fabre'faction.** *Obs. rare.* [as if ad. L. **fabrēfactiōn-em*, n. of action f. *fabrēfacĕre*, f. *fabrē* skilfully + *facĕre* to make.] The action or process of fashioning or making (a work of art).

1652 GAULE *Magastrom.* 29 O toylsome labour, in prestigious fabrefaction! **1678** CUDWORTH *Intell. Syst.* 429 The Platonists, whose Inferiour Generated Gods..were supposed to have had a stroke in the Fabrefaction of Mankind.

fabric ('fæbrɪk, 'feɪbrɪk), *sb.* Forms: 5–6 fabrike, -yke, 6–7 fabrique, (7 fabriq), 7–8 fabrick(e, 7– fabric. [a. Fr. *fabrique* (= Pr. *fabriga*, It. *fabbrica*, Sp. *fábrica*), ad. L. *fabrica*, f. *faber* worker in metal, stone, wood, etc. See FORGE *sb.*]

I. A product of skilled workmanship.

1. An edifice, a building.

1483 CAXTON *Gold. Leg.* 275/1 He had neuer studye in newe fabrykes ne buyldynges. **1538** LELAND *Itin.* II. 68 Gibbes the last Prior..spent a great summe of Mony on that Fabrike. **1666** EVELYN *Diary* 7 Sept., The august fabriq of Christ Church. **1708** J. CHAMBERLAYNE *St. Gt. Brit.* II. I. ii. (1743) 326 Fabricks..said to have been built by the Picts. **1756** NUGENT *Gr. Tour.* IV. 84 A vaulted fabric without wood or iron-work, three stories high. **1813** SCOTT *Trierm.* III. xvi, Never mortal builder's hand This enduring fabric plann'd. **1865** DICKENS *Mut. Fr.* III. vi, The ruinous fabric was very rich in the interior.

fig. **1611** SHAKS. *Wint. T.* I. ii. 429 You may as well Forbid the Sea for to obey The Moone, As..shake The Fabrick of his Folly. **1664** H. MORE *Myst. Iniq.* 91 Men..inspired..to erect the Fabrick of the Church. **1788** REID *Aristotle's Log.* ii. §2. 30 Force of genius sufficient to shake the Aristotelian fabric. **1873** BURTON *Hist. Scot.* VI. lxviii. 126 The whole fabric of his ambition was tottering.

†**2.** A contrivance; an engine or appliance. *Obs.*

1596 DRAYTON *Leg.* IV. 721 When here that fabrique utterly did faile. **1600** HOLLAND *Livy* XXV. xi. 553 When ..[the city of Tarentum] began to be assailed with fabricks. **1603** —— *Plutarch's Mor.* 1243 What need had he to use any such tragique engine, or fabricke to work such feats. **1657** REEVE *God's Plea* 40 Tiberius..there invented his detestable Fabricks of lust.

3. a. 'Any body formed by the conjunction of dissimilar parts' (J.); a frame, structure.

1633 G. HERBERT *Temple, Search* vii, Lord, dost thou some new fabrick mold Which favour winnes..leaving th' old Unto their Sinnes? **1674** OWEN *Holy Spirit* (1693) 25 This Goodly Fabrick of Heaven and Earth. **1718** PRIOR *Solomon* III. 268 All the parts of this great fabrick change, Quit their old station, and primeval frame. **1728** THOMSON *Spring* 648 Dry sprigs of trees, in artful fabric laid. **1853** KANE *Grinnell Exp.* (1856) 476 In this egg-shell fabric the Esquimaux navigator..encounters risks which, etc. **1863** P. BARRY *Dockyard Econ.* 241 The armour-plates and other necessary portions of the ponderous fabric.

b. *esp.* with reference to the animal body.

1695 LD. PRESTON *Boeth.* II. 84 The whole Fabrick of Man, Body and Soul, is dissolv'd. **1758** S. HAYWARD *Serm.* I. 1 To..examine this outward fabrick the body! *a* **1848** R. W. HAMILTON *Rew. & Punishm.* i. (1853) 49 The wonderful fabric of the human body. **1878** HUXLEY *Physiogr.* 228 The solid animal fabric returns to swell the sum of the fluids and gases.

c. *fig.*

a **1637** B. JONSON *Eng. Gramm.* I. ii, The less [letters] make the Fabrick of Speech. **1669** PENN *No Cross* xii. §10 Death ends the Proud Man's Fabrick. **1785** REID *Int. Powers* Ded., To pick holes in the fabric of knowledge wherever it is weak and faulty. **1817** J. SCOTT *Paris Revisit.* (ed. 4) 380 A substantial fabric of public strength, freedom, and opulence. **1856** SIR B. BRODIE *Psychol. Inq.* I. iii. 77 Questions arising out of it appertaining..to the whole fabric of society.

4. A manufactured material; now only a 'textile fabric', a woven stuff.

1753 HANWAY *Trav.* (1762) I. v. lxx. 318 We are every day making new fabrics. **1791** ROBERTSON *India* ii. 88 Working up its [silkworm's] productions into..a variety of elegant fabrics. **1832** G. R. PORTER *Porcelain & Gl.* 10 The fabrics produced..were wanting in most of the qualities essential to good porcelain. **1837** HT. MARTINEAU *Soc. Amer.* II. 227

The woollen fabric manufactured in these establishments. **1874** GREEN *Short Hist.* v. 218 Up to Edward's time few woollen fabrics seem to have been woven in England. **1883** *Stubbs' Mercantile Circular* 8 Nov. 982/2 The people in Nagasaki are fast going back to their old practice of spinning this class of fabric for themselves.

transf. and *fig.* **1831** BREWSTER *Nat. Magic* ii. (1833) 18 The fine nervous fabric which constitutes the retina. **1859** KINGSLEY *Misc.* (1860) II. 119 The villain of the piece.. being a rough fabric, is easily manufactured with rough tools.

II. 5. a. The action or process of framing or constructing; erection (of a building); formation (of an animal body or its parts). Now only *spec.* The construction and maintenance (of a church); = Eccl. Lat. *fabrica ecclesiæ.*

1611 COTGRAVE, *Fabrique d'vn'Eglise,* The fabricke, raparation, or maintenance of a Church. **1650** BULWER *Anthropomet.* v. 72 The.. providence of God manifested in the fabrique of the eye-lids. **1664** POWER *Exp. Philos.* I. 17 The.. prodigious skilfulness of Nature in the fabrick of so Minute an Animal. **1730** A. GORDON *Maffei's Amphith.* 43 He attributed the Fabrick of the Colosseum to him. **1757** BURKE *Abridgm. Eng. Hist.* I. ii, Britains.. so expert in the fabrick of those chariots. **1840** MILMAN *Lat. Chr.* III. IV. i. 382 The other [third] to the fabric and the poor.

b. *attrib.* in ***fabric-fund, -lands, -roll.***

1672 COWEL *Interpr., Fabrick-Lands* are Lands given to the rebuilding, repair, or maintenance of Cathedrals, or other Churches. **1726** *Dict. Rusticum* s.v. **1848** WHARTON *Law Lex., Fabric Lands,* property given towards the rebuilding or repairing of cathedrals and churches. **1859** RAINE *(title),* The Fabric Rolls of York Minster (Surtees). **1875** J. T. FOWLER *Ripon Ch. Accts.* (Surtees), Index. Fabric fund of Ripon.

6. Kind or method of construction or formation. †**a.** of things in general, buildings, instruments, etc. Also style (of architecture). *Obs.*

1644 EVELYN *Mem.* (1857) I. 82 The fabric of the Church is Gothic. **1662** STILLINGFL. *Orig. Sacr.* III. i. §16 The peculiar and admirable fabrick of the eyes. **1665** *Phil. Trans.* I. 313 If any person.. do not know the fabrick or use of any of the Instruments. *a* **1682** SIR T. BROWNE *Tracts* (1684) 6 Architectonical Artists look narrowly upon.. the fabrick of the Temple. **1690** LOCKE *Hum. Und.* IV. iii. §24 The particular Fabricks of the great masses of matter, which make up the.. frame of corporeal Beings. **1703** MAUNDRELL *Journ. Jerus.* (1721) Add. 4 The Boats are of a miserable Fabrick. **1748** *Anson's Voy.* II. vi. 190 To be well informed of the fabrick and strength of this fort. **1774** J. BRYANT *Mythol.* II. 228 They were exposed upon the waters in a machine of this fabrick.

b. of manufactured materials. Chiefly of textile articles: Texture. †Also *concr.* a particular 'make' or class (of goods).

1758 J. BLAKE *Plan Mar. Syst.* 8 Let a particular fabric of paper be made. **1764** HARMER *Observ.* XVII. ii. 77 We.. conjecture, that the tents of the Patriarchs.. were of the same fabric. **1879** CALDERWOOD *Mind & Br.* 55 One who is constantly at work amongst cloths of different fabric.

c. *fig.*

1752 HUME *Ess. & Treat.* (1777) I. 181 The fabric and constitution of our mind no more depends on our choice than that of our body. **1753** SMOLLETT *Ct. Fathom* (1784) 57/1 Fools of each fabrick, sharpers of all sorts. **1779-81** JOHNSON *L.P., Pope* Wks. IV. 106 He used almost always the same fabric of verse. **1871** EARLE *Philol. Eng. Tongue* §597 Compounds vary extremely as regards laxity or compactness of fabric.

7. *concr.* **a.** Of a textile article: The woven substance; tissue, fibre. Also *fig.*

1823 J. BADCOCK *Dom. Amusem.* 152 In following that example our bleachers destroyed the fabric of their goods. **1836** J. GILBERT *Chr. Atonem.* ix. (1852) 263 There are minds in whose fabric the ratiocinative faculty preponderates. **1842** BISCHOFF *Woollen Manuf.* II. 228 German wool is of that inferior description which enters into the fabric of low middling cloths. **1877** E. R. CONDER *Bas. Faith* i. 3 Faith in the Unseen and reverence for the Divine—are inwoven in the very fabric of our nature.

b. Occas. used for: Structural material. Now *spec.* the basic structure (walls, floor, roof) of a building.

1849 MURCHISON *Siluria* iii. 42 Lime wherewith to supply the fabric of the thicker shell of other mollusca. **1850** DAUBENY *Atom. Th.* viii. (ed. 2) 245 The chief constituent of the vegetable fabric. **1866** ROGERS *Agric. & Prices* I. xx. 503 The fabric of the mill appears to have been invariably timber. **1934** BATSFORD & FRY *Cathedrals of England* 4 The fabrics.. form in the majority of cases a remarkable patchwork of building periods. **1955** *Times* 3 May 6/4 The skilled staff needed not only to maintain the fabric of the buildings but to care for the precious pictures, furniture, and gardens. *Ibid.* 9 May 5/2 Much has been done.. since a public appeal was opened on behalf of the fabric of Norwich Cathedral, to make this noble building safe.

III. 8. A building erected for purposes of manufacture; a place where work is carried on; a factory, manufactory. *rare.*

1656-81 BLOUNT *Glossogr., Fabric,* a shop or work-house wherein any thing is framed. **1753** HANWAY *Trav.* (1762) I. II. xiv. 61 His fabric appeared as a little town, having about four hundred looms. **1777** W. DALRYMPLE *Trav. Sp. & Port.* xxxi, The Marquis.. has established a fabrick of woollen cloth. **1807** SOUTHEY *Espriella's Lett.* (1808) I. 33 There is a great fabric of carpets at Axminster. **1844** *Fraser's Mag.* XXX. 431/1 The first fabric of liqueurs which had any extensive renown was that of Montpellier.

IV. 9. *attrib.* and *Comb.,* as ***fabric glove, hat*** (sense 4); ***fabric-faired*** (sense 3), ***-printing*** (sense 4), adjs.

1897 *Sears, Roebuck Catal.* 231/1 Ladies' fabric gloves. **1906** *Westm. Gaz.* 22 Sept. 13/2 They offer great opportunities for colour schemes, those fabric hats. **1916** *To-Day* 25 Nov. 92/2 Even his warm winter gloves are made of cotton.. 'fabric' gloves, such as most men wear in the summer. **1934** *Jrnl. R. Aeronaut. Soc.* XXXVIII. 670 Fabric-faired girder designs are diminishing. **1946** *Nature* 2 Nov. 614/2 A rotational viscometer for fabric-printing thickeners. **1971** 'A. GILBERT' *Tenant for Tomb* i. 8 She.. carried a big old-fashioned tapestry bag and wore fabric gloves.

'fabric, *v.* In 7-8 **fabrick**(**e.** [f. prec. sb.] *trans.* To construct, fashion, frame, make (a material or immaterial object). Also, ***to fabric up*** = FABRICATE 1 and 1 c.

1623 FAVINE *Theat. Hon.* x. ii, That [Target] of Achilles, fabrickt by the Armourer Vulcane. **1625** BP. MOUNTAGU *App. Cæsar* II. xv. 215 Such as the Papists fabricke up unto themselves in their works of Supererogation. **1644** MILTON *Areop.* (Arb.) 74 Matters fram'd and fabric't already to our hands. **1708** J. PHILIPS *Cyder* I. 349 The polish'd Glass, whose small Convex.. shews.. how [Cheese-Inhabitants] Fabrick their Mansions in the harden'd milk. **1738** *Common Sense* (1739) II. 5 You fabrick Generals as Statuaries do Figures of Wood and Clay. **1921** *Public Opinion* 14 Oct. 375/1 All these were dreamed and fabricked out for immediate material benefit. **1924** W. A. WHITE *Woodrow Wilson* xvi. 352 This high dream of peace, that he fabricked upon the anvil of a three years' debate.

Hence †**'fabricker, 'fabricking** *vbl. sb.*

1698 R. FERGUSSON *View Eccles.* 107 The Original Authors and Fabrickers of the Word [*trimmer*] designed to Describe those.. who were neither Loyal Subjects.. nor Vigorous Patrons. *Ibid.* 116 A key of his own Fabricking.

fabricant ('fæbrɪkənt). Now *rare.* [a. F. *fabricant,* ad. L. *fabricant-em,* pr. pple. of *fabricāre* to FABRICATE.] One who fabricates, constructs, or fashions (anything); a maker or manufacturer.

1757 *Herald* (1758) I. No. 10. 161 The fabricant is taxed in the materials he uses. **1777** W. DALRYMPLE *Trav. Sp. & Port.* cxlv, The minister, in the name of the king, first fabricant. **1799** G. SMITH *Laboratory* II. 40 Every fabricant or manufacturer at Lyons, in the flowered way. **1834** LYTTON *Pompeii* 162 Woe to us fabricants of bronze. **1884** G. BADEN-POWELL in *Fortn. Rev.* 1 Nov. 641 Fabricants and refiners manage to create a large margin of 'sugar'.

†**'fabricate,** *pa. pple. Sc. Obs.* [ad. L. *fabricāt-us* pa. pple. of *fabricāre.*] (See quot.)

1755 JOHNSON s.v., When they [Scottish lawyers] suspect a paper to be forged, they say it is *fabricate.*

fabricate ('fæbrɪkeɪt), *v.* [f. L. *fabricāt-* ppl. stem of *fabricā-re,* f. *fabrica* FABRIC *sb.*]

1. a. *trans.* To make anything that requires skill; to construct, manufacture. Now *rare.*

1598 YONG *Diana* 171 Wals fabricated by artificiall hand. **1667** FLAVEL *Saint Indeed* (1754) 59 A guilty conscience.. is the devil's anvil on which he fabricates all those swords and spears. **1678** CUDWORTH *Intell. Syst.* 235 God Fabricated the Earth. **1774** PENNANT *Tour Scot. in 1772.* 10 Hinges.. and other branches of hardware are fabricated here. **1821** CRAIG *Lect. Drawing* ii. 134 Colourless Glass.. has never yet been fabricated. **1857** WHEWELL *Hist. Induct. Sc.* I. 198 He is reported to have fabricated clocks. **1872** YEATS *Growth Comm.* 247 And silk was first fabricated in that city [Tours].

†**b.** ***to fabricate about with:*** to surround as with a framework of. *Obs.*

1634 SIR T. HERBERT *Trav.* 64 This citie, the metropolis of Persia, is fabricated about with spacious gardens.

c. with immaterial object. Also *absol.*

1621 BURTON *Anat. Mel.* II. ii. III. 328 Our later Mathematitians haue.. fabricated new systemes of the World, out of their own Dedalean heads. **1783** C. J. FOX *Sp. E. India Bill* 26 Nov., He was not vain enough to think, that any bill he could fabricate would be perfect. **1864** BOWEN *Logic* ii. 43 The secret workshop in which nature fabricates cognitions and thoughts. **1875** WHITNEY *Life Lang.* ii. 19 The tens of thousands [of words] which might be fabricated.

†**d.** Used for: To produce factitiously. *Obs.*

1776 TH. PERCIVAL *Philos., Med. & Exp. Essays* III. 274 The miliary eruption is frequently fabricated by.. heating remedies and forced sweats.

e. To form (semi-finished metal stock or other manufacturing material) into the shape required for a finished product; also with the product as *obj.*

1926 R. J. ANDERSON *Metall. Aluminium* xix. 853 Aluminium, when annealed, is readily fabricated by these operations [*sc.* drawing, pressing, and spinning], but the light alloys are not so readily worked. **1935** G. E. DOAN *Princ. Physical Metall.* 1 A hundred men may be engaged in fabricating the metals which have been extracted, forming them into countless shapes, such as rails, I-beams, boiler plate, [etc.]. **1951** G. SACHS *Sheet-Metal Fabricating* i. 9 Generally, large parts in very thin metal are difficult to fabricate accurately. **1963** SIMONDS & CHURCH *Conc. Guide Plastics* (ed. 2) vii. 187 Both thermo-setting and thermoplastic materials can be fabricated into a variety of shapes and forms. **1971** *Helicopter* July 147/1 The rotor blades are fabricated from aluminium alloy sheet bonded together by means of a film adhesive.

2. In bad sense: To 'make up'; to frame or invent (a legend, lie, etc.); to forge (a document).

1779 J. MOORE *View Soc. Fr.* (1789) I. xl. 349 The whole story was fabricated. **1790** PALEY *Horæ Paul.* i. 5 An impostor who was fabricating a letter in the name of St. Paul. **1818** HALLAM *Mid. Ages* ix. (1819) 346 Every saint [had] his legend, fabricated in order to enrich the churches under his protection. **1855** MACAULAY *Hist. Eng.* IV. 391 Numerous lies, fabricated by the priests.. were already in circulation. **1873** *Act 36-7 Vict.* c. 71 §33 If any person.. wilfully fabricate in whole or in part,.. any voting paper.

Hence **fabricated** *ppl. a.,* **'fabricating** *vbl. sb.*

1630 WADSWORTH *Pilgr.* vii. 67 His Art in contriuing and fabricating of Ships, and Gallyes. **1796** A. M. JOHNSON *Monmouth* II. 65 While the secret schemes of diabolical revenge were fabricating. **1796** MORSE *Amer. Geog.* II. 542 Among the fabricated articles, are great numbers of stoves. **1796** BURKE *Let. Noble Ld.* Wks. VIII. 67 New fabricated republicks. **1805** T. JEFFERSON *Writ.* (1830) IV. 43 This fabricated flight from Richmond was not among the charges. **1853** KANE *Grinnell Exp.* xxv. (1856) 205 There is not a man.. who would have given.. the countenance of his silence to a fabricated claim.

fabrication (fæbrɪ'keɪʃən). [ad. L. *fabricātiōn-em,* n. of action f. *fabricāre* to FABRICATE.]

1. a. The action or process of fabricating (sense 1 of the vb.); construction, fashioning, manufacture; also, a particular branch of manufacture. Now *rare.*

1677 HALE *Prim. Orig. Man.* IV. i. 290 Plato.. falls into conjectures, attributing.. the Fabrication of the Body to the *Dii ex Deo* or *Angels.* **1710** BERKELEY *Princ. Hum. Knowl.* I. §62 The Fabrication of all those Parts and Organs be not absolutely necessary to the producing any effect. **1790** BURKE *Fr. Rev.* 44 The fabrication of a new government is enough to fill us with disgust. **1845** R. W. HAMILTON *Pop. Educ.* iii. (ed. 2) 37 Our woollen, cotton, and silk fabrications have drawn out an immense amount of artizans. **1863** LYELL *Antiq. Man* 10 Materials which have each in their turn served for the fabrication of implements.

concr. **1602** WARNER *Alb. Eng.* Epit. (1612) 356 Seuerus his forced vallie, with other strong.. fabrications. **1670** MOXON *Tutor to Astron. & Geogr.* (ed. 2) App. 201 A Sphear is complycated only of Lath-like Circles to represent each Orb, and is not an intire Orb as a Globe is, so that you may see the several Fabrications that are made within it. **1893** *Whitby Gaz.* 8 Dec. 2/7, I thought all our masts, funnel, and the whole fabrication, boats and all, would surely go.

b. The process of fabricating in the manufacture of finished products (see FABRICATE *v.* 1 e).

1926 R. J. ANDERSON *Metall. Aluminium* xix. 852 The fabrication of various articles from aluminium sheet makes up an important branch of the aluminium industry. **1940** J. D. JEVONS *Metall. Deep Drawing & Pressing* p. xi, The fabrication of all kinds of metal articles by the severe plastic deformation of metal sheet is a craft as ancient as that of steel-making itself. **1951** G. SACHS *Sheet-Metal Fabricating* i. 7 Frequently, a slight alteration in the geometry of a part may overcome difficulties in fabrication. **1963** SIMONDS & CHURCH *Conc. Guide Plastics* (ed. 2) vii. 188 After fabrication or molding, most plastics articles require some form of finishing. **1967** E. SLADE *Metals in Mod. World* viii. 189 Traditional metallurgical methods.. are used increasingly for the fabrication of other materials, particularly the plastics.

2. In bad sense: The action of fabricating or 'making up'; the invention (of a statement); the forging (of a document). Also *concr.* An invention; a false statement; a forgery.

1790 J. BRUCE *Source of Nile* II. 151 Fabrications of people that never have been in Abyssinia. **1819** SIR W. O. RUSSELL *Crimes & Misdemeanours* IV. xxvii. §1 The fabrication and false making of the whole of a written instrument.. will amount to forgery. **1839** THIRLWALL *Greece* I. vii. 257 What is said to have happened might have been invented, and the occasion and motives for the fabrication may be conceived. **1846** WRIGHT *Ess. Mid. Ages* II. xiii. 83 The common account of his death is a mere fabrication. **1880** T. A. SPALDING *Eliz. Demonol.* 46 Stories .. that had too inconvenient a basis of evidence to be dismissed as fabrications.

fabricative ('fæbrɪkətɪv), *a.* [f. L. stem *fabricāt-*: see FABRICATE and -IVE.] Having the power or quality of fabricating; tending to fabrication.

1793 T. TAYLOR *Orat. Julian* 142 Forms subsist in Nature fabricative, but not intellective. **1844** MARG. FULLER *Wom. 19th C.* (1862) 118 The first triad is demiurgic or fabricative, that is Jupiter, Neptune, Vulcan.

fabricator ('fæbrɪkeɪtə(r)). [a. L. *fabricātor,* f. *fabricāre*: see FABRICATE.]

1. One who or that which frames or fashions.

c **1645** HOWELL *Lett.* III. ix, The Almighty fabricator of the Universe doth nothing in vain. **1765** ELLIS in *Phil. Trans.* LV. 283 These worms appeared evidently, instead of being the fabricators of it, to have pierced their way into the soft substance. **1844** DISRAELI *Coningsby* VII. iii. 262 The grotesque genius of its fabricator. **1846** J. BAXTER *Libr. Pract. Agric.* (ed. 4) II. 413 Domestic fabricators are too apt to fail in this particular, thinking that when they have mixed together a portion of sugar and fruit their labour is done. **1860** FARRAR *Orig. Lang.* i. 26 The Deity as the fabricator of Adam's language. **1863** LYELL *Antiq. Man* ix. (ed. 3) 166 They teach us that the fabricators of the antique tools.. were all post-glacial.

2. In bad sense: One who frames a false statement or forges a document; a forger.

1795 MASON *Ch. Mus.* iii. 191 The Translator or Fabricator of the Works of Ossian. **1796** BP. WATSON *Apol. Bible* 231 Had they been fabricators of these genealogies, they would have been exposed at the time to instant detection. **1863** MISS BRADDON *Eleanor's Vict.* III. vi. 82 The fabricator of a forged will.

3. *Archæol.* A rod-shaped flint implement, perh. used in the manufacture of other flint tools. (See also quot. 1954.)

1872 J. EVANS *Anc. Stone Implem.* 367 A characteristic specimen of the tool to which I have provisionally assigned the name of 'flaking-tool' or fabricator. **1877** W. GREENWELL *Brit. Barrows* 35 Those [*sc.* articles found in barrows] of flint, include hatchets; scrapers;.. fabricators or flaking tools. **1930** *Antiquity* IV. 27 'Fabricators' are rare, borers very rare, and calcined flints ('potboilers') exceedingly scarce. **1954** S. PIGGOTT *Neolithic Cultures* x. 286 There is good evidence for regarding a large proportion

of 'fabricators' as strike-a-lights used with pyrites to produce a spark.

'fabricaˌtory, *a.* *rare*$^{-1}$. [ad. late L. *fabricātōri-us*, f. *fabricāre*: see FABRICATE and -ORY.] Tending to fabricate.

1855 *Chamb. Jrnl.* IV. 66 Neither Youth melodramatic.. nor Antiquary fabricatory.

fabricatress. [f. FABRICATOR + -ESS.] 'A female who fabricates.'

1846 WORCESTER cites LEE.

† **'fabricature.** *Obs.* Also 7 fabrycature. [f. L. stem *fabricāt-*: see FABRICATE and -URE.] The action of fabricating; construction. **b.** Method or style of construction. **c.** Structure; 'make'.

1600 DYMMOK *Ireland* (1843) 37 The scite and fabrycature of which [forte] declare Sr John Norris..an ingener. **1607** TOPSELL *Serpents* (1653) 643 In the fabricature of their Honey-combes, they [Bees] make the fashion according to the magnitude and figure of the place. **1641** *Disc. Pr. Henry* in *Harl. Misc.* (Malh.) III. 523 The fashion and fabricature of the ships. **1657** TOMLINSON *Renou's Disp.* 399 A Dragon..of such artificiall yet naturall fabricature.

fabricless ('fæbrɪklɪs), *a.* [f. FABRIC *sb.* + -LESS.] Without substance, baseless.

1905 E. F. BENSON *Image in Sand* xiv. 315 Thought with him was no vague and dreamy musing..nor..any fabricless cloud-building.

† **'fabrile**, *a.* *Obs.* [a. OF. *fabrile*, ad. L. *fabrīl-is*, f. *faber* artificer.] Of or belonging to a craftsman or his craft. ***fabrile glue***: carpenter's glue (L. *fabrile gluten*).

1611 COTGR., *Fabrile*, of, or belonging to the craft of a Smith, Mason, or Carpenter. **1661** LOVELL *Hist. Anim. & Min.* 22 The fabrile glue decoct in Water and applied, helpeth the teeth. **1664** EVELYN *Sylva* (1776) 649 Trees, fitted..for Timber and all other Fabrile employments. **1678** LITTLETON *Lat. Dict.*, Fabrile, or of Smiths work, *fabrilis*.

Fabry-Pérot (fabripero). *Physics.* The names of C. *Fabry* (1867–1945) and A. *Pérot* (1863–1925), French physicists, used *attrib.* or jointly to designate the étalon invented by them (see ÉTALON), and also an interferometer designed on the same principle but having one of the glass plates mounted so that its distance from the fixed plate may be varied.

1908 *Sci. Abstr.* A. XI. 387 A modified Fabry and Perot apparatus. **1914** *Phil. Mag.* 6th Ser. XXVII. 678 We thus have a problem very similar to that of the Fabry-Perrot [*sic*] étalon, only with an infinite number of parallel equidistant plates. **1923** GLAZEBROOK *Dict. Appl. Physics* IV. 887 The red light from a cadmium lamp and the light from an iron arc are sent simultaneously through a Fabry and Perot interferometer. **1956** *Nature* 3 Mar. 434/2 A sharp fringe pattern has been obtained by substituting a small Fabry-Perot étalon for the 'Polaroid'—calcite unit. **1970** G. K. WOODGATE *Elem. Atomic Struct.* ix. 173 He studied the hyperfine splitting of the line..with a Fabry-Perot interferometer.

fabular ('fæbjʊlə(r)), *a.* [ad. L. *fābulār-is*, f. *fābula* (see FABLE *sb.*).] Pertaining to or of the nature of a fable, fabulous.

1684 W. BAXTER tr. *Plutarch's Mor.* (1694) IV. 87 These then are most of the Heads of this Fabular Narration. **1811** LAMB *Guy Faux*, The way which we take to perpetuate the memory of this deliverance is well adapted to keep up this fabular notion. **1850** *Fraser's Mag.* XLI. 535 Simplicity..is better adapted to fabular composition.

† **'fabular**, *sb.* *Obs.* [ad. late L. *fābulārius*, f. *fabula* FABLE.] A narrator or recorder of tales or fictions.

1565 JEWEL *Def. Apol.* (1611) 279 That Great fond Fabular Simeon Metaphrastes.

fabulate ('fæbjʊleɪt), *v.* [f. L. *fābulāt-* ppl. stem of *fābulārī* to speak, f. *fābula* FABLE *sb.*]

†**1. a.** *trans.* To relate as a fable or myth. **b.** *intr.* To talk or narrate in fables. *Obs.*

1616 T. ADAMS *Serm. Jas.* iii. 8 Wks. (1629) 143 Guarded ..as..it were with Gyants in an Inchanted towre, as they fabulate. **1624** HEYWOOD *Gunaik.* I. 17 This historie..is with much nimble..witte fabulated by Ovid.

2. *trans.* To invent, concoct, fabricate.

1856 BUSHNELL *Serm. Living Subj.*, Fabulating visit and vision to express his grief.

fabu'lation. [ad. L. *fābulātiōn-em*, n. of action f. *fābulārī*: see prec.] The action of fabulating.

1727–36 BAILEY, *Fabulation*, the moralizing of fables. **1775** in ASH. **1945** D. DEVLIN in *Briarcliff Q.* Oct. 66 At last we have stored the windows away, The fabulation of my Lord's glory. **1958** *Partisan Rev. Anthol.* (1962) 474 'Fabulation'..is a process no less singular.

fabulator ('fæbjʊleɪtə(r)). [a. L. *fābulātor*, agent-n. f. *fābulārī* (see FABULATE).] One who fabulates or relates fables; a story-teller.

1604 *Aberdeen Reg.* 24 Oct. (Spalding Club) II. 264 He that happinnis to be fabulatour, to bring his candill with him. **1678** CUDWORTH *Intell. Syst.* I. iv. §17. 298 Looking upon this Orpheus, not as a meer Fanciful Poet and Fabulator. **1701** GREW *Cosm. Sacra* IV. iii. 170 An historical Point, which no Fabulator would have thought of. **1801** STRUTT *Sports & Past.* III. iii. 163 He desired the fabulator to tell him longer stories. **1841** D'ISRAELI *Amen. Lit.* (1867) 72 The great then had fabulators or tale-tellers, as royalty has now..its readers.

fabule, obs. var. FABLE *sb.* and *v.*

fabulist ('fæbjʊlɪst). [ad. F. *fabuliste*, f. L. *fābula*: see FABLE *sb.* and -IST.]

1. One who relates fables or legends; a composer of apologues.

1593 MUNDY *Def. Contraries* 12 The fabulists feigned Acteon to be turned into a Hart. **1682** DUDLEY *Light to Paradise* 93 Fortune, who..by the fabulist, is represented with a great Complaint in her mouth upon that occasion. **1757** FOOTE *Author* Prol., The Grecian fabulist, in moral lay, Has thus address'd the writers of this day. **1835** *Johnsoniana* 256 The fabulists frequently make the wolves converse with the lambs. **1874** FARRAR *Christ* 45 The fabulists of Christendom..surround Christ's boyhood with a blaze of miracle.

†**b.** A professional story-teller. *Obs.*

1605 B. JONSON *Volpone* II. i, Stale Tabarine, the fabulist. **1698** R. FERGUSSON *View Eccles.* 84 The Sallaries of Buffoons, Fabulists or Revelers.

2. One who invents falsehoods.

1625 BP. HALL *Public Thanksgiving* Wks. 1837 V. 220 Those bold Fabulists..take a course to cast themselves into that pit, whence [etc.]. **1794** PALEY *Evid.* II. iii. (1817) 87 The mind of a forger or a fabulist. **1836–7** SIR W. HAMILTON *Metaph.* (1877) I. iii. 47 The former [Heraclides] is confessed to have been an egregious fabulist. **1841** D'ISRAELI *Amen. Lit.* (1867) 151 The most ingenuous of voyagers has been condemned as an idle fabulist.

† **fabu'listic**, *a.* *Obs.* *rare*$^{-1}$. [f. prec. + -IC.] Given to be a fabulist; devoted to the composition of fables or apologues.

1630 J. TAYLOR (Water P.) *Sir G. Nonsence* Wks. II. 2/2 Esop, that old fabulisticke Phrygian.

† **'fabulize**, *v.* *Obs.* [f. L. *fābul-a* FABLE + -IZE.] **a.** *intr.* To invent fables. **b.** *trans.* To concoct, invent. **c.** To relate as legend: with sentence as *obj.* **d.** To dress up as a fable.

1612 tr. *Benvenuto's Passenger* I. i. §19. 71 Endlesly among themselves they fabulize, nourish the mistery. **1633** T. ADAMS *Exp. 2 Peter* i. 16 They did but fabulize an apish imitation of God's truth. **1738** G. SMITH *Cur. Relat.* II. 530 The Persians fabulize in their Alcoran, that [etc.] **1818** G. S. FABER *Horæ Mosaicæ* I. 251 It is utterly impossible that it [the Pentateuch] could thus grossly have fabulized.

Hence **'fabulized** *ppl. a.* **'fabulizing** *vbl. sb.* and *ppl. a.*

1819 G. S. FABER *Dispensations* (1823) I. 241 Their fabulized history. **1816** —— *Orig. Pagan Idol.* I. 315 The very wildest style of oriental fabulizing. *Ibid.* II. 502 The fabulizing monks of the holy sepulchre. *Ibid.* III. 334 A fabulizing martyrology.

† **fabulose**, *a.* *Obs.* [ad. L. *fābulōs-us*, f. *fābula*: see FABLE *sb.*] Fond of fables, myths, or enigmas; = FABULOUS I.

1677 GALE *Crt. Gentiles* III. 76 They [the Cabalists] grew so vain and fabulose that [etc.]. *Ibid.* 152 These fabulose Monkes mixe many of their own fantastic allegoric Fables therewith. **1727–36** BAILEY, *Fabulose*, feigned, full of fables.

fabulosity (fæbjʊ'lɒsɪtɪ). [ad. F. *fabulosité*, ad. L. *fābulōsitāt-em*, f. *fābulōsus*: see prec.]

1. The quality of being fabulous; fabulousness. **a.** Of persons: Fondness for narrating or inventing fables.

1599 ABP. ABBOT *Descr. World, Chaldea* (1634) 112 In their [Chaldeans'] fabulositie they would report that they had..Observations for five and twentie thousand years. **1646** SIR T. BROWNE *Pseud. Ep.* I. vi. 23 The fabulositie of those times.

b. Of a composition, narrative, etc.: Fabulous or mythical character; fictitiousness.

1603 HOLLAND *Plutarch's Mor.* 489 Some..more civilly avoiding the fabulosity of this tale say [etc.]. **1678** CUDWORTH *Intell. Syst.* 236 Plato..doth but..slily jear it, plainly insinuating the fabulosity thereof. **1741** WARBURTON *Div. Legat.* II. VI. ii. 490 He supposed the fabulosity of that [Book of Job] concluded against the real existence of the Patriarch. **1777** JOHNSON in *Mad. D'Arblay's Early Diary* 27 Mar., There is not..much of the spirit of fabulosity in this Fable.

†**2.** quasi-*concr.* Something fabulous; a fabulous statement, fable. *Obs.*

1601 HOLLAND *Pliny* II. 605 That..posterity ensuing may yet be acquainted with their fabulosities. **1681** H. MORE *Exp. Dan.* Pref. 48 The ridiculous fabulosity of Enoch and Elias their coming again in the Flesh. **1807** G. CHALMERS *Caledonia* I. Pref. 8 These form historical matters of singular interest if they be investigated from facts in contempt of fabulosity.

fabulous ('fæbjʊləs), *a.* [ad. L. *fābulōs-us*, f. *fābula*: see FABLE *sb.* and -OUS. Cf. F. *fabuleux.*]

1. a. Of a person (or anything personified): Fond of relating fables or legends, given to fabling.

Now only with sbs. like *historian, chronicler*; cf. sense 3. **1546** BALE *Eng. Votaries* II. (1551) 10 Wherof.. the fabulouse poetes reporteth [Venus] to be engendered. **1591** SHAKS. *1 Hen. VI*, II. iii. 18, I see Report is fabulous and false. **1637** R. HUMPHREY tr. *St. Ambrose* i. 26 Aristotle.. holdeth God to bee..no otherwise then the fabulous Poets have feigned. *c* **1650** COWLEY *Death Crashaw* 28 Wanton as Girls, as old Wives, Fabulous! **1805** N. NICHOLLS in *Corr. with Gray* (1843) 43 An author..never fabulous except when he gave the relations of others. **1864** BURTON *Scot Abr.* I. i. 2 Boece and our other fabulous chroniclers.

†**b.** Fond of listening to fables or stories. *Obs.*

1589 PUTTENHAM *Eng. Poesie* I. vii. (Arb.) 30 The Clergy of that fabulous age. **1669** GALE *Crt. Gentiles* I. I. ii. 12 It was Plato's Custome to hide his choicest opinions, under the figure of some Fable..lest he should..displease the fabulous people.

2. Spoken of or celebrated in fable or myth; fabled, mythical. [So L. *fabulosus.*]

1601 HOLLAND *Pliny* I. 91 Atlas, the most fabulous mountaine of all Africke. **1887** SWINBURNE *Locrine* Ded. viii, Milton's..lips have made august the fabulous air.

3. Of a narrative: Of the nature of a fable or myth, full of fables, unhistorical, legendary. ***fabulous age, period***, etc.: one of which the accounts are chiefly or entirely mythical.

1555 EDEN *Decades* 215 Such thynges as haue byn wrytten ..of the places where they growe are all fabulous and false. **1656** M. BEN ISRAEL *Vind. Judæorum* in *Phenix* (1708) II. 401, I have seen a fabulous Narrative of the Proceedings of a great Council of the Jews. **1712** PHILIPS *Distrest Mother* Pref., A Matter of Fact..far removed into the dark and fabulous Ages. **1776** ADAM SMITH *W.N.* I. xi. I. 214 The story..is in a great measure fabulous. **1855** H. REED *Lect. Eng. Hist.* iii. 78 The fabulous chronicles of those ages. **1872** YEATS *Techn. Hist. Comm.* 60 The Chinese possess..their fabulous and semi-historical periods.

4. a. Of alleged existences or facts: Belonging to fable, mythical, legendary.

1577–87 HOLINSHED *Chron.* I. 121/1 Which because in the iudgement of the most it may seeme meere fabulous, we will omit and passe ouer. **1644** MILTON *Areop.* 4 Those fabulous Dragon's teeth. **1737** CHESTERF. *Wks.* (1777) I. 70 The fabulous birth of Minerva. **1833** LYELL *Princ. Geol.* III. 330 The former existence of the Atlantis of Plato..may be true in geology, although fabulous as an historical event. **1875** JOWETT *Plato* (ed. 2) III. 69 Winged dragons and other fabulous monsters.

†**b.** Of a doctrine, error, or notion: Based on or originating in fable or fiction. *Obs.*

1602 WARNER *Alb. Eng.* Epit. (1612) 351 Our Historie auoideth not the suspition of some fabulous errours. **1651** HOBBES *Leviath.* IV. xliv. 334 Their fabulous Doctrine concerning Dæmons. **1794** PAINE (*title*), The Age of Reason, being an investigation of true and of fabulous Theology.

5. a. Resembling a fable, absurd, ridiculous. *rare.* **b.** Such as is met with only in fable; beyond the usual range of fact; astonishing, incredible. Now freq. in trivial use, esp. = 'marvellous', 'terrific'; cf. FAB.

a. 1561 T. NORTON *Calvin's Inst.* IV. 50 How vayne and fabulous is it, to iudge the Church alredy in euery part holy and spottlesse, wherof all the members are spotty and very vncleane. **1611** TOURNEUR *Ath. Trag.* II. vi, Tush! these idle dreames Are fabulous. **1853** BRIMLEY *Ess.* 278 The pretence is fabulous.

b. 1609 HOLLAND *Amm. Marcell.* 228 With a fabulous and incredible multitude [L. *cum multitudine fabulosa*]. **1822–56** DE QUINCEY *Confess.* Wks. I. 234 *foot-n.*, According to the modern slang phrase, I had..used 'fabulous' quantities [of opium]. **1852** MISS MITFORD in L'Estrange *Life* III. xiii. 237 His [Daniel Webster's] passion for fish..is something fabulous. **1857** LD. HOUGHTON in *Life* (1891) II. xii. 18 Houses..let at fabulous rents. **1859** MACAULAY *W. Pitt*, Misc. Writings (1889) 431 He found that the waste of the servants' hall was almost fabulous.

1959 *Cambr. Rev.* 30 May 571/2 Miss Mitchell, looking, one must admit, fabulous, played down her frenzy. **1962** *Radio Times* 4 Jan. 23/2, I think it's [*sc.* Salford] a fabulous place. **1963** A. ROSS *Australia 63* vii. 129 Trueman puffed at a cigarette and said he felt fabulous.

fabulously ('fæbjʊləslɪ), *adv.* [f. prec. + -LY².] In a fabulous manner or degree.

1. After the manner of a fable or fiction; as in a fable.

1598 GRENEWEY *Tacitus' Ann.* VI. vii. (1604) 131 These things are vncertaine and fabulously augmented. **1613** SELDEN *Notes on Drayton's Polyolb.* viii. (1622) 122 Giants.. fabulously supposed begotten by spirits upon Dioclesian's or Danaus' daughters. **1646** SIR T. BROWNE *Pseud. Ep.* VI. vi. 295 This they terme mythicon or fabulous, because the account thereof..is fabulously or imperfectly delivered. **1794** SULLIVAN *View Nat.* II. 467 The voyages, indeed, are fabulously narrated. **1856** LEVER *Martins of Cro' M.* 527 It would read fabulously enough.

2. In deviation from the fact; fictitiously, falsely.

1593 NORDEN *Spec. Brit., M'sex.* I. 36 As is (though as I take it) fabulouslie reported. **1608** B. JONSON *Masque at Ld. Hadington's Marriage* Induct. Wks. (1616) 934 The place from whence, as I haue been, not fabulously, informed, the ..Radcliffes..tooke their name. **1726** LEONI *Alberti's Archit.* I. 39 b, A certain Spaniard..was fabulously said to ..see the lowest Veins of Water that run under ground.

3. To a fabulous degree; greatly, immensely.

1845 S. AUSTIN *Ranke's Hist. Ref.* II. 247 His cruelties have been fabulously exaggerated. *Mod.* He is reported to be fabulously wealthy.

'fabulousness. [f. as prec. + -NESS.] The quality or state of being fabulous. **a.** Of a person: Fondness for fables; proneness to fiction or invention. **b.** Of a narrative, etc.: Resemblance to a fable; fabulous, fictitious or mythical character.

a. 1611 COTGR., *Fabulosité*, fabulousnesse, th' inuention of lyes, tales, fables, or fained reports. **1680** DODWELL *Two Lett. Advice* (1691) 169 Their [the Rabbins'] notorious fabulousness. **1711** *Brit. Apollo* III. 2/1 The Fabulousness of the Poets. **1775** JOHNSON *W. Isl. Scot.* Wks. X. 329 His [Boethius's] fabulousness, if he was the author of the fictions, is a fault for which no apology can be made.

b. 1587 GOLDING *De Mornay* xxx. 488 The fondness and fabulousness thereof appeereth in this. **1662** STILLINGFL. *Orig. Sacr.* I. vi. *heading*, The fabulousness of the Heroical

age of Greece. **1702** ECHARD *Eccl. Hist.* III. iv. 386 He afterwards wrote two letters..to show the fabulousness of the history of Susanna. **1807** G. CHALMERS *Caledonia* I. Pref. 5 The ancient history of North-Britain, whatever might be its fabulousness. **1837** ARNOLD in Stanley *Life & Corr.* (1844) II. viii. 101 To notice with a grave remark as to their fabulousness, the peculiar marvels of the stories.

faburden. *Music. Obs.* exc. *Hist.* Forms: 5 faburdon, -thon, -thyn, 6 fabourdoun, 6–7 faburthen, 6– faburden. [a. Fr. *faux-bourdon* (Ch. D'Orléans *a* 1466), i.e. *faux* false + *bourdon* BOURDON[2].]

1. 'One of the early systems of harmonizing a given portion of plain-song or a canto fermo, afterwards used as a term for a sort of harmony consisting of thirds and sixths, added to a canto fermo' (Stainer and Barrett).

14.. CHILSTON in Hawkins *Hist. Mus.* (1776) II. 228 Faburdun hath but two sightis, a thyrd aboue the plain-song in sight, the which is a syxt fro the treble in uoice; and euen wyth the plain-song in sight, the wheche is an eyghth from the treble in uoise. [**1462** W. WEY *Itin.* II. (Roxb.) 96 Cantabamus in honore Dei et beate Marie Magnificat, in faburthon. **1484** *Visitations of Southwell Minster* (Camden) 46 In cantando faburdon non servat ritum chori.] **1501** DOUGLAS *Pal. Hon.* I. xlii, In modulation hard I play and sing Fabourdoun, pricksang, discant. **1529** *Will J. Robynson* (Somerset Ho.), Preestes..whiche shall singe playn songe and faburden. **1590** J. BUREL *Queen's Entry Edin.* xx. in *Collect. Scot. Poems* II. (1709) 5 Fabourdon fell with decadence, With pricksang, and the singing plane. **1597** MORLEY *Introd. Mus.* Annot., Here is an example, first the plainsong, and then the Faburden. *a* **1789** BURNEY *Hist. Mus.* (ed. 2) II. ii. 139 What has since been called Counterpoint or in old English, Faburden.

2. a. The undersong; = BURDEN *sb.* 9.

1587 GASCOIGNE *Flowers* Wks. 94 When the descant sings in treble tunes above..let fa burthen say below I liv'd and dide for love. **1587** —— *Ferdinando* Y ij b, His mistresse liked..to sing faburden under him. **1609** *Pammelia* 70 The fourth must sing the Faburthen [Bome, bome on the first line of the stave]. **1622** R. TISDALE *Lawyer's Philos.*, Sighing a sad faburthen from my quill To thy more nimble warblings.

b. The refrain; = BURDEN *sb.* 10.

1580 LYLY *Euphues* (Arb.) 308 Least thou come in againe with thy fa-burthen. **1596** NASHE *Saffron Walden* K iv b, Hee was accustomed to make it the Fa burden to annie thing hee spake. *a* **1636** FITZ-GEFFRAY *Bless. Birthd.* (1881) 137 Be sure no better straine then this can be The sweet Faburthen, to their melodie.

3. A legend, motto.

1594 NASHE *Unfort. Trav.* 52 On his target he had a number of crawling wormes kept vnder by a blocke, the faburthen *speramus lucem.*

4. *attrib.* quasi-*adj.* ? High-sounding.

1596 LODGE *Wits Miserie* 9 *Mirabile, miraculoso, stupendo,* and such faburthen words.

†fac (fæk). *Printing. Obs.* [Short for FACTOTUM.] = FACTOTUM 2.

1841 SAVAGE *Dict. Art Printing* 221 The next descent was for the letter-founders to cast the ornament in type metal, and pierce it for general use, and these cast ornaments for letters were called Facs.

fac: see FEGS.

fa'çadal, *a. rare.* [f. next + -AL[1].] Of or pertaining to a façade or façades.

1879 [LINGHAM] *Science of Taste* v. 144 If a bye-law were made enforcing façadal uniformity in other blocks.

façade (fə'sɑːd). [a. F. *façade*, f. *face*, after It. *facciata*, f. *faccia* FACE *sb.*]

1. a. The face or front of a building towards a street or other open place, *esp.* the principal front. Also *attrib.* or as *adj.*, of an architectural design concerned with elegance, etc., in the façade of a building alone. Hence **fa'çadism**, such a practice or principle.

1656–81 in BLOUNT *Glossogr.* **1717** BERKELEY *Tour in Italy* Wks. 1871 IV. 534 We observed the façades of many noble buildings. **1756–7** tr. *Keysler's Trav.* (1760) II. 397 The inner façade was repaired by Bernini. **1839** J. L. STEPHENS *Trav. Greece, etc.* 88/1 The façade of the palace is unequalled. **1872** BROWNING *Fifine* cx, Shadow sucked the whole Façade into itself. **1933** *Archit. Rev.* LXXIV. 111 Façadism with a purpose, unlike the façadism of the new Railway Station at Milan. **1936** *Times Lit. Suppl.* 16 May 421/1 He..refuses to accept the recent revaluation of Nash and is more than tainted with 'façadism'. **1962** *Listener* 15 Nov. 806/2 A warning against façade architecture.

b. *transf.* and *fig.*

1845 DARWIN *Voy. Nat.* xviii. (1852) 407 Beneath a façade of columnar lava, we ate our dinner. **1875** E. WHITE *Life in Christ* III. xviii. (1878) 230 The whole façade of the Evangelical theology.

‖**2.** (See quot.)

1796 MORSE *Amer. Geog.* I. 754 Their estates [in Demerara] are regularly laid out in lots along the sea shore, called facades.

faccion, faccious, obs. ff. FACTION, FACTIOUS.

face (feɪs), *sb.* Also 4 faas, 4–5 fas(e, 5 faz. [a. Fr. *face*, corresp. to Pr. *fassa*, It. *faccia*:—popular Lat. *facia*, altered form of *faciēs* form, figure, appearance, hence face, visage, represented directly by Pr. *fatz*, Sp. *faz*, *haz*, Pg. *face*. The etymology of L. *faciēs* is uncertain: some scholars refer it to *facĕre* to make; others to the root *fa-* to appear, shine (cf. *fac-em* torch).

The general sense 'form, appearance', which in Latin was app. the source of the more specific use 'visage, countenance', is in many of its Eng. applications apprehended as a transferred use of the latter, and has received a special colouring from this association. On this account the more restricted sense is here placed first.]

I. 1. The front part of the head, from the forehead to the chin; the visage, countenance:

a. in man. (In *Anat.* sometimes with narrowed sense, as excluding the forehead: see quot. 1831.)

c **1290** *S. Eng. Leg.* 169/2178 More blod þar nas in al is face. **1340** HAMPOLE *Pr. Consc.* 772 Als a man waxes alde.. his face rouncles ay mare and mare. *c* **1380** *Sir Ferumb.* 2460 Vp þey sterte euerechon; & be-held him on þe fas. *c* **1400** *Lanfranc's Cirurg.* 141 The secunde chapitle of woundes of þe face. **1526** *Pilgr. Perf.* (W. de W. 1531) 3 My face thou may not se. **1601** SHAKS. *Jul. C.* II. i. 75 Their Hats are pluckt about their Eares, And halfe their Faces buried in their Cloakes. **1667** MILTON *P.L.* I. 600 His face Deep scars of Thunder had intrencht. **1707** FLOYER *Physic. Pulse-Watch* 374 Uneasiness from dryness and redness of the Face. **1759** STERNE *Tr. Shandy* I. xxi, The least hint of it was enough to make the blood fly into his face. **1762** WALPOLE *Vertue's Anecd. Paint.* (1765) I. ii. 24 Such pyramids on their heads, that the face became the center of the body. **1831** R. KNOX *Cloquet's Anat.* 95 The Face, properly speaking..extends vertically from the upper edge of the nasal bones to the chin.

b. in lower animals.

1535 COVERDALE *Job* xli. 14 Who openeth the dore of his face? for he hath horrible tethe rounde aboute. **1611** BIBLE *Ezek.* x. 14 The face of a lion, and..the face of an eagle. **1697** DRYDEN *Virg. Georg.* IV. 532 His grim Face a Bull's Resemblance bears. **1741** CHAMBERS *Cycl.*, Face,.. sometimes called bill, or beak; sometimes snout, etc. **1784** COWPER *Task* v. 785 Brutes graze the mountain-top, with faces prone. **1845** S. PALMER *Pentaglot Dict.* s.v., The face of birds comprehends the ophthalmic regions, cheeks, temples, forehead, and vertex;—of insects, all the parts situated between the labrum and prothorax.

c. *transf.* A representation of a human visage.

1488 *Ld. Treas. Acct. Scot.* (1877) I. 85 Item, a ring with a face. **1588** SHAKS. *L.L.L.* v. ii. 649 He's a..Painter, for he makes faces. **1623** WEBSTER *Duchess of Malfi* III. iii, That cardinal hath made more bad faces with his oppression than ever Michael Angelo made good ones. **1716** *Pope's Wks.*, *Basset-Table* 33 Upon the bottom [of an Equipage] shines the Queen's bright Face. **1801** *Sporting Mag.* XVIII. 100 No face but his own; a saying of one who has no money in his pocket, nor no court cards in his hand. **1832** W. IRVING *Alhambra* I. 111 Carved with fruits and flowers, intermingled with grotesque masks or faces. **1855** MACAULAY *Hist. Eng.* III. 503 Walker had arrived in London..His face was in every print shop.

d. In popular names of plants, as **face and hood, three (†two) faces in, under a (one) hood,** the heart's-ease, pansy (*Viola tricolor*); **face-in-hood,** the aconite (*Aconitum Napellus*).

1548 TURNER *Names of Herbes* (E.D.S.) 87 *Trinitatis herba* ..is called in english two faces in a hoode or panses. **1562** BULLEYN *Bk. Simples* 39 a, Paunsis, or three faces in one hodde. *a* **1700** B. E. *Dict. Cant. Crew*, *Hearts-ease*..an Herb called..Three Faces in a Hood..or Pansies. **1771** R. WARNER *Plantæ Woodford.* 185 Heart's-ease. Three Faces under a Hood. **1878–86** BRITTEN & HOLLAND *Eng. Plant-n.*, Face and Hood (*Viola tricolor*). *Ibid.*, Face-in-hood (*Aconitum Napellus*).

e. A slang term of address.

1923 WODEHOUSE *Inimitable Jeeves* xvii. 232, I ran into young Bingo Little... 'Hello, face,' I said. 'Cheerio, ugly,' said young Bingo. **1938** D. SMITH *Dear Octopus* I. 38 Come on, face—don't get mopey.

f. Used with varying contextual degrees of contempt, admiration, etc.: a person. *slang.*

1945 L. SHELLY *Jive Talk Dict.* 11/1 *Face*, a white man. **1964** *New Statesman* 10 Apr. 555/2 A 'face' is a person, usually someone worthy of admiration. **1964** *Observer* 24 May 12/5 Fashions are usually started by Faces—the name for trend-pushing Mods. **1967** J. MORGAN *Involved* 80 Now this face was the ideal man for me to have a deal with.

2. Phrases. **a.** *†from face to foot* = 'from head to foot'. † *to know no faces*: to have no respect of persons. *to have two faces*: to be guilty of duplicity; (of speech) to be ambiguous. In same sense, † *to bear or carry two faces under one hood*. *to open one's face* (*U.S. slang*): to open the mouth, to speak; *to shut one's face* (*slang*): to keep quiet (esp. *imp.*). *to laugh on the other side of one's face*: see LAUGH *v.* 1 b.

c **1475** *Pol. Poems* in *Archæol.* XXIX. 341 Two fases in a hode is neuer to tryst. **1562** J. HEYWOOD *Prov. & Epigr.* (1867) 138 Thou berest two faces in one whood. **1580** NORTH *Plutarch* (1676) 224 Icetes had carried two faces in one hood, and..was become a Traytor. **1607** SHAKS. *Cor.* II. ii. 112 From face to foot He was a thing of Blood. **1633** EARL MANCH. *Al Mondo* (1636) 24 Disease and Death know no faces. **1889** BARRIE *Window in Thrums* 196 Persons whose speech had two faces. **1893** S. CRANE *Maggie* (1896) ix. 73 Shet yer face, an' come home, yeh old fool! **1896** ADE *Artie* iii. 26 If you open your face to this lady again tonight, I'll separate you from your breath. **1899** C. ROOK *Hooligan Nights* ii. 29 'That's awright,' muttered young Alf. 'You shut yer face.' **1913** D. H. LAWRENCE *Love Poems* 53 An' stop thy scraightin', childt. Do shut thy face. **1917** U. SINCLAIR *King Coal* II. 186 The marshal bade him 'shut his face'. **1939** *Best Short Stories* 45 'Shut your daft grinning face,' growled Arthur. **1959** I. & P. OPIE *Lore & Lang. Schoolch.* x. 194 'Shut your chops', 'shut yer face'.

b. *to look (a person,* etc.) *in the face*: to confront, meet with a steady gaze that implies courage, confidence, or (sometimes) defiance; also *fig.* *to shew one's face*: to put in an appearance, to appear: *lit.* and *fig.*

1537 *Thersites* in Hazl. *Dodsley* I. 408 Appear, sir, I pray you, dare ye not show your face? **1561** NORTON & SACKV. *Gorboduc* I. i, Aurore..for love or shame Doth long delay to show her blushing face. **1566** GASCOIGNE, etc. *Jocasta* II. ii, Boldly to looke our foemen in the face. *a* **1662** HEYLIN *Laud* II. v. (1719) 20, I dare look Death in the Face, and I hope the People too. **1706** ? SWIFT *Wks.* (1883) X. 389 Where exiled wit ne'er shews its face. **1748** RICHARDSON *Clarissa* Wks. 1883 V. 56, I should be ashamed to show my face in public. **1780** COWPER *Table-t.* 321 When Tumult..dared to look his master in the face. **1841** LONGF. *Village Blacksmith* ii, He.. looks the whole world in the face, For he owes not any man. **1863** KINGSLEY *Water-bab.* vi. (1869) 250 The fairy looked him full in the face. **1867** FREEMAN *Norm. Conq.* (1876) I. iii. 118 Too clear to be misunderstood by anyone who looks the evidence in the face. **1882** STEVENSON *New Arab. Nts.* (1884) 194 He never so much as showed face at a window.

c. In advb. phr.: *face downwards* (*foremost, uppermost*), etc.: with the face in the direction indicated. (*to fall*) *face on*: = 'face downwards'.

1856 *Leisure Ho.* V. 332/1 He fell face on into the water.

d. *face to* (earlier †*and*, †*for*) *face*: looking one another in the face; also *attrib.* *face to face with*: looking in the face of, confronting; *lit.* and *fig.* *to see face to* (†*with*) *face*: 'without the interposition of other bodies' (J.), clearly. Also **face-to-face, face-to-faceness** *sbs.*, **face-to-facedly** *adv.*

a **1300** *Cursor M.* 23607 (Cott.) Þair ioi, þair gladdscip, qua can tell..face wit face þat godd to se. **1340** *Ayenb.* 88 We him ssolle yzy face to face clyerlyche. *a* **1400–50** *Alexander* 357 Make þe to se þe same gode & þi-selfe wakand Face to face all his fourme. **1535** STEWART *Cron. Scot.* II. 255 The proud Pechtis..face for face stude in thair fais sicht. **1576** FLEMING *Panopl. Epist.* 2 Of these matters..we shall talke shortly face to face. **1632** LITHGOW *Trav.* x. 490 Sir Walter Aston..spoke seriously face to face with him there-anent. **1767** GRAY in *Corr. N. Nicholls* (1843) 69, I am come..to congratulate you face to face on your good luck. **1848** MACAULAY *Hist. Eng.* I. 600 The two armies were now face to face. **1861** T. A. TROLLOPE *La Beata* I. vii. 155 The painter and the customer might never come face to face after all. **1864** KNIGHT *Passages Wrkg. Life* I. i. 105, I was..to be face to face with great public things. **1874** W. WALLACE *Logic of Hegel* xviii. p. cxxxiv, In both there is the same statement of immediacy or face-to-faceness. **1875** MANNING *Mission H. Ghost* ix. 260 We shall see God face to face. **1876** *Gentl. Mag.* Feb. 212 The applause thus..publicly and face-to-facedly showered upon it. **1879** FROUDE *Cæsar* i. 5 When we are face to face with real men. *a* **1916** H. JAMES *Sense of Past* (1917) 335 His disconcerted and practically defeated face-to-faceness with the way in which they do take it [*sc.* his modernism]. **1960** *Economist* 31 Dec. 1395/2 This biographical 'face-to-face'.

attrib. **1833** J. NYREN *Young Cricketer's Tutor* 59 He was a good face-to-face, unflinching, uncompromising, independent man. **1858** J. MARTINEAU *Stud. Chr.* 172 We are liable to lose the solemn face-to-face reality of the strife within us. **1864** J. H. NEWMAN *Apol.* 379 The face-to-face antagonist. **1865** MASSON *Rec. Brit. Philos.* iv. 319 We possess an intuitive, or face-to-face knowledge of certain properties of matter. **1949** M. MEAD in M. Fortes *Social Structure* 23 A regiment of soldiers, all from..the occident, come into face-to-face relations with non-occidental people. **1952** W. SPROTT *Social Psychol.* 257 Improved social relations in face-to-face groups were found salutary in dealing with mental illness. **1956** J. WHATMOUGH *Language* 12 There is a greater time-lag in a printed book, as in a recording, than there is in face-to-face talk. **1971** *Times* 8 Jan. 2/4 A combination of radio, correspondence courses and face-to-face teaching.

e. *Mil.* In words of command; †*faces to the right, left, faces about* = right, left, about face (cf. FACE *v.* 9 b); also *fig.* Hence, *to turn face about*, † *again.*

1598 B. JONSON *Ev. Man in Hum.* III. i, Good Captayne, faces about, to some other discourse. **1625** MARKHAM *Souldiers Accid.* 20 Faces to the right hand. Faces to the left. Faces about, or Faces to Reare. **1632** J. HAYWARD tr. *Biondi's Eromena* 77 He turned face againe with sword in hand. **1642** *Lanc. Tracts* (Chetham Soc.) 65 They..turned faces about, and began to make head against us. **1881** G. W. CABLE *Mad. Delphine* viii. 45 It had..turned him face about from the way of destruction.

f. *to throw, thrust,* etc. (something) *in* (a person's) *face. lit.* and *fig.*

1602 SHAKS. *Ham.* II. ii. 599 Who calles me Villaine? breakes my pate a-crosse? Pluckes off my Beard, and blowes it in my face? *c* **1645** HOWELL *Lett.* (1655) IV. xxi. 58 Who taints his soul may be said to throw dirt in Gods face. **1760** GRAY *Lett.* Wks. 1884 III. 53 You see him [Sterne]..ready to throw his periwig in the face of his audience. **1852** THACKERAY *Esmond* I. xiv, 'I fling the words in your face, my lord.' **1856** MRS. BROWNING *Aur. Leigh* II. Wks. VI. 76 God ..thrusts the thing we have prayed for in our face. **1884** MISS BRADDON *Ishmael* xxxi, His success was cast in his face as a reproach.

g. In various Biblical Hebraisms. *before the face of*: before, in advance of, in front of. *to set one's face*: to give a settled bearing or expression to the countenance. *to put, set one's face against*: to take up an attitude of determined hostility towards. *to set* (*one's*) *face †for, to, towards*: to take, etc. the direction of (a place); *fig.* to purpose, take the first steps *to, towards. to grind the faces of*: see GRIND *v.*[1] 2 b.

a **1300** *Cursor M.* 22757 (Cott.) Be-for þe face o þat kaiser angels sal his baner bere. *c* **1325** *Metr. Hom.* 9, I send..my messager Bifor thi face thi word to ber. *a* **1340** HAMPOLE *Psalter* xvii. 46, I sall less þaim as dust bifore þe face of wynd. **1388** WYCLIF *Lev.* xx. 3 Y schal sette faste [**1382** putte] my face aȝens hym. **1535** COVERDALE *Mark* i. 2, I sende my messaunger before thy face. [So in **1611** and

1881.] **1611** Bible *Gen.* xxxi. 21 He..set his face toward the mount Gilead. —— *2 Kings* xii. 17 Hazael set his face to goe vp to Ierusalem. —— *Isa.* l. 7 Therefore haue I set my face like a flint. **1624** Bp. Hall *Rem. Wks.* (1660) 11 Set your faces..against a whole faction of vice. **1632** Lithgow *Trav.* x. 493, I set face from Court for Scotland. **1664** Etheredge *Com. Revenge* iv. vii, Set thy face then; let me not see the remains of one poor smile. **1781** Cowper *Expost.* 457 The poorest of the flock Are proud, and set their faces as a rock. **1827** Scott *Jrnl.* (1890) II. 21, I can set my face to it boldly. *a* **1862** Buckle *Civiliz.* (1873) III. v. 469 The first duty of every one is to set his face in direct opposition to what he believes to be false. **1862** Lowell *Biglow P.* Poems 1890 II. 326 It's high time..to be settin' our faces Towards reconstructin' the national basis. **1884** *Times* (weekly ed.) 3 Oct. 14/2 We set our faces to the South.

3. a. Viewed with reference to beauty. † *to be in face*: to be looking one's best (cf. *to be in voice*). † *full of face*: ? beautiful (but perh. the meaning is = 'full faced, florid').

In the A.V. only in the Apocrypha; the translators of the canonical books always use 'countenance' in this connexion.

1591 Shaks. *Two Gent.* iii. i. 103 Say they haue Angells faces. **1608** —— *Per.* i. Induct., A female heir, So buxom blithe, and full of face. **1611** Bible *Judith* xi. 21 There is not such a woman from one end of the earth to the other..for beautie of face. **1712–4** Pope *Rape Lock* i. 79 Some nymphs there are, too conscious of their face. **1773** Goldsm. *Stoops to Conq.* i. i, Is it one of my well-looking days child? am I in face to day? **1842** Tennyson *Sisters* 2 She was the fairest in the face. **1851** Procter (Barry Cornwall) *Songs* lxxxiii. 3 No wealth had she of mind or face To win our love, or raise our pride.

b. Make-up, cosmetics; esp. in phrs. *to do* or *to put on one's* (or *a*) *face*: (of a woman) to apply cosmetics. *colloq.* (Occas. used of a bag containing cosmetic materials.)

1923 W. S. Maugham *Our Betters* i. 45 A wonderful woman who comes every morning to do my face. **1946** G. Millar *Horned Pigeon* xx. 327 She uncovered a dressing-case of..obvious costliness... 'You don't intend to leave that thing lying around?' 'Why not?..It's my face.' **1957** J. Frame *Owls do Cry* I. xiv. 62 How dare you watch me put on my face. **1961** *Guardian* 25 Sept. 3/2 My hair is wrecked and my 'face' totally removed. **1963** A. Lubbock *Austral. Roundabout* 10 My 'face', a small bag with make-up and washing things. **1966** 'C. E. Maine' *B.E.A.S.T.* v. 59 You've caught me with my face off. Give me three minutes. **1969** R. Lockridge *Murder in False Face* xiv. 183 I'll wash my hands and put on another face.

4. With reference to its position in the front of the body, or as the part presented to encounter. In many phrases, some of which merely express the notion of confronting or opposition, without any reference to the lit. sense. Cf. 2 d. **a.** *to meet* (a person) *in the face*: to confront directly. *to have the wind in one's face*; *lit.* and *fig.* *to shut the door in*, † *upon* (a person's) *face*; *lit.* and *fig.*

c **1430** Lydg. *Bochas* i. x. (1544) 15 b, She made her ordinaunce..With Zisara to meten in the face. **1632** Lithgow *Trav.* vii. 303 The Venetian Factor..shutting his gate vpon my face. **1710** *Brit. Apollo* III. 3/1 When th' Wind's in your Face, Your Wit grows apace. *a* **1732** T. Boston *Crook in Lot* (1805) 17 People ply their business with skill and industry, but the wind turns in their face. **1768** Sterne *Sent. Journ.* Wks. 1885 II. 640 'Tis shutting the door of conversation absolutely in his face. **1818** Byron *Juan* i. clxiv, The door was fasten'd in his legal face. **1888** Bryce *Amer. Commw.* I. xiv. 193 Seldom meeting them in the face or reaching a decision which marks an advance. *Mod.* A horse runs well with the wind in his face.

b. *to fly in the face of* (a person, etc.), *lit.* of a dog; *fig.* to act in direct opposition to.

1553 T. Wilson *Rhet.* (1580) 203 Lette hym have his will, and he will flie in thy face. **1610** Bp. Hall *Apol. Brownists* §13 Let him shew them a Cudgell, they flie in his face. **1689** *Tryal Bps.* 133 Shall he come and fly in the Face of the Prince? shall he say it is illegal? **1749** Fielding *Tom Jones* iii. viii, Thackum held, that this was flying in Mr. Allworthy's face. **1752** in *Scots Mag.* (1753) Oct. 494/1 It was flying in the face of the legislature itself. **1876** E. Fitzgerald *Lett.* (1889) I. 379 He has..been..apt to fly in the face of some who courted him. **1891** *Nation* 10 Dec. 440/2 He had to fly in the face of adverse decisions.

c. *in* (*the*) *face of*: (*a*) in front of, directly opposite to; (*b*) face to face with, when confronted with; (*c*) in defiance of, in direct opposition to, notwithstanding.

(*a*) **1766** T. Page *Art Shooting* 36 When a bird comes directly in your face, Contain your fire awhile. **1879** Dowden *Southey* 14 He was for the first time in face of the sea.

(*b*) **1871** Smiles *Charac.* ii. (1876) 36 In the face of bad example, the best of precepts are of but little avail. **1883** *Daily News* 31 Oct. 5/2 Not a man..would seriously advise withdrawal in the face of a Chinese invasion. **1885** *Manch. Exam.* 3 June 5/3 The difficulty of keeping up wages in the face of a drooping market.

(*c*) **1837** B'ness Bunsen in Hare *Life* I. x. 461 They now assert here, in the face of facts, that the cholera has ceased. **1848** Macaulay *Hist. Eng.* II. 276 They were convicted in the face of the letter and of the spirit of the law. **1885** *Manch. Exam.* 29 Oct. 5/3 Plans, perseveringly carried out in the face of many discouragements.

d. *to make face to*: to offer resistance to. *rare*, after Fr. *faire face à*.

1829 W. Irving *Conq. Granada* x. (1850) 74 The king and his commanders..made face to the Moors..repelling all assaults.

e. In ice-hockey and lacrosse: the act of facing off (see face *v.* 4 c). Also *face-off*.

1896 *Times* (Niagara, Ont.) 20 Feb. 1/4 In the face-off Bishop lost. **1898** H. E. Byers in W. A. Morgan '*House' on Sport* 211 The 'face' is a feature of the game [*sc.* lacrosse]. **1900** *Daily News* 29 Mar. 7/5 Kent opened proceedings with a goal by Jones immediately after the 'face'. **1900** J. C. Isard in J. H. C. Fegan et al. *Football, Hockey, & Lacrosse* 178 When the game is opening, with the face-off at the centre. **1936** *Times* 25 Jan. 5/7 Then Smith equalized from the face-off [in ice-hockey] with a long shot. **1968** *Globe & Mail* (Toronto) 15 Jan. 19/6, I lined up for a faceoff.

5. Contextually equivalent to: Sight, presence. In various phrases: **a.** *to fear, flee from*, etc. *the face of*.

a **1300** *Cursor M.* 953 (Cott.) Ʒee sal be flemed fra mi face. *c* **1325** *Metr. Hom.* 86, I salle be flemid awaye Fra Goddes faz, til pin of helle. **1611** Bible *Gen.* xxxv. 1 Thou fleddest from the face of Esau. **1781** Cowper *Retirement* 768 Judah's promised king..Driven out an exile from the face of Saul.

b. *before* or *in the face of*: before the eyes of, in the sight of. † *before faces*: in the public view, in company.

a **1300** *Cursor M.* 10460 (Gött.) Bot i him saw bifore mi face? *c* **1380** *Sir Ferumb.* 192 Þe man y trist an most forsakeþ me at my nede, & draʒþ ys swerd bi-fore my fas. *c* **1450** *St. Cuthbert* (Surtees) 846 Þai had grace, And loue before þe bischope face? **1532** More *Confut. Tindale* Wks. 532/1 Ye shoulde see the whole summe and effecte of this tale..before your face layed together. **1632** Lithgow *Trav.* viii. 370 The Prince..causing euery one of them to recite the praise of Mahomet before his face. *a* **1656** Bp. Hall *Rem. Wks.* (1660) 248 Even the most carelesse boyes will be affraid to offend in the face of the monitor. **1659** B. Harris *Parival's Iron Age* 292 Arras..was taken..before the face of thirty thousand men. **1760** Goldsm. *Cit. W.* xviii. 3 A new-married couple more than ordinarily fond before faces.

c. *to* (a person's) *face*: openly in his sight or hearing (implying frankness, effrontery or indecorum).

1553 T. Wilson *Rhet.* (1580) 188 You..gave him a frumpe even to his face. **1590** Shaks. *Com. Err.* i. i. 91 Wilt thou flout me thus vnto my face? **1638** Baker tr. *Balzac's Lett.* I. 231, I will not tell you to your face, that you are the Chrysostome of our Church. **1667** Denham *Direct. Paint.* ii. vi. 19 Men that there pick his pocket to his face. **1781** Cowper *Expost.* 283 Thy very children..curse thee to thy face. **1848** Macaulay *Hist. Eng.* II. 638 Sharp..read to their faces the whole service as it stood in the book. *Mod.* He does not like to be praised to his face.

d. *in the face of*: in the sight or hearing of, in the presence of. Also *fig.* *in the face of the sun, of day*, etc.: openly.

1398 Trevisa *Barth. De P.R.* ii. v. (1495) 31 Angels..ben stable in the face of god. **1540** *Act 32 Hen. VIII*, c. 38 §2 Mariages..contracte and solemnised in the face of the church. *a* **1618** W. Bradshaw in Spurgeon *Treas. Dav.* Ps. xc. 8 Sins..committed in deepest darkness are all one to him as if they were done in the face of the sun. **1711** Addison *Spect.* No. 112 ¶7 Pray for him in the Face of the whole Congregation. **1769** Blackstone *Comm.* IV. 283 If the contempt be committed in the face of the court, the offender may be instantly apprehended and imprisoned. **1773** Mad. D'Arblay *Early Diary* July, She does this in the fair face of day. **1845** M. Pattison *Ess.* (1889) I. 19 You will forfeit, in the face of all men, the character of faithful ministers of God. **1858** Buckle *Civiliz.* (1873) II. viii. 509 They broke open private houses..in the face of day. **1875** Jowett *Plato* (ed. 2) I. 164 You proclaim in the face of Hellas that you are a Sophist.

6. a. The countenance as expressive of feeling or character; a countenance having a specified expression.

c **1330** *Arth. & Merl.* 1138 So gretliche sche awondred was That hir chaunged blod and fas. **1576** Fleming *Panopl. Epist.* 357 They..with a smiling face promise us their benevolence. **1611** Shaks. *Cymb.* i. i. 13 They weare their faces to the bent of the kings lookes. **1611** Bible *Ezra* ix. 7 For our iniquities have we..bin deliuered to confusion of face. **1612** Webster *White Devil* iii. i, It would do well, instead of looking-glasses, To set one's face each morning by a saucer Of a witch's congealed blood. **1614** Bp. Hall *Recoll. Treat.* 616 And all this with a face of sad pietie and stern mortification. **1676** Etheredge *Man of Mode* iv. i, I..hate the set face that always looks as it would say, Come, love me. **1843** Macaulay *Lake Regillus* xii, With..haggard face to his last field he came.

b. *to make, pull a* (*crooked, pitiful, wry*, etc.) *face*: to distort the features. Hence the sb. is used *colloq.* for: A grimace.

1570 North *Doni's Mor. Philos.* (1888) III. 184 The poore Birde when he saw hir make that face to him was halfe afraide. **1602** Shaks. *Ham.* iii. ii. 263 Leaue thy damnable Faces, and begin. **1604** Middleton *Father Hubburd's T.* Wks. (Bullen) VIII. 72 The fantastical faces he coined in the receiving of the smoke. **1605** Shaks. *Macb.* iii. iv. 67 Why do you make such faces? **1713** Steele *Englishman* No. 7. 47 He will..make Faces at the Burgundian Grape. **1856** Reade *Never too late* xlv, I shall pull a long face. **1873** Dixon *Two Queens* III. xiv. viii. 113 The almoner made no faces at a dance. **1888** Mrs. H. Ward *R. Elsmere* II. ii. xviii, 'The adjective is excellent', she said with a little face. **1890** G. M. Fenn *Double Knot* I. i. 71 Making what children call 'a face', by screwing up her mouth and nose.

7. a. Command of countenance, *esp.* with reference to freedom from indications of shame; a 'bold front'; impudence, effrontery, 'cheek'. † *to put out of face*: to put out of countenance. *to* † *bear, have the face to* (do something): to be sufficiently impudent.

1537 *Thersites* in Hazl. *Dodsley* I. 401 He beareth not the face With me to try a blow. **1552** *Bk. Com. Prayer* Communion, With what face then, or with what countenaunce shal ye heare these wordes? **1601** Shaks. *Jul. C.* v. i. 11 Thinking by this face, To fasten in our thoughts that they haue courage. **1607** —— *Cor.* iv. vi. 116, I haue not the face To say, beseech you cease. **1654** Warren *Unbelievers* 85 He a man of that face and fore-head. **1719** De Foe *Crusoe* (1840) II. vi. 148 With what face can I say anything? **1735** Pope *Prol. Sat.* 36 To be grave, exceeds all Pow'r of face. **1760** Goldsm. *Cit. W.* (1840) 140 None are more blest with the advantages of face than Doctor Franks. **1821** Sir J. D. Paul *Rouge et Noir* 45 Vice itself affects propriety That puts your vulgar virtue out of face. **1839** Dickens *Let.* ? Dec. (1965) I. 624 As a family man, I really have not the face to dine out again to-day. **1848** T. Arnold *Let.* 16 June (1966) 53, I dismissed my guide with..two shillings; though the little dog had the face to ask 'sicca-penny more'. **1851** Longf. *Gold. Leg., Village Church*, I wonder that any man has the face To call such a hole the House of the Lord. **1865** Carlyle *Fredk. Gt.* V. xiv. v. 218 The new Kur-Mainz..conscious of face sufficient. **1890** *Spectator* 1 Nov., What an amount of 'face' it argues in him.

b. *to* † *push* or *show a face*: to exhibit a bold front. *to run one's face*: (*U.S. slang*) to obtain credit by impudence. Also *to travel on* or *upon one's face* (*U.S.*).

1758–65 Goldsm. *Ess.* viii, There are three ways of getting into debt: first, by pushing a face. **1827** Scott *Jrnl.* (1890) II. 6 They might have shown a face even to Canning. **1839** *Spirit of Times* 5 Oct. 368/3 The Picayune says there is a chap in New Orleans who has 'run his face so often for drinks, that it is completely worn off'. **1856** *Knickerbocker* XLVIII. 504 [I] must travel on my face after this, when I want to go through the College. **1859** *Yale Lit. Mag.* XXV. 60 (Th.), If you have not a ready tongue, and cannot travel upon your face, you had better [etc.]. **1862** Lowell *Biglow P.* Poems 1890 II. 286 Men that can run their face for drinks, an' keep a Sunday coat.

II. Outward form, appearance.

8. a. External appearance, look; also semblance *of* (anything). Formerly used both of material and immaterial objects; now *rare* except of immaterial objects in such phrases as *to adopt, carry, put on a* (*the*) *face of*. † (*to carry*) *a great face*: an appearance of importance. † *to have a face*: to have an appearance, give promise of success.

c **1381** Chaucer *Parl. Foules* 317 As Aleyn, in the Pleynt of Kynde, Devyseth Nature of aray and face. *c* **1394** *P. Pl. Crede* 670 Þei schulden nouʒt after þe face neuer þe folke demen. **1513** More in Grafton *Chron.* II. 762 His part should have the face and name of a rebellion. **1565** Jewel *Def. Apol.* (1611) 137 This tale hath some face of truth. **1631** Weever *Anc. Fun. Mon.* 771 Monuments..which beare any face of comelinesse or antiquity. **1674** R. Godfrey *Inj. & Ab. Physic* Pref., That is a thing carries a great face with it. **1692** R. L'Estrange *Josephus' Antiq.* iv. vi. (1733) 88 There was hardly any Face left of the Order, Piety and Devotion of former Times. **1754** Hume *Hist. Eng.* I. xvi. 395 France began gradually to assume the face of a regular civil government. **1760** Foote *Minor* i. Wks. 1799 I. 247 Pillory me, but it has a face. **1765** Croker, etc. *Dict. Arts & Sc.*, *Face of Plants*, among botanists, signifies their general appearance. **1782** Wesley *Wks.* (1872) XIII. 419 It carries no face of probability. **1827** Scott *Jrnl.* (1890) II. 35 Cadell explained to me a plan for securing the copyright of the novels, which has a very good face. **1860** H. Gouger *2 Years' Imprisonm. Burmah* 41, I professed my ignorance of the touch of gold and the face of silver. **1865** Bushnell *Vicar. Sacr.* i. (1866) 5 Vicarious..is a word that carries always a face of substitution. **1888** Bryce *Amer. Commw.* III. xcv. 356 The problems of the world..are always putting on new faces.

b. † *at prime face* = L. *prima facie*; *at, in, on the first face*: at the first appearance or look, at first sight.

c **1374** Chaucer *Troylus* iii. 870 This accident..was..so lyke a soth, at prime face. **1430** Lydg. *Chron. Troy* ii. xiii, At pryme face, whan he came to towne. **1563** T. Gale *Antidot.* Pref. 2 Although it seeme harde..at the first face, yet folow thou styll the counsell. **1596** Dalrymple tr. *Leslie's Hist. Scot.* (1885) 7 Naitur schawes furth Britannie all that it has at the first face. **1641** Shirley *Cardinal* iii. ii, Though at the first Face of the object your cool bloods were frighted. **1810** Syd. Smith *Wks.* (1859) I. 192/1 A narrative, which, on the first face of it, looked..much like truth. **1826** E. Irving *Babylon* I. ii. 120 In the very first face and showing of the thing.

¶ **c.** = phase *sb.* (perh. confused with that word).

1646 Sir T. Browne *Pseud. Ep.* vi. i. 278 In what face or position of the Moone, whether at the prime or full, or soone after. **1711** Shaftesb. *Charac.* ii. v. (1737) II. 322 This was not a Face of Religion I was like to be enamour'd with.

9. a. Visible state or condition; aspect. *to put a new face upon*: to alter the aspect of.

1587 Harrison *England* ii. v. (1877) i. 110 To stirre up such an exquisite face of the church as we imagine. **1592** Davies *Immort. Soul* Introd. xxxv, The Face of outward Things we find, Pleasing and fair. **1614** Bp. Hall *Recoll. Treat.* 694 Wee may reade Gods displeasure on the face of heaven. **1638** Baker tr. *Balzac's Lett.* I. 8 Lyvie..stayed not a little to consider the new face he would have put upon the Commonwealth. **1722** De Foe *Plague* (1754) 19 The Face of London was now indeed strangely alter'd. **1781** *Hist. Europe* in *Ann. Reg.* 24/2 The arrival of so many ships..caused a new face of affairs. **1820** W. Irving *Sketch Bk.* I. 215 A pensive quiet reigns over the face of nature. **1848** Macaulay *Hist. Eng.* I. 284 The traces left by ages of slaughter and pillage were still distinctly perceptible..in the face of the country.

b. Of a country: The configuration; assemblage of physical features. Also, † a description of the same.

1673 Temple *Observ. United Prov.* Wks. 1731 I. 43 Changes..made in the Face and Bounds of Maritime Countries..by furious Inundations. **1681** Cotton *Wond. Peak* (ed. 6) 309, I almost believ'd it, by the Face Our masters give us of that unknown place. **1779–81** Johnson *L.P., Addison* Wks. III. 47 Comparisons of the present face of the country with the descriptions left us by the Roman poets. **1792** Gouv. Morris in Sparks *Life & Writ.* (1832) II. 236 The military face of that country is understood with perfect exactness. **1859** Jephson *Brittany* vi. 78 The sun shone out, and I could observe the face of the country.

10. a. Outward show; assumed or factitious appearance; disguise, pretence; an instance of this; a pretext. Also, † ***to make a*** (***good, great***) ***face***; ***to set a face on***. † ***to interpret*** (***words***) ***to wicked face***: to put a bad construction upon. Now only in ***to put*** (formerly ***bear out, set***) ***a good face on*** (***a matter***): to make (a matter) look well; to assume or maintain a bold bearing (with regard to).

1382 WYCLIF *2 Cor.* v. 12 Hem that glorien in the face [so TINDALE; **1611** and **1881** appearance], and not in the herte. *c* **1489** CAXTON *Sonnes of Aymon* ix. 227 Lete vs . . bere oute a good face as longe as we ben alyve. **1533** BELLENDEN *Livy* IV. (1822) 377 He interpret thir wourdis of Posthumius to sa wikkit face, that the said Posthumius suld . . be odius . . to the hale ordoure. **1533** MORE *Apol.* xlvii. Wks. 920/2 In some place of the same dyoces . . they haue made a great face. **1542–5** BRINKLOW *Lament.* 9 b, The pore forgotten, except it be with a few scrappes and bones, sent to Newgate for a face! **1568** GRAFTON *Chron.* II. 265 They . . made good face and shewe to fight with the Englishe men. **1577** tr. *Bullinger's Decades* (1592) 95 Many . . haue the skill . . to make a face as though they loued them [friends]. **1590** H. SMITH *Wks.* (1867) II. 309 If thou . . have no cunning, but set a face on things, then take heed how you adjure these spirits. **1647** N. BACON *Disc. Govt. Eng.* I. lx. (1739) 118 [He] never invaded the liberties of the Commons by any face of Prerogative. *a* **1680** BUTLER *Rem.* (1759) I. 278 They . . set a Face of civil Authority upon Tyranny. **1722** DE FOE *Plague* (1754) 35 The very Court . . put on a Face of just Concern for the publick Danger. **1748** RICHARDSON *Clarissa* Wks. 1883 VIII. 110 That she may set the better face upon her gestation. **1867** FREEMAN *Norm. Conq.* (1876) I. iv. 231 Richer puts as good a face as he can on Hugh's discomfiture.

b. ***to save one's face***: see SAVE *v.* 8 f; also ***to save face***; ***to lose face*** [tr. Chinese *tiu lien*]: to be humiliated, lose one's credit, good name, or reputation; similarly, ***loss of face***. Hence *face* = reputation, good name.

1876 R. HART *These from Land of Sinim* (1901) App. II. 225 Arrangements by which China has lost face. **1899** *Harmsworth Mag.* June 400 That will save my face in the City. **1915** W. S. MAUGHAM *Of Human Bondage* cvii. 563 To save his face he began making suggestions for altering it, but Mrs Hodges . . advised him to show it to Miss Antonia as it was. **1915** J. LONDON *Lost Face* 33 He had lost face before all his people. **1928** GALSWORTHY *Swan Song* i. 5 They've got to save face. Saving face is the strongest motive in the world. **1929** *Times* 3 Aug. 11/3 Each wishes to concede only what can be conceded without loss of 'face'. **1945** E. WAUGH *Brideshead Revisited* 8 They . . sidled away at the approach of an officer for fear that, by saluting, they would lose face with their new mistresses. **1957** L. DURRELL *Bitter Lemons* 22 To lapse into Greek with anyone who was not a peasant would involve a loss of face. **1957** [see FAIRY-TALE]. **1958** *Times* 5 July 12/1 The importance of 'face', whether individually or collectively, in Japan. **1968** G. JONES *Hist. Vikings* II. iv. 129 Harald had lost face in his dealings with Norway.

III. The part of a thing presented to the eye.

11. The surface or one of the surfaces of anything.

a. *gen.* Chiefly in phrases orig. Hebraistic, ***the face of the earth***, ***the deep***, ***the waters***.

1340 HAMPOLE *Pr. Consc.* 4892 Þe face of þe erth sal brin with-out. **1382** WYCLIF *Gen.* vii. 3 That the seed be sauyd vpon the face of al erthe. **1553** T. WILSON *Rhet.* (1580) 176 All menne, dispersed throughout the face of the yearth. **1611** BIBLE *Gen.* i. 2 Darkenesse was vpon the face of the deepe: and the Spirit of God mooued vpon the face of the waters. **1632** LITHGOW *Trav.* III. 102 The Women of the Citty Sio, are the most beautifull Dames . . upon the face of the earth. **1665** HOOKE *Microgr.* 88 When there has been a great hoar-frost . . the . . Crystalline beard . . usually covers the face of . . bodies. **1698** KEILL *Exam. Th. Earth* (1734) 140 That great Deluge of waters which . . overflowed the Face of the whole Earth. **1791** *Ess. Shooting* (ed. 2) 230 If he is clad in a glaring colour, when the face of the country retains its verdure. **1887** FRITH *Autobiog.* I. i. 3 Such schools . . being improved off the face of the earth.

†**b.** Of a leaf in a book: = SIDE. *Obs.*

c **1575** FULKE *Confut. Doctr. Purgatory* (1577) 5, I will come to the third leafe and second face. **1579** —— *Refut. Rastel* 730 From the first face of the 64 leafe to the seconde face of the 47 leafe.

†**c.** *Astrol.* The third part of a sign of the zodiac, extending over 10 degrees in longitude. See also quot. 1819. *Obs.*

1426 *Pol. Poems* (1859) II. 139 His dwellyng place Ameddis the hevene in the thrid face. **1587** GOLDING *De Mornay* xxxiv. 543 The Moone . . was in the first face of Virgo. **1632** MASSINGER *City Madam* II. ii, She in her exaltation, and he in his triplicite trine and face. **1819** J. WILSON *Dict. Astrol.* 96 A planet is in its face when it is at the same distance from the ☉ or ☽ as its house is from their houses, and in the same succession of signs.

12. The principal side (often vertical or steeply inclined) presented by an object; the 'front' as opposed to the 'flanks'. **a.** (*a*) Of a cliff, etc.; also *Geol.* of a fault: The front or slope. (*b*) An open slope or hillside. *N.Z.* (*c*) *Golf*, the slope or cliff of a bunker.

1632 LITHGOW *Trav.* VI. 290 A goodly Village . . situate on the face of a fruitfull hill. *Ibid.* IX. 423 Wee Coasted the scurrile and Rockey face of Norway. **1751** R. PALTOCK *P. Wilkins* (1884) II. xviii. 203 Along the whole face of the rock . . there were archways. **1828** SCOTT *F.M. Perth* xiv, The tree . . had sent its roots along the face of the rock in all directions. **1839** MURCHISON *Silur. Syst.* I. xxxvi. 503 As the face of this fault sinks to the west.

1860 TYNDALL *Glac.* I. xi. 75 Our way now lay along the face of a steep incline of snow. **1865** GOSSE *Land & Sea* (1874) 388 A noble precipice, rising with a rough face almost perpendicularly from the water's edge.

1857 *St Leonard's Station Diary* 11 July in L. R. C. MacFarlane *Amuri* (1946) III. 126 Sheep seem all right as all on steep sunny faces which have partly cleared. **1947** P. NEWTON *Wayleggo* (1949) iii. 37 It was country of great open shingle faces. *Ibid.* 153 *Face*: open hillside. **1949** —— *High Country Days* xiii. 137 The stag up in the face gave tongue again.

1881 R. FORGAN *Golfer's Handbk.* 33 *Face*, . . the sandy slope of a bunker. **1897** *Encycl. Sport* I. 466/1 Shall I play it backwards, or sideways on to the grass, or try to get it over the face of the bunker nearer the hole? **1910** B. DARWIN *Golf Courses Brit. Isles* v. 105 We may be just short with our second . . and we shall be battering the bunker's unyielding face till our card is shattered and wrecked.

b. *Arch.* (*a*) The front or broadside of a building; the 'facade'. (*b*) The surface of a stone exposed in a wall. (*c*) The front of an arch showing the vertical surfaces of the outside row of voussoirs.

1611 BIBLE *Ezek.* xli. 14 The bredth of the face of the house, and of the separate place toward the East, an hundreth cubites. **1624** WOTTON *Archit.* in *Reliq. Wotton.* (1672) 17 The Face of the Building is narrow, and the Flank deep. **1664** EVELYN tr. *Freart's Archit.* 132 [The Architrave] is also frequently broken into two or three divisions, call'd by Artists Fascias or rather plain Faces. **1765** CROKER, etc. *Dict. Arts & Sc.*, *Face*, in archit., the front of a building, or the side which contains the chief entrance. *Face of a stone*, in masonry, that superficies of it which lies in the front of the work. **1848** RICKMAN *Goth. Archit.* 20 The cornice of this order, in Greece, consisted of a plain face, under the mutule. **1862** TROLLOPE *Orley F.* i. (ed. 4) 6 The face of the house from one end to the other was covered with vines and passion flowers. **1874** KNIGHT *Dict. Mech.*, *Face* (Carpentry), the front of a jamb presented towards the room. **1876** GWILT *Archit.* Gloss., *Face of a stone*, the face intended for the front or outward side of the work.

13. a. Of anything having two sides: The side usually presented outwards or upwards; the 'front' as opposed to the 'back'; the 'right' side of cloth.

1611 BIBLE *Isa.* xxv. 7 He wil destroy in this mountaine the face of the couering cast ouer all people. **1820** KEATS *Cap & Bells* xxxix. 1 They kiss'd . . the carpet's velvet face. **1831** G. R. PORTER *Silk Manuf.* 237 Diagonal lines . . across the face of the cloth. **1874** BOUTELL *Arms & Arm.* vi. 89 The hollow under the face of the boss was open towards the reverse of the shield. **1876** *Encycl. Brit.* IV. 137 That part of the anther to which the filament is attached and which is generally towards the petals, is the back, the opposite being the face. **1883** SIR E. BECKETT *Clocks, etc.* 146 The face of a wheel which turns in a gear. **1888** C. P. BROOKS *Cotton Manuf.* 127 The face of the card or the side which is in contact with the needles.

b. Of a coin or medal: The obverse; that which bears the effigy; sometimes used for either side. Hence in slang use: A coin (? *obs.*).

c **1515** *Cocke Lorelles B.* (Percy Soc.) 13 Some wente in fured gownes . . That had no mo faces than had the mone. **1588** SHAKS. *L.L.L.* v. ii. 617 The face of an old Roman coine. *a* **1700** B. E. *Dict. Cant. Crew*, *Nare-a-face-but-his-own*, not a Penny in his Pocket. **1725** *New Cant. Dict.* Ne'er-a-face. **1762** *Gentl. Mag.* 22 The . . face of this dye is truly antick. *Ibid.* 23 The face [of a coin] should have a resembling bust of his majesty. **1856** SMYTH *Roman Family Coins* 233 The portrait on the other face of the medal.

c. Of a document: The inscribed side. Hence ***on, upon the face of*** (a document, etc.): in the words of, in the plain sense of. Also ***on the face of it*** (*fig.*): on a merely superficial view, ***prima facie***; obviously, plainly.

1632 LITHGOW *Trav.* VI. 288 Their Great Seale . . locked in vpon the lower face of the Parchment. **1641** BP. HALL *Rem. Wks.* (1660) 80 Every novelty carries suspicion in the face of it. **1719** F. HARE *Ch. Authority Vind.* Pref. 8 The power and authority of the Ministers . . as it appears upon the face of Scripture. **1748** RICHARDSON *Clarissa* Wks. 1883 VIII. 186 An unprejudiced eye, upon the face of the letter, would condemn the writer of it. **1817** W. SELWYN *Law Nisi Prius* (ed. 4) II. 1248 It ought to appear on the face of the plea, that [etc.]. *a* **1832** BENTHAM *Ess. Lang.* Wks. 1843 VIII. 327 Of the history of language, no inconsiderable part remains to this day written upon the face of it. **1882** *Knowledge* II. 70 The whole theory was absurd on the face of it. **1923** 'J. J. CONNINGTON' *Nordenholt's Million* vi. 71 It certainly seemed on the face of it to be a very useless accomplishment. **1960** R. DAVIES *Voice from Attic* ii. 74 There seems, on the face of it, to be little harm in wanting to be solvent and comfortable.

d. Of a playing card: The marked or picture side.

c **1645** HOWELL *Lett.* (1891) I. III. xxxii, The King never shews his game, but throws his cards with their faces down on the table.

e. Of a dial: The surface which bears the hour marks, etc. Of a clock or watch: The dial plate (perh. with allusion to the human face).

[**1751** R. PALTOCK *P. Wilkins* (1884) II. xix. 218 If I ask it [a watch] what time of day it is, I look but in its face, and it tells me presently.] **1787** *Columbian Mag.* I. 329/1 The face of the dial will be parallel with the plane of the equator. **1837** MRS. CARLYLE *Lett.* I. 87 Not watches so much as lockets with watch faces. **1840** BARHAM *Ingol. Leg.*, *Look at the Clock*, 'Grandmother's Clock!' . . nothing was altered at all—but the Face! **1858** O. W. HOLMES *Aut. Breakf.-t.* ix. (1891) 211 He looked at . . the face of the watch,—said it was getting into the afternoon. **1877** MRS. MOLESWORTH *Cuckoo Clock* (1891) 41 Some brilliant moonbeams . . lighted up brightly the face of the clock. **1892** *N.Y. Nation* 23 June 474/3 A volume without an index resembles a clock-face without any hands.

f. Of a book: The front or fore-edge.

1876 *Encycl. Brit.* IV. 43/1 After the face [of a book] has been ploughed the back springs back into its rounded form.

14. Each of the surfaces of a solid. In a regular solid, a crystal, diamond, etc.: Each of the bounding planes.

1625 in Rymer *Fœdera* XVIII. 236 One Aggett cutt with twoe Faces garnished with Dyamonds. **1750** D. JEFFRIES *Treat. Diamonds & Pearls, Expl. Tech. Terms*, *Collet* . . the small horizontal plane, or face, at the bottom of the Brilliant. **1855** BAIN *Senses & Int.* II. ii. §11 A crystal with cut faces. **1863** HUXLEY *Man's Place Nat.* II. 80 The occipital foramen of Mycetes . . is situated completely in the posterior face of the skull. **1873** DAWSON *Dawn of Life* vii. (1875) 188 Crystalline faces occur abundantly in many undoubted fossil woods and corals. **1878** A. H. GREEN *Coal* i. 17 The faces of the block of coal on these sides are smooth and shining. **1884** BOWER & SCOTT *De Bary's Phaner. & Ferns* 177 The lateral faces . . are covered thickly with sieve-plates.

15. a. In implements, tools, etc.: The acting, striking, or working surface. In a molar tooth: The grinding surface. In a knife: The edge.

1703 MOXON *Mech. Exerc.* 4 In Fig. 5. A the Face [of a hammer]. **1791** *Ess. Shooting* (ed. 2) 345 The face of the hammer [of the gun] . . may be too hard or too soft. **1867** SMYTH *Sailor's Word-bk.*, *Face*, the edge of a sharp instrument. **1872** HUXLEY *Phys.* vi. 143 The face of the grinding teeth and the edges of the cutting teeth. **1874** KNIGHT *Dict. Mech.*, *Face* 4 b, the sole of a plane. *Ibid.*, *Face* (Gearing), that part of the acting surface of a cog which projects beyond the pitch line. *Ibid.*, *Face* (Grinding), that portion of a lap or wheel which is employed in grinding, be it the edge or the disk. **1888** *Lockwood's Dict. Terms Mech. Eng.* 133 The face of an anvil is its upper surface.

b. The striking surface of a golf-club, cricket-bat, hockey-stick, or tennis-racket; the inside of the net of a lacrosse-stick.

1881 R. FORGAN *Golfer's Handbk.* 8 The head [of a full-sized Driver] weighs 7 oz. or 8 oz., and is distinguished from those of the 'Spoon' family by its 'face' being straight and almost perpendicular. **1887** W. G. GRACE in G. A. Hutchison *Cricket* v. 49 It is much better to hold the face of the bat towards the umpire—nothing is gained by showing him the edge. **1891** H. G. HUTCHINSON *Hints on Golf* (ed. 6) 15 The maker's name gives you a fine guide to the centre of the face, which is the intended point of impact. **1897** *Encycl. Sport* I. 469/1 (*Golf*) The lofted face enables the player to start the ball straight. *Ibid.* 606/2 (*Lacrosse*) The leading string is then joined to the face of the gut by means of other pieces of gut, and the crosse is complete. *Ibid.* 613/2 (*Lawn tennis*) Avoid lop-sided or small-faced rackets, and see that the grain in the frame runs equally round the face. **1900** H. F. P. BATTERSBY in J. H. C. Fegan et al. *Football, Hockey, & Lacrosse* 85 Sticks are made up with the grain running, broadly speaking, in one of two ways: either parallel to the plane of the face, or at right angles to it. **1909** P. A. VAILE *Mod. Golf* i. 13 It is a mistake in the driver or brassie to have the face too shallow.

16. An even or polished surface.

1881 *Mechanic* §449 Where one piece [of glass] is ground against another to bring them to a face. **1888** *Lockwood's Dict. Terms Mech. Eng.* 133 The face of a casting is that surface which is turned or polished.

IV. Technical uses.

17. *Fortification.* **a.** (see quot. 1727); **b.** (see quot. 1859, and cf. BASTION).

a. 1489 CAXTON *Faytes of A.* II. xiv. 118 A proper place muste be ordeyned atte euery face of the walles for to sette gonnes. **1672** LACEY tr. *Tacquet's Milit. Archit.* iii. 4 The face which is the weakest part of the fortification, is defended by [etc.] **1727** BAILEY, *Face of a Place* is the Front, that is comprehended between the flanked Angles of the two neighbouring Bastions. **1800** WELLINGTON in Gurw. *Disp.* I. 190, I attacked it [Dummul] in three places, at the gateway and on two faces. **1849–50** ALISON *Hist. Europe* VIII. xlix. §24. 27 The efforts . . had been directed against the northern face of the fortress of Seringapatam. **1879** *Cassell's Techn. Educ.* IV. 138/1 The Raponiers . . are situated in the middle of each long face.

b. 1676 *Lond. Gaz.* No. 1119/3 About Noon, a Mine in a Face of the same Hornwork . . took Fire. **1818** JAS. MILL *Brit. India* II. v. v. 478 Having made a breach in one of the bastions [we] destroyed the faces of the two that were adjacent. **1859** F. A. GRIFFITHS *Artil. Man.* (ed. 9) 261 *The faces* of a work are those parts which form a salient angle projecting towards the country.

18. *Mil.* (See quot. 1853.)

1853 STOCQUELER *Mil. Encycl.* 101 The faces of a square are the different sides of a battalion, &c., which, when formed into a square, are all denominated faces; viz., the front face, the right face, the left face, and the rear face. **1885** *Times* (weekly ed.) 23 Jan. 3/1 This face had not quite closed up before it was attacked.

19. *Ordnance.* 'The surface of metal at the muzzle of a gun' (Knight).

1727 BAILEY, *Face* of a Gun is the Superficies of the Metal at the Extremity of the Muzzle. **1867** in SMYTH *Sailor's Word-bk.*

20. *Mining.* **a.** 'In any adit, tunnel, or stope, the end at which work is progressing or was last done' (Raymond *Mining Gloss.*).

1708 J. C. *Compl. Collier* (1845) 46 They frequently hole, or cut through from one Board to another, to carry their Air . . to the end or Face of their Boards. **1867** W. W. SMYTH *Coal & Coal Mining* 131 Supporting the roof at the immediate 'face' by temporary props. **1888** F. HUME *Mad. Midas* I. v, They . . visited several other faces of wash . . Each face had a man working at it, sometimes two.

b. 'The principal cleaving-plane at right angles to the stratification. (***driving***) ***on the face***: against or at right angles with the face' (Raymond *Mining Gloss.*). ***face on***: (see quot. 1883).

1867 W. W. SMYTH *Coal & Coal-mining* 25 Faces, running most regularly parallel. **1878** HUXLEY *Physiogr.* 238 The direction along which these joints run is often known as the face of the coal. **1883** W. S. GRESLEY *Gloss. Terms Coal-mining* 99 *Face on* . . working a mine parallel to the cleat or face.

21. *Steam-engine.* The flat part of a slide-valve; also, the corresponding flat part on a cylinder, on which the slide-valve travels.

1838 WOOD *Railr.* 346 The slide would be moved to the extremity of the face of the cylinder. **1874** in KNIGHT *Dict. Mech.*

22. *Typog.* That part of a type (or punch) which has the form of the letter. Also, The printing surface of type. *face of the page*: (see quot.). ***heavy face (numerals or type)***: having a broader outline, and printing thicker than the ordinary. ***old face (type)***: a form of Roman letter (characterized by oblique ceriphs and various other features) revived by Whittingham in 1844, and since very extensively used. See also FULL-FACE 2.

1683 MOXON *Mech. Exercises* II. 201 So placed the Face of the Letter runs less hazzard of receiving dammage. **1699** A. BOYER *Eng. & Fr. Dict.* s.v., A letter that has a good face (among printers), *un caractère qui a un bel œil.* **1787** *Printer's Gram.* 41 Kerned Letters are such as have part of their Face hang over. **1824** J. JOHNSON *Typogr.* II. 21 Short letters are all such as have their face cast on the middle of their square metal. **1853** *Caxton & Art of Printing* vii. 155 One of the heap which lies in the right position, both as regards the face being upwards, and the nick being outwards. **1871** *Amer. Encycl. Printing* 167/2 *Face of the page*, the upper side of the page, from which the impression is taken. **1875** URE *Dict. Arts* III. 1049 In this metal the face of the letter intended to be cast is sunk. **1891** J. WINSOR *C. Columbus* xxi. 524 The heavy face numerals show the successive holders of the honors of Columbus.

†23. *Card-playing.* = *face-card*: (see 27). *Obs.*

1674 COTTON *Compl. Gamester* in Singer *Hist. Cards* 347 If you have neither ace nor face, you may throw up your game.

24. *Tea trade.* (See quot.) Cf. FACE *v.* 15.

1886 *Chambers' Encycl.* IX. 323 Prussian blue..native indigo and gypsum are the real materials employed for giving the 'face' as it is called.

†25. *a face of fur*: ? a set of furs. Cf. FACE *v.* 12.

1562 HEYWOOD *Epigrams* I. lv, Cheepening of a face of furre. Into a skinners shop..in hast ran a gentilman there to espie A fayre face of fur, which he woulde haue bought.

V. *attrib.* and *Comb.*

26. General relations: **a.** attributive (sense 1), as ***face-bleach, -cosmetic, -glove, -hair, -mask, -massage, -paint, -powder, -screen, -sponge, -tissue, -towel, -veil, -wash***; (sense 12 b), as ***face-mortar, -work***; (sense 13 a), as ***face-side***; (sense 20), as ***face-line***. **b.** objective (sense 1), as ***face-levelling, -mending, -tearing*** vbl. sbs.; ***face-wringing***, ppl. a.; ***face-mender, -moulder***; (sense 6 b), as ***face-maker, face-pulling*** ppl. a. and vbl. sb.; (sense 3), as ***face-affecting*** ppl. a. **c.** locative (sense 1), as ***face-hot*** adj., ***-joy, -spot***; (sense 5), as ***face-flatterer***. **d.** instrumental, as ***face-forward, -down, -up*** (all adj. and adv.). **e.** similative, as ***face-high*** adj. and adv.

1675 COCKER *Morals* 24 *Face-affecting Lasses, Neglect their Graces, to attend their Glasses. **1907** *Daily News* 3 Sept. 2/7 A *face-bleach for removing all discolorations from the skin. **1887** CORELLI *Thelma* II. 207 Beauties.. deprived of elegant attire and *face-cosmetics. **1935** E. BOWEN *House in Paris* I. v. 75 Leopold..stared at the *face-down cards. **1962** *Gloss. Terms Automatic Data Processing* (*B.S.I.*) 90 Various terms are used to indicate the attitude in which a card is placed in the hopper... Face-up feed and face-down feed. **1859** TENNYSON *Idylls, Vivien* 822 *Face-flatterers and backbiters. **1907** *Westm. Gaz.* 11 Nov. 6/3 Accommodation for..two on large '*face-forward' seats. **1938** R. GRAVES *Coll. Poems* 152 Leaping face-forward from their high roofs. **1924** W. DEEPING *Three Rooms* ii. 11 She was..using the *face-glove with angry vigour. **1927** PEAKE & FLEURE *Peasants & Potters* ix. 122 Scanty *face-hair save for a chin tuft in the male. **1905** *Westm. Gaz.* 15 June 7/1 The ball went, *face-high, just within reach of Gregory. **1654** GAYTON *Pleas. Notes* II. iv. 49 Who, (but one that will carry no coales) would have rewarded a friend thus for his opinion, only in *Face-hot presses. **1850** MRS. BROWNING *Poems* II. 336 In your bitter world..*Face-joy's a costly mask to wear. **1650** BULWER *Anthropomet.* Pref., Crosse to that *Face-levelling designe, Thy high-rais'd Nose appeareth Aquiline. **1883** W. S. GRESLEY *Gloss. Terms Coal-mining* 99 Keep the *face line of the stall neither fully face on nor end on. **1756** COWPER in *Connoisseur* No. 138 Those buffoons in society, the Attitudinarians and *Face-makers. **1808** WOLCOTT (P. Pindar) *One more Peep at R.A.* Wks. 1812 V. 367 Forced to beg her humble bread While every face-maker can feast. **1906** *Westm. Gaz.* 26 Mar. 2/3 It is unnecessary for the operator [of oxygen-supplying apparatus] to wear any helmet or *face-mask. **1936** *Discovery* July 206/2 A liquid compound of ether..given.. from a face mask through a drop bottle. **1896** 'IOTA' *Quaker Grandmother* xxii. 259 She..would have her usual *face massage done then. **1900** *Daily News* 31 May 7/4 Departments for manicure, pedicure, and face-massage. **1745** E. HEYWOOD *Female Spectator* (1748) III. 156 Have they not their..barbers, aye, and their *facemenders too? *Ibid.* 234 Those..*facemending stratagems. **1793** SMEATON *Edystone L.* §222 The best *face mortar. **1650** BULWER *Anthropomet.* Pref., *Face-moulders who affect the grace Of a square, plain, or a smooth platter-face. **1915** *Illustr. Lond. News* 23 Jan. 120/1 Egyptian women..used..malachite, as the ingredient of a *face-paint. **1858** *Illustr. News of World* 17 Apr. 175/4 Saunders's *Face Powder..beautifies the complexion. **1879** *Chemist & Druggist* XXI. 481/1, 60 grammes of..Face Powder—a mixture of talc with a small proportion of white magnesia, coloured faintly red with cochineal. **1920** *Punch* 15 Sept. 219/1 A lady with a Russian name, no back to her gown and green face-powder. **1898** *Westm. Gaz.* 23 June 3/2 His *face-pulling man whose countenance is as clay in the hands of a sculptor. **1906** *Ibid.* 7 Sept. 3/2 By dint of much face-pulling I managed to persuade my poor muscles to put me in an upright position. **1941** KOESTLER *Scum of Earth* xiii. 134 He had performed his task, especially the face-pulling, with so much success that he eventually became second clown. **1818** KEATS *Let.* 16 Dec. (1958) II. 6, I brought from her a present of *facescreens. **1890** W. J. GORDON *Foundry* 155 The men around in face-screens and leg-guards. *c* **1790** IMISON *Sch. Art* II. 7 Prepare some..size, with which you must brush over the *face side [of a print]. **1885** LADY BRASSEY *The Trades* 311 The black bodies..made them look anything but suitable for use as *face-sponges. **1685** COOKE *Marrow Chirurg.* (ed. 4) VII. i. 270 Pimpernel cleanseth *Face-Spots. **1937** *Woman's Fair* Oct. 50/3 Try creaming it [*sc.* your face] a second time and see if the second *face-tissue comes off clean. **1951** E. TAYLOR *Game of Hide-and-Seek* I. iii. 57 Harriet..dropped screwed-up face-tissues on the floor. **1922** S. LEWIS *Babbitt* i. 6 His own *face-towel. **1925** R. A. KNOX *Viaduct Murder* vi. 59 The face-towel was distinctly mentioned in the washing-list. **1926** A. CHRISTIE *Murder of R. Ackroyd* x. 127 He wouldn't even buy new face towels, though I told him the old ones were in holes. **1962** *Face-up [see *face-down*, above]. **1930** A. CLARKE *Coll. Plays* (1963) 67 They wear the *face-veil. **1870** R. TOMES *Bazar Bk. Decorum* 29 Now we advise them to overturn into the fire all their *face-washes..and to betake themselves to soap. **1907** *Daily News* 3 Sept. 2/7 A face-wash for improving the complexion. **1911** E. FERBER *Dawn O'Hara* iii. 34 A motherly hug..enveloped me in an atmosphere of liquid face-wash, strong perfumery and fried lard. **1793** SMEATON *Edystone L.* §213 The *face work of the subordinate parts. *a* **1613** OVERBURY *Charac., Hypocrite*, A *face-wringing ballet-singer.

27. Special comb.: **face-ache**, (*a*) pain in the nerves of the face; (*b*) a mournful-looking person (also as a term of address) *slang*; **face-ague**, an acute form of face-ache, tic douloureux; **face-airing** *vbl. sb.* (*Mining*), see quot.; **face-bedded** *ppl. a.*, (a stone) placed so that the grain runs along the face; **face-bone** = CHEEK-BONE; **face bow** *Dentistry*, a calliper-like frame with adjustable attachments that is fixed round the front and sides of the head in order to take measurements of the mouth and jaws prior to making a denture; †**face-bread**, Heb. *'leḥem happānīm* = SHOW-BREAD; †**face-breadth**, extent of the face (sense 1) from side to side; **face-brick** *U.S.*, a special brick used for facing buildings, etc.; a facing-brick; also, face-work of brick; **face-card**, a playing-card bearing a face (of a king, queen, or knave) = COAT CARD; **face-centred** *a. Cryst.*, applied to a space lattice in which the lattice-points occur at the centres of the faces and the corners of unit cells; hence also to a crystal, substance, etc., having a structure based on such a lattice; **face-chuck** (*Mech.*) = *face-plate*; **face-cloth**, (*a*) 'a cloth for protecting the face of a baby'; a cloth laid over the face of a corpse; (*b*) a woollen cloth with a smooth napped surface; (*c*) a cloth for washing the face; **face-cog** (*Mech.*), one of the cogs or teeth on the 'face' of a wheel; **face cream**, a cream for the complexion; cold cream; **face cut** *Forestry* (see quot. 1957); **face-cutting** *ppl. a.*, making a plane surface; **face decoration**, decoration (of pottery) with a face or faces; so ***face-decorated*** adj.; **face flannel** = *face-cloth* (*c*), FLANNEL *sb.* 1 e; **face-fungus** *colloq.*, the hairy growth on a man's face, esp. a beard; **face-glass**, the glass window of a diver's helmet; **face-guard**, a contrivance for protecting the face, *esp.* in some industrial processes, fencing, etc.; **face-hammer** (see quots.); **face-harden** *v. trans.*, to harden the surface of (metal) by case-hardening, chill casting, or other process; so **face-hardened** *ppl. a.*, (in quot.) hard-faced; **face-joint** (see quot.); **face-knocker**, one in which the fixed portion has the form of a human face; **face-lathe** (see quots.); **face-lifting** *vbl. sb.*, a method of restoring a more youthful appearance by a surgical operation in which the skin is tightened and the wrinkles smoothed out; also *fig.* and *transf.*, e.g. the refacing of a building; hence (as a back-formation) **face-lift** *v. trans.*; also **face-lift** *sb.*, the operation of face-lifting (*lit.* and *fig.*); so **face-lifter**; **face-line**, (*a*) the alignment of the face of a structure, etc.: (*b*) *pl.* the lines or wrinkles of the face; **face-making** *vbl. sb.*, (*a*) portrait-painting; (*b*) *Obs. slang*, the begetting of children; (*c*) the pulling of faces; **face-man**, a miner who works at the face; **face-mould** (see quots.); **face-pack**, a preparation beneficial to the complexion, spread over the face and removed when dry; **face-painter**, (*a*) a painter of portraits, (*b*) one who applies paint to the face; **face-painting** *vbl. sb.*, portrait-painting; **face-physic**, *collect.* appliances for the face; **face-piece**, (*a*) (*Naut.*), see quot.; (*b*) = *face-glass*; (*c*) a mask covering nose and mouth (as used in anæsthetics) or nose and eyes (as used in diving); (*d*) a decorative appendage on a horse's bridle; **face-plan** (see quot.); **face-plate**, (*a*) (*Mech.*), an enlargement of the end of the mandrel (of a lathe) to which work may be attached for the purpose of being 'faced' or made flat; also *attrib.*, as in ***face-plate coupling***; (*b*) a plate protecting some piece of machinery; (*c*) the area corresponding to the visor in protective head-gear (of a diving- or space-suit); **face-play**, facial movement in acting, etc.; †**face-playing** *vbl. sb.*, the exhibition of feeling or sentiment by the play of the countenance; **face-presentation** (*Midwifery*), presentation face foremost in birth; **face-saver**, something that 'saves one's face' (see sense 10 b above); also **face-saving** *ppl. a.* and *vbl. sb.*; **face-shaft** (*Arch.*), see quot.; **face-stone** (*Arch.*) the slab of stone forming the face or front, esp. in a cornice, an entablature, etc.; **face-symbol** *Cryst.*, the symbol designating the face or plane of a crystal; **face-turning-lathe** = *face-lathe*; **face-urn**, an urn decorated with a face or faces; **face-value**, the amount stated on the face (of a note, postage-stamp, etc.), the apparent or nominal value; also *fig.*; **face-wall** (*Building*), front wall; **face-wheel** (*Mech.*) = *contrate-wheel* (see CONTRATE 2); also 'a wheel whose disk-face is adapted for grinding and polishing' (Knight); †**face-wind**, a wind blowing against one's face; **face-work**, the exterior of masonry, the material forming the outside of a wall or the like; **face-worker** = *face-man*.

1808 JANE AUSTEN *Let.* 26 June (1952) 203 Henry sends us the welcome information of his having had no *face-ache since I left them. **1865** DICKENS *Mut. Fr.* I. v, It gave you the face-ache to look at his apples. **1869** *Eng. Mech.* 12 Nov. 211/1 Faceache I believe to be..inflammation of the nerves. **1937** PARTRIDGE *Slang Dict.* 261/2 *Face-ache*, a C.20 jocular term of address. **1961** SIMPSON & GALTON *Hancock* 35/2 On a train..a carriageful of the most miserable-looking bunch of face-aches. **1883** W. S. GRESLEY *Gloss. Terms Coal-mining* 99 *Face airing, that system of ventilating the workings which excludes the airing of the goaves. **1863** *Archæol. Cantiana* V. 14 Jambs two feet eight inches apart, *face-bedded. **1883** *Stonemason* Jan., It is rare now for a face-bedded stone to be fixed in a building. **1801** SOUTHEY *Thalaba* VIII. ii, His cheeks were fallen in, His *face-bones prominent. **1922** JOYCE *Ulysses* 44 Raw facebones under his peep of day boy's hat. **1940** J. OSBORNE *Dental Mechanics* vi. 53 A *face bow is also used to register accurately the relationship between the upper jaw and the condyle. *a* **1656** BP. HALL *Rem. Wks.* (1660) 238 The matter and form of the ..Tables of the *Face-bread. **1651** J. F[REAKE] *Agrippa's Occ. Philos.* 271 Nine *face-bredths make a square well set man. **1807** *Independent Chron.* (Boston, Mass.) 21 Sept. 3/2 The Subscriber has been at considerable expense for several years past in the improvement of *Face Bricks..superior to the Philadelphia Bricks. **1878** *Congress. Rec.* 25 Jan. 548/1 In consequence of the limit placed upon the cost of the building, it was found necessary to adopt face-brick. **1901** R. STURGIS *Dict. Archit.* s.v. *Brick, Face Brick*, one of a superior quality used for the face of a wall. **1826** J. WILSON *Noct. Ambr.* Wks. (1855) 303 Desperate bad hauns..a haun without a *face-caird. **1888** *Sheffield Gloss.* (E.D.S.), *Face-card*, a court card. **1913** *Proc. R. Soc.* A. LXXXIX. 257 The assumption of diffraction by the *face-centred space lattice does not completely account for the pattern. **1921** *Physical Rev.* XVII. 587 Indium was found to consist of a face-centered tetragonal lattice of atoms. **1959** *Jrnl. Iron & Steel Inst.* CXCIII. 325/2 For face-centred cubic metals, notch ductility was found to be a linear function of the strain-hardening exponent. **1967** A. H. COTTRELL *Introd. Metall.* xiii. 158 There are two fully close-packed crystal structures, known as face-centred cubic (F.C.C.) and close-packed hexagonal (C.P. Hex.). **1888** *Lockwood's Dict. Terms Mech. Eng.* 133 *Face chuck, a face plate. **1602** *Accounts of Lord High Treasurer of Scotland* 97 (D.O.S.T.), Ane ribbenit *face claithe. **1685** *Inventory* in *Proc. Soc. Ant. Scotland* (1924) LVIII. 359 A parchment box wherein is 3 flanan face cloaths. **1748** RICHARDSON *Clarissa* xliv. VIII. 166 She.. seeing the coffin, withdrew her hand from mine and.. removed the *face-cloth. **1859** TENNYSON *Idylls, Guinevere* 7 The white mist, like a face-cloth to the face, Clung to the dead earth. **1898** *Westm. Gaz.* 29 Sept. 3/2 Dark plaid skirts and face-cloth coats. **1928** *Daily Express* 27 Dec. 5/2 Smooth face cloth and fox. **1930** *Chemist & Druggist* CXII. 663/1 A novelty in the way of face cloths. **1951** J. FRAME *Lagoon* 33 She would buy Nurse Harper a cake of soap and a face-cloth wrapped in cellophane. **1953** A. W. FIELDING *Stronghold* I. v. 81 Baggy breeches of royal blue face-cloth. **1968** J. IRONSIDE *Fashion Alphabet* 227 *Face-cloth.* This is a term loosely used for a face-finished, sleek, glossy, luxurious looking woollen cloth. **1833** HOLLAND *Manuf. Metal* II. 61 An axil which carries likewise another [wheel] with *face-cogs. **1906** E. ARIA *Costume* i. 1 Queen Victoria Eugénie, whose name has been snatched to honour a *face-cream. **1913** E. WHARTON *Custom of Country* III. xxi. 315 The little boy was encouraged to scatter the grimy carpet with face-creams and bunches of clippings. **1935** A. CHRISTIE *Death in Clouds* xix. 182 Jars of face cream. **1874** W. M. BAINES *Narr. E. Crewe* viii. 180 After taking off a '*face cut'. **1950** H. WILSON *My First 80 Yrs.* vii. 105 So far we had asked for 'face-cuts', the first slices off the logs with the bark adhering. **1957** *Brit. Commonw. Forest Terminol.* II. 69 *Face cut*, the waney..or thin piece of timber removed when a straight face is cut along a log or flitch on a sawbench. **1963** C. R. COWELL et al. *Inlays, Crowns & Bridges* ix. 99 The undercut formed by the bulge of the cingulum is removed, using a face-cutting inverted cone or tapered fissure diamond. **1928** PEAKE & FLEURE *Steppe & Sown* 97 Its curious pottery with face decorations reminds us of the *face-decorated handles of pots from Cemetery A at Kish in Mesopotamia. **1939** 'J. STRUTHER' *Mrs. Miniver* 47 All the accumulations on the debit side of parenthood:..the plasticine on the door-handles, the *face-flannels in the bathroom, [etc.]. **1961** A. WILSON *Old Men at Zoo* ii. 101 Scrambled eggs should be

scrambled, not cooked like a face flannel. **1907** F. Richardson *Bunkum* 316 He [*sc.* Juan de Castro] offered to pledge one of his whiskers.. He had grossly overcapitalised his *face-fungus. **1959** *Listener* 22 Jan. 183/2 Svengali..with his face-fungus and rolling eyes. **1896** *Strand Mag.* XII. 356/1 It is useless to butt the *face-glass or wildly knock your head against the inside of the helmet. *a* **1941** R. Bedford in *Austral. Short Stories* (1951) 98 The tender screwed the face-glass into the helmet. **1874** Knight *Dict. Mech.*, **Face-guard*, a mask with windows for the eyes. **1883** J. W. Mollett *Dict. Art & Archæol.* 134 *Face guard* on a helmet, a bar or bars of iron protecting the face. **1874** Knight *Dict. Mech.*, **Face-hammer*, one with a flat face. **1884** *Ibid.* IV. 324/1 *Face Hammer* (Masonry), one with one blunt and one cutting end. **1874** *Porcupine* 21 Feb. 742/3 They were seen to join in the revelry and devilry as drunkenly as the most face-hardened of their companions. **1896** *Westm. Gaz.* 28 Feb. 6/3 All thick armour is face-hardened on the Harvey principle. **1874** Knight *Dict. Mech.*, **Face-joint*, that joint of a voussoir which appears on the face of the arch. **1769** *Public Advertiser* 18 May 3/4 Iron *Face Knockers. **1884** Knight *Dict. Mech.*, **Face-lathe*, (*a*) a pattern-maker's lathe for turning bosses, core prints, and other face-work; (*b*) a lathe with a large face-plate and a slide rest adjustable in front on its own shears. Transverse usually but not necessarily. **1888** *Lockwood's Dict. Terms Mech. Eng.*, *Face lathe*, a lathe chiefly or exclusively used for surfacing. **1934** R. Macaulay *Going Abroad* xxvii. 226 What I needed..was a *face-lift... I should have a new, young, tight face. **1939** *Times* 28 Mar. 9/5 Many solidly built Victorian houses..which it should be possible to 'face lift'. **1957** *Times* 20 June 11/5 The restorers who will be face-lifting the exteriors of these historical buildings. **1957** *Times Lit. Suppl.* 11 Oct. 609/2 A special fund for preventing theatres and concert halls from becoming shabby and unattractive, or for giving them a face-lift when they are. **1942** N. Marsh *Death & Dancing Footman* i. 25 What's he like, this *face-lifter? **1952** *Time* 30 June 28 (Advt.), That's not a '*face-lift'. That's Forerunner Styling—the years-ahead design that makes other 'new' cars seem out of date. **1956** *Sunday Times* 8 Jan. 7/7 Buyers abroad complain that our manufacturers seem content merely to give their cars a face-lift instead of tackling fundamental features. **1971** *Daily Tel.* 1 Feb. 3 Rail travellers are demanding a facelift for scruffy stations with their peeling paint..and squalid lavatories. **1922** F. Courtenay *Physical Beauty* ix. 57 The 'face-raising' or '*face-lifting' process which does away with wrinkles, mouth and eyelines and sagging cheeks by literally 'lifting' off part of the old face and replacing it. **1928** *Sunday Dispatch* 16 Dec. 9/4 A youthful appearance is considered an advantage, and face-lifting is a common thing among men. **1883** Face-line [see face *sb.* 26]. **1906** *Daily Chron.* 13 July 3/3 They are the real Rembrandt. There is a deep furrow in the brow; the face-lines are bitten as by acid. **1909** *Westm. Gaz.* 6 Mar. 16/1 The work of erecting the new intermediate ribs between the old bridge and the new face-line is now in progress on all the spans. **1963** *Gloss. Mining Terms* (*B.S.I.*) I. 10 *Subsidiary survey*, an underground survey made to determine the position of a face line or goaf line or some other specific feature. **1623** Webster *Duchess of Malfi* iii. ii, 'Twould disgrace His *face-making, and undo him. **1785** Grose *Dict. Vulgar T.* I. 2 *Face making*, begetting children. **1799** Jane Austen *Let.* 8 Jan. (1952) 51 My sweet little George! I am delighted to hear that he has such an inventive genius as to face-making. **1827** P. Egan *Anecdotes of Turf* 177 If ever she committed any more sins in the *face-making* line—quod,..should be her portion. **1921** *Glasgow Herald* 21 Apr. 5 The effect of the new offer on the wages of '*face-men'. **1823** P. Nicholson *Pract. Build.* 222 *Face-mould, a mould for drawing the proper figure of a hand-rail on both sides of the plank. **1876** in Gwilt *Archit.* Gloss. **1926** *Amer. Mercury* Feb. 168 The profits of the beauty shop are dependent mainly upon the sale of..*face packs and similar preparations. **1944** M. Laski *Love on Supertax* x. 97 Women leaping from drying machines..and one from a face-pack. **1960** *Woman's Own* 19 Mar. 25/2 Face-packs twice a week improve the texture and..brighten the skin. **1697** *Dryden's Virgil* Life (1709) 16 (Jod.) Ill *facepainters, not being able to hit the true features..make amends by a great deal of impertinent land-scape and drapery. **1847** L. Hunt *Men, Women, & B.* I. xiv. 276 The highest face-painters are not the loveliest women. **1852** S. R. Maitland *Ess.* 107 *note*, 'He took me for a face-painter!' said a late eminent artist. **1706** *Art of Painting* (1744) 355 He was..a landskip-painter ..till he..fell to *face-painting. **1862** W. M. Rossetti in *Fraser's Mag.* July 73 Whose picture..shows a higher character of face-painting. **1611** Donne *Ignatius' Conclave* (1652) 129 Women tempting by Paintings and *Face-Physick. *a* **1613** Overbury *Charac.*, *Faire Milkmayd*, One looke of hers is able to put all face-physicke out of countenance. *c* **1850** *Rudim. Navig.* (Weale) 117 *Face-piece, a piece of elm, generally tabled on to the fore-part of the knee of the head, to assist the conversion of the main piece, and likewise to shorten the upper bolts, and prevent the cables from rubbing against them as the knee gets worn. **1908** *Westm. Gaz.* 21 Sept. 5/3 A big round-topped helmet that contains a small glass face-piece through which the wearer can see. **1955** J. Sweeney *Skin Diving* vii. 90 The only area of unequal pressure that can occur in a swimmer's equipment is that of his face-piece or sea mask. **1960** H. Hayward *Antique Coll.* 113/2 Face-piece horse brass. **1961** *Lancet* 22 July 214/1 Immediately after the shock the face-piece was reapplied. **1874** Knight *Dict. Mech.*, **Face-plan*, the principal or front elevation. **1841** Tredgold *Mill-work* 428 The *face-plate has four adjusting screws for securing the work. **1874** Knight *Dict. Mech. a* **1884** Knight *Dict. Mech.* Suppl. 324/1 *Face-plate*, a covering plate for an object to receive wear or shock. **1888** *Lockwood's Dict. Terms Mech. Eng.*, The term face plate is more commonly applied in the shops to the ordinary face chucks. *Ibid.*, *Face-plate coupling* = Flanged coupling. **1962** S. Carpenter in *Into Orbit* 75 We had to open up the faceplate on our helmets and squirt the food into our mouths. **1966** 'L. Holton' *Out of Depths* xvi. 158 He put the faceplate over his nose and eyes and the regulator in his mouth and took a suck of the air. **1970** F. McKenna *Gloss. Railwaymen's Talk* p. x, If you faced the fire-box you were subjected to radiant heat from the fire-box and the faceplate fittings. **1908** T. Hardy *Sel. Poems W. Barnes* p. viii, Each word of theirs [*sc.* of husbandmen] is accompanied by the qualifying *face-play which no construing can express. **1958** *Listener* 5 June 953/2 Neither text nor production was helpful: everything was bustled along with voices too loud and face-play too obvious. **1789** Burney *Hist. Mus.* IV. 319 She perfectly possessed that flexibility of muscles and features, which constitutes *face-playing. **1841** Rigby *Midwifery* iii. iii. 130 The opinion that *face-presentations were preternatural. **1941** E. Snow *Scorched Earth* ii. 19 As a *face-saver, however, Doihara was given enough support, from the Kwantung Army in Manchuria [etc.]. **1959** *Times* 4 May 3/1 An equalizer in the dying seconds and yet another face-saver in the extra time. **1922** A. Bennett *Lilian* i. iii. 19 She had been trapped beyond any chance of a *face-saving lie. **1931** *Economist* 4 Apr. 716/1 After all, 'face-saving' is common form in the politics of every country. **1957** *Observer* 10 Nov. 1/5 This satellite launching is an isolated face-saving move in a sense. **1849** *Ecclesiologist* IX. 345 The double semi-cylindrical *face-shafts, formerly running up the face of the piers. **1853** Ruskin *Stones Ven.* III. App. x. 238 The *face-stone and often the soffit, are sculptured. *Ibid.* III. 238 Arches decorated only with coloured marble, the facestone being coloured, the soffit white. **1899** W. J. Lewis *Treat. Crystallogr.* iv. 27 (*heading*) *Face symbol. **1903** *Athenæum* 17 Jan. 86/3 How to convert the face-symbols of Naumann into those of Miller. **1944** C. Palache et al. *Dana's Syst. Min.* (ed. 7) I. 36 Any face symbol (*hkl*) in the old orientation may be transformed to the new equivalent (*h'k'l'*). **1959** C. S. Hurlbut *Dana's Man. Min.* (ed. 17) ii. 32 The zone symbols are inclosed in brackets, as [*uvw*], to distinguish them from face and form symbols. **1841** Tredgold *Mill-work* 428 *Face-turning lathe. **1927** Peake & Fleure *Priests & Kings* 147 The *face-urns..do not seem to belong to the invading people who founded Hissarlik II. **1957** V. G. Childe *Dawn Europ. Civilization* (ed. 6) iii. 43 Anthropomorphic lids and jars ('face-urns'). **1878** F. A. Walker *Money* xx. 461 Some English Merchant who is bound to pay money in the United States for more than the *face-value of his claim. **1883** J. L. Whitney in *Lit. World* 8 Sept. 293/1 He must take the advertisements of publishers at their face value, and regard them as what they claim to be. **1888** *Daily News* 13 July 3/3 If postcards were sold at the face value of the stamps upon them. **1891** *Law Times* XCI. 224/1 The note is still worth its face value. **1874** Knight *Dict. Mech.*, **Face-wall*. **1833** J. Holland *Manuf. Metal* II. 191 The axle is turned round by a *face or crown wheel fixed upon the extremity of it. **1879** Cassell's *Techn. Educ.* I. 349/2 Face-wheels have their cogs or pins placed perpendicularly to the face of the wheel. *a* **1722** Lisle *Husb.* (1757) 113 A *face or back-wind signifies little. **1838** *Civil Eng. & Arch. Jrnl.* I. 330/1 What is called Flemish bond consists in the disposition of the bricks on the outside, or *face work. **1909** *Daily Chron.* 5 Aug. 1/3 The face-work of the old parapet having been re-erected. **1926** *Rep. R. Comm. Coal Ind.* 118 in *Parl. Papers* (Cmd. 2600) XIV, Persons working at the face..'*face' workers. In 1905 there were 58 face workers to 42 off-hand workers. **1957** *Economist* 23 Nov. 706/2 There are as many faceworkers in the mines as there were then.

28. With adverbs forming combs. expressing the action of the corresponding verbal combinations, as **face-off** (see sense 4 e above), **face-up**, a facing-up.

1936 *Discovery* Oct. 330/1 Here, at last, is a face-up to the relations between science and society.

face (feɪs), *v.* [f. prec. sb.]

I. To show a bold or opposing front.

†**1. a.** *intr.* To show a bold face, look big; to brag, boast, swagger. Phrase, *to face and brace*: (see brace *v.*[2]). *Obs.*

c **1440** *Promp. Parv.* 145 Facyn, or shewyn boolde face. **1509** Barclay *Shyp of Folys* 22 A fals extorcyoner Fasynge and bostynge to scratche and to kepe. **1601** Yarington *Two Lament. Traj.* iii. ii. in Bullen *O. Pl.* IV, Wilt thou..Face and make semblance..Of that thou never meanst to execute?

†**b.** In primero. (Cf. bluff, brag.) *Obs.*

1594 Carew *Huarte's Exam. Wits* viii. 112 To play well at Primero, and to face and vie, and to hold and giue ouer when time serueth..are all workes of the imagination.

†**c.** To show a false face, maintain a false appearance. *Obs.*

1570 Ascham *Scholem.* i. (Arb.) 54 To laughe, to lie, to flatter, to face: Foure waies in Court to win men grace. **1589** *Hay any Work* 39 Thou canst cog, face and lye, as fast as a dog can trot. **1591** Shaks. *1 Hen. VI*, v. iii. 142 Suffolke doth not flatter, face, or faine.

†**d.** To have a (specified) appearance. *Obs.*

1669 N. Morton *New Eng. Mem.* 106 The evil consequences thereof faced very sadly.

†**2.** *trans.* **a.** To confront with assurance or impudence; to brave, to bully. **b.** *to face a lie* (*upon*), to tell a manifest untruth (to). *Obs.*

1465 *Paston Lett.* No. 512 II. 205 My Lord of Suffolks men come..and face us and fray uppon us, this dayly. **1530** Palsgr. 542/2 Yet he wolde face me with a lye. **1533** More *Answ. Poysoned Bk.* Wks. 1131/2 He..faceth himself the lie upon me. *c* **1540** Heywood *Four P.P.* in Hazl. *Dodsley* I. 382 But his boldness hath faced a lie. **1548** Hall *Chron.* 59 b, The straunger so faced the Englisheman, that he faynted in hys sute. **1625** Bacon *Ess.*, *Truth* (Arb.) 501 For a Lie faces God, and shrinkes from Man. **1632** Massinger *Emperor of the East* v. i, I have built no palaces to face the court.

3. With advbs. **a.** *to face down, out*: to put down (a person) with effrontery, to browbeat; to controvert (an objection, the truth) with coolness or impudence; to maintain (a statement) impudently. Also with sentence as obj.: to maintain or insist to a person's face that [etc.]. *to face out of countenance*: to confront and disconcert (cf. countenance *sb.* 6 b); *to face up*: *intr.* to show a bold face; with *to*, to oppose (a person), confront (a problem, etc.). (See also quot. 1954 for use in *Boxing*.) **b.** *to face out* (a matter, etc.): to carry through by effrontery, brazen out. † *to face it out with a card of ten*: see 1 b and card *sb.*[2] 2 a. **c.** † *to face out of*: to exclude shamelessly from; also, to bully out of.

a. 1530 Palsgr. 542/2, I face one downe in a mater. **1533** More *Answ. Poysoned Bk.* Wks. 1131/2 He..scoffeth that I face out the trouth with lyes. **1580** Lupton *Sivqila* in *Polimanteia* (1881) p. xvii, And so faced out thy poore Father before our face. **1590** Shaks. *Com. Err.* iii. i. 6 Here's a villaine that would face me downe He met me on the Mart. **1667** Dryden *Sir Martin* iv. i, I'll not be faced down with a lie. **1787** Wesley in Wks. 1872 IV. 401 The clerk faced me down I had taken the coach for Sunday. **1860** Froude *Hist. Eng.* VI. 100 With Paget's help she faced down these objections.

1854 *Punch* 27 May 222/1 Is he to be faced out of countenance by a young whipper-snapper? **1920** W. Raleigh *Let.* 4 Sept. (1928) II. 519 He faced up to the paradox of man. **1925** M. A. Lowndes *Some Men & Women* 155 She was a woman who always faced up to the realities of life. **1935** *Punch* 4 Sept. 260/2 It was our duty as guardians of the children to face up to the situation. **1939** [see appease *v.* 2 c]. **1954** F. C. Avis *Boxing Ref. Dict.*, *Face up*, to square up in the approved way to an opponent. **1958** *Times* 8 Sept. 9/4 No longer does a man face a problem; he faces up to it.

b. 1543 Bale *Yet a Course* 59 Now, face out your matter with a carde of tenne. **1553** T. Wilson *Rhet.* (1580) 202 The Roscians kinsfolke have boldly adventured, and will face out their doynges. **1579** G. Harvey *Letter-bk.* (Camden) 73 To ..face it oute lustelye as sum other good fellowes doe. *a* **1619** Fotherby *Atheom.* i. xii. §2 (1622) 125 Obluctation, and facing out of the matter. **1630** B. Jonson *New Inn* i. iii, Cards of ten, to face it Out in the game. **1876** Trevelyan *Macaulay* (1876) I. i. 15 Unless they could make up their minds..to face it out.

c. *c* **1530** More *Answ. Frith* iv. Wks. 1132/2 Your false heresy, wherwith you would face our Sauiour out of the blessed sacrament. **1601** Shaks. *Twel. N.* iv. ii. 101 They .. doe all they can to face me out of my wits. *Ibid.* v. i. 91 His false cunning..Taught him to face me out of his acquaintance.

4. a. *trans.* To meet (danger, an enemy, or anything unpleasant) face to face; to meet in front, oppose with confidence or defiance. *to face the music*: see music *sb.* 11.

c **1659** B. Harris *Parival's Iron Age* 79 A great body of Nobility march..briskly on, to face that potent Emperour Osman. *a* **1680** Butler *Rem.* (1759) VIII. 7 These silly ranting Privolvans..face their Neighbours Hand to Hand. **1708** Addison *State of War* 25 We..cast about for a sufficient number of Troops to face them [the enemy] in the Field of Battle. *a* **1745** Swift (J.), They are as loth to see the fires kindled in Smithfield as his lordship; and, at least, as ready to face them. **1798** Ferriar *Illustr. Sterne* v. 150 He faced the storm gallantly. **1808** J. Barlow *Columb.* iv. 143 To face alone The jealous vengeance of the papal throne. **1842** Macaulay *Horatius* xxvii, How can man die better Than facing fearful odds? **1881** Besant & Rice *Chapl. Fleet* ii. xviii. (1883) 250 A man will face almost anything rather than possible ridicule.

b. To appear before (a city) as an enemy.

c **1645** T. Tully *Siege Carlisle* (1840) 1 They..p'ceeded ..to face Carlisle with a Rascall rout in 1643. **1677** Sir T. Herbert *Trav.* 284 A small party..with which he faced the City Walls.

c. *Ice Hockey* and *Lacrosse*. (Esp. with *off*). *intr.* To start or restart play by (the referee or linesman) dropping the puck, or ball, between the sticks of two opposing players. Also *trans.*, to place the puck, or ball, in this way.

1867 *Laws of La Crosse* 6 Should the ball lodge in any spot inaccessible to the 'crosse' it may be taken out by the hand and immediately placed on the 'crosse', but should an opponent be checking and cry 'face', it must be faced for. **1882** *Rules of Lacrosse* 15 Should the ball lodge in any place inaccessible to the crosse, it may be taken out by the hand; and the party picking it up must 'face' with his nearest opponent. **1897** *Medicine Hat* (Alta.) *News* 25 Feb. 1/6 Ben Niblock scored the first goal for Medicine Hat a few seconds after the puck was faced. **1910** [see facing *vbl. sb.* 2 b]. **1958** *Vancouver Province* 12 May 11/5 Reeve John Stolberg *faced off* the ball.

5. a. In weaker sense: To look in the face of; to meet face to face; to stand fronting. *lit.* and *fig.*

1632 Lithgow *Trav.* vii. 303 Facing the Iudge and pleading both our best. **1779** Mad. D'Arblay *Diary* Nov., If I faced him he must see my merriment was not merely at his humour. **1841** Elphinstone *Hist. Ind.* II. 275 He performed the journey..with such celerity that..he..faced his enemy..on the ninth day. **1853** Kingsley *Hypatia* ix. 110 Might he but face the terrible enchantress. **1883** *Manch. Exam.* 24 Nov. 5/2 The great problem which faces every inquirer into the causes of colliery explosions.

b. Esp. *pass.* To be confronted *with*.

1920 *Challenge* 21 May 44/2 An extrovert soldier faced with the problem of escape from war conditions.

6. To look seriously and steadily at, not to shrink from. Also, *to face the facts*; (*colloq.*) *let us* (or *let's*) *face it*: let us not shrink from recognizing some unwelcome fact(s).

1795 T. Jefferson *Writ.* (1859) IV. 116 My own quiet required that I should face it [the idea] and examine it. **1828** D'Israeli *Chas. I*, II. v. 104 A lawyer in the habit of facing a question but on one side, can rarely be a philosopher, who looks on both. **1883** S. S. Lloyd in *North Star* 25 Oct. 3/7 The need for external supplies of food..must be faced. **1911** G. B. Shaw *Getting Married* 249 You'll want half a dozen different sorts of contract. *The Bishop*: Well, if so, let us draw them all up. Let us face it. **1913** Galsworthy *Fugitive* i, We've got to face the facts. **1922** N. Angell *Press & Organiz. Society* ii. 43 Let us face the truth. **1928** Wodehouse *Money for Nothing* v. 83 John—she had to face it—was a jellyfish. **1932** —— *Louder & Funnier* 46 One has got to face facts. **1937** W. S. Maugham *Theatre* xxi. 203 But let's face it, I've never been in love with you any more than you've been in love with me. **1958** I. Murdoch *Bell* i. 11 To the pain of Paul and his friends the expression 'let's face it' ..was still frequently on her lips.

II. With reference to the direction of the face.

7. *intr.* **a.** Of persons and animals: To present the face in a certain direction; to look. *lit.* and *fig.*

1594 W. S. in *Shaks. C. Praise* 9, I know thy griefe, And face from whence these flames aryse. **1672** DRYDEN *Conq. Granada* I. i, He [the courser] sidelong bore his Rider on, Still facing, till he out of sight was gone. **1844** H. H. WILSON *Brit. India* II. 266 The 1st of the 20th, with one company of the 24th, were posted on the larger eminence, facing east and south. **1863** KINGLAKE *Crimea* (1877) II. vii. 64 He steadfastly faced towards peace. **1882** HINSDALE *Garfield & Educ.* I. 117 He faced to law and politics, to science and to literature.

b. Of things: To be, or be situated, with the face or front in some specified direction; to front. Const. *on, to.*

1776 WITHERING *Brit. Plants* (1796) IV. 71 Saucers rust-coloured, large, facing downwards. *c* **1850** *Rudim. Navig.* (Weale) 113 *Dagger*, a piece of timber that faces on to the poppets of the bilgeways. **1852** THACKERAY *Esmond* I. iii, The little chapel that faced eastwards. **1884** *Times* (weekly ed.) 29 Aug. 14/2 The village faces full to the south. **1887** *Pall Mall G.* 22 Aug. 11/2 The really picturesque side of the hall, facing on a lovely lake.

8. *trans.* **a.** Of persons and animals: To present the face or front towards; to look towards. **b.** Of a building, a country, and objects in general: To be situated opposite to, front towards.

a. 1632 LITHGOW *Trav.* VIII. 364 Facing the in-land wee marched for three dayss. **1750** JOHNSON *Rambler* No. 12 ¶15 Stand facing the light, that we may see you. **1774** GOLDSM. *Nat. Hist.* (1776) III. 216 He continues to combat..still facing the enemy till he dies. **1886** SHELDON tr. *Flaubert's Salammbô* 22 Neighing shrilly as they faced the rising sun. **b. 1670** MILTON *Hist. Eng.* II. Wks. (1847) 494/2 He gained ..that part of Britain which faces Ireland. **1705** ADDISON *Italy* (1767) 201 The side of the Palatine mountain that faces it. **1746–7** HERVEY *Medit.* (1818) 150 Yonder tree, which faces the south. **1860** TYNDALL *Glac.* I. vii. 55 A series of vertical walls..face the observer. **1885** *Manch. Exam.* 10 June 8/7 The statue..faces the principal entrance to the museum.

c. Of letterpress, an engraving, etc.: To stand on the opposite page to.

1766 *Gent. Mag.* XXXVI, *Directions for placing the plates*, The Emblematical Design..to face p. 8. **1887** *Pall Mall G.* 19 Feb. 5/9 An increased price is paid for advertisements 'facing matter'. **1890** *Ibid.* 20 Nov. 2/2 A letter from Mr. Gladstone is good, and an article from him worth several columns 'facing matter'. *Mod.* [On a plate inserted in a book] To face page 56.

d. ***to face*** (***a person***) ***with***: to put before the face of; to confront *with.*

1583 GOLDING *Calvin on Deut.* xviii. 109 It was Gods wil to humble his..people by facing them with the temple of a cursed idoll.

e. With *off.* To turn aside (*spec.* the current of a stream).

1887 RUSKIN *Præterita* II. 384 A little logwork to face off the stream at its angles.

9. *intr.* †**a.** in sense of *face about* (see b). Also *refl. Obs.*

1644 SLINGSBY *Diary* (1836) 112 Upon yͤ top of yͤ Hill they [the Scots] face and front towards yͤ prince. **1666** PEPYS *Diary* 4 June, The Duke did fly; but all this day they have been fighting; therefore they did face again, to be sure. **1691** *Lond. Gaz.* No. 2662/3 Upon their approach our men faced, and about 20 fired. **1824** MISS FERRIER *Inher.* vi, Having got to the top..he faced him.

b. Chiefly *Mil.* To turn the face in a stated direction (left, right, etc.). ***to face about, to the right about, round***: to turn the face in the opposite direction. As word of command, ***right*** or ***left about face!***

1634 MASSINGER *Very Woman* III. i, Let fall your cloak, on one shoulder—face to your left hand. **1647** N. BACON *Disc. Govt. Eng.* I. lxiv. (1739) 135 He faces about therefore and ..for Scotland he goes. *a* **1671** LD. FAIRFAX *Mem.* (1699) 51 He..made them face about, and march again into the Town. **1710** *Lond. Gaz.* No. 4675/1 He commanded them to face to the Left, in order to flank the Enemy. **1711** STEELE *Spect.* No. 109 ¶1 The Knight faced towards one of the Pictures. **1713** —— *Englishman* No. 55. 353 This elevated Machine..moved through..Cornhil: whence it faced about. **1753** HANWAY *Trav.* (1762) II. IV. iv. 115 They immediately conjectured that the place had changed masters, and faced about. **1787** *Columbian Mag.* I. 47 To the right about face! Forward march! Halt, and face to the Front! **1820** KEATS *Cap & Bells* xxxvi. 1 Then facing right about, he saw the Page. **1823** BYRON *Juan* VIII. xxviii, The rest had faced unto the right About. **1826** SCOTT *Woodst.* i, The minister..faced round upon the party who had seized him. **1841** LEVER *C. O'Malley* lxxxviii, Left face—wheel—quick march! **1844** *Regul. & Ord. Army* 261 On which the Captain is to face inwards, and the Lieutenant and Ensign face to the right. **1859** F. A. GRIFFITHS *Artil. Man.* (ed. 8) 19 Right or left about three-quarters face. **1863** KINGLAKE *Crimea* (1877) III. i. 215 These men had faced about to the front.

fig. **1645** *Liberty of Consc.* 28 In this Sir you have faced about, sure you are not As you were. **1684** BUNYAN *Pilgr.* II. Introd. 217 His Spirit was so stout No Man could ever make him face about.

10. *trans.* †**a.** To attract or direct the face or looks of. **b.** *Mil.* To cause (soldiers) to face, or present the front.

1630 LORD *Banians & Perses* 72 Certaine mimicall gestures, so as may most face the people to gaze upon them. **1667** WATERHOUSE *Fire Lond.* 181 The Judgments of God face us to humilitie. **1859** F. A. GRIFFITHS *Artil. Man.* (ed. 8) 30 The company..will be faced, and countermarched. *Ibid.* 31 The remaining companies first being faced to the right about.

11. a. To turn face upwards, expose the face of (a playing card).

1674 COTTON *Complete Gamester* in Singer *Hist. Cards* 344 He clasps these cards faced at the bottom. **1721** MRS. CENTLIVRE *Basset-Table* IV, Fac't again;—what's the meaning of this ill luck to-night? **1742** HOYLE *Whist* 10 If a Card is faced in the Pack, they must deal again, except it is the last Card. **1878** H. H. GIBBS *Ombre* 19 He places the cards before him, taking care not to face or show any of them.

b. *Post-office.* To turn (letters) with their faces in one direction.

1850 *Q. Rev.* June 75 The object..is merely to 'face' the stamped and paid letters all the same way. **1889** *Pall Mall G.* 15 Oct. 7/1 All the letters have been faced, sorted, and stamped.

III. To put a face upon.

12. a. To cover a certain breadth of (a garment) with another material; to trim, turn up. In *pass.* said of the wearer. Also, ***to face about, down.***

1561 in *Vicary's Anat.* (1888) App. vi. 189 My gowne of browne blue lyned and faced with black budge. **1592** GREENE *Art Conny-catch.* II. 2 The Priest was facst afore with Veluet. **1607** TOPSELL *Four-f. Beasts* (1673) 446 They ..face about the collars of men and womens garments. **1679** *Lond. Gaz.* No. 1378/4 A black hair Camlet Gown..faced down before, and on the Cape with Velvet. **1759** *Compl. Lett.-writer* (ed. 6) 229 Blue cloth, trimmed and faced with white. **1818** SCOTT *Hrt. Midl.* xxi, The five Lords of Justiciary, in their long robes of scarlet faced with white. **1855** W. SARGENT *Braddock's Expedition* 291 The uniform of the 44th was red faced with yellow.

absol. c **1570** *Pride & Lowl.* (1841) 20 Silke and lase..To welt, to edge, to garde, to stitche and face.

†**b.** *transf.* and *fig.* To trim, adorn, deck, furnish.

1565 JEWEL *Def. Apol.* (1611) 241 Would ye rather, for the better facing and colouring of your Doctrin, we should strike out this Forged Quodammodo. **1596** SHAKS. *1 Hen. IV*, v. i. 74 To face the Garment of Rebellion With some fine colour. **1630** B. JONSON *New Inn* I. i. Wks. (Rtldg.) 410/1 An host..who is..at the best some round-grown thing, a jug Faced with a beard, that fills out to the guests. **1645** MILTON *Colast.* Wks. (1847) 221, I saw the stuff..garnished and trimly faced with the commendations of a licenser. **1685** DRYDEN *Albion & Alb.* III. i, Rebellion..fac'd with publick Good!

13. To cover the surface either wholly or partially with some specified material.

1670 COTTON *Espernon* II. VIII. 349 The Terrass was not yet fac'd with stone. **1677** SIR T. HERBERT *Trav.* 279 With whose heads..the savage Turk faced a great Bulkwark. **1697** DRYDEN *Virg. Georg.* I. 259 Delve of convenient Depth your thrashing Floor; With temper'd Clay then fill and face it o'er. **1715** DESAGULIERS *Fires Impr.* 112 If you face the sides of the Chimney with thin Copper. **1803** *Phil. Trans.* XCIII. 85 The same bar was melted again, and was cast in sand, faced..by charcoal dust. **1856** *Jrnl. R. Agric. Soc.* XVII. II. 363 The more modern fence..is faced with stones.

14. To dress or smooth the face or surface of. Also, ***to face down.*** Also with *up.*

1848 MILL *Pol. Econ.* I. 152 One lathe..is kept for facing surfaces. **1873** TRISTRAM *Moab* vi. 111 Blocks of basalt.. some of them finely faced. **1879** *Cassell's Techn. Educ.* IV. 221/2 The body is carefully faced down till a fine even surface is produced. **1883** *Specif. Alnwick & Cornhill Rlwy.* 10 All bolt-holes to have bosses cast on them, which are to be faced up. **1889** P. HASLUCK *Model Engin. Handybk.* x. 113 If all the flange joints are faced up absolutely true. **1958** *People* (Broadway, N.S.W.) 19 Mar. 54 Primitive grinding or cutting machines to 'face up' their specimens. **1970** H. BRAUN *Parish Churches* vii. 83 From this technique develops the type of walling known as 'random rubble' which, properly faced-up.., is frequently met with in pre-medieval days.

15. To coat (tea) with some colouring substance. Also, ***to face up.***

1850 *Household Words* II. 277 The tea-leaf..is 'faced' by the French chalk, to give it the pearly appearance so much liked. **1869** E. A. PARKES *Pract. Hygiene* (ed. 3) 277 The green tea is either natural or coloured (faced) with indigo [etc.]. **1888** *Encycl. Brit.* XXIII. 101/1 Exhausted leaves were..faced up to do duty as fresh tea.

†**IV. 16.** To deface, disfigure, spoil in appearance. [? Short for DEFACE.] *Obs.*

c **1400** *Destr. Troy* 9129 Polexena..All facid hir face with hir fell teris.

facea, faceal, obs. ff. of FASCIA, FACIAL.

facecies, anglicized form of FACETIÆ.

faced (feɪst), *ppl. a.*[1] [f. FACE *v.* + -ED[1].] In senses of the verb. **a.** Of a card: That has been turned face upwards.

1674 COTTON *Complete Gamester* xv. (1680) 96 Then the bottom fac'd Cards are upwards. **1868** PARDON *Card Player* 21 Faced cards necessitate a new deal.

b. Of a body of soldiers: That has faced or turned about.

1796 *Instr. & Reg. Cavalry* (1813) 185 When the whole was halted, the proper front would be taken by the faced wing.

c. Of clothing: Turned up with another material.

1661 PEPYS *Diary* 13 June, My gray cloth suit and faced white coate. **1867** SMYTH *Sailor's Word-bk.*, *Faced*, turned up with facings on the cuffs and collars of uniforms.

d. Of a block or piece of stone: Having the surface dressed or smoothed.

1865 LUBBOCK *Preh. Times* xiii. (1878) 491 These [sling-stones] were called afai ara—faced or edged stones.

e. Of tea: That has been artificially altered in appearance, coloured.

1875 *Sat. Rev.* XL. 553/1 Consumers of 'faced' tea have taken to it for the benefit of manufacturers and importers.

faced (feɪst), *ppl. a.*[2] [f. FACE *sb.* + -ED[2].] Furnished with or having a face.

1. Of persons. †**a.** Having a face *like* (a dog, etc.). *Obs.* **b.** In combination with some defining prefix, as ***bare-, dog-, full-,*** etc., ***faced,*** for which see those words. Of a golf-club, tennis-racket, etc. (see FACE *sb.* 15 b), as ***long-faced, short-faced, small-faced, straight-faced*** adjs.

c **1500** *Bk. Maid Emlyn* in *Anc. Poet. Tracts* (Percy Soc.) 20 Faced lyke an aungell. **1576** NEWTON *Lemnie's Complex.* (1633) 110 Sowre countenanced, faced like death. **1599** MINSHEU *Dial. Sp. & Eng.* (1623) 67 The Devill..brought the blush-faced young man to the Court. **1624** FORD, etc. *Sun's Darling* II. i, Rural fellows, fac'd Like lovers of your Laws. **1632** LITHGOW *Trav.* VI. 293 We marched through a fiery faced plaine. **1634** SIR T. HERBERT *Trav.* 213 The Bats ..are faced like Monkeyes. **1710** SWIFT *Jrnl. to Stella* 23 Sept., He is a rawboned faced fellow. **1863** *Sat. Rev.* 124 Their leafy height, that winter soon Left leafless to the cold-faced moon. **1893** H. G. HUTCHINSON *Golfing* 21 These short-faced clubs. **1897** *Encycl. Sport* I. 467/2 A straight-faced club. *Ibid.* 613/2 [see FACE *sb.* 15 b]. **1909** P. A. VAILE *Mod. Golf* viii. 120 Don't choose a big-headed club, and avoid a long-faced one.

2. *faced cloth*: a fabric manufactured with a 'natural lustre'.

1889 *Daily News* 5 Oct. 7/7 Advt., Faced Cloths, warranted not to spot with rain, in all the new shades.

3. *faced card* = ***face-card, court-card.***

1794 *Sporting Mag.* III. 41 'We are all faced cards'. 'I hope..you are not all Kings'. **1847–78** in HALLIWELL. **1869** in PEACOCK *Gloss. Lonsdale* 29. **1879** in MISS JACKSON *Shropsh. Word-bk.* 138.

4. *Printing.* (See quot.)

1888 JACOBI *Printer's Vocab.* 43 Faced Rule, Brass Rule with the ordinary thin face somewhat thickened.

5. *Arch.* '***Faced work,*** thin stone, otherwise called bastard ashlar, used to imitate squared stone work. In painting, the rubbing down each coat with pumice before the next is laid on. Used also of superior plastering.' (*Arch. Dict.* 1892).

ˈfaced-lined, *a. Her.* [f. FACED *ppl. a.* + LINED *ppl. a.*] Of a garment: Having the lining visible.

1825 in BERRY *Encycl. Herald.* s.v. **1889** in ELVIN *Dict. Herald.* 57.

facel, var. of FASEL, *Obs.*, kidney bean.

faceless (ˈfeɪslɪs), *a.* [f. FACE *sb.* + -LESS.] Without a face. †**a.** Of persons: Lacking face or courage; cowardly; without a (visible) face. Hence anonymous, characterless, without identity. Also *transf.* and *fig.* **b.** Of a coin: Having the device and legend obliterated.

a. 1567 SEMPILL *Lordis Just Quarrel* in *Ballates* (1872) 30 Quhen faceles fuillis sall not be settin by. **1596** *Edward III*, I. ii. 9 Faceless fear that ever turns his back. **1727–36** in BAILEY. **1775** in ASH. **1865** G. MEREDITH *R. Fleming* I. xi. 176 Dahlia..lay..with her handkerchief across her eyes... She lay faceless. **1936** A. HUXLEY *Eyeless in Gaza* xix. 250 Those voluptuous and faceless bodies created by the stylists had actually come to assume Joan's features. **1936** M. MITCHELL *Gone with Wind* xix. 331 Always, faceless soldiers stood on the dark porch. **1953** *N.Y. Times* 4 Oct. 15/1 The 'faceless men'—about 15,000 anti-Communist Chinese and 7,800 anti-Communist North Koreans... In all their wars the Communists have regarded prisoners not as human beings but as hostages and pawns. **1959** *Observer* 28 June 15/1 The Institute of Directors was attacked as a pressure group for industry's 'faceless men'. **1960** *Times* 28 Sept. 15/4 One of those firms that has grown from a compact community into a sprawling, faceless industrial monster. **1967** *New Statesman* 29 Dec. 902/1 We shall go on being lectured and told to draw in our belts by a faceless and endlessly replaceable body of men whom [*sic*] we know quite well are not about to do anything very important with the money we save for them. **1970** *Times* 4 May 8/5 In Brussels ..as in Bonn, where there are a surprising number of faceless men, his warmth, genuine jollity and readiness to learn were refreshing.

b. 1855 *Fraser's Mag.* LI. 272 Specimens of the bronze coinage of the later empire..mostly trite and faceless, as a farthing of the reign of George III.

So **ˈfacelessness.**

1950 *Sat. Rev. Lit.* 21 Oct. 14 Joe Saul appears in the hospital..as only a voice and a white facelessness. **1961** *Times* 20 Dec. 7/1 It [*sc.* a production of *Macbeth*] claps a mask of facelessness on a tragedy.

facellite (fək-, fəˈsɛlaɪt). *Min.* Also **phacel(l)ite, phakellite.** [a. It. *facellite* (E. Scacchi 1888, in *Rend. dell'Accad. delle Sci. fis. e matemat.* (Napoli) XXVII. 486), f. Gr. φάκελ(λ)-ος bundle: see -ITE[1].] = KALIOPHILITE.

1891 *Jrnl. Chem. Soc.* LX. I. 22 Phakellite, a new mineral. **1931** *Min. Mag.* XXII. 599 The original labels with these specimens bear the name 'Facellite'..but..the chemical optical properties and the densities of fresh material from both specimens are those for kaliophilite.

†**ˈfacely,** *a. Obs.* [f. FACE *sb.* + -LY[1].] Giving a face to face view; open; transl. med.L. *faciālis.* Cf. FACIAL *a.* 1.

1605 BELL *Romish Faith* 44 The cleare and facely vision of God [*clara et facialis visio Dei*].

facely, var. of FACILELY.

facer ('feɪsə(r)). [f. FACE *v.* and *sb.* + -ER.]

†**1.** One who puts on a bold face; one who boasts or swaggers; a braggart, bully. *Obs.*

c**1515** *Cocke Lorelles B.* (Percy Soc.) 11 Crakers, facers, and chylderne quellers. **1550** LATIMER *Last Serm. bef. Edw. VI*, Wks. I. 252 Nay: there be no greater tattlers, nor boasters nor facers than they be. **1611** BEAUM. & FL. *Maid's Trag.* IV. ii, A race of idle people.. Facers and talkers.

2. *Post-office.* One who 'faces' letters (see FACE *v.* 11 b).

1850 *Q. Rev.* June 75 The act is by 'facers' called 'pigging'.

3. A blow in the face. *lit.* and *fig.*

1810 *Sporting Mag.* XXXVI. 243 Each of the pugilists exchanged.. half a dozen facers. **1819** MOORE *Tom Crib's Mem.* 24 Not to dwell on each facer and fall. **1859** J. BROWN *Rab & F.* 2 The.. shepherd.. delivered a terrific facer upon our.. middle-aged friend.

fig. **1828** *Blackw. Mag.* XXIII. 109/2 With the right lending the Catholics such a facer, that they are unable to come to time. **1872** BESANT & RICE *Ready Money M.* xviii, 'I've had a good many facers in my life'.

†**4. a.** A large cup or tankard. **b.** Such a cup filled to the brim; a bumper. *Obs.*

a. **1527** *Will T. Sparke* (Chetham Soc.) 17 Item, to my cosyn yong Thomas Smith my bowndon facer and my gilde spone.

b. **1688** SHADWELL *Sqr. Alsatia* I 1, There's a facer for you. a**1700** B. E. *Dict. Cant. Crew, Facer*, a Bumper without Liproom. **1785** in GROSE *Dict. Vulg. Tongue.*

†'**Facet**, *sb.*[1] *Obs.* Also 5 faceet, facett, faucet. [ad. (through F. *facet*) L. *facēt-us* (see FACETE *a.*) used as a proper name.] The book *Facetus de Moribus* (by some attributed to John Garland), which was used in schools as a book of instruction in behaviour.

c**1440** *Promp. Parv.* 145 Faceet, booke.. *Facetus.* c**1475** *Babees Bk.* (1868) 1 Facett seythe the Book of curtesye. a**1483** *Liber Niger* in *Househ. Ord.* 45 The Dean of the Chappell to drawe these chyldren.. as well in the schoole of facett, as in songe. [**1611** COTGR., *Facet*, a Primmer, or Grammer for a yong scholler.]

facet ('fæsɪt), *sb.*[2] Forms: 7 fascet, faucett, 8 fasset, fosset, 8–9 facette, 8– facet. [a. F. *facette*, dim. of *face*: see FACE *sb.*] A little face.

1. One of the sides of a body that has numerous faces; *orig.* one of the small cut and polished faces of a diamond or other gem, but subsequently extended to a similar face in any natural or artificial body. Cf. BRILLIANT. Also preceded by certain defining words, as ***diagonal-, skill-, skew-, star-facet***; for which see those words.

1625 BACON *Ess. Honour* (Arb.) 69 Diamonds cut with Fascets. **1647** R. STAPYLTON *Juvenal* 69 Sea-greene berill into fascets cut. **1750** JEFFRIES *Treat. Diamonds & Pearls* (1751) 35 A Brilliant whose lustre is derived from the angles, or facets, of the sides only. **1800** tr. *Lagrange's Chem.* II. 157 United with antimony, it gives a brittle metal with facets. **1808** SCOTT *Marm.* IV. xi, Above its cornice, row and row Of fair hewn facets. **1835** MARRYAT *Olla Podr.* xxiii, They polish rubies; that is, without cutting them in *facettes.* **1853** HERSCHEL *Pop. Lect. Sc.* viii. §165 (1873) The appearance of certain small obliquely posited facets on the crystal previous to polishing. **1854** HOOKER *Himal. Jrnls.* I. xv. 344 Light reflected from.. myriads of facets [of hoar-frost]. **1875** URE *Dict. Arts.* s.v. *Facetting*, Facets on gold and silver are cut and polished on revolving wheels. **1909** W. M. DAVIS *Geogr. Ess.* xxvi. 746 A triangular facet on the block front. **1937** WOOLDRIDGE & MORGAN *Physical Basis Geogr.* xvii. 257 (*heading*) The facets of relief in a landscape of multi-cycle character. *Ibid.* 258 It is the variously inclined facets of intersecting surfaces which must form the units of detailed geographical study. **1944** A. HOLMES *Princ. Physical Geogr.* xiii. 258 Isolated pebbles or rock fragments strewn on the desert surface are bevelled on the windward side until a smooth face is cut... Two or more facets may be cut.

transf. and *fig.* **1820** MAR. EDGEWORTH *Life R. Edgeworth* (1821) II. 260 That facet of the mind which it was the interest or the humour of the moment to turn outward. **1931** *Times Lit. Suppl.* 20 Aug. 625/3 Many facets of Tyrolese life. **1951** PALMER & WELLS *Fund. Libr. Class.* ii. 31 The sum total of the divisions of each aspect we shall call a facet.

2. *Anat.* **a.** A small flat and smooth articular surface of a bone.

1836 TODD *Cycl. Anat.* I. 272/1 The atlas.. is articulated with the occipital tubercle by a single concave facet. **1870** ROLLESTON *Anim. Life* Introd. 57 The ribs of the Sauria have only a single articular facet. **1881** MIVART *Cat* 228 On each side of this is an oval, convex, articular facet.

b. One of the individual parts or segments (*ocelli*) of a compound eye.

1834 MCMURTIE *Cuvier's Anim. Kingd.* 289 Compound eyes, where the surface is divided into an infinitude of different lenses called facets. **1859** DARWIN *Orig. Spec.* vi. (1873) 144 The numerous facets on the cornea of their great compound eyes form true lenses.

3. *attrib.*, as *facet-wise.* Also **facet-diamond**, a diamond whose surface is formed into facets; **facet-doublet**, a counterfeit jewel (see DOUBLET) similarly treated; **facet-flash**, a flash of light from one of the facets of a gem; in quot. *fig.*

1664 BUTLER *Hud.* II. i. 601 Grind her lips upon a mill, Until the facet doublet doth Fit their rhymes rather than her mouth. **1676** *Lond. Gaz.* No. 1207/4 Two Diamond Rings with one Faucett Diamond.. in each Ring. **1690** *Songs Costume* (Percy Soc.) 186 A saphire bodkin for the hair, Or sparkling facet diamond there. **1751** CHAMBERS *Cycl.* s.v. *Facet*, Multiplying-glasses are cut in facets or facet-wise. **1868** BROWNING *Ring & Bk.* I. 1361 Rather learn and love Each facet-flash of the revolving year!

facet ('fæsɪt), *v.* Pa. t. and pple. **faceted** (often *erron.* **facetted**). [f. prec. sb. Cf. F. *facetter.*] *trans.* To cut a facet or facets upon; to cover with facets. *lit.* and *fig.*

1870 *Echo* 17 Jan., The almond form [of the Sancy diamond] completely facetted over.. indisputably proves that it was an Indian-cut stone. **1873** BROWNING *Red Cott. Nt.-cap* 544 The liquid name 'Miranda'—faceted as lovelily As his own gift, the gem. **1874** WESTROPP *Precious Stones* 140 Heart-shaped Amethyst. Facetted on face and back. **1881** J. PAYNE *Villon's Poems* Introd. 84 He alone divined the hidden diamonds and rubies of picturesque expression, to be.. facetted into glory and beauty by the regenerating friction of poetic employment.

facete (fə'siːt), *a.*; *rare* in mod. use. Also 7 **faceit.** [ad. L. *facēt-us* graceful, pleasing, witty. Cf. OF. *facet.*]

1. = FACETIOUS. *arch.*

1603 HOLLAND *Plutarch's Mor.* 662 Pleasant demaunds and facete jests. **1621–51** BURTON *Anat. Mel.* I. ii. IV. iv, Lodovicus Suessanus a facete companion, disswaded him to the contrary. **1651–3** JER. TAYLOR *Serm. for Year* (1850) 292 A facete discourse.. can refresh the spirit. **1691** WOOD *Ath. Oxon.* I. 259 He was a man of.. a facete and affable countenance. **1762** STERNE *Tr. Shandy* VI. v, I will have him .. cheerful, facete, jovial. **1830** tr. *Aristophanes' Acharnians* 34 By Jove! these two hogs are facete ones! **1863** SALA *Capt. Dang.* II. ix. 310 Such a Ruffian.. could maintain an appearance of a facete disposition to the last.

b. *absol.*

1807–8 SYD. SMITH *Plymley's Lett.* Wks. 1859 II. 162/1 If he would.. consider the facete and the playful to be the basis of his character. **1828** *Blackw. Mag.* XXIV. 257 One or two attempts at raillery and the facete are indeed deplorable.

†**2.** After Latin usage: Elegant, graceful, polished. *Obs.*

a**1635** NAUNTON *Fragm. Reg.* (Arb.) 29 Leicester.. was much the more facete Courtier. *Ibid.* 56 He was so facete and choice in his phrase and stile. **1662** BAGSHAW in *Acc. Baxter's Suspension* 45 A man.. of so Elegant and Facete a Style.

Hence †**fa'cetely** *adv. Obs.*, in a witty or humorous manner, pleasantly. †**fa'ceteness**, the quality of being witty or humorous; 'wit, pleasant representation' (J.).

1619 BRENT tr. *Sarpi's Counc. Trent* (1676) 72 That which facetely was spoken by Erasmus. **1621** BURTON *Anat. Mel.* III. ii. II. ii. 558 As Iames Lernutius hath facetely expressed in an elegant Ode. **1636** FEATLY *Clavis Myst.* xxviii. 361 Poole facetely excused the matter. a**1656** HALES *Gold. Rem.* (1688) 170 Parables.. breed delight of hearing, by reason of that faceteness and wittiness which is many times found in them.

faceted ('fæsɪtɪd), *ppl. a.* Also 9 (*erron.*) facetted. [f. FACET *sb.* and *v.* + -ED.]

1. Of gems, etc.: Having, furnished with, or cut into facets. Also preceded by some qualifying word, as ***many-, keenly-faceted.***

1859 DARWIN *Orig. Spec.* vii. (1873) 203 The falling of a facetted spheroid from one facet to another. **1874** WESTROPP *Precious Stones* 140 Amethyst.. cushion-cut face; facetted back. **1890** *Harper's Mag.* Oct. 799/2 It is a many-faceted diamond of the purest lustre. **1890** *Daily News* 27 Jan. 3/1 It's [the electric light's] power is enormously multiplied by the facetted lens.

fig. **1864** CARLYLE *Fredk. Gt.* (1865) IV. XI. iii. 44 Friedrich.. loves the sharp facetted cut of the man. **1898** *Daily News* 30 Nov. 7/6 Not an hour.. when the uneasy faceted surface [of the sea] is not throwing back reflections of the sky. **1930** E. POUND *XXX Cantos* xx. 91 In the sunlight, gate cut by the shadow; And then the faceted air: Floating. **1944** A. HOLMES *Princ. Physical Geogr.* xiii. 258 Wind-faceted pebbles. **1959** J. D. CLARK *Prehist. S. Afr.* vi. 143 This is known as *faceted platform technique* on account of the care that was usually devoted to the preparation of the platform where the core was struck to remove the flake.

2. *Anat.* Provided with facets; see FACET *sb.*[2] 2.

1836 TODD *Cycl. Anat.* I. 770/2 The most remarkable modification of facetted eyes. **1870** ROLLESTON *Anim. Life* 22 An irregularly-shaped bony process.. forms with this smooth facetted process a cup-shaped cavity.

facetiæ (fə'siːʃiiː), *sb. pl.* Also 6 in anglicized form **facecies.** [a. L. *facētiæ*, pl. of *facētia* a jest, f. *facētus* FACETE.]

1. Humorous sayings or writings, pleasantries, witticisms.

1529 MORE *Dyaloge* I. Wks. 118/2 With folish facecies and blasphemous mockery. **1657** J. SMITH *Myst. Rhet.* 78 The merry and pleasant sayings incident hereunto are called Facetiæ. **1883** S. C. HALL *Retrospect* I. 324 Gilbert à Beckett .. contributed jokes and facetiæ weekly.

2. *Bookselling.* Pornography.

1851 MAYHEW *Lond. Labour* I. 293/2 He puts to the end of his catalogue.. two pages that he calls 'Facetiæ'... indecent books, indeed. **1913** [see EROTICA]. **1926** FOWLER *Mod. Eng. Usage* 164/1 *Facetiae*, in booksellers' catalogues, is a euphemism for obscenities. **1947** E. PARTRIDGE *Usage & Abusage* 115/1 *Facetiae* is a booksellers' euphemism for 'pornography' or 'a book with a certain amount of sexual interest' and should be avoided by anyone who is not a bookseller.

faceting ('fæsɪtɪŋ), *vbl. sb.* Also 9 (*erron.*) facetting. [f. FACET *v.* + -ING[1].] The action or process of cutting facets on gems or metals.

1875 URE *Dict. Arts, Facetting.* **1877** STREETER *Precious Stones* I. iv. 32 The Brilliant depends greatly upon the facetting for its exceeding beauty. **1877** GEE *Goldworker* xi. 180 The.. workman turning the links of gold chains between his thumb and finger.. and while.. it seems as if they are being presented in a haphazard fashion to the lap, the most perfect-shaped diamonds are being produced. This is called faceting.

facetiosity (fəˌsiːʃɪ'ɒsɪtɪ). *rare.* [f. next; see -ITY.] The quality of being facetious; in quot. quasi-*concr.*

1822 *Liberal* I. 209 The bookseller.. evidently.. laughs at the customer.. when he has the luck to get rid of some heavy facetiosity by a chance sale.

facetious (fə'siːʃəs), *a.* [ad. Fr. *facétieux* (cited from 16th c.), f. *facétie*, ad. L. *facētia* (see FACETIÆ) + -OUS.]

†**1.** [After L. *facetus.*] Of style, manners, etc.: Polished and agreeable, urbane. *Obs.*

1592 H. CHETTLE in *Shaks. C. Praise* 4 His facetious grace in writting which approoues his art.

2. Characterized by, or addicted to, pleasantry; jocose, jocular, waggish. Formerly often with laudatory sense: Witty, humorous, amusing; also, gay, sprightly. **a.** of utterances, compositions, actions, etc.

1605 CAMDEN *Rem.* 203 It was then thought facetious. a**1677** BARROW *Serm.* xiv. Wks. 1741 I. 147 Facetious speech there serves onely to obstruct and entangle business. **1722** SEWEL *Hist. Quakers* (1795) I. Pref. 11 Intermixed the serious part sometimes with a facetious accident. **1850** MRS. STOWE *Uncle Tom's C.* iv. 19 Aunty gave George a nudge with her finger designed to be immensely facetious. **1855** MACAULAY *Hist. Eng.* III. 346 Facetious messages.. passed between the besieged and the besiegers.

b. of persons, their qualities, etc.

1599 B. JONSON *Cynthia's Rev.* I. iii, My sweet facetious rascall. **1643** SIR T. BROWNE *Relig. Med.* 179, I am no way facetious nor disposed for the mirth.. of Company. **1710** HEARNE *Collect.* (Oxf. Hist. Soc.) II. 333 He was of a pleasant, facetious Temper. **1758** JOHNSON *Idler* No. 33 ¶2 Transmitted.. by a facetious correspondent. **1844** DICKENS *Mar. Chuz.* xxiv. (C.D. ed.) 251 'Oh you terrible old man!' cried the facetious Merry to herself. **1874** MICKLETHWAITE *Mod. Par. Churches* 283 The mediæval carvers were many of them facetious fellows.

facetiously (fə'siːʃəslɪ), *adv.* [f. prec. + -LY[2].] In a facetious manner.

1727–36 in BAILEY. **1731** WATERLAND *Scripture Vind.* II. 9 B. answers, very facetiously. **1749** FIELDING *Tom Jones* I. iii, Pages which certain droll authors have been facetiously pleased to call The History of England. **1838** DICKENS *Nich. Nick.* xix, Sir Mulberry Hawk leered upon his friends most facetiously. **1885** *Manch. Exam* 6 May 6/1 The private view, facetiously so-called.

facetiousness (fə'siːʃəsnɪs). [f. as prec. + -NESS.] The quality or fact of being facetious. †**a.** Polish and pleasantness of manner, urbanity (*obs.*). †**b.** Cheerful good-humour; also, wittiness, wit (*obs.*). **c.** Jocularity, jocosity.

1630 *R. Johnson's Kingd. & Commw.* 267 The Italians in facetiousnesse doe jest; That [etc.]. **1644** BULWER *Chirol.* 135 The facetiousnesse of manners and elegancies of learning. **1657** HOBBES *Stigmai of Wallis* Wks. 1845 VII. 386, I observe, first, the facetiousness of your title-page. **1757** BURKE *Abridgm. Eng. Hist.* III. ii, Relaxing with a wise facetiousness, he [William I] knew how to relieve his mind and preserve his dignity. **1836** HOR. SMITH *Tin Trump.* (1876) 362 This is a random facetiousness. a**1853** ROBERTSON *Lect.* i. (1858) 139 With dull facetiousness.

fach, fachen, obs. ff. of FETCH, FALCHION.

‖**Fach, fach** (faːx). [Ger., compartment, partition, division, shelf, *fig.* circumscribed branch of knowledge.] A line of work or business, a department of activity; (one's) métier. Also in *Comb.*, 'professional'.

1842 J. S. MILL *Let.* Nov. (1910) I. 121 The thing is not in my *fach.* **1887** W. JAMES *Let.* 6 Feb. (1920) I. 263 Wundt .. isn't a genius, he is a *professor*—a being whose duty is to know everything, and have his own opinion about everything, connected with his *Fach.* **1905** *Ibid.* 30 Apr. II. 227 These men.. are none of them *Fach-philosophers*, and few of them teachers at all. **1920** G. SANTAYANA *Char. & Opin. U.S.* v. 143 Very professional in tone and conscious of his *Fach.* **1923** *Contemp. Rev.* June 757 The Eldorado of story-tellers whose *Fach* is the portrayal of luxurious vice.

fachine, obs. f. FASCINE.

fachon, -oun, obs. ff. of FALCHION.

facia ('feɪʃ(ɪ)ə, 'fæʃ(ɪ)ə). [var. of FASCIA q.v.]

1. The tablet or plate over a shop front on which is written the name and often also the trade of the occupier. Also *attrib.* in ***facia writer, sign and facia writer.***

1881 *Instr. Census Clerks* (1885) 52 Sign and Facia writer. **1911** *Tariff Reform League: Rep. Labour & Social Cond. Germany* III. 74 A butcher's shop with this sign on the facia board. **1931** *N. & Q.* 14 Nov. 354/1 A double-fronted shop ..and the name 'Deck' in the middle of the facia.

2. The instrument panel or dashboard of a motor vehicle. Also *attrib.*, as ***facia board, panel.*** Cf. FASCIA 5.

1924 H. J. BUTLER *Motor Bodywork* xviii. 279 A front facia board of 1" stuff. **1937** *Times* 9 Oct. 9/2 The facia board is clearly planned so that the instruments are easily read by the driver. **1955** *Ibid.* 19 July 11/6 The full width of the facia. **1959** *Motor Man.* 93 A push-pull knob on the facia panel.

facial (ˈfeɪʃɪəl, -ʃəl), *a.* and *sb.* [a. F. *facial*, ad. med.L. *faciāl-is* of the face, f. *faciēs* FACE.]

A. *adj.* †1. *Theol.* In *facial sight, vision* = L. *visio facialis*: Face to face, immediate, open. *Obs.*

1609 BELL *Theoph. & Remig.* 16 The cleare and faciall vision of God. 1633 EARL MANCH. *Al Mondo* (1636) 194 Saint Steven..had a faciall sight of his Saviour. *a* 1711 KEN *Hymnarium* Poet. Wks. 1721 II. 17 You in that Beatifick Height, Had of Triunal God a facial Sight.

2. a. Of or pertaining to the face or visage; frequent in *Anat.*, as in ***facial artery, nerve***, etc.

1818 HOOPER *Med. Dict.*, *Facial nerve.* 1841 CATLIN *N. Amer. Ind.* (1844) II. lviii. 226 Facial outline of the North American Indians. 1842 E. WILSON *Anat. Vade M.* 273 The Facial artery arises a little above the great cornu of the os hyoides. 1855 THACKERAY *Newcomes* I. 213 A man of..great facial advantages. 1865 TYLOR *Early Hist. Man.* iv. 68 Biting her lips with an upward contraction of the facial muscles. 1874 WOOD *Nat. Hist.* 281 The Virginian Eared Owl.—The facial disc is brown, edged with black.

b. *Palæont.* ***facial suture*** (see quot. 1884).

1872 NICHOLSON *Palæont.* 167 The facial suture is wanting. 1884 *Syd. Soc. Lex.*, *Facial suture*, the line of division between the glabella and the free cheek on each side in a Trilobite.

c. ***facial angle***: the angle formed by two lines, one horizontal from the nostrils to the ear, the other (called the ***facial line***) more or less vertical from the nostrils to the forehead.

The facial angle above described is that of Camper; various other 'facial angles' have been subsequently proposed, and to some extent adopted in craniometry.

1822 W. LAWRENCE *Lect. Phys.* 146 The ancients..were aware that an elevated facial line..indicated a noble and generous nature. Hence they have extended the facial angle to 90°. 1845 DARWIN *Voy. Nat.* xvii. (1852) 388 From their low facial angle they [some Lizards] have a singularly stupid appearance. 1866 LIVINGSTONE *Jrnl.* (1873) I. vi. 140 Many have quite the Grecian facial angle.

d. ***facial eczema***: a disease of sheep in New Zealand.

1910 *N.Z. Jrnl. Agric.* 15 Nov. 464 The prevalence of so-called facial eczema among sheep last year. 1950 *Ibid.* Oct. 317/1 Adverse weather may temporarily change pasture to a toxic state capable of producing facial eczema in stock.

e. ***facial tissue***: a soft, absorbent kind of tissue paper; a *face-tissue*.

1930 H. RUBINSTEIN *Art Feminine Beauty* xvi. 265 Spread cream over the face, and wipe it off with a bit of clean linen or fine facial tissues. 1953 'S. RANSOME' *Drag Dark* (1954) i. 15 Box of face powder unspilled, facial tissues neatly folded.

3. Of or belonging to the visible part or surface of anything. ***facial value*** = ***face-value***.

1842 E. WILSON *Anat. Vade M.* 33 The external or facial surface, forms the anterior part of the bone. 1862 RAWLINSON *Anc. Mon.* I. vi. 371 To compensate for this monotony in its [the façade's] facial line. 1870 HOOKER *Stud. Flora* 328 Seeds..with 2 facial furrows. 1884 *Pall Mall G.* 28 June 5 The coupons can be purchased under their facial value.

†**4.** quasi-*sb.* = *facial angle. Obs.*

c 1817 FUSELI *Lect. Art* x. (1848) 526 Camper..appears to have ascertained, not only the difference of the faceal [*sic*] in animals, but that which discriminates nations.

B. *sb.* Beauty treatment for the face. Also *transf.* orig. *U.S.*

1914 G. ATHERTON *Perch of Devil* I. 84 I've got fourteen heads to dress..and most of them want a facial, too. 1932 *Kansas City Times* 26 Apr. 16 The north side of the courthouse clock is peeling... The newspaper suggests a facial. 1934 [see BEAUTICIAN]. 1937 *Time & Tide* 12 June, Why don't they dress better and have a facial occasionally? 1959 *Observer* 15 Mar. 13/5, I don't have facials now: I keep that and massage in reserve for when I get older. 1961 *Time* (Atlantic ed.) 6 Jan. 7 The Capitol dome, which has just had a dazzling, million-dollar facial, beamed down on the city.

Hence ˈ**facially** *adv.* †(*a*) Face to face. (*b*) With reference to the face.

a 1641 [D. BAKER] *Holy Pract. Devine Lover* (1657) 6 In this life only enigmaticallie..in the future facially and really. 1864 *Daily Tel.* 1 Aug., His Excellency is not facially remote from the portraits of Talleyrand.

†ˈ**faciale**, *sb. Obs.* [ad. late L. *faciālem* face-cloth, f. *faciēs* face.] A face-cloth for a corpse.

a 1300 *Cursor M.* 17693 (Gött.) His faciale, his winding clath, þar war þai left.

ˈ**faciata**, ˈ**faciate**. *Obs. rare.* [a. and ad. It. *facciata* FAÇADE.] A façade, front.

1644 EVELYN *Diary* 25 Oct., The faciata of the Court and Chapel. 1654 *Ibid.* 27 June, The faciate of this Cathedrall is remarkable for its historical carving.

faciation (feɪsɪˈeɪʃən). *Ecol.* [f. L. *faciēs* + -ATION.] A community containing more than one of the dominant species in an association (often related to climatic or geographic differences in the area of the association).

1920 F. C. CLEMENTS *Plant Indicators* 276 The grouping of consociations within the association is typical of all climaxes, and seems to warrant a special term... It has seemed desirable to definitize the term *facies* for seral groupings and to make a new word, *faciation*, for climax groupings... The two terms conform to the mutual relation seen in associes and association, consocies and consociation. 1938, 1960 [see FACIES 2 c]. 1952 P. W. RICHARDS *Tropical Rain Forest* xv. 319 Four 'faciations' of Evergreen Seasonal forest are recognized; more or less the same species occur in all of them but in different proportions.

‖**faciendum** (fækɪˈɛndəm, feɪʃ-). *Philos.* Pl. facienda. [a. L. *faciendum*, 'thing to be done', neut. of gerundive of *facĕre* to make, do.] A thing that should be done.

a 1832 BENTHAM *Ess. Logic* in *Wks.* (1841) VIII. xv. 241/1 Different assemblages of these *noscenda* and *facienda*; of these subjects or objects of *disciplines*, have received names. *a* 1866 J. GROTE *Exam. Util. Philos.* (1870) iv. 67 This is the idea of the *summum jus*, the *faciendum*, the notion of *duty*. 1958 W. STARK *Sociology of Knowledge* iii. 139 'Imaginative' thought..is neither concerned with *data*, like 'existential' thought, nor yet with *facienda*, like normative ideas.

facient (ˈfeɪʃ(ɪ)ənt), *sb. rare.* [ad. L. *facient-em*, pr. pple. of *facĕre* to do, make.] One who does anything; an actor or doer.

a 1670 HACKET *Abp. Williams* I. §77 (1693) 66 Is Sin in the Fact or in the Mind of the Facient? 1821 COLERIDGE in *Blackw. Mag.* X. 250 The shape beheld he would grant to be a making in the beholder's own brain; but the facient, he would contend, was a several and other subject.

-facient, formative element repr. L. *-facient-em* 'making', pr. pple. of *facĕre* to make, occurring in compounds as *calefacĕre, liquefacĕre, rubefacĕre, tepefacĕre*, etc., from pr. pple. of which are adapted the Eng. *calefacient, rubefacient*, etc.; on the strict analogy of these are *absorbefacient*, and similar words not formed in L.; and in loose imitation *abortifacient, calorifacient*, etc., for which L. vbs. would have been in *-ficāre*, and adjs. in *-ficus, calorific-us*. Some pronounce (ˈfeɪʃənt), but (ˈfeɪʃɪənt) or (ˈfeɪʃjənt) is more usual.

‖**facies** (ˈfeɪʃɪiːz). (Pl. facies.) [L. *faciēs*: see FACE.]

†**1. a.** Humorously for: Face, countenance. *Obs.*

1611 COTGR. s.v. *Abbé, Face d'abbé*, a jollie, fat, and red face; a fierie facies.

b. *Med.* The appearance or expression of the face.

[1684 S. BLANCARD *Physical Dict.* 128 *Facies Hyppocratica* is when the Nostrils are sharp, the Eyes hollow, the Temples low,..the Complexion pale, livid, of a leaden Colour, or Black. 1807 MORRIS & KENDRICK *Edin. Med. & Physical Dict.* II, *Facies hippocratica*, that particular disposition of the features which immediately precedes the stroke of death.] 1883 J. G. BROWN *Med. Diagnosis* (ed. 2) i. 14 There are one or two facies which stand out more prominently than the rest, and which deserve special attention. 1907 *Practitioner* Apr. 520, I can only recall one facies which at all suggested the condition of *bien-être* associated with the acquired disease. 1908 *Ibid.* Feb. 292 The facies gray. 1932 JEWELL & KAUNTZE *Handbk. Tropical Fevers* xx. 321 During the pyrexial period the face is flushed, the eyes injected (giving a typical 'ferrety' appearance to the facies). 1965 H. T. HYMAN *Differential Diagnosis* 166/1 In contrast with changes in facies, abnormalities of facial contour are relatively fixed.

2. a. *Nat. Hist.* General aspect or appearance.

1727–36 in BAILEY, *Facies* (in Botanick Writers) a face. 1872 NICHOLSON *Palæont.* 475 The general facies of the Carboniferous vegetation. 1881 J. S. GARDNER in *Nature* No. 623. 531 Not only is the facies of the flora identical, but identical species appear in both continents.

b. *Geol.* The character of any part of a formation as displayed by the fossils it contains, the composition, texture, etc., of the constituent rocks, or other differentiating qualities; also, a part of a formation having a particular character. In *Petrol.*, a mass of igneous rock that differs in some way from the main body of rock of which it is part.

1849 MURCHISON *Siluria* vi. 105 They present the uniform 'facies' of a thick, yet finely laminated, dark, dull grey shale. 1882 A. GEIKIE *Text-bk. Geol.* 615 Every well-marked formation is characterized..by a general assemblage or *facies* of organic forms. 1910 LAKE & RASTALL *Text-bk. Geol.* xvi. 285 When a geological series or system is in one district composed chiefly of limestone and in another of clays and shales, it is usual to speak of these different types of deposit as different 'facies'. 1913 J. P. IDDINGS *Ign. Rocks* II. I. i. 5 In one region the composition of a nearly homogeneous rock mass..may assume a certain local petrographical significance, while in another region it may appear only as a facies of a rock mass. 1913 HATCH & RASTALL *Petrol. Sedim. Rocks* i. 7 Each of the formations.. exhibits two very different facies, controlled for the most part by the conditions of formation. 1938 A. K. WELLS *Outl. Hist. Geol.* iii. 20 If rocks of a certain age exhibit a lateral change of lithological facies,..a change in conditions of formation is implied. 1951 J. GILLULY et al. *Princ. Geol.* xix. 517 The evidence is not only geometric. The facies of the rocks composing the thrust masses demand great travel also. 1965 G. J. WILLIAMS *Econ. Geol. N.Z.* iv. 38/1 The host-rock is a splintery siliceous bluish-grey slate with some micaceous, talcose and felsic facies. 1970 R. C. SELLEY *Anc. Sedim. Environm.* i. 4 The geometry of a sedimentary facies may be relatively easy to determine where it crops out at the surface.

c. *spec.* in *Ecol.* (See quots.)

1905 F. E. CLEMENTS *Res. Methods Ecol.* iv. 238 It is seldom..that the facies and invaders are so equally matched in height and other qualities that they remain in equilibrium. *Ibid.* 317 *Facies*, a dominant species of a formation: a distinct area controlled by it is a consocies. 1920 [see FACIATION]. 1932 FULLER & CONARD tr. *Braun-Blanquet's Plant Sociol.* ii. 25 The facies is distinguished wholly by differences in the quantity or distribution of species. 1938 WEAVER & CLEMENTS *Plant Ecol.* (ed. 2) iv. 107 The facies..is the developmental unit of the associes characterized, as is the faciation of climax vegetation, by the grouping of dominants. 1960 N. POLUNIN *Introd. Plant Geogr.* xi. 334 The seral counterpart of the faciation is the *facies*.

3. *attrib.* and *Comb.*, as *facies-change*; **facies fossil**, a fossil that is characteristic of a facies as a result of the restricted kind of environment tolerated by the original organism; so **facies fauna**, the (fossil) fauna characteristic of a facies.

1923 L. D. STAMP *Introd. Stratigr.* ix. 139 It seems that the Pendleside fauna is a 'facies-fauna' developed only under special conditions. *Ibid.* xii. 194 In Germany the 'facies-fossils' of the Muschelkalk do reappear at a much higher horizon. 1954 J. F. KIRKALDY *Gen. Princ. Geol.* xvii. 254 They [*sc.* fossils] not only date the beds, but in the case of facies faunas, give us valuable evidence as to the conditions under which the beds were formed. 1969 *Proc. Geol. Soc. Lond.* Aug. 146 Once the marker-points are adequately defined, subsequent demonstrations of facies-changes, diachronous boundaries, lacunae or similar phenomena do not affect their validity.

facile (ˈfæsaɪl, -ɪl), *a.* Forms: 5–6 facyl(l)e, 6–8 facil(l, 5– facile. [a. Fr. *facile*, ad. L. *facil-is* easy to do; also of persons, easy of access, courteous, easy to deal with, pliant, f. *facĕre* to do.]

1. That can be accomplished with little effort; = EASY 11. Now with somewhat disparaging sense. †Formerly used as predicate with inf. phrase as subject, and in phrase ***facile and easy***.

1483 CAXTON *Æsop* 97 It is facyle to scape out of the handes of the blynd. 1538 STARKEY *England* I. iv. 133 As the one ys ful of hardnes and dyffycuIty..so the other ys facyle and esy. 1577 HOLINSHED *Scot. Chron.* I. 449/1 They.. thought it easie and facile to be concluded. 1641 PRYNNE *Antip.* Epist. 4, I gathered with no facil labour, the most of those Materials. 1676 WORLIDGE *Cyder* (1691) 236 The more facile making of the linnen manufacture. *a* 1703 BEVERIDGE *Serm.* xci. Wks. 1729 II. 126 All other acts of piety will be facile and easy to him. 1856 FROUDE *Hist. Eng.* I. 357 Having won, as he supposed, his facile victory. 1876 C. M. DAVIES *Unorth. Lond.* 250 The work appears facile.

2. Of a course of action, a method: Presenting few difficulties.

1559 W. CUNINGHAM *Cosmogr. Glasse* 109 The waye is very facile, and without great laboure. 1607 TOPSELL *Four-f. Beasts* (1673) 152 Yet have they found out this facile and ready course. 1639 FULLER *Holy War* III. ii. (1647) 112 His Holinesse hath a facile and cheap way both to gratifie and engage ambitious spirits. *a* 1718 PENN *Tracts* Wks. 1726 I. 703 It will render the Magistrates Province more facil. 1807 VANCOUVER *Agric. Devon* (1813) 463 Baiting..in the manner performed on the continent, is an infinitely more economical and facile mode of administering refreshment to a jaded animal. 1860 TYNDALL *Glac.* II. ix. 271 The facile modes of measurement which we now employ.

†**b.** Easy to understand or to make use of. *Obs.*

1531 ELYOT *Gov.* I. v, As touchynge grammere there is at this day better introductions and more facile, than euer before were made. 1579 DIGGES *Stratiot.* II. vii. 47 We have by the former Rules produced this playne and facile Aequation. 1633 *Sc. Acts Chas. I*, c. 34 The short and facile grammer. 1644 MILTON *Educ.* 100 Those poets which are now counted most hard, will be both facil and pleasant. 1676 WORLIDGE *Cyder* (1691) 103 To make this curious Machine more useful and facile. 1786 T. WOOLSTON *Let.* in Fenning *Yng. Algebraists' Comp.* (1787) p. v, It having been long considered as a most facile Introduction to Algebra. 1797 MRS. A. M. BENNETT *Beggar Girl* (1813) II. 24 The harp and the piano-forte were equally facile to Rosa.

3. Moving without effort, unconstrained; flowing, running, or working freely; fluent, ready.

1605 B. JONSON *Volpone* III. ii, This author..has so modern and facile a vein Fitting the time and catching the court-ear. 1657 AUSTEN *Fruit Trees* II. 204 One man excells ..in a facile and ready expression. 1796 LD. SHEFFIELD in *Ld. Auckland's Corr.* (1862) III. 371 Your..happy facile expression in writing. 1820 L. HUNT *Indicator* No. 31 (1822) I. 246 On the facile wings of our sympathy. 1865 SWINBURNE *Atalanta* 1641 Deaths..with facile feet avenged. 1873 SYMONDS *Grk. Poets* v. 144 Stesichorus was one of those facile and abundant natures who excel in many branches of art. 1886 STUBBS *Med. & Mod. Hist.* iii. 57 To the facile pen of an Oxford man we owe the production of the most popular manual of our history.

4. Of persons, dispositions, speech, etc.: †**a.** Easy of access or converse, affable, courteous (*obs.*). **b.** Characterized by ease of behaviour.

c 1590 GREENE *Fr. Bacon* I. iii, Facile and debonair in all his deeds. 1638 FEATLY *Transubt.* 219 A young Gentleman of a facile and affable disposition. 1782 MAD. D'ARBLAY *Diary* 12 Aug., My father is all himself—gay, facile, and sweet. 1844 DISRAELI *Coningsby* III. v, Manners, though facile, sufficiently finished. 1876 HOLLAND *Sev. Oaks* x. 134 He was positive, facile, amiable.

c. Not harsh or severe, gentle, lenient, mild. Const. *to*; also *to* with *inf.*

1541 ELYOT *Image Gov.* 88 Your proper nature is mylde, facile, gentyll, and wytty. 1631 WEEVER *Anc. Fun. Mon.* 116 She was of a more facile and better inclined disposition. 1655 FULLER *Ch. Hist.* v. v. §7 Q. Elizabeth..A Princesse most facil to forgive injuries. 1670 MILTON *Hist. Eng.* Wks. 1738 II. 80 However he were facil to his Son, and seditious Nobles..yet his Queen he treated not the less honourably. 1851 SIR F. PALGRAVE *Norm. & Eng.* I. 297 The guilty sons were too happy to avail themselves of his facile tenderness.

5. Easily led or wrought upon; flexible, pliant; compliant, yielding.

1511 COLET *Serm. Conf. & Ref.* in *Phenix* (1708) II. 8 Those canons..that do learn you..not to be too facile in admitting into holy orders. 1556 LAUDER *Tractate* 251 Be nocht ouir facill for to trow Quhill that ȝe try the mater throw. *c* 1610 SIR J. MELVIL *Mem.* (1683) 103 Facil Princes ..promote them [Flatterers] above faithful Friends. 1648 J. BEAUMONT *Psyche* XVII. cxcvii, Alas, That facil Hearts

should to themselves be foes. **1671** MILTON *P.R.* I. 51 Adam and his facil consort Eve Lost Paradise. **1805** FOSTER *Ess.* II. vi. 192 The tame security of facile friendly coincidence.

b. in *Scots Law.* 'Possessing that softness of disposition that he is liable to be easily wrought upon by others' (Jam.).

1887 GRIERSON *Dickson's Tract. Evidence* §35 Proof that the granter of a deed was naturally weak and facile..has been held to reflect the burden of proving that [etc.].

c. *transf.* Of things: Easily moved, yielding, 'easily surmountable; easily conquerable' (J.).

1667 MILTON *P.L.* IV. 967 Henceforth not to scorne The facil gates of hell too slightly barrd.

†**6.** quasi-*adv.* Easily; without difficulty. *Obs.*

c **1523** WOLSEY in Fiddes *Life* II. (1726) 114 His countries, whose parts non of the Lords or Commons would soe facile inclyne unto. **1548** HALL *Chron.* (1809) 316 Whatsoever were purposed to hym they..might easely se and facile heare the same. **1560** ROLLAND *Crt. Venus* II. 80 The Muses ..mair facill ȝour mater will consaif, Fra time that thay heir ȝour enarratiue.

facilely ('fæsaılı, 'fæsılı), *adv. rare* in mod. use. Forms: 5 **facely**, 6–7 **facilie**, **-lly**, **-ly(e**, 6– **facilely**. [f. prec. + -LY^2.] In a facile manner.

1. With little exertion, labour, or difficulty; without effort or restraint; easily.

1490 CAXTON *Eneydos* xxi. 77 That thenne shalle permytte hym facely & lightly for to do his vyage safly. *c* **1565** LINDESAY (Pitscottie) *Chron. Scot.* (1728) 60 Now let us see how facilly this matter..may be brought to pass. **1611** SPEED *Hist. Gt. Brit.* IX. viii. §32 Cloyster-men..might more facilly be swayed to bend. **1677** LADY CHAWORTH, in *12th Rep. Hist. MSS. Comm.* App. v. 39 He might facilier do itt the second time in the way the House had ordered it. **1835** *Fraser's Mag.* XII. 267 The..principle, upon which the whole formerly so facilely moved, is destroyed.

†**2.** Affably, courteously, graciously. *Obs.*

1528 Fox in Pocock *Rec. Ref.* I. liii. 142 His holiness very promptly and facily had condescended unto the granting thereof. **1550** DK. NORTHUMBERLAND *Let.* 23 July in *Consid. Peace & Goodw. Prot.* 5 That your Grace may facilely condescend thereunto.

3. With (a too) ready acquiescence; without sufficient consideration, thoughtlessly.

1864 *Spectator* 25 June 740 He facilely concludes that some male animals have teats, others not. **1872** *Daily News* 28 Feb., The cheers..were no empty breath of a populace facilely beguiled by the lust of the eye.

'facileness. ? *Obs.* Also **facilnes(s**. [f. as prec. + -NESS.] The quality of being facile; easiness to be persuaded; easy good nature; pliancy.

1549 *Compl. Scot.* xi. 94 The cite of gabine, throcht there facilnes, gef hasty credit to sextus tarquinus. *Ibid.* 97 That ȝour facilnes be nocht sedusit be ther astuce and subtil persuasions. **1648** J. BEAUMONT *Psyche* XVII. cxcvii, Others they with facileness befriend! *a* **1665** J. GOODWIN *Filled w. the Spirit* (1867) 292 Some have a kind of goodness and facileness of disposition. **1727–36** in BAILEY. **1775** in ASH.

‖**facile princeps** ('fæsıli: 'prınsεps), *phr.* and *sb.* [L.] (A person who is) easily first; the acknowledged leader or chief.

1834 GREVILLE *Mem.* (1874) III. xxii. 64 In the prime of life,..*facile princeps* in the House of Commons. **1858** TROLLOPE *Three Clerks* I. ii. 33 He..soon became *facile princeps* in the list of habitual idlers. **1861** *Two Cosmos* I. vi, The *facile princeps* of the Whig Attorneys. **1863** [see GIPSIOLOGIST]. **1877** *Times* 20 Dec. 7/3 In that [*sc.* political tergiversation] he is *facile princeps*, and has left all competitors behind. *a* **1878** G. G. SCOTT *Lect. Med. Archit.* (1879) II. xvi. 253 [St. Sophia's] is *facile princeps* among structures on the pendentive domical principle. **1931** M. SUMMERS *Supernatural Omnibus* 31 Dr. M. R. James..is, with the exception of Vernon Lee, of all writers of ghost stories to-day *facile princeps.*

facilie, obs. f. FACILELY.

‖**facilis descensus Averni** ('fæsılıs de'sεnsəs ə'vεənaı), *phr.* [L. (Virgil *Æn.* VI. 126, where most witnesses read *Auerno*), *lit.* the descent of (or to) Avernus (is) easy. *Auernus* was the name of a deep lake near Puteoli, the reputed entrance to the underworld.] It is easy to slip into evil ways. Also *facilis descensus*, used as *sb. phr.*

1618 T. ADAMS *Happines of Church* II. 76 And downe a hill, for hell is a bottome. *Facilis descensus Auerni.* **1885** 'L. MALET' *Col. Enderby's Wife* VII. v. 296 *Facilus* [*sic*] *descensus Averni.* That remark was made a long time ago; but it holds good still. **1895** G. B. SHAW *Let.* 22 Apr. (1965) 525 Moral ruin followed slowly but surely—facilis descensus Averni. **1939** C. S. LEWIS *Let.* 8 May (1966) 165 *Romola* is a most purgative work on the *facilis descensus* because the final state of the character is so different from his original state and yet all the transitions are so dreadfully natural. **1946** 'D. YATES' *Red in Morning* i. 27, I took a first class in Honour Moderations. Unfortunately, shortly afterwards, I took twenty-seven pounds from the monies entrusted to my care. *Facilis descensus averni.* And I have never looked back.

facilitate (fə'sılıteıt), *v.* [f. F. *facilit-er* to render easy (= It. *facilitare*, f. *facilis* FACILE, after L. vbs. like *dēbilitāre*, etc.) + -ATE^3.]

1. a. *trans.* To render easier the performance of (an action), the attainment of (a result); to afford facilities for, promote, help forward (an action or process).

1611 COTGR., *Faciliter*, to facilitate or make easie. **1621** SIR G. CALVERT in *Fortesc. Papers* 155 It will..facilitate the present negotiation. **1670** COTTON *Espernon* I. II. 64 It.. much facilitated the Duke of Guise his Victories, to have an Enemy reduc'd to such streights before he came to engage them. **1714** LADY M. W. MONTAGUE *Lett.* lxxxvi. 141 It.. may facilitate your election. **1732** ARBUTHNOT *Rules of Diet* 278 All such things as increase and facilitate the animal or natural Motions. **1838** T. THOMSON *Chem. Org. Bodies* 102 All the alkaline bodies..facilitate the solution of picrotoxin in water. **1883** *Stubbs' Mercantile Circular* 27 Sept. 861/2 The reformed procedure..has not appreciably facilitated the progress of public business.

†**b.** To make easier or less abstruse; to simplify. *Obs. rare.*

a **1656** HALES *Tracts* (1677) 89, I thank you for.. facilitating to my understanding the scope and purpose of the XI of S^t. Mat.

¶ **2.** To lessen the labour of, assist (a person).

1646 H. LAWRENCE *Comm. Angells* 77 Which may more easily leade and facilitate us, to the consenting to such a lust. **1650** FULLER *Pisgah* II. 64 Here lived the Emims shrowdly smote by Chederlaomer, which probably did facilitate the Moabites in their victory over them. **1890** *Sat. Rev.* 6 Sept. 303/2 The author seems to aim solely at facilitating the pupil in his dealings with everyday French.

3. *Physiol.* To increase the likelihood of, strengthen (a response); to bring about the transmission of (an impulse). (Cf. FACILITATION 3.)

1906 C. S. SHERRINGTON *Integr. Action Nerv. Syst.* v. 175 Minimal electrical stimuli applied near together in point of time to the fore-limb region of the rabbit's cortex and to the skin of the crossed foot, exerted a facilitating influence, 'bahnung', on each other. **1934** E. S. ROBINSON in C. Murchison *Handbk. Gen. Exper. Psychol.* xii. 632 Extraneous, or unessential, stimuli can facilitate a given reaction as well as interfere with it. **1951** M. A. B. BRAZIER *Electr. Activity Nerv. Syst.* ix. 90 A long persisting effect set up by an initial stimulus would serve to facilitate impulses coming much later.

Hence **fa'cilitated** *ppl. a.*, **fa'cilitating** *vbl. sb.* and *ppl. a.*

1613 SHERLEY *Trav. Persia* 3 Which would haue beene.. a facillitating of any enterprise, which..that Earle was ever ..vndertaking against him. **1674** BOYLE *Excell. Theol.* II. iv. 171 Rectifying..errours..by the assistance of such facilitating helps. **1776** BENTHAM *Wks.* (1843) I. 288 These facilitating circumstances. **1876** MOZLEY *Univ. Serm.* vii. 151 Undoubtedly habit is a great facilitating principle. **1884** *Pall Mall G.* 2 Apr. 1/2 The lake district..is in no need of facilitated means of access.

facilitation (fə,sılı'teıʃən). [f. as prec. + -ATION.]

1. The action or process of facilitating or rendering easy; an instance of this.

1619 BRENT tr. *Sarpi's Counc. Trent* (1629) 769 For facilitation heereof, it [the Synod] doth renew some things decreed by the holy Canons. **1751** JOHNSON *Rambler* No. 103 ¶5 The use of their discoveries to the facilitation of commerce. **1791** NEWTE *Tour Eng. & Scot.* 102 This facilitation of conveyance would contribute much to the improvements in the northern parts of the island. **1862** T. A. TROLLOPE *Lent. Journey* ix. 134 Impediment to free locomotion was a very much more important consideration than facilitation of it.

2. A means of facilitating or helping forwards; help. Const. *to*, *towards*. Now *rare.*

1648 W. MONTAGU *Devout Ess.* I. x. §6. 118 A generall habit of sincerity, which when it is referred to religious uses, proves a facilitation towards fidelity and perseverance in them. **1823** LAMB *Corr.* (1870) 218 The impediments and facilitations to a sound belief are various.

3. *Physiol.* The increased excitability of a post-ganglionic neuron, resulting in an increased response to a physical stimulus, that is produced by conditioning of the ganglion by impluses due to other (similar or different) stimuli.

1895 E. B. TITCHENER in *Amer. Jrnl. Psychol.* VII. 80 *Bahnung*, facilitation. **1901** J. M. BALDWIN *Dict. Philos.* I. 367/2 *Facilitation*... The term has been given technical meaning as a translation of the German Bahnung (in neurology), which latter carries the idea of the preferential determination of a function..as to its pathway of discharge. **1906** C. S. SHERRINGTON *Integr. Action Nerv. Syst.* v. 176 He [*sc.* S. Exner] argues..that the seat of production of the facilitation lies in the spinal cord. **1943** J. F. FULTON *Physiol. Nerv. Syst.* (ed. 2) xx. 379 A series of inadequate stimuli may become adequate merely through repetition, and thus additional neurons become recruited through local facilitation. **1961** H. H. JASPER in D. E. Sheer *Electr. Stimul. Brain* xxxviii. 561/1 Critical areas of facilitation are in neuronal systems where there is convergence of impulses from many sources. **1968** M. MONNIER *Funct. Nerv. Syst.* I. iii. 112 A third, very prolonged facilitation effect begins 300–500 msec after the first conditioning impulse and lasts for several seconds.

facilitative (fə'sılıteıtıv), *a.* [f. FACILITATE *v.* + -IVE.] Tending to facilitate.

1864 *Glasgow Citizen* 19 Nov., Tolls are restrictive, and not facilitative.

facilitator (fə'sılıteıtə(r)). [f. FACILITATE *v.* + -OR.] One who or that which facilitates.

1824 *Ann. Reg.* 266* An apparatus for shaving which he denominates the useful and elegant facilitator. **1834** *New Monthly Mag.* XLII. 260 Steam and gas..are the grand facilitators and illuminators of the intercourse of the most distant provinces. **1871** *Pall Mall G.* 29 Mar. 11 The Washington correspondent..says the Senate is becoming the great facilitator of jobs and schemes.

†**'facilite**, *v. Obs. rare*$^{-1}$. [ad. Fr. *faciliter*: see FACILITATE.] = FACILITATE.

1604 T. WRIGHT *Passions* v. §4. 193 By this meanes profound conceit shall bee facilited, and therewith the auditors instructed..and moued. **1608** D. TUVIL *Ess. Polit. & Mor.* 86 b, The faciliting of treacherous..practises.

facility (fə'sılıtı). Forms: 6 **facilitye**, (**facillitie**, **facylytye**, **fecility**), 6–7 **facilitie**, 6– **facility**. [a. F. *facilité*, ad. L. *facilitāt-em*, f. *facilis* easy: see FACILE and -ITY.]

1. The quality, fact, or condition of being easy or easily performed; freedom from difficulty or impediment, ease; an instance of the same. Often in phr. ***with*** (***great***, ***much***, ***more***) ***facility.***

1531 ELYOT *Gov.* I. xxii, An induction..howe children.. may be trayned..with a pleasant facilitie. **1576** FLEMING *Panopl. Epist.* 383, I cannot see what you may do wyth more facilitie and easinesse. **1597** HOOKER *Eccl. Pol.* v. iii. (1611) 191 The great facilitie of their language. **1649** ROBERTS *Clavis Bibl.* ii. 20 That difficulties deterre not from the study of Scripture, there are intermingled some facilities. **1791** BURKE *App. Whigs* (ed. 3) 121 The facility with which government has been overturned in France. **1805** FOSTER *Ess.* I. ii. 17 The facility or difficulty of understanding. **1881** WESTCOTT & HORT *Grk. N.T.* Introd. §29 The relative facilities of the several experimental deductions.

2. a. in *sing.* Unimpeded opportunity for doing something. Const. *of*, *for*, *to* with *inf.* In early use also: †Means, resources (cf. FACULTY).

1519 *Four Elements* in Hazl. *Dodsley* I. 27 Ye..have had great facility Strange causes to seek. **1656** DUCHESS OF NEWCASTLE *Life Dk. Newcastle* (1886) 317 To impoverish my friends, or go beyond the limits or facility of our estate. **1659** B. HARRIS *Parival's Iron Age* 172 He found great facility everywhere and very little aversion anywhere. **1730** A. GORDON *Maffei's Amphith.* 347 The Facility of covering the Spectators with an Awning..was..not one of the least wonderful Things about the Building. **1859** MILL *Liberty* v. (1865) 60/1 The limitation in number..of beer..houses.. exposes all to an inconvenience because there are some by whom the facility would be abused. **1879** *Cassell's Techn. Educ.* I. 147 The utmost facility is allowed to the upper millstone of adjusting itself.

b. [So Fr. *facilités* from 17th c.] In *pl.* (also ***every facility***): Opportunities, favourable conditions, for the easier performance of any action. *spec.* (orig. *U.S.*), the physical means for doing something; freq. with qualifying word, e.g. ***educational***, ***postal***, ***retail facilities***; also in *sing.* of a specified amenity, service, etc.

1809 WELLINGTON in Gurw. *Disp.* IV. 357 He wishes to be permitted and to have the facilities given to him to return to France as soon as possible. **1825** MCCULLOCH *Pol. Econ.* I. 35 The facilities given to the exportation of goods manufactured at home. **1865** HUXLEY *Lay Serm.* ii. (1870) 28 Throw every facility in their way. **1872** R. G MCCLELLAN *Golden State* (1874) 373 There..was but little need of postal facilities. **1876** PATTERSON in C. M. Davies *Unorth. Lond.* (ed. 2) 250 The facilities for ordinary traffic are apt to break down. **1920** *Travel* July 42 To secure better roads, better transportation facilities. **1937** *Discovery* Nov. p. ci/1 [Film] projection facilities for approved bookings. *Ibid.*, Lunch and tea facilities. **1958** *Listener* 3 July 10/1 This 'facility', or 'rest room', as it is also variously called [in the U.S.]. **1962** *Gloss. Terms Autom. Data Proc.* (*B.S.I.*) 99 *Hold facility*,.. a means of interrupting the computing action and keeping all variables at the value they had. **1962** F. I. ORDWAY et al. *Basic Astronautics* xiii. 554 (*caption*) Multiaxis spin test inertial facility used by..astronauts. **1967** *Times Rev. Industry* Aug. 74/2 No one could have predicted..that the completed facility would have the bad luck to run head on into..a metals depression. **1969** *Lebende Sprachen* XIV. 65/2 Many other ports offer container facilities. *Ibid.* 97/1 The opening of Britain's National Giro..makes an entirely new banking facility available to the general public. **1971** *Oxf. Univ. Gaz.* 25 Feb. 708/1 The following decree adds Junior Members to the Committee for Sports Facilities.

3. a. In action, speech, etc.: Ease, freedom, readiness; aptitude, dexterity.

1532 HERVET *Xenophon's Househ.* To Rdr., His swete eloquence, and incredyble facilitie. **1596** LODGE *Wits Miserie* 57 Lilly, the famous for facility in discourse. **1602** WARNER *Alb. Eng.* Epit. (1612) 382 An ordinary care and skilfull Facilitie in collecting..their descents. **1736** BUTLER *Anal.* I. v. Wks. 1874 I. 86 We are capable..of getting a new facility in any kind of action. **1762–71** H. WALPOLE *Vertue's Anecd. Paint.* (1786) III. 103 The stranger..performed it with such facility and expedition, that [etc.]. **1841** D'ISRAELI *Amen. Lit.* (1867) 475 Spenser composed with great facility. **1875** JOWETT *Plato* (ed. 2) I. 16 Facility in learning is learning quickly.

b. Of style: Easy-flowing manner, fluency.

1588 SHAKS. *L.L.L.* IV. ii. 126 The elegancy, facility, & golden cadence of poesie. **1700** DRYDEN *Fables* Pref. *B I Both writ with wonderful Facility and Clearness. **1879** O. W. HOLMES *Motley* xv. 96 He proceeds with an increased facility of style.

†**4.** Easiness of access or converse, affability, condescension, courtesy, kindly feeling. *Obs.*

1550 VERON *Godly Saiyngs* (1846) 22 Beseching..that ye of your wont goodness & facilitie vouchsafe to accept this my rude labour. **1677** MARVELL *Let. to Mayor of Hull* Wks. I. 287 This slid over, out of their facility to an old servant. **1791** BOSWELL *Johnson* 25 Mar. an. 1776, I wondered at this want of..facility of manners. **1793** SMEATON *Edystone L.* §112 *note*, Our men were much struck..with the facility of the Portland ladies.

5. a. Easiness to be led or persuaded to good or bad, readiness of compliance, pliancy. Also *rarely* const. *to* with *inf.* Liability, readiness.

1533 MORE *Apol.* xxxvi. Wks. 900/2 Of some facylytye of hys owne good nature..easi to beleue som such as haue told him lies. **1607–12** BACON *Ess.*, *Goodness* (Arb.) 202 That is but Facilitie, or Softnesse; which taketh an honest Minde Prisoner. **1646** SLINGSBY *Diary* (1836) 181 To all which ye King yeilds, wth a facility of nature. **1702** *Eng. Theophrast.* 165 Licentiating any thing that is coarse and vulgar, out of a foolish facility. **1848** MACAULAY *Hist. Eng.* I. 169 The facility of Charles was such as has perhaps never been found in any man of equal sense. **1875** MANNING *Mission H. Ghost*

viii. 216 Those who have in time past been guilty of any sin ..have a facility to fall again.

b. in *Scots Law*.

c **1565** Lindesay (Pitscottie) *Chron. Scot.* (1778) 279 In regard of the Facility of the Earl of Arran. **1861** W. Bell *Dict. Law Scot.* s.v., As a ground of reduction, facility is quite distinct from incapacity.

c. *transf.* Of things: Flexibility. *rare.*

1856 Kane *Grinnell Exp.* xliii. 401 The swell of the ice.. transmitting with pliant facility the advancing wave.

6. Indolent ease, indifference.

1615 T. Adams *Two Sonnes* 68 They imagine that facilitie, a soft and gentle life is hence warranted. **1791** Boswell *Johnson* Advt., Those who read them with careless facility.

'facilize, *v. Obs. rare*⁻¹. [f. facile + -ize. Cf. F. *faciliser*.] *trans.* To render easy or plain.

1610 W. Folkingham *Art of Survey* I. viii. 15 It shall not bee amisse to particularize the Natures and qualities both of good and badde soyles, to the end their distinctions may be facilized.

facilles: see fasel.

faciner(i)ous: see facinor-.

†**facinerose,** *a. Obs. rare*⁻⁰. [ad. L. *facinerōs-us*, var. of *facinorōsus* (see facinorous).] = facinorous.

1727 in Bailey, vol. II.

facing ('feɪsɪŋ), *vbl. sb.* [f. face *v.* + -ing¹.] The action of the verb face.

†**1. a.** The action of boasting, swaggering, or browbeating; an instance of this, a defiance. *Obs.*

1523 *St. Papers Hen. VIII*, VI. 190 Protestations and exclamacions, with facyng crakyng and mynatorie wordes agaynst the Cardynalles. **1571** Golding *Calvin on Ps.* xii. 5 Their importunate facing and bracing in woordes. *a* **1625** Fletcher *Lover's Progress* III. vi, Leave facing, 'twill not serve you. **1647** N. Bacon *Disc. Govt. Eng.* I. lxvi. (1739) 140 This wrought..complainings in England, and facings between the Emperor and the Pope.

†**b.** *attrib.* in *facing-card* (see face *v.* and card *sb.*² 2 a): *fig.* an imposing allegation or argument. *Obs.*

a **1624** Bp. M. Smith *Serm.* (1632) 33 If yee [goe away,] for these facing-cardes of multitudes or chaire, vnhappy are ye.

2. a. *Mil.* The action of facing or turning in another direction. *facing-about*: the action of turning in the opposite direction, an instance of this. Hence *to put* (one) *through* (his) *facings*, *to go through* (*one's*) *facings*: *lit.* and *fig.* Also *transf.*

1635 Barriffe *Mil. Discip.* ix. (1643) 32 Facing is a particular turning of the Aspect from one part to another. **1662** Stillingfl. *Orig. Sacr.* III. ii. §11 After many encounters and facings about, they fell into their severall troops. **1724** De Foe *Mem. Cavalier* (1840) 232 Their facing about..put them into a great disorder. **1833** *Regul. Instr. Cavalry* I. 13 In going through the facings, the left heel never quits the ground. **1867** Trollope *Chron. Barset* I. xli. 356 Grace, not at all unwillingly, was put through her facings. **1888** C. Blatherwick *Uncle Pierce* i, Look in as you pass..and I'll put you through your facings.

b. *Lacrosse.* (See face *v.* 4 c.)

1910 *Westm. Gaz.* 22 Apr. 14/3 Facing is no longer to be regarded as a penalty.

3. The action of turning (a card) face upwards.

1674 Cotton *Complete Gamester* in Singer *Hist. Cards* 344 Lest there should be a discovery made of the facing, he palms them as much as he can.

4. a. *concr.* (chiefly in *pl.*): Something with which a garment is faced (cf. face *vb.* 12); *esp.* the cuffs and collar of a military jacket, when of a different colour from the rest of the coat.

1566 in Peacock *Eng. Ch. Furniture* 89 Two Copes the ffacyng taken of. **1607** Topsell *Four-f. Beasts* (1673) 87 Their skins are of great use through the world..for garments, facings, and linings. **1612** Barry *Merry Tricks* III. i, Tawny coats, with greasy facings. **1688** *Lond. Gaz.* No. 2368/4 The stuff having yellow Spots..with a little Silver Edging across the Facing. **1741** Richardson *Pamela* I. xx. 49, I made robings and facings of a pretty bit of printed calico. **1816** 'Quiz' *Grand Master* III. 56 His facings bore The designation of his corps. **1853** Stocqueler *Mil. Encycl.* s.v., The facings of the artillery are scarlet. **1866** Rogers *Agric. & Prices* I. xxii. 580 The silk lining or facing is used for the summer robe only.

b. *transf.* and *fig.*

1642 Wotton *Life Dk. Buckingham* 5 These Offices and Dignities..were but the facings and fringes of his greatnesse. **1642** Fuller *Holy & Prof. St.* v. viii. 388 Well may the Hypocrite afford gaudy facing. **1808** Syd. Smith *Plymley's Lett.* x, Dulness turned up with temerity, is a livery all the worse for the facings. **1862** Burton *Bk. Hunter* (1863) 46 Each shelf uniform, with its facings or rather backings, like well-dressed lines at a review.

5. The action of putting a new face on (anything); of overlaying (a building, etc.) with other material; of colouring (tea); the action of covering or protecting the face of. Cf. face *v.* 13–15.

1549 *Churchw. Acc. St. Dunstan's, Canterbury*, For fasynge of the Images in the Churche ix d. Item fasynge of the tabyll that stoode at the Awlter iiij d. **1703** T. N. *City & C. Purchaser* 52 Of Facing Timber-buildings with Bricks. **1825** Hone *Every-day Bk.* I. 1480 They [houses] are undergoing reparation by new facing. **1874** Knight *Dict. Mech.*, *Facing* 4 the covering of brick or rough stone-work with fine masonry, such as sawed freestone or marble. **1875** *Sat. Rev.* XL. 552/2 We are told that the 'facing' of tea.. does not affect its quality.

6. *concr.* **a.** A superficial coating or layer; also the material of which this is made.

1586 A. Day *Eng. Secretary* I. (1625) 110 The inner facing of his chimney Casket. **1783** T. Warton *Hist. Kiddington* (ed. 2) 67 If we suppose some assistance from an artificial facing, they must have been visible at a vast distance. **1832** W. Stephenson *Gateshead Local Poems* 32 I'll get My anvil a new facing. **1856** J. H. Walsh *Dom. Econ.* (1857) 285 Exhausted tea leaves made up with..facing. **1875** *Sat. Rev.* XL. 553/1 Green teas with a slight facing of colour. **1882** *Worc. Exhib. Catal.* iii. 52 Nickel, brass, and steel facing for printing from.

b. *esp.* The external layer of stone or other material which forms the face of a wall, bank, etc. Also the corners, door-jambs, etc. of stone employed to set off a brick building.

1823 P. Nicholson *Pract. Build.* 585 *Facings*, in joinery, those fixed parts of wood-work which cover the rough work of the interior sides of walls &c. **1841** W. Spalding *Italy & It. Isl.* I. 303 Rubble work..the facing of which with stone has chiefly disappeared. **1866** Rogers *Agric. & Prices* I. xx. 485 The older portions of..Merton College, many of which have perhaps been disfigured by modern facings. **1874** Knight *Dict. Mech.*, *Facing* (Hydraulic Engineering). **a.** Protection for the exposed faces of sea-walls and embankments..**b.** A layer of soil over the puddle, upon the sloping sides of a canal. **1876** Gwilt *Archit.* 562 Walls are most commonly built with an ashlar facing. **1884** J. T. Bent in *Macm. Mag.* Oct. 432/1 The facings and window cases of all the houses are of marble.

c. An external cover or protection.

1849 Grote *Greece* II. lxix. (1862) VI. 220 The horses also were defended by facings both over the breast and head. **1856** Kane *Arct. Expl.* II. xviii. 185 A small pane of glass, formerly the facing of a daguerreotype.

d. *Founding.* (See quot.)

1874 Knight *Dict. Mech.*, *Facing* (Founding), powder applied to the face of a mold which receives the metal. The object is to give a fine smooth surface to the casting. **1883** T. D. West *Amer. Foundry Practice* 364 Sea-coal or bituminous facing is mixed in with sands for heavy casting ..There is a limit to the percentage of facings to be mixed with the sand, which, if exceeded on the heavy castings, causes the iron to eat into the facing sand.

7. *Mining.* = cleat *sb.* 5.

1851 Greenwell *Coal-trade Terms Northumb. & Durh.*, *Facing*, a cleat. **1883** in Gresley *Coal-mining Gloss.*

8. *Brick-making.* (See quot.)

1884 C. T. Davis *Bricks, Tiles, etc.* (1889) 137 The opening through which the bricks are wheeled into the kiln, and hauled out after burning..is a 'facing'..or 'abutment'.

†**9.** The action of defacing or disfiguring; also the result of this; defacement, disfigurement. *Obs.*

c **1400** *Destr. Troy* 9215 Refresshing his face for facyng of teres.

10. *attrib.* and *Comb.*, as ***facing-bar***, ***-block***, ***-board***, ***-brick***, ***-implement***, ***-machine***, ***-pavior***, ***-tool***; **facing-loam**, **-sand** (see quot.).

1904 Goodchild & Tweney *Technol. & Sci. Dict.* 214/1 **Facing bar* or *work bar*, a smooth iron plate about 4 in. wide and the full width of the lace machine, over which the web of lace travels on its way to the roller. **1876** Gwilt *Archit.* 555 An exterior *facing block of a better manufactured brick. **1839** Ure *Dict. Arts* 843 In friable and shivery rocks there is put behind these beams..**facing boards*, which are planks placed horizontally.., set so close together as to leave no interval. **1850** Dobson *Bricks & Tiles* I. ii. 83 For *facing-bricks additional processes are employed. **1874** Knight *Dict. Mech.*, *Facing-brick* (Building), front or pressed brick. **1876** Voyle *Mil. Dict.* (ed. 3), **Facing Implements*, used for facing or renewing the vent and breech pieces of an Armstrong gun. **1881** Wylie *Iron Founding* 13 Fine or *facing loam, used to form the face of the mould. **1884** Knight *Dict. Mech.* IV. 324 **Facing Machine*..a machine for dressing the faces..of mill-stones. **1904** Goodchild & Tweney *Technol. & Sci. Dict.* 214/1 **Facing paviors*, hard burnt malms of good colour and shape. **1881** Wylie *Iron Founding* 73 This coal-dust sand is termed '*facing sand' as it..forms the face of the mould. **1884** F. J. Britten *Watch & Clockm.* 204 *Facing tool.

facing ('feɪsɪŋ), *ppl. a.* That faces.

†**1.** Bold, audacious. *Obs.*

1566 T. Stapleton *Ret. Untr. Jewel* i. 33 So outragious Untruthes, so facing falshoods. **1592** Babington *Comfort. Notes Genesis* iii. §2 Thirdly, by a bold lye of a facing Diuell shee is pulled on to her destruction. **1624** Bp. Mountagu *Gagg* Pref. 9 Who opineth..that hee may..build his salvation upon the facing impudency of every light-skirt mountebanck.

2. That is opposite to. *facing points* (*Railway*): a pair of points which open towards the approaching train. Also *attrib.* (see quot. 1889).

1849 *Builder* 3 Feb. 56/3 For the protection of the boxes for facing points from dust, rain, snow, &c. **1886** *Encycl. Brit.* (ed. 9) XX. 238 Many accidents have been caused to trains by facing-points..turning the train unexpectedly into a siding. **1889** G. Findlay *Eng. Railway* 75 The 'Facing-Point-Lock', which is a bar of iron working in connexion with facing points.

†**faci'norious,** *a. Obs.* Also 7 facinerious. [f. L. *facinor-*, also *faciner-* (see next) + -(i)ous.]

1601 Shaks. *All's Well* II. iii. 35 He's of a most facinerious spirit. **1636** Heywood *Challenge* Prol., Dukes and Kings Presented for some hie facinorious things.

facinorous (fə'sɪnərəs), *a. Obs.* exc. *arch.* Forms: 6 facynerous, 6–7 fascinorous, 7 faciner(i)ous, 6– facinorous. [ad. L. *facinorōs-us*, f. *facinor-*, also *faciner-*, *facinus* a deed, *esp.* a bad deed, f. *facĕre* to do; see -ous. Cf. OF. *facinereux*, *facinoreux*.] Extremely wicked, grossly criminal, atrocious, infamous, vile. Said both of persons and their actions. Very common in 17th c.

1548 Hall *Chron.* (1809) 381 The people havyng in their freshe memorie the facinorous acte of there kynge. **1592** in Strype *Ann. Ref.* IV. App. lxii. 95 Others they have cast into ..Newgate..among the most facinorous and vile persons. **1627–77** Feltham *Resolves* II. lxxvi. 323 The world..is not so..facinorous, as it was in times of Paganism. **1656** *Artif. Handsom.* 131 Things highly charged with sin..to a more facinorous and notorious degree. **1679** Bedloe *Popish Plot* Ep. A b, Notwithstanding all their facinorous Performances. **1721** Cibber *Perolla* Wks. 1727 IV. 314 The horrid Scroll Of Deeds facinorous. **1871** R. Ellis *Catullus* lxiii. 24 'Tis said, that father..with act impure stain'd the facinorous house.

Hence †**fa'cinorously** *adv.*, **fa'cinorousness.**

1692 tr. *Sallust* 154 Thus, by how much every one acted most facinorously, so much the more secure he thought himself. **1727–36** Bailey, *Facinorousness*, Villainy, Wickedness. **1822** Mrs. E. Nathan *Langreath* II. 267 The facinorousness of your lover. **1841** Borrow *Zincali* (1846) I. x. 103 Constantine the Great..condemned to death those who should practise such facinorousness.

facio- ('feɪʃɪəʊ), used as combining form (see -o) of L. *facies* face, as in **facioplegic** *a.*, pertaining to paralysis of the face; etc. (see quots.).

1900 Dorland *Med. Dict.* 250/2 *Faciobrachial*, pertaining to the face and arm. *Faciocervical*, affecting the face and neck. *Faciolingual*, pertaining to the face and tongue. *Ibid.* 252/1 *Facioscapulo-humeral*, pertaining to the face, scapula, and arm. **1910** Osler & McCrae *Syst. Med.* VII. 124 The facio-scapulo-humeral type [of progressive muscular dystrophy]. **1922** F. W. Price *Textbk. Pract. Med.* 1577 When the wasting begins in the face (facio-scapulo-humeral type). **1922** A. A. Stevens *Pract. Med.* 916 In a few instances recurrent facial paralysis seems to have been an accompaniment of migraine (facioplegic migraine). **1946** *Nature* 2 Nov. 612/1 Special hospital units for thoracic, facio-maxillary and head injuries.

facioun, -um, -un, obs. ff. fashion.

fack, var. of fake *sb.*¹

facon, obs. f. of falcon.

faconde, -ound, var. of facund.

‖**façon de parler** (fasɔ̃ də parle). [Fr.] A way or manner of speaking; a mere phrase or formula.

1804 W. Wilberforce *Let.* 29 Sept. in J. Aitken *Eng. Lett. XIX Cent.* (1946) 28 B.'s first letter would convey the idea of his having had in his mind from the very first the..plan ..but I believe that is only a *façon de parler*. **1806** *Edin. Rev.* Jan. 494 Philostratus..introduces the high priest of Serapis saying, (in the time of Vitellius) 'and who can alter the sacred institutions of Egypt?' Was this a mere *façon de parler*? **1813** Wellington *Disp.* (1838) X. 161, I hope that this mode of considering an omission which can easily be rectified, is only a *façon de parler*. **1886** H. G. Hutchinson *Hints Golf* 56 A mere golfing *façon de parler*. **1887** [see analysis 9 c]. **1907** W. De Morgan *Alice-for-Short* xlii. 439 Which was palpably a lie, taken literally; but was a *façon-de-parler* that passed muster, taken leniently. **1953** C. E. Bazell *Linguistic Form* i. 8 It is clearly a mere *façon de parler* when *sang* is split up into the segments i) *sing* and ii) *i* > *a*.

‖**façonné** (fasɔne), *a.* Also faconne, faconné(e. [Fr., pa. pple. of *façonner* to fashion.] Designating a material into which a design has been woven. Also as *sb.*, the material itself.

1895 *Montgomery Ward Catal.* 13/1 Pongee Faconne; width 21 inches. **1939–40** *Army & Navy Stores Catal.* 637/2 Rich black silk and velvet faconné. **1957** M. B. Picken *Fashion Dict.* 121/1 *Façonné*, French word meaning figured; used of fabrics, particularly those with scattered motifs woven in. **1971** *Daily Tel.* 19 Apr. 12/6 Lots are really battle jackets in *faconée* silk, and could be happily worn over a sleeveless dress.

†**facrere.** *Obs.* [? F. *faire croire* to make believe.] The art of 'make-believe', deception.

1393 Gower *Conf.* I. 230 First ben enformed for to lere A craft, which cleped is facrere. For if facrere come about, Than afterward hem stant no doubt.

facsimile (fæk'sɪmɪlɪ), *sb.* Pl. facsimiles. [Orig. two words, and before this cent. usually written as such, L. *fac*, imper. of *facĕre* to make + *simile*, neut. of *simil-is* like.

The form *factum simile*, occurring in quot. 1782, is often stated to be the original; but of this we find no evidence.]

†**1.** The making a copy of anything, *esp.* writing; imitation. *Obs.*

a **1661** Fuller *Worthies* (1662) III. 206 He, though a quick Scribe, is but a dull one, who is good only at *fac simile*, to transcribe out of an original.

2. a. An exact copy or likeness; an exact counterpart or representation. Also in phr. *in facsimile.*

1691 T. H[ale] *Acc. New Invent.* p. lxxxvi, A fac simile might easily be taken. *a* **1734** North *Lives* (1742) 59 He.. made what they call a fac simile of the Marks and Distances of those small Specks. [**1782** Pownall *Antiq.*, *Let. to Astle* 178 Drawings copied *per factum simile*.] **1795** Seward *Anecd.* (1796) III. 10 The annexed Engraving, a complete fac-simile. **1815** R. Wedgwood in *Commercial Mag.* (1846) I. 259 Fac-similes of a dispatch, written..in London, may with facility be written also in Plymouth, Dover..by the same person, and by one and the same act. **1824** J. Johnson *Typogr.* II. xii. 434 One of the most..ancient of those manuscripts has been printed in fac-simile. **1851** D. Wilson *Preh. Ann.* (1863) II. iv. iv. 281 The inscription is

produced in facsimile. **1868** G. STEPHENS *Runic Mon.* I. p. vi, Masterly facsimiles.

b. *transf.* and *fig.*

1801 *Med. Jrnl.* V. 191 This is a fac simile to his declaring .. that leave was given. **1817** COLERIDGE *Biog. Lit.* II. xvi. 42 Representing before them fac-similies [*sic*] of their own mean selves. **1864** CARLYLE *Fredk. Gt.* IV. viii. 371 Mirabeau's Gospel of Free-Trade .. some seventy or eighty years the senior of an English (unconscious) Facsimile.

3. *attrib.* **a.** *gen.*

1767 S. PATERSON *Another Traveller!* I. 415 The first fac simile man in Europe. **1791** *Gentl. Mag.* 27/2 A facsimile copy of the curious little miscellany. **1823** J. BADCOCK *Dom. Amusem.* 142 Much better adapted .. for fac simile writings. **1861** BERESF. HOPE *Eng. Cathedr. 19th C.* 227 Wyatt substituted facsimile plaster for stone groining in Lichfield nave. **1875** SCRIVENER *Lect. Greek Test.* 13 Those elaborate fac-simile editions of the chief codices.

b. *spec.* applied to a radio, telegraphic, or other system that scans written, printed, or photographic material and transmits signals used to produce a likeness of the original; as ***facsimile telegraph, transmission,*** etc.

1877 *Pract. Mag.* VII. 10/1 (*heading*) The Fac-simile Telegraph... An instrument which transmits by telegraph the weather maps of the Signal Service. **1927** *Marconi Short Wave Beam Syst.* 19 It [*sc.* the short wave beam system] can be used for facsimile transmission over any distance. **1935** *Sci. Amer.* Mar. 122/1 The home radio set will produce a copy of the printed material that was fed into the broadcasting machine, with picture and text reproduced in facsimile... That is what facsimile radio has in store. **1948** *New Yorker* 28 Feb. 21/3 The facsimile newspaper .. travels through the air. **1959** A. G. COOLEY in K. Henney *Radio Engin. Handbk.* (ed. 5) xxiii. 1 In a facsimile system the subject copy for transmission is scanned by a light beam, a line at a time. **1969** *Daily Tel.* (Colour Suppl.) 31 Oct. 25/1 Distribution .. is mastered .. with a centralised point in Tokyo, transmitting facsimile pages by microwave to be printed by offset all over the country.

Hence **fac'similist**, one who makes facsimiles. **fac'similize, -ise** *v. trans.*, to make a facsimile of, reproduce exactly.

1862 *Sat. Rev.* XIV. 453/2 Netherclift .. is well known as a facsimilist. **1885** *Law Times* 2 May 11/2 Inglis, an expert in handwriting and facsimilist .. said [etc.].

facsimile (fæk'sɪmɪlɪ), *v.* [f. prec. sb.] *trans.* **a.** To serve as a facsimile of; to resemble exactly. *rare.* **b.** To make a facsimile of; to reproduce.

1839 LADY LYTTON *Cheveley* (ed. 2) II. v. 163 Two .. sofas facsimiled each other at either end of the fireplace. **1862** *Sat. Rev.* XIV. 454/1 The signature .. of Louis XIV of France, as here facsimiled. **1877** A. B. EDWARDS *Up Nile* Pref. 14 Even romances and tales are .. photographed, facsimiled in chromo-lithography.

absol. **1882** *Pall Mall G.* 15 June 5/1 They are the work of the artist who adapts, and not of the photographer who facsimiles.

Hence **fac'similed** *ppl. a.*

1887 *Athenæum* 3 Sept. 313/2 With facsimiled, but uncoloured illustrations.

fact (fækt), *sb.* Also 6 fackte, factt, 6–7 facte, 7 fack. [ad. L. *fact-um* thing done, neut. pa. pple. of *facĕre* to do. First in 16th c.; the earlier adoption of the OF. form survives with narrowed sense as FEAT.]

1. A thing done or performed. †**a.** in neutral sense: An action, deed, course of conduct. Occas. = effect. Also, action in general; deeds, as opposed to words. *Obs.*

1545 JOYE *Exp. Dan.* xi. Z vij b, Let emprours and kinges folow this godly kynges fact. **1592** WEST *1st Pt. Symbol.* §2 E, Right .. is the chiefest cause of obligations, the fact of man the remote cause. **1605** P. WOODHOUSE *Flea* (1877) 13 The minde doth make the fact, or good or ill. *a* **1626** BACON *Sylva* x. 243 As they are not to mistake the Causes of these Operations; So much lesse are they to mistake the Fact, or effect. **1643** PRYNNE *Sov. Power Parl.* App. 193 The fact of him who acts the Gardian, is imputed to the Co-gardians. **1708** SWIFT *Sent. Ch. Eng. Man*, A history of facts done a thousand years ago. **1745** P. THOMAS *Jrnl. Voy.* 206 At length he committed a Fact that completed the Destruction of himself and all his Family. **1815** JANE AUSTEN *Emma* II. xii, Gracious in fact if not in word.

†**b.** A noble or brave deed, an exploit; a feat (of valour or skill). *Obs.*

1543 GRAFTON *Contn. Harding* 603 For the whiche noble facte, the kynge created hym afterwarde duke of Norfolke. **1586** MARLOWE *1st Pt. Tamburl.* III. ii, His facts of war and blood. **1605** STOW *Ann.* 481 Henry Hotespurre .. taketh prayes, exercising laudable factes. **1667** MILTON *P.L.* II. 124 He who most excels in fact of Arms. **1730** A. GORDON *Maffei's Amphith.* 321 Whether this wonderful Fact was performed in the Theatre or Amphitheatre, Xiphiline .. leaves us in doubt.

c. An evil deed, a crime. In the 16th and 17th c. the commonest sense; now *Obs.* exc. in ***to confess the fact*** and ***after, before the fact,*** in which the sense approaches that of 2.

1539 *Act 31 Hen. VIII*, c. 8 Euery such .. person .. shall be adiudged a traytour, and his facte high treason. **1551** T. WILSON *Logike* (1580) 47 To marke thynges that goe before the facte, as whether he hated the man or no. **1577** HARRISON *England* II. xi. (1877) I. 223 He is .. hanged .. neere the place where the fact was committed. **1603** *Philotus* lxxxiii, For to commit sa foull ane fack. *a* **1626** BACON *Max. & Uses Com. Law* viii. (1635) 34 Any accessary before the fact is subject to all the contingencies pregnant of the fact. **1689** *Col. Rec. Pennsylv.* I. 252 In a Provinciall Court held in ye County of Kent, where ye ffact was Committed. *a* **1715** BURNET *Own Time* (1766) I. 21 All who were concerned in that vile fact were pardoned. **1769** BLACKSTONE *Comm.* IV. 39 Accessories after the fact being still allowed the benefit of clergy in all cases. **1772** *Ann. Reg.* 95 He was carried before Justice Russell, where he confessed the fact. **1869** FREEMAN *Norm. Conq.* (1876) III. xii. 92 An absolution after the fact might be one.

†**d.** Actual guilt (as opposed to suspicion). *Obs.*

1632 MASSINGER *Emperor of East* v. ii, Great Julius would not Rest satisfied that his wife was free from fact, But, only for suspicion of a crime, Sued a divorce.

†**e.** An action cognizable, or having an effect in law. *Obs.*

a **1626** BACON *Max. & Uses Com. Law* xxi. (1635) 89 If tenant intaile discontinue, or suffer a descent, or doe any other fact whatsoever.

†**2.** The making, doing, or performing. ***in the (very) fact*** = in the (very) act. *Obs.*

1548 HALL *Chron.* 157 b, These three articles he denied either for fact or thought. **1593** SHAKS. *2 Hen. VI*, II. i. 173 Naughtie persons .. Dealing with Witches and with Coniurers, Whom we haue apprehended in the Fact. **1616** B. JONSON *Devil an Ass* III. i. Wks. (Rtldg.) 360/1 A project, for the fact, and venting Of a new kind of fucus. **1626** BACON *Sylva* §795 Those effects which are wrought .. by things in fact, are produced likewise in some degree by the imagination. **1650–3** *Dissert. de Pace* in *Phenix* (1708) II. 382 Causes .. not of our fact and our avoiding. **1712** ADDISON *Spect.* No. 311 ¶ 1, I have myself caught a young Jackanapes .. in the very Fact. **1768** GOLDSM. *Good-n. Man* I. i, I caught him in the fact. **1807–8** W. IRVING *Salmag.* (1824) 20 She was detected .. in the very fact of laughing .. at the description.

†**3.** *Math.* = FACTUM 3. *Obs.*

1673 KERSEY *Algebra* I. iv. (1725) 15 A third Quantity which is called the Product, the Fact, or the Rectangle. **1721–1800** in BAILEY.

4. a. Something that has really occurred or is actually the case; something certainly known to be of this character; hence, a particular truth known by actual observation or authentic testimony, as opposed to what is merely inferred, or to a conjecture or fiction; a datum of experience, as distinguished from the conclusions that may be based upon it.

[In class. Lat. *factum* had occasionally the extended sense of 'event, occurrence'; hence in scholastic Lat. was developed the sense above explained, which belongs to all the Romanic equivalents: Fr. *fait*, It. *fatto*, Sp. *hecho*.]

1632 J. HAYWARD tr. *Biondi's Eromena* 21 They resolved that the Admirall should goe disguised .. to assure himselfe of the fact. **1691** T. H[ALE] *Acc. New Invent.* 52 The said Commissioners are to report to this Board the Truth of the Fact. **1745** in *Col. Rec. Pennsylv.* V. 13 These Facts plainly shew that the French [etc.]. **1749** SMOLLETT *Gil Bl.* x. i, Facts are stubborn things. **1774** GOLDSM. *Nat. Hist.* (1776) VI. 154 The reader, instead of observations or facts, is presented with a long list of names. **1782** PAINE *Let. Abbé Raynal* (1791) 26 Facts are more powerful than arguments. **1809–10** COLERIDGE *Friend* (1865) 62 It is an undoubted fact of human nature, that the sense of impossibility quenches all will. **1836** THIRLWALL *Greece* II. xv. 283 One fact destroys this fiction. **1875** JOWETT *Plato* (ed. 2) III. 611 The very great advantage of being a fact and not a fiction.

b. in apposition with a following clause, or with const. *of*. Now often used where the earlier lang. would have employed a clause or gerundial phrase as subject or as the regimen of a preposition; cf. mod. use of 'the *circumstance* that'. In apposition to a following noun clause: ***the fact that..*** = the circumstance that.

1722 DE FOE *Plague* (1756) 72 Persons alive .. who can justify the fact of this. **1803** G. MOORE *Diary* 15 Jan. in R. J. Mackintosh *Mem. Sir J. Mackintosh* (1835) I. iv. 175, I would not agree to the fact that ennui prevailed more in England than in France. **1834** *Edin. Rev.* Oct. 73 The only difference between Crabbe and himself is the fact, that the one was raised from the ranks, while the other is still remaining in them with at least equal independence. **1846** MILL *Logic* I. iii. §11 The fact of resemblance between relations is sometimes called analogy. **1851** CARPENTER *Man. Phys.* (ed. 2) 244 The physiological fact of the peculiar connection between the mind and the brain. **1851** QUEEN VICTORIA *Let.* 13 Oct. in *Queen Victoria's Early Lett.* (1963) 183 The Queen of Spain ought to be made aware of the fact that among the reigning Sovereigns, the Emperors of Austria and Brazil .. etc., etc., have not got the Garter. **1957** D. J. ENRIGHT *Apothecary's Shop* 209 The fact—not a new one—that Eliot doesn't pull his punches.

¶**c.** Occas. applied *concr.* to a person, an institution, etc. (A strained use.)

1858 HAWTHORNE *Fr. & It. Jrnls.* (1872) I. 14 The first Napoleon .. one of the external facts of the past. **1877** OWEN in *Wellesley's Desp.* p. xxi, The British Empire in India was already a great fact.

d. ***the fact is***: const. with following noun clause introduced by *that* or with *that* understood.

1836 R. OWEN *Bk. New Moral World* xii. 79 The simple fact is that the institutions of society have been formed .. to oppose one part of human nature to another. **1868** TROLLOPE *He knew he was Right* (1869) II. li. 15 You can remain a few minutes longer. The fact is, I've got something I want to say to you. **1875** JOWETT *Plato* (ed. 2) I. 23 Whereas the fact is that I enquire with you into the truth. **1959** *N.Z. Listener* 12 June 4/3 The fact is that Lord Bledisloe .. did not realise that everything he said was not entirely worth two or three columns in a busy metropolitan daily.

e. ***facts and figures***: an alliterative phrase used in the sense 'precise information'.

1845 DICKENS *Chimes* iv. 48 Facts and figures! Put 'em down! **1855** *Westm. Rev.* VIII. 438 The honorable gentleman on one side of the House is liable to have his facts and figures shown up by his honorable friend on the opposite side. **1903** H. JAMES *Ambassadors* IV. ix. 80 Strether .. put him in full possession of facts and figures. **1957** J. BRAINE *Room at Top* xii. 122 The hard materialists, the men of facts and figures.

f. ***fact of life***: a (stark) reality of existence; a brute fact; freq. ***the facts of life***, spec. as a colloq. euphemism for 'knowledge of human sexual functions'.

1854 THOREAU *Walden* ii. 98, I went to the woods because I wished .. to front only the essential facts of life. **1855** RIDER HAGGARD *K. Solomon's Mines* ii. 21 Elephant hunters are a rough set of men, and don't trouble themselves with much beyond the facts of life and the ways of Kafirs. **1893** 'S. GRAND' *Heavenly Twins* I. i. 6 He snubbed Evadne promptly .. when she mentioned a fact of life... 'Only confusion comes of women thinking for themselves on social subjects,' he said. **1895** HARDY *Jude* VI. ii. 426, I told him I was going to have another child... I couldn't bear deceiving him as to the facts of life. **1902** W. D. HOWELLS *Lit. & Life* 305, I have not touched upon these facts of life without the purpose of finding some way out of the coil. **1908** K. GRAHAME *Wind in Willows* ix. 196 To-day, the unseen was everything, the unknown the only real fact of life. **1908** MRS. H. WARD *Diana Mallory* III. xx. 435 The first withdrawal of the veil which hides .. the more brutal facts of life. **1913** *MacLean's Mag.* June 123/1 The tone of all the speeches at the meeting [of the Eugenics Education Society] emphasized the need of teaching boys and girls the essential facts of life, so as to equip them for the momentous time when they choose life partners. **1930** W. S. MAUGHAM *Breadwinner* I. 14, I shall never forget when I was leaving my prep school, and Dorothy told Alfred he must tell me what she called 'the facts of life'. **1932** WODEHOUSE *Hot Water* xiii. 225 Didn't your mother ever teach you the facts of life, Mrs. G.? Because one of them is never to be too friendly to people you meet on boats. **1953** L. P. HARTLEY *Go-Between* x. 124 The facts of life were a mystery to me. **1957** G. FABER *Jowett* v. 84 It must certainly have been at St. Paul's that he became disgustedly aware of the 'facts of life'. **1959** *News Chron.* 22 Oct. 5/4 Telling a child of the facts of life and marriage was .. one of the tasks that the family .. had abdicated to the schools. **1967** *Boston Sunday Globe* 23 Apr. 20/3 The conservationists' warning that we will bury ourselves in our own trash will become a fact of life. **1969** AUDEN *City without Walls* 71 Mother, tongue-tied with shyness, Struggling to tell him The Facts of Life he dared not Tell her he knew already.

5. Often loosely used for: Something that is alleged to be, or conceivably might be, a 'fact'.

a **1729** S. CLARKE *Serm.* lxix. Wks. 1738 I. 428 It would have been absurd to alleage in preaching to vnbelievers, a Fact which itself presupposed the Truth of Christ's mission. **1793–7** *Spirit Pub. Jrnls.* (1797) I. 356 If another soldier should call you a jail-bird, and the truth of the fact be notorious. **1824** *Westminster Rev.* II. 209 This is, as usual, a false fact, supported by a supposed motive. **1831** *Blackw. Mag.* June 900/1 The poison of false notions, and, if we may use an expression which, we believe, is in Junius, false facts. **1832** BP. THIRLWALL *Remains* (1878) III. 185 But I do not mean to deny the fact. **187.** *Ibid.* 489, I am not concerned to deny the fact. *Mod.* The writer's facts are far from trustworthy.

6. a. (Without *a* and *pl.*) That which is of the nature of a fact; what has actually happened or is the case; truth attested by direct observation or authentic testimony; reality. ***matter of fact***: a subject of discussion belonging to the domain of fact, as distinguished from *matter of inference*, *of opinion*, *of law*, etc. (See also MATTER.)

1581 E. CAMPION in *Confer.* II. (1584) M b, He speaketh of a matter of fact. **1641** EVELYN *Mem.* (1857) I. 31 A .. description of the matter-of-fact. **1736** BUTLER *Anal.* I. iii. Wks. 1874 I. 50 An instance .. collected from experience and present matter of fact. **1745–9** *Rep. Cond. Sir J. Cope* 115 'It is Fact' that something uncommon was expected. **1794** PALEY *Evid.* (1825) II. 271 The evangelists wrote from fact, not from imagination. **1832** LEWIS *Use & Ab. Pol. Terms* iii. 35 To deny the power of the legislature to dispose of it [property] at pleasure, is to confound expediency and justice with fact. **1836** J. GILBERT *Chr. Atonem.* iv. (1852) 120 This case of deliverance .. from the pangs of guilt .. is fact. **1875** JOWETT *Plato* (ed. 2) I. 241 Imagination is often at war with reason and fact. **1878** HUXLEY *Physiogr.* 68 As a matter of fact we rarely, if ever, experience either.

b. ***in fact***: in reality (cf. sense 1 and *indeed*). Now often used parenthetically in an epexegetical statement, or when a more comprehensive assertion is substituted for that which has just been made. ***in point of fact***: with regard to matters of fact; also (and now usually) = in fact.

1707 ADDISON *Pres. State War* 36 If this were true in Fact, I don't see any tolerable colour for such a conclusion. **1711** SWIFT *Jrnl. to Stella* 10 Nov., Three or four great people are to see there are no mistakes in point of fact. **1732** BERKELEY *Alciphr.* II. §24 In whatever light you may consider it, this is in fact a solid benefit. **1774** GOLDSM. *Nat. Hist.* (1776) I. 38 In fact, a thousand questions might be asked .. which he would not find it easy to answer. **1818** JAS. MILL *Brit. India* II. v. ix. 712 In point of fact, the influence exerted .. has never been great. **1871** SMILES *Charac.* ii. (1876) 49 Gray was, in fact, a feminine man. **1888** A. W. STREANE *Jeremiah* 102 In point of fact Jeremiah was absent from Jerusalem. *Mod.* He is very independent—extravagantly so, in fact.

c. ***the fact (of the matter)***: the truth with regard to the subject under discussion.

1852 C. M. YONGE *Two Guardians* vi. 101 This is the fact of the matter, as Mrs. Cornthwayte would say.

d. Other phrases of assertion or rejoinder: ***(and) that's a fact*** (orig. *U.S.*): an emphatic addition to a statement stressing its truth; also ***this is a fact, that's the fact; is that a fact?***: is that so? (used esp. as a rejoinder (expecting no answer) to a statement).

1779 F. BURNEY *Diary & Lett.* Jan. (1842) I. 163, I know of nobody else that calls me so. This is a fact, Susy. **1834** *Boston* (Mass.) *Post* 5 Aug. 7/2 To this statement of facts he replied—'I was groggy, I *know*; but what I *did*, I *don't* know, that's a fact.' **1844** DICKENS *Mart. Chuz.* xxi. 259 'It may not be so easy to do it.' 'And that's a fact,' said a voice.. close in his ear. **1851** MAYHEW *London Lab.* I. 417/1 Of the *maimed beggars*, some are really deserving objects, as without begging they must starve to death; that's a fact, sir. **1860** *Cornhill Mag.* II. 254 There is old Dr. Squaretoso (he certainly was very rude to me, and that's the fact). **1899** E. W. HORNUNG *Amat. Cracksman* 202 'My name is Raffles, and we met at Milchester last year.' 'Is that a fact?' cried the Scotchman. **1909** 'I. HAY' *Man's Man* viii. 135 'We're thinking of staying here.'.. 'Is that a fact?.. Weel, I'll bide too.' **1914** WODEHOUSE *Man Upstairs* 133 A man I met to-day told me you were engaged. Is that a fact? **1923** R. MACAULAY *Told by Idiot* II. xxi. 140 Bicycle bolts are a back number, and that's a fact. **1933** M. LOWRY *Ultramarine* III. 162 Can't bloody move and that's a fact. **1960** D. LESSING *In Pursuit of English* VI. 215 There is a lot of money to be made out of the libel law. That's a fact. **1962** N. MARSH *Hand in Glove* iv. 110 'It doesn't explain,' Alleyn said, 'why the wick in the lantern's been turned hard off, does it?' 'Is that a fact!' Raikes remarked, primly.

e. Sometimes with exclamation mark: used as an emphatic assertion of the truth of a statement.

1819 BYRON *Don Juan* 115, Note 4, page 25 *They only add them all in an appendix.* Fact. There is, or was, such an edition, with all the obnoxious epigrams of Martial placed by themselves at the end. **1848** J. R. LOWELL *Biglow P.* 1st Ser. 4 Fact! it takes a sight o' cotton To stuff out a soger's chest. **1899** R. WHITEING *No. 5 John St.* xxi. 213 'Garn!' 'Fack. It was like this.' **1907** WODEHOUSE *White Feather* viii. 88 We are, really. Fact. **1964** J. DRUMMOND *Welcome, Proud Lady* xvii. 81 'You astonish me.' 'Fact.'

7. *Law.* In *sing.* and *pl.* The circumstances and incidents of a case, looked at apart from their legal bearing. ***attorney in fact***: see ATTORNEY.

a **1718** PENN *Tracts* Wks. 1726 I. 501 The Jury is judge of Law and Fact. **1892** J. M. LELY *Wharton's Law Lex.* 616/1 When a jury is sworn it decides all the issues of fact.

8. *attrib.* and *Comb.*, as ***fact-fetishism***, ***-fetishist*** sbs.; ***fact-bound***, ***-crammed*** adjs.; ***fact-collecting***, ***-cramming*** vbl. sbs.; ***fact-gathering*** vbl. sb. and ppl. adj.; **fact-finding** *ppl. a.*, that finds out facts; esp. descriptive of a committee, commission, etc., set up to discover and establish the facts of any matter; also as *vbl. sb.*, the work involved in such a process; hence (as a back-formation) **fact-find** *v. intr.*; also ***fact-finder***; **fact-proof** *a.*, impervious to facts; **fact-sheet**, a paper on which facts relevant to a particular issue are set out briefly and clearly.

1959 *Encounter* Sept. 14/2 Their determination to stay precise and *fact-bound at all costs. **1937** V. WOOLF *Years* 380 I'm good, she thought, at *fact-collecting. **1894** *Westm. Gaz.* 4 Apr. 3/1 It was a clever *fact-crammed speech. **1907** *Daily Chron.* 16 Jan. 3/2 A fact-crammed encyclopædia. **1933** DYLAN THOMAS *Let.* Sept. (1966) 25 You've got more in your little finger than they have in the whole of their fact-crammed brains. **1876** C. M. YONGE *Womankind* vi. 49 The contact with a really powerful thinking mind.. ought not to be sacrificed to mere *fact-cramming. **1964** K. WINETROUT in I. L. Horowitz *New Sociology* 149 We wind up with *fact-fetishism, with a 'social science of the narrow focus, the trivial detail, the abstracted almighty unimportant fact'. **1960** *Spectator* 7 Oct. 527 The book meets the demands of the most hardbitten *fact-fetishist. **1969** J. MANDER *Static Soc.* ix. 319 Fact-fetishists as they are, both authors belong to the.. spirit of the Enlightenment. **1953** *N.Y. Times* 8 Feb. E 1/4 Ostensibly their mission was to *fact-find on the problem of speeding the rearmament of Europe. **1927** P. H. DE KRUIF *Microbe Hunters* ii. 67 The spirit of the searcher, the *fact finder, flashed out of his eye. **1909** G. B. SHAW *John Bull's Other Island* p. x, The actual distinction between the idolatrous Englishman and the *fact-finding Irishman. **1926** B. WEBB *My Apprenticeship* vi. 287 My super-enthusiasm for fact-finding. **1927** *N.Y. Times* 18 July 41/1 A fact-finding committee under the leadership of William P. MacCracken Jr., Assistant Secretary for Aeronautics. **1958** *Punch* 16 July 72/2 Sociologically, of course, we are up against the fact-finders. Fact-finding is to estimating as photography is to painting in oils. **1959** *Times* 24 Sept. 15/1 Account of a fact-finding tour of eighteen months spent in New China. **1969** *New Yorker* 31 May 34/2 A well-known congressman.. had gone there.. on a fact-finding trip. **1943** *Amer. Antiquity* IX. 208 American archaeology is still in its intense historical, *fact-gathering stage. **1958** T. LANDAU *Encycl. Librarianship* 118/1 His fact-gathering and his several publications about libraries. **1961** J. WILSON *Reason & Morals* iii. 185 A subject [*sc.* philosophy] which is really a kind of conceptual psychoanalysis, and not a fact-gathering subject. **1909** G. B. SHAW *John Bull's Other Island* p. ix, He is never quite the hysterical, nonsense-crammed, *fact-proof, truth-terrified, unballasted sport of all the bogy panics.. that now calls itself 'God's Englishman'. **1959** *Times Lit. Suppl.* 2 Jan. 11/4 This is partly what the Americans call a *fact-sheet on the military strengths of America and Russia. **1969** *Guardian* 23 Oct. 3/2 The distribution in Congress last night of a 'fact sheet' outlining the.. steps taken by the Nixon Administration.

†**fact**, *pa. pple. Obs.* [ad. L. *fact-us*: see FACT *sb.*] Made.

1600 TOURNEUR *Transf. Metamorph.* xxvi, The flesh.. of excrementale earth is wholly fact.

factable ('fæktəb(ə)l). *Archit.* Also 'factabling. [Alteration of FRACTABLE *sb.*] = COPING *sb.* 1, FRACTABLE *sb.*

1819 P. NICHOLSON *Archit. Dict.* 290/2 Coping upon the gable end of a house, is called *factabling* in Liverpool. **1842** GWILT *Archit.* Gloss. 971 *Factabling*, the same as Coping. **1904** W. E. R. WINDSOR *Let.* (to Clarendon Press), Factable. **1940** *Chambers's Techn. Dict.* 320/1 *Factable*, a coping.

factful ('fæktfʊl), *a.* [f. FACT *sb.* + -FUL.] **a.** Of a person: Well acquainted with facts. **b.** Of a literary work: Full or consisting of facts.

1875 HELPS *Anim. & Mast.* i. 19 Our fact-full friend whips out some unpleasant fact. **1887** *Sat. Rev.* 3 Sept. 337 The cheap little collection.. seldom admits numbers which are not 'matterful and factful', as some singular people say. **1910** *Daily Chron.* 15 Jan. 3/1 Mr Hyatt has given us the most factful and clear-visioned record of the founding of Rhodesia. **1930** H. WILLIAMSON *Village Bk.* 38 Most of them are naturally factful where their money is not concerned.

'facthood. *rare.* [f. FACT + -HOOD.] The summation of all that has really occurred or is actually the case.

1945 C. S. LEWIS *Great Divorce* v. 42, I will bring you to Eternal Fact, the Father of all other facthood. **1947** —— *Miracles* xi. 107 He is the opaque centre of all existences, the thing that simply and entirely *is*, the fountain of facthood.

†**'factible** *a.*

c **1630** W. OUGHTRED in Vernon *Life Heylin* (1682) 46 The difficulty of the place of [the moon's node] I saw factible at Sea.

factice ('fæktɪs). Formerly also **factis**. [ad. G. *factis*, *faktis*, f. L. *factic-ius* artificial (f. *facĕre* to make).] Any of several friable rubber-like substances made by vulcanizing unsaturated vegetable oils and used chiefly as compounding ingredients with rubber. Also called *(rubber) substitute*, and distinguished as *brown* or *white*.

1896 *Jrnl. Chem. Soc.* LXX. I. 204 Brown '*factis*' was next tried. A sample containing 15·48 per cent of sulphur, gave.. acids containing 14·14 per cent of sulphur. **1904** W. T. BRANNT tr. *Bersch's Cellulose & Artificial Rubber* xiv. 322 Under the name *factis*, masses have for some time been.. used as a direct substitute for rubber... Factis masses vary very much in appearance. **1912** *Chem. Abstr.* 937 White factice (substitute) is made from rape-seed oil, linseed oil, or cottonseed oil. **1954** DINSMORE & JUVE in G. S. Whitby *Synthetic Rubber* xi. 412 The factices.. decrease plasticity but somewhat improve extrusion behavior.

fac'ticity. [f. FACT *sb.* + -ICITY.] The quality or condition of being a fact; factuality.

1945 W. EBENSTEIN *Pure Theory of Law* iii. 114 What is the relation between.. the law's normativity.. and its 'facticity', that is, the efficacy of the idea of the law? **1956** *Scott. Jrnl. Theol.* IX. 310 [Man's] fall is.. from a knowledge of himself as a child, not of chance and facticity, but of God; all which is to say, his fall is into *sin* which is a term not in the existentialist vocabulary. **1960** H. READ *Forms of Things Unknown* IV. xi. 183 Suddenly in the excitement of the battle the soldier loses his self, his 'facticity', his consciousness of himself as a human being, and becomes an anonymous machine. **1970** J. DONCEEL tr. *Rahner's Trinity* III. 85 It accepts the incarnation and the descent of the Spirit as two facticities connected by a rather extrinsic bond. *Ibid.*, Such mere facticity makes the incarnation smack of mythology.

faction ('fækʃən), *sb.*[1] Also 6 faccion, fac(c)yon, 8 factione. [a. F. *faction*, ad. L. *factiōn-em*, n. of action f. *facĕre* to do, make.

The L. senses are: 1. action or manner of making or doing; 2. a class (of persons) either professional or social; 3. a political party, chiefly in bad sense, an oligarchical clique. The popular F. representative of the word, which had only the first sense, appears in Eng. as FASHION.]

†**1.** A doing or making: cf. FASHION.

a. Manner of acting or behaving; an action, proceeding, course of conduct. **b.** The action of doing or making something; an instance of this. *Obs.*

a. 1559 in Strype *Ann. Ref.* I. App. viii. 22 The Pope's Factions in refusing to.. confirme those which were duely electyd to Ecclesiasticall Dignities. **1607** TOPSELL *Four-f. Beasts* (1673) 110 The factions of dogs for their own ease:—When they lie down, they turn round in a circle two or three times together. *a* **1625** BOYS *Wks.* (1629) 628 The prisoner of Jesus Christ, in bonds not for any faction of yours or fault of his owne.

b. 1612 R. SHELDON *Serm. St. Martin's* 34 Their daily new makings, productions, factions, creations.. of Christ. **1676** R. DIXON *Two Test.* 29 Faction, when a Testator declares this to be his last Will and Testament. **1689** *Foxes & Firebrands* III. 216 Either by Creation or Faction from some pre-existing matter.

2. A class, sort, or set of persons. †**a.** *gen.*

1530 *Proper Dyaloge* (1863) 13 Dyuers facciones Of collegianes monkes and chanones Haue spred this region ouer all. **1591** SHAKS. *Two Gent.* IV. i. 37 This fellow were a King, for oure wilde faction. **1606** —— *Tr. & Cr.* II. i. 130, I will.. leaue the faction of fooles. **1606** HOLLAND *Sueton.* 187 He chose.. 5000.. young men out of the commons, who beeing sorted into factions should learne certaine kinde of shouts and applauses.

b. *spec.* in *Rom. Antiq.* One of the companies or organizations of contractors for the chariot races in the circus.

1606 HOLLAND *Sueton.* 188 A chariot driver one of the greene-coate faction. **1788** GIBBON *Decl. & F.* xl. IV. 69 The blue and green factions continued to afflict the reign of Justinian. **1869** LECKY *Europ. Mor.* I. iii. 231 An enthusiastic partisan of one of the factions in the chariot races. **1882** C. ELTON *Orig. Eng. Hist.* xi. 308 The factions of the Blues and Greens were promised as many chariot-races as could be run between morning and night.

c. *Sc.* A division of a class in school; a section.

1700 *Extracts fr. Aberdeen Reg.* 23 Oct. (Burgh Record Soc. 1872) 331 Item, in tyme of prayer that each *decurio* goe to the factione under his inspectione. **1870** J. BURNS *Mem. W. C. Burns* i. 20 He fought his way steadily.. through the class till he reached.. the highest 'faction'. **1872** D. BROWN *Life J. Duncan* ii. 14 Maintaining his position in the first faction or bench,—each faction containing only four boys.

3. A party in the state or in any community or association. Always with opprobrious sense, conveying the imputation of selfish or mischievous ends or turbulent or unscrupulous methods.

1509 FISHER *Fun. Serm. C'tess. Richmond* Wks. (1876) 296 If any faccyons or bendes were made.. she.. dyde boulte it oute. **1535** JOYE *Apol. Tindale* 33 Tindals faccion and his disciples.. beleue lyke their master. **1561** T. NORTON *Calvin's Inst.* I. viii. (1634) 25 Core, Dathan, and Abiram, and all that wicked faction. **1581** W. STAFFORD *Exam. Compl.* iii. (1876) 97 What continuall warres hath the Faction of the Arrians bene the occasion of? **1640** YORKE *Union Hon.* 331 Hee.. was Chiefe of the faction of the white Rose. **1667** PEPYS *Diary* (1877) V. 4 He hath joined himself with my Lady Castlemaine's faction. **1776** GIBBON *Decl. & F.* I. xviii. 493 The public tranquillity was disturbed by a discontented faction. **1828** D'ISRAELI *Chas. I*, I. vi. 157 Religion was running into factions. **1849** LEWIS *Infl. Author.* x. *note* 385, When a party abandons public and general ends, and devotes itself only to the personal interests of its members and leaders, it is called a faction, and its policy is said to be factious. **1868** E. EDWARDS *Raleigh* I. vii. 108 The Marian faction and the Spanish faction had played into each other's hands.

b. *transf.* and *fig.*

1614 BP. HALL *Recoll. Treat.* 1063 The faction of evill is so much stronger in our nature, then that of Good. **1627** P. FLETCHER *Locusts* II. ii, The spirit and flesh man in two factions rend. **1697** DRYDEN *Virg. Georg.* IV. 94 If intestine Broils allarm the Hive.. The Vulgar in divided Factions jar.

c. In Ireland applied to certain mutually hostile associations among the peasantry, consisting usually of the members of one particular family (which gives its name to the faction) and of their relatives and friends.

1830 W. CARLETON *Irish Peasantry* II. 29 His family was not attached to any faction—and when I use the word faction, it is in contradistinction to the word party—for faction, you know, is applied to a feud or grudge between Roman Catholics exclusively. **1838** S. C. HALL *Lights & Shad. Irish Life* I. 287 There's as many as twenty of my faction at the Greybeard's stone.

4. 'Party' in the abstract; self-interested or turbulent party strife or intrigue; factious spirit or action; dissension. †*to be in faction with*: to be in league with.

1538 STARKEY *England* I. iv. 106 Ther should be facyon and partys, wyth grete ambycyon and enuy. *a* **1652** BROME *Mad Couple* II. Wks. 1873 I. 33 The Rogue's in faction with 'em. **1682** BURNET *Rights Princes* Pref. 13 An Equality among Pastors, cannot hold long without Faction. **1735–8** BOLINGBROKE *On Parties* Ded. 16 But Faction hath no Regard to national Interests. **1795** BURKE *Th. Scarcity* Wks. 1842 II. 247 Idle tales, spread about by the industry of faction. **1841** EMERSON *Lect., Conservative* Wks. (Bohn) II. 276 The man of principle.. even in the fury of faction is respected. **1860** HOOK *Lives Abps.* I. vi. 348 The popularity, which faction was obliged.. to concede.

†**b.** A factious quarrel or intrigue. *Obs.*

1593 R. HARVEY *Philad.* 18 Hurdibras allayed the factions and quarrels that he found among his people. **1623** LAUD in Ellis *Orig. Lett.* II. 263 III. 241 A faction about the choice of a newe Governour. **1661–2** PEPYS *Diary* 22 June, There are factions (private ones at Court) about Madam Palmer.

5. *attrib.* and *Comb.*, as ***faction-fight***, †***-governor***; ***faction-mad***, ***-ridden***, adjs.

1841 in S. C. HALL *Ireland* I. 427 'The *faction-fights'.. said an intelligent countryman.. 'are a'most.. gone off the face of the country'. **1890** *W. Smith's Dict. Gr. & Rom. Antiq.* (ed. 3) I. 438 Even in Rome faction fights frequently took place towards the declining period of the empire. **1639** DRUMM. OF HAWTH. *Vind. Hamiltons* Wks. (1711) 238 Hamilton was not named by a private *faction-governour. **1784** COWPER *Task* III. 673 An overbearing race That, like the multitude made *faction-mad, Disturb good order. **1888** *Pall Mall G.* 6 Oct. 1/2 The distracted and *faction ridden Republic of France.

faction ('fækʃən), *sb.*[2] [Blend of FACT and FICTION.] A literary genre in which fictional narrative is developed from a basis of real events or characters; documentary fiction; similarly, in film-making, etc.; an instance of this.

1967 in H. ATKINSON *Games* (*Publisher's note*), This is the great work of faction of 1967—fiction based on fact, the novel form of our time. **1967** *Courier-Mail* (Brisbane) 30 Dec. 7/1 An Australian has tried his hand at writing a 'faction' (half fact, half fiction) novel. **1969** *Times* 13 Dec. (Sat. Rev.) p. iii/3 Novel reviewers who complain about the mongrel genre of 'faction' books have only themselves to blame. **1977** *Time* 14 Feb. 76/2 Haley called his saga 'faction', and therefore it cannot be evaluated merely as history or merely as an entertainment. **1980** *Times* 24 Apr. 8/1 He is an exponent of the dramatized documentary, sometimes known as 'faction', a method of film-making which has been severely criticized for blurring the dividing line between truth and fiction. **1981** *Daily Tel.* 19 June 18 John Gouriet.. delivered his.. warning to the West. It took the form of his first novel, a 'faction'.. called 'Checkmate the President'. **1983** *Listener* 30 June 16/1 His Merseyside is vivid enough, every bit as 'real' as those fictionalised documentaries we are learning to call 'faction'.

†**'faction**, *v. Obs.* [f. FACTION *sb.*[1]]

1. *intr.* To act in a factious or rebellious spirit; to intrigue; to mutiny. Also *to faction it*.

1609 BP. W. BARLOW *Answ. Nameless Cath.* 45 Preaching to them, not factioning against them. **1656** S. H. *Gold. Law* 81 They need not faction it for their places, being already

plac't. **1682** SOUTHERNE *Loyal Brother* III, This rebel nature factions in my breast.

2. *trans.* To form into factions.

1656 S. H. *Gold. Law* 35 They..divided and factioned the people to the Hazard and Ruine of al.

Hence †'**factioned** *ppl. a.*, †'**factioning** *vbl. sb.*

1653 HOLCROFT *Procopius* Pref., How are they commonly so faction'd and sided, that their Relations are but their Interests. **1656** S. H. *Gold. Law* 61 Which else by such factionings and rebellions might have been endangered.

-faction, repr. L. *-factiōnem*, forming nouns of action related to vbs. in -FY; properly used only where *-fy* represents L. *-facĕre*, Fr. *faire*, as in *satisfaction*; but through confusion occasionally used (instead of -FICATION) where *-fy* represents L. *-ficāre*, Fr. *-fier*, as in *petrifaction*.

factional ('fækʃənəl), *a.* [f. FACTION *sb.*¹ + -AL¹.] Of or belonging to a faction or factions; characterized by faction.

1650 B. *Discolliminium* 16 It must be a National Necessity, and not a Partiall or Factionall. **1832** *Fraser's Mag.* IV. 647 Aiding..the independent part of society..and balancing the interested and factional parts. **1876** *Contemp. Rev.* XXVII. 973 Jews factional, fanatical, full of hopes. **1881** *Fifeshire Jrnl.* 24 Mar. 4/3 There have been two factional victories in Scotland within a brief period.

factionalism ('fækʃənəlɪz(ə)m). [f. FACTIONAL *a.* + -ISM.] A condition characterized by faction; tendency to factional differences; the factional spirit.

1904 *Nation* (N.Y.) 31 Mar. 244/1 The natural remedy for ..such fierce factionalism as the Republicans are now displaying in office, is to turn them out. **1922** *Glasgow Herald* 21 Feb. 8 Italy..suffers in her political life from the ineradicable vice of factionalism. **1926** *Contemp. Rev.* Nov. 594 The provinces would be less subject to civil factionalism if the incentive to obtain control of Peking were absent. **1955** *Times* 23 Aug. 7/5 Whether Signor Fanfani's pleas for less factionalism will succeed in reuniting the party will not be clear for some weeks. **1970** *Daily Tel.* 23 July 6 An anthology refreshingly free both of personal prejudice and that factionalism with which Scottish life and letters abounds.

b. *spec.* In Communist usage.

1935 E. BURNS *Handbk. Marxism* 835 The Party is synonymous with unity of will, which leaves no room for any factionalism or division of authority in the Party. **1954** KOESTLER *Invisible Writing* ii. 25 'Factionalism'—the formation of groups with a policy of their own—was a capital crime in the Party.

'**factionalist**, *a.* [f. FACTIONAL *a.* + -IST.] = FACTIONAL *a.*

1958 *Listener* 13 Feb. 266/2 Narrow factionalist issues which concentrate on caste, religion, and education. *Ibid.* 267/1 Instead of nationalist enthusiasm..one sees only factionalist quarrels.

factionalize ('fækʃənəlaɪz), *v.* orig. and chiefly *U.S.* [f. FACTIONAL *a.* + -IZE.] **a.** *trans.* To cause (a political party, etc.) to divide into factions; to render factional. **b.** *intr.* To split into factions, to become factional. Also '**factionalized** *ppl. a.*, '**factionalizing** *vbl. sb.*

1970 *New Yorker* 14 Nov. 189/1 A party factionalized seemingly beyond repair. **1973** *Honolulu Star-Bull.* 2 Apr. A4 With the Democrats certain to be factionalized in at least some areas, the GOP'ers feel they'll have a good chance. **1976** *Dun's Rev.* Nov. 55/3 They will continue to 'factionalize, fractionalize and fight'. **1979** *Daily Tel.* 4 Dec. 15/2 Now that the times of radical factionalising are over.. is a better moment than most to take stock. **1981** *Word* XXXII. 213 The term politicolinguistics..carries several connotations..; the factionalizing of language as an issue in a community or nation; political factions divided along linguistic lines; [etc.]. **1982** *Christian Science Monitor* 27 Dec. 16/2 Though there was a tendency for students to factionalize, there were always students good about diplomacy. **1985** *Congress. Q. Weekly Rep.* 23 Mar. 535/1 It's going to take maturity on the part of Republicans not to factionalize when he [*sc.* Ronald Reagan] departs.

factionally ('fækʃənəlɪ), *adv.* [f. FACTIONAL *a.* + -LY².] By means of faction.

1893 *Columbus Dispatch* 16 Sept., It will be their purpose to not factionally prolong the session. **1953** *N.Y. Times* 22 Feb. IV. E3 Many Democrats who long have been factionally embroiled.

factionary ('fækʃənərɪ), *a.* and *sb.* [f. FACTION *sb.*¹ + -ARY.] **A.** *adj.*

†**1.** Taking part in a quarrel or dissension; active as a partisan.

1607 SHAKS. *Cor.* v. ii. 30 Remember my name is Menenius; alwayes factionary on the party of your Generale.

2. Of or pertaining to a faction.

1877 MRS. OLIPHANT *Makers Flor.* iv. 94 Whenever he [the monk] ascended to the higher eminences of the Church, he too became..a factionary and political leader.

B. *sb.* A member of a faction; a partisan.

1555 EDEN *Decades* 62 Many occasions were sought agenst Ancisus by Vascus and his factionaries. *a* **1834** COLERIDGE *Notes on Waterland* in *Lit. Remains* IV. 245 The unmistakable passions of a factionary and a schismatic. **1854** tr. *Lamartine's Celebr. Char.*, *Cromwell* II. 201 This religious enthusiasm..transformed a body of factionaries into an army of saints.

†'**factionate**, *v. Obs.* [f. as prec. + -ATE³.]

1. *trans.* To join together in a faction, band together.

1611 SPEED *Hist. Gt. Brit.* IX. xvi. §68 Whose bodies though thus diuided, their mindes continued most firmely fáctionated.

2. *intr.* To form factions.

1642 HALES *Tract conc. Schisme* 11 Factionating and tumultuating of great and potent Bishops.

factio'neer, *sb.* [f. as prec. + -EER¹.] A member of a faction, a party-man.

c **1710** *Light to Blind* fo. 626 in *10th Rep. Hist. MSS. Comm.* App. v. 142 The factioneers must have their will. **1732** SIR C. WOGAN *Let. to Swift* 27 Feb., He [Charles II] found himself obliged to..turn cabalist and factioneer. **1806** W. TAYLOR in Robberds *Mem.* II. 139 Appoint a factioneer by any other voice than the people's, and he is ruined.

factioneer (ˌfækʃə'nɪə(r)), *v. rare.* [f. prec. sb.] *intr.* To busy oneself in factions. Hence **factio'neering** *ppl. a.*

1881 *Glasgow News* 22 Mar., The dupe of factioneering dogmatism.

†'**factioner.** *Obs.* [f. FACTION *v.* + -ER¹.] One who makes or joins a faction; a partisan.

1587 HOLINSHED *Scot. Chron.* II. 440/1 The assemblie.. did..appoint generall fastings..especiallie, when some factioner in the countrie was to moue anie great enterprise. *c* **1610** SIR J. MELVIL *Mem.* (1735) 311 He was advertised by some Factioners that the Earls of Angus, Mar, etc...had an Enterprise in Hand. **1644** in Carte *Ormonde* III. 360 Ormonde's factioners meet every night.

factionist ('fækʃənɪst). [f. as prec. + -IST.]

a. One who promotes or leads a faction. **b.** A member of a faction, partisan. Also *attrib.*

1609 BP. W. BARLOW *Answ. Nameless Cath.* 67 A Libeller by custom, a Factionist in Societie. **1625** BP. MOUNTAGU *App. Cæsar* II. xxiv. 271 Wee live with Puritans and opposite factionists. **1718** STRYPE *Life Whitgift* I. xiii. 76 He [Dr. Still]..kept a strict Hand over the growing Factionists. **1830** D'ISRAELI *Chas. I*, III. i. 5 Leaders..may degenerate into factionists. **1891** *Daily News* 31 Oct. 6/5 The Parnellites were simultaneously holding a meeting, which was addressed by the factionist leaders.

†**facti'ose**, *a. Obs. rare*⁻⁰. [ad. L. *factiōs-us*: see next.] 'Given or inclinable to faction, seditious' (1727 Bailey, vol. II.).

factious ('fækʃəs), *a.* Also 6 faccious, factiouse. [ad. F. *factieux* or L. *factiōs-us*, f. *factiōn-em*: see FACTION *sb.*¹ and -OUS.]

1. Of persons and their dispositions: Given to faction; inclined to form parties, or to act for party purposes; seditious.

1535 JOYE *Apol. Tindale* 44 Calling me vaynglorious.. sedycious, factiouse, a sower of heresyes. *a* **1568** ASCHAM *Scholem.* I. (Arb.) 76 A discoursing tong, and a factious harte. **1593** SHAKS. *2 Hen. VI*, v. i. 135 Chop away that factious pate of his. **1624** CAPT. SMITH *Virginia* III. iii. 52 We should incurre the censure of factious and seditious persons. **1750** BERKELEY *Patriotism* §42 Wks. 1871 III. 457 The factious man is apt to mistake himself for a patriot. *a* **1850** CALHOUN *Wks.* (1874) II. 62 A factious opposition sickens at the sight of prosperity. **1874** GREEN *Short Hist.* x. (1876) 742 The factious spirit, which springs from a long hold of power.

2. Of actions, utterances, etc.: Pertaining to or proceeding from faction; characterized by party spirit.

1532 MORE *Confut. Tindale* Wks. 666/1 For the settyng foorth and auauncing of hys [Tindal's] false faccious heresies. **1606** SHAKS. *Tr. & Cr.* I. iii. 191 Ajax..makes factious Feasts. **1665** BOYLE *Occas. Refl.* IV. xi. (1675) 239 His Factious indignation at the Princes faults. **1782** PRIESTLEY *Corrupt. Chr.* I. I. 109 In this factious manner was the great doctrine..established. **1803** SYD. SMITH *Wks.* (1867) I. 25 Why can factious eloquence produce such limited effects in this country? **1862** LD. BROUGHAM *Brit. Const.* ix. §2. 120 The party chiefs used the mob more effectually for their own factious and selfish purposes.

factiously ('fækʃəslɪ), *adv.* [f. as prec. + -LY².] In a factious manner or spirit; with a factious purpose; in the interest of a faction.

1591 PERCIVALL *Sp. Dict.*, *Vanderizamente*, factiously. **1637** GILLESPIE *Eng. Pop. Cerem.* III. viii. 123 Why did they carry matters so factiously and violently? **1693** *Apol. Clergy Scot.* 47 They have stubbornly and factiously Conspired against the Apostolical Hierarchy. **1796** BURKE *Regic. Peace* iii. Wks. 1802 IV. 509 The opposition, whether patriotically or factiously, contending that [etc.].

factiousness ('fækʃəsnɪs). [f. as prec. + -NESS.] The quality or state of being factious; a disposition to make factions, or act in the interest of a faction; seditiousness.

1580 SIDNEY *Arcadia* (1622) 16 A gentleman..friendly, without factiousnes. **1581** MARBECK *Bk. of Notes* 67 Some.. did with their factiousnesse trouble the Church. **1679** KID in G. Hickes *Spirit of Popery* (1680) 14, I have been.. branded with Factiousness. *a* **1710** BP. BULL *Serm. Priestly Office* Wks. 1827 I. 166 Not to add to our load..by your way-ward factiousness. **1812** G. CHALMERS *Dom. Econ. Gt. Brit.* 428 Whatever might be the factiousness, or imbecility of statesmen, on either side the Irish Channel. **1884** *Manch. Exam.* 28 Oct. 5/7 The Opposition at question time displayed more than its usual factiousness.

factis, var. FACTICE.

†'**factist.** *Obs.*⁻⁰ [ad. F. *factiste* (Cotgr.), in OF. *faitiste*, f. L. *fact-* ppl. stem of *facĕre* to make + -IST.] 'A poet or play-maker' (Coles).

1696 in COLES. Whence **1775** in ASH.

†'**factitate**, *v. Obs. rare*⁻¹. [f. ppl. stem of L. *factitāre*, freq. of *facĕre* to do, make.] *intr.* ? To work busily.

1617 LANE *Sqr.'s Tale* 116 In her selfe to factitate, and proiectes to begett of greatest great.

factitious (fæk'tɪʃəs), *a.* [f. L. *factīci-us* made by art (f. *facĕre* to make) + -OUS.]

†**1.** Made by or resulting from art; artificial.

1646 SIR T. BROWNE *Pseud. Ep.* II. i. 51 It becomes the chiefest ground for artificiall and factitious gemmes. **1685** BOYLE *Salubr. Air* 39 Beer, Ale, or other factitious drinks. **1769** *De Foe's Tour Gt. Brit.* I. 293 The Stones of which it [Stone-henge] was composed, are not factitious. **1774** J. BRYANT *Mythol.* I. 236 The one was a natural eminence.. The other was a factitious mound. **1801** J. JONES tr. *Bygge's Trav. Fr. Rep.* xv. 382 His factitious black lead pencils..are not prepared from the native ore, but a composition..of iron and sulphur.

†**2.** Of soil, etc.: Produced by special causes, not forming part of the original crust of the earth. *Obs.*

1684 T. BURNET *Th. Earth* I. 137 Those [islands] I call factitious, that are not of the same date and antiquity with the sea, but have been made..by accidental causes. **1739** LABELYE *Short Acc. Piers Westm. Bridge* 7 This Bed of Sand, Mud and Dirt, is a factitious Bed. **1794** S. WILLIAMS *Vermont* 80 Factitious soil, formed of decayed or rotten leaves. **1808** WILFORD *Sacr. Isles* in *Asiat. Res.* VIII. 298 The factitious soil of the Gangetic provinces..has been brought down by the alluvions of rivers.

3. Got up, made up for a particular occasion or purpose; arising from custom, habit, or design; not natural or spontaneous; artificial, conventional.

1678 CUDWORTH *Intell. Syst.* Pref., The Atheists Artificiall and Factitious Justice, is Nothing but Will and Words. **1748** HARTLEY *Observ. Man* I. iv. 420 The factitious ..Nature of these Pleasures. **1776** GIBBON *Decl. & F.* I. ix. 174 The use of gold and silver is in a great measure factitious. **1796** MORSE *Amer. Geog.* II. 51 Factitious wants created by luxury. **1810** BENTHAM *Packing* (1821) 67 The mass of factitious expence and delay ..with which the approaches to justice are clogged. **1848** MILL *Pol. Econ.* I. xi. §4 Its acquisition was invested with a factitious value. **1865** TYLOR *Early Hist. Man.* ii. 23 Factitious grammatical signs. **1871** FREEMAN *Norm. Conq.* (1876) IV. xviii. 106 The momentary and factitious joy which had greeted the day of William's crowning died utterly away.

Hence **fac'titiously** *adv.*, in a factitious manner. **fac'titiousness**, the quality of being factitious.

1795 *Encycl. Brit.* XIV. 478 There is no such Fear, as is factitiously pretended, of Popery and arbitrary Power. **1836-7** SIR W. HAMILTON *Metaph.* xxxiv. (1859) II. 279 Our factitiously complex..notions, are all merely so many products of Comparison. **1858** HAWTHORNE *Fr. & It. Jrnls.* II. 59 Festivity, kept alive factitiously. **1668** WILKINS *Real Char.* II. i. §3. 28 Factitiousness, artificial, technical, made. **1883** T. HARDY in *Longm. Mag.* July 257 As the day passes on..and he is still unhired, there does appear a factitiousness in the smile.

factitive ('fæktɪtɪv), *a.* and *sb. Gram.* [ad. mod.L. *factitīv-us*, irregularly f. *fact-* ppl. stem of *facĕre* to make.] **A.** *adj.* **a.** Of a verb: Expressing the notion of making a thing to be (either objectively or in thought or representation) of a certain character (*e.g.* 'to *make* a man king', 'to *call* one a fool', 'to *paint* the door green'); taking a complementary object; = FACTIVE 2. Also in ***factitive object, predicate,*** or ***accusative***, the complementary accus. governed by a factitive verb. **b.** By some grammarians used for: Causative.

1846 J. W. GIBBS *Philol. Stud.* (1857) 95 The simple infinitive was also used to denote the second object after a factitive verb. *Ibid.* 69 The factitive relation..a favorite technical term of the New or Beckerian Philology..is [etc.]. *Ibid.* 70 This second object is called the factitive object. **1871** *Public School Lat. Gram.* §110. 251 Verbs called Factitive..because they contain the idea of making by deed, thought, or word. **1877** WHITNEY *Eng. Gram.* 166.

B. *sb.* A factitive verb.

1889 in *Cent. Dict.* **1934** PRIEBSCH & COLLINSON *German Lang.* II. iii. 230 It [*sc. ver*] further forms factitives from adjectives, e.g. *verbittern*, *versüssen*.

Hence '**factitively** *adv.*

1877 WHITNEY *Eng. Gram.* 166 Even intransitive verbs are thus used factitively.

factive ('fæktɪv), *a.* [f. L. type *_factīv-us_, f. *facĕre* to make.]

†**1.** Tending or having the power to make; concerned with making. *Obs.*

1612 R. SHELDON *Serm. St. Martin's* 35 What new existencies are made of one Christ, by your productiue, creatiue, and factiue consecrations. *a* **1625** BOYS *Wks.* (1629) 206 The factiue sciences have their excellencies, specially painting and nauigation. **1649** BULWER *Pathomyot.* I. iii. 11 Factive motion is..restriction to animall actions performed by the abilitie of the Muscles.

2. *Gram.* (See quot.; = FACTITIVE.)

1880 *Public School Lat. Primer* 134 Factive Verbs are such as may be said to make..a thing to be of a certain character, by deed, word or thought..Factive Construction in the Passive becomes Copulative.

Hence †**fac'tivity**, capacity, range of activity.

a **1643** J. SHUTE *Judgem. & Mercy* (1645) 82 He perswades himselfe it is in his factivity, because another hath done it.

factlessness ('fæktlɪsnɪs). *nonce-wd.* [f. FACT *sb.* + -LESS + -NESS.] The quality of being devoid of or wanting in facts.

1887 *Sat. Rev.* 19 Nov. 708 An instance of the 'factlessness' of the book.

factoid ('fæktɔɪd), *sb.* and *a.* [f. FACT + -OID.]

A. *sb.* Something that becomes accepted as a fact, although it is not (or may not be) true; *spec.* an assumption or speculation reported and repeated so often that it is popularly considered true; a simulated or imagined fact.

1973 N. MAILER *Marilyn* i. 18/2 Factoids..that is, facts which have no existence before appearing in a magazine or newspaper, creations which are not so much lies as a product to manipulate emotion in the Silent Majority. **1977** MCKNIGHT & TOBLER *Bob Marley* v. 60 On such flimsy evidence, many is the factoid that has been created. **1982** *Listener* 11 Feb. 34/1 A vicious circle of misinformation and garbled folklore factoids. **1983** *Washington Post Mag.* 19 June 9/2 They spend their days with 'factoids'—data produced by a computer's simulation of the world as it might be. **1987** I. RUFF *Dead Reckoning* 59 A record not of the actual truth but a series of semi-fictional factoids.

B. *adj.* Of or having the character of a factoid, quasi-factual; *spec.* designating writing (esp. journalism) which contains a mixture of fact and supposition or invention presented as accepted fact.

1976 *Daily Tel.* 18 Feb. 14/3 The current television trend of 'factoid' journalism, reporting events which may have happened. **1977** *Even. Standard* 20 June 2/3 This..space mystery, presented in factoid form as a news report. **1980** *Encounter* Oct. 30/2 It is a valuable and entertaining, if partisan and factoid, chapter in the struggle to reveal the intimate secrets of the judiciary to those it exists to serve.

factor ('fæktə(r)), *sb.* Also 6–7 **factour.** [ad. Fr. *facteur*, ad. L. *factor*, agent-n. f. *facĕre* to do, make. Some of the obs. senses are immediately from L.]

I. A doer, agent.

†**1.** One who makes or does (anything); a doer, maker, performer, perpetrator; an author of a literary work. *Obs.* or *arch.*

1563 *Mirr. Mag., Hastings* xxxi, Foes of vertue, factours of all evylls. **1598** J. DICKENSON *Greene in Conc.* (1878) 116 Where vertue hath one affecter, vice hath many factors. *a* **1635** CORBET *Poems* (1807) 18 Their plays had sundry grave wise factors, A perfect diocess of actors. **1647** CLARENDON *Hist. Reb.* III. (1702) I. 141 An avow'd Factor and Procurer of that odious Judgement. **1863** MRS. C. CLARKE *Shaks. Char.* xiii. 321 To fasten upon the factor of his monster-crime its responsibility.

†**2.** A partisan, adherent, approver. *Obs.* [So in med.Lat.; Du Cange regards it as a corruption of the synonymous FAUTOR; but cf. L. *facere cum aliquo* to take a person's side.] In the latest examples with mixture of sense 1 or 3.

1502 ARNOLDE *Chron.* (1811) 177 Alle the ..whiche done ..byleuen in whichcrafte and sorsery..and their facturs. **1542–7** BOORDE *Introd. Knowl.* xvi. (1870) 165 Martyn Leuter & other of hys factours, in certayne thynges dyd take synistrall opinions. **1642** FULLER *Holy & Prof. St.* v. 400 Modern Factours for the Independent congregations. **1685** STILLINGFL. *Orig. Brit.*, Two very busie Factours in the Arian Cause. **1715** BENTLEY *Serm.* x. 365 What is he but a vile Factor to Libertinism and Sacrilege?

3. One who acts for another; an agent, deputy, or representative. Now *rare*.

1485 CAXTON *Chas. Gt.* iii. (1881) 16 The kyng..sente anone Aurelyen his factour. **1551** EDW. VI *Let.* in *Udall's Royster D.* (1847) p. xxx. *note*, Lycense to..Nicholas Udall and to his factors and assignes to prynt..the worke of Peter Marter. **1563–87** FOXE *A. & M.* (1684) III. 643 They.. Authorised..the Vicechancellor, to be the common Factor for the University. **1631** GOUGE *God's Arrows* IV. xv. 397 Parker was a kind of factor for English Seminaries and Nunnes beyond sea. *a* **1704** T. BROWN *Sat. Quack* Wks. 1730 I. 63 Death's busy factor, son of desolation. **1776** ADAM SMITH *W.N.* v. i. (1869) II. 298 These judges were a sort of itinerant factors, sent round the country for the purpose of levying certain branches of the king's revenue. **1862** MERIVALE *Rom. Emp.* (1865) IV. xxxiii. 104 The jealousy of the emperor was peculiarly sensitive in regard to every act and word of his factor at Alexandria.

fig. **1601** DENT *Pathw. Heaven* 72 All other vices are but Factors to Couetousness. **1673** S. C. *Art Complaisance* 70 Reason and honesty are too oft made factours to their avarice.

4. a. *Comm.* One who buys and sells for another person; a mercantile agent; a commission merchant. Also in *comb.*, as ***corn-, cotton-, produce-, wool-***, etc. ***factor.***

At the present time, a factor is distinguished from an ordinary agent or broker, in having actual possession of the goods he deals in, and trading in his own name (*N.E.D.*).

1491 in Arnolde *Chron.* (? 1503) 40/1 Shall ressayue the said v. C. frank of yᵉ said J. de castro and alonso or of any of them or of theyr factors. **1523** *Act 14–15 Hen. VIII*, c. 1 No person..shall sell..to any marchaunt..or to any of his.. factours..any maner of brode white wollen clothes. *c* **1592** MARLOWE *Jew of Malta* I. i, Bid my factor bring his loading in. **1683** *Lond. Gaz.* No. 1852/8 A Factor..for Norwich Hose or Stockings. **1727** A. HAMILTON *New Acc. E. Ind.* I. x. 113 Send Factors all over India to carry on trade. **1745** *De Foe's Eng. Tradesman* II. xlviii. 212 The buyers of cheese, butter, corn and malt, are called factors. **1850** W. IRVING *Mahomet* v. (1853) 26 Mahomet..was employed by different persons as..factor in caravan journeys to Syria. **1891** *P.O. London Directory* 1689/3 Corn and flour factors. See also..Malt factors..Hop factors..Seed factors.

b. One of the third class of the East India Company's servants. *Obs.* exc. *Hist.*

[**1600** *Min. Crt. Adventurers* 23 Oct. in *Cal. State Papers, E. Indies* (1862) 109 Thos. Wasse to be employed as factor. *Ibid.* 18 Nov. *ibid.* 111 Three principal factors to have each 100*l.* for equipment..four of the second sort to be allowed 50*l.*..four of the third sort 50*l.*..and four of the fourth and last sort 20*l.* each.] **1675–6** in J. Bruce *Ann. East-India Co.* (1810) II. 375 We do order, that..when the Writers have served their times they be stiled Factors. **1781** LD. CORNWALLIS *Corr.* (1859) I. 378 We..have a council and senior and junior merchants, factors and writers, to load one ship in the year. **1800** WELLINGTON in Owen *Desp.* 719 Writers or factors filling the stations of registers.

c. At Birmingham and Sheffield: A trader who buys hardware goods from the workman or 'little master' by whom they are made, usually causing his own trade-mark to be stamped upon them.

1833 J. HOLLAND *Manuf. Metal* II. 13 The operatives pressed between reduced prices and want of work, betook themselves to the factors. The factor..advanced to the workman a small sum to purchase the requisite tools.

d. *attrib.*

1858 H. VAUGHAN *Address River Usk* Pref. 18 The factour-wind from far shall bring The odours of the scattered spring. **1711** SHAFTESB. *Charac.* (1737) I. 304 Certain merchant adventurers in the letter-trade, who in correspondence with their factor-bookseller, are enter'd into a notable commerce with the world. **1880** BROWNING *Dram. Idylls* 2nd Ser. *Clive* 91 This fell in my factor-days.

5. a. One who has the charge and manages the affairs of an estate; a bailiff, land-steward. *Obs.* exc. *Sc.*

1561 T. NORTON *Calvin's Inst.* II. viii. (1634) 187 If any idle Factor or Bayliffe doe devoure his masters substance. **1640–1** *Kirkcudbr. War-Comm. Min. Bk.* (1855) 17 That he retein in his own hand his factor's fie. **1683** *Pennsylv. Archives* I. 54 Wᵐ Pickering of yʳ Province factor..to one Growden. **1722** *Wodrow Corr.* (1843) II. 672 Call for as many copies as you want..from Mr. McEwen's factor. **1804** J. BRISTED *Pedestrian Tour* I. 230 Lord Kinnaird's factor, or bailiff-steward. **1840** CARLYLE *Heroes* (1858) 326 The Steward, Factor as the Scotch call him, used to send letters and threatenings. **1885** *Act 48 Vict.* c. 16 §11 It shall not be lawful for any assessor..to be employed as a factor for heritable property or land agent.

b. A person legally appointed to manage forfeited or sequestered property. *Sc.*

1690 *Acts of Sederunt* 31 July, The factor shall be lyable for annualrent of what rents he shall recover. **1753** *Stewart's Trial* 153 The sole offence taken at Glenure, was his acting in the quality of factor on the forfeited estate of Ardshiel. **1885** R. BELL *Hand-bk. Law Scot.* §1480 To take measures for the preservation of the estate..by the appointment of a judicial factor.

c. *U.S. Law.* (See quot.)

1878 DRAKE *Attachm.* (ed. 5) §451 In Vermont and Connecticut, he [the garnishee] is sometimes called a *factor*, and the process [of garnishing], *factorizing process*.

II. 6. *Math.* One of two or more numbers, expressions, etc., which when multiplied together produce a given number, expression, etc. Also, ***common, primary, prime factor***, for which see the adjs. Used also of groups, rings, and other sets that can be produced from a given group, etc., by an analogue of division. So ***factor group***, etc. (see 9).

1673 KERSEY *Algebra* I. iv. (1725) 15 The Quantities given to be multiplied one by the other are called Factors. **1780** HUTTON in *Phil. Trans.* LXX. 408 For that *zy* may be positive, the signs of the two factors *z* and *y* must be alike. **1855** H. SPENCER *Princ. Psychol.* (1872) II. VII. i. 305 Error in either factor must involve error in the product. **1881** MAXWELL *Electr. & Magn.* I. 1 Every expression of a Quantity consists of two factors or components. **1906** W. H. & G. C. YOUNG *Theory Sets of Points* iv. 37 If the sets G_1, G_2, ..are all equivalent, and γ be their number,..or their potency in the general case, the equation $g = \gamma g_1$ is substituted for the preceding equation [sc. $g = g_1 + g_2 +$ ..]; *g* is then called the product of the factors γ and g_1. **1965** J. J. ROTMAN *Theory of Groups* iv. 58 If $G = H \times K$, *H* is called a direct factor of *G*; in additive notation, *H* is a direct summand of *G*.

7. a. *transf.* An element which enters into the composition of anything; a circumstance, fact, or influence which tends to produce a result. ***factor cost*** (see quot. 1941).

1816 COLERIDGE *Lay Serm.* 339 The reason..is the science of the universal, having the ideas of oneness and allness as its two elements or primary factors. **1845–6** TRENCH *Huls. Lect.* 1st Ser. i. 14 This Book..is so essential a factor in the spiritual life of men. **1878** GLADSTONE *Prim. Homer* 77 The first factor in the making of a nation is its religion. **1941** *Economist* 12 Apr. 489/2 There are two methods of valuation: the first at *factor cost* (that is, at what it costs to produce this output), the second at *market prices* (that is, at cost plus the indirect taxes and rates that have to be added in before the output can be sold). **1956** F. LAFITTE in A. Pryce-Jones *New Outl. Mod. Knowl.* 579 Factor-cost measurement gives a true indication of the amount of real economic resources appropriated by State 'consumption' services. **1971** *E. Afr. Jrnl.* Mar. 17/1 In 1963, agriculture, forestry and fishing contributed 8·2% of gross domestic product at factor cost.

b. *Genetics. Orig.*, a gene or other agent that is transmitted from parent to offspring and influences or determines a hereditary character; now *esp.* an agent that has not been shown to have the precise attributes usu. implied by the word 'gene'.

The sense 'gene' continues esp. in contexts that are elementary or have allusion to the historical development of genetics. For a discussion of the uses of G. *faktor, factor* by Gaertner 1849, Mendel 1865, and De Vries 1889, see R. C. Olby *Origins of Mendelism* (1966); the use in English prob. arose naturally out of sense 7 rather than as a consequence of the German.

1901 K. PEARSON in *Phil. Trans. R. Soc.* A. CXCVII. 287 Differentiation, whether due to function, position on the individual, season of production, &c., is usually connected with one or two well-marked dominating factors. **1905** BATESON & GREGORY in *Proc. R. Soc.* B. LXXVI. 581 The mode of appearance of a new type [of *Primula*] by the recombination of the factors brought in by the pure parental type. **1906** W. BATESON et al. in *Rep. Evol. Comm. R. Soc.* III. 3 The appearance of colour is due to the association, in one zygote, of two factors belonging to independent allelomorphic pairs. **1907** R. C. PUNNETT *Mendelism* (ed. 2) 23 Every zygotic cell, being formed by the fusion of two gametes, is a double structure, and contains two factors belonging to any given pair of characters. **1910** L. DONCASTER *Heredity* 136 In Mendelian inheritance, the hereditary determinant of a particular character is spoken of as the factor for that character. **1920** *Amer. Naturalist* LIV. 97 (*heading*) Are the factors of heredity arranged in a line? **1927** HALDANE & HUXLEY *Anim. Biol.* ii. 62 These units are called factors of heredity, or sometimes still more shortly the *genes*. **1949** DARLINGTON & MATHER *Elem. Genetics* ii. 40 We must then say that the two alternative determinants or factors of each kind in a zygote may be alike or different. **1958** BROCKLEHURST & WARD *Gen. School Biol.* xxii. 303 The alternative characters, round or wrinkled cotyledons and yellow or green cotyledons, are caused to develop by factors of two allelomorphic pairs. **1961** U. MITTWOCH tr. *Hadorn's Developmental Genetics* i. 1 Not all hereditary factors which obey Mendelian laws should be described as genes, and this applies particularly to lethal factors. A large number of these are due to a loss of more or less extensive pieces of chromosome.., and such deficiencies are also inherited in a Mendelian manner. **1964** D. WILKIE *Cytoplasm in Heredity* i. 1 Non-mendelian patterns of inheritance are often interpreted as demonstrating genetic control by cytoplasmic factors.

c. *Photogr.* In full ***filter factor.*** (See quot. 1921.)

1909 C. E. K. MEES *Photogr. Coloured Objects* iii. 19 If we wish to find the multiplying factor of this filter, we must consider it in relation to the sensitiveness curve of the plate. **1912** E. J. WALL *Dict. Photogr.* (ed. 9) 338 It is very important to know the number of times the exposure is to be increased; it is not a constant factor..but varies according to the light. **1921** *Photogr. Jrnl.* Apr. 168 A filter factor is the ratio of the exposure required with a given filter to the exposure without the filter. **1961** G. MILLERSON *Technique Telev. Production* iii. 40 Any filter introduces some light loss, and the working aperture has to be increased, or lighting augmented to compensate. This light attenuation is known as the filter's *factor*. A 'times four' (× 4) filter..requires four times the normal exposure.

d. *Med.* Each of several substances in the blood which are involved in the process of coagulation and have been assigned identifying (usu. Roman) numbers; ***factor VIII*** (or ***eight***), a beta globulin whose congenital deficiency is the cause of hæmophilia.

[**1903** *Zentralblatt für Physiol.* XVII. 530 Auch gibt es kein wirksames Ferment, das ohne die Mitwirkung aller dieser drei Faktoren entstände.] **1911** *Amer. Jrnl. Physiol.* XXIX. 209 Circulating blood contains normally all the necessary fibrin factors, namely, fibrinogen, prothrombin, and calcium. **1947** P. A. OWREN in *Acta Med. Scand.* Suppl. CXCIV. 76 The investigations..demonstrate that besides prothrombin, thrombokinase, calcium and fibrinogen a fifth factor is needed in order to ensure a normal course of the coagulation process. The factor which is included in the first stage of the coagulation process will be termed *Factor V*. **1954** F. KOLLER in *Blood* IX. 286 The following designations have been proposed: Factor disappearing during coagulation: Antihemophilic globulin of Cohn et al. Factor VIII. *Deficiency*: hemophilia A. **1961** [see CHRISTMAS DISEASE]. **1974** PASSMORE & ROBSON *Compan. Med. Stud.* III. xxi. 56/1 Factors II (prothrombin), VII, IX and X are all manufactured by the liver in the presence of adequate vitamin K_1. **1981** *Economist* 13 June 85/2 Several products..are likely to be made by genetic engineering including human albumin, factor eight, [etc.]. **1983** *Oxf. Textbk. Med.* II. xix. 111 A 50 per cent level of factor VIII ..is compatible with a normal haemostatic response. **1984** J. F. LAMB et al. *Essent. Physiol.* (ed. 2) iv. 85 The formation of the active form of factor X can occur..by an *intrinsic* pathway, which probably starts with activation of factor XII by collagen. **1985** *Listener* 14 Feb. 5/3 Many haemophiliacs who have received the blood-clotting substance factor eight have also become infected.

e. With defining word, as ***Falklands factor***, designating an event, etc., which may be a significant element in the outcome of a larger situation; *spec.* one which affects the position of a political party in the polls.

1982 *Washington Post* 7 May A26/4 One of the Social Democrats' four co-leaders, William Rodgers, said, 'The Falklands factor is a major one' in the disappointing showing of his party. **1986** *Observer* 4 May 4/5 With the Libyan Legacy taking over from the Falklands Factor, the only question about Thursday's local elections is the extent of Labour's gains. **1986** *Ibid.* 11 May 9/7, I did..wonder whether the Fulham Factor, or the..Kinnock Revival, would increase Labour's share at Liberal expense in West Derbyshire to the extent that the Conservatives would have an adequate majority.

8. a. ***factor of safety***: the ratio between the load which a structure or material is capable of supporting and the load which it is required to support, or between the stress which causes it to break and the stress which it is required to stand; also, the ratio between the elastic limit of the structure and the usual load. Cf. SAFETY 6.

1858 [see SAFETY 6]. **1866** W. J. M. RANKINE *Usef. Rules* 205 Factors of safety for perfect materials and

workmanship... Dead Load 2. Live Load 4. **1876** *Encycl. Brit.* IV. 296/2 In designing a girder the load which it will have to carry is multiplied by a number called the factor of safety, varying from 3 to 6. **1877** W. H. WHITE *Man. Naval Archit.* 377 Supposing a factor of safety of 8 to be taken instead of 10, the safe working load..for timber subject to compressive strains would be about three-eighths of a ton per square inch. **1891** [see SAFETY 6]. **1910** *Hawkin's Electr. Dict., Factor of safety,* 1. A term expressive of a determined limit to which materials or machines shall be subjected; the safety limit. 2. In wiring, the ratio between the breaking stress of a wire and the maximum tension to which it is subjected in overhead suspension. **1962** *B.S.I. News* Aug. 20/1 The factor of safety is really a factor of ignorance. The factor of safety becomes less as we learn more about properties and behaviour of materials. **1970** H. BRAUN *Parish Churches* x. 132 Their buildings were massive and employed a wide factor of safety to achieve moderate heights.

b. *factor of merit* (*Electr. Engin.*): a measure of the sensitivity of a reflecting galvanometer (see quot. 1922). Cf. *figure of merit* (FIGURE *sb.* 20c).

1890 W. E. AYRTON et al. in *Phil. Mag.* XXX. 84 An important..question to decide is whether the factor of merit of a galvanometer should be stated for a constant periodic time of oscillation..or for a constant controlling-field. **1922** GLAZEBROOK *Dict. Appl. Physics* II. 375/1 The accepted period being 10 seconds, it follows that for any galvanometer the Factor of Merit is 100 $D/T^2(R_G)^{1/2}$ or 100 $D/T^2(R_G)^{2/5}$, T being the period in seconds, R_G the resistance of the galvanometer, and D the deflection in millimetres at 1 metre.

9. *Comb.* **factor analysis** *Statistics*, a mathematical technique for calculating the relative importance of each of a set of factors that together are assumed to influence some observed set of values or properties; **factor group** *Math.* [tr. G. *factorgruppe* (O. Hölder, 1889)], a group G/H the elements of which are the cosets in a given group G of a normal subgroup H of G; **factor law** = *factor theorem*; **factor theorem** *Algebra*, the theorem that if $f(x)$ is a polynomial and $f(a) = 0$, then $(x - a)$ is a factor of $f(x)$, and conversely.

1931 L. L. THURSTONE in *Psychol. Rev.* XXXVIII. 406 It is the purpose of this paper to describe a more generally applicable method of factor analysis which has no restrictions as regards group factors and which does not restrict the number of general factors that are operative in producing the correlations. **1938** *Mind* XLVII. 102 The results of a factor-analysis of the abilities involved, are..to be investigated. **1946** H. CRAMÉR *Math. Methods Statistics* xxxvii. 555 In the psychological factor analysis of human ability, the variables $x_1, .., x_m$ represent the measurements of m given different variables of a person, while $u_1, .., u_n$ are more or less 'general' factors of intelligence, and $v_1, .., v_m$ are 'specific' factors, each associated with a particular ability. **1969** *Computers & Humanities* III. 145 While there are several varieties of factor analysis, each of which is designed to handle a special type of problem, they all involve rather elaborate mathematical operations. **1897** W. BURNSIDE *Theory Groups Finite Order* vii. 119 If a group has two different composition-series, the number of terms in them is the same and the factor-groups derived from them are identical except as regards the sequence in which they occur. **1965** PATTERSON & RUTHERFORD *Elem. Abstract Algebra* ii. 49 If G is a finite group of order m and H is a normal subgroup of order n, then..the factor group G/H is a finite group of order m/n. **1901** W. J. MILNE *Acad. Algebra* 104 Factor Law.—If a rational integral expression containing x reduces to zero when a is substituted for x, it is exactly divisible by $x - a$. **1908** —— *Stand. Algebra* 106 (*heading*) Factor Theorem. **1928** PALMER & MISER *Coll. Algebra* ii. 31 The factor theorem assists in factoring by giving a quick way for testing a possible factor. **1966** J. V. ROBISON *Mod. Algebra & Trig.* xi. 242 (*heading*) Remainder and factor theorems.

factor ('fæktə(r)), *v.* [f. prec. sb.]

1. *rare.* **a.** *intr.* To act as a factor or agent. In quot. *fig.* **b.** *trans.* To deal with (goods, money, etc.) as a factor; in Birmingham and Sheffield use, to procure goods as a factor does (see prec. 4c).

1611 SPEED *Hist. Gt. Brit.* IX. ix. §70. 527 The Pope..had his pipes and conducts to conuay this stench into this land, and the wealth of it backe in lieu thereof. Which was now so factoured by his Chaplaine Martin, that, etc. **1621** S. WARD *Happiness of Practice* 44 Send your Prayers and good Workes to factor there for you. **1692** [see below]. *Mod.* (*Sheffield*), He manufactures a few articles, and factors the rest.

2. a. *Math.* To resolve (a quantity) *into* factors; to express as a product of factors; = FACTORIZE *v.* 2. orig. *U.S.*

1848 J. RAY *Algebra* I. ii. 73 The principal use of factoring, is to shorten the work, and simplify the results of algebraic operations. **1859** C. DAVIES *New Elem. Algebra* iii. 79 Factor $30a^4b^2c - 6a^3b^2d^3 + 18a^3b^2c^2$. *Ans.* $6a^3b^2(5ac - d^3 + 3c^2)$. **1901** W. J. MILNE *Acad. Algebra* 93 From any expression that is to be factored, the monomial factors should usually first be removed. **1941** BIRKHOFF & MACLANE *Surv. Mod. Algebra* iv. 88 The polynomial $x^2 + 1$..cannot be factored into polynomials with rational coefficients. **1947** F. S. NOWLAN *Coll. Algebra* iii. 31 We factor 6 and 72 when we write $6 = 2 \times 3$ and $72 = 2^3 \times 3^2$. **1966** J. V. ROBISON *Mod. Algebra & Trig.* v. 109 To factor a polynomial, we express the polynomial as a product of other polynomials, called factors of the given polynomial.

b. *transf.* To resolve or decompose *into* components.

1958 G. A. MILLER in *Jrnl. Exper. Psychol.* LVI. 486/2 It is possible to show that such a finite state generator can be decomposed, or 'factored', into a set of simpler generators.

Hence '**factored** *ppl. a.*, '**factoring** *vbl. sb.* and *ppl. a.*

1633 P. FLETCHER *Purple Isl.* VIII. xlvi, A carrion-crow he is..the devil's factoring knave. **1692** SETTLE *Triumphs Lond.* Ded., Chaffering or Factoring have been thought so unnecessary Preliminaries in dealing with Sir John Fleet, that [etc.]. **1883** *Birm. Daily Post* 11 Oct., The Hardware Factoring Business. **1886** *19th Cent.* Aug. 244 Articles sold under other local designations in London and all over the world are the 'factored' work of Birmingham craftsmen.

factorable ('fæktərəb(ə)l), *a.* *Math.* [f. prec. + -ABLE.] Capable of being factorized; expressible as a product of factors.

1931 L. J. ROUSE *Coll. Algebra* iii. 37 If the trinomial is factorable we must find two numbers whose product is *ac* and whose sum is *b*. **1966** OGILVY & ANDERSON *Excurs. Number Theory* 146, 2 and 47 are examples of primes; 20 is composite, being factorable into $2 \times 2 \times 5$.

factorage ('fæktərɪdʒ). Also 7 -idge. [f. FACTOR *sb.* + -AGE. Cf. F. *factorage.*]

1. The action or professional service of a factor; the action of buying or selling (goods) on commission. Also *attrib.*

1670 SIR T. CULPEPPER *Necess. Abating Usury* 8 Trading with our own stocks, honest Partnership, and discreet Factorage. *a* **1734** NORTH *Lives* II. 367 A celebrated house of factorage in Constantinople. *a* **1834** LAMB *Mr. Liston* Misc. Wks. (1871) 406 Satisfied with the returns of his factorage. **1865** CARLYLE *Fredk. Gt.* VI. XX. vi. 143 Himself once a Preacher, but at present concerned with Factorage of Wool on the great scale.

2. Commission or per-centage paid to a factor on goods purchased or sold by him.

1613 F. ROBARTS *Revenue of Gospel* 100 Carriage, factorage, impost and custome. **1622** MALYNES *Anc. Law-Merch.* 111 Hee that exceedeth his Commission shall lose his Factoridge. **1721** C. KING *Brit. Merch.* III. 214 To engross the whole Profit of Commission and Factorage to themselves. **1809** R. LANGFORD *Introd. Trade* 70 Factorage 1*s.* per Quarter. **1852** MCCULLOCH *Dict. Comm., Factorage* ..is also frequently charged at a certain rate per cask, or other package.

†**3.** The place of business of a factor; an agency.

1679 PLOT *Staffordsh.* (1686) 108 The Cheesmongers of London have thought it worth their while to set up a Factorage here, for these commodities [butter and cheese].

4. *collect.* **a.** The whole body or assemblage of factors: see FACTOR *sb.* 5. **b.** The sum total of constituent elements: see FACTOR *sb.* 6.

1849 *Tait's Mag.* XVI. 12/1 The importance of the factorage was raised enormously in their own esteem. **1887** F. ROBINSON *New Relig. Med.* 127 These, were the factorage analyzed, might crop up as constituents seldom absent.

factordom ('fæktədəm). *rare*⁻¹. [f. FACTOR *sb.* 5 + -DOM.] The system of management by factors.

1888 *Scot. Leader* 20 Jan. 4 He lets some light into factordom that will not be relished.

† '**factoress.** *Obs.* Also 7 fact'ress. [f. as prec. + -ESS.] A female factor or agent.

1608–11 BP. HALL *Epist.* V. i. (1627) 363 Still the Deuill begins with Eue..Marcion had his factoresse at Rome. **1638** FORD *Fancies* III. iii, Your fact'ress hath been tamp'ring for my misery. **1668** R. L'ESTRANGE *Vis. Quev.* (1702) 190 These are our best Fact'resses, we have for doing Bus'nesses. **1722** *Lond. Gaz.* No. 6094/3 Mrs. Ann Harland ..Coal-Factoress.

factorial (fæk'tɔərɪəl), *a.*[1] and *sb.* [f. as prec. + -(I)AL[1].] **A.** *adj.*

1. *Math.* (See quots. and B. a.)

1837 *Penny Cycl.* IX. 155 The term factorial expression has been in some instances applied to an expression of which the factors are in arithmetical progression. **1860** BOOLE *Calc. Fin. Diff.* 6 The term in which they ['factorials' in Boole's sense] are involved is called a factorial term. **1867** GALBRAITH *Algebra* (ed. 3) 396 Factorial functions..If the function consist of equi-different factors.

2. Of or pertaining to a factor (sense 4).

1881 BLACKIE *Lay Serm.* v. 177 Large farms and factorial management have formed together an unholy alliance.

3. Of or pertaining to a factor (sense 7); *factorial analysis* = *factor analysis.*

Quot. 1845 refers to analysis by means of factorials.

[**1845** T. TATE (*title*) A treatise on factorial analysis with the summation of series; containing various new developments of functions, &c.] **1935** *Human Factor* IX. 182 With this infinite number of possible factorial analyses of any set of correlations,..a psychologist can find one which agrees with any preconceived notions he may have about the linkages between tests. **1935** R. A. FISHER *Design Exper.* vi. 111 With factorial experiments designed to make a large number of comparisons there will..usually be an ample number of degrees of freedom for the estimation of error. **1949** DARLINGTON & MATHER *Elem. Genetics* App. I. 391 *Factorial Experiment*, one in which all the treatments or agents under investigation are varied simultaneously, and combined in such a way that any derived effect of one or a group of them may be isolated and separately evaluated. **1950** COCHRAN & COX *Exper. Designs* v. 124 If all factors are independent in their effects, the factorial approach will result in a considerable saving of the time and material devoted to the experiments. **1971** *Jrnl. Gen. Psychol.* LXXXII. 53 A factorial analysis of covariance was performed on the data for delayed recall.

4. *Photogr.* Of or pertaining to the determination of the interval of time allowed after the appearance of the image and before the completion of the development of a film.

1910 *Westm. Gaz.* 29 June 16/2 If one be using a factorial system of development it is well to reduce the factor a little, using, say, seven where nine would represent the ordinary time of development.

B. *sb.* *Math.* [In F. *factorielle.*]

a. *gen.* The product of a series of factors in arithmetical progression. In later usage sometimes with wider sense: The product of a series of factors which are similar functions of a variable that changes by a constant difference in passing from any factor to the next. Cf. FACULTY 2c.

(Boole *Calc. Fin. Diff.* 6 defines the word as meaning each of the factors composing such a product, and uses *factorial term* for what other writers call a *factorial.*)

1816 HERSCHEL in *Lacroix's Diff. & Int. Calc.* App. §370 Any quantity of the form $ax^n + bx^{n-1}$ + etc. may be resolved into factorials. **1845** *Penny Cycl.* Suppl. I. 559 Arbogast.. proposed to call the different cases of $x^{n|a}$ by the name of factorials. **1867** GALBRAITH *Algebra* (ed. 3) 397 To find the difference of a factorial.

b. *spec.* The product of an integer multiplied into all the lower integers.

For example, the factorial of 6 (written symbolically $\underline{|6}$ or 6!) is $6 \times 5 \times 4 \times 3 \times 2 = 720$. Factorials are of frequent use in the investigation of Permutations and Probabilities.

1869 J. J. RAVEN *Ch. Bells Camb.* (1881) 77 The number of changes that can be rung on a peal of bells is the factorial of the number of the bells.

fac'torial, *a.*[2] *rare.* [f. FACTORY + -AL[1].] 'Pertaining to a factory; consisting in a factory'.

1864 WEBSTER refers to BUCHANAN. **1885** *Science* VI. 100 The advisability of..securing a limited district for a ..'factorial establishment' for American citizens in that region [the Kongo country].

factorially (fæk'tɔərɪəlɪ), *adv.* [f. FACTORIAL *a.*[1] + -LY[2].] By reference to factors.

1913 W. BATESON *Mendel's Princ. Heredity* (ed. 2) iv. 84 The genetic properties of the pied types can be represented factorially by regarding the pattern or distribution of the colour as due to a distinct factor or to its absence. **1935** R. A. FISHER *Design Exper.* vi. 104 The second advantage..in a factorially arranged experiment, is that, in addition to measuring the effects of the four single ingredients..it measures also the 11 possible interactions between these ingredients. **1935** L. L. THURSTONE *Vectors of Mind* ii. 73 The problem of describing factorially the variables whose experimental intercorrelations are given.

factorist ('fæktərɪst). *Psychol.* [f. FACTOR *sb.* + -IST.] One who seeks to explain intelligence as a measurable phenomenon in terms of the relations of general and specific factors in a person.

1930 C. SPEARMAN in C. Murchison *Psychologies of 1930* xviii. 339 Instead of such negations the factorists find good in everything, even in the other 'ists'. **1938** *Brit. Jrnl. Psychol.* Oct. 190 The doctrine urged by the Samplists turns out to be no other than that which has always constituted the 'main' theory of the Factorists themselves.

factorization (ˌfæktəraɪ'zeɪʃən). *Math.* [f. FACTORIZE *v.* + -ATION.] The operation of resolving a quantity into factors; also, the product of factors so obtained.

1886 G. CHRYSTAL *Algebra* I. vii. 122 Every known identity resulting from the distribution of a product of such factors, when read backwards, gives a factorisation. **1926** MILNE & ROBERTSON *Algebra for Schools* xiv. 89 The pupil is strongly advised to check his answer to any question on factorisation by multiplying the factors..to see whether their product gives the original expression. **1967** W. P. EAMES *Elem. Theory Numbers* iv. 117 Now we will show that the factorization of *f* is unique.

factorize ('fæktəraɪz), *v.* [f. as FACTORIAL *a.*[1] + -IZE.]

1. *trans.* (*U.S. Law.*) In Vermont and Connecticut, = GARNISH.

1864 in WEBSTER. **1878** [see FACTOR *sb.* 5c.].

2. *Math.* **a.** To break up (a quantity) into factors.

1886 G. CHRYSTAL *Algebra* I. vii. 133 The decomposition of $x^2 + y^2 + xy = (x + y + \sqrt{xy})(x + y - \sqrt{xy})$, which is often given by beginners when they are asked to factorise $x^2 + y^2 + xy$..is no solution of the problem of factorisation in the ordinary sense, inasmuch as the two factors contain $\sqrt{xy}$, and are therefore not rational integral functions of *x* and *y*. **1923** E. H. CHAPMAN *Elem. Algebra* xiii. 103 When we attempt to factorize an algebraic expression, we regard it as a product, and try to undo the multiplication. **1967** W. P. EAMES *Elem. Theory Numbers* iv. 117 Since *f* is a product of polynomials which can be factorized, *f* can also be factorized.

b. *intr.* To be capable of being factorized.

1914 A. G. CRACKNELL *School Algebra* xv. 199 Thus $3y(2x + a) - b(2y + c)$ does not factorise. **1939** GODFREY & TAIT *School Algebra* viii. 100 Quadratic equations will not always factorize.

factorship ('fæktəʃɪp). [f. as prec. + -SHIP.] The office or position of factor (senses 3, 4).

1599 HAKLUYT *Voy.* II. 162 What you shall doe in Turkie besides the businesse of your Factorship. **1611** COTGR., A factorship; or, the dutie and charge of a factor, *facturerie, factorerie.* *a* **1657** R. LOVEDAY *Lett.* (1663) 188 My friend.. had happily pleased my Lady L. in his Factorship. **1730–6** in BAILEY (folio). **1834** H. MILLER *Scenes & Leg.* xxiv. (1857) 342 In a few years after he had appointed him to the factorship he disposed of all his lands. **1885** *Manch. Exam.*

7 Jan. 4/6, £2,294 8*s.* 5*d.* had accumulated during his factorship.

fig. **1888** *Pall Mall G.* 2 Oct. 7/2 A class which contributes pretty largely to the factorship of immorality and sin.

factory ('fæktərɪ). Also 6–7 **factorie**. [repr. med.L. *factōria*, f. *factor*: see FACTOR *sb.* The proximate source is uncertain: the word is found in several of the Romanic langs.: It. *fattoria*, Sp. *factoría*, Pg. *feitoria* (1551 in the original of our first quot.); Fr. has *factorerie* (Cotgr. 1611), f. as FACTOR *sb.* + *-erie* -ERY; also, *factorie* app. adopted from some foreign lang. In senses 4–5 referred to the type of *factōrium* place or instrument of making (recorded in sense 'oil-press'), f. *facĕre* to make.]

1. An establishment for traders carrying on business in a foreign country; a merchant company's trading station.

1582 N. LICHEFIELD tr. *Castanheda's Conq. E. Ind.* xxi. 54 b, To the intent hee might remaine in the Factorye with the Factour. **1613** PURCHAS *Pilgrimage* VII. vii. §3. 573 Here [Sofala] the Portugals haue..a Fort and Factorie of very rich Trade. **1682** *Lond. Gaz.* No. 1692/1 The total subversion of their Factory at Amoy. **1701** *Charter Soc. Prop. Gospel*, The maintenance of clergymen in the Plantations, Colonies and Factories of Great Britain. **1772** MAD. D'ARBLAY *Early Diary* 3 Feb., He is chaplain to the British factory at St. Petersburg. **1837** W. IRVING *Capt. Bonneville* II. 84 Vancouver..the main factory of the Hudson's Bay Company. **1861** PATTISON *Ess.* (1889) I. 39 Long before..the Hanse..fixed their factories in Lisbon.

fig. **1641** MILTON *Ch. Govt.* II. 34 All those that seek to bear themselves uprightly in this their spiritual factory.

attrib. **1804** VALENTIA *Voy. & Trav.* (1809) I. vii. 372 The factory-house is a chaste piece of architecture.

†**2.** The body of factors in any one place. *Obs.*

1702 W. J. *Bruyn's Voy. Levant* vi. 18 The three Statues were..sent..by the French Factory to Paris. **1777** W. DALRYMPLE *Trav. Sp. & Port.* cxxv, I feasted..with the consul and factory.

3. a. The employment, office, or position of a factor; factorship. (Chiefly *Sc.*: cf. FACTOR *sb.* 5.) Also, ***letter of factory*** = 3 b.

1560 in Tytler *Hist. Scot.* I. xx. (1864) III. 328 No disposition of factorie shall be made by [= contrary to] his advice. **1594** *Sc. Acts Jas. VI* (1816) 64 Diuers personis.. hes maid dyuerss bandis, obligationis, lettres of factorie. **1631** T. POWELL *Tom All Trades* 35 The Merchant Royall.. comes to his Profession by travaile and Factory. **1752** G. BROWN in *Scots Mag.* (1753) Nov. 555/2 He..accepted the factory of the estate. **1869** *Act 32–3 Vict.* c. 116 §3 A conveyance..for the purposes of such estate or trust, or factory.

b. A document investing another with the authority of a factor or agent.

1640–1 *Kirkcudbr. War-Comm. Min. Bk.* (1855) 134 The factorie granted be Gilbert Browne of Bagbie to Johne Browne, merchand. **1676** W. ROW *Contn. Blair's Autobiog.* xii. (1848) 380 He..gaue a factorie to his son-in-law, to go over with Forther and agent that business.

†**4.** The action or process of making anything.

1664 BUTLER *Hud.* II. iii. 864 These reasons..are far from satisfactory, T' establish, and keep up your Factory. **1678** *Ibid.* III. ii. 1446 Gain has wonderful Effects, T'improve the Factory of Sects.

5. a. A building or range of buildings with plant for the manufacture of goods; a manufactory, workshop; 'works'.

1618 USSHER *Let. to Camden* 8 June, The Company of Stationers in London are now erecting a Factory for Books and a Press among us here. **1832** G. R. PORTER *Porcelain & Gl.* 307 The spacious factory of the manufacturer. **1878** JEVONS *Prim. Pol. Econ.* 63 Somebody must settle whether the factory is to work for..ten..or eight hours a day.

b. *transf.* and *fig.*

1618 MIDDLETON *Peacemaker* Wks. 1886 VIII. 326 Come then to the factory of Peace, thou that desirest to have life. **1682** SIR T. BROWNE *Chr. Mor.* (1716) 21 Our corrupted hearts are the Factories of the Devil, which may be at work without his presence. **1847** EMERSON *Poems, Monadnoc* Wks. (Bohn) I. 433 Factory of river and of rain; Link in the alps' globe-girding chain. **1856** —— *Eng. Traits, Univ.* ibid. II. 91 Oxford is a Greek factory. **1860** O. W. HOLMES *Prof. Breakf.-t.* x. 216 This was no common miss, such as are turned out in scores from the young-lady-factories.

c. A prison; a police station. *slang.*

1832 in *Penguin Bk. Austral. Ballads* (1964) 33 But the lass I adore, the lass for me, Is a lass in the Female Factory. **1874** M. CLARKE *His Natural Life* II. iii. 91 In the factory—a prison for females—the vilest abuses were committed. **1891** 'F. W. CAREW' *No. 747* xxxvi. 426 A stranger..whom a plain-clothes D. from the 'Factory' would most assuredly have catalogued as suspicious. **1938** F. D. SHARPE *Sharpe of Flying Squad* 330 *Factory*, the police-station.

6. *attrib.* (sense 5), as ***factory bill, boy, butter*** (*U.S.*), ***child, chimney, -girl, -hand, hooter, -inspector, lad, -man, owner*** (so ***factory-owning*** ppl. adj.), ***-people, -spinner, system, -village, whistle, worker, world***; ***factory-made*** pple. (and as *adj.* and *sb.*). Also **factory acts** (earlier *factories acts*), the statutes 42 Geo. III. c. 73 (1802), 3 & 4 Will. IV. c. 103 (1833), and various later acts, passed for the regulation of factories in the interest of the health and morals of the persons employed in them; **factory cloth** = *factory-cotton*; **factory-cotton** (*U.S.*), unbleached cotton cloth of home manufacture, as opposed to imported fabrics; also called *factory* and *domestic*; **factory farm** orig. *U.S.*, a farm organized on industrial lines; hence **factory farmer, -farming; factory floor**, the work-place of, or a forum for, industrial workers; also *attrib.*; **factory ship**, the base ship of a whaling fleet; **factory trawler** (see quot. 1962).

1832 *Rep. Comm. Lab. Children* in *Parl. Papers 1831–2* XV. 20 But since this *Factory Bill has been agitated,..the children have gathered round me..and have said..'Will you get the Ten Hour Bill?' **1833** *Blackw. Edin. Mag.* XXXIII. 443/1 Mr. John Wood..of whom the Rev. G. S. Bull..thus spoke a few days ago at a great Factory Bill meeting. *Ibid.* 444/2 He is perhaps a better judge of fat cattle ..than of lean *Factory boys and girls. **1840** F. TROLLOPE (*title*) Life and adventures of Michael Armstrong, the factory boy. **1888** *Vermont Agric. Rep.* X. 14 *Factory butter secures an average higher price than its patrons could secure if they made it at home. **1832** *Rep. Comm. Lab. Children* in *Parl. Papers 1831–2* XV. 640 Education of *factory children in England far behind Scotland. **1833** *Blackw. Edin. Mag.* XXXIII. 427 A Factory child..must be at her work..at four o'clock of a snowy winter-morning. **1848** MRS. GASKELL *Mary Barton* II. ix. 131 She..looked towards the *factory-chimneys, and the cloud of smoke which hovers over Manchester. **1933** V. SACKVILLE-WEST *Let.* 31 Jan. in *Lett. H. Nicolson* (1966) 136 Factory-chimneys line the cliff. **1873** M. HOLLEY *My Opinions* 113 Merrymac calico and *factory cloth. **1890** A. MARSHALL *Princ. Econ.* I. IV. xi. 351 Our knowledge..would be much increased..if some private persons,..or co-operative associations, would make a few careful experiments of what have been called '*Factory farms'. **1926** *19th Cent.* June 825 Factory-farms..can be multiplied or spread widely enough to affect the whole of British agriculture. **1952** *Economist* 7 June 657/1 The operators of the huge western factory farms..resist the rule that no more than 160 acres of a single owner's land can be supplied with federally financed water. *Ibid.* This so-called '160-acre limitation'..is still applied when new lands are irrigated, but *factory farmers, particularly in Texas and California, have been trying..to get Congress to repeal it. **1964** *New Statesman* 30 Oct. 649/1 Boycott factory farm food?.. Boycott factory farmers?.. The essential thing is to amend the Protection of Animals Act (1911) to cover *factory-farming techinques. **1968** *Ibid.* 5 Jan. 10/3 Under conditions of intensive 'factory' farming, a lot of animals *did* suffer from true infections. **1968** M. PYKE *Food & Society* v. 63 It is fashionable to sneer at intensive methods of livestock production; they are called 'factory farming'. **1968** *Listener* 30 May 692/2 The militant workers on the *factory floor have been voting to continue the strike until their leaders have wrung much more substantial concessions from the regime. **1971** P. WORSTHORNE *Socialist Myth* 252 Factory-floor agitation..is one of the few active pleasures which an industrial society provides for its less well-endowed members. **1832** D. JERROLD in *N. & Q.* (1963) Mar. 105/2 (*title*) The *Factory Girl. **1833** S. BRECK *Recoll.* (1877) App. 275 Factory-girls were introduced. **1845** GEO. MURRAY *Islaford* 143 Factory-girl, who..contrives to sport a cotton parasol. **1850** LYELL *2nd Visit U.S.* II. 300 There had recently been a strike of the factory girls. **1940** 'G. ORWELL' *Inside Whale* 122 The idea is to give the bored factory-girl or worn-out mother of five a dream-life. **1858** SIMMONDS *Dict. Trade*, **Factory-hand*..a person employed about a mill. **1930** D. H. LAWRENCE *Triumph of Machine*, They will hear far, far away the last *factory hooter. **1846** MCCULLOCH *Acc. Brit. Empire* (1854) I. 699 The appointment of *Factory Inspectors has been productive of the greatest advantage. **1875** E. TOWERS in *N. & Q.* (1963) Apr. 137/1 (*title*) Poor Joe the *Factory Lad. **1904** *Daily Chron.* 23 Aug. 5/4 The over-decorated *factory-made furniture of Michigan and Ohio. *Ibid.* 28 Dec. 4/5 Cheapest line of factory-mades. **1905** *Ibid.* 13 June 7/2 Practically all shoes are factory-made in the United States. **1939** S. SPENDER tr. *Toller's Pastor Hall* III. 102, I wear factory-made shoes nowadays. Not so beautiful and elegant as yours, but cheaper. **1845** BUDD *Dis. Liver* 349 The patient, a *factory-man, forty-seven years of age. **1851** *Baird's Cotton Spinner* 31 It is based upon an error, though a rather common one amongst *Factory owners. **1934** E. POUND *Eleven New Cantos* xxxiii. 13 That no factory-owner shall sit as a magistrate in cases concerning the spinning of cotton. **1949** WYNDHAM LEWIS *Let.* 6 Aug. (1963) 502 The U.S. *factory-owning class is very raw, arrogant, and ignorant. **1930** *N.Y. Zool. Soc. Bull.* Jan.–Feb. 7 (*caption*) The *factory ship *Lansing*. **1958** *Times* 12 Nov. 11/6 The cost of building a factory ship today at about £4m. is almost prohibitive for any private whaling company. **1969** N. W. PIRIE *Food Resources* v. 135 Larger vessels, such as the 43,000 ton *Vostok* which the Russians are building as a factory ship. **1856** EMERSON *Eng. Traits, Wealth* Wks. (Bohn) II. 71 Roberts destroyed the *factory spinner. **1832** *Rep. Comm. Lab. Children* in *Parl. Papers 1831–2* XV. 413 Will you state how you account for the melancholy result which you attribute to the *factory system as at present conducted? **1843** *Ainsworth's Mag.* V. 42 The factory system, the most deplorable ignorance..., have all excited attention in their turns. **1953** *World Fishing* II. 10/1 (*caption*) United States *factory trawler 'Ocean Life'. **1962** J. TUNSTALL *Fishermen* ii. 45 The factory trawler quick freezes its catch at sea. *Ibid.*, The first British factory trawler..started fishing in 1947. **1841–4** EMERSON *Ess., Poet* Wks. I. 161 Readers of poetry see the *factory-village and the railway. **1920** H. CRANE *Let.* 9 Nov. (1965) 45, I am sure I should not miss *factory whistles in Pisa or Morocco, but I frankly did miss them in Washington. **1848** MRS. GASKELL *Mary Barton* I. p. vi, The poor uneducated *factory-workers of Manchester. **1937** *Discovery* Aug. 234/2 An unskilled factory worker. **1906** *Daily Chron.* 28 May 3/4 Tired minds in a *factory-world. **1930** D. H. LAWRENCE *Nettles* 26 Hooked fishes of the factory world.

Hence **'factoryship** = FACTORSHIP.

1836 *Fraser's Mag.* XIV. 511 He who shot Sir Alexander Boswell is..duly fitted with a factoryship.

factotum (fæk'təʊtəm). [ad. med.L. *factōtum* (f. *fac*, imper. of *facĕre* to do + *tōtum* the whole) in phrases *Johannes Factotum, Dominus Factotum, Magister factotum*, which appear to be renderings in etymological equivalents of Romanic expressions = 'John Do-everything', 'Mr. Do-Everything'; cf. It. *fa il tutto*, *fattutto* of similar formation. These phrases are found in 16th c. in Eng., and *Frère Jean Factotum* (Paré *a* 1590), *Dominus Factotum* also in Fr.; their source has not yet been discovered. The word *factotum* without the prefixed words is used in German (as neuter sb.) from 16th c. (Grimm cites Fischart 1579), and in Fr. and It. from 17th c.]

1. †**a.** In L. phrases: ***Dominus factotum***, used for 'one who controls everything', a ruler with uncontrolled power; ***Johannes factotum***, a Jack of all trades, a would-be universal genius. Also *fig.* †**b.** One who meddles with everything, a busybody. **c.** In mod. sense: A man of all-work; also, a servant who has the entire management of his master's affairs.

1566 GASCOIGNE *Supposes* III. iv. (1572) 31 He had the disbursing..of al my masters affaires..he was *Magister fac totum.* [Ariosto 1525: *era fa il tutto.*] **1584** R. PARSONS *Leicester's Commw.* 65 Throughout all England my L. of Leycester is taken for *Dominus fac totum.* **1592** GREENE *Groatsw. Wit* E iv, Being an absolute *Johannes fac totum* [he] is in his owne conceit the onely Shake-scene in a Countrey. **1618** S. WARD *Serm. Exod. xviii.* 21–22, 65 Is there no mean between busibodies and tell-clockes, between *fac-totum* and *fay't neant?* **1630** B. JONSON *New Inn* II. ii, *Tip.* Art thou the dominus? *Host. Fac-totum* here, sir. **1662** FOULIS *Plots of Saints* (1674) 278 Robert Passellew..was *dominus fac totum* in the middle—and *fac nihil* towards the end—of the reign of Henry III. **1782** COWPER *Lett.* 18 Mar., The garden where I am my own fac-totum. **1824** MISS MITFORD *Village* 1st Ser. (1863) 9 The pensioner and factotum of the village, amongst whom he divides his services. **1863** MISS BRADDON *Eleanor's Vict.* III. ii. 25 A butler, or factotum,—for there was only one male servant in the house. **1940** J. H. JAGGER *English in Future* ii. 31 *Have* is another factotum, but *gets* off more lightly than *get*.

attrib. **1859** G. MEREDITH *R. Feverel* xi, The small factotum footman.

2. *Printing*: see quots.

1681 BLOUNT *Glossogr.* 255 *Fac-totum* signifies among Printers, a Border in the middle of which any Letter of the Alphabet may be put in for use, and then taken out. **1721–1800** in BAILEY. **1823** in CRABB *Technol. Dict.* **1914** R. B. MCKERROW in *Bibliogr. Soc. Trans. 1911–13* XII. 238 An ornamental block having a space in the centre for the insertion of a capital letter of an ordinary fount of type is called a 'factotum initial', or more properly a 'factotum'.

Hence **fac'totumship**, the office of a factotum.

1660 FISHER *Rusticks Alarm* Wks. (1679) 345 During the long time of their Dominus fac-totum-ship, in whole Christendom.

factrix ('fæktrɪks). *rare*$^{-1}$. [f. FACTOR *sb.*, after Lat. analogy: see -TRIX.] = FACTORESS.

1870 H. SCOTT *Fasti Scot. Eccles.* V. 204 Lady Forbes factrix for her son.

factual ('fæktjuːəl), *a.* [f. FACT *sb.*, after the analogy of ACTUAL.] Pertaining to or concerned with facts; of the nature of fact, actual, real.

a **1834** COLERIDGE *Notes Southey's Life Wesley* (1858) II. 8 That I should quench the ray and paralyse the factual nerve, by which I have hitherto been able to discriminate veracity from falsehood. **1846** WHEWELL *Syst. Morality* iii. 58 We can never present the Factual part of a Fact, separate from the Ideal part. **1846** DE QUINCEY *Antigone of Sophocles* Wks. XIV. 211 Any direct factual imitation, resting upon painted figures..would have been no art whatsoever. **1884** R. F. BURTON *Book of Sword* 201 Our factual knowledge of Mesopotamian civilisation.

absol. **1876** W. ALEXANDER *Bampton Lect.* v. (1877) 144 The facts and the history are Jewish; but there is a typical in the factual.

Hence **'factually** *adv.*, in a factual manner; as matter of fact.

1852 PULSFORD tr. *Muller's Chr. Doctr. Sin* I. 28 The universal moral condition of the human race, as it factually exists. **1884** R. F. BURTON *Book of Sword* 149 Nilotic allegories and mysteries which the vulgar understood factually and literally.

factualism ('fæktjuːəlɪz(ə)m). *Philos.* [f. FACTUAL *a.* + -ISM.] A predominant concern with facts or natural consequences, esp. in moral matters; any theory that treats facts as being of prime importance, or maintains that moral conclusions can be drawn from factual data alone.

1946 R. WELLEK in W. S. Knickerbocker *XX Cent. Eng.* 68 A false and pernicious 'historicism' is frequently connected with 'factualism'. **1961** J. WILSON *Reason & Morals* ii. 42 The contrast between Moralism and Factualism seems to take the form of a conflict.

factualist ('fæktjuːəlɪst), *a.* and *sb. Philos.* [f. as prec. + -IST.] **A.** *adj.* Of or relating to factualism; naturalistic. **B.** *sb.* One who is affected by, or adheres to, factualism.

1935 P. WHEELWRIGHT *Crit. Introd. Ethics* iii. 91 The 'factualist' fallacy, of which the 'proof' of hedonism is a prominent example. **1961** J. WILSON *Reason & Morals* ii. 39 Moralists and Factualists seem to defend their beliefs in different ways... A Factualist would perhaps say 'Easy divorce does harm to the children'. *Ibid.* 44 The Factualist metaphysic..need not grind any such axe.

factuality (fæktjuːˈælɪtɪ). [f. as prec. + -ITY.] The quality of being factual, factualness; (of representation) realism; (of facts) truth.

1887 *Christian Union* 3 Mar. 18/2 When we find these among the facts, it makes us doubt the factuality of the facts. **1922** A. N. WHITEHEAD *Princ. Relativ.* ii. 15 If for one moment I may use the inadmissible word 'Factuality', it is in some ways better either than 'fact' or 'totality' for the expression of my meaning. **1960** *Times* 15 Jan. 16/1 *The Kitchen*..begins as a study in a frightening factuality.

factualness (ˈfæktjuːəlnɪs). [f. FACTUAL *a.* + -NESS.] The state of being factual; factuality.

1906 F. VON HÜGEL *Let.* 29 Sept. in Briggs & von Hügel *Papal Comm. & Pentat.* II. 29 The massive *factualness*, the serried, interdependent ranks of fact upon fact. **1925** *Public Opinion* 14 Aug. 153/3 Even the compassionate pity they arouse does not lift the weight of their seriousness and factualness from the reader's breast. **1953** *Ess. in Crit.* III. 31 A kind of Janus word, gathering from one direction its whole factualness. **1971** *Daily Tel.* 18 June 14/3 The play element..was handled with an innocence and factualness which are the exact opposite of 'charm', let alone archness.

factum (ˈfæktəm). [a. L. *factum*: see FACT *sb.* Cf. F. *factum*.]

1. *Civil Law.* 'A person's act or deed; anything stated or made certain' (Wharton 1848).

2. A statement of facts, or of the points in a case or controversy; a memorial. [After Fr. legal use.]

1773 *Gentl. Mag.* XLIII. 587 An action was brought against M. de Voltaire, and an odious *factum* was drawn up in the printer's name. **1872** W. H. JERVIS *Gallican Church* I. xiii. 440 The curés of Paris and Rouen put forth a series of factums or memorials. **1886** *Sat. Rev.* 6 Mar. 349/1 Not..a novel nor an historical monograph, but an elaborate factum.

†**3.** *Math.* The product of two or more factors multiplied together. *Obs.*

1748 HARTLEY *Observ. Man* I. iii. 351 When the Factum of the proper Powers of all the Quantities is so. **1817** H. T. COLEBROOKE *Algebra* xvii, A factum of two unknown quantities.

facture (ˈfæktjʊə(r)). [a. F. *facture*, ad. L. *factūra*, f. *facĕre* to make. The popular Fr. form is *faiture*: see FEATURE.]

1. Now *rare.* **a.** The action or process of making (a thing). Cf. *manufacture.*

1580 BARET *Alv.* M 50 The facture, or making of a thing. **1605** BACON *Adv. Learn.* II. 41 The facture or framing of the inward parts. **1661** COWLEY *Prop. Adv. Exp. Philos.* ii, Professors Resident shall be bound to study and teach..the Facture of all Merchandizes. **1671** MAYNWARING *Anc. & Mod. Pract. Physick* 15 There is no other way of progress..but this of preparation and manual facture. **1888** WHISTLER in *Sat. Rev.* 26 May 821 A new class who discovered the cheap, and foresaw fortune in the facture of the sham.

b. The result of the action or process; the thing made; creation.

1647 J. MAYER *Comm. Eph.* ii. 10 We are his facture, created in Christ Jesus unto good works.

2. The manner or style of making (a thing); construction, make; workmanship. Now *rare.*

1423 JAS. I *Kingis Q.* l, Bountee, richesse, and wommanly facture. **1616** CHAPMAN *Homer's Hymns, To Vulcan* (1858) 109 Vulcan..whom fame gives the prize For depth and facture of all forge-devise. **1860** READE *Cloister & H.* I. 73, I thought not all the goldsmiths on earth had so much gold, silver, jewels, and craft of design and facture. **1883** *Sat. Rev.* 24 Nov. 667 The facture [of a literary work] of Mr. Lewis Morris..has been generally creditable.

‖**3.** *Comm.* = INVOICE. A Fr. sense: perh. never used in Eng.

1858 in SIMMONDS *Dict. Trade.* **1864** in WEBSTER.

4. *Painting.* The quality of the execution of a picture, esp. of its surface. (A Gallicism.)

1887 *Atlantic Monthly* LX. 510/2 He was acquiring in the Louvre his laborious and rude facture of successive *impasto.* **1936** H. READ *Surrealism* 63 Dali's neat, tight Vermeerish *facture* has its aesthetic as well as Picasso's bold, plangent, viscous brushwork. **1961** *Times* 21 Mar. 16/5 He knows exactly what makes the *facture* of a French picture interesting. **1971** *Listener* 25 Feb. 254/3 Warhol's method depends..on misregistration and over-inking and (art facture-wise) smudging, lopping, blotching.

†**ˈfactus.** *Math. Obs. rare.* [a. L. *factus* (? sc. *numerus*), pa. pple. masc. of *facĕre* to make.] The product of two or more numbers or expressions; = FACTUM 3.

1669 NEWTON in Rigaud *Cor. Sci. Men* II. 282 The factus of their denominators will be $b^5 + 10b^4 + 35b^3 + 50bb + 24b$.

facty (ˈfæktɪ), *a.* [f. FACT *sb.* + -Y^{1}.]

a. Full of facts.

1883 *Pall Mall G.* 2 Nov. 5/1 A 'facty' article on 'The Political Condition of Spain'. **1884** *Ibid.* 4 Dec. 5/1. **1890** *Ibid.* 3 Feb. 2/2.

b. Of persons: freq. implying 'deficient in emotion or imagination'.

1901 *Westm. Gaz.* 18 June 10/1 Mr. Page, most interesting because most real and 'facty' of Horace's editors. **1930** H. G. WELLS *Autocracy of Mr. Parham* II. i. 80 He was facty and explicit after the manner of his type. **1934** — *Exper. Autobiogr.* II. viii. 540 To him [*sc.* G. B. Shaw]..I have always appeared heavily and sometimes formidably facty and close-set; to me his judgements, arrived at by feeling and expression, have always had a flimsiness.

‖**facula** (ˈfækjʊlə). *Astron.* Chiefly pl. **faculæ** (ˈfækjʊliː). [L. *facula*, dim. of *fac-em*, *fax* torch.] One of the bright or luminous spots or streaks on the surface of the sun, as distinguished from the dark spots or *maculæ.*

1706 in PHILLIPS (ed. Kersey), *Facula*, a little Torch: Among Modern Astronomers, *Faculæ*, are certain Bright or Shining Parts, which they have sometimes observed upon or about the Surface of the Sun. **1794** SULLIVAN *View Nat.* II. 415 When they disappear, they are generally converted into faculæ or luminous spots. **1858** HERSCHEL *Outlines Astron.* (ed. 5) §388 Strongly marked..streaks, more luminous than the rest, called faculæ. **1881** STOKES in *Nature* No. 625. 595 Sometimes faculæ will break out at the surface of the sun where there is no spot.

facular (ˈfækjʊlə(r)), *a.* [f. prec. + -AR.] Of or pertaining to faculæ.

1882 PROCTOR in *Knowledge* II. 419 Facular streaks of great splendour can be seen. **1884** — in *Longm. Mag.* Apr. 592 Large portions of the facular regions.

†**ˈfaculence.** *Obs.*$^{-0}$ [f. next: see -ENCE.] Brightness, clearness.

1727–36 in BAILEY. **1775** in ASH.

†**ˈfaculent,** *a. Obs. rare*$^{-1}$. [ad. med.L. *faculent-us*, f. *fax* torch: cf. *lūculentus*, f. *lux.*] Giving forth light like a torch; bright, clear.

1560 ROLLAND *Crt. Venus* III. 589 Vergill..In Latin toung was most faculent, Nane mair pregnant, facund nor eminent. **1656–81** BLOUNT *Glossogr.* **1721** in BAILEY.

faculous (ˈfækjʊləs), *a.* [f. L. *facula* (see FACULA) + -OUS.] Consisting of faculæ; of the nature of faculæ.

1868 B. STEWART in *Macm. Mag.* July 251 The faculous mass seemed to be giving out its end. **1869** *Spectator* 3 July 786 The intense brilliancy of the faculous ridges.

facultate (ˈfækəlteɪt), *v. rare.* [f. L. *facultāt-em*: see FACULTY and -ATE^{3} 7.] *trans.* **a.** To invest with authority, empower. **b.** To authorize.

1648 J. GOODWIN *Right & Might* 21 Whatsoever..portendeth ruine and destruction to the lives of men..is facultated by him [God]..to transgresse a Law without guilt of sinne. **1878** BARING-GOULD *Myst. Suffering* iii. 41 The gift of life facultates the enjoyment of life.

facultative (ˈfækəlteɪtɪv), *a.* [a. F. *facultatif, -ive*, f. L. *facultātem*: see FACULTY and -ATIVE.]

1. a. Of enactments, etc.: Conveying a 'faculty' or permission; permissive as opposed to compulsory; hence of actions, conditions, etc.: Optional.

1820 *Ann. Reg.* II. 718 In forming these quotas, neither the facultative departmental centimes, nor the communal centimes shall be taken into account. **1839** W. O. MANNING *Law of Nations* v. vii. (1875) 387 Creating what is called 'occasional', 'accidental' or 'facultative' contraband. **1861** M. ARNOLD *Pop. Educ. France* 50 What was..to use a French expression, facultative to the communes, what..they did or not as they liked. **1881** *Times* 1 July 9/6 The great schools..treat classics as obligatory, and science as merely facultative. **1884** *Q. Rev.* Apr. 403 Permit even for the Latin clergy a facultative celibacy.

b. *transf.* Used by scientific and philosophical writers for: That may or may not take place, or have a specified character.

1874 LEWES *Probl. Life & Mind* I. 139 The Facultative Actions are those which..are..neither inevitably nor uniformly produced when the organs are stimulated, but..take sometimes one issue and sometimes another. **1875** H. WALTON *Dis. Eye* 621 The facultative [hypermetropia] is present when objects can be accurately seen at any distance. **1884** *Syd. Soc. Lex.*, *Facultative hypermetropia*..those cases of hypermetropia in which objects at an infinite distance can be distinctly seen both with and without convex glasses.

c. *Biol.* Not restricted to the particular function, mode of life, set of conditions, etc., implied in the context; opp. OBLIGATE *ppl. a.*

1887 H. E. F. GARNSEY tr. *De Bary's Fungi* vii. 356 Saprophytes..which have also the power of going through their course of development wholly or in part as parasites..may be called with Van Tieghem facultative parasites. **1900** B. D. JACKSON *Gloss. Bot. Terms* 98/1 *Facultative*, occasional, incidental, as opposed to *obligate*; ~ *Anaërobes*, organisms which can exist without the presence of free oxygen or air. ~ *Symbiont*, an organism which can either exist and reach maturity independently or in symbiosis with another. **1927** GWYNNE-VAUGHAN & BARNES *Struct. & Devel. Fungi* 13 A species which is usually saprophytic but capable of parasitic existence on occasion is described as a hemi-saprophyte or facultative parasite, and a form which is usually parasitic but sometimes saprophytic as a hemi-parasite or facultative saprophyte. **1935** *Discovery* Jan. 27/2 The parasitic bacteria are a large and important group in which every stage of facultative and obligate parasitism can be found. **1940** *Chambers's Techn. Dict.* 320/2 *Facultative gamete*, a zoospore which can function as a gamete. **1950** J. G. DAVIS *Dict. Dairying* 13 The following table suggests terms for describing the reaction of micro-organisms to oxygen... Facultative anaerobe, Aerophilic..Facultative aerobe, Aerophobic. **1961** *Encounter* XVI. 77 The 'facultative homosexuals'..are those men who consider themselves heterosexually 'normal' but engage on occasion in some form of homosexual intercourse.

2. Of or proceeding from a faculty.

1866 J. MARTINEAU *Ess.* I. 154 Every facultative activity that goes out from me. **1888** — *Study Relig.* I. I. i. 55 A purely inward process, viz. the play of an *a priori* facultative activity with the matter of our sensitive passivity.

Hence **ˈfacultatively** *adv.*, in a facultative manner or degree, contingently.

1877 GARNSEY tr. *De Bary's Fungi* 360 Certain facultatively parasitic..species of Moulds. **1900** [see AEROBE]. **1914** A. HARRISON *Kaiser's War* 6 It [*sc.* military monarchism] has been set forth again and again by the German professors, politicians, and spokesmen, militarily, politically, and (as they say) facultatively. **1965** *Canad. Jrnl. Linguistics* Spring 172 The *qiʔ*- allomorph of the future marker occurs facultatively before the *yi*- allomorph.

facultied (ˈfækəltɪd), *a.* [f. FACULTY + -ED^{2}.] **a.** That is accredited by a faculty. **b.** Furnished with a faculty or special capacity.

1837 WHITTOCK *Bk. Trades* (1842) 379 The facultied students from Edina. **1862** THORNBURY *Turner* II. v. 163 Turner was a great single facultied man.

†**ˈfacultive,** *a. Obs.* [f. as prec. + -IVE.] Of or belonging to the faculties.

1643 R. O. *Man's Mort.* iii. 15 This Facultive Guift, or Natures endowment. *Ibid.*, Could there be a Facultive subsistence..without its body.

facultize (ˈfækəltaɪz), *v.* [f. as prec. + -IZE.] *trans.* To endow with faculty (see FACULTY 1 c). Hence **ˈfacultized** *ppl. a.*, endowed with faculty; practical, shrewd.

1872 LITTLEDALE in *Contemp. Rev.* XX. 13 We..need what the Americans call 'facultized' women. Not merely capable women, educated women..but such as have capacity trained into practical efficiency.

faculty (ˈfækəltɪ). Forms: 4–6 **faculte**, (5 **facultee**), 5–7 **facultie**, 6– **faculty**. [ME. *faculte*, a. F. *faculté*: ad. L. *facultāt-em* power, ability, opportunity, also resources, wealth, f. *facilis* easy (cf. early L. *facul* adv. = *facile* easily).

Facultās and *facilitās* (see FACILITY) were originally different forms of the same word; the latter, owing to its more obvious relation to the adj., retained the primary sense of 'easiness', which the former had ceased to have before the classical period.]

I. 'The power of doing anything' (J.).

1. a. Of persons: An ability or aptitude, whether natural or acquired, for any special kind of action; formerly also, ability, 'parts', capacity in general. Sometimes (influenced by sense 4) used to denote a native as opposed to an acquired aptitude.

1490 CAXTON *Eneydos* xv. 59 To her youen the facultee and power for to reherce and saye alle thinges that sholde come in her mouthe. **1573** G. HARVEY *Letter-bk.* (Camden) 7 M. Lewins extemporal faculti is better than M. Becons is. **1586** A. DAY *Eng. Secretary* II. (1625) 128 The facultie and use of well writing. **1594** HOOKER *Eccl. Pol.* I. viii. 68 There is no kind of faculty or power in man or any other creature, which can [etc.]. **1605** CAMDEN *Rem.* 11 Many excelling in Poeticall facultie. **1614** BP. HALL *Recoll. Treat.* 87 Behaviour..which if a man of but common faculty doe imitate, he makes himselfe ridiculous. **1636** MASSINGER *Bashf. Lover* IV. i, The heavenly object..would..force him [Ovid] to forget his faculty In verse. **1711** STEELE *Spect.* No. 95 ¶3 This Faculty of Weeping, is peculiar only to some Constitutions. **1751** JOHNSON *Rambler* No. 141 ¶6, I devoted all my faculties to the ambition of pleasing them. **1795** MASON *Ch. Mus.* iii. 204 Music, though in one sense an Art, yet is in another a natural faculty. **1829** CARLYLE *Misc.* (1857) II. 1 Were will in human undertakings synonymous with faculty. **1836** *Johnsoniana* 238 The faculty of teaching inferior minds the art of thinking. **1853** LYNCH *Self-Improv.* iii. 68 Every self-improving man has faculty enough to become a good reader.

†**b.** A personal quality; disposition. *Obs.*

c **1565** LINDESAY (Pitscottie) *Chron. Scot.* (1728) 89 They knew the king's faculties. *c* **1610** SIR J. MELVIL *Mem.* (1683) 30 The Queen Mother knowing his [the King of Navarr's] faculty. **1613** SHAKS. *Hen. VIII*, I. ii. 73, I am Traduc'd by ignorant Tongues, which neither know My faculties nor person.

c. General executive ability, *esp.* in domestic matters. (Chiefly U.S., but *colloq.* in some circles in England.)

1859 MRS. STOWE *Minister's Wooing* I. i. 2 Faculty is Yankee for *savoir faire*, and the opposite virtue to shiftlessness. **1884** J. D. WHITING in *Harper's Mag.* Oct. 741/1 Lizzie had 'faculty', and proved a notable housekeeper.

†**2. a.** Of things: A power or capacity; an active quality, efficient property or virtue. *Obs.*

1490 CAXTON *Eneydos* i. 14 The sterres had no faculte ne power..to enlumyne the sayd place. **1526** *Pilgr. Perf.* (W. de W. 1531) 143 It passeth the faculty of our barbarous tonge to expresse ony of them. **1578** LYTE *Dodoens* II. cvi. 296 Lovage, in facultie and vertues doth not differ much from Ligusticum. **1601** SHAKS. *Jul. C.* I. iii. 67. **1620** VENNER *Via Recta* v. 87 It is..of a penetrating, cooling and detersiue faculty. **1665** *Phil. Trans.* I. 49 The Electrical faculty of Amber. **1707** *Curios. in Husb. & Gard.* 167 Nitre is of great Use..in Regard to its Faculty of contributing..to the Propagation of Plants.

†**b.** One of the 'mechanical powers'.

1641 WILKINS *Math. Magick* I. iii. (1648) 13 Of the first Mechanical faculty, the Ballance. *Ibid.* vii. 43 That which is reckoned for the fourth faculty, is the Pulley. **1663** CHARLETON *Chor. Gigant.* 60 Leaver, Roller, Wheel, Pulley, Wedge, and Screw..fundamental Faculties of Mechaniques.

c. *Math.* A function of the form $x|^{m}|^{a}$, i.e. $x(x + a)(x + 2a)(x + 3a)$.. to m factors. See FACTORIAL B a.

[Introduced *c* 1798 by Kramp, who afterwards withdrew it in favour of Arbogast's term *factorial*. The word has since been revived, but is less frequent in English than in Continental use.]

1889 CHRYSTAL *Algebra* II. 374 Any faculty can always be reduced to another whose difference is unity.

3. An inherent power or property of the body or of one of its organs; a physical capability or function.

a 1500 *Colkelbie Sow* 637 And laking teith famvlit hir faculte That few folk mycht consaue her mvmling mowth. **1543** TRAHERON *Vigo's Chirurg.* Interpr. strange Words, There ben thre faculties..whych gouerne man, and are distributed to the hole bodye..namely animal, vital, and natural. **1576** FLEMING *Panopl. Epist.* 324 The bodie, and the abilities of the same, whiche are called corporall faculties. **1607** WALKINGTON *Opt. Glass* viii. (1664) 100 The Spirits..impart a faculty to the nerves of sense, and real motion. **1615** CROOKE *Body of Man* 406 If the arteries bee dilated by a faculty, then are they contracted by their grauity. *Ibid.* 612 The Visiue Facultie..the Faculty of Hearing. **1656** BRAMHALL *Replic.* i. 5 Sensibility and a locomotive faculty are essentiall to every living creature. **1684** tr. *Bonet's Merc. Compit.* I. 9 If the Faculty of the Guts be slow..and dull, they must be involuntarily excited to motion. **1729** BUTLER *Serm.* Wks. 1874 II. 42 A man may use the faculty of speech as an instrument of false witness. **1741** CHAMBERS *Cycl.* s.v., To account for the act of digestion, they [the antient philosophers] suppose a digestive Faculty in the stomach. **1875** JOWETT *Plato* (ed. 2) III. 362 Sight and hearing, for example, I should call faculties.

4. One of the several 'powers' of the mind, variously enumerated by psychologists: *e.g.* the will, the reason, memory, etc.

(By phrenologists applied to the congenital aptitudes supposed to be indicated by the cranial 'organs' or 'bumps': e.g. 'language', 'imitation', 'constructiveness'. This use has greatly influenced popular language.)

1588 FRAUNCE *Lawiers Log.* I. i. 2 That ingraven gift and facultie of wit and reason. **1614** BP. HALL *Recoll. Treat.* 66 When we are born, who knowes whether..we shall have the faculties of reason and understanding? **1690** LOCKE *Hum. Und.* II. xxi. (1695) 126 The Understanding and Will, are two Faculties of the mind. **1726** BUTLER *Serm.* Wks. 1874 II. 27 You cannot form a notion of this faculty, conscience, without [etc.]. **1785** REID *Int. Powers* 369 The faculties of consciousness, of memory, of external sense, and of reason, are all equally the gifts of nature. **1830** MACKINTOSH *Eth. Philos.* Wks. 1846 I. 159 The Moral Faculty..is intelligibly and properly spoken of as One. **1839** LD. BROUGHAM *Statesm. Geo. III, Loughborough* (ed. 2) 44 Changes..effected while the monarch's faculties were asleep. **1859** MILL *Liberty* (1865) 34/2 No need of any other faculty than the ape-like one of imitation. **1885** F. TEMPLE *Relat. Relig. & Sc.* ii. 46 Our personality..is centred in one faculty which we call the will.

5. Pecuniary ability, means, resources; possessions, property. *sing.* and *pl.* Also *attrib.*, as in *faculty tax*.

1382 WYCLIF *Gen.* xxxi. 14 Han we eny thing of residewe in faculteis and erytage of the hows of oure fader? —— *Tobit* i. 25 Tobie is turned aȝeen to his hous, and al his faculte restorid to hym. **1490** CAXTON *How to Die* 11 Wylt thou the thynges that thou hast taken be by the restored after the value of thy faculte. **1615** CHAPMAN *Odyss.* I. 620 The faculties This house is seised of. **1649** *Alcoran* 47 Restore to them [Orphans] their faculties, and devour them not unjustly before they be of age. **1781** GIBBON *Decl. & F.* II. 28 If so heavy an expence surpassed the faculties or the inclination of the magistrates..the sum was supplied from the Imperial treasury. **1792** A. YOUNG *Trav. France* 104 The prices..are beyond their faculties and occasion great misery. **1797** BURKE *Regic. Peace* iii. Wks. VIII. 356 We raise no faculty tax. We preserve [? *read* presume] the faculty from the expence. **1889** *Cent. Dict., Faculty*... 6. In the law of divorce (commonly in the plural), the pecuniary ability of the husband, in view of both his property and his capacity to earn money, with reference to which the amount of the wife's alimony is fixed. **1894, 1965** [see *faculty theory*, sense 12 below].

II. Kind of ability; branch of art or science.

†**6.** A branch or department of knowledge. *Obs.*

In this sense the word is used to render the Med.L. *facultas* = Gr. δύναμις used by Aristotle for an art or branch of learning.

c **1384** CHAUCER *H. Fame* I. 248 To speke of love? hyt wol not be; I kannot of that faculte. *c* **1400** *Test. Love* II. (1560) 282 b/2 All the remnaunt beene no genders but of grace, in facultie of Grammar. **1494** FABYAN *Chron.* VI. ccxiv. 232 Yᵉ whiche I remytte to theym that haue experience in suche facultie. **1553** T. WILSON *Rhet.* (1580) 30 The greate learned clerkes in al faculties. **1598** F. MERES in *Shaks. C. Praise* 22 In this faculty the best among our Poets are Spencer.. Daniel, etc. *a* **1661** FULLER *Worthies* (1840) III. 335 Books written in all faculties:—Grammar..Poetry..History [etc.]. **1757** BURKE *Abridgm. Eng. Hist.* II. ii, He brought with him a number of valuable books in many faculties.

7. *spec.* One of the departments of learning at a University. Hence ***Dean of a Faculty***.

When four faculties are mentioned, those intended are Theology, Canon and Civil Law, Medicine, Arts, of which the first three were called the Superior Faculties. Logic, Rhetoric, Astrology, Surgery, Grammar, and (in the English Universities) Music are occasionally spoken of as Faculties, and degrees could be taken in them; but the Masters teaching these branches did not form distinct bodies as those mentioned in sense 9.

[*c* **1184** GIRALDUS CAMBRENSIS *De Gestis* II. i. (Rolls) I. 48 Ubinam in jure studuerit..Præceptor autem ejusdem in ea facultate. *Ibid.* II. xvi. (Rolls) I. 73 In crastino vero doctores [hospitio suscepit] diversarum facultatum omnes.] **1387** TREVISA *Higden* (Rolls) VI. 259 Whan eny man is i-congyed þere to commence in eny faculte. **1482** *Monk of Evesham* (Arb.) 97 In connyng of dyuynyte as in other lyberals facultees. **1581** MULCASTER *Positions* xxxvii. (1887) 162 This man, whom I now prefer to this degree, in this facultie. **1641** EVELYN *Mem.* (1857) I. 29 The..Professor..in Latin demanded..to what Faculty I addicted myself. **1649** J. H. *Motion to Parl., Adv. Learn.* 27 We have hardly Professours for the three principall faculties. **1835** MALDEN *Orig. Univ.* 5 This faculty [of arts] originally constituted the whole university [of Paris]; and the faculties of theology, law, and medicine, were not added till a later period. **1868** M. PATTISON *Academ. Org.* iv. 114 In colleges, properly so called, the head will be the dean of his faculty. **1875** *Edin. Univ. Calendar* 37 The Chairs of the University are comprehended in the four Faculties. The affairs of each Faculty are presided over by a Dean. **1879** M. ARNOLD *Irish Cathol.* Mixed Ess. 101 At Bonn there is a Protestant faculty of theology. **1892** *Durham Univ. Calendar* cxii, Degrees in the Faculty of Music.

8. In a more extended sense: That in which any one is skilled; an art, trade, occupation, profession. *Obs.* exc. *arch.* or *Hist.*

c **1386** CHAUCER *Prol.* 244 For unto swiche a worthy man as he Accordeth nought, as by his faculte, To haven with sike lazars acquaintance. **1494** FABYAN *Chron.* II. xlvi. 29 A cunnynge musician; the whiche, for his excellence in that facultie, was called of the Brytons God of Glemen. **1503** *Act 19 Hen. VII*, c. 11 The facultie of Bowyers [is] almoste distroyed. **1529** in *Vicary's Anat.* (1888) App. xiv. 253 No persone..shall take..any..Straunger, to occupy the facultie of Barbery or Surgery. **1576** FLEMING *Panopl. Epist.* 163 They lende listening eare, to..slaunderers..have them in high..favour, who professe that facultie. **1605** ROWLANDS *Hell's Broke Loose* 14 By facultie at first, I was a Taylour. **1675** *Art Contentm.* vii. §6. 214 We..rely upon men in their own faculty. We put our estates in the lawyer's hand, our bodies into the physician's. **1687** CONGREVE *Old Bach.* I. i, Wit, be my faculty and pleasure my occupation. **1703** T. N. *City & C. Purchaser* 208 A..Soap-boyler, dwelling without Aldgate..and..another Gentleman of the same Faculty..in Southwark. **1839** ALISON *Hist. Europe* I. ii. §66. 184 They..proposed to abolish all..crafts, faculties, apprenticeships, and restrictions of every kind. **1841** STEPHEN *Laws Eng.* I. 7 To gentlemen of the faculty of physic the study of the law is attended with some importance. **1853** MARSDEN *Early Purit.* 388 Doctors in the University and the three learned faculties.

9. a. The whole body of Masters and Doctors, sometimes including also the students, in any one of the studies, Theology, Law, Medicine, Arts.

The use of the Latin word in this sense originated at some period in the 13th cent.; quot. 1255 indicates a use intermediate between this and sense 7.

[**1255** in *Chartularium Univ. Paris* (1889) I. 278 Nos.. magistri artium..propter novum et inestimabile periculum, quod in facultate nostra imminebat. **1325** *Title of Decree in Munimenta Acad.* (Rolls) I. 117 Quod facultas artium plene deliberet de tractandis in congregatione generali.] *c* **1425** WYNTOUN *Chron.* VIII. iv. 241 Þai studyusly De matere in þare faculteis Sowcht. **1673** RAY *Journ. Low C.* 17 The several Faculties are distinguished by their Habits. **1687** *Lond. Gaz.* No. 2275/3, 24 Doctors of the several Faculties, the two Proctors, and 19 Masters of Arts. **1774** WARTON *Hist. Eng. Poetry* I. Diss. ii. 11 Louis the eleventh.. borrowed the works of the Arabian physician Rhasis, from the faculty of medicine at Paris. **1832** tr. *Sismondi's Ital. Rep.* vii. 152 The faculty of the Sorbonne..was acknowledged to be the first theological school in Europe.

b. The whole teaching staff of a college, university, or school. orig. and chiefly *U.S.*

1767 in J. Maclean *Hist. College N. Jersey* (1877) I. 292 Concurring with the Trustees of this College in the establishment and support of a Faculty. **1780** in *Docs. Revolutionary Hist. New Jersey* (1901–17) IV. 223 The trustees and Faculty are now exerting themselves with great diligence for the improvement of the seminary. **1843** *Yale Lit. Mag.* IX. 66 That was all I could ever get from him on the subject—'that the Faculty were funny fellows, very—had sent him off for laughing'. **1893** W. K. POST *Harvard Stories* 79 There are many classes and individuals..as firmly established..as the Faculty. **1902** 'G. M. MARTIN' *Emmy Lou* 264 Once one would have said with 'the teachers', but in the High School one knew them as the Faculty. **1967** *Boston Sunday Globe* 23 Apr. 3/1 Catholic University officials worked behind the scenes Saturday to find quick settlement of a student-faculty strike that virtually closed the school Thursday. **1969** *Listener* 12 June 833/1 Students and some faculty are compelling the American universities to painful self-scrutiny.

10. *transf.* The members of a particular profession regarded as one body: **a.** of the medical profession (in popular language 'The Faculty').

1511–2 *Act 3 Hen. VIII*, c. 11 Calling to them such expert persons in the said Faculties [of Physicians and Surgeons]. **1529** MORE *Comf. agst. Trib.* II. Wks. 1185/2 One of the most cunning men in yᵉ faculty. **1638** T. WHITAKER *Blood of Grape* Pref. 2 The faculty deserveth the patronage of a Prince. **1699** GARTH *Dispens.* IV. (1730) 101 A zealous Member of the Faculty. **1747** WESLEY *Prim. Physic* (1762) p. xiii, We must do something to oblige the Faculty. **1840** HOOD *Up the Rhine* 14 Fat bacon..was once in vogue amongst the Faculty for weak digestions. **1886** GILMOUR *Mongols* 186 Their own faculty have no remedy for this disease.

b. *Sc. the Faculty* (also ***the Dean and Faculty***) ***of Advocates***.

1711 *Act Faculty Edin.* 18 July in *Lond. Gaz.* No. 4887/3 The Dean and Faculty of Advocates understanding, that several malicious Reports have been rais'd. **1848** WHARTON *Law Lex., Faculty of Advocates*, the college or society of advocates in Scotland. *a* **1862** BUCKLE *Civiliz.* (1869) III. iii. 145 A great part of the Faculty of Advocates was expelled from Edinburgh.

III. Conferred power, authority, privilege.

11. a. Power, liberty, or right of doing something, conferred by law or permission of a superior. ***faculty to burden***: Sc. Law (see quot. 1809).

1534 in W. H. Turner *Select Rec. Oxford* 128 They would clere take away from the Chaunceller all faculty to banish.. eny townesmen. **1605** SHAKS. *Macb.* I. vii. 17 Duncane Hath borne his Faculties so meeke. **1681** in Picton *L'pool Munic. Rec.* (1883) I. 271 Usinge the facultie of a freeman. **1752** CARTE *Hist. Eng.* III. 345 Pole..laid aside the marks of his legatine authority and abstained from the exercise of his faculties. **1800** COLQUHOUN *Comm. Thames* viii. 259 Care has been manifested in..divesting Power of the Faculty of Abuse. **1809** TOMLINS *Law Dict.* s.v., In the Scotch law.. a faculty to burden is the power or right of charging an estate with a sum of money. **1824** J. MARSHALL *Const. Opin.* (1839) 320 The charter of incorporation..gives it [a bank] every faculty which it possesses. **1865** M. ARNOLD *Ess. Crit.* x. (1875) 422 Something anti-civil and anti-social which the State had the faculty to judge and the duty to suppress.

b. A dispensation, license: *esp. Eccl.* an authorization or license granted by an ecclesiastical superior to some one to perform some action or occupy some position which otherwise he could not legally do or hold. ***Court of Faculties***: a court having power to grant faculties in certain cases. ***Master of Faculties***: the chief officer of that court.

1533–4 *Act 25 Hen. VIII*, c. 21 §3 The Archbishop of Canterburie..shall haue power and authoritie..to giue.. dispensations, compositions, faculties, grants, rescripts [etc.]. **1591** LAMBARDE *Archeion* (1635) 11 The Court of Faculties, for Dispensations. **1607** COWEL *Interpr.* s.v., An especiall officer..called..the Master of the faculties. **1662** *Bk. Com. Prayer, Ord. Deacons* Pref., None shall be admitted a Deacon, except he be Twenty three years of age, unless he have a Faculty. **1712** PRIDEAUX *Direct. Ch.-wardens* (ed. 4) 75 The Bishop can grant Faculties for the building..of them. **1843** *Act 6–7 Vict.* c. 90 §8 The Master of the Faculties..is hereby..empowered to issue Commissions [etc.]. **1857** FROUDE *Short Stud., Monast.* (1867) 282 An abbot able to purchase..a faculty to confer holy orders. **1869** *Times* 16 Mar. 12/4 This was an application..for a faculty or license to make some alterations in the interior of the church. **1872** PHILLIMORE *Blunt's Church Law* IV. i. 263 Private rights to particular seats, conferred by a faculty, *i.e.* a license from the ordinary. **1885** MOZLEY *Remin.* II. lxxv. 70 The faculties..did not assign pews to persons..but to persons and families residing in certain houses.

IV. 12. *attrib.* **a.** (sense 11) as ***faculty-court***, ***-office***; **b.** (sense 7) as ***faculty-place***; **c.** (sense 10) as ***faculty-composition***, ***-habits***, ***-influence***; **d.** (sense 9 b) ***faculty business***, ***-full*** (sb.), ***list***, ***meeting***, ***member***; also, **faculty doctrine** = *faculty psychology*; **faculty-pew, -seat**, a pew or seat in a parish church appropriated to particular persons by a faculty: cf. sense 11; **faculty psychology**, a term for those systems of psychology in which certain mental faculties were held to be the forces and powers accountable for the phenomena of mind; so ***faculty psychologist***; †**faculty-tax**, a property or income tax; **faculty theory**, the theory of taxation according to which every man should help to bear public burdens according to his ability; **faculty wife** chiefly *U.S.*, the wife of a faculty member (see sense 9 b above), esp. one whose life revolves around faculty social functions, etc.

1877 E. S. WARD *Story of Avis* v. 51 Some pressing *Faculty business took him..to Professor Dobell's house. **1905** W. JAMES *Mem. & Stud.* (1911) v. 83 In faculty-business he might not run well in harness, but..his influence on the students would be priceless. **1790** BURKE *Fr. Rev.* Wks. V. 97 An wholly professional and *faculty composition. **1863** H. COX *Instit.* II. xi. 568 The *Faculty Court, belonging to the Archbishop of Canterbury. **1912** W. McDOUGALL *Social Psychol.* (ed. 5) 378 All these doctrines ..are forms of the '*faculty doctrine' whose fallacies have so often been exposed. **1905** W. JAMES *Mem. & Stud.* (1911) v. 84 In a university..a few undisciplinables..may be infinitely more precious than a *faculty-full of orderly routinists. **1790** BURKE *Fr. Rev.* Wks. V. 97 Professional and *faculty habits. **1791** MACKINTOSH *Vind. Gall.* Wks. 1846 III. 64 This '*faculty influence', as Mr. Burke chooses to phrase it, was not injuriously predominant. **1911** H. S. HARRISON *Queed* xviii. 218 The president sat up late going over his *faculty list. **1839** H. CASWALL *America* xii. 200 [The professors] form a body denominated the Faculty, and conduct the government of the institution by regulations and laws established by themselves in '*Faculty meetings' from time to time. **1911** H. S. HARRISON *Queed* xviii. 218 There was one man on the staff that West objected to from the first faculty meeting. **1903** W. JAMES *Mem. & Stud.* (1911) xiv. 331 The College had always gloried in a list of *faculty members who bore the doctor's title. **1715** KERSEY, *Faculty-office. **1881** *Dict. Eng. Churchm.* 354 All..pews other than *faculty pews in an ancient church are the common property of the parish. **1682** PRIDEAUX *Lett.* (Camden) 123, I hope by this you are secured of a *faculty place..and advise you to thinke of takeing your Dʳˢ degree in laws as soon as you can. **1886** *Encycl. Brit.* XX. 41/1 To free us from the mythology and verbiage of the '*faculty-psychologists'. **1909** *Cent. Dict.* Suppl. s.v. *Psychology*, C. von Wolff (1679–1754) is regarded as the typical faculty-psychologist. **1890** W. JAMES *Princ. Psychol.* I. ii. 27 Gall.. took the *faculty-psychology as his ultimatum on the mental side, and he made no farther psychological analysis. **1897** C. H. JUDD tr. *Wundt's Outl. Psychol.* 11 The faculty-psychology considered these class-concepts as psychical forces or faculties, and referred psychical processes to their alternating or united activity. **1951** J. C. FLUGEL *Hundred Years Psychol.* (ed. 2) ii. 34 Beneke equally avoids the dangers of the faculty psychology, inasmuch as the powers or 'faculties' with which he deals are not broad characteristics or abilities,..but quite specific forms of apprehension, feeling or behaviour. **1872** PHILLIMORE *Blunt's Church Law* IV. i. 263 *marg.*, No jurisdiction in *faculty seats. **1766** *Hist. Europe* in *Ann. Reg.* 45/2 Besides a *faculty-tax upon all personal estates. **1797** BURKE *Regic. Peace* iii. Wks. VIII. 356 Land and offices only excepted we raise no faculty tax. **1911** E. R. A. SELIGMAN *Income Tax* 398 The only other state in which the faculty tax lasted during the nineteenth century is South Carolina. **1894** ——

Progress. Taxation iii. 127 The *faculty theory of taxation is very old. That a man should contribute to the public burdens in proportion to his ability or faculty is a principle which dates back to the middle ages. **1896** C. C. Plehn *Introd. Public Finance* II. ii. 84 Each citizen should contribute as he is able. They claim that it is easier to measure ability than it is to measure benefit. This theory is called the faculty theory, the term 'faculty' having been found in this sense in early tax laws. **1965** J. L. Hanson *Dict. Econ. & Commerce* 169/1 *Faculty theory of taxation*, an alternative term for the 'Ability-to-pay' theory of taxation. **1962** A. Lurie *Love & Friendship* iv. 63 She had a great advantage over every other *faculty wife at Convers. **1977** *New Yorker* 8 Aug. 68/3 (Advt.), For students, retirees, faculty wives, husbands, and others, it could work out to be a pretty good deal.

† **'facund**, *sb.* *Obs.* Forms: 4–5 facound(e, facund(e, 5 faciund, faconde. [ad. F. *faconde*, semi-popular ad. L. *fācundia*, f. *fācundus* (see next).] Eloquence.

a **1340** Hampole *Psalter* xi. 4 þaire facunde & þaire skilles ere of þaim self. **1393** Gower *Conf.* III. 85 Rhetorique, whose facounde Above all other is eloquent. *c* **1400** *Destr. Troy* 3748 He was..of faciund full faire, fre of his speche. *c* **1440** *Secrees* (E.E.T.S.) 127 þe chastite of daniel, þe ffaconde of ysae. **1483** Caxton *Gold. Leg.* 346/4 The.. moste plentyuous wysedome of facunde and spekyng.

facund ('fækʌnd, fə'kʌnd), *a. arch.* Forms: 4–5 facond(e, 4–6 facound(e, 6 facunde, 6– facund. [ME. *faconde, facounde*, ad. OF. *facond*, ad. L. *fācundus* eloquent, f. *fāri* to speak.]

1. Eloquent; also *fig.*, said of beauty, etc.

c **1381** Chaucer *Parl. Foules* 521 With facound voys seyde, 'Holde your tonges there'. **1483** Caxton *Gold. Leg.* 230/1 Martha was ryght facounde of speche. **1503** Hawes *Examp. Virt.* iv. 43 [They] were endued with facounde pulcrytude. **1530** Lyndesay *Test. Papyngo* 710 ȝour facunde wordis fair. **1586** Ferne *Blaz. Gentrie* 27 Poets and excellent musicions whose braines being not moysted with the iuyce of Bacchus..be nothinge plenty nor facund. **1610** *Chester's Tri.* Joy's Speech 89 The powerfull tongue of facund Mercury. **1721–1800** in Bailey. **1859** I. Taylor *Logic in Theol.* 179 The learned and the facund Jerome..is our authority.

† **2.** Inspiring or promoting eloquence. *Obs.*

1501 Douglas *Pal. Hon.* II. xl, The facund well and hill of Helicon.

† **facundate**, *v.* *Obs.*$^{-0}$ [f. facund *a.* + -ate³.] *trans.* To make eloquent.

1656–81 in Blount *Glossogr.* **1692–1732** in Coles.

† **facundie**, *a.* *Obs. rare*$^{-1}$. [ad. L. *fācundia*.] = facund *sb.*

1447 Bokenham *Seyntys* (Roxb.) 167 For the facundye wych she oysyd there.

† **fa'cundious**, *a.* *Obs.* [f. L. *fācundia* (see facund *sb.*) + -ous. Cf. OF. *facondieux*.] Of persons: Gifted with fluent speech; eloquent, glib. Of speech: Copious, fluent.

1430 Lydg. *Chron. Troy* II. xv, Of speche ryght facundious. **1503** Hawes *Examp. Virt.* Prol. 4 O prudent Gower in langage..moost facundyous. **1534** Whitinton *Tullyes Offices* II. (1540) 102 The crafte of eloquence..[is] more facundyous. **1606** Warner *Alb. Eng.* 408 Our facundious Fooles. **1656–81** in Blount *Glossogr.* **1721–66** in Bailey.

Hence † **fa'cundiously** *adv.*, eloquently. *Obs.*

1509 Hawes *Past. Pleas.* 37 Yet Elocusion..The mater exorneth right well facundyously. **1624** Heywood *Gunaik.* II. 75 Eloquentlie to speake, and facundiouslie to delate of that thing.

fa'cundity. Also 6 facundite. [a. OF. *faconditě*, ad. L. *fācunditāt-em*, f. *fācundus*: see facund *a.* and -ity.] Eloquence.

1530 Palsgr. Epist. 8 The naturall inclination..unto eloquence and facundite. **1624** Heywood *Gunaik.* II. 76 Mercury..begets eloquence, facunditie, and elegancie of speech. *a* **1652** Brome *Queen* III. vii, Upon my facundity, an elegant construction. **1773** J. Ross *Fratricide* (MS.) II. 739 Eve..reproaches him..With suitable facundity. **1921** *Times Lit. Suppl.* 17 Feb. 110/4 Two love sequences..have a fine poetic facundity, but that is all.

facy ('feɪsɪ). *Obs.* exc. *dial.* [f. face *sb.* + -y.] Characterized by 'face'; insolent, impudent.

1605 B. Jonson *Volpone* II. ii, These..facy, nasty.. rogues. **1887** Darlington *Folk-sp. S. Chesh.* 128, 'I should ha' thowt nowt at doin' summat for him if he hadnur ha' bin so facy.'

fad (fæd), *sb.*¹ *dial.*

1825 Brockett *Gloss. N.C. Words* 66 *Fad, faud*, a bundle of straw, twelve of which make a thrave. **1863** Robson *Bards of Tyne* 135 Aw' thowt aboot the fad o' straw.

fad (fæd), *sb.*² [Etym. unknown; widely current in dialects (chiefly midland), and thence recently adopted in general use. Cf. next vb.]

1. A crotchety rule of action; a peculiar notion as to the right way of doing something; a pet project, *esp.* of social or political reform, to which exaggerated importance is attributed; in wider sense, a crotchet, hobby, 'craze'.

1834 Bp. Fraser in Hughes *Life* (1887) 14 Uncle need not fuss himself about the Doctor becoming a Bishop, as it is all a fad. **1867** Trollope *Chron. Barset* II. lxxxii. 363 She may take up some other fad now. **1881** Miss Braddon *Asph.* xxx. 339 The Engadine is the last fad of the moneyed classes. **1884** *Illust. Lond. News* 22 Nov. 491/2 Slöijd..the last new 'fad'.

2. A fussy, over-particular person. Only *dial.*

1877 in *N.W. Linc. Gloss.* **1879** Miss Jackson *Shropsh. Word-bk.* 138 'Everybody toud me as I should never stop ooth sich a noud fad.'

3. *Comb.* **fad-monger**, one who deals in fads; **fad-mongering** *ppl. a.*; **fad-mongery**.

1883 *Sat. Rev.* No. 1452. 238 Measures of the kind dear to the fadmonger. **1885** *Ibid.* 24 Jan. 104/2 The..asceticism dear to his fad-mongering friends. **1890** *Guardian* 1 Oct. 1527/3 'Fadmongery' or 'faddism' is..becoming..a rampant and ridiculous craze.

fad (fæd), *v.* Chiefly *dial.* [Belongs to prec. sb.; it is not certain which is the source of the other. Cf. fidfad *v.*], *intr.* **a.** *dial.* (see quots.). **b.** *nonce-use.* To advocate 'fads'.

1847 Halliwell, *Fad*, to be busy about trifles. **1879** Miss Jackson *Shropsh. Word-bk.* 138 'The poor owd Maister canna do much now—ony fad-about a bit.' **1890** *Sat. Rev.* 27 Sept. 383/2 We have..a warning against listening to faddists, fad they never so charmingly.

Hence **'fadding** *ppl. a.*

1864 *Field* 28 May 383 To condemn us old hands as finical, priggish, fadding.

fad: see langfad, *Obs. Sc.*, long boat.

faddish ('fædɪʃ), *a.* [f. fad *sb.*² + -ish.]

a. Of persons: Addicted or given to fads, whimsical. **b.** Of things: Of the nature of a fad.

1855 Robinson *Whitby Gloss.*, *Fondish* or *Faddish*, adj., shallow in point of intellect, whimsical. **1881** Mrs. C. Praed *Policy & P.* II. 194 Never was there such a faddish creature. **1891** *Athenæum* 31 Jan. 148/1 The faddish extremes of some composers.

Hence **'faddishness.**

1884 *Pall Mall G.* 5 Dec. 1/2 If only they give up faddishness. **1889** *Sat. Rev.* 16 Feb. 184/2 Political faddishness.

faddishly ('fædɪʃlɪ), *adv.* [f. faddish *a.* + -ly².] In a faddish or finical manner.

1928 *Collier's* 10 Nov. 35/2 The sufferer generally eats poorly and faddishly.

faddism ('fædɪz(ə)m). [f. fad *sb.*² + -ism.] Fondness for fads; a disposition to pursue fads.

1885 *Spectator* 19 Sept. 1221 It will..annihilate faddism. **1890** *Guardian* 1 Oct. 1527/3 'Fadmongery' or 'faddism'.

faddist ('fædɪst). [f. as prec. + -ist.] One who has a fad; one who indulges in fads.

1883 *St. James's Gaz.* 21 Apr. 4 The faddists will not be deterred by such a trifle as that. **1886** *Sat. Rev.* 3 Apr. 455 He is a very fair specimen of the modern faddist Radical.

'faddity. [f. as prec. + -ity.] = fad *sb.*² 1.

1892 *Sat. Rev.* 23 Jan. 92/1 It is one of the many pet little faddities of this overweening sect.

faddle ('fæd(ə)l), *v.* *Obs.* exc. *dial.* [Cf. fad *v.* and fondle, dandle, etc.]

1. *trans.* To make much of (a child), pet, caress.

1688 Miege *Fr. Dict.* 11 To faddle a Child, *caresser un Enfant*. **1721–1800** in Bailey. **1881** Evans *Leicester Words* 144 'His mother had use to faddle him a deal.'

2. *intr.* 'To trifle; to toy; to play' (J.).

1755 in Johnson. **1761** Mrs. F. Sheridan *Sidney Bidulph* I. 204, I thought..to have faddled away a good while longer. **1879** Miss Jackson *Shropsh. Word-bk.*, *Faddle-after*, to pay minute attention to a person, to be solicitous about—and complying with—fads..'Bessy's a rar' place up at the owd 'all; nuthin 'ardly to do but faddle-after the Missis'.

Hence **'faddler**, one who faddles; **'faddling** *ppl. a.*, trifling, pettifogging.

1883 J. W. Sherer *At Home & in Ind.* 8 It [the garden] was divided into faddling beds. **1884** *Pall Mall G.* 30 Oct. 5/1 The critic who gratified Mr. Stevenson by calling him a 'faddling hedonist'. **1888** *Sat. Rev.* 7 Jan. 19 It is to be hoped that it contains a much smaller percentage of faddlers.

faddle ('fæd(ə)l), *sb. dial.* or *colloq.* [f. prec. vb.]

1. Nonsense, trifling; usually fiddle-faddle.

1850 in Bamford *Gloss. S. Lanc.* **1892** Mrs. H. Ward *D. Grieve* I. 26 Oh, is they? Then I spose books is faddle.

2. (See quot.)

1881 Evans *Leicester Words*, *Faddle* sb., a fanciful person; either fastidious in trifles or devoted to some particular hobby.

faddom, obs. f. of fathom.

faddy ('fædɪ), *a.* (and *sb.*) Chiefly *dial.* and *colloq.* [f. fad *sb.* + -y.]

1. Of persons and personal attributes: Occupied with fads, particular about trifles, crotchety. Of things: Of the nature of a fad, taken up as a fad.

1824 Mrs. Sherwood *Waste Not* I. 11 She is so faddy. **1885** *Sat. Rev.* 21 Feb. 238 The local sanitary official may be crotchety and 'faddy'. **1885** *Kendal Mercury* 30 Jan. 6/4 Such a faddy thing as the planting of trees at this place. **1888** McCarthy & Praed *Ladies' Gallery* II. vii. 112 A faddy old book-collector.

2. *sb.* = fad *sb.*² 2.

1887 G. R. Sims *Mary Jane's Mem.* 239 It's bad enough to be under a real missus who is a faddy.

Hence **'faddiness.**

1865 *Cornh. Mag.* May 621 The extreme faddiness of the old falconers.

fade, *sb.*¹ [f. the vb.] **1.** The action of the vb. fade.

In quot. 1969 ***nix out on the fade*** in Surfers' slang = don't go away.

a **1300** *Cursor M.* 23513 (Cott.) Frenscip þar es, wit-vten fade [*sc.* in heuin]. **1775** Harris *Philos. Arrangem.* Wks. (1841) 301 [A slain hero and a flower just gathered have] the same drooping head, the same lifeless fade, the same relicts of a form that was once fair and flourishing. **1918** A. Stringer *House of Intrigue* ii. 27, I got so I could face a tight fade without a quaver, and do my gay-cat part in sloughing our make as easily as falling off a log. **1965** *Language* XLI. 277 Stockwell suggests that the lesser fade at the juncture between the two 'main' conjuncts can be described as an environmentally conditioned allophone of terminal fade. **1969** *Times* 25 July 5/2 Nix out on the fade with it stashed on the moke.

b. Phr. *to do* (or *take*) *a fade* (*U.S. slang*), to disappear.

1949 A. Miller *Death of Salesman* I. 57 If I'm going to take a fade the boss can call any number where I'm supposed to be and they'll swear to him that I just left. **1962** K. Orvis *Damned & Destroyed* xiv. 92 Then, pal, we'll both do a fade. **1970** H. Waugh *Finish me Off* (1971) 86 If this is a sample of her business acumen, that beauty salon will do a fast fade.

2. *Cinematogr.* and *Broadcasting.* The action or an act of 'fading' (see fade *v.*¹ 9); also, the gradual decrease or (freq. ***fade-in***) increase in the brightness or definition of a picture or the loudness of a sound. See also fade-out.

1918 H. Croy *How Motion Pictures are Made* vii. 175 It was in such experiments that the principle of fade was discovered, by means of which a scene could be made gradually to grow plainer until the full details were before the audience. This in photographic parlance came to be known as the fade-in. *Ibid.*, The second means of accomplishing a fade picture is by means of the dissolving shutter. *Ibid.*, The diaphragm fade is open to the objection that with an iris that never closes completely it is impossible to make a complete fade. **1922** L. C. Macbean *Kinemat. Studio Technique* ix. 71 The number of turns in which a 'mix' or 'fade' should be accomplished. **1937** *Printers Ink Monthly* Apr. 53/1 *Fade*, a diminishing of program volume. **1937** *Amer. Speech* XII. 101 To fade is usually the engineer's duty, reducing volume of an orchestra..while an announcer speaks into another microphone, hence a good or bad fade-in. **1960** D. Wilson *Television Playwright* 15 By means of 'mixes' and 'fades' short or long time-lapses can be established. **1962** A. Nisbett *Technique Sound Studio* ix. 153 When we talk about the fade, the first thing that springs to mind is the use to which it is put in dramatic productions: the convention is that each scene starts with a fade in, and ends with a fade out.

3. *Theatr.* The gradual brightening or dimming of the stage lighting; usu. ***fade-in*** or fade-out.

1959 W. C. Lounsbury *Backstage from A to Z* 39 *Fade in*, gradual dim up of lights or sound. **1962** *Listener* 5 July 26/3 Pointless use of fade-in and fade-out lights on a stage confusingly and ineptly split into four parts.

4. The reduction in effectiveness of the braking system of a motor vehicle, e.g. as a result of the generation of heat.

1949 G. Grant *Modern Motorcars* vi. 47 On the average car the efficiency of the linings is not greatly impaired until the brake-drum temperature reaches a critical point, where there is a noticeable falling-off of braking power. This is known as 'brake-fade', and can be a very real problem on ultra-fast cars. **1959** *Motor* 4 Mar. 163/1 Unusual design of ..brake drum..produces fade only after severe provocation. **1962** *Which? Car Suppl.* Oct. 141/1 Its brakes ..were very susceptible to fade.

5. *Comb.*, as **fade-proof** *a.*, resistant to fading.

1909 *Public Ledger* (Philadelphia) 26 June 7/6 Pure worsted serge suits—guaranteed fade-proof. **1959** *Listener* 5 Mar. 435/1 They [*sc.* the fabrics] are rot-proof and fade-proof. **1961** *Ibid.* 30 Nov. 933/1 His jokes are appreciated for their topicality, which cannot be fade-proof.

fade (feɪd), *sb.*² *dial.* [? f. fade *v.*¹] Mould (on cheese); oftener ***blue-, green-fade***.

1884 Holland *Chester Gloss.*, *Green-Fade*, blue mould in cheese. **1887** Darlington *Folk-speech S. Chesh.*, *Blue-fade*.

† **fade**, *sb.*³ *Obs.* Also 6 faid. **a.** A company of hunters. **b.** ? The leader of the hunt.

1513 Douglas *Æneis* IV. iii. 56 Quhen..the rangis and the faid on breid Dynnis throw the gravis. **1536** Bellenden *Cron. Scot.* (1821) I. 205 Quhen the faid had brocht in the wolf afore the houndis, the skry arais, and ilk man went to his gam. **1567** Sempill *Inclination of King* in *Ballates* (1872) 2 The faid also rycht feitlie could he set. **1606** Birnie *Kirk-Buriall* (1833) 25 The formest [ship]..doth fuir before with lantern and flag, as fade whom the rest should follow.

† **fade**, *a.*¹ *Obs.* Also 4 fede, 5 fadde. [Etymology unknown; the senses assigned are somewhat uncertain, and perh. the examples do not all contain the same word.]

1. Strong, doughty, brave, powerful. Also, of a thing: Great, large.

c **1320** *Sir Tristr.* 153 þe kniȝtes þat wer fade, þai dede as rohand bade. *Ibid.* 2474 In þat forest fede Tristrem hodain gan chast. *c* **1340** *Gaw. & Gr. Knt.* 149 He ferde as freke were fade. *a* **1400** *Sir Perc.* 616 Ther was no mane that durste hym lett, Thofe that he ware fadde. *Ibid.* 1165 The childe sawe that he was fade. *c* **1400** *Rowland & O.* 1420 Full fele Sarazenes felle þay fade.

2. ? Cruel, ? hostile.

a **1300** *Cursor M.* 24025 (Cott.) þe folk þat was sa fade [*v.r.* fad] O clai þai kest at him þe clote, And laiked wit him sitisote. *a* **1400** *Sir Perc.* 1440 If I sle hym, or he me, That never ȝit was fade?

fade (feɪd), *a.*² Also 3 vad, 5 faed. [a. F. *fade* vapid, insipid, dull, faded; according to M. Gaston Paris (*Mém. de la Soc. de Ling.* I. 90) repr. L. *vapidum* (see VAPID); cf. OF. *rade*:—L. *rapidum*, *maussade*:—L. *male sapidum*.

The great difficulty is the anomalous representation of L. *v* by *f*; the apparent parallel in OF. *feiz* (mod. *fois*):—*vicem* is questionable, the *f* in that case being prob. due to sentence-combination. The ordinary view that *fade* descends from L. *fatuum* foolish, also insipid (whence Pr. *fatz* fem. *fade*, in same senses), is inadmissible on phonological grounds; but it is possible that early confusion with this word may have given rise to the change of *v* into *f*. No OF. **vade* has been found: if it existed it would explain the Eng. *vade*, var. of FADE *v.*, which is otherwise difficult to account for, as the Eng. dialects that have *v* for *f* usually retain *f* in Romanic words. Cf. Fr. dial. (Lyons) *vadou* (fem. *vadoussi*), repr. L. type **vapidōsum*.]

†**1.** Of colour, etc.: Dull, pale, wan, sombre. *Obs.* exc. *arch.*

c **1290** *S. Eng. Leg.* I. 318/672 Of fade [*MS. Harl.* No. 2277 vad] colur of hard huyde. *c* **1350** *Will. Palerne* 891 þi faire hewe is al fade. **1393** GOWER *Conf.* I. 173 The nettle.. maketh hem [roses] fade and pale of hewe. *c* **1399** *Pol. Poems* (1859) II. 7 The day is gone, the nygth is derk and fade. *c* **1430** *Syr Gener.* 1288 With angry hert and colour fade. *c* **1460** *Towneley Myst.* 225 Thyn een.. lost thay have thare light And wax alle faed in fere. *c* **1500** *Blowbol's Test.* 23 in Hazl. *E.P.P.* I. 93 His evy countenaunces and his colour fade. **1854** SYD. DOBELL *Balder* xxiii. 127 Tears Grow in the fade eyes of the relict world.

†**2.** Faded, feeble, languishing, withered. *Obs.*

1303 R. BRUNNE *Handl. Synne* 3220 Proude wymmen ..þat are so foule and fade, That make hem feyrere than God hem made Wyþ oblaunchere. **13..** *Leg. Rood* (1871) 66 þare groued neuer gres, ne neuer sall, Bot euermore be.. falow, and fade. **1388** WYCLIF *Ecclus.* xi. 12 Ther is a man fade. **1540–54** CROKE *Ps.* (Percy Soc.) 30 All ben cleane put out of place That my sowle trobled, and ben fade. **1613–31** *Primer Our Lady* 18 Our sence here fraile and fade. **1752** BERKELEY *Thoughts on Tarwater* Wks. 1871 III. 493 Tar-water.. may extract.. from the clay a fade sweetishness.

‖**3.** [mod.F. *fade* (fad).] That has lost taste; insipid, commonplace, uninteresting.

Some of the early instances may be the Eng. word in fig. use of 2.

1715 M. DAVIES *Athen. Brit.* I. 195 Fade and unsavoury Anglo-saxon turns of thinking and speaking. **1775** MAD. D'ARBLAY *Early Diary* 3 Apr., Mr. Nesbit.. is a young man infinitely fade. **1813** MAR. EDGEWORTH *Patron.* (1832) I. xvi. 261 Simplicity had something too fade in it to suit his taste. **1824** *Westm. Rev.* I. 556 A picture at once crude, coarse, and *fâde* [sic]. **1834** *Fraser's Mag.* X. 102 A fade and vapid style of set-speech compliment. **1862** *Athenæum* 25 Oct. 527 Mrs. Opie['s] fade and feeble sentimentality.

Hence **'fadeness**, *Obs. rare*⁻¹. The quality or state of being 'fade'; want of vivacity, dullness.

1837 *Fraser's Mag.* XVI. 550 Emily.. was a blonde.. yet had she none of the fadeness so common to such a complexion.

fade (feɪd), *v.*¹ Forms: *α.* 4–5 fade(n, (4 fate), 5–6 faid(e, 6 feid, 4– fade; *β.* 5–6 vade. [a. OF. *fade-r*, f. *fade* FADE *a.*²]

1. *intr.* Of a flower, plant, etc.: To lose freshness and vigour; to droop, wither.

α. **1340** HAMPOLE *Pr. Consc.* 697 For a flour þat semes fayre and bright Thurgh stormes fades. *c* **1465** *12 Lett.* 45 in *Pol. Rel. & L. Poems* (1866) 2 An R for the Rose þat is fresche and wol nat fade. **1578** *Gude & G. Ball.* (1868) 83 Lyke the widderit hay sone sall they faid. **1610** NICCOLS *Winter Night* (cont. *Mirr. Mag.*) 556 The barren fields, which whilome flower'd as they would neuer fade. **1667** MILTON *P.L.* III. 360 Elisian Flours.. that never fade. **1704** POPE *Autumn* 29 Ye trees that fade when autumn-heats remove. *Ibid.* 69 The garlands fade, the vows are worn away. **1859** TENNYSON *Lotus-eaters* 82 The flower.. Ripens and fades, and falls.

β. *c* **1489** CAXTON *Blanchardyn* liv. 212 Life began to vade. **1578** LYTE *Dodoens* v. lxxix. 648 The leaves.. do not vade and perish. **1579** TOMSON *Calvin's Serm. Tim.* 613/1 The state of this worlde.. is flitting, and euer vading. **1597** GERARD *Herbal* I. xxxii. §2 (1598) 43 When the flowers be vaded, then followe the seedes.

fig. *c* **1400** *Rom. Rose* 354 Faded was al hir beaute. **1500–20** DUNBAR *Contemplatioun* iv, Thy youth, Sall feid as dois the somer flouris. **1655** *Nicholas Papers* (Camden) II. 261 Our expectation of the breach betweene the crowne of France and Cromwell.. is fadinge. **1696** TATE & BRADY *Ps.* xvi. 11 And Joys that never fade. **1828** MRS. HEMANS *Graves Household* 23 She faded 'midst Italian flowers. **1878** B. TAYLOR *Deukalion* II. iii, Honors fade unworn.

†**2.** To grow small or weak; to decline, decay, fail, or faint; to shrink. *lit.* and *fig.* *Obs.*

1388 WYCLIF *Josh.* xviii. 3 How longe faden ȝe bi cowardise. **1398** TREVISA *Barth. De P.R.* XIII. iii. (1495) 443 A manere ryuer that.. fadyth in drye weder. *c* **1450** in *Pol. Rel. & L. Poems* (1866) 114 þou art þe lufe þat neuere sal fade. **1526** *Pilgr. Perf.* (W. de W. 1531) 6 b, The heuenly rychesse, that neuer shall fade ne fayle. **1529** MORE *Comf. agst. Trib.* III. Wks. 1212 The faith shalbe at that tyme so far faded, that [etc.]. **1585** J. B. tr. *P. Viret's Sch. Beastes* C b, With the touch thereof [poyson] her heare, her eares, and nose, did fade.

†**3.** *trans.* To weaken; to deprive of freshness or vigour; to corrupt, taint. *Obs.*

c **1400** *Test. Love* I. (1560) 272/2 Ne death, ne no manner travayle hath no power myne heart so much to fade. *c* **1400** *Destr. Troy* 9188 A ffrele woman me fades. *c* **1425** WYNTOUN *Cron.* VII. i. 69 Set þow hawe fadyt þi Lawte. *c* **1440** *York Myst.* i. 132 Sum ar fallen into fylthe þat evermore sall fade þam. **1775** [see FADED *ppl. a.*].

4. *intr.* Of colour, light, or any object possessing these qualities: To lose brightness or brilliance; to grow dim, faint, or pale. Also with *away*.

α. [**1303** R. BRUNNE *Handl. Synne* 9295 Hys wrytyng was alle to-fade.] **13..** *Pearl* (Gollancz) lxxxvii. 6 A parfyt perle þat neuer fatez. **1393** GOWER *Conf.* III. 109 The mone is somedele faded. *a* **1400–50** *Alexander* 5309 'Qui fadis so þi faire hew?' said þe faire lady. **1430** LYDG. *Chron. Troy* I. vi, When the day gan faide. **1483** *Act 1 Rich. III*, c. 8 Preamb., The Colours made with the which Orchell.. faden away. *c* **1600** SHAKS. *Sonn.* xviii, Thy eternal summer shall not fade. **1718** *Freethinker* No. 63. 53 The strongest Colouring will fade. **1783–94** BLAKE *Songs Innoc., Nurse's Song* 13 Go and play till the light fades away. **1801** SOUTHEY *Thalaba* XII. xv, Dimmer now it [the flame] fades, and now is quench'd. **1860** TYNDALL *Glac.* I. xi. 74 Light.. deepening at one extremity into red, and fading at the other into a pure ethereal hue.

β. **1471** RIPLEY *Comp. Alch.* Pref. in Ashm. (1652) 127 Colour whych wyll not vade.

fig. **1792** ROGERS *Pleas. Mem.* I. 88 When nature fades and life forgets to charm. **1836** EMERSON *Nat., Prospects* Wks. (Bohn) II. 172 When the fact is seen under the light of an idea, the gaudy fable fades. **1876** E. MELLOR *Priesth.* v. 208 The old Dispensation faded away in the dawning light of the New.

5. *trans.* †**a.** To lose brilliancy of (colour). *Obs.* **b.** To cause to lose colour; to dim, dull, wither. Now *rare*.

1559 CAVILL in *Baldwin's Mirrour for Magistrates* (1563) B iv a, The fresshest colours soonest fade the hue. **1598** MARSTON *Pygmal.* iv. 154 So haue I seen the march wind strive to fade The fairest hewe that Art, or Nature made. **1658** DRYDEN *O. Cromwell* xv, No winter could his laurels fade. **1744** E. HEYWOOD *Female Spectator* (1748) I. 272 Ill-nature.. swells the lip, fades the complexion, contracts the brow. **1768–74** TUCKER *Lt. Nat.* (1852) II. 587 To brighten or fade their colours. **1839** LONGFELLOW *Hyperion* Prose Wks. (1886) II. II. iii. 81 The early autumn gives to the summer leaves a warmer glow, yet fades them not. **1864** N. HAWTHORNE *Grimshawe's Secret* xi. (1883) 133 Tapestry, or carpet.. still retaining much of the ancient colors, where there was no visible sunshine to fade them.

6. a. *intr.* To pass away or disappear gradually; vanish, die out. Also with *away*.

α. **1590** SPENSER *F.Q.* I. v. 15 He stands amazed how he thence should fade. **1610** SHAKS. *Temp.* IV. i. 155 Like this insubstantiall Pageant faded. **1797** MRS. RADCLIFFE *Italian* vii, And fades, as if into air, at my approach. **1820** W. IRVING *Sketch Bk.* I. 11, I saw the last blue line of my native land fade away. **1848** MACAULAY *Hist. Eng.* II. 134 Religious animosity.. would of itself fade away. **1856** KANE *Arct. Expl.* I. vii. 68 Headland after headland.. until they faded into the mysterious North. **1876** E. MELLOR *Priesth.* vi. 279 Other persons and things might fade from their memory.

β. **1538** STARKEY *England* I. ii. 35 Thys bodyly wele wyl sone vade and vanysch away. **1548** HALL *Chron.* 117 The glory of thenglishmen.. began.. to decay, and vade awaie in Fraunce. *a* **1555** J. PHILPOT in Pagitt *Heresiogr.* (1648) 43 To my great griefe it [a vision] vaded away.

b. humorously *transf.* To vanish mysteriously. Also, to disappear from the scene; to depart; to faint. Freq. const. *away*, *out*.

1848 THACKERAY *Van. Fair* lx. 540 Florence Scape, Fanny Scape and their mother faded away to Boulogne. **1900** ADE *More Fables* (1902) 10 The Bookie told him to Back Up and Fade and do a Disappearing Specialty. **1910** 'I. HAY' in *Granta* 11 June 12 Next moment everybody seemed to fade away. **1924** A. J. SMALL *Frozen Gold* i. 39 When that gang fades out of one camp, I hear all about it inside twenty-four hours. **1929** J. B. PRIESTLEY *Good Companions* I. ii. 63 'My wife,' Mr. Rathbury muttered, fading out. **1950** *Times* 20 Sept. 2/6 Miller, Lindwall, and Johnson have faded out of the picture. **1954** 'N. BLAKE' *Whisper in Gloom* I. iv. 60 Copper and Foxy faded.

†**c.** *trans.* (causatively). *Obs.*

1787 *Mirror* 295 Those lineaments which time.. had almost faded away from her remembrance.

7. *intr.* Of sound: to die *away* or *out*. Also, with *in*, *up*, to increase gradually in loudness from a low or inaudible level.

1879 G. B. PRESCOTT *Speaking Telephone* ix. 287 The voice increased or faded out in proportion as the telephone was directed toward or receded from the pole of the dipping needle. **1924** *Wireless Ann.* 21 Without a word of warning, the signal 'fades' to nothing. **1932** F. E. TERMAN *Radio Engin.* xiii. 488 As the signals fade in or out, the sensitivity of the receiver is varied. **1966** J. L. BERNSTEIN *Audio Syst.* v. 122 Moving the control.. causes the signal from one channel to fade out and the other to fade in. **1969** A. GLYN *Dragon Variation* ix. 282 'That's a sort of *bon voyage* present from Miami,' she said, when the orchestra finally faded out. **1971** *Daily Tel.* 30 July 13/3 'Welcome to your Sunday bumper edition of Radio Northwick Park.'.. The music fades up and Paul closes the mike for an aside to fellow programme announcer Phil.

8. *slang.* (See quots. 1942, 1964.)

1890 *Dialect Notes* I. 61 *To fade*, to bet against the player shooting. [**1912** J. W. JOHNSON *Autobiogr. Ex-colored Man* vi. 92, I was soon 'fated'. I threw the dice—seven—I had won.] **1931** D. RUNYON *Guys & Dolls* (1932) xiii. 273 Nathan Detroit's crap game is what is called.. a fading game, because the guys bet against each other rather than against the bank, or house. **1934** J. T. FARRELL *Young Manhood Studs Lonigan* (1936) xvii. 368 Weary frowned at the guy and faded ten of the fifteen. **1942** BERREY & VAN DEN BARK *Amer. Thes. Slang* §750/6 *Fade*, to cover the bet of the thrower [at dice]. **1957** W. C. HANDY *Father of Blues* xvii. 233 Lovejoy faded him for twenty-five cents. **1964** A. WYKES *Gambling* vi. 141 To 'fade' is to accept a bet.

9. a. *Cinematogr.* *trans.* To cause (a picture, etc.) to pass gradually *in* or *out*, i.e. to appear or disappear on the screen.

1918 H. CROY *How Motion Pictures are Made* vii. 177 The fourth method of fading a picture is by means of a chemical process. *Ibid.*, This shutter device for fading out a picture may be operated automatically or by hand. **1918** V. O. FREEBURG *Art of Photoplay Making* 122 The caption 'The Depths of Shame' is faded in. **1922** L. C. MACBEAN *Kinemat. Studio Technique* ix. 82 On occasions.. it is necessary.. to *fade* or *mix* titles into a scene to which they relate. **1958** R. H. BOMBACK *Handbk. Amat. Cinematogr.* II. 93 For some shots that have to be faded in or out you may be able to increase the camera speed so that each individual frame will receive less exposure. **1969** P. PETZOLD *All-in-One Cine Bk.* 27 If you can fade a scene this is the ideal answer to show the passing of time.

b. *transf.* Of radio and television transmission. Also with *up*, *down*.

1927 *Observer* 11 Sept. 21 Why can't we have the crowd noises faded in? If it is properly handled it won't interfere with the man who is reading the race. *Ibid.* 30 Oct. 26 It was faded out in the middle of Mr. Chesterton's speech. **1937** [see FADE *sb.*¹ 2]. **1937** *Discovery* Nov. 330/2 The producer of the programme making his selection of view by fading down the signal from one camera and fading up the signal from another before passing the video signal to the vision control engineer. **1958** G. BARKER *Two Plays* 22 Music.. fade in Peter's voice. **1958** *Spectator* 20 June 819/2 She had to be hurriedly faded out. **1971** *Radio Times* 7 Oct. 70/2 At the end of *Choral Evensong* (Radio 3) the organist is nearly always 'faded out'.

10. *intr.* Of the brakes of a motor vehicle (see FADE *sb.*¹ 4).

1940 *Jrnl. Research Nat. Bureau of Standards* May 543 A lining is said to fade when the coefficient of friction decreases rapidly to a low value. **1962** *Which? Car Suppl.* Oct. 120/2 The brakes still faded very badly. **1970** *New Yorker* 12 Sept. 113/2 (Advt.), Those.. front disc brakes.. right in the car's airstream to help them cool. So you can keep cool and not worry about them fading.

Hence **'fader**, an apparatus for controlling (*a*) the volume of sound in a cinematographic film, (*b*) the signal in sound or television broadcasting.

1931 B. BROWN *Talking Pictures* v. 102 The simplest type of fader.., where a variable resistance or potentiometer is placed across the output leads to the main amplifier. **1949** *Electronic Engin.* XXI. 354 The equipment consists of the recording machine and amplifier, microphones and fader unit. **1957** *Encycl. Brit.* IV. 218/2 In.. sound broadcasting, the amplified current from each microphone is connected to a fader. **1969** W. RUTHERFORD *Gallows Set* vi. 77 Terry said, 'Fade grams. And—Take One.'.. The girl at the vision mixer pulled the fader down.

†**fade**, *v.*² *Obs. rare.* [OE. *fadian*:—WGer. type **fadôjan*, f. **fada* (OHG. *vata*) state, condition; cf. OHG. *keunvatôn* to discompose, confound.] *trans.* To dispose, suit, arrange.

c **1020** *Laws of Cnut, Eccl.* xix, And word and weorc freonda ȝehwylc fadiȝe mid rihte. *c* **1400** *Sowdone Bab.* 678 He and his sone Sir Ferumbras Here goddis of golde dide fade. *c* **1475** *Partenay* Prol. 164, I.. my witte shal put to fade In-to other fourme.

fade, *v.*³ *dial.* 'To dance from town to country' (*W. Cornw. Gloss.*).

1846 *Spec. Cornish Dial.* 19 A passel of maidens.. begin'd for.. to fade so friskis.

fade, obs. Sc. form of FEUD *sb.*²

†**'fadeable**, *a.* *Obs.* [f. FADE *v.*¹ + -ABLE.] Liable to fade.

1633 T. ADAMS *Exp. 2 Peter* iii. (1865) 884 Neither Christ's honour nor our thankfulness are fadeable things.

fade-away. *U.S.* [FADE *v.*¹ 6.]

1. *Baseball.* (See quot. 1961.)

1909 *Amer. Mag.* May 31/1 Matty dropped his famous 'fade away' over the plate, and Tinker drove a long, high, line fly to left center. **1931** D. RUNYON *Guys & Dolls* (1932) x. 224, I.. cut loose with the old fadeaway. **1961** J. S. SALAK *Dict. Amer. Sports* 150 *Fadeaway*, a pitched ball that tends to slow up and drop as it reaches the plate.

2. An act of disappearance.

1911 H. S. HARRISON *Queed* v. 56 She had only pretended to die in order to make a fade-away with the gate receipts. **1912** C. MATHEWSON *Pitching in a Pinch* i. 11 Many persons have asked me why I do not use my 'fade-away' oftener when it is so effective.

faded ('feɪdɪd), *ppl. a.* [f. as FADEABLE *a.* + -ED¹.] That has lost its freshness and vigour; withered, decayed, worn out.

1580 BARET *Alv.* F. 16 Withered, faded, *flaccidus*. **1595** SPENSER *Colin Clout* 27 The fields with faded flowers did seem to mourne. **1667** MILTON *P.L.* I. 602 Care Sat on his faded cheek. **1725** POPE *Odyss.* xx. 64 Her [Nature's] faded powers with balmy rest renew. **1775** T. PERCIVAL *Philos., Med. & Exp. Ess.* (1776) III. 223 Like faded cheese. **1797** MRS. RADCLIFFE *Italian* xxxi. (1824) 705 The condition of Vivaldi, his faded appearance.. were [etc.]. **1820** KEATS *Hyperion* I. 90 Old Saturn lifted up His faded eyes. **1860** FARRAR *Orig. Lang.* vi. 116 Every language is a dictionary of faded metaphors. **1874** GREEN *Short Hist.* iv. 177 The faded glories of Arthur's Court. **1892** *Daily News* 8 Sept. 6/4 That unenviable cognomen of faded flowers.

Hence **'fadedly** *adv.*

18.. DICKENS (Webster), A dull room fadedly furnished.

fadeless ('feɪdlɪs), *a.* [f. FADE *v.* + -LESS.] That is exempt from fading or decay: unfading.

1652 BENLOWES *Theoph.* VI. xx, Flow'rs.. Which into fadeless colours flow. *c* **1722** WATTS *Reliq. Juv., Ode Death Sir T. Abney*, Come dress the bed with fadeless flowers. **1796** COLERIDGE *To J. Cottle*, May your fame fadeless live! **1852** D. M. MOIR *Leg. St. Rosalie* Poet. Wks. II. 79 Paradise, Where all is fadeless. **1854** H. MILLER *Sch. & Schm.* xvi. (1860) 177 A deathless, fadeless ray.

Hence **'fadelessly** *adv.*

1861 H. MACMILLAN *Footn. Page Nat.* 189 The robe of nature is yet fadelessly green. **1880** L. WALLACE *Ben-Hur*

121 Judah gave each . . a last look . . as if to possess himself of the scene fadelessly.

Fade-Ometer (feɪˈdɒmɪtə(r)). Also **Fade-ometer, Fadometer.** [Trade name, f. FADE *sb.*[1] or *v.*[1]: see -OMETER.] (See quot. 1925.)

1925 *Trade Marks Jrnl.* 5 Aug. 1700 *Color Fade-Ometer*, . . apparatus . . for testing the fastness of colours. Atlas Electric Devices Company . . Chicago, Illinois. **1934** *Chem. Abstr.* 7021/1 Comparison of the fading produced by the Fade-ometer . . and by sunlight . . . For short periods of time the Fade-ometer is a satisfactory substitute for sunlight in fading tests. **1940** *Chambers's Techn. Dict.* 320/2 *Fadometer*, an instrument used to determine the resistance of a dye or pigment to fading. **1951** R. MAYER *Artist's Handbk.* ii. 90 Machines such as the Fadeometer and the Weatherometer have been designed to give the equivalent of years of exposure to direct sunlight and dampness in a few hours.

ˈfade-out. [FADE *v.*[1] 6 b, 7, 9.] An act or instance of fading away or disappearing; *spec.*:

1. *Cinematogr.* and *Television.* The gradual blacking out or disappearance of a picture.

1918 H. CROY *How Motion Pictures are Made* vii. 176 Slowly the details of the picture are faded in until not only the girl's features are plain, but also the surrounding setting. The reverse of this—the gradual elimination of the scene—came to be known as fade-out. **1921** WODEHOUSE *Jill the Reckless* xviii. 276 Marriage isn't a motion-picture close-up with slow fade-out on the embrace. **1934** *Electronics* June 173/1 It is possible not only to change the focus easily so that close ups may be made, but 'zooms' and fade-outs are easily possible. **1959** *Punch* 2 Dec. 543/1 Her protector . . sadly lets her go, in time for the fadeout. **1962** *Movie* Oct. 6/2 Hitchcock makes much use of the power of the fade-out for fixing impressions in the mind of the audience.

2. *transf.* and *fig.* Disappearance; death; see also quot. 1967.

1924 A. J. SMALL *Frozen Gold* i. 39 It isn't natural for a whole tribe of stick-at-nothings to be able to do a fade-out like that. **1928** *Punch* 21 Mar. 318/1 The veriest front-row flapper knows that marriage is the 'fade-out' of love. **1930** *London Mercury* Feb. 324 Personally I don't want a sticky fade-out yet. **1937** J. R. FIRTH *Tongues of Men* xi. 132 T. S. Eliot may perhaps be one of the 'fade-out' voices of a disappearing world. **1967** *Gloss. Paper/Ink Terms for Letterpress Printing (B.S.I.)* 10 *Fade-out*, a gradual reduction in the strength of successive images, caused by the rate of removal of ink exceeding the rate of supply.

3. A temporary interruption of radio communication, caused esp. by ionospheric disturbance due to solar flares; fading.

1937 *Nature* 9 Jan. 61/2 *(heading)* Solar eruptions and radio fade-outs. *Ibid.*, Three radio fade-outs were reported later as having occurred during the morning of December 30 on short-wave . . wireless transmission. **1941** K. HENNEY *Radio Engin. Handbk.* (ed. 3) xv. 527 Ionospheric storms . . resulting in fade outs. **1959** *Daily Tel.* 16 May 1/1 The commercial possibilities of long-distance radio communication, with freedom from ionospheric fade-out and other disturbances. **1962** F. I. ORDWAY et al. *Basic Astronautics* iv. 145 *(caption)* Recorded in D layer as radio fade-out.

4. *Theatr.* The dimming of the stage lighting. (Cf. FADE *sb.*[1] 3.)

1936 I. SHAW *Bury Dead* 62 Send out the call . . . Women! *(Fadeout).* **1962** [see FADE *sb.*[1] 3].

fader, obs. and dial. f. of FATHER.

fader: see FADE *v.*[1]

fadge (fædʒ), *sb.*[1] *dial.* and *techn.* [Etymology uncertain: it is not clear whether the word is connected with FADGE *v.* Cf. OF. *fais* bundle (mod.F. *faix* burden).] A bundle of leather, sticks, wool, etc.; a bale of goods.

1588 *Wills & Inv. N.C.* (Surtees) II. 180 Three hundrethe and threttene fadges of lynte. **1596** *Ibid.* 263 One hundredthe nynty and one fadgs, or bundels, of lynt. **1808** JAMIESON, *Fadge*, a bundle of sticks. **1858** SIMMONDS *Dict. Trade*, *Fadge*, a name amongst leather sellers for a covering of undressed leather inclosing a bundle of patent or other valuable leather. **1882** *Lanc. Gloss.*, *Fadge*, a burden, part of a horse's load. **1883** *Almondbury Gloss.*, *Fadge*, a bundle of cloth, wool, &c. fitted into a pack-sheet and fastened with skewers. **1933** L. G. D. ACLAND in *Press* (Christchurch) 30 Dec. 13/7 *Wool pack.* Becomes a *bale of wool* when filled and pressed and a *fadge* when loosely filled. **1953** S. J. BAKER *Australia Speaks* iii. 60 *Fadge*, a butt of a bale or two bags sewn together, usual weight 60 lb. to 150 lb.

fadge (fædʒ), *sb.*[2] *Sc.* Also ? 6 fage. A large flat loaf or bannock.

a **1609** tr. *Iter Camerarii* ix. in Skene *Reg. Maj.* (1609) 150 b, All kindes of bread . . that is, ane fage [L. *quachetum*] symmell, wastell . . and bread of trayt. [The older text of the translation (Record ed.) omits the equivalent of *quachetum*.] **1719** RAMSAY *Ep. Hamilton* II. iii, A Glasgow capon and a fadge Ye thought a feast. *a* **1774** FERGUSSON *Farmer's Ingle* Poems (1845) 38 A crum O kebbuck whang'd and dainty fadge. **1808** in JAMIESON. **1845** *New Statist. Acc. Scot.*, *Berwickshire* 77 Cakes . . of barley meal, baked to a great thickness and called fadges.

fadge, *sb.*[3] *dial.* A short fat individual.

a **1765** *'Ld. Thomas & Fair Annet'* viii. in Child *Eng. & Sc. Pop. Ball.* (1885) III. lxxiii. 182/2, I sall hae nothing to mysell Bot a fat fadge by the fyre. **1876** in C. C. ROBINSON *Mid-Yorksh. Gloss.*

fadge, *sb.*[4] *slang.* A farthing.

1789 G. PARKER *Life's Painter* xv. 161. **1812** in J. H. VAUX *Flash Dict.* **1873** in *Slang Dict.* 157.

fadge, *sb.*[5]: see FADGE *v.*

fadge (fædʒ), *v.* Also 6–7 fadg, fagge. [Etymology unknown: first found late in 16th c.

The various uses of the word are substantially identical with those of the older FAY *v.* (:—OE. *fēȝan*), of which, however, it can neither be a variant nor a derivative by any known process. Possibly it may have been a new type formed unconsciously on the suggestion of *fay* and some word ending in *-dge*. Cf. FADGE *sb.*[1] The close correspondence of the senses with those of COTTON *v.*[1] is remarkable.]

†**1.** *intr.* Of things: To fit, suit, be suitable. Const. *dat.* or *to.* Also, to agree, fit in *with* (a thing); to agree, go down *with* (a person). *Obs.*

1578 WHETSTONE *Promos & Cass.* Pt. I. v. v, In good soothe, Sir, this match fadged frim. **1599** MARSTON *Sco. Villanie* I. i. 172 How ill his shape with inward forme doth fadge. *a* **1618** SYLVESTER *Epist.* i. 40 Ill, mee seems, that Cognizance doth fadge To such a Coate. *c* **1622** FLETCHER *Love's Cure* II. ii, These clothes will never fadge with me. *a* **1661** FULLER *Worthies* IV. (1662) 12 The Study of the Law did not fadge well with him. **1670** W. SIMPSON *Hydrol. Ess.* 43 You do not . . make it fadge to your purpose. **1681** W. ROBERTSON *Phraseol. Gen.* (1693) 708 Let men avoid what fadgeth not with their stomachs. **1711** *Brit. Apollo.* IV. 2/1 Your Rhimes ne'er will Fadge With us.

†**2.** Of persons: To do *with*, put up *with* (a thing); to agree, 'hit it', rub on (with a person).

1592 NASHE *Strange Newes* F ij, A new kind of quicke fight, which your . . slow-moving capacitie cannot fadge with. **1601** DEACON & WALKER *Spirits & Divels* 163 The Exorcist . . faggeth with me now. **1604** *Fr. Bacon's Proph.* 123 in Hazl. *E.P.P.* IV. 272 The merry Crew, That with no drinke coulde fadge, But where the fat they knew. **1639** SIR J. LENKE in *Mem. Verney Fam.* (1892) I. 209 Mistress ffaulkner and my lady do fadge. **1643** MILTON *Divorce* Pref., They shall . . be made, spight of antipathy to fadge together. **1678** BUTLER *Hud.* III. ii. 25 When they thriv'd, they never fadg'd, But only by the ears engag'd.

†**b.** To be content or willing, agree, 'make up one's mind' *to* do something. *Obs.*

1592 WARNER *Alb. Eng.* VIII. xl. (1612) 195 For it did many fadge to fight. **1644** QUARLES *Sheph. Orac.* vii, My rambling flocks would never fadge to stay Within my pastures. **1655** GURNALL *Chr. in Arm.* v. (1669) 20/1 If you cannot love naked truth, you will not fadge to go naked for truth.

3. *trans.* †To fit (the parts of) *together* (obs.). Also, *to fadge up*: to fit up, piece together. *rare.* Cf. FUDGE *v.*

1674 N. FAIRFAX *Bulk & Selv.* 75 The Watch thus fadg'd together. **1863** MRS. WHITNEY *Faith Gartney* iv. 28 Frocks 'fadged up' out of old faded breadths of her mistress's dresses.

†**4.** *intr.* To fit in with or suit the surroundings; hence to get on, succeed, thrive. Of an event: To come off. Often with indef. subject, *it, that, this, matters, things*, etc. *it won't fadge*: it won't act. *Obs.*

1573 G. HARVEY *Letter-bk.* (Camden) 142 Nothing fadgith, that with them is at variaunce. **1589** WARNER *Alb. Eng.* VI. xxix. (1612) 145 If gold but lacke in graines, the wedding fadgeth not. **1608** *Merry Devil Edmonton* in Hazl. *Dodsley* X. 230 You see how matters fadge. **1615** G. SANDYS *Trav.* 173 The Æthiopian Priest first enters (without whom, they say, the miracle will not fadge). **1639** FULLER *Holy War* v. xv. (1647) 255 Why do our English merchants bodies fadge well enough in Southern aire? **1650** R. GENTILIS *Considerations* 179 Either the seed doth not fadge and take root there, or it turnes to poyson. **1675** WYCHERLEY *Country Wife* IV. iii. 45 Well, sir, how fadges the new design? **1694** R. L'ESTRANGE *Fables* 44 The Fox . . saw it would not fadge. **1809** SCOTT in Lockhart *Life* (1839) III. 195, I shall be impatient to hear how your matters fadge. **1880** *W. Cornwall Gloss.* s.v., 'That 'ull never fadge.'

†**5.** Of persons: To make things fit; hence, to get on, succeed. *Obs.*

1611 COTGR. s.v. *Mouldre*, Let him that cannot fadge in one course, fall to another. **1630** J. TAYLOR (Water P.) *Unnat. Father* Wks. II. 136/2 He . . saw that he could not fadge there [in Holland] according to his desire. **1789** COWPER *Let.* 6 June, We . . have none but ourselves to depend on . . Well, we can fadge.

6. To make one's way; to jog along; to trudge. *rare* exc. *dial.* [Perh. a different word.]

1658 R. FRANCK *North. Mem.* (1821) 266 From hence we fadg to Ferry-Brigs. **1855** ROBINSON *Whitby Gloss.* s.v., 'He goes fadging along'. **1861** *Fraser's Mag.* Dec. 764 A man came fadging nimbly after me on a fresh ass. **1870** BARBER *Forness Folk* 3 (*Lanc. Gloss.*), I . . fadged away up Gamswell. **1876** C. C. ROBINSON *Mid-Yorksh. Gloss.* s.v., 'Thou fadges like an old horse.'

Hence **fadge** *sb.*[5] *dial.*, a slow regular motion, a jog-trot. Also *attrib.*

1873 HARLAND *Swaledale Gloss.*, *Fadge-trot*, a jog-trot. **1877** ROSS, etc. *Holderness Gloss.*, *Fadge*, a jog-trot. **1878** in DICKINSON *Cumberld. Gloss.* s.v.

†**ˈfadging,** *ppl. a. Obs.* [f. as prec. + -ING[2].] That fits, suits, etc.; well-matched.

c **1611** CHAPMAN *Iliad* XXII. 194 He . . much was joy'd that single strokes should try This fadging conflict.

fadgy (ˈfædʒɪ), *a. dial.* [f. FADGE *sb.*[2] + -Y.] Corpulent, fat, unwieldy.

1847–78 in HALLIWELL. **1877** in ROBINSON *Whitby Gloss.*

†**ˈfading, ˈfadding,** *sb. Obs.* [Etymology unknown; the Ir. *feadán* (ˈfadɔːn) pipe, whistle, has been suggested; but cf. FADE *v.*[3]] The name of a dance, app. Irish. 'With a fading' was the refrain of a popular song of an indecent character.

1611 BEAUM. & FL. *Knt. Burning Pestle* III. v, I will have him dance Fading; Fading is a fine jig. **1611** SHAKS. *Wint. T.* IV. iv. 195 He has the prettiest Loue-songs . . with such delicate burthens of Dildo's and Fadings. **1616** B. JONSON *Epigr.* xcvii, See you yond' Motion? not the old fa-ding . . But one more rare. **1633** SHIRLEY *Bird in a Cage* IV. i, Under her coats the Ball will be found, With a fading. **1672** JORDAN *Lond. Tri.* 13 To the tune of—With a Fadding.

fading (ˈfeɪdɪŋ), *vbl. sb.* [f. FADE *v.*[1] + -ING[1].]

a. The action of the vb. FADE; also, the period of decay. ***fading out***: a gradual dying out.

1579 LYLY *Euphues* (Arb.) 178 The fading of our dayes. **1617** HIERON *Wks.* II. 233 Persons . . discontinuing their attendance herein . . presently manifest a kind of slaking and fading in good duties. **1709** STEELE *Tatler* No. 95 ¶1 That fading in her Countenance. **1875** WHITNEY *Life Lang.* v. 90 We may call it an attenuation, a fading-out.

b. *Cinematogr.* (See FADE *v.*[1] 9.) Also *ppl. a.*

1918 H. CROY *How Motion Pictures are Made* vii. 176 Fading in or out is accomplished by four different methods. **1922** L. C. MACBEAN *Kinemat. Studio Technique* viii. 65 The operations of 'fading in' and 'fading out' . . are . . effected with the diaphragm. *Ibid.* 82 The film is then wound back to the beginning of the 'fading', with the lens closed. **1935** D. C. OTTLEY *Cine-Amateur's Workshop* vi. 26 The author advises a supplementary iris if fading and like effects are required.

c. Irregular fluctuations in the intensity of received radio signals as a result of varying atmospheric conditions.

1912 LEE DE FOREST *Let.* 13 Sept. in *Proc. Inst. Radio Engin.* (1930) XVIII. 1600, I think you have not considered with sufficient care what a variety of imaginable atmospheric conditions might be conceived to explain the phenomena of 'fading'. **1923** *Wireless Rev.* 23 June 128/2 Manchester and Newcastle both appear to be suffering very badly from fading. **1927** *Glasgow Herald* 1 Jan. 9 A site where interference and what is technically known as 'fading' would be reduced to a minimum. **1931** MOYER & WOSTREL *Radio Handbk.* iv. 178 Fading is probably due to the interference between radio waves which arrive at the receiver along different paths. **1953** F. LANGFORD-SMITH *Radio Designer's Handbk.* (ed. 4) xxii. 901 Where night-time fading of signals is encountered, straight vertical aerials should be used. **1968** B. P. LATHI *Communication Syst.* iii. 195 The fading is also sensitive to frequencies . . . Thus the carrier and each of the sidebands undergo different amounts of fading.

fading (ˈfeɪdɪŋ), *ppl. a.* [f. as prec. + -ING[2].] That fades, in various senses of the vb.

1535 COVERDALE *Isa.* xxviii. 1 The faydinge floure. **1576** FLEMING *Panopl. Epist.* 364 Vadeing shadowes. **1655** FULLER *Ch. Hist.* I. iv. §5 Wonder not that he . . should wish for fading Water. **1658** T. GOODWIN *Fair Prospect* 37 Like a cupboard of glasses, fair to the eye, but very brittle and fading. **1690** LOCKE *Hum. Und.* II. x. (1695) 71 The Pictures drawn in our Minds are laid in fading Colours. **1804** J. GRAHAME *Sabbath* 5 The fading flowers, That yester-morn bloom'd waving in the breeze. **1860** TYNDALL *Glac.* I. vii. 57 The fading light warned me that it was time to return. **1922** L. C. MACBEAN *Kinemat. Studio Technique* ix. 78 'Mixing' from a 'Fading-in' Title.

b. *Bot.* Of the petals: Withering before fertilization is completed.

1776 WITHERING *Brit. Plants* (1796) I. 318 Petals . . permanent, but fading.

Hence **ˈfadingly** *adv.*, **ˈfadingness**, tendency to fade.

1838 *Tait's Mag.* V. 36 The cold moonshine fadingly struggled. **18..** ? KEATS *To*—— Poems (1889) 346 Do not look so sad . . and fadingly. **1654** W. MONTAGU *Devout Ess.* xi. §3 Beautie, the fadingness whereof is the great detector of our frailtie. **1735** *Dict. Polygraphicum*, *Fadingness* is represented in painting, by a lady clad in green [etc.]. **1909** *Times Lit. Suppl.* 3 June 202/2 The quick fadingness of grass.

fadme, -om, etc., obs. ff. FATHOM.

‖**fado** (ˈfadu). [Pg., lit. 'fate'.] A Portuguese folk-song of melancholy type; also, the name given to various kinds of dance (music) and song popular in Portugal.

1902 *Jrnl. Amer. Folk-Lore* July–Sept. 165 The nearest we can get to the original significance of the word is to call the '*fado*' the laborer's song of fate; which is more than we can do with the present form, for the Portuguese indiscriminately call '*fados*' what we designate as serenades, ballads, jigs, and sailor's hornpipes. **1936** *Discovery* Dec. 396/2 The *fado*, that remarkable modern product of Portuguese popular genius. **1957** *Times Lit. Suppl.* 6 Dec. 736/3 A brilliant run-through of Portuguese poetry and prose, the inevitable chapter on the *fado*. **1969** *Times* 1 Nov. p. viii/5 The most typical way to spend an evening in Lisbon is to listen to *fados*, the traditional song of the Portuguese town worker; but make sure that you go to a genuine *fado* restaurant.

†**faˈdoodle.** *Obs. rare*$^{-1}$. Something foolish or ridiculous; nonsense.

a **1670** HACKET *Abp. Williams* II. (1692) 131 When all the stuff in the letters are scann'd, what fadoodles are brought to light.

fady (ˈfeɪdɪ), *a.* [f. FADE *v.* + -Y[1].] Tending to fade, shading off by degrees into a paler hue.

1730–6 in BAILEY (folio). *c* **1750** SHENSTONE *Ruin'd Abbey* 180 The vivid vermeil left his fady cheek. **1763** —— *Ess.* 105 Planted . . with yew-trees, then firs, then with trees more and more fady. **1775** in ASH; and in later Dicts.

fae, Sc. var. of FOE.

fæcal (ˈfiːkəl), *a.* Also 7–9 fecal. [f. L. *fæc-em*, *fæx*, dregs + -AL[1]. Cf. F. *fécal.*] Belonging to or of the nature of fæces, characterized by the

presence of fæces, as in *fæcal abscess*, *fistula*, *tumour*.

1541 R. COPLAND *Guydon's Quest. Chirurg.*, Lytell celles, wherin the fecall mater taketh forme. **1623** HART *Arraignm. Ur.* I. ii. 6 Easilier to expell the fecall excrements. **1730–6** BAILEY (folio), *Fæcal Matter.* **1775** NOURSE in *Phil. Trans.* LXVI. 438 The fæcal discharge lessened daily. **1872** HUXLEY *Phys.* vi. 155 The characteristic fæcal odour and colour. **1878** T. BRYANT *Pract. Surg.* I. 2 An abdominal tumour may be..fæcal. **1884** *Syd. Soc. Lex.*, *Fistula, fæcal*, an abdominal fistula opening into an intestine.

†**fæ'cality.** In 7 fecality. [f. prec. + -ITY.] *concr.* Fæcal matter.

1653 URQUHART *Rabelais* I. iv. 23 O the fair fecality wherewith she swelled.

fæcaloid ('fiːkəlɔɪd), *a.* [f. as prec. + -OID.] Resembling fæces.

1882 QUAIN *Dict. Med.* (Intestinal Obstruction 739), The vomit is..fæcaloid in appearance and odour.

†**fæ'cation.** *Obs.* [f. next + -ATION.]

1884 *Syd. Soc. Lex.*, *Fæcation*..a term in the older chemistry for the separation of a deposit from a fluid.

fæces ('fiːsiːz), *sb. pl.* Forms: 5–8 feces, -is, 6 fecies, fesses, (8 feeces), 7– fæces. [a. L. *fæces* pl. of *fæx* dregs.]

1. Sediment; dregs, lees, subsidence, refuse.

1460–70 *Bk. Quintessence* I. 4 Rotun fecis of wiyn. **1527** ANDREW *Brunswyke's Distyll. Waters* B vij, Euery water shold be cast upon his owne feces. **1594** PLAT *Jewell-ho.* II. 40 The Lee or fæces of yᵉ best sallet oyle. **1655** CULPEPPER *Riverius* I. ii. 13 The fecies or residents of the Powder in the bottom. **1742** *Lond. & Country Brew.* I. (ed. 4) 73 The Fæces or Sediment which causes the Fermentation to be fierce or mild. **1811** A. T. THOMSON *Lond. Disp.* (1818) 524 Set apart the liquor, that the fæces..may subside.

2. Waste matter that is discharged from the bowels; excrement.

1639 BEAUMONT & FLETCHER *M. Thomas* II. iii Do you mark the faeces? 'Tis a most pestilent contagious fever. **1732** ARBUTHNOT *Rules of Diet* 293 If there be any Acrimony in the Fæces. **1748** HARTLEY *Observ. Man* I. i. 96 The Impressions which the Aliment, Bile, and Fæces, make upon the villous Coat. **1802** *Med. Jrnl.* VIII. 369 The expulsion of the fæces. **1872** HUXLEY *Phys.* vi. 139 The residue..leaves the body as the fæces.

†'**fæcical,** *a. Obs.* [f. L. *fæc-es* + -IC + -AL¹.] = FÆCAL.

1594 PLAT *Jewell-ho.* II. 35 Hee..did..also make good vineger the fæcicall parte of thereof. *Ibid.* III. 10 Fecicall.

fæcula, fecula ('fɛkjʊlə). Pl. -æ. [a. L. *fæcula* crust of wine, dim. of *fæx*: see FÆCES. Cf. F. *fécule*.

The spelling *fecula* is now the more common, but is not in accordance with analogy, as L. words not anglicized in termination ordinarily retain their original spelling.]

1. 'The sediment or lees which subsides from the infusion of many vegetable substances, *esp.* applied to starch' (*Syd. Soc. Lex.* 1884). ***amylaceous fæcula***: starch. ***green fæcula*** (Fr. *fécule verte*): see quot. 1800.

1684 tr. *Bonet's Merc. Compit.* v. 146 It is better to use the powder of the root [of Pæony] than the fæcula. **1791** HAMILTON *Berthollet's Dyeing* II. II. II. ii. 76 The fecula remaining on the filter he compared to..Carolina indigo. **1800** tr. *Lagrange's Chem.* II. 258 Green Fecula, is extracted from the juice of vegetables: this green colour is exceedingly fugitive..The other kind, called Amylaceous Fecula, is in a great measure extracted from corn. **1810** HENRY *Elem. Chem.* (1840) II. 257 The fecula..is not dissolved, but merely suspended mechanically. **1858** CARPENTER *Veg. Phys.* §691 The bulbs generally contain a large quantity of fecula.

2. Sediment in general, dregs. *sing.* and *pl. rare.*

1816 J. SMITH *Panorama Sc. & Art* II. 385 Astringent vegetables..precipitate a fine black fecula from sulphate of iron. **1823** P. NICHOLSON *Pract. Build.* 411 Linseed oil..is ..filtered to free it from feculæ.

fæculence, -ency, -ent: see FEC-.

fæcundity, obs. f. of FECUNDITY.

faein, obs. f. of FAIN.

‖**faena** (fa'ena). *Bull-fighting.* [Sp., lit. 'task'.] (See quot. 1957.)

1927 E. HEMINGWAY *Men without Women* (1928) 43 He looked at the bull, planning his faena, his work with the red cloth that was..to make him manageable. **1957** *Times* 12 Oct. 7/7 Getting by in the bull-ring means giving the bull the least possible chance of making contact—by..cutting short a whole *faena* (the part when the matador plays the bull alone with the red cloth). **1961** H. THOMAS *Spanish Civil War* xx. 174 The amputation of the ear of a bull in honour of a matador, following a very successful *faena*.

Faenza (fa'ɛnza). Name of a city in the province of Emilia-Romagna, Italy, used, gen. *attrib.*, to designate the pottery made there in the sixteenth century. Cf. FAIENCE.

1863 W. CHAFFERS *Marks Pott. & Porc.* 105 There are two plates of the XVIIIth Century in the Sèvres Museum; one in imitation of Faenza, the other an allegory of Luther. **1885** *Encycl. Brit.* XIX. 627/2 Faenza plate (tondino), with border in deep ultramarine blues, and central coat of arms in rich orange and red. **1904** GOODCHILD & TWENEY *Technol. & Sci. Dict.* 214/1 *Faenza Ware*, a distinctive term given to a fine sort of pottery originally made at Faenza near Bologna, in Italy. **1962** *Victoria & Albert Mus. Internat. Art Treasures Exhib.* 76/1 A Faenza cylindrical drug vase with a band in the centre.

faerie, faery ('fɛəri, 'feɪəri), *sb.* (*a.*) *arch.* [A variant of FAIRY; it prob. existed in ME. (cf. OF. *faerie*), but its first known appearance is as employed *arch.* by Spenser (usually as trisyllable). In present usage, it is practically a distinct word, adopted either to express Spenser's peculiar modification of the sense, or to exclude various unpoetical or undignified associations connected with the current form *fairy*.]

1. The realm or world of the fays or fairies; fairyland, fairydom (cf. FAIRY *sb.* 1). Usually, the imaginary world depicted in Spenser's *Faery Queene*, the personages of which have little or no resemblance to the 'fairies' of popular belief.

1590 SPENSER *F.Q.* II. Introd. i, None that breatheth living aire does know Where is that happy land of Faery. **1818** SHELLEY *Rev. Islam* Ded. i, Some victor Knight of Faëry. **1835** WILLIS *Pencillings* II. xlix. 80 A grass so verdant..that it seems the very floor of faëry. **1870** MORRIS *Earthly Par.* I. II. 554 Men dreaded there to see The uncouth things of faërie.

†**2.** = FAIRY *sb.* 2. *Obs.*

1612 DRAYTON *Poly-olb.* iv. 307 The feasts that vnder-ground the Faërie did him make.

†**3.** = FAIRY *sb.* 4. *Obs.*

1590 SPENSER *F.Q.* I. iv. 15 The stout Faerie..Thought all their glorie vaine. **1591** —— *Tears of Muses* 31 The.. light-foote Faeries. **1634** MILTON *Comus* 436 No goblin or swart faery of the mine, Hath hurtful power o'er true virginity.

4. *attrib.* passing into *adj.* (never in predicative use), with sense: Of or belonging to 'faerie', resembling fairyland, beautiful and unsubstantial, visionary, unreal. Also *Comb.*, as ***faery-land***, ***-tale***; ***faery-fair***, ***-frail*** adjs.

1590 SPENSER (*title*), The Faerie Queene. *Ibid.* I. Introd. ii, Lay forth..The antique rolles..Of Faerie knights. *Ibid.* II. Introd. iv, Of faery lond yet if he more inquyre By certein signes..He may it find. **1598** SHAKS. *Merry W.* IV. vi. 20 To night at Hernes-Oke..Must my sweet Nan present the Faerie-Queene. **1652** BROME *Joviall Crew* IV. Wks. 1873 III. 417 A House..built upon Faery-Ground. **1667** MILTON *P.L.* I. 781 Faerie Elves Whose Midnight Revels..some belated Peasant sees. **1804** WORDSW. *To the Cuckoo* viii, The Earth..Again appears to be An unsubstantial faery place. **1820** KEATS *St. Agnes* viii, Hoodwink'd with faery fancy. **1839** HALLAM *Hist. Lit.* v. II. §89 The legends of Faeryland. **1868** LD. HOUGHTON *Select. fr. Wks.* 174 So faery-frail, so faery-fair. **1890** R. BRIDGES *Shorter Poems* III. v, To taste the faery cheer Of spirits in a dream.

Færoese: see FAROESE *a.* and *sb.*

fafell, var. of FAVEL, *Obs.*

faff (fæf), *v. dial.* and *colloq.* [cf. FAFFLE *v.*] *intr.* To fuss, to dither. Often with *about*. Also as *sb.*, fuss, 'flap'.

1874 S. BARING-GOULD *Yorks. Oddities* I. 179 T' clock-maker..fizzled an' faff'd aboot her, but nivver did her a farthing's worth o' good. **1888** J. DALBY *Mayroyd* III. vi. 99 A flay-crow wench, aw feathers an' faff. **1954** N. COWARD *Future Indefinite* v. 319 The Welfare Officers appeared,.. faffed about, used either too much initiative or too little, and retired in due course. **1959** 'O. MILLS' *Stairway to Murder* x. 117 It's a bad time for the villagers anyway, faffing around after the ewes. **1960** M. CECIL *Something in Common* xx. 228 Dithering about in a perpetual faff.

'**faffle,** *v. dial.* [Of echoic origin: cf. *maffle*; also dial. *faff* a puff of wind, *faff* to blow in sudden gusts.] **a.** To stutter or stammer; to utter incoherent sounds. **b.** To saunter; to fumble. **c.** Of a sail: To flap idly in the wind. **d.** = FAFF *v.*

1570 LEVINS *Manip.* 9 To Faffle, *balbutire*. *Ibid.* 127 Faffil. **1580** in BARET *Alv.* F. 19. **1781** in HUTTON *Tour to Caves* Gloss. **1869** in *Lonsdale Gloss.* s.v. **1951** AUDEN *Nones* (1952) 21 Impassive, cloaked and great on Horseback under his faffling flag. **1965** M. FRAYN *Tin Men* xxi. 113 Faffling away at whatever it was she faffled away at.

fag (fæg), *sb.*¹ [f. the vb.]

1. That which causes weariness; hard work, toil, drudgery, fatigue. *colloq.*

1780 MAD. D'ARBLAY *Diary & Lett.* 13 Apr., This was my fag till after tea. **1798** NELSON *Lett.* (1814) II. 233 As no fleet has more fag than this, nothing but the..greatest attention can keep them healthy. **1847** MRS. CARLYLE *Lett.* II. 8 Not worth the fag of going and coming. **1860** DIXON *Hist. Bacon* x. §19 The fag and contest of the world.

2. a. In English public schools, a junior who performs certain duties for a senior. Also *transf.* a drudge.

1785 R. CUMBERLAND *Observer* xcv. §3, I had the character at school of being the very best *fag* that ever came into it. **1811** L. M. HAWKINS *C'tess & Gertr.* I. 50 She..finds herself in the situation of 'a fag' at our public schools. **1841** MACAULAY *W. Hastings* Ess. (1851) 597 He [Hastings] hired Impey with a tart or a ball to act as fag. **1857** HUGHES *Tom Brown* I. viii, The..night-fags had left duty.

transf. **1813** P. HAWKER *Diary* 7 Jan. (1893) I. 66 Mr. Macintosh..a good fag. **1827** *Sporting Mag.* May 12/2 Though by no means good fags, a French chasseur will be in the field before daylight. *a* **1839** PRAED *Poems* (1864) II. 115 William Tag, Thalia's most industrious fag. **1855** THACKERAY *Newcomes* I. 171 The diminutive fag of the studio.

b. *Cricket.* A fieldsman. *Obs.*

1840 *Sporting Mag.* Aug. 332 Great Jupiter [shall be] long fag, because he can shy The ball like a thunder-bolt straight through the sky. **1897** W. J. FORD in K. S. Ranjitsinhji *Jubilee Bk. Cricket* ix. 341 The 'fags' in the out-field have their hands full indeed.

3. *attrib.* as *fag-day*, *-partner* (cf. *fagging partner* under FAGGING *ppl. a.*).

1828 AIRD in *Blackw. Mag.* Dec. 713/1 A fag partner at whist when a better fourth hand is wanting. **1885** *Pall Mall G.* 27 May 6/1 Far more exhausting than a fag day of five hours at Rugby.

†**fag** (fæg), *sb.*² *Obs.* exc. in *Comb.* and *dial.* [See FAG *v.*]

1. Something that hangs loose; a flap. In quot. *attrib.* See also FAG-END.

1486 *Bk. St. Albans* B j a, The federis at the wynge next the body be calde the flagg or the fagg federis.

2. = FAG-END in various senses.

c **1580** J. CHAPPELL *Will* in Noake *Worcestershire Relics* (1877) 34 To his sister-in-law he [a clothier] leaves a 'fagg' to make her a petticoat..to Roger Massye..a white fagg to make him a coat. *a* **1626** MIDDLETON *Changeling* III. iii, To finish (as it were) and make the fagg Of all the Revels. **1659** FULLER *App. Inj. Innoc.* I. vi. 5, I have..presented the whole Cloath of his Book..Length and Breadth, and List and Fag and all. **1775** ASH, *Fag*..the fringe at the end of a rope.

3. *dial.* **a.** An odd strip of land. **b.** Odds and ends of pasture-grass.

1880 *Times* 17 Sept. 8/5 The fags along the sides of the river are being irretrievably damaged. **1884** LAWSON *Upton Gloss.*, *Fag*, generally *Old Fag*, tufts of last year's grass not eaten down.

fag (fæg), *sb.*³ [Etymology unknown; perh. senses 1 and 2 do not belong to the same word.]

1. A 'knot' in cloth.

1464 *Act. 4 Edw. IV*, c. i, En cas que ascune autiel diversite ou Rawe, Skawe, cokell ou fagge, aveigne destre en ascun part des ditz draps. **1858** SIMMONDS *Dict. Trade*, *Fag* ..a knot in cloth.

2. A parasitic insect which infects sheep; a sheep-tick; hence a disease of sheep. Also, ***sheep-fag***. *dial. attrib.* **fag-water** (see quot.).

1789 *Projects* in *Ann. Reg.* 71 Hippobosca ovina, called in Lincolnshire sheep faggs. **1877** *N.W. Linc. Gloss.*, *Sheep-fag*, a parasitic insect that infests the wool of sheep. **1886** *S.W. Linc. Gloss.*, *Fag-water*, water mixed with arsenic and soft-soap in which sheep are dipped to kill the ticks.

fag (fæg), *sb.*⁴ *slang.* [Abbreviation of FAG-END. (Cf. FAG *sb.*² 2.)] **a.** The fag-end of a cigarette. **b.** A cheap cigarette. **c.** Any cigarette (the current use). Also *attrib.*, as **fag card**, a cigarette card; **fag hag** (see quot. 1945).

1888 *Sat. Rev.* 30 June 786/2 They..burn their throats with the abominable 'fag', with its acrid paper and vile tobacco. **1893** *Pick-me-up* 14 Oct. 45/2 Stimulants he calls 'booze' and a cigarette a 'fag'. **1898** *Eng. Dial. Dict.* s.v., Here [*sc.* at Redruth] we are often asked by youngsters to 'chuck' them 'a fag'—and whole cheap cigarettes are also often called fags. **1908** *Church Times* 7 Feb. 173/1 He gathered into a leather pouch the remains of his cigarettes, and left the room. 'What does he do with all those fags?' asked Conway. **1921** GALSWORTHY *To Let* III. viii. 284 The fag of Fleur's cigarette..fell on the grass. **1922** JOYCE *Ulysses* 70 Smoking a chewed fagbutt. **1928** GALSWORTHY *Swan Song* iv. 24 Cinemas, fags, and football matches—there would be no real revolution while they were on hand. **1942** C. BARRETT *On Wallaby* v. 97 Cobbers of the men in detention had hit upon an ingenious method of smuggling fags to them. **1945** L. SHELLY *Jive Talk Dict.* 24/1 *Fag hag*, girl chain smoker. **1959** W. GOLDING *Free Fall* ii. 49 There was the business of the fagcards. We all collected them.

fag (fæg), *sb.*⁵ *U.S. slang.* [Abbreviation of FAGGOT *sb.* 6 b.] = FAGGOT *sb.* 6 b.

1923 N. ANDERSON *Hobo* vii. 103 Fairies or Fags are men or boys who exploit sex for profit. **1931** 'D. STIFF' *Milk & Honey Route* 205 *Fagot* or *fag*, a *road kid* with homosexual tendencies. **1932** HEMINGWAY *Death in Afternoon* 298 *Maricón*, a sodomite, nance, queen, fairy, fag, etc... Interested parties..are continually proving that Leonardo da Vinci, Shakespeare, etc., were fags. **1939** R. CHANDLER *Big Sleep* xii. 90 A stealthy nastiness, like a fag party. **1957** J. KEROUAC *On Road* (1958) III. v. 206 The car belonged to a tall, thin fag. **1964** 'L. EGAN' *My Name is Death* v. 49 You can't tell the fags from outside looks.

fag (fæg), *v.*¹ [Of obscure etymology; the common view that it is a corruption of FLAG *v.* would satisfactorily account for the sense; see quot. 1486 in FAG *sb.*² 1. Cf. also FAIK *v.*³]

†**1.** *intr.* To flag, droop, decline (*lit.* and *fig.*); to fall off, swerve *from*, *into*. *Obs.* exc. *dial.*

1530 PALSGR. 543/1, I fagge from the trouthe (Lydgate): this terme is nat in our comen use. **1563–87** FOXE *A. & M.* (1596) 1017/2 His handes fagged downward. **1624** BP. HALL *True Peace-maker* 24 Woe be to those partiall Iudges..the girdle of whose equitie faggs downe on that side where the purse hangs. **1639** FULLER *Holy War* 202 Elective States.. often fagge aside into schismes and factions. **1708–11** G. MACKENZIE *Lives* (1722) III. 292 The Italian attacked him with such..Eagerness, that he began to fag, having overacted himself. **1786** *Harvest Rig* in R. Chambers *Pop. Poems Scot.* (1862) 44 They never fag. **1878** *Cumbrld. Gloss.*, *Fag*..to hang back.

2. To do something that wearies one; to work hard; to labour, strain, toil.

1772 MAD. D'ARBLAY *Early Diary* Apr., All day I am fagging at business. **1794** LD. SPENCER in *Ld. Auckland's Corr.* III. 299 Arthur Paget, on whose account I am now fagging to Berlin. **1829** SCOTT *Jrnl.* 19 Mar., I fagged at my review on Ancient Scottish History. **1859** DICKENS *T. Two Cities* II. viii, The Marquis in his travelling carriage..fagged

up a steep hill. **1862** *Sat. Rev.* 8 Feb. 144 Like giving up a problem instead of fagging on till it is solved. **1884** LAWSON *Upton Gloss., Fag*..to pull hard as at a rope.

3. *trans.* To make (one) fatigued; to tire, weary. Said of both persons and things.

1826 SCOTT *Jrnl.* 9 Apr., I worked at..correcting manuscript, which fags me excessively. **1836** E. HOWARD *R. Reefer* xxii, He would fag me desperately at cricket. **1858** B'NESS BUNSEN in Hare *Life* II. iv. 235 Correcting the vast number of sheets that have come..has fagged him too much. **1879** DIXON *Brit. Cyprus* xxvii. 269 No one cares to fag himself with talk.

4. In Public School phraseology. **a.** *intr.* To be a fag, to act as a fag; to perform certain services for another. *to fag out*: to go as fag, *esp.* in cricket, to field.

1806 J. BERESFORD *Miseries Hum. Life* (ed. 3) III. xv. 48 Fagging for a niggardly glutton. **1857** T. HUGHES *Tom Brown* I. viii, I won't fag except for the sixth. **1860** THACKERAY *Round. Papers, On a Joke* 89 The ground where you had to fag out on holidays. **1881** *Macm. Mag.* XLIII. 288/2 They must..fag out at cricket.

b. *trans.* To make a fag of; to compel to do certain offices.

1824 SOUTHEY in C. Southey *Life & Corr.* I. 138 He was not high enough in the school to fag me. **1845** ALB. SMITH *Fort. Scatterg. Fam.* xvi. (1887) 53 He was fagged in the schoolroom during the hours that he was at the mercy of his superior fellows. **1857** T. HUGHES *Tom Brown* I. viii, What right have the fifth-form boys to fag us? **1889** A. R. HOPE in *Boy's Own Paper* 699/2 He [the prefect] used to fag me to blow the chapel organ for him.

5. *Naut.* (See quots.) Cf. FAG *sb.*[2]

1841 DANA *Seaman's Manual* 104 A rope is fagged when the end is untwisted. **1867** SMYTH *Sailor's Word-bk.* 285 *Fag out*..to wear out the end of a rope or end of canvas.

6. *slang.* **a.** To beat. *Obs.* [? A distinct word; cf. FEAGUE.]

a **1700** B. E. *Dict. Cant. Crew, Fag*, to Beat. **1730–6** in BAILEY (folio). **1847–78** in HALLIWELL.

b. To smoke; to supply with a cigarette. Cf. FAG *sb.*[4] *U.S. slang.*

1926 MAINES & GRANT *Wise-Crack Dict.* 8/1 *Fag me*, give me a cigarette. **1940** *Amer. Speech* XV. 335/2 To smoke is..to fag. **1954** W. FAULKNER *Fable* (1955) 324 'Fag me again.' The corporal gave him another cigarette.

fag (fæg), *v.*[2] *dial.* Also **vag.**

1. *trans.* To cut corn with a sickle and a hooked stick; = BAG *v.*[2]

1841 *Jrnl. R. Agric. Soc.* II. I. 120 Six ridges..being fagged or cut at the ground. **1854** *Ibid.* XV. I. 213 Some farmers fag a large quantity of barley. **1875** in PARISH *Sussex Gloss.* s.v. **1888** *Berksh. Gloss.* s.v. *Vag*, 'When the straa be long, vaggin' wuts be better'n mawin' on um.'

2. *Comb.*, as *fag-hook* = *fagging-hook.*

1875 PARISH *Sussex Gloss., Fag-hook.*

Hence **'fagging** *vbl. sb.*[2] Also *attrib.*, as *fagging-hook, -stick.*

1837 *Outl. Flemish Husb.* in *Brit. Husbandry* (1840) III. II. iii. 17 Those who are accustomed to the method of fagging in use in Middlesex, Surrey,..will readily see that this scythe is only an improved fagging hook, allowing the reaper to stand upright at his work. **1844** *Jrnl. R. Agric. Soc.* V. I. 28 Little fagging or bagging..is performed except in the vicinity of the metropolis. **1854** *Ibid.* XV. I. 213 The straw is cut close to the ground with a fagging hook. **1881** *Oxford Gloss.* Supp. s.v., A hooked stick, called a faggin' stick. **1942** *Archit. Rev.* XCI. 51/1 Scythes, slash-hooks, fagging-hooks, hay-knives or turnip-knives. **1958** *Times* 16 Aug. 7/6 Fagging-hook, frostbeck, hack-hook..are some of the variations on a single agricultural theme.

†**'fagald, faggald.** *Sc. Obs.* [Corrupt form of FAGGOT.] A faggot.

1375 BARBOUR *Bruce* XVII. 615 Gret fagalds [ed. Skeat flaggatis] tharoff thai maid Gyrdyt with irne bands braid. *c* **1470** HENRY *Wallace* XI. 897 Full feill fagaldys in to the dyk thai cast. **1535** STEWART *Cron. Scot.* II. 146 Congall..Richt mony fagald all that nycht gart mak. **1829** HOGG *Sheph. Cal.* II. 18 I'm sure ony o' them's worth a faggald of thee.

fagarie, -ary, obs. ff. VAGARY.

fagdom ('fægdəm). [f. FAG *sb.*[1] 2 + -DOM.] The condition of being a fag.

1902 J. BUCHAN *Watcher by Threshold* II. ii. 118 From the anomalous insignificance of fagdom Colin climbed up the School. **1914** C. MACKENZIE *Sinister St.* II. III. xii. 734 The photographic souvenirs of Lonsdale's fagdom.

†**fage,** *v. Obs.* exc. *dial.* Also 4 **faage,** 5 **fagg,** 9 *dial.* **fadge.** [Of unknown origin; not identical with FADGE *v.*]

1. *trans.* To coax. flatter; to beguile, soothe.

c **1340** *Cursor M.* 7622 (Fairf.) Dauid come him to fage. *a* **1400–50** *Alexander* 4669 For ȝe bot fage ay þe flesche & felsen it wele. *c* **1470** HARDING *Chron.* LXVI. ii, Such subtyll meane to fage the kyng he fande.

2. *absol.* or *intr.* To coax, flatter, toady; to speak coaxingly *to.*

c **1380** WYCLIF *Serm.* Sel. Wks. I. 44 It is manere of ypocritis..to fage and to speke pleasantli to men, but for yvel entent. **1382** —— *Judg.* xiv. 15 Faage to thi man. *c* **1430** LYDG. *Bochas* I. xiii. (1554) 25 b, Women can flatter and fage. *c* **1460** —— *Order of Fools* 66 He that falsluy wul fage. **1471** RIPLEY *Comp. Alch.* v. in Ashm. (1652) 159 The Fox can fagg and fayne. **1881** EVANS *Leicestersh. Gloss., Fadge*, to 'toady', to play the parasite.

Hence †**'fager,** a flatterer; also **'faging** *vbl. sb.* and *ppl. a. Obs.* exc. *dial.*

1435 MISYN *Fire of Love* (E.E.T.S.) 20 Fagiars & bakbitars. **1483** *Cath. Angl.* 120 A Fager, *adulator.* *c* **1380** WYCLIF *Serm.* Sel. Wks. I. 56 þei spaken fagynge wordis as ypocritis doen. *Ibid.* III. 175 þis was a fagynge of þe fendus childur. *c* **1440** *York Myst.* xxx. 513 With-outen fagyng. *c* **1450** *Mirour Saluacioun* 354 Sho broght him inne with faging wordes white. **1483** *Cath. Angl.* 120 A Fagynge, *blandicia. Ibid.*, Fagynge, *blandus.* **1883** *Almondbury Gloss.*, *Fageing* or *Fagey*, deceiving, flattering, soft-sawdering.

†**'fage,** *sb. Obs.* [f. prec. vb.] The action of coaxing or deceiving; a deceit, fiction.

1420 J. PAGE *Siege Rouen* in *Archæol.* XXII. 370, I wille haue it withoute fage. *c* **1450** LYDG. *Hist. Thebes*, Hold it for no fage. **1692–1732** in COLES. **1721** in BAILEY.

fag-end (ˌfæg'ɛnd). [f. FAG *sb.*[2] + END.]

1. a. The last part of a piece of cloth; the part that hangs loose, often of coarser texture than the rest.

1721–1800 in BAILEY. **1778** *Love Feast* 21 Like base Fag-Ends will surely be cut off. **1809** TOMLIN *Law Dict.* s.v. *Fag*, The fag-end..where the weaver..works up the worst part of his materials. **1858** in SIMMONDS *Dict. Trade.*

b. Of a rope: An untwisted end.

1775 in ASH. **1808** WHITBREAD *Sp. in Ho. Commons* 22 Jan., Sooner than have surrendered the fag end of a cotton rope to England. **1840** R. DANA *Bef. Mast.* xxii. 66 There was no rust, no dirt..no fag ends of ropes.

2. *transf.* The last part or remnant of anything, after the best has been used; the extreme end, *e.g.* of a portion of space or time, a collection of persons, a written composition, volume, etc.

1613 R. TAILOR *Hog lost Pearl* in *Dodsley* (1780) VI. 329 There's the fag-end of a leg of mutton. *a* **1656** BP. HALL *Revelation Unrev.* §1 The fag-end of this last century. **1677** PLOT *Oxfordsh.* 5 This wind was the fag-end of a Hurricane. *a* **1687** COTTON *Martial* I. ii. (1695) 3 Where now a goodly terrace does extend..Was but the court's fag and expiring end. **1691** WOOD *Ath. Oxon.* II. 174 The turning out of the Fag-end of that Parliament. **1729** BERKELEY *Skel. Serm.* vi. Wks. IV. 640 The first fruits..to the devil, the fag-end, when faculty for good and evil is gone, to God. **1747** HOOSON *Miner's Dict.* Nj, The Fagg ends of a certain Lordship. **1765** STERNE *Tr. Shandy* (1802) VIII. xxxv. 199 To be wove into the fag end of the eighth volume. **1844** DICKENS *Mart. Chuz.* xlii, To..hum the fag-end of a song. **1853** C. BEDE *Verdant Green* iv, The old Kidderminster carpet..burnt into holes with the fag-ends of cigars. **1882** MISS BRADDON *Mt. Royal* I. viii. 241 Vegetating at the fag-end of England.

Hence **fag-'ender.**

1828 *Examiner* 21 Sept. 618/1 Clinging to the old rubbish of the worn-out Cabinet of former days—the fag-enders of a hated party. **1924** J. M. MURRY *Voyage* vii. 121 'There are some religious people left.' 'I don't think she'd deny that. She was only speaking of people like us—the fag-enders,' said Doherty.

fagged (fægd), *ppl. a.* [f. FAG *v.* + -ED[1].]

†**1.** Flaccid, drooping. *Obs.*

1578 BANISTER *Hist. Man* VI. 88 They incontinent become slacke, narrow together, fagde, and shorter.

2. Wearied out, excessively fatigued.

1780 MAD. D'ARBLAY *Diary & Lett.* May, I felt horribly fagged. **1841** CATLIN *N. Amer. Ind.* (1844) II. xlvii. 97 Leave him fagged out by the way-side. **1862** MRS. H. WOOD *Mrs. Hallib.* I. v. 25 You look thin and fagged. **1883** E. PENNELL-ELMHIRST *Cream Leicestersh.* 300, I have seldom seen as many fagged faces as on Saturday.

fagger ('fægə(r)). [f. FAG *v.* + -ER[1].] One who fags. **a.** One who has a junior boy as his fag at school. **b.** One who works hard.

a. **1836** E. HOWARD *R. Reefer* liv, I was the *fagged*, and not the fagger. **1885** *Academy* 6 June 393/3 It would be of some interest to ascertain his fagger's name.

b. **1833** W. JOWETT *Mem. C. Neale* (1835) 38 He had..never been a hard fagger. **1843** *Fraser's Mag.* XXVII. 45 The hardest faggers and the hardest idlers.

faggery ('fægərɪ). [f. FAG *sb.*[1] + -ERY.] The system of fagging at public schools.

1853 DE QUINCEY *Autobiog. Sk.* Wks. I. 207 Faggery was an abuse too venerable..to be touched by profane hands.

fagging ('fægɪŋ), *vbl. sb.*[1] [f. FAG *v.* + -ING[1].] The action of the vb. FAG.

1. The action of working hard or wearying oneself at something; an instance of this, hard work. Also *fagging about.*

1777 MAD. D'ARBLAY *Early Diary* (1889) II. 163 After all this fagging, Mr. Lowndes sent me word, that he..could not think of printing it [the book]. **1837** LOCKHART *Scott* (1839) I. 194 The ordinary indoor fagging of the chamber in George's Square. **1849** E. E. NAPIER *Excurs. S. Africa* II. 122 Hard knocks, hard fare, and hard fagging of every description. **1850** MRS. CARLYLE *Lett.* II. 110, I had such a fagging about last year.

2. *slang.* (See quot.)

1775 ASH, *Fagging*, a beating or thumping.

3. The system under which a junior boy acts as fag to a senior. Also *attrib.*

1824 T. MEDWIN *Convers. Byron* (1832) I. 77 Drury's kindness..enabled me to bear..fagging. **1825** C. M. WESTMACOTT *Eng. Spy* I. 42 In no fear of fagging. **1825** S. R. in Hone *Every-day Bk.* I. 1291 The *fagging* system was only to be tolerated. **1876** GRANT *Burgh Sch. Scot.* II. v. 202 For elevating the tone of the School he made use of the sixth form and of fagging.

fagging ('fægɪŋ), *ppl. a.* [f. FAG *v.* + -ING[2].] That fags, in senses of the vb.

1795 W. B. STEVENS *Jrnl.* 8 Aug. (1965) III. 279 He is the most fagging Student I ever knew and this to the exclusion of all other enjoyments. **1806** SURR *Winter in Lond.* (ed. 3) I. 20 An idle fagging partner. **1862** MRS. H. WOOD *Mrs. Hallib.* I. v. 25 Mine is a fagging profession!

faggot, fagot ('fægət), *sb.* Forms: 4 faget(t, 4–6 faggott, 5 fagatt, -ot(t, 6 fagget, *Sc.* faggat, 4–fagot, 5– faggot. See also FAGALD. [a. Fr. *fagot*, of unknown origin; cf. It. *fa(n)gotto.*]

1. A bundle of sticks, twigs, or small branches of trees bound together: **a.** for use as fuel.

a **1300** *Cursor M.* 3164 (Cott.) ȝong ysaac a fagett broght. **1398** TREVISA *Barth. De P.R.* XVII. cxlix. (1495) 703 Thornes ..ben bounde in faggottes..and brent in ouens. **1478** *Bury Wills* (Camden) 77 The price of the c fagots iijs vjd. **1578** *Gude & G. Ball.* (1868) 92 As the flame burning quhair it can find The faggat. **1649** BLITHE *Eng. Improv. Impr.* (1653) 36 Thou must take good green Faggots. **1770** GOLDSM. *Des. Vill.* 133 To pick her wintry fagot from the thorn. **1821** CLARE *Vill. Minstr.* I. 128 Goody begg'd a helping hand To heave her rotten faggot up. **1866** ROGERS *Agric. & Prices* I. xviii. 424 In all probability the fagot was of very various sizes.

†**b.** *Mil.* for use in fascines. *Obs.*

c **1400** *Sowdone Bab.* 285 Fagotis to hewe..And fille the dikes faste anoon. **1548** HALL *Chron.* 112 Castyng faggottes into the diches. **1603** KNOLLES *Hist. Turks* (1621) 1064 [He] would oftentimes..carrie a fagot..before him..for the raising of the mount. **1711** ADDISON *Spect.* No. 165 ¶3 The Black Prince..filled a Ditch with Faggots as successfully as the Generals of our Times do it with Fascines.

2. a. With special reference to the practice of burning heretics alive, *esp.* in phrase ***fire and faggot***; † ***to fry a faggot***, to be burnt alive; also, ***to bear, carry a faggot***, as those did who renounced heresy. Hence *fig.* the punishment itself.

a **1555** LATIMER *Serm. & Rem.* (1845) 277 Running out of Germany for fear of the fagot. **1621** BP. MOUNTAGU *Diatribae* 44 You deserued to fry a faggot. **1649** BP. HALL *Cases Consc.* III. v. 274 Fagots were never ordained by the Apostle for arguments to confute hereticks. **1667** POOLE *Dial. betw. Protest. & Papist* (1735) 101 You answer our Arguments with Fire and Faggot. **1721** STRYPE *Eccl. Mem.* I. viii. 86 He should go before the cross bare-headed..carrying a faggot on his shoulder. **1741–8** WATTS *Improv. Mind* I. xiv. 195 Mitres or Faggots have been the Rewards of different Persons according as they pronounced these consecrated Syllables, or not pronounced them. **1808** J. BARLOW *Columb.* IV. 206 Racks, wheels and crosses, faggots, stakes and strings. **1868** J. H. BLUNT *Ref. Ch. Eng.* I. 85 Wolsey caused them to carry a faggot to the fire..Henry placed them in the midst of actual faggots. **1888** J. GAIRDNER in *Dict. Nat. Biog.* XIII. 30/2 It is not easy to answer arguments in prison, with fire and faggots in the background.

b. The embroidered figure of a faggot, which heretics who had recanted were obliged to wear on their sleeve, as an emblem of what they had merited.

1706 in PHILLIPS (ed. Kersey). **1823** in CRABB *Technol. Dict.*

3. In wider sense. **a.** A bundle or bunch in general, *e.g.* of rushes, herbs, etc. **b.** *fig.* A 'bundle', collection (of things not forming any genuine unity).

1489 CAXTON *Faytes of A.* I. xiv. 38 Fagotis and bondellis of rede. **1545** BRINKLOW *Compl.* 25 b, Yet must he..pryuyly beare a fagot of russhes in his chamber. **1555** EDEN *Decades* 5 They founde faggottes of the bones of mennes armes and legges. **1650** W. CRADOCK in Spurgeon *Treas. Dav.* Ps. lxxxiii. 1 That he may..gather the wicked into one fagot..that they may be destroyed together. **1723** J. NOTT *Cook's & Confectioner's Dict.* BA §27 A Faggot of sweet Herbs. **1741** *Compl. Fam. Piece* I. ii. 99 A little Faggot of Thyme, Savory, and Parsley. **1742** H. WALPOLE *Corr.* (ed. 3) I. xxxviii. 154 My faggot of compliments. **1782** in Baker *Biogr. Dram.* iii. (1812) 260 A faggot of utter improbabilities. **1854** EMERSON *Lett. & Soc. Aims, Quot. & Orig.* Wks. (Bohn) III. 214 The psalms and liturgies of churches are..a fagot of selections. **1906** MRS. BEETON *Bk. Househ. Managem.* lxi. 1638 The little bunch or fagot of herbs..usually consists of two or three sprigs of parsley, a sprig of thyme, and a bayleaf. **1960** *Harper's Bazaar* Oct. 153/1 The traditional faggot of mixed herbs.

4. A bundle of iron or steel rods bound together.

1540 *Act 32 Hen. VIII*, c. 14 Item for euery last of faggottes of yron iiii. s. **1640** in Entick *London* II. 181 For a faggot of steel o 1d. **1706** PHILLIPS (ed. Kersey), *Faggot* of Steel (in Traffick) the Quantity of 120 Pound-Weight. **1721–1800** in BAILEY. **1825** J. NICHOLSON *Operat. Mechanic* 338 This is termed a faggot [of iron], being about 12 or 14 inches long, and six inches square. **1881** GREENER *Gun* 221 The bars were then..fastened into a faggot.

5. (See quot. 1851.)

1851 MAYHEW *Lond. Labour* II. 227 He..made his supper..on 'fagots'. This preparation..is a sort of cake, roll or ball..made of chopped liver and lights, mixed with gravy, and wrapped in pieces of pig's caul. **1858** SALA *Journ. due North* 308 The curious viands known in cheap pork-butchery..as Faggots. **1881** in *Oxford Gloss.* Supp.

6. a. A term of abuse or contempt applied to a woman (orig. *dial.*) Also in extended uses.

1591 LODGE *Catharos* 4 b, A filbert is better than a faggot, except it be an Athenian she handfull. **1840** BARHAM *Ingol. Leg., Grey Dolphin*, 'What's that you say, old faggot?' **1862** MRS. H. WOOD *Mrs. Hallib.* II. xxi, She..struck at me, she did, the good-for-nothing faggot! **1882** MRS. CHAMBERLAIN *W. Worc. Words* 11 *Faggit*, a term of reproach used to children. **1900** *Eng. Dial. Dict.* II. 278/2 To a stray cow: 'Come out o' that, ye old faggot.' **1922** JOYCE *Ulysses* 723 That old faggot Mrs Riordan. **1925** D. H. LAWRENCE *Refl. Death Porcupine* 176 To me she [*sc.* a cow] is fractious, tiresome, and a faggot. Yet the subtle desirableness is in her, for me. **1969** *Sunday Mirror* 9 Feb. 35 'Urry up wi' that glass o' beer, you lazy faggot!

b. A (male) homosexual. *slang* (orig. and chiefly *U.S.*).

1914 JACKSON & HELLYER *Vocab. Criminal Slang* 30 s.v. Drag, Example: 'All the fagots (sissies) will be dressed in drag at the ball tonight.' **1926** WOOD & GODDARD *Dict. Amer. Slang* 16 *Fagot*, a chorus man; an effeminate man. **1936** J. DOS PASSOS *Big Money* (1937) 273 The first thing Marge thought was how on earth she could ever have liked that fagot. **1962** H. KANE *Killer's Kiss* xxvii. 207 Duffy was no queen, no platinum-dyed freak, no screaming faggot. **1966** *New Statesman* 18 Mar. 392/3 The American word 'faggot' is making advances here over our own more humane 'queer'. **1970** *New Yorker* 28 Nov. 21/2 A gathering of homosexuals..a Jew, a Negro, a butch faggot, a nellie faggot.

†**7.** A person temporarily hired to supply a deficiency at the muster, or on the roll of a company or regiment; a dummy. *Obs.*

a **1700** B. E. *Dict. Cant. Crew, Faggots*, Men Muster'd for Souldiers, not yet Listed. **1708** *Brit. Apollo* No. 105. 4/1 You may be some Faggot to pass at a Muster. **1755** *Mem. Capt. P. Drake* II. iii. 75 The Adjutants..came to treat and settle with me about the Fagots (Men deficient of the Number of Workmen, ordered from each Regiment). **1756** LD. CHESTERFIELD *Connoisseur* CII, William, a Faggot in the First Regiment of Guards. **1802** in JAMES *Mil. Dict.*

8. = FAGGOT VOTE.

1817 SIR F. BURDETT in *Parl. Deb.* 1368 These faggots.. returned the two members to the House of Commons. **1879** *Daily News* 16 Apr. 6/6 He..had not the slightest doubt he would win, unless he were to be swamped by faggots. **1884** *Truth* 13 Mar. 374/1 The art of manufacturing fagots.

9. In various occasional uses: (see quots.).

1727 BRADLEY *Fam. Dict.* s.v., *Faggots of Oranges*, Orange-Peels turn'd or par'd very thin, in order to be preserv'd. **1867** SMYTH *Sailor's Word-bk.* 287 *Fagot*, a billet for stowing casks. **1880** *E. Cornw. Gloss., Faggot*..a secret and unworthy compromise.

10. *attrib.* and *Comb.*, as ***faggot-bearer, -boat, -flame, -maker, -making, -pile, -steel, -stick, -wood.*** Also, **faggot-brief**, a dummy brief (cf. 7); **faggot-drain**, a drain made by placing faggots at the bottom of a trench and then covering them with earth; **faggot filling-stitch** = *faggot-stitch*; **faggot-iron**, iron, in the form of bars or masses, made from welding together a faggot or pile of iron bars; †**faggot-spray**, the refuse twigs, etc., left in making faggots; **faggot-stitch**, needlework in which two pieces of material are joined together by stitching resembling the faggoting of drawn-thread work; so ***faggot-stitching***; †**faggot-waisted** *a.*, arranged in pleats like a bundle of sticks. Also FAGGOT-VOTE.

c **1515** *Cocke Lorelles B.* (Percy Soc.) 11 With lollers, lordaynes, and *fagot berers. **1616** BEAUM. & FL. *Scornful Lady* II. iii, If you 'scape with life, and take a *faggot-boat. **1859** SALA *Tw. round Clock* (1861) 97 The briefless ones.. pretend to pore over '*faggot' briefs. **1819** *Communic. Board Agric.* 245 Many of these *faggot-drains have failed. **1934** M. THOMAS *Dict. Embroidery Stitches* 182 *Sheaf filling stitch*, also known as *faggot filling stitch. **1957** M. B. PICKEN *Fashion Dict.* 121/1 *Fagot filling-stitch*, group of parallel stitches tied together at center to form a bundle. **1842** SIR A. DE VERE *Song of Faith* 243 Turkish cimeters Not fiercelier bite than Christian *faggot-flame. **1870** E. RÖHRIG *Technol. Dict.* (ed. 2) II. 219/2 **Fagot-iron, faggotted iron*, das Paketeisen, das Schroteisen. Ferraille. **1584** R. SCOTT *Discov. Witchcr.* v. i. 73 Three witches of great wealth.. assalted a *faggot-maker. **1822** T. MITCHELL *Aristoph.* I. p. l, Originally a faggot-maker, his mode of tying up bundles excited the attention of Democritus. **1826** MISS MITFORD *Village* 2nd Ser. (1863) 408 Its long open sheds for broom and *faggot-making. *Ibid.* 257 The cart-shed..and the *faggot-pile. **1664** EVELYN *Kal. Hort.* (1729) 204 Put some Rubbish of Lime-stones..*Faggot-spray, or the like, at the bottom of the Cases. **1831** J. HOLLAND *Manuf. Metal* I. 234 The article known among dealers by the appellation of *faggot steel. **1523** *Tell-Troth's N.Y. Gift* 13 Began to beelabour her..with a *faggotstick. *a* **1774** GOLDSM. tr. *Scarron's Com. Romance* (1775) II. 7 The maid followed puss, with a faggot-stick in her hand. **1903** *Daily Chron.* 13 June 8/4 A lace and canvas epaulette pelerine, the seams of which are separated by *faggot-stitch. **1928** *Sunday Express* 3 June 8 The frills, which were not more than half an inch wide, were set in with *faggot stitching. **1581** RICH *Farewel Mil. Prof.* (1846) 218 Their dublettes some-tyme *faggot wasted above the navill; sometymes cowe-beallied belowe the flanckes. **1704** *Collect. Voy.* (Church.) III. 727/2 Boats came..to fetch *Faggot-wood.

faggot ('fægət), *v.* [f. prec. Cf. Fr. *fagoter.*]

1. a. *trans.* To make into a faggot or faggots; to bind up in or as in a faggot. Also, ***to faggot up.***

1598 FLORIO, *Affascinare*..to fagot. **1641** J. JACKSON *True Evang. T.* I. 33 Hermes..with his Wife, Children, and whole family..were all faggotted together to make one great bone-fire. **1649** BLITHE *Eng. Improv. Impr.* (1653) 162 All their brush being faggoted into the Faggot. **1669** FLAVEL *Husbandry Spiritualised* (1832) 210 Growing amongst them that shall shortly be cut down and faggoted up for hell. **1721** R. KEITH tr. *T. à Kempis' Solil. Soul* ii. 132 Then shall they be faggotted together in Bundles for the Fire, who were here Companions in Drunkenness. **1786** COWPER *Let.* 8 May, The dunce..cut down and faggoted up the whole grove. **1857** LANDOR (*title*) Dry Sticks Fagoted.

b. *transf.* and *fig.*

1605 BACON *Adv. Learn.* II. viii. §5 Titles packed and fagotted vp together. **1685** *Roxb. Ball.* V. 542 He.. faggotted his Notions as they fell, And if they rhim'd and rattled all was well. *a* **1722** LISLE *Husb.* (1752) 173 The.. seeds are not..faggotted together with so strong an union. **1784** HARE *Vict. Faith* 38 Things essentially and substantially different, bundled and fagoted together for the occasion. **1882** MOZLEY *Remin.* I. lv. 352 [Newman] fagoted Hampden's pamphlet..with several other scandals..in the 'Foundations of the Faith Assailed'.

†**c.** To bind (persons) in couples; also, to bind hand and foot. *Obs.*

1607 G. WILKINS *Miseries Inforced Marriage* v, Then [they] fagotted you and the fool, your man, back to back. **1725** *New Cant. Dict., Faggot*, to bind Hand and Foot. **1721–1800** in BAILEY.

d. *Embroidery.* To ornament (needlework) by FAGGOTING; also, to join (two pieces of material) by faggot-stitch.

1900 M. E. WILKINS *Parson Lord* 117 She has hem-stitched and fagoted everything. **1904** *Daily Chron.* 3 May 5/4 They are joined with an insertion, or are faggoted together to make kimonas for morning wear.

2. *Metall.* To fasten together bars or rods of iron preparatory to reheating and welding.

1861 W. FAIRBAIRN *Iron* vi. 102 These [puddle bars] are cut up and piled regularly together or faggotted. **1879** *Cassell's Techn. Educ.* IV. 175/1 The axles should be made of the best scrap iron fagoted.

3. To set (a person) on the faggots preparatory to burning; *lit.* and *fig. rare.*

1543 JOYE *Confut. Winchester* 24 Fagetting, burninge and slaying the true professours..of gods holy word. **18..** LANDOR *Wks* (1868) II. 156 The poet is staked and faggoted by his surrounding brethren.

4. a. *intr.* To make or bind faggots.

1874 T. HARDY *Madding Crowd* II. x. 108 Heaps of white chips..showed that woodmen had been faggoting. **1879** JEFFERIES *Wild Life in S.C.* 76 After they have finished faggoting, the women rake up the fragments for their cottage fires.

†**b.** To carry or wear a faggot in token of recantation; to recant. *Obs.*

1535 SHAXTON in Strype *Eccl. Mem.* I. App. lxi. 149 Making onely his reformation in words; and neither faggoting nor..any open revocation.

5. (See quot.)

1880 *E. Cornw. Gloss., Faggot*..a man who in the wrestling ring, sells his back, is said to faggot.

fag(g)oted ('fægətɪd), *ppl. a.* [f. FAGGOT *sb.* or *v.*] Made into faggots. Spec. *faggoted iron* = *faggot-iron.*

1841 W. TEMPLETON *Locomotive Steam Engine* 29 The best wrought iron, fagoted and welded together, generally termed fagoted iron. **1870** [see *faggot-iron*]. *a* **1877** KNIGHT *Dict. Mech.* I. 823/2 Fagoted iron furnace. **1960** HORNER & ABBEY *Dict. Mech. Engin.* (ed. 8) II. 134 *Fagoted scrap*, the ends, cuttings, or remnants of wrought-iron bar and plate of the smithy and boiler shop, piled into fagots welded under the steam hammer.

faggoteer (fægə'tɪə(r)). In 9 **fagoteer.** [f. FAGGOT *sb.* + -EER[1].] One who makes faggots.

1878 *Scribner's Mag.* XVI. 117/1 If some one would only organize a phalanx of fagoteers.

†**faggoter** ('fægətə(r)). In 5 **fagoter.** [f. FAGGOT *sb.* or *v.* + -ER[1].] = prec.

1481–90 *Howard Househ. Bks.* (Roxb.) 366 To William, fagoter, for makenge of wode vj. dayes ix. d.

'faggoting, *vbl. sb.* [f. as prec. + -ING[1].]

1. The action of the vb. FAGGOT.

1837 W. B. ADAMS *Eng. Pleas. Carriages* vii. 107 The best axle-trees are formed of several flat bars of iron welded together in a mass, which process is technically called 'fagoting'.

2. In *Embroidery.* The process by which a number of threads in the material are drawn out and a few of the cross threads tied together in the middle. Hence, the work done in this manner.

1885 *Chicago Advance* 19 Feb., Bits of dainty 'fagoting'.

faggotless ('fægətlɪs), *a.* [f. FAGGOT *sb.* + -LESS.] Devoid of faggots.

1873 OUIDA *Pascarèl* I. 78 Lifting his hands, as he peered into the faggotless cupboard.

faggot-vote ('fægətvəʊt). [App. a transferred use of FAGGOT *sb.* 7, 'dummy' soldier; as many faggot-votes were often created at one time by the practice (forbidden in 7 & 8 Will. III. c. 25) of subdividing a single tenement among a number of nominal owners, the word was naturally interpreted as alluding to the primary sense 'bundle of sticks'.]

A vote manufactured for party purposes, by the transfer to persons, not otherwise legally qualified, of sufficient property to qualify them as electors.

1817 SIR F. BURDETT in *Parl. Deb.* 1368 Lord Lonsdale had conveyed to him a certain property, on which he was to vote in that borough, as, what was familiarly called a faggot vote. **1836** DISRAELI *Lett. Runnymede* 60 Notwithstanding ..your father's fagot votes. **1879** *Daily News* 16 Apr. 2/2 Attempts to tamper with the register by the introduction of what are termed faggot votes.

Hence **faggot-voter, -voting.**

1880 GLADSTONE in *Pall Mall G.* 14 July 2/1 The subject of the fagot voter. **1887** *Times* (weekly ed.) 28 Oct. 7/2 The question of faggot-voting.

faggoty ('fægətɪ), *a.* In 9 (*erron.*) **fagotty.** [f. as prec. + -Y.] **1.** Of or pertaining to faggots.

2. Of, pertaining to, or suggestive of homosexuality; homosexual. Cf. FAGGOT *sb.* 6 b.

1928 C. McKAY *Home to Harlem* I. iv. 36 And there is two things in Harlem I don't understan'. It is a bulldyking woman and a faggoty man. **1964** S. BELLOW *Herzog* 238 There was a certain faggotty prissiness in his speech. **1967** *Listener* 7 Dec. 740/3 It is..irredeemably vulgar, a vision of 'only faggoty desire'. **1968** A. BINKLEY *What shall I Cry?* 183 Albie in his faggoty silk pajamas.

Hence **faggoty-minded**, disposed to use faggots, inclined to burn opponents.

1856 VAUGHAN *Mystics* (1860) II. 5 The virulent fagotty-minded pervert Scheffler.

Fagin ('feɪgɪn). The name of a character in Dickens's 'Oliver Twist', a receiver who trained children to be thieves and pickpockets; allusively used for a thief, a trainer of thieves, or a receiver.

1847 *Punch* 2 Oct. 125 The Fagin of France after condemnation. (*Slightly altered from* 'Oliver Twist'.) **1905** *Daily Chron.* 14 Apr. 6/6 Thieves' kitchen kept by two modern Fagins... This school of crime bore outwardly the innocent semblance of a greengrocery and ice-cream shop. .. The two Fagins who conducted it were..both Italians. [**1907** *Ibid.* 17 May 3/4 The Fagin-like person who has hitherto been King of the Nile.] **1965** *Listener* 26 Aug. 292/2 The young unemployed.., the bastards.., the artful dodgers..thus have 500 Fagins to instruct them in everything from petty thievery to drug addiction. **1970** C. DRUMMOND *Stab in Back* iv. 82 In the world of receivers of stolen property a kind of system of titles prevails, starting with 'Cousin Joe', progressing upwards through 'the Uncle' to 'Father'—very important indeed, but dwarfed by..a gentleman known as 'the Fagin'.

fagine ('feɪdʒɪn). *Chem.* Also **-in.** [ad. G. *fagin* (Buchner and Herberger 1832, in J. A. Buchner's *Rep. f. d. Pharmacie* XL. 157), f. L. *fāg-us* beech + -INE[5].] An alkaloid reported to have been obtained from the nuts of the common beech *Fagus sylvatica* (but see quot. 1908).

1838 R. D. THOMSON in *Brit. Annual* 337 Fagin. **1846** LOUDON *Veget. Kingd.* 291 The husks of the common Beech-tree yield a narcotic extractive, called Fagine. **1860** *Chambers's Encycl.* I. 804/2 A volatile, narcotic, poisonous principle, called Fagine, is..found in it [*sc.* beechmast]. **1885** *Jrnl. Chem. Soc.* XLVIII. II. 676 The author [*sc.* J. Habermann]..believes that the existence of fagine as a true alkaloid cannot be doubted. **1908** HALL & DEFREN tr. *Abderhalden's Text-bk. Physiol. Chem.* vi. 114 Other bases have been isolated from various plants, which in part have been given characteristic names; e.g. amanitine, from toad-stools; fagine, from buchu seeds, etc. They are, however, all identical with choline.

fagmaster ('fægmɑːstə(r), -mæstə(r)). [f. FAG *sb.*[1] 2 + MASTER *sb.*[1]] A boy who has a junior boy as his fag; a fagger.

1876 LD. ALBEMARLE *50 Yrs. of My Life* I. v. 293 One day I had to take a pair of my fagmaster's shoes to 'Cobbler Foots' to be mended. **1895** *Q. Rev.* Oct. 283 Probably he would have been..cobbed by his fagmaster as an incorrigible toast-burner. **1920** *Blackw. Mag.* Oct. 483/2 One small boy, Harker minor,..was told by his fagmaster that he would be licked for 'fighting' as soon as he was well. **1964** *Punch* 13 May 724/2 Handling his fagmaster's amours.

†**fagnet.** *Obs. rare*$^{-1}$. Some kind of net for fishing.

1558 *Act 1 Eliz.* c. 17 §1 No Person..with any..Crele, Raw, Fagnet, Trolnet..shall take..Spawn or Fry of Eels.

†**fagong.** *Obs. rare.* [corruption of Pg. *fogão* stove.] A fire-place used on shipboard.

1772 NEWLAND in *Phil. Trans.* LXII. 90 E E [is] the fagong or fire-place. *Ibid.*, I had well secured the pot in the fagong E E.

fagopyrism (ˌfægəʊ'paɪrɪz(ə)m). *Vet.* Also as mod.L. **fagopy'rismus.** [ad. mod.L. *Fagopyr(um* (see BUCKWHEAT), f. L. *fāg-us* beech-tree + -O + Gr. πυρός wheat + -ISM.] A skin disease affecting certain white-skinned animals, caused by poisoning by buckwheat and subsequent exposure to sunlight.

1909 in WEBSTER. **1909** *Johns Hopkins Hospital Bull.* XX. 153/2 Dr. Smith said fagopyrismus was derived from Latin *fagus*, beech-tree, and Greek *pyros*, wheat, and meant poisoning from the buckwheat. The condition is not uncommon in pigs, swine, horses..which eat the grains, plant, straw, or stubble of the buckwheat. White or spotted animals are especially susceptible, and the disease is moderated by shelter or a cloudy sky. **1917** E. A. BRUCE in *Jrnl. Amer. Vet. Med. Assoc.* III. 189 (*heading*) Fagopyrismus (buckwheat poisoning) and similar affections. **1930** W. A. BILLINGS *Livestock & Poultry Dis.* xiv. 317 Fagopyrism, caused by exposure to sunlight after animals have been feeding on buckwheat. The symptoms closely resemble those of big-head. **1961** R. SEIDEN *Livestock Health Encycl.* (ed. 2) 373/1 *Photosensitization*,.. also called white-skin disease..fagopyrism.

fagot, var. of FAGGOT.

‖**fagottist** (fə'gɒtɪst). [Ger. *fagottist*, ad. It. *fagottista*, f. *fagotto*: see next.] A performer on the bassoon, bassoonist.

1886 *Sat. Rev.* 25 Dec. 836 Brandt, the celebrated fagottist at Munich.

‖**fagotto** (fa'gɔtto). *Mus.* [It. *fagotto.* Cf. Ger. *fagott.*] = BASSOON 1, 2 a.

1724 in *Explication Foreign Words in Music* 30. **1876** in STAINER & BARRETT *Dict. Musical Terms* 52.

fah, var. of FAW, *Obs.*

faham ('fɑːhəm). *Bot.* [f. the native name for the plant.] An orchid, *Jumellea* (*Angræcum*) *fragrans*, from Réunion and Mauritius, whose leaves are used, especially in France, as a substitute for tea; also, the leaves so used.

1850 *Gardeners' Chron.* 599/3 The leaves of Faham, known also by the name of Fahon or Fahum leaves, are imported from the Mauritius. *Ibid.* 600/1 Like many of the exotic orchids, the Faham is parasitic. **1858** SIMMONDS *Dict. Trade*, Faham-tea. **1861** [see BOURBON 3 c]. **1891** *Curtis's Bot. Mag.* CXVII. 7161 The popular name is variously spelled Fahame, Faham, Fahan, Fahon, Fahum, and Faam, of the origin of which I have no information.

‖**fahlband** ('fɑːlbant). *Geol.* [Ger.; f. *fahl* ash-coloured (= FALLOW *a.*) + *band* BAND, stripe.] A zone or stratum in crystalline rocks.

1880 *Sat. Rev.* 1 May 577 A succession of partly decomposed rocks known as fahlbands or rotten belts.

‖**fahlerz** ('fɑːlɛːrts). *Min.* Also **fahlertz.** [a. Ger. *fahlerz*, f. *fahl* ash-coloured, yellowish + *erz* ore.] Grey copper or copper-ore, tetrahedrite.

1796 KIRWAN *Min.* II. 148 The grey Ore from the Hartz is the real Fahlerz. **1808** SMITHSON in *Phil. Trans.* XCVIII. 57 A combination of galena and fahlertz. **1880** tr. *Wurtz' Atom. Th.* 141 The varieties of fahlerz.

fahlore ('fɑːl,ɔə(r)). *Min.* [Partially translated form of prec.] = prec.

1805 R. JAMESON *Char. Min.* II. 201 Grey Copper-Ore, or Fahl-Ore. **1872** RAYMOND *Statist. Mines & Mining* 189 Twenty men have been at work slowly developing some of the lodes of 'fahl-ore.'

fahlunite ('fɑːlənaɪt). *Min.* [f. (by Hisinger, 1808) *Fahlun*, in Sweden + -ITE.] A hydrous silicate of aluminium and iron, resulting from the alteration of iolite.

1814 T. ALLAN *Min. Nomen.* 18 Fahlunite Kars. 112 b. **1879** RUTLEY *Stud. Rocks* xiv. 298 The rock contains as accessories..hydrargillite, fahlunite, gahnite, etc.

Fahrenheit ('fɑːrənhaɪt, 'færənaɪt). The name of a Prussian physicist (1686–1736), inventor of the mercurial thermometer. Used *attrib.* and *ellipt.* to denote the thermometric scale introduced by him and still in common use in England and the U.S., according to which the freezing point of water is 32° and the boiling point 212°. Often abbreviated F; *e.g.* 20°F = '*twenty degrees* (*of*) *Fahrenheit*'.

1753 *Phil. Trans.* XLVIII. 109 The mercury stood at 240 degrees in De L'Isle; which is 72 below 0 in Fahrenheit. **1823** J. BADCOCK *Dom. Amusem.* 65 Fire-heat at 212° of Fahrenheit produced detonation.

faicte, obs. f. of FEAT.

faie: see FAY *v.*

‖**faience** (fajɑ̃s). Also 8 **fayance**, 8–9 **fayence.** [a. Fr. *faïence*, prob. an appellative use of the proper name †*Fayence*, Faenza in Italy, one of the chief seats of ceramic industry in 16th c.] 'A general term comprising all the various kinds of glazed earthenware and porcelain' (Fairholt).

Hence **fai'enced** *ppl. a.*, covered with faience.

1714 *Fr. Bk. of Rates* 152 Fayances or Earthen-Ware. **1762–71** H. WALPOLE *Vertue's Anecd. Paint.* (1786) IV. 28 Roman fayence, called Raphael's earthen-ware. **1835** MARRYAT *Olla Podr.* xiii, Every article of *fayence*. **1879** J. J. YOUNG *Ceram. Art* 41 The Chinese..seek to equal the wonderful coloring of the faience of Persia. **1883** W. H. BISHOP in *Harper's Mag.* Mar. 504/2 A Henri II. faience candlestick. **1954** KOESTLER *Invisible Writing* xii. 137 The mosaic floors and faïenced walls convey even to-day an image of perfection.

faierie, obs. form of FAIRY.

faik, *sb.* [Of obscure origin; prob. identical with FAKE *sb.*¹]

1. 'A fold of anything; as a ply of a garment' (Jam.). *Sc.*

2. = MANYPLIES.

1890 J. H. STEEL *Diseases Sheep* 119 Impaction of the faik or manyplies.

faik (fek), *v.*¹ *Sc.* [Belongs to FAIK *sb.*]

1. *trans.* 'To fold, to tuck up' (Jam.).

†**2.** To enfold, clasp. *Obs. rare*⁻¹.

1513 DOUGLAS *Æneis* x. vii. 88 Half lyfles thy fyngyrrs war sterand, Within thy neif doys gryp and faik the brand.

faik (fek), *v.*² *Sc.* Also 5 **falk**, 9 **faick.** [? Shortened form of *defaik*, DEFALK.] *trans.*

1. a. To abate, diminish, lessen. **b.** To deduct.

1445 *Burgh Records Aberdeen* 18 Feb. (Jam.), Thar sal be chosin four discrete persounes to falk the tax of men that has tholit skath oft. **1494** *Acc. Ld. High Treasurer* (1877) I. 245, Xxviij wolkis; of the quhilkis thar is to be falkyte twa wolkis of the tyme of ȝowle. **1822** GALT *Entail* I. 169 I'll no faik a farthing o' my right.

2. 'To excuse, let go with impunity' (Jam.).

1789 BURNS *2nd Ep. to Davie* iii, Gif it's sae, ye sud be licket..Sic hauns as you sud ne'er be faiket, Be hain't wha like.

faik, *v.*³ *Sc.* ? *Obs.* [Possibly the same word as FAIK *v.*¹; cf. ME. use of *fold* = falter, fail (said of the limbs). But cf. OS. *fakôn*, MDu. *vaeken* to slumber.] **a.** *intr.* Of the limbs: To fail from weariness; to cease moving. **b.** *trans. to faik never a foot*: not to cease from movement.

1768 ROSS *Helenore* (1866) 152 Her limbs they faicked under her and fell. *Ibid.* 210 The lasses..faiked ne'er a foot for height nor how. **1808–79** JAMIESON s.v., *My feet have never faikit*, I have still been in motion.

faikes (feɪks). *Geol.* Also **fakes.** (See quots.)

[**1808–79** JAMIESON, *Faik*, a stratum or layer of stone in the quarry.] **1865** PAGE *Handbk. Geol. Terms*, *Faikes* or *Fakes*, a Scotch miner's term for fissile sandy shales, or shaly sandstones. **1876** —— *Adv. Text-bk. Geol.* v. 92 Faikes, a thin-bedded shaly sandstone of irregular composition. **1882** GEIKIE *Text-bk. Geol.* II. II. §6. 158 Micaceous sand-stone—a rock so full of mica-flakes that it readily splits into thin laminae..This rock is called 'fakes' in Scotland.

faikyn, Sc. var. FAKEN *a. Obs.*, deceitful.

†**fail**, *sb.*¹ *Sc. Obs.* Also 6 **fale**, 6–8 **faill**, 8 **feal.** [? a. Gael. *fàl* a sod.]

1. 'Any grassy part of the surface of the ground, as united to the rest' (Jam.).

1513 DOUGLAS *Æneis* XII. Prol. 88 The variant vestur of the venust vaill Schrowdis the scherald fur, and euery faill.

2. 'A turf, a flat clod covered with grass cut off from the rest of the sward' (Jam.). Also turf, as a material.

1535 STEWART *Cron. Scot.* II. 146 Euerie man ane flaik sould mak of tre, And faillis delf into greit quantitie. **1536** BELLENDEN *Cron. Scot.* (1821) I. 172 He beildit ane huge wall of fail and devait. **1639** SPALDING *Troub. Chas. I* (1792) I. 173 Close it [the port] up strongly with faill and thatch. **1708** J. CHAMBERLAYNE *St. Gt. Brit.* II. III. i. (1743) 400 Every minister has fewel, foggage, faill, and diviots allowed them.

3. *Comb.* **fail-dyke**, a wall built of sods.

1536 in Pitcairn *Crim. Trials Scot.* I. 174* The overthrowing of a 'faill-dyke' built on the said lands. **17..** in Scott *Minstr. Scot. Bord.* (1803) III. 241 'Behint yon auld fail dyke, I wot there lies a new slain knight.' **1816** SCOTT *Antiq.* xx, 'Auld Edie will hirple out himsell if he can get a feal-dike to lay his gun ower.'

fail (feɪl), *sb.*² Also FAILYIE. [a. OF. *faile*, *faille*, deficiency, failure, fault, f. *faillir* to FAIL.]

1. = FAILURE 1. *Obs.* exc. in phrase ***without fail***; now used only to strengthen an injunction or a promise; formerly also with statements of fact, = unquestionably, certainly. †Also, in same sense, (*it is*) ***no fail*** (*but*), ***sans fail***: without any doubt, for certain.

1297 R. GLOUC. (1724) 245 Þer wyþoute fayle, At Eccestre strong enou hii smyte an bataylle. *c* **1330** R. BRUNNE *Chron.* (1725) 245 In luf & pes sanz faile went Edward. *c* **1385** CHAUCER *L.G.W.* 1092 *Dido*, Comaunded hire massangerys for to go The same day with outyn any fayle. *c* **1430** LYDG. *Bochas* VIII. xvii. (1544) 188 b, In Europe stant Thrace..it is no fayle. **1546** LANGLEY *Pol. Verg. De Invent.* I. xvi. 29 a, It is no fayle but it [the knowledge of medecines] was perceyued, by what thinges were wholsome, & what unwholsome. **1555** ABP. PARKER *Ps.* l, I wil no fayle deliuer thee. **1611** BIBLE *Josh.* iii. 10 The liuing God..will without faile driue out from before you the Canaanites. **1611** SHAKS. *Wint. T.* v. i. 27 Dangers, by his Highnesse faile of Issue, May drop vpon his Kingdome. **1656** *Burton's Diary* (1828) I. 176 There is no fail of justice..yet. **1678** CUDWORTH *Intell. Syst.* 128 There might be never any Fail of Generations. **1713** SWIFT *Jrnl. to Stella* 26 Feb., The meeting of parliament..will be next Tuesday..without fail. **1847** MARRYAT *Childr. N. Forest* xviii, The tailor has promised the clothes on Saturday without fail.

†**2.** = FAILURE 3. ***for fail***: in the event of failure; as a precaution against failure. *Obs.*

1477 NORTON *Ord. Alch.* ii. in Ashm. (1652) 29 Of all paines the most grevious paine, Is for one faile to beginn all againe. **1627–77** FELTHAM *Resolves* I. xci. 141 The Prince suffers in the fails of his Ambassador. **1660** SHARROCK *Vegetables* 98 Be sure you plow up..annoying weeds, and for fail let some-body, with a spade, follow the plough, to root up such as are left. *a* **1734** NORTH *Exam.* II. iv. §84 (1740) 272 They continually watched for Colours, and for Fail, made them, to affirm this.

†**3.** = FAILURE 2. *Obs.*

1647 SANDERSON *Serm.* II. 207 Overmuch sorrow..upon the fail of any earthly helps or hopes. **1654** GATAKER *Disc. Apol.* 47 Chalkie Pillars..threatning a fail, if not a fall.

†**b.** Death. *Obs. rare.*

1613 SHAKS. *Henry VIII*, I. ii. 145 How grounded hee his Title to the Crowne Vpon our faile.

fail (feɪl), *v.* Forms: 3–4 **faile-n**, (4–5 **faylen**), 3–5 **fail(l)i**, 3–6 **faille(n**, **faylle**, 3–7 **faile**, (3 **vaile**), **fayle**, **-y**, 4–6 **faly(e**, (4 **failly**, **fal(l)e**, **feile**, 6 **feyle**, **faeille**, 7 **faill**, **fall**), 3– **fail.** *Sc.* 4–6 **failȝe** (6–7 *printed* **failze**), (6 **falȝe**, 7 **failyie**), **faillie.** [a. OF. *faillir* to be wanting, miss (mod.F. *faillir* to miss, *falloir* impers. to be wanting, to be necessary) = Pr. *faillir*, *falhir*, OSp. *fallir* (in mod.Sp. replaced by the derivative form *fallecer*, f. L. type **fallescĕre*), Cat., OPg. *falir* (mod.Pg. *falecer*), It. *fallire*:—vulgar L. **fallīre* (for class. L. *fallĕre* to deceive), used *absol.* in sense 'to disappoint expectation, be wanting or defective.' The OF. verb was adopted in MHG. *vêlen* (mod.G. *fehlen*), Du. *feilen*, ON. *feila*.

In 15–17th c. in intrans. senses often conjugated with *be*.]

I. To be or become deficient.

1. a. *intr.* To be absent or wanting. Now only of something necessary or desirable (coinciding with sense 5); often in pr. pple. with sb. or pron., as ***failing this*** = 'in default of this' (see FAILING *prep.*). In early use, †To be wanting to complete a specified quantity; also *impers.*

a **1300** *Cursor M.* 1486 (Cott.) Matusale Liued..til þat nine hundret yeir war gan And seuenti, falid it bot an. *c* **1325** *E.E. Allit. P.* B. 741 What if fyue faylen of fyfty þe noumbre? *c* **1400** MAUNDEV. (1839) xvii. 182 There faylethe but 5 Degrees & an half, of the fourthe partie. *c* **1400** *Lanfranc's Cirurg.* 63 Make þat þe splentis & byndynge faile above þe wounde. *a* **1400–50** *Alexander* 4279 Forþi failis vs all infirmit[e]s of ffeuyre & of ells. **1483** CAXTON *Gold. Leg.* 284/3 The preues of the lignages were fayled. **1543–4** *Act 35 Hen. VIII*, c. 1 §6 If suche heyres shulde fayle. **1611** BIBLE *2 Sam.* iii. 29 Let there not faile from the house of Ioab one that hath an issue. **1703** MAUNDRELL *Journ. Jerus.* (1732) 128 Shaded over head with Trees, and with Matts when the boughs fail. **1878** BROWNING *La Saisiaz* 58 Failing proof then of invented trouble.

†**b.** with *dat.* of the person. *Obs.*

a **1300** *Cursor M.* 11426 (Gött.) Þaim fayled neuer drinc ne fode. *a* **1300** *Leg. Rood* (1871) 30 Þo þe work was almest ido; hem vailed a vair tre. *c* **1300** *St. Brandan* 510 Him faillede grace..his lyf to amende. **1424** *Paston Lett.* 4 I. 12 Hem fayled ropes convenient to here..purpos. **1611** BIBLE *1 Kings* ii. 4 There shall not faile thee..a man on the throne of Israel.

c. To be inadequate or insufficient. Chiefly in phrase ***time would fail***. Const. *dat.* of person.

c **1325** *E.E. Allit. P.* B. 548 Tyl any water in þe worlde to wasche þe fayly. **1548** HALL *Chron.* 244 Kyng James would make no aunswere..knowing that his power now fayled..to performe the request demaunded. **1611** BIBLE *Heb.* xi. 32 The time would faile mee to tell of Gedeon. **1614** BP. HALL *Recoll. Treat.* 612 The day would faile mee if I should [etc.].

2. a. To become exhausted, come to an end, run short. Const. *dat.* of the person; also, †*of*, *from* (a place, receptacle).

c **1250** *Old Kentish Serm.* in *O.E. Misc.* 29 Wyn failede at þise bredale. *c* **1330** R. BRUNNE *Chron.* (1725) 326 Alle þer store failed. **1382** WYCLIF *1 Macc.* iii. 29 He sawȝ, that monee failide of his tresours. *c* **1400** *Cato's Morals* 87 in *Cursor M.* App. iv, Loke þou spende mesureli, þe gode þat þou liuis bi, or ellis wille hit faile. **1596** SPENSER *F.Q.* IV. i. 43 The breath gan him to fayle. **1611** BIBLE *1 Kings* xvii. 14 Neither shall the cruse of oile faile. —— *Job* xiv. 11 The waters faile from the sea. **1653** HOLCROFT *Procopius* II. xvi. 58 Their Provisions being failed, they fed upon Hides. **1695** LOCKE *Further Consider. Money* (ed. 2) 68 Where the credit and money fail, barter alone must do. **1729** BUTLER *Serm.* Wks. 1874 II. 146 All other enjoyments fail in these circumstances. **1801** SOUTHEY *Thalaba* IV. xviii, Soon would our food and water fail us here. **1871** B. TAYLOR *Faust* (1875) II. II. iii. 124 Health is none where water fails!

b. To become extinct; to die out, lose vitality, pass away. Of an odour or sound: To die away.

c **1400** MAUNDEV. (Roxb.) xv. 68 Machometes lawe sall faile. **1463** *Bury Wills* (Camden) 18 If the office of Seynt Marie preest fayle. **1535** STEWART *Cron. Scot.* III. 393 Of him the airis maill did falȝe. **1611** BIBLE *Esther* ix. 28 These dayes of Purim should not faile from among the Jewes. **1647–8** COTTERELL *Davila's Hist. Fr.* (1678) 5 The eldest line failing. **1764** GOLDSM. *Trav.* 91 Where wealth and freedom reign, contentment fails. **1767** BLACKSTONE *Comm.* II. 239 The blood of the Kempes shall not inherit till the blood of the Stiles's fail. **1819** SHELLEY *Ind. Serenade*, The Champak's odours fail Like sweet thoughts in a dream. **1837** NEWMAN *Par. Serm.* (ed. 2) III. viii. 120 Religion seems to be failing when it is merely changing its form. **1842** TENNYSON *Vision of Sin* 24 The music..Rose again from where it seem'd to fail.

†**c.** Of a period of time or anything that has a finite duration: To come to an end, expire. *Obs.*

c **1399** LANGL. *Rich. Redeles* II. 14 Somere hem ffaylid. *c* **1477** CAXTON *Jason* 14 b, As sone as the triews shall faylle ye shal be guerdoned. **1563** GOLDING *Cæsar* (1565) 96 b, The season of the yeare mete for warrefare fayled. **1611** BIBLE *Heb.* i. 12 Thou art the same and thy yeeres shall not fayle.

†**d.** To cease to speak *of*. *Obs. rare.*

c **1650** *Merline* 1208 in Furniv. *Percy Folio* I. 460 Now let us of his mother fayle, And turne us to another tale.

3. a. 'To fall off in respect of vigour or activity' (W.); to lose power or strength; to flag, wane; to break down; *fig.* of the heart. Of the eyes, light, etc.: To grow dim.

a **1225** *Ancr. R.* 228 None deofles puffe ne þurue ȝe dreden, but ȝif þet lim ualse [*v.r.* faille]. *c* **1275** LAY. 2938 Þo holdede þe king [Leir] and failede his mihte. **1340** HAMPOLE *Pr. Consc.* I. 727 At even late he..fayles..and dwynes to noght. **1382** WYCLIF *Isa.* xiii. 7 Eche herte of a man shal wane, or faylen. **1398** TREVISA *Barth. De P.R.* III. viii. (1495) 54 The soule vegetable faylyth and at the laste whan the body deyth, it deyeth. *c* **1400** *Destr. Troy* 3549 His sight failet. **1548** HALL *Chron.* 88 His heart fayled. **1667** MILTON *P.L.* XII. 9, I perceave Thy mortal sight to faile. **1669** STURMY *Mariner's Mag.* IV. 136 Let slip thine Anchor, the Wind fails. **1743** WESLEY *Jrnl.* 20 Oct., My voice suddenly fail'd. **1820** SHELLEY *Julian* 597 The poor sufferer's health began to fail. **1833** HT. MARTINEAU *Tale of Tyne* iv. 67 The wind..failed. **1842** TENNYSON *Lady Clare* 78 Her heart within her did not fail. **1860** RAMSAY *Remin.* 1st Ser. (ed. 7) 107 In Scotland it used to be quite common to say of a person whose health and strength had declined, that he had failed. **1881** S. COLVIN *Landor* 136 That kind..old lady had been failing since the spring of 1829 and had died in October.

b. with *dat.* of the person (approaching sense 5).

a **1300** *Cursor M.* 24001 (Cott.) Gang, and steyuen, and tung, and sight, All failled me þat tide. *a* **1300** *Leg. Rood* (1871) 20 Þe strengþe him failede of is lymes. *a* **1400–50** *Alexander* 1443 All failis þam þe force. **1586** A. DAY *Eng. Secretary* II. (1625) 47 My senses did faile me. **1611** BIBLE

Luke xxi. 26 Mens hearts failing them for feare. **1678** *Trans. Crt. Spain* II. 61 If my memory fail me not. **1842** MISS MITFORD in L'Estrange *Life* III. ix. 136 His eyesight fails him now. **1871** FREEMAN *Norm. Conq.* (1876) IV. xviii. 116 The heart of Eustace failed him.

c. *dial.* To fall ill (*of*).

1875 *Sussex Gloss.* s.v., As though he was going to fail with the measles. **1876** *Surrey Provinc.*, *Fail of*, to fall ill of, to sicken with.

†**d.** To die. *Obs.* [So Sp. *fallecer.*]

1613 SHAKS. *Hen. VIII*, I. ii. 184 Had the King in his last Sicknesse faild. **1878** *Cumberld. Gloss.*, *Fail*, to die.

4. a. To prove deficient upon trial. †Of fighting men: To give way (before an enemy). Of a material thing: To break down under strain or pressure (*arch.*). Of a rule, anticipation, sign: To prove misleading.

1375 BARBOUR *Bruce* II. 393 For thar small folk begouth to failȝe, And fled all skalyt her and thar. *c* **1398** CHAUCER *Fortune* 56 In general this rewle may not fayle. *a* **1400–50** *Alexander* 1372 With þat scho [a tower] flisch noþer fayle fyue score aunkirs. *c* **1400** *Lanfranc's Cirurg.* 133 Or ellis þou schalt knowe bi þis signe þat nevere failiþ. *c* **1430** LYDG. *Min. Poems* (Percy Soc.) 47 Thyng counterfeet wol faylen [*printed* fayler] at assay. **1622** R. HAWKINS *Voy. S. Sea* xxxii. 76 Creatures..bred in..fresh Rivers die presently, if they come into Salt water..This fayleth in some Fishes. **1776** G. SEMPLE *Building in Water* 18 The second Pier of the Foot-way, failed and carried off by the Floods. **1782** COWPER *Gilpin* 95 Loop and button failing both At last it [the cloak] flew away. **1815** T. FORSTER *Atmos. Phenom.* 155 The abundance of berries in the hedges is said to presage a hard winter, but this often fails. **1855** TENNYSON *Maud.* I. xi. 2 O let the solid ground Not fail beneath my feet.

b. *to fail safe*: of a mechanical or electrical device or machine, aircraft, etc., to revert, in the event of failure or breakdown, to a condition involving no danger. Also **fail-safe** *a.*

1948 *Jrnl. R. Aeronaut. Soc.* LII. 198/1 Automatic power plant control including automatic 'fail safe' provision against mechanical trouble or power failure. **1949** *Ibid.* LIII. 179/1 What was really required was a propeller and c.s.u. combination which would fail safe. **1958** 'P. BRYANT' *Two Hours to Doom* 15 The *Failsafe* procedure, the system SAC had dreamed up to prevent any accidental attack sparking off a third world war. **1958** *Times* 20 Aug. 9/7 It is becoming accepted practice that they [*sc.* jet aircraft] must 'fail safe'. **1958** *Listener* 16 Oct. 593/1 Designers [of aircraft] learnt how to design against fatigue, and the 'fail-safe' form of design was developed. **1959** *New Statesman* 790/3 Just as atomic bombers have a technical fail-safe device which recalls them from a mission if anything goes wrong, so it is inevitable that every country will have to devise its own political fail-safe policy, designed to insulate itself from the dangers due to other countries' actions. **1962** F. I. ORDWAY et al. *Basic Astronautics* vii. 317 The component..is as fail-safe as the one tested. **1962** *Want to run a Railway?* 16 The system is designed throughout on 'fail-safe' principles—if any part of it is not working properly then signals automatically go to danger. **1971** *Daily Tel.* (Colour Suppl.) 8 Jan. 15/4 Because of the possibility of human error and total reliance on communications between pilots and controller the system will 'fail-dangerous' rather than 'fail-safe'.

5. a. Not to render the due or expected service or aid; to be wanting at need. Chiefly with *dat.* of the person, rarely with *to.* quasi-*trans.*: To disappoint, give no help to; to withold help from.

a **1300** *Floriz & Bl.* 424 Ihc schal þe failli neure mo. *a* **1300** *K. Horn* 638 Mi swerd me nolde faille. *c* **1305** *Edmund Conf.* 592 in *E.E.P.* (1862) 86 Foreward he huld þis monekes: & ne faillede hem noȝt. *c* **1330** R. BRUNNE *Chron.* (1810) 99 Sir Lowys failed nouht, his help was him redie. *c* **1420** *Anturs of Arth.* xlvi, Frettut with fyne gold, that failis in the fiȝte. *c* **1489** CAXTON *Sonnes of Aymon* I. 37 Serue the kynge..nor faylle hym not for noo thyng. **1549** *Compl. Scot.* viii. 74 The inglis men dreymis that ȝe haue failȝet to them. **1590** SIR J. SMYTH *Disc. Weapons* 3 b, Al their other weapons in fight have failed them. **1771** MRS. E. GRIFFITH tr. *Viaud's Shipwreck* 44 If it [the shattered boat] should fail me..said I to myself. **1836** KEBLE *Serm.* viii. Postscript (1848) 373 The language..fails him..in his endeavour to find words to express the greatness of the gift. *a* **1845** LYTE *Hymn*, '*Abide with me*,' When other helpers fail and comforts flee. **1871** FREEMAN *Norm. Conq.* (1876) IV. xviii. 222 Here again chronology fails us. **1881** *Daily Tel.* 28 Jan., In the afternoon the wind failed us.

†**b.** *trans.* with double *obj.* or const. *of*: To disappoint of (something due or expected). *Obs.*

c **1386** CHAUCER *Shipman's T.* 188, I wil nought faile yow my thankes. **1647** EVELYN *Mem.* (1857) III. 7 Two posts having falled me of intelligence.

II. To have a deficiency or want; to lack.

6. a. *intr.* To be wanting or deficient *in* (an essential quality or part).

c **1380** WYCLIF *Wks.* (1880) 22 Men þat failen in charite. *c* **1384** CHAUCER *H. Fame* III. 8 Though somme vers fayle in A sillable. *c* **1400** MAUNDEV. (Roxb.) xiii. 58 Bot ȝit þai faile in sum articles of oure beleue. **1556** *Aurelio & Isab.* (1608) K v, Beter to faille a litell in the justice, than to be superflue in crualte. **1655** EARL ORRERY *Parthenissa* (1676) 80 You might have fail'd in the knowledge of those particulars. **1875** JOWETT *Plato* (ed. 2) I. 114 The Dialogue fails in unity.

b. *to fail of*: = 7.

1307 *Elegy Edw. I*, x. (in Warton (1840) I. 94) Of gode knyhtes darh him nout fail. *c* **1386** CHAUCER *Shipman's T.* 248 Of siluer in thy purs shaltow nat faille. **1495** *Act 11 Hen. VII*, c. 9 §1 The King..not willing his..subgettis to faill of remedy. **1586** A. DAY *Eng. Secretary* I. (1625) 42 If I faile not of memory therein, we [etc.]. **1651** MARIUS *Adv. Conc. Bills of Exchange* 24 The drawer of the Bill was failed of his credit. **1671** R. BOHUN *Disc. Wind* 20 When the Atmosphere begins to thicken..wee seldom fail of a Wind. **1713** GAY *Guardian* No. 149 ¶17 A dancing-master of the lowest rank seldom fails of the scarlet stocking and the red heel. **1796** MORSE *Amer. Geog.* I. 150 Whenever the continent shall come to fail of timber. **1867** LONGF. *Giotto's Tower* 6 How many lives..Fail of the nimbus which the artists paint Around the shining forehead of the saint. **1884** *Manch. Exam.* 22 May 5/4 Failing of any other remedy, they grumble.

7. *trans.* To be or become deficient in; to lack, want, be without. Now *rare.*

c **1325** *E.E. Allit. P.* B. 1535 A fust faylaynde þe wryst. **1375** BARBOUR *Bruce* XVIII. 269 Thai of the host that falit met. *c* **1400** *Sowdone Bab.* 2290 He saugh the ladies so whiȝte of ler, Faile brede on here table. **1466** MARG. PASTON in *Paston Lett.* 560 II. 291 Send me word..whether ye have your last dedes that ye fayled. **1483** *Festivall* (W. de W. 1515) 22 Whan Jacob fayled corne he must nedes sende for more. **1869** FREEMAN *Norm. Conq.* (ed. 2) III. xi. 44 The Primate prayed that their chosen King might never fail the throne. **1883** JEFFERIES *Stor. Heart* vii. 115, I fail words to express my utter contempt.

†**8.** *to fail little, not much*: to have a narrow escape (of some misadventure). Const. *to* with *inf.* and *of* with gerund. Also, *to fail of*: to keep clear of, escape, miss. *Obs.*

1624 CAPT. SMITH *Virginia* I. (1629) 13 We fayled not much to have been cast away. **1653** HOLCROFT *Procopius* IV. 130 The Romans Rams..failed little to be all set on fire. **1684** *Contempl. State of Man* I. ii. (1699) 16 Croesus..failed but little of being burnt alive. **1724** SWIFT *Drapier's Lett.* iv, That pernicious Counsel of sending base money hither very narrowly failed of losing the Kingdom. **1771** GOLDSM. *Hist. Eng.* II. 216 A weak prince..seldom fails of having his authority despised.

III. To fall short in performance or attainment.

9. a. *intr.* To make default; to be a defaulter; to come short of performing one's duty or functions.

1340 *Ayenb.* 173 Yef he faileþ at his rekeninge: god nele naȝt faly at his. **1389** in *Eng. Gilds* (1870) 30 And qwo falye, schal payen thre pound of wax. **1471** EARL WARWICK in *12th Rep. Hist. MSS. Comm.* App. IV. I. 4, I pray you ffayle not now. **1535** STEWART *Cron. Scot.* III. 394 Desyrand..To mak redres als far as tha had faillit. **1551** *Act Mary* (1814) 488 Gif ony Lord..failȝeis and brekis the said act. **1611** BIBLE *Job* xxi. 10 Their bull gendereth, and faileth not. **1667** MILTON *P.L.* VIII. 534 Nature fail'd in mee. **1875** JOWETT *Plato* (ed. 2) III. 324 No one will be less likely..to fail in his religious duties.

†**b.** *trans.* To make default in; to break. *Obs.*

c **1500** *Melusine* 12 Fals kinge, thou hast fayllled thy couenaunt. *a* **1653** GOUGE *Comm. Heb.* iii. 5 It is a great crime to fail trust. **1784** COWPER *Tirocin.* 293 These menageries all fail their trust.

†**c.** To disappoint (expectation). *Obs.* Cf. 5.

1634 HEYWOOD *Lanc. Witches* I. Wks. 1874 IV. 178 Your Vncle..Hath failed your expectation. **1651** GATAKER in *Fuller's Abel Rediv.*, *Whitaker* 403 Neither did he therein either faile their estimation, or [etc.]. **1699** W. DAMPIER *Voy.* II. I. 105 Not altogether to fail the Readers expectation, I shall give a brief account.

10. a. *trans.* To leave undone, omit to perform, miss (some customary or expected action). *Obs.* exc. with *inf.* as object.

1393 GOWER *Conf.* I. 352 To mordre who that woll assente He may nought faile to repente. **1485** CAXTON *Chas. Gt.* 29 He fayllled not to doo gretely hys deuoyr in sacrifyses & oblacions. **1523** LD. BERNERS *Froiss.* I. ccxliii. 362 We commaunde you..that this be nat fayled, in as hasty wyse as ye can. **1529** WOLSEY in Ellis *Orig. Lett.* I. 102 II. 2 Fayle not therfor to be here thys nygth. **1611** BIBLE *1 Sam.* ii. 16 Let them not faile to burne the fat presently. **1719** DE FOE *Crusoe* I. v. (1840) 87 My morning Walk with my Gun, which I seldom failed. **1810** SCOTT *Lady of L.* III. xi, Burst be the ear that fails to heed. **1885** C. J. MATHEW in *Law Times' Rep.* LIII. 779/1 He failed to keep his word.

†**b.** with gerund as object. Also, *to fail of.*

1723 *Pres. State Russia* I. 105 Such corrupt Habits as could not fail producing an Aversion to him. **1749** FIELDING *Tom Jones* II. ii, Thomas..whom he had hitherto seldom failed of visiting at least once a Day.

c. With *inf.* as object, of a thing, circumstance, situation, influence: not to have the effect of, not to result in (doing something) (usu. in negative const.).

1920 *Eng. Hist. Rev.* Jan. 143 Turenne..was a protestant, a circumstance which could not fail to prejudice Louis.

†**11. a.** *intr.* To be at fault; to miss the mark, go astray, err. Const. *of, from. Obs.*

c **1290** *S. Eng. Leg.* I. 95/103 þou faillest of þin art. *a* **1340** HAMPOLE *Psalter* xi. 1 Vnnethes ere any funden þat failes noght fra halynes. **1393** LANGL. *P. Pl.* C. XXIII. 31 And *spiritus prudencie* in menye poynt shal fayle Of þat he weneþ wolde falle. *c* **1440** *York Myst.* xxiii. 210 In ȝoure faith fayland. **1538** STARKEY *England* I. iv. 119 The ordur of our law also in the punnyschment of theft..faylyth much from gud cyvylyte. **1590** SIR J. SMYTH *Disc. Weapons* 17 b, If..Mosquettiers in taking their sights, doo faile but the lengthe of a wheate corne in the height of their point.

†**b.** *trans.* To miss (a mark, one's footing, etc.). Also, *to fail of. Obs.*

1375 BARBOUR *Bruce* III. 123 He lansyt furth delyuerly, Swa that the tothir failȝeit fete. *c* **1430** *Syr Tryam.* 1220 He faylyd of hym, hys hors he hytt. **1470–85** MALORY *Arthur* IX. xxxv, The hors fayled footynge, and felle in the Ryuer. **1523** LD. BERNERS *Froiss* I. clxiii. 201 He fayled nat the Englysshe Knyght, for he strake hym. **1568** GRAFTON *Chron.* II. 338 He had thought to have lept agayne to his horse, but he fayled of the Styrop.

†**c.** *trans.* To come short of; to miss, not to obtain. Also *absol. Obs.*

1377 LANGL. *P. Pl.* B. XI. 25 þe freke þat folwed my wille failled neuere blisse. **1393** *Ibid.* C. III. 159 Gyue gold al a-boute..to notaries þat non of hem faille.

12. a. *intr.* To be unsuccessful in an attempt or enterprise. Const. *to* with *inf.*; also *in.* Said of persons; occas. of the means.

1340 HAMPOLE *Pr. Consc.* 1463 Now we fande our force, now we fail. *c* **1385** CHAUCER *L.G.W.* 1646 *Hipsiph. & M.*, He shal nat fayle The fles to wynne. **1523** LD. BERNERS *Froiss.* I. clxiii. 201 And thenglyshe knight thought to haue striken hym with his speare in the targe, but he fayled. **1609** SKENE *Reg. Maj.* 116 Albeit he faillie in probation of the remanent exceptions. **1667** MILTON *P.L.* VII. 139 Our envious Foe hath fail'd. **1732** LAW *Serious C.* viii. (ed. 2) 112 Poor Tradesmen that had fail'd in their business. **1775** BURKE *Sp. Conc. Amer.* Wks. III. 47 Conciliation failing, no further hope of reconciliation is left. **1796** H. HUNTER tr. *St.-Pierre's Stud. Nat.* (1799) II. 254 They scarcely ever fail to bring out fish. **1842** TENNYSON *Gardener's Dau.* 31 You scarce can fail to match his master-piece. **1878** JEVONS *Prim. Pol. Econ.* 60 Some occupations..can be taken up by men who fail in other work.

b. Of an action, design, etc.: To miscarry, not to succeed.

c **1394** *P. Pl. Crede* 98 My purpos is i-failed. *c* **1450** *Why I can't be a nun* 151 in *E.E.P.* (1862) 142 My techyng may not fayle. **1610** SHAKS. *Temp.* Epil. 12 My project failes. **1874** GREEN *Short Hist.* iii. 148 A revolt which failed..through the desertion of their head. **1883** SIR N. LINDLEY in *Law Rep.* 25 Ch. Div. 355 His action..would fail, and he would have to pay the costs.

c. Of crops, seeds, etc.: To be abortive or unproductive.

1297 R. GLOUC. (1724) 414 Frute faylede all þulke ȝer, & heruest late also. *c* **1325** *E.E. Allit. P.* A. 34 So semly a sede moȝt fayly not. **1611** BIBLE *2 Esdras*, Their seedes shall faile, through the blasting, and haile. **1657** AUSTEN *Fruit Trees* I. 48 Chuse not those [Grafts] that are very small, they commonly fayle. **1712** MORTIMER *Husb.* II. ii. 9 He thinks that very few [Grains] failed. **1847** TENNYSON *Princ.* 124 The year in which our olives fail'd.

d. *to fail of*: to come short of obtaining or meeting with (an object desired), or of accomplishing or attaining (a purpose, etc.). Now *rare* exc. with gerund or *vbl. sb.*

a **1225** *Ancr. R.* 404 Ase þauh a mon þet heuede longe i-swunken and failede..a last, of his hure. *c* **1315** SHOREHAM 3 Yf thou nelt nauȝt climme thos, Of hevene thou hest y-fayled. **1398** TREVISA *Barth. De P.R.* XII. iii. (1495) 412 Yf she faylyth..of the pray that she resyth to. **1470–85** MALORY *Arthur* II. x, He fayled of his stroke, and smote the hors neck. **1577** HANMER *Anc. Eccl. Hist.* (1619) 145 Some failed of the purposed end. **1646** SIR T. BROWNE *Pseud. Ep.* I. x. 39 Fayling of his first attempt to be but like the highest in heaven. **1713** STEELE *Guardian* No. 17 ¶7 His man never failed of bringing in his prey. **1737** JOHNSON *Let.* 12 July in *Boswell*, Could not fail of a favourable reception. **1815** W. H. IRELAND *Scribbleomania* 165 She never can fail of bewitching the reader. **1844** H. ROGERS *Ess.* I. ii. 83 To fail of part of the admiration due to other endowments. **1875** JOWETT *Plato* (ed. 2) IV. 249 Mere perception does not reach being, and therefore fails of truth.

13. To become insolvent or bankrupt. Said of individuals and of mercantile houses, banks, etc.

1682 SCARLETT *Exchanges* 127 If that Endorser fail and be insolvent. *a* **1734** NORTH *Lives* (1826) III. 291 Mills, with his auctioneering, atlasses, and projects, failed. **1796** *Hull Advertiser* 25 June 2/3 Twelve capital houses have failed in different parts of Italy. **1868** BENTLEY *Wealth & Politics* II. 81 Thirty-one banks failed in little more than three months.

14. a. *intr.* To be unsuccessful in an examination, to be 'plucked'. **b.** *trans.* (*colloq.*) Of an examiner: To report (a candidate) as having failed; to 'pluck'.

1884 *Pall Mall G.* 6 Mar. 11 He 'fails' them all, turns to mistress, 'Your children are perfect idiots'.

c. *trans.* To be unsuccessful in (an examination).

1906 *Westm. Gaz.* 22 Apr. 3/1 Such [*sc.* Indian] men applying for positions write, 'I am a failed B.A.'. **1909** H. G. WELLS *Tono-Bungay* III. ii. 244 He failed some dreadful examination and had to go into the militia. **1925** E. WALLACE *Mind of Mr. J. G. Reeder* v. 168 He..had a sketchy knowledge of the law (on his visiting cards was the inscription 'Failed LL.B.'). **1971** *Daily Tel.* 7 Oct. 2/2 The RIBA said that students in the five schools were failing examinations because of low teaching standards.

IV. †**15.** *trans. nonce-use.* To deceive, cheat (L. *fallĕre*).

1590 SPENSER *F.Q.* III. xi. 46 So lively and so like that living sence it fayld.

†**'failable,** *a. Obs.* [f. FAIL *v.* + -ABLE.] Liable to fail or give way; unreliable.

1561 EDEN *Arte Navig.* Pref. ¶iij b, Such signes are fayleable. **1576** *Tyde Tarryeth no Man* in J. P. Collier *Illustr. Eng. Pop. Lit.* xvi. 70 It is a thing but fayleable and vayne. **1649** BLITHE *Eng. Improv. Impr.* (1653) 129 This [plan] was yet never failable to me since I found it.

†**'failance.** *Obs.* [f. as prec. + -ANCE. Cf. OF. *faillance.*] The quality or fact of failing; failure, neglect, falling off; an instance of the same. *in failance of*: for lack of.

1612 HAYWARD *Ann. Eliz.* (Camden) 9 The fayleance whereof would eyther change or abate theyr loves. **1622** PEACHAM *Compl. Gent.* xx. (1634) 240 Such pawse..as may afforde you meanes to discerne any failance. **1667** *Decay Chr. Piety* Pref. 195 Disquisitions about our failances and aberrations. **1674** tr. *Scheffer's Lapland* xxvii. 125 They use the root of a kind of moss..or in the failance of that, the stalke of Angelica. **1686** GOAD *Celest. Bodies* I. xii. 60 What else..should make the Success equiponderate with the Failance?

failed (feɪld), *ppl. a.* Also 5 *Sc.* failȝeit, 6 *Sc.* faillit. [f. FAIL *v.* + -ED¹.]

1. Decayed, worn out. Chiefly, of a person: Impaired in health or vigour; infirm.

1490 CAXTON *Eneydos* iv. 19 A persone..nyghe alle faylled and deed. **1496** *Acc. Ld. High Treasurer* (1877) I. 324 Ane ald failȝeit preist. **1535** STEWART *Cron. Scot.* II. 683 Malcome.. The kirk of Durhame foundit of stone and lyme, That faillit wes. **1816** SCOTT *Antiq.* xxv, After striking a few strokes, he..said to his companion, 'I'm auld and failed now, and canna keep at it'. **1880** *Antrim & Down Gloss.*, *Failed*..in impaired health.

2. Unsuccessful. Also, Bankrupt, insolvent.

1655 *Nicholas Papers* (Camden) II. 344 The late failed designe. **1869** *Daily News* 4 Jan., Similar proceedings were stopped in another failed company. **1871** RUSKIN *Fors Clav.* vii. 17 If we ever..chance to catch hold of any failed bankers. **1889** *Pall Mall G.* 25 Nov. 6/2 Failed books..were sent off to the colonies.

failer ('feɪlə(r)). [f. as prec. + -ER¹.] One who fails, in senses of the vb.

1362 LANGL. *P. Pl.* A. II. 99 Fals is a faytur, a faylere or werkes. *c* **1690** *Roxb. Ball.* VII. 181 Cabbidge..of which you are no failer. **1728** in *Memorabilia Domestica* (1889) 12 To be paid by the party failer to the party performer. **1796** *Mod. Gulliver's Trav.* 159 'Tis easy! and..Wou'd give the honest failer halcyon days. **1884** BROWNING *Ferishtah* (ed. 3) 143 On his sole head, failer or succeeder, Lay the blame or lit the praise.

failer, obs. f. of FAILURE.

failȝe, obs. Sc. form of FAIL.

failing ('feɪlɪŋ), *vbl. sb.* [f. as prec. + -ING¹.]

1. The action of the vb. FAIL, in various senses; an instance of this, a failure. †*for, without* (*any*) *failing* = for, without fail (see FAIL *sb.*¹).

1382 WYCLIF *Isa.* v. 27 Ther is not failing ne trauailyng in hym. **1398** TREVISA *Barth. De P.R.* VII. xxv. (1495) 241 Rotyd moysture comyth vp of the stomak..and therof comyth..fayllynge of teeth. *c* **1410** *Sir Cleges* 375 He thowght with hym to speke Wythout any faylynge. **1526** *Pilgr. Perf.* (W. de W. 1531) 150 This..meltyng of the soule the prophet Dauid calleth a faylynge of the spiryte. **1577** B. GOOGE *Heresbach's Husb.* IV. (1586) 185 b, [Of bees] There are sundry kinges bredde for failing. **1611** BIBLE *Deut.* xxviii. 65 The Lord shall giue thee..failing of eyes, & sorrow of minde. **1622** R. HAWKINS *Voy. S. Sea* (1847) 127 The waight in the head and sterne by fayling of the water, began to open her plankes in the middest. **1671** J. COSIN *Corr.* 23 May, Your apprehension of my failing before the Great Chapter-day. **1727** CHAMBERS *Cycl.* s.v. *Bankruptcy*, A failing, breaking or stopping of payment, diminishes the merchant's credit..When a merchant, etc., fails to appear at the exchange, etc., without apparent reason, it is called a failing of presence.

2. A defect, fault, shortcoming, weakness.

1590 SIR J. SMYTH *Disc. Weapons* 21 b, All which unreadynesses, and failings. **1612** BRINSLEY *Lud. Lit.* 179 My selfe to supplie their wants and faylings. **1651** BAXTER *Inf. Bapt.* 94 Not aggravating failings, but hoping all things. **1770** GOLDSM. *Des. Vill.* 164 E'en his failings lean'd to Virtue's side. **1843** PRESCOTT *Mexico* VII. v. (1864) 459 His bigotry, the failing of the age. **1876** J. H. NEWMAN *Hist. Sk.* I. II. iv. 257 Want of firmness has been repeatedly mentioned as his [Cicero's] principal failing.

failing ('feɪlɪŋ), *ppl. a.* Also 4 failand, faylande, *Sc.* falȝeand. [f. as prec. + -ING².]

1. That fails, in the senses of the vb.

a **1300** *Cursor M.* 28844 (Cott.) Failand frute comis o þat tan. *c* **1375** *Sc. Leg. Saints, Andreas* 961 Fore þis joy falȝeand þu Ay-lestand joy has chosine nov. **1435** MISYN *Fire of Loue* (E.E.T.S.) 9 þingis transitory & faylynge. **1667** MILTON *P.L.* IX. 404 O..much failing, hapless Eve. **1719** DE FOE *Crusoe* (1840) II. xiv. 293 My never-failing old pilot..had a pistol. **1879** FROUDE *Cæsar* xiv. 204 Axes..of soft iron, fair to the eye and failing to the stroke. **1885** *Law Times' Rep.* LII. 648/2 Plowright was..in failing health.

†2. *Astron.* Of a planet: Remote *from* some fixed point. *Obs.*

c **1391** CHAUCER *Astrol.* II. §4 If [a planet] passe the bondes of thise forseide spaces, a-boue or by-nethe..they sein þat the planete is failling fro the assendent.

Hence '**failingly** *adv.*, '**failingness**.

1631 *Celestina* IV. 49 That failingnesse of force and of strength. **1847** CRAIG, *Failingly*, by failing. **1880** M. CROMMELIN *Black Abbey* I. xii. 163 The poor Tom-boy.. struggled, failingly, to join in Hector's ever-manlier pursuits.

failing ('feɪlɪŋ), *prep.* [The pr. pple. of FAIL *v.*, used either with intrans. sense in concord with the following sb. or pron. (*failing this* = 'if this fail'), or in trans. sense with the sb. etc. as object (*failing this* = 'if one fail this').] In default of.

1810 H. T. COLEBROOKE *2 Treat. Hindu Law Inher.* 225 In default of these, the heritage goes to the son of the..aunt. Or, failing him, it passes, etc. **1818** WORDSWORTH in *Wks.* 1876 I. 241 Many must have opportunities of knowing him; or failing that intimate knowledge, we require, etc. **1843** CARLYLE *Past & Present* 92 Failing all else, what gossip about one another. **1859** DASENT *Pop. Tales Norse* Introd. p. xlv, By clinging..to some king or hero..or, failing that, to some squire's family.

faille (faɪj, feɪl). Also 6 faile or fayle. [a. F. *faille* in same senses.]

†1. A kind of head-dress. *Obs.*

1530 PALSGR. 218/2 Fayle, an upparmost garment of a woman. **1694** EARL PERTH *Lett.* (Camden) 30 A faille..is a great scarf of tafita for the best, and of worsted for others.

2. A light kind of ribbed silk fabric.

faille française has a larger rib than faille proper, being thus intermediate between this and 'ottoman'. More recently the term *wool faille* has been applied to a kind of 'terry'.

1869 *Le Follet*, Feb., *Faille* is very fashionable for long dress. **1878–9** A. BARLOW *Weaving* 396 The most important of these manufactures comprise..'Failles', black. **1887** *Yng. Ladies Jrnl.* XXX. 122 The bonnet is of cream faille. **1888** *Bow Bells Weekly* 13 Jan., The train is in full folds of yellow tulle over yellow faille. **1889** *Daily News* 24 July 5/5 The finest and softest corded silk, of the sort known technically as faille française.

faille(n, failly, faillie, obs. ff. of FAIL.

failure ('feɪljʊə(r)). Also 7 failer, fayler, failour, faileur, failler, failȝour, faylor. [First in 17th c. in form *failer*, a. AF. *failer*, for F. *faillir* to FAIL; see quot. 1641, and cf. law terms like *cesser*, *trover*. Subsequently the ending was variously confused with the suffixes -OR, -OUR, -URE, but the original form did not become obsolete until the end of the century.] The fact of failing.

1. A failing to occur, be performed, or be produced; an omitting to perform something due or required; default.

[**1641** *Termes de la Ley* 154 Failer de Record est quant un Action est port envers un, & le defendant plede [etc.].. Donques il est dit pur failer de son Record.] **1643** PRYNNE *Sov. Power Parl.* I. (ed. 2) 33 There would necessarily follow ..a fayler of Justice in the highest Court of Justice. **1645** PAGITT *Heresiogr.* (1661) 307 Consecrated here in London by the Reverend Fathers of this Church, through failer of a Bishop surviving in that. **1648** FAIRFAX *Remonstrance* 31 How easie it is to finde, or pretend a failer of full performance. **1652** HEYLIN *Cosmogr.*..On the failer [*ed.* **1682** faileur] of his Line. **1673** *Essex Papers* (Camden) I. 65 Haveinge all Titular Arch Bps..comded by Proclaon to depart this Kingdom, & on their Faylor to be proceeded against. **1767** BLACKSTONE *Comm.* II. 237 On failure of the descendants of John Stiles himself, the issue of Geoffrey and Lucy Stiles, his parents, is called in. **1832** SOUTHEY *Hist. Penins. War* III. 80 To preserve to..Ferdinand VII, all his dominions, and, in his failure, to his legitimate successors. **1841** ELPHINSTONE *Hist. Ind.* I. 67 On the failure of issue.. an adopted son succeeds. **1885** *Act 48–9 Vict.* c. 72 §5 A failure of justice will take place if the leave [to appeal] is not granted.

†b. A lapse, a slight fault; a failing, infirmity. *Obs.*

a **1656** USSHER *Ann.* v. (1658) 73 Thorough failler of memory, or false copying. **1660** R. COKE *Power & Subj.* 270 In regard of the ordinary failures of the Press..the Reader is desired to correct these faults before hee begin. **1689** *Col. Rec. Pennsylv.* I. 262 An unwilling faylor and error in their proceedings. **1702** *Eng. Theophrast.* 323 This [envy] is the basest and most ungenerous of all our natural failures. *a* **1716** SOUTH *Serm.* (1737) I. viii. 299 He owed his death to ..a little inadvertency and failure of memory.

2. The fact of becoming exhausted or running short, giving way under trial, breaking down in health, declining in strength or activity, etc.

1695 WOODWARD *Nat. Hist.* iii. §1. 152 There then must needs have been an universal failure and want of Springs and Rivers all the Summer-Season. **1793** SMEATON *Edystone L.* §259 We concluded the failure had been in the Forelock of the bolt. **1841** MISS MITFORD in L'Estrange *Life* III. viii. 126 The mind gone..utter failure of intellect. **1885** *Weekly Notes* 28 Mar. 67/2 The house had become uninhabitable through the failure of the water-supply.

3. The fact of failing to effect one's purpose; want of success; an instance of this.

1643 NETHERSOLE *Proj. for Peace* (1648) 19 The failer of the timely discovery..happened..through your..default. **1667** LD. DIGBY *Elvira* v. 82, I..th'other day, could scarce o'ercome The sense of a slight failour. **1686** GOAD *Celest. Bodies* III. iv. 509 All the Exceptions and Failers will lye, upon the account of ♃. **1800** MALONE *Dryden* I. II. 505 By his failure in that work he might lose the reputation which he had gained. **1874** GREEN *Short Hist.* v. 219 The failure of his foreign hopes threw Edward on the resources of England. **1878** SEELEY *Stein* II. 327 We see efforts ending in feebleness and failure.

b. *concr.* A thing or person that proves unsuccessful.

1837 DICKENS *Pickw.* ii, This attack was a failure also. **1865** MILL in *Morn. Star* 6 July, If you elect me and I should turn out a failure. **1883** *Ch. Times* 9 Nov. 813/2 Lutheranism has been from the very first a conspicuous religious failure. **1889** *Academy* 1 June 369/1 The general result of efforts directed to this end is the production of.. educated failures.

4. The fact of failing in business; bankruptcy, insolvency.

1702 *Lond. Gaz.* No. 3791/4 Divers Failures have.. happened among the Traders in this City. **1709** STEELE *Tatler* No. 5 ¶5 The Bankers of Geneva were utterly ruined by the Failure of Mr. Bernard. **1796** *Hull Advertiser* 25 June 2/3 Two of these failures have occurred at Milan. **1861** PATTISON *Ess.* (1889) I. 41 A few years later..came the failure of the great Italian bankers.

†'**failyie**. *Sc. Obs.* Also 6 failȝe, (7 *printed* failzie). [a. OF. *faille*: see FAIL *sb.*] **a.** Failure, non-performance; also, an instance of this. **b.** Consequent liability to a penalty.

1551 *Sc. Acts Mary* (1814) 488 He sall content and pay for euerie failȝie [of ane act] ane hundreth markis. **1552** LYNDESAY *Monarche* 5760 The fraudfull failȝeis Off Schireffis, Prouestis, and of Bailȝeis. **1640–1** *Kirkcudbr. War-Comm. Min. Bk.* (1855) 40 Ane thousand merks, to be peyit to the Committie..in case of failzie. *a* **1670** SPALDING *Troub. Chas. I* (1792) II. 225 It was a snare devised to draw gentlemen under failzies.

fain (feɪn), *a.* and *adv.* Forms: α. 1 fæȝen, fæȝn, 3 fæin, fein, vein, vayn, 3–6 fayn(e, (5 faynne), 4 (fyne), 4–5 feyn(e, 4–7 faine, 5 fyene, 5–6 fane, 6 faint, (fayen, feene), (7–9 feign), 3– fain. Also compar. 3 fenre. β. 3–4 faȝe(n, 3 vawe, 4–5 fawe(n, (5 faue). [OE. *fæȝen*, *fæȝn* = OS. *fagan*, *fagin*, ON. *feginn*; allied to OE. *ȝeféon* (pa. t. *feah*), OHG. (*gi-*) *fehan* (pa. t. *fah*) to rejoice.]

A. *adj.*

1. Glad, rejoiced, well-pleased. Often in phrases, ***full fain, glad and fain***. Const. *of*; also followed by *inf.* or *subord. cl.* Now chiefly *dial.* or *poet.*

α. *Beowulf* 1633 Ferdon forð þonon feþelastum ferhþum fæȝne. *c* **888** ÆLFRED *Boeth.* xl. §5 Ic bio swiþe fæȝn ȝif ðu me lædest þider ic ðe bidde. *c* **1205** LAY. 4891 Þe duc þer fore fain wes. *a* **1300** *Cursor M.* 20452 (Cott.), I am ful fain yee ar me mid. **1340** HAMPOLE *Pr. Consc.* 4552 Of þair dede þai sal be fayn. *c* **1420** *Chron. Vilod.* 974 Bot þen was þis wrechede mon full fayne. *c* **1460** *Towneley Myst.* 84 Now in hart fulle fane. **1535** STEWART *Cron. Scot.* II. 589 He..of thair cuming wes so glaid and fane. *a* **1569** KINGESMYLL *Man's Est.* i. (1580) 7 He is very faine of the findyng of suche a fielde. **1591** SHAKS. *1 Hen. VI*, III. ii. 114 Are glad and faine by flight to saue themselues. **1640** J. DYKE *Worthy Commun.* 56 Then full faine wilt thou be to have Christ Jesus receive thy soule. **1664** *Floddan F.* vii. 65 And of his welfare all were fain. **1787** BURNS *Twa Dogs* 137 My heart has been sae fain to see them. **1801** WORDSW. *Cuckoo & Night.* xxvi, I should be wondrous fain That shamefully they one and all were slain. **1863** MRS. GASKELL *Sylvia's L.* I. 195 My master is quite fain of his company. **1876** MORRIS *Sigurd* III. 176 And fain and full was my heart.

β. **1297** R. GLOUC. (1724) 218 So þat hii mette hem þer, boþe hii were wel vawe. *c* **1380** *Sir Ferumb.* 3800 War-for y am wel fawe.

b. *Proverb.*

1471 RIPLEY *Comp. Alch.* v. in Ashm. (1652) 157 Fayre promys makyth folys fayne. **1579** LYLY *Euphues* (Arb.) 69 There may you see..the faire wordes that make fooles faine. **1829** SCOTT *Anne of G.* iv. Fine words to make foolish maidens fain.

2. Const. *to* with *inf.* Glad under the circumstances; glad or content to take a certain course in default of opportunity for anything better, or as the lesser of two evils.

α. *c* **1330** R. BRUNNE *Chron.* (1725) 28 Þei were fayn to ask pes. **1393** GOWER *Conf.* III. 230 He was faine him self to save. **1559** in Strype *Ann. Ref.* I. App. ix. 26 They were faine to patche uppe the matter with a little piece of paper clapped over the foresaid wordes. **1593** SHAKS. *2 Hen. VI*, II. i. 153, I must be faine to pawne..my Plate. **1631** GOUGE *God's Arrows* ii. §26. 170 Men were faine to eate horse-flesh. **1693** LOCKE *Education* §89. 105 Castalio was fain to make Trenchers at Basle to keep himself from starving. **1812** COMBE (Dr. Syntax) *Picturesque* XVI. (Chandos) 60 Pleas'd with the prospect he was feign To yawn, and go to sleep again. **1839** THIRLWALL *Greece* VII. liv. 52 He was fain to take shelter in a canal. **1882** MISS BRADDON *Mt. Royal* II. vi. 115 Christabel was fain to make the best of her life at Mount Royal.

β. *c* **1330** *Arth. & Merl.* 208 To fle sone he was wel fawe.

b. This passes gradually into the sense: Necessitated, obliged.

1513 MORE *Rich. III* in Grafton *Chron.* II. 785 Pinkye.. so loste his voyce, that he was fayne to leave off. **1579** FENTON *Guicciard.* II. (1599) 75 Lodowyke..was feene with teares to acknowledge his cowardize. **1676** HALE *Contempl.* I. 103 In this condition, he is fain to bear his burdensom Cross towards the place of his Execution. *a* **1682** SIR T. BROWNE *Tracts* 7 Many plants are mentioned in Scripture under such names as they are fain to be rendred by analogy. **1685** H. MORE *Paralip. Proph.* 315 A Cannon of so vast a bigness, that it was fain to be drawn by seventy yoke of Oxen. **1722** SEWEL *Hist. Quakers* (1795) I. Pref. 23, I have been fain to trust the oversight..of my work to others. **1841** D'ISRAELI *Amen. Lit.* (1867) 360 Ascham, indeed, was fain to apologise for having written in English. **1884** F. M. CRAWFORD *Rom. Singer* I. 93 He was fain to acknowledge that she was right.

3. Disposed, inclined or willing, eager. Const. †*of*, †*for*, *to* with *inf. arch.* or *dial.*

c **1205** LAY. 6994 For elchen vuele he wes fein. **1340–70** *Alex. & Dind.* 237 So it farus bi folk þat fain is to teche. *a* **1605** MONTGOMERIE *Natur passis Nurriture* 34 To fang his friendship they war fane. **1802** R. ANDERSON *Cumberld. Ball.* 32 The..sleet and snaw are nought at aw, If yen were fain to gang! **1851** GALLENGA *Mariotti's Italy* 75 The gentle and respectful behaviour of the soldiery in what they were fain to look upon as a land of conquest. **1884** W. C. SMITH *Kildrostan* 83 Vain for a man to think that he Can hide what a woman is fain to know!

†b. Apt, wont. *Obs.*

1596 SPENSER *F.Q.* IV. viii. 37 Whose steadie hand was faine his steed to guyde. **1650** JER. TAYLOR *Holy Living* i. §1. 7 To a busie man temptation is fain to climbe up together with his businesses.

†4. Well-disposed, favourable. Const. *of* or *dat.* Also in phr. ***fair and fain***. *Obs.*

c **1205** LAY. 12719 Lauer king Aldroein Ofte þe wurðe godd fæin [*c* **1275** fain]. *c* **1305** *11,000 Virgins* 134 in *E.E.P.* (1862) 69 Ourse of britaigne þo hi fonde such a creatoure, so fair & so fayne. *c* **1440** *Sir Gowther* 679 Fader, and Sone, and Holy Gost, Of owre sowles be fayne. [*a* **1850** ROSSETTI *Dante & Circ.* I. (1874) 77, I..saw Love coming towards me, fair and fain.]

B. *adv.* Gladly, willingly, with pleasure. Frequent in ***I, he,*** etc. ***would*** (†***had***) ***fain***; otherwise *Obs.* or *arch.*

α. *c* **1175** *Lamb. Hom.* 35 Ic walde fein pinian and sitten on forste and on snawe. *a* **1225** *Ancr. R.* 192 Vor uein wolde þe hexte cwemen ou. *c* **1290** *S. Eng. Leg.* 272/53, I chulle þe telle fayn. *c* **1440** *York Myst.* xx. 121 And if þou wolde neuere so fayne. **1483** CAXTON *Gold. Leg.* 430/3 The soppes

of which he fayne ete. **1513** DOUGLAS *Æneis* IX. iv. 64 To bring agane Eneas full fane thai wald. **1523** LD. BERNERS *Froiss.* I. cxxv. 151 The kyng..demaunded of them whyther they wolde faynest go. **1590** SPENSER *F.Q.* I. iv. 10 A mirrhour..Wherein her face she often vewed fayne. **1610** SHAKS. *Temp.* I. i. 72, I would faine dye a dry death. **1709** BERKELEY *Th. Vision* §86, I would fain know wherein consists that sharpness. **1801** SOUTHEY *Thalaba* X. iv, He full fain would sleep. **1858** NEALE *Bernard de M.* 32 My spirit seeks thee fain. **1874** MORLEY *Compromise* (1886) 85 Those who would fain divide the community into two great castes. **1876** MORRIS *Sigurd* III. 173 She..kisseth her sweet and fain. **1880** MISS BROUGHTON *Sec. Th.* II. vii, She had fainer not.

β. *c* **1330** *King of Tars* 1058 Ageyn the soudan he gan hyghe, And wolde hym sle ful fawe. *c* **1380** *Sir Ferumb.* 308 Þanne wolde þay wel faȝe, ȝif þei miȝt helpe to þat sir Olyuer hadde be slaȝe.

†**fain**, *sb. Obs.* [f. prec.] Gladness, joy.

c **1340** *Cursor M.* 3852 (Laud MS.) Laban then he did to calle for fayne of hym his frendis alle. *c* **1400** *Ywaine & Gaw.* 2086 Alsone als he saw him stand For fayn he liked fote and hand. *c* **1440** *Bone Flor.* 844 Syr Garcy went crowlande for fayne.

†**fain**, *v.*¹ *Obs.* Forms: 1 **fæȝenian, fæȝnian, fahnian,** 2 **faȝenien,** 3 **faȝnien, fainen,** (**fawe**), 3–6 **fayne,** (4 **feyn**), 3–7 **faine.** See also FAWN *v.* [OE. *fæȝnian, fæȝenian* (f. *fæȝen*, FAIN) = ON. *fagna*, OS. *faganôn, faginôn*, OHG. *faginôn, feginôn*, Goth. *faginôn*.]

1. *intr.* To be delighted or glad, rejoice. Const. *of* (earlier *genitive*), *on, in*; with *to* and *inf.* also, to desire, wish.

c **888** ÆLFRED *Boeth.* xxx. §1 Ne sceal he..to unȝemetlice fæȝnian ðæs folces worda. *a* **1000** *Boeth. Metr.* i. 66 Fæȝnodon ealle. *c* **1000** *Ags. Gosp.* Mark xiv. 11 Þa hi þis ȝehyrdon hi fahnodon [*c* **1160** *Hatton G.* fageneden]. *c* **1200** *Trin. Coll. Hom.* 135 Fele shule faȝenien on his burde. *c* **1205** LAY. 21843 Þa fainede swiðe folc an hirede Of Arðures cume. *a* **1240** *Ureisun* in *Cott. Hom.* 199 ȝif þu wult hit iðauien iwis he wule ðurchut fawe. *a* **1300** *E.E. Psalter* v. 12 And fayne sal alle þat hope in þe. *a* **1340** HAMPOLE *Psalter* xxxi. 14 Ffaynes in lord & glades rightwis. *c* **1380** WYCLIF *Serm.* Sel. Wks. I. 246 Clerkis shulde..feyn to be discharged of erþeli goodis. *a* **1400–50** *Alexander* 1745 Feyne all with fairnes & fayne at þou may. *c* **1450** *Mirour Saluacioun* 417 And thogh some tyme be gude the werld make man to fayne. **1596** SPENSER *F.Q.* V. xii. 36 [She] faynes to weave false tales.

b. To pretend kindness. Cf. FAWN *v.*

a **1225** *Ancr. R.* 194 Hwonne ou ne wonteð nowiht, þeonne ueineð he mid ou.

2. *trans.* To make glad. Hence to welcome (a person); also, to congratulate (const. *of*).

c **1250** *Gen. & Ex.* 1441 Eliezer..broȝt him a wif..He faȝnede hire wið milde mod. *a* **1300** *E.E. Psalter* xlii[i]. 4 God þat faines mi youthede al. *a* **1375** *Joseph Arim.* 243 þei ..faynede me wiþ wordes, Bote þei hateden me. *a* **1400–50** *Alexander* 2 Fayn wold þai here Sum farand þing efter fode to fayn þere her[t]. **1480** *Robt. Devyll* 10 Of hys companye no man us fayne.

3. To rejoice in, enjoy; also, to take to gladly, show preference for. *rare.*

1483 CAXTON *Cato* E viij, I wyl not that ye..suppose that ..synnars faynen [L. *lucrari*] theyr synnes wythout to haue ..punycyon..in thys world or in the other. **1606** WARNER *Alb. Eng.* XVI. ci. (1612) 399 The sprewsest Citie-Lads for her would faine the Countrie-aire.

Hence †'**faining** *ppl. a.*, gladsome, affectionate; also, longing, wistful.

c **1400** *Destr. Troy* 12732 Clunestra..Resayuit hym.. With a faynond fare. **1596** SPENSER *Hymns, Hon. Love* 216 His heavens queene..in his fayning eye Whose sole aspect he counts felicitye.

fain (feɪn), *v.*² Chiefly *School slang*, orig. *dial.* = FEN *v.*² Used in the expression *fains* or *fain(s I, fain it, fainit(e)s*: see quots.

1870 *N. & Q.* 4th Ser. VI. 415/2 'Fains', or 'Fain it'—A term demanding a 'truce' during the progress of any game, which is always granted by the opposing party. *Ibid.* 517/1 A boy who had 'killed' another at marbles, that is hit his marble, would call out 'Fain it', meaning 'You mustn't shoot at me in return'; or if a boy was going to shoot, and some inequality of surface was in his way, which he would have cleared away, his antagonist would prevent him by calling out 'Fain clears'. *Ibid.* 517/2 If a prefect wants anything fetched for him and does not say by whom, those who wish to get off going say 'Fain I'. **1889** BARRÈRE & LELAND *Dict. Slang, Faints* [*sic*], in vogue among schoolboys to express a wish temporarily to withdraw from participation in the particular sport or game being played. **1891** FARMER *Slang*, Fains! Fainits! Fain it! **1913** C. MACKENZIE *Sinister St.* I. I. vii. 103 He could shout 'fain I' to be rid of an obligation and 'bags I' to secure an advantage. **1927** W. E. COLLINSON *Contemp. English* 14 The custom of putting oneself out of the game altogether by crossing the fingers and saying pax! or faynights! [feinaits] or both together. **1948** J. BETJEMAN *Coll. Poems* (1958) 150 'I'd rather not.' 'Fains I.' 'It's up to you.' **1960** *Guardian* 1 July 9/7 The Englishman..could remain absolutely pax and fainites. **1969** I. & P. OPIE *Children's Games* i. 18 This rule is so embedded in children's minds that their immediate response to the proposal of a game is to cry out..'Me fains first'. *Ibid.*, He must safeguard himself by saying in one gulp, 'Let's-play-Tig-fains-I-be-on-it'.

fain(e, obs. ff. of FEIGN.

faineance ('feɪneɪəns). *rare*⁻¹. [f. FAINÉANT: see -ANCE; F. *fainéance* occurs in Montaigne.] = next.

1853 KINGSLEY *Hypatia* xxvii. 342 The mask of sneering faineance was gone.

faineancy ('feɪneɪənsɪ). [f. as prec.: see -ANCY.] The quality or condition of being a fainéant.

1854 THOREAU in Salt *Life* (1890) 156 They may be single, or have families in their faineancy. **1884** GOLDW. SMITH in *Contemp. Rev.* Sept. 316 The reduction of the House of Lords to faineancy.

‖**fainéant** (fɛneɑ̃), *sb.* and *a.* Also 7 **fainiant, faitneant, faytneant.** [F. *fainéant* (16th c. also *fait-néant*) 'do-nothing', f. *fait*, 3rd pers. sing. pres. of *faire* to do + *néant* nothing; really an etymologizing perversion of OF. *faignant* sluggard (still current as a vulgarism), pr. pple. of *faindre* to skulk: see FAINT.]

A. *sb.* One who does nothing; an idler. Often with allusion to the *rois fainéants*, 'sluggard kings', a designation of the later Merovingians.

1619 SIR D. CARLETON in *Eng. & Germ.* (Camden) 93 The two last Emperors..were both faineants. **1621** [see FACTOTUM 1]. **1672** PETTY *Pol. Anat.* (1691) 13 There are yet to spare..Casherers and Fait-neants, 220,000. **1855** H. G. LIDDELL *Hist. Rome* v. xlvi, The fainéans who had disappointed them could hardly appear in public.

B. *adj.* That does nothing; indolent, idle.

1855 MILMAN *Lat. Chr.* (1864) IX. XIV. i. 14 The fainéant Merovingians. **1868** M. PATTISON *Academ. Org.* iv. 163 The faineant aristocrat and apathetic dullard.

‖**faineantise** (fɛneɑ̃tiz). Also 7 **faitneantise.** [Fr. *fainéantise*, f. *fainéant*: see prec.] 'Do-nothingness'; indisposition to do anything; indifference, inactivity.

a **1684** LEIGHTON *Let.* in *Leisure Hour* Dec. (1874) 805 Nor would any fatigue..have degusted me so much as our ten years fai(n)tneantise has done. *a* **1734** NORTH *Exam.* (1740) 99 If the King had, by any Faineantise or Remissness, let their Line run into Opportunities. **1822** T. L. PEACOCK *Maid Marian* ix, He had..sent all King Henry's saints about their business, or rather about their no-business, their fainéantise.

‖**fainéantism(e** (fɛneɑ̃tɪzm). [f. FAINÉANT + -ISM.] = FAINEANTISE.

1873 *Bookseller* 2 July 549/1 He had little tolerance for anything like fainéantism or shirking in those about him. **1898** *Star* 3 Jan. 1/7 Old Russia, with its fainéantism, its childish superstition, its base and effeminate pleasures. **1958** *Spectator* 31 Jan. 131/1 Its unflattering implications of *fainéantisme* and unemployability.

fainer, obs. f. FEIGNER.

†'**fainhead.** *Obs.* In 4–5 **faynhed.** [f. FAIN *a.* + -HEAD.] Gladness, joy.

a **1300** *Cursor M.* 3851 (Gött.) Laban for faynhed he did to call..his freindes all. *c* **1400** *Destr. Troy* 2446 Hit shall.. fille you with faynhed.

†'**fainlessly,** *adv.* [? f. *fain*, FEIGN *v.* + -LESS + -LY². Cf. FAINTLESS.] Without attempted evasion.

1652 GAULE *Magastrom.* 261 Women..have fainelesly and willingly left their bodies and imbraced their deaths.

fainly ('feɪnlɪ), *adv. rare.* [f. FAIN *a.* + -LY.] Gladly, eagerly.

1535 STEWART *Cron. Scot.* II. 28 Lord Eolus richt fanelie did thame gyde. **1626** W. SCLATER *Expos. 2 Thess.* (1629) 221 Grace..Easily, Willingly, fainely beteemes another, any other, all others share with it in the common Saluation. ? *a* **1800** *Jolly Goshawk* ix. in Child *Eng. & Sc. Pop. Ball.* IV. 360 She's gone unto her west window And fainly aye it drew. **1850** BLACKIE *Æschylus* II. 268 Xerxes, stript of all his glory ..Fainly comes..to the bridge that links the lands.

fainness ('feɪnnɪs). Chiefly *Sc.* and *north. dial.* [f. FAIN *a.* + -NESS.] The quality or state of being fain; eagerness, gladness.

c **1300** *Cursor M.* 3851 (Cott.) Laban for fainnes did him call..his frendes all. *c* **1340** HAMPOLE *Psalter* iv. 7 þou has gifen faynes in my hert. **1535** STEWART *Cron. Scot.* II. 80 Tha..left all waist for fanenes for to flie. **1571** G. BUCHANAN *Admon. Trew Lordis* Wks. (1892) 30 Causit ye..hamiltonis to fon for faynnes. **1830** GALT *Lawrie T.* V. viii. 228 The.. bailie rubbed his hands with fidgety fainness. **1837** CARLYLE *Fr. Rev.* I. v. ix, Foulon (in his fainness)..also claps.

faint (feɪnt), *sb.* [f. FAINT *a.* and *v.*]

†**1.** Faintness. *Obs.*

a **1300** *Cursor M.* 13477 (Gött.) If þai turn ham þair wai, For þe faint sone faile sal þai. *c* **1320** *Sir Beues* 4195 Beues for ffeynt bere hym lowe. *c* **1430** *Syr Gener.* (Roxb.) 8814 For pure feint right now she sank. *a* **1533** LD. BERNERS *Huon* cxx. 430 Huon..was sore wery for faynt, for the blude that he had loste. *a* **1541** WYATT *Poet. Wks.* (1861) 149 My hope ..stumbleth straight, for feeble faint. **1600** HOLLAND *Livy* IV. xli. 165 Wearied with travaile, and faint of his woundes.

2. A swoon.

1808 SCOTT *Marm.* IV. xvi, The Saint, Who propped the Virgin in her faint. **1865** L. OLIPHANT *Piccadilly* (1870) 280 In a dead faint. **1885** R. L. & F. STEVENSON *Dynamiter* 45 The night..found me still where he had laid me during my faint.

3. *Comb.* as *faint-fit* = fainting-fit.

1795 WOLCOTT (P. Pindar) *Pindariana* Wks. 1812 IV. 190 Without a scream, a faint-fit or a kick. **1892** [see DWALM *sb.*].

faint (feɪnt), *a.* Forms: 4 (and 9 in sense 1 b) **feint,** 4–6 **fainte, faynt(e, feynt(e,** 6 *Sc.* **fant(e,** 4– **faint.** [a. OF. *faint, feint* feigned, sluggish, cowardly, pa. pple. of *faindre, feindre* (mod.F. *feindre*) to FEIGN, in early use also *refl.* to avoid one's duty by false pretences, to shirk, skulk.]

†**I.** Feigned, pretended, simulated. *Obs.*

a **1300** *Cursor M.* 19535 (Cott.) Þar-for tok he [Symon Magus] baptim faint. *a* **1340** HAMPOLE *Psalter* xl. 6 Vayn thynge & faynt spak his hert. *c* **1400** *Destr. Troy* 12591 Þo lyghers..forget a faint tale vnder fals colour. *c* **1440** *York Myst.* xxix. 229 A faynte frend myght he þer fynde. **1477** EARL RIVERS (Caxton) *Dictes* 144 He that loueth the with feynt loue. **1568** GRAFTON *Chron.* II. 93 And finished the sayde peace with an assured othe..but it semed a faynt peace, for [etc.].

b. *Law. faint action, pleading*, etc.: = 'feigned action', etc.: see FEIGNED.

1542–3 *Act 34–5 Hen. VIII*, c. 24 The saide Manour..to be recovered by fainte pleader, reddicion or other fraude or covyne. **1552** HULOET, Faynte accion, *actio exermata.* **1607** COWEL *Interpr., Faynt pleader.* **1641** *Termes de la Ley* 154 Faint pleading is a covenous, false, and collusory manner of pleading to the deceit of a third party. **1672** in COWEL *Interpr., Faynt* alias *Feynt Action.* **1818** CRUISE *Digest* (ed. 2) V. 517 A feint title.

II. Sluggish, timid, feeble.

†**2.** Avoiding exertion, shirking, lazy, sluggish.

c **1325** *Coer de L.* 2519 'Rowes on faste! who that is feynt, In evel water may he be dreynt!' **1393** GOWER *Conf.* II. 5 He ..had his thoughtes feint Towardes loves and full of slouthe. *c* **1440** *Promp. Parv.* 153 Feynt, *segnis.* **1513** DOUGLAS *Æneis* I. vii. 33 The beis..fra thair hife..Expellis ..the faynt drone be. **1680** TEMPLE *Orig. & Nat. Gov.* Misc. 53 The spirits..are rendered faint and sluggish.

3. Wanting in courage, spiritless, cowardly. *Obs.* or *arch.* exc. in *faint heart* (now associated with sense 4 b).

a **1300** *Cursor M.* 18081 (Cott.) A faint fighter me thinc er þou. *c* **1300** *K. Alis.* 7597 Haveth now non heorte feynte! *c* **1320** *Sir Beues* 1575 Ase he was mad & feint To Iesu Crist he made is pleint. **1414** BRAMPTON *Penit. Ps.* cxvi (Percy Soc.) 44 Myn herte is fals[e], feynt, and drye. *c* **1489** CAXTON *Sonnes of Aymon* viii. 184 Thoughe ye shold abyde behynde as weke men and feynte. *a* **1533** LD. BERNERS *Huon* lii. 177 Thou arte of a faynte corage. *a* **1593** H. SMITH *Wks.* (1867) II. 219 The faint spies that went to the land of Canaan. **1627** MAY *Lucan* III. (1635) 103 To send thee civill wars Having so faint a chiefe. **1702** ROWE *Tamerl.* I. i, His Party..soon grew faint. **1875** JOWETT *Plato* (ed. 2) III. 689 Faint heart never yet raised a trophy.

absol. **1814** BYRON *Lara* II. x, The fierce that vanquish, and the faint that yield. **1870** BRYANT *Iliad* I. IV. 120 He made the faint of spirit take their place.

b. *Proverb.* **1569** W. ELDERTON *Ballad, Brittains Ida* v. i, Faint heart ne'er won fair lady. **1624** MASSINGER *Parl. Love* II. iii, All hell's plagues light on the proverb That says 'Faint heart'—! But it is stale.

4. Wanting in strength or vigour. †**a.** Of persons or animals, their faculties or condition; also (rarely) of material agents: Weak, feeble; sickly, out of condition. *Obs.*

c **1350** *Will. Palerne* 785 Febul wax he & faynt. **1399** LANGL. *Rich. Redeles* III. 88 With many ffair ffowle, þouȝ þey ffeynte were. *c* **1420** *Pallad. on Husb.* III. 288 In bigger bowes fele, and fainter fewe Brannches doo traile. **1513** DOUGLAS *Æneis* VII. viii. 74 Thi vile unveildy age, Ourset with hasart hair and faynt dotage. **1535** COVERDALE *Ps.* cxlii[i]. 7 My sprete waxeth faynte. **1641** BEST *Farm. Bks.* (Surtees) 143 Barley strawe..is fownde..not altogeather soe faint as haver strawe. **1653** WALTON *Angler* 130 If I catch a Trout in one Meadow, he shall be white and faint. **1697** DRYDEN *Virg. Georg.* III. 204 If the Sire be faint, or out of Case. **1699** DAMPIER *Voy.* II. III. 36 Where the scantiest or faintest Land-winds are found. **1764** HARMER *Observ.* IV. iv. 142 A very slow faint fire.

b. Of actions, wishes, purposes: Half-hearted, languid, feeble.

1596 SPENSER *F.Q.* IV. vi. 24 Turning feare to faint deuotion. **1630** in Picton *L'pool Munic Rec.* (1883) I. 158 Many disorders growen..through..faint execucon of those lawes. **1640** HABINGTON *Edw. IV.* 183 The King..dismist the Embassadors with some faint comfort. **1728** VENEER *Sincere Penitent* Pref. 4 A faint..progress in..religion. **1735** POPE *Prol. Sat.* 201 Damn with faint praise, assent with civil leer. **1848** MACAULAY *Hist. Eng.* I. 581 A faint show of opposition from one or two peers. **1863** FR. A. KEMBLE *Resid. Georgia* 37 And found there had been some faint attempt at sweeping.

5. Producing a feeble impression on the senses or the mind; dim, indistinct, hardly perceptible: **a.** of light, sound, odour.

1660 BOYLE *New Exp. Phys. Mech.* 270 The sound grew fainter and fainter. **1665** HOOKE *Microgr.* 84 By.. Turpentine, &c. all those reflections are made more faint. **1706** PHILLIPS (ed. Kersey) s.v. *Vision, Faint Vision* is when a few Rays make up one Pencil, and tho' this may be distinct, yet it is obscure and dark. **1784** COWPER *Task* v. 59 Diligent to catch the first faint gleam Of smiling day. **1818** SHELLEY *Rosalind* 1015 The summer wind faint odours brought From mountain flowers. *a* **1839** PRAED *Poems* (1864) I. 96 Echo shrinks, as if afraid Of the faint murmur she has made. **1868** LOCKYER *Elem. Astron.* i. (1879) 10 A star of the sixth magnitude is..the faintest visible to the naked eye.

b. of a colour.

1552 HULOET, Faynte and vnperfite coloure, *dilutus color.* **1665** HOOKE *Microgr.* 74 All manner of Blues, from the faintest to the deepest. **1716** *Lond. Gaz.* No. 5468/4 Stolen ..a Faint Bay Horse. **1730** THOMSON *Summer* 1317 (1746) From her naked limbs of glowing white, In folds loose-floating fell the fainter lawn. **1816** J. SMITH *Panorama Sc. & Art* II. 724 The faintest part of the picture. **1872** BRYANT *Little People of Snow* 111 She saw a little creature..With.. faint blue eyes.

c. of markings, etc. Applied *spec.* to the lines of a pale blue or neutral tint ruled on paper as a guide for handwriting. Hence quasi-*adv.* in *ruled faint.*

d. of objects of mental perception, *e.g.* resemblance, probability, etc. Also of conceptions or representations: 'Pale' or feeble compared with the reality. Used in superl., with ellipsis of *idea, notion*.

1727 SWIFT *Gulliver* II. viii. 166 Some faint hopes of relief. **1751** JORTIN *Serm.* (1771) II. xvii. 333 The faint remembrance of the word of God. **1772** PRIESTLEY *Inst. Relig.* (1782) II. 113 We form a faint idea of [it]. **1834** PRINGLE *Afr. Sk.* x. 338 Such is a faint picture of the state of things. **1884** *Manch. Exam.* 11 June 5/3 There is not the faintest chance that [etc.]. **1961** PARTRIDGE *Slang Dict.* Suppl. 1083/1. **1962** I. MURDOCH *Unofficial Rose* ii. 27 'Where's Penny?' said Ann. 'Haven't the faintest,' said Miranda.

absol. **1840** BROWNING *Sordello* v. 417 Some first fact I' the faint of time.

6. Feeble through inanition, fear, or exhaustion; inclined to 'faint' or swoon. Const. †*of, with.*

c **1320** R. BRUNNE *Medit.* 509 þey broȝt hym to pylate, he stode ful feynt. *c* **1380** *Sir Ferumb.* 332 He ys boþe paal & feynt. **1430** LYDG. *Chron. Troy.* I. ix, Which of laboure were ful mate and feynt. *c* **1489** CAXTON *Sonnes of Aymon* ix. 249 Guycharde..was feynte and felle doun to the erthe. **1704** F. FULLER *Med. Gymn.* (1711) 30 When a Man..rises first from his sick Bed..he quickly grows faint. **1837** MAJOR RICHARDSON *Brit. Legion* II. (ed. 2) 291 He was exceedingly ..faint with the bruises he had received. **1867** DICKENS *Lett.* (1880) II. 272, I was taken so faint afterwards.

transf. **1548** HALL *Chron.* 230 b, Knowyng his treasorie.. to bee so voyde and faint.

III. 7. a. Producing faintness; sickly; †having a sickly smell. Of the atmosphere: Oppressive.

1525 LD. BERNERS *Froiss.* II. clxxvii. [clxxiii.] 530 The wether was so faynt. **1622** FLETCHER *Beggar's Bush* III. i, The white Cony skin Though it be faint tis faire to the eye. **1673** TEMPLE *Observ. United Prov.* Wks. 1731 I. 46 Warm faint Air turns in a Night to a sharp Frost. **1712** W. ROGERS *Voy.* 182 The Weather was very wet, hot and faint. **1864** SALA in *Daily Tel.* 16 Aug., I wish La Villa Ricca de Vera Cruz had not quite so faint a smell. **1870** HAWTHORNE *Eng. Note-bks.* (1879) II. 345 The atmosphere was a little faint and sickish.

b. Of food: not fresh; tainted. *local.*

1848 DICKENS *Dombey* lvii. 573 A man..chewing a faint apple. **1902** *Westm. Gaz.* 25 Oct. 2/3 This meat hadn't been trimmed. I admit it was 'faint'.

IV. *Comb.* **8. a.** with adjs. of colour, as *faint-blue, -green*, etc. **b.** parasynthetic, as *faint-breathed, -hued, -lipped, -voiced*, etc.

1598 SYLVESTER *Du Bartas* II. ii. II. Babylon 301 The faint-breath'd children Cry often Bek. **1682** SIR T. BROWNE *Chr. Mor.* 9 Persons..but pale in goodness, and faint hued in integrity. **1820** KEATS *Hyperion* III. 19 Faint-lipped shells. **1832** TENNYSON *Mariana in S.* 5 A faint-blue ridge upon the right. **1844** LD. HOUGHTON *Palm Leaves* 138 Purple and faint-green relics of the day. **1871** E. F. BURR *Ad Fidem* xiv. 284 Difficulties become faint-voiced.

9. quasi-*adv.* with ppl. adjs., as *faint-gleaming, -glimmering, -heard, -lit, -warbled*, etc.

1727–46 THOMSON *Summer* 48 The meek-ey'd morn appears..faint-gleaming in the dappled east. **1728–46** —— *Spring* 585 The long-forgotten Strain, At first faint-warbled. **1729** SAVAGE *Wanderer* III. 12 The Stars.. faintglimm'ring with remains of day. **1866** HOWELLS *Venet. Life* xvii. 260 Faint-heard refrains. **1867** R. LYTTON *Chron. & Char.*, The faint-lit cold-wall'd corridors.

faint (feɪnt), *v.* Forms: 4–5 feinte, 4–6 faynt(e, (6 fayncte), feynt(e, 5– faint. [f. FAINT *a.*; cf. the rare OF. *feintir* = sense 1.]

1. *intr.* To lose heart or courage, be afraid, become depressed, give way, flag. Now only *arch.* after Biblical uses.

c **1350** *Will. Palerne* 3638 For here fon gun feynte & felde were manye. *a* **1400** *Adam Davy's Dreams* 118 A voice me bede I ne shulde nouȝth feinte. **1526** TINDALE *2 Cor.* iv. 1 As mercy is come on us we fayncte not. **1548** HALL *Chron.* 59 b, The straunger so faced the Englishman, that he faynted in hys sute. **1653** HOLCROFT *Procopius* II. 41 The soldiers blamed each other for fainting. **1701** STEELE *Chr. Hero* III. 62 His great heart, instead of fainting and subsiding, rose and biggen'd. **1722** SEWEL *Hist. Quakers* (1795) I. III. 187 He was despised by many; yet he fainted not. **1827** KEBLE *Chr. Y.* 24th Sund. after Trin., Why should we faint and fear to live alone. **1875** JOWETT *Plato* (ed. 2) II. 478 Answer and faint not.

2. To become faint, grow weak or feeble, decline. Const. *in, of. Obs.* exc. *poet.*

c **1400** *Destr. Troy* 13918 All feblit þe freike, fainted of strenght. *c* **1450** *Crt. of Love* 460 All her ymage paynte In the remembraunce till thow begynne to faynte. **1530** RASTELL *Bk. Purgat.* II. xviii, The understandynge begynnyth to faynt. **1568** *Jacob & Esau* I. i. 31 in Hazl. *Dodsley* (1874) II. 190 Sometimes Esau's self will faint for drink and meat. **1623** BINGHAM *Xenophon* 45 If they perceiue, that you faint in courage. **1697** DRYDEN *Virg. Æneid* IX. 473 The Fires were fainting there. **1820** SHELLEY *Œdipus* II. i. 56 Loading the morning winds until they faint With living fragrance. **1866** B. TAYLOR *Poems, Odalisque*, The day, through shadowy arches fainting.

†**b.** To fall short. *Obs. rare.*

1623 BINGHAM *Lepsius' Comparison* 3 It fainteth or straieth from the marke, if you aime further off.

3. To fall into a swoon. Also with *away.*

c **1400** *Destr. Troy* 3550 He..fainted for febull, and felle to þe ground In a swyme. *c* **1440** *York Myst.* xlv. 95 Caste some watir vppon me, I faynte! **1600** SHAKS. *A.Y.L.* IV. iii. 149 And now he fainted, And cride in fainting vpon Rosalinde. **1668** ETHEREDGE *She Would if She Could* IV. i, Oh, I shall faint! **1703** MAUNDRELL *Journ. Jerus.* (1732) 107 Where Christ fainted thrice, under the weight of his Cross. **1742** WESLEY *Jrnl.* 18 Jan., As soon as she rose from prayer, she fainted away. **1847** GROTE *Greece* II. lii. (1862) IV. 421 He fainted away and fell back. **1880** OUIDA *Moths* I. 16 She could have fainted.

b. To droop, sink *into. lit.* and *fig. rare.*

1712–4 POPE *Rape Lock* IV. 34 There Affectation..Faints into airs, and languishes with pride. **1821** KEATS *Lamia* 139 A flower That faints into itself at evening hour.

4. To lose colour or brightness; to fade, die away. Const. *into.* Now *rare.*

1430 LYDG. *Chron. Troy* II. xvii, Coloures that may neuer faynte. **1594** PLAT *Jewell-ho.* III. 66 The Wines doe.. beginne to faile or faint. **1675** A. BROWNE *Ars Pictoria* 90 The next [grounds]..as they loose in their distance must.. faint..in their colours. **1708** H. PHILIPS *Cyder* II. 67 Unskill'd to tell Or where one colour rises or one faints. **1711** POPE *Let. H. Cromwell* 12 Nov., Those..figures in the gilded clouds which while we gaze long upon..the whole faints before the eye, and decays into confusion. **1873** MISS THACKERAY *Old Kensington* xv. 124 The draperies hang fainting and turning grey and brown. **1890** W. C. RUSSELL *Ocean Tragedy* III. xxxii. 193 The sky had fainted into a sickly hectic.

b. *nonce-use.* To grow dull or insensible *to.*

1669 PENN *No Cross* Wks. 1782 II. 93 We fainted to that pleasure and delight we once loved.

5. *trans.* To make faint or weak, depress, enfeeble, weaken. *Rare* in mod. use. Also impers. *it faints me.*

c **1386** CHAUCER *Man of Law's T.* 828 O luxurie..thou feyntest mannes mynde. *c* **1400** *Destr. Troy* 11162 þurgh failyng of fode..fainttes þe pepull. *c* **1420** *Pallad. on Husb.* III. 1090 Ffele I have seyn thair dammes feynt or quelle. **1509** HAWES *Past. Pleas.* XIX. xiii, Doth he not knowe how your hert is faynted? **1581** MULCASTER *Positions* iv. (1887) 22 Neither faint it [the body] with heat, nor freese it with cold. **1613** SHAKS. *Hen. VIII*, II. iii. 103 It faints me To thinke what followes. **1614** T. ADAMS in Spurgeon *Treas. Dav.* Ps. xxxv. 3 Deferred hope faints the heart. *a* **1657** LOVEDAY *Lett.* (1662) 195 It..faints my industry. **1755** GUTHRIE *Christians Gt. Interest* (1667) 113 This seriousness breaketh the man's heart, and fainteth the stoutness of it. **1858** MRS. OLIPHANT *Laird of Norlaw* III. 175 Too much joy almost fainted the heart of the Mistress. **1871** R. ELLIS *Catullus* lxiv. 216 Son, whom needs it faints me to launch full-tided on hazards.

†**b.** To make less, diminish. *Obs. rare.*

1599 MARSTON *Sco. Villanie* III. viii. 212 With incensing touch To faint his force.

faint-draw (feɪntdrɔː), *v.* [f. FAINT *a.* + DRAW *v.*] *trans.* To draw or delineate lightly.

1728 SAVAGE *Bastard* 33 You had faint-drawn me with a form alone.

fainted ('feɪntɪd), *ppl. a.* [f. FAINT *v.* + -ED[1].] †**a.** Rendered cowardly or timid. †**b.** Become weak or exhausted. **c.** Fallen into a swoon (*rare*).

c **1500** *Melusine* 140 By one only Cowarde & feynted herte is sometyme lefte & loste al a hoole werke. *a* **1533** LD. BERNERS *Huon* liii. 180 A! false faynted hert. **1614** BP. HALL *Recoll. Treat.* 124 Why doth none of his gallant nobles revive the faynted courage of their Lorde with a new cuppe? **1642** MILTON *Apol. Smect.* (1851) 296 So reviving to the fainted Common-wealth. **1847** *Fraser's Mag.* XXXVI. 32 There she lies, not fainted..but like a somnambule.

†**'fainten,** *v. Obs. rare*⁻¹. [f. FAINT *a.* + -EN[5].] *trans.* To make faint, depress, dispirit.

1612–5 BP. HALL *Contempl., N.T.* II. i, Thou wilt not be ..absent..so long as to fainten the heart.

fainter ('feɪntə(r)). [f. FAINT *v.* + -ER[1].] One who faints or gives way.

1826 SCOTT *Woodst.* xxxiii, The soldiers chosen for this service should be..no fainters in spirit. **1935** W. DE LA MARE *Early One Morning* 268 If he is not by nature a fainter he may pore over the blood.

†**'faintful,** *a. Obs.* [f. FAINT *sb.* or *v.* + -FUL.] Ready to faint; causing or indicating faintness.

1589 FLEMING *Virg. Georg.* III. 18 Faintfull and like to die. **1590** GREENE *Orl. Fur.* (1861) 98 Let them stream along my faintfull looks. **1594** LODGE *Wounds Civ. War* v. in Hazl. *Dodsley* VII. 195, I feel the faintful dews of death.

faint-heart ('feɪnthɑːt), *sb.* and *a.* [f. FAINT *a.* + HEART.] **A.** *sb.*

†**1.** The fact or condition of having a faint heart; want of spirit. *Obs.*

1580 NORTH *Plutarch* (1676) 760 They [men]..through faint-heart, and lack of courage, do change their first mind.

2. One who has a faint heart; a coward.

1870 *Daily News* 16 Nov., 'You are all fainthearts, not Frenchmen.'

B. *adj.* Faint-hearted, timid, spiritless, cowardly.

1590 MARLOWE *2nd Pt. Tamburl.* III. ii, That coward faint-heart runaway. **1596** SPENSER *F.Q.* IV. x. 17 Cowards ..And faint-heart fooles. **1870** MORRIS *Earthly Par.* II. III. 501 O faint-heart thief of love.

faint-hearted (ˌfeɪnt'hɑːtɪd), *a.* [f. as prec. + -ED[2].] Having a faint heart; wanting energy, courage, or will to carry a thing through; timid, cowardly. Also *absol.*

c **1440** *Promp. Parv.* 153 Feynt hertyd, *vecors.* **1535** COVERDALE *1 Sam.* xiii. 7 All the people were faynthartred after him. **1631** GOUGE *God's Arrows* v. xi. 421 A few white-liverd, faint-hearted soldiers. **1723** DE FOE *Col. Jack* (1840) 17, I find you are faint-hearted, and unfit for our trade. **1843** BETHUNE *Sc. Fireside Stor.* 54 Young fellows like you, are sometimes faint-hearted. **1871** FREEMAN *Norm. Conq.* (1876) IV. xviii. 145 A fainthearted..faction soon began to show itself among those of higher degree.

absol. *a* **1600** HOOKER *Eccl. Pol.* (1617) 746 The punishment threatened..to the fearful and faint-hearted. **1847** EMERSON *Repr. Men, Goethe* Wks. (Bohn) I. 395 The disadvantages of any epoch exist only to the faint-hearted.

Hence ˌ**faint-'heartedly** *adv.*, in a fainthearted manner. ˌ**faint-'heartedness**, the quality or state of being fainthearted; timidity, cowardice.

1580 HOLLYBAND *Treas. Fr. Tong, Laschement*..faint hartedly. *Ibid., Couardise*..fainthartednesse. **1605** BP. HALL *Medit. & Vows* II. §76 To finde such fainthartednes in my-selfe at the first conceit of death. **1671** H. M. tr. *Erasmus Colloq.* 110 But how many Christians dye very faint-heartedly? **1753** N. TORRIANO *Gangr. Sore Throat* 60 A Faint-heartedness..always accompanies Putrefaction and Insensibility. **1874** MOTLEY *Barneveld* (1879) II. xi. 26 Baffled..by the faintheartedness of his nominal friends. **1876** MRS. WHITNEY *Lights & Ins.* xi. 120 'It is such a responsibility to take'..I said, faint-heartedly.

fainting ('feɪntɪŋ), *vbl. sb.* [f. FAINT *v.* + -ING[1].] The action of the vb. FAINT.

1. A growing feeble or faint-hearted; depression, discouragement.

c **1400** *Destr. Troy* 13936 With fainttyng & feblenes he fell to þe ground. **1590** SHAKS. *Com. Err.* I. i. 46 Almost at fainting vnder The pleasing punishment that women beare. **1633** G. HERBERT *Temple, Love Unknown* 2 In my faintings I presume your love Will more complie, then help.

2. Swooning.

1601 HOLLAND *Pliny* XIX. v. 18 This root..[elecampane] thus confected is singular good for faintings. **1684** BUNYAN *Pilgr.* II. (1879) 176 Fetch something, and give it Mercy..to stay her fainting. **1748** HARTLEY *Observ. Man.* I. i. 40 Hence Faintings and Stupors. **1850** MRS. STOWE *Uncle Tom's C.* xxxix. 344, I meant to stop your fainting.

b. *attrib.* in *fainting fit*, a swoon.

1702 J. PURCELL *Cholick* (1714) 97 Fainting Fits, or a Syncope..will ensue. **1828** SCOTT *F.M. Perth* ii, Catharine ..was..recovered from her fainting fit. **1855** STANLEY *Mem. Canterb.* iii. (1857) 128 Often he fell into long fainting fits, which his attendants mistook for death.

fainting ('feɪntɪŋ), *ppl. a.* [f. as prec. + -ING[2].] That faints, in senses of the verb.

1558 PHAER *Æneid* VI. 361 The feble mone doth giue sometime a faynting light. **1576** FLEMING *Panopl. Epist.* 76 The Senate, whom I perceived in manner fainting and wearie. **1591** SHAKS. *1 Hen. VI*, II. v. 40 That I may kindly giue one fainting kisse. **1708** EDM. SMITH *To Mem. of J. Philips* in Anderson *B.P.* VI. 618 The fainting Dutch remotely fire. **1771** MRS. GRIFFITH tr. *Viaud's Shipwreck* 201 Yes, O Yes! she replied in an almost fainting tone. **1771** HULL *Sir W. Harrington* (1797) IV. 162 We had such trembling and almost fainting doings. **1818** SHELLEY *Lett.* 10 July, Translating into my fainting and inefficient periods, the divine eloquence of Plato's Symposium. **1855** MACAULAY *Hist. Eng.* III. 239 His eloquence roused the fainting courage of his brethren.

faintingly ('feɪntɪŋlɪ), *adv.* [f. prec. + -LY[2].] In a fainting manner; †feebly, †faint-heartedly; like one who is fainting.

1576 FLEMING *Panopl. Epist.* 41 This letter is not onely lamentably indited, but also faintingly invented. **1586** A. DAY *Eng. Secretary* II. (1625) 108 And albeit he was.. likeliest of all other to attaine the victory, yet..he faintingly withdrew. **1635** SWAN *Spec. M.* ix. §1 (1643) 470 His many knocks cause him faintingly to fall. **1839** LADY LYTTON *Cheveley* (ed. 2) I. vii. 135 Mademoiselle began to..incline her head faintingly towards his shoulder. **1844** LD. HOUGHTON *Mem. Many Scenes, Dream in Gondola* 96 A deft canoe..Faintingly rocked within a lone-some cove.

†**'faintingness.** *Obs.* [f. as prec. + -NESS.] = FAINTNESS.

1634–5 BRERETON *Trav.* (1844) 126 Save only a faintingness when I came on shore.

†**'faintise.** *Obs.* Forms: 3–5 feint-, feynt-, -ise, -yce, -yse, (4 fentesye, 5 feyntyse), 4–5 faint-, fant-, faynt-, -es(e, -is(e, -ys(e, (4 *Sc.* fayntice, 5 fentyse). [a. OF. *faintise, feintise* (mod.F. *feintise*) = Pr. *feintesa*, f. *faint, feint* feigned, sluggish, cowardly: see FAINT *a.*]

1. Deceit, dissimulation, hypocrisy, pretence.

1340 *Ayenb.* 26 Hit wes al fayntise and ypocrisie. *c* **1400** *Destr. Troy* 594 Ere he fayne any faintes. **1485** CAXTON *Chas. Gt.* 217 The kyng..dysposed hym to receyue baptym ..without fayntyse.

2. Feebleness, weakness (of body or mind); want of energy, cowardice. Cf. FAINTNESS. ***without faintise***: without flagging or flinching.

1297 R. GLOUC. (1724) 39 Muche þing, þat ys eldore loren þorw feyntyse..he wann seþþe a ȝeyn. *c* **1330** R. BRUNNE *Chron.* (1810) 176 Philip withouten fayntise did alle his trauaile. *a* **1400** *Pol. Rel. & L. Poems* 246 For feyntyce fel þat fayre fode, Nakyd he bar þat hard rode To-ward caluery. *c* **1470** HARDING *Chron.* LXXXI. viii, Thei faught without feyntise.

faintish ('feɪntɪʃ), *a.* [f. FAINT *a.* + -ISH.]

1. †**a.** Rather weak or feeble. *Obs.* **b.** Affected with a feeling somewhat like that of fainting. Also of the feeling itself.

1667 H. STUBBE in *Phil. Trans.* II. 501 Neither does all that sweat make us faintish. **1683** TRYON *Way to Health* 82 Those Cattel that feed on Grass are weak and faintish in comparison of those..fed with Hay and Corn. **1767** GOOCH *Treat. Wounds* I. 224 He continued faintish for some days. **1834** LANDOR *Exam. Shaks.* Wks. 1846 II. 267, I wax faintish at the big squat man. **1848** J. H. NEWMAN *Loss & Gain* III. ii. (1853) 288 Charles had a faintish feeling come over him. **1856** LEVER *Martins of Cro'M.* 128 A qualm of faintish sickness.

2. Rather indistinct, hardly perceptible.

1712 *Nereides* 35 The Water-Lillies are a faintish sweet. **1713** ROWE *Jane Shore* v. i, Upon her Cheek a faintish Flush

was spread. **1748** RICHARDSON *Clarissa* (1811) V. i. 4 Then in a faintish, but angry voice, 'begone from my door'. **1767** EHRET in *Phil. Trans.* LVII. 114 The young leaves..are of a faintish green. **1866** CARLYLE *E. Irving* in *Remin.* (1881) 268 To the Louvre..got rather faintish good of the pictures there.

faintishness ('feɪntɪʃnɪs). [f. prec. + -NESS.] The state or condition of being or feeling faintish; a slight tendency to faint.

1733 ARBUTHNOT *On Air* III. §vii. 48 The sensation of faintishness and debility. **1789** W. BUCHAN *Dom. Med.* (ed. 11) 221 When..faintishness..render[s] cordials necessary, we would recommend good wine. **1816** *Chron.* in *Ann. Reg.* 575, I felt myself assailed by a kind of faintishness. **1833** M. SCOTT *Tom Cringle* (1859) 206 While faintishness encreased so that I could hardly speak.

'faintive, *a. rare*$^{-1}$. [f. FAINT *v.* + -IVE.] Ready to faint; languid.

a **1813** A. WILSON *Disconsolate Wren* Poet. Wks. (1846) 96 She poured out her mane, Sae faintive, sae plaintive.

'faintless, *a.* [f. FAINT *sb.* + -LESS.] Exempt from fainting; unflagging.

1593-4 SYLVESTER *Profit of Imprisonment* 323 By faintless exercise faire Vertue to maintaine. **1664** PEPYS *Diary* (1879) III. 96 Cramp be thou faintless.

†**'faintling**, *sb.* and *a. Obs.* [f. as prec. + -LING.] **A.** *sb.* One who is faint or faint-hearted. **B.** *adj.* Faint-hearted.

1614 C. B. *Ghost of Rich. III*, Such fayntlings never yet were prest with coyne. **1712** ARBUTHNOT *John Bull* (1752) 82 Thou art such a faintling, silly creature.

†**'faintly**, *a. Obs.* [f. FAINT *a.* + -LY[1].] = FAINT in various senses.

1712 W. ROGERS *Voy.* (1718) 267 It being but a faintly food. **1771** J. FOOT *Penseroso* II. 69 Hence the spring Emits a faintly blush.

faintly ('feɪntlɪ), *adv.* [f. as prec. + -LY[2].]

†**1.** Feignedly, by way of feint or pretence, deceitfully. *Obs.*

c **1330** R. BRUNNE *Chron.* (1725) 152 Gode acord to make, forsoþe fulle fayntlie. *c* **1400** *Cato's Morals* 16 in *Cursor M.* App. iv, Fainteli for to speke..is falsid and blame. **1523** LD. BERNERS *Froiss.* I. ccxxi. 287 Some men of armes passed after fayntly. **1548** HALL *Chron.* 241 Countryes..by hym stollen and faintly conquered. **1741** MIDDLETON *Cicero* I. v. 365 Gabinius..was forced to..fight for Pompey at first faintly [L. *simulate*] and unwillingly, but at last heartily.

†**2.** In a spiritless manner, like a coward; timidly.

1297 R. GLOUC. (Rolls) 10596 Hii fouȝte feinteliche. **1387** TREVISA *Higden* (Rolls) VII. 491 What he bygynneþ frescheliche, he forsakeþ hit feyntliche as a womman. *c* **1400** *Melayne* 1419, I fro this grete Iournee Fayntly fledde a way. **1580** BARET *Alv.* W 341 Womanishlie, faintlie, fearefullie, *muliébriter*. **1643** DENHAM *Cooper's H.* 285 He faintly now declines the fatal strife.

3. In a weak, feeble, or languid manner; feebly.

c **1320** R. BRUNNE *Medit.* 572 Cryst goþ krokedly þys heuy cros vndyr, And feyntly hyt bereþ. *c* **1380** WYCLIF *Serm.* Sel. Wks. I. 180 þus moun we se how feyntli we serve to Crist. *c* **1430** *Syr Gener.* (Roxb.) 1617 Wel feyntlie she felt hir stere. **1526** *Pilgr. Perf.* (W. de W. 1531) 155 b, Perfeccyon, whiche they slowly & weykly or fayntly desyre. **1632** J. HAYWARD tr. *Biondi's Eromena* 29 Faintly kissing him, she breathed out her life. **1699** DAMPIER *Voy.* II. I. 16 The tide pressing against the stream, tho faintly. **1781** GIBBON *Decl. & F.* II. xli. 504 Their valiant promise was faintly supported in the hour of battle. **1861** *Athenæum* 29 June 854 Cavour faintly smiled.

†**b.** With hesitation, not actively or energetically, coldly, half-heartedly. *Obs.*

c **1440** *Promp. Parv.* 153 Feyntly, *segniter*. **1488** CAXTON *Chast. Goddes Chyld.* 13 Though I wyll but fayntly..my wylle is to wylle perfyghtly. **1548** HALL *Chron.* 177 They set forward the king, and..brought him to London..where he was fayntly receyved, and febly welcomed. **1627** MAY *Lucan* III. (1635) 356 Brothers faintly would 'gainst brothers fight. **1712** STEELE *Spect.* No. 468 ¶3 To praise faintly the good Qualities of those below them. **1756** C. LUCAS *Ess. Waters* III. 180 Having but Mayow..faintly on my side.

4. In a faint or almost imperceptible degree; very slightly; in faint tones; without vividness or distinctness.

1590 SPENSER *F.Q.* III. v. 24 An arrow..fayntly fluttering. **1595** SHAKS. *John* IV. ii. 227, I faintly broke with thee of Arthurs death. **1695** BLACKMORE *Pr. Arth.* III. 706 Some..faintly Blue. **1708** J. PHILIPS *Cyder* ii, The cowslip posies, faintly sweet. **1781** GIBBON *Decl. & F.* III. 149 The wide and stony beds, whose centre was faintly marked by the course of a shallow stream. **1800** tr. *Lagrange's Chem.* I. 420 This salt detonates faintly. **1849** MRS. SOMERVILLE *Connex. Phys. Sc.* xxxvii. 436 Faintly visible to the naked eye. **1892** *Law Times* XCIII. 459/1 The notice of objection is not signed by any elector, but is stamped faintly with a stamp signifying that 'Richard Mason' is the objector.

†**b.** Hardly, scarcely. *Obs.*

1529 *Supplic. to King* 50 Doo not these thinges fayntely agree with the sayenge of..Paule the Apostle. **1634** MASSINGER *Very Woman* II. ii, We have but faintly yet begun our journey. **1636** —— *Bashful Lover* III. iii, My enemy—I can faintly call him so.

faintness ('feɪntnɪs). [f. as prec. + -NESS.] The state or condition of being faint.

1. The state or condition of being without strength or exhausted; exhaustion, feebleness.

a **1440** *Sir Eglam.* 901 For feyntnes sche myght not speke a worde. **1494** FABYAN *Chron.* VI. cxcvi. 201 He bled so sore that for fayntnes he fyll from his horse. **1548** HALL *Chron.* 60 b, This miserable famyne..encreasyng so..that the stout souldiour for faintnes could skase welde his weapon. **1625** HART *Anat. Ur.* II. iv. 72 There followeth a..faintnesse of their ioynts. **1672** SANDERSON in Walton *Life* M ij a, A great bodily weakness and faintness of spirits. *a* **1717** BLACKALL *Wks.* (1723) I. 63 'Tis this faintness of their Desire which is the Cause of it's being successless. *a* **1871** GROTE *Eth. Fragm.* i. (1876) 14 The faintness or potency of the feeling.

†**b.** *transf.*

1543-4 *Act 35 Hen. VIII*, c. 10 For fayntnes of the springes..the accustomed course of the waters.. diminished. **1548** HALL *Chron.* 226 To them he explaned.. the fayntnesse & lenenesse of hys treasure.

†**c.** Of flesh: Want of firmness or solidity.

1599 MINSHEU *Dial. Sp. & Eng.* (1623) 56 Of this fertilitie proceeds the faintnesse of the flesh there.

2. The state of being faint in spirit; dejection, timorousness; inertness, slackness, sluggishness. *Obs.* exc. in *faintness of heart*, etc.

1398 TREVISA *Barth. De P.R.* XII. xxvii. (1495) 430 For his feyntnes and cowardnes the kite is ouercome of a birde that is lesse than he. *c* **1485** *Digby Myst.* iii. 280 In feyntnes I falter, for þis fray fell. **1591** SHAKS. *1 Hen. VI*, IV. i. 107 The palenesse of this Flower, Bewray'd the faintnesse of my Masters heart. **1645** MILTON *Tetrach.* Introd., They..have neglected through faintnesse the onely remedy of their sufferings. **1851** GALLENGA *Italy* 301 Faintness of heart and infirmity of purpose must naturally..be found in so vast a mass.

3. The feeling of being faint or ready to swoon.

1526 *Pilgr. Perf.* (W. de W. 1531) 253 b, He fell downe for feyntness and weyknes. **1791** MRS. RADCLIFFE *Rom. Forest* xx, The faintness is already gone off. **1828** SCOTT *F.M. Perth* xxxiv, The faintness which seemed to overpower him. **1874** LISLE CARR *Jud. Gwynne* I. i. 29 Sudden faintnesses at the last moment.

4. The quality or fact of being faint or of feebly affecting the senses; dimness or feebleness (of light, colour, outline, etc.).

1651 DAVENANT *Gondibert* III. iv. 50 It [the emerald].. will, when worn by the neglected wife, Shew when her absent Lord disloyal proves, By faintness. **1732** BERKELEY *Alciphr.* IV. §8 Littleness or Faintness..seem to have no necessary connexion with greater Length of Distance. **1824** L. MURRAY *Eng. Gram.* (ed. 5) I. 40 The faintness of the sound of this letter. **1883** F. M. CRAWFORD *Dr. Claudius* ix. 169 The faintness of the gathering twilight.

faints (feɪnts), *sb. pl.* Also 9 feints. [pl. of FAINT *a.* (quasi-*sb.*).] The impure spirit which comes over first and last in the process of distillation. Also *attrib.*

1743 MAXWELL *Sel. Trans.* 295 Is it not a great Fault among Distillers, to allow any of the Faints to run among their pure Goods? **1816** J. SMITH *Panorama Sc. & Art* II. 580 The latter part of this running being weak, is called feints. **1883** J. GARDNER *Brewer, Distiller etc.* v. 146 The remaining weak spirit that distils over, called faints, is caught separately.

attrib. **1880** *Act 43-4 Vict.* c. 24 Sched. 1, A low wines and feints charger must be connected with the still. *Ibid.* 24 §3 Spirits conveyed into a feints receiver.

fainty ('feɪntɪ), *a. Obs.* exc. *poet.* and *dial.* [f. FAINT *a.* + -Y.]

1. Faint, sickly, languid. In later use chiefly: Inclined to swoon.

1530 TINDALE *Pract. Prelates* Wks. II. 257 Faith waxed feeble and fainty. **1586** COGAN *Haven Health* lxix. (1636) 78 If a man use much Saffron, it will make him very fainty. **1648** GAGE *West Ind.* xvi. (1655) 109, I presently found my stomach fainty. **1697** DRYDEN *Virg. Georg.* II. 431 The fainty Root can take no steady hold. **1700** —— *Fables, Flower & Leaf* 381 The fainty knights..knew not where To run for shelter. **1796** COLERIDGE in Mrs. Sandford *T. Poole & Friends* (1888) I. 177 It..left me pale and fainty. **1855** SINGLETON *Virgil* I. 295 All hands..their fainty frames have flung Upon the earth. **1884** HOLLAND *Chester Gloss.* s.v. *Aitch*, Fainty aitches are fainting fits.

2. Causing or productive of faintness; sickly.

1590 T. WATSON *Eglogve Death Sir F. Walsingham* 107 Who shall recure their faintie maladies? **1600** ABP. ABBOT *Exp. Jonah* 602 A faintie sultrie blowing. **1683** TRYON *Way to Health* 86 They are apt to sweat much, whence proceeds a fainty Indisposition.

Hence †**'faintiness**.

1683 TRYON *Way to Health* 31 Green Corn or Grass.. makes such Cattle..apt to faintyness and Diseases. *Ibid.* 593 Causing a general Faintiness to attend the whole Body.

faiple, Sc. var. of FIPPLE, underlip.

fair (fɛə(r)), *sb.*[1] Forms: 4-5 feire, feyre, 4-7 faire, fayre, 5-6 fayer (6 faier), 5-7 fare, 7- fair. [a. OF. *feire* (mod.F. *foire*) = Pr. *feira*, *fiera*, *fieyra*, Sp. *feria*, Pg. *feira*, It. *fiera*:—Lat. *fēria* holiday.]

1. a. A periodical gathering of buyers and sellers, often with shows and entertainments, in a place and at a time ordained by charter or statute or by ancient custom. Freq. modified by prefixing other words, indicating the things sold, the time of year, or some special object for which the fair is held; as *cattle-*, *cheese-*, *horse-*, *ram-*, *sheep-*, etc., *fair*; *Easter-*, *Michaelmas-*, *summer-fair*. More recently also *spec.* (*a*) an exhibition, esp. one designed to publicize a particular product or the products of one industry, country, etc.; freq. with defining word pre-fixed; (*b*) = *fun fair*.

[**1292** BRITTON I. xiv. §3 Qe il facent crier la pes de eux en citez..et en feyres et en marchez.] *c* **1330** R. BRUNNE *Chron.* (1810) 328 In feire and markette þei salle seke him oute. **1393** LANGL. *P. Pl.* C. VII. 211 Ich wente to þe faire With many [maner] marchandises. **1489** *Ld. Treas. Acc. Scot.* (1877) I. 119 A blak horss boycht..in the fayre. **1548** HALL *Chron.* 122 b, The faier, on the day of Sainct Michaell the Archangell, kepte in..the toune of Caen. **1611** BIBLE *Transl. Pref.* 12 To neglect a great faire, and to seeke to make markets aftewards. **1686** *Col. Rec. Pennsylv.* I. 181 Ye freemen..of New Castle..Requesting a Fare to be kept in yt Towne twice a year. **1763** [see ROUNDABOUT *sb.* 4 b]. **1764** FOOTE *Mayor of G.* II. i, Has he not..made himself the fool of the fair. **1805** *National Intelligencer* (Washington, D.C.) 24 Apr. 3/2 Washington Fairs. It will be perceived..that.. the premiums offered, may be an inducement to graziers and farmers to bring their cattle and other effects to the city. **1818** CRUISE *Digest* (ed. 2) III. 272 Where the King grants a fair or market, the grantee shall have..a court of record. **1841** ELPHINSTONE *Hist. Ind.* I. 327 Each has its market day, and its annual fairs and festivals. **1844** *Farmers' Cabinet* 15 Oct. 73/1 New York State Fair and Cattle Show at Poughkeepsie. **1850** *New Eng. Farmer* II. 413 The State Board of Agriculture are making up a collection of samples of Indian Corn for the World's Fair [*i.e.* the International Exhibition of 1851 in London.] **1856** *Spirit of Times* 11 Oct. 95/1 The Ladies' Riding Match at the Monroe County Fair. **1857** MRS. CARLYLE *Lett.* II. 315 A mere cattle-fair; no booths with toys and sweeties. **1863** [see *book-fair* s.v. BOOK *sb.* 18 a]. **1864** P. PATERSON *Glimpses Real Life* xvii. 164 The penny-showman fights his battle of life, industriously wandering from one fair to another... At these places are usually congregated a multifarious crowd of exhibitions, swings, merry-go-rounds, Punch-and-Judys, and living skeletons. **1870** E. PEACOCK *Ralf Skirl.* II. 145 The summer fair had long gone by. **1903** *Daily Chron.* 7 Dec. 5/1 In America the word 'fair' has been preserved to describe meetings at which prizes are awarded for farm live stock. **1950** *Oxf. Jun. Encycl.* IX. 209/1 All the paraphernalia of a modern fair is carried in vans and on trailers from fairground to fairground. **1952** *Sat. Rev.* 25 Oct. 67/1 This year's Audio Fair will show a tremendous improvement in [loud-] speakers designed in the conventional way. **1968** D. BRAITHWAITE *Fairground Archit.* i. 13 The atmosphere of today's pleasure fair is far removed from the vigorous barter of primitive trading fairs. **1969** 'A. CADE' *Turn up Stone* i. 10 Michael's previous forays overseas had been limited to..an annual pilgrimage to the Frankfurt Book Fair.

b. phr. *a day after the fair*: too late.

1548 HALL *Chron.* 218 b, A daie after the faire, as the common proverbe saieth. **1676** ETHEREDGE *Man of Mode* III. i, You came a day after the fair. **1882** P. FITZGERALD *Recreat. Lit. Mag.* (1883) 55 It..would be the day after the fair.

c. *transf.* Applied to a 'bazaar' or collection of goods to be sold to raise money for a charitable purpose. Chiefly in *fancy-fair* (see FANCY *a.* 1 d), *church-fair* (*U.S.*).

1876 W. A. BUTLER *Mrs. Limber's Raffle* i. 18 A church fair, or any fair, in fact, always seems to me like a contrivance to get a great deal of money for very little value.

d. *fun of the fair*: colloq. phr., in extended use.

1852 DICKENS *Bleak Ho.* xxiv. 250 You're half the fun of the fair, in the Court of Chancery. **1899** R. WHITEING *No. 5 John St.* xi. 104 The balance, 11s. 6½d., must serve for everything—washing, food, odds and ends, household and personal. 'The fun of the fair.' **1940** 'N. BLAKE' *Malice in Wonderland* I. ii. 25, £3 10.0. inclusive of everything—all the fun of the fair, as you might say. **1954** L. MACNEICE *Autumn Sequel* x. 69 The last Fun of the fair will snap with a snap of elastic.

2. *attrib.* and *Comb.*, as *fair-booth*, *-day*, *-goer*, *-ground*, *-place*, *-stead*, *-time*, *-town*; *fair-like* adj.; *fair-wards* adv.; **fair-going** *a.*, going to a fair; **fair-keeper**, (*a*) one who has a stall, etc., at a fair; (*b*) an officer charged with the maintenance of order at a fair.

1862 H. MARRYAT *Year in Sweden* II. 385 On the village-green stand moss-grown *fair-booths. **1568** GRAFTON *Chron.* II. 431 He..tooke the towne of Peples on their *fayre day. **1678** BUNYAN *Pilgr.* 122 The Prince of Princes..went through this Town..upon a Fair-day. **1771** WESLEY *Jrnl.* 18 June, It being the fair-day. **1929** A. CLARKE *Later Poems* (1961) 19 When tide had filled the boat-rings, Few dealers could be tempted Who drank upon the fair-day. **1836** DICKENS *Sk. Boz.* I. 321 The regular *fair-goers. **1966** *Times* 28 Feb. (Canada Suppl.) p. x/3 A determined fair-goer could travel through Ontario, Quebec..and find a fair every day. **1801** BLOOMFIELD *Rural T.* (1802) 6 Many a kind *Fair-going face. **1851** MRS. BROWNING *Casa Guidi Windows* 123 The world..has grown A Fair-going world. **1741** LADY POMFRET *Let.* 21 June (1805) III. 247 The *fair-ground; which is a square enclosure, with..shops of all sorts on each hand. **1881** *Echo* 9 July 3/1 The Munster pig buyers have peremptorily refused to buy on the fair-ground of Sir Henry Becher. **1953** *Encounter* Oct. 40/1 A blue-green, rococo building..that reminds me of a fair-ground pavilion, and is a temple. **1708** *Lond. Gaz.* No. 4398/3 The *Fair-keepers resorting to the Two Fairs held in..Bristol. **1864** A. McKAY *Hist. Kilmarnock* 106 The guard, or 'fair-keepers'.. were supplied with ale, etc., at the expense of the town. **1577-87** HOLINSHED *Chron.* II. 21/2 The..*fairlike markets ..kept in Dublin. **1898** *Daily News* 28 Mar. 4/3 The shooting galleries, cocoanut 'shies' and other fair-like attractions. **1795** *Sporting Mag.* V. 39 A battle was fought in the *fair-place. **1657** REEVE *God's Plea* 166 Merchandize.. is the Nations Head-servant..sent out to all the earth, as to a generall Market, and *fairstead to buy her provisions. **1467** in *Eng. Gilds* (1870) 384 In the *feyre tyme ij d. **1602** CAREW *Cornwall* 122 a, Camelford, a market and *Fayre (but not faire) towne. **1926** W. J. LOCKE *Stories Near & Far* 298 The gradual traffic going *fair-wards passed him by.

fair (fɛə(r)), *a.* and *sb.*[2] Forms: *a.* 1 fæȝer, (fæȝir), 2 *Orm.* faȝȝerr, (3 fæier, -iȝer, -ir, faȝer, faiȝer, feiȝer), 2-6 feir, -yr, feier, -yer, 5-7 faire, -yr(e, 5 feire, -yre, 3-6 faier, -yer, (5 fayir), 4-7 far(e, 2- fair. *β.* 2-3 veir, (3 væȝer, veȝer, veieȝer), 3-4 vair, -yr. [Com. Teutonic: OE.

fæȝer = OS. *fagar*, OHG. *fagar*, ON. *fagr* (Sw., Da. *fager*), Goth. *fagrs*:—OTeut. **fagro-z*.]

A. *adj.* (In all the older senses formerly used antithetically with *foul*. This is now *obs.* or *arch.* exc. with the sbs. *weather, means*.)

I. Beautiful.

1. Beautiful to the eye; of pleasing form or appearance; good-looking. Phrases, ***fair to see*** (arch.); ***fair and free*** (obs. or arch.).

No longer in colloquial use; in literature very common, but slightly *arch.* or *rhetorical*.

a. of persons; chiefly with reference to the face; in mod. use, almost exclusively of women. Also of the body or its parts.

c **888** K. ÆLFRED *Boeth.* xxxii. §2 Swa fæȝer swa swa Alcibiades..wæs. *a* **1000** *Cædmon's Gen.* 457 Oþ-ðæt he Adam ȝearone funde..and his wif somed, freo fæȝroste. *c* **1200** ORMIN 6392 þatt an wass swiþe faȝȝerr wif. *c* **1205** LAY. 3886 He wes wis he wes fæir. *Ibid.* 25305 þa ueieȝereste wifmen. *c* **1250** *Gen. & Ex.* 2659 So faiȝer he was on to sen. **1297** R. GLOUC. (1724) 66 Fairor womman nas þo non. *Ibid.* 556 Vairore fole ne miȝt be, þan wiþ him was þere. *a* **1300** *Cursor M.* 4223 (Cott.) Ioseph..was fre and feir. *c* **1320** *Sir Beues* 538 Ne non, so faire limes hade! *c* **1385** CHAUCER *L.G.W.* 613 *Cleopatras*, Sche was fayr as is the Rose in May. **1398** TREVISA *Barth. De P. R.* v. xviii. (1495) 123 Yf the chynne be proporcyonate to the foreheed, it makyth it fare. *a* **1400–50** *Alexander* 601 þe fax on his faire hede was ferly to schawe. *c* **1435** *Torr. Portugal* 782 My dowghttyr gente That ys so feyer and fre. **1548** HALL *Chron.* 166 b, In this trobleous season..was yᵉ quene delivered at Westmynster of a fayre sonne. **1553** T. WILSON *Rhet.* (1580) 40 A Gentle-woman..faire of bodie. **1602** SHAKS. *Ham.* I. i. 47 That Faire and Warlike forme. **1667** MILTON *P.L.* IV. 324 The fairest of her Daughters Eve. **1697** DRYDEN *Virg. Georg.* IV. 760 His Head, from his fair Shoulders torn. **1810** SCOTT *Lady of L.* II. xxv, Of stature fair. **1832** TENNYSON *Sisters*, The earl was fair to see. **1864** —— *Aylmer's F.* 681 Fair as the Angel that said 'Hail!'

fig. **1871** R. B. VAUGHAN *Life T. Aquinas* II. 639 The noblest and fairest spirits of beautiful, wicked Athens.

b. Applied to women, as expressing the quality characteristic of their sex. So, ***the fair sex*** (= Fr. *le beau sexe*), ***a fair one.*** Also in comparative.

c **1440** *York Myst.* xlvi. 259 If we bynde ouȝte þat faire one in fere nowe. **1599** MINSHEU *Dial. Sp. & Eng.* (1623) 5 What from our faire neighbour? Yea Sir. Well..they are from a cleanly woman. **1638** BAKER tr. *Balzac's Lett.* II. 92, I..can by no meanes approve the ambition of your fayre neighbour. **1665** BOYLE *Occas. Refl.* v. ix. (1675) 329 Persons of the fairer sex. **1690** LOCKE *Hum. Und.* III. x. §34 Eloquence, like the fair sex, has too prevailing beauties in it to suffer itself ever to be spoken against. **1711** SHAFTESB. *Charac.* (1737) I. 331 The confessing lover..ascribes all to the bounty of the fair-one. **1726** *Adv. Capt. R. Boyle* 48 A Note..which my fair Correspondent had taken Opportunity of leaving. **1732** BERKELEY *Alciphr.* II. §24 The fair sex have now nothing to do but dress and paint. **1798** FERRIAR *Illustr. Sterne* v. 155 My fair readers must excuse me. **1800** *Med. Jrnl.* III. 442 These melancholy cases..spread a general alarm over a considerable district among the fair sex. **1825** A. CUNNINGHAM '*Wet Sheet & Flowing Sea*' 10 O for a soft and gentle wind! I heard a fair one cry. **1878** J. H. BEADLE *Western Wilds* xxix. 451 The fairer section of our party are startled at the crowds of men in the streets.

absol. with plural sense.

1700 DRYDEN *Fables, Cock & Fox* 624 What will not Beaux attempt to please the Fair? **1777** W. DALRYMPLE *Trav. Sp. & Port.* xviii, At church..the fair carry the appearance of saints.

c. of abstractions personified.

1742 POPE *Dunc.* IV. 24 There, stript, fair Rhet'ric languish'd on the ground. **1750** GRAY *Elegy, Epitaph* i, Fair science frown'd not on his humble birth. **1764** GOLDSM. *Trav.* 365 Fair Freedom, taught..to feel The rabble's rage.

d. used in courteous or respectful address. *Obs.* exc. *arch.*

c **1350** *Will. Palerne* 4596 Faire fader, bi mi feiþ folili ȝe wrouȝten. *c* **1450** *Merlin* 9 Ffeire suster ye ouȝt not to come in this place. *Ibid.* 15 Feyre sone, for youre sake shall I suffir the deth. **1483** CAXTON *Gold. Leg.* 92/3 Ha faire sires he was but late byheded. **1530** PALSGR. 218/2 Fayresyr, *beau sire.* **1568** GRAFTON *Chron.* II. 205 Ye be welcome fayre sister, with my fayre Nephew your sonne. **1588** SHAKS. *L.L.L.* v. ii. 310 Faire sir, God saue you. **1820** SCOTT *Abbot* xi, 'So much for your lineage, fair sir,' replied his companion. **1889** 'MARK TWAIN' *Connecticut Yankee* 230 Even so, fair my lord.

†**e.** of animals. Hence in Hunting use applied distinctively to a roebuck of the fifth year. *Obs.*

c **1220** *Bestiary* 734 Panter is an wilde der, Is non fairere on werlde her. **1382** WYCLIF *Jer.* xlvi. 20 The she calf fair and shapli Egipt. **1486** *Bk. St. Alban's* A vj b, This is a fayr hawke. **1535** COVERDALE *Judges* v. 10 Ye that ride upon fayre Asses. **1576** FLEMING *Panopl. Epist.* 401 A sea Gull among a sort of faire swannes. **1664** POWER *Exp. Philos.* I. 1 In it [the flea] are two fair eyes. **1728** POPE *Dunc.* II. 41 A partridge plump, full-fed and fair. **1820** SCOTT *Abbot* i, The fairest herd in the Halidome.

f. of inanimate things.

Beowulf 773 On hrusan ne feol fæger foldbold. *c* **1175** *Lamb. Hom.* 25 He..bið al swa is an eppel iheoweð, he bið wið-uten feire and frakel wið-innen. *c* **1200** *Trin. Coll. Hom.* 185 A faier bode inne to wunien. *c* **1290** *S. Eng. Leg.* I. 48/42 A fayr wode in deorsete. *a* **1300** *Cursor M.* 22511 (Cott.) þe sun..es þe fairest on to loke at middai-time. *c* **1340** *Ibid.* 2468 (Trin.) A..fair cuntre þe flom ran þourȝe feire to se. *a* **1400–50** *Alexander* 1541 On hys heued a hoge fair myter. **1495** *Act 11 Hen VII*, c. 16 Preamb., Divers tenementes and feier places bilded ther. **1526** *Pilgr. Perf.* (W. de W. 1531) 46 He brynge forth euery yere fayre floures. **1548** HALL *Chron.* 87 The fayre toune of Compaigne. **1596** SHAKS. *Tam. Shr.* Induct. i. 46 Carrie him..to my fairest Chamber. **1658** *Vestry Bks.* (Surtees) 324 He hath already a fayre and large pew in the church. **1710** HEARNE *Collect.* (Oxf. Hist. Soc.) III. 88 He presented his Majesty with a fair guilt Cup. **1719** DE FOE *Crusoe* (1858) 422 The same wicker work, but much fairer. **1799** WORDSW. '*She dwelt*' Wks. (1888) 115/1 A violet..Fair as a star, when only one Is shining in the sky. **1808** SCOTT *Marm.* I. i, Tweed's fair river, broad, and deep. **1819** SHELLEY *Cenci* v. iv. 104 Awakening earthquake, o'er whose couch Even now a city stands, strong, fair and free. **1842** BARHAM *Ingol. Leg., Ingol. Penance*, The Ingoldsby lands are broad and fair. **1849** RUSKIN *Sev. Lamps* vi. §20. 182 A fair building is..worth the ground it stands on.

g. of appearance, visible qualities, arrangement, etc.

c **1175** *Cott. Hom.* 219 Hi alle wurðon awende of þan feȝre hiwe. *c* **1340** *Cursor M.* 4225 (Trin.) þi godenes & þi feire hew. *c* **1400** *Rom. Rose* 3613 As faire semblaunt thanne shewed he me..As aforn didde he. **1535** COVERDALE *Judith* xvi. 7 Iudith..with hir fayre bewtye hath discomfited him. **1563** SHUTE *Archit.* D iij b, Ye may finde a faire diminishing as I have said before. **1867** MISS BRADDON *Rupert Godwin* I. i. 1 The Captain and his wife were both in the fairest prime of middle age.

h. In various plant names, as **fair days, grass,** the Goose-grass (*Potentilla anserina*); **fair in sight,** the Blue-bell. See also FAIR MAID.

1578 LYTE *Dodoens* II. xxiii. 175 These floures [Blue bells] be now called Fayre in sight. **1884** MILLER *Plant-n.* 42/2 Fair Grass, or Fair Days, *Potentilla anserina.*

†**2.** Of sounds, odours, etc.: Agreeable, delightful. *Obs.*

a **1000** *Cædmon's Exod.* 566 (Gr.) Seȝnas stodon on fæȝerne sweg. **13..** *E.E. Allit. P.* A. 46 A fayr reflayr ȝet fro hit flot.

†**3. a.** Desirable, reputable. *Obs.*

c **1380** WYCLIF *Sel. Wks.* III. 144 Ffeyre hit is to haue a son. *c* **1386** CHAUCER *Prol.* 212 (Harl. MS.) He hadde i-made many a faire mariage. **1393** LANGL. *P. Pl.* C. xxii. 28–9 To be cald a knyght is fair..To be cald a kyng is fairour. **1650** FULLER *Pisgah* IV. vii. 134 His two sons who slew him, got exile..too fair a reward for so foul a Patricide. **1676** ETHEREDGE *Man of Mode* II. ii, E'ne let him go, a fair riddance.

b. Of an amount, an estate, fortune, etc.: Considerable, 'handsome', liberal.

a **1240** *Ureisun* in *Cott. Hom.* 199 þu schalt me a ueir dol of heoueriche blisse. **1642** R. CARPENTER *Experience* IV. xii. 172 The imagination..performeth a faire deale more in the Table, than the painter. **1654** SIR E. NICHOLAS in *N. Papers* (Camden) II. 88 A faire fortune is come to our countryman Sir Chi. Wrey. **1848** MACAULAY *Hist. Eng.* II. 112 Scotland, since her sovereigns had succeeded to a fairer inheritance, had been independent only in name. **1859** JEPHSON *Brittany* xviii. 289 Giles, to whom a fair heritage was no less agreeable than a fair wife.

†**4.** Of language, diction: Elegant. Hence ***fair speaker.*** *Obs.*

c **1380** *Antecrist* in Todd 3 *Treat. Wyclif* 141 If hise [antichrist's] clerkis cunne speke fayre latyne. **1398** TREVISA *Barth. De P.R.* XV. lxviii. (1495) 514 Men of Grecia were fayr and moost grete spekers. *c* **1425** WYNTOUN *Cron.* IX. Prol. 10 To tret a matere in fare Dyte. *c* **1440** *Promp. Parv.* 146 Fayre spekar, *orator.* **1477** EARL RIVERS (Caxton) *Dictes* 145 It was..translated into right good and fayr englissh.

5. a. Of external manifestations, words, promises: Attractive or pleasing at the first sight or hearing; specious, plausible, flattering.

a **1000** *Cædmon's Gen.* 899 (Gr.) Me nædre beswac..þurh fæȝir word. *a* **1200** *Vices & Virtues* (1888) 11 Ic habbe beswiken min emcristen mid faire wordes. *a* **1300** *Cursor M.* 24824 (Cott.) Wit hightes fair he wan þair will. **1362** LANGL. *P. Pl.* A. II. 23 Fauuel with feir speche haþ brouȝt hem togedere. *c* **1400** *Lanfranc's Cirurg.* 173 He mote be war þat faire biheste ne veyn glorie ne coveitise ne bigile him not. **1473** WARKW. *Chron.* 7 By fayre speche..the Kynge scaped oute of the Bisshoppys handes. **1538** STARKEY *England* II. ii. 191 By hys dyssymulatyon and Fare wordys [he] was interteynyd in a long sute. **1568** GRAFTON *Chron.* II. 17 A feyre speaker, and a deepe dissembler. **1611** BIBLE *Gal.* vi. 12 Many..desire to make a faire shew in the flesh. **1653** H. MORE *Antid. Ath.* III. ix. (1712) 115 A fair Tale was made to the Pastor of the Parish. **1695** CONGREVE *Love for Love* IV. xiii, After all your fair speeches..and kissing, and hugging. **1873** BURTON *Hist. Scot.* V. lvi. 125 He has fallen away from all his fair promises. **1875** JOWETT *Plato* (ed. 2) III. 604 The Sophists have plenty of brave words and fair devices.

b. *Proverbs.*

1471 [see FAIN *a.* 1 b]. *c* **1572** GASCOIGNE *Fruites Warre* Wks. 154 Fayre wordes make fooles fayne. **1593** DRAYTON *Idea* lix, 'Fair words make fools', replieth he again. **1676** WYCHERLEY *Pl. Dealer* V. iii, Fair words butter no cabbage.

II. 6. Of complexion and hair: Light as opposed to dark.

App. not of very early origin. In the context of our first quot. 'brown' and 'foul' are treated as equivalent.

1551 T. WILSON *Logike* (1580) 34 b, I shall marrie a faire woman..a browne woman. **1554** J. WALLIS in *Songs & Ball.* (Roxb. 1860) 146 [Women are] Fearare than the flower delyce, Ruddye as the rose. **1604** SHAKS. *Oth.* I. iii. 291 Your Son-in-law is farre more Faire then Blacke. *a* **1661** FULLER *Worthies* (1840) III. 392 Negroes have their beauties as well as fair folk. **1697** DRYDEN *Virg. Past.* x. 58 Are Violets not sweet, because not fair? **1774** GOLDSM. *Nat. Hist.* (1776) II. 232 In all regions, the children are born fair, or at least red. **1803** *Med. Jrnl.* X. 547 Persons who have the fairest skin. **1864** TENNYSON *Aylmer's F.* 193 His [face]..Sear'd by the close ecliptic, was not fair.

III. Free from blemish or disfigurement.

†**7.** Of fruit, flesh, etc.: Sound, free from disease or specks. *Obs.*

c **1400** *Lanfranc's Cirurg.* 93 þe fleisch is maad fairer þan it was tofore. *c* **1450** *Two Cookery-bks.* 83 Take faire rawe parcelly. **1669** WORLIDGE *Syst. Agric.* (1681) 165 The fairest may be kept for Seed, as before of Carrots. **1671** *Eng. Rogue* IV. xi. 204 [Street cry] Fair Oranges,—Fair Lemons. *c* **1770** MRS. GLASSE *Compl. Confectioner* 6 Take the fairest and firmest pippins.

8. †**a.** Of things in general: Clean, unsoiled, unstained. Of paper: Not written upon, unused. *Obs.*

c **1420** *Liber Cocorum* (1862) 39 Put hit in cofyns þat bene fayre. *c* **1450** *Two Cookery-bks.* 82 Put þe pork on a faire spitte. **1552** *Bk. Com. Prayer* Communion, A fayre white lynnen clothe. **1660** BOYLE *New Exp. Phys. Mech.* xxxvi. (1682) 142, I took a fair glass siphon. **1703** M. MARTIN *W. Islands Scot.* 278 They [the bones] were fair and dry. **1737** WESLEY *Wks.* (1872) I. 46 A paper book; all the leaves thereof were fair, except one. **1800** HERSCHEL in *Phil. Trans.* XC. 529 The vanes are covered with a piece of fair white paper.

b. Of water: Clean, pure. Now *rare.* †Of colour: Clear, not cloudy.

c **1340** *Cursor M.* 20212 (Fairf.) Ho..wasshed hir bodi in faire water. *c* **1440** *Douce MS.* 55 fol. 10 Bray hem in a morter small with feyre water. **1577** B. GOOGE *Heresbach's Husb.* III. (1586) 121 Most Bullockes..desire a faire cleere water. **1655** CULPEPPER *Riverius* I. xi. 42 Fair water may suffice to wash the Feet. **1663** GERBIER *Counsel* 108 As red as the fairest Vermilion. **1669** STURMY *Mariner's Mag.* v. 65 Gun-powder of a faire Azure..colour is very good. **1727** A. HAMILTON *New Acc. E. Ind.* II. xxxvi. 43 A Dish of Rice boiled in fair Water. **1756** BURKE *Subl. & B.* III. xvii, The colours of beautiful bodies must not be dusky or muddy, but clean and fair. **1816** SCOTT *Antiq.* xxxvi, A glass of fair water. **1858** O. W. HOLMES *Aut. Breakf.-t.* (1883) 3 The rinsings..spoil a draught of fair water.

c. Of handwriting: Neat, clear, legible. ***fair copy***: a transcript free from corrections. Cf. CLEAN *a.* 3 c. See FAIR COPY.

1697 DAMPIER *Voy.* (1698) I. 355 This Letter was written in a very fair hand. **1709** HEARNE *Collect.* (Oxf. Hist. Soc.) II. 228 A fair copy of the Statutes. **1828** COLEBROOKE *Misc. Ess.* (1873) I. 518 Let him appoint, as scribe, one..whose hand-writing is fair, etc. **1844** DICKENS *Mart. Chuz.* I, A fair copy of his draft of the catalogue.

d. Phrase. Cf. CLEAN 3 d.

1562 J. HEYWOOD *Prov. & Epigr.* (1867) 64 Except hir maide shewe a fayre paire of heeles. **1630** WADSWORTH *Sp. Pilgr.* viii. 83, I shewed them a faire paire of heeles.

e. Of a line, curve, or surface: Free from roughnesses or irregularities; smooth, even. Now chiefly *Naut.*

1486 *Bk. St. Alban's* D ij b, Take a tame Malarde and set hym in a fayr playn. **1577** B. GOOGE *Heresbach's Husb.* I. (1586) 42 b, The floore must be fayre and smoothe made. *c* **1850** *Rudim. Navig.* (Weale) 117 *Fair*, a term to denote the evenness or regularity of a curve or line. **1888** LONGF. in *Scribn. Mag.* III. 424 Fair surfaces have fallen into neglect nowadays, our present fancy being for..wrinkled or blotchy surfaces.

9. Of character, conduct, reputation: Free from moral stain, spotless, unblemished. Also in phrase ***to stand fair.***

c **1175** *Lamb. Hom.* 137 Æuric mon þe ledeð feir lif and clene. *c* **1200** *Trin. Coll. Hom.* 85 Manie swo ledden here lif þat te biginninge was fair, and te middel fairere, and te ende alre fairest. *c* **1330** R. BRUNNE *Chron.* (1810) 14 Ailrik was..a duke of faire fame. **1676** HALE *Contempl.* I. 47 A quiet, serene, and fair Conscience. *a* **1704** T. BROWN *Two Oxford Scholars* Wks. 1730 I. 6 The poor painful priest standing fair in the Opinion of the neighbourhood. **1734** EARL OXFORD in *Swift's Lett.* (1768) IV. 64 This person..had the fairest and most unexceptionable character. **1819** SHELLEY *Cenci* III. i. 293 My fair fame. **1892** F. HALL in *Nation* (N.Y.) LV. 411/2 To the detriment of his fair fame.

10. a. Of conduct, actions, arguments, methods: Free from bias, fraud, or injustice; equitable, legitimate. Hence of persons: Equitable; not taking undue advantage; disposed to concede every reasonable claim. Of objects: That may be legitimately aimed at; often in ***fair game***, fig.; ***fair wage(s)*** (also *attrib.*). See FAIR AND SQUARE, FAIR TRADE.

c **1340** *Cursor M.* 13837 (Trin.) þo dedes to vs be not faire. *c* **1435** *Torr. Portugal* 786 Were that feyer, To make an erlles sone myn Eyer? **1641** J. JACKSON *True Evang. T.* II. 95 The fat Calfe. Whereby, in a faire parabolicall interpretation, is meant..Christ himselfe. **1647** SIR E. NICHOLAS in *N. Papers* (Camden) I. 77 L. C. doubts not of Lo. Bruces faire dealing. **1680** OTWAY *Orphan* III. i. 811 The fair Hunter's cheated of his Prey. **1690** LOCKE *Hum. Und.* III. x. (1695) 287 As fair a Man, as he..who sells several Things under the same Name. **1748** HARTLEY *Observ. Man* I. iii. 278 Words which have the fairest Right to each Class. **1790** PALEY *Horæ Paul.* Rom. ii. 18 [It] is rendered a fair subject of presumption. **1801** M. EDGEWORTH *Belinda* I. vii. 209 Quiz the doctor..he's an author—so fair game. **1816** BENTHAM *Chrestom.* 296 In that character it becomes fair game for ridicule. **1825, 1852** [see GAME *sb.* 10 b]. **1839** T. ATTWOOD *Sp. in Ho. Com.* 14 June, They only ask for a fair day's wages for a fair day's work. **1848** MACAULAY *Hist. Eng.* I. 567 The king..would fall by fair fighting and not by murder. **1854** H. ROGERS *Ess.* II. i. 10 The fairest of all controversial antagonists. **1870** MAX MÜLLER *Sc. Relig.* (1873) 150 *note*, It is but fair..to state. **1885** *Law Times* 28 Mar. 388/2 A fair account should be given. **1886** *Pall Mall G.* 27 Oct. 3/2 'Fair houses', i.e. firms where the rules of the Union are followed. **1894** S. & B. WEBB *Hist. Trade Unionism* 386 A hundred and fifty local authorities have now (1894) adopted some kind of 'Fair Wages' resolution. **1902** *Encycl. Brit.* XXXII. 692/1 The extent to which a 'fair wages clause', in some form or another, has been inserted in public contracts. **1907** *Westm. Gaz.* 3 Sept. 7/1 The committee appointed to consider the fair-wages resolution. **1909** *Daily Chron.* 11 Mar. 1/7 The Labour party's motion for a stricter fair-wage clause in Government contracts.

b. Of conditions, position, etc.: Affording an equal chance of success; not unduly favourable or adverse to either side. Phrase, ***a fair field (and no favour).***

1711 PUCKLE *Club* 22 *note*, Supposing both box and dice fair, gamesters have the peep, eclipse, thumbing. **1771**

FRANKLIN *Autobiog.* Wks. 1840 I. 60, I was now on a fair footing with them. **1845** JAMES *A. Neil* I. vii. 143 That would not matter if the ground were fair. **1873** 'MARK TWAIN' & WARNER *Gilded Age* 355 For the first time in his life his talents had a fair field. **1883** E. PENNELL-ELMHIRST *Cream Leicestersh.* 202 He..asked only for a fair field and a clear course.

c. ***fair play***: upright conduct in a game; equity in the conditions or opportunities afforded to a player; *transf.* upright conduct, equitable conditions of action generally.

1595 SHAKS. *John* v. i. 67 Shall we vpon the footing of our land, Send fayre-play-orders, and make comprimise. *Ibid.* v. ii. 118 According to the faire-play of the world, Let me haue audience. **1630** *R. Johnson's Kingd. & Commw.* A ij b, Some..name him when they quote him; and thats faire play. **1669** MARVELL *Corr.* cxxvi. Wks. 1872–5 II. 287 To give the fairest play to him. **1744** BERKELEY *Let. Tarwater* §21 Give this medicine fair play. **1824** SCOTT *Redgauntlet* xx, Fair play's a jewel. **1844** DISRAELI *Coningsby* IV. v, To prevent his fine manners having their fair play. **1882** C. M. YONGE *Unknown to Hist.* xxxvi, Fear of the future shut his eyes to all sense of justice and fair play.

d. *spec.* in games.

1856 *Spirit of Times* (N.Y.) 6 Dec. 229/1 A player must make his first base after striking a fair ball. **1867** *Routledge's Handbk. Football* 41 Knocking on and throwing forward are disallowed: in case of this rule being broken a catch from such a knock or throw shall be equivalent to a fair catch. *Ibid.* 47 A Fair Catch is a catch from a kick, or a knock on from the hand but not from the arm of the opposite side, or a throw on, when the catcher makes a mark with his heel provided no one else on his side touch the ball. **1896** KNOWLES & MORTON *Baseball* 23 If the ball falls exactly on the foul line, it is a fair hit, unless it rolls into foul territory. **1935** *Encycl. Sports* 518/1 A fair catch can be made in a player's own In-goal. **1960** E. S. & W. J. HIGHAM *High Speed Rugby* xiii. 183 The method of making a fair-catch is to make a mark on the ground with the heel as the ball is caught, and to call: 'Mark!'

e. ***fair do's***: see DO *sb.*[1] 2 c.

f. ***fair enough***, colloq. phr. implying acquiescence: 'that's reasonable'.

[**1866** TROLLOPE *Belton Est.* III. iii. 57 This was fair enough, and she..promised him that she would do her best.] **1926** WODEHOUSE *Heart of Goof* ix. 304 'I am going to ..tear him into little bits..and make him swallow himself.' 'Fair enough,' said Mr. Brown. **1934** A. CHRISTIE *Parker Pyne Investigates* 29 Wilbraham considered. 'Fair enough,' he said at last. 'I agree.' **1953** J. B. PRIESTLEY in *Best One-Act Plays 1952–53* 118 'The mistress must not press any demands upon a man who, whatever their relations may have been, is not the man she really wants, as she herself has said.' 'Fair enough.' **1958** G. BARKER *Two Plays* 18 'Why won't he come?' 'Simply because he don't want to.' 'Fair enough. Fair enough. Let's get the dinghy.' **1959** *Cambr. Rev.* 30 May 559/2 If one's employer makes plastic hot water bottles then, as far as humour goes, plastic hot water bottles will be his blind spot. Which, I came to suppose, was fair enough.

g. ***fair go***: see GO *sb.* 4 d.

11. a. Expressing moderate commendation: Free from grave objection; of tolerable though not highly excellent quality; 'pretty good'. Of amount or degree: Adequate though not ample; 'respectable'.

[**1795** BURKE *Corr.* (1844) IV. 317 The course taken by the enemy often becomes a fair rule of action.] **1860** TYNDALL *Glac.* I. xviii. 133 Fair glacier work was now before us. **1870** LUBBOCK *Orig. Civiliz.* ii. (1875) 37 Very fair drawings of animals. **1873** BLACK *Pr. Thule* xxiii. 385 A pretty fair notion of what had happened. **1874** GREEN *Short Hist.* vi. 304 Edward the Sixth, was a fair scholar in both the classical languages. **1875** HAMERTON *Intell. Life* x. v. 388 A person in fair health. **18..** R. KIPLING *Railway Folk* 56 A fair number of old soldiers.

b. In school reports, marking a passable degree of excellence.

1861 V. LUSHINGTON in *Working Men's Coll. Mag.* 149 Power to refuse the required certificate of school-attendance, unless the school is 'fair' for the purpose intended.

c. Unquestionable, absolute, complete, thorough (*dial.* or *slang*). Freq. *Austral.* and *N.Z.* See also DINK *sb.*[4] and *a.*[2], DINKUM B. *adj.*

1872 E. J. IRVING *Fireside Lays* 232 The sichts an' the soun's that we witnessed, Amaist made me greet for fair shame. **1889**, etc. Fair cop [see COP *sb.*[7] 1]. **1902** W. SATCHELL *Land of Lost* iv. 26 While it [*sc.* others' money] held out it would be a fair pour. **1916**, etc. [see COW *sb.*[1] 4 c]. **1937** N. MARSH *Vintage Murder* xxi. 174 'A fair nark' or, more emphatically, 'a fair cow' is anything inexpressibly tedious or baffling. **1944** N. COWARD *Middle East Diary* 10 They can ramp about among obscure English essayists and have a fair beano.

d. ***a fair treat***: something or someone highly enjoyable or satisfactory; also as *advb. phr. colloq.*

1898 J. D. BRAYSHAW *Slum Silhouettes* 3 The way 'e set abaht Bill was a fair treat: why, Bill couldn't git a look-in nohow. **1899** [see TREAT *sb.*[1] 5 b]. **1902** E. NESBIT *Five Children & It.* iv. 119 As Cyril said, and I can't think where he got hold of such a strange expression, 'It does you a fair treat!' **1905** H. G. WELLS *Kipps* I. iv. 80 These little Folkestone hills are a Fair Treat. **1936** 'N. BLAKE' *Thou Shell of Death* iii. 52 Miss Cavendish. You're looking a fair treat.

IV. Favourable; benign; unobstructed.

12. a. Of the weather: Favourable, not wet or stormy. Also with some notion of sense 1: Fine, bright, sunny. Now sometimes contrasted with *fine*, as 'the weather was fair, but not fine'.

c **1205** LAY. 7594 Heo hæfden swiðe fair weder. *c* **1450** *St. Cuthbert* (Surtees) 1077 His seruands on a day fayre Bare him with oute to take þe ayre. **1535** COVERDALE *Ecclus.* iii. 15 Thy synnes also shall melt awaye, like as the yse in yᵉ fayre warme wether. **1611** BIBLE *Matt.* xvi. 2 It will be faire weather: for the skie is red. *a* **1671** R. BOHUN *Disc. Wind* 122 At Surat, Malabar..and that coast of India, is the fair season till March. **1713** BERKELEY *Ess. Guardian* v. Wks. III. 161 Fair weather is the joy of my soul. **1781** COWPER *Anti-Thelypthora* 71 October..mild and fair as May. **1867** OUIDA *C. Castlemaine* (1879) 6 The morning was fair and cloudless.

†b. ***fair day, daylight*** = BROAD DAY, DAYLIGHT.

c **1450** *Merlin* 610 It was than feire day. **1523** LD. BERNERS *Froiss.* I. cclxv. 392 It was faire day or he coude get into the right waye. **1603** KNOLLES *Hist. Turks* (1621) 308 It was yet scarce fair day, when..the armies..began again the battell. **1605** SHAKS. *Lear* IV. vii. 52 Where am I? Faire day light?

c. *fig.*; esp. in phrases, † ***to make fair weather to, with***: to curry favour with. † ***to make it fair with***: to deal complaisantly with.

c **1380** WYCLIF *Sel. Wks.* III. 365 Crist..wolde not make it fair wiþ þes ordris. **1598** MARSTON *Sco. Villanie* I. 139 Ixion makes faire weather vnto love. **1625** BACON *Ess., Friendship* (Arb.) 173 Frendship maketh indeed a faire Day in the Affections, from Storme and Tempests. **1687** R. L'ESTRANGE *Answ. Diss.* 5 The Roman Catholiques are making Fair Weather with the Dissenters. **1866** CRUMP *Banking* ix. 217 For fair weather the Act of 1844 works.

13. Of the wind: Favourable to a ship's course. † ***to come fair***: to become favourable.

c **1384** CHAUCER *H. Fame* 1967 Of faire wyndes and eke of tempestes. **1593** SHAKS. *Rich. II*, II. ii. 123 The wind sits fair for news to go to Ireland. **1665** SIR T. HERBERT *Trav.* (1677) 386 So soon as the wind came fair aboard away we went. **1790** BEATSON *Nav. & Mil. Mem.* 374 To proceed..with the first fair wind. **1879** BEERBOHM *Patagonia* 1 A fair wind ..soon brought us close to our destination.

14. a. Giving promise of success; 'likely to succeed' (J.); likely, promising, advantageous, suitable. Of a star, omen: Propitious. Phrases, † ***to be, seem, stand fair for***, or ***to*** with *inf.*; ***to be in a fair way*** †***of, to***: to have a good chance of (doing, obtaining, or reaching something).

1375 BARBOUR *Bruce* XVII. 837 To se quhethir fayr war him till To ly about the toun all still. *c* **1400** *Destr. Troy* 1119 Now fraist we before how fairest wille be. *c* **1550** LLOYD *Treas. Health* (1585) 8 Ther is no better..nor no fayrer cure. **1588** SHAKS. *L.L.L.* IV. i. 10 A stand where you may make the fairest shoote. **1596** —— *Merch. V.* II. i. 20 Your selfe.. stood as faire As any commer..For my affection. **1603** KNOLLES *Hist. Turks* (1621) 113 They..let slip that so faire an opportunitie. *a* **1618** RALEIGH *Ess.* (1650) Ev, The Caliphes..obteined..a mighty Empire, which was in faire way to have enlarged. **1642** ROGERS *Naaman* 11 Many more ..who might seeme faire for it [the grace of God]. **1655** SIR E. NICHOLAS in *N. Papers* (Camden) II. 197 Cardinal Francisco Barbarini is believed to stand fair to be elected pope. **1669** BAXTER *Call to Unconverted* iv, How fair you are for everlasting salvation. **1676** WISEMAN *Surg.* v. ix. 386, I presently looked for the jugular veins..opened the fairest, and took away..a dozen ounces of blood. **1678** BUNYAN *Pilgr.* I. 29, I once was, as I thought, fair for the Cœlestial City. **1683** DRYDEN *Vind. Dk. of Guise*, The first play I undertook was the Duke of Guise, as the fairest way..of setting forth the rise of the late rebellion. **1757** BURKE *Abridgm. Eng. Hist.* Wks. 1842 II. 563 The crown, to which he had such fair pretensions. **1814** D. H. O'BRIEN *Captiv. & Escape* 101 Being at last in a fair way of succeeding. *c* **1820** SHELLEY *Homer's Hymn to Castor* 20 Fair omen of the voyage. **1822** —— *Trium. of Life* 256 The star that ruled his doom was far too fair. **1848** MACAULAY *Hist. Eng.* II. 551 A fair prospect of reaching their destination.

†b. ***a fair day***: success in battle. *Obs.*

1548 HALL *Chron.* 76 b, A famous victory and a faire daie. **1550** CROWLEY *Way to Wealth* 602 The Egiptians thought to haue had a faire day at them. **1600** HOLLAND *Livy* VI. xxxii. 239 They [the Romans]..were but only in some good hope of having a fair day of their enemies.

†c. ***to have the fairer*** (***of***): to get the better or upper hand *of. Obs.*

1375 BARBOUR *Bruce* x. 77 Thair ennymyes Had all the fayrer off the fycht. *c* **1400** *Destr. Troy* 6882 þe troiens..þe fairer of þe fyght in þe feld had. *Ibid.* 7990 If it falle me by fortune the feirer to haue.

15. Of a means or procedure, and of language: Gentle, peaceable, not violent. †Of the countenance: Benignant, kindly. †Of death: Easy, 'natural'; without violence.

In ***fair means*** the adj. can also have the sense 10, and sometimes has a mixed sense.

1340–70 *Alex. & Dind.* 45 He wolde fare wiþ his folk in a faire wise To bi-holden here hom & non harm wirke. **1548** HALL *Chron.* 176 Determining either by force or fayre meanes, to bring their purpose to a conclusion. **1603** KNOLLES *Hist. Turks* (1621) 1161 With a faire countenance, and a majestie full of mildnesse..hee..sought to appease them. *Ibid.* 1332 To seduce men either by force or faire persuasion. **1659** B. HARRIS *Parival's Iron Age* 101 Ferdinand..thought it his duty to draw, either by fair meanes or foul, all his Subjects to the Roman Catholick Religion. **1671** MILTON *Samson* 688 Not only dost..remit To life obscur'd, which were a fair dismission. *c* **1680** HICKERINGILL *Hist. Whiggism* Wks. (1716) I. 74 The Lord Treasurer Weston dyed of his fair death, flying beyond Sea. **1703** MAUNDRELL *Journ. Jerus.* (1732) 9 Try first by fair means. **1704** J. LOGAN in *Pa. Hist. Soc. Mem.* IX. 292, I have used both fair and foul words. **1832** LANDER *Adv. Niger* I. iii. 160 They..endeavoured to obtain her by fair means.

16. Free from obstacles; unobstructed, open.

1523 FITZHERB. *Husb.* §19 The waye is lyke to be fayre and drye. **1603** KNOLLES *Hist. Turks* (1621) 69 A faire breach for the Christians to enter. **1622** BACON *Hen. VII* 12 Left faire to interpretation eyther way. **1665** BOYLE *Occas. Refl.* Table of Contents, His horse stumbling in a very fair way. **1670** NARBOROUGH *Jrnl.* in *Acc. Sev. Late Voy.* (1711) I. 79 Keep the South-shore in fair view. **1682** BUNYAN *Holy War* v, They made a fair retreat. **1712** W. ROGERS *Voy.* 49 Go out on the other side..which I think is the fairest Outlet. **1768** J. BYRON *Narrative* 10 The sea making a fair breach over her. **1816** J. WILSON *City of Plague* III. iv, Keep back..so that each man may have A fair view of the pit. **1845** FORD *Handbk. Spain* I. 12 The fairest though farthest way about is the nearest way home.

17. Open to view, plainly to be seen, clear, distinct. Now chiefly *dial.*

1577 B. GOOGE *Heresbach's Husb.* IV. (1586) 157 b, The white..are alwaies the fairest marke in a Hawke, or a Bussardes eie. **1633** P. FLETCHER *Purple Isl.* v, Fair on the face [God] wrote the index of the mind. **1665** BOYLE *Occas. Refl.* IV. xix. (1675) 282 The fairer and wider Marks that may be hit in many places. **1671** GREW *Anat. Plants* I. ii. §8 Although in all places of the Root they are visible, yet most fair and open about the filamentous Extremities of some Roots. **1847** TENNYSON *Princ.* II. 305 All her thoughts..fair within her eyes. **1877** *N.W. Linc. Gloss.* s.v., Lincoln Minster's fair to see fra Barton field.

18. a. *Comb.*, chiefly parasynthetic, as, ***fair-ankled, -born, -cheeked, -coloured, -complexioned, -conditioned, -eyed, -featured, -fortuned, -fronted, -horned, -maned, -minded*** (hence ***fair-mindedness***), ***-natured, -outsided, -reputed, -sized, -skinned, -spaced, -speeched, -tongued, -tressed, -visaged, -weathered, -zoned.***

c **1624** CHAPMAN tr. *Homer's Batrachomyomachia* 148 Her *faire-anckl'd Mother. **1851** BUCKLEY *Iliad* XIV. 261 Fair-ankled Danaë. **1875** LONGF. *Pandora* VI, Zeus..like a swan flies to fair-ankled Leda! **1830** BREWSTER *Edin. Cycl.* VII. I. 49/2 The *fair born children of Negroes. **1870** BRYANT *Iliad* I. I. 9 Let the *fair-cheeked maid Embark, Chryseis. **1757** DYER *Fleece* III. 154 *Fair-colour'd threads. *a* **1773** LD. LYTTLETON *Wks.* 1776. I. 189 A very pretty, *fair-complexioned girl. **1866** CARLYLE *Remin.* I. 139 She was of the fair-complexioned..and comely type. **1634** LAUD *Wks.* (1860) VII. 92 A very honest, *fair-conditioned man. **1591** GREENE *Maidens Dreame* xi, *Fair-ey'd pity in his heart did dwell. **1630** DRAYTON *Muses Elysium, Noah's Flood* 270 The bull..to the ark brings on the fair-ey'd cow. *a* **1845** HOOD *Lamia* v. 30, I thought This fair-eyed day would never see you from me! **1850** MRS. BROWNING *Poems* II. 30 O *fair-featured maids. **1847** JAMES *Convict* iv, I was once as prosperous and as *fair-fortuned as himself. **1830** TENNYSON *Clear-headed Friend* 12 *Fair-fronted Truth shall droop not now. **1777** R. POTTER *Æschylus' Supplicants* 324 Does Jove approach her in this *fair-horn'd state? **1632** MASSINGER & FIELD *Fatal Dowry* IV. i, I..pick my choice Of all their *fair-maned mares. **1874** MORLEY *Compromise* (1886) 187 An honest and *fair-minded man's own instincts. **1853** LYNCH *Self-Improv.* iv. 96 Discipline for temper and *fair-mindedness. **1634** FORD *P. Warbeck* v. ii, Young Buckingham is a *fair-natured prince. **1637** RUTHERFORD *Lett.* lxxxviii. (1862) I. 227 A blasted and sunburnt flower, even this plastered, *fair-outsided world. **1795** J. FAWCETT *Art of War* 4 In the number rank'd Of *fair-reputed callings. **1861** HUGHES *Tom Brown at Oxf.* iv. (1889) 30 They were *fair-sized rooms..furnished plainly but well. **1827** G. HIGGINS *Celtic Druids* 98 The *fair-skinned tribe of martial Germans. **1820** KEATS *Lamia* II. 273 Now no azure vein Wander'd on *fair-spaced temples. **1567** DRANT *Horace Epist.* II. i. G iv, This *fayre-speachde queare. **1805** T. HOLCROFT *Mem. B. Perdue* I. 16 Fair-speeched gentlemen as they are. **1842** FABER *Styrian Lake* 345 He is a *fair-tongued knight. **1870** BRYANT *Iliad* I. IX. 288 Angry with me for the sake Of a *fair-tressed wanton. **1607** WALKINGTON *Optic Glass* xv. (1664) 157 He was comely and *fair-visag'd. **1630** *R. Johnson's Kingd. & Commw.* 642 The Country [Brazil]..is..*faire weathered. **1768** *Life & Adv. Sir Barth. Sapskull* I. 50 Suppose they have fair-weather'd countenances. **1725** POPE *Odyss.* XXIII. 142 *Fair-zon'd damsels form the sprightly dance.

b. Special comb. **†fair-chance**, some kind of game or lottery; **fair-curve** (see quot.); **fair-face** *a.*, of brickwork, = FAIR-FACED *a.* 3; **fair-fashioned** *a.*, *Sc.* 'having great appearance of discretion without the reality; having great complaisance of manner' (Jam.); **fair-hair**, *Sc.* = PAX(Y-WAX(Y; **fair-handed** *a.*, (*a*) †of a horse (see quot. 1614); (*b*) having well-formed hands; **Fair Hebe jug**, a jug inscribed with the words 'Fair Hebe' (see quots.); **fair-skin**, a fair-skinned person; **fair-to-middling** *a.* (also *adv.*), slightly above average; **fair-walling** (see quot. 1886); **fair-world**, 'a good time, state of prosperity' (W.).

1755 *Mem. Capt. P. Drake* II. xi. 235 A Pharaoh Table Cards, and a *Fair Chance being ready. **1775** ASH, **Fair-curve* [printed *fair-carve*]. **1823** CRABB *Technol. Dict.* s.v., A Fair-Curve, in delineating ships, is a winding line whose shape is varied according to the part of the ship it is intended to describe. **1948** *Archit. Rev.* CIV. 186 The north wall is *fair-face brick. **1816** SCOTT *Old Mort.* v, 'Hegh, sirs, sae *fair-fashioned as we are!' **1823** ELIZA LOGAN *St. Johnstoun* II. 195 'Ye are aye sae fair-fashioned..there's scarce ony saying again' ye.' **1614** MARKHAM *Cheap Husb.* 6 Observe in any wise to have them [mares] *fayre-handed, that is, good head, necke, breast, and shoulders. **1728–46** THOMSON *Spring* 528 Fair-handed Spring unbosoms every grace. [**1903** R. L. HOBSON *Catal. Eng. Pott. Brit. Mus.* 288 Jug.. in the form of a tree stump, round the base of which are figures..a man offering a nest full of eggs to a girl seated on a log, between them a scroll inscribed **Fair Hebe*..signed I. Voyez 1788.] **1912** W. CHAFFERS *Marks Pott. & Porc.* (ed. 13) 698 Some 'Fair Hebe' jugs also bear the mark of Voyez. **1929** H. READ *Staffs. Pott. Figures* 16 We do not know when he [*sc.* Voyez] returned to Staffordshire and have no evidence of his connection with Ralph Wood until 1788, which is the date of the famous 'Fair Hebe' jug... Several copies of this jug are known..they always bear Voyez's signature. **1901** KIPLING *Kim* x. 254 Besides, a Pathan is a *fair-skin. **1865** 'A. WARD' *A. Ward: His Travels* 41 The men are *fair to middling. **1884** A. DOHERTY *N. Barlow* xi. 66, I guess my wallet's fair-to-middling fat. **1900** H. GARLAND *Eagle's Heart* 223 'How'd they feed ye back

there?'..'Oh, fair to middlin'.' **1961** *Listener* 5 Oct. 527/2 A fair-to-middling detective story. **1886** *S.W. Linc. Gloss.*, *Fair-walling, the level, smoothly-built masonry or brickwork above the roughly-built foundations. *a* **1674** MILTON (W.), They think it was never *fair-world with them since.

B. *sb.*[2] [The adj. used *absol.* or *elliptically*.]

1. a. That which is fair (in senses of the adj.); the fair side or face; also in phrases, *by* (*soft and*) *fair*: by fair means. *for* (*foul nor*) *fair*: for fair words or treatment.

In the expressions *fair befall* and the like the word admits of being taken either as sb. or adv. The advb. sense is prob. original (see FAIR *adv.* 6 b), but cf. quot. 1423 below.

1393 LANGL. *P. Pl.* C. x. 85 To turne þe fayre outwarde. **1423** JAS. I *Kingis Q.* cxc, Fair and lufe befall The nychtingale. **1456** *How Wise Man taught Son* 151 in Hazl. *E.P.P.* (1864) 175 [Be] soft and fayre men make tame Hert and buk. **1483** CAXTON *G. de la Tour* (1868) 6 A lorde wolde haue a gentille woman, bi faire or be force. **1592** SHAKS. *Rom. & Jul.* I. iii. 90 'Tis much pride For faire without, the faire within to hide. **1611** —— *Cymb.* I. vi. 37 Can we not Partition make..Twixt faire, and foule? **1627–47** FELTHAM *Resolves* 429 Their blacke tongue can never spot the faire of virtue. **1749** FIELDING *Tom Jones* XV. x, Nothing short of the fair and honourable, will satisfy the delicacy of their minds. **1864** TENNYSON *En. Ard.* 529 After..frequent interchange of foul and fair.

b. *colloq.* *to see fair* = 'to see fair play'.

1837 DICKENS *Pickw.* xxv. (C.D. ed.) 218 If you will step in there..Mr. Weller will see fair. **1891** *Daily News* 11 Mar. 5/2 The police..came up to see fair between both sides.

c. *for fair*: completely, altogether. *U.S. slang.*

1900 FLYNT & WALTON *Powers that Prey* 180 They're goin' to railroad him for fair. The *World* says the police found the weapon on him. **1903** *N.Y. Times* 5 Dec. 5 'I seem to be putting my foot in it for fair,' said the green marine. **1916** H. L. WILSON *Somewhere in Red Gap* viii. 352 Pete must of [= have] been crazy for fair about that time. **1957** J. KEROUAC *On Road* (1958) I. ix. 53 Then we danced and started on the beer for fair.

d. *fair's fair*: (reciprocal) fairness is called for. *colloq.*

1898 S. WEYMAN *Castle Inn* xxiii. 231 No, but fair's fair, and if I am not in this, it is low. **1938** C. S. FORESTER *Ship of Line* ix. 118 Fair's fair..I'll spin a coin for it. **1963** C. MACKENZIE *My Life & Times* II. 161 'No, no,' said Mr Green, with a sigh of noble resignation. 'Fair's fair. They're your plums now.' **1969** *Private Eye* 25 Apr. 12 Fair's fair Eric, for cripes sake!

2. One of the fair sex, a woman; *esp.* a beloved woman. Now *arch.* or *poet.*

1423 JAS. I *Kingis Q.* lxvi, That faire vpward hir eye Wold cast. *c* **1489** CAXTON *Blanchardyn* xxiv. 84 The fayer þ[e] proude pucell. **1590** SHAKS. *Mids. N.* I. i. 182 O happie faire! Your eyes are loadstarres. **1638** FORD *Lady's Trial* III. i, The best, though call em..Faires, fines, and honies, are but flesh and blood. **1647** CRASHAW *Poems* 146 Say, ling'ring fair! why comes the birth Of your brave soul so slowly forth? **1747** *Gentl. Mag.* Apr. (*Ld. Lovat's Execution*), No fair forgets the ruin he has done. **1847** L. HUNT *Men, Women, & B.* I. x. 177 Pursuing his fair in a solitary street. **1876** BLACKIE *Songs Relig. & Life* 169 Some prouder fair hath humbled Thy proud passion.

transf. **1697** DRYDEN *Virg. Georg.* III. 202 Produce him to the Fair; And join in Wedlock to the longing Mare.

†**3.** A person with a fair complexion.

1771 T. HULL *Hist. W. Harrington* (1797) III. 1 One is a fair, the other a brunet.

†**4. a.** Beauty, fairness, good looks. Also *pl.*: Points or traits of beauty. *Obs.*

c **888** K. ÆLFRED *Boeth.* xxxii. §2 þæs lichoman fæger and his streon..maʒon beon afeorred. *c* **1200** *Trin. Coll. Hom.* 19 þe mone and þe sune wundrieð of faire. *a* **1225** *Juliana* 6 He sumchere iseh hire utnume feir. *a* **1240** *Ureisun* in *Cott. Hom.* 193 Heo neuer ne beoð sead þi ueir to iseonne. **1590** SHAKS. *Com. Err.* II. i. 98 My decayed faire, A sunnie looke of his, would soone repaire. **1599** MARSTON *Sco. Villanie* II. vii. 207 The greene meades, whose natiue outward faire Breathes sweet perfumes. **1633** P. FLETCHER *Elisa* ii, His weeping spouse Eliza..all her beauteous fairs with grief infecting.

†**b.** *Comb.*

1622 DRAYTON *Poly-olb.* Song xxviii, 388 The fayre-enamoured Flood.

fair (fɛə(r)), *adv.* Forms: 1 fæʒre; 3–4 as those of the adj. with the addition of *-e*; 5– coincident with those of the adj. [OE. *fæʒre*, f. *fæʒer*, FAIR *a.*] In a fair manner or degree.

1. In a beautiful or comely manner; agreeably, beautifully, brightly, handsomely, nobly.

a **1000** *Cædmon's Gen.* 210 (Gr.) Fæʒere leohte þæt liðe land lago yrnende. *c* **1000** ÆLFRIC *Gram.* xxxviii. (Z.) 228 Fæʒere he syngþ. *c* **1175** *Cott. Hom.* 219 þa wes þes tyendes hapes alder swiþe feir isceapen. **1393** LANGL. *P. Pl.* C. XXI. 71 Somme seiden he was godes sone þat so faire deyede. *c* **1400** *Rom. Rose* 108 Bowes blosmed feyre. *c* **1440** *Gesta Rom.* i. 3 (Harl. MS.) The goode man..faire endid his liffe. *a* **1568** ASCHAM *Scholem.* II. (Arb.) 150 The Latin tong did faire blome. **1577** B. GOOGE *Heresbach's Husb.* I. (1586) 5 So faire he bare his age, as I tooke him to be scarse fiftie. **1596** SHAKS. *1 Hen. IV*, III. i. 142 The Moone shines faire. **1600** —— *A.Y.L.* III. ii. 97 All the pictures fairest Linde are but blacke to Rosalinde. **1632** SIR R. LE GRYS tr. *Paterculus* 377 The excellent Generall..preferred things profitable before such as shewed faire. **1738** WESLEY *Psalms* i. 3 Spread out his boughs and flourish fair.

2. a. Civilly, courteously, kindly. Now only in phr. *to speak* (*a person*) *fair.*

a **1000** *Cædmon's Gen.* 2351 (Gr.) Him..fæʒere..ece drihten andswarode. *c* **1175** *Lamb. Hom.* 53 þis faʒe folc..speket..feire biforen heore euencristene. *c* **1205** LAY. 4842 Wha swa oðerne imette þer fæire hine igrætte. **1297** R. GLOUC. (1724) 90 Morice þider com, and faire was vnderfonge. *c* **1350** *Will. Palerne* 347 þemperour..comande þe couherde curteysli and fayre, to heue vp þat hende child. *c* **1450** *St. Cuthbert* (Surtees) 5346 þar come a monke and prayde him faire. *c* **1460** *How Goode Wif taught Doughter* 65 in Hazl. *E.P.P.* (1864) 184 Alle ben nought trewe that faire spekyn. *c* **1530** LD. BERNERS *Arth. Lyt. Bryt.* (1814) 87 They that speak fair, fair shall hear again. **1590** SHAKS. *Com. Err.* III. ii. 186 So faire an offer'd Chaine. **1695** CONGREVE *Love for L.* III. iii, I spoke you fair, d'ye see, and civil. **1818** SCOTT *Hrt. Midl.* xlv, The work-people..spoke him soft and fair. *a* **1866** NEALE *Hymn*, '*Christian, dost thou see them*', Christian, dost thou hear them, How they speak thee fair?

†**b.** (To keep, part) *fair*: i.e. on good terms *with*. *Obs.* or *arch.*

a **1400–50** *Alexander* 2750 He..twynnys with þaim faire. **1597** SHAKS. *2 Hen. IV*, II. i. 207 Tap for tap, and so part faire. **1641** SIR E. NICHOLAS in *N. Papers* (Camden) I. 25 His Majestie..will certainly part fayre with this people. **1671–2** SIR C. LYTTELTON in *Hatton Corr.* (1878) 80 The Spaniard and wee shall still continue faire together. **1700** DRYDEN *Palamon & Arc.* II. 164 Fair they parted till the Morrow's Dawn. **1715** *Lond. Gaz.* No. 5332/1 To keep fair with the Persian Court. **1823** SCOTT *Quentin D.* xxiii, We must keep fair with him.

3. In neat and legible handwriting; clearly, legibly, plainly.

1513 MORE *Rich. III* in Grafton *Chron.* II. 782 This Proclamacion..was..fayre written in Parchement. **1666** PEPYS *Diary* (1879) IV. 15 Up betimes to the office, to write fair a laborious letter. **1705** J. BLAIR in W. S. Perry *Hist. Coll. Amer. Col. Ch.* I. 151 A copy..which he promised as soon as it could be fair drawn out. **1774** CHESTERF. *Lett.* I. xvi. 50, I desire that you would translate and copy it fair into a book. **1832** FR. A. KEMBLE *Jrnl.* in *Rec. Girlh.* (1878) III. 187 After tea I..copied fair a speech I had been writing. **1838** CARD. NEWMAN *Lett.* (1891) II. 250, I then write it out fair for the printer.

4. Equitably, honestly, impartially, justly; according to rule. Also in phr. FAIR AND SQUARE.

c **1300** *Havelok* 224 Al was youen, faire and wel. **1603** SHAKS. *Meas. for M.* III. i. 141 Heauen shield my Mother plaid my Father faire. **1680** OTWAY *Orphan* II. vii, I can never think you meant me fair. *a* **1764** LLOYD *Dial. betw. Author & Friend* Poet. Wks. 1774 II. 14 Read their works, examine fair. **1885** *North Star* 1 July 3/2 Lord Randolph..has ever hit fair.

†**5.** In a proper or suitable manner; becomingly, befittingly. Also, *fair* and *sweetly*, *fair and well.*

1297 R. GLOUC. (1724) 446 Kyng Henry..yburede ys þere [at Reading] vayre ynou. *c* **1340** *Cursor M.* 10448 (Trin.) Leue þi bere, Cloþe þe feire. *c* **1386** CHAUCER *Chan. Yeom. Prol. & T.* 560 He hem leyde faire and wel adoun. *c* **1430** *Freemasonry* 608 Knele down fayre on bothe thy knen. **1483** CAXTON *G. de la Tour* Aj, Whiche fayre and swetely chastysed her doughters. **1523** LD. BERNERS *Froiss.* I. cccix. 467 Fayre fared, quoth the constable, we are nat in mynde to do to our enemys so moche auantage. **1526** TINDALE *2 Cor.* v. 11 We fare fayre [Luther *fahren wir schön*] with men. **1544** BALE *Chron. Sir J. Oldcastell* in *Harl. Misc.* (Malh.) I. 271 Bury them [images] fayre in the ground. *a* **1568** ASCHAM *Scholem.* I. (Arb.) 44 To ride faire, is most cumelie for him selfe. **1607** SHAKS. *Cor.* IV. vi. 118 You have crafted faire. **1665** DRYDEN *Ind. Emperor* v. ii, Stand fair, and let my Heart-blood on thee flow.

6. a. With good promise; promisingly, auspiciously; favourably, prosperously. *Obs.* exc. in *to bid*, *promise fair*: see the vbs.

1154 *O.E. Chron.* an. 1154 Nu is abbot & fair haued begunnon. **1590** SPENSER *F.Q.* II. xi. 17 Faire mote he thee. **1593** SHAKS. *Rich. II*, II. ii. 123 The winde sits faire. **1596** —— *1 Hen. IV*, v. v. 43 Since this Businesse so faire is done.

†**b.** With impers. vbs. used optatively. *fair be to you*: prosperity attend you. *fair befall, cheve, fall*: see the verbs. *Obs.* exc. *arch.*

1606 SHAKS. *Tr. & Cr.* III. i. 46 Faire be to you my Lord. **1867** JEAN INGELOW *Gladys* 306 O rare, The island! fair befall the island; let Me reach the island!

†**7. a.** Gently, quietly, without haste or violence. Chiefly in phrases, *fair and easily*, *evenly*, *softly.*

a **1000** *Menol.* (Fox) 314 He fæʒere mid wætere oferwearp wuldres cynebearn. *c* **1374** CHAUCER *Troylus* v. 347 þei take it wisely faire & softe. *c* **1430** *Pilgr. Lyf Manhode* I. cxxxv. (1869) 71 If thei [the armour] ben heuy, go faire. **1523** LD. BERNERS *Froiss.* I. xviii. 22 The oste..rode fayre and easely all the daye. **1552** HULOET, Fayre and..softly, *suspenso gradu.* **1607** TOPSELL *Four-f. Beasts* (1673) 210 The proverb is old and true, 'Fair and softly goeth far'. **1622** S. WARD *Life of Faith in Death* (1627) 63 Sometimes he followes faire and a farre off, lingers aloofe and out of sight, etc. **1653** URQUHART *Rabelais* I. xxxiii, He returned fair and softly. **1782** COWPER *Gilpin* 85 So fair and softly, John he cried. **1804** MAR. EDGEWORTH *Pop. Tales, Will* ix, Fair and softly goes far in a day.

†**b.** Moderately, not excessively. *Obs.*

c **1450** *Two Cookery-bks.* 71 Leche it faire, but not to thyn. *Ibid.* 82 Roste hem faire.

8. Evenly, on a level. Chiefly *dial.*

1708 *Lond. Gaz.* No. 4422/7 The nine Sail stood in fair with us. **1877** *N.W. Linc. Gloss.* s.v., 'Th' table doesn't stand fair.' **1882** *Daily Tel.* 4 May, The plate does not lie fair on the frames.

†**9. a.** Directly, straight, 'due (north, etc.)'. *Obs.*

c **1489** CAXTON *Sonnes of Aymon* xx. 449 Reynawd..wente fayre vpon the folke of Charlemagne. **1719** DE FOE *Crusoe* (1840) II. ii. 35, I came fair on the south side of my island. **1720** —— *Capt. Singleton* xi. (1840) 185 They stood..fair after us. *Ibid.* xv. (1840) 255 We stood away fair west.

b. With reference to a blow, etc.: 'Clean', 'full', plump, straight.

c **1340** *Gaw. & Gr. Knt.* 2229 Fayre on his fote he foundez on þe erþe. **1823** SCOTT *Quentin D.* xiv, Striking his antagonist fair upon the breast. **1891** *Blackw. Mag.* CL. 651/2 A living catapult, that if he took you fair, would knock the life out of you.

c. Completely, fully, quite. Cf. CLEAN *adv.* 5. Now *dial.*, *U.S.*, *Austral.*, and *N.Z.*

c **1330** *Amis. & Amil.* 2388 To-morn thei schull beryed ben, As thei faire ded were. *a* **1400–50** *Alexander* 2230 Som..faire fest on a fyre att þe foure ʒates. **1457** AGNES PASTON in *Past. Lett.* (1787) I. xxxv. 144, I had leuer he wer fayr beryed than lost for defaute. **1494** *Househ. Ord.* 130 When he cometh to the church..take the image and chest downe, and beare him faire into the church. **1868** ATKINSON *Cleveland Gloss.* s.v., 'It [a cat]'s fair wild.' **1897** D. MCK. WRIGHT *Station Ballads* 55, I feel fair sick. **1904** 'G. B. LANCASTER' *Sons o' Men* 88 It fair gets me down to see the poor brutes dying. **1928** J. DEVANNY *Dawn Beloved* xix. 190, I get fair sick of it. **1935** H. W. HORWILL *Dict. Mod. Amer. Usage* 125/2 *Fair*, in the sense of completely, fully, or clearly, distinctly, this word is now obs. in Eng. exc. in certain dial., but is still current in Am. **1945** *Coast to Coast 1944* 200 It fair gets my goat. **1966** J. HACKSTON *Father clears Out* 181 A cow..will come home, and, in a most flagrant manner, deposit a pat fair bang in the bail.

†**d.** Clearly, distinctly, plainly. *Obs.*

1393 LANGL. *P. Pl.* C. II. 2 þe feld ful of folke ich shal ʒow fayre shewe. *c* **1400** *Destr. Troy* Prol. 82 Here fynde shall ye faire of þe felle peopull, What Kynges þere come of costes aboute. **1628** DIGBY *Voy. Medit.* (1868) 2 The pointe of the Lizard faire in sight. **1697** DAMPIER *Voy.* (1729) I. 256 We were fair in sight of Cape Corrientes.

10. *Comb.* **a.** With *agent-nouns* and *vbl. sbs.* forming sbs., as ***fair-dealer***, ***-dealing***, ***-doing***, ***-seeming***, ***-speaking***.

1746 LOCKMAN *To First Promoter Cambrick & Tea Bills* 25 A Craft, indeed, gives some *Fair-dealers pain. **1711** SHAFTESB. *Charac.* (1737) I. 63 There is as much difference between one sort and another, as between *fair-dealing and hypocrisy. **1879** FARRAR *St. Paul* (1883) 443 Let them not be weary in *fair-doing. **1724** SAVAGE *Sir T. Overbury* I. i. 6 The Statesman's Promise, or false Patriot's Zeal, Full of *fair Seeming, but Delusion all. **1483** *Vulgaria abs Terentio* 25 b, If it wyll be wyth giffynge and *faire spekynge I shall nott be behynde.

b. With adjs., as ***fair-fierce***, ***-seemly***, ***-sweet***, and with pres. pples. forming adjs., as ***fair-applauding***, ***-blazing***, ***-blooming***, ***-boding***, ***-dealing***, ***-flowing***, ***-glaring***, ***-growing***, ***-revolving***, ***-seeming***, ***-shining***, ***-sounding***, ***-speaking***, ***-spreading***, ***-thinking***, ***-winding***.

1777 R. POTTER *Æschylus' Supplicants* 1005 The voice Of *fair-applauding fame. **1726–46** THOMSON *Winter* 312 The officious wife prepares The fire *fair-blazing. **1740** SHENSTONE *Judgm. Hercules* 339 *Fair-blooming Health surveys her altars there. **1594** SHAKS. *Rich. III*, v. iii. 227 The..*fairest boading Dreames, That euer entred in a drowsie head. **1718** *Freethinker* No. 14. 96 A *fair-dealing, honourable Merchant. **1580** SIDNEY *Arcadia* (1613) 224–5 She, *faire-fierce, to such a state me calls. **1848** CLOUGH *Amours de Voy.* III. 85 The cypress-spires by the *fair-flowing stream. **1649** G. DANIEL *Trinarch.* To Rdr. 51 The *faire-Glareing Tulip. **1870** BRYANT *Iliad* II. XXI. 291 A tall *fair-growing elm. **1708** J. PHILIPS *Cyder* II. 523 *Fair-revolving years. **1625** K. LONG tr. *Barclay's Argenis* IV. xviii. 303 Adulterate vertue, and *faire-seeming vice. **1776** 'C. MELMOTH' *Pupil of Pleasure* I. vii. Plausible exterior, fair-seeming sentiments, etc. **1920** D. H. LAWRENCE *Lost Girl* xvi. 359 Your fair-seeming face covered the schemes and vice of your true nature. **1590** SPENSER *F.Q.* I. ii. 30 *Faire-seemely pleasaunce each to other makes. **1593** SHAKS. *3 Hen. VI*, II. i. 40 Hence forward will I beare Vpon my Target three *faire shining Sunnes. **1798** *Invasion* I. 227 Unsuspicious of the treachery concealed beneath words so *fair-sounding. **1871** E. F. BURR *Ad Fidem* iii. 39 Fair-sounding terms. **1398** TREVISA *Barth. De P.R.* VI. xiii. (1495) 198 In a good wyfe byhoueth that she be *fayre spekynge. **1647** CLARENDON *Contempl. on Ps.* Tracts (1727) 517 To grapple with our fair-speaking adversaries. **1746** THOMSON *Autumn* 246 His..once *fair-spreading Family dissolv'd. **1581** SIDNEY *Astr. & Stella* lxxxii, Sweet-gard'n-nymph..most *faire-sweet, do not..banish mee. **1915** F. M. HUEFFER *Good Soldier* II. i. 108 The upright..*fair-thinking, public character. **1746** THOMSON *Summer* 1426 The matchless vale of Thames; *Fair-winding up to where the muses haunt.

c. With pa. pples. forming adjs., as ***fair-betrothed***, ***-bound***, ***-built***, ***-compacted***, ***-contrived***, ***-divided***, ***-exstructed***, ***-feathered***, ***-folded***, ***-forged***, ***-plastered***, ***-sculptured***, ***-set***, ***-sunned***, ***-told***, ***-written***.

1608 SHAKS. *Per.* v. iii. 71 This prince, the *fair-betrothed of your daughter. **1614** BP. HALL *Recoll. Treat.* 129 Some goodly *faire bound Senecaes Tragedies. **1598** SYLVESTER *Du Bartas* II. i. I. Eden 372 The *fair-built Bridge..More like a tradefull City. **1655** H. VAUGHAN *Silex Scint.* I. (1858) 49 A *faire-compacted frame. **1645** QUARLES *Sol. Recant.* 55 Thy *faire-contriv'd designes. **1746** THOMSON *Autumn* 832 The *fair-divided earth. **1647** H. MORE *Song of Soul* II. iii. III. xxiii, Those *fair extructed loads Of carvèd stone. **1607** A. BREWER *Lingua* I. i, A speech *faire fetherd could not flie. **1844** LD. HOUGHTON *Mem. Many Scenes, To Landor* 144 He..fed his heart—as thou—On storied Fiesole's *fair-folded brow. **1590** SPENSER *F.Q.* I. ii. 2 That *faire-forged spright. **1535** COVERDALE *Ecclus.* xxii. 17 Lyke as a *fayre playstred wall in a winter house. **1870** BRYANT *Iliad* I. IV. 117 Ships with..*fair-sculptured prows. **1648** HERRICK *Hesper.* I. 121 A full spread, *faire-set Vine. **1850** MRS. BROWNING *Poems* II. 300 Prayers—that upward mount Like to a *fair-sunned fount. **1548** HALL *Chron.* 153 Whiche *faire told tale, allured to hym muche people. **1700** PRIOR *Carmen Seculare* 27 Her *fair-written page.

fair (fɛə(r)), *v.* Forms: α. 1 fæʒrian, 2 feiren, 4 fairen, 5 fayre, 7– fair; β. 4 vayren. Also, see YFAIRED. [ME. *feiren*, OE. *fæʒrian*, f. *fæʒer*, FAIR. In later use directly f. FAIR *a.*]

†**1. a.** *intr.* To appear or become fair or clean.

a **1000** *Seafarer* 48 (Gr.) Bearwas blostmum nimað, byriʒ fæʒriað. *c* **1300** *K. Alis.* 2903 Mury hit is in sonne-risyng!..

Weyes fairith. **1340** *Ayenb.* 95 þis trau greneþ and uayreþ be his uirtue.

b. Of the weather: To clear; *esp.* with *away*, *off*, or *up*. *dial.* and *U.S.*

1836 E. L. WILLSON *Diary* 29 May (1929), It was still rainy; towards night it faired away. **1842** MRS. CARLYLE *Lett.* I. 182 We are to go, if it fairs, to take tea at a show place. *a* **1859** *Western Tales* (Bartlett), He..moved to the North, and whenever he see a fog risin', took to his bed, and kept it till it fair'd off. *a* **1859** *Spirit of Times* (N.Y.) (ibid.), There's going to be a nasty fog to-night,..call me if it fairs up. **1859** W. WHITE *Northumb. & Border* 448 The squall lasted for nearly two hours. When it 'faired up' the son said [etc.]. **1867** G. M. HOPKINS *Jrnl.* 29 Aug. (1959) 153 Dull, fairing in afternoon. **1868** *Times* 16 Sept. 9 The weather faired by mid-day. **1878** STEVENSON *Inland Voy.* 160 It faired as the night went on, and the moon came out of the clouds. *Ibid.* 177 The afternoon faired up. **1891** MISS DOWIE *Girl in Karp.* 148 When it rained he turned the furry side out.. when it faired, he..reversed it. **1899** T. D. PRICE *MS. Diary* 28 Apr., Rain in morning but faired up and good day. **1903** A. ADAMS *Log of Cowboy* viii. 110 The weather in the meantime had faired off. **1923** W. STEVENS *Let.* 30 Jan. (1967) 233 Later in the morning it faired off, as they say. **1951** L. CRAIG *Singing Hills* 68 He spoke of how it had weathered up considerable the day before, but it had faired up without a rain to do any good. **1960** V. WILLIAMS *Walk Egypt* (1961) II. vii. 140 He tipped his head back and scanned the sky. 'Looks like it's fairing off some.'

†**2.** *trans.* To make fair; to make clean or good-looking; to beautify. *Obs.*

c **1175** *Lamb. Hom.* 53 þus heo doð for to feiren heom seluen. *c* **1320** *Cast. Love* 876 þe rihtwys sone..fairede hir more a þousend folde. **1340** *Ayenb.* 233 þise zix leues.. uayreþ moche þe lylye of maydenhod. *a* **1450** *Knt. de la Tour* (1868) 69 Faire doughtres..holde it in youre herte that ye putte no thinge to..fayre youre uisages. *c* **1600** SHAKS. *Sonn.* cxxvii, Fairing the foul with art's false borrow'd face.

3. *Ship-building.* To make fair or level; to ascertain the correctness of curvature in the various parts of a ship; to fit the beams, plates, etc., according to the curvature. Also of an aeroplane or motor car (cf. FAIRING *vbl. sb.*²). Also with *in*, and *transf.*

1867 in SMYTH *Sailor's Word-bk.* **1869** SIR E. J. REED *Shipbuild.* viii. 154 The ship is faired by means of ribands and cross-spalls. **1879** *Cassell's Techn. Educ.* IV. 208/1 The frames..then can be faired with ease. **1922** *Encycl. Brit.* XXX. 21/1 To reduce resistance, exposed parts may be 'faired'. **1930** *Times Lit. Suppl.* 30 Mar. 231/2 The perfectly faired curves. **1934** *Flight* 25 Jan. 78 *e*/1 Now that we are familiar with metal monocoque fuselages..it is worth the trouble to fair the lines properly. **1959** *Motor* 2 Sept. 97/2 Chassis members have been faired in. **1959** B. G. D. SALT in Halas & Manvell *Technique Film Animation* 319 Movements in animation are generally 'faired'. This means that the movement in question is smoothly blended with its neighbours, no abrupt change taking place... The term 'to fair' or 'fairing'—an old craft word commonly used in the aircraft industry—is probably the most accurate available.

Hence **faired** *ppl. a.*

1933 *Jrnl. R. Aeronaut. Soc.* XXXVII. 77 Faired lines and a retractable landing carriage improved the cruising speed. **1963** *Times* 15 Jan. 12/2 The faired-in headlamps.

fair and square, *a.* and *adv.*

A. *adj.* Honest, just, straightforward. **B.** *adv.* In a just or straightforward manner, honestly; with set purpose, determinedly; completely, utterly. Also with ellipsis of 'acting' or the like = *fair dealing*.

1604 *Fr. Bacon's Proph.* 443 in Hazl. *E.P.P.* IV. 284 Faire, and square..The gamester calls fooles holy-day. **1649** CROMWELL *Lett.* cxlvi. (Carlyle) There will clearly be no living for the Portugal unless he..do that which is fair and square. **1673** WYCHERLEY *Gentl. Dancing-Master* Epil., You are fair and square in all your dealings. **1712** ARBUTHNOT *John Bull* IV. ii. 7 We'll settle it between Ourselves: Fair and Square. **1887** G. R. SIMS *Mary Jane's Mem.* 252 We're lovers all fair and square and above board. **1890** F. R. STOCKTON in *Century Mag.* 543/1 When a man sits down, fair and square, to tell a story. **1931** *Daily Express* 16 Oct. 7 Thirty years ago, American boot manufacturers opened shops right and left in this country, but British pluck and skill beat them fair and square. **1957** *New Yorker* 16 Feb. 125 The financial burden ought to be borne fair and square by the home government.

Hence **fairly and squarely** *adv.*

1638 W. CHILLINGWORTH *Relig. Prot.* IV. §19. 201 Me thinkes he hath little reason to complain, that he hath not been fairely, and squarely dealt with. **1862** *Congress. Globe* 27 Mar. 1402/2, I..doubt..the ability of these guns to remain in their position if..struck fairly and squarely by shot from the enemy. **1890** W. A. WALLACE *Only a Sister* 338, I think I can fight my own battles fairly and squarely.

fai'ration. *dial.* [f. FAIR *a.* + -ATION.] Fair play.

1861 E. WAUGH *Birtle Carter's T.* 14 Give o'er! Let's ha' fairation.

fair copy, *sb.* orig. *Law.* [See FAIR *a.* 8 c.] The condition of a document copied after final correction; also, written material transcribed after correction.

1873 TRISTRAM *Moab* viii. 158 Our depositions were now produced in fair copy.

Hence **fair-copy** *v.*, to write out in fair copy.

1819 R. WOODHOUSE *Let.* 19 Sept. in H. E. Rollins *Lett. Keats* (1958) II. 164 He then read to me Lamia, which he has half fair Copied. **1840** DICKENS *Old C. Shop* xxxiii, She could ingross fair-copy [etc.]. **1885** *Law Times Rep.* LIII. 460/2 Notice of dissolution..was left at the offices..to be fair copied.

faird, Sc. var. of FARD *v.*, to paint the face.

faird, var. of FARD Sc. motion, impetus.

Fair Deal. *U.S. Pol.* [f. FAIR *a.* 10 + DEAL *sb.*² (cf. sense 4 c, quots. 1928, 1958).] Name given to the policy of social improvement advocated by H. S. Truman, President of the U.S. 1945–53.

1949 *Time* 6 June, The Fair Deal had all but lost steerage-way.

Hence **Fair Dealer**, a proponent of this programme.

1954 *Manch. Guardian Weekly* 14 Jan. 2/3 The false premise that the Fair Dealers were ever in control of the Democratic party.

'fairess. *rare.* [f. FAIR-Y + -ESS.] A female fairy.

1674 BREVINT *Saul at Endor* 163 A Fairess, or a white witch. **1875** G. M. HOPKINS *Jrnl.* 7 Feb. in *Note-bks. & Pap.* (1937) 217, I asked Miss Jones in my Welsh lesson the Welsh for *fairy*..(she says *fairess*..for a she-fairy).

fair-faced, *a.*

1. a. Having a fair or light-coloured complexion. **b.** Of beautiful countenance.

The two senses are in many early examples not easy to distinguish.

1588 SHAKS. *Tit. A.* IV. ii. 68 (Qo.) Here is the babe as loathsome as a toade, Amongst the fairefast [ed. **1623** fairest] breeders of our clime. **1607** ROWLANDS *Famous Hist.* 56 The beauteous fair-fac'd Bride. **1689** *Lond. Gaz.* No. 2512/4 He is a low well set Man, fair faced. **1795** *Fate of Sedley* I. 130 A fair-faced son of an Eastern Sultan. **1864** J. FORSTER *Life Sir J. Eliot* I. 28 The fair-faced fiend..had received her sentence on the previous day.

2. Having a fair appearance (see FACE *sb.* 8), pretty; fair to the eye only, specious.

1595 SHAKS. *John* II. i. 417, I shall shew you peace, and faire-fac'd league. **1616** HAYWARD *Sanct. Troub. Soul* I. (1620) 9 The faire-faced shewes of the world. **1693** CONGREVE *Double-Dealer* II. viii, Tis such a pleasure to angle for fair-faced fools!

3. Of brickwork or stonework: not plastered.

1948 *Archit. Rev.* CIV. 132 (*caption*) The walls are of fair-faced brickwork, distempered. **1958** *Ibid.* CXXIII. 131 The offices are of r.c. construction with brick infill, with columns slate-faced and the edge beams fairfaced. **1970** *Interior Design* Dec. 775/1 An industrial standard of finish has been adopted with fair-faced brick partitions, exposed concrete, and granolithic floor. **1971** *Country Life* 30 Sept. 848/1 In the Tweed valley the walls are beautifully built in 'fair-faced' hand-split blue whinstone.

fair-farrand: see FARRAND.

fairfieldite ('fɛəfiːldaɪt). *Min.* [Named in 1879 by Brush and Dana after *Fairfield*, the county (in Connecticut) where it was found: see -ITE.] A hydrous phosphate of calcium, manganese, and iron.

1879 *Amer. Jrnl. Sc.* 3rd Ser. XVII. 359 Fairfieldite occurs generally in massive crystalline aggregates.

fair-ful ('fɛəfʊl). [f. FAIR *sb.*² + -FUL.] A quantity sufficient to make or fill up a fair.

1872 BROWNING *Fifine* 164 Fix into one Elvire a Fair-ful of Fifines.

fair-haired, *a.*

a. Having fair or light-coloured hair.

1626 MASSINGER *Rom. Actor* II. i, Fair-haired Calliope. **1725** POPE *Odyss.* VI. 145 The fair-hair'd Dryads of the shady wood. **1814** SCOTT *Wav.* xx, The flash of the gun cost me a fair-haired son. **1892** GARDINER *Student's Hist. Eng.* 6 The Celts were fair-haired.

†**b.** In the name of a plant (see quot).

1597 GERARD *Herbal* (1598) 102 The faire haired Iacint.

c. *fig.* Darling, favourite. (Cf. WHITE *a.* 9, WHITE BOY.)

1909 *Sat. Even. Post* 24 Apr. 26/2 The old crowd of Fair-haired Correspondent Boys who hung to the ear of President Roosevelt with viselike grip dissolved. **1918** J. W. GERARD *Face to face with Kaiserism* vii. 76 The [German] Government published a certificate in the *Official Gazette* to the effect that I was their fair-haired boy, etc. **1949** *Time* 14 Mar. 30/1 Vishinsky was Stalin's newest fair-haired boy.

† **'fairhead.** *Obs.* Forms: α. 3 faiȝered, 3–4 faired(e, fairehed(e, (3 -hid), 3–5 fair-, fayrhed(e, 4 fairheed, fayrhed, feir(e)-, 4–6 fayrehed, (5 farhed), 6 *Sc.* fairheid; β. 3–4 vair-, vayrhede. [f. FAIR *a.* + -HEAD.] Beauty.

c **1250** *Gen. & Ex.* 2666 He was ȝuð, Wið faiȝered and strengthe kuð. **1297** R. GLOUC. (Rolls) 2515 þe king.. bihuld hire vairhede. *a* **1340** HAMPOLE *Psalter* Prol., In þaim is so mykill fayrhed of vnderstandynge. **1340** *Ayenb.* 16 Liȝtbere, þe angel, vor his greate uayrhede an his greate wyt, wolde by aboue þe oþre angeles. *c* **1440** HYLTON *Scala Perf.* (W. de W. 1494) II. xlvi, The fairhede [**1533** fairnesse] of angels. **1501** DOUGLAS *Pal. Hon.* I. xxxvi, Her bewtie schane castand sa greit ane glance, All fairheid it oppresst. **1560** ROLLAND *Crt. Venus* II. 105 Thair was the flour of fairheid.

† **'fairhood.** *Obs.* = prec.

a **1587** FOXE *A. & M.* (cited in WORCESTER 1846).

fairily ('fɛərɪlɪ), *adv.* [f. FAIRY *a.* + -LY².] In a fairy-like manner.

1864 TENNYSON *Islet* 18 Fairily-delicate palaces shine.

fairing ('fɛərɪŋ), (*vbl.*) *sb.*¹ [f. FAIR *sb.* + -ING¹.]

1. A present given at or brought from a fair.

1574 HELLOWES *Gueuara's Fam. Ep.* (1577) 86 The Gentle-women that did serue her [the Empresse]..would vse their libertie in asking fayrings. **1614** B. JONSON *Barth. Fair* Prol., The Maker..hopes, to night To giue you for a Fayring, true delight. **1661** PEPYS *Diary* 31 Aug., To Bartholomew Faire..Mr. Pickering bought them some fairings. **1786** MAD. D'ARBLAY *Diary* 8 Nov., Presenting her one of my fairings. **1827** CLARE *Sheph. Cal.* 149 With kerchief full of fairings in her hand. **1883** *Longm. Mag.* Apr. 655 The lasses get their 'fairing' from the lads in gingerbread and nuts from the stalls.

b. *transf.* A complimentary gift of any kind.

1588 SHAKS. *L.L.L.* V. ii. 2 We shall be rich ere we depart, If fairings come thus plentifully in. **1668** PEPYS *Diary* 17 Sept., I..did give her five guineas as a fairing. **1727** MRS. DELANY *Life & Corr.* I. 135 A jewel box which Mrs. Tillier desires you to accept as her fairing. **1766** GOLDSM. *Vic. W.* xvii, Colin..gives her a fairing to put in her hair. **1826** MISS MITFORD *Village* 2nd Ser. (1863) 439 To our little pet, Lizzy ..she predicted a fairing.

c. *fig. to get, give (any one) his fairing*: to get, give (him) his deserts.

1785 BURNS *Death & Dr. Hornbook* xxx, Neist time we meet, I'll wad a groat, He's got his fairin'. **1818** SCOTT *Old Mort.* xxxvii 'Mackay will pit him [Claverhouse] down.. he'll gie him his fairing.' **1823** LOCKHART *Reg. Dalton* I. II. iv. 262 'Ane o' them got his fairin.'

2. Cakes or sweets sold at fairs; *esp.* gingerbread nuts. Chiefly *colloq.*

a **1774** FERGUSSON *Hallowfair* Poems (1845) 13 He'll.. creish her loof Wi what will buy her fairin To chow that day. **1888** *W. Somerset Word-bk.* s.v., Do you like fairings or comforts best?

3. ? *nonce-use.* Buying, etc., at a fair.

1887 *Cornh. Mag.* Mar. 251 The fairing was done with shivers.

4. *attrib.* and *Comb.*

1593 *Pass. Morrice* I b, Honestie knowes what the fairing-monger will saye. **1790** MAD. D'ARBLAY *Diary* Aug., I placed one of my fairing work-baskets..on a table.

fairing ('fɛərɪŋ), *vbl. sb.*² [f. FAIR *v.* 3 + -ING¹.] The action or result of making the lines of a vessel, aircraft, or motor vehicle suitable for its easy passage through water or air; the line or curvature so made, or the structure added for this purpose.

a **1865** SMYTH *Sailor's Work-bk.* (1867) 286 *Fairing*, sheering a ship in construction. Also, the draught of a ship. **1914** *Aeronaut. Jrnl.* Oct. 316 *Fairing*, a piece added to any structure to reduce its head resistance or drag. **1916** H. BARBER *Aeroplane Speaks* 137 *Fairing*, usually made of thin sheet aluminium, wood, or a light construction of wood and fabric; and bent round detrimental surface in order to give it a 'fair' or 'stream-like' shape. **1927** *Daily Tel.* 6 Sept. 11/3 The fairing of the wings into the fuselage. **1930** *Daily Express* 23 May 11/5 The fairing piece at the extreme end of the tail, which performs no actual function in the operation of the airship, was slightly damaged. **1934** *Flight* 25 Jan. 78 *e*/1 The section on lines will..apply equally well to a set of 'fairing lines' for an ordinary fairing drawing. **1936** *Times* 19 Oct. 8/4 The car, which has graceful curves and fairings to reduce wind-noise, costs £368. **1962** J. GLENN et al. in *Into Orbit* 244 *Fairing*, part of the structure of an aircraft or spacecraft which provides streamlining in order to reduce aerodynamic resistance.

b. *transf.* (see quot. 1922); also used of the movement of animated figures in cinematography.

1922 *Encycl. Brit.* XXX. 21/1 In other countries cable has continued to be used, frequently duplicated, the cables lying one behind the other with a wood 'fairing' between them. **1959** [see FAIR *v.* 3].

fairish ('fɛərɪʃ), *a.* and *adv.* [f. FAIR *a.* and *adv.* + -ISH.] **A.** *adj.* Somewhat fair.

1. Moderately good, passable.

1611 COTGR., *Bellastre*, fairish, reasonably faire, passable. **1660** in HOWELL *Lexicon.* **1847** *Illust. Lond. News* 28 Aug. 142/1, I rowed in a fairish 'eight'. **1863** W. C. BALDWIN *Afr. Hunting* 331 So ended a fairish day's sport. **1882** B. M. CROKER *Proper Pride* I. xi. 226 Sometimes..he is in fairish spirits.

b. *dial.* Tolerably well (in health); †also, merry with drink.

1756 W. TOLDERVY *Hist. Two Orphans* IV. 3 Humphry.. was now quite fairish, as he called it, and attended to nothing but spouting speeches from Shakespear's Pistol. **1876** *Oxfordsh. Gloss.* s.v., 'I be fairish.' **1888** *Berksh. Gloss.* s.v. *Vaairish*, 'I be a veelin' varish now zur'.

2. Considerable in amount; fairly large. *colloq.*

1881 *Leicestersh. Gloss.*, 'Theer's pritty feerish on 'em this turn.' **1883** D. C. MURRAY *Hearts* II. 136 Cost a fairish penny, didn't it? **1884** *Gd. Words* 229 Two fairish sized tubs.

B. *adv.* In a fair manner; to a fair degree. *colloq.* or *dial.*

1836–48 B. D. WALSH *Aristoph., Knights* I. iii, I..got laughed at pretty fairish. **1877** *Holderness Gloss.* s.v., 'Ah's gettin' on fairish wi job.' **1881** *Leicestersh. Gloss.* s.v.,'Surs! it's feerish waarm.'

Fair Isle ('fɛər aɪl). The name of one of the Shetland islands, used attrib. to designate woollen articles knitted in certain designs characteristic of the island.

1851 *Illustr. Catal. Gt. Exhib.* III. III. 585/2 Fair Isle socks, gloves, vest piece, comforter, and cap. **1923** *Queen* 25 Oct. p. i/3 (Advt.), Allover Fair Isle Jumpers. *Ibid.*, Fair Isle Knitting Yarn, in 2-ply yellow, green, blue and red. **1924** *Tourist* Winter Sports No. 20 Shetland wool with Fair Isle border. **1925** *Queen* 8 Apr. 19 Attired in her Fair Isle jersey. **1955** *Oxf. Jun. Encycl.* XI. 277/2 The well-known Fair Isle patterns in many colours are modern interpretations of.. national designs.

b. Fair Isle field mouse, a kind of mouse, an alleged (sub-)species (*Apodemus sylvaticus*

fridariensis) of the field-mouse (FIELD *sb.* 19), found in the Shetlands, of larger size than the ordinary field-mouse.

[**1906** N. B. KINNEAR in *Ann. Scot. Nat. Hist.* Apr. 68, I think the Fair Isle mice are quite entitled to be ranked as a sub-species, and therefore I propose the name of Mus sylvaticus Fridariensis.] **1915** G. E. H. BARRETT-HAMILTON *Hist. Brit. Mammals* XVII. 542 (*heading*) The Fair Isle Field Mouse. *Apodemus Fridariensis. Ibid.*, Distribution: Fair Isle and Shetland Islands, where it occurs on Yell, and possibly on Mainland. **1960** M. BURTON *Wild Animals Brit. Isles* 78 The Fair Isle or Shetland field mouse.., like the yellow-necked but without the collar.

fair-lead ('fɛəli:d). **a.** (See quot. 1860). **b.** = FAIR-LEADER. **c.** *transf.*

a. *c* **1860** H. STUART *Seaman's Catech.* 21 What do you mean by a fair lead? In reeving a rope, to be very careful to have it so led through the block or sheave aloft, that it does not cut or chafe any of the rigging, or cross any other ropes. **1867** SMYTH *Sailor's Word-bk., Fair-lead.*

b. **1869** SIR E. J. REED *Shipbuild.* xv. 290 Of late.. fair-leads or dead-eyes of malleable cast-iron have been employed.

c. **1937** *Times* 13 Apr. xvi/2 Roller fairleads at the rear end of the vehicle allow the cable to be used immediately to the rear or at any angle to the side. **1957** *N.Z. Timber Jrnl.* Feb. 45 *Fairlead*, a device of 3 or 4 rollers in the form of a U through which a cable can be carried out or reeled in from any direction for hauling logs.

Similarly **fair-leader** (see quot. 1841). **fair-leading** *vbl. sb., attrib.* in ***fair-leading block***, a block that acts as a fair-leader.

1841 R. H. DANA *Seaman's Man.* 104 *Fair-leader* a strip of board or plank, with holes in it, for running rigging, to lead through. Also, a block or thimble used for the same purpose. **1882** NARES *Seamanship* (ed. 6) 59 The falls being led.. through fair-leaders in ship's side. *Ibid.* 55 A fair-leading block stropped to it.

† **'fairlec.** *Obs.* [f. FAIR *a.*: see -LOCK.] Fairness, beauty.

a **1225** *St. Marher.* 19 Feirlec ant strencðe beoð his schrudes. *c* **1230** *Hali Meid.* 39 He ȝiueð feirlec to al þat is feir in heuene & in earðe. *c* **1320** *Cast. Love* 145 He ȝaf him .. Feirlek and freodam.

Fairlight Clay. [f. *Fairlight*, name of a town in Sussex + CLAY *sb.*] A band of shales and clays of the Wealden series extending through Kent and East Sussex.

1875 W. TOPLEY *Geol. Weald* I. i. 5 In the neighbourhood of Hastings and Fairlight, clays have been separately mapped.. and were termed 'Ashburnham Beds'... They are now called *Fairlight Clays.* **1929** P. G. H. BOSWELL in Evans & Stubblefield *Handbk. Geol. Gt. Brit.* 388 Near Hastings and Eastbourne the lower part is replaced by a lenticular mass of variegated and mottled clays, the *Fairlight Clays* (350 ft. +) with seams of lignite, sandstone and spherulitic ironstone. **1960** L. D. STAMP *Britain's Struct.* (ed. 5) xvi. 189 Fairlight Clays, grey and variegated shales and clays.

† **fair-like,** *a. Obs. rare*$^{-1}$. [f. FAIR *a.* + LIKE *a.*] In good condition; well-looking.

1662 HICKERINGILL *Apol. Distressed Innocence* Wks. (1716) I. 273 Naboth.. was too Fat and Fair-like to avoid the Shambles of these bloody Butchers.

fairly ('fɛəlɪ), *adv.* [f. FAIR *a.* + -LY^2.]

† **1.** So as to make a fair appearance; beautifully, handsomely. Also in bad sense: Speciously. *Obs.*

c **1400** MAUNDEV. (1839) xxii. 242 Alle the hoost cometh fayrely aftre him. *c* **1400** *Destr. Troy* 5142 Þai.. ferdon on fote fairly to-gedur. **1483** *Cath. Angl.* 120 Fayrly, *ornate.* **1592** SHAKS. *Rom. & Jul.* III. ii. 84 Was euer booke.. So fairely bound? **1630** *R. Johnson's Kingd. & Commw.* 131 Saint Germaines.. was very fairely builded. **1819** BYRON *Juan* III. lxxvi, To make The skin.. appear more fairly fair. **1870** MORRIS *Earthly Par.* I. I. 47 Raiment.. Most fairly woven.

b. Of writing: Neatly, elegantly. *arch.*

1594 SHAKS. *Rich. III*, III. vi. 2 The Indictment.. in a set Hand fairely is engross'd. **1717** BERKELEY *Tour in Italy* Wks. IV. 514 The book is fairly writ on vellum.

† **2.** Courteously, respectfully. *Obs.*

1590 SHAKS. *Com. Err.* v. i. 233 Fairely I bespoke the Officer To go in person with me. **1608** —— *Per.* v. i 10, I pray ye, greet them fairly.

3. With due regard to equity; candidly, impartially; without undue advantage on either side.

1676 DRYDEN *Aureng-zebe* III. i, I interpret fairly your design. **1712** STEELE *Spect.* No. 272 ¶ 1 Circumstances fairly represented in the Spectator. **1776** *Trial of Nundocomar* 25/1 The Durbar charges were not just and fairly charged. **1783** HAILES *Antiq. Chr. Ch.* iv. 72 The inferences that are fairly deducible from it. **1848** MACAULAY *Hist. Eng.* II. 375 The counsel were by no means fairly matched. **1851** DIXON *W. Penn* v. (1872) 47 In no corner of these islands were the Quakers treated fairly. **1862** STANLEY *Jew. Ch.* (1877) I. xiii. 260 Only in the light of that time can they be fairly considered.

4. Becomingly, fitly, properly, suitably; proportionably.

1596 SHAKS. *Merch. V.* I. i. 128 My cheefe care Is to come fairely off from the great debts. **1691** T. H[ALE] *Acc. New Invent.* p. xx, The Bolt-heads, &c., being fairly parcelled. **1731** ARBUTHNOT *Aliments* IV. ii. §24. 98 The Serum of the Blood is fairly substituted in its place. **1800** *Med. Jrnl.* IV. 462 His time will be fairly, and I doubt not successfully employed. **1832** HT. MARTINEAU *Homes Abroad* v. 74 You may fairly marry as soon as you like. **1892** SIR A. KEKEWICH in *Law Times Rep.* LXVII. 139/1 The facts.. may be fairly described in that manner.

b. By proper or lawful means, legitimately; opposed to *foully.*

1632 J. HAYWARD tr. *Biondi's Eromena* 145, I will kill thee fairly, as becomes a good Knight. **1709** STEELE *Tatler* No. 38 ¶ 3 [They] in decent Manner fought full fairly with their wrathful Hands. **1719** DE FOE *Crusoe* (1840) II. xi. 236 We came honestly and fairly by the ship. **1797** MRS. RADCLIFFE *Italian* iii. 23 She came fairly by her death.

† **5.** Gently, peaceably, quietly, softly. *Obs.*

c **1400** MAUNDEV. (Roxb.) xiv. 61 It standes still and rynnez noȝt, or elles bot fairely. **1590** SPENSER *F.Q.* II. vi. 40 Guyon.. with strong reason master'd passion fraile, And passed fayrely forth. **1591** SHAKS. *Two Gent.* II. v. 14 They parted very fairely in iest. **1634** MILTON *Comus* 168, I fairly step aside, And hearken.

6. Clearly, distinctly, plainly.

a **1661** FULLER *Worthies* (1840) III. 490 The door fairly set open for him by Divine Providence. **1671** GREW *Anat. Plants.* I. iii. §11 The Pores.. by the help of good Glasses, are very fairly visible. **1828** SCOTT *F.M. Perth* ii, [I] saw the bonny city lie stretched fairly before me. **1841** MIALL *Nonconf.* I. 2 It becomes dissenters fairly to avow it.

7. Completely, fully, quite, 'clean'; actually, positively, really.

In written examples it is often difficult to know whether this or the very different sense 8 is intended; but in speech this confusion is prevented by the marked difference in intonation.

1596 SPENSER *State Irel.* (1633) 9 All which they nevertheless fairely overcame. **1604** in Ellis *Orig. Lett.* II. 249 III. 216 He would wish him fairly buried before his eyes. **1653** H. COGAN tr. *Pinto's Trav.* xx. 73 They fairly tore out one anothers throats with their teeth. **1713** *Guardian* No. 42, I fairly nodded in the elbow-chair. **1766** GOLDSM. *Vic. W.* xx, I had some thoughts of fairly shipping back to England again. **1804–8** FOSTER in *Life & Corr.* (1846) I. 268, I never think of fairly sitting down for a conversation. **1823** LAMB *Elia, Poor Relation*, When he goeth away, you dismiss his chair into a corner.. and feel fairly rid of two nuisances. **1867** FREEMAN *Norm. Conq.* (1876) I. vi. 500 The star of Harold was fairly in the ascendant. **1868** M. PATTISON *Academ. Org.* v. 306 Our system.. has fairly run away with us. **1873** TRISTRAM *Moab* iv. 64 We were fairly in the trap.

8. Moderately, passably, tolerably.

1805 WORDSW. *Waggoner* I. 110, I am fairly safe to-night. **1860** TYNDALL *Glac.* I. ix. 63 The structure of the ice was fairly developed. **1863** KINGLAKE *Crimea* (1877) I. xiv. 215 He.. rode fairly to hounds. **1871** MORLEY *Voltaire* (1886) 9 People with whom the world goes fairly well materially.

9. *Comb.*, as *fairly-balanced, -fitted.*

1848 DICKENS *Dombey* (C.D. ed.) 8 They were.. a.. fairly-balanced, give-and-take couple. **1870** BRYANT *Iliad* I. IV. 115 He drew The arrow from the fairly-fitted belt.

'fair-'maid.

1. = FUMADE.

1848 C. A. JOHNS *Week at Lizard* 54 The Italians call them [salted pilchards] *fumados*.. from a corruption of this word they are universally called, in Cornwall, 'fair-maids'. **1883** *Fisheries Exhib. Catal.* (ed. 4) 128 Quarter Hogsheads of Fairmaids.

2. In various names of plants. **fair maid(s of February**, the Snowdrop, *Galanthus nivalis*; **fair maids of France, of Kent** [= Fr. *belle-pucelle*], a double-flowered variety of Crowfoot, *Ranunculus aconitiflorus.*

1776 WITHERING *Brit. Plants* (1796) II. 331 Common Snowdrop. Fair Maids of February. **1823** CRABB *Technol. Dict.* s.v. *Fair*, Fair Maid of France, the *Ranunculus aconitifolius* of Linnæus, a perennial. **1863** PRIOR *Plant-n., Fair Maids of February*, white flowers that blossom about the 2nd of that month. *Ibid., Fair Maids of France.* **1878–86** BRITTEN & HOLLAND *Plant-n.*, Fair Maids of Kent.

fairness ('fɛənɪs). [f. FAIR *a.* + -NESS.]

1. The quality or condition of being fair; beauty: **a.** in the abstract; also *concr.* something that is fair, a beautiful feature, an ornament.

c **1200** ORMIN 12253 Off hæle, off faȝȝerrnesse, Off strenncþe. *c* **1340** HAMPOLE *Prose Tr.* (1866) 39 Thare es souerayne fairenes, lyghtenes, strenghe [etc.]. **1398** TREVISA *Barth. De P.R.* VIII. xvii. (1495) 325 The mone is the fayrnes of the nyght. **1450–1530** *Myrr. our Ladye* 177 Beholdynge in hym all fayreness, all power, and all verteu. **1649** JER. TAYLOR *Gt. Exemp.* II. vii. 35 Persons of the greatest fancy, and such who are most pleased with outward fairnesses are most religious. **1856** RUSKIN *Mod. Paint.* III. IV. xvi. §14 For all fairness we have to seek to the flowers.

b. of women.

a **1000** *Liber Scint.* 168 Leas gyfu & ydel ys fæȝernyss. *a* **1225** *St. Marher.* (1862) 35 For ir feirnesse, þau ho bee comen of þrelle. **1377** LANGL. *P. Pl.* B. XII. 47 Felyce hir fayrnesse fel hir al to sklaundre. *c* **1430** *Pilgr. Lyf Manhode* I. vii. (1869) 4, I seygh a lady in my wey; of hire fairnesse she dide me ioye. **1526** *Pilgr. Perf.* (W. de W. 1531) 63 In the whiche synne they fall communly by the reason of theyr fayrnes. **1624** HEYWOOD *Gunaik.* IV. 164 The higher powers have bestowed upon you fairenesse above man. **1762–71** H. WALPOLE *Vertue's Anecd. Paint.* (1786) I. iv, The print gives .. some of her Flemish fairness. **1877** MRS. FORRESTER *Mignon* I. 54 And right royally she uses the prerogative of her fairness.

c. of men and children; *rarely* of animals. *Obs.* or *arch.*

a **1000** *Lambeth Ps.* xliv. 5 (Bosw.) Mid ðinum hiwe oððe wlite and fæȝernysse ðinre. *c* **1175** *Lamb. Hom.* 77 Sunne and mone þostreþ for his fairnesse. *c* **1250** *Gen. & Ex.* 1233 Wantede ðit child faiernesse and miȝt. **1387** TREVISA *Higden* (Rolls) I. 285 A woman.. wedded a bocher for his faireness. **1401** *Pol. Poems* (1859) II. 68 If Sathanas were transfigurid into his former fairnesse. **1535** COVERDALE *Isa.* liii. 2 When we loke vpon him, there shalbe no fayrnesse. **1608** D. T. *Ess. Pol. & Mor.* 48 The beautie and fairenesse of his eyes. **1820** KEATS *Hyperion* III. 125 The immortal fairness of his limbs.

† **d.** of inanimate things. *Obs.*

1303 R. BRUNNE *Handl. Synne* 7025 Myȝte no.. tunge telle þe feyrnesse. *c* **1325** *Prose Psalter* xlix. 12 Þe fairnes of þe felde is wyþ me. *c* **1400** *Cato's Morals* 109 in *Cursor M.* App. iv, Noȝt for þe fairnes, bot for þi nedines, loue þou þe peny. *c* **1511** *1st Eng. Bk. Amer.* (Arb.) Introd. 27 All with feders bouden for there bewtynes and fayrenes. **1583** HOLLYBAND *Campo di Fior* 305, I am not of opinion that any place can be found like to this in fairenesse. **1662** MERRETT tr. *Neri's Art of Glass* lxxxvi, A Violet colour of notable fairness. **1726** *Adv. Capt. R. Boyle* 9, I shew'd him the Money, and he soon knew the Piece.. from the particular Fairness of it.

† **e.** of speech. *Obs.*

c **1490** *Promp. Parv.* 146 (MS. K.) Fayirnesse of speche, *facundia.*

2. Of the complexion or skin: Lightness of colour.

1599 HAKLUYT *Voy.* II. 331 The whitenesse thereof [ivory] was.. thought to represent the natural fairenesse of man's skinne. **1796** MORSE *Amer. Geog.* II. 550 Ambitious of intermarrying with Persians.. on account of the fairness of their complexion. **1828** SCOTT *F.M. Perth* xv, The fairness of his skin, where it had not.. been exposed.

3. Equitableness, fair dealing, honesty, impartiality, uprightness.

c **1460** *Towneley Myst.* 195 It is best that we trete hym with farenes. **1722** *Wodrow Corr.* (1843) II. 628, I hope fairness and truth were in mine eye. **1771** *Junius Lett.* xlvi. 245 No man.. will dispute the fairness of this construction. **1802** *Med. Jrnl.* VIII. 184 We do not doubt of the fairness of the statement. **1859** MACAULAY *Biog.* (1867) 91 A show of fairness was.. necessary to the prosperity of the Magazine. **1888** BRYCE *Amer. Commw.* III. xcix. 387 The criticisms of an outspoken press rarely assail.. their [English judges'] fairness.

† **4.** Of the weather: The state of being free from storms or rain; fineness. *Obs.*

c **1440** *Promp. Parv.* 146 Fayrnesse of wedur, *amenitas.* **1580** BARET *Alv.* F 37 Fairenesse of weather: quietnesse, *serénitas.* **1743** BULKELEY & CUMMINS *Voy. S. Seas* 23 The Moon, Tides, and Fairness of Weather were more favourable to us by Night than Day.

† **5.** Courtesy. *Obs.*

c **1205** LAY. 3272 Me vnder-feng þene king: mid mochele feirnusse. *a* **1400–50** *Alexander* 1745 Feyne all with faires & fayne at þou may.

† **6.** Gentleness; only in *by, **with fairness***: by fair or gentle means. *Obs.*

c **1386** CHAUCER *Prol.* 519 To drawen folk to heven, with fairnesse, By good ensample. *c* **1400** *Beryn* 1396 Let assay efft ageyn, with ffeirnes hym to chast. **1470–85** MALORY *Arthur* IX. lxxxvii, Outher with fayrenes or foulenesse I shalle brynge hym to this courte. **1568** GRAFTON *Chron.* II. 331 The king.. will provyde some remedy for us, eyther by fayrenesse or otherwise.

fairney-cloots. *Sc.*

'The small horny substances above the hoofs, where the pastern of a horse lies, but said to be found only in sheep or goats, *Ettr. For.*' (Jam.)

1822 HOGG *Perils of Man* III. 33 'Here's a tyke wi' cloven cloots like a gait, fairney cloots and a' thegither.'

fair-pleader, -ing. *Law.* = BEAU-PLEADER.

1670 BLOUNT *Law Dict.* s.v., Neither in the Circuit of Justices, nor in Counties.. any Fines shall be taken of any Man for Fair pleading, that is, for not pleading fairly or aptly to the purpose. **1700** [see BEAUPLEADER]. **1721–1800** in BAILEY. **1848** in WHARTON *Law Lex.*

fair-sex, *v. nonce-wd.* In *to fair-sex it*: to discourse upon the fair sex.

1712 SWIFT *Jrnl. to Stella* 8 Feb., I will not meddle with the Spectator, let him fair-sex it to the world's end. **1810** W. TAYLOR in *Monthly Mag.* XXX. 346 He may fair-sex it (as Swift says) to the end.

† **'fairship.** *Obs.* [f. FAIR *a.* + -SHIP.]

a. Fairness, beauty. **b.** The personality of a 'fair lady'. Cf. BEAUTYSHIP, *ladyship.*

c **1320** *Cast. Love* 688 Ther may no man here feyrship wyte. *a* **1400** *Vernon Poems* 444 The swete face of his Lorde there.. In his feyreship he may him showen.. Of hevyn he may i-se the wydnes, The feyreshepe and the heynes. **1646** J. HALL *Poems* 11 How every wit Capers.. to fit Words to her faireships grief.

† **'fairsome,** *a. Obs. rare*$^{-1}$. [f. FAIR *a.* + -SOME.] Beautiful; in quot. *absol.*

a **1641** SIR J. SUCKLING in *N. & Q.* I. 72 Still I'll love the fairsome.

,fair-'spoken, *a.* Also 7 fairspoke. **a.** Of persons: Gifted with fair speech; courteous, pleasant; smooth-tongued.

1460 CAPGRAVE *Chron.* (Rolls) 81 He was.. fayre-spokyn, but he spak but seldam. **1530** PALSGR. 312/1 Fayre spoken .. *bein en langaige.* **1597** HOOKER *Eccl. Pol.* v. (1617) 266 Arius.. a subtlewitted and a marvellous fair-spoken man. **1647** HAMMOND *Serm., Christian's Oblig. Peace* (1649) 7 Fair-spoken sword-men.. whose words are softer than butter. **1665** DRYDEN *Ind. Emperor* II. i, Kalib, ascend, my fairspoke servant rise. **1828** LANDOR *Imag. Conv.* III. 473 He was.. fairspoken both to high and low.

b. Of words: Bland, civil.

1649 MILTON *Eikon.* Pref., These his faire spok'n words shall be heer fairely confronted.. to his.. deeds.

fair-top boot. *U.S.* [FAIR *a.* 1 f.] A boot topped with light-coloured leather.

1799 in C. Cist *Cincinnati* (1841) 159 As an illustration of fashions.. fair-top boots. **1826** *Rhode Isl. American* Let. 2 Mar. (Th.), His usual dress in the Senate is a blue coat,.. drab small-clothes, and fair-top boots. **1853** J. G. BALDWIN *Flush Times Alabama* 22 He dressed in the old-fashioned

fair-top boots and shorts. **1860** S. Mordecai *Virginia* iii. 48 His tall and burly form arrayed in fair-top boots [etc.].

ˈfair-ˈtrade.

1. a. Trade carried on legally as opposed to dealing in contraband goods. **b.** In the 18th c. also applied (in popular language) in the precisely opposite sense; a euphemistic synonym for smuggling.

1774 Burke *Amer. Tax.* (1775) 49 The contraband will always keep pace in some measure with the fair trade.

2. In recent use: The fiscal system advocated by those who consider that 'one-sided free trade' is injurious to the nation adopting such a policy, and that the principle of free trade should be applied only in dealing with nations that admit our products free.

1881 Gladstone in *Times* 8 Oct. 6/5 This he says he wants, not as protection, but in the name of fair trade. **1891** *Spectator* 21 Feb. 263/2 An excellent speech against 'Fair-trade'.

attrib. **1881** *Spectator* 10 Dec. 1558 The Fair trade question. **1882** T. H. Farrer *Free Trade v. Fair Trade* ii. 6 The programme of the Fair Trade League is not definite in its particulars. *Ibid.* ii. 8 That application is not contained in the Fair Trade programme.

Hence **fair-trader**, (*a*) one who trades fairly or legally; (*b*) one who supports the Fair-trade programme; (*c*) a smuggler (cf. fair-trade 1 b, free-trader 2). **fair-tradism**, the doctrines of a fair-trader (sense b).

1673 *Essex Papers* (Camden) I. 56 Others who have found yᵉ encouragemᵗ from yᵉ farmʳˢ of Ireland to yᵉ ruin of yᵉ fair Trader here. **1746** Lockman *To First Promoter Cambrick & Tea Bills* 27 Bid the Fair-trader..bemoan His credit lost. **1824** Scott *Redgauntlet* II. xiii. 313 Ay, Mr Alan Fairford—a good name for a fair trader. **1881** W. F. Ecroyd *Sp. at Oldham* 21 Fair Traders..wanted..an extension of real free exchange. **1884** D. Pae *Eustace* 217, I am what is called a fair trader—in other words a smuggler. **1887** *Spectator* 21 May 674/1 The Fair-traders are at their wits' end for a compromise with Free-trade. **1888** *Pall Mall G.* 26 Nov. 12/1 Fair-tradism is apparently to be brought down from national to local application.

ˈfairwater. [f. fair *v.* 3 + water *sb.*] A structure making the lines of a vessel suitable for its easy passage through water.

1910 D. W. Taylor *Speed & Power of Ships* I. ii. 125 About all that can be done for the propeller hub is to fit a conical fair-water behind it. Model experiments show that a long fair-water, say of length about twice the diameter of the propeller hub, offers materially less resistance than a short fair-water of length say about one-half the diameter of the propeller hub. **1927** G. Bradford *Gloss. Sea Terms* 62/1 *Fair water cone*, the conical cap covering the after side of the hole of a propeller which takes the end of the tail shaft. **1948** R. de Kerchove *Internat. Maritime Dict.* 250/2 *Fairwater*, 1. A conical-shaped cap fitted over the locknut at the afterend of the propeller shaft to prevent an abrupt change in the streamlines. Also called fairwater cone, propeller cap, fairwater cap. 2. Any casting or plate affixed to the hull with a view to maintaining smooth streamline flow of water. Plating fitted about the ends of shaft tubes or struts to prevent a sharp change in the direction of streamlines. **1956** *Jane's Fighting Ships 1956–7* 226 Transferred to Italy by U.S.A. after conversion to guppy-schnorkel [submarine]. Modified structure and fairwater.

ˈfairway. Also 9 fare-way. [See fair *a.* 16; the interpretation suggested by the spelling *fareway* (cf. fare *v.*) appears to be erroneous.] **a.** A navigable channel in a river or between rocks, sandbanks, etc.; the usual course or passage of a vessel on the sea or in entering and leaving a harbour.

1584 in Binnell *Descr. Thames* (1758) 62 That the fair Way be kept as deep and large as heretofore. **1675** *Lond. Gaz.* No. 1006/4 The fair way going into Plymouth Sound. **1769** Falconer *Dict. Marine* (1789), *Débacleur*, an officer whose duty it is..to keep the passage, or fair-way, open. **1858** *Adm. Reg.* in *Merc. Marine Mag.* V. 103 Sea-going vessels..at anchor in roadsteads or fairways. **1883** *Chamb. Jrnl.* 523 Clear water fareways, by which the fishermen wend a speedy course from point to point. **1893** *Daily Chron.* 4 Jan. 5/7 She was in the fairway of all steamers crossing to and from New York.

attrib. **1875** Bedford *Sailor's Pocket-bk.* v. (ed. 2) 137 Fairway buoys are plainly marked.

b. *Golf.* That part of a golf-course between a tee and putting-green which consists of short grass.

1910 B. Darwin *Golf Courses Brit. Isles* i. 18 Hillocks have risen as if by magic in the middle of the fairway. **1923** *Daily Mail* 18 Jan. 9 The maintenance staff..are busy on the fairways and teeing grounds. **1952** *Golf* ('Know the Game' series) 24/2 The player must loft the ball out, thus losing considerable distance in relation to an opponent lying on the fairway.

c. *transf.* and *fig.*

1927 *Daily Tel.* 30 Aug. 10/5 (Lawn tennis) The court..was soft and yielding near the base-lines, even if true enough in the fairway. **1931** H. G. Wells *Work, Wealth & Happiness of Mankind* (1932) xii. 574 Every member must leave his seat in the chamber and walk in queue through the fairway of one or other of two lobbies, the 'Ayes' or the 'Noes'. **1959** *Manch. Guardian* 12 Aug. 5/7, I had walked..through the forest..following the long fairways used to check fires.

ˈfair-weather, *a.*

1. Fit or suitable only for calm or fair weather.

1810 *Naval Chron.* XXIV. 69 These fair-weather birds would never put to sea. **1855** Macaulay *Hist. Eng.* III. 650 The first gale would send the whole of this fairweather armament to the bottom of the Channel. **1883** *Manch. Exam.* 26 Nov. 5/3 They are all fair-weather craft.

2. *fig.*

1736 *Pope's Lett.* 1 Oct. 1730 My Fair-weather friends of the summer are going away for London. **1748** Smollett *Rod. Rand.* iii, That there fair weather Jack (pointing to the young squire). **1828** E. Irving *Last Days* 287 What a fair-weather service there is of God! **1873** Miss Broughton *Nancy* II. 10 Am I to be only a fair-weather wife to you?

fairy (ˈfɛərɪ), *sb.* and *a.* Forms: 4 feir-, feyr-i(e, -ye, (5 fery, 6 feirie), 4–5 fai-, fayerie, -ye, (4 fayryȝe), 4–6 fair-, fayr-é, -ey, -ie, -y(e, (6 fayere, 6–7 pharie, 7 farie, phair-, pherie), 4– fairy; also faerie, -y. [a. OF. *faerie, faierie* (mod.F. *féerie*), f. OF. *fae* (mod.F. *fée*) fay *sb.*²]

A. *sb.*

†**1.** The land or home of the fays; fairy-land. *Obs.*: see faerie.

c **1320** *Orfeo* 273 The kyng of Fayré, with his route, Com to hunte all aboute. *c* **1386** Chaucer *Sqr.'s T.* 88 Though he were comen ayeyn out of ffairye. *c* **1400** Maundev. (Roxb.) xvi. 73 A sperhawke..and a faire lady of Fairye sittand þerby. **1593** Drayton *Eclogues* iii. 15 [Collin] is to *fayrie* gone a Pilgrimage. **1610** B. Jonson *Alch.* I. ii, The Doctor Sweares that you are..Allied to the Queene of Faerie.

†**2.** A collective term for the fays or inhabitants of fairyland; fairy-folk. *Obs.*

c **1320** *Orfeo* 189 Awey with the fayré sche was ynome. *c* **1350** *Will. Palerne* 230 þemperour wend witerly for wonder of þat child, þat feiȝþely it were of feyrye. *c* **1489** Caxton *Sonnes of Aymon* xiv. 337 The horse..that cam of the fery. **1525** Ld. Berners *Froiss.* II. ccxxiv. [ccxx.] 700 Suche as knowe..affyrmeth that the fayry and the nympes be moche conuersaunt there. *c* **1540** *Pilgrim's Tale* 88 Where this man walked, there was no farey..for his blessynges..did vanquyche them. **1603** *Philotus* cxxviii, Gang hence..to the Farie, With me thow may na langer tarie.

†**3.** Enchantment, magic; a magic contrivance; an illusion, a dream. *Obs.*

c **1300** *K. Alis.* 6924 That thou herdest is fairye. *c* **1310** *E.E.P.* (1862) 134 Hit nis but fantum and feiri. **1362** Langl. *P. Pl.* A. Prol. 6 Me bi-fel a ferly A Feyrie me þouhte. *c* **1430** *Pilgr. Lyf Manhode* II. xxxvi. (1869) 89, I wot not what this tokeneth, but if it be a fairye. *a* **1533** Ld. Berners *Huon* clvi. 595 To yᵉ entente that the monke shuld not begyle hym, thus by the fayrey and enchauntement.

4. a. One of a class of supernatural beings of diminutive size, in popular belief supposed to possess magical powers and to have great influence for good or evil over the affairs of man. See elf and fay *sb.*²

1393 Gower *Conf.* II. 371 And as he were a fairie. *c* **1450** *Voc.* in Wr.-Wülcker 571 *Cavni*, fayryes. **1563** Fulke *Meteors* (1640) 68 b, Those round circles..that ignorant people affirme to be the rings of the Fairies dances. **1583** Sempill *Ballates* xxxv. 210 Ane carling of the Quene of Phareis. **1650** Baxter *Saint's R.* II. (1654) 270 Hags (or Fairies) that is, such as exercise familiarity with men. **1743** Collins *Ep. to Sir T. Hanmer* 98 Twilight fairies tread the circled Green. **1813** Shelley *Q. Mab* 167, I am the Fairy Mab. **1832** W. Irving *Alhambra* I. 128 She is small enough to be a fairy, and a fairy she may be for aught I can find out. **1891** *Daily News* 30 Oct. 5/1 The first appearance of the conventional Fairy..is made in Perrault's 'Contes' (1697).

b. *fairy of the mine*: a goblin supposed to inhabit mines. (The designation is used by Milton; later writers use it as the equivalent of the German *kobold* or *gnome*.) †*fairy of the sea*: a Nereid.

1555 Eden *Decades* 12 The fayre nimphes or fayeres of the sea (cauled Nereiades). **1607** Topsell *Four-f. Beasts* (1673) 261 The Virgin lived among the Pharies of the Sea. **1634** [see faerie 3]. **18..** *Scot. Encycl.* s.v., The Germans believed in two species of Fairies of the Mines.

5. *transf.* †**a.** One possessing more than human power; an enchantress. *Obs.*

1606 Shaks. *Ant. & Cl.* IV. viii. 12 To this great faiery [Cleopatra], Ile commend thy acts.

b. A small graceful woman or child.

1838 Lytton *Alice* 21 Miss Merton was..surprised by the beauty..of the young fairy before her.

c. A male homosexual. *slang.*

1895 *Amer. Jrnl. Psychol.* VII. 216 This coincides with what is known of the peculiar societies of inverts. Coffee-clatches, where the members dress themselves with aprons, etc., and knit, gossip and crotchet; balls, where men adopt the ladies' evening dress, are well known in Europe. 'The Fairies' of New York are said to be a similar secret organization. **1923** [see fag *sb.*⁶]. **1925** F. Lonsdale *Spring Cleaning* II. 75 *Mona.* I say, what's the fairy's name? *Richard.* I have happily forgotten it for the moment! **1929** R. Hughes *High Wind in Jamaica* iv, 'Who are they?' Emily asked the Captain... 'Who are who?' he murmured absently... 'Oh, those? Fairies.' 'Hey! Yey! Yey!' cried the mate. **1945** E. Waugh *Brideshead Revisited* I. v. 102 Two girls stopped near our table and looked at us curiously. 'Come on,' said one to the other, 'we're wasting our time. They're only fairies.'

B. *adj.*

1. Of or pertaining to fairies; of the nature of fairies; enchanted, illusory, fictitious.

c **1640** Waller *To one who libelled C'tess Carlisle* iii, Hast thou not heard of fairy Arthur's shield. **1699** Bentley *Phal.* 286 His two Fairy Poets wrote Tragedies against him. **1713** *Guardian* No. 141 The fairy images of glory and honour. **1821** Shelley *Epipsych.* 193 The fairy isles of sunny lawn.

2. Resembling a fairy, fairy-like; delicate, finely formed or woven.

1788 W. Gilpin *Mount. & Lakes* II. 223 Little fairy scenes, where the parts, tho trifling, are happily disposed. **1838** Lytton *Alice* II. ii, Delicate and fairy cast of beauty. *a* **1839** Praed *Poems* (1864) I. 229 Many a fairy form I've met. **1864** Tennyson *Aylmer's F.* 91 [He] Show'd her..The little dells of cowslip, fairy palms..fairy pines. **1883** Aldrich *Ponkapog to Pesth* 243 Fairy textures from looms of Samarcand.

C. *attrib.* and *Comb.*

1. General relations: **a.** simple attrib., as *fairy-arrow*, *-book*, etc.; also in various local names for the Foxglove (*Digitalis purpurea*), *fairy-bell*, *-cap*, *-fingers*, *-glove*, *-thimble*, *-weed*; **b.** appositive, as *fairy-folk*, *-godmother*; **c.** instrumental and originative, as *fairy-born*, *-haunted*, *-pencilled* adjs.; **d.** parasynthetic and similative, as *fairy-featured*, *-fine*, *-formed*, *-like* adjs.

1864 Tennyson *Aylmer's F.* 94 What looked a flight of *fairy arrows. **1870** *Science Gossip* 1 June 135 In Anglo-Irish we call it [the Foxglove]..*fairy bell. **1850** Mrs. Browning *Poems* II. 213 A child..sleeping with dropt head Upon the *fairy-book he lately read. **1871** Palgrave *Lyr. Poems* 11 All these things..So wrought on her, though *fairy born and wild. *c* **1620** *Convert Soule* in Farr *S.P. Jas. I* (1848) 89 And for thy food eat *fairy bread. **1828** Miss Mitford *Village* 3rd Ser. (1863) 83 The prettier Irish name of that superb plant [the fox-glove], the *fairy-cap. **1681** Dryden *Sp. Friar* II. 21 These *Fayery favours are lost when not concealed. **1778** Langhorne *Owen of Carron* lxvii, The *fairy-featured vale. **1904** *Westm. Gaz.* 20 May 2/4 A wonder, a green miracle, More *fairy-fine than words can tell. **1925** C. Day Lewis *Beechen Vigil* 21 Give me your hands so fairy-fine. **1878–86** Britten & Holland *Plant-n.*, *Fairy fingers, *Digitalis purpurea* L. **1513** Douglas *Æneis* VIII. vi. 7 Nymphis and Favnis..Quhilk *fairfolkis..clepyng we. **1827** Pollok *Course T.* III, Tales Of fairy folk and sleepless ghosts. **1864** Tennyson *Aylmer's F.* 90 The *fairy footings on the grass. **1816** Byron *Ch. Har.* III. cii, Bees and birds, And *fairy-form'd and many-colour'd things. **1870** *Science Gossip* 1 June 135 Its [foxglove's] other name '*fairy glove'. **1883** Ouida *Wanda* I. 43 A very *fairy godmother. **1792** S. Rogers *Pleas. Mem.* II. 3 To view the *fairy-haunts of long-lost hours. **1603** Harsnet *Pop. Impost.* 21 The poore Wench was so *Fayrie haunted, as she durst not goe..to Ma. Dibdale hir chamber alone. **1598** Shaks. *Merry W.* IV. iv. 57 Let them all encircle him about And *fairy-like to pinch the vncleane knight. **1840** Dickens *Old C. Shop* i, So slight and fairy-like a creature. **1867** Deutsch *Rem.* (1874) 5 Hieroglyphical *fairy-lore. **1813** Shelley *Q. Mab* I. 91 Those who had looked upon the sight..Saw but the *fairy pageant. **1810** *Associate Minstrels* 105 The *fairy-penciled spray. **1884** Holland *Chester Gloss.*, *Fairies' *Petticoats*, the foxglove. **1794** Mrs. Radcliffe *Myst. Udolpho* i, Tell the Goddess of this *fairy scene. **1590** Shaks. *Mids. N.* II. ii. 1 Come, now a Roundell, and a *Fairy song. **1878–86** Britten & Holland *Plant-n.*, *Fairy Thimbles, *Digitalis purpurea* L. **1732** Berkeley *Alciphr.* VII. §25 They have exposed their *fairy ware not to cheat but divert us. **1870** *Science Gossip* 1 June 135 In Anglo-Irish we call it [the Foxglove]..*fairy weed.

2. Special Comb.: **fairies-arrow**, = elf-shot 2; **fairies' (fairy) bath**, *Peziza coccinea*; **fairy-beads** (see quot.); **fairy-bell** (see quot. 1861); **fairy bells**, a kind of musical instrument; **fairy-bird** (see quot.); **fairy (fairies') butter**, (*a*) (see quot. 1777); (*b*) *Tremella albida*; **fairy cake**, a small individual sponge cake, usu. iced and decorated; **fairy-cheeses**, *Malva rotundiflora*, from the shape of the seeds; **fairy-circle**, (*a*) = fairy-ring; (*b*) a fairy-dance; (*c*) a circle of fairies dancing; hence **fairy-circled** *a.*; **fairy-court**, the court of some fairy king or queen; **fairy-cucumber** (see quot.); **fairy-cups**, (*a*) *Primula veris*; (*b*) = *fairies' bath*; hence **fairy-cupped** *a.*; **fairy-cycle**, a small-wheeled low bicycle for children; **fairy-dance**, (*a*) = fairy-ring; (*b*) dance of the fairies, in quot. *fig.*; **fairy-dart**, = elf-shot; **fairy-eggs** (see quot.); **fairy-fingermarks** (see quot.); **fairy-flax**, *Linum catharticum*; **fairy-fly**, a minute insect which deposits its eggs in the eggs of other insects; a chalcid of the family Mymaridæ; **fairy godmother**, a fairy who acts as godmother or protector to a mortal child; also *transf.*, a benefactress; so ***fairy godfather***; also (*nonce-wds.*) ***fairy-godmother*** v. trans., ***-godmotherly*** adj.; **fairy-grass** *Briza media*; **fairy-green**, = fairy-ring; **fairy-groat** (see quot.); **fairies'-hair**, *Cuscuta epithymum*; **fairy-hammer** (see quot.); **fairy-hillock** (see quot.); **fairies-horse**, *Senecio Jacobæa*; **fairy lamp**, a lamp containing a candle; **fairy light** (usu. in pl.), (*a*) a small coloured light used in illuminations and often hung among trees; (*b*) a kind of nightlight; (*c*) perversion of 'Very light'; hence **fairy-lighted**, **-lit** adjs.; **fairy-lint**, = *fairy-flax*; **fairy-loaf** (see quot.); **fairy-martin**, Australian name for *Hirundo ariel*; **fairy-money**, money given by fairies, said to crumble away rapidly; **fairy moss**, tiny, free-floating, aquatic ferns of the genus *Azolla*; **fairy-mushroom**, a toadstool; †**fairy-nips** (see quot.); **fairy-pavements**, cubes used in Roman pavements; **fairy penguin**, the little or little blue penguin, *Eudyptula minor*, found on the southern coasts of Australasia; **fairy-pipe**, an old kind of tobacco-pipe, frequently dug up in Great Britain; **fairy**

prince, a prince of the fairies; *transf.*, an idealized person, the ideal husband-to-be; **fairy prion**, a prion, *Pachyptila turtur*, of Australasian and subantarctic coasts, with a bluish bill and bluish feet; **fairy-purse** (see quot.); **fairy queen**, the queen of the fairies; also, the player who takes the part of the fairy queen in a pantomime; such a part; **fairy-rade**, *Sc.*, the expedition of the fairies to the place where they are to hold their annual banquet; **fairy rose**, *Rosa chinensis* var. *minima*; **fairy-shrimp**, = *Chirocephalus diaphanus*, a British fresh-water crustacean; **fairy-sparks** (see quot. 1875); **fairy-stone**, (*a*) a fossil sea-urchin or echinite; (*b*) a flint arrow-head, = ELF-SHOT 2; **fairies'-table**, various fungi; **fairy (fairies')-treasure**, **-wealth**, = *fairy-money*; **fairy tern**, (*a*) *Austral.* and *N.Z.*, a small black-crowned tern; *Sterna nereis*; (*b*) a tropical white tern, *Anous* (*Gygis*) *albus*; †**fairy-walk**, = FAIRY-RING.

1794 SUTHERLAND in *Statist. Acc. Scot.* X. 15 The common people confidently assert that they [celts] are *fairies' arrows, which they shoot at cattle. **1856** C. M. YONGE *Daisy Chain* I. viii. 72 Flora..sought in the hedge-sides for some crimson '*fairy baths' to carry home. **1878–86** BRITTEN & HOLLAND *Plant-n.*, *Fairies' Bath.* **1831** J. HODGSON in Raine *Mem.* (1858) II. 222 The crinoidea or enchrinal fossil, which in Cumberland is called *fairy beads. **1861** MRS. LANKESTER *Wild Flowers* 47 The tiny white flowers [of Wood Sorrel]..are called by the Welsh '*fairy bells'. **1895** *Army & Navy Co-op. Soc. Price List* 15 Sept. 1664 Fairy Bells. **1916** E. CRUTCHFIELD in G. B. Shaw *Sham Educ.* in *Doctors' Delusions* (1931) 361 A clown was then introduced. He played the 'fairy bells' in imitation of church bells. **1885** SWAINSON *Prov. Names Birds* 204 Little Tern ..*Fairy bird (Galway). **1777** BRAND *Pop. Antiq.* (1813) II. 339 There is a substance found..in crevices of lime-stone rocks..near Holywell..which is called Menyn Tylna Teg or *Fairies Butter. So also in Northumberland the common people call a certain fungous excrescence, sometimes found about the roots of old trees, Fairy Butter. **1878–86** BRITTEN & HOLLAND *Plant-n.*, *Fairy-Butter.* **1895** *Army & Navy Co-op. Soc. Price List* 4 *Fairy Cakes... Price per lb. 0/7. **1967** R. RENDELL *New Lease of Death* v. 47 A tea trolley.. laden with home-baked pastries, strawberries in glass dishes, fairy cakes in paper cases. **1971** *Guardian* 9 Jan. 11/1 The occasional fairy cake and cuppa from Mrs. Purdie the tea-lady. **1878–86** BRITTEN & HOLLAND *Plant-n.*, **Fairy cheeses.* **1653** H. MORE *Antid. Ath.* III. xi. §1 Those dark Rings in the grass which they call *Fairy-Circles. **1711** *Acc. Distemper Tom Whigg* II. 44 Tom..trod out Fairy Circles at the Head of each Tribe. **1854** in *Proc. Berw. Nat. Club* (1873) VII. 32 In the churchyard there is a large..fairy circle. **1859** TENNYSON *Guinevere* 255 The flickering fairy-circle wheel'd and broke Flying. **1777** WARTON *Monody* Poems 7 Fancy's *fairy-circled shrine. *a* **1649** DRUMM. OF HAWTH. *Wks.* (1711) 44 To..know the sports Of foreign shepherds, fawns, and *fairy-courts. **1708** *Phil. Trans.* XXVI. 78 The Ecknite Spoke, or *Fairy Cucumber. **1878–86** BRITTEN & HOLLAND *Plant-n.*, **Fairy Cups.* **1863** BROWNING *Poems, By Fire-side* 59 The *fairy-cupped Elf-needled mat of moss. **1926–7** *Army & Navy Stores Catal.* 888/2 '*Fairy cycle'. With adjustable saddle. **1927** *Times* 6 July 13 A girl of six..riding her fairycycle. **1928** *Daily Express* 2 June 7/3 The boy was pushing his fairy cycle near his home when a collision occurred between two motor-cars, one of which killed him. **1675** EVELYN *Terra* (1776) 62 A florid green circle or *Fairy-dance at the bottom. **1798** SOTHEBY tr. *Wieland's Oberon* (1826) I. 51 The twinkling fairy-dance of light and shade. **1877** BREWER *Dict. Phrase & Fable* 284 **Fairy-darts*, flint arrowheads now called celts. **1860** J. F. CAMPBELL *Tales W. Highl.* I. Introd. 1 Fishermen ..often find certain hard, light floating objects..which they call sea-nuts..and *fairy-eggs. **1869** *Lonsdale Gloss.*, **Fairy finger-marks*, hollow marks in limestone as if fingers had been pressed upon the stones when soft. **1841** LONGF. *Wreck Hesp.* ii, Blue were her eyes as the *fairy-flax. **1903** W. F. KIRBY *Butterflies & Moths of Europe* p. xxxvi/1 The smallest of all known insects are some parasitic *Hymenoptera* belonging to the family *Mymaridæ*, which lay their eggs in those of other insects. They have elegant battledore-shaped wings, with a fringe of very long hairs... They are popularly known as '*Fairy Flies'. **1949** *Oxf. Jun. Encycl.* II. 82/2 The Fairy Flies, which include the smallest known insects, are Chalcids that spend their larval life inside the eggs of other insects, feeding on the contents. **1935** *Mademoiselle* Aug. 59/2 Acquaintance? He's my *fairy godfather. **1959** M. STEEN *Tower* I. iv. 65 The little old fairy godfather was nicely covering the sherry he offered his visitors. **1851** M. GATTY (*title*) The *fairy godmothers and other tales. **1855** C. M. YONGE *Hist. Sir Thomas Thumb* p. vii, Other fairies.. were generally women, enchantresses..and probably all the fairy god-mothers we hear of, are meant for these. **1883** Fairy godmother [see FAIRY *sb.* and *a.* C. 1]. **1909** G. K. CHESTERTON *Orthodoxy* iv. 98 Fairy godmothers seem at least as strict as other godmothers. **1959** *Listener* 18 June 1058/2 Any country which embarks on this programme will be the world's fairy godmother. **1962** *Ibid.* 26 July 146/3 Mrs Eileen J. Garrett, President of the Parapsychology Foundation of New York and fairy godmother of paranormal study. **1919** W. DEEPING *Second Youth* xxxi. 260 Miles's name had been placed upon the list some weeks ago, with Kate's name recording her sponsorship, for each accredited visitor had to be '*fairy' godmothered' by a W.M.C. member. **1900** E. T. FOWLER *Farringdons* 272 'I have found your mislaid grandfather; be a mother to him for the rest of your life!' It would give one the most delicious, *fairy-godmotherly sort of satisfaction! **1878–86** BRITTEN & HOLLAND *Plant-n.*, **Fairy grass.* **1819** *Edin. Mag.* July 19 He wha tills the *fairy green, Nae luck again sall hae. **1577–87** HARRISON *England* II. II. xxiv. 218 Some peeces [of coine]..are dailie taken vp, which they call..*Feirie groats. **1627** DRAYTON *Nymphidia* 71 In their courses make that round, In meadows..found, By them so call'd the *Fairy-ground. **1878–86** BRITTEN & HOLLAND *Plant-n.*, **Fairies' hair.* **1815** *Clan-Albin* II. 240 *note*, *Fairy-hammers are pieces of green porphyry, shaped like the head of a hatchet. **1808–79** JAMIESON, **Fairy-hillocks*..verdant knolls..from the vulgar idea that these were anciently inhabited by the fairies, or that they used to dance there. **1877** BREWER *Dict. Phrase & Fable* 284 *Fairy-hillocks.* **1878–86** BRITTEN & HOLLAND *Plant-n.*, **Fairies' Horse.* **1886** *Colon. & Ind. Exhib. Official Catal.* 166 Advt., New Patent '*Fairy' Lamps and 'Fairy' Lights. **1891** *Sale Catal. Glass Wks. Stourbridge*, Five fairy lamps. *a* **1941** V. WOOLF *Captain's Death Bed* (1950) 205 In the Amusement Compound..they light a horse-shoe of fairy-lamps above the Jack and Jill. **1871** *English Mechanic* 24 Nov. 244/2 A long crescent of *fairy-lights, glimmering on the coast-line. **1891** *Strand Mag.* Aug. (Advt.), The Queen of Lights. 'Fairy' Light. With Double Wicks. **1895** *Army & Navy Co-op. Soc. Price List* 15 Sept. 20 Night Lights... Fairy Lights, to burn in the 'Fairy Lamps'. **1925** FRASER & GIBBONS *Soldier & Sailor Words* 91 *Fairy Light*, Véry Light, named after its inventor. Véry Lights were flares or fire balls fired from a pistol, employed everywhere in the trenches and by airmen. **1927** W. E. COLLINSON *Contemp. Eng.* 98 Fairy lights (Verey lights to send up the S.O.S. or distress signals). **1955** M. HASTINGS *Cork & Serpent* vii. 86 A gay little inn with a string of fairy lights illuminating the banks of bottles behind the bar. **1968** *Listener* 12 Dec. 807/3 Even electric fairy lights are not entirely free of fire risk. **1938** *Times* 10 Jan. 10/4 *Fairy-lighted Christmas trees. **1878–86** BRITTEN & HOLLAND *Plant-n.*, **Fairy lint.* **1953** C. DAY LEWIS *Italian Visit* i. 22 Let *fairy-lit streets run wine through the veins like a ride on a scenic Railway. **1877** BREWER *Dict. Phrase & Fable* 284 **Fairy loaves*..fossil sea-urchins (echini), said to be made by the fairies. **1865** GOULD *Handbk. Birds Australia* I. 113 The *Fairy Martin is dispersed over all the southern portions of Australia. **1690** LOCKE *Hum. Und.* I. iv. (1695) 38 Such borrowed Wealth, like *Fairy-money..will be but Leaves and Dust when it comes to use. **1849** LYTTON *Caxtons* XVII. vi, Half-suspecting they must already have turned into withered leaves like fairy-money. [**1908** T. W. SANDERS *Encycl. Gardening* 163 Fairy Floating Moss (Azolla caroliniana).] **1938** F. PERRY *Water Gardening* ix. 134 The Azollas are so dainty in appearance that the English name of *Fairy Moss is no misnomer. **1968** D. BARTRUM *Water in Garden* viii. 116 *Azolla caroliniana*..is closely allied to the Ferns... The popular name of the plant is Fairy Moss. **1884** MILLER *Plant-n.* 137 Toadstool..*Fairy-Mushroom. Any of the poisonous Fungi. **1656** ADEY *Candle in Dark* 129 There be also found in Women with Childe..certain spots black and blew, as if they were pinched or beaten, which some common ignorant people call *Fairy-nips. **1787** *Archæol.* VIII. 364 Some small stone cubes..which the country people called *fairy pavements. **1848** J. GOULD *Birds of Australia* VII. 85 (*heading*) *Spheniscus undina*, Gould. *Fairy Penguin. **1901** A. J. CAMPBELL *Nests & Eggs Austral. Birds* II. 1012 The Fairy Penguin is the smallest of its singular tribe. **1966** G. DURRELL *Two in Bush* ii. 79 Fairy Penguins appeared in small groups and hopped their way up the rocks towards their nest burrows. **1867** *Chambers's Encycl.* s.v. *Tobacco-pipes*, From their smallness, some ancient tobacco-pipes are called *fairy pipes. **1840** *Fraser's Mag.* July 99/2 Caroline..had set him down for her divinity, her wondrous *fairy prince. **1911** 'I. HAY' *Safety Match* xii. 194 A purely hypothetical fairy prince, composed of equal parts of Peer of the Realm, Lifeguardsman, Mr Sandow, Lord Byron, and the Bishop of London, whom she had cherished in..her heart. **1966** J. GLOAG *Sentence of Life* xlix. 415 It was Mr Maddox this, Mr Maddox that. You'd have thought he was the fairy prince the way she carried on. **1912** G. M. MATHEWS *Birds of Australia* II. II. 217 Pseudoprion Turtur Turtur. Australian *Fairy-Prion. **1930** W. R. B. OLIVER *New Zealand Birds* 114 Fairy Prion... *Pachyptila turtur*. The Fairy Prion was first discovered in Bass Strait... The Fairy Prion in all its forms is to be distinguished from the other members of the genus by the form of the bill. **1966** G. DURRELL *Two in Bush* ii. 79 Then the Fairy Prions—delicate little swallow-like petrels—started to arrive. **1877** E. PEACOCK *Manley & Corringham Gloss.*, **Fairy-purses*, a kind of fungus..something like a cup, or old-fashioned purse. **1590** SHAKS. *Mids. N.* II. i. 9, I serue the *Fairy Queene. **1813** SHELLEY *Q. Mab* 59 The chariot of the Fairy Queen! **1859** TENNYSON *Elaine* 1248 Look how she sleeps—the Fairy Queen so fair! **1899** G. B. SHAW *Let.* 12 Oct. in J. Dunbar *Mrs. G. B. S.* (1963) xi. 187 Poor Moony Silly grinned like a fairy queen in a fifth rate pantomime. **1904** *Sat. Rev.* 14 May 620/2 In the seventies pantomime was flourishing still. Demon King and Fairy Queen..were familiar and popular things. **1810** CROMEK *Remains Nithsdale Song* 298 At the first approach of summer is held the *Fairy Rade. *c* **1820** HOGG *Woolgatherer* in *Tales & Sk.* (1837) I. 196 There have been fairy raids i' the Hope. **1848** W. PAUL *Rose Garden* II. ii. 131 Rosa... The Lawrenceana, or *Fairy Rose... In dry soils the Fairy Roses may be planted in masses. **1955** G. S. THOMAS *Old Shrub Roses* ix. 78 In 1805, at Colville's nursery in England, Parsons's Pink China gave rise to the Dwarf Pink China, a miniature Rose known in England as the Fairy Rose. **1857** A. WHITE *Brit. Crustacea* 263 The *Fairy Shrimp seems to live on dead animal or vegetable matter. **1674** RAY *S. & E.C. Words* 65 *Fairy-sparks or Shel-fire: Kent: often seen on clothes in the night. **1875** PARISH *Sussex Gloss.*, *Fairy-sparks*, phosphoric light seen on various substances in the night-time. **1646** SIR T. BROWNE *Pseud. Ep.* II. i. 53 That we call a *Fayrie stone, and is often found in gravell pits amongst us. **1791** FORD in *Statist. Acc. Scot.* I. 73 Arrow points of flint, commonly called elf or fairy stones are to be seen here [Lauder]. **1881** *Isle of Wight Gloss.*, *Fairy stones*, fossil echini. **1878–86** BRITTEN & HOLLAND *Plant-n.*, *Fairies Table or Tables, (1) *Agaricus campestris*..(2) *Hydrocotyle vulgaris*. **1925** P. MONCRIEFF *New Zealand Birds* 24 Little White Tern (*Fairy Tern). **1926** W. BEEBE *Arcturus Adv.* ix. 228 Scores of sea-birds—frigate birds, boobies, and pure white fairy terns. **1954** FISHER & LOCKLEY *Sea-Birds* i. 29 *Gygis alba*, the tropical, white, almost 'transparent' fairy tern breeds north in the Atlantic. **1966** R. A. FALLA et al. *Field Guide Birds N.Z.* 163 Fairy Terns reappear at breeding grounds in September. [**1632** MASSINGER & FIELD *Fatal Dowry* IV. i, 'Tis Fairies' Treasure.] **1698** NORRIS *Pract. Disc.* (1707) IV. 15 Every man keeps it [Religion] as a *Fairy-Treasure. **1686** *Phil. Trans.* XVI. 207 The circles in Grasse called commonly *Fairy Walkes. **1652** *Brief Char. Low Countries* 26 (Brand) She falls off like *Fairy Wealth disclosed.

fairybabe, corrupt form of FEAR-BABE, -BABY.

fairydom ('fɛərɪdəm). [f. FAIRY + -DOM.] = FAIRYLAND.

1844 R. P. WARD *Chatsworth* I. 34 The cleverest fingers in fairydom. **1884** CHILD *Eng. & Sc. Pop. Ball.* II. xxxix. 336/1 An attempt to rescue a woman from fairydom.

fairyhood ('fɛərɪhʊd). [f. as prec. + -HOOD.] **a.** The condition of being under the influence of fairies; enchanted state. **b.** Fairy nature or characteristics. **c.** *concr.* Fairies collectively.

1832 *Fraser's Mag.* V. 475 Sipping his coffee in the blessed unconsciousness of the fairyhood of his situation. **1842** MRS. BROWNING *Grk. Chr. Poets* (1863) 179 The 'Midsummer Night's Dream' displays more of the fairyhood of fairies, than the 'Paradise Lost' does of the angelhood of angels. **1844** *Blackw. Mag.* LVI. 85 The down-trodden fairyhood.

fairyism ('fɛərɪɪz(ə)m). [f. as prec. + -ISM.] **a.** The personal qualities of a fairy; fairy power. Hence *transf.* the power (of a poet) to cast a spell over a hearer or reader. **b.** The conditions of fairy existence; a resemblance to those conditions; fairyland. **c.** Belief in fairies, fairy-lore.

1715 tr. *D'Anois' Wks.* 373 The Gift of Faryism, which I receiv'd from my Birth. **1763** H. WALPOLE *Let. G. Montagu* 17 May, The air of enchantment and fairyism, which is the tone of the place. **1796** W. TAYLOR in *Monthly Rev.* XXI. 491 The miracles of fairyism. **1803** —— in *Ann. Rev.* I. 265, I would have shown you the great power of my fairyism. **1835** SIR E. BRYDGES *Milton's Comus* 182 Thomson..has not the distinctness and fairyism of Milton. **1843** *Blackw. Mag.* LIV. 26 What Rousseau..terms 'a false air of magnificence, fairyism, and enchantment'. **1877** OUIDA *Puck* xxiii. 273 In all her..winged fairyism.

fairyland ('fɛərɪlænd). [f. as prec. + LAND.] The country or home of the fairies; an enchanted land existing only in fancy. Also *attrib.*

1590 SHAKS. *Mids. N.* II. i. 60 When thou wast stolne away from Fairy Land. **1665** DRYDEN *Ind. Emperor* I. i, Methinks we walk in Dreams on Fairy Land. **17..** GRAY in *Corr. N. Nicholls* (1843) 294 King Arthur was not dead, but translated to Fairy-Land. **1832** A. EARLE *Narr. Res. N.Z.* (1966) 70 A beautiful rainbow..tinged the scene with a fairy-land effect. **1833** TENNYSON *Poems* 20 Looming like baseless fairyland. **1873** SYMONDS *Grk. Poets* vii. 231 Euripides..entered the fairyland of dazzling fancy. **1968** *Times* 15 Oct. 13/5 Wedgwood fairyland lustre, a twentieth-century ware especially sought after in America.

fairyology (fɛərɪ'ɒlədʒɪ). [f. FAIRY + -OLOGY.] The study of fairies. Hence **fairy'ologist**, one who studies fairies.

1859 M. A. DENHAM (*title*) A few fragments of fairyology. **1908** *Daily Chron.* 11 Dec. 4/4 Mr. Dion Clayton Calthrop, the 'fairyologist' of all others—to quote Mr. Tree's quaint phrase.

fairy-ring ('fɛərɪrɪŋ). [f. as FAIRY *sb.* and *a.* + RING.] A circular band of grass differing in colour from the grass around it, a phenomenon supposed in popular belief to be produced by fairies when dancing; really caused by the growth of certain fungi.

1599 B. JONSON *Ev. Man out of Hum.* Epil., Let.. turtle-footed peace dance fayrie rings About her court. **1698** NORRIS *Pract. Disc.* (1707) IV. 222 We tread the same Fairy-ring. **1791** E. DARWIN *Bot. Gard.* I. 36 So from dark clouds the playful lightning springs, Rives the firm oak, or prints the Fairy-rings. **1832** *Veg. Subst. Food* 328 The 'fairy rings' ..are found..upon dry downs. **1875** in *Sussex Gloss.*

b. *attrib.* in ***fairy-ring-champignon***, etc.

1884 MILLER *Plant-n.*, *Fairy-ring Champignon*, see Champignon. *Ibid.*, Mushroom, fairy-ring. *Marasmius oreades* and *M. urens.*

fairyship ('fɛərɪʃɪp). [f. as prec. + -SHIP; cf. *his lordship.*] The personality of a fairy.

1854 *Blackw. Mag.* LXXV. 413 Her fairyship may fairly be considered to be already sufficiently rewarded.

fairy story ('fɛərɪ ˌstɔərɪ). [f. FAIRY *sb.* and *a.* + STORY *sb.*[1]] = next.

1850 DICKENS *Dav. Copp.* xix. 193 Life was more like a great fairy story, which I was just about to begin to read, than anything else. **1859** THACKERAY *Virginians* II. xxv. 199 Our favourite fairy story-books. **1925** G. H. MULLIN *Adv. Scholar Tramp* vi. 85, I told her an abominable pack of lies —a fairy-story, as we call such fabrications on the Road. **1927** R. LEHMANN *Dusty Answer* I. i. 19 He reminded me of something fabulous—a Chinese fairy-story. **1932** E. HEMINGWAY *Death in Afternoon* Gloss. 299 s.v. *Maricón*, There are many very, very funny Spanish fairy stories. **1956** 'B. BUCKINGHAM' *Three Bad Nights* xxii. 202 Please go on with your fairy story if it amuses you. **1966** S. JACKMAN *Davidson Affair* viii. 100 You'll never persuade them to accept your fairy-story ending.

fairy-tale ('fɛərɪ teɪl). [f. FAIRY *sb.* and *a.* + TALE *sb.*; rendering F. *conte de fées.*] **a.** A tale about fairies. Also *gen.*, fairy legend, faerie. **b.** An unreal or incredible story. **c.** A falsehood. Also *attrib.* Hence **'fairy-tale-ish** *a.*

1749 H. WALPOLE *Let.* 3 May (1903) II. 369 It..was by far the..prettiest spectacle I ever saw: nothing in a fairy tale ever surpassed it. **1750** H. BROOKE (*title*) A new collection of fairy tales. **1797** J. MOSER (*title*) Moral Tales; consisting of the Reconciliation,..a Fairy Tale, in the modern style. Clementia and Malitia; a Fairy Tale, in the ancient style. **1819** KEATS *Let.* 21 Sept. (1958) II. 173 Dont forget to tell Reynolds of the fairy tale Undine. **1864** TENNYSON *Aylmer's F.* 89 He had..told her fairy-tales. **1887** RUSKIN *Præterita*

II. 244 [Shakespeare's] Henry V. is only a king of fairy tale. **1896** ADE *Artie* xiii. 117 Guess what they train on.. Cocoanut pie. That ain't no fairy tale, neither. **1900** *Daily Tel.* 4 July 10/2 Mr. Kruger..has told a Chicago journalist one of his pretty little fairy tales, the only truth in which is that some burghers are again taking up arms. **1900** E. T. FOWLER *Farringdons* xiv. 272 If I were a man I should belong to the Herald's Office. It would be such fun to be called a 'Red Bonnet' or a 'Green Griffin', or some other nice fairy-tale-ish name. **1914** *Scotsman* 16 Sept. 6/4 The Russians have neither 'landed in nor passed Great Britain on their way to France or Belgium', nor are they now on French or Belgian soil. The whole story has been a gigantic fairy tale. **1920** 'O. DOUGLAS' *Penny Plain* ix, It would be very nice and fairy-tale-ish! **1923** [see BEE[1] 5 b]. **1957** M. KENNEDY *Heroes of Clone* IV. vi. 269 Why should I back up this fairy-tale of yours, just to save your face? **1963** AUDEN *Dyer's Hand* 212 There is only one fairy-tale motif, to my knowledge, that contains an element of inner conflict. **1971** *Daily Tel.* 16 Jan. 20/3 A full moon then added its light to the fairy-tale scene.

faisable, -ible, obs. ff. of FEASIBLE.

‖**faisandé** (fɛzɑ̃de), *a.* [Fr.: pa. pple. of *faisander* to hang (game) up until it is high.] Affected, artificial, theatrical; 'spicy'.

1912 C. MACKENZIE *Carnival* xxvii. 306 The more imaginative observer would perceive in the group something unhealthy, something *faisandé*, an air of too deliberate enjoyment that seemed to imply a perfect knowledge of the limitations of human pleasure. **1930** *Times Lit. Suppl.* 21 Aug. 664/4 There is nothing *faisandé* about Irène de Bénauge; her mind is..hard, clear, clean, beneficent and unimaginative. **1958** *Observer* 1 June 15/1 He plays the part in a *faisandé* Cockney accent straight out of Bruce Bairnsfather's Old Bill cartoons.

†**fait,** *sb. Law. Obs.* [a. Fr. *fait* deed, act: see the variant FEAT.] **a.** A deed. **b.** In the translation of Perkins: Act of parties, as distinguished from operation of law.

1562 *Act 5 Eliz.* c. 14 §12 Convicted..in an Action of forger of false Faytes. **1642** tr. *Perkins' Prof. Bk.* iii. §191. 85 The difference betweene a license in fait and a license in Law. **1651** W. G. tr. *Cowel's Inst.* 182 Amongst those Obligations in writing, which wee call Faits or Deeds.

fait, obs. form of FEAT.

†**fait,** *v.*[1] *Obs.* Also 4 fayte(n. [? Back-formation from FAITOUR.]

1. *intr.* To act or speak falsely, use false pretences; to beg on false pretences.

c **1320** *Sir Tristr.* 3054 Falsly canestow fayt. **1377** LANGL. *P. Pl.* B. xv. 208 Alle suche þei faiten. **1393** *Ibid.* C. I. 43 Faytynge for hure fode.

2. *trans.* To deceive, lead astray.

c **1430** *Hymns Virg.* (1867) 76 My fleissche in ouerhope wolde me faite.

Hence 'faiting *vbl. sb.*, deceit, pretence.

1377 LANGL. *P. Pl.* B. x. 38 But þo þat feynen hem folis, and with faityng libbeth.

†**fait,** *v.*[2] *Obs.* [ad. OF. *faitier*, f. *fait*, pa. pple. of *faire* to do.] *trans.* To arrange, construct, fit.

1635-6 *Burgh Rec. Glasgow* I. 482 Hinging of the said bell and faiting all wark thairto.

‖**fait accompli** (fɛt akɔ̃pli, ˌfeɪt aˈkɒmplɪ). [Fr.] An accomplished fact; an action which is completed (and irreversible) before affected parties learn of its having been undertaken.

1845 R. FORD *Handbk. Spain* I. 337 This is now a *fait accompli*. **1872** E. BRADDON *Life in India* v. 179 After the overland route was a *fait accompli*, the rules of the services ..restricted the servants of the East India Company from enjoying much of their leave westward of the Cape of Good Hope. **1895** *Bow Bells* 16 Aug. 177/2 It will be very interesting to see..whether various other suggestions..will also become fait accompli. **1905** MRS. H. WARD *Marriage of W. Ashe* II. viii. 139 Elizabeth knew that his appearance in the conversation invariably meant a *fait accompli* of some sort. **1906** W. DE MORGAN *Joseph Vance* xxxiv. 337 And Janey knew she was herself, so that no explanation seemed necessary. A *fait accompli* has leisure to wait for an official *raison d'être*. **1955** *Times* 6 Aug. 5/2 He did not propose to proceed by surprise or stealth, or to bind his hands and renounce the prerogatives of the executive. He could give an assurance to the parties represented in the majority that the Government would never be presented with a fait accompli.

†**faite,** *v. Obs.* [aphet. f. of AFAITE.] = AFAITE 4, 5.

1362 LANGL. *P. Pl.* A. v. 49 Heo wolde vn-souwen hire smok, and setten þer an here Forte fayten hire Flesch. **1393** *Ibid.* C. IX. 30 Faite þy faucones to culle wylde foules.

†'**faiterous,** *a. Obs. rare.* [f. *faiter*, FAITOUR + -OUS.] Characterized by deceit; treacherous.

1600 HOLLAND *Livy* III. xviii. 100 Faiterous and secret mischeefe was underhand practised by the Tribunes. *Ibid.* 959 Peevish folly first and faiterous falshood afterwards.

†'**faitery.** *Obs.* Forms: 4-7 fai-, fayterie, -y(e, (4 faytrye, 6 faitry). [f. as prec. + -Y.] Fraud, deception, hypocrisy.

1377 LANGL. *P. Pl.* B. XI. 90 And wher-of serueth lawe.. if no lyf vndertoke it, Falsenesse ne faytrye. *c* **1430** *Pilgr. Lyf Manhode* II. liii. (1869) 96 Not that j sey thee thus for to putte thee in to faitourye [mistransl. Fr. *festardye* 'indolence']. *c* **1440** *Promp. Parv.* 147 Fayterye, *fictio*. **1529** MORE *Dyaloge* I. Wks. 40/1, I let passe ouer the faitry and falshed that is therin vsed. **1600** HOLLAND *Livy* XXXIV. xxiii. 867 He [Philip of Macedon] charged the Romanes with fraud and faiterie.

‖**faites vos jeux** (fɛtvoʒø), *int.* [Fr.] Place your bets (an instruction given by croupiers at a roulette game).

1867 'OUIDA' *Under Two Flags* I. ix. 183 Brains..let themselves be lulled with the monotone of '*Faites votre jeu*' [sic]. **1904** A. BENNETT *Great Man* xxv. 273 '*Faites vos jeux, messieurs*,' said the chief croupier... Yes, he was at Monte Carlo. **1922** JOYCE *Ulysses* 496 Sieurs et dames, faites vos jeux!..(Tiny roulette planets fly from his hands.) Les jeux sont faits! **1963** G. GREENE *Sense of Reality* 113 'Faites vos jeux, messieurs,' the croupiers cried. **1964** A. WYKES *Gambling* ix. 217 At the beginning of each round the croupier invites players to place their bets with the phrase *faites vos jeux*.

faith (feɪθ), *sb.* Forms: 3 feið, 3-4 feiþ, (4 feiȝþ), 3-6 feith(e, 4-5 feyth(e, 4 faiþ(e, 4-6 fayth(e, (5 fath, feth), 5-6 faithe, 4- faith. See also FAY *sb.*[1] [a. OF. *feid*, *feit* (pronounced *feið*, ? *feiþ*: see Suchier in Gröber's *Grundriss Rom. Phil.* I. 586), = Pr. *fe* (nom. *fes*), Sp., Pg. *fé*, It. *fede*:—L. *fidem*, f. root of *fīd-ĕre* to trust. The later OF. form *fei* (whence mod. F. *foi*) was also adopted in ME., and survived in certain phrases down to 16th c.: see FAY *sb.*[1]

The L. *fides*, like its etymological cognate Gr. πίστις, which it renders in the N.T., had the following principal senses: 1. Belief, trust. 2. That which produces belief, evidence, token, pledge, engagement. 3. Trust in its objective aspect, troth; observance of trust, fidelity.]

I. Belief, trust, confidence.

1. a. Confidence, reliance, trust (in the ability, goodness, etc., of a person; in the efficacy or worth of a thing; or in the truth of a statement or doctrine). Const. *in*, †*of*. In early use, only with reference to religious objects; this is still the prevalent application, and often colours the wider use.

a **1300** *Cursor M.* 3405 (Cott.) In drightin was his fayth ai fest. *c* **1340** *Ibid.* 2286 (Trin.) In maumetrie furst feiþ he [nembrot] fond. *c* **1391** CHAUCER *Astrol.* II. §4 Obseruaunces ..& rytes of paiens, in which my spirit ne hath no feith. **1398** TREVISA *Barth De P.R.* xv. lxxxvii (1495) 522 The Germans tornyd the Liuones..to the worshyp and fayth of one god. **1550** CROWLEY *Last Trump.* 151 Se that thy fayth be pitched On thy Lord God. **1680** OTWAY *Orphan* II. vii, Attempt no farther to delude my Faith. **1768-74** TUCKER *Lt. Nat.* (1852) II. 235 Such an one has great faith in Ward's pills. **1821** CHALMERS *Serm.* I. i. 18 Faith in the constancy of this law. **1837** J. H. NEWMAN *Par. Serm.* (ed. 2) III. vi. 87 To have faith in God is to surrender oneself to God. **1848** MACAULAY *Hist. Eng.* I. 168 Without faith in human virtue or in human attachment. **1855** KINGSLEY *Lett.* (1878) I. 442 There was the most intense faith in him..that Right was right.

b. Belief proceeding from reliance on testimony or authority.

1551 T. WILSON *Logike* (1580) 60 b, An historicall faithe. As I doe beleve that Willyam Conquerour was kyng of Englande. *a* **1628** PRESTON *Breastpl. Faith* (1630) 15 Faith is ..assenting to Truthes for the Authority of the Speaker. **1725** WATTS *Logic* II. ii. §9 When we derive the Evidence of any Proposition from the Testimony of others, it is called the Evidence of Faith. *a* **1873** HUXLEY in Hamerton *Intell. Life* VIII. ii. (1873) 299 The absolute rejection of authority.. the annihilation of the spirit of blind faith.

2. Phrases. *to give faith*: to yield belief *to*. *to pin one's faith to* or *upon*: to believe implicitly.

1430 *Paston Lett.* No. 14 I. 30, I prey yow to gyve feith and credence touchant this matier. **1552** ABP. HAMILTON *Catech.* (1884) 27 Fayth to be geven to the Word of God. **1556** *Aurelio & Isab.* (1608) I vij, One oughte to geve more feithe unto the secrete consentment of the soule, than [etc.]. **1653** H. COGAN tr. *Pinto's Trav.* xxxv. 140 Opinions..unto which they give so much faith, that nothing can be able to remove them from it. **1702** POPE *Dryope* 69 If to the wretched any faith be giv'n. **1710** HEARNE *Collect.* 4 Mar., Some pin..their Faith on..Hoadly. **1797** MRS. RADCLIFFE *Italian* vi, You believe..that I am willing to give faith to wonderful stories. **1812** SHELLEY *Propos. Association* Prose Wks. I. 270 Well-meaning people, who pin their faith upon their grand-mother's apronstring. **1885** *London Society* Apr. 357 The..practitioner of the old school..pins his faith to time-honoured methods.

3. *Theol.* in various specific applications. **a.** Belief in the truths of religion; belief in the authenticity of divine revelation (whether viewed as contained in Holy Scripture or in the teaching of the Church), and acceptance of the revealed doctrines. **b.** That kind of faith (distinctively called *saving* or *justifying faith*) by which, in the teaching of the N.T., a sinner is justified in the sight of God. This is very variously defined by theologians (see quots.), but there is general agreement in regarding it as a conviction practically operative on the character and will, and thus opposed to the mere intellectual assent to religious truth (sometimes called *speculative faith*). **c.** The spiritual apprehension of divine truths, or of realities beyond the reach of sensible experience or logical proof. By Christian writers often identified with the preceding; but not exclusively confined to Christian use. Often viewed as the exercise of a special faculty in the soul of man, or as the result of supernatural illumination.

1382 WYCLIF *Jas.* ii. 17 Feith, if it haue not werkes, is deed in it silf. **1526** TINDALE *Prol. Moses* Wks. 7 Fayth, is the beleuyng of Gods promises, and a sure trust in the goodnes and truth of God, which fayth iustified Abrah. **1555** EDEN *Decades* Pref. to Rdr. (Arb.) 51 Abraham the father of fayth. **1581** MARBECK *Bk. of Notes* 375 Faith..maketh God & man friends. **1651** HOBBES *Leviath.* III. xlii. 271 Faith is a gift of God, which Man can neither give, nor take away. **1690** LOCKE *Hum. Und.* IV. xviii, Faith..is the Assent to any Proposition..upon the Credit of the Proposer, as coming from God, in some extraordinary way of Communication. **1700** BURKITT *On N.T.* John i. 12 Faith is..such an affiance in Christ..as is the parent and principle of obedience to him. **1744** SWIFT *Serm. Trinity* 52 Faith is an entire Dependence upon the Truth, the Power, the Justice, and the mercy of God. **1781** COWPER *Expost.* 111 Faith, the root whence only can arise The graces of a life that wins the skies. **1830** WORDSW. *Russian Fugitive* II. xi, That monumental grace Of Faith. **1860** PUSEY *Min. Proph.* 415 The faith of which he speaks, is a real true confiding faith. **1869** GOULBOURN *Purs. Holiness* iii. 21 Faith..the faculty by which we realize unseen things.

4. That which is or should be believed.

a. A system of religious belief, e.g. *the Christian, Jewish, Mohammedan*, etc., *faith*. Also, *confession, rule of faith*, for which see those words.

c **1325** *Coer de L.* 4062 He is at the Sarezynes faith. *c* **1330** R. BRUNNE *Chron.* (1810) 24 At haly kirkes fayth alle on were boþe. **1393** LANGL. *P. Pl.* C. XVIII. 258 In a faith lyueþ þat folke, and in a false mene. *c* **1400** MAUNDEV. (1839) iii. 18 Thei varien from oure Feithe. **1485** CAXTON *Chas. Gt.* 1 The cristen feythe is affermed. **1529** MORE *Dyaloge* II. Wks. 179/1 The churche..muste..haue all one fayth. **1553** EDEN *Treat. Newe Ind.* (Arb.) 24 They haue no law written and are of no faith. **1599** SHAKS. *Much Ado* I. i. 75 He weares his faith but as the fashion of his hat. **1611** BIBLE *Jude* 3 Earnestly contend for the faith which was once deliuered vnto the Saints. **1653** H. COGAN tr. *Pinto's Trav.* viii. 21, I swear to thee by the faith of Pagan, that [etc.]. **1832** W. IRVING *Alhambra* I. 302 Are you willing to renounce the faith of your father? **1858** LD. ST. LEONARDS *Handy Bk. Prop. Law* xiii. 81 The child should be brought up in the religious faith of the father.

transf. **1878** MORLEY *Byron* Crit. Misc. 1st Ser. 224 It was perhaps the secret of the black transformation of the social faith of '89 into the worship of the Conqueror of '99.

b. *the faith*: the true religion; usually = the Christian faith. Also, without article in certain phrases, as *contrary to faith*, etc. *of faith*: part and parcel of the faith.

a **1300** *Cursor M.* 21013 (Cott.) Iacob þe mar..þe land o spaigne in fait he fest. *c* **1340** *Ibid.* 8990 (Fairf.) þat caytef kinde..made him [salamon] in þe faiþ ful fals. *a* **1375** *Joseph Arim.* 11 Joseph..hedde I-turned to þe feyþ, fifti with him-seluen. *c* **1485** *Digby Myst.* II. 240 A very pynacle of the fayth. **1555** EDEN *Decades* Pref. to Rdr. (Arb.) 50 *marg.*, The Indians subdued to the fayth. **1611** BIBLE *Transl. Pref.* 3 A manifest falling away from the Faith. **1635** PAGITT *Christianogr.* I. iii. (1636) 108 The Gospel conteineth intirely the faith. **1844** LINGARD *Anglo-Sax. Ch.* (1845) II. App. 401 Matters contrary to faith. **1867** BP. FORBES *Explan.* 39 *Art.* i. (1881) 5 The uncompounded nature of God is of faith.

c. What is believed, or required to be believed, on a particular subject. †Also *pl.* points of faith, tenets.

c **1380** WYCLIF *Sel. Wks.* III. 378 Freris perverten þo right feithe of þo sacrament of þo auter. **1513** BRADSHAW *St. Werburge* I. 1638 Prechynge..The faythes of holy chyrche. **1845** MAURICE *Mor. & Met. Philos.* in *Encycl. Metrop.* II. 632/1 We assumed the common faith of our countrymen respecting the..discipline of the Jew to be true. **1883** H. DRUMMOND *Nat. Law in Spir. W.* 276 A repetition of the Hebrew poets' faith.

†**5.** *act of (the) faith*: = AUTO DA FÉ. *Obs.*

1656 BEN ISRAEL *Vind. Judæorum* in *Phenix* (1708) II. 400 The Act of the Faith, which is ordinarily done at Toledo, was done at Madrid, Anno 1632. **1709** *Lond. Gaz.* No. 4565/1 On the thirtieth of the last Month an Act of Faith was held in this City [Lisbon] by the Inquisition.

II. Inducement to belief or trust.

†**6.** Power to produce belief, credit, convincing authority. *Obs.*

a **1638** MEDE *Ep. to Estwick* Wks. IV. 836 S. Jerom is a man of no faith with me. **1808** W. MITFORD *Hist. Greece* IV. xxxi. (app.) 124 It may not be unnecessary..towards establishing the faith of the foregoing..narrative.

†**7.** Attestation, confirmation, assurance. *Obs.*

1393 GOWER *Conf.* III. 326 To yive a more feith..In blacke clothes they hem cloth. **1556** *Aurelio & Isab.* (1608) F vj, The manney folde paines..makethe cleare faithe inoughe, that the greter follie is yowres. **1654** JER. TAYLOR *Real Pres.* xii. 27 An excellent MS. that makes faith in this particular. **1730** A. GORDON *Maffei's Amphith.* 375 Relying on the Faith of Books.

†**8. a.** Assurance given, formal declaration, pledge, promise. In phrases, *to do, make faith* (= L. *fidem facere*): to affirm, promise, give surety. *to give (one's) faith* (= L. *fidem dare*): to give assurance, pledge one's word. *on his faith*: on parole. *Obs.*

1382 WYCLIF *Prov.* xi. 15 He shal be tormetid with euel that doth feith [Vulg. *fidem facit*] for a stranger. *c* **1400** *Destr. Troy* 548 þat ȝe me faith make, In dede for to do as I desyre wille. *c* **1430** *Syr Gener.* (Roxb.) 9969 He toke feith of free and bond. **1483** CAXTON *Gold. Leg.* 223/1 Alle made fayth to other that [etc.]. **1523** LD. BERNERS *Froiss.* I. ccxi. 254 The kyng of England..trusted them on theyr faithes. **1548** HALL *Chron.* 184 b, Emongest men of warre, faith or othe, syldome is performed. **1558** BP. WATSON *Sev. Sacram.* xxviii. 178 Jane, here I geue to thee my faythe and truthe.. I wyll marrye thee. **1581** MARBECK *Bk. of Notes* 807 Faith was made to them, that..they should come safe. **1641** BAKER *Chron.* (1679) 32/2 King William..upon faith given returns to London. **1685** H. CONSETT *Prac. Spir. Courts* 265 If the Plaintiff doth personally make Faith, that [etc.].

b. *on the faith of*: in reliance on the security of.

1734 tr. *Rollin's Anc. Hist.* (1827) I. 344 [They] traded there on the faith of treaties. **1839** THIRLWALL *Greece* VII. lvii. 204 On the faith of his oath they had placed themselves in his power. **1866** CRUMP *Banking* i. 28 The bank-note is circulated entirely upon the faith of the issuing bank. **1890** SIR R. ROMER in *Law Times' Rep.* LXIII. 685/2 The plaintiff applied for shares.. on the faith of the prospectus.

III. The obligation imposed by a trust.

9. a. The duty of fulfilling one's trust; allegiance owed to a superior, fealty; the obligation of a promise or engagement.

c **1250** *Gen. & Ex.* 2187 Bi ðe feið ic oȝ to king pharaon. *c* **1330** R. BRUNNE *Chron.* (1810) 333 þe best were þan in his feith. **1389** in *Eng. Gilds* (1870) 39 The feyth þat þei owen to God. **14..** *Customs of Malton* in *Surtees Misc.* (1890) 63 He schall never clame no thyng.. bott alonly hys faythe for hys .. lande. *c* **1489** CAXTON *Sonnes of Aymon* xxv. 538 Vpon the feyth that ye owe to me. **1568** GRAFTON *Chron.* II. 78 Untill he were returned unto his fayth. **1598** W. PHILLIPS *Linschoten* in Arb. *Garner* III. 15 The Lords.. took their oaths of faith and allegiance unto Don Philip. **1671** MILTON *Samson* 987 Who to save Her countrey from a fierce destroyer, chose Above the faith of wedlock-bands. **1863** MARY HOWITT tr. *F. Bremer's Greece* I. vii. 245 To give their faith and obedience to the French monarch.

b. In many phrases, in which the sense approaches that of 8: ***to engage, pledge, plight (one's) faith***; † ***to swear, perjure one's faith***; ***to keep*** (†***hold***), ***break, violate (one's) faith***; so ***breach of faith***.

c **1320** *Seuyn Sag.* (W.) 3274 For glotonye he brake his fayth. *c* **1374** CHAUCER *Former Age* 48 Everych of hem his feith to oother kepte. *c* **1400** MAUNDEV. (1839) xii. 138 Non of hem holdethe Feythe to another. **1483** CAXTON *Cato* Bj, A man ought.. to kepe feyth unto his frendes. **1588** SHAKS. *L.L.L.* v. ii. 283 Berowne hath plighted faith to me. *c* **1592** MARLOWE *Jew of Malta* II. ii. Faith is not to be held with heretics. **1665** MANLEY *Grotius' Low C. Warres* 339 No Faith is to be held with such as differ from them. **1697** DRYDEN *Virg. Past.* viii. 25, I my Nisa's perjur'd Faith deplore. **1700** —— *Palamon & Arcite* 78 For you alone, I broke my Faith with injur'd Palamon. **1781** GIBBON *Decl. & F.* II. 129 The two princes mutually engaged their faith never to [etc.]. **1874** STUBBS *Const. Hist.* (1875) II. xv. 296 He led the way and kept faith.

10. The quality of fulfilling one's trust; faithfulness, fidelity, loyalty. †***to bear faith***: to be loyal *to*.

c **1250** *Gen. & Ex.* 2678 Ðat him sal feið wurðful ben boren. *a* **1300** *Cursor M.* 6980 (Cott.) þair faith lasted littel space, þai.. lefte þe lagh of hei drightin. *c* **1391** CHAUCER *Astrol.* Prol. 2 Alle that him feyth bereth & obeieth. **1393** GOWER *Conf.* III. 70 Thus he.. feigneth under guile feith. **1590** SHAKS. *Mids. N.* III. ii. 127 Bearing the badge of faith to proue them true. **1593** —— *2 Hen VI.* v. i, 166 Oh where is Faith? Oh, where is Loyalty? **1649** EVELYN *Mem.* (1857) III. 40 Persons of great faith to his Majesty's cause. **1741** MIDDLETON *Cicero* I. VI. 492 Illustrious for victory and faith. **1810** T. JEFFERSON *Writ.* (1830) IV. 137 Confidence .. in our faith and probity. **1844** H. H. WILSON *Brit. India* II. 166 Indignant at his want of faith.

11. ***good faith, bad faith***: = L. ***bona, mala fides***, in which the primary notion seems to have been the objective aspect of confidence well or ill bestowed. The Eng. uses closely follow those of L.

a. ***good faith***: fidelity, loyalty (= sense 10); *esp.* honesty of intention in entering into engagements, sincerity in professions, BONA FIDES.

c **1340** *Cursor M.* 6778 (Fairf.) To vse gode faiþ god vs bede. **1480** CAXTON *Chron. Eng.* ccxxv. 230 By good feyth and trust. **1824** MACKINTOSH *Sp. Ho. Com.* 15 June Wks. 1846 III. 464 They have been able to observe good faith with their creditors. **1871** BLACKIE *Four Phases* i. 37 Among what.. men.. are fellowship and good faith possible? **1885** SIR J. HANNEN in *Law Reports* 15 Q. Bench Div. 139 It is admitted that the magistrates.. acted in good faith.

b. ***bad faith***: faithlessness, treachery; intent to deceive. ***Punic*** (rarely ***Carthaginian***) ***faith*** (= L. *fides Punica*): faithlessness.

1631 MASSINGER *Believe as you List* II. ii, The Punicque faith is branded by Our enemies. **1653** H. COGAN tr. *Pinto's Trav.* xlvi. 179 The bad faith of the Chineses. **1711** STEELE *Spect.* No. 174 ⁋2 Carthaginian Faith was a proverbial Phrase to intimate Breach of Leagues. **1768–74** TUCKER *Lt. Nat.* (1852) II. 318 French faith became the same among us, as Punic faith had been among the Romans.

12. In asseverative phrases. **a.** ***in (good) faith***: in truth, really, 'sooth to say'.

c **1350** *Will. Palerne* 858 And fayn sche wold þan is feiþ haue fold him in hire armes. *c* **1386** CHAUCER *Chan. Yeom. Prol. & T.* 91 He is to wys in feith, as I bileeue. **1393** GOWER *Conf.* III. 25 In good feith to telle soth I trowe.. She wolde nought her eye swerve. *c* **1400** *Destr. Troy* 735 þou failes not in faith of a fowle end. **1513** MORE *Rich. III* in Grafton *Chron.* II. 769 In good fayth.. I would not be he that [etc.]. **1599** MINSHEU *Dial. Sp. & Eng.* (1623) 28 In faith this mule hath taken degree in Zalamanca. **1755** SMOLLETT *Quix.* (1803) 107 In good faith, we have no poor kindred now.

b. ***in faith, i' faith, faith, good faith***: used interjectionally.

c **1420** *Sir Amadace* (Camd.) xii, Nedelonges most I sitte him by. Hi-fath, ther wille him non mon butte I. **1513** MORE *Rich. III* in Grafton *Chron.* I. 781 In faith man.. I was never so sory. *c* **1530** REDFORDE *Play Wit & Sc.* (1848) 11 Do ye fle, ifayth? **1586** A. DAY *Eng. Secretary* II. (1625) 48 Faith sir.. tis but as the wiser sort doe hold opinion. **1594** SHAKS. *Rich. III*, II. iv. 16 Good faith, good faith, the saying did not hold. **1607** TOURNEUR *Rev. Trag.* v. iii, Y'faith, we're well. **1709** *Tatler* No. 110 ⁋4 Faith Isaac.. thou art a very unaccountable old Fellow. **1777** SHERIDAN *Sch. Scand.* III. i, Speak to me thus, and i'faith there's nothing I could refuse you. **1795** BURNS *For a' That* iv, Gude faith, he mauna fa' that. **1840** DICKENS *Barn. Rudge* v, I'd rather be in old John's chimney-corner, faith. **1849** JAMES *Woodman* v, Good faith, he has no choice. **1855** BROWNING *Bp. Blougram's Apol.*, Cool i'faith! We ought to have our Abbey back you see.

c. In quasi-oaths. ***by*** or ***on my, thy***, etc., ***faith, by the faith of (my body, love***, etc.). ***my faith*** (= Fr. *ma foi!*).

c **1350** *Will. Palerne* 275 Now telle me, felawe, be þi feiȝþ .. sei þou euer þemperour? *c* **1420** *Sir Amadace* (Camd.) lxi, But, be my faythe, with-outun stryue. *c* **1477** CAXTON *Jason* 36 b, By your faith seme ye good that I ought to go after him. *c* **1489** CAXTON *Blanchardyn* xxiii. 75 On my feyth ye be well the man. **1588** *Marprel. Epist.* (Arb.) 5 By my faith, by my faith.. this geare goeth hard with vs. **1600** SHAKS. *A.Y.L.* III. ii. 450 By the faith of my loue, I will. **1601** —— *All's Well* II. i. 84 Now by my faith and honour. **1798** COLERIDGE *Anc. Mar.* VII. iv, Strange, by my faith! the Hermit said. **1871** BROWNING *Pr. Hohenst.* 1421 Weapons outflourished in the wind, my faith!

¶ **13.** An alleged designation for a company of merchants.

1486 *Bk. St. Alban's* F vij a, A faith of Marchandis.

IV. 14. *Comb.* Chiefly objective, as ***faith-breach, -breaker, -philosophy, -state, -stretcher, -value***; ***faith-definition, -reformation, -tradition***; ***faith-breaking, -keeping*** sb. and adj.; ***faith-confirming, -infringing, -shaking, -sown, -starved, -straining***, †***-workful*** adjs.; ***faith-wise*** adv.; **faith-cure**, a cure wrought by means of 'the prayer of faith' (*Jas.* v. 15); whence **faith-curer, -curist**, one who believes in or practises faith-cure; **faith-fire**, *fig.* the flame of faith; **faith-healer** = *faith-curer*; **faith-healing**, healing by faith-cure; **faith-ladder** (see quot. *a* 1910); **faith-mark**, one of the leading tenets of religion; **faith-press**, the Inquisition.

1605 SHAKS. *Macb.* v. ii. 18 Now minutely Reuolts vpbraid his *Faith-breach. *c* **1440** *Promp. Parv.* 153 *Feythe breke(r), *fidifragus*. **1561** T. NORTON *Calvin's Inst.* IV. xx. (1634) 736 They are false Faith-breakers in their office. *a* **1649** DRUMM. OF HAWTH. *Hist. Jas. II* Wks. (1711) 30 They declare the king, and those that abode with him, faith-breakers. **1852** MISS YONGE *Cameos* II. xxi. 236 He was.. no faith-breaker. **1625** K. LONG tr. *Barclay's Argenis* III. vii. 174 The very instant of her *faith-breaking. **1654** GAYTON *Pleas. Notes* III. viii. 123 The.. covetous Faith-breaking Senate. **1645** QUARLES *Sol. Recant.* 56 *Faith-confirming Charity. **1885** *Century Mag.* XXXI. 274 A *faith-cure is a cure wrought by God in answer to prayer. **1888** *Pop. Sc. Monthly* XXXII. 507 The miracles claimed by the *faith-curers. **1888** *N.Y. Herald* 29 July 16/6 Great preparations are being made by the *Faith-Curists.. for their annual conference. **1665** J. SERGEANT *Sure-footing in Chr.* 209 But he will finde no such fopperies in *Faith-definitions made by the Catholick Church. **1890** MCCAVE & BREEN *Alcester Lect.* 40 Neighbouring bishops were expected to keep the *faith-fire ablaze along their frontiers. **1885** *Century Mag.* XXXI. 276 We claim that all *faith-healers should report as do our hospitals. **1885** G. ALLEN in *Longm. Mag.* VII. 85 Persons who believe in *faith-healing. **1621** BRATHWAIT *Natures Embassie* (1877) 24 A *faith-infringing Polymnestor. **1605** VERSTEGAN *Dec. Intell.* viii. 253 This was.. giuen.. in recomendation of loyaltie or *faith-keeping. **1648** FAIRFAX, etc. *Remonstrance* 30 For point of Faith-keeping.. witnesse his Accords with the Scottish Nation. *a* **1849** J. C. MANGAN *Poems* (1859) 383 The faith-keeping Prince of the Scotts. **1909** W. JAMES *Pluralistic Universe* viii. 328 In some of my lectures at Harvard I have spoken of what I call the '*faith-ladder'. *a* **1910** —— *Some Probl. Philos.* (1911) App. 224 The following steps may be called the 'faith ladder': 1. There is nothing absurd in a certain view of the world being true, nothing self-contradictory; 2. It *might* have been true under certain conditions; 3. It *may* be true, even now; 4. It is *fit* to be true; 5. It *ought* to be true; 6. It *must* be true; 7. It *shall* be true, at any rate true for *me*. Obviously this is no intellectual chain of inferences, like the *sorites* of the text-books. **1822** SYD. SMITH *Wks.* (1859) II. 8/2 When once the ancient *faith-marks of the Church are lost sight of. **1846** J. D. MORELL *Hist. View Philos.* II. vii. 311 Haumann had.. attempted to found a system of *faith-philosophy.. but it was Jacobi who first brought the faith-philosophy into repute. **1624** T. SCOTT *Lawfuln. Netherlandish War* 14 That most intolerable.. thraldome of the Inquisition, or *Faith-presse. **1665** J. SERGEANT *Sure-footing in Chr.* 233 The.. most refin'd quintessence of all *Faith-Reformation. **1896** *Westm. Gaz.* 21 Dec. 2/3 Could anything be more *faith-shaking than this halt of several weeks in the negotiations? **1844** J. G. WHITTIER *Wks.* (1898) 197/2 *Faith-sown seeds Which ripen in the soil of love. **1946** R. CAMPBELL *Talking Bronco* 69 Where *faith-starved multitudes may quarry As in a mountain, and be fed. **1896** *Amer. Jrnl. Psychol.* Apr. 315 The state of confidence, trust,.. which we have found.. in every conversion considered is the *Faith-state. **1924** W. B. SELBIE *Psychol. Relig.* 158 To induce what psychologists call the faith state may be a very great and wonderful thing if the object of faith is worthy, i.e. God or Christ. **1897** 'MARK TWAIN' *Following Equator* 172 Here are some *faith-straining figures. **1676** MARVELL *Gen. Councils* Wks. 1875 IV. 126 Those *faith-stretchers.. that put mens consciences upon the torture. **1665** J. SERGEANT *Sure-footing in Chr.* 43 A compleat and proper notion of *Faith-Tradition. **1903** G. TYRRELL *Lex Orandi* xxiii. 191 Mistakings of *faith-values for fact-values are to be ascribed to that almost ineradicable materialism of the human mind which makes us view the visible world as the only solid reality. **1869** W. P. MACKAY *Grace & Truth* (1875) 72 Salvation came intellect-wise, and not *faith-wise. **1604** BROUGHTON *Corrupt. Handl. Relig.* (1605) 93 Troup-full Gad was grauen in this *faithworkfull stone.

† **faith**, *v. Obs.* [f. prec. sb.] **a.** *intr.* To place or rest one's faith *on*. **b.** *trans.* To provide with a creed or standard of faith. **c.** To utter upon one's word of honour. **d.** To give credit to, believe, trust.

1430 LYDG. *Chron. Troy* I. vi, By whose example women may well lere How they shuld faith or trusten on any man. **1547** HOOPER *Declar. Christ* v, These decrees that papistry of late days faithed the church withal. **1553** GRIMALDE *Cicero's Offices* I. (1558) 10 It is called faithfulnes because it is fulfilled which was faithed [*quia fiat quod dictum est*]. **1570–6** LAMBARDE *Peramb. Kent* (1826) 221 He shall [not] have cause.. to faith the other [opinion] unadvisedly. **1605** SHAKS. *Lear* II. i. 72 Would the reposal of my trust.. in thee Make thy words faith'd?

† **faithed**, *ppl. a. Obs.* [f. FAITH *sb.* and *v.* + -ED.]

1. Having faith: with defining words as ***feeble-faithed, strong-faithed***, etc.

c **1374** CHAUCER *Troylus* I. 1007 They are the folk that.. strengist feithid be. **1532** MORE *Confut. Tindale* Wks. 507/2 There wer no weake conscience of feeble-faithed folk offended. **1545** JOYE *Exp. Dan.* v. 90 He is weake faithed which loueth and enbraceth the trwe doctrine.. albeit he dare not defende it openly.

2. Of a promise: Given on one's faith or word of honour.

1553 GRIMALDE *Cicero's Offices* III. (1558) 159 Hast thou thy faithed promise broke.

faithful (ˈfeɪθfʊl), *a.*, *adv.*, and *sb.* [f. FAITH *sb.* + -FUL.]

A. *adj.* † **1.** Of persons, their actions, etc.: Full of or characterized by FAITH (sense 3); believing. *Obs.* exc. absol.: see 7.

a **1300** *Cursor M.* 5348 (Cott.) Faithful abraham. **1542** BECON *Pathw. Prayer* Wks. 141 Inflame.. mens hearts with the love of faithful prayer. *a* **1555** LATIMER *Serm. & Rem.* (1845) 155 The poor faithful man is more sure of his living, than if he had the same in his chest. **1610** B. JONSON *Alch.* II. i, You are not faithfull, sir. This night, I'll change All, that is mettall, in thy house, to gold. **1611** BIBLE *Gal.* iii. 9 Faithful Abraham. **1759** DILWORTH *Pope* 66 He saw no.. difficulty for a faithful mind to believe the trinity.

2. a. Firm in fidelity or allegiance to a person to whom one is bound by any tie; constant, loyal, true. Const. *to*.

a **1300** *Cursor M.* 19799 (Cott.) þair he fand a faithful frend. *c* **1330** R. BRUNNE *Chron.* (1810) 307 So faithfulle þei bisemed Boþe erles and barons. **1393** LANGL. *P. Pl.* C. II. 15 To be faith-ful to hym he ȝaue ȝow fyue wittes. *c* **1440** *York Myst.* xxxii. 221 Full faithfull schall ȝe fynde me. **1576** FLEMING *Panopl. Epist.* 162 The chiefest and faythfullest of your favourers. **1639** DK. HAMILTON in *H. Papers* (Camden) 104 My cariage.. such as became your faithfullst servant. **1722** SEWEL *Hist. Quakers* (1795) I. Let. to King 4 No small part of his faithful subjects. **1727** DE FOE *Syst. Magic* I. iii. (1840) 80 [They] vowed themselves to be his faithful allies. **1732** POPE *Ess. Man* I. 112 His faithful dog shall bear him company. **1832** HT. MARTINEAU *Demerara* iii. 35 Be faithful to your master. **1856** GRINDON *Life* ii. (1875) 13 We must.. be faithful to His revealed law.

b. *transf.* of things.

1651 tr. *Bacon's Life & Death* 51 The Remedies faithfull to the Intentions. **1697** DRYDEN *Virg. Georg.* II. 762 His faithful Bed is crown'd with chaste Delight. **1784** COWPER *Task* III. 8 A greensward smooth And faithful to the foot. **1828** SCOTT *F.M. Perth* xxxii, Whose hand was faithful to his sword.

3. a. True to one's word or professed belief; abiding by a covenant or promise, steadfast. Const. *to*.

c **1400** MAUNDEV. (1839) xii. 139 Ffor the sarazines ben gode and feyþfulle, ffor thei kepen entierly the commaundement of the holy book Alkoran. **1594** T. B. *La Primaud. Fr. Acad.* II. 187 God is so often.. called faithfull .. because Hee neuer falsifieth His faith. **1611** BIBLE *Deut.* vii. 9 The faithfull God, which keepeth Couenant and Mercy with them that loue him. **1690** DRYDEN *Don Sebast.* v. 114 Naturally good, And faithfull to his word. **1841** LANE *Arab. Nts.* I. 100 Are ye remaining faithful to your covenant?

b. Of a covenant, promise, etc.: Containing a pledge of fidelity, binding.

c **1425** WYNTOUN *Cron.* VIII. xii. 59 Bwndyn.. wyth faythful Band To succoure þe Fredwme of Scotland. *a* **1533** LD. BERNERS *Huon* xlviii. 162, I haue made a faythfull vow. **1601** SHAKS. *Twel. N.* v. i. 117 The faithfull'st offrings.. That ere deuotion tender'd. *a* **1817** JANE AUSTEN *Northanger Abbey* (1818) II. ix. 180 'Isabella promised so faithfully to write directly.' 'Promised so faithfully!—A faithful promise! —That puzzles me.—I have heard of a faithful performance. But a faithful promise—the fidelity of promising!'

4. a. Of persons and their conduct: Conscientious, thorough in the fulfilment of duty.

c **1350** *Will. Palerne* 337 Be feiȝtful & fre & euer of faire speche. **1377** LANGL. *P. Pl.* B. VI. 253 þe freke þat fedeth hym-self With his feythful laboure. **1529** MORE *Dyaloge* III. Wks. 238/2 So faythfull a prince. **1851** CARLYLE *Sterling* III. ii. (1872) 180 Faithful assiduous studies. **1892** *Law Times* XCII. 144/2 The faithful and conscientious discharge of his duties.

b. Often used (? after *Prov.* xxvi. 6) with reference to the duty of telling unwelcome truths or giving unwelcome counsel. Chiefly *colloq.*

1655 STANLEY *Hist. Philos.* I. II. v. 17 Think not those faithful who praise all thy.. actions, but those who reprove thy faults.

5. Of persons and their actions: That may be believed or relied upon; trustworthy, veracious. †Also, of things: Reliable.

1340–70 *Alex. & Dind.* 65, I haue founde ȝou folk faiþful of speche. **1393** LANGL. *P. Pl.* C. XIX. 141 Suche a surgeyn setthen yseye was þer neuere, Ne non so faithfol fysician.

1611 BIBLE *Ps.* cxix. 138 Thy testimonies..are..very faithfull. 1678 PRIDEAUX *Lett.* (Camden) 65 The faithfullest relators..are the Grecians. 1742 FIELDING *J. Andrews* II. xvii, Unless I had much faithfuller interest, [he] advised me to give over my pretensions. 1814 SCOTT *Wav.* iii, Memoirs scarcely more faithful than romances. 1891 M. E. WILKINS *Humble Romance* 280 Her husband..did the cooking, and he was as faithful at it as a woman!

6. True to the fact or original, accurate.

1529 MORE *Dyaloge* III. Wks. 241/1 Any good verteous man hath hadde the mynde in faithful wise to translate it. 1660 H. MORE *Myst. Godl.* v. xvii. 211 This is the faithfullest Account that I can give. 1709 POPE *Ess. Crit.* 484 When the faithful pencil has design'd Some bright Idea of the master's mind. 1749 FIELDING *Tom Jones* I. vi, Mrs. Deborah..made a faithful report. 1781 COWPER *Truth* 161 In faithful memory she records the crimes. 1809–10 COLERIDGE *Friend* (1865) 59 A faithful catalogue of its many miseries! 1841 MYERS *Cath. Th.* III. §42. 159 The Latin, though..more faithful than the Septuagint, is far from being perfect. 1857 H. MILLER *Test. Rocks* iii. 153 We pronounce the map..a faithful copy.

7. *absol.* Chiefly *pl.* **a.** In sense 1 (but with some notion of 2, 3): 'True believers'; the believing members of the church; the orthodox of any religious community. Often as transl. Arab. *al-mūminūn* (genit. *-in*), the designation given by Mohammedans to those of their own faith.

father of the faithful (after *Rom.* iv. 11): Abraham. ***Commander*** or ***Father of the Faithful***: titles applied by Mohammedans to the Caliph.

1558 BP. WATSON *Sev. Sacram.* xv. 95 Hee was one of the number of the faithfull and familiars with Christ. 1563 MAN tr. *Musculus' Commonpl.* 275 The Sacraments..be giuen unto the faithful only. 1597 HOOKER *Eccl. Pol.* v. xliv. (1611) 275 The faithfull which departed this life before the comming of Christ. 1609 BIBLE (Douay) *Hist. Table* II. 1073 Seths children and other faythful were called the sonnes of God. 1635 PAGITT *Christianogr.* I. iii. (1636) 102 We beleeve the faithfull to eate Christs body. *a* 1711 KEN *Hymnotheo* Wks. 1721 III. 77 The Faithful, who retrieve baptismal Flame. 1753 CHAMBERS *Cycl. Supp.*, *Faithful*, a designation the mahometans assume to themselves. 1782 PRIESTLEY *Corrupt. Chr.* II. VI. 14 The faithful received the eucharist every Lord's day. 1840 *Comic Almanac* (Hotten) I. 248 The Sultan of Turkey..the Father of the Faithful. 1841 LANE *Arab. Nts.* I. 71 Another custom required of the faithful on this festival is the giving of alms. 1846 *Edin. Rev.* LXXXIV. 68 The Commander of the Faithful repaired..to the tomb of the Prophet. 1848 MACAULAY *Hist. Eng.* I. 159 A communion service at which the faithful might sit. *Ibid.* 555 Sufficient evidence that he was not one of the faithful [the covenanters].

†**b.** *transf.* as a slang term for drunkards.

1609 W. M. *Man in Moon* B 3/2 One of the faithfull, as they prophanely terme him..he will drinke many degrees beyond a Dutchman.

8. *Comb.*, as *faithful-hearted*.

1925 J. GREGORY *Bab of Backwoods* xix. 244 Faithful-hearted retainer.

†**B.** *adv.* = FAITHFULLY. *Obs.* in educated use.

1556 *Aurelio & Isab.* (1608) A vj, I love her..faythfuller then you. 1645 MILTON *Tetrach.* Wks. 1738 I. 233 To see Covenants of greatest moment faithfullest perform'd. 1651 SIR E. NICHOLAS in *N. Papers* (Camden) 216, I doe faithfull promise and ingage myselfe that [etc.].

C. as *sb.* A faithful person. **a.** A true believer, one of 'the faithful'. **b.** A trusty adherent.

a. 1571 HANMER *Chron. Irel.* (1633) 54 What faithfull soever being penitent, shall bee buried there. 1588 A. KING tr. *Canisius' Catech.* 15 No work of godlines suld be æstemit of ane trew faithful hard. 1849 CARD. WISEMAN *Miracles N.T.* Essays 1853 I. 188 Nor is there reason to suppose, that every simple faithful was a Thaumaturgus.

b. 1648 *British Bell-man* 2 Whilest the King and his Faithfuls retained their Places of Dominion. *Ibid.* 4 Your out-cries against those his [the king's] old faithfulls. 1890 H. M. STANLEY *Darkest Africa* II. p. xiii, The Faithfuls at Zanzibar.

†'**faithfullist.** *nonce-wd.* [f. prec. adj. + -IST.] A believer.

1653 URQUHART *Rabelais* II. Prol., You have..seen..and like upright Faithfullists, have firmly beleeved all to be true that is contained in them.

faithfully ('feɪθfʊlɪ), *adv.* [f. FAITHFUL *a.* + -LY².] In a faithful manner.

†**1. a.** With full faith, trust, or confidence; confidingly, confidently. *Obs.*

1401 *Pol. Poems* (1859) II. 107, I afferme faithfully that that is Cristis body. *c* 1450 LONELICH *Grail* xxxvii. 395 Feythfully now trosteth to me. 1552 *Bury Wills* (1850) 141 Most faythfully beleving..yᵗ my sowle..shall rest wᵗʰ Abrahᵃm. 1607 SHAKS. *Timon* III. ii. 46, If his occasion were not vertuous, I should not vrge it halfe so faithfully.

†**b.** Assuredly, in truth. *Obs.*

c 1400 *Destr. Troy* 1890 And þou faithfully a fole, & a freike mad, May be countid in this case.

2. a. With fidelity or firm allegiance; loyally, truly. ***yours faithfully***: one of the customary modes of subscribing a letter. **b.** With strict adherence to duty, conscientiously. **c.** Sincerely, truthfully.

1362 LANGL. *P. Pl.* A. VII. 64, I schal fynden hem heore fode þat feiþfulliche lyuen. *c* 1400 MAUNDEV. (Roxb.) xxv. 120 He beleueth not feithfully in God. 14.. *Pol. Rel. & L. Poems* (1866) 49 Euery wygth þat louyth feythefully. 1550 CROWLEY *Last Trump.* 154 Daniel..serued his prince fayethfully. 1588 J. UDALL *Demonstr. Discip.* (Arb.) 16 The Discipline which they receiued of Christe, they deliuered faythfully to the people. 1603 KNOLLES *Hist. Turks* (1621) 1082 Beleeve us..who love you not fainedly, but faithfully, and in deed. 1632 *High Commission Cases* (Camden) 317 He ..did..faithfullie exercise his ministery. 1705 STANHOPE *Paraphr.* II. 254 They who do their own Endeavours faithfully shall be..strengthened to do more. 1772 *Junius Lett.* lxviii. 335 Those laws..he has sworn to administer faithfully. 1781 GIBBON *Decl. & F.* III. 119 The fatal secret ..was faithfully preserved. 1787 W. PITT in G. Rose *Diaries* (1860) I. 68 Most sincerely and faithfully yours, W. Pitt. 1793 SMEATON *Edystone L.* §222 Faithfully remembering not to terminate the beating, till [etc.]. 1873 OUIDA *Pascarel* I. 61 We all went to him faithfully.

3. In strict accordance with the facts or original; accurately, correctly, exactly, truthfully.

? *a* 1400 *Morte Arth.* 1913, I wille..faythfully tellene. *c* 1400 *Destr. Troy* 654, I will you faithfully enforme how ye fare shall. 1556 LAUDER *Tractate* 524, I haue said ye veritie ..faithfullie. 1690 *Def. Rights Univ. Oxford* Pref., Thus.. do [we] faithfully keep an exact register of their contentions. 1712 *Spect.* No. 527 ¶ 2 What I have faithfully related. 1792 *Gentl. Mag.* 13/1 The church is faithfully represented in the annexed drawing. 1877 MRS. OLIPHANT *Makers Flor.* iii. 79 So came I..to judge faithfully with my proper eyes.

4. †**a.** In a convincing or assuring manner (*obs*). **b.** With binding assurances (still common *colloq.*). Cf. FAITHFUL 3 b and FAITH 7, 8.

c 1384 CHAUCER *H. Fame* 455 So feythfully to me spake he. 1525 ABP. WARHAM in Ellis *Orig. Lett.* III. I. 370 To whome I have feighfully promised not to vtter the same. 1548 HALL *Chron.* 241 b, Promisyng faithfully shortly to sende for her. 1600 SHAKS. *A. Y. L.* II. vii. 192 If that you were the good Sir Rowlands son, As you haue whisper'd faithfully you were. *a* 1817 [see FAITHFUL *a.* 3 b]. *a* 1894 *Mod.* He promised faithfully to send the book the next day. 1922 JOYCE *Ulysses* 746 And I promised him yes faithfully Id let him block me.

faithfulness ('feɪθfʊlnɪs). [f. as prec. + -NESS.] The quality of being faithful. **a.** Fidelity, loyalty (to a superior or friend); trustworthiness, conscientiousness. **b.** Strict adherence to one's pledged word; honesty, sincerity. **c.** Exact correspondence to an original or to fact.

1388 WYCLIF *Esther* vi. 3 What..meede gat Mardochee for this feithfulnesse? 1486 *Bk. St. Alban's, Her.* A v a, Cherefull to faythfulnes. *a* 1533 LD. BERNERS *Huon* lxxxii. 253 Grete petye it shalbe yf ye sholde dye for your trouth and faythfulnes. 1581 SIDNEY *Apol. Poetrie* (Arb.) 19 The beast of most..faithfulnes. 1662 STILLINGFL. *Orig. Sacr.* II. vi. §12 The truth and faithfulness of God. 1688 SOUTH *Serm.* (1704) I. xii. 517 The Band, that..supports all Compacts, is Truth and Faithfulness. 1700 BURKITT *On N.T.* Matt. x. 40–2 Our..Saviour encourages his Apostles to Faithfulness in their Office. 1783 HAILES *Antiq. Chr. Ch.* ii. 31 The faithfulness and loyalty of the Jews to the Roman government. 1869 FREEMAN *Norm. Conq.* (1876) III. xii. 191 The valour and faithfulness of the house of Geroy. 1885 *Manch. Exam.* 15 May 5/2 Persons..dependent upon each other's stability and faithfulness. *Mod.* I was exceedingly pleased with the faithfulness of the likeness.

Faithist ('feɪθɪst). [f. FAITH *sb.* + -IST.] A member of a sect whose religion is based on revelations contained in the 'Kosmon Bible' or 'Oahspe' and on angelic communications. Also *attrib.*

1885 *Santa Fé Weekly New Mexican* 23 July 4/4 Tanner has joined the new community or sect of faithists near Las Cruces, N.M. 1907 *Westm. Gaz.* 25 June 10/1 The Faithist Community, which has established a modest footing in Balham, and whose comprehensive gospel ranges from the creation of man to the 'glory and labours of the gods and goddesses of the Etherian Heavens'. 1921 *Glasgow Herald* 21 Sept. 10 Mr. F. T. A. Davies, founder of the Faithist movement in England. 1928 *Sunday Dispatch* 29 July 9/5 The Faithists originated in America. There are only two or three hundred in Great Britain—most of them in London and the Home Counties.

faithless ('feɪθlɪs), *a.* [f. FAITH *sb.* + -LESS.] Without faith.

1. a. Without belief, confidence, or trust; unbelieving. Const. †*of*, *in*.

a 1300 *Cursor M.* 6517 (Cott.) To þis fait-les lede Manna fel. 1611 BIBLE *John* xx. 27 And bee not faithlesse, but beleeuing. 1681 LUTTRELL *Brief Rel.* (1857) I. 123 The more sober sort..are not altogether faithlesse as to his innocency. 1826 E. IRVING *Babylon* II. VI. 74 Men are not now more faithless of Armageddon, than [etc.]. 1842 LOWELL *Sonnets* xvi, An old man faithless in Humanity. 1850 TENNYSON *In Mem.* cvi, The faithless coldness of the times.

b. Without religious faith; unbelieving. Of a heathen or a Jew: Without Christian faith. Also absol. ***the faithless***: unbelievers. Now *rare*.

1534 MORE *On the Passion* Wks. 1320/1 That dede doone by yᵉ faythlesse is not meritorius at al. 1548 UDALL, etc. *Erasm. Par. Rom.* Prol. sig. ††i, Else shalt thou remaine euermore faithlesse. 1590 SPENSER *F.Q.* III. iii. 34 He..shall ..holy Church with faithlesse handes deface. 1628 WITHER *Brit. Rememb.* VI. 252 As faithlesse as the Jewes, are we. *absol.* 1577 B. GOOGE *Heresbach's Husb.* III. (1586) 138 b, A great number of others imagined by the faithlesse. 1944 A. CLARKE *Coll. Plays* (1963) 217 The terrible assumption of that woman..is a warning to the faithless.

2. Destitute of good faith, unfaithful, insincere; false to vows, etc., perfidious, disloyal. Const. *to*.

1362 LANGL. *P. Pl.* A. x. 135 Fals folk and Feiþles, þeoues and lyȝers. 1399 *Pol. Poems* (1859) I. 377 The ffortune that ffallyn is to ffeitheles peple. 1613 SHAKS. *Hen. VIII*, II. i. 123 A most vnnatural and faithlesse Seruice. 1678 WANLEY *Wond. Lit. World* v. ii. §81. 478/2 A man..of a..faithless disposition. 1725 POPE *Odyss.* XIV. 322 Domestic in his faithless roof I staid. 1786 BURKE *W. Hastings* Wks. 1842 II. 214 The dangerous, faithless, and ill-concerted projects of the..council of Bombay. 1807 CRABBE *Par. Reg.* II. 142 The faithless flatterer. 1839 KEIGHTLEY *Hist. Eng.* II. 65 She had never been faithless to the royal bed.

3. That cannot be trusted or relied on; unstable, treacherous, shifting, delusive.

1603 SHAKS. *Meas. for M.* III. i. 137 Oh faithlesse Coward, oh dishonest wretch. 1738 JOHNSON *London* 239 The midnight murd'rer bursts the faithless bar. 1766 GOLDSM. *Hermit* 10 Yonder faithless phantom flies To lure thee to thy doom. 1853 KANE *Grinnell Exp.* xlix. (1856) 466 Striving to tear us from this faithless anchorage.

Hence '**faithlessly** *adv.*, in a faithless manner.

1643 PRYNNE *Treachery & Disloyalty* App. 218 Had we.. not faithlessely betrayed, but sincerely discharged the severall trusts reposed in us.

faithlessness ('feɪθlɪsnɪs). [f. prec. + -NESS.] The quality or fact of being faithless. **a.** Want of fidelity, disloyalty, perfidy. **b.** Want of good faith, insincerity. **c.** Want of religious belief; infidelity.

1605 BP. HALL *Medit. & Vows* I. §10 So great distrust is there in man..from his impotence or faithlesnes. 1726 POPE *Let. to Bethel* 9 Aug. *Lett.* (1737) 320, I..wish he had lived long enough to see so much of the faithlessness of the world, as to have been [etc.]. 1758 T. EDWARDS *Canons Crit.* (1765) 344 Sharp are the pangs that follow faithlessness. 1790 BLAIR *Serm.* III. xiii. 275 When the heart is sorely wounded by the ingratitude or faithlessness of those on whom it had leaned. *a* 1849 J. H. EVANS in Spurgeon *Treas. Dav.* Ps. lxxi. 17 The faithlessness of Abiathar, and the faithlessness of even his faithful Joab. 1849 GROTE *Greece* II. xlvii. VI. 96 Perdikkas whose character for faithlessness we shall have.. to notice. 1860 RUSKIN *Mod. Paint.* V. IX. xii. 347 Faithlessness..characteristic of this present century.

†'**faithly,** *adv. Obs.* [f. FAITH *sb.* + -LY².]

1. With fidelity, faithfully, loyally, steadfastly, truthfully.

c 1325 *Metr. Hom.* 162 Feitheli scho hir candel held aye. *c* 1330 R. BRUNNE *Chron.* (1810) 316 Of þe treus to speke. And feyþly þerto bondon. 1393 LANGL. *P. Pl.* C. XXII. 70 Faithly for to speke his furst name was Ihesus. *c* 1440 *Sir Degrev.* 541 Y shalle faythly fyeght Both in wrong and in ryght.

2. As an asseveration: In deed or truth, certainly, surely, verily.

c 1340 *Gaw. & Gr. Knt.* 1636 þis gomen is your awen.. faythely ȝe knowe. ? *a* 1400 *Morte Arth.* 4032 We are faithely to fewe to feghte with them. *a* 1400–50 *Alexander* 2279 Now faithly..fall þe so thrise, þou sall be crouned.

'**faithward,** *adv. rare.* [See -WARD.] Towards (the Christian) faith.

1886 J. M. LUDLOW in *Homilet. Rev.* Aug. 165 Almost resistless tendencies faithward..were born of his early Christian culture.

'**faithworthy,** *a.* [f. FAITH + WORTHY *a.*] Worthy of belief or trust, trustworthy. Hence '**faithworthiness**, the quality of being faithworthy (Worcester, 1846, citing *Quart. Rev.*).

a 1535 FISHER *Wks.* 433 Luther..neither is faith worthy ..nor he doth no miracles. 1671 J. WEBSTER *Metallogr.* iii. 56 Certain and faith-worthy Authors in the nearer Germany. 1772 NUGENT *Hist. Friar Gerund* I. 217 It is affirmed by a..faith-worthy author. 1861 *Daily Tel.* 26 Oct., The lady is faithworthy in her evidence as to identity. 1865 *Reader* 28 Jan. 98/2 So far as profound knowledge.. can ensure faithworthy evidence.

faitneant, -ise, obs. ff. of FAINÉANT, -ISE.

faitour ('feɪtə(r)). *Obs.* exc. *arch.* Forms; 4–7 **faytor, -tour(e, -towre, 6 fayter, feytour, 4– faitour.** [a. AF. *faitour*, OF. *faitor* doer, maker:—L. *factōr-em*: see FACTOR *sb.* The special sense of 'impostor' seems to be peculiarly AF. and Eng.; cf. OF. *faiture* sorcery, spell.]

1. An impostor, cheat; *esp.* a vagrant who shams illness or pretends to tell fortunes.

App. already obsolescent in 1568, as Grafton *Chron.* II. 598 glosses it 'as much to say as loyterer, vagabond, or begger'. Sir W. Scott often uses it *arch.*

a 1340 HAMPOLE *Psalter* xxx. 16 þai ere all faitors & ypocrites & iogulors þat desayues men. [1383 *Act 7 Rich. II*, c. 5 Governours des villes & lieux ou tielx faitours & vagerantz vendront.] *c* 1430 *Life of St. Kath.* (1884) 23 Put me in duresse as þou3 I were a faytour. 1496 *Dives & Paup.* (W. de W.) I. xxx. 69 These faytours that ben called sothe sayers. 1529 MORE *Comf. agst. Trib.* II. Wks. 1209/2 Nor to beleue euery faytor..that will saye hymselfe that he is verye sycke. 1579 SPENSER *Sheph. Cal.* May 39 Those faytours [*gloss.* vagabonds] little regarden their charge. 1624 BP. MOUNTAGU *Gagg* 104 As faitors use, you play fast and loose. 1813 SCOTT *Trierm.* II. xi, Tyrant proud, or faitour strong. 1828 —— *F.M. Perth* viii, Yonder stands the faitour, rejoicing at the mischief he has done.

b. *nonce-use.* The disease of being a 'faitour'.

c 1500 *Blowbol's Test.* 25 in Hazl. *E.P.P.* I. 93 He was infecte..With the faitour, or the fever lordeyn.

†**2.** Comb. ***faitour's grass***: Spurge, the acrid juice of which was used in malingering.

c 1440 *Promp. Parv.* 146 Faytowrys gresse, or tytymal. 1534 FITZHERBERT *Husbandry* (E.D.S.) lix, A Grasse that is called feitergrasse [ed. 1598 fettergrass].

faix, var. of FEGS *int.*

‖**faja** ('faha). [Sp.] A sash, girdle.

1841 G. BORROW *Zincali* I. II. v. 304 A faja, or girdle of crimson silk, surrounds the waist. 1897 'H. S. MERRIMAN' *In Kedar's Tents* xix. 213 About his person in the form of handkerchief and faja were..touches of bright colour. 1931 *Discovery* Dec. 392/2 (Mexico) The 'faja' (sash)..may be worn by either men or women according to style and design.

fake (feɪk), *sb.*[1] *Naut.* Also 7, 9 fack. [Of obscure origin; cf. FAKE *v.*[1]

The MHG. *vach* had the sense 'fold' in addition to those of 'appointed place, portion of space or time, compartment'; if a similar sense belonged to the etymological equivalents OE. *fæc* (recorded in sense 'space of time'), MDu. *vak* (enclosure, partition), the word might come from either source. If it be identical with the Sc. FAIK *sb.* fold, a native origin seems probable.]

(See quot. 1867.)

1627 CAPT. SMITH *Seaman's Gram.* vii. 30 Lay it [Cable] up in a round Ring, or fake, one aboue another. **1688** R. HOLME *Armoury* III. 163/2 How many Facks is in the Rope? **1730** CAPT. W. WRIGLESWORTH *MS. Log-bk. of the 'Lyell'* 14 Oct., Hauled up the Small Bower and Sheet Cables and Coiled them down again in shorter fakes. **1810** J. H. MOORE *Pract. Navig.* (ed. 18) 274 *Fack* or *Fake*. **1867** SMYTH *Sailor's Word-bk.*, *Fake*, one of the circles or windings of a cable or hawser, as it lies disposed in a coil.

fake (feɪk), *sb.*[2] *slang.* [Belongs to FAKE *v.*[2]]

1. An act of 'faking'; a contrivance, 'dodge', trick, invention; a 'faked' or 'cooked' report. Passing from *slang* to *colloq.* in the sense of 'a counterfeit person or thing'.

1827 MAGINN in *Blackw. Mag.* (Farmer), The fogle-hunter's doing. Their morning fake in the prigging lay. **1851** MAYHEW *Lond. Labour* (1861) I. 223 After that we had a fine 'fake'—that was the fire of the Tower of London—it sold rattling. **1885** *Punch* 31 Jan. 60 If I worked the theatrical fake—which I don't. **1887** *Financ. News* 24 Mar. 1/4 D..is generally regarded as the father of the testimonial fake. **1888** *N.Y. Mercury* (Farmer), Both ladies then came to the conclusion that the fortune-teller was a fake, and they decided to notify the police. **1891** *Pall Mall G.* 28 July 6/2 The abominable fakes..telegraphed to the papers by the agencies. **1899** R. WHITEING *No. 5 John St.* xxiii. 229 She went so far as to affirm her conviction that I was a 'fake'. **1927** F. LONSDALE *The Fake* III. ii. 59 If you stood at this moment to be judged by these..people, you would have earned from them that which I can only ever feel for you —everlasting contempt...you Fake! **1945** AUDEN *Coll. Poetry* 35 To think of love as a subjective fake.

2. A composition used for 'faking' (see quots.).

1866 *Islington Guardian* 3 Apr. 3/3 [Condensed milk sold to dealers to be watered down and retailed as new milk] is known in the trade under the name of 'Fake'. **1880** GEE *Goldsmith's Handbk.* x. (ed. 2) 140 Soft-soldering Fluid bears various names in the different workshops, such as 'monkey', 'fake'.

3. *attrib.* or as *adj.* Spurious, counterfeit; *spec.* used in *Jazz* of a book of music containing the basic chord-sequences of tunes.

1775 W. HOWE *Let.* 3 Dec. in *Canadian Archives* (1904) App. I. 355 So many artifices have been practiced upon Strangers under the appearance of Friendship, fake Pilots &c., that those coming out with Stores..cannot be put too much on their guard. **1890** *Stock Grower & Farmer* 15 Mar. 7/1 The farce of surveying for their fake ditch. **1892** *Boston* (Mass.) *Jrnl.* 9 June 10/2 *heading*, Another Fake Interview Denounced. **1903** *Daily Chron.* 16 June 3/4 [Amer. loq.] They were all men of position and character, who would not be connected with a 'fake' institution. **1909** *Westm. Gaz.* 16 Nov. 2/3 Swindled by a 'fake' paper, the supposed verdict being simply a prophecy of what it was likely to be. **1920** *Glasgow Herald* 17 Nov. 9 Fake whisky..the symptoms following consumption are similar to those of gastric poisoning. **1927** *Melody Maker* May 495 By blowing the instrument as though you intended to play one long note, but during this long note, changing the fingering alternately from 'legitimate' (or recognised) to fake fingering. **1933** *Mind* XLII. 34 Anyone can write a fake dictionary. **1953** X. FIELDING *Stronghold* III. i. 182 These fake Americans usually appear so scornful of what..they call 'the home-town'. **1958** *Amer. Speech* XXXIII. 225 *Bible* (the chord book, or 'fake book', which guides most small combos through this weary world). **1964** *McCall's Sewing* iv. 57/1 *Fake fur*, woven or knitted fabrics made of cotton or synthetic fibres to simulate the fur of animals. **1965** *New Yorker* 2 Jan. 46/2 Bring that fake book, please, in case they ask me to play something I recorded forty years ago. Everybody but me remembers those tunes.

fake (feɪk), *v.*[1] *Naut.* [app. f. FAKE *sb.*[1], which, however, appears much later. Cf. Sc. FAIK *v.*[1] to fold.] *trans.* To lay (a rope) in fakes or coils; to coil.

?*a* **1400** *Morte Arth.* 742 Ffrekes one þe forestayne, fakene þeire coblez. *c* **1860** H. STUART *Seaman's Catech.* 62 The chain cables and messengers are faked in the chain lockers. **1875** BEDFORD *Sailor's Pocket-bk.* viii. (ed. 2) 281 But for subsequent shots the line may be faked on the beach.

fake (feɪk), *v.*[2] *slang.* [Of obscure origin. There appears to be some ground for regarding it as a variant of the older FEAK, FEAGUE, which are prob. ad. Ger. *fegen* (or the equivalent Du. or LG.) to furbish up, clean, sweep.

In Rowland's *Martin Mark-all* 1610, *a feager of loges* is explained as meaning 'one who begs with false documents' (cf. *to fake a screeve*); and the modern *fake away* appears to correspond to the earlier *feague it away*. The colloquial and jocular uses of the Ger. *fegen* closely resemble the senses mentioned in quot. 1812: amongst those given by Grimm are 'to clear out, plunder' (a chest, purse: cf. *to fake a cly*), 'to torment, ill treat'.]

1. a. *trans.* In thieves' or vagrants' language: To perform any operation upon; to 'do', 'do for'; to plunder, wound, kill; to do up, put into shape; to tamper with, for the purpose of deception. In the last-mentioned application it has latterly come into wider colloquial use, *esp.* with reference to the 'cooking' or dressing-up of news, reports, etc., for the press. Also, with *up* or *absol.*

1812 J. H. VAUX *Flash Dict.* s.v., To *fake* any person or place, to rob them; to *fake* a person may also imply to shoot, wound, or cut; to *fake* a man *out and out*, is to kill him; a man who inflicts wounds upon, or otherwise disfigures, himself, for any sinister purpose, is said to have *faked himself*; if a man's shoe happens to pinch or gall his foot, he will complain that his shoe *fakes* his foot sadly..to *fake* your *slangs*, is to cut your irons in order to escape from custody; to *fake* your *pin*, is to create a sore leg, or to cut it, as if accidentally..in hopes..to get into the doctor's list, &c.; to *fake* a *screeve* is to write any letter or other paper; to *fake* a *screw*, is to shape out a skeleton or false key, for the purpose of *screwing* a particular place; to *fake a cly* is to pick a pocket. **1851** MAYHEW *Lond. Labour* 352 The ring is made out of brass gilt buttons..it's faked up to rights. **1885** *Sporting Times* 23 May 1/3 The chorister fair..Faked her-self up. **1885** H. P. GRATTAN in *The Stage* 10 July, A pair of shoes to fake the patchey (*Anglice* play the harlequin). **1885** *Spectator* 24 Jan. 119/2 Nine pictures out of ten in modern galleries are simply studies—'faked up'. **1887** *Times* 30 July 5/5 He now knew that..these diamonds were 'faked'. **1888** *Phonetic Jrnl.* 7 Jan. 4/2 'Faking' in newz-paper fraze meanz ..the supplying..ov unimportant detailz which may serv an exsellent purpos in the embellishment ov a despatch. **1888** 'BOLDREWOOD' *Robbery under Arms* I. xvii, The horse-brand..had been 'faked' or cleverly altered. **1896** *People* 6 Sept. 10/3 Complainant..denied that..he was accused by a lady of picking her pocket..he did not say he had 'never faked a poke' in his life. **1908** *Smart Set* Sept. 39, I knew that ..it had no curative power and I didn't want to be caught faking. **1921** G. B. SHAW *Back to Methuselah* IV. III. 203 What else could the poor old chap do but fake up an answer fit for publication?

b. *spec.* To conceal the defects of (an animal) by colouring hair or feathers.

1874 *Punch* 7 Mar. 98/1 Pr'aps he'd a come to you with him [a horse] faked up for sale. **1883** W. G. STABLES *Our Friend the Dog* vii. 60 *Faking*, dyeing, staining, clipping, or otherwise interfering with the dog's coat or appearance, to hide defects and deceive the judge or public.

c. To feign or simulate.

1941 *London Opinion* Apr. 42/1 Faking an interest in the goods displayed. **1943** E. O'NEILL *Moon for Misbegotten* III. 148, I..hid my face in my hands and faked some sobs.

2. *absol.* or *intr.* To steal (? only a literary misapprehension); also in *fake away* (see quots.).

1812 J. H. VAUX *Flash Dict.*, *Fake away, there's no down*.. go on with your operations, there is no sign of any alarm or detection. **1834** H. AINSWORTH *Rookwood* III. v, 'Nix my dolly pals fake away.' **1860** READE *Cloister & H.* III. iv. 82 They molest not beggars, unless they fake to boot, and then they drown us out of hand.

3. *intr.* Of jazz musicians: to improvise. *colloq.*

1926 *Melody Maker* Jan. 20 In those days..the dance band was not studied by the orchestrator as it is now, and one had to 'fake' saxophone and banjo parts from those of such other instruments as were catered for in the score. **1933** *Fortune* Aug. 92/3 It is no exaggeration to say that his band of fourteen can *fake* (improvise) as adroitly as the early five-piece combinations. **1944** *Spotlight* Jan. 18 There was enough good music 'faked' in those days.

Hence **faked** *ppl. a.*; **'faking** *vbl. sb.*; **'faker**, one who 'fakes' (cf. CLY-FAKER); **'fakery**, the practice of 'faking'.

a **1845** BARHAM *Ingol. Leg.*, *Lay St. Aloys.*, Nought is waking Save mischief and 'faking'. **1846** R. L. SNOWDEN *Magistrate's Assistant* 345 Umbrella menders..mushroom fakers. **1851** BORROW *Lavengro* II. iii. 29 We never calls them thieves here, but prigs and fakers. **1872** *Morning Post* 7 Nov. 3/1 Since the 'faking' of the scales in Catch-'em-Alive's year. **1885** *Daily Tel.* 1 Aug. 2 'I've turned faker of dolls and doll's furniture.' **1886** *Bicycling News* 11 June 536/2 What has been termed a 'faked' machine. **1887** *Sat. Rev.* 9 Jan. 70 The gold and vellum binding with the orange-tinted edges form a pretty piece of 'fakery'. **1892** A. C. DOYLE *Advent. S. Holmes* xiii, in *Strand Mag.* IV. No. 24. 657/2, I found him [the horse] in the hands of a faker. **1898** *Westm. Gaz.* 25 June 2/3 The profession of the faker has become quite a recognised one, and happy the man who.. shows intelligent anticipation of some important item of war news. **1934** S. R. NELSON *All about Jazz* i. 23 Chas. Washington..was the father of the fakers, as he was unable to read a note of music.

fakement ('feɪkmənt). *slang.* Also **fakeman-charley**. [f. as prec. + -MENT; the origin of the longer form is unknown.] A piece of manipulation, contrivance, 'dodge'; vaguely, a thing, 'concern'; a trimming, decoration (on an article of clothing).

1812 J. H. VAUX *Flash Dict.* s.v. *Fakeman-charley*, Speaking of any stolen property which has a private mark, one will say, there is a *fakeman-charley* on it; a forgery which is well executed is said to be a *prime fakement*; in a word, anything is liable to be termed a *fakement*, or a *fakeman-charley*, provided the person you address knows to what you allude. **1823** EGAN in *Grose's Dict. Vulg. Tongue* (ed. 3) s.v. *Tell the macers to mind their fakements*, desire the swindlers to be careful not to forge another person's signature. **1838** GLASCOCK *Land Sharks* II. 4, I see you're fly to every fakement. **1851** MAYHEW *Lond. Labour* I. 52 Pair of long sleeve Moleskin..with a double fakement down the side. *Ibid.* I. 246 Ah! once I could screeve a fakement (write a petition). **1877** *Five Years Penal Servitude* iv. 254 You worked that little fakement in a blooming quiet way.

† **'faken**, *sb. Obs.* Forms: 1 fácen, fácn, 2 facne, 3 *Orm.* fakenn. [OE. *fácen* = OS. *fêkn*, *fêcan*, OHG. *feichan* fraud, ON. *feikn* portent :—OTeut. **faikno-m.*] Fraud, guile; wickedness, crime.

c **924** *Laws of Æthelstan* i. §17 He ladige þa hand mid þe man tyhð þæt he þæt facen mid worhte. *c* **1000** *Ags. Gosp.* Matt. xxii. 18 Ða se Hælend hyra facn [*c* **1160** *Hatton*, facne] ȝehyrde, þa cwæð he. *c* **1200** ORMIN 12797 An soþ Issraelisshe mann þatt niss na fakenn inne.

† **'faken**, *a. Obs.* Forms: 1 fácne, fǽcne, 3 facen, faken, (4 foken), 5 *Sc.* faikyn. [OE. *fácne* (oftener with umlaut *fǽcne*) = OS. *fêkni* wicked, ON. *feikn* awful, monstrous:—OTeut. **faiknjo-*, f. **faikno-m*: see prec.] Deceitful, fraudulent.

c **1000** *Ags. Ps.* cv[i]. 10 Swa hi alysde lifes ealdor of heora feonda fæcnum handum. *a* **1200** *De Animo & Corpore* (ed. Phillips 1838) 8 [Þ]i tunge is ascorted þeo þe facen was. *c* **1200** ORMIN 12655 Þe frosst off fakenn trowwþe. *c* **1330** R. BRUNNE *Chron.* (1810) 194 Saladyn was fulle foken [*printed* foen, *rime-word* token], on him may non affie. *c* **1450** HENRYSON *Fables, Paddok & Mous* 58 Fair thingis oftymis ar fundin faikyn.

Hence † **'fakenliche** *adv. Obs.*, craftily.

c **1000** ÆLFRIC *Gen.* xxvii. 35 Þin broðor com facenlice and nam þine bletsunȝa. *a* **1200** *De Animo & Corpore* (ed. Phillips 1838) 8 Heo ȝeoððde fakenliche & þen feonde icwemde.

fakes: see FAIKES.

‖**faki**. [Arab. *faqīh* one learned in the law.] A title given in Africa to schoolmasters.

1872 BAKER *Nile Tribut.* viii. 112 He chanced to combine in his own person the titles of both sheik and faky. **1884** A. FORBES *Chinese Gordon* vi. 151 ['The Mahdi'] became the disciple of a faki (head dervish) who lived near Khartoum. **1892** *Blackw. Mag.* Sept. 629 Tipping the faki or schoolmaster.

fakir (fə'kɪə(r), 'feɪkɪə(r)). Forms: 7 fakier, (fuckeire, foker, -quere), 7-9 faquir, (8 fackire, fa(c)quier, foughar), 9 fakeer, faqueer, 8- fakir. [a. Arab. *faqīr* lit. 'poor, poor man'; some of the early forms may be due to the pl. *fuqarā*.]

1. a. 'Properly an indigent person, but specially applied to a Mahommedan religious mendicant, and then loosely, and inaccurately, to Hindu devotees and naked ascetics' (Yule).

1609 RO. C. *Hist. Disc. Muley Hamet* vii. C iij/2 Fokers, are men of good life, which are onely given to peace. **1638** W. BRUTON *Newes from E. Indies* 27 They are called Fuckeires. **1704** *Collect. Voy.* (Church.) III. 568/1 You shall take care to embark all the Facquiers. **1763** SCRAFTON *Indostan* (1770) 27 Bestowing a part of their plunder on.. Faquirs. **1813** BYRON *Giaour* xi, Nor there the Fakir's self will wait. **1861** DICKENS *Tom Tiddler's Gr.* i, A Hindoo fakeer's ground. **1874** MORLEY *Compromise* (1886) 178 A fakir would hardly be an estimable figure in our society.

b. *erron.* for FAKER, pronounced ('feɪkə(r)). *U.S.*

1882 in S. Poe *Buckboard Days* (1936) 99 Thieves, Thugs, Fakirs and Bunkco-Steerers. **1902** A. D. MCFAUL *Ike Glidden* xvii. 127 Each day brought its new characters, fakirs, peddlers, schemers and promoters. **1903** *N.Y. Even. Post* 31 Oct. 5 One may see at almost any of the downtown corners a street fakir selling shoestrings. **1932** E. WILSON *Devil take Hindmost* ix. 87 Some listen to a patent-medicine fakir.

2. *attrib.* and *Comb.*, as *fakir-race*; *fakir-like* adj. and adv.

1849 SOUTHEY *Comm.-pl. Bk.* Ser. II. 390 Pilgrims.. carrying bars of iron..fakir-like. **1859** I. TAYLOR *Logic in Theol.* 146 The genuine successors..of a fakir race. **1884** *Pall Mall Budget* 22 Aug. 6/2 The fakir-like devotion with which he has fixed his eyes upon..the House of Lords.

Hence **fakirism**, the system, faith, and practice of the Fakirs.

1856 KINGSLEY *Hours w. Mystics* Misc. I. 349 Hindoo mysticism..has died down into brutal fakeerism. **1883** GOLDW. SMITH in *Contemp. Rev.* Dec. 806 Fakirism is devil-worship.

'fala. *rare*[−1]. [ad. Du. *falie*.] A sort of kerchief worn in Holland.

1721 RAMSAY *Tartana* 340 May she be curst to starve in Frogland Fens, To wear a Fala ragg'd at both the Ends.

fa-la (fɑːlɑː). **a.** Used as a refrain. **b.** *Music.* A sort of madrigal or 'ballet' in vogue in the 16th and 17th c.

a. 1595 MORLEY *1st Bk. Balletts* 1, Sit we heere our loues recounting Fa la la la. **1665** EARL DORSET *Poems* (1721) 58 To all you Ladies now at Land..With a Fa, la, la, la, la. *a* **1800** COWPER *Poems, To Celia* i, No serenade to break her rest..With my fa, la, la.

attrib. **1838** J. STRUTHERS *Poet. Tales* 78 Fifths or thirds And other Crankums set and shown Many Fa la words.

b. 1597 MORLEY *Introd. Mus.* 180 Another kind of Ballets, commonlie called fa las. **1674** PLAYFORD *Skill Mus.* I. 59 Your Madrigals or Fala's of five and six Parts. **1867** MACFARREN *Harmony* ii. 55 Balletts, or Fal-las, of the end of the sixteenth century.

Falange (fa'lanxe, fə'lɑːnʒ, -'lænʒ). [Sp., PHALANX.] A Spanish political party, founded in 1933 as a Fascist movement by J. A. Primo de Rivera and merged in 1937 with traditional right-wing elements to form the ruling party, the Falange Española Tradicionalista, under General Franco. Hence **Fa'langism**; **Fa'langist** *sb.* and *a.* Cf. PHALANGIST[2] 1.

1937 *Ann. Reg. 1936* 247 The employment by the Fascist *Falange Española* of gunmen and thugs to destroy 'Bolshevism'. (The *Falange* was a comparatively insignificant group which had come to model its tactics as well as some of its ideology on those which had proved eminently successful in Italy and Germany.) **1938** *Times* 30 Sept. 13/6 They [*sc.* the Carlists] find little inspiration in the obscurities with which the more wayward Falange writers overload their meditations. **1939** R. CAMPBELL *Flowering Rifle* III. 94 Braided with scarlet arrows by the Sun, A 'Falangist' himself, if there is one! **1941** *Economist* 25 Jan.

97/1 If undiluted Falangism is to be Spain's future, foreign policy must finally fall into line. *Ibid.*, The Falange is trying to force the pace. *Ibid.*, Greater Falangist control in foreign policy. **1955** *Ann. Reg. 1954* 215 The Falangist newspaper Arriba. **1957** P. KEMP *Mine were of Trouble* i. 15 Blue, tasselled *Falange* forage caps. **1961** H. THOMAS *Spanish Civil War* I. 415 Franco took the opportunity to decree the establishment of his new party, uniting the Falange and Carlists. *Ibid.*, The Generalissimo, of course, would be the head of the new party though he had never been either a Falangist or a Carlist.

Falasha (fəˈlɑːʃə). [Amharic *falasha* exile, immigrant.] One of a group of people in Ethiopia holding the Jewish faith. Also as *collect. sing.*

1710 tr. *Tellez's Trav. Jesuits in Ethiopia* I. viii. 38 Betwixt the Emperor's Dominions and the Cafres..there are still many of these Jews, whom they there call Falaxas, which signifies, Strangers. **1790** J. BRUCE *Trav.* I. 404 The Falasha ..are a people of Abyssinia, having a particular language of their own;..they are now, and ever were, Jews. **1869** S. P. GOODHART tr. J. M. Flad (*title*) The Falashas (Jews) of Abyssinia. **1908** *Daily Chron.* 6 Mar. 3/5 Proposed School for the 'Falashas' of Abyssinia. **1908** J. HASTINGS *Encycl. Relig.* I. 165/2 The Falashas..are frequently called the Jews of Abyssinia. But they are certainly not Jews by descent... Possibly their Jewish faith is the survival of some earlier diffusion of Judaism through Abyssinia before the introduction of Christianity, as there is no record of their conversion. **1964** *Guardian* 26 Mar. 16/4 The Falasha, the so-called Black Jews of Ethiopia. **1970** ROTH & WIGODER *New Standard Jewish Encycl.* 663 *Falashas*, Abyssinian tribes observing a form of Judaism, living N. of Lake Tana.

falaterie, obs. f. of PHYLACTERY.

falau, obs. f. of FALLOW.

falaver, -ing, obs. or dial. ff. of PALAVER, etc.

‖**falbala** (ˈfælbələ). Also 8 falbeloe, fallbullow. [*Falbala*, a word found in several Romance languages from the 17th c. downwards; origin unknown. Cf. FURBELOW.] A trimming for women's petticoats, scarves, etc.; a flounce, furbelow. Also *attrib.*

1704 CIBBER *Careless Husband* I, As many blue and green Ribbons..as would have made me a Falbala Apron. **1713** STEELE *Guardian* No. 171 Freeing their fall-bullows..from the annoyance both of hilt and point. **1859** THACKERAY *Virgin.* xxxii, The girls went off..to get their best..falbalas. **1865** CARLYLE *Fredk. Gt.* xx. v, I have got my face wrinkled like the falbalas of a petticoat.

†**falc.** App. some plant.

c **1310** *Old Age* in *E.E.P.* (1862) 149 As falc i falow an felde.

falcade (fælˈkɑːd). *Horsemanship.* [a. Fr. *falcade*, ad. It. *falcata*, L. *falcāta*, fem. of *falcātus*: see FALCATE.] (See quot.)

1730–6 BAILEY, A falcade is the action of the haunches, and of the legs, which bend very low, as in corvets when a stop or half-stop is made. **1775** in ASH.

falcate (ˈfælkeɪt), *a. Anat.*, *Bot.*, and *Zool.* [ad. L. *falcāt-us*, f. *falc-em*, *falx* sickle.] Bent or curved like a sickle; hooked.

1826 KIRBY & SP. *Entomol.* (1828) III. xxix. 166 The mandibulæ of Lampyris..are falcate. **1835** LINDLEY *Introd. Bot.* (1848) II. 349 *Falcate.* **1845** —— *Sch. Bot.* v. (1858) 56 Pod..always falcate or spirally twisted. **1870** HOOKER *Stud. Flora* 273 Capsule compressed, ovate, oblique or falcate. **1879** *Cassell's Techn. Educ.* IV. 39/2 The four wings..are falcate at the tip. **1884** *Syd. Soc. Lex.*, *Falcate cartilages*, the semi-lunar cartilages of the knee-joint.

falcated (ˈfælkeɪtɪd), *a.* [f. as prec. + -ED.]

a. *Astron.* Having a sickle-shaped appearance; said of the moon or a planet when less than one half of its surface is illuminated.

1704 in HARRIS *Lex. Techn.* **1783** W. F. MARTYN *Geog. Mag.* I. Introd. 18 Mercury, on his approach to [the Sun] is falcated like the new-moon. **1867–77** G. F. CHAMBERS *Astron.* Vocab. 916 The Moon..is said to be 'falcated' when its illuminated portion is crescent-shaped.

†**b.** *Bot.* and *Zool.* = FALCATE. *Obs.*

1750 G. HUGHES *Barbadoes* 224 These are tipped with large falcated Apices. **1815** KIRBY & SP. *Entomol.* III. xxxv. 642 In Attacus Atlas the primary wings are falcated or hooked at their apex.

†**falˈcation.** *Obs.* [f. L. *falc-em* sickle: see -ATION.]

1. The condition of being falcate; *concr.* a falcate outgrowth or appendage, hook.

1646 SIR T. BROWNE *Pseud. Ep.* v. iii. 236 The Locusts have..a long falcation or forcipated tayle behinde. **1714** DERHAM *Astro-Theol.* v. i. (1715) 107 In whose [the Moon and Venus'] Falcations the dark part of their Globes may be perceived.

2. (See quot.)

1656 BLOUNT *Glossogr.*, *Falcation*, a mowing or cutting with Bill or Hook. **1721–1800** in BAILEY.

falchion (ˈfɔːlʃən), *sb.* Forms: 4–7 fach-, fauch-, fawch-, -on(e, -oun, (5 fauschune, fawchun, fouchon, fwalchon), 6–9 fauch-, faulch-, fawch-, -eon, -ion, (6 fachen, falcheon. 6–7 fau-, fawchin(e, 7 falchon, 8 faulchin), 7– falchion; also 5 fawken, 7 falcen, perh. by confusion with FALCON. [ME. *fauchoun*, a. OF. *fauchon* = It. *falcione*:—vulg. Lat. **falciōn-em*, f. L. *falci-*, *falx* sickle.]

1. A broad sword more or less curved with the edge on the convex side. In later use and in poetry: A sword of any kind.

1303 R. BRUNNE *Handl. Synne* 8645 Hys [the priest's] tung shuld be hys fauchoun. *c* **1380** *Sir Ferumb.* 2244 Lucafer..drow out a schort fachoun. *c* **1440** *York Myst.* xxxi. 246 Y trowe youre fauchone hym flaies. *a* **1533** LD. BERNERS *Huon* xlii. 141 He..toke a grete fawchon in his handes. *a* **1628** SIR J. BEAUMONT *Bosworth F.* 501 He lifts his Fauchion with a threatening Grace. **1720** GAY *Poems* (1745) I. 37 In the bright air the dreadful fauchion shone. **1808** SCOTT *Marm.* VI. xxvi, Spears shook, and faulchions flashed amain. **1852** KINGSLEY *Poems, Andromeda* 237 Curved on his thigh lay a falchion.

†**b.** ***single, double falchion, case of falchions***: various species of sword-play. *Obs.*

1708 J. CHAMBERLAYNE *St. Gt. Brit.* I. III. vii. (1743) 189 The nobility and gentry have..quarter-staff, single faulchion, double faulchion, etc. **1712** STEELE *Spect.* No. 436 ¶2 The several Weapons following, viz...Single Falchion, Case of Falchions, Quarter Staff. **1712** ARBUTHNOT *John Bull* I. v, He dreaded not old Lewis either at back-sword, single falchion, or cudgel-play.

attrib. **1489** CAXTON *Faytes of A.* II. xxvi. 138 Axes of werre facioned asswel after fawken wise as other. **1601** R. JOHNSON *Kingd. & Commw.* (1603) 159 A falcen sword after the Turkish fashion. **1667** PEPYS *Diary* (1879) IV. 330 His Knife..was with a falchion blade.

†**2.** = BILL *sb.*[1] 4 or BILL-HOOK. *Obs.*

1483 CAXTON *Gold. Leg.* 343/3 Other plowemen..folowed the wulf and with their staues and fauchons delyuerd the child hoole. **1596** DRAYTON *Legends* iii. 8 Let thy bright Fauchion lend Me Cypresse Boughes. **1664** H. MORE *Myst. Iniq.* 333 The Huntsman..with a wood-knife or faucheon at his side.

†ˈ**falchion**, *v. Obs. rare*[−1]. [f. prec. sb.] *trans.* To cut with a falchion, use a falchion upon.

1526 SKELTON *Magnyf.* 2216 Hold thy hande Or I shall fawchyn thy flesshe, and scrape the on the skyn.

Falcidian (fælˈsɪdɪən), *a.* [f. *Falcidius* + -AN.] In *Falcidian law* (*Lex Falcidia*), a law carried by P. Falcidius, which ordained that no Roman citizen should bequeath more than three-fourths of his estate away from his legal heirs. Hence ***Falcidian portion*** the fourth part thus reserved.

1656–81 in BLOUNT *Glossogr.* **1756** G. HARRIS tr. *Justinian's Inst.* II. xxii. 105 The Falcidian law was at length enacted. **1788** GIBBON *Decl. & F.* IV. xliv. 391 His successor..was empowered to retain the *Falcidian* portion.

falˈciferous, *a. Obs.*[−0] [f. L. *falc(i)-*, *falx* sickle + -FEROUS.] Carrying a sickle, scythe-bearing.

1656–81 in BLOUNT *Glossogr.* **1692–1732** in COLES.

falciform (ˈfælsɪfɔːm), *a.* [f. L. *falc-em* sickle + -(I)FORM.] Sickle-shaped, curved, hooked. Frequent in *Anat.*, as in ***falciform cartilage, ligament, process***, etc.

1766 PENNANT *Zool.* (1776) III. 236 Immediately behind this fin was another, tall and falciform. **1787** HUNTER in *Phil. Trans.* LXXVII 410 The right lobe is the largest..its falciform ligament broad. **1798** HOOPER *Med. Dict.*, *Falciform process*, the falx, a process of the dura mater, that arises from the crista galli, separates the hemispheres of the brain and terminates in the tentorium. **1836** TODD *Cycl. Anat.* I. 13 The fold which passes upwards towards the liver is falciform. **1838** *Blackw. Mag.* XLIII. 650 What a falciform..and warlike organ, leads the van of Wellington's warlike countenance!

falciparum (fælˈsɪpərəm). *Path.* [mod.L., f. L. *falc(i)-*, *falx* sickle + *-parum* (see -PAROUS).] The specific epithet of a protozoon of the genus *Plasmodium*, used *attrib.*, to designate a severe type of malaria caused by this protozoon, in which paroxysms recur at approximately two-day intervals. Also called *æstivoautumnal*, *malignant*, and *subtertian malaria*.

1930 M. F. BOYD *Introd. Malariology* ii. 49 The extent of gametocyte production appears to vary directly with the intensity of injection, at least in cases of *vivax* and *falciparum* infections. **1940** *Amer. Jrnl. Public Health* Apr. 410/1 New York City is an endemic area for the occurrence of falciparum malaria. **1952** P. F. RUSSELL *Malaria* 33 Acute falciparum malaria sometimes imitates other abdominal conditions such as pancreatitis..and acute appendicitis. **1965** *Listener* 18 Mar. 406/1 People who inherit a sickle cell gene..possess a greater resistance to falciparum malaria.

falcon (ˈfɔːlkən, ˈfɔːk(ə)n), *sb.* Forms: 3–4 faukun, 4 faucoun, -kon, -koun, 4 facoun, 4–7 faucon(e, 5–6 facon, 5–7 faw(l)con, -kon, (5 fawken), 6–8 faulcon, (7 -kon), 5– falcon. [ME. *faucon (faukun)*, a. OF. *faucon, falcun*, ad. late L. *falcōn-em*, *falco*, commonly believed to be f. *falc-*, *falx* sickle, the name being due to the resemblance of the hooked talons to a reaping-hook. Cf. It. *falcone*, Sp. *halcon*. In the 15th cent. the spelling was refashioned after Lat.]

1. *Ornith.* One of a family of the smaller diurnal birds of prey, characterized by a short hooked beak, powerful claws, and great destructive power; *esp.* one trained to the pursuit of other birds or game, usually the Peregrine Falcon (*Falco peregrinus*). In *Falconry*, applied only to the female, the male, being smaller and less adapted for the chase, is called the *tercel* or *tiercel*.

a **1250** *Owl & Night.* 101 That other ȝer a faukun bredde. **1362** LANGL. *P. Pl.* A. VII. 34 Fecche þe hom Faucons þe Foules to quelle. **1432–50** tr. *Higden* (Rolls) I. 335 Sparre-howke, ffawken, and gentille gossehawke. **1605** SHAKS. *Macb.* II. iv. 12 A Faulcon towring in her pride of place. **1653** WALTON *Angler* i. (1655) 11 It [Air] stops not the high soaring of my noble generous Falcon. **1735** SOMERVILLE *Chase* III. 94 As stoops the Falcon bold To pounce his Prey. *a* **1839** PRAED *Poems* (1864) I. 213 He laid a bet upon his falcon's flight. **1868** WOOD *Homes without H.* xxix. 561 The Great Grey Shrike was formerly used as a falcon.

b. with epithet defining the species.

1525 LD. BERNERS *Froiss.* II. xlvi, By comparyson as fawcons pelegrines. **1678** RAY *Willughby's Ornith.* 79 It is said to be lesser than a Peregrine Falcon. **1781** LATHAM *Hist. Birds* I. 54 White-rumped Bay Falcon. **1785** PENNANT *Arct. Zool.* II. 208 Plain Falcon. **1802** G. MONTAGU *Ornith. Dict.* 537 White Falcon, a name for the Jer Falcon. **1821** SELBY *Brit. Ornith.* I. 39 *Spotted Falcon*: a name for the Peregrine Falcon. **1875** W. MᶜILWRAITH *Guide Wigtownshire*, These cliffs are frequented by the Peregrine falcon.

2. A representation of a falcon.

1525 in Glasscock *Rec. St. Michael's Bp. Stortford* (1882) 39 For the scoryng..the facon and the branche before seynt mighill xiiijd. **1589** HAKLUYT *Voy.* (1600) III. 736 A..Gentleman, from whom our Generall tooke a Fawlcon of golde with a great Emeraud in the Breast thereof.

3. An ancient kind of light cannon.

[For the practice of naming species of fire-arms from birds of prey, cf. *musket*.]

1496 LD. BOTHWELL in Ellis *Orig. Lett.* I. 13. I. 31 Yᵉ provision of Ordinance..is bot litill..ij. great curtaldis..x. falconis or litill serpentinis. **1577–87** HARRISON *England*, II. xvi. (1877) 281 Falcon hath eight hundred pounds, and two inches and a half within the mouth. **1663** *Flagellum; or O. Cromwell* (1672) 103 Two demy Culverings..two Falcons. **1805** SCOTT *Last Minstr.* IV. xx, Falcon and culver on each tower. **1849** J. GRANT *Kirkaldy of Gr.* xv. 163 The royal stores furnished..falcons, or light six-pound field-pieces.

4. *Comb.* chiefly *attrib.*, as (sense 1) ***falcon-face, -fisher, -flight, -guise, -nest***; ***falcon-eyed*** adj.; ***falcon-like*** adj. and adv.; (sense 3) ***falcon shot***.

1847 TENNYSON *Princ.* II. 26 A quick brunette, well-moulded, *falcon-eyed. **1891** MISS DOWIE *Girl in Karp.* xiii. 171 He had the genuine '*falcon-face' of the Huculs. **1759** tr. *Adanson's Voy. Senegal* in Pinkerton *Voy.* (1814) XVI. 649 The *falcon-fisher..is a bird about the bigness of a goose. *a* **1835** MRS. HEMANS *Poems, Indian with dead Child*, The arrows of my father's bow Their *falcon-flight have sped. **1889** R. B. ANDERSON tr. *Rydberg's Teut. Mythol.* 60 In the Norse mythology..Freyja had a *falcon-guise. *a* **1649** DRUMM. OF HAWTH. *Elegy G. Adolphus* Wks. (1711) 54 With full plum'd wing thou *falcon-like could fly. **1852** READE *Peg Woff.* (1853) 88 To see her falcon-like stoop upon the stage. **1814** SCOTT *Ld. of Isles* IV. viii, Canna's tower..Like *falcon-nest o'erhung the bay. **1598** BARRET *Theor. Warres* V. iii. 134, 2 thousand *Falcon shot. **1600** HAKLUYT *Voy.* III. 714 It is within falcon-shot of the ships.

†ˈ**falcon**, *v. Obs. rare.* [f. prec. sb.] To hunt with falcons; to hawk.

1807 SIR R. WILSON *Jrnl.* 27 Aug., After dinner we went falconing.

falconer[1] (ˈfɔː(l)kənə(r), ˈfɔːk(ə)nə(r)). Forms: 4–6 fauconer, (4 faucounner, 4–5 faukener, -oner), 5 falconar(e, fawconer, -kener(e, 6 faconer, 6–8 faulk(e)ner, 7 faulconer, (fal-, faukner), 5– falconer. [a. OF. *fau(l)connier* (mod.F. *fauconnier*), f. *fau(l)con* FALCON *sb.*: see -ER[2].]

1. One who hunts with falcons, one who follows hawking as a sport.

c **1386** CHAUCER *Frankl. T.* 468 Thise ffauconers..with hir haukes han the heron slayn. **1593** *Bacchus Bountie* in *Harl. Misc.* (Malh.) II. 273 This youth was..a fine faulkner. *a* **1641** SUCKLING *Lett.* (1696) 93 Faulkners that can but seldom spring right Game, should [etc]. *c* **1720** PRIOR *Henry & Emma* 109 A Falk'ner Henry is, when Emma hawks. **1810** SCOTT *Lady of L.* III. xiv, The falconer tossed his hawk away. **1834** MᶜMURTRIE *Cuvier's Anim. Kingd.* 121 The Common Sparrowhawk..is employed..by falconers.

fig. **1581** J. BELL *Haddon's Answ. Osor.* 68 A malitious and hungry fawconer of titles & sillables.

2. A keeper and trainer of hawks. Also, as an official designation, ***Grand*** or †***Great Falconer***.

c **1440** *Promp. Parv.* 152 Fawkenere [PYNSON fawconer], *falconarius*. *c* **1450** *Bk. Curtasye* 563 in *Babees Bk.* 317 The chaunceler answeres..For ȝomen, faukeners, and hor horsyng. **1539** *Act 31 Hen. VIII*, c. 12 Some of his graces fauconers. **1619** SIR R. BOYLE *Diary* (1886) I. 226, I sent..a caste of marlyns..by his own ffawlconer. **1710** *Lond. Gaz.* No. 4711/2 The great Faulkner prepared a curious Artificial Firework for their Entertainment. **1797** BEWICK *Brit. Birds* (1847) I. 32 The Emperor of China in his sporting excursions..is usually attended by his grand falconer. **1848** LYTTON *Harold* VII. v, Behind him came his falconer and bard.

†ˈ**falconer**[2]. *Obs. rare.* In 6 fawconere, faulkner. [a. F. *fauconnière*, f. *faucon*: see FALCON *sb.*] A game-bag carried by falconers.

c **1570** *Pride & Lowl.* (1841) 47 It was a great bagge like a fawconere And hong upon his gyrdle by a ring. **1592** GREENE *Upst. Courtier* in *Harl. Misc.* (Malh.) II. 231 By his side, a great side pouch like a faulkner.

falconet (ˈfɔːkənɪt). Also 7 fau(l)conet. [In sense 1 ad. It. *falconetto* in same sense (= Sp.

falconete; cf. Fr. *fauconneau*), dim. of *falcone* FALCON; in sense 2 f. FALCON + -ET[1].]

1. A light piece of ordnance of various calibres, used in the sixteenth and seventeenth centuries.

1559 *Naval Report* in Froude *Hist. Eng.* (1881) VI. 168 (Culverins) minions (and) falconets. *a* **1642** SIR W. MONSON *Naval Tracts* III. (1704) 343/2 A Faulconet. The Bore 2 inches. **1647** NYE *Gunnery* 78 *Fauconets*. The mouth of the peece is 2 inches and a quarter high..the weight of the shot one pound 5 ounces. **1645** N. STONE *Enchir. Fortification* 54 A Falconet..carries a 6 pound ball. **1727** A. HAMILTON *New Acc. E. Ind.* I. x. 108 Planting little Falconets on the top of our Walls in Swivels. **1864** BURTON *Scot Abr.* II. ii. 142 With only a couple of falconets or two-pounders, as their whole artillery.

2. A pygmy falcon, especially one belonging to the genus *Microhierax*.

1851 *Cuvier's Anim. Kingd.* 180 The Crested Falconet (*Lanius frontatus*)..inhabits New Holland. *Ibid.*, The falconets have a compressed beak almost as high as long. **1883** E. W. OATES *Birds Brit. Burmah* II. 212 *Micro-hierax fringillarius*, the Black-legged Falconet. *Ibid.* 213 The Black-legged Falconet occurs in Tenasserim. **1931** *Discovery* Nov. 348/1 The black-legged falconet (which breeds in holes). **1961** O. L. AUSTIN *Birds of World* 83/2 The falconets, or pygmy falcons, of the subfamily Poliohieracinae occur in South America, Malaya, the Philippines, and Africa. **1964** FISHER & PETERSON *World of Birds* 31/2 The Falconidae include..the tiny insect-hawking falconets, not much bigger than sparrows.

'falcon-'gentle. Also 5 falcon gent. [After F. *faucon gentil.*] The female of the peregrine falcon.

1393 GOWER *Conf.* III. 147 As a gentil faucon soreth. *c* **1400** MAUNDEV. (1839) xxii. 238 Gerfacouns, sparehaukes, faukons gentyls. *c* **1435** *Torr. Portugal* 479 Torent..Get her a facon jent. **1486** *Bk. St. Alban's* D iij b, Ther is a Fawken gentill and a Tercell gentill. **1615** CHAPMAN *Odyss.* XIII. 136 Nor her winged speed The falcon-gentle could for pace exceed. **1774** GOLDSM. *Nat. Hist.* (1862) I. II. iii. 314 The falcon gentle, with which, when properly trained, they go forth on horseback.

falconine ('fælkənaɪn), *a. Zool.* [f. L. *falcōn-em* falcon + -INE.] Like a falcon or hawk, belonging to the *Falconidæ*.

In mod. Dicts.

'falconish, *a. rare.* [f. FALCON *sb.* + -ISH.] Like a falcon; proper to or characteristic of a falcon.

1587 HOLINSHED *Chron.* III. 193/1 The legat Guallo..vpon a falkonish or wooluish appetite fleeced the church. **1833** CARLYLE *Crit. & Misc. Ess.* in *Wks.* (1869) IV. 351 The vulturous and falconish character of our Isle.

falconry ('fɔːkənrɪ). [a. F. *fauconnerie*: see FALCON and -RY.] **a.** The branch of knowledge concerned with the sport of hawking, and the breeding and training of hawks. **b.** Occasionally, the practice of hawking.

a. 1575 TURBERVILLE (*title*) The Booke of Falconrie. **1626** T. H. tr. *Caussin's Holy Crt.* 62 You haue a certayne bird in the mistery of Faulconry, called the Hobby. *a* **1682** SIR T. BROWNE *Tracts* 117 The Greeks understood little or nothing of our falconry. **1828** SIR J. S. SEBRIGHT *Observ. Hawking* 1 The Art of Falconry is in danger of being entirely lost.

b. 1818 HALLAM *Mid. Ages* ix. §1 (ed. 2) III. 361 Falconry ..became from the fourth century an equally delightful occupation. **1869** GILLMORE *Reptiles & Birds* 206 Falconry afforded a..picturesque sport to the great.

falculate ('fælkjʊleɪt), *a.* [f. L. *falcula*, dim. of *falc-*, *falx* sickle + -ATE.] Resembling a little sickle in form, small and curved.

1847 TODD *Cycl. Anat.* III. 329/1 Others [of the Marsupials] are digitigrade with falculate claws.

fald, obs. f. of FOLD.

faldage ('fældɪdʒ). *Law.* [ad. law-L. *faldāgium*, f. OE. *fald*, FOLD *sb.*[1] In 16th c. anglicized as FOLDAGE.] An old privilege by which a lord of the manor could set up folds in any fields within the manor, in which his tenants were obliged to put their sheep, the object being to manure the land.

1692–1732 COLES, *Faldage*, the Lords liberty of folding his tenants' sheep. **1708** *Termes de la Ley* 330 This Faldage in some places is termed Fold-course or Free-fold. **1865** NICHOLS *Britton* II. 373 His right of faldage, i.e. to have the tenant's sheep to manure his land.

‖**fal'della.** *Obs.* [med.L., a. It. *faldella* in same sense, dim. of *falda* fold of cloth, skirt.] (See quot. 1753.)

c **1400** *Lanfranc's Cirurg.* 317 Leie þerupon faldellas wiþ white of an ey. **1753** CHAMBERS *Cycl. Supp.*, *Faldella*, a word used by some of the writers in surgery for a sort of compress made of list contorted together in several doubles.

falderal, folderol (ˌfældə'ræl, ˌfɒldə'rɒl). Also fal de rol.

1. As a meaningless refrain in songs.

1701 FARQUHAR *Sir H. Wildair* IV. ii. Wks. (Rtldg.) 554/2 Wildair [sings] Fal, al, deral! [**1864** BROWNING *Mr. Sludge* Fol-de-rol-de-rido liddle iddle-ol].

2. A gewgaw, trifle; a flimsy thing.

c **1820** HOGG *Basil Lee* in *Tales & Sk.* (1837) III. 56 'He'll flee frae ae falderall til anither a' the days o' his life.' **1879** E. GARRETT *House by Works* II. 154 That his darling might never want for fal-de-rals. **1881** MRS. C. PRAED *Policy & P.* I. 118 The little piebald is far too 'cute to trust her legs on that English fal-deral [a rickety fancy bridge].

attrib. **1861** SALA *Dutch Pict.* vi. 67 None of your fal-de-ral lavender boots, but rigid, unmistakeable shoes.

Hence ˌ**falde'ral** *v.*, in phr. *to falderal it*: to sing falderal, to sing unmeaning sounds.

1825 L. HUNT *Poems, Redi Bacchus* 426 Falderallalling it With quips and triple rhymes.

‖**faldetta** (fal'dɛtə). Also in quasi-Fr. form faldette. [It. *faldetta*, dim. of *falda*: see FALDELLA.] A combined hood and cape, worn by women in Malta.

1834 SIR F. B. HEAD *Bubbles fr. Brunnen* 191 Women, semi-shrouded in their black silk faldettes. **1866** BLACKMORE *Cr. Nowell* xii (1881) 48 A maiden with the love dream nestling beneath the bridal faldetta. **1883** C. D. WARNER *Roundabout Journ.* xiii. 119 All the Maltese ladies..wear the *faldetta* to church.

†**'faldfee.** *Obs. rare*[−1]. In 3 (?) faldfey. [app. f. OE. *fald*, FOLD *sb.*[1] + *feoh* (see FEE).] Some kind of manorial dues.

The record quoted by Blount has not been identified; it is not the *Liber Niger Scaccarii.* Possibly there is some error.

?*a* **1300** *Liber Niger* Heref. fol. 158 (Blount) W. M. tenet novem acras terræ Custumariæ in Bosbury..et debet quasdam consuetudines, viz. Tak & Toll & Faldfey. **1679** BLOUNT *Anc. Ten.* 155 This Faldfey might signify a fee or rent paid by the Tenant to his Lord for leave to fold his Sheep on his own ground. **1706** in PHILLIPS (ed. Kersey). **1809** in TOMLINS *Law Dict.* **1848** in WHARTON *Law Lex.*

†**'falding.** *Obs.* A kind of coarse woollen cloth; frieze.

c **1386** CHAUCER *Prol.* 391 In a gowne of faldyng to the kne. **1436** *Pol. Poems* (1859) II. 186 Irish wollen, lynyn cloth, faldynge..bene here marchaundyse. **1523** FITZHERB. *Husb.* §44 A pece..of faldynge, or suche a softe cloth.

attrib. **1392** *Test. Ebor.* (Surtees) I. 174 Item lego patri meo..meam armilausam, videlicet faldyng-clok.

b. A covering or garment of the same.

c **1386** CHAUCER *Miller's T.* 26 His presse i-covered with a faldyng reed. **1387** TREVISA *Higden* (Rolls) I. 353 Blak faldynges instede of mantels and of clokes. *c* **1440** *Promp. Parv.* 147 Faldynge, clothe..*amphibalus.* **1526** *Lanc. Wills* (Chetham Soc.) 13, I gyff to Alice Legh..my best typett my faldyng and my bok in the church.

†**fal'distory.** *Obs.* Also 8 faldisdory. [ad. med.L. *faldistori-um*, var. of *faldistolium*: see FALDSTOOL.] The seat or throne of a bishop within the chancel.

1675 PLUME *Life Bp. Hacket* (1865) 82 The Reverend Bishop came to the faldistory in the middle of the choir. **1722** SPARROW *Bk. Com. Prayer* 273 A Faldistory is the Episcopal Seat or Throne within the Chancel. **1768** E. BUYS *Dict. Terms Art*, *Faldisdory*, the Bishop's Seat, or Throne within the Chancel. **1848** in WHARTON *Law Lex.*

faldore, var. of FALL-DOOR.

faldstool ('fɔːldstuːl). See also FALDISTORY. [ad. med.L. *faldistoli-um*, ad. OHG. *faldstuol* lit. 'a folding seat or campstool', f. *faldan* to fold + *stuol* seat, chair: see FOLD and STOOL. Cf. FAUTEUIL. The OE. *fyldestól* has been explained as from Lat. or Rom. (with umlaut of the vowel of the first syll. due to the euphonic *i* prefixed in Romanic to a syllable beginning with *st-*) but cf. the gloss 'volumina, fyldas' in *Zeitschrift f. deutsches Alterthum*, IX. 494.]

1. *Eccl.* An armless chair used by bishops and other prelates when they do not occupy the throne or when officiating in any but their own church.

c **1050** *Abbo Glosses* in *Ztsch. f. dtsches Alt.* XXXI. 10 Forbuh ðu twyhweolne siȝe onfoh þu fyldestol [*c* **1100** fældestol]. [**1340** *Ayenb.* 239 Þer he yzeȝ ane gratne dyeuel þet zet ope ane uyealdinde stole and al his mayne aboute him.] **1849** ROCK *Ch. of Fathers* II. vi. 256 In later times..the faldstool was 'a chair of woode covered with crymsen velvet'.

2. A movable folding-stool or desk at which worshippers kneel during certain acts of devotion; *esp.* one used by the sovereign at the ceremony of coronation.

1603 *Ceremon. at Coron. Jas. I* (1685) 3 A Fald-stool, with Cushions for the King to pray at. **1685** *St. George's Day* 6 The King kneeled at a fald-stool. *a* **1693** ASHMOLE *Antiq. Berks.* (1719) I. 10 A Judge in his Robes, kneeling at a Faldstool. **1838** *Form Coronation* in Maskell *Mon. Rit.* (1847) III. 86 The Queen..kneeling at the Faldstool set for Her. **1851** KINGSLEY *Yeast* ii, She turned and prayed at her velvet faldstool. **1862** GOULBURN *Pers. Relig.* (1864) 66 When we fail to derive from Prayer comfort and satisfaction, we become cowards, and run away from the faldstool.

3. A small desk at which the Litany is appointed to be said or sung; a Litany-stool.

a **1626** BP. ANDREWES in W. Nichols *Comm. Bk. Com. Prayer* Notes (1710) 23 The Priest..(at a low Desk before the Chancel-door, called the Fald-stool) kneels and says or sings the Litany. **1838** *Form Consecration* in Maskell *Mon. Rit.* (1847) III. 90 Then followeth the Litany to be read by two Bishops..kneeling at a Faldstool. **1869** *Daily News* 22 Dec., The Litany was chanted by two of the minor canons at a faldstool. **1874** MICKLETHWAITE *Mod. Par. Ch.* 45 The small desk for the Litany to be said from, generally miscalled the Faldstool.

†**fale,** *sb.*[1] *Obs.* [Of obscure origin; it has been conjectured to be a subst. use of OE. *fǽle* dear: see FELE *a.*[2]] App. = 'comrade, fellow'.

c **1380** *Sir Ferumb.* 1845 Let anoþer ys message telle, & stond þou þer by þy fale.

‖**fale** ('faleɪ), *sb.*[2] [Samoan.] A house of the type built by the Samoans (see quot. 1959); also *transf.* (see quot. 1966).

1902 L. P. CHURCHILL *Samoa 'Uma* iii. 36 Her [*sc.* a Samoan woman's] house ceases to be *fale*, but becomes *maota*, a mansion. **1959** A. MCLINTOCK *Descr. Atlas N.Z.* 81 The Samoan *fale* with its compounded floor, open sides, and leaf-thatch roof is admirably suited to the climate [of Samoa]. **1961** C. C. MARSACK *Samoan Medley* i. 18 The houses are almost without exception the Samoan type of *fale*, a thatched roof standing on posts, open on all sides and with no interior partitions. **1966** *Courier Mail* (Brisbane) 21 Jan. 11 No grass hut here, but a luxurious six-bed holiday home... This is the first of 10 'fales'—Samoan houses—being built on..Fraser Island, off the Queensland coast... The fale is fitted with hot and cold water, [etc.].

†**fale,** *a. Obs.*

c **1325** *E.E. Allit. P.* C. 92 Þaȝ þe fader þat hym formed were fale of his hele.

fale, obs. f. of FALLOW.

fale, var. of FELE *a.*[1] *Obs.* many.

Falern(e (fə'lɜːn), *a.* and *sb.* Chiefly *poet.* [ad. L. (*vinum*) *Falern-um.*] = next.

1601 HOLLAND *Pliny* I. 420 He likewise gaue away a largesse of wine as well Chian as Falern. [**1671** MILTON *P.R.* IV. 117 Their wines of Setia, Cales, and Falerne.] **1703** J. PHILIPS *Splendid Shilling* 34 Wines, that well may vie With Massic, Setin, or renown'd Falern.

Falernian (fə'lɜːnɪən), *a.* [f. as prec. + -IAN.] Of or pertaining to the *ager Falernus* in Campania, which produced a celebrated wine. Also *absol.*, Falernian wine.

1726 AMHERST *Terræ Fil.* i. 2 Whose lady kiss'd Damon the butler behind a hogshead of falernian. *a* **1764** LLOYD *Dial.* Poet. Wks. 1774 II. 6 Gen'rous liquor..Broach'd from the rich Falernian tun. **1842** LYTTON *Zanoni* 29 Vineyards famous for the old Falernian. **1884** MRS. ROSS in *Longm. Mag.* Feb. 404 White Falernian [wine] is excellent.

falewe, obs. f. of FALLOW.

Faliscan (fə'lɪskən), *sb.* and *a.* Also -ian. [f. L. *Falisc-us* + -AN.] **A.** *sb.* **a.** A native or inhabitant of the ancient Etrurian city of Falerii. **b.** The dialect or language of Falerii and its environs, or its alphabet, of Etruscan origin. **B.** *adj.* Of or pertaining to Falerii, its inhabitants, dialect, or produce.

1600 HOLLAND *Livy* v. 197 It was the manner amongst the Faliscians, to entertaine..one that should both teach and instruct them [*sc.* their children] in schoole. **1686** tr. *Roman Hist. written in Latine by Titus Livius* VII. xvii. 183 The whole Nation of the Tuscans took Arms, and led on by the ..Faliscans, were advanced as far as Salinae. *Ibid.* 'Table', Faliscan Priests with flaming Torches. **1875** *Encycl. Brit.* I. 610/2 The second [family of Italian alphabets contains] the Latin and Faliscan... These three languages are all written from right to left, in which the Faliscan agrees with them. **1883** I. TAYLOR *Alphabet* II. 127 The Faliscan and the Latin [alphabets], wedged in between the Etruscan and the Oscan. **1932** *Times Lit. Suppl.* 21 July 530/4 The last five plates figure Italian fabrics, Faliscan, Apulian and Campanian. **1965** W. S. ALLEN *Vox Latina* iii. 64 A Faliscan inscription.

falk (fɔːk), *sb.* Also 9 faik, fauk. A name applied dial. to one of the three species of the Auk; the Razor-bill.

1698 M. MARTIN *Voy. St. Kilda* 61 The Bird, by the inhabitants called the Falk, the Rasor-Bill in the West of England. **1766** PENNANT *Zool.* (1768) II. 148 Razor-bill. The Falk. **1806** P. NEILL *Tour Orkney & Shetland* 197 Bawkie, Razor-bill, Alca Torda. In the Hebrides this bird is called Falk or faik.

falk, obs. form of FAIK *v.*[2] *Sc.*

†**'falked,** *a. Obs. rare.* = FALCATE.

1597 GERARD *Herbal* II. xxxiv. (1633) 299 Crooked or falked hawkeweed hath leaves..slightly indented.

fall (fɔːl), *sb.*[1] Forms: 3 fael, 3 *south.* væl, val, 3–7 fal, 4–7 falle, 6 faule, fawle, foll, 8–9 *Sc.* fa', faw, 3– fall. [f. FALL *v.*: cf. OFris. *fal*, *fel* masc., OS., OHG. *fal*, ON. *fall* neut. The synonymous OE. *fiell*, *fyll* (:—**falli-z*), f. same root, did not survive into ME., unless it be represented by the forms *fæl*, *væl* in Layamon.] An act or instance of falling.

I. A falling from a height.

1. a. A dropping down from a high or relatively high position, by the force of gravity. *to ride for a fall*: see RIDE *v.* 1 d.

c **1200** *Ormin* 11862 Full hefiȝ fall to fallenn. *a* **1225** *Leg. Kath.* 2322 Nis nawt grislich sihðe to seon fallen þæt þing þæt schal arisen, þurh þæt fal, a þusentfalt te fehere. **1393** GOWER *Conf.* I. 15 Betwene two stooles is the fall. **1553** T. WILSON *Rhet.* (1580) 154 An other pitiyng his fall, asked him ..how got you into that pitte? **1563** FULKE *Meteors* 8 By the fall of them [the starres], both thunder and lightning are caused. **1599** SHAKS. *Pass. Pilgr.* 136 A green plum that..falls..before the fall should be. **1667** MILTON *P.L.* I. 76 The companions of his fall..He soon discerns. **1748** F. SMITH *Voy. Disc. N.-W. Pass.* I. 151 One of them, by a Fall from the Parapet at the Top of the Factory, was killed. **1850** TENNYSON *In Mem.* xi. 14 These leaves that redden to the fall. **1851** GREENWELL *Coal-trade Terms Northumb. & Durh.* 25 *Fall*, a dropping down of the roof stone. **1860** TYNDALL *Glac.* I. xi. 84 Fixing my feet suddenly in the snow, [I] endeavoured to check his fall. **1863** KINGSLEY *Water-bab.*

297 That was all in his day's work like a fair fall with the hounds.

b. *fig.*; *esp.* a descent from high estate or from moral elevation.

c **1230** *Hali Meid.* 15 Se herre degre se þe fal is wurse. *c* **1430** *Syr Gener.* (Roxb.) 53 Min hert so high set haue I, A fall I drede to haue therby! **1526** *Pilgr. Perf.* (W. de W. 1531) 6b, Whom they moost auaunce..they..gyue them the greater fall. **1679** Burnet *Hist. Ref.* an. 1543 I. III. 326 Doctor London..did now, upon Cromwell's fall, apply himself to Gardiner. **1780** Harris *Philol. Enq.* Wks. (1841) 454 The fall of these two empires. **1827** Hallam *Const. Hist.* (1876) III. xvii. 333 The fall of the Stuarts. **1874** Green *Short Hist.* viii. 582 Puritanism..drew..a nobler life from its very fall.

c. *concr.* That which falls; also *pl.*

1742 Young *Nt. Th.* IX. 63 Nor shall the present year..spread of feeble life a thinner fall. **1844** *Jrnl. R. Agric. Soc.* V. I. 268 The short and broken [straw]..goes away in what is technically termed 'falls' or pulls. **1890** *Pall Mall G.* 11 Mar. 4/2 To clear away a 'fall', some of the blocks of coal in which were as large as trucks.

d. A descent of rain, hail, snow, meteors, etc.; the quantity that falls at one time or in a certain period. Cf. RAINFALL.

1593 Shaks. *Lucr.* 551 Some gentle gust..Hindering their [vapours'] present fall by this dividing. **1634** Sir T. Herbert *Trav.* (1638) 128 Raine in..violent irruptions: dangerous..in the fall. **1749** F. Smith *Voy. Disc. N.-W. Pass.* II. 20 A very great Fall of Hail, Snow, and Sleet. **1814** D. H. O'Brien *Captiv. & Escape* 178 The flood was very rapid from the late falls of rain. **1833** *Penny Cycl.* I. 151/1 Aërolites, when taken up soon after their fall, are extremely hot. **1858** Longf. *Children* iii, The wind of Autumn, And the first fall of the snow. **1871** Lockyer *Astron.* iii. §316. 139 Among the largest aërolitic falls of modern times we may mention the following.

concr. **1878** Huxley *Physiogr.* 63 A fall of snow thus acts like a mantle of fur thrown over the earth.

e. The coming down, approach, first part (of night, twilight, winter, etc.). *rare.* Cf. NIGHTFALL.

1655 Earl Orrery *Parthen.* (1676) 674 Fifteen thousand Horse and Foot were sent..about fall of the Night. **1661** Lovell *Hist. Anim. & Min.* 229 They are best..at the fall and dead of Winter. **1816** Keats *Poems, To my Brothers*, The love so voluble and deep, That aye at fall of night our care condoles. **1823** Byron *Juan* VII. lvi, Towards the twilight's fall.

†**f.** Shedding, effusion (of blood). *Obs.*

1599 Shaks. *Hen. V*, I. ii. 25 Neuer two such Kingdomes did contend, Without much fall of blood.

†**g.** The dropping out (of teeth). *Obs.*

1520 *Calisto & Melib.* in Hazl. *Dodsley* I. 78 Hollowness of mouth, fall of teeth, faint of going.

†**h.** The downward stroke (of a sword. etc.).

1594 Shaks. *Rich. III*, v. iii. 111 Put in their hands thy bruising irons of wrath, That they may crush down with a heavy fall The usurping helmets of our adversaries. **1604** —— *Oth.* II. iii. 324, I heard the clink and fall of swords.

2. (In early use also more fully ***fall of the leaf***.) That part of the year when leaves fall from the trees; autumn. In N. Amer. the ordinary name for autumn; in England now rare in literary use, though found in some dialects; ***spring and fall***, ***the fall of the year***, are, however, in fairly common use.

1545 Ascham *Toxoph.* I. (Arb.) 48 Spring tyme, Somer, faule of the leafe, and winter. **1599** Raleigh *Reply to Marlowe* Poems (Aldine ed.) 11 A honey tongue, a heart of gall Is fancies spring, but sorrows fall. *a* **1631** Capt. Smith *Eng. Improvement Revived* III. (1673) 59 The best time to..remove younger trees is at..the fall of the leaf. **1664** Evelyn *Sylva* (1679) 15 His..leaves..becoming yellow at the fall, do commonly clothe it all the winter. **1697** H. Kelsey *Papers* (1929) 95 Thos. Bullears boy..died of ye rivers mouth last fall. **1714** Luttrell *Brief Rel.* (1857) VI. 726 In the spring and fall he was alwaies disturbed. **1752** J. Edwards *Wks.* (1834) I. p. cxcv/1, I thank you for your letter..which I received this fall. **1767** *Quebec Gaz.* 5 Jan. 3/1 A few barrels of pickeled *cod fish*, taken..last Fall. **1826** Scott *Mal. Malagr.* i. 10 She has been bled and purged, spring and fall. **1846** J. Baxter *Libr. Pract. Agric.* (ed. 4) II. 379 The winter pruning should be performed..at the fall of the leaf. **1849** J. E. Alexander *L'Acadie* II. i. 10 A week at Loughborough in the 'fall' is delightful. **1851** Carlyle *Sterling* I. xi. (1872) 67 His first child..was born there..in the fall of that year 1831. **1862** Merivale *Rom. Emp.* (1865) VI. xlvii. 38 It was in the fall of the year..that Agrippa sailed for the East. **1864** Lowell *Biglow P.* Poet. Wks. (1879) 255 Frosts have been unusually backward this fall. **1922** C. E. Montague *Disenchantment* ix. 132 The fall of the leaf had brought, too, a sad shortage of heroes. **1936** D. McCowan *Anim. Canad. Rockies* xi. 99 In the Rockies they stay out until quite late in the fall.

fig. **1727** *Philip Quarll* (1816) 82 In the fall of life how sweet's repose.

3. a. The manner in which anything falls. **b.** *Cards.* The manner in which the cards are dealt.

1535 Coverdale *Prov.* xvi. 33 The lottes are cast in to the lappe, but their fall stondeth in the Lorde. **1885** Proctor *Whist* iv. 60 The fall of the cards in the first suit may..lead him to do so.

4. Birth or production by dropping from the parent; the quantity born or produced.

1796 *Hull Advertiser* 14 May 1/4 The largest fall of lambs this year almost ever known. **1831** Howitt *Seasons* 72 The principal fall of lambs takes place now. **1865** J. G. Bertram *Harvest of Sea* (1873) 236 The greatest fall of spawn ever known in England occurred forty-six years ago.

II. A sinking to a lower level.

5. a. A sinking down, subsidence (*esp.* of waves and the like); the ebb (of the tide). Also, the setting (of the sun, stars, etc.), *arch.*; †the alighting (of a bird). †***to be at fall***: to be in a low condition.

1571 Hanmer *Chron. Irel.* (1633) 128 The sunne..holdeth his course to his fall. **1586** A. Day *Eng. Secretary* I. (1625) 24 What rising, and deepest falls of waves..doth he there relate. **1598** Chapman *Iliad* II. 396 In their falls [fowl] lay out such throats, that [etc.]. **1607** Shaks. *Timon* II. ii. 214 Now they are at fall, want Treature. **1830** Lyell *Princ. Geol.* I. 264 The perpendicular rise and fall of the spring-tides. **1868-70** Morris *Earthly Par.* (1890) 168/2 The wide sun reddened towards his fall.

fig. **1672** Temple *Ess. Govt.* Wks. 1731 I. 104 Modes of Government have all their Heights and their Falls.

b. *Astrol.* (See quot.)

1676 Lilly *Anima Astrologiæ* 10 When a Planet is joyned to another in his Declension or Fall; that is, in Opposition to its own House or Exaltation. **1819** in J. Wilson *Dict. Astrol.* 99. **1835** in 'Zadkiel' *Lilly's Introd. Astrol.* 337.

c. *fig.* Decline, decay.

c **1645** Howell *Lett.* I. II. xv. 23 Amsterdam..rose upon the fall of this Town [Antwerp]. **1682** Otway *Venice Preserved* IV. i, Remember him that prop'd the fall of Venice. **1864** *Glasgow Herald* 12 Nov., A country that was in the utmost state of fall and degradation.

d. The decline or closing part (of a day, year, life). Also rarely, ***fall of day*** = the west.

1628 Venner *Baths of Bathe* 7 The declining or Fall of the year. **1712** Blackmore *Creation* 98 Th' adventurous merchant thus pursues his way Or to the rise or to the fall of day. **1800-24** Campbell *Poems, Caroline* II. *To Evening Star* v, Sacred to the fall of day, Queen of propitious stars. **1882** Besant *Revolt of Man* i. (1883) 8 The older pictures were mostly the heads of men, taken in the fall of life.

6. The discharge or disemboguement of a river; †the place where this occurs, the mouth.

1577-87 Harrison *Descr. Brit.* xii. in Holinshed 53 The greatest rivers, into whose mouthes or falles shippes might find safe entrance. **1705** Addison *Italy* 113 The Po..before its Fall into the Gulf..receives..the most considerable Rivers of Piemont.

7. a. The falling of a stream of water down a declivity; hence, a cascade, cataract, waterfall. Frequent in *pl.*, as in *Falls of the Clyde*, *Niagara*, etc.

1579 Spenser *Sheph. Cal.* Apr. 36 His laye..he made..And tuned it vnto the Waters fall. **1632** Lithgow *Trav.* VII. 318 The fall and roaring of Nyle. **1674** N. Fairfax *Bulk & Selv.* 185 The shallow waters that drill between the pebbles in the Falls of Guiny or Africa. **1726** Shelvocke *Voy. round World* (1757) 265 The fall of waters, which one hears all around. **1756-7** tr. *Keysler's Trav.* (1760) I. 9 Of the falls in the Rhine, near Schaffhausen. **1787** Best *Angling* (ed. 2) 30 It is good angling..at the falls of mills. **1806** *Gazetteer Scot.* (ed. 2) 92 The falls of Clyde principally interest the stranger. **1832** Ht. Martineau *Life in Wilds* ix. 116 On that fall of the stream will be our mill. **1872** Raymond *Statist. Mines & Mining* 198 The roar of the falls is heard in the distance.

†**b.** That over which water falls. *Obs.*

1749 F. Smith *Voy. Disc. N.-W. Pass.* II. 26 Some Pieces [of ice] stopped upon a Fall or Ridge of Stone.

†**c.** ***fall of a bridge***: cf. quot. 1880.

1626 Bacon *Sylva* §115 Waters, when they..are strained (as in the falls of Bridges). [**1880** Walmisley *Bridges over Thames* 6 The resistance caused to the free ebb and flow of a large body of water by the contraction of its channel produced a fall or rapid under the bridge.]

8. a. Downward direction or trend of a surface or outline; a deviation, sudden or gradual, in a downward direction from the general level; a slope or declivity.

1565-73 Cooper *Thesaurus, Abruptum*..that hath such a fal or stipenesse downe, that a man cannot go but fall downe. **1601** Holland *Pliny* II. 615 Neither doth this circle shine in the concauitie or in the fall of the gem. **1712** J. James tr. *Le Blond's Gardening* 194 A small insensible Fall should be given these Channels. **1755** Gray *Lett.* Wks. 1884 II. 265 A natural terrass three mile long..with a gradual fall on both sides. **1832** Scott *Jrnl.* (1890) II. 465 Stocked with wild animals towards the fall of the hills. **1847** Marryat *Childr. N. Forest* xxvii, The symmetrical fall of the shoulders. **1858** *Jrnl. R. Agric. Soc.* XIX. I. 188 Most of the Weald lands have a good fall for draining. **1865** Baring-Gould *Werewolves* vii. 87 The girls..saw a little fall in the ground.

b. The distance through which anything descends, whether suddenly or gradually; the difference in the levels (of ground, water, etc.).

1686 Burnet *Trav.* iv. 238 The Tarpeian Rock is now of so small a fall, that a Man would think it no great matter..to leap over it. **1712** J. James tr. *Le Blond's Gardening* 191 You..know exactly what Fall there is from the Top of the Hill..to the Bottom. **1739** Labelye *Short Acc. Piers Westm. Bridge* 11 The perpendicular Height of the Fall that might be expected under a Bridge. **1774** Goldsm. *Nat. Hist.* (1776) I. 223 Its waters are..poured down, by a fall of an hundred and fifty feet perpendicular. **1881** Salter *Guide Thames* 9 Hart's Weir..has a fall of 3 ft.

c. *Naut.* (See quots.)

1644 Manwaring *Seaman's Dict.* 38 When we mention the Falls of a ship..it is meant by the raising or laying some part of the Deck higher, or lower then the other. **1680** *Lond. Gaz.* No. 1526/4 The Adventure Pink, Dogger built, two Decks, with a Fall where the Windles stand. *c* **1850** *Rudim. Navig.* (Weale) 117 *Fall*, the descent of a deck from a fair curve lengthwise..to give height to the commander's cabin, and sometimes forward at the hawse-holes.

9. The sinking down of the fluid in a meteorological instrument. Said also of temperature, and loosely of the instrument itself.

1806 Gregory *Dict. Arts & Sc.* I. 204 The principal cause of the rise and fall of the mercury is from the variable winds. **1815** T. Forster *Atmos. Phenom.* 228 The rise of the thermometer..accompanies the fall of the barometer. **1823** Scoresby *Jrnl.* 30 The most remarkable fall of temperature I ever witnessed. **1864** *Nat. Hist. Trans. Northumb. & Durh.* I. 119 The violent falls in the barometer were not attended by corresponding disturbance of the air.

10. *Mus.* A sinking down or lowering of the note or voice; cadence.

1601 Shaks. *Twel. N.* I. i. 4 That straine agen, it had a dying fall. **1634** Milton *Comus* 251 At every fall smoothing the raven down Of darkness. **1706** A. Bedford *Temple Mus.* ix. 186 A fall in Musick, and then a rising again to the same sound. **1760** Beattie *Hermit* ii, Why..Philomela, that languishing fall? **1855** Bain *Senses & Int.* III. ii. §14 The echo of one of the falls of an old utterance. **1879** Geo. Eliot *Coll. Breakf. P.* 682 Mortal sorrows..Are dying falls to melody divine.

11. A sinking down or reduction in price, value, etc.; depreciation.

c **1555** Edw. VI *Jrnl.* (1884) 39 There was a Proclamation fighed [signed] for shortening of the fall of the Mony. **1614** Bp. Hall *Recoll. Treat.* 127 Another..hanging himselfe for the fall of the market. *a* **1687** Petty *Pol. Arith.* (1690) 99 The natural fall of Interest, is the effect of the increase of Mony. **1708** J. Chamberlayne *St. Gt. Brit.* I. II. xiii. (1743) 126 By the great fall of Monies now, the Sheriffs authority..is much diminished. **1814** *Stock Exchange Laid Open* 5 The speculator..anxiously looks for a fall. **1845** McCulloch *Taxation* II. xi. (1852) 380 The remarkable fall..in the prices of corn. **1848** Macaulay *Hist. Eng.* I. 189 A sudden fall of rents took place.

III. A falling from the erect posture.

12. A falling to the ground: **a.** of persons. *spec.* A descent to the floor in the technique of modern dancing.

a **1300** *Cursor M.* 537 (Cott.) Hijs fete him bers up fra fall. *c* **1440** *Promp. Parv.* 147 Fal, *casus, lapsus.* **1576** Fleming *Panopl. Epist.* 285 They cannot avoyd the fall whereof they be in danger. **1632** Lithgow *Trav.* III. 82 Onely apprehended by a fall in his flight. **1809** W. Irving *Knickerb.* (1861) 224 Risingh..hastened to take advantage of the hero's fall. **1853** Lytton *My Novel* III. ii, He felt the shock of his fall the more, after the few paces he had walked. **1949** Shurr & Yocom *Mod. Dance* v. 174 This fall requires a strong contraction of hip and abdominal muscles. *Ibid.* 190 The use of the floor as a momentary base in a total movement sequence of fall and recovery.

b. of a building, etc.; *fig.* of an institution, etc.

a **1300** *Cursor M.* 28853 (Cott.) A wall bateild fast wit-vten fall. **1535** Coverdale *Matt.* vii. 27 That housse..fell, and great was the fall of it. **1576** Fleming *Panopl. Epist.* 282 Some are slaine with the soudaine ruine and fall of a bancke. **1661** J. Childrey *Brit. Bacon.* 131 And the Elegies they commonly sing at their [stately Piles'] fall. **1756-7** tr. *Keysler's Trav.* (1760) II. 447 He relates the fall of one of these wooden structures at Fidena. **1841** Lane *Arab. Nts.* I. 109 The other by a fall of a house.

c. *spec.* of a wicket in Cricket.

1871 'Thomsonby' *Cricketers in Council* 30 Swiping..or rushing far out of your ground to meet the ball..are equally certain to result in the ultimate fall of your wicket. **1966** J. Arlott in B. Johnston *Armchair Cricket 1966* 9 Every run and fall of a wicket.

d. *Tennis.* (See quot.)

1900 G. E. A. Ross in A. E. T. Watson *Young Sportsman* 609 The second contact of the ball with the floor, called the *fall* of the ball, at any point where chase-lines are painted.

13. *Wrestling.* The fact of being thrown on one's back by an opponent; hence, a bout at wrestling. Phrases, ***to give, shake*** (*Sc.*), ***try, wrestle a fall***. *lit.* and *fig.* Cf. FOIL.

1553 Eden *Treat. Newe Ind.* (Arb.) 6 Not for one foyle or fal to be dismayd. **1600** Shaks. *A.Y.L.* I. ii. 216 You shall trie but one fall. **1602** Carew *Cornwall* 76a, Whosoever ouerthroweth his mate in such sort..is accounted to giue the fall. **1645** R. Baillie *Lett.* (1775) II. 111 We must wrestle a fall with some kind of creatures. **1676** Cotton *Walton's Angler* II. vi. (1836) II. 371 Let him [a fish] come, I'll try a fall with him. **1686** Dryden *Duchess of York's Paper Defended* 125 As three Foils will go towards a Fall in Wrastling. **1768** Ross *Helenore* I. 141 Fu' o' good nature..And kibble grown at shaking of a fa'. **1803** Anderson *Cumbld. Ball.* 62 At rustlin, whilk o' them dare try him a faw? **1855** Kingsley *Heroes* II. iii. (1868) 216, I must wrestle a fall with him. **1868** *Times* 14 Apr. 6/5 France..was not then ready to try a fall with Prussia. **1883** *Standard* 24 Mar. 3/7 The final falls were wrestled between Moffatt and Kennedy.

14. a. A felling of trees; *concr.* the timber cut down at one season.

1572 *Nottingham Rec.* iv. (1889) 141/29 In wyne iij. quartes..fetched..when the falle was appoynted xij d. *a* **1613** Overbury *Newes, Newes fr. verie Countrie* Wks. (1856) 176 Justices of peace have the selling of underwoods, but the lords have the great fals. **1649** Blithe *Eng. Improv. Impr.* (1652) 160 At every fall..take a good..Sampler growing of Ash or Willow. **1707** *Lond. Gaz.* No. 4373/4 The Fall of above 130 Acres of Wood Land..are to be sold. **1864** *Jrnl. R. Agric. Soc.* XXV. II. 314 Beech woods..are periodically thinned, and the fall used by wheelers and..chair-makers. **1879** Miss Jackson *Shropsh. Word-bk.* s.v., The young Squire..'e'll fall a sight of timber; an' a grand fall ther'll be.

†**b.** The roots and stumps of felled trees. *Obs.*

1785 Phillips *Treat. Inland Nav.* 40 Grubbing up the fall at fifty years, then planting again in the same place.

c. *Marl-digging.* (See quot.; cf. 19 d.)

1847 *Jrnl. R. Agric. Soc.* VIII. II. 313 They..proceed to make what are termed 'falls'..this is done by..undermining at the bottom..clay wedges shod with iron..driven in at top..and..the clay splits down perpendicularly.

15. Of a city or fortress: The fact of coming into the power of an enemy by capture or surrender.

1586 A. Day *Eng. Secretary* I. (1625) 35 Achilles and Hector, that made the fall of Troy so famous. **1776** Gibbon *Decl. & F.* (1887) IV. 499 The fall and sack of great cities. **1816** E. Baines *Hist. Wars Fr. Rev.* I. xxiv, Immediately on the fall of Mantua, Bonaparte published a proclamation to

his army. 1855 Macaulay *Hist. Eng.* III. 183 It was universally supposed that the fall of Londonderry could not be long delayed.

16. *fig.* **a.** A succumbing to temptation; a lapse into sin or folly. In stronger sense: Moral ruin.

*a*1225 *Ancr. R.* 326 þet fifte þing is muche scheome þet hit is, efter val, to liggen so longe. *a*1300 *Cursor M.* 9770 (Cott.) Adam..moght wit na chance Of his fall get gain couerance. *c*1450 tr. *T. à Kempis' Imit.* I. xxv. 37 The religiose man..is open to a greuous falle. 1503-4 *Act 19 Hen. VII*, c. 28 Preamb., The Kinges Highnes..beyng sory for eny suche untrougth and fall of eny of his subgiects. 1587 *Mirr. Mag.*, *Humber* xvi, Let my..fall..bee A glasse wherein to see if thou do swerue. *a*1656 Bp. Hall *Rem. Wks.* (1660) 415 He who before fel in over pleasing himself, begins to displease himself at his fall. 1758 S. Hayward *Serm.* xvii. 516 They see the falls of those that profess a real love for him. 1826 Disraeli *Viv. Grey.* v. xiii, The moral fall of a fellow creature!

b. *Theol.* *the fall*, *the fall of man*: the sudden lapse into a sinful state produced by Adam's transgression.

*a*1300 [see prec.]. 1553 T. Wilson *Rhet.* (1580) 42 The other Sacramentes..were applied to mans nature after the fall. *a*1656 Bp. Hall *Rem. Wks.* (1660) 359 Mans will since the fall hath of it self no ability to any Spiritual Act. 1698 Keill *Exam. Th. Earth* (1734) 189 The Theorist..ridicul'd the Scriptural relation of the Fall. 1699 Burnet *39 Art.* ix. 111 To return to the main point of the Fall of Adam. 1875 Manning *Mission H. Ghost* vi. 157 We are all conscious of the effect of the fall.

†**17.** *ellipt.* for: The cause of a fall. Cf. *to be the death of*, etc. *Obs.*

1535 Coverdale *Judg.* ii. 3, I wil not dryue them out before you, that they maye be a fall vnto you. 1594 Hooker *Eccl. Pol.* I. iv. 56 The fall of Angels, therefore, was pride. 1611 Bible *Ecclus.* v. 13 The tongue of man is his fall.

18. a. The fact of being struck down by calamity or disease, in battle, etc.; death, destruction, overthrow.

*c*1205 Lay. 635 þaet ne mihte þes kinges folc of heom fael makien. *c*1400 *Destr. Troy* 7933 þi falle I dessyre. 1595 Shaks. *John* III. iv. 141 But what shall I gaine by yong Arthurs fall? 1611 Bible *Judith* viii. 19 Our fathers..had a great fall before our enemies. 1659 B. Harris *Parival's Iron Age* 322 Now happened the fall of one of the greatest men in Europe..Oliver Cromwell. 1842 Macaulay *Lays, Lake Regillus* xxix, And women rent their tresses For their great prince's fall.

b. An arrest. *Criminals' slang.*

1893 [see *fall money* s.v. sense 29]. 1894 *Reminisc. Chief-Insp. Littlechild* xx. 204 This man..is now in prison on the Continent. The story of his last 'fall' is interesting. 1935 [see sense 18c].

c. A period of imprisonment. *Criminals' slang.*

1934 *Amer. Speech* IX. 26/2 *Fall*, v. to go to prison. n. a term in prison. 1935 N. Ersine *Underworld & Prison Slang* 35 *Fall.* 1. An arrest. 2. An imprisonment. 'That last fall got him the book.'

IV. 19. As a measure.

†**a.** The distance over which a measuring-rod 'falls'; *esp.* in *fall of the perch* (= b). *Obs.*

The general sense in the first quot. may have been merely inferred by Folkingham from the specific use.

1610 W. Folkingham *Art of Survey* II. iv. 52 *Lineal Fals.* Lineall dimensions are diuersified..as Inches, Palmes [etc.]. *Ibid.* II. vii. 59 Acres..differ in Content according to the..lineall Fall of the Pearch.

b. A lineal measure (orig. = *perch, pole, rod*), the 40th part of a furlong, varying in actual extent according to the value locally assigned to this.

App. peculiar to northern and north midland districts, where the furlong was larger than the present statute furlong.

1597 Skene *De Verb. Sign.* s.v. *Particata*, Sa meikle lande as in measuring falles vnder the rod or raip, in length is called ane fall of measure, or ane lineall fall. 1662 Dugdale *Hist. Imbanking & Draining* 165 Another [Gote] to be set fourscore falls beneath the old Sea Gote. 1869 Peacock *Lonsdale Gloss.*, *Fau'*, a rood of lineall land-measure of seven yards.

c. The square measure corresponding to the above; the 160th part of a customary acre. Now only in Scotland, where it = 36 square ells.

[1319 *Charter Conishead Priory, Lancs.* in Dugdale *Mon.* (1661) II. 425 Concessionem..de duabus acris, & tribus rodis terræ, & triginta fallis.] 1597 Skene *De Verb. Sign.* s.v. *Particata*, Ane superficiall fall of Lande..conteinis ane lineall fall of bredth and ane lineall fall of length. 1629 *Manch. Court Leet Rec.* (1886) III. 152 Adam Smith hath purchased..ffoure ffalles of land. 1760 in *Scotsman* 20 Aug. (1885) 5/3 Fourteen acres, thirty-three falls, and six ells of ground. 1827 Steuart *Planter's G.* (1828) 343 At the rate of 9d. or 10d. per Scotch Fall (which is about one fifth part larger than the English Pole or Rod). 1864 A. McKay *Hist. Kilmarnock* 303 The Green then measured eighty-seven falls.

d. *Marl-digging.* A measure of 64 cubic yards. (Perh. not in any way connected with the preceding: see 14c.)

1849 *Jrnl. R. Agric. Soc.* X. I. 27 The marl is calculated [in Lancashire] by the fall, which is 64 cubic yards.

V. A falling to one's share; a happening, occurrence.

†**20.** What befalls or happens to a person; one's fortune, 'case' or condition, lot, appointed duty, etc. *Obs.*

*c*1400 *Destr. Troy* 8117 Thy fall and þi faith is foule loste. *c*1489 Caxton *Sonnes of Aymon* xii. 304 Fowle fall have I now yf I feyne me now. *c*1489 —— *Blanchardyn* xx. 68 Held her hert..so ouer pressid wyth loue that she had to blanchardyn that she myght noo lenger hyde her falle. *a*1533 Ld. Berners *Gold. Bk. M. Aurel* (1546) P, A sodayne falle of mischaunce. 1631 Heywood *Fair Maid of West* IV. Wks. 1874 II. 393 What must my next fall be? 1721 Wodrow *Corr.* (1843) II. 557 It is my fall to go to the next Assembly. 1785-6 Burns *Address to Deil* xvi, Black be your fa! 1832-53 *Whistle-binkie* (Sc. Songs) Ser. III. 121 Fair be thy fa! my Phœbe Graeme.

†**21.** The date of occurrence (of days). *Obs.*

1583 Stubbes *Anat. Abus.* II. 66 [The almanac may be useful] to distinguish winter from sommer, spring from haruest, the change of the moone, the fall of euerie day.

†**22.** The descent (of an estate, etc.). *Obs. rare.*

1579 J. Stubbes *Gaping Gulf* D iij, Noble men..in their vsuall conveighances do marshall the fal of theyr inheritances by limitation vpon limitation.

VI. In various concrete applications.

23. An article of dress. **a.** A band or collar worn falling flat round the neck, in fashion during the seventeenth century.

1599 Marston *Sco. Villanie* III. Wks. 1856 III. 223 Under that fayre ruffe so sprucely set, Appeares a fall, a falling-band forsooth! 1608 Machin, etc. *Dumb Knt.* I. in Hazl. *Dodsley* X. 122 The French fall, the loose-bodied gown, the pin in the hair. 1640 G. H. *Wit's Recreations* No. 250 A question tis why women weare a fall. 1852 Thackeray *Esmond* III. viii, His lordship was represented in his scarlet uniform..with..a fall of Bruxelles lace. 1858 Simmonds *Dict. Trade*, *Fall*, a border of lace to the neck-part or body of a lady's evening dress.

b. A kind of veil worn by women; *esp.* one hanging from the front of the bonnet.

1611 Tourneur *Ath. Trag.* IV. i, There are those Falles and Tyres I tolde you of. 1818 Miss Ferrier *Marriage* xxiv, The Chantilly fall which embellished the front of her bonnet. 1865 *Ann. Reg.* 48 Miss Kent wore a thick fall, which almost screened her face from view.

c. In various applications: (see quots.).

1634 T. Carew *Cœlum Britannicum* 2 Mercury descends..upon his head a wreath with smal fals of white Feathers. 1688 R. Holme *Armoury* III. 258/1 Some..have..Falls or long Cufts to hang over the Hands. 1726 Shelvocke *Voy. round World* (1757) 112 The Montera or Spanish cap, made with a fall to cover their neck and shoulders. 1869 Mrs. Palliser *Lace* iv. 49 The..ladies wore their sleeves covered up to the shoulders with falls of the finest Brussels lace. *a*1921 G. H. Gibson in *Penguin Bk. Austral. Ballads* (1964) 206 He could..Chop his name with a green-hide fall on the flank of a flyin' steer. 1933 L. G. D. Acland in *Press* (Christchurch) 14 Oct. 15/7 *Fall*, a plain strip of leather at the end of the lash of a whip to which the cracker is attached.

24. a. *Bot.* in *pl.* Those parts or petals of a flower which bend downward.

1794 Martyn *Rousseau's Bot.* xiv. 155 The three outermost of these parts..are bent downwards, and are thence called falls. 1882 *Garden* 22 Apr. 284/2 The 'falls'..are pure ivory-white.

b. The long hair hanging down the faces of certain terriers.

1908 J. Maxtee *English & Welsh Terriers* 86 When the coat is sufficiently long to justify its being done, the 'fall' (as the long hair covering the face is termed by fanciers) should be plaited and tied up over the head with ribbon. 1948 B. Vesey-Fitzgerald *Bk. Dog* 996 *Fall*, the long fringe of hair overhanging the face of the Yorkshire, Skye and Clydesdale terriers.

25. The moveable front of a piano, which comes down over the key-board.

26. a. *Mech.* The loose end of the tackle, to which the power is applied in hoisting.

1644 Manwaring *Seaman's Dict.* 38 The small roapes which we hale-by in all tackles, is called the fall of the tackle. 1752 Smeaton in *Phil. Trans.* XLVII. 495 The..line, by which the draught is made..commonly called, the fall of the tackle. 1828 J. M. Spearman *Brit. Gunner* (ed. 2) 184, 7..assists..in passing the fall round the windlass. 1848 Layard *Nineveh* II. xiii. 80 The ends, or falls of the tackle..being..held by the Arabs.

b. An apparatus for lowering bales, etc.; also *Naut.* in *pl.*

1832 Marryat *N. Forster* x, Overhaul the boat's falls. 1860 [see 29 *fall-way*]. 1881 W. C. Russell *Sailor's Sweetheart* I. viii. 289 The port boat's falls were..provided with patent hooks, which sprang open and released the boat the moment she touched the water.

†**27.** An alleged name for a covey or flight (of woodcocks). *Obs.*

*c*1430 Lydg. *Hors, Shepe. & G.* 30. Hence 1486 *Bk. St. Alban's* F vj b.

VII. *attrib.* and *Comb.*

28. a. attributive (sense 2), as *fall-feed*, *-plowing*, etc. **b.** objective (sense 13), as *fall-giver*, *-taker*.

1602 Carew *Cornwall* I. 76 The fall-giuer to be exempted from playing againe with the taker. 1677 W. Hubbard *Narrative* II. 14 Offering..to pay forty Beaver Skins at the next Fall-Voyage. 1788 Franklin *Autobiog.* Wks. 1887 I. 286 The orders..for insurance..for fall goods. 1821 in Cobbett *Rur. Rides* (1885) I. 3 Whole families were frequently swept off by the 'fall-fever'. 1848 Chandler in *Jrnl. R. Agric. Soc.* IX. II. 524 All the manure from the fall-feed is left where made. 1856 Olmsted *Slave States* 663 The improvement had been effected entirely by draining and fall-plowing. 1906 *Daily Colonist* (Victoria, B.C.) 17 Jan. 1/5 The condition of the fall wheat of Alberta today is declared to be A1. 1926 *Ibid.* 18 July 2/5 Officials have been working indefatigably in their efforts to this year promote the most successful Fall Fair that this community has ever experienced. 1928 M. de la Roche *Whiteoaks* (1929) II. 27 He had a new fall overcoat of expensive English melton.

29. Special comb.: **fall-block**, either of the two lower blocks of a boat's falls; **fall-board**, a shutter hinged at the bottom; **fall-breaker** (break *v.* 28b), that which reduces the impact of a fall or the speed of falling; †**fall-bridge**, a boarding-bridge attached to the side of a ship; **fall-cloud** (see quot.); **fall-(iron) door** (see quot.); **fall-fish** (see quot.); **fall-front** *sb.* and *attrib.* = *drop-front* (s.v. drop- a); **fall-gate**, *dial.* (see quot.); **fall guy** *slang* (orig. *U.S.*), one who is easily tricked, an easy victim; one who 'takes the rap' for others, a scapegoat; **fall-leaf** *U.S.*, a table-leaf which can be let down; also *attrib.*; **fall(-)line**, (*a*) a line in the eastern United States marked by waterfalls and rapids at points where rivers cross it and forming the boundary between the Atlantic coastal plain and the Piedmont; hence in *Physical Geogr.*, any line joining points of sudden descent on rivers and representing a similar geological discontinuity (see quot. 1968); (*b*) *Ski-ing* [ad. G. *fallinie*] (see quot. 1961); **fall money** *Criminals' slang*, money set aside by a criminal for use if he should be arrested; **fall-pipe**, (*a*) the sloping inlet pipe of a water-ram; (*b*) the pipe conveying rainwater from a roof, etc., to the ground; **fall-pippin** *U.S.*, a certain variety of apple; **fall-rise** *Phonetics* (see quot. 1932); **fall-rope**, a rope used for lifting; **fall-trap** = fall *sb.*²; **fall-way** (see quot.); **fall-wind**, a sudden gust; †**fall-window** = *fall-board*; †**fall-wood**, wood that has fallen or been blown down; **fall zone** = *fall-line* (*a*).

*a*1877 Knight *Dict. Mech.* 678/1 s.v. *Davit.* When the boat is lowered the hooks of the *fall-blocks are cast off simultaneously. 1883 *Man. Seamanship for Boys* 136 Fall Blocks, for Top-Tackle Pendants. 1743 W. Ellis *Mod. Husbandm.* (1744) III. I. July 86 The Entrance [being] afterwards stopped with a *Fall-board, so that no Pole-cat..can in the least molest them. 1820 *Blackw. Mag.* June 281 A pair of fall-boards belonging to a window. 1927 *Daily Express* 31 Oct. 13/2 The competitors climb like cats to the top of a tall tower... They jump and dive eighty-five feet into *fall-breakers. 1946 W. F. Burbidge *From Balloon to Bomber* iii. 35 Leonardo da Vinci..in his manuscript *Codex Atlanticus* (*circa* 1514) described a device, aptly called a 'fall-breaker', consisting of 'a tent of chalked linen' which would enable a man to 'fall from any great height without danger to himself'. 1375 Barbour *Bruce* XVII. 419 Thai the schip on na maner Micht ger cum till the vall so neir That thair *fall-brig mycht reik thar-till. 1823 T. Forster *Atmos. Phenom.* I. §4 (ed. 3) 12 *heading*, Of the Stratus or *Fallcloud. 1837 C. V. Incledon *Taunus* 207 A *fall iron door, which answered the double purpose of door, and draw-bridge. 1812 J. Henry *Camp. agst. Quebec* 32 A delicious chub which we call a *fall-fish. 1902 W. H. Hackett *Decorative Furnit.* xiii. 160 A satinwood upright secretaire with *fall-front. 1907 *Yesterday's Shopping* (1969) 372/1 Fall front spirit stands..2-pint half cut bottles..34/0. 1929 *Times* 2 Nov. 7/5 A Louis XV. kingwood marqueterie escritoire, with..the fall-front drawer, and pigeon holes. 1955 R. Fastnedge *Eng. Furnit. Styles* iii. 87 Small walnut and marquetry fall-front writing cabinets on chests of drawers or stands. 14.. *Brome Commpl. Bk.* (1886) 165 Ony man that hath no3te hangyd his *fal-3ates at resonable tymes. 1795 Marshall *E. Norf. Gloss.* (E.D.S.), *Fall-gate*, a gate across a public road. 1886 *Chester Gloss.*, *Fall-gate*, a gate across the high road. 1906 H. Green *At Actors' Boarding House* 226, I never thought I'd be the *fall guy for such raw work as this. 1912 G. Bronson-Howard *Enemy to Society* ix. 293 We ain't goin' to be th' 'fall guys' for Steve... If we've got to do time, so has he! 1929 'C. G. Gordon' *Crooks Underworld* 118 The grafter becomes the 'fall guy', and the solicitors ensure immunity from scandal by falling back on the dignity of their profession. 1935 *Amer. Speech* X. 15/1 *Fall guy*, [formerly] one who bungles his work and usually gets caught; a clumsy thief. This word now means one who is made the goat, one who involuntarily *takes the rap* for the rest of the gang. 1946 'P. Quentin' *Puzzle for Fiends* (1947) xxi. 149 Selena..would deliver me as a fall guy to the police without batting an eye. 1956 S. Bellow *Seize Day* (1957) i. 34 Perhaps he was foolish and unlucky, a fall guy, a dupe, a sucker. 1959 'M. Ainsworth' *Murder is Catching* vi. 77 There's never been a political murder yet..without there being some sort of a fall guy, prepared in advance. 1963 *Spectator* 6 Sept. 295 Ward began to hear from friends that he was being cast for the part of fall guy (I know of no equivalent expression here) by Profumo's friends. 1854 B. F. Taylor *Jan. & June* 204 It was the old table with the *fall leaves. 1882 C. Waite *Adv. Far West* 189 [A] fall-leaf table. 1882 *Nation* (N.Y.) 13 July 33/1 It is here, at the '*fall-line', that the most available water-powers are to be found. 1902 Ld. Avebury *Scenery of Eng.* xvi. 481 A similar line along the junction of the uplands with the sea-plain is known in the United States as the 'fall-line'. 1955 *Sci. Amer.* Mar. 82/2 In the Atlantic terrace the thin edge of the sedimentary wedge reaches inland to the 'fall line' (a zone of waterfalls) on the eastern side of the Appalachian Mountains. 1961 J. S. Salak *Dict. Amer. Sports* 152 *Fall line*, the natural way down a slope—the course a rolling ball would take. On a perfect inclined plane, it would be the shortest straight line from any point on the slope to the bottom. 1968 R. W. Fairbridge *Encycl. Geomorphol.* 344/1 The term 'fall line' or 'fall zone'..has been adopted in geomorphology as a general term to identify the boundary between a more resistant crystalline upland or plateau province and a coastal plain of weak rocks. 1970 *Times* 13 Feb. 13/5 Some series of gates are ranged down the fall line—the straight line down the mountain. 1893 L. W. Moore *His Own Story* xii. 197 If any accident happened to us, Hall was to stand his part of the '*fall' money. 1929 'C. G. Gordon' *Crooks Underworld* 215 We had often discussed the matter of 'fall money'. 1888 *Lockwood's Dict. Mech. Engin.* 134 **Fall pipe*, a drive pipe. 1929 *Daily Tel.* 22 Jan. 12/4 When cornered he slid down a fallpipe. 1817-8 Cobbett *Resid. U.S.* (1822) 16 The wind is knocking down the *fall-pipins for us. 1885 Roe *Driven back to Eden* 262 Fall pippins and greenings. 1932 D. Jones *Outl. Eng. Phonetics* (ed. 3) xxxi. 282 If there are several syllables following the emphatic fall, the terminal rise is spread over these. But if there is only one unstressed syllable following, the terminal rise is compressed into it. If there is no

following unstressed syllable, the terminal rise is compressed into the same syllable as the emphatic fall; the emphatic syllable is therefore said in this case with a *fall-rise. **1962** S. STUBELIUS in F. Behre *Contrib. Eng. Syntax* 200 Rise-endings and fall-rise endings are by no means rare in statements. **1889** *Cent. Dict.*, *Fall-rope. **1891** KIPLING *Barrack-r. Ballads* (1892) 205 And the fall-rope whines through the sheave. **1933** *Times Lit. Suppl.* 18 May 350/3 Someone had..thrown the body overboard, but a fall-rope caught it by the neck. *c* **1450** HENRYSON *Uplandis Mous & Burges Mous* 90 Poems (1865) 111 Of cat, nor *fall-trap, I haif na dreid. **1837** CARLYLE *Fr. Rev.* (1872) III. VII. i. 213 Deadly gins and falltraps. **1860** BARTLETT *Dict. Amer.*, *Fall-way, the opening or well through which goods are raised and lowered by a fall. **1867** SMYTH *Sailor's Word-bk.*, *Fall-wind. **1422** *Searchers Verdicts* in *Surtees Misc.* (1890) 16 The *falle wyndow to ye streteward. *c* **1524** *Churchw. Acc. St. Mary Hill, London* (Nichols 1797) 126 Two lode of *fawle wode. **1528** *Papers Earls of Cumberland* in Whitaker's *Hist. Craven* (1812) 308 Item, 3 load of falwood and bavings, 3*s.* 4*d.* **1929** H. S. SHARP in *Science* LXIX. 545/1 The erosional surface to which it is proposed to apply the term *Fall Zone peneplane is of considerable importance. **1937** WOOLDRIDGE & MORGAN *Physical Basis Geogr.* XV. 220 The Fall Line, or, more accurately, the Fall Zone of North America, where falls and rapids mark the descent of the streams from the 'old-land' to the coastal plain. **1968** Fall zone [see *fall-line*, above].

30. With adverbs forming combs. (rarely occurring in literary use) expressing the action of the corresponding verbal combinations (FALL *v.* XI); as **fall-in** *Mil.* [FALL *v.* 88 g] (see quot. 1852); **fall-off, fall-out**, etc.

1852 R. BURN *Naval & Mil. Techn. Dict.* (ed. 2) II. 92/1 *Fall-in*, beat of drum or trumpeter's call. **1862** SALA *Accepted Addr.* 145 A ferocious fall-out about an abominable little Skye terrier. **1880** G. M. HOPKINS *Let.* 5 Sept. (1935) 109, I think the Lethe mythology of the last stanza is a fall-off and unrealises the whole. **1889** *Pall Mall G.* 23 Aug. 2/1 A steady income from advertisements makes a slight fall off in the sale of less consequence. **1915** 'I. HAY' *First Hundred Thousand* vi. 42 Here the 'fall-in' sounded. **1958** M. L. HALL et al. *Newnes Compl. Amat. Photogr.* x. 116 It [*sc.* bounce flash] produces soft, even lighting and reduces the effect of background fall-off. **1969** *Listener* 5 June 786/1 There is going to be a fall-off in orders.

fall (fɔːl), *sb.*[2] Forms: 1 fealle, 5 falle, felle, 9 *Sc.* fa, 8– fall. [OE. (*mús-*)*fealle* wk. fem. (= OHG. *falla*), f. *feallan* to FALL.] Something that falls; a trap-door, trap. Cf. PITFALL, SPRINGFALL.

[*a* **1000** *Voc.* in Wr.-Wülcker 477 *Pelx*, musfealle.] *c* **1440** *Promp. Parv.* 147 Falle, or mowstrappe, *muscipula, decipula.* **1772** T. SIMPSON *Vermin-Killer* 6 By a Fall is meant a wire door, hung at the top instead of the sides. **1802** SIBBALD *Gloss.*, *Fa*, trap for mice or rats. **1823** J. D. HUNTER *Captivity N. Amer.* 114, I had constructed several falls..in the vicinity of the beaver houses.

fall (fɔːl), *sb.*[3] [*Whale-fishing*. Perh. a local Sc. pronunciation of *whale*; in Aberdeenshire *wh* is pronounced (f).]

a. The cry given when a whale is sighted, or seen to blow, or harpooned. **b.** The chase of a whale or school of whales. ***loose fall*** (see quots. 1820 and 1867).

a. 1694 *Acc. Sev. Late Voy.* II. (1711) 156 When they see Whales..they call into the Ship, Fall, fall. **1867** SMYTH *Sailor's Word-bk., Fall! a Fall!* the cry to denote that the harpoon has been effectively delivered into the body of a whale.

b. 1820 W. SCORESBY *Acc. Arctic Reg.* II. 237 When the whole of the boats are sent out, the ship is said to have 'a loose fall' *Ibid.* II. 534 Sometimes 10 or 12 fish are killed 'at a fall'. **1867** SMYTH *Sailor's Word-bk.*, *Loose fall*, the losing of a whale after an apparently good opportunity for striking it.

fall (fɔːl), *v.* Pa. t. **fell** (fɛl); pa. pple. **fallen** (fɔːl(ə)n). Forms: *Infin.* 1 feallan, 3–5 falle(n, *south.* valle(n, 3–6 fal, (5 fale, fulle, 6 faul(e, *Sc.* faa, fawe, 8–9 *Sc.* fa', 3– fall. *Pa. t.* 1–3 féoll, 2, 3 feol, fol(l, 2–3 *south.* veol(l, 2–4 ful(l, 3 *south.* vul, 2–6 fel, 2 *south.* vel, 4–5 felle, (4 fele), 4 *south.* velle, 4–5 fil(l(e, fylle, 4 *south.* vil(l, 3– fell; *weak forms*: 4 felde, 6 falled. *Pa. pple.* 1 feallen, 4–5 fallin, -yn, (4 faleyn), 5–8 faln(e, (6 faulen), *Sc.* 6 fawin, 8 fawn, 9 fa'(e)n, 3– fallen; also 4 falle, 4–5 fal, (7 fell), 5–7 fall; also 6 *weak form* falled. [A Com. Teut. redupl. str. vb. (wanting in Gothic): OE. *feallan* = OFris. *falla*, OS. *fallan* (Du. *vallen*), OHG. *fallan* (MHG. *vallen*, mod.G. *fallen*), ON. *falla* (Sw. *falla*, Da. *falde*):—OTeut. **fallan* (pa. t. **fefall-*), perh.:—pre-Teut. **phal-n-* cognate with L. *fallĕre* to deceive; more certainly cognate is Lith. *pùlti* to fall; the Gr. σφάλλειν (if f. root *sqhel*) is unconnected.

In the intransitive senses often conjugated with *be*.]

I. To descend freely (primarily by 'weight' or gravity): opposed to 'rise'.

1. a. *intr.* To drop from a high or relatively high position. Const. †*in, into, to, on, upon*; also, *to the earth, ground.*

c **890** K. ALFRED *Metra* v. 15 (Gr.) Him on innan felð muntes mæġenstan. *a* **1000** *Crist* 1526 (Gr.) Hi sceolon raðe feallan on grimne grund. *c* **1175** *Lamb. Hom.* 61 Þe angles of heouene uolle for heore prude in to helle. *c* **1200** *Trin. Coll. Hom.* 155 Sum of þe sed ful uppe þe ston. *a* **1225** *Ancr. R.* 58 ȝif eni unwrie put were, & best feolle þer inne. *a* **1300** *Cursor M.* 24538 (Cott.) Þe tere fell o min ei. **1382** WYCLIF *Matt.* xxi. 44 Vpon whom it [this stoon] shal falle it shal togidre poune hym. *a* **1400–50** *Alexander* 509 Þis egg, or þe kyng wyst, to þe erth fallis. *c* **1430** *Syr Gener.* (Roxb.) 2866 Malachias was fal of the toure. **1526** *Pilgr. Perf.* (W. de W. 1531) 166 [The ball] mysseth the hande & falleth to the grounde. **1596** SHAKS. *Tam. Shr.* III. ii. 163 All amaz'd the Priest let fall the booke. **1601** —— *All's Well* IV. iii. 217 His braines are forfeite to the next tile that falls. **1632** LITHGOW *Trav.* v. 190 Two of our Asses fell ouer a banke. **1774** GOLDSM. *Nat. Hist.* (1776) I. 222 The water falls three hundred feet perpendicular. **1818** SHELLEY *Lett. Italy* 10 Nov., A plant more excellent than that from which they [seeds] fell. **1875** JOWETT *Plato* (ed. 2) I. 84 A stone.. fell on the deck at his feet.

b. Proverb. ***fall back, fall edge***: come what may; through thick and thin. Cf. BACK *sb.*[1] 4.

1622 MABBE tr. *Aleman's Guzman d'Alf.* I. 9 Fall backe, fall Edge, goe which way you will to worke. **1781** COWPER *Let.* 13 May. **1830** SCOTT *Jrnl.* 21 Dec., Fall back, fall edge, nothing shall induce me to publish what [etc.].

c. *fig.* esp. with reference to descent from high estate, or from moral elevation.

a **1300** *Cursor M.* 8992 (Cott.) He fell fra liue and saul hele. **1483** CAXTON *Gold. Leg.* 215/2 To exclude hem from the felicite that they fil fro. **1621–51** BURTON *Anat. Mel.* I. i. II. xi. 29 Falne from his first perfection. **1707** NORRIS *Treat. Humility* v. 199 Pride..made them..fall from goodness and happiness. **1813** BYRON *Giaour* 139 No foreign foe could quell Thy soul, till from itself it fell. **1818** CRUISE *Digest* (ed. 2) II. 469 A fruit fallen from what is the creditor's. **1890** T. F. TOUT *Hist. Eng. from 1689*, 45 In 1719 Alberoni fell through a Court intrigue.

d. of what comes or seems to come from the atmosphere (*e.g.* hail, rain, lightning, etc.), and by extension of heaven, the stars, etc.

c **1000** ÆLFRIC *Exod.* ix. 19 Se haȝol him on utan fealð. *c* **1000** *Ags. Ps.* lxxi[i]. 6 Se stranga ren fealleð on flys her. *c* **1320** *Sir Tristr.* 1936 Of snowe was fallen aschour. **1393** LANGL. *P. Pl.* C. IV. 102 Þenne falleþ þer fur on false menne houses. *c* **1400** MAUNDEV. (1839) xiv. 152 The dew of heuene ..falleð vpon the herbes. **1523** LD. BERNERS *Froiss.* I. cvi. 128 Ye stones..semed lyke thondre falled fro heuyn. **1614** BP. HALL *Recoll. Treat.* 499 What if heaven fall, say you? **1630** LORD *Persees* 44 Fire..occasioned by lightning falling on some tree. **1671** R. BOHUN *Disc. Wind* 236 Rain, falling ..by Bucket-fuls. **1842** TENNYSON *Morte d'Arthur* 262 Where falls not hail or rain or any snow. **1856** MRS. BROWNING *Aur. Leigh* III. 97 The thunder fell..and killed a wife.

e. *fig.* of calamity, disease, fear, sleep, vengeance, etc.

a **1300** *Cursor M.* 10270 (Cott.) For þis resun Es fallen on þe þis malicoun. *c* **1320** *Sir Tristr.* 2951 Maugre on me falle ȝif y þe wold slo! *c* **1346** *Prose Psalter* liv. [lv.] 4 Drede of deþ fel vp me. *c* **1400** *Lanfranc's Cirurg.* 266 Þe frenesie fil on hir. *a* **1533** LD. BERNERS *Huon* li. 171 A grete mysfortune fell apon vs. **1568** GRAFTON *Chron.* II. 16 Great moreyne fell upon brute beastes. **1611** BIBLE *Gen.* ii. 21 God caused a deepe sleepe to fall vpon Adam. **1655** FULLER *Ch. Hist.* IV. i. §20 Most fiercely fell their fury on the Dutch. **1751** JORTIN *Serm.* (1771) II. x. 200 Calamities..fall upon the good and the bad. **1860** SIR T. MARTIN *Horace* 112 Wonder fell on all. **1870** ROGERS *Hist. Gleanings* Ser. II. 48 A fiery persecution fell on the Lollards. **1886** A. SERGEANT *No Saint* II. vi. 132 A great stillness fell upon the place.

f. of darkness, night, etc.

a **1613** OVERBURY *Characters, Fair & happy milk-mayd*, When winter euenings fall early. **1771** MRS. GRIFFITH tr. *Viaud's Shipwreck* 86 Night began to fall. **1805** SCOTT *Last Minstr.* III. 24 The evening fell, 'Twas near the time of curfew bell. **1841** LONGF. *Excelsior* 1 The shades of night were falling fast. **1862** TYNDALL *Mountaineer.* ii. 11 Soft shadows fell from shrub and rock. **1885** STEVENSON *Dynamiter* 104 The night fell, mild and airless.

g. *Tennis.* (See quots.) (Cf. FALL *sb.*[1] 12 d.)

1900 G. E. A. ROSS in A. E. T. Watson *Young Sportsman* 610 Y returns the first service so that X cannot reach the ball. The marker, seeing that it 'falls' (*i.e.*, comes into contact with the floor for the second time) on the line 2, calls out 'chase 2'. **1957** *Encycl. Brit.* XIII. 793/1 A chase..is made, the goodness or the badness of which depends upon the spot on the floor which the ball touches next after its first bound. .. Thus if a ball fell on the line marked 4, he [*sc.* the marker] would call 'chase 4'.

2. To become detached and drop off. **a.** Of feathers, the hair, leaves, etc.: To drop off or out. **b.** Of clothes: To slip off.

1297 R. GLOUC. (1724) 313 He let hym myd hors to drawe ..þat þe peces ffelle of ys ffess aboute. *a* **1300** *Cursor M.* 3569 (Cott.) Þe freli fax [biginnes] to fal of him. **1530** PALSGR. 544/1 Se howe his heares fall. **1577** B. GOOGE *Heresbach's Husb.* IV. (1586) 165b, His [peacock's] taile falling everie yeere. **1611** BIBLE *Lev.* xiii. 40 The man whose haire is fallen off his head. **1852** THACKERAY *Esmond* I. ix, Her hair fell, and her face looked older. **1854** *Jrnl. R. Agric. Soc.* XV. II. 353 The foetal incisors and tushes..rarely fall before this period, notwithstanding they be worn to the gums.

fig. *a* **1400** in *Retr. Rev.* Aug. 1853. 419 Clerkyn lowe fal from me So doth ȝe lef on grofys tre. **1850** DICKENS *Child's Dream of Star* in *Househ. Words* I. 26 My age is falling from me like a garment. **1889** MRS. LYNN LINTON *Thro' Long Night* II. II. xiii. 196 Some of the quainter forms of his adopted speech were falling from him. **1890** *Univ. Rev.* May 84 My fevered mood fell from me.

3. Of objects moving vertically as on a hinge: To drop to a lower position. † ***the orloge falles***: (the hammer of) the clock strikes.

a **1400** *Relig. Pieces fr. Thornton MS.* (1866) 57 Before þat þe orloge falles, or any belles rynges. **1621** FLETCHER *Thierry & Theodoret* III. ii, The vault is ready, and the door conveys to 't Falls just behind his chair. **1808** SCOTT *Marm.* I. iv, Let the drawbridge fall. **1816** J. SMITH *Panorama Sci. & Art* I. 15 Such a hammer will, as it is technically termed, fall well. **1881** GREENER *Gun* (1888) 139 The block is..held in position by a spring stud until the hammer falls.

4. a. To drop, come or go down, in a given direction or to a required position; chiefly in *to let fall* (an anchor, curtain, sail, etc.). Also, ***to let fall*** (***a perpendicular***): to draw so as to meet a base line. Of a lash: To be brought down.

1593 SHAKS. *Rom. & Jul.* IV. i. 100 Thy eyes windowes fall. **1594** —— *Rich. III*, v. iii. 116, I let fall the windowes of mine eyes. **1626** CAPT. SMITH *Accid. Yng. Seamen* 27 Let fall your fore sayle. **1667** PRIMATT *City & C. Build.* 161 Let a Perpendicular line fall upon the Base. **1696** tr. *Du Mont's Voy. Levant* 98 Let fall a Ladder of Ropes. **1698** T. FROGER *Voy.* 69 We..let fall Anchor. **1816** PLAYFAIR *Nat. Phil.* (1819) II. 18 The perpendicular is to be let fall..from the star on the meridian. **1881** BESANT & RICE *Chapl. Fleet* I. 187 The cruel cat falling at every step upon their naked and bleeding shoulders. **1889** *Repent. P. Wentworth* II. ix. 179 The curtain fell on the fourth act.

b. To hang down, extend downwards.

1577 B. GOOGE *Heresbach's Husb.* III. (1586) 115 His mane ..falling on the right side. **1665** SIR T. HERBERT *Trav.* (1677) 365 A party-coloured Mantle which falls no deeper than the knees. **1745** P. THOMAS *Jrnl. Anson's Voy.* 337 From the Ridge of his [Zebra's] Back down to his Belly, fall several streaks of various Colours. **1890** PHILIPS & WILLS *Sybil Ross's Marriage* i. 5 Golden hair fell in great masses upon her shoulders. **1892** *Speaker* 3 Sept. 289/2 Wild rose ..falling in close exquisite veils of pink and green.

5. Of the young of animals: To be 'dropped' or born.

a **1400–50** *Alexander* 2081 Mare fersere in feld fell neuire of modire. **1532–3** *Act 34 Hen. VIII*, c. 7 Any maner yonge suckinge calfe..which shall happen to fall or to be calued. **1595** SHAKS. *John* III. i. 90 Let wiues with childe Pray that their burthens may not fall this day. **1617** MARKHAM *Caval.* I. 32 If a foale fall early in the yeare. **1711** ADDISON *Spect.* No. 121 ¶1 A Lamb no sooner falls from its Mother, but immediately [etc.]. **1844** *Jrnl. R. Agric. Soc.* V. I. 175 Calves that fall early enough to be fattened before grass time. **1864** *Ibid.* XXV. II. 296 The lambs should fall in May.

fig. **1892** *Standard* 12 Feb. 2/3 A plan which fell still-born.

6. Of speech, etc.: ***to fall from*** (***a person, his mouth***): to issue or proceed from.

1605 BP. HALL *Medit. & Vows* II. §88 It was an excellent rule that fell from Epicure. **1770** W. HODSON *Ded. Temple of Solomon* 1 Wisdom falling from his Tongue. **1813** HOGG *Queen's Wake* 182 The wordis that fell fra her muthe War wordis of wonder. **1890** *Harper's Mag.* June 45/1 Every word that fell from her lips.

II. To sink to a lower level: opposed to 'rise'.

7. a. To descend, sink *into, to.* Now only of inanimate things.

c **1400** *Lanfranc's Cirurg.* 287 Whanne þe spiritis fallip þan a mannes vertues failen. *Ibid.* 350 And þan do hem to seþing on þe fier til þe herbis falle to þe botme. **1665** HOOKE *Microgr.* 172 Flies..steady in one place of the air, without rising or falling. **1682** OTWAY *Venice Preserved* I. i, The obsequious billows fall And rise again. **1822** G. W. MANBY *Jrnl.* (1823) 31 Those immense bodies of ice the undulating swell..caused to rise and fall. *a* **1843** SOUTHEY *Inchcape Rock* 7 So little they [waves] rose, so little they fell. **1891** J. WINSOR *Chr. Columbus* 238 There were signs of clearing in the west, and the waves began to fall.

b. To get into a low state, physically or morally; to decline. † ***to fall in age***: to become advanced in years.

a **1300** *Cursor M.* 3563 (Cott.) Quen þat he bicomis alde, Til vnweild bigines to falde. *c* **1400** *Lanfranc's Cirurg.* 212 If he be feble..& his pous falle. **1530** PALSGR. 543/2 You fall in age apace. **1614** BP. HALL *Recoll. Treat.* 213 Fall'n to bee levell with their fellowes; and from thence beneath them, to a mediocrity. **1667** MILTON *P.L.* I. 84 How fall'n! how chang'd From him who..didst outshine Myriads. **1728** VENEER *Sincere Penitent* Pref. 6 How easy it may be..to fall from one wickedness to another. **1820** KEATS *Isabel* xxxii, Sweet Isabel By gradual decay from beauty fell. **1845–6** TRENCH *Huls. Lect.* Ser. II. viii. 280 We fall below our position. **1879** FARRAR *St. Paul* (1883) 49 He was ever falling and falling, and no hand was held out to help him.

†**c.** Of a bird or rider: To alight. *Obs.*

c **1400** *Destr. Troy* 13563 His broder..Fell vnto fote, & his fole esyt. **1535** COVERDALE *Judg.* i. 14 She fell from the Asse. *c* **1575** *Bk. Sparhawkes* (ed. Harding 1886) 16 That will make her fall at marke. **1619** BERT *Treat. Hawkes* 6 You may perhaps finde her folly giue her leaue to fall again vpon the ground within..twenty yards of you.

†**d.** To go down hill. *Obs. rare.*

1691 T. H[ALE] *Acc. New Invent.* 123 For the Ships ease of falling into the Sea.

†**e.** Of the sun, etc.: To go down; to sink, set. *Obs.*

1633 *R. Johnson's Kingd. & Commw.* 19 To places parellel, the Sunne neither riseth, nor falleth. **1658** T. WILLSFORD *Nature's Secrets* 37 Those Asterismes..That in the night do either rise or fall. **1669** STURMY *Mariner's Mag.* II. 85 The Sun..is descending, or as we commonly say he is fallen.

8. Of land: To slope.

1573 TUSSER *Husb.* (1878) 100 Land falling..South or southwest, for profit by tillage is lightly the best. **1634** SIR T. HERBERT *Trav.* (1638) 31 Parts [of the earth] falling into fruitfull dales. **1694** SMITH & WALFORD *Acc. Sev. Late Voy.* I. (1711) 62 Rounds up..in white Cliffs, and falls into shores. **1862** *Temple Bar Mag.* IV. 428 The high ground of the plateau falls towards this narrow strait.

9. a. Of a river or stream: To discharge itself, issue *into.*

c **1205** LAY. 1401 Þer Læire falleð i þa sæ. **1398** TREVISA *Barth. De P.R.* XIII. iii. (1495) 442 The ryuer Downow.. fallith in to the See that hyghte Ponticum. **1490** CAXTON *Eneydos* xxxiii. 122 The ryuer of tonyre..falleth there in to the see. **1613** PURCHAS *Pilgr.* v. i. 381 The Riuer Ganges.. falleth into the Gulfe of Bengala. **1705** ARBUTHNOT *Coins* (1727) 251 The Loir, and the Rivers that fall into it. **1825** *New Monthly Mag.* XV. 397 Rivers that fall into Lake Huron. **1865** F. HALL in *H. H. Wilson's Vishńu Puráńa* II. 150 A river Veńi..falls into the Kŕishńá.

†**b.** *transf.* of a road. *Obs.*

1693 *Col. Rec. Pennsylv.* I. 389 Lay ott the king's road, where it may fall into the king's old road. **1706** *Ibid.* II. 276 A Road..falling into the Road leading to Philadelphia.

10. a. Of water, flames, etc.: To subside. Of the tide: To ebb.

a **1300** *Cursor M.* 1876 (Cott.) How sal we o þis waters weit Quedir þai be fulli fallen yeit? **1340** HAMPOLE *Pr. Consc.* 1216 Þe se..Ebbes and flowes, and falles agayn. **1535** STEWART *Cron. Scot.* II. 451 Quhen that the flude war fawin. **1670** NARBOROUGH *Jrnl.* in *Acc. Sev. Late Voy.* I. (1711) 66 The Water riseth and falls perpendicular ten Feet. **1726** SWIFT *Gulliver* I. v, The tide was a little fallen. **1849** RUSKIN *Sev. Lamps* vii. §3. 185 The ocean falls and flows. **1886** SHORTHOUSE *Sir Percival* iii. 99 Flames that leaped up suddenly and fell again. **1887** *Earth and its Story* I. 331 The water suddenly rose an inch and fell again.

fig. **1632** LITHGOW *Trav.* III. 117 Not..till it [Greece] fell to the lowest ebbe. **1705** ADDISON *Italy* Ded. A 2 Their Hopes..rose or fell with Your Lordship's Interest. **1819** SHELLEY *Peter Bell the Third* IV. xxii, What though..wit, like ocean, rose and fell? **1886** *Lesterre Durant* I. v. 66 The grand music rose and fell with a flood of sound.

b. Of the wind, weather, etc.: To decrease in violence; to abate, calm down. Also in phrases, as ***it fell calm, a dead, flat calm.***

a **1300** *Cursor M.* 24942 (Cott.) Þe storm it fell. **1670** NARBOROUGH *Jrnl.* in *Acc. Sev. Late Voy.* I. 17 It fell calm this Afternoon. **1752** WASHINGTON *Barbadoes Jrnl.* (1892) 73 Ye Wind was fallen. **1840** R. DANA *Bef. Mast* x. 24 In a few minutes it fell dead calm. **1872** HOWELLS *Wedd. Journ.* 5 The storm fell before seven o'clock.

11. *fig.* Of the countenance: To lose animation; to assume an expression of dismay or disappointment. [Orig. a Hebraism.]

1382 WYCLIF *Gen.* iv. 5 Caym was greetli wroth, and therwith felle his chere. *c* **1430** *Syr Gener.* (Roxb.) 1882 Downward his chere lete he falle. **1611** BIBLE *Gen.* iv. 5 Cain was very wroth, and his countenance fell. **1718** HICKES & NELSON *J. Kettlewell* I. ii. 13 As soon as he heard the Sound of Drum or Trumpet, his Countenance did always fall. **1816** SCOTT *Antiq.* vii, The countenance of the old man fell. **1888** Q. *Troy Town.* viii. 81 Caleb's face fell a full inch.

12. To be lowered in direction, droop. Of the eyes: To be cast down.

1586 A. DAY *Eng. Secretary* II. (1625) 48 The Peacocke..stooping doune to his feet, his feathers fall with the selfesight immediatly. **1665** HOOKE *Microgr.* 118 The tender Sprouts of it, after the leaves are shut, fall and hang down. **1889** F. M. CRAWFORD *Greifenstein* II. xviii. 234 His eyes fell before her gaze.

†**13. a.** Of anything heated or swollen: To settle down. *Obs.*

1580 BARET *Alv.* F 92 The swelling falleth or asswageth. **1632** MASSINGER & FIELD *Fatal Dowry* III. i, Fall and cool, my blood! Boil not in zeal. **1665** HOOKE *Microgr.* 39 You shall find the parts of the upper Surface to subside and fall inwards. **1823** J. BADCOCK *Dom. Amusem.* 186 If blisters do not fall, lay cloths over them steeped in vinegar.

†**b.** To be worn down. *Obs. rare*$^{-1}$.

1708 *Lond. Gaz.* No. 4499/4 One..rough Stone weighing about 21 Carrats, a Point something fallen.

†**14. a.** To shrink; *esp.* of an animal or a limb, to become lean. Also ***to fall in*** or ***out of flesh.***

1530 PALSGR. 544/2, I fall out of flessche by reason of sycknesse. **1599** SHAKS. *Hen. V*, v. ii. 167 A good leg will fall. **1615** CROOKE *Body of Man* 92 His body fell to the wonted scantling. *a* **1661** FULLER *Worthies* (1662) III. 38 The cattle ..will fall in their flesh, if removed to any other Pasture. **1686** J. SMITH *Natural Time* 33 A Pendulum..not being so subject to rise and fall, as others are. **1688** R. HOLME *Armory* II. vii. 155/1 The tenth year the Temples [of a horse] fall. **17** .. SWIFT *Direct. to Servants*, The cattle are weak, and fallen in their flesh with hard riding.

†**b.** Of the complexion: To grow pale. *Obs.*

c **1369** CHAUCER *Dethe Blaunche* 564 That maketh my hewe to fal and fade.

†**15.** Of a horse: ***to fall at*** or ***on the crest***: to have the flesh or skin of the neck drooping or over-hanging. Cf. CREST-FALLEN. *Obs.*

1697 *Lond. Gaz.* No. 3303/4 Lost..one white Nag.. fallen at the Crest with the Harness. **1701** *Ibid.* 3715/4 Stolen..a Sorrel Gelding..falls on the Crest.

16. a. Of (the fluid in) a meteorological instrument: To sink to a lower point.

1658 WILLSFORD *Nature's Secrets* 154 If the water [in a weather glass] falls a degree in 6 hours. **1660** BOYLE *New Exp. Phys. Mech.* xxiii, They found the suspended mercury fall a little as they ascended the hill. **1798** tr. *J.F.G. de la Perouse's Voy. round World* II. x. 188 The barometer fell considerably. **1825** A. CALDCLEUGH *Trav. S. Amer.* I. xi. 342 The thermometer in the winter seldom falls to freezing. **1860** ADM. FITZ-ROY in *Merc. Marine Mag.* VII. 338 The quick-silver ranges, or rises and falls, nearly three inches. **1887** C. C. ABBOTT *Waste-Land Wand.* ii. 22 As I left the house the old mercury barometer was falling.

b. Of temperature: To be reduced.

1871 B. STEWART *Heat* §11 When the amount of sensible heat in a body diminishes its temperature is said to fall. **1890** *Gd. Words* Aug. 553/2 The sun's temperature..may be rising instead of falling.

17. *Music.* To sound a lower note.

1597 MORLEY *Introd. Mus.* 71 If the base rise or fall, you must not rise and fall iust as manie notes as your base did. **1674** PLAYFORD *Skill Mus.* III. 4 If your Bass should fall a seventh, it is but the same as if it did rise a second. **1706** A. BEDFORD *Temple Mus.* ix. 177 Teaching them first to rise, or fall Six or Eight Notes.

18. a. Of a price, rate, rent, weight, etc.: To decrease, diminish, or become reduced.

1580 BARET *Alv.* F 91 The price of victuall was not much fallen. **1602** CAREW *Cornwall* I. 20b, When the price of corne falleth, men generally..breake no more ground, then will serue to supplie their owne turne. **1647** COWLEY *Mistress, Bargain* i, Let no man know The Price of Beauty faln so low! *a* **1687** PETTY *Pol. Arith.* Pref., The Rents of Land are generally fall'n. **1776** ADAM SMITH *W.N.* I. v. (1869) I. 45 The price of bullion has fallen below the mint price. **1890** *Chamb. Jrnl.* 10 May 303/1 The number..has fallen from four thousand to one thousand.

b. Of articles for sale, investments, etc.: To be lowered or diminished in price or value.

1586 A. DAY *Eng. Secretary* II. (1625) 62 Wools are as yet at high rate, but I thinke shortly they will fall. **1608** BP. HALL *Vert. & Vices* II. 131 The Covetous..would despach himselfe when corne falles. **1707** CIBBER *Double Gallant* v. ii, May all the bank-stocks fall when I have bought 'em. **1713** SWIFT *Jrnl. to Stella* 6 Feb., My livings are fallen much this year. **1801** H. C. ROBINSON *Diary* I. 106 Wheat has fallen in our market from 92*s* to 30*s* the coomb. **1812** G. CHALMERS *Dom. Econ. Gt. Brit.* 466 The exchange fell below par.

III. To lose the erect position (primarily with suddenness): opposed to 'stand'.

* To become suddenly prostrate.

19. a. *intr.* To be brought or come suddenly to the ground; also, ***to fall prostrate, to the ground,*** etc.

a **1300** *Cursor M.* 11760 (Cott.) Al þair idels..fel vnto þe grund. *a* **1340** HAMPOLE *Psalter* xxi. 15 Þe iwes wend þat he sould haf fallen in till dust of ded. *c* **1340** *Cursor M.* 23695 (Trin.) Mony floures..þat neuermore shal falle ne dwyne. **1393** LANGL. *P. Pl.* C. I. 113 He ful for sorwe Fro hus chaire. *a* **1400–50** *Alexander* 849 He stumbils..& fallis. **1486** *Bk. St. Alban's* E vij b, Downe in to the steppis ther fallyn of his fete. **1556** *Aurelio & Isab.* (1608) L, The extreme sorrowe.. made her fall as almoste dede to the earthe. **1592** SHAKS. *Rom. & Jul.* IV. ii. 20, I..am enioyn'd..to fall prostrate here, And beg your pardon. **1632** LITHGOW *Trav.* III. 92 Where they fell, there they lay till the morne. **1671** R. BOHUN *Disc. Wind* 153 Trees, and sturdy Oaks..fell in this Tempest. **1694** *Acc. Sev. Late Voy.* II. (1711) 170 One may easily fall, as upon slippery Ice. **1719** DE FOE *Crusoe* (1840) II. xiii. 279 My horse fell. **1840** DICKENS *Barn. Rudge* vi, Starting aside I slipped and fell.

b. *fig.*; esp. in ***to fall to the ground***: to come to nothing; to be discredited or futile. ***to fall flat***: see FLAT *a.* 7 c.

1611 BIBLE *Prov.* xi. 28 He that trusteth in his riches, shall fall. **1634** W. TIRWHYT tr. *Balzac's Lett.* 237 Suffering that name to fall to ground. **1690** LOCKE *Govt.* I. xi. (Rtldg.) 140 The natural power of kings falls to the ground. **1795** *Hist.* in *Ann. Reg.* 126 The injurious epithets..being proofless, fell to the ground. **1825** *New Monthly Mag.* XV. 51 Falsehood is sure to fall to the ground ultimately. **1848** MACAULAY *Hist. Eng.* I. 516 The proposition fell to the ground. *Ibid.* II. 161 Who..could hope to stand where the Hydes had fallen? **1879** M. J. GUEST *Lect. Hist. Eng.* xxxiv. 346 His great hopes fell to the ground.

c. To come down *on* (the point of) a sword, etc. In the Bible translations, after Heb. use: To throw oneself *upon.*

1382 WYCLIF *1 Sam.* xxxi. 4 So Saul cauȝte his swerd and felle vpon it [**1388** felde theronne]. *c* **1400** *Lanfranc's Cirurg.* 67 He [a child] fel on þat knyf in þe former partie of þe þrote. **1611** BIBLE *1 Sam.* xxxi. 4 Therfore Saul tooke a sword, and fell upon it. **1884** [So in R.V.].

d. *Cricket.* Of the wicket: To be knocked down by the ball in bowling. (By extension, the *wicket* is now said *to fall* when the batsman is dismissed in any way.) Const. *to.* Also, of the batsman, with *to*: to be out.

1773 J. DUNCOMBE in R. Freeman *Kentish Poets* (1821) II. 365 Full fast the Kentish wickets fell. **1859** *All Y. Round* No. 13. 306 It was painful to see the Colonel's expression as the sergeant's wicket fell. **1882** *Daily Tel.* 17 May, Robinson's wicket falling to Palmer's bowling. **1882** *Australians in Eng.* 147 Grace fell to a catch at long-on. **1888** R. H. LYTTELTON in Steel & Lyttelton *Cricket* 344 Ridley again fell to Patterson, with the total at 16. **1890** *Sat. Rev.* 5 July 5/2 The sixth wicket..fell for 91.

20. Used (after Heb. idiom preserved in the Vulgate) with reference to voluntary prostration: To prostrate oneself in reverence or supplication. Const. *before, to* (a person), in early use with *dat., at,* †*to* (his feet, †hand). Also, ***to fall on one's face, knees.***

971 *Blickl. Hom.* 27 Þas ealle ic þe sylle, ȝif þu feallest to me & me weorþast. *c* **1000** *Ags. Gosp.* Luke xvii. 16 Þa cyrde he..& feoll to hys fotum. *c* **1205** LAY. 12716 Þe ærchebiscop feol [*c* **1275** fulle] to þes kinges fot. *a* **1300** *Cursor M.* 16632 (Cott.) Þai..on knes be-for him fell. *Ibid.* 25646 (Gött.) Thre kinges com of thrin land to fal þi suete sun til hand and gaf him gift. *c* **1386** CHAUCER *Man of Law's T.* 1006 Whan sche saugh hir fader..Sche..falleth him to feete. *a* **1400–50** *Alexander* 815 Lordis & othire Come to þat conquerour & on knese fallis. **1611** BIBLE *Rev.* xix. 10, I fell at his feete to worship him. **1614** BP. HALL *Recoll. Treat.* 1069 Their Governours fall on their faces to God. **1653** H. COGAN tr. *Pinto's Trav.* iii. 6 We fell on our knees before her. **1850** MRS. STOWE *Uncle Tom's C.* xxvii, 'I'm sure of it', said Tom, falling on his knees.

21. (*fig.* of 19). To succumb to attack or opposing force. **a.** Of a fortified place, *rarely*, of a ship: To be taken.

1606 SHAKS. *Tr. & Cr.* v. viii. 11 So Illion fall thou. **1632** J. HAYWARD tr. *Biondi's Eromena* 81 The forts left alone unsuccour'd, would afterwards fall of themselves. **1797** NELSON in Nicolas *Disp.* II. 343 On the quarter-deck of a Spanish First-rate..did I receive the Swords of vanquished Spaniards..thus fell these Ships. **1818** BYRON *Juan* I. lvi, When proud Granada fell. **1869** W. LONGMAN *Hist. Edw. III*, x, Stirling fell before he could advance to its relief.

b. Of an empire, government, institution, etc.: To be overthrown, come to ruin, perish.

1780 HARRIS *Philol. Enq.* Wks. (1841) 514 After a succession of centuries, the Roman empire fell. **1803** MACKINTOSH *Def. Peltier* Wks. 1846 III. 248 If it [the press] be to fall, it will fall only under the ruins of the British empire. **1818** BYRON *Ch. Har.* IV. cxlv, When falls the Coliseum, Rome shall fall; And when Rome falls—the World. **1874** GREEN *Short Hist.* i. 20 The faith of Woden.. was not to fall without a struggle. **1886** MRS. C. PRAED *Miss Jacobsen* I. i. 14 The Ministry was certain to fall in a short time.

22. a. In moral sense: To yield to temptation, to sin; *esp.* of a woman: To surrender her chastity.

a **1200** *Moral Ode* 158 in *E.E.P.* (1862) 32 It is strong to stonde longe & liht it is to falle. *c* **1340** *Cursor M.* 25812 (Fairf.) Wiþ how litel speche he moȝt haue couered mercy quen he felle. **1526** TINDALE *Rom.* xi. 9 An occasion to faul. **1604** SHAKS. *Oth.* IV. iii. 88 It is their Husbands faults If wiues do fall. **1667** MILTON *P.L.* III. 129 The first sort by their own suggestion fell, Self-tempted. **1758** S. HAYWARD *Serm.* xvii. 505 When he [David] fell so criminally and publickly with Bathsheba. **1869** *Daily News* 21 May, No girls..of any age who are suspected of having fallen. **1875** MANNING *Mission H. Ghost* i. 12 The first Adam..by sinning fell and died.

b. To become pregnant.

1722 *Session Bk. Penninghame* (1933) I. 479 The said.. Jannet..confessed that she fell with child and parted with it in May last. **1891** FARMER *Slang* II. 370/2 *Fall* (venery), to conceive. **1957** YOUNG & WILLMOTT in 'C. H. Rolph' *Human Sum* vii. 129 The expression a woman uses when she is pregnant. She says she has 'fallen'. 'We had been married eight months before I fell.'

23. a. To drop down wounded or dead; to die by violence; *rarely*, by disease. Also † ***to fall dead.***

a **1300** *St. Andrew* 104 in *E.E.P.* (1862) 101 As he homward wende He ful ded. *c* **1374** CHAUCER *Anel. & Arc.* 170 Sheo fallethe dede as any stoone. *c* **1570** *Marr. Wit & Science* v. i. in Dodsley *O. Pl.* 1874 II. 382 He..fought and fell in open field. **1592** SHAKS. *Rom. & Jul.* v. i. 62 The lifewearie-taker may fall dead. **1634** SIR T. HERBERT *Trav.* (1638) 115 A brave Prince..fell by the axe of treachery. **1703** J. SAVAGE *Lett. Antients* xliv. 106 If I had fallen in my Distemper. **1743** BULKELEY & CUMMINS *Voy. S. Seas* 75, I had no desire of falling by the Hand of Captain C. **1874** GREEN *Short Hist.* ii. 80 The greater part of the higher nobility had fallen in battle.

†**b.** To be taken ill *of* (a disease). *Obs.*

1538 HEN. VIII in *Select. Harl. Misc.* (1793) 146 Yrion of Brearton, John Cocke the pothecary, be fallen of the swett in this house. **1653** EVELYN *Mem.* 17 May, My servant..fell of a fit of apoplexy.

c. of animals. Also in *Sporting phraseol.* ***to fall to*** (***one's rifle***): to be brought down by.

1697 DRYDEN *Virg. Georg.* III. 737 By the holy Butcher, if he [Ox] fell. **1823** SCORESBY *Jrnl.* 289 Another whale..fell under our lances. **1892** H. CHICHESTER in *Dict. Nat. Biog.* XXIX. 116/1 Seven lions fell to his rifle in one day.

†**d.** *fig.* To lapse, die out, expire. *Obs.*

1523 LD. BERNERS *Froiss.* I. lxiv. 86 *heading*, The duke dyed without heyre, wherby the dyscencion [descent] fell. *a* **1715** BURNET *Own Time* II. 109 An additional excise, that had been formerly given, was now falling. **1754** ERSKINE *Princ. Sc. Law* (1809) 187 A tack..granted to a single woman, falls by her marriage.

e. *Cards.* To be captured by (a higher card).

1712 POPE *Rape of the Lock* iii. 64 Ev'n mighty Pam..now destitute of aid Falls undistinguish'd by the victor spade. **1889** 'B. W. D.' & 'CAVENDISH' *Whist* 2 A..leads knave of spades, to which nine, eight, and seven fall. *Ibid.* 58 The knave of diamonds must fall to the king.

f. *Criminals' slang.* To be arrested. Cf. FALL *sb.*[1] 18 b.

1879 *Macm. Mag.* XL. 502/2, I fell (was taken up) again at St. Mary Cray for being found at the back of a house. **1938** F. D. SHARPE *Sharpe of Flying Squad* xiv. 158 'What, has he fell *again*!' Getting caught [by the police] is always referred to as 'falling'.

g. *Criminals' slang.* To be convicted; to be sent to prison. Cf. FALL *sb.*[1] 18 c.

1893 L. W. MOORE *His Own Story* xxxiv. 447, I want you to follow my instructions when the case is tried, and if I fall I will find no fault with you. **1926** J. BLACK *You can't Win* ix. 108 If you do fall, the government don't hang a lot of prior convictions on you. **1932** 'S. WOOD' *Shades Prison House* ix. 140 A young Jew at Parkhurst who fell for three years at the game simply because he failed..of ascertaining the actual *locale* of the university of which he claimed to be an alumnus. **1934** [see FALL *sb.*[1] 18 c].

24. Phrases (with sense varying betw. 21 and 23). ***to fall a prey, sacrifice, victim to.*** *lit.* and *fig.*

1648 BOYLE *Seraph. Love* xiv. (1700) 85 Thousands fall sacrifices to the severer Attribute. *a* **1774** FERGUSSON *Drink Eclogue* Poems (1845) 52 The ox..fa's a victim to the bluidy axe. **1825** *New Monthly Mag.* XV. 523 He..fell a victim to his error. **1839** T. BEALE *Sperm Whale* 298 Brave men have at various times fallen a sacrifice to this kind of daring. **1885** *Manch. Exam.* 6 July 4/6 The..books fell a prey to the flames.

25. a. To stumble †*on, into*; to be drawn or forced *into* (danger, fire, a pit, etc.); †to be caught *in* (a snare).

c **1000** *Ags. Gosp.* Matt. xvii. 15 Oft he fylþ on fyr, & ȝelomlice on wæter. *c* **1400** *Rom. Rose* 6650 If ye fillen in her laas. **1456** *How Wise Man taught Son* 64 in Hazl. *E.P.P.* (1864) 171 Comon women..Maks ȝongmen..fulle yn danger. **1548** HALL *Chron.* 152 A man entending to avoide the smoke, falleth into the fyre. **1564** *Complaint Sinner* in Sternhold, etc. *Psalms*, The righteous man falleth now..or than In daunger of thy wrath. **1585** J. B. tr. *P. Viret's Sch. Beastes* C ij, To make them to fall into their nettes. **1611** BIBLE *Amos* iii. 5 Can a bird fall in a snare vpon the earth, where no ginne is for him? —— *Acts* xxvii. 17 They.. fearing lest they should fall into the quicksands, strake saile. **1694** F. BRAGGE *Disc. Parables* xiv. 477 He perceives not the dangers under his feet till he falls into them. **1823** SCORESBY *Jrnl.* 390 In readiness for bringing up, if we

seemed to be falling into danger. **1877** Miss Yonge *Cameos* Ser. iii. vii. 62 They fell into the ambush and were all cut off.

b. fig. *to fall into* (error, sin, etc.).

c **1175** *Lamb. Hom.* 63 God..ȝife us swa his will to donne..þat we ne fallen naut ine sunne. *a* **1300** *Cursor M.* 25400 (Cott.) Lat us in na fanding fall. **1340** Hampole *Pr. Consc.* 3438 In swa many veniel syns we falle. *c* **1449** Pecock *Repr.* ii. ix. 199 So miȝti men..fillen into ydolatrie. *c* **1500** *Lancelot* 1322 Yow art fallyng in the storng vengans Of goddis wreth. **1553** Eden *Treat. Newe Ind.* (Arb.) 10 Sayncte Augustyne..fell into a chyldishe errour. **1611** Bible *1 Tim.* iii. 6 Lest..hee fall into the condemnation of the deuill. **1649** Bp. Hall *Cases Consc.* i. vii. 64 The necessity into which you are fallen. **1711** Steele *Spect.* No. 53 ¶4 Many new Vanities which the Women will fall into. **1751** Jortin *Serm.* (1771) III. i. 21 Many persons fall into mistakes in their notions of happiness. **1875** Jowett *Plato* (ed. 2) III. 202 An error into which we have fallen.

** With the additional notion of breaking up.

26. a. Of a building, etc.: To come down in fragments.

c **1275** Lay. 15949 þine walles fulle. **1382** Wyclif *Isa.* xxi. 9 He answerde, and seide, Is falle, is falle Babilon. *c* **1450** *Merlin* 37 The toure fallith. **1563** Fulke *Meteors* (1640) 20 b, The people were faine to dwell abroad in the fields..for feare their houses would fall on their heads. **1608** D. T. *Ess. Pol. & Mor.* 64 Though the wide world, being broke, should chance to fall, Her may the ruines hurt, but not appall. **1755** *Let.* in *Gentl. Mag.* Dec. 561 At the time the city [of Lisbon] fell..on the opposite side of the river..many houses also fell. **1829** Milman *Hist. Jews* xvi. (1878) 391 One of them [towers] had fallen with its own weight.

b. Of a substance: To crumble.

1770–4 A. Hunter *Georg. Ess.* (1803) I. 30 Clay, well limed, will fall in winter.

†**c.** Of a vessel (in the body): To break down. Of a stitch: To give way. *Obs.*

1615 Crooke *Body of Man* 83 How shal it passe that way after those passages and pores are falne. **1654** Whitlock *Zootomia* 91 Let the Taylor..undertake to mend a stitch fallen in their Bodies.

27. a. *to fall in* or *to* †*mould, pieces, powder*: to break up into fragments, and drop. Similarly, *to fall in two, asunder*. In mod. use *to fall to pieces* is often *transf.* and *fig.*; cf. *go, come to pieces* (see piece).

c **1340** *Cursor M.* 22798 (Fairf.) Quen godd will sua..þat mans flexs to mold se fall. **1398** Trevisa *Barth. De P.R.* xiii. i. (1495) 438 By strengthe of grete driness therth shulde falle to powder. **1665** Hooke *Microgr.* 133 The casual slipping out of a Pin had made several parts of his Clock fall to pieces. **1697** Dampier *Voy.* (1698) I. 215 His Ship..being old and rotten fell in pieces. **1799** E. King *Munimenta Antiqua* I. 309 They fell to pieces on being touched. **1820** Scoresby *Acc. Arctic Reg.* I. 254 The whole mass falls asunder. **1832** Fr. A. Kemble *Let.* in *Rec. Girlhood* (1878) III. 214 The whole concern must collapse and fall to pieces. **1878** Morley *Carlyle* Crit. Misc. Ser. i. 200 Would it have been better..for the old belief gradually..to fall to pieces. **1882** *Standard* 9 Dec. 2/8 The crew rapidly fell to pieces.

†**b.** *to fall in two, to pieces*: (*Sc.*) to give birth to a child; cf. 40 c. *Obs.*

1781 Bentham *Wks.* (1843) X. 111 Mrs. Dunning..is just ready to fall to pieces. **1788** Picken *Poems, Edina* 43 She fell in twa wi' little din.

IV. 28. To move precipitately or with violence; to rush. *Obs.* exc. combined with preps., as in *to fall upon*, to assault (see branch X). †*to fall about* (*a person's*) *ears*: to assail suddenly with blows.

c **1400** *Destr. Troy* 2867 Other folke vpon fer fell thedur thicke. *Ibid.* 13171 þai fell to me fuersly, & my folke slogh. *a* **1400–50** *Alexander* 1133 With þat þe flammand flode fell in his eȝen. **1632** J. Hayward tr. *Biondi's Eromena* 163 Many Galleyes fall towards them so suddenly. **1660–1** Pepys *Diary* 23 Mar., His master fell about his ears and beat him.

V. To be determined to a specified position or object; to have a certain incidence.

29. a. Of a missile or moving body, a movement; also, of light, the sight, etc.: To have or take its direction; to be determined or directed; to settle or impinge. Const. *on, upon.* So also of sound, *to fall upon the ear.*

1658 Willsford *Nature's Secrets* 61 A Rain-bow..formed by the light rays of the Sun falling upon vapours..opposite unto him. **1665** Hooke *Microgr.* 74 The ting'd Rays..past through them, and fell on a sheet of white Paper. **1709** Berkeley *Th. Vision* §35 The rays falling on the pupil. **1793** Smeaton *Edystone L.* §229 She..fell upon the south reef near the highest part. **1834** Medwin *Angler in Wales* I. 290 A random spear..fell wide of him. **1865** J. G. Bertram *Harvest of Sea* (1873) 236 The spawn falls at a considerable distance from the place where it has been emitted. **1878** G. Macdonald *Phantastes* II. xvi. 53 The sound of a closing door..fell on my ear. **1886** A. Sergeant *No Saint* II. vi. 131 His eye fell..upon Cissy. **1890** *Spectator* 10 May, The dreary forest, where full light never falls. **1892** *Temple Bar Mag.* Apr. 474 The words fell solemnly on the stillness.

b. To have its eventual situation in a certain place, or on a certain object.

1570 Billingsley *Euclid* i. vii. 17 The poynt D shall fall either within the triangle ABC or without. **1589** Puttenham *Eng. Poesie* ii. (Arb.) 86 The Cesure fals iust in the middle. *Ibid.* ii. (Arb.) 92 Your sharpe accent falles vpon the last sillable. **1705** Cheyne *Phil. Princ.* §42. 245 Birds..lay their Heads under their Wings, that so the Center of the gravity..may fall upon the Foot they stand on. **1816** Playfair *Nat. Phil.* (1819) II. 17 When the perpendicular..falls within the triangle. **1875** Ouseley *Harmony* iv. 61 Causes the Semitones to fall between the 3rd and 4th.

30. Of a lot, a choice, or anything that is determined by fortune or choice: To 'light *upon*' a particular object. See also lot.

c **1330** R. Brunne *Chron.* (1810) 124 Þe lote felle on Reynere, and on his wif also. *c* **1385** Chaucer *L.G.W. 1942 Ariadne*, The lotte is fallen hym upon. **1535** Coverdale *Ps.* xv[i]. 6 The lott is fallen vnto me in a fayre grounde. **1568** Grafton *Chron.* II. 417 After a long fight the victorie fell on the Englishe part. **1605** Shaks. *Macb.* ii. iv. 30 The Soueraignty will fall vpon Macbeth. **1611** Bible *Acts* i. 26 They gaue foorth their lots, and the lot fell vpon Matthias. **1721** *Lond. Gaz.* No. 6008/1 The Election by Balloting fell upon M. d'Erlac. **1838** Thirlwall *Greece* IV. 47 The suspicion of disaffection..fell on a man of eminent talents. **1855** Macaulay *Hist. Eng.* III. 248 The choice..fell on Whig candidates. **1855** Kingsley *Heroes* ii. (1868) 241 The people stood..weeping, as the lot fell on this one and on that.

31. To come as a lot, portion, or possession; to be allotted or apportioned. Const. †with *dat.* or *to*, †*unto*; rarely *impers.* Also in phrases, *to fall to one's lot* or *share* (see lot, share).

a **1300** *Cursor M.* 4072 (Cott.) Þat blis sal þe neuer fall. *c* **1330** R. Brunne *Chron.* (1810) 142 Him felle to be þe toþer. *c* **1400** *Rom. Rose* 7343 Sich armour as to hem felle. **1475** *Bk. Noblesse* 23 Youre next enheritaunce that fille to youre sede progenitoures. **1576** Fleming *Panopl. Epist.* 35 Al-though it [victorie] fall to the lot of the better, yet [etc.]. **1586** A. Day *Eng. Secretary* ii. (1625) 28 One onely poore Farme fell to my share. *a* **1668** Denham *Progr. Learning* 12 After the Flood, Arts to Chaldæa fell. **1696** tr. *Du Mont's Voy. Levant* 127 The Commanderies..fall to 'em by right of Seniority. **1709** Steele *Tatler* No. 180 ¶1 He had an Estate fallen to him. **1742** Fielding *J. Andrews* ii. xiv, The hogs fell chiefly to his care. **1838** Thirlwall *Greece* II. 320 Many [prisoners] fell to the share of Agrigentum. **1858** Carlyle *Fredk. Gt.* (1865) I. iii. xvi. 234 The whole fighting fell to Sir Horace. **1873** Black *Pr. Thule* ix. 131 A greater treasure than falls to the lot of most men.

32. a. To come as a burden or duty. Const. *to, on, upon*; also *to* with *inf.*

1599 Minsheu *Dial. Sp. & Eng.* (1623) 59 Doe you know when we watch? This night it fals to the companie. **1694** *Acc. Sev. Late Voy.* ii. (1711) 174 The Loss or Gain falls upon the Merchants. **1841** *Jrnl. R. Agric. Soc.* II. i. 25 It falls rather to the Zoologist than to the Botanist to notice them. **1852** *Jrnl. R. Agric. Soc.* XIII. i. 2 A charge of two cents an acre..fell to be paid by the allottees. **1885** *Law Times* LXXIX. 188/2 The expense..must fall upon the purchaser.

b. Followed by *inf.* To be under the necessity, to 'have to' (be, do, etc.). *rare* in literary use; common in *north. dial.*

1845 *New Statist. Acct. Scotl.* XV. (Caithness) 16 Eminent men. Under this head falls to be noticed the late Rev. David Mackay. **1848** *Blackw. Mag.* Nov. 536 These countries would fall to be excluded. **1892** H. R. Mill *Realm of Nature* i. 3 They alone fall to be considered here.

†**33. a.** To appertain or belong; to be applicable, fitting, or proper. Const. *dat.* of indirect obj., or *for, to, till.* *Obs.*

1297 R. Glouc. (1724) 6 Þe bischopriche of Ely, þat þe yle of Ely ys, And of al Cambrugge schire, þat þerto falleþ y wys. *c* **1325** *Coer de L.* 1392 An engyne..And al the takyl that therto fel. *a* **1340** Hampole *Psalter* xii. 6 Wondirful criynge þat falles till contemplatif lyf. **1362** Langl. *P. Pl.* A. i. 50 'Þenne Reddite' quaþ God 'þat to Cesar falleþ.' *c* **1386** Chaucer *Man of Law's T.* 51 Sojourned have these marchauntz in the toun A certeyn tyme, as fel to here plesaunce. *a* **1400** *Relig. Pieces fr. Thornton MS.* (1867) 15 'Sende ȝowre callynge.' This worde falles till vs folke of religioune. *c* **1400** *Lanfranc's Cirurg.* 298 Blood-letynge..falliþ for oure craft þouȝ we for pride take it to barbouris & to wommen. *c* **1440** *York Myst.* xxxi. 338 White clothis we saie fallis for a fonned ladde. *c* **1450** *Bk. Curtasye* 640 in *Babees Bk.* (1868) 321 Speke I wylle of oþer mystere þat falles to court. **15..** *How Plowman lerned Pater Noster* 20 in Hazl. *E.P.P.* (1864) 210 He coude..daube a wall; With all thynge that to husbondry dyde fall.

†**b.** *impers.*; also quasi-*impers.* with inf. phr. or subord. cl. as subject. *Obs.*

1297 R. Glouc. (1724) 446 Þe bones..yburede ys þere vayre ynou, as vel to an kyng. *c* **1300** *Seyn Julian* 9 (Ashm. MS.) It ne ualleð noȝt to me..to be ispoused to þe. *c* **1325** *Metr. Hom.* 11 It falles to a mihty king, That messager word of him bring. *c* **1375** *Cato Major* ii. ix. in *Anglia* VII, Hit falleþ mon to spende his good. **1393** Langl. *P. Pl.* C. xix. 186 'Hit falleþ nat me to lye.' **1401** *Jack Upland, Pol. Poems* (1861) II. 20 Dede men should have but graves, as falleth it to dede men. **1428** *Surtees Misc.* 10 Als fallez a trew merchaunt to doo. **1563** B. Googe *Eglogs* (Arb.) 103 She..supped well as falleth for her state.

VI. To come casually, or without design or effort, into a certain position.

34. Of things: To come by chance; esp. † *to fall in* or *into a person's heart, mind*, etc.: to occur to (him); also, *to fall in one's* †*road, way*, etc.; rarely of a person.

c **1340** *Cursor M.* 15483 (Fairf.), How muȝt hit falle in þi hert to be-gyn suche a dede. **1413** Lydg. *Pylgr. Sowle* v. i. 71 It myghte not fall in no mans mynde fully to descryuen it. **1530** Palsgr. 544/1, I wyll nat do but as it falleth in my brayne. **1583** Hollyband *Campo di Fior* 3 There is some thing fallen I know not what into mine eyes. **1590** Sir J. Smyth *Disc. Weapons* 23 b, I will..answere as many of them [objections] as shall fall into my memorie. **1605** Bp. Hall *Medit. & Vows* ii. §44 As for riches, if they fall in my way, I refuse them not. **1624** Massinger *Renegado* ii. iv, Nor can it fall in my imagination, What wrong you e'er have done me. **1656** *Burton's Diary* (1828) I. 43 A matter of the like nature cannot possibly fall before you. **1677** Hale *Prim. Orig. Man.* i. ii. 62 A..deliberate connexing of Consequents, which falls not in the common road of ordinary men. **1751** T. Hollis in *Lett. Lit. Men* (Camden) 379 Acquainting you with any thing that fell in my way abroad. **1861** M. Pattison *Ess.* (1889) I. 35 The earliest notice on the subject which has fallen in his way.

35. Of persons. **a.** To come by chance into a certain position. Now chiefly in phrase (of biblical origin), *to fall among* (thieves, etc.).

c **1175** *Lamb. Hom.* 79 A mon lihte from ierusalem in to ierico and fol imong þoues. **1382** Wyclif *Luke* x. 30 Sum man cam doun fro Jerusalem in to Jerico, and felde among theuues. [So **1535** in Coverdale; **1611** in A.V.] **1586** A. Day *Eng. Secretary* ii. (1625) 39, I sithence fell into company. **1611** Shaks. *Cymb.* iii. vi. 76 Be sprightly, for you fall 'mongst Friends. **1634** Sir T. Herbert *Trav.* (1638) 84 [He] falls among five hundred light horse of Curroons and perishes. **1879** Miss Braddon *Clov. Foot* xxvi, I fell among thieves, and got cleaned out. **1879** M. J. Guest *Lect. Hist. Eng.* xxx. 296 The mixed company he falls into.

b. To happen, or be thrown †*into, on,* or *upon* (a period of specified character).

1633 Bp. Hall *Hard Texts* 370 Ye are now fallen into a time wherein there is much opposition to Christ. **1803** *Pic Nic* No. 2 (1806) I. 56 You are fallen on such incorrigible times. **1844** Disraeli *Coningsby* vi. ii. 226 The degenerate days on which he had fallen. **1888** M. Arnold *Ess. Crit.* Ser. ii. iii. 91 Gray, a born poet, fell upon an age of prose.

36. To come naturally, without forcing or effort. *lit.* and *fig.* † *to fall to oneself*: to regain self-control. *Obs.*

c **1400** *Lanfranc's Cirurg.* 316 In þis maner þe boon schal falle into his joinct. **1517** Torkington *Pilgr.* (1884) 22 We..fell to an Ankyr in the Rode. **1613** Shaks. *Hen. VIII*, ii. i. 35 He..something spoke in choller, ill, and hasty; But he fell to himselfe againe. **1760–72** tr. *Juan & Ulloa's Voy.* (ed. 3) II. 287 The ship will fall into her station without any difficulty. *Mod.* When the main features of your plan are settled, the details will fall into their places easily.

37. To be naturally divisible *into.*

1641 Bp. Hall *Rem. Wks.* (1660) 66 The Text falls into these parts so naturally. **1862** *Temple Bar Mag.* VI. 388 The subject..falls into four divisions. **1876** F. G. Fleay *Shaks. Manual* ii. i. 128 The plays fall distinctly into four periods.

VII. To pass suddenly, accidentally, or in the course of events, into a certain condition.

38. a. Of persons: To pass (usually, with suddenness) †*in, into,* †*to* some specified condition, bodily or mental, or some external condition or relation.

a **1225** *Ancr. R.* 224 He..feol so into unhope. *a* **1300** *Cursor M.* 19084 (Cott.) For wonder sum þai fell in suim. *Ibid.* 20496 (Cott.) All þar fell to slepe onan. *c* **1385** Chaucer *L.G.W.* 590 *Cleop.*, He was fallyn in prosperite. *c* **1430** Lydg. *Bochas* i. x. (1544) 21 a, The wretchednes that I am in fall. *c* **1489** Caxton *Sonnes of Aymon* xxii. 489 Yf thus he wylle doo I shall falle to peas. *a* **1533** Ld. Berners *Huon* li. 172, I am fallen in to pouerte and mysery. **1548** Hall *Chron.* 14 The Abbot of Westminster..fell in a sodaine palsey. *Ibid.* 32 [He] fell in suche favour with the kyng. **1568** Grafton *Chron.* II. 136 He fell to agreement with the French king. **1570–6** Lambarde *Peramb. Kent* (1826) 211 Shee fell into the travaile of childe birthe. **1655** Sir E. Nicholas in *N. Papers* (Camden) II. 298, I am fallen into an acquaintance with a most eminent Leueller. **1659** B. Harris *Parival's Iron Age* 139 These two, being both Officers of the same Master, fell to difference. **1709** Steele & Swift *Tatler* No. 68 ¶3 Some..fall into Laughter out of a certain Benevolence in their Temper. **1711** Addison *Spect.* No. 7 ¶2, I fell into a profound Contemplation. **1751** Jortin *Serm.* (1771) IV. i. 54 He fell into an agony at the thoughts of it. *a* **1862** Buckle *Civiliz.* (1873) III. iv. 192 The religious servitude into which the Scotch fell. **1879** Geo. Eliot *Coll. Breakf. P.* 377 Fall to sleep In the deep bosom of the Unchangeable. **1879** M. J. Guest *Lect. Hist. Eng.* xix. 186 Henry fell into one of his fearful rages.

b. *to fall in love*: to become enamoured. Const. *with.* Also *transf.* to become very fond of, or devoted to. (Cf. 40 c.)

1530 Palsgr. 544/2, I shall fall in love with her. **1591** Shaks. *Two Gent.* i. ii. 2 Would'st thou then counsaile me to fall in loue? **1659** J. Moxon *Tutor to Astron.* 18 To make Men fall in love with Astronomy. **1768** Mad. D'Arblay *Early Diary* (1889) I. 25 A young lady of fashion..has fallen in love with my cousin. **1837** Lytton *E. Maltrav.* 14 We must not fall in love with each other. **1866** G. Macdonald *Ann. Q. Neighb.* i. (1878) 6, I would go and fall in love..with the country round about.

39. Of things, whether material or immaterial: To pass, lapse (usually, unperceived or by neglect) †*in, into,* †*to* some specified condition, *esp.* arrears, confusion, decay, ruin, etc. Cf. 26, 27.

c **1340** *Cursor M.* 9204 (Trin.) Þat kyngdome fel in to wrake. **1530** Palsgr. 545/1 This castell falleth to ruynes euery day. **1577** B. Googe *Heresbach's Husb.* i. (1586) 35 It flowreth in June and July, and then falleth to seede. **1579** Fenton *Guicciard.* i. (1599) 8 If in this desire he had beene satisfied, the peace of Italy had not perhaps falne into so sodaine alteration and trouble. **1605** Shaks. *Macb.* v. iii. 23 My way of life Is falne into the Seare, the yellow Leafe. **1720** Ozell tr. *Vertot's Rom. Rep.* I. vii. 424 The Lex Licina fell at length into Contempt. **1761** Hume *Hist. Eng.* III. liv. 167 He found every thing fallen into such confusion. **1817** W. Selwyn *Law Nisi Prius* (ed. 4) II. 1227 The form of declaring with a continuando has fallen into disuse. **1879** M. J. Guest *Lect. Hist. Eng.* xxxi. 306 The tribute..had fallen into arrears. **1889** Mrs. C. Carr *Marg. Maliphant* II. xx. 103 The wane of the day had fallen into dusk.

40. With compl. (adj., sb., or prepositional phrase): To become (whatever the complement signifies).

The compl. usually denotes either an unfavourable condition, or one that comes in the ordinary course of events.

a. with *adj.* as complement (*e.g.* ill, lame, sick, vacant, etc.). *to fall due*: see due.

1382 Wyclif *Gen.* xxvi. 13 The man fel ryche. *a* **1400–50** *Alexander* 856 Philip falne [was] sare seke. **1530** Palsgr. 545/1 My lorde entendeth to gyve him the nexte benyfyce

that falleth voyde. *a* **1533** LD. BERNERS *Huon* clxii. 629 *heading*, To fal aquaynted with the fayre damoysel. **1607** TOPSELL *Four-f. Beasts* (1673) 241 The King fell exceeding angry. **1658** A. FOX tr. *Wurtz' Surg.* II. xi. 89 When a party is wounded in the Back..he fals lame. **1667** SIR C. LYTTLETON in *Hatton Corr.* (1878) 51 Falling very ill againe ..of feavor. **1751** SMOLLETT *Per. Pic.* vii, She fell sick of sorrow and mortification. **1820** SOUTHEY *Life Wesley* II. 414 His horse fell lame. **1858** CARLYLE *Fredk. Gt.* (1865) I. III. iii. 147 The Teutsch Ritters were fallen moneyless. **1879** FROUDE *Cæsar* xviii. 303 All the offices fell vacant together. **1889** A. SERGEANT *Luck of House* I. ix. 129 Her tongue would fall silent.

b. with *sb.* as compl. Now only in ***to fall heir***.

1591–2 LD. BACON *Let.* in Spedding *Life & Lett.* (1861) I. 116 His eldest son is fallen ward. **1606** G. W[OODCOCKE] tr. *Justin's Hist.* 29 b, At last they fal friends out of a voluntarie consent. **1627–77** FELTHAM *Resolves* I. xix. 35 'Tis gain.. that makes man fall a Traitor. **1891** *Harper's Mag.* Dec. 100/2 The elder..eventually fell heir to a certain estate.

†**c.** with *prep. phr.* as complement. *Obs.* exc. *dial.*

1508 BARCLAY *Shyp of Folys* 14 They fall out of theyr mynde. **1530** PALSGR. 544/1 He is fallen all on a sweate. **1577** B. GOOGE *Heresbach's Husb.* I. (1586) 45 b, Hey..yf it be carryed into the Loft, rotteth, and the vapour being over-heated, falleth on fyre and burneth. **1578** LYTE *Dodoens* III. xxvi. 352 Them that waxe mad or fall beside themselves. **1631** WEEVER *Anc. Fun. Mon.* 691 Leyland..fell besides his wits. **1813** PICKEN *Poems, Auld Joanna* 43 Blear-e'ed Kate had fa'n wi' bairn. **1877** E. PEACOCK *N.W. Linc. Gloss.*, *Fall wi' bairn*, to become pregnant.

d. ***to fall to be***: to come to be.

1548 UDALL, etc. *Erasm. Par. John* 42 Our mynde ought not so to be delited in the contemplacion of hye thynges that we fall to be careles of our common stocke. **1663** GERBIER *Counsel* 44 The peeres of Brick or Stone between them [window-cases], will fall to be of a fit width. *a* **1715** BURNET *Own Time* (1766) I. 443 William fell to be in ill terms with his mother. **1887** STEVENSON *Misadv. J. Nicholson* iv. 6 The memory of his faults had already fallen to be one of those old aches.

41. a. Of a benefice or its revenues: To lapse, revert to the feudal superior. †**b.** Of an office, living, holding: To become vacant. *Obs.*

1530 PALSGR. 544/1 So sone as thou cannest se any offyce fall, come aske it of the kynge. **1550** CROWLEY *Epigr.* 948 Reuersions of fermes are bought long ere they fall. **1583** *Wills & Inv. N.C.* (Surtees) II. 76 To remayne..in the manor house of Thirlwall, untill Newbiggen fall. **1665** J. WEBB *Stone-Heng* (1725) 119 He..returned into England when His Place fell. **1686** R. PARR *Life Ussher*, He.. obtained a grant of a patent..of such impropriations belonging to the Crown, as were then Leased out, as soon as they should fall. *a* **1715** BURNET *Own Time* II. 286 The Mastership of the temple was like to fall. **1796** JANE AUSTEN *Pride & Prej.* (1885) I. xvi. 68 When the living fell, it was given elsewhere. **1839** KEIGHTLEY *Hist. Eng.* II. 48 The revenues should fall to the crown. **1871** FREEMAN *Norm. Conq.* (1876) IV. xvii. 58 The new Minster was held to fall by the treason of its Abbot.

†**42.** To change, turn *to*, *into* (something worse). *Obs.*

1393 LANGL. *P. Pl.* C. XXI. 108 ȝoure fraunchise þat freo was fallen is to þraldom. **1393** GOWER *Conf.* I. 7 Love is falle into discorde. *Ibid.* III. 275 Which..From aungels into fendes felle. **1426** AUDELAY *Poems* 12 Ale the wyt of this word fallus to foly. **1586** A. DAY *Eng. Secretary* II. 18 Your writing..falleth otherwise to a manner of reproaching.

†**43.** Of the weather: To turn out, prove to be.

1633 G. HERBERT *Temple, Complaining* ii, A silly flie, That live or die According as the weather falls.

VIII. To occur, come to pass, befall, result.

†**44.** To arrive in course of time. Cf. COME *v.* 20.

1340 HAMPOLE *Pr. Consc.* 2616 In erthe sal duelle þe bodis alle, Until þat dredful day sal falle. **1340–70** *Alex. & Dind.* 323 We mowe tellen our time whan þe time fallus. **1697** DRYDEN *Virg. Georg.* IV. 337 Two Honey Harvests fall in ev'ry Year.

45. Of a special day or season: To come or occur at a stated time, or within stated limits.

1297 R. GLOUC. (1724) 277 A Seyn Austynes day yt was, as yt valþ in May. *a* **1300** *Cursor M.* 17288 + 77 (Cott.) þat friday was þair leuedy day.. But now ful selden falles it soo. *c* **1391** CHAUCER *Astrol.* II. §12 The xiij day of March fil vp-on a Saterday. **1662** STILLINGFL. *Orig. Sacr.* I. i. §20 The 11 Generation after Moses, which will fall about the time of Samuel. **1694** HOLDER *Time* viii. 101 The Vernal Equinox, which at the time of the Nicene Council fell upon the 21st of March, falls now above 10 days sooner. **1853** MAURICE *Proph. & Kings* xx. 352 The date..falling between the years 610 and 600 before Christ. **1889** *Repent. P. Wentworth* III. iv. 44 Easter fell early that year.

46. Of an event, etc.: To come to pass; to happen, to occur. *Obs.* exc. *poet.* **a.** simply; rarely with *adj.* as complement.

c **1290** *S. Eng. Leg.* I. 16/512 Mani miracle þar feol a-day. *c* **1340** *Cursor M.* 12284 (Trin.) Wherfore haue ye leten þis falle. **1382** WYCLIF *Ecclus.* xlviii. 29 He shewide thingus to come..er that thei fellen. *c* **1450** LONELICH *Grail* lvi. 64 A famyne that schold fallen in gret Bretaygne. **1523** LD. BERNERS *Froiss.* I. cxlvi. 174 Lykewise they woll deale with vs if the case fell lyke. *a* **1547** SURREY *Aeneid* II. 897 A sodein monstrous marvel fell. **1633** BP. HALL *Hard Texts* 521 The death of this cruel Tyran..shall fall about two moneths after this later period. **1764** GOLDSM. *Trav.* 57 Oft a sigh prevails, and sorrows fall. **1823** LONGFELLOW *Life* (1891) I. iii. 33, I am rather sorry that the Exhibition falls so late in the year. **1878** TENNYSON *Q. Mary* v. i, If war should fall between yourself and France.

b. with *dat.* as indirect obj., or *to*, *unto*. Also with adj. as compl. *Obs.* exc. *arch.*

c **1300** *Cursor M.* App. ii. 706 Thei comen lepand þiderwarde, and þat hem fel swiþe harde. **1375** BARBOUR *Bruce* II. 45 Sa hard myscheiff hym fell. *a* **1400–50** *Alexander* 2722 þe mare vnfryndschip þarfore fall sall þe neuire. *c* **1450** *Merlin* 10 It..neuer fill to woman saf oonly to me. *a* **1533** LD. BERNERS *Huon* vii. 15 The peteous aduenture that fell..to the two chyldren. **1583** SEMPILL *Bp. of St. Androis* in *Ballates* (1872) 218 A vengeance faa him. **18..** TENNYSON *Grasshopper* Poems (1830) 108 Shame fall 'em.

c. *impers.*; also quasi-*impers.* with subject clause. Now *rare.* Const. *dat.*, rarely with adj. as compl. † ***him fell well***: he prospered. † ***it falleth profit***: it proves profitable. † ***may fall*** (in ME. = mayhap, perhaps): see MAY.

c **1250** *Gen. & Ex.* 1521 Niðede ðat folk him fel wel. *c* **1340** *Cursor M.* 11929 (Fairf.) Hhyt fille vpon an holiday..Ihesu and othir childryn in samyn went hem by the rever to gamyn. **1375** *Cantic. de Creatione* 638 in *Anglia* I, By þe weye it fel hem hard: an addre to hem gan lepe. *c* **1375** *Cato Major* I. viii. in *Anglia* VII, Ofte falleþ þe wyf hit hateþ þat loueþ þe goode hosebande. *c* **1380** WYCLIF *Sel. Wks.* III. 431 It falleþ profyte to summe men to be bounde to a stake. *a* **1400–50** *Alexander* 2600 þof us fall now to flee we may na ferryre wend. *a* **1533** LD. BERNERS *Huon* lx. 210 So it fell that ..kinge Charlemayn sent for hym. **1611** BIBLE *2 Kings* iv. 11 It fell on a day that hee came thither. **1868–70** MORRIS *Earthly Par.* (1890) 387/2 As it fell..an elder 'gan to tell The story.

d. In phrases, ***fair fall, foul fall***: may good *or* evil befall. Also, †***fall what can, will, fall***: happen what may; through thick and thin.

a **1225** *Leg. Kath.* 1376 O, leue feren, feire is us i-fallen. *c* **1385** CHAUCER *L.G.W.* Prol. 277 My lady sovereyne..ys so good..I prey to God that ever falle hire faire. *c* **1440** *York Myst.* xvi. 50 Faire falle þe my faire sone. *a* **1450** *Knt. de la Tour* (1868) 37 Falle what wolle falle, y wol do more euelle. **1523** SKELTON *Garl. Laurel* 27 Fair fall that forster that so well can bate his hownde. **1631** MASSINGER *Emp. East* II. i, I will not come behind, Fall what can fall! **1651** BAXTER *Inf. Bapt.* 100 Fair fall to the Antinomians. *a* **1775** *Hobie Noble* i. in Child *Ballads* (1890) VII. clxxxix. 2/1 Foul fa the breast first treason bred in! **1787** BURNS *To a Haggis* i, Fair fa' your honest, sonsie face. **1860** MARTIN *Horace* 218 Foul fall the day. **1884** *Cheshire Gloss.* s.v., 'Fair-faw Johnny; he's best lad o' th' two.'

47. To come in the course of events, or of orderly treatment. Const. with *dat. infin.* ***to fall to be, to be*** (***spoken of***, etc.).

1450–1530 *Myrr. our Ladye* 34 The feaste of saynt Anyan fell to be the same tyme at Orleaunce. **1535** in Ellis *Orig. Lett.* Ser. III. I. 317 The same gentleman that toke hym may convaye hym to the forsaide place wher he shall faule to be upon monday next. **1634** SIR T. HERBERT *Trav.* 87 The Gardens fall in the next place, to be spoken of. **1639** GENTILIS *Servita's Inquis.* (1676) 872 With ease they are made, because with ease they are revoked..as it falls to be most commodious for their businesses. *a* **1715** BURNET *Own Time* (1724) I. iii. 372 A Church falling to be given in that way, the electors had a mind to choose me. **1863** BURTON *Bk. Hunter* 310 Had it fallen to be edited by a philosophical enquirer. **1879** FROUDE *Cæsar* vii. 62 The campaign of Sylla in the East does not fall to be described in this place. **1884** *Daily News* 11 Feb. 5/5 The advance would fall to be made in the driest time.

†**48. a.** To come as a consequence or result. Const. *by*, *from*, *of*, *out of*. *Obs.*

a **1300** *Cursor M.* 4520 (Cott.) Was þar nan emang ham all Cuth sai quat þar-of suld fall. **1398** TREVISA *Barth. De P.R.* VII. iii. (1495) 223 Of that ytchynge fallyth many scalles. *c* **1400** *Lanfranc's Cirurg.* 191 Icchinge & scabbe..falliþ ofte of salt metis. **1483** CAXTON *G. de la Tour* Cj, Yet shalle I saye ..how it happed..and what fylle therof. *a* **1533** LD. BERNERS *Huon* ii. 4 Wherby so many illes haue fallen. *c* **1585** R. BROWNE *Answ. Cartwright* 57 Other matters, which fall out of the former proofes. *a* **1656** BP. HALL *Soliloquies* 35 What can fall from defective causes but imperfect effects?

†**b.** To turn *to*, result *in*; to turn out, result.

a **1300** *Cursor M.* 15420 (Cott.) To þaim þat þe cheping did, it fel to mikel vnspede. *Ibid.* 29058 (Cott.) þat þi fast to saul fode mai falle. **1377** LANGL. *P. Pl.* XII. 47 Felyce hir fayrnesse; fel hir al to sklaundre. **1398** TREVISA *Barth. De P.R.* XVII. clxxxv. (1495) 727 Dronkenesse fallyth ofte in mannys slowthe and spouse brekynge. *c* **1400** *Destr. Troy* 8934 All oure fare & oure fortune hath fallyn to þe best. **1611** BIBLE *Ruth* iii. 18 Sit still..vntill thou know how the matter will fall. **1699** BENTLEY *Phal.* 211 Let the dispute about Comedy and Susarion fall as it will.

†**c.** ***fall of*** (after 'what'): To happen to, to become of. Cf. BECOME 4. *Obs.*

c **1430** *Chev. Assigne* 130 And askede hym, in good feythe what felle of þe chyldren. **1485** CAXTON *Paris & V.* 45 What shal falle of you my lady. **1525** LD. BERNERS *Froiss.* II. lxxviii. [lxxiv.] 234 No man knewe what sholde fal of theyr bodyes.

IX. Transitive senses. * *causative.*

†**49. a.** To let fall, drop; to shed (tears); to cast, shed (leaves); to bring down (a weapon, the hand, etc.). *Obs.* exc. in *Bellringing* (see quot. 1868).

1475 *Bk. Noblesse* 66 It wolde make an harde hert man to falle the teris of his yen. **1594** SHAKS. *Rich. III*, v. iii. 135 To morrow in the battell..fall thy edgelesse Sword. **1598** SYLVESTER *Du Bartas* II. ii. II. (1641) 120/2 A spark, that Shepheards Have faln..Among dry leaves. **1598** GRENEWEY *Tacitus' Ann.* I. xii. (1622) 23 Arminius wife..not once falling a teare, nor crauing fauor. **1600** SHAKS. *A.Y.L.* III. v. 5 The common executioner..Falls not the axe upon the humbled neck, But first begs pardon. **1610** —— *Temp.* II. i. 296 Fall it [your hand] on Gonzalo. *a* **1628** F. GREVILLE *Poems, Cælica* xxxvi, He had falne his Fathers Canne, All of Gold in the deepe. **1632** NABBES *Covent Garden* I. v, You've fallen my glove. **1665** G. HAVERS *P. della Valle's Trav. E. India* 2 We cast Anchor without falling our sails. **1665–76** RAY *Flora* 20 Shrubs which fall their leaves in the winter. **1808** J. BARLOW *Columb.* VII. 201 They..the sullen draw-bridge fall. **1868** DENISON *Clocks & Watches* (ed. 5) 415 In some parts of England they never raise and 'fall' the bells in order.

†**b.** *fig.* To 'drop', not to insist on. *Obs.*

a **1700** DRYDEN (J.), I am willing to fall this argument.

†**c.** To drop, give birth to (lambs, etc.). *Obs.*

1596 SHAKS. *Merch. V.* I. iii. 89 The..Ewes..did in eaning time Fall party-colour'd lambs. **1667** COLEPRESSE in *Phil. Trans.* II. 480 A White Lamb faln on a Common.

†**50. a.** To let down, lower in position or direction. ***to fall one's crest***: see CREST. *Obs.*

1692 *Capt. Smith's Seaman's Gram.* II. xxii. 135 Causing a Matross to raise or fall the Gun with an Hank-spike. **1748** RICHARDSON *Clarissa* vi. V. 82 Half rearing the lids, to see who the next-comer was; and falling them again. **1795** J. PHILLIPS *Hist. Inland Navig.* 8 Method employed..to raise or fall vessels out of one Canal into another.

†**b.** To cause to settle or subside. *Obs.*

1789 *Trans. Soc. Enc. Arts* II. 235 Throwing in a small quantity of oil to fall the froth.

†**c.** To lower (the voice), either in pitch or loudness. *Obs.*

1626 BACON *Sylva* §105 To raise or fall his Voice still by Half-Notes. **1748** DODSLEY *Preceptor* Introd. (1763) I. 44 *Emphasis* is raising the Voice, *Cadence* is falling it.

†**d.** To lower (a price, etc.); to bring down in value, depreciate; to depress (the market). Also, of land: To become worth less (rent). *Obs.*

1677 YARRANTON *Eng. Improv.* 149 The Lands fall Rents. **1691** LOCKE *Lower. Interest* Wks. 1727 II. 8 You fall the Price of your Native Commodities. **1717** NEWTON in Rigaud *Corr. Sci. Men* (1841) II. 425 In raising and falling the money, their King's edicts have sometimes varied a little. **1722** *Lett. from Mist's Wkly. Jrnl.* II. 41 The turning of Money in Stocks; and raising and falling the Market. **1790** BURKE *Fr. Rev.* 282 He falls the value of his land and raises the value of assignats.

†**51. a.** To bring or throw to the ground; to overthrow. *lit.* and *fig.* *Obs.*

c **1300** *K. Alis.* 7186 He hath take my castelis; He hath falle my torellis. **1362** LANGL. *P. Pl.* A. III. 43 Bere wel þin ernde ..Concience to falle. *c* **1420** *Sir Amadace* (Camd.) xxxviii, God may bothe mon falle and rise. **1586** A. DAY *Eng. Secretary* II. (1625) 78 By desire men are enflamed, by anger kindled, fallen by errour. *a* **1625** BOYS *Wks.* (1629) 301 The serpent doth..bruise our heele and so fall vs.

b. Of a horse: To 'throw' (its rider). *U.S.*

The wk. conjugation indicates that this is taken as another word, f. FALL *sb.*

a **1851** W. COLTON *Ship & Shore* viii. 139 The servant-boy..told how the animal had falled him three times.

c. To cut down (trees). Now *dial.*, *U.S.*, *Austral.*, and *N.Z.*

c **1386** CHAUCER *Knt's T.* 2930 The beestes and the briddes alle ffledden for fere, whan the wode was falle. *c* **1420** *Pallad. on Husb.* II. 437 Nowe make is to falle in season best. **1523** FITZHERB. *Husb.* §134 To fall the vnder wode. **1685** *Col. Rec. Pennsylv.* I. 128 A Penalty to be laid upon such as Cutt or fall Marked..trees. **1805** H. REPTON *Landscape Gard.* 75 The most beautiful places may..be formed by falling..trees. **1860** A. F. RIDGWAY *Voices from Auckland* 67 Large quantities of bush have this season been 'fallen'. *Ibid.* 67 When to fall his bush? When to burn off? **1869** J. MAY *Guide to Farming in N.Z.* 18 We had a dread of commencing to fall bush. **1875** PARISH *Sussex Gloss.* s.v., These trees are getting too thick, I shall fall a few of them next year. **1882** W. D. HAY *Brighter Britain* I. vii. 186 In felling bush, or 'falling' it, as we say here, advantage is taken of the lay of the land. **1883** E. INGERSOLL in *Harper's Mag.* Jan. 201/1 We must fall a tree straight and true. **1891** R. WALLACE *Rural Econ. Austral. & N.Z.* xv. 231 In the case of bush country the trees require to be 'fallen', and the under-scrub cut. **1941** ALLEY & HALL *Farmer in N.Z.* iv. 99 The bush was then felled, or 'falled'.

†**52.** To throw, direct, cause to impinge (*upon*).

a **1774** GOLDSMITH *Surv. Experim. Philos.* (1776) II. 235 A number of plain glasses, united to fall their rays upon the same spot, would actually burn.

** *not causative.*

†**53.** = 'To fall from', 'to fall down'. *Obs.*

c **1450** *St. Cuthbert* (Surtees) 5993 How a ȝonge man felle a tre. **1665** SIR T. HERBERT *Trav.* (1677) 201 If we miss One step, we headlong fall the precipice.

54. To have as one's share, come in for, obtain. *Obs.* exc. *dial.*

[Derived from 31, by transposition of subject and object.]

c **1400** *Destr. Troy* 2406 A mede..That ye faithfully shall falle. *a* **1568** A. SCOTT *Poems* (1820) 51 Feind a crum of the scho fawis. **1637–50** ROW *Hist. Kirk* (1842) 89 If a minister depart this life after Michaelmas, his executors shall fall that year's stipend. **1641** BEST *Farm. Bks.* (Surtees) 26 If they bee under five the procter falleth none..if there bee above five the procter falleth one. **1690** W. WALKER *Idiomat. Anglo-Lat.* 164 He heard that Dion had fallen a good estate. **1750** *Song, For a' that* in *Collect. Loyal Songs* 43 The Whigs think a' that weal is won, But Faith they ma' na fa' that. [Cf. **1795** BURNS *For a' that* iv, Guid faith he mauna fa' that.] **1889** *Manley & Corringham Gloss.*, *Fall*, to get, to receive.

X. With prep. (and prepositional phrases).

Besides the prepositions *from*, *into*, *out of*, *to*, which naturally follow *fall*, it is construed with a variety of others, for which see above: in the following combinations the sense is more or less specialized.

55. fall a ——. To set about, take to, begin (some action). Now only with vbl. sbs. in *-ing*.

Cf. *fall on* (65 a), and A *prep.*[1] 13 b.

1576 FLEMING *Panopl. Epist.* 274 Democritus..fell a laughing at what so ever he sawe done. **1635** SIBBES *Soul's Confl.* Pref. (1638) 11 Luther when he saw Melancthon.. falls a chiding of him. *a* **1644** CHILLINGW. *Serm.* ii. (1664) 43 He is scarse a man..till he fall a work. **1749** FIELDING *Tom Jones* v. vi, Mr. Jones now fell a trembling as if he had been shaken with the fit of an ague. **1867** TROLLOPE *Chron. Barset* II. liii. 101 She reined in her horse and fell a-weeping.

56. fall across ——. To come upon by chance, meet with.

1886 'HUGH CONWAY' *Living or Dead* v, I happened to fall across Estmere..in the park.

57. fall at ——. †**a.** To be drawn or pass suddenly into (debate, strife, etc.). ***to fall at square***: see SQUARE. *Obs.*

c **1400** MAUNDEV. (Roxb.) xv. 69 Thurgh drunkenness þai fall at grete wordes. **1525** *2 Proph. St. Eng.* in Furniv. *Ballads from MSS.* I. 306 Fflaunders and England shall fall at decensyoun. **1648** HERRICK *Bag of Bee* i, Two Cupids fell at odds.

†**b.** ***fall at hand.*** To be near at hand, to be going to happen. *Obs.*

1529 MORE *Comf. agst. Trib.* I. Wks. 1139/1 Greate perilles appeare here to fall at hande.

58. fall behind ——. To drop into the rear of, be outstripped or left behind by.

1856 *Titan Mag.* Nov. 443/1 A man who has fallen behind his age. **1890** T. F. TOUT *Hist. Eng. from 1689.* 12 Dutch commerce was now falling behind that of England.

59. fall down ——. a. See DOWN *prep.*

1712 BERKELEY *Pass. Obed.* §27 Suppose a prince..to fall down a precipice.

b. To descend or drop down (a river, etc.).

1699 DAMPIER *Voy.* II. I. 103 We fell down from Hean to our Ships. **1761–2** HUME *Hist. Eng.* (1806) V. lxxi. 296 The army quickly fell down the rivers and canals from Nimeguen. **1790** BEATSON *Nav. & Mil. Mem.* 310 They fell down the river, till they came up to the 7 Dutch Ships.

60. fall for ——. To be captivated or carried away by; to yield to the attractions of; (in a bad sense) to be taken in by. *slang* (orig. *U.S.*).

1903 R. L. MCCARDELL *Conversat. Chorus Girl* 28 The mayor fell for it. **1911** L. J. VANCE *Cynthia* xi. 179 There's only one sensible thing... And I think I see you falling for it. **1914** *Sat. Even. Post* 23 May 62/3, I fell for her the first time I seen her. **1916** H. L. WILSON *Somewhere in Red Gap* v. 186 Even Mis' Judge Ballard fell for it, though hers were made of severe black with a long coat. **1917** A. G. EMPEY *From Fire Step* xxii. 152 When firing my gun, I was to play my tune, and Fritz, no doubt, would fall for it, try to imitate me as an added insult. **1924** R. MACAULAY *Orphan Island* xix. 250 European critics, for ever falling for new things, would fall most certainly for this. **1926** GALSWORTHY *Silver Spoon* II. viii, 'He's fallen for Marjorie Ferrar.' '"Fallen for her"?' said Soames. 'What an expression!' 'Yes, dear; it's American.' **1929** J. J. FARJEON *Underground* xxi. 139, I held out my pocket-case, and said I'd found it on the floor of the hotel. 'Is it yours?' I asked. To my surprise, he fell for it beautifully. **1952** L. A. G. STRONG *Darling Tom* xvii. 138 So he had fallen for it, had he, the big sap? **1958** *Times Lit. Suppl.* 12 Sept. 509/4 He meets and falls for a twenty-year-old dipsomaniac.

61. fall from ——. a. See simple senses. †**b.** To drop off in opinion from; to disagree with.

c **1380** WYCLIF *Sel. Wks.* III. 342 We mai see..how þes popis fallen fro Petir, and myche more þei fallen fro Crist. **1646** SIR T. BROWNE *Pseud. Ep.* I. vii. 27 Galen..in some things hath fallen from him [Hippocrates].

c. To drop away from, forsake, revolt against; to renounce one's allegiance to, or connexion with.

1535 COVERDALE *Jer.* lii. 3 Sedechias fel from the kynge of Babilon. **1548** HALL *Chron.* 148 b, After this spousage, the Kynges frendes fell from hym. **1548–9** (Mar.) *Bk. Com. Prayer* Offices 24 Suffre vs not..to fal from thee. **1595** SHAKS. *John* III. i. 320 England, I will fall from thee. **1649** BP. REYNOLDS *Hosea* i. 37 Achitophel, a man of great wisdome fals from David. **1872** C. E. MAURICE *Stephen Langton* iv. 254 The followers of Louis were falling from him.

†**d.** To drop out of, give up (a practice or purpose); to depart from, break (a commandment).

1513 MORE in Grafton *Chron.* II. 769 Theeves..never fall from their craft, after they once fall thereunto. **1535** COVERDALE *Judg.* ii. 19 They wolde not fall from their purposes. **1542–5** BRINKLOW *Lament.* (1874) 85, I exhorte yow..to..fall from your accustomed ydolatry. **1811** CHALMERS *Let.* in *Life & Lett.* (1851) I. 243 In the..life of every individual..this commandment is fallen from.

e. = ***fall off*** (see 92 d) ***from.***

1600 E. BLOUNT tr. *Conestaggio* 290 The French admirall ..being ill intreated in this cruell fight, fell from the gallion Saint Mathew.

62. fall in (= *into*) **——.** †**a.** To come upon by chance, light upon. *Obs.*

1377 LANGL. *P. Pl.* B iv. 156, 'I falle in floreines', quad þat freke.

b. = ***fall into*** 63 d.

c **1386** CHAUCER *Frankl. T.* 236 They fille in speche. *a* **1450** *Knt. de la Tour* (1868) 26 As thei felle in talkinge.. one of hem saide. **1523** LD. BERNERS *Froiss.* I. clxix. 177 He fyll in seruyce with a man of armes. **1530** PALSGR. 544/2, I fall in aquoyntaunce with hym. **1632** J. HAYWARD tr. *Biondi's Eromena* 81 She feared..to..fall in conference with him.

c. ***to fall in hand to*** or ***with***: to set oneself to (an action), set upon (a person). See HAND.

63. fall into ——. †**a.** To come into, by chance or otherwise; to drop into. ***to fall again into***: to get back into, be restored to. *Obs.*

1523 LD. BERNERS *Froiss.* I. clxix. 207 He fell agayne into the princes love. **1698** T. FROGER *Voy.* 39 We durst not fall into the Bay till break of Day. **1709** STEELE *Tatler* No. 83 ¶1, I happened this Evening to fall into a Coffee-house near the 'Change. **1745** P. THOMAS *Jrnl. Anson's Voy.* 108 They fell into the Harbour unknown to themselves and by mere Chance, the 16th Day.

†**b.** To make a hostile descent or inroad upon. *Obs.*

1665 SIR T. HERBERT *Trav.* (1677) 244 Some Pioneers Inhabitants of Coon-sha..fell into his naked quarter. **1684** *Scanderbeg Rediv.* iv. 62 The Tartars of Dialogrod falling into the Ukrain. *a* **1715** BURNET *Own Time* (1823) I. 344 Ready either to invade them, or to fall into Flanders.

c. To take (one's place), take one's place in (the ranks, etc.). *lit.* and *fig.*

1632 J. HAYWARD tr. *Biondi's Eromena* 145 Two hundred of them falling into a close order, interposed themselves. **1888** W. J. KNOX LITTLE *Child of Stafferton* iv. 49 In a moment they all fell into their places. **1889** *Times* (weekly ed.) 13 Dec. 3/3 Negotiations were opened with the lightermen..in the hope of getting them to 'fall into line' with those unions. **1890** S. LANE-POOLE *Barbary Corsairs* I. xiv. 174 The Christian fleet was slower in falling into line.

d. To engage in, enter upon (*esp.* talk); to begin the discussion of (a subject). Also, to become the subject of (discourse).

c **1475** *Rauf Coilȝear* 90 Into sic talk fell thay. **1590** SIR J. SMYTH *Disc. Weapons* *3 They fall into argument of some such matters. **1666** PEPYS *Diary* 14 Aug., We..fell into dancing. **1673** TEMPLE *Ess. Ireland* Wks. 1731 I. 109, I know not what it was that fell into Discourse t'other Day. **1711** ADDISON *Spect.* No. 124 ¶2 We must immediately fall into our Subject. **1851** DIXON *W. Penn* xxv. (1872) 225 The merchants and craftsmen had fallen into their callings. **1889** F. PIGOT *Strangest Journ.* 163 One lady had fallen into conversation with them.

†**e.** To come within (the range of); to be taken in or grasped by. *Obs. rare.*

1586 A. DAY *Eng. Secretary* II. (1625) 16 He fell into your notice. **1613** SHAKS. *Hen. VIII*, III. ii. 340 Those things you haue done..Fall into' th' compasse of a Premunire. **1712** ADDISON *Spect.* No. 415 ¶10 The intire Concavity [of the dome] falls into your Eye at once.

f. To come under, be included among.

1586 A. DAY *Eng. Secretary* I. 90 They [letters]..doe for the most part, fall into the..Defensorie or Excusatorie kinde. **1967** E. SHORT *Embroidery & Fabric Collage* iii. 81 Curtains similarly fall into two main categories, namely opaque and transparent.

g. To comply or take up with, accommodate oneself to. Also, to have recourse to.

1714–5 ATTERBURY *Serm.* 13 Mar., We fall into all his Commands and Directions. **1788** PRIESTLEY *Lect. Hist.* v. lii. 404 The generality of nations have fallen into the method of stamping them. **1790** MAD. D'ARBLAY *Diary* June, We fell immediately into our usual Windsor life. **1890** T. F. TOUT *Hist. Eng. from 1689*, 128 The ignorant masses fell blindly into the plans of the United Irishmen.

h. To get or drop into (a habit, etc.).

1886 A. SERGEANT *No Saint* I. vii. 141 He had fallen into a trick of walking with bent head.

64. to fall off ——. a. Of an animal: To lose appetite for (food); to refuse. **b.** Of a vessel: To deviate from (her course). Cf. 92 c, g.

1745 MORTIMER in *Phil. Trans.* XLIII. 553 As soon as a Cow falls off her Meat, give her another Dose. **1839** T. BEALE *Sperm Whale* 316 [He] called out..for the helmsman to..allow the ship to fall off her course.

65. fall on ——. †**a.** To pass suddenly or break out into, set about (an action or state). *Obs.*

a **1300** *Cursor M.* 14008 (Cott.) Sco fell on suilk a grete, þat al sco was vr lauerd fete. **1513** MORE in Grafton *Chron.* II. 763 Thus should all the realme fall on a roare. **1632** LITHGOW *Trav.* VI. 262 The fellow fell on trembling. **1670** NARBOROUGH *Jrnl.* in *Acc. Sev. Late Voy.* I. (1711) 52 We fall on fitting of our Rigging and getting the Ship fit. **1737** WHISTON *Josephus' Antiq.* VI. vi. §3 If any one..fell on eating..he should be accursed.

b. *Mil.* To make a hostile descent or attack upon, join battle with; to rush upon, assault. (With *indirect passive.*)

c **1400** *Destr. Troy* 10515 Ffallys on hym fuersly, frap hym to dethe. **1548** HALL *Chron.* 214 b, He feared lest the.. commen people..would fall on hym, as one that fled away. **1667** EVELYN *Mem.* (1857) I. 26 The Dutch..were fallen on our fleet at Chatham. *a* **1715** BURNET *Own Time* (1823) I. 533 No merchants' ships should be..fallen on, till six months after a declaration of war. **1864** BURTON *Scot Abr.* I. ii. 61 Stewart..fell on the episcopal city of Elgin.

transf. and *fig.* **1662** J. DAVIES *Voy. Ambass.* 419 When the Ambassador..was pleas'd to fall on any with his ordinary Language. **1667** PEPYS *Diary* (1877) V. 179 The Parliament ..are likely to fall heavy on the business. **1711** STEELE *Spect.* No. 260 ¶1 You cannot fall on a better Subject. *a* **1715** BURNET *Own Time* II. 38 The house of Commons were resolved to fall on all the ministry. **1827** O. W. ROBERTS *Centr. Amer.* 126 A heavy sea falls on the coast. **1840** BARHAM *Ingol. Leg., Bagman's Dog*, He..fell tooth and nail on the soup and the bouilli. **1848** MACAULAY *Hist. Eng.* I. 194 They fell on him [Clarendon] as furiously as their predecessors had fallen on Strafford.

c. To come across, light upon; †to hit upon (an expedient). (With *indirect passive.*)

1596 SHAKS. *1 Hen. IV*, v. iv. 34 Seeing thou fall'st on me so luckily. **1652** SIR C. COTTERELL tr. *Cassandra* II. 107 At first he fell not on the thought of what it was. **1761–2** HUME *Hist. Eng.* (1806) V. lxix. 199 A strange expedient was fallen on to supply this deficiency. **1790** BEATSON *Nav. & Mil. Mem.* I. 96 They fell on means to heave her round. **1890** R. M. KETTLE *Old Hall* I. vi. 51 They had fallen on a thing it would be unwise to pursue.

d. To have recourse to; to make use of.

1654 WHITLOCK *Zootomia* 142 Presently they fall on that common place, how much mischiefe it [learning] may do without Grace. *a* **1715** BURNET *Own Time* (1823) I. 452 They fell on propositions of a strange nature to ruin them. **1885** STEVENSON *Dynamiter* 175 Sir George..fell on some expressions which I still remember.

e. To drop back to, resume (a position).

1809 ROLAND *Fencing* 140 After which fall on the position of the guard.

f. quasi-*impers.* with *it* introducing infinitive clause: To occur to, befall (a person). *rare.*

1842 J. H. NEWMAN *Par. Serm.* VI. viii. 108 Some persons recollect a time..when it fell on them to reflect what they were.

g. ***to fall on board***: see simple senses and BOARD *sb.* 12 e. Cf. 73 a.

1805 *Log* in Nicolas *Disp. Nelson* VII. 207 *note*, The Royal Sovereign fell on board of our starboard beam.

h. ***to fall on one's feet***: *fig.* to fare fortunately, be well provided for.

1857 TROLLOPE *Barchester T.* III. xvii. 298 It is well known that the family of the Slopes never starve: they always fall on their feet, like cats. **1886** WARNER *Their Pilgrimage* (1888) 6 Mr. King..was put in good humor by falling on his feet, as it were, in such agreeable company.

†**i.** ***to fall on shore***: to run aground. *Obs.*

1590 MARLOWE *Edw. II*, IV. vi, With sore tempests driven, To fall on shore.

†***to fall on sleep***: see ASLEEP.

66. fall through ——. To make a 'mess' of. *Sc.*

1825 JAMIESON s.v., By her foolish airs, she's fa'n through her marriage. **1826** HOGG *Meg o' Marley*, The minister's fa'en through the text An' Meg gets a' the blame o't.

67. fall to ——. †**a.** To be drawn by feeling to; to attach oneself to, become a follower of; also, to make one's peace with. *Obs.*

a **1300** *Cursor M.* 15131 (Gött.) We se þe folk alle fall till him. **1557** *K. Arthur* I. xviii, To them fell kynge Ryence of North Wales. **1611** BIBLE *1 Chron.* xii. 19 There fell some of Manasseh to David, when he came..against Saul to battle.

†**b.** To get upon (the scent); to get the scent of, track. *Obs. rare.*

c **1340** *Gaw. & Gr. Knt.* 1425 Þe howndez..fellen..fast to þe fuyt. *c* **1420** *Anturs of Arth.* i, Thay hom dyȝt into the depe dellus, Fellun to tho femalus.

†**c.** To agree with, accede to (a proposal, etc.).

1523 LD. BERNERS *Froiss.* I. clxi. 195, I wold gladly fall to any reasonable way. **1548** HALL *Chron.* 214 b, The citiezens ..fell to this pact. **1683** PENN in R. Burton *Eng. Emp. Amer.* vii, He fell to the Bounds of the Land they had agreed to dispose of, and the Price.

d. To apply or betake oneself to; to have recourse to; to take to; to begin, proceed to. With *sb.*, *inf.*, or *gerund.* Also in ***fall to it***: set to work, bestir yourself.

c **1380** *Sir Ferumb.* 647 Tel þou me..al þe soþe as þow art gent & free, & suppe schalle we to-gadre boþe falle to fiȝte a-ȝe. *a* **1400–50** *Alexander* 4587 A wolfe..Quen he has faute of his flesch he fallis to þe soile! **1526** *Pilgr. Perf.* (W. de W. 1531) 35 b, Fall to prayer and make thy peticyon to God. *a* **1568** ASCHAM. *Scholem* I. (Arb.) 32 Then will he sonest faul to beate his scholers. **1600** E. BLOUNT tr. *Conestaggio* 14 Growing to more yeeres, they fell to distrust him. **1610** SHAKS. *Temp.* I. i. 3 Speake to th' Mariners: fall too't, yarely, or we run our selues a ground. **1644** SLINGSBY *Diary* (1836) 112 In Marston corn feilds [the Parliamentary army] falls to singing psalms. **1707** *Lond. Gaz.* No. 4329/5 They fell to their Oars. **1727** SWIFT *Lett. Eng. Tongue* 18 That Licentiousness which..fell to corrupt our Language. **1853** LYTTON *My Novel* IV. xi. 187 He fell to patting the mare with great unction. **1865** KINGSLEY *Herew.* I. x. 236 He was healed instantly, and fell to religion.

e. † ***to fall to*** (food): to begin eating (it). ***to fall to work***: to begin working.

a **1400** *Sir Perc.* 1326 Thay felle to thaire fude. **1551** CROWLEY *Pleas. & Pain* 495 Fall nowe to worke for your lyueynge. **1699** DAMPIER *Voy.* II. I. 52 When this is done they fall to their Meat. I saw one of these Grave-Feasts. **1719** DE FOE *Crusoe* (1840) I. xiv. 243 He fell to work. **1817** COBBETT *Taking Leave* col. 25 The Grazier then fell to work with his stick in such a style as I never before witnessed. **1861** HUGHES *Tom Brown at Oxf.* iii. (1889) 22 The four fell to work upon the breakfast.

68. fall under ——. †**a.** To throw oneself at the feet of. *Obs.*

a **1300** *Cursor M.* 12475 (Gött.) Honurand him he fel him vnder.

b. To come or be classed under, be included in.

c **1460** FORTESCUE *Abs. & Lim. Mon.* vii, Riche furres, oþer than be wonned to fall vnder..þe yerely charges off his warderobes. **1818** CRUISE *Digest* (ed. 2) II. 281 The present limitation..does not fall under either of these heads. *c* **1865** J. WYLDE in *Circ. Sc.* I. 5 Electrotyping and Gilding..fall under this section. **1870** MAX MÜLLER *Sc. Relig.* (1873) 357 Being signs they fall under the category of language.

c. To be brought under the operation or scope of, be subjected to.

1576 FLEMING *Panopl. Epist.* 307 Them, that..passe over what soever falleth under their fingers. **1605** BACON *Adv. Learn.* I. iv. §1 To speak unto such as do fall under or near unto a popular observation. **1654** WHITLOCK *Zootomia* 222 Their *modus operandi*..doth not fall under Demonstration. **1711** ADDISON *Spect.* No. 44 ¶5 Absurdities..as ridiculous as that which falls under our present Censure. **1824** MEDWIN *Convers. Byron* (1832) II. 109 His 'Revolt of Islam' ..fell under the lash of 'the Quarterly'. **1839** G. BIRD *Nat. Phil.* Introd. 35 These..states of matter will fall under our observation.

69. fall unto ——. = *fall to*, in various senses.

1535 COVERDALE *1 Chron.* xii. 19 Of Manasses there fell certain vnto Dauid. **1587** TURBERV. *Trag. T.* (1837) 134 The Lady, somewhat hungrie, fell unto the Cates. **1611** BIBLE *2 Kings* vii. 4 Let vs fall vnto the host of the Syrians.

70. fall upon ——. †**a.** = *fall on* 65 a.

a **1300** *Cursor M.* 15580 (Cott.) Alle þe apostels þan bi-gan to fal a-pon a gret.

b. = *fall on* 65 b.

1480 CAXTON *Chron. Eng.* ccxxvi. 231 Kyng edward..fyll vpon phelip of valoys. **1568** GRAFTON *Chron.* II. 148 Sir Edward..fell sodeinly upon the hoste of..Sir Simond. **1671** NARBOROUGH *Jrnl.* in *Acc. Sev. Late Voy.* I. (1711) 132 The Commander..began to fear, lest they might be fallen upon. **1698** T. FROGER *Voy.* 33 This Bird..pearches upon some Tree..waiting till the Fish swim even with the Surface of the Water, to fall upon them. **1749** FIELDING *Tom Jones* XVI. ii, He hath fallen upon me with that stick. **1844** H. H. WILSON *Brit. India* II. 106 Some of the principal Omras urged the Nizam to fall upon the Residency.

transf. and *fig.* **1709** HEARNE *Collect.* 13 Apr., The Dr. has ..fallen upon Gronovius..But he was provok'd to it by

Gronovius's first falling upon him. **1749** Fielding *Tom Jones* xvi. iv, When I expected you would have commended me for all I have done, to be fallen upon in this manner. **1840** Dickens *Old C. Shop* x, Kit..falling upon a great piece of bread and meat. **1857** Livingstone *Trav.* xv. 278 Manenko fell upon our friends..she is a most accomplished scold.

c. = *fall on* 65 c.

1632 Lithgow *Trav.* iv. 137 At last we fell vpon a Dalmatian widdow, whose pittifull lookes..stroke my soule. **1747** in *Col. Rec. Pennsylv.* V. 99 Some Method should be fall'n upon to prevent the Evils which threaten Us. **1777** Pringle *Telescopes* 9 By the force of his..genius he fell upon this new property of light. **1837** W. Irving *Capt. Bonneville* II. 77 He..soon fell upon the track of Mr. Robert Campbell's party, which had preceded him by a day. **1862** Ld. Brougham *Brit. Const.* xiii. 189 Edward III fell upon an expedient which gave very great satisfaction to all. **1874** G. W. Dasent *Tales from Fjeld* 247 When he had walked a while, he fell upon an old wife.

†**d.** To begin upon, take up, set about. *Obs.*

1625 Burges *Pers. Tithes* 2 My Purpose is not here to fall vpon that Question. **1649** Bp. Hall *Cases Consc.* i. v. 43 Otherwise some Interloper may..fall upon the work at a lower rate, and undoe the first editor. **1701** Swift *Contests Nobles & Com.* iii, These Persons..fell violently upon advancing the Power of the People. **1741** Wesley *Wks.* (1872) I. 304 They immediately fell upon their favourite Subject.

e. To come (casually) to, take up with, adopt, have recourse to.

1633 Bp. Hall *Hard Texts* 231 He that falls rashly upon his determinations..cannot but offend. **1654** H. L'Estrange *Chas. I* (1655) 130 His Majesty fell upon Davids design..of numbering the People. **1858** Sears *Athan.* iii. v. 297 The church..had fallen upon the belief that he [Christ] was soon to appear again.

f. *Geom.* Of a line, point, etc.: To have a place upon, cover, come exactly upon.

1570 Billingsley *Euclid* i. viii. 18 The line FG may fall directly upon the line DF. **1840** Lardner *Geom.* 42 The vertex of the angle *c'* must fall upon the vertex of the angle *c*.

†**g.** To come upon, become legally chargeable to (the parish). *Obs.*

1677 Yarranton *Eng. Improv.* 150 Consider that Bank-Granaries..will be the occasion of taking infinite poor people off the Parish, and prevent others falling upon the Parish.

†**h.** = *fall back upon.*

1767 S. Paterson *Another Traveller!* I. 218 Failing of an inscription, [he] may fall upon a derivative.

†**71. fall with ——.** To come upon in due course; to meet with. Chiefly *Naut.* To make (land). *Obs.*

1556 W. Towrson in Hakluyt *Voy.* (1589) 112 The 12 of May we fell with the Isle of Lundy in the Channel of Bristoll. **1599** *Ibid.* II. i. 258 The land is very high that we fell withall. **1632** Le Grys tr. *Vell. Paterc.* 1 Teucer..falling with [*adpulsus*] Cyprus, did build..Salamina. **1646** J. Brinsley *Araignm. Pres. Schism* 1 Opening his Bible, he fell with that of the Psalmist. **1670–1** Narborough *Jrnl.* in *Acc. Sev. Late Voy.* i. (1711) 124 Expecting to fall with Indians, for I saw many Fires up in the Land. *Ibid.* 125 This Morning..I fell with a fine Sandy Bay.

72. fall within ——. To come within the influence, operation, or scope of; to be included in.

1576 Fleming *Panopl. Epist.* 228 Those things that..fall within the view of the sight. **1688** *Lett. conc. Present St. Italy* 92 This was indeed a matter that could fall within the Popes understanding. **1771** *Junius Lett.* xliv. 240 There may be instances..which do not fall within my own exceptions. **1806** *Med. Jrnl.* XV. 561 This..work would not have fallen within the notice of our department, had it not been [etc.]. **1845** M. Pattison *Ess.* (1889) I. 23 A charge..such..as should fall within this penalty. **1884** G. Denman in *Law Rep.* 29 Chanc. Div. 466 Statements..made..so recklessly as to fall within the rule of fraud.

XI. With adverbs, forming the equivalent of compound vbs. in other langs.; e.g. *to fall out* = L. *excĭdĕre*, Ger. *ausfallen.*

(The phrases *fall foul, fall short*, are for convenience placed here, notwithstanding some uncertainty in the grammatical character of the adjuncts: see foul, short, *adjs.* and *advbs.*)

73. fall aboard. a. See aboard 2 d.

c **1380** Wyclif *Serm.* Sel. Wks. I. 294 Men þat now dremen an accident wiþouten suget mai falle aborde wiþ þese foolis. **1769** Falconer *Dict. Marine* s.v. *Aboard*, To fall *Aboard* of, to strike or encounter another ship, when one or both are in motion. **1791** *Hist.* in *Ann. Reg.* 187 They fell aboard a Swedish line of battle ship.

†**b.** To make a beginning. *Obs.*

a **1680** Butler *Cat & Puss* Rem. (1759) I. 93 To lose no further Time, he fell aboard. *a* **1700** B. E. *Dict. Cant. Crew*, *Fall-a-bord*, fall on and Eat heartily.

74. fall about. a. See simple senses and about *adv.*

1874 Mrs. L. B. Walford *Mr. Smith* vii. (1876) 74, I wish you would not go falling about that way.

†**b.** To search around, cast about. *Obs.*

1632 Rutherford *Lett.* xxi. (1862) I. 86 It is high time we were..falling about to try what claim we haue to Christ.

c. *slang.* To laugh uncontrollably; to become helpless with laughter. Freq. with *laughing.*

1967 *Atlantic Monthly* Apr. 108/2, I loped across the lawn imitating Myer Layevsky. I blinked an eye at the assembled company. 'That's all the money you took in today?' And they fell about. **1968** *Crescendo* June 31/3 His witty announcing had the very receptive audience falling about. **1973** *Times* 19 Jan. 14 The thought of producing a book in that time is enough to make us fall about. **1978** *Economist* 17 June 94 Some fell about laughing. Others booed. Most were clearly alarmed. **1985** A. Guinness *Blessings in Disguise* ii. 9 The audience fell about laughing but no laughter came from me. I was in love with her.

75. fall abreast of. See 36 and abreast 4.

1886 Mrs. C. Praed *Miss Jacobsen* I. x. 205 The object of it..checked his horse and fell abreast of her.

†**76. fall adown.** See 1 and adown A. 1.

1297 R. Glouc. (1724) 401 Þe on alf [of the body] vel adoun anon, þe oþer byleuede stylle In þe sadel. *c* **1400** *Lanfranc's Cirurg.* 277 Þe stoon fallíþ adoun of þe reynes toward þe bladdre bi þe weie of þe urine. **1513** Bradshaw *St. Werburge* i. 1302 His gloues..shortly to grounde falled adowne.

fall afire. See 40 c and afire.

†**77. fall after.** Of a dream: To come true.

c **1400** *Rom. Rose* 13 To wene that dremes after falle.

78. fall asleep. See 38 and asleep 2, 3.

1393 Langl. *P. Pl.* C. xxii. 5 Ich fel eft-sones a slepe. **1553** T. Wilson *Rhet.* ii. 75/1 We..fall a slepe, when we should moste harken. **1662** J. Davies *Voy. Ambass.* 82 She ..fell asleep. **1719** De Foe *Crusoe* (1840) I. vi. 102 The fit wearing off, I fell asleep.

fall aslope. See 39 and aslope.

79. fall astern. See 36 and astern 3.

1669 Sturmy *Mariner's Mag.* iv. 160 If you sail against a Current..Swifter than the Ship's way, you fall a Stern. **1776** in Falconer *Dict. Marine.* **1833** Marryat *P. Simple* l, The boat fell astern, leaving two Spaniards clinging to the side.

80. fall away. a. See simple senses and away.

a **1300** *Cursor M.* 19691 (Cott.) Skales fell fra his eien a-wai. *c* **1400** *Lanfranc's Cirurg.* 179 If þou wolt kepe heeris þat þei schulen not falle awei. **1577** B. Googe *Heresbach's Husb* i. (1586) 39 Flowres..which falling away, leaveth behinde them little round knoppes. **1697** Dampier *Voy.* (1698) I. 112 The top of it..gradually falls away on each side with a gentle descent. **1862** Tyndall *Mountaineer.* ii. 14 Portions of snow had fallen away from the upper slope. **1889** A. C. Doyle *Micah Clarke* xxiii. 24 The breeze has fallen away to nothing.

†**b.** To cease to speak of a subject. Const. *from.*

c **1374** Chaucer *Troylus* iii. 1257 Lat us fal away fro this matere, For it suffiseth, this that seyde is here.

c. To withdraw one's support, draw off, desert, revolt. Const. *from, to.*

1535 Coverdale *2 Chron.* x. 19 Thus fell Israel awaie from the house of Dauid. **1611** Bible *2 Kings* xxv. 11 The fugitiues that fell away to the king of Babylon. **1889** A. C. Doyle *Micah Clarke* xxxiii. 362, I am surprised..that you should have fallen away from that allegiance.

d. With respect to religious belief or practice: To become a backslider; to apostatize (*from*).

1597 Hooker *Eccl. Pol.* v. xlii. 84 Some fell..away..from soundnes of beliefe. **1611** Bible *Luke* viii. 13 These..for a while beleeue, and in time of temptation fall away. **1751** Wesley *Wks.* (1872) X. 285, I believe a saint may fall away. **1824** Scott *Redgauntlet* xxi, 'O Joshua..wilt thou thus fall away from the truth?' **1867** Freeman *Norm. Conq.* (1877) I. iv. 210 Large numbers of the Normans..fell away from Christianity.

†**e.** To lose flesh or substance; to shrink. *Obs.*

1530 Palsgr. 544/1, I fall awaye, I wax leane of flesshe ..*Je descharne.* *a* **1680** Butler *Rem.* (1759) II. 446 He delights, like a fat overgrown Man, to see himself fall away. **1770** Gray *Lett.* Wks. 1884 III. 354 Mrs. Jonathan..is much fallen away.

f. To decay, pine away, perish, vanish.

1576 Fleming *Panopl. Epist.* 223 All things..when they are at their ful ripenesse, then are they most fit to fall away and pearish. **1591** Shaks. *1 Hen. VI*, iii. i. 193 Till bones and flesh and sinewes fall away. **1611** Bible *1 Macc.* iv. 32 Cause the boldness of their strength to fall away. **1711** Addison *Spect.* No. 111 ¶5 How can it enter into the Thoughts of Man, that the Soul..shall fall away into nothing, almost as soon as it is created? **1827** Longf. *Life* (1891) I. viii. 106 The cottages [are] ruinous and falling away piecemeal. **1871** R. Ellis *Catullus* li. 6 Within me Every lost sense falleth away for anguish.

81. fall back. a. See simple senses and back.

1622 Fletcher *Beggar's Bush* iii. iv, Can mens prayers.. Fall back like lazy mists? **1676** *Walton's Angler* i. xix, The.. slime which that river leaves on the banks, when it falls back into its natural channel. **1696** tr. *Du Mont's Voy. Levant* 176 A large piece of Felt..which falls back on their Shoulders. **1845** H. Rogers *Ess.* (1860) I. 144 The Church would soon have fallen back..into its ancient corruptions.

b. To step back, give way. Of troops: To retreat, retire.

1607 Tourneur *Rev. Trag.* ii. ii, Brother fall back And you shall learne some mischeife. **1612** Drayton *Poly-olb.* xii. 204 Falling backe where they Might field-room find. **1676** Etheredge *Man of Mode* iii. i, Fall back on the sudden..and break out Into a loud laughter. **1781** *Hist Eur.* in *Ann. Reg.* 16/1 That regiment being ordered to fall back on their approach. **1823** *Douglas, or Field of Otterburn* III. iii. 36 His enemies..fell back to avoid his..thrusts.

fig. **1714** Addison *Spect.* No. 556 ¶3 Nothing but an invincible Resolution..could have prevented me from falling back to my Monosyllables. **1879** M. J. Guest *Lect. Hist. Eng.* xlvi. 464 They fell back a little, too, to favouring the celibacy of the clergy.

c. Of a coast-line: To recede.

1820 Scoresby *Acc. Arctic Reg.* I. 224 The coast falls gradually back.

†**d.** To fall into arrear (in payments). *Obs.*

1786 Burke *W. Hastings* Wks. 1842 II. 88 The..nabob.. falling back in other payments in the same.. proportion.

82. fall back on, upon. a. *Mil.* To retire to. **b.** *fig.* To have recourse to (something) when other things fail.

1841 Myers *Cath. Th.* 287 The internal Evidence of Christianity..on which we must fall back. **1862** Trench *Mirac.* xxxiii. 456 A manual trade, on which to fall back in the time of need. **1864** C. M. Yonge *Trial* II. v. 103 Her own fortune had always appeared to her something to fall back on in case of want of success. **1877** Miss Yonge *Cameos* Ser. iii. xxii. 205 The rebel army fell back..upon Linlithgow. **1889** Jessopp *Coming of Friars* v. 254 Young men presumably with some private means to fall back upon.

83. fall behind, behindhand. See simple senses and behind, behindhand.

1530 Palsgr. 543/2 He is fallen behynde the hande, within this thre yere. **1885** *Manch. Exam.* 21 July 5/2 If the tenant falls behind with his instalments. **1887** Visct. Bury & Hillier *Cycling* i. 40 After about twenty miles the horse slowly but surely falls behind.

†**84. fall by. a.** To miss receiving something. **b.** *Sc.* To be mislaid. **c.** *Sc.* To be affected with any ailment, *esp.* to be confined in childbed (Jam.).

1614 T. White *Martyrd. St. George* B ij b, His arme now thrusting forth..To latch the stripes for feare of falling by. **1640** Rutherford *Lett.* ii. xxix. (1671) 491 Christ's papers of that kinde cannot be lost or fall by.

85. fall down. a. See simple senses and down.

a **1175** *Cott. Hom.* 221 Swa michte æac þe oðre þe þer fellon don. *c* **1250** *Gen. & Ex.* 2734 ȝet sal ðin pride fallen dun. **1382** Wyclif *Gen.* iv. 5 Cayn was wrooth greetli, and his cheer felde doun. *c* **1460** Fortescue *Abs. & Lim. Mon.* xvi, The estate off þe Romans..be ganne to fall doune. **1513** Douglas *Æneis* ii. viii. 6 The ancyant worthy citie doun is fall. **1632** Lithgow *Trav.* iii. 99 There fell downe a deadly storme, at the *Grecoe Leuante.* **1755** *Let.* in *Gentl. Mag.* XXV. 564 At Algazaist several walls fell down. **1809** *Med. Jrnl.* XXI. 474 When boiled..the black oxide of iron fell down in abundance. **1875** Jowett *Plato* (ed. 2) I. 183 He is ready to fall down and worship them.

†**b.** To pass down, descend. *Obs.*

1632 Lithgow *Trav.* vi. 294 Aduancing in our course, we fell downe from the hils in a long bottome.

c. Of a ship, etc.: To 'drop down' towards the sea. Also, †To sail *to. Obs.*

1598 W. Phillips *Linschoten* in Arb. *Garner* III. 24 They fall down by means of the stream. **1685** R. Burton *Eng. Empire in Amer.* xix. 194 Before he fell down to the Havana, he should touch at St. Christophers. **1754** Fielding *Voy. Lisbon* Wks. 1882 VII. 34 He ordered his ship to fall down to Gravesend. **1867** in Smyth *Sailor's Word-bk.* **1890** *Sat. Rev.* 13 Dec. 687/2 They..fell down to Ameralikfjord.

†**d.** To make a hostile descent, swoop down.

17.. *Remarks Reign Will. III* in *Select. Harl. Misc.* (1793) 490 If the troops of his most Christian majesty had fell down into the Spanish Netherlands.

†**e.** To take to one's bed; to sicken. *Obs.*

1757 B. Franklin *Lett.* Wks. (1887) II. 522, I..got fresh cold and fell down again. **1772–84** Cook *Voy.* (1790) III. 800 Our crew..began to fall down in fevers.

f. To 'come to grief', collapse, fail. Freq. with *on. slang* (orig. *U.S.*).

1873 J. H. Beadle *Undevel. West* xxxii. 704 We'll reach Sioux City by 5 o'clock if we don't fall down... But we did 'fall down' just at noon, running hard aground. **1899** J. L. Williams *Stolen Story* 223 It amazed him every time a new reporter..fell down on a story. **1928** *Publishers' Weekly* 26 May 2175 We know of many cases where we fell down on buying books written by authors that had had successful books before. **1928** *Daily Tel.* 14 Aug. 10/4 If we fall down on the job of absorbing these 10,000 men of good stock and stamina. **1953** R. Lehmann *Echoing Grove* 300, I felt I couldn't cope: I saw myself falling down on the responsibilities. **1959** *Spectator* 6 Feb. 181/2 The Congress party is falling down on the job of rallying public confidence in the present policies of the Government of India. **1961** A. Christie *Pale Horse* x. 112 Oh dear, I seem to have fallen down badly. I was so very sure.

86. fall forth. = *to fall out.*

†**a.** To drop out (*obs.*) †**b.** To happen, occur (*obs.*). †**c.** To quarrel, fight (*obs.*).

1601 Holland *Pliny* II. 138 The..teeth..will shed and fall forth of the head. **1604** T. Wright *Passions* ii. i 52 Here it falleth foorth..hee which is most studious, is best learned. **1607** Topsell *Four-f. Beasts* 464 The males often-times fall forth, for sometimes eight..males follow one lioness.

87. fall foul. a. To come into collison. Chiefly of ships. Const. *of*, †*on, upon*, †*with.*

a **1613** Overbury *Newes, Newes from Sea* Wks. (1856) 181 A mans companions are (like ships) to be kept in distance, for falling foule one of another. **1678** Phillips *Tavernier's Trav.* ii. i. 53 Both the Ships Company began to cry out, for fear of falling foul one upon another. **1745** P. Thomas *Jrnl. Anson's Voy.* 284 The Prize..fell foul with her Head on our Starboard Quarter.

b. *fig.* To clash, come into conflict (with); to get into disputes; to quarrel.

1597 Shaks. *2 Hen. IV*, ii. iv. 183 Shall wee fall foule for Toyes? **1630** M. Godwyn tr. *Bp. Hereford's Ann. Eng.* (1675) 37 Henry must of necessity fall foul with the Emperour. **1645** Cromwell *Let.* 14 Sept. (Carlyle), To avoid confusion and falling foul one upon another. **1667** Pepys *Diary* (1877) V. 156 We fell very foul. **1871** R. H. Hutton *Ess.* (ed. 2) I. 80 So that we may not..fall foul of the forces..of that infinite world.

c. To make an attack. Const. *of, on, upon.*

1611 Speed *Hist. Gt. Brit.* vii. xliv. 376 Yet fell they [the Danes] so foule vpon Essex..that the King was enforced to compound a peace. *a* **1661** Fuller *Worthies* (1840) III. 427 John Bale..falleth foul on all friars. **1700** Dryden *Fables* Pref. Wks. (Globe) 505, I have fallen foul on priesthood. **1726** Cavallier *Mem.* iv. 338, I fell foul upon them..and put them to flight. **1846** Landor *Imag. Conv.* Wks. I. 116/2 You fall foul upon our miracles and our saints. **1885** *Manch. Exam.* 13 July 5/2 The Duke then falls foul of Lord Rosebery for stating this fact.

88. fall in. a. See simple senses and in.

1867 *Jrnl. R. Agric. Soc.* III. ii. 595 A fence..to prevent any person from falling in. **1887** Stevenson *Talk & Talkers* ii. in *Mem. & Portraits* 177 He was all fallen away and fallen in; crooked and shrunken. *Mod.* Her eyes have fallen in.

b. Of a building, etc.: To drop to pieces towards the interior or inwardly. *transf.* Of a cliff: To drop in fragments into the sea.

1719 De Foe *Crusoe* v. (1840) I. 94 Thinking that the top of my Cave was falling in. 1766 Goldsm. *Vicar Wakef.* xxii, Part after part [of the roof] continuing to fall in. 1810 Shelley *Zastrozzi* i, Almost at the same instant the roof fell in. 1829 Milman *Hist. Jews* xvi. (1878) 402 During the night, the wall suddenly fell in with a terrific noise. 1869 Phillips *Vesuv.* iii. 68 The whole crater top fell in.

c. Of the mouth: To recede.

1704 *Lond. Gaz.* No. 4031/4 His Mouth falls in.

†d. To make one's way in, accidentally or otherwise; to rush in with a hostile intention. *transf.* Of the sea. Also of a ship: To take a course (to land). *Obs.*

1382 Wyclif *Dan.* xiii. 26 Forsothe the seruauntes of the hous fellen yn by the posterne. 1535 Coverdale *1 Sam.* xxvii. 10 Achis spake: Whither fell ye in to daye? 1697 Dampier *Voy.* (1698) I. 247 They..fell in among a company of Spanish soldiers..who immediately fired at them. 1715 *Lond. Gaz.* No. 5374/1 A large Boat..fell in amongst them, and took one Boat. 1748 *Anson's Voy.* II. ii. 137 This ship..had fallen in to the northward of the Island. 1772–84 Cook *Voy.* (1790) IV. 1268 These are covered by islands in the offing, so that no sea can fall in to hurt a ship.

†e. To strike in, interpose a plea. *Obs. rare.*

*a*1641 Bp. Mountagu *Acts & Mon.* iv. (1642) 291 Nicolaus..purposed to fall in for Herod in his plea against Syllæus.

f. To happen, occur, take place. Also to appear (in a narrative). Now *rare.*

1589 Puttenham *Eng. Poesie* ii. (Arb.) 99 Continue on till an other like distance fall in. 1654 H. L'Estrange *Chas. I* (1655) 75 What became of those Iesuites will fall in afterward. *a*1715 Burnet *Own Time* II. 163 An accident fell in ..which took off much from Oates's credit. 1883 Stevenson *Treasure Isl.* iv. xvii. (1886) 139 The report fell in at the same instant.

g. *Mil.* To get into line, take one's place in the ranks.

1750 R. Paltock *Peter Wilkins* II. ix. 73 Nasgig..gave Orders for the whole Body..to fall in behind me. 1841 Lever *C. O'Malley* lxv. 306 'Fall in, fall in there lads!' resounded along the line.

transf. 1815 Chalmers *Let.* in *Life* (1851) II. 21 The ministers..must fall in at every procession.

h. *trans.* To form (troops) in line; to parade. Also, usu. as a command, ***get fell in.***

1860 Russell *Diary India* (7th thous.) II. 311, I fell them [Sepoys] in against the wall. 1888 J. H. Parke in H. M. Stanley *Darkest Africa* (1890) I. xix. 464 Stanley fell in all the men. 1889 *Pall Mall G.* 2 Apr. 3/2 The marines were fallen in for rifle drill. 1930 E. Raymond *Jesting Army* iii. v. 327, I was standing with the crah'd watchin' the West Essex getting fell in. 1945 C. H. Ward-Jackson *Piece of Cake* (ed. 2) 32 '*Get fell in!*' Fall in! Common way for senior N.C.O.s to give the command. 1959 *N.Z. Listener* 10 July 4/4 It was perfectly dreadful for instance to be fallen in—or as the Navy says, to 'Get fell in'.

i. *dial.* To meet, become acquainted. Cf. 91 a.

1808 R. Anderson *Cumbld. Ball.* (1819) 163 Fifty shwort years hae flown owre us, Sin' furst we fell in at the fair.

j. To agree. Of things: To fit in. Of persons: To concur in an arrangement.

1681 H. More *Exp. Dan.* 130 So handsomely do all things fall in and agree together. 1890 T. F. Tout *Hist. Eng. from 1689*, 300 In 1871 British Columbia..also fell in on condition of a railway being built to join them with the eastern colonies.

†k. To make up a quarrel, become reconciled. *Obs.* Cf. *fall out.*

1606 Shaks. *Tr. & Cr.* iii. i. 112 *Pand.* Sheele none of him, they two are twaine. *Hel.* Falling in after falling out, may make them three. 1773 Goldsm. *Stoops to Conq.* ii. i, They fall in and out ten times a day.

†l. To give way, yield. *Obs. rare*$^{-1}$.

1667 Pepys *Diary* 27 Nov., The King is now fallen in, and become a slave to the Duke of Buckingham.

m. To come to an end, terminate. Of a debt: To become due. Of a fund: To become available. Of land, houses, etc.: To come again into the owner's disposition at the end of a lease. Of a lease: To run out.

1796 Morse *Amer. Geog.* II. 379, 600 millions of debt had fallen in. 1854 *Jrnl. R. Agric. Soc.* XV. ii. 258 Colleges are ..taking up their bad leases, and, when the lands fall in, will probably let them to respectable tenants. 1885 *Law Rep.* 30 Chanc. Div. 18 The claim..would bind those assets when they fell in. 1887 Besant *Katharine Regina* i, The inheritance fell in. 1891 *Pictorial World* 7 Mar. 295/2 The leases of a rookery in Bermondsey fell in.

89. to fall in for. To come in for, get, incur.

1853 *Jrnl. R. Agric. Soc.* XIV. ii. 465 Those pigs having flourished most which had fallen in for the lion's share. 1864 Trollope *Small House at Allington* xvi, 'I did not mean to fall in for this' said Crosbie to himself.

90. to fall in upon. To come *upon* unexpectedly; to drop in upon or visit by chance.

1793 Mrs. E. Parsons *Woman as she should be* III. 99 His creditors all fell in upon him. 1888 B. W. Richardson *Son of a Star* II. iii. 29 To fall in upon his generals and see the encampments suddenly and without notice..is the very thing that suits his versatile humour. 1890 *Century Mag.* 128/1, I am always glad when any one falls in on me like you have to-night.

91. to fall in with. a. To come upon by chance, light upon, meet with, get into company with. Also, †To arrive at (land).

1594 Shaks. *Rich. III*, iii. v. 51 After he once fell in with Mistresse Shore. 1697 Dampier *Voy.* (1698) I. 472 We fell in with a small woody Island. 1748 *Anson's Voy.* i. vii. 71 We had great expectation of falling in with Pizarro's squadron. 1780 Coxe *Russ. Disc.* 26 Possibly the time is not far distant when some of the Russian adventurers will fall in with that coast. 1795 *Hist.* in *Ann. Reg.* 30 A Polish corps..fell in with the main body of the Russians. 1833 Ht. Martineau *Cinnamon & P.* i. 5 They fell in with no other vessel till they came in sight of the shore. 1955 *Times* 11 Aug. 9/5 Senhor Alberto de Lacerda is a Portuguese writer in his late twenties, who has had the good fortune to fall in with Mr. Arthur Waley.

b. To drop into the views of, agree with (a person); to make common cause or side with.

1642 Fuller *Holy & Prof. St.* v. xiii. 409 He falls in with all his neighbours that fall out. 1708 Swift *Sacramental Test* in *Misc.* (1711) 333 The Number of Profest Dissenters ..was..something under a Dozen, and..Thirty others, who were expected to fall in with them. 1781 *Hist. Eur.* in *Ann. Reg.* 144/1 Those under its influence continually fell in with..the French party.

c. To accede to or comply with (a proposal), join in (a project).

1711 Addison *Spect.* No. 123 ⁋4 Leontine..was..prevailed upon to fall in with the Project. 1816 Chalmers *Let.* in *Life* (1851) II. 31 Falling in with such arrangements ..as your natural superiors expect you to concur in. 1879 F. W. Robinson *Coward Conscience* iii. ix, Sir John did not fall in with this suggestion.

d. To harmonize with, suit, match. Of a point, period of time, etc.: To coincide with.

1662 Stillingfl. *Orig. Sacr.* i. vi. §3 The reign of Adrastus at Sicyon falls in with that of Atreus and Thyestes at Argi or Mycenæ. 1712 J. James tr. *Le Blond's Gardening* 100 The Track..of the circular Segments, with which the Tracing-Point ought to fall in exactly. 1728 Newton *Chronol. Amended* vi. 354 His 20th year fell in with the 4th year of 83d Olympiad. 1759 Robertson *Hist. Scot.* I. iii. 239 Nothing could fall in more perfectly with her views concerning Scottish affairs. 1867 Freeman *Norm. Conq.* (1876) I. App. 677 It falls in exactly with his conduct directly after.

e. To agree, concur with (an opinion, the opinion of); to conform to; to humour. Also, To unite, join with.

1699 Bentley *Phal.* 200 With this opinion all those fall in, who assert that Comedy is more recent than Tragedy. 1705 Berkeley *Commonpl. Bk.* Wks. IV. 459 Hobbs in some degree falls in with Locke. 1793 Smeaton *Edystone L.* §127 Those..generally fall in with the popular opinion. 1860 Trollope *Framley P.* i. 3 He fell in with the views of his patroness. 1863 Mrs. C. Clarke *Shaks. Char.* iv. 101 How pleasantly he falls in with their several natures and qualities.

92. fall off. a. See simple senses and off.

1490 Caxton *Eneydos* xxxii. 121 The wax..beganne to melte and the feders to falle of. 1583 Hollyband *Campo di Fior* 51 Put thy sacchell over thy arme, that it fall not of. 1611 Bible *Acts* xii. 7 His chaines fell off from his hands. 1683 Burnet tr. *More's Utopia* (1685) 165 Who does not see that the Frauds..would all fall off? 1803 *Pic Nic* No. 1 (1806) I. 16 The mask of universal philanthropy has fallen off. 1850 *Tait's Mag.* XVII. 422/1 The drunkards fell off asleep.

b. To drop off in position; to step aside or back, withdraw. Also *fig.* †To recall an offer.

1613 Shaks. *Hen. VIII*, iv. i. 64 The..Lords, and Ladies, hauing brought the Queene To a prepar'd place..fell off A distance from her. 1636 Massinger *Bashf. Lover* ii. ii, Sweet youth, fall off. 1649 Bp. Hall *Cases Consc.* i. vi. 58 You have just reason..to fall off from the bargaine. 1710 Steele *Tatler* No. 247 ⁋5 When you had consented to his Offer, if he fell off, you would call him a Cheat. 1838 Dickens *O. Twist* lii, They fell off, one by one..the street was left to solitude.

c. *Naut.* Of a vessel: To fail to keep her head to the wind; to refuse to answer the helm. Rarely *trans.* To let (a vessel) veer from the wind.

1692 in *Capt. Smith's Seaman's Gram.* i. xvi. 76 In keeping the Ship near the Wind, these terms are used..Fall not off, Veer no more, keep her to. 1699 Dampier *Voy.* II. ii. 22 She would fall off 2 or 3 Points from the Wind. 1750 in Blanckley *Naval Expositor* s.v. *Fall.* 1841 Dana *Seaman's Manual* xii. 74 Let her have a plenty of helm, to come to and fall off freely with the sea.

d. *Naut.* To separate, part company; to move away, deviate. Of a coast-line: To trend away.

1632 J. Hayward tr. *Biondi's Eromena* 64 The Prince..fell off with a contrary wind to Fermentera. 1669 Sturmy *Mariner's Mag.* i. 20 Starboard give not fire until he fall off. 1719 De Foe *Crusoe* (1840) I. i. 14 The shore falls off to the westward towards Cromer. 1795 Nelson in Nicolas *Disp.* II. 13 As the Ship fell off, [I] gave her our whole broadside. 1892 *Eng. Illustr. Mag.* IX. 555 The vessel fell off from her course.

e. Of lovers or friends: To part company, become estranged, draw off. Of subjects: To revolt, withdraw from allegiance.

1513 More *Rich. III* in Grafton *Chron.* II. 787 Whose hart she perceyved more fervently set then to fall of for a worde. 1596 Shaks. *1 Hen. IV*, i. iii. 93 Revolted Mortimer? He neuer did fall off. 1614 Bp. Hall *Recoll. Treat.* 1046 Like as those which purposed love, when they fall off, call for their tokens backe againe. 1667 Milton *P.L.* i. 30 What cause Mov'd our Grand Parents..to fall off From their Creator. 1711 Addison *Spect.* No. 179 ⁋1 Were I always Grave, one half of my Readers would fall off from me. 1721 De Foe *Mem. Cavalier* (1840) 131 The duke of Saxony fell off, and fought against them. 1888 B. W. Richardson *Son of a Star* III. xiv. 254 He sees the..people falling off from the king.

f. To decrease in amount, intensity, or number; to diminish. Also of persons.

1605 Shaks. *Lear* i. ii. 126 Loue cooles, friendship falls off, Brothers diuide. 1749 F. Smith *Voy. Disc. N.-W. Pass.* II. 31 It was the Season of the Year for the Tides to fall off. 1827 O. W. Roberts *Centr. Amer.* 271 Towards evening..the breeze began to fall off. 1833 Macaulay *Life & Lett.* (1883) I. 304 The publishers..tell him that the sale is falling off. 1842 L. Howard *Cycle of Seasons* 19 The rain now falls off again. 1890 *Longman's Mag.* July 241 The demand for porcelain had much fallen off. 1914 W. Owen *Let.* 14 Oct. (1967) 287 If pupils fall off I shall be obliged to pack off sooner!

g. To decline in health, vigour, interest, etc.; to degenerate. Said also of health, interest, etc.

1709 Addison *Tatler* No. 148 ⁋2 Many great Families are insensibly fallen off from the Athletick Constitutions of their Progenitors. 1802 T. Beddoes *Hygëia* vii. 38 The patient fell off in flesh. 1821 Shelley *Lett. fr. Italy* 22 Oct., The 'Jungfrau von Orleans' of Schiller,—a fine play, if the fifth act did not fall off. 1848 Dickens *Dombey* xxvii, 'We have fallen off deplorably', said Mr. Carker. 1890 G. Gissing *Emancipated* II. i. xiii. 100 Her..health began to fall off.

93. fall on. †a. See 1 f and on.

1535 Coverdale *Matt.* xiv. 15 Ye night falleth on.

b. To come with violence; to make an attack, join battle. (*absol.* of 65 b.)

1387 Trevisa *Higden* (Rolls) III. 59 Whan þe Sabynes fil on. *a*1400–50 *Alexander* 2132 þai fall on freschly þe folk of þe cite. 1613 Shaks. *Hen. VIII*, v. iv. 57 They fell on, I made good my place. 1716 *Lond. Gaz.* No. 5473/1 Flanginy fell on first with the St. Lawrence. 1855 Macaulay *Hist. Eng.* III. 425 The English were impatient to fall on.

c. To set to work, begin, make a start. Now *rare*; cf. 100 c.

1677 Yarranton *Eng. Improv.* 66 We came to an agreement. Upon which I fell on, and made it..Navigable from Sturbridge to Kederminster. *a*1680 Butler *Rem.* (1759) VIII. 3 All stood ready to fall on. 1733 Fielding *Quix. in Eng.* Ded., Wit, like hunger, will be with..difficulty restrained from falling on, where there is great plenty..of food. 1890 W. Morris in *Eng. Illustr. Mag.* July 765 The squall falleth on when the sun hath arisen.

94. fall out. a. *intr.* See simple senses and out.

1577 B. Googe *Heresbach's Husb.* i. (1586) 39 The rootes standyng upwarde that the seede may fall out. 1658 Willsford *Natures Secrets* 172 There fell out of the Air such multitudes of strange..flies. 1703 Dampier *Voy.* III. 20 Tho' several of the Nails or Pegs of the Boat should by any shock fall out. 1772–84 Cook *Voy.* (1790) IV. 1451 The morning flood falling out too early.

b. *Mil.* To drop out of one's place in the ranks; to drop behind a marching body. Also *trans.*

1832 *Regul. Instr. Cavalry* iii. 60 The Farriers and Band fall out. 1844 *Regul. & Ord. Army* 180 To bring any Man who may have fallen out. 1890 *Standard* 7 Aug. 5/7 Some of the men were obliged to fall out from fatigue. 1923 Kipling *Irish Guards in Great War* I. 24 A newly appointed platoon-officer..fell them out. 1942 E. Waugh *Put out More Flags* ii. 120 Companies paraded at quarter past eight; immediately after inspection men were fallen out for the company commanders' orderly room.

†c. *Mil.* To make a sally. *Obs. rare*$^{-1}$.

1637 Monro *Expedition* ii. 25 Major John Sinclaire..not having a hundred Musketiers within the Towne in all, neverthelesse fell out with fiftie..and skirmished bravely.

d. To disagree, quarrel.

1562 J. Heywood *Prov. & Epigr.* (1867) 76 Whan theeues fall out, true men come to their goode. 1654 *Nicholas Papers* (Camden) II. 61 The Bp. of Derry and Sr Rich. Grenville are fallen extremely out. 1783 Cowper *Lett.* 2 Feb., Monarchs..fall out, and are reconciled just like the meanest of their subjects. 1879 M. J. Guest *Lect. Hist. Eng.* xvii. 159 The king and the archbishop soon fell out.

e. ***fall out with***: to quarrel *with.* Rarely in *indirect pass.*

1530 Palsgr. 545/1 Fall nat out with your frendes for a thing of naught. 1542 Udall *Erasm. Apoph.* 259 a, Pollio had aforetyme been angrye and foule out with Timagenes. *a*1659 Osborn *Luther Vind.* (1673) 403 Falshood is fallen-out with for..Love of Truth. 1771 Fletcher *Checks* Wks. 1795 II. 213 So preach that those who do not fall out with their sins may fall out with thee. 1859 Thackeray *Virgin.* iv, So this good woman fell out with her neighbours.

f. To come by chance into existence. *rare.*

1856 Mrs. Browning *Aur. Leigh* v. Poems 1890 VI. 213 If the Iliad fell out..By mere fortuitous concourse of old songs, Conclude as much too for the Universe.

g. To happen, chance, occur, arise, come to pass. Now chiefly quasi-*impers.* with subject clause. Also, *to fall out to be.*

1568 Grafton *Chron.* II. 102 It must needes fall out, that he shall have the better. 1598 Grenewey *Tacitus' Ann.* xii. x. (1622) 170 Vologeses thinking there had fell out just occasion of inuading Armenia..assembleth his power. 1627 Perrot *Tithes* 51 How often falls it out that a Parishioner..detaines some part or the whole of his tithe. 1650 Baxter *Saints' R.* iii. (1654) 13 If anything fell out amiss. 1688 *Lett. conc. Present St. Italy* 101 It fell out to be the year of Jubily, 1650. 1770 Langhorne *Plutarch* (1879) I. 344/2 The death of this great mathematician fell out in the year of Rome 542. 1848 Dickens *Dombey* vi, Thus it fell out that Biler..sought unfrequented paths.

h. To prove to be, turn out. Formerly with *adj.* as compl., or *to be*; now only with adverb of manner.

1570 T. Wilson *Demosthenes* 4 *marg.*, As things fall out, the common sort judge. 1577 B. Googe *Heresbach's Husb.* i. (1586) 15 b, Such kinde of bargainyng..maketh his accomptes seeldome fall out just. 1614 Bp. Hall *Recoll. Treat.* 71 God purposed it as it is fallen out. 1642 Rogers *Naaman* 369 If there fall out to be any defect therein. 1669 Sturmy *Mariner's Mag.* 115 If the Division doth fall out even, without any over-plus. 1705 Stanhope *Paraphr.* I. 7 When Matters so fall out that we cannot attend to Mercy and Sacrifice both. 1879 M. J. Guest *Lect. Hist. Eng.* xiv. 130 The chronicler tells how things fell out.

†i. *to fall out in*: to burst out *in*, to begin.

*a*1555 Latimer *Serm. & Rem.* (1845) 97 Zachary..fell out in praising of God.

†j. *to fall out upon*: to result from. *Obs.*

1665 J. Spencer *Vulg. Prophecies* 88 Fatal events have fallen out upon vain prophecies.

95. fall out of. a. See simple senses and out.

*c*1340 *Cursor M.* 12269 *heading* (Fairf.), Ihesus raisid a dede childe fallin out of a loft. *c*1400 *Lanfranc's Cirurg.* 93

þere schal falle out of him pecis gobetmele. **1563** Fulke *Meteors* (1640) 68 b, Quicksilver hath divers times fallen out of the clouds. **1579** Gosson *Sch. Abuse* (Arb.) 21 He fel out of heauen into Lemnos. **1856** Froude *Hist. Eng.* (1858) I. i. 62 The people..were falling out of archery practice, exchanging it for similar amusements. **1885** *Manch. Even. News* 6 July 2/2 Land has fallen out of cultivation.

†**b.** To make a raid from. *Obs. rare*⁻¹.

1535 Coverdale *2 Kings* v. 2 There had men of warre fallen out of Syria, and caried awaye a litle damsel.

c. *Mil.* (Cf. 94 b.)

1824 Scott *Redgauntlet* xv, Do you fall out of the line, and wait here with me. **1859** Jephson *Brittany* xiv. 234 The men piled arms and fell out of the ranks.

d. *to fall out of lease*: to cease to be held on lease.

1841 *Jrnl. R. Agric. Soc.* II. ii. 154 Farms which fell out of lease.

96. fall over. a. See simple senses and OVER. **b.** *Sc.* To go to sleep. †**c.** To go over *to* (the enemy).

1595 Shaks. *John* iii. i. 127 Dost thou now fall ouer to my foes? **1694** *Acc. Sev. Late Voy.* ii. (1711) 32 The Waves.. fall over with dashing and foaming. **1820** Scoresby *Acc. Arctic Reg.* I. 466 The moment life is extinct, it [a whale] always falls over on its side. **1823** Lockhart *Reg. Dalton* ii. v, Ellen Hesketh..wakened me—I had just fallen over.

d. *to fall over oneself*: (*a*) see quot. 1895; (*b*) to show great eagerness (freq. to do something), to be desperately anxious *to. colloq.*

1895 W. C. Gore in *Inlander* Dec. 113 *Fall all over one's self*, to get confused. **1904** *Brooklyn Standard Union* 2 Aug. 6 The bonafide independent element is not falling over itself to come to Parker's assistance. **1923** R. D. Paine *Comr. Rolling Ocean* 130 The thirsty outlaws fall over themselves to hand you ten or twelve dollars a quart for it. **1935** *Forres Gaz.* 30 Oct. 4/7 In your haste to 'fix up' a piece of business, have you ever 'fallen over yourself'? **1947** K. Tennant *Lost Haven* iii. 48 Why was it that..these rich coots with tons of money nearly fell over themselves grabbing at anything they could get free? **1957** *Ess. in Criticism* VII. 159 [A review] which, though it falls over itself at the end to be as nice as possible, [etc.].

e. *to fall over backwards* = *to bend over backwards* (BACKWARDS *adv.* A).

1958 B. Nichols *Sweet & Twenties* xi. 135 Even nice old ladies..fell over backwards in their efforts to stop the menace of the encroaching scissors. **1958** *Listener* 20 Nov. 848/1 There was a certain complacency, a falling over backwards to be fair. **1966** *Ibid.* 11 Aug. 190/1 In the system of trial is it correct to say, as many people say, that we fall over backwards to protect the guilty?

97. fall short. a. Of supplies: To give out, fail, become insufficient.

1694 *Acc. Sev. Late Voy.* ii. (1711) 106 Their [foxes'] Food falls but short there. **1748** *Anson's Voy.* ii. ii. 137 Apprehensions of our provisions falling short.

b. Of a shot, etc.: Not to reach the mark aimed at.

1793 Hoste in Nicolas *Disp. Nelson* I. 329 *note*, The Fort fired at us, but their balls fell short. **1848** J. Grant *Adv. of Aide-de-C.* xxxi, The bombs fell short.

†**c.** *ellipt.* for *fall short of finding*: to miss.

1688 Bunyan *Heavenly Footman* (1886) 171 Be sure thou wilt fall short the way at last.

98. fall short of. a. To fail to reach or obtain (an object, wages, etc.); to fail in performing (one's duty).

1590 Sir J. Smyth *Disc. Weapons* 21 b, The matches..fall ..short of the pannes and powder. **1629** tr. *Herodian* (1635) 111 The souldiers falling short of their hopes were extremely offended. **1793** Smeaton *Edystone L.* §101 The workmen should on no occasion fall short of the common wages of the country. **1890** H. S. Merriman *Suspense* II. v. 114 He fell lamentably short of his duty.

b. To fail of attaining to (a certain amount, degree, level, or standard); not to reach the same amount, etc. as. Also † *to fall short to*.

1596 Spenser *F.Q.* vi. iii. 5 They fall too short of our fraile reckonings. **1630** *R. Johnson's Kingd. & Commw.* 88 They.. will fall short to our expectation. **1662** Stillingfl. *Orig. Sacr.* ii. iv. §1 The other Prophets fell so much short of Moses. **1697** Dampier *Voy.* (1698) I. 202 They fell short of the number they told us of. **1711** Addison *Spect.* No. 61 ¶5 Though they excel later Writers in Greatness of Genius, they fall short of them in Accuracy. **1746** Hervey *Medit.* (1818) 113 A felicity that never falls short of the very perfection of elegance. **1845** McCulloch *Taxation* iii. iii. (1852) 467 The income..fell greatly short of the expenditure.

99. fall through. To break down, come to nought, fail, miscarry. †Rarely of persons.

1781 G. R. Clark in Sparks *Corr. Amer. Rev.* (1853) III. 324 Should we fall through in our present plans..the Consequences will be fatal. **1879** Miss Yonge *Cameos* Ser. iv. ix. 106 The charge seems to have fallen through. **1884** *Manch. Exam.* 22 May 5/1 The proposed amalgamation.. fell through.

100. fall to. †**a.** Analytical form of ME. *to-fallen* to happen, occur. *Obs.*

c **1400** *Destr. Troy* 2719 No man..ferd is of fortune till it falle to.

b. Of a gate, etc.: To shut automatically.

1889 Maartens *Sin of J. Avelingh* I. i. x. 130 The oaken door fell to behind them.

c. To set to work, make a beginning; *esp.* to begin eating; also, to come to blows. (Cf. 67 d, e.)

1593 Shaks. *Rich. II*, v. v. 98 My Lord, wilt please you to fall too? **1677** Yarranton *Eng. Improv.* 101 Let us fall too, and consider of some good things to advance the Woollen Manufactures. **1842** Dickens *Amer. Notes* ii, We fall-to upon these dainties. **1865** Parkman *Champlain* iii. (1875) 223, I have seen our curé and the minister..fall to with their fists on questions of faith. **1886** *Tip Cat* xv. 199 Dick, finding a spare rake, fell to and worked with a will.

101. fall together. †**a.** Of the eyes: To close. †**b.** To collapse, contract, shrink up. *Obs.*

a **1300** *Cursor M.* 16762 + 75 (Cott.) To-geder fell his eghen. **1654** Whitlock *Zootomia* 75 He telleth him..that the Brain is fallen close together.

c. *fall together by the ears*: see EAR 1 d.

d. *Phonetics.* To become identical.

1905 J. Wright *Eng. Dial. Gram.* p. iv, Many vowel-sounds, which are generally supposed to have fallen together in Middle English, were in reality kept apart. **1959** A. Campbell *Old Eng. Gram.* 153, *æ*, *e*, and *i* fell together in a sound written *e* in unaccented syllables.

☛ *Phrase-key.* (The prepositional combinations in X, and the adverbial combinations in XI, are not included.).

Fall *pres. conj.* (fair, foul *f.*, *f.* what can, etc.) 46 d; fall a prey, sacrifice, victim 24; *f.* about a person's ears 28; *f.* among thieves 35 a; *f.* at the crest 15; *f.* calm 10 b; *f.* dead 23; *f.* due 40 a; *f.* from a person, his mouth 6; *f.* heir 40 b; *f.* in age 7 b; *f.* in flesh 14; *f.* in (one's) heart 34; *f.* in love 38 b; *f.* in pieces 27; *f.* in two 27 b; *f.* into error, sin 25 b; *f.* into (a person's) heart, mind 34; *f.* on (one's) face, knees 20; *f.* on a sword 19 c; *f.* out of flesh 14; *f.* pregnant 22 b; *f.* profit 46 c; *f.* to be 40, 47; *f.* to earth, ground 1, 19; *f.* to (one's) lot, share 31; *f.* to mould, to pieces, powder 27; *f.* to (one's) rifle 23 c; *f.* to (one)self 36; *f.* to (one's) share 31; let fall 4.

† **'fallable**, *a. Obs.* Also 6 -ible. [f. FALL *v.* + -ABLE.] Capable of falling, liable to fall.

1548 Hall *Chron.* 177 b, The feble foundation of this fallible buildyng. **1577** tr. *Bullinger's Decades* (1592) 487 Unlesse God had made man fall-able, there had beene no praise of his workes or vertue. *a* **1656** Bp. Hall *Rem. Wks.* (1660) 371 Man, as he was creable, fallable, saveable.

† **fa'llace**, *sb. Obs.* Forms: 4–5 fallas, 5 falace, 4–7 fallace. [a. F. *fallace*, ad. L. *fallācia*, f. *fallax*: see next.]

1. Deception, trickery, falsehood; deceitfulness; an instance of the same; = FALLACY 1, 2.

a **1300** *Cursor M.* 3664 (Cott.) If mi fader þat es now blind Mai mi fallace oght vnderfind. **1388** Wyclif *Matt.* xiii. 22 The fallace of ritchessis strangulith the word. **1483** Caxton *G. de la Tour* H iv, The fallaces and vanytees of the world. **1599** Hakluyt *Voy.* II. ii. 73 Lyes and fallaces that they did write. *a* **1634** Chapman *Alphonsus* Plays 1873 III. 235 Nay without fallace they have several Beds.

2. A sophistical argument; = FALLACY 3.

1532 More *Confut. Tindale* Wks. 637/2 A goodly false foolishe fallace. **1605** Bacon *Adv. Learn.* ii. xiv. §6 Socrates ..hath exactly expressed all the fourmes of obiection, fallace and redargution.

† **fa'llace**, *a. Obs. rare*⁻¹. [a. OF. *fallace*, ad. L. *fallax* (stem *fallāci-*), f. *fallĕre* to deceive.] = FALLACIOUS.

1393 Langl. *P. Pl.* C. xvii. 231 Freres..Meuen motifs meny tymes insolibles and fallaces.

† **falla'ciloquence.** *Obs.*⁻⁰ [ad. L. *fallāciloquentia*, f. *fallāci-* (see prec.) + *loquentia* talking: see -ENCE.] Deceitful speech.

1656–81 in Blount *Glossogr.* **1721–61** in Bailey.

† **falla'ciloquent**, *a. Obs.*⁻⁰ [f. L. *fallāci-* (see FALLACE) + *loquent-em*, pr. pple. of *loquī* to speak.] Speaking deceitfully.

1730–6 in Bailey.

fallacious (fə'leɪʃəs), *a.* [f. L. *fallāci-a* (see FALLACY) + -OUS. Cf. F. *fallacieux.* In early use it appears with sense derived from that of the sb.; subsequently (in accordance with the usual tendency of adjs. in -ACIOUS) it came to be taken as the representative of L. *fallax.*]

1. Of an argument, syllogism, etc.: Containing a fallacy.

1509 Hawes *Past. Pleas.* xi. xx, Seven sophyms full hard and fallacyous Thys ydre used in preposicion Unto the people. **1651** Baxter *Inf. Bapt.* 228, I undertake to prove every Argument of his..to be vain and fallacious. **1788** Reid *Aristotle's Log.* v. §3. 116 Such fallacious syllogisms are considered in this treatise. **1864** Bowen *Logic* ix. 294 Those fallacious reasonings which are correct in form.

2. †**a.** Of persons: Deceitful (*obs.*). **b.** Of things: Deceptive, misleading.

a. 1663 Cowley *The Complaint* viii, Teach me not then, O thou fallacious Muse, The Court..t'accuse. **1769** Burke *Late State Nat.* Wks. 1842 I. 82 This author..is only slovenly and inaccurate, and not fallacious.

b. 1651 Biggs *New Disp.* ¶305 A fallacious word, signifying contrary to what it pretends. **1772–84** Cook *Voy.* (1790) VI. 2024 A very fallacious method of judging. **1856** Froude *Hist. Eng.* (1858) II. x. 434 No evidence is more fallacious than that which rests upon isolated facts.

3. That causes disappointment; mocking expectation, delusive.

1667 Milton *P.L.* ix. 1046 That fallacious Fruit. **1741** Middleton *Cicero* II. x. 385 False and fallacious hopes. **1877** Sparrow *Serm.* i. 11 Nor is it a deceitful joy..a fallacious peace.

fallaciously (fə'leɪʃəslɪ), *adv.* [f. as prec. + -LY².] In a fallacious manner.

1650 Sir T. Browne *Pseud. Ep.* Pref., We..promise no disturbance or reoppose any pen that shall fallaciously refute us. **1764** Reid *Inquiry* vi. §5. 139 That our senses fallaciously represented them [heat, colour, etc.] as being in bodies. **1884** Sir C. S. C. Bowen in *Law Rep* 28 Chanc. Div. 15 It is often fallaciously assumed that [etc.].

fallaciousness (fə'leɪʃəsnɪs). [f. as prec. + -NESS.] The quality or fact of being fallacious.

1681 H. More *Exp. Dan.* 34 The..fallaciousness of the Greek Nation. **1752** Johnson *Rambler* No. 203 ¶2 Every one has..detected the fallaciousness of hope. **1847** Hare *Vict. Faith* 44 The groundlessness and fallaciousness of a proposition.

† **fa'llacity.** *Obs.* [ad. L. *fallācitāt-em*, n. of state f. *fallax*: see FALLACE *a.*] Fallaciousness.

1664 Power *Exp. Philos.* iii. 190 The old..Aphorism of.. Nature's obscurity..the Senses fallacity. **1773** *Observ. State Poor* 49 However consistent this specious reasoning may be with..justice, its fallacity will not escape detection.

fallacy ('fæləsɪ). Forms: 5–7 falacy(e, 6–7 fallacie, (7 fallecie), 7– fallacy. [ad. L. *fallācia*, n. of quality f. *fallax* deceptive: see FALLACE *a.* First in 15th c. replacing the older FALLACE *sb.*]

†**1.** Deception, guile, trickery; a deception, trick; a false statement, a lie. *Obs.*

1481 Caxton *Reynard* (Arb.) 67 Ha reynart how wel can ye your falacye and salutacion doon. **1607** Topsell *Four-f. Beasts* (1673) 159 Then make they a narrow bridge covered with earth..that the beasts may dread no fallacy. **1671** Milton *P.R.* i. 155 Winning by Conquest what the first man lost By fallacy surpriz'd. **1749** Fielding *Tom Jones* xvi. ix, Her utter detestation of all fallacy.

2. †**a.** Deceitfulness (*obs.*). **b.** Deceptiveness, aptness to mislead, unreliability.

1641 J. Johnson (*title*), The Academy of Love, describing the Folly of younge Men and the Fallacy of Women. **1654** Whitlock *Zootomia* 220 Let us not affirm their existence, and ὅτι on the Fallacies of Sense. *c* **1800** K. White *Rem.* (1837) 381 The fallacy of human friendship. **1849** Mrs. Somerville *Connex. Phys. Sc.* xxv. 264 A consciousness of the fallacy of our senses.

3. a. A deceptive or misleading argument, a sophism. In Logic *esp.* a flaw, material or formal, which vitiates a syllogism; any of the species or types to which such flaws are reducible. Also, sophistical reasoning, sophistry. In certain phrases in the formal terminology of Logic, as *fallacy of accident* (see quots.); *fallacy of composition* (see COMPOSITION 4 b); *fallacy of division*, the fallacy that whatever is true of a whole must be true of any part or member of that whole.

Not in Wilson's *Logic* (1552) which has 'deceipt', 'deceiptfulness', as the equivalent of *fallacia* in this sense.

[**1552** R. Ascham *Let.* 12 July in H. Ellis *Orig. Lett. Lit. Men* (1843) 12 Lest the *fallax* of composicion and division.. inverte the sentence. **1562** Turner *Herbal* ii. 100 a, It is a false fallacie.. to argue from a parte to the hole. **1599** Blundevil *Logike* 166 *Fallacia Accidentis*..: which may bee englished thus: the fallax of the Accident.] **1612** Brinsley *Lud. Lit.* xvii. (1627) 208 To helpe to answer the subtilties or fallacies. *a* **1665** J. Goodwin *Filled w. the Spirit* (1867) 160, I shall..proceed to shew the fallacies and other weaknesses of those pretences. **1685** tr. *Arnauld & Nicole's Logic* III. xix. 108 To judge of a thing which only agrees with it by accident. This Sophism is call'd in Schools Fallacia accidentis, the Fallacy of the Accident. *Ibid.* 109 To pass from sence divided to sence compos'd..is call'd Fallacia Compositionis, Fallacy of Composition. *Ibid.*, To pass..from sence compos'd to sence divided..is call'd.. Fallacy of division. **1776** Adam Smith *W.N.* ii. iv. I. 357 The fallacy which seems to have misled those gentlemen. **1870** W. S. Jevons *Elem. Lessons Logic* xxi. 176 The fallacy of *accident* consists in arguing erroneously *from a general rule to a special case*, where a certain accidental circumstance renders the rule inapplicable. **1884** tr. *Lotze's Logic* 284 The commonest fallacy is ambiguity of the middle term. **1961** J. G. Brennan *Handbk. Logic* (ed. 2) x. 213 The Gambler's Fallacy may be construed as an example of the fallacy of division. **1967** *Philosophy* XLII. 7 An avoidance of the fallacy of accident or *secundum quid*.

b. Also in extended use (cf. 4, 5): *fallacy of misplaced argument* (see quot. 1942); *fallacy of misplaced concreteness* (see quots.); *fallacy of simple location*, acc. to A. N. Whitehead, an assumption that underlies the whole of science since the 17th century, viz. a form of materialism which holds that the space-time location of a material object is not dependent on reference to other space-time regions; *fallacy of the inversion of parts* (see quot. 1867); *fallacy of the perfect dictionary* (see quot. 1938).

1867 J. S. Mill *Exam. Hamilton's Philos.* (ed. 3) vii. 127 There is a mode of controversy which I do not remember to have seen in any enumeration of Fallacies, but which will some day find a place there, under some such name as the Inversion of Parts. It consists in indignantly vindicating as against your adversary the very principle which he is asserting against yourself. **1925** A. N. Whitehead *Sci. & Mod. World* (1926) iii. 64 The accidental error of mistaking the abstract for the concrete..is an example of what I will call the 'Fallacy of Misplaced Concreteness'. [*Ibid.* iv. 72 There is no element whatever which possesses this character of simple location.] **1927** B. Russell *Analysis of Matter* xxxii. 340 Dr. Whitehead..is not open to such a charge; his 'fallacy of simple location', when avoided, leads to a world-structure quite different from that of common sense and early science. **1929** A. N. Whitehead *Process & Reality* i. i. 9 The 'fallacy of misplaced concreteness'..consists in neglecting the degree of abstraction involved when an actual entity is considered merely so far as it exemplifies certain categories of thought. **1938** —— *Modes of Thought* 235 The very natural belief, that mankind has consciously entertained all the fundamental ideas which are applicable to its experience. Further it is held that human language, in single words or in phrases, explicitly expresses these ideas. I will term this presupposition, the Fallacy of the Perfect

Dictionary. **1942** R. G. COLLINGWOOD *New Leviathan* iv. 73 The fallacy of arguing about questions like this is what I call the *Fallacy of Misplaced Argument*; which may be defined as the fallacy of arguing about any object immediately given to consciousness.

4. A delusive notion, an error, *esp.* one founded on false reasoning. Also, the condition of being deceived, error.

1590 SHAKS. *Com. Err.* II. ii. 188 Ile entertaine the free'd [*Globe ed.* offer'd] fallacie. **1665** GLANVILL *Sceps. Sci.* xiii. 75 We being then thus obnoxious to fallacy in our apprehensions and judgments. **1735-8** BOLINGBROKE *On Parties* Ded. 22 When They cannot impose a Fallacy, endeavour..to hinder Men from discerning a Truth. **1825** SYD. SMITH *Wks.* (1859) II. 59/2 A vast number of absurd and mischievous fallacies. **1844** H. H. WILSON *Brit. India* I. 413 In adducing the authority of Hindu writers in favour of the doctrine, two sources of fallacy are discernible.

5. a. Sophistical nature, unsoundness (of arguments); erroneousness, delusiveness (of opinions, expectations, etc.).

1777 PRIESTLEY *Disc. Philos. Necess.* Pref. 30, I was enabled to see the fallacy of most of the arguments. **1825** MCCULLOCH *Pol. Econ.* II. 158 The returns under the population acts have shown the fallacy of these opinions. **1850** PRESCOTT *Peru* II. 193 Expectations of wealth, of which almost every succeeding expedition had proved the fallacy.

†**b.** Proneness to err, fallibility. *Obs. rare.*

1651 N. BACON *Disc. Govt. Eng.* II. xxvii. (1739) 120 Finding the fallacy of the infallible Chair, he hearkens unto other Doctors. **1796** GOUV. MORRIS in Sparks *Life & Writ.* (1832) III. 87 Experience has taught me a sincere faith in the fallacy of human opinions.

6. *Comb.*, as ***fallacy-monger***.

1849 COBDEN *Speeches* 10 When the revolutions broke out, these fallacy-mongers exclaimed.

fallage ('fɔːlɪdʒ). [f. FALL *v.* + -AGE.] The action or process of falling or cutting down trees.

1882 MAYNE REID in *N. Y. Tribune* May, The fallage is not all done at the same time.

fal-lal (ˌfæl'læl, fæ'læl), *sb.* and *a.* Also **fallol**. [One of the many reduplicating formations expressing the notion of something trivial or gaudy; cf. *knick-knack*, *gew-gaw*. The suggestion may have been given by FALBALA.]

A. *sb.*

1. a. A piece of finery or frippery, a showy adornment in dress. Chiefly *pl.*

a **1706** EVELYN (Fairholt), His dress has bows and fine fal-lalls. **1718** MRS. CENTLIVRE *Bold Stroke for Wife* II, And thou do'st really think those Fallals becometh thee? **1775** T. SHERIDAN *Art Reading* 88 One of their painted Courtezans, adorned with fripperies and fallals. **1816** SCOTT *Old Mortal.* xxxix, It was an idle fancy..to dress the honest auld man in thae expensive fal-lalls that he ne'er wore in his life. **1861** SALA *Dutch Pict.* viii. 121 New bonnets..and similar feminine fallals.

b. *fig.*

1957 *Technology* Mar. 3/4 Some people may find it rather odd, in a journal professedly devoted to training and education for industry, to come across film reviews, music notices and such fal-lals.

2. *dial.* Affectation in manner, fussy show of politeness.

1879 MISS JACKSON *Shropsh. Word-bk.*, 'I canna believe a word 'e says 'e's so much fallal about 'im.' **1887** *S. Cheshire Gloss.*, 'He's too much fallol about him to pleease me.'

3. = FA-LA.

1864 *Reader* 17 Sept. 364 The slow dance with its 'fal-lal' burthen.

B. *adj.* **a.** Affected, finicking, foppish.

1748 RICHARDSON *Clarissa* I. xlii. 291 Humouring his old fal-lal taste. **1768** MAD. D'ARBLAY *Early Diary* 17 July, I was so sick of the ceremony and fuss of these fall lall people! **1818** SCOTT *Hrt. Midl.* xxv, Your cockups and your fallal duds. **1830** H. LEE *Mem. Manager* II. vi. 9 Are no lacqueys kept to administer to idle caprices? To run on fal lal messages, or carry complimentary cards, parrots or lapdogs? **1847** A. & H. MAYHEW *Greatest Plague* vii. 87 Lo and behold! my neat, unpretending chrysalis had changed into a flaunting fal-lal butterfly.

†**b.** absol. ***to be a little upon the fal-lal***: to border on the affected.

1754 RICHARDSON *Grandison* V. xvi, The lady is a little upon the fallal.

fal-lal, *v.* [f. FAL-LAL *sb.*] *intr.* To behave or dress in an affected or finicking manner; to idle, dally, procrastinate.

1854 A. E. BARKER *Gloss. Northants.* I. 219 *Fallals*, flaunting finery. It is also used participially to a female dressed out beyond her station. 'See how she's *fallal'd* out.' **1857** TROLLOPE *Three Clerks* II. iv. 72 She can't go on fal-lalling with you, and then nothing to come of it. **1864** —— *Small Ho. at Allington* II. xvi. 161 If I was to be fal-lalling with that married woman, you wouldn't like it. **1866** —— *Last Chron. Barset* I. xxvi. 233 My wife can do very well without you fal-lalling here all day.

fallalery (fæl'lælərɪ). [f. FAL-LAL *sb.* + -ERY.] Tawdry finery, gaudy ornament.

1833 HOOD *Public Dinner* ii, Dames in the gallery, All dressed in fallallery. **1891** G. MEREDITH *One of our Conquerors* I. iv. 65 Dancing and flirting and fal-lallery.

fallalish (fæl'lælɪʃ), *a. rare.* [f. FAL-LAL *a.* + -ISH.] Somewhat fal-lal. Hence **fal'lalishly** *adv.*

1754 RICHARDSON *Grandison* (1781) V. xliii. 274 An old soul, whose whole life has been but one dream, a little fal-lal-ishly varied.

†**fa'llation.** *Obs.* Forms: 6-7 **fallacian, -ion, fallation.** [Formation not quite clear; f. FALLACY or its source, the ending being confused with -ATION; or f. FALLACIOUS, on the analogy of *suspicious, suspicion.*] = FALLACY 3.

a **1568** ASCHAM *Scholem.* II. (Arb.) 132 Tomitanus..hath expressed euerie fallacion in Aristotle, with diuerse examples out of Plato. **1588** FRAUNCE *Lawiers Log.* I. iv. 26 b, Fallacians bee eyther in the woord or in the reason. **1610** HEALEY *St. Aug. Citie of God* 309.

'**fall-away**, *sb.* [f. vbl. phrase *fall away*: see FALL *v.* 80.] †**1.** One who falls away from religion; an apostate. *Obs.*

1682 BUNYAN *Barren Fig-tree* (1684) 104 It is impossible for those Fall-a-ways to be renewed again unto repentance.

2. A falling off.

1878 B. F. TAYLOR *Between Gates* 232 On midsummer the Yo Semite is less of a fall than a fall-away. **1879** G. M. HOPKINS *Let.* 14 Aug. (1935) 86 A fall-away or diminuendo.

†'**fallax**, *sb. Obs.* [a. L. *fallax*, neut. of *fallax* deceptive, f. *fallĕre* to deceive.] = FALLACY.

1530 PALSGR. 218/2 Fallaxe or desceyt, *falace*. **1563** FOXE *A. & M.* 750, I answer to thargument, whych I do deny as a fallax. *a* **1628** F. GREVILLE *Sidney* viii. (1652) 104 That ever-betraying Fallax of undervaluing our enemies. **1669** STURMY *Mariner's Mag.* C ij b.

†**fa'llaxity.** *Obs.* [f. L. *fallax*: see FALLACE *a.* and -ITY.] = FALLACY.

c **1640** J. SMYTH *Lives Berkeleys* (1883) II. 226 Great deceit, fallaxity and crafty waies.

'**fall-back**, *sb.* [f. vbl. phrase *fall back*: see FALL *v.* 81.] For the stress on this and similar words, cf. BREAK-DOWN.

a. Something upon which one may fall back; a reserve. **b.** A falling back, depression.

1851 *Jrnl. R. Agric. Soc.* XII. II. 402 It is..advisable..to provide a 'fall-back', or adjacent stubble field into which the flock may retire at pleasure. **1853** KANE *Grinnell Exp.* xxi. (1856) 162 He would leave the Mary..to serve as a fall-back in case we should lose our vessels. **1892** *Pall Mall G.* 26 Feb. 2/1 You will have occasional months of fall-back, but that will in time be made up, and every quarter will show a steady increase.

c. *concr.* Fall-back pay.

1961 *Observer* 7 May 40/6 Men who failed to find a day's work should get a guaranteed minimum payment (the 'fall-back'). **1969** *Daily Tel.* 11 Apr. 29/3 The men are paid on the basis of the £17 'fall-back' plus piece-work, which gives them average earnings of about £30 a week.

fall-back, *a.* **1.** Of a chaise, etc.: having a back which can be let down. *U.S.*

1767 *Boston Gaz.* 12 Oct. (Th.), A Fall-back Chaise for sale. **1768** *Essex Inst. Hist. Coll.* XI. 38 He also has five fall-back chaises, one fall-back curricle. **1832** *Coll. New H. Hist. Soc.* III. 37 He was the proprietor of a fall back chaise.

2. That may be used in an emergency; *esp.* of a minimum wage paid when work is not available.

1930 *Economist* 6 Dec. 1057/2 The operatives..laid stress on the absence of any provision for a fall-back wage, and a minimum wage to provide for the contingency of under-employment. **1942** W. ROSE *Good Neighbours* iii. 23 The work lasted through the summer, and provided a fall-back job when weather conditions were unsuitable for hay work. **1959** *Times* 8 Dec. 13/6 By the time the tug strike was a few days old 5,000 dockers were without work and receiving 'fall-back' pay.

†'**fall-door.** *Obs. rare.* [f. FALL *sb.*[1] + DOOR, after Flemish *valdeure.*] A trap-door.

1481 CAXTON *Reynard* (Arb.) 27 And ther stode a faldore by, and we clymened ther up..and they that laye nexte the fyre cryden that the valdore was open.

'**fall-down**, *a.* [f. vbl. phrase *fall down*: see FALL *v.* 85.] That falls down, turned over.

1829 MARRYAT *F. Mildmay* xxiii, He appeared in a..fall-down collar. **1882** *Unif. Reg.* in *Navy List* July 493/2 *Coat.*—Blue cloth, double-breasted, fall-down collar.

fallen ('fɔːl(ə)n), *ppl. a.* For forms see FALL *v.*

1. a. That has come down or dropped from a high position.

c **1400** *Rom. Rose* 1214 White as snowe falle newe. **1776** WITHERING *Brit. Plants* IV. 154 Two distinct species grow ..on the fallen branches of trees. **1849** *Sk. Nat. Hist., Mammalia* IV. 27 Fallen acorns constitute the food of the dormouse.

b. ***fallen-stars*** Sc.: (see quot.).

1808 JAMIESON, *Fallen stars..Tremella Nostoc*, Linn.; a gelatinous plant, found in pastures &c. after rain. *Ibid.* s.v., *Sea Fallen Stars*..an animal thrown on the sea-shore in summer and autumn; *Medusa æquorea*, Linn.

2. Of the sun: Having set. *rare.*

1892 TENNYSON *Foresters* I. iii, The long bright day is done, And darkness rises from the fallen sun.

3. Of flesh, etc.: Shrunken, emaciated. ***fallen fleece***: see quot. 1892. ***fallen arch***: see ARCH *sb.* 4 b; so ***fallen instep***.

1722 DE FOE *Col. Jack* (1840) 281 Her fallen flesh plumped up. **1748** RICHARDSON *Clarissa* VI. xxx. 98 The old lines appearing strong in the..fallen cheeks. **1892** *Labour Commission* Gloss. No. 8 *Fallen Fleeces*. Fleece, wool, or mohair, taken from the dead carcases of sheep, &c., and, therefore, diseased. **1926** M. D. POST *Man Hunters* 292 *(caption)* Flat foot or a fallen arch. **1948** A. BARON *From City from Plough* 11 All the other ranks 'll have fallen arches or double ruptures. **1954** L. MACNEICE *Autumn Sequel* IX. 59 A life of fallen insteps and surplus fat.

4. That has been laid low, or brought to the ground. Also *absol.* of men. *lit.* and *fig. spec.*, of those who have died in battle.

a **1631** DONNE *Epigr.* (1652) 93 Falne Okes the Axe doth into Timber hew. **1765** H. BLAIR *Crit. Diss.* (ed. 2) 70 He professedly delights in strife and blood. He insults over the fallen. **1774** GOLDSM. *Nat. Hist.* (1776) I. 283 The branches of the fallen forest. **1819** MRS. HEMANS *Abencerrage* 56 There bleed the fallen, there contend the brave. **1825** G. R. GLEIG *Subaltern* vii. 109 Desiring..a fellow..to keep guard near one of his fallen comrades. 'I don't care for living men,' said the soldier; 'but..don't keep me beside *him*.' *a* **1835** —— *Marius* 82 Midst fallen palaces she sits alone. **1871** FREEMAN *Norm. Conq.* (1876) IV. xvii. 34 The estates of the fallen King [Harold]..were..forfeited. *Ibid.* 62 The fallen gonfanon of Harold. **1878** J. P. HOPPS *Jesus* v. 21 His delight was, to lift up the fallen. **1914** W. D. NEWTON *War* xi. 119 The corpses of the fallen were trodden and ground beneath stumbling heedless soles. **1914** *New Republic* 5 Dec. 14/2 Mr. Shaw referred to the miserable pensions that are being paid to the widows of fallen soldiers. **1917** L. BINYON *(title)* For the Fallen and other poems. **1919** *Times* 12 Nov. 16/5 The majority of the citizens willingly consented to pay a tribute to the memory of the fallen.

5. *fig.* **a.** In a moral sense: That has lost purity or innocence; ruined. ***a fallen woman***: one who has surrendered her chastity. **b.** With reference to rank, fortune, or dignity: That has come down from high estate.

a **1628** F. GREVILLE *Poems, Hum. Learning* xix, Yea of our falne estate the fatall staine Is such, as [etc.]. **1645** MILTON *Tetrach.* Wks. 1738 I. 230 God..would..not [have] sent word by Malachi in a sudden fal'n stile. **1682** *Lond. Gaz.* No. 1711/4 It was contrived by some Discontented Antimonarchical Fallen-Angel. **1712** STEELE *Spect.* No. 276 ¶1 Your Papers with regard to the fallen Part of the Fair Sex. **1751** JORTIN *Serm.* (1771) I. ii. 21 The Messiah was to restore fallen man. **1820** BYRON *Mar. Faliero* II. i, The once fall'n woman must for ever fall. **1848** MACAULAY *Hist. Eng.* III. 482 The fallen dynasty and the fallen hierarchy were restored. **1875** JOWETT *Plato* (ed. 2) III. 71 Philosophy, even in her fallen estate, has a dignity of her own.

6. Comb. ***fallen-in*** (cf. FALL *v.* 88). ***fallen-off***: (see FALL *v.* 92).

1611 SHAKS. *Cymb.* III. vii. 6 The Legions now in Gallia, are Full weake to vndertake our Warres against The falne-off Britaines. **1806** SURR *Winter in Lond.* (ed. 3) I. 188 He is ..a fallen-off branch from the good old English tree. **1900** *Westm. Gaz.* 14 Feb. 6/3 Inrush of snow and sleet through the fallen-in roof. **1938** E. BOWEN *Death of Heart* I. ii. 47 Thomas sits so fallen-in, waiting for Anna, that his clock makes the only sound in his room.

†'**fallency.** *Civil Law. Obs.* [ad. med.L. *fallentia*, f. *fallĕre* to deceive: see -ENCY.] An instance of the failure of a rule: an exception.

1603 HAYWARD *Answ. to Doleman* iv. L ij, Alexander and Felinus doe assigne fiue fallencies vnto these rules. **1660** JER. TAYLOR *Duct. Dubit.* I. Pref. 9 Socinus sets down 802 fallencies, (that's the word of the law,) concerning the contestation of suits and actions at law.

fallenness ('fɔːl(ə)nnɪs). [f. FALLEN *ppl. a.* + -NESS.] The state of being fallen; *esp.* degeneracy consequent upon the Fall.

1871 W. GRAHAM *Lect. Ephesians* vi. 364 It teaches the fallenness of our whole nature. **1912** W. H. MOBERLY in *Foundations* 283 What is important is not an historical Fall, but the fact of 'fallenness'. **1923** *Expos. Times* July 439/2 It fails to express the fallenness of man's original animalism and degradation. **1952** V. A. DEMANT *Religion & Decl. Capitalism* iv. 86 The fallenness of man consists in a certain net of evil in which mankind is caught because of his refusal to live obediently.

faller ('fɔːlə(r)). [f. FALL *v.* + -ER[1].]

1. One who falls, in various senses of the vb. Also with *adv.*, as ***faller away, off, out.***

c **1440** *Promp. Parv.* 147 Fallare, or he þat oftyn tyme fallythe, *cadax*. **1577** tr. *Bullinger's Decades* (1592) 824 He was accounted..a faller off from yᵉ true Church of God. *a* **1631** LAUD *Serm.* (1847) 13 Nor are we fallers out of the Church, but they fallers off from verity. **1725** BRADLEY *Fam. Dict.* s.v. *Rules for buying Horses*, It's a true Mark of..a perpetual Faller. **1835** COBBETT *Legacy Parsons* ii. 54 The disrespectful name of *Dissenters*; that is to say, fallers away from the true faith. **1890** *Pall Mall G.* 22 Aug. 1/2 Six riders were brought to grief..Being experienced fallers, however, nothing more serious than bruises resulted. **1964** *Cath. Gaz.* June 161/2 Most of the fallers out..tended to be..Catholics who were not deeply involved.

2. A feller of timber.

1879 MISS JACKSON *Shropsh. Word-bk.* s.v., The fallers bin on Esridge [Eastridge] coppy agen. **1905** *Terms Forestry & Logging* 37 *Faller*, one who fells trees. **1908** M. A. GRAINGER *Woodsmen of West* xiv. 84 The 'fallers' had worked along the slope. **1926** K. S. PRICHARD *Working Bullocks* ii. 23 The faller, Bob Carew, who was giving a lift on the rake. **1941** *Time* 11 Aug. 16/2 The faller (who chops and saws the tree). **1966** *Daily Colonist* (Victoria, B.C.) 4 Feb. 17/6 Mr. Peterson is employed as a faller by Butler Brothers. **1971** *Timber Trades Jrnl.* 14 Aug. 72 (Advt.), A gang of experienced fallers required for a parcel of beech and oak near Portsmouth.

3. The Hen-harrier (*Circus cyaneus*).

1885 in SWAINSON *Prov. Names Brit. Birds* 132.

†**4.** A part of a mill for scouring clothes, etc.: (see quot.). *Obs.*

1677 YARRANTON *Eng. Improv.* 107 There are Six or Eight Fallers (or Feet) which are taken and lifted up by the Axle-tree..and so fall down-right into a Box, or Chest, wherein the Cloth lyeth.

5. a. The name of various appliances in spinning machines. Also *attrib.*

1851 L. D. B. GORDON *Art Jrnl. Catal. Gt. Exhib.* p. vi **/2 As the carriage approaches the roller-beam, the spinner

gradually raises the faller-wire. **1879** *Cassell's Techn. Educ.* IV. 396/1 Along the top of the spindles stretch two wires called the 'fallers'.

b. A kind of stamp (see quots.).

a **1884** KNIGHT *Dict. Mech.* Suppl. 326/1 *Faller,* a vertical stamp in a fulling, milling, or stamping machine; usually lifted by cams and allowed to drop vertically and endwise. *Ibid.,* *Faller Machine,* a machine with vertical stamps or fallers, used in milling goods.

†fallera. *Falconry. Obs. rare*⁻¹. Also 7-8 in Dicts. **fal(l)orn, falera.** (See quots.)

1486 *Bk. St. Alban's* C iij a, When ye se that yowre hawkes clees wax white: then she has the fallera. **1692-1732** COLES, *Falorn, fall-,* a disease in hawks known by their white talons. **1721-1800** BAILEY, *Falera.*

fallibilism ('fælɪbɪlɪz(ə)m). [f. FALLIBLE *a.* + -ISM.] The principle that propositions concerning empirical knowledge cannot be proved.

c **1897** C. S. PEIRCE *Coll. Papers* (1931) I. I. iii. 61 Fallibilism..only says that people cannot attain absolute certainty concerning questions of fact. *Ibid.* 70 Fallibilism is the doctrine that our knowledge is never absolute but always swims, as it were, in a continuum of uncertainty and of indeterminacy. **1941** *Mind* L. 81 Fallibilism which denies intuitive or certain knowledge even of common-sense propositions.

'fallibilist, *a.* [f. as prec. + -IST.] Maintaining or accepting the principle of fallibilism; pertaining to or resembling fallibilism.

c **1897** C. S. PEIRCE *Coll. Papers* (1931) I. I. iii. 63 Let us look then at two or three of the grandest results of science and see whether they appear any different from a fallibilist standpoint from what they would to an infallibilist. **1941** *Mind* L. 82 That all propositions must be either logically certain or equally corrigible is a rash bifurcation of which fallibilist philosophers should surely beware.

fallibility (fælɪ'bɪlɪtɪ). [f. next + -ITY. Cf. F. *faillibilité.*] The state or fact of being fallible; liability to err or to mislead (in mod. usage limited to the former); an instance of the same.

1634 'E. KNOTT' in *Chillingworth's Relig. Prot.* iv. §14 Nothing of the Churches Visibility or Invisibility, Fallibility or Infallibility. **1677** HALE *Prim. Orig. Man.* II. i. 131 Those Evidences of Fact..have or may have their several allays and fallibilities. **1725** WATTS *Logic* II. ix. 409 Tho' there be a great deal of Fallibility in the Testimony of Men. **1775** HARRIS *Philos. Arrangem.* Wks. (1841) 353 The fallibility which sometimes attends this method of distinguishing. **1840** THACKERAY *Paris Sk.-bk.* (1872) 216 The fallibility of judges and lawyers. **1859** MILL *Liberty* i. 18 The fallibility of what is called the moral sense.

fallible ('fælɪb(ə)l), *a.* Also 6-7 **fallable.** [ad. late L. *fallibilis,* f. *fallĕre* to deceive: see -BLE. Cf. F. *faillible.*

The L. word appears in Papias (11th c.) with the active sense 'deceitful'; in late med.L. it has the passive sense 'deceivable'.]

1. Of persons or their faculties: Liable to be deceived or mistaken; liable to err.

1430 LYDG. *Chron. Troy* I. vi, I suppose her connyng was fallible. **1638** *Penit. Conf.* vii. (1657) 135 He is fallible, and often erring in judgment. **1699** BURNET 39 *Art.* xxxiii. (1700) 364 An Authority to which no fallible Body of men can have a Right. **1763** JOHNSON in Boswell *Life* (1831) I. 391 A fallible being will fail somewhere. **1855** MILMAN *Lat. Chr.* (1864) V. ix. ii. 206 The papal power..the representative of fallible man rather than of the infallible God. **1881** W. COLLINS *Bl. Robe* I. iii. 142 These rebuffs are wholesome reminders of his fallible human nature.

2. Of rules, opinions, arguments, etc.: Liable to be erroneous, unreliable.

a **1420** HOCCLEVE *De Reg. Princ.* 2867 This worldes joye is transitorie, And the truste on it slipir and fallible. **1534** MORE in Ellis *Orig. Lett.* I. 117 II. 52 The fallible opinion.. of lightsome chaungeable peple. *c* **1555** HARPSFIELD *Divorce Hen. VIII* (1878) 164 This is but a fallable argument. **1603** SHAKS. *Meas. for M.* III. i. 170 Do not satisfie your resolution with hopes that are fallible. **1643** SIR T. BROWNE *Relig. Med.* i. 23 The.. fallible discourses of man upon the word of God. **1677** W. HUBBARD *Narrative* II. 1 Uncertain and fallible Reports. **1736** BUTLER *Anal.* viii. 393 The rules..of preserving health.. are not only fallible and precarious. **1851** HERSCHEL *Stud. Nat. Phil.* III. iii. 286 A slow and painful process if rightly gone into, and a very fallible one if only partially executed.

†b. Not determinable with certainty. *Obs. rare.*

1664 POWER *Exp. Philos.* III. 166 This Angle of Variation being quite fallible, and always variable.

†3. Fallacious, delusive. *Obs. rare.*

1559 MORWYNG *Evonym.* 176 Suche waters..make a fallible image of youth.

4. quasi-*sb.* One who is fallible. *rare.*

1705 HICKERINGILL *Priest-cr.* Wks. (1716) 79 She [Queen Elizabeth] over-liv'd this infallible fallible [Pope Pius V]. **1846** G. S. FABER *Lett. Tractar. Secess. Popery* 164 All these fallibles are added up together in one sum which collectively constitute the Church.

Hence **'fallibleness** = FALLIBILITY.

1648 HAMMOND *To Ld. Fairfax* 19 The weaknesse and falliblenesse of these few principles. **1730-6** in BAILEY (folio).

fallibly ('fælɪblɪ), *adv.* [f. as prec. + -LY².] In a fallible manner.

1552 HULOET, *Fallably, subdole.* **1638** CHILLINGW. *Relig. Prot.* I. ii. §94. 87 Why does shee imploy particular Doctors to interpret Scriptures fallibly?

falling ('fɔːlɪŋ), *vbl. sb.* [f. FALL *v.* + -ING¹.] The action of the vb. FALL.

1. In intransitive senses.

c **1300** *Cursor M.* 1854 (Cott.) Abute fiue monetz was þat it stud Wit-outen falling þat fers fludd. *c* **1340** *Ibid.* 411 *heading* (Fairf.) þe fallinge of lucifer and his felawes. *a* **1450** *Knt. de la Tour* 11 She..in her fallyng cried helpe on our lady. **1533-4** *Act 25 Hen. VIII,* c. 13 §13 From the tyme of the falling of theym [lambs] unto the feast of.. Seynt John Baptyste. **1563** FULKE *Meteors* (1640) 55 b, Sleet.. beginneth to melt in the falling. **1580** HOLLYBAND *Treas. Fr. Tong, Ravallement..* a falling in price, as the falling of the market. **1621** SANDERSON *Serm.* I. 214 Vzza had better have ventured the falling, than the fingering of the ark. **1771** MRS. GRIFFITH tr. *Viaud's Shipwreck* 109 The falling of night would otherwise have forced us to lay aside our labour. **1807** T. THOMSON *Chem.* (ed. 3) II. 378 The falling of the drops of alcohol from the beak of the receiver. **1839** LONGF. *Hyperion* I. vii. (1865) 38 The silent falling of snow.

2. In various specific applications. **a.** *the falling of the leaf*: autumn. **b.** Setting (of the sun). **c.** *Pathol.* (see quot. 1884). **d.** In the barometer, etc. **e.** *Mus.* Cf. FALL *v.* 17.

a. **1503** HAWES *Examp. Virt.* i. 5 In Septembre in fallynge of the lefe.

b. **1555** EDEN *Decades* 1 Folowinge the fallinge of the sonne.

c. *c* **1400** *Lanfranc's Cirurg.* 303 For fallinge of þe maris þat is cleped dislocacioun of the maris. **1884** *Syd. Soc. Lex., Falling of the womb,* a popular term for *Prolapsus uteri.*

d. **1658** WILLSFORD *Natures Secrets* 154 The often rising and falling of the water [in a weather-glass] shews the outward Air very mutable.. and the weather unconstant. **1688** J. SMITH *Baroscope* 65 Wet and Rainy Weather come presently upon the Mercury's Falling. **1814** W. C. WELLS *Ess. Dew* 9 The falling of the mercury in the barometer. **1860** ADM. FITZ-ROY in *Merc. Marine Mag.* VII. 340 Indications of approaching changes.. are shown.. by its [the barometer's] falling or rising.

e. **1609** DOULAND *Ornith. Microl.* I. vi. 17 The falling of a Song. **1674** SIMPSON in Campion *Art of Descant* 4 *foot-n.,* If the Bass do rise more than a fourth, it must be called falling. **1706** A. BEDFORD *Temple Mus.* ix. 186 A falling..at the Beginning of a Strain.

3. In transitive senses.

1580 *Lease* in Hearne *Collect.* (Oxf. Hist. Soc.) I. 237 At every falling he will leave for every acre fallen.. twelve trees. **1699** LUTTRELL *Brief. Rel.* (1857) IV. 483 A libell against the last parliament about their falling of guineas.

†4. A depression in the soil; a hollow, declivity, slope. *Obs.*

1563 GOLDING *Cæsar* 61 b, High rockes and steepe fallings. **1580** SIDNEY *Arcadia* III. (1622) 250 Amphialus embushed his footemen in the falling of a hill. **1684** R. H. *Sch. Recreat.* 83 Observe.. the Risings, Fallings, and Advantages of the Places where you Bowl. **1712** J. JAMES tr. *Le Blond's Gardening* 21 Gardens.. having no Risings, nor Fallings.

5. *concr.* Something which falls or has fallen. **a.** A fragment (of a building); a ruin. **b.** usually in *pl.* A dropping, a windfall. Also *fig.*

a. **1382** WYCLIF *Isa.* lxi. 4 And olde fallingus thei shul rere, and thei shul restore cities forsaken. **1599** HAKLUYT *Voy.* II. I. 214 A great part of it..is.. almost couered with the aforesayd fallings.

b. **1608** *Yorksh. Trag.* I. i, Apples hanging longer.. than when they are ripe, make so many fallings. *a* **1661** HOLY-DAY *Juvenal* 180 Virro was capable of such caduca, such fallings .. such windfalls. **1687** DRYDEN *Hind & P.* III. 103 Tis the beggar's gain To glean the fallings of the loaded wain. **1847-78** HALLIWELL, *Fallings,* dropped fruit. *South.*

6. a. With adverbs, expressing the action of the vbl. combinations under FALL *v.* XI.

1440 *Promp. Parv., Fallynge downe, idem est quod Fallynge evylle.* **1580** HOLLYBAND *Treas. Fr. Tong, Catarrhe ..* the Catarre or fallyng downe of humours. **1607** SHAKS. *Timon* IV. iii. 401 The falling from of his Friendes. **1611** BIBLE *2 Thess.* ii. 3 That day shall not come, except there come a falling away first. **1659** B. HARRIS *Parival's Iron Age* 200 They.. observed the falling back of the French. **1712** W. ROGERS *Voy.* 315 Numbers.. are lost by the falling in of the Earth. **1748** RICHARDSON *Clarissa* VII. v. 26 All her falling away, and her fainting fits. **1878** L. P. MEREDITH *Teeth* 181 The falling away of the gums after extraction.

b. *falling off*: the action of the vb. *fall off* (FALL *v.* 92); decadence, defection, diminution.

1602 SHAKS. *Ham.* I. v. 47 Oh Hamlet, what a falling off was there. **1709** STEELE & ADDISON *Tatler* No. 111 ¶4 A Falling off from those Schemes of Thinking. **1802** T. BEDDOES *Hygëia* vii, Should it be accompanied by falling off in flesh. **1834** *Brit. Husb.* III. 60 A falling off of the milk is immediately noticed. **1837** WHITTIER *Barclay of Ury* xv, Hard to feel the stranger's scoff, Hard the old friend's falling off. **1883** E. PENNELL-ELMHIRST *Cream Leicestersh.* 155 The grey showed no falling off from his previous form.

c. *falling out*: the action of the vb. *fall out* (FALL *v.* 94), disagreement, quarrel; also **†**tending. Also *falling in (with)*: the action of the vb. *fall in* FALL *v.* 88, 91); opp. *falling out.*

1568 GRAFTON *Chron.* II. 97 This fallyng out of king John with.. Geoffrey Archebishop of Yorke. **1586** W. WEBBE *Eng. Poetrie* (Arb.) 56 The falling out of verses together in one like sounde, is commonly called.. Ryme. **1667** PEPYS *Diary* (1877) V. 194, I have heard of a falling out between my Lord Arlington.. and W. Coventry. **1741** RICHARDSON *Pamela* III. 337 We had a sad Falling-out t'other Day. **1838** DICKENS *Lett.* 16 Jan. (1965) I. 355 It almost seems as if we had had a mortal falling out. I hope we shall have a lasting falling in again, soon. **1847** TENNYSON *Princess* I. 251 Blessings on the falling out That all the more endears. **1919** H. CRANE *Let.* 13 Dec. (1965) 26 He has had a falling out with Amy Lowell, but a falling in with T. S. Eliot by way of compensation.

d. *falling-short*, the action of the vbl. phr. *fall short of* (FALL *v.* 98): failure, insufficiency; inability to reach.

1857 F. L. OLMSTED *Journey through Texas* p. viii, Certain fallings-short from the standard of comfort and of character in older communities are inevitable. **1916** A. BENNETT *These Twain* xi. 221 His life seemed to be a life of half-measures, a continual falling-short. **1936** *Discovery* Oct. 308/2 'My predecessors,' he said, 'have spoken of the shortcomings of the active world—to me they are but the fallings short of science.'

7. = FELLING *vbl. sb.* 1. Also *attrib.,* in *falling axe, rope, saw, wedge.* Now *N. Amer., Austral.,* and *N.Z.*

1388 WYCLIF *Ps.* lxxiii. 6 Thei castiden down it with an ax, and a brood fallinge ax. **1580** [see sense 3]. **1678** *New Castle (Delaware) Court Rec.* (1904) 362, 3 falling axses. **1866** J. MURRAY *Descr. Province Southland* III. 29 For the falling, cross-cutting and splitting of his posts and rails, he will find it of advantage again to get a mate. **1875** G. C. DAVIES *Rambles School Field-Club* viii. 67 A 'falling rope'.. that men attach to the top of a tree when they wish to cut it down. **1905** *Terms Forestry & Logging* 37 *Falling ax,* an ax with a long helve and a long, narrow bit, designed especially for felling trees. *Falling wedge,* a wedge used to throw a tree in the desired direction, by driving it into the saw kerf. **1943** R. E. SWANSON *Rhymes Lumberjack* 12 So huge they were (both cedar and fir) that days were spent in their falling. **1946** F. DAVISON *Dusty* xvii. 200 [He] came to know as much as a distant observer could of the business of falling, hauling and sawing pine logs. **1960** *Citizen* (N. Vancouver) 10 Mar. 10/1 Swinging balance and cut of keen falling-saw Bite of falling-axe, tap of falling-wedge.

8. *falling-in-love* [FALL *v.* 38 b, LOVE *sb.*¹ 7 f], the state of becoming enamoured.

1859 *Nat. Rev.* Oct. 375 In the first place, a fighting period; and in the next place, a falling-in-love period. **1923** J. S. HUXLEY *Ess. Biologist* vii. 271 The commonest example is 'falling in love', where the simple sex-instinct becomes intertwined with other instincts. **1963** AUDEN *Dyer's Hand* IV. iv. 222 The traditional symbol in Western Literature for this kind of personal choice is the phenomenon of falling-in-love.

falling ('fɔːlɪŋ), *ppl. a.* [f. as prec. + -ING².]

1. That falls, in various senses of the vb.

a **1300** *Cursor M.* 27581 (Cott.) þe standand fall, þe falland rise. **1611** BIBLE *Isa.* xxxiv. 4 All their hoste shall fall downe .. as a falling figge from the fig tree. **1613** SHAKS. *Hen. VIII,* III. ii. 333 Presse not a falling man too farre. **1661** J. CHILDREY *Brit. Bacon.* 170 The high Hils.. break of the storms and falling Snow. **1695** CONGREVE *Love for L.* Prol., One falling Adam, and one tempted Eve. *a* **1711** KEN *Hymns Evang.* Poet. Wks. 1721 I. 86 Dark Prophecies predict our falling State. **1717** LADY M. W. MONTAGUE *Lett.* (1763) II. xxix. 29 My Caftan.. is a robe.. with very long strait falling sleeves. **1762** FALCONER *Shipwr.* I. 490 The vessel parted on the falling tide. **1781** GIBBON *Decl. & F.* III. 148 The weakness of the falling empire. **1833** HT. MARTINEAU *Vanderput & S.* vi. 99 Hein's frowning brow and falling countenance. **1843** LYTTON *Last Bar.* I. iv. 28 The long throat and falling shoulders. **1848** MILL *Pol. Econ.* III. xxiv. §3 The speculative holders are unwilling to sell in a falling market. **1858** in *Merc. Marine Mag.* V. 12 Kate Hooper.. had strong.. winds.. with falling barometer. **1874** KNIGHT *Dict. Mech.* I. 852/2 The Peabody gun.. has a falling breech-block.

2. *Prosody.* Of a foot, rhythm, etc.: Decreasing in stress, having the ictus at the beginning. *falling diphthong*: see DIPHTHONG *sb.* note. Also *Comb.,* as *falling-rising.*

1844 BECK & FELTON tr. *Munk's Metres* 8 A rhythm which begins with the arsis, and descends to the thesis, is called falling or sinking. **1924** H. E. PALMER *Gram. Spoken Eng.* I. 13 Falling-Rising Nucleus-tone. **1964** R. H. ROBINS *Gen. Ling.* iii. 111 Falling-rising tones.

3. *Astrol. falling houses* (see CADENT *a.* 2).

1594 BLUNDEVIL *Exerc.* IV. xxxvi. (ed. 7) 493 Those that go next before any of the foure principall Angles, are called falling houses.

4. *falling-in*: that slopes inwards from below.

1887 *Sci. Amer.* 2 July 11/2 Yachts with the falling-in top-sides of a man of war.

5. Syntactical Combinations. **a.** *falling-†disease,* †*-evil* (see EVIL 7 b), †*-ill, -sickness* (now rare) = EPILEPSY; also humorously for 'a fall', and *fig.*; *falling-weather* (*dial.* and *U.S.*) applied to weather in which rain, snow, or hail falls or may be expected.

The Eng. expressions for epilepsy are after L. *morbus caducus*; cf. Ger. *fallende sucht.*

a **1225** *Ancr. R.* 176 Fallinde vuel ich cleopie licomes sicnesse. **1527** ANDREW *Brunswyke's Distyll. Waters* C v, An ounce is good for them that haue the fallynge sekenesse. **1607** TOPSELL *Four-f. Beasts* (1673) 171 The gall of a Ferret is commended against the Falling disease. **1652** *Woman's Universe* in Watson *Collect. Scots Poems* III. (1711) 101 Hippocrates.. Could never cure her Falling-ill, Which takes her when she pleases. **1706** PHILLIPS (ed. Kersey), *Falling Evil,* a Disease which sometimes happens to Horses, being no other than the Falling-sickness. **1733** FRANKLIN *Poor Richard's Almanac* 6 Windy and falling weather. **1760** WASHINGTON *Diaries* I. 112 The morning.. promised much rain or other falling weather. **1780** in *Coll. New H. Hist. Soc.* IX. 176 Cloudy but no falling weather. **1838** C. GILMAN *Recoll. Southern Matron* xxv. 172 It looks like falling weather, and my old drab will come in well to-day. **1843** SIR T. WATSON *Lect. Physic* (1871) I. 630 Its [epilepsy's] common designation is the *falling sickness*; or, more vaguely, fits. **1859** BARTLETT *Dict. Amer.* (ed. 2) s.v. *Weather,* 'We are going to have falling weather', means that we are going to have rain, snow or hail. **1884-** in dial. glossaries (Gloucester, Hereford, Warwick, Worcester). **1919** H. L. WILSON *Ma Pettengill* v. 165 Will you look at that mess of clouds? I bet it's falling weather over in Surprise Valley.

b. in various other Combs., as **falling-band** = FALL *sb.*[1] 23 a; **falling collar**, a wide collar which lies flat; †**falling-door** = *folding-door*; †**falling-gate** = *falling-sluice*; †**falling-hinge**, one by which a door, etc. rises vertically when opened; **falling leaf**, an aerobatic manœuvre in which an aeroplane is stalled and sideslipped while losing height; also *attrib.* and *transf*; **falling-mould**, *Arch.* (see quot.); **falling-sluice** (see quot.).

1598 *Falling-band [see FALL *sb.*[1] 23 a]. **1637** EARL OF CORK *Diary* in Sir R. Boyle *Diary* Ser. I. (1886) V. 39 Sent me this daie..6 laced ffalling bands and vi pair of cuffes sutable. **1862** *Revised Regs. Army U.S.* 478 A sack coat.. made loose, without sleeve or body lining, *falling collar, inside pocket on the left side. **1866** MRS. GASKELL *Wives & Daughters* I. vi. 62 Two boys, in the most youthful kind of jackets and trousers, and falling collars. **1753** HANWAY *Trav.* I. II. xxxiv. 231 The Divan, or open hall, is in the centre, and shuts in with *falling-doors. **1801** *Hull Navig. Act* 2559 Two clear openings..in which shall be placed *falling gates. **1783** *Trans. Soc. Arts* I. 320 A *falling hinge. **1918** H. BARBER *Aerobatics* 51 (*caption*) *Falling Leaf. **1935** H. G. WELLS *Things to Come* IX. 82 Aeroplane looping the loop—then the falling leaf trick. **1957** BANNERMAN *Birds Brit. Isles* VI. 314 When performed at the lower altitudes the technique is often the individual 'falling-leaf', but at higher altitudes the birds rush downwards together and the formation is not broken. **1970** H. KRIER *Mod. Aerobatics & Precision Flying* ii. 56 The falling leaf is a series of checked spins, in which the airplane is allowed to fall off first to the right and then to the left, or vice versa. **1876** GWILT *Archit.* Gloss., *Falling Moulds, the two moulds applied to the vertical sides of the railpiece, one to the convex, the other to the concave side, in order to form the back and under surface of the rail and finish the squaring. **1846** BUCHANAN *Technol. Dict.*, *Falling-sluice, a..flood-gate, in connection with mill-dams..self-acting or contrived to fall down of itself in the event of a flood.

falling-star (ˈfɔːlɪŋstɑː(r)). [f. FALLING *ppl. a.* + STAR.] A meteor; a shooting star.

1563 FULKE *Meteors* (1640) 8 b, Thus much for the shooting or falling starres. **1690** T. BURNET *Th. Earth* III. 98 The last sign we shall take notice of is that of Falling Stars. **1759** MILLER in *Phil. Trans.* LI. 258 This meteor..moved with less rapidity than falling-stars commonly do. **1836** MACGILLIVRAY *Humboldt's Trav.* x. 127 He found falling stars more frequent in the equinoctial regions.

fall-less (ˈfɔːllɪs), *a.* [f. FALL *sb.*[1] + -LESS.] Having no fall (in various senses).

1897 F. THOMPSON *New Poems* 49 Then leaf, and flower, and falless [*sic*] fruit Shall hang together on the unyellowing bough. **1910** *Daily Chron.* 2 Feb. 8/2 The Indian..was nearly always the aggressor in the eighty minutes' fall-less wrestling which took place.

fallocque, obs. f. of FELUCCA.

Fallopian (fəˈləʊpɪən), *a. Anat.* [f. *Fallopi-us* (latinized name of an Italian anatomist 1523–1562) + -AN.] Used in the names of certain anatomical structures reputed to have been discovered by Fallopius, as in ***Fallopian aqueduct***, ***arch***, ***canal***, ***ligament***, ***tube***: see quots.

1706 PHILLIPS (ed. Kersey), *Fallopian Tubes*. **1754–64** SMELLIE *Midwif.* I. 113 The Fimbria of the Fallopian tube. **1831** R. KNOX *Cloquet's Anat.* 55 There is a hole..which terminates the Fallopian aqueduct, and transmits the facial nerve from the interior of the cranium. **1860** MAYNE *Expos. Lec.*, *Fallopian tubes*, two canals inclosed in the peritoneum ..communicating from the sides of the *Fundus Uteri* to the ovaries. **1877** BURNETT *Ear* 88 The fallopian canal, appears at first as a simple broad groove in the tympanum. **1884** *Syd. Soc. Lex.*, *Fallopian arch*, a name for Poupart's ligament.

Fallot (ˈfæləʊ). [Name of Étienne Louis Arthur *Fallot* (1850–1911), French physician.] ***Fallot's tetralogy***, a form of congenital heart disease in which four abnormalities occur together, freq. accompanied by cyanosis.

The condition had been previously described by a number of writers before Fallot published his description in 1888.

1927 *Amer. Heart Jrnl.* III. 85 A case of pulmonary stenosis, dextroposition of the aorta, and septal defects (not strictly Fallot's tetralogy) in a man who lived to be fifty-two. **1970** *New Scientist* 26 Mar. 625/1 Techniques and results for the treatment of Fallot's tetralogy—a particularly difficult type of blue baby with which to deal.

fall-out, *sb.* [f. vbl. phr. *fall out*: see FALL *v.* 94.] Radioactive refuse of a nuclear bomb explosion; the process of deposition of such refuse. Also *attrib.*, *Comb.*, *transf.*, and *fig.*

[**1946** *Effects of Atomic Bombs at Hiroshima* (*Home Office*) vi. 15 The fall of a small fraction of the radioactive fission products.] **1950** *Effects of Atomic Weapons* 35 When the violence of the disturbance due to the bomb has subsided, the contaminated dirt particles gradually fall back to earth, giving rise to the phenomenon known as the *fall-out*. **1952** *N.Y. Times* 17 Aug. E9/6 Nevertheless, a good deal of radioactive stuff is picked up and carried by the wind and deposited all over the country... So far there have been no dangerous concentrations of radioactive 'fall-out', as it is called, that is outside of the proving grounds in Nevada. **1954** *Time* 20 Dec. 66/3 The most recent H-bomb test (by the Russians) was made in Siberia about three months ago, but the fall-out of fear and worry that the H-bomb tests have caused has by no means died away. **1955** *Times* 19 July 8/5 An hour after the explosion, radio-active 'fall-out' material would be dropping 20 miles away. **1957** *Economist* 5 Oct. 16/2 A temporary cessation within the Labour party of personal bomb explosions and consequent deadly fall-out. **1961** *Guardian* 16 Sept. 7/1 Fallout-laden clouds. **1961** *John o' London's* 28 Sept. 345/1 The make-it-yourself fallout shelter. **1964** *Listener* 3 Dec. 865/2 The wasteful method of technical fall-out, of just hoping for ideas to seep through. **1965** *Sunday Times* (Colour Suppl.) 31 Oct. 35/1 After the A.D. 79 eruption this fallout [of ashes, etc.] buried Pompeii in a matter of hours. **1969** *Times* 2 Sept. 10/3 Two Japanese fishermen died after fall-out had reached their vessel.

fallow (ˈfæləʊ), *sb.* Forms: 3–4 **falwe**, 5 **falghe**, (**valwe**), 5–6 **falow(e**, 6–7 **fallowe**, 6– **fallow**. See also FAUCH *sb.* [The relation between this and the cognate FALLOW *a.*[2] and *v.* is not quite clear. The OE. *fælȝing*, glossed *novalia* ('fallows') and *occas.* ('harrows') in *Corpus Glossary*, seems to imply a vb. **fealȝian* (= FALLOW *v.*), f. **fealh*, recorded in pl. *fealȝa* harrows, implements for breaking clods (*occas.* Epinal Gl.). The sb. and adj., which have not been found in OE., were either f. *fealh* or f. the vb. Cf. OHG. *felga* harrow, mod.Ger. (Sanders) and East Fris. *falge* fallow (sb.), *falgen* to break up ground, plough. As FALLOW *a.*[1] was used to denote the colour of exposed soil, it is probable that some confusion may have arisen at an early date between the two words.]

†**1.** A piece of ploughed land; also *collect.* ploughed land in general, arable land. *Obs.*

c **1300** *Havelok* 2509 Thei..drowen him unto the galwes, Nouth bi the gate, but ouer the falwes. *c* **1386** CHAUCER *Wife's Prol.* 656 Who..pricketh his blind hors over the falwes. *c* **1440** *Promp. Parv.* 148 Falow, lond eryd, *novale*. *c* **1450** *Lat. & Eng. Voc.* in Wr.-Wülcker 618 *Varratum, i. novale*, valwe. **1483** *Cath. Angl.* 121 Falghe (Falowe A.), *terra sacionalis*. *a* **1535** FISHER *Wks.* (1876) I. 365 He must treade vppon the fallowes. **1599** SHAKS. *Hen. V*, v. ii. 54 All our Vineyards, Fallowes, Meades, and Hedges..grow to wildnesse. **1713** ROWE *Jane Shore* II. i, Around it Fallows, Meads, and Pastures fair.

2. Ground that is well ploughed and harrowed, but left uncropped for a whole year or more; called also ***summer fallow***, as that season is chosen for the sake of killing the weeds. ***green***, ***cropped***, or ***bastard fallow***: one from which a green crop is taken.

1523 FITZHERB. *Husb.* §13 Euery good housbande hath his barleye falowe..lyenge rygged all the..wynter. **1552** HULOET, Fallowe or tylthe of land, called the somer fallowe or tylth, *veruactum*. *c* **1611** CHAPMAN *Iliad* XIII. 628 So close to earth they plow The fallow with their horns. **1707** MORTIMER *Husb.* ii. 38 The best Ploughs to plow up Lays or Summer Fallows with. **1784** COWPER *Task* IV. 315, I saw far off the weedy fallows smile With verdure not unprofitable. **1805** R. W. DICKSON *Pract. Agric.* I. x. 369 Green fallows or what are termed fallow crops such as beans, peas, cabbages [etc.]. **1810** SCOTT *Lady of L.* I. xxxi, The lark's shrill fife may come At the daybreak from the fallow. **1813** SIR H. DAVY *Agric. Chem.* (1814) 353 A summer fallow, or a clean fallow, may be sometimes necessary in lands over-grown with weeds. **1889** WRIGHTSON *Fallow & Fodder Crops* 5 The superiority of cropped over naked fallows.

3. The state of being fallow; an interval during which land is allowed to lie fallow.

1523 FITZHERB. *Husb.* §17 So shal he mucke all his landes ouer at euerye seconde falowe. *Ibid.* §34 That is vsed, where they make falowe in a fyelde euery fourthe yere. **1797** BILLINGSLEY *Agric. Somerset* 177 Ten or twelve successive crops of wheat, without an intervening fallow. **1858** J. B. NORTON *Topics* 211 To withhold the land from cultivation ..with the view of making it, by a fallow, doubly profit-able the next year. **1866** GEO. ELIOT *F. Holt* 5 They resisted the rotation of crops and stood by their fallows.

fig. **1772** BURKE *Corr.* (1844) I. 356 Your fallow adds to your fertility. **1796** —— *Regic. Peace* i. Wks. VIII. 140 Unless the fallow of a peace comes to recruit her [France's] fertility.

4. *attrib.* Of or pertaining to a fallow; *esp.* grown on a fallow, as in ***fallow-crop***, ***-hay***; and in local names for the Wheatear (*Saxicola œnanthe*), as ***fallow-chat***, ***-finch***, ***-lunch***, ***-smich***, ***-smiter***, from its frequenting fallows. Also **fallow-break**: see BREAK *sb.* 12; **fallow-field**: see quot. 1851.

1678 RAY *Willughby's Ornith.* 233 The Fallow-Smich, in Sussex the Wheat-ear. **1706** PHILLIPS (ed. Kersey), *Oenanthe*, the Wheat-ear..In Warwickshire it is call'd a Fallow-smiter. **1753** CHAMBERS *Cycl. Supp.*, Fallow-finch. **1787** WINTER *Syst. Husb.* 153 Beans are a good fallow crop. **1821** CLARE *Vill. Minstr.* I. 182 Nor wilt thou fallow-clods disdain. **1834** D. LOW *Pract. Agric.* v. 161 The culture of fallow-crops. **1843** YARRELL *Brit. Birds* I. 254 The Wheat-ear or Fallowchat. **1851** *Gloucestersh. Gloss.*, *Fallow-field*, a common. **1885** *Encycl. Brit.* (ed. 9) I. 338 A large portion of the fallow-break can thus be dressed with home-made manure. **1885** SWAINSON *Prov. Names Brit. Birds* (E.D.S.) 9 Wheatear..Fallow-finch; Fallow-smich; or Fallow-lunch.

fallow (ˈfæləʊ), *a.*[1] Forms: 1 falu, fealo, -u, 3 falau, (3–4 *inflected* falewe), 4 fale, -u, -we, 4–6 falow(e, 6 fallo, 6– fallow. See also FAUCH *a.* [OE. *falu*, *fealo*, *fealu*, pl. *fealwe* = OS. *falu*, (MDu. *vale*, mod. *vaal*), OHG. *falo* (mod. Ger. *fahl*, *falb*), ON. *fǫlr*, pl. *fǫlvar*:—OTeut. **falwo-*, prob. cognate with Gr. πολιός grey, L. *pallēre* to be pale.]

1. Of a pale brownish or reddish yellow colour, as withered grass or leaves. *Obs.* exc. of the coat of an animal; now chiefly in FALLOW-DEER.

Beowulf 865 (Gr.) Fealwe mearas. *a* **1000** *Riddles* xvi. 1 (Gr.) Hais is min hwit and heafod fealo. *c* **1205** LAY. 18449 Pendragun and his cnihtes..sluȝen ȝeond þan feldes falewe lockes. *Ibid.* 27468 Blod ut ȝeoten, ueldes falewe wurðen. *a* **1300** *Cursor M.* 1263 (Cott.) Þe falau slogh sal be þi gate. *c* **1325** *Coer de L.* 461 On in atyr blak Com prickande ovyr the falewe feld. *c* **1386** CHAUCER *Knt.'s T.* 506 His hewe falow [*Corpus* falwe] and pale as Asshen colde. **1494** FABYAN *Chron.* VII. 667 Many a dere both rede and falowe to be slayne before them. **1547** BOORDE *Brev. Health* lxxiii. 25 An urine that is falowe lyke the heare of a falowe beast. **1598** SHAKS. *Merry W.* I. i. 91 How do's your fallow Greyhound, Sir. **1667** *Lond. Gaz.* No. 185/4 A Fallow Dog..lost about a Fort-night since. **1727** BRADLEY *Fam. Dict.* s.v. *Hart*, The Coats and Colours of this noble Beast..are usually of three several sorts, viz. Brown, Red, and Fallow. **1759** tr. *Adanson's Voy. Senegal* 24 His belly was of a pale blue, and his back fallow. **1865** *Athenæum* No. 1954. 484/1 The horn of a fallow-ox.

2. *absol.* (quasi-*sb.*), as the name of a colour.

1741 *Compl. Fam. Piece* II. i. 289 Those that are of a lively red Fallow have a black List down..their Backs.

3. *Comb.*, as ***fallow-coloured***.

1688 *Lond. Gaz.* No. 2347/4 Lost or stolen..a fallow coloured Bitch. **1825** HONE *Every-day Bk.* I. 983 The fallow-coloured dog was taken away.

fallow (ˈfæləʊ), *a.*[2] Forms: 5–6 falow(e, 6 fallowe, 6– fallow. [See FALLOW *sb.*]

Of land: frequent in phrases, *to lie*, *to lay fallow*. **a.** That is uncropped for the current year. **b.** Uncultivated. †**c.** Fit for tillage; ploughed ready for sowing (*obs.*). **d.** *transf.* and *fig.*

a. ? *c* **1475** *Hunt. Hare* 12 He fond a hare full fayr syttand Apon a falow lond. **1523** FITZHERB. *Husb.* §18 He that hath a falowe felde. **1611** COTGR., *Nouvellis*, fallowes; ground that lies fallow euerie other yeare. *a* **1689** NAVARETTE *China* in *Churchill's Coll. Voy.* (1732) I. 52 The land in China never lies fallow. **1846** MCCULLOCH *Acc. Brit. Empire* (1854) I. 473 There appears to have been little or no fallow land. **1875** LYELL *Princ. Geol.* II. III. xlii. 457 We are..compelled to let it lie fallow the next [year].

b. *c* **1460** *Towneley Myst.* 98 The tylthe of oure landes lyys falow as the floore. **1599** SHAKS. *Hen. V*, v. ii. 44 Her fallow Leas..The Darnell, Hemlock, and ranke Femetary, Doth root vpon. **1611** BIBLE *Jer.* iv. 3 Breake vp your fallow ground, and sow not among thornes. **1716** ADDISON *Freeholder* No. 40 ¶4 The soil must lie fallow. **1797** MAD. D'ARBLAY *Lett.* Dec., He is like a fallow field..one that has been left quite to itself. **1870** BRYANT *Iliad* II. XVIII. 226 A broad fallow field Of soft rich mould.

c. **1530** PALSGR. 218/2 Faloweland, *terre labourable*. **1580** BARET *Alv.* F. 103 The Fallowe field, or that is tilled redy to be sowen. *a* **1627** HAYWARD *Edw. VI* (1630) 32 The ridges of the fallow field lay traverse.

d. **1642** FULLER *Holy & Prof. St.* III. xiii. 183 The head.. hath lain fallow all night. **1673** *Ess. Educ. Gentlewom.* 33, I suppose you do not intend to lay Fallow all Children that will not bring forth Fruit of themselves. **1752** FOOTE *Taste* I. Wks. 1799 I. 11 Then I lay fallow—but the year after I had twins. **1827** HARE *Guesses* Ser. II. (1873) 459 Fields of thought seem to need lying fallow. **1842** TENNYSON *Audley Court* 77 The fallow leisure of my life. **1850** KINGSLEY *Alt. Locke* xxxvii, My heart lay fallow for every seed that fell.

†**ˈfallow**, *v.*[1] *Obs.* Forms: 1 fealuwian, fealewian, fealwian, 3–4 falewe(n, 3 falewi, falwy, falowen, (*south. dial.* 3 valewen, valuwen, 4 valouwe), 4–5 falwe, 4–6 falow. [OE. *fealuwian*, *fealewian*, *fealwian*, f. *fealo*, *fealu* FALLOW *a.*[1] Cf. OHG. *falewên*.] **a.** To become pale or yellow; hence, to fade, wither. **b.** Of the face, etc.: To blanch, grow pale.

a. *a* **1000** *Salomon & Sat.* 313 (Gr.) Lytle hwile leaf beoð grene, þonne hy eft fealewiað. *c* **1205** LAY. 16414 Faȝeden þa feldes & þat gras falewede. *a* **1310** in Wright *Lyric P.* 89 Falewen shule thy floures. *a* **1400** *Leg. Rood* (1871) 132 Mi fruit..is fouled and falwed. **1584** T. BASTARD *Chrestoleros* II. xiv. (1598) 35 Here lies a bounch of haire deepe falowed.

fig. *a* **1225** *Ancr. R.* 132 Þe blisse of heouene þet neuer ne valeweð auh is euer grene. *a* **1310** in Wright *Lyric P.* xv. 50 Y-cast in care, Y falewe as flour. *c* **1375** *Sc. Leg. Saints, Johannes* 175 Florysand a quhile ȝe be, þat ȝe ma eftirwart falow.

b. *c* **1205** LAY. 30987 Faleweden nebbes. *a* **1300** *E.E. Poems* (1862) 20 His [Christ's] fair lere falowiþ. **1340** *Ayenb.* 81 Þis uayrhede..fayleþ and ualouweþ ase þet flour of þe uelde. *a* **1400** *Death & its Precursors* 15 in *Rel. Ant.* I. 65 His hew shal falewen. *c* **1440** *Sir Gowther* 62 Al falwyd hire faire chere.

fallow (ˈfæləʊ), *v.*[2] Forms: 4 falewe(n, 5 falwe, (valwe), 5–6 falowe(n, 6 fallo(we, 6– fallow. See FAUCH *v.* Also in *Comb.*, TWIFALLOW, TRIFALLOW, etc. [? OE. **fealȝian*: see FALLOW *sb.*]

1. *trans.* To plough or break up (land); to prepare for sowing. Also rarely, ***to fallow up***.

13.. *Chron. Eng.* 94 in Ritson *Met. Hom.* II. 274 Hy falewede erthe, and feolden wode. *c* **1440** *Promp. Parv.* 148 Falwe londe (falowen P.), *novo*. *c* **1450** *Lat. & Eng. Voc.* in Wr.-Wülcker 618 *Varro*, valwe londe. **1523** FITZHERB. *Husb.* §4 He setteth it in the vttermoste nycke, that is beste for falowynge. **1591** HARINGTON *Orl. Fur.* Pref. (1634) ¶5 To heare one of my ploughmen tell how an acre of wheat must be fallowed and twyfallowed. **1604** ANT. SCOLOKER *Daiphantus* (1880) 37 Ile fallow vp the wrinkles of the earth. **1767** A. YOUNG *Farmer's Lett. People* 263, I fallowed and ploughed two acres of light gravelly land. **1846** J. BAXTER *Libr. Pract. Agric.* (ed. 4) II. 239 Fifth year, tares, which should be fed on the ground, and immediately fallowed for backward turnips or rape.

2. To plough and break up (land) without sowing (it), for the purpose of destroying weeds, etc., and for mellowing the soil; to lay fallow. Also *absol.*

14.. in *Walter of Henley's Husb.* (1890) 46 In aprell it is good seasone to falowe land. **1523** FITZHERB. *Husb.* §8 If thou haue any leys, to falowe or to sowe otes vpon. **1616** SWIFT & MARKH. *Countrie Farme* 20 He shall breake vp or fallow that Earth which he intends to keepe tilth the yeare following. **1741** *Compl. Fam. Piece* III. 522 Fallow your Wheat Land, which will kill the Weeds, and mellow the Ground. **1780** A. YOUNG *Tour Irel.* I. 172 Scarce any fallow, a few sow clover. **1886** HOLLAND *Chester Gloss.*

fig. *a* **1764** CHURCHILL *Journey* 27 Genius.. Must, to ensure his vigour, be laid down, And fallow'd well. **1855** DE MORGAN in Graves' *Life Sir W. R. Hamilton* (1889) II. 501 A teacher who does not either fallow or sow another crop is sure to get into mere routine.

fallow, Sc. f. of FELLOW *sb.*, FOLLOW *v.*

fallow, obs. f. FELLOE, FELLY.

fallow-deer ('fæləʊ'dɪə(r)). [f. FALLOW *a.*[1] + DEER.] A species of deer (*Cervus dama* or *Dama vulgaris*) smaller than the stag or *red* deer. So called from its colour. Also *fallow-buck, doe.*

15.. *Adam Bel* 469 We haue slaine your fat falow der. **1548** THOMAS *Ital. Gram. & Dict., Dama*, a valow deere. **1697** DRYDEN *Virg. Georg.* III. 623 With Cries of Hounds, thou mayst.. chase the fallow Deer. **1720** GAY *Poems* (1745) I. 77 Made of the skin of sleekest fallow deer. **1851** LONGF. *Gold. Leg.* IV. *Refectory*, The cells hung all round with the fells of the fallow-deer.

fallowed ('fæləʊd), *ppl. a.* [f. FALLOW *v.*[2] + -ED[1].] In the senses of the vb.

1551 TURNER *Herbal* I. (1568) D ij b, In the corne feldes and in fallowed landes. **1607** TOPSELL *Four-f. Beasts* (1673) 62 Oxen.. must also be accustomed to draw.. a plough in fallowed ground. **1735** SOMERVILLE *Chase* II. 132 O'er the fallow'd Ground How leisurely they work. **1805** R. W. DICKSON *Pract. Agric.* I. x. 368 Crops.. produced on fallowed lands.

fig. **1607** WALKINGTON *Opt. Glass* 84 In the meane time wee will lay in mortgage a peece of our fallowed invention.

fallowing ('fæləʊɪŋ), *vbl. sb.* [f. FALLOW *v.*[2] + -ING[1].]

1. The action or operation of ploughing and breaking up land; an instance of this.

c **1450** *Lat. & Eng. Voc.* in Wr.-Wülcker 618 *Varracio*, valwynge. **1532** HERVET *Xenophon's Househ.* (1768) 63 Falowynge and stirryng of the grounde, helpeth very moche to the sowynge. **1577** B. GOOGE *Heresbach's Husb.* I. (1586) 40 At the first fallowing they marle the grounde. **1669** WORLIDGE *Syst. Agric.* (1681) 35 These several Ploughings or Fallowings are very advantageous to Ground in several respects. **1789** *Trans. Soc. Encourag. Arts* I. 139 [The field] had received two fallowings.

2. The method or system by which land is ploughed, etc, and then allowed to lie uncropped for a time; an instance of this. Also *bare-, summer-fallowing.*

1669 J. WORLIDGE *Syst. Agric.* (1681) 9 For the same reason are the Summer-Fallowings advantageous to the Husbandman, not only for the destroying of the weeds. **1765** A. DICKSON *Treat. Agric.* III. (ed. 2) 392 With the assistance of fallowing, [the land] carries very good crops. **1777** NIMMO *Stirlingshire* 434 The advantages which that.. soil must derive from summer fallowing. **1807** VANCOUVER *Agric. Devon* (1813) 143 When fallowing, or a preparation for rotting the green sward, is intended. **1881** *Daily News* 4 June 5/5 A.. quantity of land set apart for bare fallowing.

'fallowist. *nonce-wd.* [f. FALLOW *sb.* or *v.* + -IST.] One who favours or follows the practice of fallowing land.

a **1832** SIR J. SINCLAIR (in Webster 1832), A controversy .. between.. the fallowists and the anti-fallowists.

fallowness ('fæləʊnɪs). [f. FALLOW *a.* + -NESS.] The condition of being fallow; idleness.

a **1631** DONNE *To R. Woodward* Poems (1633) 74 So affects my muse now, a chast fallownesse. **1855** SINGLETON *Virgil* II. 114 Regions rife In thorns by fallowness.

fally ('fɔːlɪ), *a. rare.* [f. FALL *sb.* + -Y.] Full of falls or shallow rapids.

1802 W. TAYLOR in Robberds *Mem.* I. 413 The rills [are] too fally to float a canoe.

†**'falsage.** *Obs. rare*$^{-1}$. [f. FALSE *v.* + -AGE.] Deceit, falsehood.

a **1400** *Cov. Myst.* (Shaks. Soc.) 39, I am.. cursyd of God ffor my ffalsage.

†**'falsart.** *Obs. rare*$^{-1}$. In 3 *pl.* **falsarz.** [a. OF. *falsart, faussart, fauxart.* f. *faux*:—L. *falx, falcem* sickle. Cf. mod.F. *faucard, fauchard.*] A bill-hook.

c **1380** *Sir Ferumb.* 966 þay caste til hem gleyues & launce, falsarz & feþerd dart.

†**'falsary.** *Obs.* Forms: 5-7 **falsarie**, 6 **falsery**, *Sc.* **falsar**, 7- **falsary**. [ad. late L. *falsārius*, f. *falsus* FALSE.]

1. One who falsifies, or fraudulently alters (a document, etc.); a falsifier.

1435 in *Bp. Gray's Register, Lincoln* 173 Falsaries of þe popes lettres. **1565** JEWEL *Repl. Harding* (1611) 176 The Bishop of Rome.. was.. found an open Falsarie, for.. the Canons of his making disagreed from the very Originals. **1612** T. JAMES *Corrupt. Script.* IV. 29 A falsarie is hee that in writing addeth. or detracteth, or altereth any thing fraudulently. *a* **1734** NORTH *Exam.* Pref. (1740) p. xiv, A Writer of his own Time cannot avoid being partial, that is, a wilful Falsary. **1828** C. WORDSWORTH *Charles I* 213 Gauden.. an habitual impostor and falsary.

b. One who forges a document; a forger.

1579 FULKE *Heskins' Parl.* 79 He that did forge this Epistle.. was.. an impudent falsarie. **1590** DAVIDSON *Repl. Bancroft* in *Wodr. Soc. Misc.* (1844) I. 507 If this be not to play the falsarie forger.. let the chaplain himself be judge. **1678** *Acts of Sederunt* 31 July They will proceed against and punish these persons as falsaries and forgers of writes. **1697** BENTLEY *Ep. Socrates* (1836) II. 189 The ground for our falsary to forge this Epistle.

2. A false or deceitful person.

1573 G. HARVEY *Letter-bk.* (Camden) 141 O that there were a wyndowe in to y[e] breastes of such falsaryes. **1652** GAULE *Magastrom.* 331 A falsary, and an intruder into his secrets.

false (fɔːls, fɒls), *a.*, *adv.*, and *sb.* Forms: 1-7 **fals**, (3 *Orm.* **falls**, 4 **falsse**, 3-4 **vals(e)**, 4-7 **falce**, (5 **fauce**, 6 **falls, faulse, fawse**), 8-9 *Sc.* **fause**, 7, 9 *dial.* **fause, -sse**, 3- **false.** [late OE. *fals* adj. and sb., ad. L. *fals-us* false (neut. *fals-um*, used subst. in sense fraud, falsehood), orig. pa. pple. of *fallĕre* to deceive; cf. ON. *fals* sb. The adj. is found in OE. only in one doubtful instance (see sense 13); its frequent use begins in the 12th c., and was prob. due to a fresh adoption through the OF. *fals, faus* (mod.F. *faux* = Pr. *fals*, Sp., Pg., It. *falso*). The continental Teut. langs. adopted the word in an altered form: MHG. *valsch.* mod.G. *falsch* (cf. OHG. *gifalscôn* to falsify), OFris. *falsch*, Du. *valsch*, late Icel. (15th c.) *falskr*, Da., Sw. *falsk*.

The etymological sense of L. *falsus* is 'deceived, mistaken' (of persons), 'erroneous' (of opinions, etc.). The transition to the active sense 'deceitful' is shown in phrases like *falsa fides* 'breach of trust, faithlessness', where the sb. has a subjective and an objective sense. In mod.Eng. the sense 'mendacious' is so prominent that the word must often be avoided as discourteous in contexts where the etymological equivalent in other Teut. langs. or in Romanic would be quite unobjectionable. Some of the uses are adopted from Fr., and represent senses that never became English.]

A. *adj.* **I.** Erroneous, wrong.

1. a. Of opinions, propositions, doctrines, representations: Contrary to what is true, erroneous.

c **1200** ORMIN 10024 To trowwenn wrang o Godd þurrh þeȝȝre fallse lare. *a* **1225** *Juliana* 65 Forlore beo þu reue wið false bileaue. *c* **1380** WYCLIF *Sel. Wks.* III. 250 Falce undirstondinge of þe lawe of Crist. *c* **1384** CHAUCER *H. Fame* III. 982 Were the tydynge sothe or fals. *c* **1400** *Lanfranc's Cirurg.* 267 Summen seien þat a womman mai be cured for to kutte off al þe brest & þat is al fals. **1483** CAXTON *G. de la Tour* E v b, Of whiche two sonnes cam first the paynyms and the fals lawe. **1551** T. WILSON *Logike* (1580) 3 To knitte true argumentes, and unknitte false. *a* **1568** ASCHAM *Scholem.* I. (Arb.) 81 Corrupt maners in liuinge, breede false iudgement in doctrine. **1592** DAVIES *Immort. Soul* XXXII. lv. (1714) 125 How can that be false, which every Tongue.. affirms for true? **1631-2** *High Commission Cases* (Camden) 228 This man is to be for his false doctrines.. sharply censured. **1652** CULPEPPER *Eng. Physic.* 107 [He] affirms that eating nuts causeth shortness of breath, than which nothing is falser. **1670** NARBOROUGH *Jrnl.* in *Acc. Sev. Late Voy.* I. (1711) 83 The Draughts are false.. for they do not make any mention of the several Islands. **1695** DRYDEN tr. *Dufresnoy's Art Painting* Pref. p. xxvi, The Persons, and Action of a Farce are all unnatural, and the Manners False. **1725** WATTS *Logic* I. iii. §4. 66 When I see a strait staff appear crooked while it is half under the Water, I say, the Water gives me a false Idea of it. *a* **1797** MASON *Hymn* Wks. 1811 I. 467 Impious men, despise the sage decree, From vain deceit, and false philosophy. **1831** BREWSTER *Newton* (1855) II. xxiv. 358 False systems of religion have.. been deduced from the sacred record. **1848** MACAULAY *Hist. Eng.* I. 279 It may perhaps correct some false notions.

b. *Law.* Of a judgement or verdict.

1634 SANDERSON *Serm.* II. 293 In the courts of law.. false verdicts, false judgments. **1768** BLACKSTONE *Comm.* III. 34 A writ also of false judgment lies to the courts at Westminster to rehear and review the cause. *Ibid.* 402 A jury of twelve men gave a false verdict.

c. *Arith.* *false position*: the rule also called simply POSITION, q.v.

2. Not according to correct rule or principle; wrong. **a.** *Gram.* Now somewhat *arch.* exc. in *false concord*, a breach of any of the rules for the 'agreement' of words in a sentence; ***false quantity***, an incorrect use of a long for a short vowel or syllable, or *vice versâ.*

1551 T. WILSON *Logike* (1580) 3 A Grammarian is better liked, that speaketh true & good Latine, than he y[t] speaketh false. **1580** BARET *Alv.* F 110 False verses, *carmina vitiosa.* **1588** *Marprel. Epist.* (Arb.) 38, I write false Englishe in this sentence. **1654** WHITLOCK *Zootomia* 450 In the Peoples Construing Booke, the Acts of those above them have alwayes some false Latine in them. **1709-10** GIBSON in *Lett. Lit. Men* (Camden) 237 To.. correct the false spellings, &c. **1711** ADDISON *Spect.* No. 59 ¶3 This Poet avoiding.. a false Quantity. **1837** LOCKHART *Scott* lx, A false quantity which his [Scott's] generosity may almost be said to have made classical. **1872** F. HALL (*title*) Recent Exemplifications of False Philology.

b. *Music.* Of a note: Not in tune, wrong in pitch, also *fig.* Also, ***false cadence*** (see quot. 1888). ***false fourth, fifth***, etc.: a fourth, fifth, etc. when not perfect. ***false intonation***: (*a*) the production of an unnatural or improper quality of tone; (*b*) singing or playing out of tune. ***false relation***: the separation of a chromatic semitone between two parts. Also, see quot. 1869. ***false string***: a badly woven string, which produces an uncertain and untrue tone.

1592 DAVIES *Immort. Soul* XXXII. xvi. (1714) 115 If false Accords from her false Strings be sent. **1597** MORLEY *Introd. Mus.* 72 Shew me.. which be the true notes, and which false. **1626** BACON *Sylva* §171 A Lute-String, if it be .. Unequall in his Parts.. we call False. **1674** PLAYFORD *Skill Mus.* III. 35 The fifth yields a false fourth, and the sixth a false fifth. **1817** BYRON *Beppo* xxxii, Some false note's detected flaw. **1830** TENNYSON *Poems* 102 If ye sing not, if ye make false measure, We shall lose eternal pleasure. **1869** OUSELEY *Counterp.* ii. 9 By a false relation is meant the simultaneous, or immediately successive, sounding of a note of the same name, but accidentally altered pitch. **1876** *Academy* 9 Sept. 253/1 The minutest.. examination [of an actress's part] will hardly discover a false note or a dropped stitch. **1888** STAINER & BARRETT *Dict. Mus. Terms* 66 When the last chord of the phrase is other than the tonic chord and is preceded by that of the dominant, the cadence is said to be interrupted, false or deceptive. *Ibid.* 164 False or feigned music was that in which notes were altered by the use of accidentals. **1917** T. S. ELIOT *Prufrock* 19 Inside my brain a dull tom-tom begins.. That is at least one definite 'false note'. **1932** *Week-end Rev.* 13 Aug. 188/2 This episode, with its rather sentimental sequel, seems to strike a false note in the story.

c. *Drawing.*

1715 J. RICHARDSON *Painting* 134 If the Perspective is not just the Drawing of that Composition is false.

d. *Law.* ***false imprisonment***: the trespass committed against a person by imprisoning him contrary to law, or by any restrictive action or influence.

1386 *Rolls Parlt.* III. 225/1 The forsaid Nichol'.. destruyed the kynges trewe lyges.. bi false emprisonement. **1768** BLACKSTONE *Comm.* III. viii. 127 To constitute the injury of false imprisonment there are two points requisite; 1. The detention of the person; and, 2. The unlawfulness of such detention. **1880** T. E. HOLLAND *Jurispr.* xi. 111 A man has a right to go where he pleases,.. and anyone who prevents him from so doing, whether by constraint actually applied, or by such show of authority or force as has an effect on the will equivalent to actual constraint, is said in English law to be guilty of 'false imprisonment'. **1891** *Law Times' Rep.* LXIII. 690/2 An action to recover damages for false imprisonment.

e. *Her.* (See quots.)

1730-6 BAILEY (folio), *False Arms* [in Heraldry] are those wherein the fundamental rules of the art are not observed. **1864** BOUTELL *Heraldry Hist. & Pop.* xii. 81 An Orle is blazoned as a 'false escutcheon', by the early Heralds. **1889** ELVIN *Dict. Her.*, An Annulet [is blazoned] as a False Roundel. A Cross voided, as a False Cross.

f. Of a horse: (see quot.). ***false gallop***: see GALLOP.

1833 *Regul. Instr. Cavalry* I. 56 In cantering to the right, a horse leading with the two near legs is 'false'. **1884** E. L. ANDERSON *Mod. Horsemanship* vi. 27 If it [the horse] turn to the right when the left legs are taking the advanced steps, it is false in its gallop.

g. Of a card: (see quot.).

1879 'CAVENDISH' *Card Ess.* 163 A card [played] contrary to rule in order to take in the adversary.. is technically called a false card.

h. ***false point*** (POINT *sb.*[1] C. 6): a mistaken act of pointing by a game-dog. Hence ***false-pointing*** vbl. sb., ***false-point*** vb.

1954 BANNERMAN *Birds Brit. Isles* III. 214 Ring-ouzels.. possess an exceptionally strong scent. They are a frequent cause of 'false point' in gun-dogs.. a Border terrier often winding the sitting bird at a greater distance than he would a snipe or woodcock. **1960** *Times* 24 Sept. 9/1 On scenting game they [*sc.* setters] halt.. close enough.. to avoid 'false-pointing'. **1965** P. WAYRE *Wind in Reeds* iii. 38 The best of dogs can false-point.

3. Of a balance, measure: Not truly adjusted, incorrect. Also, Of play: Unfair. Of dice: Loaded so as to fall unfairly. †***false point***: a stroke of deceit; a trick.

c **1340** *Cursor M.* 27274 (Fairf.) Fals weȝt & mette againe þe lagh in lande is sette. *c* **1480** J. WATTON *Spec. Chr.* 30 b, Usyng of fals weghts or mesuring. *a* **1529** SKELTON *Dyuers Balettys* Wks. 1843 I. 26 Ware yet.. of Fortunes double cast, For one fals poynt she is wont to kepe in store. **1551** T. WILSON *Logike* (1580) 3 Those which plaie with false Dice, & would make other beleve y[t] thei are true. **1611** BIBLE *Prov.* xx. 23 A false ballance is not good. *a* **1631** DONNE *Poems* (1633) 62 Men.. Who know false play, rather then lose, deceive. **1634** SANDERSON *Serm.* II. 293 False weights, false measures, false thumbs.. in the markets and shops. **1781** COWPER *Convers.* 22 If it weigh the importance of a fly, The scales are false. **1812** *Sporting Mag.* XXXIX. 91 Causing two grooms to lose 15*l.* by false play. **1818** BYRON *Ch. Har.* IV. xciii, All things weigh'd in custom's falsest scale.

4. Of shame, pride: Arising from mistaken notions.

1791 MRS. RADCLIFFE *Rom. Forest* i, A false pride had still operated against his interest. **1802** MAR. EDGEWORTH *Moral T.* (1816) I. viii. 61 True and false shame.

5. ***false position*** (F. *fausse position*): a position which compels a person to act or appear in a manner inconsistent with his real character or aims.

1830 *Q. Rev.* Jan. 120 It [taking tithes in kind] places them [the clergy] in what the politicians call 'a false position', with respect to the community at large.

6. (*to make*) ***a false step*** (= Fr. *faux pas*): a misplaced step, a stumble; hence *fig.* an unwise or improper action; formerly *spec.* a woman's lapse from virtue. ***false start***: a wrong start in a race; often *transf.* and *fig.*

1700 S. L. tr. *Fryke's Voy. E. Ind.* 207, I.. unfortunately made a false step, and tumbled down again into the Boat. **1709** POPE *Ess. Crit.* 602 False steps but help them to renew the race. **1756** NUGENT *Gr. Tour* I. 114 Such young women as have made a false step. **1815** *Racing Calendar* 102 Industry.. was distanced by having been pulled up soon

after starting, in consequence of a repeated cry of 'false start'. **1823** F. CLISSOLD *Ascent Mont Blanc* 20 A false step might have swept us below into an immense crevasse. **1850**, etc. [see START *sb.*² 5]. **1854** J. R. PLANCHÉ *Camp at Olympic* 13 Because I fling your follies in your face, And call back all the false starts of your race. **1875** JOWETT *Plato* (ed. 2) III. 231 If he has taken a false step he must be able to retrieve himself. **1957** G. RYLE in M. Black *Importance of Lang.* (1962) 149 It was a tragically false start.

7. Defective, not firm or solid. **a.** Farriery. ***false quarter*** [= Fr. *faux quartier*]: (see quots.).

1523 SKELTON *Garl. Laurel* 504 Some lokyd full smothely and had a fals quarter. **1614** MARKHAM *Cheap Husb.* I. lv. (1668) 64 Infirmities of hoofs, as false quarters, loose hoofs. **1706** PHILLIPS (ed. Kersey), False Quarter is a Rift.. seeming like a piece put in, and not all entire. **1879** J. LAW *Farmer's Vet. Adviser* 379 False quarter..is similar to a sand-crack in appearance but caused by..destruction of the secreting structure at the top of the hoof.

b. *Arch.*

1728 R. MORRIS *Ess. Anc. Archit.* 87 What a false Bearing, or rather what Bearing at all has it? **1876** GWILT *Archit. Gloss.* s.v., *Bearing wall or Partition*..when [the partition is] built in a transverse direction, or unsupported throughout its whole length, it is said to have a false bearing, or as many false bearings as there are intervals below the wall or partition.

II. Mendacious, deceitful, treacherous.

In senses 8–10 the phr. *false as hell* was formerly common.

8. a. Of a statement: Purposely untrue; mendacious. Frequently in ***to bear*** (†***speak***) ***false witness***: to testify falsely.

c **1175** *Lamb. Hom.* 13 Ne spec þu aȝein þine nexta nane false witnesse. *c* **1290** *S. Eng. Leg.* I. 40/223 Betere is trewe dede þane fals word. *a* **1300** *Cursor M.* 26234 (Cott.) Fals wijtnes and trouth breking. *c* **1340** *Ibid.* 4635 (Trin.) He was prisounde wiþ fals reede. *c* **1374** CHAUCER *Troylus* I. 593, I have..for trew or fals report..ilovede the al my lyve. **1377** LANGL. *P. Pl.* B. II. 80 To bakbite, and to bosten, and bere fals witnesse. *a* **1553** UDALL *Royster D.* V. i, See that no false surmises thou me tell. **1611** BIBLE *2 Kings* ix. 12 And they said, It is false. *c* **1630** JACKSON *Signs Time* Wks. (1673) II. VI. 380 False-witness-bearing, and Coveting their Neighbours Goods, are far more rife amongst us than they were. **1639** FULLER *Holy War* IV. vi. (1647) 177 Afterwards this report was controlled to be false. **1678** EARL OF ARRAN in *Lauderdale Papers* (1885) III. lxv. 100 He found all to be false as hell. **1813** LD. ELLENBOROUGH in *Ho. Lords* 22 Mar., The accusation is as false as hell in every part! **1818** SCOTT *Hrt. Midl.* xxiii, She came to bear false witness in her sister's cause. **1833** CRUSE *Eusebius* I. vii. 32 Neither of the gospels has made a false statement.

b. *Law.* ***false issue***, an issue introduced by counsel in order to conceal the real issue; ***false pretences***, misrepresentations made to convey a false impression. Also ***false representation***.

1757 *Act 30 Geo. II* c. 24 §1 All persons who knowingly and designedly, by false pretence or pretences, shall obtain ..money, goods, wares or merchandizes, with intent to.. defraud any person..of the same. **1778** P. THICKNESSE *Year's Journey* (ed. 2) I. iii. 32 He may indeed say..that obtaining money by false pretences is better than forging. **1831** J. BANIM *Smuggler* I. xi. 253 Made prisoners in it, upon false pretences. **1836** *Mag. Dom. Econ.* I. 92 Indictable for obtaining money under false pretences. **1858** False representation [see REPRESENTATION 4]. **1861** *Act 24 & 25 Vict.* c. 96 §88 It shall be sufficient in any Indictment for obtaining or attempting to obtain any such Property by false Pretences to allege that the Party accused did the Act with Intent to defraud, without alleging an Intent to defraud any particular Person. **1903** *Westm. Gaz.* 12 June 10/1 Mr. Robson: Then your lordship does not specify any false issues that you say I raised? His Lordship: The false issue you raised was whether or not the uncle was justified in going to the detective to find out the wife's residence instead of going to the father, and there were hours in the Divorce Court occupied upon that point. **1907** *Daily Chron.* 28 Aug., When charged he pleaded guilty to three charges of obtaining goods on false pretences. **1959** JOWITT *Dict. Eng. Law* I. 781/2 It is now practically immaterial whether a prisoner is indicted for false pretences or for larceny.

9. Of a person or his speech: Uttering or expressing what is untrue; mendacious. (In *false prophet* the sense varies between this and 13 b).

a **1225** *Ancr. R.* 68 Þat þe witnesse ne preoue heom ualse. *c* **1325** *Metr. Hom.* 99 Thai..said that Crist was fals prophete. **1340** HAMPOLE *Pr. Consc.* 3366 Sacrilege, and fals wittenessyng. *c* **1380** WYCLIF *Wks.* (1880) 284 Falce gloseris maken goddis lawe derk. **1382** —— *Mark* xiii. 22 Fals Cristis and fals prophetis schulen ryse vp. **1545** JOYE *Exp. Dan.* iii. 32 Dauid..abhorreth soche false accusers. **1560** BIBLE (Genev.) *Mal.* iii. 5, I will be a swift witnes agaynst false swearers. **1611** SHAKS. *Wint. T.* III. ii. 32 Innocence shall make False Accusation blush. **1662** STILLINGFL. *Orig. Sacr.* II. v. §5 There may be false Prophets as well as true. **1687** CONGREVE *Old Bach.* IV. iii, My face is a false witness, and deserves to be pilloried. **1822–56** DE QUINCEY *Confess.* Wks. 1890 III. 395 O just and righteous Opium! that to the chancery of dreams summonest, for the triumphs of despairing innocence, false witnesses.

10. a. Of persons, their attributes or actions: Deceitful, treacherous, faithless. Formerly often pleonastically, expressing detestation, with sbs. like *traitor*, *treason* (now only *arch.*). Const. †*of*, *to*, †*unto*.

c **1205** LAY. 31422 Þa rad forð a þan felde falsest alre kinge. *a* **1225** *Ancr. R.* 128 Ase vox is best falsest. *c* **1230** *Hali Meid.* 15 Þah þi fleschliche wil fals beo. **1297** R. GLOUC. (1724) 385 Þys false byssop Ode. *a* **1300** *Cursor M.* 11530 (Cott.) He was traitur, fals in fai. *c* **1489** CAXTON *Sonnes of Aymon* xxvi. 565 Now are deed the sones of foulques of moryllon by theyr false wyt. *a* **1533** LD. BERNERS *Huon* lxxxvii. 275 This Angelars was false and a traytoure. **1559** *Mirr. Mag., Dk. Suffolk* xix, My dedes..Wer shortly after treasons false estemed. **1590** MARLOWE *Edw. II*, II. iii, Never was Plantagenet False of his word. **1591** SHAKS. *Two Gent.* IV. iv. 141 Though his false finger haue prophan'd the Ring. **1663–72** WOOD *Life* (Oxf. Hist. Soc.) I. 471 False to his trust. **1676** SOUTH *Serm. Worldly Wisdom* (1737) I. ix. 349 False as hell, and cruel as the grave. **1709** STEELE *Tatler* No. 105 ¶3 She had been false to his Bed. **1742** POPE *Dunc.* IV. 93 They..false to Phœbus, bow the knee to Baal. **1794** *Song 'Stay, my Willie'* in *Burns' Wks.* (1857) IV. 117 When this heart proves fause to thee. **1815** SCOTT *Guy M.* i, 'Get up, ye fause loon.' **1855** MACAULAY *Hist. Eng.* IV. 231 He might be false to his country, but not to his flag. **1865** DICKENS *Mut. Fr.* I. ii, I banish the false wretch.

†**b.** *transf.* Of ground, a foundation, etc.: Treacherous, insecure. *Obs.*

1590 SPENSER *F.Q.* I. xi. 54 An huge rocky clifft, Whose false foundacion waves have wash't away. **1697** DRYDEN *Virg. Past.* III. 147 Graze not too near the Banks, my jolly Sheep, The Ground is false. **1692** R. L'ESTRANGE *Fables* liv. 55 The Heart of Man is like a Bog, it looks Fair to the Eye, but when we come to lay any Weight upon't, the Ground is False under us.

†**11.** ***false trust***: breach of trust [= L. *falsa fides*, where *falsa* is merely pple.]. *Obs. rare.*

1649 BP. HALL *Cases Consc.* I. vii. 71 The..goods miscarried, either by robbery or false trust.

12. a. Of things, indications, appearances: Fallacious, deceptive. Of a medium of vision: That distorts the object looked at; so in †***false glass, mirror, spectacles. false colour*** (fig.): cf. COLOUR *sb.* 2 d, 12, 13.

1531 [see COLOUR *sb.* 2 d]. **1580** BARET *Alv.* F 111 A false glasse, *speculum mendax*. **1605** BP. HALL *Medit. & Vows* II. §79 When they wil needs have a sight of their own actions, it showes them a false glasse to looke in. **1641** J. JACKSON *True Evang. T.* II. 146 The Devill makes us false spectacles. **1658** WOMOCK *Exam. Tilenus* A, You seem to magnifie the riches of the divine Grace: but when we come strictly to examine it, 'tis by a false glass. **1734** POPE *Ess. Man* IV. 392 Wit's false mirror held up Nature's light; Shew'd erring Pride. **1768** BLACKSTONE *Comm.* III. 391 The true import of the evidence is duly weighed, false colours are taken off. **1848** MACAULAY *Hist. Eng.* I. 173 Looking on all that passed at home..through a false medium. **1855** BAIN *Senses & Int.* II. iii. §7 So false is the appetite for sleep, that [etc.].

†**b.** ***false door, postern*** (= F. *fausse porte*): a secret door or postern. *Obs.*

c **1489** CAXTON *Sonnes of Aymon* viii. 190 Yf ye doo assaille the castell, they shall yssue oute at the fauce posternes. **1552** HULOET, Ffalse posterne or backe dore. **1627** R. ASHLEY *Almansor* 44 King Almansor entered sometimes into this Hospitall by a false doore. **1768** J. BYRON *Narr. Patagonia* (ed. 2) 237 They have a false door to the alcove.

III. Spurious, not genuine.

13. Counterfeit, simulated, sham.

a. Of things, *esp.* of metal, money, jewels: Counterfeit, spurious. Of a document: Forged.

c **1000** *Voc.* in Wr.-Wülcker 183 *Paracaraximus*, fals pening [Possibly a compound of the sb., like ON. *falspeningr*]. *a* **1225** *Ancr. R.* 182 False gold vorwurðeð þerinne [fure]. *a* **1300** *Cursor M.* 28395 (Cott.) A-mang myn oþer wark vn-lele haf i oft forged fals sele. **1340** *Ayenb.* 26 Of guod metal hy makeþ uales moneye. *c* **1400** *Lanfranc's Cirurg.* 293 Þou schalt..do awei al medicyns þat ben false. **1558** W. TOWRSON in Hakluyt *Voy.* (1589) 121 The suspition which we gathered of their false charter parties. **1609** SKENE *Reg. Maj.* 121 The wreits..can not prove against him, because they are fals. **1649** BP. HALL *Cases Consc.* I. vii. 64 Criples that pretend false soares. **1730–6** BAILEY (folio), *False Diamond*, one that is counterfeited with glass. **1856** RUSKIN *Mod. Paint.* III. IV. iii. §12 *note*, An artificial rose is not a 'false' rose, it is not a rose at all. **1867** SMYTH *Sailor's Word-bk.* 288 False Papers frequently carried by slavers and smugglers. **1885** *Catholic Dict.* s.v., *False decretals*, the collection ostensibly made by Isidorus Mercator, in the middle of the ninth century.

b. Prefixed to personal designations: Pretended, that is not really such; *esp.* in ***false god, prophet***.

a **1175** *Cott. Hom.* 237 Þurh false godes þe ælc þiode ham selfe macede. *c* **1200** *Trin. Coll. Hom.* 83 Þese ben false cristene. *c* **1250** *Meid. Maregrete* iii, He levede on þe false godes. **1382** WYCLIF *Baruch* vi. 58 It is beter a kyng for to be schewynge..a profitable vesselle..than fals goddis [**1560** BIBLE (Genev.) *ibid.*, Then such false gods]. **1552** HULOET, Ffalse messenger..ffalse prophet. **1870** (*title*), False Heir and other Choice Stories for the Young.

c. with the name of an author: = 'Pseudo-'.

1868 FREEMAN *Norm. Conq.* II. 629 The false Ingulf.

d. Of hair, teeth, etc.: Artificially made or adapted. Also ***false eyelashes, nose***, and in more general sense.

1591 PERCIVALL *Sp. Dict.*, *Cabelléra*, a false heare, or peruke. **1634** SIR T. HERBERT *Trav.* 168 Hired women, who for five houres space..howle bitterly, teare their false haire [etc.]. **1795** E. WYNNE *Diary* 31 Dec. (1937) II. 59 The poor Man has a dozen false teeth in his mouth. **1817** BYRON *Beppo* lxvi, One has false curls. **1836** DICKENS *Sk. Boz* I. 329 Gentlemen..with..false noses. **1873** *Young Englishwoman* Oct. 518/2 Will the Editor kindly say if there is anything revolting in wearing false teeth? **1885** *Pall Mall G.* 16 Apr. 3/2 The false teeth are nothing but animal teeth attached to the human teeth by means of small gold plates. **1902** *Encycl. Brit.* XXXII. 605/1 Where pheasants exist in any number, a 'false covert' of spruce and fir loppings should be made at the point to which it is desirable to force the birds. **1939** L. MACNEICE *Autumn Jrnl.* xv. 57 False eyelashes and finger-nails of carmine. **1954** —— *Autumn Sequel* xxiii. 141 That Christmas should be white Is something we go on with, like false noses.

e. ***false face***: a mask. Also, a deceiver, a hypocrite.

1818 SCOTT *Rob Roy* ix, His fause-face slipped aside. **1833** M. SCOTT *Tom Cringle* xi. (1859) 248 A white false-face or mask of a most methodistical expression. **1893** STEVENSON *Catriona* xxv. 104 That false-face, Prestongrange; I think shame to own to you that I was ever trusting to a lawyer.

f. ***false key***: a skeleton key, picklock.

1701 *Lond. Gaz.* No. 3708/3 A false Key, and a Steel, were left by the said Murderers. **1833** J. HOLLAND *Manuf. Metal* II. 267 False keys, and all other counterfeit means of opening locks.

g. Of attributes or actions: Feigned, counterfeited, spurious.

c **1600** SHAKS. *Sonn.* lxxii, Least your true loue may seeme falce. **1697** DRYDEN *Virg. Æneid* II. 197 False tears true pity move. **1709** POPE *Ess. Crit.* 25 So by false learning is good sense debased.

h. *Law.* ***false action*** = 'feigned action': see FEIGNED. ***false plea*** = sham plea.

1706 PHILLIPS (ed. Kersey), *False Action* = Faint Action. **1848** WHARTON *Law Lex.* 246/2 *False plea.*

i. *Photogr.* ***false image***: an extra image made on the plate by a defective lens at the same time as the image proper.

1892 *Photogr. Ann.* II. 39 Another troublesome fault is what is called a ghost, or false image. **1918** *Photo-Miniature* XV. Mar. (Gloss.), *False Image*, an extra image, usually unsharp and often inverted, which a defective (doublet) lens will give on the plate at the same time as the image proper.

14. a. *Nav.* and *Mil.* Counterfeited for the purpose of deception; feigned, pretended; as in ***false attack, lights, ports, signal***. Also in phrases (often *fig.*), †***to show false colours, under false colour(s*** (see COLOUR *sb.* 6 b); ***to hang out false colours*** (see COLOUR *sb.* 7 d).

c **1400** Fals colour [see COLOUR *sb.* 6 b]. **1677** *Lond. Gaz.* No. 1179/2 One towards Mount Azine, which some look upon to be only a false Attack. **1697** DAMPIER *Voy.* (1698) I. 252 Had we enter'd the Port upon the false signal, we must have been taken or sunk. **1765–93** BLACKSTONE *Comm.* I. (ed. 12) 294 Putting out false lights in order to bring any vessel into danger. **1769** FALCONER *Dict. Marine*, *Faux sabords*, false ports, painted in a ship's side, to deceive an enemy. **1784** MAD. D'ARBLAY *Diary* 30 Dec., A letter..which seems to shew her gay and happy. I hope it shows not false colours. **1809** ROLAND *Fencing* 102 Various small motions made without longing, are termed false attacks. **1853** STOCQUELER *Mil. Dict.* 25/2 *False attack*, a feigned or secondary movement in the arrangements of an assault, intended to divert the attention of an enemy from the real or principal attack. **1867** SMYTH *Sailor's Word-bk.* 288 To sail under false colours..is an allowable stratagem of war. **1874** MORLEY *Compromise* (1886) 172 If men go through society before marriage under false colours.

b. ***false fire***: †(*a*) a blank discharge of firearms (*obs.*); (*b*) a fire made to deceive an enemy, or as a night-signal.

1633 T. JAMES *Voy.* 26 We shot and made false fires. **1642** SIR E. DERING *Sp. on Relig.* xvi. 86 Artillery men, though.. nimble with false fires, are not immediately compleated into true-Souldiers. **1711** A. DUNCAN *Mariner's Chron.* (1805) III. 289 Night coming on we lost sight of our consort, and made several false fires. **1720** DE FOE *Capt. Singleton* viii. (1840) 140 We made false fire with any gun that was uncharged, and they would walk off as soon as they saw the flash. **1805** NELSON in Nicolas *Disp.* (1846) VII. 57 We have found the comfort of blue lights and false fires in the Mediterranean. **1853** STOCQUELER *Mil. Dict.* 101/2 When an army is about to retire from a position during the night, false fires are lighted in different parts of the encampment to impose upon the enemy's vigilance.

c. ***false alarm***: an alarm without foundation, given either purposely to deceive or under misapprehension of danger. Now often *transf.* or *gen.*

1579 GOSSON *Sch. Abuse* 32 That is a vain brag, & a false alarme. **1594** [see ALARM *sb.* 8]. **1770** JOHNSON *False Alarm* 3 One of the chief advantages derived by the present generation from the improvement and diffusion of Philosophy, is..exemption from false alarms. **1802** C. JAMES *Milit. Dict.* s.v. *Alarm*, False-Alarms, are strategems of war, frequently made use of to harrass an enemy, by keeping them perpetually under arms. **1834** tr. *Jacquemont's Journ. India* I. 214 My pistols and watch were almost in his way; but, disturbed..by some noise or false alarm, he had not time to choose. **1847** A. BRONTË *Agnes Grey* xvii, There was 'no need to be in such agitation about the matter—it might prove a false alarm after all'. **1873** *Gentl. Mag.* X. 587 The false alarm..was made the occasion of a discussion.., which ended in the Lord Mayor advising his civic brethren to wait and see. **1900** *Daily News* 7 Dec. 3/2 Any day the giving of a false alarm might cause the deaths of persons endangered by fire, and whom the Brigade did not reach in time. **1931** H. MUTSCHMANN *Gloss. Americanisms* 22/1 *False Alarm*, a divorced woman.

15. Improperly so called. (Prefixed, like *quasi-* or *pseudo-*, to form names of things bearing a deceptive resemblance to those properly denoted by the sb.) **a.** in various sciences and technical uses: see quots.

1594 False ribbes [see BASTARD *a.* 5 c]. **1741** A. MONRO *Anat. Bones* (ed. 3) 222 The Five inferior of each Side are the *False* [Ribs]. **1774** GOLDSM. *Nat. Hist.* (1776) IV. 245 Immediately on quitting the real womb, they creep into the false one. **1776** SEIFERTH tr. *Gellert's Metal. Chym.* 14 It [Yellow Quartz] is called..after its colour..false topaz. **1807–26** S. COOPER *First Lines Surg.* (ed. 5) 248 When all the coats of an artery are wounded, ruptured, or perforated by ulceration, the tumour is called a false aneurism. **1833** LYELL *Princ. Geol.* III. 175 This diagonal arrangement of the layers, sometimes called 'false stratification'. **1854** *Poultry Chron.* I. 488 On inspecting the windpipe from the root of the tongue, I found congestion and swelling of the glottis and rima glottidis, but no false membrane such as I should have found in a child. **1866** *Treas. Bot.*, *False bark*, that layer on the outside of the stem of an Endogen, which consists of cellular tissue into which fibrous tissue passes obliquely. **1869** J. R. S. CLIFFORD in *Eng. Mech.* 24 Dec. 3457 At the sixth [segment] we come to what have been called the 'false legs' [of caterpillars]. **1873** T. H. GREEN *Introd. Pathol.* (ed. 2) 265 In croup the exuded materials

coagulate principally upon the surface of the membrane, where, together with the newly-formed cellular elements, they form the false membrane. **1880** *Encycl. Brit.* XII. 180/2 Immediately within the opening of the nostril [of a horse], the respiratory canal sends off on its upper and outer side a diverticulum or blind pouch (called 'false nostril') of a conical form. **1881** MIVART *Cat* viii. 229 The superior or false vocal cords. **1882** CAULFEILD & SAWARD *Dict. Needlew.*, *False hem*, this is applied to a fold-over at the extreme edge of any portion of dress or other article.. which has the appearance of a hem.. but is not one. **1883** *Man. Seamanship for Boys* 97 Cardinal Points... False Points. So called because they borrow their names from the two points between which they come. **1883** *Encycl. Brit.* XV. 235/2 Such a point is called a false north pole, and we see that the existence of two true north poles necessitates the existence of a false north pole. **1886** *Ibid.* XXI. 404/2 These portions go on growing in a direction at an angle with the previous one, but still in contact, and thus produce the 'false-branching' to which the *Cladothrix* owes its name. **1888** *Lockwood's Dict. Mech. Engin.* s.v. *False Water*, When steam is generated very rapidly in a boiler, the immediate effect is a rapid rising of the water level in the gauge cocks, due to the increase in volume caused by admixture of steam. This sudden increase is termed false water. **1890** G. H. WILLIAMS *Crystallography* 212 False planes, apparent crystal faces, whose position is not that of true crystal planes, may be produced by oscillatory combination. **1902** *Encycl. Brit.* XXXIII. 99/2 *False Station.* —— When the theodolite cannot for any reason be placed over the centre of a station, if the distance be measured, and the theodolite reading of it be noted, the observed angles may be reduced to what they would be at the centre of the station. False stations have frequently to be made in practice. **1932** D. C. MINTER *Mod. Needlecraft* 132 False hem machined on. **1948** *New Biol.* V. 14 Colonies such as those of *Gloeotrichia* and *Rivularia* originate by a process known as false branching, in which one part grows out at a break in the filament. **1960** B. SNOOK *Eng. Hist. Embroidery* 106 False quilting, worked through two thicknesses of fabric without padding, was also used.

b. in popular or literary names of plants (sometimes rendering mod.L. names formed with *pseudo-*).

1578 False Rewbarbes [see BASTARD *a.* 5 b]. **1597** GERARDE *Herbal* Index, False Mercurie. **1854** THOREAU *Walden* (1937) 182 The *celtis occidentalis*, or false elm. **1861** MISS PRATT *Flower. Pl.* VI. 50 False Brome-grass. **1861** *Chambers' Encycl.* s.v. *Bottle-gourd*, The common bottle-gourd, or false calabash, is a native of India. *Ibid.* s.v. *Locust Tree*, The locust-tree of America is also called the false acacia, or thorn acacia. **1878–86** BRITTEN & HOLLAND *Plant-n.*, False Parsley. **1940** E. STEP *Wayside &c. Trees* 23 The Sycamore, Great Maple, or False Plane (*Acer pseudoplatanus*).

†**c.** ***false nail***: ? = AGNAIL 3. *Obs.*

1818 *Art Preserv. Feet* 335 False nails.. arise from a want of due attention to the parts surrounding the nail.

d. *Phys.* ***false conception***: a spurious conception, in which a shapeless mass is produced instead of a fœtus.

1611 DONNE *Anat. World* sig. B4v, And false-conceptions fill the generall wombs. **1662** R. MATHEW *Unl. Alch.* §87. 121 It.. brought from her an abortive or false conception. **1697** DRYDEN *Virg. Georg.* III. 441 They shed A slimy Juice, by false Conception bred. **1889** WAGSTAFFE *Mayne's Med. Voc.* 94 *False Conception*, an imperfect impregnation or blighted ovum.

e. ***false grain***: a fresh crop of small sugar crystals formed during the process of sugar manufacture when syrup is introduced into the crystallizing pans in order to increase the size of the crystals already formed.

1900 S. P. SADTLER *Hand-bk. Industr. Org. Chem.* (ed. 3) 132 The process of admitting successive portions of fresh syrup after the 'grain' has once formed is used in the development of large crystals. It must be used with judgment though, or the new syrup starts a new set of minute crystals, making what is called 'false grain'. **1959** *Chambers's Encycl.* V. 200/2 If more sugar is held in the solution than that given by the super-solubility curve, a fresh crop of nuclei or a 'false grain' will result.

f. ***false killer***, a name of the whale, *Pseudorca crassidens*, which partly resembles the KILLER (sense 2); ***false scorpion*** = *pseudo-scorpion* (PSEUDO- 2).

1875 *Encycl. Brit.* II. 281/2 The impression inevitably created on a comparison of the true and false scorpions is that the latter are little scorpions without tails. **1937** NORMAN & FRASER *Giant Fishes, Whales & Dolphins* II. xiii. 294 In the genus *Pseudorca*.. there is only one species admitted, *P. crassidens*, the False Killer Whale. It is nearly related to the true Killer, but many external differences distinguish the two forms from each other. **1949** *Oxf. Jun. Encycl.* II. 140/1 False Scorpions owe their name to the possession of a pair of large, claw-like 'pedipalpi' or specialized feelers, like those of the Scorpions; but they lack the Scorpion's tail and sting. **1959** A. HARDY *Fish & Fisheries* xv. 288 The false killer, *Pseudorca crassidens*, is entirely black and might perhaps be mistaken for the pilot whale.

16. †**a.** ***false colour***: in water-colour painting, a lighter tint of any of the recognized colours (*obs.*). **b.** ***false dyes, colours*** (= Fr. *teint faux*): fugitive as opposed to permanent dyes.

1573 *Art of Limning* 4 Azure or Byze. His false coloure, Two parts azure and one of cereuse. *Ibid.* 11 Lay.. First thy false colours and after thy sadd. **1816** J. SMITH *Panorama Sc. & Art* II. 527 Dyes of the second class, are called false or little dyes. **1842** BISCHOFF *Woollen Manuf.* II. iii. 80 Two branches, namely, that of permanent colours, and that of false or fugitive colours.

c. ***false dawn, morning, sunrise*** [tr. Arab. *ṣubḥ kāḏib*]: a transient light which precedes the true dawn by about an hour, a phenomenon common in the East. Also *fig.*

1832 J. MORIER *Zohrab* i. 6 Do tell me.. whether that be the dawn or the false dawn? **1868** E. FITZGERALD *Omar* (ed. 2) ii. 1 Before the phantom of False morning died. **1879** E. ARNOLD *Lt. Asia* v. 112 Then slept he.. But rose e'er the False-Dawn. **1924** E. WHARTON (*title*) Old New York. False Dawn. **1928** *Daily Express* 23 Aug. 8/3 A flickering false-sunrise. **1946** K. TENNANT *Lost Haven* (1947) i. 29 When the false dawn came, it was a pale thing compared to the moon-light. **1963** *Times* 16 Jan. 3/3 We are thus back to where we were before the excitement of Melbourne and the optimism of the week that followed. That seems now like a false dawn.

17. (Chiefly *Mech.*) Subsidiary, supplementary; substituted for or serving to supplement the thing properly or chiefly denoted by the name. **a.** ***false bottom***: a horizontal partition in a vessel; also, a partition built close to the bottom, as in a box or trunk. Also in *Mining* and *Metallurgy* (see quot. 1881). ***false core*** (see CORE *sb.*[1] 8).

1596 HARINGTON *Metam. Ajax* (1814) 117 You shall make a false bottom to that privy that you are annoyed with—either of lead or stone. **1626** BACON *Sylva* (1627) v. 127 Take a Vessel, and.. make a false Bottom of course Canvasse. **1641** FRENCH *Distill.* i. (1651) 5 A false bottom where the Quick-silver must lye. **1800** M. EDGEWORTH *Parent's Assist.* (ed. 3) III. 132 This box has a false bottom—it holds only three quarters as much as it ought to do. **1823** J. BADCOCK *Dom. Amusem.* 146 Each vat is to have a false bottom, made with cross bars, or stout wicker work. **1843** C. & J. HOLTZAPFFEL *Turning* I. 338 The term false-core is employed by the brass founder to express the same thing as the drawback of the iron founder. The former calls every loose piece of the mould not intended for holes, a false core. **1875** [see CORE *sb.*[1] 8]. **1881** D. C. DAVIES *Metall. Min. & Mining* 413 False Bottom.. a loose plate put into the stamp box; a floor of iron placed in a puddling machine; a bed of drift holding auriferous drift, and overlying the bed of the latter that usually lies on the bed rock. **1907** MCWILLIAM & LONGMUIR *Gen. Foundry Practice* xii. 95 In light work these removable parts of a mould are termed 'false cores', and in heavy work 'drawbacks'. **1933** MCLACHLAN & OTTO in W. J. Kearton *Engin. Educator* (ed. 2) II. 606/2 Part of a mould forming an internal shape, whether loose or not, is usually referred to as a 'cod', while a loose part of a mould forming some external part of it, is generally referred to as a 'false-core' or 'drawback'.

b. *Shipbuilding.* Of things temporarily attached to the real or true part to assist or protect it, as in ***false keel, keelson, post, rail, stay, stem, stern, stern-post***. Also in ***false deck***, a grating or the like supported above the main deck by the 'close fights'.

1626 CAPT. SMITH *Accid. Yng. Seamen* 14 A grating, netting or false decke for your close fights. **1627** —— *Seaman's Gram.* xi. 53 Another keele vnder the first.. wee call a false Keele. *Ibid.*, Fix another stem before it [the stem], and that is called a false stem. **1709** *Lond. Gaz.* No. 4521/2 Having our.. Back-stays cut to pieces; as also our Main and False-stay. **1769** FALCONER *Dict. Marine* (1789) C iv b, The false post.. serves to augment the breadth of the stern-post. *c* **1850** *Rudim. Navig.* (Weale) 117 *False keel. Ibid.*, *False rail*, a rail fayed down upon the upper side of the main, or upper rail of the head. **1860** SMYTH *Sailor's Word-bk.*, *False kelson* or Kelson Rider.

c. *Gunmaking.*

1875 'STONEHENGE' *Brit. Sports* I. I. xi. §2. 33 The false-breech is cut away more than I like it. **1880** *Encycl. Brit.* XI. 280/1 A pair of barrels.. abutting against a false breech. **1881** GREENER *Gun* 262 A false pin is screwed into the lever, which, when removed, will leave an aperture through which the breech-pin must be extracted.

d. *Arch.* in ***false pillar, roof*** (see quots.). ***false ceiling***, a dummy ceiling fixed below the genuine one (e.g. to accommodate wires, conduits, etc.).

1552 HULOET, Ffalse roufe of a chambre, house, seller, or vault. **1611** PERKINS *Cases Consc.* (1619) 143 The other which was most outward, and lesse weightie might be vpholden by lesser proppes, which Artificers in that kind call by the name of false-pillars. **1849–50** WEALE *Dict. Terms*, *False roof*, the space between the ceiling and the roof above it. **1870** BREWER *Dict. Phr. & Fable* 285/2 *False ceiling*, the space between the garret ceiling and the roof. **1874** MICKLETHWAITE *Mod. Par. Churches* 213 The main pipes should.. be in the false roof. **1937** *Archit. Rev.* LXXXI. 63 (*caption*) The entrance hall from the living room, showing again the curved screen wall with its false ceiling.

B. *adv.*

†**1.** Untruly. With *to speak*, *swear*. *Obs.* or *arch.*

1303 R. BRUNNE *Handl. Synne* 776 3yf þou euere swore.. Yn any tyme fals or wykkedly. *c* **1380** WYCLIF *Sel. Wks.* III. 345 Whanne Petre.. swore fals for a wommans vois. *a* **1400–50** *Alexander* 298 Þar haue þai fals spoken. **1613** SHAKS. *Hen. VIII*, II. iv. 136 Let him in naught be trusted, For speaking false in that. **1621** LADY M. WROTH *Urania* 202 He vow'd, nothing should make him answere false.

2. Improperly, wrongly. Of an arrow's flight: In the wrong direction; erringly. Of music: Out of tune, incorrectly. *Obs.* or *arch.*

1591 SHAKS. *Two Gent.* IV. ii. 59 The Musitian.. plaies false.. So false that he grieues my very heart-strings. **1596** —— *1 Hen. IV*, I. ii. 74 Thou judgest false. **1608** —— *Per.* I. i. 124 If it be true that I interpret false. **1815** MOORE *Lalla R.* (1824) 139 False flew the shaft, though pointed well.

3. Faithlessly, perfidiously. Chiefly in *to play (a person) false*: to cheat in play; *fig.* to betray.

1590 SHAKS. *Com. Err.* II. ii. 144 If.. thou play false, I doe digest the poison of thy flesh. **1593** —— *2 Hen. VI*, III. i. 184 Beshrew the winners, for they play'd me false. **1596** —— *Merch. V.* I. ii. 48 His mother plaid false with a Smyth. **1611** —— *Cymb.* III. iv. 117 Mine eare Therein false strooke, can take no greater wound. **1825** A. W. FONBLANQUE in *Westm. Rev.* IV. 402 Sheridan played false to his political friends on this occasion. *a* **1859** MACAULAY *Hist. Eng.* (1872) V. xxiv. 24 They had their fears that Lewis might be playing false.

C. *sb.*

†**1.** Fraud, falsehood, treachery. In early use *esp.* counterfeiting (of coin), forgery. *Obs.*

c **1000** ÆLFRIC *Gen.* xliv. 7 Hwi tihþ ure hlaford us swa micles falses? *a* **1016** *Laws of Æthelred* vi. §32 þæt an mynet gange ofer ealle þas þeode buton ælcon false. **1154** *O.E. Chron.* an. 1124 Hi hafden fordon eall þæt land mid here micele fals. *c* **1200** ORMIN 7334 Crist forrwerrpeþþ falls & flærd. *c* **1300** *Cursor M.* 19254 (Edin.) þu leies.. and a3te haue wand wiþ fals þe hali gaste to fand. *a* **1375** *Joseph Arim.* 208 Wiþ-outen faute oþ er faus. *c* **1400** *Destr. Troy* 8109 Now art þou trewly hor traitour, & tainted for fals!

2. One who or that which is false. †**a.** *ellipt.* for 'false person'. *Obs.*

a **1300** *Cursor M.* 4412 (Cott.) Ioseph.. þat suikeful fals, þat fole lichour. *c* **1340** *Ibid.* 17473 (Trin.) Alle false shul fare on þat wise. *c* **1400** *Destr. Troy* 12355 Eneas.. wold haue dungyn hym to deth, & deiret þe fals.

†**b.** What is false; falsehood. *Obs.* exc. as absol. use of the adj.

c **1380** WYCLIF *Sel. Wks.* III. 345 Men moten.. take ofte fals as bileve. *a* **1592** GREENE *Jas. IV* (1861) 213 Such reports more false than truth contain. **1603** SHAKS. *Meas. for M.* II. iv. 170 My false, ore-weighs your true. *a* **1680** BUTLER *Rem.* (1759) I. 224 Science.. Conveys, and counterchanges true and false. **1812** SIR H. DAVY *Chem. Philos.* 13 Truths.. were blended with the false.

c. Something that is false; untruth; false appearance. *Obs.* exc. *arch.*

1584 T. BASTARD *Chrestoleros*, He.. hath put a false upon thy face. **1786** tr. *Swedenborg's Chr. Relig.* §273 His Understanding is full of Falses. **1884** TENNYSON *Becket* III. iii, Earth's falses are heaven's truths.

†**3.** *Fencing.* = FEINT. *Obs.*

1637 NABBES *Microcosm.* in Dodsley *O. Plays* IX. 122 Mar's fencing school, where I learn'd a mystery that consists in.. thrusts, falses, doubles.

D. *Comb.*

1. Of the adj.: **a.** With agent-nouns forming sbs., as ***false-buller, -coiner***; †***false writer***, (*a*) one who writes incorrectly; (*b*) a forger. Also (not with agent-noun); ***false-innocence*** (also ***false-innocent*** adj.) cf. FAUX-NAÏF *sb.* and *a.*

a **1300** *Cursor M.* 29306 (Cott.) Fals bullers [see FALSE *v.* 1]. **1440** *Promp. Parv.* 148 False wryter, *plastographus.* **1580** BARET *Alv.* F 109 A false writer.. *mendosus scriptor. Ibid.*, A false coiner, *adulterator monetæ.*

1928 D. H. LAWRENCE *Woman who rode Away* 272 Her eyes especially were warm and naïve and false-innocent. **1938** R. GRAVES *Coll. Poems* 187 Their false-innocence assaulting her, Breaching her hard heart.

b. With pa. pples., forming adjs. chiefly parasynthetic, as ***false-biased, -bottomed, -eyed, -faced, -faithed, -fingered, -fronted, -grounded, -hearted*** (whence ***false-heartedness***), ***-necked, -principled, -tongued, -visored***.

1654 WHITLOCK *Zootomia* 450 For our Equalls, what they say or do.. what is good, we make Casuall, or *false Byassed. **1654** H. L'ESTRANGE *Chas. I* (1655) 25 You have.. upon *false-bottomed suggestions endeavoured to distain his [the king's].. honour. **1645** QUARLES *Sol. Recant.* 55 Then banish *fals-ey'd mirth. **1607** SHAKS. *Cor.* I. ix. 44 Let Courts and Cities be Made all of *false-fac'd soothing. *a* **1959** E. MUIR *Coll. Poems* (1960) 291 But why was our old friend Everyman Among this false-faced company? **1601** CHESTER *Love's Mart.* cv. (1878) 71 *False-faithed Scotland. **1648** GOODWIN *Youngl. Eld.* Ess. 4 *Fals-fingered men. **1889** A. R. HOPE in *Boy's Own Paper* 3 Aug. 697/2 The *false-fronted frump. **1649** ROBERTS *Clavis Bibl.* 341 His confutation, of their *false-grounded opinion. **1571** GOLDING *Calvin on Ps.* lv. 21 Yᵉ *falseharted folk bear in their mouth hony dipped in poison. **1685** BAXTER *Paraphr. N.T.* Matt. xii. 39 A false-hearted People that will not be convinced by Miracles. **1847** EMERSON *Poems, To Rhea* Wks. (Bohn) I. 402 When love has once departed From the eyes of the false-hearted. **1571** GOLDING *Calvin on Ps.* xli. 7 To utter the *falsehartednesse assoone as they come out of the doores. **1889** *The Voice* (N.Y.) 16 May, The.. false heartedness of the temperance Republicans. **1892** *Academy* 24 Sept. 270 *False-necked vases are represented in the tomb of Ramessu III. **1837** HT. MARTINEAU *Soc. Amer.* III. 94 The brand of contempt should be fixed upon any.. *false principled style of manners. **1910** W. DE LA MARE *Three Mulla-Mulgars* 41 Oh, these *false-tongued Mulgars! **1563** FOXE *A. & M.* 1355/2 The dark and *falsceuisured kingdom of Antichrist.

2. Of the adv.: **a.** With pr. pples., forming adjs., as ***false-boding, -creeping, -glozing*** (see GLOZING), ***-judging, -lying, -persuading, -speaking, -warbling***; with vbl. sbs., forming sbs., as ***false-contracting, -dealing, -enditing, speaking, -promising, -writing***.

1594 SHAKS. *Rich. III*, I. iii. 247 *False boding Woman, end thy frantick Curse. **1598** SYLVESTER *Du Bartas* II. i. III. *Furies* 746 Theeving, *False-contracting, Church-chaffering [etc.]. **1593** SHAKS. *Lucr.* 1517 Jealousy itself could not mistrust *False-creeping craft. **1702** C. MATHER *Magn. Chr.* I. ii. (1852) 51 This *false-dealing proved a safe-dealing for the good people. *c* **1480** JOHN WATTON *Spec. Chr.* 30 b, *Fals Enditing. **1633** G. HERBERT *Temple, Dotage* i, *False glozing pleasures. **1686** SOUTH *Serm.* (1737) II. ix. 347 A false glossing parasite would.. call his fool-hardiness valour. **1839** HALLAM *Hist. Lit.* viii. I. §50 A very *false-judging pedantry. **1562** TURNER *Herbal* II. 70 b, A *falslying good lesse man. **1682** OTWAY *Venice Preserved* IV. i. 56 Thanks to thy tears and *false perswading love. **1684** —— *Atheist* I. i, There's.. *False-promising at Court. *c* **1600** SHAKS. *Sonn.* cxxxviii, Simply I credit her *false-speaking tongue. **1884** tr. *Lotze's Logic* 286 False-speaking is wrong in itself. **1728–46** THOMSON *Spring* 992 *False-warbling in his cheated ear.

b. With pa. pples., forming adjs., as ***false-derived, -fed, -found, -gotten, -imagined, -persuaded, -pretended, -purchased, -spoken, -sworn, -tinctured, -whited, -termed, -written.***

1597 SHAKS. *2 Hen. IV*, IV. i. 190 Euery..*false-deriued Cause. **1680** H. MORE *Apocal. Apoc.* 69 They shall not be *false-fed..by deceitful Teachers. *a* **1558** Q. MARY in Foxe *A. & M.* (1684) III. 14 Seditions have been nourished..by printing of *false found books. **1460** in *Pol. Rel. & L. Poems* (1866) 260 *Fals goten good. *c* **1625** MILTON *Death Fair Infant* 72 Her *false-imagined loss cease to lament! **1605** SHAKS. *Lear* I. iv. 254 (Qo.), I should be *false persuaded I had daughters. **1553** BALE *Gardiner's De vera Obed.* Pref. Bv, *False pretended supremacie. **1530** *Form Greater Excommun.* in Maskell *Mon. Rit.* II. 299 All tho ben acursed ..that use wytingly suche *false purchased letters. **1843** CARLYLE *Past & Pr.* (1858) 142 *False-spoken, unjust. **1569** J. SANFORD tr. *Agrippa's Van. Artes* 2b, A *falsesworne Marchaunte. **1729** SAVAGE *Wanderer* II. 391 *False-term'd honour. **1706** WATTS *Horæ Lyricæ* II. (1808) 169 The cruel shade apply'd..a *false tinctur'd glass. **1641** MILTON *Ch. Govt.* II. iii. (1851) 173 A *false-whited, a lawnie resemblance of her. **1755** CARTE *Hist. Eng.* IV. 93 Names *false-written as Artherus for Arthurus.

c. With verbs, forming verbs, as ***false-brood, -colour, -feed, -play, -point, -preen, -promise***; (whence ***false-brooding***, etc., vbl. sbs.).

1948 *Brit. Birds* XLI. 237 He '*false-brooded' by crouching in any convenient depression nearby. *Ibid.* 243 In the same way false-brooding occurs as a substitute activity when uncertainty arises within the bird's mental framework. **1817** COLERIDGE *Biog. Lit.* (1847) II. 170 Genius neither distorts nor *false-colours its objects. **1948** *Brit. Birds* XLI. 12 She then inserts her bill into that of the male and symbolic '*false-feeding' follows in which food is not actually passed. **1961** D. NETHERSOLE-THOMPSON in Bannerman *Birds Brit. Isles* X. 313 After oystercatchers have copulated, they may preen or 'false preen', feed rapidly or 'false feed', peck at the ground, curtsey. **1606** SHAKS. *Ant. & Cl.* IV. xiv. 19 The Queene..has *false plaid my Glory Vnto an Enemies triumph. **1892** *Field* 7 May 695/1 They kept on *false pointing and backing..Ivybridge did little else but false point. **1949** *Brit. Birds* XLII. 7 On one or two occasions the *false-preening by the male, mentioned by Makkink, was observed at this stage. **1961** False preen. [see *false feed*]. *a* **1618** SYLVESTER *Cup of Consolation* 22 Smiling Hope..*False-promiseth long Peace and plenty too.

3. Special comb.: †**false-back** *a.*, ? treacherously retreating; **false-bedded** *a.*, **-bedding** *Geol.* (see quots. 1876, 1887); †**false-cup**, a kind of drinking cup; **false ebony** (see quots.); †**false-heart** *a.* = *false hearted* (see *Comb.* 1); **false-muster**, an incorrect statement of the number of men in a regiment or a ship's company; **false-nerved** *a. Bot.*, having no vascular tissue; **false nest** (see quot.); **false twist** *Textiles* [TWIST *sb.*[1] 4] (see quot. 1960), also *attrib.*; whence ***false-twist*** *v.* intr. and ***false-twisting*** *ppl. a.*; †**false-winged** *a. Arch.* = *pseudo-dipteral.*

1633 P. FLETCHER *Purple Isl.* XI. xlviii, The *false-back Tartars fear with cunning feign. **1876** PAGE *Adv. Text Bk. Geol.* v. 91 Sandstones are said to be *false-bedded when their strata are crossed obliquely by numerous laminæ. **1884** *Nature* 13 Nov. 32 The lower zone of false-bedded grits. **1876** WOODWARD *Geol.* (1887) 13 *False-bedding..is a feature produced in shallow water by currents and tidal action, whereby beds are heaped up in irregular layers without any approach to horizontality or continuity. **1877** A. H. GREEN *Phys. Geol.* iv. §1. 124 False-bedding e.g. Current-, Cross-, or Drift-Bedding. **1708** MOTTEUX *Rabelais* v. xxxiv. (1737) 152 *False-Cups, Tumblers. **1892** C. M. YONGE *Old Woman's Outlook* v. 96 The inside heart wood [of the laburnum] is so black as to be called *false-ebony. **1911** *Encycl. Brit.* XVI. 32/1 The heart wood of the laburnum is of a dark reddish-brown colour, hard and durable, and takes a good polish... The laburnum has been called false ebony from this character of its wood. **1593** SHAKS. *2 Hen. VI*, v. i. 143, I am thy King, and thou a *false-heart Traitor. **1752** A. MURPHY *Gray's-Inn Jrnl.* (1756) I. 116 No. 17 There are besides several Faggots, and *False-musters, which the General thinks proper to connive at. **1954** BANNERMAN *Birds Brit. Isles* III. 354 This species [wren] builds '*false' nests in the vicinity of the nest which is eventually to hold the eggs..some naturalists considering that they are for the purpose of roosting in, but this is denied by others who consider they are merely the result of the male's craze for building. **1866** *Treas. Bot.*, *False-nerved, when veins have no vascular tissue, but are formed of simple elongated cellular tissue; as in mosses, seaweeds, etc. **1960** *Textile Terms & Defs.* (ed. 4) 62 **False twist*, turns inserted in opposite directions and in equal numbers in adjacent elements of yarn..characterized by its temporary nature. *Ibid.*, The false-twisting element, through which the yarn or sliver passes. **1965** *Guardian* 31 Mar. 17/1 False-twist version of acetate yarn. *Ibid.*, The idea of false-twisting acetate yarns. **1715** LEONI *Palladio's Archit.* (1742) II. 20 This Temple was..*false-wing'd.

†**false**, *v. Obs.* Forms: 3 falsie-n, (fausie-n), 3–7 false(n, (5 -yn), 3–4 *south. dial.* valse(n, 4–5 falshe, 4–6 fals, 6 falce. [a. OF. *false-r* (mod.F. *fausser*):—late L. *falsāre*, f. *fals-us*: see FALSE *a.* Cf. ON. *falsa.*] To be or make false.

1. a. *intr.* Of a thing: To prove unreliable; to fail, give way.

c **1205** LAY. 23967 þe helman his hæuede and his hereburne gon to falsie [*c* **1275** fausie]. *a* **1225** *Ancr. R.* 228 Vor none deofles puffe ne þurue ȝe dreden, bute ȝif þet lim ualse. *Ibid.* 270 ȝif he mei underȝiten þet ower bileaue falsie.

b. *trans.* To cause to fail or give way; to foil (a weapon).

a **1225** *Ancr. R.* 292 Godes stronge passiun falsie þes deofles wepnen. *a* **1240** *Sawles Warde* in *Cott. Hom.* 255 Ne mei..ne na wone falsi min heorte. *c* **1275** *Luue Ron* 124 in *O.E. Misc.* 97 Ne may no Mynur hire vnderwrote, ne neuer false þene grundwal. *c* **1320** *Seuyn Sag.* (W.) 2125 The fir.. falsed the siment, and the ston.

2. *trans.* To counterfeit (money); to forge (a document).

a **1300** *Cursor M.* 29308 (Cotton Galba) Fals bulleres..þat falses þe papes sele. **1303** R. BRUNNE *Handl. Synne* 5362 ȝyf þou dedyst euere þy myghte To false a chartre. *c* **1450** MYRC 709 All that falsen the popes lettres. **1480** CAXTON *Chron. Eng.* cl. 131 A clerk had falshed the kynges money. **1493** *Festivall* (W. de W. 1515) 193, I denounce..all those that fals the kynges standarde. **1553** T. BECON *Reliq. Rome* (1563) 240a, All thoe that false the Popes Bull.

3. To falsify, make untrue; to introduce falsehood into; to corrupt.

c **1380** WYCLIF *Sel. Wks.* III. 434 Men moten.. pacientliche dispose hem to deye for Crist, and fals not þe gospel for favor of men. *c* **1386** CHAUCER *Miller's Prol.* 66, I mote reherse Hir tales alle..Or elles falsen som of my matere. **1450–1530** *Myrr. our Ladye* 54 They that clyppe away from the money of goddes seruice, eny wordes or letters or syllables, & so false yt from the trew sentence. **1598** SYLVESTER *Du Bartas* II. ii. II *Babylon* 473 Those scattered Masons Had falsed it [Adam's language] in hundred thousand fashions.

4. To be or prove false to. **a.** To break, violate (one's faith, word, etc.). Const. *dat.* of person.

1303 R. BRUNNE *Handl. Synne* 11191 Men falsen here trouþes. *c* **1386** CHAUCER *Sqr.'s T.* 619 He..hath his trouthe falsed. **1480** CAXTON *Chron. Eng.* xxii. 20 These couenauntes sholde neuer be broke ne falsed. *a* **1533** LD. BERNERS *Huon* cxx. 429 Then shall I false her my promyse. **1563** B. GOOGE *Eglogs* vii. (Arb.) 57 When fyrst she falst her troth to me. **1624** HEYWOOD *Captives* II. i. in Bullen *O. Pl.* IV, That false their faythes. **1923** HARDY *Coll. Poems* (ed. 2) 596 Past regretting Loves who have falsed their vow.

b. To play false to (a person); to betray, deceive. Also *absol.*

c **1374** CHAUCER *Troylus* v. 1053 Ther made neuere womman more wo Than she, when that she falsed Troylus. *c* **1420** LYDG. *Temple of Glass* 63 Medee..was falsed of Iason.

c. *absol.* and *intr.* To defraud, deal falsely.

1393 GOWER *Conf.* II. 301 To falsen and to ben unkinde. *c* **1450** MYRC 709 All that falsen or use false measures. *a* **1541** WYATT *Poet. Wks.* (1861) 163 Never yet..Intended I to false, or be untrue.

d. ? *refl.* To betray one's trust. (Doubtful: the word may be adj.)

1611 SHAKS. *Cymb.* II. iii. 74 'Tis Gold..makes Diana's Rangers false themselues.

5. To maintain to be false, impugn. ***to false*** (*a doom*): in Sc. Law 'to deny the equity of a sentence, and appeal to a superior court' (Jam.).

a **1225** *Juliana* 69 Ah false swa hare lahe. *a* **1400** *Cov. Myst.* (Shaks. Soc.) 241 Thus xal I false the wordys that his pepyl doth testefy. *c* **1400** *Apol. Loll.* 60 In mennis lawe oft men falsen domis, & appelen þer fro. *c* **1430** *Pilgr. Lyf Manhode* I. lxxxv. (1869) 49 Thine argumentes, that seist i have falsed and repreued thy gretteste principle. **1469** *Act Parl. Jas. III* (1814) 94 The dome gevin in the Justice are of Drumfress..& falsit and againe callit be maister Adam cokburn forspekar..was weile gevin & evil again callit. **1609, 1708** [see FALSING *vbl. sb.* below].

6. ***to false a blow***: to make a feint.

1590 SPENSER *F.Q.* II. v. 9 Sometimes he strook him strayt, And falsed oft his blowes t'illude him with such bayt. **1594** [see FALSING *vbl. sb.* below].

Hence **falsed** *ppl. a.*, **'falsing** *vbl. sb.* and *ppl. a.*, in senses of the verb. ***falsing of dooms***: (see FALSE *v.* 5).

a **1225** *Ancr. R.* 72 þurh swuch chastiement haueð sum ancre arered bitweonen hire & hire preost..a valsinde luue. *c* **1340** *Gaw. & Gr. Knt.* 2378 Lo! þer þe falssyng, foule mot hit falle! *c* **1400** *Destr. Troy* 11330 Falsyng & flatery. *a* **1541** WYATT *Poet. Wks.* (1861) 30 Yet shall they shew your falsed faith. **1590** SHAKS. *Com. Err.* II. ii. 95 Not sure in a thing falsing. **1594** J. G. (*title*) tr. Grassi's True Arte of Defence, with a Treatise of Deceit or Falsinge. **1594** DANIEL *Compl. Rosamond* xxi, The adulterate beauty of a falsed cheek. **1599** MARSTON *Sco. Villanie* I. iii. 181 Hence, ye falsed, seeming Patriotes. **1609** SKENE *Reg. Maj.* Table 70 Falsing of Domes (reduction of decreiteis) sould be done incontinent be the partie agains quhom they are given. *a* **1641** BP. MOUNTAGU *Acts & Mon.* (1642) 544 That falsed Homily. **1708** J. CHAMBERLAYNE *St. Gt. Brit.* II. III. x. (1743) 432 Edinburgh ..assisted the Chamberlain in the falsing of dooms.

false-bray: see FAUSSE-BRAY.

false-card, *v. intr.* To play a false card (FALSE *a.* 2 g); esp. in *Bridge*, to play a card other than the normal one, so as to mislead an opponent. So **false-carding** *vbl. sb.*

1589 W. WARNER *Alb. Eng.* VI. xxx. 132 Nay, be it that he should espie false carding, what of it? **1902** J. B. ELWELL *Bridge* 82 The dealer false-cards so that the adversaries will not know that he holds the queen. **1923** *Daily Mail* 23 June 6 A simple case of false-carding is where declarer holding ace, king of a suit led by an opponent takes the first trick with the ace in order to convey the idea that he does not possess the king... Many players false-card without rhyme or reason. **1939** N. DE V. HART *Bridge Players' Bedside Bk.* xxii. 79 The declarer executed his simple piece of false-carding on the edge of an abyss. **1960** T. REESE *Play Bridge with Reese* xxxii. 112 Unless both opponents were false-carding in spades they are 4–4.

†**'falsedict.** *Obs.* [A parallel formation to VERDICT, by the substitution of *false* for the first member.] An untrue deliverance or utterance.

1579 FULKE *Heskins' Parl.* 499 Wee will not take the verdicte or rather the falsedict at his mouth. **1616** B. PARSONS *Mag. Charter* 23 A verdict..is a falsedict, if [etc.].

†**'falsedom.** *Obs.* [f. FALSE *a.* + -DOM.] Treachery, untruth; a falsehood.

1297 R. GLOUC. (Rolls) 852* *note*, þe vnkunde suikedom [*v.r.* falsedom]. *a* **1300** *Siriz* 65 in Wright *Anecd. Lit.* 4 Ne con ich saien non falsdom. **1303** R. BRUNNE *Handl. Synne* 2748 ȝyf he swere fals, or falsdom bede.

falsehood ('fɔːls-, 'fɒlshʊd). Also †**falsehead.** Forms: α. 3–6 fals(e)-, (4 falce-, fauls- *south dial.* vals-), hed(e, -ed, (4 -ede, -heed, -id, 5 -hedd, 6 -heade), 6–7 -head. β. 4–6 fals- (6 false-) hod(e, (4 *Sc.* -ade), 6– falsehood. [f. FALSE *a.* + -HEAD, -HOOD.]

†**1.** As an attribute of persons: Falseness, deceitfulness, mendacity, faithlessness. *Obs.*

1297 R. GLOUC. (1724) 454 Of falshede, ne of trecherye, in þe worl hys per nys. *a* **1340** HAMPOLE *Psalter* xi. 2 Sothfastnes is lessed & falshede waxis. *c* **1440** *Generydes* 1539 A sotilte To hide your falshede. **1534** LD. BERNERS *Huon* lxxxii. 253 Me thynke he is full of falshede for I se none other but he purchaseth for your deth.

2. Want of conformity to fact or truth; falsity. Now almost always implying intentional falsity.

c **1340** *Cursor M.* 22865 (Trin.) Mony wenen þat ben not wise þat þat flesshe shal not hool vprise. þat to wene is but falshede. *c* **1440** *Generydes* 5221 Ffalshede and trougth is euer atte debate. **1530** RASTELL *Bk. Purgat.* I. viii, Truthe and falshed be two contraryauntes. **1611** BIBLE *Job* xxi. 34 In your answeres there remaineth falshood. **1742** JOHNSON *L.P., Sydenham*, The falshood of this report. **1793** BEDDOES *Scurvy* 46 He has..shewn the falsehood of the conclusion. **1809–10** COLERIDGE *Friend* (1865) 20 The shameless assertion, that truth and falsehood are indifferent in their own natures.

b. That which, or something that, is contrary to fact or truth; an untrue proposition, doctrine, belief, etc.; untrue propositions, etc. in general.

1393 GOWER *Conf.* III. 136 Logique hath eke in his degree Betwene the trouthe and falshode The pleine wordes for to shode. *c* **1449** PECOCK *Repr.* III. xiv. 373 Out of a treuthe folewith not a falshede. **1691** HARTCLIFFE *Virtues* 289 Such Minds, as shall have as clear Conceptions of Falshoods, as they have of Truths. **1845** S. AUSTIN *Ranke's Hist. Ref.* II. 278 Truth would be suppressed together with falsehood. **1847** HELPS *Friends in C.* (1854) I. 6 Each age has to fight with its own falsehoods. **1861** M. PATTISON *Ess.* (1889) I. 32 It would be easy..to exaggerate this truth..into a falsehood.

†**c.** An error, mistake (in writing); a slip of the pen. *Obs. rare.*

c **1440** *Promp. Parv.* 148 Falsheed yn boke, for yvel wrytynge, *menda.*

3. Deception, falsification, imposture; a forgery, counterfeit. *Obs.* or *arch.*

1340 *Ayenb.* 40 Notaryes þet makeþ þe ualse lettres, and.. to uele oþre ualshedes. *c* **1394** *P. Pl. Crede* 616 þanne [he].. fyeþ on her falshedes þat þei bifore deden. **1667** MILTON *P.L.* IV. 122 Hee..Artificer of fraud..was the first That practisd falshood under saintly shew. *Ibid.* IV. 812 No falshood can endure Touch of Celestial temper.

4. The intentional making of false statements; lying. (Occasionally with wider sense adopted from ancient philosophy: see quot. 1810.)

1662 STILLINGFL. *Orig. Sacr.* I. iv. §10 Herodotus was.. suspected of falshood. **1797** MRS. RADCLIFFE *Italian* xvi, Add not the audacity of falsehood to the headlong passions of youth. **1810** BENTHAM *Packing* (1821) 135 Your logical falsehood is—where, for example, you speak of a thing which is not true as if it were true, whether you think it true or not: your ethical falsehood is—where you speak of a thing as true, believing it not to be true, whether it be really true or not. *a* **1839** PRAED *Poems* (1864) II. 394 Fraud in kings was held accurst, And falsehood sin was reckoned. **1841** LANE *Arab. Nts.* I. 24 Falsehood is permitted by their religion. **1875** JOWETT *Plato* (ed. 2) V. 74 He who loves involuntary falsehood is a fool.

5. An uttered untruth; a lie. Also, false statements, uttered untruth, in general.

c **1290** *S. Eng. Leg.* 42/288 Alas, alas, þe deolfole cas: to heore so muche falshede! *c* **1380** WYCLIF Sel. Wks. III. 140 He seies, as blaspheme falsehed þat he makes medeful to slee Cristen men. *c* **1450** *Gesta Rom.* xlix. 223 (Harl. MS.) He with his sotil cautellis & falshedes blindithe & disseyuithe þe soule. **1593** SHAKS. *Rich. II*, IV. i. 39, I will turne thy falshood to thy hart, Where it was forged, with my Rapiers point. **1794** MRS. RADCLIFFE *Myst. Udolpho* xii, Why did you accuse me of having told a falsehood. **1849** RUSKIN *Sev. Lamps* ii. §15. 42 To cover brick with cement, and to divide this cement with joints that it may look like stone, is to tell a falsehood. **1856** FROUDE *Hist. Eng.* (1858) I. iv. 314 A small element of truth may furnish a substructure for a considerable edifice of falsehood.

†**6.** *Arith. rule of falsehood* = 'False Position': see POSITION. *Obs.*

1542 RECORDE *Gr. Artes* (1575) 439 The rule of Falsehode, whiche beareth his name..for that by false numbers taken at all aduentures, it teacheth howe to finde those true numbers that you seeke for.

7. *Sc. Law.* (See quot.): in mod. law books for the older FALSET.

1699 SIR G. MACKENZIE *Laws Cust. Scot.* xxvii. 134 *Falsum*, Falshood..a fraudulent suppression, or imitation of Truth, in prejudice of another. **1773** in J. ERSKINE *Instit. Law Scot.* IV. iv. §66. **1861** in W. BELL *Dict. Law Scot.* 378/2.

8. *Comb.*, as ***falsehood-free, -monger.***

1839 LADY LYTTON *Cheveley* (ed. 2) I. xii. 293 What will not those falsehood-mongers, the poets, have to answer for. **1850** MRS. BROWNING *Poems, Exile's Return* iii, How change could touch the falsehood-free And changeless thee!

†**'falseleke.** *Obs. rare*[-1]. [f. FALSE *a.*: see -LOCK.] Falsehood.

a **1310** in Wright *Lyric P.* viii. 32 To fet y falle hem feole, for falsleke fifti folde.

†'**falsely**, *a. Obs. rare*⁻¹. In 4 falsly. [f. FALSE *a.* + -LY¹.] False, deceptive.
a **1310** in Wright *Lyric P.* viii. 31 My fykel fleishe, mi falsly blod.

falsely (fɔːls-, fɒlslɪ), *adv.* Forms: 3-5 fals(e)liche, (4 falslich, -lik, -lyche, valsliche), 3-5 falsli, 3-8 falsly, 4- falsely. [f. FALSE *a.* + -LY².]
1. In violation of truth; untruthfully.
1303 R. BRUNNE *Handl. Synne* 726 Whan þou falsly by hym swerest. *c* **1320** *Sir Tristr.* 3054 Falsly canestow fayt. **1651** HOBBES *Leviath.* II. xxvi. 146 A man is accused falsly of a fact. **1841-4** EMERSON *Ess., Spir. Laws* Wks. I. 66 When a man..has base ends, and speaks falsely.
2. Erroneously, incorrectly, wrongly.
a **1300** *Cursor M.* 23131 (Cott.) Falsli es he cristen calld. *c* **1400** MAUNDEV. (1839) xii. 134 Thei seyn that the cristene men..beleeven folyly and falsly that Iesu Crist was crucyfyed. **1563** WINZET *Vincent. Lirin.* xxvi. Wks. 1890 II. 54 Science falslie so callit. **1597** MORLEY *Introd. Mus.* 183 Such things as I haue either left out or falsely set downe. *a* **1627** SIR J. BEAUMONT *Answ. Metrodorus* in *Poems* (1869) 240 All states are good, and they are falsly led, Who wish to be vnborne. **1727-38** GAY *Fables* I. x, How falsly is the spaniel drawn! **1809-10** COLERIDGE *Friend* (1865) 128, I have falsely represented his principles.
3. Wrongfully. **a.** Unjustly. for no sufficient cause, without justification. **b.** Dishonestly, fraudulently.
1303 R. BRUNNE *Handl. Synne* 5347 3yf þou..falsly purchasede..þat ys grete synne. *c* **1330** —— *Chron.* (1810) 235 Gascoyne & Normandie, þat þe kyng of France chalanges falsly. **1389** in *Eng. Gilds* (1870) 5 Enpresoned falslich by enme. *c* **1430** *Pilgr. Lyf Manhode* II. xiv. (1869) 80 Thou mesurest falsliche, and stelest folkes corn. **1602** MARSTON *Antonio's Rev.* II. iii. Wks. 1856 I. 98, I must die falsely. **1666** DRYDEN *Ann. Mirab.* 675 Success, which they did falsly boast. **1711** ADDISON *Spect.* No. 170 ¶7 For such who are treated ill and upbraided falsely.
4. Deceitfully, treacherously.
a **1225** *Ancr. R.* 208 Falsliche igon to schrifte. *a* **1300** *Cursor M.* 818 (Gött.) Þe feind..falsli bigiled adam. *c* **1394** *P. Pl. Crede* 693 A fewe Folwen fully þat clop, but falsliche þat vseþ. **1401** *Pol. Poems* (Rolls) II. 41 Falselier than the fende. *c* **1489** CAXTON *Sonnes of Aymon* xiv. 341 Kyng yon, that so falsli hath betrayed vs. **1503-4** *Act 19 Hen. VII*, c. 34 Preamb., Persones falsly and traiterously ymagynyng..the deth..of the Kinge. **1605** CAMDEN *Rem.* (1637) 253 John..falsely and unnaturally revolted unto the French king. **1742** YOUNG *Nt. Th.* vii. 478 The third witness..falsly promises an Eden here.
†5. Improperly. *Obs.*
1393 LANGL. *P. Pl.* C. x. 270 Ful meny fayre flus falsliche wasshe! **1483** CAXTON *G. de la Tour* E vij b, The daughters of Moab were falsly engendryd and goten. **1529** MORE *Dyaloge* III. Wks. 208/1 The churche fell sodeinly down..was falsely wrought. **1594** SHAKS. *Rich. III*, v. iii. 251 A base foule Stone, made precious by the soyle Of Englands Chaire, where he is falsely set.

falsen ('fɔːls(ə)n, 'fɒls(ə)n), *v. rare.* [f. FALSE *a.* + -EN⁵.] *trans.* To make false or unreal.
1888 M. ARNOLD in *19th Cent.* Apr. 482 The whole action of our minds is hampered and falsened.

falseness ('fɔːls-, 'fɒlsnɪs). Also 4-7 falsnes(s(e, 4-8 false- (*south. dial.* vals-) nesse. [f. FALSE *a.* + -NESS.] The quality of being false.
1. Contrariety to fact; want of reality or truth; falsehood, unreality. †Also quasi-*concr.* anything false.
1303 R. BRUNNE *Handl. Synne* 1497 3yf he deme fals iuggement, þere falsnes ys, he shalle be shent. **1340** *Ayenb.* 256 Ualsnesse me ne ssel zigge. **1398** TREVISA *Barth. De P.R.* III. vi. (1495) 52 Racio or reason demyth bitwene..sothe and falsnesse. **1597** SHAKS. *Lover's Compl.* 105 His rudeness..Did livery falseness in a pride of truth. **1655** SIR E. NICHOLAS in *N. Papers* (Camden) II. 170, I noe whit repent me of the Collogne newes I sent you, since I was..confident of the falsnes. **1847** C. G. ADDISON *Contracts* II. vii. §1 He..did not know of the falseness of the affirmation at the time it was made. **1877** MRS. FORRESTER *Mignon* I. 6 The falseness of its illusions.
2. Deceitfulness, duplicity, imposture. Also quasi-*concr.* a deceit, an imposture.
c **1330** R. BRUNNE *Chron.* (1810) 265 He sent vnto þe pape, &..a new falsnes did schape. *c* **1386** CHAUCER *Can. Yeom. Prol. & T.* 423 His infinite falsenesse Ther coude no man writen. *c* **1449** PECOCK *Repr.* I. i. 7 Se ȝe that no man bigile ȝou bi..veyn falsnes. **1513** *Act 5 Hen. VIII*, c. 4 §1 The said Deceits and Falseness. **1568** GRAFTON *Chron.* II. 196 He was..arreigned and judged for his falsenesse. **1649** BP. REYNOLDS *Hosea* ii. 71 The falsenes..of our corrupt hearts. **1732** WATERLAND *Christ. Vind.* 38 They that reject Superstition in Theory, and yet retain it in Life..do but expose their own Folly and Falseness. **1846** TRENCH *Mirac.* xx. (1862) 329 Another part of his falseness was, that [etc.].
3. Faithlessness, inconstancy, treachery. Also an instance of this.
c **1330** R. BRUNNE *Chron.* (1810) 55 Falsnes brewes bale. **1393** LANGL. *P. Pl.* C. XIX. 173 Falsnesse ich [Iesus] fynde in þy [Iudas] faire speche. *c* **1470** HENRY *Wallace* I. 39 It was lost with tresoune and falsnes. **1523** LD. BERNERS *Froiss.* I. cclxxx. 171 a, He wolde make y traytours derely abye their falsnesse. **1658** *Whole Duty Man* iv. §8. 40 Some inward guilt of falseness, for which that oath must be the cloak. **1709** PRIDEAUX *Lett.* (Camden) 203 Beeing for his falsenesse in the management of that trust broken and discarded. **1876** BANCROFT *Hist. U.S.* IV. x. 386 His predecessor..had recorded their falseness and cruelty.
†4. The fact of failing or 'giving way'. *Obs.*
1552 HULOET, Falsenes of herte, *demissio.* **1580** BARET *Alv.* F 111 A falsenesse of heart, and feeble courage.

†'**falser**. *Obs.* Also 6 falsor. [f. FALSE *v.* + -ER¹. Cf. F. *fausseur.*]
1. A falsifier, forger, counterfeiter.
1340 *Ayenb.* 62 Ha ssel by demd ase ualsere. **1388** WYCLIF *Jas.* Prol., The whiche [enuyous men] pronouncen me to be a falsere. **1450-1530** *Myrr. our Ladye* 53 Falsers of the kynges money are punysshed by deth.
2. One who acts falsely; a deceiver.
1579 SPENSER *Sheph. Cal.* Epil., To teach the ruder shepheard how..from the falsers fraude his folded flocke to keepe. **1597** LYLY *Wom. in Moone* IV. i, Detested falsor! *a* **1637** B. JONSON *Hue & Cry after Cupid*, We hope ye'll not abide him, Since ye hear this falser's play.

†'**falsery**. *Obs.* Also 6-7 falsary. [a. OF. *falserie*, f. *fals* FALSE *a.*] Deception, falsification, falsehood.
1594 *2nd Rep. Dr. Faustus* in Thoms *Prose Rom.* (1858) III. 397 The good emperor..came now to make him amends for his pretty falsery. **1639** GENTILIS *Servita's Inquis.* (1676) 889 That Tribunal, to which that falsary [calumniation of an accused person] hath not born respect. *a* **1670** M. CASAUBON *Treat. Spirits* (1672) 214 This Gassendus thinks is enough to prove Plutarch's falsary.

†'**falseship**. *Obs.* In 3 falschipe, 4 felsship. [f. FALSE *a.* + -SHIP.] The quality of being false.
a. Untruthfulness. **b.** Dishonesty, deceit.
c **1230** *Hali Meid.* 26 Ah ichulle scheawen hit al wið falschipe ismeðet. **14..** in *Pol. Rel. & L. Poems* (1866) 222 Glosinge and felsship beon riue.

'**falsesome**, *a. Obs.* exc. *Sc. rare.* Also 9 *Sc.* fause-. [f. FALSE *a.* + -SOME.] Deceitful, untrue.
1533 MORE *Debell. Salem* i. Wks. 932/1 So many falsesome sayes in that sedicioμse boke. **1883** *Edin. Even. Expr.* 2 May 2/3 Of fausesome ways thou'st taen a scunner.

†'**falset**¹. Chiefly *Sc. Obs.* Also 4 falsat, 5 falssett. [app. a. OF. *falset* (Godef. s.v. *faussé*):—late L. *falsātum*, neut. pa. pple. of *falsāre*: see FALSE *v.*] Falsehood, treachery, fraud; an instance of this. In Scots Law = FALSEHOOD (see quot. 1609).
1375 BARBOUR *Bruce* xv. 122 Falsat euirmar Sall haue..euill ending. **1482** *Certificate* in *Surtees Misc.* (1890) 40 To put down all falssett and untrewit. **1555** *Sc. Acts Mary* (1597) §44 Mony falsettes daylie done within this realme be Notars. **1569** J. SANFORD tr. *Agrippa's Van. Artes* 161 This then standeth in force..although there appeare erroure or falset. **1609** SKENE *Reg. Maj.* 69 The generall crime of falset, conteines vnder it sundrie speciall crimes. As false Charters or Writtes, false money, false measures, false wechts. *Ibid.* 128 He quha is convict of falset in weghts.

†**falset**², anglicized form of FALSETTO.
1707 J. STEVENS tr. *Quevedo's Com. Wks.* (1709) 59 A young Man singing..with such a Voice, as seem'd not to come from Heaven..it was a Falset. **1782** BURNEY *Hist. Mus.* II. iv. 374 The other just come from Rome—sings in Falset. **1796** —— *Memoirs Metastasio* II. 174 A great player on the violin in falset.

‖**falsetto** (fal'sɛtto, fɒl'sɛtəʊ). Also 8 *erron.* falsetta. [It., dim. of *falso* FALSE. Cf. F. *fausset.*]
1. A forced voice of a range or register above the natural; the head voice.
1774 WALPOLE *Let. Earl Strafford* 11 Nov., There is a full melancholy melody in his [Leoni's] voice, though a falsetta. **1799** YOUNG in *Phil. Trans.* XC. 142 The same difference..takes place between the natural voice and the common falsetto. **1843** *Penny Cycl.* XXVI. 419/1 The term basso falsetto has been proposed to designate this voice [a feigned lower voice], but the term lower falsetto is more accurate. **1855** SMEDLEY *H. Coverdale* lvii. 390 'To whom do I refer?' repeated her husband in the highest note of his shrill falsetto. **1879** GROVE *Dict. Mus.* 501/2 The male counter-tenor, or alto voice, is almost entirely falsetto.
fig. **1796** BURKE *Regic. Peace* i. Wks. 1808 VIII. 103 The mock heroick falsetto of stupid tragedy. **1814** SCOTT *Drama* (1874) 186 All is tuned to the same smooth falsetto of sentiment. **1875** SWINBURNE *Ess. & Studies* 249 Much of the poem is written throughout in falsetto.
2. One who sings with a falsetto voice.
1789 BURNEY *Hist. Mus.* IV. 44 You are pleased..to compare the *falsetti* of former times with the *soprani.* **1884** NIECKS *Dict. Mus. Terms, Falsetto*, a singer who sings soprano or alto parts with such a voice.
3. *attrib.*
1826 MISS MITFORD *Village* Ser. II. (1863) 276 A sort of falsetto tone in her speech. **1854** BUSHNAN in *Circ. Sc.* (*c* 1865) I. 286/2 The falsetto voice has more of a humming character. **1876** FOSTER *Phys.* III. vii. (1879) 605 The vocal cords are seen to be wide apart when falsetto notes are uttered. **1889** *Spectator* 9 Nov. 623/2 The last sentence..seems to us to go perilously near making a falsetto conscience out of the antipathies of strait-laced men.
Hence **fal'settist**, one who sings in falsetto.
1889 *Harper's Mag.* LXXVII. 73 Soprano falsettists were once common enough in France. **1892** *Daily News* 28 July 6/2 The Italian tenor..is an 'incomparable falsettist'.

falsework ('fɔːlswɜːk). [f. FALSE *a.* 17 + WORK *sb.* 10.] A temporary framework or support put up while the main structure is being built and afterwards removed.
1874 KNIGHT *Dict. Mech.* I. 824/2 *False-works*..construction works to enable the erection of the main works. **1930** *Engineering* 18 Apr. 503/3 All substructure and false work were removed. **1954** *Archit. Rev.* CXVI. 336 It was decided to..avoid covering the whole interior with falsework. **1958** *Times* 19 June 10/6 The falsework supporting the unfinished sixth span of the bridge collapsed.

falsidical (fɒl'sɪdɪkəl), *a. rare*⁻¹. [as if f. L. *falsidic-us* falsehood-telling (f. L. *falsum* falsehood + *dic-* weak stem of *dīcĕre* to speak) + -AL¹: on the analogy of VERIDICAL.] Suggesting as true what is really false; falsehood-telling.
1886 MYERS *Phantasms of Living* II. 284 Illusory (or falsidical) hallucinations.

falsies ('fɔːlsɪz), *sb. pl. colloq.* (orig. *U.S.*). [f. FALSE *a.* + -IE.] A padded brassière; breast-pads. Also *transf.*
1943 *N.Y. Post* 6 Oct. 42/3 'Falsies'..the term for the pads that convert them [*sc.* nightclub chorus girls] from 32s to 34s. **1946** *Life* 14 Oct. 35 'Falsies', padded rubber or cloth brassières worn to augment movie actresses' bosoms. **1957** R. HOGGART *Uses of Literacy* viii. 210 'Falsies', the most popular new feature in all the sex-joke magazines. **1958** M. DICKENS *Man Overboard* vii. 105 The secretary slouched in..her falsies pushing out her sweater like cardboard cones. **1964** J. S. HUXLEY *Ess. Humanist* 58 My American friends tell me that falsies are now obtainable for the other side of the female anatomy—false bottoms, in fact.

falsifiability (ˌfɔːlsɪfaɪə'bɪlɪtɪ). *Philos.* [f. FALSIFIABLE *a.* + -ITY.] The quality or fact of being falsifiable. Also *attrib.*
1937 *Philos. Sci.* IV. 26 We may take Popper's principle of falsifiability as an example. **1945** *Mind* LIV. 119 The concepts of absolute and of relative verifiability (and falsifiability) are of an entirely different character. **1959** *Cambr. Rev.* 30 May 567/2 Whether or not the verifiability criterion is a criterion of the meaningfulness of a statement or of the scientific character of a statement, the defects which it has in either case can be reproduced *quid pro quo* for the falsifiability criterion. **1965** J. D. NORTH *Measure of Universe* xiv. 295 Not all propositions can have an inherent degree of falsifiability.

falsifiable ('fɒlsɪfaɪəb(ə)l), *a.* [f. FALSIFY *v.* + -ABLE. Cf. F. *falsifiable.*] That may be falsified.
1611 COTGR., *Falsifiable*, which may be falsified, adulterated, forged, sophisticated. **1685** COTTON tr. *Montaigne* II. 412 The senses are the soveraign Lords of his knowledge, but they are uncertain and falsifiable in all circumstances. **1862** F. HALL *Hindu Philos. Syst.* 252 The Vedántins believe the world to be falsifiable. **1959** *Cambr. Rev.* 30 May 568/2 Suppose now that a statement was meaningful if and only if it was falsifiable. **1964** W. P. ALSTON *Philos. Lang.* iv. 70 We should also note the specially wide sense in which the positivists use 'verifiability'. In this use, it is really equivalent to the disjunction 'verifiable or falsifiable', that is, 'capable of being established as true or false'.

†**fal'sific**, *a. Obs.* [ad. L. *falsific-us*, f. *fals-us* false + *-ficus* making: see -FIC.] 'Making false, falsifying, dealing falsely' (Bailey 1736).

falsification (ˌfɒlsɪfɪ'keɪʃən). [n. of action f. late L. *falsificāre* to FALSIFY: see -ATION.]
1. The action of rendering (something) false; fraudulent alteration (of documents, of weights or measures, etc.); misrepresentation, perversion (of facts); counterfeiting; an instance of the same.
1565 JEWEL *Repl. Harding* iv. §15. 251 He..shoareth vp a ruinous mater with the falsification of his Doctours. **1594** HOOKER *Eccl. Pol.* III. §5. 137 By falsification of the wordes, wittingly to endeuour that anything may seeme diuine which is not. **1607** TOPSELL *Four-f. Beasts* (1673) 38 Some adulterate Castoreum..this is a falsification discernible. **1630** J. TAYLOR (Water P.) *Wks.* II. 36, I am accused for lies and falsifications. **1682** SCARLETT *Exchanges* 351 If there were..ground of suspicion that the Figures were altered, its still the same; but..If the Falsification were so neat, that it could not so easily be discerned..then [etc.]. **1706** COLLIER *Refl. Ridic.* 77 Affectation is the falsification of the whole Person. **1799** S. TURNER *Anglo-Sax.* (1836) I. III. iii. 176 Their..manifest falsifications both of manners and history. **1833** LAMB *Elia* (1860) 358 By a wise falsification, the great masters of painting got at their true conclusions. **1868** E. EDWARDS *Raleigh* I. xxvi. 655 The falsification of date.
2. The showing (something) to be groundless.
1885 *Manch. Exam.* 12 Dec. 5/2 The complete falsification of these confident assurances.
b. *Equity.* 'The showing an item of charge in an account to be wrong' (Webster 1864, citing Story).
1845 J. W. SMITH *Man. Equity* 163 The proving an item to be wrongly inserted is a falsification.

falsificator (ˌfɒlsɪfɪ'keɪtə(r)). [agent-n. f. late L. *falsificāre* to FALSIFY.] One who deals in falsification; a falsifier.
1609 T. MORTON *Answ. Higgons* To Rdr. 1 Lest thou shouldest stumble vpon me, as vpon a Falsificator. **1638** FEATLY *Transubst.* 203 You must say you tooke up your quotations upon trust, or els confesse you are a falsificator. **1883** *St. James's Gaz.* 8 Nov., The audacious falsificators print with old-fashioned type upon hand-made paper.

falsifier ('fɔːlsɪfaɪə(r), 'fɒlsɪfaɪə(r)). [f. FALSIFY *v.* + -ER¹.] One who falsifies.
1532 MORE *Confut. Tindale* Wks. 679/2 Lyars and falsefiers of scripture. **1675** BAXTER *Cath. Theol.* II. I. 283 Dare you deny that these were my words? If you do you are a falsifier. **1682** SIR T. BROWNE *Chr. Mor.* 54 Diogenes..in his younger days was a falsifier of money. **1724** A. COLLINS *Gr. Chr. Relig.* 144 It is unjust to accuse the Evangelists and Apostles with being falsifyers. **1878** *N. Amer. Rev.* CXXVII. 131 A wilful falsifier of history.

†'**falsify**, *sb. Fencing. Obs.* [f. next vb. (sense 7).] The action of 'falsifying' a blow; a feint.
1621 QUARLES *Argalus & P.* (1678) 116 Amphialus..let flie A down-right blow; but with a falsifie Reverst the stroke. **1635** SHIRLEY *Coronat.* I. i, A falsify may spoil his cringe, Or making of a leg.

falsify ('fɔːlsɪfaɪ, 'fɒlsɪfaɪ), *v.* Also 5–7 **falsifie**, 6 **falcefy**, **falsefye**, **-ifye**. [ad. Fr. *falsifier*, ad. late L. *falsificāre*, f. L. *falsific-us* making false, f. *falsus* FALSE: see -FY.]

1. *trans.* To make false or incorrect. **a.** To alter fraudulently; to introduce false matter into or give an incorrect version of (a document, etc.).
1502 *Ord. Crysten Men* (W. de W. 1506) IV. viii. 188 To falsefye the lettres of the pope. **1527** R. THORNE in Hakluyt *Voy.* (1589) 256 Those they haue falsefied of late purposely. **1651** HOBBES *Leviath.* III. xxxiii. 204 They did not therefore falsifie the Scriptures. **1741** tr. *D'Argens' Chinese Lett.* v. 28 Funeral Orations had contributed very much to falsify History. **1831** BREWSTER *Newton* (1855) II. xx. 237 He..falsified the document by the substitution of a paragraph. *a* **1832** MACKINTOSH *Rise & Fall Struensee* Wks. 1846 II. 396 Accused..of having falsified the public accounts.

b. To give a false account of; to misrepresent.
1630 PRYNNE *Anti-Armin.* 118 Which falsifies the eternal truth. *a* **1641** BP. MOUNTAGU *Acts & Mon.* (1642) 152 Aemylius Probus mistook, or falsifies Thucydides. **1711** STEELE *Spect.* No. 252 ¶1 Good-breeding has made the Tongue falsify the Heart. **1847** EMERSON *Repr. Men, Napoleon* Wks. (Bohn) I. 379 He sat..in his lonely island, coldly falsifying facts and dates.
absol. **1779** JOHNSON 10 Oct. in *Boswell*, Lord Bathurst did not intentionally falsify. **1824** DIBDIN *Libr. Comp.* 510 Not that Johnson designedly falsified. **1868** BROWNING *Ring & Bk.* I. 217, I falsified and fabricated.

†**c.** To assert falsely. *Obs.*
1606 G. W[OODCOCKE] tr. *Ivstin* 24 b, How they might take away his life, either by treason to be falsified against him, or [etc.].

†**d.** To adulterate. Also of disease: To corrupt, vitiate. *Obs.*
1562 *Act 5 Eliz.* c. 11 §1 Divers..Persons..diminish, impair and falsify the Monies and Coins current within this Realm. **1634** W. TIRWHYT tr. *Balzac's Lett.* 385 Those who..falsifie Merchandizes. **1656** BEN ISRAEL *Vind. Judæorum* in *Phenix* (1708) II. 421 Verdigrease..all falsify'd with earth. **1658** A. FOX *Wurtz' Surg.* III. vi. 233 By diseases the joint water or radical humor is falsified.

e. To make (a balance or standard) untrue.
1611 BIBLE *Amos* viii. 5 Falsifying the balances by deceit. *a* **1848** R. W. HAMILTON *Rew. & Punishm.* viii. (1853) 404 We are not compelled to falsify our standards.

f. To alter or pervert from correct rule.
1589 PUTTENHAM *Eng. Poesie* II. (Arb.) 94 There can not be..a fowler fault, then to falsifie his accent to serue his cadence. **1841** D'ISRAELI *Amen. Lit.* (1867) 475 He [Spenser] falsified accentuation, to adapt it to his metre.

g. To make unsound.
1868 M. PATTISON *Academ. Org.* 6 An unhappy spirit..falsified the relation between the parties.

¶**h.** Used by Dryden in avowed imitation of It. *falsare*: (see quot.).
1697 DRYDEN *Virg. Æneid* IX. 1093 His ample shield Is falsify'd, and round with jav'lins fill'd. *Ibid., note*, I use the word falsify in this place to mean that the shield of Turnus was not of proof against the spears and javelins of the Trojans.

†**2. a.** To produce a counterfeit of; to counterfeit. **b.** To get up in imitation of something else. *Obs.*
a. 1601 HOLLAND *Pliny* II. 613 After that crystall was once found out, they deuised to sophisticat and falsifie other gems therewith. **1699** M. LISTER *Journ. Paris* 124 They stampt and falsified the best ancient Medals so well.
b. 1589 PUTTENHAM *Eng. Poesie* III. xxv. (Arb.) 310 The Lapidarie [counterfeits] pearles and pretious stones by glasse and other substances falsified, and sophisticate by arte.

3. To declare or prove to be false.
c **1449** PECOCK *Repr.* I. x. 50 To falsifie this present xij^e conclusioun. **1570–6** LAMBARDE *Peramb. Kent* (1826) 221 He shall have cause neither to falsifie the one opinion lightly nor [etc.]. **1805** T. JEFFERSON *Writ.* (1830) IV. 42 No man can falsify any material fact here stated. **1849** STOVEL *Canne's Necess.* Introd. 9 Relinquishing all claim to respect by falsifying their own affirmations. **1876** MOZLEY *Univ. Serm.* i. (1877) 23 The rights of conscience belong so much to the morality of society now, that they must falsify any moral creed opposed to them.

b. *esp.* in *Law* (see quots.). *to falsify a doom* (Sc.): = *to false a doom*; see FALSE *v.* 5.
1574 tr. *Littleton's Tenures* 33 a, It shall not lye in the mouthe of the tenaunte to falsifye or defete the recoverie which was againste his Lord. **1628** COKE *On Litt.* 104 b, To falsifie in legall understanding is to prove false, that is, to avoid or..to defeat. **1642** tr. *Perkins's Prof. Bk.* v. §382. 165 His wife shall falsifie this recovery in a writ of dower. **1817** W. SELWYN *Law Nisi Prius* (ed. 4) II. 945 The sentence was conclusive evidence to falsify the warranty. **1854** J. W. SMITH *Man. Equity* 210 To give liberty to..falsify the account.

c. To fail in fulfilling, or prevent the fulfilment of (a prediction, expectation, etc.).
1596 SHAKS. *1 Hen. IV*, I. ii. 235 By so much shall I falsifie mens hopes. *a* **1719** ADDISON *Evid. Christ.* viii. (1730) 66 Jews and Pagans united all their endeavours..to baffle and falsify the prediction. **1851** W. COLLINS *Rambles beyond Railw.* vii. (1852) 124 The prognostications of our Cornish friends were pleasantly falsified. **1884** *L'pool Daily Post* 10 July 5 To consider..whether we are contented to falsify his high regard for us.

†**4.** *intr.* To make a false representation or statement; to deal in falsehoods. *Obs.*
1629 tr. *Herodian* (1635) 112 Iulian was contemned by the Souldiery, for falsifying with them. **1646** SIR T. BROWNE *Pseud. Ep.* I. ii. 6 His wisdome will hardly permit him to falsifie with the Almighty. **1702** *Eng. Theophrast.* 338 The practice of falsifying with men will lead us on insensibly to a double-dealing with God himself. **1748** RICHARDSON *Clarissa* (1811) III. xxxiii. 197 Would you either falsify or prevaricate? **1777** SHERIDAN *Sch. Scand.* II. ii, To propagate a malicious truth wantonly is more despicable than to falsify from revenge.

†**5.** *trans.* To prove false to, fail to keep; to break, violate (one's faith, word, etc.). *Obs.*
1532 MORE *Confut. Tindale* Wks. 585/1, I shall..finde Tindal himself so good a felow, as to falcefy his own wordes here & beare a poore man company. **1590** GREENE *Never too Late* (1600) 111 Æneas..falsified his faith to Dido. **1670** MILTON *Hist. Eng.* v. Wks. (1851) 204 Falsifying that Oath, by night with all the Horse they had..stole to Exeter.

†**6.** *intr.* To prove faint; to fail, give way. *Obs.*
1668 PEPYS *Diary* 27 Aug., My heart beginning to falsify in this business.

†**7.** *Fencing.* To feign (a blow); to make (a blow) under cover of a feint. Also *absol. Obs.*
1595 SAVIOLO *Practice, Rapier & Dagger* i, If you perceiue..that he go about to falsifie vpon you..put your selfe in your ward. **1600** FAIRFAX *Tasso* VI. xlii. 102 Now strikes he out, and now he falsifieth. **1611** BEAUM. & FL. *King & No King* I. i, Tigranes falsified a blow at your Leg, which you..avoided. **1625** K. LONG tr. *Barclay's Argenis* II. x. 94 One of them making offer at his necke with a Halbert, and falsifying his blowe, hit him under the short ribbe. *a* **1680** BUTLER *Rem.* (1759) I. 219 As th' are wont to falsify a Blow.

Hence '**falsified** *ppl. a.*, '**falsifying** *vbl. sb.* and *ppl. a.*
1577 tr. *Bullinger's Decades* (1592) 978 They do defile and blemish the wordes of God which deck them with strange and falsified titles. **1603** KNOLLES *Hist. Turks* (1638) 292 Your falsified faith. **1648** MILTON *Tenure Kings* (1650) 2 With the falsifi'd name of Loyalty, to colour over base compliances. **1886** *Pall Mall G.* 1 July 6/1 The falsified prediction is a good omen.
1565 JEWEL *Def. Apol.* II. 178 Lies, Corruptions, and Falsifieinges. **1601** R. JOHNSON *Kingd. & Commw.* (1603) 78 Cloth, which by reason of exceeding falsifying and deernesse of ours, growth every day into more and more request. **1652** URQUHART *Jewel* Wks. (1834) 222 He shewed such excellent dexterity in warding the other's blows, slighting his falsifyings. **1680** BOYLE *Produc. Chem. Princ.* Pref. 14 Purifying it..from the falsifying alloy. *a* **1700** B. E. *Dict. Cant. Crew*, *Feinting* or *Falsifying*.

†**fal'siloquence.** *Obs. rare.* [f. L. *falsiloqu-us* (f. *falsus* false + *loquī* to speak) + -ENCE.] False speaking; deceitful speech.
1710 E. WARD *Vulg. Brit.* XI. 121 Adorn'd instead of Sense With Trappings of Falsiloquence. **1736** in BAILEY.

†'**falsimony.** *Obs.*^{−0} [ad. L. *falsimōni-a*, f. *falsus* FALSE.] 'Falsity, falseness' (Bailey 1736).

'**falsish** *a. rare.* [f. FALSE *a.* + -ISH.] Somewhat false.
1873 BROWNING *Red Cott. Nt.-cap* 1497 There exists A falsish false, for truth's inside the same, Truth that's only half true, falsish truth.

falsism ('fɔːlsɪz(ə)m, 'fɒlsɪz(ə)m). [f. FALSE *a.* + -ISM.]
1. a. 'An assertion or statement, the falsity of which is plainly apparent' (W.). **b.** A platitude that has not even the merit of being true.
The word owes its meaning to the antithesis with *truism*; hence the two-fold application.
1835 J. S. MILL *Diss. & Disc.* (1859) I. 109 This *dictum*..is, as Coleridge would say, a falsism. **1840** *Ibid.* 209 Books like Mr. Colton's 'Lacon'—centos of trite truisms and trite falsisms pinched into epigrams. **1847** LEWES *Hist. Philos.* (1853) 160 If so, it is a truism, if not, a falsism. **1855** —— *Goethe* II. VI. vii. 313 The ideas are no longer novel; they appear truisms or perhaps falsisms.

2. *nonce-use.* Falsity of representation, conceived as erected into a systematic principle of art.
1883 M. BLIND *Life Geo. Eliot* 68 Realism is thus the basis of all Art, and its antithesis is not Idealism but Falsism.

falsity ('fɔːlsɪtɪ, 'fɒlsɪtɪ). Forms: 4 **falste**, **falsite**, 5 **-etee**, 6–7 **-itie**, (7 **fauxitie**), 6– **falsity**. [a. OF. *falseté* (mod.F. *fausseté*), ad. L. *falsitās*, f. *falsus* FALSE: see -ITY.]

1. The quality or condition of being false. **a.** Contrariety or want of conformity to truth or fact. Also an instance of this.
1579 FULKE *Confut. Sanders* 577 Between veritie & falsitie there is no meane. **1655–60** STANLEY *Hist. Philos.* (1701) 27/2 He [Solon] absolutely forbad him to teach or act Tragedies considering their falsity unprofitable. **1767** WILKES *Corr.* (1805) III. 89 His lordship had not said a word to prove the falsity of any one sentence. **1879** GLADSTONE *Glean.* II. i. 3 He..denounced the falsity of the doctrine which was inculcated there.

b. Untruthfulness, deceitfulness, insincerity.
1603 I. C. in *Shaks. C. Praise* 57 Cressids falsitie. **1665** MANLEY *Grotius' Low C. Warres* 943 Accusations of ingratitude and falsity. **1879** FARRAR *St. Paul* (1883) 235 A Greece which had lost its genius and retained its falsity.

c. Spurious or counterfeit character.
1678 R. BARCLAY *Apol. Quakers* v. §16. 146 Socrates was informed by it..of the Falsity of the Heathen's Gods.

2. Something that is false. **a.** An untrue proposition, doctrine, or statement; an error or falsehood. Also in generalized sense, that which is untrue; false opinion or statement, error, falsehood.
1557 *N.T.* (Genev.) *Epist.* *iv, In lyes and falsitie ther is no suche consent and concorde. *a* **1661** FULLER *Worthies* III. 57 God forbid, that this Authors fauxities should make us undervalue this worthy King. **1776** PAINE *Com. Sense* (1791) 24 The most barefaced falsity ever imposed upon mankind. **1833** MARRYAT *P. Simple* (1863) 428 A preamble, composed of every falsity that could be devised.

b. A counterfeit, sham. *rare.*
1780 MAD. D'ARBLAY *Lett.* 22 Jan., This, as Miss Waldron said of her hair, is all a falsity.

†**3.** False or treacherous conduct; treachery, fraud. *Obs.*
c **1330** R. BRUNNE *Chron.* (1810) 247 Dilexit Sir Adam gilerie & falste. *c* **1430** *Pilgr. Lyf Manhode* II. cxxvi. (1869) 123 Flaterye j am cleped bi my name..eldere douhter to falsetee. **1581** LAMBARDE *Eiren.* IV. xxi. (1588) 625 Unlawfull taking of money for doing his office, or of such other falsitie.

‖**falso bordone** ('falso bor'done). *Mus.* [It. *falso* false + *bordone* BOURDON².] = FABURDEN.
1740 GRASSINEAU *Mus. Dict.* **1801** T. BUSBY *Dict. Mus.* sig. G4 *Falso bordone*, a term applied in the early days of descant to such counterpoint as had either a drone bass, or some part constantly moving in the same interval with it. **1876** [see *basso ostinato*]. **1961** *Listener* 5 Oct. 535/3 The solemn falsobordoni of Monteverdi's *Dixit Dominus*.

Falstaffian (fɒl'stæfɪən), *a.* [See -IAN.] Characteristic of or resembling Falstaff, a fat, humorous, jovial knight in Shaks. *Hen. IV*, *Hen. V*, and *Merry Wives*. Also, resembling the 'ragged regiment' recruited by Falstaff (*Hen. IV*, III. ii).
1808 R. K. PORTER *Trav. Sk. Russ. & Swed.* (1813) I. i. 12 Clothing is issued to them [the Danish soldiery] once in three years; and..you can easily imagine what a Falstaffian array they are in by the time their new wardrobe comes round. **1856** OLMSTED *Slave States* 411 Wrapped up to a Falstaffian rotundity in flannels and furs. **1880** *Harper's Mag.* LX. 676 He unwillingly tramped into Santa Fe at the head of his Falstaffian band.

†'**falsy**, *v. Obs.* = FALSE *v.* 4 a.
1626 L. OWEN *Spec. Jesuit.* (1629) 20 To equiuocate and falsie their oaths and faiths.

falt, obs. form of FAULT.

faltboat ('fæltbəʊt). Also in G. form **faltboot**. [partial tr. of G. *faltboot* collapsible boat, f. *falten* to fold + *boot* boat.] A folding boat (see FOLDING *ppl. a.* 2). Hence '**faltbooting** *vbl. sb.*
1926 *Blackw. Mag.* Feb. 241/1 Crossing the English Channel is one of many adventurous voyages in 'Falt-boots'. *Ibid.* 254/1 'Faltbooting'..is a fine weather employment. **1936** *Times Lit. Suppl.* 20 June 525/3 The still growing popularity of the *faltboat*, besides revolutionizing canoeing itself, has produced a small library of books on the sport.

falter, var. of FAULTER, *Obs.*, defaulter.

falter ('fɔːltə(r), 'fɒltə(r)), *v.*¹ Forms: 5 **faltir**, 6 (in Fisher **flalter**, **floghter**), **folter**, 6–9 **faulter**, (7 **foulter**), 7 **felter**, 4– **falter**. [Of obscure etymology.
The current view, which connects the word with *fault*, is untenable, on the ground that *falter* has always been written with the *l*, and is so pronounced in the dialects in which it occurs, whereas in *fault* the *l* is an etymologizing insertion, which rarely occurs in spelling before 16th c., and was not pronounced, even by educated speakers, till much later. (But it is not unlikely that association with *fault* may have coloured the recent use of the word.) It seems possible that sense 1, 'to stumble', may have been developed from the sense 'to be entangled' (FALTER *v.*²). On the other hand it is noteworthy that ME. *falde-n*, FOLD *v.* is used of the limbs and the tongue in the sense 'to give way, fail, falter'; perh. *falter* may be a frequentative of *fald-en*, formed irregularly through the influence of approximately synonymous vbs. like *balter*, *totter*, *welter*.]

1. Of a person or his steps; also of a horse: To stumble, stagger; to walk with an unsteady gait.
c **1340** *Gaw. & Gr. Knt.* 430 Nawþer faltered ne fel þe freke..Bot styþly he start forth vpon styf schonkes. *c* **1485** *Digby Myst.* (1882) III. 280 In feyntnes I falter. **1561** T. NORTON *Calvin's Inst.* II. vii. (1634) 159 Hee beginneth..to shake and folter. **1603** KNOLLES *Hist. Turks* (1621) 87 Which [mare] now suddenly faultring under him. **1639** T. DE GRAY *Compl. Horsem.* 30 If you doe perceive him to felter with any of his feet. **1781** COWPER *Truth* 537 Faltering, faint and slow. **1795** T. JEFFERSON *Writ.* (1859) IV. 119, I have laid up my Rosinante in his stall, before his unfitness for the road shall expose him faultering to the world. **1821** BYRON *Sard.* v. i, The dispirited troops..had seen you fall, and falter'd back. **1878** *Masque Poets* 35 Thou guidest steps that falter on alone.

b. Of the limbs: To give way, totter.
c **1386** CHAUCER *Man of Law's T.* 674 O messager, fulfild of dronkenesse, Strong is thy breth, thy lymes faltren ay. **1447** BOKENHAM *Seyntys* (Roxb.) 179 Hys leggys to faltryn gunne sodeynly. **1531** ELYOT *Gov.* I. xvii, Where the water hath come to his [the horse's] bely, his legges hath foltred. **1672** WISEMAN *Wounds* I. ix. 120 He felt his legs faulter. **1797** MRS. RADCLIFFE *Italian* i. (1826) 4 In descending the last steps..the foot of the elder lady faltered.

c. Of the tongue: To fail to articulate distinctly; to speak unsteadily (see 2).
a **1533** LD. BERNERS *Gold. Bk. M. Aurel.* xlviii. (1539) 93 a, His tonge faultred, and his handes shoke. *a* **1535** FISHER *Wks.* (1876) I. 356 Thy tongue flaltereth in thy mouth. **1671** R. BOHUN *Disc. Wind.* 148 Wee find the tongue more apt to falter.

2. To stumble in one's speech; to speak hesitatingly or incoherently; to stammer. Of the voice, speech, etc.: To come forth incoherently.

c **1440** *Promp. Parv.* 148 Faltryn yn þe tunge, *cespito, vel lingua cespitare.* **1530** PALSGR. 544/1, I falter in my speakyng, as one dothe that is dronken. *Je baboye.* **1565** GOLDING *Ovid's Met.* III. (1593) 63 She foltred in the mouth as often as she spake. **1602** MARSTON *Antonio's Rev.* IV. iii. Wks. 1856 I. 124 Her speach falters. **1672** MARVELL *Reh. Transp.* I. 114 He..faulters in this discourse. **1768** H. WALPOLE *Hist. Doubts* 92 He did not faulter, nor could be detected in his tale? **1791** MRS. RADCLIFFE *Rom. Forest* vi, The words of welcome faltered on his lips. **1804** J. GRAHAME *Sabbath* 687 His voice soon faltering stops. **1821** MRS. HEMANS *Dartmoor* 288 When holy strains..falter on its tongue. **1859** TENNYSON *Guinevere* 301 Even in the middle of his song He falter'd.

b. *trans.*; with quoted words as obj.

1842 TENNYSON *Gardener's D.* 230 She..made me most happy, faltering, 'I am thine'. **1884** POE *Eustace* 69 'Why would you have Ralph discharged?' she faltered.

c. *to falter forth* or *out*: to utter hesitatingly or with difficulty; to stammer forth. Also (*poet.*), To breathe out (the soul) by gasps.

1762 *Gentl. Mag.* 73, I faultered out my acknowledgements. **1813** BYRON *Corsair* I. i, While gasp by gasp he falters forth his soul. **1855** MACAULAY *Hist. Eng.* IV. 532 She..faltered out her commands that he would sit down. **1868** MILMAN *St. Paul's* 305 The Dean faltered out that he meant no harm.

3. To waver, lose steadfastness; to flinch, hesitate in action from lack of courage or resolution. Also of courage, hopes, resolve: To give way, flag.

1521 FISHER *Wks.* (1876) I. 313 That we floghter not in the catholike doctryne. *a* **1568** ASCHAM *Scholem.* (Arb.) 128 The hier they flie, the sooner they falter and faill. *a* **1677** BARROW *Serm.* Wks. 1716 I. 11 All other principles..will soon be shaken and faulter. **1697** DAMPIER *Voy.* (1729) I. 2 If any Man faultred in the Journey over Land he must expect to be shot to death. **1752** HUME *Ess. & Treat.* (1777) II. 452 It made them faulter and hesitate. **1802** MAR. EDGEWORTH *Moral T.* I. xii, His hopes..began to falter. **1818** JAS. MILL *Brit. India* II. IV. v. 168 A part of the army faultered considerably. **1859** TENNYSON *Enid* 1361 Nor let her true hand falter, nor blue eye Moisten, till she had lighted on his wound. *a* **1864** I. TAYLOR (W.), Here..the power of distinct conception of space and distance falters. **1872** MISS BRADDON *To Bitter End* I. xvii. 291 The girl's spirits did not falter. **1874** GREEN *Short Hist.* ii. §4. 77 The citizens.. faltered as William..gave Southwark to the flames.

†**b.** To fail in strength, collapse. *Obs.*

1799 *Med. Jrnl.* I. 18 Until the patient in a close room faulters and sinks. [**1886** ELWORTHY *W. Somerset Gloss.*, *Faltery*, to show signs of old age; to break up in constitution.]

c. *transf.* Of inanimate things: To move as if irresolutely or hesitatingly; to tremble, quiver. Also of a breeze: To flag.

The later examples are all from U.S. writers; to an English reader the use in the quot. from Irving sounds incorrect, that in the two others justifiable though unusual.

1745 P. THOMAS *Jrnl. Anson's Voy.* 152 Trade Wind blows..within 60 or 70 Leagues of the Mexican Shore, where they say it sometimes falters, but oftner reaches to within 30 Leagues. **1810** [see FALTERING *ppl. a.*]. **1832** W. IRVING *Alhambra* II. 240 He..began to nod, and his staff to falter in his hand. **1848** LOWELL *Indian Summer Reverie* i, When falling leaves falter through motionless air. **1874** MOTLEY *Barneveld* II. xvii. 227 The ancient Rhine as it falters languidly to the sea.

d. *dial.* Of a crop: To fail.

1863 *Dorset Gloss.* s.v., 'I be a-feärd the teäties will falter.'

Hence **'faltered** *ppl. a.*, **'faltering** *vbl. sb.*

1706 EARL BELHAVEN *Sp. in Sc. Parlt.* 5 Are our Eyes so Blinded? Are our Ears so Deafned? Are our Tongues so Faltered? *a* **1800** T. BELLAMY *Beggar Boy* (1801) III. 42 In a voice, faltered by surprize..he eagerly demanded their business. **1614** MARKHAM *Cheap Husb.* (1623) 65 The signes are a foltering in his fore legges. **1621** LADY M. WROTH *Urania* 172 Some thing made those faulterings in my talke. **1722** SEWEL *Hist. Quakers* (1795) I. IV. 290 He..hath long watched for my faultering. **1823** LAMB *Elia* Ser. I. xi. (1865) 89 He has no falterings of self-suspicion. **1871** *Standard* 23 Jan., There were occasional natural falterings.

†**'falter,** *v.*² *Obs. rare.* [perh. var. of FELTER *v.*, to be felted, matted, f. OF. *feltre, faultre* felt. But cf. OIcel. *faltra-sk* 'to be cumbered, *faltra-sk við e- t.* to be puzzled about a thing' (Vigf.).] *intr.* To become entangled, catch.

c **1450** *St. Cuthbert* (Surtees) 6038 Þe whele faltird in his clathes þat ware lange and syde.

falter ('fɔːltə(r)), *v.*³ Also 7 **faulter, foulter,** 9 *dial.* **faughter, fauther.** [? a. OF. **faltrer* (recorded form *fautrer*) to strike, beat.] *trans.* To thrash (corn) a second time in order to cleanse it and get rid of the awn or beard, etc.; hence, to cleanse.

1601 HOLLAND *Pliny* XVIII. x, They haue much ado..to thresh it cleane and falter it from the huls and eiles. **1649** BLITHE *Eng. Improv. Impr.* (1652) 182 Then foulter and beat the husk again. **1681** HOUGHTON *Lett. Husbandry* 64 In choosing Barly..the Malster looks that it be..clean faltered from haines. **1788** in MARSHALL *E. Yorksh. Gloss.* **1876** in ROBINSON *Whitby Gloss.*

Hence **'faltering** *vbl. sb.* (in *Comb.*).

1847-78 HALLIWELL, *Faltering-irons.* **1869** PEACOCK *Lonsdale Gloss.*, *Faughtering-iron*, an iron used to knock off the beards of barley when thrashed.

falter ('fɔːltə(r), 'fɒltə(r)), *sb.* [f. FALTER *v.*¹] A faltering or quavering, unsteadiness.

1834 C'TESS MORLEY *Dacre* I. xi. 233 With a slight falter in her voice. **1880** MRS. FORRESTER *Roy & V.* I. 74 She fancied she heard a falter in Viola's tones.

b. A faltering or quavering sound.

c **1842** LOWELL *Rhœcus* Poems (1844) 121 Far away..The falter of an idle shepherd's pipe.

falter, var. of FELTER.

faltering ('fɔːltərɪŋ, 'fɒltərɪŋ), *ppl. a.* [f. FALTER *v.*¹ + -ING².]

1. That falters; in senses of the vb.: **a.** of a person, the limbs, etc.

1549 COVERDALE *Erasm. Par. Heb.* xii. 12 Your weake and foltryng knees. **1667** MILTON *P.L.* IX. 846 Oft his [Adam's] heart..Misgave him; hee the faultring measure felt. **1744** AKENSIDE *Pleas. Imag.* III. 210 With faultering feet. **1820** KEATS *St. Agnes* xxii, Her faltering hand upon the balustrade. **1884** J. COLBORNE *Hicks Pasha* 178 The poor fellow then staggered on with faltering step.

b. of the voice, tongue, accent. Also of a person speaking, a breeze.

1590 SPENSER *F.Q.* III. xi. 12 Swelling throbs empeach His foltering tongue. **1642** MILTON *Apol. Smect.* (1851) 253 Speaking deeds against faltering words. **1741** MIDDLETON *Cicero* I. iv. 318 In broken, faultering accents. **1773** GOLDSM. *Stoops to Conq.* v, The faultering gentleman, with looks on the ground. **1810** SCOTT *Lady of L.* II xiv, My dull ears Catch no faltering breeze. **1878** *Masque Poets* 80 The small sweet voices of the night Begin in faltering music to awake.

2. quasi-*adv.* = FALTERINGLY.

a **1741** CHALKLEY *Wks.* (1749) 191 He spoke very low and faultering.

'falteringly, *adv.* [f. prec. + -LY².] In a faltering manner, hesitatingly.

1611 COTGR., *Brutivement*, brutishly, rudely..also faulteringly. **1768** *Woman of Honor* III. 222 He had.. faulteringly acquainted me, that the keys of his closet..were under his bed's-head. **1797** MRS. RADCLIFFE *Italian* xxvi, 'May not a witness summon persons before the tribunal..' continued Vivaldi, falteringly. **1852** HAWTHORNE *Blithedale Rom.* ix. (1885) 87 She ran falteringly.

faltour, var. of FAULTER, *Obs.*, defaulter.

falu, obs. f. of FALLOW.

falucca, faluke, obs. ff. of FELUCCA.

‖**falun** (falœ̃). *Geol.* Usually in *pl.* [F.] (See quot. 1865.)

1833 LYELL *Princ. Geol.* III. 203 The *faluns* and associated strata are of slight thickness. **1865** PAGE *Geol. Terms* (ed. 2), *Faluns*, a French provincial term for the shelly Tertiary..strata of Touraine and the Loire.

Falunian (fə'l(j)uːnɪən), *a. Geol.* [f. prec. + -IAN.] The distinctive epithet of the group of strata represented by the faluns; upper Miocene.

1851 RICHARDSON *Geol.* (1855) 321 The falunian, subapennine, and diluvial stages of both continents. **1863** LYELL *Antiq. Man* xxii. 430 The mollusca of the Falunian or Upper Miocene strata of Europe.

falutin, *sb.* and *a.* = HIGHFALUTIN *sb.* and *a.*

1921 T. R. GLOVER *Pilgrim* viii. 118 He does not use of the Church the splendid language of Paul, still less the falutin of some second century Christians. **1928** *Observer* 12 Feb. 17/5 The Swarajists..would have..sought to flout Parliament with falutin phrases.

‖**falx** (fælks). Pl. **falces.** [L. *falx* scythe or sickle.] **1.** *Anat.* A process of the *dura mater*, sometimes called *falx cerebri. falx cerebelli* (see quot. 1860).

1706 PHILLIPS (ed. Kersey), *Falx*..one of the Processes.. of the..Dura Mater. **1741** A. MONRO *Anat. Bones* (ed. 3) 83 In it a little Process of the *Falx* is lodged. **1800** *Phil. Trans.* XC. 435 There is a bony falx of some breadth. **1855** HOLDEN *Human Osteol.* (1878) 119 The 'crista galli', which gives attachment to the falx cerebri. **1860** MAYNE *Expos. Lex.*, *Falx Cerebelli*..term for a triangular portion of the *dura mater*..separating the two lobes of the cerebellum. **1874** JONES & SIEV. *Pathol. Anat.* 231 The falx is occasionally found cribrated.

†**2.** *Zool. Obs.* Each of the paired cheliceræ of spiders; sometimes used to mean only the basal section of a chelicera (see quot. 1889) and in this sense = PATURON.

1848 J. BLACKWALL in *Trans. Linn. Soc.* (1852) XXI. 37 The instruments employed by the *Araneidea* to seize and destroy their prey are improperly denominated mandibles ..I propose..to name them falces. **1866** E. F. STAVELEY *Brit. Spiders* ii. 12 Below the eyes and above the mouth is a pair of jaw-like organs, known as the falces. **1885** H. O. FORBES *Nat. Wand. East. Archipelago* III. vi. 216 With the rapidest motion..it [*sc.* a spider] flashed its falces into my flesh. **1889** H. C. MCCOOK *Amer. Spiders* I. i. 22 Each mandible is composed of two parts, the base or falx and the fang... The falx is covered with hair, especially near the base, and at the apex is formed into a toothed groove or sheath into which the fang is folded down when at rest. **1904** W. H. HUDSON *Green Mansions* xx. 288 He [*sc.* a spider] might come stealthily back at night to plunge his long, crooked falces into my throat.

falx, var. of FAULX, *Obs.*

falye, *Sc.* **falȝe,** obs. f. of FAIL.

fam (fæm), *sb. slang.* [Short for FAMBLE *sb.*] = FAMBLE in various senses. Also in *Comb.* as **fam-grasp** *v.*, *intr.* and *trans.*, to shake hands, make up a difference (with); **fam-snatcher.**

1692-1732 COLES, *Fam grasp*, agree with. *a* **1700** B. E. *Dict. Cant. Crew*, *Famgrasp*, to agree. **1789** G. PARKER *Life's Painter* 180 Fam, a gold ring. **1812** J. H. VAUX *Flash Dict.*, *Fam*, the hand. **1819** MOORE *Tom Crib's Mem.* 28 Delicate fams which have merely Been handling the sceptre. **1828** P. EGAN *Finish to Life in London* xiv. (1871) 309 To Jerry Hawthorn, Esq., I resign my fam-snatchers—i.e. my gloves.

fam (fæm), *v.* [f. prec. sb.] *trans.* To feel or handle.

1812 in J. H. VAUX *Flash Dict.*

faman, obs. f. of FOEMAN.

famatinite (fə'mætɪnaɪt). *Min.* [Named by Stelzner 1873 from the *Famatina* mountains in the Argentine Republic: see -ITE.] An antimonial variety of enargite.

1875 DANA *Min.* App. ii. 20 Famatinite, Stelzner. **1879** WATTS *Dict. Chem.* VIII. 3rd Suppl. I. 733.

†**fa'mation.** *Obs.* [? Aphetic f. DEFAMATION, DIFFAMATION; but cf. FAME *v.*¹ 4.] Defamation.

c **1325** *E.E. Allit. P.* B. 188 Fals famacions & fayned lawez. *c* **1325** *Rembrun* xxiii, Ich wile þat Y ben hanged & drawe Boute Y defende me wiþ þe lawe Of þis famacioun.

famble ('fæmb(ə)l), *sb. slang.* [perh. f. FAMBLE *v.* in its (probable) original sense 'to grope, fumble'.]

1. A hand.

1567 HARMAN *Caveat* 87 He tooke his Iockam in his famble. **1622** FLETCHER *Beggar's Bush* II. i, Last we clap our fambles. **1673** R. HEAD *Canting Acad.* 19 White thy fambles. **1815** SCOTT *Guy M.* xxviii, If I had not helped you with these very fambles (holding up her hands).

†**2.** A ring. *Obs.*

1688 SHADWELL *Sqr. Alsatia* II, Look on my finger.. here's a Famble. **1691** *Lond. Gaz.* No. 2715/4 A small Famble, made up of two little Diamonds, and 4 or 5 Rubies.

†**3.** = FAMBLER b. *Obs.*

1673 R. HEAD *Canting Acad.* 192 The thirteenth a Famble, false Rings for to sell.

†**'famble,** *v. Obs.* Also 4 **famelen.** [Of obscure origin; the word may originally have had the sense 'to grope, FUMBLE'; cf. Sw. *famla*, Da. *famle* to grope, metathetic form of ON. *falma* (Icel. *fálma*), cogn. with OE. *folm* hand.]

1. *intr.* To speak imperfectly; to stammer, stutter.

14.. in *Pol. Rel. & L. Poems* (1866) 224 His tonge shal stameren, oþer famelen. **1611** COTGR., *Beguayer*, to famble, fumble, maffle in the mouth. **1706** PHILLIPS (ed. Kersey), *Famble*, to Faulter or Stammer in Speech. **1721-1800** in BAILEY. **1886** *S.W. Linc. Gloss.*, He fambles so in his talk.

2. (See quot.)

1877 PEACOCK *N.W. Linc. Gloss.*, *Fambling*, eating without an appetite.

Hence **'fambling** *vbl. sb.*, **'fambling** *ppl. a.*

1611 COTGR., *Begayement*, a fambling or maffling in the mouth. *Ibid.*, *Begué*..fambling, fumbling, maffling in the mouth. *a* **1693** URQUHART *Rabelais* III. xxvi. 216.

†**'famble-,cheat.** *slang. Obs.* Also **fambling cheat.** (See quots.)

1567 HARMAN *Caveat* 82 A fambling chete, a rynge on thy hand. **1610** ROWLANDS *Martin Mark-all* E ij b, Fambling cheates, Rings. **1692-1732** COLES, *Famble Cheats*, rings or gloves. Cant. **1721-1800** in BAILEY.

'famble-,crop. *dial.* [Cf. FAMBLE *v.* 2.]

a **1825** FORBY *Voc. E. Anglia*, *Famble-crop*, the first stomach in ruminating animals.

†**'fambler.** *Obs.* [f. FAMBLE *sb.* + -ER.] **a.** A glove. **b.** (see quot. 1725).

1610 ROWLANDS *Martin Mark-all* E ij b, Famblers, a paire of Gloues. **1725** *New Cant. Dict.*, *Famblers*..Villains that go up and down selling counterfeit Rings, &c.

fame (feɪm), *sb.*¹ Also 3 **fam,** 6 **fayme.** [a. F. *fame*, ad. L. *fāma* report, fame, = Gr. *φήμη* (Dor. *φᾱμᾱ́*) f. root *fā-*, *φᾱ-* (OAryan **bhā-*) in L. *fārī*, Gr. *φάναι* to speak.]

1. a. That which people say or tell; public report, common talk; a particular instance of this, a report, rumour. Now *rare.*

c **1300** *Cursor M.* 8750 (Gött.) Of þis dome sua spredd þe fam, þat all spac of þis king salamon. **1387** TREVISA *Higden* (Rolls) I. 71 Me schal trowe olde fame, þat is nouȝt wipseide. **1388** WYCLIF *1 Sam.* ii. 24 It is not good fame which Y here. **1482** *Monk of Evesham* (Arb.) 47 Not verely certifide of so soroful a fame and happe. **1513** MORE in Grafton *Chron.* II. 758 As the fame runneth. *a* **1626** BACON *Ess.*, *Fame* (Arb.) 580 Mucianus undid Vitellius by a Fame, that he scattered. **1679** *Hatton Corr.* (1878) 199, I heare this only from publicke fame. **1730-6** BAILEY (folio) s.v., Common Fame's seldom to blame. **1747** FRANKLIN *Ess.* Wks. 1840 III. 20 The very fame of our strength..would be a means of discouraging our enemies. **1818** JAS. MILL *Brit. India* III. VI. i. 38 *note*, The King, whose zeal for Mr. Hastings was the object of common fame. **1855** MACAULAY *Hist. Eng.* III. 163 At the fame of his approach, the colonists..retreated northward.

b. (quasi-) personified.

1393 GOWER *Conf.* I. 350 Fame with her swifte winges Aboute fligh and bare tidinges. *a* **1547** SURREY *Æneid* IV. (1557) Ej/2 A mischefe Fame.. That mouing growes, and flitting gathers force. **1548** HALL *Chron.* 11 These monasticall persones..toke on them to..regester in the boke of fame, noble actes. **1703** MAUNDRELL *Journ. Jerus.* (1721) 137 On each side of the Eagle is describ'd a Fame likewise upon the Wing. **1828** SCOTT *F.M. Perth* xvi, I would thou couldst clear him of other charges, with which fame hath loaded him.

†**c.** *without fame*: ? = 'without fable', certainly. *Obs.*

c **1430** *Hymns Virg.* 116 Alle things sche trowith without fame That goddis lawe techith truthe to be. *c* **1450** *Guy Warw.* (C.) 108 Segwarde was..A trewe man, wythowten fame.

2. a. The character attributed to a person or thing by report or generally entertained; reputation. Usually in good sense.

a **1225** *Ancr. R.* 222 Heo schal..þenchen þe lesse of God and leosen hire fame. **1297** R. GLOUC. (1724) 367 Þer nas prince in þe al worlde of so noble fame. **1375** BARBOUR *Bruce* IX. 574 A knycht..Curtass [and] fair and of gude fame. **1387** TREVISA *Higden* (Rolls) VI. 281 His virtues passed his fame. **1456** *Pol. Poems* (Rolls) II. 183 Allas! why dede wee these offence, Ffully to shende the olde Englisshe fames. **1548** HALL *Chron.* 169 This is the most spot that was..ever moste to be caste in the Dukes fame. **1662** PETTY *Taxes* 58 Such whose fames are yet entire. **1708** J. CHAMBERLAYNE *St. Gt. Brit.* II. II. iii. (1743) 366 They ought to..enquire into her former and present fame. **1800–24** CAMPBELL *Poems, Adelgitha* i, A valiant champion..slew the slanderer of her fame. **1848** M. ARNOLD *Bacchanalia* Poems 1877 II. 136 Many spent fames and fallen nights.

b. *house of ill fame*: see HOUSE.

3. a. The condition of being much talked about. Chiefly in good sense: Reputation derived from great achievements; celebrity, honour, renown.

c **1290** *S. Eng. Leg.* 27/26 On of heom: þat was of grete fame. *a* **1340** HAMPOLE *Psalter* viii. 1 þe coy and þe fame of þi name ihesu. *c* **1450** *St. Cuthbert* (Surtees) 19 A man of mykil fame. **1553** EDEN *Treat. Newe Ind.* (Arb.) 5 The fame of Achilles. **1634** MASSINGER *Very Woman* v. iv, Tho' the desire of fame be the last weakness Wise men put off. **1711** POPE *Temp. Fame* 505 Fame...that second life in others' breath. **1816** BYRON *Ch. Har.* III. cxii, Fame is the thirst of youth. **1848** MACAULAY *Hist. Eng.* I. 295 Bands which had long sustained..the fame of English valour.

†**b.** With adj. in pejorative sense. *Obs. rare.*

a **1300** *Cursor M.* 2476 (Cott.) þe land of sodome..was in an iuel fame. **1651** *Life Father Sarpi* (1676) 42 This Father himself..was also in a sinister fame.

†**c.** *concr.* One who constitutes the fame of a place; its 'glory'. *Obs. rare.*

c **1590** MARLOWE *Faust.* Wks. (Rtldg.) 122/2 The learned Faustus, fame of Wittenberg.

†**4.** Evil repute, infamy. *Obs.*

c **1325** *Poem Times Edw. II*, 111 in *Pol. Songs* (Camden) 328 Thise gode men fallen oft in fame. *c* **1375** *Cato Major* II. xxiii. in *Anglia* VII, þei ben two wikked vices And bringe men ofte in fame. *c* **1425** *Seven Sag.* (P.) 3413 The fame that on me hys broght. **1592** DANIELL *Compl. Rosamond* (1717) 37 Fame finds never Tomb t'inclose it in.

5. *Comb.*: **a.** objective, as *fame-catcher*, *-seeker*, *-spreader* sbs.; *fame-achieving*, *-destroying*, *-getting*, *-giving*, *-thirsting*, *-thirsty*, *-worthy* adjs.; **b.** instrumental, as *fame-blazed*, *-crowned*, *-ennobled*, *-favoured*, *-sung* adjs.; **c. fame-flower** (see quot. 1891).

1601 CHESTER *Love's Mart.* cx. (1878) 71 *Fame-atchieving Arthur. *c* **1611** CHAPMAN *Iliad* XVI. 57 Take thou my *fame-blaz'd arms. **1682** HICKERINGILL *Black Non-Conformist* Wks. (1716) II. 3 Let *Fame-catchers mind their stops. **1811** MARIANA STARKE *Beauties C.M. Maggi* 36 Dear, classic soil, whence *fame-crown'd Tasso sprang. **1899** R. ST. BARBE *In Mod. Spain* 34 The fiddler with his *fame-destroying *mañana* theme. **1777** POTTER *Æschylus' Furies* (1779) II. 294 To grace their *fame-ennobled arms with victory. **1893** E. SULLIVAN tr. *Dante's Comedy* II. 4 Rescue me from her, *fame-favoured bard. **1879** T. MEEHAN *Native Flowers & Ferns U.S.* II. 55 Terete talinum... Thus Rafinesque proposed to call it *Phemeranthes* or '*Fame-flower'. **1891** *Cent. Dict.* s.v. *Talinum.* *T(alinum) teretifolium*, a native of the United States from Pennsylvania to Colorado and southward, a low tuberous-rooted perennial, growing on rocks and exceptional in its cylindrical leaves, has been called *fame-flower* from the transitoriness of its elegant purple petals. **1941** R. S. WALKER *Lookout* 47 It appears on the sandstones at Rock City..and travels all the way to the southern extremity... This is fame-flower. **1820** SHELLEY *Let.* 20 Apr. (1964) II. 185 Atoms of the *fame-getting..whirlwind. **1756** CAMBRIDGE *Fakeer* 51 In retirement he sigh'd for the *fame-giving chair. **1886** W. GRAHAM *Social Problem* 20 Men, not self-seekers, nor *fame-seekers. **1552** HULOET, *Fame spreader, *famiger*. **1649** G. DANIEL *Trinarch., Hen. V*, ccxlviii, Let not that Day, *fame-sung, fill up the mouth of Honour. **1598** SYLVESTER *Du Bartas* II. ii. II. Babylon 486 *Fame-thirsting wits that toyl..to trick their gracious stile. **1605** *Play Stucley* in Simpson *Sch. Shaks.* (1878) 219 Portingales *fame-thirsty king. **1610** HEALEY *St. Aug. Citie of God* 655 Athens..was more famous then *fame-worthy. **1855** SINGLETON *Virgil* I. 146 Fame-worthy shepherd from Amphrysus.

†**fame**, *sb.*² *Obs. rare.* In 6 fayme. [ad. F. *faim*:—L. *fam-em*, *fames* hunger.] Want of food, hunger.

a **1533** LD. BERNERS *Huon* cxlviii. 560, I haue bene in yᵉ presone to bere meet to yᵉ..presoners, who cryeth out for fayme.

fame (feɪm), *v.* Now *rare.* [a. OF. *fame-r*, f. *fame* FAME *sb.*¹; cf. med.L. *fāmāre.*]

†**1.** *trans.* To tell or spread abroad, report. *Obs.*

1303 R. BRUNNE *Handl. Synne* 3654 3yf he þat cunseyl fyrþer fame. **1483** *Cath. Angl.* 122 To Fame, *famare.* **1555** ABP. PARKER *Ps.* xx, His prayse to fame. **1671** tr. *Palafox's Conq. China* i. 7 It is famed, that they were both Generals in the Emperour of China's Armies. **1681** W. ROBERTSON *Phraseol. Gen.* (1693) 575 It was famed and reported frequently to him.

2. To report (a person or thing) *as*, *for*, *to be* (so and so), also *to do* (so and so). Chiefly in *passive*, to be currently reported or reputed.

c **1325** *E.E. Allit. P.* B. 275 He watz famed for fre þat fe3t loued best. *c* **1384** CHAUCER *H. Fame* III. 690 Ye wolde, Ben famed good, and nothyng nolde Deserue why. *a* **1400–50** *Alexander* 2387 Alexander is..famyd For ane of þe curtast kyng þat euir croune werid. **1550** BALE *Apol.* 68 b, Samuel shulde be famed abroad to haue bene promysed and borne by myracle. **1593** SHAKS. *3 Hen. VI*, IV. iv. 26 Your Grace hath still beene fam'd for vertuous. **1615** G. SANDYS *Trav.* 175 This is famed to be the houshold Monument of certaine of the Kings of Iuda. **1638** FORD *Lady's Trial* I. iii, One however maskt In colourable privacie, is fam'd The Lord Adurnse's pensioner, at least. **1646** BUCK *Rich. III*, III. 82 That Richard..should fame king Edward the fourth a bastard. **1671** MILTON *Samson* 1094 Thou art famed To have wrought..wonders with an ass's jaw! **1820** KEATS *Ode to Nightingale* viii, The fancy cannot cheat so well As she is fam'd to do. **1881** DUFFIELD *Don Quix.* III. xxiii. 141 She was..not so beautiful as she was famed.

3. To make famous: **a.** To spread abroad the fame of, render famous by talk; to talk of.

1388 WYCLIF *Matt.* ix. 31 But thei..diffameden [*v.r.* famyden] hym thorou al that lond. *c* **1400** *Cato's Morals* 42 in *Cursor M.* App. iv. 1669þat þou be nane of þese þat men famis in fable. **1606** SHAKS. *Tr. & Cr.* II. iii. 254 Be..thy parts of nature Thrice fam'd beyond, beyond all erudition. **1616** B. JONSON *Epigr.* I. xliii, Her foes enough would fame thee in their hate. **1635** A. STAFFORD *Fem. Glory* (1869) 137 When we desire to fame some other maid. **1814** BYRON *Corsair* I. ii, His name on every shore Is famed and feared.

†**b.** To render famous by some quality, deed, etc. Said also of the quality or deed. *Obs.*

a **1552** LELAND *Collect.* (1725) I. II. 549 Syr Knight, ye be cum hither to fame your Helmet. **1592** GREENE *Poems* 31 The..cedars trees, Whose stately bulks do fame th' Arabian groues. **1613** W. BROWNE *Brit. Past.* II. iv, Of holy Ursula (that fam'd her age). *c* **1665** MRS. HUTCHINSON *Mem. Col. Hutchinson* 3 In that magnanimity and virtue, which hath famed this island.

4. To spread an ill report of (a person); to defame. [Perh. short for DEFAME, DIFFAME: but cf. FAME *sb.*¹ 4.]

1393 LANGL. *P. Pl.* C. IV. 232 þow hast famede me foule by-fore þe kynge here. *c* **1430** *Syr Tryam.* 21 False and fekylle was that wyght, That lady for to fame. ? *c* **1475** *Sqr. lowe Degre* 392 Yf it may be founde in thee, That thou them fame for enmyte.

†**5.** *nonce-use.* *to fame it*: to become famous.

a **1625** FLETCHER *Hum. Lieutenant* II. ii, Do you call this fame? I have famed it; I have got immortal fame, but I'll no more on't.

†**fame**, *v.*² *Obs. rare.* [f. L. *fam-es* hunger. Cf. OF. *afamer.*] *trans.* To famish, starve. Hence '**famyt** *ppl. a.*

c **1330** R. BRUNNE *Chron.* (1810) 122 Steuen wille vs traueile, & famen vs to dede. *a* **1400** *Cov. Myst.* (1841) 105 Thyn ffamyt folke with thi ffode to fede.

fame, obs. f. of FOAM.

famed ('feɪmd), *ppl. a.* [f. FAME *v.*¹ + -ED¹.]

1. That is much talked about, known by report; †alleged by report; rumoured.

a **1533** LD. BERNERS *Gold. Bk. M. Aurel.* xiii. (1553) B v/1 There haue been diuers sonnes of Rome..famed throughout the worlde. **1701** ROWE *Amb. Step-Moth.* II. i, The fam'd Vertue of our Ancestors. **1741** MIDDLETON *Cicero* II. VIII. 131 Complaining so heavily of..the famed acts of his [Cicero's] Son in law.

2. Celebrated, renowned, famous. Now *arch.* exc. as predicate (const. *for*).

1593 SHAKS. *3 Hen. VI*, II. i. 156 Were he as famous and as bold in Warre As he is fam'd for Mildnesse, Peace, and Prayer. **1676** D'URFEY *Mad. Fickle* III. i, This Scull was..brought thither by a fam'd Antiquary. **1710** STEELE *Tatler* No. 228 ¶2 A Man so famed for Astrological Observations. **1748** WASHINGTON *Jrnl.* 18 Mar., We..call'd to see yᵉ fam'd Warm Springs. **1812** BYRON *Ch. Har.* II. xlvi, In famed Attica such lovely dales Are rarely seen. **1837** HAWTHORNE *Amer. Note-Bks.* 8 July (1883) 52 A corpulent, jolly fellow, famed for humour. **1881** W. ALLINGHAM in *Macm. Mag.* XLIV. 228 He grew Famedest monk of all the monastery.

b. with prefixed adv.

1796 BURKE *Regic. Peace* iv. Wks. IX. 30 The ever-famed 'last week of October'. **1828** SCOTT *F.M. Perth* x, The descendant of the far-famed James of Douglas. **1870** MORRIS *Earthly Par.* III. IV. 89 He..Lies quiet and well famed.

fameful ('feɪmfʊl). [f. FAME *sb.* + -FUL.] Full of fame, famous, renowned.

1591 SYLVESTER *Du Bartas* I. iii. 377 Whose foaming stream strives proudly to compare..with Fame-full'st Floods that are. *a* **1606** J. DAVIES *Bien Venu* 140 Occasion such, As now rich Opportunity doth giue To make you Fame-full.

famelen, var. of FAMBLE. *Obs.*

fameless ('feɪmlɪs), *a.* [f. as prec. + -LESS.] Without fame or renown; undistinguished.

1598 SYLVESTER *Du Bartas* II. Ded. to A. Bacon 6 My fame-lesse Name doom'd to oblivion. **1646** G. DANIEL *Poems* Wks. 1878 I. 47 When I, vnto the fameles Devia, now Vtter my song. **1796** SOUTHEY *Joan of Arc* x. 304 Nor few, nor fameless, were the English Chiefs. **1848** *Tait's Mag.* XV. 105 Earth's unknown heroes..sink to a fameless grave.

Hence '**famelessly** *adv.*

1847 in CRAIG.

†**fa'melic**, *a. Obs.* [ad. L. *famēlic-us* hungry, f. *fames* hunger. Cf. F. *famélique.*] Pertaining to hunger; in quots.: Exciting hunger, appetizing.

1614 B. JONSON *Barth. Fair* III. i, It were a sin of obstinacy ..to..resist the good titillation of the famelic sense, which is the smell. **1651–3** JER. TAYLOR *Serm. for Year* (1678) 112 The famelick smells of Meat.

†**fa,meli'cose**, *a. Obs. rare.* [ad. L. *famēlicōs-us*, f. *fames*: see prec.]

1730–6 BAILEY (folio), *Famelicose*, often or very hungry. **1775** in ASH.

famelist, var. of FAMILIST.

famell, obs. f. FEMALE.

famen, Sc. var. of FOEMEN.

Famennian (fə'mɛnɪən), *a. Geol.* Also **Fammenian**, †**Famennien.** [ad. F. *Famennien* (J. Gosselet 1879, in *Ann. Soc. géol. du Nord* VI. 396), f. *Famenne*, name of a district of western Belgium.] Name of the upper of the two stages constituting the Upper Devonian in Europe; of or pertaining to this stage or the geological period during which it was deposited. Also *absol.*

1882 [see FRASNIAN *a.*]. **1888** J. PRESTWICH *Geol.* II. 581 Famennian system. **1893** A. GEIKIE *Text-bk. Geol.* (ed. 3) 787 In Brittany also, Devonian strata are found, including representatives of the Famennian groups with Cypridinas and Goniatites. **1895** J. D. DANA *Man. Geol.* (ed. 4) 627 In the Eifel, the three divisions, the Rhénan, Eifelian and Famennian are well developed. **1909** H. B. C. SOLLAS tr. *Suess's Face of Earth* IV. 61 Five species of Avicula (Leptodesma) which the Chemung stage possesses in common with the Famennian of Belgium. **1931** GREGORY & BARRETT *Gen. Stratigr.* vi. 96 In Spain and Portugal the Devonian is widely developed and includes a full succession from Siegenian to Famennian. **1963** D. W. & E. E. HUMPHRIES tr. *Termier's Erosion & Sedimentation* x. 208 At Ben-Zireg near Colomb-Béchar..banks of Devonian rocks are enclosed in the Visean... They form a *Wildflysch*, resting on Fammenian lime-stones.

†'**famer.** *Obs.* [f. FAME *v.* + -ER.] One who brands with infamy.

1646 W. SHEPHEARD (*title*), The Famers Famd.

†'**famicide.** *Obs.*⁻⁰ [f. L. *fām-a* FAME *sb.* + -CIDE.] A destroyer of one's reputation, slanderer.

1656–81 in BLOUNT *Glossogr.* **1721–1800** in BAILEY.

†**fa'migerate**, *v. Obs.*⁻⁰ [f. ppl. stem of L. *fāmiger-āre*, f. *fāma* FAME *sb.* + *ger-ĕre* to carry.] *trans.* To report abroad. Also †**famige'ration** *Obs.* **fa'migerous** *a. Obs.*

1623–6 COCKERAM, *Famigerate.* **1692–1732** COLES, *Famigeration*, a divulging, reporting abroad. **1730–6** BAILEY (folio), *Famigerous*, carrying news, tales, &c.

'**familary**, *a.* = FAMILIAR.

c **1450** *Abce of Aristotill* 6 in *Q. Eliz. Acad.* 66 Be not to fers, to familary, but frendli of chere.

‖**familia** (fə'mɪlɪə). Pl. **familiæ.** [See FAMILY *sb.*] (See quots.)

1708 *Cowel's Law Dict.*, *Familia*, is sometimes taken by our Writers for a Hide, sometimes called a Manse, sometimes Caracuta, or a Plough-land, containing as much as one Plough and Oxen can till in one year. **1729** G. JACOB *New Law-Dict.*, *Familia*, signifies all the Servants belonging to a particular Master; but in another Sense, it is taken for a Portion of Land, sufficient to maintain one Family. **1883** *Encycl. Brit.* XX. 712/2 With the Christian emperors the last traces disappeared of the old conception of the *familia* as an aggregate of persons and estate subject absolutely to the power and dominion of its head. **1912** J. A. WILLIS tr. *Marucci's Christ. Epigr.* 6 Nearly all the cognomens of the most illustrious familiae, as the Scipiones, ..the Cicerones, etc., have been already explained by ancient writers. **1933** E. K. CHAMBERS *Eng. Folk-Play* 226, I do not think that the relation of father and sons indicates anything beyond the relation of the leader of the revel to his *familia* or troop. **1965** D. WHITELOCK in Bessinger & Creed *Medieval & Linguistic Stud.* 223 It is..very likely that when Aldred, bishop of Worcester, became archbishop of York in 1060, some members of his familia went with him.

familial (fə'mɪlɪəl), *a.* [a. F. *familial*, f. L. *familia* family + -AL.] **a.** *Med.* Occurring among members of a family, hereditary.

1900 GOULD *Pocket Med. Dict.* (ed. 4) 249 *Familial*, pertaining to a family. **1903** *Amer. Jrnl. Psychol.* July–Oct. 100 The chronic constitutional type, said to be to a large extent familial. **1910** *Practitioner* June 809 It is a familial defect rather than an acquired disease. **1925** H. CUSHING *Osler* I. 432 Instances in which the disease [*sc.* Angina Pectoris] has shown hereditary or familial tendencies. **1964** S. DUKE-ELDER *Parsons' Dis. Eye* (ed. 14) xviii. 259 A somewhat similar macular degeneration beginning between the ages of twelve and fourteen is seen as a rare familial disease (Stargardt's Disease). **1971** *Nature* 14 May 97/1 Such particles were readily detected in the milk of 60% of American women with a familial history of breast cancer.

b. Of, pertaining to, or characteristic of a family.

1903 E. C. PARSONS tr. *Tarde's Laws of Imitation* vii. 252 The essentially familial character which this people [*sc.* the Chinese] has retained. **1907** *Daily Chron.* 6 June 4/4 The parental or familial attitude towards education. **1919** CONRAD *Arrow of Gold* IV. ii. 163 A remote ideal which yet may belong to his familial tradition. **1929** M. JOSEPHSON *Zola* pl. facing 492 A Familial Scene in the Garden of Zola's English Retreat. **1953** J. B. CARROLL *Study of Lang.* ii. 62 A technique for inferring, from statistical comparisons of language systems, estimates..of their probable familial relationships. **1957** V. W. TURNER *Schism & Continuity in Afr. Society* viii. 238 The kinship basis of a village.. represents a compromise between familial and lineal principles of organization.

Hence **fa'milially** *adv.*, in a familial manner.

1953 J. B. CARROLL *Study of Lang.* ii. 25 Features of languages can be studied comparatively, whether these languages are familially related or not.

familiar (fə'mɪlɪə(r), -ljə(r)), *a.* and *sb.* Forms: 4-6 famuler(e, (4 -iar, 5 -ier, -yer), famil-, famyler, -iar(e, -ier(e, -yar(e, -yer, 5-6 fameliar, -yar, 6-7 famillar, 4- familiar. [a. OF. *familier, famelier, famulier* (mod.F. *familier*), ad. L. *familiār-is*, f. *familia*: see FAMILY.]

A. *adj.*

1. a. Of or pertaining to one's family or household. (Now *rare*, and with mixture of other senses.) †Of an enemy: That is 'of one's own household': *lit.* and *fig.* †Of habits: Pertaining to one's family life, private, domestic.

c **1386** CHAUCER *Merch. T.* 540 O famuler fo, that his service bedith! *c* **1400** *Test. Love* II. 343/1 Nothyng is werse ..than..a famyliar enemye. **1534** MORE *On the Passion* Wks. 1294/1 The false treason of his familier enemy. **1548** HALL *Chron.* 205 Either the familier enemies abidyng at home, or the extravagant fooes, lyngeryng beyonde the sea. **1568** GRAFTON *Chron.* II. 105 Commaunded..neyther..his awne familier houshold to doe him anye kinde of service. **1779-81** JOHNSON *L.P.*, *Prior* Wks. III. 143 His private character and familiar practices. **1862** STANLEY *Jew. Ch.* (1877) I. ii. 35 Abram was dwelling..in the midst..of his familiar circle.

†b. Of titles, heraldic bearings, etc.: Belonging to a family. *Obs.*

1646 BUCK *Rich. III*, II. 45 Yet neither of these foure legitimate children..were permitted to the princely familiar Title of Lancaster. *Ibid.* 46 [The Heralds]..assign'd him.. a shield of familiar Ensignes, the armes of France border'd with an Orle of Normandy or Guyen.

2. Of persons and their relations: On a family footing; extremely friendly, intimately associated, intimate. Const. †*till*, †*to*, *with*.

c **1340** HAMPOLE *Prose T.* (1866) 7 He apperyde till ane þat was famyliare till hym in hys lyfe. *c* **1386** CHAUCER *Prol.* 215 Ful wel..familiar was he With frankeleins over al in his countree. *c* **1450** *St. Cuthbert* (Surtees) 1508 Herefriðe.. was familier to cuthbert neest. **1450-1530** *Myrr. our Ladye* p. lviii, She was moch famylyer wyth Seint Birgette in hyr lyfe. *c* **1585** R. BROWNE *Answ. Cartwright* 28 Priuate famillar felloshippe. **1642** FULLER *Holy & Prof. St.* v. xix. 438 Every one was..pleased..because he might be so familiar with the Prince. **1751** JOHNSON *Rambler* No. 160 ¶6 Time and intercourse have made us familiar. **1831** ARNOLD *Let.* in Stanley *Life & Corr.* (1844) I. ii. 37 Be as familiar with them as you possibly can. **1847** J. WILSON *Chr. North* (1857) II. 9 A familiar and privileged guest.

†b. Of knowledge: Intimate. *Obs.*

1761 HUME *Hist. Eng.* II. xxxvi. 285 She had attained a familiar knowledge of the Roman and Greek languages.

c. In a bad sense. Unduly intimate. Const. †*to*, *with*. Now only with advbs. like *too*, *over*.

c **1450** tr. *Th. à Kempis' Imit.* I. viii, Be not familier to eny womman. **1494** FABYAN *Chron.* VI. ccx. 224 Emma..was accused to be famulyer with the bysshop of Wynchester. **1514** BARCLAY *Cyt. & Uplondyshm.* (Percy Soc.) 2 Aboute all London there was no propre prym But longe tyme had ben famylyer with hym. **1605** CAMDEN *Rem.* (1636) 279 A poore man found a Priest over familiar with his wife.

d. ***familiar angel***: a guardian angel. ***familiar †devil, spirit***: a demon supposed to be in association with or under the power of a man.

14.. *Prose Legends* in *Anglia* VIII. 146 Hir famylier aungel þet hadde hir in kepynge. **1460** CAPGRAVE *Chron.* (1858) 25 That same familiar devel. **1565** STOW *Chron.* 107b, A familiar spirit which hee had..in likenesse of a Catte. *a* **1641** BP. MOUNTAGU *Acts & Mon.* vii. §143 (1642) 473 People, who..had familiar spirits attending on them. *a* **1707** BEVERIDGE *Wks.* II. (R.), They..called over them that had familiar spirits, in the name of our Lord Jesus. **1876** GEO. ELIOT *Dan. Der.* III. xxvii, No familiar spirit could have suggested to him more effective words.

†e. *transf.* Of a plant: Adapted to relations *with*. *Obs. rare.*

1721 R. BRADLEY *Wks. Nat.* 38 Mistletoe..can never be made familiar enough with the Earth to take Root, or grow in it.

3. Of animals: Accustomed to the company of men; domesticated, tame, on a domestic footing *with*.

1483 CAXTON *Gold. Leg.* 263/2 He had one [hound] moche famylyer whiche boldly wold take brede for the borde. **1598** SHAKS. *Merry W.* I. i. 21 It is a familiar beast to man. **1600** J. PORY tr. *Leo's Africa* II. 213 Serpents so familiar with men, that at dinner-time they wil come like dogs and cats. **1721** R. BRADLEY *Wks. Nat.* 71 This year..several ..[snakes] have been familiar about the House. **1784** COWPER *Task* v. 423 Till the pampered pest Is made familiar. **1849** *Sk. Nat. Hist., Mammalia* III. 56 The tapir is occasionally domesticated and becomes..familiar.

fig. **1604** SHAKS. *Oth.* II. iii. 313 Good wine, is a good famillar Creature, if it be well vs'd.

†4. Of food, etc.: Congenial, suitable. *Obs.*

1620 VENNER *Via Recta* (1650) 90 Womans milk is best, because it is most familiar unto mans bodie. **1626** BACON *Sylva* §61 Poysons haue beene made by some, Familiar. **1661** LOVELL *Hist. Anim. & Min.* 106 Roe-buck. The flesh is..familiar to mans body.

5. Of persons: Well or habitually acquainted, having a close acquaintance or intimate knowledge. Of a person's manner: Resulting from close association. Const. *with*.

1508 FISHER *Wks.* (1876) 278 Who that wyl not make his remembraunce famuler with them [the perylles of hell]. **1726-7** SWIFT *Gulliver* II. vii, He was amazed, how so.. groveling an Insect as I..could entertain such inhuman Ideas, and in so familiar a manner. **1732** POPE *Ess. Man* II. 219 Familiar with her [vice's] face We first endure, then pity, then embrace. **1848** MACAULAY *Hist. Eng.* I. 332 Men familiar with all ancient and modern learning. **1861** M. PATTISON *Ess.* (1889) I. 31 An assembly..with whose incapacity we are familiar.

6. Of things: Known from constant association; pertaining to every-day knowledge, well-known. Const. *to*, †*with*.

1490 CAXTON *Eneydos* xxix. 112 As we see by example famyler whan [etc.]. **1576** FLEMING *Panopl. Epist.* 105 Such pointes as to you are familiar. **1581** R. GOADE in *Confer.* III. (1584) X ij, This place of Tertull..is a knowen and familiar place. **1612** BRINSLEY *Lud. Lit.* ix. (1627) 145 Untill the Latine be as familiar to the Scholler as the English. **1690** LOCKE *Hum. Und.* II. i. §22 It begins to know the Objects, which being most familiar with it, have made lasting Impressions. **1756** C. LUCAS *Ess. Waters* III. 298 An experiment familiar to nurses. **1793** J. WILLIAMS *Calm Exam.* 44 To simplify our laws, and render them more familiar with our comprehension. **1818** SCOTT *Rob Roy* i, I will..endeavour to tell you nothing that is familiar to you already. **1873** H. SPENCER *Stud. Sociol.* viii. 180 The contradictions..become by-and-by familiar, and no longer attract his attention.

b. Of every-day use, common, current, habitual, ordinary, usual. Const. *to*.

1599 SHAKS. *Hen. V*, IV. iii. 52 Familiar in his mouth as household words. **1614** RALEIGH *Hist. World* v. vi. §10 The familiar custome, among Princes..of violating Leagues. **1690** LOCKE *Hum. Und.* I. iii. §9 It is familiar among the Mingrelians..to bury their Children alive. **1711** ADDISON *Spect.* No. 135 ¶10 All ridiculous Words make their first Entry into a Language by familiar Phrases. **1780** COWPER *Progr. Err.* 509 With such fine words familiar to his tongue. **1836** J. GILBERT *Chr. Atonem.* iii. (1852) 75 The practice of impeaching the wares of others..is too familiar with mankind. **1866** ROGERS *Agric. & Prices* I. xxv. 618 Wine was an article of general and familiar supply.

†c. Homely, plain; hence, easily understood.

1529 MORE *Dyaloge* I. Wks. 156/1 The very straunge familiar fassyon thereof. **1588** SHAKS. *L.L.L.* I. ii. 9 *Brag.* How canst thou part sadnesse and melancholy! *Boy.* By a familiar demonstration of the working. **1606** —— *Tr. & Cr.* III. iii. 113, I doe not straine it at the position, It is familiar; but at the Authors drift. **1694** ADDISON *Eng. Poets* 139 He [Montague] unreins His verse, and writes in loose familiar strains.

†7. Of persons, their actions, etc.: Affable, courteous, friendly, sociable. *Obs.*

c **1385** CHAUCER *L.G.W.* 1602 Now was Jason..goodly of his speche, and famulere. *c* **1430** *ABC of Aristotle* in *Babees Bk.* (1868) 11 F to fers, ne to famuler, but freendli of cheere. **1529** MORE *Dyaloge* III. Wks. 225/2 If they [men] be familier we call them light. If they be solitarye we call them fantastike. *a* **1555** LATIMER *Serm. & Rem.* (1845) 76 Christ ..was a good familiar man..he came to men's tables when he was called. **1632** LITHGOW *Trav.* IX. 416 Here I found euery where kind and familiar people. *a* **1656** USSHER *Ann.* VII. (1658) 802 Whereupon one in a familiar banquet.. promised Caius, that [etc.]. **1742** POPE *Dunc.* IV. 497 Bland and familiar to the throne he came. **1751** JOHNSON *Rambler* No. 89 ¶12 In his unbended and familiar intervals.

8. Free, as among persons intimately acquainted, unceremonious; occas. Too free, taking liberties *with*; also in ***to make familiar with***.

c **1386** CHAUCER *Shipman's T.* 31 In his hous as familiar was he, As it possible is any friend to be. **1485** CAXTON *Paris & V.* (1868) 88 That ye suffyr hym soo famylyer with you. **1645** HOWELL (*title*) Epistolæ Ho-Elianæ. Familiar Letters, domestic and foreign. **1687** T. BROWN *Saints in Uproar* Wks. 1730 I. 79 There's no stopping your licentious tongue, otherwise you wou'd not make so familiar with the head of the Church. **1712** STEELE *Spect.* No. 526 ¶2 It does look a little familiar, but I must call you *Dear Dumb.* **1712** ARBUTHNOT *John Bull* IV. v, As if I had been familiar with your reputation. **1786** W. THOMSON *Watson's Philip III* (1793) II. v. 110 He..was indulged at all times, with familiar access to his person.

†b. *adv.* = FAMILIARLY.

1803 tr. *Le Brun's Monsieur Botte* III. 28 A person..who continues to treat me so shockingly familiar.

9. *Comb.*, as ***familiar-fond, -mannered*** adjs.

1857 W. COLLINS *Dead Secret* II. VI. iii. 264 The ladies she is familiar-fond with. **1876** GEO. ELIOT *Dan. Der.* VI. xlviii, A coarse, familiar-mannered man.

B. *sb.*

1. A member of a person's family or household (*obs.* in general sense). In the Roman Catholic Church, a person who belongs to the household of the Pope or a bishop, and renders domestic but not menial services.

1460 *Burgh Rec. Peebles* 9 June (1872) 137 The said Sir Thomas Kenedy was in the Kyngis respit at the byschof of Sanct Andoris has of the Kyngis as famelyar tyl hym. **1536** SIR R. MORYSON in Strype *Eccl. Mem.* I. App. lxxii. 175 We princes wrot ourselves to be familiars to popes. **1541** BECON *News out of Heaven* Early Wks. (1843) 40 A mans own household and familiars shall be his most enemies. **1548** HALL *Chron.* 244b, To him, and his servauntes and familiers a fre and a general Pardon. **1632** LITHGOW *Trav.* VI. 268 Their victuals are brought dayly to them by their familiars. **1885** *Catholic Dict.*, s.v. The nephews..of a bishop..in order to be considered his familiars, must render him real service. *Ibid.*, The familiars of the Pope..enjoy many privileges.

b. An officer of the Inquisition, chiefly employed in arresting and imprisoning the accused.

1560 FRAMPTON *Narr.* in Strype *Ann. Ref.* I. xx. 239 This done, we took our journey towards Sevil; the familiar..and his man well armed. *c* **1645** HOWELL *Lett.* (1650) I. 246 When the said Familiar goes to any house..all doors..fly open to him. **1781** GIBBON *Decl. & F.* III. 245 Many of the Castillans, who pillaged Rome, were familiars of the holy inquisition. **1825** J. NEAL *Bro. Jonathan* III. 441 If my familiars have done their duty, he is on his way to the scaffold. **1855** MOTLEY *Dutch Rep.* II. iii. (1866) 165 It [the 'Holy Office']..having its familiars in every house.

transf. **1821** SOUTHEY *Lett.* (1856) III. 227, I do not like to embody myself as a political Familiar.

2. A person with whom one has constant intercourse, an intimate friend or associate.

c **1374** CHAUCER *Boeth.* I. iv. 18 For whiche þing oon of þi familers not vnskilfully axed þus. ȝif, etc. **1494** FABYAN *Chron.* VI. cci. 208 Hugh Capet..was his famulyer and chief counceler. **1504** LADY MARGARET tr. *T. a Kempis' Imit.* IV. xiii, Thou, my god, art closed & hyd in councell of thy famyliars. *a* **1569** KINGESMYLL *Man's Est.* xi. (1580) 70 Thou whom I have chosen..one of my twelve familiars. **1640** BP. HALL *Episc.* II. x. 139 A co-partner and a deare fameliar of..St. Peter and St. Paul. **1669** PENN *No Cross* ix. §10 It weans thee off thy Familiars. **1859** GEO. ELIOT *A. Bede* 14 Retaining her maiden appellation among her familiars.

b. One intimately acquainted with (a thing).

1875 LOWELL *Wordsw.* Prose Wks. 1890 IV. 399 The life-long familiar of the mountains.

3. A familiar spirit, a demon or evil spirit supposed to attend at a call.

1584 R. SCOT *Discov. Witchcr.* III. xv. 65 A flie, otherwise called a divell or familiar. **1633** FORD *Broken H.* III. iv, You have..a familiar That posts i' th' air for your intelligence? **1748** SMOLLETT *Rod. Rand.* (1812) I. 249 She paid me a visit ..to be introduced to my familiar. **1812** SOUTHEY *Omniana* II. 250 The old belief in familiars. **1866** ALGER *Solit. Nat. & Man* III. 152 Our familiar is..a nimble and tricksy spirit, like Puck.

transf. and *fig.* **1819** BYRON *Juan* II. xlix, Twelve days had Fear Been their familiar, and now Death was here. **1830** GALT *Lawrie T.* I. vii. (1849) 22 The garret was alive with musquitoes, domestic familiars. **1836** *Backwoods of Canada* 51 Vile familiars to the dormitory kept us from closing our weary eye-lids. **1867** LOWELL *Rousseau* Prose Wks. 1890 II. 250 He..keeps a pet sorrow, a blue-devil familiar, that goes with him everywhere. **1867** J. H. STIRLING in *Fortn. Rev.* Oct. 379 Style..is one of De Quincey's familiars.

familiarism (fə'mɪlɪərɪz(ə)m). [f. FAMILIAR *a.* + -ISM.] A mode of expression usual only in familiar language; a colloquialism.

1765 *Patriotism, a Mock-heroic* (ed. 2) Index, Familiarisms and vulgarisms. **1787** W. MARSHALL *Norfolk* II. To Rdr. 9, I thought it prudent to do away some of the familiarisms of the original minutes. **1803** W. TAYLOR in *Monthly Mag.* XIV. 506 *Would-be.* This familiarism deserved record.

†fa'miliarist. *Obs. rare.* [f. as prec. + -IST.] One who is an authority on familiar spirits.

1726 DE FOE *Hist. Devil* (1840) 246 That learned familiarist Mother Hazel.

familiarity (fə,mɪlɪ'ærɪtɪ). Forms: 4 famularite, -iarite, familarite, 5-7 familiaritie(e, -ie, -iarte, (5 -yaryte), famyliarite, (6 -tie, 7 -ty, 5 -tye, 6 -yaryte), 6- familiarity. [a. F. *familiarité*, ad. L. *familiāritāt-em*, f. *familiāris*: see FAMILIAR and -ITY.] The quality or state of being familiar.

†1. The quality proper to the head of a household, hospitality. *Obs. rare.*

a **1483** *Liber Niger* in *Househ. Ord.* 18 Hardeknoute may be called a fader noreshoure of familiaritie.

†2. The quality proper to a member of the family; hence, behaviour due from a retainer or a familiar friend, devotion, fidelity. *Obs.*

c **1440** *Secrees*, Largesse engendrys ffamiliarite, þat ys trew seruice. **1526** *Pilgr. Perf.* (W. de W. 1531) 17b, All this he dyd to gyue us an occasyon of reuerent familiarite. **1548** HALL *Chron.* 172 The duke of Yorke ledde the Quene with great familiaritie to all mens sightes. **1576** FLEMING *Panopl. Epist.* 116 A man ful of familiaritie and courteous acquaintance.

†3. Suitableness, fitness (of food, etc.). *Obs.*

1551 TURNER *Herbal* I. (1568) Mvja, A certayne familiaritie that is betwene their natures. **1646** SIR T. BROWNE *Pseud. Ep.* III. xxi. 159 There is..required in the aliment a familiarity of matter.

4. The state of being very friendly or intimate, friendly intercourse; intimacy *with* (a person).

c **1450** tr. *T. à Kempis' Imit.* III. xlii, þese folke comeþ not ..to þe grace of my iocunde familiarite. **1533** BELLENDEN *Livy* I. (1822) 87 Nocht alanerlie had he familiarite with the saidis princes of Latinis. **1588** J. UDALL *Demonstr. Discip.* (Arb.) 27 The louing familiarity that should be betwixt the minister and his people. **1664** MARVELL *Corr.* Wks. 1872-5 II. 174 The old familiarity and kindness betwixt the two Kings. **1727** DE FOE *Syst. Magic* I. iv. (1840) 111 When this familiarity is once obtained with the evil spirit. **1761** HUME *Hist. Eng.* II. xxvii. 127 [He] resolved to introduce Wolsey to the young prince's familiarity. **1880** L. STEPHEN *Pope* iii. 61 Pope was not disinclined to pride himself upon his familiarity with the great.

b. Undue intimacy.
1387 TREVISA *Higden* (Rolls) VII. 163 He [Edward]..his owne moder for suspecte famuliarite and homlynes deprived of al hire goodes. **1600** J. PORY tr. *Leo's Africa* II. 206 If any of them offer to have familiaritie with their wiues, they punish him most seuerely.

†**c.** *concr.* A familiar person or persons. Also *collect.*, a circle of intimate friends or connexions.
a **1635** NAUNTON *Fragm. Reg.* (Arb.) 43 A Lady of great honour, of the Kings familiarity. **1643** MILTON *Divorce* Wks. 1738 I. 201 The leaving of Parents, or other familiarity whatsoever. **1665** J. WEBB *Stone-Heng* (1725) 125 Such frivolous Reasons..as unto all judicious Men, even those of his own Familiarity, are ridiculous.

5. Close or habitual acquaintance *with* (a thing); constant practical knowledge, habituation.
1601 SHAKS. *All's Well* v. ii. 3 When I haue held familiaritie with fresher cloathes. *a* **1732** ATTERBURY (J.), We contract at last such an intimacy and familiarity with them, as makes it difficult and irksome for us to call off our minds. **1841** ELPHINSTONE *Hist. Ind.* I. 305 The familiarity occasioned by the daily sight of its ceremonies. **1854** BREWSTER *More Worlds* xvii. 256 Our daily familiarity with the ordinary phenomena of life.

6. Absence of ceremony, free or unrestrained intercourse, *esp.* with inferiors. Proverb, ***Familiarity breeds***, † ***brings***, † ***creates contempt***.
c **1380** WYCLIF *Wks.* (1880) 44 Haue þei so muche famularite or homlynesse. **1477** EARL RIVERS (Caxton) *Dictes* 40 Hyt behoueth a kyng to..be conuersant amongis them [his people] without ouermoche famylyarite. **1548** UDALL, etc. *Erasm. Par. John* 34 a, Familiaritie bringeth contempte. **1599** MINSHEU *Dial. Sp. & Eng.* 65/2 Much familiaritie oftentimes breedes contempt. **1647** CLARENDON *Hist. Reb.* I. (1843) 15/1 Olivarez had been heard to censure very severely the duke's familiarity..towards the prince. **1667** EVELYN *Publ. Employment* in Misc. Wks. (1835) 535 Familiarity creates contempt. **1797** MRS. RADCLIFFE *Italian* vii, To allow him an unusual degree of familiarity in conversation. **1876** MISS BRADDON *J. Haggard's Dau.* II. 102 Jim greeted his stepmother with frank familiarity.

b. An instance of familiar behaviour in action, speech, or expression; something allowed or justified only on the ground of intimacy. Usually in *pl.*
1641 J. JACKSON *True Evang. T.* III. 180 Any other noble, and lawfull familiarities of intimacie, and deerenesse. **1697** COLLIER *Ess. Mor. Subj.* I. (1709) 33 If you Confound these two Relations [of Master and Servant] by lavish and indiscreet Familiarities, you destroy the Respect. **1821** LAMB *Elia* Ser. I. *New Year's Eve*, Misbecoming familiarities inscribed upon your ordinary tombstones. **1875** MRS. RANDOLPH *W. Hyacinth* I. 10 Too great [awe] to allow of his being guilty of a familiarity.

7. *Astrol.* (See quot.)
1819 J. WILSON *Dict. Astrol.* 99 *Familiarities*, called also configurations or aspects.

familiarization (fəˌmɪlɪəraɪˈzeɪʃən). [f. next + -ATION.] The action of familiarizing in various senses; an instance of this.
1755 H. T. CROKER *Orl. Fur.* I. Pref. 6 By familiarization we reduce the force of formidable objects. **1765** MISS C. TALBOT in Miss Carter *Lett.* (1809) III. 126, I would..read to it with proper familiarisations the most striking parts. **1836** T. HOOK *G. Gurney* II. i, A constant familiarization with such scenes. **1888** SWEET *Eng. Sounds* 45 The familiarization of foreign words.

familiarize (fəˈmɪlɪəraɪz), *v.* [f. FAMILIAR *a.* + -IZE.] *trans.* To make familiar.
1. *trans.* To make (a thing, *rarely* a person) familiar or well-known.
a **1639** WOTTON *Let., Reliq. Wotton.* (1672) 478 Intending ..to familiarize it [final resignation of ourselves] between us as much as I can. **1774** WARTON *Hist. Eng. Poetry* xxi. (1840) II. 271 Wethamstede..being desirous of familiarising the history of his patron saint to the monks of his convent. **1846** JOYCE *Sci. Dial.* i. 2 Your drawing compasses may familiarize to your mind the idea of an angle. **1875** W. S. HAYWARD *Love agst. World* 14 Horses and hounds recognized that shout, familiarized to them by many a good run.

†**b.** To render familiar or accustomed; to divest of strangeness.
1608 SYLVESTER *Du Bartas* 630 Long continuance and custome..Familiarizing so the fit, that..one may almost forget it. **1711** ADDISON *Spect.* No. 159 ¶3 The Genius smiled upon me with a Look of..Affability that familiarized him to my Imagination. **1768** JOHNSON *Pref. Shaks.* Wks. IX. 245 Shakespeare..familiarizes the wonderful. **1779** COWPER *Let.* Wks. 1837 XV. 45 Long habit and custom are able to familiarize to us things much more disagreeable than this.

2. a. To put (a person) on a footing of intimacy. (*rare.*) †**b.** To render (a person's manner) familiar or affable. (*obs.*) **c.** *refl.* and *intr.* for *refl.* To adopt a familiar and courteous demeanour. Also in a bad sense: 'To make oneself cheap'. Now *rare*.
a. **1754** RICHARDSON *Grandison* V. xvii. 96, I should be glad..to be familiarized to the Ladies of your family. **1858** HAWTHORNE *Ancestral Footstep* (1883) 501 Middleton on his arrival..is familiarized at the Hospital.
b. **1709** STEELE *Tatler* No. 127 ¶9 For the Cure of this particular Sort of Madness [haughtiness] it will be necessary to..familiarize his Carriage by the Use of a good Cudgel. **1761–2** HUME *Hist. Eng.* (1806) V. lxxi. 321 It was very difficult for him..to soften or familiarize it [his address].
c. **1685** *Gracian's Courtier's Orac.* 163 He that familiarizes himself, presently loses the Superiority that his serious air gave him. **1697** *C'tess D'Aunoy's Trav.* (1706) 22 She at length familiariz'd herself, and told me, 'Twas not through fear of anything else but of displeasing me. *a* **1734** NORTH *Lives* II. 418 He..familiarized with his equals, and gave no offence to his inferiors. **1748** RICHARDSON *Clarissa* (1811) IV. 157 We had familiarized to each other long ago. **1886** *Harper's Mag.* Aug. 377 Captain T. Cook..is another type of the reserved man who does not familiarize with the passengers.

3. To bring into familiar or common use; to popularize. Now *rare*.
1752 JOHNSON *Rambler* No. 208 ¶11, I have familiarized the terms of philosophy by applying them to popular ideas. **1779–81** —— *L.P., Pope* Wks. IV. 74 This mode of imitation, in which the ancients are familiarised, by adapting their sentiments to modern topicks. **1807** W. TAYLOR in *Ann. Rev.* V. 563 The discussion served to familiarize the words congress, general government [etc.]. **1834** BRAYLEY *Graph. & Hist. Illust.* Pref., It was my wish to familiarize Archæological inquiries.

b. To give a familiar form to (a name).
1804 W. IRVING *Life & Lett.* (1864) I. vi. 94 An invincible propensity to familiarize the names of people.

4. To accustom (a person, one's mind, etc.) *to*, †*into*, or *to do* (something); to habituate. Now *rare*.
1646 SIR J. TEMPLE *Irish Rebell.* 7 They began to..suffer ..their English followers to familiarize themselves into their beastly manners and customes. **1734** *Mem. Geo. Psalmanazar* 214 To..exert my talents in..familiarising myself to this pretended Formosan language and character. **1830** HERSCHEL *Stud. Nat. Phil.* 22 By familiarising us..to walk uprightly. **1833** J. H. NEWMAN *Lett.* (1891) I. 483 To familiarise the imagination of the reader to an Apostolical state of the Church. **1848** —— *Loss & Gain* 239 Intending to familiarize my parishioners to it by little and little.

b. To make (a person or oneself) well acquainted, or to feel at ease, at home *with*.
a **1687** PETTY *Pol. Arith.* i. (1691) 17 He is familiarized with Hardships and Hazards. **1741** J. LAWRY & H. HEATON *Athenian Lett.* (1792) I. 147 Having familiariz'd myself much of late with the hieroglyphical imagery. **1815** MOORE *Lalla R.* Pref. (1850) 10 To..familiarise myself with its various treasures. **1856** FROUDE *Hist. Eng.* (1858) I. ii. 98 Wolsey..familiarized Henry with the sense that a reformation was inevitable. **1863** TYNDALL *Heat* iii. 61 My object here is to familiarise your minds with the general conception of atomic motion.
absol. **1834** FONBLANQUE *Engl. under 7 Administr.* (1837) III. 23 The first effect may be to startle; but the second will be to familiarise.

†**5.** To domesticate, tame (an animal). Cf. FAMILIAR *a. Obs.*
1634 W. TIRWHYT tr. *Balzac's Lett.* 205 Since we are forced to live among savage creatures, wee had neede..to familiarise..them. **1682** NORRIS *Hierocles* 35 Which is the method men take to tame and familiarize wild beasts.

Hence **faˈmiliarized** *ppl. a.*, **faˈmiliarizer**, one who familiarizes, **faˈmiliarizing** *ppl. a.*, **faˈmiliaˌrizingly** *adv.*
1654 WHITLOCK *Zootomia* 241 This familiarized Book [Bible]. **1726–7** SWIFT *Gulliver* III. vii, I soon grew so familiarized to the sight of spirits that..they gave me no emotion at all. **1832** LANDER *Adv. Niger* I. v. 215 Their faces had become familiarized to us. **1872** PROCTOR *Ess. Astron.* iii. 37 In the less dignified *rôle* of a familiariser he was not successful. **1876** BLACK *Mad-cap V.* viii. 73 She would have got familiarised with us, and stayed on indefinitely. **1890** J. H. STIRLING *Gifford Lect.* x. 179 Jehovah, whom German and French Writers have taken of late, degradingly and I suppose familiarisingly, to call Jahve.

familiarly (fəˈmɪlɪəlɪ), *adv.* [f. FAMILIAR *a.* + -LY².] In a familiar manner.
†**1.** After the manner of a domesticated animal.
1550 THOMAS *Ital. Gram., Domesticamente*, familiarely or homely. **1607** TOPSELL *Four-f. Beasts* (1673) 101 Ptolomeus Philadelphe..having a hinde-calf..brought it so familiarly tame, that [etc.]. **1651** W. G. tr. *Cowel's Inst.* 59 If any shall happen to be made tame, and by custome goe familiarly in and out.

2. Like one who has an intimate acquaintance (with either persons or things); intimately.
14.. *Prose Legends* in *Anglia* VIII. 162 Familierly taghte of þe holy goste. **1548** HALL *Chron.* 66 The kyng of England ..them honorably embraced and familierly kissed. **1675** HOBBES *Odyssey* (1677) 231 Great Minos..used with great Chronides Familiarly of old to sit and chat. **1748** HARTLEY *Observ. Man* II. iii. 287 Two ill Men can scarce become known to each other familiarly. **1809–10** COLERIDGE *Friend* (1865) 113 Lord Chancellor Bacon..was familiarly acquainted with all the secrets of personal influence. **1865** *Sat. Rev.* 5 Aug. 169/2 The..desirableness of doctors or lawyers being brought more familiarly together.

†**b.** In a bad sense: With undue freedom. *Obs.*
1603 KNOLLES *Hist. Turks* (1638) 68 Her whom his aged father..had too familiarly vsed.

3. As an every-day matter or matter of course; commonly, usually. *Obs.* exc. with words implying knowledge.
1576 FLEMING *Panopl. Epist.* 226 Using themselves familiarly to such foule enormities. **1621–51** BURTON *Anat. Mel.* I. ii. II. iii. 77 There be..too that familiarly drink Seawater. **1674** BOYLE *Excell. Theol.* II. iv. 178 The familiarly visible stars. **1781** GIBBON *Decl. & F.* III. 202 Scenes with which he was familiarly conversant. **1879** *Cassells Techn. Educ.* I. 207 The form of crane..most familiarly known is that which is called the jib-crane.

†**b.** In every-day language or manner, easily.
1561 T. NORTON *Calvin's Inst.* IV. 69 These two places, which I haue..familiarly..expounded. **1607** TOPSELL *Four-f. Beasts* (1673) 266 More..perspicuously..and familiarly..expressed by them. *c* **1660** J. HARRINGTON *Valerius & Publ.* To Rdr. (1700) 475 There is nothing..I so much desire as to be familiarly understood.

4. Without ceremony, in a free and easy manner, unceremoniously.
c **1425** WYNTOUN *Cron.* VIII. v. 42 He..wyth þame spak famylyarly. **1568** GRAFTON *Chron.* II. 810 [The Duke] exhorted him familierly..to say whatsoever he thought. **1678** DRYDEN *Limberham* v. i, We'll banish all Pomp and Ceremony, and live familiarly together. **1712** TICKELL *Spect.* No. 410 ¶1 She saluted him very familiarly by his Name. **1821** LAMB *Elia* Ser. I. *Valentine's Day*, Our familiarly pious ancestors. **1875** T. W. HIGGINSON *U.S. Hist.* viii. 56 Called familiarly by the name of 'Pilgrims'.

familiarness (fəˈmɪlɪənɪs). [f. as prec. + -NESS.]
1. = FAMILIARITY 4–6. Now *rare*.
1612 BRINSLEY *Lud. Lit.* 262 The familiarnes of the matter. *a* **1645** R. HEYWOOD *Observ. & Instr.* III. lxii. (1869) 55 Neuer was of familiarnes Contempt esteem'd the proper childe. **1730–6** in BAILEY (folio), *Familiarness*. **1789** MAD. D'ARBLAY *Diary* Apr., She does not choose such sort of familiarness. **1854–6** PATMORE *Angel in Ho.* I. II. XII. (1879) 251 So near a touch Affirms no mean familiarness.

†**2.** Suitableness. *Obs. rare*.
1617 HIERON *Wks.* II. 182 The fitness of the rite to represent that to which it hath reference, and the familiarnesse of it for their vnderstanding.

†**faˈmiliary**, *a. Obs. rare*⁻¹. [f. L. type **familiāri-us*, f. *familia*: see FAMILY and -ARY².] Pertaining to the control of a family; domestic.
1643 MILTON *Divorce* II. xxi, It pleas'd God..to make him [Henry VIII] the beginner of a reformation..by first asserting into his familiary power the right of just divorce.

†**faˈmilic**, *a. Obs.* In 7 familique, -elique, -ellick. [f. FAMILY + -IC; prob. arising from a misunderstanding of FAMELIC; cf. med.L. *liber famelicus* account-book of domestic expenditure, *famelica cura* domestic management (Pertz *Scriptt.* XXV. 676).] Pertaining to a family; also, domestic, familiar.
1660 WATERHOUSE *Arms & Arm.* 47 Their familique Banners. **1676** SHADWELL *Virtuoso* II, A domestick animal.. a Mangy Spaniel; and a less famellick creature..a Sound Bull Dog. **1684** OTWAY *Atheist* I. i, With as grave, a fatherly, famelique countenance as ever I saw.

†**faˈmilical**, *a. Obs. rare*⁻¹. [f. as prec. + -ICAL.] Of or belonging to a family; family.
1660 WATERHOUSE *Arms & Arm.* 48 Arms in National Standards, and familical Ensigns or Banners.

familism (ˈfæmɪlɪz(ə)m). Also 7 familyism. [f. L. *famil-ia* FAMILY + -ISM.]
1. The doctrine and practice of the Familists.
1642 CANNE in J. Ball *Answ.* I. 112 It is familisme for him to say..I will have in my selfe a secret meaning from the rest. **1648** *Protest of Ministers* in Miall *Congregationalism Yorks.* (1868) 49 We are resolved..never to consent to the toleration of..Familyism..or any other heresies. *a* **1716** SOUTH *Serm.* (1717) V. 148 The Devil found it requisite.. to set up his Standard in Familism or Enthusiasm. **1765** T. HUTCHINSON *Hist. Mass. Bay* I. 117 His principles were the very dregs of familism.

2. In Fourier's socialistic philosophy: The feeling existing between members of a family; fraternity.
1848 *Tait's Mag.* XV. 705 The propensity to group embraces love, friendship, ambition, and a fourth passion called familism.

familist (ˈfæmɪlɪst). Also 7 famel-, famul-, famylist. [f. as prec. + -IST.]
†**1.** The head of a family, a family-man. *Obs.*
1612 W. PARKES *Curtaine Dr.* 7 Then hath he descended ..from Families to euery particular Famulist. **1615** BEDWELL *Moham. Imp.* II. §70 Mohammed was a good familist. **1658** OSBORN *Adv. Son* 70 If you will needs be a Familist, and Marry.

†**2.** One of the same family or household. *Obs.*
1631 BRATHWAIT *Whimzies, Zealous Brother* 119 Controversies which he secretly commenceth amongst his owne familists. **1638** HEYWOOD *Wise Woman* II. Wks. 1874 V. 304 If you come to live in our house, and be a Familist amongst us.

3. A member of the sect called the *Family of Love*; see FAMILY 7.
1592 NASHE *P. Pennilesse* B 3 Like the Anabaptists and adulterous Familists. **1634** CANNE *Necess. Separ.* (1849) 132 The cursed Familists do hold that religion standeth not in outward things. *a* **1716** SOUTH *Serm.* (1717) V. 151 See, with what Contempt the Father of the Familists, Henry Nicolas, casts off the Use and Authority of it [Scripture]. **1853** MARSDEN *Early Purit.* 391 The familists did not escape the watchful vigilance of the privy council.

‖**familistère** (familistɛr). [Fr.] = FAMILISTERY.
1880 *Encycl. Brit.* XI. 265/2 A palatial *familistère* with accommodation for 400 families. **1886** *Sci. Amer. Suppl.* 10 July 8761/3 In 1859 Godin put up a large building, called the '*familistère*', for the accommodation of 300 families, adding a theater, school-house, etc. **1899** *Daily News* 15 Sept. 3/2 The famillistère [*sic*] founded by M. Goudin at Guise.

familistery (fæmɪˈlɪstərɪ). *rare.* [ad. F. *familistère*, f. *famille*, f. L. *familia* (see FAMILY), formed by substituting *famili-* for the first member of the word *phalanstère*.] The abode of a community living together as one family.
1865 *Reader* No. 145. 399/3 The 'Familistery', or Workman's Home. **1886** *Pall Mall G.* 5 Oct. 5/2 Familistères, reading rooms, museums..will ensue spontaneously.

†**fami'listic**, *a. Obs.* [f. FAMILIST + -IC.] **a.** Of or pertaining to the Familists or Familism. **b.** Pertaining to a family or household.

a. **1646** PAGITT *Heresiogr.* (ed. 3) 90 A fourth holds.. Familisticke Tenets. **1667** H. MORE *Div. Dial.* Schol. (1713) 566 This Man possessed with Familistic dotage.
b. **1660** WATERHOUSE *Arms & Arm.* 42 The certain rise of familistique distinctions.

†**fami'listical**, *a. Obs.* [f. prec. + -AL[1].] **a.** = FAMILISTIC a.; **b.** = FAMILISTIC b.

a. **1653** GAUDEN *Hierasp.* 306 They labour..to turn the solidity of Truth..into nothing but Familisticall whimseys. **1702** C. MATHER *Magn. Chr.* II. iv. (1852) 124 The suppression of an antinomian and famalistical faction.
b. **1660** R. COKE *Power & Subj.* 15 Theological virtues relate to the attaining of Eternal happiness: Moral, Humane, and Familistical, to the conservation of society and peace in their several places.

Hence †**fami'listically** *adv.*

1653 BAXTER *Meth. Peace Consc.* 24 [We] put false interpretations on the plainest precepts of Christ..and Familistically turn them into Allegories.

‖**famille** (famij). [Fr. = family.] **a.** Phr. ***famille de robe***: a family founded by a lawyer; a legal family (in pre-Revolutionary France). (See ROBE *sb.* 4 b.)

1857 J. W. CROKER *Ess. Fr. Rev.* iv. 161 Pierre Louis Rœderer, born about 1756 of a respectable *famille de robe.* **1881** A. I. THACKERAY *Mme de Sévigné* ii. 10 A..gentle heiress belonging to a respectable *famille de robe.*

b. ***famille jaune***, Chinese enamelled porcelain of which the predominant colour is yellow; so also ***famille noire, rose, verte***, in which the predominant colour is, respectively, black, red, and green.

1872 LADY C. SCHREIBER *Jrnl.* (1911) I. 145 C. S. espied a bowl and cover of the 'famille verte' like the jars we acquired at Cadiz. **1876** *Ibid.* 456 Went up to Le Roy's, to look after some Famille Verte beakers. **1898** W. G. GULLAND *Chinese Porc.* I. 174 *Famille verte.* So called from the decoration being chiefly in green enamel. *Ibid.* 192 *Famille rose.* So named from a rose tint in greater or lesser quantity being employed in the decoration. **1900** F. LITCHFIELD *Pott. & Porc.* 114 The high value placed upon a really fine specimen of the '*famille noire*'. **1903** *Daily Chron.* 7 July 2/7 A large famille-rose cistern. **1904** E. DILLON *Porcelain* 106 We may probably associate with the beginning of this reign [*viz.* of Kien-lung (1735–1795)].. the first use of the *rouge d'or* which has given its name to a well-known class of porcelain—the *famille rose.* **1945** W. B. HONEY *Ceramic Art China* ii. 149 Enamelled Wares of the K'ang Hsi Period (1662–1722)... Big vases with green, black, and yellow grounds, are often of noble form... These coloured grounds of the *famille noire*, *famille jaune*, etc., are much sought after by European and American collectors. **1962** *Oxf. Univ. Gaz.* 30 May 1280/1 Eight pieces of porcelain, export ware, *famille rose*, Chinese, 19th century. **1969** *Guardian* 16 July 18/1 Rarer examples of famille noire or jaune which were made under the Ch'ing Dynasty.

family ('fæmɪlɪ), *sb.* Forms: 5 **famylye**, (*Sc.* **famyle**), 5–6 **famyll(e**, 5–7 **familie**, 6 **famelie, -ly, famuly, famylie**, *Sc.* **famell**, 7 **familly**, 6– **family**. [ad. L. *familia* household, f. *famulus* servant.]

I. †**1. a.** The servants of a house or establishment; the household. *Obs.* exc. in ***family of servants***.

?*a* **1400** *Chester Pl.* (Shaks. Soc.) I. 213 You are my desciples, and of my familie. **1641** *Disc. Pr. Henry* in *Harl. Misc.* (Malh.) III. 522 His family..consisted of few less than five-hundred. **1707** SLOANE *Jamaica* I. 46 The proprietor keeps a large family for its defence. **1722** DE FOE *Plague* (1840) 10, I was a single man..but I had a family of servants. **1794** GODWIN *Cal. Williams* 39 Mr. Tyrrel.. proposed..to take him into his family, and make him whipper-in to his hounds.

†**b.** The retinue of a nobleman or grandee. *Obs.*

1548 HALL *Chron.* 171 b, The Kyng, the Quene with all their familie, shortly folowed. **1609** SKENE *Reg. Maj.* 45 Na Prelat, Erle, nor Barron..sal ryde with ane greater familie (number) of men and hors.

c. The staff of a high military officer or (in India) state official.

1808 ELPHINSTONE *Let.* 5 Sept. in Colebrooke's *Life* I. 185 Mr. Seton..waived his right to nominate my family. **1809** JAS. MOORE *Camp. Spain* 72 The Staff Officers of Sir John Moore's family. **1856** J. W. COLE *Mem. Brit. Gen. Penin. War* II. viii. 84 The officers of his family..fell in with the same humour.

d. *Rom. Ant.* A troop, school (of gladiators).

1863 WHYTE MELVILLE *Gladiators* I. 62 You look as if you belonged to the family yourself.

2. a. The body of persons who live in one house or under one head, including parents, children, servants, etc.

1545 JOYE *Exp. Dan.* iv. 48/1, I Nebucadnezar, happye and prosperouse in my familie. **1631** *Star Chamb. Cases* (Camden) 44 His family were himself and his wife and daughters, two mayds, and a man. *a* **1729** S. CLARKE *Serm.* (1730) II. iii. 51 Representing..all Orders of intelligent Beings, as the Family of God. **1794** MRS. RADCLIFFE *Myst. Udolpho* ii, I am going to prayers with my family. **1859** JEPHSON *Brittany* ii. 10 The difference between people who live in Society and people who live in the family.

b. ***Happy Family***: a collection of birds and animals of different natures and propensities living together in harmony in one cage.

1844 in P. T. Barnum *Sixty Years Recollections* (1889) 120 [At Coventry] we visited an exhibition called the 'Happy Family'. **1890** *Evening News* 4 Dec. 4/5 He was..on his way home with his 'Happy Family'.

3. a. The group of persons consisting of the parents and their children, whether actually living together or not; in wider sense, the unity formed by those who are nearly connected by blood or affinity. ***Holy Family***: see quot. 1875.

1667 MILTON *P.L.* x. 216 As Father of his Familie he clad Thir nakedness. **1796** H. HUNTER tr. *St. Pierre's Stud. Nat.* (1799) III. 589 We pass..through the love of our family.. to love Mankind. **1829** JAS. MILL *Hum. Mind* (1869) II. xxii. 218 The group which consists of a Father, Mother and Children, is called a Family. **1875** TYRWHITT in *Dict. Chr. Antiq.* I. 661 *Family*—The Holy. The subject which bears this title in modern art is generally a group consisting of the Virgin Mother, bearing the Sacred Infant, of St. Joseph, and frequently of the younger St. John Baptist and occasionally of St. Elizabeth.

b. A person's children regarded collectively.

1732 POPE *Ep. Bathurst* 382 Seldom at Church..But duly sent his family and wife. **1876** MISS BRADDON *J. Haggard's Dau.* xxx. 280 'I'm a man with a long fambly.' *Mod.* He has a large family.

4. a. Those descended or claiming descent from a common ancestor: a house, kindred, lineage.

c **1425** WYNTOUN *Cron.* VIII. iv. 304 Amang his Kyn and his Famyle. **1513** DOUGLAS *Æneis* XI. viii. 136 The famell and kynrent of Volsca. **1581** MARBECK *Bk. of Notes* 708 Plinie affirmeth also, that..ther was a Famuly that would go vpon a great fire, & not be touched therewith. **1593** SHAKS. *3 Hen. VI*, I. i. 65 Let vs assayle the Family of Yorke. **1599** —— *Hen. V.* II. ii. 129 Come they of Noble Family? **1671** MILTON *P.R.* III. 168 By strong hand his [Maccabeus'] family obtain'd..the crown. **1734** POPE *Ess. Man* IV. 213 Go! and pretend thy family is young. **1804** J. GRAHAME *Sabbath* (1839) 15/2 Every great merchant and money-dealer wishes to be the founder of what is called a family. **1868** FREEMAN *Norm. Conq.* (1876) II. ix. 268 The abbey of Coventry..still kept in the family.
fig. **1775** SHERIDAN *Duenna* II. iii, The beggars are a very ancient family in most kingdoms.

b. (Man, woman, etc.) ***of family***: of noble or gentle descent.

a **1763** SHENSTONE *Ess., External Figure* Wks. 1764 II. 60 If dress be only allowable to persons of family, it may [etc.]. **1762–71** H. WALPOLE *Vertue's Anecd. Paint.* (1786) III. 32 He..married a beautiful English-woman of family. **1777** W. DALRYMPLE *Trav. Sp. & Port.* lx, Three troops..each consisting of 200 men, who are all men of family. **1810** BENTHAM *Packing* (1821) 146 People of no 'family'.

c. In wider sense: A race; a people or group of peoples assumed to be descended from a common stock.

1583 STANYHURST *Aeneis* I. (Arb.) 25 You to me ful promist..That Roman famely should spring from the auncetrye Troian. **1842** PRICHARD *Nat. Hist. Man* 468 The Tamanacs, who belong to the same family, live on the right bank of the Orinoco. **1848** MACAULAY *Hist. Eng.* (ed. 5) I. i. 18 By the mixture of three branches of the great Teutonic family with each other.

5. *transf.* and *fig.* (with mixed notion of 3 and 4). A brotherhood or group of individuals or nations bound together by political or religious ties.

1611 BIBLE *Eph.* iii. 15 The Father of our Lord Iesus Christ, Of whom the whole family in heauen and earth is named. **1650–3** *Dissert. de Pace* in *Phenix* (1708) II. 348 Of all the Familys and Societys of Christians, they are most hated. *a* **1865** E. EVERETT (W.), The States of Europe were by the prevailing maxims of its policy, closely united in one family. **1875** MANNING *Mission H. Ghost* ix. 253 They [the apostles] subdued the..Greeks..the..Romans, and our.. forefathers into one family.

6. a. A group or assemblage of objects, connected together and distinguished from others by the possession of some common features or properties.

a **1626** BACON *Sylva* §354 There be two Great Families of Things;..Sulphureous and mercurial. **1731** POPE *Ep. Burlington* IV. 96 With all the mournful family of Yews. **1741** *Chambers' Cycl.* s.v. *Curves*, Family of Curves. **1762** J. PRIESTLEY *Theory Lang.* viii. 117 The Eastern tongues of that genus, or family as we may call it. **1796** HUTTON *Math. Dict.* I. 353 *Family of curves* is an assemblage of several curves of different kinds, all defined by the same equation of an indeterminate degree. **1813** BAKEWELL *Introd. Geol.* (1815) 457 The classification of simple minerals into families. **1875** FORTNUM *Majolica* viii. 65 Persian, Damascus, Rhodian, and Lindus wares, composing a large family. **1875** WHITNEY *Life Lang.* xii. 228 We have called a certain body of languages a family, the Indo-European. **1950** F. GAYNOR *Encycl. Atomic Energy* 157 A radioactive series, also called radioactive family, is a group of radioactive isotopes, each of which is the product of the radioactive decay of the preceding one.

b. In modern scientific classification: A group of allied genera. (Usually, a 'family' is a subdivision of an 'order'; but in the 'natural system' of botanical classification the two words are, so far as cotyledonous plants are concerned, synonymous: English botanists chiefly using 'order', while in French Jussieu's term *famille* is retained.) (In Botany 'family' is now used, as in Zoology, for a division of an order, and has therefore superseded the term 'natural order'; e.g. order Rosales, family Rosaceæ. Also *spec.* in Ecology.)

1753 CHAMBERS *Cycl. Supp.* s.v., The bream and the herring, though very different in genus, may yet be brought into the same Family. **1831** J. DAVIES *Manual Mat. Med.* 223 *Rest-harrow*, of the family *Leguminosæ.* **1858** CARPENTER *Veg. Phys.* §19 Several genera may, in like manner, be united into a family. **1880** GRAY *Struct. Bot.* ix. §1. 325 Family in botany is synonymous with order. **1881** MIVART in *Nature* No. 615. 337 The order *Lacertilia* is made up of a certain number of large groups, each of which is called a family, which family is again composed of genera. **1916** B. D. JACKSON *Gloss. Bot. Terms* (ed. 3) 143/2 *Family*..a group of genera, formerly styled *Order.* **1916** F. E. CLEMENTS *Plant Succession* vii. 139 A family is a group of individuals belonging to one species. It often springs from a single parent plant. **1951** G. H. M. LAWRENCE *Taxon. Vascular Plants* iv. 46 An order of plants is composed of one or more families... The family usually represents a more natural unit than any of the higher categories. **1960** N. POLUNIN *Introd. Plant Geogr.* xi. 334 The seral equivalent is the *family*, derived from the multiplication and gregarious growth of a single immigrant.

7. ***family of love***: a sect which originated in Holland, and gained many adherents in England in the 16th and 17th c.; they held that religion consisted chiefly in the exercise of love, and that absolute obedience was due to all established governments, however tyrannical.

1579 J. KNEWSTUB (*title*), A Computation of monstrous and horrible heresies..embraced of a number, who call themselves the Familie of Love. **1606** *Sir G. Goosecappe* II. i. in Bullen *O. Pl.* (1884) III. 38 You are either of the familie of Love, or of no religion at all. **1645–62** PAGITT *Heresiogr.* (ed. 6) 105 This sect of the family of love..are so called because..their love is so great that they may join any congregation. **1667** H. MORE *Div. Dial.* Schol. (1713) 568 Being lately informed by an Elder of the Family..that they of their Family that were regenerated..became Christs.

8. *slang.* **a.** The thieving fraternity. See 11, ***family-man***.

1749 *Bamfylde Moore-Carew* (Farmer), No member of the Family. **1812** J. H. VAUX *Flash Dict.* s.v., Thieves, sharpers, and all others who get their living upon the cross, are comprehended under the title of '*The Family*'. **1838** GLASCOCK *Land Sharks* II. 100 This house..was a favourite resort of the Family.

b. *spec.* (The members of) a local organizational unit of the Mafia. orig. and chiefly *U.S.*

1954 FEDER & JOESTEN *Luciano Story* ii. 50 'There's trouble in the family,' he was informed by these delegates. To Mafiosi, it was never 'the club' or 'our mob' or anything but 'the family'. **1967** *N.Y. Times* 9 May 38 A Mafia family is a group of individuals who are not necessarily blood relatives. **1970** 'J. MORRIS' *Candywine Devel.* xiv. 166, I think Mr. Vestucci represents certain family interests in Candywine. **1984** *Times* 29 Oct. 5/2 His execution had been decided by the 'Commission' composed of the local heads of Mafia families.

II. ***attrib.*** (***adj.***) and ***Comb.***

9. Simple *attrib.*, passing into an *adj.* **a.** Of or pertaining to the family or household; domestic. Also, of unexceptionable nature, suitable for all the members of a family.

1602 FULBECKE *Pandectes* 47 Such familie-seruantes or retinue as to be agreeable..to his dignitie. **1641** HINDE *J. Bruen* 66 This Gentleman knew right well, that family exercises were the very goads and spurs unto godlinesse. **1685** BAXTER *Paraphr. N.T.* Matt. vi. 5 Publick Church Prayer, and Family-Prayer are as great duties as secret Prayer. **1694** F. BRAGGE *Disc. Parables* xiii. 438 These Family-devotions at the beginning and close of the day. *a* **1732** T. BOSTON *Crook in Lot* (1805) 23 Such was the crook made in David's lot, through his family-disorders. **1768** *Woman of Honor* II. 178 If this sordid..family-spirit does not soon meet with an effectual check. **1801** M. EDGEWORTH *Belinda* I. xii. 370 She was in hopes that these terrible family quarrels might be made up. **1807** R. SOUTHEY *Lett. from Engl.* vi. 47 To paint the family group is out of my power. **1807** (*title*) The Family Shakespeare. **1817** *Blackw. Mag.* I. 63/2 She..assented to his proposal of having the usual family-worship in her bedroom. **1818** CRUISE *Digest* (ed. 2) II. 157 It was a family affair. **1845** *Edin. Rev.* LXXXII. 407 The development of domestic feelings and family life. **1853** MRS. GASKELL *Let.* ? Feb. (1966) 223 About Ruth one of your London librarians..has had to withdraw it from circulation on account of 'its being unfit for family reading'. **1859** F. C. L. WRAXALL tr. *Robert-Houdin's Memoirs* I. viii. 154 The family tickets gave admission to four persons at half price. **1874** (*title*) Cassell's Family Magazine. **1875** JOWETT *Plato* (ed. 2) III. 329 Tell us something about their family life. **1889** J. K. JEROME *Three Men in Boat* i. 6 If I was a co-operative stores and family hotel combined, I might be able to oblige you. **1902** H. JAMES *Wings of Dove* i. 15 Show family feeling by seeing what I'm good for. **1926** A. MØLLER tr. *Pedersen's Israel* I. II. 376 A dissolution of the family-unity. **1933** *Discovery* Dec. 381/2 The..trend of policies since the war has been to break these [*sc.* estates of eastern Europe] up into single family units. **1937** M. BORDEN *Black Virgin* x. 188 She was new to the house, if not to family rows. **1940** *Illustr. Lond. News* CXCVI. 608/3 'Family' cars that have been laid up indefinitely. **1960** J. B. PRIESTLEY *Lit. & Western Man* vii. 76 *The School for Scandal* might be described as a Restoration comedy.., without the impudent indecencies, and so entirely suitable for family entertainment. **1960** *Guardian* 22 July 4/6 Much of the output..[is] unsuitable for 'family viewing'.

b. In tradesmen's signs, advertisements, and the like; ***family butcher, grocer, druggist***, etc: originally one who supplies commodities for household use, as opposed, *e.g.* to one who supplies them to ships or the army. ***family hotel***: one which claims to be especially for the reception of families.

c. Of or pertaining to a certain family, lineage, or kindred.

1699 M. LISTER *Journey to Paris* 101 He shewed me the Catalogue of Authors..alphabetically disposed by Family Names. *a* **1715** WYCHERLEY *Ess. agst. Pride & Ambit.*, As if nobility consisted alone in being entitled to..have the family plate graved with a coat of arms. **1769** GRAY *Let.* Poems (1775) 365 Ridale-hall, the family-seat of Sir Michael Fleming. **1771** SMOLLETT *Humph. Cl.* III. 182, I was..

engaged in a family partie. **1773** MELMOTH *Cato* Remarks 171 Securing to the heir..a sufficient part of the family-estate to support his rank and station. **1775** G. WHITE *Let.* 2 Oct. in *Selborne* (1789) 195 The name of their [gypsy] clan is *Curleople*..may not this family-name..be the very name they brought..from the Levant? **1780** *Mirror* 25 Apr. 401 The little family-history I am going to relate. **1795** tr. *C.P. Moritz's Travels* 116, I saw..sundry little family parties, walking arm in arm along the banks of the Thames. **1803** BEDDOES *Hygëia* x. 59 A family disposition to insanity. **1813** JANE AUSTEN *Pride & Prejudice* III. xviii. 314 The comfort and elegance of their family party at Pemberley. **1818** *Art Preserv. Feet* 200 Sometimes accidental causes, produce what has been termed a family toe, partly in consequence of its being hereditary. **1829** H. FOOTE *Compan. to Theatres* 36 Private boxes,..family ——. **1846** C. BRONTË *Professor* (1857) II. xxv. 242 He..would dwell on the past times of his house, on his family history. **1901** C. MORRIS *Life on Stage* xv. 203 A short time after that, she sat one evening in Mr. Ellster's family box. **1925** O. JESPERSEN *Mankind, Nation & Individual* ix. 172 The Araukans carefully conceal their personal-name from strangers: in their presence they are called by their family-name. **1967** N. FITZGERALD *Affairs of Death* i. 6 You have the family face at its best. **1969** M. LASKI *Jane Austen & her World* 9 Sir Thomas Leigh..had sheltered Charles I at Stoneleigh Abbey in Warwickshire, the family seat of the younger, ennobled branch of the family.

10. Phrases. **a.** *in a* (or †*the*) *family way*: in a domestic manner; with the freedom of members of the same family: without ceremony. Also † *in family* (= F. *en famille*).

1709 STEELE & ADDISON *Tatler* No. 136 ¶1 His Wife is the Daughter of an honest House, ever bred in a Family-Way. **1768** *Woman of Honor* I. 87 Dining together, in family. **1784** *Lett. to Honoria & Marianne* II. 64 She would..stay some time with them, quite in the family way. **1789** G. KEATE *Pelew Isl.* 107 At the house of this Chief they were received quite in a family way. *a***1809** J. PALMER *Like Master like Man* (1811) I. 193 You'll find all in the family way. **1854** J. S. C. ABBOTT *Napoleon* (1855) II. xii. 214 We should have discussed our interests in a family way. **1859** THACKERAY *Virgin.* II. x. 74 Why don't we ask him and his ladies to come over in a family way and dine with some other plain country gentlefolks?

b. (*to be*) *in the family way*: pregnant. Also *to put in the family way*: to make pregnant.

1796 MRS. E. PARSONS *Myst. Warn.* I. 90 The Countess was again in the family way. **1840** LADY C. BURY *Hist. of Flirt* xxvi, Esther is in the family-way. **1875** JOWETT *Plato* (ed. 2) III. 62 The wives..will have a fine easy time when they are in the family way. **1898** *Sessions Paper* Feb. 266, I did not put his wife in the family way. *a***1935** T. E. LAWRENCE *Mint* (1955) II. ix, There's only one thing..that the Air Force can't do: put us in the family way.

11. Special Comb.: *family portrait*; *family-oriented* adj.; **family allowance**, an allowance paid by the state to parents who have a specified number of children; also any similar allowance paid by an employer to employees with families; in N.Z. called *family benefit*; **family Bible**, a large copy of the Bible for use at family prayers (its fly-leaves often contain a 'family register' or record of the birth of children, etc.); **family-boat** (see quot. 1883); **family circle**, the company of persons and their children, and other relatives and friends, who are inmates in the household; **family coach**, a large closed carriage capable of containing a whole family; also, a certain game of forfeits, in which a story of the adventures of a 'family coach' is related; **family compact**, (*a*) a treaty made in the eighteenth century between the Bourbon dynasties of France, Spain, and the Two Sicilies for common action, *esp.* against England and Austria; (*b*) the name applied to the governing class, esp. the officialdom, of Upper Canada in the first part of the 19th cent.; **family council**, a meeting of the members of a family to decide questions relating to their common interest; *spec.* see *family-meeting*; also *transf.*; **family-disease** (see quot.); **family doctor**, a general practitioner (traditionally regarded as a friend and adviser to the family on other than medical matters); hence **family-doctor** *v. trans.*; **family-government**, (*a*) the government of a family; (*b*) the system in which each family stands alone as a political unit; **family-head** (see quot.); **family-likeness**, a resemblance such as may be looked for in members of the same family; also *fig.*; **family-living**, a benefice in the gift of the head of the family; † **family-lovist** [f. *family of love* (see 7) + -IST], = FAMILIST 3; **family-man** , a man with a family; also (*a*) one who leads a domestic or homely life; (*b*) *slang* a thief; also a 'fence' (cf. sense 8); **family-meeting**, in *Louisiana* and *Quebec*, a council of at least five relations which meets before a public notary to give advice concerning a minor or other person; **family-picture**, (*a*) a painting representing a family; (*b*) a picture handed down as an heirloom; **family-piece**, (*a*) a composition relating to the doings of a family; (*b*) = prec. (*a*); **family planning**, the use of various methods of birth control to limit the size of a family; freq. used *attrib.* of an association, centre, etc., from which medical advice and information about contraception are obtainable; **family practitioner** = *family doctor*; **family resemblance** = *family-likeness*; **family room** *N. Amer.*, a living- or recreation room; **family skeleton** = SKELETON *sb.* 1 b; **family-tree**, a genealogical tree; also a diagrammatic representation of the relationship of specified languages.

1924 E. F. RATHBONE *Disinherited Family* v. 193 *Family allowances in an extremely rudimentary form were started in France in 1890 by the Railway Companies. **1928** *Britain's Industr. Future* (*Lib. Ind. Inq.*) III. Argt. 139 The minimum wage should be fixed for each industry..; the introduction of Family Allowances may be found desirable by industries to which they are suited. **1928** *Manch. Guardian Weekly* 6 Jan. 5/2 A living wage laid down by the State, to pay which industry must be reorganised by State action, family allowances, [etc.]. **1958** *New Statesman* 11 Jan. 29/1 The most vital and cherished social services—family allowances, school meals, welfare food and welfare milk. **1970** *Times* 4 May 9/6 It is for the Government to make an immediate increase in family allowances. **1955** D. O. W. HALL *Portrait of N.Z.* ix. 179 A *family benefit of 10/- weekly is paid the mother for every child below 16 years (up to 18 years if still at school) without any means test. **1740** RICHARDSON *Pamela* II. 359 Good Books, such as a *Family-Bible, a Common-Prayer. **1781** JOHNSON *Lett. Dr. Patten* 25 Sept., This Lexicon..might become a concomitant to the Family Bible. **1908** *Daily Chron.* 20 June 3/1 A regimental record of the family-bible kind. **1822** J. FLINT *Lett. Amer.* 73 The craft, called *family boats. **1883** W. C. RUSSELL *Sailors' Lang.*, Family boats, the name given to smacks worked by members of the same family. **1809** H. MORE *Cœlebs* I. 347 Being agreeable..in one's own *family circle. **1709** *Lond. Gaz.* No. 4522/2 That Coach was preceded by his Majesty's *Family-Coaches. **1852** E. WARNER *Wide W. World* 82 They played the Old Family Coach. **1761** *Hist. Europe* in *Ann. Reg.* 52/2 The only reply was, that the King of Spain had thought proper to renew his *family compacts. **1828** *Toronto Public Library MSS. B104* 153 The measures to be adopted to relieve this province from the evils which a family compact have brought upon it. **1899** J. P. TAYLOR *Cardinal Facts Canad. Hist.* 119 About this time [1820] the 'Family Compact' is said to have been formed in Upper Canada. **1965** *Kingston* (Ont.) *Whig-Standard* 9 Jan. 9/8 He wrested the leadership of the old Family Compact from the Anglican Tories of muddy York and made it into the Conservative party. **1853** MRS. GASKELL *Cranford* iii. 51 The state of the remainder wine was examined into in a *family council. **1902** *Little Folks* 251/1 Ted called a family council in his carpentering shed. **1965** *Guardian* 25 Aug. 5/1 The under-16s..will be dealt with by *Family Councils*—appointed by local authorities and composed of social workers, teachers, doctors, and others experienced in dealing with children. **1884** *Syd. Soc. Lex.*, *Family diseases*, diseases proceeding from heredity. **1846** R. FORD *Gatherings from Spain* xvii. 228 Most Spaniards who can afford it have their *family or bolster doctor, the *Medico de Cabecera*. **1943** A. CHRISTIE *Moving Finger* viii. 92 He spoke in a comfortable family-doctor kind of way. **1952** 'C. BRAND' *London Particular* v. 56 Fat old Tedward, who had family doctored her since she was born. **1715** DE FOE *Fam. Instruct.* I. v. (1841) I. 106 We must set up a *family-government entirely new. **1803** SYD. SMITH *Wks.* 1859 I. 29/2 In politics, they appear to have scarcely advanced beyond family-government. **1867** SMYTH *Sailor's Word-bk.*, **Family-head*, when the stem was surmounted with several full-length figures. **1766** GOLDSM. *Vicar* I. i. 8 A *family likeness prevailed through all..they had but one character. **1824** MEDWIN *Convers. Byron* (1832) I. 94 In his women..there is little family-likeness. **1883** CLODD in *Knowl.* 24 Aug. 115/1 The family likeness of those Indian folk-tales to those [European ones] given above. **1798** JANE AUSTEN *Northang. Abb.* (1833) II. vii. 144 It is a *family living. **1883** READE *Many a Slip* in *Harper's Mag.* Dec. 132/2 Joe was ordained priest, took the family living. **1589** NASHE *Martins Months Minde* To Rdr. Wks. 1883 I. 165, I meddle not here with the Anabaptists, *Family louists, Machiauellists, nor Atheists. **1788** G. A. STEVENS *Adv. Speculist* I. 221 Gamesters, Gamblers or *Family-men. **1856** EMERSON *Eng. Traits, Ability* Wks. (Bohn) II. 44 These private reserved mute family-men. **1846** SNOWDEN *Mag. Assistant* 342 Thieves: Family-men. **1859** W. COLLINS *Q. of Hearts* (1875) 17 I'm a family man myself, with grown-up daughters of my own. **1856** BOUVIER *Law Dict. U.S.* (ed. 6), **Family-meeting*. **1949** M. MEAD *Male & Female* 460 A multi-disciplinary approach to *family-oriented treatment of illness. **1965** M. BRADBURY *Stepping Westward* v. 265, I thought England was a family-oriented society. **1762–71** H. WALPOLE *Vertue's Anecd. Paint.* (1786) I. 147 The *family-picture of the consul Mejer. **1712** HUGHES *Spect.* No. 525 ¶8 One of the most agreeable *family-pieces of this kind I ever met with. **1762–71** H. WALPOLE *Vertue's Anecd. Paint.* (1786) II. 192 Mr. Willett..has a small family-piece of Dr. Hibbard, physician, his wife and five children. **1826** SCOTT *Provinc. Antiq., Seton Chapel*, It is a family-piece, comprehending the Lord Seton, his lady, and four children, painted..by Sir A. More. **1939** *Family Planning Assoc., 9th Ann. Rep.* 1 Objects... To advocate and promote the provision of facilities for scientific contraception so that married people may space or limit their families. **1945** *Lancet* 3 Mar. 294/1 Growing numbers of women attending 'family planning' centres. **1957** *Listener* 26 Sept. 467/2 Family planning..will not spread in the villages until someone invents a contraceptive which is easy, very cheap, and does not require privacy. **1970** *Times* 30 Apr. 12/8 It was members of this committee [*sc.* Birth Control Investigation Committee] who persuaded Lady Denman to form what is now the Family Planning Association to coordinate the work. **1814** JANE AUSTEN *Mansf. Park* I. ix. 174 Of pictures there were abundance, and some few good, but the large part were *family portraits. **1902** A. CONAN DOYLE *Hound of Baskervilles* xiii. 297 A study of family portraits is enough to convert a man to the doctrine of reincarnation. **1931** *N. & Q.* 20 June 447/2 Is not the fifteenth century too early for family portraits? **1846** DICKENS *Dombey* i. 4 'Mr. Pilkins here, who from his position of medical adviser in this family—no one better qualified to fill that position, I am sure.' 'Oh!' murmured the *family practitioner. **1858** *Sat. Rev.* 29 May 566/1 A peculiar and remarkable writer, whose style showed little or no *family resemblances with that of any living author. **1901** A. E. TAYLOR *Probl. Conduct* iii. 151 The family resemblance which all systems of judgments of approbation exhibit. **1953** G. E. M. ANSCOMBE tr. *Wittgenstein's Philos. Investigations* §67, I can think of no better expression to characterize these similarities than 'family resemblances'. **1853** *Harper's Mag.* VI. 443 The first night of my arrival I was honored with a spare *family room. **1884** W. D. HOWELLS *S. Lapham* xix. 356 Indicating the family-room, he added, 'She's in there.' *Ibid.* xxv. 461 He heard talking in the family room. **1968** *Globe & Mail* (Toronto) 3 Feb. 11/5 (Advt.), Every home includes a log burning fireplace and a separate family room. **1850** THACKERAY *Pendennis* II. xxi. 208 That ugly closet..in which, according to the proverb, the *family skeleton is locked up. **1881** Family skeleton [see SKELETON *sb.* 1 b]. **1936** C. DAY LEWIS *Friendly Tree* v. 74 Evelyn and Richard glanced at each other with embarrassment. There was some family skeleton peeping out here. **1961** *Guardian* 23 Mar. 9/2 Family skeletons are being brought out of the German cupboard. **1807** R. SOUTHEY *Lett. from Engl.* lx. 368 An English Esquire would as soon walk abroad in his grandfather's wedding suit, as suffer the *family Tree to be seen in his hall. **1864** THACKERAY *D. Duval* i. (1869) 1, I once drew a fine family tree of my ancestors. **1933** BLOOMFIELD *Lang.* xviii. 311 The comparative method thus shows us the ancestry of languages in the form of a family tree. *Ibid.*, The earlier students of Indo-European did not realize that the family-tree diagram was merely a statement of their method. *Ibid.* 318 The older family-tree theory of linguistic relationship.

'familyish, *a.* [f. as prec. + -ISH.] In *nonce-uses*: **a.** Recalling family associations. **b.** Exhibiting the full force of family ties, 'clannish'.

1824 *New Monthly Mag.* XI. 439 Snooksville had a very familyish sound. **1891** *Harper's Mag.* Aug. 420/2 They're a very familyish sort of family.

famine ('fæmɪn), *sb.* Forms: 4–6 **famin**, **famyn(e**, 4– **famine**. [a. F. *famine* = Pr. *famina*, f. late L. type **famina*, f. *fames* hunger.]

1. a. Extreme and general scarcity of food, in a town, country, etc.; an instance of this, a period of extreme and general dearth.

1362 LANGL. *P. Pl.* A. VII. 309 Famyn schal a-Ryse þorw Flodes and foul weder. **1494** FABYAN *Chron.* VI. clxxxvi. 186 By reason wherof ensued a great famyne. **1555** EDEN *Decades* 20 The violent famine dyd frustrate all these appoyntmentes. **1651** HOBBES *Leviath.* II. xxvii. 157 If in a great famine he take the food by force. **1776** GIBBON *Decl. & F.* I. 285 A long and general famine was a calamity of a more serious kind. **1860** EMERSON *Cond. Life, Fate* Wks. (Bohn) II. 315 Famine..war..and effete races, must be reckoned calculable parts of the system of the world.

fig. **1644** MILTON *Areop.* (Arb.) 72 Should ye..bring a famin upon our minds.

b. personified.

1610 *Histrio-m.* VI. 16 Thin Famine needs must follow Poverty. **1784** COWPER *Task* II. 185 He calls for Famine, and the meagre fiend..taints the golden ear.

2. *transf.* An extreme dearth or scarcity of something specified, material or immaterial.

1611 BIBLE *Amos* viii. 11, I will send a famine in the land, not a famine of bread..but of hearing the words of the Lord. **1634** SIR T. HERBERT *Trav.* 184 These negroes..have no famine of Natures gifts and blessings. **1681** R. KNOX 19 *Years' Captivity* in Arb. *Garner* I. 400, I..lamented under the famine of God's Word and Sacraments. **1888** *L'pool Daily Post* 26 June 4/8 The threatened water famine. **1889** *Pall Mall G.* 7 Nov. 3/3 The perennial talk of an ivory famine has as yet come to nothing.

3. Want of food, hunger; hence, starvation.

*c***1386** CHAUCER *Pard. T.* 123 And schold hir children sterve for famyn. *c***1450** *Merlin* 224 The Citee..was right stronge, that nothynge ne dowted, saf only for famyn. **1586** T. B. *La Primaud. Fr. Acad.* 510 That ancient and usuall punishment of famine. **1605** SHAKS. *Macb.* v. v. 40 If thou speak'st false, Vpon the next Tree shall thou hang aliue Till Famine cling thee. **1773** *Observ. State Poor* 8 More really die of famine than those who are found. **1837** W. IRVING *Capt. Bonneville* III. 101 Their horses..had recovered from past famine and fatigue.

4. Violent appetite, as of a famished person; chiefly *fig.*

1393 GOWER *Conf.* III. 32 Of love the famine I fonde..To fede. **1600** DEKKER *Fortunatus* Wks. 1873 I. 169 The famine of base gold Hath made your soules to murders hands be sold. **1667** MILTON *P.L.* II. 847 Death Grinnd horrible a gastly smile, to hear His famine should be fill'd. **1858** MIDDLETON *Shelley* I. xvii. 168 He..shall never cease thirsting, but, striving ever to quench his thirst..shall only render it so much the more the famine of his nature.

5. *Comb.*: **a.** simple attributive, as *famine-blight*, *-prices*, *relief* (cf. RELIEF[2] 4 a), *-wolf*; **b.** instrumental, as *famine-hollowed*, *-pinched*; **famine-bread**, a species of lichen (*Umbilicaria arctica*); **famine-fever**, (*a*) typhus; (*b*) relapsing fever.

1845 MRS. NORTON *Child of Islands* (1846) 111 *Famine-blights that swept from east to west. **1887** *Encycl. Brit.* (ed. 9) XXII. 409 The so-called '*famine-bread'..which has maintained the life of so many arctic travellers. **1876** OUIDA *Winter City* iii. 45 Is it not a *famine fever which never comes near a well-laden table? **1877** ROBERTS *Handbk. Med.* (ed. 3) I. 132 Relapsing fever prevails generally during periods of famine, and has hence been called famine-fever. **1822** BYRON *Werner* I. i. 119 This..*famine-hollow'd brow. **1856** KANE *Arct. Expl.* II. xxi. 206 These *famine-pinched wanderers of the ice. **1847** *Builder* 29 May 256/2 The *famine prices of provisions. **1856** EMERSON *Eng. Traits, Wealth* Wks. (Bohn) II. 75 Bread rose to famine-prices. **1876** *Correspondence on Famine in W. & S. India* I. 13 in *Parl. Papers* 1877 (C. 1707) LXV. 1 In my letter of 25th August last..I pointed out the necessity of starting *famine

relief works. **1963** *Listener* 17 Jan. 108/2 Such young people seek their own expression in such positive forms of political action as work projects and famine relief. **1891** *Pall Mall G.* 30 Sept. 7/1 Russia at present is..anxious to muzzle the *famine wolf.

† **'famine,** *v. Obs.* [f. prec. sb.]

1. *trans.* To distress with famine; to kill or subdue with hunger; to starve.

1520 *Caxton's Chron. Eng.* VI. 69 b/2 He was put in the castell Aungell, and was famyned to dethe. **1523** LD. BERNERS *Froiss.* I. ccccviii. 711 The flemynges thought by this siege to famyne them within.

2. *intr.* To suffer, or die of, hunger; to starve.

1553 EDEN *Treat. Newe Ind.* (Arb.) 31 For wante of vitayles and foode, they begonne to famyne. **1596** BELL *Surv. Popery* III. x. 412 It grieueth him to behold others famine.

Hence † **'famined** *ppl. a. Obs. rare.*

1622 H. SYDENHAM *Serm. Sol. Occ.* (1637) 178 Rather.. than sacrifice the remainder of a famin'd body to an honourable death.

famish ('fæmɪʃ), *v.* Forms: 5–6 famyssh, (5 -ysch, 6 -esh, -eszsh, -ishe, -issh, -ysh), 6– famish. [alteration of FAME *v.*², after vbs. in -ISH. Cf. AFFAMISH.]

1. *trans.* To reduce to the extremities of famine and hunger; to starve. Also, † *to famish away.*

a **1400–50** *Alexander* 1496 þare suld my folk for defaute be famyscht for euire. **1489** CAXTON *Faytes of A.* II. iii. 96 The other cartagiens that kepte the said townes..were famysshed. **1493** *Festivall* (W. de W. 1515) 100 Tytus laye so sore to the cyte that he famysshed theym. **1535** COVERDALE *Joel* i. 20 The shepe are fameszshed awaye. **1593** SHAKS. *2 Hen. VI*, I. iii. 175, I danc't attendance on his will Till Paris was besieg'd, famisht, and lost. **1659** B. HARRIS *Parival's Iron Age* 91 Spinola before Breda..seeing no means to take it by force, resolved to famish it. **1790** BURKE *Fr. Rev.* Wks. V. 250 The regicides whom he [Henry IV] hanged after he had famished Paris into a surrender. **1871** R. ELLIS *Catullus* xxi. 3 All..that shall ever in after years be famish'd.

fig. **1546** *Supplic. of Poore Commons* (E.E.T.S.) 64 They would famysh the soules of the residue. *c* **1645** HOWELL *Lett.* (1892) II. 379 Some Females..to feed their Pride..will famish Affection. *c* **1766** BURKE *Tracts Popery Laws* Wks. 1842 II. 445 Whose quality it is to famish the present hours. **1817** SHELLEY *Pr. Athanase* I. 38 Those false opinions which the harsh rich use To blind the world they famish for their pride.

2. To kill with hunger, starve to death. Also, *to famish to death.*

c **1440** *Bone Flor.* 875 So longe logyd the sege there, That they wythynne nere famysched were. *a* **1533** LD. BERNERS *Huon* I. 169 He was nere famyshyd for lake of sustenaunce. *a* **1649** DRUMM. OF HAWTH. *Hist. Jas. I.* Wks. (1711) 5 Robert..had famished to death the king's brother David, in the castle of Falkland. **1720** DE FOE *Capt. Singleton* vii. 130 We were in a most dreadful apprehension of being famished to death. **1797** MRS. RADCLIFFE *Italian* vii, Paulo bewailed the probability of their being famished.

† **b.** To deprive (a person) *of* anything necessary to life. *Obs. rare.*

1667 MILTON *P.L.* XII. 78 Where thin Aire Above the Clouds will..famish him of Breath, if not of Bread.

3. *intr.* **a.** To suffer the extremity of want of food; to be intensely hungry. Const. *for.*

1535 COVERDALE *Isa.* ix. 20 Yf a man do turne him to the right honde he shal famesh. **1607** SHAKS. *Cor.* I. i. 5 You are all resolu'd rather to dy then to famish. **1680** BAXTER *Answ. Stillingfl.* lxxiii. 93 They..reproach them as covetous that will rather beg than sin or famish. **1813** SHELLEY *Q. Mab* III. 104 Not one wretch Whose children famish..rears an arm. **1826** DISRAELI *Viv. Grey* VI. i, One of the most hungry mortals that ever yet famished.

fig. **1844** BROWNING *Colombe's Birthday* I. Poems 1887 II. 183 Sir Chynet, You famish for promotion.

† **b.** To die of starvation, perish from want of food. Also, *to famish with hunger. to famish a dog's death. Obs.*

1530 PALSGR. 545/1, I famysshe for honger, *je affame.* **1551** CROWLEY *Pleas. & Pain* 260 If the pore famyshed for lacke of fode. **1607** SHAKS. *Timon* II. ii. 91 Thou shalt famish a Dogges death. **1670** MILTON *Hist. Eng.* v. (1851) 217 A small Iland where many of them famish'd. **1683** DRYDEN *Art. Poetry* iv. 186 Now none famish who deserve to eat. **1796** MORSE *Amer. Geog.* I. 118 They had all miserably famished with hunger.

Hence † **'famisher,** one who famishes (sense 1); **'famishing** *vbl. sb.*, **'famishing** *ppl. a.*

1553 BALE *Gardiner's De vera Obed.* B j, This hathe ben a famysher of the Kinges souldiours. *c* **1489** CAXTON *Sonnes of Aymon* i. 21 It was imprenable but only by famyshynge. **1786** BURKE *W. Hastings* Wks. 1842 II. 126 Sundry documents concerning the famishing..of the women and children of the late sovereign. **1836** W. IRVING *Astoria* I. 16 Their stomachs injured by occasional famishing. **1577** tr. *Bullinger's Decades* (1592) 174 Darius..shutteth vp Daniels enemies in the same denne, to bee torne in peeces by the famishing beastes. **1836** W. IRVING *Astoria* III. 77 The poor famishing wanderers.

famished ('fæmɪʃt). *ppl. a.* [f. prec. + -ED¹.] In senses of the vb. Also in *comb.*, as *famished-looking* adj.

a **1450** *Knt. de la Tour* (1868) 28 The pore pepille..lene and famisshed for hunger. **1591** SHAKS. *1 Hen. VI*, I. ii. 7 The famisht English..Faintly besiege vs one houre in a moneth. *a* **1682** SIR T. BROWNE *Tracts* 59 Poor and half famished fellows despised him. **1781** GIBBON *Decl. & F.* III. 167 The famished host of Radagaisus was in its turn besieged. **1828** MISS MITFORD *Village* Ser. III, (1863) 467 A long, lean, famished-looking boy. **1869** FREEMAN *Norm. Conq.* (1876) III. xii. 138 Some rode on famished horses.

fig. **1633** G. HERBERT *Temple, Longing* i, With sick & famisht eyes..To thee my sighs..ascend. **1877** BRYANT *Poems, Third of November* 1861 vi, Howling, like a wolf, flies the famished northern blast.

famishment ('fæmɪʃmənt). Now *rare.* [f. as prec. + -MENT.]

1. The state, condition, or process of being famished or starved; an instance of this, hungry appetite. Also †a means of starving.

c **1470** HARDING *Chron.* XLIV. iii, For drede of famyshement He treated with the duke Androgeus. **1563–87** FOXE *A. & M.* (1596) 66/2 Eugenia..was assailed with.. famishment in prison. **1611** SPEED *Hist. Gt. Brit.* IX. i. §29 Hee caused the Earle by famishment to yeelde vp his Fort. **1667** *Answ. West to North* 13 The bane of Traffick, and the famishment of the poor Handicrafts man. **1727–36** in BAILEY. **1847** A. H. CLOUGH *Poems & Pr. Rem.* (1869) I. 279 The sky..in Ireland looks upon famishment and fever. **1855** SINGLETON *Virgil* II. 107 He with mad famishment, Three gullets opening snaps up that was thrown.

† **b.** *fig. Obs.*

1569 CROWLEY *Soph. Dr. Watson* i. 206 Not to be pertaker of the mysticall supper at all, is a famishment and death. **1610–11** J. DAVIES *Wittes Pilgrimage* V ij b, Laugh and bee fatt, sith al you touch is gold, Though that foode your Soules famishment affordes.

† **2.** = FAMINE *sb.* 1. *Obs.*

1526 TINDALE *Luke* iv. 25 Greate fammisshment was troughoute all the londe. **1557** N. T. (Genev.) *Mark* xiii. 8 Earthquakes..and famishementes and troubles.

Fammenian, var. FAMENNIAN.

famon, obs. f. of FOEMAN.

† **fa'mose,** *a. Obs.* [ad. L. *fāmōs-us*, f. *fāma* (see FAME).] = FAMOUS.

1432–50 tr. *Higden* (Rolls) I. 181 In whom grete Constantine erecte ij. famose chirches. *c* **1449** PECOCK *Repr.* I. v. 27 Bicause such speche is famose in vce. *c* **1530** in *Pol. Rel. & L. Poems* (1866) 46 Famose poetys of antiquite. **1562** *Register of St. Andrews Kirk Session* (1889) I. 182 Befoyr ane curat and famos wytnes. **1581** MULCASTER *Positions* xxvi. (1887) 103 The famosest knight, of the fellowship. *c* **1625** WHITELOCKE *Lib. Fam.* (Camden) 13 A reader..that was reputed the famosest in that language about the towne. **1727–36** in BAILEY.

† **fa'mose,** *v. Obs.* exc. *arch.* Also 6–7 famoze, 7 famoize. [f. prec. adj.] = FAMOUS *v.* 1.

1590 TARLTON *News Purgat.* (1844) 53 That merrye Roscius..that famosed all comedies so with his pleasant and extemporall invention. **1631** WEEVER *Anc. Fun. Mon.* 687 The red crosse, by which Saint George the Tutelar Saint of all Englishmen is famozed. ? **1650** *Don Bellianis* 55 Our Prince, that is no lesse famosed then he. **1845** HALLIWELL *Fairy Mythology* p. viii, Robin Goodfellow was famosed in every old wives' chronicle for his mad merry pranks.

Hence † **fa'mosed** *ppl. a. Obs.*

1583 STANYHURST *Aeneis* III. (Arb.) 80 Possesseth Pyrrhus thee spouse of famosed Hector? **1600** TOURNEUR *Transf. Metamorph.* lxv, This noble conquest made him famoized. **1613** W. BROWNE *Brit. Past.* II. i. (1772) 27 The halcyon famosed For colours rare.

† **fa'mosity.** *Obs. rare*⁻¹. [ad. F. *famosité*, ad. L. *fāmōsitāt-em* ill fame, f. *fāmōsus*, see FAMOSE *a.*] Celebrity, notoriety, renown.

1535 STEWART *Cron. Scot.* III. 110 Ane Williame of greit famositie. **1727–36** in BAILEY

‖ **fa'moso.** *rare*⁻¹. [It. *famoso*, ad. L. *fāmōsus*: see FAMOSE *a.*] A notorious person.

1663 *Flagellum; or O. Cromwell* (1672) 9 Fate..had decreed..unhappy Birth of this Famoso.

famous ('feɪməs), *a.* Forms: 4–5 famows(e, 4–6 famouse, 5 famus, 4– famous; superl. 6 famoust, 6– famousest. See also FAMOSE. [a. AF. *famous*, OF. *fameus* (mod.F. *fameux*), ad. L. *fāmōs-us*, f. *fāma*: see FAME and -OUS.]

1. Celebrated in fame or public report; much talked about, renowned. Const. *for.* Also † *famous of renown.*

a. of persons, their attributes, etc.

? *a* **1400** *Morte Arth.* 3304 Ffamows in fferre londis, and floure of alle kynges. *c* **1450** *St. Cuthbert* (Surtees) 6421 At mailros boisill', a famus man. **1512** *Act 4 Hen. VIII*, 91 His moste noble fadre of famouse memorye. **1589** PUTTENHAM *Eng. Poesie* III. xix. (Arb.) 242 The famoust Queene that euer was. **1641** MILTON *Reform.* I. (1851) 15 The..Councel of Nicæa, the first and famousest of all the rest. **1697** DRYDEN *Virg. Georg.* III. 191 The..old Stallion..Famous in his Youth for Force and Speed. **1756–7** tr. *Keysler's Trav.* (1760) III. 387 The body of this famous cardinal lies at Rome. **1832** W. IRVING *Alhambra* II. 154 The famous Italian singer Farinelli. **1833** TENNYSON *Blackbird* 16 The melody that made thee famous once, when young.

b. of things.

c **1385** CHAUCER *L.G.W.* 1440 *Hipsiph. & Medea*, This famous tresore. **14..** *Epiph.* in *Tundale's Vis.* (1843) 103 To see this ster most famows of renown. **1587** GOLDING *De Mornay* xxii. 338 There also was her famousest Temple. **1665** MANLEY *Grotius' Low C. Warres* 255 Steeneberg, famous of old for a Harbour. **1674** BOYLE *Excell. Theol.* I. iii. 83 The famous answer given by an excellent Philosopher. **1748** *Anson's Voy.* I. ii. 16 This Island of Madera..is famous ..for its excellent wines. **1782** COWPER *Gilpin* 4 A train band captain eke was he Of famous London town. **1850** McCOSH *Div. Govt.* II. i. (1874) 117 The three famous laws of Kepler. **1868** Q. VICTORIA *Life Highl.* 35 The stream of which [the Tummel] is famous for salmon.

c. Phr. *famous last words* (cf. WORD *sb.* 25 b): a remark or prediction likely to be proved wrong by events.

1948 PARTRIDGE *Dict. Forces' Slang* 67 *Famous last words*, a catch-phrase rejoinder to such fatuous statements as 'Flak's [*sc.* Anti-aircraft fire is] not really dangerous'. **1948** *Shell Aviation News* CXVII. 9/1 Leopoldville is easy to find because you cannot miss the Congo River. (Famous last words!) **1962** J. CANNAN *All is Discovered* iv. 89 'Why... It's nothing.' 'Famous last words.'

† **2.** Of good repute, reputable. *Sc. Obs.*

1555 in Balfour *Practicks* (1754) 145 Twa or thré of his nichtbouris, famous and unsuspect men. **1683** *Act Justiciary* 8 Aug. in Wodrow *Hist. Suff. Ch. Scot.* (1721) II. 309 For proving of this, adduced several famous witnesses.

† **3. a.** In a bad or neutral sense: Notorious. *Obs.* exc. *arch.*

1388 WYCLIF *Matt.* xxvii. 16 He hadde tho a famous man boundun, that was seid Barrabas. **1606** SHAKS. *Ant. & Cl.* I. iv. 48 Menacrates and Menas famous Pyrates. **1680** MORDEN *Geog. Rect.* (1685) 452 That famous infamous English Rebel Stuckley. **1691** TILLOTSON *Serm. 1 John* iv. 9 Sermons 1704 II. 460 The Death of the Cross..was the Death of famous [*later edd.* infamous] Malefactours. **1728** MORGAN *Algiers* I. iv. 160 The Infamously famous Count Julian. **1817** COBBETT *Wks.* XXXII. 367 A famous falsehood, which has appeared in the Morning Post. **1837** CARLYLE *Fr. Rev.* (1872) II. v. ii. 174 Make the name of Mountain famous infamous to all times and lands.

† **b.** Of utterances, etc.; after L. *famosus*: Libellous, slanderous. *Obs.*

1543 in Balfour *Practicks* (1754) 537 That na maner of man mak, write, or imprent ony..writingis..famous or sclanderous to ony persoun..under the pane of death. **1589** PUTTENHAM *Eng. Poesie* I. xxiv. (Arb.) 62 Vntrue and famous libels.

† **4.** That is matter of common talk; common, ordinary, usual. *Obs.*

1528 PAYNEL *Salerne's Regim.* B iv, Coler vnnaturall..is called famous or notable: by reason hit is ofte engendred. **1672** BAXTER *Bagshaw's Scand.* ii. 9 Analogous..words..are to be taken in the most common or famous sense. **1680** MORDEN *Geog. Rect.* (1685) 43 Their mention is very frequent and famous during the race of the French Kings of the Caroline Line. **1727–44** LEWIS *Pecocke* 17 Taking the word *preach* in its most famous signification.

5. Used (chiefly *colloq.*) as an emphatic expression of approval: Excellent, grand, magnificent, splendid, 'capital'.

a **1700** EVELYN *Diary* 13 Nov. an. 1695 (1955) V. 223 Famous & very chargeable Fireworkes. **1798** SOUTHEY *Battle Blenheim* 36 'But every body said', quoth he, 'That 'twas a famous victory'. **1800** M. EDGEWORTH *Parent's Assistant* (ed. 3) V. 147 'There's to be the most *famous* doings, that ever were heard of upon the Downs here,.. Lady Diana Sweepstakes, you know, is a *famous* rider, and archer.' **1836** *Backwoods of Canada* 141 My Irish maid.. soon roused up famous fires, and set the house in order. **1890** *Spectator* 6 Sept. 308/2 It is a famous place for a fair. **1966** *Times* 9 Nov. 1/1 Both parties..were ready to claim a famous victory in the early hours of tomorrow.

† **famous** ('feɪməs), *v. Obs.* exc. *arch.* See also FAMOSE *v.* [f. prec. adj.]

1. *trans.* To make famous. † **a.** To render celebrated, earn celebrity for (*obs.*). **b.** Of a writer, etc.: To celebrate (*arch.*).

1590 LODGE *Euphues' Gold. Leg.* in Halliwell *Shaks.* VI. 11 To famous that house..shewe thy resolution to be peremptorie. **1622** PEACHAM *Compl. Gentl.* 74 The wooden dove of Archytas, so famoused..by Agellius. **1633** BP. HALL *Hard Texts* 508 This empire was famoused..by an eminent King. **1691** WOOD *Ath. Oxon.* I. 465 Men.. worthily famoused on this side, and beyond the Sea. **1873** LOWELL *Among my Bks.* Ser. II. 306 The heroic uncle, whose deeds..were properly famoused by the boy Homer.

† **2.** To cause to be generally reputed *for. Obs.*

1614–15 W. BROWNE *Inner Temple Masque* 26 From whose continuall store such pooles are fed, As in the land for seas are famoused. **1615** T. ADAMS *Two Sonnes* 75 Our eldest, whom we have famoused for our sole and entire heirs.

Hence **'famoused** *ppl. a.*; **'famousing** *vbl. sb.*

1606 FORD *Honor Tri.* (1843) 15 That famoused trophy. **1607** ROWLANDS *Famous Hist.* 5. We toyl so much in other Nations praise, That we neglect the famousing of our own. **1665** SIR T. HERBERT *Trav.* (1677) 50 Men famoused for vertue.

famously ('feɪməslɪ), *adv.* [f. as prec. + -LY².]

† **1.** In a famous or celebrated manner, renownedly. *Obs.*

1579 FULKE *Confut. Sanders* 670 Rome doeth set foorth the merites of Peter and Paule the more famously and solemnly. **1594** SHAKS. *Rich. III*, II. iii. 19 This land was famously enrich'd With politike graue Counsell. **1684** WINSTANLEY in *Shaks. C. Praise* 400 He became so famously witty. **1727–36** BAILEY, *Famously*, renownedly.

† **2.** In or by common talk; commonly, openly. Also, in bad sense: Notoriously. *Obs.*

1553 EDEN *Treat. Newe Ind.* (Arb.) 32 *Molucca* so famously spoken of for the great abundaunce of swete spices. **1592** NASHE *Intercepting of Cert. Lett.* G iij, [Stannyhurst] had neuer been praisd by Gabriel for his labour, if therein hee had not bin so famously absurd. **1630** *R. Johnson's Kingd. & Commw.* 277 Which story is famously knowne in Cambridge. **1637** R. HUMPHREY tr. *St. Ambrose* Pref., It notoriously appeareth, and famously to their eternall infamy brands the Papists. **1701** GREW *Cosm. Sacra* IV. ii. §32 They looked on the Particulars, as Things famously spoken of. **1727** A. HAMILTON *New Acc. E. Ind.* II. xxxiv. 18 The Town is famously infamous for a Seminary of female Lewdness.

† **b.** Publicly; so that the fact may be widely known *Obs.*

1563–87 FOXE *A. & M.* (1684) 709/1 The said John Hus shall be famously deposed and degraded from his priestly Orders.

3. *colloq.* Excellently, splendidly, capitally. Cf. FAMOUS *a.* 5.

1607 SHAKS. *Cor.* I. i. 37, I say vnto you what he hath done Famouslie, he did it to that end. **1671** *Lond. Gaz.* No. 544/4 The *City of Argiers*..is famously carved and painted in her stern, being a new stout Ship. **1746** in *Leisure Hour* (1880) 119, I had the terrible mortification of seeing a horse of Willy's famously beat. **1841** LYTTON *Nt. & Morn.* I. i, I've contrived it famously. **1858** RAMSAY *Remin.* v. (ed. 18) 119 We get on famously.

famousness ('feɪməsnɪs). [f. as prec. + -NESS.] The state of being famous. †**a.** The fact or state of being well-known (*obs.*). **b.** Celebrity, renown.

a. 1605 A. WOTTON *Answ. Pop. Articles* 13 The perpetuall visibility, and famousnesse in the world. **1677** CARY *Chronol.* I. I. I. vi. 16 The famousness and long continuance of the *Annus Æquabilis* in civil use among them.

b. 1548 UDALL, etc. *Erasm. Par. Luke* i. 27 Not by famousnesse of name, nor portlynesse of life. **1675** J. SMITH *Chr. Relig. Appeal* I. 28 The future famousness of a Stage-Player. **1726–36** in BAILEY. **1801** MAR. EDGEWORTH *Belinda* vii, In point of famousness, I'd sport my 'Random' against all the books that ever were..written. **1873** MRS. WHITNEY *Other Girls* xvi (1876) 212 She had taken in the housemaid and small-boy view of famousness.

famp (fæmp). *Geol.* [Of unknown etymology; originally *dial.* (north of England).] 'An indurated wavy calcareous shale' (Phillips) found among limestone rocks. Also *attrib.*, ***famp-bed***.

1836 PHILLIPS *Geol. Yorksh.* II. 28 On which is a 'famp' bed. *Ibid.*, Black beds intermixed with 'famp' and nodules of chert. **1875** URE *Dict. Arts* II. 325 *Famp* is a siliceous bed, composed of very fine particles. **1881** RAYMOND *Mining Gloss.*, *Famp*, Newc., soft, tough, thin shale beds.

†**'fample**, *v. Obs. rare*⁻¹. *trans.* Sense uncertain; in the context, To put (food) into a child's mouth.

c **1230** *Hali Meid.* 37 Hu muchel ha schule at eanes in his muð famplen nowðer to muchel ne to lutel.

famulary ('fæmjʊlərɪ), *a. rare.* [ad. L. *famulāris*, f. *famulus* servant: see -ARY.] Of or belonging to servants.

1840 G. RAYMOND in *New Monthly Mag.* LIX. 245 The famulary group was increased by sundry other servants.

†**'famulate**, *v. Obs.*⁻⁰ [f. L. *famulāt-* ppl. stem of *famulārī*, to be a servant, f. *famulus* servant.] 'To serve' (Cockeram 1623–6).

†**'famulative**, *a. Obs. rare*⁻¹. [f. as prec. + -IVE.] Having the attribute of serving.

1678 CUDWORTH *Intell. Syst.* 45 By means whereof..(as they pretend) the divine creative power is made too cheap.. as being famulative alwaies to brutish..lusts.

famuler, obs. f. of FAMILIAR.

†**'famulist**. *Obs.* [f. L. *famul-us* + -IST.

The genuineness of this word is very doubtful. In the Latin registers of Oxford colleges, the designation *famulus* appended to a name meant sometimes one of the college servants (who used to be regularly matriculated) and sometimes a poor student who entered college as a servant to another undergraduate. Most probably *famulist* is merely a blunder for this word; but it may possibly have been jocularly current as an anglicized form of it.]

1818 TODD s.v. *Famulate*, The word *Famulist* is in use at Queen's College in Oxford for an inferior member of it. **1846** in WORCESTER; and in some later Dicts.

‖**famu'lorum**. [L. genitive pl. of *famulus* a servant.] The name given to a prayer in the Mass for the Commemoration of the living, beginning '*Memento, Domine, famulorum famularumque tuarum*'.

c **1380** ? WYCLIF *Eng. Wks.* (1880) 134 Here special preiere, as famulorum & benefactorum. —— *Sel. Wks.* III. 441 þai say furst..one Famulorum saide of a frere is better þen a Pater noster. **1401** *Pol. Poems* (Rolls) II. 104 Wel I wote that alle ȝe gate never a peny, with the pater-noster, but with ȝoure famulorum..ȝe gete many poundes.

‖**famulus** ('fæmjʊləs). Pl. famuli. [L. *famulus* servant.] An attendant; *esp.* on a scholar or a magician.

1837 CARLYLE *Fr. Rev.* (1872) III. III. iii. 112 The Magician's Famulus got hold of the forbidden Book, and summoned a goblin. **1852** THACKERAY *Esmond* I. v, Faithful little famuli see all and say nothing.

famy, obs. Sc. f. FOAMY.

†**'famylous**, *a. Obs. rare.* [ad. OF. *fameilleux*, *famelleus*, f. L. *fames* hunger.] Famished, hungry, starved.

c **1475** *Partenay* 6258 To socour nedy and tho famylous.

fan (fæn), *sb.*¹ Forms: *α.* **1 fann**, (**fon**, *Northumb.* **fonnæ**), **4–7 fann(e**, **4– fan**. *β.* **5–7 vanne**, **7– van**. [OE. *fann*, str. fem., ad. L. *vannus*, fem., = sense 1 a. Cf. F. *van*.]

1. An instrument for winnowing grain.

a. A basket of special form (also, earlier, a sort of wooden shovel) used for separating the corn from the chaff by throwing it into the air. *Obs.* exc. *Hist.*

a **800** *Corpus Gloss.*, *Uanna*, fon. *c* **950** *Lindisf. Gosp.* Luke iii. 17 His fonnæ *vel* windȝefonnæ. *c* **1000** *Ags. Gosp.* ibid., His fann ys on his handa. *a* **1100** *Gerefa* in *Anglia* IX. 262 Fanna, trogas, æscena. *c* **1386** CHAUCER *Miller's T.* 129 Strouted as a ffanne large and brode. *c* **1440** *Promp. Parv.* 148 Fann to clense wythe corne, *vannus*. **1573** TUSSER *Husb.* (1878) 35 Flaile, strawforke and rake, with a fan that is strong. **1616** SURFL. & MARKH. *Country Farme* 88 The Corne scattered from the Fanne. **1654** TRAPP *Comm. Ps.* xiii. 8 Chaff will get to the top of the Fan; when good Corn ..lieth at the bottom of the heap. **1718** POPE *Iliad* v. 612 As when, on Ceres' sacred floor, the swain Spreads the wide fan to clear the golden grain. **1875** JOWETT *Plato* (ed. 2) III. 635 The grain shaken and winnowed by fans. **1889** ELVIN *Dict. Heraldry* p. xlix, Winnowing-basket..Fan or Vane.

β. *c* **1450** *Lat. Eng. Voc.* in Wr.-Wülcker 570 *Capisterium*, a vanne [or a Seve]. **1601** HOLLAND *Pliny* II. 100 Rushes so big, that they will serue to make sieues, rangers, and vans. **1610** HEALEY *Vives' Comm. St. Aug. Citie of God* (1620) 239 There was also the Vanne, which is otherwise called the creele. **1725** POPE *Odyss.* XI. 158 A shepherd..the Oar surveys, And names a Van. **1791** COWPER *Odyss.* XI. 157 Who shall name The oar..a van.

b. Any kind of contrivance to blow away the chaff; a fanner; a fanning or winnowing-machine.

c **1669** WORLIDGE *Syst. Agric.* (1681) 325 A Fan is an instrument that by its motion artificially causeth Wind: useful in the Winnowing of Corn. **1677** PLOT *Oxfordsh.* 259 They..do it..with the fan at home, I mean the leaved fan; for the knee fan..[is] not in use amongst them..But the wheel fan saves a mans labor. **1707** MORTIMER *Husb.* viii. 117 For the cleansing of Corn..is commonly made use of.. a Fan with Sails. **1768** *Specif. of Meikle & Mackell's Patent* No. 896 A fan to blow out the gross chaff [in a grain dressing machine]. **1836** HEBERT *Engineer's Encycl.* I. 489 *Fan*..a rotative blowing machine, consisting of vanes turning upon an axis, used for winnowing corn.

c. *transf.* and *fig.* Sometimes with allusion to Matt. iii. 12.

1559 T. BRYCE in Farr *S.P. Eliz.* (1845) I. 172 When William Nicoll..Was tryed with their fiery fan. **1570–6** LAMBARDE *Peramb. Kent* (1826) 70 The fire and fan of iudgment and discretion. **1606** SHAKS. *Tr. & Cr.* I. iii. 27 Distinction with a lowd and powrefull fan, Puffing at all, winnowes the light away. **1612** T. TAYLOR *Comm. Titus* i. 15 He hath sought to purge his floore by sundry fannes of afflictions. **1667** MILTON *P.L.* v. 269 He..with quick Fann Winnows the buxom Air.

†**d.** Applied to things resembling a winnowing fan (sense 1 a) in shape (see quots.). *Obs.*

In the Chaucer passage the word is commonly supposed to mean 'quintain'.

c **1386** CHAUCER *Manciple's Prol.* 42 Now sweete sire, wol ye Iusten atte ffan. ? *a* **1500** tr. *Vegetius* in *Promp. Parv.* 148 Olde werriours were wont to iuste with fannes, and pley with the pil, or the pale. *Ibid.*, [Young soldiers ought to have] a shelde made of twigges sumwhat rounde, in maner of a gredryn, the whiche is cleped a fanne.

e. (See quot.; = FANFUL). *dial.*

1863 MORTON *Cycl. Agric.* Gloss., *Fan* (Camb.) of chaff, 3 heaped bushels.

†**2.** An instrument for blowing a fire; *lit.* and *fig.*

1530 PALSGR. 218/2 Fanne to blowe with, *estovillon*. **1594** HOOKER *Eccl. Pol.* Pref. 10 The contradiction of others is a fanne to inflame that love.

3. An instrument for agitating the air, to cool the face, etc. with an artificial breeze. **a.** A fan to be held in the hand.

A common kind, and the one always referred to in transferred senses relating to shape, is constructed so as to admit of being folded up in small compass, its form when unfolded being that of a sector of a circle.

1555 EDEN *Decades* 154 A fanne of golde and an Idole. **1599** B. JONSON *Cynthia's Rev.* III. ii, For the least feather in her bounteous fan. **1641** 'SMECTYMNUUS' *Answ.* §2 (1653) 5 Their daughters walking in Cheapeside with their fannes and farthingales. **1727** SWIFT *Gulliver* II. v. 139 The ladies gave me a gale with their fans. **1760–72** tr. *Juan & Ulloa's Voy.* (ed. 3) I. 32 Fans..made of a very thin kind of palm in the form of a crescent, having a stick of the same wood in the middle. **1837** DICKENS *Pickw.* ii, The widow dropped her fan. **1841–71** T. R. JONES *Anim. Kingd.* (ed. 4) 307 The posterior pair [of wings] are folded up lengthways like a fan. **1850** LAYARD *Nineveh* xiii. 325 Two eunuchs holding fans over the head of the monarch.

†**b.** = PUNKAH. *Obs.*

1696 tr. *Du Mont's Voy. Levant* 133 Fans..hung at the Ceiling..There is also a small silken cord fasten'd to it, and drawn thro' a Hole into the Anti-Chamber, where a Servant is placed to keep the Machine playing. These Fans are usually hung over a Couch, or Bed.

4. *poet.* A wing. [? After It. *vanni* pl.]

α. **1640** FULLER *Joseph's Coat* (1867) 238 The shame-faced birds..Did hold their other fan before their eye. **1700** DRYDEN *Fables, Cock & Fox* 770 Then stretch'd his feather'd fans with all his might. **1818** KEATS *Endym.* I. 764 The fans Of careless butterflies.

β. **1667** MILTON *P.L.* II. 927 His Sail-broad Vannes He spreads for flight. **1791** E. DARWIN *Bot. Gard.* I. 163 You [Sylphs]..the airy surge, Mix with broad vans. **1816** WORDSW. *Poems Sentim. & Reflect.* xxv, Ravens spread their plumy vans. **1830** TENNYSON *Love & Death* 8 Love.. spread his sheeny vans for flight.

5. a. Anything spread out in the shape of a fan (sense 3 a); *e.g.* a leaf, the tail of a bird, the delta at the mouth of a river, fan-like tracery in a roof.

1599 T. M[OUFET] *Silkwormes* 3 Then fig-tree fannes uppon their shame they wore. **1692** R. L'ESTRANGE *Fables* ccxxxiv. 204 The Peacock spreads his Tail, and Challenges the Other, to shew him such a Fan of Feathers. **1807** SOUTHEY *Espriella's Lett.* I. 142 On the upper story live peacocks are spreading their fans. **1815** RICKMAN in *Smith's Panorama Sc. & Art* I. 163 The squares were filled with fans, &c. of small tracery. **1856** MISS MULOCK *J. Halifax* i. 6 The large brown fan of a horse-chestnut leaf. **1871** TYNDALL *Fragm. Sc.* (1879) I. vi. 211 A fan of beams, issuing from the hidden sun, was spread out. **1879** SIR G. SCOTT *Lect. Archit.* II. 218 The interstices between the fans are filled up in various ways. **1883** *Daily News* 25 June 2/1, I..detect a strain of the tendon in the fan of the off fore-heel.

β. **1821** JOANNA BAILLIE *Met. Leg.*, *Calum* xvi, As the deep vans [of the palm leaf] fall and rise.

b. = *fan-light*.

1844 ALB. SMITH *Adv. Mr. Ledbury* xxviii. (1886) 85 There was a light over the fan of the door.

c. *Organ-building* (see quot.).

1880 HOPKINS in Grove *Dict. Mus.* II. 598 s.v. *Organ*, A long arm of iron, called a fan, extending horizontally in front of the vertical draw-rods.

d. *Physical Geogr.* A fan-shaped or conical alluvial deposit formed by a stream or river where its bed becomes less steep (e.g. at the edge of a plain); *esp.* a deposit of little height and gentle slope (cf. CONE *sb.*¹ 1 d). Also *attrib.*, as ***fan-delta***, ***-terrace***.

1864 J. VON HAAST *Rep. Form. Canterbury Plains* 19 Thinking that giving such a name [*sc.* 'delta'] to the alluvial accumulations of the rivers in this island, showing some peculiarities, would impart an erroneous impression, Dr. Hector and myself, in drawing up a synopsis of the geological formations of New Zealand, have adopted for the formation of those subaerial accumulations the expression 'Fan', for those of regular water-courses; and of 'Half-cone', for those of intermittent mountain torrents, and we shall for the future use these two expressions. **1873** *Q. Jrnl. Geol. Soc.* XXIX. 446 At the mouth of each of these [gorges] are alluvial fans, which project out into the flat of the river-alluvium. *Ibid.* 447 The fan is properly a flat cone, having its apex at the mouth of the ravine. **1883** *Proc. R. Physical Soc. Edin.* VII. 290 In this paper *lateral* delta terraces will be referred to as fan terraces. **1884** DAWSON in *Leisure Hour* Aug. 492/1 A great mass of similar matter was projected from it in a fan or delta. **1890** GILBERT in *U.S. Geol. Survey Monogr.* I. 81 The 'alluvial fan' of Drew is the 'alluvial cone' of American Geologists, and there would be some reason for preferring 'fan' to 'cone' if it were necessary to employ a single term only. It is convenient to use them as synonyms, employing 'cone' when the angle of slope is high and 'fan' when it is low. **1902** in Ld. Avebury *Scenery of Eng.* 482 The vale of Neath contains a series of such cones or 'fans' of gravel. **1920** *Nature* 13 May 322/2 The wind-worn grains of magnetite brought northward from the great fan-deltas of the Adour system. **1948** *Proc. Prehist. Soc.* XIV. 34 These alluvial fans extend right down to the sea. **1965** A. HOLMES *Princ. Physical Geol.* (ed. 2) xviii. 551 There are all gradations from wide fans 10–100 miles across that are usually nearly flat.., through fans of moderate width and inclination.., to relatively small steep-sided cones..built of the coarser debris brought down by short torrential streams.

6. A rotating apparatus (analogous to the later forms of winnowing fan: see 1 b) usually consisting of an axle or spindle, with arms bearing flat or curved blades: **a.** for producing a current of air as a means of ventilation, etc.

1835 URE *Philos. Manuf.* 380 The effect of one of Fairbairn and Lillie's four-guinea fans upon a large factory is truly admirable. **1854** RONALDS & RICHARDSON *Chem. Technol.* (ed. 2) I. 314 A fan, by which heated and compressed air could be supplied to the ash-pit. **1869** E. A. PARKES *Pract. Hygiene* (ed. 3) 131 A powerful fan is used to drive air into some of the wards. **1881** RAYMOND *Mining Gloss.*, *Fan*, a revolving machine, to blow air into a mine (pressure-fan)..or to draw it out (suction-fan).

b. for regulating the throttle-valve of a steam-engine. Also called *fan-governor*.

1887 EWING in *Encycl. Brit.* (ed. 9) XXII. 509 The Allen governor..has a fan directly geared to the engine.

c. in a windmill (see quot.).

1825 J. NICHOLSON *Operat. Mechanic* Gloss. 776 *Fan*, small vanes or sails to receive the impulse of the wind, and ..to keep the large sails of a smock wind-mill always in the direction of the wind. **1874** in KNIGHT *Dict. Mech.*

d. (see quot.); also *fan-fly*.

1825 J. NICHOLSON *Operat. Mechanic* Gloss. 776 *Fan*..an instrument..to decrease speed by its action on the air.

e. *Soap-manuf.* (see quot.).

1885 CARPENTER *Manuf. Soap* vi. 158 An important adjunct to a soap-copper..for preventing the contents from boiling over..is called a fan, and..it consists essentially of a rotating paddle, whose blades just touch the top of the boiling mass.

f. In a motor vehicle, an apparatus for sending a current of cold air over the radiator. Also *attrib.*, as **fan belt**, the belt which transmits torque to the fan from the engine.

1900 *Motor-Car World* May 178/2 The motor..is cooled by means of a fan driven from the periphery of the fly-wheel. **1904** GOODCHILD & TWENEY *Technol. & Sci. Dict.* 215/1 *Fan cooling*, a small fan, worked by the motor, is sometimes used to drive a current of cool air on to the outside of the cylinder to keep it cool. **1909** *Westm. Gaz.* 27 Apr. 4/1 The cylinders had kept so cool by the fan-blower that I could almost keep my hand on the combustion head. **1912** *Motor Man.* (ed. 14) iii. 64 An alternative method which avoids the use of a separate fan, is provided by fan-vaned arms in the fly-wheel. **1921** *Daily Colonist* (Victoria, B.C.) 19 Oct. 6/1 (Advt.), We recommend that you carry a spare fan belt of genuine leather. **1939** J. HARRISON *Motor-Cars To-day* vi. 82 Under conditions where slow speed is combined with heavy pulling, such as when climbing a hill, there would be a risk of over-heating if it were not for the fan. **1956** 'T. B. D. SERVICE' *Ford Cars* v. 114 It may be necessary, after extended mileage, to replace a fan belt. **1963** BIRD & HUTTON-STOTT *Veteran Motor Car* 175 The Vivinus.. voiturette had a fan-assisted air-cooled engine. **1963** R. F. WEBB *Motorists' Dict.* 95 *Fan cooling*. This is necessary for any air-cooled engine that is placed in an enclosed engine compartment.

7. a. The flukes or lobes of the whale's tail. **b.** *Naut.* The screw used in propelling vessels; a single blade of the same. Also *attrib.* in ***two-fan***. **c.** *Angling.* A similar apparatus on spinning-bait.

1785 *Specif. of Bramah's Patent* No. 1478 Fig. 25. A is a wheel..made with fans on its extremity like the water wheel of a mill..The fans will then act as oars and force the ship forward. **1859** J. S. MANSFIELD in *Merc. Marine Mag.* (1860) VII. 15 Her engines..worked a two-fan screw. *Ibid.* 17 The *Prince* was supplied with a three-bladed fan. **1867** F. FRANCIS *Angling* iv. (1880) 120 The other end of the brass [of the spinning bait] has fixed on it a pair of wings or fans, on the Archimedean screw principle.

†**8.** Confused with FANE *sb.*[1], VANE. **a.** A pennon. **b.** A weathercock. *Obs.*

c **1375** BARBOUR *Troy-bk.* I. 229 With fannys ande banneres wpone hight Aboue standande. *c* **1475** *Voc.* in Wr.-Wülcker 805 *Hic cherucus*, a fanne [cf. *Promp. Parv.* 148 Fane of a stepylle, *cherucus*]. **1650** B. *Discolliminium* 49 A red high-crown'd Cap on his head, with..a Fan or weather-cock on the top of it.

†**9.** The motion of the air caused by or as by a fan. *Obs.* [Properly a distinct word: f. the vb.]

1606 SHAKS. *Tr. & Cr.* v. iii. 41 The captiue Grecian fals Euen in the fanne and winde of your faire Sword.

10. *attrib.* and *Comb.* **a.** simple attributive (sense 3 a), as ***fan-exercise***, ***-form***, ***-stick*** (whence ***fanstick-maker***), ***-wind***; ***fan-like***, ***-wise*** adj. and adv.; ***fan-fashion*** adv.; (sense 6) as ***fan-blast***, ***-blower***, ***-house***, ***-shaft***, ***-ventilator***, ***-wheel***. **b.** attributive in the sense of resembling a fan in shape, as ***fan-coral***, ***-crest***, ***-hoop***, ***-jet***, ***-leaf***, ***-shell***. **c.** objective, as ***fan-bearer***, ***-maker***, ***-painter***, ***-painting***, ***-tearer***; ***fan-bearing*** adj. **d.** parasynthetic and similative, as ***fan-crested***, ***-leaved***, ***-nerved***, ***-pleated***, ***-shaped***, ***-veined*** adjs.

a. 1875 *Encycl. Brit.* III. 552 *Fan blast machines are frequently employed..to urge the fire of steam boilers. **1847** *Rep. Comm. Patents 1846* (U.S.) 84 The *fan blowers now used in steamboats for blowing the fires in the furnaces are generally made from two to three feet in diameter. **1874** KNIGHT *Dict. Mech.*, *Fan-blower*, a blower in which a series of vanes fixed on a rotating shaft creates a blast of air. **1867** OUIDA *C. Castlemaine* (1879) 2 Practising the *Fan exercise. **1853** KANE *Grinnell Exp.* xxxv. (1856) 319 This expanded, *fan-fashion, as it rose. **1871** *Figure Training* 110 The toes ..spread widely, and in *fan form, out. **1888** *Pall Mall G.* 26 Jan. 7/1 The *fanhouse was partly destroyed. **1816** SOUTHEY *Poet's Pilgrimage* IV. 46 Where loftiest trees High o'er the grove their *fan-like foliage rear. **1836** TODD *Cycl. Anat.* I. 688/1 The arms..are separated one from the other, fan-like. **1686** *Lond. Gaz.* No. 2149/4 Two *Fan-sticks, Carved curiously with hollow work. **1761** *Gentl. Mag.* XXXI. 498 The ladies began to count their fan sticks. **1723** *Lond. Gaz.* No. 6170/9 Edward Bunn..*Fan-Stick-maker. **1874** KNIGHT *Dict. Mech.*, **Fan-ventilator*. **1842** BRANDE *Dict. Sc.* s.v. *Fan*, The force of the current created by the *fan wheel. **1578** BANISTER *Hist. Man* VII. 94 A *fanwynde to the hart, to coole the same. **1882** T. FOSTER in Proctor *Nature Studies* 55 Feathers radiating *fanwise from each of the fore-limbs. *Ibid.* 56 The fan-wise and rounded arrangement of the wing-feathers.

b. 1806 *Gazetteer Scot.* (ed. 2) 178 Great quantities of sponge and *fan-coral are annually thrown ashore. **1881** *Rep. Geol. Expl. N. Zealand* 67 This fan-coral bed. **1883** MOLLETT *Dict. Art*, **Fan-crest* Her., an early form of decoration for the knightly helm. **1756** COWPER *Connoisseur* cxxxiv, Mrs. Mayoress..came sidling after him in an enormous *fan-hoop. **1884** KNIGHT *Dict. Mech.* IV. 326 **Fan-jet*, a form of nozzle for watering-pots and engines having a fan or spoon shaped lip. **1869** A. R. WALLACE *Malay Archip.* xvii. 422 It is probably the Livistona rotundifolia of botanists, and is the most complete and beautiful *fan-leaf I have ever seen. **1879** LADY C. SCHREIBER *Jrnl.* 1 Dec. (1911) II. 248 He had come to England and brought some fan leaves.

c. 1877 A. B. EDWARDS *Up Nile* viii. 205 The King, attended by his *fan-bearers, returns in state. **1596** DRAYTON *Mortimeriados* Tj, No Apish *fan-bearing Hermophradite. **1710** *Lond. Gaz.* No. 4781/3 Mr. Lewis Fortin, *Fanmaker. **1858** SIMMONDS *Dict. Trade*, *Fan-maker*, a manufacturer of ladies' fans. *Fan and Sky-light Maker*, a manufacturer of semi-circular windows and glazed roofs. **1723** *Lond. Gaz.* No. 6188/10 John Gibbons..*Fan-Painter. **1879** *Encycl. Brit.* (ed. 9) IX. 28 Rosalba Carriera was..a fan painter of celebrity in the 17th century. *Ibid.*, Cano de Arevalo..devoted himself to *fan painting. **1695** CIBBER *Love's Last Shift* III, An eternal *Fan-tearer, and a constant Persecutor of Womankind.

d. 1799 BARTON, *Fragm. Nat. Hist. Pennsylv.* 2 *Mergus cucullatus* *Fan-crested-Duck. **1834** CAUNTER *Orient. Ann.* v. 85 The *fan-leaved palm. **1884** *Syd. Soc. Lex.*, **Fan-nerved*, having the nerves radiating like a fan from one point as in some leaves and insects' wings. **1873** *Young Englishwoman* June 286/1 *A fan-pleated flounce. **1892** *Pall Mall G.* 19 May 1/3 Fan-pleated bows of lace. **1776** WITHERING *Brit. Plants* (1796) IV. 337 Grows exactly like the Boletus versicolor..*Fan-shaped; scarcely ½ an inch diameter. **1807** BRITTON *Architect. Antiq.* I. (King's Coll. Chapel) 8 They appear in the fan-shaped tracery, or groining of the inner surface. **1850** LYELL *2nd Visit U.S.* II. 134 The swamp palmetto..raises its fan-shaped leaves. **1866** *Treas. Bot.* s.v., **Fan-veined*, when the veins or ribs are disposed like those of a fan.

e. In various *attrib.* uses relating to the ventilation of a mine by means of a fan.

1875 URE *Dict. Arts* III. 1069 The fan is driven by a small ..engine K, connected to a crank on the end of the fan-shaft B. **1883** W. S. GRESLEY *Gloss. Coal-mining* 101 *Fan drift*, a short tunnel leading from a short distance from the top of the upcast shaft to the fan chamber or casing in which the fan runs, along which the whole of the return air is drawn by the fan... *Fan shaft*. 1. A shallow pit-shaft sunk beneath a fan connecting it with the fan drift. 2. The upcast shaft where a fan is in use. **1906** *Daily Colonist* (Victoria, B.C.) 14 Jan. 10/3 Firemen, engineers, fanmen and pumpmen..had their wages increased on November 1. **1908** *Westm. Gaz.* 9 Mar. 7/4 The fan-drift connecting the present down-cast pit with the existing fan has at last been completed. **1921** *Dict. Occup. Terms* (1927) §047 *Fan boy*, *fan man*,..turns handle of small ventilating fan to ventilate heading not served by main air current. **1927** *Daily Tel.* 7 June 12/5 The dismissal of three fanmen who refused to do certain work. **1963** *Gloss. Mining Terms* (*B.S.I.*) II. 10 *Fan drift*, an airway leading from a mine shaft, or airway, to a fan. *Ibid.*, *Fan shaft*. 1. The ventilating shaft to which a mine fan is connected. 2. The spindle on which a fan impeller is mounted.

f. *Geol.* Used *attrib.* and in *Comb.* to denote an arrangement of strata in a series of folds which incline outwards from the central fold, the axes of the folds being likened to the diverging lines of a fan.

1882 A. GEIKIE *Text-bk. Geol.* VII. 917 The inward dip and consequent inversion..lead up to the fan-shaped structure, where the oldest rocks of a series occupy the centre and overlie the younger masses. **1902** *Encycl. Brit.* XXVIII. 652/2 The peculiar arrangement in mountains known as fan-structure may be produced by the continued compression of a simple anticline. **1937** WOOLDRIDGE & MORGAN *Physical Basis Geogr.* v. 68 Before the recognition of recumbent folds or nappes..the Alps were usually interpreted as showing 'fan-folding'.

11. Special comb.: **fan-banner**, a fan-shaped banner; **fan belt**, see 6 f; **fan-bonnet**, a bonnet so called from its shape; **fan consonant**, a consonant pronounced with the edges of the tongue more extended than is usual in making analogous sounds, as in the Arabic 'emphatic' consonants; **fan cooling**, see 6 f; **fan dance**, a solo dance in which the performer uses a fan or fans, esp. to conceal her nudity; hence *fan dancer*; **fan-delta**, see 5 d; **fan draught**, a system of supplying air in boiler furnaces by means of mechanically driven fans; **fan flat**, the flat [FLAT *sb.*[3] 10 b] in which the fans for ventilating the boiler room of a ship are situated; **fan-fly** = FAN *sb.* 6 d; **fan-forge** (see quot.); **fan-frame** (see quot.); **fan-governor** (see FAN *sb.* 6 b): **fan-groining**, *Arch.* = *fan-tracery*; **fan heater**, a heater containing an electric fan that forces air over an electrically-heated element into a room or other place; **fan-jet (engine)**, a jet engine in which additional thrust is provided by cold air drawn by a fan through a duct surrounding the rest of the engine, which is used to drive the fan; also (as *fan-jet*), an aeroplane having such engines; = TURBO-FAN; **fan-lift** *a. Aeronaut.*, fitted with fans to assist the vertical take-off of an aircraft; **fan marker** *Aeronaut.*, a radio marker beacon that transmits a fan-shaped beam; **fan-mount** [= Fr. *monture d' éventail*], the frame upon which a fan is mounted; **fan-palm**, a name applied to palms having fan-shaped leaves; **fan-plant**, the palmetto; **fan-print**, a design printed upon a fan; **fan-shade**, a shade for a lamp, etc., in form like a circular fan; **fan-steam-engine** (see quot.); **fan-tracery**, *Arch.* (see quot. 1842); **fan-training**, *Horticulture*, a method of training fruit trees on a trellis or wall, in the form of a fan; so **fan-trained** *a.*; **fan-tree**, (*a*) = *fan-palm*; (*b*) a tree spread out in the form of a fan (in quot. *attrib.*); **fan-vaulting** = *fan-tracery*; **fan-window** (see quot.); **fan-work** = *fan-tracery*; **fan worm**, any of various annelids of the families Sabellidæ and Serpulidæ. Also FAN-LIGHT, FAN-TAIL.

1835 WILLIS *Pencillings* I. xviii. 128 The immense *fan-banners of peacocks' feathers. **1774** *Westm. Mag.* II. 484 Black *Fan Bonnets. **1902** H. SWEET *Primer Phonetics* (ed. 2) 36 *Fan (spread) consonants..are modifications of point and blade consonants. [**1908** —— *Sounds Eng.* 45, *tl*, *dl* occur in Irish English as substitutes for þ, ð respectively; in them the fan modification is supplemented by a slight raising of the back of the tongue.] **1879** *Fan dance [see DANCE *sb.* 2]. **1951** T. RATTIGAN *Who is Sylvia?* II. 248 I'd better get Babs to do her fan dance—if she's still vertical. **1936** R. E. SHERWOOD *Idiot's Delight* I. 22 Shirley is the principal, a frank, knowing *fan dancer. **1894** W. H. WHITE *Man. Naval Archit.* (ed. 3) xiv. 561 *Fan draught is also of great value under unfavourable conditions, such as hot weather, calms, or following winds. **1909** *Westm. Gaz.* 15 May 2/2 A monstrous wave..poured into the *fan-flat. **1923** *Man. Seamanship* II. xvii. 285 The fans are situated on an enclosed fan flat from which they draw their air. *Ibid.*, Access to the boiler rooms is arranged through the fan flats. **1868** DENISON *Clocks & Watches* (ed. 5) 28 The simplest of all the methods of regulating the velocity of the train..is the *fan-fly. **1884** KNIGHT *Dict. Mech.* IV. 326 **Fan-forge* a transportable form of forge and fan. **1884** *Encycl. Brit.* (ed. 9) XVII. 834 The *fan-frame [of an organ] is a set of backfalls having one set of ends close together, usually corresponding to the keys; the other ends are spread widely apart. **1881** C. A. EDWARDS *Organs* 71 The communication ..effected by..the fan-frame movement. **1879** SIR G. SCOTT *Lect. Archit.* II. 222 *Fan groining [is] itself a purely English invention. **1961** I. MURDOCH *Severed Head* vi. 48 He dangled his long broad-nailed hand in front of his new *fan heater. **1970** *Bodl. Libr. Rec.* VIII. 173 Cold air is deflected from the entrance by three 3kw fan heaters. **1963** *Sat. Rev.* 20 July 14 (Advt.), In 1961, American Airlines introduced a new engine called the *fan-jet—with 30% more power than ordinary jets. **1963** *N.Y. Times* 15 Sept. p. xx7/3 The fan-jet engines..have turbine blades spaced for a minimum of sound. **1967** N. E. BORDEN *Jet-Engine Fund.* 47 Fanjets, as they are called by some of the commercial airlines, and turbofans are one and the same thing. **1968** *Daily Colonist* (Victoria, B.C.) 10 Nov. 9/6 The nose gear of an Alaska Airlines 727 fanjet was severed Saturday afternoon when the plane collided with a moose as the plane came in for a landing. **1961** *Flight* LXXX. 504/2 Jet and *fan lift aircraft appear to offer good range-speed-payload performance where substantial range is required and where hovering requirements are at a minimum. **1961** *Aeroplane & Astronaut.* CI. 791/1 Two VTOL test-bed aircraft using the G.E. J85-5 fan-lift engine. The complete programme, which covers two years and will cost $10.5 million, includes the construction of the two fan-lift airframes by Ryan at San Diego. **1948** *Shell Aviation News* CXXIV. 8/2 Written examinations are required on radio facilities in the New York area, including radio ranges, homing facilities, *fan markers and let down procedures on the heavily congested La Guardia airport. **1753** *Scots Mag.* May 215/1 So inconsiderable an implement as a *fan-mount. **1865** BROWNING *Poems* I. 22 To carry pure death in..a fan-mount. **1820** T. GREEN *Universal Herbal* I. 284/2 *Chamærops Humilis.* Dwarf *Fan Palm. **1839** MARY HOWITT *Humming-bird* 12 They flit about..through the fan palm tree. **1840** F. D. BENNETT *Whaling Voy.* II. 345 *Corypha umbraculifera*..Fan Palm..It resembles the common Fan Palm, or Palmyra, of the East Indies. **1885** LADY BRASSEY *The Trades* 177 It is sometimes called the fan-palm, because travellers use the leaves as fans. **1884** MRS. HOUSTON *Yacht Voy. Texas* II. 11 Frequent tufts of the *fan-plant; as it is here called. **1860** FAIRHOLT *Costume* (ed. 2) s.v. *Fan*, I have some *fan-prints of various similar subjects. **1867** J. HOGG *Microsc.* I. iii. 160 One of the old-fashioned *fan-shades will be found useful. **1874** KNIGHT *Dict. Mech.*, **Fan-Steam-engine*. The action of this steam is the inverse of that of the fan. The outer annular casing.. discharges [steam] from its inner surface in tangential jets upon the scoop-shaped blades which are attached to a rotating shaft. **1815** RICKMAN in *J. Smith's Panorama Sci. & Art* I. 164 We now come to a new and most delicate description of roof, that of **fan-tracery*. **1842** BLOXHAM *Gothic Architecture* 196 A very rich and peculiar description of vaulting is one composed of pendant semi-cones covered with foliated panel-work, called *fan-tracery*. **1871** ROBINSON *Loudon's Horticulturist* viii. 325 *Fan-training is chiefly adapted for trees trained against walls. **1880** S. WOOD *Tree Pruner* 5 A well-developed *fan-trained Peach-tree. **1835** BROWNING *Paracelsus* v. 138 Light strippings from the *fan-trees. **1846** BAXTER *Libr. Pract. Agric.* (ed. 4) II. 379 The fruit-tree method [of pruning] in which the plant is spread out in the fan-tree manner. **1835** R. WILLIS *Archit. Middle Ages* 83 This appears to be the first step towards *fan-vaulting. **1874** KNIGHT *Dict. Mech.*, **Fan-window* (*Arch.*), a semicircular window with radial sash. **1801** *Beauties Eng. & Wales* I. 48 The vast arched roof..with its voluminous stones displaying all the elegance of *fan-work. **1833** W. BARNES *Gent. Mag. Lib. Topog.* III. (1893) 314 Four fan-work groins. **1851** *Fan-worm [see SABELLA]. **1963** R. P. DALES *Annelids* 15 The most specialized tube-dwellers are the sabellid and serpulid fan-worms.

fan, *sb.*[2] Also 7 fann, phan. [Abbrev. of FANATIC. Re-formed in 19th c.] **1.** A fanatic; in mod.E. (orig. *U.S.*): a keen and regular spectator of a (professional) sport, orig. of baseball; a regular supporter of a (professional) sports team; hence, a keen follower of a specified hobby or amusement, and *gen.* an enthusiast for a particular person or thing.

1682 *New News from Bedlam* 13 The Loyal Phans to abuse. *Ibid.* 40 To be here Nurs'd up, Loyal Fanns to defame, And damn all Dissenters on purpose for gain. **1889** *Kansas Times & Star* 26 Mar., Kansas City base-ball fans are glad they're through with Dave Rowe as a ball club manager. **1896** ADE *Artie* xvii. 158 I'm goin' to be the worst fan in the whole bunch. **1901** *Dialect Notes* II. 139 *Fan*, a base ball enthusiast; common among reporters. **1914** *Daily Express* 3 Oct. 3 First League football 'fans' in London can have a joyous time to-day. **1915** *Film Flashes* 13 Nov. 1 It is quite usual for a picture 'fan' to come out of one theatre and immediately cross the road to another. **1919** W. T. GRENFELL *Labrador Doctor* (1920) iv. 56 Among my acquaintances there were not a few theatre fans. **1921** A. W. MYERS *20 Yrs. Lawn Tennis* 142 This was sheer spectacular tennis, dear to the hearts of the American 'fans'. **1925** H. V. MORTON *Heart of London* 93 The fight fans howling like a pack of hungry wolves. **1928** S. VINES *Humours Unreconciled* xiii. 168 What about..your League of Nations and disarmament fans? **1950** *Manch. Guardian Weekly* 4 May 15/4 The Water Department..had received..'good-natured' complaints from base-ball fans about the washing-out of two days' play.

2. *Comb.* **fan club**, a group formed by the devotees of some hero, 'star', etc.; **fan letter**, a letter from an admirer to a celebrity; **fan magazine**, a journal specializing in some common object of devotion or in well-known personalities; **fan mail**, the letters sent to a celebrity by his or her followers.

1941 V. FAULKNER in *Sat. Even. Post* 6 Sept. 37/3 Sleepy Hollow, the name Desire had selected for her residence from a contest held by her fan club. **1959** 'O. MILLS' *Stairway to Murder* v. 51, I believe she's the President of your Fan Club. **1932** WODEHOUSE *Louder & Funnier* 41 How many fan-letters did you get last week? **1937** W. S. MAUGHAM *Theatre* x. 82 She was naturally polite and it was, besides, a principle with her to answer all fan letters. **1928** *Amer. Speech* III. 364 It was picked up from a 'fan-magazine'. **1951** *Life* 21 May 130/2 'Fanzines', or fan magazines, which are usually small mimeographed publications devoted to amateur STF, criticism and gossip. **1924** *Motion Pict. Mag.* June 43 (*title*) The business of fan mail. **1937** AUDEN & MACNEICE *Lett. fr. Iceland* 17 A poet's fan-mail will be nothing new. **1955** R. BANNISTER *First Four Minutes* xiv. 194 It was the beginning of a fan mail and of invitations to open bazaars that have continued ever since.

Fan (fæn), *sb.*[3] and *a.* Also **Fang.** [Fr. *Fan*, presumably ad. Fan *Pangwe*.] **A.** *sb.* **a.** A member of an African people in the Ogowe basin in western equatorial Africa. **b.** The Bantu

language of this people. **B.** *adj.* Of or pertaining to this people or their language.

1861 P. B. DU CHAILLU *Expl. & Adv. Afr.* vii. 65 He..set off to a Fan village. *Ibid.* 67 Great crowds of *Fan*..came to see me. **1865** *Trans. Ethnol. Soc. Lond.* III. 37 It is proposed thus to write the very nasal nasals of the Fan language. **1879** *Encycl. Brit.* X. 3/2 The Fan, whose name appears under the various forms of Fanwe, Panwe, Phaouin, and Paouen, are newcomers to the Gaboon district. **1883** R. N. CUST *Sk. Mod. Lang. Afr.* II. xii. 413 As we advance into the Interior, we find only two leading Languages, the Fan, spoken by the invading Oshiba, and the Benga. **1897** M. KINGSLEY *Trav. W. Afr.* xiv. 319 A young Fan man has to fend for himself. *Ibid.* 322 Fan pottery, although rough and sunbaked, is artistic in form. **1911** J. FRAZER *Golden Bough* (ed. 3) I. vi. 349 Thus in the Fan tribe the strict distinction between chief and medicine-man does not exist. The chief is also a medicine-man and a smith to boot; for the Fans esteem the smith's craft sacred, and none but chiefs may meddle with it. **1936** *Discovery* June 172/1 The area of the Western Bantu includes..in the west [the home of] such renowned cannibals as the Fang; it also includes the territory of considerable and highly organised kingdoms, such as the medieval kingdoms of the Kongo and the Balunda, and the later Bushongo Empire. **1962** *Listener* 12 Apr. 630/1 The Fan villages.

fan (fæn), *v.* Forms: 1 fannian, 4–5 *south. dial.* **vannien, vanne,** 6 **fane,** 6–7 **fann(e,** (7 **phan**), 5– **fan.** [f. FAN *sb.*[1] Cf. F. *vanner*.]

1. *trans.* To winnow (corn, etc.). †Also *fig.*

c **1000** *Liber Scint.* lx. (1889) 186 Na fanna [L. *ventiles*] þu þe on ælcum winde. **1340** *Ayenb.* 139 Oure lhord ssel uanni his corn ate daye of dome. *c* **1440** *Promp. Parv.* 149 Fanne corne, or oþer lyke, *vanno.* **1523** LD. BERNERS *Froiss.* I. ccclxxxi. 640 Their tenantes ought..to bring home theyr cornes, and some to threshe and to fanne. **1631** GOUGE *God's Arrows* i. §15. 21 Men when they fan their corne cannot do it so thorowly cleane. **1853** SOYER *Pantroph.* 42 They take white oats..they are fanned, cleaned, and carried to a mill. **1884** C. H. FARNHAM in *Harper's Mag.* Feb. 400/2 We..fan grain.

absol. **15..** *How Plowman lerned Paternoster* in Hazl. *E.P.P.* I. 218 He coude eke sowe and holde a plowe.. Thresshe, fane, [etc.].

fig. **1611** SHAKS. *Cymb.* I. vi. 177 The loue I beare him, Made me to fan you thus. **1612** T. TAYLOR *Comm. Titus* i. 15 Let vs then..fanne ourselues. **1671** FLAVEL *Fount. Life* xiii. 38 Satan will fan thee not to get out thy Chaff.

b. To winnow away (chaff); to drive away or scatter like chaff. Chiefly with *away, out. lit.* and *fig.*

c **1430** *Two Cookery-bks.* 7 þan fan owt þe holys. **1639** AINSWORTH *Annot. Ps.* cvi. 27 To sell their seed among the heathens, and to fan them in the land. **1641** SANDERSON *Serm.* II. 11 They may fan away the chaff from the wheat. **1644** H. PARKER *Jus Pop.* 67 Phanning out of our way such advantages as the Royalists may seem to lay hold of. **1653** MILTON *Ps.* i. 11 As chaff, which, fanned, The wind drives, so the wicked shall not stand In judgement. **1818** KEATS *Endym.* I. 818 To fan And winnow from the coming step of time All chaff of custom. **1879** A. W. TOURGÉE *Fool's Err.* xxvii. 261 Whoever got 'fanned out'—it was always our own folk that did it. **1908** A. RUHL *Other Americans* x. 151 One dreams of..a Broadway policeman marching down upon them leisurely with a nightstick and fanning them away.

c. To sweep away as by the wind from a fan.

1820 SCOTT *Abbot* ii, To fan the flies from my ladie's face while she sleeps. **1821** CLARE *Vill. Minstr.* I. 29 Fanning the sere leaf far upon the leas. **1872** BLACK *Adv. Phaeton* xxx. 397 You could have fanned her out of the way with a butterfly's wing.

2. *intr.* †To make a fan-like movement; to flap. †Of a bird: To flutter. Of the wind: To blow. Now *rare.*

c **1325** *E.E. Allit. P.* B. 457 [þe rauen] fongez to þe flyȝt, & fannez on þe wyndez. *c* **1400** MAUNDEV. (Roxb.) vii. 25 þe fewle..fannez with his wenges ay till þe forsaid thinges be sett on fire. **1526** *Pilgr. Perf.* (W. de W. 1531) 202 b, With her wynges she fanneth..vnto she haue kyndled in them fyre. **1599** SHAKS. *Hen. V,* IV. i. 212 Fanning in his face with a Peacocks feather. **1671** R. BOHUN *Disc. Wind* 99 They [winds] begin insensibly to fanne, and agitate the Air. **1699** DAMPIER *Voy.* II. III. 27 These Sea-Breezes do commonly rise in the Morning..in half an Hour's time..it fans pretty briskly. **1889** 'MARK TWAIN' *Yankee at Crt. K. Arthur* I. 67 To feel the cold uncanny night breezes fan through the place.

b. To be wafted gently along; to move as by a gentle beating of the wings (*rare*). Also, to move smartly; to clear *out* (*U.S. slang*).

1622 WITHER *Mistr. Philar.* (1633) 629 Such Downe As in time of Molting, fanns From the breasts of silver Swanns. **1853** KANE *Grinnell Exp.* ix. (1856) 66 We managed to fan along at a rate of two knots an hour. **1874** JOHNS *Brit. Birds* 52 The Barn Owl..fans its way onwards with its down-fringed wings. **1902** O. WISTER *Virginian* xv. 168 This hyeh train?.. Why, it's been fanning it a right smart little while. **1904** *Leslie's Monthly Mag.* Aug. 421/2 He saw I was drunk, and fanned out, me shootin' at him with every jump. **1927** W. R. JAMES *Cow Country* viii. 230 Todd..stuck to his seat and fanned his pony on out to the open.

3. *trans.* To move or drive (the air) with a fan. Const. *dat.*, also *in, upon.* Also, to stir (water) in this way; hence *intr.* or *absol.*

c **1440** *Gesta Rom.* lxxxvii. 408 (Add. MS.) [The ape] toke vp the clothes, and fanned hem wynde. **1594** MARLOWE & NASHE *Dido* IV. iv, Cupids hover in the Air, And fan it in Aeneas lovely face! **1633** EARL MANCH. *Al Mondo* (1636) 26 Breath, which nature fannes upon it for a while. **1801** SOUTHEY *Thalaba* IV. xv, The birds of heaven..fann'd around him The motionless air of noon. **1886** *Outing* (U.S.) VIII. 161/1 The trout..is balancing himself on the hard sandy bottom, his fins slowly fanning the water. **1898** *Daily News* 15 June 4/7 It is commonly in steady weather that you see the trout with their heads a quarter of an inch beneath the surface, and with their tails fanning expectantly.

b. To move like a fan; to wave. *arch.*

1637 MILTON *Lycidas* 40 The willows..Shall now no more be seen, Fanning their joyous leaves to thy soft lays. **1740** DYER *Ruins Rome* 374 The gourd and olive fan Their am'rous foliage.

4. To drive a current of air upon, with or as with a fan: **a.** with the object or effect of cooling. Also *to fan into* (*slumber*).

1605 SHAKS. *Macb.* I. ii. 50 The Norweyan Banners flowt the skie, And fanne our people cold. **1653** H. COGAN tr. *Pinto's Trav.* viii. 23 He made one of his followers to fan me with a ventilow for to refresh me. **1711** STEELE *Spect.* No. 80 ¶3 Fanned into Slumbers by successive Hands of them [Slaves]. **1725** BERKELEY *Proposal* Wks. III. 221 The air in Bermuda is perpetually fanned and kept cool by sea-breezes. **1821** KEATS *Isabel* xxvii, Where Arno's stream..still doth fan Itself with dancing bulrush. **1832** TENNYSON *Eleänore* 9 Thy bounteous forehead was not fann'd With breezes from our oaken glades. **1863** MRS. OLIPHANT *Doctor's Fam.*, Mrs. Fred..took up her handkerchief and..began to fan her.. cheeks.

b. with the object or result of kindling a flame; chiefly *fig.* Const. *into, to.*

1607 SHAKS. *Cor.* III. iii. 127 Let..Your Enemies, with nodding of their Plumes Fan you into dispaire. **1649** JER. TAYLOR *Gt. Exemp.* II. Ad. Sec. xi. 27 (Prayer) A coale from thy altar fann'd with the wings of the holy Dove. **1709** W. KING *Ovid's Art of Love* XIV. 67 By slow Degrees he fans the gentle Fire. **1821** SHELLEY *Hellas* 60 Its unwearied wings could fan The quenchless ashes of Milan. **1828–40** TYTLER *Hist. Scot.* (1864) I. 146 He [Edward II] employed his ambassadors..to fan the dissensions between them. *a* **1859** MACAULAY *Hist. Eng.* V. 102 His almost imperceptible spark of life had been..fanned into a..flickering flame. **1887** C. C. ABBOTT *Waste-Land Wand.* iv. 96 The little fire..was fanned by a passing breeze to a lively flame.

5. Of a breeze, etc.: To blow gently and refreshingly upon, as if driven by a fan; to cool; *rarely* of a person: To breathe upon.

1590 SHAKS. *Mids. N.* III. ii. 142 High Taurus snow, Fan'd with the Easterne winde. **1605** *Tryall Chev.* v. i. in Bullen *O. Pl.* (1884) III. 339 The coole winds have fand the burning Sunne. **1635** A. STAFFORD *Fem. Glory* (1869) 15 Only Zephirus was let loose to fanne the Pinke. **1668** CULPEPPER & COLE *Barthol. Anat.* II. i. 316 The heat of the parts is fanned, cooled and tempered. **1704** POPE *Windsor For.* 194 Pants on her neck, and fans her parting hair. **1798** COLERIDGE *Anc. Mar.* VI. xii, It fanned my cheek Like a meadow-gale of spring. **1812** J. WILSON *Isle of Palms* I. 11 The sea, I ween, cannot be fann'd By evening freshness. **1862** MERIVALE *Rom. Emp.* (1865) IV. xxxiv. 149 Terraces, fanned by cool breezes from the sea.

6. To spread out like a fan. **a.** *trans. Naut.* To widen. Also, *to fan out* (see quot. 1871). **b.** *intr.* for *refl. to fan out*: to expand in rays, to assume a fan-like shape. Also *fig.* and (*U.S.*) to make a display.

a. 1867 SMYTH *Sailor's Word-bk.*, *Fanning*, the technical phrase for breadthening the after part of the tops. Also, widening in general. **1871** *Amer. Encycl. Printing, Fanning Out*..spreading out the upper part of the paper somewhat in the resemblance of a fan.

b. 1592 R. D. *Hypnerotomachia* 11 A prodigious winged horse..his wings fanning out. **1860** BARTLETT *Dict. Amer.*, To *Fan out*, to make a show at an examination. **1861** THORNBURY *Turner* I. 314 What Orient splendour of colour, fanning out far beyond towards Ithaca. **1926** *Hutchinson's Best Story Mag.* Nov. 59/1 His black tangle of beard, fanning over his knees ruffled in the wind. **1943** F. S. HERMAN *Dynamite Cargo* xi. 95 The warship screen fanned out and closed in. **1962** *Times* 25 Apr. 16/6 There fan out from the incident..not changes of attitude..but a series of comments on the nature of priestly vocation. **1965** *Electronics Weekly* 1 Dec. 17/5 Generating stations.. interconnected by..transmission feeders fanning out to reach principal load centres.

7. *slang.* **a.** *trans.* To beat; to rate soundly. **b.** To feel, handle. Also = FRISK *v.* 4 a.

1785 GROSE *Dict. Vulg. Tongue* s.v., I fanned him sweetly, I beat him heartily. **1862** MAYHEW *Lond. Labour* (ed. 2) IV. 319 Joe..had fanned the gentleman's pocket, i.e. had felt the pocket and knew there was a handkerchief. **1887** TRISTRAM in *Eng. Illust. Mag.* Dec. 228 Fanning them, which in the tongue of coachmen, is whipping them. **1916** E. TITUS *I Conquered* vi. 84 His quirt fell... He fanned his pony again, and the beast grunted in his struggles for increased speed in the climbing. **1918** C. E. MULFORD *Man fr. Bar-20* ix. 100 Cussed if I wouldn't 'a' give six pesos, U.S. to 'a' seen that cougar a-fannin' you! **1927** E. WALLACE *Feathered Serpent* xvii. 216 Legally no policeman has the right to 'fan' a prisoner until he gets into the police station. **1931** L. STEFFENS *Autobiogr.* I. II. v. 213 You wonder why we fan these damned bums, crooks, and strikers with the stick. **1946** J. IRVING *Royal Navalese* 74 *To fan*, to search a person quickly for symptoms of concealed contraband articles, firearms, etc.

8. *N. Amer.* Of a pitcher in baseball: to cause (a batter) to strike out.

1909 in WEBSTER. **1912** C. MATHEWSON *Pitching in a Pinch* v. 101 He fanned the next two men. **1970** *Globe & Mail* (Toronto) 28 Sept. 19/4 The Indian lefthander..has fanned more than 300 hitters.

b. *intr.* Of a batter: to strike out.

1886 *Outing* (U.S.) July 477/2 The man who..'fans out' or 'pops one up'. **1945** *This Week Mag.* 21 Apr. 10 He fanned in a pinch and the opposition booed.

fan, irregular pa. t. of FINE, to end.

fan, obs. and dial. var. of FAWN *v.*

‖**fanā** (fə'nɑː). [a. Arab. *fanā'*.] The Sufi doctrine of annihilation (see quots.).

1867 E. H. PALMER *Oriental Mysticism* v. v. 67 Further than this he cannot go, but pursues his habit of self-denial and contemplation until his death, which is, however, merely looked upon as a total re-absorption into the Deity, forming the consummation of his Journey, the last stage, designated *Faná*, Extinction. **1911** *Encycl. Brit.* XXVI. 31/2 The step to pantheism was first decisively taken by the great Persian Sūfī, Abū Yazīd (Bāyezīd)..(d. A.D. 874), who introduced the doctrine of annihilation (fanā), *i.e.* the passing away of individual consciousness in the will of God. **1956** E. WOOD *Yoga Dict.* 153/1 In the end the constant thought or remembrance..of God, will lead to union..with Him, in which there will be passing away (*fana*) of all human qualities or nature.

†**'fanacle.** *Obs. rare*$^{-1}$. [App. meant for a dim. of L. *fānum* FANE.] A small temple, shrine.

1594 W. PERCY *Coelia* (1877) 17 One day I went to Venus Fanacle.

Fanagalo ('fɑːnaga'lɔː). Also **Fanakolo, -kalo.** [f. the common phr. *fana ga lo* = 'like this' in the *lingua franca* of southern African mines (see below), f. Zulu *fana* be like + *ka* poss. prefix Class 1a + *lo* demonstr. Classes 1 and 3.] A *lingua franca* of southern Africa, made up of elements of Zulu/Xhosa, English, and Afrikaans. Formerly called *Kitchen Kaffir* or *Mine Kaffir*.

The word *kaffir* being regarded as derogatory by Africans, the new name *Fanagalo* came to be adopted by mining authorities and other employers.

1947 J. D. BOLD *Dict. & Phr.-Bk. Fanagalo* 6 The appelation *Fanagalo* probably derives from *kuluma fana ga lo* meaning 'to speak like this'. **1951** *Cape Argus* 19 Jan. 8 'Fanakolo', the *lingua franca* of the mine compounds of South Africa. **1952** L. MARQUARD *Peoples & Policies S. Afr.* ii. 35 A more or less regularized version of this ['Kitchen Kaffir'] called Fanakolo, is used as the *lingua franca* on the gold-mines. **1956** A. G. MCRAE *Hill called Grazing* xii. 126 He spoke the lingua franca of all South African natives, the so-called Fana-ka-lo.

†**fanal** ('feɪnəl). *Obs.* exc. *arch.* Also 6 **fanell,** 9 **phanal.** [a. Fr. *fanal*, It. *fanale*, med.L. *fanāle*, *fanālis*, f. Gr. φανός lantern, f. φαν- stem of φαίνειν to show.] **a.** A beacon, a lighthouse. **b.** A (ship's) lantern.

1471 RIPLEY *Comp. Alch.* IV. in Ashm. (1652) 147 As shyneyng fanells. **1632** J. HAYWARD tr. *Biondi's Eromena* 90 Seeing her with three fanals or lanthornes. **1766** SMOLLETT *Trav.* 133 On the right hand..there is an elegant fanal or light house. **1848** BROWNING *Sordello* IV. 395 He flashes like a phanal,—all men catch The flame!

‖**fanam** (fʌ'nɑːm). Also 6 **fanan, -on,** 9 **fanom.** [Corruption of Malayālam and Tamil *paṇam*, f. Skr. *paṇa* wealth.] A small coin, formerly the usual money of account in South India.

'No longer used in British India; in some native states gold and silver fanams are still current; in Travancore the former is worth ¼ and the latter ⅕ of a rupee' (*N.E.D.*, 1895).

[**1510** VARTHEMA *Itin.* in Ramusio *Navig.* (1588) I. 159 b, Batte anchora moneta d'argento chiamato fanon.] **1555** EDEN *Decades* 233 This Fanan, is also a kynde of money which is in value, one ryale of syluer. **1704** *Collect. Voy.* (Church.) III. 822/2 A Fanam is only 5*d.* tho they have Golden and Silver Fanams. **1792** GARROW in *Phil. Trans.* LXXXVIII. 409 The stone is..paid for at the Pollam, in the gold fanam. **1803** WELLINGTON in Gurw. *Desp.* I. 452 Their pay shall be a gold fanam for every day they do not work, and two gold fanams for every day they do. **1883** S. MATEER *Gospel in S. India* 148 A woman has given 100 fanams to provide two good globe lamps.

Fanar, Fanariot(e, varr. PHANAR, PHANARIOT.

fanatic (fə'nætɪk), *a.* and *sb.* Forms: α. 6 **fanatike,** 6–8 **-ick(e,** 7 **-ique,** 7– **fanatic.** β. 6 **phanatik,** 6–8 **ic(k,** 7 **-ique.** [ad. L. *fānātic-us*, f. *fānum* temple: see -ATIC. Cf. Fr. *fanatique*.]

A. *adj.*

†**1. a.** Of an action or speech: Such as might result from possession by a deity or demon; frantic, furious. Of a person: Frenzied, mad. *Obs.*

1533 BELLENDEN *Livy* IV. (1822) 356 This uncouth and terribil buschement..ruschit..with phanatik and wod cours on thare inemyis. *c* **1534** tr. *Pol. Verg. Eng. Hist.* (Camden) I. 71 Such fanatike and fond observations. **1626** MINSHEU *Ductor* (ed. 2), *Fanatick*, mad, franticke, also inspired with a prophetical furie. **1634** SIR T. HERBERT *Trav.* (1638) 221 Some think..the torryd Zone, the fierie sword; and such other fanatick fancies. **1641** BAKER *Chron.* 148 A fanatick fellow..gave forth, that himselfe was the true Edward. **1655–60** STANLEY *Hist. Philos.* (1701) 494/2 Persons Divinely inspired, and Fanatick. **1721–1800** in BAILEY.

b. *Comb.*

1603 CHETTLE *Eng. Mourn. Garment* in *Harl. Misc.* (1793) 202 They are..proud, fanatick-spirited counterfeits. **1926** W. J. LOCKE *Stories Near & Far* 225 A bearded, fanatic-eyed..figure. **1932** W. FAULKNER *Light in August* xx. 447 Fanaticfaced country preachers.

2. Of persons, their actions, attributes, etc.: Characterized, influenced, or prompted by excessive and mistaken enthusiasm, *esp.* in religious matters.

1647 CLARENDON *Hist. Reb.* IV. (1702) I. 266 The Lord Mayor..Opposing all their Fanatick humours..grew to be reckon'd in the First Form of the Malignants. **1659** BP. WALTON *Consid. Considered* 169 Papists, Atheists, and fanatic persons. **1659–60** MONK *Sp.* 6 Feb. in Wood *Life* (Oxf. Hist. Soc.) I. 303 Be careful neither the cavalier nor phanatique party have yet a share in your civil..power. *a* **1680** BUTLER *Rem.* (1759) I. 215 All our lunatic fanatic Sects. **1704** SWIFT *T. Tub* i. 26 The two principal qualifications of a Phanatic Preacher are [etc.]. **1774**

PENNANT *Tour Scot. in 1772.* 58 The cloisters..fell victims to fanatic fury. **1850** W. IRVING *Mahomet* x. (1853) 39 The Fanatic legions of the desert. **1883** *Manch. Exam.* 30 Oct. 5/5 Banded..in fanatic and violent opposition to the measure.

B. *sb.*

†**1.** A mad person. In later use: A religious maniac. *Obs.*

c **1525** *Robin Hood* 160 Fool, fanatick, baboon. **1655** M. CASAUBON *Enthusiasme* 7 One Orpheus, a mere fanatick. **1806** *Med. Jrnl.* XV. 213 Dr. G[all] gave..hints how to treat fanatics, by using topical remedies and poultices.

2. a. A fanatic person; a visionary; an unreasoning enthusiast. Applied in the latter half of the 17th c. to Nonconformists as a hostile epithet.

1644 ABP. MAXWELL *Sacrosancta Regum Majestas* 44 *Gratia gratum faciens*, Saving Grace, as some fanatickes and fantastickes fondly imagine. **1657** JOHN GAULE *Sapient. Justif.* 11 Enthusiasts, Anabaptists, Fanaticks, and Familists. **1660** FULLER *Mixt. Contempl.* (1841) 212 A new word coined, within few months, called fanatics..seemeth well..proportioned to signify..the sectaries of our age. **1660** PEPYS *Diary* 15 Apr., Since Lambert got out of the Tower, the Fanatiques had held up their heads high. **1709** EVANS in Hearne *Collect.* 10 Nov., D. Sacheverel.. thunderd..against yᵉ phanaticks. **1780** HARRIS *Philol. Enq.* (1841) 430 Henry the Fourth of France..was unexpectedly murdered by a wretched fanatic. **1859** KINGSLEY *Sir W. Raleigh* I. 20 The man of one idea, who works at nothing but that..sacrifices everything to that; the fanatic in short. **1883** FROUDE *Short Stud.* IV. iii. 269 The Jews..were troublesome fanatics whom it was equally difficult to govern or destroy.

b. A fanatical devotee *of*.

1790 BURKE *Fr. Rev.* Wks. V. 66 Those exploded fanaticks of slavery.

c. *Comb.*

1707 E. WARD *Hud. Rediv.* (1715) II. ix, To show, tho' conquer'd, they abhor (Fanatick like) all sov'reign Pow'r. **1722** SEWEL *Hist. Quakers* (1795) II. VII. 62 Robinson's mischievous intent to go a fanatick hunting.

Hence †**fa'naticness** *Obs.*, fanaticalness.

1662 J. SPARROW tr. *Behme's Rem. Wks., Complexions* 17 Which is Phrenzie, Madnesse and Phanatiquenesse. **1665** J. SERGEANT *Sure-Footing* 108 The denying Tradition is a proper..disposition to Fanatickness.

fanatical (fə'nætɪkəl), *a.* [f. prec. + -AL¹.]

†**1.** Possessed by a deity or by a devil; frantic, mad, furious. *Obs.*

1568 GRAFTON *Chron.* II. 538 A fanaticall Enchaunteresse [Joan of Arc]. **1581** SAVILE *Tacitus' Hist.* (1612) 82 The Æduans..with some of Vitellius Cohortes, discomfited that fanaticall multitude. *a* **1633** AUSTIN *Medit.* (1635) 89 Those Phanaticall women of the Gentiles.

†**b.** Characteristic of a possessed person. *Obs.*

1600 HOLLAND *Livy* xxxix. 1031 The men shaking & wagging their bodies too and fro after a fanaticall fashion. **1603** —— *Plutarch's Mor.* 1345 Certaine fanaticall cries and voices.

2. = FANATIC *a.* 2.

1550 BALE *Apol.* 96 A Christen mannis obedyence standeth not in the fulfyllyng of fanaticall vowes. **1589** COOPER *Admon.* 201 The Anabaptists, and some other phanaticall spirits. **1634** SANDERSON *Serm.* II. 283 That phanatical opinion..that no ecclesiastical person might lawfully exercise any secular power. **1669–70** MARVELL *Corr.* cxxxix. Wks. 1872–5 II. 307 Fox, a teacher of some fanaticall people in Wiltshire, did conventicle there. **1732** BERKELEY *Alciphr.* VI. §25 As fanatical as any Quietist or Quaker. **1841** ELPHINSTONE *Hist. Ind.* II. 289 The present quarrel orginated in a fanatical spirit, which had sprung up, many years before. **1876** GEO. ELIOT *Dan. Der.* III. xlvi. 308, I call a man fanatical when..he..becomes unjust and unsympathetic to men who are out of his own track.

†**b.** In a weaker sense: Extravagant. *Obs.*

1588 SHAKS. *L.L.L.* v. i. 20, I abhor such phanaticall phantasims.

†**3.** Of or pertaining to the 'fanatics' or Nonconformists. *Obs.*

1678 HICKES in Ellis *Orig. Lett.* II. 318. IV. 46 Many of the fanatical party..hope that the Commons..will grow jealous of these military proceedings. *a* **1695** WOOD *Life* (1848) 245 Mr. John Fairclough..a non-conforming minister, was buried in the fanatical burial place, near the Artillery yard London. **1703** DE FOE *Shortest Way with Dissenters* Misc. 421 The phanatical Party of this Land.

Hence **fa'natically** *adv.*, in a fanatical manner. **fa'naticalness**, the quality or state of being fanatical; fanaticism.

1672 CRESSY (*title*), Fanaticism fanatically imputed to the Catholick Church by Doctour Stillingfleet. **1792** BURKE *Petit. Unitarians* Wks. x. 57 Men..furiously and fanatically fond of an object. **1833** KEBLE *Serm.* vii. (1848) 157 Those who maintain, profanely and fanatically, that the State.. ought not to be of any religion. **1856** FROUDE *Hist. Eng.* (1858) I. v. 422 The populace of France were fanatically catholic. **1668** WILKINS *Real Char.* II. 290 To which the notion of fierceness or fanaticalness is opposed.

fanaticism (fə'nætɪsɪz(ə)m). Also 7–8 **phanaticism.** [f. FANATIC + -ISM.]

†**1.** The condition of being, or supposing oneself to be, possessed. *Obs.*

1711 SHAFTESB. *Charac.* (1749) I. 36 Fanaticism, as it was used by the Antients in its original sense, for an 'Apparition' transporting the mind.

2. The tendency to indulge in wild and extravagant notions, *esp.* in religious matters; excessive enthusiasm, frenzy; an instance, a particular form, of this.

1652 GAULE *Magastrom.* 133 Were not those the times to broach and vent their fanaticisms and impostures with more licentiousness and impunity? **1685** BAXTER *Paraphr. N.T., I John* i. 6, 7, Is it not Phanaticism to talk of Fellowship with God? **1769** ROBERTSON *Chas. V*, VI. VI. 106 The large infusion of fanaticism mingled with its regulations should be imputed to Loyola its founder. **1813** SCOTT *Rokeby* VI. xxvii, Dark Fanaticism rent Altar, and screen, and ornament. **1837** CARLYLE *Fr. Rev.* III. III. i, This battle of Mountain and Gironde..is the battle of Fanaticisms and Miracles. **1880** DIXON *Windsor* III. xx. 197 A sour fanaticism, which he mistook for piety.

b. In a weaker sense: Eagerness or enthusiasm in any pursuit.

1855 BAIN *Senses & Int.* III. iv. §21 The fanaticism that prompts to endless attempts was found in..Kepler.

fanaticize (fə'nætɪsaɪz), *v.* Also **fanaticise.** [f. as prec. + -IZE.]

1. *trans.* To infect with fanaticism; to render fanatical, make a fanatic of; to infuriate.

1812 W. TAYLOR in *Monthly Rev.* LXVII. 148 The Duke ..accused the parliamentary zealots of having fanaticized the assassin. **1848** CLOUGH *Amours de Voy.* I. 106 These, that fanaticized Europe. **1860** *Sat. Rev.* X. 357/2 The object is..to fanaticize the mob against the day of trial.

2. *intr.* To act as a fanatic.

1715 M. DAVIES *Athen. Brit.* I. 269 Take heed least a worse Prophecy..overtake them..for fanaticizing and rejecting the express Words of Scripture. **1837** CARLYLE *Fr. Rev.* III. III. ii, A man..fighting and fanaticising amid a Nation of his like. **1883** *Brit. Q. Rev.* Oct. 403 He loves humanity as a whole too truly to fanaticise for a class.

Hence **fa'naticized** *ppl. a.*

1827 SOUTHEY *Hist. Penins. War* II. 186 About two hundred, whom the French praised in reality...by calling them the most fanaticised, etc. **1873** *Contemp. Rev.* XXI. 912 A party of men honest but fanaticized.

†**'fanatism.** *Obs.* [ad. F. *fanatisme.*] = FANATICISM.

1680 *Refl. late Libel on Curse-ye-Meroz* 38 Whimsies, Fancies, Fopperies, and Phanatismes. **1686** *Popery Anatomis'd* 15 All mixture of Calvinism and Fanatism. **1797** *Hist.* in *Ann. Reg.* 78/2 That was the moment pitched upon to..reorganize the power of fanatism. **1800** T. JEFFERSON *Writ.* (1859) IV. 311 The persecutions which fanatism and monarchy have excited against you.

†**fanc.** *Obs. rare*⁻¹. [a. OF. *fanc* (mod.F. *fange*).] Mud.

1340 *Ayenb.* 251 Þe ilke welle ne uelþ naȝt þane fanc [*printed* fauc] ne þe erþe..of þise wordle.

‖**fanchon** (fɑ̃ʃɔ̃). [Fr., dim. of name *Françoise.*] A kerchief. Also *fanchon bonnet, cap* (see quots.).

1872 *Young Englishwoman* Nov. 611/1 This pretty light fanchon is knitted with white and red Shetland wool. **1928** 'BRENT OF BIN BIN' *Up Country* xvi. 275 They had elegant bonnets richly ornamented, fançon-shaped behind. **1957** M. B. PICKEN *Fashion Dict.* 122/1 *Fanchon (kerchief) bonnet*, bonnet resembling a diagonally folded kerchief. Popular in Victorian period. **1960** CUNNINGTON & BEARD *Dict. Eng. Costume* 76/1 *Fanchon*, 1830's on. A small kerchief for the head, the term being chiefly used for the lace trimming falling about the ears of a day cap or outdoor bonnet. *Ibid.*, *Fanchon cap*, 1840's to 1860's. A lace or tulle cap with side pieces covering the ears, or sloping down to them.

‖**fanchonnette** (fɑ̃ʃɒnɛt). [f. as prec. + -ETTE.] (See quots.)

1845 E. ACTON *Mod. Cookery* xvi. 432 *Fanchonnettes*.. Roll out..puff paste..cover it..with peach or apricot jam ..roll a second bit of paste..and lay it carefully over the other. *Ibid.* 433 This is not the form of pasty called by the French *fanchonnettes*. **1861** MRS. BEETON *Bk. Househ. Managem.* xxvii. 660 Fanchonnettes, or Custard Tartlets. **1958** W. BICKEL tr. *Hering's Dict. Cookery* 682 *Fanchonnettes*, tartlet moulds lined with puff paste, filled with almond cream, half baked, covered with meringue mixture.

fanciable ('fænsɪəb(ə)l), *a.* [f. FANCY *v.* + -ABLE.] That may be fancied; *spec.* of a person: sexually attractive (to another).

1934 in WEBSTER. **1981** *Spectator* 31 Oct. 14/3 Fanciable, actually, in circumstances less *folklorique*. **1982** BARR & YORK *Official Sloane Ranger Handbk.* 127/2 Your virginal (well, fresh and young) attendants, his dashing fanciable ushers. **1986** *Times* 12 May 11/7 Impolite men are not the least bit fanciable.

fancical ('fænsɪkəl), *a. rare* exc. *dial.* [f. FANCY *sb.* + -IC + -AL¹.] = FANCIFUL.

1671 *True Nonconf.* 244 Praying in words, specially extemporary and various, is..fancical. **1676** T. MACE *Musick's Monument* xxiv. 128 After they have Compleated Their Tuning, They will..fall into some..Fansical Play. **1864** J. BROWN *Jeemes* 12 'What kind of weaver are you?' 'I'm in the fancical line'.

fancied ('fænsɪd), *ppl. a.* [f. FANCY *v.* + -ED¹.]

1. Formed or portrayed by the fancy; existing only in the fancy; imaginary.

1568 T. HOWELL *Newe Sonets* (1879) 137 Thier fancied feares. **1651** HOBBES *Leviath.* III. xxxiv. 212 By Angel was understood a fancyed Voice. **1719** DE FOE *Crusoe* (1840) II. xvi. 324 The fancied felicity which he enjoyed. **1795** SOUTHEY *Vis. Maid of Orleans* III. 271 With eye more dangerous Than fancied basilisk. **1869** FREEMAN *Norm. Conq.* (1876) III. xiii. 307 Supporting their native sovereign in the pursuit of his fancied rights.

†**2. a.** Contrived to suit the fancy or whim; *esp.* of dress; = FANCY *a.* 1. **b.** Artistically designed. Cf. FANCY *v.* 3. *Obs.*

a. **1688** PRIOR *Ode Ex.* iii. 14 vi, Fancy'd Rules and Arbitrary Laws. **1775** JOHNSON *Let. Mrs. Thrale* 21 June, Floating on the Thames in a fancied dress. **1781** HAYLEY *Tri. Temper* VI. 42 The gracious earl..Has plann'd..A fancied ball, a private masquerade. **1796** MORSE *Amer. Geog.* II. 612 Striped and fancied silks. **1796** *Ned Evans* I. 92 A casimir waistcoat with a fancied pattern of silk embroidery round the button-holes.

b. **1709** STEELE *Tatler* No. 142 ¶5 His Seals are curiously fancied, and exquisitely well cut. **1782** MISS BURNEY *Cecilia* I. iv, The prettiest fancied [buckles] I ever saw.

3. That one has taken a liking or fancy for; favourite.

1589 WARNER *Alb. Eng.* VI. xxix. (1612) 144 A braue Esquire of Wailes, That tide her fancie to his forme, till fancied forme preuailes. **1640** FULLER *Joseph's Coat* viii. (1867) 185 What the Corinthians spake of their fancied preachers. **1873** BROWNING *Red Cott. Nt.-cap* 245 Till beverage obtained the fancied smack. **1887** *Daily News* 15 Nov. 3/5 Molynoo..beat the more fancied Bloodstone.

4. Of an animal: see FANCY *v.* 9.

1876 *Encycl. Brit.* IV. 249/2 The wide differences observable in 'fancied' animals.

fancier ('fænsɪə(r)). [f. FANCY *v.* + -ER².] One who fancies, in senses of the vb.

1. One who fancies or imagines.

1828 MACAULAY *Hallam, Ess.* (1889) 53 People who, in their speculations in politics, are not reasoners, but fanciers.

2. One who makes tasteful designs.

1856 RUSKIN *Mod. Paint.* III. IV. xiv. §11. 203 Their.. most brilliant fanciers were employed in..embroidering the robe.

3. One who has a liking for, and a critical judgement in, some class of curiosities, plants, animals, etc. Chiefly with prefixed sb., as in ***dog-, flower-, pigeon-fancier.***

1765 JOHNSON *Shaks.* I. 155 Some now call that which a man takes particular delight in his *Fancy*. *Flower fancier* for a florist, and *Bird fancier* for a lover and feeder of birds are colloquial words. **1769** S. PATERSON *Another Trav.* II. I. 152 It is also true that Dutchmen, generally speaking, are fanciers. **1773** BARRINGTON in *Phil. Trans.* LXIII. 280 Some of the nightingale fanciers..prefer a Surry bird to those of Middlesex. **1824** W. IRVING *T. Trav.* I. 247 We have oddity fanciers among our ladies of rank. **1859** SALA *Tw. round Clock* (1861) 167 Dog-fanciers..in many cases might with as much propriety answer to the name of dog-stealers. **1861** DELAMER *Fl. Gard.* 34 The fourth year..the fancier may look out for a prize or two. **1867** TEGETMEIER *Pigeons* iii. 25 Numerous varieties of pigeons..are known to naturalists and fanciers.

attrib. **1891** *Leeds Merc.* 3 Oct. 12/2 A 'fancier Judge'.

fanciful ('fænsɪfʊl), *a.* [f. FANCY *sb.* + -FUL.]

1. a. Characterized by the possession of fancy (*rare*). **b.** In disparaging sense: Disposed to indulge in fancies; whimsical.

1695 WOODWARD *Nat. Hist. Earth* I. 63 Some fanciful Men have expected nothing but Confusion and Ruin. **1713** STEELE *Englishman* No. 7. 45 A fanciful Fellow..amuses himself with the Woods and Mountains which he discovers in the Skies. **1727** POPE, etc. *Art of Sinking* 83 A careful and fanciful pattern-drawer. **1817** COLERIDGE *Biog. Lit.* 43 Milton had a highly imaginative, Cowley a very fanciful mind. **1874** MICKLETHWAITE *Mod. Par. Churches* 6 Fanciful people..sometimes gave mystical interpretations to the arrangements.

absol. **1676** GLANVILL *Ess.* vi. §6. 17 Not only the Melancholick and the Fanciful, but the Grave and the Sober.

2. a. Characterized by or displaying fancy in design; fantastic, odd in appearance; **b.** suggested by fancy; imaginary, unreal.

a **1627** HAYWARD *Edw. VI.* 88 How foolish and fancifull were they [buildings]. **1642** FULLER *Holy & Prof. St.* II. vi. 71 He affects not phancy-full singularity in his behaviour. **1697** DRYDEN *Virg. Past.* Pref. (1721) I. 75 With all our fanciful Refinements. **1767** J. BYRON *Voy. round World* 186 The other circumstances they have mentioned..appear to be merely fanciful. **1823** SCOTT *Peveril* xxxix, The fanciful and singular female..had one of those faces which are never seen without making an impression. **1828** —— *F.M. Perth* xi, She wears a petticoat..I would it were..of a less fanciful fashion. **1852** MRS. STOWE *Uncle Tom's C* xv, A variety of fanciful diseases. **1868** M. PATTISON *Academ. Org.* v. 193 The claims of Art..cannot be set aside as fanciful.

3. quasi-*adv.* = FANCIFULLY.

1775 JOHNSON *Let. Mrs. Thrale* 23 June, I hope you.. were dressed fine and fanciful.

fancifully ('fænsɪfʊlɪ), *adv.* [f. prec. + -LY².] In a fanciful manner.

1664 H. MORE *Antid. Idolatry* To Rdr., What conceited old man is this..that talks thus phancifully? **1741** WARBURTON *Div. Legat.* II. I. iv. §4. 148 Hieroglyphic symbols fancifully adapted by Analogy. **1801** S. & HT. LEE *Canterb. T.* IV. 396 Carriages fancifully ornamented. **1809** PINKNEY *Trav. France* 2 Eliab..fancifully believed himself to be ill-treated. **1885** SIR J. W. CHITTY in *Law Times' Rep.* LIII. 80/2 A word newly or fancifully applied.

fancifulness ('fænsɪfʊlnɪs). [f. as prec. + -NESS.] The quality of being fanciful.

1667 H. MORE *Div. Dial.* IV. xxiv. (1713) 347 Some.. suspecting such Interpretations of overmuch Phancifulness. **1677** HALE *Prim. Orig. Man.* II. v. 168 Transported with too much fancifulness. **1818** *Bp. Horne's Wks.* (ed. 2) I. Pref. p. xi, Charges him [the bishop] with fancifulness and presumption. **1857** W. COLLINS *Dead Secret* v. iii. (1861) 218 A..fancifulness in her execution of the music.

fancify ('fænsɪfaɪ), *v.* [f. FANCY *sb.* + -FY.] *trans.* †**a.** To have a fancy for; to like (*obs.*). †**b.** To fancy, imagine (*obs.*). **c.** To imagine the existence of. **d.** To make fanciful.

1656 EARL MONM. *Advt. fr. Parnass.* 441 The prime vertues that she most fancified in her Frenchmen. **1748** RICHARDSON *Clarissa* (1811) VI. 344 The good she ever delighted to do, and fancified she was born to do. **1890** *Sat.*

Rev. 8 Mar. 291/1 Much study of the 'Ivory Gate' had ..'fancified' his own views.

Hence **fancifi'cation**, **'fancified** *ppl. a.*

1845 TRAIN *Hist. Isle of Man* II. 359 *note*, This fancified island has been bound to the bottom of the ocean. **1937** *New Republic* 24 Feb. 74 The constant elaboration, figures of speech, conceits, fancifications, involutions, not seldom characteristic of Elizabethan writing. **1960** V. PACKARD *Waste Makers* (1961) xi. 124 The trend in color went right back to white, with some venturing into fancification with tracery effects. **1962** *Spectator* 14 Dec. 941 Their elusive and often fragmented fancifications.

fanciless ('fænsılıs), *a.* [f. FANCY *sb.* + -LESS.] Of persons, compositions, etc.: Destitute of fancy.

1753 ARMSTRONG *Taste* 185 A pert, or bluff important wight, Whose brain is fanciless. **1789** BURNEY *Hist. Mus.* IV. 546 These [compositions]..are fanciless, and no more fit for one instrument than another. **1800–24** CAMPBELL *Poems, View St. Leonard's* 53 Who can be so fanciless as to feel no gratitude. **1863** KINGLAKE *Crimea* II. 162 Fanciless men. **1868** BROWNING *Ring & Bk.* I. 144 In this book lay absolutely truth, Fanciless fact.

fancy ('fænsı), *sb.* and *a.* Forms: *α.* 5–6 **fansey**, 6–8 **fansie, -ye**, 6–7 **fancie, -ye**, 6– **fancy**. *β.* 6–8 **phansy(e, -cie, -cy**, 6–9 **phansie**. [A contraction of FANTASY; cf. the forms *fantsy*, *phant'sy* under that word.] **A.** *sb.*

†**1.** In scholastic psychology: = FANTASY *sb.* 1.

[*c* **1400**, **1509**: see FANTASY *sb.* 1.] **1594** HOOKER *Eccl. Pol.* I. vi. (1632) 56 Beasts..in actions of sense and phancie go beyond them [men] . **1722** WOLLASTON *Relig. Nat.* v. 101 We know matters of fact by the help of..impressions made upon phansy.

†**2.** A spectral apparition; an illusion of the senses. Cf. FANTASY *sb.* 2. *Obs.*

[*c* **1360–1576**: see FANTASY *sb.* 2.] **1609** HOLLAND *Amm. Marcell.* XIV. xi. 25 Dreadfull spectres and fansies skreaking hideously round about him. **1659** B. HARRIS *Parival's Iron Age* 10 Forrests, where are sometimes heard great illusions, and phancies.

3. Delusive imagination; hallucination; an instance of this; = FANTASY 3.

1597 HOOKER *Eccl. Pol.* II. 732 The righteous..may have their phancies; they may..conceive worse of their own estate than reason giveth. **1693** tr. *Emilianne's Hist. Monast. Ord.* xv. 157 Phancies of a deluded mind. **1727** DE FOE *Syst. Magic* I. iv. (1840) 107 The vision appeared to his fancy. **1840** DICKENS *Barn. Rudge* i, That may be my fancy. **1856** STANLEY *Sinai & Pal.* ii. (1858) 156 Which..claims to be founded not on fancy..but on Fact.

4. a. In early use synonymous with IMAGINATION (see FANTASY 4); the process, and the faculty, of forming mental representations of things not present to the senses; chiefly applied to the so-called creative or productive imagination, which frames images of objects, events, or conditions that have not occurred in actual experience. In later use the words *fancy* and *imagination* (esp. as denoting attributes manifested in poetical or literary composition) are commonly distinguished: *fancy* being used to express aptitude for the invention of illustrative or decorative imagery, while *imagination* is the power of giving to ideal creations the inner consistency of realities. Often *personified*.

1581 T. HOWELL *Deuises* (1879) 229 The flaming dartes, That Fancie quickly burne with quenchlesse fyre. **1632** MILTON *L'Allegro* 133 Sweetest Shakespeare, Fancy's child. **1662** GLANVILL *Lux Orient.* Pref. 5 What..dangerous opinions soever their phancies might give birth to. **1676** HOBBES *Iliad* Pref. (1686) 5 In Fancy consisteth the Sublimity of a Poet. **1712** ADDISON *Spect.* No. 411 ¶2 The Pleasures of the Imagination or Fancy (which I shall use promiscuously). **1713** C'TESS WINCHELSEA *Misc. Poems* 217 Wand'ring Wishes, born on Phancy's Wings. **1785** REID *Int. Powers* 374 Fancy may combine things that never were combined in reality. **1811** COLERIDGE *Lect.* (1856) 45 When the whole pleasure received is derived from an unexpected turn of expression, then I call it wit; but when the pleasure is produced..by an image which remains with us..I call it fancy. **1822** HAZLITT *Table-t.* II. x. 221 Fancy colours the prospect of the future. **1845** L. HUNT *Imag. & Fancy* 2 Poetry..embodies and illustrates its impressions by imagination, or images of the objects of which it treats..It illustrates them by fancy, which is a lighter play of imagination, or the feeling of analogy coming short of seriousness. **1851** RUSKIN *Mod. Paint.* II. III. II. iii. §7 The fancy sees the outside..The imagination sees the heart and inner nature, and makes them felt. **1861** M. PATTISON *Ess.* (1889) I. 39 That ocean-horse in which the poetic fancy of the sea-roving Saxons saw an emblem of their high-prowed vessels.

b. A mental image.

1663 BP. PATRICK *Parab. Pilgr.* 257 The very fancy of them [enjoyments] is delightful. **1798** COLERIDGE *Ode to France* i, Oft, pursuing fancies holy, My moonlight way o'er flowering weeds I wound.

5. a. Inventive design; an invention, original device or contrivance. Cf. FANTASY 4 d.

1665 SIR T. HERBERT *Trav.* (1677) 223 Adorned with..fancies of Arabic Characters. **1670** NARBOROUGH *Jrnl.* in *Acc. Sev. Late Voy.* I. (1711) 57 The model I imagine is to record our Ship..This Fancy we let alone untouched. **1692** R. L'ESTRANGE *Josephus' Antiq.* XII. ii. (1702) 322 The graving work..being the Phancy of a Foliage of the Vine. *c* **1710** C. FIENNES *Diary* (1888) 168 Severall good fancy's of human and animals. **1867** F. FRANCIS *Angling* xii. (1880) 438 This fly [Salmon fly] is Mr. Blackwall's own fancy.

†**b.** *esp.* in *Music*, a composition in an impromptu style. *Obs.* Cf. FANTASIA, FANTASY 4 e.

1577 T. DAWSON (*title*), The Workes of a young Wyt, trust vp with a Fardell of Prettie Fancies. **1597** SHAKS. *2 Hen. IV*, III. ii. 342 He..sung those tunes to the over-scutched huswives that he heard the carmen whistle, and sware—they were his fancies, or his good-nights. **1663** PEPYS *Diary* 27 May, Mr. Gibbons being come in..to musique, they played a good Fancy. **1691** WOOD *Ath. Oxon.* I. 848 He was..much admired for his composition of Fancies of various parts. **1789** BURNEY *Hist. Mus.* III. vii. 408 John Jenkins a voluminous composer of Fancies for viols. **1823** CRABB *Technol. Dict.* I, *Fancies*, lively little airs.

†**c.** *pl.* 'The ornamental tags, etc., appended to the ribbons by which the hose were secured to the doublet' (Fairholt). *Obs.*

a **1652** BROME *Mad Couple* Prol., I've a new Suite, And Ribbons fashionable, yclipt Fancies.

6. A supposition resting on no solid grounds; an arbitrary notion.

1471 RIPLEY *Comp. Alch.* v. in Ashm. (1652) 149 To know the truth, and fancies to eschew. **1539** TAVERNER *Erasm. Prov.* (1552) 18 Menne myght loke upon it, and talke theyr fansies of it. **1590** SIR J. SMYTH *Disc. Weapons* 25 Rather upon fancie, than upon anie souldiour lyke reasons. **1672** MARVELL *Reh. Transp.* Wks. II. 58 After this I had another phansie..not altogether unreasonable. **1783** HAILES *Antiq. Chr. Ch.* ii. 33 This fancy is very ancient, for Orosius hints at it. **1809–10** COLERIDGE *Friend* (1865) 142 As wild a fancy as any of which we have treated.

7. a. Caprice, changeful mood; an instance of this, a caprice, a whim. Also *concr.* a whimsical thing.

1579 G. HARVEY *Letter-bk.* (Camden) 86 A foolish madd worlde, wherein all thinges ar overruild by fansye. **1646** SIR T. BROWNE *Pseud. Ep.* II. iv. 82 Cardans Mausoleum for a flye, is a meere phancy. **1676** LISTER in *Ray's Corr.* (1848) 124 The addition of the French names would have been but a fancy. **1717** LADY M. W. MONTAGUE *Lett.* II. xlvii. 40 His wife's..expenses are no way limited but by her own fancy. **1787** BENTHAM *Def. Usury* i. 2 A fancy has taken me just now to trouble you with my reasons. **1848** MACAULAY *Hist. Eng.* II. 46 The antipathy of the nation to their religion was not a fancy which would yield to the mandate of a prince. **1860–1** FLO. NIGHTINGALE *Nursing* 43 Such cravings are usually called the 'fancies' of patients. **1878** *Masque Poets* 80, I have a fancy we go out to-day.

†**b.** Fantasticalness. *Obs.*

1588 SHAKS. *L.L.L.* I. i. 171 This childe of fancie that Armado hight. **1602** —— *Ham.* I. iii. 71 Costly thy habit as thy purse can buy; But not exprest in fancie; rich, not gawdie. **1823** BYRON *Juan* XI. xvii, A real swell, Full flash, all fancy.

8. a. Capricious or arbitrary preference; individual taste; an inclination, liking, *esp.* in phrases ***to have, take a fancy for, to***; † ***to have no fancy with***; ***to take, catch the fancy of***.

1465 *Paston Lett.* No. 530 II. 243, I have non fansey with some of the felechipp. **1541** *Act 33 Hen. VIII* c. 21 In case it fortune..the king..should take a fancie to anie woman. **1553** T. WILSON *Rhet.* (1580) 200 Speake muche, according to the nature and phansie of the ignoraunt. **1577** B. GOOGE *Heresbach's Husb.* III. (1586) 114 b, Hee that hath a fansie to breed Horse. **1600** J. PORY tr. *Leo's Africa* II. 315 Each..would interpret the opinions of Mahomet according to their owne fancie. **1662** J. DAVIES *Voy. Ambass.* 314 The Persians have a great fancy to Black hair. **1682** WHELER *Journ. Greece* I. 36 Phansie took us to see the Fortress. **1700** S. L. tr. *C. Fryke's Voy. E. Ind.* 82 The Admiral had a mighty fancy to go over. **1848** MACAULAY *Hist. Eng.* II. 433 The..tune caught the fancy of the nation. **1866** G. MACDONALD *Ann. Q. Neighb.* xxxi. (1878) 533 What could have made Miss Crowther take such a fancy to the boy? **1884** W. C. SMITH *Kildrostan* 86 Have you no fancy To ride the white steeds?

†**b.** *spec.* Amorous inclination, love. *Obs.*

1559 *Mirr. Mag., Dk. of Clarence* xii, Knowing fansie was the forcing rother, Which stiereth youth to any kinde of strife, He offered me his daughter to my wife. **1579** LYLY *Euphues* (Arb.) 81 Philautus was..neuer loued for fancie sake. **1596** SHAKS. *Merch. V.* III. ii. 63 Tell me where is fancie bred. **1712** ARBUTHNOT *John Bull* III. iii, 'Fancy is free', quoth Peg.

9. Taste, critical judgement in matters of art or elegance.

c **1665** MRS. HUTCHINSON *Mem. Col. Hutchinson* 23 He was..genteel in his habit, and had a very good fancy in it. **1705** ADDISON *Italy* 11 Palaces..built with an excellent Fancy. **1713** SWIFT *Cadenus & Vanessa*, I'll undertake, my little Nancy In flounces hath a better fancy. **1748** C'TESS SHAFTESBURY in *Priv. Lett. Ld. Malmesbury* I. 72 A buff-coloured damask, trimmed with a good deal of fancy. **1857** RUSKIN *Pol. Econ. Art* 42 They possess..sense of colour, and fancy for form.

†**10.** 'Something that pleases or entertains' (J.).

1590 SIR J. SMYTH *Disc. Weapons* 39 All such as are..not carried with toyes, fancies, and new fashions. **1712** MORTIMER *Husbandry* II. 204 London-Pride is a pretty Fancy for borders. **1721** CIBBER *Love's Last Shift* IV, A particular nice Fancy, that I intend to appear in.

†**11.** An alleged name for the pansy. *Obs.*

1712 tr. *Pomet's Hist. Drugs* I. 120 Fancy, in English, is a kind of Violet.

12. ***the fancy***: collect. for those who 'fancy' a particular amusement or pursuit. **a.** *gen.*, as applied to bird-, book-fanciers, etc.

1735 J. MOORE *Columbarium* 40 These Pigeons by their Flight afford an admirable Satisfaction, to those Gentlemen of the Fancy that have time to attend them. **1830** DE QUINCEY *Bentley* Wks. 1863 VI. 57 *note*, A great book sale..had congregated all the *Fancy*. **1889** *Sat. Rev.* 22 June 772/1 Pigeon-fanciers are called the Fancy.

b. *esp.* The prize-ring or those who frequent it.

1807 SOUTHEY *Lett. fr. Eng.* (1951) lxxi. 451 The Amateurs of Boxing, who call themselves *the Fancy*. **1811** SOUTHEY *Let.* 11 Oct. (1856) II. 236 I have fibbed the 'Edinburgh' (as the 'fancy' say) most completely. **1848** THACKERAY *Bk. Snobs* xiv. (1869) 64 Mr. William Ramm, known to the Fancy as the Tutbury Pet. **1873** H. SPENCER *Stud. Sociol.* viii. (ed. 6) 187 Among leaders of 'the fancy', it is an unhesitating belief that pluck and endurance are the highest of attributes.

attrib. **1811** SOUTHEY *Let.* 6 Mar. (1856) II. 215, I am in high condition, to use a fancy phrase.

c. The art of boxing; pugilism. Also, sporting in general.

1820 BYRON *Let. to Murray* 12 Nov., One of Matthew's passions was 'the Fancy'. **1841** DE QUINCEY *Plato's Rep.* Wks. IX. 236 When the 'fancy' was in favour. **1851** MAYHEW *Lond. Labour* (1861) III. 5 He..is always..at home..to discuss the Fancy generally. **1889** *Standard* 28 Oct., Modern displays of 'the Fancy'.

13. The art or practice of breeding animals so as to develop points of conventional beauty or excellence; also one of these points. Sometimes with qualifying word prefixed, as ***pigeon-fancy***.

1889 *Sat. Rev.* 22 June 772/2 The peculiar fancy affecting him [the carrier] is to have wattles and excrescences round his eyes and beak. **1889** *Standard* 23 Oct., The layman uninitiated in the mysteries of 'fancy'.

attrib. **1862** HUXLEY *Lect. Wrkg. Men* 105 Birds which fly long distances..and are..used as carriers are not carriers in the fancy sense. **1876** *Encycl. Brit.* IV. 249/2 The less important art of fancy breeding. **1889** *Sat. Rev.* 22 June 772/2 A pouter graces the frontispiece, using the word 'grace' in the Fancy sense.

14. a. = various combs. of the adj. Often = ***fancy cake*** (below, C. 1).

1841 *Week in Wall Street* 82 A very large portion of the stocks termed 'fancies', are entirely worthless in themselves. **1851** *Beck's Florist* 140 Pelargoniums, both 'Fancies' and common kinds, were produced..Mr. Ambrose's Fancy..was..distinguished. **1862** *Times* 17 Feb., Ordinary cloths and fancies moved off alike slowly. **1891** *Confectioners' Union* 15 Oct. p. iii (Advt.), Fondant, Jellies, Gelatine goods,..and other Fancies. *Ibid.* 15 Nov. 633/2 The room where Christmas fancies are being packed by a small army of girls. **1894** E. SKUSE *Compl. Confect.* 110 There are a great number of fancies made from grain sugars, sold about Christmas time. **1968** M. BRAGG *Without City Wall* I. xix. 191 Jars of jam being given by the ladies, a box of teacakes and fancies by Agnes.

b. = *fancy-roller*; see C 2 b.

1864 *Specif. Barraclough's Patent* No. 1581. 5 The rollers *c* are the 'fancies' before named. **1873** E. LEIGH *Cotton Spinning* I. 144 The surface of the 'fancy' runs in the same direction as the cylinder only a little faster. **1876** W. C. BRAMWELL *Wool-Carder* (ed. 2) viii.

B. *attrib.* and *Comb.*

1. General relations: **a.** Simple attrib. (sense 4) as ***fancy-fit, -freak, -woof***; (sense 12 b, c) as ***fancy-lay*** [see LAY *sb.*].

1855 BROWNING *Men & Wom., In a Balcony* 101 This wild girl (whom I recognise Scarce more than you do, in her *fancy-fit). **1884** —— *Ferishtah* (1885) 4 A *fancy-freak by contrast born of thee. **1819** *Tom Crib's Memorial* App. 43 We, who're of the *fancy-lay. *a* **1845** HOOD *Irish Schoolmaster* xvi, Weaves a *fancy-woof, Dreaming he sees his home.

b. objective, as ***fancy-feeding, -lighting, -stirring, -taking, -weaving*** ppl. adjs.; ***fancy-monger, -weaver***; ***fancy-spinning*** vbl. sb.

1599 SANDYS *Europæ Spec.* (1632) 162 Their..*fancy-feeding flatterers shall all shrinke from them. **1857** WILLMOTT *Pleas. Lit.* xxi. 132 The *fancy-lighting damsels of Dryden. **1600** SHAKS. *A.Y.L.* III. ii. 381 If I could meet that *Fancie-monger, I would giue him some good counsel. **1962** W. NOWOTTNY *Lang. Poets Use* iv. 91 Gaunt tries to comfort him with something like the *fancy-spinning of Richard. **1835** WILLIS *Pencillings* II. xlv. 58 The Egyptian bazaar has been my..*fancy-stirring lounge. **1855** *National Rev.* July 57 The great features..which make society..remarkable, *fancy-taking. *a* **1845** HOOD *Compass* xvii, To eye of *fancy-weaver Neptune..seem'd tossing in A raging scarlet fever! **1884** *Athenæum* 6 Dec. 725/2 A certain *fancy-weaving dervish.

c. instrumental, originative, and adverbial, as ***fancy-baffled, -blest, -born, -borne, -bred, -built, -caught, -driven, -fed, -formed, -framed, -grazing, -guided, -led, -raised, -struck, -stung, -topped, -waistcoated, -woven, -wrought*** ppl. adjs.

1645 QUARLES *Sol. Recant.* iv. 21 Thy false affections may rise up, and shake Thy *fancy-baffled Judgment. **1759** GOLDSM. *Polite Learning* vii. Wks. 1881 II. 44 The *fancy-built fabric is styled for a short time very ingenious. **1631** T. POWELL *Tom All Trades* 174 The young Factor being *fancy-caught. **1844** LD. HOUGHTON *Palm Leaves* 131 They wandered, *fancy-driven. **1850** TENNYSON *In Mem.* lxxxiv. 24 So shall..pining life be *fancy-fed. **1654** GATAKER *Disc. Apol.* 68 *Fancie-formed pictures. **1647** CRASHAW *Poems* 53 He his own *fancy framed foe defies. **1852** *Meanderings of Mem.* I. 79 The *fancy-grazing herds of freedom's pen. **1645** QUARLES *Sol. Recant.* vii. 36 *Fancy-guided motion. **1777** J. MOUNTAIN *Poetical Reveries* (ed. 2) 20 *Fancy-led th' ideas ran. **1873** LONGF. *Wayside Inn, Emma & Eginhard* 88 Love-letters thought the poet fancy-led. **1798** SOTHEBY tr. *Wieland's Oberon* (1826) I. 80 Now, reader, *fancy-rais'd, as swells thy mind. **1773** J. HOME *Alonzo* IV, If we stay here we shall be *fancy-struck. **1822** HAZLITT *Table-t.* Ser. II. vii. (1869) 149 Our ears are *fancy stung. **1875** *Atlantic Monthly* Jan. 70 She has two tall *fancy-topped chimneys. **1909** *Daily Chron.* 7 Aug. 4/7 He of the well-dressed, *fancy-waistcoated order. **1785** WARTON *Ode New Year* i. 9 Fable's *fancy-woven vest. **1801** *Lusignan* IV. 147 A *fancy-wrought spectre.

2. Special comb.: **fancy-bloke**, *slang*, = FANCY MAN; **fancy Dan** *slang* (orig. *U.S.*), a dandy; a

showy but ineffective worker or sportsman; **fancy-fit** *v. trans.*, to fit (with a garland) to one's fancy; **fancy-free** *a.*, free from the power of love; **fancy-girl** *colloq.* = *fancy-woman*; **fancy-loose** *a.*, ready to roam at will; **fancy-piece** = *fancy girl, woman*; **fancy-sick** *a.*, love-sick; **fancy-woman**, a kept mistress (cf. FANCY MAN).

1846 R. L. SNOWDEN *Magistrate's Assistant* 344 A *fancy bloak. **1943** *Amer. Speech* XVIII. 107 *Fancy Dan (a pitcher good in practice but sour in a game; also a dressy player). **1950** J. DEMPSEY *Championship Fighting* ii. 12 The amateur and professional ranks today are cluttered with ..'fancy Dans'. **1950** A. LOMAX *Mr. Jelly Roll* (1952) 49 Then you could observe the fancy Dans, dressed fit to kill. **1960** T. MCLEAN *Kings of Rugby* xi. 168 Wellington's strong and experienced men..knew too much about defensive play to be gulled by Fancy-Dan stuff. **1820** KEATS *Lamia* II. 220 Each, as he did please, Might *fancy-fit his brows. **1590** SHAKS. *Mids. N.* II. i. 164 The Imperiall Votresse passed on, In maiden meditation *fancy free. **1840** THACKERAY *Paris Sk.-bk.* (1869) 98 They walk, fancy-free, in all sorts of maiden meditations. **1892** P. H. EMERSON *Son of Fens* xv. 131 We allust call our scythes arter our *fancy-gels or our wives. **1930** A. P. HERBERT *Water Gipsies* xxii, Let's hear the rest now—out with it! You been his fancy-girl? **1969** 'M. INNES' *Family Affair* ix. 101, I thought this fellow might paint a man's fancy girls—see? **1850** MRS. BROWNING *Poems* II. 320 My thoughts..for earth too *fancy-loose. **1821** P. EGAN *Life in London* I. iii. 47 Or even *smiled* with indifference at the rolls of *soft* which his most captivating **fancy-piece* drew from him repeatedly. **1590** SHAKS. *Mids. N.* III. ii. 96 All *fancy sicke she is, and pale of cheere, With sighes of loue. *a* **1704** R. L'ESTRANGE (J.), When we come to the fancy-sick, there's no cure for it. **1823** JOANNA BAILLIE *Poems* 219 To thee the lover, fancy-sick, will sigh. **1812** J. H. VAUX *Flash Dict.*, A woman who is the particular favourite of any man, is termed his **fancy woman*, and *vice versa*. **1892** *Daily News* 1 Mar. 2/4 He brought home a female, whom he introduced as his 'fancy woman'.

C. *adj.* [Developed from the attrib. use of the sb.; scarcely occurring in predicative use.]

1. a. Of a design varied according to the fancy; 'fine, ornamental', in opposition to 'plain'; as in ***fancy basket, cake, trimming***, etc. Also FANCY DRESS, FANCY WORK.

1751 H. GLASSE *Art Cookery* (ed. 4) App. 333 A few Astertion Flowers stuck here and there looks pretty..but Lemon, and all those Things are entirely Fancy. *a* **1761** GRAY *Lett.* Wks. 1884 III. 118 They [wall papers] are all what they [the shops] call fancy. **1788** W. MARSHALL *Yorksh.* (1796) I. 116 The fancy farm-houses..I purposely pass over. **1834** MEDWIN *Angler in Wales* II. 211 He had for field duty two fancy uniforms. *a* **1839** LONGF. *Hyperion* II. ix, A very tall man with fiery red hair and fancy whiskers. **1842** TENNYSON *Vis. Sin* 102 Fish are we that love the mud, Rising to no fancy-flies. **1866** MRS. WHITNEY *L. Goldthwaite* ix, To grow intimate over tableau plans and fancy stitches. **1883** E. INGERSOLL in *Harper's Mag.* June 78/1 'Fancy' flour differs from the ordinary superfine in that the middlings are ground through smooth rollers. **1893** E. HÉRISSÉ *Art of Pastry Making* ii. 8 (*heading*) Fondant icing ..for icing fancy pastry-cakes. *Ibid.* xiii. 97 (*heading*) Fancy ornamental meringues. (Meringues décorées.) **1912** —— *Ibid.* (new ed.) ii. 20 Dip in the fancy cakes or pastry with the point of a penknife or fork. **1960** *Good Housek. Cookery Bk.* (ed. 5) 387/1 Small iced fancy cakes... Cut the cake into fancy shapes before icing.

b. *Printing.* (see quots.)

1871 *Amer. Encycl. Printing* s.v. *Job Letter*, Job Letter may be conveniently divided into Plain, Fancy, Text, and Script. **1888** C. T. JACOBI *Printers' Voc.* 42 *Fancy rules*, rules other than plain ones of various designs. *Fancy types*, founts of type of various kinds used for jobbing purposes.

c. Of flowers, grass, etc.: Particoloured, striped.

1793 G. WASHINGTON *Let.* Writings 1891 XII. 378 From the fancy grass..I have been urging for years..the saving of seed. **1851** *Beck's Florist* 139 Mr. Ayres shewed his fancy Pelargonium. **1893** *Webbs Spring Catal.* 65 Webbs' Fancy Pansy. *Ibid.* 80 Perpetual fancy Carnation.

d. *ellipt.* That deals in, or is concerned with the sale of, fancy goods. ***fancy fair***: see FAIR *sb.*[1] 1 c. Also ***fancy shop***.

1821 *Blackw. Mag.* X. 4 Haberdashers and others in the fancy line. **1835** DICKENS *Sk. Boz.* (1836) I. 136 Flaming accounts of some 'fancy fair in high life'. **1840** H. COCKTON *Life Valentine Vox* xxv. 178 A placard..which announced that a Fancy Fair and a Fete Champetre were about to take place. **1844** J. COWELL *30 Yrs. among Players* (1845) I. vi. 15/2 His address..was at a handsome fancy-shop in George-street. **1848** THACKERAY *Van. Fair* l, She buys a couple of begilt Bristol boards at the Fancy Stationers. **1863** J. C. JEAFFRESON *Sir Everard's Dau.* 113 A chattel for which a fancy-upholsterer in London would ask a strangely large number of pounds. **1876** *World* V. 17 A fancy-fair is one of the diversions of a London Season. **1885** *Bookseller* 5 Mar. 317/2 A good Fancy Trade. **1911** A. BENNETT *Hilda Lessways* I. iii. 24 She went straight into Dayson's little fancy shop.

e. ***fancy ball*** = *fancy dress ball* (see FANCY DRESS *sb.*). Also ***fancy dance***.

1800 M. EDGEWORTH *Parent's Assistant* (1848) III. 285 How fine we are!..one might fancy one's-self..at a fancy ball. **1825** C. M. WESTMACOTT *Eng. Spy* II. 24 A grand fancy ball was to take place at the Argyle Rooms. **1827** J. CONSTABLE *Let.* 10 Oct. (1962) 237 To day..a Garden Promenade—and fancy dance in a temporary pavilion. **1836** HAWTHORNE *Amer. Note-bks.* (1883) 34 A Fancy Ball, in which the prominent American writers should appear, dressed in character.

f. ***fancy goods*** (cf. 1 d).

1792 *Columbian Centinel* (Boston, Mass.) 12 May, A large and extensive assortment of staple and fancy goods. *a* **1828** D. WORDSWORTH *Tour Continent* in *Jrnls.* (1941) II. 73 Stalls and shops of jewelry, millinery and fancy goods of all sorts. **1860** DICKENS in *All Year Round* 28 Jan. 321/1, I..have rather a large connexion in the fancy goods way. **1933** *Archit. Rev.* LXXIV. 16/3 A manufacturer of fancy goods and hand-bags remarks that, 'we study the public taste while we try to originate'.

2. a. Added for ornament or extraordinary use.

1794 *Rigging & Seamanship* I. 169 *Fancy-line* is a rope used to overhaul the brails of some fore and aft sails. **1841** R. H. DANA *Seaman's Man.* 104 *Fancy-line*, a line rove through a block at the jaws of a gaff, used as a downhaul. **1874** MICKLETHWAITE *Mod. Par. Churches* 77 To increase the list of fancy and solo stops [in an organ].

b. ***fancy roller*** (in a Carding-engine): see quots.

1850 *Specif. E. Leigh's Patent* No. 13027. 2 Thirdly in the employment of a 'fancy roller' for partially stripping the main cylinder, such roller being only partially clothed with card. **1873** E. LEIGH *Cotton Spinning* I. 144 For heavy carding a fancy roller, which is a roller that overruns the periphery of the cylinder, is sometimes used with advantage ..[It] lifts the cotton that would otherwise get wedged in the wire of the cylinder, and thereby admits heavy carding.

3. Calling forth or resulting from the exercise of fancy or caprice. **a.** Of an action: Capricious, whimsical.

1646 PAGITT *Heresiogr.* (ed. 3) 118 Their own fancy presumption they call..justifying faith. *a* **1820** W. IRVING *Sketch Bk., Stratford-on-Avon* (1865) 330 The Avon.. made a variety of the most fancy doublings. **1821** *Blackw. Mag.* X. 417 Many a fancy flam was proposed. **1837** DICKENS *Pickw.* xix, As a display of fancy shooting, it was extremely varied and curious.

b. Of a price, rent, etc.: Estimated by caprice, rather than by actual value. So ***fancy stocks*** (cf. FANCY *sb.* 14).

a **1838** MACAULAY *Life & Lett.* (1883) II. 28 The fancy price which a peculiar turn of mind led me to put on my liberty. **1848** J. R. BARTLETT *Americanisms* 132 Fancy Stocks. A species of stocks which are bought and sold to a great extent in New York..Nearly all the fluctuations in their prices are artificial. **1874** MICKLETHWAITE *Mod. Par. Churches* 312 They will give a fancy price for a work by a Leighton. **1874** R. TYRWHITT *Sketch. Club* 197 To take a moor at a fancy rent. **1888** T. E. HOLLAND in *Times* 18 Aug. 8/4 The bombardment of an unfortified town..for the purpose of enforcing a fancy contribution or ransom.

c. Of an animal or bird: Of a kind bred for the development of particular 'points' or qualities. Also in ***fancy-farm***: an experimental farm.

1810 *Sporting Mag.* XXXVI. 10 A great many sorts of fancy-pigeons. **1818** SCOTT *Hrt. Midl.* xlii, To engage him ..to superintend his fancy-farm in Dumbartonshire. **1851** MAYHEW *Lond. Labour* II. 54 A dog recommended by its beauty, or any peculiarity..is a 'fancy' animal. **1880** *Gainsburgh Times* 20 Feb. in *N.W. Linc. Gloss.*, 'What sort of a dog was it?'..'A fancy dog'. **1881** J. C. LYELL *Fancy Pigeons* Introd., Fancy pigeons from the lofts of well-known breeders.

d. ***fancy franchise***: one based on an arbitrarily determined qualification (see quot. 1868).

1859 *Hansard Commons* 28 Feb. 1025 [John Bright *loq.*] I say, all these fancy franchises are absurd. **1868** *Chambers' Encycl.* X. 695/2 The dual vote was early abandoned, and its abandonment involved that of the 'fancy' franchises..they proposed to give votes to all who paid £1 annually in direct taxes (not including licences), who belonged to certain of the better educated professions, or who had £50 in a savings-bank or in the funds. **1889** *Tablet* 21 Dec. 983 Fancy franchises were also abandoned.

e. ***fancy religion*** (see quot.).

1925 FRASER & GIBBONS *Soldier & Sailor Words, Fancy religion*, a very old Service colloquial term in both Navy and Army for a creed or denomination not Church of England, Roman Catholic, or Presbyterian, before the War the three authorized creeds.

4. Based upon or drawn from conceptions of the fancy (*sb.* 3), as ***fancy picture, piece, portrait, sketch***.

1800 MAR. EDGEWORTH *Belinda* (1832) II. 2 This picture is not a fancy-piece. *c* **1811** FUSELI *Lect. Art* iv. (1848) 437 The Phantasiæ of the ancients..modern art..in what is called Fancy-pictures, has..debased. **1844** WHITTIER *Two Processions* Prose Wks. 1889 III. 116 The caricature of our 'general sympathizers'..is by no means a fancy sketch. **1870** EMERSON *Soc. & Solit., Art.* Wks. (Bohn) III. 20 In sculpture, did ever anybody call the Apollo a fancy piece? **1873** ROGERS *Orig. Bible* i. (1875) 36 We..look at this wonderful character as a fancy portrait.

5. Applied to a person who is fancied or who fancies himself: mostly synonymous (but in some expressions with slang overtones) with FANCY MAN a, or *fancy-woman*. Cf. also *fancy-girl* (sense B. 2 above).

1891 KIPLING *Light that Failed* v. 73 'E brought some most remarkable fancy young gentlemen up 'ere. **1905** H. ELLIS *Stud. Psychol. Sex* IV. 235, I..told her again I had no money. She..said, 'That does not matter... I want you to be my fancy boy.' **1934** T. S. ELIOT *Rock* i. 12 One o' them fancy lads—a good soldier and fond o' the ladies—but a great one for 'is church. **1938** E. BOWEN *Death of Heart* III. iv. 381 Eddie had been warned..that one could not go to all lengths as Mrs. Quayne's fancy boy. **1942** BERREY & VAN DEN BARK *Amer. Thes. Slang* §452. 3 *Dandy*,..fancy pants. **1967** 'M. HUNTER' *Cambridgeshire Disaster* viii. 52 Some puffed-up fancy pants..said something which made the barmaid laugh.

fancy ('fænsɪ), *v.* Also *α.* 6 fancie, 6–7 fansie, 8 fansy. *β.* 6–7 phancie, -cy, (6 phansie). [f. prec. sb. Cf. the older FANTASY *v.*]

I. With reference to mental conception.

1. *trans.* **a.** To frame in fancy; to portray in the mind; to picture to oneself; to conceive, imagine. Also (with notion of FANCY *sb.* 3), to suppose oneself to perceive.

1646 SIR T. BROWNE *Pseud. Ep.* IV. xii. 215 Severall nations and ages do fancy unto themselves different years of danger. *a* **1661** FULLER *Worthies* (1840) I. 110 It [Berkshire] may be fancied in a form like a lute. **1713** SWIFT *Cadenus & Vanessa*, She fancies musick in his tongue. **1748** HARTLEY *Observ. Man* I. iii. 327 Fansying to our-selves a confused Heap of Things. **1769** *Junius Lett.* xx. 97 The author is..at liberty to fancy cases, and make..comparisons. **1860** THACKERAY *Four Georges* i. (1862) 31, I fancy a considerable shrewdness..in his ways.

absol. *c* **1698** LOCKE *Cond. Underst.* §31 If all our Search has yet reach'd no farther than simile..we rather fancie than know.

b. with simple complement, or *to be*: To imagine (a person, oneself, a thing) to be (so and so).

1662 STILLINGFL. *Orig. Sacr.* III. iv. §6 Some have fancyed the earth to bee as one great animal. **1696** tr. *Du Mont's Voy. Levant* 61, I fansi'd my self restor'd from Death to Life. **1728** YOUNG *Love Fame* iii. Wks. (1757) 109 What most we wish, with ease we fansy near. **1833** HT. MARTINEAU *Vanderput & S.* i. 11 Learning to fancy himself better than he is. **1856** KANE *Arct. Expl.* II. xxii. 218, I could have fancied it a walrus. **1869** J. MARTINEAU *Ess.* II. 64 He fancies himself not in the senate, but on the bench.

†**c.** with *inf.* as *obj.* *Obs.*

1726 J. M. tr. *Tragic. Hist. Chev. de Vaudray* 157 He, at last, fancy'd to have found the Mystery of it. **1754** A. MURPHY *Gray's Inn Journal* (1756) II. 194 No. 83, I fancied to myself to see my amiable Country-women engaged in a deep Debate.

d. with *obj.* and *inf.* or object clause. Also, †To represent imaginatively.

1551 BP. GARDINER *Explic. true Cath. Fayth* 137 Fansinge that as one waue in the water thrusteth away an other, so doth one fourme an other. **1630** *R. Johnson's Kingd. & Commw.* 64 The figure of Europe is fancied to resemble a Queene. **1638** BAKER tr. *Balzac's Lett.* II. 64 Imployments, in which I fancy in my minde, we may spend our time. **1654** tr. Scudery's *Curia Politiæ* 5 A device..which fansied me to passe beyond Hercules's Pillars. *a* **1682** SIR T. BROWNE *Tracts* (1683) 107 He is aptly phancied even still revengefully to pursue his hated Wife. **1791** MRS. RADCLIFFE *Rom. Forest* x, She almost fancied she heard voices swell in the storm. **1845** M. PATTISON *Ess.* (1889) I. 7 We read Bingham, and fancy we are studying ecclesiastical history.

e. In *colloq.* use often in the imperative as an exclamation of suprise. Also *absol.*

1813 JANE AUSTEN *Let.* 6 Nov. (1932) II. 90 Very snug, in my own room, lovely morn[g], excellent fire, fancy me. **1834** MEDWIN *Angler in Wales* I. 159 Fancy me boxed up in the narrow vehicle. **1850** E. RUSKIN *Let.* 9 Feb. in M. Lutyens *Effie in Venice* (1965) I. 139 But, only fancy, the Thousands and Thousands of wax lights. **1859** LANG *Wand. India* 13 Fancy we three meeting again in the Himalaya mountains! **1861** THACKERAY *Round. Papers, On being found out* 126 Fancy all the boys in all the school being whipped. **1881** GRANT WHITE *Eng. Without & Within* xvi. 388 Fancy, now! [in England] a very common expression of surprise. *a* **1943** R. G. COLLINGWOOD *Idea Hist.* (1946) v. 270 Whom is she shielding? Either her father or her young man. Is it her father? No: fancy the rector! **1971** E. MCGIRR *No Better Fiend* 83, I did the 'fancy that!' line of patter.

†**f.** ***to fancy out***: to represent by an image; to exemplify. *Obs. rare.*

1669 STURMY *Mariner's Mag.* VI. 105 The two later Motions are fancied out unto us, by a Man turning a Crane-Wheel, or Grind-stone 365 times round, while a Worm.. creeps once round the contrary way.

2. To believe without being able to prove; to have an idea *that*. Frequently in ***I fancy***: I rather think.

1672 SIR C. LYTTELTON in *Hatton Corr.* (1878) 99, I phancy the Dukes match wth y[e] Archduchesse is a little dulld. **1790** T. JEFFERSON *Writ.* (1859) III. 162 This day, I fancy, will determine whether we are to be removed to Philadelphia or not. **1825** COBBETT *Rur. Rides* (1885) II. 33 The estate is, I fancy, theirs yet. **1883** F. M. PEARD *Contrad.* xviii, We fancy she is engaged to a Mr. Atherton.

3. To liken (a thing) in fancy †*to*; to transform (it) *into*. *rare.*

1646 BUCK *Rich. III.* Ded., I fancy them to our shaddowes. **1801** SOUTHEY *Thalaba* IV. ix, Hast thou never, in the twilight, fancied Familiar object into some strange shape? **1868** LOWELL *Witchcraft* Prose Wks. 1890 II. 356 The first child that ever bestrode his father's staff, and fancied it into a courser.

†**4.** To arrange in or according to fancy, or with artistic taste; to contrive, devise, design, plan.

1624 MASSINGER *Parl. Love* IV. ii, Something I must fancy, to dissuade him From doing sudden violence on himself. **1635** SWAN *Spec. M.* v. §2 (1643) 136 They [painters] fashion diversly according to their skill in phancying the laying of their colours. **1665** SIR T. HERBERT *Trav.* (1677) 145 The figure of a Horse preparing to defend himself against a Lion; but so rarely fancied as gains the Sculptor praise. **1716** LADY M. W. MONTAGUE *Lett.* (1763) I. vii. 32 Furniture..so well fancied and fitted up. *a* **1759** GOLDSM. *The Bee* No. 2 *On Dress*, Clothes..fancied by the artist who dresses the three battalions of Guards. **1759** B. MARTIN *Nat. Hist. Eng.* I. 298 The mourning Pallases at the Base of it [a martial Figure] are both well fansied and well adapted.

†**5.** To allot or ascribe in fancy. *Obs.*

a **1643** W. CARTWRIGHT *Ordinary* IV. ii, I fancy'd you a beating. **1646** SIR T. BROWNE *Pseud. Ep.* I. vi. 23 To fancy wings unto Dædalus. **1647** N. BACON *Disc. Govt. Eng.* I. lvi. (1739) 103 Fame hath fancied him that Title.

6. To have a good conceit of, plume oneself upon (oneself, one's own actions or qualities). *colloq.*

1866 *Daily Tel.* 20 Jan. 8/1 He ogles, he 'fancies himself'. **1886** H. CONWAY *Living or Dead* viii, I was conceited and fancied my game at whist.

II. With reference to fondness or liking.

†7. a. To be to the fancy of; to please. b. To attach by 'fancy' or liking *to*. *Obs. rare.*

1566 PAINTER *Pal. Pleas.* (1890) III. 431 The sauourous fruict..fansied the sensuall taste of Adams Wyfe. *c* **1590** GREENE *Fr. Bacon* (1630) 17 Fast fancied to the Keepers bonny Lasse.

8. To take a fancy to; to entertain a liking for; to be pleased with; to like. **a.** with *obj.* a person. (In early use often = to be or fall in love with.)

1545 UDALL, etc. *Erasm. Par. Luke* i. 54 The people of Israel..as a people more derely beloued and fansyed. **1568** GRAFTON *Chron.* II. 225 She went as simply as she might, to thentent that the king should not phansie her. **1596** SHAKS. *Tam. Shr.* II. i. 12, I neuer yet beheld that speciall face, Which I could fancie, more then any other. **1614** RALEIGH *Hist. World* I. i. §8. 199 Ninus..fancied her so strongly, as, (neglecting all Princely respects) he took her from her husband. **1663–4** DRYDEN *Rival Ladies* I. ii, I do not think she fancies much the man. **1838** MRS. CARLYLE *Lett.* I. 95 Carlyle breakfasted with Moore..and fancied him.

absol. **1588** GREENE *Perimedes* 53 Sheepheards can fancie, but they cannot saye. **1601** SHAKS. *Twel. N.* II. v. 29 Should shee fancie, it should bee one of my complection. **1713** SWIFT *Cadenus & Vanessa*, Five thousand guineas in her purse! The doctor might have fancy'd worse.

b. with *obj.* a thing; also †with *inf.* as *obj.*

1598 B. JONSON *Ev. Man in Hum.* I. i, Not to spend Your coyne on euery bable, that you phansie. **1644** MILTON *Areop.* (Arb.) 39 Burning..what they fansied not. **1669** A. BROWNE *Ars Pict.* App. (1675) 24 One phansies to draw Pictures by the Life. **1727** POPE, &c. *Art of Sinking* 119 Throw all the adventures you fancy into one tale. **1852** MRS. STOWE *Uncle Tom's C.* xx, Miss Ophelia was uneasy that Eva should fancy Topsy's society so much. *Mod.* The patient may eat anything that he fancies.

c. To view (a horse) favourably as a likely winner of a race.

1922 JOYCE *Ulysses* 391 A racing-horse he fancied. **1923** WODEHOUSE *Inimitable Jeeves* xi. 116 Ocean Breeze is fancied, as I am told the expression is, for a race which will take place..at Goodwood.

III. **9.** To breed (animals or birds); to grow (plants) so as to develop in them conventional 'points' of beauty. Also, *simply* to breed.

1851 MAYHEW *Lond. Labour* I. 15 Pigeons are 'fancied' to a large extent. **1876** [see FANCYING *vbl. sb.*].

Hence **'fancying** *vbl. sb.*, the action of the verb in various senses; also *concr.* something that one fancies.

1662 PETTY *Taxes* 6 Civil wars are..caused by peoples fansying that [etc.]. *a* **1729** S. CLARKE *Serm.* I. (1738) xl. 252 A childish..imagination, that God is pleas'd with their.. fansying that they believe they know not what. **1758** FRANKLIN *Let.* Wks. 1887 III. 8 Another of my fancyings.. a pair of silk blankets. *a* **1839** PRAED *Poems* (1864) II. 184 The fancyings of fancy costumes. **1876** *Encycl. Brit.* IV. 249/2 'Fancying' is not governed by rules identical with those which regulate breeding for economic purposes. **1889** *Athenæum* 16 Nov. 667/3 The excellent fancying of the little 'genteel' colony in Bankside.

fancy bread. [FANCY *sb.* and *a.* C. 1.] Bread not of the ordinary texture, size, and weight of the standard 'household' and 'cottage' loaves.

1801 *Times* 9 Mar., Germans, who make what they call French or fancy bread, particularly to please the appetites of foreigners. **1841** *Guide to Trade, Baker* 65 Fancy bread, ginger-bread, buns, rolls, muffins and crumpets, etc. **1853** *Fraser's Mag.* June. XLVII. 680/2 A large assortment of fancy breads. **1904** *Westm. Gaz.* 23 Aug. 4/1 Fancy bread is for the future to be defined as that which is 'made up into separate rolls, twists, or other shapes, each of which is less than one pound in weight'. **1908** J. KIRKLAND *Mod. Baker* II. xxvii. 165 The greatest diversity of opinion prevails amongst bakers as to what is fancy bread. The rough interpretation of the term as recognized by the Bread Laws is: Bread that cannot readily be mistaken for plain bread. The distinguishing mark..is some difference in shape or glaze: but the baker..makes it include all sorts which involve more labour in manufacture, or entail greater cost for materials.

fancy dress, *sb.*

1. A costume arranged according to the wearer's fancy, usually representing some fictitious or historical character. Also *attrib.* in *fancy dress ball.* Also *fig.*

1770 MAD. D'ARBLAY *Early Diary* 10 Jan., I was soon found out by Miss Lalause, who..had on a fancy dress.. much in the style of mine. **1808** *Monthly Pantheon* I. 76 Bending branches press In many folds blithe nature's fancy dress. *a* **1831** MACAULAY *Life & Lett.* (1883) I. 225 The fancy-dresses were worn almost exclusively by the young ladies. **1844** G. W. KENDALL *Narr. Santa Fé Exped.* II. 51 Such variety of costume..would put to the blush..any.. fancy-dress procession ever invented. **1882** *Let.* 8 Aug. in A. Nathan *Costumes by Nathan* (1960) iv. 60 They would be required for a Fancy Dress Ball the week of the 4th September. **1915** A. D. GILLESPIE *Let.* 8 June (1916) 187 A fancy dress dance given there by the Germans on Christmas Eve. **1919** D. ASHFORD *Young Visiters* vi. 52 Is it a fancy dress party he asked. **1922** C. E. MONTAGUE *Disenchantment* ii. 26 London..was grotesque with a kind of fancy-dress ball of non-combatant khaki. **1938** L. MACNEICE *Mod. Poetry* 39, I realize that this piece [*sc.* The Lady of Shalott], though dressy, is fancy-dress at its best.

2. A dress with ornamental trimming.

1826 DISRAELI *Viv. Grey* I. i, His curly locks, and his fancy dress.

fancy dress, *v. rare*⁻¹. *trans.* To array or clothe in a fancy dress.

1878 *Masque Poets* 226 Nothing can exceed a woman's tact in fancy-dressing both herself and fact.

Hence **fancy dressed** *ppl. a.*, **fancy dressing** *vbl. sb.*

1837 DICKENS *Pickw.* xv, Never was such ingenious posturing, as his fancy-dressed friends exhibited. **1848** THACKERAY *Van. Fair* lii, Pitt Crawley..reprobated in strong terms the habit of play acting and fancy dressing.

fancy'ette. *nonce-wd.* A little fancy.

a **1834** COLERIDGE *Marginalia* in *Blackw. Mag.* CXXXI. (1882) Jan., 125 [Two Fancyettes, as Coleridge names them, at the end of a volume of Fichte].

fancy man. **a.** A man who is fancied; a sweetheart. **b.** *pl.* = *the fancy* (see FANCY *sb.* 12 b). **c.** *slang.* A man who lives upon the earnings of a prostitute.

a. 1835 MARRYAT *Jac. Faithf.* xliii, One day the sergeant was the fancy man, and the next day it was Tom. **1847–78** HALLIWELL s.v. *Fancy*, A sweetheart is still called a fancy-man.

b. 1847–8 H. MILLER *First Impr.* xiv. (1857) 247, I should have succeeded in astonishing the 'fancy-men'. **1870** EMERSON *Soc. & Solit.* x. 213 Fancy-men, patrons of the cock-pit and the ring.

c. 1811 *Lex. Balatron.*, *Fancy man*, a man kept by a lady for secret services. **1818** 'A. BURTON' *Adv. Johnny Newcome* iii. 154 The Sweepers e'en, were *fancy men!* **1821** P. EGAN *Tom & Jerry* 42 Although One of the Fancy, he was not a fancy-man. **1851** MAYHEW *Lond. Labour* I. 178 The women of the town buy of me..for themselves and their fancy men. **1890** *Spectator* 6 Dec. 825/2 They will bear from the 'fancy-man' any usage, however brutal. **1891** T. HARDY *Tess* III. v. xli. 26 Though your fancy-man was so up about it. **1922** JOYCE *Ulysses* 48 Her fancyman is treating two Royal Dublins. **1960** D. LESSING *In Pursuit of English* vi. 217 My mother's married that fancy man and he's already started to treat her bad. **1966** B. NAUGHTON *Alfie* i. 12 You won't get one husband in ten feels any thanks to the wife's fancy man for the happiness he brings to the marriage.

'fancy work. **a.** Ornamental, as opposed to plain, work, *esp.* in needlework, crochet, knitting, or the like; *rarely*, a piece of such work. Also *fig.*

1810 F. CUMING *Sk. Tour Western Country* xxvi. 163 Boarders instructed in..embroidery..and any other fashionable fancy-work. **1816** JANE AUSTEN *Emma* I. iii. 39 His..claim on her to leave her neat parlour hung round with fancy-work whenever she could. **1842** F. D. BENNETT *Whaling Voy.* II. 91 Their domestic manufactures are chiefly..fancy works, executed with the split leaves of the fan-palm. **1864** C. M. YONGE *Trial* II. xvi. 308, I admired the pattern, and Blanche inspected it..hoping to convert me to a fancy-work-woman. **1866** MRS. GASKELL *Wives & Dau.* xiv. (1867) 142 You don't do fancy-work! **1896** E. TURNER *Little Larrikin* xxiii. 206 A pair of slippers bought at a fancy-work shop. **1907** *Times Lit. Suppl.* 12 July 217/3 The importance and the novelty of their matter seem to prevent any excessive rhetoric; they cannot afford the time for fancy work. **1929** *Daily Express* 7 Nov. 19/1 They cut out all fancy work and went straight ahead for goal. **1954** F. C. AVIS *Boxing Ref. Dict.* 38 *Fancy work*, 'clever' movements of the hands and body intended to impress the onlookers, but often merely a waste of energy.

b. *slang.* In phrase '*to take in fancy work*: to be addicted to secret prostitution' (Farmer).

†fand, fond, *sb. Obs.* [f. next vb.] **a.** The action of trying; trial, proof, experience. **b.** The state of being tried; a trial, a temptation.

a. *c* **1250** *Gen. & Ex.* 336 Of ðis fruit wile ic hauen fond. *a* **1300** *Cursor M.* 4333 (Cott.) Sco broght him [Joseph] to þe fand. *Ibid.* 24364 (Cott.) Hard faand i þar-of fand.

b. *a* **1300** *Cursor M.* 25175 (Cott.) Þat thoru ouer cuming o þat faand He mai þe mede haf ai last[and]. **1451** *Pol. Poems* (Rolls) II. 230 Yef the commyns of Englonde Helpe the kynge in his fonde.

†fand, fond, *v. Obs.* Forms: α. 1 fandian, -iȝan, 2–3 fandien, 2–4 fondien, 3–5 fond(e(n, *south. dial.* vonden, -ien, (3 feonden), 3–4 faand, (faunde), 4–5 fand(e, *Sc.* faynd, 4–5 found(e, (5 foond, fownd(e). β. 1 ȝefan-, ȝefondian, 3 i(y)vonden, ifonden. [OE. *fandian*, *ȝefandian* = OFris. *fandia*, OS. *fandôn* to tempt, visit (Du. *vanden* to visit a woman after her confinement), OHG. *fantôn* to visit (the mod.G. *fahnden*, to raise hue and cry, is commonly believed to be identical in spite of unsolved phonetic difficulties).

The pa. t. and pa. pple. occas. appear in contracted forms *fond* (16th c.), *fonte* (14th c.).]

1. *trans.* To put to the proof, try, test (a person or thing); to make trial of (one's strength, skill); to taste (food, etc.); in early use with *gen.*

c **893** K. ÆLFRED *Oros.* I. xii. §4 Þæt þæm weorce nanum men ær ne ȝerise bet to fandianne þonne þæm wyrhtan þe hit worhte. *c* **1000** *Ags. Gosp.* Mark viii. 11 And þa ferdon ða pharisei..and his fandedon. *c* **1205** LAY. 25842 Þat he fehten mihte and fondien [*c* **1275** fondie] hine seolue. *Ibid.* 30092 Heore maines heo uondeden wel ueole siðen. *c* **1230** *Hali Meid.* 29 To fonde þe hweðer þu beo treowe. *a* **1300** *Cursor M.* 2902 (Cott.) Mani man..þam-self can noþer faand [*Gött.* fonde] ne feil. **1340–70** *Alisaunder* 107 Now fares Philip þe free too fonden his myght. **1375** BARBOUR *Bruce* VI. 618, I will..se quhat fors that thai can faynd. ? *a* **1400** *Morte Arth.* 3372 Fonde of the fyneste, thow freliche byerne. *a* **1400–50** *Alexander* 681 Quod Alexander to þis athill as he his arte fandis. *c* **1460** *Towneley Myst.* 36 My servand I will found and frast.

absol. *a* **1300** *Cursor M.* 542 Þe erth [gis man] þe tast, to fele and faand.

b. With sentence as *obj.*: To prove, try to find out, see.

a **1000** *Runic Poem* 25 (Gr.) Garsecȝ fandað, hwæðer ac hæbbe æðele treowe. *a* **1000** *Cædmon's Gen.* 2410 (Gr.) Ic wille fandiȝan nu..hwæt þa men don. *c* **1205** LAY. 2949 Ic wille fondien whulchere beo mi beste freond. *c* **1250** *Gen. & Ex.* 5946 Ic sal fonden and sen Quat tiding so it cam on ðe niȝt. *c* **1300** *Harrow. Hell* 68 Forte..fonden how we pleyen here. *c* **1440** *York Myst.* xx. 264, I schall thynke on þam wele to ffonde what is folowand.

c. To examine, scan.

13.. *Pearl* xv. (Gollancz) Her figure fyn quen I had fonte.

d. To 'tempt', 'prove' (God). In early use const. *gen.* after OE.

c **1175** *Lamb. Hom.* 93 Hwi iwearð hinc swa þet ȝit dursten fondian godes. *a* **1300** *E.E. Psalter* cv[i]. 14 Þai fanded God in drines. **1375** BARBOUR *Bruce* XII. 364 Thai faynd god all too gretumly.

2. To endeavor to lead into evil; to tempt.

c **1175** *Lamb. Hom.* 67 He fondede god solf mid his wrenche. *c* **1200** ORMIN 5945 He þurrh þe laþe gast Wass siþþenn fandedd þriȝȝess. *c* **1275** *Passion* 28 in *O.E. Misc.* (1872) 38 For to beon yuonded of sathanas þen olde. **1340** *Ayenb.* 15 Zuo heþ þe dyeuel diuerse maneres..to uondi þe uolk. *c* **1375** *Sc. Leg. Saints, Andreas* 167 Scho me fandyt besily To syne with hyr in lichory. **1393** LANGL. *P. Pl.* C. xv. 120 In whiche flood þe feend fondeþ man.

b. In good or neutral sense: To try to induce (to do something).

c **1425** WYNTOUN *Cron.* VI. xviii. 276 He hym fandyde..of Scotland to tak þe crowne.

3. **a.** To have experience of, deal with (a person); to have (carnal) acquaintance with. **b.** To make experiment with (a thing); to prove, try. **c.** *absol.* To have experience (of something implied).

a **1175** *Cott. Hom.* 239 God þurh his mucele milce ne letes us nefer fandie. *c* **1200** *Trin. Coll. Hom.* 224 Hadde he fonded sume stunde, he wolde seggen oðer. *c* **1320** *Sir Tristr.* 860 Ȝongling..Foles thou wendest to fand. *a* **1330** *Roland & V.* 470 So hard he was to fond. **1340–70** *Alisaunder* 740 Hee..fonded hur fleshlych or hee fare wolde. *c* **1420** *Pallad. on Husb.* I. 1137 But malthes colde in other crafte thou founde. *Ibid.* III. 551 Cannetes nowe with craftes may be fande. *c* **1450** *Mirour Saluacioun* 741 Marie fande first the avowe of gloriouse maydenhede.

4. To enquire; to seek, look for; to enquire into (a matter); to search (a place), explore (a track). Also const. *of*, to enquire about, hence, to care for.

a **1225** *Ancr. R.* 104 Of smelles..ne uond ich nout mucheles. *c* **1340** *Cursor M.* 6441 (Trin.) Þis ille folk was wantoun to fonde þat moyses hadde vndir honde. *Ibid.* 10840 (Trin.) Þis aungel sende þe trinite..Nazareth þe toun to fond. *a* **1400–1450** *Alexander* 4871 Þat þan fonde all þe flote fiftene dayis. *c* **1420** *Chron. Vilod.* 640 Þey..vondeden þ' place, and made hit ryde Tyll [etc.]. *c* **1425** WYNTOUN *Cron.* VII. ix. 369 Þai fayndyd of þis þe kyngis wille.

b. *absol.* To ask.

1340–70 *Alisaunder* 1054 Leeue fader..fonde I, mee tell The sterre þat yee staren on sticketh it in heuin.

5. To attempt, try. Const. *to* with *inf.*

a **1225** *St. Marher.* 10 Þene acursede gast þet feondeð to fordo me. **1297** R. GLOUC. (1724) 455 Ȝe stallewardes knyȝtes, þat..þes kyng vondeþ bryng to noȝte. *c* **1300** *Cursor M.* 21224 (Cott.) Mani oiþer men in strijf Fanded for to folu his lijf. **1375** BARBOUR *Bruce* I. 42 The barnage..fayndyt fast To cheyss a king. **1387** TREVISA *Higden* (Rolls) VII. 7 Elsynus bisshop of Wynchestre..fondede to have þe see. *c* **1450** *St. Cuthbert* (Surtees) 1750 Let vs fande som helpe to gett. **1494** FABYAN *Chron.* VII. 304 He fondyd to put yᵉ prerogatyue..from y munkys. **1590** SPENSER *F.Q.* III. vii. 26 For in the sea to drowne herselfe she fond, Rather then of the tyrant to be caught.

absol. *c* **1340** *Gaw. & Gr. Knt.* 565 What may mon do bot Fonde?

b. To busy oneself.

c **1350** *Will. Palerne* 1682 In þe kechene..arn crafti men ..þat fast fonden alday to flen wilde bestes.

6. To attempt, undertake (a deed). Also with sentence as *obj.*: To take care, see (that).

Beowulf 2454 Þonne se an hafað þurh deaðes nyd dæda ȝefondad. *a* **1300** *Beket* 676 He wende him..into the see passage forto fonde. **1307** *Elegy Edw.* I. v, Thou hevedest sunne, That thou the counsail woldest fonde, To latte the wille of kyng Edward To wend to the holy londe. ? *a* **1400** *Morte Arth.* 656 Ffaunde my fforestez be ffrythede. *c* **1400** *Melayne* 1401 Thou fayles of that thou fande. *a* **1440** *Sir Degrev.* 120 He was in the holy lond, Dede of armes for to ffond. *a* **1455** HOLLAND *Houlate* xlvii, Ȝaipe, thocht he ȝong was, to faynd his offens.

7. To acquit oneself (well); also with refl. pron.

c **1470** HENRY *Wallace* IX. 1273 Thai had..fayndyt thaim rycht weill. *Ibid.* X. 1026 A..knycht..fayndyt weill amang his enemys keyn.

8. To go, proceed; also with refl. pron. = FOUND *v.*¹

a **1340** *Cursor M.* 12978 (Cott.) Apon þe heist fell he faand. *a* **1400–50** *Alexander* 2671 Þan fandis he furth in-to þe fild. *c* **1440** *York Myst.* xviii. 149 Fande þe furthe faste for to flee. *c* **1650** *Sir Lambewell* 517 in Furniv. *Percy Folio* I. 160 A softly pace her palfray fand.

fand, obs. pa. t. of FIND.

fandang (fæn'dæŋ) *dial.* [See next.] See quot.

1876 ROBINSON *Whitby Gloss.* (E.D.S.), *Fandangs*..the fanciful adornments in personal attire, trinkets.

Hence **fan'dangous** *a.* Pompous, showy.

1797 MRS. A. M. BENNETT *Beggar Girl* (1813) III. 277 A parcel of nonsense about jukes and lords, and them sort of fandangus trumpery.

fandangle (fæn'dæŋg(ə)l). *colloq.* [An arbitrary formation; perh. suggested by next.] Fantastic ornament; nonsense, tomfoolery.

1835 *Southern Lit. Messenger* I. 361 What is the use of all these fandangles of lace? **1880** *World of Cant* xxiv. 196 A girl is sure to keep up some of the old fandangle of her mother. **1887** JESSOPP *Arcady* viii. 232 A solo with no end of shakes and trills and fandangles.

fandango (fænˈdæŋgəʊ). [a. Sp. *fandango*; alleged to be of negro origin.]

1. a. A lively dance in ¾ time, very popular in Spain and Spanish America.

17.. ELIZ. CARTER *Lett.* (1808) 138 You are twirled round in the *fandango* of the world. **1774** MAD. D'ARBLAY *Early Diary* (1189) I. 286 Upon my word, the fandango, like the allemande, requires sentiment, to dance it well. **1812** S. ROGERS *Voy. Columbus* v. 146 With gipsy maid Dancing Fandangos in the chestnut shade. **1863** OUIDA *Held in Bondage* (1870) 56 Scores of Castillian girls I have seen doing the fandango.

b. *Mus.* A tune to which the fandango is danced.

1800 H. WELLS *Constantia Neville* (ed. 2) I. 258 Spanish ladies, with guittars..who never had read of a fandango. **1851** MAYNE REID *Scalp Hunt.* lviii, The music commences. It is a merry air—a fandango. **1866** ENGEL *Nat. Mus.* i. 10 Gluck adopted in his ballet 'Don Juan' a well-known Spanish fandango.

c. *fig.*

1841 *Congress. Globe* App. 25 Jan. 153/2 All the fool Federal fandangoes that disgraced the country. **1894** *Monthly Packet* Feb. 152 The hippopotamus does not indulge in these fandangoes. **1928** BLUNDEN *Undertones of War* xix. 197 The usual free-verse fandango of brick mounds and water-holes.

2. A social assembly for dancing, a ball.

In 18th c. common in English use; now only *U.S.*, or with reference to foreign countries.

1760–72 tr. *Juan & Ulloa's Voy.* (ed. 3) I. 39 One of the most favourite amusements of the natives here, is a ball, or Fandango. **1766** C. ANSTEY *Bath Guide* xiii. 14 She loves an Assembly, Fandango, or Rout. **1785** COWPER *Faithful Bird* 33 Satisfied with noise, Fandango, ball, and rout! **1854** BARTLETT *Mex. Boundary* I. xviii. 429 A perpetual fandango was thus kept up day and night.

3. = FANDANGLE. *rare.*

1856 MISS MULOCK *Halifax* x. (1859) 109 No fripperies or fandangos of any sort.

4. *attrib.*, as ***fandango-bird, -dancer.***

1809 *Tales of Other Realms* I. 94 We quitted the *fandango dancers* in disgust. **1871** J. F. HAMILTON in *Ibis* 305 The natives [of Brazil] call them Fandango birds, and say that they are in the habit of performing a dance.

fanˈdango, *v. nonce-wd.* To dance a fandango.

1834 BECKFORD *Italy* II. 364 Thirteen or fourteen couples started..and fandangoed away.

†ˈfander, ˈfonder. *Obs.* [f. FAND *v.* + -ER¹.] A tempter.

c **1340** *Cursor M.* 25369 (Cotton Galba) Fals fanders [we] here haue thrin. **1340** *Ayenb.* 116 Þe dyeuel is þe uondere.

†ˈfanding, ˈfonding, *vbl. sb. Obs.* [f. FAND *v.* + -ING¹.]

1. The action of trying. **a.** A testing or putting to the proof; a trial.

a **1300** *Cursor M.* 7231 (Gött.) Ofte in fanding men findes sua [etc.]. *c* **1400** *Gamelyn* 147, I ne did it noght broþer but for a fondyng. *c* **1450** *St. Cuthbert* 2493 And send him fandyngs many ma. **14..** *Jhesu* 20 in Furniv. *Ballads from MSS.* I. 320 Brettyng of benes & fondyng of foles.

b. A trying to do or find out something; an attempt, experiment.

a **1000** *Cædmon's Gen.* 1452 (Gr.) He..of earce forlet.. haswe culufran on fandunga. *a* **1300** *Cursor M.* 17756 (Cott.) All þair fanding was for noght. *c* **1340** *Ibid.* 23776 (Fairf.) Wiþ-outen ani fonding of fliȝt. **1375** BARBOUR *Bruce* IV. 691 Thai..maks fanding Off things to cum to haiff knawing.

2. Temptation.

c **1000** ÆLFRIC *Interr. Sigewulfi* (Mac Lean) lxix, He wyle þæt hi beon þe ȝeþungenran on þære fandunge. *c* **1175** *Lamb. Hom.* 69 Þet ure leue beo ure sceld aȝein þes fondes fondunge. *a* **1300** *Cursor M.* 25111 (Cott.) Lede þou vs in na fanding. *a* **1340** HAMPOLE *Psalter* xvii. 32 In þe i sall be outreft fra fandynge. **1377** LANGL. *P. Pl.* B. XIV. 298 Þe fyfte is..a frende in alle fondynges. **1426** AUDELAY *Poems* 21 Fore one fonding of the fynd fulfyl your forward. **1496** *Dives & Paup.* (W. de W.) x. iii. 374/1 The fende..stange..Adam.. with his wycked fondynge.

3. ? A tempting of Providence. Cf. FAND *v.* 1 d.

1375 BARBOUR *Bruce* III. 289 For-owt fayntice or yheit fayndíng.

ˈfandom. orig. *U.S.* [f. FAN *sb.*² + -DOM.] The world of enthusiasts for some amusement or for some artist; also in extended use.

1903 *Cincinnati Enquirer* 2 Jan. 3/1 (*heading*) Fandom puzzled over Johnsonian statements. **1928** *Publishers' Weekly* 30 June, Ty Cobb, the idol of baseball fandom. **1958** *Times* 13 Sept. 7/6 The same editor calculates that at least half his British writers have been recruited from 'fandom'. **1963** *Philos. Rev.* LXXII. 520 Morality has or ought to have its fandom.

†fane, *sb.*¹ *Obs.* Also 5 **fayne,** 5–6 **phane,** 7 **faine;** and see VANE. [Common Teut.: OE. *fana* wk. masc. = OFris. *fana*, OS. and OHG. *fano* (Ger. *fahne*), Goth. *fana*, ON. (*gunn-*) *fani* (Da. *fane*, Sw. *fana*; the mod.Icel. *fáni*, 'buoyant, high-flying person', is unconnected).]

1. A flag, banner, pennant.

a **1000** *Boeth. Metra* i. 10 Fana hwearfode scir on sceafte. *c* **1325** *Coer de L.* 3893 They trumpyd and her baners displaye Off sylk, sendel, and many a fane. **1459** *Test. Ebor.* II. (Surtees) 227 A grete salte salar gilte with banars and fanes. **1503** HAWES *Examp. Virt.* iii. 31 The towres..With fanes wauerynge in the wynde. **1671** R. BOHUN *Disc. Wind* 72 The Fanes of ships. **1712** *Lond. Gaz.* No. 5051/3 Ensigns, Jacks, Pendants and Fanes. **1806** *Naval Chron.* XV. 194 On the fane of her fore-mast, is the date.

2. A weathercock. See VANE.

c **1386** CHAUCER *Clerk's T.* 940 O stormy poeple..ever untrewe..and chaungyng as a fane. **1483** *Cath. Angl.* 122 A Fayne of a schipe..ubi a weder coke. *c* **1510** BARCLAY *Mirr. Gd. Manners* (1570) Biv, Varying as fanes erect vnto the winde. ? **1635** GLAPTHORNE *Lady Mother* III. i. in Bullen *O. Pl.* (1883) II. 142 Light faines erected on the tops Of lofty structures. **1773** J. NOORTHOUCK *Hist. London* 611 The turret..from its top rises a ball that supports the fane.

fane (feɪn), *sb.*² *poet.* Also 7 **fawne,** 5–7 **phane.** [ad. L. *fān-um* temple.] A temple.

14.. LYDG. *Lyfe of our Ladye* (Caxton) Hj, To haue answer.. How long this fane ryal of asyse..sholde last. **1430** —— *Chron. Troy* II. xiii, In this phane..they knele. **1563–87** FOXE *A. & M.* (1596) 107/1 The idolatrous temples and phanes. **1637** HEYWOOD *Dial.* iv. 62 The phane Where the two brothers deify'd remain. **1727–46** THOMSON *Summer* 769 Where palaces, and fanes, and villas rise. **1814** SCOTT *Ld. of Isles* IV. x, To old Iona's holy fane. **1850** TENNYSON *In Mem.* lvi, Man, her last work..built him fanes of fruitless prayer.

transf. and *fig.* *a* **1618** SYLVESTER *Du Bartas, Panaretus* 656 Long live the Story Of Valiant Princes in the Fane of Glory. *a* **1839** PRAED *Poems* (1864) II. 54 The fane where Fashion dwells, 'Lyce's Academy for Belles'.

Hence **†faned** *ppl. a.* [+ -ED²], having a fane; enshrined.

1633 FORD *Love's Sacr.* II. ii, Such..as might well become The shrine of some fan'd Venus.

fane (feɪn), *sb.*³ *Obs.* (See quots.)

c **1000** *Sax. Leechd.* II. 138 Drenc wiþ feondseocum men, of ciricbellan to drincanne..fane, finul [etc.]. **1597** GERARDE *Herbal* Supp. to Gen. Table, *Fane*, white Flower deluce. **1878** BRITTEN & HOLLAND *Plant-n.*, *Fane*..some white-flowered Iris, but we cannot determine the species.

fane (feɪn), *sb.*⁴ *Sc.* [Cf. Sw. *fan* the devil.] An elf, a fairy.

1806 TRAIN *Poet. Reveries, Witch Inverness* 100 Kate was haunted wi' a fane. *Ibid.* 27 Every fane..in thy breast.

fane, Sc. f. of FAIN, FEIGN.

fane, obs. f. of FAN *sb.*

fane, Sc. pa. t. of FINE *v.* to finish.

faneer, obs. f. of VENEER.

‖fanega (faˈneːga). Also 7 **hanega.** [Sp. *fanega*, also *hanega*.]

1. A Spanish measure of quantity, usually equal to a bushel or a bushel and a half.

1502 ARNOLD *Chron.* 158 He promysed him of whete and barly xxv. fanegas. **1600** J. PORY tr. *Leo's Africa* II. 372 Everie Hanega of corne that is ground in Fez. **1760–72** tr. *Juan & Ulloa's Voy.* (ed. 3) II. 285 The fanega costs here only ten or twelve rials, or two dollars. **1850** B. TAYLOR *Eldorado* vii. (1862) 65 We purchased half a fanega—a little more than a bushel—of wheat, for $5.

2. A measure for land.

1852 TH. ROSS tr. *Humboldt's Trav.* I. xv. 478 In this country five thousand three hundred coffee-trees are generally planted in a fanega of ground.

fan-fan (ˈfænˈfæn). [Formed by repeating the first syllable of FANNY *sb.*] A pet dog.

1834 *Fraser's Mag.* X. 169 The noble now upon his fan-fan spends Revenues large; her puppies are his friends.

fanfarade (fænfəˈreɪd). *rare.* [f. next + -ADE.] = FANFARE.

1883 R. BROWN in *Fortn. Rev.* 1 Sept. 386 Ushered into the world with a louder fanfarade of literary trumpeters. **1884** BLACKMORE *Hist. Sir F. Upmore* I. 319 The infectious fanfarade of the great Rogue's March.

‖fanfare (ˈfænfɛə(r), fænˈfɛə(r), fɑ̃fɑːr). Also 6 **famphar,** 7 *erroneously* **farfara.** [Fr. *fanfare* perhaps an echoic word.] **a.** A flourish, call, or short tune, sounded by trumpets, bugles, or hunting-horns.

1769 GRASSINEAU *Mus. Dict.* App. 20 (T.) *Fanfare,* [is] a sort of military air or flourish..performed by trumpets, and imitated by other instruments. **1816** SCOTT *Old Mort.* xi, Amid the fanfare of the trumpets. **1863** LONGF. *Falc. Federigo* 221 Fanfares by aërial trumpets blown. **1887** GROVE *Dict. Mus.* IV. 470 They [horns] were used..for playing merry fanfares..when the huntsmen..returned home.

b. *transf.* and *fig.*

a **1605** MONTGOMERIE *Welcome Ld. Semple* 40 My trompet, to, sall sound The famphar of thy fame. **1628** LE GRYS tr. *Barclay's Argenis* 159 The farfaras of Drummes and Trumpets. **1676** TEMPLE *Let. to King* Wks. 1731 II. 425 After all his Fanfares about a separate Peace. **1878** L. W. M. LOCKHART *Mine is Thine* II. xxiv. 130 The harsh fanfares of forced laughter.

c. A style of bookbinding decoration developed in Paris in the 16th century in which a continuous interlaced ribbon, bounded by a double line on one side and a single on the other, divides the whole surface on both covers into symmetrical compartments of varying shapes and sizes.

1895 J. W. ZAEHNSDORF *Short Hist. Bookbinding* 22 A development of the 'fanfare' sprays of foliage. *Ibid.*, The graceful ornamentation known as 'fanfare' is attributed to the Eves... The name of 'fanfare' was given to this style of work in the last century, when Charles Nodier had a volume entitled 'Les Fanfares et Corvées Abbadesques' bound for him by Thouvenin. **1936** *Times Lit. Suppl.* 13 June 493/4 The popular attribution of *fanfare* bindings to Nicolas and Clovis Eve is..shown to be..untenable. **1959** *Chambers's Encycl.* V. 489/1 All bindings in the so-called 'fanfare' style ..have an all-over pattern of ribbons, bounded on one side by a double and on the other by a single line. **1969** *Times* 25 Feb. 16/1 (Advt.), A fine Parisian fanfare binding and other decorated book bindings.

Hence **ˈfanfare** *v. intr.*, to sound a fanfare.

1860 RUSSELL *Diary India* II. 237 As we moved the Trumpets fanfared the Drums rattled.

‖fanfaron (ˈfænfərɒn), *sb.* (*a.*). Also 7 **fanfaroone, -rrone,** 8 **-ran,** 9 **-roon.** [F. *fanfaron*, f. *fanfare*.]

1. A blusterer, boaster, braggart.

1622 MABBE tr. *Aleman's Guzman d'Alf.* II. 62 They should not play the Fanfarrones. **1694** R. L'ESTRANGE *Fables* 137 There are fanfarons in the tryals of wit too, as well as in feats of Arms. **1754** H. WALPOLE *Lett. H. Mann* (1834) III. cclviii. 78 An excellent fanfaron, a Major Washington. **1861** SALA *Dutch Pict.* xix. 297, I..always set him down as a vapouring fanfaroon.

b. Const. *of.* One who makes a parade *of* something; a trumpeter *of.*

1857 FONBLANQUE *Life & Lab.* (1874) 273 He is a little fanfaron of his virtues. **1880** MCCARTHY *Own Times* I. ii. 27 He became the fanfaron of vices which he never had.

c. *attrib.* or *adj.* Braggart, boastful.

1670–98 LASSELS *Voy. Italy* I. Pref., He must not follow them in all their Phantastical and fanfaron clothings. **1716** M. DAVIES *Athen. Brit.* III. *Diss. upon Pallas Anglic.* 21 These Fanfaran or Thrasonick Romists. **1831** *Soc. Life Eng. & France* ii. 74 Blood..seems to have been a sort of fanfaron assassin.

¶**2.** = FANFARE.

1848 LYTTON *Harold* II. IX. ii. 298 Amidst a loud fanfaron of fifes and trumpets.

fanfaronade (ˌfænfærəˈneɪd, fɑ̃farɔnad), *sb.* Also 9 **fanfaronnade, -arronade.** [ad. F. *fanfaronnade*, f. *fanfaron.* Cf. Sp. *fanfarronada.*]

1. Boisterous or arrogant language, boastful assertion, brag; ostentation; an instance of this.

1652 URQUHART *Jewel* Wks. (1834) 217 The Gasconads of France, Rodomontads of Spain, Fanfaronads of Italy. *a* **1745** SWIFT *Pref. Bp. Sarum's Intro.* Wks. 1841 I. 379 b, The bishop copied this proceeding from the fanfaronade of Monsieur Bouffleurs. **1784** BAGE *Barham Downs* II. 259 He damned her ingratitude; She, his fanfarronade. **1789** MRS. PIOZZI *Journ. France* I. 24 [It] diverted me..by the fanfaronades that it contained. **1814** SCOTT *Diary* 24 Aug., He seems to..act..like a chief, without the fanfaronade of the character. **1865** KINGSLEY *Herew.* xii. (1866) 165 They outvied each other in impossible fanfarronades.

¶**2.** = FANFARE.

1812 *Examiner* 12 Oct. 652/2 The fanfarronade..of the favourite Hussars. **1861** DUTTON COOK *P. Foster's D.* i, So much by way of a fanfaronade before the showman pulls the strings.

Hence **ˌfanfaroˈnade** *v. intr.*, to bluster, swagger. **ˌfanfaroˈnading** *vbl. sb.* and *ppl. a.*

1837 CARLYLE *Fr. Rev.* II. I. viii. 58 With ceremonial evolution and manœuvre, with fanfaronading..they made oath..to stand faithfully by one another. *Ibid.* II. VI. viii. 422 Fanfaronading emigrants. **1878** BAYNE *Purit. Rev.* v. 157 His professed contempt for impossibility was useful only for fanfaronading purposes.

fanfaˈrrado. *nonce-wd.* = FANFARE.

1824 GALT *Rothelan* III. 230 My arrival was announced to the ducal court with a great fanfarrado.

fanfoot (ˈfænfʊt). Pl. **fanfeet, fanfoots.** [f. FAN *sb.*¹ + FOOT *sb.*] **a.** A collectors' name for a moth of the family Hypeninæ. **b.** A gecko of the genus *Ptyodactylus*, having fan-shaped toes; also called ***fan-footed gecko.***

1832 J. RENNIE *Butterfl. & Moths* 146 Polypogon..The Common Fan-foot..The Clay Fan-foot. **1863** W. SMITH *Dict. Bible* II. s.v. *Lizard*, The Fan-Foot Lizard (*Ptyodactylus Gecko*). **1933** *Proc. Zool. Soc.* II. 764 The Fan-foot is abundant and distributed widely in Palestine. *Ibid.* 765 A Fan-footed Gecko brought in from the desert was turned loose in my room. **1961** R. SOUTH *Moths Brit. Isles* (ed. 2) I. 393 The fan-foot (*Zanclognatha tarsipennalis* Treit.). *Ibid.* 394 The small fan-foot (*Zanclognatha nemoralis* Fab.). *Ibid.* 395 The dotted fan-foot (*Zanclognatha cribrumalis* Hübn.). The clay fan-foot (*Paracolax derivalis* Hübn.). *Ibid.* 396 The common fan-foot (*Herminia barbalis* Clerck).

†ˈfanfreluche, *v. Obs.* Also 7 **fanferluche.** [ad. F. *fanfrelucher* in same sense.] *intr.* To trifle; to act wantonly. Also, ***to fanfreluche it.***

1653 URQUHART *Rabelais* II. xxiii, They..jumd and fanfreluched at every fields end. *a* **1693** *Ibid.* III. xxxi. 265 By dufling and fanferluching it..Thirty times a day.

fanful (ˈfænfʊl). [f. FAN *sb.* + -FUL.] As much as a fan [FAN *sb.* 1 a] will contain.

1806–7 A. YOUNG *Agric. Essex* (1813) I. 110, 3 corn fansful of chaff each horse per week, at 6*d.* per fanful.

fang (fæŋ), *sb.* Also 7 **phang(e.** [OE. *fang*, cogn. with OFris. *fang* m., ON. *fang* n., MHG. *fang*, *vanc* m., repr. OTeut. *fango-, f. root of *fanhan (see FANG *v.*).]

I. The act or fact of catching or seizing.

†1. a. A capture, catch. Also a tight grasp, a grip. ***in fang with:*** in the embrace, under the protection of. (Cf. ON. *í fang*, in one's arms.)

a **1400–50** *Alexander* 1725 In fang with my faire godis. *c* **1470** HENRY *Wallace* XI. 1219 King Eduuard was rycht fayn off that fang. **1597** J. PAYNE *Royal Exch.* 41 Whome he once gettethe with full fange into his gripinge clowches he howldeth faster than catt the mowce. **1600** SHAKS. *A.Y.L.* II. i. 6 The Icie phange And churlish chiding of the winters winde.

b. *Sc.* In phrase *to lose the fang*: 'to miss one's aim, to fail in an attempt' (Jam.). Also of a pump (see quot.).

1825 JAMIESON Suppl. I. s.v., A pump well is said to lose the fang when the water quits the pump.

2. *concr.* That which is caught or taken; captured game; booty, plunder, spoils (*obs.* exc. *Sc.*). Hence, in *Sc. Law* of a thief: ***caught, taken with the fang***.

1016 *O.E. Chron.* (Laud MS.), [Hi] fang woldon fon. *a* **1300** *Cursor M.* 3728 (Cott.) Was þou not at me right now, And fedd me wit þi fang i trau? *Ibid.* 15434 (Cott.) Quen.. Iudas þus receiued had his fang. *c* **1340** *Ibid.* 4801 (Fairf.) Quen ȝe fondyn haue ȝour fange. **1609** SKENE *Reg. Maj.* 71 Gif ane man apprehends in his house ane theif, with the fang of the thift. **1728** *Biggar Council Proceedings*, The fangs (plunder) being found in his house. **1790** MORRISON *Poems* 110 Snap went the sheers, then in a wink, The fang was stow'd behind a bink.

II. An instrument for catching or holding.

†**3.** A noose, trap. In quots. *fig.* *Obs.*

1535 STEWART *Cron. Scot.* I. 470 The Britis fled, and wes fane of that fang To leif the Romanis in the thickest thrang. **1794** *Piper of Peebles* 277 The Laird was fairly in a fang, An' naething for him now but hang.

4. a. A canine tooth; a tusk. In *pl.* applied *gen.* to the teeth of dogs, wolves, or other animals remarkable for strength of jaw.

1555 EDEN *Decades* 187 Theyr fanges or dogge teeth. **1613** HEYWOOD *Silver Age* III. 157 These phangs shall gnaw vpon your cruded bones. *a* **1700** DRYDEN *Ovid* VIII. 535 The fatal Fang drove deep within his Thigh. *a* **1771** GRAY *Poems, Descent of Odin* 10 Eyes that glow, and fangs that grin. **1808** *Med. Jrnl.* XIX. 58 This is done by inserting his [a leech's] three fangs into the skin. **1867** EMERSON *May Day, etc.* Wks. (Bohn) III. 439 Wolves shed their fangs.

fig. **1601** SHAKS. *Twel. N.* I. v. 196 By the verie phangs of malice, I sweare I am not that I play. *a* **1633** AUSTIN *Medit.* (1635) 191 Fast in the Iron fangs of that Foxe Herod. **1794** FOX *Sp.* 21 Jan. Wks. 1815 V. 159 The relentless fangs of despotism. **1827** HALLAM *Const. Hist.* (1876) I. i. 28 Sufficient to bring him within the fangs of the recent statute. **1867** TROLLOPE *Chron. Barset* II. lii. 89 Having strong hopes.. that Grace's father might escape the fangs of justice.

b. In various transferred uses: (see quots.).

1694 *Acc. Sev. Late Voy.* II. (1711) 123 The Phangs of a Tooth-drawer. **1776** MICKLE tr. *Camoens' Lusiad* VII. 282 The anchor's moony fangs. **1789** *Trans. Soc. Encourag. Arts* VII. 193 The fangs on the fliers are alternately driven. *a* **1825** FORBY *Voc. E. Anglia*, *Fang*, a fin. From the fancied resemblance of their pointed ends to long teeth. **1853** KANE *Grinnell Exp.* xlvi. (1856) 423 The water-line was toothed with fangs of broken ice. **1878** BROWNING *La Saisiaz* 14 Fangs of crystal set on edge in his demesne.

†**c.** *pl.* The mandibles of an insect. *Obs.*

1609 C. BUTLER *Fem. Mon.* (1634) 102 The matter thereof [of wax] they gather from flowers with their Fangs. **1713** WARDER *True Amazons* (ed. 2) 3 Her [a Bee's] Fangs, or Mouth, wherein are her Teeth.

d. The venom-tooth of a serpent; also the claws, provided with poison-ducts, which terminate the chelicerae of a spider.

1800 *Med. Jrnl.* IV. 295 The punctures made by the poisonous fangs were evident. **1802** PALEY *Nat. Theol.* xii. §1 The fang of a viper..is a perforated tooth. **1855** KINGSLEY *Heroes* II. 206 Where are your spider's fangs? **1862** DARWIN *Fertil. Orchids* v. 220 Each horn is tubular, like an adder's fang. **1875** CAMBRIDGE in *Encycl. Brit.* (ed. 9) II. 294 The channel [of the poison] running completely through the fang [in a spider].

fig. **1809–10** COLERIDGE *Friend*, The serpent fang of this error. **1849** ROBERTSON *Serm.* Ser. I. xiii. 224 The fang of evil pierces the heel of the noblest as he treads it down.

e. *colloq.* A human tooth. Also *Comb.* and *fig.*

1840 DICKENS *Old C. Shop* iii, The few discoloured fangs gave him the aspect of a panting dog. **1891** FARMER *Slang* II. 374/1 *Fang-faker*, a dentist. **1919** W. H. DOWNING *Digger Dial.* 22 'To put in the fangs'—to demand money, etc. **1936** WODEHOUSE *Laughing Gas* v. 57 Possibly because they were old dental college chums,..these two fang-wrenchers shared a common waiting-room. **1943** HUNT & PRINGLE *Service Slang* 31 *Fang farrier*, dentist. **1957** 'N. CULOTTA' *They're Weird Mob* (1958) viii. 109 Jimmy got himself some bread and butter and an open tin of jam. 'Yer good on the fang, mate,' said Joe.

†**5. a.** A claw or talon. *Obs.*

Although this sense would appear on etymological grounds likely to have existed, it seems to rest solely on the authority of the Dicts. Possibly it may have been wrongly inferred from figurative applications of sense 4, in which the pl. is often equivalent to 'clutches', 'grasp', with little or no conscious allusion to the literal use.

1731 J. K. *New Eng. Dict.* (ed. 3), *Fang*, a claw. **1749** B. MARTIN, *Fangs*, claws. **1755** JOHNSON, *Fang*, the nails, the talons.

†**b.** (See quot.)

1768 E. BUYS *Dict. Terms Art*, *Fangs*, (in *Botany*) the shoots or tendrils by means of which one Plant takes hold of another.

6. The pointed tapering part of anything which is embedded in something else. **a.** A spike; the tang of a tool.

1769 FALCONER *Dict. Marine* (1776), *Dog*, a sort of iron hook, or bar, with a sharp fang at one end, so formed as to be easily driven into a plank. **1823** P. NICHOLSON *Pract. Build.* 222 *Fang*, the narrow part of the iron of any instrument which passes into the stock. **1887** *S. Cheshire Gloss.*, *Fang*, a prong, *e.g.* a yelve-fang.

b. The root of a tooth; one of the prongs into which this divides.

1666 *Phil. Trans.* I. 381 That Tooth..which had not a phang like other Cutters. **1803** *Med. Jrnl.* X. 365 If the fangs were capable of an increase by the ossific inflammation. **1872** HUXLEY *Phys.* vi. 142 One or more fangs which are embedded in sockets.

†**c.** A prong of a divided root. *Obs.*

1664 EVELYN *Kal. Hort.* (1729) 200 Take out your Indian Tuberoses, parting the Off-sets (but with care, lest you break their Fangs). **1727** BRADLEY *Fam. Dict.* s.v. *Anemone*,[Sifting earth upon the bed] till..there remain only above ground the Fangs of these young Anemones.

III. Technical uses.

7. *Naut.* **a.** A rope leading from the peak of the gaff of a fore-and-aft sail to the rail on each side (used for steadying the gaff). Now usually VANG.

1513 DOUGLAS *Æneis* V. xiv. 8 Now the lie scheit, and now the luf, thai slak, Set in a fang, and threw the ra abak. **1769** FALCONER *Dict. Marine* G iv, The mizen-yard is furnished with *fangs*, or vangs in the room of braces.

b. *pl.* The valves of a pump-box. [Cf. 1 b.]

1867 in SMYTH *Sailor's Word-bk.*

8. *Mining.* (See quots.) [Derbyshire dialect: perh. a separate word. Also WINDFANG.]

a **1661** FULLER *Worthies* I. 230 A Spindle, a Lampturne, a Fange. **1747** HOOSON *Miner's Dict.* G iv b, *Fange* is a Place ..which is left as we drive along the Drift, on purpose to carry Wind along with us. **1802** MAWE *Mineral. Derbysh.* Gloss., *Fang*, a case made of wood, &c., to carry wind into the mine. **1836** R. FURNESS *Medicus Magus* 51 [The devil] quite rusty with the smoke, Fled up the Fang. [Here app. used for 'chimney'.] *Ibid.* 69 (Glossary) *Fang*, a passage made for conducting air after the miner.

IV. 9. *attrib.* and *Comb.*: **fang-bolt**, a bolt having a spiked nut or washer, used for attaching iron to wood.

1876 J. W. BARRY *Railway Appliances* ii. 73 Fang-bolts consist of bolts long enough to pass through the sleepers, with a screw cut on the lower end to fit a wide flat nut, having on it fangs or short spikes. **1915** C. J. ALLEN *Mod. Brit. Perm. Way* 60 Whereas this type of fang-bolt has in all three separate parts—bolt, nut, and washer—it will be noticed that the Great Southern and Western and Great Eastern fang-bolts..consist of the bolt and a fanged nut only.

fang (fæŋ), *v.*[1] Now *arch.* or *dial.* Forms: α. Inf. 1–2 **fón**, 3 **fo-n**; pa. t. 1–4 **feng**, (3 **fang**, *south.* **veng**, **venk**, 4 **feyng**), 3–5 **fong(e**, (5 **fone**), 8 *south.* **vung**; pa. pple. 1 **fangen**, 3 **fon**, 5 **fonge**. β. Inf. 3 *Orm.* **fangenn**, 3–6 **fong(e(n**, (3 **foangen**), 4–6 **fange**, (**fannge**, **fonnge**), 5 **fangyn**, (6 **fangue**), 7 **phang**, *south.* **vang**, 3– **fang**; pa. t. and pa. pple. 4–5 **fonged**, **-ett**, **-id**, **-it**, *Sc.* **fangit**, 4– **fanged**. [Com. Teut.: OE. *fón*, redupl. str. vb. corresp. to OFris. *fâ*, OS. *fâhan*, OHG. *fâhan* (MHG. *vâhen*, mod.Ger. (poet) *fahen*), ON. *fá* (Da. *faae*, Sw. *få*), Goth. *fāhan*:—OTeut. **fanhan*, pret. *fefang-*, pa. pple. *fangano-*. About 1200 the stem *fang-* of the pa. pple. appears as a present-stem (inf. *fangen*), and gradually supersedes the older form; a similar change has taken place independently in the other Teut. langs.: cf. Du. *vangen*, mod.HG. *fangen*, late Icel. *fanga* (Da. *fange*, Sw. *fånga*). The weak pa. t. and pa. pple., which are peculiar to English, appear first in 14th c.; the original strong forms seldom occur after the 15th c.]

†**1.** *trans.* To lay hold of, grasp, hold, seize; to clasp, embrace. *Obs.*

c **1200** ORMIN 3733 Mann mihhte himm fon & pinenn. *a* **1300** *Cursor M.* 17723 (Cott.) Symeon..iesus tuix his handes fang. *a* **1400–50** *Alexander* 2971 Felly fangis it [a torche] in his fist. *c* **1400** *Ywaine & Gaw.* 299, I wil him fang With mi fingers. *a* **1450** *Le Morte Arth.* 1796 In hys hand a swerd he fone. *c* **1470** HENRY *Wallace* II. 425 Sodanly in armys he coud him fang.

b. To catch (fish); to take in a snare. Also *fig.* *Obs.* exc. *arch.*

c **900** *Bæda's Hist.* I. i. §1 Her beoþ oft fangene seolas & hronas. *a* **1225** *St. Marher.* 3 As þe fuhel þe is fon i þe fuheleres grune. *a* **1450** *St. Cuthbert* (Surtees) 5480 Of þat fysche þat þai þus fang. *c* **1450** HENRYSON *Mor. Fab.* 69 Might wee that herring fang. **1637** GILLESPIE *Eng. Pop. Cerem.* IV. viii. 36 He hath..fanged himselfe faster in the snare. **1850** BLACKIE *Æschylus* II. 185 May Até Fang them in her hopeless snare! **1877** —— *Wise Men* 206 A little child ..Can fang a stickleback with pin for hook.

†**c.** To seize upon (booty); to catch, apprehend, get into one's power (a person); to capture (a city), to seize (lands, possessions). *Obs.* exc. *arch.*

1016 *O.E. Chron.*, Hi fang woldon fon. *c* **1325** *Metr. Hom.* 80 He might this ilk nonne fange To slake his lust. ? *a* **1400** *Morte Arth.* 425 Ffaunge the fermes in fatthe of alle þa faire rewmes. *c* **1400** *Destr. Troy* 956 His goddis..hym grace lent The flese for to fonge. *c* **1440** *York Myst.* xix. 128 May I þat faitour fange. *c* **1450** *Mirour Saluacioun* 56 The toure of Baris..was so verray stronge That all the werld fro two men with force moght noght it fonge. *c* **1450** *St. Cuthbert* (Surtees) 5744 þat na thefe suld him [a horse] fang. *c* **1470** HARDING *Chron.* CXXXIX. iv, To assayle the citee, and haue fongid With might of menne. **1522** SKELTON *Why not to Court* 1157 [He] wyll..streitly strangle us, And he may fange us. **1570** LEVINS *Manip.* 23 To Fangue, *comprehendere.* **1607** DEKKER & WEBSTER *Northw. Hoe* I. Wks. 1873 III. 10 Hee's in the lawes clutches, you see hee's fanged. **1607** SHAKS. *Timon* IV. iii. 23 Destruction phang mankinde. **1691** WOOD *Ath. Oxon.* II. 327 Death fang'd the remnant of his lugs. **1922** G. BLAIR *Haunted Dominie* 21 O what shall then betide me, when Death shall fang my shoulders.

absol. **1638** SHIRLEY *Mart. Soldier* in Bullen *O. Pl.* (1882) I. 242 It has ever beene my profession to fang and clutch and to squeeze.

†**d.** To get, get at, obtain, procure. Also, to get together, collect. *Obs.*

1340–70 *Alex. & Dind.* 552 For ensample, bi my sawe soþ mow ȝe fonge Of iubiter. *a* **1400–50** *Alexander* 2059 Amonta þe miȝtfull his men þan he fangis. *c* **1400** *Melayne* 984 Go fonnge the another fere. *c* **1440** *York Myst.* xxvi. 16 Ther fanged I my fame. **1513** DOUGLAS *Æneis* VI. ix. 138 Furth renting all, his fude to fang full fane. **15..** *Childe of Bristowe* 33 Hazl. *E.P.P.* (1864) 112 He rought not whom he begiled, worly good to fong. **1560** ROLLAND *Crt. Venus* II. 3 He him bethocht for to fang sum defence. *a* **1605** MONTGOMERIE *Natur Passis Nuriture* 34 To fang his friendship they war fane.

†**e.** *to fang up*: 'to pluck up' (the heart); to 'take up', interrupt sharply. *Obs.*

a **1400–50** *Alexander* 988 Fange vp ȝour hertis. *Ibid.* 2197 þan fangis him vp þe fell kyng a fuyll feyned laȝtir.

2. To receive, accept. **a.** To receive as a gift, or as one's due; to earn as wages; also, to accept as one's lot. *Obs.* exc. *dial.*

Beowulf 2989 He þam frætwum feng. *c* **1000** *Sal. & Sat.* 686 (Gr.) Foh hider to me burh and breotone bold to ȝewealde rodora rices. *c* **1200** ORMIN 5390 Seoffne ȝifess þatt man foþ Off Haliȝ Gastess hellpe. *c* **1205** LAY. 6240 Ah eower monradene ic wulle fon. **1258** *Proclam. Hen. III*, Riȝt for to done and to foangen. *c* **1325** *E.E. Allit. P.* B. 540 þe fowre frekez of þe folde fongez þe empyre. *c* **1394** *P. Pl. Crede* 836 It mot ben a man of also mek an herte þat myȝte ..þat Holly Gost fongen. *c* **1400** *Ywaine & Gaw.* 2642 Wha juges men with wrang, The same jugement sal thai fang. *c* **1475** *Partenay* 2423 When thes Barons thys answere had fong. **1482** in *Eng. Gilds* (1870) 313 Euery seruant that ffangyth wagys, schalle [etc.]. **1846** *Spec. Cornish Dial.* 27 But ded'st fang any money? as a body may say.

†**b.** *to fang cristendom*: to receive baptism, become Christian. Also, of Christ, ***to fang mennishe*** or ***mankind***: to assume human nature. *Obs.*

c **1200** *Trin. Coll. Hom.* 133 God fundede from heuene to eorðe to fongen mennisshe. **1297** R. GLOUC. (1724) 73 He willede anon in hys herte to fonge Cristendom. *c* **1375** *Sc. Leg. Saints, Magdalena* 242 Howe mane-kynd þat he can fange. *c* **1386** CHAUCER *Man of Law's T.* 279 Sche wold reney hir lay, And cristendam of prestes handes fonge.

†**c.** To receive as a guest; to welcome. *lit.* and *fig.* *Obs.*

c **1275** LAY. 13378 He..hehte þe beste cnihtes..þreo hundred him come to and he ȝam wolde wel fon. *c* **1400** *Destr. Troy* 366 He fongid þo freikes with a fine chere. *c* **1418** *Pol. Poems* (Rolls) II. 247 Fals beleve is fayn to fonge The lewde lust of lollardie. *c* **1430** *Pol. Rel. & L. Poems* (1866) 209 þe modir þat wolde deeþ fong. **1578** *Scot. Poems 16th C.* (1801) 130 Sa blyth as bird my God to fang.

3. = TAKE in various uses; *esp.* with obj. *arms*, *counsel*, *leave*, *a name*, *one's way*; to undertake (battle). Also const. *to*, *unto*, *to be*: To take (a person or thing) *for* (a purpose).

a **1000** *Cædmon's Gen.* 287 (Gr.) Mid swilcum mæȝ man ræd ȝeþencean fon. *c* **1205** LAY. 22878 Elc þer feng water & clæd. **1290** *Beket* 7 in *S. Eng. Leg.* I. 106 Gilbert Bekat.. him bi-þouȝte þe Croiz for-to fo In-to þe holie land. *c* **1314** *Guy Warw.* (A.) 1122 Armes y fenge for loue of [þe]. *c* **1330** *Amis & Amil.* 970 Pray him..That he the batail for ous fong, Ogain the steward. *c* **1340** *Gaw. & Gr. Knt.* 1556 Hir leue fayre con scho fonge. **1393** GOWER *Conf.* I. 245 Straught unto Kaire his wey he fongeth. *c* **1394** *P. Pl. Crede* 786 þei schulden..mene-mong corn bred to her mete fongen. *a* **1400–50** *Alexander* 805* (Dublin MS.) Frist of my faire foles fang þe a hundreth. *Ibid.* 3186 þe name of an Emperoure ne wald he neuire fange. *a* **1420** HOCCLEVE *De Reg. Princ.* 3831 Yf that a man outrageousli hem [wynes] fonge, They birien witte. **1420** *Siege Rouen* in *Archæol.* XXI. 67 As they satte here mete to fonge. *c* **1440** *Bone Flor.* 1831 They went Florence to leman have fonge. *c* **1460** *Towneley Myst.* 133 Let us fownde a slepe to fang. **1567** SEMPILL *Ballates* i. (1872) 2 Zit neuer did sho se his maik in France Off royall bluid to fang to be hir feir.

4. *intr.* To seize, lay hold, take hold *on*; to take *to*, betake oneself *to*, turn *to*, proceed *to* or *against*; to set upon, attack.

Beowulf 1542 Heo..him toȝeanes feng. **855** *O.E. Chron.*, And þa fengon his ii sunu to rice. *a* **1000** *Byrhtnoth* 10 (Gr.) þa he to wæpnum feng. *c* **1200** *Trin. Coll. Hom.* 181 Ðe honde foð to..alle þinge þe hire beð biheue. *c* **1205** LAY. 659 þe mete forð iwat for þer fengen feole to. *Ibid.* 1707 [Heo] fusden to þa Freinscan & heo hem to ȝan fengen. *Ibid.* 5909 þa odere..fengen heom to-ȝæinenes. *Ibid.* 27176 þæt whenne Rom-leoden þer comen riden þat heo uengen heom on. *Ibid.* 31785 þeos feng to his riche after his fader daiȝe. *c* **1320** *Cast. Love* 895 Wiþ-outen eny meþ on me heo foþ. *c* **1325** *E.E. Allit. P.* B. 457 He [þe rauen] fongez to þe flyȝt. ? *a* **1400** *Morte Arth.* 3309 He fongede faste one þe feleyghes [of a wheel]. *a* **1400–50** *Alexander* 1990 Fyne, fole, of þi fare, & fange to þi kythis. *c* **1420** *Metr. St. Kath.* (Halliw.), Yonge to Cryste sche can to fonge. **1880** *W. Cornwall Gloss.* s.v., 'I don't fang to your notions.'

5. To engage *on*, set about, begin *on*; to begin, commence *to do* (something).

c **888** K. ÆLFRED *Boeth.* XXXIX. §4 Ic ȝetiohhod hæfde on oðer weorc to fonne. *a* **1000** ÆLFRIC *Interr. Sigewulfi* (Mac Lean) xxi, We foð nu on þa axunge þar we hi ær forleton. *a* **1225** *St. Marher.* 22 þe feondes..fengen to ȝeien Margarete meiden..leowse ure bondes. *c* **1275** *Woman of Samaria* 4 in *O.E. Misc.* (1872) 84 He venk to prechie. *c* **1306** *Execution Fraser* 89 in *Pol. Songs* (Camden) 216 Nou ichulle fonge ther ich er let Ant tellen ou of Frisel.

b. With *on* adv.: To begin. Cf. ONFANG *v.* = Ger. *anfangen*. *Obs.*

c **1205** LAY. 31415 ȝet ich þe suggen wulle ane sunder rune hu þu mihte fon on þat hit ne buð nauere undon. *a* **1225** *St. Marher.* 5 þe edle meiden..feng on þeos bone. *a* **1225**

Juliana 10 He feng on to tellen him hu his dohter droh him from deie to deie. *a* **1250** *Owl & Night.* 179 And fo we on mid riȝte dome.

†**6.** To promise, resolve, undertake. Const. with *inf.* (or its equivalent). *Obs.*

c **1175** *Lamb. Hom.* 61 God us ȝefe in horte to fon þet we ne þenchen ufel to don. *a* **1400** *Cov. Myst.* (1841) 243 To do penawns loke that ȝe ffonge. *c* **1400** *Destr. Troy* 599, I shall fonge you to forther, & my faith holde.

b. *to fang to*: to be sponsor for. *dial.*

[**994** *O.E. Chron.*, Se cyning Æþelræd his onfeng æt bisceopes handa.] *c* **1420** *Chron. Vilod.* 558 Seynt Ede hurre self was redy tho þer, To fonge to þe child as he had y teyȝt. **1674** RAY *S. & E.C. Words* 80 He vangd to me at the Vant. **1746** *Exmoor Scolding* 8 Whan tha vung'st to.. Rabbin. **1888** ELWORTHY *W. Som. Word-bk.* 797 When the paa'sn come there wad-n nobody vor to vang to un.

†**7.** *intr.* To take one's way, go, proceed; also, to swerve *from*. *Obs.*

c **1400** *Song Roland* 577 In Cristis name let us furthe fonge. *c* **1456** *Turnament of Tottenham* 193 in Percy *Reliq.*, He saw Tyrry away wyth Tyb fang. **1522** *World & Child* in Hazl. *Dodsley* I. 257 *Conscience.* Manhood, will ye by this word stand? *Manhood.* Yea, Conscience.. I will never from it fong. **1536** BELLENDEN *Cron. Scot.* I. Proheme (1821) 13 The fatall hors did throw thair wallis fang.

fang (fæŋ), *v.*^{2} [f. FANG *sb.*]

1. *trans.* To strike one's fang or fangs into. Of an anchor: To 'bite' with its fluke. *rare.*

1808 J. BARLOW *Columb.* VII. 216 And with thin moony anchors fang the coast. **1839** BAILEY *Festus* (1854) 531 What though sin, Serpent-like, fanged her.

2. *to fang a pump*, (loosely) *a well*: to give (it) a grip of the water; to prime. Cf. FANG *sb.* 1 b, 7 b. Also *fig.*

1819 *Blackw. Mag.* V. 654 To fang a well signifies to pour into it sufficient liquid to set the pump at work again. **1826** J. WILSON *Noct. Ambr.* Wks. 1855 I. 19 If the wall's fanged I'll bring up a gush with a single drive. **1867** in SMYTH *Sailor's Word-bk.* **1883** W. C. SMITH *N.C. Folk* 181 Little he read, and what he did Was mostly sermons to 'fang his pump'.

Fang, var. FAN *sb.*^{3} and *a.*

fanged (fæŋd), *a.* [f. FANG *sb.* + -ED^{2}.] Furnished with fangs; in various senses of FANG *sb.*

1602 SHAKS. *Ham.* III. iv. 203 My two school-fellows,— Whom I will trust as I will adders fang'd. **1670** MILTON *Hist. Eng.* II. (1851) 44 Chariots phang'd at the Axle with Iron Sithes. *a* **1709** WATTS *Horæ Lyr.* II, *Victory of Poles* 65 A ridge of knotty oaks Deep fang'd. **1791** COWPER *Iliad* x. 424 As two feet hounds sharp fang'd. **1794** COLERIDGE *Destiny of Nations* xiii, The night was fanged with frost. **1816** KIRBY & SP. *Entomol.* (1843) II. 34 They will make their fanged jaws meet at the very first stroke. **1820** KEATS *St. Agnes* xvii, They be more fang'd than wolves and bears. **1889** ELVIN *Dict. Herald.* Plate xlii, 52 Fanged tooth.

†**'fanger.** *Obs.* [f. FANG *v.* + -ER^{1}.] **a.** One who takes another under his protection, a guardian. **b.** One who catches or captures. **c.** That with which one catches hold (*e.g.* a tooth).

a **1300** *E.E. Psalter* iii. 4 Laverd, mi fanger [L. *susceptor*] art þou. *a* **1455** HOLLAND *Houlate* xiv, The Scarth [was] a fische fangar. **1612** DEKKER *If it be not good* Wks. 1873 III. 313 All the craft in that great head of yours cannot get it out of my fangers. **1763** DEL PINO *Sp. Dict.*, *Dientes caninos*, the eye-teeth, or fangers.

fanging ('fæŋɪŋ), *vbl. sb.* [f. as prec. + -ING^{1}.]

1. The action of the verb FANG in various senses. †**a.** The action of standing sponsor (*obs.*). **b.** The action of earning wages; in pl. *concr.* earnings. (*dial.*)

1493 *Festivall* (W. de W. 1515) 167 b, Thrughe fongynge of chyldren at the fonte. **1846** *Spec. Cornish Dial.* 46 Why a spent all hes fangings laste Saturda nite.

2. *Mining.* (A main of) air-pipes used for ventilation in mines. Cf. FANG *sb.* 8.

1747 HOOSON *Miner's Dict.* H, That expense may be spared, and Air enough taken along by Fanging. **1875** URE *Dict. Arts* s.v. *Fang*, Sometimes the term *a fanging* is applied to a main of wood-pipes.

fangish ('fæŋɪʃ), *a.* [f. as prec. + -ISH.] Of the nature of a fang; piercing.

c **1825** BEDDOES *Poems, Israelite amid Philistines* 102 A curse.. Fangish enough to reach the quick of earth!

fangle ('fæŋg(ə)l), *sb.*^{1} Also 6 **fangel**, 7 *south. dial.* **vangle.** [This and FANGLE *v.*^{2} app. arose from a mistaken analysis of NEWFANGLED, later form of *newfangle* 'eager for novelty'. As *newfangled* was said both of persons and of their actions or productions, it came to be diversely interpreted to mean either 'characterized by new fashions or crotchets' or 'newly fashioned or fabricated'.]

1. *new fangle*: a new fashion or crotchet; a novelty, new invention. (Always in contemptuous sense.) Now *rare.*

1548 UDALL, etc. *Erasm. Par. 1 Tim.* iv. 6 Full growen age, which is not wonte easily to swerue into newe fangles. **1579** LYLY *Euphues* (Arb.) 116 A Pedlers packe of new fangles. **1670** MAYNWARING *Physician's Repos.* 122 That Physician.. departs from the primitive Practice, for a new fangle and fashion of Prescribing. **1869** TROLLOPE *He knew* lxxxix. (1878) 494 She would still scorn the new fangles of the world around her. **1881** GRANT WHITE *Words & Uses* (ed. 3) 334 New fashions and fangles of dress, of manners, and of speech.

†**2.** A fantastic, foppish, or silly contrivance; a piece of finery; foppery, fuss. *Obs.*

1583 GREENE *Mamillia* I. Wks. 1881 II. 19 There was no Feather, no fangle, Gem, nor Jewell.. left behinde. *c* **1600** *Time's Alteration* in Chambers *Pop. Lit.* I. 247 French fashions then were scorned, Fond fangles then none knew. **1642** MILTON *Apol. Smect.* (1851) 315 If God loathe the best of an Idolaters prayer, much more the conceited fangle of his prayer. **1654** GAYTON *Pleas. Notes* IV. ix. 230 What fangle now, thy thronged guests to winne. **1695** KENNETT *Par. Antiq.* Gloss. s.v. *Fannatio*, Fangles or vangles properly the baubles or playthings of children that are proud to be new fangled.

†**'fangle**, *sb.*^{2} *Obs. rare.* [? cf. Ger. (dial.) *fankel* spark; also, a sort of demon.] ? A spark.

1649 G. DANIEL *Trinarch. Hen. IV*, clxii, [Glendower] fraught wth some Rudiments of Art And strooke with fangle of his Countriman, The boasted Merlin. *Ibid.* cclviii, There may we find wth out the fangle which Fires the dry touch of Constitution.

'fangle, *sb.*^{3} *Anglo-Irish.* [? a. Ir. *fainneall* 'a handful of straw for thatching' (O'Reilly).] (See quot.)

1863 *Dublin Univ. Mag.* Oct. 438 The parties returning home, probably by the light of fangles. *Ibid.*, *note*, Fangles .. were long irregular cones of straw, tied at short intervals with twigs or slight straw bands. Being set on fire.. they burned slowly, and were very useful in dark nights.

†**'fangle**, *v.*^{1} *Obs. rare*$^{-1}$. In 5 **fangel.** [? cf. Ger. dial. *fankeln* to trifle.] *intr.* ? To trifle.

a **1400** *Tutivillus* 14 in *Rel. Ant.* I. 257 For his love that ȝou der boȝth Hold ȝou stil and fangel noȝth.

'fangle, *v.*^{2} *Obs.* exc. *dial.* [See FANGLE *sb.*^{1}] *trans.* Contemptuously used for: To fashion, fabricate; to trick out. Also, *to new fangle*: to dress up anew.

1615 J. TAYLOR (Water-P.) *Siege Jerusalem* Wks. (1630) 10/2 Such gibrish, gibble-gabble, all did fangle [at Babel]. **1641** MILTON *Prel. Episc.* (1851) 90 Not hereby to.. new fangle the Scripture. **1755** CARTE *Hist. Eng.* IV. 136 Such was their zeal for a new religion of their own fangling. **1762** *Songs Costume* (Percy Soc.) 240 If I give a charm 'Tis so metamorphos'd by your fiddling and fangling. **1881** MISS JACKSON *Shropsh. Word-bk.* s.v., 'Er bonnit wuz fangled all o'er ooth ribbints.

†**'fangled**, *ppl. a. Obs.* [f. FANGLE *sb.*^{1} + -ED^{2}.] Characterized by crotchets or fopperies.

1587 M. GROVE *Pelops & Hipp.* (1878) 48 Mens minds wer not so fangled then as now they doe appeare. **1611** SHAKS. *Cymb.* v. iv. 134 Be not, as is our fangled world, a Garment, Nobler then that it couers. **1727** in BAILEY.

fanglement ('fæŋg(ə)lmənt). [f. FANGLE *v.*^{2} + -MENT.] The action of fangling or fashioning; hence, something fashioned or made, an invention, a contrivance.

a **1670** HACKET *Abp. Williams* I. §108 (1692) 97 He adventur'd to maintain Orthodox Religion against old Corruptions and new Fanglements. **1866** BLACKMORE *Cradock Nowell* xiii. (1881) 53 Round-about foreign fanglements. **1888** ELWORTHY *W. Somerset Word-bk.* 797 These here new-farshin vanglements 'bout farmerin' an' that.

fangless ('fæŋlɪs), *a.* [f. FANG *sb.* + -LESS.]

a. Without fangs, toothless. **b.** Of a tooth: Having no fang or root.

a. **1597** SHAKS. *2 Hen. IV*, IV. i. 218 His power, like to a Fanglesse Lion, May offer, but not hold. **1823** *Blackw. Mag.* XIV. 81 A sort of fangless viper. **1868** GEO. ELIOT *Sp. Gipsy* IV. 302 A lion in fangless infancy.

fig. **1790** J. WILLIAMS *Shrove Tuesd.* (1794) 29 Rebellion fangless grinn'd on Brunswick's pride. **1795** *Jemima* II. 198, I should dread the consequence of his iniquity even in that almost fangless situation. **1887** SWINBURNE *Locrine* IV. i. 105 So shall fear, mistrust, and jealous hate Lie foodless, if not fangless.

b. **1835–6** TODD *Cycl. Anat.* I. 114/2 The mouth.. furnished with.. fangless.. teeth.

fanglet ('fæŋlɪt). [f. as prec. + -LET.] A little fang or tooth.

1843 J. DAYMAN *Inferno of Dante* xxv. 159 Then either cheek with poisoned fanglets stung.

fanglomerate (fæn'glɒmərət). *Geol.* [f. FAN *sb.*^{1} 5 d + CON)GLOMERATE *sb.*] A rock consisting of comparatively erosion-resistant fragments of various sizes deposited in an alluvial fan and consolidated into a solid mass.

1912 A. C. LAWSON in *Bull. Geol. Soc. Amer.* XXIII. 72 (*heading*) Fanglomerate, a detrital rock at Battle Mountain, Nevada. **1933** *Geogr. Jrnl.* LXXXI. 156 The gravel was then consolidated into conglomerates and fanglomerates. **1957** F. J. PETTIJOHN *Sedimentary Rocks* (ed. 2) xiii. 630 This facies appears to consist of fanglomerates deposited near the boundary fault scarps and of channels, floodplains, and swamp deposits in the more remote areas.

‖**fango** ('fæŋgəʊ). [It., mud, dirt: cf. FANC.] A kind of mud obtained from the thermal springs at Battaglia in the Veneto in Italy, used in the treatment of gout, rheumatism, and other ailments. So **fango'therapy.**

1900 GOULD *Pocket Med. Dict.* (ed. 4) 249 Fango. **1903** DORLAND *Med. Dict.* (ed. 3) 264/1 *Fangotherapy*, treatment by the application of fango. **1904** E. RUTHERFORD *Radio-Activity* 363 'Fango'—a fine mud obtained from hot springs in Battaglia, Northern Italy. **1905** *Jrnl. Balneology* Jan. 5 The annual visits of several patients to Italy for the sole purpose of taking a course of fango-packs. **1906** *Christian World* 22 Mar., I have just returned from a trial of 'Fango' at the Royal Hotel and Baths, Matlock Bath. **1906** *Punch* 2 Feb. 161/1 The Italians are rightly proud of their [spa] muds (do they not still send us Fango?). **1913** J. LINDSAY *Gout* xxxi. 204 Peat, mud, fango, and similar semi-solid baths are of therapeutic value on account of their thermal action. **1940** B. I. COMROE *Arthritis* xxvii. 332 In some spas, fango is used extensively. *Ibid.* 333 Fango therapy produces marked hyperemia of the skin.

fangot ('fæŋgət). [ad. It. *fangotto*, var. of *fagotto* bundle, FAGGOT.] A quantity of wares, *esp.* raw silk, from 1 to 3 cwt.

1673 *Lond. Gaz.* No. 841/4 Lost.. out of a Close Lighter at Brewers Key, one Fangot of White Cyprus Silk. **1708** *Ibid.* No. 4472/4, 4 Fangotts of Italian Raw Silk. **1721–1800** in BAILEY. **1768** in E. BUYS *Dict. Terms Art.*

fangy ('fæŋɪ), *a.* [f. FANG *sb.* + -Y^{1}.] Having a number of fangs; divided into fangs; resembling fangs.

1847 *Jrnl. R. Agric. Soc.* VIII. II. 292 It makes the roots fangy. **1859** SALA *Gaslight & D.* x. 120 A fangy range of teeth.

†**'fanikin.** *Obs. rare*$^{-1}$. [a. MDu. *vaneken* (Flem. *vaenken*, Kilian), dim. of *vane* (now *vaan*): see FANE *sb.*^{1} and -KIN.] A small flag or banner.

1539 in Pitcairn *Crim. Trials Scot.* I. *298 Fanikynnis, Ansenȝeis, stramaris, and banaris.

fanion ('fænjən). [a. Fr. *fanion*, f. as *fanon* (see FANON).] See quots.

1706 PHILLIPS (ed. Kersey), *Fanion*, a Banner carry'd by a Servant belonging to each Brigade of Horse and Foot at the Head of the Baggage. **1721–1800** in BAILEY. **1867** SMYTH *Sailor's Word-bk.*, *Fanions*, small flags used in surveying stations, named after the bannerets carried by horse brigades.

fank (fæŋk), *sb.*^{1} *Sc.* [a. Gael. *fang, faing* = Ir. *fang* in same sense.] A sheep-cot or pen.

1812 P. GRAHAM *Agric. Stirling* xiv. 294 It is necessary to enclose the whole flock in the pen or fank. **1827** J. ANDERSON *Ess. State Soc. Highlands* 127 Bargains were concluded at the homes and fanks of the farmers. **1883** W. C. SMITH *N.C. Folk* 219 When he came to byre or fank.

fank, *sb.*^{2} *Sc.* [Cf. FANG *sb.* 7.] A coil of rope; a noose.

1825–80 in JAMIESON. **1826** SCOTT *Jrnl.* (1890) I. 255 He .. is a prince of Bores, but.. like the giant Pope.. he can only sit and grin at Pilgrims.. and is not able to cast a fank over them as formerly.

fank (fæŋk), *v. Sc.* [f. FANK *sb.*^{1}] *trans.* To put (sheep) in a fank; to pen up (Jam.). Hence **fanked** *ppl. a.*, penned up; in quot. *transf.* of a sword: Set fast in the sheath.

? *a* **1600** *Death of Parcy Reed* xxviii. in Child *Eng. & Sc. Ball.* (1890) VII. cxciii. 27/6 Brave Parcy raised his fankit sword, And felld the foremost to the ground. **1923** *Glasgow Herald* 19 Nov. 7 Days.. set apart for fanking the sheep.

fankle ('fæŋk(ə)l), *v. Sc.* [f. FANK *sb.*^{2}: see -LE.] *trans.* To tangle, entangle; to entrammel (a horse, etc.) with a rope; hence, *to get fankled*: *fig.* to lose the thread of a discourse (see Jamieson s.v.).

c **1450** HENRYSON *Lyon & Mons* xxxiv. in *Evergreen* I. 196 Our ryal Lord.. now is fast heir fanklet in a Cord. **1826** J. WILSON *Noct. Ambr.* Wks. 1885 I. 103 My long spurs.. never got fankled.

fan-light ('fænlaɪt). A fan-shaped window over a door; sometimes applied loosely to any window over a door. Also *attrib.*

1819 *P.O. Lond. Direct.* 220 M'Namar, E., Metal Fan-light manuf. **1838** DICKENS *Nich. Nick.* iv, In shape resembling the fan-light of a street door. **1886** STEVENSON *Dr. Jekyll* ii. (ed. 2) 26 At the door of this [house].. now plunged in darkness except for the fan-light. **1888** GWILT *Encycl. Arch.* 766 Fanlight frames over doors.

fannell ('fænəl), *Obs.* exc. *Hist.* Also 6 **phanelle.** [ad. med.L. *fanul-a* (Wr.-Wülck. 649) or *fanonellus* (Du Cange), dim. of *fano* (see FANON).] = FANON 1.

1530 PALSGR. 218/2 Fannell for a preestes arme, *fanon.* **1566** in Peacock *Eng. Ch. Furniture* (1866) 29 Item vestmentes copes crosses aulbes phanelles. **1672** J. DAVIES *Rites Durham* 16 Stoles and Fannels. **1830** *Beauties of Isle of Thanet* I. 51 On his left side.. is seen the end of the fannel or maniple.

¶App. taken as dim. of FAN or FANE: A small screen or fan.

1555 *Fardle Facions* II. viii. 167 For that thei sette muche by beautie, thei cary aboute with theim phanelles [Lat. text *umbrellas*] to defende them fro the sonne.

fanner ('fænə(r)). [f. FAN *sb.* or *v.* + -ER^{1}.]

1. One who fans. †**a.** One who winnows grain with a fan. *Obs.*

c **1515** *Cocke Lorell's B.* (Percy Soc.) 10 Repers, faners and horners. **1654** TRAPP *Comm. Ps.* xiii. 8. 600 Good corn.. falls low at the feet of the Fanner.

b. One who fans (himself or another person) with a fan.

1888 *Bow-Bells Weekly* 18 May, The present Emperor of China when he was a baby had.. twenty-five fanners. **1890**

Daily News 15 Feb. 6/4 Which caused a draught almost sufficient to blow the fanner quite away.

2. = FAN *sb.*[1] 1 b. *lit.* and *fig.* Also, in later use, an appliance forming part of this.

1788 *Specif. Meikle's Patent* No. 1645. 3 Below the harp a pair of fanners may be placed so as to separate the corn from the chaff. **1799** J. ROBERTSON *Agric. Perth* 99 Fanners for cleaning grain have been long used by the most industrious of the farmers. **1800** *Farmers Mag.* (Edinb.) I. 159 James Meikle who went to Holland in 1710..brought over a winnowing machine or what is commonly called a pair of fanners. **1828** *Blackw. Mag.* XXIII. 841/2 How from the fanners of his genius would the cock-chaffers of Cockneys fly like very chaff indeed! **1853** *Jrnl. R. Agric. Soc.* XIV. II. 291 The grain, after leaving the mill fanners, is put through hand-fanners preparatory to measuring.

b. *U.S.* (see quot.).

1890 *Dialect Notes* (Boston, U.S.) II. 58 *Fanner*, an open basket dishing out from the bottom upwards..Originally it was used to separate the chaff from the wheat.

3. (See quots.)

1874 KNIGHT *Dict. Mech.*, *Fanner*, a blower or ventilating fan. **1858** SIMMONDS *Dict. Trade*, *Fanner*..a cooling apparatus.

4. A kind of hawk so called from the fanning motion of its wings. Also *vanner-hawk*.

1875 PARISH *Sussex Gloss.*, *Fanner*, a hawk. **1885** SWAINSON *Prov. Names Birds* 140 Kestrel..Vanner hawk, Windfanner.

fanning ('fænɪŋ), *vbl. sb.* [f. FAN *v.* + -ING[1].] The action of the vb. FAN.

1. The action of fanning or winnowing (corn).

1577 B. GOOGE *Heresbach's Husb.* I. (1586) 43 The.. fannyng and wynnowing in Sommer. *a* **1679** T. GOODWIN *Wks.* V. II. 144 Others take this fanning (Luke iii. 16, 17) for that discovery which shall be made at the day of judgment. **1879** FARRAR *St. Paul* II. vii. I. 123 'All the fanning in the world will not make you [a cornfield] so remunerative as commerce', said Rabh.

b. *concr.* The siftings of tea.

1870 *Daily News* 16 Nov., Common fannings mixed with broken stalks.

2. The action of moving the air with or as with a fan; an instance of this.

1528 PAYNELL *Salerne's Regim.* Tiv, The fier, without fannynge of the aier, is schoked and quenched. **1696** tr. *Du Mont's Voy. Levant* 133 Where a Man may lie and enjoy the Pleasure of Fanning as long as he pleases. **1715** DESAGULIERS *Fires Impr.* 41 Fanning..makes that Air feel cold or cool, which is otherwise warm. **1852** D. MOIR *Hymn to Night Wind* Poet. Wks. II. 381 The delightful fannings of thy wing!

3. The action of blowing gently as with a fan; an instance of this; a breeze.

1712 BUDGELL *Spect.* No. 425 ¶1 The Fanning of the Wind rustling on the Leaves. **1764** GRAINGER *Sugar Cane* 562 The first glad fannings of the breeze. **1818** KEATS *Endym.* II. 664 Exhal'd asphodel, And rose, with spicy fannings interbreath'd, Came swelling forth.

4. = *fan-tracery* (see FAN *sb.*[1] 11).

1851 RUSKIN *Stones Ven.* I. xxix. §4, I would rather..have a plain ridged Gothic vault..than all the fanning..and foliation that ever bewildered Tudor weight.

5. Also *fanning-out*: the action of spreading out like a fan (cf. FAN *v.* 6); an instance of this.

1883 W. C. RUSSELL *Sailor's Lang.*, *Fanning*, widening the after-part of a ship's top. **1889** GEIKIE in *Nature* 19 Sept. 488/1 The fanning-out of the ice on its southward march.

6. *Comb.*, as *fanning-machine*, *-mill*. (= FAN *sb.*[1] 1 b.)

1747 *Gent. Mag.* XVII. 438 A Fanning Mill, used in Silesia, for cleaning of corn from tares, &c. **1842** BRANDE *Dict. Sc.*, *Fanning-machine*. **1874** KNIGHT *Dict. Mech.*, *Fanning-mill*.

'fanning, *ppl. a.* [f. as prec. + -ING[2].] That fans, in senses of the verb. *lit.* and *fig.*

c **1340** *Gaw. & Gr. Knt.* 181 Fayre fannand fax vmbefoldes his schulderes. **1555** LATIMER *Serm. & Rem.* (1845) 442 Fear not the fanning wind. *a* **1700** DRYDEN *Cymon & Iphig.* 104 The fanning wind upon her bosom blows. **1725** POPE *Odyss.* VI. 284 Inhaling freshness from the fanning breeze. **1818** BYRON *Ch. Har.* IV. xliv, My bark did skim The bright blue waters with a fanning wind. **1867** SMYTH *Sailor's Word-bk.*, *Fanning-breeze*, one so gentle that the sail alternately swells and collapses.

fanny ('fænɪ), *sb.*[1] *dial.* (See quot.)

1892 *Labour Commission* Gloss. No. 3, *Fanny*, a local term, a corruption of fanner or fanblower; that is, a wheel with vanes fixed on to a rotating shaft enclosed in a case or chamber to create a blast of air. It is used in the scissor-grinding industry.

fanny ('fænɪ), *sb.*[2] *Naut.* [? The female name.] A tin for holding anything to be drunk; a mess-kettle.

1904 *Daily Chron.* 11 Aug. 3/2 Many total abstainers drawing their grog and leaving it in the 'fanny' for the benefit of the mess. **1923** *Man. Seamanship* (*H.M.S.O.*) II. 35 A full set of mess utensils, consisting of, mess kettle.. fanny (metal tin 1½ gallons). **1925** FRASER & GIBBONS *Soldier & Sailor Words*, *Fanny*, a name for the receptacle holding the bluejackets' 'tot' of rum. **1926** *Blackw. Mag.* Dec. 823/2 On board a British man-of-war the same..vessel is called a 'fanny'.. Tea made in a billy or fanny is the best to be had. **1943** C. S. FORESTER *Ship* i. 13 The 'mess-traps' about which he had worried, the 'fannies' of soup. **1952** G. HACKFORTH-JONES *Dangerous Trade* xxv. 175 Send a fanny full of hot tea while you are about it.

Fanny, *sb.*[3] The word formed by the initials of *F*irst *A*id *N*ursing *Y*eomanry accommodated to the form of the name *Fanny*.

1918 [see F.A.N.Y. (F III. 3)].

fanny, *sb.*[4] *slang* [Orig. unknown.]

1. = BACKSIDE 3. (orig. and chiefly *U.S.*).

1928 HECHT & MACARTHUR *Front Page* II. 115 Parking her fanny in here. **1930** N. COWARD *Private Lives* I, You'd fallen on your fanny a few moments before. **1937** T. RATTIGAN *French without Tears* II. i. 44 That's it. Progress. *Kit.* Progress my fanny. **1946** R. CAMPBELL *Talking Bronco* 29 Ere you came back to serenade the sentry, Who thanks you with this bayonet in your fanny! **1949** E. POUND *Pisan Cantos* lxxx. 95 And three small boys on three bicycles Smacked her young fanny in passing. **1953** 'R. GORDON' *Doctor at Sea* i. 16 Move over, Second, and let the Doctor park his fanny. **1959** M. STEEN *Woman in Back Seat* II. vii. 284 Classy, isn't it [*sc.* a cardigan]?—that little roll round the fanny. **1960** 'N. SHUTE' *Trustee from Toolroom* iv. 82 I'd never be able to think of John and Jo again if we just sat tight on our fannies and did nothing.

2. The female genitals. (Chiefly British English.)

1879 *Pearl* I. 82 You shan't look at my fanny for nothing. **1889** BARRÈRE & LELAND *Dict. Slang* I. 354/2 *Fanny* (common), the fem. pud. **1939** JOYCE *Finnegans Wake* 204 Two lads in scoutsch breeches went through her..before she had a hint of a hair at her fanny to hide or a bossom to tempt a birch canoedler. **1980** E. JONG *Fanny* I. xv. 120 'Madam Fanny,' says he, obliging me, but with the same ironick Tone. 'D'ye know what that means in the Vulgar Tongue?'.. 'It means the Fanny-Fair,..the Divine Monosyllable, the Precious Pudendum, [etc.].'

fanny ('fænɪ), *v. slang.* [Orig. unknown.] *trans.* To deceive or persuade by glib talk. Also as *sb.*, glib talk, a tall story.

1933 G. INGRAM *'Stir'* v. 65 'Spin a regular fanny to the "Croaker"', advised Smith. **1936** 'J. CURTIS' *Gilt Kid* xiii. 134 He would spin her a fanny about the marriage laws. **1942** G. KERSH *Nine Lives Bill Nelson* ii. 12 A Guardsman comes to Bill with some Fanny about needing some cash. **1949** *John o' London's* 4 Mar. 123/3 'Fannied' a 'Pitch', that is, got together a larger crowd and told them of the excellence of the play to be seen inside. **1965** A. PRIOR *Interrogators* viii. 147 They could not fanny Norris into thinking they believed he might have been out to a woman.

Fanny Adams ('fænɪ 'ædəmz). [The name of a young woman who was murdered *c* 1867.]

1. *Naut. slang.* **a.** Tinned meat. **b.** Stew.

1889 BARRÈRE & LELAND *Dict. Slang*, *Fanny Adams* (naval), tinned mutton. **1927** *Blackw. Mag.* Feb. 259/2 'Fanny Adams' (or preserved mutton) brought from the ship. **1962** W. GRANVILLE *Dict. Sailors' Slang* 46/1 *Fanny Adams*, general nautical slang for stew or hash.

2. *slang.* Freq. prec. by *sweet*: nothing at all. Cf. *F.A.* (F III. 3).

Sometimes interpreted as a euphemism for 'sweet fuck all' in the same sense.

1919 W. H. DOWNING *Digger Dial.* 22 *F.A.*, 'Fanny Adams', or 'Sweet Fanny Adams'—nothing; vacuity. **1930** BROPHY & PARTRIDGE *Songs & Slang 1914–18* 123 F.A. Sometimes lengthened into Sweet F.A. or bowdlerized into Sweet Fanny Adams. Used to mean 'nothing' where something was expected. **1949** J. R. COLE *It was so Late* 61 What do they do? Sweet Fanny Adams!

fanon ('fænən). Forms: α. 5 fanen, -one, -oun, -un, *Sc.* fannowne, 6 fannom, (*Sc.*) -oun, fawnon, 6–8 fannon, 5– fanon. β. 6 phanon. [Fr. *fanon*, ad. med.L. *fanōn-em*, *fanō* banner, napkin, a. OHG. *fano*, Goth. *fana*: see FANE *sb.*[1]]

1. An embroidered band, corresponding with the stole, but shorter, originally a kind of napkin, attached to the left wrist of the officiating priest or celebrant, and of the deacon and subdeacon at mass; a maniple.

1418 *Bury Wills* (Camden) 3, j. fanon. **1496** *Dives & Paup.* (W. de W.) VIII. viii. 331/2 The fanon betokneth bounds of his [Christ's] hondes. **1500–20** DUNBAR *Fenyeit Freir* 55 On him come nowthir stole nor fannoun. **1536** in *Antiq. Sarisb.* (1771) 197 Two Tunicles and three Albes; with divers Stoles and Fannons. **1571** GRINDAL *Articles*, Whether all Vestments..Stoles, Phanons, Pixes [etc.]..be vtterly, defaced..and destroied. **1844** LINGARD *Anglo-Sax. Ch.* (1858) II. ix. 69 The usual episcopal vestments, the amice..fanon, etc.

2. (See quots.)

1844 PUGIN *Gloss. Eccl. Ornament* 120 Georgius says that the fanon or phanon worn by the Pope, is the same as the orale, and is a veil of four colours in stripes. **1849** ROCK *Ch. of Fathers* I. v. 466 The Roman pontiff..vested..in what is called the fanon now but formerly the 'Orale'.

fanship ('fænʃɪp). [f. FAN *sb.*[2] + -SHIP.] The state or quality of being a 'fan'.

1928 *Weekly Disp.* 20 May 17, I, who left fanship..when I was seventeen..started out on the goose chase for Menjou. **1959** P. BULL *I Know Face* xi. 197, I showed him my fanship was genuine by the comprehensive collection I had of his records.

fant, var. f. FAUNT *Obs.*, child.

fant(e, obs. f. of FAINT *a.*, FONT.

fantabulous (fæn'tæbjʊləs), *a. slang.* [Blend of FANT(ASTIC *a.* + F)ABULOUS *a.*] Of almost incredible excellence.

1959 *N.Z. Listener* 9 Jan. 4/2 Air travel—it's fantabulous. **1961** *She* Sept. 59/2 There's BMC's fantabulous service depot, where owners and cars alike get real kid-glove/red-carpet treatment. **1968** *Punch* 6 Mar. 352/3 A cat involved in a court of law May fairly be called fantabulous. **1971** *Sunday Express* (Johannesburg) 28 Mar. (Home Jrnl.) 4/2 Since the bust up of the fantabulous group, it's been George who's been doing most of the slogging.

fantad, var. FANTOD.

fan-tail ('fænteɪl), *sb.* [f. FAN *sb.*[1] + TAIL.]

1. A tail or lower end in the shape of a fan.

1728 SWIFT *Ladies at Sot's Hole*, We who wear our wigs With fan-tail and with snake. **1862** *Jrnl. R. Agric. Soc.* XXIII. 214 Turning the butt-end [of a sheaf] upwards, spreading out the ears, and making a sort of 'fantail'.

2. A variety of the domestic pigeon, so called from the form of its tail. Also *fantail-pigeon*.

1735 J. MOORE *Columbarium* 54 They [pigeons] are call'd by some Fan-Tails. **1767** S. PATERSON *Another Trav.* II. 148 The..fan-tails and the..powters are of my breed! **1840** DICKENS *Barn. Rudge* (1849) 2/1 Runts, fantails, tumblers, and pouters. **1859** DARWIN *Orig. Spec.* i. (1878) 16 The fantail has thirty or even forty tail feathers, instead of twelve or fourteen. **1884** MAY CROMMELIN *Brown-Eyes* i. 3 The grazing deer, and the proud fantail pigeons.

3. A genus (*Rhipidura*) of Birds found in Australia and New Zealand.

1848 in MAUNDER *Treas. Nat. Hist.* **1860** A. S. ATKINSON *Jrnl.* 27 Oct. in *Richmond-Atkinson Papers* (1960) I. 645 Found a fantail nest (young ones) & a riroriro's with two young ones & an egg. **1882** W. L. BULLER *Man. Birds N.Z.* 26 The Pied Fantail, ever flitting about with broadly-expanded tail.., is one of the most pleasing and attractive objects in the New Zealand forest. **1935** J. GUTHRIE *Little Country* xxiii. 356 A fantail perched on a twig near them and flirted its feathers.

4. a. *Mech.* A kind of joint. Cf. *dove-tail*.

1858 in SIMMONDS *Dict. Trade*.

b. = FAN *sb.*[1] 6 c.

1934 *Archit. Rev.* LXXVI. 166/3 The elaborate invention of an ingenious Scot, by name Meikle, who, in 1750, conceived a method of turning the mill automatically so that the 'sails', 'sweep', 'arms'—whatever pet name you care to employ—always faced the wind. It—the invention—was known as a 'fantail', and consisted of a fan of six to ten blades... Mounted on a spindle, and so arranged that if the wind should veer slightly, it strikes the 'fan-tail' which turns the mill through appropriate gearing until such time as the sails face the wind again. **1949** K. S. WOODS *Rural Crafts Eng.* II. iv. 74 By these three inventions—automatic sails, fan-tail, and governor—the wind itself has been used to counteract its own fickle and varying moods in man's service.

c. *Naut.* 'The projecting part of the stern of a yacht or other small vessel when it extends unusually far over the water abaft the stern post' (*Cent. Dict.* 1889); so extended to larger craft. (Cf. OVERHANG *sb.*)

1882 *Harper's Mag.* LXIV. 174/2 The stalactites of ice.. at the start lent the wheel and 'fan-tail' a novel beauty. **1943** J. STEINBECK *Once there was War* (1959) 206 The boat.. threw out a curving V of wake and boiled the water a little under the fantail. **1948** R. DE KERCHOVE *Internat. Mar. Dict.* 252/2 *Fantail stern*, a type of yacht stern in which the shell planking or plating sweeps up to a sharp point to join the deck planking... This type of stern has been almost abandoned in recent years. **1955** C. S. FORESTER *Good Shepherd* 70 Krause strode out on the wing of the bridge as the..gun at the fantail went off. **1957** *Jane's Fighting Ships 1957–58* 424 The aircraft crane on the fantail has not the capacity to handle heavy boats.

5. (See quot. 1874.)

1858 in SIMMONDS *Dict. Trade*, *Fantail*, a joint; a gas burner. **1874** KNIGHT *Dict. Mech.*, *Fan-tail*..a form of gas-burner in which the burning jet has an arched form.

6. *attrib.*, as *fan-tail-hat*, also, simply, *fan-tail*, a coal-heaver's hat, a sou'wester; *fan-tail gentleman*, a wearer of such a hat, a coal-heaver.

1810 *Sporting Mag.* XXXVI. 243 The two fan-tail Gentlemen soon gave in. **1850** P. CROOK *War of Hats* 47 Those heavers, too, of coals, with smutted face And fantail hats. **1877** J. GREENWOOD *Dick Temple* II. vii. 220, I fancy I see you..with knee-breeches and calves and a 'fantail', shouldering an inky sack.

Hence **fan-tail** *v. intr.* Of a whale: To work its tail like a fan. **fan-tailed** *a.*, having a fan-tail.

1812 H. & J. SMITH *Rej. Addr.*, *Arch. Atoms* 154 The dustman..doffs his fan-tail'd hat. **1851** H. MELVILLE *Whale* xxxvi. 179 Does he fan-tail a little curious before he goes down? **1868** WOOD *Homes without H.* xi. 211 A rather pretty bird the Fan-tailed Warbler.

fan-tan ('fæntæn). [Chinese *fan t'an* repeated divisions.] A Chinese gambling game, in which a number of small coins are placed under a bowl and the players then bet as to what will be the remainder when the pile has been divided by four. Also *attrib.*

1878 LADY BRASSEY *Voy. Sunbeam* xxiii. 401 A few natives playing at fan-tan. **1888** *Pall Mall G.* 16 May 2/1 At their fan-tan tables lads of ten..years of age may be seen gambling away their pence. **1888** *Times* (weekly ed.) 19 Sept. 15/4 The home of fantan..is the Portuguese colony of Macao.

†**'fantaser.** *Obs. rare*[−1]. [f. *fantase*, FANTASY *v.* + -ER[1].] A fancier; one who is in love with (some one).

a **1547** SURREY *Descr. Restless State* 145 A fantaser thou art of some, By whom thy wits are overcome.

fantasia (fanta'zia, fæn'tɑːzɪə, -'teɪ-). [a. It. *fantasia* (see FANTASY), lit. 'fancy', hence 'an instrumental composition having the appearance of being extemporaneous' (Tommaseo).]

1. a. *Mus.* 'A composition in a style in which form is subservient to fancy' (Stainer and Barrett).

1724 *Explic. Foreign Words in Music* 30 Fantasia, is a Kind of Air, wherein the Composer..has all the Freedom and Liberty allowed him for his Fancy or Invention, that can

reasonably be desir'd. **1776** SIR J. HAWKINS *Hist. Music* IV. iv. 47 His [Hilton's] Compositions were for the most part Fantasias for the viols and organ. **1815** *European Mag.* July 46/1 The first movement, termed 'Fantasia'..is a most spirited..effort. **1879** GROVE *Dict. Mus.* I. 503/1 Fantasia..was the immediate predecessor of the term Sonata.

b. *transf.* and *fig.*

1818 E. BLAQUIERE tr. *Pananti's Narr. Res. Algiers* xix. 367 These excesses called *fantasias*, or paroxysms of passions. **1880** J. H. SHORTHOUSE *J. Inglesant* xxvi. 372 Wandering amid this brilliant fantasia of life, Inglesant's heart smote him. **1896** 'J. O. HOBBES' (*title*) The Herb-Moon. A Fantasia. **1919** G. B. SHAW *Heartbreak House* p. xlix, Heartbreak House: a Fantasia in the Russian manner on English themes. **1921** D. H. LAWRENCE *Sea & Sardinia* 41 Every wretched bit of would-be extra chic is called a fantasia. **1922** —— (*title*) Fantasia of the Unconscious. **1935** H. G. WELLS *Things to Come* v. 33 Long lines of steel-helmeted men. Lorries full of men. Lorries full of shells. Great dumps of shells. A fantasia of war material in motion. **1957** T. S. ELIOT *On Poetry & Poets* 83 A suspension of the action in order to enjoy a poetic fantasia: these passages are really less related to the action than are the choruses in *Murder in the Cathedral.*

‖**2.** The It. word is current in the Levant and North Africa, in the senses: **a.** Ostentation, pomp, self-importance; **b.** A kind of Arab dance; also, an exhibition of evolutions on horseback by a troop of Arabs.

1838 SPARKS *Biog.* IX. Eaton viii. 263 But they must have a consul with less fantasia. **1859** WRAXALL tr. *R. Houdin* II. viii. 239 Our captain had arranged for us the surprise of a fantasia. **1873** TRISTRAM *Moab* ii. 28 A capital 'fantasia' or Arab dance..round our camp fire.

fantasied, phantasied ('fæntəsɪd), *ppl. a.* [f. FANTASY *sb.* and *v.* + -ED.] **a.** Framed by the fancy; imaginary. Now *spec.* in *Psychol.* **b.** Filled with (strange, new) fancies or imaginations (so OF. *fantasié*). **c.** Characterized by phantasy; dreamy, imaginative. **d.** Full of fancies or caprices; whimsical.

a. **1561** T. NORTON *Calvin's Inst.* II. xiv. (1634) 230 A fantasied Ghost is thrust in place of the Manhood. **1613** PURCHAS *Pilgrimage* VI. xi. 521 Phantasied dangers. **1960** I. BENNETT *Del. & Neur. Childr.* iii. 69 Lying to support fantasied exploits. **1963** *New Society* 21 Nov. 11/1 Fantasied wishes for power. **1969** *Sunday Times* (Colour Suppl.) 9 Feb. 9/3 A double image of marriage as stability, and unfulfilled romantic passion as the chivalric myth..kept socially chaste and fantasied longings in their proper place.

b. **1590** SIR J. SMYTH *Disc. Weapons* 2 b, These our such new fantasied men of warre. **1595** SHAKS. *John* IV. ii. 144, I finde the people strangely fantasied.

c. **1882** SHORTHOUSE *J. Inglesant* II. ii. 54 The alluring world of phantasied melody which Vanneo had composed.

d. **1883** C. F. WOOLSON *For the Major* iv, Mr. Dupont was conducting himself after his usual fantasied fashion.

†**fan'tasious,** *a. Obs. rare*$^{-1}$. In 5 **fantasyouse.** [a. OF. *fantasieus*, f. *fantasie*: see FANTASY *sb.* and -OUS.] Full of fancies, capricious.

c **1489** CAXTON *Blanchardyn* iii. 17 The dyuerse..conclusyons that his fantasyouse wylle dyde present by fore hym.

fantasist ('fæntəsɪst). [f. FANTASY + -IST.] One who 'weaves' fantasies.

1923 *Glasgow Herald* 10 May 6 Wilde, a chartered fantasist. **1927** E. M. FORSTER *Aspects of Novel* vi. 141 The other novelists say 'Here is something that might occur in your lives', the fantasist 'Here is something that could not occur'. **1928** *Observer* 1 Jan. 5/2 The Fantasists or Special Geniuses! *Ibid.* 2 Sept. 5 There is, I believe, no agreement among statisticians as to the number of H. G. Wells's. There are the sociologist and the fantasist and the novelist and the prophet. **1934** E. BOWEN *Cat Jumps* 190 Mrs. Letherton-Channing could countenance a diluted reality but could not suffer a fellow fantasist. **1960** *Guardian* 21 Sept. 7/1 Pictures that vary in mood between the poetry of a fantasist and the illusionism of a surrealist.

fantasize ('fæntəsaɪz), *v.* [f. FANTASY + -IZE.] **a.** *intr.* = FANTASY *v.* 1 c.

1926 *Spectator* 13 Mar. 455/2 Certainly one may fantasize to one's own taste. **1960** *Guardian* 28 Sept. 11/2 Only when they listened to each other could one fantasize about their mood.

b. *trans.* To visualize fancifully, to represent in the fancy.

1950 LONDON & CAPRIO *Sexual Deviations* xiii. 593, I used to put my penis between my legs so that nothing but the hair of the pubic region showed and would thus fantasize how my sister looked when I did the peeping. **1961** E. HUNTER *Mothers & Daughters* I. 59 The men were..fantasizing the entire crew in dress uniform. **1968** *Sunday Sun* (Baltimore) 3 Nov. D1/6, I always fantasized myself as a James Dean type.

Hence **'fantasized** *ppl. a.*

1964 *Spectator* 8 May 632/2 The manner and matter of these various charges seem to belong to his own fantasised world.

fantasm(a, etc.: see PHANTASM(A, etc.

fantasque (fæn'tæsk), *a.* and *sb.* Also 8 **fantask.** [a. Fr. *fantasque*:—L. *fantasticus.*]

A. *adj.* Fanciful, fantastic; curious. *rare.*

1701 C. BURNABY *Ladies Visiting Day* I. i, A clean Napkin and a plain Dish is my Feast; Garnish and Ornament are fantask. **1844** MRS. BROWNING *Poems, Drama Exile* I. 52 Twelve shadowy signs of earth, In fantasque apposition. *Ibid., Ho. Clouds* II. 226 The fantasque cloudlets.

†**B.** *sb.* Fancy, whim. *Obs.*

1698 VANBRUGH *Prov. Wife* III. iii, *Lady Brute*..There is not upon earth so impertinent a thing as women's modesty. *Belinda.* Yes, Men's Fantasque, that obliges us to it. **1703** STEELE *Tend. Husb.* II. i, I have a Scribbling Army-Friend, that..will hit the Nymph's Fantasque to a Hair.

fantassin ('fæntæsɪn). [a. Fr. *fantassin*, ad. It. *fantaccino*, dim. of *fante* foot-soldier.] (See quot. 1835.)

1835 LYTTON *Rienzi* IX. i, Two hundred fantassins, or foot-soldiers, of Tuscany. **1853** *Tait's Mag.* XX. 534 Fierce Isolani's fantassins. **1860** RUSSELL *Diary India* II. 253 Quaint fantassins with matchlock, musket, tulwar, and bow.

fantast, phantast ('fæntæst). [ad. med.L. *phantasta*, Gr. φανταστής, agent-n. f. φαντάζειν, φαντάζεσθαι. In Gr. the word meant (in accordance with the primary sense of the active verb) 'an ostentatious person, boaster': see next. Cf. Ger. *fantast, phantast*, which is the source of the modern use.]

1. A visionary, a dreamer; a flighty, impulsive person.

1588 J. H[ARVEY] *Disc. Probl.* 128 O vain Phantasts and fond Dotterels! **1804** COLERIDGE in *Lit. Rem.* (1836) II. 413 A quiet and sublime enthusiast with a strong tinge of the fantast. **1855** LEWES *Goethe* (1864) 494 She is one of those phantasts to whom everything seems permitted.

2. A fantastic writer; one who aims at eccentricity of style.

1873 F. HALL *Mod. Eng.* 171 Fantasts and contortionists like Mr. Carlyle.

fantastic (fæn'tæstɪk), *a.* and *sb.* Forms: *α.* 4 **fantastik,** 5–7 **fantastike, -tyke, -tique, -tyque,** 6–8 **fantastick(e,** 7– **fantastic.** *β.* 6–8 **phantastick(e,** 6 **phantastike,** 7 **phantastique.** 7– **phantastic.** [ad. med.L. *fantastic-us*, late L. *phantasticus*, a. Gr. φανταστικός, f. φαντάζειν to make visible (middle voice φαντάζεσθαι, in late Gr. to imagine, have visions): see FANTASY. Cf. Fr. *fantastique.*

The form *phantastic* is no longer generally current, but has been casually used by a few writers of the 19th c., to suggest associations connected with the Gr. etymology.]

A. *adj.*

1. †**a.** Existing only in imagination; proceeding merely from imagination; fabulous, imaginary, unreal (*obs*). **b.** In mod. use, of alleged reasons, fears, etc.: Perversely or irrationally imagined.

α. *a* **1387** TREVISA *Higden* (Rolls) V. 279 What is i-seide..of Merlyn has fantastik getynge. *Ibid.* VIII. 63 Kyng Arthures body [was founden] þat was i-counted as it were fantastik. **1529** MORE *Supplic. Soulys* Wks. 338 A very fantastike fable. **1627** F. E. *Hist. Edw. II* (1680) 11 His fantastique Happiness. **1721** SWIFT *South Sea* viii, He longs to rove in that fantastick scene. **1775** HARRIS *Philos. Arrangem.* Wks. (1841) 299 A fourth sort..may be called fantastic, or imaginary; such as centaurs. **1816** J. WILSON *City of Plague* I. i, I could smile at such fantastic terrors. **1876** M. ARNOLD *Lit. & Dogma* 157 His hearers and reporters were sure to verse it on their own fantastic grounds also.

β. **1678** CUDWORTH *Intell. Syst.* 481 All those other phantastick Gods, were nothing but Several Personal Names. **1742** YOUNG *Nt. Th.* i. 94 My soul phantastic measures trod O'er fairy fields.

†**2.** Pertaining to, or of the nature of, a phantasm. *Obs.*

α. **1483** CAXTON *Gold. Leg.* 19/2 He shewed that he was veryly rysen..by etyng openly, and by no art fantastyke. **1491** —— *Vitas Patr.* (W. de W. 1495) I. xlii. 68 a/1 [I am] noo thynge fantastyque, but a sparcle of fyre; Asshes, and flesshe. **1598** YONG *Diana* 127 A meere dreame, or some fantastick illusion. **1624** FLETCHER *Rule a Wife* IV. iii, Is not this a fantastic house we are in, And all a dream we do? **1648** BP. HALL *Rem. Wks.* (1660) 198 One will allow of his humanity..another will allow a divine soul with a fantastick body.

β. **1635** A. STAFFORD *Fem. Glory* (1869) 145 That He had a phantasticke Body, not made of his Mothers Flesh. **1691-8** NORRIS *Pract. Disc.* IV. 377 Aery Banquets, Phantastick Food. *a* **1716** SOUTH *Serm.* (1741) VII. 16 An aerial phantastic body.

†**3.** Of or pertaining to phantasy, in its various psychological senses (see FANTASY *sb.* 1, 4) as denoting either the faculty (and act) of apprehending sensible objects, or that of imagination; imaginative.

1483 CAXTON *Cato* F viij b, By cogytacyon or thynkyng fantastyke and by illusyon of the deuyll. **1592** DAVIES *Immort. Soul* xx. ii. (1599) 47 [Phantasie] in her Ballance doth their values trie, Where some things good, and som things il do seeme..in her phantasticke eye. **1649** JER. TAYLOR *Gt. Exemp.* Pref. ¶43 There is as much phantasticke pleasure in doing a spite, as in doing revenge. **1678** CUDWORTH *Intell. Syst.* 29 The different Phancies in us, caused by the respective Differences of them..Which Phancies or Phantastick Idea's are [etc.]. **1793** T. TAYLOR *Sallust* viii. 38 The irrational soul..is sensitive and phantastic life.

†**b.** Of poetry: Concerned with 'phantasy' (Gr. φαντασία) or illusory appearance. *Obs.*

[See Plato *Sophistes* xxiii, li. In quot. 1581 the word may be merely a transliteration of Gr. φανταστική.]

1581 SIDNEY *Apol. Poetrie* (Arb.) 54 Mans wit may make Poesie, (which should be *Eikastike*, which some learned haue defined, figuring foorth good things,) to be *Phantastike*: which doth contrariwise, infect the fancie with vnworthy obiects. **1669** GALE *Crt. Gentiles* I. III. i. 18 Phantastic Poesie is that, which altogether feigns things.

4. Of persons, their actions and attributes: †**a.** Having a lively imagination; imaginative (*obs.*). **b.** Fanciful, impulsive, capricious, arbitrary; also, foppish in attire. Now in stronger sense: Extravagantly fanciful, odd and irrational in behaviour.

α. **1488** CAXTON *Chast. Goddes Chyld.* xix. 50 Whether he haue a sadde knowyng or felinge or elles a soden wytte or fantastyk. **1591** SHAKS. *Two Gentl.* II. vii. 47 To be fantastique, may become a youth Of greater time then I shall shew to be. **1628** WITHER *Brit. Rememb.* II. 1 Let no fantastique Reader now condemne Our homely Muse. **1683** TRYON *Way to Health* 577 The..fantastique Directions of ignorant Physitians. *c* **1760** SMOLLETT *Ode to Indep.* 100 And all her jingling bells fantastic Folly ring. **1790** BURKE *Fr. Rev.* 312 The fantastick vagaries of these juvenile politicians. **1847** EMERSON *Repr. Men, Montaigne* Wks. (Bohn) I. 350 Great believers are always reckoned..impracticable, fantastic, atheistic.

β. **1600** E. BLOUNT tr. *Conestaggio* A iij b, He that talking of a young gentleman, shoulde say, that he was phantasticke, cholericke, amorous..doth hym no wrong. **1702** STEELE *Funeral* II, I have long..bore with your Phantastick Humour.

5. Arbitrarily devised. Now *rare.* Cf. FANCY *a.*

1658 BRAMHALL *Consecr. Bps.* iii. 29 They say..the..Protestant Bishops..were consecrated..by a new phantastick forme. **1846** TRENCH *Mirac.* i. (1862) 115 Phantastic and capricious miracles. **1876** HUMPHREYS *Coin-Coll. Man.* xxvi. 396 Occasionally fantastic variations of well-known inscriptions occur.

6. Having the appearance of being devised by extravagant fancy; eccentric, quaint, or grotesque in design, conception, construction, or adornment.

α. **1616** R. C. *Times' Whistle* III. 1077 Drusus, that fashion-imitating ape, Delights to follow each fantastic shape. **1728** YOUNG *Love Fame* iii. Wks. (1757) 107 The masquerade's fantastic scene! **1750** GRAY *Elegy* xxvi, Yonder nodding beech, That wreathes its old fantastic roots so high. **1841** SPALDING *Italy & It. Isl.* II. 221 Vaulted halls adorned with the usual fantastic arches. **1856** STANLEY *Sinai & Pal.* i. (1858) 30 The Arab traditions..are too fantastic to be treated seriously. **1871** B. TAYLOR *Faust* (1875) I. vi. 109 The witch with fantastic gestures draws a circle.

β. **1618** WITHER *Motto, Nec Curo*, Each phantastique Garb our Gallants weare. *a* **1713** ELLWOOD *Autobiog.* (1714) 242 Written in such an affected and phantastick stile.

b. Arbitrarily used by Milton for: Making 'fantastic' movements (in the dance); hence in later allusions to Milton's phrase. So in Comb. ***fantastic-footed.***

1632 MILTON *L'Allegro* 33 Trip it as you go On the light fantastic toe. *a* **1790** WARTON *On Approach of Summer* 59 Haste thee, Nymph! and hand in hand..Bring fantastic-footed Joy. **1826** DISRAELI *Viv. Grey* v. xv, Mr. St. Ledger..prided himself..on his light fantastic toe.

7. In trivial use: excellent, good beyond expectation. *colloq.*

1938 M. ALLINGHAM *Fashion in Shrouds* xi. 175 Oh, Val, isn't it *fantastic*?..It's amazing, isn't it? **1971** *New Statesman* 5 Feb. 176/3 A friend tells me of a recent experience..which really does rate that over-worked adjective, fantastic. **1973** *Brand New Monty Python Papperbok* (1986) 27 For the past seventeen weeks Janet has been on a fantastic package tour to Malaga. **1987** *Los Angeles Times* 5 Sept. v. 2/3 'Only..very nice?' he asked woefully. 'Oh, it's great! I mean, it's fantastic!'

B. *sb.*

1. One who has fanciful ideas or indulges in wild notions. *Obs.* exc. *arch.*

α. **1598** MARSTON *Pygmal.* III. 148 Thou art Bedlam mad..And glori'st to be counted a fantastick. **1621** QUARLES *Div. Poems, Esther* (1717) 111 Power..to perverse fantasticks if conferr'd..spurs on wrong. **1706** E. WARD *Hud. Rediv.* (1715) I. vii, The Church-men justly growl to see..that the Force of Toleration..Should set each canting proud Fantastick Above their Courts Ecclesiastick. **1882** SHORTHOUSE *J. Inglesant* II. xv, A Fantastic, whose brain was turned with monkish fancies.

β. **1630** BRATHWAIT *Eng. Gentl.* (1641) 3, I would be glad to weane this Phantasticke from a veine of lightnesse.

fig. **1675** G. R. tr. *Le Grand's Man Without Passion* 132 Opinion is the Fountain, this Fantastick which seduceth our understanding, etc.

†**2.** One given to fine or showy dress; a fop. *Obs.*

a **1613** OVERBURY *Charac.*, A Phantastique, An Improvident young Gallant. **1628** MILTON *Vacation Exerc.* 20 Trimming..which takes our late fantasticks with delight. *a* **1680** BUTLER *Rem.* (1759) II. 131 A Fantastic is one that wears his Feather on the Inside of his Head.

†**3.** A fanciful composition. *Obs.*

1641 G. H. (*title*), Wits Recreations, Containing..Variety of Fancies and Fantasticks.

†**4.** Power of fancy or imagination. *Obs.*

1764 *Public Advertiser* 31 May in *N. & Q.* 3rd Ser. IV. 385 It [Mozart's playing] surmounts all Fantastic and Imagination.

5. That which is fantastic, strange, eccentric or odd.

1908 *Daily Chron.* 17 Mar. 3/3 The tradition of the fantastic which has clung to the memory of Buckingham.

fantastical (fæn'tæstɪkəl), *a.* and *sb.* [f. FANTASTIC *a.* and *sb.* + -AL[1].] **A.** *adj.*

†**1.** = FANTASTIC *a.* 1. *Obs.*

a. *c* **1485** *Digby Myst.* (1882) IV. 1545 My wordes wer not fantasticall..I told youe no lesinge. **1529** MORE *Conf. agst. Trib.* II. Wks. 1182/2 With this fantastical fear of hers, I wold be loth to haue her in myne house. *c* **1530** *Pol. Rel. & L. Poems* (1866) 43 Than me thynkithe y see youre likenes: Hit is nat so, it is fantasticalle. *a* **1680** BUTLER *Rem.* (1759) I.

61 Our Pains are real Things, and all Our Pleasures but fantastical.

β. *a* **1533** FRITH *Disput. Purgat.* (1829) 160 A place that.. more properly confuteth this phantastical purgatory, than doth this same text. **1684** BURNET *Th. Earth* II. 100 When anything great is represented to us, it appears phantastical. **1728** T. SHERIDAN *Persius* vi. (1739) 99 *note*, Tertullian.. runs the phantastical Genealogy thus.

†**b.** Of opinions: Irrational, baseless. (Passing into sense 6.) *Obs.*

α. *a* **1546** JOYE in Gardiner *Declar. Art. Joye* (1546) 53 He ..conceyueth a certayne fantasticall opinion therof [of fayth]. **1711** SHAFTESB. *Charac.* (1737) II. I. III. §2. 52 Which only false Religion or fantastical Opinion.. is able to effect.

β. **1555** EDEN *Decades* Pref. to Rdr. (Arb.) 53 Mysshapened with phantastical opinions. **1599** HAYWARD *1st Pt. Hen. IV.* 91 He said that the lawes of the realme were in his head..by reason of which phantasticall opinion, he destroyed noblemen.

†**2.** = FANTASTIC 2. Chiefly in *fantastical body* in reference to the heresy of the Docetæ. *Obs.*

α. **1533** FRITH *Answ. More* (1829) 174 Fantastical apparitions. **1563–87** FOXE *A. & M.* (1684) III. 308 Ye make of it [the Sacrament] a thing so fantastical, that ye imagine a Body without Flesh. **1728** EARBERY tr. *Burnet's St. Dead* I. 220 That the Body of Christ upon Earth was a fantastical one, as the Gnosticks held.

β. **1555** RIDLEY *Wks.* 200 Marcion.. said that Christ had but a phantastical body. **1642** R. CARPENTER *Experience* II. vii. 185 Hee did not take a phantasticall body in the Incarnation.

†**b.** Of colours: = EMPHATICAL 5. *Obs.*

1666 HOOKE *Microgr.* 168 These colours are onely fantastical ones. **1704** J. HARRIS *Lex. Techn.*, *Phantastical Colours*, such as are exhibited by the Rainbow, Triangular Glass Prism, the Surface of very thin Muscovy Glass, &c.

†**3.** = FANTASTIC *a.* 3. *Obs.*

1526 *Pilgr. Perf.* (W. de W. 1531) 125 His lyghtes be euer eyther fantasticall or els corporall. **1589** PUTTENHAM *Eng. Poesie* I. viii. (Arb.) 35 Euen so is the phantasticall part of man..a representer of the best images..to the soule. **1647** H. MORE *Song of Soul* II. II. II. xxxv, The Orb Phantastick must exert All life phantasticall.

†**b.** Pertaining to the passion of love. See FANCY 8 b. *Obs. rare*⁻¹.

1594 H. WILLOBIE in *Shaks. C. Praise* 7 Sodenly infected with the contagion of a fantasticall fit.

4. = FANTASTIC 4.

α. **1531** ELYOT *Gov.* I. i, They be nat in commune (as fantasticall foles wolde haue all thyngs). **1589** WARNER *Alb. Eng.* VI. xxxi. (1612) 157 Loue is Fantasticall in Women. **1616** SURFL. & MARKH. *Country Farme* 671 The herne is.. very fantasticall, as not giuen to stay in any place, but such as pleaseth him verie well. **1702** *Eng. Theophrast.* 311 The gratifying of a fantastical Appetite. **1791** HAMILTON *Berthollet's Dyeing* II. II. vi. 307 The fantastical changes of the fashion. **1862** MRS. OLIPHANT *Last Mortimers* I. v. 27 A pretty fantastical young girl.

β. **1555** EDEN *Decades* 314 Many iudged hym phantasticall. **1621–51** BURTON *Anat. Mel.* II. iii. II. 319 An affected phantastical carriage. **1693** SIR T. P. BLOUNT *Nat. Hist.* 129 The..vain and phantastical abuse of this Stinking Weed. **1711** STEELE *Spect.* No. 30 ¶2 The Oxonians are phantastical now they are Lovers.

†**5.** = FANTASTIC 5. *Obs.*

a **1618** RALEIGH *Mahomet* (1637) 24 The care and use of his fantasticall Law.

6. = FANTASTIC 6.

α. **1599** SHAKS. *Much Ado* II. i. 79 The first suite is hot and hasty like a Scotch jigge (and full as fantasticall). **1789** BURNEY *Hist. Mus.* III. ii. 111 Canons..in triangular and other fantastical forms. **1830** D'ISRAELI *Chas. I*, III. viii. 177 A portrait which, however fantastical, may still bear some remarkable resemblances.

β. *a* **1613** OVERBURY *A Wife* (1638) 166 Our new phantasticall building. **1711** STEELE *Spect.* No. 151 ¶5 An Occasion wherein Vice makes so phantastical a Figure.

†**B.** *sb.* One who has fanciful ideas or notions.

1589 PUTTENHAM *Eng. Poesie* I. viii. (Arb.) 34 Who so is studious in th' Arte [of Poesie]..they call him in disdayne a phantasticall. **1616** J. DEACON *Tobacco tortured* 57 Alas poore Tobacco..thou that hast bene hitherto accompted.. the Fantasticals foretresse.

fantasticality (fæn,tæstɪˈkælɪtɪ). Also 7 **phan-**. [f. prec. + -ITY.] Fantastical character or quality; eccentricity, grotesqueness, oddity.

1592 G. HARVEY *Four Lett.* iii, An epitome of fantasticality. **1606** *Sir G. Goosecappe* III. i. in Bullen *O. Pl.* (1884) III. 43 Our Lords are as farr beyond them..for person..as they are beyond ours for phantasticality. **1824** *New Monthly Mag.* XII. 154 A little fantasticality here and there, but upon the whole exquisite! **1878** T. SINCLAIR *Mount* 275 He is not quite sure..about the fantasticality of these etymologies.

b. *concr.* and quasi-*concr.* Something that is fantastical; a crotchet, whim.

1631 R. H. *Arraignm. Whole Creature* xv. §3. 263 The Fantasticalites of their bodyes. **1840** CARLYLE *Heroes* (1858) 329 The Song he [Burns] sings is not of fantasticalities. **1858** CARLYLE *Fredk. Gt.* (1865) I. I. iii. 23 Ceremonials, and troublesome fantasticalities. **1887** SAINTSBURY *Hist. Elizab. Lit.* vii. 284 The graceful fantasticalities of Lyly.

fantastically (fænˈtæstɪkəlɪ), *adv.* Also 6–7 **phantastically**. [f. as prec. + -LY².]

†**1.** Through the exercise of the fancy or imagination. *Obs.*

1526 *Pilgr. Perf.* (W. de W. 1531) 124 b, Somtyme as it were an aungell of lyght: somtyme visybly, somtyme fantastically. **1691–8** NORRIS *Pract. Disc.* (1711) III. 121 My Soul fantastically joins with it.

†**2.** In a phantasmal or unreal manner. *Obs.*

1543 BECON *New Year's Gift* Early Wks. (1843) 318 All this was not fantastically done, but truly and unfeignedly. **1577** tr. *Bullinger's Decades* (1592) 64 Our Lord suffered in very deed, and not phantastically to the appearance onely.

†**3.** Fabulously, fictitiously. *Obs.*

1547 J. HARRISON *Exhort. Scottes* B viij a, As Welshe and Scottishe Poetes, haue phantastically fayned. **1577–87** HOLINSHED *Chron.* I. 91/1 Arthur, of whom the trifling tales of the Britains..fantasticallie do..report woonders.

4. According to one's fancy; capriciously, arbitrarily.

1547–64 BAULDWIN *Mor. Philos.* (Palfr.) 63 He cannot be a true seruer of God, which serueth Him..fantastically, and in hipocrisie. **1663** COWLEY *Disc. Govt. O. Cromwell* Wks. (1669) 59 Though it may seem to some fantastically, yet was it wisely done. **1701** GREW *Cosm. Sacra* II. iv, One cannot so much as fantastically choose, even or odd. **1829** I. TAYLOR *Enthus.* iv. (1867) 79 The righteous God deals with mankind not fantastically. **1885** *Law Times* LXXIX. 78/1 Any fantastically coined word.

5. In a fanciful or odd manner; grotesquely, oddly, strangely.

1597 SHAKS. *2 Hen. IV*, III. ii. 334 A forked Radish, with a Head fantastically caru'd vpon it. **1662** J. DAVIES *Voy. Ambass.* 129 Wooden hats, fantastically painted. **1796** MORSE *Amer. Geog.* I. 747 Beads and feathers, fantastically arranged. **1813** BYRON *Giaour* 302 The silver dew In whirls fantastically flew. **1852** MISS YONGE *Cameos* I. xlii. 365 Their dress was..fantastically gay.

fantasticalness (fænˈtæstɪkəlnɪs). Also 7 **phantasticalness**. [f. as prec. + -NESS.] The quality, condition, or fact of being fantastical.

†**1.** The condition of being subject to phantasms.

1547 BOORDE *Brev. Health* II. 27 Fantasticalnes, or collucion, or illusyons of the deuyll.

2. Addiction to strange fancies; eccentricity, oddity; an instance of this.

1581 MULCASTER *Positions* xlv. (1887) 297 Is that point in suspition of any noueltie or fantasticallnes to haue wymen learned? **1630** *R. Johnson's Kingd. & Commw.* 266 Their.. phantasticalnesse in apparall. **1653** H. COGAN tr. *Pinto's Trav.* lviii. 229 Six little Girls danced with six of the oldest men..which seemed to us a very pretty fantasticalness. *c* **1698** LOCKE *Cond. Underst.* §34 We are taught to cloath our minds..after the fashion in vogue, and it is accounted fantasticalness..not to do so. **1821** SOUTHEY in *Life* (1849) I. 39 Their mother was plainly crazed with hypochondriacism and fantasticalness. **1871** HAWTHORNE *Septimius* (1879) 119 The fantasticalness of his present pursuit.

3. Absurd unreality.

1847 DE QUINCEY *Schlosser's Lit. Hist.* Wks. VIII. 55 Chloes and Corydons—names that proclaim the fantasticalness of the life with which they are..associated.

†**4.** Capriciousness, whimsicality; waywardness.

1583 GOLDING *Calvin on Deut.* xxiii. 139 The wicked Fantasticalnesse of men in worshipping the sunne. **1678** OTWAY *Friendship in F.* IV. i. The fantasticalness of your appetite.

fantasticate (fænˈtæstɪkeɪt), *v.* [f. FANTASTIC + -ATE³.] †**a.** *trans.* To conceive or represent in the fancy; to fancy (*obs.*). **b.** *intr.* To frame fantastic notions. *rare.*

1600 F. WALKER *Sp. Mandeville* 66 a, Wee call the thinges ..which are fantasticated and represented in the fantasie, Fancies. **1624** DARCIE *Birth of Heresies* xii. 53 Brunus.. fantasticates, that by the Maniple is inferred the Messalian Priests speciall care to driue away bad affections. **1880** VERN. LEE *Belcaro* x. 282 Instead of enjoying, we fantasticate in theory.

c. *trans.* To render fantastic.

1936 P. FLEMING *News from Tartary* 19 Half a dozen pierrettes and apaches..suitably fantasticated our unserious departure. **1962** *Listener* 5 July 4/1 We had a terrific opportunity in the nineteenth century to elaborate and fantasticate our social structure. **1966** *Punch* 16 Mar. 393/2 The novel..gives an amusing account, duly fantasticated, of his arrival in London.

Hence **fanˈtasticated** *ppl. a.*; **fanˈtasticating** *vbl. sb.*

1880 VERN. LEE *Belcaro* vii. 179 His subtle and fantasticating style of art. **1892** *Pall Mall G.* 7 Jan. 3/1 This illimitable fantasticating in a vacuum. **1960** *Guardian* 16 June 8/3 Highly fantasticated, and sustained with brilliantly executed tricks. **1964** W. GOLDING *Spire* vi. 124 The fantasticated, eight foot fall of the lights. **1971** *Daily Tel.* 15 Apr. 6/8 Mr West has a racy, impressionistic, fantasticated style that is most engaging.

fantastiˈcation [f. FANTASTICATE *v.* + -ION¹]

a. Fantastic speculation. **b.** = PHANTASTRY a.

1880 VERN. LEE *Belcaro* i. 13 All the wonderful fantastications of art philosophers. **1929** C. MORGAN *Portrait in Mirror* iv. 211 Richard..would laugh, too, at my folly and be unable to consider it as anything but a boy's fantastication of life. **1931** *Punch* 28 Oct. 471/2 Mr Alan Napier had a well-written part in the *Venetian Ambassador* and brought the man to life, his habitual fantastications being reasonably in the picture. **1955** *Times* 15 July 4/4 His gay fantastication of nature in delicate pinks and greens of a truly theatrical effect plays a great part in the preposterous idyll of the lovers' day in the country. This fantastication includes all sorts of recklessly idiotic birds and snails and kite-flying cows. **1969** *Daily Tel.* 23 July 19/1 This scene comes off well. There is a regrettable lack of high elegance, of aristocratic fantastication, in the proceedings.

fantasticism (fænˈtæstɪsɪz(ə)m). [f. as FANTASTICATE *v.* + -ISM.]

†**1.** The doctrine that there is no objective reality; subjectivism. *Obs.*

a **1688** CUDWORTH *Immut. Morality* IV. vi. (1731) 286 But I have not taken all this Pains only to Confute Scepticism or Phantasticism.

2. The following of arbitrary fancy in art or speculation.

1846 RUSKIN *Mod. Paint.* I. II. VI. i. §14 In all the trees of the merely historical painters, there is..fantasticism and unnaturalness of arrangement. **1868** J. H. STIRLING in *N. Brit. Rev.* Dec. 382 Speculation..without experiment, yields phantasticism.

†**fanˈtasticize**, *v.* *Obs. rare*⁻¹. In 7 **fantastiquize**. [f. FANTASTIC *a.* + -IZE.] *intr.* To throw oneself into fantastic or strange attitudes.

1603 FLORIO *Montaigne* II. iii. (1632) 193 To rave and fantastiquize, as I doe, must necessarily be to doubt.

†**fanˈtasticly**, *adv.* *Obs.* = FANTASTICALLY.

1599 B. JONSON *Cynthia's Rev.* II. i, He is neither too fantastickly melancholy, or too rashly cholerick. **1619** DRAYTON *Idea* Ded., A Libertine! fantasticly I sing!

fanˈtasticness. Now *rare.* [f. FANTASTIC *a.* + -NESS.] = FANTASTICALNESS.

1549 *Compl. Scot.* Prol. 16 Al sic termis procedis of fantastiknes ande glorius consaitis. **1661** PRYNNE *Exam. Exuberances Bk. Com. Prayer* 31 To adorn our Bodies in a modest..manner; without..fantastickness. **1825** LD. COCKBURN *Mem.* (1860) 78 When looking at an Oak-tree, you dwell..on the Fantasticness of the Branches.

†**fanˈtastico.** *Obs.* [It.; corresp. to FANTASTIC.] An absurd and irrational person.

1597 SHAKS. *Rom. & Jul.* II. iv. 30 (Qo. 1) Limping antique affecting fantasticoes [*fol.* 1623 *ed.* phantacies] these new tuners of accents. **1600** DEKKER *Fortunatus* Wks. 1873 I. 117, I have..seene fantasticoes.

†**fantastry**, obs. var. PHANTASTRY.

fantasy, phantasy (ˈfæntəsɪ), *sb.* Forms: *α.* 4–7 **fantasi(e, -ye, -azie, -aisie, -aysie, -esi(e, -esy(e, -essy, (5 fantsy, fayntasie, feintasy), 5–6 fantosy, 6–7 fantacie, -y,** 4– **fantasy**. *β.* 6– 8 **phantasie**, (6 **-esie**, 6–7 **phant'sie, -'sy**), 6– **phantasy**. [a. OF. *fantasie* (Fr. *fantaisie*), (= Pr. *fantazia*, Sp., Pg. *fantasia*, It. *fantasia*), ad. L. *phantasia*, a. Gr. φαντασία lit. 'a making visible', f. φαντάζειν to make visible, f. φαίνειν to show.

The senses of φαντασία from which the senses of the word in the mod. langs. are developed are: 1. appearance, in late Gr. esp. spectral apparition, phantom (so L. *phantasia* in Vulg.); 2. the mental process or faculty of sensuous perception; 3. the faculty of imagination. These senses passed through OF. into Eng., together with others (as delusive fancy, false or unfounded notion, caprice, etc.) which had been developed in late L., Romanic, or Fr. The shortened form FANCY, which apparently originated in the 15th c., had in the time of Shakspere become more or less differentiated in sense. After the revival of Greek learning, the longer form was often spelt *phantasy*, and its meaning was influenced by the Gr. etymon. In mod. use *fantasy* and *phantasy*, in spite of their identity in sound and in ultimate etymology, tend to be apprehended as separate words, the predominant sense of the former being 'caprice, whim, fanciful invention', while that of the latter is 'imagination, visionary notion'.]

1. In scholastic psychology: †**a.** Mental apprehension of an object of perception; the faculty by which this is performed. *Obs.*

[*a* **1382** ORESME in Meunier *Ess. sur Oresme* 179 Il entent par fantasie apprehension ou cognoissance sensitive des choses presentes.]

α. *c* **1400** *Lanfranc's Cirurg.* 113 þat place [þe brayn] is propre instrument of ymagynacioun þe which resceyveþ þinges þat comprehendiþ of fantasie [*res a phantasia comprehensas*]. **1509** HAWES *Past. Pleas.* XXIV. ii, These are the v. wyttes remeuing inwardly..common wytte.. ymaginacyon, Fantasy, and estymacyon..And memory. **1675** BAXTER *Cath. Theol.* II. I. 76 Sense perceiveth sweetness by tast or smell, light and pulchritude by sight and fantasie.

β. *a* **1618** RALEIGH *Rem.* (1664) 126 According to the diversity of the eye, which offereth it unto the phantasie. **1655–60** STANLEY *Hist. Philos.* (1701) 478/2 It is..likely, that all living Creatures which have Eye-balls oblique and narrow..have a peculiar phantasie of Objects. **1669** A. BROWNE *Ars Pict.* (1675) 40 Light..is the cause..whereby coloured things are seen, whose Shapes and Images pass to the phantasie.

†**b.** The image impressed on the mind by an object of sense. *Obs.*

c **1340** HAMPOLE *Prose Tr.* (1866) 14 When the resone es cleryde fra all..fygours and fantasyes of creatures. **1596** CAREW *Huarte's Exam. Wits* xi. 155 Memorie supplieth none other office..than..to preserue the figures and fantasies of things.

†**2.** A spectral apparition, phantom; an illusory appearance. *Obs.*

c **1325** *Song of Yesterday* 30 in *E.E.P.* (1862) 134 þis worldly blis. Is but a fykel fantasy. **1398** TREVISA *Barth. De P.R.* IX. xxv. (1495) 362 Moo fantasyes ben seen by nyghte than by daye. **1401** *Pol. Poems* (Rolls) II. 46 Somme fantasie of Fiton hath marrid thi mynde. *c* **1425** WYNTOUN *Cron.* VI. xviii. 31 þe fantasy þus of hys Dreme Movyd hym mast to sla hys Eme. **1530** PALSGR. 172 *Phantosme*, a fantosy. *a* **1533** LD. BERNERS *Huon* xxi. 64 All is but fantesey and enchauntementes. **1535** STEWART *Cron. Scot.* III. 365 Trowand that tyme it wes ane phantasie. *a* **1583** GRINDAL *Fruitful Dial.* Wks. (1843) 59 No bread..but certain fantasies of white and round.

3. a. Delusive imagination, hallucination; the fact or habit of deluding oneself by imaginary perceptions or reminiscences. ? *Obs.*

α. **1340–70** *Alisaunder* 384 For fere, ne fantasie faile they nolde. *c* **1374** CHAUCER *Troylus* V. 1535 This fool of fantasie [*sc.* Cassandra]. **1574** R. SCOT *Hop Gard.* (1578) 60 Such as haue Mountaynes in fantasie and beggery in possession. **1602** SHAKS. *Ham.* I. i. 54 You tremble and look pale: Is not

this something more then Fantasie? **1658** S. SIMPSON *Unbelief* ix. 66 They thought it was but meer fantasie and imagination.

β. *a* **1533** FRITH *Disput. Purgat.* (1829) 83 Making..the elders..to wander in phantasies. **1654** *Case of Commonwealth* 50 If we falter, or be mis-led through phant'sie. **1675** BROOKS *Signal Presence of God* 20 Raising such a phantasy in the Lyons that they looked upon Daniel ..as on one that was a friend unto them. **1753** SMOLLETT *Ct. Fathom* (1784) 11/1 He will..be sometimes misled by his own phantasy.

b. A day-dream arising from conscious or unconscious wishes or attitudes.

1926 G. COSTER *Psycho-Analysis* ii. 35 The term *phantasy* is much used in analytical psychology, and the fact that its technical meaning differs subtly from its colloquial one leads to some confusion. A phantasy is a day-dream in which desire, unfulfilled in the world of reality, finds an imaginary fulfilment or satisfaction. **1957** P. LAFITTE *Person in Psychol.* ix. 120 The Rorschach test invites him to enact his very vaguest fantasies, as when he sees pictures in the fire or on the wall.

4. a. Imagination; the process or the faculty of forming mental representations of things not actually present. (Cf. FANCY *sb.* 4.) Also *personified*. Now usually with sense influenced by association with *fantastic* or *phantasm*: Extravagant or visionary fancy.

In early use not clearly distinguished from 3; an exercise of poetic imagination being conventionally regarded as accompanied by belief in the reality of what is imagined.

α. **1589** GREENE *Menaphon* (Arb.) 41 The Idea of her person represents it selfe an object to my fantasie. **1602** MARSTON *Ant. & Mel.* III. Wks. 1856 I. 35 The soules swift Pegasus, the fantasie. *a* **1631** DONNE *Elegie* Poems (1633) 153 When you are gone, and Reason gone with you, Then Fantasie is Queene. **1831** CARLYLE *Sart. Res.* (1858) 52 Ever in my distresses..has Fantasy turned, full of longing to that unknown Father. **1870** LOWELL *Among my Bks.* Ser. I. (1873) 176 Imagination, as it is too often misunderstood, is mere fantasy, the image-making power common to all who have the gift of dreams.

β. **1553** T. WILSON *Rhet.* (1567) 17 a, Nature is a righte that phantasie hath not framed. **1672–3** MARVELL *Reh. Transp.* II. 130 You have attracted by force of phantasy some extraordinary Spirit to your assistance. **1704** NEWTON *Opticks* I. II. viii. 120 By the power of phantasy we see Colours in a Dream. **1831** LYTTON *Godolph* xxvii, Volktman himself, in the fulness of his northern phantasy, [could not] have sculptured forth a better image. **1837–8** SIR W. HAMILTON *Logic* ii. (1870) III. 22 We may view it in phantasy as black or white. **1855** MILMAN *Lat. Chr.* (1864) IX. XIV. vii 258 *note*, Their union with the Deity was.. through the phantasy.

b. A mental image.

1823 LAMB *Elia* Ser. I. *Grace before meat*, To the temperate fantasies of the famished Son of God. *a* **1853** ROBERTSON *Serm.* Ser. III. vi. 81 Our creative shaping intellect projected its own fantasies. **1876** GEO. ELIOT *Dan. Der.* VI. xlviii, Fantasies moved within her like ghosts.

c. A product of imagination, fiction, figment.

1362 LANGL. *P. Pl.* A. I. 36 Iapers and Iangelers.. Founden hem fantasyes. **1399** *Pol. Poems* (Rolls) I. 371 If ȝe ffynde ffables or ffoly ther amonge, or ony ffantasie yffeyned that no ffrute is in. **1688** R. HOLME *Armoury* III. 147/1 Centaurs, Satyrs, Griffins, &c. [are] Forced Figures.. Fiction or Fantacy..to express a Novelty.

d. An ingenious, tasteful, or fantastic invention or design.

α. *c* **1440** *Gesta Rom.* xxxii. 123 (Harl. MS.) A silkyne gyrdil, sotilly i-made; for the damyselle comunely lovithe swiche fantasys. **1542** RECORDE *Gr. Artes* (1561) Y vj a, Some questions of thys rule maye be varied above 1000 waies; but I would have you forget suche fantasies, tyll a time of more leysure. **1848** DICKENS *Dombey* xxiii, There was a monstrous fantasy of rusty iron.

β. **1542–3** *Act 34–5 Hen. VIII*, c. 1 Balades, plaies, rimes, songes, and other phantasies. **1821** KEATS *Isabel* xlvii, A soiled glove, whereon Her silk had played in purple phantasies.

e. *esp.* in *Music*; a fantasia. (Cf. 6.)

1597 MORLEY *Introd. Mus.* 181 The..chiefest kind of musick which is made without a dittie is the fantasie, that is, when a musician taketh a point at his pleasure, and wresteth and turneth it as he list. **1674** PLAYFORD *Skill Mus.* I. x. 34 This is called the Dupla or Semibreve Time..its Mood..is usual in Anthems, Fantasies, &c.

f. A genre of literary compositions.

1949 (*title*) The Magazine of Fantasy and Science Fiction. **1954** M. F. RODELL *Mystery Fiction* ii. 4 Mysteries belong to the vast category of escape fiction. Westerns, 'romances', historical novels, and fantasies (other than satires) all belong in the same category. **1955** F. BROWN *Angels & Spaceships* 9 Fantasy deals with things that are not and cannot be. Science fiction deals with things that can be, that some day may be.

5. a. A supposition resting on no solid grounds; a whimsical or visionary notion or speculation.

Now more emphatically contemptuous than FANCY *sb.*

α. *c* **1400** *Destr. Troy* 2669 His olde fader fantasi þai filet in hert. *c* **1440** *Generydes* 4652 Leve all these fantesies..ye shall not fynde it thus. **1526** *Pilgr. Perf.* (W. de W. 1531) 166 b, The mynde..is moost apte to..wauerynge fantasyes aboute dyuerse thynges. **1665** MANLEY *Grotius' Low C. Warres* 953 The Minds of the common People would be divided, according as any one would teach his Fantasies. **1876** WHITNEY *Sights & Ins.* II. xiv. 443 All that would be to them less than fancy—mere fantasy. **1878** MORLEY *Vauvenargues* Crit. Misc. 20 Many pernicious and destructive fantasies.

β. **1586** COGAN *Haven Health* ccxliii. (1636) 306 Vaine.. is their phantasie that thinke it ungodly to flee from..the plague. *a* **1610** HEALEY *Epictetus Man.* (1636) 30 Keepe thy minde firme against all such phantasies. **1858** R. A. VAUGHAN *Ess. & Rev.* I. 6 Not a phantasy in religion..but might there soar or flutter.

†**b.** *in my fantasy*: = 'as I imagine'; modestly used for 'in my opinion'. *Obs.*

α. **1543** RECORDE *Gr. Artes* (1561) L j, And yet in my simple fantasy these thinges offer them-selves..to be studied for aboute progression. **1570–6** LAMBARDE *Peramb. Kent* (1826) 191 In mine own fantasie it wanteth not the feete of sound reason to stand upon.

β. **1570–6** LAMBARDE *Peramb. Kent* (1826) 237 There standeth a Towne yet called Sturmere, which (in my phantasie) sufficiently mainteineth the knowledge of this matter.

6. Caprice, changeful mood; an instance of this; a caprice, whim. †Often in *at, after, according to, upon one's own fantasy* (*obs.*).

α. *a* **1450** *Knt. de la Tour* 23 Alle good women..aught to leve all suche fantasyes. **1490** CAXTON *Eneydos* vi. 25 His wyf ..he loued..of fyne loue wythout fayntasie. **1519** *Interl. Four Elem.* in Hazl. *Dodsley* I. 7 Every man after his fantasy Will write his conceit. **1598** BARRET *Theor. Warres* V. i. 146 Whosoeuer shall kill his souldier vpon his owne fantasie, without iust cause. **1649** MILTON *Eikon.* xi. (1851) 420 The Kingdom..must depend in great exigencies upon the fantasie of a Kings reason. **1679–1714** BURNET *Hist. Ref.*, It was..out of no light fantasy..that he thus refused it. **1814** SCOTT *Ld. of Isles* VI. xvii, Fate plays her wonted fantasy.. with thee and me. **1883** C. F. WOOLSON *For the Major* iv, Little ways..considered to belong to the 'fantasies of genius'.

β. **1548** HALL *Chron.* 137 b, The Dolphyn tooke upon hym, the rule..orderyng causes..after his awne.. phantasie. **1624** CAPT. SMITH *Virginia* III. v. 55 Our strength and labours were idely consumed to fulfill his phantasies.

†**7.** Inclination, liking, desire. *Obs.*

α. *c* **1374** CHAUCER *Former Age* 51 The lambyssh poeple.. Hadden no fantesye to debate. *c* **1386** —— *Miller's T.* 5 Al his fantasye Was torned for to lerne astrologye. *c* **1450** *Merlin* 213 Soche a fantasie fill in his herte that he cowde not it remeve. **1462** *Paston Lett.* No. 435 II. 83 If..ther be sent swhyche downe to tak a rewyll as the pepyll hathe a fantsy in. **1535** STEWART *Cron. Scot.* II. 158 Throw fantasie of this Roxiana, Of hir sic plesour he had. **1599** HAKLUYT *Voy.* I. 4 He fell into a fantasie and desire to..know how farre that land stretched. *a* **1618** RALEIGH *Rem.* (1644) 83 Every man prefers his fantasie in that appetite, before all other worldly desires.

β. **1563–87** FOXE *A. & M.* (1596) 65/1 Diuerse men [worship] diuerse gods; so as euerie one hath in himselfe a mind or phantasie to worship.

8. *attrib.* and *Comb.*, as *fantasy-building* vbl. sb. and ppl. a.; *fantasy-life, -world.*

1938 *Tablet* 1 Jan. 20/2 Now it is very strange that these judgments of her contemporaries should fit in so exactly with the present day estimate of Teresa as a fantasy-building neurotic.., unable at times to distinguish between imaginative and objective reality. **1959** H. READ *Conc. Hist. Mod. Painting* vii. 287 An immense effort to rid the mind of that corruption which, whether it has taken the form of fantasy-building or repression..constitutes a false witness to sensation or experience. **1937** 'M. INNES' *Hamlet, Revenge!* i. 12 They have their tenure in remaining—remote, jewelled and magical—a focus for the fantasy-life of thousands. **1960** C. DAY LEWIS *Buried Day* 22 It is said that an only child develops a particularly vivid fantasy-life. **1920** T. P. NUNN *Education* vii. 83 Prefers his fantasy-world to reality. **1955** A. C. SMITH *Speaking Eye* vi. 63 The other chairs were littered with film magazines... The fantasy world of sex.

fantasy ('fæntəsɪ), *v.* Forms: *α.* 5–7 **fantasie, -ye,** 5–6 **fantesye,** 6 **fantase, -aise,** 7 **fant'sy,** 5– **fantasy.** *β.* 6–7 **phantasie, -y,** (6 **phantasey,** 7 **phantacy, -zy**), 9 **phantasy.** [a. OF. *fantasie-r*, f. *fantasie* FANTASY *sb.*]

1. a. *trans.* = FANCY *v.* 1; rarely, *to fantasy with oneself.*

c **1430** LYDG. *Bochas* Prol. 3 Men of craft may..Fantasien in their inward sight Devises newe. **1543** GRAFTON *Contn. Harding* 496 Dreames..his awne feare fantesieth. **1547–8** *Ordre of Communion* 1 Euery manne phantasying and deuisyng a sondery waie by hymself. **1563–87** FOXE *A. & M.* (1684) II. 23/1 It was not the same very present Body of Christ, as the Priests did phantasie. *a* **1577** SIR T. SMITH *Commw. Eng.* (1609) 5 As wise men have..fantasied foure simple bodies which they call elements. **1603** KNOLLES *Hist. Turks* (1621) 182 The image of the yong gentleman was well phantazied in her brain. **1818** KEATS *Endym.* 509 A dream.. so phantasied. **1855** MOTLEY *Dutch Rep.* II. 17 He fantasied in his imagination a kind of religion, half Catholic, half Reformed. **1949** M. MEAD *Male & Female* xii. 262 Behind that schoolgirl complexion..could be phantasied many sorts of conditions. **1960** *20th Cent.* Dec. 519 It is ludicrous to fantasy 'disinventing' the hydrogen bomb. **1970** *New Society* 31 Dec. 1157/1 The long-termers only occasionally fantasy or talk with each other about various styles of 'making-out' on release.

b. with *obj.* and *inf.* or object clause.

1430 LYDG. *Chron. Troy* I. ii, Day by day cast and fantesyeth How his venim may..Upon this Jason be fully execute. **1562** TURNER *Herbal* II. 51 a, Som dyd phantasey one thyng to be the cause and som an other. **1582** BENTLEY *Mon. Matrones* 77 Fantasing with themselves that I doo it.. of hatred. **1661** BOYLE *Style of Script.* 51 The Syrian Leper ..vainly fant'sied, that Gods appointment could not put a difference between things that knew no other.

c. *absol.* or *intr.*

1548 UDALL, etc. *Erasm. Par. John* x. 13 He fantasieth thus; In case thei go to wracke, what than?

†**2.** *trans.* To wear the appearance (φαντασία) of. *Obs. rare*⁻¹.

c **1611** CHAPMAN *Iliad* XXIII. 60 At every part the form did comprehend His likeness; his fair eyes, his voice, his stature, every weed His person wore, it fantasied.

†**3.** To take a fancy or liking to; to be favourably inclined to; to fall in love with. Also with *inf.*, to 'take it into one's head' (to do something). Cf. FANCY *v.* 8. *Obs.*

1548 HALL *Chron.* 194 b, He..favored her suyte, but muche more phantasied her person. **1553** T. WILSON *Rhet.* 4 b, As if one should phantasy to praise a Gose before any other beast. **1592** WARNER *Alb. Eng.* VII xxxiv. (1612) 168 Death, late feared, now she fantaseth. **1641** PRYNNE *Antip.* 79 That he [the King] should neither phantacy nor regard the serious Petition of the importunate Commons.

absol. **1560** BECON *Treat. Fasting* xi. Wks. II. 89 b, Nether do they direct their fastes vnto any godly end, but as euery one fantasieth, so do they fast.

4. *intr.* To play fantasias; to extemporize. *rare* (but often in Carlyle).

1840 CARLYLE *Wks.* (1858) II. 323 He [Hoffmann] could fantasy to admiration on the harpsichord. **1858** —— *Fredk. Gt.* II. x. vi. 650 Fantasying on the flute in an animated strain.

Hence **'fantasying** *vbl. sb.*

1543 RECORDE *Gr. Artes* (1561) Z v b, You should..not have taken a question of your owne fantasying. **1555** L. SAUNDERS *Let.* in Coverdale *Lett. Martyrs* (1564) 184 The fantasing of the flesh-pottes of Egypte. **1607** *Schol. Disc. agst. Antichrist* II. ix. 135 We are charged with a Corinthian fantasying of mens persons. **1932** O. D. LEAVIS *Fiction & Reading Public* I. iii. 54 A habit of fantasying will lead to maladjustment in actual life. **1960** I. BENNETT *Del. & Neur. Childr.* iii. 69 'Bouts' of lying and fantasying to get other boys into trouble.

fantekyn, var. f. FAUNTEKIN *Obs.*

†**'fanterie.** *Obs.* [a. OF. *fanterie*, ad. It. *fanteria* f. *fante* foot-soldier (literally boy, short for *infante* = INFANT cf. FAUNT).] Infantry; *pl.* foot-soldiers.

a **1577** GASCOIGNE *Fruits War* clii. in *Wks.* (1587) 146 Fiue ..bands of English Fanteries. **1601** HOLLAND *Pliny* I. 128 Trusting vpon their Cauallery and Fanterie, wherein they are strong.

Fanti ('fæntɪ), *sb.* and *a.* Also **Fante, Fantee.** [Native name.] The name of a Negro people inhabiting Ghana, and their language; a member of this people. Also *attrib.*

1819 T. E. BOWDICH *Mission to Ashantee* 344, I have heard about half a dozen words in the Fantee, which might be said to be not unlike the same nouns in the Welsh language. *Ibid.* 345 The Fantee word *umpa* (*true, indeed*). [**1868** CARR & BROWN (*title*) Mfantsi grammar.] **1875** [see ASHANTI]. **1879** *Encycl. Brit.* X. 756/1 Fante dialects are spoken, not only in Fanti proper, but in Afutu or the country round Cape Coast. *Ibid.*, A Fanti..can converse without much difficulty with a native of Aquapem or Ashantee. *Ibid.*, The Aquapem, which is based on the Akem but has imbibed Fanti influences. **1923** [see AKAN *a.* and *sb.*]. **1955** P. STREVENS *Papers in Lang.* (1965) ix. 115 The Kwa Larger Unit, comprising such languages as Twi, Ga, Fante, Ewe, Yoruba and Ibo. **1962** [see ASHANTI].

b. Phr. *to go fantee*: to join the natives of a district and conform to their habits.

1885 KIPLING *Departmental Ditties* (1886) 59 'Went Fantee'—joined the people of the land. Turned three parts Mussalman and one Hindu. **1887** —— *Plain Tales fr. Hills* (1888) 23 He was perpetually 'going Fantee' among natives. **1906** *Daily Chron.* 9 Aug. 8/5 Caluna, too, had 'gone fanti', and was raiding and pillaging. **1930** CHESTERTON *Four Felons* 190 He was a white man, or whitish man, who had gone fantee, and wore nothing but a pair of spectacles.

fantigue (fæn'tiːg). *dial.* Also **fanteag(ue, fanteeg, fantique.** [Cf. FANTAD.] A state of anxiety or excitement; an instance of this, *esp.* a fit of ill-humour.

1825 *Univ. Songster* ii. 142 Don't put yourselves in a fantique. **1837** DICKENS *Pickw.* xxxviii, 'Involving our precious governor in all sorts o' fanteegs.' **1866** MRS. H. WOOD *Elster's Folly* I. v. 117 You need not have put yourself in a fantigue. **1879** MISS JACKSON *Shropsh. Word-bk.*, The Missis is in a pretty fantaig. **1882** *W. Worcestersh. Gloss.*, 'E's allus on with some uv 'is fanteagues.'

‖**fantoccini** (fantot'tʃini). Also 8 **fantocine,** 9 *vulgar* **fantosceny.** [It. pl. of *fantoccino*, dim. of *fantoccio* puppet, f. *fante* boy, servant, etc.: see FANTERIE.]

1. *pl.* Puppets made to go through certain evolutions by means of concealed strings or wires.

1791 BOSWELL *Johnson* (1816) I. 396 The exhibition of the Fantoccini in London. **1842** DICKENS *Amer. Notes* (1850) 60/1 Are there no Punches, Fantoccini, Dancing dogs..or even Barrel-organs? **1876** BESANT & RICE *Gold. Butterfly* xxx. (1884) 227 As awkward as a pair of fantoccini.

2. A dramatic representation in which these are the performers; a marionette show.

1771 MRS. J. HARRIS in *Priv. Lett. Ld. Malmesbury* (1870) I. 212, I was much pleased with the 'Fantocine' I saw last night. **1817** MAR. EDGEWORTH *Harrington* (1832) 132 He had refused to go..to the Fantoccini. **1851** MAYHEW *Lond. Labour* (1861) III. 60 'The Fantoccini', he said, is the proper title of the exhibition of dancing dolls.

attrib. **1817** HAZLITT *Char. Shaks.* (1838) 220 The fantoccini exhibition. **1822** —— *Table-t.* II. xii. 274 A little fantoccini figure..playing a number of fantastic tricks before the audience.

fantod ('fæntæd). Also **fantad.** [? An unmeaning formation suggested by FANTASTIC, FANTASY, etc.: cf. *fantigue.*] A crotchety way of acting; a fad.

1839 C. F. BRIGGS *Adv. H. Franco* I. 249 You have got strong symptoms of the fantods. **1867** SMYTH *Sailor's Word-bk.*, *Fantods*, a name given to the fidgets of officers. **1880** MRS. PARR *Adam & Eve* xxxii. 440 I'd do the trick, if

I was she, 'fore I'd put up with such fantads from you. **1881** *Leicestersh. Gloss., Fantodds*, 'megrims', 'mulligrubs', a stomach-ache; a fit of the sulks or other slight indisposition, mental or bodily. **1884** 'MARK TWAIN' *Huck. Finn* xvii, These was all nice pictures,..but I didn't somehow seem to take to them, because..they always give me the fan-tods. **1886** BARNES *Dorset Dial.* 63 *Fantod*, a fuss, fidget. 'She's always in a fantod about Meary'. **1910** *Sat. Westm. Gaz.* 1 Jan. 6/1 Sundays inside of a house gives you the fan-tods. **1920** GALSWORTHY *In Chancery* I. v, You mustn't get into a fantod, it'll never do. **1935** J. MASEFIELD *Box of Delights* viii. 220 'I say,' Kay said, 'what a place!' 'It gives me the fantods,' Peter answered. 'I don't like the place.'

Hence **'fantod** *a.*, Fidgetty, restless.

1887 in *Kent Gloss.* **1883** W. C. RUSSELL *Sailor's Lang., Fantod*, A fiddling officer who is always bothering over small things.

fantom, obs. form of PHANTOM.

fanzine ('fænzi:n). orig. *U.S.* [f. FAN *sb.*² + MAGA)ZINE.] A magazine for fans, esp. those of science fiction.

1949 *New Republic* 17 Jan. 16 *Fantasy Commentator*, perhaps the best of the fanzines, once ran a history of fan magazines. **1950** *N.Y. Times* 7 May VII. 26/4 The fantasy writers..now in California..are busily forming societies, printing and circulating special fan magazines—'fanzines' is the term. **1951** [see *fan magazine* s.v. FAN *sb.*² 2]. **1957** P. MOORE *Science & Fiction* 90 So much for the official science-fiction magazines... There remain the amateur publications, known as 'fanzines'.

faon, obs. form of FAWN.

†**fap**, *a. Obs.* Drunk, intoxicated.

1598 SHAKS. *Merry W.* I. i. 183 The Gentleman had drunke himselfe out of his fiue sentences..And being fap, sir, was (as they say) casheerd. **1818** J. BROWN *Psyche* 44 Getting daily fap with ale.

fapes: see FEABERRY *dial.*, gooseberry.

fapesmo (fɑ:'pɛzməʊ). *Logic.* A mnemonic word for that supposed indirect mood of the first figure of syllogisms in which the major premiss is universal and affirmative, the minor universal and negative, and the conclusion particular and negative. (Later seen to be, by changing the order of the premisses, the fourth-figure mood FESAPO.)

1599 BLUNDEVIL *Logike* 121 Barbara: Celarent: Darii: Ferio: Baralipton Celantes: Dabitis: Fapesmo: Frisesomorum. **1685, 1849** [see DABITIS]. **1884** J. N. KEYNES *Formal Logic* III. iv. 199 Similarly Fapesmo and Frisesomorum (the Fesapo and Fresison of Figure 4) have no corresponding direct moods.

faquir, var. of FAKIR.

‖**far**, *sb. Obs.* [Latin.] A coarse kind of wheat; spelt.

c **1420** *Pallad. on Husb.* XII. 1 Novembre wol with whete & far besowe. **1601** HOLLAND *Pliny* II. 138 As for the bearded wheat Far, there is a certaine worme breeding in it like to a moth. **1624** MIDDLETON *Game at Chess* v. iii, Cockles from Chios, frank'd and fatted vp With *Far* and *Sapa*, Flower and cockted Wine.

far (fɑ:(r)), *adv.* Forms: 1–4 feor(r, (3 *south.* veor), 2–3 (9 *dial.*) fur, 3–6 for, (3 forre), 2–6 fer(r(e, 3–4 *south.* ver(re, (2 fir, 3 fear, feȝer, feir, 4 fere, 5 feer), 3–7 farr(e, (4–7 fare), 3– far. *Compar.* 1 fier(r, fyr(r, 2, 4 fir, 3–4 (9 *dial.*) fur, 4–5 furre, fyrre, 7 furr, 5 far, 2–6 ferrer, (4–6 ferrere), 2–3 ferror, 4–7 farrer, 5–6 farrar. *Superl.* 1 fyrrest, 3–5 ferrest, 3–6 farrest, (4 furrest, 7 farst). [OE. *feor(r* corresponds to OFris. *fir*, OS. *fer* (Du. *ver*), OHG. *fer*, ON. *fiarre*, Goth. *fairra*:—OTeut. **ferr-* (the OTeut. form of the suffix is not determinable with certainty; a distinct but synonymous type appears in OS. and OHG. *ferro*, MHG. *verre*), f. OTeut. root *fer-*:—OAryan *per-*, whence Gr. πέρᾱν, Skr. *paras*, beyond.

The forms with final *-e* in 13–14th c. belong etymologically to the derivative FERREN; subsequently the monosyllabic *ferre*, *farre*, is a mere variant spelling of *fer*, *far*. The OE. comparative *fierr*, *fyrr* (:—**ferriz*) began in 12th c. to give place to a new formation on the positive, *ferrer*, *-or*; this survived till the 17th c. in the form *farrer*; after that period the comparative and superlative remained only in dialects, being superseded in educated use by *farther*, *farthest*: see FARTHER.]

1. At a great distance, a long way off. Const. *from*, (colloq.) *off*. Also with advbs. *away*, *off*, *out*.

a. in space.

c **900** *Bæda's Hist.* I. i. §3 We witan heonan noht feor oþer ealond. *c* **1025** *Interl. v. Rule St. Benet* I. 85 þa eallunga feor synd on ȝeswince. *c* **1205** LAY. 543 Achalon heihte an flum þe nes noht feor from heom. *a* **1300** *Cursor M.* 4933 (Cott.) Theues..of a cuntre þat heþen es far. **1340** HAMPOLE *Pr. Consc.* 7650 Ilk planete es ferrer þan other fra us. *c* **1380** WYCLIF *Sel. Wks.* III. 184 Sum ferrer and sum nerrer. *c* **1420** *Sir Amadace* (Camd.) xvi, A marchand of this citè Was fer oute in a-nothir cuntre. *c* **1440** *Promp. Parv.* 156 Fer, or fer a-way, *procul*. *c* **1485** *Digby Myst.* (1882) IV. 112, I was not farre hence. **1490** CAXTON *Eneydos* x. 40 Whiche caused grete fere and drede vnto the countreys nygh neyghbours and also ferre of. **1549** *Compl. Scot.* vi. 80 He vil see ane schip farrar on the seye. **1550** CROWLEY *Epigr.* 211 A Spittlehouse, no farre from where his dwelling was. **1647** H. MORE *Song of Soul* II. ii. II. iii, Things near seem further off; farst off, the nearest at hand. **1697** DRYDEN *Virg. Georg.* IV. 17 The painted Lizard, and the Birds of Prey..be far away. **1711** STEELE *Spect.* No. 63 ¶7 Not far from these was another Set of merry People. **1808** SCOTT *Marm.* II. i, Far upon Northumbrian seas. **1875** JOWETT *Plato* (ed. 2) I. 10 He is likely to be not far off himself. **1879** J. BURROUGHS *Locusts & Wild H.* (1884) 263 The Green Mountains..seen careering along the horizon far to the south-west.

b. *far and near* or *nigh*: in every part, everywhere. *far or near*: anywhere. *far nor near*: nowhere.

a **1000** *Crist* 390 (Gr.) Feor and neah. *c* **1175** *Lamb. Hom.* 137 To..beon iwurðegede fir and neor. *a* **1250** *Owl & Night.* 921 East and west, feor and neor. *a* **1300** *Cursor M.* 17288 + 213 (Cott.) Marie..loked farre & neghe. *c* **1430** *Hymns Virg.* (1867) 107 þere is no man feer ne neer. **1587** TURBERV. *Trag. T.* (1837) 96 The brute was blowne abrode both farre and nye. [**1629** (see 5).] **1631** GOUGE *God's Arrows* iii. §67. 305 Memorable matters, worthy to be knowne farre and neare. **1667** MILTON *P.L.* VI. 295, I..have sought thee farr and nigh. *a* **1704** R. L'ESTRANGE (J.), I have been hunting..far and near..to find out a remedy. **1797** MRS. RADCLIFFE *Italian* xiii, But I could see nothing of them far or near.

c. in past time. Cf. FAR-OFF.

1362 LANGL. *P. Pl.* B. xv. 226 In a freres frokke he was yfounde ones Ac it is ferre agoo in seynt Fraunceys tyme. **1611** SHAKS. *Wint. T.* IV. iv. 442 Farre then Deucalion off.

d. *fig.* with reference to unlikeness, alienation of feeling, etc. Often elliptically in phrase (*so*) *far from* ——*ing* (used when something is denied and something opposite asserted). Also interjectionally, *far from it.*

1534 WHITINTON tr. *Tullyes Offices* I. C v, This maner is as ferre distaunt from offyce..that [etc.]. **1611** BIBLE *Ps.* lxxiii. 27 They that are farre from thee, shall perish. **1648** BOYLE *Seraph. Love* xix. (1700) 116 Gods love is so far from resembling the usual sort of Friends. *a* **1661** FULLER *Worthies* I. 150 So far from imitating the industry of their Ancestors..that [etc.]. **1840** DE QUINCEY *Essenes* III. Wks. 1890 VII. 166 So far..from shocking his [the Jew's] prejudices..the error of the early Christians would lie the other way. **1873** BLACK *Pr. Thule* xiv. 221 It was in a far from unfriendly fashion. **1874** DASENT *Tales from Fjeld* 128 He was not far off losing both wit and sense. *Ibid.* 154 He was not far off being half-dead of thirst. **1882** WICKSTEED tr. *Kuenen's Hibbert Lect.* III. 127 The truly religious tone..not unmixed, indeed, far from it, but unmistakable.

e. Phrases. *far be it from* (*me*, etc.): a form of deprecation = 'God forbid that (I, etc.).' *I'll be far* (*enough*) *if*, etc.: a strong negation or refusal (*vulgar*). *far to* †*find*, *seek*: (*a*) hard to discover, out of the way; (*b*) of persons: at a loss.

1382 WYCLIF *Gen.* xliv. 17 Josephe answerde, Fer be it fro me, that Y thus do. **1393** LANGL. *P. Pl.* C. XI. 77 Beþ þre fayre vertues and beeþ nauht ferr to fynde. **1576** FLEMING *Panopl. Epist.* 163 Bee it farre from me to utter any such speache. **1667** EARL OF CARDIGAN in *12th Rep. Hist. MSS. Comm.* App. v. 9 Farre be it from me..to enter into dispute with your Lordship. **1709** STEELE *Tatler* No. 148 ¶4 Far be it that I should attempt to lessen the Acceptance which Men of this Character meet with in the World. **1752** FOOTE *Taste* II. Wks. 1799 I. 23 I'll be fur enough if it en't a May-game. **1836** J. GILBERT *Chr. Atonem.* viii. (1852) 225 Far, infinitely far, be such imputation from our thoughts. **1874** GLADSTONE in *Contemp. Rev.* Oct. 667 If instances must be cited, they are not far to seek. **1879** GEO. ELIOT *Theo. Such* xvi. 285 Many minds..are far to seek for the grounds of social duty. **1888** *Sheffield Gloss.* s.v., 'I'll be far if I do' means 'I will not.'

2. a. To a great distance; to a remote place. *far and wide*: see WIDE *adv.* 1 b.

c **825** *Vesp. Psalter* ix. 22 Tohwon dryhten ȝewite ðu feor. *c* **1205** LAY. 1720 He ferde to feor ut from his iueren. *c* **1250** *Gen. & Ex.* 2616 Wilt ðu, leuedi, ic go fear out. *c* **1350** *Will. Palerne* 2781 To fle..fer away from þe see. *c* **1450** *St. Cuthbert* (Surtees) 2184 Farrer fra men to be remoued. **1601** WEEVER *Mirr. Martyrs* D ij, I wisht the popes dominion Might stretch no furr than Callis Ocean. **1610** SHAKS. *Temp.* II. i. 110 She..is so farre from Italy remoued. **1667** MILTON *P.L.* XI. 727 He ceas'd Contending, and remov'd his Tents farr off. **1774** GOLDSM. *Nat. Hist.* (1776) IV. 329 A..habitation, from which it seldom ventures far.

b. To a great distance in various directions; over a large area; widely.

c **1200** *Vices & Virtues* (1888) 45 Carite sprat his bowes on bræde and on lengðe swiðe ferr. *c* **1400** *Destr. Troy* 216 þi fame shall goo fer. *c* **1440** *York Myst.* xi. 80 So sall þe folke no farrar sprede. **1692** J. BARNES *Pref. Verses* in E. Walker *Epictetus' Mor.*, An Heathen, far for vertue Fam'd.

†**c.** *to cast far*: to make far-reaching plans. (Cf. FAR-CASTER.) So *to bethink far*. Obs.

a **1300** *Cursor M.* 8269 (Cott.) Ferr and depe he vmbithoght. *c* **1394** *P. Pl. Crede* 485 Fer he [þe devell] casteþ toforn þe folke to destroye.

3. To or at an advanced point of progress. **a.** in space. (Down to the 15th c. the vb. *go* is often omitted after *will*, *shall*, *may*, *can*, etc.)

a **1300** *Fragm. Pop. Sc.* (Wright) 210 Whan the sonne hath thider i-drawe the mist thurf hire hete, Hit ne mai no fur for the colde. *a* **1300** *Cursor M.* 17288 + 392 (Cott.) Iesus made hom semblant as he wald ferrer goo. *c* **1330** R. BRUNNE *Chron.* (1810) 308 Ferrere mot he nouht, Scotland forto se. *c* **1386** CHAUCER *Friar's T.* 89 Sayde this yiman, 'Wiltow fer to day?' *c* **1400** *Lanfranc's Cirurg.* 303 It is sett undir a mannes ers to drawe out þe emeroides þat sittiþ hed fer yn. *c* **1450** *St. Cuthbert* (Surtees) 6091 Ay þe ferrer þat he gase. *c* **1460** *Towneley Myst.* 276 No far thou shalle. **1583** STUBBES *Anat. Abus.* II. 1 How farre purpose you to trauell this way. **1709** STEELE & ADDISON *Tatler* No. 114 ¶1 We were now got pretty far into Westminster. *a* **1801** R. GALL *Tint Quey* Poems 173 Here, or we gae farer ben, Aiblins it's fitting to let ken To them wha reads, that [etc.]. **1814** SOUTHEY *Roderick* III, We travell'd fast and far. **1845** tr. *Sue's Wandering Jew* xvii. 86 Long bamboos which are driven far into the ground.

b. *fig.* with reference to progressive action or condition: To a great length or degree. *far gone*: in an advanced stage; see also GO *v.* 48 f. *to go far to* (produce a certain effect): to tend greatly. †*to speak a person far*: to go to great lengths in his praise.

a **1300** *Cursor M.* 11011 (Gött.) Bot elizabeth was ferrer gane. **1360–80** WYCLIF *Tracts* xxii. (1879) 311 þei shewen ferrere how þei ben disciplis of fals pharisees. *c* **1430** *Chev. Assigne* 311, I kan sey no furre. **1545** BRINKLOW *Compl.* 8 This matter is so farre gone, that there is no remedy. **1576** FLEMING *Panopl. Epist.* Q iij b, Least by presuming to farre, I should loose my selfe. **1579** TWYNE *Phisicke agst. Fortune* II. xc. 278 a, Who is so mad..vnlesse he be to farre gone, that standeth not in feare of them? **1579** FULKE *Heskins' Parl.* 382 Maister Heskins store is farre spent. **1611** SHAKS. *Cymb.* I. i. 24 You speake him farre. **1668** HALE *Pref. Rolle's Abridgm.* 3 Where the subject of any Law is single..prudence..may go far at one Essay to provide a fit law. **1704** SWIFT *T. Tub* Apol., When these two enter far into the composition of any work. **1709** STEELE *Tatler* No. 34 ¶4 There's no carrying a Metaphor too far, when a Lady's Charms are spoke of. *a* **1715** BURNET *Own Time* (1823) I. 377 To do all they could to hinder him to engage too far. *c* **1813** MRS. SHERWOOD *Stories Ch. Catech.* iv. 19 Both..very tipsy..one..so far gone, that she could not walk straight. **1818** CRUISE *Digest* (ed. 2) IV. 233 This was going too far. **1845** McCULLOCH *Taxation* II. x. (1852) 361 This high duty..went far to enable the distillers to fix the price of spirits. **1847** GROTE *Greece* II. xlvii. (1862) IV. 191 The Corinthians had gone too far..to admit of listening to arbitration. **1875** JOWETT *Plato* (ed. 2) I. 46 You are already far gone in your love.

c. in time. †With genitive, *far days*, *nights*: late in the day or night (cf. Gr. πόρρω τῆς ἡμέρας, τῆς νυκτός); in later use also *far-day*, *-night* (cf. 8 c).

a **1400–50** *Alexander* 3900 Be þai had fyneschid þis fiȝt was ferre in with euyn. *c* **1440** *Generydes* 66 A man right ferre in age. *a* **1450** *Knt. de la Tour* (1868) 45 She happed to abide so longe on a sonday that it was fer dayes. **1533** BELLENDEN *Livy* I. (1822) 135 He wes waik, and fer run in yeris. **1561** T. HOBY tr. *Castiglione's Courtyer* K iij b, It was farre in nighte. **1577–87** HOLINSHED *Chron.* III. 1148/2 It is far nights. **1602** *2nd Pt. Return fr. Parnass.* III. ii. (Arb.) 42 But the day is farre spent, M. Recorder. **1631** *Celestina* VIII. 98 O how farre daies is it? **1662** J. DAVIES *Voy. Ambass.* 278 It was far-night ere we got away. **1732** BERKELEY *Alciphr.* II. §26 The day being now far spent. **1870** E. PEACOCK *Ralf Skirl.* III. 2 Far gone as the day was. **1885** *Manch. Exam.* 10 Sept. 5/5 A heavy downpour which continued far into the night.

4. By a great interval, widely. **a.** of separation in place; *fig.* of estrangement or alienation.

c **1400** *Rom. Rose* 3483 His mercy was to ferre bihynde. **1548** GEST *Pr. Masse* I v a, The heaven saínctes who be farrer distanted..from us then..London..from Cambredge. **1568** GRAFTON *Chron.* II. 12 These two Sees were farre asonder, that is to say, Caunterbury and Yorke. **1603** KNOLLES *Hist. Turks* 649 Following not far after himself. **1697** DRYDEN *Virg. Georg.* III. 306 He..leaves the Scythian Arrow far behind. **1730–46** THOMSON *Autumn* 1284 Far distant from their native soil. **1813** SCOTT *Rokeby* I. xvii, Mortham's lord grew far estranged From the bold heart with whom he ranged.

b. qualifying adjs., advbs., or their equivalents, implying excess, defect, or variation from a standard. †In 16–17th c. often prefixed to adjs. or advbs. of negative import, as in *far unfit* = far from fit.

a **1375** *Joseph Arim.* 552 þei were weri of-fouȝten and feor ouer-charged. **1521** FISHER *Wks.* (1876) 348 This man gothe fer wyde from the streyght waye. **1555** PHILPOT *Let.* in Coverdale *Lett. Martyrs* (1564) 229 God knoweth it is written far uneasily. **1564** GRINDAL *Fun. Serm. Emp. Ferdinand* Rem. (1843) 29 Preparations afore death..far out of square. **1614** R. TAILOR *Hog hath lost Pearl* in Dodsley *O. Pl.* (1780) VI. 390 Then my Lord, your father is far impatient. **1631** WEEVER *Anc. Fun. Mon.* 532 A match thought farre vnfit for such a man. **1835** SIR J. ROSS *Narr. 2nd Voy.* xli. 545 We were often far underfed. **1875** JOWETT *Plato* (ed. 2) I. 207 They were not far wrong.

c. of inequality or unlikeness. Often with comparatives or superlatives; sometimes more emphatically *far* (*and*) *away*. Also with vbs., as *to differ*, *exceed*, *excel*, etc. *far other*: widely different. †*to distinguish far*: to make a wide distinction.

c **900** *Bæda's Hist.* III. xiv. §2 Feor on oþre wisan. *a* **1400–50** *Alexander* 3922 A beste..Ferre fersere þan an olifaunt. **1496** *Act 12 Hen. VII*, c. 6 They be sold far under the Price that they be worth. **1545** JOYE *Exp. Dan.* v. 75 a, He passed farre his grandfather in synne. **1562** J. HEYWOOD *Prov. & Epigr.* (1867) 20 Ye be better fed then taught farre awaie. **1563** SHUTE *Archit.* D i a, Which differeth not farre from the declaration of Vitruuius. **1587** GOLDING *De Mornay* xxiv. 373 One that beheld a farre other beauty..and tasted a farre other pleasure than of the worlde. **1593** SHAKS. *Lucr.* 81 Which far exceeds his barren skill to show. **1611** BIBLE *Transl. Pref.* 2 A farre most excellent weight of glory. **1646** DK. HAMILTON in *H. Papers* (Camden) 124 No Englishman will..hold..that Scotland must be satisfied with it, farre leese that it be of the Scots framing. **1667** MILTON *P.L.* IX. 862 To answer and resound farr other Song. *a* **1687** PETTY *Pol. Arith.* i. (1691) 26 In France..the Hugonots are..far the greatest Traders. **1695** WOODWARD *Nat. Hist. Earth* (1723) 9 Of this various Matter..the far greatest Part of the Terrestrial Globe consists. **1709** STEELE *Tatler* No. 92 ¶1 With us it is far otherwise. **1719** DE FOE *Crusoe* II. vi. 156 You will allow it to consist with me, as a Roman, to distinguish far between a Protestant and a Pagan. **1743** J. MORRIS *Serm.* ii. 53 Paul uses this argument to prove

charity far preferable. **1773** MAD. D'ARBLAY *Early Diary* (1889) I. 187 The delight..more far away than I have ever received. **1852** *Democratic Rev.* 11 Far and away the greatest. **1880** T. A. SPALDING *Eliz. Demonol.* 22 A slight surrender of principle was a far surer road to success. **1880** TROLLOPE *Duke's Children* I. xxi. 253 He was far-and-away the cleverest of his party. **1883** W. E. NORRIS *Thirlby Hall* xxxiv, You are far and away the greatest scoundrel I ever saw. **1885** *Law Reports* 29 Ch. Div. 528 The testator's estates were..incumbered..to an amount far beyond their value.

†**5.** From a remote source. *Obs.* exc. in Comb.: see FAR-FETCHED, etc.

1629 MAXWELL tr. *Herodian* (1635) 65 For this purpose all kinde of wilde beasts were brought farre and neere. **1697** tr. *C'tess D'Aunoy's Trav.* (1706) 34 Here's the Etymology of a Word drawn far enough.

6. Preceded by *as, how, so, thus*, the word (like many other quantitative advbs. and adjs.) often undergoes a change of meaning, the notion of definite quantity being substituted for the primary notion of great quantity. Hence the following modifications of the preceding senses:

a. To or at a definite distance.

c **1250** *Gen. & Ex.* 1238 Bi al-so fer so a boȝe mai ten ðor sat his moder. *a* **1300** *Cursor M.* 506 (Cott.) How farr es in to hell pitte. **1711** ADDISON *Spect.* No. 42 ¶4 When there is a Battle in the Hay-Market Theatre, one may hear it as far as Charing-Cross. **1860** TYNDALL *Glac.* I. xxvii. 215, I had not thought it possible to see so far through so dense a storm.

b. Up to or at a particular point of advance. Also, *as far as that goes* (used to express disagreement) = on the contrary; *as far as, so far as* [so *sb.* 35], in so far as it concerns (me, etc.); as for.

a **1300** *Cursor M.* 2253 (Cott.) Now we haue vs sped sa ferr. *c* **1489** CAXTON *Sonnes of Aymon* ii. 60 Sith that it is soo ferre come that ye wyll not here vs, we shall kepe owr peas. **1535** COVERDALE *1 Chron.* xvii[i]. 16 Who am I? and what is my house, yᵗ thou hast broughte me thus farre? **1611** BIBLE *Jer.* li. 64 Thus farre are the words of Ieremiah. **1626** BACON *Sylva* §105 If a Man would endeuour to raise or fall his Voice..as farre as an Eighth. **1724** DE FOE *Mem. Cavalier* (1840) 172 The king was almost as far as Banbury. **1833** CRUSE *Eusebius* I. v. 29 Thus far Josephus. **1841** ELPHINSTONE *Hist. Ind.* I. 469 Menander..went on as far as the Isamus. **1855** THACKERAY *Newcomes* I. 221 She could make an ormolu bracelet go as far as another woman's emerald clasps. *Mod.* So far no great harm has been done. **1905** A. LANG *Adv. among Bks.* 231 As far as that goes..most of you were highly favoured. **1926** H. W. FOWLER *Mod. Eng. Usage* 170/1 *As* or *so far as x* cannot be used as short for *as far as x goes* or *so far as concerns x*. **1939** H. S. CANBY *Thoreau* xiv. 217 The cabin..was in perfect condition so far as frame and covering until 1868. **1960** J. F. KENNEDY in *U.S. News & World Report* 26 Sept. 76/1 As far as whether I could attend this sort of a function in your church..then I could attend.

c. To a certain extent or degree. *as far as* (*I*, etc.) *see him*: normally in contexts implying distrust.

a **1300** *Cursor M.* 16386 (Cott.) Sacles es he sa feir se sum i can. *c* **1400** *Rom. Rose* 2209 Hated bothe of olde and yong, As fer as Gaweyn the worthy, Was preised for his curtesie. **1477** EARL RIVERS *Dictes* (Caxton) 1 As fer as my wrecchednes wold suffyse. **1577** B. GOOGE *Heresbach's Husb.* III. (1586) 116 The bay [horse] is most of price as farre as I see at this daye. **1579** LYLY *Euphues* (Arb.) 191 For thou ..wilt not permit any (as farre as in thee lyeth) to be well employed. **1601** J. MANNINGHAM in *Shaks. C. Praise* 45 A Citizen gaene soe farr in liking with him. **1606** J. DAY *Ile Guls* C2 Wil you trust him? Yes as farre as I see him. **1638** DK. HAMILTON in *H. Papers* (Camden) 18 How fare I shall be abill to prevall uith him I can not yett tell. **1651** HOBBES *Leviath.* I. viii. 35 He may be so farre a good man, as to be free from giving offence. **1751** JORTIN *Serm.* (1771) I. iii. 46 Such persons may so far conduce to the temporal prosperity of a nation. **1821** J. Q. ADAMS in C. Davies *Metr. Syst.* III. (1871) 119 But this law so far as it prescribed a new bushel, had never been executed. **1835** THIRLWALL *Greece* I. 423 To decide how far he deserved it. **1848** TROLLOPE *Kellys & O'Kellys* I. i. 15 He knows what he's about, and isn't the man to thrust a Protesthant half as far as he'd see him. **1875** JOWETT *Plato* (ed. 2) V. 427 Let us endeavour to ascertain how far we are consistent with ourselves. **1969** 'A. GILBERT' *Missing from Home* xiii. 205 'She doesn't trust us as far as she can see us,' Charlie remarked.

7. quasi-*sb.* **a.** † *of, on far*: see AFAR. † *upon far*: at a distance. *from far*: at a distance (cf. FERREN). *by far*: by a great interval (= sense 4); see BY 18 b. *in so far*: to such an extent.

a **1300** *Cursor M.* 6655 (Cott.) Þam thoght him hornd apon farr. *Ibid.* 13457 (Cott.) Fra ful ferr can þai til him seke. *Ibid.* 27643 (Cott.) Sin es fowler þan any deuil in hell by fer. *c* **1380** WYCLIF *Serm.* Sel. Wks. I. 17 Sum of hem comen fro ferre. *c* **1400** MAUNDEV. (Roxb.) xix. 86 To þat ymage men commez fra ferre in pilgrimages. **1513-75** *Diurn. Occurrents* (1833) 276 Thair wes the greiter slauchter be over far maid vpoun the Inglis. **1647** H. MORE *Philos. Devot.* 43 Lo! from farre I you salute. **1737** WHISTON *Josephus' Antiq.* I. xix. §10 Thus far of his apology was made. **1764** GOLDSM. *Trav.* 28 That, like the circle bounding earth and skies, Allures from far. **1871** SMILES *Charac.* x. (1876) 282 By far the largest class of readers. **1888** BRYCE *Amer. Commw.* I. viii. 104 Eloquence..imagination..or extent of knowledge, are all in so far a gain to him that [etc.].

†**b.** *to have far to*: to have a long way to go to, be far from. *Obs.*

1377 LANGL. *P. Pl.* B. XIX. 477 Þe vyker had fer home & faire toke his leue. **1393** *Ibid.* C. XII. 196 Folwe forþ þat fortune wol; thou hast ful fer to elde.

8. Combinations.

a. When *far* (in senses 1-5) qualifies a ppl. adj. used attributively, it is usually hyphened, thus giving rise to an unlimited number of quasi-compounds, as *far-beaming, -branching, -embracing, -extending, -flying, -going, -ranging, -travelled*, etc.

1533 MORE *Answ. Poysoned Bk.* Wks. 1047/1 Making one perfit person and one farpassing perfyt person of God and man together. **1596** SPENSER *State Irel.* 2 The manner rather of desperate men farre driven. **1598** CHAPMAN *Iliad* I. 19 Far-shooting Phœbus. **1601** YARINGTON *Two Lament. Traj.* III. ii. in Bullen *O. Pl.* IV, I will..live in some far-removed continent. *a* **1649** DRUMM. OF HAWTH. *Poems* Wks. (1711) 31 These saphyre far-extending heights. **1688** *Addr.* in *Lond. Gaz.* No. 2536/1 Your far distanced New England Subjects. **1725** POPE *Odyss.* XIX. 127 O Queen! whose far-resounding fame, Is bounded only by the starry frame. **1735** SOMERVILLE *Chase* I. 272 Their Arms Far-gleaming, dart the same united Blaze. **1779-81** JOHNSON *L.P., Swift* Wks. III. 404 Variegated by far-sought learning. **1784** COWPER *Task* I. 184 Mighty winds That sweep the skirt of some far-spreading wood. **1812** BYRON *Ch. Har.* II. xli, Leucadia's far-projecting rock of woe. **1820** KEATS *St. Agnes* xxix, Far-heard clarionet. **1827** HARE *Guesses* (1859) 69 Expressing profound and farstretching thoughts in the simplest words. **1852** J. A. ROEBUCK *Hist. Whig Min.* II. 32 The view was exceedingly offensive to the far-going reformers. **1854** *Excelsior* II. 128 His venerable and far-travelled friend. **1857** RUSKIN *Pol. Econ. Art* 139 Consider what a far-branching, far-embracing good you have wrought. **1864** ENGEL *Mus. Anc. Nat.* 232 Far-spread popularity. **1870** tr. *F. Marion's Wonderful Balloon Ascents* I. i. 5 The far-flying comets. **1905** *Westm. Gaz.* 9 Sept. 2/3 Far-travelled tourists. **1923** KIPLING *Irish Guards in Great War* I. 5 One single far-ranging rifle-bullet. **1939** *War Illustr.* 4 Nov. 283/3 Far-flying squadrons over home waters and foreign seas had splendidly maintained our cause. **1959** E. H. CARR *Socialism in one Country* II. xix. 201 The intellectuals whose far-ranging thought had provided the inspiration of the revolution. **1969** *Jane's Freight Containers 1968-69* 240/3 Far-going mechanisation and cost-reduction is rendered possible.

b. *rarely* in similar quasi-comb. with *vbl. sbs.*, as *far-flashing, -withdrawal*.

1822 SHELLEY *Hellas* 331 The far-flashing of their starry lances Reverberates the dying light of day. **1866** HOWELLS *Venet. Life* xvii, Their..strange effect of far-withdrawal.

c. Special combinations: **far-apart** *a.*, at a great distance (from); **far-being** *vbl. sb.*, the state of being at a distance; †**far-born** *a.*, born long ago; **far-darter**, one who sends darts to or from a great distance; **far-darting** *a.*, esp. as epithet of Apollo, the *far-darter*; †**far-day**, the latter part of the day [cf. 3 c]; **far-distant** *a.*, at a great distance; **far-eastern** *a.*, belonging to the extreme east; **far-eyed** *a.*, = FAR-SIGHTED *a.*; **far-farer** (*rare*), = *far-goer*; **far-foamed** *a.*, fringed with foam for a great distance; **far-goer**, one who goes far, *lit.* and *fig.*; **far-gone** *a.*, advanced to a great extent; **far-northern** *a.*, lying in the extreme north; **far-point** (*Optics*), the extreme range; **far-seeing** *a.*, = FAR-SIGHTED 1; **far-seen** *a.*, seen at a distance; also *Sc.* = FAR-SIGHTED; **far-shot** *a.* = *far-shooting*; **far-southern** *a.*, at the extreme south; **far-thinking** *a.*, = FAR-SIGHTED *a.* 1; †**far-went** *a.*, that has wended or travelled far; **far-western**, belonging to the extreme west.

1865 *Punch* 27 May 215/1 What, Sir, is the object of a railway? To do away with distance, and bring *far-apart scenes within the easy reach of all. **1955** E. BOWEN *World of Love* xi. 222 The sky..let fall far-apart tepid drops. **1580** SIDNEY *Arcadia* (1622) 124 The desolation of the *far-being from comfort. **1672** WYCHERLEY *Love in Wood* III. i, Nine-and-thirty years old, mistress? I'd have you to know I am no *far-born child. **1598** CHAPMAN *Iliad* I. 91 This is cause why heaven's *Far-darter darts These plagues amongst us. **1868** MORRIS *Earthly Par.* (1870) I. II. 500 Dimly he remembered ..the sight Of the Far-darter. **1849** THOREAU *Week on Concord* 199 And near at hand the *far-darting glances of the god. **1851** BUCKLEY *Iliad* 4 The wrath of Apollo, the far-darting king. **1871** WHITMAN *Passage to India* (1872) 6 The far-darting beams of the spirit! **1655** H. VAUGHAN *Silex Scint.* I. 74 *Far-day sullies flowres. **1793** J. BARLOW in *Amer. Poems* I. 86 *Far-distant land. **1936** *Mind* XLV. 549 Modern astronomical researches into far-distant stars. **1913** A. FORTESCUE *Lesser Eastern Churches* ii. 36 Edessa certainly was the chief see of *far-eastern Christendom. *a* **1882** EMERSON *Wks.* (1883) IX. 258 The height of Fancy's *far-eyed steep. **1903** HARDY *Dynasts* I. VI. i. 109 The wariness That marks your usual far-eyed policy. **1861** DASENT *Burnt Njal* II. 354 Thorwald Kodran's son, the *far-farer. **1820** KEATS *Hyperion* II. 172 Murmurs, which his first endeavouring tongue Caught infant-like from the *far-foamed sands. **1841** GEN. P. THOMPSON *Exerc.* (1842) VI. 358 The party which the *far-goers at least of the deliberants, believe to be the least undeserving of the two. **1778** *Conquerors* 39 As drunken men who brave the dang'rous fight O'er sparkling glasses in the *far-gone night. **1831** T. L. PEACOCK *Crotchet Castle* xvi, Which the far-gone innamorato found irresistible. **1856** KANE *Arct. Expl.* I. xxiii. 309 The temperature of these *far-northern regions. **1876** BERNSTEIN *Five Senses* 72 The *far-point of the eye. **1837** LONGF. *Voices Night* (1843) 42 The Poet..*far-seeing. **1848** LYTTON *Harold* VIII. ii, Though wise and farseeing, Harold was not suspicious. **1943** W. S. CHURCHILL *End of Beginning* 240 The wise, far-seeing appeals of the American President. **1730-46** THOMSON *Autumn* 790 From lofty Caucasus *far seen by those, Who in the Caspian..toil. **1827** KEBLE *Chr. Y.* Monday bef. Easter, Two silent nights and days In calmness for His far-seen hour He stays. **1615** CHAPMAN *Odyss.* VIII. 453 Useful Mercury And *far-shot Phœbus. **1856** KANE *Arct. Expl.* I. xxiii. 228 Commodore Wilkes in his *far-southern discovery of an Antarctic continent. **1937** B. H. L. HART *Europe in Arms* XV. 211 They can hardly fulfil such a *far-thinking role. **1609** BP. W. BARLOW *Answ. Nameless Cath.* 191 The Gibeonites came to Iosua like *far-went Trauellers. **1589** PUTTENHAM *Arte Eng. Poesie* 121 [Northern English] is not so Courtly..as our Southerne English is, no more is the *far Westerne mans speach.

far (fɑː(r)), *a.* Forms: 1-4 feor(r, 2-6 fer, 3-7 farr, 5-7 farre, 3- far. *Compar.* 1 fyrra (fem. and neut. *-e*), 3-4 fyrre, furre, 3-6 ferre(r(e, 3 ferror(e, *south.* verrore, 4-7 farrer. *Superl.* 1 fyrrest, 3-5 ferrest, 3-6 farrest. [OE. *feorr* = OFris. *fer, fir*, OS. *fer*, OHG. *fer*:—WGer. type **ferro-*. As the adj. does not occur in Gothic or ON., it is prob. derived from the adv.]

1. Remote: **a.** in space; chiefly of countries or places; occas. of persons, etc. *the far east, north, west, south*: the extreme eastern, etc. parts of a region, or of the world. Cf. FAR WEST. †*far absence*: absence in a distant part.

a **1000** *Wife's Complaint* 47 (Gr.) Feorres folclondes. *a* **1225** *Leg. Kath.* 1565 Into þe ferreste ende of Alixandre. *a* **1300** *Cursor M.* 4820 (Cott.) Wee are o farr cuntre, Of a land hait chanaan. **1340** *Ayenb.* 204 Huerof yealde filozofes hem uledden in-to uerre stedes in-to dezert. **1382** WYCLIF *Joel* iii. 8 They shule selle hem to Sabeis, a fer folc. *c* **1450** *Mirour Saluacioun* 1643 Thick ffolewastoure son..departid to ferre lande. *c* **1489** CAXTON *Sonnes of Aymon* xxviii. 585 Folke cam..from ferre ways for to seke hym. **1548** HALL *Chron.* 101 b, The Englishemen consideryng..the farre absence of their frendes. **1553** EDEN *Treat. Newe Ind.* (Arb.) 8 To returne home from these farre countreys. *a* **1605** MONTGOMERIE *Misc. Poems* (1886) xxxii. 38 Far foullis hes ay fair fethers, sum will say. **1682** DRYDEN *Mac Fl.* 131 To far Barbadoes on the western main. **1808** J. BARLOW *Columb.* I. 45 A far dim watch-lamp's thrice reflected beam. **1822** SHELLEY *Hellas* 813 What hearest thou? *Mahmud.* A far whisper. **1839** BAILEY *Festus* (1854) 56 It is fear which beds the far to-come with fire.

absol. *c* **1386** CHAUCER *Prol.* 494 To visite The ferrest in his parish.

b. *fig.* of remoteness or difference in time, relationship, or nature.

1531 ELYOT *Gov.* II. vi. (1557) 100 A vice moste ugly, and farrest from humanitee. **1583** HOLLYBAND *Campo di Fior* 309 How farre this fielde is to that which bordereth upon it. **1630** CRASHAW *Poems* 129 Pulling far history Nearer. **1859** TENNYSON *Elaine* 799 Sir Torre..Past up the still rich city to his kin His own far blood. **1860** HAWTHORNE *Marb. Faun* (1879) II. xx. 200 So many far landmarks of time.

c. *the far end*, †*the far*: the very end, or extremity; the last stage (of life, strength, or resources). Now only *dial.*

c **1400** *Destr. Troy* 78 In this shall faithfully be founden to the fer ende, All þe dedis. *Ibid.* 8272 The next tym þou noyes me, þou neghis to þe fer. **1637** RUTHERFORD *Lett.* clxxxiii. (1862) I. 447 What standeth beyond the far-end of my sufferings..He knoweth. **1790** W. COMBE *Devil upon Two Sticks in Eng.* (1817) II. 58 Whose..love of pleasure will soon get to the far-end of a moderate fortune. **1855** ROBINSON *Whitby Gloss.*, He seems almost at the far end. **1888** *Sheffield Gloss.* s.v. *Far end*, 'Ah'm ommast at t' far end.'

2. Extending to a distance, long. *far traveller*: one who comes from or goes to a distance. †(*a person*) *of a far fetch*: far-reaching, far-sighted. †*far way*: a long way, by far.

c **1340** *Cursor M.* 11385 (Laud.) For els might not tho thre haue rawght to ride so farre wai, And come to cryst thilk day. **1393** LANGL. *P. Pl.* C XVII. 51 Of wyt and wysedome þat fer way is bettere Than richesse. **1508** FISHER *Psalms* N vj b, Her grete & ferre Journey. **1550** COVERDALE *Spir. Perle* xxix, A merchant-man maketh far voyages and great journeys. **1574** HELLOWES *Gueuara's Fam. Ep.* (1577) 314 Some men so euill and of so farre a fetch, that [etc.]. **1605** VERSTEGAN *Dec. Intell.* ii. (1628) 30 A verie farre way from Africa. **1624** GATAKER *Transubst.* 204 Far travellers may lye by authority. **1820** SCOTT *Monast.* xxix, You could not miss the road..it was neither far way nor foul gate. **1830** GEN. P. THOMPSON *Exerc.* (1842) I. 287 It would not be a far stretch of intellect to infer.

†**b.** Of authority: Extensive.

c **1400** *Apol. Loll.* 29 God ȝaue him no farrer power.

†**c.** Of a difference in kind or value: Great. *Obs.*

1509 FISHER *Fun. Serm. C'tess Richmond* Wks. (1876) 304 This shall be a farre dyfference. **1631** WEEVER *Anc. Fun. Mon.* 578 Valued, at a farre vnder rate, to bee worth..ten pound.

†**d.** Of a person: Advanced (in age or knowledge). *Obs.*

c **1340** *Cursor M.* 15124 (Trin.) Þis ihesus..was so wis & so fer in lore. **1591** SPENSER *M. Hubberd* 218 As one farre in elde.

3. The remoter of two; in early use also in the comparative. † *the far side* (of a horse, etc.): the off or right-hand side. *the fur ahin* (Sc.): the hind right-hand (horse) in a team of four.

Prob. *far* here represents the original compar. form *fyrre*.

c **1400** *Rowland & O.* 1227 With him Rowlande and Olyvere Appon the ferrere syde. *c* **1400** *Destr. Troy* 9054 Priam the prise kyng..was feghtyng in the feld on the fer syde. **1486** *Bk. St. Albans* D j b, Iff yowre hawke nym the fowle at the fer side of the Ryuer..Then she sleeth the fowle at the fer Jutty. **1540** *Act 32 Hen. VIII*, c. 17 The farre ende of high holborn. **1617** MARKHAM *Caval.* II. 4 The white fore-foote, on the right side, commonly cald the farre side. **1641** BEST *Farm. Bks.* (Surtees) 12 To give them [lambes].. the botte on the farre buttocke. **1724** *Lond. Gaz.* No. 6294/3 The Coronett of the far Hoof before. **1768** STERNE *Sent. Journ.* 95 She sat in a low chair on the far side of the shop. **1786** BURNS *Inventory* 20 My fur ahin's a wordy beast. **1883** STEVENSON *Treasure Isl.* III. xiv. 110 On the far side of the open stood one of the hills.

†**far**, *v. Obs.* exc. *dial.* Also 1 feorran, 3–5 fere, ferre, 4 *south. dial.* verri, *pa. pple.* yverred. [OE. *feorran, fyrran* = OHG. *firren*, ON. *firra*:—OTeut. type **firrjan*, f. **ferr-*, FAR *a.*]

trans. To put far off, remove. In *mod. dial.* only in the expression of a wish (see quots.). Const. *from*; rarely with double *obj.*

Beowulf 156 Grendel..ne wolde wið manna hwone feorhbealo feorran. *a* **1300** *E.E. Psalter* lxxxvii. 19 Neghburgh and frend fered þou fra me. **1340** *Ayenb.* 240 þe stat of religion ssel by zuo yuerred uram þe wordle þet [etc.]. *c* **1380** *Sir Ferumb.* 3625 Richard was noȝt so ferred ys fon, þat hy hym þo ne seȝe. *c* **1430** *Pilgr. Lyf Manhode* II. lxviii. (1869) 101 Thouh thou were forveyed other ferred from thi wey. **1855** MRS. GASKELL *North & S.* xvii, Pooh, wench! latter days be farred! **1863** —— *Sylvia's L.* (ed. 2) I. 189, I wish the man were farred who [etc.].

b. *refl.* and *intr.* for refl.

a **1225** *Ancr. R.* 76 He furseð (note ? firres [*printed* firnes]) him awei urommard ure stefne. *c* **1315** SHOREHAM 164 God wyste wel that man schold..uerry [*printed* nerry] Fram alle healthe. **1340** *Ayenb.* 178 þe uoȝel him uerreþ..uram þennes huer me brekþ his nest.

far, obs. f. of FAIR and *Sc.* f. FARE *sb.* and *v.*

far, obs. var. of FARROW, young pig.

ˌ**far-a'bout**, *adv.* and *sb.*

A. *adv.* †**a.** To a great distance around, everywhere (*obs.*). †**b.** At a great distance (*obs.*). †**c.** Far astray, out of the way (*obs.*). **d.** By far, very much (*dial.*).

c **1300** *Cursor M.* 21821 (Cott.) Thoru him i regned ferr a-bute. *c* **1450** *Pol. Poems* (Rolls) II. 241 Wherfore concord ys put feer abowte. **1483** *Cath. Angl.* 128 Ferre a-boute, *multum distans a via regia.* **1848** A. B. EVANS *Leicestershire Words* 35 Oh! that's the nearest way, fur-about.

†**B.** *sb.* A digression, wandering. *Obs.*

1639 FULLER *Holy War* v. xxix. (1647) 280 But what need these farre-abouts?

farad ('færəd). *Electr.* [short f. FARADAY.]

1. a. Suggested (but apparently not used) as a name for a unit of charge, equal to approximately $9{\cdot}5 \times 10^{-10}$ coulomb.

The unit was defined as the charge on either plate of a capacitor that has plates one square metre in area spaced one millimetre apart and charged to the voltage of a Daniell cell, there being dry air between the plates.

1861 CLARK & BRIGHT in *Electrician* 9 Nov. 4/2 The farad, or unit of quantity, is as small a one as is likely to be required in practice... One hundred farad, if allowed to pass through a very sensitive galvanometer, produce a visible motion of the needle.

b. A unit of charge (equal to the present microcoulomb) and also of capacitance (equal to the present microfarad). *Disused.*

1868 *Rep. Brit. Assoc. 1867* 488, 10^5 EMF, acting on a circuit of 10^{13}, will pass in one second 10^{-8} absolute units of quantity; and similarly, 10^5 EMF will charge a condenser of absolute capacity equal to 10^{-13} absolute units with 10^{-8} absolute units of quantity... Mr. Clark calls the unit of quantity thus defined (10^{-8}) one Farad, and similarly says that the unit of capacity has a capacity of one Farad, it being understood that this is the capacity when charged with unit electromotive force (10^5). **1868** L. CLARK *Elem. Treat. Electr. Measurement* vii. 44 The farad is that quantity of electricity which, with an electromotive force of one volt, would flow through a resistance of one megohm in one second. **1875** J. T. SPRAGUE *Electricity* v. 156 Microfarad = Microveber/Volt = $10^{-8}/10^5 = 10^{-13}$. The microfarad here represents what is usually called the farad.

2. The practical unit of capacitance (now incorporated into the International System of Units), being the capacitance of a capacitor in which a charge of one coulomb raises the potential difference between the plates by one volt. (Orig. also used as a unit of charge, equal to the present coulomb.)

1873 J. C. MAXWELL *Electr. & Magn.* II. IV. x. 244 The quantity of electricity which flows through one Ohm under the electromotive force of one Volt during one second, is equal to the charge produced in a condenser whose capacity is one Farad by an electromotive force of one Volt. **1874** *Phil. Trans. R. Soc.* CLXIV. 1 Certain multiples have been adopted in practice and have received names, and are now in almost universal use among electricians. These units are:.. Capacity.—The Farad, equal to 10^{-7} absolute electromagnetic units. *Ibid.* 2 The measure of quantity is the same as that of electrostatic capacity, and in practice generally receives the same name, although it has been sometimes called the 'Weber'; the weber or farad quantity is equal to 10^{-2} absolute units. Electrical currents are defined as currents of so many farads per second. **1881** *Electrician* 24 Sept. 297/2 At the meeting [of the Paris Electrical Congress] the report of the First Section on Electrical Units was received, and the following resolutions adopted:—..7. The name farad will be given to the capacity defined by the condition that a coulomb in a farad gives a volt. **1881** MAXWELL *Electr. & Magn.* II. 246 The practical unit of capacity is called the Farad. **1882** *Electrician* 15 July 205/2 The unit of static quantity is a *farad*, or that quantity which, if discharged through one ohm in one second, would give a veber current. **1892** *Gloss. Electrical Terms* in *Lightning* 3 Mar. Supp. 7 The *Farad* is the capacity of a conductor in which the electrical pressure is raised one volt by the addition of one coulomb. **1894** *Rep. Brit. Assoc. 1894* 122 Governments represented by the delegates of this International Congress of Electricians .. are .. recommended to formally adopt as legal units of electrical measure the following... As a unit of capacity the international farad, which is the capacity of a condenser charged to a potential of one international volt by one international coulomb of electricity. **1925** BRYANT & CORRELL *Alternating-Current Circuits* ii. 51 The farad is too large a unit for most considerations, and the microfarad is more common, there being 1,000,000 microfarads in 1 farad. **1947** *Jrnl. Inst. Electr. Engineers* XCIV. I. 342/1 From the 1st January, 1948, the units employed will be those derived from the centimetre, gramme and second, i.e. the so-called 'absolute' units... One international farad = 0·99951 'absolute' farad. **1958** W. C. MICHELS in Condon & Odishaw *Handbk. Physics* IV. v. 55/1 Precision standards are readily available in decade values from 10^{-3} ohm to 10^6 ohms, from 10^{-10} farad to 10^{-5} farad, and from 10^{-4} henry to 10 henrys.

faradaic (færə'deɪɪk), *a.* [f. *Faraday* (see prec.) + -IC.] Used as a distinctive epithet of inductive electricity and of the phenomena pertaining to it.

1875 H. C. WOOD *Therap.* (1879) 37 When the faradaic current elicits a response it should always be employed. **1881** D. E. HUGHES in *Nature* XXIII. 522 There is a Faradaic induction of 50° at both poles. **1885** *Lancet* 26 Sept. 568 Sensation and faradaic contractility were normal.

faradaism ('færədeɪɪz(ə)m). [f. as prec. + -ISM.] = FARADISM.

1886 *Pall Mall G.* 1 Apr. 16/1 Induced Electricity, or Faradaism.

Faraday ('færədeɪ). The name of Michael *Faraday* (1791–1867), English scientist, used: **1.** *attrib.* or in the possessive to designate certain phenomena observed, apparatus invented, and principles enunciated by him.

Faraday cage, an earthed metal screen surrounding a piece of equipment to protect it from external electrostatic interference; **Faraday's constant** = FARADAY 2; **Faraday('s) dark space**, in a discharge tube the dark space observed between the positive column and the negative glow when the pressure is moderately low; also called the *second dark space*; **Faraday('s) disc**, a metal disc in which an e.m.f. is induced when it is made to rotate in a magnetic field parallel to the axis of rotation; **Faraday effect**, the rotation of the plane of polarization of light or other electromagnetic waves when transmitted through certain substances in a magnetic field that has a component parallel to the direction of transmission; **Faraday('s) ice-pail experiment**, an experiment used to demonstrate certain principles of electrostatic induction; **Faraday's law**, any of two or three laws; (*a*) when the magnetic flux linking a circuit changes, an e.m.f. is induced in the circuit proportional to the rate of change of the flux linkage (the *law of induction*); (*b*) the amount of any substance deposited or liberated during electrolysis is proportional to (i) the quantity of charge passed and (ii) the equivalent weight of the substance (the *law(s) of electrolysis*); (quot. 1850 refers to a different phenomenon); **Faraday's line**, a line of force of a magnetic field; **Faraday tube**, a tube of force of an electrostatic field, defined so that one tube arises from a unit charge.

1916 G. KAPP *Princ. Electr. Engin.* I. vii. 103 All the transforming apparatus is in a building which is a huge Faraday cage... If the building should be struck by lightning this would momentarily acquire a high potential, but nothing inside it would be damaged. **1955** A. HUXLEY *Let.* 27 Aug. (1969) 761 Harry, the Dutch sculptor,..goes into trances in the Faraday cages. **1971** *Physics Bull.* Jan. 46/2 Ions leave the oscillator through a rectangular slot along the cathode and parallel to the wires and are collected in a Faraday cage. **1931** PAGE & ADAMS *Princ. Electr.* vi. 201 As the atomic weight of hydrogen is 1·008 and its valence is unity, *F*, called Faraday's constant, is the number of coulombs required to liberate 1·008 grams of hydrogen. **1893** T. O'C. SLOANE *Stand. Electr. Dict.* 249 *Faraday's Dark Space*, a non-luminous space between the negative and positive glows, produced in an incompletely exhausted tube through which a static discharge..is produced. **1958** C. G. WILSON *Electr. & Magn.* xii. 365 At a pressure of 10^{-2} mm. Hg. or less, the Faraday Dark Space and Negative Glow disappear and the Crooke's [*sic*] Dark Space almost fills the tube. **1886** J. A. FLEMING *Short Lect. Electr. Artisans* ii. 36 (*caption*) Faraday's Disk Induction Machine. **1962** CORSON & LORRAIN *Introd. Electromagn. Fields* 530 Consider the Faraday disk or, as it is also called, the homo-polar generator. **1889** O. LODGE *Mod. Views Electr.* xv. 278 The only substance in which the Faraday effect is large, is iron. **1966** *McGraw-Hill Encycl. Sci. & Technol.* V. 181/1 The Faraday effect is particularly simple in substances having sharp absorption lines, that is, in gases and in certain crystals. **1888** A. GRAY *Absol. Measurem. Electr. & Magn.* I. i. 24 The results of Faraday's ice-pail experiments..are direct consequences of the following general proposition regarding closed conductors. **1953** E. R. PECK *Electr. & Magn.* i. 35 In the Faraday ice-pail experiment, a charged metal ball is suspended by an insulating string inside a closed metal pail which is initially uncharged and is insulated except for a wire connecting it to an electroscope indicating the potential of the pail. **1850** *Phil. Mag.* 3rd Ser. XXXVII. 245 Faraday's law..may be illustrated by some very curious although extremely simple experiments. **1881** *Jrnl. Chem. Soc.* XXXIX. 286 The more experimental methods were refined, the more completely were the exactness and generality of Faraday's law [of electrolysis] confirmed. **1886** J. A. FLEMING *Short Lect. Electr. Artisans* ii. 31 We are able to group under one law all the effects so far described, and the expression of this is called Faraday's law of Induction. **1904** R. A. LEHFELDT *Electro-chem.* I. i. 3 Faraday's two laws may be conveniently summed up in one statement..96600 coulombs are required for the deposition of one gram equivalent of any substance. **1954** W. E. ROGERS *Introd. Electr. Fields* xi. 307 The interrelations of a circuit with its magnetic flux are investigated most easily by relating the induced emf to the currents which produce the flux, rather than by using Faraday's law directly. **1857** *Rep. Brit. Assoc. 1856* 12 (*heading*) On a method of drawing the theoretical forms of Faraday's lines of force without calculation. **1911** *Encycl. Brit.* XVII. 323/1 Faraday's lines not only show the direction of the magnetic force, but also serve to indicate its magnitude or strength in different parts of the field. **1893** J. J. THOMSON *Recent Res. Electr. & Magn.* 3 The Faraday tubes either form closed circuits or else begin and end on atoms. **1959** *Chambers's Encycl.* XIV. 8/1 The number of Faraday tubes in unit area was called the displacement by Maxwell.

2. As a name for the quantity of electric charge required to flow to deposit or liberate one gramme-equivalent of any element during electrolysis, viz. approximately 96,490 coulombs. (Usu. with lower-case initial letter.)

1904 R. A. LEHFELDT *Electro-chem.* I. i. 3 This fundamental quantity of electricity, which occurs constantly in all writings on electro-chemistry, is called by the Germans a 'faraday', a term which we in England may very well adopt. **1940** S. GLASSTONE *Physical Chem.* xii. 872 One faraday of electricity liberates 16·8 liters of gas at S.T.P. **1958** HAMER & WOOD in Condon & Odishaw *Handbk. Physics* IV. ix. 140/2 The measurements of the faraday by electrochemical methods involve the measurement of the absolute current, the time, and the mass of material reacted.

faradic (fə'rædɪk), *a.* [ad. Fr. *faradique* (Duchenne 1851), f. *Faraday*.] = FARADAIC.

1878 A. HAMILTON *Nerv. Dis.* 275 Duchenne reports two cures by the faradic current. **1884** in *Syd. Soc. Lex.*

faradine, var. f. of FARANDINE.

faradism ('færədɪz(ə)m). [a. F. *faradisme*, f. *Faraday*: see -ISM.] Inductive electricity; the application of this for therapeutic purposes.

1876 GROSS *Dis. Bladder* 97 Electricity, in the form of galvanism or faradism, should not be neglected as a local stimulant. **1884** in *Syd. Soc. Lex.*

faradization (ˌfærədaɪ'zeɪʃən). [f. next. + -ATION.] The action of faradizing; the application of induced currents of electricity to the body.

1867 *Chambers' Encycl.* s.v. *Tabes dorsalis*, For this disease Duchenne recommends Faradisation. **1875** H. C. WOOD *Therap.* (1879) 292 Faradization of the diaphragm.

faradize ('færədaɪz), *v.* [ad. F. *faradiser* (Duchenne), f. *Faraday*: see -IZE.] *trans.* To stimulate by means of faradic currents.

1864 S. W. MITCHELL, etc. *Gunshot Wounds* 138 It is the muscle itself, and not the nerve, which we desire to faradize.

Hence **'faradizer**, an instrument for faradizing.

farage, var. of FARRAGE, *Obs.*

faraginous: see FARR-.

farand, etc.: see FARRAND.

†**'farandine.** *Obs.* Also 7 fara-, faren-, farin-, farran-, ferrandine, farrender, far(r)endon, farwendine, 8 farandain. [a. F. *ferrandine*, said to be f. *Ferrand* name of the inventor *c* 1630 (Littré *Suppl.*).] **a.** A kind of cloth used in the seventeenth century, made partly of silk and partly of wool or hair. **b.** A dress made of this material. Also *attrib.*

1663 PEPYS *Diary* 28 Jan., Her new ferrandin waistecoate. **1666** *Lady Hatton* in *Hatton Corresp.* (1878) I. 50 Farrender for a gowne. **1668** SEDLEY *Mulberry Gardens* v. i, I must..wear black farandine the whole year about. **1672** WYCHERLEY *Love in Wood* v, I know a great Lady that cannot follow her husband abroad..because her Farrandine is so ragged. **1685** *Lond. Gaz.* No. 2078/4 Six Bredths of Peach-Colour Faradine. **1673** FOUNTAINHALL in *Suppl. Dec.* (1826) III. 2 Farandains..are part silk, part hair.

†**faran'dinical**, *a. Obs. rare*$^{-1}$. [f. FARANDINE + -ICAL.] Of the nature of farandine; hence, second-rate, worthless. Cf. the use of *bombast, fustian, linsey-woolsey.*

1675 T. DUFFETT *Mock Tempest* I. i. 4 You louzy farandinical Sots, Reputation!

†**'farandman.** *Sc. Law. Obs.* Also 7 fairandman. [f. *farand*, obs. pr. pple. of FARE to travel + MAN.] A stranger, a traveller.

The *law of farandman* provided that a pedlar, not residing within the shrievalty, should have the right of bringing to trial, 'within the third flowing and ebbing of the sea', any person who had committed theft or felony against him.

[*c* **1205** LAY. 4262 Alken farinde mon ȝef slaht oþer hæfde þeofðe idon.] **14..** *Fragmenta* in *Sc. Stat.* I. App. v. 726 Partis striffande be þe law of farandman or pipuderous. **1597** SKENE *De Verb. Sign., Farandman*..ane stranger or Pilgrimer. **1609** —— *Reg. Mag., Burrow Lawes* clx, The law of Fairandman, or Dustifut.

‖**farandole** (farɑ̃dol). Also **farandola.** [Fr. *farandole*, ad. mod.Pr. *farandoulo* in same sense; It. *farandola.* Cf. Sp. *farándula* troop of travelling comedians.] A Provençal dance,

generally in $\frac{6}{8}$ time; the music which accompanies this dance, or any music written to its peculiar rhythm. Also *fig.*

1876 STAINER & BARRETT *Dict. Mus. Terms* 164/2 *Farandola*, a dance popular among the peasants of the South of France and the neighbouring part of Italy. It is performed by men and women taking hands, and forming a long line, and winding in and out with a waving motion. **1890** A. J. C. HARE *S.E. France* viii. 341 Here the peasants still dance the farandola. **1904** *Athenæum* 2 Apr. 426/3 Mr. Chesterton's farandole of farce may easily be wrongly praised.

‖**farang** (fa'raŋ). [Thai *fa⁴-rang⁴* white race of people, ad. FRANK *sb.*¹; cf. FERINGHEE.] The Thai term for a foreigner, esp. a European.

[**1852** F. A. NEALE *Narr. Res. Capital of Kingdom of Siam* vii. 109 'What!' said he, 'do you Franks dare to break the laws of this country, and set my authority in defiance?'] *a* **1861** H. MOUHOT *Trav. Indo-China* (1864) I. iii. 126 The priests were much surprised to see a 'farang' (foreigner) in their pagoda, but some trifling gifts soon established me in their good graces. **1873** F. VINCENT *Land of White Elephant* xv. 184 Notice was sent to His Excellency of the arrival of the 'farangs' (foreigners). **1967** *Listener* 10 Aug. 170/3 'In those days,' said one of the old waiters, 'we had many, many *farangs*.'

farant, var. FERRAUNT *obs.*, iron-gray.

farash, obs. form of FERASH.

far-away (fɑːrə'weɪ, 'fɑːrəweɪ), *a.*, *adv.* and *sb.* [f. FAR *adv.* + AWAY.] **A.** *adj.*

1. Situated at a great distance; remote: **a.** in space; **b.** in time; **c.** in relationship.

1816 SCOTT *Antiq.* xxix, 'Relics..fetched frae far-awa' kirks.' **1818** —— *Rob Roy* xiv, 'Pate's a far-awa' cousin o' mine.' **1851** H. MELVILLE *Whale* xxvi. 126 This far-away domestic memory of his young wife and child. **1876** GEO. ELIOT *Dan. Der.* III. xli. 324 Far-away ancestors. **1883** STEVENSON *Treasure Isl.* III. xiii. (1886) 107 They..gave a cheer that started the echo in a far-away hill. **1891** E. PEACOCK *N. Brendon* I. 56, I am really most gravely interested in these far-away matters.

2. a. Of a look, eye: Directed to a distance, absent, dreamy.

1881 *Dr. Gheist* 204 That far-away look so characteristic of the human face when under the dominion of an all-absorbing idea. **1886** HALL CAINE *Son of Hagar* I. ii, The girl kneeled with far-away eyes.

b. Of a voice: sounding faint as if from a distance.

1897 M. KINGSLEY *Trav. W. Africa* x. 216 A quaint, falsetto, far-away sort of voice. **1900** H. LAWSON *On Track* 83 Then he commenced to speak—..to talk in that strange, absent, far-away tone that awes one. **1926** *Glasgow Herald* 30 Sept. 5, I heard his voice sounding in a far-away and curious tone.

Hence **far-awayness**, the state or fact of being far away, remoteness.

1888 *Univ. Rev.* II. 569 The far-awayness of Europe. **1888** *Athenæum* 13 Oct. 480/3 The presence is to be remarked of (as it were) 'far-awayness' of touch [in a picture].

B. *adv.* See FAR *adv.*

C. *sb.* **1.** What is far away; distant parts; the 'dim distance'.

1823 HOOD *Ode Autumn* v, In the hush'd mind's mysterious far away. **18..** LONGF. *To the Stork* i, O Stork! that dost wing thy flight from the far-away!

2. Part of a cinema film taken at a distance, as distinguished from a 'close-up'. ? *Obs.*

1926 B. MAINE *Receive It So* 29 Seeing that for nine-tenths of the house these things appeared as 'far-aways', the whole point of them was lost, because the essence of a 'close-up' is that you should see a tear drop or a stamp licked, and for the moment nothing else.

'far-back, *a.* and *sb.* [f. FAR *adv.* + BACK *a.*]

A. *adj.* **1.** Ancient.

1869 *Atlantic Monthly* XXIII. 200 As of the far-back days the poets tell. **1890** CHILD *Eng. & Sc. Ball.* VII. ccix. 126/2 Some far-back reciter of the Scottish ballad.

2. Remote in space; inaccessible.

1900 *Daily News* 4 Oct. 6/1 The jackals and other denizens of the far-back forests. **1934** A. RUSSELL *Tramp-Royal in Wild Australia* xx. 131 Station men in the far-back parts of Australia.

B. *sb.* **1.** (See quot.) *slang.*

1889 BARRÈRE & LELAND *Dict. Slang* I. 354/2 *Far back* (tailors), an indifferent workman or an ignorant person.

2. The most remote districts or back settlements.

1926 *Spectator* 11 Sept. 370/1 It [*sc.* Australia] is no longer a pioneering country, except in the far-back.

'far-be'tween, *a.* Occurring at long intervals; infrequent. (Chiefly in predicative use, after Campbell's echo of Blair's phrase.)

1743 R. BLAIR *Grave* 589 Its Visits Like those of Angels' short, and far between. **1797** CAMPBELL *Pleas. Hope* II. 372 Like angel-visits, few and far between. **1836–9** DICKENS *Sk. Boz, Elect. Beadle* I. 37 Occasions for their coming into direct collision are neither few nor far between. **1861** F. W. ROBINSON *No Church* I. 48 Travellers being so few and far between. **1873** SYMONDS *Grk. Poets* x. 312 These pines are few and far between; growing alone or in pairs they stand like monuments upon the hills.

†**far-cast**, *v. Obs.* [f. FAR *adv.* + CAST *v.*] *trans.* To cast to a distance off; in derivatives *fig.*

a **1340** HAMPOLE *Psalter* i. 5 Dost þe whilk wynd fercastis fra þe face of þe erth. *Ibid.* xxx. 28, I am ferkasten fra þe clere syght of þi fairhede.

†Hence **far-cast** *sb.*, the action or quality of casting (one's thoughts) to a distance; forethought, shrewdness, cunning. Cf. CAST *sb.* VI and VII. **far-'caster**, one who exercises forethought. **far-'casting** *vbl. sb.*, forethought, cunning. **far-'casting** *ppl. a.*, scheming, shrewd.

c **1400** *Destr. Troy* 1447 Lo, how fortune is felle & of fer caste. *Ibid.* x. 4351 The fynde, with his falshed & his fer cast ..onswaret the pepull. *Ibid.* VIII. 3950 Wise of his dedis, In fele thinges forwise, & a fer-caster. *c* **1400** *Maundev.* (1839) xx. 219 Of malice and of fercastynge þei passen all men vnder heuene. **1387** TREVISA *Higden* (Rolls) VI. 23 Machometus was a wonderful man and fer castynge. **1480** CAXTON *Chron. Eng.* clxii 146 He was a fell man and a subtil enuious and ferre castynge. **1567–83** *Leg. Bp. Sanctandrois* 43 in *Sempill Ball.* 201 Then finding out ane new far cast [*printed* fas cast].

farce, *sb.*¹ Forms: 4–5 fars, 7–8 farce. [a. OF. *farce*, f. *farcir*, *farsir*:—L. *farcīre* to stuff.] Force-meat, stuffing.

? *c* **1390** *Form of Cury* (1780) 75 Make a Coffyn an ynche depe & do þe fars þerin. *c* **1430** *Two Cookery-bks.* 45 Take of the fars, and lay on þe cake. **1727** BRADLEY *Fam. Dict.* s.v. *Calves Ears*, They must be..unsew'd when ready, but so as the Farce may not fall out. **1796** MRS. GLASSE *Cookery* vi. 116 Make a farce with the livers minced small. **1823** CRABB *Technol. Dict.*, *Farces*, meat chopped small, and well spiced. **1904** *Daily Chron.* 4 May 10/5 The hollow should be filled with a rich veal farce.

farce (fɑːs), *sb.*² Also 6–7 farse, 6 *Sc.* farsche. [a. (in 16th c.) F. *farce*, app. a metaphorical use of *farce* stuffing: see prec.

The history of the sense appears to be as follows: In the 13th c. the word (in latinized form *farsa*, *farsia*) was applied in France and England to the various phrases interpolated in litanies between the words *kyrie* and *eleison* (e.g. 'Kyrie, *genitor ingenite, vera essentia*, eleison'); to similar expansions of other liturgical formulæ; and to expository or hortatory passages in French (sometimes in rime) which were inserted between the Latin sentences in chanting the epistle. (The related vb. L. *farcire*, OF. *farcir* to stuff, hence to 'pad out', interlard, was used in the same connexion in the expressions *epistola farcita*, *un benedicamus farci*. See Du Cange s.vv. *Farsa*, *Farsia*, and Burney *Hist. Music* II. 256.) Subsequently the OF. *farce*, with similar notion, occurs as the name for the extemporaneous amplification or 'gag', or the interludes of impromptu buffoonery, which the actors in the religious dramas were accustomed to interpolate into their text. Hence the transition to the modern sense is easy. (The Eccl. Lat. *farsa*, *farcire*, referred to above, have been anglicized by mod. writers on liturgical antiquities as FARSE *sb.* and *v.*)]

1. a. A dramatic work (usually short) which has for its sole object to excite laughter.

[**14..** *La Vie de St. Fiacre* in *Mysterès inédits* 15ᵐᵉ *Siécle* (1837) I. 332 Cy est interposé une farsse.] **1530** PALSGR. 17 Suche as writte farcis and contrefait the vulgare speche. **1530** LYNDESAY *Test. Papyngo* 41 In ballatts, farses, and in plesand playis. **1668** PEPYS *Diary* 31 July, To the King's House, to see the first day of Lacy's 'Monsieur Ragou'..a farce. **1726** AMHERST *Terræ Fil.* xliv. 235 Excellent farces so frequently..perform'd in her [Oxford's] convocation-house. **1824** W. IRVING *T. Trav.* I. 274 A tragedy, pantomime, and farce, were all acted in the course of half an hour.

b. That species of the drama which is constituted by such works.

1676 DRYDEN *Epil. Etheredge's Man of Mode* 3 Those Nauseous Harlequins in Farce may pass. **1717** LADY M. W. MONTAGUE *Let.* 1 Jan., The scenes were pretty, but the comedy itself such intolerable low farce. **1756** HURD *Provinces of Drama* Introd. *Wks.* (1811) II. 30 By *Farce* I understand, that species of the drama 'whose sole aim and tendency is to excite Laughter'. **1877** A. W. WARD in *Encycl. Brit.* VII. 438/1 English comedy seemed inclined to leave to farce the domain of healthy ridicule.

2. Something as ridiculous as a theatrical farce; a proceeding that is ludicrously futile or insincere; a hollow pretence, a mockery.

1696 tr. *Du Mont's Voy. Levant* 296 The Farce is too gross and visible. **1704** PRIOR *Ladle* 139 A Ladle..is what I want ..you have pray'd ill; what should be Great you turn to Farce. **1705** W. WOTTON *Defense* 57 'Tis all with him a Farce and all a Ladle, as a very facetious Poet says. **1762** STERNE *Tr. Shandy* v. xv, Unless every one's Life and Opinions are to be looked upon as a farce. **1791** BURKE *Corr.* (1844) III. 255 It is quite a farce to talk of his liberty. **1824** W. IRVING *T. Trav.* I. 246 The buzz of notoriety and the farce of fashion. **1888** BRYCE *Amer. Commw.* III. lxxxix. 204 These delegates..duly went through the farce of selecting and voting for persons already determined on by the King.

3. *attrib.* and *Comb.*, as *farce-scribbler*, *-trager*, *-writer*; *farce-like* adj.

a **1683** OLDHAM *Horace his Art Poet.* 362 in *Some New Pieces* (1684) 19 Satyrs..Whose Farce-like Gesture, Motion, Speech, and Meen Resemble those of modern Harlequin. **1695** DRYDEN tr. *Du Fresnoy's Art Painting* Pref. p. xxvi, Farce-Scribblers make use of the same noble invention [laughter], to entertain Citizens. **1710** C. GILDON *Life T. Betterton* 174 Nay, after these our very Farce Writers deserve more Esteem. **1850** KINGSLEY *Alt. Locke* xxxvii, Those miserable, awful farce tragedies of April and June. **1859** H. MORLEY *Jrnl.* 5 Nov. (1866) 240 Reasons which a farce-writer is entitled to regard as sufficient.

farce (fɑːs), *v.*¹ *Obs.* or *arch.* Also 4–9 farse, (5 faarce, 5–6 fars). [ad. OF. *farsir* (Fr. *farcir*) = Pr. *farsir*:—L. *farcīre* to stuff.] To stuff, to fill full of something. Const. *with.*

†**1. a.** *trans.* In cookery: To stuff (an animal, a piece of meat) with force-meat, herbs, etc. *Obs.*

13.. *Medical Receipts* in *Rel. Ant.* I. 51 Farse the catte within als thu farses a gos. *c* **1430** *Two Cookery-bks.* 41 Broche þin Pygge; þen farce hym. **1530** PALSGR. 545/2 This conye is well farced. **1586** BRIGHT *Melanch.* xxxix. 252 Pigge ..farced with sage. **1613** PURCHAS *Pilgrimage* II. xviii. 173 If any farse a henne, the needle must be threeded the day before. **1727** BRADLEY *Fam. Dict.* s.v. *Breast of Veal*, Farce it between the Skin and small Ribs. **1736** BAILEY *Househ. Dict.* 235 To farce Cucumbers.

absol. **1501** DOUGLAS *Pal. Hon.* II. li. 1231 Martiall was cuik till roist, seith, farce and fry.

†**b.** *to farce together*: to make into force-meat. *Obs.*

1653 B. *Discolliminium* 46 Polcatts Lites, and Hedge-hoggs Livers..farced together with the galls of Wizards.

†**2.** In embalming (see quots.). *Obs.*

1563 *Homilies* II. *Idolatry* III. (1859) 264 They bury dead bodies farced with spices. **1665** SIR T. HERBERT *Trav.* 325 Some used to embalm..the belly..farced with cassia.

†**3.** To cram (the stomach, etc., oneself) with food. Also, To fill out (what is lean or shrunken).

1375 BARBOUR *Bruce* IX. 398 With gud morsellis [thai] farsis thair panch. **14..** *Prose Legends* in *Anglia* VIII. 154 She was..farsed wiþ goostly fodes. **1513** DOUGLAS *Æneis* VIII. Prol. 52 A gus..To fars his wame full. **1599** B. JONSON *Ev. Man out of Hum.* v. v, If thou would'st farce thy leane ribbes with it too, they would not rub out so many doublets. *a* **1632** T. TAYLOR *God's Judgem.* I. I. ix. (1642) 20 Never ceasing to farse his greedy throat with continuall sustenance. **1669** *Address Young Gentry England* 39 They farse themselves with the most exquisite delicacies.

†**4.** *gen.* To cram *full of*; to pack; also, to overlay thickly. *Obs.*

c **1386** CHAUCER *Prol.* 233 His typet was ay farsud ful of knyfes. **1569** STOCKER *Diod. Sic.* III. xiii. 124 b, A couer.. made of cowe hides farsed with wolle. **1577** HELLOWES tr. *Gueuara's Chron.* 60 The ayre seemed to be farsed or compound with dust. **1583** STANYHURST *Æneis* I. (Arb.) 31 When they [bees]..cels ar farcing with dulce and delicat hoonnye. **1607** TOPSELL *Four-f. Beasts* (1673) 137 His capcase farsed with things of great value. **1611** SPEED *Hist. Gt. Brit.* IX. viii. (1632) 563 A Helmet of excellent proofe full farsed with Mayle. **1634** T. JOHNSON *Parey's Chirurg.* XI. iii. (1678) 278 The wound must..be inlarged..that so there may be free passage..for such things as are farced..therein.

5. *fig.*; *esp.* To season, 'spice' (a composition, speech). Also with *up*. (Cf. FARSE *v.*)

a **1340** HAMPOLE *Psalter* xvi. 11 þai held þaire pride farsid in felonyse. *c* **1385** CHAUCER *L.G.W.* 1369 *Hipsiph. & Medea*, Wordes farsed with plesaunce. *c* **1400** *Apol. Loll.* 49 Stoffid and farsid wiþ gold. **1406** HOCCLEVE *La Male Regle* 13 Farsid was I with hertes gladnesse. *c* **1555** HARPSFIELD *Divorce Hen. VIII* (1878) 116 The book..is farced with many untruths. **1577–87** HOLINSHED *Chron.* I. 84/1 With what stuffe our old historiographers haue farced vp their huge volumes. **1599** B. JONSON *Cynthia's Rev.* Induct., Stale apothegmes..to farce their Scenes withall. **1631** MASSINGER *Believe as You List* III. ii, Farce thy lean ribs with hope. **1678** OWEN *Mind of God* viii. 233 Such notable sayings are many of our late Criticks farced withal. **1830** D'ISRAELI *Chas. I*, III. xi. 243 Their invectives were well farced for the gross taste of the multitude. **1834** SOUTHEY *Let.* in H. Taylor *Autobiog.* (1885) I. xvi. 280 Farcing it [a book]..with quotations.

†**6.** To stuff or force (something) *into* something else; also *to farce in*; in quots. *fig.* Also to force (something) *through* (a strainer). *Obs.*

c **1420** *Liber Cocorum* (1862) 30 Take mustarde..Stomper hit in a morter fyne, And fars hit þurghe a clothe of lyne. **1579** FULKE *Heskins' Parl.* 257 He farceth in another slaunder of vs. **1613** PURCHAS *Pilgrimage* IV. iv. 361 Other prodigious miracles he farseth into his storie.

7. = FARSE *v.*

1857 *Ecclesiologist* XVIII. 204 A very curious farced Epistle. **1894** *Athenæum* 28 July 128/2 A peculiar feature in the recitation is the 'farcings' of each psalm, *i.e.*, the introduction of sentences, generally giving some application of the psalm to Christ. **1895** *Liturgy of Holy Apostles Adai & Mari* 1 There is no farcing at feasts, but a Hallelujah is said. **1907** *Mod. Philol.* IV. 585 None of these gradual variations caused legend or farced epistle to become anything other than legend and farced epistle.

Hence **'farced** *ppl. a.* in senses of the vb.

c **1420** *Liber Cocorum* (1862) 36 Pygges farsyd. *c* **1430** *Two Cookery-bks.* 41 Capoun or gos farced. **1549** CHALONER *Erasmus on Folly* I ij a, Well farsed tables. **1599** SHAKS. *Hen. V*, IV. i. 280 The farsed Title running 'fore the King. **1725** BRADLEY *Fam. Dict.* s.v. *Carp*, Farced Carps.

†**farce**, *v.*² *Obs.* [Cf. prec. 4 and FARD.] *trans.* To paint (the face).

c **1400** *Rom. Rose* 2285 Farce not thi visage. *c* **1430** LYDG. *Bochas* I. xiv, To shere my berde, and farce my vysage With oyntments..To make it souple.

farce, obs. f. FORCE *v.*² and ³.

farcedom ('fɑːsdəm). *nonce-wd.* [f. FARCE *sb.*² + -DOM.] Farcical spirit or style.

1842 MRS. BROWNING *Grk. Chr. Poets* 148 The broad farcedom of the earlier, however episcopal writers.

†**'farcement.** *Obs. rare*⁻¹. [f. FARCE *v.*¹ + -MENT. Cf. OF. *farcement.*] Forcemeat, stuffing.

1627–77 FELTHAM *Resolves* I. xciii. 145 They often spoil a good dish with..unsauoury farcements.

farcer ('fɑːsə(r)). [f. as prec. + -ER¹. Cf. F. *farceur.*] One who writes or acts a farce.

1791–1823 D'ISRAELI *Cur. Lit.* (1859) II. 132 These were rather the low humour of the Mimes, than of the Atellan Farcers. **1813** J. FORSYTH *Remarks Excurs. Italy* 300 *note*, [Some] consider Punch as a lineal representation of the Atellan farcers. **1813** W. TAYLOR in *Monthly Rev.* LXX. 459 When a nation has once produced a great farcer.

farcere, var. of FARSURE, *Obs.*, stuffing.

‖**farcetta** (far'sɛtə). *rare*⁻¹. [as if ad. It. *farsetta*, dim. of *farsa* FARCE *sb.*²] A short farce.
1835 *Musical Library* II. Supp. 48 After this came an exceedingly laughable Farcetta.

‖**farceur** (fɑːsœːr). [F. *farceur*, f. *farcer* to act farces, f. *farce* sb.] **a.** A joker, wag.
1781 G. SELWYN *Let.* 27 Dec. in *15th Rep. Hist. MSS. Comm.* (1897) App. VI. 553 Such *farceurs* as are in opposition. **1828** J. P. COBBETT *Tour Italy* (1830) 8 This wag, or *farceur*, as his countrymen would call him..'Aha' exclaimed the farceur. **1877** LOCKHART *Mine is Thine* xvii. (1878) II. 21 That rattling talker and farceur. **1884** *Standard* 30 Jan. 5/4 Mr. Barnum is a chartered farceur.
b. An actor or writer of farces.
1889 in *Cent. Dict.* **1957** *Listener* 10 Oct. 581/2 His company are accomplished farceurs.
c. *attrib.*, as ***farceur pianist***.
1910 V. TREE *Let.* 30 Sept. in *Castles in Air* (1926) I. 34 He is a splendid *farceur* pianist.

†**'farcic**, *a. Obs. rare*⁻¹. [f. FARCE *sb.*² + -IC.] = FARCICAL *a.*¹ I.
1763 *Brit. Mag.* IV. 437 All the farcic droll'ry to suspend.

farcical ('fɑːsɪkəl), *a.*¹ [f. as prec. + -AL¹.]
1. Of or belonging to farce; of the nature of farce.
1716 GAY *What d'ye Call it* (ed. 3) Pref., They deny the characters to be farcical, because they are actually in nature. **1744** AKENSIDE *Let. to Dyson* Poems (1845) 276 A Dutch tragedy..farcical beyond anything in Aristophanes. **1818** FOSTER in *Life & Corr.* (1846) II. 4 A farcical and operatic cast. **1877** DOWDEN *Shaks. Prim.* vi. 65 The Comedy of Errors is Shakespere's one farcical play.
2. Resembling farce; extremely ludicrous; that is matter only for laughter; absurdly futile.
1739 CIBBER *Apol.* (1756) I. 63 Vice and farcical folly. **1796** *Campaigns* 1793–4 I. I. ix. 83 Fine farcical shew and parade. **1821** EDGEWORTH *Mem.* I. 69 My farcical marriage and more farcical divorce. **1865** CARLYLE *Fredk. Gt.* VI. XVI. iii. 162 Nor is Death a farcical transaction.
Hence **'farcically** *adv.*, in a farcical manner. **'farcicalness**, farcical quality.
a **1779** LANGHORNE (T.), Images that are farcically low. **1836** T. HOOK *G. Gurney* I. 54 That disposition to treat high and serious subjects farcically. **1864** WEBSTER, *Farcicalness*.

farcical ('fɑːsɪkəl), *a.*² [f. FARCY + -IC + -AL¹.] Pertaining to the farcy.
1762 STERNE *Tr. Shandy* V. i, I wish..that every imitator had the farcy..and that there was a farcical house, large enough to hold..them. **1847** YOUATT *Horse* xv. 317 A mare had been the subject of farcical enlargements.

farcicality (fɑːsɪ'kælɪtɪ). [f. FARCICAL *a.*¹ + -ITY.] Farcical quality; an instance of this.
1849 THACKERAY *Lett.* 3 Sept., [I] laughed..but it was at pure farcicality, not at wit. **1865** *Daily Tel.* 29 May, The farcicalities of the actors were..tragically interrupted. **1883** *Pall Mall G.* 14 Dec. 3/1 An exercise the farcicality of which shocks even reverent sceptics. **1888** *Sat. Rev.* 9 June 707 A mixture..of risky but pardonable farcicalities.

farcied ('fɑːsɪd), *ppl. a.* [f. FARCY + -ED².] Affected with farcy.
1830 A. W. FONBLANQUE *England Under 7 Administr.* (1837) II. 50 Sir Robert, the best, but farcied and touched in the wind. **1891** *Daily News* 30 Oct. 6/2 To render the slaughter of farcied..horses compulsory. **1892** *Ibid.* 28 July 7/2 Eight horses, all glandered and some farcied..in a stable.

†**'farciful**, *a. Obs. rare*⁻¹. [f. FARCE *sb.*² on false analogy of *fanciful.*] Ludicrous, farcical.
1731 MEDLEY *Kolben's Cape G. Hope* I. 326 He had been several times diverted with her farciful extravagancies.

farcify ('fɑːsɪfaɪ), *v.* [f. FARCE *sb.*² + -(I)FY.] *trans.* To turn into a farce.
1834 SIR F. B. HEAD *Bubbles fr. Brunnen* 86 They..farcify below stairs the 'comedy of errors' which they catch an occasional glimpse of above. **1837** *Blackw. Mag.* XLI. 173 Covent-Garden has had the vigour to farcify it for the merriment of mankind.

†**'farcilite.** *Min. Obs.* [f. FARCE *sb.*¹ + -(I)LITE.] Pudding-stone; conglomerate.
1799 KIRWAN *Geol. Ess.* 133 The calcareous Farcilite..is formed of rounded calcareous masses..cemented by a calcareous cement. **1811** PINKERTON *Petral.* I. 139 From their composition, they come under the denomination..of farcilites.
Hence **farci'litic** *a.*, consisting of farcilite.
1799 KIRWAN *Geol. Ess.* 256 Farcilitic mountains are..common in the north of Scotland.

†**'farciment.** *Obs.* [as if ad. L. **farcīment-um*, f. *farcīre* to stuff.] Stuffing; seasoning.
1657 TOMLINSON *Renou's Disp.* 160 Pastyes, Puddings, many farciments and biscake. **1681** tr. *Willis' Rem. Med. Wks.* Vocab., *Farciments*, stuffings or fillings of anything.

†**far'ciminous**, *a. Obs. rare.* [f. L. *farcīmin-um* farcy (f. *farcīre*: see FARCE *v.*¹) + -OUS.] Of the nature of farcy.
1607 TOPSELL *Four-f. Beasts* (1673) 60 The humors which annoy the body of oxen are many..the fourth is farciminous, wherein this whole body breaketh forth into mattry bunches. **1748** tr. *Vegetius' Distemp. Horses* 9 There are seven species of this Maul. This moist..and the farciminous.

†**'farcin.** *Obs.* exc. *dial.* (in form *fashion*). Forms: 5 farseyn, 6–7 farcion, -yon, fashion, 6 farcine, -yn, 7–8 farcin. Also in *pl.* 6 fassones, 6–8 fashions. [a. Fr. *farcin*:—L. *farcīminum*: see prec.] = FARCY I.
a **1425** *Bk. Hunting* xiii. (MS. Bodl. 546 fol. 52 b), Fleyng manyew..comeþ moste comuneliche a boute þe houndes ers and yn hure legges þan yn any oþer places as þe farsyn. **1523** FITZHERB. *Husb.* §93 The farcyon is an yll soraunce. **1568** TURNER *Herball* III. 17 The farcye or fassones. *a* **1592** GREENE & LODGE *Looking Glass* Dram. Wks. (1831) I. 67 If a horse have outward diseases as the spavin..or fashion we let him blood. **1610** MARKHAM *Masterp.* II. iii. 392 The farcy (of our ignorant Smiths called the Fashions). **1686** *Lond. Gaz.* No. 2158/4 A black brown Colt..very full of Knots, like the Fashions. **1727** BRADLEY *Fam. Dict.* s.v., The Farcin in Horses is the same as the Small-pox is in Men.
attrib. **1667** *Lond. Gaz.* No. 211/4 A fine light Bay Stone-horse..having some Fashion spots upon him.
b. A farcy-bud.
1453 *Paston Lett.* No. 188 I. 255 Hese hors hath j. farseyn and grete rennyng sorys. **1617** MARKHAM *Caval.* II. 22 Foule Farcions and other cankerous sores.

†**'farcinate**, *v. Obs.* [f. L. *farcināt-* ppl. stem of *farcināre* to stuff.] *trans.* To cram, fill, stuff: **a.** (a place) with something; **b.** (the stomach) with food.
1634 SIR T. HERBERT *Trav.* 25 Their too much farcinating and late ore-charging their stomackes with fresh victuall. *Ibid.* (1638) 318 Each Varella farcinated with ugly..Idolls. **1775** in ASH.

farcing ('fɑːsɪŋ), *vbl. sb.* [f. FARCE *v.*¹ + -ING¹.]
1. The action of the vb. FARCE, in various senses; an instance of this.
c **1540** *Surr. Northampton Priory* in France *Addit. Narr. Pop. Plot* 36 Continual ingurgitations and farcyngs of our carayne Bodies. **1611** FLORIO, *Farsata*, a farcing or stuffing of meat.
fig. **1602** CAREW *Cornwall* 75 b, It ministered some stuffe to the farcing of that fable.
2. *concr.* Stuffing, forcemeat.
1532 MORE *Confut. Tindale* Wks. 614/2 Neuer was there puddyng stuffed so full of farsynge. **1568** *Hist. Iacob & Esau* IV. v. in Hazl. *Dodsley* II. 236 Good herbs..To make both broth and farcing. **1677** *Compleat Servant-Maid* 107 Take out the farsing and put it in a dish.
3. *attrib.*
1615 MARKHAM *Eng. Housew.* (1660) 68 A bunch of the best farcing herbs. **1648** HERRICK *Hesper.* I. 235 He who lookes Shall find much farcing Buckram in our Books.

farcinous ('fɑːsɪnəs), *a.* [f. FARCIN + -OUS.] 'Relating to, or being affected by farcy' (*Syd. Soc. Lex.*).

far-come (fɑːkʌm), *a.* [f. FAR *adv.* + COME *ppl. a.*] That has come from a distance.
.... *Laws Ine* xx. Feor cumen [*MS.* cuman; *v.r.* -cund] man. **1590** SPENSER *F.Q.* I. iii. 32 His ship farre come. **1675** HOBBES *Odyssey* XIV. 399 His far-come friend to entertain withal. **1819** L. HUNT *Indicator* No. 7 (1822) I. 53 Gilbert Becket took to his arms..his far-come princess.

†**'farcost.** *Obs.* Also 3 ferr cost, fare-, *south.* varecoste, 4 fercest, 7 fercost. [ad. ON. *farkostr*, f. *far* journey, ship + *kostr* means, condition (Da. and Sw. *farkost*).]
1. A kind of boat or ship.
1284 in GILBERT *Hist. & Mun. Doc.* Ireland (Rolls) 190 De qualibet navi que vocatur Farecost 8d. *a* **1300** *Cursor M.* 24885 (Cott.) Þaa þat in þat ferr cost fard. ? *a* **1400** *Morte Arth.* 743 Wyghtly one þe wale thay wye up þaire ankers, In floynes and fercestez, and Flemesche schyppes. **1455** *Will of Rawlyn* (Somerset Ho.), Dimidium vnius le Farecost vocat le Kateryn. **1597** SKENE *De Verb. Sign.* s.v. *Fercosta*, Ane Fercost..is inferior in birth and quantity to ane schip. **1609** —— *Reg. Maj., Stat. Alex. II.* 19 Anie schip or fercost, or other veschell.
2. Condition, welfare; *pl.* circumstances.
c **1205** LAY. 30735 Brien hine gon fræine of his fare-coste. *Ibid.* 32028 Vnder þissen uare-coste he sumnede ferde.

farctate ('fɑːkteɪt), *a. Bot.* [f. L. *farct-us*, pa. pple. of *farcīre* to stuff + -ATE².] 'Stuffed, crammed or full; without vacuities' WEBSTER 1832 (citing Martyn, who app. has only the L. *farctus*).

farcy ('fɑːsɪ), *sb.* Also 5–6 farsy(e, 7 farsey, farcie, 8 fassee. [variant of FARCIN.]
1. A disease of animals, *esp.* of horses, closely allied to glanders.
1481–90 *Howard Househ. Bks.* (Roxb.) 400 Medesyn for a horse that had the farsy xij. d. **1552** HULOET, *Farsye*..a sore vpon a beast or horse. **1614** MARKHAM *Cheap Husb.* I. xlix. (1668) 61 For the Farcy..with a knife slit all the knots..and then rub in the Medicine. **1710** *Lond. Gaz.* No. 4674/8 Has had the Fassee. **1713** DERHAM *Phys. Theol.* II. vi. 5 An Horse troubled with Farcy..cured himself of it in a short time by eating Hemlock. **1847** YOUATT *Horse* viii. 185 Farcy is intimately connected with glanders. **1869** E. A. PARKES *Pract. Hygiene* (ed. 3) 115 Glanders and farcy are less frequently caught in knackeries than in stables.
b. = *farcy-bud.*
1684 *Lond. Gaz.* No. 1989/4 The Horse has a Sore or Farcy on the Off-side. **1770** *Monthly Rev.* 135 Horses..sent to the salt marshes..Leave there their glanders and their farcies.
2. The same disease as communicated to men.
1762 STERNE *Tr. Shandy* V. i, I wish from my soul, that every imitator..had the farcy. **1865** *Morning Star* 4 Jan., A cabman died of 'acute farcy'.
3. *attrib.* and *Comb.*, as ***farcy humour, sore, ulcer***; **farcy bud**, one of the small tumours which occur during the progress of farcy; **farcy button** = prec., *esp.* applied where there is little thickening of connective tissue; **farcy cords, farcy pipes**, the hardened lymphatic vessels found in most cases of farcy; †**farcy horse** = *farcied horse*: see FARCIED *ppl. a.*
1533 *Surtees Misc.* (1890) 34 That no man put eny farcy horsses..of the commen. **1802** BLAINE *Outlines Veterinary Art* (1816) 411 Every diffused swelling..even ossifications and ligamentary enlargements are termed farcy humours. **1842** T. H. BURGESS *Man. Diseases Skin* 182 The matter..of a farcy-bud will produce glanders. **1878** T. BRYANT *Pract. Surg.* I. 76 Tumours or a knotty condition of the subcutaneous glands, called 'farcy buds'.

farcy ('fɑːsɪ), *v. nonce-wd.* [? ad. Fr. *farcir*: see FARCE *v.*] *trans.* To stuff.
1830 S. J. BARRINGTON *Pers. Sk. Own Times* (ed. 2) II. 186 Poetry, with which the publishers were crammed and the public farcied.

†**fard, faird**, *sb.*¹ *Sc. Obs.* Also 6 farde, 7 ferd. [Prob. identical with ME. FERD:—OE. *fyrd, fierd*, etymologically a verbal abstract f. *faran* FARE *v.* to go, though recorded only in the sense expedition, army.] Motion, rush, impetus. Hence, Impetuosity, ardour; a violent onset.
1513 DOUGLAS *Æneis* VI. xi. 12 He persavis..comand throw gresy sward His derrast son Enee with hasty fard. **1536** BELLENDEN *Chron. Scot.* x. viii. Ee ij a/1 King Feredech ..ruschit with sic farde amang his ennymes, that he was excludit fra his awin folkis. **1563** WINZET *Four Scoir Thre Quest.* §33 *Margin. note*, At this place..Iohne Knox maid a fel farde. **1639** R. BAILLIE *Let.* 28 Sept. *Lett. & Jrnls.* (1775) I. 170 Well understanding that the ferd of our hot spirits could not long abide in edge. **1681** COLVIL *Whigs Supplic.* I. 85 None gained by those bloody fairds But two three Beggers who turn'd Lairds. **1714** RAMSAY *Elegy J. Cowper* 45 E'en tho' there was a drunken laird To draw his sword and make a faird In their defence.

†**fard** (fɑːd), *sb.*² *Obs.* exc. *arch.* [a. Fr. *fard* (OF. *fart* masc., *farde* fem.); of obscure etymology; Diez refers it to OHG. *gi-farwit* coloured, painted (fem. *givarida*, glossed *fucata*), pa. pple. of *farwjan* to colour.] Paint (*esp.* white paint) for the face.
1540 PALSGR. tr. *Acolastus* I. i, A certain gay glosse or farde, such as women paynte them with. **1629** Z. BOYD *Last Battell* II. 959 Fard and foolish vaine fashions of apparell are but Bawds of allurement to vncleannesse. **1766** SMOLLETT *Trav.* 160 Rouge and fard are more peculiarly necessary in this Country. **1791** J. WHITAKER *Review of Gibbon* 4 The skeleton of history, not merely..animated with life..but.. rubbed with Spanish wool, painted with French fard. **1889** F. BARRETT *Under Strange Mask* II. x. 8 The enamels and fards employed to conceal the mark of Time's finger.
fig. **1587** *Mirr. Mag., Locrinus* xxvii, Though yee coloure all with coate of ryght No fayned fard deceaues or dimmes his sight. **1663** SIR G. MACKENZIE *Religious Stoic* viii. (1685) 75 The fard of Eloquence. **1839** THACKERAY *2nd Lect. Fine Arts*, Why will he not stick to copying her majestical countenance instead of daubing it with some..fard of his own?

†**fard** (fɑːd), *v. Obs.* Also 7 *Sc.* faird, feard. [ad. F. *fard-er*, f. *fard*: see prec.]
1. *trans.* To paint (the face) with fard, to hide defects and improve the complexion.
a **1450** *Knt. de la Tour* (1868) 69 A lady..that folke said she popped and farded her. *c* **1620** Z. BOYD *Zion's Flowers* (1855) 69, I farded have my face with fard most rare. **1653** A. WILSON *Jas. I.* 56 That Beauty..so farded and sophisticated with some Court Drug.
absol. **1584** HUDSON *Du Bartas' Judith* in *Sylvester's Du Bartas* 738 He frisles and he fards, He oynts, he bathes.
2. *transf.* and *fig.* To embellish or gloss over (anything).
1549 *Compl. Scot.* Prol. 16, I thocht it nocht necessair til hef fardit ande lardit this tracteit vitht exquiste termis. **1606** BIRNIE *Kird-Burial* (1838) 11 Our funerals wherewith wi but feard death. **1637** GILLESPIE *Eng. Pop. Cerem.* III. ii. 31 The..inveagling trinkets, wherewith the Romish Whoore doth faird..her self. **1674** PETTY *Disc. Dupl. Proportion* A v, Euphonical Nonsence, farded with formality. **1816** SCOTT *Old Mort.* xxi, Nor will my conscience permit me to fard or daub over the causes of divine wrath.
Hence †**'farded** *ppl. a.* †**'farding** *vbl. sb.*, the action of the vb. FARD, the effect produced by this. †**'farding** *ppl. a.*
1637 RUTHERFORD *Lett.* lxxxii. (1862) I. 208 This farded and overgilded world. *a* **1651** CALDERWOOD *Hist. Kirk* (1678) 458 They..mask a feigned heart with the vail of fairded language. *a* **1763** SHENSTONE *Economy* II. 140 The farded fop, and essenc'd beau. **1545** RAYNOLD *Byrth Mankynde* Prol. (1634) 6 Vtterly abhorring and defying all farding, painting, and counterfeit cast colours. **1681** COLVIL *Whigs Supplic.* (1751) 153 Like fairding on a face that's wrinkled. **1637** GILLESPIE *Eng. Pop. Cerem.* Ep. A iij, Her comely countenance is miscoloured with the farding lustre of the mother of Harlotes.

fard, obs. f. FEARED, afraid.

†**'fardage.** *Obs.* [a. Fr. *fardage* (= Sp. *fardaje*, Pg. *fardagem*, It. *fardaggio*), f. *farde*: see FARDEL.]
1. The impedimenta of an army, baggage.
1578 T. N. tr. *Conq. W. India* 116 Cortes departed with his army in good order, and in the midst of them went the fardage and artillerie. **1600** HOLLAND *Livy* XLII. lxiv. 1153 Perseus..putting his fardage and carriage before.

†**2.** = DUNNAGE.

(Used in charter parties about 1860; now *obs.* among English shippers.)

fardel ('fɑːdəl), *sb.*[1] *arch.* Forms: 4-6 **fardele**, 4-7 **far-, ferdel(l(e**, (6 **ferdle**), 5 **fardille**, 6-7 **farthel(l(e**, 6-9 **fardle**, (7 **fardal**), 3- **fardel**. [a. OF. *fardel* (later *fardeau*), dim. of *farde* burden, cognate with Sp., Pg. *fardo*.

It has been suggested that the source of the Rom. word is Arab. *fardah*: see Devic s.v.]

1. a. A bundle, a little pack; a parcel. Also *collect.* Occas. in *pl.* Baggage (of a company of men).

a **1300** *Cursor M.* 5004 (Cott.) þai..did þair fardels be vndon. *Ibid.* 24947 (Gött) Wid all þair fardel and þair fere þai com till land. **1375** BARBOUR *Bruce* III. 432 Sum..on his bak ber a fardele. **1388** WYCLIF *Ruth* ii. 9 Also if thou thirstist go to the fardels and drynke watris. *a* **1400-50** *Alexander* 5136 Foure hundreth Olifaunts in fere þis fardille to bere. *c* **1485** *Digby Myst.* (1882) I. 273 This ferdell of gere I ley vp my bakke. *a* **1533** LD. BERNERS *Huon* lii. 176 He promysed to serue me and to bere my fardel. **1557** N. T. (Genev.) *Acts.* xxi. 15 We trussed vp our fardeles and went vp to Ierusalem. **1611** SHAKS. *Wint. T.* IV. iv. 783 There lyes such Secrets in this Farthell and Box, which none must know but the King. **1681** EVELYN *Diary* (1827) IV. 259 Tis not easy to imagine the infinite fardles of papers. **1759** STERNE *Tr. Shandy* II. ix, A little diminutive pony..under such a fardel. *c* **1817** HOGG *Tales & Sk.* V. 228 You are to walk behind Lady Jane, and carry her fardel. **1853** LYTTON *My Novel* (1856) 262 The tinker..resumed his fardel, and followed Leonard to the town.

b. The omasum, or third stomach, of ruminants. Also *fardel-bag*.

1862 *Chambers's Encycl.* IV. 245/1 Fardel-bound, a disease of cattle and sheep, consists of impaction of the fardel bag. **1908** *Animal Managem.* 16 The..'manyplies' or 'fardel' (omasum).

2. *fig.* **a.** A collection, 'lot', parcel (of immaterial things).

1526 *Pilgr. Perf.* (W. de W. 1531) 24 Suche..sentences as we haue gathered of holy fathers..togyder, as in one fardell. **1614** BP. HALL *Recoll. Treat.* 459 What is their Alcoran, but a fardle of foolish impossibilities? **1667** H. MORE *Div. Dial.* III. xix. (1713) 219 This fictitious Fardel of Transubstantiation. *a* **1703** BURKITT *On N.T. Rom.* xi. 2 Let them prove that their fardles of traditions were delivered to the church from the mouth of the apostles. **1873** H. ROGERS *Orig. Bible* i. 49 *note*, A fardel of myths.

b. *esp.* A burden or load of sin, sorrow, etc.

c **1380** WYCLIF *Sel. Wks.* III. 208 þe fardel of his wickidnesse. **1483** CAXTON *Gold. Leg.* 119/3 Goo fro me thou fardel of synne. **1576** FLEMING *Panopl. Epist.* 356 His fardle of troubles. **1644** HERRICK *Hesper.* (1844) II. 124 None sees the fardel of his faults behind. **1818** BYRON *Ch. Har.* IV. clxvi, These fardels of the heart. **1835** LYTTON *Rienzi* x. viii, Who can..sit tamely down to groan under the fardel of the Present?

†**3.** That in which something is wrapped; a wrapping, wrapper. *Obs.*

1388 WYCLIF *Ezek.* xxvii. 24 In fardels of iacinct and of clothis of many colours. **1600** J. PORY tr. *Leo's Africa* II. 249 About their heads they lap such fardels of linnen, as they seeme comparable to the heads of Giants. **1649** G. DANIEL *Trinarch., Hen. V*, cccxxix, In a Petty-Coat Wrapt, a night fardle.

4. *attrib.* and *Comb.* **fardel-bound** *a.*, costive; so as *sb.*, a condition in cattle and sheep in which food is retained in the folds of omasum.

1587 TURBERV. *Trag. T.* v. 313 Jewels for to save, Trusst up in fardell wise. **1825** LOUDON *Encycl. Agric.* 976 Costiveness also brings on a colic in them, called clue bound, fardel bound, etc. **1844** H. STEPHENS *Bk. Farm* II. 155 The fardlebound of cattle and sheep is nothing more than a modification of the disease in horses called stomach-staggers, which is caused by an enormous distention of the stomach. **1862** [see 1 b]. **1892** *Pall Mall G.* 23 Sept. 6/2 An emancipation of all down-trodden, fardel-bearing..slaves.

†**'fardel**, *sb.*[2] *Obs.* Also 7 *Sc.* **ferdall, farthel**. Also FARTHINGDEAL and *Sc.* FARL. [repr. OE. *féorða dǽl* fourth part; see FOURTH *a.* and DEAL *sb.*] A fourth part of anything. ***fardel of land*** (see quots. 1641, 1706). Also in *pl.* Quarters, pieces, fragments.

c **1440** *Gaw. & Gol.* 1019 The scheld in fardellis can fle, in feild away fer. **1627** *Dumbarton Burgh Rec.* in J. Irving *Hist. Dumbartonshire* (1860) 483 It is..ordanit..that thair be onlie four kaiks in the pek, and thrie ferdalls in ilk kaik onlie. **1641** NOY *Compl. Lawyer* (1651) 57 Two Fardells of Land make a Nooke of Land, and two Nookes make halfe a Yard of Land. *c* **1666** W. SUTHERLAND in Wodrow *Hist. Suff. Ch. Scot.* I. App. 101, I..bought a Farthel of Bread and a Mutckin of Ale. **1706** PHILLIPS (ed. Kersey), *Fardel of Land*, the fourth part of a Yard-land. **1883** SEEBOHM *Eng. Village Community* 57 There were also holders of fardels or quarter-virgates, and half-fardels or one-eighth-virgates.

†**'fardel**, *sb.*[3] In 6 **ferdele, fardell**. Also FOREDEAL. [a. Du. *voordeel* advantage.] Profit.

1523 HEN. VIII in Strype *Eccl. Mem.* I. 45 Whereby..shall ensue grete advantage and ferdele to the common affairs of the Kings grace. **1569** SIR T. GRESHAM in Ellis *Orig. Lett.* II. 183 II. 318 Her Highnes maie paie it bie the waie of exchaung..to her gret fardell and profit.

†**'fardel**, *v.* *Obs.* Also 6-7 **fardle**, 7 **fardell**, 7-8 **farthel(l**. [f. prec. *sb.*; cf. OF. *fardeler*, and see FARL, FURDLE, FURL *vbs.*]

1. *trans.* To make into a bundle; *fig.* in quots. Also *to fardel up*.

1594 CAREW *Huarte's Exam. Wits* i. (1596) 10, I haue alwaies held it an errour, to heare many lessons of diuers matters, and to carry them all home fardled vp together. **1660** FISHER *Rustick's Alarm* Wks. 443 Prophesies, Psalms, Proverbs, Parables..found and fardelled together. **1701** BEVERLEY *Apoc. Quest.* 33 So that all I can suppose, is, that it is Fardled up in the Four First Trumpets.

2. *Naut.* = FURL.

1582 N. LICHEFIELD tr. *Castanheda's Conq. E. Ind.* 72 b, The Captaine generall commanded..to fardle vp their sprits sailes. **1598** BARRET *Theor. Warres* II. i. 21 This Ensigne..if fardled vp, all they are to do in the like order. **1630** DRAYTON *Muses Elizium* VII. 98 A pretty handsome Packe, Which she had fardled neatly at her backe. **1704** J. HARRIS *Lex. Techn.*, *Farthell, Farthelling*; is the same with what the Seamen now call *Furl* or *Furling*.

†**'fardellage.** *Obs.* [ad. OF. *fardelage*, f. *fardeler* to pack up, f. *fardel* FARDEL *sb.*[1]] A package.

1489 CAXTON *Faytes of A.* I. xiii. 34 Baggage and fardellages must be taken.

farden, obs. and dial. var. of FARTHING.

farder, obs. var. of FARTHER *a.*, *adv.*, and *vb.*

fardin(g, fardin(g-, see FARTHING, etc.

†**'fardlet.** *Obs.* Also 5 **fardelet**. [ad. OF. *fardelet*, dim. of *fardel*, FARDEL *sb.*[1]] A little bundle.

1413 LYDG. *Pilgr. Sowle* II. xliii. (1859) 49 Justyce..hadde me bitake my sorry fardelet. **1611** COTGR., *Fardelet*, a fardlet, a little fardle.

'far-down, *sb.* and *a.* **A.** *sb.* (Also **far-downer**.) An Irish-American belonging to a family which emigrated from the north of Ireland. *U.S.*

1834 *Amer. Railroad Jrnl.* III. 384/1 The parties arrayed against each other are known as the *Fardowns* and the *Corkonians*. *a* **1837** R. J. BRECKINRIDGE *Memoranda* (1845) I. 29 This city [*sc.* Cork] gives name to one of those bloody factions, which under the appellations of *Corkonians* and *Fardowns* divide the lowest classes of Irish Catholics in that distant land [*sc.* U.S.A.]. **1857** *Spirit of Times* 21 Feb. 405/2 They formed into two hostile factions, called Corkonians and Far-Downers. **1899** *Echo* 9 Mar. 1/2 Down in that quarter of Chicago you can hear all the 'various accents of Ireland, from the awkward brogue of the "far-downer" to the mild and aisy Elizabethan English of the Southern Irishman'.

B. *adj.* Situated or existing far below.

1911 FLETCHER & KIPLING *School Hist. Eng.* vii. 134 The far-down shark Shoots glimmering on his ways. **1949** BLUNDEN *After Bombing* 49 In the far-down street That Statue watched the laughing markets meet.

†**fardredeal.** *Obs.* $rare^{-1}$. [? f. FARTHER + DEAL *sb.*; cf. FARDEL *sb.*[3]] ? Advantage.

1521 PACE in *St. Papers Hen. VIII*, I. 36 The Frenche Kynge..is at a greate fardredeal.

†**'fardry.** *Obs.* In 5 **fardrye**. [ad. OF. *farderie*, f. *farde*: see FARD and -RY.] The action of painting the face, the effect produced by this.

c **1430** *Pilgr. Lyf Manhode* III. xlviii. (1869) 161 This fauce visage is cleped Fardrye, with which whan j am eelded and bicome riueled..j make me shynynge in despite of nature.

fare (fɛə(r)), *sb.*[1] Forms: 1 **fær, faru** (*inflected* **fare**), 3-4 **far**, 4-5, 8 **fair**, 4-6 **fayr(e**, 5-6 **faire**, (6 **faier**, 4, 8 **phare**), 2- **fare**. [Orig. two words, both f. root of FARE *v.*: OE. *fær* str. neut. = OHG. and ON. *far*:—OTeut. **faro(m*, and OE. *faru* str. fem. = OFris. *fare*, MHG. *var*. ON. *fǫr*:—OTeut. **farâ*.]

I. †**1. a.** A going, journeying; course, passage, way; voyage. *Obs.*

c **1000** *Ags. Gosp.* Luke ii. 44 Anes dæʒes fær. *c* **1005** *Byrhtferth's Handboc* in *Anglia* VIII. 305 Hyt byð ʒeradlic þæt we ascrutnion his fare. **1154** *O.E. Chron.* an. 1120 And on þam fare wurdon adrincene þæs cynges twegen sunan Willelm and Ricard. *c* **1200** *Vices & Virtues* (1888) 137 Ðare muchele burʒh ðe ʒelaste ðrie daiʒes fare. *c* **1205** LAY. 4092 Suððen he turnde his fare. *c* **1250** *Gen. & Ex.* 3179 Almost redi was here fare. *a* **1300** *Cursor M.* 4754 (Cott.) þat flum þat rennes þar Til ioseph hus it has þe fare. *c* **1325** *E.E. Allit. P.* C. 98 Fyndez he a fayr schyp to þe fare redy. **1375** BARBOUR *Bruce* IV. 627 God furthir vs in-till our fair! *a* **1400-50** *Alexander* 2250 A Jentill man..Foloʒes þare fare ai on fote. **1557** *Tottell's Misc.* (Arb.) 133 The ioyfull fare, the end of strife. **1596** SPENSER *F.Q.* v. x. 16 Nought the morrow next more stay his fare. **1613-6** W. BROWNE *Brit. Past.* II. iii. 70 Her Dolphins..plyde So busily their fares on every side. **1751** CHAMBERS *Cycl.*, *Fare*, a voyage or passage.

†**b.** An expedition. ***herring-fare***: a voyage to catch herrings. *Obs.*

a **1000** *Cædmon's Exod.* 554 (Gr.) Fullesta mæst, se ðas fare lædeþ. **1154** *O.E. Chron.* an. 1128 Se firste fare was on Urbanes dæi. **1387** TREVISA *Higden* (Rolls) I. 141 After þis phare was pees in Scythia. **1530** PALSGR. 825/1 A heryng fare, *pescher des harencz*.

†**c.** Equipment for a journey; rigging out (of a ship); apparel, belongings. *Obs.*

c **1320** *Sir Tristr.* 926 Fair was his schip fare. **1393** GOWER *Conf.* I. 119 He in all his proude fare, Unto the forest gan to fare. *a* **1400-50** *Alexander* 3694 Of fethirhame & alle fare, as feetely enjoyned. *c* **1475** *Rauf Coilʒear* 419 Sa saw he quhair the Coilʒear come with all his fair.

2. † **a.** A road, track (*obs.*). **b.** *spec.* The track of a hare or rabbit (*obs.* exc. *dial.*). † **c.** A ferry (*obs.* $rare^{-1}$; perh. merely suggested by Ger. *fahr* in the original).

1509 HAWES *Past. Pleas.* xxxv. xxi, Ye had forsaken The lowe vale, and up the craggy fayre..the hye waye had taken. **1610** FLETCHER *Faithf. Sheph.* IV. i, Not a Hare Can be started from his fare. **1612** DRAYTON *Poly-olb.* xvi. 269 Coming in her course to cross the common fare. **1762** tr. *Busching's Syst. Geog.* IV. 548 A fare over the Mosel and Tarforst. **1879** *Shropshire Word-bk.*, *Fare*, a track, as of a rabbit.—*Oswestry*.

†**3.** A number of persons prepared for a journey; a troop, multitude. Also, a swarm (of flies). *Obs.*

c **1205** LAY. 3904 Swulc fare of fleoʒen her was. *Ibid.* 30666 Brien bonnede his fare. **1297** R. GLOUC. (1724) 52 þe emperour say, þat ys fare nas noʒt þere. *a* **1300** *Cursor M.* 12763 (Cott.) þe Iues tiþand of him [John] hard, And of his far þat he wit fard. *c* **1400** *Destr. Troy* 11069 þai folowest fast on þe fare, with hor fell dynttes Dang hom to dethe.

transf. **1634** W. TIRWHYT tr. *Balzac's Lett.* 324, I have observed among man onely a fare of flatteries, fooles and Cheaters.

4. † **a.** A passage or excursion for which a price is paid; hence **b.** Cost of conveyance (now only of persons; formerly also of goods); passage money.

c **1425** WYNTOUN *Cron.* VI. xviii. 226 þare suld nane pay mare þan foure pennys for þare fare. **1514** FITZHERB. *Just. Peas* (1538) 194 b, These articles to be kept upon payne to forfayt treble the fare. **1535** COVERDALE *Jonah* i. 3 He payde his fare, and wente aborde. **1570-6** LAMBARDE *Peramb. Kent* (1826) 438 Making the whole fare (or passage) worth foure shillings. *c* **1620** Z. BOYD *Zion's Flowers* (1855) 8 Most willingly I'le pay thereof the fare. **1765** FOOTE *Commissary* I. Wks. 1799 II. 8 What's your fare? **1767** *Babler* II. No. 76. 57 That person..who cannot..take an eighteen-penny fare in occasional sedan. **1806-7** J. BERESFORD *Miseries Hum. Life* (1826) IV. xxviii, Being asked by the coachman three or four times his fare. **1864** SKEAT *Uhland's Poems* 49 Boatman, come, thy fare receive.

5. a. The passenger, or (now *rarely*) company of passengers, that engages a vehicle plying for hire.

[Presumably transf. from 4 b; certainly so apprehended in present use.]

1562 J. HEYWOOD *Prov. & Epigr.* (1867) 205 Thy fares ouer the water thou shouldst row. **1630** J. TAYLOR (Water P.) *Fearful Summer* Wks. I. 60/2 Those..water-men..land their fares in Heaven or Hell. **1696** *Lond. Gaz.* No. 3149/4 The Fare was taken up in Grivell-Street, and set down in Channel-Row. **1712** STEELE *Spect.* No. 498 ¶2 A hackney-coachman..set down his fare, which..consisted of two or three very fine ladies. **1798** CANNING, etc. *Loves of Triangles* in *Anti-Jacobin* (1852) 124 'Shoot we the bridge!' the exulting fare reply. **1823** BYRON *Juan* x. lxxi, Germany, wherein they muddle Along the road, as if they went to bury Their fare. **1841** S. C. HALL *Ireland* I. 69 Elevating what serves for a whip if they think a fare is approaching. **1876** SAUNDERS *Lion in Path* xvii, For his fare two persons.

b. †The 'load' (of an animal). *Obs.* Also U.S. The cargo of a vessel; a load or 'catch' of fish.

1600 HEYWOOD *1 Edw. IV*, 39 Drive Dun and her faire softly downe the hill. **1707** in *Essex Inst. Hist. Coll.* XLII. 165 Loosing their last faires of fish. **1792** J. BELKNAP *Hist. New Hampsh.* III. 214 The fish of the summer and fall fares is divided into two sorts. **1831** A. SHERBURNE *Mem.* (ed. 2) x. 217 The old gentleman had just arrived from the ocean with a fare of fish. **1875** J. G. HOLLAND *Sevenoaks* xi. 139 The whalers had returned with scantier fares year after year. **1884** E. E. HALE *Fort. Rachel* ii. 15 Stopping to telegraph to his partner..of the fare taken. **1886** *Harper's Mag.* Dec. 105/1 He come by with his fare o' fish, an' hove to to see what I was gittin. **1904** *N.Y. Even. Post* 18 June, The prices brought by the 'fares', which are..cargoes of fresh or salted fish.

II. †**6. a.** Mode of proceeding, bearing, demeanour; appearance, aspect. *Obs.*

1297 R. GLOUC. (Rolls) 2743 þo he adde ysywed me longe in þisse fare. *a* **1300** *Cursor M.* 24375 (Cott.) þair tender fare For child þat þai ha born. *c* **1325** *E.E. Allit.* P. B. 861 Your fare is to strange. *c* **1420** *Anturs of Arth.* xli, He foundes into the freke with a fresche fare. **1508** DUNBAR *Goldyn Targe* 225 On syde scho lukit with a fremit fare. **1521** *St. Papers Hen. VIII*, VI. 84 She wold bee gladder of peax, then she maketh fayre of. **1540** HYRDE tr. *Vives' Instr. Chr. Wom.* (1592) X vj, Let the wife..shew example of sober fare.

†**b.** A proceeding, action; 'doings'; hence, fighting. *Obs.*

1340-70 *Alex. & Dind.* 1096 þe sawe þat ʒe sente to segge of ʒoure fare. **1393** LANGL. *P. Pl.* C. XXI. 130 Ich haue ferly of þis fare in faith. *c* **1400** *Destr. Troy* 7442 Furse was þe fare þo fyn men betwene. *c* **1440** *York Myst.* ix. 90 This fare wille I no lenger frayne. *c* **1450** MYRC 332 Songe and cry and suche fare, For to stynte þow schalt not spare. *a* **1548** *Thrie Priests Peblis* in Pinkerton *Scot. Poems* I. 38 Allace..this is ane haisty fair.

†**c.** Display, pomp; commotion, uproar, fuss.

a **1300** *Cursor M.* 13212 (Cott.) þai ledd his licam vte o tun, Til sebastin wit mikel far. *c* **1330** R. BRUNNE *Chron. Wace* (Rolls) 16263 He made gret fare ffor þat Osewy was nought þare. **1375** BARBOUR *Bruce* xx. 126 Swa did he [Croune his ʒoung sone] With gret fair and solempnite. **1387** TREVISA *Higden* (Rolls) I. 419 Wawes of þe see..brekeþ in þare Wiþ suche noyse and fare. *c* **1400** *Gamelyn* 199 Why makestow this fare? *c* **1425** *Seven Sag.* (P.) 698 Baucillas, lat be thy fare. *c* **1440** *Promp. Parv.* 150/1 Fare, or boost, *jactancia, arrogancia*. *c* **1475** *Rauf Coilʒear* 149 The King..maid ane strange fair.

†**7.** Condition, state, welfare; state of things, prosperity, success. ***what fare?*** what is the state of things? (cf. *what cheer?*). *Obs.*

c **1250** *Gen. & Ex.* 2771 For te loken hirdnesse fare. *a* **1300** *Cursor M.* 4238 (Cott.) Leue we now iacob in þis care To tell of ioseph and his fare. **1340-70** *Alex. & Dind.* 150 For miche wildnede þe weiʒht to witen of here fare. *c* **1375** *Cato Major* II. xvii. in *Anglia* VII, Of oper mennes euel fare Envye makeþ him gleo. *a* **1400-50** *Alexander* 2019 Fra þat I fraist haue þat faire of my faire lady. *Ibid.* 3257 þi wale gode..fully feld alle þe fare þat falle suld on erthe. **14..** in *Tundale's Vis.* (1843) 77 He askede hur of hur fare. **1549** LATIMER *4th Serm. bef. Edw. VI* (Arb.) 118 He knoweth hys fare by thys—he is eyther in joye or in payne. **1593** SHAKS.

3 Hen. VI, II. i. 95 How now faire Lords? What faire? What newes abroad? *c* **1611** CHAPMAN *Iliad* xv. 214 Add thy care, O Phœbus..that this so sickly fare Of famous Hector be recur'd.

8. Food, regarded with reference to its quality; supply or provision of food, regarded as abundant or scanty. †*to make a fare*: ? to provide plentifully (cf. 6 c). *bill of fare*: see BILL 10.

c **1205** LAY. 10236 Her wes unimete fare a þissere folc riche. *c* **1340** *Gaw. & Gr. Knt.* 537 He made a fare on þat fest, for þe frekez sake. **1375** BARBOUR *Bruce* XVI. 46 He maid thame mekill fest and far. *c* **1475** *Rauf Coilȝear* 112 Heir is bot hamelie fair. **1531** ELYOT *Gov.* III. xxii, The excesse of fare is to be iustly reproued. **1579** SPENSER *Sheph. Cal.* Jan. 44 Whose knees are weake, through fast and euill fare. **1667** MILTON *P.L.* IX. 1028 After such delicious Fare. **1730–46** THOMSON *Autumn* 191 Careless of to-morrow's fare. **1774** PENNANT *Tour Scot. in 1772*, 212 Their daily wretched fare, limpets and perriwinkles. **1816** SCOTT *Tales Landl.* Ser. I. Introd., Such fare as the mountains of your own country produce. **1874** LISLE CARR *Jud. Gwynne* I. ii. 62 Such homely dainties were not 'company fare'.

fig. *a* **1592** H. SMITH *Serm.* (1866) II. 168 What is the fare? Peace, joy, righteousness. **1651** DAVENANT *Gondibert* II. I. 61 Truth we grudge her as a costly fare. *a* **1679** GURNALL in Spurgeon *Treas. Dav.* Ps. cxix. 132 This is no more than family fare, what thou promisest to do for all that love thee. **1693** DRYDEN *Juvenal* xiv. 389 So few there are, Who will conform to Philosophick fare. **1727** DE FOE *Prot. Monast*, iv, I shall have Neighbours Fare.

III. 9. *attrib.* and *Comb.* (sense 4 b), as ***fare-board***, ***-card***, ***-stage***; ***fare-free***, ***-paying***, adjs. Also **fare indicator**, an instrument for registering the fares paid in a public conveyance; †**fare-maker**, a boaster.

1897 *Daily News* 10 July 9/2 Labels on the outside [of buses] announced that the fares were sixpence or one shilling for any distance, and in each case the painted *fare-board was replaced by a printed paper. *Ibid.*, If omnibus proprietors wished to charge special fares they must go to the expense of having a special *fare card painted. **1893** *Daily News* 5 Apr. 3/3 All the world knows that he is travelling *fare free. **1892** *Pall Mall G.* 14 Nov. 2/3 A *fare-indicator for cabs. *c* **1440** *Promp. Parv.* 150 *Fare makere, or bostowre, *jactator*. **1928** *Daily Tel.* 16 Oct. 12/4 The first company of *farepaying passengers to cross the Atlantic by airship. **1926** *Year's Work Eng. Stud. 1924* 31 We have seen it [*sc.* a book] devoured on the top of a tram to the oblivion of *fare-stages.

fare (fɛə(r)), *sb.*² *Obs.* exc. *dial.* [f. FARE *v.*²; see FARROW *sb.*] A litter of pigs.

1557 TUSSER *100 Points Husb.* lv, The losse of one fare of thy sowe is greater, then losse of two calues of thy kowe. **1674–91** RAY *S. & E.C. Words* 97 A Fare of Pigs is so many as a Sow bringeth forth at one time. **1736** BAILEY *Housh. Dict.* 341 When a sow has brought a fare of pigs. **1787** in GROSE *Prov. Gloss.* Suppl. **1847** in HALLIWELL.

†**fare**, *sb.*³ *Obs.* Also 8 phare. [ad. It. *faro* in same senses, ad. L. *pharus*, Gr. φάρος PHAROS.] The name of a promontory (marked by a lighthouse) at the entrance of the Strait of Messina. Hence, the strait itself. More fully ***The Fare of Messina***.

1628 DIGBY *Voy. Medit.* (1868) 26 A shippe plying to gett into the fare of Messina. **1720** *Lond Gaz.* No. 5827/1 Before they could get out of the Phare. **1730–6** BAILEY (folio), *Fare*, a watch-tower at sea, as the Fare of Messina. **1739** *Encour. Sea-f. People* 38 He stood in about the Point of the Fare towards Messina.

†**fare**, *sb.*⁴ *Obs.* [Belongs to FARE *v.*³] A certain game at dice.

1530 [see FARE *v.*³]. **1847** in HALLIWELL.

fare (fɛə(r)), *v.*¹ Pa. t. and pa. pple. fared. Forms: *Inf.* 1–2 faran, 2–5 faren (*Orm.* farenn), 4–5 faryn, 3–4 *south.* vare, veare, 4– 5 far, 6 farre, 4–7 fair, fayr(e, (5–6 faar(e, 6 faer), 3– fare. *Pa. t.* (*str.*) 1 fór, 2–3 for (*south.* vor), 4–5 fore, (4 fer, foure, 4–5 foore), 4–7 fur(e, 6 *Sc.* fuir(e, 8 *Sc.* foor. *Pa. pple.* (*str.*) 1–4 faren, 3–5 farin, -yn, 4–6 farn(e, fare, (5 fairen). *Pa. t.* and *pa. pple.* (*weak*) 5 faryd, 6 fard(e, (7 feared), 6– fared. [A Com. Teut. str. vb.: OE. *faran*, pa. t. *fór*, pa. pple. *faren*, corresponds to OFris. *fara*, *fôr*, *faren*, OS. *faran*, *fôr*, (*gi*)*faran* (Du. *varen*, *voor*, *gevarn*), OHG. *faran*, *fuor*, (*gi*)*faran* (MHG. *var(e)n*, *vuor*, *gevar(e)n*), ON. *fara*, *fór*, *farenn* (Da. *fare*, *foer*, *faret*, Sw. *fara*, *for*, *farit*), Goth. *faran*, *fôr*, *farans*:—OTeut. **faran*, *fôr*, *farano-*, f. pre-Teut. **por-*, *pōr-*, f. Aryan root **per*, *por*, *pər* to pass through, whence many derivatives in all the Aryan langs.: cf. Sk. *par*, *pṛ* to carry through or across, Gr. πόρος way, passage, ford, L. *portāre* to carry; also the words mentioned under FAR, FOR.

The change from the strong to the weak conjugation seems to have been due in part to the influence of the derivative vb. FERE, which in Eng. had the same sense, though in the other Teut. langs. its equivalent expressed the transitive sense 'to carry'. In this sense this vb. became obsolete before 14th c.; but its pa. t. and pa. pple. *ferd(e* (in northern dialects also *fard(e)* continued in use, virtually serving as inflexions of *fare*. The irregular wk. vb. thus produced (*fare*, *ferd*) became regular (*fare*, *fared*) before the 16th c. The strong pa. t., already comparatively infrequent in ME., seldom appears after 15th c. exc. in Sc.; of the strong pa. pple. we have no examples after 16th c.]

I. To go, travel.

1. *intr.* To journey, travel, make one's way. Now *arch.* or *poet.* †In early use occas. with cognate obj. ***to fare a voyage, a way*** (cf. *wayfarer*, *-ing*).

971 *Blickl. Hom.* 15 Nu we faraþ to Gerusalem. **1154** *O.E. Chron.* an. 1135 On þis gære for se King Henri ouer sæ. *c* **1205** LAY. 2412 Alch mon mihte faren ȝend hire lond þaih he bere ræd gold. *a* **1300** *Cursor M.* 3295 (Cott.), I am a man farand þe way. *c* **1314** *Guy Warw.* (A.) 1101 Nov is Gij to Warwike fare. *c* **1350** *Will. Palerne* 5079 He had ferrest to fare. **1375** BARBOUR *Bruce* XI. 530 To the castell thai thoucht to fair. *c* **1450** MYRC 265 Whenne they doth to chyrche fare. **1530** LYNDESAY *Test. Papyngo* 100 Quhare euer I fure, I bure hir [the bird] on my hande. **15..** *Sir A. Barton* in *Surtees Misc.* (1890) 64 Nor a Burgesse voy(a)ge we der not farre. **1590** SPENSER *F.Q.* I. i. 11 Resolving forward still to fare. **1609** HEYWOOD *Brit. Troy* xv. lvi, Eneas, madly Faring Through flames. **1664** *Flodden F.* i. 5 And how he fared was into France. **1667** MILTON *P.L.* II. 940 On he fares..half on foot, Half flying. **1725** POPE *Odyss.* x. 683 Sadly they fared along the sea-beat shore. **1794** BURNS *There was a lass* ii, O'er the moor they lightly foor. **1837** CARLYLE *Fr. Rev.* III. I. iv, Abbé Sicard, with some thirty other Nonjurant Priests ..fare along the streets. **1855** M. ARNOLD *Poems*, *Resignation* 69 Through the deep noontide heats we fare.

fig. **1837** CARLYLE *Fr. Rev.* II. v. v, Altars..changing to the Gobel-and-Talleyrand sort, are faring by rapid transmutations to—shall we say, the right Proprietor of them?

2. In wider sense = GO. †**a.** of persons, *lit.* ***to let fare***: = to let go. *Obs.*

a **1123** *O.E. Chron.* an. 1101 þa heofod men heo betwenan foran. *a* **1300** *Cursor M.* 3935 (Cott.) þe angel badd [iacob] lete him far. *c* **1385** CHAUCER *L.G.W.* 2209 *Ariadne*, She.. kyssed..The steppes of hys fete, there he hath fare. *a* **1400–50** *Alexander* 5549 Sum..farand as bestis. ? *c* **1475** *Sqr. lowe Degre* 739 To morowe ye shall on hunting fare. **1590** SPENSER *F.Q.* I. iii. 15 One knocked at the dore, and in would fare.

†**b.** *fig.* *Obs.*

a **1225** *St. Marher.* 6 He of wreððe for neh ut of his iwitte. **1552** LYNDESAY *Monarche* 5325 First wyll I to the Scripture fare.

†**c.** To depart from life; to die. *Obs.*

c **1175** *Lamb. Hom.* 115 He scal faran to þan eche liue for his treowscipe. *c* **1200** *Vices & Virtues* (1888) 15 Ær ðane he of ðese liue fare. *c* **1220** *Bestiary* 731 Hise loðe men sulen to helle faren. *a* **1225** *Leg. Kath.* 1393 Hwi ne hihe we for to beon i-fulhtnet..ear we faren henne? *a* **1300** *Cursor M.* 2356 (Cott.) His fader was farn o liue. *Ibid.* 25441 (Cott.) Fast i fund to fare. *c* **1330** *Arth. & Merl.* 70 Out of this warld y most fare. **1340–70** *Alex. & Dind.* 330 We..leue þat þe soule..schal fare to blisse. **1377** LANGL. *P. Pl.* B. VII. 98 Whan he shal hennes fare.

†**d.** ***to fare on***: to rush upon, assault. *Obs.*

1535 STEWART *Cron. Scot.* (1858) I. 10 He..fuir on thame with sic a felloun force.

†**e.** Of a liquid, a stream: To flow, 'run'. Of immaterial things, *esp.* time: To go, pass, proceed. *Obs.* or *arch.*

c **1250** *Gen. & Ex.* 2153 Ðe vii. fulsum ȝeres faren. *a* **1300** *Cursor M.* 1034 (Cott.) Flummes farand in fer landes. *c* **1400** *Destr. Troy* 149 A fame þat fer in fele kynges londes. *a* **1400–50** *Alexander* 3901 Foure houres full farne & þe fifte neghes. **15..** *Smyth & Dame* 327 in Hazl. *E.P.P.* III. 213 That bloud out gan fare. **1827** HOOD *Hero & L.* xciv, The crystal skin Reveals the ruby tide that fares within.

f. ***to fare astray*** (†***misliche, amiss***): = to go astray. *Obs.* or *arch.*

c **1175** *Lamb. Hom.* 119 He scal misliche faran on monie gedwilþan. *c* **1425** *Seven Sag.* (P.) 2337 Why and whare-fore hyt hys, That ȝoure syght fareth amys. *Ibid.* 2756 Thou levest wykked concel iwys, That makes the fare amys. **1596** SPENSER *Hymn Heav. Love* xxviii. (1611), When we fared had amis. *a* **1849** J. C. MANGAN *Poems* (1859) 119 Is it earthly music faring astray.

†**g.** To 'go', range, have a place. *Obs. rare*⁻¹.

1704 J. LOGAN in *Pa. Hist. Soc. Mem.* IX. 293 The fields and boats fare before schools or books.

†**h.** To 'go', pass, change into something else.

1398 TREVISA *Barth. De P.R.* v. lxv. (1495) 183 Whan the water heetyth, therof comyth whytnesse as it faryth in foom.

3. rarely *trans.* †**a.** To tread (under foot). **b.** Of a horse: To take (a person) along.

c **1460** *Towneley Myst.* 120 Under my feete I shalle thaym fare, Those ladys that wille [not] lere my lare. **1867** CARLYLE *Remin.* (1881) II. 139 Ourselves two alone in the world, the good [pony] 'Larry' faring us.

II. With reference to behaviour or condition.

†**4.** To 'go on', behave, conduct oneself, act.

a **1300** *Cursor M.* 11807 (Gött.) þat wili wolf, þat for sua fals. *Ibid.* 16762 + 41 (Cott.) Mony grete clerkez..Seghen þe son fare soo. **1340** HAMPOLE *Pr. Consc.* 599 He..fares als an unresonabel beste. *c* **1400** *Destr. Troy* 654, I will you faithfully enforme how ye fare shall, Your worship to wyn. **1470** MALORY *Arthur* XX. xii, Ye fare as a man that were aferd. **1563–87** FOXE *A. & M.* (1596) 65/1 He fared as one out of his wits. **1697** DRYDEN *Virg. Æneid* VII. 534 Thus fares the Queen, and thus her fury blows Amidst the crowd.

†**b.** To 'go on' impetuously, rage, rail (*against*). *Obs.* Cf. FARE *sb.*¹ 6 c.

1603 HOLLAND *Plutarch's Mor.* 98 One who being bidden to reade..a poore seely Epigram..taketh on and fareth against the paper wherein it is written. **1609** —— *Amm. Marcell.* XVI. iv. 60 Constantius having intelligence hereof, fared and fumed. *Ibid.* XVI. xi. 73 They fared and raged above their wonted manner.

†**c.** With prep. *by*, *with*: To deal with, treat, *esp.* in ***to fare fair*** or ***foul with***. Also in indirect passive. ***to fare with oneself***: to behave. *Obs.*

1340–70 *Alex. & Dind.* 266 Wiþ him fare as a fol þat failede his wittus. *c* **1386** CHAUCER *Pars. T.* ¶825 So faren they by wommen. *a* **1450** *Knt. de la Tour* (1868) 25 It is gret drede to fare foule with hem in suche materes. **1470–85** MALORY *Arthur* VII. xxiii, Dame Lyones..soo faryd with her self as she wold haue dyed. **1483** *Vulgaria abs Terentio* 9 b, He is a man..that few men can..faare wyth all. **1493** *Festivall* (W. de W. 1515) 34 b, Whan they se him [Christ] so foule faren with. **1526** TINDALE *2 Cor.* v. 11 We fare fayre with men. **1614** RALEIGH *Hist. World* II. v. vi. §3. 621 Demetrius..fared very angerly with his brother.

†**d.** ***to fare with*** (a thing): to make use of, employ, possess; to live upon (food). *Obs.*

a **1340** HAMPOLE *Psalter* ci. 9 My fas..sware þat it is ypocrisy þat i fare with. **1340–70** *Alex. & Dind.* 202 Fode for to fare wiþ. *Ibid.* 242 To witen of þe wisdam þat ȝe wiþ faren. *Ibid.* 618, & al þe weihes in þis word scholde wiþ fare. *a* **1400–50** *Alexander* 2944 Quat faris þou with?

5. †**a.** Followed by *as though*, *as if*, that; To act so as to cause an expectation or belief; to pretend. Also ***to let fare***. *Obs.*

1483 *Vulgaria abs Terentio* 17 b, If thou be wyse fare as thowe thou knowist nott. *a* **1535** MORE *De Quat. Noviss.* Wks. 73/2 It maketh the stomak wamble, and fare as it would vomit. **1548** UDALL, etc. tr. *Erasm. Paraph. John* vii. 19, 20 They let fare as if they thought the multitude did not knowe their wickednes. **1570–6** LAMBARDE *Peramb. Kent* (1826) 301 He would..fare in shew as though he would have flowne in their faces. **1573** G. HARVEY *Letter-bk.* (Camden) 11 Thai fare that this singulariti in philosophi is like to grow to a shrode matter. **1633** D. ROGERS *Treat. Sacraments* I. 121 Doe ye fare, as if the Lord bade yee come hither?

b. To seem likely, bid fair. *dial.* (With *inf.* it is often little more than a periphrasis for the finite vb.)

1849 DICKENS *Dav. Copp.* xlvi, 'How do you fare to feel about it, Mas'r Davy?' **1869** *Lonsdale Gloss.*, 'She [a cow] fares a cauving.' **1876** *Whitby Gloss.*, His ailment fares to go hard with him. **1883** *19th Cent.* Oct. 595 Fares as if they mos' of 'em goes up country. **1884** *Mehalah* i. 7 When she fares to say or do a thing, there is no staying tongue or hand. **1888** RIDER HAGGARD *Col. Quaritch* III. v. 77 The skilly.. do fare to take the skin off your throat.

6. *impers.* To 'go'; to happen; to turn out. *Occas.* with *well*, *ill*, etc. Const. †*by*, *with*.

c **1230** *Hali Meid.* 7 Sekerliche swa hit fareð. **1340–70** *Alex. & Dind.* 795 So it fareþ by ȝou folk þat fillen ȝou siluen. **1481** CAXTON *Reynard* (Arb.) 89 He forgeteth that one wyth that other and so faryth by me. **1586** COGAN *Haven Health* ccxiii. (1636) 223 It fareth by them as it doth by a lampe. **1655–60** STANLEY *Hist. Philos.* (1701) 31/2 It fares alike with good and bad. **1671** MILTON *P.R.* III. 443 So fares it when with truth falsehood contends. **1713** SWIFT *Frenzy of J. Denny*, Beware..that it fare not with you as with your predecessor. **1850** TENNYSON *In Mem.* xliv, How fares it with the happy dead?

7. To 'get on' (well or ill); to experience good or bad fortune or treatment.

c **1000** ÆLFRIC *On N.T.* (Gr.) 20 Hu mæȝ se man wel faran, þe [etc.]. *a* **1300** *Cursor M.* 11900 (Cott.) Send him quar he faris werr. **1375** BARBOUR *Bruce* III. 548 The king then..speryt..How thai..had farne. **1382** WYCLIF *3 John* 2, I make preyer, thee for to entre, and fare welsumly. *c* **1450** *Merlin* 71 He farith well and is in hele. *c* **1460** *Towneley Myst.* 62 For we fare wars than ever we fowre. **1535** STEWART *Cron. Scot.* II. 6 How he fuir that tyme..It war ouir lang..to tell. **1587** TURBERV. *Trag. T.* (1837) 10 Remember how fonde Phæton farde. **1607** HIERON *Wks.* I. 193 His children had their heads cut off, and all his race feared the worse for his sake. **1612** ROWLANDS *Knaue of Harts* 41 The world did wrangle for their wealth, And Lawyers far'd the better. **1703** POPE *Thebais* 520 So fares a sailor on the stormy main. **1711** ADDISON *Spect.* No. 130 ¶1 Fearing that his Poultry might fare the worse for it. **1755** *Mem. Capt. P. Drake* I. vii. 50 Colonel Tatton..kindly asked me..how I fared of my Wound. **1784** COWPER *Task* IV. 341 Ill fares the traveller now. **1829** LYTTON *Disowned* 6 How fares your appetite? **1848** MACAULAY *Hist. Eng.* I. 161 Sculpture fared as ill as painting. **1871** FREEMAN *Norm. Conq.* (1876) IV. xvii. 77 We shall see hereafter how he fared on his errand.

Phrase. **1614** BP. HALL *Recoll. Treat.* 412 That ancient check of going far and faring worse. **1862** STANLEY *Jew. Ch.* I. ii. 38 We may go much farther and fare much worse.

8. *spec.* To be (well or ill) entertained with food; to feed (*well*, *ill*, *hardly*, *sumptuously*, etc.).

1393 LANGL. *P. Pl.* C. VI. 8 Whenne ich hadde myn hele ..and louede wel fare. **1532** MORE *Confut. Tindale* Wks. 651/2 Saynt John..fasted and fore hard. **1607** SHAKS. *Timon* III. vi. 37 Feast your eares with the Musicke awhile: If they will fare so harshly. **1611** BIBLE *Luke* xvi. 19 A certaine rich man..fared sumptuously euery day. **1666** PEPYS *Diary* (1879) IV. 215, I do not think they fared very hard. **1712** STEELE *Spect.* No. 479 ¶3, I fared very well at dinner. **1774** GOLDSM. *Nat. Hist.* (1776) VII. 324 No animal fares more sumptuously. **1856** KANE *Arct. Expl.* I. xv. 169 Our breakfast, for all fare alike, is hard tack.

9. Used in imperative with *well*, as an expression of good wishes to a parting friend, or as a mere formula in recognition of parting; = FAREWELL *int. arch.* **a.** with the person as *subj.* (see sense 7). †Also *occas.* in infinitive.

1377 LANGL. *P. Pl.* B. XIII. 180 Frendes, fareth wel. *c* **1386** CHAUCER *Wife's T.* Prol. 501 Let him farwel, God give his soule rest. *c* **1440** *York Myst.* xvii. 204 Fares wele, ȝe be bygilid. **1533** GAU *Richt Vay* (1888) 109 Fair now veil. **1551** ROBINSON tr. *More's Utop.* (Arb.) 166, I byd you moste hartely well to fare. **1582** T. WATSON *Centurie of Loue* i. (Arb.) 37 Well fare the life..I ledde ere this. **1611** BIBLE *Acts* xv. 29 Fare ye well. **1826** BEDDOES *Let. to B. Procter* Poems 171 Fare, as you deserve it, well. **1859** TENNYSON *Elaine* 692 A diamond is a diamond. Fare you well. A thousand times!

b. *impers.* (see sense 6) with *dat.*

1671 H. M. tr. *Erasm. Colloq.* 544 If they prefer gain before godliness, fare them well. **1676** HOBBES *Iliad* xx. 321 Fare him well. **1816** BYRON *Fare thee well* i, For ever, fare thee well. *a* **1839** PRAED *Poems* (1864) I. 247 Beloved, fare thee well! **1877** *Holderness Gloss.*, *Fares-te-weel*: fare thee well.

†**III. 10.** To ache, throb. *dial.* ? *Obs.*

[Perh. etymologically 'to go on', rage: cf. 4 b.] **1781** in HUTTON *Tour to Caves* Gloss. **1847** in HALLIWELL.

IV. In phraseological combination with advbs.

†**11. fare about.** To go about, set oneself. *Obs.*

1563 J. PILKINGTON *Burn. Paules Ch.* v. sig. Q ij, Theym that fare about to doe agaynste the ordinance of God.

12. fare forth (analytical form of OE. *forðfaran*). See FARE *v.*¹ and FORTH.

a. To go forth, depart, start.

c **1200** *Trin. Coll. Hom.* 225 To heueriche hie sulle fare forð mid ure drihte. **1375** BARBOUR *Bruce* III. 345 All hyr cumpany, Lap on thar horss, and furth thai far. *c* **1400** *Melayne* 206 Rowlande.. Fares forthe with Baners brade. **1647** H. MORE *Song of Soul* I. I. xxvi, Like Doves so forth they fore. **1727–38** GAY *Fables* I. I. xiv. 5 Forth he fares, all toil defies. **1853** KINGSLEY *Hypatia* xxi. 258 Before sunrise .. Raphael was faring forth gallantly.

†**b.** To go on, advance, with respect either to space or time. In the latter sense also quasi-*impers.*

1340–70 *Alex. & Dind.* 939 Whan he is fare so forþ fer in his age. *c* **1350** *Will. Palerne* 3260 It was forþ [to] niȝt faren bi þat time.

†**c.** To go by, pass away. *Obs.*

a **1225** *Leg. Kath.* 1629 Pinen, þe fare forð in an hondhwile.

†**13. fare up.** To get up. *Obs.*

a **1400–50** *Alexander* 545 þan faris scho vp and farkis furth a fute or tway.

fare, *v.*² *Obs.* [var. of FARROW *v.*] *intr.* Of a sow: To litter. Hence **'faring** *ppl. a.*

1573 TUSSER *Husb.* (1878) 74 Sow ready to fare. *Ibid.*, Good faring sow.

†**fare,** *v.*³ *Obs.* To play at the game called 'fare': see FARE *sb.*⁴ *Obs.*

1530 PALSGR. 545/2, I fare, I playe at a game so named (at the dyse). **15..** *Jack Juggler* in Hazl. *Dodsley* II. 115 A corner.. Where boys were at dice, faring at all; When Careaway with that good company met, He fell to faring withouten let.

fare, obs. var. FEAR *v.*

Far East. [FAR *a.* 1 a, EAST *sb.*] The extreme eastern regions of the Old World, esp. China and Japan.

[**1616** T. ROE *Let.* 17 Jan. (1899) I. 113 Load-stones heere are none. They are in the farre East Countries.] **1852** J. H. NEWMAN *Second Spring* 29 The great St. Francis opened the way to the far East. **1894** G. N. CURZON *Problems of Far East* i. 7 No introduction is needed in presenting the Far East to an English audience. **1898** *Westm. Gaz.* 1 Jan. 2/3 The Emperor's Far-East policy. **1906** *Q. Rev.* Jan. 287 The main interest of Great Britain in the Far East. **1911** *Ibid.* July 245 The great conflict which for many months bathed the Far East in blood weakened Russia in Europe. **1931** *Sat. Rev.* 21 Nov. 645 Apparently they cannot leave the Far East alone. **1950** *Sci. News* XV. 126 The rhesus negative characteristic is almost unknown in the Far East.

So **Far-Eastern** *a.*, of or belonging to the Far East.

1888 *Peel City Guardian* 14 July 7/4 One firm has the monopoly of this Far-Eastern *pari mutuel.* **1900** *Black & White Budget* 25 Aug. 649/1 The Far Eastern question is a new one to American diplomacy.

fareden, var. of FOREDEN, ME., enmity.

†**'fare-fee.** *Obs. rare.* [f. FARE *v.* + FEE *sb.*²] A fee paid on quitting a tenancy.

1523 [see FAREWELL B 2].

†**'farelet.** *Obs. rare*⁻¹. See quot. [Perh. a mistake for FORCELET.]

1602 FULBECKE *Pandectes* 43 He that couenanteth to defend a castell or farelet is not bound, if warre bee raised through his fault, to whome hee made the couenant.

farendine, var. of FARANDINE, *Obs.*

farer ('fɛərə(r)). Also 6 *Sc.* farar. [f. FARE *v.* + -ER¹.] A traveller. Chiefly with defining sb., as SEAFARER, WAYFARER, etc.

[**1513** DOUGLAS *Æneis* v. xiii. 30 The wind.. followit fast the se fararis behynd.] **1881** *Century Mag.* XXIII. 52 Open as the highway to all farers.

fareway, var. f. of FAIRWAY.

farewell (fɛə'wɛl). *int.* Also *sb.* (*a.*) and *adv.* Forms: 4–6 farwel(l(e, 4–8 farewel, (5 fayrwell, 6 fairewell, fearewele), 5– farewell. [The phrase *fare well* (see FARE *v.* 9) treated as one word.]

A. *int.*

1. An expression of good wishes at the parting of friends, originally addressed to the one setting forth, but in later use a mere formula of civility at parting; Goodbye! Adieu! Now *poet.* or *rhetorical*, and chiefly implying regretful feeling.

1377 LANGL. *P. Pl.* B. xi. 41 'ȝee, farewel phippe!' quod fauntelte. *c* **1440** *York Myst.* xli. 458 Fayrwell! Godson, thowe grant vs thy blyssng. **1509** HAWES *Past. Pleas.* xvi. vii, Fare well, she sayde, for I must parte you fro. **1601** SHAKS. *All's Well* II. i. 36, I am your accessary, and so farewell. **1697** DRYDEN *Virg. Georg.* IV. 718 And now farewel. **1821** BYRON *Mar. Fal.* IV. i, Farewell! we meet no more in life!—Farewell. **1871** R. ELLIS *Catullus* xlvi. 9 Farewell company true, my lovely comrades.

2. *fig.* An expression of regret at leaving anything, or a mere exclamation = Goodbye to, no more of. Also *farewell to*, and *farewell it.*

c **1385** CHAUCER *L.G.W.* Prol. 39 Whan.. that the floures ginnen for to springe Farwel my book and my devocioun! *c* **1386** —— *Knt's T.* 1902 Farewel physike; go bere the man to cherche. ? *c* **1475** *Sqr. lowe Degre* 941 Farewell golde, pure and fyne; Farewell velvet, and satyne. **1584** R. SCOT *Discov. Witchcr.* III. ii. 33 All the vertue thereof is gone, and farewell it. **1659** B. HARRIS *Parival's Iron Age* 139 And if she yeilded, farewel Bavaria. **1697** DRYDEN *Virg. Past.* VIII. 82 Farewell ye secret Woods, and shady Groves. **1766** FORDYCE *Serm. Yng. Wom.* (1767) I. v. 193 Farewel to real friendship, farewel to convivial delight! **1784** COWPER *Task* I. 247 So farewel envy of the peasants' nest.

†**b.** Proverb, *farewell fieldfare*; said to one of whom the speaker wishes to see no more, with allusion to the fieldfare's departure northward at the end of winter. *Obs.*

c **1374** CHAUCER *Troylus* III. 812 The harme is don, and farewel feldyfare. *c* **1400** *Rom. Rose* 5513.

c. In the name of a plant (see quot.).

1878–86 BRITTEN & HOLLAND *Plant-n.*, Farewell Summer, *Saponaria officinalis* L... From its flowering in the months of August and September.

B. *sb.*

1. a. The *int.* used *subst.* as a name for itself, and hence for any equivalent, as in *to say farewell to.* With this has now coalesced the originally distinct use in *to bid farewell*, where *farewell* represents historically the *infinitive*, not as elsewhere the *imperative*, of the vbl. phrase. **b.** An utterance of the word 'farewell'; any expression or act equivalent to this; a parting salutation, formal leave-taking, adieu.

1393 GOWER *Conf.* II. 268 But farewell she was ago Unto Pallas. **1526** TINDALE *Acts* xviii. 21 Bad them feare well. **1570** NORTH *Doni's Mor. Philos.* (1888) IV. 229 For a farewell.. he will yerke out behinde and put him in daunger of his life. **1587** JANES in *Hakluyt's Voy.* III. 113 But we, little regarding their curtesie, gaue them the gentle farewell, and so departed. **1633** FORD *Broken H.* IV. iv, She.. begg'd some gentle voice To tune farewel To life and griefs. **1684** BUNYAN *Pilgr.* II. 12 So their Visitor bid them farewel. **1710** ADDISON *Whig Exam.* No. 1 ¶14, I take my farewel of this subject. **1758** S. HAYWARD *Serm.* xvi. 490 He was going to bid all things here an everlasting farewel. **1770** GOLDSM. *Des. Vill.* 367 Fondly look'd their last, And took a long farewell. **1838** LYTTON *Alice* 53 She had wept her last farewell on her mother's bosom. **1850** TENNYSON *In Mem.* cxxiii, I cannot think the thing farewell. **1880** OUIDA *Moths* I. 116, 'I came to bid you farewell', he said softly. **1884** *Illust. Lond. News* 1 Nov. 410/2 The 'farewells'.. of actors and singers are not always to be depended on.

†**2.** A payment on quitting a tenancy. *Obs.*

1523 FITZHERB. *Surv.* 25 b, The tenant.. shall make a fyne with the lorde for his dep[ar]tyng.. and it is called a farefee or a farewell.

†**3.** *transf.* An after-taste, twang. *Obs.*

1634 SIR T. HERBERT *Trav.* 183 The Jacke.. leaves a clammy farewell in the mouth, but addes a double benefit to the stomacke. **1648** SANDERSON *Serm.* II. 245 Temporal advantages of wealth [etc.].. have a very ill farewel with them at the last. **1759** BOYER *Fr. & Eng. Dict.* s.v., This wine has a sad farewell with it.

4. *attrib.* passing into an adj.: Pertaining to a farewell, accompanying or signifying a farewell. (In this use the stress is variable: most commonly *'farewell.*)

a **1711** KEN *Hymns Evang.* Poet Wks. 1721 I. 182 He num'rous Farewell-Blessings on them pour'd. **1712** ADDISON *Spect.* No. 445 ¶2 Writers, who have taken their Leave of the Publick in farewel Papers. **1713** TICKELL *Prospect of Peace* 41 The hardy Vet'ran.. Leans on his Spear to take his farewell View. **1769** FALCONER *Dict. Marine* (1789), *Coup de partance*, a farewell gun. **1822–56** DE QUINCEY *Confess.* (1862) 108 A few final or farewell farewells. **1856** KANE *Arct. Expl.* I. x. 115, I accompanied them with my dogs as a farewell escort for some miles. **1932** E. HEMINGWAY *Death in Afternoon* xix. 249 He is.. giving a final series of farewell performances. **1938** M. ALLINGHAM *Fashion in Shrouds* viii. 120, I wanted to make sure that he was coming down on Saturday to Ramillies' farewell party. **1959** N. MAILER *Advts. for Myself* (1961) 267 To announce a farewell appearance then be on the scene again the following week is to ooze all the ebbing charm.. of the desperate old actor. **1971** R. BUSBY *Deadlock* xv. 224 You could say it was his farewell performance.

b. applied to the point where one 'bids farewell to' or parts from a person or thing.

1669 STURMY *Mariner's Mag.* A ij, The Lizard being the farewel Cape to most Ships that sail out of the British Seas. **1865** PAGE *Handbk. Geol. Terms* (ed. 2), *Farewell Rock.* The familiar term in the South Welsh coal-field for the Millstone Grit, because on striking it the miner bids fare-well to all workable seams of coal.

†**C.** *adv.* (cf. ADIEU *adv.* 1) *to go farewell*: to go away, be dismissed. *Obs.*

c **1391** CHAUCER *Astrol.* II. §23 Let A & F [two stars] go farwel til agayns the dawenyng a gret while.

farewell (fɛə'wɛl), *v.* Also 7 farwell. [f. prec.] **a.** *trans.* To take leave of, bid or say good-bye to; spec. *Austral.* and *N.Z.*: to honour a departing or retiring person or persons at a ceremonial occasion. **b.** *intr.* To say good-bye.

1580 SIDNEY *Arcadia* (1622) 93 She brake from their armes.. And fare-welling the flocke, did homeward wend. **1606** tr. *Rollock's Lect. on 1 & 2 Thess.* I. xxvi. 325 After tryell if thou findst it [his doctrine] sound.. keep it; if not, faire-well it. *a* **1657** R. LOVEDAY *Lett.* (1663) 28 It put some doubts to flight that you had farewell'd Barningham. *a* **1693** URQUHART *Rabelais* III. xliii. 356 Pantagruel.. farewell'd.. the President. **1885** R. F. BURTON *1001 Nights* I. 122 She farewelled me with her dying eyes. **1902** J. H. M. ABBOTT *Tommy Cornstalk* 235 The North Terrace and the railway station had farewelled us with more delightful fervour than even if we had been an Australian Eleven driving round in drags. **1930** *Tribune* (Melbourne) 15 May 2/3 A popular priest. Fr. Hyland farewelled. **1931** *Auckland Star* 22 Mar., Opportunity was taken to farewell the Rev. E. Drake and Mrs. Drake.

fare-you-well. *U.S. colloq.* [f. phr. *fare you well*, FARE *v.*¹ 9.] *to a fare-you-well*: to the last point; to the utmost degree; completely.

1884 G. W. CABLE *Dr. Sevier* II. liv. 173 And then it means a house.., and milk, anyhow, till you can't rest, and buttermilk to fare-you-well. **1910** W. M. RAINE *B. O'Connor* 77 The little cuss has got me bluffed to a fare-you-well. **1911** R. D. SAUNDERS *Col. Todhunter* i. 3 The fight's begun, and we've got to rally around old Bill Strickland to a fare-you-well. **1924** W. M. RAINE *Troubled Waters* x. 101 'Who is boss of the round-up this year?'.. 'Rowan is, and believe me he worked us to a fare-you-well. He's some driver, Mac is.' **1943** S. LEWIS *Gideon Planish* x. 95 You can lambast Brother Rood to a fare-you-well.

‖**farfalla.** *Obs. rare.* [It. *farfalla* a candle-fly or moth.] (See quots.)

1607 SYLVESTER *Du Bartas* II. iv. II. (1641) 208/1 [New Farfalla] in her radiant shine, Too-bold, I burn these tender wings of mine. **1626** COCKERAM, *Farfalla*, a Candle-Fly.

far-famed ('fɑː,feɪmd), *a.* [f. FAR *adv.* + FAMED *ppl. a.*] That is famed to a great distance; well-known, widely celebrated.

1624 MASSINGER *Parl Love* II. iii, The far-famed English Bath. **1725** POPE *Odyss.* x. 162 Stern Æetes came The far-fam'd brother of th' enchantress dame. **1818** COBBETT *Pol. Reg.* XXXIII. 539 That far-famed sanctuary of the laws. **1855** KINGSLEY *Heroes* v. (1868) 66 The far-famed slayer of the Gorgon. **1867** LADY HERBERT *Cradle L.* vii. 168 This was the far-famed valley of Eshcol.

‖**farfel** ('fɑːfəl). Also farfal, ferfel. [Yiddish *farfal, farfil, ferfel* sb. pl., ad. MHG. *varveln* sb. pl. noodles, noodle soup.] Ground or granulated noodle dough.

1892 I. ZANGWILL *Childr. Ghetto* (1893) I. i. 49 In Jewish cookery.. *Ferfel*.. are *Lockschen* [like vermicelli] in an atomic state. **1925** *Jewish Encycl.* IV. 256/1 Lokshen consists of flour and eggs made into dough.. then cut into long strips... Cut into small squares, these strips are called 'farfil'. *Ibid.* 257/2 Teigachz, or pudding.. is usually made from rice, noodles, 'farfel' (dough crumbs). **1960** A. E. BENDER *Dict. Nutrition* 5 Farfals are ground, granulated or shredded [alimentary pastes].

†**'far-fet,** *a. Obs.* [f. FAR *adv.* + *fet*, pa. pple. of FET *v. Obs.*]

1. = FAR-FETCHED 1.

1579 LYLY *Euphues* (Arb.) 93 Farre fet and deere bought is good for Ladyes. **1581** SIDNEY *Astr. & Stella* (1622) 536 Those far-fet helpes. **1613** BEAUM. & FL. *Honest Man's Fort.* III. iii, Your far-fet viands please not My appetite. **1671** MILTON *P.R.* II. 401 Others.. Whose pains have earn'd the far-fet spoil.

2. = FAR-FETCHED 2.

1533 MORE *Answ. Poysoned Bk.* Wks. 1123/2 In.. hys farre fet reason, neyther is hys maior true, nor hys argument toucheth not the matter. **1580** SIDNEY *Arcadia* III. (1590) 360 Therewith he told her a farre-fet tale. *a* **1680** BUTLER *Rem.* (1759) II. 116 For Metaphors, he uses to chuse the.. most far fet that he can light upon.

3. as *sb.* (See quot.) *rare*⁻¹.

1589 PUTTENHAM *Eng. Poesie* III. xvii. (Arb.) 193 The figure *Metalepsis*, which I call the *farfet*, as when we had rather fetch a word a great way off then to vse one nerer hand to expresse the matter aswel and plainer.

†**far-fetch,** *sb. Obs.* [Back-formation from FAR-FETCHED.]

1. A deeply-laid or cunning stratagem.

a **1562** G. CAVENDISH *Life Wolsey* (1827) 129 Ye may see .. how she can compass a matter to work displeasure by a far fetch. **1566** GASCOIGNE & KINWELMARSH *Jocasta* II. i, This minde of mine Doth fleete full farre from that farfetch of his. **1678** BUTLER *Hud.* III. ii. 1584 Jesuits have deeper Reaches In all their Politick Far-fetches.

2. Fondness for far-fetched ideas.

1813 W. TAYLOR *Eng. Synonyms* (1856) 64 Wieland had too fine a smell; his reader must be practised, to be aware of his far-fetch.

3. *attrib.* or *adj.* = FAR-FETCHED.

1603 SIR C. HEYDON *Jud. Astrol.* xviii. 365 Had he neuer printed it, this farre-fetch deriuation had neuer beene dearely bought.

†**far-fetch,** *v. Obs. rare.* [f. as prec.] *trans.* To derive in a far-fetched manner.

1639 FULLER *Holy War* IV. ii. (1647) 168 It seemeth a forced and overstrained deduction, to farrefetch the name of Tartars from an Hebrew word. **1870** LOWELL *Among my Bks.* Ser. I. (1873) 193 There is such a difference between far-reaching and far-fetching. **1929** D. H. LAWRENCE *Pornogr. & So On* (1936) 16 Poetry more and more tends to far-fetch its word-meanings.

far-fetched ('fɑːfɛtʃt, fɑː'fɛtʃt), *ppl. a.* [f. FAR *adv.* + FETCHED; cf. FAR-FET.]

1. Brought from far. *Obs.* exc. *arch.* †Of a pedigree: Traced from a remote origin.

1583 STUBBES *Anat. Abus.* I. (1879) 33 Farrefetched and deare boughte is good for Ladyes, they say. **1586** COGAN *Haven Health* clxxxvii. (1639) 169 Indian pearles be greatest and more desired as being far fetched. **1634** W. WOOD *New Eng. Prosp.* Ded., The first fruites of my farre-fetcht experience. **1647** CLARENDON *Hist. Reb.* VI. (1703) II. 162 A far fetch'd Pedigree, through so many hundred years. **1658**

W. BURTON *Itin. Anton.* 20 Oysters..conveyed thence to Rome, among other farfetcht Dainties. **1769** *De Foe's Tour Gt. Brit.* I. 254 According to the old Saying, Far-fetch'd, and dear bought, is fittest for the Ladies. **1784** COWPER *Task* I. 243 He..brings his bev'rage home, Far-fetch'd and little worth. **1870** MORRIS *Earthly Par.* III. IV. 71 She reached her fine strong hand anear The far-fetched thing.

†**b.** Devious, circuitous. (Cf. *to fetch a compass.*)

a **1656** BP. HALL *Rem. Wks.* (1660) 48 Others by secret and far-fetch't passages escaped home.

2. Of an argument, notion, simile, etc.: Studiously sought out; not easily or naturally introduced; strained.

1607 TOPSELL *Four-f. Beasts* (1673) 99 Democritus and other..give other reasons, but..they seem to be far fetched. **1647** COWLEY *Mistress, Wish* iv, Pride and Ambition here, Only in far-fetch'd metaphors appear. **1732** BERKELEY *Alciphr.* II. §1, I shall not trouble you with authorities, or far-fetched arguments. **1844** H. ROGERS *Ess.* (1860) I. 76 Some far-fetched conceit, or unpardonable extravagance. **1869** TROLLOPE *He Knew* lxxxi. (1878) 450 Far-fetched ideas respecting English society.

Hence **far-'fetchedness**, the state or fact of being far-fetched.

a **1849** POE *Browning* Wks. 1864 III 415 A certain far-fetchedness of imagery. **1866** *Times* 6 Apr. 5 No excuse for extreme quaintness, oddity, and far-fetchedness.

far-flung, *a.* [FAR *adv.* 8 a.] 'Flung', 'cast', or extended far or to a great distance.

1895 *Times* 14 Oct. 8/1 To the far-flung fenceless prairie. **1897** KIPLING *Recessional* i, Lord of our far-flung battle-line. **1902** *Daily Chron.* 31 Jan. 3/5 The tangled, far-flung story of the once semi-Royal house of Douglas. **1925** B. N. ODELL in E. F. Norton *Fight for Everest, 1924* 292 A far-flung head tributary of the Dzakar Chu. **1927** H. E. FOSDICK *Pilgr. Palestine* (1928) i. 23 This far-flung vista of the land he loved. **1933** A. G. MACDONELL *England, their England* xi. 197 He was in favour of..the immediate launching of twenty new cruisers to protect the trade routes of our far-flung Empire. **1960** *Times* 20 Apr. 14/7 The efficiency and self-sufficiency of this far-flung French outpost.

far-forth, *adv.*: see FAR and FORTH; also 5 ferthforthe. Now usually as two words.

†**1.** To a great distance or extent; far, far on.

c **1470** HARDING *Chron.* lxxii. (1812) 120 She ferforth with childe was then begonne. **1483** CAXTON *G. de la Tour* C vij, And it was thenne ferforthe on the day. *c* **1500** *Melusine* xix 106 These tydings were ferfourth brought in the land, that Vryan knew of it. **1590** SPENSER *F.Q.* III. ix. 53 The humid night was farforth spent. **1858** M. PORTEOUS *Souter Johnny* 30 Farforth to range.

†**b.** quasi-*adj.* ***farforth day***: late in the day, 'high-day'. *Obs.*

c **1440** HYLTON *Scala Perf.* (W. de W. 1494) II. xxxii, The soules that are in this state are not all lyke ferforth. *c* **1450** *Merlin* 282 It is so ferforth that it is to late for vs to repente. **1560** INGELEND *Disob. Child* in Hazl. *Dodsley* II. 312 In my bed, Until it were very far-forth day.

2. To a definite degree, or distance; in phrases, ***how, so, or thus far-forth, as or so far-forth as, so far forth that.***

†**a.** in reference to distance or advanced position in space, time, or order. *Obs.*

c **1340** *Cursor M.* 22711 *heading* (Trin.), Now we be þus ferforþ come. **1430** LYDG. *Chron. Troy* I. vi, So ferforthe as this my lyfe may endure. **1526** TINDALE *Luke* xxii. 51 Soffre ye thus farre forthe. **1570–6** LAMBARDE *Peramb. Kent* (1826) 117 He gave also..the royaltie of the water on each side, so farre foorth as..a man might cast a short hatchet out of the vessell unto the banke.

b. in reference to degree or extent. Now only in phrase ***so far forth***, with sense 'to the specified extent and no more'.

1297 R. GLOUC. (Rolls) 9204 Alle þes were aȝen þe kinge, as verþuorþ as hii couþe. *c* **1340** *Cursor M.* 1585 (Trin.) þe fende wende..þat al mankynde shulde han ben his So ferforþ þat god not myȝt [etc.] *c* **1384** CHAUCER *H. Fame* III. 792 As fer forthe as I han my arte. **1413** LYDG. *Pilgr. Sowle* I. xxvii. (1859) 31 Crist..soo ferforth remitted his rigour. **1464** *Paston Lett.* No. 486 II. 152 As fertheforthe as I kan undyrstand yet, they shall have grase. **1533** HEYWOOD *Pard. & Friar* in Hazl. *Dodsley* I. 207 Many a man so far-forth lacketh grace. **1549** COVERDALE *Erasm. Par. Rom.* Argt., Knowyng well how farfurth his disciples, had nede of lyght meate. **1610** SHAKS. *Temp* I. ii. 178 Know thus far forth, By accident most strange, bountifull Fortune..hath mine enemies Brought to this shore. **1635** PAGITT *Christianogr.* I. iii. (1636) 179 [They] are so farre forth orthodox that they retain a saving profession. **1690** LOCKE *Govt.* II. ii. §2 Every Offence..may..be also punished equally, and as far forth as it may in a Commonwealth. **1827** WHATELY *Logic* IV. i. §1 Induction..so far forth as it is an argument, may, of course, be stated Syllogistically.

Hence, **far 'forthly** *adv. Obs.*, to a great or definite extent; also, entirely, excellently.

1362 LANGL. *P. Pl.* A. VIII. 158 Dowel on Domesday Is digneliche [*v.r.* ferforþliche] I-preiset. *c* **1374** CHAUCER *Troylus* III. 52 God wote for I have, As ferforthly as I have kunnyng, Bene youres. *c* **1430** *Life St. Kath.* (1884) 19 So ferforthly that alle creatures schal haue neede to hym. ? **1481** CAXTON *Orat. G. Flamineus* F iv, That knyght whiche avaunced himself most ferforthly..in the bataylle. **1494** FABYAN *Chron.* V. cxl. 127 The people..was wonderfully mynysshed..so ferforthlye, that..the quicke bodyes suffysed not to bury the ded.

†'**farger**, *sb. Obs.* ? A kind of false dice.

1591 GREENE *Disc. Coosnage* (1859) 38 Their Cheates, Bard-dice, Flattes, Fargers..and many others.

fargite ('fɑːgaɪt). *Min.* [f. (Glen) *Farg* in Fifeshire + -ITE.] (See quots.)

1868 DANA *Min.* (ed. 5) 427 *Fargite* is a red natrolite from Glen Farg, containing..about 4 p. c. of lime. **1883** HEDDLE in *Encycl. Brit.* (ed. 9) XVI. 423 Fargite, consisting of two equivalents of natrolite and one of scolecite.

†'**fargood.** *New England. Obs.* ? An outrigger.

1726 PENHALLOW *Ind. Wars* (1859) 53 But having no fargood, and their boat a dull sailor, ours gained on them so much, that [etc.]. *Ibid.* 54 The enemy making too near the wind (for want of a fargood) came to stays several times.

'**far-hand**, *sb. Sc.* [? f. FAR *a.* + HAND.

But perhaps a corruption of *farand*, northern pr. pple. of FARE to travel; cf. FARANDMAN.]

The condition or standing of an artisan who seeks employment away from home. Only in phrase ***at far-hand***, and *attrib.*

1820 CLELAND *Rise & Progr. Glasgow* 32 Fee for a Stranger, or what is called at far-hand. *Ibid.* 38 The Crown receives Three Pounds for the stamp on the Far-hand tickets. *Ibid.*, The Far-hand entrants are exempted from bucket-money.

farina (fə'raɪnə, fə'riːnə). See also FERINE, FARINHA. [a. L. *farina*, f. *far* corn. Cf. F. *farine.*]

1. The flour or meal of any species of corn, nut, or starchy root.

[**1398** TREVISA *Barth. De P.R.* XVII. lxvii. (1495) 643 Mele is properly called farina whan the corne is well grounde. **1577** B. GOOGE *Heresbach's Husb.* I. (1586) 29 The Meale was called Farina.] **1800** tr. *Lagrange's Chem.* II. 265 The farina of wheat does not give carbonate of lime by incineration. **1846** J. BAXTER *Libr. Pract. Agric.* (ed. 4) II. 133 Two scruples of the farina of the Croton nut should be given in a little gruel. **1876** HARLEY *Mat. Med.* 316 Starch is the farina of seeds and soft cellular roots and stems.

b. A powdery substance, dust.

1707 *Curios. in Husb. & Gard.* 33 A white substance which we call Farina (Meal) to nourish the new-born Plant. **1764** J. GRAINGER *Sugar Cane* IV. 534 *note*, Small seeds, covered with a red farina. **1783** J. C. SMYTH in *Med. Commun.* I. 194 Some have the surface covered with a fine white powder, or farina. **1823** J. BADCOCK *Dom. Amusem.* 32 Rub off the farina, should any adhere.

c. A preparation of maize used for puddings.

2. In various scientific uses. **a.** *Bot.* = Pollen.

1721 BRADLEY *Wks. Nat.* 27 The Farina of each..Plant. **1770–4** A. HUNTER *Georg. Ess.* (1803) I. 486 Impregnated by the farina of the male [plant]. **1861** *Sat. Rev.* 15 June 619 The bee and its congeners..by carrying the fructifying farina from flower to flower, convert flowers into fruit.

b. *Chem.* A fine white powder obtained from cereals, the potato, etc.; starch.

1813 SIR H. DAVY *Agric. Chem.* i. (1814) 11 Farina or the pure matter of starch. **1830** M. DONOVAN *Dom. Econ.* I. 345 This white matter will at length subside: it may be collected on a filter and dried: it is then starch or farina.

c. *Entom.* A mealy powder found on some insects.

1828 STARK *Elem. Nat. Hist.* II. 327 Body cylindrical, brown, covered with farina.

d. *Geol.* ***fossil farina*** (see quot. 1859).

1816 P. CLEAVELAND *Min. & Geol.* (ed. 2) I. 170 Fossil farina..appears in thin, white crusts..attached to the lateral or lower surfaces of beds of shell limestone, &c. **1859** PAGE *Handbk. Geol. Terms, Fossil Farina*, a mealy-looking infusorial or microphytal earth—the Berg-mahl of the Swedes and Laplanders.

3. *Comb.* **farina-boiler**, *U.S.*, a utensil used for cooking farinaceous articles. (*Cent. Dict.*)

farinaceous (færɪ'neɪʃəs), *a.* [f. L. *farīnāce-us*, f. *farīna* (see prec.) + -OUS. Cf. F. *farinacé.*]

1. Consisting or made of flour or meal.

1656 [see FARINOUS]. **1755** *Gentl. Mag.* XXV. 8 It cannot be absolutely affirmed to be merely farinaceous, but it does not appear to be compounded of any animal substance. **1807–26** S. COOPER *First Lines Surg.* (ed. 5) 81 During the symptomatic fever, a mild, vegetable farinaceous diet is proper. **1866** LIVINGSTON *Jrnl.* (1873) I. xi. 278 Their farinaceous food creates a great craving for fish.

2. Containing or yielding flour or starch: starchy.

1667 *Phil. Trans.* II. 485 A Farinaceous or Mealy Tree, serving to make bread of it. **1732** ARBUTHNOT *Rules of Diet* 322 Their Aliment ought to be light, of farinaceous vegetables. **1830** M. DONOVAN *Dom. Econ.* I. 217 The greater fineness of the meal, and the less solubility of its farinaceous part. **1873** E. SMITH *Foods* 156 This large class of farinaceous seeds.

3. Of a mealy nature, resembling meal in texture or quality.

1664 *Phil. Trans.* I. 10 One is a kind of Crystalline Stone, and almost all good Lead: the other not so rich and more farinaceous. **1796** WITHERING *Brit. Plants* IV. 13 The granulations of the crust much larger, but equally soft and farinaceous. **1807** J. E. SMITH *Phys. Bot.* 81 The root becomes farinaceous, tasteless and inert. **1870** HOOKER *Stud. Flora* 343 Cotyledons thick, fleshy or farinaceous.

4. Having a mealy appearance. **a.** Finely comminuted, powdery; now only *Path.*: see quot. 1884.

1664 POWER *Exp. Philos.* I. 47 This farinaceous Seed of Wort. **1884** *Syd. Soc. Lex., Farinaceous*, in Medicine, the term is applied to epidermal exfoliations which are pale and very minute, so as to resemble flour.

†**b.** Covered with farina or fine dust. *Obs.*

1646 SIR T. BROWNE *Pseud. Ep.* III. xv. 141 All farinaceous or mealy winged animals, as Butter-flies, and Moths. **1668** WILKINS *Real Char.* 126 Crane Fly. Farinaceous wings; being covered with a mealy substance easily coming off upon a touch. **1829** LOUDON *Cyclop. Plants* 1016–7 Farinaceous outside, pink inside.

5. Characterized by flour: ***farinaceous city, colony***, playful names for Adelaide and South Australia, from the large export of wheat.

1873 TROLLOPE *Austral. & N.Z.* II. 184 [Adelaide] has also been nicknamed the Farinaceous City. **1902** *Daily Chron.* 7 May 7/1 Before emigrating to the 'farinaceous colony'.

farinaceously (færɪ'neɪʃəslɪ), *adv.* [f. prec. + -LY^{2}.] **a.** In a farinaceous manner: see quot. 1840. **b.** In the direction of or with an inclination towards farinaceous food.

1840 PAXTON *Bot. Dict., Farinaceously Tomentose*, covered with a mealy kind of down. **1853** *Fraser's Mag.* XLVII. 680 So farinaceously disposed were the guests..that the introduction of a cake..would frequently spur a jaded appetite to new efforts.

farinar, obs. form of FOREIGNER.

farination (færɪ'neɪʃən). *rare*$^{-1}$. [f. FARINA + -ATION.] The action of making into flour.

1859 R. F. BURTON *Centr. Afr.* in *Jrnl. Geog. Soc.* XXIX. 401 It is hard, waxy, and unfit for farination.

farine: see FARINHA.

†**farined**, *a. Obs. rare*$^{-1}$. [f. F. *farine* (= FARINA) in spec. sense powder for the complexion + -ED^{2}.] Powdered.

1664 EVELYN *Sylva* (1776) 230 Our effeminate Farined Gallants.

faring ('fɛərɪŋ), *vbl. sb.* [f. FARE *v.* + -ING^{1}.]

1. The action of the vb. FARE; journeying, travelling; an instance of the same.

1594 CAREW *Huarte's Exam. Wits* i. (1596) 8 This faring, that a man takes from his owne Country. **1633** P. FLETCHER *Elisa* I. xxi, Through this troubled faring..I guiltlesse past. **1837** CARLYLE *Fr. Rev.* III. II. vi, His deplorable farings and voyagings draw to a close.

2. Condition or state; *esp.* a passing condition of body. *dial.*

1811 L. M. HAWKINS *C'tess & Gertr.* II. 103 One woman asked another how her husband fared..and was answered, that he had strange farings. **1857** WRIGHT *Dict. Obs. & Provinc. Eng., Fareings*, feelings, symptoms. *East.* **1882** WHITTIER *Poems, An Autograph* xiii. 54 Age brings me no despairing Of the world's future faring.

3. *concr.* Entertainment, fare; in *pl.* made dishes.

1655 MOUFET & BENNET *Health's Improv.* (1746) 328 Broths, Pottage, Farings, Sauces. **1681** COLVIL *Whigs Supplic.* (1751) 125 Watered meal of oats..we prefer..To all the king of Babel's faring. **1803** C. CAUSTIC *Terrible Tractoration* III. (ed. 2) 122 Who cook up most delicious farings From cheese rinds.

b. ***to get one's faring***: see FAIRING *sb.* 1 c.

1846 L. S. COSTELLO *Tour to & fr. Venice* 253, I am..glad to see how the old demon gets his faring.

†'**faring**, *ppl. a. Obs.* [f. as prec. + -ING^{2}.] That has a specified condition or state; (well-, better-, best-) conditioned. (Cf. FARRAND.)

c **1386** CHAUCER *Frankl. T.* 204 Oon of the beste farynge man on lyue. *c* **1430** *Syr Gener.* (Roxb.) 4119 He is..a wel faring king. **1470–85** MALORY *Arthur* VIII. x, She thouȝt she sawe neuer..a better farynge knyght. **1557** *K. Arthur* (Copland) VI. i, He hadde neuer seen..so wel faryng a man.

faringee, var. of FERINGHEE.

†'**faringly**, *adv. Obs.* [f. prec. + -LY^{2}.] Like one in a specified condition; in a (well-, ill-, etc.) conditioned manner.

c **1440** *Partonope* 6735 The Sowdan..forth past Throw the Reynes wele farynglj. **1530** PALSGR. 830/1 All yll faryngly, *tout mausadement.*

‖**farinha** (fa'riɲə). Also 8 farina, and in anglicized form farine. [Pg. *farinha*:—L. *farīna*: see FARINA.] = CASSAVA 2.

1726 SHELVOCKE *Voy. round World* 52 Boiling the water and soaking a quantity of this Farina in it. **1863** BATES *Nat. Amazon* I. 28 Both are products of the same root, tapioca being the pure starch, and farinha the starch mixed with woody fibre. **1870** DASENT *Ann. Eventful Life* (ed. 4) i. 44 Salt-fish, and farine, and ale-wives. **1893** *Act 56–7 Vict.* c. 88 Sched. I, An extraordinary quantity of manioc, or cassada, commonly called farinha.

attrib. **1743** BULKELEY & CUMMINS *Voy. S. Seas* 170 Two Bags of Farine Bread.

farinose (ˌfærɪ'nəʊs), *a.* and *sb.* [ad. L. *farīnōs-us*; see FARINOUS.]

A. *adj.* Yielding farina; also *Bot.*, *Zool.*, and *Path.* (see quot. 1845).

1727 BAILEY (vol. II), *Farinose*, full of meal, mealy. **1845** S. PALMER *Pentaglot Dict., Farineux*..farinose: an epithet employed to designate..2. in Botany and Zoology the parts, or organs, of Plants and of Insects which..are sprinkled with a white powder, resembling farina: 3. in Pathology a species of herpetic eruption. **1856** LINDSAY *Brit. Lichens* 42 The soridia..give it [a thallus]..a farinose or mealy appearance.

B. *sb. Chem.*

1882 VINES *Sach's Bot.* 57 At every point of a starch grain both constituents occur together; if the granulose is extracted, the farinose remains behind as a skeleton.

Hence ˌ**fari'nosely** *adv.*

1840 PAXTON *Bot. Dict., Farinosely-tomentose*, covered with a mealy kind of down. **1847** in CRAIG.

farinous ('færɪnəs), *a.* ? *Obs.* [ad. L. *farīnōs-us*, f. *farīna*; see FARINA and -OUS. Cf. F. *farineux*.] **a.** Containing farina. **b.** Covered with a white mealy substance.

1656 BLOUNT *Glossogr.*, *Farinaceous* or *Farinous*, mealy or full of meal, bemealed, beflowred. 1727 BRADLEY *Fam. Dict.* s.v. *Age*, If you are troubled with farinous or running Tetters. 1742 *Lond. & Country Brew.* I. (ed. 4) 12 The farinous Part loses a great deal of its essential Salts.

farinulent (fə'rɪnjʊlənt), *a.* *Entom.* [ad. L. *farinulent-us*. f. *farīna*: see FARINA and -ULENT.] 'Covered with minute dots resembling white or yellow powder, or with a fixed whitish powder on a dark surface' (*Cent. Dict.*).

‖**fario** ('fɛərɪəʊ). [L. *fario* salmon-trout.] (See quot. 1753.)

[*a* 1672 WILLUGHBY *Icthyogr.* 189 Ausonii ætate maximi & seniores Salmones dicebantur, mediæ magnitudinis & ætatis Sariones aut Fariones.] 1753 CHAMBERS *Cycl. Supp.*, *Fario* in Zoology, a term for a salmon when about half-grown. 1854 BADHAM *Halieut.* 7 They are all poached farios.

farish ('fɑːrɪʃ), *a.* *dial.* Also farrish. [f. FAR *a.* + -ISH.] Somewhat far. Only in phr. ***farish on.***

1855 ROBINSON *Whitby Gloss.*, 'We're getting farish on in years.' 1869 *Lonsdale Gloss.*, *Farrish on*, advanced in years; also nearly intoxicated. 1877 *N.W. Linc. Gloss.* s.v. *Farish on.* 'He's farish on by this time; I should say he'll be i' Lunnun by three o'clock.'

'**farkleberry.** *U.S.* = SPARKLEBERRY.

1765 J. BARTRAM *Diary* 11 July in *Trans. Amer. Philos. Soc.* (1942) XXXIII. 14/1 Trees which naturaly [*sic*] grows there is.. very fine long-leaved pine pitch pine yapon fartle [*sic*] berry chinkapin. 1829 A. EATON *Man. Bot.* (ed. 5) 344 *Vaccinium arboreum*, farkleberry. 1856 A. GRAY *Man. Bot.* (ed. 2) 248 *Vaccinium arboreum*, the Farkleberry, a tall species of this section, with evergreen leaves, probably extends northward into Virginia. 1942 L. R. TEHON *Fieldbk. Nat. Illinois Shrubs* 232 The Farkleberry ranges in dry sandy soils in open woods from Virginia to Florida and westward into Texas. 1951 *Dict. Gardening* (R. Hort. Soc.) IV. 2186/2 Subgenus Batodendron has only one species, *V. arboreum*, the Farkleberry or Sparkleberry, which forms a large bush or small tree with campanulate flowers, included anthers, and dry hard berries.

farl (fɑːl), *sb.* *Sc.* Also 8 farle, 9 farrel. [Contraction for FARDEL *sb.*[2]] Originally, the fourth part of a thin cake made either of flour or oatmeal; now applied to a cake of similar kind and size, whether quadrant-shaped or not.

1724 RAMSAY *Tea-t. Misc.* (1733) I. 91 Sowens, and farles, and Baps. 1787 BURNS *Holy Fair* vii, An farls bak'd wi' butter. 1830 SCOTT *Leg. Montrose* iii, I have tasted no food since daybreak but a farl of oat-cake.

†**farl**, *v.* *Obs.* In 7 farle. [Contraction for FARDEL; cf. FURL.] = FARDEL *v.*

1622 FLETCHER & MASSINGER *Sea Voyage* I. i, Farle up all her Linnery.

†'**farland**, *a.* *Sc.* *Obs.* [f. FAR *a.* + LAND.] Coming from a distance; foreign.

a 1595 SIR J. MAITLAND *Admon. Mar* 36 in *Maitland Poems* (1830) App. 125 Farland fules seime to haif fedderis fair. 1606 BIRNIE *Kirk-Buriall* (1833) 33 Marchants.. whose vent was to furnish the far land Jewes.

farland, obs. form of FORELAND.

farleu ('fɑːljuː). *Law.* Also farley, farlieu. [Etymology unknown.] (See quot. 1670.)

1670 BLOUNT *Law Dict.*, *Farley* or *Farleu.* In the Mannor of West-slapton in Com. Devon, if any Tenant die possessed of a Cottage, by custome he must pay sixpence to the Lord for a farley which probably may be in liew of a Heriot; for in some Mannors Westward, they difference Farleu as the best good from Heriot the best Beast. 1706 in PHILLIPS (ed. Kersey). 1851 *N. & Q.* 25 Oct. 317 Devonshire leases for lives often reserve a money payment on the death of each life as a 'heriot' or 'farlieu'.

farley, -i(e, -ik, -y(e: see FERLY.

farlot, var. of FIRLOT.

†'**farly**, *adv.* *Obs.* [f. FAR + -LY[2].] Far, to a great extent or distance.

c 1460 *Towneley Myst.* 298 Farlee may we fownde and fare For myssyng of oure master Iesus. 1555 ABP. PARKER *Ps.* cvi, God sware unto them all that he would.. sparple them, as runnegates in countries farly wyde.

†**farm**, *sb.*[1] *Obs.* Forms: 1 feorm (*Northumb.* færm), 2 ferm, 3 *south.* veorme, 4 form, 5 farme. [OE. *feorm* str. fem.:—prehistoric **fermâ*.

Not found outside Eng., and no satisfactory Teut. etymology has been proposed. On the assumption that the primary sense was 'fixed portion of provisions, ration', it would be admissible to regard the word as a. late L. *firma*, and so ultimately identical with FARM *sb.*[2] In Domesday Book *firma unius noctis* is equivalent to *anes nihtes feorme* of quot. *c* 1122 below; and mediæval Lat. writers in England used *firma* in the sense of 'banquet'. If the hypothesis of its Latin origin be correct, the word must have been adopted at a very early date: it occurs frequently in the oldest poetry. The derivative *feormian* to feed, is found in the *Corpus Glossary a* 800 ('*fovet*, feormat, broedeþ', the corresponding OHG. gloss. '*formot*, fofet' in *St. Gall. MS.* 913 may be derived from an OE. source, the vb. being otherwise unknown in OHG.]

Food, provision; hence, a banquet, feast.

Beowulf 451 No ðu ymb mines ne þearft lices feorme leng sorȝian. *a* 900 *Charter* xli. in *O.E. Texts* (1885) 449 Hio forȝifeð fiftene pund for ðy ðe mon ðas feorme ðy soel ȝelæste. *c* 1000 *Ags. Gosp.* Matt. xxii. 4 Nu ic ȝegearwode mine feorme, mine fearras and mine fuȝelas synt ofsleȝne. *c* 1122 *O.E. Chron.* (Peterborough) an. 777 Cuðbriht geaf þone abbote .l. punde.. & ilca ȝear anes nihtes feorme. *c* 1200 *Trin. Coll. Hom.* 11 At ferme and at feste. *c* 1205 LAY. 14426 þæt þe king makede ueorme swiðe store. 1387 TREVISA *Higden* (Rolls) VII. 217 ȝif he wolde come to his form he schulde have salt mete i-now. *a* 1500 *Chaucer's Dreme* 1752 This hasty farme had bene a feast.

farm (fɑːm), *sb.*[2] Forms: 3–7 ferm(e, (5 feerme, fereme, 6 fearme), 5–7 farme, (8–9 *Hist.* ferm, *pseudo-arch.* feorm), 6– farm. [a. F. *ferme*:—med.L. *firma* fixed payment, f. *firmāre* to fix, settle, confirm, f. *firmus* FIRM *a.* (The med.L. word, by a different application of the etymological sense, means also 'confirmation of a document, signature'; so Sp. and It. *firma*: see FIRM *sb.*)]

†**1.** A fixed yearly amount (whether in money or in kind) payable as rent, tax, or the like (as opposed to a rent, tax, etc., of variable amount, *e.g.* one calculated at a certain proportion of the produce). Also ***rent and farm.*** *Obs.*

a 1400 in *Eng. Gilds* (1870) 350 Euerych gret hows in wham me workeþ þe qwyltes, shal to þe ferme v.s. by þe ȝere. *c* 1440 *Promp. Parv.* 156 Feerme, a rent, *firma.* *c* 1450 *Bk. Curtasye* 596 in *Babees Bk.* (1868) 319 Of þe resayuer speke wylle I, þat fermys resayuys wytturly. 1463 *Bury Wills* (1850) 19, I wyl eche of hem alle haue iiij*d.* to drynkke whanne they pay her ferme. 1463 M. PASTON in *Paston Lett.* No. 975 III. 431 They.. haskyd hem rent and ferme and they seydyn they had payed you. 1487 *Churchw. Acc. Wigtoft, Lincolnshire* (Nichols 1797) 84 Robert Peby oweth for ferme of a salt-panne of 16 stone of lede 1*s.* 2*d.* 1527 *Bury Wills* (1850) 118 The yearlie ffearme of iij acres londe. 1552 ABP. HAMILTON *Catech.* (1884) 11 Takaris of ouir mekil mail or farme to the herschipe of the tenentis. 1642 PERKINS *Prof. Bk.* xi. §751. 329 If a man be bounden unto 1*s.* in 100*£* to grant unto him the rent and farme of such a mill. 1700 TYRRELL *Hist. Eng.* II. 814 All.. Tythings shall stand at the old Farm, without any Increase. 1767 BLACKSTONE *Comm.* II. 320 The most usual and customary feorm or rent.. must be reserved yearly on such lease.

2. a. A fixed yearly sum accepted from a person as a composition for taxes or other moneys which he is empowered to collect; also, a fixed charge imposed on a town, county, etc., in respect of a tax or taxes to be collected within its limits. Cf. FARM *v.* *Obs.* exc. *Hist.*

c 1386 CHAUCER *Prol.* 252 b (Hengwrt) He was the beste beggere of his hous: [And yaf a certeyn ferme for the graunt]. 1565 *Act 8 Eliz.* c. 12 §1 The said Aulneger.. standeth charged with the Payment of a great annual Farm to the Queens Majesty for the said Aulnege. 1647 N. BACON *Disc. Govt. Eng.* I. lxvii. (1739) 172 The King.. raised the values of the Farm of Counties granted to the Sheriffs. *a* 1715 BURNET *Own Time* (1766) II. 184 He got undertakers to offer at a farm of the whole revenue. 1861 RILEY *Liber Albus* 39 One half of the ferm of the City due to the King. 1876 FREEMAN *Norm. Conq.* V. xxiv. 439 He [the Sheriff] paid into the Exchequer the fixed yearly sum which formed the farm of the shire.

b. The letting-out of public revenue to a 'farmer'; the privilege of farming a tax or taxes. *Obs.* exc. *Hist.*

1667 PEPYS *Diary* 3 Aug., I find them mighty hot.. against the present farm of the Customes. 1765 SMOLLETT *Trav.* (1766) II. 198 [The French King] has the revenue of the farms. 1825 T. JEFFERSON *Autobiog.* Wks. 1859 I. 86 The oppressions of the tithes, the tailles, the corvees, the gabelles, the farms and the barriers. 1885 EDWARDS in *Encycl. Brit.* (ed. 9) XIX. 580 The first farm of postal income was made in 1672.

c. The body of farmers of public revenues.

1786 T. JEFFERSON *Writ.* (1859) I. 547 A late contract by the Farm has [etc.]. *Ibid.* 568 They despair of a suppression of the Farm.

3. a. In certain phrases, senses 1 and 2 pass into the sense: The condition of being let at a fixed rent; now only with reference to revenue, the condition of being 'farmed out'. †***at, in farm; to have, hold, let, put, set, take,*** etc., †***in, out*** or †***forth to, to farm.*** Cf. med.L. *ad firmam, accipere, recipere, committere, locare.*

1297 R. GLOUC. (Rolls) 7773 He sette is tounes & is londes to ferme wel vaste. *Ibid.* 8566 Hor londes & hor rentes þe king huld in is honde & oþer wile to ferme tok. 1303 R. BRUNNE *Handl. Synne* 2409 ȝyf þou haue a þyng yn ferme. 1377 LANGL. *P. Pl.* B. XVI. 16 *Liberum arbitrium* hath þe londe to ferme. 1432–50 tr. *Higden* (Rolls) VII. 433 Venerable Anselme.. deposed mony abbottes and putte þeire places to ferme. 1439 *E.E. Wills* (1882) 115 The wich I hold to ferme of the mayster and couent. *c* 1440 *Promp. Parv.* 157 Fermyn or take a þynge to ferme, *firmo, vel ad firmam accipio.* *c* 1461 *Paston Lett.* No. 432 II. 79, I must selle or lete to ferme all that I have. 1523 FITZHERB. *Surv.* 9 So dothe y profyte ryse to the lordes, wheder they go by way of improuement or set to ferme. 1524 *Churchw. Acc. St. Giles, Reading* 20 In rents at ferme. 1557 HAKLUYT *Voy.* (1599) I. 314 A Cursemay, which the Emperour sometime letteth out to farme. 1568 GRAFTON *Chron.* II. 126 Quene Hithe taken of the king in farme. 1602 FULBECKE *Pandectes* 73 The Publicanes had Salt in farme. *a* 1618 RALEIGH *Rem.* (1644) 83 Letting the Realm to farm to mean persons. 1660 MARVELL *Corr.* xiii. Wks. 1872–5 II. 41 The Excise we hear is to be lett to farme. 1709 J. JOHNSON *Clergym. Vade M.* II. (1731) 141 That no bishop, clergyman, or monk, do take to farm any estate or office. 1776 ADAM SMITH *W.N.* v. ii. (1869) II. 501 Taxes upon consumable commodities.. may be let in farm for a rent certain. 1785 BURKE *Sp. Nabob Arcot's Debts* Wks. IV. 273 Districts which were in a condition to be let to farm. 1844 H. H. WILSON *Brit. India* I. 383 The lease of a district in farm. 1845 MCCULLOCH *Taxation* Introd. (1852) 30 Government may let them in farm for a rent certain.

fig. 1554 LATIMER *Serm. & Rem.* (1845) 274 Your learning is let out to farm.

b. in the operative words of a lease.

1765 *Act 5 Geo. III*, c. 26 Preamb., His late Majesty.. did .. demise, lease, and to farm-lett.. all those houses. 1818 CRUISE *Digest* (ed. 2) IV. 68 The words demise, lease, and to farm let, are the proper ones to constitute a lease.

†**4.** A lease. *Obs.*

a 1500 *Fragmenta Collecta* c. 24 in *Sc. Stat.* I. 369 It is well lefful till him till giff or to sell his ferm to quham soeuer he likis. 1596 SPENSER *State Irel.* (1633) 58 It is a great willfullnes in any such Land-lord to refuse to make any longer farmes unto their Tenants. 1647 N. BACON *Disc. Govt. Eng.* I. xxxi. (1739) 47 Hence the Leases so made were called Feormes or Farmes.

5. a. Originally, a tract of land held on lease for the purpose of cultivation; in mod. use often applied without respect to the nature of the tenure. Sometimes qualified by sb. prefixed, as ***dairy-, grass-, poultry-farm.***

1523 FITZHERB. *Husb.* §123 Though a man.. shall haue hys farme .xx. yeres. 1553 N. GRIMALD tr. *Cicero's Duties* 135 b, If they who offer to sell a good farme [L. *villa*], etc. 1579 RASTELL *Expos. Terms Law* 91 Farme or ferme is the chiefe mesuage in a village or towne.. vsed to be let for terme of lyfe, yeares, or at will. 1611 BIBLE *Matt.* xxii. 5 But they.. went their wayes, one to his farme, another to his merchandize. 1667 MILTON *P.L.* IX. 448 The pleasant Villages and Farmes. 1737 POPE *Hor. Epist.* II. ii. 259 There mingled farms and pyramids appear. 1817 W. SELWYN *Law Nisi Prius* (ed. 4) II. 676 Proceeding by ejectment to turn him out of the farm. 1874 GREEN *Short Hist.* ix. 693 The farms of Lothian have become models of agricultural skill.

b. Extended to tracts of water devoted to the breeding or rearing of some animals, *gen.* with qualification, as ***fish-farm, oyster-farm, terrapin-farm,*** etc. (see first terms).

1866 *Chambers's Jrnl.* 22 Sept. 601/1, I saw no farm of mussels. 1962 *Daily Tel.* 4 Apr. 12/3 The cultivation of an underwater 'farm' on a one-by-three mile area of sea.

c. Extended to storage installations.

1955 *N.Y. Times* 20 Feb. 20/4 Each farm.. consists of several storage tanks with a pump house. 1958 *Globe & Mail* (Toronto) 10 Oct. 20/4 Tankers have piped ashore $29\frac{1}{2}$ million gallons of gasoline and oil products into the tanks of three storage farms.

6. A farm-house.

1596 SPENSER *F.Q.* IV. iv. 35 As when two greedy Wolves doe breake by force Into an heard, farre from the husband farme. 1598 HAKLUYT *Voy.* I. 577 Farmes or granges which conteine chambers in them. 1600 HOLLAND *Livy* VII. xiii. 1401 *note*, Neere unto this causey Cæsar had a ferme or mannor house. *Mod.* Mr. Smith lives at the White Farm at the end of the village.

7. A place where children are 'farmed'.

1869 GREENWOOD *Curses Lond.* iii. 45 There can be no question that he has a better chance.. than.. at the 'farm.'

8. *slang.* The prison infirmary. ***to fetch the farm*** = to be ordered infirmary diet and treatment. Cf. *farmery*, FERMERY.

1879 'TICKET-OF-LEAVE MAN' *Convict Life* vii. 167 After his conviction.. he can 'fetch the farm', which is thieves' language for obtaining admission to the infirmary. *a* 1889 *Evening News* (Barrère & Leland), The dodges which would take place to 'fetch the farm'. 1900 *Pall Mall Gaz.* Oct. 202 The 'farm'.. in ordinary prison vernacular, the synonym for the hospital. *Ibid.* 203 To 'fetch the farm' was, and still is, the current slang equivalent for getting round the doctor.

9. *attrib.* and *Comb.* **a.** Simple attributive (sense 5), as ***farm-account, farm-bailiff, -boy, -building, -cart,*** †***-carle, -gate, -holding, implement, -kitchen, -labour, -labourer, -life, -produce, -rent, -servant, -stock, -woman, -work,*** etc.

1551 *Richmond. Wills* (Surtees) 72 My.. wyfe.. shall have full enterest in all suche fermeholding as I have in ferme and occupation at this daye. 1655 SIR E. NICHOLAS in *N. Papers* (Camden) II. 349 The most revenue being farme rents. 1813 J. SINCLAIR *Syst. Husbandry Scotl.* (ed. 2) II. App. 173 Gentlemen farmers, who.. are not aware, of the real state of their farm accounts. 1816 *Farmer's Mag.* XVII. 477 Other labourers.. dependent upon farm-work.. are without employment. 1818 COBBETT *Pol. Reg.* XXXIII. 170 The low price of farm produce. 1825 LOUDON *Encycl. Agric.* §7064 Farm-servants [in Angus] live chiefly on oatmeal. 1825 LOUDON *Encycl. Agric.* 737 In the adjustment of farm labor, the great art is to divide it as equally as possible throughout the year. 1831 W. HOWITT *Bk. Seasons* 105 In farm-kitchens.. hear a chirping of chickens. 1834 D. LOW *Elem. Pract. Agric.* 630 Farm gates have sometimes been made wholly of hammered iron. ?1842 LANCE *Cottage Farmer* 26 The decided advantages of employing oxen in general farm work. 1844 H. STEPHENS *Bk. Farm* I. 18, I have confidence of giving such an *exposé* of farm implements as will surpass every other work of the kind. *Ibid.* III. 1349 The next, and one of the most important books, is the Farm-account book. 1845 HIRST *Poems* 77 The farm boy with his shining spade. 1859 W. COLLINS *Q. of Hearts* (1875) 44 The Farm-lands stretched down gently into a beautiful rich valley. 1860 G. E. STREET in *Archaeol. Cantiana* III. 99 *note*, The farm-buildings near the church. 1863 D. G. MITCHELL *My Farm Edgewood* 17 The economies of a quiet farm-life. 1864 J. C. ATKINSON *Stanton Grange* xxvi. 286 So much the better, if he could.. get the inmates to put him into one of their farm-carts on some straw. 1875 W. MCILWRAITH *Guide Wigtownshire* 132 Some of the villagers are.. farm labourers. 1890 *Daily News* 31 Jan. 5/5 The need for some farm-labour training on the part of the emigrants. 1891 ATKINSON *Last of Giant Killers* 86 The farm-carle had been gone a long time. 1891 HARDY *Tess* II. xxi. 12 A farm-woman would be the only sensible kind of wife for him. 1905

Westm. Gaz. 6 May 10/2 We see the children playing in the farm-kitchen. **1915** D. H. LAWRENCE *Rainbow* i. 2 The heated, blind intercourse of farm-life. **1960** *Farmer & Stockbreeder* 1 Mar. 58/1 The total January farm-gate deliveries of 148½m gallons.

b. Special comb.: **farm-court** = FARM-YARD; **farm-crossing**, a railway-crossing from one part of a farm to another; †**farm-dish**, a fixed quantity of ore payable as rent for copper mines; cf. *toll-dish*; **farm-furrowed** *a.*, *nonce-wd.*, cut up into farms; **farm-hand**, any person that works on a farm; **farm-instructor**, a teacher of agriculture; **farm-meal**, *Sc.*, meal given in payment of rent; **farm-office**, usually *pl.*, the out-buildings on a farm; †**farm-place** = FARM *sb.* 6; **farm-room**, ? a rented room or a leasehold; **farm-stock**, the cattle, etc., implements, and produce of a farm; **farm-stocking**, the cattle on a farm; **farm-store** = *farm-produce*. Also FARM-HOLD, FARM-HOUSE, FARM-STEAD, FARM-STEADING, FARM-YARD.

1860 MISS YONGE *Stokesley Secret* xiv. (1881) 329 He could look down into the *farm-court. **1858** REDFIELD *Law of Railways* (1869) I. 488 Cattle-guards at *farm-crossings. **1713** *Lond. Gaz.* No. 5141/4 To treat about further Setts of the same [Copper-Works] for Years at a Toll or *Farm-Dish. **1857** EMERSON *Poems, Monadnoc* 332 This..*Farm-furrowed, town-incrusted sphere. **1843** *Cultivator* X. 85 In unpropitious weather for out door employment your *farm hands can go to threshing out grain. **1878** W. WHITMAN *Specimen Days* (1883) 108 He was about the best specimen of a young country farm-hand I ever knew. **1884** S. E. DAWSON *Handbk. Canada* 9 *Farm-instructors are appointed to teach the Indian adults..to till their lands. **1811** G. S. KEITH *Agric. Aberdeenshire* vii. §4. 244 Before 1782, the *farm meal was commonly paid of this inferior oats. **1807** SIR R. C. HOARE *Tour in Ireland* 55 They have convenient *farm-offices for their cattle. **1825** LOUDON *Encycl. Agric.* §7039 The farm-offices..consisting of a barn, cow and ox sheds and hog-sties. **1526** TINDALE *Matt.* xxii. 5 They..went their wayes: won to his *ferme place. **1650** S. CLARKE *Eccl. Hist.* (1654) I. 6 He was persuaded to betake himself to a certain Farm place. **1633** RUTHERFORD *Lett.* xxvi. (1848) 54 An inheritance in this world (God forgive me, that I should honour it with the name of an inheritance, it is rather a *farm-room). **1860** A. MORRIS in Borthwick *Amer. Reader* 78 Exclusive of *farm-stock. **1828–40** TYTLER *Hist. Scot.* (1864) I. 230 The chamberlain should..levy an annual tax upon the crops and *farm-stocking. **1848** CLOUGH *Bothie* ix. 93 Market-carts..bringing in..Flower, fruit, *farm-store.

farm, *v.*¹ *Obs.* exc. *dial.* Forms: 1 feormian, 2 fermien, 5–7 ferm(e, (4 feorm), 7– farm. [OE. *feormian*, of unknown etymology; cf. OHG. *â-fermi* 'squalor' (*Ahd. Glossen* I. 177).] *trans.* To cleanse, empty, purge.

c **1000** *Ags. Gosp.* Luke iii. 17 He feormað his bernes flore. **1382** WYCLIF *1 Kings* x. 2 Thow shalt fynde two men byside the sepulcre of Rachel..feermynge greet dichis. **1401** *Pol. Poems* (Rolls) II. 44 Haue we not to..ferme the dikes. **1440** J. SHIRLEY *Dethe K. James* (1818) 16 To clense and ferme the said privay. **1530** PALSGR. 548/1, I ferme a siege or privy, *Jescure*. **1608** ARMIN *Nest Ninn.* (1842) 30 The fellow sat a long houre farming his mouth. **1881** *Oxford Gloss.* Supp. s.v., 'Farm out th' 'en-us ŏŏl ee?'

farm (fɑːm), *v.*² Forms: 5–7 ferme, 6–7 farme, 7– farm. [f. FARM *sb.*²]

1. *trans.* To take or hold for a term at a fixed payment. †**a.** To rent (land, etc.). *Obs.*

c **1440** *Promp. Parv.* 157 Fermyn, or take a þynge to ferme. **1530** PALSGR. 548 1, I haue fermed his house and al the lande he hath in this towne, *jay prins a ferme* [etc.]. **1602** SHAKS. *Ham.* IV. iv. 20 (Qo.) To gain a little patch of ground..To pay five ducats, five, I would not farm it. **1695** BP. PATRICK *Comm. Gen.* 259 Abram..farmed..some ground of them. **1703** MAUNDRELL *Journ. Jerus.* (1721) Add. 10 The Valley is farm'd of the Grand Signior at 1200 Dollars per Annum.

fig. absol. **1641** MILTON *Prel. Episc.* (1851) 88 To betake them..to..that..overgrowne Covert of antiquity thinking to farme there at large roome.

b. To take the fees, proceeds, or profits of (an office, tax, etc.) on payment of a fixed sum.

1569 J. PARKHURST *Injunctions*, None of you shall ferme one cure..within this Dioces. **1606** HOLLAND *Sueton.* Annot. 12 These Publicanes, so called for that they fermed their Cities revenewes. **1639** FULLER *Holy War* v. xxvii. (1647) 276 The Guardian farmeth the Sepulchre of the Turk at a yearly rent. **1667** PEPYS *Diary* (1879) IV. 427 The two women that farm the well. **1738** JOHNSON *London* 58 Let such..Collect a tax, or farm a lottery. **1861** M. PATTISON *Ess.* (1889) I. 41 The Tidemann farmed..the tin-mines belonging to the Duchy of Cornwall.

transf. **1888** *Daily News* 19 Sept. 3/1 Colonel Mapleson..as he could get no one to farm him..had..to farm others, and he became an impresario.

2. To let another during a specified term on condition of receiving a specified payment. Also, *to farm out*.

a. To lease or let (land) to a tenant. Now *rare*.

1593 SHAKS. *Rich. II*, I. iv. 45 We are inforc'd to farme our royall Realme. **1695** KENNETT *Par. Antiq.* Pref. 3 The Lands were farm'd out for near the full Rent in money. **1721** STRYPE *Eccl. Mem.* II. iii. 264 To raise money for the King, by farming out his lands. **1847** JAMES *Convict* vi, Is not the land you cultivate your own, as much or more than his that he farms to others?

b. To lease or let the proceeds or profits of (customs, taxes, tithes, an undertaking) for a fixed payment.

1602 *2nd Pt. Return fr. Parnass.* III. i. (Arb.) 35 My promise for farming my tithes at such a rate. **1672** PETTY *Pol. Anat.* 362 The customs..yielded anno 1657, under 12000*l.* but was farmed anno 1658, for above thrice that sum. *a* **1704** T. BROWN *Two Oxford Scholars* Wks. 1730 I. 9 If I be minded to farm out my Tythes. **1817** COLERIDGE *Biog. Lit.* 274 The concern should be farmed to some responsible individual. **1845** MᶜCULLOCH *Taxation* Introd. (1852) 31 Any attempt to farm taxes on income..would excite the most violent clamour. **1879** FARRAR *St. Paul* (1883) 249 Augustus had farmed the copper-mines to Herod the Great.

c. To let the labour of (†cattle, persons) for hire.

1607 TOPSELL *Four-f. Beasts* (1658) 55 Other buy Kie to farme them out to other. **1777** ROBERTSON *Hist. Amer.* (1778) I. III. 182 They farmed out the Indians. **1783** BURKE *Sp. Fox's E. India Bill* Wks. IV. 83 They have..continued to farm their subjects..to that very nabob.

transf. **1790** BOSWELL in *Mad. D'Arblay's Diary* Oct., I would farm you out myself for double, treble the money!

3. a. To contract for the maintenance and care of (persons, an institution, etc.) at a stipulated price. Also *to farm out*.

1666 PEPYS *Diary* (1879) IV. 100 A proposal made heretofore to farm the Navy. **1773** *Observ. State Poor* 39 The patrons of the practice of farming workhouses. **1791** BENTHAM *Panopt.* II. 82 Oh, but this contract-plan—it's like farming the poor. **1838** DICKENS *O. Twist* (1850) 3/1 The parish authorities..resolved, that Oliver should be 'farmed'. **1862** W. W. STORY *Roba di R.* iii. (1864) 34 The support of these..criminal slaves is farmed out..to some responsible person at the lowest rate that is offered.

b. With *out*. To send (a university student) to a tutor outside his own college.

1959 *Camb. Rev.* 7 Mar. 399/1 Politics is often taught by history tutors or by research students; there is a great deal of 'farming out' which naturally undermines the purpose of the tutorial system. **1961** *New Statesman* 28 Apr. 669/3 One term 'farmed out' with a man tutor taught me more both of my subject and of its relation to other subjects and to life than I learned from several terms with women tutors.

4. To cultivate, till.

1806 *Gazetteer Scot.* (ed. 2) 88 Many of the proprietors farm their own estates. **1841** ELPHINSTONE *Hist. Ind.* II. 179 He farmed a small spot of land belonging to a Bramin astrologer. **1846** MᶜCULLOCH *Acc. Brit. Empire* (1854) I. 557 The different degrees of skill and economy with which they are farmed.

5. *intr.* To follow the occupation of a farmer; to till the soil.

1719 DE FOE *Crusoe* (1840) II. i. 6, I farmed upon my own land. **1807** CRABBE *Village* I. 40 Fields and flocks have charms For him that gazes, or for him that farms.

6. *trans.* and *intr.* In *Cricket*, of a batsman: to contrive to receive the majority of the balls bowled.

1955 I. PEEBLES *Ashes* xii. 125 Maddocks was run out..when trying to farm the strike. **1963** *Times* 23 May 4/3 Richardson..went belligerently on..'farming' skilfully.

Hence **farmed** *ppl. a.*

1888 *Daily News* 11 Dec. 4/6 A drop of 14 per cent. had occurred in labourers' wages over the farmed surface of England. **1889** *Ibid.* 25 Nov. 5/3 The survivor of the farmed children.

†**'farmable**, *a. Obs.* Also 7 farmeable. [f. prec. + -ABLE.] That may be farmed or leased.

1611 COTGR., *Affermable*..farmeable, leasable, lettable. **1727–36** in BAILEY. **1775** in ASH.

farmacie, -y, obs. forms of PHARMACY.

†**'farmage.** *Obs.* Also 7 fermage. [a. F. *fermage*: see FARM *sb.* and -AGE.] **a.** The system of farming taxes, tithes, etc. **b.** Leasehold tenure. *to let in farmage*: to let on lease. **c.** see quot. 1611. **d.** Cost of cultivation.

1528 ROY *Rede me* (Arb.) 102 They do by farmage Brynge the londe into a rearage. **1530** *Proper Dyaloge* (1863) 12 Which to gentillmen they let in farmage. **1611** COTGR., *Fermage*, farmage: the profit made of, reuenue comming in by, a farme. **1650** ELDERFIELD *Tythes* 123 It seems they were willing to deduct the charge of the Fermage before they marked the Tythes.

farman, var. FIRMAN.

†**farme**, *sb.* [prob. dial. var. of FORM.] A 'shape' for a pudding.

1623 MARKHAM *Countr. Content.* II. i. 68 Then put thereto at least eight yelks of Egges, a little Pepper, Cloves, Mace [etc.]..and then fill it vp in the Farmes according to the order of good housewiferie. *Ibid.* 69 When all is mixt well together..fill it into the farmes.

†**'farmer**¹. *Obs.* Forms: 5 fyrmar, 6 fermer, fermourer. [f. FARM *v.*¹ + -ER¹.] One who cleanses or purifies. In comb. *gong-farmer*. *Obs.*

c **1440** *Promp. Parv.* 203 Goonge fyrmar [*v.r.* gonge-fowar], *cloacarius*. *c* **1515** *Cocke Lorell's B.* (Percy Soc.) 3 Than came a gonge fermourer, Other wyse called a masser scourer. *Ibid.* 11 Stynkynge gonge fermers.

farmer² ('fɑːmə(r)). Forms: 4–7 fermour(e, (5 fermowre), 5 farmor, 5–7 fermer, -or, 6 farmar, -our, fermar, 6– farmer. Also 6–7 *Sc.* FERMERER. [a. AF. *fermer* (Britton), F. *fermier*:—med.L. *firmārius*, f. *firma*: see FARM *sb.*² Now usually apprehended as agent-n. f. FARM *v.*² + -ER¹; some mod. uses may be properly regarded as belonging to this formation and not to the older word.

In the early recorded forms the suffix *-er* has been replaced by *-our*, so that the word apparently corresponds to the synonymous med.L. *firmātor*, one who takes something on lease (Du Cange), agent-n. f. *firmāre* in sense to contract for, become responsible for.]

1. a. One who undertakes the collection of taxes, revenues, etc., paying a fixed sum for the proceeds.

c **1385** CHAUCER *L.G.W.* Prol. 358 Hym oughte nat be..crewel As is a fermour to don the harm he can. **1420** *E.E. Wills* (1882) 52 My goodez that is..in þe fermors handes off my rent. **1491** *Act 7 Hen. VII*, c. 14 The Bailly fermour or receivour..for the tyme of the seid Kyng. **1569** J. PARKHURST *Injunctions*, No Parson Vicar, propriatorie or fermer of any benefice, doe [etc.]. **1587** FLEMING *Contn. Holinshed* III. 1539/1 Thomas Smith..farmer of hir majesties customs inwards. **1641** *Art. Impeachm. Bp. M. Wren* in Rushw. *Hist. Coll.* (1692) III. I. 354 He..sold..the profits of his Primary Visitation..and for the better benefit of the Farmer, set forth a Book. **1642** PERKINS *Prof. Bk.* i. §5. 3 If a Monke bee farmour unto the Kings Majestie. **1659** B. HARRIS *Parival's Iron Age* 205 Questioning the Farmers of the Custom-house, for levying Tunnage and Poundage. **1706** T. HEARNE *Collect.* 16 Feb., The Priests and Tyth Farmers. **1719** W. WOOD *Surv. Trade* 114 These Commodities being under Monopolies in France, the Farmers of them took [etc.]. **1788** PRIESTLEY *Lect. Hist.* v. lxiii. 508 Taxes are raised..by means of farmers who advance the money as it is wanted. **1838–42** ARNOLD *Hist. Rome* III. xlii. 57 He might go out as a farmer of the taxes to Sicily. **1864** H. AINSWORTH *John Law* I. v. 98 Contractors, speculators, farmers of revenues, and others.

b. *Mining.* The lessee of 'the lot and cope of the king' (see COPE *sb.*³ 3).

1653 MANLOVE *Lead Mines* 3 Then one half meer at either end is due And to the Lord or Farmers doth accrew. *Ibid.* 5 See that right be done..Both to the Lord, and Farmers, on the Mine.

c. The lessee of a government monopoly.

1662 J. DAVIES *Voy. Ambass.* 194 The King of Persia farms out the fishing..which brings him in..many times more than the Farmers make thereof.

†**2.** *gen.* One who rents or has a lease of anything; a lessee. *Obs.*

1523 *Act 14–5 Hen. VIII*, c. 13 Every owner, fermer, and occupier of the said weres.

3. *spec.* One who rents land for the purpose of cultivaton; = *tenant farmer*. Now chiefly as a contextual application of 5.

1487 *Act 4 Hen. VII*, c. 16 The Occupier and Fermer of them..to be discharged against his Lessor of the Rent. **1523** FITZHERB. *Husb.* §123 Though a man be but a farmer, and shall haue hys farme .xx. yeres. **1577** HARRISON *England* II. v. (1877) I. 133 The yeomen are for the most part farmers to gentlemen.

†**4.** One who cultivates land for the owner; a bailiff, steward. *Obs.*

1382 WYCLIF *Luke* xvi. 1 Ther was sum riche man, that hadde a fermour, ethir a baily. **1526** *Pilgr. Perf.* (W. de W. 1531) 281 They shall haue yᵉ kyngdome of heuen, not as baylyes or fermers, but as possessyoners. **1579** LYLY *Euphues* (Arb.) 145 Architas..sent for his farmour, vnto whome hee sayde, if I [etc.]. **1580** BARET *Alv.* F 146 Fermer, or gouernour of a ferme, *villicus*.

5. a. One who cultivates a farm, whether as tenant or owner; one who 'farms' land, or makes agriculture his occupation.

1599 T. M[OUFET] *Silkwormes* Ded., Meaner Theams beseeme a Farmers quill. **1647** CLARENDON *Hist. Reb.* I. (1843) 40/2 Many gentlemen and farmers, had..good farms..of their own inheritance. **1666** WOOD *Life* (Oxf. Hist. Soc.) II. 86 Many fermers broke..corne being soe cheap. **1771** SMOLLETT *Humph. Cl.* II. 18 July, I eat like a farmer. **1813** SIR H. DAVY *Agric. Chem.* (1814) 15 The general experience of farmers had long before convinced the unprejudiced. **1849** COBDEN *Speeches* 2 We appear here as the farmers friends.

b. *dial.* The eldest son of the occupier of a farm.

a **1825** FORBY *Voc. E. Anglia* s.v., One labourer would ask another, 'Did my master set out that job?' And would be answered, 'No, my master didn't, but the farmer did'.

6. a. One who undertakes to perform (a specified work or service) at a fixed price.

1865 *Morn. Star* 26 June, It might be the interest of the farmer [of the permanent way] to starve the repairs..as much as possible.

b. One who undertakes the charge of children for a fixed sum. Usually *baby-farmer*.

1838 DICKENS *O. Twist* (1850) 83/1 'It's very much blotted, sir', said the farmer of infants. **1869** GREENWOOD *Seven Curses Lond.* iii. 45 It is to the 'farmers'' interest..to keep down their expenditure in the nursery. *Ibid.* iii. 57 Anyone however ignorant..may start as a baby farmer.

7. *slang.* **a.** An alderman.

1848 DUNCOMBE *Sinks of Lond.* Gloss. **1859** MATSELL *Vocabulum* s.v. (Farmer).

b. A hare (*Kent*).

c. An ignorant rustic; a stupid or gauche person.

1864 HOTTEN *Slang Dict.* (ed. 3) 131 *Farmer*..this term..In London..is used derisively of a countryman, and denotes a farm-labourer, clodpole. **1903** A. H. LEWIS *Boss* 263 Me fadder aint such a farmer as to go leavin' his address wit' no one.

d. (See quots.) *Naut. slang.*

1886 R. BROWN *Spunyarn & Spindrift* vi. 89 I'm a farmer to-night, and means to have a quiet and peaceful night's rest. *Ibid.*, A sailor calls himself a farmer when he has neither wheel nor look-out during a night. **1933** P. A. EADDY *Hull Down* viii. 179, I was a 'farmer' that night,..not having any wheel or look-out.

8. *Comb.* **a.** Simple attributive, as ***farmer-boy, -commonwealth, -proprietary.*** **b.** Similative, as ***farmer-like, farmer-looking*** adjs.

1851 *Literary Gaz.* 27 Dec. 924/3 His burly form and uncouth, farmer-looking appearance. **1854** G. W. CURTIS *Lit. & Soc. Ess.* (1894) 5 The farmer-boy—sweeping with flashing scythe through the river meadows. **1868** BRIGHT in *Star* 14 Mar., Would it not be possible..to establish to some extent..a farmer proprietary throughout the country? **1874** GREEN *Short Hist.* i. 3 Each little-farmer-commonwealth was girt in by its own border. **1891** *Daily News* 10 Sept 2/1 A field whose profusion of weeds would have sorely exercised the farmer-like soul of Mr. Poyser. **1957** J. KEROUAC *On Road* (1958) iv. 24 The standard North Dakota farmer-boy hat.

c. ***farmer's*** (or ***farmers'***) ***lung***, a pulmonary disease resulting from sensitization to fungal spores from mouldy hay, etc.

1945 *Brit. Med. Jrnl.* II. 716/1 *Farmer's lung*..is clinically and radiologically a fairly well characterized disease..commonly believed to be a kind of pulmonary mycosis. **1962** *Lancet* 26 May 1108/2 The test is..often the most convenient way of distinguishing sarcoidosis from..carcinomatosis, pneumoconiosis, or 'farmer's lung'. **1970** *Daily Tel.* 8 Oct. 9/8 Farmers' lung, a rare disease caused by mouldy hay, killed Mr Joseph Bradley.

farmerage ('fɑːmərɪdʒ). *nonce-wd.* [f. FARMER² + -AGE.] The body of farmers collectively.

1828 MISS MITFORD *Village* Ser. III. (1863) 493 The whole farmerage and shopkeepery of the place, with a goodly proportion of wives and daughters, came pouring in apace.

farmeress ('fɑːmərɪs). [f. FARMER² + -ESS.] **a.** A woman who farms land. **b.** A farmer's wife.

1672 EVELYN *Mem.* (1857) II. 80 A gallant widow brought up a farmeress. **1792** A. YOUNG *Trav. France* 171 She was an excellent farmeress. **1870** MISS BROUGHTON *Red as Rose* I. 265 The farmeresses and yeomen's wives of the Melford district.

farmerette (fɑːmə'rɛt). orig. and chiefly *U.S.* [f. FARMER² + -ETTE.] A woman or girl who farms land; a farmeress.

1918 *Independent* (N.Y.) 14 Sept., The farmerettes are producing food which creates the bodies and minds of mankind. **1923** *Daily Mail* 15 Aug. 2/4 Girl Farmers' Popularity... The organisers of the fair heard that the 'farmerettes' were coming. **1963** M. MCCARTHY *Group* iv. 72 Gag up a sketch about the milk strike with some farmerettes in straw hats.

farmer-general. [tr. F. *fermier-général.*] One who, under the old French monarchy, 'farmed' the taxes of a particular district.

1711 *Fr. Bk. of Rates* 126 The said Farmer-General, or his Clarks. **1768** STERNE *Sent. Journ.* (1778) II. 159 *Paris*, The farmer-general was just as inquisitive about our taxes. **1821** T. JEFFERSON *Autobiog.* Writings I. 90 A mitigation of the monopolies of our tobacco by the Farmers-general.

transf. **1790** MAD. D'ARBLAY *Diary* Oct., I am no farmer-general. **1892** *Daily News* 28 Apr. 5/1 The right to sell programmes at 6d. is farmed out..and the farmer is often a farmer-general whose privilege includes a whole batch of theatres.

farmerhood ('fɑːməhʊd). [See -HOOD.] The state of being a farmer.

1890 *Times* 19 June 9/3 A man..cannot glide into complete farmerhood by the easy and imperceptible gradations which the Committee seem to contemplate.

farmering ('fɑːmərɪŋ), *vbl. sb. dial.* [f. FARMER² + -ING¹.] The business of a farmer.

1888 in ELWORTHY *W. Somerset Word-bk., Farmering*, farming as a pursuit.

farmering ('fɑːmərɪŋ), *ppl. a.* [f. as prec. + -ING².] Engaged in the occupation of a farmer.

1883 C. READE in *Harper's Mag.* June 96/1 A farmering man wants to have four eyes.

farmerish ('fɑːmərɪʃ), *a.* [f. as prec. + -ISH.] Somewhat resembling a farmer.

1882 J. S. LLOYD *We Costelions* II. ix. 49 There was one farmerish looking lad.

†**'farmerly,** *a. Obs.* [f. as prec. + -LY¹.] Like a farmer.

a **1674** CLARENDON *Hist. Reb.* IX. (1703) II. 513 Some Farmerly Men..which had good reputations of affection..to the King's Service. **1727** in BAILEY vol. II. **1793** W. JONES (of Nayland) *Let. John Bull, Esq.* 2 Thomas Bull is a plain farmerly man, given up to the business of his calling.

†**'farmership.** *Obs.* [f. as prec. + -SHIP.] The state or occupation of being a farmer, or steward; stewardship.

1551 UDALL, etc. *Erasm. Par. Acts* ii, The lucky first fruites that the Ghospel brought forth for his rent and fermership. **1624** GEE *Foot out of Snare* 85 Giue an account of thy Farmer-ship.

farmery ('fɑːmərɪ), *sb.* [f. FARM *sb.* + -ERY.]

1. The buildings, yards, etc., belonging to a farm.

1656 S. HOLLAND *Don Zara* (1719) 8 The first thing therefore debated on by our Don was (as an Inquisitor) what food the Farmery afforded. **1787** W. MARSHALL *Norfolk* I. 81 The farmeries of Norfolk are..large and convenient. **1851** J. J. MECHI *2nd Paper Brit. Agric.* 30 Our present ill-arranged farmeries. **1891** *Daily News* 2 July 8/1 A farmery and three cottages.

2. = FARMING 2.

1801 W. TAYLOR in *Monthly Mag.* XII. 579 A rustic and rusticating fashion for farmery.

'farmery, *a.* [f. FARMER² + -Y³.] Farmer-like.

1861 THORNBURY *Turner* I. 312 Makes his cheese with farmery care.

farmery, var. of FERMERY, *Obs.*

farmhold ('fɑːmhəʊld). [f. FARM *sb.*² + HOLD *sb.*] A quantity of land held and cultivated as a farm.

1449 *Plumpton Corr.* 68 He thinks to have the farm-hould for 2vijˢ. viiiᵈ. in one yeare; but he shall not. **1504** *Plumpton Cor.* 184, I will not lett Tho. Croft wife..occupie her fermeald. **1567** *Wills & Inv. N.C.* (Surtees) I. 275, I geue to my wyf Agness..the leas of my fremhold during hir lyf naturall. **1628** COKE *Littleton* 5 a, A fearme is called in Lancashire a fermeholt. **1774** T. WEST *Antiq. Furness* (1805) 151 Grants, fermholds, annuities, corridies. **1882** G. ORNSBY *York* 27 Under a corrupted form it [the name Jacobi villa] probably still survives in the appellation of a farmhold.

'farm-,house. [f. FARM *sb.*² + HOUSE.] **a.** The chief dwelling house attached to a farm.

'In this word and FARM-YARD the Dicts. mark the principal stress on the first syllable; but in England this pronunciation is unusual, exc. when the word is *attrib.*' (*N.E.D.*, 1895).

1598 SHAKS. *Merry W.* II. iii. 91, I will bring thee where Mistris Anne Page is, at a Farm-house a Feasting. **1603** B. JONSON *Sejanus* IV. i, Tiberius sitting at his meat, In a farm-house they call Spelunca. **1711** T. HEARNE *Collect.* (Oxf. Hist. Soc.) III. 103 The great Farm-House call'd Chilswell Farm. **1820** W. IRVING *Sketch Bk.* (1859) 46 Every antique farm-house..is a picture.

b. *attrib.* and *Comb.*

1835 W. IRVING *Tour on Prairies* xxv. 267 Regaling themselves with savoury anticipations of farm-house luxuries. **1845** E. ACTON *Mod. Cookery* (ed. 2) xi. 245 Leg of Suffolk farm-house pork. *Ibid.* 261 Common farm-house sausages are made with nearly equal parts of fat and lean pork. **1851** MRS. GASKELL *Let.* May (1966) 836 Mary says she enjoyed the farm house bread. **1879** JEFFERIES *Wild Life in S.C.* 142 The farm-house garden. **1903** LD. R. GOWER *Rec. & Reminisc.* xv. 138 All the furniture of the simplest and most farmhouse-like kind. **1955** *Times* 10 May 12/3 Farmhouse cheese probably represents in the popular mind the difference between 'home made' and mass-produced cheese. **1960** *Farmer & Stockbreeder* 8 Mar. 57/1 Farmhouse-gate sales are considerable. **1969** J. FREDMAN *Fourth Agency* vii. 55 We'd all break for a farmhouse tea of hot buttered scones at four o'clock.

farming ('fɑːmɪŋ), *vbl. sb.* [f. FARM *v.*² + -ING¹.] The action of the vb. FARM.

1. The action or system of farming (out) or letting out to farm (the revenue, etc.).

1591 PERCIVALL *Sp. Dict.*, *Arrendamiento*, letting, ferming. **1672** PETTY *Pol. Anat.* 360 This and other practices of farming..hath been a great trade in Ireland. **1786** BURKE *W. Hastings* Wks. XII. 121 The farming out of the defence of a country..could have no real object but to enrich the contractor at the Company's expense. **1845** MCCULLOCH *Taxation* Introd. (1852) 31 Bentham..has endeavoured to show that farming is in every case the preferable mode of collection. **1877** DOWDEN *Shaks. Prim.* vi. 88 His farming of the realm.

2. The business of cultivating land, raising stock, etc.; agriculture, husbandry.

1733 W. ELLIS (*title*), Chiltern and Vale Farming explained. **1767** A. YOUNG *Farmer's Lett. People* 294 When I am told that farming answers to gentlemen..I never believe it. **1819** *Edin. Rev.* XXXII. 464 Capital..expended on what is called high farming. **1878** JEVONS *Primer Pol. Econ.* 90 As agriculture becomes more a science, farming will require greater skill.

3. *attrib.* and *Comb.* Simple attributive (sense 1), as ***farming-system***; (sense 2), as ***farming-country, -interest, -land, -life, -operation, -plan, -regulation***; **farming-office** = *farm-office*; **farming-stock,** the live stock and produce of a farm.

a **1764** LLOYD *Spirit Contradiction* Poet. Wks. 1774 II. 144 Friend Jerkin..rented, on the farming plan Grounds at much greater sums *per ann.* **1776** ADAM SMITH *W.N.* I. xi. (1869) I. 152 The ordinary profits of farming-stock in the neighbourhood. **1792** A. YOUNG *Trav. France* 131 A very..commodious house, with farming-offices, on the most ample and solid scale. **1799** *Morning Post* in *Spirit Publ. Jrnls.* (1800) III. 10 Any bye-laws or farming-regulations. **1828–40** TYTLER *Hist. Scot.* (1864) I. 240 *note*, The farming operations of ploughing and harrowing. **1845** MCCULLOCH *Taxation* II. iv. (1852) 202 The farming interest was far more depressed after the peace. **1872** RAYMOND *Statist. Mines & Mining* 287 Large areas of farming and garden land.

farming ('fɑːmɪŋ), *ppl. a.* [f. as prec. + -ING².] That farms, in senses of the vb.

1551 EDW. VI. *Disc. Ref. Abuses* in *Lit. Rem.* (Roxb.) II. 482 True gentlemen (I meane not theis ferming gentlemen, nor clarking knightes). **1885** EDWARDS in *Encycl. Brit.* (ed. 9) XIX. 580 It put a board of postmasters in room of a farming postmaster-general.

farmlet ('fɑːmlɪt). [f. FARM *sb.*² + -LET.] A little farm.

1881 *Athenæum* 9 Apr. 490/2 They retire from business, buy a farmlet..and resolve to live happily ever after. **1936** F. CLUNE *Roaming round Darling* i. 3 A general store, a row of workmen's cottages, and a few farmlets chucked in, constitute the altered town. **1952** J. STEINBECK *East of Eden* ii. 9 The owned and fought-over farmlets of Europe. **1963** *Punch* 13 Nov. 718/3 The Minister..giving extra support..to his own farmlets.

'farmost, *a.* [f. FAR + -MOST; irreg. superlative of FAR.] Farthest; most remote.

1618 BOLTON *Florus* III. v. 179 From off..the farmost watch-towre of the Northerne world. **1700** DRYDEN *Sigismonda & Guiscardo* 264 Within the farmost entrance of the Grot. **1885** W. TOWERS *Poems* 15 (E.D.D.), He sought the barn's farmost end. **1920** H. D. SHAWCROSS *Road-Wanderer* x. 120 The farmost end is seen crowned by a vision of distant hills.

farm-stead ('fɑːmstɛd). [f. FARM *sb.*² + STEAD.] A farm with the buildings upon it, a homestead. Also *attrib.*

1807 G. CHALMERS *Caledonia* I. III. vii. 401 *note*, A farm-stead, named Camus-ton. **1870** RAMSAY *Remin.* vi. (ed. 18) 203 Mr. Dunlop..passed a farm-stead. **1870** MORRIS *Earthly Par.* III. IV. 88 The raven hanging o'er the farm-stead gate.

farm-steading ('fɑːm,stedɪŋ). [f. prec. + -ING¹.] = prec.

1839 *Penny Cycl.* XV. 507/1 It [a kind of rat] establishes colonies in farm-steadings. **1873** SMILES *Huguenots Fr.* III. vi. (1881) 490 The present structure being merely part of a small farmsteading.

'farm-wife. Also **farmwife.** [f. FARM *sb.*² + WIFE *sb.*] A farmer's wife.

1880 W. D. HOWELLS *Undiscovered Country* 261 The growth of the bargaining passion in the wary farm-wives. **1907** *Daily Chron.* 21 Oct. 8/1 The farm-wife from the Ghyll stepped softly in. **1954** W. FAULKNER *Fable* (1955) 331 Above them stood the farmwife.

farmy ('fɑːmɪ), *a.* [f. FARM *sb*² + -Y.] Marked by the presence of farms.

1818 L. HUNT *Sonnet, Hampstead*, A leafy rise, with farmy fields in front. **1857** MRS. GORE *Two Aristocracies* I. xv. 262 A fair landscape stretching far into the distance—farmy fields and stretching parks.

'farm-,yard (with regard to the stress see FARM-HOUSE). The yard or inclosure attached to a farm-house or surrounded by farm-buildings. Also *attrib.*

1748 RICHARDSON *Clarissa* Wks. 1883 V. 258 In this very farmyard. **1788** W. MARSHALL *Yorksh.* (1796) I. 361 Farm-yard Management. **1807** *Med. Jrnl.* XVII. 354 He soon came out, and crossing the farm yard, attacked a bullock. **1846** J. BAXTER *Libr. Pract. Agric.* (ed. 4) II. 50 Guano..'a most powerful auxiliary to farm-yard manure'. **1856** EMERSON *Eng. Traits, Lit.* Wks. (Bohn) II. 103 The English muse loves the farmyard.

farm-yardy ('fɑːmjɑːdɪ), *a.* [f. FARMYARD + -Y¹.] Of, pertaining to, or resembling a farm-yard.

1928 GALSWORTHY *Swan Song* I. xii. 93 Things are much better..than they were—not nearly so stuffy and farmyardy.

farnesol ('fɑːnəsɒl, -səʊl). *Chem.* [a. G. *farnesol* (Haarmann & Reimer 1902, in (German) *Patentschrift 149603*), f. mod.L. *farnes-iana*, epithet of a species of Acacia, f. the name of Odoardo *Farnese* (1573–1626), Italian cardinal + -OL. 1.] A terpenoid alcohol, $C_{15}H_{25}OH$, that occurs in various essential oils and is used in the preparation of scents.

1904 *Jrnl. Chem. Soc.* LXXXVI. I. 514 *Farnesol*, $C_{15}H_{26}O$, a new sesquiterpene alcohol, is obtained from various acacia oils, from musk oil, and from lime-tree blossom oil. **1949** T. F. WEST et al. *Synthetic Perfumes* iii. 29 Pure farnesol appears to the casual observer to be an almost odourless oil. **1961** *New Scientist* 2 Nov. 279/2 A relatively simple organic compound, farnesol (an open-chain terpene alcohol), has the same effects on immature insects as extracts of natural juvenile hormone. **1970** V. B. WIGGLESWORTH *Insect Hormones* iv. 68 Farnesol is..an intermediate in the biosynthesis of cholesterol and of carotenoids; although it had rather low juvenile hormone activity in insects..the natural hormone might well be a related isoprenoid compound.

farness ('fɑːnɪs). [f. FAR + -NESS.]

1. The state or fact of being far; remoteness. Also *occas.* of sight: Far-reachingness. Now *rare.*

1398 TREVISA *Barth. De P.R.* III. xxi. (1495) 69 The syȝte demyth a grete sterre but smalle..for fernesse of place. **1580** NORTH *Plutarch* (1676) 650 Fearing the farness of the journey. **1605** VERSTEGAN *Dec. Intell.* ii. (1628) 29 Here is no neerenesse of affinitie at all, but as much farnesse as needeth to be. **1621** LADY M. WROTH *Urania* 29 By reason of the farrnesse from the Court. **1876** BANCROFT *Hist. U.S.* V. lx. 208 Farness of sight and fixedness of belief. **1883** S. A. BROOKE in *Homilet. Monthly* Dec. 152 In their farness from the strife and trouble of men.

†**b.** Amount of distance. *Obs.*

1523 *St. Papers Hen. VIII*, IV. 1 Every bataile an arrowe shotte from the other, and all like fernes from the Englisshe armye. **1674** N. FAIRFAX *Bulk & Selv.* 78 Having nearnesses or farnesses betwen each other.

2. *concr.* Distant parts. (*from, in*) ***the farness***: 'the distance'. *arch.*

1571 GOLDING *Calvin on Ps.* lxv. 6 Thou that art the hope..of the farnesse of the sea. *a* **1849** J. C. MANGAN *Poems* (1859) 263 In the farness lay the moonlight on the Mountains of the Nile. **1855** *Fraser's Mag.* LI. 94 From the farness, To the castle..rode a knight in flashing harness.

†**'farnet.** *Obs.* Also fernet, farned. [? a. ON. *fǫru-neyte* company of travellers.] A band, company, train of attendants.

a **1300** *Cursor M.* 24947 (Cott.) Wit al þair farnet and þair fere þai com til land. *c* **1340** *Ibid.* 6070 (Fairf.) þe farned [C. fernet] þar-wiþ [þe lambe] salle be fedde.

‖**far niente** (far nj'ɛnte). [It., lit. 'to do nothing.'] Idleness. (Usu. in phr. DOLCE FAR NIENTE.)

1819 T. HOPE *Anastasius* II. vii. 132, I determined..to indulge in the supreme pleasure of the Italians—the *far niente*. **1857** TROLLOPE *Barchester T.* I. ix. 118 The *far niente* of her Italian life had..brought her to regard a state of inactivity as the only earthly good. **1894** 'M. O'RELL' *John Bull & Co.* xxxii. 271 Allow him to pass his life in the softest of *far nientes*.

farn(t)ic(k)le, -ed, var. FERNTICLE, -ED, *dial.*

faro[1] ('fɛərəʊ). Forms: 8–9 **pharaoh**, *erron.* **pharoah, pharo**, (8 **pharaon, farro**), 8– **faro**. [f. PHARAOH, after F. *pharaon*, It. *faraone*.

Why the name was given is not clear; some mod. Dicts. assert that one of the cards used in the game formerly bore the picture of Pharaoh.]

1. A gambling game at cards, in which the players bet on the order in which certain cards will appear when taken singly from the top of the pack.

1739 *Act 12 Geo. II*, c. 28 §1 Games of the Ace of Hearts, Pharaoh, Basset and Hazard. **1748** H. WALPOLE *Corr.* (ed. 3) II. cxc. 233 Silver-pharaoh and whist for the ladies that did not dance. **1797** *Chron.* in *Ann. Reg.* 14/2 Convicted in the penalty of £50 each for playing at the game of Faro. **1842** BARHAM *Ingol. Leg.*, *Black Mosquetaire*, He Lost large sums at faro. **1859** THACKERAY *Virgin.* xxvii, Preferring smoke and faro to fresh air.

2. *attrib.* and *Comb.*, as ***faro-player***, ***-table***, ***-winnings***; **faro bank**, (*a*) a gaming-house where faro is played; (*b*) the banker's deposit of money against which the other players put their stakes; **faro banker**, the proprietor of a faro bank; **faro dealer**, the dealer in a game of faro.

a **1735** ARBUTHNOT *Harmony in Uproar* Misc. Wks. 1751 II. 34 The Tricks of a Faro-Table or a Bowling-Green. **1756** MRS. CALDERWOOD *Jrnl.* (1884) 187 Mr. Hay's profit is from the..farro bank. **1795** WOLCOTT (P. Pindar) *Hair Powder* 236 Let..stately Cumberland [pinch] her faro winnings. **1796** *Hull Advertiser* 21 May 2/4 The threatening notice taken by the Lord Chief Justice of the Ladies' Faro Tables. **1798** *Sporting Mag.* XI. 7 The villany of a female Faro Banker. **1801** MAR. EDGEWORTH *Belinda* iv, Mrs. Luttridge..being a great faro-player. **1856** *Harper's Mag.* Dec. 68/2 A grim, imperturbable faro-dealer. **1877** MORLEY *Crit. Misc.* Ser. II. 52 Kill time..at lansquenet and the faro bank. **1952** S. KAUFFMANN *Philanderer* (1953) iv. 64 Cameron..had once been a faro dealer in a gambling house.

‖**faro**[2] ('faro). [F. *faro*.] A kind of beer made chiefly at Brussels and in its neighbourhood.

1848 THACKERAY *Van. Fair* xxxi. 266 A mug of Faro at the bench of a beer-house on the road to Laeken. **1864** *Daily Tel.* 17 Mar., You stop on the road to drink faro. **1865** *Ibid.* 28 Nov. 7/3 Faro and brown beer flowed almost for the asking. **1960** *Spectator* 25 Nov. 831 This Belgian beer..[is] called *lambic* or *faro*, and the books all say it's light and rather bitter.

faröelite ('fɑːrəʊɪlaɪt). *Min.* [f. (by Heddle) *Faröe* where it was found + -LITE.] A variety of Thomsonite occurring 'in spherical concretions, consisting of lamellar radiated individuals, pearly in cleavage' (Dana).

1858 GREGG & LETTSOM *Min.* 157 Faröelite may rank as a distinct species.

Faroeman ('fɛərəʊmæn, 'færəʊmæn). = FAROESE *sb.* a.

1898 *Blackw. Mag.* Aug. 246/1 The ancestors of the Faroemen were Norwegians. **1905** T. N. ANNANDALE *Faroes* 2 The taxes are collected by sheriffs, who are always native Faroemen. *Ibid.* 3 The Faroeman is by nature peaceable.

Faroese (fɛərəʊ'iːz, færəʊ'iːz), *a.* and *sb.* Also **Faröese, Færoese, Feroese**. [f. *Faröe* + -ESE, after Sw. *Föräarna*, Da. *Færøerne* Faröe islands = Icel. *Færeyskr* Faroese (adj.), f. *Færeyjar* Faröe islands, f. *fær* sheep + *ey* island.] **A.** *adj.* Of or pertaining to the Faröe Islands, an autonomous dependency of the kingdom of Denmark situated between Great Britain and Iceland, their inhabitants, or the language spoken by them. **B.** *sb.* **a.** A native or inhabitant of the Faröe Islands. **b.** The language of the Faröe Islands, which is a variety of Norse.

1851 *Illustr. Catal. Gt. Exhib.* III. III. 552/1 Faroese and Danish St. Luke. **1855** *Narr. Cruise Yacht Maria* i. 15 Immediately after we anchored, a Feroese gentleman came on board. *Ibid.* ii. 25 The Feroese are very long-lived. **1898** J. RUSSELL-JEAFFRESON *Faröe Isl.* i. 15 The religion of the Faröese..is Lutheran. *Ibid.* v. 99 The child cried out in Faröese, 'Nüg me up.' *Ibid.* 103, I collected..as many of the old Faröese proverbs as I came across. **1908** W. G. COLLINGWOOD *Scand. Brit.* 259 The 'Norn' is shown to be fairly pure Norse, with a very slight sprinkling of Danish, Færoese, Frisian and English words. *Ibid.* 260 Phonetic changes like those in Icelandic and Færoese. **1953** *New Biol.* XV. 57 A Faeroese shearwater, with a nestling. **1969** *Guardian* 13 Aug. 4/8 The enterprise and success of their Faroese neighbours is an irksome example to the Shetlanders. **1969** *Language* XLV. 570 In languages like Faeroese or Danish..sonorants may be completely voiceless after tenues. **1969** J. WOOD *Three Blind Mice* iii. 42 Taking on two belligerent Faroese. **1970** *Sruth* (Inverness) 10 Dec. 6/1 Frederick Petersen, author of the Faroese national anthem.

far-off ('fɑːr'ɒf, -ɔː-), *a.* [f. FAR *adv.* + OFF *adv.*, formerly written as two words.]

1. Far distant, remote. **a.** In space. **b.** In time. **c.** In relationship.

a. 1590 SHAKS. *Mids. N.* IV. i. 194 Like farre off mountaines turned into Clouds. **1632** MILTON *Penseroso* 74, I hear the far-off Curfeu sound, Over some wide-water'd shore. **1794** MRS. RADCLIFFE *Myst. Udolpho* vii, The far-off low of cattle. **1816** J. WILSON *City of Plague* II. i. 199 Our far-off friends. **1840** DICKENS *Barn. Rudge* II. xiv, The far-off places in which he had been wandering. **1855** MILMAN *Lat. Chr.* (1864) IX. XIV. viii. 280 Their humble posture of far off adoration.

b. 1850 TENNYSON *In Mem.* i, Who shall..stretch a hand thro' time to catch The far-off interest of tears? **1875** JOWETT *Plato* (ed. 2) III. 78 The far-off result of the working of many minds in many ages. **1877** A. B. EDWARDS *Up Nile* i. 18 Those far-off days of Cheops and Chephren.

c. 1828 MISS MITFORD *Village* Ser. III. (1863) 90, I..am but a far-off kinswoman.

d. Other *fig.* uses, e.g. of thoughts, looks, etc.

1849 *Hogg's Weekly Instructor* III. 313/1 The far-off thoughts of earthly love and beauty. **1870** W. MORRIS *Earthly Par.* III. 462 Scarce happy 'neath his far-off moody gaze. **1876** *Mr. Gray & his Neighbours* II. 41 Alice Gray was very pale, and with that far-off look in her eyes, which those who are to die young have more than others. **1922** C. E. MONTAGUE *Disenchantment* i. 8 The far-off, longed-for ideal of smartness. **1948** L. MACNEICE *Holes in Sky* 21 The Painter's little daughter, far-off-eyed. **1959** T. S. ELIOT tr. *St. J. Perse's Anabasis* 37 My soul engaged in far-off matters.

2. absol. ***in the far off***: in the distance.

1866 C. M. YONGE *Dove in Eagle's Nest* I. xii. 230 There will be freedom in rushing at last into the great far-off! **1884** SALA *Journ. due South* I. xxv. (1887) 339 The eternal but subdued resonance of Niagara in the far-off. **1932** V. MCNABB in *God's Way of Mercy* (1937) xxi. 186 Faith brings the far-off very near, and makes the very little large.

Hence **far-offness**, the state or fact of being far-off, distance.

1873 R. S. CANDLISH *Serm.* v. 93 My..helpless far-offness from God. **1877** MALLOCK *New Republic* IV. ii. II. 208 But ah! the weariness, the far-offness of it all.

Faroish ('fɛərəʊɪʃ, 'færəʊɪʃ), *a.* Now *rare*. [f. *Faröe* + -ISH[1].] = FAROESE *a.* Also **Farish** ('fɛərɪʃ, 'færɪʃ) *a.*

a **1889** CHILD *Ballads* I. 315 (Cent. Dict.), The Swedish ..Danish, and Faroish ballads. **1898** *Blackw. Mag.* Aug. 245 A collection of Farish ballads. **1905** T. N. ANNANDALE *Faroes* 14 It is only some fifty or sixty years since Farish began to be written. *Ibid.* 131 A Farish cottage is generally clean, an Icelandic farmhouse is almost as often airless, filthy, and verminous.

‖**farol** (fə'rəʊl). [Sp., lit. lantern.] In *Bullfighting*, a movement in which the bullfighter draws the bull by passing the cloak back rapidly over his own head.

1932 E. HEMINGWAY *Death in Afternoon* i. 18 In bullfighting..it is the picturesqueness..of farols and molinets. *Ibid.* xv. 169 The different ways of using the cape, the gaonera, the mariposa, the farol. **1957** A. MACNAB *Bulls of Iberia* vi. 61 In the *farol*, he flings both arms upwards and the cape swirls up above his head, with the bull sometimes rearing up spectacularly in an effort to reach it.

‖**farouche** (faruʃ). Also *Sc.* **farouchie**. [Fr. *farouche*, of unknown origin; the received connexion with L. *ferōcem* cruel is untenable.] Sullen, shy and repellent in manner.

1765 H. WALPOLE *Lett. H. Mann.* (1857) IV. 412 The King..has great sweetness in his countenance instead of that farouche look which they give. **1814** BYRON in Moore *Life & Lett.* (1832) III. 56 It is too farouche; but..my satires are not very playful. **1855** MRS. GASKELL *North & S.* xliv, She has been very farouche with me for a long time. **1880** OUIDA *Moths* I. 298 She is a little farouche.

farouchely (fa'ruːʃlɪ), *adv.* [f. FAROUCHE *a.* + -LY[2].] In a farouche manner.

1931 A. POWELL *Afternoon Men* v. 52 The boy, an ill-conditioned youth..stood farouchely clasping and unclasping his hands. **1967** *Listener* 31 Aug. 267/2 Gillespie ..farouchely ambles across the platform.

far-out, *a.* [f. FAR *adv.* + OUT *adv.*]

a. Remote, distant.

1887 J. SERVICE *Life Dr. Duguid* 84 A faur oot freen of John Paiks' father. **1888** 'R. BOLDREWOOD' *Robb. under Arms* I. xvii. 232 These far-out back-of-beyond places. *Ibid.* III. xv. 215 The far-out squatters that were stocking up new country in Queensland. **1929** D. H. LAWRENCE *Pansies* 100 Yet even waste, grey foreshores, sand, and..far-out clay Are sea-bed still.

b. Of jazz: of the latest or most progressive kind. More generally, avant-garde, far-fetched; excellent, splendid. orig. *U.S.*

1954 *Time* 8 Nov. 70 Jazz lingo becomes obsolescent almost as fast as it reaches the public ear... A daring performance was 'hot', then 'cool', and now is 'far out'. **1956** M. STEARNS *Story of Jazz* (1957) xviii. 232 There were too many choices in 'far-out' harmony. **1959** *Listener* 1 Oct. 542/3 Cute, gone, far-out little girls. **1960** *Melody Maker* 31 Dec. 6/3 Oliver Cool is the pseudonym of singer Larry Ellis, who found he won more success when he adopted the 'far-out' monniker. **1962** *Listener* 29 Nov. 911/2 In the spread of serialism, we are faced with another and greater neo-classical craze, the most far-out of all. **1963** K. AMIS *One Fat Englishman* iii. 36 She was..several times more attractive than her with-it off-beat far-out co-religionist deserved. **1970** *Sci. Jrnl.* May 47/2 Talking with computers, so much a far-out idea when this journal discussed IBM's work on it four years ago, now seems quite straightforward.

†'**farrage**. *Obs.* Also 7 **farage**. [a. F. *farrage*, ad. L. *farrāgo*: see FARRAGO.]

1. Fodder for cattle. Also *attrib.*, as ***farrage rye***.

1609 HOLLAND *Amm. Marcell.* XXIII. ii. 220 In those countries such kinds of farage are mowed up. **1659** TORRIANO, *Farrāggine*, dredge, bollimong, or farage rye.

2. = BULLIMONG I.

[**1578** LYTE *Dodoens* IV. vii. 459 *Farrago* is none other thing but barley, otes, and suche lyke graynes mingled togither.] **1601** HOLLAND *Pliny* XVIII. xvi. 573 That kind of dredge or farrage..ought to be sowne very thicke.

3. = FARRAGO b.

1698 F. B. *Modest Cens.* 29 A farrage of jejune Learning.

†**fa'rraginary**, *a.* *Obs. rare*[−1]. [f. L. *farrāgin-*, FARRAGO + -ARY.] Confused, miscellaneous.

1538 LATIMER *Let.* 25 Aug. in *Serm. & Rem.* (1845) 401 This foolish farraginary scribbling.

farraginous (fə'reɪdʒɪnəs), *a.* [f. as prec. + -OUS.] Miscellaneous, indiscriminate, 'hotchpotch'. Also of a person: That makes a hotch-potch.

1615 [see BULLIMONG 1 b]. **1646** SIR T. BROWNE *Pseud. Ep.* I. iii. 10 A farraginous concurrence of all conditions, tempers, sex, and ages. **1669** W. SIMPSON *Hydrol. Chym.* 103 The stomach..becomes tantaliz'd by the farraginous mixtures of concretes. **1765** WARBURTON *Div. Legat.* IV. iv. §6 Notes (ed. 4) 131 The great farraginous body of Popish rites and ceremonies. **1799** KIRWAN *Geol. Ess.* 226 In some [mountains] different species [of stone] are jumbled together, these I call faraginous. *a* **1843** SOUTHEY *Doctor* cxxii. (1862) 301 The Laureate has somewhere in his farraginous notes..a story of certain Polish physicians who [etc.]. **1863** READE in *All Year Round* 3 Oct. 123/2 Bailey was one of the farraginous fools of the unscientific science.

farrago (fə'reɪgəʊ). Also 8–9 **farago**. [a. L. *farrāgo* mixed fodder for cattle, hence *fig.* a medley, confused mixture, f. *farr-*, *far* spelt, corn.] A confused group; a medley, mixture, hotchpotch.

†**a.** of material things or of persons. *Obs.*

1632 B. JONSON *Magn. Lady* I. vii, Hee..holds..their causes, a farragoe, Or a made dish. **1677** HALE *Prim. Orig. Man.* II. iii. 149 The People were a Farrago, collected and gathered out of the neighbouring Nations. **1789** G. WHITE *Selborne* (1853) II. xxx. 245 Among this farrago also were to be seen some maggots.

b. of immaterial things.

1637–50 ROW *Hist. Kirk* (1842) 371 A strange miscellanie, farrago, and hotch-potch of Poperie, Arminianisme, and what not. **1783** POTT *Chirurg. Wks.* II. 7 Ancient surgery was..loaded with a farrago of external applications. *a* **1827** CANNING *Poet. Wks.* (1827) 41 No longer we want This farrago of cowardice, cunning, and cant. **1876** C. M. DAVIES *Unorth. Lond.* 120 A farrago of the Lord's Prayer, the Litany of the Church of England, and the extemporaneous effusion of Dr. Cumming himself.

'**farrand, farrant**, *a.* *Sc.* and *north. dial.* Also 4 **farand(e**. [prob. an application of *farande*, northern pr. pple. of FARE *v.*[1]; cf. the sense 'to suit, befit' of ON. *fara*; also quots. s.v. FARING *ppl. a.*]

†**1.** Of a person: Well-favoured, comely, handsome. *Obs.*

13.. *E.E. Allit. P.* B. 607 If þay [wyȝeȝ] wer farande & fayre to beholde. **1375** BARBOUR *Bruce* II. 514 Othir ladyis fayr and farand.

2. Of things: Becoming, dignified, pleasant.

13.. *E.E. Allit. P.* A. 864 Lest les þou leue my talle farande. *c* **1340** *Gaw. & Gr. Knt.* 101 Vch farand fest. **1882** in *Lanc. Gloss.*

3. Having a specified appearance, disposition, or temperament. With qualifying word prefixed, as ***auld-***, ***evil-***, ***fair-***, ***fighting-***, ***foul-***, ***well-farrand***.

a **1400** *Sir Perc.* 848 Siche ille farande fare. *c* **1440** *Ipomydon* 282 So goodly a man and wele farand. *a* **1455** HOLLAND *Houlate* 153 Thai apperit to the Pape..Fair farrand and fre. **1513** DOUGLAS *Æneis* VII. viii. 147 Sum the maist semyly farrand personage Tystis to the feild. **1635** D. DICKSON *Pract. Wks.* (1845) I. 88 A sore matter for a sinner to be corrected and yet to go light-farrand under it. **1674–91** RAY *N.C. Words* s.v. *Farand*, *Fighting-Farand*, in a fighting humor. **1816** SCOTT *Antiq.* xlii, 'Ochiltree, is very skeely and auld farrant about mony things.' **1830** GALT *Lawrie T.* I. viii. (1849) 29 'Ye're an auld farrant chappy.'

farrandly, farrantly ('færəndlɪ, -tlɪ), *adv.* *Sc.* and north *dial.* [f. FARRAND, -ANT + -LY[2].] Pleasantly, handsomely, splendidly.

c **1325** *E.E. Allit. P.* C. 435 Farandely on a felde he fettelez hym to bide. **1613** T. POTTS *Disc. Witches* (Chetham Soc.) K b, What is yonder that casts a light so farrandly. *c* **1750** J. COLLIER (Tim Bobbin) *Wks.* 49 Yo coom'n farrantly off. **1865** B. BRIERLEY *Irkdale* I. 100 Hoo wouldno behave so farrantly, if hoo yerd what I're talkin' abeawt.

farrantly ('færəntlɪ), *a.* *north. dial.* Also 8–9 **far-, farrently**. [f. FARRANT *a.* + -LY[1].]

1. Of a person. **a.** Comely, handsome, good-looking. **b.** Genteel, respectable.

1674 RAY *N.C. Words* 17 *Farantly*, handsome. **1790** MRS. WHEELER *Westmld. Dial.* (1821) 20 Whya hang thee, thau er farrantly enuff tae leak at. **1794** MRS. DARWALL *Poems* I. 95 Five farently youths for her wished their prime. **1867** *Cornh. Mag.* XV. 731 So took up wi' a farrantly whench.

2. Of a thing: Becoming, fit, proper.

c **1750** J. COLLIER (Tim Bobbin) *Wks.* 72 There's none sitch farrantly tawk abeawtr'. **1839** *Cumbrld. & Westm.*

Dial. 13 Tae spin tow for bord claiths en sheets.. wod hev been mitch mair farently then ritin books. **1855** E. WAUGH in *Harland's Lanc. Lyrics* 136 A farrantly bargain he'd be.

farrash, var. FERASH.

far-reaching (stress variable), *a.* [f. FAR *adv.* 8 + REACHING *ppl. a.*] That reaches far; extensive (*lit.* and *fig.*); exerting an influence or producing an effect which extends far in space or time.

1824 NEWMAN *Poems, To H. E. N.* xii, The dusky heath far-reaching. **1849** J. R. LOWELL *To W. L. Garrison* 18 in *Poet. Wks.* (1891) 116 Rome's far-reaching bolts. **1860** RUSKIN in *Cornhill Mag.* Sept. 284 That which seems to be wealth may be only the gilded index of far-reaching ruin. **1874** H. SIDGWICK *Meth. Ethics* 245 A fundamental conflict of ideas, which appears more profound and far-reaching in its consequences the more we examine it. **1894** *Pop. Sci. Monthly* XLIV. 572 Geology formed a subject of far-reaching importance. **1900** *Daily News* 1 Mar. 2/1 A number of far-reaching caves. **1913** J. G. FRAZER *Psyche's Task* (ed. 2) 168 Such mental variations, with all their far-reaching train of social consequences. **1950** L. S. THORNTON *Revelation & Mod. World* v. 149 This far-reaching continuity of revelation. **1971** *Guardian Weekly* 24 Apr. 5/1 The implications of the new controversy are far-reaching.

Hence **far-'reachingly** *adv.*; also **far-'reachingness**.

c **1850** BAGEHOT *To R. C. Ch.* iii. in *Wks.* (1915) I. 12 With hand of power and thoughts of light, As Britain seas, far-reachingly. **1893** *Harper's Mag.* May 821 The most far-reachingly beneficial expression of this fostering policy. **1901** S. BUTLER in H. F. Jones *Mem.* (1919) I. 264, I was oppressed and scared by the far-reachingness and daring of what I had done.

farreate ('færiːeɪt), *a. Rom. Antiq.* [ad. L. *farreāt-us* pa. pple. of *farreāre*, f. *farreum* cake of spelt-bread, neut. of *farreus*: see FARREOUS.] **a.** Of persons: United in marriage by the offering of spelt-bread (see CONFARREATION). **b.** Of marriage: = CONFARREATE *a.*

1880 MUIRHEAD *Gaius* I. §112 No person is elected to the office.. unless born of farreate parents. *Ibid.* Digest 545 No one.. who was not the issue of a farreate marriage.

farreation (færiː'eɪʃən). *Rom. Antiq.* [ad. L. *farreātiōn-em* the use of spelt-bread in marrying, f. as prec.] = CONFARREATION.

1656 in BULLOKAR; **1818** in TODD; and in mod. Dicts.

farrel, dial. form of FARL.

†**farrement.** *Obs. rare.* Also **farment.** [a. OF. *ferrement*:—L. *ferrāment-um* implement of iron.] In *pl.* Iron fittings.

1440 J. SHIRLEY *Dethe K. James* (1818) 15 The farrements of the chaumbur wyndos.. wer.. strongli sowdid yn the stonys with moltyne lede. **1458** *Yatton Ch.-wardens' Accts.* (Som. Rec. Soc.) 100 For.. farmentes, hokys, and other thynges to the chorche euce.

farrender, -ine, -on, var. of FARANDINE, *Obs.*

farreous ('færɪəs), *a. Med.* [f. L. *farre-us* made of corn, f. *far* corn + -OUS.] (See quot.)

1884 *Syd. Soc. Lex.*, *Farreous*, scurfy; applied to the urine when it deposits a branny sediment.

farrier ('færɪə(r)), *sb.* Forms: 6-8 ferrier, farriar, (7 farrior, -yer), 6- farrier. [a. OF. *ferrier*:—L. *ferrārius*, f. *ferr-um* iron, in med.L. (often *ferrus*) horseshoe.

The synonym FERROUR, current in Eng. in 14-16th c., is a different formation.]

1. One who shoes horses; a shoeing-smith; hence, also one who treats the diseases of horses.

1562 *Act 5 Eliz.* c. 4 §3 The.. Crafts.. of.. Smiths, Farriers. **1622** F. MARKHAM *Bk. War* v. ii. §6 An excellent Smith or Farryer who shall euer be furnished with Horse-shooes, nayles, and drugges, both for inward and outward applycations. **1718** QUINCY *Compl. Disp.* 80 Essential Oil is much in use amongst our Farriers. **1751** SMOLLETT *Per. Pic.* (1779) I. xvii. 146 Blacksmith and ferrier. **1821** SCOTT *Kenilw.* x, The light stroke of a hammer as when a farrier is at work. **1872** YEATS *Techn. Hist. Comm.* 178 Farriers or shoeing smiths appeared first in Germany.

2. An official who has care of the horses in a cavalry regiment. Also *farrier-major*, *corporal-*, *serjeant-farrier*.

1832 *Regul. Instr. Cavalry* III. 60 The Farriers and Band fall out. **1844** *Regul. & Ord. Army* 373 The Troop Farrier is carefully to examine each foot of every Horse. **1868** *Ibid.* ¶317 The Farrier Major is liable to be reduced for misconduct to the rank and pay of Farrier. **1885** *Ibid.* 279 Serjeant-farriers at home (including corporal-farriers of the Household Cavalry) are required to train men to become efficient as shoeing smiths. *Ibid.* 281 The services of the farrier quartermaster-serjeant are to be placed entirely at the disposal of the veterinary surgeon.

†**3.** With sb. prefixed, as *sergeant-*, *yeoman-farrier* = FERROUR 3. *Obs.*

1647 HAWARD *Crown Rev.* 33 Three Yeomen ferriers. **1711** *Lond. Gaz.* No. 4791/4 John Willis, late Sergeant-Farrier.

4. *Comb.*, as *farrier-like* adj.

1809 *Med. Jrnl.* XXI. 308 Relieving them [strictures] in some scientific way; not by the Farrier-like.. methods too commonly practiced.

farrier ('færɪə(r)), *v. rare.* [f. the sb.]

1. *trans.* To treat (an animal) as a farrier does.

1814 *Selby & M. Weighton Road Act* ii. 7 Beasts.. returning from being shoed or farriered.

2. *intr.* To practise farriery.

Hence **'farriering** *vbl. sb.*, the action of the vb.

1707 MORTIMER *Husb.* 154 The Art of Farriering and Cow-leeching. *a* **1873** LIVINGSTONE in *Boy's Own Paper* (1889) 7 Sept. 778/3 Carpentering, gun-mending, farriering.

farriery ('færɪərɪ). [f. as prec. + -Y³.] The art of the farrier; now = veterinary surgery.

1737 BRACKEN (*title*), Farriery Improved. **1760** GOLDSM. *Cit. W.* lxxxvi, Several of the great here.. understand as much of farriery as their grooms. **1821** SCOTT *Kenilw.* xiii, His extraordinary practice in farriery. **1880** MISS BRADDON *Just as I am* xxxix, They were acquainted with the elements of farriery.

farro, obs. form of FARO.

farrow ('færəʊ), *sb.* Also 1 faerh, fearh, 3 far, 8-9 *dial* farry. Cf. FARE *sb.*² [OE. *fearh* str. masc. corresp. to OS. **farh* (whence diminutive MLG. *ferken*, Du. *varken*), OHG. *farh*, *farah* (MHG. *varch*; diminutive OHG. *farhelîn*, MHG. *verkel*, mod.G. *ferkel*):—OTeut. **farho-z* boar:—pre-Teut. **porkos* = Gr. πόρκος, L. *porcus*: see PORK.]

†**1.** A young pig. *Obs.*

a **700** *Epinal Gloss.* 811 *Porcellus*, faerh. *a* **1100** *Ags. Voc.* in Wr. Wülcker 321 *Porcellus*, fearh. *c* **1300** *K. Alis.* 2441 Heo.. flodeden, so faren in feld.

transf. **1820** BYRON *Morg. Mag.* lxiii, Another, to revenge his fellow farrow, Against the giant rush'd.

2. An act or instance of farrowing. [Properly another word; f. the vb.]

1601 HOLLAND *Pliny* I. 229 One sow may bring at one farrow twenty pigges. **1869** *Daily News* 8 Dec., Mr. Lynn and his man.. proved the dates of the farrows.

3. Hence *concr.* A litter of pigs; occas. in sing. (after Shakspere) with numeral to indicate the number of young.

1577 B. GOOGE *Heresbach's Husb.* III. (1586) 149 b, If you will have two farrowes in one yeere. **1605** SHAKS. *Macb.* IV. i. 65 Powre in Sowes blood, that hath eaten Her nine Farrow. **1607** TOPSELL *Four-f. Beasts* (1673) 519 The Lavinians were much troubled about the signification of such a monstrous farrow. **1787** HUNTER in *Phil. Trans.* LXXVII. 236 In that time she had eight farrows.. and had in all seventy-six pigs. **1826** in *Sheridaniana* 313 A fine Chinese sow and nine farrow. **1869** BLACKMORE *Lorna D.* xvii, Two farrows of pigs ready for the chapman.

4. Of the sow: *in* or *with farrow*: with young.

1577 B. GOOGE *Heresbach's Husb.* III. (1586) 150 So shall the damme. bee sooner with farrowe againe. **1884** *Farm & Home* 25 Oct. 275/2 Boars do not usually pay much attention to sows in farrow.

5. *attrib.*, as *farrow-sow*.

1871 B. TAYLOR *Faust* (1875) I. xxi. 182 She rides upon a farrow-sow.

farrow ('færəʊ), *a.* Chiefly *Sc.* Forms: 5 *Sc.* ferow, 6-8 *Sc.* furrow, 7- farrow. [Of unknown derivation; *farrow cow* corresponds formally to Flemish *verwekoe*, *varwekoe* (De Bo), in 16th c. '*verrekoe*, taura' (Kilian), which means a cow that has ceased to be capable of producing offspring.]

Of a cow: That is not with calf (see quots.). Also in *to be*, *go* or *run farrow*. *farrow-farrow*, barren in two successive seasons.

1494 *Act. Dom. Conc.* 363 Twa ferow ky. **15..** *Depredations in Argyll* 51 (Jam.) Sex furrow cows. **1688** R. HOLME *Armoury* II. 173/2 A Farrow Cow is a Cow that gives Milk in the second year after her Calving, having no Calf that year. **1725** RAMSAY *Gent. Sheph.* III. iii, My faulds contain twice fifteen furrow nowt. **1856** AIRD *Poet. Wks.* 193 Farrow, ill-haired, and lean. **1879** *Mem. Ochiltree* 52 If the same animal had no calf the following year, she was farrow-farrow.

fig. **1674** N. FAIRFAX *Bulk & Selv.* 19 Whatever is big with or positive of eternity, cannot go farrow, or be privative of real entity.

farrow ('færəʊ), *v.* Forms: 4-6 *Sc.* ferrie. (6 farowe), 7-9 *dial.* farry, 4- farrow. Also 3 iveruwe, 4 yvarȝe; and see FARE *v.*² [f. FARROW *sb.*]

1. *trans.* Of a sow: To bring forth (young).

a **1225** *Ancr. R.* 204 Þus beoð þeos pigges ieuruwed. **1513** DOUGLAS *Æneis* III. vi. 72 A grete sow fereit of grysis thretty heid. **1614** MARKHAM *Cheap Husb.* (1623) 126 Many Sowes.. will deuoure their Pigges when they haue farro'd them. **1760** GOLDSM. *Cit. W.* lviii, A sow.. farrowed fifteen pigs at a litter. **1828-40** TYTLER *Hist. Scot.* (1864) I. 137 The English sow had farrowed her pigs.

fig. **1823** LAMB *Lett.* (1888) II. 60 If Evelyn could have seen him, he would never have farrowed two such prodigious volumes.

2. *intr.* To produce a litter.

1340 *Ayenb.* 61 Þe zoȝe huanne hi heþ yuarȝed wel bleþeliche byt men ycloped mid huyt. **1375** BARBOUR *Bruce* XVII. 701 On the wallis thai can cry, 'That thair sow feryt wes thair!' **1535** STEWART *Cron. Scot.* III. 342 For that same sow I haif ordand sic draf.. Sall gar hir ferrie sone at the midsyde. **1601** HOLLAND *Pliny* VIII. li. 229 Swine.. farrow commonly twice a yeere. *a* **1658** FORD, etc. *Witch Edmonton* v. ii, To cast her Pigs a day before she would have farried. **1727** SWIFT *Baucis & Philemon*, Thought whose sow had farrow'd last. **1838-42** ARNOLD *Hist. Rome* I. i. 2 She laid down and farrowed, and her litter was of thirty young ones.

†**b.** Of other animals. (See also FARROWING *ppl. a.*) *Obs. rare.*

1580 HOLLYBAND *Treas. Fr. Tong*, *La Muette*.. the place where a Hare doth farrow.

Hence **'farrowed**, **'farrowing** *ppl. adjs.*, **'farrowing** *vbl. sb.* Also *attrib.*

1583 STANYHURST *Æneis* III. (Arb.) 83 Her mylckwhit farroed hoglings. **1510-20** *Compl. too late maryed* (1862) 8 A farrowynge bytche. **1398** TREVISA *Barth De P.R.* XIX. lxiii. (1495) 899 A sowe is moost thicke in farowynge tyme. **1577** B. GOOGE *Heresbach's Husb.* III. (1586) 149 b, Her farrowing times are so divided for the nonce. **1607** TOPSELL *Four-f. Beasts* (1673) 518 Barly.. at the farrowing causeth an easie and safe pigging.

‖**farruca, Farruca** (fa'ruka). [Sp., fem. of *farruco* Galician or Asturian, f. *Farruco* nickname of *Francisco* Francis.] A local Spanish dance.

[**1914** T. & M. W. KINNEY *Dance* vi. 127 *La Farruca*, *el Tango*, and *el Garrotin*, the most popular *Flamenco* dances at present, preserve to admiration the Gipsy qualites. *Ibid.* 130 La Farruca probably exploits more completely than any of its fellows the varied resources of the *Flamenco*.] **1931** C. RICE *Dancing in Spain* i. 28 The three dances which constitute the nucleus of the modern flamenco school are the Tango, the Garrotín, and the Farruca. *Ibid.* ii. 52 Of all the dances of Spain it is the Farruca which provides a man with the fullest opportunity of displaying his powers. **1958** *Times* 8 Oct. 6/3 This [*sc.* a suite of songs and dances] was rather too long, but it included a Farruca from Mr. Paco Ruiz. **1967** 'LA MERI' *Sp. Dancing* (ed. 2) ix. 121 Forty years ago I danced farruca and bulerias with the gitanas and was taken for one of them.

†**'farry**, *v. Obs.* [Back-formation from FARRIER, taken as agent-n. in -ER¹.] = FARRIER *v.* 1. Hence **'farrying** *vbl. sb.*, in quot. *farring*.

1807 *Beverley & Kexby Road Act* 6 Horses.. going to be.. farried. **1825** *Beverley Lighting Act* ii. 17 Shoe, bleed, kill or farry any horse. **1678** E. R. (*title*), The Experienced Farrier; or Farring Completed, in two books Physical and Chyrurgical.

‖**farsang** ('fɑːsæŋ). Also in Arab. form **farsakh.** [Pers. *farsang*: see PARASANG.] 'A Persian measure of distance—the *Parasang* of the ancients—about four miles' (H. H. Wilson *Gloss. Ind. Terms*).

1613 PURCHAS *Pilgrimage* (1864) 65 From hence they reckon their way by farsangs. **1753** HANWAY *Trav.* (1762) I. III. xxxiii. 154 We travelled three farsangs over mountains. **1864** PUSEY *Lect. Daniel* iii. 119 A reservoir.. 40 farsangs in circumference. **1889** *Times* (weekly ed.) 13 Dec. 8/1 A distance of 12 farsakhs, or 48 miles.

farse (fɑːs), *sb. Eccl. Antiq.* [A mod. adaptation of med.L. *farsa* (see FARCE *sb.*²)] An amplificatory phrase inserted into a liturgical formula; also, each of the hortatory or explanatory passages in the vernacular interpolated between the Latin sentences in chanting the lesson or epistle.

1842 HOOK *Church Dict.* 296 The subdeacon first repeated each verse of the epistle or *lectio*, in Latin, and two choristers sang the Farse, or explanation.

farse (fɑːs), *v. Eccl. Antiq.* Also FARCE *v.*¹ (sense 7). [ad. OF. *farsir*, in pa. pple. latinized as *farcitus*: see FARSE *sb.*] *trans.* To amplify (a liturgical formula) by the insertion of certain words; to provide (an epistle) with a 'farse' or interpolated vernacular comment. Also, to insert (a passage) by way of 'farse'.

1877 J. D. CHAMBERS *Divine Worship* 320 The 'kyrie' was simple, not farsed.. Between each kyrie is farsed.. one of the ten Commandments.

transf. **1875** H. T. KINGDON *Fasting Communion* 11 A wonderful instance of 'farsed' history.

farse, obs. form of FARCE.

†**'farset.** *Obs. rare*⁻¹. A casket, small case.

1639 HORN & ROB. *Gate Lang. Unl.* l. §552 Store-houses to keep things in, are chests [hutches], coffers.. cases, caskets, farsets, little boxes. Hence **1671** in SKINNER *Etymol. Ling. Angl.*

Farsi ('fɑːsiː), *sb.* (*a.*). Also **Fārsī, Farsee.** [a. Pers., f. *Fārs*, the Arabic name for the region of Pars in Iran: see PARSEE and PERSIAN *a.* and *sb.*] **a.** = PARSEE 2. **b.** The Persian name for the modern Persian language; cf. PERSIAN *sb.* 2. Also *attrib.* or as *adj.*

1878 *Chambers's Encycl.* VI. 426/1 The transition from the ancient to the modern Persian is formed by the Parsee, or, as the Arabs call it, Farsi, in use from 700 to 1100 A.D. **1926** *Ibid.* VIII. 39/1 The present or modern Persian (which is invariably called Farsi by the modern Persians). **1951** N. B. JOPSON *Persian Lang.* 8 In the old province of Fars, where Fārsī (or Pārsī), the language of Persia, originated. **1962** *Whitaker's Almanack 1963* 907 Persian, or Farsi, the language of Iran, and of some other areas formerly under Persian rule, is an Indo-European tongue with many Arabic elements added. **1979** *Observer* 25 Nov. 5/5 One of the aides is the Press Secretary, who presents Farsi translations.. of British Press reports. **1980** *Times Lit. Suppl.* 5 Sept. 972/4 The disgusting state of the walls of the London Underground stations, defaced by slogans in Farsee or Arabic characters. **1984** *Bull. British Soc. Middle Eastern Studies* XI. 123 It may still not be too late to put an end to the grotesque affectation of applying the name 'Farsi' to the language which for more than five hundred years has been known to English-speakers as Persian.

far-sight. Ability to see far. Also *attrib.* and *fig.*

1887 *Christian Union* 12 May 22/1 With keen far-sight, with indomitable energy. **1889** *Pall Mall G.* 15 June 2/2 A far-sight machine, by means of which he [Edison] hopes to be able to increase the range of vision by hundreds of miles. **1927** V. McNabb *Cath. Ch. & Philos.* iii. 117 Anyone who would deny that reason had such insight and far-sight as to discern God.

far-sighted (fɑːˈsaɪtɪd), *a.* [f. FAR *adv.* + SIGHT + -ED².] Furnished with a capacity for distant vision.

1. *fig.* Looking far before one; forecasting, shrewd, prudent.

1641 Milton *Ch. Govt.* Wks. 1738 I. 75 The fair and far-sighted eye of his natural discerning. **1768–74** Tucker *Lt. Nat.* (1852) II. 262 To man she has given understanding, far-sighted faculty. **1853** Kane *Grinnell Exp.* xv. (1856) 116 This far-sighted commander had..salted down..many of these birds. **1865** Tylor *Early Hist. Man.* xi. 303 A few far-sighted thinkers.

2. *lit.* Able to see objects at a distance more clearly than those near at hand.

1878 *Encycl. Brit.* VIII. 820/1 This kind of eye is called hypermetropic, or far-sighted.

Hence **far-sightedly** *adv.*, in a far-sighted manner. **far-sightedness**, the state of being far-sighted. *lit.* and *fig.*

1860 Mill *Repr. Govt.* (1861) 138 Any measure..truly, largely, and far sightedly conservative. **1884** *Times* (weekly ed.) 20 June 5 The mother country must show herself farsightedly liberal. **1824–9** Landor *Imag. Conv.* (1846) II. 243 Verily our Prophet did well and with far-sightedness in forbidding the human form..to be graven. **1881** Le Conte *Monoc. Vision* 48 This defect is often called..far-sightedness.

†**ˈfarsure.** *Obs. rare.* Also 5 farcere, farsor. [ad. L. *farsūra*, f. *farcīre* to stuff.] = FARCE *sb.*¹

1381 in S. Pegge *Form of Cury* (1780) 100 Make a Farsure and fil ful the skyn. *c* **1420** *Liber Cocorum* (1862) 26 Of alle þo thynges þou make farsure. **14..** *Noble Bk. Cookry* (Napier 1882) 116 Tak pork and hennes flesh and good pouders and make a farsor ther of.

farsyn, var. of FARCIN, *Obs.* farcy.

fart (fɑːt), *sb. Not in decent use.* Also 5 fert(e, fartt, 5–6 farte. [f. the vb.; cf. OHG. *firz, furz*, mod.G. *farz*, ON. *fretr.*] **1. a.** A breaking wind. Often in *let* (†*let flee*) *a fart.*

c **1386** Chaucer *Miller's T.* 620 This Nicholas anon let flee a fart. **14..** *Madman's Song* in *Rel. Ant.* I. 260 Onys I fley and let a fert. **1562** J. Heywood *Prov. & Epigr.* (1867) 21, I shall geat a fart of a dead man as soone As a farthyng of him. **1650** Bulwer *Anthropomet.* 220 The Guineans are very careful not to let a fart. **1728** Swift *Dial. Mad. Mullinix & Timothy* In doleful scenes that break our heart Punch comes, like you, and lets a f—t. **1825** Thurlow *Ess. Wind* 6 There are five or six different species of farts.

†**b.** As a type of something worthless. *Obs.*

c **1460** *Towneley Myst.* 16 Bi alle men set I not a farte. **1642** in Picton *L'pool Munic. Rec.* (1883) I. 233 Hee..cared not a f—'t for it. **1685** Crowne *Sir Courtly Nice* v, A fart for your family.

c. A contemptible person.

1937 in Partridge *Dict. Slang* 267/1. **1968** J. Sangster *Touchfeather* xi. 121 I'm supposed to be non-operational. What does the silly old fart want? **1971** *Ink* 24 July 5/1 Marty Feldman said to the judge as he left the witness stand, 'I don't think he even knew I was here, the boring old fart.'

†**2.** A ball of light pastry, a 'puff'. *Obs.* [Cf. F. *pet* 'beignet en boule.']

1552 Huloet, Fartes of Portingale, or other like swete conceites, *collybia.*

fart (fɑːt), *v. Not now in decent use.* Also 3 verten, 4 farten, 5 farton, 6 farte. [Common Teut. and Indo-germanic: OE. **feortan* = OHG. *ferzan* (MHG. *verzen*, and with ablaut variants *vurzen, varzen*, mod.G. *farzen*), ON. *freta*:—OTeut. **fertan*:—OAryan **perd-* (Skr. *pard. pṛd*, Gr. πέρδειν, Lith. *pérdzu*, Russ. *perdet'*; the L. *pēdere* is unconnected).]

1. *intr.* To break wind (see BREAK *v.* 47).

c **1250** *Cuckoo Song*, Bulluc stertep, bucke uertep. *c* **1386** Chaucer *Miller's T.* 152 He was somdel squaymous Of fartyng. *c* **1440** *Promp. Parv.* 150 Farton, *pedo.* *c* **1532** Dewes *Introd. Fr.* in Palsgr. 941/1 To farte or to burste, *crepiter.* **1610** B. Jonson *Alch.* I. i, I fart at thee. **1740** Gray *Lett.* Wks. 1884 II. 59 Now they are always in a sweat, and never speak, but they f—t.

fig. [after L. *oppedere.*]

1580 Baret *Alv.* F 149 To fart against one: and Metaphoricè, To denie with a lowd voice, *oppedere.* **1671** H. M. tr. *Erasm. Colloq.* 503, I cannot sufficiently admire, that there are not some men who fart against those men.

2. *trans.* To send forth as wind from the anus.

1632 Massinger *Maid of Hon.* IV. iv, Tho' the devil fart fire, have at him! **1710** *Brit. Apollo* III. 3/1 What is meant, when we say, a Man Farts Frankinsence.

3. *intr.* To fool *about* or *around*; to waste time.

1900 in *Eng. Dial. Dict.*, Go bon tha! thoo's allus farten aboot, thoo's warse ner a hen wi' egg. **1937** Partridge *Dict. Slang* 267/1 *Fart about*, to dawdle; to waste time; play about. **1964** P. Larkin *Jill* (ed. 2) 223 They scuffled for a few moments, knocking over a pile of books and papers. 'Don't fart about,' said Patrick wearily. **1968** H. C. Rae *Few Small Bones* II. v. 115 Now don't fart about, Birnie, or I'll get angry. **1969** J. Wainwright *Big Tickle* 173 Look! It's important. Stop farting around.

Hence ˈ**farted** *ppl. a.* ˈ**farter**, one who breaks wind. ˈ**farting** *vbl. sb.*, in quot. used *attrib.* ˈ**farting** *ppl. a.*

c **1440** *Promp. Parv.* 150 Fartare. *Ibid.* Fartynge, *peditura, bombizacio.* **1580** Hollyband *Treas. Fr. Tong*, *Cest vn gros ..vesseur*, a great farter. **1583** Stubbes *Anat. Abus.* II. (1882) 35 The same starching [brothell] houses (I had almost said farting houses) do serue the turn. **1648** Herrick *Hesper.* I. 216 The farting tanner. **1653** Urquhart *Rabelais* (1694) II. xxvii. 166 Are your Farts so fertil?..here be brave farted Men. **1660** Howell *Lex. Tetraglot.*, A Farter, *peteur.* *a* **1687** C. Cotton *Poet. Wks.* (1765) 9 He was..the loud'st of Farters.

farth, alleged synonym of FARROW *sb.* 2.

1688 R. Holme *Armoury* II. 134/1 The young ones..of a sow..are called a Farth, a Farrow of Pigs.

farthendele, var. of FARTHINGDEAL. *Obs.*

farther (ˈfɑːðə(r)), *adv.* and *a.* Forms: 3–6 ferder, ferdre, 4 ferþer(e, 4–6 ferthere, 4–8 farder, 5– farther. [ME. *ferþer* (whence by normal phonetic development *farther*) is in origin a mere variant of FURTHER, due prob. to the analogy of the vb. *ferþren*:—OE. *fyrðrian* to FURTHER. The primary sense of *further, farther* is 'more forward, more onward'; but this sense is practically coincident with that of the comparative degree of *far*, where the latter word refers to real or attributed motion in some particular direction. Hence *further, farther* came to be used as the comparative of *far*; first in the special application just mentioned, and ultimately in all senses, displacing the regular comparative *farrer*. In standard Eng. the form *farther* is usually preferred where the word is intended to be the comparative of *far*, while *further* is used where the notion of *far* is altogether absent; there is a large intermediate class of instances in which the choice between the two forms is arbitrary.]

A. *adv.*

1. More forward; to or at a more advanced point. **a.** in space, or in a course of procedure or development.

a **1300** *Cursor M.* 6831 (Gött.) Help him or þu ferþer wend. *c* **1320** *Sir Tristr.* 1491 He no may ferþer far. **1398** Trevisa *Barth. De P.R.* IV. iii. (1495) 81 The kynde dryenesse of the erthe suffryth not the fletynge reeses of the see passe ferder. *c* **1400** *Destr. Troy* 11748 Thou art no farder..thy fame for to lose, þan I my lyffe were leuer leue in þe plase. *c* **1460** *Towneley Myst.* 276 We may no farther walk. **1508** Fisher *Wks.* (1876) 281 Or we procede ony ferder. **1548** Hall *Chron.* 161 b, The capitaines folowed no farther the chace. **1616** R. C. *Times' Whistle* II. 845 The foole Was never farther than the grammer schoole. **1695** Woodward *Nat. Hist. Earth* i. (1723) 5 Having little Prospect of..carrying on these observations any farther. **1703** Moxon *Mech. Exerc.* 130, I shall run no farther into this Argument. **1883** Ht. Martineau *Charmed Sea* i 5 If you can bear your load no farther, say so. **1876** Gladstone *Homeric Synchr.* 12, I wish..to carry the affirmative portion of my propositions greatly farther.

b. in time: Longer.

1548 Forrest *Pleas. Poesye* 26 As Ferdre in reigne grue their contynuance. **1640–1** *Kirkcudbr. War-Comm. Min. Bk.* (1855) 42 Until the next Committie day, and farder during thair plessor. **1711** Addison *Spect.* No. 120 ¶5 Some Creatures cast their Eggs as Chance directs them, and think of them no farther. **1802** Mar. Edgeworth *Moral T.* (1816) I. vii. 45 Then we need argue no farther.

c. *farther gone*: at a more advanced stage.

1708 Swift *Sacramental Test* Wks. 1824 VIII. 355 The Observator is..farther gone of late in lyes than his Presbyterian brother.

2. To a greater extent, more completely.

1513 More in Grafton *Chron.* II. 774 Yet feare I no farther then the law feareth. **1585** James I *Ess. Poesie* (Arb.) 21 Not doubting..but you will accept my..trauellis in good parte, (sen I requyre no farder). **1610** Shaks. *Temp.* I. ii. 33 Sit downe For thou must now know farther. **1789** Bentham *Princ. Legisl.* xvii. §7 Punishment cannot act any farther than in as far as the idea of it..is present in the mind.

3. In addition, also, besides, moreover.

c **1380** Wyclif *Sel. Wks.* III. 345 Se we ferþer hou þis stiward may erre in ordenaunce of the Chirche. **1413** Lydg. *Pilgr. Sowle* IV. xxviii. (1483) 75 He knoweth al thynge, therfore there is nought ferther to seken by discours. **1486** *Certificate* in *Surtees Misc.* (1890) 46 And ferder entenditte to examyne in that behalve. **1562** Winzet *Cert. Tractates* i. Wks. 1888 I. 13 Farder, sen all man hes this word reformatioun in mothe..we [etc.]. **1652** Milton in *Four C. Eng. Lett.* 99 And have this farder, which I thought my parte to let you know of, that [etc.]. **1719** De Foe *Crusoe* II. i. 2 Nay farther, the common Motive of foreign Adventures was taken away. **1794** *Fletcher's Wks.* VII. Pref. 6 The Reader is farther requested, to remember that [etc.].

4. To or at a greater distance; by a greater interval. *to wish* (*any one*) *farther.*

c **1380** Wyclif *Serm.* Sel. Wks. II. 107 Ech man shulde sue him or ferþere or nerþere. **1489** Caxton *Fayttes of A.* IV. xvii. 280 It is ferder from the lyght more than eny of the other colours be. **1578** Lyte *Dodoens* I. lii. 76 The leaves be ..standing farder asunder one from another. **1586** Cogan *Haven Health* (1636) 135 Flesh of a drie complexion is better neere calving time than farder from it. **1766** Goldsm. *Vic. Wakef* xiv. (1806) 71 He could hop on one leg farther than I. **1782** Mad D'Arblay *Diary* 12 Aug., Miss Plauta..only wished the maid farther for never finding us out till we began to be comfortable without her. **1821** Keats *Isabel* iii, He would catch Her beauty farther than the falcon spies. **1847** Halliwell s.v., I'll be farther if I do it, i.e. I won't do it. **1876** J. Parker *Paracl.* I. vii. 106 Can anything be farther from theology..than stone-cutting?

5. *Comb.*, as ***farther-spreading*** adj.

1876 Geo. Eliot *Dan. Der.* IV. liii. 90 The expression of something..with..farther-spreading roots.

B. *adj.*

†**1.** Prior, anterior; front; = FURTHER *a.* 1. *Obs.*

1398 Trevisa *Barth. De P.R.* V. ii. (1495) 104 Kynde settith in the eyen in the ferder and the ouer partie of the beest. **1534** Whitinton *Tullyes Offices* I. (1540) 16 Where as there be two maners of contencions..the ferther is appropried unto man, the seconde unto wylde beestes. *Ibid.* III. 117 Of the two farther maners Panecius did declare in thre bookes. Of the thyrde maner he wrote [etc.].

2. More extended, going beyond what already exists or has been dealt with, additional, more.

c **1520** Sir W. Godolphin in Ellis *Orig. Lett.* III. II. 218, I coud not macke no fferder serche. **1548** Hall *Chron.* 117 b, Avoydyng farther effusion of christen bloud. **1641** Hinde *J. Bruen* xlvi. 146 For the clearing of this point, and the farther satisfaction of such as delight therein. **1704** Swift *T. Tub* Apol., There is one farther objection made by those who have answered this book. **1768** Goldsm. *Good-n. Man* IV. i, For fear he should ask farther questions. **1802** Mar. Edgeworth *Moral T.* (1816) I. 209 The king took no farther notice of what had happened. **1837** Dickens *Pickw.* xii, Down he sat without farther bidding.

3. a. More distant, remoter.

1568 Grafton *Chron.* II. 332 The farther syde of London. **1598** Grenewey *Tacitus' Ann.* 83 The Hierocæsarienses fetchte their matter from a farther beginning. **1651** Hobbes *Leviath.* III. xxxiv. 207 To hinder them from a farther prospect. **1675** Ashmole *Diary* (1774) 348 Great pain in my farther tooth, on the left side of my upper jaw. **1743** Pope *Thebais* 420 Whose ghost..Expects its passage to the farther strand. **1754** Sherlock *Disc.* (1759) I. xiv. 367 These Gifts were subservient to a farther end.

b. ***Farther East*** = FAR EAST.

1876 *Fraser's Mag.* Jan. 1/2 There came another thunderclap tending once more to direct men's eyes from the near to the farther East. **1902** A. T. Mahan *Retrospect & Prospect* 160 It is..the principal sea route between Europe and the Farther East.

farther (ˈfɑːðə(r)), *v.* Now *rare.* Also 7 farder. [The regular phonetic descendant in standard Eng. of ME. *ferþre-n*: see FURTHER *v.*]

trans. To help forward, promote, favour, assist (an action, movement, etc., rarely, † a person); = FURTHER *v.*

a **1000–1390** [For examples of the forms with *fer-* (OE. *fyr-*) see FURTHER *v.*]. **1570** North *Doni's Mor. Philos.* (1888) III. 197 That I might..farther and aduance my poore familie. **1605** Carew in *Lett. Lit. Men* (Camden) 100, I praie that yow wilbe pleased to farder the motion. **1651** Hobbes *Govt. & Soc.* i. §2. 6 Though the benefits of this life may be much farthered by mutuall help. **1703** Mrs. Centlivre *Bean's Duel* I. ii, I love mischief so well, I can refuse nothing that farthers that. **1846** Ruskin *Mod. Paint* II III. I. xv. §9 It has been said..that the sense of beauty never farthered the performance of a single duty.

absol. **1579** Digges *Stratiot.* v. 10 This..is sufficient for Division, more woulde rather discourage than farther. **1669** A. Browne *Ars Pict.* (1675) 9 The more the capacity is wanting, the more my Labour will farther, when need requireth.

†ˈ**fartherance.** *Obs. rare.* [f. FARTHER *v.* + -ANCE.] = FURTHERANCE.

1785 Paley *Mor. Philos.* (1818) II. 329 Conduce to the fartherance of human salvation.

†ˈ**fartherer.** *Obs.* [f. as prec. + -ER¹.] = FURTHERER.

1494 [see CONDUCTRICE]. **1633** Stafford *Pac. Hib.* (1821) vi. 289 Florence was not onely forward in his owne person but also a fartherer of others. **1655** Fuller *Hist. Camb.* §13. 47 A great favourer and fartherer of the truth.

†**farthermore**, *adv.* and *a. Obs.* Forms: see FARTHER and -MORE. [var. FURTHERMORE, q.v.]

A. *adv.* = FURTHERMORE in various senses.

a **1300** *Cursor M.* 10238 (Gött.), I bidd þe cum na ferþermare. *c* **1380** Wyclif *Sel. Wks.* III. 431 Fferþermor we shal suppose þat bodyliche abyte..makiþ not men religiose. *c* **1400** *Rom. Rose* 3926, I shalle repente ferthermore, For the game goth alle amys. **1450–1530** *Myrr. Our Ladye* 199 Farthermore the prophetes were sory. **1488** Caxton *Chast. Goddes Chyld.* ii. 7 Some causes of his wythdraweng I wyll shew now or I wryte ferder more of ony matere. **1535** Stewart *Cron. Scot.* III. 112 Now fardermoir in that mater till mute, Tha passit all onto the yle of Bute.

B. *adj.* More remote; = FARTHER *a.* 3.

1610 Holland *Camden's Brit.* I. 643 The hithermore is called Tullie..the farthermore is named Barry.

farthermost (ˈfɑːðəməʊst), *a.* [var. of FURTHERMOST: cf. FARTHER.] Farthest, most remote or distant.

1618 Bolton *Florus* II. v. 90 The Illyrians..inhabit at the farthermost roots of the Alpes. **1705** *Lond. Gaz.* No. 4145/4 She..is lame on the farthermost Shoulder. **1856** Kane *Arct. Expl.* I. xix. 237 The farthermost expansion of Smith's Strait.

farthest (ˈfɑːðɪst), *a.* and *adv.* Also 4 ferþest, ferdest, 5–7 fardest. [var. of FURTHEST; used as superlative of FAR: see FARTHER.]

A. *adj.*

1. Most distant or remote. Also with *off.*

1377 Langl. *P. Pl.* B. v. 239 þe ferthest ende of norfolke. **1398** Trevisa *Barth De. P.R.* IV. i. (1495) 78 The fyre that is ferdest from the myddle of the erthe. **1474** Caxton *Chesse* 156 The fardest ligne of theschequer. **1549** Latimer *4th Serm. bef. Edw. VI* (Arb.) 121 He was a manne the fardest

frome the feare of God that euer I knewe. **1597** HOOKER *Eccl. Pol.* v. xli. (1611) 266 Which wee..imagine to be fardest off. **1622** MALYNES *Anc. Law-Merch.* 222 The Prouerbe is true, That he who is farthest from his goods, is neerest to his losse. **1671** MILTON *P.R.* III. 397 And that time for thee Were better farthest off. **1726** tr. *Gregory's Astron.* I. 11 If it be most Direct and farthest off the Earth. **1777** SIR W. JONES *Poems & Ess.* 179 The farthest limits of the kingdom. **1823** H. J. BROOKE *Introd. Crystallogr.* 31 With the edge at which those planes meet, the farthest from you.

2. Extending to the greatest distance, longest.

1633 T. JAMES *Voy.* 109 In Nauigation, the farthest way about. **1878** STEVENSON *Inland Voy.*, It was the farthest piece of travel accomplished.

3. absol. ***at (the) farthest***: **a.** of space: At the greatest distance. **b.** of future time: At latest. **c.** of degree: At the outside.

1596 SHAKS. *Merch. V.* II. ii. 122 Let it be so hasted that supper be readie at the farthest by fiue of the clocke. **1661** COWLEY *Prop. Adv. Exp. Philos.*, Within one, two or (at farthest) three miles of London. **1670** NARBOROUGH *Jrnl.* in *Acc. Sev. Late Voy.* I. (1711) 33 When I was at the farthest ..I could not see any sign of People. **1765** CHESTERF. *Lett.* cccli. (1774) IV. 221 You may depend upon what I promised you, before Midsummer next, at farthest.

B. *adv.* To or at the greatest distance. Also with *off*.

1598 YONG *Diana* 174 Sometimes striuing who could smite a stone fardest with them. **1607** TOURNEUR *Revenger's Trag.* IV. I iij, Here's the comfort my Lord.. When it seemes most it threatnes fardest off. **1667** MILTON *P.L.* I. 247 Fardest from him is best Whom reason hath equald.

b. *Comb.* forming the superlatives of compounds of FAR *a.*

1580 SIDNEY *Arcadia* (1622) 282 In the farthest-fet construction. **1879** E. ARNOLD *Lt. Asia* 10 The wisest one, The farthest-seen in Scriptures.

farthing ('fɑːðɪŋ), *sb.* Forms: 1 **feorðung**, 2 **feorþing**, 2–3 **ferþing**, **-yng**, 3–4 *south* **verþ-**, **verthing**, 3–6 **ferthing**, **-yng(e**, 4–6 **ferdyng(e**, 6 **farthinge**, **-yng(e**, 6–8 **fardin(g**, **-yng**, 9 *dial* **farden**, **-in**, 6– **farthing**. [OE. *féorðing, féorðung*, f. *féorð-a* FOURTH; corresp. to ON. *fiórðungr*, of which it may possibly be an adoption.] A quarter of some particular denomination of money or measure.

1. a. The quarter of a penny; the coin representing this value. (Until 17th c. chiefly a silver coin; subsequently of copper alloys; then of bronze.) In translations of the N.T. used for the two Roman coins *as* and *quadrans*, respectively the tenth and the fourth part of a *denarius*.

c **950** *Lindisf. Gosp.* Mark xii. 42 Tuoȝe stycas þæt is feorðung penninges. —— *Luke* xxi. 2 Gesæh ðonne an widua ðorfondlico sendende mæslenno feorðungas tuoeȝ. *c* **1290** *S. Eng. Leg.* I. 129/800 To ȝelden ech ferþing. **1335** *Act 9 Edw. III*, II. c. 3 Que nul esterling, maille ne ferthing soit fondu pour vessel. **1340** *Ayenb.* 193 Þe poure wyfman þet ne hedde bote tuaye uerþinges þet hi offrede to þe temple. *c* **1430** *How Good Wijf tauȝte Douȝtir* 184 in *Babees Bk.* (1868) 46 Ne þerfore spende neuere þe more of a ferthing. **1502** *Ord. Crysten Men* (W. de W. 1506) II. xviii. 136 Unto yᵉ last ferdynge. **1520** *Caxton's Chron. Eng.* VII. (1520) 91 b/1 The kynge ordeyned that the sterlyng halfpeny and ferthyng sholde go throughout al his lande. **1562** J. HEYWOOD *Prov. & Epigr.* (1867) 165 She thinkth hir farthing good syluer. **1611** BIBLE *Matt.* x. 29 Are not two Sparrowes solde for a farthing? **1642** [see BRASS *sb.* 7]. **1667** E. CHAMBERLAYNE *St. Gt. Brit.* I. (1684) 11 A small piece of copper, called a Farthing. **1688** *Lond. Gaz.* No. 2407/4 The new Tin Farthings..are to be delivered out at the Tinn Office in Bishopsgate-street. **1749** FIELDING *Tom Jones* VI. xiii, Here, then..take every farthing I am worth. **1849** ROBERTSON *Serm.* Ser. I. ii. (1866) 32 A miser..hoards farthings. **1866** G. MACDONALD *Ann. Q. Neighb.* xxxii. (1878) 556 Nor can you touch one farthing of her money.

†**b.** ***under farthing***: marked with a farthing.

1715 *Lond. Gaz.* No. 5365/4 Sheep..gabel'd on the Left Ear, the Right Ear under Farthing.

2. *transf.* †**a.** A very small piece of anything. *Obs.* Hence **b.** *fig.* A very little, 'an atom', 'a bit', *esp.* in ***not to care*** or ***matter a farthing***.

a. *c* **1386** CHAUCER *Prol.* 134 In hire cuppe was no ferthing sene Of grees.

b. *c* **1400** *Destr. Troy* 8884 Hit neuer fortherit me a ferthing to fylsy my goodes. **1550** CROWLEY *Last Trump* 828 Thou knowest not therbi to make the sicke man one farthinge better. **1647** WARD *Simp. Cobler* 43 It matters not a farthing whether he be Presbyterian or Independent. *a* **1707** PRIOR *The Ladle* 18 Else all these Things we toil so hard in, Wou'd not avail one single Farthing. **1712** STEELE *Spect.* No. 522 ¶6 The gentleman who has told her he does not care a farthing for her. **1872** BLACK *Adv. Phaeton* xxv. 347 Declared that he did not care a brass farthing.

†**3.** ***farthing (of gold)***: **a.** A quarter noble; also *farthing noble*. (The AF. statute of 1421 has *ferling*.) **b.** A quarter royal (see quot. 1494).

1463 *Bury Wills* (1850) 15, I beqwethe to..Davn John Wulfpet..a ferthing of gold. **1494** FABYAN *Chron.* VII. 655 This yere [1464–5] was a newe coyne ordeyned by the kynge ..namyd the royall..in value of .x. shillynges, the halfe royall .v.s. and the ferthynge .ii. s. vi. d. **1529** RASTELL *Pastyme* (1811) 220 [In 1351] the kynge stablysshed his coyne..and ordayned that..a noble of golde shulde go for halfe a marke and xx.d for a farthynge of gold, and xii of those farthynges of golde dyd way an ounce.

†**4.** The name of various measures of land: **a.** ? The quarter of a hide; = VIRGATE; cf. FARDEL *sb.*² **b.** ? The quarter of a virgate. **c.** ? The quarter of an acre, a rood (see quot. 1669 for *farthing-land* in 5 b). *Obs.*

a **1000** *Exon Domesday* fol. 356 Oltredus..reddidit gildum pro iii uirg. et iii ferdin' et dim. **1602** CAREW *Cornwall* 36 a, Commonly thirtie Acres make a farthing land, nine farthings a Cornish Acre, and four Cornish Acres, a Knight's fee. *c* **1630** RISDON *Surv. Devon* §68 (1810) 65 Moyhun was seized of three rods and three farthings of land.

5. *attrib.* and *Comb.* **a.** *attrib.* Costing or valued at a farthing, as ***farthing-candle***, whence ***farthing-candle-light***, ***farthing-fee***, ***-loaf***. Also *objective*, as ***farthing-coiner***. Also as quasi-*adj.*, trivial, almost valueless, unworthy of respect or notice.

c **1300** *Havelok* 878 He..bar þe mete to þe castel, And gat him þere a ferþing wastel. *c* **1350** *Eng. Gilds* (1870) 354 3if þe ferþingloff is in defawte of wyȝte ouer twelf pans. **1463** *Bury Wills* (1850) 28 As moche ferthyng white breed as comyth to iiij s. ij d. **1524** *Test. Ebor.* (Surtees) V. 181 To every man and woman and childe of the contrie a farddyng loof. **1596** J. DEE in *Recorde's Gr. Artes* II. 324 Directly against it [the price of wheate] in the second columne you may find the waight of the farthing white loafe. **1597–8** BP. HALL *Sat.* I. iv. 2 Strayning his tip-toes for a farthing fee. **1631** *Star Chamb. Cases* (Camden) 84 Then was..read the severall confessions of the 2 farthing coyners. **1673** E. PEARSE *Best Match* vii. §5. 76 Not so much as the light of a Farthing-Candle is to the light of the Sun. **1691** tr. *Emilianne's Frauds Romish Monkes* 247 Her sisters would never be at a Farthing charge to procure Prayers for her. **1795** WOLCOTT (P. Pindar) *Wks.* (1812) IV. 180 A sun with us..yields to every Farthing Candle. **1817** BYRON *Beppo* xliii, That sort of farthing candlelight which glimmers When reeking London's smoky caldron simmers. **1848** GARNETT *Ess.* 120 The farthing-candle style of the notes. **1864** *Sat. Rev.* 9 July 66 The farthing, as first issued, was called a farthing token. **1893** STEVENSON *Catriona* v. 58 They each made me a little farthing compliment. **1896** BELLOC *Verses & Sonnets* 25 His farthing honours.

b. Special comb., as **farthing-boat**, a boat on which the fare is a farthing; **farthing-cut**, a mark with which horses were branded by the owner; **farthing-gleek**, see GLEEK; **farthing-land** (see quots.); †**farthing-man**, *Sc.*, some official of a guild; **farthing-noble**, the fourth part of a noble; **farthing-office**, the office from which farthings were issued; **farthing-shop**, one where articles priced at a farthing are sold; **farthing-trout**, a name of the Samlet or Parr.

1832 W. STEPHENSON *Gateshead Local Poems* 58 She took the *farthing boat. **1691** *Lond. Gaz.* No. 2694/4 Stolen or strayed..one black Nag..with a *farthing cut in the near Ear. **1711** *Ibid.* No. 4877/4 A farthing Cut on his Left Ear. *a* **1652** BROME *Mad Couple well Matched* II. i, At Post and Pare, or *Farthing gleeke. **1602** CAREW *Cornwall* 36 a, Commonly thirtie acres make a *farthing land. **1669** WORLIDGE *Syst. Agric.* (1681) 325 A Farding Land, or Farundale of Land, is the fourth part of an Acre. **1882** C. ELTON *Orig. Eng. Hist.* 193 Three kinds of land, Assart, Farthing-land and Cotman-land. **15..** *Stat. Gild* in Balfour *Practicks* 77 Quhen the Alderman, Thesurare, *Farthing-man or Dene..convene the gild brether for the commoun affairis. **15..** *Chron. Gr. Friars* (Camden) 5 The nobylle, half noblyle, and *ferdyng-nobylle. **1672** *Lond. Gaz.* No. 714/4 The *Farthing-Office..for the delivering out of Farthings will be open on Tuesdays only. **1889** *Pall Mall G.* 6 Sept. 3/1 The *farthing shop is in Dorset-street. **1865** COUCH *Fishes Brit. Isl.* IV. 245 Samlet..*Farthing trout.

farthingale ('fɑːðɪŋgeɪl). Forms: 6 **farthyngall**, 6–8 **fardingal(l**, 7 *Sc.* **fartigal**, 7–8 **farthingal**, 7– **fard-**, **farthingale**. *β.* 6–8 **vardingal(e**, 6 **verdynggale**, 7 **verdingal(e**, (**vertingale**, **virdingal**). [ad. OF. *verdugale*, *vertugalle*, corruption of Sp. *verdugado* a farthingale, f. *verdugo* rod, stick. (So called because distended by cane hoops or rods inserted underneath.)]

A frame-work of hoops, usually of whalebone, worked into some kind of cloth, formerly used for extending the skirts of women's dresses; a hooped petticoat. **farthingale chair**, a seventeenth-century chair with a wide seat, a low straight back, and no arms.

1552 LATIMER *Serm. Gospels* iii. 166, I warrant you they had bracelets and verdynggales and such fine gere. **1607** DEKKER *Westw. Hoe* I. Wks. 1873 II. 282 To learne how to weare a Scotch Farthingale. **1673** RAY *Journ. Low C.* 499 The Women wear great Vardingales, standing..far out at each side. **1753** L. M. tr. *Du Boscq's Accomplish'd Woman* I. 124, I cannot esteem those who part with regret from their high-heads and vardingales. **1776** FOOTE *Bankrupt* II, Her majesty's old fardingale is not more out of fashion. **1830** J. G. STRUTT *Sylva Brit.* 47 The maids of honour had just stripped off their fardingales. **1860** READE *Cloister & H.* I. 280 Whatever he was saying or doing, he stopped short at the sight of a farthingale. **1904** P. MACQUOID *Hist. Eng. Furnit.* vii. 179 The chair..is an early example of what was termed a farthingale chair. **1955** *Oxf. Jun. Encycl.* XI. 51/1 The 'farthingale chairs' designed for ladies wearing the wide skirts..no longer had solid backs, but upholstered rectangular backs raised above the seats on turned supports.

attrib. **1711** J. DISTAFF *Char. Don. Sacheverelli* 4 A large Fardingale Petticoat.

Hence **'farthingaled** *a.*, having a farthingale.

1873 MISS BROUGHTON *Nancy* I. 19 Like the faithful, ruffed and farthingaled wife on a fifteenth century tomb.

farthing-bag ('fɑːðɪŋbæg). *dial.* Also 8 **farding-bag**. See quots.

a **1722** LISLE *Husb.* (1752) 248 They quite choaked up their first stomach called the farding bag. **1879** MISS JACKSON *Shropsh. Word-bk.*, *Farthing-bag*, the second stomach of a cow. 'Ers bund i'the farthin' bag.

†**'farthingdeal.** *Obs.* Forms: 5 **forthingdole**, 6–7 **farthendele**, 7–8 **fardingdeal(e**, **farthingdole**, **far(r)undell**. [repr. OE. *féorðan dǽl*, accus. of *féorða dǽl* fourth part: see FOURTH and DEAL *sb.* Cf. HALVENDEAL, THIRDENDEAL. The first element was afterwards regarded as a form of FARTHING.]

1. *gen.* A fourth part.

a **1400–50** *Alexander* 3844 Als fast as þai þe forthing-dole had of þe flode past.

2. *spec.* **a.** The fourth part of an acre; a rood.

1542 RECORDE *Gr. Artes* (1575) 208 A Rod of lande, whiche some call a roode..some a Farthendele. **1600** T. HYLLES *Arith.* 67 a, A farthendele or roode of lande. **1607** COWEL *Interpr.*, *Farding deale* alias Farundell of land signifieth the fourth part of an acre. **1692–1732** in COLES. **1721–1800** in BAILEY. **1835** *Rep. Muncipal Corporations Comm.* II. App. 1248 The remaining..acres are divided into quarter acres, called 'farthingdoles'.

b. See quot.; = FARTHING 4 b.

c **1640** J. SMYTH *Lives Berkeleys* (1883) I. 156 Quarter of a yard land called a farrundell.

farthingless ('fɑːðɪŋlɪs), *a.* [f. FARTHING *sb.* + -LESS.] Without a farthing; destitute.

1834 *Blackw. Mag.* XXXV. 695 You being farthingless.

farthingsworth ('fɑːðɪŋzwəθ). [f. as prec. + -WORTH.] As much as is bought or sold for a farthing, a very small amount. Also *fig.*

c **1325** *Poem Times Edw. II*, 100 in *Pol. Songs* (Camden) 328 A prest..That can noht a ferthingworth of god. *c* **1380** WYCLIF *Sel. Wks.* II. 515 Þe kyng may not take fro hem an halfpeny ne ferþingworþ. **1393** LANGL. *P. Pl.* C. VII. 360 A ferthyng-worth of fynkelsede. **1579** LANGHAM *Gard. Health* (1633) 519 A farthingworth of bruised Licoras. **1719** DE FOE *Crusoe* (1840) II. v. 108 Not one farthing's-worth of service.

‖**fartlek** ('fɑːtlɛk). [Sw., f. *fart* speed + *lek* play.] A method of training for middle- and long-distance running, in which the athlete runs over country, mixing fast with slow work.

1952 *Scholastic Coach* XXI. VII. 20 The answer that finally emerged was 'fartlek'—the Swedish system of training. **1957** DUNCAN & BONE *Oxf. Pkt. Bk. Athletic Training* (ed. 2) iii. 23 Fartlek is a pleasant..form of wind sprints across country. *Ibid.*, The essence of a successful fartlek session is enjoyment in hard but varying work. **1958** *Times* 18 Aug. 3/1 He was out training..and was using the Fartlek or run-as-you-please training which originated from Sweden in the early 1940s. **1968** B. TULLOH *Tulloh on Running* v. 46 *Fartlek*, meaning 'speed play'..is a continuous run in which patches of fast striding are interspersed with jogging.

†**'farture.** *Obs.* [ad. L. *fartūr-a*, f. *fart-*, ppl. stem of *farcīre* to stuff.] = FARSURE, stuffing.

1657 TOMLINSON *Renou's Disp.* 87 As Saliture and Farture rather seem to appertain to a cooks (shop).

farundell: see FARTHINGDEAL.

far-welted ('fɑːwɛltɪd), *a. dial.* Also **far-**, **fow-**, **welter'd**. [f. WELT *v.*, a. ON. *velta* to overturn; the first element is perh. ON. *fár* harm, mischief, as in *fár-veikr* very ill.] (See quots.)

1870 TENNYSON *North. Farmer, New Style* viii, An 'e ligs on 'is back.. Woorse nor a far-welter'd [*footnote*, Or fow-welter'd] yowe. **1877** *N.W. Linc. Gloss.*, *Farwelted*, overthrown; said of sheep.

farwendine, var. of FARANDINE *Obs.*

Far West. *N. Amer.* [f. FAR *a.* 1 a + WEST *sb.*¹] A term applied to regions in the Rocky Mountains and along the Pacific coast. Formerly applied to areas lying west of the earliest settlements, i.e. to what is now the *Middle West*.

1830 *Deb. Congress U.S.* 8 May 920/2 Sir, I am from the West, although not from the 'far, far West'. **1832** *Ibid.* Feb. 290 Some of the descendants of illustrious families have gone to the far West. **1835** *Southern Lit. Messenger* I. 615, I do not believe that the prairies of the 'far West' can exhibit more luxuriant fields of corn. **1836** *Bytown* (Ottawa) *Gaz.* 13 Oct. 3/2 Being in the 'far West' at the time. **1843** 'R. CARLTON' *New Purchase* I. 2 In a part of what was, at the time of this journey, the Far West. **1845** *Globe* (Toronto) 14 Oct. 1/3 The..'Far-West'..what was formerly known as such is not now even thought of in connexion with that term. **1880** A. A. HAYES *New Colorado* (1881) vii. 108 Surely this is at variance with the traditions of the Far West. **1890** HOWELLS in *Harper's Mag.* Nov. 965 The great plains..in the far West. **1948** *N.Y. Star* 30 June 18/1 The cities of the Midwest, Far West and East. **1968** J. W. WATSON *N. Amer.* (ed. 2) xxi. 683 The Far West..gained from the battle which the Mid-West had fought for the growth of domestic industry.

Hence **Far-Wester**, **Far Westerner**, a settler in, or inhabitant of, the Far West; **Far-Western** *a.*, of or belonging to the Far West.

1843 'R. CARLTON' *New Purchase* I. 112 True honest-hearted far westers unadulterated by foreign or domestic scum. **1844** BP. S. WILBERFORCE *Hist. Amer. Ch.* (1846) 341 The peculiar services of a far-western clergyman. **1845** *Knickerbocker* XXVI. 283 There is a county in one of our far-western states which numbers just four whigs. **1862** G. C. STRONG *Cadet Life at West Point* 125 The far-Westerner ..declared his intention of being a lifelong bushfighter against the Indians. **1874** B. F. TAYLOR *World on Wheels*, etc. I. vi. 50 Such touches of border-life give a Far Western train a character of its own. **1887** C. B. GEORGE *40 Yrs. on Rail* xi. 234 The hearty 'Wall stranger', with which a Far Wester greets his neighbor on the train, immediately does away with reserve. **1948** *Pacific Discovery* May–June 15/1

The cloud that Far Westerners near the coast see most frequently is the advection fog. **1952** A. Huxley *Let.* 14 Aug. (1969) 651 A series of soliloquies having Far Western places as their source and excuse.

†**'fary.** *Sc. Obs.* Also farie. Cf. FEERY-FARY. [? Related to FARE *sb.* 6 c.] A state of tumult or consternation.

1500-20 Dunbar '*Full oft I muss*' 39 Lat us..evir be reddy and addrest, To pass out of this frawfull fary. **1501** Douglas *Pal. Hon.* Prol. 107 Amyd the virgultis all in till a fary, As feminine so feblit fell I down. **1513** —— *Æneis* x. xiv. 31 Meȝentius..baith hys handis in that sammyn steyd Towart the hevin vphevis in a fary.

fary (Levins 1570), var. of FARROW *v.*

†**fas.** *Obs.* (*Since OE. only Sc.*) Also 6 fasse, fæs. [OE. *fæs*, *fas* str. neut., cogn. with OHG. *faso* m., *fasa* f. (MHG. *vase*), also MHG. *vaser*, mod.G. *faser*, of same meaning.]

1. A border, fringe.

c **950** *Lindisf. Gosp.* Matt. ix. 20 Wif..ȝeneolecde..and ȝehran fas wedes his. **1474** *Ld. Treas. Accts. Scot.* (1877) I. 22 Item vj vnce of silk for fassis. **1501** Douglas *Pal. Hon.* I. xxxiv, Fas, nor uther frenzies, had it none. **1560** Rolland *Crt. Venus* I. 137 With fassis fyne nane fairer mycht be found.

2. As the type of something worthless.

1508 *Ballad* in *Golagr. & Gaw.* sig. b v, Sik gouuernance I call noucht vvorth a fasse. **1513** Douglas *Æneis* iv. Prol. 155 Scant worth a fas.

‖**fasces** ('fæsi:z), *sb. pl.* [L. *fascēs* (sing. *fascis* bundle) in same sense.]

1. A bundle of rods bound up with an axe in the middle and its blade projecting. These rods were carried by lictors before the superior magistrates at Rome as an emblem of their power.

1598 Grenewey *Tacitus' Ann.* I. iii. (1622) 5 The fasces or knitch of rods. **1713** Swift *The Faggot*, In history we never found The consuls' fasces were unbound. **1879** Froude *Cæsar* xxiii. 401 The consular fasces, the emblem of the hated Roman authority.

b. *Her.* As a badge.

1889 Elvin *Dict. Her.* s.v. *Fascis*, The Fasces are now frequently given to those who have held magisterial offices.

2. *transf.* and *fig.* **a.** The ensigns of authority or power, *esp.* in ***to take, lay down, resign the fasces***, hence also, authority.

1619 Beaum. & Fl. *Valentinian* v. v, He must take the fasces. **1666** Dryden *Ann. Mirab.* 199 The Duke..shook aloft the Fasces of the Main. **1673-95** Wood *Life* (1848) 184 The senr. proctor..laid down the fasces of his authority. **1797** Burke *Let. Affairs Irel.* Wks. 1812 V. *321 You must submit your fasces to theirs. **1792** S. Rogers *Pleas. Mem.* I. 292 Diocletian's self-corrected mind The imperial fasces of a world resigned. **1827** Macaulay *Machiav.* Ess. (1854) 49/2 He pines for..the fasces of Brutus.

†**b.** The punishments threatened by the fasces; flogging or beheading. *Obs.*

1641 R. Brooke *Eng. Episc.* II. vii. 109 That Tragedy, whose Epilogue was Flame and Fagot, or at least the *Fasces* to younger men.

c. *humorously.* The birch rod.

1762 Foote *Orator* I. Wks. 1799 I. 197 The fescues and fasces..have been..consigned to one, or more matron in every village.

fascet ('fæsɪt). A tool used to introduce glass bottles into the annealing oven.

1662 Merrett *Neri's Art of Glass* 364 *Fascets* are Irons thrust into the bottle to carry them to anneal. **1753** in Chambers *Cycl. Supp.* **1825** in W. Hamilton *Hand-bk. Terms Art & Sc.*

‖**Fasching** ('fæʃɪŋ). [G.] (See quot. 1963.) Also *transf.*

1911 R. Brooke *Let.* Mar. (1968) 287 München in Carnival..these smooth, baggy, tired faces in the streets with the watery obstinacy 'It is *Fasching*. We are Enjoying ourselves' in the eye. **1928** *Daily Express* 3 Jan. 8/5 The 'Fasching', or carnival season. **1963** *Guardian* 21 Feb. 9/5 In Munich we are in the middle of Fasching, which is the South German word for what the Rhineland calls carnival. It began on Epiphany (January 6) and lasts until Shrove Tuesday. **1965** *New Statesman* 19 Mar. 465/1 Cardiff, more than ever, staged a secular *Fasching*. International rugby matches in Wales have always been the occasion for carnival. **1970** *Sat. Rev.* 12 Sept. 64 Fasching starts soon after New Year's Day and holds Munich in its thrall until Ash Wednesday.

Fasci ('faʃi), *sb. pl.* [It., pl. of *fascio* bundle, burden, assemblage, group:—pop.L. *fascium* for L. *fascis* bundle: see FASCES.] Groups of men organized politically, such as those (*fasci dei lavoratori*) in Sicily *c* 1895, and those of the Fascisti (e.g. the *fascio interventista* of 1915).

1902 *Encycl. Brit.* XXIX. 649/1 To produce in Sicily a discontent of which Socialist agitators took advantage to organize the workmen of the towns and the peasants of the country into groups known as *fasci*. **1921** *Public Opinion* 20 May 464/3 The first Fasci (composed of ex-soldiers) began to show signs of resistance and opposition to the Communists. **1922** *Q. Rev.* Jan. 144 A considerable proportion of the poet's legionaries in Fiume was drawn from the Fasci in different Italian towns. **1959** E. J. Hobsbawm *Primitive Rebels* iii. 42 The great peasant rising of 1894—the *Fasci Siciliani*—saw it [*sc.* the Mafia] on the side of reaction, or at best neutral... Even then it was observed that the rise of the Fasci had diminished the hold of *Mafia* on the peasants.

fascia ('fæʃɪə, 'feɪʃ(ɪ)ə). Pl. fasciæ. In architectural uses also **-as**. Forms: 7 **fasia, facea**, 8 **facio, -tio**, 9 **facia** (with English plural), 6- **fascia**. [a. L. *fascia* in senses 1 and 2.]

†**1.** in *Lat.* sense: A band, fillet. *Obs.*

1587 T. Underdown tr. *Heliodorus* 85 Cariclia tied a part of her fascia that was foule, about her head. **1594** Drayton *Ideas* Wks. (1748) 399 Poor rogue [Cupid] go pawn thy fascia and thy bow. **1606** B. Jonson *Hymenæi* Wks. (Rtldg.) 554/2 A Veile..bound with a Fascia of severall coloured silkes.

2. *Archit.* **a.** Any long flat surface of wood, stone or marble, *esp.* in the Doric order, the band which divides the architrave, and in the Ionic and Corinthian orders, each of the three surfaces into which the architrave is divided. (Hence the use explained under FACIA.)

1563 Shute *Archit.* D ij a, The lowest Fascia..the second Fascia..the third Fascia. **1663** Gerbier *Counsel* (1664) 71 Beades in the Fasia, cut at round. **1703** T. N. *City & C. Purchaser* 13 A broad Plinth, or Fatio. **1766** Entick *London* IV. 81 The present edifice [is] built partly with brick, and stone faceas. **1769** De Foe *Tour Gt. Brit.* I. 169 This Work ..is crowned with a Facia and Torus of wrought Stone. **1827** G. Higgins *Celtic Druids* Introd. p. 46 One [Round Tower] at Ardmore has fasciæ at the several stories, which all the rest..seem to want. **1881** F. Young *Every man his own Mechanic* §1354 To the ends of the rafters a facia should be nailed. **1909** H. G. Wells *Tono-Bungay* I. iii. 100 The bright little shop still saying 'Ponderevo' with all the emphasis of its fascia. **1963** *Gloss. Build. Terms* (*B.S.I.*) 23 *Fascia*, a long and relatively narrow upright face at eaves or cornice or over a shop front. **1971** *Guardian* 21 July 11/5 In worn-out Upper Street..gaudy fascias brighten up derelict façades.

†**b.** A ceiling coved on two opposite sides only.

1613-39 I. Jones in Leoni *Palladio's Archit.* (1742) I. 39 A Fascia is the same as a Conca, and terminates to the wall. **1715** *Ibid.* (1721) I. 83 The Hall is arch'd with a Fascia.

3. *Anat.* **a.** A thin sheath of fibrous tissue investing a muscle or some special tissue or organ; an aponeurosis.

1788 H. Watson in *Med. Commun.* II. 268 Tendinous expansions, or Fasciæ..support the muscles. **1804** Abernethy *Surg. Obs.* 30 A tumour formed apparently beneath the fascia of his thigh. **1807** Morris & Kendrick *Edinb. Med. & Physical Dict.* II, *Fascia lata*, a strong tendinous expansion..to surround the muscles of the thigh. **1840** G. Ellis *Anat.* 413 The palmar fascia and the transverse ligament of the metacarpal bones. **1854** Owen *Skel. & Teeth* (1855) 3 The temporal fascia in the turtle. **1876** Duhring *Dis. Skin* 24 The superficial fascia of muscles. **1961** *Lancet* 5 Aug. 318/1 Connective tissue (fascia lata). **1967** G. M. Wyburn et al. *Conc. Anat.* vi. 156 The fascia lata is attached above to the pelvis and inguinal ligament and below to the condyles round the knee joint.

b. The substance of which this is composed.

1881 Mivart *Cat* 133 This muscle is only covered by skin and fascia.

4. Any object, or collection of objects, that gives the appearance of a band or stripe.

a. *Astron.* The belt of a planet. **b.** *Conchol.* A row of perforations. **c.** *Bot.*, *Zool.*, and *Ornith.* A band of colour. **d.** *Her.* = FESSE.

a. 1704 J. Harris *Lex. Techn.*, *Fasciæ*, in the Planet Mars, are certain Rows of Spots, parallel to the Equator of that Planet, which looks like Swathes or Fillets wound round about his Body. **1825** W. Hamilton *Hand-bk. Terms Art & Sc.*, *Fasciæ*, the belts seen on the discs of the superior planets.

b. 1877 Huxley *Anat. Inv. Anim.* ix. 571 The ambulacra ..are not arranged in fasciæ.

c. 1752 Sir J. Hill *Hist. Anim.* 152 There are three brown fasciæ running over it of considerable breadth. **1826** Kirby & Sp. *Entomol.* (1828) III. xxxii. 302 The secondary wings are black with an orange fascia near the posterior margin. **1839** Jardine *Brit. Birds* II. 80 An ill-defined ochraceous fascia across the vent.

d. 1880 *Encycl. Brit.* XI. 694/2 The Fess, fesse, fascia, is a strip placed horizontally across the middle of the field.

5. *attrib.* (in sense 2 and in the sense of FACIA 2), as ***fascia-board, -panel.***

1924 H. J. Butler *Motor Bodywork* 482/2 Fascia boards. **1925** W. Deeping *Sorrell & Son* i. 9 Painted in white letters on a black fascia-board 'John Verity—Dealer in Antiques'. **1957** 'N. Shute' *On Beach* i. 21 He could hardly remember what the fascia panel looked like or on which side the seat adjustment lever lay.

fascial ('fæʃɪəl), *a.*[1] *rare*⁻¹. [f. FASC-ES + -(I)AL.] Of or pertaining to the (Roman) fasces.

1832 in Webster. **1855** Singleton *Virgil* II. 148 Dost thou list..the fascial rods, Recovered, to behold?

fascial ('fæʃɪəl), *a.*[2] *Anat.* [ad. L. *fasciālis*: see FASCIA and -AL[1].] Of or pertaining to the fasciæ; aponeurotic.

fasciate ('fæʃɪət), *a.* [ad. late L. *fasciāt-us*, pa. pple. of *fasciāre* to swathe, f. *fascia*: see FASCIA.] *Bot.* = FASCIATED.

fasciate ('fæʃɪeɪt), *v.* [f. late L. *fasciāt-* ppl. stem of *fasciāre*: see prec.] *trans.* To bind with or as with a fascia. Also, ***to fasciate together***.

1658 Sir T. Browne *Gard. Cyrus* ii, The armes not lying fasciating or wrapt up, after the Grecian manner. **1664** Evelyn *Sylva* (1776) 543 The fatal prediction of..accidents fasciating the boughs and branches of trees. **1677** Plot *Oxfordsh.* 148 A broad flat stalk, as if there were several of them fasciated together.

fasciated ('fæʃɪeɪtɪd), *ppl. a.* [f. FASCIATE *v.* + -ED[1]. Cf. Fr. *fascié*.]

1. *Bot.* See quot. 1835.

1835 Lindley *Introd. Bot.* (1848) II. 382 *Fasciated* [is] when several contiguous parts grow unnaturally together into one. **1868** Darwin *Anim. & Pl.* I. x. 365 The flower-stem [of the Cockscomb] is wonderfully 'fasciated' or compressed.

b. *Crystallog.* Massed together.

1811 Pinkerton *Petral.* II. 133 Very small crystals, elegantly fasciated in various directions.

†**2.** Of a roof: Coved on two opposite sides only: see FASCIA 2 b. *Obs.*

1715 Leoni *Palladio's Archit.* (1721) I. 79 The Arches of the..Rooms near the Galleries, are fasciated.

3. Marked with bands or stripes; striped.

1752 Sir J. Hill *Hist. Anim.* 152 The bluish, fasciated Porcellana. **1766** Pennant *Zool.* (1777) IV. 119 Red fasciated with black or white, along the spires. **1798** —— *Hindoostan* II. 204 The columns are ribbed and near their tops doubly fasciated. **1801** Latham *Hist. Birds* 2nd Supp. 312 Fasciated Sandpiper.

fasciation (fæsɪ'eɪʃən). [a. F. *fasciation*: see FASCIA and -ATION.]

1. The binding up of a limb, etc., with bandages.

1650 Bulwer *Anthropomet.* xix. 190 By their constant and foolish Fasciation the Bones..may be incurvated. **1704** J. Harris *Lex. Techn.*, *Fasciation* is a binding of Swathes about a Limb that is to be cured. **1889** Wagstaffe *Mayne's Med. Voc.*, *Fasciation*, the binding up of a diseased or wounded part with bandages.

†**b.** *concr.* A bandage. *Obs.*

1658 Sir T. Browne *Gard. Cyrus* ii. 107 Even Diadems.. were but fasciations, and handsome ligatures, about the heads of Princes. **1658** —— *Hydriot.* i. 5 The fasciations and bands of death.

2. The process of becoming fasciated; also, fasciated condition (see FASCIATED 1).

1677 Plot *Oxfordsh.* 148 The fasciation..being as it were an attempt for two stalks. **1881** J. Gibbs in *Science Gossip* No. 203. 254 The growth of several buds from the same node..does not often give rise to fasciation of the branches.

fascicle ('fæsɪk(ə)l). Also 7 fasickle. [ad. L. *fasciculus* dim. of *fascis*: see FASCES.]

1. A bunch, bundle. Now only in scientific use. Formerly also *fig.*

1622 F. Markham *Bk. War* IV. v. 138 This Fasickle or bundle of vertues. **1792** *Char.* in *Ann. Reg.* 46/2 The middle fascicle of hair..is wrapped in a large quill of silver. **1846** Dana *Zooph.* (1848) 368 Lamellæ arranged in groups or fascicles. **1877** Coues *Fur. Anim.* vii. 198 The hairs of the tail..grow..in somewhat isolated fascicles.

b. *spec.* in *Bot.* A cluster of leaves or flowers with very short stalks growing closely together at the base; a tuft. Also, a bunch of roots growing from one point.

a **1794** Sir W. Jones *Select Ind. Plants* Wks. 1807 V. 113 Each blossom, that opens in the fascicle. **1835** Lindley *Introd. Bot.* (1848) I. 320 *Fascicle*, a term..synonymous with compound corymb. **1872** Oliver *Elem. Bot.* II. 246 In Larch..and Cedar..the acicular leaves are numerous, in dense fascicles. **1880** Gray *Struct. Bot.* v. 147 An umbel.. is sometimes called a Fascicle.

c. *Anat.* = FASCICULUS 1 c.

1738 Stuart *Muscular Motion* iii. 44 A fascicle or bundle of..small muscular fibres. **1839** Todd *Cycl. Anat.* III. 600/1 The nerve-tubes separate from the primary trunk into smaller fascicles. **1845** Todd & Bowman *Phys. Anat.* I. 71 The tendons are for the most part implanted by separate fascicles into distinct depressions in the bones.

2. A part, number, 'livraison' (of a work published by instalments); = FASCICULUS 2.

1647 Mayne *Serm. Vind.* 19 In the next fascicle, you say ..that I maintain some things. **1858** Carlyle *Fredk. Gt.* II. x. ii. 606 Suhm translates; sends it to him..fascicle by fascicle, with commentaries. **1887** *Homeop. World* 1 Nov. 521 The Sixth Fascicle completes this beautiful work.

fascicled ('fæsɪk(ə)ld), *ppl. a. Bot.* [f. prec. + -ED.] = FASCICULATE a.

1792 Roxburgh *Asiatic Res.* III. 470 Flowers Papilionaceous..fascicled. **1830** Lindley *Nat. Syst. Bot.* 247 Leaves..sometimes fascicled in consequence of the non-development of the branch. **1840** Paxton *Bot. Dict.*, *Fascicled-whorled*, arranged in parcels but forming a whorl, or circle. **1880** Gray *Struct. Bot.* iii. §1. 31 *note*, Fascicled Roots are those which form in clusters. **1882** Vines *Sachs' Bot.* 379 Fascicled branches.

fascicular (fə'sɪkjʊlə(r)), *a.* [f. FASCICUL-US + -AR.]

†**1.** (See quot.) *Obs.*

1656-81 Blount *Glossogr.*, *Fascicular*, belonging to a bundle or fardel. **1721-1800** in Bailey.

¶ With allusion to FASCES.

1866 Sala *Barbary* 28 A fascicular bundle of canes of which a Roman lictor might have been proud.

2. Pertaining to, or of the nature of, a fascicle. **a.** *Bot.* Also, ***fascicular tissue***, 'a term which includes all the varieties of cellular tissue of plants which are collected into bundles or fascicles' (*Syd. Soc. Lex.*, 1884).

1840 Paxton *Bot. Dict.*, *Fascicular*, arranged in bundles or parcels. **1884** Bower & Scott *De Bary's Phaner. & Ferns* 400 Whether the accompanying fibrous strands belong to the 'fascicular tissue' or to the 'ground tissue'.

b. *Geol.* and *Min.*

1805-17 R. Jameson *Char. Min.* (ed. 3) 238 Fascicular.. when the fibres diverge only on one side. **1816** P. Cleaveland *Min.* ii. 54 The fibres may be..fascicular, like

a bundle of rods confined at one extremity. **1879** RUTLEY *Stud. Rocks* xii. 237 Confused, fascicular, radiating aggregates.

c. *Anat.*

1845 TODD & BOWMAN *Phys. Anat.* I. 70 Fascicular flattened bands, more or less expanded.

Hence **faˈscicularly** *adv.*, in a fascicular manner.

17.. KIRWAN (cited in Webster); **1847** in CRAIG.

fasciculate (fəˈsɪkjʊlət), *a.* [f. as prec. + -ATE².] Arranged in a fascicle; fascicle-like; growing or occurring in a bunch, bundle, or tuft. **a.** *Bot.* **b.** *Zool.* **c.** *Path.*

a. 1794 MARTYN *Rousseau's Bot.* xxvii. 412 The roots are ..fasciculate. **1861** H. MACMILLAN *Footnotes fr. Nature* 46 Its branches are fasciculate and disposed around the stem in spirals. **1872** OLIVER *Elem. Bot.* I. vii. 80 Leaves tufted in this way are said to be fasciculate [as in Pine].

b. 1846 DANA *Zooph.* iv. (1848) 83 When the branches are laterally in contact, as in the Columnariæ..fasciculate forms result. **1870** ROLLESTON *Anim. Life* Introd. 117 A fasciculate rather than an arborescent arrangement.

c. 1847–9 TODD *Cycl. Anat.* IV. 119/2 The 'fasciculate' variety of cancer.

Hence **faˈsciculately** *adv.*

1840 PAXTON *Bot. Dict.*, *Fasciculately-tuberous*, roots composed of parcels of tubers. **1846** DANA *Zooph.* (1848) 308 Corallum with unequal lamellæ, fasciculately interrupted.

† **faˈsciculate**, *v.* *Obs.*⁻⁰ [f. L. *fascicul-us* + -ATE³.] *trans.* 'To tie up into a bundle or fascicle' (Blount *Glossogr.* 1656–81).

1708–32 in COLES.

fasciculated (fəˈsɪkjʊleɪtɪd), *ppl. a.* [f. prec. + -ED¹.] In various scientific uses = FASCICULATE.

1777 HUNTER in *Phil. Trans.* LXVII. 611 The fasciculated surfaces in the heart. **1788** tr. *Swedenborg's Wisd. Angels* v. §366. 345 The Fibres..successively collect themselves into Nerves, and when they are fasciculated or become Nerves [etc.]. *a* **1798** PENNANT *Zool.* (1812) IV. xxxiii. 185 Asterias, or sea star, with twelve broad rays.. roughened with fasciculated long papillæ on the upper part. **1835–6** TODD *Cycl. Anat.* I. 140/1 The muscular system consists of reddish and whitish fasciculated fibres. **1853** TH. ROSS *Humboldt's Trav.* III. xxvi. 115 We found some [veins] ..full of small fasciculated crystals of rutile titanite. **1854** S. THOMSON *Wild Fl.* I. (ed. 4) 29 The fasciculated or bundled [root]..we see in the bird's-nest orchis.

fasciculation (fəˌsɪkjuːˈleɪʃən). [f. FASCICULATE *v.*: see -ATION.] **a.** The state of being fasciculate. **b.** That which is fasciculated. **c.** *Physiol.* [f. FASCICUL(US.] Uncoordinated twitching of a muscle, esp. that involving the simultaneous contraction of whole bundles or fasciculi of muscle fibres.

1938 *Brain* LXI. 321 This phenomenon, commonly called 'fibrillation', but more properly called 'fasciculation', may therefore represent the intermittent involuntary discharge of single nerve impulses by an abnormal motor neurone. *Ibid.* 322 In the few seconds following the movement fasciculation is more rapid in that particular unit. **1959** H. GRUNDFEST in J. Field *Handbk. Physiol.: Neurophysiol.* I. v. 164/1 The disorganized contraction of muscles, frequently but incorrectly termed 'fasciculation', is due to the initial excitatory effect of the synaptic depolarization. **1963** *Lancet* 19 Jan. 130/1 With decamethonium muscle fasciculation was only slight, whereas with suxamethonium it was severe and long lasting.

fasciculato-, combining form of FASCICULATE, occas. prefixed to other adjs. to indicate a fasciculate form or arrangement.

1846 DANA *Zooph.* (1848) 404 Fasciculato-glomerate: tubes of the coralla cylindrical. **1866** *Treas. Bot.*, *Fasciculato-ramose*, when branches or roots are drawn closely together so as to be almost parallel.

fascicule (ˈfæsɪkjuːl). [a. F. *fascicule*, ad. L. *fasciculus*: see FASCICULUS.]

† **1.** (See quot.) *Obs.*

1699 EVELYN *Acetaria* (1729) 152 *Fascicule*, a reasonable full Gripe, a Handful.

2. = FASCICLE 2, FASCICULUS 2.

1880 G. ALLEN in *Academy* 24 Jan. 58/2 Mr. Spencer will obtain more readers for separate fascicules..than he is likely to find for his thicker volumes. **1880** *Nature* XXI. 453 Three large octavo volumes in double column, which will appear by fascicules of 300 to 400 pages.

3. = FASCICULUS 1 c.

1745 PARSONS *Muscular Motion* i. 22 Many Filaments, or tendinous Fibres, which are parallel to one another in every little Bundle or Fascicule.

fasciculite (fəˈsɪkjʊlaɪt). *Min.* [f. FASCICULE + -ITE.] Tufted fibrous hornblende.

1823 HITCHCOCK in *Amer. Jrnl. Sc.* VI. 226 So..striking an instance do these exhibit of the fascicular structure of minerals that I..have denominated them Fasciculite. **1884** DANA *Min.* 240 The fasciculite of Hitchcock is merely this tufted hornblende.

‖ **fasciculus** (fəˈsɪkjʊləs). Pl. fasciculi. [L. *fasciculus*, dim. of *fascis*: see FASCES.]

1. = FASCICLE 1; chiefly in scientific use.

1816 KIRBY & SP. *Entomol.* (1843) I. 344 These pale-blue fasciculi Mr. Blackwell found to proceed from two additional spinners. **1823** SCORESBY *Jrnl.* 77 Every spine consisted of a fasciculus of needles. **1836–7** SIR W. HAMILTON *Metaph.* xxxiv. (1859) II. 286 Our cognitions comprehend different fasciculi of notions. **1865** *Daily Tel.* 28 Oct. 4/6 To see Lord Palmerston..fumble with a fasciculus of papers. **1874** tr. *Lommel's Light* 20 A small conical fasciculus [of rays of light] traverses the aperture.

b. *Bot.* = FASCICLE 1 b.

1857 HENFREY *Bot.* §135 The fasciculus is a cymose collection of nearly sessile flowers. **1889** WAGSTAFFE *Mayne's Med. Voc.*, *Fasciculus*, a handful, as of flowers, leaves, roots.

c. *Anat.* 'A bundle of fibres, chiefly applied to nerve structures' (Wagstaffe).

1713 CHESELDEN *Anat.* Introd. (1726) 3 Nerves are Fasciculi of cylindrical fibres. **1797** M. BAILLIE *Morb. Anat.* (1807) 21 The fasciculi of the muscular fibres. **1881** MIVART *Cat* 125 Each fasciculus being furnished by a membranous envelope.

2. = FASCICLE 2.

1844 LINGARD *Anglo-Sax. Ch.* (1858) I. vii. 281 He collected entire psalms..in eight separate fasciculi. **1872** ELLACOMBE *Ch. Bells Devon* vii. 161 An elegant folio fasciculus descriptive of the bell and shrine. **1880** *Athenæum* 29 May 699 We have received the first fasciculus of a new monthly periodical in Hebrew.

fasciitis (fæʃɪ-, fæsɪˈaɪtɪs). *Path.* Also fascitis (fæʃ-, fæˈsaɪtɪs). [f. FASCI(A + -ITIS.] Inflammation of a fascia.

1893 DUNGLISON *Dict. Med. Sci.* (ed. 21) 424/1 Fascitis. **1940** B. I. COMROE *Arthritis* xlii. 611 The main therapeutic attack upon plantar fascitis includes..use of a rubber pad to protect the heel, procaine injections into the plantar fascia.. and removal of focal infection. **1961** *Lancet* 30 Sept. 740/1 The term plantar fasciitis was used to describe a condition characterised by painful feet. **1966** R. W. EVANS *Histol. Appearances of Tumours* (ed. 2) i. 5 Nodular fascitis is not a tumour but a fibroblastic proliferation.

† **fasciˈnade.** *Obs. rare.* [f. FASCINE + -ADE: cf. *stockade*, *palisade*.] (?) A defensive work composed of fascines.

1736 LEDIARD *Marlborough* III. 171 A Bridge of Hurdles and Planks..by which their Fascinades were join'd.

† **fascinage.** *Obs. rare*⁻¹. [a. F. *fascinage*, f. *fascine*: see FASCINE *sb.*] = prec.

1715 *Lond. Gaz.* No. 5347/1 A great part of the Fascinage had been torn away by the Rhine.

fascinate (ˈfæsɪneɪt), *v.* [f. L. *fascināt-* ppl. stem of *fascināre* to enchant, f. *fascinum* spell, witchcraft. Cf. F. *fasciner*.]

† **1.** *trans.* To affect by witchcraft or magic; to bewitch, enchant, lay under a spell. *Obs.*

1598 B. JONSON *Ev. Man in Hum.* IV. ix, I was fascinated, by Jupiter: fascinated: but I will be unwitch'd, and reveng'd, by law. **1621–51** BURTON *Anat. Mel.* I. ii. III. ii. 96 Why do witches and old women, fascinate and bewitch children? **1657** TOMLINSON *Renou's Disp.* 108 Such as.. promise to fascinate and cure stinking breaths.

2. † **a.** To cast a spell over (a person, animal, etc.) by a look; said *esp.* of serpents. **b.** In later use disconnected from the notion of witchcraft: To deprive of the power of escape or resistance, as serpents are said to do through the terror produced by their look or merely by their perceived presence.

1641 J. JACKSON *True Evang. T.* I. 17 Man is a..Basilisk ..fascinating with an envious eye the prosperity of his neighbour. **1845** TODD & BOWMAN *Physiol. Anat.* I. xii. 390 The serpent fascinates its prey, apparently by the power of his eyes. **1848** MACAULAY *Hist. Eng.* II. 582 James.. remained at Whitehall, fascinated..by the greatness and nearness of the danger, and unequal to the exertion of either struggling or flying. **1857** H. REED *Lect. Eng. Poets* II. xii. 124 The pet dove of the castle fascinated in the forest by a serpent.

3. *fig.* † **a.** To enslave (the faculties), the judgement of (a person) (*obs.*). **b.** To attract and retain the attention of (a person) by an irresistible influence. **c.** Now usually, To attract and 'hold spellbound' by delightful qualities; to charm, enchant.

a. 1651 *Reliq. Wotton, Disp. Buckhm. & Essex* 54 A certain innate wisdom and vertue..with which he..fascinated all the faculties of his incomparable master. **1789** BENTHAM *Princ. Legisl.* xviii. §44 *note*, Aristotle, fascinated by the prejudice of the times, divides mankind into..freemen and ..slaves.

b. 1847 EMERSON *Repr. Men, Napoleon* Wks. (Bohn) I. 378 He delighted to fascinate Josephine..in a dim-lighted apartment by the terrors of a fiction. **1862** BURTON *Bk. Hunter* (1863) 111 The eye of the Ancient Mariner fascinated the wedding guest.

c. 1815 MOORE *Lalla R.* (1824) 30 Illum'd by a wit that would fascinate sages. **1832** LYTTON *Eugene A.* I. v, The gay Ellinor was fascinated into admiration. **1874** MORLEY *Compromise* (1886) 23 They so fascinated the imagination.. that [etc.].

absol. **1875** EMERSON *Lett. & Soc. Aims, Eloquence* Wks. (Bohn) III. 189 This power [eloquence]..fascinates and astonishes.

fascinated (ˈfæsɪneɪtɪd), *ppl. a.* [f. prec. + -ED¹.] In senses of the vb.

1706 PHILLIPS (ed. Kersey), *Fascinated*, bewitched. **1768** STERNE *Sent. Journ.* (1775) I. 56 (*Paris*) Tilting at it like fascinated knights. **1810** SOUTHEY *Kehama* V. xii, Her fascinated eyes. **1817** —— *Life* (1850) IV. 233 Are they rendered absolutely helpless by fear, like a fascinated bird?

fascinatedly (ˈfæsɪneɪtɪdlɪ), *adv.* [f. FASCINATED *ppl. a.* + -LY².] In a fascinated manner.

1894 M. DYAN *All in Man's Keeping* I. vi. 103 The lady stared fascinatedly on. **1949** T. BONNET *Mudlark* (1950) vi. 65 Mr. Brown performed again,..watched fascinatedly by Wheeler. *a* **1953** E. O'NEILL *Touch of Poet* (1957) II. 69 She stares at him fascinatedly—then blurts out with impulsive admiration.

fascinating (ˈfæsɪneɪtɪŋ), *ppl. a.* [f. FASCINATE *v.* + -ING².] That fascinates, in senses of the vb. Now chiefly, Irresistibly attractive, charming.

1648 W. MOUNTAGUE *Devout Ess.* I. xix. §5. 353 Such temptations and fascinating vanities. **1794** SULLIVAN *View Nat.* I. 9 Bewitching and fascinating flowers. **1869** J. MARTINEAU *Ess.* II. 111 M. Cousin's fascinating lectures on the history of philosophy.

Hence **ˈfascinatingly** *adv.*

1835 *Tait's Mag.* II. 538 Our enamel smilingly and fascinatingly displayed. **1870** *Temple Bar Mag.* XXIX. 191 Heroines..lovely..and fascinatingly attired.

fascination (fæsɪˈneɪʃən). [ad. L. *fascinātiōn-em*, n. of action f. *fascināre* to FASCINATE.]

1. The casting of a spell; sorcery, enchantment; an instance of this, a spell, incantation. *Obs.* exc. *Hist.*

1605 BACON *Adv. Learn.* II. xi. §3. 46 Fascination is the power and act of Imagination intensiue vpon other bodies. **1615** CROOKE *Body of Man* 60 We deny that fascination or bewitching is done onely by sight. **1626** DONNE *Serm.* cxxxix. V. 488 When Elijah used that holy Fascination upon Elisha to spread his mantle over him. **1681** GLANVILL *Saddücismus* I. 1 The odd Phænomena of Witchcraft and Fascination. **1702** C. MATHER *Magn. Chr.* I. iv. (1852) 66 They began to suspect that the Indian sorcerers had laid the place under some fascination. **1855** SMEDLEY *Occult Sciences* 204 A belief in Fascination..appears to have been very generally prevalent in most ages and countries.

† **b.** The state of being under a spell. *Obs.*

1651 J. F[REAKE] *Agrippa's Occ. Philos.* 101 Fascination is a binding, which comes from the spirit of the Witch, through the eyes of him that is bewitched, entering to his heart. **1767** FAWKES *Theocritus* VI. *note*, The antients imagined that spitting in their bosoms three times..would prevent fascination.

2. The action and the faculty of fascinating their prey attributed to serpents, etc.

1796 MORSE *Amer. Geog.* I. 219 They [Rattle Snakes] are supposed to have the power of fascination in an eminent degree. **1848** LYTTON *Harold* I. i, The fascination of the serpent on the bird held her mute and frozen.

b. The state of being so fascinated.

1831 BREWSTER *Nat. Magic* iii. (1833) 43 Mrs. A. described herself as at the time sensible of a feeling like what we conceive of fascination.

3. Fascinating quality; irresistibly attractive influence; an instance or mode of this.

1697 EVELYN *Numism.* ix. 301 Unaccountable Fascination, or other material Quality of Mastering Spirits. **1784** COWPER *Task* VI. 101 Some to the fascination of a name Surrender judgment hoodwinked. *a* **1806** K. WHITE *My own Charac.* 42 in *Rem.* (1816) I. 29, I..can't withstand you know whose fascination. **1816** J. SCOTT *Vis. Paris* (ed. 5) 209 A Frenchwoman..will ever be felt..to be a creature of fascination. **1843** PRESCOTT *Mexico* (1820) I. 185 The career thus thrown open had all the fascinations of a desperate hazard. **1847** EMERSON *Repr. Men* Wks. (Bohn) I. 283 Like a master..drawing all men by fascination into tributaries. **1860** HAWTHORNE *Transform.* I. xix. 203 The perilous fascination which haunts the brow of precipices.

fascinative (ˈfæsɪneɪtɪv), *a.* [f. FASCINATE *v.* + -IVE.] Disposed or tending to fascinate.

1855 BAILEY *Mystic* 96 Vipers..That fascinative seek the tender breasts Of wilful maids, and sing their souls to sleep. **1874** M. COLLINS *Transmigr.* I. vii. 119, I acknowledged Lady Diana's marvellous fascinative force.

fascinator (ˈfæsɪneɪtə(r)). [a. L. *fascinātor*, agent-n. f. *fascināre* to FASCINATE. Cf. F. *fascinateur*.] One who fascinates. **a.** A magician. **b.** A charming or attractive person.

a. 1750 tr. *Leonardus' Mirr. Stones* 52 Nor does this happen merely from the sight, but from—the soul of the fascinator. **1862** LYTTON *Str. Story* II. 147 The dread Fascinator from whom it had been taken.

b. 1838 DICKENS *Nich. Nick.* xvii, The demdest little fascinator in all the world. **1885** MABEL COLLINS *Prettiest Wom.* i, Sacha was considered an irresistible fascinator.

c. A head shawl worn by women, either crocheted or made of a soft material. orig. *U.S.*

1878 K. D. WIGGIN *Let.* 20 Dec. in N. A. Smith *K. D. Wiggin* (1925) 35 Mother crocheting a fascinator. **1897** *Sears, Roebuck Catal.* 305/1 Ladies' Fascinator, made of good quality Shetland yarn..colors, pink and white. **1908** *Scribner's Mag.* Feb. 177 A scant worsted 'enchanter' or 'fascinator', I think she called it, thrown over her head and shoulders. **1909** *Daily Chron.* 8 Dec. 9/4 A lovely shawl of eider, Shetland, or any fine wool..can be utilised as a fascinator, or shoulder wrap. **1949** R. HARVEY *Curtain Time* 110 The ladies in their furred evening cloaks..with snowflakes caught in their lacy fascinators. **1969** *New Yorker* 29 Nov. 59/2 Doris, in a pink cloak trimmed with swansdown and a candy-striped fascinator over her dark head, stepped out.

fascinatress (ˈfæsɪneɪtrɪs). [f. prec. + -ESS. Cf. F. *fascinatrice*.] A fascinating woman.

1878 H. JAMES *Daisy Miller* 42 'She's an enchantress..a charmer', I said, 'a fascinatress'.

fascine (fæˈsiːn), *sb.* Also 8 fachine, 9 facine. [a. F. *fascine*, ad. L. *fascina*, f. *fascis* a bundle.]

1. *Mil.* A long cylindrical faggot of brush or other small wood, firmly bound together at short intervals, used in filling up ditches, the construction of batteries, etc. Usually in *pl.*

a **1688** SIR T. MORGAN *Relat. Progr. France* (1699) 14 The major-general..ordered the two battalions..each man to take up a long fascine upon their musquets and pikes. **1692**

Lond. Gaz. No. 2807/2 Orders are given to provide a great number of Fascines, in order to storm the Castle of Ebernburg. **1776** C. LEE in Sparks *Corr. Amer. Rev.* (1853) I. 158 They are employed in making fascines..for constructing three redoubts. **1801** WELLINGTON in Gurw. *Desp.* I. 361 They ought to be provided with facines to fill a part of the ditch. **1880** KINGLAKE *Crimea* VI. ix. 241 Of round-shot, of gabions and fascines.

b. *transf.* in various non-military uses, *esp.* in *Civil Engineering*.

1712 E. COOKE *Voy. S. Sea* 412 He..made a Sort of floating Island of Fascines, Earth, and other Materials. **1723** *Pres. State Russia* I. 351 A large Dike or Peer made of Fachines and Earth. **1852** BURNELL *Rudim. Hydraulic Engineering* II. 94 The lower part of the majority of wooden jetties is..covered either by a mass of concrete, of loose stones, or of fascines. **1866** LEE tr. *Keller's Lake Dwell. Switz.* 70 The upper beds of fascines..lock into one another at the ends and form one continuous mass.

2. *transf.* and *fig.*

1844 H. ROGERS *Ess.* (1860) III. 121 This fascine of citations..is in truth nothing to the purpose. **1870** H. MACMILLAN *Bible Teach.* iv. 70 The pine is a natural fascine or fortification against the ravages of the elements.

3. *attrib.* **a.** Suitable for fascines, as *fascine-stick*. **b.** Consisting or made of fascines, as *fascine-battery*, *-bridge*, *-platform*; **fascine-dwelling**, a lacustrine habitation supported on fascines; hence *fascine-dweller*; **fascine-horse** (see quot.).

1748 SMOLLETT *Rod. Rand.* xxxiii. (1804) 213 A body of sailors who made themselves masters of..the *fascine batteries. **1857** S. OSBORN *Quedah* xii. 150 When clearing away the jungle to construct the fascine battery. **1796** STEDMAN *Surinam* I. iv. 82 To throw a *fascine bridge over the marsh. **1882** R. MUNRO *Anc. Scot. Lake-dwellings* 12 The civilisation of the *fascine-dwellers. **1866** LEE tr. *Keller's Lake Dwell. Switz.* 69 The *fascine dwellings seem only to have been adopted in lakes of small depth and extent. **1859** F. A. GRIFFITHS *Artil. Man.* (ed. 9) 254 *A *fascine horse* is formed with two pickets..driven about 1 foot obliquely into the ground, so as to cross each other at right angles 2 feet above the surface of the earth; and they are fastened together at their point of meeting with cord. **1866** LEE tr. *Keller's Lake Dwell. Switz.* 72 This gentleman..noticed..parts of a *fascine platform. **1870** *Daily News* 18 Oct., The country..affording withies for binding and *fascine sticks to any extent.

Hence **fa'scine** *v. trans.* to fill up with fascines.

1870 *Daily News* 29 Nov., The pioneers had..fascined the track.

fascinery (fæ'siːnərɪ). [f. FASCINE *sb.* + -ERY.] (See quot.)

1856 BREES *Terms Archit. etc.*, *Fascinery*, a description of cradling or hurdle-work, employed to retain earth.

† **'fascinous**, *a. Obs. rare.* [f. L. *fascin-um* witchcraft + -OUS.] 'Caused or acting by witchcraft or enchantment' (J.).

1666 G. HARVEY *Morb. Angl.* xix. (1672) 38, I shall not here undertake the task of discussing the possibility of fascinous Diseases.

fasciola (fæsɪ'əʊlə). *Anat.* [L., small bandage.] In full *fasciola cinerea*. A thin layer of grey matter that forms the posterior continuation of the dentate gyrus in the hippocampal formation of the brain; the *gyrus fasciolaris*. (See also quot. 1882.) Hence **fa'sciolar** *a.*, of or pertaining to the fasciola.

1848 QUAIN *Elem. Anat.* (ed. 5) II. 724 The grey matter in the floor of the fourth ventricle has been named fasciolæ cinereæ. **1882** WILDER & GAGE *Anat. Technol.* 478 Fasciola. .. The somewhat thickened margin of cinerea along the fimbria. In man the ventral portion has commonly been called *fascia dentata*; in the cat, however, there is no denticulation, and the name fascia is certainly misleading; hence the senior author proposed to employ *fasciola* for the whole. **1889** *Cent. Dict.* III. *Fasciolar*, pertaining to the fasciola, or fascia dentata of the brain. **1954** T. L. PEELE *Neuroanat. Basis Clin. Neurol.* xxiii. 502 Posteriorly, the dentate gyrus is continuous through the fasciolar gyrus below and behind the splenium with the supracallosal gyrus. **1962** E. C. CROSBY et al. *Correl. Anat. Nerv. Syst.* vii. 422 Although the main mass of the hippocampus terminates in the region central to the splenium of the corpus callosum, strands of hippocampal tissue (usually gyrus dentatus) extend, as fasciola cinerea, around the splenium to continue into the induseum griseum.

fasciole ('fæsɪəʊl). *Zool.* [f. prec.] One of the bands of minute tubercles, bearing modified spines, in spatangoid sea-urchins.

1850 E. FORBES *Brit. Organic Rem.* III. plate x. 2 A fasciole of tertiary spines. **1888** ROLLESTON & JACKSON *Forms Anim. Life* 558 Clavulæ, found only in *Spatangideæ*, are minute spines,..attached to minute tubercles which form regular bands known as *fascioles* or *semitæ*. **1962** D. NICHOLS *Echinoderms* viii. 100 Clavulae..occur in special bands called *fascioles*, diagnostic of the order Spatangoida.

fascioliasis (ˌfæsɪə'laɪəsɪs). *Path.* [mod.L., f. *Fasciola*, name of a genus of trematode worms, f. L. *fasciola* small bandage + -IASIS.] Infection with the liver-fluke, *Fasciola* (*Distoma*) *hepatica*; liver-rot.

1890 J. H. STEEL *Treat. Dis. Sheep* v. 140 Hence to all intents and purposes we may deal with rot as fascioliasis, i.e. the pathological state which results from fluke invasion. **1968** G. LAPAGE *Vet. Parasitol.* (ed. 2) xvii. 338 About 200 cercariae will produce acute fascioliasis in a rabbit, but much depends on the nutritional state of the host. **1968** E. J. L. SOULSBY *Helminths, Arthropods & Protozoa Domesticated Animals* 23 The fluke is cosmopolitan in its distribution, and is the cause of fascioliasis (liver fluke disease, liver rot), especially in sheep and cattle.

Fascism ('fæʃɪz(ə)m, occas. 'fæsɪz(ə)m). Also in It. form **Fascismo** (faʃ'ʃizmo), and with small initial. [ad. It. *fascismo*, f. *fascio* bundle, group: see FASCI and -ISM.] The principles and organization of Fascists. Also, *loosely*, any form of right-wing authoritarianism.

1921 *19th Cent.* July 148 The Fascismo was born in the provinces, where the extremistic menace was stronger. **1922** *Q. Rev.* Jan. 148 A section of the Press..now veered completely round to the cause of Fascism. The Fascist terror increased in intensity. **1923** *Contemp. Rev.* Jan. 44 We do not want Fascismo in this country. *Ibid.* Nov. 557 Fascism in Germany will never be more than one of several factors. **1925** *Weekly Westm. Gaz.* 10 Jan. 320/2 The outrages which have been associated with Fascism have gradually alienated much of the support which it won two years ago. **1934** tr. *K. Heiden's National Socialism* xvii. 354 The electoral victories all over Europe with which the Labour Parties have replied to German Fascism. **1936** *Discovery* Dec. 378/1, I have strongly criticised modern education and the methods of handling youth generally as inculcating excessive respect for authority and thereby conducing to the growth of Fascism. **1939** A. COBBAN *Dictatorship* v. 124 In March 1919..Fascism was still..a revolutionary and socialist movement, hostile to the monarchy, to finance, and to parliamentary government, demanding social reform and workers' control, but separated from the other branches of the socialist movement by its intense nationalism. **1965** L. VENNEWITZ tr. *Nolte's Three Faces Fascism* II. ii. 87 Maurras was the first man in Europe who as a thinker and a politician drove conservatism beyond the limits dividing it from incipient fascism. **1971** *Tablet* 26 June 616/2 (*title*) The ghost of Fascism.

Fascist ('fæʃɪst, occas. 'fæsɪst), *sb.* and *a.* Also in It. form **Fascista** (faʃ'ʃista) and with small initial. Pl. **Fascists, Fascisti** (faʃ'ʃisti). [ad. It. *Fascista*, formed as prec.: see -IST.] One of a body of Italian nationalists, which was organized in 1919 to oppose communism in Italy, and, as the *partito nazionale fascista*, under the leadership of Benito Mussolini (1883–1945), controlled that country from 1922 to 1943; also *transf.* applied to the members of similar organizations in other countries. Also, a person having Fascist sympathies or convictions; (*loosely*) a person of right-wing authoritarian views. Hence as *adj.*, of, pertaining to, or characteristic of Fascism or Fascists.

1921 *Times* 1 Jan. 9/6 The *Fascisti* are certainly paying back..the Socialists in matters of violence. **1921** *Glasgow Herald* 30 Mar. 9 A party of Fascisti from Perugia visiting Citta di Castello burned the Labour Bureau. **1921** *Public Opinion* 20 May 464/1 For the moment the Fascisti are acting as a sort of Government bodyguard for the elections and Fascist candidates find a place..on the Government lists. **1922** *Daily Mail* 17 Nov. 7 Signor Mussolini, the Fascist leader, to-day made his first speech in the Chamber. **1923** [see BLACKSHIRT]. **1928** *Outlook* 26 May 645/2 Indeed, I cannot help wondering whether the suggestion does not originally emanate from the British Fascists. **1929** H. S. WALPOLE *Hans Frost* ii. 146 At Venice..a Fascist official at the railway station had been abominably vulgar. **1931** J. S. HUXLEY *What dare I Think?* vii. 231 The Fascist dictatorship. **1936** M. PLOWMAN *Faith called Pacifism* 74 Fascists in all countries are obliged openly to acknowledge their reliance upon war as a means of policy. **1936** *S.P.E. Tract* XLVI. 204 Does not their enthusiasm [for the study of stylistic perfection], when compared with other forms of fascist and fanatical activities, seem almost innocuous? **1938** *Ann. Reg. 1937* 320 The foreign policy of Fascist Italy. **1940** AUDEN in *I Believe* 30, I cannot see how a Socialist country could tolerate the existence of a Fascist party any more than a Fascist country could tolerate the existence of a Socialist party. **1940** N. MITFORD *Pigeon Pie* iii. 39 Luke was an awful old fascist. **1960** S. M. LIPSET *Political Man* v. 133 Fascist ideology, though antiliberal in its glorification of the state, has been similar to liberalism in its opposition to big business, trade-unions, and the socialist state. **1961** H. THOMAS *Spanish Civil War* viii. 70 José Antonio Primo de Rivera..gradually emerged as the Leader of all the Spanish Young Fascists. *Ibid.* 71 The Socialists..were described by [Communist] party jargon as 'social fascists'. **1963** *Times* 27 Mar. 10/2 As the main body of demonstrators began to move away,..screams of 'Fascist pigs' and 'Gestapoism' continued. **1969** *Times* 17 Nov. 10/4 Taunts of 'Sieg Heil', 'Fascists', and the occasional smoke bomb from youthful demonstrators were bound to invite trouble. **1971** *E. Afr. Jrnl.* Mar. 28/1 The international fascist alliance had already found 'an adventure'. **1971** *Tablet* 26 June 616/2 In remoter mountain villages there are still a few..slogans which..survived..the collapse of Fascist rule.

Hence **ˌfasci'zation, ˌfascisti'zation**, the action or process of making Fascist. Also **'fascistize** *v. trans.*

1925 *Glasgow Herald* 20 May 10 The complete 'fascistisation' of Italy. **1937** A. HUXLEY *Ends & Means* v. 36 Belief in our ideal postulates has acted as a brake on fascization. **1940** *Ann. Reg. 1939* 196 This Charter [the Fascist School Charter] has for its object to 'fascistise' entirely the three classes of instruction. To 'fascistise'..is 'to give the school a social and political content' of a certain type. **1955** H. HODGKINSON *Doubletalk* 50 This is part of the process of 'fascistisation' or move from bourgeois democracy to full fascism. **1965** L. VENNEWITZ tr. *Nolte's Three Faces Fascism* I. i. 7 Mussolini's theory of the imminent fascistization of the world undoubtedly seems prejudiced and vague.

Fascistic (fæ'ʃɪstɪk, fæ'sɪstɪk), *a.* Also **fascistic**. [f. prec. + -IC.] Of or pertaining to Fascism or Fascists; having Fascist ideals. So **Fa'scistically** *adv.*

1928 *Daily Express* 2 Oct. 9 Mussolini is taking every possible measure to ensure that the children..grow up feeling 'Fascistically'—the word is good current Italian. **1935** *Mind* XLIV. 208 Why should not some Fascistic professor of physiology succeed in discovering some drug or mode of life that would extend indefinitely the organism's power to repair itself, and so to stave off death? **1947** *Ibid.* LVI. 187 One need not wonder that the same man should be a Socialist and also fascistically inclined. **1951** E. MITTELHOLZER *Shadows move among Them* III. vii. 306 Why should you consider it Fascistic to get rid of a man who has proved himself a hopeless crime-addict? **1962** R. B. FULLER *Epic Poem on Industrialization* 58 Witness its panicky Fascistic plotting.

fascitis, var. FASCIITIS.

† **fase.** *Obs.* [ad. L. (Vulg.) *phase*, a. Heb. *pesaḥ* passover.] The passover.

1388 WYCLIF *Ex.* xii. 21 Take a beeste by ȝoure meynees and offre ȝe fase [1382 paske]. *Ibid.* 43 This is the religioun of fase [1382 phask].

fase, obs. form of *foes*, pl. of FOE.

† **'fasel**, *sb. Obs.*$^{-0}$. In 5 fasylle. [f. next.] A ravelling, a shred.

1440 *Promp. Parv.* 150/2 Fasylle of clothe (or other lyke, P.), *fractillus*.

† **'fasel**, *v. Obs. rare.* Also 6 fasyll, 7 fazle. [Cf. Ger. *faselen*, Du. *vezelen*, cogn. with OE. *fæs* FAS.] *intr.* To ravel. Also, *to fasel out*.

c **1440** *Promp. Parv.* 150/2 Facelyn as clothys (faselyn P.), *villo*. **1530** PALSGR. 546/1 My sleeve is fasylled. **1643** T. GOODWIN *Child of Light* 58 Which hath fazled and entangled this controversy.

† **fasels**, *sb. pl. Obs.* Forms: 6 faselles, facilles, 7 phaselles, faceles, fasells, fesels, 7– fasels. [ad. L. *faseoli*, pl. of *faseolus* in same sense. Cf. OF. *faseles*.] **a.** Chick pease: see CHICK-PEA. **b.** Kidney-beans: see BEAN *sb.* 3.

1558–68 WARDE tr. *Alexis' Secr.* 71 a, A kind of litle graine called in Latine *faseoli*, in Englishe *facilles* and cyche peason. **1562** TURNER *Herbal* II. 86 a, Phasiolus may be called in Englishe *faselles* untill we can fynd a better name for it. **1601** HOLLAND *Pliny* I. 496 The Pulse named Dolychos, which is Fasels or Kidney beanes. **1616** SURFL. & MARKH. *Country Farme* 147 Fasels or long Pease. **1628** MAY *Virgil's Georg.* I. 247 Disdain not Fesels, or poor Vech to sow. **1693** URQUHART *Rabelais* III. viii. 68 Pease, Beans, Fasels [etc.].

fash (fæʃ), *sb.*[1] *Sc.* and *north. dial.* [f. FASH *v.*[1]] Trouble, vexation; bother, inconvenience; also, something that gives trouble. *to take* (*the*) *fash*: to take (the) trouble, to be at the pains.

1794 BURNS *Addr. to Toothache* iv, Of a'..The tricks o' knaves, or fash o' fools, Thou bear'st the gree. **1808** ELIZ. HAMILTON *Cottagers of Glenburnie* (ed. 2) 150 We have never ta'en the fash to put it by. **1816** SCOTT *Old Mort.* iv, 'Clergy and captains can gie an unco deal o' fash in thae times.' **1832–53** *Whistle-binkie* (Sc. Songs) Ser. III. 111 Weel kennin' it [cash] only wad breed me mair fash. **1855** ROBINSON *Whitby Gloss.*, *Fash*, trouble, inconvenience. **1861** RAMSAY *Remin.* Ser. II. 175 When there's ony fash or trouble, The deevil a thing you'll do at a'. **1868** G. MACDONALD *R. Falconer* II. 252, 'I didna think ye wad hae ta'en sae muckle fash.'

fash (fæʃ), *sb.*[2] *dial.* [? var. of FAS, OE. *fæs*.] A fringe; anything resembling a fringe.

It is doubtful whether the first quot. belongs here: the word might be a. OF. *faisse*:—L. *fascia* band.

1558 *Richmond. Wills* (Surtees) XXVI. 128 A fashe of silke and sewed withe gold. **1847–78** in HALLIWELL. **1877** *Holderness Gloss.*, *Fash*, the long hair of a horse's legs.

b. *dial.* The tops of carrots, turnips or mangolds.

c **1750** J. COLLIER (Tim Bobbin) *Lanc. Dialect* Gloss., *Fash*, the tops of turnips, etc. **1847** in HALLIWELL.

c. A rough edge or ridge left on nails, cast bullets, etc.

1831 J. HOLLAND *Manuf. Metal* I. 215 The perfection of cut nails, consists principally in the shank being..free from fash. *Ibid.* 335 The teeth [of the saw] are severally filed to a sharp point, and the wiry edges, or fash..completely removed. **1867** SMYTH *Sailor's Word-bk.*, *Fash*, the mark left by the moulds upon cast bullets. **1888** *Sheffield Gloss.*, *Fash*, a burr or roughness on anything.

Hence **fash** *a.*, hairy.

1877 *Holderness Gloss.*, 'His legs is varry fash.'

fash (fæʃ), *v.*[1] Chiefly *Sc.* and *north. dial.* Also 6–7 fasch(e, fashe (? 6 fach). [a. OFr. *fascher* (Fr. *fâcher*).]

1. *trans.* To afflict, annoy, trouble, vex. Also, to give trouble to, bother, weary. Also *refl.* and *to fash one's beard, head, thumb*: to take trouble.

1533 BELLENDEN *Livy* v. (1822) 393 The Veanis war sa faschit be continuall ambicioun and desire of honouris. **1556** J. HEYWOOD *Spider & F.* lvii. 128 Behold.. How thordinance lieth flies fer and ner to fach..how euerie peece ..Hath a spider gonner with redy fired mach. **1637** RUTHERFORD *Lett.* cxlv. (1862) I. 342 Fash Christ (if I may speak so) and importune Him. **1723** *Wodrow Corr.* (1843) III. 45 Be not fashed if you miss a letter. **1725** RAMSAY *Gent. Sheph.* III. ii, Howe'er I get them, never fash your beard. **1823** GALT *Entail* III. ii. 21 Ne'er fash your head wi' your father's dodrums. **1824** SCOTT *Redgauntlet* Let. xi, 'Never fash yoursel' wi' me..but look to yoursel'.' **1861** RAMSAY *Remin.* Ser. II. 125 What gars your horse's tail wag that way?

it's fashed wi a wakeness. **1871** C. GIBBON *Lack of Gold* ii, He..never fashed his thumb about his debt. **1874** HELPS *Soc. Press.* iv. (1875) 60 People fash themselves about..dim and distant dangers. **1876** *Whitby Gloss.* s.v., 'Deeant fash your beard anent it.'

2. *intr.* for *refl.* To weary, be annoyed; to bother or trouble oneself; to take trouble. Const. *of.*

1585 JAMES I. *Ess. Poesie* (Arb.) 74 Then woundred I.. how they did them selfis so farr begyle, To fashe of tyme. **1597** MONTGOMERIE *Cherrie & Slae* 597 Of our fellowschip ȝou fasche. *Ibid.* 1435 For feir folk maun not fash. **1721** J. KELLY *Collect. Scot. Proverbs* 390 You soon fash of a good office. *a* **1810** TANNAHILL *Poems* (1846) 70 Wha..wad fash to scribble, Expecting scorn for a' his trouble? **1821** GALT *Ann. Parish Dalmailing* 229 The dinner was a little longer of being on the table than usual, at which he began to fash. **1886** STEVENSON *Kidnapped* xviii. 178 'They didnae stop to fash with me!'

Hence **fashed**, *ppl. a.* Troubled, worried.

1597 MONTGOMERIE *Cherrie & Slae* 296 The mair I wrestlit with the wynd, The faschter still myself I fynd.

fash (fæʃ), *v.*² *dial.* [f. FASH *sb.*²] To cut off the tops (of turnips, etc.).

1882 *Lanc. Gloss.*, *Fash*, to pare, to cut off. **1884** *Chesh. Gloss.*, Fashing turnips is generally done by piecework.

fashen. *Sc.* Also feshen, foshen. [pa. pple. of FETCH *v.*]

1768 ROSS *Helenore* iii. 123 Just as their ain, she's fashen up, an' ta'en For Dick's ae dather, now by ilka ane.

fashery ('fæʃərɪ). *Sc.* and *north.* Also 6 fascherie, -ery, (faschrie, fashrie), 7–9 fasherie. [ad. OF. *fascherie* (Fr. *fâcherie*), f. *fascher* (*fâcher*) to FASH.] Annoyance, trouble, vexation, worry; also something that causes worry. *rare* in *pl.*

1553 Q. KENNEDY *Compend. Tractive*, We geve nocht occasioun of fascherie to the Redare. **16..** in *Poet. Misc.* (1845) 33 My muse began to tire, Through daily faschery of my owne affaires. *a* **1605** MONTGOMERIE *Sonn.* v. 3 With frostis of fashrie frozen is that heet. **1621** MOLLE *Camerar. Liv. Libr.* III. vi. 167 Fence the mind from the fasheries and troubles that molest it. **1725** *Wodrow Corr.* (1843) III. 173 Nobody gives you so much fashery. **1820** SCOTT *Monast.* iv, You kirk-folk make sic a fasherie. **1876** *Whitby Gloss.*, *Fashery*, all kinds of 'botheration'. **1882** STEVENSON *Men & Bks.* 389 Not without some cross and fashery of mind and body.

fashion ('fæʃən), *sb.* Forms: 4 facioun, -un(e, 4–5 fasoun (4 -zoun), 4–6 *Sc.* fassoun, (-s)sowne), 5–6 facion(e, -cyon, -oun, (-ssion, -oun, -s)syon(e, 5 fasceon, -schyoun, 6 facon, -son, -sson(e, fastyon, fachion, -scyon, -shin, -sshon, -s)shyon, -szshion, fayssyon), 6– fashion. [a. OF. *façon*, *fazon*, ONF. *fachon* (mod. Fr. *façon*) = Pr. *faisso*, It. *fazione* (the Sp. *faccion* is of learned origin):—L. *factiōn-em*, n. of action f. *facĕre* to make: see FACTION *sb.*]

†**1.** The action or process of making. Hence, the 'making' or workmanship as an element in the value of plate or jewellery. *Obs.*

1463 *Mann. & Househ. Exp.* 154 Ffor the fasyon of the same schene, v. marc. **1575–6** *Act 18 Eliz.* c. 15 This they [Goldsmythes] take not above the rate of xij d. for the ounce of Golde (besides the fashion). **1590** SHAKS. *Com. Err.* IV. i. 29 The..chargefull fashion..doth amount to three odde Duckets more. **1594** T. B. *La Primaud. Fr. Acad.* II. 393 Of the fashion of a childe in the wombe, and how the members are framed. **1664** PEPYS *Diary* (1879) III. 62 They judge the fashion to be worth above 5*s.* per oz. more. **1761–2** HUME *Hist. Eng.* (1806) III. App. iii. 630, 14 or 15 thousand pounds weight [of silver plate], which, besides the fashion, would be [etc.].

2. a. Make, build, shape. Hence, in wider sense, visible characteristics, appearance. Said both of material and of immaterial things. *arch.* † *out of fashion*: out of shape.

Some of the earlier instances may belong to 2 c.

a **1300** *Cursor M.* 22322 (Cott.) Fair in faciun for to sei. *c* **1320** *Sir Beues* 2155 Me wolde þenke be his fasoun, þat hit were Beues of Hamtoun. *c* **1350** *Will. Palerne* 402 A dere damisele..of all fasoun þe fairest. **14..** *Tundale's Vis.* 2062 A crowne Off gold that was of semyly faschyown. **1440** *Promp. Parv.* 150/2 Fassyone, or factyone, forme of makynge, *forma, formefactura, formefactio.* *c* **1511** *1st Eng. Bk. Amer.* (Arb.) Introd. 35/1 There be dyuers people of fason in our lande..there be people that haue the body of a man and the hede lyke a dogge. **1526** TINDALE *Luke* xii. 56 Ye can skyll of the fassion of the erth, and of the skye. **1551** ROBINSON tr. *More's Utop.* I. (Arb.) 31 Vnder the line equinoctiall..all thynges bee..out of fassyon, and comelinesse. **1562** TURNER *Herbal* II. 85 a, Phalaris..hath a sede..whyte in fasshon. **1581** MULCASTER *Positions* xxx. (1887) 111 If the infirmitie in fashion be casuall..exercise.. will make that streight, which was croked. **1611** BIBLE *Luke* ix. 29 The fashion of his countenance was altered. **1615** CROOKE *Body of Man* 20 He inquireth into the nature and fashion of euery Bone. *a* **1661** FULLER *Worthies* (1840) II. 261 This county, in fashion, is like a bended bow. **1784** COWPER *Task* I. 21 A massy slab, in fashion square or round. **1793** BURKE *Rem. Policy Allies* Wks. 1842 I. 591 The fashion of some constitution which suited with their fancies. **1865** SWINBURNE *Poems & Ball., Before Parting* 21, I know..The fashion of fair temples tremulous With tender blood. **1877** L. MORRIS *Epic Hades* II. 221, I knew not The fashion of his nature.

†**b.** Spoken of as an attribute, that may be imparted and possessed; form as opposed to matter.

1576 LAMBARDE *Peramb. Kent* (1826) p. v, The craftesman that bringeth it to fashion. **1577** B. GOOGE *Heresbach's Husb.* IV. (1586) 185 b, The..common sort [of bees] when they begin to have fashion, are called Nimphes. **1594** T. B. *La Primaud. Fr. Acad.* II. 394 The seede..receiueth not fashion presently vpon the conception, but remaineth for a time without any figure. **1614** BP. HALL *Recoll. Treat.* 897 When wee have matter, wee can give fashion: thou gavest a being to the matter, without forme.

†**c.** Face, features. *Obs.*

[A very common use in OF.; perh. associated with *face.*]

c **1300** *Cursor M.* 21319 (Cott.) Matheu o man he has facium, Luce has of ox. *c* **1430** *Pilgr. Lyf Manhode* III. xxxviii. (1869) 155 She shadwde hire visage and hire facioun vnder hire hood.

3. a. A particular make, shape, style, or pattern. Somewhat *arch.*

c **1325** *Song Merci* 41 in *E.E.P.* (1862) 119, I made þe Mon ..Of feture liche myn owne fasoun. *a* **1450** *Le Morte Arth.* 2531 Galeis grete of fele fasowne. **1522** *Bury Wills* (Camden) 116 A quarte wyne pott of the olde fasshon. **1576** FLEMING *Panopl. Epist.* 299 Two standing cuppes of silver, differing from the fashion of this time. **1611** BIBLE *Transl. Pref.* 9 The very Romane Seruice was of two fashions, the New fashion, and the Old. **1699** DAMPIER *Voy.* II. I. 62 Besides, our fashions of Utensils differ mightily from theirs. **1714** J. FORTESCUE-ALAND *Pref. Fortescue's Abs. & Lim. Mon.* 32 The Author..puts in his Franco-Germanick, of the Latin fashion. **1848** MACAULAY *Hist. Eng.* I. 464 A limited monarchy after the modern fashion. **1849** JAMES *Woodman* iv, Spreading out at the edges in the fashion of a basin.

b. *esp.* with reference to attire: a particular 'cut' or style. Cf. 8 c, 9.

1529 *Supplic. to King* (E.E.T.S.) 52 Somtyme cappe, somtyme hoode; nowe the Frenshe fasshyon, nowe the Spanyshe fasshyon. **1605** SHAKS. *Lear* III. vi. 84, I do not like the fashion of your garments. *a* **1674** CLARENDON *Surv. Leviath.* (1676) 81 To wear his Clothes of that fashion which he likes best. **1838** LYTTON *Alice* 6 Her dress..of no very modern fashion.

†**c.** A device, material or immaterial. *Obs.*

1560 WHITEHORNE *Arte Warre* (1573) bij a, Against this fashion they haue used to make a fashion like unto a paire of sheres. **1597** MONTGOMERIE *Cherrie & Slae* 1363 Se first quhat fashion may be fund To pacifie his pains.

4. Kind, sort. Now *rare.* Also † *in fashion to*: of a kind to.

1562 TURNER *Herbal* II. 73 b, Suche fasshon of figure is not in a Mirt-berry. **1591** SHAKS. *Two Gent.* v. iv. 61 Thou friend of an ill fashion. **1596** —— *Merch. V.* I. ii. 23 This reason is not in fashion to choose me a husband. **1608** —— *Per.* IV. ii. 84 Gentlemen of all fashions. **1611** COTGR., *Panier*..a fashion of Trunke made of Wicker. **1874** MORLEY *Compromise* (1886) 87 Consider the difference between these two fashions of compromise.

5. a. Manner, mode, way, *esp.* in *after,* †*of, in,* †*on, this, such a, my, his,* etc. *fashion.* rare in *pl.*

13.. *E.E. Allit. P.* A. 1100, & coronde wern alle of þe same fasoun. **1375** BARBOUR *Bruce* XVII. 300 Palȝeonis Be stentit on syndry fassownys. *c* **1489** CAXTON *Sonnes of Aymon* xiv. 351 To hevy a bourdon for to lede of this facyon. **1539** in *Vicary's Anat.* (1888) App. iii. 173 [They] passed through the Cytie in good ordre after A warlike facion. **1567–83** *Sempill Ball.* 98 Ay selling caill, The best fassoun I may. **1602** SHAKS. *Ham.* I. iii. 111 He hath importun'd me with loue, In honourable fashion. **1633** BP. HALL *Hard Texts* 358 We doe, in all fashions of sorrow bemoane ourselves. **1654** tr. *Scudery's Curia Pol.* 7, I have governed my Subjects in such a fashion that [etc.]. **1715** DE FOE *Fam. Instruct.* I. v. (1841) I. 109 After quite another fashion. **1822** LAMB *Elia* Ser. I. *Distant Corr.*, Subjects serious in themselves, but treated after my fashion, non-seriously. **1860** TYNDALL *Glac.* I. viii. 58 In zigzag fashion..I continued to ascend.

b. In depreciatory sense, *after, in, a* or *some fashion*: somehow or another, in a sort, tolerably, not too well.

1614 BP. HALL *Recoll. Treat.* 459 Whom yet Rome harbors, and, in a fashion, graces. **1860** G. MACDONALD *Ann. Q. Neighb.* i. (1878) 5 Work..which I can do after some fashion. **1869** TROLLOPE *He Knew* xvi. (1878) 89 Providence..has made me a lady after a fashion.

†**c.** A method of doing anything. *Obs.*

1556 *Aurelio & Isab.* (1608) K viij, And this is the fachone be the whiche al the reames and dominions..I presently do posseade, have beane gotten. **1577** B. GOOGE *Heresbach's Husb.* I. (1586) 42 b, To wynnowe it after the olde fashion with the winde. **1614** BP. HALL *Recoll. Treat.* 404 To say nothing of the fashion of their Cures. **1674** PLAYFORD *Skill Mus.* I. xi. 39 A good fashion of singing. **1743** *Lond. & Country Brew.* II. (ed. 2) 134 He would I believe alter his Mind and Fashion.

6. a. Mode of action, bearing, behaviour, demeanour, 'air'. Now *rare.*

1447 BOKENHAM *Seyntys* (Roxb.) 29 Be what similat facyoun Meche peple to his favour he drew. *a* **1535** MORE *De Quat. Noviss.* Wks. 76/1 With som good grace and pleasant fashion. **1601** ? MARSTON *Pasquil & Kath.* I. 237 He..takes a whiffe with gracefull fashion. **1719** D'URFEY *Pills* (1872) IV. 304 She keeps her cruel Fashion. **1851** THACKERAY *Eng. Hum.* ii. (1858) 81 With such a grace, with such a fashion.

b. *pl.* Actions, gestures, 'ways'. Now *rare.*

1569 J. ROGERS *Gl. Godly Loue* 182 With spiteful wordes and wanton fashions. **1580** NORTH *Plutarch* (1676) 28 He.. gave himself in fashions to be somewhat like a Tyrant. **1605** BACON *Adv. Learn.* II. ix. 37 Whose eyes do dwell on the faces and fashions. **1852** MRS. STOWE *Uncle Tom's C.* xxxvi, He shall beg my pardon, and promise better fashions.

†**7.** Outward action or ceremony; a mere form, pretence. *Obs.* exc. in Sc. phrase, *to make fashion*: to make a show, pretend.

1571 GOLDING *Calvin on Ps.* xl. 7 Worshipping God slyghtly for fashyon sake. **1596** SHAKS. *Merch. V.* IV. i. 18 Thou but leadest this fashion of thy mallice To the last houre of act. **1637** RUTHERFORD *Lett.* No. 119 (1862) I. 296 The memory of his love maketh me think Christ's glooms are but for the fashion. **1653** URQUHART *Rabelais* II. xxii, Panurge made the fashion of driving them [i.e. dogs] away. **1816** SCOTT *Antiq.* xvi, He..only just pits a bit on the plate to make fashion.

8. a. A prevailing custom, a current usage; *esp.* one characteristic of a particular place or period of time.

c **1489** CAXTON *Sonnes of Aymon* xxvi. 544 A knighte.. presented..a fayr knyff, after the facyon of the londe. **1583** STUBBES *Anat. Abus.* D vij, How unseemelie..a fashion that is, let the wise judge. **1599** SHAKS. *Much Ado* I. i. 98 The fashion of the world is to auoid cost. **1614** BP. HALL *Recoll. Treat.* 870 Ingenuously, as his fashion is. **1764** GOLDSM. *Trav.* 279 The mind still turns where shifting fashion draws. **1814** SCOTT *Ld. of Isles* III. xxiv, Let every man Follow the fashion of his clan! **1821** J. Q. ADAMS in C. Davies *Metr. Syst.* III. (1871) 125 The old fashion of 140 gallons..to the butt..was then restored. *a* **1839** PRAED *Poems* (1864) I. 366 New follies come, new faults, new fashions. **1876** MOZLEY *Univ. Serm.* i. 7 As a fashion of thought the idea..has.. passed away.

†**b.** In *pl.* often = 'Manners and customs' (of nations), 'ways' (of men); chiefly in phrases, *to know, learn, see (the) fashions.* Obs.

1555 WATERMAN (*title*) The fardle of facions. **1599** MINSHEU *Dial. Sp. & Eng.* (1623) 36, I will dye and live with thee Peter, for thou knowest fashions. **1658–9** *Burton's Diary* (1828) IV. 164 Any that come among you to see fashions. *a* **1716** SOUTH *Serm.* (1737) VI. v. 196 To see the country, and to learn fashions (as the word goes). **1721** STRYPE *Eccl. Mem.* II. II. v. 287 The king had sent him [Barnaby Fitz-Patric] thither to remain in his [the French king's] court to learn fashions.

c. *spec.* with regard to apparel or personal adornment.

1547 BOORDE *Introd. Knowl.* xiv. (1870) 159, I wyll not chaunge my olde fathers fashyon. **1576** PETTIE *Pal. Pleas.*, New fashions in cutting of beardes. **1596** SHAKS. *Tam. Shr.* III. ii. 72 'Tis some od humor pricks him to this fashion, Yet oftentimes he goes but meane apparel'd. **1654** WHITLOCK *Zootomia* 225 Fashions crosse the Seas as oft as the Packet Boat. **1713** STEELE *Guardian* No. 10 ¶4 An opportunity to introduce fashions amongst our young gentlemen. **1833** HT. MARTINEAU *Brooke Farm* viii. 105 To dress themelves in Miss Black's fashions. **1859** JEPHSON *Brittany* xv. 241 A tall stout man, dressed in country fashion. **1865** WRIGHT *Hist. Caricature* vi. (1875) 103 During the feudal ages, the fashions in France and England were always identical.

9. a. Conventional usage in dress, mode of life, etc., *esp.* as observed in the upper circles of society; conformity to this usage. Often personified, or quasi-personified.

(The first quot. may belong to 2 or 6.)

1602 SHAKS. *Ham.* III. i. 161 The glasse of Fashion, and the mould of Forme. **1632** LITHGOW *Trav.* v. 205, I am.. become a courtly Tobacconist; more for fashion then for liking. **1711** SHAFTESB. *Charac.* (1737) III. 288 The man of quality..must, for fashion-sake, appear in love. **1739** CIBBER *Apol.* (1756) I. 71 Taste and fashion with us have always had wings. **1781** COWPER *Expostulation* 38 As Int'rest biass'd knaves, or fashion fools. **1793** BEDDOES *Catarrh* 169 To break the spell of Fashion would be an atchievement. **1806** *Med. Jrnl.* XV. 91 Fashion, that destroying angel. **1829** LYTTON *Devereux* II. vii, Some better object to worship than the *capricieuse* of fashion. **1865** *Pall Mall G.* 1 Aug. 10/2 Fashion and *bon ton* are by no means the same thing. **1892** *Daily News* 23 Apr. 3/5 Fashion is the all-absorbing subject.

b. Fashionable people; the fashionable world.

1807–8 W. IRVING *Salmag.* (1824) 161 Days..When heart met heart in fashion's hall. **1873** BROWNING *Red Cott. Nt.-cap* 125 Paris fashion's blame.

c. high fashion (chiefly *attrib.*), haute couture; also *transf.*

1958 *Sunday Times* 19 Oct. 25/1 'Line for line' copies of French models are the current high fashion rage in New York. **1959** *Observer* 22 Mar. 3/8 Now that high fashion has overtaken the circular, manufacturers have two kinds of worry. **1959** *News Chron.* 10 Aug. 6/5 The high-fashion hats seen in Paris. **1963** *Listener* 28 Feb. 370/1 The Educational Board of the R.I.B.A. now finds its stodgy, nineteenth-century type syllabus at least partly in tune with the high fashion of the day.

10. *the fashion*: **a.** The mode of dress, etiquette, furniture, style of speech, etc., adopted in society for the time being. *to lead, set the fashion*: to be an example in dress, etc., for others to follow. *to be in the fashion*: to adopt the accepted style.

1568 GRAFTON *Chron.* II. 34 A scarlet Robe with a hoode (as the fashion then was). **1601** ? MARSTON *Pasquil & Kath.* I. 276 Her loue is..as vnconstant as the fashion. **1604** JAS. I *Counterbl.* (Arb.) 105 It is come to be the fashion. **1612** ROWLANDS *Knaue of Harts* 13 Let vs haue standing Collers, in the fashion. **1710** STEELE *Tatler* No. 77 ¶1 Alexander the Great had a wry Neck, which made it the Fashion in his Court, to carry their Heads on one Side. **1762** GOLDSM. *Nash* 10 Several persons qualified to lead the fashion both by birth and fortune. **1794** NELSON in Nicolas *Disp.* (ed. 2) I. 474 It is the fashion to say it would have been difficult to make a breach. **1838** DE MORGAN *Ess. Probab.* Pref. 7 It was then very much the fashion..to publish results and conceal methods. **1840** DICKENS *Barn. Rudge* xvi, The fashion being of course set by the upper class.

b. The person or thing that it is fashionable to admire or discuss.

1790–1811 COMBE *Devil upon Two Sticks* (1817) II. 217, I should not be tempted to marry him, if he were not the fashion. **1824** MEDWIN *Convers. Byron* (1832) I. 55, I was the fashion when she first came out. **1837** MISS MITFORD in L'Estrange *Life* III. v. 78 Another book..is much the fashion.

11. *in, out of (the) fashion*: in, out of, vogue or customary use, *esp.* in polite society; according or contrary to the customary rule or standard. Also *to bring, come, grow into, go out of fashion.*

1601 SHAKS. *Jul. C.* v. v. 5 Slaying is the word, It is a deed in fashion. **1601** —— *All's Well* I. i. 170 Virginitie like an olde Courtier, weares her cap out of fashion. **1603** FLORIO *Montaigne* (1632) 505 The Hungarians did very availefully bring them [war-coaches] into fashion. **1608** W. SCLATER *Malachy* (1650) 103 Sins, when they are grown into fashion, are swallowed up as no sins. **1614** BP. HALL *Recoll. Treat.* 684 Shall nothing but our soules be out of the fashion? **1630** *R. Johnson's Kingd. & Commw.* 55 Let him..take heed, that the apparell he weares, be in fashion in the place where he resideth. **1719** D'URFEY *Pills* (1872) V. 154 Would you be a man in Fashion? **1728** W. CLELAND *Let. Publisher Pope's Dunciad* 19 Out of power, or out of fashion. **1782** PRIESTLEY *Corrupt. Chr.* II. IX. 157 Solitary pilgrimages were..much in fashion. **1848** MACAULAY *Hist. Eng.* I. 179 The decorous gravity which had been thirty years before in fashion at Whitehall. **1850** *Tait's Mag.* XVII. 532 1 Little dogs that had come into fashion. **1880** MISS BRADDON *Just as I am* vii, Aunt Dora's gowns..were always in the fashion.

12. (*man, woman*) *of fashion*: †**a.** (In early use often more fully *of high, great, good fashion.*) Of high quality or breeding, of eminent social standing or repute. [Cf. sense 4 and OF. *gens de (bonne) façon.*] This gradually merges into the current sense b. That moves in upper-class society, and conforms to its rules with regard to dress, expenditure, and habits.

c **1489** CAXTON *Blanchardyn* xlviii. 187 They..defended theym vygoryously, as men of highe facion. **1597** SIR R. CECIL in Ellis *Orig. Lett.* I. 234 III. 43 A Gentleman of excellent fashion. *a* **1618** RALEIGH *Apol.* 7 It is strange that men of fashion and Gentlemen should so grosly bely their owne knowledge. *c* **1675** *Househ. Ord.* 354 Persons of good fashion..that have a desire to see us at dinner. **1702** W. J. *Bruyn's Voy. Levant* x. 37 Greeks of Fashion, who are not for herding with the Populace. **1752** HUME *Ess. & Treat.* (1777) I. 204 Augustus was obliged..to force men of fashion into the married state. **1755** E. MOORE in *World* No. 151 (1772) III. 278 A woman cannot be a woman of fashion till she has lost her reputation. **1766** GOLDSM. *Vic. W.* xxi, Intimacy with people of the best fashion. **1800** MRS. HERVEY *Mourtray Fam.* II. 76 A person of her fashion and figure. **1824** MEDWIN *Convers. Byron* (1832) II. 50, I..was in favour with Brummell (and that was alone enough to make a man of fashion).

13. *attrib.* and *Comb.* **a.** Simple attrib. *fashion-artist, -designer, -journal, -letter, magazine, mania, -model* (so *-modelling* vbl. sb.), *show*; *fashion-conscious* adj.

1903 A. BENNETT *Truth about Author* x. 120, I could instruct a *fashion-artist. **1951** M. MCLUHAN *Mech. Bride* 75/2 Mallarmé and Joyce refused to be distracted by the *fashion-conscious sirens of contents and subject matter. **1960** *Guardian* 15 July 8/2 The fashion-conscious visitor to Paris. **1909** *Westm. Gaz.* 15 Mar. 5/1 The very red about which *fashion-designers are decided. **1905** E. WHARTON *House of Mirth* II. ix. 432 The newspapers, the *fashion-journals. **1894** E. L. SHUMAN *Steps into Journalism* 154 Jennie June..who is known all over the country for her syndicate *fashion letters. **1903** A. BENNETT *Truth about Author* x. 120 A Paris fashion-letter. **1879** M. E. BRADDON *Vixen* II. xiv. 256 Your *trousseau* should be..described in the *fashion magazines. **1966** H. YOXALL *Fashion of Life* viii. 75 The majority of middle-aged women still have distressingly little sense of style... For them the fashion magazines might just as well not exist. **1829** *Westm. Rev.* XI. 399 This practice of blushing for unmodish friends.. belongs to the *fashion-mania. **1962** *John o' London's* 22 Mar. 291/1 An ageing *fashion-model. **1970** P. MOYES *Who saw her Die?* i. 12 She was thirty-three years old, with the figure of a fashion model. **1964** C. BARBER *Present-Day Eng.* v. 118 *Fashion-modelling has been built up..as the ideal career. **1938** *Collier's* 8 Jan. 13 This is, believe it or not, a *fashion show.

†**b.** Forming with preceding adj. a quasi-adj. or adjectival phrase. *Obs.*

1677 HALE *Prim. Orig. Man.* I. i. 4 What fashion Cloaths the Roman officers..used. **1712** E. COOKE *Voy. S. Sea* 85 The great Square..has old Fashion Houses on the East and South Sides.

c. Forming with a preceding sb. or adj. an adverbial phrase. Cf. -WISE.

[**1494** FABYAN *Chron.* VII. 313 He had deuysed newe engynes after towerre facion.] **1633** P. FLETCHER *Purple Isl.* IV. xxxii, Made like an Ivie leaf, broad-angle-fashion. **1670** NARBOROUGH *Jrnl.* in *Acc. Sev. Late Voy.* I. (1711) 66 Flint stones, neatly made broad Arrow-fashion. **1710** *Lond. Gaz.* No. 4748/4 A Silver Hungary Water Bottle Flask fashion gilt. **1721** BAILEY, *Capon Fashion* [in Archery], the same as Bob-tail. **1796** MRS. GLASSE *Cookery* xviii. 295 Take the leg of a..small beef..and cut it ham-fashion. **1809–12** MAR. EDGEWORTH *Absentee* ix, Laying the outer-most part of your feather this fashion next to your hook. **1867** FREEMAN *Norm. Conq.* (1876) I. App. 624 The tardy bridal was done Christian fashion. **1886** R. C. LESLIE *Sea-painter's Log* 216 Picked up the puppy, holding it baby fashion in his arms.

d. objective, as *fashion-following* sb., *fashion-fancying* adj.; instrumental, as *fashion-bound, -driven, -favoured, -fettered, -led, -minded, -ridden* adjs.

1949 KOESTLER *Insight & Outlook* xxi. 297 Implicit, sophisticated, or *fashion-bound forms of artistic expression. **1891** KIPLING *Light that Failed* iv. 69 The easy applause of a *fashion-driven public. **1896** *Westm. Gaz.* 2 July 4/3 *Fashion-favoured stuffs. **1647** WARD *Simp. Cobler* 25 These *fashion-fansying wits Are empty thinbrain'd shells. **1887** *Pall Mall G.* 26 Sept. 11/2 *Fashion-fettered fops. **1621** S. WARD *Happin. Pract.* (1627) 43 Sabbath-breaking, and *fashion-following. **1784** COWPER *Tiroc.* 779 Whom do I advise? the *fashion-led. **1938** *Chatelaine* Oct. 2/1 The upward sweep has become of intense importance to the *fashion-minded. **1940** *Manch. Guardian Weekly* 30 Aug. 142 British manufacturers are continually producing new samples to meet the requirements of the most fashion-minded overseas wearers. **1897** G. B. SHAW *Let.* 28 May (1965) 770 The silly visionary *fashion-ridden theatres.

14. Special comb.: **fashion-book**, a book describing and illustrating new fashions in dress; **fashion-fly**, *fig.* one who sports in the beams of fashion; **fashion house**, a business establishment for the display and sale of high-quality clothes; **fashion-paper**, a journal of fashionable life; esp. a journal specializing in current fashions in dress; **fashion-picture**, a representation of fashionable costumes; **fashion piece**, *Naut.* (see quots.); **fashion plate**, 'a pictorial design showing the prevailing style or new style of dress' (W.); also applied to other kinds of fashionable display; **fashion-timber**, = *fashion-piece*. Also FASHION-MONGER.

1840 *Fiddle Faddle Fashion Book* 8/1 To depart from *Fashion* in a *Fashion-Book* is so shocking a thing that we tremble at the very idea of it. **1853** MRS. GASKELL *Cranford* vii. 134 Three or four handsomely bound fashion-books ten or twelve years old. **1907** B. M. CROKER *Company's Servant* viii. 74, I have brought back..a fashion-book, ribbons, gloves, and lots of sweets. **1868** LD. HOUGHTON *Select. fr. Wks.* 63 Many a careless *fashion-fly. **1958** *London Mag.* Dec. 33 A woman of character and elegance who ran a *fashion house on one of the streets near Central Park. **1970** D. WHEATLEY *Gateway to Hell* iv. 44 She..became the top model in a leading fashion house. **1885** E. D. GERARD *Waters Hercules* xxx, She snatched up the *fashion-paper. **1901** F. H. BURNETT *Making of Marchioness* I. i. 4 You might get on to one of the second-class fashion-papers to answer ridiculous questions about house-keeping or wall-papers or freckles. **1913** KIPLING *Lett. of Trav.* (1920) 246 She showed me what looked like a fashion-paper print of a dress-stuff. **1925** L. P. SMITH *Words & Idioms* iii. 127 Even in fashion-papers we read of 'creations' in millinery. **1884** *Sat. Rev.* 14 June 780/1 The subject..is a mere *fashion-picture. **1627** CAPT. SMITH *Seaman's Gram.* ii. 2. From it [the Stern-post] doth rise the two *fashion peeces, like a paire of great hornes. **1704** J. HARRIS *Lex. Techn., Fashion-pieces* are those two Timbers which describe the breadth of the Ship at the Stern. **1830** MARRYAT *King's Own* xlix, My..fashion pieces were framed out. *c* **1850** *Rudim. Navig.* (Weale) 117 *Fashion-pieces*, the timbers..fashioning the after-part of the ship in the plane of projection, by terminating the breadth and forming the shape of the stern. **1851** A. O. HALL *Manhattaner* 21 She unrolls the *fashion plate. **1859** L. WILMER *Press Gang* 332 Fashion-plate magazines. **1864** WEBSTER, *Fashion plate.* **1891** *Stamp Collector* Dec. 48 The latest philatelic 'fashion plates' tell us that the new idea of collecting postal cards is to collect them direct from the countries issuing them. **1908** *Westm. Gaz.* 26 May 4/2 Altering the outline of each new season's model, with the result that the preceding ones are..rendered old-fashioned. .. We do not want the fashion-plate methods to become general amongst motor-constructors. **1967** D. YARWOOD *Eng. Costume* (ed. 3) viii. 211 We now have innumerable fashion plates and magazines.

fashion ('fæʃən), *v.* Forms: 5 facioun, 6 facion, -yon, fation, fasshion, 7 fashon, 6– fashion. [f. prec. sb.; cf. F. *façonner.*]

1. *trans.* To give fashion or shape to; to form, mould, shape (either a material or immaterial object). Also, *to fashion out.*

1413 LYDG. *Pilgr. Sowle* IV. xxx. (1483) 78 That this statua be faciound duely and fourmed as it sholde. *c* **1500** *Melusine* 50 Tentes..so meruayllously facyoned. **1551** T. WILSON *Logike* (1580) 45 Leather when it is made or fashioned for the foote, is called a Shoe. **1608** D. T. *Ess. Pol. & Mor.* 66 b, To polish and fashion out his then rough-hewen fortune. **1611** BIBLE *Job* xxxi. 15 Did not one fashion vs in the wombe? **1690** LOCKE *Hum. Underst.* II. ii. §2 Every one.. who shall go about to fashion in his Understanding any simple Idea. **1697** DRYDEN *Virgil, Life* (1721) I. 41 A course Stone is presently fashion'd. **1713** GAY *Fan* I. 112 *Poems* (1720) I. 35 Here the loud hammer fashions female toys. **1812** H. & J. SMITH *Rej. Addr.* (1813) 83 Our stage is so prettily fashion'd for viewing. **1838** LYTTON *Alice* 28 Young people fashion and form each other. **1863** LYELL *Antiq. Man* 18 Fragments of rude pottery, fashioned by the hand. **1878** *Musque Poets* 76 The wish I might have fashioned died In dreams.

†**b.** Said of the constituent parts of anything.

1668 CULPEPPER & COLE *Barthol. Anat.* I. xx. 51 A Cavity fashioned by the *Os sacrum*, the Hip and Share-bones.

†**c.** To make good-looking; to beautify. *Obs.*

1557 *N.T.* (Genev.) Epist. **j, He was disfigured to fashion vs, he dyed for our life.

2. a. To form, frame, make. *rare.*

c **1549** *Hist. Lucres* A ij b, Her browes bente, facioned with fewe heares. **1608** D. T. *Ess. Pol. & Mor.* 46 b, Favonnus.. had reason..to fashion them this reply. **1840** CARLYLE *Heroes* (1858) 304 Many have to perish, fashioning a path through the impassable. **1863** LONGF. *Wayside Inn* Prel. 275 The instrument..was fashioned of maple and of pine. **1880** E. KIRKE *Garfield* 13 Bringing his saw and jackplane again into play, he fashioned companies..out of maple blocks.

†**b.** To contrive, manage. *Obs.*

c **1540** *Pilgr. T.* 79 in Thynne *Animadv.* App. i. 79 Then could he fation in the best wyce many a deynte dyche. **1590** SHAKS. *Mids. N.* III. ii. 194 They haue conioyned..To fashion this false sport. **1596** —— *1 Hen. IV*, I. iii. 297 You, and Dowglas..As I will fashion it, shall happily meete. **1604** —— *Oth.* IV. ii. 242 His going thence, which I will fashion to fall out betweene twelue and one.

3. To give a specified shape to; to model *according to, after,* or *like* (something); to form †*into* (the shape of something); to shape *into* or *to* (something). Also *refl.* and †*intr.* for *refl.*

1526 TINDALE *Rom.* viii. 29 Fasshioned unto the shape of his sonne. *a* **1585** ABP. SANDYS *Serm.* (1841) 421 We are exhorted to fashion ourselves according to that similitude and likeness which is in him. **1599** SHAKS. *Much Ado* III. iii. 142 Fashioning them [the Hotblouds] like Pharaoes souldiours. **1634** SIR T. HERBERT *Trav.* 151 Coines.. fashioned like point-aglets. **1672–3** GREW *Anat. Plants* II. ii. §31 The Mould; about which, the other more passive Principles gathering themselves, they all consort and fashion to it. **1774** J. BRYANT *Mythol.* I. 467 This they fashioned to a conical figure. **1796** H. HUNTER tr. *St. Pierre's Stud. Nat.* (1799) II. 149 Some of them are fashioned into the figure of shells. **1809** PINKNEY *Trav. France* 242 Chairs fashioned according to the designs. **1866** ROGERS *Agric. & Prices* I. xx. 508 A smith to fashion his steel into picks or awls. **1872** BAGEHOT *Physics & Pol.* (1876) 216 Communities which are fashioned after the structure of the elder world.

b. With complement or complementary obj.

1591 SHAKS. *1 Hen. VI*, III. iii. 65 When Talbot hath.. fashion'd thee that Instrument of Ill. **1605** —— *Lear* I. ii. 200 All with me's meete, that I can fashion fit.

†**4.** To change the fashion of; to modify, transform. With compl. *like*, or const. *to*. *Obs.*

1528 TINDALE *Obed. Chr. Man* 97 b, When a man fealeth ..him selfe..altered and fascioned lyke vnto Christe. **1547** *Homilies* I *Falling from God* I. 1859 84 Be fashioned to him in all goodness requisite to the children of God. **1576** FLEMING *Panopl. Epist.* 382 Fashion yourselfe to sobernesse. *a* **1592** H. SMITH *Serm.* (1866) 312 Fashion thyself to Paul. **1601** SHAKS. *Jul. C.* II. i. 220 Send him but hither, and Ile fashion him. **1611** BIBLE *Phil.* iii. 21 Who shall change our vile bodie, that it may bee fashioned like vnto his glorious body. **1753** FOOTE *Eng. in Paris* Epil. Wks. 1799 I. 31 His roughness she'll soften, his figure she'll fashion.

†**b.** To counterfeit, pervert. *Obs.*

1599 SHAKS. *Much Ado* I. iii. 31 It better fits my bloud to be disdain'd of all, then to fashion a carriage to rob loue from any. **1599** —— *Hen. V*, I. ii. 14 God forbid..That you should fashion, wrest, or bow your reading.

5. To give (a person or thing) a fashion or form suitable *to* or to do (something); to accomodate, adapt *to*. Also *refl.* and *intr.* for *refl.* Now *rare.*

1526 TINDALE *1 Cor.* ix. 22 In all thynge I fasshioned my silfe to all men. **1591** SHAKS. *Two Gent.* III. i. 135 How shall I fashion me to weare a cloake? **1599** —— *Much Ado* v. iv. 88 A halting sonnet..Fashioned to Beatrice. **1608** D. T. *Ess. Pol. & Mor.* 88 b, There are some that fashion themselves to nothing more, then how to become speculative into another. **1612** BREREWOOD *Lang. & Relig.* vi. 50 It was spoken corruptly, according as the peoples tongues would fashion to it. **1613** SHAKS. *Hen. VIII*, IV. ii. 50 This Cardinall.. fashion'd to much Honor From his Cradle. **1623** MASSINGER *Dk. Milan* II. i, Lies..fashion'd to so damnable a purpose. **1630** *R. Johnson's Kingd. & Commw.* 529 We fashion our selves to extoll the ages past. **1770** GOLDSM. *Des Vill.* 146 Doctrines fashioned to the varying hour. **1871** TYNDALL *Fragm. Sc.* (1879) II. i. 3 These priests fashioned that which they did not understand to their respective wants and wishes.

†**b.** To present the form of; to represent. *Obs.*

1590–6 SPENSER (*title*), The Faerie Queene, Disposed into twelve books fashioning XII Morall vertues.

c. *intr.* To bring oneself, 'have the face' (to do something). *dial.* (Cf. quot. 1591 in 5.)

1847 E. BRONTE *Wuthering Heights* (1858) 11 Aw wonder how yah can faishion to stand theear i' idleness. *Ibid.* 29 She did fly up, asking how he could fashion to bring that gipsy brat into the house. **1883** *Almondbury & Huddersf. Gloss.*, 'Why don't you go and ask him for it?' 'I cannot fashion'.

6. *Naut.* (See quot.) *Obs.*

1769 FALCONER *Dict. Marine* (1789) C iv b, The knees.. fashion the transoms to the ship's side. [*Ibid. supra*: The knees which connect the beams to the sides.]

fashion, var. of FARCIN *Obs.*, farcy.

fashionability (,fæʃənə'bɪlɪtɪ). [f. next: see *-bility*, -ITY.] = FASHIONABLENESS.

1839 G. DARLEY *Introd. Beaum. & Fl. Wks.* I. 30 Fashionability is a kind of elevated vulgarity. **1881** BLACK *Beautiful Wretch* I. 28 There was far too much flimsiness and fashionability about their social circle.

fashionable ('fæʃənəb(ə)l), *a.* and *sb.* [f. FASHION *v.* and *sb.* + -ABLE.]

A. *adj.*

†**1.** Capable of being fashioned, shaped, or moulded. Const. *to, unto.* Of a damaged article: Capable of being brought into shape. *Obs.*

1607 HIERON *Wks.* I. 238 Hee that..can endure the hewing, and groweth more and more fashionable vnto good things. **1611** SPEED *Hist. Gt. Brit.* IX. xvi. (1632) 835 Nine yeares olde, a most fashionable and waxen age for all impression. **1614** JACKSON *Creed* III. viii. Wks. II. 256 Peter's..power by them [keys]..to exclude all that were not fashionable to this rock and corner stone. **1623** ROWLANDSON *God's Bless.* 27 Could the iron be pliable and fashionable to the minde of the smith. **1656** in Picton *L'pool Munic. Rec.* (1883) I. 152 Some cups are broken and not fashionable.

†**b.** Conformable *to*. *Obs.*

1657 R. CARPENTER *Astrology* 15 It is most fashionable to Reason, That Job, by Musick..understands [etc.].

†**2.** Pertaining to outward form or ceremony; merely formal. *Obs.* (Cf. FASHION *sb.* 7.)

1614 BP. HALL *Recoll. Treat.* 612 A fashionable observation of the outwarde Letter. **1633** —— *Hard Texts* 110 His fashionable disciples..went away from him. *a* **1656** —— *Soliloquies* 73 Not that we should..fall suddenly into a fashionable devotion. **1616** S. WARD *Coale from Altar* (1627) 47 No maruell if his seruice be formall and fashionable. *Ibid.* 82 To confess the truth of the fashionable Christian.

†**3.** Of a good fashion or appearance; goodlooking, stylish. Also, *fashionable-like*. *Obs.*

1630 *R. Johnson's Kingd. & Commw.* 135 We have fashionable attendance. **1663** Gerbier *Counsel* D iij a, Some of them Bear-like-whelps (by licking and smoothing) have gotten some fashionable like shape. **1719** De Foe *Crusoe* I. 244 A Cap..made of a Hare-skin, very convenient and fashionable enough. **1720** *Lond. Gaz.* No. 5865/4 A light dapple grey Nag..fashionable and full aged.

4. a. Of persons: Observant of or following *the fashion*; dressing or behaving in conformity with the standard of elegance current in upper-class society.

1606 Shaks. *Tr. & Cr.* iii. iii. 165 A fashionable Hoste.. slightly shakes his parting Guest by th' hand. **1609** W. M. *Man in Moone* (1849) 42 A finicall fellow he is, and very fashionable. **1738** Chesterf. *Common Sense* 11 Feb. No. 16 Taste is now the fashionable Word of the fashionable World. **1816** *Remarks Eng. Mann.* 86 Nor do I believe a less fashionable man would have paid any attention. **1845** *Florist's Jrnl.* 139 A numerous and fashionable company. **1892** *Speaker* 30 July 141/1 Reviewers are apt to be.. slavishly fashionable in adjectives.

absol. **1790** Han. More *Relig. Fash. World* (1791) 1 The polite and the fashionable.

b. Of things, *esp.* dress: Conformable to fashion; in accordance with prevailing usage; of the kind in vogue among persons of the upper class. Of immaterial things: Approved by custom, generally accepted, current (now in depreciatory sense).

1608 W. Sclater *Malachy* (1650) 103 It..was grown so fashionable, that it seemed to be no sin. **1639** Fuller *Holy War* iii. vi. (1840) 125 His..attire more fashionable. **1650** —— *Pisgah* ii. viii. 177 Such chariots were..fashionable in their fights. **1665** Glanvill *Scep. Sci.* Add. to R. Soc. 62 The eminence of your condition will..make philosophy fashionable. **1668** Rokeby *Let.* 6 Oct. in *Mem.* (Surtees) 17 A rideing cloake of ye best worsted camlett of a fashionable sorte. **1700** Dryden *Fables, Pygmalion* 45 Fashionable robes her person deck. **1781** Gibbon *Decl. & F.* III. 229 The fashionable opinions of the court. **1823** Lamb *Elia* (1860) 157 A newer and more fashionable mansion. **1825** J. Neal *Bro. Jonathan* II. 329 A fashionable dress. **1848** Macaulay *Hist. Eng.* I. 515 Artificial ringlets clustering in fashionable profusion round his shoulders. **1866** Geo. Eliot *F. Holt* 119 His illusions..were not of a fashionable sort.

5. a. Of, pertaining to, or characteristic of persons of fashion. **b.** Treating of the world of fashion. **c.** Frequented or patronized by people of fashion.

a. 1712 Steele *Spect.* No. 504 ¶4 These rascals..carried it with a fashionable haughty air. **1790** Han. More *Relig. Fash. World* (1791) 221 That mode of life emphatically distinguished by the appellation of fashionable. **1884** J. Hall *A Chr. Home* 75 A hollow and conventional 'fashionable life'.

b. 1831 Carlyle *Sart. Res.* (1858) 169 Nor are Sacred Books wanting to the Sect [of the Dandies]; these they call Fashionable Novels. **1882** Pebody *Eng. Journal.* xi. 78 The *Morning Post*..made a name for itself by its fresh and sparkling paragraphs of Court and fashionable gossip.

c. 1815 tr. *Duc de Levis's Engl. 19th Cent.* i. 170 Ranelagh pleases them much: it is even called *fashionable* [*orig.* il recoit même l'épithète de *fashionable*]. **1838** Emerson *Nat.*, *'Lit. Ethics* Wks. (Bohn) II. 214 In fashionable or political saloons. **1839** Hood *Up the Rhine* 43 The Waal branch of the fashionable river. **1848** Dickens *Dombey* xviii, Burgess & Co.,—fashionable tailors (but very dear). **1877** Johnston *Dict. Geog.* 1234/1 Scarborough..is now the most fashionable watering-place on the N.E. coast. **1881** Lady Herbert *Edith* 1 And drew up at a door in a fashionable quarter.

B. *sb.* A fashionable person. Chiefly in *pl.*

a **1800** T. Bellamy *Beggar Boy* (1801) I. 178 All the fashionables in town. **1800** H. Wells *Constantia Neville* I. 240 That he was merely a fashionable, she could not believe. **1800** *Sporting Mag.* XV. 265 Our fair fashionables. **1834** Medwin *Angler in Wales* II. 150 Fashionables of all countries. **1848** Thackeray *Van. Fair* xlix, A very pleasing and witty fashionable. **1883** Mrs. Lynn Linton *Girl of Period* II. 11 She will probably end her days as a frantic Fashionable.

fashionabledom ('fæʃənəb(ə)ldəm). *rare.* [f. prec. + -dom.] The fashionable world.

1859 Sala *Tw. round Clock* (1861) 338 A grand entertainment..given in Fashionabledom.

'fashionableness. [f. as prec. + -ness.]

†**1.** Superficiality, formality. Cf. fashionable 2.

1608–11 Bp. Hall *Epist.* iii. iii. 43 All which that Babylonish religion shifteth off with a careless fashionablenesse. **1612–5** —— *Contempl.* N. T. *Bloody Issue* Wks. (1634) II. 139 Outward fashionablenesse comes into no account with God; that is onely done which the soule doth.

2. †**a.** Elegance, attractiveness (*obs.*). **b.** The quality or state of being in vogue or in conformity with fashion.

1640 Fuller *Joseph's Coat* iii. (1867) 128 (To give the world..her due) she hath for the time a kind of a pleasing fashionableness. **1661** Boyle *Style of Script.* 187 A Fashionableness which within a short while will perhaps be Ridiculous. **1699** Locke *Educ.* §37 This outside fashionableness of the Taylor or Tire-woman's making. **1776** Adam Smith *W.N.* i. xi. (1869) I. 165 The fashionableness and scarcity of the wine. **1841** Hor. Smith *Moneyed Man* I. iv. 95 The ultra-fashionableness of a professed *elegante*.

fashionably ('fæʃənəblı), *adv.* [f. as prec. + -ly².] In a fashionable manner.

†**1.** With respect to the fashion or external form; outwardly, superficially, in appearance. (Cf. fashionable 2.) *Obs.*

1614 Bp. Hall *Recoll. Treat.* 85 How fewe are there, that doe otherwise than fashionably professe him [Christ]. **1615** Stephens *Satyr. Ess.* (ed. 2) 336 A Pettifogging Atturny.. may take bribes from both parties, and please both fashionably. **1628** Bp. Hall *Contempl.* IV. xii. 74 Neither doth Saul goe fashionably to worke, but does this service heartily. **1656** *Artif. Handsom.* 25 Those many arts..of dressing and adorning, which..ingenuity..had found out, and fashionably used.

2. Conformably to the prevailing fashion or usage, *esp.* that current in upper-class society.

1628 Earle *Microcosm.*, *Serving Man* (Arb.) 83 A Seruing man..is cast behind his master as fashionably as his sword and cloake are. **1711** Shaftesb. *Charac.* ii. ii. ii. (1737) II. 148 However fashionably we may apply the Notion of good Living. *a* **1716** South *Serm.* (1737) II. vi. 215 He might so fashionably and genteelly..have been duelled or fluxed into another world. *Ibid.* VI. iii. 94 A rotten, fashionably-diseased body. **1781** Cowper *Hope* 92 A mind, not yet so blank, or fashionably blind. **1820** W. Irving *Sketch Bk.* (1849) 125 They were dressed fashionably, but simply.

†**'fashional,** *a. Obs.* Also fashionall. [f. fashion *sb.* + -al¹.] = fashionable 2 and 3.

1617 Donne *Serm.* cxlvii. VI. 15 False and Fashional Christians. **1618** *Ibid.* cxxxiii. V. 389 The fashional man that will do as he sees great men do. *a* **1631** —— *Lett.* (1633) 360, I think it now most seasonable and fashionall for mee to breake. **1629** Gaule *Holy Madn.* 98 The fine Flourishes of his Fashionall Rhetoricke.

†**'fashionary,** *a. Obs. rare*⁻¹. [f. fashion *sb.* + -ary.] Formal; = fashionable 2.

a **1640** W. Fenner *Sacrifice of Faithfull* (1648) 176 Your formall repentance..your fashionary prayers.

†**'fashionate,** *ppl. a. Obs.* [f. fashion *v.* + -ate².] **a.** Fashioned or formed after an image or model. **b.** Well formed, perfect.

1593 B. Barnes *Parthenophil* Madrigal xxii, That figure fashionate Which in the jetty mirror lurks. **1593** Lodge *Will. Longbeard* Addr. to Rdr., Men are in thraldome to their fashionate manners. **1609** Dekker *Gull's Horne-bk.* (1812) 94 Your mediterranean isle [middle aisle of St. Paul's] is then the only gallery wherein the pictures of all your true fashionate and complemental gulls are..hung up.

†**'fashionative,** *a. Obs.* Also 6 fascionative. [f. fashion *sb.* and *v.* + -ative.] **a.** ? Prone to fantastic behaviour, affected. **b.** Tending to fashion or form; formative *of*.

1584 Lodge *Alarum* 18 b, It is idlenesse that maketh amorous; it is idlenesse that maketh fascionative. *a* **1693** Urquhart *Rabelais* iii. xlii. 348 A Third Act, fashionative of another Member.

fashioned ('fæʃənd), *ppl. a.*¹ [f. fashion *v.* + -ed¹.] **a.** Wrought into fashion or shape; formed with art or skill. *Rarely* of persons. Used esp. of stockings that are shaped to fit the contours of the leg. Cf. *full-fashioned*, *fully-fashioned* adjs.

1535 Coverdale *Isa.* xlii. 16 Let them conuerte..that.. saye to fashioned ymages: ye are oure godes. **1691** Locke *Lower. Interest* Wks. 1727 II. 83 Fashion'd Plate sells for more than its Weight of the same Silver. **1807** Sir R. Wilson *Jrnl.* 9 July in *Life* (1862) II. viii. 305, I had expected to see a gentleman, but I never saw one less fashioned. **1829** Carlyle *Misc.* (1857) II. 86 A character is a completely fashioned will. **1881** J. Paton in *Encycl. Brit.* XII. 299/2 It was necessary to seam them [stockings] up the selvages of web shaped on the frame (fashioned work). **1887** C. A. Moloney *Sk. Forestry W. Afr.* 26 Fashioned wood. **1895** *Montgomery Ward Catal.* 300/2 Ladies' lisle finished hose, patented seams, fashioned ankles. **1909** *Daily Chron.* 13 Apr. 5/2 Fashioned hosiery. **1919** *Ladies' Home Jrnl.* May 56 Burson Fashioned Hose..without seams.

b. preceded by adv. of manner.

1496 [see evil *adv.* 8 c]. **1710** *Lond. Gaz.* No. 4691/4 Florence O'Donoughue..a..clean Limb'd and well-fashioned Man. **1769** *Dublin Merc.* 16–19 Sept. 9/1 Black-Nose..has given such proof of his getting the finest fashioned foals. **1835** Lytton *Rienzi* i. i, Less warlike or worse fashioned weapons.

fashioned ('fæʃənd), *ppl. a.*² Also Sc. fawsont. [f. fashion *sb.* + -ed²] Having or provided with a fashion (*i.e.* an appearance, manner, or shape) of a peculiar kind. Only in parasynthetic combinations as ***honest-***, ***long-***, ***many-***, ***what-a-fashioned***; also old-fashioned. ***extension-fashioned*** (nonce-wd.): possessed of the property of extension.

1577 B. Googe *Heresbach's Husb.* i. (1586) 10 A newe and a strange fashioned Mill of your owne devise. **1581** Sidney *Apol. Poetrie* (Arb.) 58 Many, and many-fashioned Gods. **1633** T. Stafford *Pac. Hib.* xiii. (1821) 631 Thus may your honour see what a fashioned warre, I doe conceiue to bee least in charge. **1668** Culpepper & Cole *Barthol Anat.* i. vii. 14 The Peritonæum..is like a Bladder, or a long-fashioned Egg. **1674** N. Fairfax *Bulk & Selv.* 64 One figure being as much extension fashion'd as another. **1787** Burns *Twa Dogs* 142 Decent, honest fawsont folk.

fashioner ('fæʃənə(r)). [f. fashion *v.* + -er¹.] One that fashions; one that gives fashion or shape to; a creator, maker.

1548 Udall, etc. *Erasm. Par. 1 Cor.* xi. 11 The man is principall doer and fashioner. **1615** tr. *De Monfart's Surv. E. Indies* Pref. B j a, The Fashioner of this work. *a* **1673** J. Caryl in Spurgeon *Treas. Dav.* Ps. cxxxix 14 God is the.. fashioner of us all. **1809** Mrs. J. West *The Mother* (1810) 224 Fancy, fashioner of ills Most horrible. **1820** Scott *Monast.* xxxvii, A fashioner of doublets. **1864** Sir. F. Palgrave *Norm. & Eng.* III. 27 A new era of which he was ..the fashioner.

b. One who makes articles of dress; a tailor costumier, modiste. *Obs.* or *arch.*

[Cf. F. *façonnier*, 'ouvrier qui travaille aux ouvrages façonnés' (Littré).]

1625 B. Jonson *Staple of N.* v. i, Where is my Fashioner ..Linener, Perfumer, Barber? **1706** Phillips (ed. Kersey), *Fashioner*, as the Queen's Fashioner, or Taylor. **1771** Smollett *Humph. Cl.* (1815) 254 Mr. Coshgrave, the fashioner in Shuffolk Street. **1826** Scott *Mal. Malagr.* i. 52 Those humble fashioners..went to work by measuring the person of their customer. **1858** Simmonds *Dict. Trade, Fashioner*..a tailor. **1859** R. F. Burton *Centr. Afr.* in *Jrnl. Geog. Soc.* XXIX. 323 Fashion and its fashioners.

fashioning ('fæʃənıŋ), *vbl. sb.* [f. as prec. + -ing¹.]

1. The action of the vb. fashion; an instance of this.

1580 Baret *Alv.* F 161 A fashioning of a thing, *formatura*. **1594** T. B. *La Primaud. Fr. Acad.* ii. 399 The conception and fashioning of man. *a* **1600** Hooker *Eccl. Pol.* (1617) 673 Earnest exhortations..for my better fashioning unto good correspondence and agreement. *a* **1628** Preston *New Covt.* (1634) 337 It is the inward fashioning of every man's apprehension that makes him happy. *a* **1635** Naunton *Fragm. Reg.* (Arb.) 35 Art and Nature had spent their excellencies in his fashioning. **1861** W. F. Collier *Hist. Eng. Lit.* 141 The occasional dressing of leather and fashioning of gloves. **1884** *Littell's Living Age* CLXI. 67 A mind that ruled the fingers' fashionings.

attrib. **1847** Emerson *Poems, Monadnoc* Wks. (Bohn) I. 435 Wax their fashioning skill betrays.

b. *spec.* (See quot.) Also *attrib.*, as ***fashioning-needle***, ***-point***.

1874 Knight *Dict. Mech.*, *Fashioning-needle*, one of the needles in a knitting-machine which lift loops from some of the bearded needles and transfer them to others, in order to widen or narrow the work. **1892** *Labour Commission* Gloss., *Fashioning*, the process of shaping the stocking-leg and foot, also the shirt-sleeve and pant-leg, and back. This is done by hand by means of small points with which some of the loops are removed to narrow the stocking or pant at the ankle..In the steam-work these fashioning points are forced through the material by pressure.

2. Style in which a thing is fashioned. Also *concr.*

1870 F. R. Wilson *Ch. Lindisf.* 81 Stones of Norman fashioning. **1885** S. O. Jewett *March Island* xiv, A fair young girl of..flower-like fashioning. **1887** Hall Caine *Deemster* xl. 261 Beehives of a rude fashioning. **1890** S. J. Duncan *Social Departure* 412 Rich fashionings in wood and precious metals.

†**3.** The action or habit of following fashions (of dress). *Obs. rare*⁻¹.

1654 Whitlock *Zootomia* 173 As much Pride might be in affected Gravity, as in changeable fashioning.

fashioning ('fæʃənıŋ), *ppl. a.* [f. as prec. + -ing².] That fashions.

1674 N. Fairfax *Bulk & Selv.* 111 A fashioning or plastick spring of lifesomness.

fashionist ('fæʃənıst). [f. as prec. + -ist.]

1. A follower of the fashions; one who conforms to the prevailing style of dress; a fashion-monger.

1616 Chapman *Homer's Hymns* Epil., For ostentation humble truth still flies, And all confederate fashionists defies. **1750** E. Smith *Compleat Housewife* Pref., The Israelites grew Fashionists, and would have a King. **1850** Lyell *2nd Visit U.S.* II. 15 'There go two of our fashionists', pointing to two gaily-dressed ladies, in the latest Parisian costume.

2. One who prescribes or sets the fashions. *rare*⁻¹.

1815 Milman *Fazio* (1821) 27 Signior Dandalo, the court fashionist.

fashionize ('fæʃənaız), *v. rare*⁻¹. [f. as prec. + -ize.] *trans.* To make (a garment) fashionable; to alter (clothes) according to the fashion.

1824 *Blackw. Mag.* XV. 450 His taste compelled him to send this suit to his tailor every month to be fashionized.

fashionless ('fæʃənlıs), *a.* [f. fashion *sb.* + -less.] Without fashion or shape.

1581 Mulcaster *Positions* vi. (1887) 43 Misshapen and fashionles. **1589** Fleming *Virg. Georg.* iii. 48 Fashionlesse, illfauoured, vnhandsome lies the land With heaps of snow. **1833** Whittier *Proselytes* Prose Wks. 1888 I. 309 We grapple with the fashionless air. **1860** Ld. Lytton *Lucile* ii. vi, The fashionless cloud of far time.

†**'fashionly,** *a. Obs. rare*⁻¹. [f. as prec. + -ly¹.] ? Subject to the sway of fashion.

1613 Purchas *Pilgrimage* viii. ix. (1614) 784 Thou.. mightest see as Monster-like fashions at home, and more fashionly monster of thy selfe.

'fashion-monger. [f. fashion *sb.* + monger.] One who studies and follows the fashion or fashions.

1599 Marston *Sco. Villanie* 166 Each quaint fashion-monger, whose sole repute Rests in his trim gay clothes. **1624** Heywood *Gunaik.* vi. 298 Wild fashion-mongers, and fantasticke gallants. **1782** *European Mag.* I. 247 A knot of fashion-mongers assembled in the drawing room of a

French dancer. **1826** Miss Mitford *Village* Ser. II. (1863) 425 A thrifty fashion-monger.

Hence †**fashion-monging** *ppl. a.*

1599 Shaks. *Much Ado* v. i. 94 Fashion-monging boyes.

fashious ('fæʃəs), *a. Sc.* and *north. dial.* Forms: 6 fa(s)cheous, (7 fachius), 6–7 faschious, (8 fachious), 9 fash(e)ous, 7– fashious. [ad. OF. *fascheux* (Fr. *fâcheux*), f. *fascher* (*fâcher*) to fash.] Causing or giving anxiety or trouble; tiresome, vexatious, *rarely* of a person.

1536 Bellenden *Cron. Scot.* (1821) I. p. xlv, It were bot ane faschious and vane laboure. **1599** Jas. I Βασιλ. Δωρον (1603) 125 To free mens heads..from the fashious thoughts on their affaires. *a* **1662** R. Baillie *Lett. & Jrnls.* (1775) I. 221 The way of proceeding was fashious both to ours and the English commissioners. **1789** Burns *Let. to Jas. Tennant* 56 For, faith, they'll aiblins fin' them fashious. **1811** Scott *Let.* 25 Aug. in *Lockhart*, Wearing on as easily as this fashious world will permit. **1876** *Whitby Gloss.*, A fashous kind of a body.

fasiane, obs. var. of pheasant.

fasing, obs. form of facing.

†**faskidar.** *Sc. Obs.* A name applied to the Northern Gull.

1703 M. Martin *Descr. Western Isl.* 73 The Bird Faskidar [is] about the bigness of a Sea-maw of the middle size. **1766** Pennant *Zool.* (1770) IV. 25 The arctic gull is..the Faskidar of Martin.

fasola ('fɑːsɒlɑː, -səʊl-). *Mus.* [f. fa *sb.* + sol *sb.*² + la *sb.*] (See quot. 1964.)

1933 G. P. Jackson (*title*) White spirituals... The story of the fasola folk. *Ibid.* 3 Ask any real country person..about fasola singers, and he will very likely be able to direct you to one of them. **1933** *Times Lit. Suppl.* 13 Apr. 257/1 Conventions held..for 'fasola' singing. **1956** M. Stearns *Story of Jazz* (1957) viii. 126 Yankee singing masters invaded rural areas with their 'fasola' and 'shape-note' systems of reading music. **1964** *Conc. Oxf. Dict. Mus.* 320/1 *Lancashire Sol-fa.* A modern name for a system of sight-singing more properly called 'Old English Sol-fa', since it was universally used in England from at least the early 17th c. and its latest textbook appeared in 1879. It is a method of solmization applied to the normal staff notation; the first 3 notes of every major scale are called *fa-sol-la*, and so are the second 3 notes, the remaining note being called *mi*... In the Amer. Colonies (and later the U.S.A.) it was called *Fasola* or, sometimes (from the special notation there used), *Patent Notes.*

fason, -oun, -owne, obs. ff. fashion.

fassaite ('fæseɪaɪt). *Min.* Also fassait. [Named in 1796 by Dolomieu, and in 1817 by Werner, after *Fassa* (in the Tyrol) where it was found: see -ite.] †**a.** Foliated zeolite (*obs.*). **b.** A variety of pyroxene, containing a little alumina in addition to the elements of sahlite.

1814 T. Allan *Min. Nomen.* 46 Foliated zeolite..Fassait. *Ibid.* 5 Fassaite of Werner is a variety of augite.

fasse: see fas.

fassee, obs. form of farcy.

†**fasse-phierre.** *Herb. Obs.* = samphire.

1710 London & Wise *Compl. Gard.* (1719) 316 He should likewise plant in Borders of the same Walls, his Fasse-phierre, or Samphire.

fasset, obs. form of facet, faucet.

fasshin, -sshon, s)shyon, obs. ff. fashion.

†'**fassion.** *Obs.* In 5 facyon, fassyone. [ad. med.L. *fassiōn-em* (Papias), f. L. *fatēri* to confess.]

c **1440** *Promp. Parv.* 150/2 Fassyone, or knowlechynge [facyon, P.], *fassio, confessio.*

fassion, -oun, -(s)syon(e, Sc. fassoun, (-s)sowne, obs. ff. fashion.

fassone, var. of farcin *Obs.*, farcy.

fast (fɑːst, -æ-), *sb.*¹ Also 3–6 faste, *Orm.* fasste. [Early ME. *faste*, prob. a. ON. *fasta* (Da. *faste*, Sw. *fasta*), = OS. *fasta*, OHG. *fasta* (MHG. *vaste*), f. OTeut. *fastêjan* to fast. The OE. synonym was *fæsten*: see fasten *sb.*]

1. An act or instance of fasting: **a.** as a religious observance, or as an expression of grief.

c **1200** Ormin 11329 All wiþþutenn mete & drinnch Heold Crist hiss fasste þære. *a* **1300** *Cursor M.* 6523 (Cott.) But sum o þaim þis fast forsoke, And þai þis riche manna toke. *c* **1400** Maundev. (1839) xii. 134 The seke men be not constreyned to þat fast. **1546** Langley *Pol. Verg. De Invent.* vi. iii. 116 a, He kepeth not the true fast whyche forbeareth flesh, or forgoeth his supper. **1557** N. T. (Genev.) *Acts* xxvii. 9 Because also the tyme of the Fast was now passed. **1633** Ford *'Tis Pity* i. iii, I have..even starv'd My veins with daily fasts. **1700** S. L. tr. *C. Fryke's Voy. E. Ind.* 350 We kept a Fast in our Ship, to beg God's assistance. **1851** Ht. Martineau *Hist. Peace* (1877) III. iv. xiv. 133 The day appointed for a general fast. **1857** Buckle *Civiliz.* I. viii. 515 The reformed clergy..appointed a public fast.

fig. *a* **1300** *Cursor M.* 29031 (Cott.) Þe thrid es better þan þe twa wit gastli fast all giltes for-ga. **1545** Brinklow *Compl.* 57 The Scripture teacheth what true fast is..that is to say; To lett them out of bondage which be in danger..to deale thy bread to the hungry, &c. [See *Isa.* lviii. 6.]

b. in general. *to break* (*one's*) *fast*: see break *v.* 9 c.

c **1440** *Promp. Parv.* 151/1 Faste of abstynence, *jejunium.* **1669** Dryden *Tyran. Love* ii. i, She's..refus'd to cast One glance to feed me for so long a fast. **1671** Milton *P.R.* ii. 247 That fast To virtue I impute not. **1843** Hood *Song of Shirt* v, I hardly fear his terrible shape..It seems so like my own, Because of the fasts I keep.

†**c.** The action of fasting; abstinence from food. Also *personified. Obs. rare.*

[*a* **1300, 1545**: see 1 *fig.*] **1603** Shaks. *Meas. for M.* i. ii. 130 Surfet is the father of much fast. **1632** Milton *Penseroso* 46 Spare Fast, that oft with gods doth diet. **1795** *Montford Castle* I. 13 Ate with a voracity obviously the result of pining fast.

2. A day or season appointed for fasting.

a **1300** *Cursor M.* 6570 (Cott.) Qua held þe fast mang oþer men? **1565** Calfhill *Answ. Treat. Crosse* v. 125 b, That whiche bred in the Church a miserable schisme..the Easter fast. **1611** Bible *Jonah* iii. 5 The people of Nineueh.. proclaimed a fast. **1732** Law *Serious C.* i. (ed. 2) 13 All the Feasts and Fasts of the Church. **1847** S. Austin *Ranke's Hist. Ref.* III. 75 In March 1552, the people of Zurich broke the fast and ate eggs and meat. **1852** Hawthorne *Blithedale Rom.* xvi. (1883) 477 Except on..the Fourth of July, the autumnal cattle-show, Thanksgiving, or the annual Fast.

3. *attrib.* and *Comb.*, as *fast-book*, *-sermon*; †**fast-lost** *a.*, lost through a fast; **fast-mass**, Shrovetide; †**fast-spittle** = *fasting-spittle*; **fast-week** *Sc.*, the week preceding the celebration of the Sacrament, and including the fast-day. Also fast-day, Fast-gong.

1607 Shaks. *Timon* ii. ii. 180 Feast won, fast lost. **1637** Laud *Sp. Star-Chamb.* 14 June 20 The Prayer for seasonable weather was purged out of this last Fast-booke. **1681** Chetham *Angler's Vade-m.* (1689) 52 The stinging of Hornets is cured by..applying outwardly Cow-dung and Fast-spittle. **1681** Wood *Life* (Oxf. Hist. Soc.) II. 514 Mr. Birch..preached the fast sermon at St. Marie's. **1866** *Chambers' Encycl.* s.v. *Shrovetide*, These days were sometimes called..Fast-mass. **1891** J. M. Barrie *Little Minister* (1892) iii. 21 A garret in which the minister could sleep if he had guests, as during the Fast week.

fast (fɑːst, -æ-), *sb.*² *Naut.* Also 5 fest. [ME. *fest*, a. ON. *fest-r*, f. *festa* to fasten, f. *fast-r* fast *a.* In mod.Eng. assimilated to the adj.] A rope, etc. by which a ship or boat is fastened to a wharf.

c **1440** *Promp. Parv.* 158/1 Fest or teyynge of a schyppe, or bootys, *scalamus.* **1678** Littleton *Lat. Dict.*, Fast..rope to fasten a boat or ship, *prymnesium.* **1763** S. T. Janssen *Smuggling laid open* 222 The Captain..employed..His Majesty's Officer..to cast off his Fasts, fastened on Shore. **1840** R. H. Dana *Bef. Mast* xxix. 104 The topsails were at the mast-head, the fast just ready to be cast off. **1856** Kane *Arct. Expl.* I. iii. 35 We succeeded in changing our fasts to another berg. **1863** in Robson *Bards of Tyne* 246 While their keel's at the fest.

†**2.** = anchor-hold¹. *Obs.*

1638 T. Jackson *Creed* ix. xv. Wks. 1673 II. 984 The cable [may be] very strong, when the fest or Anchor-hold is slippery. *Ibid.* ix. xix. II. 998.

fast (fɑːst, -æ-), *sb.*³ [The adj. used *absol.* or *ellipt.*] Something that is fast or fixed; *spec.* (see quots.).

1836 Polwhele *Corn.-Eng. Voc.* 76 *Fast.* The fast is the understratum supposed never to have been moved or broken up since the creation. **1853** Kane *Grinnell Exp.* x. (1856) 73 Forming an icy margin or beach known technically as the 'land ice', or 'the fast'. **1883** Gresley *Coal-Mining Gloss.*, *Fast*, the first hard bed of rock met with after sinking through running sand or quick ground.

†**fast**, *sb.*⁴ *Obs.* [ad. Fr. *faste*, ad. L. *fastus.*] Arrogance, pompousness.

1673 *Phil. Trans.* VIII. 6027 He examines..the Fast and Gravity of the Spanish language. **1762–71** H. Walpole *Vertue's Anecd. Paint.* i. Wks. 1798 III. 27 Perhaps the generous sentiment implied in his motto..contained more true glory than all the Fast couched under Louis's [XIV] emblem of the sun.

fast (fɑːst, -æ-), *a.* Forms: 1–2 fæst, 2 fest, 3 *Orm.* fasst, 4 *south. dial.* vest, 4–6 faste, 3– fast. [Com. Teut.: OE. *fæst* corresponds to OFris. *fest*, OS. *fast* (Du *vast*), OHG. *festi* (MHG. *veste*, mod.HG. *fest*), ON. *fastr*; prob. repr. OTeut. **fastu-* (the word having, like other adj. *u* stems, passed into the *o* and *i* declensions), cogn. with Goth. *fastan* to keep, guard, observe.]

I. Firm.

1. a. Firmly fixed in its place; not easily moved or shaken; settled, stable. *Obs.* or *arch.* exc. as said predicatively of something fixed as in a socket (*e.g.* a nail, a post), where the sense approaches 4.

c **888** K. Ælfred *Boeth.* xii, Se þe wille fæst hus timbrian ne sceall he hit no settan upon þone hehstan cnol. *c* **1000** *Sax. Leechd.* III. 268 Ealle mæst hi [steorran] synd fæste on þam firmamentum. *c* **1374** Chaucer *Anel. & Arc.* 313 Als fast As in a tempest is a roten mast. *c* **1400** *Lanfranc's Cirurg.* 321 It is necessarie þat þe patient ligge also stille as he mai wiþouten remevyng til þe boon be fast. **1535** Coverdale *1 Chron.* xvii. [xvi.] 30 He hath made the compase of the world so fast, that it can not be moued. **1576** Fleming *Panopl. Epist.* 179 If you lay not such a fast foundation. **1656** Ridgley *Pract. Physick* 291 Pain of the Colick is moveable; of the stone, fast. **1674** N. Fairfax *Bulk & Selv.* 74 A great heap of fast and loose bodies hudled up together. **1765** A. Dickson *Treat. Agric.* v. (ed. 2) 159 In lands..where the fast stones have been carefully digged out. **1820** Scoresby *Acc. Arctic Reg.* II. 264 It was ready to drop out. Some.. expressed a wish that the harpoon were better fast. **1858** J. Martineau *Stud. Chr.* 36 Structures hollowed in the fast mountain. **1871** Morley *Voltaire* iv. (1886) 161 Something ..which sets a fast gulf between them and those who are.. irredeemably saturated with corruption.

b. In immaterial sense; *esp.* Of a person, his attributes, feelings, etc.: Not easily turned aside, constant, firm, steadfast. Now only in *fast foe* (arch.), *fast friend*; in the latter the adj. is commonly apprehended in sense 4.

c **900** *Bæda's Hist.* iv. iii. §4 Þonne eode he to cirican..& on sealmsonge fæste moode awunade. *c* **1200** *Trin. Coll. Hom.* 119 Þe holi gost..alihte hem of brihtere and of festere bileue þe hie hedden er. *c* **1340** Hampole *Psalter* i. 1 He is man þ^t is fast & stabile ageyns ese. **1340** *Ayenb.* 116 Vayre zuete uader make oure herten ueste an stedeuest. *a* **1400–50** *Alexander* 4616 We þat fourmed is & fast. **1485** Caxton *Paris & V.* 69 He had alle waye faste byleue in our Lord. **1508** Fisher *Wks.* (1876) 271 A fast hope and confydence that he had in prayer. **1513** More in Grafton *Chron.* II. 778 Catesby..founde him [Hastings] so fast..that [etc.]. **1607** Shaks. *Cor.* ii. iii. 192 If he should still malignantly remaine Fast Foe to th' Plebij. **1611** Speed *Hist. Gt. Brit.* ix. xix. §23. 716 He had beene fast vpon the part of King Henry, while that part was in wealth. **1697** Dampier *Voy.* (1698) I. 158 The Indian neighbourhood..were our fast friends, and ready to receive and assist us. **1793** Burke *Cond. Minority* Wks. 1842 I. 621 England must be the fast friend, or the determined enemy, of France. **1833** Ht. Martineau *Loom & Lugger* ii. v. 91 We shall..be fast friends. **1878** Browning *La Saisiaz* 68 There's the nice distinction 'twixt fast foes and faulty friends.

†**c.** Pleonastically. *fast and sure*: well assured, certain. *Obs.*

1522 Skelton *Sp. Parrot* 504, I make the faste and sure. *c* **1550** Bale *K. Johan* (Camden) 20, I wyll not breke yt, ye may be fast and suer.

d. †Of sleep: Deep, sound, unbroken. Of persons: = *fast asleep. Obs.* exc. *dial.*

1592 Shaks. *Rom. & Jul.* iv. v. 1 Fast I warrant her. **1605** —— *Macb.* v. i. 9 All this while in a most fast sleepe. **1743** Fielding *Journey* i. i, She was in a fast sleep. **1762** Foote *Orators* ii. Wks. 1799 I. 211 Smoke the justice, he is as fast as a church. **1861** H. Kingsley *Ravenshoe* xli, 'They waked we sharp enough; but as for she! she's fast.'

e. *fast aground, ashore*: (of a vessel) fixed on the ground, the shore. *fast asleep*: fixed in sleep, sound asleep, in a deep sleep.

In these phrases *fast* seems to have been originally the grammatical predicate; now it is usually apprehended as an adv. qualifying *aground, ashore, asleep.*

1555 T. Haukes in Foxe *A. & M.* (1631) III. xi. 260 The old Bishop..was fast asleepe. *c* **1620** Z. Boyd *Zion's Flowers* (1855) 12, I see a man..Hard fast asleepe. **1725** De Foe *Voy. round World* (1840) 331 Running fast aground. **1751** Smollett *Per. Pic.* ii, We were fast ashore before you knew anything of the matter. **1771** —— *Humph. Cl.* (1846) 329 In half an hour I was fast asleep in bed. **1837** Dickens *Pickw.* viii, The fat boy, for once, had not been fast asleep. **1867** Smyth *Sailor's Word-bk.*, *Fast aground*, immoveable or high and dry.

f. Of a colour: That will not quickly fade or wash out; permanent. Also *fast-colour* attrib.

1658 W. Sanderson *Graphice* 80 Fast and firm colours, as Umber, Oke. **1840** F. D. Bennett *Whaling Voy.* II. 92 Its texture is strong and neat; its colours are fast. **1884** I. Levinstein in *Manch. Exam.* 6 Oct. 4/5 The fastest red dye known on cotton. **1939** H. G. Wells *Holy Terror* i. iii. 72 There's that fool Lord Horatio Bohun and his purple shirts —mauve shirts really they are, for he never had the wit to get his shirts fast colour. *Ibid.* iii. iii. 317 We are the Revolution from the West and all fast-colour Revolutions come out of the West. **1962** *B.S.I. News* June 10/1 There is a good deal of loose use of expressions such as 'guaranteed fast colours' and 'fast colours', without any indication of what the colours are fast to—and without even any recognition that a colour that is fast to light is not necessarily fast to washing, and *vice versa.* **1962** J. T. Marsh *Self-Smoothing Fabrics* xviii. 298 Since 1952–53 there has been an increasing use of vat dyes with thermo-setting resins on cotton, for fast-colour work has become a particularly important factor in the U.S.A.

g. *fast line* (Surveying): see quot. *hard and fast line*: see hard *a.*

1807 Hutton *Course Math.* II. 73 When a line is measured whose position is determined..it is called a *fast line.*

h. Of an organism: resistant to the stain-removing or toxic action of a (specified) agent. Used chiefly in *Comb.* preceded by the name of the agent. (Cf. fast *a.* 1 f.)

1904 [see *acid-fast* adj.]. **1907** *Jrnl. R. Inst. Public Health* XV. 453 The atoxyl-fast strain is also resistant to a number of substances related to atoxyl. **1949** E. J. Pulaski in S. A. Waksman *Streptomycin* xxxiv. 491 Wide variation in susceptibility is observed and initially strepto-mycin-fast organisms are found. **1951** A. Grollman *Pharmacol. & Therapeutics* i. 26 By subjecting susceptible organisms to inadequate doses of a drug it is possible to render them 'drug fast'. **1964** M. Hynes *Med. Bacteriol.* (ed. 8) v. 48 An 'acid-fast' organism is one which when stained resists decolourization with 25 per cent sulphuric acid. *Ibid.*, The smegma bacillus..is acid-fast, but not alcohol-fast.

†**2. a.** Firmly or closely knit together, compact, dense, solid, hard. *Obs.* exc. *dial.*

c **1000** *Sax. Leechd.* I. 114 Ðeos wyrt..bið cenned..on fæstum stowum. *c* **1200** Ormin 1602 Wiþþ fasst & findiȝ laf & harrd. **1398** Trevisa *Barth De P.R.* xvii. ii. (1495) 598 Trees that ben moost sad and faste. **1581** Marbeck *Bk. of Notes* 1038 Then is hayle ingendered, because ye thing is become more fast. **1601** Holland *Pliny* xvi. xl, The Cherrie tree wood is firme and fast. **1609** C. Butler *Fem. Mon.* i. (1623) C j, The stuffe [new Fustian] is so fast that it holdeth the sting. **1661** J. Childrey *Brit. Bacon.* 16 Tin is a fast metal, and not apt to dissolve. **1765** A. Dickson *Treat.*

Agric. (ed. 2) 316 The half of the earth, *e f*, with the fast land below, is thrown into the furrow E F. **1805** SCOTT *Last Minstr.* IV. xvii, In close array and fast. **1881** *Leicestersh. Gloss.*, This ere bread cuts so fasst.

†**b.** Of style: Compact, terse. *Obs.*

a **1568** ASCHAM *Scholem.* II. (Arb.) 113 If Osorius would.. translate Demosthenes, with so straite, fast, and temperate a style in latine, as he is in Greeke.

c. Frozen. *N. Amer.* ? *Obs.*

1706 *Boston News-Letter* 21 Jan. 2/2 New York Jan. 7th.. Hudsons River was froze over and continued fast several days. **1743** J. ISHAM *Obs. Hudsons Bay* (1949) XII. 179 The Lakes and Rivers near the ocean some affirm, are fast all the Summer. **1796** E. DRINKER *Jrnl.* 23 Dec. (1889) 296 Clear and very cold. Wind N.W. The river fast to day. **1854** in *Beaver* (1924) Dec. 31 We have had the pleasure of seeing the river fast this morning.

†**3.** Of a fortress: Strong. Of a place or district: Secure against attack or access. *Obs.* Cf. FASTNESS.

c **900** *Bæda's Hist.* III. xvi, Seo burȝ wæs to þon fæst þæt [etc.]. *c* **1205** LAY. 9775 Sone he gon faren..in to Ex-chæstre, þa burh wes þa fæstre. **1571** HANMER *Chron. Irel.* (1633) 113 They found the country fast with woods, bogges, and paces trenched. **1596** SPENSER *State Irel.* (1633) 100 Robbers and Outlawes..lurking in Woods and fast places. **1633** T. STAFFORD *Pac. Hib.* vii. (1821) 86 A strong and fast Countrey.

4. a. Firmly attached to something else; that cannot easily escape or be extricated; fixed to the spot; *lit.* and *fig.* Said both of persons and things.

c **1400** *Lanfranc's Cirurg.* (MS.A) 352 Presse hem þat þei bicome fast togidere. *a* **1400–50** *Alexander* 747* (Dublin MS.) In rapes fast for ryfyng of bernes. *c* **1440** *Promp. Parv.* 151/2 Fast, or festyd be clevynge to, or naylynge, *fixus, confixus.* **1535** COVERDALE *Ps.* lxxvii[i]. 8, I am so fast in preson, that I can not get forth. **1603** KNOLLES *Hist. Turks* 685 Being..almost fast in the deep mud. **1659** B. HARRIS *Parival's Iron Age* 86 France..by keeping herself fast with them..hath drawn no small advantages from them [Swiss]. **1682** MILTON *Hist. Mosc.* v, I am now fast in your Country. **1700** S. L. tr. *C. Fryke's Voy. E. Ind.* 41 The Hook struck into his Throat, and had him fast. **1772–84** COOK *Voy.* (1790) VI. 2236 Captain King..remained fast till the return of the boat. **1806–7** J. BERESFORD *Miseries Hum. Life* (1826) I. Introd., If you and your mind and your nerves are such fast cronies. **1827** SCOTT *Jrnl.* (1890) II. 13 Mr. Scrope, who is fast with the gout. **1833** TENNYSON *Poems* 120 We must bind And keep you fast, my Rosalind. **1878** H. PHILLIPS *Poems fr. Sp. & Germ.* 16 Prisoner fast was Virgil taken.

b. Of a knot, band, etc.: Firmly tied, not easily loosed. Also *fig.* of an alliance, etc.

1553 T. WILSON *Rhet.* (1580) 40 For that faste kinred and aliaunce, which is betwixt us. **1583** HOLLYBAND *Campo di Fior* 21 Tye the latcheth of a loose knot, and not of a fast one. **1641** MILTON *Ch. Govt.* Wks. 1738 I. 63 Our Prelates..have enter'd into fast League with the principal Enemy against whom they were sent. **1724** R. FALCONER *Voy.* (1769) 232 To lie still as if their Chains were fast.

c. *to make fast*: to bind, connect, or fix firmly. In nautical use also *absol.*

c **1340** *Cursor M.* 16684 (Trin.) Abouen his heed..a bord was made fast. *c* **1400** *Lanfranc's Cirurg.* 174 Þer ben maad fast wiþ þe ballokis .ij. vessels. **1526** TINDALE *Acts* xvi. 24 Which iayler..made their fete fast in the stockes. **1627** CAPT. SMITH *Seaman's Gram.* v. 22 In stead of tying, sea men alwayes say, make fast. **1697** DAMPIER *Voy.* (1698) I. 17 [He] took the end of a Line, and made it fast about his Neck. **1748** F. SMITH *Voy. Disc. N.-W. Pass.* I. 45 Captain More ..made fast to another Piece [of ice]. **1835** MARRYAT *Jac. Faithf.* vii, Make the boat fast, there's a good lad. **1872** C. GIBBON *For the King* i, The horses were made fast in one corner of the court.

fig. *a* **1310** in Wright *Lyric P.* ix. 37 Betre is make forewardes faste, then afterward to mene ant mynne. **1553** T. WILSON *Rhet.* (1580) 144 A Gentleman, being handfasted to a Gentlewoman..afterwardes lost her, being made faster to another manne, then ever she was to hym. **1560** ROLLAND *Crt. Venus* IV. 469 Ȝe man mak fast that salbe to ȝow laid.

d. *fig.* In a perplexity or difficulty; 'in a fix'. *to be fast for*: to be in want of. *dial.*

1863 MRS. TOOGOOD *Yorksh. Dial.*, I sent to borrow your saddle, for I..was fast for one. **1877** *Cheshire Gloss.*, 'I've getten fast amang it.' **1883** *Almondbury Gloss.*, 'Why don't you get on with your job?' 'Nay, Au'm fast.'

e. *Whale-fishing.* Of the whale: Having a harpoon sticking in it. Also of the boat, to which the harpoon is attached. Cf. *fast-boat, -fish, -ship* (see 11).

1820 SCORESBY *Acc. Arct. Reg.* II. 320 Whether the fish, at the time of being harpooned by the second ship, was fast or loose? **1823** —— *Jrnl.* 444 Amongst this run of fish, the king George was fast to three. **1839** T. BEALE *Sperm Whale* 181 The immense creature almost flew..throwing tons of spray high into the air, shewing that he was 'fast.'

f. Constipated; costive. *Obs.* exc. *dial.*

c **1000** *Sax. Leechd.* I. 74 Gif mannes innoð to fæst sy. **1877** *N.W. Linc. Gloss.*, *Fast*, costive.

5. Of a door, window, etc.: Close shut, bolted, or locked. Also, *to make* (a door, etc.) *fast.*

c **1305** *Edmund Conf.* 416 in *E.E.P.* (1862) 82 Make faste þe dore after þe. *c* **1320** *Cast. Love* 876 Thorgh the fast ȝate he con in teo, At the owt-goyng he lette hit fast be. *c* **1425** *Seven Sag.* 1355 (P.) The wyf fonde the dore faste. **1562** J. HEYWOOD *Prov. & Epigr.* (1867) 160 He that cumth last make all fast. **1623** MASSINGER *Dk. Milan* v. ii, I'll first make fast the door. **1748** RICHARDSON *Clarissa* Wks. 1883 VI. 290, I thought I heard her coming to open the door..but it was only to draw another bolt, to make it still the faster. **1832** HT. MARTINEAU *Hill & Valley* i. 9 He..walked round the cottage to see that the windows were fast. **1853** KINGSLEY *Hypatia* xxviii. 359 The door..was fast. With a single blow he burst it open.

6. a. Gripping, tenacious. Const. *of. Obs.* exc. in *to take fast hold* (*of*).

c **1510** MORE *Picus* Wks. 5/2 A meruelouse fast memorie. **1608** BP. HALL *Char. Virtues & V.* II. 76 He greets his friend ..with..so fast a closure, that [etc.]. **1611** BIBLE *Prov.* iv. 13 Take fast hold of instruction. **1625** BACON *Ess., Gardens* (Arb.) 557 Roses Damask & Red are fast Flowers of their Smels. **1662** J. DAVIES *Voy. Ambass.* 272 These Conductors ..laid..fast hold on their hands. **1724** R. FALCONER *Voy.* (1769) 62 Laying fast hold of the Skirt of my Waistcoat.

†**b.** Close-fisted, mean, niggardly. *Obs.*

c **1175** *Lamb. Hom.* 143 Þa feste Men þa þet mei lutel to wreche. *a* **1300** *Pop. Science* 275 A slouȝ wrecche and ferblet, fast and loth to ȝeve his god.

7. *Mining.* **a.** In *fast country, ground*, applied to that part of the bed of minerals which lies next the rock (cf. 4).

1671 *Phil. Trans.* VI. 2096 The (then real but now imaginary) surface of the Earth, which is termed by the Miners, the Shelf, Fast Countrey or Ground that was never moved in the Flood. *Ibid.* 2099 When we come to the Shelf or Fast Countrey. **1753** CHAMBERS *Cycl. Supp.*, Fast Ground or Fast Country.

b. *fast end, wall* (see quots.). Cf. 1.

1851 GREENWELL *Coal-trade Terms Northumb. & Durh.* 25 *Fast Wall*, a sheth wall; the wall in which, at the top or bottom of a course, the bearing up or bearing down stopping is placed. **1881** RAYMOND *Mining Gloss.*, *Fast-end*..a gangway with rock on both sides. **1883** GRESLEY *Coal min. Gloss.*, *Fast End*, the limit of a stall in one direction.

II. Rapid.

[This sense was app. developed first in the adv., and thence transferred to the adj.: see FAST *adv.*]

8. a. Of action, motion, or progress: Quick, swift. Hence of an agent: (*a*) Moving quickly; (*b*) Imparting quick motion to something. *fast and furious*: see FURIOUS *a.* 1 d.

[In the first quot. the sense may be 'strong, vigorous' (cf. 1, 2 and the *adv.* 1 d).]

a **1300** *Cursor M.* 7169 (Cott.) Sampson..gaue a braid sa fers and fast, þat all þe bandes of him brast. **1552** HULOET, Fast wryter, *impiger scriba.* **1594** SHAKS. *Rich. III*, III. i. 103 Idle Weeds are fast in growth. *c* **1610** SPEED in *Lett. Lit. Men* (Camden) 109 With a fast eye you had overune it. *a* **1627** MIDDLETON *Chaste Maid* v. i, A fair, fast, legible hand. **1662** J. DAVIES tr. *Mandelslo's Trav. E. Ind.* 120 A hundred Boats, all which row for the fastest. **1712** SWIFT *Jrnl. to Stella* 12 Dec., I am slower, but MD is faster. **1788** FRANKLIN *Autobiog.* Wks. 1887 I. 287 His ship..foul to a degree that must necessarily hinder her fast sailing. **1837** DICKENS *Pickw.* xiv, The vixenish mare with the fast pace. **1837** APPERLEY *The Road* (1851) 32 The average price of horses for fast coaches. **1886** *Manch. Exam.* 7 Jan. 5/2 The want felt in Lancashire of a good fast bowler. **1886** T. HOPKINS *'Twixt Love & Duty* xli, The fast train was exchanged for a local one. **1888** STEEL *Cricket* iii. 164 It is strange that English first-class cricket is so devoid of really fast bowling.

b. Coming in quick succession. *freq.* in Shelley; otherwise *rare.*

1815 SHELLEY *Alastor* 533 For as fast years flow away The smooth brow gathers. *a* **1822** —— *Coliseum* Ess. & Lett. (Camelot) 59 Like the fast drops of a fountain.

c. Of a clock or watch: Indicating a time more advanced than the true time.

1840 *Penny Cycl.* XVII. 405/1 In an observatory it is always desirable that a clock should..be slow rather than fast. *Mod.* My watch is fast. 'It is six by my watch.' 'I think you must be fast.'

d. *Photogr.* Needing only brief exposure (emulsion, film); shortening the necessary exposure time (lens); providing a brief exposure time (shutter).

1902 A. WATKINS *Photogr.* 115 The folded focussing cloth can be held in front of the lens before drawing the slide. Probably half the subjects usually taken with a fast shutter would be better done in this way. **1923** *Brit. Jrnl. Photogr. Alm. 1924* 165 (Advt.), Ilford Roll Films... Exceptionally fast. **1939** HENNEY & DUDLEY *Handbk. Photogr.* viii. 214 In all the common methods of specifying film speed, the larger numerical units indicate the faster..emulsions. **1958** *Amat. Photographer* 31 Dec. 914/2 The benefits of a fast lens are greatest with a 35-mm camera. **1968** A. DIMENT *Gt. Spy Race* vii. 107 It was a good, fast film and I worked the re-wind lever like the bolt on a rifle.

e. Used in nuclear physics to denote various processes, devices, etc., that involve *fast neutrons* (see sense 11), as *fast breeder* (*reactor*), a breeder reactor that is a fast reactor; *fast fission*, the fission of a nucleus by a fast neutron; *fast pile, reactor*, a nuclear reactor in which fission is caused primarily by fast (unmoderated) neutrons.

1945 H. D. SMYTH *Gen. Acct. Devel. Atomic Energy Mil. Purposes* viii. 79 The enhancement may be taken into account by multiplying the original number of neutrons N by a factor ϵ which is called the fast-fission effect or the fast-multiplication factor. *Ibid.* 91 The original fast neutrons are slightly increased in number by fast fission. **1947** *Sci. News Let.* 6 Sept. 147 'Fast reactor' uses man-made plutonium. **1949** *Nucleonics* Dec. 40 The 'fast' pile, in which the neutrons produce fission at practically the same energy at which they themselves are released by fission. **1954** *Wall St. Jrnl.* 11 Oct. 3/4 There are two more experimental reactor types to be built under the A.E.C.'s present plans—a so-called homogeneous reactor and a 'fast breeder' reactor. **1954** *Sci. Amer.* Dec. 39/1 The homogeneous reactor and the fast breeder represent the boldest explorations among the five reactor projects. **1957** *Technology* July 184 Remoteness was considered essential for the site of an experimental fast-breeder reactor. In this respect, Dounreay was ideal. **1964** A. SALMON *Nuclear Reactor* iii. 31 The fast reactor cannot use natural, or near natural, uranium because inelastic scattering by the ^{238}U reduces the mean neutron energy into a region where fast fissions are not sufficient to overcome the losses due to leakage of neutrons from the reactor and to capture in the ^{238}U. **1968** *New Scientist* 1 Feb. 230/2 Most industrialized countries are growing enthusiastic..about fast reactors, which they foresee as the next successful breed of nuclear power generators.

9. Adapted to, or productive of, quick movement. **a.** With reference to locomotion or transport. **b.** *Cricket* and *Football.* Said of the ground when hard and dry. **c.** *Billiards.* Said of a table of which the cushions are very elastic.

a. **1857** B. TAYLOR *North. Trav.* 245 As it was not a 'fast' station, we were subject to the possibility of waiting two or three hours for horses. *Mod.* A fast line (of railway).

b. **1888** STEEL *Cricket* iii. 150 Finishing his stroke as he would do on a fast wicket. **1891** *Field* 7 Mar. 345/3 The ground [at a football match] was very fast.

c. **1873** BENNETT & CAVENDISH *Billiards* 21 By a moderately fast table is meant one on which if a player strikes a ball as hard as he can, it will run five times the length of the table.

10. a. Of persons: Living too fast (see FAST *adv.* 7); extravagant in habits; devoted to pleasure, dissipated; usually implying a greater or less degree of immorality. Also in *fast life, living*, etc. **b.** Often applied to women in milder sense: Studiedly unrefined in habits and manners, disregardful of propriety or decorum. **c.** Of language, etc.: Characteristic of 'fast' people. **d.** Of a place: Inhabited or frequented by 'fast' people.

1745 E. HEYWOOD *Female Spect.* (1748) II. 273 In deep consultation..how to repair the defects of age and fast living. **1841** J. T. HEWLETT *Parish Clerk* I. 179 All the fast men were anxious to make their acquaintance. **1852** L. OLIPHANT *Journey to Katmandu* 191 Lucknow is a fast place. **1856** F. E. PAGET *Owlet Owlst.* 140 If a fast young lady be detestable anywhere, what must she be in a country parsonage? **1861** HUGHES *Tom Brown at Oxf.* i. (1889) 2 The college was decidedly fast. **1870** RAMSAY *Remin.* v. (*ed.* 18) 119 I never heard..all these fast terms. **1874** BURNAND *My Time* xxiii. 203 My lot was cast in a fast set.

III. 11. *Comb.* and locutions: **fast back, fastback**, (*a*) in *Bookbinding*, a back that adheres to the sheets as distinguished from a loose back or spring back; (*b*) orig. *U.S.*, on a motor car; a back that slopes in one continuous line from the top of the car to the rear bumper; hence, such a car; freq. *attrib.*; **fast-boat**, a whaling-boat which has made itself fast to a whale, *i.e.* has harpooned it; **fast buck** *U.S.* [BUCK *sb.*^{8}], a quickly earned dollar; †**fast-fingered** *a.* = CLOSE-FISTED; **fast fish**, a whale which has been harpooned and is therefore *fast* to the boat; **fast-footed** *a.*, (*a*) *Cricket*, denoting the action or method of keeping the back foot immobile in batting; (*b*) fast-moving, speedy of foot; **fast-freight**, *U.S.* (Railways), goods for rapid transportation, whence *fast-freight-line*; **fast-gated** *a.*, *dial.* going at a rapid rate; **fast-goer**, one who goes fast; †**fast-hand** *v.*, to grasp tightly; †**fast-handed** *a.* = CLOSE-FISTED; **fast-hold**, (*a*) a stronghold; *lit.* and *fig.*; (*b*) confinement, durance; **fast ice**, ice covering sea-water but usually attached to land (cf. FAST *sb.*^{3} and FAST *a.* 2 c); **fast lane**, (*a*) a traffic lane, usu. that farthest from the outer edge of a motorway or dual carriageway, intended for drivers who wish to overtake slower cars; (*b*) *fig.*, esp. denoting a glamorous or highly-pressured lifestyle; freq. in phr. *in the fast lane* and *attrib.*; **fast neutron**, a neutron with kinetic energy greater than some arbitrary value, esp. one that has not been slowed down by the action of a moderator after being produced by the fission of a nucleus; **fast one** *slang* (orig. *U.S.*), esp. in phrases, as *to pull* (or *put over*) *a fast one*, to take unfair advantage by (rapid) action of some sort; **fast-pulley**, also in *fast and loose pulley* (see quots.); **fast ship**, a ship which has secured a particular whale, by means of its boats; **fast-shot** (see quot.); **fast store** *Computers* (see quot. 1962); also called *fast-, quick-access storage*; **fast track** orig. *U.S.*, (*a*) *Horse-racing*, a race-track on which the going is dry and hard, enabling the horses to race at high speed; (*b*) a hectic place or post, esp. in business; a route to rapid advancement or development; (*c*) as *adj.*, (i) high-flying; suitable for rapid promotion; (ii) chiefly *U.S.*, of planning, construction, etc.: accelerated; **fast tracker** *U.S.*, a high-flyer; an ambitious or thrusting person; **fast worker** *colloq.*, one who makes rapid progress, used esp. in amatory contexts. Also FAST AND LOOSE.

1912 A. J. PHILIP *Business of Bookbinding* xv. 181 Books which are to have leather backs are now individually examined and tested to find out which should have *fast backs and which open backs. **1965** *Economist* 7 Aug. 552/2 The 1600 [Volkswagen car] is given a 'fast' (or sharply sloping) back. **1968** *Autocar* 14 Mar. 27/1 German fastback fitted with new fully automatic transmission. **1969** *Guardian* 7 Oct. 5/4 A fastback family saloon. **1820** SCORESBY *Acc. Arctic Reg.* I. 480 It frequently drags the *fast-boat with

such speed through the water, that it is . . soon out of sight. **1839** T. Beale *Sperm Whale* 165 Those in the 'fast' boat haul themselves gently towards the whale. **1949** *New Yorker* 5 Nov. 82 Tryin' to hustle me a *fast buck. **1969** *Observer* 23 Nov. 7/1 A friend who made a fast buck out of selling dirty postcards. **1971** *Publishers' Weekly* 22 Mar. 33 In recent years, the Norman Rockwell kind of vision has been sullied by cynical, fast-buck door-to-door operators. **1607** Hieron *Wks.* I. 339 How *fast fingered and close handed are they, when any thing should come from them to a good purpose? **1820** Scoresby *Acc. Arctic Reg.* II. 244 The first effort of a '*fast-fish' or whale that has been struck, is to escape from the boat. **1897** *Encycl. Sport* I. 228/2 The '*fast-footed' style of hitting. **1907** *Westm. Gaz.* 21 Aug. 7/1 To play right over it in attempting a fast-footed drive. **1960** T. McLean *Kings of Rugby* xi. 143 Watson, who had not been conspicuously fast-footed as Faull made his run, restored his reputation [etc.]. **1881** *Chicago Times* 12 Mar., The Commercial Express *Fast-Freight line. **1875** Waugh *Old Cronies* iv. in *Tufts Heather* (1892) I. 221 A *fast-gated spendthrift. **1837** Dickens *Sk. Boz* 2nd Ser. 42 [His] great aim . . was to be considered as a 'knowing card', a '*fast-goer'. **1885** Miss Braddon *Wyllard's Weird* I. vii. 183 In a hunting country, the fast-goers generally get together. **1632** J. Hayward tr. *Biondi's Eromena* 104 She perceived it was a woman who *fast-handing a little plancke, floted on the sea. **1611** Speed *Hist. Gt. Brit.* Proeme, Nature in those gifts hath beene both liberall . . and prodigall, though Fortune as sparing and *fast handed against me. **1622** Bacon *Hen. VII* 207 The King also beeing fast handed, and loth to part with a second Dowrie. **1802** *Hatred* III. 152 A banditti . . secured themselves from punishment by retiring to this *fast hold. **1832** *Fraser's Mag.* V. 566 The wild cat, the fox, and the badger, are almost entirely exterminated from their fastholds. **1870** *Daily News* 8 Sept. 6 When the last fast-hold of priestly influence is rapidly disappearing in the West. **1932** *Geogr. Rev.* XXII. 81 The relative lightness and flatness of the sea ice over the entire length of our flight classified it as belonging to the pack-ice zone intermediate between the polar cap ice of the central basin and the *fast ice of the coastal shelves. **1956** *Nature* 31 Mar. 599/2 About five thousand Emperor penguins were found on the fast-ice in an adjoining bay. . . A few days after arrival the sea ice on which the penguins had been nesting broke up. **1966** T. Wisdom *High-Performance Driving* xi. 111 One is frustrated on a motor-way by the driver ahead in the '*fast' lane (if only he appreciated that it is the *overtaking* lane). **1971** K. Royce *Concrete Boot* x. 120 I'd been batting away on the fast lane, peering ahead . . through the cars in front of me. **1978** *Detroit Free Press* 16 Apr. (Parade) 20/4 The image usually associated with the superjet, 'fast lane' set. **1981** *Christian Science Monitor* 9 Oct. 14 (*heading*) Cambodian united front talks in fast lane to nowhere. **1984** *Tampa* (Florida) *Tribune* 5 Apr. 4D/1 Nero's sense of humor compensates for any drudgery in his fast-lane schedule. **1933** *Physical Rev.* XLIV. 236 (*heading*) Disintegration of neon nuclei by *fast neutrons. **1945** H. D. Smyth *Gen. Acct. Devel. Atomic Energy Mil. Purposes* vi. 53 The program would provide the theoretical and experimental data required for the design of a fast-neutron chain-reacting bomb. **1956** A. H. Compton *Atomic Quest* i. 55 It was the fast neutrons coming directly from the atom's fission that would take part in an atomic explosion; in the controlled reaction where a moderator was used, it was the slow neutrons that were most important. **1968** *New Scientist* 8 Feb. 305/1 Experiments in fast-neutron therapy have so far concentrated mainly on animals. **1923** H. C. Witwer in *Cosmopolitan* Nov. 98/1 He's trying to put over a *fast one! **1932** J. Sayre *Rackety Rax* xiii. 103 Brick pulled a fast one in the St. Mary's game. **1932** Wodehouse *Hot Water* xvii. 282 The thought that a girl capable of thinking up a fast one like that should be madly throwing herself away on Blair Eggleston . . was infinitely saddening. **1933** J. G. Cozzens *Cure of Flesh* II. 157 You never know when they may pull a fast one on you. **1937** R. Stout *Red Box* ix. 127 There was a chance you were putting over a fast one. **1943** H. Bolitho *Combat Report* 107, I said . . that they must not try to pull a fast one on me. **1943** Hunt & Pringle *Service Slang* 31 *A Fast One*: (a) any remark giving rise to Thought. (b) a trick, especially one calculated to shift the onus. 'Pulling a fast one' on your associates is very much the same as 'putting one over' on them. **1953** R. Lehmann *Echoing Grove* 250 [Amer. loq.] The last thing I meant was to try and pull a fast one, but I guess that's what I'm doing. **1958** 'A. Gilbert' *Death against Clock* 96 Mad to think they can pull a fast one . . over the whole community. **1856** Brees *Terms Archit., etc.*, **Fast and loose pulleys*, a very simple . . contrivance for disengaging and re-engaging machinery, consisting of two pulleys. One pulley is fixed on an axle, another, having a bush, is loose. The band conveying the motion may consequently be shifted from one pulley to the other at pleasure. **1874** Knight *Dict. Mech.*, *Fast-pulley* (Machinery), one keyed to the shaft so as to revolve therewith. **1820** Scoresby *Acc. Arctic Reg.* II. 250 These signals serve to indicate . . the exclusive title of the '*fast-ship' to the entangled whale. **1846** Brockett *Gloss. N. Country Words* (ed. 3) 161 When a shot has discharged without disturbing the coal . . it is said to be a **fast shot*. **1955** *Scope Electronic Computers in Office* (Office Managem. Assoc.) 36 The *fast store has a capacity of 390 forty binary digit words. **1962** *Gloss. Terms Autom. Data Proc.* (*B.S.I.*) 64 *Fast store*, an imprecise term referring to a store whose access time is relatively short. **1964** T. W. McRae *Impact of Computers on Accounting* i. 8 Apart from these historical or backing stores we need a fast access store for handling that part of the data which is being currently processed by the computer. **1934** R. S. Dowst *Playing the Races* 175 **Fast track*, a track in condition to permit maximum speed. **1965** R. M. Nixon in *N.Y. Times Mag.* 25 Apr. 14/4 New York . . is a place where you can't slow down—a fast track. Any person tends to vegetate unless he is moving on a fast track. **1968** *Bulletin* (Sydney) 3 Feb. 22/2 The 'fast track' men want to go some place in the corporation. **1968** T. Ainslie *Compl. Guide Thoroughbred Racing* vii. 108 Information about the running styles, preferred distances, [etc.] . . of most horses is based on fast-track performances. **1970** *Archit. Rec.* CXLVIII. 91/1 Unit theory design is a synthesis of concepts: the module (structural or functional), the systems approach . . and the 'fast track' approach to programing, design and construction. **1984** *Business Rev. Weekly* Feb. 29/3 There are not enough signs now that the US is entering this fast track. **1984** *Times* 15 Dec. 7/1 Many a thrusting young manager or fast-track public servant has had his hopes dashed. **1977** *Fortune* June 160/2 Some of the *fast trackers seem so preoccupied with getting ahead that they don't always notice the implications of what they do. **1982** Peters & Waterman *In Search of Excellence* viii. 265 He almost always put his fast-trackers in the tiny divisions. **1921** S. Ford *Inez & Trilby May* xii. 212 The dark stranger is getting a bit free. He is patting Inez on the arm. . . 'One of these *fast workers, I take it,' says I. **1929** J. B. Priestley *Good Companions* II. v. 373 He had had two while some fellows . . had not been able to secure a single drink. . . He was undoubtedly a fast worker. **1961** I. Murdoch *Severed Head* xxiii. 195 'I'm going to get married.' . . 'Admit you're a fast worker!' **1965** 'R. Foley' *Suffer a Witch* (1966) v. 95 And you had dinner with him practically the next evening? . . He seems to be a fast worker.

fast (fɑːst, -æ-), *adv.* Forms: 1 **fæste**, 3 **fæste, feste**, *south. dial.* **væste, veste**, 3–6 **faste**, 3 *Orm.* **fasste**, *south. dial.* **vaste**, 3– **fast**; *comp.* 1 **fæstor**, 3 **fæstre**, *south. dial.* vastre, 3– faster. [OE. *fæste* = OS. *fasto* (Du. *vast*), OHG. *fasto* (MHG. *vaste* firmly, fixedly, closely, quickly, mod.G. *fast* almost), ON. *fast*:—OTeut. **fastô*, f. *fastu-* FAST *a.*]

1. a. In a fast manner, so as not to be moved or shaken; *lit.* and *fig.*; firmly, fixedly. Often with *stand*, *sit*, *stick*, etc. †***to sit fast upon***: to insist upon.

c **900** *Bæda's Hist.* II. xiii, þa sceat he mid þy spere, þæt hit sticode fæste on þæm heriȝe. *c* **1205** Lay. 9562 Heore grið heo setten fæste. *c* **1300** *Beket* 1306 Whan ech man of the lond faste aȝen him is. *c* **1400** *Lanfranc's Cirurg.* 188 It wole make hise heeris longe & make hem sitte faste. **1526** *Pilgr. Perf.* (W. de W. 1531) 8b, Persones that . . stycke fast in theyr owne blynde fantasy. **1535** Coverdale *Ps.* xxxiii. 9 For . . loke what he commaundeth, it stondeth fast. **1563–87** Foxe *A. & M.* (1684) III. 112 Whose faith may be the faster fixed on Gods verity. **1566** T. Stapleton *Ret. Untr. Jewel* I. 37 He sitteth so fast upon the bare wordes. **1611** Bible *1 Cor.* xvi. 13 Stand fast in the faith. **1726** Shelvocke *Voy. round World* (1757) 202 Their fire had little or no effect. All stood fast with us. **1777** H. Gates in Sparks *Corr. Amer. Rev.* (1853) I. 548, I have seen the Mohawk River fast frozen on the 10th of November. **1789** Cowper *Ann. Mem.* 1789. 45 The symbol of a righteous reign Sat fast on George's brows again. **1815** Scott *Paul's Lett.* (1839) 124 Stand fast, 95th . . we must not be beat. **1843** Macaulay *Lays Anc. Rome, Virginia*, No cries were there, but teeth set fast. **1879** F. W. Robinson *Coward Conscience* I. i, Stick fast to the hand-rail.

b. ***to sleep fast***: to sleep soundly.

(For *fast asleep* see FAST *a.* 1 e.)

c **1200** *Trin. Coll. Hom.* 201 Sume men slapeð faste and sume nappeð. **1297** R. Glouc. (Rolls) 2780 In eiþer [stone] a dragon þer inne slepe vaste. *c* **1381** Chaucer *Parl. Foules* 94 Tooke rest, that made me to slepe faste. **1483** Caxton *G. de la Tour* F viij, Whyle he fast slept she cutte awey the heerys of his heede. **1557** *K. Arthur* (W. Copland) VI. i, So syr Launcelot slepte passyng fast. **1667** Milton *P. L.* IX. 182 Him fast sleeping soon he found. **1758** Johnson *Let.* 9 Jan., I must have indeed slept very fast. **1819** Byron *Juan* II. xcix, The day before fast sleeping on the water, They found a turtle. **1844** Mrs. Browning *Sonnets, Comfort*, He sleeps the faster that he wept before.

†**c.** Expressing fixity of attention, effort, or purpose: Earnestly, steadily, diligently, zealously.

c **1200** Ormin 9241 Menn himm sohhtenn fasste to, Forr himm to seon & herenn. *c* **1300** *Havelok* 2148 Þanne bihelden he him faste. *c* **1325** *Poem Times Edw. II*, 57 The clerkes of the cuntré wolen him faste wowe. **1375** Barbour *Bruce* I. 42 The barnage . . Assemblyt thaim, and fayndyt fast To cheyss a king thar land to ster. *Ibid.* IV. 616 Eftyr the fyr he lukyt fast. **14..** *Tundale's Vis.* 2053 Tundale lystenyd fast and logh. *c* **1430** *Syr Tryam.* 65 Syr Marrok, hys steward, Was faste abowtewarde To do hys lady gyle. **1533** Bellenden *Livy* (1822) 413 The army at Veos desirit fast to have thare money for thare wageis. **1535** Coverdale *Judith* x. 23 She loked fast vpon him, & fell downe vpon the earth. **1593** Shaks. *2 Hen. VI*, V. ii. 21 Thou art so fast mine enemie. **1644** Milton *Areop.* (Arb.) 69 Others as fast reading, trying all things.

†**d.** Expressing vigour in action: Stoutly, strongly, vigorously. *Obs.*

1297 R. Glouc. (1724) 399 Hii . . bysegede þe cyte, & asaylede vaste. *c* **1320** *Sir Tristr.* 2783 Tristrem as aman, Fast he gan to fiȝt. **1375** Barbour *Bruce* XIII. 129 Be thai [presit] . . A little fastar . . thai discumfit soyn sall be. *c* **1420** *Anturs of Arth.* xlvii, Fast he foundes atte his face With a squrd kene. *c* **1450** Myrc 1627 Wepeth faste and ys sory. **1570** Buchanan *Chamæleon* Wks. (1892) 51 Albeit Chamæleon . . ragit neuir sa fast the contrait was concludit.

2. a. With firm grasp, attachment, or adhesion; so as not to permit of escape or detachment; tightly, securely. Often with *bind*, *hold*, etc. *lit.* and *fig.* See also HOLD *v.*

c **888** K. Ælfred *Boeth.* xxxv. §2 Swiþe fæste to somne ȝelimed. *c* **1200** *Trin. Coll. Hom.* 103 Þe man þe halt faste his sinne . . he is demd fro heuene to helle. *c* **1205** Lay. 15337 Þa wes Uortigerne væste ibunden. *c* **1220** *Bestiary* 212 And feste ðe forðward fast at thin herte, ðat tu firmest higtes. *c* **1300** *St. Brandan* 93 With bole huden stronge y-nou y-nailed therto faste. **1340** Hampole *Pr. Consc.* 684 This es the leef that hanges noght faste. *c* **1400** *Lanfranc's Cirurg.* 315 Þan take faste þe boon & drawe it to his place aȝen. **1480** Caxton *Chron. Eng.* ccxlii. 283 Kyng Richard was deposed and was kept fast in hold. **1542–3** *Act 34–5 Hen. VIII*, c. 6 Pinnes . . such as shal . . haue the heads soudered fast to the shanke. **1576** Fleming *Panopl. Epist.* 308 Something to hold fast, among many thinges that I have read. **1596** Shaks. *Merch. V.* II. v. 53 Fast binde, fast finde, A prouerbe neuer stale in thriftie minde. **1667** Milton *P.L.* VI. 543 Let each . . gripe fast his orbed Shield. **1685** *Lond. Gaz.* No. 2095/3 All the Ships in the Downs Ride fast. **1771** Mrs. Griffith tr. *Viaud's Shipwreck* 31 Clinging fast to the side of our vessel. **1816** J. Wilson *City of Plague* II. iii. 290 Fear binds us fast to guilt. **1838** Thirlwall *Greece* II. 306 To exhort them to choose and hold fast the good. **1850** Mrs. Browning *Rom. of Page*, And wedded fast were we.

†**b.** *fig.* Of a command or prohibition: Strictly.

c **1310** *St. Swithin* 76 in *E.E.P.* (1862) 45 His men faste he bad þat hi ne scholde him burie noȝt in church. **13..** *E.E. Allit. P.* B. 1147 To defowle hit euer vpon folde fast he forbedes. **1535** Coverdale *Jer.* xxxv. 14 The wordes . . are fast and surely kepte.

†**c.** Of defence or concealment: Securely. *Obs.*

1481 *Bk. St. Albans* E iv b, In moore or in moos he hidyth hem fast. **1535** Coverdale *2 Macc.* xii. 13 A cite, which was very fast kepte with brydges.

d. With passive notion: So as to be unable to move. ***to stick fast***: often *fig.* to be nonplussed, unable to get any further.

1526–34 Tindale *Acts* xxvii. 41 The foore parte stucke fast and moved not. **1635** Laud *Wks.* (1860) VII. 174 When he saw the man and his horse stuck fast in the quagmire. **1768** J. Byron *Narr. Patagonia* 15 Providentially we stuck fast between two great rocks. **1847** Marryat *Childr. N. Forest* xxi, Many of them stuck fast . . and attempted to clear themselves in vain. **1850** W. B. Clarke *Wreck of Favorite* 68, I found my limbs completely set fast from the intensity of the cold.

†**e.** quasi-*int.* (See quot.) *Obs.*

1720 Strype in *Stow's Surv. Lond.* I. xxix. 250/1 [The charter of the Fraternity of St. George, 1537, ordained] that in Case any Person were shot . . by any of these Archers, he was not to be . . molested, if he had immediately before he shot, used that common Word, *Fast*.

3. In a close-fitting manner; so as to leave no opening or outlet. Often with additional notion of security.

c **1205** Lay. 15320 Þa ȝæten heo tunden uaste. *c* **1340** *Cursor M.* 2788 (Trin.) Faste þe dores gon he bare. *c* **1400** Maundev. (Roxb.) ii. 7 Þe Iews . . sett a coroun on his heued and thrast it þeron so fast þat þe blude ran doune. *c* **1430** *Two Cookery-bks.* 27 Do it ouer þe fyre & hele it faste. **1600** J. Pory tr. *Leo's Africa* II. 167 Each one of these cels is shut fast with a little doore. **1667** Milton *P.L.* IV. 190 Some rich Burgher whose substantial dores, Cross-barrd and bolted fast, fear no assault. **1781** Cowper *Hope* 658 While Bigotry . . His eyes shut fast, his fingers in his ears. **1850** Kingsley *Alt. Locke* xxxvii, Crossthwaite had kept his face fast buried in his hands. **1850** B. Taylor *Eldorado* iv. (1862) 36 With their hats pulled fast over their brows. **1854** H. Miller *Footpr. Creat.* i. (1874) 2 Fast jammed in between a steep hill and the sea.

4. a. Of proximity; *lit.* and *fig.* Close, hard; very near. Now only in ***fast beside***, ***fast by*** (arch. or poet.), and with vbs. expressing following, where the sense approaches 6.

c **1275** Lay. 9 Faste by Radistone. *c* **1325** *Song Yesterday* 68 in *E.E.P.* (1862) 135 To-ward vr ende we drawe ful fast. *c* **1340** *Cursor M.* 15782 (Trin.) Wiþ þat word . . þei bigon to awake And him faste aboute biset. *c* **1400** Maundev. (1839) xxi. 228 The See that touched & was fast to the mount. *c* **1400** *Destr. Troy* 326 Ther were fyldes full faire fast þere besyde. *c* **1420** *Palladius on Husb.* VIII. 169 If Aust be fast nygh September. *c* **1425** *Seven Sag.* 3009 (P.) Faste by hym he hyr sete. **1526** *Pilgr. Perf.* (W. de W. 1531), Whiche worlde . . decaynge draweth fast to an ende. **1590** Spenser *F.Q.* I. xii. 25 Fast before the king he did alight. **1603** Knolles *Hist. Turks* (1621) 1117 A mill fast without the town. **1667** Milton *P. L.* II. 725 The Snakie Sorceress that sat Fast by Hell Gate. **1679–1714** Burnet *Hist. Ref.* I. II. 48 Lautrech with the French army lay still fast about Bononia. **1704** Pope *Windsor For.* 314 And, fast beside him, once-fear'd Edward sleeps. **1729** Savage *Wanderer* v. 399 The Globe of Light Drops sudden; fast pursued by Shades of Night. **1790** Beatson *Nav. & Mil. Mem.* 394 Which brought the vessels in our rear fast up. **1801** Wordsw. *Cuckoo & Nightingale* xx, The next bush that was me fast beside. **1821** Keats *Lamia* 17 Fast by the springs . . Were strewn rich gifts. **1869** Freeman *Norm. Conq.* (1876) III. xi. 72 Fast on its appearance had followed the troubles of the reign of . . Eadward.

b. ***fast upon*** or ***on***: near upon (a specified quantity). Cf. Ger. *fast* almost. *Obs.* exc. *dial.*

1583 Golding *Calvin on Deut.* xxx. 177 After he had gone about with them a fortie yeres or fast vpon it. **1600** Holland *Livy* XXIX. 735 So there were . . killed in the place . . fast upon a thousand. **1869** *Lonsdale Gloss.*, 'I gev fast on ten pounds for her.'

†**5.** Closely, at once, immediately. ***as fast as***: as soon as (cf. 6). *Obs.*

a **1300** *Cursor M.* 823 (Gött.) Als fast as þai had don þat sinne, Bigan all vr baret to biginne. *c* **1386** Chaucer *Can. Yeom. Prol. & T.* 552 Whan he cometh, as fast schul ye see A wonder thing, which ye saugh never er this. *a* **1400–50** *Alexander* 3944 Þan come a fliȝtir in of fowls, as fast as it dawid. *c* **1400** *Lanfranc's Cirurg.* 322 It is necessarie as faste þat a mannes rigboon is out of þe joynct þat it be brouȝt yn aȝen anoon. **1428** *Surtees Misc.* (1890) 9 Was done afterwarde als her fast folowys. *c* **1440** *Lay Folks Mass Bk.* (MS. C.) 56 Say a paternoster and an ave fast þereon. **1645** Hammond *Pract. Catechism* I. iii. 50 He . . gave evidence of his fidelity as fast as occasions were offered. **1724** R. Falconer *Voy.* (1769) 231 My Opinion was to execute it as fast as ever we could. **1782** Cowper *Gilpin* 117 And still as fast as he drew near, 'Twas wonderful to view, How [etc.].

6. a. Quickly, rapidly, swiftly.

For the development of this sense from the primary sense 'firmly', cf. 1 d, 4, 5, and expressions like 'to run hard'. It does not appear that this sense is recorded in OE., but it belongs to MHG. *vaste*, ON. *fast*.

c **1205** Lay. 7986 He warnede alle his cnihtes . . & fusden an veste. **1297** R. Glouc. (1724) 401 Þo þe Cristyne yt vnderȝete, aȝen hii wende vaste. *a* **1300** *Cursor M.* 3866 (Cott.) It was ferli . . How fast þai multiplid þar. **1340** Hampole *Pr. Consc.* 4003 Takens, war-thurgh he may understande, þat þe day of dome es fast comande. *c* **1450** *St. Cuthbert* (Surtees) 7437, I prayde my felowes fast to ryde. **1548** Hall *Chron.* 113b, The Frenchemen . . fled into the toune so faste, that one letted the other to entre. **1585** J. B. tr. *P. Viret's Sch. Beastes* B viij b, Men doo not so fast breake them, as she repaireth and amendeth them. **1632** Lithgow

Trav. VI. 298 The Camell..hath a most slow and lazy pace ..neither can he goe faster although he would. **1688** J. SMITH *Baroscope* 71 The Mercury then generally Rises very fast of a sudden. **1719** DE FOE *Crusoe* (1840) I. xv. 268, I found he..would make it go almost as swift and fast again as I could. **1776** ADAM SMITH *W.N.* I. xi. (1869) I. 264 The rate of profit..is..highest in the countries which are going fastest to ruin. **1814** SCOTT *Ld. of Isles* II. xiii, Barendoun fled fast away. **1876** TREVELYAN *Macaulay* II. 2 His health was breaking fast. **1893** SIR L. W. CAVE in *Law Times* XCV. 26/1 The frequent applications to commit for contempt of court are fast bringing the law itself into contempt.

b. In quick succession; one close upon another.

1591 SHAKS. *1 Hen. VI*, III. i. 82 The Bishop and the Duke of Glosters men..Doe pelt so fast at one anothers Pate, That [etc.]. **1610** —— *Temp.* I. ii. 281 Where thou didst vent thy groanes As fast as Mill-wheeles strike. **1647** CLARENDON *Hist. Reb.* I. (1843) 22/2 His honours had grown faster upon him than his fortunes. **1771** MRS. GRIFFITH tr. *Viaud's Shipwreck* 169 My tears fell faster than his. *a* **1822** SHELLEY *Song for Tasso* 12 My thoughts come fast.

c. Readily, with alacrity. *Obs.* exc. in colloq. phrase ***fast enough***.

c **1420** *Anturs of Arth.* xviii, Thou dele fast of the gode, To tho that fales the fode. *c* **1477** CAXTON *Jason* 30 They.. attended frely and fast a fote. **1553** T. WILSON *Rhet.* (1580) 2 The one affirmyng for his parte, and the other deniyng as faste againe for his parte. **1598** SHAKS. *Merry W.* IV. i. 69 Hee teaches him to hic and to hac; which they'll doe fast enough of themselues. **1642** MILTON *Apol. Smect.* (1851) 314, I cannot but admire as fast what they think is become of judgement, and tast in other men. *Mod.* He would do it fast enough, if you paid him for it.

7. ***to live fast***: **a.** to expend quickly one's vital energy; **b.** to live a dissipated life. Cf. FAST *a.* 10.

a. 1700 DRYDEN *Char. Good Parson* 9 Of sixty years he seemed; and well might last To sixty more, but that he lived too fast. **1711** SHAFTESB. *Charac.* (1737) I. 126 As if they liv'd the fastest who took the greatest pains to enjoy least of life. **1851** CARPENTER *Man. Phys.* (ed. 2) 78 Cold-blooded animals live much faster..at high temperatures, than at low; so that they die much sooner.

b. 1699 T. BROWN *Colloq. Erasm.* iv. 26 Living very fast, as they say, [he] has brought his Noble to Nine-pence. **1754** *World* 19 Sept. ¶2 He has lived rather fast formerly. **1820** W. IRVING *Sketch Bk.*, *J. Bull* (1865) 389 They fear he has lived too fast.

8. Comb. with ppl. adjs. and (rarely) vbl. sbs.

a. (sense 1) as ***fast-dyed, -grounded, -rooted*** (whence ***fast-rootedness***), ***settled***, ppl. adjs.

1541 COVERDALE *Old Faith* ix, The only true, old, undoubted, and fast-grounded faith. **1587** GOLDING *De Mornay* Ep. Ded. 1 In the world we see a stedie and fast-setled order. **1832** TENNYSON *Lotos-Eaters* 83 The flower.. Fast-rooted in the fruitful soil. **1853** LYNCH *Self-Improv.* ii. 31 The fast-rootedness of religious vitality. **1888** *Daily News* 19 Nov. 2/7 The fast-dyed black goods retain their popularity.

b. (sense 2) as ***fast-anchored, -bound, -plighted*** ppl. adjs.; †***fast-fancied***, attached firmly by fancy.

1580 BARET *Alv.* F 181 Fast bound or tied, *religatus*. *c* **1590** GREENE *Fr. Bacon* v. 79 Thou com'st in post from merry Fressingfield Fast-fancied to the Keepers bonny lass. **1627** DRAYTON *Agincrt.* ccxxviii. 2032 His fast plighted troth. **1633** FORD *'Tis Pity* v. v, Our fast-knit affections. **1784** COWPER *Task* II. 151 Were they the wicked above all, And we the righteous, whose fast-anchored isle Moved not? **1814** BYRON *Hebr. Mel.*, *Destr. Jerusalem* ii, The fast-fettered hands. **1823** SCOTT *Peveril* III. iii. 56 The darbies are the fetlocks—the fast-keepers my boy—the bail for good behaviour. **1842** MANNING *Serm.* xxv. (1848) 382 There still remains with us a fast-cleaving and mysterious evil. **1871** B. TAYLOR *Faust* (1875) II. III. 193 Bring I thee Fast bound in welded fetters the knave.

c. (sense 3) as ***fast-closed, -locked, -shut***, ppl. adjs.

1595 SHAKS. *John* II. i. 447 Our fast closed gates. *a* **1649** DRUMM. OF HAWTH. *Poems* (1711) 18 A fast-shut prison. **1907** *Academy* 27 July 717/1 Some fast-locked gate. **1931** R. CAMPBELL *Georgiad* ii. 46 Nor glide a ghost around each fast-shut door.

d. (sense 6) as ***fast-sailing***, vbl. sb.; ***fast-falling, -going, -sailing***, etc., ppl. adjs.; (sense 10 of adj.) ***fast-going*** ppl. a.

1593 SHAKS. *3 Hen. VI*, I. iv. 162 Euen my Foes will shed fast-falling Teares. **1593** —— *Rich. II*, III. iv. 34 Goe thou, and like an Executioner Cut off the heads of too fast growing sprayes. **1622** DRAYTON *Poly-olb.* xxiii. 187 A good fast feeding grass, most strongly that doth breed. **1757** DYER *Fleece* IV. 603 Fast-gath'ring tempests. **1800** NELSON in Nicolas *Disp.* IV. 200 A fast-sailing Polacca of about 70 Tons. **1820** SCORESBY *Acc. Arctic Reg.* II. 338 That valuable property of a ship, called fast-sailing. **1820** KEATS *Ode to Nightingale* 49 Fast-fading violets cover'd up in leaves. *a* **1822** SHELLEY *Bigotry* I. 3 The fast-fleeting hind. **1822** in Cobbett *Rur. Rides* (1885) I. 96 The fast-sinking Old Times newspaper. *a* **1835** MRS. HEMANS *Penitent's Offering* Poems (1875) 496 That fast-flowing rain of tears. **1866** TROLLOPE *Belton Est.* I. iii. 81 She was a fast-going girl. **1870** DICKENS *E. Drood* ii, The fast-darkening scene. **1892** *Pall Mall G.* 12 Oct. 5/1 The fast-going autumn. **1901** *Daily News* 23 Feb. 6/7 The awkwardness inseparable from fast-growing young creatures who have not yet attained perfect command of their limbs. **1910** *Westm. Gaz.* 24 June 12/2 The river has been very thick and fast-running. **1935** B. RUSSELL *Relig. & Sci.* vi. 159 It *might* happen that..all the fast-moving particles got to one side. **1952** C. DAY LEWIS tr. *Virgil's Aeneid* v. 115 The fast-swimming Tritons. **1957** *Times Lit. Suppl.* 25 Oct. 646/2 *De Luxe Tour* careers along, where the other novels meander. It is fast-moving, slick and professional. **1960** *Farmer & Stockbreeder* 16 Feb. Suppl. 23/1 A completely healthy fast-growing herd of pigs. **1964** G. H. HAGGIS et al. *Introd. Molecular Biol.* vii. 203 Ultra-fine genetic analyses using fast-breeding micro-organisms. **1971** *Engineering* Apr. 31/1 With such a fast-growing market there is always a danger of people with little knowledge of vending producing machines which, in the long term, could damage the image.

9. Special Comb. **fast-forward** *a.*, designating accelerated forward motion of a tape, etc., esp. to reach a particular place in a recording; hence (unhyphened) as *sb.*, (the facility for) fast-forward motion; also as *v. intr.* and *trans.*, to move rapidly forward through (the contents of a tape, etc.) by using the fast-forward facility.

1948 *Audio Engin.* Oct. 15/3 Very high rewind and fast-forward modes of operation have been provided. **1955** *Wireless World* July 335 (*caption*) Main control knob with seven positions:—(1) 'off', (2) amplifier only, (3) fast forward, (4) fast rewind. **1974** *Stereo Rev.* Mar. 71/2 To return to a specific point on the tape you must fast-forward along through the entire loop. **1983** *Listener* 13 Jan. 34/2 Some car tape-players offer rewind and fast forward, like a domestic tape-deck. **1985** *Marxism Today* May 34/1 People with the technology use it to avoid commercial breaks..by fast-forwarding material recorded off-air.

† **fast**, *v.*[1] *Obs.* Forms: 1 fæstan, 3–5 fest(e(n, -yn, 3–4 fasten, 5–6 faste, 5– fast. *Pa. t.* 3–5 fest, 4 fast-, fested, -id, -yd, 5–7 fasted. *Pa. pple.* 3–5 fest(e, 4 fast(e. [OE. *fæstan* (rare; also in compounds *ʒe-*, *oð-befæstan*), corresp. to OFris. *festia*, OS. *festian* (Du. *vesten*), OHG. *fasten*, *festan* (MHG. *festen*), ON. *festa* (Da. *fæste*, Sw. *fästa*):—OTeut. **fastjan*, f. **fast-u-* FAST *a.*

Before *st*, *ft*, the umlaut of *a* in OE. was *æ* (instead of *ę*), and in ME. dialects this is divergently represented by *a* and *e*. The wide prevalence of the form *fest(en* in ME., however, is prob. in part due to Scandinavian influence.]

1. To make fast to something; to attach with bonds or nails; to bind together. Const. *on*, *till*, *to*, *unto*. **a.** with reference to material things. Also, ***to fast up*** (a wound): to bind up.

c **1220** *Bestiary* 462 Ðe spinnere..festeð atte hus rof hire fodredes. *a* **1300** *Leg. Gregory* (Schulz) 110 Þan ſche hadde ..in þe cradel fast him fest. *a* **1300** *Cursor M.* 1728 (Gött.) [Noe] himself festid [*Fairfax* feste] bath band and lace. *c* **1330** R. BRUNNE *Chron.* (1810) 272 Fire þei fest on it alle, & brent it [þe rede haule] þat et felle. **1340** HAMPOLE *Pr. Consc.* 5275 Þe neyles þat hym thurgh hand and fote Til þe hard rode tre fast fested. **1382** WYCLIF *Ezek.* xxx. 21 Boundyn in clothis and fastid..with smale lynnen clothis. *c* **1440** *Syr Gener.* (Roxb.) 2717 On his legges thou doo fest Strong fetures. **1523** FITZHERB. *Surv.* xxv. (1539) 48 To faste the teme to the same. **1549** COVERDALE *Erasm. Par. Gal.* 14 Jesus Christ was for your sakes faste vpon the crosse. **1593** *Rites & Mon. Ch. Durh.* (Surtees) 4 Which cord was all fest together..over the cover. **1615** W. LAWSON *Orch. & Gard.* III. x. (1668) 29 Cover your wound, and fast it up. **1626** CAPT. SMITH *Accid. Yng. Seamen* 27 Fast you[r] Anchor with your shanke painter. **1665** G. HAVERS *P. della Valle's Trav. E. India* 348 At the foot of that Cross three Nails, to signifie those which fasted our Saviour unto it.

b. with reference to immaterial things.

c **1220** *Bestiary* 553 Wo so festeð hope on him, he sal him folgen to helle dim. *a* **1340** HAMPOLE *Psalter* xii. 1 A perfit man..has..fested þaim [desires] in ihesu crist. **1568** T. HOWELL *Arb. Amitie* (1879) 94 Firmely fast thy fayth on him, that's true continually.

c. *refl.* and *intr.* for *refl.* With *on*, *to*: To attach oneself to, take hold of, seize upon. Cf. *to fasten on*.

c **1250** *Gen. & Ex.* 3797 A fier maȝti ðat folc fest on. *c* **1300** *Cursor M.* 26782 (Cott.) Þai þaim to þair filthes fest. **1340** HAMPOLE *Pr. Consc.* 6772 Nedders þat on þam sal fest. *c* **1420** *Avow. Arth.* vii, Ther was non so hardy Durste on the fynde fast. **14..** *Kyng & Hermit* 475 in Hazl. *E.P.P.* (1864) I. 32 Ther is no dere in this foreste And it [an arrow] wolde onne hym feste, Bot it schuld spyll his skale.

d. To make fast in wedlock; to betroth, wed. Const. *to*, *with*.

c **1300** *Sat. Kildare* in *E.E.P.* (1862) 155 He is sori of his lif þat is fast to such a wif. **1377** LANGL. *P. Pl.* B. II. 123 Þow hast fest hire to fals. *c* **1430** *Syr Tryam.* 643 They schulde faste hur with no fere.

2. To fix in something else; to fix firmly; to establish, settle, in material or immaterial sense; and with sentence as *obj.*

c **950** *Lindisf. Gosp.* Luke xxiii. 46 In hondum ðinum..ic fæsto [*commendo*] gast minne. *c* **1250** *Gen. & Ex.* 1524 Ðor wurð wið him trewðe fest Abimalech. **1297** R. GLOUC. (1724) 150 Þat ich hym wolde myd trewþe siker faste on honde. *a* **1300** *Cursor M.* 21013 (Gött.) Iacob þe mare..þe land of spaigne in faith he fest. **1382** WYCLIF *Ex.* xv. 17 Lord, thi seyntuarye, that thin hondes fastiden. *c* **1400** *Ywaine & Gaw.* 1989 His shelde bifor his face he fest. *c* **1440** *Secrees, Prose Version* (E.E.T.S.) A kynge, þat yn vnite and obedience haþ confermed and fastyd þe louable poeple of Inde. *c* **1460** *Towneley Myst.* 91 Then wold I we fest This mete who shalle into panyere kest. **1664** *Floddan Field* ix. 81 His folks could hardly fest their feet.

b. To plant, bring or drive home (a blow). Of the sun: To send forth (a ray).

a **1300** *Cursor M.* 23385 (Cott.) Als suith als sunn mai fest fra est his lem vnto þe west, als suith mai þou cum þider. *c* **1330** R. BRUNNE *Chron.* (1810) 190 A stroke on him he fest. *c* **1330** *Arth. & Merl.* 5986 So strong was Caulang verrament That King Arthour myht fest no dint.

c. *refl.* ***to fast oneself of***: to confirm oneself in.

c **1220** *Bestiary* 182 Feste ðe of stedefastnesse and ful of ðewes.

3. To confirm (a covenant); to pledge (faith, etc.).

a **1300** *Cursor M.* 5725 (Cott.) For forward þat he wit þam fest His ei of reuth he on þam kest. **1306** *Sir Simon Fraser* 41 in *Pol. Songs* (Camden) 214 To the kyng Edward hii fasten huere fay. *c* **1340** *Cursor M.* 2691 (Trin.) Þis couenaunt was faste wiþ þis. *a* **1450** *Le Morte Arth.* 3324 Yiff we may not oure forwardys faste. *c* **1470** HENRY *Wallace* XI. 540 Passand thai war..Till Inglismen thair fewte for to fest.

Hence **'fasted** *ppl. a.*

c **1440** *Promp. Parv.* 151/1 Fast, or bowndyn, or festyd, *vinctus*. *Ibid.* 158/1 Festyd, or teyyd fast to a thynge, *fixus*.

fast (fɑːst, -æ-), *v.*[2] Forms: 1–2 fæstan, 2 fæsten, 2–3 festen, 3–4 *south. dial.* vesten, 3–4 fasten. *Orm.* fasstenn, 4–5 fastyn, faste, *south. dial.* vaste, 4– fast. *Pa. t.* 1 fæstte, 2–3 feste, 4 faste, 7 fast, 3 fastede, 4–5 fastid, *Sc.* fastit, 4– fasted. *Pa. pple.* 3 ifaste, *south. dial.* i-, y-vast, 4 fast, fasten, 4–5 fastid, *Sc.* fastyt, 4– fasted. [Com. Teut.: OE. *fæstan* = OFris. *festia*, MDu., mod.D. *vasten*, OHG. *fastên* (MHG. *vasten*, mod.G. *fasten*), ON. *fasta* (Da. *faste*, Sw. *fasta*), Goth. *fastan*:—OTeut. **fastêjan*. The Goth. word has also the sense 'to keep, to observe', of which the sense 'to fast' was originally a specific application; cf. med.L. *observare* 'to fast'. In accordance with this presumed derivation, the ecclesiastical use of the word is here placed first, though the wider sense 2 appears in OE. and in all the modern Teut. langs.]

1. a. *intr.* To abstain from food, or to restrict oneself to a meagre diet, either as a religious observance or as a ceremonial expression of grief.

971 *Blickl. Hom.* 27 Þæt ure Drihten æfter þæm fulwihte fæstte. *c* **1050** *Byrhtferth's Handboc* in *Anglia* VIII. 311 Þon sceal man fæstan on þam ærran sæternes dæge. *c* **1175** *Lamb. Hom.* 29 Ic wulle gan to scrifte and forleten and festen þer fore. *a* **1225** *Ancr. R.* 20 Hwon ȝe vesteð ine winter. **1340** *Ayenb.* 50 God him hat ueste. *c* **1400** MAUNDEV. (Roxb.) iii. 10 Þai fast noȝt þe Seterday na tyme of þe ȝere. **1483** CAXTON *G. de la Tour* A vj, Yf ye may not faste the thre dayes. **1542** BECON *Potation for Lent* Early Wks. (1843) 107 He also teaches us the true..manner of fasting. **1600** SHAKS. *A.Y.L.* III. v. 58 But Mistris..downe on your knees And thanke heauen, fasting, for a good mans loue. *a* **1711** KEN *Serm.* Wks. (1838) 163 When he fasted, his diet was afflicting, such as became a mourner. **1782** PRIESTLEY *Corrupt. Chr.* II. VIII. 129 Some persons fasted before Easter. **1842** J. H. NEWMAN *Par. Serm.* VI. i. 1 We fast by way of penitence.

fig. *a* **1300** *Cursor M.* 27916 (Cotton Galba) To fast fro all syn. **1634** SIR T. HERBERT *Trav.* (1638) 259 Prosper's saying, That to fast from sinne, is the best fast.

b. with mention of the kind of spare diet permitted. Const. *on*; †formerly also *in*, *to*, *with*, and quasi-*trans.* in phrase ***to fast bread and water***.

c **1305** *Edmund Conf.* 24 in *E.E.P.* (1862) 71 Ofte heo ȝaf hem mede For to faste þane fridai to watere & to brede. **1375** BARBOUR *Bruce* XI. 383 Thai fastit bred and vattir ilkone. *a* **1450** *Knt. de la Tour* 12 [She] fasted..two tymes in brede and water. **1562** J. HEYWOOD *Prov. & Epigr.* (1867) 100 Thou rather wouldest..fast bread and water. **1588** SHAKS. *L.L.L.* I. i. 303 You shall fast a Weeke with Branne and water. **1844** LINGARD *Anglo-Sax. Ch.* (1858) II. x. 120 He fasted on bread, herbs, salt, and water.

2. a. *gen.* To go without food. †Also (contextually) to go without drink. Const. *from*.

c **1000** *Sax. Leechd.* I. 200 Genim ðysse sylfan wyrte leaf, syle etan fæstendum. *c* **1220** *Bestiary* 126 [Ðe neddre] fasteð til his fel him slakeð. *c* **1300** *Havelok* 865 Two days þer fastinde he yede. *c* **1340** *Cursor M.* 17345 (Trin.) Fro mete & drinke for to fast. *c* **1400** MAUNDEV. (1839) v. 58 He [a camel] may well faste fro drynk 2 dayes or three. **1606** SHAKS. *Ant. & Cl.* II. vii. 108, I had rather fast from all, foure dayes then drinke so much in one. **1607** TOPSELL *Serpents* (1608) 780 She must either quench her thirst with that, or fast. **1657** W. RAND tr. *Gassendi's Life of Peiresc* ii. 220 If he should fast all day from eating and drinking. **1671** MILTON *P.R.* II. 284 Fasting he went to sleep, and fasting wak'd. **1796** MRS. GLASSE *Cookery* xv. 265 Drink half a pint in the morning fasting. **1855** MILMAN *Lat. Chr.* (1864) II. III. vi. 90 The monk..was enjoined to fast rather than partake of food abroad.

transf. **1525** LD. BERNERS *Froiss.* II. cci. [cxcvii.] 615 The doughter of Fraunce..this fyue or syxe yere..shall nat be able to kepe hym company..he hath answered..that.. thoughe he faste a season, he shall take it well a worth. **1611** SHAKS. *Wint. T.* IV. iv. 612 Not a counterfeit Stone, not a Ribbon..to keepe my Pack from fasting.

b. Irish Antiq. ***to fast against, upon*** (a person): said with reference to the custom of sitting without food or drink at the door of a debtor, or any person who refused to satisfy some lawful demand.

1865 HANCOCK tr. *Senchus Mor.* I. 115, I deem it right that they be fasted upon before distress shall be taken from them. **1873** W. K. SULLIVAN *O'Curry's Anc. Irish* I. Introd. 283 Where the defendant was a *Rig*, the plaintiff was obliged to 'fast' upon him..before he made his distress. **1887** W. STOKES tr. *Tripartite Life St. Patrick* I. 219 Patrick..went to the king..And fasted against him.

c. quasi-*trans.* in various nonce-uses.

1596 SHAKS. *Tam. Shr.* I. i. 109 Their loue is not so great ..but we may blow our nails together, And fast it fairely out. **1668** ETHEREDGE *She would if she could* IV. ii, Thou shoud'st fast thyself up to a Stomach now and then.

d. *trans.* To cause to fast or be without food.

1854 *Poultry Chron.* I. 15 Before they are killed, they should be fasted at least fourteen hours. **1970** *Nature* 24 Oct 383/1 The animals were then fasted, one group for 4–6 days, another for 13 days. **1971** *Ibid.* 5 Feb. 420/2 They [*sc.* rats] ..were fasted about 48 h before use.

†**3.** *trans.* To pass (time) fasting; to keep or observe (a day, etc.) as a time of abstinence. Also, ***to fast out***. *Obs.*

c **1275** *Passion of our Lord* 30 in *O.E. Misc.* 38 þo he hedde heom [fourty dawes] yuast þo luste hym ete. *a* **1300** *Cursor M.* 6558 (Cott.) Haf yee þe dais al fasten vte þat i bad ar i me went? *c* **1340** *Ibid.* 12921 (Fairf.) Til he haue fasted his lentyn-tide. **1553** BECON *Reliques of Rome* (1563) 168 Telesphorus.. appoynted firste of all, Lente to be fasted. *a* **1681** WHARTON, *Fasts & Fest.* Wks. (1683) 30 The Ember Weeks.. are four.. and anciently Wednesday, Friday, and Saturday, in each Fasted.

fast and (†or) loose.

a. An old cheating game (see quot. 1847).

1578 WHETSTONE *Promos & Cass.* I. II. v. At fast or loose, with my Giptian, I meane to haue a cast. **1621** B. JONSON *Gipsies Metamorph.* Song i, Leave pig by and goose, And play fast and loose. **1678** BUTLER *Hud.* III. ii. 392 Had forc'd his Neck into a Nooze, To shew his play at Fast and Loose. **1847** HALLIWELL, *Fast-and-loose*, a cheating game played with a stick and a belt or string, so arranged that a spectator would think he could make the latter fast by placing a stick through its intricate folds, whereas the operator could detach it at once.

b. *fig.* ***to play (at) fast and loose***: to ignore at one moment obligations which one acknowledges at another; to be 'slippery' or inconstant.

1557 *Tottel's Misc.* (Arb.) 157 [Title of Epigram] Of a new maried studient that plaied fast or loose. **1595** SHAKS. *John* III. i. 242 Play fast and loose with faith. **1630** *R. Johnson's Kingd. & Commw.* 369 The French playing fast and loose with their Salick Law. **1712** STEELE *Spect.* No 320 ¶1 A little.. playing fast and loose, between Love and Indifference. **1829** *Westm. Rev.* X. 185 Doctrines.. which play at fast and loose with truth and falsehood. **1860** THACKERAY *Lovel the Wid.* vi. (1869) 252 She had played fast and loose with me.

c. Hence, shiftiness, inconstancy.

1648 MILTON *Tenure Kings* Wks. 1738 I. 319 The fast and loose of our prevaricating Divines. **1692** BENTLEY *Boyle Lect.* 217 An eternal vicissitude of fast and loose.

attrib. **1855** MOTLEY *Dutch Rep.* VI. iii. (1866) 821 The English Queen.. had.. almost distracted the provinces by her fast-and-loose policy.

fast-day. [f. FAST *sb.*[1] + DAY; cf. *fasten-day* s.v. FASTEN *sb.*] A day to be observed as a fast.

In some New England States *spec.* the day appointed every spring by the governor for fasting. ***sacramental fast-day*** (Scotland): a fast observed on one day in the week preceding the yearly or half-yearly Communion Sunday; until about 1886 business was generally suspended on these days as on Sundays.

c **1340** *Cursor M.* 27210 (Fairf.) In halitide or fast-day. **1643** in Clarendon *Hist. Reb.* (1704) II. 289 Stir them up, the next Fast-day to the chearful taking of it. **1724** R. FALCONER *Voy.* (1769) 232 It was some Fast-day with them. **1841** TRENCH *Parables* xxix. (1864) 479 Moses appointed but one fast-day in the year.

attrib. **1866** LOWELL *Commencement Dinner* Poems 1890 IV. 256 A Fast Day discourse.

fasted ('fɑːstɪd, -æ-), *ppl. a.* [f. FAST *v.*[2] + -ED[1].] That has gone without food: said of animals. Only in ***fasted weight***: the weight of an animal in a fasting condition.

1852 *Jrnl. R. Agric. Soc.* XIII. I. 192 The fasted live weight. **1855** *Ibid.* XVI. I. 64 The proportion of dead or carcass weight, calculated both to the un-fasted and the fasted live-weight, are given.

†**'fasten,** *sb. Obs.* exc. in *Comb.* FASTENS-EEN, FASTEN TUESDAY, *dial.* Forms: 1–2 **fæsten fæstan,** (*Northumb.* **fæstern**), 1–3 **festen, vesten,** 3 **fasten, fastin,** (**fastim**), 4– (see FASTENS-EEN). [OE. *fæsten* str. neut.:—OTeut. type **fastunjo-m*, f. **fast-êjan* to FAST. Similar but not exactly equivalent derivatives are OS *fastunnia* str. fem., Goth. *fastubni* str. neut. The ONorthumb. form *fæstern* (cf. *éfern, wéstern* = WS. *æfen, wésten*) is the source of the Sc. *fastryn, fastern*, etc.: see FASTENS-EEN.]

1. Fasting; an act of fasting; = FAST *sb.*[1] 1.

c **825** *Vesp. Psalter* cviii. [cix.] 24 Cneow min ȝeuntrumad sind fore festenne. **971** *Blickl. Hom.* 37 Halȝiaþ eower fæsten & medeme lac bringaþ Drihtne. *c* **1000** *Ags. Gosp.* Matt. xvii. 21 Soþlice þis cynn ne byþ ut-adryfen buton þurh ȝebed and fæsten. *c* **1175** *Lamb. Hom.* 37 Ne lipnie ȝe no al to eower festene ȝif ȝe maȝen eni oðer god don. *a* **1225** *Ancr. R.* 138 Vesten, wecchen & oðre swuche.. beoð mine sacrefises. *a* **1300** *Cursor M.* 28627 (Cotton Galba) Ogains pride praier may rise, fastin for flesli couatyse.

2. = FAST *sb.*[1] 2.

a **725** *Laws Withræd* §14 Gif mon his heowum in fæsten flæsc ȝefe. *c* **1050** *Byrhtferth's Handboc* in *Anglia* VIII. 311 þæt ymbren fæstan byð on þissum monðe. *c* **1200** *Winteney Rule St. Benet* (1888) 83 þa bec synd to syllanne on anginne fæsten[es].

3. *Comb.*, as ***fasten-day, -tide, -time.***

a **900** *Charter* xxxvii. in *O.E. Texts* (1885) 444 Gif hit þonne festendæȝ sie. *a* **1035** *Sec. Laws of Cnut* §47 Yfel bið þæt man riht fæsten-tide ær mæle ete. *a* **1225** *Ancr. R.* 318 Ich hit dude inne leinten, ine uestendawes, holidawes. *a* **1300** *Cursor M.* 27210 (Cott.) Halitide or fastim dai. *Ibid.* 28464 (Cott.) Bath lenten tide and fasten day oft haue i broken gain my lay. *Ibid.* 29071 (Cott.) Yee hele yur aun fastintide. *Ibid.* 29083 (Cott.) þai held noght fastin time.

fasten ('fɑːs(ə)n, -æ-), *v.* Forms: **fæstnian, festnian,** 3 *south.* **væstn(i)en,** *Orm.* **fesstnenn,** 3–4 **festnen, fastnen, festni,** *south.* **vestni,** 3–6 **festne, festen, festin,** 5 **festyn, feston,** 4–8 **fastne,** 6 *Sc.* **fessin, -ynn, fassinn,** 4– **fasten.** Also with prefix 1–2 **ȝe-,** 2–4 *pa. t.* and *pa. pple.* **i-, y-.** [OE. *fæstnian* = OFris. *festna*, OS. *fastnôn*, OHG. *fastinôn, festinôn* (MHG. *festenen*, mod.G. *festnen*), to make firm, bind fast (cf. also ON. *fastna* to plege, betroth, Da. *fastne* to consolidate, Sw. *fastna* intr. to stick fast):—OTeut. **fastinôjan*, f. **fast-u-* FAST *a.* See -EN[5].]

To make fast (cf. senses of the adj.).

†**1. a.** *trans.* To make firm or stable; to establish, settle, confirm. ***to fasten the feet***: to give or obtain sure foothold. *Obs.*

a **1175** *Cott. Hom.* 221 þa ȝefestnede se ælmihti god þa nigen angle wærod. *c* **1200** *Trin. Coll. Hom.* 57 þe holie man is ned þat he [? *insert* bie] festned on his holinesse. *a* **1225** *Leg. Kath.* 2011 To festnin ham in treowe bileaue. *a* **1300** *E.E. Psalter* xcii[i]. 1 He festned werld of erthe al. **13..** *E.E. Allit. P.* C. 273 þer he [Ionas] festnes þe fete. *c* **1340** *Cursor M.* 27898 (Fairf.) Alle þat euer festenis witte drunkenis scailis hit. *a* **1400** *Prymer* (1891) 38 So in syon y was fastned. **1535** COVERDALE *Song Sol.* viii. 8 Yf she be a tower, we shal festen her with bordes of Cedre tre. —— *Ecclus.* xl. 25 Golde and syluer fasten the fete [Vulg. *est constitutio pedum*]. *a* **1569** KINGESMYLL *Comf. Afflict.* (1585) F iv, The faithful are fastened and confirmed therein most unfaignedly. **1643** *Plain English* 22 Men walking among Quagmires, know not where to fasten a foot.

†**b.** To make sure, confirm, ratify (an agreement). *Obs.*

a **900** *Charter* xli. in *O.E. Texts* 448 Ic abba ȝeroefa ðis write & festnie mid kristes rodetacne. *a* **1000** *Byrhtnoth* 35 (Gr.) We willað wið þam golde grið fæstnian. *a* **1175** *Cott. Hom.* 219 þa þe hi alle hafeden þisne red betwuxe ham ȝefestnod. *c* **1205** LAY. 29061 Ȝif hit þi wille weore.. þas spechen uæstnien. *a* **1225** *Ancr. R.* 62 Ich habbe ivestned, seið Job, foreward mid min eien. **13..** *E.E. Allit. P.* B. 327 Bot my forwarde with þe I festen on þis wyse. **1382** WYCLIF *Jer.* xxxv. 16 Fastneden therfore the sonus of Jonadab [Vulg. *Firmauerunt igitur filii Ionadab*], sone of Recab, the heste of their fader. *c* **1425** WYNTOUN *Cron.* VI. xii. 80 In-to þat place, Quhare festnyd all þare Cownandis was. **1553** T. WILSON *Rhet.* (1580) 41 Matrimonie, whiche the creatour of all thynges did.. fasten and make holy.

†**2. a.** To make firm or solid; to strengthen, harden. *Obs.*

c **1400** *Lanfranc's Cirurg.* 52 þis medicyn fastneþ þe place & defendiþ him fro putrefaccions. *c* **1440** *Giraldus' Hist. Irel.* (E.E.T.S.) 22 Lasers to clense, paralys to festnen, y-dropesie.. to helen. *c* **1440** *Secrees, Prose Version* (E.E.T.S.) 149 Mete and drynke þat he was costomed to byfore norisshed by, & þat has festnyd his substance. **1577** B. GOOGE *Heresbach's Husb.* II. (1856) 106 The force of the aire in Winter doth fasten and make sounde the Trees.

†**b.** *intr.* To become firm; to 'set'. *Obs.*

1660 *England's Monarchy Freest State in World* 7 How is it probable.. that any Government.. can ever subsist and fasten, without an exorbitant and all-devouring power.. to uphold.. it. **1726** LEONI tr. *Alberti's Archit.* I. 36b, Buildings.. are taken with the Frost.. before ever they have fasten'd. **1730** A. GORDON *Maffei's Amphith.* 285 The rough part of them fastens very well with Mortar.

†**c.** *trans.* To fortify. *Obs.*

1387 TREVISA *Higden* (Rolls) II. 109 Edward þe Eldere fastened a castel at the Mamcestre in Norþumberlond.

†**3. a.** To make fast (in fetters); to set fast, render unable to move. *Obs.*

a **1000** *Andreas* 49 (Gr.) Hie þam halȝan þær handa ȝebundon and fæstnodon. *a* **1300** *E.E. Psalter* lxviii. 3 [lxix. 2], I am festened in slime depe. **1632** LITHGOW *Trav.* V. 223 Such.. deep carouses of wine that both hee and I were almost fastned in the last plunge of understanding.

b. *intr.* To become fast or unable to move.

1742 YOUNG *Nt. Th.* VI. 397 We leap at stars, and fasten in the mud. **1853** KANE *Grinnell Exp.* x. (1856) 71 We fastened in the ice.

4. a. *trans.* To make fast to something else; to attach, more or less securely, by a tie or bond of any kind. Const. *to*, occas. *on, upon*; also with advbs. *on, together, up.* Formerly often, now rarely, with immaterial object.

c **1175** *Lamb. Hom.* 121 Mid irenen neilen he wes on þere rode ifestned. *c* **1200** *Vices & Virtues* (1888) 95 To hire bieð ifastned alle ðe raftres of ðe hali mihtes. *a* **1225** *St. Marher.* 19 Festne wið fulht mi sawle to þe seoluen. **1340** *Ayenb.* 221 Hy byeþ y-uestned to-gidere be spoushod. **1398** TREVISA *Barth. De P.R.* IV. iii. (1495) 82 Moysture.. fastnyth the partyes togider. *c* **1400** *Destr. Troy* 2849 þai.. festonit the flete. *c* **1450** *Mirour Saluacioun* 3498 Hevenly thinges and erthly hym liked eft festyn to gidere. **1483** *Act 1 Rich. III*, c. 8 Preamb., Dyers.. upon the Lists of the same Clothes festen and sowe great Risshes. **1552** ABP. HAMILTON *Catech.* (1884) 77 Samekil is the lufe of God & our nychbour fessinit and linkit togiddir. **1590** SHAKS. *Com. Err.* I. i. 86 My wife and I, Fastned our selues at eyther end the mast. **1662** J. DAVIES tr. *Mandelslo's Trav. E. Ind.* 10 To fasten and cement them together. **1696** *Col. Rec. Pennsylv.* I. 497 Men that are fastned to the Country by visible estates. **1759** tr. *Adanson's Voy. Senegal* 74 When they saw it [my hair], really fastened to my head. **1796** JANE AUSTEN *Pride & Prej.* (1885) II. v. 185 The chaise arrived, the trunks were fastened on. **1837** DICKENS *Pickw.* iv, Fastened up behind the barouche was a hamper. **1840** E. HOWARD *Jack Ashore* III. xv, He consented to be again fastened up, but he walked about as much as the limits of his chain would permit. **1849** JAMES *Woodman* vii, The visitor proceeded to fasten his horse to a large iron hook. **1852** MOTLEY *Corr.* (1889) I. v. 137 The canvas.. had been fastened on a pole.

b. *absol.* or *intr.* To make one's boat fast. In whale-fishing: ***to fasten to*** (see quot. 1820); also in *indirect pass.*

1700 S. L. tr. *C. Fryke's Voy. E. Ind.* 207 As soon as we could come to fasten by her [the Ship's] side. **1820** SCORESBY *Acc. Arctic Reg.* II. 534 Each boat 'fastens to', or strikes a distinct fish. **1839** T. BEALE *Sperm Whale* 46 'Fastened to'.. means, when a harpoon with a line attached is fixed in his body. *Ibid.* 165 The two boats that have not yet 'fastened'.. give chase.

5. a. To bind (a servant, an apprentice) by a contract or agreement (*dial.*); cf. *fastening penny.* †**b.** To join in a contract *with* (obs.).

1362 LANGL. *P. Pl.* A. II. 51 In Mariage.. To beo fastnet with fals. **1425** *Sc. Acts, 1st Parl. Jas. I* c. 20 þe schiref sall assigne xl dais to sic ydil men to get þaim masteris, or to festyn þaim to leful craftes. **1632** LITHGOW *Trav.* VIII. 353, I fastned Iohn Browne with him to accompany his returne. *Mod.* (Sheffield) He's a sort of a prentice, but he's not fastened.

6. To attach together the parts of (a fabric or structure). *Obs.* exc. *Naut.*

1562 TURNER *Baths* 16 a, They that are.. not well fastened together, ought not to tarye so long in the bath. **1609** SKENE *Reg. Maj., Chalmerlan Air* c. 27 §2 They festen and bindes them not with lether or glew. **1646** SIR T. BROWNE *Pseud. Ep.* II. iii. 71 Their ships are fastned not with Iron but wood. **1860** *Merc. Marine Mag.* VII. 284 A ship fastened with yellow metal.

7. a. To make fast, secure (a tie, band); to secure (an article of dress), *e.g.* with a clasp, pins, buttons, etc. Also, with pregnant sense, ***to fasten*** (a person) ***in*** a garment.

a **1300** *Cursor M.* 1728 (Cott.) [Noe] he self festnid bath band and lace. *c* **1350** *Will. Palerne* 1720 Sche.. festened hire in þat fel wiþ ful god þonges. **1600** J. PORY tr. *Leo's Africa* ii. 24 The corners of which mantle are.. fastened about their shoulders. **1696** tr. *Du Mont's Voy. Levant* 130 Breeches fasten'd with Buttons. **1727** DE FOE *Hist. Appar.* iv. (1840) 31 No chain can bind him, but the chains fastened on him by Heaven. **1767** J. BYRON *Voy. round World* 51 Skins.. fastened about their necks by a thong.

b. ***to fasten off*** (a thread): to fix with a knot or extra stitches.

1893 *Mrs. Leach's Fancy-work Basket* May 146/2 Run ribbon through holes.. and fasten it off at wrist with neat bow.

c. *intr.* To admit of being fixed or fastened.

1850 F. E. SMEDLEY *F. Fairlegh* iv, The macintosh.. fastening round the neck with a hook and eye. **1924** A. D. SEDGWICK *Little French Girl* II. viii, A dark silk dress fastening at the breast with a great old clasp of wrought gold.

8. a. *trans.* To make fast (a door, etc.) with a latch, bolt, etc., or (an envelope, etc.) with a seal. Hence, ***to fasten*** (a person or animal) ***in*** or ***out.*** Also with ***up.***

1749 FIELDING *Tom Jones* VIII. vi, I will fasten the door. **1764** LLOYD *Rhyme* 153 Colts.. Clapt up and fasten'd in the pound. **1797** MRS. RADCLIFFE *Italian* xii, I have not caused this gate to be fastened. **1801** SOUTHEY *Thalaba* IX. xxii, Her ears are closed with wax, And her prest finger fastens them. **1819** BYRON *Juan* I. cxxxvi, The door was fastened. **1833** HT. MARTINEAU *Tale of Tyne* vi. 103 The lattice was not quite fastened. **1860** TYNDALL *Glac.* I. xxvii. 216 The rooms were swept.. the shutters fastened. **1868** ATKINSON *Cleveland Gloss.*, *To fasten out*, to turn the Moor-sheep to the moor for the season, excluding them for good from the enclosed land. **1908** J. S. FLETCHER *Paradise Crt.* v. ii, Was he.. to be fastened up there like a rat in a trap for—how long?

b. *intr.* To admit of being closed with fastenings.

1829 SCOTT *Old Mort.* Note x, The iron hasps [of the window].. fastened in the inside. **1862** G. MACDONALD *D. Elginbrod* II. xxiv, He could find no fastening upon it [*sc.* a door]. 'No doubt,' thought he, 'it does fasten, in some secret way or other.'

†**9.** To close (the hands, teeth) with a grip. ***to fasten hold***: to take hold firmly. *Obs.*

1530 LYNDESAY *Test. Papyngo* 354 Fassinnyng ȝour fingaris faste. **1585** T. WASHINGTON tr. *Nicholay's Voy. Turkie* IV. xxx. 153 To the end their adversaries should fasten the lesse hold upon them. **1596** SPENSER *F.Q.* V. iv. 15 This threasure.. well I proue.. To be this maides with whom I fastned hand. **1599** MINSHEU *Dial. Sp. & Eng.* (1623) 51 Two hands fastned together, alwaies hath beene a token of friendship. **1607** TOPSELL *Serpents* (1653) 750 When it once biteth and fasteneth teeth, it never letteth go.

10. a. To fix or hold securely in position; to make fast (what is loose).

a **1300** *Cursor M.* 8223 (Cott.) Bot þat þa wandis þan had rote, þat festind ware in erde sua fast. *c* **1400** *Apol. Loll.* 86 Festining it wiþ irne þat it fal not. *c* **1400** *Lanfranc's Cirurg.* 156 For to fastne þe schuldre þis boon rostral is putt in maner of a wegge. *c* **1440** *Gesta Rom.* I. i (Harl. MS.) þis nigromancien.. fastenyd it [ymage] in þe wall afore him. **1578** LYTE *Dodoens* II. lxxxv. 264 Axen of Rosemarie burnte, doth fasten loose teeth. **1662** J. DAVIES *Voy. Ambass.* 24 A great Cross, fasten'd in a great piece of timber. **1703** MOXON *Mech. Exerc.* 223 Pitch the other sides to be Turned flat carefully against the Hole.. fastning them with Wax. **1821** SHELLEY *Boat on Serchio* Poems (1891) 586/2 Sit at the helm—fasten this sheet.

b. with immaterial object; also with *inf.* as *obj.*

c **1200** ORMIN Ded. 219 He wollde fesstnenn swa Soþ trowwþe i þeȝȝre brestess. *ibid.* 2441 Icc hafe fesstnedd i min þohht To libbenn i clænnesse. **1393** LANGL. *P. Pl.* C. XIII. 9 Freres wollen.. fastne þe in here fraternite. *c* **1430** *Hymns Virg.* (1867) 26 Fastne þere in þee my þouȝt. **1513** MORE *Rich. III.* Wks. 45/1 Suche euyll oppinyon once fastened in mennes heartes. **1611** SHAKS. *Wint. T.* II. iii. 15 He.. Fasten'd, and fix'd the shame on't in himselfe. **1683** *Pennsylv. Archives* I. 74 Time will.. fasten things as they are and should be. **1818** CRUISE *Digest* 481 When once a trust is sufficiently created, it will fasten itself upon the estate.

c. ***to fasten down***: to fix (a thing) so as to prevent its rising: *fig.* to fix definitely.

1731 MEDLEY *Kolben's Cape of G. Hope* I. 68, I have.. rescued the character of the Hottentots from the brutish stupidity to which it has been fastened down by all the authors. **1876** GLADSTONE in *Contemp. Rev.* June 12 To fasten down its sense, the affix 'Evangelical' may suffice. *Mod.* The lid of the box is fastened down.

†**d.** *intr.* To take hold; to attach oneself; to make one's abode. *Obs.*

c **1400** *Destr. Troy* 1429 Of a sparke unspied..May feston vp fyre. **1590** SPENSER *F.Q.* III. ii. 26 The Damzell well did vew his Personage And liked well, ne further fastned not, But went her way. **1625** FLETCHER & SHIRLEY *Nt.-Walker* I. i, A very pretty girl she was..But he was too wise to fasten. *a* **1657** R. LOVEDAY *Lett.* (1663) 258 We are here in London, where I think we shall fasten for most part of this ensuing Summer. **1742** YOUNG *Nt. Th.* iii. 531 We.. Spring from our fetters; fasten in the skies.

†**11.** *trans.* To deliver effectively (a blow); to imprint (a kiss). Const. *on. Obs.*

c **1500** *Lancelot* 850 Strokis festnit in the shelde. **1531** ELYOT *Gov.* I. xvi, Or he coulde fasten on the other any violent stroke. **1613** PURCHAS *Pilgrimage* IV. vii. (1614) 370 A mutuall kisse..is fastened on the cheeke. **1632** J. HAYWARD tr. *Biondi's Eromena* 170 Wee could never come once to fasten a blow on him. **1633** T. STAFFORD *Pac. Hib.* II. xxiii. 243 I could never fasten a salley yet upon him, but with losse to myselfe. **1697** DRYDEN *Virgil* Ded. Ej, Cou'd he fasten a blow..when not suffer'd to approach.

12. In various fig. applications of senses 4, 7, 10: To fix (something) *upon* (a person, etc.).

a. To direct (feelings, thoughts, attention, etc.) intently or keenly towards.

a **1400** *Prymer* (1891) 53 Y schal fastne myn eyen op on þe. *c* **1450** *Mirour Saluacioun* 793 Hire hert vpwards on heven was festined nyght & day. **1568** E. TILNEY *Disc. Mariage* B vj, If she once fasten hir eyes on a nother, he shall enjoy hir. **1603** SHAKS. *Meas. for M.* III. i. 203 Fasten your eare on my aduisings. **1611** BIBLE *Luke* iv. 20 The eyes of all.. were fastened on him. **1633** BP. HALL *Hard Texts* 320 To that man whose heart is fastned upon thee. **1840** DICKENS *Old C. Shop* xli, The attention of the sly little fiend was fastened upon them. **1850** HAWTHORNE *Scarlet L.* Introd. (1883) 50 My eyes fastened themselves upon the old scarlet letter. **1885** *Manch. Exam.* 10 July 572 A madman armed with a knife, upon whom a steady eye must be fastened.

b. To fix (a nickname, imputation, etc.) *on* a person; to impute or attach to.

1615 STEPHENS *Satyr. Ess.* (ed. 2) 38 Thinke how little paines Doth fasten credit upon lucky straines. **1638** WILKINS *New World* ii. (1707) 20 Some of the Ancients have fasten'd strange Absurdities upon the Words of the Scripture. **1672** CAVE *Prim. Chr.* I. v. (1673) 12 To form and fasten this charge upon them. *Ibid.* III. v. (1673) 368 The story..fastened upon Philip the Emperor. *a* **1674** CLARENDON *Surv. Leviath.* (1676) 304 He hath not been able ..to fasten the least reproch upon them. **1722** SEWEL *Hist. Quakers* (1795) I. Pref. 18 To fasten doctrines upon them which they never approved. **1855** MACAULAY *Hist. Eng.* III. 310 Those very Londoners..now fastened on the prince.. the nickname of Butcher.

†**c.** To induce acceptance of (a gift, etc.); to propose (a health). *Obs.*

1604 SHAKS. *Oth.* II. iii. 50 If I can fasten but one Cup vpon him. **1615** STEPHENS *Satyr. Ess.* (ed. 2) 256 If you fasten a guift upon him, his thankes bee liberall. **1632** LITHGOW *Trav.* x. 431, I neuer saw one..to pledge or present his Maiesties health; but as many other healths as you list; they will both fasten, and receiue from you. **1673** RAY *Journ. Low C.* 435 We could scarce fasten any more upon them. **1726** *Adv. Capt. R. Boyle* 354, I did not know how to fasten a Present upon Mr. Ratcliff.

d. To impose (something unwelcome) on a person. Now chiefly in ***to fasten a quarrel upon***: to drag into a quarrel against his inclination. Also with *to*.

1663 DRYDEN *Wild Gallant* II. i, He..could never fasten a quarrel upon you. **1682** *Enq. Elect. Sheriffs* 8 Endeavouring..to fasten such a Sheriff upon them. **1718** *Freethinker* No. 41. 294 Divert her Malice by fastening a new Spark upon her. **1797** GODWIN *Enquirer* I. vi. 36 No practice..fastened upon us by decrees and penalties. **1855** MACAULAY *Hist. Eng.* III. 325 The..Macdonalds.. fastened a succession of quarrels on the people of Inverness. **1861** HUGHES *Tom Brown at Oxf.* v. (1889) 36 He..had fastened himself upon him. **1881** C. E. L. RIDDELL *Sen. Partner* xxxv, One of the nephews..insisted on fastening himself to Mr. Snow.

e. = FIX *v.* 6 c.

1881 C. E. L. RIDDELL *Sen. Partner* xvi, Fastening her kinsman with a cold steely eye.

13. *intr.* ***to fasten on, upon*** : †**a.** to obtain a firm hold upon, become fixed on (*obs.*); **b.** to seize on, lay hold of; to single out for attack or censure; to avail oneself eagerly of (a pretext, etc.).

a **1225** *Leg. Kath.* 1180 O godd..ne mei nan uuel festnin. *c* **1230** *Hali Meid.* 15 þe fiends arrow..ne wundeð þe nawt bute hit festni oþe. **1513** MORE in Grafton *Chron.* II. 783 No colour could fasten upon these matters. **1590** SHAKS. *Com. Err.* II. ii. 175, I will fasten on this sleeve of thine. **1607** ROWLANDS *Famous Hist.* 48 Experience often hath..taught, that when advantage I do see, To fasten on occasion and begin. **1647** N. BACON *Disc. Govt. Eng.* I. xl. (1739) 60 Yet could not that custom fasten upon the Saxons. **1662** J. DAVIES *Voy. Ambass.* 57 They break down the houses adjoyning..that it [fire] may not fasten on other more solid structures. **1726** *Adv. Capt. R. Boyle* 230 An English Mastiff..had the Impudence to fasten upon my Rival by the Arm. **1844** THIRLWALL *Greece* VIII. 389 The senate.. viewed Perseus as a prey, on which it resolved to fasten. **1844** STANLEY *Arnold* (1858) I. ii. 25 One object on which our..imaginations may fasten. **1847** L. HUNT *Men, Women, & Books* I. II. 20 He is fastened upon by the man with the bundle. **1855** MOTLEY *Dutch Rep.* II. vii. (1866) 282 The whole mob..fastened upon the company of marble martyrs. **1875** JOWETT *Plato* (ed. 2) IV. 285 Sickness..has fastened upon him.

fastened ('fɑːs(ə)nd, -æ-), *ppl. a.* [f. prec. + -ED[1].]

†**1.** Settled, confirmed. *Obs.*

1596 SPENSER *Hymns, Heav. Beaut.* 289 They..in their fastened mynd All happie ioy and full contentment fynd. **1605** SHAKS. *Lear* II. i. 79 O strange and fastned Villaine.

†**2.** Rendered firm in consistency. *Obs.*

1625 HART *Anat. Ur.* I. ii. 23 The which [excrement] being..somewhat fastened or stiffe.

3. Fixed or bolted together. In *comb.*, as ***copper-, iron-fastened*** (see the sbs.).

1803 R. PERING in *Naval Chron.* XV. 60 Iron-fastened ships. **1860** *Merc. Marine Mag.* VII. 284 The copper-fastened vessel will obtain the best rate.

fastener ('fɑːs(ə)nə(r), -æ-). [f. as prec. + -ER[1].]

1. One who fastens or makes fast.

1755 in JOHNSON. **1798** JANE AUSTEN *Northang. Abb.* (1838) II. vii. 142 The possibility of the door's having been at first unlocked, and she herself its fastener.

2. That which serves to fasten anything.

1792 MARY WOLLSTONECR. *Rights Wom.* iv. 151 Individuality of character, the only fastener of the affections. **1874** W. CROOKES *Dyeing & Calico-printing* 323 The modified Gallipoli oil acts..as fastener of the red lake. **1884** *Birm. Weekly Post* 15 Nov. 3/7 The fastener [of a trap-door] was not properly adjusted. **1892** *Law Times' Rep.* LXVII. 163/1 Small hooks or fasteners on the metal busks of the corsets.

†**3.** One who fastens *on* something. *Obs.*

1628 EARLE *Microcosm., Plain country Fellow* (Arb.) 49 He is a terrible fastner on a piece of Beefe.

†**4.** *slang.* A warrant for arrest. *Obs.*

a **1700** B. E. *Dict. Cant. Crew, Fastner*, c. a Warrant. **1785** in GROSE *Dict. Vulg. Tongue.*

fastening ('fɑːs(ə)nɪŋ, -æ-), *vbl. sb.* [f. as prec. + -ING[1].]

1. The action of the vb. FASTEN in various senses.

a **1400** *Relig. Pieces fr. Thornton MS.* 8 Matrymoyne..es lawefull festynnynge be-twyx man and woman. **1605** TIMME *Quersit.* III. 192 Of all fastnings or closing up of glasses..the seale of Hermes is most noble. **1691** T. H[ALE] *Acc. New Invent.* 24 Firm and unwasted as at their first fastening. **1793** SMEATON *Edystone L.* §244 The fastening of the circle of stones..upon their respective cubes. **1850** W. B. CLARKE *Wreck Favorite* 33 There is no fastening of the shaft or stock into the socket.

b. *attrib.* ***fastening penny*** (dial.): a small sum of money paid on hiring a servant, to secure the agreement. Cf. FASTEN *v.* 5.

1872 *Gentl. Mag.* Nov. 578 A bargain was struck, and considered thoroughly binding by the acceptance on the part of the servant of what was called 'the fastening penny'.

†**2.** The condition of being fastened; **a.** of being set on a firm basis. **b.** ***in fastening*** = in prison.

a **1340** HAMPOLE *Psalter* 502 Thorgh whaim oþere ere broght til stabilnes & festyngynge. **1375** BARBOUR *Bruce* xv. 309 He [Iohn of Lorn] wes lang tyme in festnyng.

3. *concr.* That which fastens or makes secure; that which connects one person or thing with another, or secures (a person or thing) in position; †that which confirms or establishes.

c **1175** *Lamb. Hom.* 67 þos ilke bode wisliche þing of oðre is ful festning. *a* **1340** HAMPOLE *Psalter* xvii[i]. 1 Lord my festynynge. **1480** CAXTON *Chron. Eng.* cclvii. 126 The chirch dores were shytte with keyes and with other fastnynge. **1611** BIBLE *Hab.* ii. 11 The stone shall crie out of the wall, and the beame [*marg. note* fastening] out of the timber shall answere it. **1769** *Public Advertiser* 18 May 3/4 Brass Sash Fastenings. **1850** PRESCOTT *Peru* II. 340 Pizarro, unable..to adjust the fastenings of his cuirass, threw it away. **1869** C. GIBBON *R. Gray* v, Crummie was not likely to break from her fastenings. **1885** *Law Reports* 15 Q. Bench Div. 316 A bar..was kept in its position by means of a fastening.

fig. **1633** G. HERBERT *Temple, Confession* iv, Smooth open hearts no fastning have.

'fastening, *ppl. a.* [f. as prec. + -ING[2].] That fastens, in various senses of the vb.

1621 S. WARD *Happin. Practice* (1627) 1 The fastening Nayle of the chiefe Master of the Assemblies. **1821** BYRON *Cain* I. i, In his eye There is a fastening attraction. **1828–40** TYTLER *Hist. Scot.* (1864) II. 221 His tent..was of silk; the fastening chains were richly gilt. **1865** SWINBURNE *Atalanta* 970, I shall have..no face of children born Or feeding lips upon me or fastening eyes For ever.

fastenment ('fɑːs(ə)nmənt, -æ-). *dial.* [f. as prec. + -MENT.] A fastening of any kind.

1877 *Auctioneer's Catal.* (Church Stretton) Door-fastenments. **1879** MISS JACKSON *Shropsh. Word-bk.*, 'Put a fas'nment o' the brew-'us door.'

Fastens. Also 7 fastins. [short for next.]

1616 *Chron. Snathense* in *Jrnl. Statist. Soc.* XXI. 413 To be paid betwixt Candlemas and Ffastins. **1876** *Mid-Yorksh. Gloss., Fastens*, Shrovetide.

Fastens-een, -eve, -even. *Sc.* and *north. dial.* Also 4 fast(e)ryn(gs-, 5–6 fasteringis-, 6 fasterns-, -trin-, -tron-, 8 fasten-, 8–9 fasting(s-, 9 fasterns-. [f. OE. *fæstenes*, gen. of *fæsten* FASTEN *sb.* + EVEN or EVE.] The eve or day before the fast (of Lent); Shrove-Tuesday.

1375 BARBOUR *Bruce* x. 372 On the fasteryn evyn rycht In the begynnyng of the nycht. **1496** *Ld. Treas. Accts. Scot.* (1877) I. 319 The vij day of Februare was Fasteringis evin. **1565** in Picton *L'pool Munic. Rec.* (1883) I. 35 Fasten's eve or Shrovetide. **1674–91** RAY *N.C. Words*, Fastens-Een or Even. *c* **1750** J. COLLIER (Tim Bobbin) *Lanc. Dialect* Wks. (1862) 68 Feersuns een, on it matter't naw mitch. **1780** M. LONSDALE *Th' Upshot* ii. in *Jollie's Sketch of Cumberland Manners* (1811) 5 An upshot lang an' sair To keep up fassen's-even. **1785** BURNS *Ep. to J. Lapraik* 7 On fasten-een we had a rockin. **1834** H. MILLER *Scenes & Leg.* xxviii. (1857) 416 On Fasten's-eve,—the Schoolmaster..would call on the boys to divide, and choose for themselves 'Head-stocks'.

Fasten(s)-Tuesday. Also 9 *dial.* **fassans, -ens.** [see prec.] = prec.

1585 *Nottingham Rec.* (1889) IV. 211 Betwene thys and Fastens Tuysdaye nexte cummyng. **1858** C. B. ROBINSON *Jrnl. Statist. Soc.* XXI. 413 Shrove Tuesday being called Fastins Tuesday. **1877** *Holderness Gloss., Fassans-tuesda*, Shrove Tuesday.

faster ('fɑːstər, -æ-). Also 5 fastare. [f. FAST *v.* + -ER[1].] One who fasts or abstains from food.

a **1300** *Cursor M.* 27684 (Cott.) [þis] man es gret faster. *c* **1440** *Promp. Parv.* 151/1 Fastare, *jejunator, jejunatrix.* *a* **1450** *Knt. de la Tour* 13 It is a blessed thinge to faste, for the more harme it doth the faster, the more is the merit. **1560** BECON *Treat. Fasting* 79 b, A certayne monke..was counted the greatest and deuoutest faster in all those quaters. **1662** GUNNING *Lent Fast* 199 Such fasters I cannot better resemble, then to the ancient blood-thirsty Tyrants. **1712** SWIFT *Jrnl. Stella* 16 Jan., This being fast day, Dr. Freind and I went into the city to dine late, like good fasters. **1807** MILNER *Martyrs* I. ii. 58 *note*, A man..of a strict life and a great faster. **1880** *Daily News* 27 July 5/5 The faster's condition physically during the day was remarkably encouraging.

fast food. orig. *U.S.* Also **fast-food, fastfood.** [f. FAST *a.* + FOOD *sb.*] **a.** Used *attrib.* with reference to catering outlets where foods are kept hot and ready to serve, or partially prepared so that they can be served quickly.

1951 *Fountain & Fast Food Service* Oct. 39/1 The partners have become old hands at spotting the type of conventioneer that will patronize their fast food service. **1960** *Fast Food* July 17/2 Fast food type restaurants do the lion's share of business for breakfast and noon meals eaten out. **1968** *N.Y. Times* 23 June III. 2/3 Another star performer in the fast-food field has been A-G Foods, which ..operates a string of quick-service restaurants. **1975** *New Yorker* 14 Apr. 80/1 Supermarkets and fast-food shops are gaining great ground. **1978** *Tucson Mag.* Dec. 6/3 Nothing but a glorified, garlic-flavored fastfood operation with the poorest example of Italian cuisine. **1984** *Verbatim* X. III. 20/2 Fastfood eateries often dispense plastic 'silverware'.

b. The type of food served in these restaurants; convenience food which can be prepared quickly at home.

1954 (*title*) Fountain and fast food. **1960** *Fast Food* Feb. 48/1 Delicate scallops are *really* fast food..because they come ready to cook. **1977** *Times* 6 June 2/5 'Fast food' requires no preparation by the customer. Traditional 'fast food outlets' like fish-and-chip shops are being superseded by Chinese, Indian, Kebab and fried chicken houses. **1980** *Guardian* 24 May 19/8 Fastfoods have managed to get rid of their junk tag and cash in on new attitudes to leisure. **1985** *Times* 11 Nov. 3/4 (*heading*) £1,000 for a British fast food.

†**Fast-gong.** *Obs.* [f. FAST *sb.* + ME. *gong*, act of going, see GANG. Cf. ON. *fǫstugangr.*] Shrove-Tuesday; = FASTINGONG. Also *attrib.* in **Fastgong-tide** (spelt after Norfolk pronunciation *fasguntide*), Shrove-tide.

c **1440** *Promp. Parv.* 151/1 Fast gonge, or schroffetyde, or gowtyde, *carniprivium.* **1674–81** BLOUNT *Glossogr.*, *Fasguntide* or Fastingtide, Shrovetide, so called in Norfolk, being the time when the Fast of Lent begins.

‖**fasti** ('fæstaɪ). [Lat. *fastī*, pl. of *fastus* (*dies*) a 'lawful' day, a day on which the courts sat: hence as under.]

a. *Rom. Ant.* A calendar or calendars, indicating the lawful days for legal business, and also the festivals, games, anniversaries of historical events, etc., connected with each day of the year. ***consular fasti*** (L. *fasti consulares*): the register of the events occurring during the official year of a pair of consuls; the series of such registers. **b.** *transf.* A chronological register of events; annals, chronological tables or lists of office-holders.

1611 B. JONSON *Catiline* v. iv, Let it [this day] be added to our Fasti. *a* **1670** HACKET *Abp. Williams* I. §26 (1693) 20 Like Consuls that acted nothing, and were useful for nothing but to have the Fasti known by their Names. **1691** WOOD (*title*), Athenæ Oxonienses..To which are added the Fasti or Annals, of the said University. **1734** E. CORSINI (*title*), Fasti of the Archons of Athens. **1786** HAN. MORE *Florio* 967 Still, in Life's Fasti, you presume Eternal holidays will come. **1814** *Edin. Rev.* XXIV. 245 A country [the U.S.]..whose fasti are consecrated to record our cruelties and defeats. **1880** C. T. NEWTON *Art & Archæol.* 15 Roman coins are not Fasti..yet the labour of numismatists has made [them] almost the best authority for the chronology of the Roman empire.

†**fa'stidiate,** *v. Obs. rare.* [f. L. *fastīdium* (see next) + -ATE.] *trans.* To feel a disgust for, loathe.

1618 SIR S. D'EWES *Autobiog.* I. (1845) vii. 106 Bury school..I began to fastidiate, and be weary of the sweet and happy life I there led.

†**fastidie.** *Obs. rare.* [a. OF. *fastidie*, ad. L. *fastīdium* in same senses.] **a.** Pride, haughtiness. **b.** Scorn, disdain.

1536 E. HARVEL in Ellis *Orig. Lett.* II. 118 II. 77 My minde enclinith..to..give ope the worldly fastidie to them *qui ambiunt honores.* **1538** in Strype *Eccl. Mem.* I. App. lxxxiii. 218 Which when it [the general council] shal take effect.. must needs make him great dishonor, great fastidie.

†**fastidiose,** *a. Obs.*⁻⁰ = FASTIDIOUS.

1727-36 in BAILEY. **1775** in ASH.

fastidi'osity. *rare*⁻¹. [f. L. *fastīdiōs-us* (see FASTIDIOUS) + -ITY.] Fastidiousness. (In quot. humorously pedantic.)

1704 SWIFT *T. Tub* v. (1750) 74 His epidemical Diseases being Fastidiosity, Amorphy and oscitation. **1775** in ASH.

fastidious (fæ'stɪdɪəs), *a.* [ad. L. *fastīdiōs-us*, f. *fastīdium* loathing: see -OUS. Cf. Fr. *fastidieux.*]

†**1.** That creates disgust; disagreeable, distasteful, unpleasant, wearisome. *Obs.*

1531 ELYOT *Gov.* I. ix, That thinge for the whiche children be often tymes beaten is to them..fastidious. **1582** HESTER *Secr. Phiorav.* II. xxiii. 102 A fastidious Ulcer. **1630** *R. Johnson's Kingd. & Commw.* 193 A fastidious and irksome companion. *a* **1677** BARROW *Serm. Wisdom* in *Beauties of B.* (1846) 9 Folly is..fastidious to society. *a* **1734** NORTH *Lives* II. 399 His partner, whose usage was.. fastidious to him.

†**2. a.** That feels or is full of disgust; disgusted.

1534 MORE *On the Passion* Wks. 1312/1 Hee hadde of theym so muche, that he was full thereof, fastidious and wery. **1678** CUDWORTH *Intell. Syst.* 81 All desire of Change and Novelty, argues a Fastidious Satiety.

†**b.** Full of pride; disdainful; scornful. *Obs.*

c **1440** *Foundation Barts Hosp.* (E.E.T.S.) 15 A lamentable querell, expressynge..whate fastidious owtbrekyngys hadde temptid hym. **1623-6** COCKERAM, *Fastidious*, disdainfull, proud. **1634** SIR T. HERBERT *Trav.* (1638) 189 Regardlesse of the rodomantadoes of the fastidious Pagan. **1631** B. JONSON *New Inn, Ode* 7 Their fastidious vaine Commission of the braine. **1744** YOUNG *Night Thoughts* VI. 551 Proud youth! fastidious of the lower world. **1791** BOSWELL *Johnson* (1816) II. 277 (an. 1773) We see the Rambler with fastidious smile Mark the lone tree. **1796** C. MARSHALL *Garden.* xxii. (1813) 447 Those who have much practical skill..slight what is written upon subjects of their profession, which is a fastidious temper.

†**c.** *transf.* Of things: 'Proud', magnificent.

1638 SIR T. HERBERT *Trav.* 62 One of them [Courts] fastidious in foure hundred porphirian pillars. *Ibid.* 102 Temples of Idolatry..once lofty in fastidious Turrets.

3. Easily disgusted, squeamish, over-nice; difficult to please with regard to matters of taste or propriety.

1612-5 BP. HALL *Contempl.*, *O.T.* XIX. x, A fastidious choice of the best commodities. **1647** WARD *Simp. Cobler* 77, I hold him prudent, that in these fastidious times, will helpe disedged appetites with convenient condiments. **1691** RAY *Creation* Pref. (1704) 7 Fastidious Readers. **1784** COWPER *Task* I. 513 The weary sight, Too well acquainted with their smiles, slides off Fastidious. **1848** MACAULAY *Hist. Eng.* II. 266 People whom the habit of seeing magnificent buildings ..had made fastidious. **1853** TRENCH *Proverbs* 3 A fastidious age..and one of false refinement. **1865** LIVINGSTONE *Zambesi* xvii. 342 Though being far from fastidious, refused to eat it. **1877** BLACK *Green Past.* xlii. (1878) 338 The society..was not at all fastidious in its language.

fastidiously (fæ'stɪdɪəslɪ), *adv.* [f. as prec. + -LY².] In a fastidious manner; †disdainfully; squeamishly, with excessive scrupulousness of taste.

1624 GATAKER *Transubst.* 42 Fastidiously and childishly ..full of Logicke rules. **1654** HAMMOND *Acc. Cawdrey's Triplex Diatribe* v. §17 Discriminating themselves proudly and fastidiously from other men. **1790** BURKE *Fr. Rev.* 33 The legislature..fastidiously rejected the fair and abundant choice..presented to them. **1841** D'ISRAELI *Amen. Lit.* (1867) 128 Critics fastidiously rejecting what they deem the antiquated. **1880** DISRAELI *Endym.* I. xxi. 193 A couple of grooms, who sat with..unmoved countenances, fastidiously stolid amid all the fun.

fastidiousness (fæ'stɪdɪəsnɪs). [f. as prec. + -NESS.] The quality of being fastidious.

†**1.** Loathing, disgust. *Obs.*

1533 ELYOT *Cast. Helthe* (1541) 28 b, Sowthistle..causeth fastidiousness or lothsomnesse of the stomake. **1599** A. M. tr. *Gabelhouer's Bk. Physicke* 267/2 Excepte it..get a fastidiousnes therof [pappe]. **1632** LITHGOW *Trav.* x. 425 After I had..escaped infinite dangers..excessive fastidiousnesse, unspeakable adversities. **1807** COXE *Austria* I. 67 Rhodolph observing their fastidiousness, rose from table.

†**2.** Disdainfulness, haughtiness, pride. *Obs.*

1613 R. C. *Table Alph.* (ed. 3) *Fastidiousnesse*, disdainfulnesse. **1649** JER. TAYLOR *Gt. Exemp.* III. §14. 52 He reproved the fastidiousnesse of the Pharisee.

3. Disposition to be easily disgusted; squeamishness; over-niceness in matters of taste or propriety.

1661 BOYLE *Style of Script.* 202 More Discerning Times ..will Repair the Omissions and Fastidiousnesse of the Present. **1784** J. BARRY *Lect. Art* vi. (1848) 207 Fastidiousness, and a useless and too critical nicety, may be expected to increase. **1824** DIBDIN *Libr. Comp.* 745 The fastidiousness of criticism may object to the frequent repetition. **1869** J. MARTINEAU *Ess.* II. 98 Any nice inquiry ..would be a misplaced fastidiousness.

fastidium (fæ'stɪdɪəm). *rare.* [a. L. *fastīdium*; see FASTIDIE.] Disgust; 'ennui'.

a **1734** NORTH *Lives* I. 159 The fastidium, upon this occasion contracted..diverted his mind from..such projects. **1885** MRS. H. WARD tr. *Amiel's Jrnl.* (1889) 277 How is *fastidium* to be avoided?

†'**fastigate,** *v. Obs.*⁻⁰ [f. L. *fastīgāt-* ppl. stem of L. *fastīg-āre* to make pointed.]

a. *trans.* To make pointed. **b.** *intr.* To become pointed.

1623-6 in COCKERAM. **1656** in BLOUNT *Glossogr.* **1732** in COLES.

fastigiate (fæ'stɪdʒɪət), *a.* [f. L. *fastīgi-um* summit of a gable, top, vertex + -ATE². Cf. F. *fastigié.*]

1. Sloping up or tapering to a point like a cone or pyramid. †**a.** of a hill = FASTIGIATED. *Obs.*

1662 RAY *Three Itin.* ii. (Ray Soc.) 148 That noted hill.. the top whereof is fastigiate like a sugar loaf.

b. *Bot.* Having flowers or branches whose extremities form a tapering or cone-like outline.

1835 LINDLEY *Introd. Bot.* (1848) II. 382. **1836** *Penny Cycl.* V. 252 Fastigiate, when the branches of any plant are pressed close to the main stem, as in the Lombardy poplar. **1870** HOOKER *Stud. Flora* 349 *Taxus fastigiata*..(Irish or Florence-court yew) is a fastigiate variety.

c. *Entom.* Of the elytra: Tapering to a point.

1848 in MAUNDER *Treas. Nat. Hist.* Gloss.

2. †**a.** *Bot.* Formerly applied (after F. *fastigié*) in the sense 'having a horizontal surface at the top', as in an umbel or corymb. *Obs.*

[The use app. originated in a misunderstanding, the L. *fastigium* being interpreted as 'roof'.]

1793 in MARTYN *Lang. Bot.* s.v. **1794** —— *Rousseau's Bot.* xxviii. 445 The latter tree..having a fastigiate, or flat top. **1860** in MAYNE *Expos. Lex.* s.v.

b. Hence, of a zoophyte: = CORYMBED.

1846 DANA *Zooph.* (1848) 175 *Mussa fastigiata.* Fastigiate: disks usually nearly circular.

Hence **fa'stigiately** *adv.*

1840 PAXTON *Bot. Dict.*, *Fastigiately-branched*, the branches becoming gradually shorter from the base to the apex. **1884** in *Syd. Soc. Lex.*

fastigiate (fæ'stɪdʒɪeɪt), *v.* [f. as prec. + -ATE³.] *trans.* To make pointed at the top like a gable. **b.** *intr.* To taper to a point.

1656 BLOUNT *Glossogr.*, *Fastigiate*, to raise up, or grow up to a sharp top. **1732** in COLES.

Hence **fa'stigiated** *ppl. a.*, formed like a cone or ridge; 'roofed, narrowed up to the top' (Johnson 1773). †**fastigi'ation**, 'a making or growing sharp at the top like a pyramid' (Phillips 1662).

1647 H. MORE *Song of Soul* Notes 381 Day will hang in the sky many thousand miles off from us, fastigiated into one conicall point. **1668** WILKINS *Real Char.* II. v. §4. 146 Hawks..noted for having a fastigiated or rising head. **1730-6** in BAILEY (folio). **1840** in HUMBLE *Dict. Geol. & Min.*

†**fa'stigious,** *a. Obs.* [f. L. *fastīgi-um* + -OUS.] Like a fastigium; with gables. Also *fig.* Pretentious.

1670 G. H. *Hist. Cardinals* I. III. 94 They thought the Title too eminent and fastigious [orig. *sollevato*] for them. **1697** EVELYN *Acc. Architects* (1723) 50 The ancients dwellinghouses being generally flat at the top, Julius Cæsar being the first whom they Indulg'd to raise his Palace in this Fastigious manner.

‖**fastigium** (fæ'stɪdʒɪəm). [L.]

1. The apex or summit; *spec.* in *Arch.* the ridge of a house.

1677 HALE *Contempl.* II. 125, I have now arrived to the very Fastigium, the very highest point of this Mountain. **1706** PHILLIPS (ed. Kersey), *Fastigium*, the top or height of any Thing: In Architecture, the ridge of a House. **1825** W. HAMILTON *Hand-bk. Terms Arts & Sc.*. *Fastigium*..the summit, apex or ridge of a house, or pediment.

2. The gable end (of a roof); a pediment.

1849 J. WEALE *Dict. Terms*, *Fastigium*, the pediment of a portico. **1876** in GWILT *Archit.* Gloss.

3. a. *Pathol.* The acme or highest state of intensity (of a disease). **b.** *Anat.* (see quot. 1884).

1876 *Wagner's Gen. Pathol.* 619 The period of the fastigium, the complete development of the fever. **1884** *Syd. Soc. Lex.*, *Fastigium*, the upper and posterior angle of the fourth ventricle lying between the upper border of the posterior medullary velum and the posterior border of the anterior medullary velum.

†'**fasting,** *vbl. sb.*¹ *Obs.* [f. FAST *v.*¹ + -ING¹.]

1. The action of the vb. FAST¹; also *attrib.*

1398 TREVISA *Barth. De P.R.* XVII. xxv. (Tollem. MS), Cipris is a medicinal tre of couenable and fastynge vertu. *c* **1440** *Promp. Parv.* 158 Festynge to a thynge, *confixio.* **1660** HEXHAM, *De anckers aen den timmer*, a fasting of ankers to the Timber.

b. *fasting penny* (dial.): = 'fastening penny'; see FASTENING 1 b.

1691 RAY *N.-C. Words*, Festing-penny.

2. = FASTENING 3.

a **1400-50** *Alexander* 2590 It stonaid þam all For ferd þe festing suld faile.

fasting ('fɑːstɪŋ, 'fæst-), *vbl. sb.*² [f. FAST *v.*² + -ING¹.]

1. The action of the vb. FAST; abstinence from food; an instance of this.

c **1175** *Lamb. Hom.* 207 Ich bide þe..bi his eadi festunge iþe wildernesse. *c* **1250** *Old Kent. Serm.* in *O.E. Misc.* (1872) 28 Si mirre signefiet uastinge. **1340** *Ayenb.* 33 Be uestinges and be wakinges. **1480** CAXTON *Chron. Eng.* ccix. 191 He was so feble for his moch fastyng that he was dede almost. **1579** FULKE *Heskins' Parl.* 530 Although fasting for merite bee iustly punishable by statute. **1642** FULLER *Holy & Prof. St.* v. viii. 388 Even fasting it self is meat and drink to him. **1840** DICKENS *Old C. Shop* viii, Corporal punishment, fasting, and other tortures and terrors. **1873** W. K. SULLIVAN *O'Curry's Anct. Irish* I. Introd. 283 A *Trosca* or fasting was made by the plaintiff going to the defendant's house, and remaining there for a certain time..before making his distress.

†**2.** A season of abstinence from food, a fast.

1382 WYCLIF *Acts* xxvii. 9 And whanne now seylinge was not sykir, for that fasting passide, Poul coumfortide hem. **1398** TREVISA *Barth. De P.R.* IX. iii. (1495) 347 The fastynge of springynge tyme is the fyrst weke of Lente. **1483** CAXTON *G. de la Tour* A vj b, The fastynges that she had kept. **1656** *Artif. Handsom.* 81 He bids the Jewes, even in their fastings, to use it.

3. *attrib.*, as *fasting-weeds*; **fasting blood sugar**, the concentration of sugar in the blood after a period of fasting; **fasting-spittle**, the saliva that is in the mouth before one's fast is broken. Also FASTING-DAY.

1460-70 *Bk. Quintessence* 19 Mortifie it wiþ fastynge spotil. **1607** TOPSELL *Serpents* (1653) 607 If the fasting spittle of a Man fall into the jaws of a Serpent, he certainly dyeth thereof. **1648** HERRICK *Hesper. Fairie Temple* 104 Their Holy Oyle, their Fasting-Spittle, Their sacred Salt. **1654** TRAPP *Comm. Esther* v. 1 She laid aside her fasting-weeds, and put on her best. **1818** *Art Preserv. Feet* 146 Rubbing them with fasting spittle. **1927** *Practitioner* Feb. 116 If the fasting blood sugar is above 0·14 per cent., especially if it is in the neighbourhood of 0·2 per cent. or over, then diabetes is clearly established. **1968** J. ANDERSON in W. G. Oakley et al. *Clinical Diabetes* xxvi. 689 In uncomplicated hypo-thyroidism the fasting blood sugar is usually normal but may occasionally be low.

fasting ('fɑːstɪŋ, 'fæst-). *ppl. a.* [f. as prec. + -ING².] That fasts, *lit.* and *fig.*

c **1440** *Promp. Parv.* 151 Fastynge, *jejunus, impransus.* *c* **1470** HENRY *Wallace* v. 1034 For fastand folk to dyne gud tym war now. **1525** LD. BERNERS *Froiss.* II. ccxli. [ccxxxviii.] 745 Sir, are ye fastynge? *a* **1592** H. SMITH *Serm.* (1866) II. 213 Yet doth the non-resident keep his benefice fasting. **1595** SHAKS. *John* III. i. 260 A fasting Tyger. **1847** EMERSON *Poems, Initial Love* Wks. (Bohn) I. 456 Inquisitive, and fierce, and fasting.

Hence †'**fastingly** *adv.*, in a fasting manner, abstemiously, sparingly. *Obs.*

c **1460** J. RUSSELL *Bk. Nurture* 667 Furst speke..For frutes a-fore mete to ete þem fastyngely. **1566** DRANT *Horace Sat.* vi. H viij b, My frende why lyke you still To lyve in countrye fastynglye uppon a craggie hill? **1616** BEAUM. & FL. *Wit without Money* IV. v, You shall..not dine neither, but fastingly.

'**fasting-day.** [f. FASTING *vbl. sb.* + DAY. Cf. *fasten-day.*] = FAST-DAY.

a **1300** *Cursor M.* 29056 (Cotton Galba) þe thing þat þou þiself suld ett if it no fasting day þan ware. **1398** TREVISA *Barth. De P.R.* IX. iii. (1495) 347 In eche of thise foure tymes ben thre fastynge dayes. *c* **1430** *Two Cookery-bks.* 17 Do it in fastyng dayis & serue it forth. **1552** *Bk. Com. Prayer* Communion, Any holye dayes or fasting daies. **1656** TRAPP *Comm. 1 Cor.* vii. 5 Fasting-days are soul-fatting days. *a* **1711** KEN *Man. of Prayers* Wks. (1838) 424 All the fasting I advise you to, is only to some fasting-day. **1850** A. J. STEPHENS *Bk. Com. Prayer* II. 1150 Notice..of the fasting days..is commonly neglected.

†'**Fastingong.** *Obs.* Forms: 4-6 **fastyngong(e**, (5 **fastyngon**), 5 **fastyngange.** Also, corruptly, 6 **festigam.** [f. FAST *sb.*¹ + *ingong*, INGANG; cf. ON. *fǫstu-inngangr.*] = SHROVE TUESDAY. Also *Fastingong Eve, Fastingong Tuesday.*

1389 in *Eng. Gilds* (1870) 69 Yᵉ sonneday next after Fastyngonge. *c* **1442** in Blomefield *Hist. Norfolk* II. 111 John Gladman..on Tuesday in the last ende of Cristemesse viz. Fastyngonge Tuesday made a Disport with hys Neyghbours..coronned as Kyng of Crestemesse. *c* **1470** HARDING *Chron.* CCXXXVII. ii, Southward came thei..vpon the fastyngange eue. **1477** SIR J. PASTON in *Lett.* No. 786 III. 174 Wretyn at London..the Fryday a for Fastyngong. **1530** PALSGR. 804/1 At Fastyngonge, *a Quaresme prennant.*

Hence **Fastingong Sunday** = Shrove Sunday.

1450 *Paston Lett.* No. 78 I. 110 All the tenawntes ben chargyd to pay al her rent..be Fastyngong Sonday. **1541** R. BARNES *Workes* (1573) 222/2 The Thursday before Festigam Sonday.

fastish ('fɑːstɪʃ, 'fæst-), *a.* [f. FAST *a.* + -ISH.] Somewhat fast.

1854 S. PHILLIPS *Ess. fr. Times* Ser. II. 330 A short, stout, empty, good-natured, and over-dressed—in other words a 'fastish' young man. **1873** MISS BRADDON *Str. & Pilgr.* II. ii. 167 Fastish noblemen. **1884** *Lillywhite's Cricket Ann.* 115 A useful bowler, fastish as a rule.

'**fastland.** [f. as prec. + LAND; after Ger. *festland.*] The mainland, as distinguished from islands; the continent.

1883 *Chamb. Jrnl.* 524 The irregular banks of these islands shielded them from all outlook from the fastland.

† **'fastlings**, *adv. Sc. Obs. rare*⁻¹. [f. FAST *adv.* + -LING with advb. genitive *-s.*] ? Almost, nearly. (Cf. FAST *adv.* 4 b.)
a **1600** A. SCOTT *May* iv, Now all sic game is fastlings gone But gif it be amangs clovin Robbyns.

fastly ('fɑːstlɪ, 'fæst-), *adv. arch.* [f. FAST *a.* + -LY².] Now replaced by FAST *adv.*]
† **1.** In a fixed or steady manner. *Obs.*
c **888** K. ÆLFRED *Boeth.* xxxix. §7 Sio nafa.. færþ micle fæstlicor..ðonne þa felȝan. *a* **1225** *Ancr. R.* 234 Þet tu þer-efter þe wisluker wite him, hwon þu hauest ikelht him: & te uestluker holde. **1340** *Ayenb.* 166 Hit be-houeþ þet he hym hyealde vestliche ine his wylle. **1549–62** STERNHOLD & H. *Ps.* xxiv. 2 For he hath fastly founded it aboue the sea to stand.
† **2.** Firmly, unwaveringly, steadfastly; with confidence. *Obs.*
c **1175** *Lamb. Hom.* 115 He scal..festliche winnan wið onsiȝendne here. *c* **1200** *Trin. Coll. Hom.* 77 Cumen festliche to ure saule leche and unhelen him ure sake wundes. *c* **1205** LAY. 13000 Imong þan eorlen he stod & fastliche hit wið-soc. *c* **1350** *Prose Psalter* 196 Þe which bot if ich man haue bileued trewlich & fastelich. *c* **1440** HYLTON *Scala Perf.* (W. de W. 1494) III. xiii, Put forth fastely all thy good dedes to hym in as moche as they be good. **1513** MORE in Grafton *Chron.* II. 766 The Lord Hastinges..perswaded the lordes to beleve that the Duke of Glocester was sure & fastly faithfull to his prince. **1581** MARBECK *Bk. of Notes* 306 Faith, that fastlie beleeveth sinnes to be forgiven freelie by Christ.
† **b.** Without intermission or cessation. *Obs.*
971 *Blickl. Hom.* 47 Gif þa lareowas þis nellaþ fæstlice Godes folce bebeodan. *a* **1000** ÆLFRIC *Judg.* iv. 24 Hiȝ fæstlice weoxon. *c* **1175** *Lamb. Hom.* 237 Of þe folce we siggeð þat hit cumþ fastlice.
† **3.** Closely, securely. *Obs.*
c **1050** *Lat. & A.S. Glosses* in Wr.-Wülcker 354 *Artius*, fæstlicor. **1526** *Pilgr. Perf.* (W. de W. 1531) 90 Cleue to his mercy & goodnes the more fastly. **1591** SYLVESTER *Du Bartas* I. v. (1641) 42/2 A score of Anchors held her fastly bound. **1646** SIR T. BROWNE *Pseud. Ep.* III. xxv. 174 At the first littering their eyes are fastly closed. **1800** *Epist. to Sir W. Farquhar* in *Spirit Publ. Jrnls.* (1801) IV. 175 Men, who love their places..And fastly hold them with unblushing faces. **1817** J. SCOTT *Paris Revisit.* (ed. 4) 305 Their desires might bind them fastly to the Imperial cause.
4. Quickly, rapidly, speedily; hence, readily. Now *rare*.
c **1205** LAY. 27774 Forð heo gunnen fusen..& fastliche heom to buȝen. **1597** SHAKS. *Lover's Compl.* 61 Towards this afflicted fancy fastly drew. *c* **1645** T. TULLY *Siege of Carlisle* (1840) 13 Seeing them come fastly to her house. *a* **1806** K. WHITE *Rem.* II. 84 The sand of life Ebbs fastly to its finish. **1859** CORNWALLIS *New World* I. 207 The life of the child was fastly on the wane.

fastness ('fɑːstnɪs, 'fæst-). [f. as prec. + -NESS.]
I. The quality or state of being fast.
1. The quality or state of being firmly fixed; fixedness, stability. †Also, firm attachment.
c **888** K. ÆLFRED *Boeth.* xxxii. §2 Behealdaþ nu..ða fæstnesse þisses heofenes. **1340** *Ayenb.* 107 Þet no þing þet moȝe beualle ne moȝe ous ondo of þe ilke uestnesse ne of þise grace. *c* **1400** *Lanfranc's Cirurg.* 49 If þat ilke pece haue no fastnes to þe hool boon do þat pece awey. *a* **1400–50** *Alexander* 3259 (Dubl.) Suld not be funde in hym fastnes. **1523** FITZHERB. *Husb.* §139 The wynde is lykely to blowe it besyde the heed, for it hath no fastnes in the wode. **1603** FLORIO *Montaigne* I. ix. (1632) 16 Falsehood, which therein can have no such footing or setled fastnesse. **1677** GILPIN *Dæmonol.* (1867) 429 His words be so far from the fastness of nails that they shall be as wind. **1886** E. KNECHT tr. *Benedikt's Coal Tar Colours* III. 201 Shades..characterised by their extreme fastness.
† **b.** Fidelity, loyalty, firm adherence. Const. *to*.
c **1577** STANYHURST *Epitaph Baron of Louth* (Arb.) 151 Thee fastnesse of foster brotherhod. **1648** SYMMONS *Vind. Chas. I*, 331 Your tender care, and constant fastness to our Soveraign.
† **2.** Close alliance. *Obs. rare.*
a **1631** SIR R. COTTON *Advice* in Rushw. *Hist. Coll.* I. 471 Nothing can prevent the Spanish Monarchy, but a Fastness of those two Princes.
† **3.** The quality or state of being compact or close; density, solidity. Also of style: Conciseness, pithiness. *Obs.*
1555 *Fardle Facions* I. ii. 30 This earth then brought by yᵉ heate of the sonne into a more fastenesse. *a* **1568** ASCHAM *Scholem.* (Arb.) 114 To bring his style, from all lowse grosnesse, to soch firme fastnes in latin, as is in Demosthenes in Greeke. **1621** AINSWORTH *Annot. Ps.* xix. 11 Solid gold, called Paz, which hath the name of strength, fastnesse, or solidity. **1660** SHARROCK *Vegetables* 17 They think to hinder their quick descent by the fastness of the ground. **1666** J. SMITH *Old Age* (1752) 103 The fastness and fulness of the flesh. **1673–4** GREW *Anat. Trunks* II. vii. §4 Its Fastness [depending] on the closeness of the true Wood.
† **4.** Capacity for gripping tightly or retaining; tenacity, retentiveness. *Obs.*
1552 HULOET, Fastnes, *tenacia, tenacitas.* **1581** MULCASTER *Positions* v. (1887) 27 We finde also in them [children], as a quickenes to take, so a fastnesse to retaine.
† **5.** Security from invasion, difficulty of access; safety, strength. *Obs.* Cf. 9.
1596 SPENSER *F.Q.* v. x. 18 To those fennes for fastnesse she did fly. **1600** DYMMOK *Ireland* (1843) 23 It is very hard to hurt him, by reason of the fastnes of his cuntry. **1697** DRYDEN *Virg. Æneid* IX. 940 The Foes had left the fastness of their Place.
6. Rapidity, swiftness.
a **1642** SIR W. MONSON *Naval Tracts* IV. (1704) 452/1 Our..Ships have..advantage..by reason of their Fastness by a Wind. **1727–36** BAILEY, *Fastness*, swiftness. **1871** SIR H. HOLLAND *Recoll.* (1872) 268 The increased fastness of living, incident to all classes and occupations of men.
7. Of persons: The quality of being 'fast' in manners, talk, or mode of living. Cf. FAST *a.* 10.
1859 MRS. CARLYLE *Lett.* III. 1 There is a growing taste for fastness. **1863** *Lond. Rev.* 31 Jan. 126/1 Her fastness is more impulsive and less calculating, very much the result merely of animal spirits and impatience of restraint. **1881** C. NEW *Serm.* 101 Fastness is not manliness, but emptiness and weakness. **1889** H. JAMES *London Life* xi. 211 Putting an appearance of 'fastness' upon her.
II. Concrete senses.
† **8.** That which fastens or keeps fast.
a. Support, help. **b.** A fastening. *Obs.*
a. 1382 WYCLIF *Ps.* xxiv. [xxv.] 14 Fastnesse is the Lord to men dredende hym. *a* **1400** *Prymer* (1891) 109 Oure lord is a fastenesse to hem that dredith hym.
b. 1676 WORLIDGE *Cyder* (1691) 117 Weights of..lead, with rings, cords or other fastnesses to them. **1879** MISS JACKSON *Shropsh. Word.-bk.*, 'That theer bull's bin 'ilin the dur o' 'is place, an' bruk the fas'ness.'
9. A place not easily forced; a stronghold, fortress.
c **1000** ÆLFRIC *Gram.* ix. §12 (Z.) 41 *Munimen*..fæstnys. **1586** J. HOOKER *Girald. Irel.* in Holinshed II. 157 They..ouertooke them at a fastenes fast by the woods side. **1650** CROMWELL *Let.* 30 July (Carlyle), They would rather tempt us to attempt them in their fastness. **1748** *Anson's Voy.* II. i. 121 Separate herds..which inhabit distinct fastnesses. **1844** H. H. WILSON *Brit. India* III. 341 A strong and almost inaccessible fastness at Bandi.
fig. **1864** LOWELL *Fireside Trav.* 200 In the impregnable fastness of his great rich nature he [the Roman] defies us.

† **fastrede**, *a. Obs. rare.* In 1 **fæstræd**, 3 **fastrede**. [OE. *fæstræd*, f. *fæst*, FAST *a.* + *ræd* purpose.] Firm in purpose, inflexible, steadfast.
Beowulf 610 Gehyrde on Beowulfe folces hyrde fæstrædne ȝeþoht. *c* **888** K. ÆLFRED *Boeth.* xix, Se wisa & fæstræda Cato. *a* **1250** *Owl & Night.* 211 He is nu ripe and fastrede Ne lust him nu to none unrede.

† **fasts**, *sb. pl. Obs. rare.* [Anglicized form of FASTI; cf. F. *fastes*.] Annals, records.
1705 *Phil. Trans.* XXV. 2019 Two Ages after the same Fasts were compos'd by King Atlas.

† **'fastship.** *Obs. rare.* [f. FAST *a.* + -SHIP.] The quality of gripping tightly; parsimony.
a **1225** *Ancr. R.* 202 Simonie: Gauel: Oker: Uestschipe of ȝeoue, oðer of lone. *Ibid.* 276 Vestschipe salue [is] ureo heorte.

'fast-talk, *v. colloq.* Chiefly *U.S.* [f. FAST *adv.* + TALK *v.*] *trans.* To persuade by eloquent or deceitful talk.
1946 *Richmond* (Virginia) *News Leader* 29 Mar. 1/3 A marine private who fast-talked a Japanese bank president out of 587,800 yen. **1950** J. S. REDDING *Stranger & Alone* xxii. 225 He wasn't going to let some cracker lawyer..cheat and fast-talk Nan out of it. **1959** C. WILLIAMS *Man in Motion* x. 126 Purcell and Stedman deliberately fast-talked the liquor store man into an identification. **1960** *Sunday Express* 18 Dec. 17/6 Gantry hits the road again, to fast-talk himself into whatever good bet lies round the next bend. **1969** J. BURMEISTER *Hot & Copper Sky* iii. 64, I fast-talked my way into a bottle after..the party broke up.

† **'fastuose**, *a. Obs.*⁻⁰ [ad. L. *fastuōs-us*: see FASTUOUS.] = FASTUOUS.
1727 in BAILEY vol. II.

† **fastu'osity.** *Obs.* [f. L. *fastuōs-us* (see FASTUOUS) + -ITY.] The quality of being fastuous; haughtiness, ostentation, pomposity.
1656–81 in BLOUNT *Glossogr.* **1678** CUDWORTH *Intell. Syst.* I. i. §45. 53 That new Modle of Ethicks, which hath been obtruded upon the World with so much Fastuosity. **1680** H. MORE *Apocal. Apoc.* 25 The excessive pride and fastuosity of the Idolatrous Hierarchy. **1685** —— *Illustr. Dan.* xi. 45 Either a solid Greatness..or a tumid Fastuosity and affected Greatness. **1730–6** in BAILEY (folio).

fastuous ('fæstjuːəs), *a.* Now *rare.* [ad. L. *fastuōs-us*, f. *fastus* haughtiness, arrogance: see -OUS. Cf. F. *fastueux*.] Haughty, arrogant, pretentious, ostentatious.
a **1638** MEDE *Paraphr. 2 Pet.* iii. 3, Wks. 1672 III. 616 That supposed fastuous style of Sapores King of Persia to Constantius the Emperour, *Rex Regum*, etc. **1653** HAMMOND *On N.T.* Mark vii. 22 Fastuous and vain-glorious behaviour. **1707** COLLIER *Refl. Ridic.* 101 A pompous display of a fastuous Learning. **1786–8** J. WILLIAMS *Child. Thespis* 132 Too fastuous for exquisite passion's digression, Too fair for a hero. **1836** M. J. CHAPMAN in *Fraser's Mag.* XIV. 22 Let no man, With vain conceit and fastuous humour swelling, Sneer idly. **1888** *Sat. Rev.* 6 Oct. 418/1 The..fastuous *vates* of dysentery.
Hence **'fastuously** *adv.*, in a fastuous manner. **'fastuousness**, the quality of being fastuous.
a **1677** BARROW *Serm. 2 Tim.* iii. 2 Wks. 1686 III. 318 Demeaning our selves insolently and fastuously toward them. **1728** R. NORTH *Mem. Musick* (1846) 123 He behaved himself fast[u]ously; no person must whisper while he played. **1649** JER. TAYLOR *Gt. Exemp.* I. Add. §5. 58 Diogenes trampled upon Plato's pride with a greater fastuousnesse and humourous ostentation. *a* **1677** BARROW *Pope's Suprem.* (1680) I. iv. 66 Then there was no fastuousness in the Church. **1752** T. BIRCH *Life Tillotson* 430 He had nothing of pride or fastuousness.

fastyon, obs. form of FASHION.

'fasure. *Obs.* Also fasor, fassure. [? a. AF. *faisure*, f. *faire* to make.] Fashion, form.
13.. *E.E. Allit. P.* A. 431 That freles fleȝe of hyr fasor. *Ibid.* 1083 So ferly þer-of watz þe fasure [*printed* falure]. *c* **1400** *Destr. Troy* 3956 Polidamas..[was a] ffaire man of fassure [*MS.* faffure] & of fyn strenght. [But is *faffure* a form of *favour*?]

fasyll(e, var. of FASEL, *Obs.*

fasyon(e, faszshion, obs. forms of FASHION.

† **fat** (fæt), *sb.*¹ *Obs.* Forms: 1 fæt(t, 2–4 fet, *south.* vet, (3 feat), 4–8 fatt(e, 5–7 fate, (5 faat), 4– fat. See also VAT. [OE. *fæt* str. neut., corresp. to MLG., Du. *vat*, OHG. *faȥ* (MHG. *vaȥ*, mod.G. *fass*), ON. *fat* (Da. *fad*, Sw. *fat*):—OTeut. *fato-m* :—Teut. root **fat-* (:—pre-Teut. **pod-*, *pōd-*) to hold, contain; cf. OFris. *fatia*, MDu. *vatten*, OHG. *faȥȥôn* (MHG. *vaȥȥen*, mod.G. *fassen*) to grasp; also, Lith. *pudas* (:—*pōdos*) vessel; OE. *fetel*, OHG. *feȥȥil* (MHG. *veȥȥel* sword belt, mod.G. *fessel*, fetter), ON. *fetell* band.]
1. a. In early use *gen.* A vessel.
Beowulf 2761 Geseah..he..fyrnmanna fatu. *c* **950** *Lindisf. Gosp.* John ii. 7 Gefylleð ȝie ða fatto of uætre. *a* **1000** *Elene* 1026 (Gr.) Heo þa rode heht..in seolfren fat locum belucan. *a* **1000** ÆLFRIC *Gen.* xl. 11 And ic nam þa winberian & wrang on þæt fæt and sealde Faraone. *c* **1050** *Gloss.* in Wr.-Wülcker 347 *Acerra*, fæte oððe gledfæte. *a* **1225** *St. Marher.* 18 Þe reue..bed..bringen forð a uet ant fullen hit of wettre.
fig. c **1230** *Hali Meid.* 13 Þe uertu þat halt ure bruchele feat þat is ure feble flesch..in hal halinesse. **1340** *Ayenb.* 231 Hi bereþ a wel precious tresor ine a wel fyebble uet.
b. *spec.* A vessel of silver, or other metal, of a particular form; *esp.* one to contain holy-water.
c **1330** *Arth. & Merl.* 1054 A fende..pelt me in an holy fat. **1454** *Test. Ebor.* (Surtees) II. 175 A gylted cop called a fate covered. **1484** *Churchw. Acc. Wigtoft Boston* (Nichols 1797) 79 For saudryng of the holy water fatte. **1536** in *Antiq. Sarisb.* (1771) 198 A Fat of Silver for holy water. **1571** GRINDAL *Injunct. Clergie & Laytie* Biv, The Churchwardens..shall see..that all..Holy water stocks or Fattes..be utterly defaced.
2. A vessel of large size for liquids; a tub, a dyer's or brewer's vat, a wine cask. Cf. VAT.
In the A.V. *esp.* the vat in which grapes are trodden.
[*a* **1225** *St. Marher.* 17 Saloman þe wise..bitunde us in ane tunne, ant comen babilones men..ant breken þæt feat. **13..** *E.E. Allit.* P. B. 802, I schal fette yow a fatte your fette for to wasche.] *c* **1400** *Sowdone Bab.* 3152 Kinge Charles..bade him ordeyne a grete fat To baptyse the Sowdone yne. **1469** *Bury Wills* (Camden) 46 The occupier..shall haue his wetyng of his barly in the fate of the seid Denyse duryng maltyng tyme. **1483** CAXTON *Gold. Leg.* 100 3 [He] made hym to be caste in to a fatte or a tonne full of hote oylle. **1538** BALE *Thre Lawes* 447 Whan ale is in the fatt. **1565** GOLDING *Ovid's Met.* II. (1593) 27 Harvest smeard with treading grapes late at the pressing fat. **1606** SHAKS. *Ant. & Cl.* II. vii. 122 In thy Fattes our Cares be drown'd. *a* **1610** HEALEY *Theophrastus* To Rdr., A great water-pot like a Diers fat, or chaldron. **1678** J. PHILLIPS *Tavernier's Trav.* v. viii. 219 The golden Fat out of which they take the water. **1725** BRADLEY *Fam. Dict.* s.v. *Wine*, The Liquor..should stand in the Fatt about fifteen days. **1755** MAGENS *Insurances* I. 521, 5 Fatts red Wine £1661: 16.
b. Proverb.
1583 BABINGTON *Commandm.* vi. (1637) 53 They would have every fatte..stand on his owne bottome. **1678** BUNYAN *Pilgr.* I. 37 Every Fatt must stand on his own bottom.
3. A cask or barrel to contain dry things. Occas. more explicitly, ***dry-fat***.
1540 *Act 32 Hen. VIII*, c. 14 For the freight of a drie fatte of the biggest sort .vi. s. viii. d. sterling. **1622** R. HAWKINS *Voy. S. Sea* (1847) 134 Our pipes and fatts of bread. *c* **1647** A. WHEELOCKE in *Lett. Abp. Ussher* (1686) 546 The Lambeth Books..as yet..remain in Fats, or great Chests. *a* **1680** BUTLER *Rem.* (1759) I. 227 Wares, That come in dry Fats o'er from Francfort Fairs. **1688** R. HOLME *Armoury* III. 260/1 All Goods..in Barrels, Hogsheads, Fats, Chests or Packs. **1715** tr. *D'Anois' Wks.* 386 The Fairy..return'd with a huge Fat full of Feathers. **1812** J. SMYTH *Pract. Customs* 37 Battery, in fats.
4. Used as a measure of capacity (see quots.).
1413 *Act 1 Hen. V*, c. 10 Un mesure use deins la dicte Citee appelle le Faat. **1433** *Act 11 Hen. VI*, c. 8 Une vessell appelle le Fat, que conteient viij busselx dez blees ou un autre bussell mys a ycell pur une quartier. **1600** HEYWOOD *Edw. IV*, I. III. i, I would give..a fat of leather, to match her to some justice. **1607** COWEL *Interpr.*, Fate or Fat: is a great wooden vessell..vsed..to measure mault by, containing a quarter. **1660** *Act 12 Chas. II*, c. 4 Sched. s.v. *Books*, The basket or maund, containing 8 bales or 2 fats. **1706** PHILLIPS (ed. Kersey), *Fat* of Ising-glass, a Quantity from Three Hundred Weight and a quarter to Four Hundred Weight. **1866** ROGERS *Agric. & Pr.* I. x. 166 This measure [of 9 gallons] called a fatt was prohibited by statute.
5. *Comb.*
1483 *Cath. Angl.* 123/2 A Fattmaker, *cuparius.*

fat (fæt), *a.* and *sb.*² Forms: 1 fǽt(t, 2–4 fet(t(e, *south.* vet(te, 3–7 fatt(e, 3 *south.* vat(te, (4 faat), 4– fat. [OE. *fǽtt*, corresp. to OFris. *fat*, MDu., Du., MLG. *vet* (mod.G. *fett* adopted from LG.), OHG. *feiȥȥit* (MHG. *veiȥet*, *veiȥt*, mod.G. *feist*):—OTeut. **faitido-*, pa. pple. of **faitjan* to fatten (OHG. *veiȥȥen*, ON. *feita*), f. **faito-* adj. fat, represented by OS. *feit*, MHG.

veiz, ON. *feitr* (Da. *fed.*, Sw. *fet*); the existence of the primary adj. in OE. cannot be proved, as the form *fæt* in MSS. is prob. only a variant spelling of *fǽtt*.]

A. *adj.*

I. With respect to bulk or condition.

1. Of an animal used for food: Fed up for slaughter, ready to kill, fatted.

c **1000** *Ags. Gosp.* Luke xv. 27 þin fæder of-sloh an fæt [*c* **1160** *Hatton Gosp.* fet] celf. *a* **1300** *Cursor M.* 3643 (Cott.) O kyddes fatt þou fett me tuin. **1382** Wyclif *Isa.* xxv. 6 A feste of fatte bestes. *c* **1386** Chaucer *Prol.* 349 Ful many a fat partrich hadde he in mewe. *c* **1400** Maundev. (1839) xvii. 179 3if thei [the children] ben fatte, þei eten hem anon. *c* **1420** *Liber Cocorum* (1862) 38 Sethe a mawdelarde þat fat is þenne And cut in peses. *c* **1440** *Promp. Parv.* 151/2 Fat fowle, or beste, mestyde to be slayne, *altile.* **1552** Huloet, Fatte by feading, as in a francke or penne, *altilis.* **1719** De Foe *Crusoe* (1840) II. iv. 79 The party concluded it was to see whether he or she was fattest and fittest to kill first. **1849** Ld. Houghton in *Life* (1891) I. x. 439 Fat beasts sold for the price they were bought lean. **1890** *Daily News* 21 Nov. 5/3 Animals which..have won prizes as 'fat', that is to say, as ripe for the butcher.

2. a. Of animals or human beings, their limbs, etc.: In well-fed condition, plump; well supplied with fat (see B).

c **893** K. Ælfred *Oros.* iv. xiii. §5 Ge sindon nu utan fætte & innan hlæne. *a* **1000** *Deut.* xxxi. 20, & þonne hiȝ etaþ & fulle beoþ & fætte. *c* **1175** *Lamb. Hom.* 81 [He] luueð his sunnen alse deð þet fette swin þet fule fen to liggen in. *a* **1225** *Ancr. R.* 138 Hit regibbeð anon, ase uet kelf & idel. **1297** R. Glouc. (1724) 429 Ballede he was, & þycke of breste, of body vat also. *a* **1300** *Cursor M.* 4566 (Gött.) þe seuen of þaim..were selcuth fat and fair ky. **1393** Langl. *P. Pl.* C. x. 208 Faitours in frere cloþynge hadde fatte chekus. *c* **1450** *Merlin* 227 Her flessh whitter than snowe, and was not to fatte ne to sklender. **1598** Shaks. *Merry W.* v. v. 14 A Windsor Stagge, and the fattest (I thinke) i'th Forrest. **1626** Bacon *Sylva* §899 The Beare, the Hedge-hog..wax Fat when they Sleepe. **1668** Davenant *Man's the Master* ii. i, The chief reason why I am not fat is..because I am in love with three of our neighbours' maids. **1731** Arbuthnot *Aliments* vi. 190 You may see in an Army forty thousand Foot-Soldiers without a fat Man. **1774** Goldsm. *Nat. Hist.* (1776) V. 45 Their bodies are fat and muscular. **1864** P'cess Alice in *Mem.* (1884) 78 My fat Baby..is a great darling. **1883** Gilmour *Mongols* (1884) 108 The Mongols like to be careful of their camels, even when they are fat and strong.

absol. *c* **1205** Lay. 19445 Ne durste þær bilæuen na þæ uatte no þe læne.

b. In unfavourable sense: Overcharged with fat, corpulent, obese.

a **1000** *Riddles* xli. 105 (Gr.) Mara ic eom and fættra, þonne amæsted swin. *c* **1400** *Destr. Troy* 3068, A necke.. nawþer fulsom, ne fat, but fetis & round. *c* **1400** *Lanfranc's Cirurg.* (MS. B) 5 Of seknesse of a wommans tetys to grete to fatte oþere to lene. **1494** [see corpulent 2]. **1598** Shaks. *Merry W.* iv. v. 25 There was..an old fat woman euen now with me. **1646**, **1791** [see corpulency 2]. **1856** Mrs. Carlyle *Lett.* II. 294 So fat a man one rarely sees.

c. *fig.*

1526 *Pilgr. Perf.* (W. de W. 1531) 173 b, He is fatte of my benefytes and good dedes. **1558** Bp. Watson *Sev. Sacram.* i. A j b, By the Sacramente..wee are nourished to everlastyng life, and made fatte with God. **1596** Shaks. *Merch. V.* i. iii. 48, I will feede fat the ancient grudge I beare him. **1596** —— *1 Hen. IV*, iii. ii. 180 Aduantage feedes him fat, while men delay. **1611** Bible *Prov.* xi. 25. **1620** May *Heir* i. i. in Hazl. *Dodsley* XI. 515 'Twill feed me fat with sport, that it shall make.

d. *fig.* in vulgar phrase *to cut up fat*: see cut *v.* 60 k.

e. Of larger size than is usual; large in comparison with others of the same species.

1877 *Encycl. Brit.* VII. 368/2 The Fat Dormouse (*Myoxus glis*) is larger than the British species. **1877** A. B. Horton in C. A. Moloney *Sk. Forestry W. Afr.* (1887) 38 Nuts well supplied with flesh, or what is technically called 'fat nuts'.

f. *fat herring* = matie.

1863 [see matie]. **1883** F. M. Wallem *Fish Supply Norway* 15 The Norwegian fat herring is considered to be the very best herring in the world. **1967** *Oceanogr. & Marine Biol.* V. 436 The 'fat' herring fishery, exploiting one-to-four-year-old, adolescent fish.

3. a. *transf.* Of things: Thick, full-bodied, substantial; *spec.* of printing types. Also † *to beat fat* (Typog.): see quot. 1683. †Of the voice: Full.

c **1250** *Gen. & Ex.* 2104, vii eares wexen fette of coren. **1398** Trevisa *Barth. De P.R.* xix. cxxxi. (1495) 942 The voyces ben fatte and thycke whanne moche spyryte comyth out as the voys of a man. **1578** Lyte *Dodoens* ii. xlii. 200 The white lillie his leaues be..somewhat thicke or fat. **1596** Shaks. *1 Hen. IV*, i. ii. 141 There are..Traders riding to London with fat Purses. **1676** Moxon *Print. Lett.* 5 The.. Draughts of the Letters will shew him what parts of a Letter must be fat or lean. *Ibid.* 7 The *Stem* or Broad stroke in a Letter is called the *Fat stroke.* **1683** Moxon *Dict. Printing, Beat Fat*, If a Press-man Takes too much Inck with his Balls, he Beats Fat. The Black English Faced Letter is generally Beaten Fat. **1787** Winter *Syst. Husb.* 247 The leaves of the seeds..appeared twice as fat or thick. **1841** Savage *Dict. Printing, Fat Face* or *Fat Letter* is a letter with a broad stem. **1867** G. P. Marsh in *Nation* 3 Jan., The substitution of full-faced—I have heard it called *fat* by printers..small letter for capitals.

b. *Naut.* (see quot. 1704).

1627 Capt. Smith *Seaman's Gram.* ii. 4 If it [the Tuck] lie too low it makes her haue a fat quarter. **1704** J. Harris *Lex. Techn.* s.v., If the Trussing in, or Tuck of a Ships Quarter under Water, be deep: They say she hath a Fat Quarter. **1867** in Smyth *Sailor's Word-bk.* s.v.

II. With respect to the component parts.

4. a. Containing much fat, oil, etc.; consisting of fat, greasy, oily, unctuous. *to cut it (too) fat*: lit. referring to a slice of meat, *fig.* (vulgar) to make a display. See cut *v.* 8 *b.*

c **1000** *Ags. Ps.* lxxx. 15 [lxxxi. 16] He hi fedde mid fætre lynde, hwæte and huniȝe. *c* **1200** Ormin 995 Bræd.. smeredd wel wiþ elesæw & makedd fatt & nesshe. **1377** Langl. *P. Pl.* B. xii. 264 þe larke..of flesch, by fele folde fatter and swetter. *c* **1440** *Promp. Parv.* 159/1 Fet, or fatte, as flesshe and oþer lyke, *pinguis.* **1577** B. Googe *Heresbach's Husb.* iii. (1586) 147 Fatt and newe Milke. **1597** Shaks. *2 Hen. IV*, v. v. 143 If you be not too much cloid with Fat Meate. **1607** Topsell *Four-f. Beasts* (1673) 332 It shall be needful..to use some fat broth. **1638** Rawley tr. *Bacon's Life & Death* (1650) 7 Mixed with Tallow or any Fat Thing. **1662** J. Davies *Voy. Ambass.* 201 The Milk..is so fat, that it makes a Cream two fingers thick. **1701** Addison *Lett. Italy* 134 The fat Olive. **1824** Mrs. Cameron *Marten & Scholars* vii. 43 This nice fat cheese which brother gave me. **1836** W. Irving *Astoria* II. 205 Which he began to sniff, pronouncing them 'fat and tender'. **1836–9** Dickens *Sk. Boz* Scenes ix, Promenading about..with surprising dignity, or as the gentleman in the next box facetiously observes, 'cutting it uncommon fat'. **1842** *Comic Almanac* 49 A goose, even tailors have, who cut it fat.

†**b.** *transf.* Of figs: Full of juice, juicy. *Obs.*

1398 Trevisa *Barth. De P.R.* v. xv. (1495) 121 Leues of trees in whyche is fatte humour fallith not. *c* **1400** *Lanfranc's Cirurg.* 212 Medle þerwiþ fatte figis. **1656** Ridgley *Pract. Physick* 292 Take fat Figs 12 oz.

c. Of an actor's part, offering abundant opportunity for skill, display, etc.; of speeches, etc., impressive, effective.

1758 W. Toldervy *Hist. Two Orphans* III. 157 He..sings as many fat songs as the best man in the Garden. **1901** C. Morris *Life on Stage* xix. 139 What is vulgarly known today as a 'fat' part, 'fat' meaning lines sure to provoke applause. **1929** Wodehouse *Gentleman of Leisure* xv. 119 True acting part, the biggest in the piece, full of fat lines.

d. Of wood: Resinous (*U.S.*); also †of amber. Of coal: Bituminous.

1697 Dryden *Virg. Past.* viii. 74 Fat Amber let the Tamarisk distill. **1831** Macculloch *Syst. Geol.* II. xliv. 356 A resinous plant such as fir..would produce a fatter coal than an oak, because the resin itself is converted into bitumen. **1836** *Backwoods of Canada* 234 The resinous substance called fat-pine being usually found in places where the living pine is least abundant. **1856** Olmsted *Slave States* 335 The room was filled with smoke of the fat light-wood. **1877** Dodge *Hunting Grounds Gt. West* xxxvi. 393 They [the Indians] procured some 'fat' pine knots. **1883** Gresley *Gloss. Coal Mining Terms, Fat Coals*, those which contain volatile, oily matters.

5. Of mould, clay, etc.: Containing much soluble or plastic matter; having a 'greasy' feeling to the touch; sticky. Of limestone: Containing much lime, and few impurities; hence, Pure.

1502 Arnolde *Chron.* 168 Yᵉ erthe muste..be neyther too fat ne to grauelly. **1546** *St. Papers Hen. VIII*, XI. 335 The grounde of the countrey..is so fatte, that if it rayne there three dayes..the ordinaunce wolde sticke..in the myre. **1563** Fulke *Meteors* (1640) 14 b, A Comet is an Exhalation ..fat and clammie, hard compact like a great lumpe of pitch. **1611** Bible *Song 3 Child. 22 marg.*, Naphtha, which is a certaine kind of fat and chalkie clay. **1697** Dryden *Virg. Georg.* iii. 687 Fat Pitch, and black Bitumen, add to these. **1703** Moxon *Mech. Exerc.* 238 A fat Earth full of Allom. **1787** Winter *Syst. Husb.* 332 It appeared very fat between the fingers. **1794** Kirwan *Min.* I. 116 The distinction of fat and meagre limestones. **1843** Portlock *Geol.* 682 The fat clay..is mixed with a meagre or sandy clay.

†**6.** Full of stimulating elements, rich. *Obs.*

1707 *Curios. in Husb. & Gard.* 268 Fat, warm and subtile Nourishments. **1797** Wolcott (P. Pindar) *Livery of London* Wks. 1812 III. 441 Pine-apples ne'er grow on cold raw clay But fat manure.

7. Of fluids: Charged with solid or extraneous particles. †**a.** Of water: Thick, turbid.

1387 Trevisa *Higden* (Rolls) III. 259 Fatte water. **1587** Harrison *England* ii. vi. (1877) i. 160 The fattest standing water is alwaies the best. **1607** Topsell *Serpents* (1653) 744 This Serpent is bred in fat waters and soils. **1713** *Phil. Trans.* XXVIII. 233 When the Water is fattest and fullest of Foam.

†**b.** Of wine or ale: Fruity, full-bodied, sugary.

1609 Bible (Douay) *Ezek.* xxvii. 18 The Damacene was thy merchant..in fatte wine. **1632** Lithgow *Trav.* iii. 102 These Cloysters haue a brauer life for good cheare [and] fat Wines..than any..Friers can elsewhere find. **1816** Scott *Antiq.* xi, A species of fat ale.

c. Of air, mist, etc.: Charged with moisture or odours; dense. *rare.* †Of a room: Full of dense air.

1596 Shaks. *1 Hen IV*, ii. iv. 1 Come out of that fat roome. **1659** Lovelace *Poems* (1864) 186 When a fat mist we view, we coughing run. **1697** Dryden *Virg. Past.* viii. 91 Make fat with Frankincense the sacred Fires. **1837** Emerson *Addr., Amer. Schol.* Wks. II. 189 Public and private avarice make the air we breathe thick and fat.

†**d.** See quot. *Obs.*

1683 Moxon *Dict. Printing, Fat Ashes*, Founders call their Ashes Fat, if they are considerably Heavy, because then they have much Mettle in them.

8. *fat oil* or *oils*: in various senses (see quots.).

c **1790** Imison *Sch. Art* II. 37 Take four ounces of fat oil, very clear, and made of good linseed oil. **1838** T. Thomson *Chem. Org. Bodies* 433 Fat oils become solid by long exposure. **1875** J. C. Wilcocks *Sea Fisherman* 179 *Train-oil*, a name given to it on the spot to distinguish it from whale, or seal oil..called *fat-oil.* **1877** Watts *Dict. Chem.* IV. 179 Fat or fixed oils..resemble one another in not being capable of distilling without decomposition.

III. With reference to the amount of produce or supply.

9. Yielding or capable of yielding excellent and abundant returns. **a.** Of land: Fertile, rich.

1393 Langl. *P. Pl.* C. xiii. 224 On fat londes and ful of donge foulest wedes groweth. *c* **1420** *Pallad. on Husb.* i. 72 To see thi lande..fatte and swete. **1562** Turner *Herbal* ii. 112 b, The fat ground. **1672** Cave *Prim. Chr.* i. i. (1673) 5 The blood of Christians making the Churches soil more fat and fertile. **1777** Robertson *Hist. Amer.* (1783) II. 98 The roots..multiply amazingly with the heat of the climate in a fat soil. **1827** Pollok *Course T.* iii, Turned fat lands To barrenness. **1851** D. Jerrold *St. Giles* xi. 103 The broad, fat fields of Kent lay smiling in the sun.

b. of a source of income (*e.g.* a benefice, office).

c **1380** Wyclif *Sel. Wks.* III. 519 3if þe benefice be faat. **1581** Mulcaster *Positions* xli. (1887) 250 To leaue his old poore place for a fatter rowme. **1642** Milton *Apol. Smect.* (1851) 305, I would wish him the biggest and the fattest Bishoprick. **1710** Steele *Tatler* No. 228 ¶1 A worthy Gentleman has lately offered me a fat Rectory. **1852** Thackeray *Esmond* i. iii, 'Church! priesthood! fat living!' **1883** *American* VI. 38 Congress as the creator of fat jobs. **1884** *Manch. Exam.* 17 Nov. 5/3 His fat sheriffship.

c. of a dispute or suit at law.

1644 Milton *Educ.* (1738) 136 The promising and pleasing thoughts of litigious terms, fat contentions, and flowing fees. **1646** J. Cooke *Vind. Law* 26 A recreation which they have..to recreate the spirit of the Judges and Advocates, which they call a Fat case. **1858** Carlyle *Fredk. Gt.* (1865) I. iii. xiii. 219 Never was such a Lawsuit—so fat an affair for the attorney species.

†**d.** Of a prisoner: That can pay a good ransom. *Obs. rare.*

1548 Hall *Chron.* 123 b, So with greate riches, and fatte prisoners, he returned again to Paris.

e. *Typog. fat take, fat work*, in type-setting, work or a piece of work especially profitable to the compositor who works by the piece. Hence, *fat page*: one having many blank lines or spaces.

10. Well supplied with what is needful or desirable. †**a.** Of a person: Affluent, wealthy. *Obs.*

1611 Bible *Ps.* xcii. 14 They [the righteous] shalbe fat, & flourishing. *a* **1700** B. E. *Dict. Cant. Crew, Fat Cull*, a rich fellow. *a* **1716** South (J.) Persons grown fat and wealthy by a long and successful imposture. *a* **1764** Lloyd *Fam. Epistle fr. Hanbury's Ho.* 19 Mark the fat Cit, whose good round sum, Amounts at least to half a Plumb.

b. Of things: Abundant, plentiful; *esp.* of a feast, pasture, etc. Also, Well-stocked.

1563 *Homilies* ii. *Gluttony & Drunkenness* (1859) 306 He that loveth wine and fat fare shall never be rich. **1577** Holinshed *Chron.* I. 185 The best and fattest pasturages. **1596** Dalrymple tr. *Leslie's Hist. Scot.* v. (1887) 267 Finalie he returnes with a fatt praii. **1611** Bible *Ezek.* xxxiv. 14 In a fat pasture shall they feede. **1677** Yarranton *Eng. Improv.* 28 Scotland is a thin and lean Kingdom..England is a fat Kingdom. *a* **1790** Franklin *Way to Wealth*, A fat kitchen makes a lean will.

c. *a fat lot*: a large amount, a great deal: always *ironical* and implying 'very little, hardly anything'. Similarly *a fat chance*, implying 'hardly any opportunity (or possibility)'; also (N.Z.) *a fat show.*

1892 I. Zangwill *Childr. Ghetto* (1893) i. ii. 24 'I von't sell you no more tickets,' said Sugarman... 'A fat lot I care,' said Becky, tossing her curls. **1899** C. J. C. Hyne *Further Adv. Capt. Kettle* i. 5 Shows what a fat lot of influence this État du Congo has got. **1906** F. Metcalfe *Side Show Studies* 99 The Proprietor..suggested sending the announcement..to the papers. 'A fat chance I'd stand of having it printed,' he grumbled. **1908** 'I. Hay' *Right Stuff* vi. 83 Rot! Fat lot you know about it, Dilly. **1914** D. H. Lawrence *Widowing Mrs. Holroyd* iii. 72 Some women could have lived with him happy enough. An' a fat lot you'd have thanked me for my telling. **1916** J. S. Clouston *Two's Two* ix. 69 'And a fat lot of good they'll be!' scoffed Archibald. **1922** S. Lewis *Babbitt* v. 63 Fat chance! **1933** W. S. Maugham *Sheppey* iii. 75 Fat chance I've got of going to France now. **1936** Wodehouse *Laughing Gas* viii. 88 A fat chance, of course. I should have known his psychology better. **1947** A. Vogt in D. M. Davin *N.Z. Short Stories* (1953) 374 The men from the mill..had a fat chance of getting in [to the pub] before that [6 p.m.]. **1948** D. Ballantyne *Cunninghams* (1963) i. xii. 63 It would be corker if he could go outisde with Carole Plowman... Fat show! **1951** E. Coxhead *One Green Bottle* i. 23 Idiot, thought Cathy. Fat lot you know. **1962** *Coast to Coast 1961–62* 87 You're a fat lot of help to me, moping about alone all the time. **1967** B. Wright tr. *Queneau's Between Blue & Blue* xix. 208 Fat lot of use it was me getting my posterior frozen for a whole night to do my host a favour.

IV. 11. Displaying the characteristics of a fat animal; slow-witted, indolent, self-complacent.

1588 Shaks. *L.L.L.* v. ii. 268 Wel-liking wits they haue, grosse, grosse, fat, fat. **1602** —— *Ham.* i. v. 32 Duller should'st thou be then the fat weede That rots it selfe in ease ..Would'st thou not stirre in this. **1611** Bible *Isa.* vi. 10 Make the heart of this people fat, and make their eares heauy, and shut their eyes. *a* **1616** Beaum. & Fl. *Wit without Money* i. i, Grounding their fat faiths upon old country proverbs. **1790** Burke *Wks.* (1871) II. 373 The fat stupidity and gross ignorance. **1819** Shelley *Peter Bell* iv. xxi, With loose fat smile, The willing wretch sat winking there. *a* **1854** J. Wilson (W.), How could it enter into his fat heart to conceive [etc.]. **1879** *Temple Bar Mag.* No. 227 A fat smile of complacent wisdom on his face.

V. 12. With the senses mixed.

c **1325** *Poem Times Edw. II* 188 in *Pol. Songs* (Camden) 332 The frere wole to the direge, if the cors is fat. **1596** Shaks. *1 Hen. IV*, ii. iv. 559–60 *Sher.* A grosse fat man. *Car.* As fat as Butter. **1611** Bible *Ps.* cxix. 70 Their heart is as fat as grease. **1642** Fuller *Holy & Prof. St.* v. xix. 437 These countreys were fat enough to be stewed in their own liquour. *a* **1732** Gay *Songs & Ball., New Song on New Similies*, My cheeks as fat as butter grown.

VI. Combinations.

13. Parasynthetic (chiefly in sense 2), as ***fat-arsed***, ***-backed***, ***-barked***, ***-beneficed*** (sense 9), ***-brained*** (sense 2 or 11), ***-cheeked***, ***-eyebrowed***, ***-fleshed***, ***-hearted*** (sense 2 or 11), ***fat-hipped***, ***-kidneyed***, ***-legged***, ***-paunched*** (sense 2b), ***-rumped***, ***-tailed*** adjs. Also FAT-FACED, FAT-WITTED.

1891 J. S. FARMER *Slang* II. 377/1 **Fat-arsed*, broad in the breech. **1923** D. H. LAWRENCE *Kangaroo* xvi. 351 Slaving to keep this marvellous Empire going, with its.. fat-arsed hypocritical upper classes. **1607** A. BREWER *Lingua* III. ii. in Hazl. *Dodsley* IX. 386 Your.. *fat-backed.. drones. **1616–61** HOLYDAY *Persius* 297 'Armes, and the man I sing.' Perchance you'l dare To call this frothy, *fat-bark'd [L. *cortice pingui*]? **1634** 'E. KNOTT' *Charity Maintained* I. vi. §21 Such *fat-beneficed Bishops. **1597** DRAYTON *Mortimeriados* 69 *Fat-braind Fleamings. **1580** HOLLYBAND *Treas. Fr. Tong, Joufflu*, *fat cheeked. **1591** PERCIVALL *Sp. Dict.*, *Fat eie browed. **1863** MISS POWER *Arab. Days & N.* 109 Those '*fat-fleshed' fair ones. **1607** HIERON *Wks.* I. 230 The *fat-hearted Israelites. **1921** D. H. LAWRENCE *Let.* 26 Mar. ? (1962) II. 647 The *fat-hipped soft fellow we saw at Anticoli last year. **1596** SHAKS. *1 Hen. IV*, II. ii. 5 Peace ye *fat-kidney'd Rascall. **1719** D'URFEY *Pills* VI. 351 Glud [sic] Kate and *fat legged Lissey. **1891** R. KIPLING *City Dreadf. Nt.* 72 Quaint houses, with fat-legged balustrades on the roofs. **1563** FOXE *A. & M.* 1691/2 The *fat panched bishop. **1842** BISCHOFF *Woollen Manuf.* II. 289 The head is like that of the *fat-rumped [sheep]. *Ibid.* II. 320 The Doomba, or *fat-tailed sheep of Cabool.

14. Special comb., as **fat-back** *U.S. local*, a strip of fat from the back of a pig; **fat-bird**, a name (*a*) of the Guacharo *Steatornis caripensis*; (*b*) of the Pectoral Sandpiper *Actodromas maculata* (U.S.); **fat cat** *slang* (orig. and chiefly *U.S.*), a political backer; also *transf.*; **fat crab** *U.S.*, a crab ready to shed its shell; **fat-face**, (*a*) a term of abuse; (*b*) *Typog.* less commonly **fat letter** (see quot. 1841), and *attrib.*; **fat-fed** *a.*, fed up to fatness: of a man, full-fleshed; also *transf.*; **fat-guts**, one having a big belly, used as a term of abuse, also *attrib.*; **fat-headed**, (*a*) having a fat head; (*b*) dull, stupid; **fat-headedness**, stupidity; **fat lamb** *N.Z.*, a lamb bred to be exported as refrigerated meat; **fat-lute** (see quot.); **fat-rascal** (see quots.); †**fat-sagg** *a.*, hanging down with fat; **fatstock, fat-stock**, marketable live-stock; **fat-tail**, a fat-tailed sheep; †**fat-ware**, cattle fatted for market; **fat-wood** *U.S. local* = LIGHTWOOD^2 a. Also, FAT-HEAD.

1903 *Sears, Roebuck Catal.* (ed. 113) 18/1 Clear back pork. This pork is made from the *fat backs of prime hogs, is free from lean and bone. **1932** E. CALDWELL *Tobacco Road* i. 8 Salty soup Ada had made by boiling several fat-back rinds in a pan of water. **1941** A. F. RAPER *Sharecroppers All* 24 The great majority bring for lunch cold baked 'taters' and sandwiches of soda biscuits and fat back. **1928** F. R. KENT *Pol. Behavior* vi. 59 These capitalists have what the organization needs—money to finance the campaign. Such men are known in political circles as '*Fat Cats'. **1949** *Sat. Rev. Lit.* 16 Apr. 4 Hollywood celebrities, literary fat cats. **1960** *Economist* 8 Oct. 157/2 Methods of exhorting [*sic*] money which.. harry so-called 'fat-cats'—rich supporters—to an extent which looks like cruelty to animals. **1966** *New Statesman* 21 Jan. 78/3 The kind of balance-sheet fat cats who characterise the worst side of ITV. **1971** *Flying* Apr. 34/1 Those who view the business jet as a smoke-belching, profit-eating chariot of the fatcat. **1905** W. P. HAY in *Rep. Bureau Fisheries 1904* (U.S.) 411 The individual bearing it [*sc.* a narrow white line] is classed as a '*fat crab', or more vulgarly as a 'snot'. **1741** RICHARDSON *Pamela* (1824) I. 179 Answer me, *fat-face! **1841** SAVAGE *Dict. Printing, Fat Face* or *Fat Letter* is a letter with a broad stem. **1871** *Amer. Encycl. Printing, Fat-face Letter*, Letter with a broad face. **1607** TOPSELL *Four-f. Beasts* 181 This kind of Dog.. is mighty, grosse, and *fat fed. **1616** *Trav. Eng. Pilgr.* in *Harl. Misc.* (Malh.) III. 329 Fat-fed friars. **1648** HERRICK *Hesper.* I. 204 The fat-fed smoking temple. **1596** SHAKS. *1 Hen. IV*, II. ii. 32 Peace ye *fat guttes, lye downe. **1682** N. O. *Boileau's Lutrin* IV. 278 Till fat-guts Everard open'd, and quite marr'd it. **1853** HICKIE tr. *Aristoph.* (1872) II. 536 Pray sit down here, you fat guts. *c* **1510** *Gest Robyn Hode* II. 38 With that cam in a *fat-heded monke. **1603** H. CROSSE *Vertues Commw.* (1878) 99 The lazie Monkes, and fat-headed Friers. **1748** RICHARDSON *Clarissa* Wks. 1883 VIII. 188 This I leave to thy own fat-headed prudence. **1768** *Life & Adv. of Sir Barth. Lapskull* II. 66 The fat-headed majority, intoxicated by the fumes of excess. **1820** W. IRVING *Sketch Bk., Christmas Dinner* (1865) 276 A fat-headed old gentleman next him. **1883** W. BROMLEY DAVENPORT in *19th Cent.* Sept. 402 A few obese fat-headed carp. **1840** A. BUNN *Stage* I. 272 Such is the *fat-headedness of *John Bull*. **1891** KIPLING *Light that Failed* viii, The fat-headedness of deliberately trying to do work that will live. **1915** WODEHOUSE *Something Fresh* iii, If you want any further proof of your young man's fat-headedness, mark that. **1891** R. WALLACE *Rural Econ. Austral. & N.Z.* xxvii. 369 Any of the various breeds or crosses now in the country [*sc.* N.Z.] will supply suitable mothers for *fat lambs, provided they are good milkers. **1923** *N.Z. Jrnl. Agric.* 20 Jan. 50 Which breed of sheep is best for fat-lamb production? **1928** R. G. STAPLEDON *Tour Austral. & N.Z.* viii. 58 Fat lambs are also largely produced on a Romney basis. **1956** G. BOWEN *Wool Away!* (ed. 2) xii. 147 On the flat country.. fat-lamb and mutton production predominate. **1858** SIMMONDS *Dict. Trade*, **Fat-lute*, a mixture of pipeclay and linseed oil for filling joints. **1868** ATKINSON *Cleveland Gloss.*, **Fat-rascal*, a kind of rich tea-cake compounded with butter or cream.. and with currants intermingled. **1606** MIDDLETON *Black Bk.* Wks. 1886 VIII. 12 With her *fat-sagg chin hanging down like a cow's udder. **1880** *Trans. Illinois Dept. Agric.* X. 65 The success of the *Fat Stock Show. **1906** *Daily Colonist* (Victoria, B.C.) 30 Jan. 5/4 It was decided to hold a fat stock sale in this city in the middle of March. **1907** R. WALLACE *Farm Live Stock Gt. Brit.* (ed. 4) 281 Steers slaughtered at the Smithfield Fat-Stock Show. **1912** *Jrnl. Bath & West & Southern Counties Soc.* 5th Ser. VI. v. 175 For many years the Middle Whites carried off the highest awards at the fat stock shows. **1955** *Times* 13 July 12/5 The fatstock marketing scheme had been working successfully for the past 12 months. **1888** *Castle Line Handbk. S.A.* 55 (Pettman), The *fat-tails held their own for many years. **1909** WEBSTER, *Fatwood*, any pine wood full of pitch. **1601** HOLLAND *Pliny* XVII. xxiv, These forsooth they feed in mue, and franke them up like *fat-ware, with good corn-meale. **1938** M. K. RAWLINGS *Yearling* vii. 67 She unbanked the fire on the hearth and threw on *fat-wood. **1963** *Times* 19 Mar. 10/7 All kinds of wood, including fat-wood.

B. *sb.*^{2}

1. a. The adj. used *absol.* The fat part of anything. †Rarely in *pl.*

1393 LANGL. *P. Pl.* C. XXII. 280 That cast for to kele a crokke and saue þe fatte aboue. **1535** COVERDALE *Lev.* xvii. 6 Burne the fat for a swete sauoure vnto the Lord. *c* **1540** in *Vicary's Anat.* (1888) App. ix. 222 Take the fatte of capons or hennys. **1616** SURFL. & MARKH. *Country Farme* 31 He shall make prouision of Fats, or of the marrowes of the bones of Mutton. **1667** MILTON *P.L.* XI. 439 Then sacrificing, laid The Inwards and thir Fat.. On the cleft Wood. **1796** MRS. GLASSE *Cookery* xiv. 238 Pour the fat out of the pan. **1890** MRS. BEETON *Cookery Bk.* 19/1 Droppings of fat and gravy.. fall from the roast meat.

b. *pl.* or (in *attrib.* use only) *collect. sing.* Fat cattle or sheep. *Austral.* and *N.Z.*

1886 C. SCOTT *Sheep-farming* 137 Sheep intended for the fat market. **1894** A. ROBERTSON *Nuggets* 132 What say ye to him goin' to Melbourne to see the flock o' fats sold at the Flemington Yards? **1907** W. H. KOEBEL *Return of Joe* 20 The only different thing you'll see, I hope, will be a larger mob of fats. **1921** H. GUTHRIE-SMITH *Tutira* xxxvi. 362, I remember.. watching the well-known dealer, Andrew Grant, picking 'fats'. **1936** I. L. IDRIESS *Cattle King* ix. 77 Drovers with their plants were coming in increasing numbers to drove to distant markets the growing herds of 'fats'. **1954** B. MILES *Stars my Blanket* xxiii. 199 Their four-year-olds.. will be trucked to the factories as 'fats'. **1969** *Sunday Mail Mag.* (Brisbane) 5 Oct. 2/1 We were mustering fats along the channels of Cooper's Creek.

2. In various *transf.* senses: †**a.** The soft part of a fruit or tree.

1575 TURBERV. *Faulconrie* 278 Anoynting the ende of the borowed feather in the fatte of a figge. **1577** B. GOOGE *Heresbach's Husb.* II. (1586) 110 The fat, the softest and the woorst part of the tree.

†**b.** *the fat of glass*: = Fr. *suin de verre*, SANDIVER, GLASS-GALL. *Obs.*

1578 LYTE tr. *Dodoens' Herbal* 116 That which.. swimmeth upon the stuffe whereof Glasses are made, is now called in Shoppes *Axungia vitri*: in English, the fatte or floure of Glasse.

c. The richest or most nourishing part of anything; the choicest produce (of the earth). Hence also, Plenty, superabundance. *Obs.* exc. in phrase ***(to eat, live on) the fat of the land.***

1570–6 LAMBARDE *Peramb. Kent* (1826) 223 This Realme.. wanted neither the favour of the Sunne, nor the fat of the Soile. **1611** BIBLE *Gen.* xlv. 18 Ye shall eat the fat of the land. —— *Deut.* xxxii. 14 The fat of kidneis of wheat. **1623** MASSINGER *Bondman* I. ii, In this plenty, And fat of peace. **1640** J. DYKE *Worthy Commun.* 188 The fat and moysture of the earth. **1661** LOVELL *Hist. Anim. & Min.* Introd., Sulphurs, which are the fat of the earth. **1832** L. HUNT *Poems* Pref. 9 We have the poetry.. of the 'fat of the land' in Thomson. **1857** TROLLOPE *Three Clerks* xiv, For thirteen years he has lived on the fat of the land.

d. Phr. ***a bit of fat***: (an instance of) good fortune; (an opportunity for) profit. *colloq.*

1923 BREWER *Dict.* 419/2 *A bit of fat*, an unexpected stroke of luck; also, the best part of anything. **1936** J. CURTIS *Gilt Kid* ii. 19 'Where did you graft in Wandsworth?' 'Cleaner.' 'Blimey, that was a bit of fat for you, wasn't it?' 'Yeah, but you couldn't pinch no grub.' **1951** P. BRANCH *Wooden Overcoat* i. 6 He had been acquitted... Cor! What a bit o' fat! I got away with it!

3. a. The oily concrete substance of which the fat parts of animal bodies are chiefly composed; any particular variety of this substance. Often modified by a sb. prefixed, as *beef-*, *candle-*, *cow-*, *mutton-*, *ox-*, etc. *fat*. **b.** *Chem.* Any of a class of organic compounds of which animal fat is the type.

1539 in Rogers *Agric. & Prices* III. 285/4, 1593 Ludlow. Candle fat $12\frac{3}{4}$ lb. @/$2\frac{1}{4}$. **1552** HULOET, Fatte or grease, *sagina*. **1731** ARBUTHNOT *Aliments* ii. 44 This Membrane separates an oily Liquor call'd Fat. **1774** GOLDSM. *Nat. Hist.* (1776) IV. 4 The muscles of the body are very strong, and without fat. **1841–71** T. R. JONES *Anim. Kingd.* (ed. 4) 848 But, beneath the skin, fat has been accumulated in prodigious quantities. **1860–1** FLO. NIGHTINGALE *Nursing* 50 Butter is the lightest kind of animal fat. **1884** *Athenæum* 12 Apr. 465/1 Fats were dear in the early time. **1884** *Syd. Soc. Lex., Fat*, a greasy substance consisting of carbon, hydrogen, and a little oxygen.. Fats are contained in both plants and animals and are compounds of glycerin with acids, chiefly palmitic, oleic, or stearic. **1891** *Brit. Med. Jrnl.* Suppl. 78/1 Fats are digested with the expenditure of a small amount of energy.

c. Phrases: † ***to lick the fat from the beard of***: to forestall the results of (a person's) enterprise or industry. † ***the fat flits from (a man's) beard***: he lets go the advantage he has gained. ***(all) the fat is in the fire***: in early use expressing that a design has irremediably failed; now used when some injudicious act has been committed that is sure to provoke a violent explosion of anger. ***to chew the fat***: see CHEW *v.* 3 g.

1548 HALL *Chron.* 169 b, Other.. marchantes.. sore abhorryng the Italian nacion, for lickyng the fat from their beardes, and taking from them their accustomed livyng. **1562** J. HEYWOOD *Prov. & Epigr.* (1867) 6 Than farewell riches, the fat is in the fire. *Ibid.* 7 Blame me not to haste, for feare.. the fat cleane flit fro my berde. **1579** SPENSER *Sheph. Cal.* Sept. 123 But they that shooten neerest the pricke Sayne, other the fat from their beards doen lick. **1644** ORMONDE *Let.* in Carte *Life* (1735) III. 281, I hear nothing of the armes, ammunition or provisions, without all which all the fat is in the fire. **1797** WOLCOTT (P. Pindar) *Livery of London* Wks. 1812 III. 449 Should we once complain The fat will all be in the fire. **1850** CARLYLE *Latter-d. Pamph.* iv. 4 The fat in the fire will be a thing worth looking at.

4. The habit of body marked by the deposition of fat; corpulence, obesity.

1726 *Adv. Capt. R. Boyle* 45 The two first [women] were very handsom, a little inclining to Fat.

5. In the phraseology of various trades or occupations, applied to especially lucrative kinds of work. †**a.** (See quot. *a* 1700). **b.** *Printing* (see quot. 1841). **c.** *Newspaper* (see quot. 1890). **d.** *Theatrical*, a part with good lines and telling situations, which gives the player an opportunity of appearing to advantage.

a. *a* **1700** B. E. *Dict. Cant. Crew, Fat*, the last landed, inned or stow'd of any sort of Merchandize.. so called by the several Gangs of Water-side-Porters. **1785** in GROSE *Dict. Vulg. Tongue*.

b. **1796** GROSE *Dict. Vulg. Tongue* (ed. 3), *Fat* amongst printers means void spaces. **1841** SAVAGE *Dict. Printing, Fat*, with compositors, short pages, blank pages, and light open matter: with pressmen, light forms, forms that require one pull at wooden presses.

c. **1890** *Answers* 6 Dec. 24 If he [the liner] has a piece of 'fat' (that is, a good piece of exclusive news).

d. **1812** *Dramatic Censor 1811* 440 Mr Dowton.. did not exhibit any propensity to give us too much of the *fat*. **1883** *Referee* 18 Mar. 2/4 They have nothing to do, all the fat having been seized by Terry. **1885** W. C. DAY *Behind the Footlights* 116 Lest any of his 'fat' should be lost through the self grimaces of his fellow comedian. **1933** P. GODFREY *Back-Stage* iii. 36 An expression which is likely to puzzle the uninitiated is the term 'fat'. Theatrical 'fat' is determined not by the size of the part, but by its effectiveness.

6. *attrib.* and *Comb.* **a.** attrib., as ***fat-basis***, ***-cell***, ***-corpuscle***, ***-deposit***, ***-drop***, ***-gland***, ***-globule***, ***-granule***, ***-mass***, ***-vesicle***; ***fat-like*** adj.

1847–9 TODD *Cycl. Anat.* IV. 129/1 Growths of *fat-basis. **1845** G. E. DAY tr. *Simon's Anim. Chem.* I. 355 Some.. presented a resemblance to conglomerate *fat-cells. **1847–9** TODD *Cycl. Anat.* IV. 96/1 Deposition of peculiar altered *fat-corpuscles. *Ibid.*, The relationship of *fat-deposit to the morbid changes in Bright's disease. **1841–71** T. R. JONES *Anim. Kingd.* (ed. 4) 44 Dark globules, resembling *fat-drops. **1866** *Chambers's Encycl.* s.v. *Skin*, The sebaceous or *fat glands. **1846** G. E. DAY tr. *Simon's Anim. Chem.* II. 326 *Fat-globules were detected under the microscope. **1847–9** TODD *Cycl. Anat.* IV. 130/2 We have occasionally seen *fat granules in these tumours. **1709** BLAIR in *Phil. Trans.* XXVII. 95 A *fat-like Substance. **1872** G. M. HUMPHRY *Obs. Myol.* 5 In addition to the four *fat-masses disposed with the longitudinal series of vessels are four deep fat-masses lying beneath the four lateral muscles. **1845** TODD & BOWMAN *Phys. Anat.* I. iii. 82 The *fat vesicle of the human subject.

b. objective, as ***fat-engendering***, ***-formation***, ***-former***, ***-forming***, ***-reducing***, ***-splitting*** adjs.

1883 *Knowl.* 20 July 34/2 *Fat-engendering repose. **1909** *Daily Chron.* 8 July 6/4 *Fat-formation in the body.. is not to be regarded as a mere accretion or addition of the fat we consume to the tissues of the frame. **1886** C. SCOTT *Sheep-farming* 41 A ton of good linseed cake contains of *fat-formers 1508 lbs.; of flesh-formers, 582 lbs. **1893** F. F. MOORE *I forbid Banns* xxxiv, She knew the flesh-formers from the fat-formers, and partook of both. **1848** *Rep. Comm. Patents 1847* (U.S.) 116 With respect to the *fat-forming principle.. the proportions of the different parts of the grain stand thus. **1883** *Knowl.* 27 July 49/2 Dangerous *fat-reducing systems. **1890** BILLINGS *Med. Dict.*, **Fat-splitting ferment*, steapsin. **1907** *Practitioner* Aug. 320 The steapsin, or fat-splitting ferment of the pancreatic juice. **1955** J. G. DAVIS *Dict. Dairying* (ed. 2) 181 Tributyrin is extremely bitter, and certain fat-splitting bacteria may cause bitterness by producing this substance.

c. Special combs., as **fat-body**, in arthropods, esp. insects, and amphibians: a mass consisting of connective tissue and globules of fat, forming a reserve store of nutritious matter; **fat boy** (see quots.); **fat-cake** (see quots. 1865, 1898); **fat-free** *a.*, free from fat; **fat-gude**, *Shetland dial.* (see quot.); **fat-liquor**, a mixture of soap and oil used in leather manufacture for softening hides; also as *vb.*; so **fat-liquored** *ppl. a.*, **-liquoring** *vbl. sb.*; **fat-soluble** *a.*, soluble in fats or oils; **fat-trap**, a device for catching fat in drains, etc.

1869 A. S. PACKARD *Study of Insects* 37 In the larva of insects is found the *corpus adiposum*, or *fat-body, in the form of large lobes of fat-cells. **1927** HALDANE & HUXLEY *Anim. Biol.* iv. 113 In the frog fat is stored in special fat-bodies. **1964** V. B. WIGGLESWORTH *Life of Insects* ix. 136 It may be the 'fat body' or the blood that is coloured. **1940** *Chambers's Techn. Dict.* 324/1 **Fat boys* or *fatters*, boys or men employed to lubricate axles of tubs or wagons and rollers of haulage gear. **1955** *Evening News* 28 Sept. 3/8 *Fat Boy*, a boy who greases wagon-axles and does odd jobs in a quarry. **1839** 'T. TREDDLEHOYLE' *Sum Thowts abaght Nan Bunt's Chresmas Tea-Party* 19 A great pile of muffins an *fat-cake browt up at table. **1865** W. HOWITT *Hist. Discov. Austral.* II. 15 Fat-cakes, made of flour, and fried in their pan, a bush dainty. **1898** MORRIS *Austral Eng., Fat-cake*, a ridiculous name sometimes applied to *Eucalyptus leucoxylon*. **1953** P. ABRAHAMS *Return to Goli* vi. 200 After this we had fat-cakes and coffee. **1869** E. A. PARKES *Pract. Hygiene* (ed. 3) 160 The dog and the rat can live on *fat-free

meat alone. **1860** BALFOUR *Odal Rights & Feudal Wrongs* 114 **Fatgude*, a term used in Zetland for the Butter or Oil paid to the Donatary. **1903** L. A. FLEMMING *Pract. Tanning* 22 The leather is then ready to be stained or colored, *fat-liquored, put out on the grain and treated in the finishing operations. *Ibid.* 127 The leather treated with it [*sc.* palmetto] takes even cooling and carries the fat-liquor well. **1931** WILSON & MERRILL *Anal. Leather* xi. 395 In both fat liquoring and finishing, most of the fatty constituents of the soap are absorbed by the leather. **1945** MCLAUGHLIN & THEIS *Chem. Leather Manuf.* xxiv. 723 Soap emulsions are used in some special cases for fatliquoring leather. *Ibid.* 739 It [*sc.* egg yolk] clarifies the fatliquor and.. gives a drier, or a less oily and greasy feel, to the surface of the leather. *Ibid.* 742 A sample of fatliquored, chrome-tanned calf skin. **1922** *Encycl. Brit.* XXXII. 932/1 These [vitamins] are (1) the anti-scorbutic factor; (2) the water-soluble B.; (3) the *fat-soluble A. **1926** J. S. HUXLEY *Ess. Pop. Sci.* viii. 88 Fat-soluble vitamin A. **1956** *Nature* 21 Jan. 123/2 The chlorinated compounds which are fat-soluble and chemically stable tend to accumulate in the fatty tissue. **1884** *Health Exhib. Catal.* 55/1 Gullies and *Fat-Traps.

‖**fat** (fat, fa), *sb.*³ [Fr., a stupid, conceited person, f. Pr. *fat* stupid, ignorant, f. L. *fatuus*: see FATUOUS *a.*] A presumptuous, conceited dandy; a fop.

1832 F. TROLLOPE *Dom. Manners* I. xx. 333 'Monsieur,' said my young *fat*, with an indescribable grimace. **1853** C. BRONTË *Villette* I. xiv. 265, I took my revenge on this 'fat', by making him as fatuitous as I possibly could. **1876** GEO. ELIOT *Dan. Der.* III. v. xxxv. 316 How that *fat* Deronda can bear looking at her.

fat (fæt), *v.* Forms: 1 **fǽttian**, 3 *south.* **vetten**, 4 **fatten**, 4–6 **fatte**, (5 **faat**, 6 **fate**), 3, 6– **fat**. [OE. *fǽttian*, f. *fǽtt* FAT *a.*]

†**1.** *trans.* As lit. rendering of Heb. *dishshēn*, Vulg. *impinguare*: To anoint, 'make fat' (the head); to load (an altar) with fat. *Obs.*

c **1000** *Ags. Ps.* xxii[i]. 5 Ðu faettades in ele heafud min. *a* **1300** *E.E. Psalter* xxii[i]. 5 Þou fatted in oli mi heved ywhit. **1382** WYCLIF *Ecclus.* xxxv. 8 The offring of the riȝtwis fatteth the auter. **1698** NORRIS *Pract. Disc.* IV. 114 The Sacrifices with which they fatted their Altars.

†**b.** To bedaub with fat or grease; hence, *transf.* to cover thickly. *Obs. rare.*

a **1661** HOLYDAY *Juvenal* iii. 42 Durt fats my thighs.

2. *intr.* To grow or become fat. Also ***to fat up***.

a **1225** *Ancr. R.* 128 Nout ase swin ipund ine sti uorte uetten & forte greaten aȝein þe cul of þer eax. **1398** TREVISA *Barth. D.P.R.* v. xli. (1495) 158 Yf the mylte mynysshyth and fadyth, the body fattyth. **1577** B. GOOGE *Heresbach's Husb.* IV. (1586) 161 The harder they [fowl] lie, the sooner they fatte. **1607** TOPSELL *Four-f. Beasts* (1673) 466 If they fat of their own accord, it hath been found that the tail of one of these Sheep have weighed ten or twenty pound. **1794** WASHINGTON *Lett.* Writings 1892 XIII. 24 The hogs which have been fatting. **1807** VANCOUVER *Agric. Devon* (1813) 355 Proper time being allowed, [they] will commonly fat to six score per quarter. **1825** COBBETT *Rur. Rides* 467 They were fatting on the grass.

fig. *c* **1000** *Ags. Ps.* lxiv. 13 [lxv. 12] Faettiað endas woestennes. *a* **1300** *E.E. Psalter* ibid., Fat sal faire of wildernes. *c* **1300** *Song Husbandm.* 32 in *Pol. Songs* (Camden) 151 Falsshipe fatteth. **1596** J. NORDEN *Progr. Pietie* (1847) 139 The heaviness of sin, wherein they lie fatting in all delights. **1631** R. H. *Arraignm. Whole Creature* xv. §1. 251 Vanities, on which our Prodigall eates, but neyther feeds, fils, nor fats.

3. *trans.* To make fat, fatten; usually, to feed (animals) for use as food. Also ***to fat up***.

13.. *E.E. Allit. P.* B. 56, & my fêdde foulez [arn] fatted with sclaȝt. *c* **1420** *Pallad. on Husb.* I. 562 To faat hem is avayling and plesaunte. **1515** BARCLAY *Egloges* i. (1570) A vj/3 When they [our hogges] be fatted by costes and labour. **1561** T. NORTON *Calvin's Inst.* IV. 137 b, A heard of swine: which they [Anabaptistes] fondly faine to haue ben fatted vp by the Lord. **1612** DEKKER *If it be not good* Wks. 1873 III. 275 Churles.. fat their rancke gutts whilest poor wretches pine. *a* **1633** LENNARD tr. *Charron's Wisd.* III. xiii. §5 (1670) 436 The.. presence of the Master, saith the Proverb, fatteth the horse and the land. **1769** GRAY *Jrnl. in Lakes* Wks. 1884 I. 278 Numbers of black cattle are fatted here. **1774** GOLDSM. *Nat. Hist.* (1776) V. 172 The first who fatted up the peacock for the feasts of the luxurious. **1877** BARING-GOULD *Myst. Suffering* 48 His ideal of beauty.. was woman fatted on milk till she could not walk.

absol. *c* **1440** *Secrees, Prose version* (E.E.T.S.), þese fattys and moystes: Rest of body, gladnesse of wyl [etc.]. **1584** LYLY *Campaspe* I. ii, [Apelles] proueth that muche easier it is to fatte by colours, and telles of birdes that haue beene fatted by paynted grapes.

fig. *c* **1386** CHAUCER *Sompn. T.* 172 Who so wol preye, he moot.. fatte his soule and make his body lene. **1553** *Short Catech.* in *Liturgies, etc. Edw. VI* (Parker Soc.) 525 If they be watered, and fatted with the dew of Gods word. **1633** G. HERBERT *Temple, Odour* ii, This broth of smells, that feeds and fats my minde.

b. *refl. lit.* and *fig.*

1567 DRANT *Horace Epist.* iii. C vj, A long deuoued cowe Which graseth here.. And fattes her selfe for you. **1603** KNOLLES *Hist. Turks* (1621) 43 Fatting themselves with great and gainfull offices. **1679** PENN *Addr. Prot.* II. v. (1692) 179 She.. hath fatted herself with the Flesh of Saints.

c. Said of the food.

c **1400** *Lanfranc's Cirurg.* 61 Dieting þat fattiþ & makiþ him glad. **1528** PAYNEL *Salerne's Regim.* Q iij b, The substance or meate of cheries.. fattethe the bodye. **1633** J. FISHER *Fuimus Troes* Prol. in Hazl. *Dodsley* XII. 451 Making your huge trunks To fat our crows. **1708** J. CHAMBERLAYNE *St. Gt. Brit.* I. I. iii. (1743) 24 Knot-grass.. its long knots will fat swine. **1829** *Bone Manure, Rep. Doncast. Com.* 25 This improved and fatted the sheep.

absol. **1528** PAYNEL *Salerne's Regim.* G ij, Grene chese nourysheth and fattethe.

d. *trans.* In the manufacture of leather, to smear over with fat-liquor.

1903 L. A. FLEMMING *Pract. Tanning* 166 The leather is now treated as usual, and fatted or oiled.

4. ***to fat off***: to fatten for sale or slaughter.

1789 *Trans. Soc. Encourag. Arts* (ed. 2) II. 90 Bull steers.. fed with hay during the labouring part of their lives.. then fatted off. **1850** *Jrnl. R. Agric. Soc.* XI. II. 679 Decided to fat off the wethers as early as possible.

5. To enrich (the soil) with nutritious and stimulating elements; to fertilize.

1562 TURNER *Herbal* II. 52 b, Horned clauer.. fatteth the grownde. **1594** BLUNDEVIL *Exerc.* v. (ed. 7) 564 The floud Nilus, which by his inundations doth yeerely.. fatte the country of Egypt. *a* **1639** W. WHATELEY *Prototypes* I. iv. (1640) 30 If the sheepes dung did not fat the ground. **1648** GAGE *West Ind.* xviii. (1655) 135 Which with the ashes left after the burning fatteth the ground. **1808** J. BARLOW *Columb.* v. 660 Till Austria's titled hordes, with their own gore, Fat the fair fields they lorded long before.

fatal (ˈfeɪtəl), *a.* Also 4 **fathel**, 5–6 *Sc.* **fatell**, 6–7 **fatall**. [ad. L. *fātāl-is*, f. *fātum* FATE. Cf. Fr. *fatal.*]

†**1.** Allotted or decreed by fate or destiny; destined, fated. Const. *to*, *unto*. *Obs.*

c **1374** CHAUCER *Troylus* v. 1 The fathel destyne, That Joves hath in disposicioune. *c* **1430** LYDG. *Bochas* IV. xiv. (1554) 114 a, Was neuer seine prince nor princesse That more proudly toke their fatal death. **1513** DOUGLAS *Æneis* XI. Prol. 178 Prynce Enee, That, for his fatale cuntre, of behest Sa feill dangeris sustenit. *c* **1610** SIR J. MELVIL *Mem.* (1683) 67 It appeared to be fatal to him, to like better of flatterers.. than plain speakers. **1658** ROWLAND *Moufet's Theat. Ins.* 909 Obnoxious to.. very much rain, a thing fatall to Islands. **1663–78** BUTLER *Hud.* I. iii. 530 It was Still fatal to stout Hudibras.. when least He dreamt of it to prosper best. **1667** MILTON *P.L.* II. 104 With perpetual inrodes to allarme, Though inaccessible, his fatal Throne. **1713** BENTLEY *Collins' Freethinking* I. xxvi. 142 It is fatal to our author ever to blunder when he talks of Egypt.

†**2.** Condemned by fate; doomed. Const. *to.*

1509 HAWES *Past. Pleas.* VII. ii, More lyker.. Unto a place which is celestiall, Than to a certayne mancion fatall. *c* **1592** MARLOWE *Massacre at Paris* I. iv, Now have we got the fatal, straggling deer Within.. a deadly toil. **1602** WARNER *Alb. Eng.* x. liv. (1612) 242 The Guizian Scot Fatall to Seaes of blood. *a* **1634** RANDOLPH *Amyntas* IV. viii, A fatall oake, at which great Jove Levels his thunder. **1668** DAVENANT *Man's the Master* III. i, She, whose fatal and unexperienc'd heart too soon believ'd thy many oaths.

3. Of the nature of fate; resembling fate in mode of action; proceeding by a fixed order or sequence; inevitable, necessary.

1605 CAMDEN *Rem.* 33 As though.. fatall necessitie concurred.. with voluntary motion in giving the name. **1610** HEALEY *St. Aug. Citie of God* v. ix. (1620) 198 Euery cause is not fatall, because there are causes of chance, nature and will. **1663** J. SPENCER *Prodigies* (1665) 134 Nature is a blind and fatal Agent. **1751** JORTIN *Serm.* (1771) II. i. 14 We must not charge our transgressions upon a fatal necessity. **1863** HAWTHORNE *Our Old Home* 114 What a hardy plant was Shakspeare's genius, how fatal its development. **1874** MIVART in *Contemp. Rev.* Oct. 776 'Instinct' is 'fatal' but *blind*.

4. Concerned or dealing with destiny. Of agents: Controlling the destinies of men. (***the***) ***fatal dames, ladies, sisters***: the Fates, or Parcæ. ***the fatal thread***: that supposed to be spun by the Fates, determining the length of a man's life; so ***fatal web, fatal shears***.

1447 BOKENHAM *Seyntys* (Roxb.) 8 Not to hastyly My fatal threed a sundyr smyte. **1552** HULOET, Fatal ladies, *parcæ*. *a* **1592** R. D. *Hypnerotomachia* 9 b, Abiding the proofe of their paine and the cutting in Sunder of their fatall thread. **1622** FLETCHER *Spanish Curate* IV. v, Fatall Dames, that spin mens threds out. **1624** HEYWOOD *Gunaik.* I. 45 The Parcæ (or fatall Goddesses) are three. **1704** S. DALE in *Lett. Lit. Men* (Camden) 210 Death cut the fatal thread of life. **1708** POPE *Ode St. Cecilia* 94 How wilt thou now the fatal sisters move? *a* **1721** M. PRIOR *Turtle & Sparrow* 56 Nor Birds nor Goddesses can move The just Behests of Fatal Jove. **1880** BREWER *Reader's Hand-bk.* 323/2 The three Fatal Sisters were Clotho, Lachesis, and Atropos.

†**b.** Prophetic. *Obs.*

1503 HAWES *Examp. Virt.* vii. 129 Poetes that were fatall. **1509** —— *Past. Pleas.* VIII. iii, They [the poets].. Pronounced trouthe under cloudy figures, By the inventyon of theyr fatall scriptures. **1614** RALEIGH *Hist. World* II. 393 They.. taking direction.. from the fatall Bookes, burned alive two men. **1635** COWLEY *Davideis* I. 917. As he [Balam] went his fatal Tongue to sell.

†**c.** Foreboding or indicating mischief; ominous.

1590 MARLOWE *2nd Pt. Tamburl.* IV. iii, The black and fatal ravens. **1591** SHAKS. *1 Hen. VI*, III. i. 195 Now I feare that fatall Prophecie. **1628** WITHER *Brit. Rememb.* 35 Such fatall fowles As croking Ravens. **1658** WILLSFORD *Natures Secrets* 173 For seven nights after his death, there was heard hideous howling.., fatal Birds screaking in their Cities. *Ibid.* 188 These fatal Meteors are great motives to humble Man, to make him repent.

5. Fraught with destiny; fateful. Often with mixture of 6 or 7.

c **1386** CHAUCER *Man of Law's T.* 163 The woful day fatal is come. *c* **1430** LYDG. *Bochas* I. viii. (1544) 13 Her father had fatal heere.. the which did him assure Manly to fyght ayeinst his mortal foone. *c* **1470** HENRY *Wallace* IV. 294 With out respyt cummyn was thair fatell houris. **1548** HALL *Chron.* 115 The fatall daie of her obstinacie was come. **1612** MONNIEPENNIE *Abr. Chron.* in *Misc. Scot.* I. 7 Who transported the marble fatall chayre to Westminster. **1667** MILTON *P.L.* II. 725 The Snakie Sorceress.. kept the fatal Key. **1713** ADDISON *Cato* I. iii, What anxious moments pass between The birth of plots, and their last fatal periods. **1828** SCOTT *F.M. Perth* xix, The fatal spot where the unlucky Bonnet-maker's body was lying. **1863** KINGLAKE *Crimea* (1876) I. xi. 179 In these same fatal days the Emperor Nicholas did much to bring his good faith into question.

6. Producing or resulting in death, destruction, or irreversible ruin, material or immaterial; deadly, destructive, ruinous. Const. *to.* Also in phrase ***to prove fatal (to)***.

1514 BARCLAY *Cyt. & Uplondyshm.* (Percy Soc.) 10 That fatal fruyte which kyndled all theyr care. **1685–8** *Roxb. Ball.* VII. 454 O that my sorrows were ended, by the most fatalest hand. **1692** DRYDEN *St. Evremont's Ess.* 24 Suspicions fatal to the merit of Strangers. **1732** ARBUTHNOT *Rules of Diet* iv. 369 A Palsy.. when it seizeth the Heart, or Organs of Breathing, [is] fatal. **1759** ROBERTSON *Hist. Scot.* I. II. 87 His death was fatal to the Catholic religion. **1781** COWPER *Charity* 144 A stroke as fatal as the scythe of Death. **1791** MRS. RADCLIFFE *Rom. Forest* i, A removal in her present state must be fatal. **1803** *Med. Jrnl.* X. 315 Influenza.. is by no means a fatal disease. **1838** THIRLWALL *Greece* V. 80 The Spartan power had suffered a fatal blow. **1862** H. SPENCER *First Princ.* I. ii. §14 To carry away this conclusion.. would be a fatal error. *Mod.* A fatal accident occurred on Monday.

b. Of a weapon, bait, etc.: Sure to kill, deadly.

1599 SHAKS. *Hen. V*, V. ii. 17 Your eyes which hitherto haue borne In them.. The fatall Balls of murthering Basiliskes. **1774** GOLDSM. *Nat. Hist.* (1776) VII. 293 A crooked sting.. that fatal instrument which renders this insect so formidable. **1879** JEFFERIES *Wild Life in S.C.* 358 A gudgeon is a fatal bait. Nothing is so certain to take.

7. The hyperbolical use of the word in sense 6 gives rise to a weakened sense: Causing serious harm, disastrous, gravely mischievous.

Cf. F. *fatal*, which is often used in a trivial manner unknown in English.

1681 DRYDEN *Abs. & Achit.* 146 By their Monarch's fatal mercy grown, From Pardon'd Rebels, Kinsmen. **1758** S. HAYWARD *Serm.* xvii. 513 Incredible, did not fatal experience too much shew it. **1794** S. WILLIAMS *Vermont* 181 Wars had also a fatal influence on population. **1845** CARLYLE *Cromwell* (1871) I. Introd. 42 To develop itself in other still fataler ways. **1855** MACAULAY *Hist. Eng.* IV. 371 Never would such disasters have befallen the monarchy but for the fatal law which [etc.]. **1862** MRS. BROWNING *Last Poems, Ld. Walter's Wife* x, Now, you no longer are fatal, but ugly and hateful.

8. *Comb.* with pr. and pa. pples., as ***fatal-looking***; also (quasi-*adv.*) in ***fatal-boding***, ***-plotted***.

1588 SHAKS. *Tit. A.* II. iii. 47 Giue the King this fatall plotted Scrowle. **1594** LODGE *Wounds Civ. War* III. i. in Hazl. *Dodsley* VII. 149 The screech-owl chants her fatal-boding lays. **1839** CARLYLE *Chartism* i, Brandishing pike and torch (one knows not in which case more fatal-looking).

†**9.** *sb.* in *pl.* Fatal persons or things. ***the three Fatals***: the three Fates or Parcæ. *Obs.*

1560 ROLLAND *Crt. Venus* II. 556 The thre fatales. *Ibid.* II. 985 Thir Fatallis thre.. bad me pas, stand to my destinie. **1652** GAULE *Magastrom.* 162 Providence is in the ordering of casuals as well as fatals.

fatalism (ˈfeɪtəlɪz(ə)m). [f. prec. + -ISM. Cf. Fr. *fatalisme*, It. *fatalismo.*]

1. The belief in fatality; the doctrine that all things are determined by fate; a particular form of this doctrine.

In early use not distinguished from 'the doctrine of necessity', i.e. the doctrine that all events take place in accordance with unvarying laws of causation. In strict etymological propriety, and in the best modern usage, it is restricted to the view which regards events as predetermined by an arbitrary decree.

1678 CUDWORTH *Intell. Syst.* 6 We shall oppose those three Fatalisms.. as so many false Hypotheses of the Mundane System. **1733** BERKELEY *Th. Vision* §6 Pantheism, Materialism, Fatalism are nothing but Atheism a little disguised. **1774** FLETCHER *Hist. Ess.* Wks. 1795 IV. 20 Fatalism, in which the greatest Infidels unanimously shelter themselves. **1829** LYTTON *Devereux* II. v, You are.. a believer in the fatalism of Spinosa. **1876** L. STEPHEN *Eng. Thought 18th Cent.* (1881) I. 298 Fatalism assumes what necessity excludes, the existence of an arbitrary element in the universe.

2. Acquiescence in the decree of fate; submission to everything that happens as inevitable.

a **1734** NORTH *Lives* III. 61 *marg.*, A Turk convinced against fatalism. **1835** THIRLWALL *Greece* I. vi. 194 The fatalism of the Greeks was very remote.. from the dogma. **1871** MORLEY *Carlyle* Crit. Misc. (1878) 188 This acquiescence which is really not so far removed from fatalism.

fatalist (ˈfeɪtəlɪst). [f. as prec. + -IST. Cf. Fr. *fataliste.*]

1. One who holds the doctrine of fatalism; one who believes that all things happen by inevitable necessity.

1650 R. GELL *Serm.* 8 Aug. 38 The most notorious Fatalists. **1722** WOLLASTON *Relig. Nat.* v. 105 They [the ancients] were generally fatalists. **1887** T. FOWLER *Princ. Morals* II. ix, The Fatalist, as distinguished from the Determinist, imagines himself to be completely at the mercy of some external power.

2. One whose conduct is regulated by fatalism; one who accepts every event as an inevitable necessity.

a **1734** NORTH *Lives* III. 61 It is commonly known that the Turks are fatalists. **1763** SCRAFTON *Indostan* (1770) 115 Those who know what strong fatalists these eastern people are. **1848** MACAULAY *Hist. Eng.* II. 185 The confidence which the heroic fatalist placed in his high destiny. **1883** OUIDA *Wanda* I. 202 'What a fatalist you are.'

3. *attrib.* or *adj.* = next.

1843 J. MARTINEAU *Chr. Life* (1867) 407 Every Fatalist.. scheme destroys merit. **1850** KINGSLEY *Alt. Locke* i, He preached 'higher doctrine', i.e., more fatalist and antinomian than his gentler colleague. **1865** *Cornh. Mag.* Apr. 403 The fatalist resignation..now quieted him. **1874** LADY HERBERT *Hübner's Ramble* II. ii. (1878) 513 The moral basis of society lies in a fatalist submission.

fatalistic (feɪtəˈlɪstɪk), *a.* [f. prec. + -IC.] Of, pertaining to, or of the nature of fatalism.

1832 COLERIDGE *Table-t.* (1835) II. 29 Are you a Christian, and talk about a crisis in that fatalistic sense? **1838** *Blackw. Mag.* XLIV. 240 The fatalistic forces of nature. **1859** GEO. ELIOT *A. Bede* 197 A fatalistic view of jug-breaking. **1861** THORNBURY *Turner* (1862) I. 12 The doctrine of innate tendencies they deride as..fatalistic.

Hence **fataˈlistically** *adv.*, in a fatalistic manner; according to the fatalistic doctrine; like a fatalist.

1856 DOVE *Logic Chr. Faith* v. i. §2. 267 Power..working fatalistically for given ends. **1884** J. PARKER *Apost. Life* III. 53 The point at which life itself is despised as compared with what he..fatalistically calls his 'course'.

fatality (feɪˈtælɪtɪ). [ad. F. *fatalité*, ad. late L. *fātālitātem*, f. *fātālis* FATAL: see -ITY.]

1. a. The quality or condition of being predetermined by or subject to fate or destiny; subjection to fate, as attributed to the universe generally; the agency of fate or necessity, conceived as determining the course of events.

a **1631** DONNE in *Select.* (1840) 83 We banish from thence, all imaginary fatality. **1665** GLANVILL *Sceps. Sci.* 29 To suppose every action of the Will to depend upon a previous Appetite or Passion is to destroy our Liberty, and to insert a Stoical Fatality. **1678** CUDWORTH *Intell. Syst.* 7 The Will of Man..may contract upon it self such Necessities and Fatalities, as it cannot upon a suddain rid it self of at pleasure. **1692** BENTLEY *Boyle Lect.* i. 12 The blind impulses of Fatality and Fortune. **1702** *Eng. Theophrast.* 276 Marriages are governed..by an over-ruling fatality. **1736** BUTLER *Anal.* I. vi. 147 A Fatality supposed consistent with what we certainly experience does not destroy the proof of an intelligent author and Governor of nature. **1768–74** TUCKER *Lt. Nat.* (1852) I. 583 An irresistible force, a something we cannot explain nor account for its existence.. we call a fatality.

b. *fig.*

1699 BENTLEY *Phal.* 299 There was..a kind of Fatality in his Errors. **1822** HAZLITT *Table-t.* Ser. II. iv. (1869) 83 There is a fatality about our affairs. **1834** MEDWIN *Angler in Wales* II. 61 The Viceroy..as fatality would have it, was struck.

c. A decree of fate.

1763 TUCKER *Freewill* §42. 192 If he sows oats in his field, does he think anything of a fatality against his reaping wheat or barley?

d. That which a person or thing is fated to; a destined condition or position, a destiny.

1589 PUTTENHAM *Eng. Poesie* II. (Arb.) 124, I took them both for a good boding, and very fatallitie to her Maiestie. **1603** FLORIO *Montaigne* II. xxix. (1632) 398 Our fatalitie which it lieth not in us to avoyde or advance. **1648** STERRY *Clouds* 35 He cannot discerne..the Fatality of Persons and Kingdomes. **1692** R. L'ESTRANGE *Fables, Old Man & Lion* 95 All the Father's Precaution could not Secure the Son from the Fatality of Dying by a Lyon. **1860** W. COLLINS *Wom. White* x. 52 A fatality that it was hopeless to avoid.

¶ **e.** Used for: Belief in fatality; fatalism.

1674 HICKMAN *Quinquart. Hist.* (ed. 2) 14, I do not find him..charged with Fatality.

2. The condition of being doomed by fate; predestined liability to disaster.

1654 SIR E. NICHOLAS in *N. Papers* (Camden) II. 116 Ther is a strange fatality..attends all our intentiones and designes. **1769** *Junius Lett.* viii. 33 There [is] a fatality attending every measure you are concerned in. **1871** H. AINSWORTH *Tower Hill* III. v, A sad fatality had attended her family. **1873** SYMONDS *Grk. Poets* vii. 190 The fatality attending an accursed house.

3. The quality of causing death or disaster; fatalness; a fatal influence.

1490 CAXTON *How to Die* 21 Sathanas wyth all his cruelle fatallytees. **1646** SIR T. BROWNE *Pseud. Ep.* IV. xii. 208 7. times 9. or the yeare of sixty three..is conceived to carry with it, the most considerable fatality. **1706–7** FARQUHAR *Beaux' Strat.* II. i, Love and Death have their Fatalities. **1793** E. DARWIN in Beddoes *Lett. Darwin* 62 Young men and women..if they knew the general fatality of their disease..would despond. **1839** BAILEY *Festus* xviii. (1848) 185 Thy beauty hath fatality. **1856** KANE *Arct. Expl.* I. xx. 245 The insidious fatality of hot countries.

4. a. A disastrous event; a calamity, misfortune.

1648 EVELYN *Mem.* (1857) III. 19 This was the tragedy of Tuesday..Since this fatality, some talk of an inclination in Surrey to associate. **1678** MARVELL *Growth Popery* Wks. I. 463 Their interviews are usually solemnized with some fatality and disaster. **1815** W. H. IRELAND *Scribbleomania* 254 *note*, Fatalities to which the human race is liable. **1868** E. EDWARDS *Raleigh* I. v. 83 A long series of fatalities ended in the wreck of two ships.

b. A disaster resulting in death; a fatal accident or occurrence. *attrib.*, as ***fatality figure, rate.***

1840 BARHAM *Ingol. Leg., Look at Clock*, The shocking fatality Ran over, like wild-fire, the whole Principality. **1861** *Times* 7 Oct., The only fatalities were the five above mentioned, while a large number were more or less injured. **1897** *Daily News* 8 Jan. 6/2 What is called the fatality rate, that is to say, the proportion of deaths to cases, varies considerably in the case of diphtheria. **1912** *Maclean's Mag.* Feb. 433 The 'fatality' figures in Toronto..are as follows. **1966** *Lancet* 24 Dec. 1372/2 The daily fatality-rate..shows a peak on the second day in all the groups. **1971** *Brit. Med. Bull.* XXVII. 27/1 The most likely explanation seemed to be a change in the fatality-rate.

fatalize (ˈfeɪtəlaɪz), *v.* [f. FATAL + -IZE.] **a.** *intr.* To incline to fatalism. **b.** *trans.* To render subject to fate or inevitable necessity. Hence **ˈfatalized, ˈfatalizing** *ppl. adjs.*

1834 G. S. FABER *Prim. Doctr. Election* (1836) p. lii, Melancthon..expressly rejected the fatalising Scheme. *Ibid.* 155 The fatalising dogmatism. **1876** J. MARTINEAU *Hours Th.* (1877) 85 The Universe would be without a God a fatalised organism. **1888** —— *Study of Religion* I. II. i. 243 Its ways seem fatalised.

fatally (ˈfeɪtəlɪ), *adv.* Also 7 **fatallie.** [f. as prec. + -LY².] In a fatal manner.

1. As decreed by fate; in a predestined manner.

1574 *Petit. to Q. Eliz.* 22 Mar. in *Cal. State Papers, Colonial* 1574–1660. 1 Sundry rich and unknown lands fatally reserved for England. **1601** ?MARSTON *Pasquil & Kath.* II. 33 Fatally predestinate To consecrate it selfe vnto your loue. **1661** *Origen* in *Phenix* I. 54 The inferior Spirit of the World acts not by choice but fatally. **1725** POPE *Odyss.* XIV. 82 He trod so fatally the paths of Fame. **1880** VERN. LEE *Belcaro* vii. 195 Inevitably, fatally..the work..must be the ideal of all purely devotional art.

2. In a deadly or disastrous manner: **a.** Destructively, with destructive results.

1599 SHAKS. *Hen. V*, II. iv. 54 When Cressy Battell fatally was strucke. **1635** COWLEY *Davideis* III. 584 Backward the Winds his active Curses blew, And fatally round his own Head they flew. **1812** H. R. in *Examiner* 4 May 283/2 A few yards of rope, which, by an unlucky snap, might..convince them too fatally of their mortality. **1859** C. BARKER *Associative Principles* iii. 66 These wars operated fatally upon the noble order of knighthood.

b. Ruinously, by or with disastrous results.

1663 COWLEY *Verses & Ess.* (1669) 21 Which like an Anti-Comet here Did fatally to that appear. **1757** JOHNSON *Rambler* No. 177 ¶8 How fatally human sagacity was sometimes baffled. **1793** BURKE *Conduct of Minority* Wks. 1842 I. 621 It is fatally known, that [etc.]. **1800** FOSTER in *Life & Corr.* (1846) I. 125, I must be fatally wrong. **1828** D'ISRAELI *Chas. I*, III. ii. 65 The possible dangers which afterwards were so fatally realized. **1866** HOWELLS *Venet. Life* (1883) II. xvii. 98 The Venetian fine lady..fatally hides her ankles in pantalets.

c. With death as the result, *esp.* of disease, ***to end, terminate fatally.***

1809 *Med. Jrnl.* XXI. 278 The attack..terminated fatally. **1837** HT. MARTINEAU *Soc. Amer.* III. 56 Those who fight the most frequently and fatally are the French creoles. **1882** *Med. Temp. Jrnl.* L. 56 Many of the cases..ended fatally.

fatalness (ˈfeɪtəlnɪs). [f. as prec. + -NESS.] The quality of being fatal.

1. 'Invincible necessity' (J.).

1755 in JOHNSON; and in mod. Dicts.

2. a. Disastrous nature. **b.** Destructive or deadly quality.

1651 *Reliq. Wotton.* B8/2 Master Cuffe being then a man of no Common note..for the fatalness of his end. **1652** SPARKE *Prim. Devot.* (1663) 76 Whether for their readiness cheapness, fatalness, I argue not..but with stones destroyed they this servant of..Jesus Christ.

‖**fata Morgana** (ˈfɑːtə mɔːˈgɑːnə). [It. *fata* a fairy; *Morgana*, sister of the British legendary hero Arthur, app. located in Calabria by the Norman settlers.] A kind of mirage most frequently seen in the Strait of Messina, attributed in early times to fairy agency. Also *fig.*

1818 R. JAMIESON in *Burt's Lett. N. Scotl.* II. xxiii. 111 In mountainous regions, deceptions of sight, fata morgana, &c. are more common. **1851** CARLYLE *Sterling* I. viii. 78 He [Coleridge] preferred to create logical fatamorganas for himself on this hither side. **1892** *Daily News* 17 May 5/4 A fata Morgana seen last autumn near..Karlova.

attrib. **1829** CARLYLE *Misc.* (1857) II. 61 Cloud mountains, and fatamorgana cities.

†**ˈfatary.** *Obs. rare*⁻¹. [f. FATE *sb.* + -ARY¹.] One who foretells fates.

1652 GAULE *Magastrom.* 147 Why doe our fataries and fortunaries so confound them..in their prognostications?

†**faˈtation.** *Obs. rare.* [f. FATE *sb.* + -ATION.] The exercise of inevitable and irresistible influence.

1652 GAULE *Magastrom.* xviii. §6. 148 If there be necessitating and enforcing fatation upon things. *Ibid.* xviii. §19. 154 What fatation, or fatall necessitation to man, among all these?

†**fatch,** *sb. Obs.* [var. of VETCH.]

1545 RAYNOLD *Byrth Mankynde* (1564) C viij, Let her chawe in her mouth very small a fewe fatches. **1547** RECORDE *Judic. Ur.* 47 In bygnesse of a small fatche, and red coloured, which you mai cal therfore red fatches, bycause of their lykenesse. **1575** TURBERV. *Faulconrie* 365 Berries as bygge as pease or fatche.

fatch, obs. form of FETCH *sb.* and *v.*

fate (feɪt), *sb.* [ad. L. *fātum*, lit. 'that which has been spoken', neut. pa. pple. of *fārī* to speak. The primary sense of the L. word is a sentence or doom of the gods (= Gr. θέσφατον); but it was subsequently used as the equivalent of the Gr. μοῖρα, which, originally meaning only a person's 'lot' or 'portion', had come to express the more abstract conception explained below (sense 1), and its personification as a mythological being.

Cf. OF. *fat(e*, Pr. *fat*, It. *fato*, Pg. *fado*, Sp. *hado*. (The pl. *fāta* gave rise in popular L. to the fem. sing. *fāta* fairy: for the Rom. forms of this see FAY *sb.*) The immediate source of the Eng. word is doubtful. Chaucer uses it in *Troylus* (where he translates from Boccaccio's Italian), but in rendering the Latin of Boethius he uses only *destiné*.]

1. a. The principle, power, or agency by which, according to certain philosophical and popular systems of belief, all events, or some events in particular, are unalterably predetermined from eternity. Often *personified.*

The OE. synonym was *wyrd*: see WEIRD.

c **1374** CHAUCER *Troylus* v. 1550 The fate wold his soule shold vnbodye. **1610** SHAKS. *Temp.* I. i. 32 Stand fast good Fate to his hanging. **1655–60** STANLEY *Hist. Philos.* (1701) 191/1 Concerning Fate, Plato held thus: All things are in Fate, yet all things are not decreed by Fate. **1667** MILTON *P.L.* II. 232 When everlasting Fate shall yield To fickle Chance. **1678** CUDWORTH *Intell. Syst.* 161 Fate, and the Laws or Commands of the Deity, concerning the Mundane Oeconomy..being really the same thing. **1701** ROWE *Amb. Step-Moth.* I. i, Fate, Or somewhat like the force of Fate was in it. **1770** J. LOVE *Cricket* 24 Jove, and all-compelling Fate. **1777** PRIESTLEY *Philos. Necess.* Pref. 25 Fate was some-thing that even the gods often endeavoured..to resist. **1807** CRABBE *Par. Reg.* I. 106 We..Fate's fixed will from Nature's wanderings learn. *a* **1848** R. W. HAMILTON *Rew. & Punishm.* viii. (1853) 345 The idea of fate sets us free from the sense of blame. **1875** FARRAR *Silence & V.* i. 11 What is He but a vast formless Fate?

b. *fig.*

1588 SHAKS. *L.L.L.* v. ii. 68 So pertaunt like would I o'resway his state That he shold be my foole, and I his fate. **1701** ROWE *Amb. Step-Moth.* IV. i, I am Fate in Persia And Life and Death depend upon my Pleasure.

2. *Mythol.* **a.** The goddess of fate or destiny; in Homer Μοῖρα. **b.** *pl.* In later Greek and Roman mythology, the three goddesses supposed to determine the course of human life (Gr. Μοῖραι, L. *Parcæ, Fata*).

In Gr. the three Fates are called Clotho, Lachesis, and Atropos; these names were adopted by Latin poets, but the mythologists give as native names Nona, Decuma, and Morta.

1590 SHAKS. *Mids. N.* v. i. 199 *Pir.*.. Like Limander am I trusty still. *This.* And [I] like Helen till the Fates me kill. **1709** POPE *Jan. & May* 193 Bless the kind fates, and think your fortune rare. **1794** SULLIVAN *View Nat.* V. 338 Thread, which is spun by the fates in one part uniform and strong, in another weakened. **1828** SCOTT *F.M. Perth* xxx, Your slightest desires seem a law to the Fates. **1847** TENNYSON *Princ.* ii. 443 We three Sat muffled like the Fates.

3. That which is destined or fated to happen. **a.** *gen.* Also in *pl.* Predestined events. ***as sure as fate***: see SURE *adv.* 4 a.

1667 MILTON *P.L.* VII. 173 What I will is Fate. So spake th' Almightie. **1697** DRYDEN *Virg. Georg.* III. 738 Th' inspected Entrails cou'd no Fates foretel. **1732** POPE *Ess. Man* I. 73 Heav'n from all creatures hides the book of fate. **1849** JAMES *Woodman* vii, Tis the best way of meeting fate. **1865** CARLYLE *Fredk. Gt.* XVI. i, There lay in the fates a Third Silesian War for him.

b. Of an individual, an empire, etc.: The predestined or appointed lot; what a person, etc. is fated to do or suffer.

c **1374** CHAUCER *Troylus* v. 209 He curseth..His byrthe, hym self, his fate, and ek nature. **1559** *Mirr. Mag., Dk. of Clarence* lv, To flye theyr fate. **1603** B. JONSON *Sejanus* I. ii, How blest a fate were it to us. **1647** CLARENDON *Hist. Reb.* II. (1843) 57/2 By a very extraordinary fate [he had] got a very particular interest..in many worthy men. **1668** LADY CHAWORTH in *12th Rep. Hist. MSS. Comm.* App. v. 10 Mr. Ho..deserves a better fate. *a* **1717** BLACKALL *Wks.* (1723) I. 25 It has been commonly their Fate to fare hardlier. **1848** MACAULAY *Hist. Eng.* I. 164 The general fate of sects is to obtain a high reputation for sanctity while they are oppressed. **1848** W. H. BARTLETT *Egypt to Pal.* iv. (1879) 68 A noteworthy comment on the fate of human pride.

c. In etymological sense: An oracle or portent of doom.

1850 MRS. BROWNING *Poems* II. 50 The solemn knell fell in with the tale of life and sin, Like a rhythmic fate sublime.

4. a. What will become of, or has become of (a person or thing); ultimate condition; destiny. Often in ***to decide, fix, seal one's fate. a fate worse than death***: see DEATH *sb.* 17 b.

1768–74 TUCKER *Lt. Nat.* (1852) I. 584 The lover waits for the decision of his mistress to fix his fate. **1793** SMEATON *Edystone L.* §322 Anxiety for the fate of the Edystone. **1797** MRS. RADCLIFFE *Italian* xii, If she is now discovered her fate is certain. **1838** LYTTON *Leila* I. ii, The base misers.. deserve their fate. **1841** ELPHINSTONE *Hist. Ind.* II. 581 It only remained to the brothers to decide on the fate of its tenant. **1856** FROUDE *Hist. Eng.* (1858) I. ii. 163 He was obliged to bear the..fate of a minister, who..had thwarted the popular will. **1888** BRYCE *Amer. Commw.* III. xc. 246 More of it may share the same fate. **1891** E. PEACOCK *N. Brendon* II. 142 Plumer's fate was sealed.

b. Death, destruction, ruin.

c **1430** LYDG. *Bochas* III. xxvi. (1554) 97 b, Cirus was passed into fate. **1635** SHIRLEY *Coronat.* IV, Will you assist, and run a fate with us. **1643** DENHAM *Cooper's H.* 114 In the Common Fate, The adjoyning Abby fell. **1701** ROWE *Amb. Step-Moth.* I. i, Thousand vulgar fates Which their Drugs daily hasten. **1852** MISS YONGE *Cameos* I. xl. 345 Their fate has been well sung by Lord Houghton.

c. An instrument of death or destruction. *poet.*

1700 DRYDEN *Iliad* I. 74 He..Feather'd Fates among the Mules and Sumpters sent. **1715–20** POPE *Iliad* I. 68 Hissing fly the feather'd fates.

5. *attrib.* and *Comb.* **a.** simple attrib., as *fate-spell*; also *fate-like* adj.; **b.** objective, as *fate-*

denouncing*, *-foretelling*, *-scorning ppl. adjs.; **c.** instrumental, as ***fate-environed*, *-fenced*** (implied in *fate-fencedness*), ***-folden*, *-furrowed*, *-menanced*, *-stricken*** adjs.

1708 OZELL tr. *Boileau's Lutrin* 48 The Bird of Night With *Fate-denouncing Outcries takes his Flight. **1835** TALFOURD *Ion* II. i, Why should I waste these *fate-environ'd hours. **1827** HARE *Guesses* (1859) 80 His own *fate-fencedness, or, as he would call it, his luck. **1880** W. WATSON *Prince's Quest* (1892) 93 An enchanted sea From all the world *fate-folden. **1777** POTTER *Æschylus* 173 The *fate-foretelling seer, Amphiaraus. **1804** J. GRAHAME *Sabbath* 329 Relentless Justice! with *fate-furrow'd brow! **1860** O. W. HOLMES *Elsie V.* xv, The expression of the creatures [rattlesnakes] was..*fate-like. **1834** WRANGHAM *Homerics* 7 Knew'st thou what misfortunes lie, *Fate-menaced, on thine homeward way. **1850** MRS. BROWNING *Poems* II. 282 Proud Œdipus, *fate-scorning. *a* **1618** SYLVESTER *Sonnets* iv, Vnder that *Fate-spell onely are fore-showne Eternall praises. **1866** SWINBURNE *Poems & Ballads* (1868) 172 Our greatest from his throne *Fate-stricken, and rejected of his own.

d. fate-line *Palmistry*, a line in the palm of the hand supposed to indicate a person's fate in worldly affairs.

1889 K. ST. HILL *Gram. Palmistry* II. 43 When the Fate Line is tortuous..it is a sign of misfortune, or bad character. **1945** E. BOWEN *Demon Lover* 103 Dirt engraved the fate-lines in Mary's palms.

fate (feɪt), *v.* [f. prec. sb.]

†**1.** *trans.* To ruin irrevocably. *Obs.*

c **1400** *Destr. Troy* 5091 A fame [may] be defoulede, & fatid for euer.

2. To preordain as by the decree of fate. Const. *to* and *to* with *inf.* *Obs.* exc. in *pass.* in sense: To be appointed or destined by fate. Often quasi-*impers.* with subject clause.

1601 SHAKS. *All's Well* IV. iv. 20 Heauen..hath fated her to be my..helper to a husband. **1610** —— *Temp.* I. ii. 129 A treacherous Armie leuied, one mid-night Fated to th' purpose. **1725** POPE *Odyss.* IV. 248 Fated to wander. **1828** D'ISRAELI *Chas. I*, I. i. 4 It was fated that England should be the theatre of the first of a series of Revolutions. **1860** EMERSON *Cond. Life*, *Fate* Wks. (Bohn) II. 310 Whatever is fated, that will take place. **1867** LADY HERBERT *Cradle L.* v. 152 The breathing-time..was fated to be of short duration.

†**b.** *ellipt.* To destine to death. *Obs.*

1788 COWPER *Stanzas for* 1788. 18 Could I prophetic say Who next is fated.

fate, obs. form of FAT *v.*, FEAT.

fated ('feɪtɪd), *ppl. a.* [f. FATE *sb.* and *v.* + -ED.]

1. Appointed, decreed or determined by fate.

1715–20 POPE *Iliad* I. 282 Thy injured honor has its fated hour. **1821** JOANNA BAILLIE *Met. Leg.*, *Wallace* xvii, Each upon his fated day. **1864** PUSEY *Lect. Daniel* v. 239 God's judgments were not..a mere fated thing.

2. Doomed to destruction.

1817 CHALMERS *Astron. Disc.* i. (1852) 38 A blazing comet may cross this fated planet. **1855** MACAULAY *Hist. Eng.* IV. 14 Cavalry..were fast approaching the fated city.

3. 'Invested with the power of fatal determination' (J.).

1601 SHAKS. *All's Well* I. i. 232 The fated skye Giues vs free scope.

4. Controlled, guided, or driven on by fate.

1801 SOUTHEY *Thalaba* II. xxii, The fated Fire moved on. **1817** BYRON *Manfred* II. ii, Fated in thy sufferings. **1827** POLLOK *Course T.* VII. 448 The fated crew..warred Against the chosen saints. **1870** MORRIS *Earthly Par.* I. I. 303 He purified His fated hands of that unlooked-for guilt.

¶**5.** Of armour: Made proof by spells, charmed. *rare*$^{-2}$.

[Suggested by Ariosto's *armi fatate*; the It. *fatare* to render proof by spells, to charm, corresponds to OF. *faer*:—popular L. *fātāre*, f. *fāta* fairy (see FAY *sb.*); but the etymological notion as apprehended by Dryden was prob. 'protected as by a decree of Fate'.]

1697 DRYDEN *Virg. Æneid* Ded., His fated Armour was only an Allegorical Defence. *Ibid.* VIII. 716 Bright Vulcanian Arms, Fated from force of Steel by Stygian charms.

6. Preceded by some qualifying adv.: Having a particular fate or destiny. *rare* exc. in ILL-FATED.

a **1721** PRIOR *Epil. to Phædra* 25 Her aukward Love indeed was oddly fated; She and her Poly were too near related.

fateful ('feɪtfʊl), *a.* [f. FATE *sb.* + -FUL.]

1. Of a voice or utterance: Revealing the decrees of fate; prophetic of destiny.

1715–20 POPE *Iliad* XIX. 466 Then ceas'd for ever, by the Furies ty'd, His fate-full voice. **1794** COLERIDGE *Melancholy*, A mystic tumult and a fateful rhyme. **1850** CARLYLE *Latter-d. Pamph.* i. (1872) 28 That fateful Hebrew Prophecy. **1863** LONGF. *Wayside Inn* II. Prel. 105 The fateful cawings of the crow. **1878** B. TAYLOR *Deukalion* II. v. 84 The fateful words, 'Rise Brother'.

2. Fraught with destiny, bearing with it or involving momentous consequences; decisive, important. Chiefly of a period of time.

1800 COLERIDGE *Death of Wallenstein* III. viii, A fateful evening doth descend upon us. **1850** W. IRVING *Mahomet* ix. (1853) 35 The fateful banner of Khaled. **1861** *Romance of a Dull Life* xiii. 97 Each minute seemed fateful to her. **1884** ROE *Nat. Ser. Story* xii. in *Harper's Mag.* Nov. 907/1 A fateful conference..was taking place.

3. Marked by the influence of fate; controlled as if by irresistible destiny.

1876 S. A. BROOKE *Eng. Lit.* 130 The Bride of Lammermoor, as great in fateful pathos as Romeo and Juliet. **1885** *Pall Mall G.* 17 Feb. 6/2 That fateful inability to review their position. **1891** *Times* 14 Feb. 7/5 Peasants.. begin..their..wanderings from place to place in an aimless, fateful sort of way. **1891** E. PEACOCK *N. Brendon* I. 229 As fateful as a Greek tragedy.

4. Bringing fate or death; deadly; = FATAL 6.

1764 J. GRAINGER *Sugar Cane* IV. 174 Nor fateful only is the bursting flame. **1798** CANNING & HAMMOND *Progr. Man* in *Anti-Jacobin* No. 16 Resounds the fateful dart. **1808** J. BARLOW *Columb.* IV. 316 The soldier's fateful steel.

5. Having a remarkable fate; of eventful history.

1886 G. T. STOKES *Ireland & Celtic Church* (1888) 108 *note*, This fateful book is said to be still in existence.

Hence '**fatefully** *adv.*, in a fateful manner. '**fatefulness**, the quality of being fateful.

1863 S. HIBBERD in *Intell. Observer* III. 439 If she [the bee] is so fatefully mechanical as to build and furnish a cell without knowledge of what it is. **1865** CARLYLE *Fredk. Gt.* XVII. iii, Those fatefully questionable months. **1882** *Pall Mall G.* 1 Dec. 3 Assigning much mock fatefulness to Sir Crimson Fluid. **1886** *Athenæum* 20 Feb. 274 A whimsical air of fatefulness.

'**fateless,** *a.* *rare.* [f. FATE *sb.* + -LESS.] Without fate; in which fate has no existence.

1881 J. THOMSON *Vane's Story, Weddah & O.* IV. xxxv, Fateless Heaven.

fat-faced, *a.* [f. FAT *a.* + FACE + -ED^{2}.] Having a fat face. **a.** Of persons. †Also *fig.* (nonce-use) of land, with allusion to the sense FAT *a.* 9a, fertile. **b.** *Printing*, as ***fat-faced Egyptian*** (see FAT *a.* 3).

1632 LITHGOW *Trav.* v. 231 The curling playnes of fat-fac'd Palestine. **1782** *George Bateman* II. 2 A short, thick-set, fat-faced man. **1840** DICKENS *Barn. Rudge* ix, A fat-faced puss she is. **1863** HAWTHORNE *Our Old House* (1883) 30 A.. fat-faced individual came into my private room.

fath, obs. and dial. form of FAITH.

Fatha, Fatheh, varr. FATIHAH.

†**fathe.** *Obs.* *rare*$^{-1}$. See quot.

a **1387** *Sinon. Barthol.* Introd. (1882) 3 De dolore pectoris qui anglice dicitur fathe.

†**fathead.** *Obs.* *rare*$^{-1}$. [f. FAT *a.* + -HEAD.] = FATNESS.

c **1250** *Gen. & Ex.* 1547 Heuene dew, and erðes fetthed.

fat-head. [f. FAT *a.* + HEAD.]

1. One having a fat head; a stupid dolt.

1842 BARHAM *Ingol. Leg.*, *Nursery Reminisc.* 7 You little Fat-head, There's a top, because you're good. **1885** MRS. RIDDELL *Mitre Court* xix, He is a fathead—a great blundering John Bull.

2. a. A labroid fish *Semicossyphus* or *Pimelometopon pulcher*. **b.** A cyprinoid fish *Pimephales promelas*, the Blackhead or Blackheaded Minnow. (*Cent. Dict.*)

fat-hen ('fæt,hɛn). A name for certain plants of the Goosefoot tribe, *Chenopodium Bonus-Henricus* and *Atriplex patula*. Also, in Australia, applied to various species of *Chenopodium* and *Atriplex* which are eaten as vegetables.

1795 *Trans. Soc. Encourag. Arts* XIII. 204 Chickweed, fumitory, fat-hen, and persicaria. **1847** LEICHHARDT *Jrnl.* II. 40 The fat-hen..grew abundantly on the reedy flats. **1853** G. JOHNSTON *Nat. Hist. E. Bord.* 172 Atriplex patula, *Fat Hen.* **1863** in PRIOR *Pop. Names Brit. Plants* (1879) 75. **1880** *Blackw. Mag.* Feb. 182 Fathen [*pr.* falhen] (a kind of indigenous spinach). **1889** MRS. CAMPBELL PRAED *Romance of a Station* 46 To gather fat-hen, to do duty as cabbage.

father ('fɑːðə(r)), *sb.* Forms: 1–3 **fæder** (1 **-yr**), **feder**, (3 **feader**), 2–6 **fader**, (3 *Orm.* **faderr**), (*south. dial.* 3 **væder**, **veder**, 3–4 **vader**), 3–4 **fadre**, 4–5 **fadir(e**, **-ur(e**, **-yr**, 4 **faþer**, 6– **father**. [Com. Teut. and Aryan: OE. *fæder* corresponds to OFris. *feder*, *fader*, OS. *fadar*, *fader* (LG., Du. *vader*, *vaar*), OHG. *fater* (MHG. and mod.G. *vater*), ON. *faðer*, *-ir* (Sw., Da. *fader*, *far*), Goth. *fadar* (found only *Gal.* iv. 6, the ordinary word being *atta*):—OTeut. *fader*, ?*fadēr*:—OAryan *pə'tēr* (*pə'ter-*, *pətr-*). whence Skr. *pitṛ*, Gr. πατήρ, L. *pater*, OIr. *athir*.

The spelling in our quots. is uniformly with *d* until 16th c., exc. that *faþer* occurs sporadically in the Cotton and Göttingen MSS. of the *Cursor Mundi* (*a* 1300); but the pronunciation (ð) may have been widely current in the 15th c. or even earlier; in 14–15th c. the spelling with *-der* is very common in words like *brother*, *feather*, *leather*, though this spelling cannot in all cases be supposed to indicate that the writers pronounced the words with (d). The mod.Eng. *-ther* (ðə(r)) for OE. *-der*, *-dor* in *father* and *mother* is often wrongly said to be due to the analogy of *brother*, or to Scandinavian influence; it is really the result of a phonetic law common to the great majority of Eng. dialects; other examples in standard Eng. are *gather*, *hither*, *together*, *weather*. At present nearly all dialects pronounce *father* and *mother* with (ð) as in standard Eng.; in various parts of the north of England and the north Lowlands (d), alveolar or dental, is sometimes heard. The representation of OE. *æ*, *a* by (ɑː) in this word is anomalous; the only parallel case, setting aside the class of instances in which (ɑː) and (æ) vary, is *rather*. Among the chief variant pronunciations in dialects are ('faðər, 'feːðər) (by writers of dialect books often spelt *faither*, *feyther*), ('fiːðə(r), *Sc.* 'feðər) etc.

In OE. the genitive had the two forms *fæder* (cf. OS. *fader*, OHG. *fater*, ON. *fǫður*) and *fæderes*. The uninflected form survived in occasional use down to the 15th c.]

1. a. One by whom a child is or has been begotten, a male parent, the nearest male ancestor. Rarely applied to animals.

c **825** *Vesp. Psalter* xxvi[i]. 10 Forðon feder min & modur min forleorton mec. *c* **1000** ÆLFRIC *Deut.* xxiv. 16 Ne slea man fæderas for suna gylton. *c* **1200** *Trin. Coll. Hom.* 165 Ðe sune wussheð þe fader deað ar his dai cume. *c* **1290** *S. Eng. Leg.* I. 14/457 He liet..maken him king of al is fader lond. *c* **1350** *Will. Palerne* 241 A kowherde, sire..is my kynde fader. *c* **1400** *Rom. Rose* 4863 Whanne fader or moder arn in grave. **1473** WARKW. *Chron.* 10 Herry Percy, whos fadere was slayne at Yorke felde. **1571** LYNDESAY *MS. Collect.*, The litill bĩrdis straikis thair fader in the face with thair wingis. **1597** MONTGOMERIE *Answ. Ingliss Railar* 12 Brutus ..Quha slew his fader howping to succeid. **1670** G. H. *Hist. Cardinals* II. II. 144 Ginetti..proved his Fathers own Son. **1753** HANWAY *Trav.* (1762) I. II. xiv. 62 For a son to call his father by that endearing name. **1884** TENNYSON *Becket* v. ii, His father gave him to my care.

b. *fig.* (Quots. 1597^{2} and 1802 have given rise to proverbial phrases.)

1398 TREVISA *Barth. De P.R.* XVII. i. (1495) 591 Aristotle sayth that the erthe is moder and the sonne fader of trees. **1577** B. GOOGE *Heresbach's Husb.* II. (1586) 75 b, So shall the branch [when grafted] live, being both nourished by his olde Mother, and his newe Father. **1597** SHAKS. *2 Hen. IV*, I. i. 8 Eu'ry minute now Should be the Father of some Stratagem. *Ibid.* IV. v. 93 Thy wish was Father (Harry) to that thought. **1604** JAS. I. *Counterbl.* (Arb.) 102 The foure Complexions, (whose fathers are the foure Elements). **1802** WORDSW. *Rainbow*, The child is father of the man. **1859** KINGSLEY *Misc.* (1860) I. 7 He..too often makes the wish father to the thought.

c. (More explicitly ***spiritual father***.) The teacher to whom a person owes his religious life.

1382 WYCLIF *1 Cor.* iv. 15 If ȝe han ten thousandis of litle maistris in Crist Jhesu, but not manye fadris. **1769** H. VENN in *Life* (1835) 152 A lady said to me, 'You, sir, are my spiritual father'. *a* **1858** BP. D. WILSON in Bateman *Life* (1860) II. 208 As our Father Scott used to say.

d. Proverbs.

1549 LATIMER *3rd Serm. bef. Edw. VI* (Arb.) 97 Happye is the chylde, whose father goeth to the Deuyll. **1616** SURFL. & MARKH. *Country Farme* 400 This is it which some vtter in a prouerbe, That he that will plant his father, must cut off his head. *c* **1645** HOWELL *Lett.* (1650) II. 118 He will be a wise child that knows his right father.

e. Colloquially extended to include a father-in-law, stepfather, or one who adopts another as his child (more fully ***adoptive father***).

1592 SHAKS. *Rom. & Jul.* IV. i. 2 My Father Capulet will haue it so. **1599** —— *Much Ado* IV. i. 24 Stand thee by Frier, father.. Will you with free and vnconstrained soule Giue me this maid your daughter. **1605** —— *Macb.* IV. ii. 63 If you would not [weep for him] it were a good signe, that I should quickely haue a new Father. **1798** COLEBROOKE tr. *Digest Hindu Law* (1801) III. 147 Sons inferior to these..claim the family of their adoptive father.

f. Applied *transf.* to the relative or friend who 'gives away' a bride. Also ***father-in-church***.

1599 SHAKS. *Much Ado* v. iv. 15 You must be father to your brothers daughter, And giue her to young Claudio. **1719** DE FOE *Crusoe* (1840) II. vii. 174, I was father at the altar..and gave her away. **1871** MRS. H. WOOD *Dene Hollow* vi, 'I shall want you to stand father-in-church to this young lady,' said Geoffrey to the clerk.

g. Used colloquially by a wife addressing or referring to her husband.

1855 DICKENS *Dorrit* (1857) I. ii. 12 'Never mind, Father, never mind!' said Mrs. Meagles. **1917** D. CANFIELD *Understood Betsy* (1922) iii. 61 'It's gathering,' said Aunt Abigail... 'Father'll churn it a little more till it really comes.' **1960** C. WATSON *Bump in Night* iv. 40 If anyone was to blame it was Mr Biggadyke. He nearly lost father his job over that business.

h. ***the father and mother of a***: used colloquially to indicate extreme severity, exceptionally large size, etc. Also (esp. *Austral.* and *N.Z.*), ***the father of a***.

1892 KIPLING *Many Invent.* (1893) 45 It would ha' bin my duty..to give you the father an' mother av a beltin. **1892** —— *Lett. of Travel* (1920) 41 The father and mother of all weed-spuds. **1908** SOMERVILLE & 'ROSS' *Further Exper. Irish R.M.* viii. 197 There's been the father and mother of a row down there between old Sir Thomas and Hackett. **1930** *Bulletin* (Sydney) 3 Dec. 21/3 ''Twas the father of a lickin' I intended for ye, Skinny, for the way ye hoofed it awhile ago,' he said. **1938** N. MARSH *Artists in Crime* xiii. 202 You've led Bathgate into the father and mother of a row for talking out of school. **1947** 'A. P. GASKELL' *Big Game* 119 Harry threatened to give him the father of a hiding. **1948** D. W. BALLANTYNE *Cunninghams* II. xi. 177 The local side got the father of a hiding. **1954** G. SMITH *Flaw in Crystal* 139 They've allowed me to arrange the father and mother of a credit overdraft with the banks. **1958** L. A. G. STRONG *Treason in Egg* vii. 143 There's the father and mother of a message on the paper. I can't understand it. **1960** *Punch* 13 July 47/2 The stage is set for the father and mother of a row.

i. In conjunctive phrases: ***father-child*, *-daughter*, *-son***.

1949 M. MEAD *Male & Female* xvi. 326 A father-daughter household is not as disapproved [etc.]. **1958** *Listener* 21 Aug. 263/2 The father-son relationship is necessarily permanent. **1960** C. DAY LEWIS *Buried Day* vii. 142 Pathetic attempts to revive the old father-child relationship.

2. A male ancestor more remote than a parent, *esp.* the founder of a race or family, a forefather, progenitor. In *pl.* ancestors, forefathers. So in Scriptural phr. ***to be gathered*, †*to be put to*** or ***sleep with one's fathers***: to be dead and buried. Also loosely for 'a man of old', 'a patriarch'.

c950 *Lindisf. Gosp.* Luke i. 55 Suæ ʒesprecen wæs to fadores usra. c1000 *Ags. Gosp.* Matt. iii. 9, & ne cweþað betwux eow we habbað abraham us to fæder. c1200 *Trin. Coll. Hom.* 226 Vre foremes faderes gult we abugeð alle. 1377 LANGL. *P. Pl.* B. III. 126 ȝowre fadre she felled þorw fals biheste. 1382 WYCLIF *Judg.* ii. 10 Al that generacioun is gedrid to her fadris. —— *1 Kings* i. 21 Whanne my lord kyng shal sleep with his faders. c1400 MAUNDEV. (1839) vi. 66 The Sarazines.. han the place in gret reuerence for the holy fadres, the patriarkes þat lyȝn þere. a1440 *Found. St. Barthol.* 34 He decessid, and was put to his fadres. 1538 STARKEY *England* I. i. 19 Theyr cyuyle ordynance and statutys, deuysyd by theyr old Fatherys in eury secte. 1611 BIBLE *Acts* xiii. 36. 1671 MILTON *P.R.* I. 351 God who fed Our fathers here with manna. 1791 COWPER *Yardley Oak* 144 One man alone, the father of us all, Drew not his life from woman. 1848 MACAULAY *Hist. Eng.* I. 20 Nor were the arts of peace neglected by our fathers during that stirring period.

3. a. One who institutes, originates, calls into being; a constructor, contriver, designer, framer, originator. Also one who gives the first conspicuous or influential example of (an immaterial thing). ***the Fathers*** (U.S.): the framers of the constitution.

Often in designations of Biblical origin. ***the Father of Lights***, etc.: applied to God. ***the father of faith, of the faithful***: Abraham. ***the father of lies*** (after John viii. 44): the Devil.

1362 LANGL. *P. Pl.* A. I. 14 He is Fader of Fei. 1382 WYCLIF *Jas.* i. 17 The fadir of liȝtis. 1555 EDEN *Decades* Pref. to Rdr. (Arb.) 51 Abraham the father of fayth. 1588 *Marprel. Epist.* (Arb.) 31 Iohn Cant. was the first father of this horrible error in our Church. 1669 WORLIDGE *Syst. Agric.* (1681) 114 In Germany no young Farmer is permitted to Marry.. till he.. hath planted, and is a father of such a stated number of Wallnut Trees. 1700 DRYDEN *Fables* Pref. Wks. (Globe) 499 He [Chaucer] is the father of English poetry. 1748 RICHARDSON *Clarissa* Wks. 1883 VI. 275 Hannibal was called the father of warlike stratagems. 1795 *Hull Advertiser* 14 Nov. 3/3 Dr. Hooper the father of the canal. 1825 J. NEAL *Jonathan* II. 5 The Father of Lies himself. 1829 SCOTT *Jrnl.* (1890) II. 290 Words.. sung by the Fathers of the Reformation. 1844 SIR D. GOOCH *Diaries* (1892) 54, I may.. I think, claim to be the father of express trains. 1867 SMYTH *Sailor's Wordbk.*, *Father*, the dockyard name given to the person who constructs a ship of the navy. 1875 JOWETT *Plato* (ed. 2) I. p. ix, To represent Plato as the father of Idealism. 1888 BRYCE *Amer. Commw.* II. xli. 105 In 'the days of the Fathers'.

b. pl. ***the Fathers*** (***of the Church***): the early Christian writers; usually applied to those of the first five centuries, but by some extended further. ***Apostolical Fathers***: see APOSTOLICAL.

1340 *Ayenb.* 155 Ase zayþ þe boc of collacions of holy uaderes. 1549 (Mar.) *Bk. Com. Prayer* Pref., If a manne woulde searche out by the auncient fathers. 1588 SHAKS. *L.L.L.* IV. ii. 153 As a certaine Father saith. a1641 BP. MOUNTAGU *Acts & Mon.* iii. §54 (1642) 200 To this discourse of Basil, other Fathers agree. 1710 PRIDEAUX *Orig. Tithes* 141 Irenaeus and Origen, and other Fathers. 1776–81 GIBBON *Decl. & F.* xlvii. *note*, The Greek as well as the Latin fathers. 1839 LONGF. *Hyperion* IV. vii, I gazed with rapture on the vast folios of the Christian Fathers. 1887 LOWELL *Democr.* Prose Wks. 1890 VI. 14 A Father of the Church said that property was theft many centuries before Proudhon was born.

4. a. One who exercises protecting care like that of a father; one who shows paternal kindness; one to whom filial reverence and obedience are due. (In OE. applied to a feudal superior.)

a1000 *O.E. Chron.* an. 924 Hine ʒeces þa to fæder & to hlaforde Scotta cyning. 1382 WYCLIF *Job* xxix. 16 Fader I was of pore men. 1460 EARL OF MARCHE in Ellis *Orig. Lett.* I. 5. I. 9 Oure.. ryght noble lorde and ffadur. 1591 SHAKS. *1 Hen. VI*, III. i. 98 A Father of the Common-weale. 1627 MASSINGER *Gt. Dk. Florence* I. ii, For her love I will be a father to thee. 1787 H. KNOX *Let.* 19 Mar. Washington's Writ. 1891 XI. 123 *note*, The glorious republican epithet, The Father of your Country. 1867 FREEMAN *Norm. Conq.* (1877) I. iii. 143 It was meant to assert that Scots.. owed no duty to Rome.. but only to their Father and Lord at Winchester.

b. with reference to patronage of literature.

1513 DOUGLAS *Æneis* I. Prol. 85 Fader of bukis, protectour to science. 1837–9 HALLAM *Hist. Lit.* I. v. I. §17. 339 Francis I. has obtained a glorious title, the Father of French literature.

c. Applied to a religious teacher or counsellor (cf. 6).

1393 LANGL. *P. Pl.* C. I. 120 Ȝe sholde be here fadres, and techen hem betere. c1465 *Eng. Chron. 28 Hen. VI* (Camden 1856) 64 There thay slow him horribly, thair fader and thair bisshoppe. 1655 FULLER *Ch. Hist.* IX. vii. §13 He was commonly called Father Gilpin. 1757 in Sidney *Life of S. Walker* (1838) 281 Dr [*dear*] Father in the Lord. 1828 GRIMSHAWE *Mem. of L. Richmond* (1829) 132 He was regarded by them [the communicants] as a father. 1833 in Sidney *Life of R. Hill* (1834) 408 The minister who read the .. service, substituted the word father for that of brother.

d. ***like a father***: in a paternal, authoritative, or severe manner.

1830 J. K. PAULDING *Chron. Gotham* 64 If she wont listen to reason, I will talk to her like a father. 1922 JOYCE *Ulysses* 316 Talking to him like a father, trying to sell him a secondhand coffin. 1926 F. W. CROFTS *Insp. French & Cheyne Myst.* vi. 74 James talked to him like a father and he seemed to swallow it all down.

5. a. Applied to God, expressing His relation to Jesus, to mankind in general (considered either as His offspring, as the objects of His loving care, or as owing Him obedience and reverence), or to Christians (as His children by regeneration or adoption). Also applied to heathen gods.

c825 *Vesp. Psalter* lxxxviii[i] 27 He ʒeceð mec feder min ðu earð god min. c1000 *Ags. Gosp.* Matt. xxiii. 9 An ys eower fædyr se þe on heofonum ys. c1200 *Vices & Virtues* (1888) 25 And [he] steih in to heuene, and sitt on his fader swiðre. a1225 *Ancr. R.* 10 Þe is also federleas þet haueð þurh his sunne vorlore þene Veder of heouene. c1386 CHAUCER *Pars. T.* ¶57 He haþ agilte his fader celestial. 1470–85 MALORY *Arthur* XVII. xv, Ioye and honour be to the fader of heuen! 1533 GAU *Richt Vay* To Rdr. (1888) 3 Grace marcie and pece of god our fader. 1562 WINȜET *Last Blast* Wks. 1888 I. 41 The lauchfull vocatioun of His Heuinlie Fader. 1775 HARRIS *Philos. Arrangem.* Wks. (1841) 322 Through which relation they are called his offspring, and he their Father. 1821 SHELLEY *Prometh. Unb.* I. 354 Most unwillingly I come, by the great Father's will driven down To execute a doom of new revenge. 1843 MACAULAY *Lays Anc. Rome, Horatius* lix, O Tiber! father Tiber, To whom the Romans pray. 1865 TENNYSON *En. Ard.* 785 Uphold me, Father, in my loneliness A little longer! 1871 MORLEY *Voltaire* (1886) 2 Some.. austere step-son of the Christian God, jealous of the divine benignity.. of his father's house.

†**b.** Applied to Christ. *Obs. rare.*

1470–85 MALORY *Arthur* XVII. xiv, Fayr fader ihesu Cryste I thanke the. [Hence 1859 TENNYSON *Guinevere* 558 Our fair father Christ.]

c. *Theol.* ***(God) the Father***: the First Person of the Trinity.

c1000 *Ags. Gosp.* John xiv. 26 Se haliʒe frofre gast þe fæder sent on minum naman. c1175 *Lamb. Hom.* 53 Þe feder and þe sune and þe halie gast iscilde us þer wið. a1300 *E.E. Psalter* i. Gloria, Blisse to þe Fadre and to þe Sone, And to þe Hali Gaste. c1450 MYRC 459 Leue on fader and sone and holy gost. 1548 tr. *Luther's Chiefe Articles Chr. Faythe* A vj b, The Holy Goost from the Father and the Sonne procedynge. 1737 POPE *Hor. Epist.* II. i. 102 And God the Father turns a School-divine. 1851 NEALE *Mediæv. Hymns* 127 Honour, laud, and praise addressing To the Father and the Son.

6. Ecclesiastical uses.

a. The title given to a confessor or spiritual director. Also explicitly ***spiritual*** and (*arch.*) ***ghostly father*** (but the former, in Eng., has more usually the sense 1 c).

a1300 *Cursor M.* 27857 (Cott.) O scrift þon do þi faders rede, sua þat þi saul mai ai be quite. *Ibid.* 28077 (Cott.) Til ouer lauerd crist and þe, mi gastli fader, yeild i me. 1393 GOWER *Conf.* I. 104 Min holy fader, so I will. 1526 *Pilgr. Perf.* (W. de W. 1531) 9 b, Takynge penaunce of our goostly father for our transgressyon & synne. 1677 LADY CHAWORTH in *Hist. MSS. Comm.* 12th Rep. App. v. 43 The D[uchess] of Portsmouth.. has promised it to her ghostly father. 1805 SCOTT *Last Minstr.* II. vi, Penance, father, will I none.

b. A priest belonging to a religious order or congregation. Also the title given to the superior of a monastic house in relation to those subject to his rule.

1571 HANMER *Chron. Irel.* (1633) 48 He.. became father of the Monkes of Saint Hilarie. 1603 SHAKS. *Meas. for M.* III. ii. 11 'Blesse you good Father Frier. 1711 ADDISON *Spect.* No. 164 ¶3 A Father of a Convent. 1739 GRAY *Jrnl. in France* Wks. 1884 I. 244 It [the Chartreuse] contains about 100 Fathers, and Freres together. 1756–7 tr. *Keysler's Trav.* (1760) III. 278 S. Maria di Galiera is a beautiful church, and belongs to the fathers of the oratory. 1848 MACAULAY *Hist. Eng.* II. 99 The skill and care with which those fathers [Jesuits] had.. conducted the education of youth.

c. Applied to bishops. ***Right Reverend, Most Reverend Father in God***: the formal designation respectively of a bishop and an archbishop.

1508 *Fisher's Seuen Penit. Ps.*, This treatyse.. was.. compyled by the ryght reuerente fader in god Iohan Fyssher .. bysshop of Rochester. 1521 (*title*), The sermon of Iohan the bysshop of Rochester made.. by the assignement of the moost reuerend father in god the lord Thomas Cardinall of Yorke. 1594 SHAKS. *Rich. III*, III. vii. 61 He is within; with two right reuerend Fathers Diuinely bent to Meditation. 168. S. HOLLINGWORTH in *MS. Bodl. Rawl. Lett.* LIX. fol. 190 To the Right Reuerant father in God His Grac Willam Lord Arch Bishshop of Canterbery. 1848 MACAULAY *Hist. Eng.* II. 354 He had yielded to the intreaties of the fathers of the Church. 1869 FREEMAN *Norm. Conq.* (1876) III. xii. 89 The Pope and the assembled Fathers. *Mod.* The most Reverend Father in God (William), by Divine Providence Lord Archbishop of Canterbury.

d. ***the Holy Father***: the Pope.

c1400 MAUNDEV. (1839) xxxi. 314, I.. schewed my lif to oure holy fadir the Pope. a1562 G. CAVENDISH *Life Wolsey* App. (1827) 519 They.. by force imprisoned our holy Father the Pope.

e. As a prefix to the name of a priest. Also abbreviated F., Fr.

Formerly, as still in Continental use, restricted to the regular clergy (see b). In the nineteenth century this became the customary English mode of designating a Roman Catholic priest, even among those not of his own communion: but some secular priests still refused the title as incorrect, preferring to be addressed as 'The Rev. A. B.' The abbreviated forms are seldom used exc. by Roman Catholics.

As the prefix 'Father' was in the 16th c. used only with the names of members of religious orders, its use was of course not continued in the reformed Church of England. 'Of late years the title has been applied, among a section of the High Church party, to Anglican priests, and some prominent members of that section are very commonly designated by it' (*N.E.D.*). Now quite commonly used in High Church circles.

1529 MORE *Dyaloge* Wks. 140 The good Scottish freer father Donold. 1719 DE FOE *Crusoe* (1840) II. xiii. 265 Father Simon was courteous. 1741 CHALLONER *Missionary Priests*, The same year were banished Father William Weston, S.J., Father John Roberts, O.S.B., Mr. Antony Wright and Mr. James West, priests. 1890 *Dublin Rev.* XXIV. 236 Our readers do not need to be told who Father Faber was.

7. At Cambridge: see quots.

1574 M. STOKYS in Peacock *Stat. Cambridge* App. A. (1841) p. vi, The Father shall enter hys commendacions of hys chyldren. 1772 JEBB *Remarks* 20 The students enter.. preceded by a Master of Arts.. who on this occasion is called the Father of the College to which he belongs. 1803 *Gradus ad Cantabrigiam*, *Father*, one of the Fellows of a College.. who.. attends all the examinations for Bachelor's Degree, to see that.. justice is done to the men of his own College. 1884 DICKENS *Dict. Cambridge* 34 Then the Senior Wrangler.. is presented to the Vice-Chancellor by his Father (or Prælector) and receives his degree on his knees.

8. a. A respectful title given to an old and venerable man, and (with personification) to a river.

1559 CUNNINGHAM *Cosmog. Glasse* A iv b, How often doth father Moses in his . V. bookes, make mention of Babilon. 1607 SHAKS. *Cor.* v. i. 3 He call'd me Father. 1704 POPE *Windsor For.* 197 In vain on father Thames she calls for aid. 1742 GRAY *Eton Coll.* 21 Say, Father Thames.. Who foremost now delight to cleave With pliant arm thy glassy wave? 1815 SOUTHEY *Old Man's Comforts* 1 You are old, Father William, the young man cried.

b. ***Father Christmas***: the personification of Christmas as a benevolent old man with a flowing white beard, wearing a red sleeved gown and hood trimmed with white fur, and carrying a sack of Christmas presents. ***Father Time***: see TIME *sb.* 25.

1658 J. KING (*title*) Examination and Tryall of Old Father Christmas. a1800 in J. Brand *Pop. Antiq.* (1813) I. 373 Lordings, in these realms of pleasure Father Christmas yearly dwells. 1860 *Christmas Tree* 189 'Tis now, when once more from his lair Old Father Christmas issues forth. *Ibid.* 190 Hail, Father Christmas! Come, and bring Thine ancient merriment and glee. 1864 *Chambers's Bk. of Days* II. 740/2 Old Father Christmas, bearing, as emblematic devices, the holly bough, wassil-bowl, etc. 1919 *Punch* 24 Dec. 538 Uncle James (who after hours of making up rather fancies himself as Father Christmas). 1940 *Economist* 20 Jan. 93/1 A Father Christmas State,.. which weakly allowed its citizens to believe that wealth came from him not them. 1968 C. CHAUNDLER *Everyman's Bk. Anc. Customs* II. 180 December the sixth is the feast day of St. Nicholas,.. in Britain we usually call him Santa Claus, or Father Christmas.

9. a. The oldest member of a society, etc. (Chiefly, with reference to duration of membership; occas. with reference to age.) ***Father of the City***, the senior alderman of the City of London.

1705 HEARNE *Collect.* 13 Sept., Sr Robert Clayton.. Alderman, the Father of yt City. 1837 APPERLEY *The Road* (1851) 61 Mr. Warde the father of the field, may.. be called the father of the road also. 1855 DICKENS *Dorrit* vi, You'll be the Father of the Marshalsea. 1880 *Athenæum* 18 Dec. 820/1 Sir Edward Sabine, now in his ninety-second year, is the father of the Society. 1893 *Daily Tel.* 8 July 7/3 The Right Hon. C. P. Villiers, M.P., 'Father of the House of Commons', was robbed of his watch on Thursday.

b. ***Father of the Chapel***: see CHAPEL 10.

1683 MOXON *Printing* xxv. 356 The Oldest Freeman is Father of the Chappel. 1888 in JACOBI *Printer's Vocab.*

c. Hence, The presiding member, or president; also, The leading individual of a number. Phr. ***Father of waters***, etc.; in later *U.S.* use *spec.* the Mississippi.

1600 J. PORY tr. *Leo's Africa* I. 13 They call Abagni the father of rivers. 1704 POPE *Windsor For.* 219 Thou too, great father of the British floods! 1759 JOHNSON *Rasselas* i. 1 The mighty emperour, in whose dominions the Father of Waters begins his course. 1763 tr. *Le Page du Pratz' Hist. Louisiana* I. II. i. 202 By some savages of the North it is called Meact-Chassipi, which literally denotes, the ancient Father of Rivers, of which the French have, by corruption, formed Missisipi. 1771 SMOLLETT *Humph. Cl.* (1846) 251, I will take your place.. and think myself happy to be hailed 'Father of the Feast'. 1808 T. ASHE *Travels* III. xxxviii. 173 Throughout this great water, this Father of Floods, as the Indians calls [*sic*] it, in some places, islands are seen sinking into annihilation. 1813 *Niles' Weekly Reg.* V. Suppl. 176/2 The Mississippi is the Nile of America. The aborigines who resided on its banks, called it Mechaseba, or Father of waters. 1818 H. B. FEARON *Sk. Amer.* 257 The facilities of export afforded by those 'fathers of waters', the Ohio, Mississippi, and Missouri. 1836 J. HALL *Statistics of West* iii. 46 The traveler is struck with the magnitude.. of the stream which has been so appropriately called, the Father of waters. 1878 B. F. TAYLOR *Between Gates* 23 Fox river, Rock river, Mississippi, the old Father of them all. 1917 J. F. DALY *Life A. Daly* 64 A voyage down the Father of Waters in war times. 1949 *New Orleans Times-Picayune Mag.* 27 Mar. 7 With summer approaching, the unique craft will start slipping down Father of Waters.

10. a. *pl.* (rarely *sing.*) The leading men or elders of a city or an assembly.

1590 T. FENNE *Frutes* 57 A grave father of Carthage who boldlie stood foorth. 1697 DRYDEN *Æneid* I. 9 From whence the Race of Alban Fathers come. 1776–81 GIBBON *Decl. & F.* xlvii. ¶13 The fathers.. of the council were awed by this martial array. *Ibid.* II. 93 A council of senators, emphatically styled the Fathers of the City. 1828 SCOTT *F.M. Perth* vii, They were.. the fathers of the city. 1837 HAWTHORNE *Twice Told T.* (1851) II. ii. 34 The Selectmen of Boston, plain, patriarchal fathers of the people.

b. *esp.* The senators of ancient Rome. Sometimes ***Conscript Fathers***: see CONSCRIPT *a.* 1. Also used for: The Patricians.

1533 BELLENDEN *Livy* II. (1822) 158 The samin yere deceissit Meninius Agrippa, quhilk wes lufit baith with the Faderis and small pepill. 1588 SHAKS. *Tit. A.* III. iii. 1. Heare me graue fathers. 1741 MIDDLETON *Cicero* I. v. 382 The authority of the Fathers, and the interests of the

Republic. **1843** MACAULAY *Lays, Regillus* viii, The Fathers of the City Are met in high debate. —— *Horatius* xxxiii, The Tribunes beard the high, And the Fathers grind the low.

11. *attrib.* and *Comb.* **a.** appositive (sense 1), as ***father-bird, -dog, -fool, -symbol, -widower***; (sense 1 b) as ***father-cause, -fount, -grape, -stock, -tree***; (sense 5) as ***Father-God***; (sense 6) as ***father-abbot, -confessor, -director, -jesuit, -preacher, -saint***; (sense 9) as ***father-poet, -ruffian***; **b.** attrib., as ***father-sentiment, -strength***. **c.** objective, as ***father-slayer***; also ***father-sick*** adj.

1797 MRS. RADCLIFFE *Italian* xi, The ceremony began with the exhortation of the *Father-Abbot. **1795** COWPER *Pairing Time* 56 Soon every *father bird and mother Grew quarrelsome. **1646** SIR T. BROWNE *Pseud. Ep.* I. i. 1 The first and *father cause of Common Error. **1756–7** tr. *Keysler's Trav.* (1760) I. 295 The admonitions of his *father-confessor. **1797** MRS. RADCLIFFE *Italian* x, He who appeared to be the *Father-director of the pilgrimage. **1862** H. MARRYAT *Year in Sweden* I. 459 The *father-dog was kept tame. **1864** TENNYSON *Aylmer's F.* 390 One of these old *father-fools. **1884** J. HALL *A Chr. Home* 46 The *Father-fount of nature. **1875** W. P. MACKAY *Grace & Truth* 213 Christians have been made sons of such a *Father-God. **1842** TENNYSON *Will Waterproof* 7 Such [port] whose *father-grape grew fat On Lusitanian summers. **1630** WADSWORTH *Sp. Pilgr.* iii. 14 Obedience the Students are bound to bestow vpon *Father Iesuites. **1711** SHAFTESB. *Charac.* (1737) I. 243 Before the age of Homer or till such time as this *father-poet came into repute. **1691** tr. *Emilianne's Frauds Romish Monks* 277 The one half of the Alms.. belongs to the *Father-Preacher. **1814** SCOTT *Ld. of Isles* III. xxix, The *Father-ruffian of the band. **1842** SIR A. DE VERE *Song of Faith* 108 Hear holy lessons from the *Father-Saints. **1920** T. P. NUNN *Education* xii. 146 The mother-sentiment appears, to be followed.. by the *father-sentiment. **1927** B. MALINOWSKI *Sex & Repress. Savage Soc.* 43 Soon the typical father-sentiment is formed, full of contradictory emotions. **1748** RICHARDSON *Clarissa* III. lix. 281 So *father-sick! so family-fond! **1483** *Cath. Angl.* 120 A *Fader slaer, *patricida*. **1598** SYLVESTER *Du Bartas* II. ii. III. Colonies 526 From fruitfull loyns of one old *Father-stock. **1871** B. TAYLOR *Faust* (1875) II. III. 206 The child in that bright season gaineth The *father-strength. **1922** *Internat. Jrnl. Psychoanal.* III. 206 A totem is, of course, as we know from Freud, a *father-symbol. **1605** SYLVESTER *Du Bartas* II. iii. I. Vocation 139 Fruits that.. have a vertue given.. to draw their *father-tree to heav'n. **1845** MRS. NORTON *Child Isl.* (1846) 132 The *Father-widower.. Strokes down his youngest child's long silken hair.

12. Special combinations: **father-better** *a. Sc.*, better than one's father [cf. ON. *fǫður-betringr* sb.]; †**father-breeder** = *father-forger*; **father-complex** (see COMPLEX *sb.* 3); **father-dust**, the fructifying powder in the anther of flowers; = POLLEN; **father-figure**, one who is regarded as having some of the characteristics of a father; also **father-image, -imago** (see IMAGO); **father-fixation** [FIXATION 3 b], a fixation on one's father; hence *father-fixated* adj.; **father-forger**, one who counterfeits writings of the Fathers; **father-general**, the head or chief of the Society of Jesus; †**father-queller**, a parricide; **father-right** [G. *vaterrecht*], the supremacy of the father in a family in which descent follows the male line; **father-rule**, the rule of the father of a family as distinguished from the rule of the male relatives of the mother where descent follows the female line; patriarchy; **Father's Day** orig. *U.S.*, 'A day for recognition of the respect and gratitude felt by children toward their fathers, commonly observed on the third Sunday in June. Father's Day was originated by Mrs. John Bruce Dodd of Spokane and proclaimed by the governor of Washington in 1910 but was not widely observed until twenty-five years later' (Webster 1950); more recently observed also in Britain; **father-substitute, -surrogate**, a person to whom the attachment of a child is directed in place of the father; **father-waur** *a. Sc.*, 'worse than one's father' (Jam.); cf. *father-better*, and ON. *fǫður-verringr* sb. Also in syntactical combinations of the uninflected genitive, **father-brother, -sister**, *Sc.*, a paternal uncle, paternal aunt; FATHER-KIN.

1645 R. BAILLIE *Lett.* (1841) II. 295 Her glowming sonne, whom I pray God to bless, and make *father-better. **1624** GATAKER *Transubst.* 103 Under his name our Popish *Father-breeders have of late set out a many of Sermons and Treatises. **1513** DOUGLAS *Æneis* VI. vi. 37 We stand content.. That ay remane the chaist Proserpyna Within hir *faderis broderis boundis and ring. **1609** SKENE *Reg. Maj.* 33 The father brother of the fathers side. **1916** C. E. LONG tr. *Jung's Coll. Papers Analyt. Psychol.* iii. 174 As a pious and obedient daughter.. Sarah has brought about the usual sublimation and cleavage of the *father-complex and on the one side has elevated her childish love to the adoration of God, on the other has turned the obsessive force of her father's attraction into the persecuting demon Asmondi. **1922** D. H. LAWRENCE *England, my England* 20 Let the psychoanalysts talk about father complex. It is just a word invented. **1950** J. STRACHEY tr. *Freud's Totem & Taboo* iv. 143 The same contradictory feelings which we can see at work in the ambivalent father-complexes of our children and of our neurotic patients. **1943** *Greeley* (Colo.) *Daily Tribune* 5 June 5/5 Governor Vivian proclaimed Sunday, June 30, as *Father's Day. **1956** A. HUXLEY *Adonis & Alphabet* 169 Mother's Day and, despite the growing absurdity of poor Poppa, Father's Day were instituted. **1963** *New Yorker* 15 June 82 And, what an inspired idea for Father's Day! **1728–46** THOMSON *Spring* 540 From family diffused To family, as flies the *father-dust, The varied colours run. **1934** M. BODKIN *Archetypal Patterns in Poetry*, Index 338/2 *Father-figure, -imago. **1955** D. HUDSON in *Forgotten King* (1960) 200, I was conscious of William Ewart Gladstone as a father-figure of looming.. import. **1957** *Ann. Reg. 1956* 168 President Eisenhower.. was also something of a 'father figure' whose personality inspired such confidence as often to serve as a substitute for a policy. **1958** *Sunday Times* 1 June 6/4 Samuel Beckett (a father-figure: his 'Murphy' (1938) constantly echoes in today's fiction). **1970** *New Society* 5 Mar. 396/3 Later this was changed to grandfather so that a lost father-figure could be hauled in by the back hairs as an excuse. **1961** *Times* 20 Sept. 16/5 The *father-fixated daughter. **1930** *Amer. Jrnl. Psychiatry* 864 The reverse of course is equally true of the woman with a so-called *father-fixation who marries not so much a husband as a father symbol. **1939** G. GREENE *Confid. Agent* I. ii. 86 I'm not romantic. This is what's called a father-fixation. **1624** GATAKER *Transubst.* 64 Our Popish *Father-forgers have set out divers things. **1587** FLEMING *Contn. Holinshed* III. 1326/1 Their *father generall deliuering them what he hath in office. **1679** OATES *Myst. Iniq.* 16 All these.. do serve as Intelligencers to the Father General. **1937** *Harper's Monthly Mag.* Nov. 569/2 Mr. Martin questions whether the labours of the Shamans and witch doctors in creating the perfect '*father image' have not been a little overdone. **1956** E. L. MASCALL *Christ. Theol. & Nat. Sci.* vi. 217 As soon as he [*sc.* Freud] had convinced himself that the idea of God was the projection of a father-image in a wish-fulfilment. **1916** B. M. HINKLE tr. *Jung's Psychol. of Unconscious* I. iii. 55 Difficulties develop in the capacity for erotic expression, which may be reduced analytically to disturbances through a repressive attempt at resuscitation of the father image, or the '*Father-Imago'. **1923** E. JONES *Ess. Appl. Psycho-Analysis* 79 The figure of Polonius may be thus regarded as resulting from 'decomposition' of the paternal archetype... He is but a substitute for the step-father, i.e. a father *imago*. **1943** *Horizon* Oct. 252 Dramas of the soul which aspired either to destroy or reach beyond the traditional father-imago. *c* **1440** *Promp. Parv.* 145 *Fader Qwellare, *patricida*. **1561** DAUS tr. *Bullinger on Apoc.* (1573) 22 b, A most arrant father queller. *a* **1641** BP. MOUNTAGU *Acts & Mon.* iv. §52 (1642) 280 They would never endure Father-quellers to rule over them. **1899** F. W. MOORE tr. *Gumplowicz's Outl. Sociol.* I. 53 He [*sc.* J. Lippert] goes on to show the rising '*father right'. **1907** *Folk-Lore* June 245 The passage from motherright to fatherright. **1955** M. GLUCKMAN *Custom & Conflict in Afr.* iii. 73 The two contrasting types of kinship system, extreme father-right and extreme matriliny, are built up on the same principle: the link of mother to child. **1899** F. W. MOORE tr. *Gumplowicz's Outl. Sociol.* III. 112 It is recognized that mother-rule everywhere gave place to *father-rule. **1597** SKENE *De Verb. Sign.* s.v. *Eneya*, The *father sister and her bairnes suld succeede. **1938** F. L. LUCAS *Delights of Dictatorship* ii. 46 The hysteria that can find in the Head of that State [*sc.* the U.S.S.R.] a dream-husband, a *father-substitute,.. a God. **1949** E. COXHEAD *Wind in West* vi. 156 He had almost detached himself from Mother... Transference to a father-substitute was plainly the next stage. **1950** J. STRACHEY tr. *Freud's Totem & Taboo* iv. 148 The totem may be the *first* form of *father-surrogate. **1957** N. FRYE *Anat. Criticism* 165 The fury with which these characters are baited.. shows that they are father-surrogates.

father ('fɑːðə(r)), *v.* [f. prec. sb.]

1. *trans.* To be or become the father of; to beget.

1483 *Cath. Angl.* 120 To Fadyr, *genitare*. **1583** STANYHURST *Æneis* I. 285 By Mars fiery fathered twins. **1591** F. SPARRY tr. *Cattan's Geomancie* 81 If the childe be right fathered. **1605** SYLVESTER *Du Bartas* II. iii. I. Vocation 997 Ismael.. lives, to father mighty Progenies. **1611** SHAKS. *Cymb.* IV. ii. 26 Cowards father Cowards, & Base things Syre Bace. **1877** S. LANIER *Poems, Florida Sunday* 103, I am one with all the kinsmen things That e'er my Father fathered. **1884** TENNYSON *Becket* III. iii. 132 Had I fathered him I had given him more of the rod than the sceptre.

b. *fig.* To originate, bring into existence; to be the author of (a doctrine, statement, etc.).

1548 GEST *Pr. Masse* D iij/1 The true meanyng of them who fathered the Canon. **1601** HOLLAND *Pliny* I. 91 When some grave personage fathereth a lie. **1842** TENNYSON *Love & Duty* 7 Shall Error in the round of time Still father Truth? **1850** KINGSLEY *Alt. Locke* vii, As wild Icarias.. as ever were fathered by a red Republic.

2. To appear or pass as, or acknowledge oneself, the father of; †to adopt.

c **1400** MAUNDEV. (Roxb.) xxxi. 142 On þis wise may þai fader anoþer mannez childe. **1589** WARNER *Alb. Eng.* VI. xxx. (1612) 148 Who so the Childe shall git.. Vulcan.. shall father it. **1678** DRYDEN *True Widow* Prol. 32 He's a sot, Who needs will father what the parish got. **1722** DE FOE *Col. Jack* (1840) 213, I would father no brats that were not of my own getting. **1855** MACAULAY *Hist. Eng.* III. 8 The charge of.. fathering a supposititious child.

fig. **1737** POPE *Hor. Epist.* II. ii. 170 Use will father what's begot by Sense.

b. To appear or acknowledge oneself as the author of; to adopt; to take the responsibility of. Also †To represent oneself as the owner of.

1591 HORSEY *Trav.* App. (Hakluyt Soc.) 282 They shall not.. father any other mens goods but their owne. **1634** CANNE *Necess. Separ.* (1849) 242 The report goes that he was not the.. author of it, but another did it, and got him to father it. **1662–3** J. BIRKENHEAD *Assembly-Man* To Rdr., Unwilling to father other mens sins. **1727** SWIFT *To Earl of Oxford*, Men of wit, Who often father'd what he writ. **1827** SCOTT *Jrnl.* (1890) II. 25 A singular letter from a lady, requesting I would father a novel of hers. **1855** MACAULAY *Hist. Eng.* IV. xx. 498 By these two distinguished men Paterson's scheme was fathered. Montague undertook to manage the House of Commons, Godfrey to manage the City. **1870** SPURGEON *Treas. Dav.* Ps. xliv. *heading*, No other writer should be sought for to father any of the Psalms, when David will suffice.

3. To act as a father to, look after; †to carry out (a law).

1577 tr. *Bullinger's Decades* (1592) 192 Suppose.. there were no magistrate to execute and as it were to father those lawes. **1611** SHAKS. *Cymb.* IV. ii. 395, I good youth And rather Father thee, then Master thee. **1892** *Pall Mall G.* 3 May 3/1 The way in which Khama fathers his people.

4. †**a.** To trace the father of. *Obs.* **b.** ***to father oneself***: to indicate one's paternity. *Obs.* exc. *dial.*

1599 SHAKS. *Much Ado* I. i. 111 The Lady fathers her selfe: be happie Lady, for you are like an honorable father. **1680** BURNET *Rochester* 14 A Child is fathered sometimes by its resemblance. **1878** *Cumbrld. Gloss.* s.v. *Fadder*, A child having features resembling those of its father 'fadders it sel'.

fig. **1808** SCOTT in *Lockhart* xviii, This spirited composition as we say in Scotland fathers itself in the manliness of its style.

5. To name or declare the father of (a child). With const. *on, upon*: To fix the paternity of (a child) *on* or *upon*; to affiliate to.

1570 LEVINS *Manip.* 78/1 To Father, *patrem nominare*. **1611** SPEED *Theat. Gt. Brit.* i. 2/1 Brute should have had more sons fathered on him. **1625** K. LONG tr. *Barclay's Argenis* II. xxii. 141 Neptune, upon whom.. our Ancestors have fathered all the men of extraordinary huge stature. **17..** *Young Tamlane* 67–8 Father my bairn on whom I will, I'll father nane on thee. **1885** *Daily News* 13 Mar. 7/3 He advised her to father her child. *Ibid.*, He had asked her to father it upon the gardener.

6. *fig.* of 5. To name the author of. *rare.* With const. †*of, on, upon*: To ascribe (some thing) to (a person) as his production or work; to attribute the authorship of (something) *to* (a person).

1542 UDALL *Erasm. Apoph.* I. xxii. 11 This saiying.. is fathered on Socrates. **1548** GEST *Pr. Masse* I viij, The canones whiche the catholiques father of yᵉ apostles. *c* **1590** CARTWRIGHT in *Presbyt. Rev.* Jan. 1888 120 Especially if these be ther workes which are fathered of them. *a* **1635** NAUNTON *Fragm. Reg.* (Arb.) 37 It is a likely report that they father on him. **1764** FRANKLIN *Narrative* Wks. 1887 III. 269 To father the worst of crimes on the God of peace. **1865** LIVINGSTONE *Zambesi* xix. 398 And coolly fathered the traffic on the Missionaries.

b. *to father* (a thing) ***upon*** (something else): to trace to (something) as a source or origin; to lay to the account of.

1608 *Yorksh. Trag.* I. iii, Fathering his riots on his youth. **1680** BOYLE *Scept. Chem.* VI. 433 Such Phantastick and Unintelligible Discourses.. father'd upon such excellent Experiments. **1702** *Eng. Theophrast.* 270 We father upon love several dealings and intercourses in which it is not concerned. **1774** FLETCHER *Fict. & Gen. Creed* Pref. Wks. 1795 III. 313 The principle on which such a doctrine might be justly fathered.

c. *loosely*, const. *on, upon*: To put upon, impose upon, attach to.

1816 KIRBY & SP. *Entomol.* (1828) II. xvii. 47 This interpretation has been fathered upon them. **1874** H. R. REYNOLDS *John Bapt.* iii. §1. 147 *note*, Some attempt to father on the Christian Church the limitations and orders of the Jewish priesthood. **1885** *Law Times* LXXIX. 190/2 The word 'land' is to bear the meaning which is fathered upon it by sub-sect. 10 (i.).

†**7.** With complement: To assert to be (something) in origin; to declare to have been originally.

1606 WARNER *Alb. Eng.* XIV. lxxxiii. (1612) 346 The Scots.. do father it The Stone that Iacob.. Did sleepe vpon. **1620–55** I. JONES *Stone-Heng* (1725) 13 Jeffrey Monmouth.. was the first.. that father'd Stone-Heng their Monument.

†**'father-,age**. *Obs.* [f. FATHER *sb.* + AGE.]

a. The time of life when one is a father; hence, a mature age. **b.** An age earlier than the present, a period gone by.

1596 Q. ELIZ. *Let.* in Tytler *Hist. Scot.* (1864) IV. 350 Were it in the nonage of a prince, it might have some colour; but in a Father-age it seemeth strange. **1633** P. FLETCHER *Purple Isl.* I. ix, Tell me, ye Muses, what our father-ages Have left succeeding times to play upon.

fathered ('fɑːðəd), *ppl. a. rare.* [f. as prec. + -ED².] Provided with or having a father.

1601 SHAKS. *Jul. C.* II. i. 297 Thinke you, I am no stronger than my Sex Being so Father'd, and so Husbanded? **1605** —— *Lear* III. vi. 117 That which makes me bend makes the king bow, He childed as I father'd! **1856** MRS. BROWNING *Aur. Leigh* VI. 648 Not much worse off in being fatherless Than I was, fathered.

fatherhood ('fɑːðəhʊd); also †**fatherhead**. Forms: α. 4–5 fader-, -ir-, -ur-, -yr-, -hed(e, -heed, 5 fatherhed(e, 6 (fathered), *Sc.* fatherheid, 6–7 fatherhead. β. 5 fader-, -ir-, -hode, -hood, (fathyrod), 6 fatherhode, -hoode, 6– fatherhood. [f. FATHER *sb.* + -HOOD, -HEAD.]

1. a. The attribute of being a father; the relation of a father to a child; paternity. Also in spiritual sense.

c **1380** WYCLIF *Sel. Wks.* III. 179 Frute of such fadurhede schal be joye of heven. **1579–80** NORTH *Plutarch* (1676) 21 Patres Conscripti, which is a name of Father-head. *a* **1647** FILMER *Patriarcha* i. §9 (1884) 19 The right of fatherhood. **1759** JOHNSON *Let. to Simpson* in *Boswell*, In his refusal to assist you there is neither good nature, fatherhood, nor wisdom. **1866** GEO. ELIOT *F. Holt* (1868) 119 I'll lay hold of them by their fatherhood.

transf. **1889** *Boys' Own Paper* 23 Mar. 400/1 The fatherhood of the game [stool-ball] to cricket is unmistakable.

b. applied to God in his relation to mankind.

1611 PERKINS *Cases Consc.* (1619) 368 He beares in his person the image of Gods paternitie, or father-hoode. *c* **1620** DONNE *Serm.* xxxviii. 380 Now we consider God in a two-fold Paternity a two-fold Fatherhood. **1830** E. IRVING in Mackintosh *Life* II. 477 We pray for those orphans who have been deprived of their parents and are now thrown on the fatherhood of God. **1876** A. SWANWICK in *Contemp. Rev.* June 116 This conception of the universal Fatherhood of God..has changed..the aspect of the world.

c. with especial reference to *Eph.* iii. 15 after the Vulgate rendering (*paternitas*).

1382 WYCLIF *Eph.* iii. 15 Oure Lord Jhesu Crist, of whom ech fadirheed in heuenes and in erthe is named. **1583** GOLDING *Calvin on Deut.* xxxvi. 214 We heare that all fatherhoode proceedeth of God. **1588** A. KING tr. *Canisius' Catech., Prayers* 36 To the Father..frome quhome al fatherheid in heauen and earth is named.

¶**d.** *confused use.* The attribute of having a certain father.

1846 KEBLE *Lyra Innoc., Children Like Parents* 7 To descry The welcome notes of fatherhood, In form, and lip, and eye. **1878** GROSART *H. More's Poems* Mem. Introd. 41/1 His conception of our common Fatherhood and Brotherhood was Christ-like.

e. The position of being the 'father' or oldest member of a society, esp. of the House of Commons.

1899 *Daily News* 24 Apr. 7/3 The House decided informally that the Fatherhood rested with whoever had been longest in the House. **1907** *Westm. Gaz.* 23 May 2/3 The 'Fatherhood' of Sir Henry Campbell-Bannerman.

2. The relation of an author, originator, or perpetrator. *rare.*

1871 H. B. FORMAN *Our Living Poets* 462 Any more than Silisco and Ruggiero..lack..fatherhood to fine sayings. **1885** *Manch. Exam.* 26 Jan. 5/1 To adopt the fatherhood of such atrocities is an easy way of obtaining credit.

†**3.** Authority of or as of a father in various senses; paternal authority, headship. *Obs.*

c **1460** *Play Sacram.* 894 And in fatherhed that longyth to my dygnyte Vn to yowr grefe I wylle gyf credens. **1563-87** FOXE *A. & M.* (1596) 195/2 Yet had Becket no cause to claime fatherhood ouer the King. **1610** BP. CARLETON *Jurisd.* 4 Others..content to allowe the Pope's Fatherhood in spirituall matters. **1645** MILTON *Tetrach.* (1851) 165 Shall fatherhood, which is but man, for his own pleasure dissolve matrimony? **1690** LOCKE *Govt.* I. ii. (1694) 5 We might have had an entire Notion of this Fatherhood, or Fatherly Authority.

†**4.** The personality of a father; in ***thy, your,*** etc. ***fatherhood(s,*** a form of address, denomination, or title given: **a.** to ecclesiastics, *esp.* those of high rank. ***His Holy Fatherhood,*** the Pope. *Obs.*

c **1400** MAUNDEV. (1839) xxxi. 314 And [I] besoughte his holy fadirhode, þat my boke myghte be examyned. **1483** CAXTON *Gold. Leg.* 247/1 What thyng is in me yt hath displesyd thy faderhede. **1534** *Hildebrand* (W. de W.) A vj, Althoughe he haue fulfylled the penaunce of thy fatherhode enjoyned. **1546** BALE *Eng. Votaries* II. (1550) 22 b, Gregory the vj..had nothynge left hym, to sustayne hys owne holy fathered..but the bare offerynges and a fewe rentes there besydes. **1614** BP. HALL *Recoll. Treat.* 870 Sixe whole books, should, by their father-hoods of Trent, be..imperiously obtruded upon God, and his Church. **1641** PRYNNE *Antip.* 113 Never to make an end, till both parties hath given some possessions to his Holy Father-head. *a* **1661** FULLER *Worthies* III. 147 He reproved Pope Sergius his fatherhood, for being a father indeed to a Base Child.

b. to God.

c **1485** *Digby Myst.* (1882) III. 904 That my prayour be reswondable to þi fathyrod In glory. **1531** TINDALE *Exp. 1 John* 22 His fatherhed geueth pardon frely.

c. to a literal father; hence *gen.* to persons having a claim to respect.

c **1450** HENRYSON *Mor. Fab.* 46 Not to displease your Fatherhood. **1461** *Paston Lett.* No. 410 II. 39, I submytt me lowlely to your good faderhood. **1608** MIDDLETON *Trick to Catch Old One* I. iv, Now to the judges, 'May it please your reverend honourable fatherhoods.' **1682** BUNYAN *Holy War* 256 If what we have said shall not by thy Father-hood be thought best.

'fathering, *vbl. sb.* [f. FATHER *v.* + -ING[1].] The action of the vb. FATHER; an instance of this.

1549 COVERDALE *Erasm. Par. Rom.* i. 1 A fauourable and gentle fatheryng. *Ibid.* 6 Ye Romaines are..by adopcion & fatheryng, called all to the..Surname of Iesus Christe. **1894** 'G. EGERTON' *Discords* 60 The want-wit inconsistency that forgives the man that begat the brat and treats with pitiless scorn the helpless result of his fathering. **1894** *Athenæum* 24 Feb. 238/3 The fathering of bairns. **1894** G. DU MAURIER *Trilby* III. VII. 19 Taffy..was equal to any burden or responsibility all this instinctive young fathering might involve. **1903** *Daily Chron.* 16 Oct. 3/4 There was too much fathering. The settlers were fathered by their priests, fathered by their King. **1920** H. G. WELLS *Outl. Hist.* 122 The divine fathering and birth of Amenophis III. **1969** J. ROWE *Yours by Choice* (rev. ed.) vii. 54 Some people..look upon the fathering of an out-of-wedlock child as the 'wild oats' normally sown by young men about town.

father-in-law ('fɑːðərɪnlɔː). Also 5 fadyr in, yn, lawe, faderlaw, 6 fatherlaw. [App. *in law* = in Canon law. Cf. BROTHER-IN-LAW.]

1. The father of one's husband or wife.

c **1385** CHAUCER *L.G.W.* 2272 *Philomene*, Un-to his fadyr in lawe gan he preye. **1467** *Mann. & Househ. Exp.* 172 John Hobes and is faderlaw. *a* **1533** LD. BERNERS *Huon* lxiv. 221 Gerard called to hym his father in law, his wyfes father. **1598** CHAPMAN *Iliad* III. 187 The fairest of her sex replied: Most reverend father-in-law, Most loved, most fear'd. *a* **1704** T. BROWN *Eng. Sat.* Wks. 1730 I. 25 This ungenerous father-in-law..discreetly hanged himself. **1843** BETHUNE *Sc. Fireside Stor.* 51 We are before the door of your intended father-in-law.

fig. **1650** B. *Discolliminium* 15 Pretended Necessity [is] the Father-in-law of intended iniquity.

2. = STEPFATHER. Now commonly regarded as a misuse.

1552 HULOET, Father in lawe, *vitricus.* **1594** SHAKS. *Rich. III*, v. iii. 81 All comfort that the darke night can affoord, Be to thy Person, Noble Father in Law. **1598** GRENEWEY *Tacitus' Ann.* III. vi. (1622) 72 A..band of alliance..betwixt the father in law, and his wiues children. **1748** RICHARDSON *Clarissa* IV. xxiii. 122 Nancy could not bear a father-in-law. **1773** GOLDSM. *Stoops to Conq.* I. ii, Father-in-law has been calling me a whelp and hound. **1838** DICKENS *Nich. Nick.* iv, I am not their father, I'm only their father-in-law. **1876** GEO. ELIOT *Dan. Der.* lvi, I did not like my father-in-law to come home.

Hence **father-in-law** *v. nonce-wd.*, to call (a man) father-in-law.

1749 FIELDING *Tom Jones* XV. v, I'll teach you to father-in-law me.

†**'fatherkin.** *Obs.* [OE. *fæder cyn* (= ON. *fǫður kyn*), f. *fæder*, genit. of *fæder* FATHER + *cyn* KIN. OE. had also *fæd(e)ren cyn*, where the former word is an adj.] Descent by the father's side.

O.E. Chron. an. 755 §3 And hiera ryht fæder cyn gæþ to Cerdice. [*a* **1000** *Crist.* 248 (Gr.) Nu we areccan ne magon þæt fædrencynn.] *c* **1440** *Promp. Parv.* 145 Fadyrkyn, or modyrkyn, *parentela.* **1556** J. HEYWOOD *Spider & F.* xxxix. 71 From which grownd..by my fatherkin I will not starte.

fatherland ('fɑːðəlænd). [f. FATHER *sb.* + LAND.]

1. The land of one's birth, one's country. †*in fatherland*, at home (opp. to *abroad*). Cf. MOTHER-COUNTRY.

1623 WODROEPHE *Marrow Fr. Tongue* 270, I thanke my lucke that hath caused me to find here my Countryman, and one of my Fatherland. **1635** T. ODELL (*title*), A brief and short Treatise called the Christian's Fatherland. **1683** F. ELLIS *Let.* in *Hedges' Diary* (1887) 120, I hope..to meet with much better [Justice] in Father-Land for ye inexpressable damage done me. **1799** W. TAYLOR in *Monthly Mag.* VII. 399 Through thee alone the father-land is dear. **1840** GEN. P. THOMPSON *Exerc.* (1842) V. 130 Returning to their fatherland in peace. **1873** SYMONDS *Grk. Poets* v. 138 Stesichorus acknowledged an Ionian colony for his fatherland.

b. Used to translate the Dutch or German *vaderland, vaterland.* ***the Fatherland***: now usually = Germany.

1672 TEMPLE *Ess. Govt.* Wks. 1731 I. 100 The Dutch..instead of our Country, say our Father-land. **1791-1823** D'ISRAELI *Cur. Lit.* (1858) III. 31 The glorious history of its independence under the title of *Vaderlandsche Historie*—the history of Father-land. **1839** W. CHAMBERS *Tour Holland* 9/1 The attachment which the Dutch show to their Vaderland, or Fatherland, as they commonly term it. **1864** *Macm. Mag.* Oct. 433 Its [Tübingen's] famous University ..more identified with the spiritual..development of Germany than any other single institution in the Father-land. **1874** MORLEY *Compromise* (1886) 6 A German has his dream of a great fatherland.

2. The land of one's fathers; mother-country.

1822 W. IRVING *Braceb. Hall* I. 13 The ancient and genuine characteristics of my father land. **1831** *Blackw. Mag.* Sept. 528/2 They [the Americans] look to a dreadful breaking-up of those old establishments, under the shelter of which have grown..the liberties of their 'father-land' [Great Britain].

Hence **'fatherlandish** *a.* [+ -ISH], of, or pertaining to, one's fatherland.

1832 tr. *Tour Germ. Prince* III. x. 279 Two genuine Nürnberg housewives, dressed in their fatherlandish caps. *Ibid.* IV. ii. 117 The immoveable and unchangeable fatherlandish friend,—the majestic Mont Blanc.

'fatherlandless, *a.* [tr. G. *vaterlandslos.*] Unpatriotic.

1898 *Daily News* 11 July 3/4 A Conservative Deputy at Dirschau lately called five Liberal electors who voted for the Polish candidate 'Vaterlandlose gesellen' (unpatriotic 'Fatherlandless' fellows). **1915** T. F. A. SMITH *Soul of Germany* 274 Every Socialist, in my opinion, means an enemy to Empire and Fatherland. They are the Fatherlandless enemies of the divine order of things.

'father-'lasher. The name of two species of sea-fish, *Cottus bubalis* and *scorpius.*

1674 RAY *Collect. Words, Fishes* 104 *Father-lasher*, Cornubiensibus pueris dictus: Scorpæna Bellony. **1740** R. BROOKES *Art of Angling* II. xx. 125 The Father-lasher..when full-grown does not exceed nine Inches in length. **1863** COUCH *Fishes Brit. Isl.* II. 9 The Father-lasher, or Sting-fish, will live long out of the water.

fatherless ('fɑːðəlɪs), *a.* [See -LESS.

In the OE. *feadur-léas* the first element is the normal form (not elsewhere occurring) corresponding to ON. *fǫður* genitive of *faðer*; the word is therefore not in origin a true compound, but a syntactic combination; cf. ON. *fǫðurlauss.*]

1. Having no father.

c **1205** LAY. 21897 þu hauest..vre children imaken faderlese. *a* **1225** *Ancr. R.* 10 Helpen widewen & federlease children. *a* **1340** HAMPOLE *Psalter* ix. 42 þe fadirles barn. *c* **1450** *Merlin* II. 35 Sholde ye not haue sought the fadirles childe. **1549** *Bk. Com. Prayer* Litany, That it may please thee to..provide for the fatherlesse children and widows. **1594** SHAKS. *Rich. III.* II. ii. 64 Our fatherlesse distresse was left vnmoan'd. **1600** HOLLAND *Livy* II. 76 The commonwealth was half fatherlesse as it were, for the losse of a Consull. **1719** J. RICHARDSON *Sc. Connoisseur* 127 We can be satisfied we are not..exposed here in a Fatherless World. **1801** SOUTHEY *Thalaba* I. ii, The widow'd mother and the fatherless boy. **1873** SYMONDS *Grk. Poets* vii. 229 How shall I, Brotherless, friendless, fatherless, alone, Live on?

absol. *c* **1000** *Ags. Ps.* xciii. [xciv.] 6 Widwan & wrecan of-sloȝun & feadur-lease of-sloȝun. *c* **1300** *Havelok* 75 To þe faderles was he rath. **1382** WYCLIF *Jas.* i. 27 Pupilles, that is, fadirles or modirles or bothe. **1611** BIBLE *Ps.* lxviii. 5 A father of the fatherlesse. *c* **1737** DODSLEY *Epit. Q. Caroline* Misc. (1777) 227 Ask the cries of the Fatherless, they shall tell thee. **1813** SHELLEY *Q. Mab* III. 28 Hearest thou not The curses of the fatherless?

2. Of a book, etc.: Without a known author; anonymous. *Obs.* exc. with intentional metaphor.

1611 BEAUM. & FL. *Philaster* IV. ii, There's already a thousand fatherless tales amongst us. **1641** R. BROOKE *Eng. Episc.* II. i. 67 A fatherlesse Treatise of Timothy's Martyrdome. **1732** *London Mag.* I. 78 To call that a fatherless Story. **1803** *Pic Nic* No. 14 (1806) II. 261 She humanely adopted several fatherless essays..that were wandering about the world.

Hence **'fatherlessness,** fatherless condition.

1727-36 in BAILEY. **1832** in WEBSTER; and in later Dicts.

fatherlike ('fɑːðəlaɪk), *a.* and *adv.* [f. as prec. + -LIKE.] Like a father.

A. *adj.*

†**1.** Resembling one's father. *Obs.*

c **1425** WYNTOUN *Cron.* VII. vi. 135 Fadyre-lyk in all hys Dedis. **1614** R. WILKINSON *Paire Serm.* 11 It were well for the child, if it were not so fatherlike..as it is.

2. Having the aspect and bearing of a father.

1887 *Pall Mall G.* 5 Apr. 2/1 One of the most loveable and father-like men I have ever seen.

3. Such as is proper to a father; such as a father would do; fatherly.

1570 LEVINS *Manip.* 122 Fatherlike, *paternus.* **1581** MARBECK *Bk. of Notes* 138 This manner of breaking of bread was verie fatherlike and commendable among the elders of olde time. *a* **1641** BP. MOUNTAGU *Acts & Mon.* iv. §67 (1642) 296 He gave them father-like education. **1654** FULLER *Comm. Ruth* (1868) 127 Young men will herupon take occasion..to despise their..father-like authority. **1681** W. ROBERTSON *Phraseol. Gen.* (1693) 1079 This is right father-like. **1876** *Whitby Gloss., Faather-like*, fatherly.

B. *adv.* As a father, in a fatherly manner.

1604 DRAYTON *Owl* 539 How father-like he gives affliction bread. **1675** BROOKS *Gold. Key* Wks. 1867 V. 567 Observe how fatherlike he melts and mourns over them. **1834** H. F. LYTE *Hymn, 'Praise my Soul,'* Father-like he tends and spares us. **1864** TENNYSON *En. Ard.* 154 The feeble infant..Whom Enoch took..and fondled fatherlike.

fatherliness ('fɑːðəlɪnɪs). [f. FATHERLY *a.* + -NESS.] The quality of being fatherly; fatherly character, function, or feeling.

1551 CHEKE *Matt.* Let. iv. (1843) 116 His fatherlines in life, his authoritee in knowlege. **1662** J. CHANDLER *Van Helmont's Oriat.* 147 Although a fleshly Father doth give of his own, whence the name of Paternity or fatherliness is given unto him. **1727-36** in BAILEY. **1820** L. HUNT *Indicator* No. 16 (1822) I. 124 Ah, young gentleman, said he (for so he called me in the fatherliness of his age). **1856** *Lit. Churchman* II. 90/1 The fatherliness of God, as distinguished from His justice.

fatherling ('fɑːðəlɪŋ). (Only in nonce-uses.) [f. FATHER *sb.* + -LING.] A little father. Used **a.** as an affectionate mode of address; **b.** in contempt.

1625 USSHER *Answ. Jesuit* 282 These bastard fatherlings in their Nicene Creed, did not onely insert this clause..but, etc. **1826** *Blackw. Mag.* XX. 847 In what nation..but the German, does a daughter address her father as her 'dear little fatherling'?

father-long-legs. = DADDY-LONG-LEGS (the cranefly, and long-legged spider).

1796 MORSE *Amer. Geog.* I. 226 *Father Long Legs*, Phalangium. Several species. **1808** *Sporting Mag.* XXXI. 169 A spider, or a father long legs. **1856** MISS YONGE *Daisy Chain* II. xxii. (1879) 600 Mary climbs like a cow, and Ethel like a father-long-legs.

fatherly ('fɑːðəlɪ), *a.* [OE. *fæderlic*, f. *fæder*, FATHER + *-lic*: see -LY[1].]

†**1.** Of or pertaining to a (natural or spiritual) father; paternal. *Obs.*

1599 SHAKS. *Much Ado* IV. i. 75 By that fatherly and kindly power, That you haue in her. **1626** L. OWEN *Spec. Jesuit.* (1629) 33 Of his owne meere fatherly and Apostaticall motion. *a* **1633** LENNARD tr. *Charron's Wisd.* I. xlvii. §3 (1670) 174 Now this fatherly power..is almost of it self lost and abolished.

†**b.** Of or pertaining to ancestors; ancestral. Hence also, Venerable. *Obs.*

a **1000** *Elene* 431 (Gr.) þy læs..þa fæderlican lare [sien] forlæten. **1581** SIDNEY *Apol. Poetrie* (Arb.) 48 Poetrie is..of most fatherly antiquitie. **1634** CANNE *Necess. Separ.* (1849) 154 Ecclesiastical decrees, constitutions, provincial and synodal statutes, fatherly customs.

2. Resembling a father: †**a.** In age, hence, venerable (*obs.*). **b.** In character or demeanour.

1577 NORTHBROOKE *Dicing* (1843) 19 That place is more fitte for such olde fatherly men as you are, than for such yong men as I am. **1583** STUBBES *Anat. Abus.* II. (1882) 71 The bishops are graue, ancient, and fatherlie men. **1777** MAD. D'ARBLAY *Early Diary* (1889) II. 277 How friendly, and fatherly, sweet soul! **1832** L. HUNT *Sir R. Esher* (1850) 89 A gentleman..who..having no children is so fatherly as to take care of the children of others. **1867** O. W. HOLMES *Guardian Angel* iv. (1891) 47 He had been fatherly with Susan Posey.

3. Of the feelings and conduct: Such as is proper in or from a father; natural to a father; paternal.

c **1440** *Gesta Rom.* lii. 232 (Harl. MS.) Crist..hathe to vs a fadirlye affeccion. **1482** *Monk of Evesham* (Arb.) 28 Y.. thankid him that he wolde white safe to chaste me..in a fadyrly chastment. **1526** *Pilgr. Perf.* (W. de W. 1531) 198 The father of heuen shewed hymselfe in a fatherly voyce, sayenge. **1533** GAU *Richt Vay* (1888) 86 Lat vsz knaw thy faderlie lwiff. **1623** JAS. I in Ellis *Orig. Lett.* I. 283. III. 141 With my fatherlie blessing. **1649** BP. HALL *Cases Consc.* III. iv. 264 Humbly to submit yourselfe to his fatherly directions. **1776** FOOTE *Bankrupt* II. Wks. 1799 II. 122 Perhaps it was a fatherly weakness. **1801** SOUTHEY *Thalaba* x. xiii, 'Twas fear, Fatherly fear and love. **1828** D'ISRAELI *Chas. I*, I. ii. 16 The fatherly admonition was received in silence.

fatherly ('fɑːðəlɪ), *adv.* [f. FATHER *sb.* + -LY².] In a fatherly manner, as a father; with a father's care and affection.

a **1500** *Orol. Sap.* in *Anglia* X. 364, I am so fadirly admonestid. **1589** *Pasquil's Return* D ij, Exhorting him fatherlie to giue ouer that course. *a* **1723** I. MATHER *Vind. New Eng.* in *Andros Tracts* II. (1869) 27 God hath for a while Fatherly Chastised them by those Rods. *c* **1848** LOWELL *Changeling*, I cannot lift it up fatherly, And bliss it upon my breast. **1853** MRS. BROWNING *Poems, Runaway Slave*, The sky..That great smooth Hand of God stretched out On all his children fatherly.

fathership ('fɑːðəʃɪp). [f. FATHER *sb.* + -SHIP.] **a.** The position, state or relation of a father; paternity, fatherhood. †Also in ***His Fathership***: the personality of an ecclesiastical father.

1583 GOLDING *Calvin on Deut.* lxxx. 489 Let vs beware of such maner of fathership. **1670** G. H. *Hist. Cardinals* I. II. 60 His Fathership. **1755** JOHNSON, *Paternity*, fathership; the relation of a father. **1809** SOUTHEY *Lett.* (1856) II. 168 After the fathership, and sonship, and all the other ships have been exhausted. **1871** *Sat. Rev.* 15 Apr. 457 There was not a throne which did not acknowledge in his [the Pope's] fathership the palladium of its liberty and strength. **1875** M. COLLINS *Blacksmith & Scholar, etc.* (1876) III. 107 The man whose fathership she disowned. **1890** T. W. ALLIES *Peter's Rock* 468 The civil bond sprung from a spiritual fathership.

b. = FATHERHOOD I e.

1899 *Westm. Gaz.* 28 Dec. 3/3 The 'Fathership' falls upon Lord Templemore. **1901** *Ibid.* 22 Apr. 1/1 The successor of the late Mr. Villiers in the 'fathership' of the House of Commons. **1910** *Ibid.* 16 Feb. 2/3 Mr. Balfour..lost his chance of the 'Fathership' by a like accident.

fathogram ('fæðəʊgræm). [f. FATHO(METER + -GRAM.] A tracing, made by an echo-sounder, representing the varying depth of water beneath a moving vessel.

1950 *Internat. Hydrogr. Rev.* XXVII. 56 If both vessels operate their echo sounders..the depth record may be almost impossible to interpret. Diagonal streaks across the fathogram are an indication of interference. **1953** J. Y. COUSTEAU *Silent World* xii. 124 My mind leaped back to the recording of the deep scattering layer. The coincidence of the whale's lunch and the lines drawn on the fathogram may have been entirely fortuitous. **1966** SHEPARD & DILL *Submarine Canyons* ii. 19 The inverted V that often appears on a fathogram below the crossing of the canyon profile may indicate the true depth of the canyon floor.

†'**fatholt**. *Sc. Obs. rare.* [? a. Du. *vathout*, f. *vat* cask + *hout* wood.] ? Staves for casks.

1543 *Aberd. Reg.* V. 18 (Jam.), xij hundreth fatholt at fourty sh. the hundreth.

fathom ('fæðəm), *sb.* Forms: 1 **fæðm**, **fædm**, 2–4 **fedme**, 4 **feþme**, **fademe**, 3 **fadim**, (**fadum**, **fathum**, *south.* **veðme**), 4–5 **fadme**, 4–6 **fadom(e**, 5–6 **fadam(e**, **fathem**, (*Sc.* **fadowme**, **fawdom(e**, 5 **fadmen**, **fadym**, *south.* **vathym**, **veth(e)ym**, 6 **faddam**, **feddom**, *Sc.* **faldom**, **faudom**, *south.* **vadome**), 6 **fatham(e**, 6–7 **fathome**, 7 **faddom(e**, 7– **fathom**. [OE. *fæðm* str. masc. (also fem.) corresponds to OFris. *fethm* sing., OS. *fathmôs* pl., the two arms outstretched (Du. *vadem*, *vaam*, measure of 6 feet), OHG. *fadum* cubit (mod.G. *faden* measure of 6 feet), ON. *faþmr* (Icel. *faðmr*, Da. *favn*, Sw. *famn*) the outstretched arms, embrace, bosom, also measure of 6 feet:—OTeut. **faþmo-z*, cognate with Goth. *faþa*, MHG. *vade* enclosure, f. Teut. root *feþ-*, *faþ-*:—pre-Teut. *pet-*, *pot-*, whence also Gr. πέταλος spreading, broad, πεταννύναι to spread out.

Formally identical with this word are the MDu. *vadem*, OHG. *fadum*, *fadam* (MHG. *vadem*, *vaden*, mod.G. *faden*), thread; cf. OWelsh *etem* in same sense. Possibly the two widely divergent senses of the type **faþmo-* may be explained as different applications of the etymological sense 'stretching out'.]

†**1.** In *pl.* The embracing arms; in *sing.* = BOSOM I b. OE. only.

a **1000** *Riddles* xxvii. 25 (Gr.) Freonda þy ma þa..hi lufan fæðmum fæste clyppað. *a* **1000** *Andreas* 825 (Gr.) Ða..het lifes brytta..englas sine, fæðmum ferigean..leofne.

†**b.** *fig.* Grasp, power. *Obs.*

Beowulf 1210 Ʒehwearf þa in Francna fæðm feorh cyninges. *a* **1000** *Crist* 1486 (Gr.) Þe ic alysde me feondum of fæðme. **1607** MIDDLETON *Michaelm. Term* Induct., I grasp best part of the autumnian blessing In my contentious fathom. **1622** FLETCHER *Prophetess* II. i, He beleeves the earth is in his fadom.

†**c.** The object of embrace, the 'wife of thy bosom'. *Obs. rare*⁻¹.

1602 DEKKER *Satiromastix* Wks. 1873 I. 209 Thy Bride.. She that is now thy fadom.

2. †**a.** A stretching of the arms in a straight line to their full extent. Also in ***to make a fathom***.

1519 HORMAN *Vulg.* 29 The length..fro the both toppys of his myddell fyngers, whan he maketh a vadome. **1607** TOPSELL *Four-f. Beasts* 717 The first of these hornes..being of the length of my fadome. **1646** SIR T. BROWNE *Pseud. Ep.* IV. v. 191 The extent of his fathome..is equall unto the space between the soale of the foot and the crowne. **1785** BURNS *Halloween* xxiii. *note*, Take an opportunity of going.. to a bean-stack, and fathom it three times round. The last fathom of the last time you will catch in your arms the appearance of your future conjugal yoke-fellow.

b. *fig.* Breadth of comprehension, grasp of intellect; ability. *Obs.* exc. *arch.*

1604 SHAKS. *Oth.* I. i. 153 Another of his Fadome, they haue none. **1827** T. HAMILTON *Cyril Thornton* (1845) 89 This..is beyond my fathom to determine.

3. A measure of length.

†**a.** The length of the forearm; a CUBIT. *Obs.*

c **1000** ÆLFRIC *Gloss.* in Wr.-Wülcker 158/10 *Cubitum*, Fæðm betwux elboȝan and handwyrste. *c* **1000** —— *Gen.* vi. 15 Þreo hund faþma biþ se arc on lenȝe. *a* **1175** *Cott. Hom.* 225 An arc þreo hund fedme lang. *c* **1205** LAY. 27686 Þat sper þurh ræhte fulle ane ueðme. *a* **1300** *Cursor M.* 21532 (Gött.) He right depe had doluen dare, Ma þan tuenti fadim or mare. *c* **1440** *Promp. Parv.* 145 Fadme, or fadyme, *ulna*.

b. The length covered by the outstretched arms, including the hands to the tip of the longest finger; hence, a definite measure of 6 feet (formerly for some purposes less: see quot. 1751), now chiefly used in taking soundings (but see quot. 1968).

a **800** *Corpus Gloss.*, *Passus*, faeðm, *uel* tueȝen stridi. *c* **1300** *K. Alis.* 546 His taile was fyve fedme long. *c* **1400** *Rom. Rose* 1393 These trees were sette..One from another in assise Five fadme or sixe. *c* **1450** *Merlin* 31 This tour is iij or iiij fadom of height. *a* **1490** BOTONER *Itin.* (Nasmith 1778) 175 Arches of x vethym yn hyth. **1496** *Ld. Treas. Acct. Scot.* (1877) I. 291, vj fawdome of smal pailȝoune tow, ilk fawdome ij d. **1526** TINDALE *Acts* xxvii. 28 The ship-men.. sounded and founde it .xx. feddoms. **1580** BARET *Alv.* F 199 As big as four men could compasse with their armes, or foure fathom broade. **1610** SHAKS. *Temp.* I. ii. 396 Full fadom fiue thy Father lies. **1643** WINTHROP *Jrnl.* (1790) 325 They..presented the court with twenty-six fathom more of wampom. **1688** R. HOLME *Armoury* III. 163/2 The deepness of Water is sounded by Faddoms. **1748** *Anson's Voy.* III. ii. 219 We could not find ground with sixty fathom of line. **1751** CHAMBERS *Cycl.* s.v., There are three kinds of fathoms ..The first, which is that of men of war, contains six feet; the middling, or that of merchant ships, five feet and a half; and the small fathom, used in fluyets, fly-boats, and other fishing-vessels, only five feet. **1814** SCOTT *Ld. of Isles* III. xx, 'Where lies your bark?' 'Ten fathom deep in ocean dark!' **1865** LIVINGSTONE *Zambesi* ix. 197 We..handed him two fathoms of cotton cloth. **1878** HUXLEY *Physiogr.* 176 The Gulf Stream itself is not more than 100 fathoms deep. **1968** *Guardian* 26 Apr. 1/1 The fathom..is to disappear from British Admiralty charts. In future sea depths will be marked in metres.

†**c.** (See quots.; perh. some error.) *Obs.*

1692–1708 COLES, *Fathom*, three Feet in length. **1751** CHAMBERS *Cycl.* s.v., Fathom is..used in several countries, particularly Italy, for the common yard or ell.

d. in *pl.* Depths. *lit.* and *fig.* Also in *fig.* expressions ***fathoms deep***, ***fathoms down***; cf. 6.

1608 MIDDLETON *Trick to Catch Old One* III. i, Swallow up his father..Within the fathoms of his conscience. **1611** SHAKS. *Wint. T.* IV. iv. 502 All..the profound seas, hides In vnknowne fadomes. **1880** MISS BRADDON *Just as I am* xviii, You will sink fathoms deep in my respect.

4. *Mining* (see quot. 1881).

1778 W. PRYCE *Min. Cornub.* Gloss. 320/1 Work in the Cornish Mines, is generally performed by the fathom. **1872** RAYMOND *Statist. Mines & Mining* 315 [Cost of] stoping $12 or $18 per fathom [of ore]. **1881** —— *Mining Gloss.*, A fathom of mining ground is six feet square by the whole thickness of the vein.

5. A certain quantity of wood; now, a quantity 6 ft. square in section, whatever the length may be.

1577 HARRISON *England* II. xxii. (1877) I. 340 Our tanners buie the barke..by the fadame. **1669** WORLIDGE *Syst. Agric.* (1681) 317 A Fathom of Wood is a parcel of Wood set out, six whereof make a Coal Fire. **1681** BLOUNT *Glossogr.*, When a Ship is past service they saw the wood of it in length, and sell it by the fathom, which is six foot, two broad, and six high. **1835** *Tariff Tables* in McCulloch *Dict. Commerce* 1133 Lathwood in pieces under 5 feet in length, per fathom, 6 feet wide and 6 feet high [duty] £4 5*s.* *od.*; 12 feet long or upwards, per fathom, 6 feet wide and 6 feet high, £13 12*s.* *od.* **1875** T. LASLETT *Timber & Timber Trees* 252, 18000 fathoms of firewood were imported into London in 1874.

6. *attrib.* and *Comb.*, as ***fathom lot***; **fathom-deep** *a.* = *fathoms deep* (see 3 d), excessively deep; **fathom-fish** *western N. Amer.* = OOLAKAN; **fathom health**, a health (drunk) fathoms deep; **fathom line**, the line used in testing the depth of the sea in fathoms; also *fig.*; **fathom-proof** (*nonce-wd.*), unfathomable; **fathom-tale** (*Mining*), a fixed sum for every fathom excavated; **fathom-wood** [cf. Sw. *famnved*, Ger. *fadenholz*] (see quot. 1867).

1835 *Edin. Rev.* Apr. 75 *Fathom-deep in murders and debaucheries. **1850** TENNYSON *In Mem.* x. 18 If..the roaring wells Should gulf him fathom-deep in brine. **1849** A. ROSS *Adv. Oregon River* (1904) vi. 109 To prepare them [*sc.* the ulichans] for a distant market, they are laid side by side, head and tail alternately, and then a thread run through both extremities links them together, in which state they are dried, smoked, and sold by the fathom, hence they have obtained the name of *fathom-fish. **1897** E. COUES *New Light Greater Northwest* II. 787 Another name of these 'smelts' was fathom-fish, given because they were strung on strings and sold by the fathom. **1600** DEKKER *Gentle Craft* Wks. 1873 I. 71 Carowse mee *fadome healths to the honour of the shoomakers. **1596** SHAKS. *1 Hen. IV*, I. iii. 204 The deepe, Where *Fadome-line could neuer touch the ground. **1816** BYRON *Pr. of Chillon* vi, The fathom-line was sent From Chillon's snow-white battlement. **1821** SHELLEY *Epipsych.* 90 The brief fathom-line of thought or sense. **1792** *Elizabeth Percy* I. 91 As if he thought what passed, a smooth surface, but not *fathom-proof. **1881** RAYMOND *Mining Gloss.*, *Fathom-tale..probably arises from the payment for such work by the space excavated, and not by the ore produced. **1867** SMYTH *Sailor's Word-bk.*, *Fathom-wood*, slab and other offal of timber, sold at the yards, by fathom lots.

fathom ('fæðəm), *v.* Forms: 1 **fæðmian**, 3 **fadme**, 4 **faþme**, 6–7 **fadom(e**, **fathame**, 7 **fathome**, 7– **fathom**. [OE. *fæðmian* = OHG. *fademôn*, ON. *faþma* (Icel. *faðma*, Da. *favne*, Sw. *famna*) :—OTeut. **faþmôjan*, f. **faþmo-* FATHOM *sb.*]

1. *trans.* To encircle with extended arms.

c **1300** *Havelok* 1295 And mine armes weren so longe, That I fadmede, al at ones, Denemark, with mine longe bones. **1637** POCKLINGTON *Altare Chr.* 91 It contained too many Cubits for him to..fathome it round about. **1646** J. HALL *Horæ Vac.* 71 No man ought to graspe more then he can well fathome. **1775** in ASH. **1810** J. HODGSON *Let.* in Raine *Mem.* (1857) I. 65 Ten trunks each more than I can fathom. **1828** SCOTT *Jrnl.* II. 187 Trees..so thick that a man could not fathom them.

transf. and *fig.*

Beowulf 3133 Hie..leton..flod fæð mian frætwa hyrde. *a* **1000** *Andreas* 1574 (Gr.) Wæter fæðmedon. **1626** MASSINGER *Rom. Actor* v. i. Caesar..in his arms Fathoming the earth. **1644** DIGBY *Nat. Bodies* Ded. (1658) 15 Flashy wits..cannot fadom the whole extent of a large discourse.

†**b.** To clasp or embrace (a person). ***to fathom together***: to embrace mutually. *Obs.*

13.. *E.E. Allit. P.* B. 399 Frendez fellen in fere faþmed to-geder. *c* **1440** *Promp. Parv.* 145 Fadmyn (fadomyn, P.), *ulno*. **1629** T. ADAMS *Fatall Banket, Shot* Wks. 1861 I. 242 Lascivious Delilahs..fadomed him in the arms of lust.

2. Of two or more persons: To encircle by extending the arms in line, with the view of measuring the girth. *Obs.* exc. *arch.*

1555 EDEN *Decades* 68 Seuen men..with theyr armes streached furthe were scarsely able too fathame them [trees] aboute. **1652–62** HEYLYN *Cosmogr.* III. (1682) 148 Stocks of Vines..as big in bulk as two men can fathom. **1724** R. FALCONER *Voy.* (1769) 135 Mr. Musgrave and I could but just fathom it. **1874** DASENT *Tales fr. Fjeld* 261 We will fathom it [a tree] and then we shall soon see.

b. Of one person: To measure in fathoms by means of the two outstretched arms. *rare.*

1680 *Play-bill* in Rendle & Norman *Inns Old Southwk.*, He [the Gyant] now reaches ten foot and a half, fathoms near eight feet, spans fifteen inches. **1785** BURNS [see FATHOM *sb.* 2 a].

†**3.** *intr.* ***to fathom about***: to try what the arms will take in; to grope *about*. *Obs. rare.*

13.. *E.E. Allit. P.* C. 273 Þer he festnes þe fete & fathmez aboute, & stod vp in his stomak.

4. *trans.* To measure with a fathom-line; to ascertain the depth of (water); to sound.

1634 BRERETON *Trav.* (1844) 5 Fathoming the depth of the water over against Brill, we found [etc.]. **1665** SIR T. HERBERT *Trav.* (1677) 253 In other places..[the Ocean] never hitherto has been fathomed. **1721–1800** in BAILEY. **1860** MAURY *Phys. Geog. Sea* xiii. §563 Attempts to fathom the ocean, both by sound and pressure.

fig. **1613** HIERON *Spirit. Sonne-ship* ii. *Serm.* 372 This loue, to bee Sonnes, who can fadome it? **1642** R. CARPENTER *Experience* v. xvii. 314 O God, who can fadome thy eternity? **1681** DRYDEN *Abs. & Achit.* 742 To sound the depths and fathom..The Peoples hearts. **1732** BERKELEY *Alciphr.* VI. §17 An abyss of wisdom which our line cannot fathom. **1875** HAMERTON *Intell. Life* VIII. i. 281 A..French nobleman whose ignorance I have frequent opportunities of fathoming.

b. To get to the bottom of, dive into, penetrate, see through, thoroughly understand.

1625 MASSINGER *New Way* v. i, The..statesman.. believes he fathoms The counsels of all Kingdoms on the earth. **1686** J. SMITH *Baroscope* 91 Causes..very difficult for Human Wit to Fathom. **1748** *Anson's Voy.* III. ix. 400 There was some treachery designed him, which he could not yet fathom. **1781** MAD. D'ARBLAY *Diary* May, [His] character I am at this moment unable to fathom. **1839** KEIGHTLEY *Hist. Eng.* I. 443 He could conceal his own designs and fathom those of others. **1853** C. BRONTË *Villette* xxxvii. (1876) 416, I saw something in that lad's eye I never quite fathomed.

5. *intr.* To take soundings. *lit.* and *fig.* Also, †***to fathom into***: to enquire into.

1607 TOURNEUR *Rev. Trag.* I. iii, And deeply fadom'd into all estates. **1751** R. PALTOCK *P. Wilkins* (1884) I. 84 When fathoming, I could find no bottom. **1855** MILMAN *Lat. Chr.* (1864) III. VI. ii. 389 The philosopher..went fathoming on ..in the very abysses of human thought. **1878** BROWNING *La Saisiaz* 72, I can fathom by no plummet-line sunk in life's apparent laws.

fathomable ('fæðəməb(ə)l), *a.* [f. FATHOM *v.* + -ABLE.] **a.** Capable of being fathomed or sounded.

1697 DAMPIER *Voy.* (1698) I. 531 Southward of all the Soundings, or fathomable ground. **1727** in BAILEY vol. II.

b. *fig.* Comprehensible; intelligible.

1633 AMES *Agst. Cerem.* II. 178 These [arguments].. seeming more fadomable. **1647** BP. HALL *Satan's fiery darts quenched* III. vi. 303 Things..not fadomeable by reason.

1781 MAD. D'ARBLAY *Diary* 26 June, Mr. Crutchley.. continues the least fathomable.. of all men I have seen. **1896** *Daily News* 27 May 6/6 No doubt, if the mystery of these rays is fathomable, he will fathom it.

fathomer ('fæðəmə(r)). Also 6–7 **fadomer**, 7 **feathomer**. [f. as prec. + -ER[1].]

1. One who fathoms: in the senses of the vb.

1598 FLORIO, *Scandagliatore*.. a fadomer of the sea. **1616** LANE *Sqr.'s T.* IX. 25 Time, the feathomer of wittes and spoile. **1660** HOWELL *Lex. Tetragl.*, A Fadomer, *toiseur*. **1790** COWPER *Iliad* I. 726 Fathomer of my conceal'd designs.

2. An instrument for ascertaining the depth of the sea (see quot.).

1823 *Mechanic's Mag.* No. 4. 59 The object of the Fathomer is to obtain soundings without heaving-to.

Fathometer (fæ'ðɒmɪtə(r)). Also **fathometer**. [f. FATHO(M + -METER.] An instrument for the determination of the depth of the sea by measuring the time taken by a sound-wave to reach the bottom and return.

1925 *Hydrographic Rev.* II. II. 140 (*heading*) The 'Fathometer' of the Submarine Signal Co. of Boston. This apparatus, also based on the same principle as that of Fessenden, differs.. by the particular feature only, *viz.* the angle to be measured is observed by means of a lighted index ..which is illuminated when it receives the reflected acoustic signal. **1927** S. H. LONG *Navigational Wireless* xi. 149 Another method of determining the sounding of a ship consists of a piece of apparatus.. called the 'Fathometer'. This instrument is based on the principle of emitting a sound wave from a sound transmitter, casuing this wave to be reflected from the sea-bed, and receiving the reflected sound wave on a receiver. **1937** *Geogr. Jrnl.* XC. 543 Her echo-sounding device (known in the U.S.A. as the Fathometer). **1971** *Islander* (Victoria, B.C.) 14 Mar. 10/3 The speedometer and log was helpful in establishing position and the fathometer very useful when entering an unfamiliar anchorage.

'fathoming, *vbl. sb.* [f. FATHOM *v.* + -ING[1].]

1. The action of encircling with the arms.

c **1440** *Promp. Parv.* 145 Fademynge, *ulnacio*. **1630** DONNE *Serm.* lxxii. 736 A net is a large thing past thy Fadoming if thou cast it from thee, but if thou draw it to thee, it will lie upon thy arme.

2. The action or process of ascertaining the depth (of the sea, etc.).

1642 ROGERS *Naaman* 181 The fadoming of so bottomelesse depth. **1727** *Philip Quarll* 79 Very expert in the Art of Fathoming.

b. *attrib.*, as *fathoming-line*.

a **1800** COWPER *Comm. Milton's P.L.* II. 934 A fathoming-line.. for the purpose of sounding an abyss. **1874** H. R. REYNOLDS *John Bapt.* vi. §1. 364 The prophet here plunged his fathoming line into a deep ocean.

fathomless ('fæðəmlɪs), *a.* [f. as prec. + -LESS.]

†**1.** That cannot be clasped with the arms. *Obs.*

1606 SHAKS. *Tr. & Cr.* II. ii. 30 Wil you.. buckle in a waste most fathomlesse With spannes and inches?

2. That cannot be measured with a fathom line; of measureless depth. Often of a metaphorical 'abyss'.

1638 G. SANDYS *Paraphr. Div. Poems* Ex. xv, God, in the fathomlesse Profound, Hath all his choice Commanders drown'd. **1644** MILTON *Educ.* (1738) 126 Fathomless and unquiet deeps of controversy. **1647** CLARENDON *Hist. Reb.* I. (1843) 6/2 That fathomless abyss of reason of state. **1801** SOUTHEY *Thalaba* VII. vi, Adown.. Plunge the whole waters; so precipitous, So fathomless a fall. **1830** TENNYSON *Ode to Memory* iii, The half-attain'd futurity, Tho' deep not fathomless. **1871** E. F. BURR *Ad Fidem* xv. 293 Passing up through fathomless azure.

3. *fig.* That cannot be penetrated or fully understood; incomprehensible. Cf. FATHOM *v.* 4 b.

1645 MILTON *Tetrach.* (1851) 184 Heer lies the fadomles absurdity. **1713** YOUNG *Last Day* I. 229 Oh joys unmix'd, and fathomless delight! **1883** E. CLODD in *Knowl.* 15 June 352/2 The fathomless mystery of the universe. **1891** *Spectator* 14 Feb., His ignorance.. is fathomless.

Hence **'fathomlessly** *adv.*

1822 BRYON *Werner* IV. i. 506 His death was fathomlessly deep in blood. **1878** *Masque Poets* 29 The smile so fathomlessly bland.

†**'faticane**. *Obs. rare*[−1]. [ad. L. *fātican-us*, f. *fāti-* comb. form of *fātum* FATE + *canĕre* to sing.] A singer of fate; a prophet.

1652 GAULE *Magastrom.* 162 What fatuous thing is fate, then, that is so obvious.. as for the faticanes to foretell?

fatidic (feɪ'tɪdɪk), *a.* Now *rare*. [ad. L. *fātidic-us*, f. *fāti-* comb. form of *fātum* FATE + *dic-* weak root of *dīc-ĕre* to speak.] Of or concerned with predicting fates; prophetic.

1671 J. DAVIES *Sibylls* I. xviii. 48 The Fatidick Books. **1692** J. EDWARDS *Remarkable Texts* 310 The earth become old, so that the fatidick virtue was worn out. **1721–36** in BAILEY. **1844** T. MITCHELL *Sophocles* I. 72 *note*, A verb applicable to fatidic purposes. **1861** in *Jrnl. Sacred Lit.* XIV. 175 When Moses, in the fatidic spirit, foretold the future prosperity of Israel.

fatidical (feɪ'tɪdɪkəl). [f. L. *fātidic-us* (see prec.) + -AL[1].] **a.** = prec. **b.** Of persons, trees, etc.: Gifted with the power of prophecy.

a. 1607 TOPSELL *Serpents* (1653) 685 This Beast is.. indued.. with a fatidical or prophetical geographical delineation. *a* **1652** J. SMITH *Sel. Disc.* vi. 209 To understand what is spoken.. in this fatidical passion. **1697** POTTER *Antiq. Greece* II. xvi. (1715) 335 Urns, into which the Lots or Fatidical Verses were thrown. **1721–1800** in BAILEY. **1829** CARLYLE *Misc.* (1857) II. 98 The fatidical fury spreads wider and wider. **1855** SMEDLEY *Occult Sciences* 331 A tablet, on which certain fatidical verses were written.

b. 1641 BRIGHTMAN *Predict.* 2 Our ancient Prophets, Bards, and fatidicall Vaticinators. *c* **1645** HOWELL *Lett.* (1688) IV. 486 The Ancients write of some Trees, that they are Fatidical. **1652** GAULE *Magastrom.* 255 Fatidical Mars. **1864** W. BELL in *N. & Q.* V. 442 One of those fatidical women, who.. ruled the destinies of the nation.

Hence **fa'tidically** *adv.*

a **1693** URQUHART *Rabelais* III. xxv. 210 As fatidically, as under the Emperor Valence.

fatidicate (feɪ'tɪdɪkeɪt), *v. rare.* [f. as prec. + -ATE.] *intr.* To declare or predict fates. Hence **fa'tidicating** *vbl. sb.*, in quot. used *attrib.*

1867 J. B. ROSE tr. *Virgil's Æneid* 229 Carmenta deified Fatidicating power.

†**fa'tidicency**. *Obs. rare*[−1]. [f. as prec. + -ENCY.] A method of foretelling fate; divination.

a **1693** URQUHART *Rabelais* III. xix. 154 Let us make trial of this kind of Fatidicency.

fatiferous (feɪ'tɪfərəs), *a.* [f. L. *fātifer* (f. *fāti-* comb. form of *fātum* FATE + *-fer* producing) + -OUS.] Fate-bringing; deadly, mortal, destructive.

1656 in BLOUNT *Glossogr.* **1755** in JOHNSON; whence in mod. Dicts.

fatigability (fætɪgə'bɪlɪtɪ). Also **fatiguability** (fəˌtiːg-). [f. FATIGABLE: see -ILITY.] Susceptibility to fatigue.

1908 W. MCDOUGALL *Introd. Soc. Psychol.* iv. 119 Differences in respect to fatigability and rapidity of recuperation. **1919** J. A. HADFIELD in B. H. Streeter *Spirit* III. 79 A man's fatiguability is tested by tying a weight to his finger [etc.]. **1964** L. MARTIN *Clinical Endocrinol.* (ed. 4) iii. 112 Some degree of muscular weakness and increased fatiguability exists in most cases of thyrotoxicosis.

'fatigable, fa'tiguable, *a.* [a. OF. *fatigable*, ad. L. *fatīgābilis*, f. *fatīgāre* to FATIGUE.] **a.** Capable of being fatigued; easily tired. †**b.** Wearying, tiring. *Obs.*[−0]

a. 1608 MIDDLETON *Fam. Love* III. ii, *Lip.* Indefatigable, boy, indefatigable. *Shr.* Fatigable, quoth you? **1853** RUSKIN *Stones Ven.* III. iii. §26. 127 An imperfect, childish, and fatigable nature.

b. 1656 BLOUNT *Glossogr.*, *Fatigable*, wearying or tyring.

Hence **'fatigableness, fa'tiguableness**.

1727 in BAILEY vol. II. **1856** RUSKIN *Mod. Paint.* III. IV. x. §18 That other character of the imagination, fatiguableness.

†**'fatigate**, *pa. pple. Obs.* [ad. L. *fatīgāt-us*, pa. pple. of *fatīgāre* to FATIGUE.] Fatigued.

1471 RIPLEY *Comp. Alch.* Admon. in Ashm. (1652) 191, I was fatygate. **1530** LYNDESAY *Test. Papyngo* 474 My wytt bene waik, my fyngaris faitegate. **1531** ELYOT *Gov.* I. vii, Suffre nat the childe to be fatigate with continuall studie. **1607** SHAKS. *Cor.* II. ii. 121 His doubled spirit Requickened what in flesh was fatigate.

†**'fatigate**, *v. Obs.* [f. L. *fatīgāt-* ppl. stem of *fatīgāre* to FATIGUE.] = FATIGUE *v.* 1.

1535 BONNER *Let.* in Burnet *Hist. Ref.* II. 177 The Party adverse, which.. goeth about to fatigate and make weary the Consistory of the disputations. **1549** *Compl. Scot.* vi. 37 The lang conteneuation of studie.. did fatigat my rason. **1577** HELLOWES *Gueuara's Chron.* 309 The Romans were fatigated.. with warres. **1622** SIR R. HAWKINS *Observations* (1878) 127 With which extreame heate the bodie fatigated, greedily desireth refreshing. *a* **1652** J. SMITH *Sel. Disc.* VI. 249 This kind of divine inspiration.. did.. [not] fatigate and act upon the imagination. **1749** FIELDING *Tom Jones* IV. 197 She will soon be fatigated with the journey.

Hence **'fatigated** *ppl. a.*

1552 HULOET, Fatigated, *defatigatus*. **1625–6** PURCHAS *Pilgrims* II. 1837 These sweet seasoned Songs of Arcadian Shepherds.. did recreate my fatigated corps. **1632** LITHGOW *Trav.* VI. 297 Fatigated travellers.

†**fati'gation**. *Obs.* Also 6 **-acion, -acyon**. [a. OF. *fatigation*, ad. L. *fatīgātiōn-em*, n. of action f. *fatīgāre* to FATIGUE.]

1. The action of fatiguing; an instance of this.

a **1529** SKELTON *Image Ipocr.* II. 393 Other like vexations; As with.. Fatigations.. And dissimulations, With like abbominations. **1535** *Act 27 Hen. VIII*, c. 3 Without frustrate or wilful delay.. or any other maner of fatigacion.

2. The state of being fatigued; weariness.

1504 W. ATKINSON tr. *à Kempis' Imit.* I. xviii, These sayntes.. have served God.. in great fatigacion. **1570** FOXE *A. & M.* I. 882/1 Cyprus and Albania, whiche he after long fatigation of siege, at length ouercame. *a* **1652** J. SMITH *Sel. Disc.* VI. iv. (1821) 215 He speaks of those fatigations that Daniel complains of. **1720** STRYPE *Stow's Surv.* (1754) I. I. xxiii. 144/2 Keeping watch.. as they had many times.. been compelled, to their great Fatigation and unquieting.

fatiguable, var. of FATIGABLE.

fatigue (fə'tiːg), *sb.* [a. Fr. *fatigue* fem., f. *fatiguer*: see next. Cf. Sp. *fatiga*, It. *fatica* fem.]

1. a. Lassitude or weariness resulting from either bodily or mental exertion.

1719 DE FOE *Crusoe* I. 323 It having been a Day of great Fatigue to me. **1776** *Trial of Nundocomar* 32/2 Imminent danger of expiring from fatigue. **1843** PRESCOTT *Mexico* VII. iii. (1864) 434 Extremities of famine and fatigue. **1874** MORLEY *Compromise* (1886) 8 The mortal fatigue that seizes catholic societies after their fits of revolution.

b. The condition of weakness in metals or other solid substances caused by cyclic variations in stress. Now esp. as ***metal fatigue***.

1854 BRAITHWAITE in *Proc. Inst. Civil Eng.* XIII. 463 Many.. accidents on railways.. are to be ascribed to that progressive action which may be termed the ' fatigue of metals'. **1874** KNIGHT *Dicts. Mech.* I. 827/1 To fatigue is ascribed the breaking of car-axles. **1885** *Engineering* 10 July 31 The law of the fatigue and refreshment of metals. **1905** [see *Fatigue test* 4 below]. **1913** *Sci. Amer.* Suppl. 13 Dec. 372 (*heading*) A recently installed fatigue testing machine. **1937** *Discovery* July 194/2 The fatigue resistance of some metals. **1949** *Jrnl. R. Aeronaut. Soc.* LIII. 788/2 A ray of hope that non-ferrous alloys could be developed which would show similar features in lack of 'fatigue-memory' to the ferritic steels. **1955** *Times* 8 July 5/1 Her Royal Highness drove across the airfield to see a Bristol Britannia airliner undergoing metal fatigue tests in a water tank. **1966** *McGraw-Hill Encycl. Sci. & Technol.* II. 284/2 The only examples of a fatigue fracture in bone are those seen usually in military training,.. in which a soldier not previously used to repetitive exercise is forced to march 30 or 40 miles in a single day.

c. *Physiol.* A condition of muscles, organs, or cells characterized by a temporary reduction in power or sensitivity following a period of prolonged activity or stimulation.

1872 J. H. BENNETT *Text-bk. Physiol.* ii. 83 (*heading*) Muscular fatigue. **1876** *Kirkes' Hand-bk. Physiol.* (ed. 9) xix. 586 *Fatigue of muscle.*—A muscle becomes rapidly exhausted from repeated stimulation. **1888** M. FOSTER *Text Bk. Physiol.* (ed. 5) I. 149 The sense of fatigue of which, after prolonged or unusual exertion, we are conscious in our own bodies.. cannot be taken as an adequate measure of the actual fatigue of the muscles. **1891** A. D. WALLER *Introd. Human Physiol.* xii. 448 Negative after-images are the most obvious sign of retinal—or properly speaking—of retino-cerebral fatigue. **1932** S. DUKE-ELDER *Text-bk. Ophthalmol.* I. xxiv. 969 The lowered visual acuity which is readily demonstrable on continued observation.. is due to fatigue in mental or even general bodily processes... Of retinal fatigue there seems to be no evidence. **1949** E. G. WEVER *Theory of Hearing* xii. 322 The specificity of the fatigue effect.. is studied by exposing the ear to one tone and then testing with various other tones above and below. **1966** *Lancet* 12 Mar. 585/2 True muscular fatigue and what, for want of a better term, must be called tiredness are plainly different.

†**d.** *Mech.* ***fatigue of elasticity***: a decrease in the elasticity of a material after a long period or repeated applications of stress, followed by a gradual recovery after the stress is removed; also ***elastic fatigue***. *Obs.*

1877 W. THOMSON in *Encycl. Brit.* VII. 802/1 Experimental exercises.. brought to light some very remarkable and interesting results,.. showing also a very remarkable fatigue of elasticity, according to which a wire which had been kept vibrating for several hours or days through a certain range came to rest much quicker when left to itself than when set in vibration after it had been at rest for several days and then immediately left to itself. **1895** *Proc. R. Soc.* LXVIII. 136 In every case, overstrain has produced a like fatigue of elasticity, and elastic recovery has followed during an interval of some days or weeks of rest. **1899** *Nature* 6 July 239/2 Experiments on an iron wire.. showed distinct fatigue of elasticity. **1899** W. WATSON *Text-bk. Physics* xix. 205 This phenomenon is referred to as elastic fatigue. **1920** A. E. H. LOVE *Treat. Math. Theory Elasticity* (ed. 3) iv. 117 An analogous property of bodies is that to which Lord Kelvin has called attention under the name 'fatigue of elasticity'. **1922** *Proc. Physical Soc.* XXXV. 165 In his own experience of electrometers elastic fatigue appeared to be due mainly to the attachment at the two ends of the suspension wire.

e. The reduction of the efficiency of an (esp. luminescent) material during use or exposure.

1904 *Philos. Trans. R. Soc.* A. CII. 443 At pressures below, say, a tenth of an atmosphere, zinc showed little or no signs of fatigue when illuminated by ultra-violet light. **1949** G. F. J. GARLICK *Luminescent Materials* vii. 187 The saturation of the screen material by electrons at low voltages .. results in a fatigue of the material.

2. That which causes weariness; †fatiguing labour, 'trouble' (*obs.*); a fatiguing duty or performance, labour, toil.

1669 TEMPLE *Let. to Pr. Tuscany* Wks. 1731 II. 196 The glorious Fatigues which have hitherto been the Diversion of your Highness. **1691** WOOD *Ath. Oxon.* II. 644 When the Treaty for the delivery of it [Oxon] up for the use of the Parliament was in agitation, he [Rushworth] was often posting to London upon intermessages and fatigues. **1695** WOODWARD *Nat. Hist. Earth* I. (1723) 37 A Question.. which hath.. given no small Fatigue to Learned Men. **1712** W. ROGERS *Voy.* 364 The Governour's Deputy.. had the Fatigue to get our Provisions together. **1780** BURKE *Corr.* (1844) II. 381 The fatigues of the election are over. **1844** H. H. WILSON *Brit. India* II. 305 The men were much distressed by.. the fatigues of their previous march. **1866** GEO. ELIOT *F. Holt* (1868) 12 Sight had become one of the day's fatigues.

3. a. The extra-professional duties of a soldier, sometimes allotted to him as punishment for misdemeanour; an instance of this.

1776 A. WARD in Sparks *Corr. Amer. Rev.* (1853) I. 191, I.. have ordered all the men, not on actual duty, to turn out upon fatigue every day. **1844** *Regul. & Ord. Army* 275 The levelling of ground in the vicinity of the Camp or Barracks, and making communications between different parts of them, are duties of fatigue. **1881** *Through the Ranks to a Commission* 57 For the two weeks that I was a private I took my turn at the daily fatigues.

b. Short for *fatigue party*, and in *pl.* for *fatigue-dress*.

1836 J. Hildreth *Dragoon Campaigns Rocky Mts.* i. vii. 51 We have not yet received our uniforms.. but even in our 'fatigues', we make an imposing appearance when mounted. 1876 Voyle & Stevenson *Milit. Dict.* 135/2 *Fatigue*..a party of soldiers told off for any other duty than a dress parade necessitates. 1892 W. G. Browne in *19th Cent.* Nov. 850 Change into stable fatigues. 1966 D. F. Galouye *Lost Perception* viii. 85 Clad in ill-fitting and occasionally torn fatigues, the soldiers were a vivid contrast to the flawlessly uniformed Guardsmen. 1967 *Boston* (Mass.) *Herald* 5 Apr. 59/3 The generals..in their 'pressed fatigues and shining stars'. 1970 *Daily Tel.* 6 Oct. 4/4 A Palestinian major, dressed in jungle green fatigues.

4. *attrib.* and *Comb.*, as ***fatigue-blouse***, ***-cap***, ***frock***, ***-jacket***, ***trousers***, ***-uniform*** (= *fatigue-dress*); ***fatigue-man***; **fatigue-call**, the call to fatigue-duty; **fatigue-dress**, the dress worn by a soldier on fatigue-duty; also *transf.*; **fatigue-duty** = FATIGUE *sb.* 3; **fatigue limit**, the (presumed) value of the fatigue strength for an infinite number of cycles of stress; also called *endurance limit*; **fatigue-party**, a party of soldiers on fatigue-duty; **fatigue products, stuff, substances** [tr. G. *ermüdender Stoff*, *ermüdende Substanz* (J. Ranke *Tetanus* (1865) xiv. 329, xviii. 450)], an accumulation of toxic material formerly held to result from excessive muscular activity and to be the cause of fatigue; **fatigue range**, the maximum variation in stress that a material can be subjected to for a large or infinite number of cycles of stress without its failing from fatigue; **fatigue strength**, half the value of the fatigue range of a material for a given (large) number of cycles of stress, esp. when the mean stress is zero; also called *endurance strength*; **fatigue test**, a test carried out on a material or part to determine its behaviour under cyclic variations of stress and esp. its fatigue strength; also as *vb.*; so ***fatigue testing*** vbl. sb.; **fatigue testing machine**, a machine for performing fatigue tests; **fatigue-work** = FATIGUE *sb.* 3.

1890 *Century Mag.* Aug. 617/2 A thin *fatigue blouse. 1861 R. A. Wise *Let.* 9 Jan. in *Wm. & Mary Coll. Q.* 2nd Ser. XVIII. 197 Their uniform is to be home spun pantaloons and a red flannel shirt and a *fatigue cap. 1914 E. A. Powell *Fighting in Flanders* vi. 139 Small, round, visorless fatigue-caps. 1833 Marryat *P. Simple* xvi, A soldier in his *fatigue dress. 1847 Emerson *Repr. Men, Goethe* Wks. (Bohn) I. 387 He had put off a gay uniform for a fatigue dress. 1879 Escott *England* II. 213 The black gown is the fatigue dress of judges. 1873 Burton *Hist. Scot.* I. ii. 72 The soldier never slept till he had done his *fatigue-duty. 1803 M. Lewis *Jrnl.* (1905) VIII. 233, 20 *Fatigue Frocks or hunting shirts. 1847 in H. Howe *Hist. Coll. Ohio* 490 It was at night..and they [*sc.* the soldiers] were dressed in fatigue frocks. 1852 Lever *Daltons* II. iv. 35 A creature that..carries a bread bag over its shoulder through the streets in a *fatigue jacket. 1911 *Proc. Inst. Mech. Engin.* Oct. 884 As far as he could ascertain, there was no relationship between *fatigue limits and the ordinary elastic limits. 1959 *Chambers's Encycl.* IX. 326/2 When a metal is subjected to many millions of cycles of alternating or vibrating stress, below the elastic limit, but above the so-called 'fatigue' limit, it eventually breaks by 'fatigue'. 1774 J. Andrews *Let.* 28 Sept. (1886) 57 A number of **fatigue* men with hand barrows. 1871 L. W. M. Lockhart *Fair to See* III. xxxi. 49 *Laissez-aller* hospital orderlies and sluggish 'fatigue-men'. 1957 M. K. Joseph *I'll soldier no More* (1958) xiii. 255 Tino and a couple of fatigue-men have sweated in the cookhouse. 1840 De Quincey *Casuist. Rom. Meals* Wks. 1863 III. 271 A *fatigue party of dustmen sent upon secret service. 1844 *Regul. & Ord. Army* 2 A..Fatigue-Party, is not entitled to exemption from a Tour of Duty. 1860 Russell *Diary India* II. xvi. 304 The men of a fatigue party ..were emptying out shot. 1909 *Westm. Gaz.* 8 June 9/2 To eliminate from the muscles what pathologists know as '*fatigue products'. 1935 Winton & Bayliss *Human Physiol.* (ed. 2) i. 17 It was at one time supposed that a specific physiological mechanism was at the root of the state of fatigue, which was attributed to the action of products of activity, 'fatigue products', circulating in the blood. 1922 Glazebrook *Dict. Appl. Physics* I. 179/2 A determination of the *fatigue range occupied a very long time. 1954 L. E. Benson in W. R. Osgood *Residual Stresses in Metals* 81 With mild steel..the upper limit of the fatigue range of stress (with zero mean stress) is approximately equal to the yield point. 1912 *Min. Proc. Inst. Civil Engin.* CLXXXVIII. i. 10 There only remained the investigation of the effects of the high speed on the *fatigue strength of the specimens. 1959 Crandall & Dahl *Introd. Mech. Solids* v. 221 The fatigue strength of 2024-T4 aluminium alloy, when tested as unnotched bars, is about 30,000 psi for 10^6 cycles and 24,000 psi for 10^7 cycles. 1971 *Engineering* Apr. 38/1 These bronzes ..have a very good fatigue strength. 1885 W. Stirling tr. *Landois' Text-bk. Human Physiol.* II. x. 667 The cause of fatigue is probably the accumulation of decomposition products, '*fatigue stuffs' in the muscular tissue. 1905 *Jrnl. Iron & Steel Inst.* LXVII. 488 It is not easy to definitely compare the tensile and *fatigue tests in this case. 1955 Fatigue test [see 1 b]. 1959 Sines & Waisman *Metal Fatigue* vii. 167 Any part design which differs greatly from standard practice should be carefully *fatigue-tested before it is adopted for service. 1905 *Jrnl. Iron & Steel Inst.* LXVII. 486 The *fatigue testing-machines were of Wöhler's cantilever type. 1908 *Ibid.* LXXVI. 70 The chief object of fatigue-testing was to discover the existence or non-existence of a relation between the elastic properties of a material and its resistance to fatigue. 1813 *Niles' Weekly Reg.* III. 295/2 *Fatigue trowsers. 1890 *Illust. Lond. News* Christmas No. 2/1 A grey *fatigue-uniform. 1846 *Aide Mémoire Mil. Sci.* I. 521 Fascine pickets are..usually considered *fatigue-work. 1889 Wolseley in *Times* 15 Feb. 12/3 Fatigue work, such as carrying coals.

fatigue (fə'tiːg), *v.* [ad. F. *fatiguer* (= Pr., Sp. *fatigar*, It. *faticare*), ad. L. *fatīgāre*, f. stem **fati-* (in *ad-fatim* enough), prob. meaning 'yawning'; cf. FATISCENT.]

1. *trans.* a. 'To tire, weary; to harass with toil; to exhaust with labour' (J.).

1693 *Lond. Gaz.* No. 2911/3 Many false Allarms to harass and fatigue their Men. 1725 De Foe *Voy. round World* (1840) 345 Five of them..extremely fatigued themselves in pursuing them [cattle]. 1784 Cowper *Task* iv. 706 Heroes and their feats Fatigued me. 1848 Lytton *Harold* vi. vii, Thou fatiguest thyself in vain. 1863 Fr. A. Kemble *Resid. in Georgia* 34 My morning's work had fatigued me.

b. To induce a condition of fatigue in (a muscle, organ, etc.): see FATIGUE *sb.* 1 c.

1872 J. H. Bennett *Text-bk. Physiol.* ii. 83 The muscles of a strong man are not so easily fatigued as those of a weak one. 1885 W. Stirling tr. *Landois' Text-bk. Human Physiol.* II. x. 668 Loads may be suspended to perfectly passive muscles without fatiguing them. 1896 W. P. Lombard in W. H. Howell *Amer. Text-bk. Physiol.* ii. 97 It is doubtful whether nerves are fatigued by the process of conduction. 1954 Wever & Lawrence *Physiol. Acoustics* ix. 157 The ear is strongly fatigued with a tone of a certain frequency..and then is stimulated with two primary tones of adjacent frequencies.

2. a. To weaken by straining; to strain (a mast).

1794 *Rigging & Seamanship* II. 273 Augmenting the number of sails..at the risque of fatiguing the masts. 1869 Sir E. J. Reed *Shipbuild.* v. 83 To render the angle-iron frames less fatigued.

b. *trans.* To weaken by the application of a periodically varying stress; to induce fatigue in (FATIGUE *sb.* 1 b, d).

1899 J. A. Ewing *Strength of Materials* iii. 56 A piece which has been fatigued by many variations of stress. 1905 *Jrnl. Iron & Steel Inst.* LXVII. 491 A broad face of a specimen of oblong section is polished, and the specimen is then fatigued. 1925 Timoshenko & Lessels *Appl. Elasticity* xvi. 464 The material, after being fatigued, showed an increase in angular strain when frequency of alternation was decreased. 1962 A. J. Kennedy *Processes Creep & Fatigue in Metals* v. 298 The fracture hardness was lower for copper specimens fatigued at 20×10^3 p.s.i. than for those fatigued at 16×10^3 p.s.i.

†3. *intr.* To undertake fatigue.

1697 Collier *Ess. Mor. Subj.* ii. (1709) 163 Age is not vigorous enough for Business and Fatiguing.

fatigued (fə'tiːgd), *ppl. a.* [f. prec. + -ED[1].] a. Wearied. b. Strained by over-pressure.

1791 Cowper *Iliad* v. 947 His arm failed him fatigued. 1820 Keats *Eve St. Agnes* xxvii, The poppied warmth of sleep oppress'd Her soothed limbs, and soul fatigued away. 1856 Olmsted *Slave States* 12 Struck with her fatigued appearance, he made some inquiries. 1869 [see FATIGUE *v.* 2].

c. Worn, shabby. Also *fig.*

1774 F. Burney *Diary* 20 Feb. (1907) I. 285 These two subjects he wore thread-bare; though indeed they were pretty much fatigued, before he attacked them. 1894 *Daily News* 22 Jan. 5/1 Preferring a fatigued brown calf binding to a new suit of leather for 'Tom Jones'. 1897 *Ibid.* 20 Nov. 8/3 The renovation of a dress that has seen some wear, and consequently has that fatigued appearance.

d. Affected with, or characterized by, a condition of fatigue (FATIGUE *sb.* 1 b, c, d).

1853 W. Brinton tr. *Valentin's Text Bk. Physiol.* xv. 381 It is probable that, even during life, a fatigued muscle is more yielding than when fresh and vigorous. 1877 M. Foster *Text Bk. Physiol.* 65 A muscle, even within the body, after prolonged action is fatigued. 1885 W. Stirling tr. *Landois' Text-bk. Human Physiol.* II. x. 667 In order to obtain the same amount of work from a fatigued muscle, a much more powerful stimulus must be applied to it. 1899 J. A. Ewing *Strength of Materials* iii. 56 A period of rest in a 'fatigued' piece tends to restore elasticity. 1931 E. H. Salmon *Materials & Structures* I. xviii. 540 It was concluded that, as a result of mere repetition of loading, a material became less capable of resistance, or, as it was termed, *fatigued*. 1949 E. G. Wever *Theory of Hearing* xii. 324 The fatigued ear resembles an ear that is suffering from nerve deafness. 1967 J. Y. Mann *Fatigue of Materials* iii. 13 The relative areas of the fatigued zone and the zone of final static failure..can provide information relating to the general stress level on the plane of fracture.

fatigueless (fə'tiːglɪs), *a.* [f. FATIGUE *sb.* and *v.* + -LESS.] Without fatigue; unwearying; tireless.

1818 J. Brown *Psyche* 42 Endow'd them with fatigueless care. 1879 Jefferies *Wild Life in S.C.* 132 Riders upright and fatigueless. 1889 Talmage *Serm.* in *The Voice* 2 May, The angels are a fatigueless race.

fatiguesome (fə'tiːgsəm), *a.* [f. as prec. + -SOME.] Of a fatiguing nature; wearisome.

a 1734 North *Exam.* iii. vii. §16 (1740) 515 The Attorney General's Place is very nice and fatiguesome, and the other quiet. 1746 Turnbull *Justin* xxvii. iii. 218 Antiochus was overcome the second time; and after a fatiguesome flight of several days, came at last to [etc.]. 1827 *Blackw. Mag.* XXI. 475 His 'Excursion' would hae been far less fatigue-some.

fatiguing (fə'tiːgɪŋ), *ppl. a.* [f. FATIGUE *v.* + -ING[2].] That causes fatigue; wearisome.

1708 Luttrell *Brief Rel.* (1857) VI. 322 Vendosme..by fatiguing marches gained the Dender on the 5th. 1774 Goldsm. *Nat. Hist.* (1776) IV. 189 It would be fatiguing.. to go through a particular description. 1833 J. Rennie *Alph. Angling* 64 A heavy [trouting] rod is..fatiguing. 1860 Tyndall *Glac.* i. xi. 77 The most fatiguing position.

Hence **fa'tiguingly** *adv.*, in a fatiguing manner.

1807 Southey *Espriella's Lett.* II. 241 The most unpleasant part of this expedition, fatiguingly steep as it was. 1840 T. Hook in *New Monthly Mag.* LVIII. 155 They dance quadrilles fatiguingly. 1871 Le Fanu *Checkmate* II. ix. 93 [She] was..most fatiguingly well up in archæology. 1880 Miss Bird *Japan* II. 149 One makes one's way fatiguingly along soft sea sand.

‖**Fatiha(h)** ('fɑːtɪha). Also **Fatha**, **Fatheh**, **Fattah**, **Fattha**. [Arab. *fātiḥa*, *fatḥa* opening, f. *fataḥa* to open.] The short first sura of the Koran, used by Moslems as a prayer.

1821 G. F. Lyon *Narr. Trav. N. Afr.* ii. 74 Some one of Mukni's men cries out 'The Fattha!' (or first chapter of the Koran), every one joining in that prayer. *Ibid.* iii. 94 We sometimes met people on our road, who invariably at parting recited the Fatha. 1824 J. Morier *Hajji Baba* III. i. 20 The *Fatheh* (the first chapter of the Koran) was repeated by all present. 1863 *Chambers's Encycl.* V. 818/1 Immediately after the introductory fattah or exordium, follows the longest chapter. 1883 E. Arnold *Pearls of Faith* xlv, 'Gabriel! why stay'st thou me?'..'Since at this hour the Fâtihah should be read.' 1916 J. R. Harris *Testimonies* i. v. 41 He begins his discourse with an imitation of the Fatha, or opening chapter of the Koran. 1959 *Chambers's Encycl.* VIII. 255/2 The *suras* do not stand in historical order. The first, the Fatiha, is a short prayer, much used by the Moslems.

†**fa'tiloquency.** *Obs.* $rare^{-1}$. [f. as next: see -ENCY.]

a 1693 Urquhart *Rabelais* iii. xxv, By Gastromancy, which kind of ventral Fatiloquency was..used in *Ferrara*.

fatiloquent (feɪ'tɪləkwənt), *a.* [f. L. *fāti-*, comb. form of *fātum* FATE + *loquent-em* speaking; after L. *fātiloquus*.] Declaring fate, prophetic.

1656-81 in Blount *Glossogr.* *a* 1693 Urquhart *Rabelais* iii. xxi. 182 Fatiloquent Southsayers. 1885 Betham-Edwards in *All Year Round* No. 854 N.S. 76 A voice fatiloquent.

†**fa'tiloquist.** *Obs.* $rare^{-1}$. [f. L. *fātiloquus* (see prec.) + -IST.] One who declares or foretells fates; a fortune-teller.

1652 Gaule *Magastromancer* 145 Fatiloquists..taken from talking they know not what. 1727-36 in Bailey.

†**fatiloquy.** *Obs.*$^{-0}$ [ad. L. *fātiloqui-um*, f. *fātum* FATE + *-loquium* speaking, f. *loquī* to speak.] Soothsaying.

1623-6 in Cockeram.

Fatimite ('fætɪmaɪt), *a.* and *sb.* Also **Fat(h)emite**, **Fathimite**, **Fatimid(e**. [f. Arab. *Fāṭima* (see below) + -ITE[1].] A. *adj.* Descended from Fatima, the daughter of Mohammed by his first wife, Khadija. B. *sb.* A descendant of Fatima and her husband, Ali; a member of the Arabian dynasty which ruled in parts of northern Africa from A.D. 908 to 1171, and during some of that period in Egypt and Syria. Also *attrib.*

1727-38 Chambers *Cycl.*, Fathimites, or Fathemites. 1797 *Encycl. Brit.* III. 4/2 He [*sc.* Obeidallah] pretended to be descended in a right line from Fatema..for which reason ..the Arabs called him and his descendants Fatemites. *Ibid.*, Abul Kasem, son to the Fatemite khalif Al Mohdi. *Ibid.* VII. 177/1 Fathemites, Fatemites, or Fathimites. 1838 *Penny Cycl.* X. 207/1 Obeidallah, the first Fatimide caliph. 1872 H. A. Rawes *God in His Works* iii. 55 The kingdoms of the Fatimites. 1883 *Encycl. Brit.* XVI. 587/1 With the reign of Moktadir is connected one of the greatest events in the history of the Caliphate, the foundation of the Fátimite dynasty. 1897 *Daily News* 8 Apr. 8/1 In 1072 the Holy City was possessed by the Fatimite Caliph of Egypt. 1902 *Daily Chron.* 20 June 4/2 The Fatimid Caliphate. 1940 *Burlington Mag.* Nov. 152/1 There seems to be no connection between Fatimid art and the miniature painting of the Mamluks. 1951 S. Runciman *Hist. Crusades* I. i. ii. 31 He realized the Fatimites were more dangerous enemies than their Abbasid rivals. *Ibid.* v. i. 267 The coast line from the middle Lebanon to the Fatimid frontier.

fatiscence (fə'tɪsəns). *Geol.* [f. next: see -ENCE.] The condition of being open in chinks or clefts.

c 1784 Kirwan cited by Webster 1828.

fatiscent (fə'tɪsənt), *a.* [ad. L. *fatiscent-em*, pr. pple. of *fatiscĕre* to open in chinks or clefts, f. **fati-* yawning: see FATIGUE *v.*] Having chinks or clefts; cracked.

1807 Headrick *Arran* 51 Fatiscent granite. 1916 B. D. Jackson *Gloss. Bot. Terms* (ed. 4) 144/1 *Fatiscent*, cracked, or gaping open. 1957 Snell & Dick *Gloss. Mycology* 57/2 *Fatiscent*, disappearing; breaking up.

†'**fatist.** *Obs.* [f. L. *fāt-um* or Eng. FATE + -IST.] = FATALIST.

1615 J. Stephens *Ess. & Char., Worthy Poet* 154 Hee is an enemy to Atheists; for he is no Fatist.

fatless ('fætlɪs), *a.* [f. FAT *sb.* + -LESS.] Without fat or greasy matter.

1825 *Blackw. Mag.* XVIII. 155 A mere wafer of fatless ham..constituted a breakfast. 1872 Huxley *Phys.* vi. 137 Four pounds of fatless meat.

fatling ('fætlɪŋ), *sb.* [f. FAT *v.* + -LING; cf. *nursling*.] A calf, lamb, or other young animal fatted for slaughter. Also *transf.*, of a person.

1526-34 Tindale *Matt.* xxii. 4 Beholde, I have prepared my dynner; myne oxen, and my fatlinges are kylled, and all things are redy. 1570 Bryon in Farr *S.P. Eliz.* (1845) II. 335 My fatlings then I'll tender, And offrings to thee make. 1611 Bible *Isa.* xi. 6 The calfe and the yong lion, and the

fatling [shall lie down] together. **1725** POPE *Odyss.* VIII. 53 Twelve fatlings from the flock. *a* **1861** T. WINTHROP *John Brent* (1883) vii. 58 'Well, boys!' said the unpleasant fatling, approaching again. **1877** BRYANT *Poems Sella* 303 The herd Had given its fatlings for the marriage feast.

attrib. **1870** BRYANT *Iliad* I. IX. 275 Chines of a sheep and of a fatling goat.

fatling ('fætlɪŋ), *a. rare.* [dim. of FAT *a.* (see -LING), suggested by prec. sb.] Small and fat.

1847 TENNYSON *Princ.* VI. 122 The babe..began..to..reach its fatling innocent arms And lazy, lingering fingers.

fatly ('fætlɪ), *adv.* [f. as prec. + -LY[2].]

†**a.** Grossly, greasily. †**b.** Plentifully. **c.** To a great extent, largely. **d.** Like a fat person, clumsily.

1515 BARCLAY *Egloges* iv. (1570) C v/1 Some beast agayne still leane and poore is seene, Though it fatly fare within a medowe greene. **1611** COTGR., *Graissement*, fatly, grossely, greasily. **1866** WHIPPLE *Char. & Charac. Men* 322 An old dowager lady, fatly invested in commerce and manufactures. **1866** HOWELLS *Venet. Life* xi. 160 Renaissance angels and cherubs in marble..fatly tumbling about on the broken arches of the altars. **1873** MISS BROUGHTON *Nancy* I. 132 Largely, fatly, staringly plain.

fatner, obs. form of FATTENER.

fatness ('fætnɪs). [f. as prec. + -NESS.]

1. The quality or state of being fat.

a. The condition of having the flesh interspersed with fat; plumpness, fullness of flesh, corpulence.

c **1000** *Ags. Ps.* xvi[i]. 9 Hi habbaþ ealle heora fætnesse.. utan bewunden. *c* **1400** *Lanfranc's Cirurg.* 86 If þat þe bodi ..ben mene bitwene fatnes & lenenes þat is neiþer to fatt ne to leene. **1581** MULCASTER *Positions* xvii. (1887) 76 Wrastling..taketh awaie fatnesse, puffes, and swellinges. **1653** WALTON *Angler* 187 Eeles have all parts fit for generation..but so smal as not to be easily discerned, by reason of their fatness. **1756** C. LUCAS *Ess. Waters* I. 177 We can account for the extraordinary fatness of cooks, butchers, and other persons. **1885** *Truth* 28 May 850/1 Fatness alone prevented her from continuing to shine as a lyric star.

fig. **1602** SHAKS. *Ham.* III. iv. 153 In the fatnesse of this pursie times, Vertue it selfe, of Vice must pardon begge.

†**b.** *Typogr.* Breadth or thickness. *Obs.*

1676 MOXON *Print Lett.* 23 Measure the Fatness of the left hand Arch of e.

c. Of a tree: Oiliness; juiciness. Of the soil: Unctuous nature; hence, fertility, luxuriance. *Obs.* or *arch.* exc. *U.S.*

1382 WYCLIF *Rom.* xi. 17 Fatnesse of the olyue tree. **1555** EDEN *Decades* 4 The greate moystenesse and fatnesse of the grounde. **1611** BIBLE *Gen.* xxvii. 28 God giue thee of the dew of heauen, and the fatnesse of the earth. *a* **1735** ARBUTHNOT (J.), By reason of the fatness and heaviness of the ground, Egypt did not produce metals. **1814** J. TAYLOR *Arator* (ed. 2) 172 This [*sc.* using bottom lands for tillage and grazing] is owing to the extreme fatness of the soil. **1849** E. BRYANT *California* ii. 23, I never saw a soil indicative of a higher degree of fatness. **1887** MORRIS *Odyss.* XI. 93 Then about his vineyard's fatness where the mother of wine doth abound. **1891** HARDY *Tess* II. III. xxiv. 34 The oozing fatness and warm ferments of the Var Vale.

fig. **1526** *Pilgr. Perf.* (W. de W. 1531) 162 Makynge it to encrease in a spirituall fatnes of deuocyon.

†**2.** That which makes fertile; a fertilizing property or virtue; fertilizing matter. *Obs.*

c **1420** *Pallad. on Husb.* XII. 7 Valey ther hilles fattenesse hath rest. **1563** FULKE *Meteors* (1640) 16 Comets..betoken ..barrennesse..because the fatnesse of the earth is drawn up, whereof the Comet consisteth. **1611** BIBLE *Ps.* lxv. 11 Thy paths drop fatnesse. **1692** BENTLEY *Serm.* 5 Dec. 29 Water..to..feed the Plants of the Earth with..the fatness of Showrs. **1738** WESLEY *Hymns, Eternal Wisdom, Thee we praise* vii, They sink and drop Their Fatness on the ground.

†**3. a.** *concr.* A greasy or oily substance, fat. *Obs.*

c **1000** *Ags. Ps.* xvi[i]. 11 Fætnysse heora hi beclysdon. **1398** TREVISA *Barth. De P.R.* v. lxiii. (1495) 181 In the beest is fatnesse that is callyd Adeps, Aruina wythout. *c* **1400** *Lanfranc's Cirurg.* 257 Summe seien þat þe fatnes of grene froggis..haþ vertu for to make men heere. *c* **1430** *Stans Puer* 39 in *Babees Bk.* (1868) 29 In ale ne in wyn with hond leue no fatnes. **1450-1530** *Myrr. our Ladye* (1873) 113 The fatnesse of oyle may not burne, tyl a weyke or matche be put therto. **1641** FRENCH *Distill.* iii. (1651) 71 There will distill into the receiver a fatness. **1697** DRYDEN *Virg. Georg.* II. 547 Whose offer'd Entrails shall..drip their Fatness from the Hazle Broach.

fig. *a* **1400** *Prymer* (1891) 90 As wiþ grece and fatnesse fyld be my soule. **1561** T. NORTON *Calvin's Inst.* I. 4 This is the iuste vengeance of God, to drawe a fatnesse ouer their hartes. **1611** BIBLE *Ps.* lxiii, My soule shall be satisfied as with marrow and fatnesse.

†**b.** In the soil, etc.: An unctuous substance; an unctuous layer or deposit. *Obs.*

1577 B. GOOGE *Heresbach's Husb.* I. (1586) 20 b, A kinde of pith and fatnesse of the earth..called *Marga. Ibid.* 43 b, The fatnesse that the water leaves behinde it. **1626** BACON *Sylva* §355 Earth and Water..mingled by the helpe of the Sunne, gather a nitrous Fatnesse. **1715** tr. *Pancirollus' Rerum Mem.* II. ii. 283 Chalky Earth..beaten and steeped in Water, affordeth a Cream or Fatness on the Top.

†**4.** The richest of best part of anything. *Obs.*

c **1000** *Ags. Ps.* lxxx[i]. 17 Of fætnysse hwætes. *c* **1300** *E.E. Psalter* cxlvii. 14 And with fattnes of whete filled þe wele. **1644** G. PLATTES in Hartlib *Legacy* (1655) 176 Cities, which ..devoured the fatness of the whole Kingdom. **1665** DRYDEN *Ind. Emperor* I. ii, Those ghostly kings would..all the Fatness of my Land devour.

Fatso ('fætsəʊ). *slang.* [presumably f. *fat* with addition of pl. *s* + -O[2].] Used humorously or derisively as a nickname for a fat person.

1944 R. D. BOYER in P. Gammond *Duke Ellington* (1958) I. 28 The other card players looked over and in succession asked, 'How's it going, Pops?' 'Getting anywhere, Sandhead?' and 'You sending 'em, Fatso?' **1962** L. DEIGHTON *Ipcress File* v. 32, I began to envy Fatso his sausage sandwiches. **1964** E. LACY *Pity Honest* iv. 97 Fatso glanced at me with disgust.

fattable ('fætəb(ə)l), *a. rare.* In 9 fatable. [f. FAT *v.* + -ABLE.] Capable of being fatted.

1859 KINGSLEY *Misc.* II. 145 Pigs being as greedy and fatable under Free-trade..as they were under Protection.

Fattah, Fattha, varr. FATIHAH.

fatted ('fætɪd), *ppl. a.* Somewhat *arch.* [f. FAT *v.* + -ED[1].] In senses of the vb.; now only, fattened.

[*to kill the fatted calf*: proverbially used with reference to *Luke* xv.]

1552 HULOET, Fatted or dressed with fatte, *adipatus, a, um.* **1580** BARET *Alv.* F 215 A fatted hogge, *saginatus porcus.* **1611** BIBLE *1 Kings* iv. 23 Beside.. fallow Deere, and fatted foule. **1647** COWLEY *Mistress, The Welcome* i, Go, let the fatted Calf be kill'd. **1660** HEXHAM, *Gemest landt*, Dunged or Fatted land. **1725** POPE *Odyss.* IX. 49 The fatted sheep. **1870** BRYANT *Iliad* I. II. 54 Agamemnon Offered a fatted ox of five years old. **1875** JOWETT *Plato* (ed. 2) III. 51 Pictures of the lean dogs and the fatted sheep.

fatten ('fæt(ə)n), *v.* [f. FAT *a.* + -EN[5].]

1. *trans.* To make fat or plump. Also *to fatten up.* Usually: To feed (animals) for market, make fit to kill. Const. *on.*

1552 HULOET, Fatten or make fatte, *crasso.* **1622** MASSINGER *Virg. Mart.* II. i, You snatch the meat out of the prisoner's mouth, To fatten harlots. **1632** LITHGOW *Trav.* III. 95 Wandring Laton..In spight of Juno, fatned with Joves balme. **1745** tr. *Columella's Husb.* VIII. i, Such fowls as are shut up in coops, and fattened. **1777** MAD. D'ARBLAY *Early Diary* (1889) II. 284 His legs..have been fattened up by the gout. **1849** COBDEN *Speeches* 3 His idea seems to be that men in time of peace were only being fattened up for a speedy slaughter. **1853** SOYER *Pantroph.* 165 To fatten turkeys..give them mashed potatoes [etc.]. **1873** TRISTRAM *Moab* viii. 148 Myriads of larks in combined flocks fattening themselves upon them.

absol. **1650** BULWER *Anthropomet.* 241 All Bodies may be made lean; but it is impossible to fatten, where, etc.

b. Said of the food.

c **1590** GREENE *Fr. Bacon* x. 59 Whose battling pastures fatten all my flockes. **1665** SIR T. HERBERT *Trav.* (1677) 299 Wine and Music fattens them [Persian women]. **1781** GIBBON *Decl. & F.* III. 213 The forests of Lucania, whose acorns fattened large droves of wild hogs. **1834** *Brit. Husb.* III. xiii. 59 The same food is given..to fatten cows or oxen.

c. *transf.* and *fig.* *to fatten into*: to bring into a certain state by pampering (*rare*). *to fatten out*: to drive out by fattening.

1566 DRANT *Hor. Sat.* II. vi, I..praye him..to fatten all I haue, excepte my witte alone. **1634** SIR T. HERBERT *Trav.* (1638) 235 Choosing rather to fatten themselves by a contented Notion, than by curious inquisition to perplex their other recreations. **1784** COWPER *Task* IV. 504 The excise is fattened with the rich result Of all this riot. **1840** ARNOLD *Let.* in Stanley *Life* (1881) II. ix. 163 It is then quite too late to try to fatten them [men] into obedience. **1848** LOWELL *Biglow P.* Poems 1890 II. 36 John Bull has suffered the idea of the Invisible to be very much fattened out of him.

2. *intr.* To grow or become fat. Const. †*in, on.* †Of a letter type: To become thicker. *Obs.*

1676 MOXON *Print Lett.* 49 The Belly fattens downwards. **1693** DRYDEN *Juvenal* xiv. 210 The good Old man and Thrifty Husewife spent Their Days in Peace, and Fatten'd with Content. **1712** GRANVILLE *Poems* 100 Tygers and Woves shall in the Ocean breed, The Whale and Dolphin fatten on the Mead. **1745** E. HEYWOOD *Female Spectator* (1748) III. 132 They..rejoice and fatten in the blood of slaughtered millions. **1755** in *World* No. 113 ⁋12, I therefore propose to you that..we severally endeavour.. you to fatten, and I to waste. **1790-1811** COOMBE *Devil upon Two Sticks* (1817) III. 271 After having, for some years, fattened in the ruin of others, he was at length ruined himself. **1813** SHELLEY *Q. Mab* I. 273 The meanest worm That..fattens on the dead. **1854** *Jrnl. R. Agric. Soc.* XV. I. 252 The ewes readily fatten.

b. *fig.*

1638 BAKER tr. *Balzac's Lett.* II. 13 Methinkes..shee fattens and grows gracefull with these prayses you give her. **1761-2** HUME *Hist. Eng.* (1806) IV. lvii. 357 Such persons, who fatten on the calamities of their country. **1813** SHELLEY *Q. Mab* III. 108 Those gilded flies That, basking in the sunshine of a court, Fatten on its corruption! **1867** FREEMAN *Norm. Conq.* (1876) I. v. 318 Foreigners who..were to fatten on English estates and honours.

3. *trans.* To enrich (the soil) with nutritious or stimulating elements; to fertilize.

1563 FULKE *Meteors* (1640) 50 The river Nilus, whose overflowings doe marveylously fatten the earth. **1583** STUBBES *Anat. Abus.* II. (1882) 44 They are not ignorant also ..what kind of dung is best to fatten the same againe. **1697** DRYDEN *Virg. Georg.* I. 661 Just Heav'n thought good To fatten twice those Fields with Roman blood. **1709** SWIFT *Merlin's Prophecy*, One kind of stuff used to fatten land is called Marle. **1809-10** COLERIDGE *Friend* (1865) 190 Genuine philanthropy, which, like the olive tree..fattens not exhausts the soil from which it sprang.

transf. and *fig.* **1697** DRYDEN *Juvenal Sat.* III. 112 Obscene Orontes..fattens Italy with foreign Whores. **1707** *Curios. in Husb. & Gard.* 259 How efficacious Water is, when it has been fatten'd and heated by Dung. **1842** TENNYSON *Golden Year* 34 Wealth..shall slowly melt In many streams to fatten lower lands.

fattened ('fæt(ə)nd), *ppl. a.* [f. prec. + -ED[1].] That has been made fat.

1613-6 W. BROWNE *Brit. Past.* II. i. 92 Full of well-fleec'd Flockes and fatned Droves. **1725** POPE *Odyss.* IV. 318 Where prolific Nile With various simples clothes the fattened soil. **1872** YEATS *Techn. Hist. Comm.* 63 Fattened hogs of five years old are mentioned by Homer.

fattener ('fæt(ə)nə(r)). [f. as prec. + -ER[1].]

a. One who or that which makes fat. **b.** One that grows fat. **c.** With adj.: An animal that fattens (early, late, slowly, etc.).

1611 COTGR., *Graissier*..a Grasier, or fattener of cattell. *a* **1735** ARBUTHNOT *Mart. Scribl.* (1742) 14 The wind was at West; a wind on which that great Philosopher bestowed the Encomiums of Fatner of the earth [etc.]. **1817** T. L. PEACOCK *Melincourt* xl, Fatteners on public spoil. **1852** *Jrnl. R. Agric. Soc.* XIII. I. 193 Their character as rapid and early fatteners. **1884** W. WREN in *Pall Mall G.* 14 May 11/1 There is a difference between crammers and chicken fatteners.

fattening ('fæt(ə)nɪŋ), *vbl. sb.* [f. as prec. + -ING[1].] The process of making fat or becoming fat. Also the action of thickening (a type).

1614 MARKHAM *Cheap Husb.* VII. xxi. (1668) 124 Peacocks being..seldome..eaten, it mattereth not much for their fatning. **1623-6** COCKERAM II, A Fattening..*sagination.* **1676** MOXON *Print. Lett.* 32 The Fatning is made by setting off 5 on either side the Centre. **1846** J. BAXTER *Libr. Pract. Agric.* (ed. 4) II. 114 Nothing contributes more to expedite the fattening of cattle, than moderate warmth.

fattening ('fæt(ə)nɪŋ), *ppl. a.* [f. as prec. + -ING[2].] That fattens. **a.** That makes fat. **b.** That grows fat.

a. 1697 DRYDEN *Virg. Georg.* I. 119 Load with fat'ning Dung thy fallow Ground. **1866** B. TAYLOR *Poems, Mondanim* 255 Fed by fattening rains. **1876** FOSTER *Phys.* II. v. (1879) 395 Sugar or starch..is always a large constituent of ordinary fattening foods.

b. 1697 DRYDEN *Virg. Past.* VI. 6 Apollo..bade me feed My fatning Flocks. **1790-1811** COOMBE *Devil upon Two Sticks* (1817) VI. 185 An occasional sermon for the service of fattening ignorance, or idle opulence. **1804** EARL LAUDERD. *Publ. Wealth* (1819) 178 Cattle and sheep of a peculiar fattening kind.

fatter ('fætə(r)). [f. FAT *v.* + -ER[1].] **a.** One who makes fat. †Said also of the food. †**b.** With adj. prefixed: An animal that grows fat (quickly, etc.). Also †*fatter up.*

1528 PAYNEL *Salerne's Regim.* G ij, Grene chese..is a nourisher and a fatter. **1671** H. M. tr. *Erasm. Colloq.* 71 This Hen..hath..had a niggardly fatter of her up. **1806** W. TAYLOR in *Ann. Rev.* IV. 83 Where food is plentiful the Java hog is the quickest fatter. **1882** *Athenæum* 26 Aug. 271/2 Those who..buy up lean chickens for the fatter's coop.

fattily ('fætɪlɪ), *adv.* [f. FATTY *a.* + -LY[2].] As by a morbid deposition of fat. Only in *fattily-degenerated.*

1886 *Syd. Soc. Lex.* s.v. *Heart, degeneration of, fatty*, The fattily-degenerated heart is often enlarged and dilated.

fattiness ('fætɪnɪs). [f. FATTY + -NESS.] The quality or condition of being fatty.

1572 J. JONES *Bathes of Bath* II. 14 b, Some man will saye ..that fattines is not in all waters. **1574** NEWTON *Health Mag.* 26 Fattinesse in meate. **1603** HOLLAND *Plutarch's Mor.* 659 Even salt it selfe hath a certeine fattinesse and unctuosity in it. **1638** tr. *Bacon's Nat. Hist.* II. 40 We are to come next to the oleosity or fattiness of them. **1870** A. W. WARD tr. *Curtius' Hist. Greece* I. I. i. 29 Excessive fleshiness and fattiness of body were equally rare.

†**b.** *concr.* Grease. *Obs.*

1601 HOLLAND *Pliny* II. 308 The sweat or fattinesse of vnwashed wooll.

fatting ('fætɪŋ), *vbl. sb.* [f. FAT *v.* + -ING[1].]

1. The action or process of making (an animal or person) fat.

1577 B. GOOGE *Heresbach's Husb.* IV. (1586) 165 b, M. Aufidius Surco, who first beganne the fatting of this Foule. **1681** W. ROBERTSON *Phraseol. Gen.* (1693) 668 He is a mere glutton, born for the fatting of his belly. **1792** *Trans. Soc. Encourag. Arts* (ed. 2) III. 45 [They] gained the first three weeks of fatting, two pounds and a quarter each per diem.

†**2.** The process of growing or becoming fat.

1594 SHAKS. *Rich. III*, I. iii. 314 Clarence..is well repayed: He is frank'd vp to fatting for his paines. **1650** BULWER *Anthropomet.* 242 Three causes..which impede the fatting of Man. **1772** *Ann. Reg.* 106/1 The fatting in the valuable parts of the body.

3. The process of enriching (land) or making (it) fertile or fruitful.

1600 SURFLET *Countrie Farme* I. xv. 93 The dung put aside for the fatting of the medowes. *a* **1617** HIERON *Wks.* II. 464 Salt..is very good for the fatting of the earth.

4. *attrib.*, as **fatting-house**, a place in which to fat animals; **fatting-land**, land suitable for fatting animals; **fatting-stock**, stock for fatting.

1580 BARET *Alv.* F 214 A fatting-house, *saginarium.* *a* **1722** LISLE *Husb.* (1752) 251 It is best to have the sides of the fatting-house open. **1834** *Brit. Husb.* II. 490 The value of fatting land being different. **1861** *Times* 27 Sept., The requisite fatting stock.

fatting ('fætɪŋ), *ppl. a.* [f. as prec. + -ING[2].]

a. That makes fat. **b.** That is growing or being made fat.

1533 ELYOT *Cast. Helthe* (1539) 88 a, The diete of fattinge thinges dothe nourishe abundantly. **1602** MIDDLETON *Blurt, Master Constable* IV. ii, I've fatting knavery in hand. **1767** A. YOUNG *Farmer's Lett. People* 86 Fed off..by some fatting sheep. **1825** COBBETT *Rur. Rides* 458 A stout horse will eat much more than a fatting ox. **1865** *Jrnl. R. Agric. Soc.* 2nd

Ser. I. 255 We believe in it [the pulper] for the young fatting animal.

fattish ('fætɪʃ), *a.* [f. FAT *a.* + -ISH.]

a. Somewhat fat; fairly supplied with fat. †**b.** Somewhat greasy or unctuous. *Obs.*

a. *c* **1369** CHAUCER *Dethe Blaunche* 954 She had..armes ever lith, Fattish, fleshy, nat great therewith. **1577** B. GOOGE *Heresbach's Husb.* IV. 161 For fatting, the best are those [poultry] that have the skinnes of theyr neckes thicke and fattysh. **1668** CULPEPPER & COLE *Barthol. Anat.* III. ix. 149 In the Lobe it is so mingled with Flesh, that it becomes..fattish, fleshy and spungy. **1815** J. W. CROKER in *Croker Papers* (1884) I. iii. 65 Talleyrand..is fattish for a Frenchman. **1864** CARLYLE *Fredk. Gt.* (1865) IV. II. iii. 58 The jolly Ambassador..Camas, a fattish man.

b. **1589** FLEMING *Virg. Georg.* III. 51 Pitch of trees on Ida hill, and fattish wax with grease. **1610** W. FOLKINGHAM *Art of Survey* I. x. 32 Clay mixed with a viscous and fattish Earth. **1671** J. WEBSTER *Metallogr.* xiii. 216 Thin plates of white silver in a fattish stone. **1726** LEONI tr. *Alberti's Archit.* I. III. 49a, The fattish sort [of mortar] is more tenacious than the lean.

Hence '**fattishness**, the quality of being fattish.

1662 H. STUBBE *Ind. Nectar* iii. 28 The body of the water..did shine with a visible Fattishnesse.

fattrels ('fætrɪlz), *sb. pl. Sc.* [ad. F. *fatraille* 'trash, trumpery, things of no value' (Cotgr.).] Ribbon-ends.

1786 BURNS *To a Louse* 20 Now haud you there, ye're out o' sight, Below the fatt'rils, snug and tight. **1788** E. PICKEN *Poems* Gloss. 231 *Fattrels*, ribbon-ends, &c.

fatty ('fætɪ), *a.* and *sb.* [f. FAT + -Y[1].]

A. *adj.* **1. a.** Resembling fat, of the nature of fat, unctuous, oleaginous, greasy.

1398 TREVISA *Barth. De P.R.* XVI. lxxiv. (1495) 577 Yf a stone is not fatty it woll all to fall by maystry of drynesse. **1563** FULKE *Meteors* (1640) 64b, These liquors concreat, that be moist and not fatty. **1616** SURFLET & MARKH. *Country Farme* 548 The bread vvhich is made thereof is..fattie, slymie, heauie. **1731** ARBUTHNOT *Aliments* vi. 194 Spirit of Nitre will turn Oil of Olives into a sort of fatty Substance. **1851** CARPENTER *Man. Phys.* (ed. 2) 160 The fatty matters must be received back into the blood. **1879** *Cassell's Techn. Educ.* III. 398 The fatty ink employed.

†**b.** Besmeared with fat; greasy. *Obs. rare*$^{-1}$.

1572 HULOET (ed. Higgins) s.v. *Fat*, The boye handled the pot with his fatty [*vnctis*] fistes.

†**2.** Of animals, their limbs: Full of fat, plump, well-fed. Of a leaf: Full of sap; juicy. *Obs.*

1552 HULOET, Fatte or Fattye, *adeps.* **1589** FLEMING *Virg. Bucol.* VI. 16 A shepheard it behooues To feed his fattie sheepe. **1601** HOLLAND *Pliny* II. 216 The leaues be whiter and fattier.

3. Full of fertilizing matter. Of soil: Fat, rich.

1590 SPENSER *F.Q.* I. i. 21 As when old father Nilus gins to swell..His fattie waves doe fertile slime outwell. **1855** SINGLETON *Virgil* I. 113 For fatty lands These fit, for lighter those.

4. Consisting of or containing fat; adipose.

1615 CROOKE *Body of Man* VI. v. 353 The fatty veine called *Adiposa.* **1804** ABERNETHY *Surg. Obs.* 30, I have known several fatty tumours growing at the same time. **1861** HUME tr. *Moquin-Tandon* II. I. 41 The Fatty or Adipose Tissue consists of vesicles..filled with an oily fluid. **1884** *Syd. Soc. Lex., Fatty ligament*, a synonym of the *Mucous* ligament of the knee-joint. *Fatty membrane*, the subcutaneous areolar tissue which contains the fat. A *Fatty tumour* is a mass of soft yellow fat, generally enclosed in a..thin fibrous capsule.

5. Marked by morbid deposition of fat, tending to the production of fat, *esp.* in ***fatty degeneration*** (see quot.) ***fatty heart*** or ***kidney*** = fatty degeneration of the heart or kidney.

1866 A. FLINT *Princ. Med.* (1880) 55 In fatty infiltration of a cell, the protoplasm is displaced by the fat. **1877** ROBERTS *Handbk. Med.* (ed. 3) II. 51 Fatty Degeneration is sometimes a part of a general tendency to fatty changes. **1884** *Syd. Soc. Lex., Fatty degeneration*, that condition in which a part or the whole of any tissue or organ is replaced by fat. **1886** *Pall Mall G.* 16 Aug. 14/1 He..dies within a few years from inertia or fatty heart.

6. ***fatty oil***: = fixed oil. ***fatty acid; fatty acid series***: see quot. ***fatty series***: the open-chain group of carbon compounds; the aliphatic series.

1831 J. DAVIES *Manual Mat. Med.* 364 Catapucia Oil..a fatty oil, extracted from the seeds of the *Euphorbia lathyris*, Lin. **1863–72** WATTS *Dict. Chem.* I. 616 *Fatty acids* or *Soap acids.* **1868** HOBLYN *Dict. Terms Med.* (ed. 9), *Fatty Acids*, a group of acids extracted from fats and fixed oils in the process of saponification. The *fatty acid series* is a term synonymous with the *acetic series of acids.* **1872** *Jrnl. Chem. Soc.* XXV. 682 A method of forming the nitro-compounds of the fatty series. **1878** HUXLEY *Physiogr.* 119 Its fatty acids form insoluble salts with the lime. **1926** H. G. RULE tr. *Schmidt's Textbk. Org. Chem.* I. 69 The numerous compounds classified under this title [*sc.* aliphatic or fatty compounds] may be regarded as derived from the hydrocarbon methane... Since the common animal and vegetable fats similarly fall under this heading, the whole series is frequently known as the aliphatic or fatty series.

B. *sb.* A fat person: esp. as a nickname.

1797 B. WYNNE *Diary* 3 Mar. (1937) II. x. 170 His wife is a poor miserable thing, the daughter a good looking fatty. **1882** R. RICHARDSON *Trav. Medit.* II. xix. 266 Well-built fatties, with double mouldings in the neck and chin. **1891** FARMER *Slang, Fatty*, a jocular epithet for a fat man; a comic endearment for a fat woman. **1919** *Holiday Ann. 1920* 120/1 Fatty Wynn was busy... Arthur Augustus..wondered whether Fatty, engrossed by the cake, would think of looking out on the platform. **1960** V. NABOKOV *Invitation to Beheading* x. 101 Cincinnatus..followed every step of the nimble fatty. **1971** *Petticoat* 17 July 32/1 Success stories connected with slimming are few and far between, so any fatties who might be reading this—take note of this tale!

†**fatuant**, *a. Obs. rare*$^{-1}$. [ad. L. *fatuant-em*, pr. pple. of *fatuārī*: see FATUATE *v.*] Behaving fatuously, foolish, silly.

1641 D. HOLLIS in Rushw. *Hist. Coll.* III. (1692) I. 316 A Sorrow not womanish and fatuant, but accompanied with Indignation, and vigorous magnanimous Resolution.

†'**fatuate**, *ppl. a. Obs.* [ad. L. *fatuāt-us*, pa. pple. of *fatuārī*: see next.] Used as equivalent to the later FATUATED.

1601 B. JONSON *Poetaster* V. iii, *Crisp.*—O—oblatrant—furibund—fatuate—strenuous. **1678** R. R[USSELL] *Geber* II. I. II. iii. 47 Their heads are fatuate and void of Humane Reason.

fatuate ('fætjʊeɪt), *v. arch.* [f. L. *fatuāt-* ppl. stem of *fatuārī* to talk foolishly, f. *fatuus* foolish.] *intr.* To become silly, to act foolishly.

Hence '**fatuated** *ppl. a.*, rendered fatuous.

1656–81 BLOUNT *Glossogr., Fatuate*, to play the fool. **1692–1708** in COLES. **1721–1800** in BAILEY. **1848** *Blackw. Mag.* LXIV. 464 Full-grown infant pumpkins, fatuated, empty of anything solid or digestible.

fatuism ('fætjʊɪz(ə)m). [ad. F. *fatuisme*, f. L. *fatu-us*: see FATUOUS and -ISM.] = FATUITY 2.

1884 in *Syd. Soc. Lex.*

fatuitous (fə'tju:ɪtəs), *a.* [f. L. *fatuit-ās* (see FATUITY) + -OUS.] Characterized by fatuity.

a **1734** NORTH *Lives* II. 129 The extremity of fatuitous madness. **1849** C. BRONTE *Shirley* xxix. 427, I may be the most fatuitous..of men. **1869** RUSKIN *Queen of Air* i. 59 In proportion to the degree in which we become narrow in the ..conception of our passions..their expression by musical sound becomes broken, fatuitous, and at last impossible.

Hence **fa'tuitousness**.

1727 in BAILEY vol. II.

fatuity (fə'tju:ɪtɪ). [ad. F. *fatuité* = Pr. *fatuitat*, ad. L. *fatuitātem*, f. *fatuus* foolish.]

1. Folly, silliness, stupidity. Now chiefly (? after 2) in stronger sense: Crass stupidity, 'idiotic' folly; mental blindness caused by 'infatuation'.

The F. word, being associated with its etymological cognate *fat* fop, has usually the sense of 'conceited folly, silly affectation'; this sense, if it occurs in Eng., is only a Gallicism.

1648 *Eikon Bas.* v. 28 It had argued..extream fatuitie of minde in Mee, so far to binde My own hands at their request. **1660** WATERHOUSE *Arms & Arm.* 53 They descend to the fatuity of bringing wild beasts into their Gods and Emperours places. **1797** MRS. RADCLIFFE *Italian* xxiii. (1824) 660 He confounded delicacy of feeling with fatuity of mind. **1812** H. & J. SMITH *Rej. Addr.* x. (1873) 93 The applause of unintellectual fatuity. **1859** THACKERAY *Virgin.* lxxxv, O strange fatuity of youth! **1878** LECKY *Eng. in 18th C.* I. i. 10 Attacked with a strange fatuity the very Church on whose teaching the monarchical enthusiasm mainly rested.

b. Something fatuous; that which is fatuous.

1538 BALE *Thre Lawes* 1386 In vayne worshyp they teachynge mennys fatuyte. **1887** F. HALL in *Nation* (N.Y.) XLIV. 141/2 Star-gazing..and kindred futilities and fatuities.

2. Idiocy, mental imbecility, dementia. Now *rare.*

1621–51 BURTON *Anat. Mel.* I. i. III. iii. 34 If..the animal spirits are..cold, [follows] fatuity and sottishness. *a* **1676** HALE *Hist. Placit. Cor.* (1736) I. iv. 29 Ideocy or *fatuity à nativitate.* **1707** FLOYER *Physic. Pulse-Watch* 93 The Ancients imputed Fatuity to the Refrigeration of the Head. **1748** HARTLEY *Observ. Man* I. iii. 391 A species of Madness; as Fatuity or Idiotism is. **1779** JOHNSON *Lett. Mrs. Thrale* 6 Apr., Death is dreadful, and fatuity is more dreadful. **1797** M. BAILLIE *Morb. Anat.* (1807) 434 He has met with this appearance in cases of fatuity. **1884** in *Syd. Soc. Lex.*

fatuoid ('fætjʊɔɪd). [ad. mod.L. *fatua* (H. Nilsson-Ehle 1921, in *Hereditas* II. 401), f. L. *fatuus* (see FATUOUS) + -OID.] A variant form of cultivated oat, partially resembling the wild oat (*Avena fatua*).

1922 C. V. B. MARQUAND in *Bull. Welsh Plant Breeding Station* C. II. 4 (*heading*) The 'wild base' type, or 'Fatuoid-mutation' of Cultivated Varieties. **1930** *Times Lit. Suppl.* 30 Oct. 894/4 Fatuoids are forms resembling the wild oat that appear occasionally in cultivated varieties of oat. **1957** *Encycl. Brit.* XVI. 665/1 Fatuoids or false wild oats have been observed in nearly all cultivated varieties. Fatuoid kernels also drop to the ground as in the case of wild oats.

†**fatu'osity.** *Obs. rare*$^{-1}$. [as if f. L. **fatuōs-us*, f. *fatuus* FATUOUS + -ITY.] = FATUITY.

1681 GLANVILL *Sadducismus* I. 90 Which opinion..is stiffly held..not without some Fatuosity and Superciliousness.

fatuous ('fætjʊəs). *a.* [f. L. *fatu-us* foolish, silly, insipid + -OUS.]

1. Of persons, their actions, feelings, utterances, etc.: Foolish, vacantly silly, stupid, besotted.

1633 STRUTHER *True Happines* 20 Mathematicians are fatuous. **1652** GAULE *Magastrom.* 162 What fatuous thing is Fate. **1665** GLANVILL *Sceps. Sci.* xiii. 73 We pity, or laugh at those fatuous extravagants. **1844** LEVER *T. Burke* ix, A fatuous, stupid indifference to everything. **1864** H. AINSWORTH *John Law* I. iv, The veteran courtier, fatuous as he was, was not duped by professions of regard. **1877** MORLEY *Crit. Misc.* Ser. II. 277 The fatuous commonplaces of a philosophic optimism. **1878** BOSW. SMITH *Carthage* 33 Roman Senate, in their fatuous disregard for intellect.

2. That is in a state of dementia or imbecility; idiotic. Now *rare* exc. in *Sc. Law.*

1773 ERSKINE *Inst. Law Scot.* I. vii. §48. 139 Fatuous persons, called also idiots..who are entirely deprived of the faculty of reason and have an uniform stupidity and inattention in their manner and childishness in their speech. **1842** M'GLASHAN *Sheriff Courts Process* §441 When a fatuous or furious person has been cognosced. **1868** *Act 31–2 Vict.* c. 100 §101 Such person shall be deemed insane if he be furious or fatuous.

3. ***fatuous fire***: = IGNIS FATUUS. So ***fatuous light, vapour***, etc.

1661 A. BROME *Epist., New Year's Gift*, Those fatuous Vapors, whose false light Purblinds the World. *a* **1668** [see FATUUS]. **1839** BAILEY *Festus* xxxii. (1848) 354 The fatuous fire Of man's weak judgment. **1857–8** SEARS *Athan.* iv. 31 A fatuous light that shall lead him astray.

†**4.** In Lat. sense. Tasteless, insipid, vapid.

1608 D. T. *Ess. Pol. & Mor.* 8b, Truth and Knowledge..where-with whatsoever is not seasoned, is fatuous and unsavourie. **1624** DONNE *Devotions* 25 Instantly the tast is insipid and fatuous.

Hence '**fatuously** *adv.*, in a fatuous manner; '**fatuousness**, the quality or fact of being fatuous; imbecility, stupidity.

1876 J. WEISS *Wit, Hum. & Shaks.* v. 154 The fair maid [Ophelia] who must be the tenant of this grave so fatuously dug. **1882** MISS BRADDON *Mnt. Royal* i, Such wild youths, she told herself, fatuously, generally make the best men. **1874** MORLEY *Compromise* (1886) 27 In both orders alike there is only too much of this kind of fatuousness. **1884** *Westmorland Gaz.* 1 Nov. 5/1 The..fatuousness of the policy..pursued in South Africa.

'**fatuus.** *rare*$^{-1}$. Short for IGNIS FATUUS.

a **1668** DENHAM *Progr. Learning* 160 Thence Fatuus fires and Meteors take their birth. **1820** COTTLE *Expost. Let. Ld. Byron* 165 To..turn aside Whoe'er may take thy fatuus for a guide.

fat-witted, *a.* [f. FAT *a.* + WIT + -ED[2].] Of slow wit, dull, 'thick-headed'.

1596 SHAKS. *1 Hen. IV*, I. ii. 2 Thou art so fat-witted..that thou hast forgotten to demand that truely, which thou wouldest truly know. **1797** J. LAWRENCE in *Monthly Mag.* XLVI. 215 Grave and pious, or fat-witted sophisters. **1803** SYD. SMITH *Wks.* (1859) I. 62/1 If they are endowed, professors become fat-witted. **1863** HAWTHORNE *Our Old Home* (1883) I. 374 These..lawyers, slow-paced and fat-witted as they must needs be.

faubourg (fobur). Forms: 5 **faubourgh, fabo(u)r**, 6 **faubor, (foubour), (fourbourg)**, 7–8 **fauxburgh**, 7–9 **fauxbourg**, 9 **fauberg**, 7– **faubourg**. [late ME. *faubourg, fabo(u)r*, a. F. *faubourg.* From the 15th c. to the beginning of the 17th c. the word was more or less naturalized, esp. in Scotland; it is now used only as foreign, with Fr. pronunciation or (more frequently) semi-anglicized as ('fəʊbʊə(r), -bʊəg).

Littré considers *faubourg*, formerly also spelt *faux-bourg* (= 'false borough') to be a corruption of the earlier-recorded synonym *forsbourg* (f. *fors* outside + *bourg* borough), which is the source of some of the Eng. forms given above. The word *faubourg, faux-bourg*, seems not to be known in F. before 15th c., but its existence in 1380 is implied by L. *falsus burgus* in a charter cited by Du Cange. Its origin may possibly be found in the MHG. *phâlburgere* (also spelt *falborgere*), which according to German scholars originally meant 'burghers of the pale', i.e. 'persons living outside the city wall but within the palisade'; it afterwards denoted a special class of non-resident burghers, having only partial civic rights. The word occurs frequently in the imperial charters of 13–14th c., sometimes latinized as *phalburgenses*; and a charter of 1365, according to a French translation given by Laguille (1727) speaks of 'des faux bourgeois dits en allemand Pfalbourguers'. From these facts it seems not unlikely that *faubourg, faux-bourg*, may have been evolved from *phalburgensis* or its punning translation *falsus burgensis, faux bourgeois.*]

A portion of a town or city, lying outside the gates; a suburb. (In Paris the name is still retained by various parts of the city which were originally suburbs, but have long been included within the walls.)

1470, 1489 [see FABOR]. **1483** CAXTON *Gold. Leg.* 308/4 The other kepe the cytees the townes the castellys and the faubourghs. **1523** LD. BERNERS *Froiss.* I. ccclxv. 596 Theyr foreryders went to the faubories of Sence. **1582–8** *Hist. Jas. VI* (1825) 6 Neir the toun wall and fauxbourg thereof. **1608** LD. HERBERT *Trav. fr. Paris* in *Life* (1886) 90 *note*, You must conceive they're..come To Fourbourgs St. Germans. **1655** SIR E. NICHOLAS in *N. Papers* (Camden) II. 315 My lo. of Buckingham lyes here in these fauxbourgs. **1739** GRAY *Jrnl. in France* Wks. 1884 I. 243 A charming view..just before you come to Lyons, of the Fauxbourgs of that City. **1830** R. CHAMBERS *Life Jas. I*, I. 40 The Canongate, one of the fauxbourgs of Edinburgh. **1877** D. M. WALLACE *Russia* xxiii. 355 At the further end of this fauberg stood a fortified tower.

faucal ('fɔ:kəl), *a.* and *sb.* [f. L. *fauc-ēs* (see FAUCES *sb. pl.*) + -AL[1].] **A.** *adj.* Of or pertaining to the fauces or throat. In phonology applied chiefly to certain deep guttural sounds, *esp.* in the Semitic languages.

1864 in WEBSTER. **1876** T. DOUSE *Grimm's L.* App. A. 179 Its more usual affinity being for the faucal *â*. **1883** I. TAYLOR *Alphabet* I. III. §3. 180 The 'faucal breaths' as well as the linguals, are characteristic of the Semitic languages. **1884** *Syd. Soc. Lex., Faucal*, relating to, or arising in connection with, the *Fauces.*

B. *sb.* A faucal sound.

1883 I. TAYLOR *Alphabet.* I. III. §3. 180 '*Ayin* is the most difficult of the faucals. *Ibid.* I. III. §3. 181 *Cheth*.. a 'fricative faucal', was a strongly marked continuous guttural sound produced at the back of the palate.

faucalize ('fɔːkəlaɪz), *v.* [f. FAUCAL *a.* + -IZE.] *trans.* To add a faucal element to (a sound).

1919 H. H. JOHNSTON *Comp. Stud. Bantu & Semi-B. Lang.* I. ii. 36 The slurring of *g* or the faucalizing of *w.* **1920** *Man* XX. 14 How do you faucalise *w*?

‖**fauces** ('fɔːsiːz), *sb. pl.* Also 6 faulses. [Latin.] See also FAUX.

1. *Anat.* The cavity at the back of the mouth, from which the larynx and pharynx open out.

1541 R. COPLAND *Guydon's Quest. Chirurg.*, Demaunde. Whereof serueth the encla, and the amygdales and faulses and where are they sette? **1746** R. JAMES *Introd. Mouffet's Health's Improv.* 3 The alimentary Mass.. is thrust towards the Fauces. **1805** *Med. Jrnl.* XIV. 114 Without producing much affection of his salivary glands and fauces. **1878** HABERSHON *Dis. Abdomen* (ed. 3) 33 The anterior fauces are greatly narrowed.

transf. **1800** HURDIS *Fav. Village* 17 E'er he pours into the distant deep, Through the wide fauces of yon hiant cliffs.

2. a. *Bot.* The throat of a calyx, corolla, etc. **b.** *Conch.* That portion of the first chamber of a shell which can be seen from the aperture.

1840 PAXTON *Bot. Dict.*, *Fauces*, the gaping part of monopetalous flowers.

faucet ('fɔːsɪt), *sb.*[1] Forms: 5 faucett, fawcet(t, 5–6 fawset, 6 faucete, -set, (fasset, faulsed, -set), 7 faucit, -sset, 7–8 fosset, (forset), 4– faucet. [a. F. *fausset* (in sense 1); of unknown etymology.]

†**1.** A peg or spigot to stop the vent-hole in a cask or in a tap; a vent-peg. *Obs.*

c **1430** *Wyclif's Job.* xxxii. 19 (MS. V.) Lo! my wombe is as must with out faucet [**1388** spigot] *ether a ventyng* that brekith newe vessels. **1616** SURFL. & MARKH. *Country Farme*, To giue it [ayre] when the fosset is halfe out. **1632** B. JONSON *Magn. Lady* II. i, With a faucet or peg. **1741** *Compl. Fam. Piece* I. v. 266 Give it Vent.. with a Hole made with a Gimblet; into which put a Peg or Faucet.

2. A tap for drawing liquor from a barrel, etc. Now *dial.* and *U.S.*

Formerly more fully *spigot and faucet*, denoting an old form of tap, still used in some parts of England, consisting of a straight wooden tube, one end of which is tapering to be driven into a hole in the barrel, while the other end is closed by a peg or screw. The peg or screw when loosened allows the liquor to flow out through a hole in the under side of the tube. Properly, the *spigot* seems to have been the tube, and the *faucet* the peg or screw (as still in the Sheffield dialect); but in some examples the senses are reversed, and each of the words has been used for the entire apparatus. In the U.S. *faucet* is now the ordinary word for a tap of any kind.

?*a* **1400** *Morte Arth.* 205 Vernage.. In faucetez of fyne golde. *a* **1483** *Liber Niger* in *Househ. Ord.* 77 He asketh allowaunce for tubbys, treyes, and faucettes. **1468** *Paston Lett.* No. 549 II. 268 For claretts and fawcetts vi d. **1530** PALSGR. 740/1 Our men be to thrustye to taryе tyll their drinke be drawen with a faulsed. **1549** CHALONER *Erasmus on Folly* G iv b, He founde a backe faulset set in his wyne vessell. **1630** RANDOLPH *Aristippus* (1652) 16 Thi Nose like a Fausset with the Spicket out. **1719** D'URFEY *Pills* (1872) I. 285 In spite of his Spigot and Faucet, The States-man must go to old Nick. **1780** VON TROIL *Iceland* 190 A hole in the rock, which is shut with a spigot and faucet. **1881** MISS LAFFAN in *Macm. Mag.* XLIV. 379 This was furnished with a half-dozen faucets, which could be turned on at will. **1888** *Sheffield Gloss.*, *Faucet*, a wooden tap-screw for a barrel. **1890** *Harper's Mag.* Apr. 751 The dripping of the water from the faucet in the sink sounded sharp and distinct.

fig. **1568** T. HOWELL *Arb. Amitie* A ij. *To Lady Talbot*, It is.. more commendable to learne to suppresse thy tongue, then to seeke the fasset to set abroch the same. **1640** BROME *Sparagus Gard.* III. iv. Wks. 1873 III. 160 In every man there are all humours to him that can find their faussets.

†**b.** A contemptuous appellation for a tapster.

1614 B. JONSON *Barth. Fair* II. ii, My chayre, you false faucet you. *Ibid.* II. iii, Speake in thy faith of a faucet.

3. Used as a synonym of ADJUTAGE.

a **1774** GOLDSM. *Surv. Experim. Philos.* (1776) I. 407 The contrivance of the fosset or ajutage.

4. *U.S.* (See quot.)

1874 KNIGHT *Dict. Mech.*, *Faucet*, the enlarged end of a pipe to receive the spigot end of the next section.

5. *attrib.* and *Comb.*, as *faucet-hole*, *-seller*. Also U.S. **faucet-joint** (see quot.).

1607 SHAKS. *Cor.* II. i. 79 Hearing a cause betweene an Orendge wife and a Forset-seller. **1688** R. HOLME *Armoury* III. iii. 108/1 *Tap* is the Forset hole made in the head of the Barrel to draw the Liquor out. **1874** KNIGHT *Dict. Mech.*, *Faucet-joint*, 1. An expansion-joint for uniting two parts of a straight metallic pipe, which is exposed to great variations of temperature. 2. One form of breech-loader in which the rear of the bore is exposed by the turning of a perforated plug.

†**'faucet, 'fauset,** *sb.*[2] *Obs.* [Corruption of FACET.] = FACET. Also applied to a faceted stone. *Comb.* **faucet-cut**, cut like a facetted stone.

1684 R. WALKER *Nat. Exper.* 131 The fausets (*i.e.*) those [diamonds] that are ground of their own Octoedral Figure, seldom or never failed. **1685** *Lond. Gaz.* No. 2028/4 Lost.. a little Drap containing one large Stone.. and three little Faucets weighing about two Grains and half each. **1712** *Ibid.* 5055/3 The 2 Side-drops faucet-cut.

fauch, faugh (fɑːx), *sb.* Chiefly *Sc.* Also 9 *north.* fauf, fawf. 'A single furrow, out of lea; also the land thus managed, Ang.' (Jam.); = FALLOW *sb.* 2 and 3. Also attrib. *faugh sheep*, sheep fed on a fallow.

15.. *Scotish Field* in *Percy's* Folio MS. I. 228 On the broad hills we busked our standards, And on a faugh vs beside. **1641** BEST *Farm. Bks.* (Surtees) 17 Well happed sheepe are the best for an hard faugh. *Ibid.* 27 Our faugh sheepe doe not afforde soe fine a wooll. **1736** RAMSAY *Sc. Prov.* (1807) 16 Farmers faugh gar lairds laugh. **1792** G. S. KEITH in *Statist. Acc. Scotl.* II. 535 Their outfields and fauchs are rated at from 3*s.* to 10*s.* **1794** R. MICHIE *ibid.* X. 239 The faughs are a part of the outfield never dunged. **1876** *Whitby Gloss.*, Fauf, a fallow. **1883** *Almondbury Gloss.* s.v. *Fauf*, A 'potato fauf' is when the land is ready for the sets, and also after the crop has been taken out.

†**fauch,** *a.*[1] *Sc. Obs.* Also 6 fawch. [From the sense app. a variant of FALLOW *a.*[1]; the abnormal form may be due to association with FALLOW *a.*[2], of which *fauch* (see next) is the normal representative in Sc.] = FALLOW *a.*[1] 1.

1513 DOUGLAS *Æneis* VIII. i. 74 A linȝe wattry garmond dyd hym vaill, Off colour fauch [L. *glauco*]. *Ibid.* XII. Prol. 108 Sum grece, sum gowlis.. Blanchit or brovne, fawch ȝallow mony ane.

fauch (fɑːx), *a.*[2] Chiefly *Sc.* Forms: 8 **faugh,** 9 *north.* **fauf,** 6 **fauch.** [Northern var. of FALLOW *a.*[2] (:—OE. *fealh-).] = FALLOW *a.*[2]

1513 DOUGLAS *Æneis* VI. vi. 68 Amang the fauch rispis harsk and star. *c* **1565** LINDSAY (Pitscottie) *Chron. Scot.* (1814) 499 It was in ane fauch eard and rid land quhair they moved for the tyme. **1688** R. HOLME *Armoury* III. 73/1 Faugh ground, or ground lying Faugh.. the same to Fallow. **1721** RAMSAY *Wks.* (1848) III. 56 He likes best To be of good faugh riggs possesst. **1876** *Mid. Yorksh. Gloss.* s.v. *Fauf*, 'A fauf-field', a fallow-field. **1876** *Whitby Gloss.* s.v. *Fauf*, To 'lie fauf' as when the soil is left to mellow.

fauch, faugh, *v.* Chiefly *Sc.* Also 6 faucht, 9 *north.* fauf. [var. of FALLOW.] *trans.* To fallow (ground).

15.. *Aberdeen Reg.* (Jam.), Sayand at [= that] hewald nocht eir nor faucht his land sa air in the yeir. **1703** THORESBY *Let. to Ray* 27 Apr. Yorksh. Wds. (E.D.S.), *Faugh.* **1799** A. JOHNSTONE in *Statist. Acc. Scotl.* XXI. 139 A part of folding ground, enriched by the dung of sheep and of cattle.. or fauched (a kind of bastard fallow) and manured by a little compost dung, bore three, four or five crops. **1810** CROMEK *Rem. Nithsdale Song* (1880) 69, I brawlie can faugh yere weel-ploughed lea. **1855** ROBINSON *Whitby Gloss.*, *Faugh*, to fallow. **1883** *Almondbury Gloss.* s.v., They say a man is faufing his land when he is cleaning it with no crop on it.

faucheon, -ion, -on, var. ff. of FALCHION.

faucial ('fɔːʃ(ɪ)əl, -ʃəl), *a.* [as if f. L. *fauci-*, *faucēs* (see FAUCES) + -AL[1]. Cf. FAUCAL.]

a. Of or pertaining to the fauces. Of a sound: Proceeding from the fauces. **b.** *Bot.* Pertaining to the fauces or 'throat' of a flower.

1807 *Ann. Reg.* 932 That hoarse faucial noise before mentioned. **1840** POE *W. Wilson* Wks. (1864) I. 423 My rival had a weakness in the faucial or guttural organs. **1845** LINDLEY *Sch. Bot.* v. (1858) 60 Stamens.. arising from the outside of an annular faucial disk.

faucitis (fɔː'saɪtɪs). *Path.* [f. FAUC-ES + -ITIS.] Inflammation of the fauces.

1875 H. C. WOOD *Therap.* (1879) 50 In faucitis, the strength of the solution [Nitrate of Silver] may vary from fifteen to thirty grains. **1884** in *Syd. Soc. Lex.*

faucon(e, -oun, -onet, obs. ff. FALCON, -ET.

faucylle, obs. form of FOCILE.

faud, dial. form of FOLD.

faudom, obs. Sc. form of FATHOM.

faue, obs. form of FAIN *a.*

†**'faufel(l.** *Obs.* [a. Arab. *faufel.*] = ARECA.

1594 BLUNDEVIL *Exerc.* v. vi. (ed. 7) 545 That Indian tree which is called Faufell. **1693** *Phil. Trans.* XVII. 684 The Betel and Faufel (the first of the Pepper, the latter of the Palm kind). *Ibid.* 766 The Indians chew the Leaves instead of Betel with the Faufel or Arequa. **1755** JOHNSON, *Faufel*, the fruit of a species of the palm-tree. And in later Dicts.

faugh (fɔː). *int.* Also 6 fah, 6–7 foh, 7 fough. An exclamation of abhorrence or disgust.

1542 UDALL tr. *Erasm. Apoph.* 320 b, All yᵉ coumpaignie.. crying foh at suche a shamefull lye. *c* **1597** NASHE *Let.* in Grosart *Wks.* I. Introd. 64 Had I beene of his [Sir J. Harrington's] consayle, he shold have sett for the mott, or word before it [H.'s *Ajax*], Fah! **1599** B. JONSON *Cynthia's Rev.* III. ii, Fough, he smells all lamp-oyle. *a* **1679** LD. ORRERY *Guzman* iv, Faugh, What an unsavory Smell assaults my Nose! *c* **1680** HICKERINGILL *Hist. Whiggism*, Wks. 1716 I. 108 Foh! no more of them. **1700** FARQUHAR *Constant Couple* I. ii, Faugh, the nauseous fellow! he stinks of poverty already. **1832** W. IRVING *Alhambra* I. 291 'A monkey! faugh!.. I hate the nauseous animal'. **1864** THACKERAY *D. Duval* vii, Faugh! the wicked little beast!

faugh, var. of FAUCH.

fauȝt, fauht(e, obs. ff. *fought*; see FIGHT *v.*

faughter, dial. f. of FALTER *v.*[3]

faughter, var. of FAULTER *sb. Obs.*, a defaulter.

faughty, obs. form of FAULTY.

fauhn, obs. form of FAWN *v.*

faujasite ('foːʒəsaɪt). *Min.* [Named after *Faujas de Saint-Fond*, French geologist: see -ITE.]

1844 DANA *Min.* 524 Faujasite occurs in square octahedrons. **1863–72** WATTS *Dict. Chem.* II. 617 *Faujasite*, a silicate occurring, together with black augite in the mandelstein of the Kaiserstuhl in Baden.

faul(e, obs. form of FALL.

fauld, Sc. and dial. form of FOLD.

fauld (fɔːld). *Min.* [Perh. = *fauld*, Sc. var. of FOLD.] (See quot.)

1874 KNIGHT *Dict. Mech.* I. 827/2 *Fauld*, the tymp-arch or working arch of a furnace. **1881** in RAYMOND *Min. Gl.*

Faulknerian (fɔːk'nɪərɪən), *a.* [-IAN.] Of or pertaining to (the writings of) William Faulkner (1897–1962), American novelist.

1951 *Yale Rev.* XLI. II. p. viii/2 Another book with Faulknerian echoes. **1960** *Encounter* Aug. 74/1 A Faulknerian family disaster. **1961** *Times* 12 Jan. 15/5 Mr. Faulkner's style is as Faulknerian as ever. **1966** S. MARCUS *Other Victorians* i. 17 The prevailing tone of this book.. is resonant of danger, doom, and disaster (to strike a Faulknerian note).

fault (fɔːlt, fɒlt), *sb.* Forms: 3–7 (8, 9 *dial.*) faut(e, (5 fauute, fauȝt), 4–6 fawt(e, 5–7 falt, faulte, 5– fault. [ME. *faut(e*, a. OF. *faute* fem. (also *faut* masc.) = Pr., Sp., Pg., It. *falta*:—popular Lat. *fallita, a failing, coming short, f. *fallitus, popular Lat. pa. pple. of *fallěre*: see FAIL *v.*

The earliest recorded spelling in Fr. is *faute*; the etymological *l* was inserted by some writers in 15–17th c., and this example was followed in Eng. (our first certain instance being in the MSS. of Barbour written in 1487–9); from 17th c. the standard spelling has been *fault*, but in Pope and Swift it rimes with *thought*, *wrought*, and Johnson 1755 says that in conversation the *l* is generally suppressed. In many dialects the pronunciation is still (fɔːt).]

†**1. a.** Deficiency, lack, scarcity, want *of* (something specified). *rare* in *pl.* Also used *absol.* (like *want*) = want of food or necessaries. *Obs.*

a **1300** *Cursor M.* 4504 (Cott.) Man þat.. thoru his welth, na fautes felis. *Ibid.* 5385 (Cott.) Faut o bred was in þat tide. **1340–70** *Alex. & Dind.* 303, & whan we faren to fed we finde no faute. **1375** BARBOUR *Bruce* IX. 318 [He] has the castell tan, Throu falt of vach. *c* **1450** HENRYSON *Mor. Fab.* 60 The Fowles faire for falt they fell off feete. *c* **1450** *St. Cuthbert* (Surtees) 7628 He fande faute of honeste. **14..** *Pol. Rel. & L. Poems* (1866) 95 The pore, for faute late þem not spylle! **1523** LD. BERNERS *Froiss.* I. clix. 193 They had gret faut in their hoost of vitayle. **1591** CONINGSBY *Siege of Rouen* in *Camden Misc.* (1847) I. 30 You would have thoughte there had bene noe faulte of men.

†**b.** The amount deficient (in an account). *Obs.*

1665 PEPYS *Diary* 20 Mar., He.. is ready to lay down in ready money the fault of his account.

c. *for* (*the*) *fault of*: in default of; in the absence of; through deficiency or want of. Also without *for* (after F. *faute de*). Now *arch.*

c **1290** *S. Eng. Leg.* I. 397/154 His fon haueþ moch of his lond for þe faute of þe y-nome. *c* **1330** *Arth. & Merl.* 7834 Ded me weren leuer by Ihesus Than he starf for faut of ous. *c* **1386** CHAUCER *Sqr.'s T.* 435 She swouned.. for faute of blood. *c* **1420** *Pallad. on Husb.* IV. 699 For faute of that gete other thinges goode. **1480** *Bury Wills* (1850) 56 For the favte of sweche issue the remandyre therof to the next heyre. *a* **1533** LD. BERNERS *Gold. Bk. M. Aurel.* (1546) N iij, Rome is fallen.. not for faute of money and armes. **1597** SHAKS. *2 Hen. IV*, II. ii. 45 One it pleases me, for fault of a better, to call my friend. **1620** *Frier Rush* 30 His Masters shoone.. for faut of greasing.. were very hard. **1685** *Gracian's Courtiers Orac.* 221 Seriousness is wanting, for fault of which great qualities have no lustre in them. **1794** BURNS *Gane is the day*, We'll ne'er stray for faute o' light. **1867** EMERSON *Poems* (1914) 252 And, fault of novel germs, Mature the unfallen fruit. **1874** SWINBURNE *Bothwell* (1882) II. xiv. 195 Though it be evil made for fault of time.

†**2.** Default, failing, neglect. *without* (*any*) *fault* (= Fr. *sans faute*): without fail; hence, for a certainty. Cf. FAIL *sb.* 1. *Obs.*

c **1325** *Coer de L.* 1214 Thou schalt.. have.. folk inowe with thee; In us schall no fawte bee. **1389** in *Eng. Gilds* (1870) 34 Who-so.. be nouthe þere.. he schal paie a pound of wax for is faute. *c* **1477** CAXTON *Jason* 45 b, If ye wole telle me your name with out any faute, I shal telle yow myn also. *c* **1489** —— *Sonnes of Aymon* ix. 215 Now shall they be honged to morowe wythoute fawte. *c* **1500** *Melusine* 318 My swete loue.. there shal be no fawte of it. **1502** *Bury Wills* (Camden) 92 For fawte of thithing and offryng nectly-gently forgotyn iij s. iiij d. **1523** LD. BERNERS *Froiss.* I. xviii. 22 Your ennemies.. be within iii. myle of you.. ther shall ye fynde them without faulte. **1587** MASCALL *Govt. Cattle* (1627) 182 They are bred by euill meate, and fault of drinking good water.

3. A defect, imperfection, blameable quality or feature. **a.** in moral character. (Expressing a milder censure than *vice*.)

1377 LANGL. *P. Pl.* B. XI. 209 Ne vnder-nym nouȝte foule for is none with-oute faute. *c* **1400** *Apol. Loll.* 100 We are not so sikir þat we be wiþ out faut, error, and vnkunning. *c* **1420** *Chron. Vilod.* 1226 In me fforsothe no fauȝt þer nys. **1587** *Mirr. Mag.*, *Porrex* vii, Can I excuse my selfe deuoide of faut. **1642** FULLER *Holy & Prof. St.* IV. xiv. 308 That godly King.. had some defects, but few faults. **1784** FRANKLIN *Autobiog.* Wks. 1840 I. 113 A benevolent man should allow a few faults in himself. **1785** BURNS *Epist. to J. Lapraik* xvii, There's ae wee faut they whiles lay to me, I like the lasses. *a* **1846** LANDOR *Imag. Conv.* Wks. 1846 I. 464 Great men too often have greater faults than little men can find room for.

1857 LIVINGSTONE *Trav.* ii. 44 His independence and love of the English were his only faults.

b. in physical or intellectual constitution, appearance, structure, workmanship, etc.

c **1320** *Seuyn Sag.* (W.) 120 The fairest man.. Withouten faute fra heid to fote. **1538** STARKEY *England* II. i. 26 The commyn fautys and mysordurys of the same. **1599** MINSHEU *Dial. Sp. & Eng.* (1623) 57 The women generally.. have three faults.. litle eies, great mouthes, and not very smooth skin. **1651** HOBBES *Leviath.* II. xvii. 86 Do not see.. any fault, in the administration of their common businesse. **1675** VILLIERS (Dk. Buckhm.) *Ess. Poetry* 74 Where can one [song] be seen without a fault? **1713** SWIFT *Cadenus & Vanessa* 603 She own'd the wandering of her thoughts, But he must answer for her faults. **1884** tr. *Lotze's Logic* 197 An essential fault of the Pythagorean theory.

c. In phrase *to a fault* (qualifying an adj.): to such an extent that it becomes a fault; excessively, extremely.

1752 *Scots Mag.* xv. 41/1 This was good-natur'd to a fault. **1762** GOLDSM. *Nash* Wks. 1881 IV. 89 She was.. generous to a fault. **1849** D. G. MITCHELL *Battle Summer* (1852) 140 His dress is plain to a fault.

d. Comm. ***with all faults*** (now sometimes abbreviated 'A.F.' or 'Job A.F.'): with all defects, *i.e.* the seller will not be answerable for them.

1716 *Lond. Gaz.* No. 5400/4 To be taken away with all Faults. **1894** *Times* (Weekly ed.) 22 June p. iii/4 A first folio Shakespeare, imperfect, and sold with all faults, realized £255.

†**4.** An unsound or damaged place; a flaw, crack; *Mil.* a gap in the ranks. *Obs.*

1514 BARCLAY *Cyt. & Uplondyshm.* (Percy Soc.) 9 Stoppe all the holes where thou can fautes se. **1595** SHAKS. *John* IV. ii. 33 Patches set vpon a little breach Discredite more in hiding of the fault. **1609** C. BUTLER *Fem. Mon.* iii. (1623) G iij, First, lift vp the stalls.. then setting them downe againe.. mend all brackes and faults about them. **1698** SIR T. MORGAN *Progr. in France* in *Select. Harl. Misc.* (1793) 388 Major Morgan, observing the enemy mending faults, and opening the intervals of the foot, to bring horse in.

5. Something wrongly done. Phrase, ***to commit*** (rarely ***do, make***) ***a fault***. **a.** In moral sense: A dereliction of duty; a misdeed, transgression, offence. Also *occas.* Delinquency in general, 'something wrong'.

13.. *E.E. Allit. P.* B. 177 For fele fautez may a freke forfete his blysse. *a* **1450** *Knt. de la Tour* (1868) 66 Forto clense her of sertaine fauutes that she had done. **1514** BARCLAY *Cyt. & Uplondyshm.* (Percy Soc.) 3 Faustus.. To them imputynge grete fautes. **1550** CROWLEY *Last Trump* 753 Winke not at faltes. **1611** BIBLE *Gen.* xli. 9, I doe remember my faults this day. **1748** BUTLER *Serm.* Wks. 1874 II. 310 Distresses.. brought upon persons by their own faults. *a* **1853** ROBERTSON *Serm.* Ser. III. xvii. 219 A restless, undefinable sense of fault. **1875** JOWETT *Plato* (ed. 2) III. 250 A fault which is most serious, I said; the fault of telling a lie.

b. A failure in what is attempted; a slip, error, mistake. Now somewhat *rare*; 'lady teachers often use it in marking school exercises (after F. *faute*)' (*N.E.D.*). In early use *esp.* †a clerical error or misprint.

1523 LD. BERNERS *Froiss.* I. Author's Pref., If any faute be in this my rude translacyon. **1559** W. CUNNINGHAM *Cosmogr. Glasse* A iij b, If faultes escape.. with penne spedely amende it. **1583** HOLIBAND *Campo di Fior* 359 Leave more space betwene both lines. That there maye be place to mende your faultes. **1633** *E. Campion's Hist. Irel.* (at end), Faults escaped. **1701** DE FOE *True-born Eng.* Pref., The Book is Printed; and tho I see some Faults, 'tis too late to mend them. **1725** WATTS *Logic* III. iii, There must be some fault in the deduction. **1774** GOLDSM. *Grecian Hist.* II. 35 The other army.. had made another fault, not less considerable. **1845** GRAVES *Rom. Law* in *Encycl. Metrop.* 775/1 The.. faults of the Florentine MS. are corrected.

c. *spec.* in *Rackets* and *Tennis.* A faulty stroke; a stroke in which the server fails to make the ball fall within the prescribed limits.

1599 CHAPMAN *Humorous Day's Mirth* E ij, I gaue him fifteene and all his faults. **1611** COTGR., *Bisque*, a fault at Tennis. **1679** SHADWELL *True Widow* I, We'll play with you at a bisk, and a fault, for twenty pound. **1886** H. F. WILKINSON *Encycl. Brit.* XX. 210/2 (*Rackets*), Two consecutive faults put a hand out. **1888** J. MARSHALL *ibid.* XXIII. 182/2 (*Tennis*), It is a fault if the service be delivered from the wrong court.

6. a. *to find* (*a*) *fault*: to discover or perceive a fault (senses 3–5) *in* a person or thing. **b.** Hence, idiomatically, ***to find fault*** (***with***, †***at***): to express dissatisfaction (with), criticize unfavourably, censure.

a. *a* **1375** *Lay Folks Mass Bk.* App. iv. 479 Faute þer-Inne ȝif þat he fynde Mak no scornynge me be-hynde. *c* **1400** *Rom. Rose* 3837 Grete faute in thee now have I founde. *c* **1440** *York Myst.* xx. 183 Fautez nowe are founden fele. **1563–7** BUCHANAN *Reform. St. Andros* Wks. (1892) 9 Geif the regent find falt quhairof the nomenclator has nocht advertysit hym. **1711** ADDISON *Spect.* No. 29 ¶3 The only Fault I find in our present Practice. **1841** LANE *Arab. Nts.* I. 63 If he find any fault in her within three days.

b. *c* **1400** *Destr. Troy* 4850 Rule vs by rightwisnes.. þat no fawte with vs founden be. **1588** J. UDALL *Diotrephes* (Arb.) 6 Finding faut with him for one thing or another. **1593** *Tell-Troths N.Y. Gift* 9 A man will finde fault without cause. **1611** BIBLE *Mark* vii. 2 When they saw some of his disciples eate bread with defiled.. hands, they found fault. **1656** *Artif. Handsom.* (1662) 4 Eyes.. over-curious to find fault at Art. **1741** MIDDLETON *Cicero* (ed. 3) III. XI. 257 You find fault with me. **1776** BENTHAM *Fragm. Govt.* Wks. 1843 I. 230 If nothing is ever to be found fault with, nothing will ever be mended. **1875** JOWETT *Plato* (ed. 2) I. 161, I am not given to finding fault. **1892** T. W. ERLE in *Law Times* XCIII. 417/2 No fault was found with my suggestions.

7. a. With reference to persons: Culpability; the blame or responsibility of causing or permitting some untoward occurrence; the wrong-doing or negligence to which a specified evil is attributable. ***to be in*** (†***one's***, †***the***) ***fault***: to be to blame. † ***to lay, put*** (***a***) ***fault*** †***in, upon***: to impute blame to. † ***to bear the fault***: to bear the blame. ***it is my*** (***his***, etc.) ***fault***: I am (he is, etc.) the person to blame for what has happened.

1377 LANGL. *P. Pl.* B. x. 103 And leyden fautes vpon þe fader þat fourmed vs alle. *c* **1475** *Rauf Coilȝear* 290 He will be found in his fault. that wantis. **1530** CROME in Strype *Eccl. Mem.* III. App. x. 20, I doo nott putt fawte in no man. **1530** PALSGR. 429/2, I am.. in the faute that a thyng is a mysse, *jay tort.* **1559** *Mirr. Mag., Northumbld.* xix, This was my hap, my fortune, or my fawte. **1600** E. BLOUNT tr. *Conestaggio* 206 To lay the faulte upon Anthony. **1665** BOYLE *Occas. Refl.* IV. xi. (1845) 235 Their Superiours are in the fault. **1700** S. L. tr. *C. Fryke's Voy. E. Ind.* 349 The Master was in all the fault. **1715** DE FOE *Fam. Instruct.* I. v. (1841) I. 96 Lay the fault on me. **1726–31** TINDAL *Rapin's Hist. Eng.* (1743) II. XVII. 675 Who are in the greatest faults. **1735** POPE *Ep. Lady* 73 Let Blood and Body bear the fault. **1756–7** tr. *Keysler's Trav.* (1760) I. 319 All is lost, but not through any fault of mine. *a* **1839** PRAED *Poems* (1864) II. 22 When weak poets go astray, 'The stars are more in fault than they'. **1848** DICKENS *Dombey* ii, It will be our own faults if we lose sight of this one. **1884** F. M. CRAWFORD *Rom. Singer* I. 1 It was not any fault of mine.

¶ Incorrectly in plural, by the attraction of poss. adj. referring to two or more persons.

1738 *Common Sense* (1739) II. 242 Where this happens, it is their own Faults. **1774** MITFORD *Ess. Harmony Lang.* 228 It is our own faults if we err greatly.

b. The defect, the 'something wrong' (in things, conditions, etc.) to which a specified evil is attributable. (Phrases as in a.)

1375 BARBOUR *Bruce* III. 298 Giff.. he thar-off failȝe, The fawt may be in his trawailȝe. **1590** SIR J. SMYTH *Disc. Weapons* 21 By the negligence of the Harquebuziers.. or by the fault of the touch-boxes. **1656** H. PHILLIPS *Purch. Patt.* (1676) 15 The fault lies in those false rules and customs. **1803** T. BEDDOES *Hygeia* XI. 15 Rich sauces eaten in profusion.. are very frequently in fault. **1807** *Med. Jrnl.* XVII. 244 The fault.. is not in the practitioner but in the patient. **1859** TENNYSON *Geraint & Enid* 1115 Creatures voiceless thro' the fault of birth.

8. a. *Hunting.* A break in the line of scent; loss of scent; a check caused by failure of scent. † ***cold fault***: cold or lost scent. ***to be, †fall at*** (***a***) ***fault***: to overrun the line of scent owing to its irregularity or failure; to lose or be off the scent or track. ***to hit off a fault***: to recover a lost scent.

1592 SHAKS. *Ven. & Ad.* 694 The hot scent-snuffing hounds.. have singled.. the cold fault cleanly out. **1607** TOPSELL *Four-f. Beasts* (1673) 107 Suddenly the hounds fell at a fault. **1637** SHIRLEY *Lady of Pleasure* II. ii, Give him leave To follow his own nose.. while he hunts In view,—he'll soon be at a fault. **1687** CONGREVE *Old Bach.* v. i, Your blood-hound has made out the fault. **1749** FIELDING *Tom Jones* x. vi, Bad hounds.. never hit off a fault them-selves. **1781** BECKFORD *Hunting* (1802) 163 If a long fault make his [the huntsman's] assistance necessary. **1888** *Times* 10 Oct. 5/5 They [bloodhounds] are at fault.. by overrunning the line. **1888** P. LINDLEY *ibid.* 16 Oct. 10/5 The hound.. took up the stale trail.. without a fault.

b. fig. ***at fault***: puzzled, at a loss.

[**1626** WOTTON in *Reliq. Wotton.* (ed. 3) 550 We are.. at a fault, in the Hunter's term.] **1833** HT. MARTINEAU *Loom & Lugger* I. v. 87 One's conscience being at fault, an appeal to the law must settle the matter. **1840** R. H. DANA *Bef. Mast* i. 1 My little knowledge of a vessel was all at fault. **1861** T. L. PEACOCK *Gryll Grange* ii, There was sufficient diversity in the characters of the rejected to place conjecture at fault. **1886** SHORTHOUSE *Sir Percival* iv. 121 The walls and courts.. were so full of.. relics of the past that the wisest antiquarians were at fault.

c. ***at fault***, not equal to the occasion, in the position of having failed.

Formerly considered an incorrect use. 'With still greater impropriety, it is (according to Mr. Fitzedward Hall) frequently employed by American and occasionally by Eng. writers in the sense of "in fault"' (N.E.D.).

1876 L. STEPHEN *Eng. Thought* I. vi. 324 The many difficulties in nature.. when made the groundwork of an argument.. imply that the creator has been at fault. **1935** *Discovery* July 206/1 Sometimes it was the glaze.. which was at fault. **1947** MULGAN & DAVIN *Introd. Eng. Lit.* xiii. 167 The natural presumption is that it is not his already proved skill that is at fault but rather the nature of the theories.

9. *Geol.* and *Mining.* **a.** A dislocation or break in continuity of the strata or vein. Also, a flaw or dislocation in ice. Cf. F. *faille.*

1796 *Phil. Trans.* 351 They discovered.. a fault.. in the strata. **1813** BAKEWELL *Introd. Geol.* (1815) 263 Faults generally decline a little from a vertical position. **1830** LYELL *Princ. Geol.* I. 43 The faults and dislocations of the strata. **1847** ANSTED *Anc. World* vi. 108 Every coal-field is.. split asunder and broken into small fragments by.. 'faults'. **1860** TYNDALL *Glac.* II. xxvii. 392 The [ice] beds were bent, and their continuity often broken by faults. **1863** LYELL *Antiq. Man* (ed. 3) 199 A valley.. follows a line of fault in the chalk. **1883** W. S. GRESLEY *Gloss. Terms Coal Mining* 103 There are several kinds of faults, e.g. Faults of Dislocation; of Denudation; Upheaval; Trough Fault; Reverse or Overlap Fault; Step Fault. **1925** N. E. ODELL in E. F. Norton *Fight for Everest, 1924* 314 That the ice above the Trough was undergoing severe stress was apparent not only from its foliation, but also from the faults—'flaws' or 'tear-faults'—that had been extensively developed in this area.

b. (See quot.)

1881 RAYMOND *Mining Gloss.*, In coal-seams, sometimes applied to the coal rendered worthless by its condition in the seam (slate-fault, dirt-fault, etc.).

10. *Telegr.* An imperfect insulation; the condition of being in contact with anything which impairs or weakens the current; a leakage.

1863 CULLEY *Handbk. Pract. Telegr.* iv. 64 These faults are called 'earth' and 'contact'. *Ibid.* iv. 65 Suppose.. a fault to occur connecting the wire to the earth.. This leak will lessen the total resistance.

11. *Comb.* Chiefly objective, as ***fault-finder*** sb.; ***fault-finding*** sb. and adj.; ***fault-hunting*** adj.; attrib. (sense 9) ***fault-fissure, -line, -plane, zone.*** Also **fault-block**, a mass of displaced rock (sometimes of extensive area) bounded by or between two faults; **fault breccia**, breccia resulting from movement along a fault, a *crush-breccia* or *fault-rock*; **fault-line scarp**, a scarp produced secondarily along a fault-line by erosion, etc.; **fault-line valley**, a valley along a fault-line; **fault-reader**, one who can trace the correspondence of strata interrupted by a fault; **fault-rock** (see quots.); **fault-scarp**, a scarp directly produced by throw at a fault; **fault-slip**, the smooth surface of the fractured rocks in some types of faults; **fault-stuff** (see quot.); **fault-vein**, a mineral vein filling a fault; **fault-vent**, a volcanic vent occurring at a fault.

1897 W. B. SCOTT *Introd. Geol.* xiii. 248 If two parallel dislocations hade toward each other, they form a trough fault and include a wedge-shaped *fault block. **1925** N. E. ODELL in E. F. Norton *Fight for Everest, 1924* 242 At one point in the gorge a fault block had been turned through 90°. **1968** W. A. PRICE in R. W. Fairbridge *Encycl. Geomorphol.* 794 Fault-block origin for the Old Crow lakes is supported by the large square drainage patterns with which the lakes are associated. **1891** *Q. Jrnl. Geol. Soc. Lond.* XLVII. 322 An interesting feature in the Packhouse Hill section is a metamorphosed *fault-breccia, which intervenes between the Lower and Middle Coldwell beds. **1969** C. R. LONGWELL et al. *Physical Geol.* xvii. 413 Rocks adjacent to a fault can be crushed into irregular pieces, forming fault breccia. **1561** T. HOBY tr. *Castiglione's Courtyer* Epist. C ij b, I confesse to my *faultfinders. **1581** SIDNEY *Apol. Poetrie* (Arb.) 49 Fault-finders.. wil correct the Verbe, before they vnderstande the Noune. **1852** ROBERTSON *Serm.* Ser. IV. xxxv. (1863) 273 Social faultfinders, who are ever on the watch for error. **1622** DAVIES *Orchestra* lxv, Correspondence.. That no *fault-finding eye did ever blame. **1626** BERNARD *Isle of Man* 20 He.. liveth upon fault-finding. **1630** M. GODWYN tr. *Bp. Godwyn's Ann. Eng.* 43 The most fault-finding could not complaine of any want in that kinde. **1865** MISS MULOCK *Chr. Mistake* 90 Small backbitings and fault-findings. **1855** J. R. LEIFCHILD *Cornwall Mines* 87 In some instances.. the *fault-fissures are open. **1903** A. GEIKIE *Text-bk. Geol.* (ed. 4) 372 Another remarkable instance of the.. fault-fissure type was furnished by the great Japanese earth-quake of 28th October 1891. **1612** CHAPMAN *Widowes T.* in Dodsley *O. Pl.* (1720) VI. 210, I must.. be sure to give no hold to these *fault-hunting enemies. **1869** PHILLIPS *Vesuv.* vii. 197 On such a *fault-line atmospheric vicissitude has been effective. **1911** *Encycl. Brit.* XXVII. 622/1 The removal of the weak strata along one side of the fault line, leaving the harder strata on the other side in relief; such scarps are known as '*fault-line scarps'. **1935** *Geogr. Jrnl.* LXXXVI. 362 They may mistake fault-line scarps for fault scarps. **1968** R. W. FAIRBRIDGE *Encycl. Geomorphol.* 349/2 A fault-line scarp.. is a cliff that is subparallel to the fault trace, but is so modified by erosion that it does not reflect the fault plane in any way. **1913** W. M. DAVIS in *Bull. Geol. Soc. Amer.* XXIV. 207 They should be called by some special name, such as *fault-line valleys, as here suggested. **1963** A. N. STRAHLER *Earth Sciences* xxxiv. 598 Streams occupying fault lines are classed as subsequent streams... Their valleys may be termed subsequent valleys, or, more specifically, fault-line valleys. **1889** O. FISHER *Physics of Earth's Crust* (ed. 2) xx. 263 A '*fault-plane' or 'thrust-plane'. **1900** *Geogr. Jrnl.* XVI. 466 Inclined fault-planes with down-throw towards one trough. **1913** *Bull. Geol. Soc. Amer.* XXIV. 166 A fault surface is the surface of fracture; it is rarely plane, but where it is without notable curvature over any area it may be called a fault plane for that area. **1939** *Proc. Prehist. Soc.* V. 107 A spring issuing from the Chalk at the fault-plane. **1891** R. KIPLING *City Dreadf. Nt.* 85 A good '*fault-reader'.. must more than know geology. **1877** A. H. GREEN *Phys. Geol.* ix. §4. 365 Fragments of the adjoining rocks mashed and jumbled together, in some cases bound into a solid mass called fault-stuff or *fault-rock. **1882** GEIKIE *Text Bk. Geol.* IV. vi. 524 The line of fracture is marked by a belt or wall-like mass of fragmentary rock, known as 'fault rock'. **1897** W. B. SCOTT *Introd. Geol.* xiii. 248 It is comparatively seldom that the upthrow side of a fault is left standing as a line of cliffs; when such is the case, the cliffs form a *fault scarp. **1960** L. D. STAMP *Britain's Struct.* (ed. 5) xxiii. 229 One of the finest examples of a fault-scarp to be found anywhere—the great wall of the Highlands overlooking a valley excavated in Old Red Sandstone rocks. **1883** GRESLEY *Gloss. Terms Coal Mining*, *Fault-slip. **1811** J. FAREY *Agric. Derbysh.* I. i. §3. 120 Extraneous matters filling the Fault.. I shall call them *Fault-stuff. **1877** [see *fault-rock* above]. **1886** J. PRESTWICH *Geol.* I. xviii. 309 Mineral veins may be divided into fissure-veins, *fault-veins, and.. quartz-veins. **1903** *Nature* 3 Sept. 413/2 During the geological periods when the fault-vent continued intermittently active. **1931** C. M. NEVIN *Princ. Struct. Geol.* iv. 78 Frequently, the displacement caused by faulting may be spread over a number of closely spaced adjacent fractures, instead of being confined to one surface, in which case a *fault zone is formed. **1944** A. HOLMES *Princ. Physical Geol.* vi. 79 Sometimes, instead of a single fracture, there are two or more, forming a strip consisting of a sheet of crushed rock of variable thickness. This is distinguished as a fault zone, and the shattered material within is called a fault breccia. **1970** *Encycl. Brit.* VII. 861/1 The bottom of the well was located in a fault zone.

fault (fɔːlt, fɒlt), *v.* Forms: 4–6 faut(e(n, fawt(e, 6 faulte, 6–7 falt, 9 *Sc.* faut, 6– fault. [f. prec. sb.; cf. OF. *fauter*, which may be the source in the older senses.]

†**1.** *intr.* To be wanting or absent. Const. *dat.*

c **1375** *Sc. Leg. Saints, Laurentius* 778 þat was to þat ilke end: Gyf ocht fawtyt, It til amend. **1377** LANGL. *P. Pl.* B. IX. 66, I fynde þat holicherche Shulde fynden hem þat hem fauteth. **1398** TREVISA *Barth. De. P.R.* XIX. i. (1495) 860 Yf lyghte lackyth and fawtyth: the qualyte of colour is not seen. *c* **1460** *Launfal* 200 Today to cherche y wolde have gon, But me fawtede hosyn and schon. **1525** LD. BERNERS *Froiss.* II. xxx. 87 Here fauteth company.

†**2.** To be deficient *in*, to be lacking *in*. *Obs.*

1504 ATKINSON tr. *De Imitatione* III. xxxix, Worldlye wyse men fawteth in thy wysdome, good lorde. **1579** E. K. in *Spenser's Sheph. Cal.* Epist., Minding to furnish our tongue in this kind, wherein it faulteth. **1586** A. DAY *Eng. Secretary* I. (1625) A iij, I will blush for mine errors, where I fault in ability I will shew you my will. **1606** HOLLAND *Sueton.* Annot. 11 Hee faulted in common civilitie.

†**3. a.** *trans.* To stand in need of, lack, want, be deficient in. *Obs.*

1377 LANGL. *P. Pl.* B. IX. 66 Foles þat fauten Inwitte. *a* **1400–50** *Alexander* 2710 A thing.. parnes þe wyngis, And fautis þe fethirhames. **1470–85** MALORY *Arthur* III. i, I fawte l [knyghtes], for so many haue ben slayne. *c* **1475** *Partenay* 6379 She noght fauteth þat haue shold A lady.

absol. **1475** *Bk. Noblesse* 31 Be this way the ost may never faut.

†**b.** *impers.* = Fr. *il faut*. To be needful. *Obs.*

1502 *Ord. Crysten Men* (W. de W.) v. iii. 377 It fauteth not for to ymagen that they ben lesse ferefull in hell.

†**4. a.** *intr.* To come short of a standard; to make default, fail. *Obs.*

14.. tr. *Leges Quatuor Burgorum* c. 19 in *Sc. Stat.* (1844) I. 336 Gif he faltis twyis he sall be chastyte twyis for his forfaute. Gif he faltis thryse [etc.]. **1486** *Stanley's Ord. Lichfield Gild* 12 If the seid.. persons wyl absent them-self .. [they] shal pay ij pownd of wax; and as ofte as ony of them so fawteth after iij times monysshed, to be discharged. **1545** ASCHAM *Toxoph.* (Arb.) 36 If shotinge faulte at any tyme, it hydes it not.. but openly accuseth and bewrayeth it selfe. *c* **1611** SYLVESTER *Du Bartas* (1621) II. iv. IV. Decay 512 Let not our Fervour fault, Through length of Siege. *a* **1677** MANTON *Serm.* Wks. (1871) II. 187 He hath exceedingly failed and faulted in his duty.

†**b.** quasi-*trans.* To fail or omit *to* (do something); to miss (one's aim). *Obs.*

1522 *St. Papers Hen. VIII*, VI. 103 Wherin His Grace shall not faulte to indevour Hymself after his best power. **1527** KNIGHT in J. S. Brewer *Henry VIII*, xxviii. (1884) II. 224 The contents whereof I shall not fault to follow according unto your Grace's pleasure. **1591** *Troub. Raigne K. John* (1611) 53 Ile mend the fault, or fault my aime.

5. a. *intr.* To commit a fault, to do or go wrong, hence sometimes, to sin. *Obs.* exc. *arch. rarely* quasi-*trans.* with neut. pron. as *obj.* Const. *against*, *to*, *toward*. Also *rarely*, *to fault it*.

c **1400** *Apol. Loll.* 66 He fautid be error & be vnkunning. *a* **1400–50** *Alexander* 2659 'Quat has he fauted?' quod þe frek. *c* **1450** HENRYSON *Mor. Fab.* 74, I faulted neuer to you truelie. **1483** CAXTON *G. de la Tour* cxxx. 182 Men shalle saye that she fawted in dede. **1548** UDALL, etc. *Erasm. Par. Luke* xv. 132 Whatsoeuer I haue faulted, I haue faulted against him alone. **1549** *Compl. Scot.* xiv. 122 I exort ȝou.. that gyf ony of ȝou hes faltit contrar ȝour comont veil.. that ȝe correct ȝour selfis. **1602** WARNER *Alb. Eng.* IX. xliv. (1612) 211 They.. die in lingring Torments, who Fault to their Inquisition. *a* **1603** T. CARTWRIGHT *Confut. Rhem. N.T.* (1618) 27 He that marrieth another, faulteth against the former wife. **1625** B. JONSON *Staple of News* II. i, And where my dogs have faulted, Remove it with a broom. *a* **1632** T. TAYLOR *God's Judgem.* I. I. xxii. (1642) 86 The people of Cæsarea faulted greatly when.. they called King Herod a god. **1647** WARD *Simp. Cobler* 88 Poore Coblers well may fault it now and then, They're ever mending faults for other men. **1825** SCOTT *Talism.* xx, He hath foully faulted towards me, in failing to send the auxiliary aid he promised. **1871** BROWNING *Balaust.* 96 Had I died for thee I had faulted more.

†**b.** of things. *Obs.*

1602 WARNER *Alb. Eng.* X. lx. (1612) 265 Somewhat somewhere faulteth. **1608** BP. HALL *Char. Virtues & V.* II. 101 Everie thing faulteth either in too much or too little.

†**6.** To make a mistake, be in error, blunder.

1530 PALSGR. 546/2 It is no marvayle thoughe I faulte yet, I am but a begynner. *c* **1550** CHEKE *Matt.* xviii, Yᵉ greak fauteth heer in yᵉ nomber. **1624** BEDELL *Lett.* vi. 95 Hee faults himselfe in the same kinde, that hee imputes to another. **1692** *Covt. Grace Conditional* 47 If they faulted in any thing about the Matter in controversie, it was in giving too much to Faith. **1765** CHESTERF. *Lett.* (1890) 178 His tongue stammering and faulting.

7. a. *trans.* To find fault with, to blame or censure. Also † *to fault (a person) with* or *that*: to charge with, find fault with because.

1559 BALDWIN *Mirr. Magistr.* (1563) vi. b, Or shal I fault the fates that so ordayne? **1585** ABP. SANDYS *Serm.* (1841) 53 If it fall upon his head, let him fault himself. **1590** T. WATSON *Eglogue death Sir F. Walsingham* 276 (Arb.) 169 My mind.. gins fault hir giuing place to sorrows sourse. **1633** T. ADAMS *Exp. 2 Peter* ii. 4 The lion was faulted by the lioness, that his breath stank. **1677** CARY *Chronol.* II. II. I. iii. 193 Josephus is to be faulted, for saying that it was in the 25th year. **1791** WOLCOTT (P. Pindar) *Rights of Kings* Wks. 1812 II. 415 Fault the poor Flesh and quarrel with the Fish. **1842** S. LOVER *Handy Andy* xxi, What's that you're faulting now? is it my deal seats without cushions? **1859** MRS. F. TROLLOPE *Petticoat Govt.* 161 Her manner.. could not, to use an American phrase, be 'faulted'. **1866** LOWELL *Biglow P.* Introd., The Americanisms with which we are faulted. **1957** *Listener* 9 May 736/1 One can fault the English for their indifference over long periods to Scottish susceptibilities. **1965** *New Statesman* 30 Apr. 670/2 The Hall Green Conservatives can be faulted for selecting him. **1971** *Wall Street Jrnl.* (Eastern ed.) 19 July 1/3 The.. report ... faults Agriculture Secretary Clifford Hardin for failing to take over state meat-inspection services that have failed to satisfy federal requirements.

b. To impugn or mark as faulty.

1585 ABP. SANDYS *Serm.* (1841) 233 Any deformity.. in the body of a naked man.. is soon espied and faulted. **1635** SHELFORD *Learned Disc.* 54 God's house is abused by them which bring hither hawks and dogs, which is faulted in our Church-homilie. **1665** J. SERGEANT *Sure Footing* 58 If Protestants faulted not the Rule. **1882–3** J. J. MOMBERT in Schaff *Encycl. Relig. Knowl.* I. 736 Twenty-nine passages.. faulted by Lawrence as incorrect. **1958** *Spectator* 6 June 740/3 His final conclusion at least cannot be faulted. **1961** *Times* 11 May 17/2 Perhaps some scholar will fault a detail.

8. *Hunting.* To put (a hound) at fault; to throw off the scent. *rare.*

1873 W. S. MAYO *Never again* xii. 164 A way! By which we'll fault their staunchest hound.

9. *Geol.* and *Mining. trans.* Chiefly *pass.* To cause a fault (see FAULT *sb.* 9) or break of continuity in; to dislocate; now also *intr.* ***to fault down*** or ***through***: to depress (part of a stratum), to drive (part of it) *through* (another) with the result of causing a fault.

1849 MURCHISON *Siluria* vii. 139 It is faulted on the north-west against Old Red Sandstone. **1863** DANA *Man. Geol.* 111 If the stratum were inclined at 15° without faulting, it would stand as in fig. D. **1872** W. S. SYMONDS *Rec. Rocks*, Black slates at Llandeilo are faulted through the Caradoc beds. **1879** RUTLEY *Stud. Rocks* ii. 8 Portions of the already solidified crust were faulted down or depressed. **1883** *Science* I. 101 An undulation which has overturned the folds, and has faulted them in some places. **1927** *Daily Express* 5 July 11/4 A geological inexactitude which appears to have faulted or slipped from peaceful churchyard surroundings to a boisterous life in the ocean waves.

fig. **1837** SIR F. PALGRAVE *Merch. & Friar* ii. (1844) 39 Correct reasoning would suddenly be faulted, as it were, by a vein of wild credulity.

faultage (ˈfɔːltɪdʒ). *Geol.* [f. FAULT *sb.* 9 + -AGE.] Faults considered collectively, faulting.

1899 *Geogr. Jrnl.* XIII. 272 Well-marked lines of faultage going down to the bases of the mountains.

faulted (ˈfɔːlt-, ˈfɒltɪd), *ppl. a.* [f. FAULT *sb.* and *v.* + -ED.] Having faults.

1. Having faults of character, faulty.

1608 MACHIN *Dumb Knight* III. i. in Hazl. *Dodsley* X. 157 A maid so faulted seldom proves good wife.

2. *Geol.* Cf. FAULT *sb.* 9.

1858 GEIKIE *Hist. Boulder* xi. 228 The contorted and faulted strata. **1863** DANA *Man. Geol.* 727 The inequality of the faulted parts of the veins. **1881** E. HULL in *Nature* XXIII. 289 Durness limestone and its faulted position.

†**3.** Reproached as faulty, impugned. *Obs.*

1628 BP. HALL *Old Relig.* xvi. §2 (1633) 40 Our Saviour.. tells him.. That these faulted Traditions were of old.

†ˈ**faulter.** *Obs.* Forms: 6 faltar, -our, faughter, (faultor, 7 faultour, fawter), 6–9 *Sc.* fauter, -or, 6–8 faulter. [f. FAULT *v.* + -ER¹, and *-our*, -OR; OF. had *fautier* adj. guilty.] One who commits a fault; a culprit, delinquent, offender.

1535 STEWART *Cron. Scot.* II. 544 Of sic faltouris thair haif tha brocht fyve hunder. **1556** J. HEYWOOD *Spider & F.* xxiv. 10 The faughter.. To saue his lyfe, apealth to be repride. **1602** *Henley in Arden Rolls*, A Presentment of all the ffaultes and fawters 13 Octʳ. 1602. **1634** HEYWOOD *Mayden-head well Lost* II. Wks. 1874 IV. 120 Punish the faulter, and the innocent saue. **1708** J. CHAMBERLAYNE *St. Gt. Brit.* I. II. ix. (1743) 81 To the Lord High Admiral belongs.. the goods of Pirates, Felons, or Capital Faulters. *a* **1796** BURNS *Here's his health in Water* 2 Tho' he be the fautor.. Yet here's his health in Water. **1840** *Whistle-binkie* (1890) I. 253 I'se no be sic a fauter.

faulter, obs. form of FALTER *v.*¹, ³.

faulter, -our, bad forms of FAUTOR.

faultful (ˈfɔːlt-, ˈfɒltfʊl), *a.* [f. FAULT *sb.* + -FUL.] Faulty, culpable.

1591 *Troub. Raigne K. John* (1611) 65 Such meteors were the Ensignes of his wrath, That hast'ned to destroy the faultfull towne. **1593** SHAKS. *Lucr.* 715 So fares it with this fault-full Lord of Rome. **1621** LADY M. WROTH *Urania* 36 You are the children of men, and like them fault-full. **1856** RUSKIN *Mod. Paint.* III. IV. ix. §4 The limiting lines between virtuous contentment and faultful carelessness. **1876** J. ELLIS *Cæsar in Egypt* 313 Thy mercy much exceedeth, As our faultful nature needeth.

Hence ˈ**faultfully** *adv.*, in a faultful manner.

1859 RUSKIN *Arrows* I. 199, I have been myself faultfully answerable for this too eager hope in your mind.

faultily (ˈfɔːlt-, ˈfɒltɪlɪ), *adv.* [f. FAULTY + -LY².] In a faulty manner.

1. In a defective manner; defectively, imperfectly, incorrectly.

1577 tr. *Bullinger's Decades* (1592) 42 Philosophie doth.. faultily teach many thinges touching God. **1580** HOLLYBAND *Treas. Fr. Tong, Incorrectement*, faultily. **1609** DOULAND *Ornith. Microl.* 69 Many of those Priests.. does read those things.. so faultily, that they doe not onely hinder the deuotion of the faithfull, but also [etc.]. **1711** HEARNE *Collect.* (Oxf. Hist. Soc.) III. 125 The Inscriptions are also most faultily taken. **1888** *N. Amer. Rev.* Feb. 198 However faultily preached.. these Indians had heard the one Gospel which must save the world.

b. = 'To a fault.' See FAULT *sb.* 3 c.

1855 TENNYSON *Maud.* II. 6 Faultily faultless.

2. In a blamable manner; blamably, culpably.

1591 PERCIVALL *Sp. Dict.*, *Criminalmente*, faultely. **1661** BOYLE *Style of Script.* (1675) 221 If they be not faultily indisposed to receive impressions from it. **1768–74** TUCKER *Lt. Nat.* (1852) II. 590 A man may be faultily scrupulous, as well as laudably conscientious. **1773** MRS. CHAPONE *Improv. Mind* (1774) I. 186 Depend upon it the corruption has.. been faultily indulged.

faultiness (ˈfɔːlt, ˈfɒltɪnɪs). [f. as prec. + -NESS.] The quality or state of being faulty.

1. The quality or state of having blemishes or defects; defectiveness, imperfection. † ***to faultiness***: = 'to a fault' (see FAULT *sb.* 3 c.).

1530 PALSGR. 219/1 Fautynesse, *favtuseté*. **1561** T. NORTON *Calvin's Inst.* III. 263 Theyr good workes are but begonne and sauoring of the faultinesse of the flesh. **1606** SHAKS. *Ant. & Cl.* III. iii. 33 *Cle.* Bear'st thou her face in mind? is't long or round? *Mess.* Round, euen to faultinesse. **1678** CUDWORTH *Intell. Syst.* (1808) II. 331 The first atheistic instance of the faultiness of things. **1726** SHELVOCKE *Voy. round World* (1757) 326 The faultiness of our ship. **1793** BEATTIE *Moral Sc.* I. i. §11. 182 Pleased, or displeased, according to the degree of excellence or faultiness. *a* **1846** LANDOR *Imag. Conv.* Wks. (1846) I. 69 Adducing a few instances of faultiness in Byron.

2. The quality or state of having moral blemishes, of being in fault or to blame; depravity, viciousness, culpability, guilt.

1571 GOLDING *Calvin on Ps.* xxv. 21 As though David requyre to bee preserved cleere from all faultynesse. **1628** DIGBY *Voy. Medit.* (Camden) 31 Such as I could not free him from much faultinesse. **1818** MRS. SHELLEY *Frankenst.* i. (1865) 63 My father would be unjust if he ascribed my neglect to vice, or faultiness on my part. **1868** BROWNING *Ring & Bk.* VI. (1889) II. 242, I bow my head.. Break myself up in shame of faultiness.

faulting (ˈfɔːlt-, ˈfɒltɪŋ), *vbl. sb.* [f. FAULT *v.* + -ING¹.]

1. The action of the vb. FAULT in various senses; an instance of this. *Obs.*

c **1450** tr. *De Imitatione* III. lix, Nature compleineþ sone of fautyng & of greuaunce. **1622** W. WHATELY *God's Husb.* 127 Some grosse outward faultings therein. *a* **1665** J. GOODWIN *Filled w. the Spirit* (1867) 155 His faulting of the translation .. doth not at all commend his skill in the original. **1679** KING in G. Hickes *Spirit of Popery* 50 So much silence and fauting even amongst Ministers.

2. *Geol.* The process of producing faults, dislocation of strata; an instance of this.

1849 DANA *Geol.* xiii. (1850) 574 In the faulting of a rock. **1863** LYELL *Antiq. Man* 345 The most wonderful shiftings and faultings of the beds are observable.

faulting (ˈfɔːlt-, ˈfɒltɪŋ), *ppl. a.* [f. as prec. + -ING².] That faults. **a.** That commits faults.

b. That is at fault. See FAULT *sb.* 8.

1566 PAINTER *Pal. Pleas.* I. Pref. 8 Faulting fooles and youthly heades. **1837** BROWNING *Strafford* IV. ii, Pym's faulting bloodhounds scent the track again.

†ˈ**faultive,** *a.* *Obs.* In 5 faltive. [a. F. *fau(l)tif, -ive*; see FAULT *sb.* and -IVE.] Faulty.

1496 *Seal of Cause* in Pennecuik *Blue Blanket* (1722) 14 Quhair it beis fundyn faltive, to forbid the samyne.

faultless (ˈfɔːlt-, ˈfɒltlɪs), *a.* [f. FAULT *sb.* + -LESS.] Free from fault.

1. Without defect, imperfection, or blemish; irreproachable. Said with reference to moral character, physical or intellectual qualities, workmanship, beauty, etc.

13.. *E.E. Allit. P.* B. 794 Of alle feturez ful fyn & fautlez boþe. *c* **1340** *Gaw. & Gr. Knt.* 640 Fyrst he watz funden fautlez in his fyue wyttes. *a* **1674** CLARENDON *Hist. Reb.* IX. (1843) 577/1 A very faultless young man. **1709** POPE *Ess. Crit.* 253 Whoever thinks a faultless piece to see, Thinks what ne'er was, nor is, nor e'er shall be. **1770** *Junius Lett.* xxxix. 203 A faultless, insipid equality. **1853** KANE *Grinnell Exp.* xii. (1856) 88 A singularly beautiful bird, faultless in its purity of white. **1868** FREEMAN *Norm. Conq.* (1876) II. x. 506 The faultless model of a ruler. **1883** GILMOUR *Mongols* xxxi. 358 Resplendent in yellow coats and faultless hats.

2. That has committed no fault; that is not to blame; guiltless, innocent. *Obs.* exc. with mixture of sense 1.

1513 MORE in Grafton *Chron.* II. 758 Finally were he faultie or faultlesse, attainted was he by Parliament. *c* **1540** *Order in Battayll* C iij b, As well for the fault-lesse, as the gyltie. **1624** FAIRFAX *Godfr. of Boulogne* III. 39 For our sinnes he faultlesse suffered paine. **1697** DRYDEN *Virg. Georg.* III. 710 Take the Traytor's Head, E'er in the faultless Flock the dire Contagion spread. [**1855** MACAULAY *Hist. Eng.* IV. 305 Rochester.. expressed a wish to be informed of the grounds on which the Admiral had been declared faultless.]

†**b.** *occas. transf.* Not caused by any fault. Also in ***faultless pardon***, a pardon for an alleged offence never committed. *Obs.*

1556 J. HEYWOOD *Spider & F.* ii. 151 To take all fautles falles, reioisinglie. **1597** HOOKER *Eccl. Pol.* V. lx. (1611) 317 In whome there is no other defect beside his faultlesse lacke of baptisme. **1752** CARTE *Hist. Eng.* III. 575 Obliging the most deserving of his subjects to ask a faultless pardon.

faultlessly (ˈfɔːlt-, ˈfɒltlɪslɪ), *adv.* [f. prec. + -LY².] In a faultless manner.

†**a.** Blamelessly (*obs.*). **b.** Without flaw or blemish; irreproachably, perfectly.

1610 HEALEY *St. Aug. Citie of God* 127 Give thus much leave to a poore woman, in tender affection, faultlessly to bewaile her spouse. **1856** FROUDE *Hist. Eng.* (1858) II. viii. 245 The fidelity of the clansmen to their leaders was faultlessly beautiful. **1880** OUIDA *Moths* II. 362 She is faultlessly

made. **1893** C. H. Herford in *Bookman* June 83/2 No doubt the translation is faultlessly correct.

faultlessness ('fɔːlt-, 'fɒltlɪsnɪs). [f. as prec. + -NESS.] The quality or condition of being faultless. †**a.** Freedom from blame; blamelessness (*obs.*). **b.** Freedom from defect or blemish.

1580 Sidney *Arcadia* (1622) 429 The wrong..you doe vnto me, to thinke me..so childish, as not to perceiue your faithfull faultlesnesse. **1754** Edwards *Freed. Will* iv. iii. (ed. 4) 292 Our ideas of excusableness or faultlessness. **1818** Hazlitt *Eng. Poets* iv. 99 His excellence is by no means faultlessness. *a* **1853** Robertson *Serm.* Ser. ii. 197 Perfection is more than faultlessness. **1858** Doran *Crt. Fools* 4 Venus..proud in the conviction of her faultlessness.

'**faultress.** *rare.* [fem. of FAULTER: see -ESS.] A female offender.

1838 J. Struthers *Poetic Tales* 16 Faultress dire to laws above.

'**faultsome,** *a. rare.* [f. FAULT *sb.* + -SOME.] Full of faults, faulty.

1891 R. Kipling in *Lippincott's Mag.* Jan. 95, I like that fault. Be more faultsome.

faulture ('fɔːlt-, 'fɒltjʊə(r)). *rare*⁻¹. [f. FAULT *v.* + -URE.] A failing; in quot. *concr.* Decayed remnants.

1820 Keats *Hyperion* (First Version) i. 70 What I had seen..Seem'd but the faulture of decrepit things To that eternal domed monument.

†'**faultworthy,** *a. Obs. rare.* [f. FAULT *v.* + WORTHY.] Deserving of blame, blameworthy, culpable.

1586 Ferne *Blaz. Gentrie* To Gentl. Inner Temple, Such things which..he iudgeth faultworthy. *a* **1656** Bp. Hall *Revelation Unrevealed* § 11 In both which extremes these last times have been too faultworthy.

faulty (fɔːlt-, 'fɒltɪ), *a.* Forms: 4–5, 9 *dial.* fauty, 4–5 fawty(e, 5 fawte, 6 fawtie, fautye, 6–7 faultie, (6 faulte), 7 faultye, 7– faulty. [f. as prec. + -Y¹, perh. after F. *fautif.*]

1. Containing faults, blemishes or defects; defective, imperfect, unsound.

a. of material things.

1435 Misyn *Mending of Life* 108 So þow settis þi-self on a fawte grounde. *c* **1450** *St. Cuthbert* (Surtees) 4082 þe walles of cuthbert oratory he fande þaim mekil fawty. **1530** Palsgr. 312/1 Fautye as fruite is that is nat sownde. **1577** *Nottingham Rec.* IV. 171 Many stretes is owte of order for mendyng vere faulte. **1643** Prynne *Open. Gt. Seal* 21 Some of the seales for ill cloathes, to have *faultie* engraven in them. **1697** Dampier *Voy.* (1698) I. 443 Here they made a new Boltsprit..our old one being very faulty. **1697** Dryden *Virgil, Life* (1721) I. 29 He [the colt] came of a faulty Mare. **1759** tr. *Duhamel's Husb.* ii. i. (1762) 115 To pluck up the faulty ears as fast as they appeared. **1846** Greener *Sc. Gunnery* 187 If a barrel be faulty, or locks inferior. **1862** Huxley *Lect. Wrkg. Men* 47 Faulty as these layers of stone in the earth's crust are, defective as they necessarily are as a record. **1887** *S. Chesh. Gloss.* s.v. *Fauty*, 'These tatoes bin turnin up very fauty.' **1888** *Berksh. Gloss., Vauty*, anything ..with part decayed is so described.

b. of immaterial things.

1380 Wyclif *Wks.* (1880) 364 God takiþ þis ordenance in his chirche as..in no wise fawtye. **1535** Joye *Apol. Tindale* 27 Whether my correccion..be a diligent correccion, and Tindales translacion fautye or no. **1551** T. Wilson *Logike* (1580) 34 b, It is a faultie argument. **1649** W. Dugdale in *Lett. Lit. Men* (Camden) 174 If Mr. Leicester do knowe it [my comparing of Domesday] to be faultye..that I will not deny. **1744** Berkeley *Siris* §68 The origin of the gout lies in a faulty digestion. **1789** Burns *Let. to Miss Williams*, Where the expression seems to be perplexed or faulty. **1830** Mackintosh *Eth. Philos.* Wks. 1846 I. 185 Those..may consistently blame the faulty principle, and rejoice in its destruction.

2. Of persons, their qualities, etc.: Having imperfections or failings; apt to do wrong or come short of duty.

1574 tr. *Marlorat's Apocalips* 40 The cause why our affections are faultie, is for that they runne headlong, and haue no stay of themselues. **1621** Bp. Hall *Heaven upon Earth* §5 Our best endeuour is.. faulty. **1712** Budgell *Spect.* No. 506 ¶6 The ladies are generally most faulty in this particular. **1729** Butler *Serm.* Pref. Wks. 1874 II. 21 To forgive injuries..so peculiarly becomes an imperfect, faulty creature. **1748** Richardson *Clarissa* (1811) I. iii. 14 His reputed faulty morals. **1878** Browning *La Saisiaz* 68 The nice distinction 'twixt fast foes and faulty friends.

3. †**a.** That has committed a fault, error, or offence; guilty of wrong-doing (*obs.*). **b.** That is in fault or to blame (for some undesirable results).

13.. *E.E. Allit. P.* B. 741 Quat if faurty be fre and fauty þyse oþer Schalt þow schortly al schende & schape non oþer. **1380** Wyclif *Wks.* (1880) 364 Ellis men mosten say þat God is and was fawty in ordenance of boþe his lawis. **1389** in *Eng. Gilds* (1870) 72 Qwat man or woman be fawty, he schal paye ..*di. li.* wax. *c* **1440** *York Myst.* xl. 130 A! fooles þat are fauty and failes of youre feithe. **1481** Caxton *Reynard* (Arb.) 5 Reynard..knewe hym self fawty and gylty in many thynges. **1509** Barclay *Shyp of Folys* (1570) 54 Howebeit I knowe my wordes shall suche greue, As them selfe knoweth fawtie and culpable. **1556** *Aurelio & Isab.* (1608) B vj, What soever person that were founde faultie of like errour. **1611** Beaum. & Fl. *Maid's Trag.* i. i, Thou art faulty; I sent for thee..Thou cam'st not. **1614** *Henley-in-Arden Rolls*, Wee Doe present william Kerbee shoomaker ffaulty. **1682** *Enq. Elect. Sheriffs* 19 How often hath the City been more faulty to divers of our former Kings. **1777** Howard *Prisons Eng.* (1780) 196 Workshops for faulty apprentices. **1812** H. & J. Smith *Rej. Addr.* 102 As it now stands, 'one fiddle' among many, the faulty individual will I hope escape detection. *absol.* **1533** More *Debell. Salem* Wks. 985/1 Yf he would compare the fauty wyth the fauty. **1614** Bp. Hall *Recoll. Treat.* 759 It is an old policy of the faulty, to complaine first.

4. Of the nature of a fault; censurable, wrong.

1548 Udall, etc. *Erasm. Par. Col.* ii. 18 A faultie humbleness it is, through Angels to loke for that whiche shuld of Christ himselfe be asked. **1699** Burnet *39 Art.* xxii. 247 No reserve is made in Scripture for this [*sc.* Idolatry] as being faulty only because it was applied wrong. **1851** Hussey *Papal Power* ii. 66 Thus Rome grew now by means of whatever was faulty in the Church. **1869** Goulburn *Purs. Holiness* Pref. 11 A faulty habit of mind.

B. *quasi-adv.* = FAULTILY *adv.*

1754 Richardson *Grandison* (1781) II. xix. 208 What an humbling thing is the consciousness of having lived faulty.

faulty, var. of FOUGHTY *a.*, musty.

†**faulx.** *Obs.* Also falx. [a. OF. *faulx*, Fr. *faux* in *faux de corps* small of the back.] A trick in wrestling; a grip round the 'small of the back'.

1602 Carew *Cornwall* 76 a, Many sleights and tricks appertaine hereunto ['wrastling']..such are the Trip, fore-Trip, Inturne, the Faulx, forward and backward. **1612** Drayton *Poly-olb.* i. 6 They practise..The forward, backward, falx.

faun (fɔːn). *Myth.* Also 6–7 fawn. [ad. L. *Faunus*, proper name of a god or demigod worshipped by shepherds and farmers, and identified with the Gr. Pan; also in pl. *fauni* (cf. Gr. *Παῦνες*), a class of similar deities. (Chaucer's *fauny* is the L. plural.)]

1. One of a class of rural deities; at first represented like men with horns and the tail of a goat, afterwards with goats' legs like the Satyrs, to whom they were assimilated in lustful character.

c **1374** Chaucer *Troylus* iv. 1544 On satiry and fawny more and lesse, þat halue goddes ben of wildernesse. *c* **1386** —— *Knt.'s T.* 2070 Nimphes, Faunes, and Amadriades. **1579** Spenser *Sheph. Cal.* July 77 Here han the holy Faunes resourse. **1631** Massinger *Emp. East* iii. iii, The poets' dreams of lustful fauns and satyrs. **1728** Swift *Let.* 14 Sept. in Wks. (1841) II. 105 The muses and the fawns..will crown you with joy. **1830** Scott *Demonol.* iv, These silvans, satyrs and fauns. **1850** Tennyson *In Mem.* cxviii, Arise and fly The reeling Faun, the sensual feast.

2. *attrib.* and *Comb.*, as ***faun-breeze, -face; faun-faced, -like, -loved, -twinkling*** adjs.

1925 E. Sitwell *Troy Park* 44 The elegant faun-breeze. *a* **1930** D. H. Lawrence *Etruscan Places* (1932) 16 His face is a faun-face, not deadened by morals. *Ibid.* 17 They can't survive, the faun-faced men. **1902** W. B. Yeats *Celtic Twilight* 75 The faun-like feet. **1962** I. Murdoch *Unofficial Rose* xxxiv. 325 That particular faun-like grace which fades later. **1881** Wilde *Poems* 69 Faun-loved Heliconian glades. **1929** Blunden *Near & Far* 64 Sunshine of vital gold, faun-twinkling groves.

faun, obs. form of FAWN.

fauna ('fɔːnə). Pl. faunæ; also faunas. [mod.L. *fauna*, an application of the pr. name of a rural goddess, the sister of Faunus (see FAUN); used by Linnæus in the title of his work *Fauna Suecica* (1746), a companion volume to his *Flora Suecica* (1745). Cf. FLORA.]

1. A collective term applied to the animals or animal life of any particular region or epoch.

1771 *Let.* in G. White *Selborne* (1876) 143 He should be able to account for the..manner of life of the animals of his own Fauna. **1828** Fleming *Hist. Brit. Anim.* Pref. 7 A few additions were afterwards made to this division of the British Fauna by Ray. **1844** *Vest. Creat.* (ed. 4) 99 Fossils do not form the sole memorials of the extraordinary fauna of this age. **1846** McCulloch *Acc. Brit. Empire* (1854) I. 133 The fauna of tropical America. **1851** Richardson *Geol.* (1855) 448 The crustacea were represented in the carboniferous fauna. **1859** Darwin *Orig. Spec.* xii. (1873) 323 A narrow isthmus now separates two marine faunas. **1877** Le Conte *Elem. Geol.* (1879) 155 There are.. geographical faunae and florae and geological faunae and florae.

2. A treatise upon the animals of any geographical area or geological period.

1885 A. Newton in *Encycl. Brit.* (ed. 9) XVIII. 16 A rapid survey of the ornithological works which come more or less under the designation of 'Faunæ'.

'**faunal,** *a.*¹ *rare.* [f. FAUN + -AL¹.] Of or pertaining to a Faun, or to Fauns.

1592 R. D. *Hypnerotomachia* 97 b, Horned faunes.. solemnising their faunall feasts. **1849** *Fraser's Mag.* XXXIX. 105 A pastoral, or rather 'faunal', sketch.

'**faunal,** *a.*² [f. FAUN-A + -AL¹.] Of or pertaining to the fauna of a country.

1877 Le Conte *Elem. Geol.* (1879) 161 The whole earth has been divided into six principal faunal regions. **1884** *Athenæum* 10 May 602/2 Their faunal distribution. **1889** Aplin *Birds Oxfordsh.* Pref., The series of county faunal works.

faunally ('fɔːnəlɪ), *adv.* [f. FAUNAL *a.*² + -LY².] As regards the fauna of a district or epoch.

1872 *Amer. Naturalist* VI. 342 These two regions are as diverse faunally as they are in physical features. **1904** *Science* 5 Feb. 235/1 Faunally the same species characterize the lower and upper members of the Portage. **1949** *New Yorker* 17 Sept. 24 For the last hundred years, faunally and florally speaking, all has been silence.

faund(e, obs. form of *found*, pa. t. of FIND.

fauness ('fɔːnɪs). *nonce-wd.* A female faun.

1890 *Sat. Rev.* 11 Oct. 437/1 The fauness or satyress.. grows a little monotonous.

†'**faunic,** *a. Obs.*⁻⁰ [as if ad. L. **faunic-us*, f. *Faunus*: see FAUN and -IC.] (See quot.)

1674–81 Blount *Glossogr.*, *Faunick* (*faunicus*), wild, woodish, rude. **1692–1732** in Coles.

faunist ('fɔːnɪst). [f. FAUN-A + -IST.] One who studies or treats of the fauna of a country or district.

1766 Pennant *Zool.* (1768) I. 173 The critical Faunist may possibly censure us. **1813** G. Low *Fauna Orcad.* Pref. 10 To assist the young Orkney Faunist in classing. **1851** *Fraser's Mag.* XLIII. 253 The male *mugil*..was caught as faunists are in the habit of catching male moths.

faunistic (fɔː'nɪstɪk), *a.* [f. prec. + -IC.] Of or pertaining to a faunist; hence, relating to a fauna. ***faunistic position***: the place in a fauna assigned by a faunist to a certain animal.

1881 *Nature* 25 Aug. XXIV. 379 The definition of their faunistic position and geographical distribution. **1890** *Ibid.* 17 Apr. XLI. 556 A number of faunistic papers in the Journal of the Linnean Society.

faunistical (fɔː'nɪstɪkəl), *a.* [f. prec. + -AL¹.] = prec. Hence **fau'nistically** adv., in a faunistical manner, as a faunist would.

1885 *Athenæum* 8 Aug. 179/1 Specialists of different orders and families..treat the subject faunistically.

faunizone ('fɔːnɪzəʊn). *Geol.* [f. FAUN(A + -I- + ZONE *sb.*] A zone (cf. ZONE *sb.* 7) characterized by a particular assemblage of fossils.

1902 S. S. Buckman in *Geol. Mag.* IX. 557 Faunizones are the successive faunal facies exhibited in strata.

faunological (fɔːnəʊ'lɒdʒɪkəl), *a.* [f. next + -IC + -AL¹.] Of or pertaining to faunology.

1884 *Nature* 31 July XXX. 326 Faunological and systematic zoological work.

faunology (fɔː'nɒlədʒɪ). *rare.* [f. FAUNA + *-ology*: see -LOGY.] That department of zoölogy which treats of the geographical distribution of animals.

†**faunsere.** *Obs. rare*⁻¹. [app. a corruption of OF. *vaussure* (= mod.F. *voussure*).] A vaulted roof.

1460 *Lybeaus Disc.* 1817 The rof abone unlek, And the faunsere [*v.r.* fasoure, vasure] ek, As hyt wolde asonder.

faunship ('fɔːnʃɪp). [f. FAUN + -SHIP.] The attribute of being a faun.

1860 Hawthorne *Marb. Faun* xii. (1883) 128 The fact of his faunship being otherwise so probable.

†**faunt.** *Obs.* Also 4 fant, fawnt. [Aphetic form of OF. *enfaunt*, *enfant*: see INFANT. The shortened form has not been found in Fr., but It. has the corresponding *fante* boy, servant, foot-soldier, whence Ger. *fant*.] An infant, a child, a young person.

13.. *E.E. Allit. P.* A. 161 At þe fote þer-of [i.e. of þe crystal clyffe] þer sete a faunt. **1382** Wyclif *Lev.* xii. 3 The eiȝt day the fawnt shal be circumcidid. *a* **1400–50** *Alexander* 4629 For quilk a frek is bot a fant þan is he first simple.

†'**fauntekin.** *Obs.* Forms: 4 faun-, fawnt(e)kyn(e, 5 fantekyn. [dim. of FAUNT: see -KIN.] A little child, an infant.

1377 Langl. *P. Pl.* B. xiii. 213, I shal dwelle as I do my deuore to shewen, And conformen fauntekynes. **1393** *Ibid.* C. xi. 182 Fauntekynes and fooles. ? *a* **1400** *Morte Arth.* 845 He has fretyne..als fele fawntekyns of freeborne childyre! *c* **1440** *Gesta Rom.* lxi. 260 (Harl. MS.) Whanne I was a fantekyn, I was fonde in a toune, in a cradyl.

†'**fauntelet.** *Obs.* [Aphetic f. OF. *enfantelet*: see FAUNT and -LET.] A little child.

1393 Langl. *P. Pl.* C. xii. 310 'ȝe, farewel fyppe', quath fauntelet.

†'**fauntelte.** *Obs.* [A badly-formed abstract noun from prec.] Childishness.

1377 Langl. *P. Pl.* B. xv. 146 Withouten fauntelte or foly.

†**fauntempere.** *Obs. rare*⁻¹. A dish in old cookery.

c **1430** *Two Cookery-bks.* 19 Fauntempere—Take Almaunde mylke, & floure of rys, Sugre [etc.].

Fauntleroy ('fɔːntlərɔɪ). The name of the hero of Frances Hodgson Burnett's novel *Little Lord Fauntleroy* (1885), used *attrib.* to designate the style of dress or hair (for boys) which the book popularized; also applied, often ironically, to a child of the gentle nature of the book's hero. (The phr. ***Little Lord Fauntleroy*** is also used.)

1911 L. Stone *Jonah* ii. i. 149 A Fauntleroy velvet suit. **1913** F. H. Burnett *T. Tembarom* xiii. 153 Who's this Fauntleroy in the lace collar? **1923** [see AFTER-LIFE 2]. **1929** T. Wolfe *Look Homeward, Angel* (1930) viii. 93 Fat Fauntleroy curls. **1933** *N. & Q.* 18 Mar. 193/1 Lace collars were sometimes worn with velvet suits before..1886. Mrs. Hodgson Burnett is understood to have invented the Fauntleroy costume by adding a sash and lace collars and cuffs to these suits. **1933** Dylan Thomas *Let.* Oct. (1966) 35

Myself aged seven—thick-lipped, Fauntleroy-haired. **1942** D. POWELL *Time to be Born* (1943) viii. 181 Some little Lord Fauntleroy who had just found out there were rotters in the world. **1950** A. WILSON *Such Darling Dodos* 34 The creature would be dressed in a velvet suit and fauntleroy collar. **1959** *Sunday Times* 9 Aug. 3/7 Brixtonites could not imagine why so many little local boys were walking about in 'Little Lord Fauntleroy' suits.

faunule ('fɔːnjuːl). *Ecol.* Also **faunula**. [mod.L., dim. of FAUNA.] The fauna of a specified small habitat, *esp.* a group of fossils from one small area.

1909 in *Cent. Dict.* Suppl. **1928** *Amer. Midland Naturalist* Jan. 21 A zonule is the stratum or strata which contain a faunule. **1936** *Proc. Prehist. Soc.* II. 166 This faunule indicates very damp conditions and it probably represents a willow-alder marsh. **1938** CARPENTER *Ecol. Gloss.* 308 *Faunula*, the entire animal population of a small unit area. **1953** *Breviora* XII (*title*) A cave faunule from western Puerto Rico.

faurd, Sc. pronunc. of *favoured*; only in compounds, as ***ill-***, ***well-faurd***.

fause, Sc. and dial. form of FALSE *a.*

'fause-house. *Sc.* [f. *fause*, Sc. f. of FALSE *a.* + HOUSE.] A hollow made in a corn-stack, with an opening on the side most exposed to the wind, for the purpose of drying the corn.

1785 BURNS *Halloween* x, Nell had the fause-house in her min', She pits herself and Rob in.

† **'fausen,** *sb. Obs.* Also 6 **valson**, 7 **valsen**, 9 *dial.* **fazen**. A kind of eel. Applied variously to a fresh or salt-water eel, and to a small or large eel (see quots). Also *fausen-eel*.

1547 BOORDE *Brev. Health* lxxxvii. 35 b, Take the fatnes of a valson ele. **1602** CAREW *Cornwall* (1733) 31 Of Eeles there are two sorts: the one Valsen, of best taste, comming from the fresh riuers .. the other, bred in the salt water & called a Conger Eele. *c* **1611** CHAPMAN *Iliad* XXI. 190 The wave-sprung entrails, about which fausens and other fish Did shoal. *c* **1640** J. SMYTH *Hundred of Berkeley* (1885) 319 A fauson, or great fat eele. **1688** R. HOLME *Armoury* II. 325/1 An Eel [is] first a Fausen, then a Grigg. **1708** MOTTEUX *Rabelais* IV. lx, Fausens, and Griggs. **1887** *Kent Gloss.*, *Fazen* adj. The *fazen* eel is a large brown eel, and is so called at Sandwich in contradiction to the silver eel.

† **'fausen,** *a. Obs.*

1591 *Troub. Raigne K. John* (1611) 53 The Friars chest filld with a fausen Nunne. **1654** GAYTON *Pleas. Notes* II. v. 57 Fausen sluts, like Bartholomew Faire pig-dressers.

fauserite ('fɔːsəraɪt). *Min.* [Named by Breithaupt (1865) from *Fauser* name of a gentleman at Pesth + -ITE.] (See quots.)

1868 DANA *Min.* 645 Fauserite .. From Herrengrund in Hungary. **1879** WATTS *Dict. Chem.* VI. 611 *Fauserite*, a native magnesio-manganous sulphate.

fauson, obs. form of FASHION.

† **'fausonry.** *Obs.* Also 7 **fauxonry**. [ad. OF. *faussonerie*, *fauxonerie*, f. *faussoner* to deceive, f. *faus* FALSE.] Fraud, in the legal sense; falsification of deeds or measures, coining false money, etc.

1647 N. BACON *Disc. Govt. Eng.* I. lxii. (1739) 121 Felonies, of Manslaughter .. and Fausonry, are to be punished with loss of Member and Estate. *Ibid.* 122 Fauxonry is of several degrees or kinds .. as *falsifying the King's Charter* .. *falsifying of Money* .. or *falsifying of Measures.*

faussebraie, -braye (fosbrɛ). *Fortif.* Forms: α. 5 **fawce-**, **fawese-**, (6 **faws-**) **braye**, 9 **fausse-braie**, 7– **fausse-braye**. β. 7–8 **false-bray**, (7 **falsbray**). [a. F. *fausse-braie*, f. *fausse*, fem. of *faux* false + *braie*: see BRAYE.] An artificial mound or wall thrown up in front of the main rampart. In early use, a covered way.

α. *c* **1489** CAXTON *Sonnes of Aymon* iii. 77 A fawcebraye vpon a roche, thrughe yᵉ whiche reynawde .. wente oute vnder couerte. *Ibid.* vi. 149 Also he made yᵉ portcolisse, fawesebrayes, & barbacanes well defensable. **1523** *St. Papers Henry VIII*, IV. 38 Having noo bulwarkes nor fawsbrayes. **1688** CAPT. J. S. *Fortification* 57 The onely end of this Faussebray, is the defence of the Moat. **1767** STERNE *Tr. Shandy* IX. xi, All its trumpery of saps, mines .. fausse-brays, and cuvettes. **1828** NAPIER *Penins. War* X. vii. (Rtldg.) II. 74 A second wall, about 12 feet high, called a *fausse braie* .. surrounded the first. **1855** SMEDLEY *Occult Sciences* 211 *note*, One of the pinnacled battlements of the fausse-braye.

β. **1604** E. GRIMSTONE *Hist. Siege Ostend* 34 Others .. were in the False Bray. **1667** *Lond. Gaz.* No. 212/2 Our men are now busily employed in placing new Palisados upon the Falsbray. **1702** W. J. *Bruyn's Voy. Levant* xi. 51 One may more properly call that of the outward Wall a False-bray, or Under-Bulwark.

attrib. **1812** WELLINGTON in Gurw. *Desp.* VIII. 551 Having escaladed the fausse braie wall.

† **fausse-brayed,** *ppl. a. Obs.* [f. prec. + -ED².] Provided with a fausse-braye.

c **1530** LD. BERNERS *Arth. Lyt. Bryt.* (1814) 187 A hous .. wel bolwarked and fausbrayed.

faussee, var. of FOSSEÉ, *Obs.*

faus(s)et, obs. form of FAUCET.

faust (fɔːst), *a. rare.* [ad. L. *faust-us*, f. *favēre* to favour.] Happy, lucky.

1692–1732 in COLES. **1721–1800** in BAILEY. **1890** E. JOHNSON *Rise of Christendom* 73 The Emperor .. ascending the Capitol amidst faust acclamations in the Hebrew, Greek, and Latin tongues.

fausted, var. of FORSTID.

Faustian ('faʊstɪən), *a.* [-IAN.] Of or pertaining to Johann *Faust* (in Latinized form Johannes Faustus), a wandering astrologer and necromancer who lived in Germany *c* 1488–1541 and was reputed to have sold his soul to the Devil: later, the hero of dramas by Marlowe and Goethe. Also *absol.*

1876 *Gentl. Mag.* XVI. 211 The sombre Faustian grandeur of this piece. **1931** *Times Lit. Suppl.* 21 May 404/4 The Faustian idea of eternal striving. **1941** *Amer. Speech* XVI. 178 Man is seen to characterize himself as the Faustian, with his soul constantly aspiring upward, the higher the better. **1943** *Scrutiny* XI. 270 The combination of the Faustian urge and faith in progress with outstanding intellectual ability explains the respect .. felt for Bacon. **1958** J. CAREW *Wild Coast* vii. 100 The world of .. the written word, the Faustian conflict. **1964** S. BELLOW *Herzog* 234, I would never grasp the Christian and Faustian world idea.

† **'faustitude.** *Obs.*⁻⁰ [as if ad. L. **faustitūdo*, f. *faustus*: see FAUST.] 'Good luck'.

1721–1800 in BAILEY.

† **'faustity.** *Obs.* [ad. L. *faustitāt-em*, f. *faustus* (see FAUST).] 'Good luck, happiness'.

1656–81 in BLOUNT *Glossogr.* **1729** M. RALPH *Misc. Poems* 243, I send you Health .. And length and faustity of Days.

faut(e, var. of FAULT.

‖ **faute de mieux** (fot də mjø). [Fr.] For want of something better; *attrib.*, used for lack of an alternative.

1766 CHESTERFIELD *Let.* 13 June (1774) II. 501 The seals .. were offered first to Lord Egmont, then to Lord Hardwicke; .. but, after their going a begging for some time, the Duke of —— begged them, and has them *faute de mieux.* **1828** LYTTON *Pelham* xxxii, At seven o'clock, up came a *cotelette pannée—faute de mieux*, I swallowed the composition. **1865** 'OUIDA' *Strathmore* ii, Still they were better than nothing, and were peppered *faute de mieux* that day. **1885** W. JAMES *Let.* 5 Feb. (1920) I. 238 This position .. is a *parti pris* and a *pis aller*,—*faute de mieux*,—to continue the Gallic idiom. **1941** AUDEN *New Year Let.* III. 50 And finds romantic, faute de mieux, The sad nostalgie des adieux. **1949** KOESTLER *Insight & Outlook* xii. 172 This *faute de mieux* procedure may seem to be a confirmation of the Freudian thesis.

fauterer ('fɔːtərə(r)). [f. *fauter*, for FAUTOR + -ER.] = FAUTOR.

a **1662** in Heylyn *Laud* (1668) I. 98 Thou art the fauterer of all Wickedness. **1817** MAR. EDGEWORTH *Ormond* vi. (1832) 60 Father Jos was by no means .. a friend or fauterer of sir Ulick.

‖ **fauteuil** (fotœj). [a. F. *fauteuil*, f. OF. *faudeteuil*, *faldestoel*:—med.L. *faldistolium* FALDSTOOL.] **a.** An arm-chair.

1744 GRAY in Gosse *Life* (1882) 74 Squatted me into a fauteuil. **1771** H. WALPOLE *Lett. Cntess. Ossory* (1857) V. 324 The mountain-gods .. pulling their fauteuils across a continent. **1813** *Examiner* 1 Feb. 71/2 Sofas, *fauteuils*, *console*-tables, girandoles. **1866** MRS. H. WOOD *St. Martin's Eve* xxiv. (1874) 299 Her grandmamma's fauteuil.

b. Popularly pronounced ('fəʊtɪl). A seat in a theatre, an omnibus, etc., designed to resemble an armchair; *spec.* = STALL *sb.*¹ 5 c.

1859 SALA *Twice round Clock* 253 The stalls... Those comfortable *fauteuils.* **1901** *Playgoer* 15 Oct. 38/1 Fine *fauteils* for sixpence; or stage box seats for ninepence. **1925** A. P. HERBERT *Laughing Ann* 37 Oh, I likes a bit of enjoyment on a Friday, I like to sit in the fautles an' be grand. **1931** *Morning Post* 20 Aug. 8/3 With their covered-in tops, resilient springs, and voluptuous *fauteuils*, the latest omnibuses have become so attractive that one often feels .. disinclined to get off. **1970** *Wykehamist* 11 July 498/2 The *real* critic .. settles down in his luxurious fauteuil on the lower slopes of the Theatre Workshop Parnassus to have a good laugh.

c. The seat of a member of the French Academy; hence, membership of the Academy.

1883 *Standard* 23 Aug. 5/2 The number of Academic *fauteuils* would be fixed. **1920** *Glasgow Herald* 28 Apr. 9 The creation .. of the class of Senior Academicians, whose fauteuils automatically become vacant.

† **'fautive,** *a. Obs. rare.* [f. L. type **fautīvus*, f. *favēre* to favour.] Tending to favour, favourable. Const. *of*, *to*.

1667 WATERHOUSE *Fire Lond.* 37 Such instances as were by wise men observed Fautive of its progress. *Ibid.* 110 No corner of the .. Land to be fautive to it or polluted by it.

fautor ('fɔːtə(r)). Forms: 4–7 **fautour(e**, (6 **fauctour**), 5–6 **fawter**, **-or**, **-our**, 6–7 **fauter**, 4, 6– **fautor**. Also 6–7 *erron.* **faulter**, **-or**, **-our**. [ad. F. *fauteur*, ad. L. *fautor*, f. *favēre* to favour.] One who favours; a favourer.

1. An adherent, partisan, supporter, abettor.

c **1330** R. BRUNNE *Chron.* (1810) 209 Him and his fautours he cursed euerilkon. **1387** TREVISA *Higden* (Rolls) IV. 443 But Symon and Iohn, with here fautoures, stopped þe wayes al aboute. *c* **1450** *St. Cuthbert* (Surtees) 8356 With þair fautours all in fere. **1527** in Fiddes *Wolsey* II. (1726) 141, I shall .. never more .. hide .. such heresies .. nor their auctors or fawtors. **1559** *Mirr. Mag.*, *Worcester* xx, For princes faultes his faultors all men teare. **1603** KNOLLES *Hist. Turks* (1621) 693 This matter was with great heat debated .. either part having great faultours. **1713** DERHAM *Phys. Theol.* V. i. 312 Cartes .. hath been thought by some to have been a Fautor of Atheism. **1786** H. TOOKE *Purley* (1798) I. 398 His lordship and his fautors will do well to contend stoutly .. for their doctrine of language. **1832** AUSTIN *Jurispr.* (1879) I. vi. 289 [Hobbes] is not of the apologists and fautors of tyranny. **1890** E. JOHNSON *Rise Christendom* 472 Montalembert, the great fautor and defender of the monks.

† **2.** A protector, patron. *Obs.*

1460 CAPGRAVE *Chron.* 304 The archbishop .. cursed him for contumacie, and great fautoure of heretikes. **1548** W. PATTEN *Expedition Scot.* Ded. in Arb. *Garner* III. 52 His most benign fautor and patron. **1605** CAMDEN *Rem.* (1637) 346 Humphrey, Duke of Glocester, a noble fautor of good letters. *c* **1611** CHAPMAN *Iliad* I. 441 O thou that all things seest, Fautor of Chrysce. **1686** GOAD *Celest. Bodies* II. xii. 321 He [a star] is the Fautor of Serenity. **1691** WOOD *Ath. Oxon* I. 24 By the favour of his Patron, and fautor of his Studies .. he was .. made Scholar or Pastor.

fautorship ('fɔːtəʃɪp). [f. prec. + -SHIP.] The fact or condition of being a fautor; partisanship.

1863 ALFORD *Grk. Test.* (ed. 5) I. Prolegomena 76 The comparative absence of blind fautorship of the received text. **1888** H. C. LEA *Hist. Inquisition* I. 167 This final effort .. was naturally construed as fautorship of heresy.

† **'fautress.** *Obs.* [f. as prec. + -ESS.] A female fautor: **a.** a patroness; **b.** an instigator.

1596 DRAYTON *Legends* iii. 313 The only Fautresse of all Noble Arts. **1621** G. SANDYS *Ovid's Met.* III. (1626) 48 Mans Fautresse, Pallas .. stood by. **1703** ROWE *Ulyss.* III. i. 1125 Pallas, the Fautress of my Master's Arms. **1717** GARTH *Ovid* Ded., He comes from Banishment to the Fautress of Liberty. **1732** in COLES.

† **'fautrix.** *Obs.* [a. L. *fautrix*, fem. of *fautor* (see FAUTOR). Cf. F. *fautrice.*] = prec.

1582 T. WATSON *Centurie of Loue* xcii, Melissa mother is, and fautrix to the Bee. **1621** G. SANDYS *Ovid's Met.* VIII. (1669) 153 Him Pallas, fautrix of good wits, sustains. **1630** M. GODWYN tr. *Bp. Hereford's Ann. Eng.* III. 325 The Queen .. was so exact a fautrix of justice.

fauve (fəʊv). Also with capital initial. [Fr., lit. 'wild beast'.] A member of a movement in painting, chiefly associated with Henri Matisse (1869–1954), which flourished in Paris from 1905, and which is mainly characterized by a vivid use of colour. Also *attrib.* or as *adj.*, and *transf.* Hence (as adj.), of a bright or vivid colour. So **'fauvism** [F. *fauvisme*], the practice of this style of painting; **'fauvist(e)** [F. *fauviste*], an adherent of fauvism; also as *adj.*

The name was coined by the French art critic Louis Vauxcelles at the Autumn Salon of 1905; coming across a quattrocento-like statue in the midst of works by Matisse and his associates, he remarked, 'Donatello au milieu des fauves!'

1915 WYNDHAM LEWIS in *Blast* July 23/1 May the mortality amongst Cubists, Carnivorists, Fauvists and Vorticists at the front be excessive. *Ibid.* 77/2 Mr. Adeney, in pallid and solidified landscapes, brings us back to the 'Fauves'. **1922** *Encycl. Brit.* XXXII. 6/1 Symbolism and Fauvism. *Ibid.* 6/2 The application of the *fauviste* recipe to the painting of fashionable Parisian society. **1932** *Times* 12 Mar., He was one of the group of Scottish painters who threw in their lot with the 'Fauves' .. and .. the result was a rather interesting blend of fauviste and Glasgow School characteristics. **1942** *Burlington Mag.* Feb. 51/2 The quasi-primitiveness of Gauguin or the Fauvistes. **1953** *Ann. Reg. 1952* 380 'The Pool of London', a colourful painting by André Derain from his *fauve* period. **1958** *Observer* 15 June 15/2 Ann Jellicoe and N. F. Simpson, the most disturbing of *fauve* humorists. **1959** *Listener* 8 Oct. 565/1 The truly decisive break to France, to Matisse and liberation by the Fauves. **1959** H. READ *Conc. Hist. Mod. Painting* ii. 34 In Paris the painters who reacted against Impressionism were known as 'les fauves' (the wild beasts), a name first used as a witticism by the critic Louis Vauxcelles at the time of the Autumn Salon of 1905. The name was apt because the means used by these painters were decidedly violent. **1960** *Guardian* 14 Nov. 7/3 The fauvist intensity of her colour —the red and yellow .. conflicting hotly with the virulent greens. **1960** *New Left Rev.* Nov.–Dec. 59/1 It seems probable that [Picasso's] *Les Demoiselles* was designed .. as a counterblast to recent trends in fauvism. **1967** *Vogue* June 101 Striking fauve flowered coat.

fauvel, var. of FAVEL, *Obs.*

‖ **fauvette** (fovɛt). [F. *fauvette*, f. *fauve* fallow.] The name given by French writers to a family of Warblers, and adopted by Bewick.

1797 BEWICK *Brit. Birds* I. 209 The Fauvette. Pettichaps (*Motacilla hippolais*, Lin., *La Fauvette*, Buff.). *Ibid.* 212 The lesser Fauvette. Passerine Warbler. *Ibid.* 213 The Winter Fauvette. Hedge Warbler. *Ibid.* 216 This disposition .. is common to all the Fauvettes. **1802** G. MONTAGU *Ornith. Dict.*, Fauvette (*Sylvia hortensis*, Bechstein). **1839** MACGILLIVRAY *Hist. Brit. Birds* II. 345 *Sylvia Hortensis*, the Garden Warbler .. Fauvette .. Garden Fauvet.

‖ **faux** (fɔːks). *rare.* [Assumed nom. sing. to L. *fauces*; the sing. has classical authority only in the ablative.] = FAUCES in various senses.

1828 KIRBY & SP. *Entomol.* I. 293 The sweet fluid which many of them (plants belonging to Dionæa, Drosera, &c.) secrete near the faux. **1856** HENSLOW *Dict. Bot. Terms*, *Faux* (the gorge), the throat.

‖ **faux bonhomme** (fo bɔnɔm). [F. *faux* false + *bonhomme* simple good-natured man.] A sly,

shifty person who assumes an open and good-natured manner.

1916 W. S. MAUGHAM *Writer's Notebk.* (1949) 113 He looks at you benignly through gold-rimmed spectacles. The *faux bon homme.* **1932** *Sunday Times* 13 Mar. 6/2 The monster [Iago] in the guise of *faux bonhomme.* **1934** G. B. SHAW *On Rocks* I. 204 *The Oxford youth*... Stow all this fo bunnum business, Chavender... *Sir Arthur.* Oh, faux bonhomme, of course. **1958** *Observer* 25 May 14/1 Smiling the perpetual sweet smile of the *faux-bonhomme.*

‖**faux-bourdon** (foburdɔ̃). [Fr.] = FABURDEN.

1879 in GROVE *Dict. Mus.* I. 509/1. **1937** C. DAY LEWIS *Starting Point* 66 One reed-like liquid tenor..danced and swayed into a faux-bourdon. **1942** *Scrutiny* XI. 11 The enormous influence exerted by English methods on the Continental voice-leading is evident in the wide-spread adoption of the faux bourdon style. **1967** *Times* 23 Feb. 10/6 Part-writings, suggested medieval organum or sometimes faux-bourdon techniques.

fauxety, -ity, obs. forms of FALSITY.

‖**faux-naïf** (fonaif), *sb.* and *a.* [F. *faux* false + NAÏF *a.*] **A.** *sb.* A person who pretends to be simple or unaffected and adopts a childish or naïve manner. **B.** *adj.* **a.** Of a work of art: self-consciously or meretriciously simple and artless. **b.** Of a person: affectedly simple or naïve; pretendedly ingenuous.

1941 *Fortune* July 111 Gibbs..is a *faux-naïf*: he pretends to have no social graces. **1952** W. PLOMER *Museum Pieces* 28 Mother loves to pretend to be extremely simple. She's a *fausse naïve.* **1958** *Listener* 3 July 31/3 As music, 'Catulli Carmina' uses the same naive technical procedures as the earlier 'Carmina Burana', but here they have degenerated into *faux-naïf* mannerism. **1958** *Times Lit. Suppl.* 21 Nov. p. ii/4 *Faux-naïf* pictures..the kind calculated to raise a snigger among grown-ups and fury in the young. **1961** *Times* 13 May 5/2 That terrible affliction of the folk-singer, the faux-naïf. **1964** G. SIMS *Terrible Door* xxvi. 140 The *fauxnaif* would have been dumped..in Poole Harbour. **1970** *Times* 18 Apr. p. iv/2 The language is faultlessly faux-naif—a recreation of the idioms of a child's thinking.

fauxonry, var. of FAUSONRY. *Obs.*, fraud.

‖**faux pas** (fo pɑ). [Fr. *faux* false + *pas* step.] A false step, *fig.*; a slip, a trip; an act which compromises one's reputation, *esp.* a woman's lapse from virtue. Cf. *false step* in FALSE *a.* 6.

1676 WYCHERLEY *Pl. Dealer* v. i, Before this faux pas, this trip of mine, the world could not talk of me. **1762** FOOTE *Lyar* I. Wks. 1799 I. 288 A firework..well designed? *Sir J.* Superb. *Y. Wild.* And happily executed? *Sir J.* Not a single faux pas. **1763** *Brit. Mag.* IV. 350 Terræ Filius..taxes them with any faux-pas, or irregularities, they may have committed. **1823** BYRON *Juan* XIV. lx, Foreigners don't know that a *faux pas* In England ranks quite on a different list. **1840** BARHAM *Ingol. Leg., Acc. New Play*, His Lordship ..Conceiv'd that his daughter had made a *faux pas.*

‖**faux-prude.** *Obs.* [Fr.; *faux* FALSE and *prude* PRUDE.] A man who simulates prudishness.

1676 ETHEREDGE *Man of Mode* IV. i. Wks. (1888) 323 In Paris the mode is to flatter the prude, laugh at the faux-prude.

fav. *Racing.* Also fav. (with point). Abbrev. (usu. written) of FAVOURITE, FAVORITE sb. 1 b, as in the results of a horse-race.

Quot. 1960 prob. requires the pronunc. (feɪv).

1935 *Daily Mail* 3 June 14/5 Vicar's Cross (6-4, fav.). **1955** *Ibid.* 2 May 11/4 1954: Jack Magic, 8-13 (H. M. Jones). 4-9 fav. S. Ingham. **1960** P. CAMPBELL *Come here till I tell You* 81 The Clonmel fellas is puttin' one in to knock over the fav. **1976** *Daily Record* (Glasgow) 4 Dec. 28/2 Falcons Boy 11-6 M Salaman fav, and Roman Rock, 11-2, R Greenway 5. **1985** *Sun* 29 Oct. 26/2 Pokerfayes (8-2), 6-1 jt-fav.

†**fa'vaginous**, *a. Obs.* Also 7 faviginous. [f. L. *favus* honeycomb; perh. on false analogy of *farraginous*, or of L. *fabaginus*, *oleaginus.*] Formed like or resembling a honeycomb in appearance; cellular.

1658 SIR T. BROWNE *Gard. Cyrus* II. 515 A like ordination there is in the favaginous Sockets..of the noble flower of the sunne. **1686** PLOT *Staffordsh.* 201 A third [membrane].. faviginous like a hony-comb or tripe, without. **1692-1708** COLES, *Favaginous.* **1884** in *Syd. Soc. Lex.*

fave (feɪv), *sb.* and *a. slang* (orig. *U.S.*). Abbrev. of FAVOURITE, FAVORITE *sb.* and *a.*, used esp. in show business. ***fave rave*** adj. and sb., of popular music(ians), films, etc.: (designating) a special favourite.

1938 *Variety* 16 Mar. 44/4 Lester Harding, heavy fave here, clicks with pop songs. **1940** *Ibid.* 3 Apr. 38/2 They give off okay on fave comedy oldies such as 'Horsie Keep Your Tail Up.' **1964** *Jackie* 11 Jan. 8/2 Her fave one is a thin strip of leather. **1967** *Melody Maker* 16 Dec. 10/7 Smith's quartet version with Stan Getz was one of the fave rave records of the period. **1973** *Times* 30 July 15 The American fan magazine market, always at the ready to replace a current fave rave. **1977** *Sounds* 9 July 18/2 I reckon 'Violation' has already found a place in my end-of-the-year-faves listing. **1982** *Washington Post* 26 July C1/1 Art Laffer, the Reaganauts' fave moneyman, threw his curve at the American Meat Institute just recently. **1986** *Pony* Sept. 4/1 Have you always longed to ask your fave riders some really stupid questions? **1987** *Face* Apr. 47/2 These new recruits may have allied themselves to Smithdom's cause because their former faves, Echo & The Bunnymen for instance, haven't delivered.

†'**favel**, *a.* and *sb. Obs.* Forms: 4 fauvel, fawvelle, 5 favel(l)e, (favyll), 6 favell, 4-6 favel. [a. OF. *fauvel*, f. *fauve* fallow-coloured, a. Teut. **falwo-*: see FALLOW *a.*[1]

The OF. word had all the uses found in Eng., so that there is no ground for treating sense 3 of the sb. as a distinct word, though it is possible that it may have been associated by some ME. writers with OF. *favele* idle talk, cajolery:—L. *fābella*, dim. of *fābula* FABLE. The phrase 'to curry Favel', OF. *estriller, torcher Fauvel*, comes from the *Roman de Fauvel* (1310), the hero of which is a counterpart of Reynard the Fox (see P. Paris, *MSS. Bibl. du Roi* I. 306); it has been adopted in Ger. as *den fahlen hengst streichen.* It is not clear whether before the date of this poem a 'fallow' horse was proverbial as the symbol of dishonesty; the same notion is found in German, 'to ride the fallow horse' (*den fahlen hengst reiten*—recorded from 15th c.) having the sense 'to play an underhand game, act deceitfully'.]

A. *adj.* Of a horse: = FALLOW *a.*[1] (The exact colour denoted by the adj. in early use is uncertain.)

c **1489** CAXTON *Sonnes of Aymon* i. 33 There came rydynge a messager vpon a horse fauell.

B. *sb.*

1. As the proper name of a fallow-coloured horse.

c **1325** *Coer de L.* 2320 Two stedes found the kyng Richard, That one hight Favel, that other Lyarde. *c* **1330** R. BRUNNE *Chron.* (1810) 175 Siþen at Japhet was slayn fauuelle [*printed* fanuelle] his stede. *c* **1375** *Morte Arthur* 2766 One ffawuelle [*printed* ffawnelle] of ffryselande to fferaunt he rydys.

2. The fallow horse proverbial as the type of fraud, cunning, or duplicity. Only in phrase *to curry favel*: see CURRY *v.* 5 a.

3. Hence used as a mere personification of cunning or duplicity.

1362 LANGL. *P. Pl.* A. II. 6 Boþe Fals and Fauuel and al his hole Menye! **1406** HOCCLEVE *La Male Regle* 223 O thow, fauele, of lesynges auctour. **14..** *Kyng & Hermit* 157 in Hazl. *E.P.P.* (1864) I. 19 Were I oute of my hermyte wede, Off my favyll I wold not drede. **1522** SKELTON *Why not to Court* 92 Favell is false forsworne. **1576** R. EDWARDS *Parad. D. Devices* (1578) I iij, O favell false, thou traitor borne, what mischief more might thou devise!

‖**favela** (fa'vela). [Pg.] In Brazil, a shack, shanty; a slum: usu. in pl. *favelas*, a collection of improvised huts, a shanty town.

Hence **fave'lado**, a person dwelling in a favela.

1961 G. MIKES *Tango* 18 In the midst of all this beauty and elegance, you discover the *favelas*... The *favela* is a wretched, ramshackle, filthy hut run up out of sticks, rotting planks, dirty rags and cardboard, as a rule in less than twenty-four hours... The *favelas* have no electricity (unless, as frequently happens, an enterprising favelado manages to tap an electric cable). **1962** *Guardian* 5 Oct. 13/4 A Sao Paulo *favela*, one of those slum shanty towns. **1964** 'M. E. CHABER' *Six who Ran* (1965) iv. 57 We have a little house in the *favelas.* **1964** W. MCCORD in I. L. Horowitz *New Sociol.* 427 They hastily retreated to the city's healthier quarters, leaving the suffering *favelados* unchanged. **1969** J. MANDER *Static Soc.* ii. 81 We cannot admire Rio's skyline for the squalid *favelas* nestling between her sugar-loaf hills.

‖**favella** (fə'vɛlə). *Bot.* Pl. -æ. [mod.L.; used by J. G. Agardh (*Kongl. Vetensk. Acad. Handl.* for 1836, p. 43); his description and drawing suggest that he intended *favellæ* to stand for 'small beans', in which case the word would be an incorrect dim. of L. *faba* bean, influenced by the F. form *fève.*] See quot. 1884.

1857 [see next]. **1867** J. HOGG *Microsc.* II. i. 274 When such a fruit is wholly external..it is called a favella. **1884** *Syd. Soc. Lex., Favella*, a form of the conceptacular fruit of florideous Algæ in which the spores are collected into spherical masses which lie on the outer surface of the frond.

favellidium (fævɪ'lɪdɪəm). *Bot.* [f. (by J. G. Agardh 1842) FAVELLA + Gr. dim. ending -ιδιον (improperly used, as no diminutive sense was intended.] See quots.

[**1842** AGARDH *Algæ* 60 Sunt sporæ numerosæ in glomerulum arcte congestæ, pericarpio hyalino.. circumdatæ; has *Favellidia* appellavi.] **1857** BERKELY *Cryptog. Bot.* §144. 170 Thus by the evolution of one cell, a favella..is formed; by the evolution of several detached but adjacent mother-cells, a compound favella or favellidium results. **1867** J. HOGG *Microsc.* II. i. 273 Such a fruit is called a favellidium and occurs in Halymenia. **1884** *Syd. Soc. Lex., Favellidium* (dim. of *Favella*), a form of the conceptacular part of a florideous Alga, in which the spores are collected into spherical masses, which lie entirely embedded in the substance of the frond, as in Halymenia; or project somewhat, as in Gigartina.

faveolate (fə'viːəleɪt), *a.* [f. mod.L. *faveolus*, dim. of *favus* honeycomb + -ATE[3]. Cf. F *faveolé.*] Honeycombed, cellular.

1866 in *Treas. Bot.* **1884** in *Syd. Soc. Lex.*

faveolus (fə'viːələs). Pl. -i. [mod.L., dim. of *favus* honeycomb.] A small depression, like a cell of a honeycomb.

1882 *Encycl. Brit.* XIV. 562/1 The apothecia of several calcicole lichens..have the power..of forming minute faveoli in the rocks. **1963** J. H. KENNETH *Henderson's Dict. Biol. Terms* (ed. 8) 199/2 *Faveolus*... A small depression or pit; alveola.

faverel ('fævərəl). [var. of next.] A name of various plants. **a.** An onion. **b.** *Draba verna*, whitlow-grass. **c.** See quot.

a. 1597 GERARDE *Herbal* App., Fauerell is *Cepea.* **1847-78** HALLIWELL, *Faverel*, an onion. *Linc.*
b. 1770 SIR J. HILL *Herb. Brit.* II. 249 *Draba verna.* Whitlow Faverel. **1878-86** BRITTEN & HOLLAND *Plant-n.*, Faverel..*Draba verna.*
c. 1884 MILLER *Plant-n., Faverell*, an old name for *Veronica Anagallis.*

†'**faverole.** *Obs.* [a. OF. *faverolle* (in Normandy the broad bean, *faba vulgaris*).] A name of various plants: see quots.

c **1265** *Voc. Names Plants* in Wr.-Wülcker 555 *Fabaria*, fauerole. **1597** GERARDE *Herbal* App., *Fauerole* is water Dragons. **1878-86** BRITTEN & HOLLAND *Plant-n.*, Faverole ..*Calla palustris* L. **1884** MILLER *Plant-n., Faverole*, an old name for *Arum Dracunculus.*

Faverolle(s) ('fævərɒl, fævə'rəʊl). [Prob. f. the place-name *Faverolles*, in the department of Seine-et-Oise, France.] One of a breed of domestic fowls originated in France by crossing light Brahmas or Dorkings with Houdans.

1902 L. WRIGHT *New Bk. Poultry* 457/1 Faverolles have for some time been common in the northern part of France, where they were regarded as simply useful fowls. *Ibid.* 457/2 The colour of the Salmon Faverolles cock is quite different from that of the hen. **1957** *Encycl. Brit.* XVIII. 378/2 The Faverolle is a French breed with feathered shanks; in England the Salmon Faverolle is crossed extensively with the Light Sussex for roaster production.

†**fa'vificous**, *a. Obs.* [f. L. **favific-us* (f. *fav-us* honeycomb + *-ficus* making: see -FIC) + -OUS.] That makes combs.

1668 WILKINS *Real Char.* II. v. §2. 126 Maggots or Worms that are Favificous; or making of Combs. **1670** *Phil. Trans.* V. 2066 They are probably the favificous and gregarious kind.

†**faviform** ('feɪvɪfɔːm), *a. Obs.* [f. L. *fav-us* a honeycomb + -FORM.] Formed or shaped like a honeycomb, honeycombed; *esp.* in *Surg.* (see quot. 1753).

1753 CHAMBERS *Cycl. Suppl., Faviform*, in surgery, a term used to express certain ulcers, which when pressed upon with the finger emit a sanies thro' several small holes. **1775** in ASH. **1884** in *Syd. Soc. Lex.*

favillous (fə'vɪləs), *a.* [f. L. *favill-a* hot ashes + -OUS. Cf. OF. *favilleux.*] Consisting of or resembling ashes.

1650 SIR T. BROWNE *Pseud. Ep.* v. xxii. 231 The avolation of the light and favillous particles. **1775** in ASH.

favism ('feɪvɪz(ə)m). *Path.* Also fabism, fa'bismus. [ad. It. *favism-o*, f. *fava* broad bean (f. L. *faba* bean) + -ISM.] A hereditary form of anæmia manifested only after contact with broad beans.

1903 DORLAND *Med. Dict.* (ed. 3) 263/1 *Fabism*, a disease of Italy caused by eating of the bean *Vicia faba.* **1933** *Jrnl. Amer. Med. Assoc.* 28 Oct. 1389/1 Favism (fabism) is a syndrome caused by inhalation from bean plants when in blossom or by ingestion of the beans. **1935** WHITBY & BRITTON *Disorders of Blood* xiii. 241 Fabismus is a hæmolytic anæmia which occurs in Italy from eating beans. **1962** *Lancet* 15 Dec. 1274/1 This enzyme deficiency is commonest among Mediterranean people, but recently favism has been reported in 3 patients of British stock, and biochemical evidence of the defect was found in 12 of their relatives.

‖**fa'vissa.** Pl. favissæ. [L. *favissæ* pl. underground cellars near the temples, used as store-houses.] (See quot.)

1730-6 BAILEY (folio), *Favissa* [with Antiquaries], a hole, pit, or vault under ground, wherin some rarity of great value was kept. **1893** *Nation* 19 Jan. LVI. 53/2 The favissæ of temples, the vaults in which were buried..'ex-votos'.

favonian (fə'vəʊnɪən), *a.* [ad. L. *favōniān-us*, f. *Favōnius* the west wind.] Of or pertaining to the west wind; hence, favourable, gentle, propitious.

1656-81 in BLOUNT *Glossogr.* **1742** YOUNG *Nt. Th.* vi. 686 Soft Spring, with breath Favonian. **1771** FLETCHER *Checks* Wks. 1795 II. 267 The favonian breathings and sighs which attended his preaching and prayers. *a* **1821** KEATS in *Life & Lett.* (1848) II. 263 Softly tell her not to fear Such calm favonian burial! **1854** W. JOHNSON *Ionica* (1858) 78 Thou Shoulds't breathe upon that pallid brow Favonian airs of mirth and glee.

†**fa'vonious**, *a. Obs.*—[0] [f. L. *Favōni-us* the west wind + -OUS.] Of or pertaining to the west wind.

1692-1732 in COLES.

Favonius (fə'vəʊnɪəs). *poet.* or *Myth.* [a. L. *Favōnius* the west wind, f. *favēre* to favour.] The west wind, Zephyr.

1549 *Compl. Scot.* vi. (1872) 61 The feyrd cardinal vynd is callit fauonius or occidental. **1634** HABINGTON *Castara* I. (Arb.) 37 If to the torrid Zone her way she bend Her the coole breathing of Favonius lend. **1742** YOUNG *Nt. Th.* ii. 242 Favonius, breathe still softer, or be chid.

‖**favori** (favɔri). [Fr.] = FAVOURITE *sb.* 3. Usu. in pl.

1801 C. WILMOT *Jrnl.* 3 Dec. (1920) 9 Their noses.. peeping out of a bush of black Beard, Moustaches, Favori

and ringlets. **1831** DISRAELI *Young Duke* II. xix. 248 His beard, his mustachios, his whiskers, his *favoris*. **1864** G. A. SALA *Quite Alone* I. i. 4 Fawn-coloured *favoris*.

favose (fəˈvəʊs), *a. Bot.* and *Path.* [as if ad. L. **favōs-us*, f. *favus* honeycomb.] (See quots.)

1840 PAXTON *Bot. Dict.*, *Favose*, pitted, like the cells of a honeycomb. **1866** in *Treas. Bot.*

Hence faˈvosely *adv.* (see quots.).

1840 PAXTON *Bot. Dict.*, *Favosely-scrobiculate*, excavated in little pits or hollows. **1847** CRAIG, *Favosely*, in the manner of a honeycomb.

favosites (fævəˈsaɪtiːz). *Geol.* Also anglicized as ˈfavosite. [mod.L. (Lamarck) f. **favōsus*: see prec.] A genus of fossil zoophytes, resembling a honeycomb in appearance.

1832 in WEBSTER. **1845** *Penny Cycl.* Suppl. I. 566 *Favosites*, a genus of fossil Zoophyta, common in the Silurian strata of Norway and Wales. **1846** DANA *Zooph.* iv. §62 (1848) 65 The Pocilloporæ, Favosites, and many Cyathophyllidæ.

faˌvoso-, combining form of FAVOSE, occas. prefixed to other adjs. to indicate a favose form.

1866 *Treas. Bot.*, *Favoso-areolate*, divided into spaces resembling the cavities of honeycomb. *Ibid.*, *Favoso-dehiscent*, appearing honeycombed after dehiscence.

favour, **favor** (ˈfeɪvə(r)), *sb.* Also 4–6 favore, favoure (5–6 fawoure, favowre, 6 favower, faveour), 5–6 favyr, faver, 6 favur, (5 fawer, fayver), 9 *dial.* favver. [ME. *favor*, *-our*, a. OF. *favor*, *-our* (mod.F. *faveur*) = Pr. and Sp. *favor*, It. *favore*:—L. *favōre-m*, f. *favēre* to regard with goodwill, side with, show kindness to, protect. As in other words with the same ending, the spelling with *-our* is preferred in the British Isles, while in the U.S. *-or* is more common.]

1. a. Propitious or friendly regard, goodwill, *esp.* on the part of a superior or a multitude. *to find favour in the eyes of* (orig. a Hebraism): to gain the goodwill of. †Formerly also with *a* and *plural*: A liking, preference. † *to have a favour to*: to have a liking or regard for.

to curry favour: corruption of *to curry favel*; see CURRY *v.* 5 b, and FAVEL *sb.* 2.

a **1340** HAMPOLE *Psalter* xxiv. 3 þai doe wickidly, to get þaim þe fauour..of þis warld. *c* **1380** WYCLIF *Sel. Wks.* III. 434, & fals not þe gospel for favor of men. *c* **1400** *Destr. Troy* 5419 The Mirmydouns his men, þat mekill ioy hade, And fayuer of þat fre, þen any folke ellis. **1526** TINDALE *1 Cor.* xvi. 23 The favoure of the lorde Jesus Christ be with you all. **1535** COVERDALE *Ps.* xliii[iv]. 3 Thou haddest a fauoure vnto them. [So in **1611**.] **1551** ROBINSON tr. *More's Utop.* I. (Arb.) 56 An other woulde haue the fauoure of the Swychers wonne with money. **1584** POWEL *Lloyd's Cambria* 94 To procure him the Kings Fauour. **1601** SHAKS. *Twel. N.* I. iv. 7 Is he inconstant sir, in his fauours. **1611** BIBLE *Esther* v. 8, I haue found fauour in the sight of the king. **1641** DK. HAMILTON in *H. Papers* (Camden) 106 Your Ma^ty..of whose..favour I have had so manie..testimonyes. **1700** DRYDEN *Theodore & Honoria* 19 He..found no favour in his lady's eyes. **1781** GIBBON *Decl. & F.* III. 247 Such assiduous zeal secured the favour of the saint. **1807** CRABBE *Hall of Just.* 74 His favour was my bliss and pride. **1823** SCOTT *Quentin D.* x, His young Life-guardsman, for whom he seemed to have taken a special favour. **1838** THIRLWALL *Greece* V. 309 The oration..opens with a congratulation on the favour of heaven. **1866** G. MACDONALD *Ann. Q. Neighb.* xiii. (1878) 271 To create a favour toward each other.

b. Approving disposition towards a thing; inclination to commend, sanction, or adopt.

1827 POLLOK *Course T.* IX. 521 The first and highest place In Fancy's favour. **1862** H. MARRYAT *Year in Sweden* II. 247 St. Brita's onion found..great favour in their sight. **1884** tr. *Lotze's Metaph.* 154 Those who looked with favour on his enterprise.

c. Objectively. (*to be, stand high,* etc.) *in a person's favour*: in his good graces. Also *in, out of favour, to bring into favour*, etc.

1514 BARCLAY *Cyt. & Uplondyshm.* (Percy Soc.) p. xliii, Thou mayst suspect and trowe Him more in favour and in conceipt then thou. **1526** *Pilgr. Perf.* (W. de W. 1531) 7 b, Familiar & great in fauour with prynces. **1548** [see FALL *v.* 38]. **1568** GRAFTON *Chron.* II. 293 The king of Navarre..was out of the french kings favour. **1580** BARET *Alv.* F 251 To bring one in fauour with a man, *insinuare aliquem alteri.* **1676** LADY CHAWORTH in *Hist. MSS. Comm.* 12th Rep., App. v. 28 She is still highly in favour. **1688** MIEGE *Fr. Dict.* s.v. *Bring*, I'll bring you again into his favour. **1701** DE FOE *True-born Eng.* I Fools out of Favour grudge at Knaves in Place. **1848** MACAULAY *Hist. Eng.* I. 447 Rochester..stood high in the favour of the King. **1860** ADLER *Fauriel's Prov. Poetry* ii. 21 The various kinds of Provençal poetry were not in equal favour among the Castilians. **1876** J. H. NEWMAN *Hist. Sk.* I. I. iv. 216 As slaves, or as captives..they were taken into favour by the dominant nation.

†**d.** The object of favour; a favourite. *Obs.*

1387 TREVISA *Higden* (Rolls) VI. 413 Elfleda favour of citezeynes [L. *favor civium*] and drede of enemyes. **1667** MILTON *P.L.* III. 664 Man, His chief delight and favour.

†**e.** The action of favouring; patronage *of* an object. *Obs. rare*$^{-1}$.

1692 TEMPLE *Ess. Anc. & Mod. Learn.* in *Misc.* II. (ed. 3) 65 The favour of learning was the humour..of the age.

2. a. Exceptional kindness; gracious or friendly action due to special goodwill, and in excess of what may be ordinarily looked for. †*for favour*: out of goodwill, freely.

The envelope of a letter sent by hand occasionally bears the words 'By favour of Mr. ——' (the friend who conveys the letter).

13.. *E.E. Allit. P.* A. 967 Of þe lombe I haue þe aquylde For a syȝt þer of þurȝ gret fauor. *c* **1460** FORTESCUE *Abs. & Lim. Mon.* vi, For the ffauour þat we do to the persones þat kepe ham, wich ffauoure þe Scottis do not. **1509** FISHER *Fun. Serm. C'tess Richmond* Wks. (1876) 299 The good deserueth ..to haue fauoure shewed vnto them. **1580** BARET *Alv.* F 251 For fauour, *gratiosè.* **1769** *Phil. Trans.* LIX. 199 *note*, A crocodile, which I lately saw by the favour of Mr. John Hunter. **1818** SCOTT *Hrt. Midl.* xxxviii, I have a friend.. who will..do me so much favour.

b. An instance of this; something conceded, conferred, or done out of special grace or goodwill; an act of exceptional kindness, as opposed to one of duty or justice. (Now also in ironic *colloq.* usage.)

1590 SHAKS. *Com. Err.* I. i. 23 Doe me the fauour to dilate at full, What haue befalne of them. **1608–11** BP. HALL *Medit. & Vows* II. §23 So shal I..accept of small favours with great thankfulnes. **1667** ANNE WYNDHAM *King's Concealm.* (1681) 56 A Gentleman..desired the favour of him, that he would please to step forth. **1714** FORTESCUE-ALAND *Pref. Fortescue's Abs. & Lim. Mon.* 39 He had extraordinary Favours shewn him from his Prince. **1780** COWPER *Table-t.* 268 Religion, richest favour of the skies. **1814** D. H. O'BRIEN *Captiv. & Escape* 13 We were allowed to mix with the officers..as a great favour. **1864** TENNYSON *En. Ard.* 284, I came to ask a favour of you. **1875** JOWETT *Plato* (ed. 2) III. 309, I wish that you would do me the favour of considering temperance first. **1959** [see DROP *v.* 4 c]. **1962** N. MARSH *Hand in Glove* v. 149 'Look,' Leonard drawled, 'do me a favour and get the hell out of this, will you?' **1963** J. T. STORY *Something for Nothing* i. 20 'Shouldn't you get an accountant to sort it out?' 'Do me a favour,' Albert said. 'It was getting an accountant that got me into all this.' **1969** *Guardian* 14 May 1/2 Was she hoping to get engaged during the year of the tour? 'Good God, no, do us a favour.'

c. A complimentary term for: Communication, letter. (Now, at least in England, almost confined to commercial correspondence.) Also explicitly in † *the favour of your letter*.

c **1645** HOWELL *Lett.* I. IV. viii, Since I was beholden to you for your many Favours in Oxford I have not heard from you. **1679** PEPYS *Let. to Dk. York* 9 June, The..excuse of my no earlier owing the favour of your Royal Highness's, by Captain Sanders. **1706** WALSH in *Pope's Lett.* (1735) I. 56 At my return..I receiv'd the favour of your Letter. **1738** FRANKLIN *Let.* 13 Apr. Wks. 1887 I. 476, I have your favors of the 21st of March. **1751** T. SHARP in *Lett. Lit. Men* (Camden) 374 Last post brought me the favour of yours of the 2^d inst^t. **1786** T. JEFFERSON *Writ.* (1859) II. 3 Your favor of June the 14th is come to hand. **1816** SCOTT *Let. to Terry* 12 Nov. in *Lockhart*, I have been shockingly negligent in acknowledging your repeated favours. **1865** MARSH in *Longfellow's Life* (1891) III. 56, I received your favor of April 8.

d. Euphemistically. Formerly also *the last favour* (= Fr. *les dernières faveurs*).

1676 WYCHERLEY *Pl. Dealer* v. iii, She..granted you the last favour, (as they call it). **1695** CONGREVE *Love for L.* III. xiv, You think it more dangerous to be seen in Conversation with me, than to allow some other Men the last favour. **1824** MEDWIN *Convers. Byron* (1832) I. 87 One who had bestowed her favours on many.

3. Kind indulgence.

a. Leave, permission, pardon. Chiefly in phrases, *by, with* (your, etc.) *favour*; *by the favour of*. Also, *under favour*: with all submission, subject to correction. *Obs.* or *arch.*

1580 BARET *Alv.* F 255 Sauing your displeasure..or, with your fauour. **1588** SHAKS. *L.L.L.* III. i. 68 By thy fauour.. I must sigh in thy face. **1590** SWINBURNE *Testaments* 287 If the wife..depart from her husband, without his good fauour. **1611** B. JONSON *Cataline* I. i, With fauour, 'twere no losse, if't might be enquir'd What the Condition of these Armes would be. **1613** SHAKS. *Hen. VIII*, I. i. 168 Pray giue me fauour Sir. **1622** CALLIS *Stat. Sewers* (1647) 21 Under the favor of these books. **1662** STILLINGFL. *Orig. Sacr.* I. i. §20 (ed. 3) 21 By the favour of so learned a man, it seems probable. **1699** BENTLEY *Phal.* 135 Under favour, I say it's an *Anapæst.* **1700** DRYDEN *Cock & Fox*, With your Favour, I will treat it here. **1750** G. JEFFREYS in *Duncombe's Letters* (1773) II. 253 Under favour, poetical justice is so far from being 'a chimera', that [etc.]. **1823** SCOTT *Quentin D.* xv, Under favour, my Lord..the youth must find another guide.

†**b.** 'Lenity, mildness, mitigation of punishment' (J.); an instance of this, a lenient act. *Obs.*

c **1460** FORTESCUE *Abs. & Lim. Mon.* v, To shewrigoure þer as fauour awght to be shewid. *c* **1475** *Rauf Coilȝear* 902 Now faindis to haue fauour with thy fleichingis. **1535** COVERDALE *Josh.* xi. 20 And no fauoure to be shewed vnto them. **1596** *Merch. V.* IV. i. 386 Prouided..that for this fauour He presently become a Christian. **1659** B. HARRIS *Parival's Iron Age* 136 Prisoners..put to ransom, by a singular favour of the Prince of Orange. **1726** SWIFT *Gulliver* vii, I could not discover the Lenity and Favour of this Sentence. **1780** BURKE *Sp. at Bristol* Wks. 1842 I. 267 Who..would construe..doubtful appearances with the utmost favour.

†**c.** An indulgence, privilege. *Obs.*

1634 *Documents agst. Prynne* (Camden) 26 Hee should not have the favour to aunswere it in this Courte. **1639** tr. *Du Bosq's Compl. Woman* A ij b, A favour reserved to few, to become witnesses of a vertue so extraordinary. **1646** SIR E. NICHOLAS in *N. Papers* (Camden) 67 She is proffered the favour..of continuinge a tennant. **1659** PEARSON *Creed* (1839) 310 Those..had not the favour of a sepulchre. **1737** WHISTON *Josephus' Hist.* IV. v. §3 At length..they had the favour to be slain.

4. Partiality towards a litigant, competitor, etc.; personal sympathies as interfering with justice. *challenge to the favour* (Law): see CHALLENGE *sb.* 3.

1393 GOWER *Conf.* III. 179 The Sampnites to him brought A somme of gold and him besought To don hem favour in the lawe. **1413** LYDG. *Pilgr. Sowle* I. xxxii. (1859) 36 Withoute fauour iuge the trouthe. **1482** *Eng. Gilds* (1870) 318 Awe noe fawer more to one than to a nother. **1632** MASSINGER *Maid of Hon.* v. ii, Not swayed or by favour or affection. *a* **1677** BARROW *Serm.* Wks. 1716 II. 83 Favour.. to their own habitual depravations of nature. **1839** in Bouvier *Law Dict.* 447 Nor shall you [the Grand Jury] leave any one unpresented for fear, favour, affection.

5. Aid, support, furtherance, whether proceeding from persons or things. *Obs.* exc. in phrases (now somewhat rare) *by, under* (*the*) *favour of*.

c **1400** *Destr. Troy* 1746 We haue..ffele fryndes and fauer out of fer londys. **1434** MISYN *Mending of Life* 128 Our gostely ee..þat light in it-self as it is..may not se, & ȝitt it felys it þat it is þere, qwhils it haldis with it favyr & heet of þatt light vnknawen. **1523** FITZHERB. *Husb.* §66 At winter he [the calfe] wyll be bygge ynoughe to saue hym selfe amonge other beastes, with a lyttell fauoure. **1580** BARET *Alv.* F 249 He hopeth that by the fauour of some man, he may be holpen in this crime. **1633** T. STAFFORD *Pac. Hib.* ix. (1821) 116 The Armie..in attempting the Castle, without the favour of the Cannon, must have endured great losse. **1653** H. COGAN tr. *Pinto's Trav.* 10 By the favor of daylight we perceived a great many sails. **1699** DAMPIER *Voy.* II. II. 46 Under favour of this Supposition, the Privateers marched through the Streets. **1726** SHELVOCKE *Voy. round World* (1757) 319 By the favour of thick weather, and a hard gale of wind, they got clear. *c* **1850** *Arab. Nts.* (Rtldg.) 626 By favour of six good rowers..we arrived at my country house. **1854** J. S. C. ABBOTT *Napoleon* (1855) II. xxix. 537 He begged permission, under favor of the night, to surprise the Bellerophon.

6. in favour of (= Fr. *en faveur de*). Used as a prep. in various senses. **a.** In defence or support of; on behalf of; on the side of. *to be in favour of*: to be on the side of, to be disposed to support or advocate.

1556 *Aurelio & Isab.* (1608) I, Hoo well have you spoken in the favoure of the wemen. **1653** H. COGAN tr. *Pinto's Trav.* xlviii. 185 They..resolved to write a letter in favour of us to the old Queen. **1782** PRIESTLEY *Corrupt. Chr.* I. I. 97 Thirty six of the bishops present were in favour of it. **1848** MACAULAY *Hist. Eng.* II. 155 He attempted to interest in his favour those Roman Catholics.

b. To the advantage of. (Rarely, † *in favour to.*) Also *Comm.* with reference to a bill, etc.: So as to be payable to.

1556 *Aurelio & Isab.* (1608) G vij, Them that in their owne favour hathe approuved and made the lawes. **1640–1** *Kirkcudbr. War-Comm. Min. Bk.* (1855) 86 Ane act, allegit purchasit in his favores be Mr. John Diksone. **1654** tr. *Scudery's Curia Pol.* 13 When such an accident happeneth, it is usually in favour to those extraordinary persons in whom [etc.]. **1776** *Trial of Nundocomar* 23/2 Bollakey Doss drew a draught on Benares in favor of Lord Clive. **1818** CRUISE *Digest* (ed. 2) VI. 58 Trusts, in favour of his wife and children. **1852** SIR H. DOUGLAS *Milit. Bridges* (ed. 3) 377 There remains a balance of strength in favour of the bridge.

†**c.** In consideration of, for the sake of. *Obs.*

1605 CAMDEN *Rem.* (1637) 46 One Regilianus..got the Empire there, onely in favour of his name.

d. Out of a preference for.

1893 *Law Times* XCV. 109/2 Builders..have refused land in Middlesex in favour of land in a non-register county.

7. a. (*concr.* of 1.) Something given as a mark of favour; *esp.* a gift such as a knot of ribbons, a glove, etc., given to a lover, or in mediæval chivalry by a lady to her knight, to be worn conspicuously as a token of affection.

1588 SHAKS. *L.L.L.* v. ii. 130 Hold, Rosaline, this favour thou shalt wear. **1592** GREENE *Groat'sw. Wit* (1617) 14 She ..returned him a silke Riband for a fauour, tyed with a Truelouers knot. **1594** MARLOWE & NASHE *Dido* III. Wks. (Rtldg.) 261/2 Favours of more sovereign worth Than Thetis hangs about Apollos neck. **1712** *Spectator* No. 436 ¶6 That custom of wearing a mistress's favour on such occasions [fencing contests] of old. **1842** BROWNING *My last Duchess*, My favour at her breast. **1864** KIRK *Chas. Bold* I. II. iii. 508 A time when he should..wear her favors in the tilting-field.

b. A ribbon, cockade, or the like, worn at a ceremony, e.g. *a bride's, coronation, wedding favour*, in evidence of goodwill; also, a similar decoration worn as a party-badge.

1599 SHAKS. *Hen. V*, IV. vii. 160 Here Fluellen, weare thou this fauour for me, and sticke it in thy Cappe. **1667** PEPYS *Diary* 20 Feb., Observing Sir W. Pen's carrying a favour to Sir W. Coventry, for his daughter's wedding. *a* **1693** URQUHART *Rabelais* III. xxx, I will send you..the Bride's Favour. **1702** LUTTRELL *Brief Rel.* (1857) V. 166 The motto of the coronation favours was, God has sent our hearts content. **1741** H. WALPOLE *Corr.* (ed. 3) I. ix. 27 The city shops are full of favours. **1771** SMOLLETT *Humph. Cl.* (1815) 254 A bride's favour..he now wore in his cap. **1825** C. M. WESTMACOTT *Eng. Spy* I. 34 Choice of jackets, hats, and favors. **1859** JEPHSON *Brittany* xi. 183 He wears in his button-hole a favour of blue, green, and white ribbons.

8. That which conciliates affection or goodwill; attractiveness, comeliness, beauty; an attraction, charm. *Obs.* exc. *arch.*

c **1300** *K. Alis.* 2844 An harpour..made a lay of gret favour. **13..** *E.E. Allit. P.* A. 428 Bot ho hir passed in sum favour. *c* **1430** *Hymns Virg.* (1867) 126 A woman..With fauour in here face far passynge my reson. **1513** DOUGLAS *Æneis* XII. vii. 25 Wyth quhais [Japis'] favour vmquhile strangly caucht, This God Appollo glaidly has hym taucht. *c* **1585** *Faire Em* I. 228 Not very fair, but richly deck'd with favour; A sweet face. *a* **1592** GREENE & LODGE *Looking Glasse* (1861) 124 Now ope, ye folds, where queen of favour

sits. 1611 BIBLE *Ecclus.* xl. 22 Thine eye desireth fauour and beautie. 1630 *R. Johnson's Kingd. & Commw.* 91 The general contentment, which our English women afford, without sophisticate and adulterate favours. 1847 HELPS *Friends in C.* (1854) I. 116 It takes away much of the favour of life.

9. a. Appearance, aspect, look. Now *arch.* or *dial.*

c1450 HENRYSON *Mor. Fab.* 34 The fauour of thy face.. is foule and disfigurate. a1529 SKELTON *Poems agst. Garnesche* 9 The favyr of your face Is voyd of all grace. 1551 ROBINSON tr. *More's Utop.* I. (Arb.) 29 A man..whome, by his fauoure and apparell..I iudged to bee a mariner. 1595 SHAKS. *John* v. iv. 50, I do loue the fauour..Of this most faire occasion. 1650 FULLER *Pisgah* I. viii. 23 Palestine.. tricked and trimmed with many new Cities, had the favour thereof quite altered. 1657 W. RAND tr. *Gassendi's Life of Peiresk* I. A 8 a, It was your pleasure also to learn the favour of his Countenance from his Picture. 1863 MRS. C. CLARKE *Shaks. Char.* viii. 197 He is the 'counterfeit presentment' of his sister in external favour.

b. The countenance, face. *arch.*

1525 LD. BERNERS *Froiss.* II. ccxlvii. [ccxliii.] 759 He was lyke kynge Richarde in fauoure. 1581 C. T. in Farr. *S.P. Eliz.* (1845) II. 396 My fauour is harde, My body croukte. 1603 KNOLLES *Hist. Turks* (1621) 861 Courrours were sent out..with certain notes also of the favour of the man. 1676 *Lond. Gaz.* No. 1126/4 He is of low stature, and thin favor. 1691 RAY *Creation* II. (1704) 439 By their virtuous behaviour compensate the hardness of their Favour. 1822 B. CORNWALL *Poems, Love cured by kindness*, I..know Whence comes this noble favour. 1875 TENNYSON *Q. Mary* v. ii, What makes thy favour like the bloodless head Fall'n on the block?

†c. A feature. *Obs.*

1596 SHAKS. *1 Hen. IV*, III. ii. 136, I will..staine my fauours in a bloody Maske. 1598 DRAYTON *Heroic. Ep.* iii. 23 In thy Face, one Favour from the rest I singled forth. 1655 DIGGES *Compl. Ambass.* 343 The Gentleman..is void of any good favour, besides the blemish of the small pocks.

d. Family likeness. Cf. FAVOUR *v.* 8. *dial.*

Mod. dial. (Staffordshire), I knew her by favour, as soon as I saw her.

10. *Comb.* **†favour-currier** = CURRY-FAVOUR; **favour-currying** *ppl. a.*: see CURRY *v.*; **†favour-ribbon**, a ribbon worn as a love-token.

1831 T. L. PEACOCK in *Examiner* 14 Aug., Long floods of favour-currying gabble. 1855 KINGSLEY *Westw. Ho!* (1889) 13/2 They train the lads up eaves-droppers and favour-curriers. 1762–71 H. WALPOLE *Vertue's Anecd. Paint.* (1786) II. 291 Drinking, and dipping their favour-ribbands in the wine.

favour, favor ('feɪvə(r)), *v.* Forms: 4 favore, favure, 4–6 faver, 4–7 favoure, (5 favoryn, favir, *Sc.* fawowr), 9 *dial.* favver, 5– favour, favor. [a. OF. *favorer*, med.L. *favōrāre*, f. *favōr-em*: see FAVOUR *sb.*]

1. a. *trans.* To regard with favour, look kindly upon; to be inclined to, have a liking or preference for; to approve.

1340–70 *Alex. & Dind.* 740 Whi fauure ȝe..falce godus? c1400 *Destr. Troy* 13950 When Vlixes..persayuit, þat he to Circes was son..He fauort hym more faithly. 1535 COVERDALE *2 Macc.* xiv. 24 He loued Iudas euer with his hert, and fauoured him. 1580 BARET *Alv.* F 251 Not fauouring learning, not minding, *auersus a Musis*. 1626 BACON *Sylva* v. §495 Men fauour Wonders. 1662 STILLINGFL. *Orig. Sacr.* II. iv. §4 Josephus seems to favour the division of the City into three parts. 1780 HARRIS *Philol. Enq.* Wks. (1841) 485 The doctrines they most favoured. 1793 BURKE *Conduct of Minority* Wks. 1842 I. 620 That party which Mr. Fox inclined most to favour. 1841 LANE *Arab. Nts.* I. 113 God favour and preserve him. 1873 BURTON *Hist. Scot.* V. lx. 285 It was one of the difficulties in the case to find what religion he favoured.

b. In film-making and broadcasting (see quots.).

1960 O. SKILBECK *Film & T.V. A.B.C.* 52 *Favour*, deliberately to turn the mike or camera to face one artist more than another. 1960 D. DAVIS *Gram. Telev. Prod.* 60 *Favour*, to see more of one person's face than that of another person in the same shot. 1970 *Amateur Photographer* 22 Apr. 84/2 Because of its strong directional properties a cardioid microphone will have to follow the actors around and be pointed at them when they speak. This is called 'favouring' and must be done gently without transmitting vibrations along the boom pole.

2. a. To show favour to; to treat kindly; to countenance, encourage, patronize; †to indulge (oneself, a feeling).

1362 LANGL. *P. Pl.* A. III. 81 Rynges with Rubyes þe Regratour to fauere. c1380 WYCLIF *Sel. Wks.* III. 489 Faveriden hem in þese open errouris. c1475 *Rauf Coilȝear* 903 Now haue I ferlie, gif I fauour the ocht. a1533 LD. BERNERS *Gold. Bk. M. Aurel.* (1546) K j b, Yf she be good, he ought to fauer her, that she may be the better. 1549 COVERDALE *Erasm. Par. Rom.* vii. 7 This wyse therfore fauoryng my selfe, I was in manner ignoraunt. 1553 T. WILSON *Rhet.* (1580) 78 Man onely..ceaseth not to favour his sorowe. 1568 GRAFTON *Chron.* II. 22 William..favoured them by giftes and easy lawes. 1611 BIBLE *Ps.* cii. 13 The time to fauour her..is come. 1655 SIR E. NICHOLAS in *N. Papers* (Camden) II. 193, I beseech you..fauor me soe much as to hint unto his Maty my misfortune. 1736 BUTLER *Anal.* II. vi, If there be a strong bias within..to favour the deceit. 1806 *Med. Jrnl.* XV. 112 If he will 'favor me', by perusing my last communication. 1857 WHEWELL *Hist. Induct. Sc.* I. 210 The former [John the Grammarian] was favoured by Amrou, the conqueror of Egypt. 1870 MAX MÜLLER *Sc. Relig.* (1873) 38 No religion..would have favoured the idea.

†b. To indulge with permission (to do something). *Obs.*

c1400 *Destr. Troy* 5101 A fole to be fauoret folili to speke. 1605 *Play Stucley* in Simpson *Sch. Shaks.* (1878) I. 160 What her bashfulness Conceals from you, favour me to disclose.

c. To indulge or oblige (a person) *with* something. ***I am favoured with***: often used as a courteous form of acknowledgement.

c1374 CHAUCER *Boeth.* I. i. 4 Fortune..fauored[e] me wiþ ly3te goodes. 1655–60 STANLEY *Hist. Philos.* (1701) 14/2 The manner of his death gave Laertius occasion to favour him with this Epigram. 1717 WODROW *Corr.* (1843) II. 308, I am favoured with yours of the 10th August. 1793 T. TWINING in *Country Clergym. 18th C.* (1882) 185 A lady.. was asked to 'favour us with a song'. 1829 LYTTON *Devereux* II. v, Fielding twice favoured me with visits. 1832 HT. MARTINEAU *Life in Wilds* iv. 48 Agriculture has..been favoured with many privileges. 1842 A. COMBE *Physiol. Digestion* (ed. 4) p. xxiv, Having..been early favoured with a copy of the original work.

†3. *intr.* To show favour *to*, *unto*. *Obs.*

1393 GOWER *Conf.* II. 77 She to nouther part favoureth. 1548 HALL *Chron.* 98 b, All those that have..favoured unto his said uncle of Winchester.

4. a. *trans.* To treat with partiality. Also, to side with, take the part of.

c1350 *Will. Palerne* 1171 Heiȝh king of heuene for þi holy name, ne fauore nouȝt so my [fo]. c1425 WYNTOUN *Cron.* VIII. xxviii, He fawowryd þe Part, þat langyd Schyr Alysawndyr Mowbray. a1533 LD. BERNERS *Gold. Bk. M. Aurel.* (1546) B iij b, I shall haue many wylle fauoure me in the same. 1580 BARET *Alv.* F 251 He fauoured Cateline. 1635 N. R. *Camden's Hist. Eliz.* Introd., Margaret of Alencon..favoured the Protestan's Religion. a1680 BUTLER *Rem.* (1759) I. 23 Uncertain which o' th' two to favour. 1734 tr. *Rollin's Anc. Hist.* (1827) I. 170 Antigonus suspecting.. that he favoured Cassander. *Mod.* The examiner was accused of having favoured his own pupils.

b. *Comm.* In market reports of a commodity: To be at prices favourable to (buyers, sellers).

1890 *Daily News* 8 Jan. 2/6 Oats favour buyers.

5. a. To aid, support; to show oneself propitious to.

1595 T. MAYNARDE *Drake's Voy.* (Hakluyt Soc.) 23 God favoringe me, they [the Spanish ships] would have bin mine. 1601 MARSTON *Pasquil & Kath.* I. 258 Fortune fauours fooles. 1783 WATSON *Philip III*, II. (1839) 65 They were secretly favoured by Henry IV. 1793 BURKE *Corr.* (1844) IV. 143 If Providence should..favour the allied arms. 1885 *Manch. Exam.* 21 May 6/1 The willingness of the House.. to favour its progress.

absol. 1393 GOWER *Conf.* III. 213 Wel the more God favoureth, Whan he the comun right socoureth. 1435 MISYN *Fire of Love* II. ii, Criste favirand. 1563 B. GOOGE *Eglogs* (Arb.) 99 Fortune fauoures not and al thynges backward go. 1697 DRYDEN *Eneid* I. 522 A Name, While Fortune favour'd, not unknown to Fame. 1878 BROWNING *La Saisaiz* 27 Had but fortune favored.

b. Of a circumstance, fact, etc.: To lend confirmation or support to (a belief, doctrine, *rarely*, a person); to point in the direction of.

1526 *Pilgr. Perf.* (W. de W. 1531) 210 The sentence also of the prophete Osee fauoureth moche (as me semeth) that it sholde be so. 1655 FULLER *Ch. Hist.* I. iv. §9 This relation is favoured by the name of Litchfield. 1659 HAMMOND *On Ps.* xxvii. 12 The sense favours them there. 1710 STEELE *Tatler* No. 209 ¶1 Every Circumstance..favoured this Suspicion. 1772 *Junius Lett.* lxviii. 337 His opinion.. appears to favour you. 1808 *Med. Jrnl.* XIX. 105 Seems to favour the opinion of Mr. Pott. 1884 LD. SELBORNE in *Law Times' Rep.* 19 Apr. 229/2 Those cases which favour the doctrine. 1887 C. C. ABBOTT *Waste-Land Wand.* ii. 22 Every indication favored rain.

6. Of circumstances, weather, etc.: To prove advantageous to (a person); to be the means of promoting (an operation or process); to facilitate.

1634 SIR T. HERBERT *Trav.* 12 That night not favouring us, we cast anchor. 1699 DAMPIER *Voy.* II. II. 29 The Wind favours them. 1709 ADDISON *Tatler* No. 97 ¶2 The Silence and Solitude of the Place very much favoured his Meditations. 1710 —— *Whig Exam.* No. 4 No one Place about it weaker than another, to favour an Enemy in his Approaches. 1786 W. THOMSON *Philip III*, v. (1793) II. 115 The darkness of the night favoured the enterprise. 1833 LYELL *Princ. Geol.* III. 210 The argillaceous stratum..by its yielding nature, favoured the waste and undermining of the..limestone. 1862 ANSTED & LATHAM *Channel Isl.* III. xvi. (ed. 2) 379 They had been favoured by the wind. 1875 BRYCE *Holy Rom. Emp.* i. (ed. 5) 10 The unity of the Empire ..had favoured the spread of Christianity.

absol. a1440 *Found. St. Barthol.* 44 Marchauntys of fflaundrys..fauer ng the see, purposid to Lundone.

7. To deal gently with; to avoid overtasking (a limb); to ease, save, spare. Now *colloq.* (esp. in stable parlance) and *dial.*

1526 *Pilgr. Perf.* (W. de W. 1531) 263 Fauour thy body. 1589 R. HARVEY *Pl. Perc.* (1590) 16 A Preacher..must haue his reader at his elbow, to fauor his voice. 1617 MARKHAM *Caval.* II. 42 When a horse doth stand but firme vpon.. three feete..fauoring the other. 1667 PEPYS *Diary* (1877) V. 361 Walking in the dark, in the garden, to favour my eyes. 1711 BUDGELL *Spect.* No. 150 ¶12 A thread-bare loose Coat ..which..he wore to keep himself warm, and not to favour his under Suit. a1745 SWIFT (Worc.), He [a painter] has favoured her squint admirably. 1792 OSBALDISTONE *Brit. Sportsman* 228/2 He will set his foot on the ground warily, and endeavour to favor it. 1840 DICKENS *Old C. Shop* i, This habit..favours my infirmity. 1837 C. M. GOODRIDGE *Voy. S. Seas* (1843) 55 This [oil-can]..favoured our other cooking apparatus. 1884 *Upton Gloss.*, 'He seems to favour the off foreleg.'

8. To resemble in face or features; rarely, to resemble generally, have the look of. Now *colloq.*

1609 B. JONSON *Case is Altered* III. iii, This young lord Chamont Favours my mother. 1690 W. WALKER *Idiomat. Anglo-Lat.* 176 He favours you in the face. 1712 STEELE *Spectator* No. 398 ¶1 The Gentleman favoured his Master. 1824 L. MURRAY *Eng. Gram.* (ed. 5) I. 431 'The manager, in countenance, favoured his friend'. It should have been, 'resembled his friend'. 1866 S. LAYCOCK in Harland *Lanc. Lyrics* 191 Tha favvers thi dad! 1867 WAUGH *Dulesgate* 19 'Conto make 'em eawt?' 'Nawe..but they favour'n Todmorden chaps'.

favourable, favorable ('feɪvərəb(ə)l), *a.* [ad. F. *favorable*, ad. L. *favōrābilis*, f. *favor*: see FAVOUR and -ABLE.]

†1. a. Winning favour; hence, pleasing, agreeable, beautiful, comely. *Obs.*

In some examples the word may owe its shade of meaning to FAVOUR *sb.* 8 'beauty', or 9 'appearance, countenance'; cf. *personable*.

1398 TREVISA *Barth. De P.R.* XIX. lv. (1495) 896 Hony is full fauourable and lykynge to the taste and to ete. c1430 LYDG. *Chorle & Byrde* (Roxb.) 12 Hit maketh men.. fauorable in euery mannes sight. a1529 SKELTON *Anc. Acquaintance* 8 Of all your feturs fauorable to make tru discripcion. 1590 SPENSER *Muiopotmos* 20 Of all the race.. Was none more favourable, nor more fair, Than Clarion.

†b. Admissible, allowable. *Obs.*

1666 BOYLE *Orig. Formes & Qual.* (1667) 31 Bodies may be said, in a very favourable sense, to have those Qualities we call Sensible.

2. a. That regards with favour (a person, project, opinion, etc.); inclined to countenance or help; well-disposed, propitious. Const. *to*, *upon*, †*of*.

1340 HAMPOLE *Pr. Consc.* 1344 Til þam þe world es favorabel. c1374 CHAUCER *Anel. & Arc.* 15 Be favorable eek, thou Polymia. 1441 *Plumpton Corr.* p. lix, Such as were favorable of their said malicious purpose. 1494 FABYAN *Chron.* I. xvii, Ye goddes were to hym so fauourable, that he slewe moche of the people of his brother and compellyd hym to fle. 1548–9 (Mar.) *Bk. Com. Prayer* Offices 34 b, Bee fauourable to thy people. 1596 SHAKS. *Tam. Shr.* IV. v. 40 Happier the man whom fauorable stars A lots thee for his louely bedfellow. 1651 HOBBES *Leviath.* III. xxxiii. 204 They would surely have made them more favorable to their power. 1667 MILTON *P.L.* v. 507 O favourable spirit..Well hast thou taught the way that might direct Our knowledge. 1749 BERKELEY *Word to Wise* Wks. III. 451 It is to be hoped this Address may find a favourable reception. 1827 O. W. ROBERTS *Centr. Amer.* 37 The Indians..are particularly favourable to the English. 1871 FREEMAN *Norm. Conq.* (1876) IV. xviii. 123 King Swegen was lending a favourable ear to their prayers.

†b. Gracious (said of a superior); kindly, obliging. *Obs.* exc. *arch.*

1502 ARNOLDE *Chron.* 159 Unto the most holyest and fauorablist Prince in erthe. 1530 HEN. VIII in Ellis *Orig. Lett.* I. 106. II. 17 To have the favorable and lovyng assistance of the noble men. 1597 SHAKS. *2 Hen. IV*, IV. v. 2 Vnlesse some dull and fauourable hand Will whisper Musicke to my wearie Spirit. 1642 I. BASIRE in *Evelyn's Mem.* (1857) III. 3 To give you thanks for your favourable communication. a1822 SHELLEY *Homer's Hymn to Moon* 25 Hail Queen, great Moon..Fair-haired and favourable [Gr. πρόφρον.]

†c. Of a reader or hearer: Disposed to interpret generously. *Obs.*

1611 SPEED *Hist. Gt. Brit.* IX. xii. (1632) 696 Polydor Virgil must haue a warie and fauourable Reader. 1655–60 STANLEY *Hist. Philos.* (1701) 65/2 Herein Damachus had need of favourable hearers.

†3. Showing undue favour, partial. Const. *to*.

c1384 CHAUCER *H. Fame* III. 389 One said that Omer made lies..And was to the Greekes favourable. 1393 GOWER *Conf.* III. 225 Thus was the steward favourable, That he the trouthe plein ne tolde. c1460 FORTESCUE *Abs. & Lim. Mon.* xv, And to make hem also ffauorable and parcial.

4. a. Of an opinion, report, etc.: That is in favour of, approving, commendatory.

1655 FULLER *Ch. Hist.* III. iv. §23 The favourablest expression of him falls from the pen of Roger Hoveden. 1712 STEELE *Spect.* No. 268 ¶8 If you would be so far my Friend as to make a favourable Mention of me in one of your Papers. 1725 DE FOE *Voy. round World* (1840) 253 Giving a favourable account of the place. 1781 COWPER *Conversation* 764 That great defect would cost him..Men's favourable judgment. 1833 LAMB *Elia* (1860) 247 To institute..favourable comparisons. 1879 *Cassell's Techn. Educ.* I. 335 Most favourable reports of the arm.

†b. Tending to palliate or extenuate. *Obs.*

1697 DRYDEN *Juvenal* viii. 350 Since none can have the favourable Thought That to Obey a Tyrant's Will they Fought. 1772 *Junius Lett.* lxviii. 336 Favourable circumstances, alleged before the judge, may justify a doubt whether the prisoner be guilty or not.

5. a. Of an answer, etc.: That concedes what is desired. Of appearances: Boding well, hopeful, promising.

1734 M. PHILIPS in *Swift's Lett.* (1768) IV. 73 [His answer] was as favourable as I could well wish for. 1781 GIBBON *Decl. & F.* III. 61 The eunuch..soon returned with a favourable oracle. 1828 SCOTT *F.M. Perth* xxi, I trust they have assumed a favourable aspect. 1875 W. S. HAYWORD *Love agst. World* 77 How eagerly I hope for a favourable answer.

b. Of a patient's condition, progress, etc.: satisfactory; favouring recovery.

1903 *Westm. Gaz.* 8 July 7/1 Seeing that his condition was so favourable. 1970 J. L. GIBBONS in *Med. Ann.* 278 Favourable prognostic signs were the presence of mild symptoms..and a stable premorbid personality.

6. Attended with advantage or convenience; facilitating one's purpose or wishes; advantageous, helpful, suitable. Said *esp.* of the weather, etc.

c1460 FORTESCUE *Abs. & Lim. Mon.* xii, Thai haue not so much ffredome in thair owne godis, nor be entreted by so ffauerable lawes as we be. 1548 HALL *Chron.* 175 b, The Wynd [was] so favourable to the Erles purpose. 1555 EDEN

Decades 245 The fauourable influence of the heauen and the planettes. **1659** B. HARRIS *Parival's Iron Age* 38 This was the first battle of this age, which proved favourable to the Hollanders. **1659** *London Chanticleers* xii. in Hazl. *Dodsley* XII. 350 Or a favourable spider drop into the cream, and drown himself, that he may poison them. *a* **1674** CLARENDON *Hist. Reb.* (1703) II. viii. 364 A place very favourable for the making Levies of Men. **1745** BUTLER *Serm.* Wks. 1874 II. 282 Incapacity and ignorance must be favourable to error and vice. **1774** PENNANT *Tour Scot. in 1772*, 325 Sail with a favourable breeze. **1850** McCOSH *Div. Govt.* II. iii. (1874) 230 The cultivation of virtuous affections is favourable to the health. **1866** CRUMP *Banking* vii. 153 The term 'favourable'..state of the exchanges. **1877** LADY BRASSEY *Voy. Sunbeam* ix. (1878) 146 Make the passage under favourable circumstances. **1930** *Economist* 20 Dec. 1158/2 The official returns indicate that the balance of 'current items', visible and invisible, is much less 'favourable' than before the war.

favourableness ('feɪvərəb(ə)lnɪs). [f. prec. + -NESS.] The quality or state of being favourable. †**a.** Kindliness, leniency (*obs.*). **b.** Suitability. **c.** Eulogistic or approving character.

a. **1545** UDALL *Erasm. Par. Luke* xvi, He..exhorted theim to a more larger fauourablenesse. **1571** GOLDING *Calvin on Ps.* xlvii. 5 The universall favorablenesse wherwith he embraceth all mankynd. **1625-8** *Camden's Hist. Eliz.* III. (1688) 441 Her favourableness in taking Contributions. **1656** *Artif. Handsom.* 199 To the favorablenesse of your Laps future censure..be pleased to add the favour of your pardon. **1727-31** in BAILEY vol. II.

b. **1775** ADAIR *Amer. Ind.* 457 The favourableness of the soil. **1790** PRICE in Burke *Fr. Rev.* 79, I mean the consideration of the favourableness of the present times to all exertions in the cause of liberty. **1820** SCORESBY *Acc. Arctic Reg.* II. 251 The speedy capture of a whale depends on..the favourableness of situation and weather.

c. **1832** HT. MARTINEAU *Homes Abroad* iv. 51 The favourableness of their report.

favourably, favorably ('feɪvərəblɪ), *adv.* [f. as prec. + -LY².] In a favourable manner.

1. a. With favour or kindness; graciously, indulgently.

1388 WYCLIF *Prol.* xi, We moun fauorably excuse hire [Judith] fro deedly synne in this doinge. *c* **1425** WYNTOUN *Cron.* VI. viii. 25 He..tretyd þe Scottis favorably. **1494** FABYAN *Chron.* VII. 314 He had fauourably harde his proctours. **1509** FISHER *Fun. Serm. C'tess Richmond* Wks. (1876) 298 Why lokest thou fauourably vpon them that despyse the? **1611** BIBLE *Wisd.* vi. 16 She..sheweth herselfe fauourably vnto them in the wayes. **1665** BOYLE *Occas. Refl.* Introd. Pref. (1845) 25 The Thoughts, which have been the favourabliest entertain'd by the Readers of my other Books. **1729** BUTLER *Serm.* Wks. 1874 II. 130 Men..judge too favourably..where themselves and their own interest are concerned. **1781** GIBBON *Decl. & F.* III. 98 Hippo had been less favourably treated than the other cities of the province. **1883** A. ROBERTS *O.T. Revision* ii. 29 It has a claim to be fairly and even favourably considered.

†**b.** With undue favour or partiality. *Obs.*

1430-50 tr. *Higden* (Rolls) I. 339 Som men feyneþ and fauorabliche seiþ þat Seynt Patryk clensed þat lond of.. venemous bestes. **1609** SKENE *Reg. Maj., Stat. Robert III* 52 Inquisitions taken favorablie, and be ignorant persons.

2. In favourable terms, or with a favourable result; to the credit or advantage of a person or thing.

1655 SIR E. NICHOLAS in *N. Papers* (Camden) II. 239, I doe not wonder they write favourably of their Protectors affaires. **1783** HAILES *Antiq. Chr. Ch.* iv. 116 Epictetus had ..spoken favourably of the Christians. **1872** RAYMOND *Statist. Mines & Mining* 17 Inyo was mentioned favorably in last year's report. **1885** *Manch. Exam.* 6 Sept. 5/2 Clemenceau's decision and vigour..contrast favourably with the timid and half-hearted utterances of M. Brisson.

3. *Comb.*

1854 H. H. WILSON tr. *Rig-veda* II. 158 Creator of the Maruts, favourably-minded towards us, grant us those blessings which are most dear to thee. **1952** C. P. BLACKER *Eugenics* ix. 219 A modest claim..is made..that wastage among favourably-assessed parachutists proved smaller than among those unfavourably assessed.

favoured ('feɪvəd), *ppl. a.*¹ [f. FAVOUR *v.* + -ED¹.] In senses of the vb. Often used for: Favoured by Nature, fortune, or Providence; having unusual advantages or blessings.

Treaties often contain a clause providing that each of the contracting powers shall allow to the other all the advantage, with regard to customs duties, permission to trade, etc., that are granted to 'the most favoured nation' (also in *attrib. phr.*).

1725 POPE *Odyss.* VII. 273 Oft with some favour'd traveller they stray. **1758** SMOLLETT *Hist. Eng.* (1800) II. 245 The same privileges that France granted to the most favoured nation. **1805** W. SAUNDERS *Min. Waters* 112 One of those choice and favoured spots. **1805** WORDSW. *Waggoner* IV. 29 The rude shepherd's favoured glance. **1848** MACAULAY *Hist. Eng.* I. 416 There were more favoured districts. **1891** *Daily News* 6 May 4/8 The favoured explanation of this action was [etc.]. **1902** *Encycl. Brit.* XXVII. 164/1 By extending to a third nation privileges granted to particular countries, the most favoured nation article began to be framed. **1909** *Westm. Gaz.* 17 Aug. 2/1 Having secured a most-favoured-nation clause in her commercial treaty with China in 1896. **1928** *Manch. Guardian Weekly* 26 Oct. 328/2 In the agreement will be two main clauses dealing with most-favoured-nation treatment.

favoured ('feɪvəd), *ppl. a.*² Also *Sc.* fa'ard, fa'rd, faurd. [f. FAVOUR *sb.* + -ED².]

1. Having an appearance or features, etc. (see FAVOUR *sb.* 9) of a specified kind. Only in parasynthetic combinations as *black-*, *crab-*, *evil-*, *hard-*, *ill-*, *well-favoured*, etc.: see these words.

2. Having or provided with favours or rosettes (see FAVOUR *sb.* 7 b). Only in *comb.*

1850 TENNYSON *In Mem.* Conclusion 90 Those white-favour'd horses wait.

favouredly ('feɪvədlɪ), *adv.* [f. FAVOURED *ppl. a.* + -LY².] In comb., as *evil-*, *ill-*, or *well-favouredly*: see these words.

favouredness ('feɪvədnɪs). [f. as prec. + -NESS.] The quality or state of having a specified appearance or look. Only in *evil-*, *ill-*, *well-favouredness*: see these words.

favourer ('feɪvərə(r)). Also 6 *Sc.* favorar. [f. FAVOUR *v.* + -ER¹.] One who favours.

1. One who countenances, encourages, or sides with another; a well-wisher, friend, or follower.

1483 *Cath. Angl.* 124/1 A Fauerer, *favtor.* **1495** *Act 11 Hen. VII*, c. 64 Preamb., The same persones..were adherentis, assistencis, confederatis, favowrers. **1535** COVERDALE *1 Macc.* vii. 7 Let him be punished with all his frendes and fauourers. **1632** LITHGOW *Trav.* III. 84 He was a great favourer of the French Nation. **1691** LUTTRELL *Brief Rel.* (1857) II. 318 Being supposed a favourer of King James. **1741** RICHARDSON *Pamela* IV. 62 That modest Freedom..which..some of my Favourers attribute to me. **1876** LYTTON *Pausanias* 49 A favourer of the Persians.

†**b.** Const. *to, towards. Obs.*

1547-64 BAULDWIN *Mor. Philos.* (Palfr.) 56 They are not ..faithfull fathers, friends, and fauourers to their country. **1586** R. CARVYLE in Ellis *Orig. Lett.* II. 225 III. 119 A favorer towards the mayntenaunce of peace and amitie.

†**c.** A patron; = FAUTOR 2.

1625 K. LONG tr. *Barclay's Argenis* II. xxi. 138 Go, Souldiers, with the gods your favourers, and subdue those men. **1741** MIDDLETON *Cicero* II. vii. 18 A particular favorer, and Patron of Ariobarzanes.

2. One who supports or promotes a movement, opinion, project, etc.; a furtherer, promoter.

1542-5 BRINKLOW *Lament.* (1874) 91 Those whiche saye they be the favorers of the Gospell. **1605** BACON *Adv. Learn.* I. vii. §4 (1873) 53 Learned, or singular favourers and advancers of learning. **1662** H. MORE *Philos. Writ.* Pref. Gen. (1712) 23 They were no enemies to the opinion of the Soul's Prae-existence, but rather favourers thereof. **1703** J. SAVAGE *Lett. Antients* clxx. 394 Whether Matters will be refer'd to any favourer of Peace. **1792** MAD. D'ARBLAY *Diary* V. VII. 304 The French Revolution, of which she is a favourer. **1875** TENNYSON *Q. Mary* I. v, They think me favourer of this marriage.

†'**favouress.** *Obs. rare.* [f. FAVOUR-ER + -ESS.] A female favourer.

1616 HAKEWILL *Answ. Dr. Carier* 184 A principal favouresse of the Protestant religion. **1660** HEXHAM, *Een gunneresse*, a Favouresse.

favouring ('feɪvərɪŋ, -vrɪŋ), *ppl. a.* [f. FAVOUR *v.* + -ING².] That favours, in senses of the vb.

1586 A. DAY *Eng. Secretary* I. (1625) 52 Your entirely favouring and carefull loving friends. **1606** SHAKS. *Ant. & Cl.* IV. viii. 23 Thy fauouring hand. **1633** T. JAMES *Voy.* 6 With the first fauouring winde, we proceeded. **1763** SIR W. JONES *Caissa* Poems (1777) 137 As favouring lots ordain. **1807** CRABBE *Library* 104 Here the poet meets his favouring muse. **1807** WORDSW. *White Doe* VII. 262 To Bolton's sacred Pile On favouring nights, she loved to go. **1875** WHITNEY *Life Lang.* ii. 14 As fast as..favoring circumstances enable him to do so.

Hence '**favouringly** *adv.*, in a favouring manner.

1829 LYTTON *Disowned* II. ii. (ed. 3) 21 The ancient servant, on whom four years had passed lightly and favouringly.

†'**favourish,** *v. Obs. rare*⁻¹. [a. OF. *favoriss-* lengthened stem of *favorir* to FAVOUR.] *trans.* **a.** = FAVOUR *v.* **b.** To bring into favour *with.*

1490 CAXTON *Eneydos* xii. 45 The goddes in their destynacyes haue fauourisshed the well with Iuno.

Hence †'**favourished** *ppl. a.*, favoured.

1556 *Aurelio & Isab.* F v, Youre colouers that you gaue to yowre favorishede [*printed* fauoirshede] knightes.

favourite, favorite ('feɪvərɪt), *sb.* and *a.* Also 6 favorit, 7 faforeite, favoret. [a. OF. *favorit* (Cotgr.), var. of *favori*, pa. pple. of *favorir* to favour; = It., Sp., and Pg. *favorito.*]

A. *sb.*

1. a. A person or thing regarded with peculiar favour, one preferred above others. Const. *of, with.*

1583 STANYHURST *Æneis* I. (Arb.) 18 This Iuno fearing, and old broyls bluddye recounting, Vsd by her Greeke fauorits. **1667** MILTON *P.L.* IX. 175 This new Favorite Of Heav'n, this Man of Clay. **1769** *Junius Lett.* viii. 38 There is another man, who is the favourite of his Country. **1781** T. GILBERT *Relief Poor* 9 Some of these Parish Officers are too apt to gratify themselves and their Favourites. **1796** JANE AUSTEN *Pride & Prej.* (1885) II. ix. 205 Their cousin Jane.. was the general favourite. **1802** WORDSW. *To the Daisy* 80 Thou not in vain Art Nature's favorite. **1838** LYTTON *Leila* II. i, The king smiled slightly at the ardour of the favourite of his army. **1839** LONGF. *Hyperion* II. vii, Of all operas, this was Flemming's favorite. **1876** MOZLEY *Univ. Serm.* vii. 155 Some persons are..favourites of heaven.

b. *spec.* in *Racing*, etc. The competitor or competing animal generally favoured or 'fancied', as being most likely to win.

1813 *Examiner* 12 Apr. 240/1 By the 3d round, Carter became the favourite (as it is termed). **1857** G. LAWRENCE *Guy. Liv.* iv. 26 All the favourites were out of the race early. **1860** O. W. HOLMES *Elsie V.* ii. 7 He was a student of mark —first favorite of his year, as they say of the Derby colts.

2. One who stands unduly high in the favour of a prince, etc.; one chosen as an intimate by a superior. Const. †*to.*

1599 SHAKS. *Much Ado* III. i. 9 Like fauourites, Made proud by Princes. **1642** FULLER *Holy & Prof. St.* IV. i. 237 A Favourite is a Court-diall, whereon all look whilest the King shines on him. **1660** T. FORD *Theatre of Wits* 36 The Duke of Suilli was a Favourite to Henry the 4th. **1671** MILTON *P.R.* IV. 95 Committing to a wicked Favourite All publick cares. **1776** GIBBON *Decl. & F.* I. xvii. 443 He bestowed on his favourites the palaces which he had built. **1874** GREEN *Short Hist.* iv. §5 The favourite [Piers Gaveston] was a fine soldier.

3. A curl or lock of hair hanging loose upon the temple: worn in the seventeenth and eighteenth centuries. [Cf. F. *favoris* whiskers.]

1690 *Songs Costume* (Percy Soc.) 189 Frelange, Fontagne, favorite. **1720** GAY *Espousals* 74 in *Poems* II. 376 Sooner I would..with immodest fav'rites shade my face. **1753** HOGARTH *Anal. Beauty* vi. 78 They [curls]..ill deserved the name of 'favourites'.

†**4.** = FAVOURER 1. *Obs.* [perh. apprehended as if f. FAVOUR *sb.* + -ITE.]

1585-7 T. ROGERS *39 Art.* Pref. (1607) 12 They have prevailed but too much already with their too credulous favourites. **1589** R. HARVEY *Pl. Perc.* 12 Neither the breeders nor faorites of discord. **1591** SHAKS. *1 Hen. VI*, IV. i. 190 This factious bandying of their Fauourites.

B. *adj.* **1. a.** (Not regarded as an adj. by Johnson, who places quots. 1711 and 1725 under the sb.) Regarded with especial favour, liking, or preference; beloved, chosen, favoured above others.

1711 ADDISON *Spect.* No. 262 ¶9 Every particular Master in this Art [criticism] has his favourite Passages in an Author. **1725** POPE *Odyss.* I. 402 So Fathers speak..Their sage experience to the fav'rite child. **1747** GRAY (*title*), Ode on the Death of a Favourite Cat. **1816** BYRON *Ch. Har.* III. xxxix, When Fortune fled her spoiled and favorite child. **1830** FR. A. KEMBLE *Let.* in *Record of a Girlhood* (1878) II. iii. 106 Portia is my favouritest of all Shakespeare's women. **1870** E. PEACOCK *Ralf Skirl.* 52 Their favourite anecdotes had all been told.

b. *favorite son*: *U.S.* (*a*) 'a commendatory title given to George Washington' (D.A.E.); (*b*) 'a man who has endeared himself to a particular country or state, used esp. of a candidate for high office favored by the constituency or political leaders of the state from which he comes' (D.A.E.). Also *transf.*

1788 R. PLATT in F. Moss *Amer. Metropolis* (1897) I. ii. 266 Motto: Freedom's favorite son. **1789** *N.Y. Daily Gaz.* 1 May 426/1 Washington, the favourite son of liberty, and deliverer of his country. **1806** J. MILNER in C. L. Lewis *Romantic Decatur* (1937) viii. 85 That country welcomes your return to her bosom. She hails you as one of her favorite sons. **1835** D. CROCKETT *Life Van Buren* 198 The views and wishes of your 'favorite son'. **1888** BRYCE *Amer. Commw.* II. III. lxx. 552 A Favourite Son is a politician respected or admired in his own State, but little regarded beyond it. **1962** *Guardian* 27 Nov. 9/1 The rumbustious campaigning of Bavaria's 'favourite son', the Federal Minister of Defence, Herr Strauss. **1963** *Ibid.* 22 Jan. 8/6 The Leeds constituency parties are..open-minded about their candidates, not reserving places for some trade union's favourite son.

2. *favourite sentence* attrib. (see quot. 1964).

1933 BLOOMFIELD *Lang.* xi. 171 Certain forms [of sentence-type] are favorite sentence-forms. *Ibid.* 172 In English we have two favorite sentence-forms. One consists of actor-action phrases—*John ran away*.. The other consists of a command..*Be good!* **1942** BLOCH & TRAGER *Outl. Ling. Analysis* v. 74 Let us look briefly at the English actor-action construction. The most striking thing about it is its universality: it is the favorite-sentence type of English. **1964** R. H. ROBINS *Gen. Ling.* vi. 232 The patterns common to large numbers of the sentences of a language may be called its favourite sentence types.

favouritism ('feɪvərɪtɪz(ə)m). [f. prec. + -ISM. Cf. F. *favoritisme.*]

1. A disposition to show, or the practice of showing, favour or partiality to an individual or class, to the neglect of others having equal or superior claims; undue preference.

1763 WILKES *Corr.* (1805) I. 82 The declared..enemies of ..favouritism. **1796** BURKE *Corr.* IV. 409 We conduct war upon the principles of favouritism. **1814** D'ISRAELI *Quarrels Auth.* (1867) 261 Truth will always prevail over literary favouritism. **1880** ADYE in *19th Cent.* No. 38. 695 Young men were appointed by favouritism, or interest.. more than from any proved capacity or talent.

2. The state or condition of being a favourite; favour. Also, of a race-horse: Relative position in public favour.

1808 COBBETT *Pol. Reg.* XIV. 691 Faction and favouritism are the high roads to power. **1823** BYRON *Juan* X. v, We left our hero, Juan, in the *bloom* Of favouritism. **1853** G. JOHNSTON *Nat. Hist. E. Bord.* I. 220 As the productiveness of one sort declines, a newer starts into favouritism. **1880** W. DAY *Racehorse in Training* xvi. 158 She..would have had as good a right to favouritism for any race as Lady Elizabeth herself. **1893** *Westm. Gaz.* 8 June 5/2 Her [a mare's] favouritism went back to the 10 to 1 mark.

ˈfavouritize, *v. rare.* [f. as prec. + -IZE.] *intr.* To practise favouritism. Hence **ˈfavouritizing** *ppl. a.*

1861 *Cornh. Mag.* Feb. 222 A job-loving, favouritizing senior.

†**ˈfavourize**, *v. Obs.* Also favo(u)rise. [ad. F. *favoriser*, f. *faveur*: see FAVOUR *sb.* and -IZE.] = FAVOUR *v.* Hence **ˈfavourizing** *vbl. sb.*

1585 T. WASHINGTON tr. *Nicholay's Voy. Turkie* I. xvii. 19 b [They] aided and favorised all the enterprises of the Emperour. **1599** A. M. tr. *Gabelhouer's Bk. Physicke* 185/2 Without favorisinge the childe anye thinge therin. **1606** HOLLAND *Sueton.* Annot. 29 Factions..favourizing this or that colour of the Chariotters. **1624** *Brief Inform. Affairs Palatinate* 16 He would not faurize them with one good word toward the Emperour.

†**ˈfavourless**, *a. ? Obs.* [f. FAVOUR *sb.* + -LESS.] Without favour. **a.** Not showing favour, unpropitious. **b.** That has no attractiveness or beauty.

1509 BARCLAY *Shyp of Folys* (1570) 166 O cruell death, O fury fauourlesse. **1590** SPENSER *F.Q.* II. ix. 7 Such happinesse Heven doth to me envy, and fortune favourlesse. **1594** MARLOWE & NASHE *Dido* III. i, *Dido.* Is not Æneas fair and beautiful? *Anna.* Yes; and Iarbas foul and favourless. *a* **1605** POLWART *Flyting w. Montgomerie* 618 Whose fauourlesse phisnomie doth dewlie declare His vices.

†**ˈfavourous**, *a. Obs.* [f. as prec. + -OUS. Cf. OF. *favo(u)reux.*] **a.** Full of favour, obliging. **b.** Adapted to win favour, pleasing.

c **1485** *Digby Myst.* (1882) III. 673 To wype my fete þou wer nat so faworus. **1560** ROLLAND *Crt. Venus* I. 591 Lufe is facound: and lufe is fauorous. *Ibid.* IV. 110 With humbill hart..and fassounis fauorous. **1597** BRETON *Wit's Trenchmour* Wks. (1879) 9/2 When women were wont to be kind-harted, conceits in men were verie fauourous. **1775** ASH (citing CHAUCER), *Favirous*, favourable.

†**ˈfavoursome**, *a. Obs. rare.* [f. as prec. + -SOME.] That is an object of favour; acceptable.

1599 B. JONSON *Cynthia's Rev.* IV. iii, Pray Phœbus, I proue favoursome in her fair Eyes.

favous (ˈfeɪvəs), *a. rare.* [f. L. *fav-us* honeycomb + -OUS.] **a.** Resembling a honeycomb. **b.** Resembling the disease *favus*.

1677 GREW *Anat. Seeds* i. §10 (1682) 196 Its Surface favous, like that of Poppy. **1884** in *Syd. Soc. Lex.*

favower, -owre, obs. forms of FAVOUR.

favrile (fæˈvriːl). [Formed as a trade name by L. C. Tiffany (1848–1933), the inventor of the glass, in 1894, from FABRILE *a.*] A kind of glass characterized by rich colouring, iridescence, and enamelling.

1902 *Encycl. Brit.* XXIX. 8/1 The so-called 'Favrile' glass of Messrs. Tiffany of New York owes its effect entirely to surface colour and lustre. **1920** E. BOK *Autobiogr.* (1921) xxii. 226 Just as the ancient Egyptians and Persians had used glazed brick and tile, set in cement, as their form of wall decoration, so Mr. Tiffany had used favrile glass, set in cement.

‖**favus** (ˈfeɪvəs). *Path.* [L. *favus* honeycomb.] A contagious disease of the skin, characterized by pustules, so called from its resemblance to a honeycomb. Also *attrib.* Hence **ˈfavic** *a.*, of, pertaining to, or characteristic of this disease.

[**1398** TREVISA *Barth. De P.R.* VII. iii. (1495) 223 Constantine callyth suche a scabbe *fauum*, an hony combe, for suche whelkes haue smalle holes, out of whiche matter comyth as hony out of the hony combe.] **1706** PHILLIPS (ed. Kersey), *Favus*..an Ulcer, mattery Sore or Scab. **1806** *Med. Jrnl.* XV. 168 The favus, when it happens on the face, and the vesications behind the ears, often arise from the same cause. **1884** *Syd. Soc. Lex.*, *Favus*, a contagious disease of the skin. **1892** G. T. JACKSON *Dis. Skin* 226 The favic fungus was found implanted upon the mucous membrane of the stomach. **1958** *New Biol.* XXVII. 55 *Trichophyton schoenleinii*..gives rise to favic lesions in man.

favver, favyr, dial. and obs. ff. FAVOUR.

faw (fɔː), *sb.* [Application of *Faa*, the surname of a tribe of Scotch gipsies; prob. a cognomen originally identical with next adj.] A gipsy. Also *attrib.*, as ***faw gang***, a gang of gipsies.

1756 *Jarrow Par. Reg.*, Francis Heron, king of yᵉ Faws, bur. 13 Jan. **1777** BRAND *Pop. Antiq.* (1849) III. 100 Gipsies still continue to be called 'Faws' in the N. of England. **1825** BROCKETT *N.C. Words* 69 *Faw-gang*, a company of riffraff. **1827** MACKENZIE *Hist. Newcastle* II. 767 *note*, Tinkers, cloggers..egglers, and others of that worthy race called Faws. **1869** *Lonsdale Gloss.*, *Faw-gang*..a gang of rogues and beggars.

†**faw**, *a. Obs.* Forms: 1 faaȝ, fáȝ, 2 foaȝ, fogh, 3 fah, foh, *south.* vaȝ, 4 fowe, 4– faw. [OE. *fáȝ*, *fáh* = OHG. *fêh*, Goth. *faihs*:—OTeut. **faiho-z*:—pre-Teut. **poiko-s*, cognate with Gr. ποικίλος particoloured. (The mod.Eng form would normally be **fow* or **fough*; *faw* is from northern dialects.)]

1. Coloured, stained, streaked; particoloured, variegated. Also in *Comb.* as ***gold-faw***.

a **700** *Epinal Gloss.* 61 Arrius [*varius*]: faaȝ. *Beowulf* 1631 Laȝu drusade wæter under wolcnum wæl dreore faȝ. *c* **1000** *Sax. Leechd.* II. 124 Ram ȝeallan þone faȝan cnua on niwe ealo. *c* **1150** *Semi-Sax. Voc.* in Wr.-Wülcker 542 *Fuluus, uel flauus*..fouh. *c* **1175** *Lamb. Hom.* 53 þas faȝe neddre bitacneð þis faȝe folc þe wuneð in þisse weorlde..Witeð eow þet ȝe ne beo noht þe foaȝe neddre. *c* **1205** LAY. 24653 Sum hafde gode grene æc, and alches cunnes fah claδ. *Ibid.* 30984 Gold-uaȝe sceldes scanden bilifes. *c* **1440** *Gaw. & Galaron* ii. 13 in Pinkerton *Scot. Poems* (1792) III. 218 Ferly fayr wes the feild, flekerit and faw, With gold and goulis in greyne. **1513** DOUGLAS *Æneis* VIII. x. (1839) 500 The God of bestis and of feildis faw.

b. In the plant-name **fawthistle** (*lit.* coloured thistle), the card thistle or teasel. *Obs.*

1483 *Cath. Angl.* 124/1 Fawthistelle, *labrum veneris*.

c. Of objects that reflect light: Bright, glancing, gleaming, twinkling.

c **1000** *Ags. Ps.* lxxxviii[i]. 36 Fultum þu him afyrdest faȝan sweordes. ? *a* **1400** *Morte Arth.* 747 The pryce schippez..fondez wyth fulle saile ower the fawe ythez.

2. quasi-*sb.* The adj. used *absol.* coupled with *gray*. A species of fur, *e.g.* ermine (see quot. *a* 1200). Cf. OF. *vair et gris*.

a **1200** *Moral Ode* 361 Ne scal þer beo fou ne grei ne cunig ne ermine. *c* **1275** *Doomsday* 28 in *O.E. Misc.* 164 Moni of thisse riche that wereden foh and grei. *c* **1314** *Guy Warw.* (A.) 4174 Gij him schred in fou & gray. *c* **1320** *Sir Tristr.* 1220 þai raft me fowe and griis, And þus wounded þai me.

faw, dial. and Sc. form of FALL *v.*

faw, obs. form of FAIN, FEW.

fawcebraye, obs. form of FAUSSEBRAYE.

fawcet(t, -set, obs. forms of FAUCET.

fawching, -chyn, obs. forms of FALCHION.

1582 N. LICHEFIELD tr. *Castanheda's Conq. E. Ind.* 25 b, Their enimies..were cutting of it [the gabell] with their wood-kniues or fawchings.

fawcht, Sc. form of FOUGHT.

fawconer(e, obs. forms of FALCONER[1] and [2].

fawd. *dial.* Also faud. [Of obscure origin; cf. FAD *sb.*[1], FEALD; also *fawdom*, Sc. var. of FATHOM.] A bundle.

1641 BEST *Farm. Bks.* (Surtees) 18 Wheare you see that the water gets yssue..yow may thrust in and ramme downe fawdes of strawe. **1876** *Whitby Gloss.*, *Faud*, a truss of straw; as much as the two arms will compass.

fawd, fawdom(e, obs. Sc. ff. FOLD, FATHOM.

fawe(n, -er, obs. forms of FAIN, FAVOUR.

fawesebraye, obs. f. of FAUSSEBRAIE, -BRAYE.

fawf, var. of FAUCH *sb. Sc.*

fawkener(e, obs. forms of FALCONER.

fawkenet, obs. form of FALCONET.

15.. in *Beauties of Thanet* (1830) II. 34 After the dischardge of ii fawkenets..the forte was won.

fawn (fɔːn), *sb.*[1] Forms: 4–5 foun(e, (5 fowen), 5 faon, 5–7 fawne, 6–7 faun(e, 5– fawn. [a. OF. *faon*, also *foun*, *feon*:—med.L. **fētōn-em*, f. *fœtus* offspring.]

†**1.** A young animal, cub. *Obs.*

[**1274** *Grands Chron. S. Denis* (*Rer. Gall. & Franc. Script.* (1818) XVII. 354) Jones fauns de bestes sauvages.] **1481** CAXTON *Myrr.* II. vi, This beest hath but ones yong fawnes. *a* **1603** JAS. I *Psalm* xxix. 6 Lyke to the faune of unicornis Will leape when he doth speik. **1603** OWEN *Pembrokeshire* I. xv. (1892) 127 The Fawne [of a seal] at the first is white.

2. A young fallow deer, a buck or doe of the first year. ***in fawn*** (said of the doe): pregnant.

c **1369** CHAUCER *Dethe Blaunche* 429 Of founes, soures, bukkes, does Was ful the wode. *c* **1400** MAUNDEV. (Roxb.) xxxi. 143 Dappeld and spotted, as it ware founez of daes. **1486** *Bk. St. Albans* E iv a, And ye speke of the Bucke the fyrst yere he is a fawne. **1535** COVERDALE *Jer.* xiv. 5 The Hynde shal forsake the yonge fawne..because there shalbe no grasse. **1667** MILTON *P.L.* IV. 404 As a Tiger, who by chance hath spi'd..two gentle Fawnes at play. **1774** GOLDSM. *Nat. Hist.* (1776) III. 137 The fawns continue to follow the deer eight or nine months in all. **1810** SCOTT *Lady of L.* III. ii, The doe awoke, and to the lawn..led her fawn. **1872** BAKER *Nile Tribut.* ii. 38 The does are now in fawn. *fig.* **1609** HEYWOOD *Brit. Troy* XV. xxxii, That her commensed spleene may be withdrawne From them, whose violence spar'd not her Fawne.

3. Short for *fawn-colour* (see 4).

1881 C. C. HARRISON *Woman's Handiwork* III. 165 Among colors in which most of the stuffs mentioned may be had, are seal-brown, nut-brown and fawn. **1892** *Pall Mall G.* 17 Mar. 1/2 A Russian costume in fawns made of fancy crépon. *Ibid.* 22 Sept. 1/3 Slight moustache and hair of a fawn that we associate rather with Caledonia than the Netherlands. **1914** [see BEAVER[1] 2 c]. **1971** P. D. JAMES *Shroud for Nightingale* v. 170 The thick winter coat in fawn was of good quality. *Ibid.* vii. 220 His fawn polo-neck sweater.

4. *attrib.* and *Comb.*, as ***fawn-skin***; also ***fawn-brown, -eyed, -like, -pink*** adjs; **fawn-colour**, a light yellowish brown (hence ***fawn-coloured*** adj.); **fawn foot** (see quots.).

1800 tr. *Lagrange's Chem.* II. 177 They acquire a strong *fawn-brown tint. **1865** GOSSE *Year at Shore* 79 Light olive, fawn-brown..or pure white. **1800** tr. *Lagrange's Chem.* II. 284 Of a red, inclining to *fawn-colour. **1844–57** G. BIRD *Urin. Deposits* (ed. 5) 133 From the palest fawn-colour to the deepest amber. **1803** DAVY in *Phil. Trans.* XCIII. 261 They gave dense *fawn-coloured precipitates. **1891** E. PEACOCK *N. Brendon* II. 391 The little fawn-coloured bullocks. **1895** J. R. LOWELL *Last Poems* 34 Seraph strong to soar, or *fawn-eyed elf. **1938** S. SPENDER *Trial of Judge* 16 The gross-lipped fawn-eyed nigger-skinned Hook-nosed intellectual Petra. **1950** H. L. EDLIN in *Wood* XV. 373/1 **Fawn foot*, swelling at the end of an axe helve, to give a better grip, shaped like a fawn's foot. **1953** A. JOBSON *Household & Country Crafts* xvii. 166 Some characteristic bill-hooks with the funniest little kick of a handle, like the spurs of a fighting-cock (I believe they are technically known as fawnfeet, and assuredly they are taken out of the hedgerow). **1838** LYTTON *Leila* I. iv, That elastic and *fawn-like grace. **1862** SHIRLEY *Nugæ Crit.* iii. 152 Little cousin Annie, with her shy fawn-like glances. **1909** *Daily Chron.* 29 Apr. 7/3 Tourterelle is a subdued *fawn-pink. **1927** D. H. LAWRENCE *Mornings in Mexico* 30 It [*sc.* the village] lies..tilted on the fawn-pink slope. **1513** DOUGLAS *Æneis* VII. vii. 126 Sum wer cled in pilchis of *foune skynnis. **1774** J. BRYANT *Mythol.* I. 10 Many allusions about a fawn, and fawn-skin, in the Dionusiaca. **1864** SWINBURNE *Atalanta* 1389 Their leaves that nod Round thy fawnskin.

†**fawn**, *sb.*[2] *Obs.* [f. FAWN *v.*[1]]

1. An act of fawning; a servile cringe, a wheedling courtesy.

1590 GREENE *Never too late* (1600) 48 Infida..plied Francesco with her flattering fawnes. **1601** B. JONSON *Poetaster* V. i, Thy..wholesome sharpnesse..pleaseth Cæsar, more than servile fawnes. **1633** P. FLETCHER *Poet. Misc.* 78 Will rave and chide..But soon to smiles and fawns turns all his heat. *a* **1657** R. LOVEDAY *Lett.* (1663) 146 The fawnes of Fortune. **1744** E. HEYWOOD *Female Spectator* (1746) I. 131 You may know him by..a servile fawn on all who can..contribute to exalting him.

2. = FAWNER. *rare*$^{-1}$.

1635 BRATHWAIT *Arcad. Pr.* 80 Had he plaid buffoun, Fawn or knave.

fawn (fɔːn), *v.*[1] Forms: 4 faghne, fayn, 4–7 fawne, 4, 6–8 faun(e, (4 fauhne), 5 fawnyn, 6 *Sc.*, 9 *dial.* fan, 5– fawn. See also FAIN *v.*[1] [app. a variant, with specialized sense, of FAIN *v.*[1] to rejoice. The OE. forms *fæȝnian* and *fahnian* (whence respectively *fain* and *fawn*) are derived from different forms of the adj., viz. OE. *fæȝen*, whence *fain* adj., and OE. *faȝen*, whence ME. *fawe*.

Prof. Sievers suggests that the divergent forms are due to suffix-ablaut (*-in*, *-an*, *-un*) in primitive OE.]

1. *intr.* Of an animal, *esp.* a dog: To show delight or fondness (by wagging the tail, whining, etc.) as a dog does.

a **1225** [see FAWNING *vbl. sb.* 1.] **1377** LANGL. *P. Pl.* B. xv. 295 þere ne was lyoun ne leopart..þat ne fel to her feet, and fauned with þe tailles. **1398** TREVISA *Barth. De P.R.* XVIII. iv. (1495) 751 A lambe..fawnyth wyth hys taylle whan he hath founde his moder. *c* **1440** *Promp. Parv.* 152/1 Fawnyn as howndys, *applaudo*. **1593** SHAKS. *Lucr.* 421 As the grim lion fawneth o'er his prey. **1611** DEKKER *Roaring Girle* Wks. 1873 III. 215 He can both fawne like a Spaniell, and bite like a Mastiue. **1667** MILTON *P.L.* IX. 526 Oft he bowd His turret Crest..Fawning. **1675** HOBBES *Odyssey* (1677) 209 The old dog Argus..fauned with his tail, but could not rise. **1791** COWPER *Odyssey* XVI. 11 Thy dogs bark not, but fawn on his approach. **1865** SWINBURNE *Poems & Ball.*, *Satia te Sanguine* 54 A tame beast..fawns to be fed.

b. ***to fawn on, upon***: (of a dog, etc.) to show delight at the presence of; to lavish caresses on, to caress.

1477 EARL RIVERS (Caxton) *Dictes* 41, I barke upon the fooles and fawne upon the wysemen. **1533** T. WILSON *Rhet.* (1580) 196 The Lion..fauned gently upon hym. *a* **1605** MONTGOMERIE *Descr. Vane Lovers* 42 A Dog..will..fan on him vha givis him fude. **1632** J. HAYWARD tr. *Biondi's Eromena* 193, I wondered to see her [a Deere] so gently fawne upon me without any feare. **1776** ADAM SMITH *W.N.* I. ii, A puppy fawns upon its dam. **1841** LANE *Arab. Nts.* I. 49 The calf..came to me, and fawned upon me. **1861** HUGHES *Tom Brown at Oxf.* iii. (1889) 28 Jack [the dog]..was fawning on him as if he understood every word. *fig.* **1573** TUSSER *Husb.* cxiv. (1878) 216 Though Fortune smiles, and fawnes vpon thy side. **1600** HOLLAND *Livy* IV. xlii. (1609) 166 It was no long time that fortune fawned upon the Æquians. **1796** BURKE *Let. noble Ld.* Wks. 1842 II. 271 In the same moment fawning on those who have the knife half out of the sheath.

†**c.** quasi-*trans.* To wag (the tail). *Obs.*

a **1300** *Cursor M.* 12354 (Cott.) þas oþer leons..honurd him faunand þair tail.

†**2.** *trans.* = *to fawn on* (sense 1 b): To caress; to pat (the head of a dog). *Obs.*

a **1300** *Cursor M.* 12333 *heading* (Gott.), þe leonis fauned iesus. *c* **1340** *Gaw. & Gr. Knt.* 1919 Hor houndez þay þer rewarde, Her hedez þay fawne & frote. *c* **1375** *Sc. Leg. Saints, Eufemia* 183, & faynand hir þare talis knet. **1483** CAXTON *Gold. Leg.* 294/4 They ranne to this hooly vyrgyne in fawnynge her.

3. *intr.* To affect a servile fondness; to court favour or notice by an abject demeanour. Const. *on*, *upon* (a person, his looks, etc.).

a **1310** [see FAWNING *vbl. sb.* 2.] *c* **1440** LYDG. *Secrees* Prol. 675 Smothe afore folk to fawnyn and to shyne. *c* **1510** MORE *Picus* Wks. 16/1 If the worlde fawne vpon the. **1576** FLEMING *Panopl. Epist.* 171 Such as fawne on them with flatterie. **1577** tr. *Bullinger's Decades* (1592) 225 By fawning on his angrie lookes she turnes them into smiles. **1612** T. TAYLOR *Comm. Titus* iii. 3 Nor further fawned [they] vpon God then to get out of his hands. **1692** E. WALKER *Epictetus' Mor.* xxxi, Nor flatter, fawn, forswear, assent or lie. **1823** LAMB *Lett.* (1888) II. 62 How the knave fawned when I was of service to him! **1857** BUCKLE *Civiliz.* I. vii. 398 Even our greatest writers prostituted their abilities by fawning upon the prejudices of their patrons. **1865** KINGSLEY *Herew.* x, They fawn on a damsel with soft words. **1879** DIXON *Windsor* I. xii. 118 He stooped to fawn where he was used to smite.

†**b.** ***to fawn upon*** (a thing, an object of desire): to aspire to. *Obs. rare*$^{-1}$.

1634 Ford *P. Warbeck* v. i, Could I be England's queen, —a glory, Jane, I never fawn'd on.

†**4.** *trans.* To cringe to (a person). *Obs. rare.*

*a*1568 Ascham *Scholem.* I. (Arb.) 83 Though, for their priuate matters they can follow, fawne, and flatter noble Personages.

fawn (fɔːn), *v.*² [f. fawn *sb.*¹; cf. OF. *faoner.*]

1. *intr.* To bring forth young. Now only of deer.

1481 Caxton *Myrr.* II. vi, They [lionesses] come to fede their fawnes the iii day after they haue fawned. 1530 Palsgr. 546/2 Haue your dere fawned yet? 1679 Blount *Anc. Tenures* 91 Because the Dear did then fawn, or bring forth their young. 1721–1800 in Bailey. 1942 J. M. Dowsett *Romance Eng. Forests* ix. 243 No hogs were allowed in the chase during the fence month when the does were fawning. 1951 D. M. Stenton *Eng. Soc. Early Middle Ages* iii. 107 The forest was closed for hunting because the beasts were supposed to be fawning.

2. *trans.* Of deer: To bring forth (a fawn).

1576 Turberv. *Venerie* 141 The Bucke is fawned in the end of May. 1618 Earl of Cork in *Sir R. Boyle's Diary* Ser. I. (1886) I. 192 The firste fawn that was fawned in my Park.

Hence **'fawning** *vbl. sb.*

1598 Manwood *Lawes Forest* xi. §2 (1615) 81 When that our Agistors doe meete together for the fawning of our wilde beasts. 1685 R. Brady tr. *John's Charter of Forests* §7 in *Hist. Eng.* App. 141 The third Swainmote shall be holden.. concerning the fawning of our Does.

fawn, obs. form of faun.

fawner ('fɔːnə(r)). [f. fawn *v.*¹ + -er¹.] One who fawns, cringes, or flatters; a toady.

*c*1440 *Promp. Parv.* 146/1 Faynare, or flaterere, *adulator.* 1553 T. Wilson *Rhet.* 106 b, Flatterers, fawners, and southers of mennes saiynges. 1685 *Gracian's Courtiers Orac.* 156 All the Fawners..are so many Monsters of impertinence. *a*1715 Burnet *Own Time* (1766) I. 68 His diary..represents him as an abject fawner on the Duke of Buckingham. 1812 Southey *Omniana* II. 322 Certainly he was no fawner. 1864 E. Sargent *Peculiar* I. 289 He..began to play the fawner once more.

†**'fawnery.** *Obs.* [f. prec. + -y.] The bearing or tricks of a fawner; flattery, sycophancy.

1661 K. W. *Conf. Charact., Temporizer* (1860) 51 This puppet of policy differs from the foregoing spanniel of fawnery only in time and degrees.

fawney ('fɔːnɪ). *slang.* [a. Irish *fáin(n)e* ring.]

1. A finger-ring.

1812 J. H. Vaux *Flash Dict., Fawney*, a finger-ring. 1834 H. Ainsworth *Rookwood* III. v, Fogles and fawnies soon went their way. 1851 Mayhew *Lond. Labour* I. 423 He wears a stunning fawny on his finger.

2. a. = *fawney rig.* ***to go on the fawney***: to practise the fawney-rig. **b.** One who practises the fawney-rig.

1781 G. Parker *View Society* II. 167 There is a large shop in London where these kind of rings are sold, for the purpose of going on the Fawney. *Ibid.*, The Fawney says, ' I dare say some poor woman [etc.]'. 1789 —— *Life's Painter* 174, *Fawny*, an old, stale trick, called ring-dropping.

3. *Comb.*, as ***fawney-dropper, -dropping***; **fawney-bouncing**, selling rings for a pretended wager; **fawney-bouncer**; **fawney-rig** (see quot.).

1781 G. Parker *View Society* II. 166 The Fawney rig. 1823 Egan *Grose's Dict. Vulgar Tongue, Fawney rig*, a common fraud thus practised:—a fellow drops a brass ring, double gilt, which he picks up before the party meant to be cheated, and to whom he disposes of it for less than its supposed, and ten times more than its real, value. 1851 Mayhew *Lond. Labour* I. 351, I do a little in the Fawney dropping line. 1857 'Ducange Anglicus' *Vulg. Tongue* 39 Fawney droppers gammon the flats and take the yokels in.

Hence **'fawneyed** [-ed²], ringed.

1812 J. H. Vaux *Flash Dict., Fawnied* or *fawney-fam'd*, having one or more rings on the finger. 1834 H. Ainsworth *Rookwood* III. v, My fawnied famms.

†**'fawnguest.** *Obs.* [? f. fawn *v.* + guest.

Possibly an etymologizing spelling of some dialect word. Nashe was an East Anglian; can the word be identical with *fangast*, given by Sir T. Browne without interpretation in his list of words peculiar to that region (*Misc. Tr.* viii. 146)? Hickes (*Ags. Gr.* 1689), however, says that in Norfolk *a fangast wench* meant 'virginem viro jam nunc maturam et virum quasi expetentem'.]

a. A fawning parasite, a sycophant, toady. Also *attrib.* **b.** One who robs or swindles another under the guise of friendship.

1592 Nashe *Strange Newes* Wks. B iv/1 Nuntius, a Fawneguest Messenger twixt Maister Bird and Maister Demetrius. 1596 —— *Saffron Walden* T iii/1 He may be a fawn-guest in his intent neuertheles. 1602 Rowlands *Greene's Ghost* (1880) 15 There be certaine mates called Fawneguests, who..will..say..a friend of yours..gaue me this bowed sixpence to drinke a quart of wine with you for his sake. *Ibid.*, Such Fawneguests were they, that [etc.].

fawning ('fɔːnɪŋ), *vbl. sb.* [f. fawn *v.* + -ing¹.] The action of the vb. fawn.

1. Said of animals: see fawn *v.*¹ 1.

*a*1225 *Ancr. R.* 290 Spit him amidde þe bearde.. þet.. fikeð mid dogge uawenunge. *a*1300 *Cursor M.* 12350 (Cott.) Abute his fete þe quilpes ran..And wit þair fauning mad him cher. 1382 Wyclif *Tobit* xi. 9 With the faunyng of his tail he iozed. *c*1400 *Ywaine & Gaw.* 2002 The lyoun wald noght fyght, Grete fawning made he to the Knyght. 1601 Shaks. *Jul. C.* III. i. 43 Low-crooked curtsies, and base Spaniell fawning. 1607 Topsell *Four-f. Beasts* (1673) 109 The lower and stiller [voice of a dog] is called 'whining', or 'fawning'. 1665 Boyle *Occas. Refl.* III. vii. (1845) 159 With ..how many Fawnings, does he [a dog] court me to fling it him? 1844 Lowell *Columbus* Poems 1890 I. 153 O days whose memory tames to fawning down The surly fell of Ocean's bristled neck!

2. Cringing, servile flattery or homage; an instance of this.

*a*1310 in Wright *Lyric P.* iv. 23 Fyth of other ne darth he fleo, that fleishshes faunyng furst for-eode. 1382 Wyclif *Judith* xiv. 13 Vagio..made fawnyng with his hondis. 1533 Udall *Flowers Latine Speaking* (1560) 67 b, Nor suffre our selues to be wonne..with faunyng. 1592 Wyrley *Armorie* 145 Let no man..To highlie of her [Fortune's] lended faunings bost. 1766 Goldsm. *Vic. W.* xxxi, No fawning, sir ..cried the baronet. 1862 Ld. Brougham *Brit. Const.* i. 3 A spirit of fawning and truckling towards those in authority.

fawning ('fɔːnɪŋ), *ppl. a.* [f. as prec. + -ing².]

1. That fawns or shows pleasure or fondness as a dog does; caressing, fondling. Said also of the arm, tail, or tongue.

*c*1340 *Cursor M.* 12354 (Trin.) þese oþere leouns.. honoured him wiþ faunyng tail. 1509 Hawes *Past. Pleas.* I. xvi, When that these grayhoundes had me so espied, With faunyng chere of great humilitie In goodly haste they fast unto me hyed. *a*1569 Kingesmyll *Godly Advise* (1580) 1 The subtile fanyng spaniell. 1621 G. Sandys *Ovid's Met.* I. (1626) 13 She..Hung on his necke with fawning armes. 1697 Dryden *Virg. Georg.* IV. 741 Fierce Tigers couch'd around, and loll'd their fawning tongues. *c*1750 Shenstone *Colemira* 7 The fawning cats compassionate his case And purr around. 1842 J. H. Newman *Par. Serm.* (ed. 2) V. viii. 120 As a king giving names to fawning brutes.

fig. 1635 Quarles *Embl.* I. vi. (1718) 25 Let wit or fawning fortune vie their best.

b. quasi-*adv.*

1387 Trevisa *Higden* (Rolls) I. 237 þe nyȝtyngale.. Twytereþ wel fawnyng Wiþ full swete song in þe dawenyng. 1398 —— *Barth. De P.R.* XII. xxiii. (1495) 428 The byrde Kaladrius settyth his syghte on hym and beholdyth hym as it were faunynge and playsynge.

2. Showing servile deference, cringing, flattering.

1585 Abp. Sandys *Serm.* (1841) 137 Drunkenness is a fawning devil, a sweet poison. 1650 Hubbert *Pill Formality* 81 The fauning Parasite, and Saint-seeming devil. 1701 *Lond. Gaz.* No. 3708/1 Edward Troupe..with a fawning Scotch-like Tone. 1769 *Junius Lett.* xxxv. 164 A fawning treachery against which no prudence can guard. 1838 Lytton *Leila* I. v, The voice..smoothed into fawning accents of base fear. 1857 Buckle *Civiliz.* I. xi. 652 A fawning and hypocritical race.

fawningly ('fɔːnɪŋlɪ), *adv.* [f. prec. + -ly².] In a fawning manner: **a.** Caressingly, joyfully. **b.** Cringingly, flatteringly, servilely.

a. 1790 Bewick *Quadrupeds* (1807) 358 The sagacious animal..leapt fawningly against the breast of a man.

b. 1591 Harington *Orl. Fur.* 332 *note*, Those Princes.. that (as is said of them) ' Never see lookes, but fawninglie disguised'. 1654 Trapp *Comm. Matt.* xii. 38 They [i.e. the Pharisees] had nothing to say for themselves, but fawningly to call him Master. *a*1711 Ken *Edmund* Poet. Wks. 1721 II. 178 Lucifer..Strove fawningly t' attract good Edmund's Ear. 1855 Macaulay *Hist. Eng.* III. 401. 'It was set down in my instructions', answered Jeffreys, fawningly, 'that I was to show no mercy to men like you.'

fawningness ('fɔːnɪŋnɪs). [f. as prec. + -ness.] A fawning disposition or demeanour; cringing behaviour, servility.

1673 O. Walker *Educ.* ii. 20 It is much easier to bend a naturall mis-inclination to its neighbour virtue..as.. fawningnes to complaisance. 1827 De Quincey *Murder* Wks. IV. 45 I'm for peace, and quietness, and fawningness, and what may be styled knocking-underness.

fawnish ('fɔːnɪʃ), *a.* [f. fawn *sb.*¹ 3 + -ish¹.] Somewhat fawn, resembling fawn in colour.

1895 *Daily News* 31 May 2/1 The rest of the dress being a negation in fawnish cream colour. 1909 M. B. Saunders *Litany Lane* I. i, Looming out of the fawnish mist shone the great golden glory of the world.

fawnsome ('fɔːnsəm), *a. dial.* [f. fawn *v.* + -some.] Of an animal: Disposed to fawn; showing fondness.

1863 Mrs Toogood *Yorksh. Dial.*, The calf..is grown so fawnsome it will follow us like a dog. 1873 *Swaledale Gloss.*, *Fansome* adj., winsome.

fawntekyn, var. fauntekin *Obs.*, an infant.

fawny ('fɔːnɪ), *a.* [f. fawn *sb.* + -y.] Of a colour: Inclining to fawn.

1849 *Beck's Florist* 260 Madame Angelina, that most unique Rose in its creamy fawny tints. 1882 *Garden* 1 Apr. 223/1 The sepals are of a pale fawny yellow.

fawoure, obs. form of favour.

fawse, obs. and dial. form of false *a.*

fawsont, Sc. var. fashioned.

fawt(e, obs. forms of fault.

†**fax**, *sb.*¹ *Obs.* Forms: α. 1 feax, *north.* fæx, 1–2 fex, 3–6 **fax**, (5 faxe, 6 facts, 7 faix, ? 6 *pl.* fassis). β. 3 væx, vax(e. [OE. *feax* = OFris. *fax*, OS. and OHG. *fahs* (MHG. *vahs*), ON. (and mod.Norw.) *fax.* The word occurs in the proper names *Fairfax, Halifax.*]

1. The hair of the head.

Beowulf 2967 Swat ædrum sprong forð under fexe. *c*900 *Bæda's Hist.* II. xvi, He..hæfde blæc feax. *c*1000 *Sax. Leechd.* I. 110 Wiþ þæt ðæt mannes fex fealle. *c*1205 Lay. 24843 [Heo] luken heom bi uaxe [*c*1275 þan heere] and laiden heom to grunde. *a*1300 *Cursor M.* 7244 (Cott.) Thoru his fax his force was tint. *c*1375 *Sc. Leg. Saints, Martha* 7 Scho was far of fax and face. *c*1440 *Bone Flor.* 1545 Then they lowsyd hur feyre faxe, That was yelowe as the waxe. 1513 Douglas *Æneis* II. vi. 51 His fax and berd was fadit quhar he stuide. 1548 Hall *Chron.* 10 b, Yᵉ fassis of their head set ful of new devised facuns. 1560 Rolland *Crt. Venus* I. 915 With countinance and facts virginall. 1606 Holland *Sueton.* Annot. 30 a, Whose lokes and faix were so slicke and glib with sweet oyles, that they shone againe. [1610 —— *Camden's Brit.* I. 723 Fax in the old English tongue signifieth the haire of the head.]

2. *derisively.* The face.

[Perhaps a misunderstanding of the obsolete word as preserved in poetic phrases; some other Sc. examples in 16th c. would admit of a similar interpretation.]

1513 Douglas *Æneis* VIII. Prol. 32 The fillok hir deformit fax wald haue a fair face.

fax (fæks), *sb.*² *Comm.* [Abbrev. of facsimile *sb.*] Facsimile, facsimile telegraphy. Also, a facsimile copy obtained in this way. Freq. *attrib.*

1948 *Time* 12 Jan. 62/3 The big news about 'fax' was that, technically, the bugs were pretty well worked out of it. 1957 *Editor & Publisher* 13 Apr. 57/1 (*heading*) Contrast cut from fax pix. 1969 *Pop. Electronics* Feb. 33/1 The facsimile process (or 'fax' as it is called in the trade) has had its ups and downs. 1971 D. M. Costigan *Fax* p. vii, Probably the most impressive thing about facsimile (fax, for short)..is its enormous potential. 1972 *Sci. Amer.* Sept. 140/3 Futurists predict that a 'fax' terminal in the home or business office may someday supplement or even replace the mail carrier. 1976 *New Scientist* 30 Sept. 683/1 If the letter is put—by hand—on to a facsimile ('fax') machine for transmitting, this is acceptable, too. But it is equally possible for the computer to generate the fax signals electronically. 1980 J. McNeil *Spy Game* xvii. 179, I want a fax of the passport photo wired from Washington. 1984 *Times* 21 Feb. 25/1 STC Business Systems has launched a new fax machine equipped with automatic transmissions and stacking systems... It is claimed that it can transmit an A4 page across the world in 15 seconds. 1984 *Daily Tel.* 28 Nov. 8 (Advt.), NEFAX is UK and European brand leader in fax.

Hence as *v. trans.*, to transmit (a document, etc.) in facsimile by scanning it and transmitting the resulting signal by wire or radio for use in reproducing the document at the receiving end.

1979 *Datamation* Aug. 75/3 (*heading*) Who will fax the mail? 1983 *Library Assoc. Rec.* Nov. 406/1 The BLLD had installed a couple of machines and was prepared to fax requests to any library which had the necessary hardware to receive it, and was prepared to pay. 1984 *Sunday Times* 11 Mar. 69/1 Stories edited by journalists are sent by facsimile transmission—'faxed'—across Europe to the printing works. 1986 *Bookseller* 3 Oct. 1422/2 Titles not in stock are gathered by the central computer and listed by publisher in ISBN sequence before being faxed, telexed or skypacked to the individual publishers.

†**faxed**, *a. Obs.* [f. prec. + -ed²; cf. ON. *faxiðr.*] Having hair, hairy. ***faxed star***: a comet, from the resemblance of its tail to hair.

891 *O.E. Chron.* (Parker MS.), Same men cweþaþ on Englisc þæt hit [cometa] sie feaxede steorra. *a*1259 Matthew Paris *Chron. Maj.* an. 891 (Rolls) I. 428 Cometa apparuit quæ Anglice *Vexede sterre* nuncupatur. [1605 Camden *Rem.* (1636) 26 The old English..could call a Comet a Fixed [*sic*] starre; which is all one with *Stella crinita.*] 1851 *Cumbrld. Gloss.*, Faxed Star.

fay (feɪ), *sb.*¹ *Obs.* or *arch.* Forms: 4 fei, feye, fai, 4–6 fey, 4–7 fay, 5 fa, 4–6 faye, 6 foy. [ad. later OFr. *fei*:—earlier *feit, feid*: see faith. *Feith*, faith was the original, and became the ordinary, Eng. form: but *fey, fay* also passed into Eng. from contemporary Fr. *a* 1300, and was for a time almost as common as the earlier form, especially in certain senses, and in phrases such as *par fay, by my fay* = OFr. *par fei, par ma fei.*]

1. Religious belief; = faith *sb.* 1–4.

*a*1300 *Cursor M.* 7562 (Cott.), I haue in drightin fest mi fai. *c*1315 Shoreham *Poems* (1849) 139 Her-to accordeth oure fay. *c*1320 R. Brunne *Medit.* 18 þat ys preved by crystes feye. *a*1375 *Lay Folks Mass Bk.* App. iv. 117 þou schalt be founden, I þe fay Hoseled. 14.. *Pol. Rel. & L. Poems* (1866) 253 Ellis faileþ al oure fay. ? 14.. *Chester Pl.* (1847) II. 116 Newe tonges shall have to preach the faye. *a*1420 Hoccleve *De Reg. Princ.* 332 Mannes resoun may not preve our fey. *c*1450 Myrc 362 For who so beleueth in the fay. 1590 Spenser *Sheph. Cal.* Sept. 107 Both of their doctrine and of their faye. 1596 Spenser *F.Q.* v. viii. 19 That neither hath religion nor fay.

2. Credit, authority; = faith *sb.* 6.

*c*1374 Chaucer *Boeth.* IV. ii. 112 For as moche as þe fey of my sentence shal be þe more ferme and haboundaunt.

3. Promise, assurance; = faith *sb.* 8.

*a*1300 *Cursor M.* 11530 (Cott.) He [heroude] was traitur, fals in fai. *c*1380 *Sir Ferumb.* 2046 þar-to sche sykerede þanne hure fay, to help hem be hure miȝte. *c*1385 Chaucer *L.G.W.* 1847 *Lucrece*, They answerde alle unto hire fey.

4. Allegiance; = faith 9; also in ***to hold, keep, owe, swear (one's) fay***; = faith *sb.* 9 b.

*c*1290 *S. Eng. Leg., St. Dominic* 246 Bi þe fei, þat i schal to þe. *c*1320 *Sir Tristr.* 318 þmariner swore his faye. 1375 Barbour *Bruce* XIII. 545 [He] held him lelely his fay. *c*1425 Wyntoun *Cron.* VIII. xli. 59 þe Folk come to þe Fay. *c*1450 Henryson *Mor. Fab.* 53 For to pray That..Lords keepe their fay Vnto their Soueraigne King. 1590 Spenser *F.Q.* II. x. 41 Did foy and tribute raise.

b. ***to be at, to take til (to) any person's or persons' fay***: to be in, to take into allegiance or subjection to him or them.

a **1300** *Cursor M.* 12984 (Cott.) þe kinges all ar at mi fai. **1375** BARBOUR *Bruce* XIII. 404 Bothwell..then at yngliss mennys fay Wes. *c* **1425** WYNTOUN *Cron.* VIII. xli. 85 He tuk þame til þe Scottis Fay: Til hym þare Athis of þat made þai.

5. Fidelity; = FAITH *sb.* 10. Also *to bear fay.*

c **1300** *Havelok* 255 Alle þe englis dede he sweren þat he shulden him ghod fey beren. **1377** *Pol. Poems* (Rolls) I. 215 So fikel in heare fay, That selden iseiȝe is sone forȝete. *a* **1529** SKELTON *Dk. Albany* 437 In loyalte and foy Lyke to Ector of Troy.

6. In asseverative phrases: **a.** *in* (*good*) *fay*; = FAITH *sb.* 12 a.

c **1300** *K. Alis.* 6952 He..thoughte in god fay. *c* **1340** *Cursor M.* 13603 (Trin.) He is oure son þei seide in fay. **1423** JAS. I *Kingis Q.* lix, Here is, in fay, the tyme. *c* **1475** *Rauf Coilȝear* 88 In gud fay, Schir, it is suith that ȝe say. *c* **1532** DEWES *Introd. Fr.* in *Palsgr.* 1046 In good fay I thanke our Lorde. *Mod. dial.* (Devon.) Iss fay!

b. In quasi-oaths. *by, upon my* (etc.) *fay*: = FAITH *sb.* 12 c. Also in Fr. form, (*par*) (*ma*) *fay.*

a **1300** *Cursor M.* 13593 (Gött.) 'A prophete', said he, 'bi mi fay'. *c* **1300** *Harrow. Hell* 81 Par ma fey! ich holde myne Alle tho that bueth heryne. *c* **1386** CHAUCER *Wife's T.* 201 If I say fals, sey nay, upon thy fey. —— *Clerk's T.* Prol. 9 Tel us som mery tale, by your fay. —— *Pars. T.* ⁋793 Par fay the resoun of a man tellith him [etc.]. *c* **1460** *Play Sacram.* 589 Betwyn Douyr & Calyce..dwellth non so cunnyng be my fey. *c* **1460** *Towneley Myst.* (Surtees) 36 Ma fa! sone I hope he shalle. **1547** GARDINER in Strype *Cranmer* II. (1694) 76 To say [etc.]..by my faye is overfar out of the way. **1808** SCOTT *Marm.* I. xxii, Nephew, quoth Heron, by my fay. **1849** JAMES *Woodman* x, By my fay, the place seems a fortress instead of an abbey.

fay (feɪ), *sb.*[2] Also 6 *in Fr. form* **fée**, 8 **faye**, *pl.* 7 **faies**. [ad. OF. *fae, faie* (Fr. *fée*) = Pr. and Pg. *fada*, Sp. *hada*, It. *fata*:—Com. Rom. *fāta* fem. sing., f. L. *fāta* the Fates, pl. of *fātum* FATE.] = FAIRY 4. Also *attrib.* and *Comb.*

1393 GOWER *Conf.* I. 193 My wife Constance is fay. [*a* **1533** LD. BERNERS *Huon* cxliv. 536 The noble quene Morgan le faye.] **1570** B. GOOGE *Pop. Kingd.* II. (1880) 15 a, As pleaseth him that fightes with Fées. **1633** B. JONSON *Tale Tub* II. i, You'd have your daughters and maids Dance o'er the fields like faies to church. **1746** COLLINS *Dirge in Cymbeline* Poems (1771) 97 The female fays shall haunt the green. *a* **1839** PRAED *Poems* (1864) I. 177 Be she a Fiend, or be she a Fay, She shall be Otto's bride to-day. **1873** G. C. DAVIES *Mount. & Mere* xiv. 113 Which needed but little imagination to transfer them into fays and water sprites. **1904** *Westm. Gaz.* 14 Sept. 2/3 Watching wild swans by some fay-haunted pool. **1962** *Listener* 12 Apr. 647/1 When she made formal use of figures in her landscapes, they were somewhat mannered, almost fay children.

fay (feɪ), *sb.*[3] Forms: 8–9 **feigh**, 9 **fay**, **feagh**, **fee**. [f. FAY *v.*[2]] The clearings from the surface; the surface soil, the dross of metals.

1747 HOOSON *Miner's Dict.* Mj, This [the Limp] the Washers use for to throw off the Feigh from the Ore out of the Sive. **1802** MAWE *Mineralogy* 204 *Feigh*, Newc. Refuse washed from the lead-ore. **1839** MURCHISON *Silur. Syst.* I. iii. 40 Fee, pronounced 'Fay', a red rubbly thin-bedded rock, with some marl. **1884** *Cheshire Gloss., Fay, Fee*, the surface soil in contradistinction to the sub-soil. **1893** SURVEYORS' INSTITUTION *Professional Notes* V. 66 They commenced removing the surface soil, or 'fey'.

fay (feɪ), *sb.*[4] Abbrev. of OFAY.

1927 *Amer. Mercury* Aug. 393 'What a lot of 'fays!' I thought, as I noticed the number of white guests. **1946** MEZZROW & WOLFE *Really Blues* (1957) 62 He was the first fay boy I ever heard who mastered this vital foundation of jazz music. **1966** *Publ. Amer. Dial. Soc.* 1964 XLII. 44 *Fay* is commonly used by Negroes to designate Caucasians.

fay (feɪ), *v.*[1] Forms: 1 **fég-an**, 3–4 **feȝen**, 3 **feien**, (**fien**), *south.* **veien**, 4 **fey**, *south.* **vie**, 5 **fye**, 6 **faie**, 5– **fay**. [OE. *féȝ-an* = OS. *fôgian* (Du. *voegen*), OHG. *fuogen* (MHG. *vüegen*, mod.G. *fügen*):—OTeut. **fôgjan* to fit, adapt, join (cf. OFris. *fôgia*, which differs in conjugation), f. **fôg-* (cf. OHG. *fuoga*, mod.G. *fuge* fitting together, joining), ablaut-form of Teut. root *fag-* in *fag-ro-* FAIR *a.*]

†**1. a.** *trans.* To fit, adapt, or join (whether in material or immaterial sense); to put together, add, compose; to fix or fasten in position. *Obs.*

a **1000** *Riddles* xxvi. 9 (Gr.) Heo..feȝeð mec on fæsten. *c* **1000** *Sax. Leechd.* III. 206 Herculem ȝesihð freo[n]dscipe feȝð. *c* **1200** *Trin. Coll. Hom.* 25 Ure fader shop us and feide þe lemes to ure licame. *Ibid.*, Forþi we clepeð him fader for þat he us feide here. *c* **1200** ORMIN 11501 Forr manness bodiȝ feȝedd iss Off fowwre kinne shaffte. *Ibid.* 11523 3iff þu feȝesst þreo wiþþ þreo þa findesst tu þær sexe. *a* **1225** *Ancr. R.* 78 Vordi ueieð Isaie hope & silence boðe togederes. *Ibid.* 396 Ure Louerd..to-tweamede his soule urom his bodie vorto ueien ure boðe togederes.

†**b.** ? To fit, furnish *with. Obs.*

c **1205** LAY. 649 He lette makien enne dic..& feiede heo mid þornen.

†**c.** *to fay upon long*: to fix at a distant point (in time); to postpone. *Obs.*

c **1400** *Destr. Troy* 5616 The ferrer þat we fay our fare opon longe, The more we procure our payne.

†**2. a.** *intr.* To suit; to match *with. Obs.*

c **1300** *Agst. Pride Ladies* in *Pol. Songs* (Camden) 154 The bout and the barbet wyth frountel shule feȝe.

b. *U.S.* Of a coat: To fit. *to fay in*: to fit into its place; also *trans.* to fill up (a gap).

1847 D. P. THOMPSON *Locke Amsden* vii. 138, I have no notion of spoiling sense to make it fay in with book rules. **1866** LOWELL *Biglow P.* Poems 1890 II. 374 Ther' 's gaps our lives can't never fay in. **1868** MRS. WHITNEY *P. Strong* xi. (1869) 128 One of the things that fayed right in. **1889** FARMER *Americanisms*, 'Your coat fays well.' **1906** P. LOWELL *Mars & its Canals* 347 The explanation of the canals as threads of vegetation fays in with the one which has been found to meet the requirements of the blue-green areas.

3. To suit, do, go on favourably, succeed. *Obs.* exc. *dial.*

c **1300** *Beket* 658 That ne vieth nothing. *c* **1425** *Seven Sag.* 2981 (P.) That may nouȝt fay And he se the with hys eye.. He wyl knowe the anoon righte. **1542** UDALL *Erasm. Apoph.* II. 336 b, This waye it will not frame ne faie, Therefore must we proue another waye. **1863** BARNES *Dorset Gloss.*, 'Things dont fay as I should wish em.' **1886** T. HARDY *Mayor of Casterbridge* xx, It came to pass that for 'fay' she said 'succeed'.

4. *Ship-building*, etc. [Special uses of 1, 2.] **a.** *trans.* To fit (a piece of timber) closely and accurately *to* (another). **b.** *intr.* Of the timber: To fit close, so as to leave no intervening space.

a. 1754 M. MURRAY *Shipbuilding* 188 *Fay*..to fitt two pieces of wood so as to join close together. The plank is said to fay to the timbers when it bears, or lies close to all the timbers. **1769** FALCONER *Dict. Marine* (1789) C iv b, The wing-transom..is fayed across the stern-post, and bolted to the head of it. **1775** FALCK *Day's Diving Vessel* 5 Two-inch planks..were fayed and nailed to all the timber of the external frame. **1867** in SMYTH *Sailor's Word-bk.*

b. 1794 *Rigging & Seamanship* I. 23 The mast where it fays is paid over with soft tar. *c* **1850** *Rudim. Navig.* (Weale) 102 The butts are rabbeted, and must fay close. **1867** SMYTH *Sailor's Word-bk.*, The plank is said to fay to the timbers, when it lies so close to them that there shall be no perceptible space between them.

Hence **fayed** *ppl. a.*; **'faying** *vbl. sb.*, the action of the vb.; also *attrib.*

1748 F. SMITH *Voy. Disc. N.-W. Pass.* I. 133 The House was..built of Logs of Wood laid one on the other, with two Sides plain or fayed, that they might be the closer. *c* **1200** *Trin. Coll. Hom.* 25 Swo digeliche hit al dihte þat on elch feinge is hem on sene. *a* **1225** *Ancr. R.* 78 þis is nu þe reisun of þe veiunge. **1858** SIMMONDS *Dict. Trade, Faying* in maritime phraseology, the union of two pieces so close that no intervening space occurs. **1869** SIR E. J. REED *Shipbuild.* x. 193 The rivet-holes shall be punched from the faying surfaces. *Ibid.* xvii. 338 Care being taken to punch from the faying-side.

fay, feigh (feɪ), *v.*[2] Forms: 3 **fæȝen, fæien, fegen, feȝen**, 4–5 **fyen**, 6 **fie**, 7 **fea**, 7–8 **fee**, 4, 7–9 **fey**, 7–9 **feigh**, **fay**. [a. ON. *fǽgja* to cleanse, polish:—OTeut. type **fǽgjan*. ON. had also a synonymous parallel derivative from same root, *fága* (= MDu. *vâgen*:—OTeut. type **fǽgôjan*) whence the Eng. FOW *v.* The ON. words appear to be related by ablaut to Du. *vegen*, MHG. *vegen*, mod.G. *fegen*, to polish, clean, sweep.

In South Yorkshire it rimes with *weigh* (weɪ), not with *day, way, say* (deː, weː, seː); perh. the best spelling is *feigh*.]

trans. To clean, cleanse, polish; to clear away (filth, etc.). Now only *dial.* in specific applications: To clean out (a ditch, pond); to pare away (surface soil); to clean (seed); to winnow (corn).

c **1205** LAY. 7957 Heo..fæȝeden heoren wepnen. *Ibid.* 8057 þe king..hehten [? hehte] heom alle..fæien heore steden. *c* **1220** *Bestiary* 210 Feȝ ðe ðus of ði brest filde. *c* **1350** in *Archæologia* XXX. 353 þis drinke xal fyen fro þi herte Glet & rewme. ? *a* **1400** *Morte Arth.* 1114 He feyed his fysnamye with his foule hondez. **1573** TUSSER *Husb.* (1878) 54 At midnight trie foule priuies to fie. *Ibid.* 133 Choised seede to be picked and trimlie well fide. **1600** HOLLAND *Livy* XXI. xxxvii. (1609) 414 Such a deale of snow there was to be digged, faied, and thrown out. **1621** BURTON *Anat. Mel.* I. ii. IV. vi, To empty jakes, fay channels, carry out durt [etc.]. **1641** BEST *Farm. Bks.* (Surtees) 4 Oates threshed and feyed. *Ibid.* 52 Fey up dursed corne, and lye strawe on the floores. **1674** RAY *N.C. Words, Fee*, to winnow. *Fey, Feigh*, to do any thing notably. To fey meadows is to cleanse them: to fey a pond, to empty it. **1704** in Picton *L'pool Munic. Rec.* (1886) II. 59 Hee has already fey'd and ring'd yᵉ seller and enclosed a garden. **1796** PEGGE *Anonym.* (1809) 91 *To fee*, or *to feigh*, as they speak in Derbyshire, is to cleanse; so *to fee out* is to cleanse out. **1813** CULLUM *Hist. Hawsted & Hardwick* Gloss., To *fay* or *fey* a pond or ditch, to clean by throwing the mud out of it. **1864** F. GREVILLE in *Field* 29 Oct., The pond had not been cleaned out, (or as we say in Norfolk, fyed out)..for fifty-five years. **1876** *Mid-Yorksh. Gloss.*, 'Fey that hedge bottom out.' **1876** *Whitby Gloss., Fay*, to fan, to winnow with the natural wind. **1887** *S. Cheshire Gloss., Fee* to remove the surface soil, e.g. to obtain marl, sand, &c.

Hence **'faying** *vbl. sb.*; used *attrib.* in **faying-cloth**, ? a winnowing cloth.

1641 BEST *Farm. & Acct. Bks.* (Surtees) §2. 115 An old coverlette..and a feyinge cloth for to lye upon them.

†**fay**, *v.*[3] *Obs.* In 3 **feahen, feaȝen**. [Only in southern ME.; a Scandinavian origin is therefore unlikely, so that the word can hardly be identified with prec.; the sense also differs. Perh. repr. OE. *fǽȝan* ('fæhit pingit' Epinal Gl.; cf. *afǽȝan* to depict), f. *fáh* coloured, FAW.] *trans.* ? To adorn.

a **1225** *Ancr. R.* 58 Al ȝet þet falleð to hire [þet þe feaȝeð hire C.]. *c* **1230** *Hali Meid.* 45 Feahe þi meidenhad wið alle gode þeawes.

Hence **'faying** *vbl. sb.*

c **1230** *Hali Meid.* 43 Nis ha nawt in claðes ne in feahunge utewið.

fay, obs. form of FOE.

fay, obs. var. of FEY *a.*, fated to die.

fayalite ('feɪəlaɪt). *Min.* [Named by Gmelin in 1840 after *Fayal*, one of the Azores: see -ITE.] A silicate of iron and other bases, found in Fayal and elsewhere.

1844 DANA *Min.* 586 Fayalite of Gmelin, from the Azores. **1879** RUTLEY *Stud. Rocks* xiii. 263 A mineral which, in chemical composition, is allied to the iron-olivine, fayalite.

fayd, var. of FADE *v.*[2] to suit; in quot. *intr.*

14.. *Wedding of Sir Gawain* 214 in Furniv. *Percy Folio* I. 109 'Thys may nott fayd', said Gawen.

fayence, var. of FAIENCE.

†**'fayer.** *Obs.* exc. *dial.* Also FOWER. [f. FAY *v.*[2] + -ER[1].] One who cleanses.

1611 COTGR., *Escureur*..a scowrer, cleanser; feyer. *Ibid.* s.v. *Fi-, Maistre fifi*..feyer of priuies.

Fayettism ('feɪɛtɪz(ə)m). [ad. F. *Fayettisme*, f. (*La*) *Fayette*: see -ISM.] The doctrine and practice of the followers of La Fayette.

1793 BURKE *Policy of Allies* Wks. VII. 138 Fayetteism, Condorcetism, Monarchism, or Democratism. **1794** ABBE BARRUEL *Hist. Clergy during French Rev.* (1795) 227 All the known friends of Fayettism. **1848** W. H. KELLY tr. *L. Blanc's Hist. Ten Y.* I. 313 Unhappy men immolated on pretence of Fayétism.

†**'fayful**, *a. Obs.*$^{-0}$ [f. FAY *sb.*[1] + -FUL.] = FAITHFUL. Hence †**'fayfully** *adv.*, in a faithful manner. **a.** Loyally. **b.** Reliably.

? *a* **1400** *Morte Arth.* 1715 Thay hafe the furthe forsette alle of þe faire watyre, That fayfully of force feghte us byhowys. **1426** AUDELAY *Poems* 10 Fayfully wrytyn in hole wryt.

fay-land ('feɪlænd). [f. FAY *sb.*[2] + LAND *sb.*[1]] The land of the fays, fairy-land.

1870 MORRIS *Earthly Par.* I. II. 622 For some green summer of the fay-land light Tripping she went.

fayler, -or, obs. forms of FAILURE.

†**fayles.** *Obs.* [The writer of *Ludus Anglicorum* (see quot. *c* 1330) connects the word with FAIL *v.*; the game being usually decided by the *failure* of one of the players to make a throw that would enable him to move. Godef. has two examples of the OF. phrase *jouer a la faille*, which, though figurative, may contain an allusion to this game.] An obsolete form of Back-gammon.

c **1330** *Ludus Anglicorum* in *Royal MS.* 13. A. xviii. 158 a, Est et alius ludus qui vocatur Faylys. [The game is described at length.] **1598** B. JONSON *Ev. Man in Hum.* III. iii, Hee'll play at Fayles, and Tick-tack.

†**fayllard**, *a.* (quasi-*sb.*) *Obs. rare*$^{-1}$. [? AF. f. Fr. *faillir*: see FAIL *v.* Cf. Fr. *babillard*, etc.] That fails or offends; offending, delinquent.

c **1310** in *Rel. Ant.* I. 145 No wily lufe na clerc fayllard.

fayme, fayn(e, obs. ff. FAME, FAIN, FEIGN.

faynd, *v. Sc. Obs.*: see FAND.

fayre, obs. f. FAIR, FARE.

fayrey, -ie, -y(e, obs. ff. FAIRY.

fayssyon, obs. form of FASHION.

fayt(te, obs. form of FEAT.

fayte(n, fayth(e, fayto(u)r: see FAIT-.

Fayum ('feɪjuːm). The name of a province in upper Egypt, used *attrib.* to designate articles discovered there. Also **Fayumic** ('feɪjuːmɪk), a dialect of Coptic.

1902 *Encycl. Brit.* XXV. 497/2 *Fayum Gospel Fragment.*—This small fragment contains two sayings of Christ and one of Peter. *Ibid.* XXVII. 727/2 The main divisions of Christian Coptic as recognized and named at present are: Sahidic... Fayumic; [spoken] in the Fayum (formerly named wrongly 'Bashmuric'..) [etc.]. **1937** *Burlington Mag.* July 53/2 Comparison of Karanis and other Fayum glasses with those from the other areas of marketing. **1948** R. H. PFEIFFER *Introd. to O.T.* (1952) 115 Portions of the Scriptures are also preserved..in Fayumic. **1961** M. LEVY *Studio Dict. Art Terms* 49 *Fayum portrait*, intensely realistic portraits of deceased persons painted by the artists of Fayum..usually on mummy cases. The portraits belong to the first four centuries of the Christian era.

fayver, obs. form of FAVOUR.

†**'fazart**, *sb.* (*a.*) *Obs. Sc.* Also 6 **faizard**, **fasert**. [Of unknown etymology; according to Jamieson *faizard* is used in some parts for a hermaphrodite fowl.]

1. A coward, dastard.

1597 MONTGOMERIE *Cherrie & Slae* 377 To fazarts, hard hazarts Is deid or they cum thair. *Ibid.* 632 3on faizardis durst not..Clim vp the craig.

2. *attrib.* or *adj.* Cowardly, dastardly.

1508 KENNEDY *Flyting w. Dunbar* 517 Fowmart, fasert, fostirit in filth and fen.

faze (feɪz), *v.* orig. *U.S.* Also **feaze** (fiːz). [Var. of dial. FEEZE *v.*[1]] *trans.* To discompose, disturb.

a. 1830 *Western Monthly Rev.* III. 357 They were too well up to these things to be fazed by a little cold lead. **1843** 'R.

CARLTON' *New Purchase* I. xix. 174 This didn't *faze* me, only I steps back for my old camlit cloak. **1859** *Harper's Weekly* 16 July (Th.), Such a stomach that even a dram of nitric acid would not faze it. **1890** *Dialect Notes* (Boston, U.S.A.) *Notes from Louisiana* II. 70 'You didn't faze him' = you did not disturb him. **1890** *Columbus* (Ohio) *Dispatch* 22 July, This blow, altho' a fearful one, did not 'faze' me. **1953** F. ROBB *Sea Hunters* ii. 17 Although Cope might be only a fishing skipper no gilded plutocrat was going to faze him. **1961** *Coast to Coast 1959–60* 89 Perrot became an anodized schoolmaster, a disciplinarian no boy could faze. **1963** 'V. LUCAS' *Bell Jar* ii. 19 Walking has never fazed me. **1971** *Listener* 8 Apr. 435/2 It never really fazed me that much. I don't know why it didn't.

β. **1906** *Springfield Weekly Republ.* 27 Dec. 1 The gentlemen at the head of the Standard oil trust will not be feazed or troubled a bit by these revelations. **1907** C. E. MULFORD *Bar-20* ix. 96 I've bit on so many of them rumours that they don't feaze me no more. **1916** 'B. M. BOWER' *Phantom Herd* ix. 143 That..rather feazed the Happy Family for a few minutes. **1938** [see BATTLE-AXE 4].

faze, obs. var. FEAZE *v.*

‖**fazenda** (fa'zɛndə). Also fazende. [Pg. *fazenda* = Sp. *hacienda*.] An estate or large farm. Also the home-stead belonging thereto.

1825 A. CALDCLEUGH *Trav. S. Amer.* II. xvii. 185 The few fazendas in the neighbourhood were..occupied in pressing the sugar cane. **1845** DARWIN *Voy. Nat.* ii. (1873) 24 On such fazêndas as these the slaves pass happy lives. **1846** G. GARDNER *Trav. Brazil* 522 The Fazenda of Padre Correa is situated in a hollow surrounded by bare hills.

‖**fazendeiro** (fazɛn'deiro). In quot. fazendero. [Pg.; f. *fazenda* (see prec.).] One who owns or occupies a fazenda.

1825 A. CALDCLEUGH *Trav. S. Amer.* II. xvii. 243 Few fazenderos used the same piece of land for more than two consecutive years.

fazle, var. of FASEL *v. Obs.* to ravel.

fazoun, obs. form of FASHION.

fe, obs. form of FEE.

feaberry ('fi:bəri, 'feɪbəri). *dial.* Forms: α. 6 feaberrie, 7, 9 fe-, 9 fa-, fae-, fayberry, 7- feaberry. β. 7–9 *pl.* feab(e)s, 9 fabes, fapes, feaps. γ. *pl.* 7 thebes, thepes, 9 thapes. [Possibly corruption of **theve berry*, f. ME. THEVE:—OE. *þéfe* prickly shrub (in *þéfe-þorn*) + BERRY; the shortened form *thebes* appears to preserve the original initial. Cf. DAYBERRY (perh. a variant).]

A gooseberry; in Norfolk applied only to the unripe fruit (Forby). Also *attrib.*

1597 GERARDE *Herbal* 1143 In English Gooseberrie, Gooseberrie bush, and Feaberrie Bush in Cheshire, my natiue countrie. **1611** COTGR., *Groiselles*, gooseberries; thornberries; fea-berries. **1615** MARKHAM *Eng. Housew.* (1660) 76 The best sauce for green Geese is the juyce of Sorrel and Suger mixt together with a few scalded Feberries. **1674** RAY *S. & E.C. Words* 65 Feabes or Feaberries: Gooseberries, Suff. Thebes in Norfolk. **1706** PHILLIPS (ed. Kersey), *Feabs* or *Fea-berries*, a Country-Word for Goose-berries. *a* **1825** FORBY *Voc. E. Anglia*, *Fapes* s. pl. gooseberries. Variously called also *feaps*, *feabs*, *fabes* and *thapes*; all abbreviations of feaberries..On that day [the Guild-day] a fape-tart is an indispensable regale at every table. **1855** E. WAUGH *Lanc. Life* (1857) 104 'Fayberry cake'..or such like homely buttery-stuff.

feable, obs. f. FEEBLE; and var. of FIABLE, *Obs.*

fead, **feadary**, obs. Sc. ff. FEUD *sb.*², FEUDARY.

feague (fi:g), *sb.*¹ *dial.* Also 7 feak. [Cf. Du. *feeks* of same meaning, referred by native etymologists to the vb. *vegen* (see FEAGUE *v.*). Also cf. ME. VECKE.] (See quot. 1781.)

1664 BOLD *Poems* 134 Three female idle feaks who long'd for pig's head. **1781** HUTTON *Tour to Caves* Gloss., *Feague*, a dirty, sluttish, idle person. **1869** in *Lonsdale Gloss.*

†**feague**, *sb.*² *Obs. rare*⁻¹. [? f. FEAGUE *v.*] In phr. *by fits and feags* = 'by fits and starts'.

1600 ABBOT *Exp. Jonah* 171 Neither that we apprehend grace, by fits or feags as we are urged by any present thing.

†**feague**, *v. Obs.* Also 7 fegue, 8 feag. [Prob., as suggested in Bailey 1721, this and the earlier recorded variant FEAK *v.*¹ (and the later FAKE *v.*) are ad. Ger. *fegen* lit. to polish, furbish, sweep (for the jocular applications see Grimm s.v.), or the equivalent Du. *vegen*. But there may be mixture of a native word; cf. FEAK *v.*³]

1. *trans.* To beat, whip. Also *fig.*

[**1589–1598**: ? Implied in BUMFEAGE.] **1668** ETHEREDGE *She Would if she Could* IV. ii, Let us even go into an Arbour, and then feague Mr. Rakehell. **1681** OTWAY *Soldier's Fort.* v, Curs, keep off from snapping at my heels, or I shall so feague ye. **1691** *Rabshakeh Vapulans* 5 Well—on my Faith, he feagues these Black-coat Sparks. **1721–1800** BAILEY, *Feag*, to beat with Rods, to whip.

2. To 'do for', 'settle the business of'; = FAKE *v.*

1668 ETHEREDGE *She Would if she Could* III. iii, Oh my little rogue..how I will turn, and wind, and fegue thy body [in a dance]! *Ibid.*, 'Tis with a bottle we fegue her. **1671** CROWNE *Juliana* I, I hope the Cardinal will feague 'um all. **1672** WYCHERLEY *Love in Wood* I. i, Sly intrigue, That must at length the jilting widow fegue. **1690** D'URFEY *Collin's Walk London* I. 6 Had not th' Times his honour fegu'd. *Ibid.* II. 84 When Cataline a league Had made, the Senators to fegue.

b. (See quot.) Cf. FAKE *v.*

1785 GROSE *Class. Dict.* s.v., To feague a horse, to put ginger up a horse's fundament, to make him lively and carry his tail well.

3. *to feague away*: to set in motion briskly. Also *fig.* To agitate (a point) in one's thoughts. Also, *to feague it away*: to work at full stretch. (Cf. *to fake away*.)

1671 SHADWELL *Humourist* III, Come in..and fegue your violins away, fa, la, la, la. **1672** VILLIERS (Dk. Buckhm.) *Rehearsal* (1714) 55 When a knotty point comes, I lay my head close to it..and then I fegue it away i' faith. **1691** SHADWELL *Scowrers* III. iii, Come out..I'll feague thee [partner in a dance] away. **1829** SCOTT *Jrnl.* (1890) II. 240 From that hour [three] till ten..I was feaguing it away.

†'**feaguer**. *Obs.* [f. prec. in unrecorded sense = FAKE *v.*; cf. FAKER.] See quot.

1610 ROWLANDS *M. Mark-all* C iij, A Feager of Loges, one that beggeth with false passes or counterfeit writings.

feak (fi:k), *sb.* [Perh. related to FEAK *v.*³; possibly a sing. inferred from *feax*, FAX *sb.*¹, mistaken for a pl.] A dangling curl of hair.

1548 THOMAS *Ital. Gram.*, *Ciocca*, a feake, or quantitie of heare. **1598** MARSTON *Pygmal.* Sat. i. 138 He that..Can dally with his Mistres dangling feake, And wish that he were it. **1600** ABP. ABBOT *Exp. Jonah* 593 It doth not become thee to go with such feakes and lockes. **1650** BULWER *Anthropomet.* ii. (1653) 72 If anything be lopped off their feaks or foretops.

†**feak**, *v.*¹ *Obs.* [var. of FEAGUE *v.*] *trans.* To beat, to thrash.

1652 J. HEYWOOD *Prov. & Epigr.* (1867) 117 The foole was feakt for this.

Hence '**feaking** *vbl. sb.*; in quot. *attrib.*

1601 CORNWALLYES *Ess.* xxiv, Being without his feaking sticke, he is without himselfe.

feak (fi:k), *v.*² *Falconry.* Cf. FEAT *v.* 2. [ad. Ger. *fegen* to cleanse, sweep.] **a.** *intr.* Of a hawk: To wipe the beak after feeding. **b.** *trans.* To wipe (the beak); also, to wipe the beak of.

c **1575** *Perfect Bk. Kepinge Sparhawkes* (ed. Harting 1886) 19 They must..haue tyme to feake. **1618** LATHAM *2nd Bk. Falconry* 146 When she hath fed, feaked, and reioyced. **1686** BLOME *Gentl. Recreat.* II. 48 When she [your Hawk] hath Fed, say she Feaketh her Beak and not wipeth it. **1852** R. F. BURTON *Falconry in Valley Indus* iii. 28, I..gently pulled her off the pelf, feaked and hooded her.

feak (fi:k), *v.*³ *dial.* Also 9 feek. [Cf. FIKE *v.* and ON. *fjúka* to drift, fly away, and its causative *feyka* to blow, drive away, to rush.]

1. *trans.* To twitch, jerk, pull smartly.

1548 THOMAS *Ital. Gram.*, *Dichiomare*..to feake the heare awaie. **1879** MISS JACKSON *Shropsh. Word-bk.*, 'I know w'en our Maister's in a bad 'umour, fur e' al'ays feaks 'is wescut down.'

2. *intr.* (See quots.)

1775 ASH, *Feake* (v. int. in the Scotch dialect), to flutter, to be officiously busy, to be idle. **1811** *W. Riding Gloss.*, *Feak*, to fidget, to be restless or busied about trifles. **1878** *Cumbrld. Gloss.*, *Feek*, to be uneasy or anxious.

†'**feal**, *sb. Sc. Obs.* Also 6 feeall, feall, 7 fiell. [In sense 1 perh. originally a subst. use of next adj., with the sense 'one who owes fealty'; but it appears to have been interpreted as if f. FEE *sb.*² or *v.* + -AL¹, and this derivation prob. gave rise to the other senses. Cf. OF. *fieal* pertaining to a fief (f. *fié* = *fief*), and med.L. *fealiter* (Du Cange) = *feodaliter* 'by feudal law'.]

1. a. A feudal tenant, vassal, liegeman. **b.** A servant 'feed' or hired for a term.

a **1572** KNOX *Hist. Ref.* Wks. (1846) I. 123 The Cardinallis baner was that day displayed, and all his feeallis war charged to be under it. *c* **1575** *Balfour's Practicks* (1754) 127 All tenentis..haldand landis of ane Baron, sould swear..that thay sall be leill fealis to him. **1663** SPALDING *Troub. Chas. I* (1851) II 280 Commanding all prenteissis, seruandis, fiellis, not to change their maisteris.

2. The condition of being held in fee.

1478 *Acts Lords of Council* (1839) 10 þe persones that has the landis in the Levenax in feale of þe lord Glammys. **1630–56** SIR R. GORDON *Hist. Earls Sutherld.* (1813) 253 John Gray of Skibo had the lands of Ardinch in fiall from John..Earle of Sowtherland.

3. A payment due to the lord of the fee; also *gen.* a periodical payment, stipend, pension.

1543 *Sc. Acts Q. Mary* (1814) 439/1 To gidder with þe fealis of þe chantorie and denrie of Glasgw..pertenying to þe said lord for his fee. **1581** *Sc. Acts Jas. VI* (1814) 245 Exceptand..the gift and feall grantit by ws till..Gilbert Prymrois..for all the dayis of his lyf. **1607** JAS. VI *MS. Let. to Ld. Scone* (Jam.), There being a particular yeirlye feall appointed to him for the discharge of the said office.

attrib. **1581** *Sc. Acts Jas. VI* (1814) 236 The saidis abbot and convent ar nocht able to pay the feall thride of the said abbay according to the first assumptioun.

feal (fi:l), *a. arch.* [a. OF. *feal*, altered form (by substitution of suffix: see -AL¹) of *feeil*:—L. *fidēlem* faithful, f. *fidēs* faith.] Faithful, firm in allegiance, constant.

1568 A. SCOTT in *Bannatyne Poems* 251 Prent the wordis..Quhilkis ar nocht skar, to bar on far frae bowrdis, Bot leale, bot feale, may haell, avaell thy Grace. *c* **1575** *Balfour's Practicks* (1754) 243 Ane tenent..sould..say..Hear ze, my Lord, I sall be leill and feal to zou. **1603** J. SAVILE *Salut. Poem Jas. I* in Arb. *Garner* V. 636 France, and froward Ireland..Are feal subjects to your royal hand. **1706** PHILLIPS (ed. Kersey), *Feal*, the Tenants by Knights-Service us'd to swear to their Lord to be Feal and Leal, i.e. Faithful and Loyal. **1814** SCOTT *Wav.* xix, His right feal, trusty, and well-beloved cousin. **1827** —— *Jrnl.* (1890) II. 15 My old and feal friend James.

feal (fi:l), *v. north. dial.* Also 4–5 fele. [A northern and north midland word, a. ON. *fela* to hide, also to commit, commend = Goth. *filhan* to hide, bury:—OTeut. **felhan*, str. vb. (pret. *falh-*, pa. pple. **folgano-*). In ME. and mod. dialects always conjugated weak.

App. equivalent in form, though the relation in sense is obscure, are OE. *féolan* (*fealh*, *folgen*) to stick fast, to reach, attain, OHG. *felahan* to put together. The compound vb. OE. *bi-féolan* to entrust, commit, command, corresponds in form and sense to OFris. *bifella*, OS. *bifelhan* (Du. *bevelen*), OHG. *bifelahan* (MHG. *bevelhen*, mod.G. *befehlen*).]

trans. To hide, conceal.

c **1325** *Metr. Hom.* 3 In al thing es he nouht lele That Godes gift fra man will fele [printed *sele*]. *Ibid.* 12 For his [Christ's] Godhed in fleis was felid Als hok in bait. ? *a* **1400** *Morte Arth.* 3237 Thurghe that foreste I flede..ffor to fele me for ferde of tha foule thyngez. *c* **1460** *Towneley Myst.* 67 My counsellars so..No wyt from me ye fele. **1570** LEVINS *Manip.* 207/30 To Feale, *velare, abscondere.* **1664** *Flodden F.* VII. 1899 The smothering smoak the light so feald, That neither Army other saw. **1674** RAY *N.C. Words* (1691) 17 He that feals can find. **1721–1800** in BAILEY. **1873** in *Swaledale Gloss.*

feal, var. of FAIL *sb.*¹, q.v. Chiefly in the law-phrase *feal and divot*: see DIVOT.

feald. *dial.* [? var. of FOLD; cf. FAD, FAWD.] A bundle of straw.

? **14..** *Carle of Carlile* 239 in *Sir Gawayne* (1839) 264 Had itt not beene for a feald of straw Kayes backe had gone in 2.

feale, obs. form of FEEL.

fealty ('fi:əltɪ). Forms: 4–6 feaute, (5 feauty, 6 feautie), 4–5 feute(e, 4–6 fewt(e(e, (5 fewthe, fewtye), 4–7 fealtie, -ye, (5 fealtee, feaulte, 6 -ie), 6- fealty. [ad. OF. *feaute*, *feaulte*, *fealte* = Pr. *fealtad*, *fedeltat*:—L. *fidēlitāt-em*, f. *fidēlis* faithful, f. *fidēs* FAITH.]

1. The obligation of fidelity on the part of a feudal tenant or vassal to his lord.

1375 BARBOUR *Bruce* I. 427 Schir byschop..Gyff thow wald kep thi fewte Thou maid nane sic speking to me. *c* **1460** J. RUSSELL *Bk. Nurture* 1204 þey haue knowleche of homages, seruice, and fewte. **1587** FLEMING *Contn. Holinshed* III. 1362/1 From all debt or dutie of fealtie. **1593** SHAKS. *Rich. II*, V. ii. 45, I am..pledge for his..fealtie to the new-made King. **1765** BLACKSTONE *Comm.* I. 367 This obligation on the part of the vasal was called his *fidelitas* or fealty. **1814** SCOTT *Ld. of Isles* III. viii, Each bent the knee To Bruce in sign of fealty. **1842** TENNYSON *Morte D'Arthur* 75 Not rendering true answer, as beseem'd Thy fëalty.

2. The recognition of this obligation (see quot. 1635). Also *pl.* Frequent in phrases *to do*, *make*, *receive*, *swear*, etc. *fealty*.

c **1300** *K. Alis.* 2911 Alle heo duden him feuté. *c* **1330** R. BRUNNE *Chron.* (1810) 3 Ine toke his feaute of alle þat lond helde. **1387** TREVISA *Higden* (Rolls) VII. 95 To whom [Swane] þe men..þat dwelled at þe norþ side of Watlyng strete gefen ostage and sworen feutee. *c* **1400** *Ywaine & Gaw.* 3762 Sho sal hald hir land of the, And to the tharfor mak fewte. **1475** *Bk. Noblesse* 38 Prince Edwarde..received theire homages and feutees..in the name of King Edwarde .iij^d. *c* **1489** CAXTON *Sonnes of Aymon* xxvi. 571 They of the londe receyved him to be their lorde & made to him fewt & homage. **1523** FITZHERB. *Surv.* 12 These tenauntes maye holde their landes by..fealtie. **1533–4** *Act 25 Hen. VIII*, c. 20 §5 Making..othe & feautie only to the kinges maiestie. **1614** RALEIGH *Hist. World* II. 416 Solomon..received fealtie of all the Princes and People of the Land. *a* **1626** BACON *Max. & Uses Com. Law* (1635) 32 Fealty is to take an oath upon a book, that hee will bee a faithfull Tenant to the King. **1682** BURNET *Rights Princes* v. 149 The Bishops were also obliged to swear fealty to the Prince. **1855** MILMAN *Lat. Chr.* (1864) IV. VII. ii. 58 Where there was no fealty there could be no treason. **1862** LD. BROUGHAM *Brit. Const.* xi. 146 The vassal swore to his baron fealty absolutely.

attrib. **1851** SIR F. PALGRAVE *Norm. & Eng.* I. 359 Henceforward, though *Lotharius Imperator* might appear in Charter or Diploma and the fealty-form be preserved to him, his sovereignty in Italy was gone.

3. *transf.* and *fig.*

c **1530** *Hickscorner* in Hazl. *Dodsley* I. 173 We all to him [God] owe fealty and service. *a* **1536** *Calisto & Melibæa* ibid. I. 54 The more to God ought I to do fealty. **1591** SHAKS. *Two Gent.* II. iv. 91 Be-like that now she hath enfranchis'd them Vpon some other pawne for fealty. **1667** MILTON *P.L.* III. 204 Man disobeying Disloyal breaks his fealtie. **1681–6** J. SCOTT *Chr. Life* (1747) III. 276 The Church..makes a visible Profession of Fealty to him. **1717** E. FENTON *Homer Odyss.* XI. in *Poems* 94 Studious to win your Consort, and seduce Her from chaste Fealty to Joys impure. **1866** FELTON *Anc. & Mod. Gr.* I. v. 82 The most advanced minds acknowledged their fealty to the old master [Homer].

feam, Sc. var. of FOAM.

feamality: see FEM-.

feance, obs. form of FIANTS.

feane, obs. var. of FEIGN.

fear (fɪə(r)), *sb.*¹ Forms: 1 fǽr, fér, 3–6 fere, 3 fer, 4–5 feer(e, 6 *Sc.* feir, 5–7 feare, 7- fear. Also

2, 5 fore. [OE. *fǽr* (the rare southern ME. *fore* may represent a variant **fár*; cf. *swár = swǽr*) str. masc., sudden calamity, danger, corresponds to OS. *fâr* ambush (MDu. *vaer*), and except for the difference of declension to MDu. *vâre* fem. fear (cf. mod.Du. *gevaar* neut. danger), OHG. *fâra* fem. ambush, stratagem, danger (MHG. *vâre*; cf. MHG. *gevǽre* fem. and neut., mod.G. *gefahr* fem.), ON. *fár* neut. misfortune, plague; the sb. (:—OTeut. **fǽro-z, fǽro(m, fǽrâ*) is not recorded in Goth., which however has the derivative *fêrja* lier in wait.

The base *fǽr-* (:—pre-Teut. *pêr-*) is prob. one of the ablaut forms of the Aryan root *per* to go through (see FARE *v.*¹), but the genesis of the sense is not clear; the current comparison with Gr. πεῖρα, L. *periculum* trial, attempt, risk, seems to be misleading.]

† 1. In OE.: A sudden and terrible event; peril.

Beowulf 1068 Hie se fær beȝeat. *a* 1000 *Cædmon's Exod.* 452 (Gr.) Wæron Egypte eft oncyrde, fluȝon forhtiȝende, fær onȝeton.

2. a. The emotion of pain or uneasiness caused by the sense of impending danger, or by the prospect of some possible evil.

Now the general term for all degrees of the emotion; in early use applied to its more violent extremes, now denoted by *alarm, terror, fright, dread*. In 14th c. sometimes pleonastically *dread and fear*.

c 1175 *Lamb. Hom.* 97 Hi..wið-utan fore godes blisse bodedan. *c* 1290 *S. Eng. Leg.* I. 82/15 He ne bi-lefte for no fere. *c* 1340 *Cursor M.* 2914 (Trin.) Into þe felde he drouȝe for feer. **1398** TREVISA *Barth. De P.R.* XII. xxxiv. (1495) 434 The ostryche maye not see the horse wythout fere. *c* **1400** MAUNDEV. (Roxb.) xxxi. 140 Fals hert myght noȝt bere þe grete drede and fere þat þai had. **1490** CAXTON *Eneydos* xv. 61 O Jupyter, hast thou..determyned..to gyue vs tremoure and feere. **1562** J. HEYWOOD *Prov. & Epigr.* (1867) 9 Feare may force a man to cast beyonde the moone. **1588** A. KING tr. *Canisius' Catech.* 17 He..may..without al feir say [etc.]. **1611** BIBLE *Ex.* xv. 16 Feare and dread shall fall vpon them. **1671** MILTON *P.R.* III. 206 Where no hope is left, is left no fear. **1725** WATTS *Logic* I. VI. §12 We are in Danger of it [Passion], it raises our fear. **1776** GIBBON *Decl. & F.* I. 303 Fear has been the original parent of superstition. **1809-10** COLERIDGE *Friend* (1865) 107 A contract..might be entered into through fear. **1875** MANNING *Mission H. Ghost* x. 265 Fear without fortitude degenerates into timidity.

b. *personified.*

1590 SPENSER *F.Q.* III. xii. 12 Next him was Feare, all arm'd from top to toe. *a* **1650** MAY *Old Couple* II. (1658) 13 Then fear steps in, and tells me [etc.]. **1747** COLLINS *Ode Passions* 17 First Fear his hand..Amid the chords bewilder'd laid. **1817** COLERIDGE *Poems* 69 Pale Fear Haunted by ghastlier shapings.

c. An instance of the emotion; a particular apprehension of some future evil.

a **1616** BEAUM. & FL. *Knt. of Malta* II. v, Tender, and full of fears, our blushing sex is. **1701** DE FOE *True-born Eng.* 2 With needless Fears the..Nation fill. **1874** MORLEY *Compromise* (1886) 36 The old hopes have grown pale, the old fears dim. **1879** MISS BRADDON *Clov. Foot* ix, You need have no such fear.

d. A state of alarm or dread. Chiefly in phrase *in fear*; also, † *to put in* (a) *fear, to fall into fear*.

1297 R. GLOUC. (1724) 402 þo þe Saracens yt yeore, hii were somdel in fere. **1535** COVERDALE *Esther* xiv. 19 Delyuer me out of my feare. **1581** PETTIE *Guazzo's Civ. Conv.* III. (1586) 159 b, They..make it a sport to put their children in feare. **1623** BINGHAM *Xenophon* 13 They, and Menon himselfe, were put in a feare. **1653** HOLCROFT *Procopius* I. 17 The Barbarians..fell into feare and disorder. **1691** tr. *Emilianne's Frauds Romish Monks* 390 She continued..in deadly fears. **1736** BUTLER *Anal.* I. iii, This state of fear being itself often a very considerable punishment. **1771** MRS. GRIFFITHS tr. *Viaud's Shipwreck* 200, I set out forthwith..in fear and trembling.

3. This emotion viewed with regard to an object; the state of fearing (something).

a. Apprehension or dread of something that will or may happen in the future. Const. *of, to* with *inf.*; also with clause introduced by *that* or *lest*.

a **1300** *Body & Soul* 172 in *Map's Poems* [MS. Laud 108, fol. 200] Ne þorte us haue friȝt ne fer that God ne wolde his blisse us sent. **1538** STARKEY *England* I. ii. 43 He..for Fere of daungerys runnyth into a relygyous house. **1568** GRAFTON *Chron.* II. 355 They are ever in feare to lose that they have. **1647** CHAS. I *Let. in Antiquary* I. 97 The feare of your being brought within the power of the army. **1848** MACAULAY *Hist. Eng.* I. 459 The..king might..without any fear of opposition from England, proceed to annex Brabant. **1884** *Manch. Exam.* 20 May 5/2 The fears of a general crisis are passing away.

b. *esp.* in phrase *for fear*, where in mod. use the sense of the sb. is often weakened; thus *for fear of* = 'in order to avoid or prevent'; *for fear that* or *lest* (also *colloq.* with ellipsis of the conj.) = 'lest'.

When *fear* in these locutions is intended to have its full sense, *through* or *from* is now usually substituted for *for*.

c **1340** *Cursor M.* 1908 (Trin.) But ȝitt bode he seuen dayes in rest For fere lest any damnyng brest. *c* **1489** CAXTON *Sonnes of Aymon* xxii. 481 Wene ye that I shall do but ye saye for fere of deth? **1583** STUBBES *Anat. Abus.* II. (1882) 95 To depart..in the time of plague..for feare of infection. **1597** MONTGOMERIE *Cherrie & Slae* 360, I was affrayd to mount sa hich, For feir to get ane fall. **1600** HOLLAND *Livy* XLIX. Epit. (1609) 1238 To depart out of those quarters..for feare to bee murdered. **1678** *Trial of Ireland, Pickering, & Grove* in Howell *St. Trials* (1816) VII. 95 Grove would have had the bullets to be champt, for fear that [etc.]. **1693** DRYDEN *Juvenal* x. 534 Must we not Wish, for fear of wishing Ill? **1749** FIELDING *Tom Jones* XII. xi, It is good to

be charitable to those sort of people, for fear what may happen. **1791** 'G. GAMBADO' *Ann. Horsem.* ix. (1809) 104, I, for fear of the worst, took to my heels.

c. Apprehensive feeling towards anything regarded as a source of danger, or towards a person regarded as able to inflict injury or punishment.

1340-70 *Alex. & Dind.* 346 We ne haue fere of no fon þat faren wiþ-oute. **1382** WYCLIF *Gen.* ix. 2 And ȝoure feer..be vpon alle the beestis of erthe. *c* **1420** *Chron. Vilod.* 3295 For þe grete fore [*rime-word* euermore] þe whyche he had þo pere of þis virgyn Seynt Ede. *c* **1489** CAXTON *Sonnes of Aymon* iii. 80 But he could do none otherwyse, for feere of Charlemayn. **1600** J. PORY tr. *Leo's Africa* II. 9 He stood in feare of the people of Tunis. **1841** LANE *Arab. Nts.* I. 92, I have an enemy of whom I am in fear.

d. A mingled feeling of dread and reverence towards God (formerly also, towards any rightful authority).

Wyclif has always *drede* in this sense. The distinction between *servile* and *filial fear* (see quot. 1860), in Lat. *timor servilis, filialis*, is stated (as already generally current) by Thomas Aquinas, *Summa* II. II. xix.

c **1400** *Solomon's Bk. Wisdom* 42 Wite þi douttren with eye wel, þat þai haue of þe fere. **1535** COVERDALE *Ecclus.* ii. 6 Holde fast his feare, and growe therin. **1548-9** (Mar.) *Bk. Com. Prayer* 75 A perpetuall feare..of thy holy name. **1599** SHAKS. *Much Ado* II. iii. 200 He..vndertakes them with a most Christian-like feare. **1607** HIERON *Wks.* I. 130 There is a..slauish feare, and a sonlike feare. **1611** BIBLE *Ps.* cxi. 10 The feare of the Lord is the beginning of wise-dome. **1729** BUTLER *Serm.* Wks. 1874 II. 82 He is..under no other force..than the fear of God. **1851** RUSKIN *Mod. Paint.* II. III. I. xiv. §27 That sacred dread of all offence to him, which is called the Fear of God. **1860** PUSEY *Min. Proph.* 598 Fear is twofold; servile, whereby punishment, not fault, is dreaded; filial, by which fault is feared. **1875** MANNING *Mission H. Ghost* xi. 295 Holy fear is the beginning of the obedience of the Children of God.

e. Phrases: *to put* (occas. *rub*) *the fear of God into*, to terrify (into submission); *without fear or favour*, impartially.

1890 *Macm. Mag.* Jan. 230/2 Rub the fear of God into the people. **1905** H. G. WELLS *Let.* 13 Aug. in D. L. Moore *E. Nesbit* (1933) xii. 214 Bland might like to come over when Clodd is here, and help me put the fear of God into him. **1906** *Independent Rev.* X. 110 He [*sc.* Dr. Johnson] judged authors as if they were criminals in the dock, answerable for every infraction of the rules and regulations laid down by the laws of art, which it was his business to administer without fear or favour. **1930** A. BENNETT *Imperial Palace* 479 When she's my wife I'll put the fear of God into her. **1956** A. WILSON *Anglo-Saxon Att.* I. i. 4 If you have grievances..send your problems to John Middleton. He will investigate your case without fear or favour. **1959** *Punch* 16 Dec. 614/3 If I may say so without fear or favour. **1960** 'J. WYNDHAM' *Trouble with Lichen* III. ix. 119 We put the fear of God into the girls over that kind of thing.

4. Solicitude, anxiety for the safety of a person or thing. Also in phrase (*for, in*) *fear of one's life*.

1490 CAXTON *Eneydos* xlix. 142 He lept in to one of the shippes..for grete feer of his lyffe. **1580** SIDNEY *Arcadia* (1622) 68 Then care, not feare, or feare, not for themselues, altered..the countenances of the..Louers. **1611** BIBLE *2 Macc.* xv. 18 The..principall feare, was for the holy Temple. **1862** *Sat. Rev.* XIV. 569/2 At a later period, when wandering, in fear of his life, over Italy [etc.].

5. In various objective senses.

a. Ground or reason for alarm. Chiefly in phrase (*there is*) *no fear*; now often used as an exclamation. The usual sense of *no fear* is now 'not likely', 'certainly not'.

1535 COVERDALE *Ps.* liii[i]. 5 They are afrayed, where no feare is. **1634** MASSINGER *Very Woman* III. i, Give him but sage and butter..And there's no feare. **1699** W. HACKE *Collect. Orig. Voy.* IV. 7 No fear but they might get 2 or 3 thousand Dollards per man. **1800** [see PHO, PHON *int.*]. **1817** A. CONSTABLE *Let.* 25 Dec. in *J. Constable's Corr.* (1962) 167 Being very clean, and good temper'd, she hop'd there was no fear of her suiting you. **1861** *Times* 25 May, 'Is there any fear, Captain?' **1887** *Money Dutch Maiden* (1888) 338 He will never go hence..no fear. **1930** A. BENNETT *Imperial Palace* xii. 73, I invite you to dinner! And in his own hotel! No fear! **1966** J. B. PRIESTLEY *Salt is Leaving* xii. 172 No fear! I wouldn't be found dead in Birkden.

† b. Intimidation. *Obs.*

1426 in *Surtees Misc.* (1890) 8 Witht oute distresse or fere done to him.

† c. Capability of inspiring fear, formidableness.

1601 SHAKS. *Jul. C.* II. i. 190 There is no feare in him; let him not dye. **1654** GODDARD in *Introd. Burton's Diary* (1828) I. 46 Our wars will have much more reputation and fear, when..a whole nation will not consent to a war lightly.

† d. An object of fear; something that is, or is to be, feared. In the Bible occas. by a Hebraism, the object of (a person's) religious reverence, the God of (his) worship.

1535 COVERDALE *Prov.* x. 29 The waye of the Lorde..is a feare for wicked doers. **1561** DAUS tr. *Bullinger on Apoc.* (1573) 204 Therfore let God be our feare. **1607** HEYWOOD *Woman killed* Wks. 1874 II. 100 The rumor of this feare stretcht to my eares. **1611** BIBLE *Gen.* xxxi. 53 Iacob sware by the feare of his father Isaac. — *Prov.* i. 26, I wil mocke when your feare commeth. **1667** MILTON *P.L.* IX. 285 His [Satan's] fraud is then thy fear.

6. Comb. a. objective with adj. as *fear-free*; with pr. pple., as *fear-inspiring*; **b.** instrumental with pa. pples., as *fear-broken, -created, -depressed, -driven, -dulled, †-fled, -froze, -palsied, -pursued, -shaken, -shook, -smitten, -stirred, -stricken, -spurred,*

-surprised, -tangled, -taught; **fear-blast** *v.*, to blast (a person) with fear; **fear instinct**, the instinctive tendency to be afraid; **fear paroxysm**, a paroxysm caused by fear; **fear-struck, -strucken**, struck with or overwhelmed by fear; **fear-worship**, worship resulting from fear.

1593 NASHE *Four Lett. Confut.* 74, I *fearblaste thee.. with the winde of my weapon. **1647** FULLER *Good Th. in Worse T.* (1841) 106 Soldiers' hearts might be *fear-broken by the score of their sins who were no soldiers. **1777** POTTER *Æschylus* 190, Seven agst. Th.*, Is this a tale of *fear-created woe? **1597** DANIEL *Civ. Wars* II. x, *Fear-depressed envie. **1901** 'L. MALET' *Hist. R. Calmady* v. ix. 460 Some *fear-driven hurrying ghost. **1938** W. DE LA MARE *Memory* 9 The *fear-dulled eyes in the pallid face. **1611** SYLVESTER *Du Bartas* II. iv. III. *Schisme* 901 Each man hies Vnto the tents of *fear-fled Enemies. *a* **1679** EARL ORRERY *Guzman* 11 Cannot you give me another [charm] to make me *Fear-free? **1791** E. DARWIN *Bot. Gard.* I. 123 The demon.. Springs o'er the *fear-froze crew with Harpy-claws. **1812** CRABBE *Dumb Orators* Tales i, An awe-compelling frown, and *fear-inspiring size. **1904** W. M. GALLICHAN *Fishing Spain* xii. 118 Tragic dreams of this strange, fear-inspiring flood. **1908** W. MCDOUGALL *Introd. Soc. Psychol.* iv. 94 The *fear-instinct has..a special perceptual inlet that renders it excitable by the sound of the cry of fear. **1923** D. H. LAWRENCE *Kangaroo* xvi. 335 The herd instinct, for example, is of many sorts. It has two main divisions, the fear-instinct, and the aggressive instinct. **1811** SHELLEY *Let.* 11 Jan. (1964) I. 38 Wild horror the *fear-palsied Earth is astounding. **1842** SIR A. DE VERE *Song of Faith* 252 Fear-palsied, and his mind scarce half awake. **1890** W. JAMES *Princ. Psychol.* II. xxiv. 419 A certain amount of timidity obviously adapts us to the world we live in, but the *fear-paroxysm is surely altogether harmful to him who is its prey. **1798** SOTHEBY tr. *Wieland's Oberon* (1826) I. 53 Nor ceas'd the wight to scamper, *fear-pursu'd. **1625** K. LONG tr. *Barclay's Argenis* v. xvi. 381 Then came Selenissas death.. into his *feare-shaken mind. *a* **1756** COLLINS *Ode on Highlands* 119 His *fear-shook limbs have lost their youthful force. **1870** BRYANT *Iliad* II. xvii. 190 Idomeneus, *fear-smitten, lashed The long-maned steeds. *c* **1626** *Dick of Devon* II. v. in Bullen *Old Pl.* II. 42 Some of the *feare-spurrd villaines Were overturnd by slaughter in their flight. **1921** W. DE LA MARE *Veil* 87 To the *fear-stirred heart And the ancient dread Of man. **1906** B. VON HUTTEN *What became of Pam* x. 176 The girl, *fear-stricken..knelt down. **1636** MASSINGER *Bashf. Lover* II. v, Let not..these thick woods give sanctuary to the *fear-stricken hares. **1776** MICKLE tr. *Camoens' Lusiad* 53 The Moors start, fear-struck, at the horrid sound. **1870** BRYANT *Iliad* II. xxi. 282 Fear-struck, yet hoping to avoid the doom. **1613** DRUMM. OF HAWTH. *Cypress Grove* Wks. (1711) 124 Why shouldst thou be *fear-strucken..for thy parting from..thy body. **1602** SHAKS. *Ham.* I. ii. 203 He walkt, By their opprest and *feare-surprized eyes. **1870** MORRIS *Earthly Par.* II. III. 149 His hope *fear-tangled..bound his eyes full fast. **1649** G. DANIEL *Trinarch., Hen. IV*, ccxl, The *feare-taught Politicks Evade the Force, by yeilding to the Power. **1849** H. MAYO *Truths Pop. Superst.* vi. 85 Somnambulism..has had no *fear-worship. **1865** *Proc. Amer. Phil. Soc.* X. 145 To learn the language of Fear-worship we must go back to the very beginning.

fear, *sb.*² = FIAR *sb.*

fear (fɪə(r)), *v.* Forms: 1 fǽran, 3 fǽren, *Orm.* fǽrenn, 3-6 fere, (4 fyre, 5 ferin, -yn, feyre), 3, 6 (*Sc.*) feir, 4-5 feer(e, 4-6 feare, (6 feair), 7 fare, 6- fear. [OE. *fǽran* (:—**fǽrjan*) wk. vb. to terrify, f. *fǽr* (see FEAR *sb.*¹); parallel derivatives in other Teut. langs., with senses varying according to those of the primary *sb.*, are OS. *fârôn* to lie in wait; MDu. *vaeren* to fear; OHG. *fârên*, to plot against, to lie in wait, to endeavour after (MHG. *vâren* in same senses, also, rarely, to fear); ON. *fǽra* to taunt, slight.]

I. 1. *trans.* To inspire with fear; to frighten. *Obs.* exc. *arch.* or *vulgar.*

c **1000** ÆLFRIC *Deut.* i. 18 þa bodan us færdon. *c* **1200** ORMIN 675 He wile himm færenn. *a* **1225** *Ancr. R.* 230 Auh heo neuede þo none leaue, bute one uort to affeóren [*v.r.* fearen] him. **1340** HAMPOLE *Pr. Consc.* 6429 For þe mynde of þam myght men feer. *c* **1400** *Sowdone Bab.* 59 Here Bugles boldely for to blowe, To fere the beestis. **1485** CAXTON *St. Wenefr.* 20, I sawe a vysyon whiche moche fered me. **1548** HALL *Chron.* 166 Women in Fraunce to feare their yong children, would crye, the Talbot commeth. **1593** SHAKS. *3 Hen. VI*, V. ii. 2 Warwicke was a Bugge that fear'd vs all. **1641** MAISTERTON *Serm.* 16 An old-wifes tale, fit for nothing but to fear fools. *c* **1665** *Roxb. Ball.* VII. 524 Our King must have Seamen..most stout His enemies' hearts for to fear. **1801** MACNEILL *Poet. Wks.* (1844) 46 If thy slumber's sweet..no dangers can fear me. **1820** KEATS *Isabella* viii, I would not..fear Thine eyes by gazing. **1872** LEVER *Ld. Kilgobbin* xviii, Devil fear her!

† b. *it fears me*: = I am afraid. *Obs.*

1503 HAWES *Examp. Virt.* Prol. 2 It fereth me sore for to endyte. **1646** *Burd. Issach. in Phenix* (1708) II. 287 It feareth me besides, that God is punishing our present Sins. **1813** HOGG *Queen's Wake* 67 It fearis me muckil ye haif seen Quhat good man never knew.

2. With pregnant sense.

† a. To drive away by fear, frighten away, scare (*esp.* birds or animals). Chiefly with *away*. *Obs.*

c **1420** *Pallad. on Husb.* I. 147 Eddres to sleyn & foules oute to fere is. **1504** ATKYNSON tr. *De Imitatione* III. xxxvii, Fere away the euyll bestes. **1577** NORTHBROOKE *Dicing* (1579) 45 b, If there were nothing else to feare them away from this play. **1603** SHAKS. *Meas. for M.* II. i. 2 A scar-crow..to feare the Birds of prey. **1613** DENNYS *Secrets of Angling* II. in Arb. Garner I. 174 There some great fish doth fear the rest away. **1614** RALEIGH *Hist. World* II. IV. ii. §7. 152 A Swallow flew about his head..and could not be feared from him. *a* **1631**

DONNE *The Storm* 52 Wks. 1873 II. 5 Some..would seeme there, With hydeous gazinge, to feare away Feare.

†**b.** To deter from a course of conduct, etc. Const. *from*; also occas. followed by *that...not*.

c **1380** WYCLIF *Wks.* (1880) 109 (*title*) *Speculum de Antichristo*, Hou anticrist & his clerkis feren trewe prestis fro prechynge of cristis gospel. **1393** LANGLAND *P. Pl.* C. XVIII. 285 Eueriche busshope..sholde... Feden hem [hus peple]..and fere hem fro synne. **1530** TINDALE *Gen.* Prol. Wks. I. 399 The ensamples..are written to fear the flesh, that we sin not. **1531** FRITH *Judgm. Tracy* 251 He doth..fear us from putting any confidence in our own works. **1539** TAVERNER *Erasm. Prov.* (1552) 3 To feare hym that he..shulde not prouoke S. Hierom. **1583** BABINGTON *Commandm.* (1588) 135 Shall it not feare vs from so foule a custome? *a* **1632** T. TAYLOR *God's Judgem.* I. I. v. (1642) 184 Their example feared not the Cornishmen from rebelling.

†**c.** To drive by fear *to*, *into*. *Obs.*

1563 FOXE *A. & M.* 788a, It should somwhat touche them to be sene by werynes of pryson to feare him to it. **1646** J. HALL *Poems* I. 68 Nor will I..Lillies feare Into a Iandise.

II. To feel fear; to regard with fear.

3. *refl.* (cf. 1 b) To be afraid. †Formerly const. *of*. Now only *arch.* in phrase *I fear me*.

1393 GOWER *Conf.* I. 294 (Fairfax MS.) So lowde his belle is runge..That of þe noise..Men feeren hem..Welmore þan þei don of þonder. **1530** PALSGR. 547/2, I feared me alwayes that it wolde be so. **1590** MARLOWE *Edw. II*, II. iv, I fear me he is slain. **1608** S. WARD in *Abp. Ussher's Lett.* (1686) 26, I fear me, he will hardly get Copies. **1856** R. A. VAUGHAN *Mystics* (1860) I. 167, I fear me that..some..earthly love mingles with his friendship. **1859** TENNYSON *Lancelot & Elaine* 966 A flash, I fear me, that will strike my blossom dead.

4. *intr.* in same sense.

†**a.** *to fear of* (rarely *at*): = sense 5.

c **1400** *Destr. Troy* 1929 We fors not his frendship, ne fere of his hate. **1509** BARCLAY *Shyp of Folys* (1874) I. 173 He or she that mariage doth breke May fere of deth eternall whan they dye. *c* **1600** SHAKS. *Sonn.* cxv, Fearing of love's tyranny. **1606** G. W[OODCOCKE] tr. *Hist. Ivstine* 97a, The men..which feared not at the command of King Phillip.

b. with dependent clause: To feel alarmed or uneasy *lest* (something should happen).

(Closely approaching the trans. use with clause; cf. 7b.)

c **1489** CAXTON *Sonnes of Aymon* xx. 455 He feered sore leste Reynawde sholde make to deye rychard of normandy. **1559** W. CUNNINGHAM *Cosmogr. Glasse* 38, I ever feare lest th' Earth..should fall to the other part of the Heavens. **1691** tr. *Emilianne's Obs. Journ. Naples* 135 Fearing lest some Insurrection might be caus'd. **1823** F. CLISSOLD *Asc. Mt. Blanc* 20, I..feared lest I should drop down.

c. *simply*. (Blends with the absol. use of senses 5 and 7.) Phrase (colloq.), ***never fear***: = 'there's no danger of that'.

1588 SHAKS. *L.L.L.* I. ii. 108 If she fear..By this [pale white cheekes] you shall not know. *c* **1590** MARLOWE *Faust.* Wks. (Rtldg.) 100/1 'Tis but a surfeit; never fear, man. **1611** BIBLE *Gen.* l. 19 And Ioseph saide vnto them, Feare not. **1651** HOBBES *Govt. & Soc.* i. §2. 7 To..take heed, provide so that they may not fear. **1798** COLERIDGE *Anc. Mar.* IV. ii, Fear not thou wedding guest! **1800** COGAN *Philos. Treat. Passions* I. ii. (1802) 102 As soon as we cease to fear, we begin to hope. **1838** LYTTON *Lady of Lyons* II. i, I'll find the occasion, never fear! **1888** MRS. PARR *Runaways* in *Longm. Mag.* Apr. 640 I'm not going to blab on myself—never fear! **1893** MORLEY in *Westm. Gaz.* 19 Apr. 3/2 Those only see aright into the future of civilised communities who hope—not those who fear.

5. *trans.* To regard with fear, be afraid of (a person or thing as a source of danger, an anticipated event or state of things as painful or evil).

c **1460** FORTESCUE *Abs. & Lim. Mon.* x, Ther shulde non off hem growe to be like vnto hym; wich thynge is most to be fered of all þe worlde. **1477** EARL RIVERS (Caxton) *Dictes* 97 Thoo that sawe not yesterday Alexander ferede him gretely, and now thoo that see him fereth him not. **1530** PALSGR. 547/2 He feareth me above all the men lyvynge. **1563** GOLDING *Cæsar* 30b, They feared not the enemy, but the narrownes of the wais. **1611** BIBLE *2 Esdras* xii. 13 It shall be feared aboue all the kingdomes that were before it. *a* **1618** RALEIGH *Rem.* (1664) 116 To fear the losse of the bell, more than the losse of the steeple. **1667** MILTON *P.L.* IX. 282 His violence thou fearst not. **1697** DRYDEN *Æn.* x. 1261 Nor Fate I fear, but all the Gods defy. **1841** LANE *Arab. Nts.* I. 92 Every..person whom thou fearest. **1885** CLODD *Myths & Dr.* II. iii. 155 What man cannot understand he fears.

transf. *c* **1489** CAXTON *Sonnes of Aymon* vi. 149 It [y^e castell] fered no sawtyng on no side of it.

b. with *inf.* (*vbl. sb.*, etc.) as object: To hesitate (*to* do something) through fear of the consequences; †*to fear offence* = to fear to offend.

1603 FLORIO *Montaigne* 563 As if he feared to attediate..us. **1700** DRYDEN *Cymon & Iphig.* 114 He..would have spoke, but..found his want of Words, and fear'd Offence. **1794** MRS. RADCLIFFE *Myst. Udolpho* xliv, Dorothee..feared to obey. **1799** tr. *Diderot's Natural Sin* ii. 26 You feared disturbing our tranquillity.

6. To regard with reverence and awe; to revere. Now only with *God* as obj.; formerly in wider sense.

a **1400** *Prymer* (1891) 101 Gretly is thi word fyred. **1526** TINDALE *Eph.* v. 33 Lett the wyfe see that she feare her husbande. **1593** SHAKS. *Rich. II*, II. i. 52 This..Wombe of Royall Kings, Fear'd by their breed. **1611** BIBLE *Ps.* ciii. 13 The Lord pitieth them that feare him. **1715** DE FOE *Fam. Instruct.* I. i. (1841) I. 10 If you fear God..as your father. **1827** POLLOK *Course T.* IV. 135 Who..feared nought but God.

7. To have an uneasy sense of the probability of (some unwelcome occurrence in the future); to apprehend. Opposed to *hope for*.

1597 SHAKS. *2 Hen. IV*, I. i. 87 He that but feares the thing, he would not know Hath..knowledge from others eyes, That what he feard, is chanc'd. **1759** JOHNSON *Rasselas* xxviii, If they have less to fear, they have less also to hope. **1861** M. PATTISON *Ess.* (1889) I. 47 London had ceased to fear a foreign foe.

b. with *subord. clause.* To be afraid *that* (something will be or is the case). In negative sentences the clause may be introduced by *but* or *but that* = that..not. Also with direct obj. and *to be* or simple complement; *rarely*, with *inf.* as *obj.* Also *parenthetically*.

1526 *Pilgr. Perf.* (W. de W. 1531) 16b, I feare sore that many chrysten people..do as the chyldren of Israel dyd. *a* **1533** LD. BERNERS *Huon* lxi. 212 Fere not but ye shalbe wel payed. **1593** SHAKS. *3 Hen. VI*, V. vi. 12 The Theefe doth feare each bush an Officer. **1638** BAKER tr. *Balzac's Lett.* I. 25 Never feare that I will impaire his ill nights. **1658–9** *Burton's Diary* (1828) IV. 47, I fear they are troubled with King's evil. **1667** MILTON *P.L.* I. 628 What power of mind..could have fear'd, How such united force of Gods..could ever know repulse. **1692** tr. *Zingis* 11 He feared with reason to be unable to do any thing for Zingis. **1726** *Adv. Capt. R. Boyle* 47, I fear'd it would be..two hundred Pounds. **1771** MRS. GRIFFITH tr. *Viaud's Shipwreck* 255, I fear much that of the sixteen persons..three only of us have survived. **1848** MACAULAY *Hist. Eng.* II. 225 He might do so without fearing that the Five Mile Act would be enforced. **1857** TROLLOPE *Three Clerks* v, I fear we are all in your black books. **1863** FR. A. KEMBLE *Resid. in Georgia* 16 The account..will hardly, I fear, render my letters very interesting.

8. a. †*trans.* (Perh. originally const. *dat.*: cf. L. *timere alicui*). To be apprehensive about, to fear something happening to (*obs.*). **b.** In same sense *intr.*; const. *for*, †*of*.

1526 TINDALE *Gal.* iv. 11, I feare off you, lest I have bestowed on you laboure in vayne. *c* **1530** LD. BERNERS *Arth. Lyt. Bryt.* (1814) 213 Arthur fered his horse, lest that the lyon shokle haue slayne hym. **1594** SHAKS. *Rich. III*, I. i. 137 His Physitians feare him mightily. **1611** TOURNEUR *Ath. Trag.* V. i, If any roote of life remaines within 'em..feare 'em not. **1651** N. BACON *Disc. Govt. Eng.* II. i. (1739) 6 The people..feared their own Free-holds. **1686** DRYDEN *Horace* I. xxix. 10 Let the greedy merchant fear For his ill-gotten gain. **1695** PRIOR *Ode death Q. Mary* 47 So much she fears for William's life. **1841** LANE *Arab. Nts.* I. 11, I fear for thee that the same will befal thee. **1853** KANE *Grinnell Exp.* xxxiii. (1856) 284 *note*, We feared for his recovery.

†**c.** In 18th c., when the vb. was conjugated negatively, a following negative was often illogically omitted, so that the vb. seems to mean: To apprehend the non-occurrence of (some event).

a **1699** STILLINGFL. *Serm.* Wks. 1710 I. 619 We need not fear a gracious answer. **1747** S. FIELDING *Lett. David Simple* I. ii. 63, I liked him, and was so accustomed to the Addresses of every Man by whom I was seen, that I did not at all fear his immediately becoming one of my Train. **1771** T. HULL *Sir W. Harrington* (1797) IV. 211 If I apply for it, I don't fear its being granted.

†**9.** To regard with distrust; to doubt. *Obs.*

1578 T. N. tr. *Conq. W. India* 16 The governour feared the wisedome and courage of his kinsman. **1607** TOPSELL *Serpents* (1653) 681 If a bird it tast..It dies assured death, none need it fear. **1730–6** BAILEY (folio), *Fear*..to doubt or question.

fear(e, var. of FERE, *Obs.*, and of FEIR, *Obs. Sc.*

fearable ('fɪərəb(ə)l), *a. rare.* [f. FEAR *sb.*¹ + -ABLE.] Giving cause for fear; to be feared.

1886 B. W. RICHARDSON in *Asclepiad* III. 187 Is virus from a poisoned animal less fearable?

†**fear-babe.** *Obs.* Also 7 *erron.* **fairybabe.** [f. FEAR *v.* + BABE.] A thing fit only to frighten a baby. Cf. SCAREBABE.

1580 SIDNEY *Arcadia* (1622) 299 As for their shewes & words, they are but feare babes. **1621** BURTON *Anat. Mel.* I. iii. II. ii, All the bugbeares of the night, and terrors and fairybabes of tombes..are before their eyes.

feard, feare, obs. Sc. ff. of FARD *v.*, FARE.

feared (fɪəd), *ppl. a.* Forms: 3–6 fer(e)d, (3 ferid, 5 fard, feerd, 6 *Sc.* feired, ferit), 4–6 ferde, 5–7 feard, (4, 6 *comp.* and *superl.* fearder, -est), 8– *dial.* feart, 6– feared. [f. FEAR *v.* + -ED¹.]

†**1.** Affected with fear, frightened, afraid; timid. Const. *of, for*, indicating either the cause of fear, or less frequently (= about) the object of concern; with *inf.* = afraid *to* (do something). *Obs.* exc. *dial.*

a **1300** *Cursor M.* 1834 (Gött.) [þai] war nohut fered of his manace. *c* **1330** R. BRUNNE *Chron. Wace* (Rolls) 1998 Of þeym boþe was he nought ferd. *c* **1340** *Cursor M.* 2423 (Fairf.) þe kinge was ferde for goddis grame. *c* **1380** WYCLIF *Sel. Wks.* III. 394 Puple wolde be ferde to dwelle in his servise. *c* **1386** CHAUCER *Nun's Pr. T.* 566 The veray hogges So fered were for berking of the dogges. *c* **1400** *Ywaine & Gaw.* 2566 Whoso es ferd i rede he fle. *c* **1400** *Destr. Troy* 13842 The..kyng [was] of his lyf feerd. *c* **1449** PECOCK *Repr.* 550 So..Ferd forto trespace. *c* **1450** LONELICH *Grail* lv. 450 The swerd, Of whiche many men was aftyr ferd. **14**..*Chester Pl.* (1847) II. 91 Fearder I never was. **1534** MORE *On the Passion* Wks. 1322/1 That passyon..of which he was so ferd. **1578** *Ps.* cxxviii. in *Gude & G. Ball.* 113 Of thy hand labour thow sall eit, be not feird. *a* **1605** POLWART *Flyting w. Montgomerie* 788 Feard flyar..I sall dunt whill I slay thee. **1650** BAXTER *Saints' R.* III. xiii. (1662) 506 Conscience grows feared. **1698** LISTER in *Phil. Trans.* XX. 247 They..would have cropen away in a feared manner. **1715** *Wodrow Corr.* (1843) II. 67 A few such feared fools, as I am reckoned hereabout. **1812** H. & J. SMITH *Rej. Addr.* ix. (1873) 84 What are they fear'd on? **1816** SCOTT *Antiq.* xxxix, 'I'm maist fear'd to speak to him.' **1828** HOOD *Lamia* iii. 40 Jove! I was feared. **1869** C. GIBBON *R. Gray* iii, 'You'll no be feart to sail on a Friday.' **1891** E. ARNOLD *Lt. of World* 82 Thyself More feared of Cæsar than of wrongfulness.

†**2.** Apprehensive, having an uneasy foreboding. Chiefly with clause introduced by *lest* or *that*; rarely const. *to* with *inf. Obs.* exc. *dial.*

1440 *Plumpton Corr.* 155 He is feard lest they wyll not appeare without a suppena. *c* **1450** *Merlin* 27 He was ferde to lese his londe. *c* **1460** *Towneley Myst.* (Surtees) 116, I am fulle fard that we tary to lang. *a* **1535** MORE *Sargeant & Frere* 233 in Hazl. *E.P.P.* III. 127 Yet was this man well fearder than, lest he the frier had slaine. **1884** J. PURVES in *Gd. Words* Nov. 767/1 'Wives are feared a man gets another sweetheart in six months' time away fra' hame.'

3. In senses of FEAR *v.* 5 and 7: Regarded with fear; anticipated or suspected with uneasiness; †apprehensively supposed to be such.

1599 SANDYS *Europæ Spec.* (1632) 74 Their professed and feared Enemies. *a* **1618** RALEIGH *Prerog. Parl.* Ep. Ded. (1628) 2 The fear'd continuance of the like abuse. **1663** J. SPENCER *Prodigies* (1665) 83 Addresses to divert a feared..displeasure of the Deity. **1719** *Wodrow Corr.* (1843) II. 451 The feared stand the success of the gospel is at. **1762** FALCONER *Shipwr.* II. 380 Pondering in their minds each fear'd event. **1890** *Daily News* 8 Sept. 6/7 Feared loss of a Liverpool ship.

Hence †'**fearedly** *adv.*, fearfully, timidly.

c **1470** HENRY *Wallace* VII. 255 Ferdly scho ast, 'Allace! quhar is Wallace?'

†'**fearedness.** *Obs.* Also 3–5 **ferd(e)nes(s(e**, (3 **feredness**, 4 **ferdnis**, 6 *Sc.* **feirdnes**). [f. prec. + -NESS.] The condition of being frightened or afraid; terror, fear. Also, *rarely*, a cause of fright.

a **1300** *Cursor M.* 3996 (Gött.) Man þat þu wil helpe in nede, Ne thar him neuer na ferednes drede. **1340** HAMPOLE *Pr. Consc.* 2231 Hym in-to wanhope for to bring..thurgh þe ferdnes þat he sal tak. *c* **1400** MAUNDEV. (Roxb.) xxxi. 139 We ware mare deuote..for ferdeness of deuils þat appered till vs. *c* **1450** tr. *Girald. Hist. Ireland* 10 The slaght of þese fewe be ferdenesse to many. *c* **1450** HENRYSON *Mor. Fab.* 83 Hee for fearednesse hes fyled vp the way. **1488** CAXTON *Chast. Goddes Chyld.* 18 Horryble sightes and dredefull ferdnes of wycked spirytes come to some.

fearely, var. of FERLY *a. Obs.*, strange.

fearer ('fɪərə(r)). [f. FEAR *v.* + -ER¹.] One who fears.

1535 COVERDALE *John* ix. 31 Yf eny man be a fearer of God..him heareth he. *a* **1601** C'TESS PEMBROKE *Ps.* cxix. H, With thy fearers all I hold, Such as hold thy biddings best. **1630** *R. Johnson's Kingd. & Commw.* A iij, The Italians..are fearers of the Spanish greatnesse. **1814** SOUTHEY *Lett.* (1856) II. 350 Calvert was a great fearer..all through the contest. **1844** WARDLAW *Lect. on Prov.* (1869) I. 25 The true fearers of God are sadly in the minority.

fearful ('fɪəfʊl), *a.* Forms: 4–5 ferful(l, (4 fervol), 4–6 fereful(l, feerful(l, 4–7 fearefull, 6–7 fearfull(e, 6– fearful. [f. as prec. + -FUL.]

I. *objectively.*

1. Causing fear; inspiring terror, reverence, or awe; dreadful, terrible, awful.

1340–70 *Alisaunder* 291 þei lete flie to þe flocke ferefull sondes. **1382** WYCLIF *Gen.* xxviii. 17 And [Iacob] dredynge seide, Howe feerful is this place! *c* **1400** *Destr. Troy* 7731 This feerfull freike frusshet into batell. **1461** *Paston Lett.* No. 400 II. 25 She shuld be..put in ferfull place, in shortyng of hyr lyve dayes. *a* **1533** LD. BERNERS *Huon* xlii. 140 When he was in dyspleasure, he had a fearfull chere. **1563** W. FULKE *Meteors* (1640) 10b, A flying Dragon..very fearefull to looke upon. **1611** BIBLE *Deut.* xxviii. 58 Feare this glorious and fearefull Name, the Lord Thy God. *a* **1694** TILLOTSON (J.), That fearful Punishment..shall be inflicted on them. **1741** RICHARDSON *Pamela* (1824) I. 98 My fearfullest danger! **1792** S. ROGERS *Pleas. Mem.* I. 43 At midnight's fearful hour. **1848** W. H. KELLY tr. *L. Blanc's Hist. Ten Y.* II. 90 M. de Choulot..made him take a..fearful oath.

†**b.** Const. *to, unto.*

1548 HALL *Chron.* 166 As his person was fearfull..to his adversaries present: so his name. **1625** PURCHAS *Pilgrims* II. 1475 They [Apes] are fearefull..to Birds that make their nests in Trees. **1658** CLEVELAND *Rustick Rampant* Wks. (1687) 418 A Glorious King, fearful to your Enemies.

c. *Comb.*; adverbially as in *fearful-sounding*.

1611 SYLVESTER *Du Bartas* II. iv. III. *Schisme* 1065 If thou their metall by that touch-stone try Which fearfull-sounding from thy mouth doth fly.

2. Applied to bad or annoying things in intensive sense. Cf. *awful, terrible, dreadful*, etc.

1634 SIR T. HERBERT *Trav.* 39 The..fearefull stench of the unburied bodies. **1811** LAMB *Guy Faux*, They make a fearful outcry against the violation of every principle of morality. **1860** TYNDALL *Glac.* I. xvi. 112 He complained of fearful thirst. **1884** *Christian Commw.* 21 Feb. 440/1 Their fearful departures from Apostolic practice.

b. *dial.* Enormous in quantity.

1877 *N.W. Lincolnsh. Gloss.*, 'There's a fearful lot o' apples t' year.'

c. *adv.* = FEARFULLY. *Obs.* in educated use; in some dialects merely intensive = AWFUL.

1634 SIR T. HERBERT *Trav.* 8 In Angola the people are fearfull blacke. **1790** MRS. WHEELER *Westmld. Dial.* (1821) 66 He leakt es if he wor fearful weel pleast. **1862** HAMERTON *Painter's Camp* I. 42 'You see theyve heard tell..'at there's a feefil 'ansome young chap.'

II. *subjectively.*

3. Frightened, timorous, timid, apprehensive.

a. *simply*. Now somewhat *rare*.

c1374 Chaucer *Troylus* II. 450 Criseyde..was þe ferfulleste wyght That myght be. 1398 Trevisa *Barth. De P.R.* XVIII. vi. (1495) 752 The female lambes ben..more ferefull than the male. c1489 Caxton *Sonnes of Aymon* xv. 361 'Ha, thef..how ferfull thou art now.' 1586 Marlowe *1st Pt. Tamburl.* I. ii, With their fearful tongues they shall confess. a1628 Sir J. Beaumont *Bosworth F.* 783 Gain thou some Hours to draw thy fearful Breath. 1653 Walton *Angler* 52 Chubs..be a very fearful fish. 1672 Dryden *Conq. Granada* II. I. ii, But now my fearful people mutiny. 1702 Addison *Dial. Medals* x. (1727) 45 Th' impatient Greyhound..Bounds..to catch the fearful Hare. 1773 Mrs. Chapone *Improv. Mind* (1774) I. 111 Women are more fearful than men. 1827 Keble *Chr. Year, 3rd Sunday in Lent*, It was a fearful joy..To trace the Heathen's toil. 1831 Mrs. Shelley *Swiss Peasant* in '*Keepsake*' 125 His fearful family would count in agony the hours of his absence.

absol. c1400 *Prymer* (E.E.T.S.) 30 Seynte marie..helpe feerful, and refresche þe soreuful.

b. Const. *of* (also *to* with inf.), or with clause introduced by *lest* or *that*.

c1360 *Vern. MS. Min. Poems* 524 Þe lattor þou art of good worching þe more feruol þou shalt be of bi-ginnyng. c1400 *Beryn* 2971 Beryn and his company wer..ferefull howe to spede. 1605 Shaks. *Lear* I. iv. 225, I..now grow fearefull..That you protect this course. 1612 Davies *Why Ireland, etc.* 270 The Irish are more fearefull to offend the Law. 1630 *Johnson's Kingd. & Commw.* 101 Somewhat fear-full of our desperate wanderers. 1665 Hooke *Microgr.* 207 As a man blindfolded would do his hands when he is fearfull of running against a wall. 1725 Pope *Odyss.* VI. 173 Fearful to offend..At awful distance he accosts the maid. 1791 Mrs. Radcliffe *Rom. Forest* x, Adeline was fearful of observation. 1798 Webbe in Owen *Wellesley's Desp.* 5, I am fearful that..an attack upon him now is more likely to end in discomfiture. 1827 Hallam *Const. Hist.* (1876) I. iv. 204 This great minister's knowledge of the queen's temper..made him sometimes fearful to act. 1850 Kingsley *Alt. Locke* i, She would have led me in a string..so fearful was she lest I should be polluted. 1879 Low *Afghan War* iii. 279 The Afghan chief, fearful of trying an assault, determined to invest the place.

†c. Anxious, concerned; with *about*, *of* indicating the object of anxiety or concern.

1535 Coverdale *1 Sam.* iv. 13 His herte was fearfull aboute ye Arke of God. 1590 Marlowe *2nd Pt. Tamburl.* III. v, Thou art fearful of thy army's strength. 1593 Shaks. *3 Hen. VI*, v. vi. 87 Edward shall be feareful of his life.

4. Of looks, words, etc.: Indicating or giving signs of fear or terror.

1535 Coverdale *2 Esdras* iii. 3, I beganne to speake fearfull wordes to the most hyest. 1594 Shaks. *Rich. III*, v. iii. 181 Cold fearefull drops stand on my trembling flesh. 1638 Chillingw. *Relig. Prot.* I. i. §7. 35 A wavering and fearful assent. 1791 Mrs. Radcliffe *Rom. Forest* ii, Adeline..threw a fearful glance around. 1814 Southey *Roderick* XIII. 119 Hasty, yet faltering in his fearful speech.

†5. Cautious, wary. *Obs.*

1526 *Pilgr. Perf.* (W. de W. 1531) 56 Fearefull in prosperytees and pacyent in aduersytees. 1640 Bp. Reynolds *Passions* ix, It is fit that..considering the deceitfulnesse of things..we should bring a fearful judgement. 1781 Gibbon *Decl. & F.* III. xlviii. 58 The march of the reinforcement was tardy and fearful. 1791 Burke *App. Whigs* Wks. VI. 98 Our courts cannot be more fearful..than prudent.

6. Full of awe or reverence.

1597 Hooker *Eccl. Pol.* v. lxvii. (1611) 359 A kinde of fearefull admiration at the heauen. 1602 F. Davison in Farr *S.P. Eliz.* (1845) II. 323 That I to thy name may beare Fearfull loue. 1879 Farrar *St. Paul* (1883) 332 Paul saw in him the spirit of loving and fearful duty.

fearfully ('fɪəfʊlɪ), *adv.* [f. prec. + -ly^2.]

I. *objectively*: With communication of fear.

1. So as to cause fear; dreadfully; terribly.

1526 *Pilgr. Perf.* (W. de W. 1531) 245 b, The..impenitent synners..be..drawen downe to hell moost terribly or feerfully. 1586 Cogan *Haven Health* ccxli. (1636) 272 That hee bee not waked sodainely and fearefully. 1605 Shaks. *Lear* IV. i. 77 There is a Cliffe, whose..bending head Lookes fearfully in the confined Deepe. 1641 Hinde *J. Bruen* xlvi. 148 This wicked fellow..within three dayes died most fearefully. 1821 Shelley *Adonais* lv, I am borne darkly, fearfully, afar. 1828 Scott *F.M. Perth* xxv, I was yesterday fearfully undeceived.

2. To a fearful extent or degree. Often hyperbolically as a mere intensive: cf. fearful 2.

1835 Dickens *Let.* 16 Dec. (1965) I. 106 This place is fearfully dull, and I have seen neither a newspaper or a book since I came down here. 1838 —— *Nich. Nick.* ii, Smoking fearfully. 1862 Sir B. Brodie *Psychol. Inq.* II. iii. 95 The evils arising from the use of alcohol have been fearfully aggravated by the invention of distillation. 1878 Smiles *Robt. Dick* vii. 76 It was fearfully warm. 1878 Mrs. H. Wood *Pomeroy Ab.* I. 25 Dinner? that's right, I am fearfully hungry.

II. *subjectively*: With a feeling of fear.

3. In a manner indicating fear; timidly, in fear.

1548 Udall, etc. *Erasm. Par. Matt.* iii. 7 They demaunde of him fearfully what he thinketh best for them to do. 1602 Marston *Antonio's Rev.* v. iii, I might observe The graver statesmen whispering fearefully. 1658 Cleveland *Rustic Rampant* Wks. (1687) 501 The Abbot..fearfully summons in his Friends to guard him. 1730 Wesley *Wks.* (1830) I. 8 Walk as prudently as you can, though not fearfully. 1832 Marryat *N. Forster* xix, A black head was seen to rise..fearfully out of the fore-scuttle.

†4. a. In a state of apprehension or uneasiness; anxiously. b. Cautiously, with hesitation. *Obs.*

1586 A. Day *Eng. Secretary* II. (1625) 28 This pure living (once in manner lost, afterwards recovered and yet stil fearefully kept). 1598 Barret *Theor. Warres* v. i. 147 Whosoeuer shall..march slow or fearefully. c1610 Sir J. Melvil *Mem.* (1683) 18 The Spaniards..compelled our foot to retire fearfully. 1727 Bradley *Fam. Dict.* s.v. *Hunt*, His old Hounds..will hunt leisurely and fearfully.

fearfulness ('fɪəfʊlnɪs). [f. as prec. + -ness.]

1. The quality of inspiring fear; dreadfulness.

1535 Coverdale *2 Macc.* xv. 23 Sende now also thy good angell before vs (o Lorde) in the fearfulnesse..of thy mightie arme. 1585 T. Washington tr. *Nicholay's Voy. Turkie* II. xv. 50 A great Earthquake..with horrible fearfulnesse and damage. 1831 Pote *Assassins of Paradise* 18 Its very fearfulness the sound endeared. 1846 Trench *Mirac.* xxix. (1862) 410 He beheld death in all its fearfulness.

2. The quality or state of being affected with fear; timidity, timorousness. Const. *of*.

1494 Fabyan *Chron.* VI. clxxxi. 180 The lordes..went vnto the kynge..and blamed as they durste his ferefulnesse. 1535 Coverdale *Ezek.* xxx. 13 A fearfulnesse will I sende in to the Egipcians londe. 1562 Turner *Baths* 8 These bathes..are good for fearfulnes of the hart. 1597 Hooker *Eccl. Pol.* v. §47 Is it credible that..our professed fearefulness to ask anything..should be noted for a popish error. 1651 Davenant *Gondibert* III. I. 232 With a Lover's fearfulness he spake. 1666 South *Serm.* 25 Nov., A third thing..is fearfulness of..bold, popular offenders. 1727 Swift *Gulliver* II. iii. 125, I was frequently rallied..on account of my fearfulness. 1841 Myers *Cath. Th.* IV. §46. 411 We cannot but be protected from all fearfulness of spiritual despotism.

fearing ('fɪərɪŋ), *vbl. sb.* [f. fear *v.* + -ing^1.] The action of the vb. fear. a. The being in fear or dread, †an instance of this. †*to have in fearing*: to be in dread of. b. The action of distrusting or doubting; †an instance of this.

In the Lancashire dialect used *collect.* for ghosts, fairies, goblins, etc. By dialect writers spelt *fe(e)orin.*

1562 J. Heywood *Prov. & Epigr.* (1867) 44 Decaie of cleane sweepyng folke had in fearyng. 1633 P. Fletcher *Purple Isl.* VIII. x. 109 Sending often back his doubtfull eye By fearing taught unthought of treacherie. a1662 Heylin *Laud* (1668) I. 113 Long he had not been in Spain, when there were many fearings of him in the Court of England. 1682 N. O. *Boileau's Lutrin* III. 126 Poor Hobhowchin puts you in this fearing.

fearing ('fɪərɪŋ), *ppl. a.* [f. as prec. + -ing^2.] That fears; often in comb. with prefixed object, as in *ghost-*, *God-fearing*: see the sbs.

1837 Ht. Martineau *Soc. Amer.* III. 14 The aristocratic is..the fearing, while the democratic is the hoping, party.

Hence '**fearingly** *adv.*, †(*a*) in a terrifying manner (*obs.*); (*b*) with fear, timidly.

1556 J. Heywood *Spider & F.* lviii, Which shall make thant ieperd much by affection..to comfort spiders spightfully Rather then discomfort them thus fearingly. 1820 Keats *Lamia* 247 Not with cold wonder fearingly But Orpheus-like. 1845 R. W. Hamilton *Pop. Educ.* viii. (ed. 2) 198 The Conformist..fearingly doubted its consequences.

†'**fearlac.** *Obs.* Also 3 far-, ferlac, 4 ferlak. [f. fear *sb.*^{1} (? or *v.*): see -lock.] Fear, terror.

a1225 *Ancr. R.* 306 Kume uorð þer efter ferlac. a1225 *Leg. Kath.* 39 Þurh fearlac of eisfule þreates. c1320 *Cast. Love* 672 Ne haþ he ferlak for no fo.

fearless ('fɪəlɪs), *a.* [f. fear *sb.*^{1} + -less.] Without fear.

1. a. Unaffected by fear; bold, intrepid. Const. *of*; *rarely*, with *inf.*

a1400-50 *Alexander* 4993 Ȝone is a fereles foule. 1591 Spenser *Tears of Muses* 303 Feareles..To tumble. 1603 Shaks. *Meas. for M.* IV. ii. 151 A man..fearelesse of what's past, present, or to come. a1639 W. Whately *Prototypes* I. xxi. (1640) 249 He..hath a bold audatious fearlesse heart. 1709 Steele *Tatler* No. 65 ⁋2 The Hero stood as fearless as if invulnerable. 1784 Cowper *Task* I. 15 The hardy chief..Fearless of wrong, repos'd his weary strength. 1820 Keats *St. Agnes* xxxix, Arise! my love and fearless be. 1870-4 Anderson *Missions Amer. Bd.* III. xiii. 218 The fearless missionary spent ten days with these 'deceitful and bloody' men.

†b. Without doubt about; confident *of*. *Obs.*

1634 Sir T. Herbert *Trav.* 78 He was fearelesse of his establishment in his Fathers Royalties.

c. Of the bearing, demeanour, etc.: Showing no sign of fear.

1803 Mackintosh *Def. Peltier* Wks. 1846 III. 242, I have said, a fearless defence. 1815 —— *Sp. in Ho. Com.* 27 Apr. ibid. 317 The uncourtly and fearless turbulence of this House. 1848 W. H. Bartlett *Egypt to Pal.* v. (1879) 116 The Hebrew historian moves over it with a fearless step. 1875 Jowett *Plato* (ed. 2) I. 430 His mien and his language were..noble and fearless.

†2. a. Not regarded with fear. b. Giving no cause for fear, free from danger. *Obs.*

1599 Sylvester *Miracle Peace* xxix, Scap't from ship-wrack..and..shiuering on the feareless bank. 1600 Holland *Livy* xxv. xxxviii. (1609) 578 Men are least..secured against that which fortune saith is fearelesse. 1614 Bp. Hall *Recoll. Treat.* 988 He [God] can..make him [Satan] if not usefull, yet fearelesse. 1745 Warburton *Serm. 1 Pet.* ii. 17 p. 8 So..will an honourless King promote the Worship of a fear-less God.

3. *Comb.* Parasynthetic, as *fearless-eyed*, *-looking*, *-seeming*.

1925 J. Gregory *Bab of Backwoods* x. 127 Bright-eyed, quick-eyed, fearless-eyed. 1864 J. A. Grant *Walk across Africa* vi. 91 There are also wild-cats..very bold, fearless-looking creatures. 1915 D. H. Lawrence *Rainbow* xii. 314 A fearless-seeming, clean type of modern girl.

fearlessly ('fɪəlɪslɪ), *adv.* [f. prec. + -ly^2.] In a fearless manner; boldly, intrepidly.

1585 Abp. Sandys *Serm.* (1841) 441 Happy is he who can fearlessly stand before the Son of God. 1685 Baxter *Paraphr. N.T.* Matt. x. 27 What I speak to you alone..that publish fearlesly to all the World. 1774 Pennant *Tour Scotl. in 1772*, 327 In the eagerness of the chace will fearlessly spring over. 1838 Dickens *Nich. Nick.* viii, Mrs. Squeers waged war..openly and fearlessly. 1856 Kane *Arct. Expl.* I. xxix. 399 The Esquimaux dog..encounters the wolf fearlessly.

fearlessness ('fɪəlɪsnɪs). [f. as prec. + -ness.] The quality or state of being without fear; boldness, intrepidity. Const. *of*.

1614 Bp. Hall *Recoll. Treat.* 110 Their fearelessenesse of earthquakes and deaths argued the truth of their religion. 1628 Wither *Brit. Rememb.* III. 672 Faith hath pow'r to teach men fearlesnesse. a1665 J. Goodwin *Filled w. the Spirit* (1867) 23 The devil..filling them with..fearlessness of God. 1736 Butler *Anal.* I. ii, There is..a certain fearlessness, with regard to what may be hereafter. 1752 Johnson *Rambler* No. 194 ⁋9 They proceed not from confidence of right, but fearlessness of wrong. 1801 Southey *Thalaba* IV. xxv, All within Was magic ease, and fearlessness secure. 1839 W. Chambers *Tour Holland* 14/1 That..fearlessness of consequences..leads to positive crime. 1893 C. H. Pearson *Nat. Life & Char.* 278 The old trick of thought that regards fearlessness in word and act as the true virtue of the man.

'**fearling.** *nonce-wd.* A creature that fears.

1837 Wheelwright tr. *Aristophanes, Birds* I. 216, I am a Libyan bird, the Fearling called.

fearn(e, obs. and dial. form of fern.

†'**fearnothing.** *Obs. rare.* = fearnought 1.

1725 *Lond. Gaz.* No. 6380/13 Charles Banton..Spinner and Carder for Fearnothing.

fearnought ('fɪənɔːt). [f. phrase: fear *v.* (in imperative) + nought.]

1. A stout kind of woollen cloth, used chiefly on board ship in the form of outside clothing in the most inclement weather, also as a protective covering or lining for the outside door of a powder magazine, the portholes, etc. Cf. dreadnought *sb.* 1.

1772-84 Cook *Voy.* (1790) I. 31 A Magellanic Jacket made of a thick woollen stuff called Fearnought. 1794 *Sporting Mag.* III. 193 The wadding..is made of..fearnaught or shepherd's cloth. 1836 Sir J. Ross *Narr. 2nd Voy.* viii. 110 A skreen lined with fearnought. 1859 F. Griffiths *Artil. Man.* (1862) 210 A wooden plug covered with fearnought.

attrib. 1772-5 Cook *Voy.* (1777) I. I. ii. 20, I..gave to each man the fearnought jacket and trowsers allowed them. 1825 J. Neal *Bro. Jonathan* II. 77 A ragged fear-naught great-coat. 1882 Nares *Seamanship* (ed. 6) 96 It is passed through fearnought shoots.

2. *dial.* (See quot.)

1883 *Almondbury Gloss.* (E.D.S.), *Fearnought*, a machine for mixing wool, shoddy, and mungo before putting upon the condenser.

3. A drink to keep up the spirits.

1880 L. Wallace *Ben-Hur* IV. x. 231 This is the fear-naught of the tentmen.

fearsome ('fɪəsəm), *a.* [f. fear *v.* or *sb.*^{1} + -some.]

1. Fear-inspiring; frightful, dreadful.

1768 Ross *Helenore* 3722 The foremost looks a fearsome chiel. 1816 Scott *Old Mort.* xxxii, War's a fearsome thing. 1842 Barham *Ingol. Leg.*, *Nell Cook*, The masons three..saw a fearsome sight. 1871 M. Collins *Mrq. & Merch.* I. viii. 236 Iron fencing..with fearsome spikes at the top.

Comb. 1815 Scott *Guy M.* xxxix, 'A muckle stoor fearsome-looking wife she was as ever I set een on.'

¶2. ? *erron.* Timid, apprehensive, frightened.

1863 A. Fonblanque *Tangled Skein* III. 205, I was..fearsome of this very danger. 1871 B. Taylor *Faust* (1875) I. viii. 120 I'm but a silly, fearsome thing!

Hence '**fearsomely** *adv.*, in a fearsome manner. (*a*) So as to excite fear. ¶(*b*) Timidly. '**fearsomeness**, the quality of being fearsome. (*a*) Dreadfulness; terror. ¶(*b*) Timidity.

1876 B. L. Farjeon *Love's Victory* ii, He looked about him fearsomely. 1883 *Daily News* 5 July 5/2 A prisoner..as fearsomely exciting as the elegant baron of fiction. 1891 T. Hardy *Tess* I. xii, The fact..lent Tess's supposed position, by its fearsomeness, a far higher fascination. 1893 *Black & White* 11 Mar. 286/2 The women..were hiding fearsomely in their innermost rooms. 1893 *Daily News* 6 June 3/4 There is even a fearsomeness in her expression, as if she dreaded to move.

†'**feasance.** *Obs.* Also 6 fesaunce. [ad. AF. *fesance*, *-aunce*, *faisaunce* (Fr. *faisance*), f. *faire* to do. Cf. malfeasance, nonfeasance.] The doing or execution of a condition, obligation, feudal service, etc.

1538 tr. *Littleton's Tenures* v. 76 a, This is nat proued that the fesaunce of the condycion..oughte to be made vppon the lande. 1642 tr. *Perkins' Prof. Bk.* x. §673. 292 For the scowring of a ditch or for the covering of a house..he shall not have an assise because they lie only in feasance. 1741 T. Robinson *Gavelkind* i. 3 Under this Term [Gavel] were comprehended all Socage Services whatsoever which lie in Render or Feasance.

'**feaser.** A provincial name for the Arctic Gull (Montagu *Ornith. Dict.* 1866).

†'**feasetraw.** *Obs.* Also feas-, festraw(e. [A corruption of *festue*, fescue, influenced by straw.] = fescue (see quots.).

1595 G. Markham *Trag. Sir R. Grinuile* xxiii, [She] with her eyes festrawe points a Storie. 1611 Florio, *Festuca*, a feskue or feasetraw that children vse to point their letters. 1638 Featley *Struct. in Lyndomastigem* I. 198 To set up a

man of straw, and push him downe with a festraw. **1648** tr. *Senault's Paraphrase upon Job* 408 Those Stones..make as little impression upon his body, as a feastraw would which the hand of a childe should push. **1660** S. FISHER *Rusticks Alarm* III. iii. 98 A..Type, Figure, Festraw, or Finger, that points [etc.].

feasibility (ˌfiːzɪˈbɪlɪtɪ). [f. next + -ITY.] The quality or fact of being feasible.

1. a. Capability of being done; practicability.

1624 T. JAMES in *Abp. Ussher's Lett.* (1686) 308 If he did turn away his mind wholly from Chelsey, I durst presume of more fasibility [*sic*] and possibility here of doing good. *Ibid.* 331 To give proof of the faisibility [*sic*] of the Work to the common profit of the Church. **1652** HEYLIN *Cosmogr.* App. 196 The Excellency and feasibility of his invention. *a* **1678** WOODHEAD *Holy Living* (1688) 162 The alike easiness and faisibility of all things unto him. **1725** BRADLEY *Fam. Dict.* s.v. *Stone*, According to the different circumstance of Difficulty or Feasibility of it. **1860** FROUDE *Hist. Eng.* VI. 519 They changed their minds on the feasibility of their enterprise.

b. quasi-*concr.* Something feasible.

1646 SIR T. BROWNE *Pseud. Ep.* I. v. 17 Men often swallow ..fesibilities for possibilities [*read* possibilities for fesibilities], and things impossible for possibilities.

†**2.** Capability of being made. *Obs.*

1655 in *Ref. Commonw. Bees* 33 My confident Assertion of the fecibility of *Aqua vitæ* out of grain unmalted.

3. *attrib.*, as *feasibility study.*

1959 *Times* 14 Jan. 2/5 Feasibility studies of new reactor systems. **1969** *Daily Tel.* 14 Feb. 23/2 Initially, the consortium is to make a two-year 'feasibility' study. **1971** *Guardian* 8 May 3/7 Britain is helping with a feasibility study for rice growing.

feasible (ˈfiːzɪb(ə)l), *a.* Forms: 5 faysyble, fesable, 6 fays-, feac-(7 feice-)able, 6–7 faisable, fesible, 7 fac-, fæs-, fa(i)s-, fe(a)cible, feizable, -ible, foisible, 7–8 feas(e)-, feazable, -ible, 7– feasible. [a. OF. *faisable, -ible*, f. *fais-* impf. stem of *faire* (:—L. *facĕre*) to do: see -BLE.]

1. Of a design, project, etc.: Capable of being done, accomplished or carried out; possible, practicable.

c **1460** FORTESCUE *Abs. & Lim. Mon.* ix, Such an enterprise is the more feseable. **1587** RALEIGH *Let. to Ld. Burghley* in *N. & Q.* (1864) V. 207 The matter and service will be very fesible. **1647** WARD *Simp. Cobler* (1843) 63 To an infinite power all things are equally faisable. *a* **1687** PETTY *Pol. Arith.* (1690) 114 It is..a very feasible matter for [England]..to gain the Universal Trade of the whole Commercial World. **1787** MAD. D'ARBLAY *Diary* Dec., This seemed a most feasible way of producing some variety in our intercourse. **1822** HAZLITT *Table-t.* Ser. II. iv. (1869) 89 The mind..runs back to what was so..feasible at one time. **1875** J. H. BENNET *Winter Medit.* I. vii. 200 We are so ready..as a nation, to go to any feasible expense to obtain what we want.

absol. **1874** MORLEY *Compromise* (1886) 111 It is the natural product of the political spirit, which is incessantly thinking of..the immediately feasible.

2. Of things in general, also of persons: Capable of being dealt with successfully in any way, either in a material or immaterial sense.

Cf. Sc. '*Feasible*, neat, tidy. Roxb.' (Jam.)

1611 SPEED *Hist. Gt. Brit.* IX. xii. 122 Paris..not being fesible, he retires into Britaine to refresh his Armie. **1614** BP. MOUNTAGU *Gagg* To Rdr. 3 [I] am like enough to draw you my Parishioners with me, at least to make you more feasable, then otherwise you would be. **1624** —— *Let.* 22 Nov., in *Bp. Cosin's Corresp.* (1869) I. 27 Yet is it [the living] feisable for a good exchaunge. **1649** BLITHE *Eng. Improv. Impr.* (1653) 48, I know all Lands are not so Fecible as others are. **1727** BRADLEY *Fam. Dict.*, *Corn-Setting Engine*, a very easy and most feasible Instrument. **1839** JAMES *Louis XIV*, II. 87 The whole place was so feasible. **1856** MRS. CARLYLE *Lett.* II. 307, I should so like a Scotch-woman, if I could get any feasible Scotchwoman. **1866** MACGREGOR *1000 Miles in Rob Roy Canoe* 5 The difficulty was to find..what rivers were at once feasible to paddle on and pretty to see. **1889** E. C. DOWSON *Let.* 3 Feb. (1967) 33, I have suggested Swinburne & Pater, Lang, Oscar Wilde & Lady Dilke as the most feasible.

3. Of a proposition, theory, story, etc.: Likely, probable.

Hardly a justifiable sense etymologically, and (probably for that reason) recognized by no Dict., though supported by considerable literary authority.

1656 HOBBES *Six Lessons* Wks. 1845 VII. 323 A proposition uttered, to the end to have it..examined whether it be true or not true, faisable or not faisable. **1726** *Adv. Capt. R. Boyle* 57 Now Mirza kept the Key of the Gate, so that my Story was feazable enough. **1767** H. BROOKE *Fool of Qual.* xvii, 'As you say, James', cried Mr. Fenton, 'this account seems pretty feasible'. **1833** LYELL *Princ. Geol.* III. 105 The only feasible theory..that has yet been proposed. **1856** DOVE *Logic Chr. Faith* v. i. §2. 277 There might be some feasible doubts as to whether [etc]. **1865** LIVINGSTONE *Zambesi* v. 129 It seems feasible that a legitimate..trade might take the place of the present unlawful traffic.

†**4.** As *sb.* in *pl.* Things feasible. *Obs.*

1661 GLANVILL *Sceps. Sci.* xii. 114 We conclude many things within the list of Impossibilities, which yet are easie Feasables.

Hence **ˈfeasibly** *adv.*, in a feasible manner; **ˈfeasibleness**, the quality or fact of being feasible, feasibility.

1649 BLITHE *Eng. Improv. Impr.* (1653) 86 Improve it by Floating, which may very Feazibly be done according to the direction of the fourth..Chapter. **1722** COLLIER *Ess.* (1725) IV. 331 They have made the Project look feasibly, and contriv'd Ways and Means to prevent Discovery. **1633** T. JAMES *Voy.* 107 The faiseablenesse of the Action intended. **1736** CARTE *Ormonde* II. 177 The feasableness of the offers which had been made of seizing Glocester. **1860** HOLLAND *Miss Gilbert* i, A demonstration of the feasibleness of infant instruction.

feasor: see TORT-FEASOR.

feast (fiːst), *sb.* Forms: 3–6 fest(e, 4–6 feaste, feest(e, (6 *Sc.* feist), 9 *dial.* veast, 6– feast. [a. OF. *feste* (Fr. *fête*) = Pr., Pg., It. *festa*, Sp. *fiesta*:—Com. Rom. *festa* fem. sing., a. L. *festa* festal ceremonies, neut. pl. of *festus* adj. festal; but the Lat. word equivalent to *feast* was *festum*, the neut. sing. of this adj.

The L. *festus* is prob. a ppl. formation containing the same root as *fēria* (:—older **fēsia*): see FAIR *sb.*]

1. A religious anniversary appointed to be observed with rejoicing (hence opposed to a *fast*), in commemoration of some event or in honour of some personage. ***the feast***, in the N.T. *esp.* the Passover.

movable feasts: those (viz. Easter and the feasts depending on it) of which the date varies from year to year; opposed to ***immovable feasts***, such as Christmas, the Saints' Days, etc.

a **1225** *Ancr. R.* 22 ȝif hit beo holiniht vor þe feste of nie lescuns þet kumeð amorwen. *c* **1275** *Passion* 85 in *O.E. Misc.* 39 As hit neyhlechet to heore muchele feste. **1297** R. GLOUC. (1724) 441 Hys Ester feste. *c* **1340** *Cursor M.* 10428 (Trin.) Men shulde..fair cloþing on hem..take for her heȝe feestes sake. *c* **1380** WYCLIF *Serm.* Sel. Wks. II. 238 þei holden wel þis feeste. **1411** *Rolls of Parlt.* III. 650/1 The Saterday neghst after the fest of Seint Michael. *c* **1470** HENRY *Wallace* XI. 352 He said, it was bot till a kyrkyn fest. **1526** TINDALE *Luke* xxii. 1 The feaste of swete breed drue nye whiche is called ester. *a* **1550** *Christis Kirke Gr.* vi, For honor of the feist. **1570–6** LAMBARDE *Peramb. Kent* (1826) 124 As the Romanes did their feast of Fugalia, or chasing out of the Kings. **1611** BIBLE *Ex.* xii. 14 You shall keepe it a feast by an ordinance for euer. **1740** GRAY *Lett.* Wks. 1884 II. 85 Corpus Christi Day, the greatest feast in the year. **1796** H. HUNTER *St. Pierre's Stud. Nat.* (1799) III. 308 It is the feast of Jupiter. **1825** FOSBROKE *Encycl. Antiq.* (1843) II. 651/2 A principal feast was made..in commemoration of the return of warmth and the sun. **1885** *Catholic Dict.*, *Feasts of the Church*, Days on which the Church joyfully commemorates particular mysteries of the Christian religion or the glory of her saints.

b. ***double feast*** (L. *festum duplex*): the designation given to the most important class of feasts in the Roman Catholic church; for the (disputed) origin of the name see Cathol. Dict. s.v. *Feast*.

a **1225** *Ancr. R.* 70 Euerich urideie..holdeð silence bute ȝif hit beo duble feste. *c* **1500** ARNOLD *Chron.* (1811) 68 On sondayes and other solempne and double festys.

c. A village festival held annually, originally on the feast of the saint to whom the parish church is dedicated (cf. Fr. *fête de village*), but now usually on a particular Sunday of the year, and the one or two days following. In some places called *wakes* or *revels*.

In England the village 'feast,' where it continues to be observed, is the great annual occasion (second to or rivalling Christmas) for family gatherings and the entertainment of visitors from a distance.

1559 *Mirr. Mag.*, *Worcester* xvii, Whan I should have gone to Blockam feast. **1821** CLARE *Vill. Minstr.* I. 33 Statute and feast his village yearly knew. **1857** HUGHES *Tom Brown* I. ii, The great times for back-swording came round ..at the feast. *Ibid.*, The Vale 'veasts' were not the common statute feasts. **1864** W. BARNES in *Macm. Mag.* Oct. 476 At the feäst, at the cool evenentide, I walk'd on wi' you.

†**2.** A gathering for pleasure or sports; a fête.

1485 CAXTON *Paris & V.* (1868) 13 The kyng..made his maundement that they al shold come wyth theyr armes and hors for to Iouste..and they that shold do best in armes.. they shold haue the prys and the worshyp of the feste. *c* **1489** —— *Sonnes of Aymon* vii. 175 They sholde kepe well the feest, that noo noyse nor noo stryffe were there made.

3. A sumptuous meal or entertainment, given to a number of guests; a banquet, *esp.* of a more or less public nature. Also a series of such entertainments. ***to make a feast***: to give a banquet. †***to hold a feast***: to give or join in a banquet.

c **1200** *Trin. Coll. Hom.* 11 Untimeliche eten alehuse and at ferme and at feste. *c* **1275** LAY. 14425 þe king makede feste [**1205** ueorme]. *a* **1300** *Floriz & Bl.* 78 Anon me him tiþinge tolde þat þe admiral wolde feste h[olde]. *c* **1350** *Will. Palerne* 5074 þe fest of þat mariage a moneþ fulle lasted. *c* **1386** CHAUCER *Clerk's T.* 954 Ful besy was Grisilde in every thing, That to the feste was appertinent. **1389** in *Eng. Gilds* (1870) 4 þe brethren and sustren..shul..hold togeder ..a fest. *c* **1400** *Destr. Troy* 205 He cast hym full cointly be cause of this thyng, In a Cite be-syde to somyn a fest. *a* **1400–50** *Alexander* 480 þis dere kynge..Had parreld him a proude feste of princes & dukis. **1523** LD. BERNERS *Froiss.* I. lxxxi. 103 The nexte day she made them a great feest at dyner. **1607** SHAKS. *Timon* III. vi. 75 Make not a Citie Feast of it, to let the meat coole, ere we can agree vpon the first place. **1678** LADY CHAWORTH in *Hist. MSS. Comm.* 12th Rep. App. v. 53 The Duke of Yorke comes to towne to the Artillery feast to-day. **1682** BUNYAN *Holy War* (1785) 165 Mr. Carnal Security did again make a feast for the town of Mansoul. **1779–81** JOHNSON *L.P.*, *Savage* Wks. III. 344 Savage..was..distinguished at their public feasts. **1814** BYRON *Corsair* II. i, Seyd, the Pacha, makes a feast to-night.

†**b.** Hence *rarely*: The company at a feast.

a **1400–50** *Alexander* 492 All þe fest was a-ferd & oþ ire folke bathe.

4. An unusually abundant and delicious meal; something delicious to feed upon; *fig.* an exquisite gratification, a rich treat. ***to make a feast***: to enjoy a good meal, eat luxuriously (*of*, *upon*).

1393 GOWER *Conf.* III. 30 Eke min ere hath over this A deinty feste. *c* **1440** *York Myst.* xv. 44 Say felowes, what! fynde yhe any feest Me falles for to haue parte, parde! **1526** *Pilgr. Perf.* (W. de W. 1531) 290 b, They attayne to greater feestes, and more..haboundaunt ioye of the spiryte. **1562** J. HEYWOOD *Prov. & Epigr.* (1867) 85 Folke saie, enough is as good as a feast. **1645** QUARLES *Sol. Recant.* viii. 43 This makes thy morsell a perpetuall Feast. **1719** DE FOE *Crusoe* (1840) I. xv. 266 And make a feast upon me. **1739** GRAY *Lett.* Wks. 1884 II. 48 Two eunuchs' voices, that were a perfect feast to ears that had heard nothing but French operas for a year. *a* **1744** POPE *Imit. Hor. Epist.* I. vii. 25 Pray take them, Sir—Enough's a Feast. **1822** SHELLEY *Hellas* 1025 The death-birds descend to their feast. **1823** LAMB *Elia* Ser. I. *Distant Corr.*, The moment you received the intelligence my full feast of fun would be over. **1851** HAWTHORNE *Ho. Sev. Gables* xix. (1883) 338 He would make a feast of the portly grunter. **1865** M. ARNOLD *Ess. Crit.* vi. (1875) 247 How little of a feast for the senses. **1870** DICKENS *E. Drood* iii, We had a feast.

†**5.** Rejoicing, festivity. *Obs.*

c **1300** *St. Brandan* 75 We seide hem that we hadde i-beo in alle joy and feste, Bifore the ȝates of Paradys. *c* **1315** SHOREHAM (Percy Soc.) 148 Ac nys no blysse ne no feste [*printed* seste] Aȝeyns the joye of conqueste Thet hys thorȝ god. **1644** MILTON *Educ.*, Living out their days in feast and jollity. **1667** —— *P.L.* VI. 167 Ministring Spirits, traind up in Feast and Song.

6. ***to make feast*** (= Fr. *faire fête*): **a.** To make merry, rejoice; in later use with narrower sense, to enjoy a delicious repast, to feast. *arch.*

a **1225** *Ancr. R.* 222 He..bringeð hire on to..a last makien feste. *c* **1300** *Seyn Julian* 33 To gadere hi made gret feste. **1375** BARBOUR *Bruce* XIX. 730 The scottis folk..maid fest and far, And blew hornys and fyres maid. **1483** CAXTON *Gold. Leg.* 188/1 As sone as thy salutacyon entrid in to myn eerys the chylde..made joye and feste. *a* **1533** LD. BERNERS *Huon* vii. 16 My hert is not very joyfull to synge nor to make fest. **1870** MORRIS *Earthly Par.*, *Cupid & Psyche* (1890) 107/1 Come, sister, sit, and let us make good feast! **1881** TENNYSON *Cup* ii. Poems (1889) 762/2, I would that every man made feast to-day Beneath the shadow of our pines!

†**b.** To show honour or respect *to*, make much of (a person). Cf. Fr. *faire fête à*. Also *absol.* To pay one's court. *Obs.*

1340 *Ayenb.* 156 þe lhord..him froteþ and makeþ him greate feste. *c* **1369** CHAUCER *Dethe Blaunche* 638 With his hede he maketh feste. *c* **1400** *Rom. Rose* 5064 She..laugheth on hym, and makith hym feeste. *c* **1450** *Merlin* 88 He.. merveiled why the kynge made hym soche grete feeste. *a* **1533** LD. BERNERS *Huon* lvi. 189 His doughter came to hym to make him feest.

7. *attrib.* and *Comb.* **a.** simple attrib., as ***feast-cake, -companion, -guest, -house, -night, -rite, -robe***; ***feast-famous*** adj. **b.** objective, as ***feast-goer***; ***feast-finding*** adj.

1857 HUGHES *Tom Brown* I. ii, Every household.. managed to raise a '*feast-cake'. *a* **1610** HEALEY *Theophrastus* (1636) 40 His *feast-companions. **1591** SYLVESTER *Du Bartas* I. v. 143 Dainty Salmons, Chevins thunder-scar'd, *Feast-famous Sturgeons. **1593** SHAKS. *Lucr.* 817 *Feast-finding minstrels. **1552** HULOET, *Feast-gestes which be inuited to the banquet or feast. **1857** HUGHES *Tom Brown* I. ii, The frighted scurrying away of the female *feast-goers. **1483** *Cath. Angl.* 128/2 A *Fest house, *conuiuarium*. **1539** CRANMER in Strype *Life* II. (1694) 246 Every alehouse and tavern, every feasthouse. **1820** KEATS *St. Agnes* xx, This *feast-night. **1725** POPE *Odyss.* x. 404 Shall I be led To share thy *feast-rites. **1594** HOOKER *Eccl. Pol.* III. (1617) 94 Keeping on his *feast-robe onely.

8. Special comb.: †**feast-bed**, a couch for reclining at meals, a triclinium; **feast-day**, a day on which a feast (senses 1–3) is held; **feast-maker**, the giver of a feast; **feast-master**, one who presides at a feast; **feast-won** *a.*, won by a feast.

a **1661** HOLYDAY *Juvenal* 268 Lazing on their *feast-beds. *a* **1300** *Cursor M.* 13131 (Cott.) Saint Ion al-wais in prisun lai, Til it com on a *fest dai. **1382** WYCLIF *1 Macc.* i. 41 The feestdays therof ben turned in to mournyng. *c* **1400** MAUNDEV. (Roxb.) viii. 30 þai drink na wyne comounly, bot on hegh feste days. **1611** BIBLE *Amos* v. 21, I despise your feast dayes. *a* **1746** HOLDSWORTH *On Virgil* (1768) 138 On the feast-day of Castor and Pollux. **1870** DICKENS *E. Drood* xiii, It would never do to spoil his feast-days. **1551** ROBINSON tr. *More's Utop.* Epist. (Arb.) 26 Geuyng no thankes to the *feaste maker. *a* **1661** HOLYDAY *Juvenal* 50 It [the word *trechedipna*] is sometimes taken for the feast-maker. **1610** HEALEY *St. Aug. Citie of God* 521 Doth not the Bridegroome turne all the *feast-maisters..out of his chamber. **1870** MORRIS *Earthly Par.* III. IV. 188 Then needs must the feast masters strive Too pensive thoughts away to drive. **1607** SHAKS. *Timon* II. ii. 180 *Feast won, fast lost.

feast (fiːst), *v.* Forms: 3–5 fest(e(n, -in, -yn, 4 feaste, 5 feest, 6 feasten, 6– feast. [ME. *festen*, ad. OF. *fester* (Fr. *fêter*), f. *feste* FEAST *sb.*]

1. *intr.* To make or partake of a feast, fare sumptuously, regale oneself. Also with *on*, *upon*, and ***to feast it***.

c **1300** *K. Alis.* 1578 Teller of jeste is ofte myslike Ribaud festeth also with tripe. *c* **1385** CHAUCER *L.G.W.* 2157 *Ariadne*, There festen they, there dauncen they and synge. **1483** *Cath. Angl.* 128/2 To Feste. **1590** SHAKS. *Com. Err.* IV. iv. 65 Did this Companion..Reuell and feast it at my house to-day[?] **1627–77** FELTHAM *Resolves* I. xxviii. 48 When the Sun-bak'd Peasant goes to feast it with a Gentleman. **1691** HARTCLIFFE *Virtues* 71 They honour a Martyr by feasting on his Festival. **1819** SHELLEY *Cyclops* 365 The Cyclops..Now feasts on the dead. **1859** TENNYSON *Enid* 1136 Geraint..bad the host Call in..his friends And feast with these in honour of their Earl.

fig. *c* **1600** SHAKS. *Sonn.* xlvii, With my loves' picture then my eye doth feast. **1768** *Verse of Oxford Newsman* in *Oxford*

Sausage (1822) 177 At length we change our wonted note And feast, all winter, on a vote. **1825** LYTTON *Falkland* 13, I have, as it were, feasted upon the passions. **1871** G. MEREDITH *H. Richmond* xxv. (1887) 226 The princess..let her eyes feast incessantly on a laughing sea.

†**b.** To keep holiday, give oneself to pleasure; to enjoy oneself. *Obs.*

1608 SHAKS. *Per.* I. iv. 107 Feast here awhile, Until our stars that frown lend us a smile.

c. *to feast away*, to drive away by feasting; to pass (time) in feasting.

1621 BP. HALL *Heaven upon Earth* §6 Feast away thy cares. **1733** FIELDING *Don Quix. in Eng.* II. v, Then hungry homeward we return, To feast away the night.

2. *trans.* To provide a feast for, regale. Also *refl.*

1340–70 *Alisaunder* 978 Whan hee is fare fro fight his folke for too feaste. **1377** LANGL. *P. Pl.* B. xv. 335 Religious þat riche ben shulde rather feste beggeres þan burgeys. **1470–85** MALORY *Arthur* I. xxi, The kynge and all..that were fested that day. **1570–6** LAMBARDE *Peramb. Kent* (1826) 256 The Lorde Bartholomew..magnificently feasted there the Queene. **1602** MARSTON *Antonio's Rev.* v. v, Here lies a dish to feast thy fathers gorge. **1651** DAVENANT *Gondibert* III. v. 80 Hope, the worlds..standing Guest, Fed by the Rich, but feasted by the Poor. **1725** DE FOE *Voy. round World* (1840) 179 Our men might be said not to refresh but to feast themselves here with fresh provisions. **1849** JAMES *Woodman* v, Arrangements made for feasting the number of forty in the stranger's hall. **1863** GEO. ELIOT *Romola* I. xx, The guests were all feasted after this initial ceremony.

fig. *c* **1300** *Havelok* 2938 Hauelok..bigan..His denshe men to feste wel With riche landes. **1393** LANGL. *P. Pl.* C. XVII 318 *Fiat-uoluntas-tua* festeþ hym eche day. **1607** SHAKS. *Timon* III. vi. 36 Feast your eares with the Musicke awhile. **1653** WALTON *Angler* 46 A companion that feasts the company with wit and mirth. **1701** FARQUHAR *Sir H. Wildair* v. v, We'll charm our ears with Abel's voice; feast our eyes with one another. **1749** FIELDING *Tom Jones* XII. xiii, With the Gypsies he had feasted only his understanding. **1816** J. WILSON *City of Plague* III. i. 163, I know not why My soul thus longs to feast itself on terror. **1818** JAS. MILL *Brit. India* II. IV. vii. 256 To feast the Company with the most flattering accounts of the state of their affairs. **1857** WILLMOTT *Pleas. Lit.* xi. 45 Pope, at twelve feasted his eyes in the picture galleries of Spenser.

3. In a more general sense: To entertain hospitably and sumptuously.

1490 CAXTON *Eneydos* xiii. 48 She doeth make grete appareylles for to feeste Eneas ryghte highely. **1548** HALL *Chron.* 184 b, They were of Philippe, duke of Bourgoyne, wel receyved and fested. **1600** E. BLOUNT tr. *Conestaggio* 30 The Duke of Medina Sidonia feasted the King, with chasing of buls. **1601** SHAKS. *Twel. N.* III. iv. 2 How shall I feast him? What bestow of him?

Hence **'feasted** *ppl. a.* **'feasting** *ppl. a.*

c **1440** *Promp. Parv.* 158/1 Festyd, or fed wythe goode mete and drynke, *convivatus.* **1652** BENLOWES *Theoph.* IV. lii. 58 That I may enter with thy feasted friends. **1674** DRYDEN *State Innocence* 17 All these are ours, all nature's excellence Whose tast or smell can bless the feasted sence. **1592** SHAKS. *Rom. & Jul.* v. iii. 86 Her beautie makes This Vault a feasting presence full of light.

feasten ('fiːst(ə)n), *a. rare.* [f. FEAST *sb.* + -EN[4].] Made for a feast.

1891 *Athenæum* 10 Oct. 486/3 The admirable collection of feasten and ceremonial cakes.

feaster ('fiːstə(r)). [f. FEAST *v.* + -ER[1].]

†**1.** The giver of a feast, host, entertainer. *Obs.*

c **1425** *Festivals Church* 294 in *Leg. Rood* (1871) 220 Neuer festour fedde better. **1548** UDALL, etc. *Erasm. Par. Matt.* xiv. 18 A feaster and a feader of the bodies. **1587** TURBERV. *Trag. T.* (1837) 40 The feaster prayde eche one to take his place. **1611** COTGR., *Festivant*, a feaster or feast maker.

2. One who is in the habit of feasting; a luxurious liver.

a **1633** AUSTIN *Medit.* (1635) 84 Thou shalt have more Ioy ..then the worldly Feasters have. *a* **1661** HOLYDAY *Juvenal* 50 Implying, that the Romans once plain and thrifty were now become feasters. **1670** MILTON *Hist. Eng.* I. Wks. (1847) 482/2 Lud was hardy, and bold in war; in peace, a jolly feaster. **1725** POPE *Odyss.* III. 401 While lawless feasters in thy palace sway. **1806** W. TAYLOR in *Ann. Rev.* IV. 231 The pampered feaster.

3. One who partakes of a feast; a guest.

1813 SCOTT *Rokeby* III. xiv, Among the feasters waited near, Sorrow. **1870** MORRIS *Earthly Par.* III. IV. 187 What music on the feasters fell.

feastful ('fiːstfʊl), *a. arch.* [f. as prec. + -FUL. The formation was prob. first suggested by the sound of FESTIVAL *a.*; cf. FESTYFUL.]

1. Occupied in or addicted to feasting; of the nature of feasting; festive. †*feastful day*: originally = festival day, but in late examples the adj. has the general sense.

a **1440** *Found. St. Bartholomew's* II. i. 35 Whan the goldyne path of the son reducid to vs the desirid ioyes of festfull celebrite. **1447** BOKENHAM *Seyntys* (Roxb.) 49 Upon a festful day Clepyd of the temple the dedycacyoun. **1553** BECON *Reliques of Rome* (1563) 75* The feastful day of the Epiphanye. **1645** MILTON *Sonnet* ix. 12 The Bridegroom and his feastful friends Pass to bliss. **1671** —— *Samson* 1741 The virgins also shall, on feastful days, Visit his tomb with flowers. **1725** POPE *Odyss.* I. 117 His herds and flocks in feastful rites devour. *Ibid.* IV. 901 They rise, and to the feastful hall remove. **1849** J. STERLING in *Fraser's Mag.* XXXIX. 416 For this he bade to smile The feastful city with all joy's excesses. **1870** MORRIS *Earthly Par.* IV. 346 So fell the noisy day to feastful night.

2. Filled with feasting, full of food and wine.

1810 LAMB *Poems, Salome*, The feastful monarch's heart was fired.

feasting ('fiːstɪŋ), *vbl. sb.* [f. FEAST *v.* + -ING[1].] The action of the vb. FEAST in various senses; an instance of this.

c **1374** CHAUCER *Troylus* III. 1669 He spendith iustith and makith festynges. **1377** LANGL. *P. Pl.* B. XI. 188 ȝowre frendes wil..fonde ȝow to quite ȝ owre festynge and ȝowre faire ȝifte. **1538** STARKEY *England* I. iii. 95 For ther was neuer so grete festyng and bankettyng. **1665** MANLEY *Grotius' Low C. Warres* 13 The Commons, whose whole study was Merchandizing and feasting. **1710** *Lond. Gaz.* No. 4659/2 Publick Feastings have been made at Court twice every Week. **1774** J. BRYANT *Mythol.* III. 133 They were giving themselves up to feasting and jollity. **1840** THIRLWALL *Greece* VII. lix. 339 Ptolemy celebrated his second deliverance..by sacrifices and feastings.

attrib. **1563** *Homilies* II. *Place & Time Prayer* II. (1859) 350 Come..and cheerfully enter into Gods feastinghouse. **1641** BROME *Joviall Crew* II. Wks. 1873 III. 389 The Master of your Feast and feasting-House.

feastings even, erron. form of FASTENS EEN.

feastivity, obs. form of FESTIVITY.

†**'feastly**, *a. Obs. rare.* [f. FEAST *sb.* + -LY[1].] Festive, fond of feasting, jolly.

c **1386** CHAUCER *Sqr.'s T.* 273 A..feestlych man as fressh as May.

†**'feastly**, *adv. Obs.* In 3 festelike. [f. as prec. + -LY[2].] As men do at a feast; merrily.

c **1250** *Gen. & Ex.* 3407 Ietro..at wið moysen festelike.

feastraw(e: see FEASETRAW.

'feastress. *rare.* A female feaster.

1836–48 B. D. WALSH *Aristoph.* 9 *note*, The plays of the Feastresses and the Frogs.

feat (fiːt), *sb.* Forms: 4–7 fait(e, -yt(e, 4–6 fete, (4 fet), 5 faytte, 5–6 faicte, feacte, fett(e, feet(e, feit, (6 fayth), 5–7 feate, 6, 9 *Sc.* fate, 6– feat. [a. OFr. *fait, fet* (later *faict*):—L. *factum*: see FACT *sb.*]

†**1.** In neutral sense: An action, deed, course of conduct; = FACT *sb.* 1 a. Also *feats and deeds. to do, perform* or *work the feat*: to 'do the deed'. *to work one's* (*full*) *feat*: to effect one's full purpose.

c **1420** *Chron. Vilod.* 2464 To Wylton he bytte ȝow gon To parforme þe fette. **1491** CAXTON *Vitas Patr.* (W. de W. 1495) I. ix. 13 b/2 Saynt Iherom..prayed that he wold recounte to hem of his faytes & his dedes. **1503–4** *Act 19 Hen. VII*, c. 34 Preamb., Dyvers feetis betwen theym conseyved and conspired. **1538** LELAND *Itin.* IV. 6 Of the which [treasoure] ..he tooke a certein part..to a Feete at his own Pleasure. *a* **1555** RIDLEY *Wks.* (1843) 65 Thou..shalt be lawfully called to do thy feat and to play thy part. **1576** *Tyde Tarryeth no Man*, Thy money is English, which must worke the feate. **1577** HOLINSHED *Chron.* II. 310 To come to their succours in time, and yer the English-men had wrote their full feat. **1587** TURBERV. *Trag. T.* (1837) 101 He that had resolvde.. to..doe his feate, and home agayne. **1630** *R. Johnson's Kingd. & Commw.* 34 Where numbers..and weapons have not..prevailed, there hath money alone done the feat. **1659** B. HARRIS *Parival's Iron Age* 7 The Tartars..as soon as they have done their feat..betake themselves to their heels. **1678** BUTLER *Hud.* III. i. 511 If you have perform'd the Feat The Blows are visible. **1732** POPE *Hor. Sat.* II. ii. 15 If then plain bread and milk will do the feat, The pleasure lies in you, and not the meat.

†**b.** Action in general; overt action; deeds, as opposed to words. *by way of feat* (Law; = F. *par voie de fait*): by violence. *Obs.*

1362 LANGL. *P. Pl.* A. I. 160 James þe gentel bond hit in his Book, þat [Fey] withouten [fait] Is febelore þen nouȝt. *a* **1400–50** *Alexander* 4366 All þare fete..in falshede it endis. **1426** *Oath of Lords* in Hall *Chron.* (1809) 135 Not suffer that any of the saied parties..procede or attempte by waye of feit against the kynges peace. *Ibid.*, Redressyng all such maner of procedyng by waie of feit or force. **1560** *Proude Wyues Pater Noster* 35 in Hazl. *E.P.P.* IV. 152, I can nought gete of him by fete nor wyle.

†**c.** A business transaction. *Obs.*

1588 J. MELLIS *Briefe Instr.* F iv b, Put your feates downe .. aparte in a leafe..after your doing.

d. *by feat of*: by the agency of, by dint of. *Obs.* exc. *arch.*

1489 CAXTON *Faytes of A.* I. i. 1 Executed by fayt of dyligence and witte. **1805** SCOTT *Last Minstr.* I. xi, Men said, he changed his mortal frame By feat of magic mystery.

2. An exceptional or noteworthy act or achievement; *esp.* a deed of valour; a noble exploit. Often in *feat of arms*. Now somewhat *arch.*, and with some mixture of 3.

a **1400–50** *Alexander* 3105 All þe feete at oure fadirs in þe fold hade. **1485** CAXTON *Paris & V.* 9 Knyghtes redy to do fayte of armes. *c* **1507** *Justes Moneths May & June* 182 Hazl. in *E.P.P.* II. 127 Noble actes and faytes mercyall Shall be had in remembraunce immortall. **1555** ABP. PARKER *Ps.* cvi. 305 Noble faytes in Egypt done. **1585** JAS. I *Ess. Poesie* (Arb.) 67 Martiall and knichtly faittis of armes. **1611** BIBLE *Judith* xi. 8 Thou onely art..wonderfull in feates of warre. **1642** R. CARPENTER *Experience*, A peece of sanctified and blessed waxe, which shall..make the Devill runne, and doe many such feates. **1667** MILTON *P.L.* II. 537 With feats of Arms From either end of Heav'n the welkin burns. **1813** SCOTT *Trierm.* II. xxvi, For feats of arms as far renown'd As warrior of the Table Round. **1843** LYTTON *Last Bar.* I. i, Those personal feats..dazzled the populace. **1856** STANLEY *Sinai & Pal.* iii. (1858) 161 Othniel performed the feat of arms that won him the daughter of Caleb.

†**b.** *man* or *folk of feat*: man *or* folk of deeds or might. Cf. Fr. *gens de fait.*

c **1500** *Melusine* 119 They were folke of faytte and of grete enterpryse. *Ibid.* 211 Prysouners..al men of estate & faytte.

3. An action displaying dexterity or strength; a surprising trick, a 'tour de force'.

1564 *Brief Exam.* ******, Among the Painims..men are able to worke theyr feates. **1614** BP. HALL *Recoll. Treat.* 989 Hee had rather send for his magicians to worke feates. **1682** S. PORDAGE *Medal Rev.* 281 The jugling feat Is plainly seen. **1770** GOLDSM. *Des. Vill.* 22 Sleights of art and feats of strength went round. **1822** IMISON *Sc. & Art* I. 22 Feats of balancing. **1826** J. WILSON *Noct. Ambr.* Wks. 1855 I. 240 What tricks did the imps perform? They werena tricks, they were fates. **1867** LADY HERBERT *Cradle L.* vi. 155 A wonderful feat of architectural skill.

†**4.** An evil deed; a crime. *Obs.* = FACT *sb.* 1 c.

1481 CAXTON *Godfrey* 224 This fals turk..had don this feet. **1490** —— *Eneydos* iv. 20 The blody faytte vpon me doon by the false..Plasmator. **1559** *Mirr. Mag., Dk. Clarence* xii, Towarde his feat to set me more on fire.

†**5.** A kind of action; one of the operations practised in any art or profession; also, in more comprehensive sense, a department of action, a pursuit, employment, art or profession. *the feat of merchandise*: mercantile business. (*the*) *feat of war*: warfare. *feats of war*: military duties or exercises. *Obs.*

c **1400** *Destr. Troy* 10039 Wise men in werr..Of all fetis enfourmyt, þat to fight longit. *c* **1500** ARNOLDE *Chron.* (1811) 80 Freemen ocupied a bowte the faite of marchandise in ferre contreis. **1511–2** *Act 3 Hen. VIII*, c. 5 §1 To serve the Kyng..in feit of Warre. **1531** ELYOT *Gov.* I. viii. (1537) 24 By the feate of portraiture..a capitayne maye dyscriue the countrey of his aduersary. **1539** CRANMER in Strype *Life* II. (1694) 243 The smith..will not sell..the tools of his occupation. For then how should hee work his feat? **1540** *Act 32 Hen. VIII*, c. 42 §3 Suche persones..exercise barbari, as washynge, or shauyng, and other feates thervnto belongyng. **1555** *Act 2–3 Ph. & M.* c. 11 §4 No..Weaver.. shall..exercise the Feat or Mystery of a Tucker. **1574** J. DEE in *Lett. Lit. Men* (Camden) 38 A good boke or Instrument for Perspective, Astronomy, or som feat of importance. **1577** tr. *Bullinger's Decades* III. i. 268/1 The feate of merchandising is no where condemned throughout the holye Scriptures. **1600** HOLLAND *Livy* XXI. xxv. (1609) 407 A nation unskilfull altogether in the feat of assaulting townes. **1648** MILTON *Tenure Kings* (1650) 57 They.. practise feats in the Artillery-grounds. **1652** NEEDHAM tr. *Selden's Mare Cl.* 498 People..using and exercising the craft and feat of Fishing.

†**6.** The art, knack, or trick of doing anything.

c **1386** CHAUCER *Clerk's T.* 373 Grisildis..Coude all the fete of wifly homliness. *c* **1400** *Destr. Troy* 1529 Masons ..þat mykull fete couthe. **1548** UDALL, etc. *Erasm. Par. Mark* iii. 27 None knewe better the feate howe to worke mischiefe. **1553** *Short Catech.* in *Liturgies, etc.* (1844) 496 More..than that I, by any feat of utterance, may easily express it. **1599** NASHE *Lenten Stuffe* (1871) 107 They want the right feat, how to salt and season them. **1633** FORD *Love's Sacr.* I. ii, I have got the feat on't. **1681** GLANVILL *Sadducismus* II. 39 These Men having..the Feat..of Colouring, Painting and Fucussing.

†**7.** Fact, actuality. In phrases: *the feat of*: the facts that relate to. *in, of feat*: in fact. *Obs.*

13.. *E.E. Allit. P.* B. 1106 Hit ferde freloker in fete in his fayre honde. *a* **1400–50** *Alexander* 30 Þai..Of þe fold & of þe firmament wele þe fete cuthe. **1436** *Pol. Poems* (Rolls) II. 182 Than shulde worshyp unto oure noble be, In feet and forme to lorde and magesté. *c* **1477** CAXTON *Jason* 13 Alway in feet ye haue refused him. **1481** —— *Myrr.* III. iv. I vij b, Will ye thenne after see the fait of the mone. **1490** —— *Eneydos* iv. 18 To haue knowleche of this myracle and of alle the faytte therof. *c* **1500** *Melusine* 184 Of faytte theire was grete scarmysshing and grete losse.

†**b.** *upon the feat of* (Fr. *sur le fait de*): on the subject of, concerning. *Obs.*

1483 CAXTON *Gold. Leg.* 427/1 Gyuyng counceyll to the sowles upon the fayte of theyr conscyence. **1483** —— *G. de la Tour* (1868) 167 Ones it befell to Syre Foucques delaual, as he told me vpon the fayt of this Ensample. *c* **1489** —— *Blanchardyn* xxiii. 76 The proude pucelle..spake..vpon the faytte of her werre.

8. *Comb.* objective, as *feat-worker.*

1617 PURCHAS *Pilgrimage* IV. xviii. §5 (ed. 3) 504 Tumblers, and other feat-workers.

feat (fiːt), *a.* and *adv. Obs.* exc. *arch.* and *dial.* Forms: 4–6 fete, 6 feet(e, (fette, fait, feacte), 6–7 feate, 5– feat. [a. OF. *fait* made:—L. *factus*, pa. pple. of *facĕre* to make.

In Fr. the word seems always to have retained its distinctly ppl. sense. But *fait pour* (lit. 'made for') is now used in much the same way as *feat for, to* (sense 1).]

A. *adj.*

1. Fitting, suitable, proper. Const. *for, to.*

c **1325** *Coer de L.* 3024 Mete and drynk that is nought fete To hys body. **1555** EDEN *Decades* 181 A name very feete and agreable to many of them. **1562** J. HEYWOOD *Prov. & Epigr.* (1867) 73 Shewyng him selfe a new man, as was feet. **1570** DEE *Math. Pref.*, At tymes fete, and in places convenient. **1575** LANEHAM *Let.* (1871) 14 This place..of nature iz foormed so feet for the purpose.

2. Of speech or action (hence of speakers or agents): Apt, apropos; smart, adroit. Of movements: Dexterous, graceful.

1519 HORMAN *Vulg.* Q iij b, The feat conueyans of a speche that soundeth well to the eare. **1532** MORE *Confut. Tindale* Wks. 421 He commeth furth with his fete proper taunte. **1557** *Tottell's Misc.* (Arb.) 157 Who hath plaied a feater cast Since iuglyng first begoon? **1579** LYLY *Euphues* (Arb.) 46 Their wit..forgeth them some feat excuse to cloake their vanitie. **1593** *Bacchus Bountie* in *Harl. Misc.* (Malh.) II. 273 This youth was a feate fellow and a fine faulkner. **1611** SHAKS. *Cymb.* v. v. 88 Neuer Master had A Page..So feate. *a* **1625** FLETCHER *Night-walker* III. vi, She speaks feat English. **1647** JER. TAYLOR *Dissuas. Popery* II. Introd., His reasoning, and deducing from those principles

such feat conclusions. *a* **1699** STILLINGFL. (J.), That feat man at controversy. **1714** GAY *Sheph. Week* Monday 49 The featest maid That e'er at wake delightsome gambol play'd. **1719** CIBBER *Love in a Riddle* II. i, Shew your Skill, and who's the featest Fellow! **1787** GROSE *Provinc. Gloss.* s.v., A feit felly, a dexterous fellow. **1851** S. JUDD *Margaret* III. (1871) 380 With featest strokes she drives forward her canoe.

3. Of dress, etc.: Becoming, well fitting, neat, elegant. Hence of the wearer: Neatly attired.

c **1430** LYDG. *Min. Poems* (Percy Soc.) 37 Feat was hir array. *c* **1450** *Crt. of Love* 1087 Patens faire and fete. **1560** *Proude Wyves Pater Noster* 47 in Hazl. *E.P.P.* IV. 153 Women.. Go feete and fresshe and trymme in theyr gere. **1610** SHAKS. *Temp.* II. i. 273 Looke how well my Garments sit vpon me, Much feater than before. **1613** WITHER *Epithal.* Juvenil. (1633) 364 In your neat'st and feat'st adorning. **1880** in *Antrim & Down Gloss.*

4. Neat in form or appearance, pretty, 'nice', elegant.

a **1471** *MS. Cantab.* Ff. ii. 38, f. 48 (Halliw.) Ye fele ther fete, so fete ar thay. **1519** HORMAN *Vulg.* T'v, She wereth corked slippers to make hir tal and feet. *a* **1536** *Calisto & Melib.* in Hazl. *Dodsley* I. 62 Her mouth proper and feat. **1594** PLATT *Jewell-ho.* III. 7 Small and feate Leaden vveightes. **1607** TOPSELL *Four-f. Beasts* (1673) 229 The Sarmatican kind of Horses is feat and well fashioned. **1623** BINGHAM *Xenophon* 60 A woman of the featest fashion. **1708** *Brit. Apollo* No. 93. 3/2 To what Use, can I put this feat Creature? **1785** BURNS *Halloween* iii, Lasses feat, an' cleanly neat.

5. Affected, finikin.

1540 HYRDE tr. *Vives' Instr. Chr. Wom.* (1592) Kij, She shal not.. use hir voyce to be feat and nice. *a* **1647** *Ess. on Death* in *Bacon's Wks.* (Spedding) VI. 603, I hold such to be but feat boldness, and them that dare commit it, to be vain. **1693** SHADWELL *Volunteers* II, 'Tis the featest finical fellow, I ever saw! **1705** HICKERINGILL *Priest-cr.* I. (1721) 44 Would Pinkethman.. screw his Chaps into such feat Grimaces. **1709** STEELE *Tatler* No. 66 ¶ 11, I proposed to flux him; but Greenhat answer'd, That if he recovered, he'd be as prim and feat as ever he was.

6. *Comb.*, as ***feat-bodied***, ***-looking*** adjs.

1613 BEAUM. & FL. *Coxcomb* III. iii, This is a feat-bodied thing I tell you. **1877** *N.W. Linc. Gloss.* s.v., 'She's a feat-lookin' lass.'

B. *adv.* In a 'feat' manner.

a **1455** *Houlate* 518 To fecht for the faith fete. **1514** BARCLAY *Cyt. & Uplondyshm.* (Percy Soc.) 27 That can gambauld or daunce feat and gent. **1597** SHAKS. *Lover's Compl.* 48 Letters.. With sleided silk feat and affectedly Enswath'd.

†**feat**, *v.* *Obs.* Also 5 fete, feete. [f. the adj. Cf. OF. *faitier*, FAIT *v.*²]

1. *trans.* To equip, furnish, make fit.

a **1400-50** *Alexander* 4632 We ere fetid full faire, & hes oure fyue wittis. **1613** P. FORBES *Comm. Revelat.* xv. 151 The preachers are feated by swallowing of the little booke. *Ibid.* 152 These Ministers of the last wrath are feated and prepared to this great execution.

b. ***to feat oneself forth***: to display oneself.

a **1400-50** *Alexander* 3989 He feetis him forth in his force & in his faire hiȝte.

2. *Falconry.* = FEAK *v.*² (of which it may be a corruption).

1508 FISHER *Wks.* (1876) 154 There she [the sparowe] wypeth and feteth her byl. **1575** TURBERV. *Faulconrie* 120 You must.. feate hir beake and cope hir reasonably.

3. ? To constrain to propriety.

1611 SHAKS. *Cymb.* I. i. 49 [He] Liu'd in Court.. A sample to the yongest: to th' more Mature, A glasse that feated them.

Hence '**feated** *ppl. a.*, suited. '**feating** *vbl. sb.*

1606 BIRNIE *Kirk-Buriall* vii, We mumchance and mourgean in such dilicate duilles, better feated for wowing nor woing. **1682** N. O. *Boileau's Lutrin* III. Argt., Yet for all's Feating, The proof of th' Pudding's seen i' th' eating.

featеous, var. form of FEATOUS *a.*, *Obs.*

feather ('fɛðə(r)), *sb.* Forms: α. 1, 2 feðer, 3 *south.* veðer, 2-5 feþer(e, -ir, 4-6 feder, 5 fedder, 5 fedyr, 4-6 fether, 6- feather. β. 1 fiðer(e, fyðer(e, 2 fi-, fyðer, 2, 4 fyþer. [Com. Teut. OE. *feðer* str. fem. = OS. *fethara* (Du. *veder*, *veer*), OHG. *fedara* (MHG. *veder*(*e*, mod.G. *feder*), ON. *fiǫþr* (Icel. *fjöðr*, Da. *fjeder*, Sw. *fjäder*):—OTeut. **feþrā*:—pre-Teut. **petrā* fem., corresponding (exc. as to declension) to Gr. πτερόν wing, f. root **pet-*, whence Skr. *pat*, Gr. πέτεσθαι to fly. With this word in ME. was to some extent confounded its derivative *fiðere* neut., wing (:—pre-Eng. type **fiþrjo-m*), the examples of which are therefore placed here.]

I. As an appendage.

1. a. One of the epidermal appendages of a bird, usually in the form of a central shaft or midrib, of a horny nature, in part tubular, for the rest square in section and solid, fringed on either side with a 'vane', *i.e.* a row of thin narrow plates mutually adpressed (the 'barbs'), which form a rounded outline at the end. Often preceded by some qualifying word, as *contour-*, *covert-*, *pin-*, *quill-* etc. *feather*. In *Pl.* also Plumage.

a **1000** *Phœnix* 145 (Gr.) þriwa ascæceð feðre flyhthwate. *a* **1225** *Ancr. R.* 140 Ase brid þet haueð lutel uleschs & monie ueðeren. *a* **1250** *Owl & Night.* 1668 Ne schal.. a wrecche feþer on ow bileve. **1393** LANGL. *P. Pl.* C. xv. 173 þe pokok and þe popeiay with here proude federes. **1440** *Promp. Parv.* 152/2 Fedyr, *penna*, *pluma*. **1508** FISHER *Wks.* (1867) 154 She proyneth & setteth her feders in ordre. **1655** MOUFET & BENNET *Health's Improv.* (1746) 171 The best part of a Duck are his Feathers. **1748** F. SMITH *Voy. Disc. N.-W. Pass.* I. 155 The whole Feathers (excepting the Pinion Feathers, and the large Feathers of the Tail) are double. **1870** YEATS *Nat. Hist. Comm.* 309 A feather consists of three parts, the quill, the shaft, and the vane.

b. In various *fig.* expressions: †***two feathers out of a goose***: a very small part of anything. †***to gain more feathers***: (of a rumour) to assume larger proportions. ***to make the feathers fly***: to cause a disturbance, to 'stir up' someone. †***to pick feathers off (a person)***: to plunder. †***to pull the feathers off (a person's fame)***: to detract from. ***to smooth one's rumpled feathers***: to recover one's equanimity. ***to find a white feather in one's tail***; ***to mount, show the white feather***: (in allusion to the fact, that a white feather in a game-bird's tail is a mark of inferior breeding) to perceive, show signs of cowardice. ***to crop the feathers of***: to strip of bravery and pomp. ***you could*** (or ***might***) ***have knocked me*** (etc.) ***down with a feather*** (and similar expressions): used hyperbolically = I was much surprised, astounded, etc.

c **1430** LYDG. *Bochas* I. xii. (1544) 24 a, Of his good fame she gan the feders pull. **1600** HOLLAND *Livy* IX. xxxviii. (1609) 342 The brute.. got more feathers still as it flew. **1677** YARRANTON *Eng. Improv.* 24 All that is, desired is but two Feathers out of their Goose. *Ibid.* 25 The Lawyers Objections are only made.. that they may pick some more Feathers off him. **1741** RICHARDSON *Pamela* I. vii. 13, I was so confounded at these Words, you might have beat me down with a Feather. **1825** *On Bull-baiting* I. (*Houlston Tracts* I. xxvii. 4), I've long guess'd.. that we should find a white feather in thy tail. **1825** J. NEAL *Bro. Jonathan* I. iv. 94 If my New York master.. had hold o' him; he'd make the feathers fly. *Ibid.* II. xxiii. 339 When they are at home.. how the feathers fly! **1827** POLLOK *Course T.* v. 1001 Vanity, With a good conscience pleased, her feathers cropped. **1829** SCOTT *Jrnl.* 15 April, No one will defend him who shows the white feather. **1843** [see sense 10 a]. **1849** DICKENS *Barn. Rudge* lix, '——' said Simon, as he smoothed his rumpled feathers. **1853** LYTTON *My Novel* III. IX. xiii. 69 You might have knocked them down with a feather! **1856** READE *Never too late* xvi, You.. tempt a.. sick creature to mount the white feather. **1924** C. MACKENZIE *Heavenly Ladder* v. 75 At present you could knock me down on a feather, as old Mrs. Geary used to say, I'm that overgone by it all. **1930** W. S. MAUGHAM *Cakes & Ale* vii. 89 When I.. saw Rosie standing there, you could 'ave knocked me down with a feather. **1970** *Globe & Mail* (Toronto) 26 Sept. 5/5 You could have knocked me over with a feather.

c. *Proverb.*

1714 MANDEVILLE *Fab. Bees* (1725) I. 130 Fine feathers make fine birds.

d. *transf.*

1784 COWPER *Task* v. 26 The bents.. fledged with icy feathers, nod superb. **1821** SHELLEY *Prometh. Unb.* IV. 221 Its plumes are as feathers of sunny frost.

2. a. *collect.* Plumage; also *transf.* (of plants); and in *fig.* sense: Attire, 'get-up'. ***all fowls in feather*** = birds of all feather.

c **1400** *Destr. Troy* 343 All fowles in ffether fell þere vppon. *a* **1400-50** *Alexander* 5604 þar fand þai bridis.. Of feþir fresch as any fame. *a* **1634** RANDOLPH *Amyntas* II. iii, What's their Feather? **1842** TENNYSON *Talking Oak* 269 All grass of silky feather grow. **1842** G. DARLING in *Proc. Berw. Nat. Club* II. 10 Which proved to be the male in tolerable feather and condition. **1855** THACKERAY *Newcomes* II. 34, I saw him in full clerical feather.

b. In *fig.* phrases. ***in fine, good, high***, etc. ***feather***: in good condition of health, spirits, etc. ***in full feather***: see quots. Of the weather: ***high feather*** = brilliant condition. †***a man of (the first) feather***: one of (very) showy parts. ***to cut out of all feather***: to take all 'the shine' out of.

1592 NASHE *P. Penilesse* Wks. (Grosart) II. 78 You shall heare a Caualier of the first feather. **1667** DRYDEN *Maiden Queen* v. i, A man of garniture and feather is above the dispensation of the sword. **1781** G. SELWYN *Let.* in *15th Rep. Hist. MSS. Comm.* App. VI. (1897) 505 He [*sc.* C. J. Fox] is in high feather. **1834** W. N. GLASCOCK *Naval Sketch-Bk.* 2nd Ser. I. 149 A lady in full feather approached the sentinel on the sward. **1844** DICKENS *Mart. Chuz.* (Househ. ed.) 416/2 Todgers's was in high feather. **1852** R. S. SURTEES *Sponge's Sp. Tour* xiii. 65 Our friend.. was now in good feather; he had got a large price for his good-for-nothing horse. **1855** DICKENS *Dorrit* xxxii, I'm in wonderful feather. **1855** J. E. COOKE *Ellie* 476 No words can describe the serene effulgence of the Heartsease appearance, when in full feather, and high spirits. **1860** HOTTEN *Slang Dict.* 138 *In full feather*, rich. *a* **1865** SMYTH *Sailor's Word-Bk.* (1867) 327 *Full feather*, attired in best dress or uniform. **1865** SCOTT in *Reader* No. 121. 452/3 She cut me out of all feather. **1873** EDWARDES & MERIVALE *Life Sir H. Lawrence* I. 389 Havelock in great feather showed us round the fields of battle. **1878** T. HARDY *Return of Native* i. (1879) 10 In summer days of highest feather. **1886** BARING-GOULD *Court Royal* xxiv, Never was Mr. Rigsby in finer feather than at Court Royal. **1886** *Graphic* 30 Jan. 130/2 Watty, by reason of his office [of butler], was of course always 'in full feather'.

c. Description of plumage; species (of bird). Often *transf.* in phrases ***of the same, that, every***, etc. ***feather***: = of the same, etc. kind or character. Proverb, ***birds of a feather flock together***.

1581 J. BELL *Haddon's Answ. Osor.* 300 A Byrd of the same feather. **1599** MINSHEU *Sp. Gram.* 83 Birdes of a feather will flocke togither. **1607** SHAKS. *Timon* I. i. 100, I am not of that Feather, to shake off My Friend when he must neede me. **1608** DAY *Hum. out of Br.* IV. iii, A whole brood of signets, and all of a feather. **1611** COTGR. s.v. *Alaine*, A bird of his owne feather. **1645** RUTHERFORD *Tryal & Tri. Faith* (1845) 60 Fowls of a feather flock together. **1650** R. STAPYLTON *Strada's Low C. Warres* v. 121 Many of the Covenanters were birds of the same feather. **1665** J. SPENSER *Vulg. Prophecies* 70 He knows good men are soonest decoyed by those which seem of a feather with themselves. **1767** S. PATERSON *Another Traveller!* II. 48 Four hundred and fifty of them.. will be of the misjudging feather. **1827** POLLOK *Course T.* v. 328 Birds of social feather, helping each His fellow's flight. **1829** CARLYLE *Misc.* (1857) I. 272 Literary quacks of every feather. **1878** BROWNING *La Saisiaz* 4 Ferns of all feather.

†**3.** Used in *pl.* for: Wings. *Obs.* [Cf. L. *pennæ*; the pl. *feðera* was so used in OE., but some of the examples in 12-14th c. prob. belong to OE. *fiðere* wing.]

c **850** *Martyrology Fragm.* in *O.E. Texts* (1885) 177 þa hi bæron to heofonum mid hiora fiðra flyhte. *c* **888** K. ÆLFRED *Boeth.* xxxvi. §2 Ic hæbbe swiþe swifte feþera. *c* **1000** *Ags. Gosp.* Matt. xxiii. 37 Swa seo henn hyre cicenu under hyre fyþeru [*c* **1160** *Hatton* fiþera] ȝegaderað. *c* **1200** *Vices & Virtues* (1888) 101 Vnder ðare scadewe of ðine fiðeres. *c* **1290** *S. Eng. Leg.* I. 64/357 And feþerene to beren eow up-on heiȝ. *a* **1340** HAMPOLE *Psalter* xvii. 12 He flow abouen þe feþirs of wyndes. *c* **1450** *De Imitatione* III. xxiii, ȝeue me feders of very liberte. **1535** COVERDALE *2 Sam.* xxii. 11 He.. appeared vpon the fethers of the wynde. **1595** SHAKS. *John* IV. ii. 174 Be Mercurie, set feathers to thy heeles. **1614** RALEIGH *Hist. World* I. 146 Josephus gave all Noah's children feathers, to carry them far away.

fig. *c* **1374** CHAUCER *Boeth.* IV. i. 110, I shal ficche feþeres in þi þouȝt. **1593** SHAKS. *Lucr.* 1216 Fleet-wing'd duty with thought's feathers flies. **1595** *Drake's Voy.* (Hakluyt Soc.) 4 Hee hath feathers to fly to the toppe of his high desires.

4. A feathered animal; a bird. Also *collect.* Feathered game.

1601 SHAKS. *Twel. N.* III. i. 71 Like the Haggard, checke at euery Feather. **1684** R. H. *School Recreat.* 136 Your Setting-Dog must.. love naturally to hunt Feathers. **1875** 'STONEHENGE' *Brit. Sports* I. I. vii. §7. 106 The true Sussex may easily be kept strictly to feather. **1887** *Pall Mall G.* 24 Aug. 13/2 He wandered.. slaying whatever of fur and feather came in his way.

II. As a detached object.

5. a. Simply; also *pl.* as a commodity.

c **1000** *Sax. Leechd.* I. 234 Smyre mid nire [i.e. niwre] feþere. **13..** *E.E. Allit. P.* B. 1026 For.. folde þer-on a lyȝt fyþer & hit to founs synkkez. *c* **1400** MAUNDEV. (Roxb.) xii. 50 If men caste a fether þerin, it synkez to þe grund. *c* **1440** *Anc. Cookery* in *Househ. Ord.* (1790) 469 And with a feder sprinke and spot the congour. **1593** SHAKS. *3 Hen. VI*, III. i. 84 Looke, as I blow this Feather from my Face. **1608-11** BP. HALL *Medit. & Vows* II. §25 The Larke.. while it playeth with the feather.. is caught in the Fowlers-net. **1614** —— *Recoll. Treat.* 413 That was but as the fowlers feather, to make mee stoope. **1745** *De Foe's Eng. Tradesman* xxvi. (1841) I. 266 The feathers also from the same country. **1800** tr. *Lagrange's Chem.* II. 422 Feathers.. give nearly the same products as hair. **1841-44** EMERSON *Ess.*, *Prudence* Wks. (Bohn) I. 99 Everything in nature, even motes and feathers, go by law.

b. *Proverb.*

1861 A. LEIGHTON *Curious Storied Traditions* Ser. II. 263 There's aye feathers where the doo [doves] roosts.

†**6.** A pen. *Obs.*

c **1000** *Ags. Gosp.* Luke xvi. 6 Nim þine feðere & site hraðe & writ fiftiȝ. *c* **1205** LAY. 49 Feþeren he [Laȝamon] nom mid fingren. **1781** S. C. KING in *Med. Obs. & Inq.* (1784) VI. XXII. 231, I send you a feather or pen.. extracted from the œsophagus of a man.

7. A portion, or (*sing.* and *pl.*) portions, of a feather attached to the base of an arrow, to direct its flight. Also *collect.*

a **1631** DRAYTON *Robin Hood*, Their arrows finely paired, for timber and for feather. **1661** BOYLE *Style of Script.* 90 Those Historical Circumstances.. are like the Feathers that wing our Arrows. **1748** RICHARDSON *Clarissa* Wks. 1883 VIII. 406 The barbed dart.. sticks not in their hearts.. up to the very feathers. **1825** FOSBROKE *Encycl. Antiq.* (1843) II. xiii. 689/1 They required nimble strong arrows, with a middling feather. **1874** BOUTELL *Arms & Arm.* viii. 134 The shafts of these arrows were provided, near their base, with feathers, or with strips of leather.

8. a. As a personal decoration; a plume, *esp.* in ***ostrich-feather***. Also collect. ***Prince of Wales' feathers***, also ***the feather***: the plume of three ostrich feathers, first adopted as a crest by the Black Prince. ***flush feather***: see quot. 1823.

1473 WARKW. *Chron.* 14 He.. wered ane estryche feder. **1536** WRIOTHESLEY *Chron.* (1875) I. 51 Hattes of blake velwett and whyte feethers. **1613** SHAKS. *Hen. VIII*, I. iii. 24 They must.. leaue those remnants Of foole and Feather. **1615** J. STEPHENS *Satir. Ess.* (ed. 2) 211 Hee stickes a feather in his Hat. **1742** YOUNG *Nt. Th.* viii. 429 Not in the feather, wave it e'er so high.. Is glory lodg'd. **1802** WOLCOTT (P. Pindar) *Gt. Cry Little Wool* Wks. 1812 V. 166 The tradesmen.. proud of the feather. **1804** WINDHAM *Sp. Additional Force Bill* 5 June in *Sp.* 1812 II. 229 The volunteers have.. feathers as high.. as those of the regular troops. **1823** CRABB *Technol. Dict.*, *Feather* (*Mil.*), an ornamental mark worn by officers and soldiers on their caps and hats.. the *flush feather*, a straight smooth feather worn by officers on the staff. **1887** *Pall Mall G.* 27 Sept. 11/1 The Prince of Wales's feathers stand separate.

b. Phrases: ***a feather in the cap, hat***: a decoration, mark of honour, *lit.* and *fig.* (also *ellipt.*); also †the badge of a fool; hence †***Jack with the feather, a plume of feathers***, for a trifling person. †***to shake, wag the feather***: to make a display of one's honours.

1581 PETTIE *Guazzo's Civ. Conv.* Pref. (1586) A vj b, Though a man shake the feather after the best fashion, and take upon him never so biglie, hee [etc.]. **1588** SHAKS. *L.L.L.* IV. i. 96 What plume of feathers is hee that indited this Letter. *a* **1633** *Flodden F.* xii. in Child *Ballads* III. VI.

clxviii. 353 Jack with a feather was lapt all in leather. **1655** FULLER *Ch. Hist.* v. iv. §17 He wore a feather in his cap, and wagg'd it too often. *a* **1700** B. E. *Dict. Cant. Crew* s.v., He has a Feather in his Cap, a Periphrasis for a Fool. **1734** DUCHESS OF PORTLAND *Let. to Miss Collingwood* in *Autob. Mrs. Delany* I. 511 My Lord.. esteems it a feather in his hat, that [etc.]. **1736** LEDIARD *Life Marlborough* III. 370 A Feather in his Cap, was the least that was expected for him. **1818** BYRON *Juan* I. cxcix, Their favour in an author's cap's a feather. **1825** M. CONSTABLE *Let.* 2 May in *J. Constable's Corr.* (1962) 220, I expect your *Barge Horse* will do wonders for you—only think of the Medal, what a *feather* it is. **1874** HELPS *Soc. Press.* v. 70 It is always a feather in my cap when [etc.]. **1958** *Times* 22 Oct. 14/1 Had Slater collected these two feathers to go with yesterday's collection he would have had a memorable match. **1968** J. F. STRAKER *SIN & Johnny Inch* 211 Strip off if you feel like it; I reckon this has been quite a feather.

9. In *pl.* As material for filling bedding, etc.

1649 G. DANIEL *Trinarch., Rich. II*, clxxviii, Richard.. Sleeps on the feathers which himselfe had drest.

10. a. Referred to as an object almost without weight, and capable of being moved with the greatest ease.

1562 J. HEYWOOD *Prov. & Epigr.* (1867) 35 Than shall we see two men beare a fether. **1611** SHAKS. *Wint. T.* II. iii. 154, I am a Feather for each Wind that blows. **1728** POPE *Dunc.* II. 44 A brain of feathers and a heart of lead. *a* **1839** PRAED *Poems* (1864) I. 232 Folly's breath.. would not stir a feather. **1843** HOOD *Forge* II. xvi, Fit for knocking down with a feather. **1852** MRS. STOWE *Uncle Tom's C.* vii, She felt the weight of her boy as if it had been a feather. **1872** BLACK *Adv. Phaeton* xxii. 307 Tita, who weighs about a feather and a half.

b. Hence: Anything of little strength or importance; a very small amount, a trifle. † *(to be pleased) to a feather*: to a nicety.

1601 SHAKS. *All's Well* v. iii. 232 You boggle shrewdly, euery feather starts you. **1659** *Burton's Diary* (1828) IV. 376 They must be pleased to a feather. **1675** TRAHERNE *Chr. Ethics* xxv. 390 A straw and a feather shall forfeit all the obligations in the world, in some tempers. *a* **1700** B. E. *Dict. Cant. Crew, Titter*, to Laugh at a Feather. **1794** T. JEFFERSON *Writ.* (1859) IV. 112 Rising at a feather against our friends.

c. = FEATHER-WEIGHT. *to ride a feather*: see quot. 1823.

1760 HEBER *Horse Matches* ix. 20 Mr. Turner's bay.. 5 years old, carrying a feather. **1822** *Examiner* 232/2 Dr. Ph-ll-m-re, very light, a feather, took the field on his new rat-tail mare. **1823** 'J. BEE' *Dict. Turf, etc.*, Boys under six stone are said to 'ride a feather'.

III. Something resembling a feather.

11. a. On human beings: A tuft or ridge of hair standing more or less upright. **b.** On horses: (see quot. 1803). Also on other animals.

a. *c* **1530** LD. BERNERS *Arth. Lyt. Bryt.* (1814) 301 Arthur and Bawdwin.. shoke theyr eares to put awaye the fethers fro their heyre. **1580** BARET *Alv.* F 320 *Feather*.. the curled bush of frizled haire (wherewith lustie gallants of late would seeme to counterfeit this iollie feather. **1841** S. WARREN *Ten Thousand a Year* II. v, What's a feather?.. You see, sir, 'tis when a small lot of hair on a gent's head will stick up, do all we can to try and get it down. **1851** *Blackw. Mag.* June 680 He wore his hair cropped close, except just in front, where it formed what the hair-dresser called a feather.

b. **1580** BLUNDEVIL *Art of Riding* I. ii. 2 The Horse that hath an Ostrich feather.. on his forehead.. can neuer be euill Horse. **1598** FLORIO, *Circhiello*, that which is called a feather in a horse. **1617** MARKHAM *Caval.* II. 6 Euery horse.. hath a feather in his forehead. **1682** *Lond. Gaz.* No. 1692/4 A light Grey Nag.. a Feather in the.. Neck. **1737** H. BRACKEN *Farriery* (1757) II. 7 Feathers, or different Turnings of the Hair, in several parts of a Horse's body. **1803** W. TAPLIN *Sport Dict.* 248 Feather. The Centrical division, and different directions, of the surrounding hair in a horse's forehead is so called: they are also frequently seen upon the neck.. the mane, and.. the hind quarters, and are considered natural ornaments. **1878** C. HALLOCK *Hallock's Amer. Club List & Sportsman's Gloss.* p. iv/2 *Feather*, the long, flowing hairs which adorn the legs of a dog. **1884** W. G. STABLES *Our Friend the Dog* vii. 60 *Feather*, the long hair on chest, legs, and tail, &c., of some breeds. The hair generally. **1897** *Outing* (U.S.) XXX. 413/1 The coat [of the Russian wolfhound] is long.., forming a liberal 'feather' upon the legs, chest, belly and hindquarters. **1914** *N.Z. Farmer* Apr., Although the General Trend of the hair [*sc.* on the part between the hock and the vulva of a cow] is in an ascending direction there are variations on certain points where changes in the direction of the growth makes the hair stand up on ridges, sometimes forming figures. These variations are called feathers. There are in all seven feathers. 1 The Oval feather. 2 The Buttock feather. 3 The Babine feather. 4 The Vulvous feather. 5 The Bastard feather. 6 The Thigh feather. 7 The Dart feather. **1942** 'M. INNES' *Daffodil Affair* I. 30 'A nice dog,' Appleby said... Mr. Gee swung round. 'Dish-faced,' he said... 'Cow-hocked. No feather. Apple-headed. Pily'. **1954** E. MEGARGEE *Dog Dict.* 47 There is abundant feather on the chest, belly, hindquarters, and legs [of a field spaniel].

c. The foamy crest of a wave. Cf. CUT *v.* 38 b.

1838 *Civil Eng. & Arch. Jrnl.* I. 272/1 The feather only of each wave would be seen. **1896** *Daily News* 10 July 3/6 White feathers from their bows.

d. (See quot. 1928.)

1928 *Papers Mich. Acad. Sci. Arts & Lett.* X. 292 *Feather*, the wake or ripple left by a protruding periscope. The 'feather' was often visible when the periscope was not. **1943** 'T. DUDLEY-GORDON' *Coastal Command* 28 You may pass by the tell-tale feather of a periscope.

12. A blemish or flaw having a feather-like appearance: **a.** in the eye; **b.** in a precious stone.

1847 LEVER *Knt. of Gwynne* xxxix. 335 He had only one [eye], there was a feather on the other. **1866** MISS BRADDON *Lady's Mile* 190 She had learned to discover a 'feather' in a fifty-guinea emerald ring. **1879** —— *Vixen* III. 293, I don't think there is a feather in one of the stones.

13. *Confectionery.* One of the degrees in boiling sugar. Also *the great, little feather*: see quots. Cf. Fr. *à la (grande, petite) plume*.

1827 JARRIN *Italian Confectioner* (ed. 3) 3 Confectioners.. have seven essential.. bases of their art.. 4. La plume, the feather. *Ibid.* 4 The larger and greater quantity of bubbles, when blown through the skimmer, are the large feather. *Ibid.* 9 Boil to the feather some of the same clarified sugar. *Ibid.* 60 Clarify a pound of loaf sugar, boil it to the large feather. **1829** *Ibid.* 177 Take a pound of clarified sugar, boil to the little feather. **1883** *Workshop Receipts* Ser. II. 152 For the 'feather,' dip the skimmer again into the sugar, and blow through the holes as before.

†**14.** *Swedish feather*: see quot. *Obs.*

1652 URQUHART *Jewel* Wks. (1834) 243 Staves with iron pikes at both ends, commonly called Swedish feathers.

15. In various phrases: *(to wear) the bull's feather*: see BULL 11 b. *Naut. to cut a feather*: see CUT *v.* 38 b. In quot. *fig.* To move briskly.

1684 T. GODDARD *Plato's Demon* 317 Men who.. have not the skill to cut a feather, very often dance themselves into that noose. **1822** SCOTT *Pirate* xxxiv, He shambles about.. as well as ever he did—for Jack could never cut a feather.

16. In various technical uses.

a. A longitudinal rib added to a shaft, etc. to increase its strength.

1823 BUCHANAN *Millwork* 263 Apply the feathers merely to prevent bending in the middle. **1839** R. S. ROBINSON *Naut. Steam Eng.* 63, Z is a strengthening feather, under the crank frame. *Ibid.* 65 From the eye run six strong arched radii or feathers, terminating in a ledge. **1842–76** GWILT *Encycl. Archit.* §1629 d, Transverse ribs or feathers on cast iron beams are to be avoided.

b. *Mining* and *Quarrying.* (see quot.)

1865 J. T. F. TURNER *Slate Quarries* 13 A hole is jumped in the block [of slate] near the edge; in this, two slightly curved pieces of iron are placed (the 'feathers'), having the concave surfaces toward each other, between them is inserted an iron punch; this is forcibly hammered in, and breaks the stone asunder. **1883** GRESLEY *Gloss. Terms Coal-Mining, Feathers.* [Describes a similar contrivance in coal mines.]

c. A projection on a board, implement, or piece of machinery; *esp.* one intended to fit into some other part. Cf. FIN.

1765 A. DICKSON *Treat. Agric.* (ed. 2) 212 The firm earth.. is opened by the feather of the other sock. **1874** KNIGHT *Dict. Mech.* I. 828/1 *Feather*, a slip inserted longitudinally into a shaft or arbor, and projecting as a fin therefrom so as to fit a groove. *Ibid., Feather*, a tongue on the edge of a board. **1884** F. J. BRITTEN *Watch & Clockm.* 237 There is a feather in the straight part of the mandrel hole.

d. *Salt-works.* (see quot.)

1753 CHAMBERS *Cycl. Supp., Mid-Feather* in the English salt-works, the name given to a sort of partition placed in the middle of the furnace.. This partition divides the body of the furnace into two chambers.

e. *dial.* 'A linch-pin; a pin used to keep machinery tight' (*N.W. Linc. Gloss.* 1877).

1908 *Westm. Gaz.* 28 May 4/2 The gear-wheels are mounted on shafts, each having four 'feathers'.

IV. [Properly a distinct word: f. the vb.]

17. *Rowing.* The action of feathering. See FEATHER *v.* 11.

1865 *Pall Mall G.* 16 May 10 Oxford and Cambridge styles used to be palpably different to the eye by the height of the feather. **1884** *St. James's Gaz.* 28 Mar. 6/2 The feather was cleaner than that of Cambridge. **1885** *Manch. Guard.* 28 Mar. 6/6 The feather is exquisitely even, and this is the best point in their rowing.

V. *attrib.* and *Comb.*

18. General combinations: **a.** simple attrib., as *feather boa, -bolster, -brush, club, -embroidery, -fan, -flower, -guise, -merchant, -pattern, -plume, -tract*. **b.** objective, as *feather-beater, -cleanser, -dresser, -drier, -finisher, -seller*; *feather-bearing* adj. **c.** instrumental, as *feather-cinctured, -clouded, -tasselled* adjs. **d.** parasynthetic and similative, as *feather-legged, -light, -like, -nerved, -soft, -tailed, -thick, -veined, -white, -witted*, adjs.; *feather-wise* adv.

c **1050** *Glosses* in Wr.-Wülcker 465 *Penniger*, *feþerberend. **1881** MIVART *Cat* 377 The feather-bearing side of the hand. **1855** H. CLARKE *Dict.*, **Feather-beater*, feather cleanser. **1895** *Army & Navy Co-op. Soc. Price List* 15 Sept. 1041 Black and Coloured *Feather Boas. **1902** *Queen* 15 Feb. Advt. 2nd sheet, Lace Berthes and Feather Boas. **1533** in Rogers *Agric. & Prices* III. 573/4 *Feather bolster 5/-. **1856** W. COLLINS *After Dark* Yellow Mask III. v, He was dusting his favourite busts.. with a *feather-brush when she came in. **1757** GRAY *Progress of Poesy* II. ii, Their *feather-cinctur'd Chief, and dusky Loves. **1829** GEN. P. THOMPSON in *Westm. Rev.* XI. 229 Some feather-cinctured sage. **1605** SYLVESTER *Du Bartas* II. iii. IV. Captains 747 His *feather-clouded Crest. **1899** R. WHITEING *No. 5 John St.* x. 101 A *Feather Club is an institution for supplying our womenkind with.. ostrich plumes for their hats. **1647** HAWARD *Crown Rev.* 26 *Feather-dresser: Fee—13. 6. 8. **1858** SIMMONDS *Dict. Trade, Feather-dresser. Ibid.*, **Feather-drier.* **1843** PRESCOTT *Mexico* (1850) I. 299 Beautiful mantles of the *plumaje*, or *feather embroidery. **1864** TENNYSON *Aylmer's F.* 289 Cooling her false cheek with a *featherfan. **1886** BESANT *Children of Gibeon* II. vi, Sign-writers, *feather-finishers and the like. **1858** SIMMONDS *Dict. Trade*, **Feather-flowers*, artificial flowers made of feathers.. used by ladies for head ornaments and for fancy plumes. **1889** R. B. ANDERSON tr. *Rydberg's Teut. Myth.* 60 In the Norse mythology several goddesses.. have.. *feather-guises. **1872–4** L. WRIGHT *Poultry* xi. 129 The chickens were *feather-legged. *c* **1837** HOOD *Ode to My Son* i, With spirits *feather-light. **1776** WITHERING *Bot. Arrangem. Vegetables* 680 Little *feather-like shoots rising single from the base of the leaves. **1807** T. THOMSON *Chem.* (ed. 3) II. 270 Long, slender, flat, feather-like crystals. **1858** SIMMONDS *Dict. Trade*, **Feather-merchant*, an importer or wholesale dealer in feathers. **1840** PAXTON *Bot. Dict.*, **Feather-nerved*, the nerves disposed like the feathers of a pen. **1883** W. G. COLLINGWOOD *Philos. Ornament* iv. 85 Barbaric annulets, zigzags, *feather-patterns, are found upon early vases. **1885** A. M. CLERKE *Pop. Hist. Astron.* 83 *Feather-plumes or *aigrettes*. **1755** JOHNSON, **Featherseller*, one who sells feathers for beds. **1923** E. SITWELL *Bucolic Comedies* 38 The goose-girl smoothed down her *feather-soft Breast. **1883** F. M. CRAWFORD *Mr. Isaacs* ii, Small head, small feet, and *feather-tailed. **1883** *Gd. Words* 113 Gorgeous articles of native dress *feather-tasseled, shell-fringed, coral-beaded. **1884** BROWNING *Ferishtah* (1885) 122 Snow, *feather-thick, is falling while I feast. **1878** BELL *Gegenbauer's Comp. Anat.* 419 The arrangement also of these first rudiments of the feathers in definite areas (*feather-tracts, pterylia). **1861** BENTLEY *Manual Bot.* 152 **Feather-veined*.. In these the midrib gives off lateral veins which proceed at once to the margins and are connected by numerous branching veinlets. **1876** H. BALFOUR in *Encycl. Brit.* (ed. 9) IV. 110 Veins going directly to the margin and forming feather-veined leaves (Oak and Chestnut). **1883** W. C. RUSSELL *Sailor's Lang.*, **Feather-white sea*, said of the sea when covered with foam. **1600** HOLLAND *Livy* x. xxix. (1609) 373 b, Opposing their targuets before them, raunged and joined one over another *featherwise. **1930** W. DE LA MARE *On Edge* 295 That black-eyed, painted-up, *feather-witted little Italian Countess.

19. a. Special comb.: **feather-alum**, see ALUM *sb.* 4; **feather ball**, a golf-ball stuffed with feathers (cf. FEATHERY *a.* 4); **feather-bird** *dial.*, the Whitethroat (*Sylvia cinerea*); **feather-boarding**, a covering of boards which thin off towards the lower edge, and overlap like a bird's feathers; **feather-bog**, a quagmire, *dial.* (Halliwell 1847); **feather-brain**, a person with a light or weak brain, whence also a light or weak brain; **feather-brained** *a.*, foolish, giddy; **feather-cling**, *Sc.*, a disease among cattle; **feather-cloth** (see quot.); †**feather-cock**, a coxcomb; **feather-curler**, one employed in curling feathers; †**feather-driver**, (*a*) = QUILL-DRIVER, (*b*) 'one who cleanses feathers by whisking them about' (J.); **feather-duster**, a brush made of feathers, used for dusting; **feather-eyed**, ? having a 'feather' (12 a) in one's eye; **feather-foot**, a foot as light as a feather, in quot. *fig.*; †**feather-glory** *nonce-wd.*, light and transitory glory; **feather-heeled** *a.* = FEATHER-FOOTED; **feather-joint** (see quot.); †**feather-lock**, *Sc.*, a spring-lock; **feather-mail**, the dress of feathers resembling a coat of mail worn by the Indians of Mexico, prior to the Spanish conquest; **feather-monger**, one who deals in feathers, also *transf.* of a bird; **feather-mosaic**, patterns worked in feathers; **feather-ore** *Min.* (see quot. 1863); **feather-painting**, the art of using feathers of various colours in place of pigments; **feather-pated** *a.* = FEATHER-HEADED; †**feather-peeper**, ? tips of feathers decorating a headdress; **feather-pie** (see quot.); **feather-poke**, (*a*) a bag of feathers, (*b*) applied to the Willow Warbler (*Phylloscopus trochilus*), the Long-tailed Titmouse (*Acredula rosea*), and the Wren (*Motacilla troglodytes*), perhaps from the appearance of their nests; **feather-process** (see quot.); **feather-pulp**, the pulp or matrix from which the feather is formed; **feather-shot copper** (see quot.); **feather-spray** (see quot.); **feather-spring**, the spring in a gun-lock which causes the *sear*, which holds the hammer at full or half cock, to catch in the notch of the tumbler; †**feather-staff**, a light kind of halbert; **feather-star**, a star-fish (*Comatula rosacea*); **feather-stick**, a stick covered with feathers; **feather-top**, nickname of a parrot (also *attrib.* = next); **feather-topped** *a.*, (of a wig) frizzed at the top (see FEATHER *sb.* 11); **feather-tuft**, an edible mushroom, *Clavaria cristata* (Hay *Brit. Fungi* (1887) 234); †**feather-wife**, a woman whose duty it was to prepare feathers for use; †**feather-worker**, one who prepares feathers. Also FEATHER-BED, FEATHER-EDGE, FEATHER-FOOTED *a.*, etc.

a **1693** URQUHART *Rabelais* III. lii. 425 Do not here instance in competition with this Sacred Herb the *Feather Allum. **1863–72** WATTS *Dict. Chem.* II. 617 *Feather-alum*, a name applied to native hydrated sulphate of aluminum.. and to native iron-alum or halotrichite.. both of which occur in delicate fibrous crystals or masses. **1893** H. G. HUTCHINSON *Golfing* 4 All this went on before the days of gutta-percha. Men played with '*feather balls'—that is, balls of leather stuffed.. tightly with feathers. **1885** SWAINSON *Prov. Names Brit. Birds* 23 *Feather bird. **1846** WORCESTER (citing LOUDON), **Feather-boarding.* **1839** CARLYLE *Chartism* x. 181 Poor palpitating *featherbrain. **1888** W. S. GILBERT *Yeom. of Guard* (1889) I. 7 Thou hast a feather-brain. **1941** A. L. ROWSE *Tudor Cornwall* xi. 269 Perhaps.. it was his feather-brains which saved his head. **1820** SCOTT *Monast.* xvi, Such a *feather-brained coxcomb as this. **1841** EMERSON *Lect., Conservative* Wks. (Bohn) II. 269 Your opposition is feather-brained and over-fine. **1799** *Highland Soc. Ess.* II. 218 **Feather Cling*.. is occasioned by want of water in very dry summers or in the hard frosts of winters. **1882** CAULFEILD & SAWARD *Dict. Needlework*,

*Feather Cloth, a mixture of cloth and feathers woven together. **1612** tr. *Benvenuto's Passenger* 19 Muskats, syrenists, *feather-cockes. **1881** *Instr. Census Clerks* (1885) 79 *Feather..Curler. **1895** *Daily News* 4 Apr. 5/6 Earning fifteenpence a day as a feather-curler. **1593** NASHE *Four Lett. Confut.* K 1 b, The onely *feather-driuer of phrases and putter of a good word to it when thou hast once got it. **1713** DERHAM *Phys. Theol.* VI. vii. 152 note, A Feather-Driver who had these Bladders filled with the fine Dust or Down of Feathers. **1858** SIMMONDS *Dict. Trade*, **Feather-duster.* c **1600** DAY *Begg. Bednall Gr.* II. ii, So *feather-ey'd ye cannot let us passe in the kings high way? **1821** CLARE *Vill. Minstr.* I. 209 The breeze with *feather-feet, Crimping o'er the waters sweet. a **1626** BP. ANDREWES *Serm.* (1856) I. 31 Glory, not like ours here *feather-glory. ?**16..** *Songs Lond. 'Prentices* (Percy Soc.) 66 The *feather-heel'd wenches that live by their owne. **1840** HOOD *Up the Rhine* 100 The wit of the Germans is not feather-heeled. **1874** KNIGHT *Dict. Mech.*, **Feather-joint*, a mode of joining the edges of boards by a fin or feather let into opposite mortises on the edges of the boards. **1478** *Act. Audit.* 82 That Schir Jhone..pay for..a *fethir lok xviii d. **1843** PRESCOTT *Mexico* (1850) I. 363 The like colours on the *feather-mail of the Indians, showed that they were the warriors of Xicotencatl. **1599** NASHE *Lenten Stuffe* 51 Some fowler with his nets, as this host of *fether mungers were getting up to ride double, inuolued or intangled them. **1767** S. PATERSON *Another Traveller!* II. 147 The open-hearted feather-monger. **1843** PRESCOTT *Mexico* (1850) I. 153 The arts of working in metals, jewelry, and *feather-mosaic. **1767** SEIFERTH tr. *Gellert's Metal. Chem.* 41 *Feather ore consists of the smallest capillary-like feathers. **1863-72** WATTS *Dict. Chem.* II. 617 *Feather ore*, this name is applied to the capillary form of native sulphantimonite of lead. **1843** PRESCOTT *Mexico* (1850) I. 123 Count Carli is in raptures with a specimen of *feather-painting which he saw in Strasbourg. **1820** SCOTT *Ivanhoe* xxxiv, The *feather-pated giddy mad-men. **1757** MRS. DELANY *Life & Corr.* (1861) III. 467 Madame Godineau in a round card cap of black lace ..it was a pity '*feather-peepers' were not added to the cap. a **1825** FORBY *Voc. E. Anglia*, **Feather-pie*, a hole in the ground, filled with feathers fixed on strings, and kept in motion by the wind. An excellent device to scare birds. **1559** *Wills & Inv. N.C.* (Surtees) 170 Two *feder poks, two payre of harne sheits, two couerletts. **1831** W. HOWITT *Bk. Seasons* Apr. 91 The little willow-wren builds an oval nest after the fashion of the common wren and the feather-poke. **1837** BYWATER *Sheffield Dial.* (1877) 193 It's just loik thrustin yer hand up to't rist into a feather poke nest. **1877** *N.W. Linc. Gloss.*, When it snows we say 't'owd woman is shackin' her feather-poke'. **1885** SWAINSON *Prov. Names Brit. Birds* 26 Willow warbler..Feather poke. *Ibid.* 32 British Long-tailed Titmouse..Feather poke. **1888** *Sheffield Gloss.*, *Feather poke*, the wren. **1878** BELL *Gegenbauer's Comp. Anat.* 419 The first sign of the feather is the growth of the knobs into papilliform processes (*feather-processes). **1859** TODD *Cycl. Anat.* V. 480/1 On the surface of the *feather-pulp a series of ridges are developed. **1869** *Eng. Mech.* 31 Dec. 388/1 Bean..and *feather shot copper [is made] by pouring [melted copper] into cold water. **1867** SMYTH *Sailor's Word-bk.*, **Feather spray*, such as is observed at the cutwater of fast steamers, forming a pair of wing feathers. **1807** *Sporting Mag.* XXIX. 207 Mr. Meredith's pistol had no *feather spring. **1833** *Regul. Instr. Cavalry* I. 95 The Recruit..is to take it..near the lock, his little finger touching the feather-spring. **1622** F. MARKHAM *Bk. War* IV. iv. 135 The only weapons for a Captaine, are a faire *Feather-staffe in the time of Peace. **1862** ANSTED *Channel Isl.* II. ix. (ed. 2) 237 The *feather-star (*Comatula rosacea*), represents the crinoids. **1824** BURCHELL *Trav.* II. 579 The *feather-stick often renders the natives important service. **1775** D. GARRICK *Bon Ton* Prol., The Tyburn scratch, thick club, and Temple tye, The parson's *feather-top, frizz'd broad and high! **1891** *Scott. Leader* 24 Oct. 4 The antique feather-top screamed the same phrases twelve months ago at Mr. Colston. **1785** MRS. BENNET *Juv. Indiscretions* (1786) I. 185 His nice *feather-top-wig. **1774** FOOTE *Cozeners* I. Wks. 1799 II. 158 His wig..white as a curd, *feather-topped, and the curls as close as a cauliflower. **1788** V. KNOX *Winter Even.* III. VII. i. 4 Divest them of their feather-topt wigs, their gowns and cassocks. **1867** LADY LLANOVER *Good Cookery* 53 As soon as the feathers were dry, they were taken away by the *featherwife. **1552** HULOET, *Fetherworcker, *plumarius*.

b. In various plant-names as **feather-bow** = FEVERFEW; **feather-columbine** (see quot. 1878-86); **feather-fern** (see quot. 1882); **feather-foil**, the water violet (*Hottonia palustris*); **feather-grass**, a perennial feather grass (*Stipa pennata*); **feather-moss**, the name of a genus (*Hypnum*) of British mosses; **feather-top wild campion** (see quot. 1597); **feather-top grass** (see quot. 1878-86); **feather-wood** (see quot. 1884).

1880 *E. Cornwall Gloss.*, **Feather bow*, fever few, *Matricaria parthenium*. **1878-86** BRITTEN & HOLLAND *Plant-n.*, *Feather..Columbine..A frequent book-name for *Thalictrum aquilegifolium* L. an old-fashioned garden plant. **1882** FRIEND *Devon. Plant-n.*, *Feather Fern, *Spiræa Japonica* L. **1776** WITHERING *Bot. Arrangem. Vegetables* 115 **Featherfoil.* **1861** MISS PRATT *Flower. Pl.* IV. 219 Common Water-Violet, or Featherfoil. **1875** *Anderida* I. viii. 155 His paddle..hung in the stems of water-crowfoot and featherfoil. **1776** WITHERING *Bot. Arrangem. Vegetables* 44 **Feathergrass.* **1861** MISS PRATT *Flower Pl.* VI. 66 Order Gramineæ..(Common Feather-grass). **1776** WITHERING *Bot. Arrangem. Vegetables* 680 **Feathermoss*, Hypnum. **1854** STARK *Brit. Mosses* 228 *Hypnum Trichomanoides* ..(Blunt Fern-like Feather Moss). *Ibid.* 229 *Hypnum Complanatum*..(Flat Feather Moss). **1597** GERARDE *Herbal* I. vi. §2. 8 In English a Bent, or *Feather-top grasse. *Ibid.* II. cxxi. §9. 385 *Lychnis Plumaria*, *Fethertop wilde Campion. **1678** LITTLETON *Lat. Dict.* s.v. *Princes*, Feather-top grass. *Gramen tomentosum arundinaceum.* **1878-86** BRITTEN & HOLLAND *Plant-n.*, Feathertop Grass, *Calamagrostis Epigejos.* **1884** A. NILSON *Timber Trees N.S.W.* (Index) 135 *Featherwood, Polyosma Cunninghamii. Saxifrageæ. **1927** *Blackw. Mag.* Oct. 464/1 The delicate green tracery of the graceful featherwoods and celery-top pines. **1947** R. H. ANDERSON *Trees N.S.W.* (ed. 2) 218 In addition to the Opossum Wood and the Featherwood there are four related species belonging to the same family (*Escalloniaceae*).

feather ('fɛðə(r)), *v.* Forms: 4-5 feder, -ir, -yr, 6 fedder, 4 feþer, 4-6 fether, 6- feather. Also with prefix 1 **ʒefiðerian**; pa. pple. (senses 1,2) 3 **iviðered**, 4 **yfeþered**, 6 **yfethred**. [OE. *ʒefiðrian*, f. the sb., to which it has been assimilated in form from 14th c.]

I. To cover or furnish with feathers.

†**1.** *trans.* To give wings to; to 'wing' for flight. *lit.* and *fig. Obs.*

c **888** K. ÆLFRED *Boeth.* xxxvi. §1 Ic sceal ærest þin mod ʒefiðerian. **1387** TREVISA *Higden* (Rolls) VII. 223, I not by what craft he feþered his feet and his hondes, for he wolde flee in Dedalus his wise. **1534** WHITTINTON *Tullyes Offices* III. (1540) 160 Oh stable truthe: faythfulnesse fethered to flye to heuen. c **1611** CHAPMAN *Iliad* II. 139 Horse slaughter'd horse, Need feather'd flight. **1634** FORD *P. Warbeck* III. i, The Cornish..flew Feather'd by rage. a **1647** R. LOVEDAY *Lett.* (1662) 204 The Polonian Story..perhaps may feather some tedious hours. c **1825** BEDDOES *Poems, Second Brother* II. ii, Blessings of mine Feather your speed!

2. To fit (an arrow) with a feather.

a **1225** *Ancr. R.* 60 Ase earewe þæt is iviðered. c **1380** *Sir Ferumb.* 2728 Dartes y-feþered wiþ bras. c **1400** *Rom. Rose* 942 Ten brode arrowes held he there..But they were..feathered aright. **1530** PALSGR. 547/1, I feder a shafte, as a fletcher doth. a **1577** GASCOIGNE *Wks.* (1587) 185 Be his flights yfethred from the goose Or peacocks quils. **1599** HAYWARD *1st Pt. Hen. IV*, 60 The King having feathered these arrowes against his owne brest, passed foorth [etc.]. **1668** DRYDEN *Evening's Love* I. ii, Cupid's arrow was well feathered. **1712** ARBUTHNOT *John Bull* III. v, An arrow feathered with his own wing. **1821** BYRON *Sardan.* IV. i. 90 Shaft-heads feather'd from the eagle's wing.

fig. a **1340** HAMPOLE *Psalter* xvii. 16 His aruys, that is his apostles..for thai ere feþerid wiþ vertus. **1393** LANGL. *P. Pl.* C. XXIII. 118 Manye brode arwes, Were fetherede with faire by-heste! **1631** MASSINGER *Believe as you list* II. ii, All arrowes in thy quiver feathered with Sclanders. **1665** J. SPENCER *Vulg. Prophecies* 77 Language, feathered with soft and delicate phrases, and pointed with pathetical accents. **1721** RAMSAY *Cupid thrown into S. Sea* iv, With transfers a' his darts were feather'd. **1835** LYTTON *Rienzi* III. iii, Whose arrow was not feathered by sadness.

3. a. To clothe or provide with feathers; to furnish with plumage; to deck or adorn with, or as with, feathers; to form a feather-like covering or adornment for.

1483 *Cath. Angl.* 124/2 To Fedyr, *pennare, plumare.* **1525** LD. BERNERS *Froiss.* III. xlii. 54/2 These gentell byrdes had pyte on hym and fethered hym agayne. **1618** N. FIELD *Amends for Ladies* v. ii, A branch of willow feathering his hat. **1622** BACON *Hen. VII*, 111 The King cared not to plume his Nobilitie..to feather himselfe. **1810** SCOTT *Lady of L.* I. xiv, A wildering forest feathered o'er His ruined sides. **1833** HT. MARTINEAU *Cinnamon & Pearls* i. 19 With more than her usual fancy did she feather with cocoa-nut leaves the poles of bamboo. a **1843** SOUTHEY *Doctor* iii. (1862) 14 A craggy hill, feathered with birch, sheltered it from the north. **1864** BURTON *Scot Abr.* I. iii. 140 He sought to feather his hat with..French plumage. **1878** BELL *Gegenbauer's Comp. Anat.* 134 The stalk..retains some of its primitive character by being feathered.

†**b.** To decorate (a person) with the projecting feather of an arrow; hence to pierce, wound. Also, To bury (an arrow) up to the feather. *Obs.*

1415 *Pol. Poems* (Rolls) III. 125 Thei felle to grownde, Here sydes federed. **1577** HARRISON *England* II. xvi. (1877) I. 279 An other [arrow should haue beene] fethered in his bowels. **1589** GREENE *Menaphon* (Arb.) 38 A man of meane estate..being feathered with Cupidis bolt.

†**c.** *Pass.* To be covered with white waves.

1749 F. SMITH *Voy. Disc. N.-W. Pass.* II. 251 The Sea was feathered with a strong Tide.

4. *refl.* and *intr.* for *refl.* Of a bird: To get its feathers, to become fledged. ? *Obs.* exc. *dial.*

c **1450** *Bk. Hawkyng* in *Rel. Ant.* I. 298 Thou seist hym [your young hawk] hym begyn to feder. **1486** *Bk. St. Albans* A ij a, When they bene vnclosed and begynneth to feder any thyng of lengthe. **1577** B. GOOGE *Heresbach's Husb.* IV. (1586) 169 They that meane to fatte Pigions..doo sever them when they be newly feathered. **1659** D. PELL *Improv. Sea* 118 The Vulture..beholds her young to thrive and feather. **1790** A. WILSON *Discons. Wren* Poet. Wks. (1846) 98 A' safe and weel about our nest, An' them quiet feath'ring laid!

5. To cover with feathers, **a.** internally: To line with feathers, in phr. ***to feather one's nest***: to avail oneself of opportunities for laying up wealth, to enrich oneself.

1583 STUBBES *Anat. Abus.* II. (1882) 38 By this meanes..they feather their nests well inough. **1612** T. TAYLOR *Comm. Titus* i. 7 Yet all this worke is neglected, that his owne neast may be well feathered. **1658** OSBORN *Jas. I* Wks. (1673) 514 He might have feathered his Family better than he did. **1753** SMOLLETT *Ct. Fathom* (1784) 41/2 His spouse..was disposed to feather her own nest, at the expence of him and his heirs. **1876** F. E. TROLLOPE *Charming Fellow* III. xii. 149 Maxfield has feathered his nest very considerably.

b. externally: To coat with feathers; more fully, ***to tar and feather*** (see TAR *v.*).

1774 FOOTE *Cozeners* III. Wks. 1799 II. 194 You wanted to send me to be feathered abroad. **1829** W. H. MAXWELL *Stories of Waterloo, F. Kennedy* 205 The population were amusing themselves..in..feathering tithe proctors.

†**6.** Of a cock: To cover with outspread feathers; to tread. *Obs.*

c **1386** CHAUCER *Nun's Pr. T.* 357 He fetherid Pertelote twenty tyme, And trad as ofte. **1700** DRYDEN *Fables, Cock & Fox* 70 Ardent in love..He feather'd her a hundred times a day.

†**7.** ? To touch with or as with a feather; to touch lightly. *Obs. rare*$^{-1}$.

a **1225** *Ancr. R.* 200 þer ich feðri on, awurðeð tene oðer tweolue.

II. To present or give (to anything) the appearance of feathers.

8. a. *intr.* To move, wave or float like feathers; to grow, extend in a feathery form.

1770 T. WHATELY *Mod. Gardening* 197 A noble wood crowns the top, and feathers down to the bottom of a large, oval, swelling hill. **1797** G. COLMAN *Br. Grins, Maid of Moor* iii, The snow came feathering down. **1820** SCOTT *Monast.* ii, Little patches of wood and copse..feathering naturally up the beds of empty torrents. **1857** S. OSBORN *Quedah* xxiv. 356 The graceful palm, the plantain, and pandanus..feathering over the edge of a beetling cliff, as if they were ostrich-plumes. **1864** TENNYSON *En. Ard.* 540 Her full-busted figure head Starred o'er the ripple feathering from her bows. **1881** BLACKMORE *Christowell* iv, Like the wave and dip of barley feathering to a gentle July breeze.

b. *U.S.* Of cream: To rise upon the surface of tea, etc. like small flakes or feathers.

1860 BARTLETT *Dict. Amer.*, The cream feathers. **1889** in FARMER *Americanisms.* **1890** *Critic* 21 June 314/1 To keep cream from feathering in hot weather.

c. *trans.* To send *up* feather-wise. *rare.*

1861 THORNBURY *Turner* (1862) I. 222 Where..Vesuvius feathers up its quiet plume of pure white smoke.

9. Of a flower (chiefly, a tulip), ***to be feathered***: to be marked with feather-like lines.

1833 HOGG *Suppl. on Florists' Flowers* 31 When a Tulip is feathered with dark purple. **1881** *Gard. Chron.* XVI. 748 The outer segments variously feathered with dark purple.

10. *trans.* To cut (wood, etc.) down gradually to a thin edge. Cf. FEATHER-EDGED *a.*

1782 EDGEWORTH in *Phil. Trans.* LXXIII. 138 An arm of deal, feather-edged, and supported by stays of the same material, feathered in the same manner. **1794** VINCE *ibid.* LXXXV. 44 Pieces of lead with the edges feathered off.

11. a. ***to feather an oar***: to turn it as it leaves the water at the end of a stroke, so that it may pass through the air edgeways.

a **1740** [see FEATHERING *ppl. a.* b.] **1774** in Hone *Every-day Bk.* II. 1062 He feather'd his oars with..skill. **1847** J. WILSON *Chr. North* I. 248 We to-day shall feather an oar.

absol. **1825** L. HUNT *Bacchus in Tuscany* 857 Boaters, who know how to feather, Never get tired. **1861** HUGHES *Tom Brown at Oxf.* xiii. (1889) 121 This wind will make it very rough..Mind you feather high.

b. To fix (paddle-boards) so as to offer the least resistance while entering and leaving the water. (Cf. FEATHERING *ppl. a.* b.)

1848 *Rep. Comm. Patents 1847* (U.S.) 71 Improvements in the mode of feathering the floats of paddle wheels.

c. *trans.* To rotate (the blades of a propeller) so that they are parallel to the direction of motion and offer the least resistance to the water or air when not driven. Hence, on a rotating-wing aircraft (or helicopter): to vary the angle of incidence of (the blades).

1883 A. E. SEATON *Man. Marine Engin.* xv. 298 Yachts and ships which are required to sail as well as steam, cannot well do the former when the screw is stopped, unless some means be adopted of feathering the blades. **1909** F. T. JANE *All World's Air-Ships* 52/1 The blades can be feathered, and either propeller feathered independently of the other. **1921** S. W. BARNABY *Marine Propellers* (ed. 6) iii. 58 In a twin-screw ship screws that can be feathered fore and aft by internal mechanism will be found advantageous. **1940** *Flight* 15 Aug. *e*/2 Should a power unit in a multi-engined aircraft suddenly fail..it is a great advantage to be able to feather the airscrew. **1947** *Times* 2 Sept. 2/5 After gaining height the piston engines were switched off and their airscrews feathered. **1955** LIPTROT & WOODS *Rotorcraft* v. 44 Displacement (or lag) therefore causes any movement about the flapping hinge..to 'feather' the blade, that is change its incidence. **1967** C. H. BARNES *Shorts Aircraft since 1900* 358 For the first time a fully loaded Sunderland could be flown safely with two airscrews feathered on the same side.

d. *intr.* Of a propeller: to assume a 'feathered' position (see FEATHERED *ppl. a.* 8 b).

1933 *Jane's Fighting Ships* 228 Variable pitch propeller on inner shaft which 'feathers' when Turbines only are used. **1951** *Engineering* 9 Mar. 301/2 Propellers of aircraft..so built that they could 'feather'.

III. In various uses.

12. *Shooting.* To knock a few feathers from (a bird) without killing.

1890 PAYNE-GALLWEY *Let. Young Shooters* 137 You would have shot 'well behind', and not even feathered the tail of a cock-pheasant. **1892** *Field* 9 Apr. 524/1 Mr. Mervyn Watts..feathered a strong bird from No. 2 trap.

13. *Hunting.* **a.** Of a hound: To make a quivering movement with the tail and body, while searching for the trail. **b.** Of the huntsman (see quot. 1884).

1803 *Spirit Public Jrnls.* (1804) VII. 111 The leading hound, beginning to feather. **1839** F. D. RADCLIFFE *Noble Science* ix. 163 See that old bitch how she feathers—how her stern vibrates with the quickened action of her pulses. **1861** G. F. BERKELEY *Sportsm. W. Prairies* 310 At last Druid began 'to feather'..on the traces of a deer. **1884** JEFFERIES *Red Deer* vii. 118 The harbourer likes to 'feather'—to set the hounds direct on the trail. **1892** *Field* 7 May, In a lot of oats Saul feathered about, but could not find.

'feather-'bed.

1. A bed stuffed with feathers.

c **1000** *Ælfric's Voc.* in Wr.-Wülcker 124 *Culcites*, feþerbed. c **1275** LAY. 17443 For nou ʒe mawe heom hebbe ase feþer-beddes. c **1369** CHAUCER *Dethe Blaunche* 251 Of

downe of pure dowves whyte I wil yive him a fether-bed. 1480 *Wardr. Acc. Edw. IV* (1830) 130 Beddes called federbeddes stuffed with downe with their bolsters v. 1535 STEWART *Cron. Scot.* II. 445 All fedder beddis forbiddin wes also. 1648 PRYNNE *Plea for Lords* 37 The Duke..was smothered to death with a featherbed. 1749 WESLEY *Acc. School Kingswood* 6 All their Beds have Mattresses on them, not Feather-beds. 1828 SCOTT *F.M. Perth* v, Make interest with your feather-bed till day-break.

fig. 1837 CARLYLE *Fr. Rev.* I. III. viii. 134 Such bolsters and huge featherbeds of Promotion. 1870 LOWELL *Study Wind.* (1886) 328 He has smothered the..simplicity of Chaucer under feather-beds of verbiage. 1952 *Economist* 16 Aug. 386 Feather beds for farmers have been a feature of post-war Europe.

2. a. The Willow Warbler (*Phylloscopus trochilus*); also of the Whitethroat (*Motacilla sylvia*).

1854 BAKER *Gloss. Northampton* I. 224 *Featherbed*, the White-throat. 1885 SWAINSON *Prov. Names Brit. Birds* 26 *Willow warbler*..Feather bed (Oxon).

b. *pl.* (*sing.* constr.). A stonewort (genus *Chara*); a bed of stoneworts.

1807 F. PURSH *Jrnl. Bot. Excursion* 4 Aug. (1923) 50 The Creek was coverd at its bottom with Chara, which the boatmen call Feather beds. 1851 A. WOOD *Class-Bk. Bot.* (ed. 23) II. 637 *C[hara] vulgaris*... Feather-beds... It appears in dense tufts, like a soft bed, undulating with the motion of the water.

3. *attrib.* and *Comb.* **a.** attrib., as ***featherbed-campaigner, -captain, job, landing, practice, rule, -soldier, treatment, -warrior***; **b.** objective, as ***featherbed-maker***. Also **featherbed-lane**, *slang* (see quot.).

1888 *Times* (weekly ed.) 2 Nov. 8/3 We want no *feather-bed campaigners. 1692 HICKERINGILL *Good Old Cause* Wks. 1716 II. 529 Is it because some *Feather-bed Captains sell such Ware? 1938 *San Francisco Examiner* 3 June 25/1 But he does feel that '*featherbed jobs'..should be abolished. 1942 A. M. LOW *Parachutes* xi. 201 The most comfortable landing is said to be in a young plantation of pines... The firemen..call these '*featherbed landings'. *a*1700 B. E. *Dict. Cant. Crew*, *Feather-bed-lane, any bad Road. *c*1515 *Cocke Lorell's B.* (Percy Soc.) 9 Bed-makers, *federbed makers, and wyre drawers. 1922 L. F. LOREE *Railroad Freight Transportation* vii. 625 The annual cost of these so-called '*feather-bed' practices. 1934 *Railway Age* XCVII. 858/2 Restrictive rules, sometimes called '*featherbed rules'. 1837 MAJOR RICHARDSON *Brit. Legion* i. (ed. 2) 20 Our position..has certainly not been that of *feather-bed soldiers. 1958 *Times Rev. Industry* Sept. 98/1 Strange to give some industries '*feather-bed' treatment. 1872 BLACK *Adv. Phaeton* xxiii. 325 Each *feather-bed warrior who rides from Knightsbridge to Whitehall.

feather-bedding, *vbl. sb.* [f. FEATHER-BED + -ING.] (The action of) making comfortable by favourable, esp. economic or financial, treatment; the state of being so treated; *spec.* the employment of superfluous staff. Hence, as a back-formation, **featherbed** *v. trans.*, to provide with, esp. economic, advantages; so **featherbedded** *ppl. a.*; also **feather-bedder**, one devoted to physical or intellectual comfort.

1921 *Bull. Bureau Business Res., Harrow* 25 Feather bedding, getting pay for work not done. 1928 G. COOKE *Theory Mus.* iii. 33 This movement has certainly produced a harshening of our music which should even satisfy those who most object to the feather-bedding of the Victorians. 1943 *Reader's Digest* Mar. 26/2 For the unions, featherbedding has become an established business procedure. 1949 G. FREEDLEY in Andrews & Trilling *Internat. Theatre* 41 This has brought about a tight departmentalising which has 'feather-bedded' union practices. 1950 *Hansard Commons* 7 Mar. 183 Examples of gross feather bedding both in Government service..and in private industry. *Ibid.* 20 Apr. 426 He can rely on this party ..not to feather bed..the farmers. 1952 M. MCCARTHY *Groves of Academe* (1953) iv. 74 A certain number of seasoned nonconformists and dissenters, sexual deviants, feather-bedders, alcoholics, impostors. 1954 *Daily Tel.* 6 Feb. 4/7 'Featherbedded farmer' is surely one of the most ludicrous phrases ever coined. 1958 *Economist* 11 Jan. 131/1 The unions have been able to impose feather-bedding and under-employment. 1962 J. CANNAN *All is Discovered* vi. 149 Those feather-bedded farmers with their sprays and their fertilisers. 1971 *Daily Colonist* (Victoria, B.C.) 17 Feb. 5/5 Why does he..call us the 'social elite featherbedded on the taxpayers' money'?

'feather-bone. [f. FEATHER *sb.* + BONE: after *whalebone*.] (See quot.)

1887 *Chicago Advance* 17 Feb. 112 *Feather-bone*.. prepared from the quills of geese and turkeys, is largely taking the place of whalebone in the manufacture of whips [etc.].

featherdom ('fɛðədəm). [f. as prec. + -DOM.] The realm of feathered creatures.

1885 *Harper's Mag.* Dec. 80/1 May they not be gathering the latest news from all featherdom?

feathered ('fɛðəd), *ppl. a.* [f. FEATHER *sb.* and *v.* + -ED.]

1. a. Of birds, animals, etc.: Provided with or having feathers. Phr. ***feathered friend***: a bird (used sentimentally or ironically). Also in parasynthetic comb., as ***black-, hard-, pen-, well-feathered*** adjs.

[*c*1150 *Eadwine's Psalter* (E.E.T.S.) lxxvii. 27 Fuglæs ȝefeðerede.] *a*1300 *Cursor M.* (Cott.) 15991 Þe cok lepe vp ..federd fayrer þan be-forn. *c*1300 *K. Alis.* 5406 Hy weren blake fethered on the wombe. *a*1440 *Found. St. Bartholomew's* I. vi, The vision of the federyd beiste. 1577 GOOGE *Heresbach's Husb.* (1586) 163, I wil not refuse to shew you somwhat also of my feathered cattle. 1684 R. H. *School Recreat.* 131 See that he [the cock] be sound, hard feather'd. 1708 PRIOR *Turtle & Sparrow* 263 My children then were just pen-feather'd. 1721 R. BRADLEY *Wks. Nature* 85 Thus have I remark'd what is most observable in the feathered Tribe. 1769 J. WALLIS *Nat. Hist. Northumberland* I. ix. 311 The young being surprized.. when they are near full feathered. 1840 F. D. BENNETT *Whaling Voy.* II. 242 The legs are..feathered to the feet. 1876 SMILES *Sc. Natur.* vii. (ed. 4) 105 A feathered wanderer flew by. 1933 E. A. ROBERTSON *Ordinary Families* xiv. 294, I did not write one letter about 'our feathered friends' which was not published. 1953 E. SIMON *Past Masters* I. iii. 35 We keep chickens..and so far our feathered friends are letting us down badly. 1967 *Guardian* 4 Feb. 14/8 The British farmers'..war against our furred and feathered friends might be an enormous mistake.

transf. 1797 MRS. RADCLIFFE *Italian* xii, One of the supporting cliffs..was in deep shade, but the other, feathered with foliage. 1851 H. MAYO *Truths in Pop. Superst.* (ed. 2) 25 An abrupt craggy ridge, feathered with underwood.

b. Pertaining to or consisting of animals with feathers.

*a*1605 MONTGOMERIE *Natur Passis Nuriture* 53 Fra sho with fedrit flesh was fed. 1611 COTGR. s.v. *Matinée*, The Fox that sleepes a mornings meets with no feathered break-fasts. 1889 (*title of periodical*), The Feathered World.

2. That is, or seems to be, supplied with wings; winged, fleet.

1587 TURBERV. *Trag. T.* 100 b, The God that feadreth [*sic*] is and blinde. 1596 SHAKS. *1 Hen. IV*, IV. i. 106, I saw young Harry..Rise from the ground like feathered Mercury. 1608 —— *Per.* v. ii. 15 In feather'd briefness sails are fill'd. 1636 R. DURHAM in *Ann. Dubrensia* (1877) 56 Those Grey-hounds, which with feather'd feete, Fly ore your pleasant downes. *a*1658 CLEVELAND *Poems* 43 (L.) Nor think..our feathered minutes may Fall under measure. 1792 S. ROGERS *Pleas. Mem.* I. 62 The feathered feet of Time. 1865 LOWELL *Poet. Wks.* (1879) 429 Yet sometimes feathered words are strong.

3. Of an arrow: Fitted with a feather. Of a wound: Inflicted by an arrow.

*c*1000 ÆLFRIC *Gloss.* in Wr.-Wülcker 143 *Sagitta, uel spiculum*, ȝefyðerad flaa. 1513 DOUGLAS *Æneis* x. v. 82 Als swyft as ganze or fedyrit arrow fleis. 1579 in W. H. Turner *Select. Rec. Oxford* 403 Syxe sheffe of goode arrowes, well fethered hedds. 1697 DRYDEN *Virgil* (1806) IV. 161 Across the shoulders came the feather'd wound; Transfix'd, he fell. 1715–20 POPE *Iliad* I. 68 He twang'd his deadly bow, And hissing fly the feather'd fates below. 1825 COLERIDGE *Aids Refl.* (1848) I. 53 The arrows of satire feathered with wit.

4. Adorned with a feather or plume of feathers.

1624 *Trag. Nero* IV. i. in Bullen *O. Pl.* I. 63 The feather'd man of Inde. 1631 T. POWELL *Tom All Trades* 170 Your feathered Gallant of the Court. 1752 A. MACDONALD in *Scots Mag.* July (1753) 338/1 Allan was..dressed in a blue side-coat..and feathered hat. 1813 SCOTT *Trierm.* II. xxiii, Their feather'd crests alone Should this encounter rue.

5. Furnished or ornamented with something resembling a feather or feathers: **a.** of animals. Cf. FEATHER *sb.* 11.

1686 *Lond. Gaz.* No. 2195/4 A black Brown Gelding.. Feather'd of each side the Neck. 1721 BRADLEY *Wks. Nature* 137 Moths have their Antennæ short and feathered.

b. *Archit.* Cf. FEATHERING *vbl. sb.* 2 b.

1845 *Ecclesiologist* IV. 14 *note*, A very rich canopied monument, with..double feathered arch. 1848 RICKMAN *Goth. Archit.* 90 The arch..is richly feathered.

c. of a plough-share. Cf. FEATHER *sb.* 16 c.

1765 A. DICKSON *Treat. Agric.* (ed. 2) 215 Giving it a.. feathered sock. 1799 J. ROBERTSON *Agric. Perth* 95 In land, which is free of stones, the feathered share is preferred.

6. a. Of leaves or petals, timber, etc.: Having feather-like markings.

1610 W. FOLKINGHAM *Art of Survey* I. iii. 7 High grounds produce wood of a more beautiful-feathered and better graine. 1833 HOGG *Suppl. Florists' Flowers* 31 [A tulip with certain markings is called] a feathered Bybloemen or feathered Rose.

b. Of plants, branches, etc.: Formed or arranged like feathers; having feather-like hairs or tufts; feather-like.

1578 LYTE *Dodoens* II. vii. 155 A littell crownet, out of the whiche the small feathered leaues do grow. 1776 WITHERING *Brit. Plants* (1796) I. 224 Summits..reflected, feathered. 1783 WATSON *Philip III* (1839) 359 Fir trees, whose close and feathered branches intwined with one another. 1820 KEATS *Hyperion* I. 9 The feathered grass.

7. In various names of **a.** flowers and **b.** moths.

a. 1578 LYTE *Dodoens* II. vii. 156 Single Gillofers..are called in Englishe by diuers names, as..feathered Gillofers. 1823 CRABB *Technol. Dict.*, The..feathered Columbine, the *Thalictrum aquilegifolium*. 1878–86 BRITTEN & HOLLAND *Plant-n.*, Feathered Gillofers, *Dianthus plumarius*.

b. 1839 WOOD *Index Entomol.* 28 *Eulepia grammica*, feathered Footman. *Ibid.* 51 *Heliophobus Leucophæus*, feathered Ear. *Heliophobus popularis*, feathered Gothic. 1869 E. NEWMAN *Brit. Moths* 289 The Feathered Brindle (*Aporophyla australis*). *Ibid.* 399 The Feathered Ranunculus (*Epunda Lichenea*). 1870 WOOD *Common Moths Eng.* 50 The Feathered Thorn (*Himera pennaria*).

8. a. Of an oar or paddle: That is or has been turned so as to 'feather': see FEATHER *v.* 11.

1812 J. WILSON *Isle of Palms* II. 417 As if the lightly feather'd oar..could take them to the shore. 1866 F. W. BREAREY *Remarks upon Aërial Navigation* in *Rep. Brit. Assoc. 1865* II. 17 The downward blow of paddles made of bamboo and silk, if returning feathered for each succeeding stroke, would enable him to effect this. 1891 *Daily News* 15 Sept. 3/4 The swish of feathered oars upon the water.

b. Of the propeller of an aircraft: having the blades turned about their axes so as to be in line with the air-flow. Cf. FEATHER *v.* 11 c.

1935 *Jrnl. R. Aeronaut. Soc.* XXXIX. 1026 The feathered propeller has only about 3 per cent. of the drag of the normal airplane. 1940 *Flight* 15 Aug. e/2 In the 'fully feathered' position the airscrew blades are turned round until the average torque exerted by the windmilling blades becomes nearly zero. 1970 H. A. TAYLOR *Airspeed Aircraft since 1931* 117 The prototype was controllable, with the propeller of the critical engine feathered.., down to speeds as low as 110kt.

9. *Sugar-boiling.* Cf. FEATHER *sb.* 13.

1706 PHILLIPS (ed. Kersey), *Feathered Boiling of Sugar*.. is when after several Boilings, the Artist blows thro' the Holes of the Skimmer..till thick and large Bubbles flying up on high, the Sugar is become Feathered.

10. ***feathered-shot*** (see quot.). Cf. *feather-shot copper*, FEATHER *sb.* 19.

1881 RAYMOND *Mining Gloss.*, *Feathered-shot*, copper granulated by pouring into cold water.

'feather-'edge, *sb.* [f. as prec. + EDGE.] The fine edge of a board, etc. that thins off to one side, so as to resemble a wedge in section.

1785 ROY in *Phil. Trans.* LXXV. 396 A line..being brought to coincide with the feather edge.

attrib. 1616 *MS. Acc. St. John's Hosp., Canterb.*, For saing of fetheredg bourd. 1703 T. N. *City & C. Purchaser* 40 *Feather-edge*..a sort of Bricks..thinner at one edge, than they are at the other. 1703 MOXON *Mech. Exerc.* 160 *Feather-edge*, Boards, or Planks, that have one edge thinner than another are called *Feather-edge* stuff. 1874 KNIGHT *Dict. Mech.*, *Feather-edge File*, a file with an acute edge. 1883 *Hendon Times* 5 May 5/2 Quantity of shop-shutters, feather-edge boards, cupboard fronts.

'feather-'edge, *v.* [f. prec. sb.] *trans.* To cut to a feather-edge, produce a thin edge upon. Also *transf.* to turn (oneself) sideways.

1799 JAS. WILSON *Mission. Voy. S. Seas* p. xlix, The planks being feather-edged, and lapped over. 1800 HERSCHEL in *Phil. Trans.* XC. 306 The slip of wood at their back..was feather-edged towards the stove. 1854 THOREAU *Walden* i. 49 The boards were carefully feather-edged and lapped. 1890 W. C. RUSSELL *Ocean Trag.* II. xxiv. 249 Tell your mad relative to feather-edge himself. He is all front.

'feather-'edged, *a.* [f. as prec. + -ED².]

1. Having one edge thinner than the other, so that the section is wedge-shaped. Also quasi-*adv.*

1703 T. N. *City & C. Purchaser* 131 That thick feather-edg'd-board, generally nail'd round the Eaves of a House. 1713 WARDER *True Amazons* (ed. 2) 115 Two Boards slit feather-edg'd will cover the House. 1785 ROY in *Phil. Trans.* LXXV. 396 Two feather-edged pieces of brass. 1806 A. YOUNG *Agric. Essex* (1813) I. 198 Mr. Rogers' Norfolk ploughs lay their furrows quite flat; but the Essex ones feather-edged. 1812 J. SMYTH *Pract. Customs* (1821) 282 The officers are to understand that the term feather-edged is applicable to such Slabs only as are rendered feather-edged by the natural convexity of the tree. 1861 J. H. WALSH *Horse* xxxii. 567 The disadvantages..of the feather-edged shoe.

2. Of ribbons, etc.: Having a tufted edge.

featheret ('fɛðərɪt). [f. as prec. + -ET¹.] A small feather.

1882 JEFFERIES *Bevis* I. xii. 212 Dowl is the fluff, the featherets no finger can remove.

'featherfew. Forms: 4 feþerfoy, 5 federfu, fedyrfoy, 6–8 fetherfew, 7– featherfew. [Corrupted var. of FEVERFEW.] The popular name of *Pyrethrum Parthenium*.

*c*1325 *St. Patrick's Purg.* cxlvii, Mint, feþerfoy and eglentere. *c*1440 *Promp. Parv.* 152/2 Fedyrfu, or fedyrfoy, herbe, *febrifuga*. 1587 MASCALL *Govt. Cattle* (1627) 99 If beasts bee sicke yee shall giue them madder, long pepper, the barke of a walnut tree, with fetherfew. 1683 TRYON *Way to Health* 552 Herbs..of a strong bitter Quality, as Wormwood, Featherfew, Tansie, and the like. *c*1759 *Roxb. Ball.* VII. 57 Here's fetherfew, gilliflowers and rue. 1863 R. PRIOR *Plant-n.*, *Featherfew*..the feverfew..from confusion of name with the feather foil. [An erroneous statement.]

'feather-'footed, *a.* **a.** Having feet covered with feathers. **b.** *fig.* Moving silently and swiftly.

a. 1580 HOLLYBAND *Treas. Fr. Tong.*, *Coulon*, or *pigeon Pattu*, fether-footed doues or pigeons. 1868 DARWIN *Anim. & Pl.* I. viii. 295 There is a feather-footed breed.

b. 1565 GOLDING *Ovid's Met.* II. 31 He bad the fether-footed houres go harnesse in his horse. 1637 HEYWOOD *Dial.* iii. Wks. 1874 VI. 137 Swift feather-footed Time. 1731 A. HILL *Adv. Poets* xxiii, Fancy's light Dwarfs! whose feather-footed Strains, Dance..through a Waste of Brains! 1797 MRS. A. M. BENNET *Beggar Girl* (1813) II. 110 The feather-footed Rosa..darted along the paddock. 1839 BAILEY *Festus* xx. (1848) 231 Soft as a featherfooted cloud on Heaven.

†**'featherham.** *Obs.* Forms: 1 feðerhama, -homa, 2 feþerhome, 5 *Sc.* fetherham, fethrame, 6 *Sc.* fedderame, fed(d)rem, -rum, fethreme. [OE. *feðer-hama*, f. *feðer* FEATHER *sb.* + *hama* a covering.] A covering or appendage of feathers; plumage, wings.

*a*800 *Corpus Gloss.* 1984 *Talaria* feðrhoman. *a*1000 *Cædmon's Gen.* 670 (Gr.) Geseo ic him his englas ymbe hweorfan mid feðerhaman. *c*1175 *Lamb. Hom.* 81 Her he uette feþer-home and wenge. *c*1470 HARDING *Chron.* xxv. iii, Afterward a Fetherham he dight, To flye with wynges as he could beest descerne. 1513 DOUGLAS *Æneis* IV. v. 93 Slyd with thi feddrame, to ȝone Troiane prence. 1570 *Sempill Ball.* xiii. (1872) 77 Tak tho feddrum of the Craw In syne of wo and dolour. 1606 BIRNIE *Kirk-Buriall* (1833) 23 It wold make our craw-down fedrum fal.

ˈfeather-head. **a.** An empty or light head. **b.** A silly, empty-headed person.

a. 1845 CARLYLE *Cromwell* (1857) I. 88 To me, in my poor feather-head, [he] seemed a somewhat unhandy gentleman. **b. 1831** CARLYLE *Sart. Res.* (1858) 154 Show the haughtiest featherhead, that a soul higher then himself is actually here. **1878** T. SINCLAIR *Mount* 19 Our periodical featherheads do not know that we dwell in the modern land of Canaan. **1878** TENNYSON *Q. Mary* v. i, A fool and featherhead.

attrib. **1886** W. GRAHAM *Social Problem* 190 Mere feather-head folly.

ˈfeather-ˈheaded, *a.* [f. prec. + -ED².]

1. Empty-headed, hare-brained, silly.

1647 WARD *Simp. Cobler* 30 Many Gentlemens..estates are deplumed by their feather-headed wifes. **1716** CIBBER *Love Makes Man* II. ii, Ah! thou hast miss'd a Man..so far above this feather-headed Puppy. **1876** GEO. ELIOT *Dan. Der.* IV. liv. 106 Some feather-headed lady or gentleman. **1881** IRVING in *Macm. Mag.* XLV. 305 It was little more than a conceited and feather-headed assumption.

2. Having a feathery top. *rare.*

1821 CLARE *Vill. Minstr.* II. 173 Feather-headed grasses.

featheriness (ˈfɛðərɪnɪs). [f. FEATHERY + -NESS.] **a.** Feathery state or condition. **b.** Lightness, fickleness.

1689 W. BATES *Sure Trial Uprightness* 130 There is such a levity and featheriness in our Minds. **1838** *Blackw. Mag.* XLIV. 612 Pulling off bright wings, and destroying the lustrous featheriness. **1892** L. F. DAY *Nature in Ornament* iv. 53 The very featheriness of its flower-heads.

feathering (ˈfɛðərɪŋ), *vbl. sb.* [+ -ING¹.]

1. a. The action of the vb. FEATHER in various senses.

1640 BP. HALL *Chr. Moder.* 8/1 That bird of whom Suidas speaks, which dies in the very act of his feathering. **1775** BURKE *Corr.* (1844) II. 26 North Carolina is left out.. because it furnishes tar for feathering. **1875** SHARPE in *Encycl. Brit.* (ed. 9) II. 372 This king [Henry V of England] directed the sheriffs of counties to take six wing-feathers from every goose for the feathering of arrows. **1878** BESANT & RICE *Celia's Arb.* iv. (1887) 35 Rowing their short, deep stroke, without any feathering, but in perfect time.

b. *Arboriculture* (see quot.)

1827 STEUART *Planter's G.* (1828) 237 What the workmen call 'the feathering', that is, the position of the capillary rootlets upon the primary rootlets or branches, which are always found pointing outwards from the body of the Tree.

c. The action of feathering the floats of a paddle-wheel or the blades of a propeller (see FEATHER *v.* 11 b, c); also, an angular motion of a revolving rotor blade about its pitch, producing a continual variation in its pitch. Also *attrib.*

1850 *Rep. Comm. Patents 1849* (U.S.) 47 Many applications have been made based upon alleged novelties in the feathering of the vertical float paddle wheel. **1909** A. E. SEATON *Screw Propeller* xi. 162 Flat blades..have been tried on propellers where complete feathering..is required for efficient sailing. **1955** J. SHAPIRO *Princ. Helicopter Engin.* iii. 173 In most rotors the blades are constrained in pitch by the control linkage and the problem of evaluating free feathering motion does not arise. **1962** *Gloss. Aeronaut. Terms (B.S.I.)* v. 16 *Feathering hinge*, a blade pivot which allows the blade pitch angle to be varied. **1970** A. C. KERMODE *Flight without Formulae* 202 Feathering means turning the blades so that, when the propeller is stopped, they offer the least resistance.

d. Of cream: see FEATHER *v.* 8 b.

1928 *Jrnl. Dairy Sci.* XI. 249 The formation of a flocculent coagulum, known as feathering, when sweet cream is added to hot coffee, is a problem of considerable commercial importance. *Ibid.*, The acidity of the product is an important factor in the feathering phenomenon. **1955** J. G. DAVIS *Dict. Dairying* (ed. 2) 465 *Feathering of cream*, a term applied to the flocculation of fat, etc., on the surface of tea or coffee, particularly with homogenised milk.

e. The spreading of ink on paper, resulting in printed or written matter having a blurred appearance.

1942 J. GRANT *Lab. Handbk. Pulp & Paper Manuf.* 120 To prevent the spreading (or 'feathering') of writing ink on paper. **1959** *New Scientist* 23 Apr. 930/1 This [*sc.* an ink containing an additive] could be used in concentration and still did not cause feathering. **1963** KENNEISON & SPILMAN *Dict. Printing* 63 *Feathering*...may be caused by using an unsuitable paper or ink.

2. a. In various concrete senses: The plumage of birds; the feather of an arrow; feather-like structure in the coat of an animal.

1530 PALSGR. 219/1 Fedderyng of a shafte. **1721** BRADLEY *Wks. Nature* 57 The Beauty of whose Shells..is as remarkable as the diversity of Feathering in Birds. **1856** KANE *Arct. Expl.* I. xxi. 268 The ptarmigan shows a singular backwardness in assuming the summer feathering. **1875** G. W. DASENT *Vikings* I. 46 An arrow on which a golden thread was twisted in the feathering. **1885** *Century Mag.* XXXI. 121 His [the Irish setter's] coat..where it extends into what is technically known as feathering, is like spun silk in quality. **1891** J. L. KIPLING *Beast & Man in India* viii. 199 In Indian horse lore the set of these featherings..ending sometimes in circles or whorls, are all mapped out like currents on a mariner's chart.

b. *Archit.* (see quot. 1842–76).

1816 J. SMITH *Panorama Sc. & Art* I. 132 The parts of tracery are ornamented with small arches and points, which is called feathering or foliation. **1842–76** GWILT *Encycl. Archit.* Gloss., *Featherings*, the cusps, plain or decorated, at the ends of a foil in tracery. **1854** J. L. PETIT *Archit. Studies France* 84 Some windows of a single light, with a free trefoil feathering in the head.

c. *Gardening.* A feather-like marking or pencilling in a flower.

1833 HOGG *Suppl. Florists' Flowers* 25 The feathering elegant and various, heavy and light, close in some [Tulips], and slightly broken in others. **1882** *The Garden* 28 Jan. 67/1 The outer surface..suffused with purple featherings.

3. *attrib.*

1858 O. W. HOLMES *Aut. Breakf.-t.* vii. (1891) 165, I have established a pair of well-pronounced feathering-calluses on my thumbs. **1867** J. HOGG *Microsc.* II. ii. 407 Whereby a 'feathering movement' is effected.

feathering (ˈfɛðərɪŋ), *ppl. a.* [f. as prec. + -ING².] **a.** That feathers; in senses of the vb.

1789 W. GILPIN *Wye* 93 The ruins..with the feathering foliage. **1839** M. F. OSSOLI in *Mem.* (1862) I. 260 His wit is so truly French in its..sparkling, feathering vivacity. **1848** LYTTON *Arthur* III. xxvii, Where o'er the space the feathering branches bend.

b. Of an oar, paddle-wheel, float, etc.: see FEATHER *v.* 11.

a **1740** TICKELL (W.), The feathering oar returns the gleam. **1867** SMYTH *Sailor's Wd.-bk.*, *Feathering-paddles.* **1869** SIR E. J. REED *Shipbuild.* xv. 278 Feathering paddle-wheel shafts are sometimes carried on brackets secured to the ship's side. **1874** KNIGHT *Dict. Mech.*, *Feathering Paddle-wheel*, a wheel whose floats have a motion on an axis, so as to descend nearly vertically into the water and ascend the same way, avoiding beating on the water in the descent and lifting water in the ascent.

c. Of the propeller of a ship or an aeroplane: see FEATHER *v.* 11 c.

1885 A. E. SEATON *Man. Marine Engin.* (ed. 4) xv. 298 A feathering screw. **1909** *Westm. Gaz.* 18 Mar. 4/2 The feathering propeller..for airship work will no doubt appeal ..as a means whereby the pitch can be altered. **1909** A. BERGET *Conquest of Air* II. ii. 141 We have obtained the longitudinal stability of the aeroplane by the use of the 'feathering tail'. **1939** *Flight* 28 Sept. p. *h*, Blade root cuffs are being fitted by the Curtiss concern to their electrically controlled, fully feathering airscrew. **1968** A. J. JACKSON *Blackburn Aircraft* 465 Four Hercules engines installed as self-contained power plants driving 14-ft diameter four-bladed Rotol constant-speed, feathering and reversible-pitch airscrews.

featherless (ˈfɛðəlɪs), *a.* [f. FEATHER *sb.* + -LESS.] Without feathers, in various senses.

c **1400** *Beryn* 1764 To shete a fethirles bolt. **1483** *Cath. Angl.* 124/2 Fedyrles or with owtyn feders, *inplumis.* *c* **1510** BARCLAY *Mirr. Gd. Manners* (1570) F iv, Yonge fetherlesse foules streyght taken from the nest. **1590** W. VALLANS *Tale two Swannes*, A haunted ducke..Was taken up all fetherlesse and bare. **1640** HOWELL *Dendrologia, Rhenusium* 74 That featherlesse bird, which went about to begge plumes of other birds to cover his nakednesse. **1658** CLEVELAND *Rustic Rampant* Wks. (1687) 407 Some with Bows and featherless Arrows. *a* **1845** HOOD *To Hahnemann* iv, A featherless cocked-hat adorns his head. **1850** LYELL *2nd Visit U.S.* II. 223 Plato's definition of a man, 'bipes implume', 'a featherless biped'.

Hence **ˈfeatherlessness**, the state of being without feathers.

1727 in BAILEY vol. II.

featherlet (ˈfɛðəlɪt). [f. as prec. + -LET.] A small feather.

1834 SOUTHEY *Doctor* Pref. 41 The episodes and digressions fringe [the story] like so many featherlets. **1866** *Morn. Star* 19 Dec., A fine bird, with..a tail of magnificent red, flecked by some snow-white featherlets.

[**featherly.** Error for FEATHERY.

[**1650** SIR T. BROWNE *Pseud. Ep.* II. i. (ed. 2) 55 Some feathery particle of snow.] **1773** JOHNSON, *Featherly*, resembling feather [quoting 'Brown' with the reading 'featherly']. Hence in **1828–32** WEBSTER, and some later Dicts.]

†**ˈfeather-maker.** *Obs.* One who dresses feathers; one who deals in feathers or plumes.

1580 HOLLYBAND *Treas. Fr. Tong.*, *Vn plumassier*, a fether maker. **1620** ROWLANDS *Pair Spy-knaves* (1872) 8 Point the Feather-maker not to faile To plume my head with his best Estridge tayle. **1681** *Lond. Gaz.* No. 1655/4 His Majesties Feather-maker (who dwels in the Pall-Mall).

ˈfeatherman. [f. FEATHER *sb.* + MAN.] One who deals in feathers or plumes.

1621 B. JONSON *Gipsies Metamorph.* Wks. (Rtldg.) 626/1 With Feathermen and Perfumers. *a* **1634** RANDOLPH *Muses Looking-glasse* I. ii, And you sweet Featherman, whose ware though light Oreweighs your Conscience. **1724** SWIFT *Reasons agst. Exam. Drugs*, The several trades..which depend on ours..such as that of hearses, coaches, coffins.. feather-men and bell-ringers. *c* **1813** MRS. SHERWOOD *Stories Ch. Catech.* xxi. 202 Mother was so busy with that feather-man, that it was of no use to ask her to hear me.

ˈfeather-stitch. A kind of stitch in ornamental needlework, producing a decorated zigzag line. (See quot. 1882)

1835 *Court Mag.* VI. xiii/1 Indian muslin pelerine, embroidered in feather-stitch. **1882** CAULFEILD & SAWARD *Dict. Needlework*, *Feather Stitch.* The two varieties of this stitch are the Opus Plumarium of ancient writers, used..for filling in Embroideries worked in silk and crewels upon silk, cloth, and serge materials, and Feather and Double Feather Stitch used to make the ornamental lines that decorate underlinen [etc.].

attrib. **1876** ROCK *Text. Fabr.* viii. 81 This was aptly called 'feather-stitch' work.

Hence **ˈfeather-stitch** *v.* **feather-stitching** *vbl. sb.* (in quot. *concr.*)

1884 *Draper's Price List*, Longcloth, scallop, feather stitched. **1891** MISS DOWIE *Girl in Karp.* xii. 149 The.. feather-stitching on my pink shirt.

ˈfeather-ˌtongue, *v. trans.* To provide with a tongue or projection for fitting into a groove. Cf. FEATHER *sb.* 16 c.

1851 *Beck's Florist* 50 For the bottom, the boards are placed lengthways, ploughed and feather-tongued, and bolted together with ⅜ bolts and nuts. **1858** *Skyring's Builders' Prices* 27 Three inch deal..feather-tongued.

ˈfeather-ˌtongued, *a.* [f. FEATHER *sb.* + TONGUE + -ED².] Of a person: Light-tongued; talkative.

a **1618** SYLVESTER *Job Triumphant* 205 The light-foot, feather-tongued Dame Had far and wide spred..the fame Of Job's Misfortunes.

ˈfeather-weight.

1. That which has the weight of a feather; hence, a very small thing.

1838 DICKENS *O. Twist* (1850) 283/1 He turned..to observe the effect of the slightest featherweight in his favour. **1885** A. M. CLERKE *Pop. Hist. Astron.* 108 The feather-weight of his carelessness, however, kicked the beam. **1915** F. M. HUEFFER *Good Soldier* I. vi. 88 Leonora lifted her up—she was the merest feather-weight—and laid her on the bed. **1932** D. C. MINTER *Mod. Needlecraft* 161/1 Now..tweeds and cloths are manufactured in featherweights.

2. *Racing.* The lightest weight allowed by the rules to be carried by a horse in a handicap. Hence sometimes applied to the rider.

1812 *Sporting Mag.* XXXIX. 136 The animals rode a feather weight. **1858** *Jockey Club Rules* in *Blaine's Rural Sports* (1870) 376 A feather weight shall be considered 4 st. 7 lb. **1883** E. PENNELL-ELMHIRST *Cream Leicestersh.* 132 [He] was going like a youth and a feather-weight.

fig. **1860** MOTLEY *Netherl.* I. 313 Burghley and Walsingham..were no feather-weights, like the frivolous Henry III.

3. *Boxing.* Applied to a pugilist who is very light, as distinguished from a *heavy-*, *middle-*, or *light-weight*. Also *attrib.*

1889 E. B. MICHELL *Boxing* 147 The boundary between heavy and middle weight, down to feather-weight (9 stone). **1928** *Daily Express* 2 Oct. 17/7 The world's feather-weight boxing title. **1933** WODEHOUSE *Heavy Weather* ix. 143 Getting a featherweight Boxing blue at Cambridge.

4. A light make of bicycle. (*Disused.*)

1901 *Morning Leader* 18 Dec. 6/2 Cycling Gossip. The topic at the moment undoubtedly is the new feather-weight fashion. **1902** *Daily Chron.* 17 May 8/6, I had these featherweights also in mind when I said that 'makers have not catered especially for light riders'. **1908** *Ibid.* 3 Aug. 6/6 Green's mount was a featherweight Raleigh.

5. *Paper.* (See quots.)

1905 *Daily Chron.* 28 June 3/2 A 'feather-weight' laid paper of a durable kind is employed. *a* **1912** *Paper Terminol.* (*Spalding & Hodge*) ii. 9 *Featherweight*, antique laid or wove light handling book papers. They are manufactured mainly from esparto, are very loosely woven, and of extreme bulk. The bulkiest are entirely unloaded. **1957** *N.Z. Timber Jrnl.* Feb. 45/2 *Feather weight paper*, a very light antique book paper of woven esparto. **1966** H. WILLIAMSON *Methods Bk. Design* (ed. 2) xviii. 290 Thick, fluffy, feeble, antique featherweight papers..are still widely used to give books a deceptive bulk.

So **ˈfeather-weighted** *ppl. a.*, trifling, unimportant; **ˈfeatherweight** *a.* = *feather-weighted* ppl. adj.; weak.

1870 LOWELL *Among my Bks.* Ser. I. (1873) 274 Finding that he can make those feather-weighted accidents balance each other. **1885** A. EDWARDS *Girton Girl* II. x. 147 It would do your cousin a vast deal of good to run away from that feather-weight husband of hers. **1958** *Times* 5 Nov. 13/1 He [*sc.* André Masson] remains..one who can just rely enough on Parisian elegance and flair to be shamelessly pretty and featherweight for much of the time.

ˈfeather-work. [f. as prec. + WORK.] **a.** The art of working in feathers; also *concr.* (see quot. 1882). **b.** = FEATHER-STITCH.

a. 1665 J. WEBB *Stone-Heng* (1725) 217 Their Curiosity in Feather-works was such, that it surpasseth all Credit and Belief. **1707** FUNNELL *Voy.* v. 113 The Natives..are very expert in Feather-work. **1784** MRS. MONTAGU *Let.* 3 Feb. in *Lady of last Cent.* (Doran 1873) 326 My great piece of feather-work is not yet compleated. **1843** PRESCOTT *Mexico* (1850) I. 32 Cotton dresses, and mantles of featherwork, exquisitely made. **1882** CAULFEILD & SAWARD *Dict. Needlework*, *Feather Work*..consists of covering buckram or other stiff foundations with birds' feathers arranged in designs and sewn entirely over the foundation.

b. 1872 O. SHIPLEY *Gloss. Eccl. Terms* 339 A certain kind of needlework is called in ancient inventories 'opus plumarium' or feather-work, from the way the stitches overlie each other like the feathers on a bird.

attrib. **1864** SALA in *Daily Tel.* 23 Dec., That wondrously variegated featherwork tapestry which the old Aztecs used to work such marvels in.

feathery (ˈfɛðərɪ), *a.* (and *sb.*) [f. as prec. + -Y.]

1. a. Of birds: Clothed with feathers; feathered.

1634 MILTON *Comus* 346 Might we but hear..the.. village cock Count the night-watches to his feathery dames. **1753** DODSLEY *Agriculture* I. 241 His feathery subjects in obedience flock Around his feeding hand. **1800** HURDIS *Fav. Village* 125 Beneath my chair Sit budge, a feathery bunch. **1884** *Pall Mall G.* 17 Mar. 12/2 The..bird.. joins once more in feathery society.

b. Of a dog: Curly-haired.

1889 *Pall Mall G.* 12 Aug. 6/1 Groups of feathery setters ..strain on their couplings.

2. a. Fringed, tipped, or flecked with something feather-like.

1792 S. ROGERS *Pleas. Mem.* I. 220 The beacon's glimmering height That faintly tipt the feathery surge with

light. **1826** MRS. HEMANS *Forest Sanctuary* I. iii, Sighing through the feathery canes. **1876** MISS BRADDON *J. Haggard's Dau.* II. 25 Silver arrows of pale summer moonlight pierced the feathery pine-branches. **1884** F. D. MILLET in *Harper's Mag.* Sept. 520/1 The sky..feathery and soft in texture.

b. Of the voice: Husky.

1881 J. GRANT *Cameronians* I. iii. 42 Sir Piers, whose voice had become..somewhat 'feathery'.

3. Resembling feathers or plumes. **a.** in appearance: Feather-like, plume-like, *esp.* of snow.

1580 C'TESS PEMBROKE *Ps.* cxlviii, Yon feathery snowes from wynters nests. **1650** SIR T. BROWNE *Pseud. Ep.* II. i. (ed. 2) 55 Which seems to be some feathery particle of snow. **1791** COWPER *Iliad* XII. 336 As the feathery snows Fall frequent. **1807** J. E. SMITH *Phys. Bot.* 300 The feathery appendages to the seeds of Dandelion. **1853** KANE *Grinnell Exp.* xxxv. (1856) 323 The prolongations..passed into detached feathery clouds. **1870** HOOKER *Stud. Flora* 180 Valeriana..Calyx-limb..developing into a feathery deciduous pappus. **1888** MISS BRADDON *Fatal Three* I. i, Diamond stars trembling amongst her feathery golden hair.

b. in lightness. Hence of immaterial things: Light, fickle. Of material things: Light, flimsy.

1601 ? MARSTON *Pasquil & Kath.* I. 281 So turnes her feath'rie fancie to and fro. **1699** W. BATES *Spir. Perfect. Unfolded* xii. 420 Our Resolutions are Light and Feathery. **1865** DICKENS *Mut. Fr.* II. vi, Blowing the feathery ash from his cigar. **1871** R. ELLIS *Catullus* lxiv. 63 Holds not her yellow locks the tiara's feathery tissue.

c. *humorously.* Of a feather-dealer.

1813 MOORE *Post-bag* (ed. 8) 54 Fine and feathery artizan..Make for me a prince's plume.

4. Of golf-balls: stuffed with feathers. Also as *sb.*

1891 R. FORGAN *Golfer's Handbk.* 34 The so-called 'feathery' variety of golf balls exclusively held the field. These 'featheries' were made of leather, stuffed with feathers.

featish ('fi:tɪʃ), *a.* [Altered form of ME. *fetis* (see FEATOUS) with the ending assimilated to the suffix *-ish*.] †**a.** Elegant, neat (*obs.*—^{0}: see FEATOUS and next word). **b.** *dial.* Pretty good, tolerable, considerable; fairly well in health.

1825 J. BRITTON *Beauties of Wiltsh.* III. 373 'How do you do?'..'Featish'. **1877** *N.W. Linc. Gloss.* s.v., 'There's a featish crop o' pears upo' that tree.' *Ibid.*, 'They be featish liars i' Swillin'ton.' **1888** *Berksh. Gloss.* s.v. *Veatish*, 'Ther be a veatish lot on um.' *Ibid.*, 'I be got rid o' the doctor, an' be a-veelin' quite veatish like now.'

Hence †**featishness**. *Obs.* neatness.

1530 PALSGR. 219/1 Featysshnesse, propernesse, *feactise*.

†'**featless**, *a. Sc. Obs.* [f. FEAT *sb.* + -LESS; cf. FECKLESS.] Inept, silly.

1599 JAS. I *Βασιλ. Δωρον* 162 A featless arrogant conceit of their greatness. **1721** J. KELLY *Scott. Proverbs* 104 Featless Folk is ay fain of other.

featly ('fi:tlɪ), *adv.* and *a.* Somewhat *arch.* [f. FEAT *a.* + -LY^2.] **A.** *adv.*

1. Fitly, properly, suitably, aptly; neatly, elegantly.

13.. *E.E. Allit. P.* B. 585 He þat fetly in face fettled alle eres. *a* **1400** *Cov. Myst.* (Shaks. Soc.) 135 Feetly with helpe sche can consent To set a cokewolde on the hye benche. *c* **1420** *Pallad. on Husb.* VIII. 142 Clense it feetly wel. **1539** TAVERNER *Erasm. Prov.* (1552) 55 Gellius applyeth this prouerbe very featlye to these grosse and rude men. **1591** FLORIO *Sec. Fruites* 63 You will haue it [wine] smelling sweetelie, coloured featly. **1606** BIRNIE *Kirk-Buriall* iii, The giuing vp of the godlies ghost may featlie be compared to three things. **1671** EACHARD *Observ. Answ. Cont. Clergy* 62 We are bluntly told..not neatly and featly. **1831** CARLYLE *Sart. Res.* I. viii. (1858) 33 Frills and fringes, with gay variety of colour, featly appended. **1855** ROBINSON *Whitby Gloss.*, 'It was all done varry feitly.'

†**b.** Exactly, precisely. *Obs.*

a **1450** *Bk. St. Albans, Fishing* (1883) 8 Bynd hem to gydur fetely so þat þe cropp may justly entur alle in to þe seyd hole. **1549** COVERDALE *Erasm. Par. Gal.* iv. 29 In this also the allegorie featly agreeth. **1674** N. FAIRFAX *Bulk. & Selv.* 74 A curious frame of well-ranged bulks so featly set together.

2. Cleverly, deftly, skilfully.

1436 *Pol. Poems* (Rolls) II. 172 Thynges wyth whiche they fetely blere oure eye. **1532** MORE *Confut. Tindale* Wks. 488/2 He..feately conuayed himself out of the frying panne, fayre into the fyre. **1609** C. BUTLER *Fem. Mon* vi. (1623) O iij, Sweets, which the Bees featly draw from them. **1787** GROSE *Provinc. Gloss., Feitly*, dexterously. *c* **1800** K. WHITE *Christiad* xvi, In homely guise I featly framed My lowly speech. **1888** G. H. RADFORD *Occasional Verses*, Let the gentle angler stand..And featly cast his specious fly.

b. With reference to movements, *esp.* dancing: With graceful agility, nimbly.

c **1340** *Gaw. & Gr. Knt.* 1758 þe lady..fetly hym kyssed. **1611** SHAKS. *Wint. T.* IV. iv. 176 She dances featly. **1635** BROME *Sparagus Garden* III. ix, How featly she holds up the neb to him! **1704** POPE *Jan. & May* 620 So featly tripp'd the light-foot ladies round. **1806** J. GRAHAME *Birds Scot.* 9 Featly ath wart the ridge she runs. **1812** BYRON *Ch. Har.* I. lxxiii, Their chargers featly prance. **1835** WILLIS *Pencillings* I. xxx. 215 His..wife..danced as featly as a fairy. **1842** BARHAM *Ingol. Leg., Ingol. Penance* II, Featly he kisseth his Holiness' toe. **1870** LOWELL *Stud. Wind.* 181 The Sapphic ..moves featly to our modern accentuation.

†**3.** Oddly, strangely. (Cf. FEAT *a.* 5.) *Obs.*

1674 N. FAIRFAX *Bulk & Selv.* 29 If my soul does not thus featly stick out of my body. **1727** BAILEY vol. II, *Featly*, oddly, after an unusual or uncouth manner.

B. *adj.* Graceful. Of a dress: Neat, well-fitting.

1801 MOORE *Ring* iii, Some the featly dance amused. **1822** W. IRVING *Braceb. Hall* (1845) 269 Her dainty person clad in featly cloak.

Hence '**featliness**, featly quality; gracefulness.

1843 LYTTON *Last Bar.* IV. vi, The admirable 'featliness' of the Count de la Roche..was rivalled only by the more majestic grace of Edward.

featness ('fi:tnɪs). [f. as prec. + -NESS.]

1. Elegance, shapeliness, spruceness, trimness.

1576 FLEMING tr. *Caius' Dogs* in Arb. *Garner* III. 248 Featness with neatness hath neighbourhood enough. *c* **1615** *Lives Women Saints* 25 The featnesse..of the bodie..is the fouling..of the soule. **1652** WHARTON tr. *Rothman's Chiromancy* Wks. (1683) 532 The Lines and other Signatures, are..by their Featness more perspicuous. **1699** BOYER *Fr. & Eng. Dict.* s.v., Featness..*propreté*.

†**b.** Nicety. *Obs.*

1577–87 HOLINSHED *Chron.* II. 12/2 The language carrieth such difficulty with it..for..the curious featnes of the pronunciation, that, etc.

†**2.** 'Oddness, uncouthness' (Bailey, folio, 1730–6).

†'**featous**, *a. Obs.* Forms: α. 4–5 fetis(e, -ys(e, 5 fetyce, 6 *Sc.* fettis; see also FEATISH. β. 5 fet(e)ous, 6 feytous, (feat-, fetus(se), feateous, 6–7 feat(u)ous, 7 fetuous. [ME. *fetys*, a. OFr. *fetis*, *feitis*, *faictis*, f. L. *facticius*: see FACTITIOUS. In 15–17th c. the ending was confused variously with the suffixes *-ish*, *-ous*, *-eous*, *-uous*, and the word seems to have been apprehended as a derivative of FEAT *a.*, to which in later use it approximates in sense.]

1. Of persons and their limbs: Well-formed, well-proportioned, handsome.

13.. *E.E. Allit. P.* B. 174 Fetyse of a fayr forme, to fote & to honde. **1340–70** *Alisaunder* 188 Fetise nailes. *c* **1386** CHAUCER *Pard. T.* 150 In comen tombesteres Fetis and smale. *c* **1400** *Rom. Rose* 829 He was..So faire, so jolly, and so fetise. *c* **1440** *Promp. Parv.* 159/2 Fetyce, or praty, *parvunculus*. **1477** MARG. PASTON in *Lett.* No. 809 III. 215 I ham waxse so fetys that I may not be gyrte in no barre of no gyrdyl that I have. **1535** STEWART *Chron. Scot.* 23865 This king..Thre sonis had baith fettis, fair and fyne.

b. Of things: Skilfully or artistically fashioned; hence, in wider sense, elegant, handsome, becoming. Often of dress.

c **1386** CHAUCER *Prol.* 157 Full fetise was hire cloke. *c* **1400** *Rom. Rose* 532 This dore..was so fetys and so lite. *Ibid.* 1133 In clothyng was he ful fetys. *c* **1460** J. RUSSELL *Bk. Nurture* 66 Wyne canels..of box fetice & fyne. **1566** DRANT *Horace Sat.* i. 83 Those that teache in schooles, With.. featusse knacks will lewre the little fooles. **1570** —— *Serm., Easter Wk.* 220 b, Ye thinke it fine and featous to be called roses..and Lilies. **1648** HERRICK *Hesper.* I. 126 Upon this fetuous board doth stand Something for shew-bread.

2. 'Dexterous.'

1755 in JOHNSON.

†'**featously**, *adv. Obs.* [f. prec. + -LY^2.]

1. With respect to attire, or ornamentation: Beautifully, handsomely, elegantly.

13.. *E.E. Allit. P.* B. 1462 þe coperounes of þe canacles þat on þe cuppe reres, Wer fetysely formed out in fylyoles longe. **1377** LANGL. *P. Pl.* B. II. 162 Fauel [sat] on a flat[er]ere fetislich atired. **1513** DOUGLAS *Æneis* IV. v. 163 Fetisly stekit with prynnit goldin thredis. *c* **1540** *Pilgr. T.* 180 His bottis sat cleyn and claspyd feytuosly. **1605** DRAYTON *Eglogs* iv. 142 A hood..Ywrought full featuously.

2. With reference to actions: Cleverly, dexterously, nimbly, properly. Of speech: Elegantly, with correctness and propriety.

c **1350** *Will Palerne* 98 þe herdes wif..fetisliche it [þat child] baþede, & wrouȝt wiþ it as wel as ȝif it were hire owne. *c* **1386** CHAUCER *Prol.* 124 Frenche she spake ful fayre and fetisly. *c* **1400** *Beryn* 141 The ffrere feynyd fetously the sprynngil for to hold. **1595** SPENSER *Prothal.* 27 They..cropt full feateously The tender stalkes. **1611** BEAUM. & FL. *Knt. Burning Pestle* IV. v, While hobby-horse doth foot it featuously.

featuous, var. form of FEATOUS *a. Obs.*

featural ('fi:tjʊərəl), *a.* [f. FEATURE *sb.* + -AL^1.] Of or pertaining to the features.

1883 G. MACDONALD *Donal Grant* I. vi. 50 There was no featural resemblance between the two faces.

Hence '**featurally** *adv.*, with regard to features.

1804 *Monthly Mag.* XVIII. 4 Never were cases more featurally distinct.

feature ('fi:tjʊə(r)), *sb.* Forms: 4–5 fetour(e, 4–6 feture, feyture, 5 fetur, (fay(c)ture, fetture, fe(i)ter, feetour, 6 feuter, fewter, 7 feauture), 6– feature. [a. OF. *feture*, *faiture* (= Pr. *faitura*, *factura*):—L. *factūra*: see FACTURE.]

1. a. Make, form, fashion, shape; proportions, *esp.* of the body; a particular example of this. *Obs.* exc. *arch.*

c **1325** *Song of Mercy* 41 in *E.E.P.* (1862) 119, I made þe Mon..Of feture liche myn owne fasoun. **14..** *Why I can't be a Nun* 134 ibid. 141, I beholde welle her feture. *c* **1410** *Sir Cleges* 11 He was a man of hight stature, And therto full fayr of feture. **1526** *Pilgr. Perf.* (W. de W. 1531) 306 b, In all feyture of body..I was moost lyke vnto thy Grace. **1600** DYMMOK *Ireland* (1843) 5 Horses of a fine feature. **1613** PURCHAS *Pilgrimage* VI. i. (1614) 558 Apes..twice as bigge in feature of their limmes. *a* **1661** FULLER *Worthies* (1840) II. 501 The king fell much enamoured of her feature. **1671** H. M. tr. *Erasm. Colloq.* 320 A woman appeared to him in his sleep, in a wonderful feature. **1684** T. HOCKIN *God's Decrees* 328 Pleasantness..is very visible in the complexion and feature of true Religion. **1820** KEATS *Hyperion* III. 88 An image, huge of feature as a cloud. **1875** TENNYSON *Q. Mary* I. i, Courtenay..of splendid feature.

†**b.** Good form or shape; comeliness. *Obs.*

1594 SHAKS. *Rich. III*, I. i. 19, I, that am..cheated of Feature by dissembling Nature. **1594** PARSONS *Succession to Engl. Crown* Ep. Ded., His excellent partes of lerning, wit, feuter of body, curtesie [etc.].

†**c.** *concr.* Something formed or shaped; a form, shape, creation. *Obs.* Cf. CREATURE I.

1483 CAXTON *Gold. Leg.* 256/2 Alle fetures and creatures prayse the moder of lyghte. **1601** B. JONSON *Poetaster* II. i, No doubt of that, sweet feature. *a* **1618** SYLVESTER *Arctophilos' Epist. to Arctoa* 84 Nature..Adorns her shop still with the matchlesse feature. **1667** MILTON *P.L.* X. 279 So sented the grim Feature, and upturn'd His Nostril wide into the murkie Air.

†**d.** As a term of contempt: = CREATURE. [So OF. *faiture*; in Eng. perh. confused with FAITOUR.]

c **1460** *Towneley Myst.* 60 Fature, for thy sake, Thay shalbe pent to pyne. *Ibid.* 120 To felle those fatures I am bowne. **14..** *Chester Pl.* (1847) II. 162 Fye on thee, feature, fie on thee.

†**2. a.** In *pl.* The elements which constitute bodily form; the build or make of the various parts of the body. Hence in *sing.* with distributive adj. **b.** *concr.* A part of the body; a limb. *Obs.*

13.. *E.E. Allit. P.* B. 794 Alle feturez ful fyn & fautlez boþe. **1393** LANGL. *P. Pl.* C. VII. 46 Prout of my faire fetours. **1447** BOKENHAM *Seyntys* Introd. (Roxb.) 5 Hyr oo foot is Both flesh and boon..Men may behoden eche feture Ther of saf the greth too only. *c* **1460–70** *Compl. Criste* 200 in *Pol. Rel. & L. Poems* 172, I sende the bodyly helthe.. fayrenes and also feturs fele. **1508** FISHER *Wks.* (1876) 240 How many lacke theyr armes..and other fetures of theyr bodyes. **1599** WEEVER *Epigr.* IV. xxii. E vj, Their rosie-tainted features cloth'd in tissue. **1726** SWIFT *Gulliver* IV. vii. 103, I agreed in every Feature of my Body with other Yahoos, except, etc. **1752** YOUNG *Brothers* IV. i, Shall I stab Her lovely image stampt on every feature?

3. In narrower sense. **a.** In *pl.* and distributively: The lineaments of the face, the form or mould of its various parts. Also *collect.* in *sing.*

c **1350** *Will. Palerne* 857 Wanne..meliors miȝt se his face, sche þout..þat leuer hire were haue welt him at wille þan of þe world be quene, So faire of all fetures þe frek was. **1393** GOWER *Conf.* III. 255 The fetures of her face In which nature had alle grace. **14..** *Epiph.* in *Tundale's Vis.* 112 They began to behold..hys feyr face Consyduryng hys feturis..With grett insyght. **1603** KNOLLES *Hist. Turks* (1621) 12 Under such simple and homly feature, lay..a most subtil..wit. *a* **1639** T. CAREW *Poems* Wks. (1824) 4 That rich treasure Of rare beauty and sweet feature. **1766** FORDYCE *Serm. Yng. Wom.* (ed. 4) II. xiii. 225 Men of sensibility desire in every woman soft features. **1842** PRICHARD *Nat. Hist. Man* 222 The features of the *Tschuk-tschi*..pronounce them of American origin. **1887** T. A. TROLLOPE *What I remember* I. xvi. 331 [He] equalled him in .. refinement of feature.

fig. *a* **1680** BUTLER *Sat. Hum. Learn.* II. Rem. 1759 I. 223 Words are but Pictures..To draw the..Features of the Mind. *a* **1788** MICKLE *Siege Marseilles* I. i, Oft..have I beheld A little, wayward, giddy levity Show its capricious features. **1827** POLLOK *Course T.* V. 738 Redeeming features in the face of Time. **1868** FREEMAN *Norm. Conq.* (1876) II. vii. 25 Tenderness for animals is no unusual feature in the portraits of holy men.

b. *concr.* Any of the parts of the face; the eye, nose, mouth, forehead, or chin.

1828 SCOTT *F.M. Perth* ii, There was daring..in the dark eye, but the other features seemed to express a bashful timidity. **1847** EMERSON *Poems, Visit* Wks. (Bohn) I. 404 Say, what other metre is it Than the meeting of the eyes? Nature poureth into nature Through the channels of that feature. **1858** HAWTHORNE *Fr. & It. Jrnls.* II. 23 Hitting the poor Venus another..blow on that unhappy feature.

4. *transf.* A distinctive or characteristic part of a thing; some part which arrests the attention by its conspicuousness or prominence.

a. Of material things.

1692 DRYDEN *St. Euremont's Ess.* 164 Examine separately each feature of the Picture. **1791** BURKE *French Affairs* Wks. 1842 I. 570 The several kingdoms..have..some features which run through the whole. **1815** ELPHINSTONE *Acc. Caubul* (1842) II. 225 The grand feature of the country is the Indus. **1866** CRUMP *Banking* x. 220 These Irish rings possessed..the features of a true coinage. **1871** B. STEWART *Heat* §362 Another feature of the locomotive is the blast-pipe. **1874** MICKLETHWAITE *Mod. Par. Churches* 186 String courses or other architectural features.

b. In various specific applications: (*a*) Applied to a person, esp. a professional entertainer.

1801 T. FREMANTLE *Let.* 1 May in A. Fremantle *Wynne Diaries* (1940) III. 54 Living on such very friendly terms with all the leading features in the Squadron. **1838** *Actors by Daylight* I. 123 Covent Garden was advertised to open, and Miss Fanny Kemble announced as the *feature*.

(*b*) A distinctive or prominent article or item in a newspaper, magazine, etc.

1855 GEO. ELIOT in *Westm. Rev.* VIII. IV. 438 The Press has no band of critics who..are on the watch for a slip or defect in the preacher, to make a 'feature' in their article. **1933** H. G. WELLS *Shape of Things to Come* I. §9 93 A daily paper..would..have found itself vigorously outdone by more richly endowed competitors, able because of their wealth to buy up all the most attractive features. **1959** *Times* 5 May 13/5 (Advt.), Nowadays it's not so much news as features; features or comment.

(*c*) A feature film. So ***feature-length*** attrib. Also in *Broadcasting*, a feature programme.

1913 [see 4f]. **1921** A. C. LESCARBOURA *Cinema Handbk.* (1922) i. 23 *Feature*, a pictured story, a plurality of reels in length. *Ibid.* x. 351 Paralleling all this is the filming of short features for the news and magazine films. **1930** J. B. PRIESTLEY *Angel Pavement* iv. 177 Then came the film of the evening, the star feature. **1932** *N.Y. Times* 10 Apr. Mag. 22/3 In England there is more chamber music, more serious drama,..fewer 'educational features'. **1938** I. BARRY in Bardèche & Brasillach *Hist. Film* 388 Since the advent of sound, feature-length travel and documentary pictures produced commercially have been less evident than formerly. **1941** *B.B.C. Gloss. Broadc. Terms* 20 *News Feature*, programme in which news is presented in radio-dramatic form. **1954** *Economist* 11 Sept. Suppl. 11/1 A BBC feature depicting Folland Aircraft and the Gnat brought a host of small buying orders for Folland shares into the market. **1956** *Ann. Reg. 1955* 385 The first feature-length cartoon film, *Animal Farm*. **1965** *Listener* 20 May 746/3 There is a Robert Mulligan going the circuits as a second feature to *Good Neighbour Sam*.

(*d*) *Philol.* (See quots. 1942 and 1957.)

1926 *Language* II. 157 Different morphemes may be alike or partly alike as to vocal features. **1942** *Ibid.* XVIII. 7 It turns out that some things..are constantly associated in groups of two or more, one appearing wherever the others do. Where this is true, the two or more elements clearly constitute a single unit, one of the minimum units into which the utterances of the range may be analyzed. These units are termed *features*. **1948** *Ibid.* XXIV. 33 Some distinctively different segments contain a distinctive combination, or one or more distinctive components in common. The distinctive aspects or components of a segment constitute one or more *features* of the segment. We use the term 'feature' for what is commonly called a distinctive feature of a sound. Features are said to occur in segments; segments are said to contain features. **1952** R. JAKOBSON et al. (*title*) Preliminaries to speech analysis: the distinctive features and their correlates. *Ibid.* i. 3 The listener is obliged to choose either between two polar qualities in the same category..or between the presence and absence of a certain quality... The choice between the two opposites may be termed distinctive features. **1957** *Trans. Philol. Soc. 1957* 122 Referring to the *two ways of discriminating* elements in the flow of speech—the one, which distinguishes elements as successive (segmentation), and the other, which distinguishes elements as successive or simultaneous (substitution): we establish *two fundamental types of element*—(i) such as *can* be isolated by segmentation, to be called '*segments*', and (ii) such as *cannot* be, to be called '*features*'. **1968** CHOMSKY & HALLE *Sound Pattern Eng.* 66 Our tentative assumption is that the segmental features and the boundary features fall into distinct sets.

(*e*) *Mil.* A topographically noteworthy point or area.

1944 *Daily Tel.* 15 May, They have also taken five more hill features and three towns. **1956** J. MASTERS *Bugles & Tiger* xviii. 229 M. L. sent my company..up the hill and spread the others out..on smaller features.

c. Of immaterial things.

a **1822** LD. CASTLEREAGH *Speech*, The feature on which this question chiefly hinges. **1835** MARRYAT *Jac. Faithf.* viii, The principal feature in him was lightness of heart. **1875** A. R. HOPE *Schoolboy Friends* 163 A great feature of the day were the recitations.

d. *attrib.*

1792 BURNS *Let. to G. Thomson* 8 Nov., The emphasis, or what I would call the feature-notes of the tune. **1853** LYNCH *Self-Improv.* vi. 145 A feature-mark, a seminal speciality.

e. Relating to a linguistic feature (sense 4 b (*d*) above).

1953 C. E. BAZELL *Linguistic Form* i. 2 Sufficient evidence is also provided by the analogical extension of a feature-alternation to phonemes for which it was previously unknown. *Ibid.* 3 It is misleading to describe feature-analysis as 'analysis in depth'. **1964** *Language* XL. 221 Particularly important for an understanding of the decoding process would be experimentation with 'feature opposition'. **1967** *Word* XXIII. 218 Feature analysis in the area of morphological categories is indeed very old, probably at least as ancient as Aristotle.

f. Special Combs. **feature film**, the principal film in a programme; so ***feature picture***; **feature programme**, a programme based on one central theme; **feature writer**, one who writes a special feature (sense 4 b (*b*) above) in a newspaper, magazine, etc; so ***feature editor***, ***story***, etc. The pl. form *features* is also used.

1911 D. S. HULFISH *Cycl. Motion-Pict. Work* II. 200 (*caption*) Feature Films. **1912** HARRINGTON & FRANKENBERG *Essentials Journalism* vi. 62 It may not be amiss..to speak briefly of the work of trained 'feature' writers. *Ibid.* 294 A feature story is one in which the news element is made subordinate. **1913** *Moving Picture Ann. 1912* 15 The rapid growth of what has come to be known as the 'feature film'..characterizes the year 1912... Features rather than 'first runs' became the popular cry. **1913** *Technical World* XIX. 464 Sunday feature pictures, sports, and advertising are all made in this dark room. **1913** *Writer's Bull.* Oct. 101/2 Here is a little suggestion to those who write feature articles. **1927** *Melody Maker* May 523/1 Fox-trots..occur frequently in feature pictures to accompany dancing. **1928** *B.B.C. Handbk. 1929* 60 Particular attention..is being paid to what have been called 'feature programmes'—composite programmes in which the aid of music and the spoken word is asked to evoke a mood, or to present an idea. **1929** F. A. POTTLE *Stretchers* (1930) 318 The editor-in-chief of the *Flare*, Cpl. Herbert M. Davidson..was, until recently, feature editor of the Chicago *Daily News*. **1938** *Ann. Reg. 1937* 371 Feature films, that is films of 3,000 feet or more, showed only a trifling increase. **1938** *Encycl. Brit. Bk. Yr.* 122/1 During 1937, dramatic productions in the studios showed a considerable development of 'feature programmes', dealing with such subjects as the history of journalism,..Hadrian's Wall, the anti-slavery movement..and the Duchy of Cornwall. **1938** E. WAUGH *Scoop* I. v. 85 The other agencies are sending feature men. **1939** 'N. BLAKE' *Smiler with Knife* v. 78 One of the *Daily Post* feature-writers. **1956** Features-producer [see B.B.C.]. **1957** C. BROOKE-ROSE *Langs. Love* v. 48 The literary types..with families to support on a regular out-put of criticism, non-fiction books..and long feature programmes for the B.B.C. **1957** *Times Lit. Suppl.* 8 Nov. 670/4 She persuades the great Arthur Brisbane, of the New York *World*..to hire her, and becomes a first-class journalist, feature-writer and columnist herself. **1958** *Punch* 1 Jan. 80/2 At the cinema trailers usually precede feature films by at least one week. **1958** *New Statesman* 25 Jan. 107/1 Success tempts the American novelist to become a kind of Public Relations Officer ad-libbing into feature journalism. **1969** *Listener* 8 May 660/2 The death last week of Joe Burroughs removes one more of the small corps of features pioneers whose common link was..a belief that all radio is one art. *Ibid.* 5 June 811/3 (Advt.), Features Editor—to be responsible for the quality of the words of the features pages.

feature (ˈfiːtjʊə(r)), *v.* [f. prec. sb.]

1. *trans.* To resemble in features; to favour; *esp.* with reference to family likeness or resemblance. Now chiefly *dial.*

1755 JOHNSON, *To feature*, to resemble in countenance. **1859** GEO. ELIOT *A. Bede* v. xxxviii, 'Ye feature him, on'y ye're darker.' **1879** MISS JACKSON *Shropsh. Word-bk.* s.v., Ben faichurs 'is faither, but all the rest favour the mother's side. **1881** J. HAWTHORNE *Fort. Fool* I. xx, She featured her mother's family more than her father's.

2. a. To affect, or mould the features of. **b.** To stand as a feature or distinctive mark upon.

1810 CRABBE *Borough* iv, Fear, hope, dismay..featured every face. **1832** DE QUINCEY *Charlemagne* Wks. XIII. 160 Differences by which they are severally marked and featured. **1863** KINGLAKE *Crimea* (1877) V. i. 85 Knolls and ridges which featured the landscape. **1878–9** S. LANIER *Remonstr.* 3 Forbear To feature me my Lord by rule and line.

3. To sketch the features of; to outline, picture, portray. Also, To impress the features of *upon* (something).

1791–1823 D'ISRAELI *Cur. Lit.* (1859) II. 62 The characters cannot be very minutely featured. **1822** BEDDOES *Bride's Tragedy* II. iv, Something in the air..Featured its ghastly self upon my soul. **1864** *Reader* 19 Mar. 351 Which some keen spirits are already featuring to themselves.

4. a. To exhibit as a 'feature'; to make a special feature or display of, make a special attraction of. orig. *U.S.*

1888 *St. Louis Globe-Democrat* 29 Apr. (Farmer), The biggest thing I saw at the wedding was a lot of glass-ware and block tin knives and forks, which were featured in one of the rooms. **1906** *Westm. Gaz.* 24 Sept. 9/3 The way in which Miss Clifford had been 'featured' and 'billed' in preference to herself. **1907** *Times* (weekly ed.) 28 June 402 Every day for weeks past it has 'featured' articles..on the Japanese question. **1928** *Publishers' Weekly* 12 May 1932 You will know then why so many booksellers feature Macaulay books. **1928** G. B. SHAW *Intell. Woman's Guide Socialism* 444 The Government posters 'feature' precisely the same epithets. **1929** *Times* 1 Aug., The Louvre, Oxford-circus, are featuring coats and skirts and top coats for Scotland in new designs. **1938** E. WAUGH *Scoop* I. v. 86 [Newspaperman loq.] They're featuring me as a special service.

b. *spec.* To exhibit as a prominent feature in a play, film, etc.

1897 *Metropolitan Mag.* (N.Y.) Nov. 383/2 A company that includes in addition to the 'featured' members, [etc.]. **1919** J. BUCHAN *Mr. Standfast* xiii. 245 Were you ever a cinema actor, Dick?..'Featuring Mary Lamington.' How does the jargon go? **1923** *Westm. Gaz.* 22 Jan., Balzac's 'The Eternal Flame', featuring Miss Norma Talmadge. **1927** *Daily Chron.* 29 Mar. 6 She said she had been 'featured' in 22 or 23 different pieces in America. **1928** *Manch. Guardian Weekly* 7 Dec. Suppl. p. ix/1 A handsome middle-aged gentleman featuring himself through five acts. **1936** *Amer. Speech* XI. 220 Is the actor to be *starred* or merely *featured*? If *starred*, the program, the signs outside the theater, and all advertising will read, 'X in Hamlet'. If *featured*, it will be, 'Hamlet with X'.

5. *intr.* To be a feature (*in*); to participate or play an (important) part in.

1941 *London & N.E. Railway Mag.* Mar. 55/1 Tea..featured frequently in early newspaper advertisements. **1965** *Listener* 9 Sept. 371/1 At the University Physiological Laboratory in Cambridge cats feature in some of the fundamental research. **1968** *Courier-Mail* (Brisbane) 25 Nov. 5/3 The man also admitted 'featuring' at the Toowong Cemetery in black magic rites. **1968** R. GITTINGS *John Keats* ii. 30 The uncles and aunts who feature so largely in the memories of many orphan children. **1976** *Times* 21 May 4/2 Libraries and the youth service feature prominently in many of the local authority cuts. **1984** F. FORSYTH *Fourth Protocol* II. xiv. 252 The habitual practice when Soviet illegals enter a country by ship is that they do *not* feature on the crew list.

Hence **ˈfeaturing** *vbl. sb.*; in quot. *concr.*

1865 CARLYLE *Fredk. Gt.* VI. XVI. vii. 202 Documents and more explicit featurings.

featured (ˈfiːtjʊəd), *ppl. a.* [f. FEATURE *sb.* and *v.* + -ED.]

†**1.** Fashioned, formed, shaped. Usually preceded by adv. of manner, as *evil, fair, fine, ill, well featured*, for which see those words. *Obs.*

c **1500** *Three Kings Sons* 111 They were passing well fetured. *c* **1540** J. HEYWOOD *Four P.P.* in Hazl. *Dodsley* I. 376 O prince of hell! Feutred in fashion abhominable. **1543** GRAFTON *Contn. Harding* 468 Richard duke of Gloucestre..was..euill feautered of lymmes. **1575** LANEHAM *Let.* (1871) 51 The rich ring..without the fayr fewtered fynger, iz nothing. **1627** HAKEWILL *Apol.* I. iii. §3. 32 Horses better featured..then now. **1633** BP. HALL *Hard Texts* 279 Thy nose..is..featured like some curious Turret.

†**b.** Well-formed; comely, beautiful. *Obs.*

1567 TURBERV. *Ovid's Epist.* 10, I at natures hand no featurde face could gaine. **1587** —— *Trag. T.* (1837) 63 Their feitured limmes bedeckt. **1602** WARNER *Alb. Eng.* X. lix. (1612) 257 Love-worth Maacha..baire To Dauid featred Absalom. **1774** LANGHORNE *Country Justice* I. 123 In the free Eye, the featur'd Soul display'd, Honour's strong Beam.

2. a. Shaped into features. **b.** Expressed by features or external form.

1742 YOUNG *Nt. Th.* ix. 70 The well-stain'd canvas, or the featur'd stone. *a* **1779** LANGHORNE *Studley Park* Poems (Chalmers) 418 Let..From Jones's hand the featur'd marble glow. **1794** MATHIAS *Purs. Lit.* (1798) 349 Each strange form in motley masquerade, Featur'd grimace, and impudence pourtray'd. **1841** HOR. SMITH *Moneyed Man* III. ii. 50 Her smile was a featured sunbeam. **1850** LYNCH *Theo. Trin.* xii. 231 Our earth, the featured Definite Has meanings all divine.

3. Furnished with or having features of a certain cast, usually preceded by some qualifying word.

1790 PENNANT *London* (1813) 302 Angelic faces..featured with impudence. *a* **1759** GOLDSM. *Voltaire* Wks. 1881 IV. 43 The Marquis d'Argent was graceful in person, regularly featured. **1850** EB. ELLIOTT *More Verse & Prose* I. 18 Who is that small Napoleon-featur'd pleader? **1861** W. F. COLLIER *Hist. Eng. Lit.* 405 That hard-featured..old forester.

featureless (ˈfiːtjʊəlɪs), *a.* [f. as prec. + -LESS.]

1. Without good features; ugly. *rare.*

c **1600** SHAKS. *Sonn.* xi, Let those whom Nature hath not made for store, Harsh, featureless, and rude, barrenly perish. **1860** *Sat. Rev.* IX. 831/1 A guard of featureless barbarians.

2. Wanting facial features. Also, Having no marked or prominent feature.

1825 COLERIDGE *Aids Refl.* (1848) I. 224 The other [face of Janus]..maimed, featureless, and weather-bitten. **1835** LYTTON *Rienzi* VI. ii, Featureless spectres..they seemed in their shroud-like robes. **1868** LD. HOUGHTON *Select. fr. Wks.* 203 The statued form of Beauty..Now prostrate, powerless, featureless and cold. **1875** JOWETT *Plato* (ed. 2) III. 66 Indiscriminate lovers..turn blemishes into beauties..the featureless are faultless.

3. *transf.* Without any prominent mark or point of interest; uninteresting.

1839 MURCHISON *Silur. Syst.* I. ii. 22 The low and featureless form of the ground. **1871** *Sat. Rev.* 29 Apr., The absolutely featureless country house of George III.'s reign. **1879** FARRAR *St. Paul* (1883) 717 Not recognising a single land-mark on the featureless shore. **1891** *Punch* Christmas No. 7/2 The month [of March] will be so featureless.

b. Of business, *esp.* on the stock market: Giving no occasion for remark; uneventful.

1879 *Standard* 21 May 2/1 Business in Discount to-day was absolutely featureless. **1885** *Manch. Exam.* 1 Apr. 4/1 Canadian Pacific shares were featureless.

Hence **ˈfeaturelessness**.

1883 MRS. BISHOP *Sk. Malay Penin.* ii. in *Leisure Hour* 21/1 Yet with all this..featurelessness..Malacca is very fascinating.

featurely (ˈfiːtjʊəlɪ), *a.* [f. FEATURE *sb.* + -LY[1].] Having strongly marked features; characteristic; typical.

c **1819** COLERIDGE in *Lit. Rem.* (1836) II. 133 More intellectually vigorous and more featurely warriors of Christian chivalry. **1853** LYNCH *Self-Improv.* iii. 59 Chaucer..giving us the featurely expression of his own age.

Hence **ˈfeatureliness**.

1818 COLERIDGE in *Lit. Rem.* (1836) I. 117 Don Quixote's leanness and featureliness. **1867** BAGEHOT *Eng. Constit.* v. 124 The picturesqueness, the featureliness, of society diminishes.

featurette (ˈfiːtjʊərət, fiːtjʊəˈrɛt). [f. FEATURE *sb.* 4 a (*c*) + -ETTE.] A short feature film. Also *transf.*

1942 *Variety* 28 Jan. 8 This Roach featurette is not quite up to par of other issues in the series. **1957** M. KENNEDY *Heroes of Clone* I. i. 16 I've sold a little screen play. Nothing important. A featurette. **1959** HALAS & MANVELL *Technique Film Animation* xvii. 147 Disney's *Man in Space*—a featurette which was an excellent piece of documentary science fiction. **1960** *Guardian* 21 Nov. 7/2 Correspondents who write reports in the older tradition, rather than featurettes. **1970** *Oxford Times* 25 Dec. 17 (Advt.), A Walt Disney cartoon featurette. Wind in the Willows.

featy (ˈfiːtɪ), *a.* [f. FEAT *a.* + -Y[1].]

†**a.** Neat, pretty (*obs.*). **b.** Handy, clever, wide-awake (*rare*).

1621 MOLLE *Camerar. Liv. Libr.* II. i. 73 The featie conceits this Epitaph sheweth to have. **1844** *Camp of Refuge* I. 101 A maiden of Alftrude's degree could not travel..without a featy handmaiden attendant upon her.

Hence **ˈfeatily** *adv.*, in quot. = FEATLY 2 b.

c **1630** in Risdon *Surv. Devon* §225 (1810) 239 They..foot it on the grass as featily.

†**feauges.** *Obs. rare*[−1].

1624 CAPT. SMITH *Virginia* v. 180 Many that went abroad, through weaknesse were subiect to be suddenly surprized with a disease called the Feauges, whiche was neither paine nor sicknesse, but as it were the highest degree of weaknesse.

feaver, -our, etc.: see FEVER.

feawd, obs. form of FEUD *sb.*[1], enmity.

feawterlocke, obs. form of FETTERLOCK.

feaze (fiːz), *v.*[1] *Obs.* exc. *Naut.* Forms: 6 faze, 9 faize, 8- feaze. [In some way related to OE. *fæs* (see FAS) fringe; possibly as a naut. term f. MDu.

vese, *veze* fringe, frayed edge, which is related by ablaut to the OE. word.]

1. a. *trans.* To unravel (a rope), etc. **b.** *intr.* Of a rope or thread: To unravel at the end. Also of a stick: To wear rough at the end.

1568 SIR T. SMITH *De recta Ling. Angl. Script.* 31 b, Fäz, *in fila diducere* [Smith's 'fäz' = *faze*; cf. 'gäz' = gaze]. *a* **1577** GASCOIGNE *Dan Bartholomew* Wks. (1587) 83, I find it [a bracelet] fazed almost quite in sunder. **1647** FARINGDON *Serm.* Pref. 28 The Schoolmen did feaze and draw it out, and then made it up into knots. **1721–1800** BAILEY, *Feazing* [Sea Term] is the Ravelling out of a Cable, or any great Rope at the Ends. **1813** W. LESLIE *View Nairn* Gloss., *Feaze*, to have the woof at the end of a piece of cloth or ribband rubbed out from the warp. **1825** JAMIESON, 'That thread 'll no go through the eye of the needle; its a' feazed at the point.' 'Get a verrule put to your staff, the end o't's a' faiz'd.' **1867** SMYTH *Sailor's Word-bk.*, *Feaze*, to untwist, to unlay ropes; to tease, to convert it into oakum.

2. *intr.* (see quot.)

1813 W. LESLIE *View Nairn* Gloss. 454 *Feaze*, to have the edge of a razor.. turned to a side, instead of being blunted by use.

Hence **'feazings** *vbl. sb. pl.*; *Sc.* **fais-**, **faizins**.

1825 JAMIESON, *Faizins*, *Faisins*. **1867** SMYTH *Sailor's Word-bk.*, *Feazings*, the fagging out or unravelling of an unwhipped rope.

†feaze, *v.*² *Obs. rare*⁻¹. (See quot.)

1641 BEST *Farm. Bks.* (Surtees) 97 Such olde sheepe and lambes as doe shoote are to be.. feased, i.e. to have all the woll under theire tayle.. clipped away.

feaze, *v.*³, var. FAZE *v.*

feaze, var. of FEEZE *sb.*

feble, obs. form of FEEBLE.

febre, obs. form of FEVER.

febricitant (fɪˈbrɪsɪtənt), *a.* and *sb.* Now *rare.* [ad. L. *febrīcitant-em*, pr. pple. of *febrīcitāre* (see next). Cf. F. *fébricitant.*]

A. *adj.* Affected with fever; feverish.

1599 A. M. tr. *Gabelhouer's Bk. Physicke* Contents 111, All Agues, and all Febricitant diseases, as is, the Rose, the Plague. **1670** *Phil. Trans.* V. 2079 A Fœtus febricitant whilst in the womb. **1884** *Syd. Soc. Lex.*, *Febricitant.*

†B. *sb.* One who is affected with fever. *Obs.*

1541 R. COPLAND *Galyen's Terapeutyke* 2 D iij b, Vj. C. tymes haue we asshed many febricitans incontinent after yᵉ fyrste actes [*read* acces]. **1650** BULWER *Anthropomet.* xxii. 245 The Amplifying force.. which formeth out in length the Bones of Febricitants, as wax.

†fe'bricitate, *v. Obs.*⁻⁰ [f. L. *febrīcitāt-* ppl. stem of *febrīcitāre* to have a fever, f. *febris* fever.] *intr.* To be ill of a fever.

1656–81 in BLOUNT *Glossogr.* **1721–1800** in BAILEY.

†fe,brici'tation. *Obs. rare*⁻¹. [n. of state f. L. *febrīcitāre*: see prec. and -ATION.] The state of being in a fever, feverishness.

1584 T. BASTARD *Chrestoleros* xv. 11 Phisition Mirus talkes of saliuation Of Tophes and Pustules and Febricitation. **1663–76** BULLOKAR, *Febricitation.* **1727** in BAILEY vol. II.

febricity (fɪˈbrɪsɪtɪ). [ad. L. *febrīcitāt-em*, n. of state f. *febrīcitāre*: see FEBRICITATE and -ITY.] The state of having a fever or being feverish.

1873 BROWNING *Red Cott. Nt.-cap* 174 In those three months' febricity Which followed.

febricose (ˌfiːbrɪˈkəʊs), *a.* [ad. L. *febricōs-us*, f. *febris* a fever.] 'Feverish' (*Syd. Soc. Lex.*).

febricula (fɪˈbrɪkjʊlə). *Med.* [a. L. *febrīcula*, dim. of *febris* a fever. Cf. F. *fébricule.*] A slight fever, of short duration.

1746 SIR R. MANNINGHAM (*title*), The symptoms, nature, causes, and cure of the febricula.. commonly called the nervous or hysteric fever. **1785** FRANKLIN *Lett.* Wks. 1840 VI. 528 Many find themselves affected by that febricula, which the English alone call a cold. **1834** J. FORBES *Laennec's Dis. Chest* (ed. 4) 204 This febricula.. is not usually followed by any mischief.

febricule (ˈfɛbrɪkjuːl). Anglicized form of FEBRICULA.

1887 R. L. STEVENSON in *Longman's Mag.* I. 679 A febricule when I digest.

febriculose (fɪˈbrɪkjʊˌləʊs), *a. Med. rare.* [ad. L. *febrīculōs-us*, f. *febrīcula*: see FEBRICULA]

1727 in BAILEY vol. II. **1884** *Syd. Soc. Lex.*, *Febriculose*, having a slight fever, relating to a Febricula.

Hence **febricu'losity**. *rare.*

1727 BAILEY vol. II, *Febriculosity*, the same as Febricitation. **1884** *Syd. Soc. Lex.*, *Febriculosity*, feverishness.

†fe'briculous, *a. Obs. rare.* [ad. L. *febrīculōs-us*: see prec. and -OUS.] Slightly feverish.

1656–81 BLOUNT *Glossogr.*, *Febriculous*, that hath or is subject to a Feaver. Whence **1692–1732** in COLES.

†'febrient, *a. Obs. rare*⁻¹. [ad. late L. *febrient-em*, pr. pple. of *febrīre* to have a fever.] Feverish, sickening of a fever.

1651 BIGGS *New Disp.* ⁋248 An infant of a year old, who is dentient and febrient.

febrifacient (fiːbrɪˈfeɪʃ(ɪ)ənt), *a.* and *sb.* [f. L. *febri-* (*febris*) fever + -FACIENT.]

A. *adj.* Fever-producing.

1803 T. BEDDOES *Hygëia* XI. 48 The fermentations from which the febri-facient effluvia spring. **1884** in *Syd. Soc. Lex.*

B. *sb.* Something that produces fever.

1832 in WEBSTER (citing BEDDOES).

febriferous (fɪˈbrɪfərəs), *a.* [f. L. *febri-*, *febris* fever + -FEROUS.] Producing fever.

1874 DUNGLISON, *Febriferous*, fever-bearing, as *a febriferous locality.* **1884** in *Syd. Soc. Lex.*

febrific (fɪˈbrɪfɪk), *a.* [ad. F. *febrifique* (Cotgr.), f. L. *febri-*, *febris* fever + *-fic-us* making: see -FIC.] **a.** Producing fever. **b.** = FEVERISH.

1710 T. FULLER *Pharm. Extemp.* 203 A Febrific Glyster. **1749** FIELDING *Tom Jones* VIII. iii, The aliment.. will aggravate the febrific symptoms. **1766** CHESTERF. *Lett.* IV. 242 The febrific humour fell into my legs. **1832** in WEBSTER. **1884** in *Syd. Soc. Lex.*

febrifugal (fɪˈbrɪfjʊgəl, fɛbrɪˈfjuːgəl), *a.* [f. next + -AL¹.] Adapted to mitigate or subdue fever; anti-febrile.

1663 BOYLE *Nat. Philos.* II. v. x. 212 Nor the mixture hath been.. noted for any Febrifugal Vertues. **1853** *Chamb Jrnl.* XX. 28 The remedies prescribed were depletory and febrifugal. **1870** BENTLEY *Bot.* (ed. 2) 483 The plants of this order have.. febrifugal properties.

febrifuge (ˈfɛbrɪfjuːdʒ), *a.* and *sb.* [a. F. *fébrifuge*, f. (on L. type **febrifugus*) L. *febri-*, *febris* fever + *fug-āre* to drive away.]

A. *adj.* = FEBRIFUGAL.

1707 *Curios. Husb. & Gard.* 235 Perriwinkle is vulnerary, astringent and febrifuge. **1725** N. ST. ANDRÉ in *Lond. Gaz.* No. 6349/3 Testaceous Powders and Febrifuge Juleps. **1803** DAVY in *Phil. Trans.* XCIII. 268 Barks supposed to be possessed of febrifuge properties. **1860** PIESSE *Lab. Chem. Wonders* 171 Nearly all the bitter plants are called febrifuge from their power to cure fever.

B. *sb.* A medicine adapted to drive away or to reduce fever; hence, a cooling drink.

1686 W. HARRIS tr. *Lemery's Chym* (ed. 3) 487 Divers other ingredients, thought to be Febrifuges. **1744** BERKELEY *Siris* §7 It hath been found an admirable febrifuge. **1860** READE *Cloister & H.* IV. 305 The grand febrifuge of anchorites—cold water. **1861** G. F. BERKELEY *Sportsm. W. Prairies* vi. 96 He had however some effervescing lemonade, so I contented myself with that febrifuge.

transf. and *fig.* **1815** SCOTT *Guy M.* viii, Chanting a rhyme which she believed sovereign as a febrifuge. **1851** RUSKIN *Stones Ven.* (1874) I. App. 364 Geometry seems to have acted as a febrifuge. *a* **1859** DE QUINCEY in H. A. Page *Life* I. iii. 34 The rough febrifuge which this awaking administered.

†febrifugous, *a. Obs.* Also 8 **febrifugious**. [f. as prec. + -OUS.] = FEBRIFUGAL.

1683 W. HARRIS *Pharmacologia* xii. 177, I have generally thought it Necessary to give some such.. Febrifugous draught. **1725** BRADLEY *Fam. Dict.* s.v. *Quinquina*, The resinous febrifugious substance of this Barke.

febrile (ˈfiːbrɪl, ˈfɛbrɪl), *a.* [a. F. *fébrile*, ad. L. *febrīlis*, f. *febris* fever.] **†a.** Of a person: Affected by, or suffering from, fever (*obs.*). **b.** Of or pertaining to fever; produced by or indicative of fever; feverish.

1651 BIGGS *New Disp.* ⁋194 Teach Physitians to fear how they expose their febrile patients. **1666** G. HARVEY *Morb. Angl.* ii. (1672) 6 The Febril heat continuing its aduction upon the dryer fleshy parts, changes into a Marcid Feaver. **1749** FIELDING *Tom Jones* VIII. iii, The acidity occasioned by the febrile matter. **1783** POTT *Chirurg. Wks.* II. 137 Calculated.. to quiet the febrile heat. **1794** SULLIVAN *View Nat.* IV. 255 We were.. all in a febrile state. We could not eat. **1844** KINGLAKE *Eothen* v. 69 The febrile irritation of the frame.

Hence **fe'brility**, the state of being febrile, feverishness. **†'febrilous** *a. Obs. rare*⁻¹. = FEBRILE b.

1873 R. BARNES *Dis. Women* 96 There is a state of febrility, .. of swimming of the eyes. **1878** T. BRYANT *Pract. Surg.* I. 54 In proportion as the local process is less acute.. there is less attendant febrility. **1651** BIGGS *New Disp.* ⁋194 Their febrilous essence of heat.

†'febris. *Obs.* Also 5 **febrys**, 6 **febres**. [a. L. *febris* fever.] A fever.

1483 CAXTON *Gold. Leg.* 230/3 Al that yere she was seke and laboured in the febrys. **1527** ANDREW *Brunswyke's Distyll. Waters* II. A ij, It [Sorell water] is good for the hote ague or febres. **1535** STEWART *Cron. Scot.* II. 219 Vter that tyme.. Into the Walis seik in the febris la.

Febronian (fɛˈbrəʊnɪən), *a.* and *sb.* [f. *Febrōnius* + -AN.] Of or pertaining to (Justinus) Febronius; a pseudonym under which J. N. von Hontheim of Treves wrote in the 18th century, maintaining the independence of national churches. Also *sb.*, a follower of Febronius.

Hence **Fe'bronianism**, the doctrine thus maintained.

1856 *Literary Churchman* II. 66/1 The extract on the Erastianism, or 'Febronianism', of Austria is as follows. **1882** SCHAFF *Encycl. Relig. Knowl.* I. 722 In harmony with the Febronian principles. **1884** ADDIS & ARNOLD *Cath. Dict.* 346/2 The Pope's power was to be reduced to that which Febronians supposed him to have exercised in the first three centuries. **1885** *Catholic Dict.* 244/2 *Febronianism*.. may be roughly described as an exaggeration of Gallicanism. *Ibid.* 346/1 The notorious Church reforms of Joseph II may be fairly called Febronian. **1895** *19th Cent.* Nov. 797 Protestants of the sixteenth and seventeenth centuries were succeeded by Febronians and Jansenists in the eighteenth.

February (ˈfɛbruːərɪ). Forms: 3 **feoverel**, **-rer**, 3–5 **fever(r)er**, **-yer(e**, (3 **-ȝeer**), 4–5 **feverȝere**, (5 *Sc.* **feveryher**), 4–6 **feverel(l(e**, (4 **-yl**), 4–7 **februar**, (9 *Sc.* **febewar**), 4 **februari**, 6–7 **februarie**, (6 **febrewary**), 7–8 **februeer**, (7 **-ere**), 4– **February**. Also abbrev. **Feb.** [ME. *feverer*, ad. OF. *feverier*, = Pr. *febrier*, Cat. *febrer*, Sp. *febrero*, Pg. *fevereiro*, It. *febbraio*:—popular L. **febrārius*, L. *februārius*, f. *februa* pl. (*februum* sing. a word of Sabine origin signifying purification), the Roman festival of purification, held on the 15th of this month. The ME. form *feverel* appears to be of Eng. origin, the dissimilation being parallel to that in *laurel* from *laurer*. It is noteworthy that Welsh has the form *chwefrawl*, *-ol* (the L. type of which would be **februālis*), beside *chwefrawr*, *-or* repr. L. *februārius*. The later forms are taken directly from Lat. or refashioned after Lat.]

1. The second month of the year, containing twenty-eight days, except in bissextile or leap year, when it has twenty-nine.

[*a* **1000** *Menologium* (Gr.) 18 Swylce emb feower wucan þætte solmonað siȝeð to tune, butan twam nihtum; swa hit ȝetealdon ȝeo, Februarius fær, frode ȝesiþas.] *a* **1225** *Juliana* 78 Oþe sixtenðe dei of feouereles moneð. **1297** R. GLOUC. (Rolls) 8238 In þe monþe of feuerer. **1398** TREVISA *Barth. De P.R.* IX. x. (1495) 354 Olde errour of nacyons.. halowed .. February to the nether goddes. *c* **1450** *St. Cuthbert* (Surtees) 7099 Of feuerȝere þe fift kalend. *c* **1470** HENRY *Wallace* VII. 1 In Feuerȝher befell the sammyn cace, That Inglismen tuk trewis with Wallace. **1588** A. KING tr. *Canisius' Catech.* Hiij, S. Matthias day yᵗ 24 of februar. *a* **1660** WHARTON *Disc. Years, etc.* Wks: (1683) 83 February *à Februo*, that is to sacrifice, because then the Romans sacrificed to Pluto.. for the Souls of their Ancestors. **1745** tr. *Columella's Husb.* 464 The xx of February Leo (the Lion) ceases to set. *a* **1810** TANNAHILL *Feberwar* Poet. Wks. (1846) 157 Thou cauld gloomy Feberwar, O gin thou wert awa'. **1867** O. W. HOLMES *Old Vol. of Life* (1891) 135 A warm day in February is a dream of April.

b. *personified.*

1398 TREVISA *Barth. De P.R.* IX. x. (1495) 355 Februari is paynted as an olde man sittynge by the fyre. **1821** SHELLEY *Dirge for Year* Poems (1891) 568/2 February bears the bier. **1863** R. CHAMBERS *Bk. of Days* I. 202 February comes in like a sturdy maiden, with a tinge of the red hard winter apple on her hardy cheek.

2. Proverbs. ***February fill-dike***: a popular appellation indicating the prevalence of either rain or snow in this month.

1557 TUSSER *100 Points Husb.* cii, Feuerell fill dyke, doth good with his snowe. **1573** —— *Husb.* xxxvii. (1878) 87 Feb, fill the dyke With what thou dost like. **1633** B. JONSON *Tale Tub* I. i, Februere Doth cut and shear. **1670** RAY *Prov.* 40 All the moneths in the year curse a fair Februeer. *Ibid.*, February fill dike, Be it black or be it white; But if it be white, It's the better to like. **1787** BEST *Angling* 165 The Welchman had rather see his dam on the bier, Than see a fair Februeer. **1889** ALLAN *Weather Wisdom* 15 If in February there be no rain, 'Tis neither good for hay nor grain.

3. *attrib.*; ***February red***, a kind of fly.

1599 SHAKS. *Much Ado* V. iv. 41 What's the matter? That you haue such a Februarie face. **1867** F. FRANCIS *Angling* vi. (1880) 200 The February red.. belongs to the Perlideæ. **1870** MORRIS *Earthly Par.* (1890) 422/2 Late February days.

†'februate, *a. Obs. rare*⁻¹. [ad. L. *februāt-us* pa. pple. of *februāre*: see next.] Only in ***a day februate***, one devoted to purification.

1610 HEALEY *St. Aug. Citie of God* 675 Hee.. calleth this feast day, a day februate, that is a day of purgation, etc.

†'februate, *v. Obs.*⁻⁰ [f. L. *februāt-* ppl. stem of *februāre* to purify, f. *februum* a means of purification.] 'To purge souls by sacrifice or prayer' (Blount *Glossogr.* 1656–81).

febru'ation. Now *rare.* [ad. L. *februātiōn-em*, n. of action f. *februāre*: see prec.] A ceremonial purification or cleansing.

a **1652** J. SMITH *Sel. Disc.* ii. 37 Those charms and februations anciently in use upon the appearing of an eclipse. **1663** J. SPENCER *Prodigies* (1665) 172 To reconcile his peevish and touchy Greatness by some Februations. **1721–1800** in BAILEY. **1876** MARTIN tr. *Keil's Comm. Ezek.* I. 207 The passing of children through fire without either slaying or burning; a februation by fire.

†fec. *Obs.* since 12th c. [OE. *fæc*, corresp. to OFris. *fek*, *fak*, OS. *fac* (MLG., Du. *vak*), OHG. *fah* (MHG. *vach*, mod.G. *fach*); the continental sense is chiefly 'compartment', 'bounded space'. The normal mod.Eng. form would be *fack*.] A definite interval in space or time; a limited distance, fixed period.

c **1000** *Ags. Gosp.* Luke xxiv. 13 On þæt castel þæt wæs on fæce [L. *in spatio*] syxtiȝ furlanga fram hierusalem. *a* **1175** *Cott. Hom.* 231 Hi bi ene féce to his curt come sceolde. *Ibid.* 235 Eft bine fece and þes lare and laȝe swiðe acolede þurh manifeald sénne.

fecal, feces, etc.: see FÆCAL, etc.

fecche, var. of *fetch*, obs. and dial. f. of VETCH.

fech(e, obs. form of FETCH *v.*

feche, obs. forms of FISH, FITCH.

fecher, obs. form of FISHER[1].

fechia ('fɛtʃ(ɪ)a). Also 8 in Ital. form feccia. [a. It. *feccia*:—vulgar Latin **fēcia*, altered form of L. *fæc-em* (*fæx*): see FÆCES.] Dregs of wine.
1704 *Lond. Gaz.* No. 4037/7 The.. Goods left unsold.. will be lowered to the following Prizes.. the good Sherries to 18*l.* per But; the Feccia to 24*s.* per C.
attrib. **1812** J. SMYTH *Pract. Customs* (1821) 33 Fechia Ashes are the ashes of the grape-vine.

Fechner ('fɛçnə(r)). The name of Gustav Theodor *Fechner* (1801–87), the founder of German experimental psychology, used in the possessive to designate laws, etc., formulated by him in attempting to establish a quantitative relationship between degrees of physical stimulation and the resulting sensation.
1874 J. SULLY *Sensation & Intuition* 62 Fechner's law accurately defines this relation. **1876** *Mind* I. 455 It is thus quite possible to give a physical interpretation to Fechner's law without implying anything 'inconceivable'. **1887** G. T. LADD *Elem. Physiol. Psychol.* v. 366 The significant addition which Fechner has made to Weber's law consists in the assumption that all just observable differences are equally great. It is therefore also called 'Fechner's law'. **1892** VAN LIEN & BEYER tr. *Ziehen's Physiol. Psychol.* 54 The logarithmic formula of Fechner's Law. *Ibid.* 55 The undoubted advantage of being able to explain or account for Fechner's Formula entirely in accordance with the spirit of the natural sciences. **1909** C. S. MYERS *Text-bk. Exper. Psychol.* 86 When a white sector upon a black ground is very slowly turned on the colour wheel, a series of black bands in the form of radii may be observed on that part of the white surface which first stimulates the eye... With somewhat more rapid rotation, especially under bright illumination, various colours, called Fechner's colours, may be visible on the white surface. **1931** *Brit. Jrnl. Psychol.* July 19 *Phenomenal Regression and Fechner's Difference Law*... This law.. is that if a – b = b – c, then A/B = B/C.. if a – b represents the sense distance corresponding to the presentation of the stimulus A with B, and b – c the sense distance similarly resulting from the stimuli B and C. **1951** S. H. BARTLEY in S.S. Stevens *Handbk. Exper. Psychol.* 981/2 Fechner's paradox is the sensory result when two eyes are independently exposed to *unequal* amounts of light. **1970** C. W. SAVAGE *Measurement of Sensation* viii. 298 Until it is shown that the nature of sensations and the nature of measurement make such a discovery impossible, we cannot conclude that Fechner's law is meaningless.

Fechnerian (fɛç'nɪərɪən), *a.* [See -IAN.] Relating to G. T. *Fechner* (see prec.).
1890 W. JAMES *Princ. Psychol.* I. xiii. 549 The Fechnerian *Maasformel* and the conception of it as an ultimate 'psychophysic law' will remain an 'idol of the den', if ever there was one. **1909** *Westm. Gaz.* 15 May 4/2 These Fechnerian ideas. **1942** *Psychol. Rev.* XLIX. 140 The Fechnerian logarithmic relationship is not appreciably distorted, in cases of intensity transmission, by being reflexly transformed into motor response of an involuntary character.

fecht, Sc. var. of FIGHT.

fecial, var. of FETIAL.

fecifork ('fiːsɪfɔːk). *Entom.* [f. L. *fæci-* (see FÆCES) + FORK.] (See quot.)
1826 KIRBY & SPENCE *Entom.* IV. 353 *Fecifork* (*Fæcifurca*), the anal fork on which the larvæ of *Cassida*, etc., carry their fæces.

feck (fɛk), *sb.*[1] *Sc.* and *north. dial.* Also 5–6 fek, 6 fecc, fect. [app. aphetic f. EFFECT *sb.*]
†**1.** = EFFECT 2 b. The purport, drift, tenor, or substance (of a statement, intention, etc.). Sometimes coupled with *form*. ? *Obs.*
With first quot. cf. Chaucer *Merch. T.* 153 Theffecte of his entente.
c **1500** *Lancelot* 2938 This is the fek of our entent. **1535** STEWART *Cron. Scot.* II. 684 In forme and fect as it wes wont to be. *c* **1550** A. SCOTT in Sibbald *Chron. Scot. Poetry* III. 148 Wald ye foirsé the forme, The fassoun, and the fek, Ye suld it fynd inorme, With bawdry yow to blek. **1600** HEYWOOD *1 Edw. IV*, IV. iv, So the feck.. of all your long purgation.. is no more.. but the King wants money.
2. [Cf. EFFECT 1 b.] Efficacy, efficiency, value; hence, vigour, energy.
1535 STEWART *Cron. Scot.* II. 617 Quhilk semis weill to be Of lytill fecc or ȝit auctoritie. **1597** MONTGOMERIE *Cherrie & Slae* 631 Thay ar maire faschious nor of feck. **1789** BURNS *Elegy on 1788*, 22 Eighty-eight.. gied you.. E'en monie a plack, and monie a peck, Ye ken yoursels, for little feck. **1811** WILLAN *W. Riding Gloss.*, *Feck*, might, activity, zeal, abundance. **1823** GALT *R. Gilhaize* III. 169 Your laddie there's owre young to be o' ony fek in the way o' war.
3. Amount, quantity. ***the (most) feck***: the bulk, greatest part, 'practically the whole'.
The corresponding sense of EFFECT *sb.* was not recognized in its proper place in this Dictionary, but an example of it prob. occurs in Chaucer *Fr. Tale* 153 'My purchas is theffect of al my rente', which may be rendered 'My gains are the *feck* of all my income'.
c **1470** HENRY *Wallace* VIII. 700 Swa sall we fend the fek of this regioun. **1535** STEWART *Cron. Scot.* II. 526 The lordis ..for the most fect, Amang thame self held Donewald suspect. *a* **1774** FERGUSSON *Leith Races* Poet. Wks. (1845) 35 Great feck gae hirplin hame like fools, The cripple lead the blind. **1794** BURNS *Carle of Kellyburn Braes* 53, I hae been a devil the feck o' my life. **1822** W. J. NAPIER *Pract. Store-Farm.* 266 'I hope you have lost none.' 'No mony.' 'What feck, think ye?' **1824** SCOTT *Redgauntlet* xxiii, 'Naething will be said.. for.. the feck of three hours.' **1876** *Whitby Gloss.* s.v., 'He did t' feck o' t' wark.' *Ibid.*, 'There's a rare feck on't.' **1887** STEVENSON *Merry Men* 139 'He had a feck o' books wi' him—mair than had ever been seen before in a' that presbytery.

†**feck**, *sb.*[2] *Obs.* Also fack. [var. of FAIK *sb.*] One of the stomachs of ruminants; ? the omasum or manyplies.
1701 GREW *Cosmol. Sacra* I. v. 29 Three Stomachs: the Panch, the Read and the Feck. **1736** PEGGE *Kenticisms* (E.D.S.), *Fack* of a bullock; that stomach that receives the herbage first, and from whence it is resumed into the mouth to be chew'd. **1887** in *Kent Gloss.*

feck (fɛk), *v. slang.* [Origin unknown.] *trans.* To steal; see also quot. 1809.
1809 G. ANDREWES *Dict. Slang & Cant*, *To feck*—to look out, to discover the best means of obtaining stolen goods. **1880** JAMIESON II. 200/2 *To feck*, to attain by dishonourable means, Loth[ian]. **1916** JOYCE *Portrait of Artist* (1964) 40 They had fecked cash out of the rector's room. **1922** —— *Ulysses* 268 Fecking matches from counters. **1962** E. O'BRIEN *Lonely Girl* i. 9 'Feck any samples?'.. 'How could I take samples with him sitting there in the car?'

fecket ('fɛkɪt). *Sc.* An under waistcoat.
1795 BURNS *To Mr. Mitchell* iv, [Death] gat me by the fecket, And sair me sheuk. **1810** AINSLIE *Tam o the Balloch* in *Pilgr. Land Burns* 242 Wi a fecket sae ful, an' a stocking sae stent. **1851** *Glasgow Past & Present* I. 138 Flannels and feckets will festoon all the windows.

feckful ('fɛkfʊl), *a.* Also 7 fectful. [f. FECK *sb.*[1] + -FUL.] Efficient, vigorous, powerful.
1596 DALRYMPLE tr. *Leslie's Hist. Scot.* (1885) 108 Gif he be feckful, and haue grace to correct maneris in wicked persones. **1606** tr. *Rollock's Lect. 2 Thess.* iv. ii. 49 Wher boldnes in preaching the Gospell is, there is effectualnes in it, & the man who hes this boldnes, is a fectfull man. **1678** R. MACWARD *Let.* in *Scots Worthies* (1826) 429 He was the most faithful, feckful compassionate and indefatigable elder. **1721** RAMSAY *To Will. Starrat* 27 Feckfu folks can front the bauldest wind. **1722** W. HAMILTON *Life Wallace* III 28 Great room he made.. Till mony a feckful Chiel that Day was slain. **1811** WILLAN *W. Riding Gloss.*, *Feckful*, strong and brawny.
Hence **'feckfully** *adv.*
1723 M. WARD *Contendings* 153 That great man of God, who hath so faithfully, so fectfully, and so zealously served his Generation.

feckins: see FEGS.

feckless ('fɛklɪs), *a.* Also 7 fectless. Originally *Sc.* and *north. dial.*, but now not infrequent in literary use. [f. as prec. + -LESS.] Of things: Ineffective, feeble, futile, valueless. Of persons, their actions and attributes: Destitute of vigour, energy, or capacity; weak, helpless.
1599 JAS. I *Βασιλ. Δωρον* (1682) 33 A fecklesse arrogant conceit of their greatnes and power. *a* **1605** MONTGOMERIE *Sonn.* xix. 4 Their feckles flyting is not worth a flie. **1619** Z. BOYD *Last Battell* (1629) 242 My Faith is both faint and fectlesse. **1632** RUTHERFORD *Lett.* (1862) I. 91 Let others take their silly, feckless heaven in this life. *a* **1774** FERGUSSON *Hallowfair* Poet. Wks. (1845) 15 Wi' that he gat anither straik.. That gart his feckless body ache. **1823** CARLYLE *Early Lett.* II. 252, I am so feckless at present that I have never yet had the heart to commence it. **1855** MRS. GASKELL *North & S.* xxxvii, I'm a poor black feckless sheep—childer may clem for aught I can do. **1869** TROLLOPE *He Knew* vii. (1878) 41 They're feckless, idle young ladies.
Hence **'fecklessly** *adv.*, in a feckless manner; **'fecklessness**, the state of being feckless; want of energy, feebleness.
1862 T. A. TROLLOPE *Marietta* II. iv. 71 Lamely, fecklessly, incapably. **1637** RUTHERFORD *Lett.* (1862) I. 362 Love over-looketh blackness and fecklessness. **1893** *Athenæum* 21 Jan. 82/3 Great general fecklessness and want of resource in not trying to save the ship after she took the ground.

feckly ('fɛklɪ), *adv. Sc.* and *north. dial.* [f. as prec. + -LY[2].]
†**1.** Effectually, indeed. *Obs.*
c **1680** [F. SEMPILL] *Banishm. Poverty* in Watson *Collect.* I. 14 Her.. kindness which I fectlie fand, Most ready still for my behoof.
2. For the most part, mostly; almost. Also ***maist feckly***.
a **1774** FERGUSSON *Poet. Wks.* (1845), Auld age maist feckly glowers right dour Upon the ailings o' the poor. **1786** BURNS *Inventory* 29 Wheel carriages I hae but few, Three carts, and twa are feckly new. **1846** *Ball. & Songs Ayrshire* Ser. I. 112 Tho' she's feckly twice my age I lo'e her best o' ony. **1891** H. HALLIBURTON *Ochil Idylls* 90 Nae doot its feckly wrang to lee.

feck(s): see FEGS.

fecky, see FIKIE, *Sc.*

†**fect**, *v. Obs. rare.* Aphet. var. of INFECT.
1541 R. COPLAND *Guydon's Quest. Chirurg.* Q ij b, Yf the father were fecte. **1558–68** WARDE tr. *Alexis' Secr.* 43 a, A very good remedie.. to drive it away after he is fected with it.

†**'fectually**, *adv. Obs.* Aphetic variant of EFFECTUALLY.
c **1485** *Digby Myst.* (1882) III. 643, I telle þe fectually I have thynges to seyn to þe.

fecula: see FÆCULA.

feculence ('fɛkjʊləns). Also 8 feculance. [a. F. *féculence*, ad. L. *fæculentia*, f. *fæculentus*: see FECULENT.]
1. The quality or state of being feculent; foulness. In quot. *fig.*
1860 *Sat. Rev.* 7 Apr. 433/2 The fulness, as well as the feculence, of the mercantile body.
2. *concr.* Feculent matter; dregs, lees, dross, scum. Also (now chiefly) in stronger sense, filth. *lit.* and *fig.*
a **1648** DIGBY *Closet Open.* (1617) 97 It is not amiss that some feculence lie thick upon the Ale. **1662** R. MATHEW *Unl. Alch.* §24. 17 How forcibly Nature will throw out the feculence. **1708** J. PHILIPS *Cyder* (1807) 60 Contriv'd To draw th' earth's purest spirit, and resist Its feculence. **1742** YOUNG *Nt. Th.* ii. 589 All feculence of falsehood long thrown down. **1794** SULLIVAN *View Nat.* V. 365 Slaves of dulness and ignorance, who drudge in feculence. **1802–3** tr. *Pallas' Trav.* (1812) I. 86 Calcareous constituents, which may be easily recognized in the feculence or foam of the sea. **1854** BADHAM *Halieut.* 116 Eel.. often taste of the weeds and feculence where they dwell. **1855** FARADAY in B. Jones *Life* (1870) II. 363 Near the bridges the feculence rolled up in clouds.
b. = FÆCES 2.
1733 CHEYNE *Eng. Malady* II. vii. §3 The Peristaltick Motion, so necessary.. [to] the Expulsion of the Feculence.

†**'feculency.** *Obs.* Also 7 feculancy, fœculency. [ad. L. *fæculentia*: see prec. and -ENCY.]
1. = FECULENCE 1.
1651 BIGGS *New Disp.* ¶85 Mortality, feculency, and turbulency. **1671** J. WEBSTER *Metallogr.* viii. 122 Nothing of impure sulphureous fœculency. **1679** J. GOODMAN *Penit. Pardoned* III. v. (1713) 347 Spiritual Bodies.. raised and sublimed from this drossy feculency.
2. = FECULENCE 2; *lit.* and *fig.* In *pl.* Impurities.
1607 TOPSELL *Serpents* (1653) 811, I cold never as yet finde.. drossy matter, or other feculency. **1655–87** H. MORE *App. Antid.* (1712) 215 The feculency of urine, that sinks to the bottom of the glass. **1680** BOYLE *Scept. Chem.* VI. 418 That crust or dry feculancy.. called Tartar. **1772** JACKSON in *Phil. Trans.* LXIII. 6 The reciprocal attraction of the particles of isinglass and the feculencies of the beer. **1822** BURROWES *Cycl.* X. 287/1 The liquor sometimes thickens too fast to permit the feculencies to rise in the scum.

feculent ('fɛkjʊlənt), *a.* Also 6 feaculent, 7–9 fæculent. [a. Fr. *féculent*, ad. L. *fæculentus*, f. *fæc-*, *fæx*: see FÆCES and -ULENT.]
1. Containing or of the nature of fæces or dregs; abounding with sediment or impurities; thick, turbid. Now usually with stronger sense: Laden or polluted with filth; foul, fetid.
1471 RIPLEY *Comp. Alch.* III. in Ashm. (1652) 140 Feculent feces. **1578** BANISTER *Hist. Man* v. 81 The grosse and feaculent part of blood. **1607** TOPSELL *Serpents* (1608) 71 Any feculent or dreggy refuse. **1686** GOAD *Celest. Bodies* III. iii. 445 A misty Air, Fog and Fæculent. *a* **1703** BURKITT *On N.T.* Rev. xxii. 1 A river, not of muddy or feculent water, but clear as crystal. **1777** HOWARD *Prisons Eng.* (1780) 8 Air which has performed its office in the lungs, is feculent and noxious. **1804** *Med. Jrnl.* XII. 469 The evacuation of fæculent matter.
fig. **1653** EVELYN *Mem.* (1857) I. 300 Such feculent stuff. **1660** WATERHOUSE *Arms & Arm.* 200 Heralds.. distinguishable from the fæculent plebs.. by their gay Coats. *a* **1734** NORTH *Exam.* II. v. §93 (1740) 373 Every Word here is feculent and stinks. **1866** *Lond. Rev.* 4 Aug. 130/1 The most feculent corruptions of modern civilization.
†**2.** Covered with fæces; filthy. *Obs.*
1590 SPENSER *F.Q.* II. vii. 61 Both his handes most filthy feculent.

feculite ('fɛkjʊlaɪt). *Chem.* [f. FÆCULA + -ITE.] (See quot.)
1884 *Syd. Soc. Lex.*, *Feculite*, a term given to pulverulent vegetable substances.. which are soluble in hot water, and when treated with nitric acid yield oxalic and malic acids.

Feculose ('fɛkjʊləʊz, -s). *Chem.* Also feculose. [f. FÆCUL(A + -OSE[2].] Proprietary name for an acetylated starch made by heating dry starch with glacial acetic acid and formerly used as a substitute for gelatine and vegetable gums.
1903 *Trade Marks Jrnl.* 29 July 820 *Feculose.* Chemical Substances used in Manufactures. The Firm of William Wotherspoon, Glenfield Starch Works. **1909** *Jrnl. Soc. Chem. Industry* 31 Mar. 291/1 Feculose is also employed in making ju-jubes and other sweets. **1920** CROSS & BEVAN *Text-bk. Paper-Making* (ed. 5) 309 'Feculose'.. is being employed in increasing quantities as a substitute for gelatine. **1966** H. WILLIAMSON *Methods Bk. Design* (ed. 2) xviii. 298 Less expensive papers are sometimes tub-sized with feculose. **1967** KRUGER & RUTENBERG in Whistler & Paschall *Starch* II. xv. 375 The dry-heating procedure for 'Feculose' probably could not compete today with other methods of preparing low D.S. acetates.

fecund ('fɛkʌnd, 'fiːkʌnd), *a.* Forms: 5–7 fecond, 5 fecounde, 7 foecund, 6– fecund. [a. F. *fecond*, ad. L. *fēcundus* fruitful. In the 16th c. the spelling was refashioned after Lat.]
1. a. Of animals, the earth, etc.: Capable of producing offspring or vegetable growth abundantly; prolific, fertile.
In recent use distinguished from FERTILITY (see quot. 1904). Cf. FECUNDITY. Otherwise somewhat *arch.*
c **1420** *Pallad. on Husb.* I. 77 Make a dyche, and yf the moolde abounde And wol not in agayne, it is fecounde. *Ibid.* I. 985 That wol make all fecundare On every side. **1537** tr. *Latimer's 2nd Serm. bef. Convocation* i. 42 He was so fecund

a father, and had gotten so many children. **1671** GREW *Anat. Plants* I. iv. App. (1682) 33 Thorns, from the outer and less fecund Part. **1676** *Phil. Trans.* II. 594 Animals fecond enough. **1678** CUDWORTH *Intell. Syst.* 489 The most Benign and Fecund Begetter of all things. **1721** BRADLEY *Wks. Nature* 30 The Nourishment and Growth of the Embrio Seed after its Germe is made fecund. **1904** *Brit. Med. Jrnl.* 23 Apr. 769 A difference is drawn between fecundity and fertility. Thus women of Irish birth in Australia are less fecund than women born either in New South Wales or in Scotland, but they are more fertile. In other words fewer Irish women have children, but to those who are fecund more children are born.

b. *transf.* and *fig.*

c **1400** *Test. Love* III. (1560) 294/2 Al your workes be cleped fecond. **1793** J. WILLIAMS *Authentic Mem. Warren Hastings* 54 The most considerable..of Mr. Burke's political apophthegms seem to quit their fecund parent.. when they are matured. **1849** RUSKIN *Sev. Lamps* vi. §4. 166 This is..fecund of other fault and misfortune. **1854** *Fraser's Mag.* XLIX. 19 The printing presses of Paris..so prolific and fecund in all kind of fruit. **1884** *Sat. Rev.* 14 June 784/2 The most brilliant and fecund era in the history of music.

2. Producing fertility, fertilizing. Cf. FECUNDITY 5.

1686 GOAD *Celest. Bodies* II. x. 289 We are troubled with Aquatique Signs, as if our Aspect was most Foecund. **1827** J. F. COOPER *Prairie* II. xv. 28 Which yielded, in return for the fecund gift, a scanty growth of grass.

Hence **ˈfecundness**, the state of being fecund. **1727** in BAILEY vol. II.

fecundate (ˈfɛkəndeɪt, ˈfiːkəndeɪt), *v.* [f. L. *fēcundāt-* ppl. stem of *fēcundāre*, f. *fēcundus* fruitful.] *trans.* To render fruitful or productive.

a **1631** DONNE *Serm.* xxxi. 304 He..actuates and fecundates our Soules. **1648** W. MOUNTAGUE *Devout Ess.* II. iv. §4 (1653) 77 These meditations..may..fecundate ev'n the best mould they fall upon. **1850** NEALE *Med. Hymns* (1867) 110 Paradise..is fœcundated With the waters irrigated From these rills. **1863** *Jrnl. Pract. Med. & Surg.* Oct., Fresh researches may possibly fecundate this ingenious application. **1870** LOWELL *Among my Bks.* Ser. I. (1873) 203 Even the Trouvères..could fecundate a great poet like Chaucer.

absol. **1646** SIR T. BROWNE *Pseud. Ep.* VII. vii. 352 It may be thought that Mandrakes may fecundate since Poppy hath obtained the Epithite of fruitfull.

b. *esp.* To make the female (individual or organ) fruitful by the introduction of the male element; to impregnate.

1721 BRADLEY *Wks. Nature* 31 Guarded with Petals or other Membranes; and yet are fecundated by the Dust of Male Flowers. **1781–7** R. WATSON *Chem. Ess.* V. 144 The eastern practice of fœcundating the female palm tree. **1796** DE SERRA in *Phil. Trans.* LXXXVI. 503 The germen..is probably fecundated through its receptaculum. **1876** DARWIN *Cross-fertil.* i. 7 Nature has something more in view than that its own proper males should fecundate each blossom.

Hence **ˈfecundated** *ppl. a.* **ˈfecundating** *vbl. sb.* **ˈfecundating** *ppl. a.*

1796 DE SERRA in *Phil. Trans.* LXXXVI. 502 Which opens itself afterwards to let loose the fecundated seeds. **1800** *Med. Jrnl.* III. 259 The heart is the first visible object in the punctum saliens of the fecundated egg. **1872** PEASLEE *Ovar. Tumours* 12 The fecundated ovum increases in size while traversing the oviduct. **1677** HALE *Prim. Orig. Man.* IV. ii. 300 The Fecundating Principle. **1721** BRADLEY *Wks. Nature* 101 It must necessarily happen that the fecundating Spirit is dissipated. **1813** W. TAYLOR in *Monthly Rev.* XC. 452 This fecundating force, this power of prompting efforts at reproduction is possessed by every writer. **1880** HUXLEY *Crayfish* i. 39 The fecundating material itself is a thickish fluid. **1884** *Syd. Soc. Lex.*, *Fecundating corpuscles*, the spermatozoa. *Fecundating dust*, the pollen of plants.

fecundation (fɛ-, fiːkənˈdeɪʃən). [n. of action f. L. *fēcundāre*: see prec. and -ATION.] The process of fecundating; fertilization, impregnation.

1541 R. COPLAND *Guydon's Quest. Chirurg.*, Or that ye make fecondacyon. **1646** SIR T. BROWNE *Pseud. Ep.* VII. vii. 350 A common conceit, that Rachel requested these plants as a medicine of fecundation. **1721** BRADLEY *Wks. Nature* 31 This Fecundation is done by the help of the Wind, which conveys the prolifick Dust into the Tubes of the Pestils. **1851** CARPENTER *Man. Phys.* (ed. 2) 486 Every-thing indicates that the contact of the Spermatozoon with the Ovulum is the one thing needful in the act of fecundation.

fecundator (ˈfɛ-, ˈfiːkən,deɪtə(r)). [agent-n. f. L. *fēcundāre*: see FECUNDATE. Cf. F. *fécondateur*.] One who or that which fecundates.

1883 B. W. RICHARDSON *Field of Disease* III. I. vii. 789 There may the filarial disease exist, with the mosquito as the fecundator and carrier.

fecundatory (fɪˈkʌndətərɪ), *a.* [f. FECUNDATE- + -ORY.] Of or pertaining to fecundation.

1839 *Fraser's Mag.* XX. 208 The heavens, light, and fire, or the fecundatory powers of nature.

† **feˈcundify**, *v. Obs. rare.* [f. FECUND + -(I)FY.] = FECUNDATE.

1730–6 in BAILEY (folio). **1763** *Nat. Hist.* in *Ann. Reg.* 82/2 The eggs are deposited almost immediately after they are fecundified.

fecundity (fɪˈkʌndɪtɪ). [ad. L. *fēcunditāt-em* fruitfulness, f. *fēcundus*: see FECUND and -ITY. Cf. F. *fécondité*.]

1. Of female animals: The faculty of reproduction, the capacity for bringing forth young; productiveness.

In recent use distinguished from FERTILITY, esp. in demographic use.

1447 BOKENHAM *Seyntys* (Roxb.) 50 Whan thou..hast fecundyte Than schul thy yiftes acceptable be. **1607** TOPSELL *Four-f. Beasts* (1673) 217 The fœcundity of the beast that beareth them. **1727** BRADLEY *Fam. Dict.* s.v. *Bee*, His Fecundity is such almost throughout the Year, that [etc.]. **1775** JOHNSON *Tax. no Tyr.* 7 They multiply with the fecundity of their own rattlesnakes. **1856** GRINDON *Life* ix. (1875) 112 The most astonishing examples of fecundity occur among fishes and insects. **1866** J. M. DUNCAN *Fecundity* 3 By fertility or productiveness I mean the amount of births as distinguished from the capability to bear... By fecundity I mean the demonstrated capability to bear children; it implies the conditions necessary for conception in the women of whom its variations are predicated... In short, fertility implies fecundity, and also introduces the idea of number of progeny; while fecundity simply indicates the quality without any superadded notion of quantity. **1904** [see FECUND *a.* 1 a]. **1922** A. M. CARR-SAUNDERS *Pop. Problem* ii. 51 Fecundity is measured by the number of ripe ova produced. **1936** *Discovery* Sept. 297/2 The ratio of fertility (actual production of children) to fecundity (child-bearing capacity). **1964** GOULD & KOLB *Dict. Soc. Sci.* 265/2 Fertility in modern demographic usage relates to the actual frequency of births and carries no overtones of ability to have children. For the latter concept fecundity or reproductive capacity are now used.

2. *Bot.* The faculty or power of germinating.

1691 RAY *Creation* (1714) 300 Some seeds that retain their Fecundity forty Years. **1884** *Syd. Soc. Lex.*, *Fecundity*..in Botany, the capacity of a seed for germination.

3. Of the earth: The quality of producing abundantly; fertility.

c **1420** *Pallad. on Husb.* I. 57 Ffecunditee thowe see thus in this lande. **1432–50** tr. *Higden* (Rolls) I. 320 The..fecundite or plentuosenes of the soyle. **1548** HALL *Chron.* Hen. VII an. 12. 41 a, The Cornyshe men inhabityng the least parte of the realme..and without all fecunditee, compleyned and grudged greatly. **1622** T. SCOTT *Belg. Pismire* 2 The Earth ..prevented thy desires with overflowing fecunditie. **1718** J. CHAMBERLAYNE *Relig. Philos.* (1730) II. xx. §7 It [the Earth] has never failed, nor entirely lost its Foecundity. **1843** PRESCOTT *Mexico* IV. vii. (1864) 251 The marvellous fecundity of the soil.

4. Productiveness in general, the faculty or power of being fruitful, fertility: **a.** of material things.

1555 EDEN *Decades* 266 It noryssheth the fecunditie of thynges generate. **1662** J. DAVIES tr. *Mandelslo's Trav.* 137 This fecundity lasts all night, till the returne of the Sunne makes both the flowers and leaves drop off. **1721** BRADLEY *Wks. Nature* 102 That Fecundity, which..antient Physicians..attributed to a Sympathy, or Love among Trees. **1796** H. HUNTER tr. *St. Pierre's Stud. Nat.* (1799) I. 573 It is not the heat of the Tropics which gives to this tree a fecundity so constant, and so varied. **1836** MACGILLIVRAY tr. *Humboldt's Trav.* xiv. 181 A few drops of a vegetable fluid impress us with an idea of the..fecundity of nature. **1855** MILMAN *Lat. Chr.* (1864) II. III. vi. 93 The monks seemed to multiply with greater fecundity than the population of the most flourishing cities.

b. of immaterial things.

1621 DONNE *Serm.* xliii. 427 The Fecundity of the words. **1691** RAY *Creation* (1714) 18 A demonstrative Proof of the.. feccundity of His Wisdom and Power. **1789** BENTHAM *Princ. Legisl.* xii. §17 The mischief..is..in point of fecundity pregnant to a degree that baffles calculation. **1824** W. IRVING *T. Trav.* II. 54 The extreme fecundity of the press. **1842** H. ROGERS *Ess.* I. i. 10 That fecundity of fancy, which can adorn whatever it touches.

5. The capacity for making fruitful or productive, fertilizing power.

1642 H. MORE *Immortal. of Souls* III. iii. 169 The fixed sunne..through his fecundity Peoples the world. **1680** MORDEN *Geog. Rect.* (1685) 443 The River Nilus is famous for its Greatness and Fœcundity. **1860** PUSEY *Min. Proph.* 144 The ancients thought that the waters of the Nile must have some power of fecundity. **1868** PEARD *Water-Farm.* xii. 120 The fecundity of 'the springs'.

fecundize (ˈfɛ-, ˈfiːkəndaɪz), *v.* [f. FECUND + -IZE.] = FECUNDATE.

1828 WILSON in *Blackw. Mag.* XXIV. 652 It fecundizes the imagination with poetic forms.

† **feˈcundous**, *a. Obs.* Also 7 fecundious. [f. as prec. + -(I)OUS.] = FECUND.

1630 J. TAYLOR (Water P.) *Wks.* I. 103 The..fecundious fat of the Goose's Axungia. **1737** M. GREEN *Spleen* 408 The press from her fecundous womb Brought forth the arts of Greece and Rome.

Fed, fed, *sb. U.S.* [Short for *federalist*.]

1. = FEDERALIST *sb.* 2.

1788 [see ANTI-FED]. **1801** [see ANTI *sb.*]. **1807** W. IRVING *Life & Lett.* (1864) I. xii. 187, I had three or four good Feds sprawling around me on the floor. **1848** *Campaign Flag* (Maysville, Ky.) 24 Mar. 1/1 The feds have got to polling the passengers on steam-boats again. **1947** *West. Pennsylvania Hist. Mag.* Mar.–June 22 There were few marriageable men left in the narrow confines to which the aristocratic 'Feds' had limited themselves.

2. An official of the federal government; *spec.* a member of the U.S. Federal Bureau of Investigation. *slang.*

1916 A. STRINGER *Door of Dread* iv. 53 Seein' Kestner and yuh'd told me the Feds had ev'rything fixt, I give him the glassy eye. **1935** *Lit. Digest* 22 June 38 'G Men' have also been called 'feds'. **1955** *Publ. Amer. Dial. Soc.* XXIV. 47 Anyway, the Feds got the letter where I sent him $400.

† **fed, fede**, *a.* and *sb. Obs.* Also fedd, feid, *pl.* fede, -es, -is. [app. repr. OE. **ȝefǽȝed* (weak decl. **ȝefǽȝda, -e*), pa. pple. of *ȝefǽȝan* (early ME. *ifæien, iveien* to set at variance: see I-FAY *v.*), f. *ȝefá*: see FOE.]

A. *adj.* At variance, hostile.

c **1250** *To Fortune* in *Old Eng. Misc.* 86 Wyþ freomen þu art ferly feid. *a* **1300** *Cursor M.* 8535 (Cott.) Cartage..to rome was euer fede.

B. *sb.* An enemy; *spec.* the fiend, devil.

a **1300** *Cursor M.* 7935 (Cott.) 'þat man,' he said, 'es godds fed.' *Ibid.* 12948 (Gött.) þan said þe lauerd to þe fede 'Man mai noght liue allane wid brede'. *Ibid.* 23746 (Cott.) Again vr fedes thrin to strijf, vr flexs, þis werld, and þe warlau.

fed, obs. form of FEUD *sb.*[1], enmity.

fed (fɛd), *ppl. a.* [Pa. pple. of FEED *v.*] In various senses of the vb. **a.** Supplied with food; hence, nourished; *lit.* and *fig.* Chiefly with adv. prefixed, as ***highly, well fed***; also in comb. with prefixed sb., as in ***bacon-, bounty-, grass-, rump-, stall-fed***, etc. (see the sbs.). †**b.** = FATTED (*obs.*).

a. 1483 *Cath. Angl.* 124/2 Fedd, *pastus, cibatus.* **1579** FULKE *Heskins' Parl.* 389 One of the feeid and fed seruants of yᵉ Pope. **1601** SHAKS. *All's Well* II. ii. 3, I will shew my selfe highly fed. *Ibid.* II. iv. 39 A good knaue ifaith, and well fed. **1621** LADY M. WROTH *Urania* 378 His fed imagination ..is so soone made to sterue againe. **1887** RUSKIN *Præterita* II. 235 A clear dashing stream, not ice fed, but mere fountain and rainfall. **1892** R. KIPLING *Barrack-r. Ballads* (ed. 2) 140 To the cod and the corpse-fed conger-eel.

b. 1535 COVERDALE *Luke* xv. 27 Thy father hath slayne a fed calfe because he hath receaued him safe and sounde. **1549** *Compl. Scot.* vi. 39 The fox folloult the fed geise. *a* **1623** W. PEMBLE *Worthy Rec. Lord's Supper* (1628) 61 The blood of bullocks, and fat of fed beasts.

fed, *pa. pple.* Slang phr. *to be fed up*: to be surfeited or disgusted (*with*), bored or tired to breaking-point. So **fed-up** *a.* Also with emphasizing expressions, as ***fed to the (back) teeth, fed to death***. Also without *up*.

[**1882** F. ARNOLD *Three-Cornered Essays* (1886) 4 Fed up to the eyelids, it is no care to him that there are other people all otherwise than so well off.]

1900 *Westm. Gaz.* 13 Nov. 2/3 It may be quite true that, to use an expression often heard in South Africa just now, the men are 'fed up' with the war. **1906** *Daily Chron.* 22 Mar. 9/5, I am about 'fed-up' over this motor-car. **1914** *Even. News* 19 Sept. 4/1 We have also seen hundreds of German prisoners, mostly looking 'fed up'. **1916** 'BOYD CABLE' *Action Front* 32 'I'm just about fed up with him,' said Gunner Donovan bitterly. **1921** W. S. MAUGHAM *Circle* III. 100, I should be fed to the teeth with you sometimes. **1921** WODEHOUSE *Indiscretions of Archie* i. 11 I've never done anything much in England, and I fancy the family were getting a bit fed. **1922** A. S. M. HUTCHINSON *This Freedom* IV. iv. 293 Oh, those sickening scarves and things, they were eternally knitting, that wasn't war work. It was fun at first. They were fed to death with doing them now. **1924** A. J. SMALL *Frozen Gold* iii. 78 He had the air of a man who was utterly and finally fed-up with the eternal effort of keeping the upper hand of the worst. **1928** *Strand Mag.* July 4 Her aspect was that of a girl who is fed to the teeth. **1929** D. G. MACKAIL *How Amusing* 342 It made me feel pretty fed with the old boy. **1946** P. LARKIN *Jill* 30 I'm getting definitely fed..with them all. **1955** *Times* 15 June 9/2 A major relief to a frankly fed-up and frustrated nation. **1958** M. ALLINGHAM *Hide my Eyes* x. 99 She's been getting fed to the teeth. Edna has been pestering her. **1961** 'G. HYTHE' *Death of Scapegoat* I. iii. 87 The skipper's gettin' fed to the back teeth. **1963** I. FLEMING *On H.M. Secret Service* ii. 21 He was fed to the teeth with chasing the ghost of Blofeld.

Hence **fed-upness** (stress variable).

1928 D. L. SAYERS *Unpleasantness at Bellona Club* iii. 22 Job gone—health gone—no money..general fedupness. **1961** *Times* 4 May 13/4 A state of acute 'browned-offness' or 'fed-upness'.

‖**Fedai** (ˈfɛdɑːiː). Pl. fedai, fedais. The Pers. forms also occur. [Pers. *fidā'ī* (pl. *fidā'iyān*) devotee, zealot, one who risks his life in a cause.] = ASSASSIN 1.

1875 *Encycl. Brit.* II. 723/1 When the sheikh required the services of any of them, the selected *fedais* were intoxicated with *hashish*. **1909** *Westm. Gaz.* 15 Feb. 2/1 Thousands of them became 'fedai', men ready to sacrifice themselves for the common good. **1921** *Glasgow Herald* 13 Sept. 7 Seventeen Fedai, otherwise reckless desperadoes, are stated to have been specially brought to Constantinople for the purpose of committing murders. **1958** J. A. BOYLE tr. *Juvaini's Hist. World-Conqueror* II. 739 *Fidā'ī*, the term applied to the emissaries of the Isma'ilis, the Assassins. **1969** A. J. ARBERRY *Relig. Middle East* II. 626 Manfred Halpern speaks of the Muslim Brethren in Egypt, Syria and elsewhere, together with movements like *Fidā'iyān-i-Islām* in Persia.

fedam, obs. form of FEYDOM.

† **ˈfedarie.** *Obs.* Also fœdarie, federarie. [var. of *feodary* FEUDARY, q.v.; but used by Shaks. in sense due to erroneous association with L. *fœdus*: see FEDERAL.

The form *federarie*, which would be a correctly formed derivative of *fœdus*, but occurs only in a single passage of the First Folio, is perhaps a misprint or a scholarly correction, as the usual form *fedarie* suits the metre better. The Second Folio and most subsequent edd. read *feodarie, -y*, in all the passages.]

A confederate, accomplice.

1603 SHAKS. *Meas. for M.* II. iv. 122 Else let my brother die, If not a fedarie but onely he Owe, and succeed thy weaknesse. **1611** —— *Cymb.* III. ii. 21 Art thou a Foedarie for this Act? **1611** —— *Wint. T.* II. i. 90 Shee's a Traytor, and Camillo is A Federarie with her.

‖**fedayeen** (fɛda'jiːn), *sb. pl.* Also **-yin**. [Colloq. Arab. *fidāʼiyīn*, pl. of Class. Arab. *fidāʼī* one who undertakes perilous adventures.] Arab guerrillas operating against the Israelis.

1955 *Time* 12 Sept. 34/2 Small groups of Arab raiders carried the fight deep into Israel. Known as *Al Fedayeen* (Self-Sacrificers), the sneaker-shod guerrillas are recruited from Palestinian Arab refugees. **1956** *Time* 23 Apr. 33/3 It was the fedayeen (self-sacrificers), members of specially trained Arab assassin squads, who had crept north from the Egyptian-held Gaza strip. **1956** *Economist* 17 Nov., The only answer to fedayeen tactics is reprisals. **1960** *Spectator* 4 Mar. 311 Several rightly critical references are made to Egyptian fedayeen raids on Israel. **1969** *Times* 20 Nov. p. iv/5 Everywhere in Jordan the tourist will see *fedayin* bristling with arms. **1970** *Daily Tel.* 22 Jan. 18 Once again it was activity by the *fedayeen*, not by regular Jordanian forces, in attacking Israeli settlements that triggered the reprisal.

‖**feddan** (fɛ'dɑːn). Also **fedan**. [Arab. *fadán*, *faddán* a yoke of oxen; an acre.] An Egyptian measure of land, a little more than an English acre in extent.

a **1817** BURCKHARDT *Arabic Prov.* (1830) 134 A piece of ground comprising seventeen feddáns. **1877** M'COAN *Egypt as it is* ix. 183 The small proprietors who own from fifty to several hundred feddans. **1882** *Standard* 13 Oct. 5/4 Two hundred thousand fedans or acres of land.

† **'feddle**, *sb. Obs.* In 5 fedill, 7 fedle. [perh. repr. (with some change of sense) OE. *fédels* fatted bird, f. *fédan* to FEED.] One who is made much of; a pet, favourite. Also *attrib.*

[*a* **800** *Corpus Gloss.* A 467 *Altilia*, foedils. *c* **1000** *Suppl. Ælfric's Voc.* in Wr.-Wülcker 190 *Altilis*, fedels.] *a* **1400-50** þar fand þar bridis..of feþir fresch as any fame, as ere þir fedill dowfis, þat [etc.]. **1611** COTGR., *Bedaud*, a fedle, minion, fauourite. *Ibid.*, *Cochonner*..make a fedle of. *a* **1693** URQUHART *Rabelais* III. xviii. 146 It will be my dainty Fedle-darling.

† **'feddle**, *v. Obs. rare.* [f. prec. sb.] (See quot.)

1611 COTGR., *Cadeler*, to cocker, pamper, fedle, cherish, make much of. *Ibid.*, *Mignoter*, to dandle, feddle.

Hence † **'feddled** *ppl. a.* † **'feddling** *vbl. sb.*

1611 COTGR., *Cadelé, -ée*, cockered, pampered, fedled, cherished. *Ibid.*, *Mignotise*, a dandling, fedling, cockering.

feddom, obs. form of FATHOM.

fede, var. of FADE *a.*[1], and FEUD *sb.*[1], enmity.

feder, obs. form of FATHER, FEATHER.

federacy ('fɛdərəsɪ). [f. late L. *fœderātus* FEDERATE *ppl. a.*, after CONFEDERACY; see -ACY.]

1. The state of being joined by a treaty; an instance of this, an alliance. *rare.*

1647 WARD *Simp. Cobler* 32 Forreigne federacies. **1692-1732** in COLES. **1855** SINGLETON *Virgil* II. 240 Dardania's chosen chiefs Have come entreating fed'racy of arms.

2. A body of federated states; = CONFEDERACY 3.

1803 *Edin. Rev.* I. 354 To render Europe a united whole within itself..a great federacy. **1862** BROUGHAM *Brit. Const.* iv. 58 The central government in a Federacy is of necessity feeble.

federal ('fɛdərəl), *a.* and *sb.* Also 7-8 **fœderal**. [a. F. *fédéral*, f. L. type **fœderāl-is*, f. *fœder-*, *fœdus* covenant (:—pre-Lat. **bhoidhes-*) cognate with *fidēs* FAITH.] **A.** *adj.*

1. † **a.** *gen.* Of or pertaining to a covenant, compact, or treaty. *Obs.*

1660 STILLINGFL. *Iren.* I. iv. (1662) 91 The sprinkling of the blood which was the main thing intended here as a fœderal rite. **1701** GREW *Cosm. Sacra* III. iv. 113 The Romans compell'd them..contrary to all Fœderal Right and Justice..to part with Sardinia. **1789** G. WHITE *Selborne* (1853) 336 Not so the sage: inspired with pious awe He hails the federal arch. **1825** T. JEFFERSON *Autobiog.* Wks. 1859 I. 15 Our connection had been federal only, and was now dissolved by the commencement of hostilities.

b. *spec.* (*Theol.*) Pertaining to or based upon the Covenant of Works, or Covenant of Grace. Also, Constituting or expressing a covenant entered into by an individual with God. See COVENANT *sb.* 8.

federal theology: the system based on the doctrine of covenants made by God with Adam as representing mankind, and with Christ as representing the Church. *federal head*: = covenant-head (COVENANT *sb.* 10 b), applied to Adam and Christ.

1645 USSHER *Body Div.* (1647) 418 There is a fœderall sanctity, or externall and visible holinesse at least in children of believing parents. **1649** JER. TAYLOR *Gt. Exemp.* II. viii. 71 Our restitution and accesse to the first fœderall condition. **1673** *True Worsh. God* 30 The Sacrament of Christs Body and Blood..being a Fæderal Banquet. **1737** WATERLAND *Eucharist* 424 The Service of the Holy Communion carries in it something of a federal Nature, is a kind of covenanting or stipulating Act. *a* **1800** COWPER *On Milton's P.L.* Wks. 1837 XV. 339 Christ becomes the federal head of his church. **1878** *Encycl. Brit.* (ed. 9) VI. 91 As one of the leading exponents of 'federal' theology, he [Cocceius] spiritualized the Hebrew Scriptures to such an extent that [etc.].

2. a. Of or pertaining to, or of the nature of, that form of government in which two or more states constitute a political unity while remaining more or less independent with regard to their internal affairs.

This sense arises from the contextual meaning of phrases like *federal union*, in which the adj. was originally used in sense 1 a.

[**1707** SETON *Sp. in Sc. Parlt.* in *Parl. Hist.* VI. App. 142 Sweden and Denmark were united by a fœderal compact under one monarch.] **1777** ROBERTSON *Hist. Amer.* (1783) II. 197 The celebrated league, that united the Five Nations in Canada into a federal republic. **1787** J. BARLOW *Oration* 4 July 8 The establishment of a permanent fœderal system. **1832** LEWIS *Use & Ab. Pol. Terms* x. 88 A federal government is when an union is formed between several States. **1837** CALHOUN *Wks.* III. 166 The party who believed that this was a Federal Republic. **1851** HT. MARTINEAU *Hist. Peace* (1877) III. v. xii. 449 The scheme of constituting a federal union of the British North American provinces. **1874** STUBBS *Const. Hist.* (1875) I. ii. 26 There was not..any federal bond among the several tribes.

b. Of or pertaining to the political unity so constituted, as distinguished from the separate states composing it.

1789 T. JEFFERSON *Writ.* (1859) II. 576 They have passed a bill rendering every person holding any federal office incapable of holding at the same time any State office. **1796** WASHINGTON *Let.* Writings 1892 XIII. 342 One or other of the proprietors in the Federal City. **1844** THIRLWALL *Greece* VIII. lxi. 83 The federal sovereignty resided in the general assembly. **1876** MATHEWS *Coinage* xxi. 198 It was not until several years after the declaration of Independence (1776) that a Federal coinage was issued. **1891** *Speaker* 11 July 36/1 Into both federal and cantonal legislation the Referendum has been introduced.

3. *U.S. Hist.* **a.** Favouring the establishment of a strong federal, i.e. central government.

1788 *Lond. Mag.* 21 [The people of Massachusetts] forward in promoting the fœderal interest. **1789** T. JEFFERSON *Writ.* (1859) II. 576 Everywhere the elections are federal. **1796** MORSE *Amer. Geog.* I. 587 Marylanders..are in general very federal. **1839** CALHOUN *Wks.* III. 391 He [Hamilton] is the..impersonation of the national or Federal School..as Jefferson is of the State Rights Republican School. **1888** BRYCE *Amer. Commw.* II. III. liii. 332 The disappearance of the Federal party between 1815 and 1820 left the Republicans masters of the field.

b. In the American Civil War of 1861-65: Of or pertaining to the Northern or Union party, or its supporters, troops, etc.

1861 O. W. HOLMES *Pages fr. Old Vol. Life* (1891) 2 A sad disaster to the Federal army. **1863** DICEY *Federal St.* II. 241 The stories of the barbarities and cruelties inflicted by the Confederates on Federal prisoners. **1878** *N. Amer. Rev.* CXXVI. 258 A loud Federal cheer was heard, proving Jackson to be hard pressed.

4. a. United in a league, allied, confederated. *rare.*

1867 J. B. ROSE tr. *Virgil's Æneid* 105 No fleet of mine was federal 'gainst Troy.

b. Applied to a non-political association of quasi-autonomous units.

1911 *Encycl. Brit.* XXII. 293/2 A loose union, called the 'Federal Council of the Reformed Churches in America', was formed in 1894. **1954** *Times Lit. Suppl.* 5 Feb. 93/1 The geography and diverse character of Wales made a federal university of scattered colleges a necessity.

B. *sb.* Chiefly *pl.* One on the side of the Union in the American Civil War of 1861-65; *esp.* a soldier in the Northern army.

1861 *Daily Dispatch* (Richmond, Va.) 24 July 3/5 The federals advanced gradually among the masked batteries. **1870** A. H. STEPHENS *Hist. War betw. States* II. xxiii. 582 Two grand campaigns were now again clearly developed by the Federals. **1871** SIR S. NORTHCOTE *Life, Lett. & Diaries* (1890) II. 38 Timidly putting in a plea for a few flowers to two or three graves of Federals also.

federalism ('fɛdərəlɪz(ə)m). [ad. F. *fédéralisme*, f. *fédéral*: see FEDERAL and -ISM.] The federal principle or system of political organization (see FEDERAL *a.* 2 a); advocacy of this principle. In U.S. *Hist.* the principles of the Federal party: see FEDERAL 3 a.

1793 BURKE *Policy of Allies* Wks. VII. 133 We see every man that the jacobins chuse to apprehend..conveyed to prison..whether he is suspected of royalism, or federalism, moderantism, democracy royal, or [etc.]. **1804** SOUTHEY in *Ann. Rev.* II. 207 Federalism would have been too loose a tie. **1843** WHITTIER *Democr. & Slavery* Prose Wks. 1889 III. 112 State after state revolted from the ranks of federalism. **1844** SIR J. GRAHAM in *Croker Papers* (1884) III. xxiii. 20 In Ireland..Federalism..with growing discontent, is gaining ground. **1876** H. C. LODGE in *N. Amer. Rev.* CXXIII. 116 The chapter on 'The Treasury and Federalism'.

federalist ('fɛdərəlɪst), *sb.* [ad. F. *fédéraliste*: see FEDERAL and -IST.]

1. One who advocates or supports federalism or federal union.

1792 *Explan. New Terms* in *Ann. Reg.* p. xv, Federalists, or friends to a federal union; such as that..among the United States of America. **1794** BURKE *Pref. Brissot's Addr.* Wks. VII. 318 The Girondin faction on this account received also the name of federalists. **1851** GALLENGA *Italy* II. xii. 436 The federalists in Switzerland have only yesterday baffled both those evil powers. **1863** FAWCETT *Pol. Econ.* II. x. (1876) 275 The federalists say that if all the productive societies are in direct connection with the Central Wholesale Society a [etc.].

2. *U.S. Hist.* A member or supporter of the Federal party. See FEDERAL *a.* 3.

1787 MADISON in *Federalist* No. 10 Cherishing the spirit and supporting the character of Federalists. **1837** HT. MARTINEAU *Soc. Amer.* II. 30 The federalists are the great patrons of commerce. **1888** BRYCE *Amer. Commw.* II. III. liii. 325 The advocates of a central national authority had begun to receive the name of Federalists.

3. *attrib.*

1801 W. DUPRÉ *Neolog. Fr. Dict.* 117 Federalist motions and intrigues. **1837** HT. MARTINEAU *Soc. Amer.* III. 289 The federalist merchants and lawyers consider the clergy so little fit for common affairs as to call them a set of people between men and women. **1876** *N. Amer. Rev.* July 130 The Federalist party was a very remarkable political organization.

Hence **federa'listic** *a.*, inclined to federalism.

1862 *Parthenon* 26 July 398 Before 1848, Italy was more 'federalistic' than unitarist.

federalization (ˌfɛdərəlaɪ'zeɪʃən). [f. next + -ATION.] Tha action of federalizing or the state of being federalized.

1864 in WORCESTER (citing STILES). **1885** *Pall Mall G.* 29 June 12/2 This advantage they will gain by the federalization of the fleet. **1890** *Spectator* 2 Aug., Obviously the people of San Salvador do not desire federalisation.

federalize ('fɛdərəlaɪz), *v.* [f. FEDERAL *a.* + -IZE.] **a.** *trans.* To make federal, unite in federal union. **b.** To decentralize; to take from the central authority and hand over to federal bodies in the state, or to federal states in a union.

1801 W. DUPRÉ *Neolog. Fr. Dict.* 116 *Fédéraliser*, to federalize; to form confederacies, or factions, as that of the Brissotines, or Girondistes. **1847** CRAIG, *Federalize*, to unite in compact, as different states; to confederate for political purposes. **1885** *Pall Mall G.* 29 June 12/1 Advice which may be condensed into one short sentence—Federalize the fleet. **1885** *Manch. Exam.* 6 July 5/2 We are asked to federalise our institutions. **1889** *Times* 30 Oct. 8/2 He was not likely to suppose that we could federalize a part of a realm.

Hence **'federalized**, **'federalizing** *ppl. adjs.*

1884 *Pall Mall G.* 4 Apr. 11/2 He established in Australia 300 federalized branches of the National League. **1889** *Spectator* 9 Nov. 627/2 The federalising revolution even Mr. Morley himself ridicules.

federally ('fɛdərəlɪ), *adv.* [f. FEDERAL *a.* + -LY[2].] In a federal manner. **a.** *Theol.* On the basis or faith of a covenant. **b.** After the manner of a federation.

1644-5 in Scobell *Acts & Ord.* I. (1658) 83 They are Christians and fœderally holy before Baptism. **1692** BURNET *Past. Care* viii. 94 A share in all which is there Federally offered to us. *a* **1703** BURKITT *On N.T.* Matt. xxii. 33 Their souls are yet alive, fœdrally alive unto God. **1843** J. MARTINEAU *Chr. Life* (1867) 142 A company of nations, federally bound of God.

† **federalness** ('fɛdərəlnɪs). *Obs. rare.* [f. as prec. + -NESS.] The state of being federal; federal character.

1727 in BAILEY vol. II.

federarie: see FEDARIE, *Obs.*

federate ('fɛdərət), *a.* and *sb.* [ad. L. *fœderāt-us*, pa. pple. of *fœderāre*: see next.]

A. *adj.* Federated, confederate, allied, in league.

1710 SHAFTESB. *Adv. to Author* II. §2. 83 Those compos'd of federate Tribes, or mix't Colonys. **1766** WARBURTON *Alliance betw. Church & State* II. iii. (ed. 4) 194 In a federate Alliance, the two Societies still subsist intire. **1808** G. EDWARDS *Pract. Plan* i. 3 The possibility of the maritime superiority of France, and her federate powers. **1855** SINGLETON *Virgil* II. 427 [Me,] who have followed Trojans' fed'rate arms. **1885** *Pall Mall G.* 28 Oct. 2/1 There may..be the greatest inequality between the federate States.

B. *sb.* **1.** One of the parties to a covenant.

1671 FLAVEL *Fount. Life* iii. 6 Redemption..differs from the Covenant of Grace..in regard of the Federates.

2. *French Hist.* Used as a translation of Fr. *fédéré*. **a.** A member of one of the armed associations formed during the first French Revolution, or during the Hundred Days in 1815, or a member of the Commune in 1871. **b.** A deputy to the Fête of the Federation, July 14, 1790.

1792 *Hist.* in *Ann. Reg.* 49 They invited armed federates, as they were called, in July 1791, to Paris. **1837** CARLYLE *Fr. Rev.* II. I. xi, From all points of the compass, Federates are arriving. **1871** *Echo* 12 Apr. 3 It seems to me that the Government of Versailles has all along taken a wrong estimate of the federates of the Commune.

federate ('fɛdəreɪt), *v.* [f. L. *fœderāt-* ppl. stem of *fœderāre*, f. *fœder-*, *fœdus*: see FEDERAL.]

a. *intr.* To enter into a league for a common object. **b.** *trans.* To band together as a league; to organize on a federal basis.

1837 CARLYLE *Fr. Rev.* II. I. viii, Thus, at Lyons..we behold as many as fifty, or..sixty thousand, met to federate. **1884** *Pall Mall G.* 22 Nov. 1/2 We shall be compelled to grant Home Rule, and Home Rule will drive us irresistibly to federate the empire. **1884** J. DOUGLAS in *19th Cent.* Dec. 854 A strong recommendation to federate, which came from a Royal Commission..at Melbourne. **1885** LOWE *Bismarck* II. 162 Did the Chancellor himself, too, dream of federating the Continent against England?

Hence **'federated** *ppl. a.*; **'federating** *ppl. a.*

1814 WELLINGTON in Gurw. *Desp.* XII. 43 To hold them as dependent or federated states rather than as colonies. **1883** W. WESTGARTH in *Pall Mall G.* 22 Oct. 2/1 Although annexation is refused to Queensland, to a federated Australasia it would be allowed. **1885** *Ibid.* 10 Jan. 1/2 The mutual consent of the federating communities.

federation (fɛdəˈreɪʃən). [a. F. *fédération*, ad. L. *fœderātiōn-em*, n. of action f. *fœderāre*: see FEDERATE *v.* and -ATION.]

1. The action of federating or uniting in a league or covenant. Now chiefly *spec.* the formation of a political unity out of a number of separate states, provinces, or colonies, so that each retains the management of its internal affairs; a similar process applied to a number of separate societies, etc.

1721–1800 BAILEY, *Federation*, a Covenanting. **1867** FREEMAN *Norm. Conq.* (1876) I. iii. 98 There must have been, if not centralization, at any rate something like federation. **1888** SIR C. G. DUFFY in *Contemp. Rev.* Jan. 27 If federation of the colonies be partly accomplished.

b. *Federation of the (British) Empire, Imperial Federation*: a proposed readjustment of the relations between the various parts of the empire, by which the colonies would have shared with the mother country the control and the cost of all measures taken for the safety and well-being of the empire as a whole.

1885 MRQ. LORNE (*title*), Imperial Federation. **1886** *Pall Mall G.* 16 June 11/1 A paper was read by Sir George F. Bowen on 'The Federation of the British Empire'..He adopted Mr. Forster's definition of..Imperial Federation —viz., such a union of the mother country with her colonies as would keep the British Empire one State in relation to other States, through the agency of an organisation for common defence, and a joint foreign policy.

2. A society or league formed for joint action or mutual support; now chiefly, a body formed by a number of separate states, societies, etc., each retaining control of its own internal affairs.

Often in names of political societies and trade-unions, as, the Miners' Federation, the National Liberal Federation, the Social Democratic Federation, the Shipping Federation.

1791 BURKE *App. Whigs* Wks. VI. 126 Is he obliged..to keep any terms with those clubs and federations? **1855** MACAULAY *Hist. Eng.* xix. 325 The Batavian federation. **1859** HELPS *Friends in C.* Ser. II. I. Addr. to Rdr. 5 There would be a federation amongst the sensible..people. **1861** M. PATTISON *Ess.* (1889) I. 40 All this was in the century preceding the formation of the Hanseatic federation. **1865** H. KINGSLEY *Hillyars & Burtons* lxii, The Australian Federation..need not despair of finding a casus belli among themselves. **1892** *Daily News* 14 Mar. 5/8 In Durham the Federation means the union of the Durham collieries.

3. *attrib.*

1837 CARLYLE *Fr. Rev.* II. IV. ix, Our sublime Federation Field is wetted..with French blood. **1893** *Westm. Gaz.* 8 Apr. 5/2 At an evening meeting Shipping Federation cards and books..were burnt.

Hence **fedeˈrationist**, an advocate of federation.

1865 *Pall Mall G.* 27 Apr. 5 The object of the Federationists. **1887** *Athenæum* 28 May 703/1 The federationist leaves this problem 'outside the discussion'.

federatist (ˈfɛdərətɪst). [f. FEDERATE *v.* + -IST.] = FEDERATIONIST.

1884 J. DOUGLAS in *19th Cent.* Dec. 853 The Imperial Federatists.

federative (ˈfɛdərətɪv), *a.* [f. L. *fœderāt-* (see FEDERATE *v.*) + -IVE. Cf. F. *fédératif, -ive.*]

†**1.** Of or pertaining to the formation of a covenant, league, or alliance. *Obs.* exc. *Hist.*

1690 LOCKE *Govt.* II. §146 This [power] contains the Power of..Leagues and Alliances..and may be called Federative. **1790** BURKE *Fr. Rev.* 227 The power to which our constitution has exclusively delegated the federative capacity of this kingdom. **1874** GREEN *Short Hist.* ix. §9 (1876) 697 The Scotch proposals of a federative rather than a legislative union were set aside.

2. Of or pertaining to a federation; forming part of a federation; of the nature of a federation.

1781 GIBBON *Decl. & F.* lxx. (1828) VIII. 395 A vast..idea of uniting Italy in a great fœderative republic. **1825** T. JEFFERSON *Autobiog.* Wks. 1859 I. 78 Our first essay, in America, to establish a federative government had fallen..very short of its object. **1846** GROTE *Greece* II. iv. II. 430 Argos, with the federative cities attached to her. **1851** GALLENGA *Italy* 39 This federative work developes..difficulties.

3. Inclined to form federations.

1885 E. C. STEDMAN in *Century Mag.* XXIX. 506 The numberless corporations of the federative Saxon race. **1886** *Blackw. Mag.* CXXXIX. 582 They acquire..a sort of clannish and federative spirit.

Hence ˈ**federatively** *adv.*

1823 SOUTHEY *Hist. Penins. War* I. 51 All the inferior powers..had contracted..federatively and individually, an alliance with the Emperor Napoleon. **1851** SIR F. PALGRAVE *Norm. & Eng.* I. 89 The authorities and tribunals federatively combined in our political constitution. **1854** ST. ANDRÉ *Land of Refuge* 55 Any established body not federatively constituted.

federator (ˈfɛdəreɪtə(r)). [f. FEDERATE *v.* + -OR.] One who or that which makes a federation; one who takes part in a federation.

1879 J. MARTINEAU *Ess.* (1891) IV. 271 It's [*sc.* religion's] power..as a federator of nations..is freely admitted. **1901** *Wide World Mag.* VI. 472/2 Professor Bickerton himself paying on the same scale as any other Federator.

†ˈ**federatory**, *a. Obs. rare*⁻¹. [f. as FEDERATIVE *a.* + -ORY.] = FEDERATIVE I.

1692 *Covt. Grace Conditional* 56 When God for his part performs the federatory action.

†ˈ**federed**, *ppl. a. Obs. rare*⁻¹. [ad. L. *fœderātus*: see FEDERATE *a.* and -ED¹.] Allied or leagued together.

1382 WYCLIF *Prov.* xvii. 9 Who with an other sermoun reherceth, seuereth the federed.

federo-, used by Jefferson as combining form of FEDERAL: see quots.

1786 T. JEFFERSON *Writ.* (1859) II. 12, I had applied that [appellation] of Federo Americans to our citizens. **1804** *Ibid.* (1830) IV. 16 A bastard system of federo-republicanism [i.e. a mixture of Federalist and Republican principles].

†**fediˈfraction.** *Obs. rare*⁻¹. [as if ad. L. **fœdifractiōn-em*, f. *fœdus* compact + *-fractiōnem* a breaking. Cf. next.] Breach of covenant.

1650 B. *Discolliminium* 45, I..shall be allowed the full benefit of all the..plenipotentialities and fedifractions that I ..can devise.

†**feˈdifragous**, *a. Obs.* [f. L. *fœdifrag-us* (f. *foedus* compact + root of *frangĕre* to break) + -OUS.] Compact-breaking, faithless, perfidious.

1600 ABP. ABBOTT *Exp. Jonah* 359 Perfidious, and fedifragous, and barbarous Princes. **1651** *C. Love's Case* 53 Such desultory and fedifragous practices.

absol. **1632** VICARS tr. *Virgil's Æneid* XII. 384 Jove..whose thunders great Do truces tie, fright the fedifragous.

fedill, earlier form of FEDDLE *sb. Obs.*

†ˈ**feding.** *Obs. rare.*

1506 *Ord. Chr. Men* (W. de Worde) I. iii. 33, I the commande..acursed spyryte fedynge [*spiritus immunde*] that thou go thy wayes. **1551** *Gray's N. Y. Gift* in Furnivall *Ball. fr. MSS.* I. 419 They clerelye deface vs with theire popishe fedynges [*rime-wd.* proceedynges].

†ˈ**fedity.** *Obs.* Also 6 feditee, 7 fœdity. [ad. L. *fœditāt-em*, f. *fœdus* foul: see -ITY.]

1. Foulness, impurity, loathsomeness, whether moral or physical.

1542 UDALL in *Lett. Lit. Men* (Camden) 6 Xenocrates.. began sumwhat to declare of the feditee of riot and drunkeness. *a* **1619** FOTHERBY *Atheom.* I. xi. §4 (1622) 116 All these delicacies..when they come into the belly, they are wrapt vp together, in one and the same fœdity. **1649** BP. HALL *Cases Consc.* IV. x. (1654) 375 The fœdity and unnaturalness of the match. *a* **1656** USSHER *Ann.* (1658) 342 Being conscious..of the feditie of his own desire. **1657** TOMLINSON *Renou's Disp.* 186 The..fedity of the skin. **1721–1800** in BAILEY.

2. *pl.* Foul or disgusting practices.

1539 LATIMER *Serm. & Rem.* (1845) 417 When comperites doth shew what fedities doth grow. **1640** BP. HALL *Episc.* I. ii. 9 All the superstitions and fœdities of the Romish Religion. **1675** J. SMITH *Chr. Relig. Appeal* II. 23 Charging them..with the devouring of their own Children ..and many other fedities. **1755** G. LAVINGTON *Moravians compared* 65 Some Fedities common amongst the Gnosticks, not fit to be named.

fedme, feþme, obs. forms of FATHOM.

fedora (fɪˈdɔːrə). *orig. U.S.* [f. *Fédora*, title of a drama (1882) by Victorien Sardou (1831–1908).] A low soft felt hat with a curled brim and the crown creased lengthways. Also *attrib.*

1895 *Montgomery Ward Catal.* 274/3 For ease, comfort and style, the soft Fedora hats lead all others. **1897** *Sears, Roebuck Catal.* 232/3 Our Young Men's Special Nutria Fur Fedora... Men's Full Shaped Fedora Hat. **1910** *N.Y. Even. Post.* 21 Apr., The fedora dented at wrong angles. **1916** S. LEACOCK *Moonbeams* ii. 23 There was no use in my having bought a sage-green fedora in Broadway. **1925** L. BROMFIELD *Possession* ix. 46 He took off..his brown fedora hat. *Ibid.* xvii. 100 In place of a warm skating cap he wore a Fedora hat pulled over his ears. **1926** *Daily Colonist* (Victoria, B.C.) 17 July 1/7 Men's Straw Fedora Shape Hats... A comfortable every-day hat for the hot Summer days; made in Fedora styles with black ribbon. **1930** *Punch* 26 Feb. 236 He carried a cheap black fedora in his hand. **1937** *Times* 11 Aug. 15/5 Soft hats of tweed and jersey material have stitched brims and fedora-shaped crowns. **1952** WODEHOUSE *Pigs have Wings* ii. 40 The investigations he has been making into the bumping off of the man in the green fedora.

fedylle, obs. form of FIDDLE.

†**fee**, *sb.*¹ *Obs.* Forms: 1 fioh, féo, 1–3 feoh, 3–4 feo, 3 *south.* veo, 2–3 feh, 2 *Orm.* fehh, 2–6 fe, (3 fæi, feih), 5–7 fie, (6 *Sc.* fye), 3–7 fee. [Common Teut. and Aryan: OE. *feoh, fioh, féo*, str. neut., corresp. to OFris. *fia*, OS. *fehu* cattle, property (Du. *vee* cattle), OHG. *fihu, fehu* cattle, property, money (MHG. *vihe, vehe*, and mod.Ger. *vieh* has only the sense cattle), ON. *fé* cattle, property, money (Da. *fæ* cattle, beast, Sw. *fä* beast), Goth. *faihu* property, money:—OTeut. **fehu*:—OAryan **péku-*, whence also Skr. *paçu* masc., L. *pecū* neut. cattle (cf. L. *pecūnia* money).]

1. Live stock, cattle, whether large or small. *wild fee*: deer.

c **900** K. ÆLFRED *Laws* xlii, Gif þe becume oðres monnes ȝiemeleas fioh on hand..ȝecyðe hit him. *a* **1000** *Salomon & Sat.* 23 (Gr.) Feoh butan ȝewitte. *c* **1250** *Gen. & Ex.* 783 Ðo sente he after abram..And gaf him lond, and aȝte, and fe. *a* **1300** *Cursor M.* 1059 (Cott.) Þis abel was a hird for fee. **1375** BARBOUR *Bruce* x. 151 Ane That husband ves, and vith his fee Oftsis hay to the peill led he. *c* **1450** HENRYSON *Mor. Fab.* 80 The keiper of the fie For verie woe woxe wanner nor the weid. ? *a* **1500** *True Thomas* 67 in Jamieson *Pop. Ballads* II. 15, I ride after the wilde fee; My raches rennen at my devys. **1535** STEWART *Cron. Scot.* III. 343 Distroyit war all bowis, flokis and fie.

2. Movable property in general; goods, possessions, wealth.

c **888** K. ÆLFRED *Boeth.* xiv. §2 þa unȝesceadwisan neotena ne wilniaþ nanes oþres feos. *c* **1000** *Ags. Ps.* cviii. [cix.] 11 His feoh onfon fremde handa. *c* **1175** *Lamb. Hom.* 109 þe feorðe unþeu is þet þe riche mon..bihude his feh. *c* **1205** LAY. 4429 þe king him ȝette..feoh & færde. *c* **1275** *A Luue Ron* 70 in *O.E. Misc.* (1872) 95 Cesar riche of wordes feo. *c* **1330** *Arth. & Merl.* 418 He..bad he schuld cum him to help And he schuld haue half his fe. *c* **1460** *Towneley Myst.* 28 Do get in oure gere, oure catalle and fe, In to this vesselle here. **1526** SKELTON *Magnyf.* 1993 Alasse, where is nowe my golde and fe? **1596** DRAYTON *Legends* iv. 74 Whose labour'd Anvile only was His Fee.

3. Money.

Beowulf 1380 Ic þe þa fæhðe feo leaniȝe. *c* **870** *Codex Aureus* 5 in *O.E. Texts* (1885) 175 Mid uncre claene feo. *c* **900** *Bæda's Eccl. Hist.* III. xiv. [xix.] (1891) 216 Forðon ȝif þu þisses monnes fea [*pecunia*] in his synnum deades ne onfenge, ne burne his wiite on þe. *c* **1000** *Ags. Gosp.* Matt. x. 9 Næbbe ȝe gold ne seolfer ne feoh on eowrum bigyrdlum. *c* **1175** *Lamb. Hom.* 91 þa..salden heore ehte and þet feh bitahten þam apostles. *c* **1200** ORMIN 15968 He selleþþ Haliȝ Gast forr fe. *c* **1205** LAY. 9176 He miðte æt-halden heore feoh þe Julius her fatte. *a* **1225** *Ancr. R.* 326 Vor sunne is þes deofles feih þet he ȝiueð to gauel. *a* **1300** *Floriz & Bl.* 25 Floriz ne let for ne feo To finden al þat neod beo. *c* **1425** WYNTOUN *Cron.* VII. viii. 754 Corrupte..wyth þe kyng of Inglandis Fe. **1677** *Lovers Quarrel* 30 in Hazl. *E.E.P.* II. 254 God give you good of your gold, she said, And ever God give you good of your fee.

4. *Comb.* **fee-house**, (*a*) in OE., a treasury, (*b*) a cattle-shed.

c **1000** *Ælfric's Voc. Sup.* in Wr.-Wülcker 184 *Ærarium*, feohhus. **1483** *Cath. Angl.* 125/1 A Feehouse, *bostar*.

fee (fiː), *sb.*² Forms: 4–5 fe, feo, fey, 6 fie, 3– fee. *Pl.* 3 fez, 3–4 feez, 5 fese, 5–6 feeze, 6 feas, feis, 4– fees. See also FEU, FEUD *sb.*², FIEF *sb.* [a. AF. *fee, fie* = OF. *fé, fié*, **fiet* (app. implied in *fiez* pl.), *fief, fieu, fiu*, Pr. *feo, feu, fieu*, It. *fio* (prob. from Fr. or Pr.; the Langobardic Lat. *faderfium* is a compound of Teut. *fehu* FEE *sb.*¹), med.L. *feodum, feudum* (first cited by Du Cange from a charter of Charles the Fat, A.D. 884), also *fevum, feum, fedium*, in Sicily *fegum*.

The mutual relation of the various Romanic and med.L. forms is somewhat obscure. According to some scholars, *fief* is a vbl. sb. f. *fiever* to grant in fee, f. *fieu*, which, as well as the other forms of the sb., descends from *feodum* or its Teut. source. The ultimate etymology is uncertain. A prevalent view is that the word is f. OHG. *fehu* cattle, property, money (= FEE *sb.*¹), + *ôd* wealth, property. This must be rejected, because such an etymology could directly yield no other sense than that of 'movable property', which is very remote from the sense of *feodum* as used in early records, viz. usufruct granted in requital of service (often opposed to *alodis*, originally meaning 'inheritance'); cf. the synonyms, Ger. *lehen*, OE. *lǣn* (the same word as Eng. *loan*), and L. *beneficium*, i.e. something granted to a subject by the kindness of his lord. A more tenable theory is that the OF. *fiu* is an adoption of the Teut. *fehu* in the contextual sense of 'wages, payment for service'; the Rom. word certainly had this meaning (see branch II below), and it is conceivable that the feudal sense is a specific application of it. The *d* of the L. forms, *feudum, feodum*, however, is left unexplained by this hypothesis; some regard it as a euphonic insertion (comparing It. *chiodo* nail from vulgar L. **clo-um* from *clavum*); others think that it is due to the analogy of *allodium*; and others suppose *feudum* to be a vbl. sb. f. *feudare* = *feum dare*; but each of these views involves serious difficulties. It is not impossible that two originally distinct words may have been confused. A conjecture proposed by Prof. Kern, and approved by some German jurists, is that *feodum* represents an OHG. **fehôd*, related to the vb. *fehôn*, which is recorded only in the sense 'to eat, feed upon', but is supposed on etymological grounds to have had the wider meaning 'to take for one's enjoyment'. This would account fairly well for the sense, but involves too much hypothesis to be accepted with confidence. It is curious, if the word be of Teut. formation, that there is no direct proof of its having existed in any Teut. language, nor is it found even in the L. text of the Frankish laws.]

I. 1. a. *Feudal Law.* An estate in land (in England always a heritable estate), held on condition of homage and service to a superior lord, by whom it is granted and in whom the ownership remains; a fief, feudal benefice. †*to take* (a person's) *fee*: to become his vassal. Now only *Hist.*

ecclesiastical fee (L. *feodum ecclesiasticum*): one held by an ecclesiastical person or corporation, and not owing any but spiritual service. *knight's fee, lay fee*: see KNIGHT *sb.*, LAY *a.*

[**1292** BRITTON III. ii. §1 Plusours maneres des feez sount et de tenures.] *c* **1330** R. BRUNNE *Chron.* (1810) 63 Þerfor vnto þam tuo he gaf Griffyns feez. *c* **1400** *Melayne* 1371 Allas..That ever I tuke thi fee! **1473** WARKW. *Chron.* 23 A generalle resumpcion of alle lordschippes..and feys grawntede be the Kynge. **1767** BLACKSTONE *Comm.* II. 105 Feodum, or fee, is that which is held of some superior, on condition of rendering him service. **1836** BAINES *Hist. Lanc.* III. 204 The great fee or lordship of Pontefract was vested in them. **1844** WILLIAMS *Real Prop.* (1877) 43 The word *fee* anciently meant any estate feudally held of another person. **1863** H. COX *Instit.* II. xi. 583 [Of the Counties Palatine] there remain now only those of Lancaster and Durham..the latter formerly an ecclesiastical fee belonging to the Bishop of Durham.

b. Phrases, (*as*) *in* or *of fee* (= L. *in*, *de feudo*, *ut in feudo*): by a heritable right subject to feudal obligations. Now only *Hist.* Also *transf.* and *fig.*

[**1292** BRITTON I. xxi. §4 Autres qe il ne avoint en lour demeyne cum de fee.] *c* **1330** R. BRUNNE *Chron.* (1810) 86 William þe Conqueror his ancestres & he Held with grete honour Normundie in fe Of alle kynges of France. *c* **1470** HENRY *Wallace* x. 977 Schyr Amer hecht he suld it haiff in hyr Till hald in fe and othir landis mo. **1491** *Act 7 Hen. VII*, c. 12 §5 That every recovery so had be as gode..as if the King were seised of the premisses in his demesne as of fee. **1494** FABYAN *Chron.* VI. ccxvii. 236 To..holde it [the lande] of hym as in fee. **1587** GOLDING *De Mornay* xx. 305 Sith we hold all things of him [God] in fee, we owe him fealty and homage. **1852** MISS YONGE *Cameos* (1877) II. v. 57 The sovereignty of the provinces he now held in fee were made over to him.

2. a. *Common Law.* An estate of inheritance in land. Also in phrases as in 1 b. (A fee is either a FEE-SIMPLE or a FEE-TAIL; but *in fee* is usually = 'in fee-simple'.)

In Eng. Law theoretically identical with sense 1, all landed property being understood to be held feudally of the Crown. In the U.S. the holder of the fee is in theory as well as in fact the absolute owner of the land.

1535 STEWART *Cron. Scot.* II. 700 The baronie he gaif To Durhame kirk in heretage and fie. **1628** COKE *On Litt.* III. iv. §293. 189 It is to be vnderstood that when it is said..that a man is seised in fee..it shall be intended in fee simple. **1764** BURN *Poor Laws* 184 To purchase lands in fee. **1809** J. MARSHALL *Const. Opin.* (1839) 126 Peck..covenanted that Georgia..was legally the owner in fee of the land in question. **1818** CRUISE *Digest* (ed. 2) I. 160 If a woman, tenant in tail general, makes a feoffment in fee, and takes back an estate in fee. *Ibid.* VI. 265 Here the fee was expressly given to the trustees. **1827** JARMAN *Powell's Devises* II. 149 An estate of which the devisor was mortgagee in fee. **1844** WILLIAMS *Real Prop.* (1879) 43 A fee may now be said to mean an estate of inheritance. **1858** POLSON *Law & L.* 197 Seized in fee.

b. *fig.* esp. in phrase *to hold in fee*, to hold as one's absolute and rightful possession.

a **1553** UDALL *Royster D.* III. iv. (Arb.) 52 One madde proprietie these women haue in fey, When ye will, they will not. **1639** G. DANIEL *Ecclus.* xxiv. 64 My ffee [A.V. inheritance] Is sweeter then Virgin-Combes. *a* **1674** MILTON *Sonn.* xii, Which after held the sun and moon in fee. **1802** WORDSW. *On Extinction Venet. Rep.*, Once did she hold the gorgeous East in fee. **1846** TRENCH *Mirac.* Introd. (1862) 38 Powers..such rather as were evidently his own in fee. **1850** TENNYSON *In Mem.* lxxix. I know thee of what force thou art To hold the costliest love in fee.

c. *base fee*: see BASE *a.* 11. Also (see quot.).

1883 F. POLLOCK *Land Laws* 108 The curious kind of estate created by the conveyance in fee-simple of a tenant in tail not in possession, without the concurrence of the owners of estates preceding his own, is called a *base fee*.

d. In s.w. dialect. (See quots.)

c **1630** RISDON *Surv. Devon* §91 (1810) 87 This town consisteth of three parts, the fee, the manor, and the borough; the fee is of such freeholders and gentlemen as do dwell in Devonshire. **1880** *W. Cornw. Gloss.*, *Fee*, freehold property. 'Our house is fee'.

e. *at a pin's fee*: at the value of a pin.

1602 SHAKS. *Ham.* I. iv. 65, I doe not set my life at a pin's fee. **1865** CARLYLE *Fredk. Gt.* VI. XVI. x. 260 The present Editor does not..value the rumour at a pin's fee.

3. A territory held in fee; a lordship.

[**1292** BRITTON III. ii. §1 Qe les seignurs des fez eyent les gardes de lour feez.] **1413** LYDG. *Pilgr. Sowle* IV. xxvi. (1483) 72 Vnder thy lord god as chyef lord of the fee. *c* **1430** *Syr Tryam.* 1056, Xij fosters..that were kepars of that fee. **15..** *Adam Bel* 56 in Hazl. *E.P.P.* II. 162 Forty fosters of the fe These outlawes had y-slaw. **1741** T. ROBINSON *Gavelkind* v. 49 The Tenements within the Fee were not departible. **1851** TURNER *Dom. Archit.* II. Introd. 20 It [the castle] was the chief place of his honour or fee. **1869** LOWELL *Singing Leaves* 84 My lute and I are lords of more Than thrice this kingdom's fee.

transf. **13..** *E.E. Allit. P.* B. 960 Þat folk þat in þose fees [cities of the Plain] lenged. *c* **1425** WYNTOUN *Cron.* VI. ii. 49 Sum hethyn man..Mycht usurpe Crystyn Feys.

†4. a. The heritable right to an office of profit, granted by a superior lord and held on condition of feudal homage. Only in phrases *in*, *of*, *to fee*. **b.** The heritable right to a pension or revenue similarly granted. *Obs.*

a. [**1292** BRITTON I. xii. §9 Et defendoms a touz ceux qi cleyment aver garde des prisouns en fee.] **1375** BARBOUR *Bruce* XI. 456 Schir robert of Keth..wes Marshall of all the host of fee. *c* **1470** HENRY *Wallace* VII. 1026 In heretage gaiff him office to fee Off all Straithern and schirreiff off the toun. **1670** BLOUNT *Law Dict.* s.v., The word Fee is sometimes used..for a perpetual *right incorporeal*; as to have the keeping of Prisons..in Fee. **1700** tr. *Charter of Edw. I*, in Tyrell *Hist. Eng.* II. 820 No Forester..who is not a Forester in Fee..shall take Chiminage.

b. [**1292** BRITTON II. x. §2 Une autre manere de purchaz est que home fet de annuel fee de deners ou de autre chose en fee.] **1823** CRABB *Technol. Dict.*, *Fee*..a rent or annuity granted to one, and his heirs, which is a *fee personal*.

†5. a. Homage rendered, or fealty promised, by a vassal to a superior. Also, employment, service.

c **1330** R. BRUNNE *Chron.* (1810) 145 Þe moneth of Nouembre..com kyng William..& þer 3ald him his fee. **1486** *Certificate* in *Surtees Misc.* (1890) 49, I..accept hyme to be of my fee and counesell. **1596** SPENSER *F.Q.* VI. x. 21 Venus Damzels, all within her fee.

†b. *to be at a*, *in fee of*, *to*, *with*: to be in the pay or service of, under an obligation to; hence, to be in league with. Also, *to have* (*one*) *in fee*: to retain, hold in one's service. *Obs.*

1529 S. FISH *Supplic. Beggars* 8 Are not all the lerned men in your realme in fee with theim. **1590** WEBBE *Trav.* (Arb.) 34 Beeing then in yeerely fee to the King of Spaine. **1600** HOLLAND *Livy* XLII. v. (1609) 1118 In fee as it were with him, in regard of many courtesies and gracious favours received at his hands. **1633** BP. HALL *Hard Texts* 324 As if ye were at a fee with death and Hell. **1703** T. N. *City & C. Purchaser* 208 Some of those Bricklayers that are in Fee with 'em. **1756** NUGENT *Gr. Tour* IV. 33 He will endeavour to carry you to his own favourite house, which has him in fee.

II. Denoting a payment or gift.

[This branch is commonly referred to FEE *sb.*[1], but the AF. is *fee*, and the med.L. *feodum*, both in England and on the continent; cf. It. *fio.* The two sbs., however, being coincident in form, were certainly confused, and in many instances it makes no difference to the sense whether the word is taken as *sb.*[1] or as *sb.*[2] Senses 6–8 seem to have been influenced by branch I; sense 9 agrees with a continental use of *feodum*.]

†6. A tribute or offering to a superior. *Obs.*

c **1369** CHAUCER *Dethe Blaunche* 266 This..god..May winne of me mo fees thus Than ever he wan. *a* **1400–50** *Alexander* 4466 Þan fall 3e flatt on þe fold, with fees þaim adoures. *Ibid* 5139 Foure hundreth fellis 3it to fee. **1602** DEKKER *Satiromastix* Wks. 1873 I. 253 Knees Are made for kings, they are the subjects Fees.

7. a. The sum which a public officer (? originally, one who held his office 'in fee': see 4 a) is authorized to demand as payment for the execution of his official functions.

[**1292** BRITTON I. xii. §7 Ne ja par defaute de tiel fee ne soit nul prisoun plus detenu.] *c* **1450** *Bk. Curtasye* 598 in *Babees Bk.* (1868) 319 Sex pons þer-fore to feys he takes. **1494** *Nottingham Rec.* III. 279 To the Chaumberlens for theire fese xxvjs. viijd. **1529** *Act 21 Hen. VIII*, c. 5 §6 Any such Ordynary..shall nat in any wyse take for the same above the fees lymytted by this Acte. **1546** *Mem. Ripon* (Surtees) III. 25 To the Auditor for his Fee xiiijs. iiijd. **1581** LAMBARDE *Eiren.* III. i. (1588) 333 Two Justices of Peace, may license such as be delivered out of Gaoles, to beg for their fees. **1593** SHAKS. *2 Hen. VI*, III. ii. 217, I should rob the Deaths-man of his Fee. **1609** SKENE *Reg. Maj.* 2 The fie of the seale, ten pounds. **1680** *Tryal & Sent. Eliz. Cellier* 18, I came to pay the Clerk of the Council his Fees..I was obliged to pay the Fees my self at the Council. **1727** SWIFT *Descr. Morning*, The turnkey now his flock returning sees, Duly let out a-nights to steal for fees. **1817** W. SELWYN *Law Nisi Prius* (ed. 4) II. 936 The captain had paid an extra fee in order to procure his clearances. **1858** KINGSLEY *Poems, Earl Haldan's Dau.* 6 The locks of six princesses Must be my marriage fee. **1868** FREEMAN *Norm. Conq.* (1877) II. x. 471 The greedy secular clergy refused the first sacrament except on payment of a fee.

b. Extended to denote the remuneration paid or due to a lawyer, a physician, or (in recent use) any professional man, a director of a public company, etc. for an occasional service.

1583 STUBBES *Anat. Abus.* II. (1882) 16 The lawiers I would wish to take lesse fees of their clients. **1644** MILTON *Educ.* Wks. (1847) 99/1 Litigious terms, fat contentions, and flowing fees. **1655** CULPEPPER *Riverius* Epigram, Who spend Their Life in Visits, and whose Labors end in taking Fees. **1727–38** GAY *Fables* II. ix. 21 The fee gives eloquence its spirit. **1791** BOSWELL *Johnson* an. 1784 (1847) 800/2 Physicians..generously attended him without accepting any fees. **1802** MAR. EDGEWORTH *Moral T.* (1816) I. vi. 34 What fee, doctor..shall I give you for saving his life? **1863** P. BARRY *Dockyard Econ.* 48 Few of them [Lawyers] are proof against a fee. **1856** EMERSON *Eng. Traits, Voy. Eng.* Wks. II. 11 The remuneration [for public lectures] was equivalent to the fees at that time paid in this country for the like services.

c. The sum paid for admission to an examination, a society, etc.; or for entrance to a public building. Also, ***admission-*, *court*, *entrance-fee***.

1389 in *Eng. Gilds* (1870) 88 He schal..payen his fees and sythyn for hys entres. **1891** *Cambridge Univ. Calendar* 22 A fee of £2 2*s.* is paid to the Common Chest by every student on each admission to a Special Examination. **1893** *Oxford Univ. Calendar* 30 University Museum. Open..to visitors (without fee) from 2 p.m. to 4 p.m.

d. Terminal payments for instruction at school.

1616 R. C. *Times' Whistle* iv. 1428 For duble fees A dunce may turne a Doctour. **1841** W. SPALDING *Italy & It. Isl.* III. 358 Private schools are taught, for small fees, by..priests. **1876** GRANT *Burgh Sch. Scotl.* II. 467 In 1746 the council [of Kirkcaldy] enact that the fees shall be paid quarterly.

†8. a. A perquisite allowed to an officer or servant (*esp.* a forester, a cook or scullion). ***fee of a bullock***: see quot. 1730. *Obs.*

c **1386** CHAUCER *Knt.'s T.* 945 Thus hath here lord..hem payed Here wages and here fees for here servise. **1474** *Househ. Ord.* 32 The larders hath to theire fees the neckes of mutton twoe fingers from the heade. [*a* **1490** BOTONER *Itin.* (Nasmith 1778) 371 Et ipse emebat de cocis lez feez.] **1486** *Bk. St. Albans* F iv a, The Right shulder..Yeueth to the foster for that is his fee. **1557** *Order of Hospitalls* H ij b, The Butler..You shall have no manner of Fees, but your ordinarie wages. **1579** TOMSON *Calvin's Serm. Tim.* 831/2 The ofscouringes or fees of the kitchen. **1593** SHAKS. *3 Hen. VI*, III. i. 23, I, heere's a Deere, whose skins a Keepers Fee. **1603** KNOLLES *Hist. Turks* (1621) 833 Certain young men..snatcht it [food] hastily up as their fees, and like greedie Harpies ravened it downe in a moment. **1730–6** BAILEY (folio), *The Fee of a Bullock*, the bones of a bullocks thighs and shoulders, having the meat cut off (but not clean) for salting for victualling ships.

†b. A warrior's share of spoil; a dog's share of the game. *Obs.*

c **1340** *Gaw. & Gr. Knt.* 1622 He com gayn, His feez þer for to fonge. **14..** *Venery de Twety* in *Rel. Ant* I. 153 The houndes shal be rewardid with the nekke and with the bewellis, with the fee. **1616** SURFL. & MARKH. *Country Farme* 697 The hare being killed, it will be good to giue the dogs their fees, the better to incourage them.

transf. **1659** B. HARRIS *Parival's Iron Age* 101 The Clergy hath ever served as Fee, or prey to the seditious.

†c. Any allotted portion. *Obs.*

1573 TUSSER *Husb.* (1878) 73 Giue sheepe to their fees the mistle of trees. *Ibid.* 78 In pruning and trimming all maner of trees, reserue to ech cattel their properly fees. **1633** G. HERBERT *Temple, Discharge* v, Onely the present is thy part and fee. **1642** H. MORE *Song of Soul* I. II. xiii, There Psyche's feet impart a smaller fee Of gentle warmth.

9. A fixed salary or wage; the pay of a soldier. Also *pl.* Wages. *Obs.* exc. *Sc.* or *Hist.*

c **1400** MAUNDEV. (1839) xv. 170 He that kepethe him [a sacred ox] hath every day grete fees. **1533** GAU *Richt Vay* (1888) 16 They that haldis thair seruandis feis fra thayme. **1535** STEWART *Cron. Scot.* II. 133 Men of weir that wald tak meit and fie. **1637–50** ROW *Hist. Kirk* (1842) 149 Mr. Bruce..hes 40 crounes monethlie for his intertainment, and 500 crounes of fie. **1686** G. STUART *Joco-Ser. Disc.* 26 Ye shall nev'r crave twice of me The smallest Penny of your Fee. **1724** RAMSAY *Tea-t. Misc.* (1733) II. 194 Her fee and bowntith in her lap. **1773** ERSKINE *Inst. Law Scot.* III. vi. §7. 507 Servants fees..being given that they may maintain themselves in a condition suitable to their service..cannot be arrested. *a* **1810** TANNAHILL *Poems* (1846) 103 For I hae wair'd my winter's fee. **1878** SIMPSON *Sch. Shaks.* I. 10 Holding the post of King's standard-bearer, with the fee of six shillings and eight pence a day.

10. †a. A prize, a reward. *Obs.*

c **1400** *Destr. Troy* 2400 The fairest of þo fele shull þat fe haue. *c* **1470** HENRY *Wallace* XI. 460, 'I wald fayn spek with the'..'Thow may for litill fe.' *a* **1541** WYATT in *Tottell's Misc.* (Arb.) 81 Chance hath..to another geuen the fee Of all my losse to haue the gayn. **1596** SPENSER *F.Q.* IV. x. 3 Yet is the paine thereof much greater then the fee. **1605** SYLVESTER *Du Bartas* II. iii. II. *Fathers* 91 Thy God, thy King, thy Fee, thy Fence I am. **1633** G. HERBERT *Temple, Businesse* viii, Two deaths had been thy fee.

b. An occasional gift, a gratuity, given in recognition of services rendered. Phrase, ***without fee or reward***.

a **1592** GREENE *Geo.-a-Greene* Wks. (Rtldg.) 267/1 Fetch me A stand of ale..this is for a fee to welcome Robin Hood. **1768** FOOTE *Devil on 2 Sticks* 11, It is a part of the world where a fee is never refused. **1832** W. IRVING *Alhambra* II. 90 'God forbid', said he, 'that I should ask fee or reward for doing a common act of humanity'. **1863** HAWTHORNE *Our Old Home* (1884) 145 The attendants..expect fees on their own private account. **1873** TRISTRAM *Moab* xv. 291 The not unacceptable fee of a kid-skin of fresh butter.

†c. In bad sense: A bribe. *Obs.*

1549 COVERDALE *Erasm. Par. 2 Pet.* ii. 15 Being corrupt with wicked fee. **1595** SHAKS. *John* II. i. 170 Drawes those heauen-mouing pearles from his poor eies Which heauen shall take in nature of a fee. *c* **1643** MILTON *Sonn.*, *To Lady Marg. Ley*, Unstain'd with gold or fee.

III. *attrib.* and *Comb.*

11. General relations (in senses 7–10).

a. attrib., as *fee-system*, *-table*, *-theatre*. **b.** objective, as *fee-payer*, *-seeker*; *fee-catching* vbl. sb.; *fee-charging*, *-checking*, *-gathering* (also *vbl. sb.*), *-paying*, *-yielding* adjs. **c.** instrumental, as *fee-fed* adj.

1810 BENTHAM *Packing* vii. (1821) 184 A mere pretence for *fee-catching. **1897** *Daily News* 2 Mar. 2/6 They did not know the number of *fee-charging schools..as distinguished from the general elementary system of the country. **1959** I. & P. OPIE *Lore & Lang. Schoolch.* xiii. 298 The private fee-charging establishments. **1810** BENTHAM *Packing* vii. (1821) 187 So *fee-checking an innovation. **1808** —— *Sc. Reform* 71 *Fee-fed lawyers always excepted. *Ibid.* 9 The Technical or *Fee-gathering system. **1828** *Edin. Rev.* XLVIII. 468 Fee-gathering is the real foundation on which the laws of England have been framed! **1832** AUSTIN *Jurispr.* (1879) II. xxxix. 703 The profession would not be merely venal and fee-gathering. **1931** *Times Educ. Suppl.* 15 Aug. 321/2 The entrance examination for *fee-payers. **1893** *Daily News* 12 July 5/1 *Fee-paying schools. **1890** *Ibid.* 7 June 2/1 Lawyers and other *fee-seekers. **1891** *Ibid.* 23 Nov. 2/1 The *fee system seems to me one of the most outrageous and indefensible. **1812** J. QUINCY in *Life* 244 If..we..mete out contributions for national safety by our *fee-tables. **1808** BENTHAM *Sc. Reform* 8 Sale of a *fee-yielding office.

12. Special comb. **† fee-buck**, ? a buck received as a perquisite; **fee-estate** (see quot.); **fee-expectant**: see EXPECTANT *a.* 3, **†fee-Gloucester**, a Cornish tenure; **fee-fund** (see quot.); **†fee-grief**, a grief that has a particular owner; **fee-liege** (see LIEGE); **†fee-Morton**, a Cornish tenure (cf. *fee-Gloucester*); **†fee-penny**, an earnest of a bargain; **†fee-pie** (in humorous phrase *to eat fee pie*, ? to receive bribes); **fee-royal** (see ROYAL). Also FEE-FARM, FEE-SIMPLE, FEE-TAIL.

a **1643** W. CARTWRIGHT *Siege* IV. ii, You..Put of your Mercer with your *Fee-buck for That season. **1775** ASH, **Fee-estate*, lands or tenements for which some service..is paid to the chief lord. **1651** tr. *Kitchin's Jurisdictions* (ed. 2) 301 If it [land in frank-marriage] were given to them in taile to have to them and their heirs, they have taile and *fee expectant. **1861** W. BELL *Dict. Law Scot.*, **Fee-fund*..the dues of Court payable on the tabling of summonses..etc., out of which the..officers of the Court are paid. **1602** CAREW *Cornwall* 38 b, They pay in most places onely fee-Morton releefes which is after fiue markes the whole Knights fee..whereas that of *fee-Gloucester is fiue pound. **1605** SHAKS. *Macb.* IV. iii. 196 Is it a *Fee-griefe Due to some single brest? **1695** G. RIDPATH (*title*) Sir T. Craig's Scotland's Soveraignty Asserted..against those who maintain that Scotland is a Feu, or *Fee-Liege of England. **1602** CAREW *Cornwall* 38 b, *Fee-Morton..so called of John Earle first of Morton. **1552** T. GRESHAM in Strype *Eccl. Mem.* II. App. C. 147 When the Kings Majesties father did first begin..to take up money upon interest..he took his *feepeny in merchandize. *a* **1640** DAY *Peregr. Schol.* (1881) 72 Saieing he was a wise Justice to eate *fee-pie with his

clarke. **1483** Caxton *Gold. Leg.* 145/2 He gaf to them.. the *fee ryall of that buscage.

†**fee**, *sb.*³ *Obs.* Also 5 fey. [a. OF. *fee*, *feie* (F. *foie*).] The liver.

14.. *Noble Bk. Cookry* (1882) 96 Tak and dight the pouche and the fee of a pik. *c* **1450** *Two Cookery-bks.* (1888) 101 Kepe the fey or the lyuer, and kutte awey the gall.

fee (fiː), *v.*¹ Also *Sc.* 4-6 fey, 5-6 fei, 6 fie. [f. fee *sb.*²]

†**I. 1.** *trans.* ? To invest with a fief; ? to grant as a fief. *Obs.*⁻⁰

1483 *Cath. Angl.* 124/2 To Fee, *feoffare.*

II. (From senses 7-10 of the sb.)

2. *trans.* To give a fee to. *to fee away* (nonce-use): to induce by a fee to go away.

a **1529** Skelton *Ware the Hauke* 151 So the Scribe was feed. **1601** ? Marston *Pasquil & Kath.* i. 278 He that fees me best, speeds best. **1716** Swift *Phillis*, Suppose all parties now agreed, The writings drawn, the lawyer fee'd. **1803** *Med. Jrnl.* IX. 62 The Governor and a few others.. chose to fee us for attendance in their respective families. **1806-7** J. Beresford *Miseries Hum. Life* (1826) iv. xxvii, You cannot drive or even fee them away as they are paid for torturing you by some barbarians at the next door. **1859** *All Year Round* No. 35. 203, I had.. feed the steward. **1884** *Times* (weekly ed.) 12 Sept. 14/2 You must fee the waiter when you give the order.

absol. **1806-7** J. Beresford *Miseries Hum. Life* (1826) v. xix, After having fee'd very high for places at Mrs. Siddon's benefit. **1884** *Times* (weekly ed.) 12 Sept. 14/2 At the hotel the guest who does not fee in advance soon finds the zeal of the waiters fall off.

3. To engage for a fee; *Sc.* to hire, employ (servants, etc.); †*transf.* to make use of (an occasion).

c **1470** Henry *Wallace* ix. 40 Semen he feyt and gaiff thaim gudlye wage. **1529** Lyndesay *Compl.* 39 The father of Fameill.. Quhilk.. Feit men to wyrk in his Wyne ȝaird. *a* **1572** Knox *Hist. Ref.* i. Wks. 1846 I. 39 Greadynes of preastis not onlie receave false miracles, bot also thei cherise and fies knaiffs for that purpoise. **1598** Shaks. *Merry W.* ii. ii. 204, I haue.. fee'd euery slight occasion, that could but nigardly giue mee sight of her. **1701** Penn in *Pa. Hist. Soc. Mem.* IX. 78 A lawyer sends me word he is offered to be feed against me. *a* **1810** Tannahill *Poems* (1846) 12 That day ye feed the skelpor Highland callan. **1806-7** J. Beresford *Miseries Hum. Life* (1826) xxi. xvi, Learning to box too—i.e. feeing a great raw-boned fellow to thresh you as long as he can stand over you. **1876** Smiles *Sc. Natur.* viii. (ed. 4) 149 Young lads and lasses came in from the country to be feed, and farmers.. came in to fee them.

†**b.** In a bad sense: To bribe. *Obs.*

1375 Barbour *Bruce* v. 485 *heading*, Heire the Inglis knycht feys a tratour. **1535** Stewart *Cron. Scot.* I. 515 How Nathologus feyit ane Man to follow Dorus.. for to slay him. **1616** R. C. *Times' Whistle* vi. 2537 Fee but the Sumner, and he shall not cite thee. **1727** De Foe *Protest. Monast.* vii, Without Feeing the Journalists or Publishers. *c* **1800** K. White *Clift. Gr.* 318 Should honours tempt thee, and should riches fee.

4. *intr.* for *refl.* To hire oneself.

a **1810** Tannahill *Poems* (1846) 17 Blythe was the time when he fee'd wi' my Father, O, Happy war' the days when we herded thegither, O. **1875** G. Macdonald *Sir Gibbie* xviii. 100 They would not fee to it [a situation] for any amount of wages.

fee (fiː), *v.*² *Mining.* See quot.

1883 Gresley *Gloss. Coal Mining, Fee*, to load up the coal, etc., in a heading into tubs.

fee, var. of fay *sb.*³

†ˈ**feeable**, *a. Obs.* Also 5 feable, feble. [f. fee *sb.*² + -able.] Subject to fees. In quots., That may be taken as a perquisite (see fee *sb.*² 8).

1461 *Liber Niger* in *Househ. Ord.* 73 When thenges byn of wyne and vesseals feble or perused. **1469** *Ibid.* 95 The remanent to be feable. *Ibid.*, The panyers of sea-fisshe to be feeable; and their fees to be divided to the yoman groomes and pages. **1847-78** Halliwell (citing Hall), *Feable*, subject to fees.

feeb (fiːb). *U.S. slang.* [Short for feeble-*minded*.] A feeble-minded person; a 'dumb' person.

1914 *Bookman* XXXIX. 432/1 Feeb? Oh, that's feeble-minded. I thought you knew. We're all feebs in here. **1931** W. Faulkner *Sanctuary* (1932) i. 8, I cook. I cook for crimps and spungs and feebs. Yes, I cook. **1968** E. Fenwick *Disturbance on Berry Hill* vii. 51 'He really is the sweetest guy,' Georgia said wistfully. 'Sometimes I envy that pretty little feeb of his. Suppose if I played dumber I could get one too.'

†**feeˈbility.** *Obs. rare.* In 5 febylyte, febylte. [f. feeble *a.*; see *-bility*, -ity.] = feebleness.

1413 Lydg. *Pilgr. Sowle* ii. iii. (1859) 54 By their owne flesshely febylyte. *c* **1450** Capgrave *St. Kath.* (E.E.T.S.) 180/166 Þat god hymself no þing wrothe schuld be.. wyth þi febylte.

feebily, obs. form of feebly *adv.*

feeble (ˈfiːb(ə)l), *a.* and *sb.* Forms: 2-6 feble, (4 febele), 3-5 febul(l(e, 3-6 fieble, (4 fyble, 6 fybull), 4-6 feable, febil(l, -yl(e, 7 feoble, 6- feeble. *Compar.* 3 feblore; *Superl.* 4 fyebleste, 6 feobleste. [a. OF. *feble*, *fieble*, *foible* (mod. *faible*), later forms of *fleible* weak:—L. *flēbilis* that is to be wept over (cf. flebile *a.*), f. *flēre* to weep. Cf. Pr. *feble*, *fible*, *freble*, Sp. *feble*, Pg. *febre*, It. *fievole* of same origin and meaning.]

A. *adj.*

1. Of persons or animals, their limbs or organs: Lacking strength, weak, infirm. Now implying an extreme degree of weakness, and suggesting either pity or contempt. †Const. *of*, also *to* with *inf.*

c **1175** *Lamb. Hom.* 47 Þa bi-com his licome swiðe feble. *a* **1225** *Ancr. R.* 276 Auh wostu hwat awilegeð monnes feble eien þet is heie iclumben? **1297** R. Glouc. (Rolls) 7665 Þe deneis no mete ne founde.. & so þe feblore were. *c* **1305** *St. Christopher* 216 in *E.E.P.* (1862) 65 Þu ert wel feble to fiȝte. *c* **1320** *Seuyn Sag.* 3450 (W.) He was lene and febil of myght. *a* **1340** Hampole *Psalter* xxxvii. 15 As aran þan þe whilk na thynge is febiler. *c* **1400** *Lanfranc's Cirurg.* 311 If the patient be maad feble wiþ medicyns laxativis. *c* **1450** *St. Cuthbert* (Surtees) 3607 He was so febill he myght noȝt ga. **1483** Caxton *G. de la Tour* C viij b, And this lady felt herself al wery and feble of the aduysyons. *a* **1529** Skelton *Bouge of Court* Prol. 27 His heed maye be harde, but feble his brayne. *a* **1533** Ld. Berners *Huon* liv. 182 Huon was mounted on his lene feble horse. **1611** Bible *Gen.* xxx. 42 The feebler were Labans. *c* **1630** Milton *Passion* 45 Though grief my feeble hands up lock. **1764** Goldsm. *Trav.* 147 The feeble heart. **1829** Hood *Eugene Aram* xiv, A feeble man and old. **1841-4** Emerson *Ess.*, *Prudence* Wks. (Bohn) I. 100 Bring them hand to hand, and they are feeble folk.

absol. *a* **1225** *Ancr. R.* 220 Þus ure Louerd spareð a uormest þe ȝunge & þe feble. *c* **1425** Wyntoun *Cron.* viii. xviii. 92 Rycht oft makis þe febil wycht. **1808** *Med. Jrnl.* XIX. 424 If acidity be troublesome, as often happens to the feeble and dyspeptic.

†**2. a.** Of things: Having little strength; weak, frail, fragile; slight, slender. Of a fortress, etc.: Having little power of resistance. *Obs.*

1340 *Ayenb.* 227 Hit is grat wonder þet hi lokeþ zuich ane fieblene castel ase hare fyeble body. *c* **1384** Chaucer *H. Fame* iii. 42 This were a feble fundament. **1387** Trevisa *Higden* (Rolls) I. 235 Hem semede þat þe legges were to feble for to bere suche an ymage. *c* **1400** *Lanfranc's Cirurg.* 322 The firste boon in a mannes necke is bounden with manye feble ligaturis. *c* **1400** Maundev. (1839) vii. 80 Before the Chirche of the Sepulcre, is the Cytee more feble than in ony other partie. *c* **1470** Henry *Wallace* xi. 1010 Thus semblyt thai about that febill hauld. **1540** *Act 32 Hen. VIII*, c. 18 Some houses be feble and very lyke to fall downe. **1697** Dryden *Virg. Georg.* i. 163 The Stem, too feeble for the freight. **1776** Withering *Brit. Plants* (1796) II. 16 Bunches lateral.. stem feeble.

absol. **1393** Gower *Conf.* I. 24 The feble meind was with the strong So myghte it nought wel stonde long.

b. *spec.* with reference to a sword. [ad. F. *faible*: see B. 4.]

1684 R. H. *School Recreat.* 57 The feeble, weak or second Part is accounted from the Middle to the Point. **1809** Roland *Fencing* 35 The fort part of your blade against the feeble part of your adversary's.

3. Lacking intellectual or moral strength.

c **1200** *Trin. Coll. Hom.* 191 He.. al te-secheð þat þone þe was er swo fieble. **1377** Langl. *P. Pl.* B. xv. 341 Wherfore folke is þe feblere and nouȝt ferme of bilieue. *a* **1400-50** *Alexander* 1710 He þoȝt him sa feble, He dressis to him in dedeyne.. a ball.. þe barne with to play. *c* **1440** *York Myst.* xxiii. 169 Ȝe ffebill of faithe! folke affraied. **1526** *Pilgr. Perf.* (W. de W. 1531) G b, We sholde not be ignoraunt, feble & weyke in these.. thynges. **1639** Dk. Hamilton in *H. Papers* (Camden) 77, I shall neuer proue false or feeble. **1692** Bentley *Serm.* 3 Oct. 29 Though we be now miserable and feeble, yet we aspire after eternal happiness. **1828** Carlyle *Misc.* (1857) I. 105 He was feeble and without volition. *a* **1859** Macaulay *Misc. Writ.* (1860) II. 107 Rigid principles often do for feeble minds what stays do for feeble bodies.

†**4. a.** Wanting in resources; ill-supplied, poor. Const. *of*. *Obs.*

c **1314** *Guy Warw.* (A.) p. 448 (lxxxiv. 10) A feble lord þou seruest. **1375** Barbour *Bruce* xvi. 355 Tharfor he thoucht the cuntre was Febill of men. **1523** Ld. Berners *Froiss.* I. ccccxlviii. 791 The Duke of Aniowe began to wax feble, bothe of men and of money.

†**b.** Of a grant of money, a meal: Scanty. *Obs.*

1494 Fabyan *Chron.* vii. 509 The sayd .iii. astatys ordeynyd a more feble money than they before hadde made. **1562** Turner *Baths* 12 a, Ye may go to a feable diner. *c* **1590** Greene *Fr. Bacon* ix. 246, I knew not of the friars feeble fare.

†**5. a.** Of inferior quality, poor, mean. Often said of clothing, food, dwelling, etc. *Obs.*

c **1275** *Lutel Soth Serm.* 41 in *O.E. Misc.* 188 Boþe heo makeþ feble heore bred and heore ale. *c* **1290** *S. Eng. Leg.* I. 15/484 Vpon a seli asse he rod: in feble cloþes also. *c* **1340** *Cursor M.* 23100 (Trin.) For here is febul abidynge. **1377** Langl. *P. Pl.* B. xv. 343 Þe merke of þat mone is good ac þe metal is fieble. *c* **1420** *Pallad. on Husb.* i. 292 And fewe or feble grapes in the same Have growe. *c* **1470** Henry *Wallace* vi. 452 The man kest off his febill weid off gray.

†**b.** Of a period, event, etc.: Miserable, illstarred, unhappy. *Obs.*

1297 R. Glouc. (Rolls) 6125 Febleliche he liuede al is lif, & deyde in feble deþe. ? *a* **1400** *Chester Pl.* (Shaks. Soc.) I. 224 In feable tyme Christe yode me froo. *c* **1400** *Destr. Troy* 1438 Ffele folke forfaren with a ffeble ende.

†**c.** In moral sense: Mean, base. *Obs.*

c **1250** *Gen. & Ex.* 1072 Wicke and feble was here ðoȝt. *c* **1440** *Gesta Rom.* xvii. 60 (Add. MS.) To fulfille her wille in feble dede.

6. Wanting in energy, force, or effect.

a. of natural agents, powers, qualities, or operations.

1340 Hampole *Pr. Consc.* 745 For-whi þe complection of ilk man Was sythen febler þan it was þan. *c* **1340** *Cursor M.* 1996 (Trin.) Now is for synne & pride of man þe erþe feblere þen hit was þan. *c* **1400** *Lanfranc's Cirurg.* 221 Þan I tastide hir pous & it was wondir feble. *Ibid.* 353 In feble men.. þou muste use feble medicyns. **1595** Shaks. *John* v. iv. 35 The old, feeble, and day-wearied Sunne. **1671** R. Bohun *Wind* 14 Air alone might seeme able to create but a very feeble and languid Wind. **1700** Dryden *Fables, Palamon & Arcite* i. 164 Some faint Signs of feeble Life appear. **1719** London & Wise *Compl. Gard.* v. iii. 99 We may have some feeble Branches on them. **1794** Mrs. Radcliffe *Myst. Udolpho* iv, Her light was yet too feeble to assist them. **1806** *Med. Jrnl.* XV. 438 A feebler action of the poison. **1847** James *Woodman* v, He has but feeble health.

b. of the mind, thoughts, etc.

1393 Langl. *P. Pl.* C. ii. 183 Þat feith with-oute fet ys febelere þan nouht. *c* **1400** Maundev. (Roxb.) xx. 92 My feble witte. **1535** Coverdale *2 Esdras* v. 14 My mynde was feble and carefull. **1590** Shaks. *Com. Err.* iii. ii. 35 My earthie grosse conceit: Smothred in errors, feeble, shallow, weake. **1651** Hobbes *Leviath.* iii. xxxiv. 214 My feeble Reason. **1836** J. Gilbert *Chr. Atonem.* ix. (1852) 278 The thought of danger would possess but feeble power to resist temptation.

c. of actions, feelings, utterances, etc.

c **1340** *Cursor M.* 14849 (Fairf.) A feble counsail ȝe do to dragh. **1393** Gower *Conf.* II. 318 That was a feble dede of armes. *c* **1400** *Destr. Troy* 3189 When the lede hade left of his speche, Fele of þe folke febull it thughten. **1580** Baret *Alv.* F 348 Feeble orations made to the people, without spirit or life. **1591** Shaks. *Two Gent.* ii. vii. 10 A true-deuoted Pilgrime is not weary To measure kingdomes with his feeble steps. **1697** Dryden *Virg. Æneid* viii. 621 Feeble are the Succours I can send. **1738** Wesley *Psalms* ii. iv, Shall all their feeble Threats deride. **1801** Southey *Thalaba* i. xvii, Grief in Zeinab's soul All other feebler feelings over-power'd. **1818** Jas. Mill *Brit. India* II. iv. v. 166 The brilliancy of the exploit had no feeble attractions for the imagination of Clive. **1840** Thirlwall *Greece* VII. 281 A feeble attempt was made by two generals. **1862** Ld. Brougham *Brit. Const.* xii. 164 The feeble conduct which lost Normandy. **1876** Trevelyan *Macaulay* II. iii. 66 He proceeded to reply with a feeble and partial argument.

7. Of an effect, phenomenon, etc.: Faintly perceptible, indistinct.

1860 Tyndall *Glac.* i. iii. 30 The effect became more and more feeble, until.. it almost wholly disappeared. **1896** Tait *Rec. Adv. Phys. Sc.* ix. 215 The feeble bands which cross the comparatively dark space between the spectra.

8. quasi-*adv.* = feebly.

1768-74 Tucker *Lt. Nat.* (1852) I. 202 Every one's experience may convince him how feeble she [reason] acts unless [etc.].

9. *Comb.*, parasynthetic, as, ***feeble-bodied***, ***-eyed***, ***-framed***, ***-hearted***, ***-minded*** (whence ***feeble-mindedness***), ***-winged***.

1774 Goldsm. *Nat. Hist.* VII. viii. 180 The viper.. is but a slow, *feeble-bodied animal. **1814** Wordsw. *Excursion* viii. 208 Those gigantic powers.. have been compelled To serve the will of feeble-bodied Man. **1600** Fairfax *Tasso* v. xii. 5 Weake Cupid was too *feeble eide To strike him sure. **1808** Cobbett *Pol. Reg.* XIV. 193 The law gives him so much power over the poor *feeble-framed creature. **1550** Bale *Image Both Ch.* i. ii. D iv b, If thou be *feble harted saye, lorde encrease my fayth. **1836** J. H. Newman in *Lyra Apost.* (1849) 150 Ere it reach Heaven's gate, Blows frustrate o'er the earth thy feeble-hearted prayer. **1534** Tindale *1 Thess.* v. 14 Comforte the *feble mynded. **1892** *Daily News* 1 Mar. 3/3 The desirability of better provision being made for the care of 'feeble-minded' women. **1908** *Rep. R. Comm. Feeble Minded* VIII. 324 in *Parl. Pap.* (Cd. 4202) XXXIX. 159 'Feeble-minded', *i.e.*, persons who may be capable of earning a living under favourable circumstances, but are incapable from mental defect existing from birth or from an early age: (*a*) of competing on equal terms with their normal fellows; or (*b*) of managing themselves and their affairs with ordinary prudence. **1963** Barnard & Lauwery's *Handbk. Brit. Educ. Terms* 93 *Feeble-minded*, a term usually applied to those whose I.Q. is between 55 and 69. **1619** W. Sclater *Expos. 1 Thess.* (1630) 481 The Nature of *feeble-mindednesse. **1846** Worcester (citing E. Irving), *Feeble-Mindedness.* **1634** Ford *P. Warbeck* i. ii, Your goodness gives large warrants to.. My *feeble-wing'd ambition.

B. *sb.*

1. A feeble person.

(Quots. 1631 and 1826 refer to *K. Hen. IV*, iii. ii. 179.)

1340 *Ayenb.* 148 Þe guode man and þe wyse bereþ and uor-bereþ alneway þe foles and þe fiebles. [**1631** T. Powell *Tom All Trades* (New Shaks. Soc.) 157 The Taylor, who.. had thrust himselfe in amongst the Nobilitie.. and was so discovered, and handled.. from hand to foot, till the Gaurd delivered him at the great Chamber door, and cryed, 'farewell, good feeble!' **1826** Disraeli *Viv. Grey* iv. i, The most forcible of feebles.] **1833** J. S. Mill *Let.* 10 July (1963) XII. 166 The consequence is they must take the *feebles.* **1844**, **1896** [see forcible feeble].

†**2.** Weakness, feebleness. *Obs.*

Only in phrase *for feeble*, which may be explained as ellipsis = 'For feeble that one is'; the substantival character of the sense is thus doubtful.

c **1325** *Coer de L.* 778 That him ne thorst yt not wyte, For febyl his dynt to smyte. *c* **1400** *Destr. Troy* 8704 Suche a sorow full sodenly sanke in his hert, þat he fainted for feble. *a* **1400-50** *Alexander* 4280 Ne for na febill at we fele.

3. = foible 1.

1678 Mrs. Behn *Sir Patient Fancy* i. i, You shall find 'em sway'd by some who have the luck to find their feebles. **1694** R. L'Estrange *Fables* ccccxcvi. (ed. 6) 543 Every Man has his Feeble. **1823** Byron *Juan* xv. xxii, Modesty's my forte, And pride my feeble.

4. *Fencing.* The portion of a sword from the middle to the point; = foible 2.

1645 *City Alarum* 1 Ther's no good fencing without knowledge of the feeble of your Sword. **1776** G. Semple *Building in Water* 54 Like taking a Sword in the feeble of the Point. **1877** *Blackie's Pop. Encycl.* III. 325/2 It should always be the care of the swordsman to receive the feeble of the enemy's weapon on the forte of his own.

feeble (ˈfiːb(ə)l), *v.* Forms: 3 febli-en, (febly), fieble, 4-5 febil(l, (5 -yl), 4-6 feble, (5 febel, febl-

yn), 6 feable(n, 6–7, 9 feeble. [f. the adj.; OF. had *foiblir* (*flebir*), and *foibloier* (*feibloier*).]

1. *intr.* To become or grow feeble. Now *arch.*

*a*1225 *Ancr. R.* 368 Leste hore licome feblie to swuðe. **1297** R. GLOUC. (Rolls) 7785 King willam.. bigan to febli vaste. **1375** BARBOUR *Bruce* II. 384 On thaim! On thaim! thai feble fast! **1496** *Dives & Paup.* (W. de W.) I. viii. 39/1 In token that they ben endlesse & elden not, ne feble not. **1889** 'MARK TWAIN' *Connecticut Yankee* 181 Sir Gawaine's strength feebled and waxed passing faint.

†**2.** *trans.* To make feeble; to enfeeble, weaken. *Obs.* exc. *arch.*

*a*1340 HAMPOLE *Psalter* xvii. 40 Þai ere noght febild my steppis. *c*1380 WYCLIF *Sel. Wks.* III. 408 Þei shulde not feble Þes rewmes. *c*1449 PECOCK *Repr.* II. vi. 175 Thou infirmyst and feblist.. the euydencis. **1450–1530** *Myrr. our Ladye* 49 Woman what menest thou with thy great wepynge so to feble thy syght. **1546** PHAER *Bk. Childr.* (1553) S v a, When a child neseth out of measure.. the brayn and vertues animal be febled. **1590** SPENSER *F.Q.* I. viii. 23 And her [a castle's] foundation forst, and feebled quight. **1614** MARKHAM *Cheap Husb.* II. xxxix. (1668) 83 A Shrew Mouse ..if it only run over a Beast, it feebleth his hinder parts. **1646** E. F[ISHER] *Mod. Divinity* i. (1752) 27 His Understanding was both feebled and drowned in darkness. **1831** *Mirror* XVII. 162/1 Every blow Is feebled with the touch of woe.

Hence '**feebled** *ppl. a.*; '**feebling** *vbl. sb.* and *ppl. a.*

1566 GASCOIGNE & KINWELMARSH *Jocasta* V. ii, Then with hir feebled armes, she doth enfolde Their bodies both. **1597** MONTGOMERIE *Cherrie & Slae* 226 My feiblit eyis grew dim. **1621** FLETCHER *Wild-Goose Chase* I. iii, 'Tis true, you're old and feebled. **1633** W. STRUTHER *True Happin.* 128 It is good that the body finde sometimes this feebling by the vigorous worke of the spirit. **1624** *Trag. Nero* III. vi. in Bullen *O. Pl.* I. 59 Peoples love Could not but by these feebling ills be mov'd. **1632** LITHGOW *Trav.* x. 461 Least by an impatient Minde, and feebling Spirit, I become my owne Murtherer.

feebleness ('fiːb(ə)lnɪs). [f. as prec. + -NESS.] The state or quality of being feeble (in the various senses of the adj.); an instance of this.

*a*1300 *Cursor M.* 28679 (Cott.) Þis man.. for-sakes penance neuer Þe lese, and legges febulnes of flexse. **1340** HAMPOLE *Pr. Consc.* 1514 Þe mare in malys and febelnes Þe kynd of ayther trobled es. **1477** EARL RIVERS (Caxton) *Dictes* 134 Wrath cometh of feblenesse of courage. **1517** TORKINGTON *Pilgr.* (1884) 39 Our Savior.. for very febylnesse fell.. to the grounde. **1533** MORE *Debell. Salem* Pref. 7 b, The feblenesse of his answere shal appere. **1568** GRAFTON *Chron.* II. 107 King Richarde walking unwisely aboute the Castell, to espie the feblenesse thereof. **1683** BURNET tr. *More's Utopia* (1684) 79 Women.. deal in Wool and Flax, which sute better with their feebleness. **1794** S. WILLIAMS *Vermont* 135 The feebleness of the weapons. **1809–10** COLERIDGE *Friend* (1865) 190 It is feebleness only which cannot be generous without injustice. **1860** GEN. P. THOMPSON *Audi Alt.* III. cxxv. 80. Committing himself to the fashionable feeblenesses. **1884** *L'pool Mercury* 22 Oct. 5/4 His grand defect lay in feebleness of will.

b. *concr.* (nonce-use).

1860 GEO. ELIOT *Mill on Fl.* III. 120 Ready to strike that daring feebleness from the stool.

†'**feebler.** *Obs. rare*⁻¹. [f. FEEBLE *v.* + -ER¹.] One who or that which makes feeble or weak.

1586 BRIGHT *Melanch.* xxxviii. 245 Excessive joy.. a great feebler of melancholick persons.

feebless. *Obs.* exc. *arch.* Forms: 3–4 feblesce, 3–5 feblesse, 4 fie-, fyeblesse, 6 feeblesse, 9 feebless. [a. OF. *feblesce, foiblece*, mod.F. *faiblesse*, f. *feble, foible* FEEBLE *a.*] Feebleness, infirmity; infirm health.

1297 R. GLOUC. (1724) 442 Þe kyng hyre fader was old man, & drou to feblesse. *c*1315 SHOREHAM 18 Ine tokne of febleste [*read* -esce] of hiis goste. **1340** *Ayenb.* 33 Zuo Þet he ualÞ ine fyeblesse and ine zuiche ziknesse. *c*1374 CHAUCER *Boeth.* IV. ii. 112 Yif so be Þat goode be stedfast Þan sheweÞ Þe fieblesse of yuel al openly. **1485** CAXTON *Chas. Gt.* 81 For feblesse he fyl to the erthe. **1596** SPENSER *F.Q.* IV. viii. 37 Great feeblesse.. did oft assay Faire Amoret that scarcely she could ride. **1866** J. B. ROSE tr. *Ovid's Fasti* VI. 932 The hours unreined old age and feebless bring.

feebling ('fiːblɪŋ). [f. FEEBLE *a.*: see -LING¹.] A weakling, a feeble person.

1887 H. A. BEERS *Outl. Sk. Amer. Lit.* vii. 273 [Henry James] has exhibited types of the American girl, the American business-man, the æsthetic feebling from Boston. **1896** *Westm. Gaz.* 13 June 2/1 To shriek with horror at them, the sign of a feebling. **1914** S. BARING-GOULD *Ch. Revival* 151 The Church was supplied with feeblings as candidates for Orders.

feeblish ('fiːblɪʃ), *a.* [f. FEEBLE *a.* + -ISH.] Somewhat feeble.

1674 R. GODFREY *Inj. & Ab. Physic* 68 They that are weakly, tender, and feeblish. **1832** WILSON in *Blackw. Mag.* XXXII. 865 Performers with feeblish faces that must frown. **1857** HUGHES *Tom Brown* II. v, He.. is feeblish.. about the knees. **1882** CARLYLE in *Century Mag.* XXIV. 23 Rather a feeblish kind of County-Town.

†'**feeblish,** *v. Obs.* Forms: 4 febliss, 4–6 feblis(s)h, 6 feeblysh, 5–7 feeblish. [a. OF. *febliss-, lengthened stem of *feblir (recorded forms *foiblir, flebir*), f. *feble*: see FEEBLE *a.*] *trans.* To render feeble, weak, or infirm; to enfeeble; = FEEBLE *v.* 2.

1375 BARBOUR *Bruce* XIV. 349 With hungyr he thoucht thame to Febliss. **1477** EARL RIVERS (Caxton) *Dictes* 64 Alle thinges be amunysshed & feblisshed by Iniustice. **1528** PAYNEL *Salerne's Regim.* C iij b, They assende and gether to gether feblysshynge the guttes. **1599** HAKLUYT *Voy.* II. I. 68 All Christendome was sore decayed and feeblished by occasion of the warres betweene England and France.

Hence '**feeblishing** *vbl. sb.*

1580 BARET *Alv.* F 346 Feeblishing, *infirmatio.* **1634** H. R. *Salernes Regim.* 116 Except yee dread great feeblishing of Nature.

†'**feeblishment.** *Obs.* [f. as prec. + -MENT.] Enfeeblement.

1548 HALL *Chron.* 157 b, Whiche promise he caused to bee performed.. to the.. feblishement of the Duchy.

feeblose, *a. rare*⁻¹. [f. FEEBLE *a.* + -OSE.] Rather feeble; weakly.

1882 J. BROWN *John Leech, etc.* 267 Peter had a gentle, sweet, though feeblose.. strain of poetic feeling.

feebly ('fiːblɪ), *adv.* Forms: 3 febleliche, -like, 3–4 febliche, (5 febiliche), 4 febilly, (5 -ylly), 4–6 febly, (4 febli, 5 feabli), 6 feablelye, feebelye, 7 feably, 7– feebly. [f. FEEBLE + -LY².] In a feeble manner.

†**1.** In a sorry manner or plight; inefficiently, insufficiently, niggardly, poorly, scantily. *Obs.*

*c*1290 *S. Eng. Leg., Edmund Conf.* 112 Ake fébleliche hire spedde, For seint Eadmund hadde ane smate ȝeorde. **1297** R. GLOUC. (Rolls) 6125 Febleliche he liuede al is lif & deyde in feble deÞe. *c*1300 *Havelok* 418 Feblelike he gaf hem cloÞes. *c*1300 *Beket* 1178 Such a man.. So febliche wende over lond. *a*1450 *Knt. de la Tour* (1868) 30, Y holde hym that dothe it but febly conseled. *c*1450 HENRYSON *Mor. Fab., Upl. Mous* 37, Poems (1865) 109 Ane sober wane, Of fog and fairn full febillie wes maid.

2. In a weak, ineffective, or half-hearted manner, without strength, energy, or force; weakly. Of sight: Dimly.

*c*1320 *Sir Tristr.* 3050 Febli Þou canst hayte. *a*1340 HAMPOLE *Psalter* cxlv. 1, I may noght stand now bot febilly. *c*1400 *Lanfranc's Cirurg.* 67 Þe pouse began to appere febiliche. **1483** *Cath. Angl.* 124/2 Febylly, *debeliter, imbecilliter.* **1533** MORE *Debell. Salem* I. xiv. 104 b, He hath ..defended.. his boke.. wythe myche worke full febly. **1548** HALL *Chron.* 177 He was fayntly receyved, and febly welcomed. **1591** SPENSER *Ruins of Rome* 221 Ye see huge flames.. Efsoones consum'd to fall downe feebily. **1607** SHAKS. *Cor.* II. ii. 87 The deeds of Coriolanus Should not be vtter'd feebly. **1682** DRYDEN *Mac Fl.* 197 Thy gentle numbers feebly creep. **1757** FOOTE *Author* II, Which were as feebly resisted. **1856** KANE *Arct. Expl.* I. xix. 232, I.. see feebly in prospect my recovery. **1875** JOWETT *Plato* (ed. 2) IV. 275 In dreaming we feebly recollect.

3. In a small degree, slightly, poorly.

1830 LYELL *Princ. Geol.* I. 133 Others feebly represented in our own country. **1838** T. THOMSON *Chem. Org. Bodies* 698 The acids act but feebly upon caoutchouc.

4. *Comb.*, as *feebly-toiling* adj.

1845 MRS. NORTON *Child of Islands* (1846) 179 The feebly-toiling heart that shrinks appalled.

feed (fiːd), *sb.* Also 5–7 fe(e)de, [f. the vb.]

1. a. The action of feeding; eating, grazing; also, the giving of food; an instance of this.

1576 TURBERV. *Venerie* 114 The feeding of an hart or such like.. is called the feede. **1614** BP. HALL *Recoll. Treat.* 1112 Long forbearance whereof [meates] causes a surfet, when wee come to full feede. *a*1626 BACON *Max. & Uses Com. Law* iv. (1635) 23 Pasture answerable to the feed of so many Deere as were upon the ground. **1686** GOAD *Celest. Bodies* I. ii. 3 Birds coming late from Feed. **1833** HT. MARTINEAU *Brooke Farm* iii. 40 He should pay for the feed of his cow. **1873** W. B. TEGETMEIER *Poultry Bk.* xxix. 370 Five or six [pellets] are given at one feed for each bird.

b. Phrases. *at feed*: in the act of eating or grazing. *out at feed*: turned out to graze. *to be off one's feed* (of animals, and *colloq.* or *slang* of persons): to have no desire for food; to have lost one's appetite. (*to be*) *on the feed* (said of fish): (to be) on the look out for food; also, (to be) eating.

1621 LADY M. WROTH *Urania* 275, I like a Deare at feede, start vp for feare. **1680** OTWAY *Orphan* v. ix. 2231 All his little Flock's at feed before him. **1816** JAMES *Milit. Dict.* (ed. 4) 156 A horse that is off his feed. **1823** LAMB *Elia* (1860) 21 The cattle, and the birds, and the fishes, were at feed about us. **1834** MEDWIN *Angler in Wales* II. 166 Towards evening he set out on the feed. **1862** HORLOCK *Country Gentleman* 172 Jack.. was quite off his feed. **1867** F. FRANCIS *Angling* iv. (1880) 108 The fish are well on the feed. **1871** BROWNING *Balaust.* 1317 And pipe.. Pastoral marriage-poems to thy flocks At feed. **1879** MOSELEY *Notes on Challenger* ii. 30 A shoal of porpoises on the feed. **1888** *Berksh. Gloss.* s.v. *Vead*, A horse is said to be 'out at ve-ad' when turned into a meadow to graze.

2. †**a.** A grazing or causing (cattle) to graze; also, the privilege or right of grazing (*obs.*). †**b.** Feeding-ground; pasture land (*obs.*). **c.** Pasturage, pasture; green crops.

1573 TUSSER *Husb.* xvi. (1878) 34 Pasture, and feede of his feeld. **1594** NORDEN *Spec. Brit., Essex* (Camden) 10 Ther is wᵗin the Nase.. Horsey Ilande, verie good for feede. **1600** SHAKS. *A.Y.L.* II. iv. 83 His Coate, his Flockes, and bounds of feede Are now on sale. **1667** MILTON *P.L.* IX. 597 For such pleasure till that hour At Feed or Fountain never had I found. **1712** PRIDEAUX *Direct. Ch.-wardens* (ed. 4) 30 The ..Feed of the Church-yard is the Minister's. **1795** BURKE *Thoughts Scarcity* Wks. 1842 II. 254 The clover sown last year.. gave two good crops, or one crop and a plentiful feed. **1858** BARTLETT *Dict. Amer.* 144 Tall feed, i.e. high grass. **1864** TENNYSON *North. Farmer* (Old Style) x, Theer warnt not feäd for a cow. **1879** MISS JACKSON *Shropsh. Word-bk.*, 'I hanna sid more feed o' the groun' fur many a 'ear.' **1888** *Berksh. Gloss.* s.v. *Vead*, Green crops for sheep, as turnips, swedes, rape, etc., are called 've-ad'.

3. a. Food (for cattle); fodder, provender.

1588 SHAKS. *Tit. A.* IV. iv. 93 (Qo.) As the one is wounded with the bait, the other [sheep] rotted with delicious feed [honey-stalks]. **1878** *Cumbrld. Gloss., Feed*, provender for cattle. **1884** F. J. LLOYD *Sc. Agric.* 243 There arose the necessity of providing them with feed. **1884** *Milnor* (Dakota) *Teller* 13 June, J.D. is prepared to grind all kinds of Feed.

b. An allowance or meal (of corn, oats, etc.) given to a horse, etc. Also *Milit.* in ***short-feed, heavy-horse-feed, light-horse-feed*** (see quot. 1823).

1735 SHERIDAN in *Swift's Lett.* (1768) IV. 117, I can give your horses.. a feed of oats now and then. **1749** FIELDING *Tom Jones* XII. xiii, Prepare them [horses] for their journey by a feed of corn. **1823** CRABB *Technol. Dict.*, A *short feed* is a portion less than the regulated quantity. *Heavy-horse-feed*, a larger proportion given to the heavy dragoons, in distinction from *Light-horse-feed*, which is given to the hussars and the light horse. **1859** F. A. GRIFFITHS *Artil. Man.* (ed. 9) 220 One feed of oats in the nose-bag. **1885** G. MEREDITH *Diana* I. viii. 176 The mare'll do it well.. She has had her feed.

c. Also, food, fare (for human beings). *U.S. colloq.*

1818 H. B. FEARON *Sk. Amer.* 194, I guess whiskey is all the feed we have on sale. **1835** *Knickerbocker* V. 304 A John Smith lives next door, to whom half my choice rounds and sirloins, selected personally in the market,—for I love good feed,—are sent without distinction. **1867** S. HALE *Lett.* (1919) 27 The cook is French and feed delicious. **1898** E. N. WESTCOTT *David Harum* 283 You want a change o' feed once in a while, or you may git the colic.

4. *colloq.* A meal; a sumptuous meal; a feast. Cf. FEAST, SPREAD. Also, a full meal.

1808 *Sporting Mag.* XXXII. 122 A feed now and then at the first tables. **1830** SOUTHEY in *Q. Rev.* XLIII. 14 It is the custom to entertain a distinguished visitor with what, in the South Seas, as in modern London, is called a feed. **1839** MARRYAT *Diary in Amer.* Ser. I. II. 228 'Will you have a feed or a check?' **1853** KANE *Grinnell Exp.* xli (1856) 375 What a glorious feed for the scurvy-stricken ships! **1862** SALA *Accepted Addr.* 193 Snug little feeds preparatory to the grand banquet. **1875** *Chamb. Jrnl.* No. 133. 66 Little boys.. having a feed of ice-cream.

5. a. The action or process of 'feeding' a machine, or supplying material to be operated upon.

1892 P. BENJAMIN *Mod. Mech.* 663 The Hoe automatic tension brake for graduating the feed of the paper to the exact speed of the machine.

b. The material supplied; also the amount supplied; the 'charge' of a gun.

1839 R. S. ROBINSON *Naut. Steam Eng.* 59 A cock by which the engineer can regulate the feed to the quantity required. **1869** *Eng. Mech.* 31 Dec. 389/1 By carrying less feed, less power may suffice. **1881** KNIGHT *Dict. Mech.* IV. 330/2 The actual feed to the boiler is regulated by a controlling cock. **1881** *Times* 24 Feb., The time was taken in which the guns could be cleaned and could fire three 'feeds'. **1883** *Daily News* 12 Dec. 2/5 The length of the feed is determined by the clutch.

c. Short for *feed gear, feed-pump*, etc.; a feeder.

1839 R. S. ROBINSON *Naut. Steam Eng.* 139 The water would fall lower and lower in the boiler, if not replaced by the feed. **1879** *Cassell's Techn. Educ.* IV. 340/2 The oil.. falls.. on the wool as it passes along the 'feed' to the teasing cylinder. **1957** *Encycl. Brit.* IX. 561/2 The feed for controlling the movement of the writing fluid [in a fountain pen] is made of plastic or of hard rubber.

d. *Theatrical slang.* = FEEDER 11. Also in extended and *attrib.* uses.

1929 J. B. PRIESTLEY *Good Companions* II. i, Joe over there ..is as good a feed as you could wish for. *Ibid.*, You couldn't want a better dancer... The only thing is, he won't feed. I never struck a worse feed. **1936** N. COWARD *To-night at 8.30* I. 94, I don't count—I'm only a feed. **1958** OSBORNE & CREIGHTON *Epitaph G. Dillon* II. 61, I suppose I give you what is known as the 'feed' line now. **1958** *Listener* 7 Aug. 189/1 He [*sc.* the interviewer] can lure his victim into a false sense of confidence with the easy-paced, perfectly staightforward, guileless 'feed' question. *Ibid.* 28 Aug. 311/1 English voices.. are nearly always used as 'feeds' for knowledgeable Americans [in broadcast discussions]. **1961** *John o' London's* 14 Sept. 307/2 Cantinflas, together with his feed-man Charamusca.

6. *attrib.* and *Comb.* **a.** simple attributive, (sense 3 and 3 b) as ***feed-bag, -bin, consumption, -crop, -house, -lot, -mill*** (U.S.), ***-rack, -stable, -station, -stuff, -yard***; (sense 5) as ***feed-bar, cistern, feed-cock, -dog*** [DOG *sb.*¹ 7], ***-hole, -pipe*** (also ***feed-pipe-cock, -strainer, -strum***), ***-pump.*** **b.** objective, (sense 3) as ***feed-chopper, -crusher, -cutter***; (sense 5) as ***feed-heating, -roller.***

1840 C. MATHEWS *Politicians* I. ii. 16 You prefer to be mystified more after the manner of a cartman's horse with his head in a *feed bag. **1874** KNIGHT *Dict. Mech.* I. 828/2 *Feed-bag*, a nose-bag for a horse or mule, to contain his noonday feed or luncheon. **1906** E. DYSON *Fact'ry 'Ands* v. 54 The bloke that comes canoodlin' here gets that in his feed-bag! **1962** *Punch* 4 July 30/1 The notion that viewers would like to see celebrities at their feed-bags. **1873** *Young Englishwoman* Mar. 131/2 The *feed bar and stitch mechanism are inclosed in a box. **1876** J. S. INGRAM *Centenn. Exposition* ix. 298 The radiating arms.. act against the feed-bar. **1898** M. DELAND *Old Chester Tales* 250 The open space between the stalls and the *feed-bins should be the stage. **1903** *Cincinnati Enquirer* 9 May 14/1 He got a motor for the corn sheller and *feed chopper. **1916** H. L. WILSON *Somewhere in Red Gap* vii. 304 Rex II [beagle] didn't get in till next day and looked like he'd come through a feed chopper. **1838** *Civil Engin. & Arch. Jrnl.* I. 237/2 The whole circle of pipes and vessels described, is supplied with water from the *feed cistern. **1967** *Gloss. Sanitation Terms* (*B.S.I.*) 14 *Feed cistern*, a cistern for supplying cold water to

a hot water system. **1833** B. SILLIMAN *Man. Sugar Cane* 56 It is drawn up into the vacuum pans..by the *feed cocks. **1883** W. C. RUSSELL *Sailors' Lang.* 49 *Feed-cock*, a cock near the bottom of a marine boiler for regulating the supply of water to the boiler. **1909** *Westm. Gaz.* 27 Aug. 2/3 Barley.. or other meal, which..form so large a factor in the *feed consumption of this country. **1891** *Daily News* 14 May 5/1 '*Feed' crops. **1881** KNIGHT *Dict. Mech.* IV. 527/2 **Feed-crusher*, a mill for flattening grain to render it more easily masticated. **1874** *Ibid.* I. 829/1 **Feed-cutter.* **1883** E. INGERSOLL in *Harper's Mag.* Jan. 207/1 He grinds all day at the feed-cutter. **1961** *Observer* 28 May 33/2 Its [*sc.* a sewing-machine's] *feed-dog tended to cockle nylon. **1961** *Which?* Nov. 285/1 Normally the feed dog feeds material directly towards or away from you. **1892** P. BENJAMIN *Mod. Mech.* 284 Power developed without *feed-heating. **1874** J. W. LONG *Amer. Wild-Fowl Shooting* 37 A quick loading flask, i.e., one having a large *feed-hole to the charger, should also be used. **1892** *Cooley's Cycl. Pract. Receipts* I. 300/2 Another complete but empty hive with open feed-hole, placed below an over-full one. **1961** C. H. DOUGLAS-TODD *Pop. Whippet* iii. 37 It [*sc.* the kennel-building] must incorporate the *feed-house..and the room..where all the 'paper work'..may be carried out. **1889** *Las Cruces* (New Mex.) *News* 16 Nov., [The new lower rate] allows Kansas feeders to ship from this territory or Arizona to their *feed lots. **1911** H. QUICK *Yellowstone Nights* vi. 165 Two boys.. had met in Allen's feed-lot to fight a duel. **1964** *Punch* 25 Nov. 807/1 They're..unlikely to..nest in electric fences, feedlots and barbed wire. **1884** *Milnor* (Dakota) *Teller* 13 June, A Steam *Feed-Mill..to grind all kinds of Feed. **1829** *Nat. Philos.* (Useful Knowl. Soc.) *Hydraulics* ii. 13 The stop-valve, covering the top of the *feed-pipe. **1839** R. S. ROBINSON *Naut. Steam Eng.* 59 At the end of each feed pipe is a cock. **1849–50** WEALE *Dict. Terms* 182/2 **Feed-pipe cocks*, those used to regulate the supply of water to the boiler of a locomotive engine. *Ibid.*, **Feed-pipe strainer*, or *strum*, a perforated, half-spherical piece of sheet iron..placed over the open end of the feed-pipe. **1839** R. S. ROBINSON *Naut. Steam. Eng.* 109 The engine supplies itself with water by a pump communicating with the hot well, called a *feed pump. **1854** RONALDS & RICHARDSON *Chem. Technol.* (ed. 2) I. 273 A small working cylinder..can be placed upon the top of the boiler to work the grate and the feed-pump. **1874** KNIGHT *Dict. Mech.* I. 830/2 **Feed-rack*, a stock-feeding device with grain-trough and hay-rack under shelter, which sometimes is extended to the stock also. **1836** URE *Cotton Manuf.* II. 17 The willowed cotton..is carried forward..to the *feed-rollers [of the blowing machine]. **1877** H. C. HODGE *Arizona* 154 Tucson has..four *feed and livery stables. **1902** O. WISTER *Virginian* ii. 13, I took its dimensions, twenty-nine buildings in all,—..one feed stable, and..others. **1910** W. M. RAINE *B. O'Connor* 106 Jay Hardman's place, a tumble-down *feed-station on the edge of town. **1856** *Porter's Spirit of Times* 4 Oct. 74/3 But a few years since our whole supplies of bread and *feed-stuffs [in Calif.] were drawn from abroad. **1909** 'O. HENRY' *Roads of Destiny* ix. 157 There was a feedstuff famine in Mexico. **1957** *Times* 2 Dec. p. ii/3 the post-war period.. until 1953 when feedstuffs were derationed. **1969** *Daily Tel.* 18 Dec. 18/1 The animal feedstuffs market. **1879** *Chicago Tribune* 14 May 7/4 The *feed-yards in Chicago are extensive. **1911** H. QUICK *Yellowstone Nights* iv. 109 One, two, three farmsteads we passed, with its white house hidden in trees, low hog-houses, its feed yards.

7. Special combinations: **feed-apron** = *feed-cloth*; **feed-bed**, (*a*) a feeding place (of rats); (*b*) the level surface along which the supply passes to the machine; **feed-block** (see quot. 1902); **feed-board**, a board on a printing machine to hold sheets of paper fed to the machine; **feed check valve** (also *feed check* ellipt.), a valve placed between the feed-pipe and the boiler, to prevent return of feed-water; **feed-cloth**, a revolving cloth which carries the cotton or other fibre into a spinning, carding or other machine; **feed collector** (see quot.); **feed-door**, the door through which the furnace is supplied with fuel; the furnace door; **feed-floor** *U.S.*, a floor off which cattle, etc., can eat food; **feed-'forward** [after FEEDBACK], (*a*) the use of calculated or presumed future states of a process to provide criteria for its adjustment or control; anticipatory control; (*b*) the modification of the output signal of a circuit by a part of the input signal that has not passed through the circuit; **feed gear**, the mechanism of feed-motion; **feed-hand** (see quot.); **feed-head**, (*a*) a cistern of water for supplying the boiler from above; (*b*) *Founding* (see quot. 1874); **feed-heater** = *feed-water-heater*; **feed horn**, a horn-shaped section of waveguide mounted in front of an aerial and used to direct a signal into it for transmission or to receive a detected signal from it; **feed-motion**, a contrivance for giving a forward movement to material in a machine; **feed-mouth** = *feed-door*; **feed-rod** = *feeding-rod*; **feed-room** *U.S.* and *N.Z.*, a room in which food for animals is stored; **feed-screw** (see quot.); **feedstock** orig. *U.S.*, 'raw material supplied to a machine or processing plant (as pulpwood to a paper mill)' (Webster 1961); also *transf.*; **feed-strip**, a cartridge belt for a machine gun; **feed-table**, a table indicating the food values of fodders; **feed-tank, -trough**, a tank or trough containing a supply of water for a locomotive; a supply trough; also, a tank containing drinking-water; *U.S.* a trough in which food for animals is placed; **feed-tub**, the supply vessel of an evaporator; **feed-wheel** (see quot.); **feed-wire** = FEEDER 10. Also FEED-WATER.

1836 URE *Cotton Manuf.* II. 16 The *feed-apron is about eight feet long. **1899** J. SOUTHWARD *Mod. Printing* III. ix. 108 The *feed board rises, the lays drop, and the grippers take the sheet. **1917** R. A. PEDDIE *Outl. Hist. Printing* 33 These machines print single sheets on both sides during their traverse from the feed-board to the delivery board. **1967** KARCH & BUBER *Offset Processes* ix. 372 The back paper-feed control..lever..permits the paper to feed on to the feedboard. **1876** *Forest & Stream* 7 Dec. 278/3 We shortly espy a '*feed-bed' in the edge of the marsh. **1889** *Pall Mall G.* 15 Oct. 7/1 Each letter in its passage along the feed-bed of the machine strikes a lever. **1895** H. T. LUKIN *Maxim Machine Gun* 11 What keeps the extractor at its highest until the cartridge is drawn from the *feed block? *Ibid.* 21 When loading for rapid fire, the crank handle is turned over to buffer spring twice and the belt is pulled through the feed block. **1902** *Encycl. Brit.* XXX. 401/2 The feed-block through which the belt of cartridges is fed to the gun. **1928** C. F. S. GAMBLE *N. Sea Air Station* xvi. 295 A left-hand feed-block, which was instantly interchangeable with the right-hand feed-block. **1895** *Daily News* 17 Dec. 3/5 To repair *feed check valve. **1908** *Westm. Gaz.* 25 Apr. 2/3 Off they went into the stokehole, where the Third put two of them to mind the feed-checks. **1836** URE *Cotton Manuf.* II. 16 The..cotton is..spread upon the *feed-cloth of the cards. **1902** *Encycl. Brit.* XXVI. 284/1 A horizontal cross-tube of square section, called a *feed collector, which extends the whole width of the [marine water-tube] boiler. **1872** *Rep. Vermont Board Agric.* I. 635 The ore..is landed at the feed door of the furnace. **1881** KNIGHT *Dict. Mech.* IV. 327/2 **Feed-door.* **1868** *Rep. Iowa Agric. Soc. 1867* 104 Put them [*sc.* hogs] in small yards with a good plank *feed-floor. **1952** I. A. RICHARDS in *Cybernetics: Trans. of Eighth Conf., 1951* 54 You have no doubt fed forward enough to see that what I am going to talk about from now on is *feed-forward. I am going to try to suggest its importance in describing how language works. **1961** E. J. BAGHDADY *Lect. Commun. Syst. Theory* xix. 505 The feedforward operation ..can be extended so that the amplifier bridges two or more cascaded narrow-band limiters. **1963** *Engineering* 6 Dec. 726/3 Anticipatory (feed-forward) control predicts the effect of input variables on output variables by solving transfer equations. **1888** *Lockwood's Dict. Mech. Engin.* 136 *Feed*, the amount or distance of the transverse of a lathe or other machine cutter taken transversely to the depth of the cut. The term is also applied to the *feed gear itself. **1895** *Daily News* 27 July 3/1 The torpedo boat destroyer Ferret, which broke down..owing to the defective working of her automatic feed gear. **1874** *Ibid.* I. 829/2 **Feed-hand*..a rod by which intermittent rotation is imparted to a ratchet-wheel. **1849–50** WEALE *Dict. Terms* 182/2 **Feed head.* **1874** KNIGHT *Dict. Mech.* I. 829/2 *Feed head*..the metal above and exterior to the mold which flows into the latter as the casting contracts. **1864** WEBSTER, *Feed-heater. **1885** *Marine Engineer* 1 Apr. 14/2 Although with the same area exposed, the feed-heater must be heavier..yet area for area the feed-heater must be much more efficient. **1952** *Electronics* May 126/3 The main beam from the scanner did not vary with *feed-horn rotation when the horn dimension was equal to three and to four-channel widths. **1962** F. I. ORDWAY et al. *Basic Astronautics* vi. 293 Radio energy from the antenna enters the feed horns. **1874** KNIGHT *Dict. Mech.* I. 830/1 **Feed-motion.* **1833** B. SILLIMAN *Man. Sugar Cane* 34 An opening into the furnace, called the *feed-mouth, for the supply of fuel and the regulation of the fire, is left. **1887** A. W. TOURGÉE *Button's Inn* 142 A great towel..hung inside the *feed-room door. **1923** 'K. MANSFIELD' *Doves' Nest* i, There it stayed..beside the feed-room door. **1939** —— *Scrapbook* 2 Every morning I went across to the feed-room where he cleaned father's boots. **1874** KNIGHT *Dict. Mech.* I. 830/2 **Feed-screw* (*Lathe*), a long screw employed to impart a regular motion to a tool-rest or to the work. **1932** BOEHTLINGK et al. tr. *Sachanen & Tilicheyev's Chem. & Tech. of Cracking* viii. 330 The hot oil pump circulates the clean *feed stock from the base of the bubble tower through the heater. **1958** *Times* 15 July 4/6 The erection of the first plant producing gas for town use from oil feedstocks. **1963** *Economist* 28 Sept. 1140/2 These..techniques..extended to use petroleum feedstocks. **1969** *New Scientist* 30 Jan. 233/3 Para-xylene, an essential feedstock in the manufacture of polyester fibres. **1969** *Sci. Jrnl.* Mar. 25/2 A gas centrifuge designed to separate the lighter uranium-235 isotope from the bulk uranium-238 (in the form of gaseous uranium hexafluoride feedstock). **1969** *Times* 1 July 5/8 Molten rocks might occur and thus provide feedstock for volcanoes. **1902** *Encycl. Brit.* XXX. 404/2 The breech-block..driving a cartridge in front of it out of the *feed-strip. **1886** C. SCOTT *Sheep-farming* 33 He can only examine the *feed tables.. and guess at the quality of his own fodders. **1886** *Marine Engineer* 1 Feb. 283 Storage-tanks..being connected by pipes to the small *feed-tanks situated above the boiler. **1923** *Man. Seamanship* (H.M.S.O.) II. 26 *Fresh Water Service.* The shipwright officer is responsible for this service (except supplies to the feed tanks). **1845** A. WILEY in *Indiana Mag. Hist.* (1927) XXIII. 212 To come with their wagons, and grain, and hay, and *feed troughs and watering buckets. **1854** J. R. BARTLETT *Pers. Narr. Explor. Texas* II. 12 All [the wagons] had to be provided with feedtroughs. **1867** *Rep. Iowa Agric. Soc.* (1868) 148 Our market is in the feed-troughs. **1889** G. FINDLAY *Eng. Railway* 108 A tender picks up water from the feed-trough while in motion. **1878** *Rep. Vermont Board Agric.* 109 The *feed tub will be high enough for the sap to run from that to the evaporator. **1874** KNIGHT *Dict. Mech.* I. 831/1 **Feed-wheel*, a continuously or intermittingly revolving wheel or disk which carries forward an object or material. **1881** *Ibid.* IV. 363/1 A plate on the feed wheel holds up the coal when the box is again brought forward. **1903** *Work* 1 Aug. 412/3 A *feed wire..will connect with the wires of the netting.

feed (fiːd), *v.* Pa. t. and pa. pple. fed. Forms: *Inf.* 1–2 fēdan, (1 *Northumb.* foedan), 2 feden, 3 *south.* veden, 2, 5 feyde, 3–4 feode, 3–6 fede, *south.* vede, 4–7 feede, 6 feade, 6– feed. *Pa. t.* 1 fēdde, *pa. pple.* fēded, fēdd; *pa. t.* and *pa. pple.* 3–5 fedde, (3 feedd, fad), 4 *south.* vedde, 4–5 feed, 9 *dial.* feeded, 4– fed. [OE. *fēdan* = OFris. *fêda*, OSax. *fôdean* (Du. *voeden*), OHG. *fuotan* (MHG. *vüeten*), ON. *fœða* (Da. *föde*, Sw. *föda*), Goth. *fôdjan*:—OTeut. **fôđjan*, f. **fôđ-â-*: see FOOD.]

1. a. *trans.* To give food to; to supply with food; to provide food for. Often followed by †*of*, *on*, *with* (a specified food).

c **950** *Lindisf. Gosp.* Matt. vi. 26 Eower fæder se heofunlica foedeþ þa [heofun fuȝlas]. *c* **1000** *Ags. Ps.* lxxx[i]. 1 b, He hi fedde mid fætre lynde hwæte. *a* **1175** *Cott. Hom.* 233 He us is..feder for he us fett. *c* **1205** LAY. 8944 He hine lette ueden ..ær he him bi-uoren come. **1297** R. GLOUC. (1724) 375 He ..made yt al forest & lese, þe bestes vorto fede. *c* **1340** *Cursor M.* 13372 (Trin.) Þe folke..was fed of breed & flesshe. *c* **1450** *Bk. Hawkyng* in *Rel. Ant.* I. 296 Fede your hawke and sey not geve here mete. **1592** DAVIES *Immort. Soul* XVI. i. (1714) 71 The Body's Life with Meats and Air is fed. **1648** SIR E. NICHOLAS in *N. Papers* (Camden) 115 Seeke for some allowance..to feede us. **1714** NELSON *Life Bp. Bull* §76. 437 About sixty necessitous People..were fed with Meat. **1756–7** tr. *Keysler's Trav.* (1760) II. 205 Gregory..was feeding twelve indigent men. **1798** WEBBE in Owen *Wellesley's Desp.* 9, I doubt whether there are any well-grounded expectations that they could feed themselves. **1835** URE *Philos. Manuf.* 394 The Leeds people are better fed. **1842** A. COMBE *Physiol. Digestion* (ed. 4) 142 Dogs fed on oil or sugar..become diseased. **1848** MACAULAY *Hist. Eng.* I. 314 It was not yet the practice to feed cattle in this manner.

b. To suckle (young); in OE. also *absol.*

c **950** *Lindisf. Gosp.* Matt. xxiv. 19 Wæ uutedlice ðæm berendum & foedendum in ðæm daȝum. *a* **1300** *Cursor M.* 5640 (Cott.) Þis womman..It [þe childe] fedd til it cuth spek and gang. **1530** PALSGR. 547/1 This bytche fedeth her whelpes. **1821** R. TURNER *Arts & Sc.* (ed. 18) 170 Pelias.. was fed by a mare. **1888** ELWORTHY *W. Somerset Word-bk.*, *Feed*, to suckle.

c. To put food into the mouth of (*e.g.* a child, a sick person, a fowl).

c **1440** *Promp. Parv.* 152/2 Feede chyldryn wythe pappe mete, *papo.* **1611** COTGR., *Appasteler*, to feed by hand, or with the hand; or, as a bird feeds her yong. **1638** MARKHAM *Farewell to Husbandry* 162 The Bitter is ever best to be fed by the hand, because when you have fed him, you may tie his Beake together. **1748** W. CADOGAN *Ess. Nursing* 19 A sucking Child should be fed..once with the Broth, and once with the Milk. **1872–4** L. WRIGHT *Poultry* 79 The fowl when fed is..held with both hands under its breast. **1882** J. W. ANDERSON *Med. Nursing* iv. (1883) 73 A patient..will not have the feeding cup, and yet must be fed in some such way. **1893** H. D. TRAILL *Social England* I. Introd. 54 His meal might be served up to him on costly dishes, but he fed himself with his fingers. *Mod.* He is so weak that he cannot feed himself.

d. To graze, pasture (cattle, sheep, etc.).

1382 WYCLIF *Gen.* xxxvii. 13 Thi britheren feden [**1388** kepen, **1611** feed] sheep in Sichemys. **1757** HOME *Douglas* II. i, My name is Norval; on the Grampian Hills My father feeds his flocks.

e. *feed-the-dove.* A Christmas game mentioned in *Brand's Pop. Antiq.* I. 278.

f. In slang phr. *to feed the bears*, to receive a ticket or pay a fine for a traffic offence: see BEAR *sb.*[1] 1 e. orig. and chiefly *U.S.*

1975 *Heavy Duty Trucking* May 33/2 Don't feed any of them cotton-pickin' bears there, guy. **1976** *CB Mag.* June 83/2 Truckers say warning each other of speed traps is their only defense against having to 'feed the bears' or collect a ticket from Smokey. **1980** S. BRAITHWAITE *CB in GB* 29 *Feed the bears*, get a speeding ticket.

2. *fig.* of 1. Const. as above.

a. simply; *esp.* in spiritual sense.

971 *Blickl. Hom.* 57 Seo saul, ȝif heo ne bið mid Godes worde feded. *c* **1200** *Trin. Coll. Hom.* 215 Eche heȝe dai [þe hodede sholde] fede mid godes worde þe hungrie soule. *c* **1380** WYCLIF *Sel. Wks.* III. 500 Þe soule is fedde wiþ charite. **1435** MISYN *Fire of Love* 58 Chosyn sawlis..with heuenly likynge is feed. **1579** FULKE *Heskins' Parl.* 274 A spirituall meate, to feede vs into eternall life. **1697** DRYDEN *Virg. Georg.* III. 767 He grinds his Teeth In his own Flesh, and feeds approaching Death. **1882** E. P. HOOD in *Leisure Hour* Apr. 225 The logic of satire has often been fed on fear.

b. To gratify, minister to the demands of (a person's vanity, desire of vengeance, or other passion); to sustain or comfort (a person) with (usually, fallacious) hopes. Cf. FOOD *v.* †*to feed forth, up* (earlier *to food forth*): to beguile, keep (one) quiet, with flattery, etc.; = AMUSE *v.* 4, 6.

c **1400** *Rom. Rose* 5428 She [Fortune]..fedith hym with glorie veyne. **1475** *Bk. Noblesse* (1860) 53 The said maister ..fedde hem forthe withe sportis and plaies tille [etc.]. **1530** PALSGR. 547/1 You haue fedde me forthe with fayre wordes longe ynoughe. **1577** NORTHBROOKE *Dicing* (1843) 141 [He] ..so continueth feeding himselfe with looking for the chaunge of the dice. **1594** SHAKS. *Rich. III*, IV. i. 65 To feed my humor, wish thy selfe no harme. **1602** MARSTON *Antonio's Rev.* I. i. Wks. 1856 I. 76 This morne my vengeance shall be amply fed. **1603** KNOLLES *Hist. Turks* 656 Craftily feeding him with the hope of libertie. *Ibid.* (1621) 114 Feeding him up with faire words. **1666** TEMPLE *Let. to Bp. of Munster* Wks. 1731 II. 15 He seems to feed himself and his Friend with the Hopes of a speedy Peace. **1726** LEONI *Alberti's Archit.* I. 66 a, Others, feeding themselves with great hopes of times to come. **1856** EMERSON *Eng. Traits, Wealth* Wks. (Bohn) II. 73 All that can feed the senses and passions..is in the open market.

c. in phrases, *to feed one's eyes, to feed one's sight.* Also, of the tongue, *to feed the ear.*

1590 SPENSER *F.Q.* II. vii. 4 In his lappe a masse of coyne he told, And turned upside downe, to feede his eye..with his huge threasury. **1625** BACON *Ess., Masques*, The Alteration of Scenes..feed and relieue the Eye. **1634** SIR T. HERBERT *Trav.* (1638) 159, I found few [monuments] to feed my eyes upon. **1641** J. JACKSON *True Evang. T.* I. 26 He fed his eyes by being a spectator of those wickednesses. **1738** WESLEY *Hymns, 'Who's this, who like the Morning'* ii, His

Tongue the Ear with Musick feeds. **1813** SCOTT *Trierm.* III. xix, The knight With these high marvels fed his sight.

†**d.** *to feed with money*: to bribe. *Obs.*

1567 J. HAWKYNS *Let. Sir W. Cecil* in *State P.* Dom. Eliz. 44. 13 They were by the Merchaunts fedd soe plentefully with mony. **1580** NORTH *Plutarch* (1676) 190 Anytus was the first that fed the Judges with Money.

3. a. *intr.* (rarely †*refl.* in same sense). To take food; to eat. Of persons now only *colloq.* Const. as in 1.

1387 TREVISA *Higden* (Rolls) VI. 19 þe corn..þerof þe colver ofte schulde fede hym self. **1486** *Bk. St. Albans* C viij a, She fedith on all maner of flesh. **1526** *Pilgr. Perf.* (W. de W. 1531) 5 b, The shale of the nut to be broken that he may fede of the cornell. **1556** *Aurelio & Isab.* (1608) N, Of hir delicate fleshe they [the Lions] fedde them. **1635** N. R. *Camden's Hist. Eliz.* II. 130 He fed hard at supper on sallats. **1703** POPE *Thebais* 686 Devouring dogs..Fed on his trembling limbs. **1719** DE FOE *Crusoe* (1840) I. x. 173 It was a good while before they [kids] would feed. **1757** CHESTERF. *Lett.* IV. cccxxii. 96 Go pretty often and feed with him. **1834** MCMURTRIE *Cuvier's Anim. Kingd.* 145 The ostrich feeds on grass. **1850** L. HUNT *Autobiog.* II. xvii. 252, I did wrong at that time not to 'feed better'. **1861** HUGHES *Tom Brown at Oxf.* i. (1889) 8 No one feeds at the high table except the dons.

b. transf. *to feed on* (a person): to live at his expense.

1733 POPE *Ess. Man* III. 61 All feed on one vain patron.

c. *fig.*

1540 CRANMER *Wks.* I. 25 Many holy martyrs..did daily feed of the food of Christs body. **1581** SIDNEY *Apol. Poetrie* (Arb.) 20 Whose milk..enabled them to feed..of tougher knowledges. **1599** *Warn. Faire Wom.* II. 1380 The people's eyes have fed them with my sight. **1612** ROWLANDS *Knaue of Harts* 29 On others miseries and woes, I feede. **1768** W. GILPIN *Ess. Prints* 10 The eye..may be pleased..by feeding on the parts separately. **1769** SIR W. JONES *Pal. Fortune* Poems (1777) 16 Grant me to feed on beauty's rifled charms. **1827** POLLOK *Course T.* IX, Disappointment fed on ruined Hope. **1883** *Standard* 20 July 5/1 Cholera feeds upon impurities of every sort.

4. *trans.* To yield or produce food for; to be, or serve as, food for (*lit.* and *fig.*). *to feed the fishes*: see also FISH *sb.*[1] 1 c.

a **1300** *Sarmun* li. in *E.E.P.* (1862) 6 þe siȝte of god him sal fede. **1393** GOWER *Conf.* III. 26 Suche is the delicacie Of love, which min herte fedeth. **1577** B. GOOGE *Heresbach's Husb.* I. (1586) 38 b, Fodder..very good to feede both cattel & Poultrye. **1669** WORLIDGE *Syst. Agric.* (1681) 28 One Acre of this Grass will feed you as many Cows as six Acres of other common Grass. **1697** DRYDEN *Virg. Georg.* III. 812 The Water-Snake, whom Fish and Paddocks fed. **1891** FARMER *Slang* II, *To feed the fishes*, to be drowned.

absol. **1665** SIR T. HERBERT *Trav.* (1677) 23 The air feeds not.

5. a. To supply with nourishment; to nourish, cause to grow, support, sustain.

a **1000** *Boeth. Metr.* xxix. 70 (Gr.) Se..metod..fet eall þætte groweð wæstmas on weorolde. *a* **1300** *Seven Sins* 33 in *E.E.P.* (1862) 19 Is fule bodi fede mid is siluir and is gold. **1398** TREVISA *Barth. De P.R.* IV. ix. (1495) 93 By the benefyce of blode al the lymmes of the body preuayle and be fedde. **1593** SHAKS. *Lucr.* 1077 A mountain-spring that feeds a dale. **1697** DRYDEN *Virg. Georg.* II. 486 Be mindful ..With Store of Earth around to feed the Root. **1719** WATTS *Hymns* I. xlviii, God..feeds the strength of every Saint. **1759** tr. *Duhamel's Husb.* I. i. (1762) 3 The trees had been fed by other roots. **1784** COWPER *Task* III. 662 Some [flowers] clothe the soil that feeds them. **1801** SOUTHEY *Thalaba* I. xxii, The ebony..A leafless tree..With darkness feeds its boughs of raven grain. **1837** DISRAELI *Venetia* I. ii, A rich valley, its green meads fed by a clear and rapid stream.

fig. **1626** BACON *Sylva* §114 Musick feedeth that disposition of the Spirits which it findeth. **1875** JOWETT *Plato* (ed. 2) III. 132 Poetry feeds and waters the passions.

†**b.** To nurture, bring up. *Obs.*

c **1320** *Sir Tristr.* 287 Fiftene ȝere he gan him fede. *c* **1400** *Destr. Troy* 623 Your-selfe..þe fresshist and fairest fed vpon erthe.

6. a. To fill with food, to pamper; to fatten, make fleshy; occas. of the food. *dial. to feed (full and) high, to feed up*: to supply or obtain with rich and abundant food.

1552 HULOET, Feade fatte in a francke or penne, *altilis.* Feade full, *saburratus.* **1630** *R. Johnson's Kingd. & Commw.* 79 This choice [the Steere] is altogether exempted from labour, and fed up for food. **1697** DRYDEN *Virg. Georg.* III. 319 Feed him full and high. **1788** W. MARSHALL *Yorksh.* Gloss., 'I mean to feed him,' I intend to fat him. **1823** J. BADCOCK *Dom. Amusem.* 62 A small dog..not to be fed too high. **1877** *N.W. Linc. Gloss.* s.v., He feeds five-an'-twenty steers every summer. **1886** *S.W. Linc. Gloss.* s.v., Milk will feed anything quicker than water. **1913** W. OWEN *Let.* 23 Apr. (1967) 185 Congratulations on the success of your feeding me up. —— *Let.* 6 Nov. 207 Began to 'feed up' today, but the difficulty is tremendous; i.e. of getting foods. *a* **1951** J. K. EWERS in *Austral. Short Stories* (1951) 335 I'll just help Larry feed up.

fig. **1596–1620** [see FAT *a.* 2 c]. **1874** MOTLEY *Barneveld* I. vii. 323 He remained in Paris,—feeding fat the grudge he bore to Barneveld.

b. *to feed off*: to fatten (an animal) for sale or slaughter.

1852 *Jrnl. R. Agric. Soc.* XIII. I. 224 The owner..feeds off a large number of sheep..annually. **1854** *Ibid.* XV. I. 112 The hoggets are..fed off before New Year.

c. *fig.* †With *on* adv.: To encourage the growth of (*obs.*). *to feed into*: to bring into by pampering. Also, (*Theat. slang*) *to feed a part*: to fill it out by the addition of details or incidents of minor importance; also, *trans.* and *intr.*, to supply another character with cues. (Cf. FEEDER 11, FEED *sb.* 5 d.)

1580 NORTH *Plutarch* (1676) 91 Publicola..was very diligent..to feed on further and encrease the same [sedition]. **1843** CARLYLE *Past & Pr.* (1858) 95 Fed into gigantic bulk. **1892** *Pall Mall G.* 22 Dec. 2/3 After this, endless complications all centreing on Mr. Penley—feeding the part would be the stage term. **1921** N. B. TARKINGTON *Let.* 21 Apr. (1959) 55 I've built it..craftily..so that the part isn't ever visibly 'fed'. **1929** [see FEED *sb.* 5 d]. **1929** D. G. MACKAIL *How Amusing* 66 I've had laughs I've earned, and laughs the other fellow's earned by my feeding him. **1968** *Listener* 11 July 59/3 The rest of the cast loll around, feeding the soloist with helpful questions.

†**d.** To give 'body' to (a liquor). *Obs.*

1667 DRYDEN *Wild Gallant* v. iii, Your vintners feed their hungry wines. **1742** *Lond. & Country Brew.* I. (ed. 4) Pref., Receipts for feeding, fining, and preserving Malt-Liquors.

e. *Tanning.* To give 'substance' to. Also, *intr.* of the leather: To gain substance; to thicken.

1882 J. PATON in *Encycl. Brit.* XIV. 389/2 The [kid] skins are..'fed' with yolk of eggs and salt. **1884** *Health Exhib. Catal.* 38 This rest allows the leather to 'feed'.

f. *intr.* To grow fat. *dial.*

1727 BAILEY vol. II, *Feeding*..growing in Flesh by eating. **1796** W. MARSHALL *Midland Counties* Gloss., *Feed*, to grow fat. **1877** *N.W. Linc. Gloss.* s.v., I nivver seed onybody feed like ——.

g. *Football*, etc. To give a pass to.

1889 BARRÈRE & LELAND *Dict. Slang* s.v., To *feed*, to support. **1897** *Encycl. Sport* I. 417/2 The way in which he can aid his side in attacking is by passing to, or, as it is called, feeding his forwards.

h. *slang. trans.* and *intr.* To tire or bore (cf. FED *pa. pple.*).

1933 G. HEYER *Why shoot a Butler?* iii. 47 Anyone can have the super motor boat as far as I'm concerned. Joan, too. She bars it completely, which feeds Brother Basil stiff. **1940** M. MARPLES *Pub. Sch. Slang* 77 'It's *feeding*, isn't it?' (i.e. calculated to make one *fed-up*).

i. To accompany (a musician, esp. a jazz musician); *spec.* to play accompanying chords for (a jazz soloist); also, to provide (an accompaniment.) *colloq.* (orig. *U.S.*).

1949 L. FEATHER *Inside Be-Bop* II. 59 The guitar..is employed like the piano to 'feed' or 'bop' the soloists by 'comping' with irregularly accented chords. **1955** in M. Stearns *Story of Jazz* (1957) xviii. 237 Lennie feeds his chords off the beat by use of irregular accents. **1958** P. GAMMOND *Decca Bk. Jazz* xii. 140 The pianist fed a progression of relevant chords in a manner which gave the soloist the greatest impetus.

7. a. To keep (a reservoir, watercourse, etc.) supplied; to supply (a fire, etc.) with fuel.

1582 in W. H. Turner *Select. Rec. Oxford* 426 Water cowrses..to feede youre pondes. **1596** SHAKS. *Merch. V.* III. ii. 266, I haue ingag'd..my friend to his meere enemie To feede my meanes. **1611** —— *Cymb.* I. vi. 110 The smoakie light That's fed with stinking Tallow. **1667** MILTON *P.L.* I. 68 A fiery Deluge, fed With ever-burning Sulphur unconsum'd. **1705** ADDISON *Italy* 274 The warm Springs that feed the..Baths. **1758** *Elaboratory laid open* 8 This manner of feeding the fire will be found a very great convenience. **1818** SCOTT *Hrt. Midl.* vi, The mob fed the fire with whatever they could find. **1869** E. A. PARKES *Pract. Hygiene* (ed. 3) 319 Cisterns at the top of every barrack should feed the ablution rooms. **1875** LYELL *Princ. Geol.* II. III. xlix. 608 Islands..large enough to feed small rivers. **1878** BOSW. SMITH *Carthage* 428 Cisterns..were fed..by the aqueduct of which they formed the termination.

b. To supply (a machine, a workman) continuously with material to work upon. Also *intr.* of the material: To pass in (to a mill).

1669 WORLIDGE *Syst. Agric.* (1681) 51 The Corn feeds not until you set the same [Engine] down again. *Ibid.* 52 In case you drive apace it feeds apace. **1707** MORTIMER *Husb.* 277 The breadth of the bottom of which [hopper] must be..near as long as the Rowlers, that it may not feed them too fast. **1808** J. BARLOW *Columb.* II. 503 She..fed The turning spindle with the twisting thread. **1879** GEO. ELIOT *Impressions of Theophrastus Such* xvii. 302 Each new machine needs a new appliance of human skill to construct it, new devices to feed it with material. **1891** FARMER *Slang* II, *To feed the Press*, to send up copy slip by slip. **1961** [see DAMP *a.* 4]. **1969** *Guardian* 18 Nov. 13/1 It is still cheaper to feed the meters (illegally) all day than pay the high price of off-street parking.

absol. **1676** BEAL in *Phil. Trans.* XI. 584 Two ordinary Labourers..(the one feeding, and the other grinding).

c. To relay or supply electrical signals or power to, esp. as part of a larger network or system.

1894 A. T. SNELL *Electric Motor Power* iv. 137 They.. feed the distributing network with current at a pressure of about 100 volts. **1952** E. A. LAPORT *Radio Antenna Engin.* ii. 132 It is necessary to feed each line with the potential that will transmit the proper amount of power down each line. **1966** *McGraw-Hill Encycl. Sci. & Technol.* XI. 251/2 Along the route there are Bell system offices, which feed local stations.

8. a. To cause to be eaten by cattle; to use (land) as pasture. Often with complementary adj. or adv. *to feed bare, close, down, off.*

a **1651** SIR RICHARD WESTON in *Hartlib's Legacy* (1655) 242 You may then feed the ground with Cattel all the Winter, as you do other ground. *Ibid.* 243 As it springs again, feed it with Cattel. **1652** ARNOLD BEATI in *Hartlib's Legacy* (1655) 139 It is very easie, by mowing or feeding it [corn] down with Cattel, to prevent it. **1669** WORLIDGE *Syst. Agric.* (1681) 23 As soon as you have fed it bare, then is it best to over-flow. *Ibid.* 28 The best Husbandry is to graze it, or feed it [grass] in Racks. **1707** MORTIMER *Husb.* 29 Take care to feed it [the grass] close before the Winter. **1807** R. PARKINSON *Experienced Farmer* I. 409 If he cannot feed it [Buck-wheat] off with some cattle. **1850** *Jrnl. R. Agric. Soc.* XI. II. 430 The crop being well grown, it only remains to feed it well off.

b. To deal out (food) *to* animals. Also with *out*, and with ellipsis of indirect object. Similarly, to supply (food) *to* (a person, etc.).

1818 in *Trans. Ill. State Hist. Soc. 1910* 158 They either have to feed out their corn or their cattle get very poor. **1852** *Trans. Mich. Agric. Soc.* III. 145, I feed almost every thing, hay, oats, straw, [etc.]. **1868** *Rep. Iowa Agric. Soc. 1867* 148 Corn is husked and cribbed and fed out to stock. **1883** P. E. GIBBONS in *Harper's Mag.* Apr. 652/1 Mangel-wurzel..is fed to the cows in winter. **1893** K. D. WIGGIN in *Atlantic Monthly* Feb. 184/1 He has been feeding bread and butter to the dog. **1904** *Grand Rapids Even. Press* 2 June 3 The professor..fed snake sandwiches to his college class at a party. **1911** R. W. CHAMBERS *Common Law* viii. 237 Rita.. fed them bits of cassava and crumbs of cake. **1946** *Harper's Mag.* Oct. 311/1 Now and then my father would have to borrow money to 'feed-out' the steers. **1961** NEW ENG. BIBLE *Matt.* vii. 6 Do not feed your pearls to pigs.

c. *transf.* (Cf. 7.) To supply continuously (material to be consumed or operated upon). Also, *to feed down*: to bring (a tool) down, gradually as required.

1860 PIESSE *Lab. Chem. Wonders* 82 Gold is fed into a vessel containing aqua regia. **1864** WEBSTER s.v. *Drill-press*, The tool B rotates and is fed down by hand or automatically. **1869** *Eng. Mech.* 19 Mar. 574/1 The wood is fed to the saw by means of a..roller. **1881** KNIGHT *Dict. Mech.* IV. 744/2 The string..is fed from a tin canister. **1883** H. TUTTLE in *Harper's Mag.* Nov. 824/2 The wet sand..is fed into the opening. **1884** W. H. RIDEING *ibid.* May 895/1 Long..tubes ..feed them to exquisitely adjusted scales.

†**d.** *Stock-exchange.* To deal *out* (stock) in portions. *Obs.*

1814 *Stock Exchange Laid Open* 28 Feeding out stock to less dealers.

e. *to feed back* (*Electr.* and *Cybernetics*): (i) to return (a fraction of an output signal) to an input of the same or a preceding stage of the circuit, device, process, etc., that produced it. Also *transf.* Chiefly in *pass.* (Cf. FEEDBACK.)

1921 *Wireless World* 10 Dec. 571/2 The magnified oscillations are fed back again into the grid circuit. **1940** *Nature* 7 Sept. 321/2 The pencil draws a curve and after an interval the information expressed by this curve is fed back to the machine. **1952** *New Biol.* XIII. 54 Information about this error must be 'fed-back' into the machine and cause it to alter its condition in such a direction as will diminish the error. **1960** O. SKILBECK *Film & TV Terms* 52 Part of an amplifier's own output may be deliberately fed back to reduce inherent sound distortion.

(ii) In *transf.* sense also used *intr.* of a result or effect of a process: to return as feedback; to affect or modify the process that brought it about.

1940 *Amateur Radio Handbk.* (ed. 2) iv. 65/2 Care should be taken..so that no output of this I.F. beat oscillator feeds back to the input of the I.F. amplifier. **1945** *Jrnl. Franklin Inst.* CCXL. 266 The *y*-shaft is driven by the output of integrator II and feeds back to drive the input of the function unit. **1960** R. W. MARKS *Dymaxion World of B. Fuller* 23/2 Since the benefits keep feeding back into the system, such techno-economic patterns are infinitely regenerative. **1964** M. A. K. HALLIDAY et al. *Linguistic Sci.* x. 275 The experience from the teaching of English to foreign learners is feeding back..to the teaching profession in Britain. **1966** *Rep. Comm. Inquiry Univ. Oxf.* I. 56 There are also advances in social studies, at postgraduate level, that are likely to feed back into undergraduate work.

f. *intr. to feed through*, to produce an effect elsewhere; to have consequences, esp. in the economy. Const. *in, into,* or *to.*

[**1975** *Business Week* 3 Nov. 25/2 When the cycle bottoms out, a slackening in the pace of inventory liquidation.. involves a boost in orders, production and employment— elements that feed through the economy.] **1979** *Economist* 24 Nov. 98/1 Not all of that [*sc.* inflation] will feed through, because raw materials and fuel make up only part of industry's costs. **1981** *Economist* 7 Feb. 64 The J-curve effect of West Germany's devaluation against the dollar should soon start to feed through in higher export volumes. **1982** *Ibid.* 27 Nov. 36/2 The results..suggested that the trade balance in manufactured goods would initially improve by £540m if devaluation did not feed through to higher wages. **1983** *Times* 16 Feb. 14/5 The increase in the speculative metals was led by gold, and it fed through into copper. **1983** *Ibid.* 14 Mar. 11/6 There is bound to be some time lag before the results feed through.

9. a. Of cattle: To eat, eat off, feed upon. Also, *to feed down, off.*

1725 POPE *Odyss.* IV. 452 A tim'rous hind..feeds the flow'ry lawns. **1858** *Jrnl. R. Agric. Soc.* XIX. I. 206 The fifty-two cows had..more than they could feed down. **1883** JEFFERIES *Nature near London* 237 The sheep have fed it too close for a grip of the hand. **1891** *West. Morn. News* 14 Sept., A crop of swedes..is again fed off by sheep.

b. *to feed down*: to eat off the food of.

1887 *Pall Mall G.* 20 Oct. 13/2 'Bunny'..feeds down the sheep.

feed (fiːd), *ppl. a.* [f. FEE *v.* + -ED[1].]

†**1.** Bound to feudal service. Only in *feed man*: see FEEDMAN. *Obs.*

2. Paid by fees; hired; bribed; *Sc.* employed for wages.

1579 FULKE *Heskins' Parl.* 389 One of the feeid and fed seruants of yᵉ Pope. **1601** SHAKS. *Twel. N.* I. v. 303, I am no feede poast, Lady; keepe your purse. **1602** MARSTON *Antonio's Rev.* IV. i. Wks. 1856 I. 117 When will the Duke hold feed Intelligence? **1628** VENNER *Baths of Bathe* (1650) 363 Such are his fee'd Agents. **1709** *Lond. Gaz.* No. 4562/4 [He] is Brother-in-Law to John Herstone of the Feed Gunners belonging to the Office of Ordnance. **1816** SCOTT *Old Mort.* xxxviii, She's no a fee'd servant. **1887** *Pall Mall G.* 2 Mar. 11/4 One of the fee'd speakers.

feed, obs. Sc. form of FEUD *sb.*[1], enmity.

feedable ('fi:dəb(ə)l), *a.* [f. FEED *v.* + -ABLE.] Capable of being fed. †**a.** That may be eaten off or grazed (*obs.*). **b.** That may be fed (with something).
1649 BLITHE *Eng. Improv. Impr.* iii. 12 Nor is [the land] grazable and feedable so soon. **1858** MISS MULOCK *Th. ab. Wom.* 44 A kissable, scoldable, sugar-plum feedable plaything.

'feedback, feed-back, *sb.* [f. FEED *v.* + BACK *adv.*] **a.** *Electr.* The return of a fraction of the output signal from one stage of a circuit, amplifier, etc., to the input of the same or a preceding stage; ***positive, negative feedback***, tending to increase, decrease, the amplification, etc.; also, a signal so returned.
1920 *Wireless Age* VIII. 27/1 An inductive feed-back in relation to the secondary system generates local oscillations. **1923** *Daily Mail* 19 May 4 The feed-back circuit. **1946** *Nature* 9 Nov. 670/1 The signal to noise ratio was increased by the application of positive feed-back to the tuned circuit. **1949** *Electronic Engin.* XXI. 358/3 To obtain the maximum stabilising effect it is desirable to take the feedback from the output and apply it at the input in the correct phase for degeneration. **1962** M. G. SAY *Newnes Conc. Encycl. Electr. Engin.* 289/1 The feedback principle is applied in electronic amplifiers, process controls and accurate servo-mechanisms.
b. *transf.* The modification, adjustment, or control of a process or system (as a social situation or a biological mechanism) by a result or effect of the process, esp. by a difference between a desired and an actual result; information about the result of a process, experiment, etc.; a response.
1943 *Philos. Sci.* X. 19 Purposeful active behavior may be subdivided into two classes: 'feed-back' (or 'teleological') and 'non-feed-back' (or 'non-teleological'). **1945** *Jrnl. Franklin Inst.* CCXL. 265 The shaft motion produced as the result of a sequence of operations is connected back into the sequence, a process called 'feed-back'. **1955** *Times* 31 Aug. 9/4 Only by constant 'feed-back' from the receptor can one ascertain how far a message has been understood rightly. **1959** J. L. M. TRIM in Quirk & Smith *Teaching of English* iii. 84 In..a lecture..the live speaker has a reaction, a 'feed-back' from the listeners, and..he can adjust his speech accordingly. **1962** *Listener* 30 Aug. 303/2 The feed-back from technology..has resulted in the production of more powerful and discriminating instruments. **1968** *Times* 6 Dec. 19/2 The production of both hormones seems to be regulated on a feedback mechanism by the level of calcium in the blood. **1970** *Sci. Amer.* Mar. 68/3 The brain has to receive feedback from the muscles and joints to correct the program of impulses directed to the motor apparatus. **1971** *Frendz* 5 Aug. 20/1 We began to get a fairly good feedback from most people who know about it and it looked as though the concerts would be good scenes.

feed-box ('fi:dbɒks). [f. FEED *sb.* + BOX *sb.*[2]] **a.** A box for containing fodder. **b.** A box containing the feeding apparatus of a machine.
1836 E. L. WILLSON *Diary* 21 May (1929), I..stood behind the wagon and held to the feed box. **1886** C. SCOTT *Sheep-Farming* 80 A number of small feed boxes, suitable for feeding the ewes in the pens. **1895** *Pall Mall Gaz.* 26 June 2/3 As if he had his nose in a feed-box and was looking for something nice. **1902** *Encycl. Brit.* XXX. 404/1 The platform on the top of the feedbox [of a machine gun] through which the teeth of the smaller feed-wheel project. **1947** *Time* 3 Feb. 20/3 Each tried to butt the other out of the feedbox.

feeder ('fi:də(r)). [f. FEED *v.* + -ER[1].] One who or that which feeds.
1. a. One who feeds or supplies food to (a person or animal); formerly often in contemptuous use, one who maintains (a parasite, a spy, etc.).
1579 TWYNE *Phisicke agst. Fort.* I. lxiv. 88 b, Often calling his Feeder by his name, and the better to perswade hym, flatteryng hym with [etc.]. **1616** *Rich Cabinet* 130 The horsse remembers..his feeder. **1653** MILTON *Hirelings* Wks. (1851) 387 Idleness, with fulnes of Bread, begat pride and perpetual contention with thir Feeders the despis'd Laity. **1683** *Loyal Observator* 11 His feeders..have..put him upon another jobb. **1725** POPE *Odyss.* XIV. 461 Those who..Blaspheme their feeder. **1826** DISRAELI *Viv. Grey* II. xv, Your Playing-up toady, who, unconscious to its feeder, is always playing up to its feeder's weaknesses. **1834** *Brit. Husb.* I. viii. 203 The feeder should be provided with an elastic ramrod. **1865** KINGSLEY *Herew.* (1866) I. x. 229, I am Hereward, the land-thief—sea-thief—the feeder of wolf and raven. **1868** GEO. ELIOT *Sp. Gipsy* 269 A handsome steed.. Neighs to new feeders.
b. *Sport.* A trainer (of cocks or horses). ? *Obs.*
1781 P. BECKFORD *Hunting* (1802) 57, I have inquired of my feeder..how he mixes up his meat. **1810** *Sporting Mag.* XXXVI. 55 The long main between the gentlemen of Staffordshire, Gosling feeder, and the gentlemen of Lancashire, Gilliver feeder, was won by the former.
c. *transf.* and *fig.*
1597 SHAKS. *2 Hen. IV*, v. v. 66 The Tutor and the Feeder of my Riots. **1616** HAYWARD *Sanct. Troub. Soul* I. ii. (1620) 30 The comforts thereof are..feeders thereof with sweet poison. **1634** M. SANDYS *Prudence* 176 Flattery..is the poysoning of Mans vnderstanding, the Feeder of humors. **1824** LAMB *Elia* II. *Blakesmoor in H——shire*, The solitude of childhood..is the feeder of love. **1849** *The Florist* 319 Numerous fibrous roots..act as feeders. **1867** SMYTH *Sailor's Word-bk.* 291 *Feeders*, in pilot slang, are the passing spurts of rain which feed a gale. **1887** GARNSEY tr. *De Bary's Fungi* 358 The plant or animal on which a parasite lives is termed its host or feeder.

2. a. One who or that which eats or takes food; an eater; usually with adj. prefixed, as *large, quick*, etc. Also, *feeder upon* (a specified food).
1562 J. HEYWOOD *Prov. & Epigr.* (1867) 106 Thone beyng an eater greedy and greate, Thother a weake feeder. **1612** WOODALL *Surg. Mate* Wks. (1653) 392 He..was a very large feeder. **1646** SIR T. BROWNE *Pseud. Ep.* II. vi. 98 The missell thrush, or feeder upon misseltoe. **1655** WALTON *Angler* (ed. 2) 277 He [the barbel] is a curious feeder. **1718** ROWE tr. *Lucan* 302 The rav'nous Feeders riot at their ease. **1733** CHEYNE *Eng. Malady* II. vii. §2 (1734) 186 No..full Feeder was ever opened, but he was found with some gross Fault in his Liver. **1798** R. PARKINSON *Experienced Farmer* I. 175 They [Downs Sheep] are..quick feeders. **1847** F. PARKMAN *Oregon Trail* xxv. (1872) 352 The carcass was completely hollowed out by these voracious feeders. **1885** CLODD *Myths & Dr.* II. iv. 165 The New Zealanders..were systematic feeders on human flesh.
b. One who eats at another's expense; a person dependent upon another for his food; a servant.
1600 SHAKS. *A.Y.L.* II. iv. 99, I will your very faithfull Feeder be. *a* **1625** FLETCHER *Nice Valour* III. i, Now servants he has kept, lusty tall feeders.
c. *transf.* Of a plant; also of a flame.
1799 J. ROBERTSON *Agric. Perth* 133 The latter [potato] being a more tender feeder. **1878** BROWNING *Poets Croisic* I Flame the stealthy feeder! **1882** *The Garden* 4 Feb. 87/3 The Fig..is a gross feeder.
d. *pl.* Cattle for feeding off or fattening.
1796 W. MARSHALL *Midland Counties* Gloss., *Feeders*.. fatting cattle. **1881** *Chicago Times* 1 June, Stockers and feeders were dull.
e. *dial.* One who grows abnormally fat.
1886 *S.W. Linc. Gloss.*, The whole family of them are feeders.
3. An instrument, organ, or appliance for feeding (senses 1 and 2): **a.** a spoon (*slang*); a child's feeding bottle; a bib; **b.** *Entom.* one of the organs composing the mouth-parts.
a. 1811 *Lexicon Balatronicum*, *Feeder*, a spoon. *To nab the feeder*; to steal a spoon. **1821** D. HAGGART *Life* (ed. 2) 69, I do not remember what became of the feeders. *Ibid.* 73, I bought two wedge table-feeders. **1886** *S.W. Linc. Gloss.*, *Feeder*, a child's bib; also a feeding-bottle, or cup with a lip. **1895** *Montgomery Ward Catal.* 80/1 Children's Feeders.. fancy printed designs...Size 10 × 12. **1932** D. C. MINTER *Mod. Needlecraft* 246/1 *Feeder*. Oblong 9" × 12" with neck hollowed out..plaited cord sewn on for tying. **1966** *Price List* (Olney Amsden & Sons) 1 Bibs and Feeders. Plastic.. Feeders..12/- dozen.
b. 1826 KIRBY & SPENCE *Introd. Entom.* IV. 308 Feeders retracted (*Trophi retracti*) when in a perfect mouth the *Trophi* are not capable of being much pushed out or drawn in. Feeders retractile, when..the Trophi can be considerably pushed forth or drawn in.
4. a. One who attends to the feeding of a flock; a herdsman, shepherd. ? *Obs.*
1611 BIBLE *Gen.* iv. 2 Abel was a keeper [*margin* feeder] of sheep. **1710** PHILIPS *Pastorals* v. 9 When, with the Flocks, their Feeders sought the Shade. **1807** G. CHALMERS *Caledonia* I. II. vi. 309 They had only advanced..from being hunters, to being feeders of flocks.
b. *fig.*
a **1400-50** *Alexander* 2961 Is þis nogt Philip son þe firs þe fedare of grece? **1413** LYDG. *Pilgr. Sowle* IV. xxix. (1859) 62 O thou wretchyd herd and fals feder of the hows Israel. *c* **1430** *Life St. Kath.* (1884) 98 He ys my God my louer and my feder. **1597** HOOKER *Eccl. Pol.* v. lxxxi. (1611) 438 They are commanded to bee..leaders, feeders, superuisors amongst their owne. **1659** TORRIANO, *Pastóre*..a Pastor or a Preacher, as it were a Feeder of souls.
5. a. One who feeds up or fattens (an animal), *esp.* one whose business it is to feed cattle for slaughter.
c **1430** *Pilgr. Lyf Manhode* I. iv. (1869) 2 A foulere oþer a feedere of briddes. **1669** WORLIDGE *Syst. Agric.* (1681) 176 In fatting of Geese..The Jews.. are esteem'd the skillfullest Feeders that be. **1893** *Daily News* 15 Feb. 5/8 The trade would become paralysed and both feeders and labourers suffer immensely.
†**b.** *humorously.* A crammer, tutor. *Obs.*
1766 GOLDSM. *Vic. W.* vii, Mr. Thornhill came with..his chaplain and feeder. **1787** *Gentl. Mag.* LVII. 869/2 A Feeder, by which is meant a person who..crams into the head of a candidate for a degree certain ideas which [etc.]. [**1848** DICKENS *Dombey* Mr. Feeder, B.A].
6. a. A stream which flows into another body of water; a tributary; also *attrib.*, as ***feeder-stream***.
1795 J. PHILLIPS *Hist. Inland Navigation* Addenda 94 To make navigable the cut or feeder from the town of Wendover, to join the canal at Bulbourne. *Ibid.* 97 No water to be taken from the feeders of the river Witham. **1800** MRS. HERVEY *Mourtray Fam.* IV. 249 An immense torrent.. becoming one of the feeders of the Lake. **1826** J. WILSON *Noct. Ambr.* Wks. 1855 I. 48 Just as I had cleared the feeder-stream..up springs a reindeer. **1832** *Act 2-3 Will. IV*, c. 65 §5 The point at which a burn or feeder joins a loch. **1878** HUXLEY *Physiogr.* 37 The Kennet..is one of the main feeders of the Thames.
transf. and *fig.*
1817 J. SCOTT *Paris Revisited* (ed. 4) 12 The downfall of great states has usually been produced by a disregard of the sources of alienation, and the feeders of discontent. **1861** MAX MÜLLER *Sc. Lang.* ii. 49 Dialects have always been the feeders rather than the channels of a literary language. **1868** J. H. BLUNT *Ref. Ch. Eng.* I. 71 As a feeder to this great college, Wolsey founded another. **1893** *Times* 27 Apr. 9/5 The Post office actually increases the business of the banks by acting as a feeder.
b. *spec.* 'A water course which supplies a canal or reservoir by gravitation or natural flow' (W.).
1825 *Beverley Lighting Act* ii. 11 Canal, aqueduct, feeder, pond. **1837** WHITTOCK *Bk. Trades* (1842) 201 The feeder is constructed so as to promote a current in its waters to the head of the reservoir. **1866** *Cornhill Mag.* Mar. 367 Another sweet-water canal, which is to be an essential feeder of the principal channel.
c. In wider sense: A centre or source of supply. In quots. *fig.*
1817 COLERIDGE *Lay Serm.* 377 Our religious opinions, out of which..all our other opinions flow, as from their spring-head and perpetual feeder. **1872** O. W. HOLMES *Poet. Breakf.-t.* iii. (1891) 80 The sources from which a man fills his mind,—his feeders, as you call them.
attrib. **1892** *Pall Mall G.* 26 Sept. 5/1 Looking down.. from the edge of the great glacier-feeder basin.
d. A branch road, railway line, air service, etc., linking outlying districts with the main lines of communication. Freq. *attrib.* (see 12).
1855 *Chicago Times* 25 Jan. 2/3 This road has many lateral roads as feeders to it. **1858** SIMMONDS *Dict. Trade*, *Feeder*, ..a branch railway, running into the main-trunk line. **1882** *Daily Tel.* 8 Nov. 5/7 It is proposed to construct lines of a less substantial character, to act as feeders to the main lines. **1902** *Encycl. Brit.* XXIX. 445/1 The construction..of branch [railway] lines..forming feeders. **1904** BELLOC *Old Road* 105 It was a branch track..one of the many 'feeders' which confuse the record of the Old Road. **1961** *Guardian* 29 Apr. 12/1 The airport [at Birmingham] will act as a feeder for Manchester and London.
7. *Mining.* **a.** A smaller lode falling into the main lode or vein.
1728 NICHOLLS in *Phil. Trans.* XXXV. 403 Small Branches opening into them in all Directions; which are by the Miners term'd, the Feeders of the Load. **1805** MUSHET *ibid.* XCV. 165 Towards the feeder it seemed loose and crumbly. **1869** R. B. SMYTH *Goldfields Victoria* 610 *Feeder*, a spur falling into a reef increasing..its size and richness.
b. An underground spring or runner of water.
1702 SAVERY *Miner's Friend* 35 When once you know how large your feeder or spring is. **1789** BRAND *Newcastle* II. 679 They know when any feeder of water is pricked. **1892** *Daily News* 16 Mar. 5/7 Abnormally heavy feeders of water.
c. A stream of gas escaping through a fissure in the ground; a blower.
1881 in RAYMOND *Mining Gloss.* **1883** in GRESLEY *Coal-mining Terms* 104.
8. One who or that which supplies material for consumption or elaboration.
a. One who 'feeds' material to a machine.
1676 BEAL in *Phil. Trans* XI. 584 By this..may two workmen, and one feeder, grind 20 bushels of Apples in an hour. **1835** URE *Philos. Manuf.* 155 The person who attends this machine..is called the feeder. **1886** *Pall Mall G.* 18 June 5/1 On a raised platform stands the feeder, with his spade, and it is his duty to shovel the quartz into the hopper. **1888** JACOBI *Printers' Voc.* 43 *Feeder*, the lad who lays on the sheets in a printing machine.
b. The player who tosses the ball to the batsman (in 'Rounders' and similar games). Hence, the name of a particular game resembling rounders.
1844 *Boy's Treasury* 17 The players next toss up for the office of feeder. *Ibid.* 18 This game [Rounders] differs from feeder only in the following particulars. **1875** 'STONEHENGE' *Brit. Sports* III. I. iv. §1. 686 The feeder is allowed to feign a toss of the ball.
c. An apparatus or a portion of an apparatus, often in the form of a hopper, into which the material to be treated is placed in order to be supplied to the machine in regulated quantities.
1669 WORLIDGE *Syst. Agric.* (1681) 51 Observe whether it will hold out..and accordingly proceed and rectifie the Feeder. **1823** J. BADCOCK *Dom. Amusem.* 79 The feeder, which coming from an air-tight vessel..full of oil, it drops slowly into the centre of the iron vessel. **1870** *Public Opinion* 16 July 81 The new feeder is a single-acting plunger pump. *a* **1877** KNIGHT *Dict. Mech.* I. 829/1 *Feeder*,..a device with fingers which take the top sheet from a pile and lead it into the press where it is printed, [etc.]. Also a device by which blanks are taken successively from a pile and carried into an envelope-machine, [etc.]. **1892** P. BENJAMIN *Mod. Mech.* 859 Automatic..feeder..to feed the grain easily. **1940** *Chambers's Techn. Dict.* 326/1 *Feeder*, a mechanical appliance for supplying broken rock or crushed ore..to some form of crusher or concentrator.
d. The lower chamber in an organ bellows which supplies the upper chamber or reservoir with wind.
1852 SEIDEL *Organ* 36 The lower one, called the feeder.. when pressed down, produces the wind. **1870** E. J. HOPKINS *Organ* 14.
e. *Naut.* A reserved compartment between decks for filling up the vacancy in the hold caused by the settling down of grain, etc.
1890 *Daily News* 10 Dec. 5/8 The cargo was secured in the usual way..seven large feeders in the 'tween-decks.
9. *Metal-casting.* **a.** (See quot. 1858.) Also *attrib.*, as ***feeder-head***. **b.** 'The opening made in a foundry mould for the introduction of the feed rod' (Lockwood).
1858 SIMMONDS *Dict. Trade* 149/2 *Feeder*..a large head or supply of fluid iron to a runner or mould in heavy castings. **1892** *Lockwood's Dict. Mech. Engin. Terms* 136 *Feeder head* ..a mass of metal which has been utilised for feeding a mould. **1928** W. RAWLINSON *Mod. Foundry Op. & Equip.* xviii. 255 For heavy castings, a feeder (or feeders) of suitable size and shape..is employed, this feeder being located to connect to the top of the casting or to the part of thickest section. **1928** *Jrnl. Iron & Steel Inst.* CXVII. 404 A refractory-lined feeder head is invariably used. **1958** *Ibid.* CLXXXIX. 263/2 It is generally held that the feeder head is useful because products of flotation from the ingot body rise into that part, which is eventually scrapped. **1960** R. LISTER *Decorative Cast Ironwork* ii. 24 Another reason for the presence of the sprue and pouring basin is to provide a reservoir to ensure that there is sufficient metal to fill out

every part of the mould cavity. For the same reason a riser, feeder, feeding head, or shrink head may be used.

10. *Electrical Engineering.* **a.** A heavy untapped main for carrying electrical energy to a distribution point or system. **b.** A branch-wire to supply a house, etc. An electrical connection between an aerial and a transmitter or receiver of electro-magnetic waves.

1886 G. KAPP *Electric Transm. Energy* viii. 213 Another kind of junction..is the so-called 'junction safety catch box', designed for connecting so-called 'feeders' with certain points in the network of mains. **1892** *Electrical Engineer* 16 Sept. 287/2 The Northampton Electric Light and Power Company have equal weights of distributing mains and feeders. **1928** STERLING & KRUSE *Radio Man.* xiv. 529 The single wire transmission line type of feeder requires that the feeder be connected to the antenna at a voltage loop. **1930** H. P. SEELYE *Electrical Distribution Engin.* vi. 82 In the general distribution in the built-up districts of a large town or city, it is usually advantageous to divide the territory served into distinct feeder areas. **1954** E. MOLLOY *Radio & Telev. Engin. Ref. Bk.* xxi. 24 Co-axial and twin feeders in general communication use for television reception will reduce the signal by about half (6 db) if 200 ft. is used. **1962** *B.S.I. News* Sept. 21 Two-pin connectors for balanced television feeders. **1968** 'E. MCBAIN' *Fuzz* xii. 188 Into this substation ran high-voltage supply cables ('They're called feeders,' Ahmad said) from a switching station.

11. *Theatrical.* (See quot. 1886.)

1866 W. DAVIDGE *Footlight Flashes* xvii. 220 Not a scene that wasn't a complete feeder from beginning to end. **1886** *Stage Gossip* 70 A part or character that is constantly giving cues for another character to 'score off' or 'cannon off' is known as a 'feeder'. **1957** *Oxf. Compan. Theatre* (ed. 2) 106/1 The comedian..was assisted also..by..the straight man or 'feeder', who was dressed in perfect evening attire.

12. *attrib.* and *Comb.* (sense 6 d) ***feeder airport, line, liner, plane, railway, road, service***; **feeder ear**, a metal fitting attached to a tramway contact wire. Also, **feeder-head** (see sense 9 a), **-stream** (sense 6).

1962 *Aeroplane* CIV. 13/1 Colchester industrialist, Mr. Geoffrey Woods has purchased the disused R.A.F. airfield at Wormingford and is to hold it in trust for the town for future development as a 'feeder' airport. **1970** *Daily Tel.* 10 July 12 The Plymouth City Council is proposing to construct a 'feeder' airport in a beautiful situation only a mile from the edge of the town. **1924** ROGET *Dict. Electr. Terms* 87/2 *Feeder ear*, a special type of trolley wire ear to which a feeder is connected. **1895** *Westm. Gaz.* 6 June 6/2 The policy of building what are known as feeder lines is one that is much advocated by politicians who take an active interest in the future of India. **1903** EARL OF CROMER in *Daily Chron.* 30 Jan. 5/5, I want feeder lines to Kassala. **1922** *Flight* XIV. 198/1 Once the airship service was started, branch or feeder lines operated with aeroplanes or seaplanes would be established almost at once. **1969** *Jane's Freight Containers 1968–69* 452/1 Lighter feeder-line transport in production and world-wide service. **1946** *Aeroplane Spotter* 16 Nov. 266/1 Twenty de Havilland Doves have been ordered by the Argentine Government; these will be used as 'feeder liners', operating in conjunction with the Vickers Vikings operating the main routes. **1949** *Flight* 24 Nov. 683 The C.A.S.A. group in Spain has developed the Type 201 Alcotan, as a feederliner and crew trainer. **1971** J. STROUD *World's Airliners* xiii. 109 Switzerland has produced a successful feederliner. **1934** *Flight* 15 Feb. 148/2 The company will operate without a Government subsidy and will employ..two feeder planes. **1959** *Observer* 8 Nov. 5/1 You start at a roundabout..on a strange feeder road..only two lanes in width. **1961** *Architect & Building News* 21 June 813 It is possible to drain traffic smoothly away into great feeder roads and motorways. **1933** *Meccano Mag.* Feb. 111/1 'Feeder' air services are now being operated in conjunction with both the Indian and African Empire air mail services. **1934** *Jrnl. R. Aeronaut. Soc.* XXXVIII. 508 Small in total prospect, but first in present availability, comes airport feeder service. Vertical flight would enable air travellers to take off from the centre of the city for transfer to air liners at the outlying airports. **1958** *Times* 21 Apr. 14/5 Special road feeder services were provided on numerous occasions for long distance rail excursions. **1971** *Nature* 19 Feb. 518/2 The best arrangement yet for using super-sonic transports—a shuttle service between Newfoundland or Maine and Ireland, with subsonic feeder services from the terminals.

feeding ('fiːdɪŋ), *vbl. sb.* [f. as prec. + -ING¹.]

1. The action of the vb. FEED, in its various senses.

c **897** K. ÆLFRED *Gregory's Past.* v. 42 Sio feding ðara sceapa. *c* **1320** R. BRUNNE *Medit.* 39 Þe fyrst ys a bodly fedyng. **14..** *Epiph.* in *Tundale's Vis.* 120 Thys day is named Phagyphanye..For thys word *phagy*..Is seyd of fedyng. *c* **1475** *Babees Bk.* (1868) 7 In youre fedynge luke goodly yee be sene. **1526** *Pilgr. Perf.* (W. de W. 1531) 137 Pamperyng..our bodyes by..moche fedyng of delycate meates and drynkes. **1676** RAY *Corr.* (1848) 122 Skill in the feeding..of singing-birds. **1725** SLOANE *Jamaica* II. 285 According to its feeding on venemous or not venemous food, 'tis wholesome or poysonous. **1803** DAVY in *Phil. Trans.* XCIII. 272 The feeding of leather in the slow method of tanning. **1837** DICKENS *Pickw.* viii, There was not a gleam of ..anything but feeding in his whole visage. **1879** GEO. ELIOT *Theo. Such* i. 15 A feeding up into monstrosity. **1897** *Encycl. Sport* I. 404/2 Many aver that..Alan Rotherham was the first to reduce the art of feeding to a science. **1929** J. B. PRIESTLEY *Good Companions* II. i. 253 This feeding I'm talking about..is a name in the profession for working up to gags.

2. a. *concr.* That which is eaten; food. Now *rare.*

1398 TREVISA *Barth. De P.R.* XVIII. i. (1495) 736 Some beestys gadre store of mete and fedynge. *c* **1440** *Promp. Parv.* 152/2 Fedynge, or fode, *pastum.* **1532–3** *Act 24 Hen. VIII*, c. 3 Beoffe, mutton, porke, and veale..is the common feedyng of..poore persons. **1581** MULCASTER *Positions* xxxvii. (1887) 148 Will ye let the fry encrease, where the feeding failes? **1653** WALTON *Angler* 148 His [the Pike's] feeding is usually fish or frogs. **1866** *Handy Horse Bk.* 20 So should the horses feeding be augmented by one-third.. more than usual.

†**b.** *to take feeding* (*of*): to feed (upon). In quot. *fig.*

c **1500** *Melusine* 298 Her of whom myn eyen toke theire fedyng.

†**c.** Nourishment, sustenance. *Obs.*

1547 BOORDE *Brev. Health* Pref. 4 Consider if..the sickenes in the exterial partes have any fedynge from the interial partes.

3. Grazing-ground or pasture land; pasturage, feeding-ground. *Obs.* exc. *dial.*

c **1430** *Pilgr. Lyf Manhode* II. cix. (1869) 116 He..ouerthroweth here feedinges [*pasturaux*]. **1467** *Bury Wills* (1850) 47 Alle the landys, medewes, pasturys, and fedyngys callyd Southwode. **1554–5** *Act 2–3 Phil. & Mary* c. 3 Lands or feedings, apt for milch kine. **1627** SPEED *England* iii. §4 Kent ..in some things hath the best esteeme: as in..feedings for Cattell. **1669** WORLIDGE *Syst. Agric.* (1681) 31 The Spring and Autumn feeding, whereon six or eight Cattle usually grazed. **1768** BOSWELL *Corsica* i. (ed. 2) 40 Sheep..have fine feeding. **1840** SPURDENS *Suppl. Voc. E. Anglia* s.v., 'You turned your horse into my feeding.'

4. *attrib.* and *Comb.* **a.** simple attrib., as ***feeding-barley, -cake, -cock, -ground, -habit, -hole, -house, -land, -linseed, -machine, -metal, -pipe, -place, -room, -stuff, -trough, -vessel, -work.***

1884 *York Herald* 19 Aug. 7/2 *Feeding foreign barley. **1883** *Encycl. Brit.* XV. 511/1 *Feeding cakes, pulse, and other..feeding stuffs. **1827** FAREY *Steam Engine*, 369 Regulate the *feeding cocks..so as to give the requisite supply. **1847** MARRYAT *Childr. N. Forest* xiv, It is all good *feeding-ground. **1933** *Brit. Birds* XXVII. 4 Until something exact is known of its distribution and numbers no correct interpretation of its *feeding-habits can be made. **1959** E. F. LINSSEN *Beetles Brit. Is.* I. 55 The effect of feeding-habits—environment and type of food—on larvae. **1868** F. H. JOYNSON *Metals* 71 In this country the *feeding hole of the furnace is generally closed. **1901** *Feilden's Mag.* IV. 436/2 With a steeper inclination..to a 'feeding-hole' for the admission of refuse from the platform above. **1807** VANCOUVER *Agric. Devon* (1831) 87 A gentleman..is judiciously distributing his *feeding-houses..over all the highest parts of his farms. **1873** TEGETMEIER *Poultry Bk.* xxix. 370 Supply a bed of clean straw in the feeding-house. **1886** *S.W. Linc. Gloss.*, *Feeding land, grazing land. **1887** *Daily News* 28 June 2/5 Not much business passing in *feeding linseed. **1873** J. RICHARDS *Wood-working Factories* 142 *Hand-feeding machines. **1891** *Lockwood's Dict. Mech. Engin. Terms* 136 The *feeding metal is..supplied in small quantities. **1669** WORLIDGE *Syst. Agric.* (1681) 52 Just behind the Share and *Feeding-pipe. **1611** BIBLE *Nahum* ii. 11 Where is..the *feeding place of the yong Lions? **1907** *North Amer. Rev.* CLXXXVI. 18 Another cheap feeding-place—the 'Miners' Restaurant'. **1910** *Blackw. Mag.* Mar. 614/1, I was wet, miserable, and tired, so I passed into the common *feeding-room. **1883** *Feeding-stuffs [see *feeding-cake*]. **1825** J. NICHOLSON *Operat. Mechanic* 403 The flax is fed or supplied in handsfull on the *feeding-trough. **1867** 'T. LACKLAND' *Homespun* II. 170 It will pay you well to feed your beast..in the feeding-trough under the shed. **1942** W. FAULKNER *Go down, Moses* 227 Corrals and feeding-troughs. **1859** LUARD in *Archæol. Cant.* II. 8 *Feeding-vessels for the chickens. **1682** HICKERINGILL *Black Non-Conformist* Wks. (1716) II. 144 This necessary *feeding-work of a good Shepherd.

b. Special comb., as **feeding board** = *feed-board* (FEED *sb.* 7); **feeding-bottle**, a glass bottle for supplying artificial food to infants; also *attrib.* in figurative sense; **feeding-box**, (*a*) a compartment in which a horse is placed to be fed; (*b*) in *hot air feeding-box*, an appliance for 'feeding' hot air to a stove; **feeding-cloth** = *feedcloth*; **feeding-cup** (see quot.); **feeding-drum**, a drum used for feeding certain kinds of furnaces; **feeding-engine, -head, -needle** (see quots.); **feeding-piece**, grazing ground; **feeding-rod**, a small metal rod used for keeping an open passage in a casting during the process of feeding; †**feeding-stead**, a pasture; **feeding-time**, (*a*) a time for taking food; meal-time; (*b*) *dial.* genial or growing weather (for crops); (*c*) the time at which animals in captivity are fed (recent examples of sense (*a*) usually have joc. allusion to (*c*)); **feeding-trace**, a track showing where animals have obtained food; **feeding-tube** (see quot.).

1892 J. SOUTHWARD *Princ. & Progress Printing Machinery* v. 29 The *feeding board, at first, consisted of merely a board like a desk, attached to the upper part of the machine. **1919** C. T. JACOBI *Printing* xxix. 301 To perform this correctly the second side in printing should be laid to the reverse end of the feeding-board. **1951** S. JENNETT *Making of Books* (1964) vii. 99 At the front of the machine is the feeding board, a large wooden surface sloping gently down towards the base of the cylinder. **1858** SIMMONDS *Dict. Trade* 149/2 *Feeding-bottle. **1884** *St. James' Gaz.* 2 Feb. 3/1 Napoleon foresaw the results of this feeding-bottle policy. **1887** *Hackney Gaz.* 9 Feb. 2/7 Fitting up infant's feeding-bottles. **1883** *Encycl. Brit.* XV. 511/1 When the manure is made in *feeding-boxes. **1884** *Health Exhib. Catal.* 65/1 Grates..with..hot air feeding box. **1821** *Specif. of Barker & Harris's Patent* No. 4574. 4 The material [fur] to be cleared being taken off the feeding cloth or endless web. **1882** J. W. ANDERSON *Med. Nursing* iv. (1883) 73 See that the *feeding cup and all vessels used for food are kept clean. **1884** *Syd. Soc. Lex.*, *Feeding-cup*, a vessel with a spout for the feeding of a sick person whilst lying down. Also, an oblong shallow vessel with a tubular end, to which a teat can be affixed for the artificial feeding of young children. **1854** RONALDS & RICHARDSON *Chem. Technol.* (ed. 2) I. 151 As each scraper comes in turn under the *feeding-drum, the coal which has fallen between each of them will be carried forward. **1874** KNIGHT *Dict. Mech.* I. 830/1 **Feeding engine*, a supplementary engine for feeding the boiler, when the main engine is stopped. *Ibid.*, **Feeding-head* (Founding), an opening in a mould..which supplies metal as the casting contracts. **1831** BREWSTER *Nat. Magic* xi. (1833) 289 A *feeding-needle [in the tambouring machine] which by a circular motion round the working-needle, lodged upon the stem of the latter the loop of the thread. **1796** W. MARSHALL *Midland Counties* Gloss, **Feeding-piece.* **1892** *Lockwood's Dict. Mech. Engin. Terms* 136 **Feeding-rod.* **14..** *Voc.* in Wr.-Wülcker 600 *Pascua*, a *ffedyngstede. **1832** *Chambers's Edinb. Jrnl.* I. 77/1 He had some reason to believe the Lion of the North..was best worth seeing at *feeding time. **1844** S. BAMFORD *Pass. Life Radical* v. 27 A howl as wild and remorseless as that from a kennel of hounds at feeding time. **1844** LADY STANLEY *Let.* 8 Dec. in N. Mitford *Ladies of Alderley* (1938) 105 It is the very large family altogether & especially feeding time that is oppressive. **1887** *S. Cheshire Gloss.*, 'It's a rare feedin' time for th' turmits.' **1888** *Illust. Lond. News* Christmas No. 11/1 A bell rang. There's feeding-time, we'd best go down. **1961** A. WILSON *Old Men at Zoo* i. 10, I had become quite deaf to the customary loud orchestra of a whole Zoo... I registered the feeding times only subliminally. **1856** KANE *Arct. Expl.* II. iii. 38 The numerous *feeding-traces [of rabbits] among the rocks. **1884** *Syd. Soc. Lex.*, **Feeding tube*, an elastic tube ..which is passed into the stomach.

feeding ('fiːdɪŋ), *ppl. a.* [f. as prec. + -ING².] That feeds.

†**1.** That nourishes; nutritious. *Obs.* exc. *dial.*

1398 TREVISA *Barth. De P.R.* II. ix. (1495) 37 This one mete..very fedynge is founden. **1651** in *Hartlib's Legacy* (1655) 101 It [Lucern] is much more feeding than any other Hay. **1660** SHARROCK *Vegetables* 136 A fat, rich, deep, moist, and feeding soil. *a* **1722** LISLE *Husb.* (1757) 422 The feedingest ground makes the toughest timber. **1877** *Holderness Gloss.* s.v., 'Whotmeeal's a varry feedin thing.'

2. a. That is taking food; of an animal: Grazing.

1824 H. DAVY *Diary* July (1836) v. 213 The Danes and Holsteiners appear to be rather *fat headed*, and a feeding and smoking people. *a* **1861** CLOUGH *Poems, Ite Domum Saturæ* 22 Doth he sometimes in his slumbering see The feeding kine. **1879** JEFFERIES *Wild Life in S.C.* 275 A feeding flock. **1888** *Daily News* 7 Sept. 5/2 Feeding trout generally keep within casting distance from the shore.

b. *transf.* Of a gale or storm: That increases gradually in violence, or in its effects. Sometimes hyphened. Also *fig.*

1641 R. BAILLIE *Lett. & Jrnls.* (1846) I. 352 This is a feeding storme. **1819** *Caled. Mercury* 30 Dec. (Jam.), We had a pretty copious fall of snow. At one time everything seemed to portend what is called a feeding-storm. **1826** SCOTT *Jrnl.* (1890) I. 76 This seems to be a feeding storm, coming on little by little. **1828** *Craven Dial.*, *Feeding-storm*, a continuance or succession of snow, daily feeding or adding to what is already on the ground. **1867** SMYTH *Sailor's Word-bk.* 291 *Feeding-gale.*

†**3.** That eats away; corrosive. *Obs. rare.*

1750 tr. *Leonardus' Mirr. Stones* 221 It cures feeding and malignant Ulcers.

4. That keeps up the supply (of a river, machine, etc.).

1833 N. ARNOTT *Physics* (ed. 5) II. 106 The feeding snows are more abundantly dissolved. **1835** URE *Philos. Manuf.* 154 Cardings introduced in pairs at the feeding rollers. **1867** SMYTH *Sailor's Word-bk.* 291 Feeding-part of a tackle, that running through the sheaves, in opposition to the standing part.

†'**feedman.** *Obs.* Also 5–6 feod(e)man. [f. FEED *ppl. a.* + MAN.] **a.** One holding a FEE (*sb.*²); a vassal. **b.** A soldier serving for pay.

c **1460** FORTESCUE *Abs. & Lim. Mon.* xvii, He shall haue than a greter myght..than he hath nowe off all his oþer ffeed men. **1465** *Paston Lett.* No. 532 II. 248 Doo warne owr ffeede men and servaunts..that they be ther thann in owr leverey. **1485** *Plumpton Corr.* p. xcvi, 38 Knyghts of his feedmen. **1555** BRADFORTH in Strype *Eccl. Mem.* III. App. xlv. 131 Lettres touching my Lord Pagette, that he shoulde be the Kinges feode man. **1565** JEWEL *Def. Apol.* (1611) 476 The Emperour is a Vassall or a Feedman of the Church of Rome. **1722** BP. WILSON in Keble *Life* xv. (1863) 484 With ..intention of lessening the Governor's authority..over the Feedmen in the Garrisons.

'**feed-water.** A supply of water for the boiler of an engine. Also *attrib.* and *Comb.*, as ***feed-water-apparatus, -heater, -pump, -purifier.***

1862 *Reports of Juries, Exhibition* 1862 v. 5 A medal was awarded to Mr. Bateson for his feed-water heating apparatus. **1867** in SMYTH *Sailor's Word-bk.* **1875** BEDFORD *Sailor's Pocket-bk.* vi. (ed. 2) 210 The feed water passes through a coiled pipe in a cistern. **1886** *Auckland Weekly News* 26 June 32/4 The boiler..has a feed-water-heater. **1892** P. BENJAMIN *Mod. Mech.* 284 Feed-Water Evaporators.

fee-farm ('fiːfɑːm). *Law.* Also *Sc.* FEU-FARM. [a. AF. *fee-ferme*, OF. *feuferme*, *fiofferme*; Anglo-Lat. (12th c.) had *feudofirma*, *feudifirma*, and the phrase *firmam in feudo tenere*; in continental use occur *feudum firmum*, *feudalis firma*, *firma feudata*; see FEE *sb.*² and FARM *sb.*²]

1. That kind of tenure by which land is held in fee-simple subject to a perpetual fixed rent, without any other services; the estate of the tenant in land so held; rarely, the land itself.

It is a debated question whether a fee-farm merely implies a perpetual rent of any kind, or whether it should be confined to a perpetual rent-service, or to a perpetual rent-charge equivalent to at least a fourth of the value of the land.

[**1114** *Charter* in *Chr. Mon. Abingdon* (Rolls) II. 110 Quoddam pratum..in firma perpetuo habendum pro xx solidis reddendis unoquoque. **1292** BRITTON I. i. §6 Si la fraunchise ne soit graunté en fee ferme..par nous. *Ibid.* III. ii. §8 Fee fermes sount terres tenuz en fee a rendre pur eux par an la verreye value, ou plus ou meyn.] *c* **1460** FORTESCUE *Abs. & Lim. Mon.* x, In grete lordshippes, maneres, ffee ffermys, and such other demaynes. **1494** FABYAN *Chron.* VII. 438 He grauntyd to the cytezyns the fee ferme of London for .ccc. li. **1555** EDEN *Decades* 249 Such as had the same in fee ferme. **1627** SPEED *England* xxviii. §7 Hurstingston..was the Fee-farme of Ramsey Abbey. **1643** in *Select. Harl. Misc.* (1793) 304 The king is forced to set many of his lands to fee-farm. **1650** WELDON *Crt. Jas. I*, 60 Hee [Salisbury] would make them buy Books of Fee-farmes. **1652** EVELYN *Mem.* (1857) I. 289 What was in lease from the Crown..he would secure to us in fee-farm.

fig. **1606** SHAKS. *Tr. & Cr.* III. ii. 53 How now, a kisse in fee-farme? **1678** MARVELL *Growth Popery* Wks. 1875 IV. 326 Were not all the votes as it were in fee-farm, of those that were intrusted with the sale?

2. The rent paid for an estate so held.

1399 LANGL. *Rich. Redeles* IV. 4 Alle his ffynys ffor ffautis ne his ffee ffermes. *c* **1520** in Fiddes *Wolsey* II. (1726) 26 Towchyng the mynyshyng of our Fee farme enenst the lorde of Ruteland. **1598** MANWOOD *Lawes Forest* xxi. §4 (1615) 201 Paying unto the King a certain fee ferme or rent for yᵉ same. **1682** *Enq. Elect. Sheriffs* 32 King John..granted..to the Citizens..the Sheriffwick of London and Middlesex..by the fee-farm of 300*l.* per Annum.

3. *attrib.* esp. in ***fee-farm-rent***.

1638 SIR R. COTTON *Abstr. Rec. Tower* 12 Their abilities will settle the Fee-farme rent. **1710** *Lond. Gaz.* No. 4702/3 To be sold a Fee-Farm-Rent of 20*l.* per Annum. **1855** MILMAN *Lat. Chr.* (1864) V. IX. vi. 287 The fee farm payment to Rome. **1881** *Act 44–5 Vict.* c. 49 §34 The land commission shall..dispose of all fee farm rents for the time being vested in them. **1882** EARL OF BELMORE in *19th Cent.* July 126 By way of fines and fee-farm grants.

Hence **fee-farming** *vbl. sb.*, the action or practice of putting out to fee-farm.

1549 LATIMER *6th Serm. bef. Edw. VI* (Arb.) 168 He hath inuented fee fermyng of benefices.

fee-farmer (ˈfiːfɑːmə(r)). *Law.* Also *Sc.* FEU-FARMER. [a. AF. *feefermer*, OF. *feufermier*, med.L. *feudifirmārius*, f. *feudifirma*: see FEE-FARM.] One who holds a fee-farm.

1468 in Rolle *Abridgment* (1668) 150 Les Fee-farmers del Roy. **1511–2** *Act 3 Hen. VIII*, c. 23 Preamb., Fermours, Feefermours, Officers and Occupiers. **1591** in Hearne *R. Brunne* (1810) 418 Her majesties fee-farmer.

fig. **1609** J. DAVIES *Holy Roode* cxxvii, As when bright Phebus..And his Fee-farmer Luna, most are parted.

fee-faw-fum (fiːfɔːfʌm). Also 7 fie foh fumme, 8 fe fi fo fum, 7–9 fee fa fum.

1. The first line of doggerel spoken by the giant in the nursery tale of 'Jack the giant killer' upon discovering the presence of Jack.

1605 SHAKS. *Lear* III. iv. 188 His word was still fie, foh, and fumme, I smell the blood of a Brittish man. **1711** *Chap-bk., Jack & the Giants* 11, Fe, Fi, Fo, Fum I smell the Blood of an English Man.

2. a. An exclamation indicating a murderous intention. **b.** Nonsense, fitted only to terrify children. Also *attrib.*

1690 DRYDEN *Amphitryon* II. i, The bloody villain is at his fee, fa, fum, already. **1811** *Lexicon Balatronicum*, I am not to be frightened by fee, faw, fum. **1825** MACAULAY *Milton* Ess. 1854 I. 12 They have..none of the fee-faw-fum of Tasso and Klopstock. **1830** A. FONBLANQUE *Eng. under 7 Administ.* (1837) II. 10 The fee-fa-fum style of rhetoric. *a* **1850** M. F. OSSOLI *At Home & Abroad* (1860) 400 It is they who invent all the 'fe, fo, fum' stories about Italy. **1855** BROWNING *Men & Wom.* I. *Lover's Quarrel* 16 The valiant Thumb Facing the castle glum And the giant's fee-faw-fum! **1890** *Review of Reviews* II. 538/2 This is all fee-faw-fum.

3. Used to express 'a blood-thirsty person'.

1678 DRYDEN *Limberham* V. i, That Fe-fa-fum of a Keeper wou'd have smelt the Blood of a Cuckold-maker. **1824** MISS FERRIER *Inher.* xiv, I feel so much of the fee, fa, fum about me, that I can scarcely ask you to trust your-self with me.

Hence **fee-faw-fumish** *a.*

1846 GEO. ELIOT *Let.* in *Life* ii. 81 The note in this proof sounds just as fee-fo-fumish as the other.

feeing (ˈfiːɪŋ), *vbl. sb. dial.* and *Sc.* [f. FEE *v.*¹] The hiring of servants for a fee. ***feeing market***, hiring market; a general semi-annual gathering of farm hands for the purpose of hiring themselves out for the next six months.

1865 W. H. L. TESTER *Poems* 127 I'll tell ye a' About the Friday's feein'. **1875** W. ALEXANDER *Sks. Life among my Ain Folk* 220 On the feeing market night he had taken Baubie home to Briggies'. **1891** A. GORDON *Folks o' Carglen* iii. 66 In the little town of Kail..there were three great hiring markets for farm-labourers in the course of the year. These were the 'feein' Friday',..'hairst Monday'... By ten or eleven o'clock a huge concourse of people anxious to be 'feed'..had assembled. **1897** *Westm. Gaz.* 29 May 10/1 The Inverness Feeing Market the other day..was like a military pageant... The recruiting sergeants were alert and busy. **1930** *Times Lit. Suppl.* 18 Dec. 1086/3 Hawked at fairs and feeing-markets.

feel (fiːl), *sb.* Also 3, 5 fele, 5–6 *Sc.* feill. [f. next vb.]

1. a. The action of feeling; an instance of this, in senses of the vb.; in quots. †a sounding of a person's intentions, etc. (*obs.*); the perceiving (something) by sensation. *rare.*

1461 *Paston Lett.* No. 415 II. 50, I dede a gode fele to enquer..whan the seid Yelverton shuld go to London. **1832** L. HUNT *Sonn.* Poems (1832) 208 Catching your heart up at the feel of June.

†**b.** A tentative suggestion, hint. *Obs.*

a **1470** HENRY *Wallace* x. 923 Off Gyane, thus, quhen Wallace hard a feill, 'No land', he said, 'likit him halff so weill.'

†**2.** *Sc.* and *north.* **a.** Consciousness, sensation. **b.** Apprehension, sense, understanding, knowledge.

a **1240** *Wohunge* in *Cott. Hom.* 285 þe muchele swetnesse of þe reaues me fele of pine. *a* **1300** *Cursor M.* 547 (Cott.) Man has his fele, O thyng man liks, il or welle. *a* **1400–50** *Alexander* 850 Has þou na force in þi fete ne fele of þi-selfe? *c* **1470** HENRY *Wallace* II. 14 Thocht Inglis men thar of had litill feille. *c* **1500** *Lancelot* 2854 That..was knycht that had most feill. **1560** ROLLAND *Crt. Venus* I. 467 Of that Text thow hes bot litill feill. **1603** *Philotus* cxxvii, Hes thow not tint thy feill.

3. The sense of touch. Now only in *to the feel.*

a **1300** *Cursor M.* 17017 (Cott.) Hering, sight, smelling and fele, cheuing er wittes five. **1812** SIR H. DAVY *Chem. Philos.* 180 It is harsher to the feel. **1874** *Contemp. Rev.* XXIV. 433 A rough texture to the feel. **1883** G. C. DAVIES *Norfolk Broads* xxxi. (1884) 237 It [the bed-eel]..is firm to the feel.

4. A feeling or sensation, mental or physical. (For quot. 1966, cf. FEELING *vbl. sb.* 7 c.)

1737 H. WALPOLE *Corr.* (1820) I. 16 With all sorts of queer feels about me. **1788** MAD. D'ARBLAY *Diary & Lett.* IV. IV. 194, I put aside the disagreeable feel of exciting that wonder. **1818** KEATS in *Life & Lett.* I. 120 Among multitudes of men I have no feel of stooping. **1833** HT. MARTINEAU *Tale of Tyne* vi. 117 To tell by the feel when the sun was going down. **1879** BROWNING *Ivàn Ivànovitch* 225 The feel of the fang furrowing my shoulder! **1891** F. W. BAIN *Antichrist* v. 216 The skilful batter, in cricket, plays every ball as it comes to him in a slightly different way: and he cannot tell another man how to do it because it is not in his *idea*, but in his *feel*. **1939** I. BAIRD *Waste Heritage* i. 3 It sounded hysterical, as though it had picked up the feel of what was going on around it. **1962** A. NISBETT *Technique Sound Studio* viii. 140 It is worth while practising with this and getting the feel of the timing. **1966** *Observer* 10 July 6/3 He can't, he [*sc.* a stockbroker] says, 'get the feel of the market'.

5. As a quality of a material object: The kind of (tactual or vague organic) sensation which it produces.

1739 S. SHARP *Surg.* xxvii. 135 We must judge then by the Feel of the Surface of the Bone. **1789** MRS. PIOZZI *Journ. France* II. 376 The general feel of the air is very mild. **1794** *G. Adams's Nat. & Exp. Philos.* I. App. 543 Fixed oils..possess..2. An unctuous feel. **1805** W. SAUNDERS *Min. Waters* 40 That rough and harsh feel to the fingers and tongue, which characterises the insipid hard waters. **1864** MRS. GATTY *Parables fr. Nature* Ser. IV. 155 Twinette was on the cold pavement. But she didn't like the feel of it at all. **1882** EDNA LYALL *Donovan* xx, It reminded him of the feel of little Dot's tiny fingers. **1931** *Economist* 4 Apr. 720/2 The coxswain on duty at the moment of emergency had not had the opportunity to learn the 'feel' of the ship. **1958** *Which?* I. II. 25/2 The car's steering..was slightly 'numb', with undesirably little road feel. **1962** *Times* 4 Jan. 3/5 Angus played a neat, economical game, appearing to have the feel of the court.

6. *slang.* An instance of 'feeling up' (cf. FEEL *v.* 1 f). Also *Comb.*

1932 J. T. FARRELL *Young Lonigan* vi. 228 Wouldn't it have been nice to have had her there..and have a feel-day. **1934** J. O'HARA *Appointment in Samarra* (1935) vi. 168 And that husband of hers, that Harvey. Trying to give me a feel under the table. **1939** JOYCE *Finnegans Wake* 95 Fine feelplay we had of it mid the kissabetts frisking in the kool kurkle dusk of the lushiness. **1969** 'J. FRASER' *Cock-pit of Roses* xviii. 143 She let me have a quick feel. **1970** 'ZENO' *Grab* iv. 35, I gave her a feel, and she pulled away.

7. *Comb.* of the vb. stem, as ***feel-horn*** (rare⁻¹) = FEELER 3 [after Ger. *fühlhorn*].

1770 J. R. FORSTER tr. *Kalm's Trav. N. Amer.* I. 134 Their antennæ or feel-horns were as long as their bodies.

feel (fiːl), *v.* *Pa. t.* and *pa. pple.* felt (fɛlt). Forms: *Infin.* 1 félan, 3–4 felen, (5 feelen), 3–5 fell, 3, 5–6 *Sc.* feil(l, (6 feild), 3–6 fele, 3–4 *south.* vele, 4–5 felyn, feyle, (5 feyll), 4–7 feele, (6 feale, 8 feell), 4, 6– feel. *Pa. t.* and *pa. pple.* 3 feild, fielde, 3–6 feld(e, 4–5 fe(e)lid, felyd(e, 4–6 feeled, 3–7 felte, 3– felt. Also with prefix (*esp.* in pa. t. and pa. pple.) 1–2 ȝe-, 2–3 i-, y-. [Com. WestGer.; OE. *félan* (also *ȝefélan*) corresponds to OFris. *fêla*, OS. *gifôlian* (Du. *voelen*), OHG. *fuolen* to handle, grope (MHG. *vüelen*, mod.G. *fühlen* to feel), Da. *föle* to feel (prob. adopted from some LG. source):—WGer. type **fôljan*, f. root *fôl*:—OAryan *pāl-*, *pl-*, occurring in OE., OS. *folm*, OHG. *folma* hand, Gr. *παλάμη*, L. *palma*, Skr. *pāṇi*, OIr. *lám* (:—**plāma*).]

I. To examine or explore by touch.

1. a. *trans.* To handle (an object) in order to experience a tactual sensation; to examine by touching with the hand or finger.

c **893** K. ÆLFRED *Oros.* I. vii. (Sweet) 38 þysþernes..swa ȝedrefedlic þæt hit man ȝefelan mihte [*tenebras crassitudine palpabiles*]. **1388** WYCLIF *Gen.* xxvii. 22 Whanne he hadde feelid hym, Isaac seide [etc.]. *c* **1400** *Lanfranc's Cirurg.* 208 If þou felist þe place wiþ þi fyngir. **1548** HALL *Chron.* 195 b, By king Edward, which loved well both to loke and to fele fayre dammosels. **1611** BIBLE *Judg.* xvi. 26 Suffer mee, that I may feele the pillars. **1632** J. HAYWARD tr. *Biondi's Eromena* 15 You neede feele no other pulse than my heart. **1662** J. DAVIES tr. *Olearius' Voy. Ambass.* 108 He was felt, and found to be Circumcis'd. *Ibid.* 409 The maids..were not shy of being seen, nor of having their hair felt. **1776** *Trial of Nundocomar* 33/1, I felt his pulse. **1828** SCOTT *F.M. Perth* xvii, 'Let me feel your pulse, dear Ramorny.'

b. In wider sense: to try by touching, *e.g.* with a stick or the foot; to move or lift gently and cautiously by way of trial.

1833 *Regul. Instr. Cavalry* (1844) 48 By feeling the bit gently with the bridle-hand, the horse is to be made to step back. **1867** F. FRANCIS *Angling* vii. (1880) 279 Feeling the fish..consists in raising the point of the rod so as to tighten the line sufficiently to enable you to feel the 'tug, tug, tug', made by the fish in detaining the worm. **1883** GRESLEY *Gloss. Terms Coal Mining, Feel* (S.S.), to examine the roof of a thick seam of coal with a long stick or rod by poking and knocking upon it. **1886** R. C. LESLIE *Sea-painter's Log* 161 Feeling first one line and then another for a bite.

c. *to feel* (†*out*) *one's way*: to find one's way by groping; to proceed by cautious steps. *lit.* and *fig.*

1436 *Polit. Poems* (Rolls) II. 165 Kynge Edwarde..felde the weyes to reule well the see. **1638** CHILLINGW. *Relig. Prot.* I. ii. §144. 108 While we have our eyes, we need not feele out our way. **1688** MIEGE *Fr. Dict.* s.v. *Feel*, A blind Man that feels his Way with a Stick. **1818** BYRON *Ch. Har.* IV. lxxxi, We but feel our way to err. **1862** G. MACDONALD *D. Elginbrod* II. xxviii, An aging moon was feeling her path somewhere through the heavens. **1879** FROUDE *Cæsar* xiv. 217 Cæsar..feeling his way with his cavalry.

d. *to feel out*: to ascertain the configuration of (something) as if by touch. Also, to search *out*, to ascertain, by feeling or testing.

1835 A. B. LONGSTREET *Georgia Scenes* 242 These [chills] I had to bear for the space of a minute or two before I could *feel out* my hat. **1892** H. R. MILL *Realm of Nature* xi. 188 The form of the floor of the ocean has thus been gradually felt out point by point. **1928** *Publishers' Weekly* 9 June 2376, I cannot stress enough..the necessity of feeling out the possibilities of a book before giving a large order.

†**e.** To grope after. *fig.* (Merely a literalism of translation). *Obs.*

1382 WYCLIF *Acts* xvii. 27 To seke God, if perauenture thei felen [L. *attrectent*] hym eyther fynden. **1535** COVERDALE *Acts* xvii. 27 That they shulde seke the Lorde, yf they mighte fele and fynde him.

f. *slang.* To caress the genital parts of (a person). Usu. const. *up*. Cf. FEEL *sb.* 6.

1930 J. DOS PASSOS *42nd Parallel* I. 75 She's awful hot. Jez I thought she was going to feel me up. **1957** J. KEROUAC *On Road* (1958) II. xi. 175 We used to get next to pretty young daughters and feel them up in the kitchen. **1968** M. RICHLER *Cocksure* xvi. 92 He literally bumped into Ziggy feeling up the prettiest girl at the party in a dark damp corner. **1970** S. ELLIN *Man from Nowhere* i. 9 We're supposed to be married. He might wonder about it if I let him feel you up in front of me without showing I didn't like it.

2. *absol.* and *intr.* **a.** To use the hand or finger as an organ of touch. Const. *at*, *of* (now only *dial.* and U.S.), †*to.*

1599 SHAKS. *Hen. V*, II. iii. 26 Then I felt to his knees, and so..vpward, and all was..cold. **1626** BACON *Sylva* §352 The part [of Wood] that shineth, is..somewhat soft, and moist to feel to. **1751** R. PALTOCK *P. Wilkins* xlvii. (1883) 140/2 There were many large heaps of ore lying, which I felt of. **1780** CHARLOTTE BURNEY in *F. Burney's Early Diary* (1889) II. 289 One Character came to feel of it [his mask]. **1864** E. SARGENT *Peculiar* II. 262 Josephine..felt of the bosom of Clara's dress till [etc.]. **1878** N. H. BISHOP *Voy. Paper Canoe* 99 Crowds of people came to feel of the canoe.

b. To search for something with the hand (or other tactile organ); to put out the hands, etc. to discover one's position or find one's way; to grope. Const. *after*, *for*. Also with *about*.

1382 WYCLIF *Isa.* lix. 10 As withoute eȝen we han felid. **1530** PALSGR. 547/2 Fele this way alonge by the wall, tyll you come to the wyndowe. **1577** B. GOOGE *Heresbach's Husb.* III. (1586) 133 Take the Taile, and feele betwixt every joint. *Ibid.* III. 136 Let him..feele for the blaines, or blisters. **1611** BIBLE *Acts* xvii. 27 If haply they might feele after him, and finde him. **1726** *Adv. Capt. R. Boyle* 22 Putting my Hand in my Pocket to feel for something else. **1771** MRS. GRIFFITH tr. *Viaud's Shipwreck* 192, I searched all my pockets..opened all our parcels..and looked and felt in every fold of them. **1838** T. BEALE *Sperm Whale* 46 Moving the tail slowly from side to side..as if feeling for the boat. **1864** TENNYSON *En. Ard.* 774 Feeling all along the garden-wall, Lest he should..tumble. **1868** J. H. BLUNT *Ref. Ch. Eng.* I. 294 The king began to feel about for further augmentations of his revenue. **1904** P. F. WARNER *How we recovered Ashes* xiii. 253 He again got Clem Hill feeling for the ball.

†**c.** *to feel of*: ? to handle, administer. *to feel together*: to come into contact. *Obs.*

c **1400** *Apol. Loll.* 30 It is necesari to hem..to fele of þe sacraments of God. *c* **1450** *Merlin* 38 As soone as these dragons felen to-geder thei will fighten strongely.

3. With *subord. clause*: To try to ascertain by handling or touch. †Formerly sometimes also with material obj.

a **1300** *Cursor M.* 3693 (Cott.) Latte me fele, If þou be he i luue sa wele. *Ibid.* 18695 (Cott.) Thomas þou fele and se Quer I me self or noght it be. *c* **1400** *Lanfranc's Cirurg.* 270 þou miȝt fele in what place þei goon in. **1611** BIBLE *Gen.* xxvii. 21 Come neere..that I may feele thee..whether thou bee my very sonne Esau, or not. **1648** J. BEAUMONT *Psyche* III. lix, Three times he..felt How to unbuckle his out-shined Belt. *Mod.* The surgeon felt if any bones were broken.

4. *fig.* To test or discover by cautious trial; to 'sound' (a person, his feelings or intentions).

a **1300** *Cursor M.* 2902 (Cott.) Mani man, for ouer-wele, þam-self can noþer faand ne feil. *c* **1460** *Towneley Myst.* (Surtees) 174 Bot yit some fawt must we feylle, Wherfor that he shuld dy. **1465** *Paston Lett.* No. 520 II. 221 Fele what he menyth. **1476** *Ibid.* No. 771 III. 154, I shall ffele hym. **1548** HALL *Chron.* 213 b, Thei had felte the myndes and ententes, of the rude people. **1581** SAVILE *Tacitus' Hist.* II. lxiii. (1519) 90 Adding..that to that purpose he had felt the cohort. **1605** SHAKS. *Lear* I. ii. 94 He hath writ this to feele my affection to your Honor. **1664** SIR C. LYTTELTON in

Hatton Corr. (1878) 41 To feele the French how they will concerne themselves between us and yᵉ Dutch. 1938 N. Coward *Operette* I. ix. 87 Play slowly at first until you feel the house.

5. *Milit.* **a.** *trans.* To examine by cautious trial the nature of (the ground), the strength of (an enemy). **b.** intr. *to feel for*: To try to ascertain the position or presence of.

a. 1793 Bentinck in *Ld. Auckland's Corr.* III. 47, I mentioned my wish of feeling that ground to Lᵈ. Loughborough. 1839 Napier *Penins. War* VI. vii. (Rtldg.) I. 316 Loison felt the Portuguese at Pezo de Ragoa. 1848 J. Grant *Adv. Aide-de-camp* vii, Order Colonel Kempt to throw forward the whole of his light infantry..to 'feel' the enemy.

b. 1839 Napier *Penins. War* VII. ii. (Rtldg.) I. 334 Syveira ..had orders to feel..for the enemy. 1847 *Infantry Man.* (1854) 96 An advanced guard..must proceed with.. precaution if feeling for an enemy.

II. To perceive, be conscious.

6. a. *trans.* To have the sensation of contact with; to perceive by the sense of touch.

1393 Langl. *P. Pl.* C. xx. 145 Al þat þe fyngres and þe fust ..felen and touchen. 15.. *Frere & Boye* 91 in Ritson *Anc. Pop. Poetry* 38 Whan he the bowe in honde felte. 1538 Starkey *England* I. i. 20 Thos thyngys wych we se, fele, or her. 1545 Brinklow *Compl.* 19 The lawyer can not vnderstond the matter tyl he fele his mony. 1580 J. Frampton *Monarde's Dial. of Yron* 155 b, Pouder..that being taken between the fingers is [not] felt between them. 1638 Baker tr. *Balzac's Lett.* I. 67, I am glad..that I can lay hold of something, I can feele. 1724 R. Falconer *Voy.* (1769) 52 It shaked its Tail to and fro..all the while it felt the water. 1771 Mrs. Griffith tr. *Viaud's Shipwreck* 86, I felt under my naked foot..some hard substance or other. 1869 Tennyson *Pelleas & E.* 428 Back as a hand that pushes thro' the leaf To find a nest and feels a snake, he drew.

b. In wider sense: To perceive, or be affected with sensation by (an object) through those senses which (like that of touch) are not referred to any special 'organ'; to have a sensation of (*e.g.* heat or cold, a blow, the condition of any part of the body, etc.). Slang phr. *to feel the draught*: to be seriously incommoded; to feel insecure, esp. financially.

a 1000 *Riddles* xxvi. 9 (Gr.) Heo..feleð sona mines ȝemotes. 1297 R. Glouc. (1724) 185 Þo kyng Arture yt [þe dunt] yuelde. *a* 1605 Montgomerie *That his hairt is woundit* 17, I the force thairof [a darte] did feild. 1639 tr. *Du Bosq's Compl. Woman* II. 82 We feele a wound, not knowing the hand which strikes us. 1662 J. Davies tr. *Olearius' Voy. Ambass.* 63 We..felt not the cold. 1665 Hooke *Microgr.* 142 A Nettle is a Plant so well known..that it needs no description; and there are very few that have not felt as well as seen it. 1705 Bosman *Guinea* (1721) 394 A stiff Gale, which prevents our feeling the Heat of the Sun. 1840 F. D. Bennett *Whaling Voy.* II. 265 The hand holding the inflated animal, feels a constant boring motion of the spines. 1925 *Westm. Gaz.* 27 Apr., When the wind changed it might be the Conservative Party which would be feeling the draught. 1941 N. Marsh *Surfeit of Lampreys* vii. 103 'Did he go bust?'..'I don't think so, Curtis. Must have felt the draught a bit.' 1966 *Listener* 9 June 831/2 With only so much national advertising to go round.., the oldest commercial stations are feeling the draught as well. 1970 *Financial Times* 13 Apr. 13/3 If the BSC or the bigger firms in the private sector felt the draught and turned their attention to smaller orders, the lesser firms could suffer badly—to the point of extinction.

c. with clause, or obj. with inf. (not preceded by *to*) or complement: To know by sense of touch or organic sensation.

c 1386 Chaucer *Knt.'s T.* 362 The deth he feleth thurgh his herte smite. 1398 Trevisa *Barth. De P.R.* IX. viii. (Tollem. MS.), Watres of depe pittes..beþ felid more hoot in wynter þan in somer. 1526 *Pilgr. Perf.* (W. de W. 1531) 119 Whan we may fele our pulses bete quikly. 1534 Tindale *Mark* v. 29 She felt in her body that she was healed of the plage. 1568 Grafton *Chron.* II. 274 When the Genowayes felt the Arrowes pearcyng thorough their heades, armes and breastes. 1726 *Adv. Capt. R. Boyle* 13 He felt the blood trickle about his Legs. 1753 Chambers *Cycl. Suppl.* s.v., In the manage, they say to *feel* a horse in the hand; that is, to observe that the will of the horse is in the rider's hand. 1771 Mrs. Griffith tr. *Viaud's Shipwreck* 239 One of the men.. cried out that he felt him still warm. 1839 T. Beale *Sperm Whale* 65 A Sardinian captain bathing..felt one of his feet in the grasp of one of these animals.

d. *to feel one's feet, legs, wings*: *fig.* to be conscious of one's powers; to be at one's ease.

1579 E. K. in *Spenser's Sheph. Cal.* Ep. Ded., So flew *Virgile*, as not yet well feeling his wings. 1881 *Daily Tel.* 27 Dec., It was not until the last act that he 'felt his legs'. 1889 *Farmer's Mag.* Dec. 217 Trees put in now cannot be expected to succeed as well as those that are already beginning to 'feel their feet'.

e. *absol.* and *intr.* To have or be capable of sensations of touch, etc.

1340 *Ayenb.* 154 Þet ech serui of his office..Ase þe eȝen to zyenne; þe yearen, to hyere..þe honden and al þet body to vele. 1601 Holland *Pliny* X. lxxi, Even oisters and the earth-wormes, if a man touch them, doe evidently feele. 1631 D. Widdowes *Nat. Philos.* (ed. 2) 49 About this time [at thirty dayes] the Childe beginneth..to feele. 1643 J. Steer tr. *Exp. Chyrurg.* iii. 8 The under skinne..hardly feeleth, though it bee pricked with a Lancet. 1800 Wordsw. *Hart-leap Well* II. xxi, The meanest thing that feels. 1887 W. James in *Mind* Apr. 184 If the skin felt everywhere exactly alike.

f. *to feel into* (see quots.).

1912 [see empathy]. 1919 M. K. Bradby *Psycho-Analysis* xviii. 239 He feels himself into the mind of the man or woman..he is studying. 1933 H. Read *Art Now* I. 50 We do not necessarily humanise the rising column or the graceful vase which we contemplate: we feel into their shape..and react to..its rhythmic convolution; and so we invent the word empathy.

g. *to feel no pain*: to be insensibly drunk. *slang.*

1947 C. Morley *Ironing Board* (1950) 116 At the table with three men who were feeling no pain. 1965 B. Sweet-Escott *Baker St. Irreg.* iii. 94 There were a great many Anglo-Russian parties, a vast quantity of vodka was drunk, and twice I saw senior Russian officers being carried out of the room evidently feeling no pain.

7. To perceive by smell or taste. *Obs.* exc. *dial.*

c 1220 *Bestiary* 510 Whan he it felen, he aren faȝen. *a* 1300 *Cursor M.* 3695 (Gött.) Quen he had felt his smell and clath. *Ibid.* 23456 (Cott.) In this lijf has man gret liking..suete spiceri to fell and smell. *c* 1350 *Will. Palerne* 638 Haue ȝe.. feled þe sauor. 1393 Gower *Conf.* III. 281 He shall weel felen ate laste, That it is sowre. *c* 1460 *Towneley Myst.* (Surtees) 43 Com nere son and kys me, That I may feyle the smelle of the. 1535 Coverdale *Dan.* iii. 27 There was no smell of fyre felt vpon them. 1575 J. Still *Gamm. Gurton* I. ii, To feele how the ale dost tast. 1604 Jas. I *Counterbl.* (Arb.) 112 By his own election he would rather feele the sauour of a Sinke. 1624 Capt. J. Smith *Virginia* I. 2 They felt a most dilicate sweete smell. 1706 W. Storr in *Yorksh. Archæol. Jrnl.* VII. 51 It was a very lothsome smell to feell all over the lordship. 1782 Sir J. Sinclair *Observ. Scot. Dial.* 83 You complain much of that tannery, but I cannot say I feel it. 1846 J. Taylor *Upper Canada* 101 My conductor exclaiming, 'I feel the odour of the spring'. 1861 E. Waugh *Birtle Carter's Tale* 7 There's that bit o' pickle i' th cubbort..Fotch it eawt, an' let him feel at it. 1870 Ramsay *Remin.* (ed. 18) 118, I feel a smell of tea. 1884 *Eastern Morn. News* 19 Apr., He felt a nasty smell.

†**8.** To perceive mentally, become aware of. *Obs.* [After L. *sentire.*] Const. as in 6 b, c.

a 1000 *Riddles* vii. 8 (Gr.) Hi þæs felað. 1377 Langl. *P. Pl.* B. xv. 29 And whan ich fele þat folke telleþ my furste name is sensus. *a* 1400–50 *Alexander* 3257 Þi wale gode þat..fully feld all þe fare þat fall suld on erthe. 1463 *Paston Lett.* No. 467 II. 126 As I feele hym disposed I schall send your maystreship answer. *c* 1470 Henry *Wallace* II. 435 With full glaid will to feill thai tithings true. *Ibid.* VI. 289 The queyne feld weill how that his purpos was. 1483 Caxton *Gold. Leg.* 340/4 Whanne he [Bede] felt [*printed* fete] this He reuoked hit in his rectrections.

9. a. To be conscious of (a subjective fact); to be the subject of, experience (a sensation, emotion), entertain (a conviction).

c 1290 *S. Eng. Leg.* I. 76/196 Grete feblesse he fielde. *c* 1385 Chaucer *L.G.W.* Prol. 106 In myn herte I feele yet the fire, That made me to ryse er yt wer day. *c* 1400 *Lanfranc's Cirurg.* 88 Þanne þe sike man schal fele to greet heete & brennynge. *c* 1435 *Torr. Portugal* 2537 Off care no thyng they ffeld. 1535 Coverdale *2 Chron.* vi. 29 Yf eny man fele his plage and disease. 1592 Shaks. *Ven. & Ad.* 311 [She]..scorns the heat he feels. 1634 W. Tirwhyt *Balzac's Lett.* 309, I have not at all felt the emotion I shewed. 1717 Pope *Eloisa* 366 He best can paint 'em [woes] who shall feel 'em most. 1798 Ferriar *Illustr. Sterne* ii. 25 Francis I. felt a curiosity to hear his book read. 1816 Byron *Ch. Har.* II. lxxxiii, Mankind have felt their strength. 1876 J. H. Newman *Hist. Sk.* I. I. i. 44 Timour..felt some misgivings about his past course.

b. with clause, or obj. with infinitive or complement.

c 1200 *Trin. Coll. Hom.* 93 Gif he feleð þat he is wurðe þerto þenne understonde he þat husel. *a* 1225 *St. Marher.* 7 Ne felestu þi flesch al toloken. *c* 1325 *Metr. Hom.* 30 He asked him hou he him felid. *c* 1325 *Song Know Thyself* 45 in *E.E.P.* (1862) 131 Ȝif þou fele þe syker and sounde. *c* 1449 Pecock *Repr.* 243 Ech of these men feelid weel in himsilf that he hadde nede for to have help and reuling. 1583 Hollyband *Campo di Fior* 37 Feelest thou thy selfe well? *c* 1590 Marlowe *Faust.* Wks. (Rtldg.) 99/1, I feel Thy words to comfort my distressed soul! 1600 E. Blount tr. *Conestaggio* 42 Feeling himselfe die by degrees. 1732 Pope *Ep. Cobham* I. 263 You..Shall feel your ruling passion strong in death. 1771 Mrs. Griffith tr. *Viaud's Shipwreck* 49 We felt ourselves warm and comfortable. 1810 Bentham *Packing* (1821) 173 He would..feel himself running counter to that which [etc.]. 1881 C. Gibbon *Heart's Problem* iii. (1884) 33 Maurice felt his eyes dazzled by a blaze of light.

c. *intr.* (for earlier *refl.*) with *complement.* To have the sensation of being (what is predicated); to be consciously; to regard oneself as. *to feel (quite) oneself*: to seem to oneself to have one's accustomed health or powers. *to feel up to* (one's work, etc.): see up.

1816 J. Wilson *City of Plague* I. i. 89 Now, that your soul feels strong, let us proceed. 1847 Marryat *Childr. N. Forest* xvii, I feel indebted to you for the service you have rendered me. 1865 Mrs. H. Wood *Mildred Arkell* I. ix, I don't feel myself. 1878 Besant & Rice *Celia's Arb.* xl. (1887) 295, I, for my part, felt small. 1884 *Graphic* 30 Aug. 231/1, I did not feel up to much fatigue.

d. *intr.* with *adv.* or *adj.* To entertain a certain sentiment, be in a particular frame of mind. Also with *as if* ——, *like.*

a 1340 Hampole *Psalter* cxxx. 3 *Si non humiliter senciebam* ..if i not mekly felyd: bot i heghid my soul. That is if i had not meke felyng. 1771 Mrs. Griffith tr. *Viaud's Shipwreck* 58 While we were asunder, we felt as if a limb was wanting. 1801 Southey *Thalaba* I. iv, She felt like one Half-waken'd from a midnight dream of blood. 1819 Shelley *Cenci* IV. ii. 18 How feel you to this work? 1839 T. Beale *Sperm Whale* 174 The captain felt certain that he was going to 'sound'.

e. In various expressions, *colloq.* or *vulgar. to feel like* (doing something): to have an inclination for (? orig. *U.S.*; now common). *to feel to* (do something): (*a*) to feel or imagine that one does; (*b*) *U.S.* to feel inclined to do.

1829 *Virginia Lit. Museum* 30 Dec. 458 *Like*..is also used, as follows, in the south: 'I do not feel like eating'. 1836 *Going to Service* xii. 141 People would take liberties with her, and I should feel to have to take care of her. 1864 Bartlett *Dict. Amer.* 144 To feel to do a thing. 1865 Grant in *Century Mag.* Nov. (1889) 142/2, I now feel like ending the matter.. before we go back. 1891 A. Forbes in *19th Cent.* Dec. 1018 In reading which one feels to hear the turmoil of the battle. 1944 M. Laski *Love on Supertax* viii. 82 I'll go straight home. I don't feel exactly like a street-corner meeting. 1970 W. J. Burley *To kill a Cat* ii. 45 They had a drink together, then Helen said that she felt like bed.

10. To have passive experience of, undergo consciously. †Also *intr.* const. *of* (in OE., genitive case; see quot. *a* 1000 in 6 b).

a 1225 *Ancr. R.* 178 Ȝif eni ancre is þet ne veleð none uondunges. *a* 1300 *Cursor M.* 19372 (Gött.) Þat þai moght of na torfer fele. *c* 1300 *Beket* 2250 Lutel ese he miȝte vele. 1375 Barbour *Bruce* I. 304 He wes worth na seyle, That mycht of nane anoyis feyle. 1393 Gower *Conf.* II. 32 So feleth he ful ofte guile [i.e. finds himself deceived], Whan that he weneth siker to stonde. *c* 1430 *Hymns Virg.* (1867) 106 Let þi neiȝhebor..of þi frendschupe fele. *c* 1440 *York Myst.* x. 78 This is a ferly fare to feele. *c* 1475 *Rauf Coilȝear* 97 So fell ane wedder feld I neuer. 1563 J. Pilkington *Burn. Paules Ch.* Aiij, They haue felde great calamities. 1614 Bp. Hall *Recoll. Treat.* 398 Wee fell upon a Cappucine novise..His head had now felt the razor, his backe the rodde. 1634 Sir T. Herbert *Trav.* 93 [He] had his head cut off, and felt a terrible reward for his Apostasie. 1767 *Byron's Voy. r. World* 6 The inhabitants feel little inconvenience from heat and cold. 1818 Shelley *Revolt of Islam* VIII. vii. 8 The stings Of death will make the wise his vengeance feel. 1840 F. D. Bennett *Whaling Voy.* I. 5 We felt the first influence of the N.E. trade-wind, in lat. 21° N.

absol. 1548 Hall *Chron.* 14 So the comon Proverbe was verified, as you have done, so shall you fele.

11. To be consciously affected in condition by (a fact or occurrence); to be sensibly injured or benefited by.

a. *simply.* †**b.** with obj. and complement.

1375 Barbour *Bruce* XIII. 13 Thair fais feld thair cummyng weill. *c* 1430 *Syr Gener.* (Roxb.) 756, I wil doo my parte, ye shul it fele. *a* 1440 *Found. St. Bartholomew's* 53 Hym ȝe shall feill most prompte helper In this present perill. *c* 1470 Henry *Wallace* v. 514 He is on lyff, that sall our natioune feill. 1883 *Manch. Guardian* 18 Oct. 4/7 The storm of Tuesday appears to have been felt very severely on the Western coasts.

12. *transf.* and *fig.* Of inanimate objects: To be influenced or affected by; to behave as if conscious of. Of a ship: *to feel her helm* (see quot. 1867).

1559 W. Cunningham *Cosmogr. Glasse* 11 Or descending to lowe, th' earth of heat shall fele the flame. 1591 Raleigh *Last Fight Rev.* (Arb.) 19 The shippe could neither way nor feele the helme. 1601 Holland *Pliny* II. 628 Orites..will abide the fire and feele no harme therby. 1611 Bible *Ps.* lviii. 9 Before your pots can feele the thornes, he shall take them away. 1660 Sharrock *Vegetables* 12 The lesse of the winter the Cabbage..feels, the more subject 'tis to caterpillars. 1694 *Acc. Sev. Late Voy.* II. (1711) 33 The Ships do not feel these smaller Waves but only the great ones. 1697 Dryden *Virg. Georg.* I. 448 Earth feels the Motions of her angry God. 1732 Pope *Ess. Man* I. 167 That never air or ocean felt the wind. 1822 Shelley *Faust* II. 12 The hoar pines already feel her breath. 1867 Smyth *Sailor's Word-bk., Feel the helm*, To have good steerage way, carrying taut weather-helm, which gives command of steerage. Also said of a ship when she has gained headway after standing still and begins to obey the helm.

13. To be emotionally affected by (an event or state of things).

1600 E. Blount tr. *Conestaggio* 271 They doe feele with greater griefe an other mans profite, then their owne losse. 1726 *Adv. Capt. R. Boyle* 1, I was too young to feel my loss. *a* 1774 Goldsm. *Epit. T. Parnell* 3 What heart but feels his sweetly moral lay. 1861 M. Pattison *Ess.* (1889) I. 38 Rudolf..felt deeply the tragical loss of his favourite son. 1882 Miss Braddon *Mt. Royal* II. ix. 171 It was her candour which he felt most keenly.

14. *intr.* To have the sensibilities excited; *esp.* to have sympathy *with*, compassion *for* (a person, his sufferings, etc.).

1605 Shaks. *Macb.* IV. iii. 7 It resounds As if it felt with Scotland. 1613 Beaum. & Fl. *Honest Man's Fort.* IV. ii, How heavy guilt is, when men come to feel! 1761 Churchill *Rosciad* (ed. 3) 638 Those who would make us feel, must feel themselves. 1809 Wellington in Gurw. *Desp.* IV. 525 No man can see his army perish by want without feeling for them. 1815 Byron *Stanzas for Music, 'There's not a joy'*, Oh! could I feel as I have felt or be what I have been. 1849 Macaulay *Hist. Eng.* II. vii. (ed. 5) 213 A moderate party.. had always felt kindly towards the Protestant Dissenters. 1893 *Speaker* 20 May 557/2 The Archbishop..and his colleagues feel very strongly on the subject of the attack upon the Welsh Church.

15. Expressing a belief or judgement. Const. either with direct object, subord. clause, or obj. with complement or infinitive (preceded by *to.*)

†**a.** *generally.* To believe, think, hold as an opinion. After L. *sentire. Obs.*

1382 N. Hereford, etc. in Lewis *Life Wyclif* (1820) 257 We were required to seyne what we felyde of diverse conclusions. *c* 1400 *Apol. Loll.* 87 Iuel þei felid of God, tenting to idols. *c* 1449 Pecock *Repr.* III. xix. 412 Thouȝ y feele thus, that the clergie, etc. 1482 *Monk of Evesham* (Arb.) 47 What schulde y thinke or fele of hym more worthior than not for to pray for him. 1544 Bale *Chron. Sir J. Oldcastell* in *Harl. Misc.* (Malh.) I. 260 That I should other-wyse fele and teach of the sacramentes. *Ibid.* 262 How fele ye thys artycle?

b. Now only with notions derived from other senses: To apprehend or recognize the truth of (something) on grounds not distinctly perceived; to have an emotional conviction of (a fact).

1613 Shaks. *Hen. VIII*, IV. ii. 91 Garlands..which I feele I am not worthy yet to weare. 1807 Crabbe *Par. Reg.* II. I. 142 Phœbe..felt she gave delight. 1853 I. Taylor *Spir.*

Despot. vi. 245 They felt that a religion..demanded a watchful control. **1861** TROLLOPE *Barchester T.* xxxii, She felt that she might yet recover her lost ground. *Mod.* The proposed legislation was felt to be inexpedient.

III. 16. Used (like *taste, smell*) in quasi-passive sense with complement: To be felt as having a specified quality; to produce a certain impression on the senses (*esp.* that of touch) or the sensibilities; to seem.

1581 PETTIE *Guazzo's Civ. Conv.* II. (1586) 92 The hande ..feeling to bee rough. **1665** HOOKE *Microgr.* 139 The substance of it feels..exactly like a very fine piece..of Chamois leather. **1694** *Acc. Sev. Late Voy.* II. (1711) 165 If it feels heavy..then we give him more Rope. **1768** J. BYRON *Narr. Patagonia* 263 The weather was extremely cold, and felt particularly so to us. **1825** A. CALDCLEUGH *Trav. S. Amer.* II. xvii. 185 The air felt chilly. **1844** LADY FULLERTON *Ellen Middleton* ix, It felt to me as if the air had grown lighter. **1862** MRS. BROWNING *Poems, Mother & Poet* vi, Then one weeps, then one kneels! God, how the house feels! **1885** E. GARRETT *At Any Cost* iv. 66 Not then could she under-stand how it felt to lie wakeful at nights.

feel, obs. form of VEAL.

c **1400** *Lanfranc's Cirurg.* 275 He mai ete fleisch of .iij. daies poudringe & he mai ete feel.

feelable ('fiːləb(ə)l), *a.* [f. FEEL *v.* + -ABLE.] That may or can be felt. †**a.** Sensible, perceptible, manifest (*obs.*). **b.** *nonce-use.* That is matter of emotion or sensibility.

c **1440** HYLTON *Scala Perf.* (W. de W. 1494) II. xxviii, By dyuers sykynes or by felable tourment of the fende. *a* **1500** *Orol. Sap.* in *Anglia* X. 358 Vndir a felable ensaumple I schalle ȝ eue the þe misterie of this doctrine. **1530** TINDALE *Answ. More* IV. xii, He uttereth his feelable blindness. **1570** in LEVINS *Manip.* 114. **1883** HUXLEY in *Nature* XXVII. 397 All things *feelable,* all things which stir our emotions, come under the term of art.

Hence **'feelably** *adv.*, in a feelable manner; perceptibly, manifestly (*obs.*).

c **1375** *Sc. Leg. Saints* Thomas 392 By þre ensampile schawit he Felably quhow ma þis be. *c* **1440** HYLTON *Scala Perf.* (W. de W. 1494) II. xx, Vntyll a soule can feleably noughte hymself.

feeld(e, obs. form of FIELD.

feele, var. of FELE *a. Obs.* many.

feeler ('fiːlə(r)). [f. FEEL *v.* + -ER[1].] One who or that which feels.

1. One who feels or perceives by the senses, *esp.* by the touch.

1526 *Pilgr. Perf.* (W. de W. 1531) 258 The smellers or felers therof. **1611** SHAKS. *Cymb.* I. vi. 101 This hand.. whose touch would force the Feelers soule To'th'oath of loyalty. **1674** N. FAIRFAX *Bulk & Selv.* 47 All hearers deaf, all feelers numb. **1840** *Tait's Mag.* VII. 706, I was one of the best feelers of a silk that ever entered Snuggs' shop.

2. a. One who is the subject of feeling or emotion. †**b.** One who knows (anything) by his own feelings (*obs.*). **c.** One who experiences or has to bear (something disastrous or painful).

1611 WOTTON *Let. to Sir E. Bacon* in *Reliq. Wotton.* (1672) 399 Of my longing to see you, I am a better feeler than a describer. **1779** JOHNSON *Let. to Mrs. Thrale* 8 Nov., If she be a feeler, I can bear a feeler as well as you. **1814** GEN. P. THOMPSON *Exerc.* IV. 24 We are to be the main feelers of the consequences. **1870** LOWELL *Study Wind.* 207 He was not a strong thinker, but a sensitive feeler.

3. a. *Biol.* One of the organs with which certain animals are furnished, for trying by the touch objects with which they come in contact, or for searching for food; a palp.

1665 HOOKE *Microgr.* 194 There are two other jointed and brisled horns, or feelers, in the forepart of the head. **1721** R. BRADLEY *Wks. Nat.* 55 Those Antenæ, or Feelers, which we observe in Lobsters. **1768** G. WHITE *Selborne* xviii. (1789) 52 The upper jaw [of the loach]..is surrounded with six feelers, three on each side. **1774** GOLDSM. *Nat. Hist.* VII. 327 The ant-lion seizes it with its feelers, which are hollow. **1843** OWEN *Invertebr. An.* xiii. 155 The mouth [of the Cirripedia] is provided with a broad upper lip, with two palps or feelers. **1880** W. B. CARPENTER in *19th Cent.* No. 38. 617 Many of these are provided with enormously long and delicate feelers or hairs.

b. *transf.* and *fig.*

1865 MERIVALE *Rom. Emp.* VIII. lxvi. 235 Her ships were the feelers with which she touched on Greece and Italy. **1874** BLACKIE *Self-Cult.* 61 [Atheists] can..fasten their coarse feelers upon nothing but what they can finger.

c. *slang.* That with which one feels; the hand.

1877 *Five Years' Penal Serv.* 259 In a week or two a man can bring his hooks and feelers into full working trim again.

4. a. One sent out to 'feel' the enemy; a scout. Cf. FEEL *v.* 3 b.

1847 *Infantry Man.* (1854) 105 These patrols must be preceded by *feelers.* **1876** VOYLE *Milit. Dict., Feelers.*

b. *transf.* A proposal or hint put forth or thrown out in order to ascertain the opinions of others.

1830 GEN. P. THOMPSON *Exerc.* (1842) I. 288 The feeler which they have put out. **1858** FROUDE *Hist. Eng.* III. xv. 273 Cromwell had thrown out feelers in the various European courts. **1886** 'H. CONWAY' *Living or Dead* v, 'It will cost a great deal if I fit them up as I like,' I said as a feeler.

attrib. **1889** *Pall Mall G.* 30 May 6/3 The project has gone no further than the feeler circular.

c. *Racing.* A trial race.

1883 *Standard* 21 May 2/1 Osborne, journeyed from Manchester..with the express purpose of having a 'feeler' on Mr. Adrian's colt.

5. a. A thin metal strip made to a stated thickness, used to measure narrow gaps or clearances and usu. forming one of a set. More fully *feeler gauge.*

1931 D. GARNETT *Grasshoppers Come* 6 While Wright was tracing out the cause of an intermittent miss on the starboard magneto of a Gipsy engine and was toying with a pair of feeler gauges. **1935** T. E. LAWRENCE *Lett.* (1938) 856 A set of Power feeler gauges, as supplied in tool kits. **1967** E. CHAMBERS *Photolitho-Offset* xv. 231 The lock nuts and adjusting screws are released in order that, for example, a 0·006 in. feeler can just be inserted between the bearers on both sides of the cylinders.

b. A device which moves a control lever in the weaving of artificial silk.

1927 T. WOODHOUSE *Artif. Silk* 131 When the weft is nearly exhausted in the shuttle, an electric circuit is completed; this causes a single feeler under the circular magazine to move a control lever which ensures that the next chance of weft will place in the shuttle a bobbin with the same kind of weft as that just finished.

feeless ('fiːlɪs), *a.* [f. FEE *sb.*[2] + -LESS.] Without a fee or fees; not bringing, paying, or yielding fees; not receiving fees.

1740 SOMERVILLE *Hobbinol* II. 260 In Shoals they come, Neglected feeless Clients. **1825** LD. COCKBURN *Mem.* ii. 145 He could not tell a story without disclosing his power [i.e. of mimicry], a feeless faculty. **1848** LYTTON *Harold* VII. v, Feeless went he now from man to man. **1852** LD. COCKBURN *Jeffrey* I. 179 His practice..included the whole of our Courts, Civil, Criminal, and even ecclesiastical, the most fee-less of them all. **1886** *Pall Mall G.* 23 Sept. 2/1 There is any number of formalities to be gone through, the first of which consists in sending the fee-less child home. **1892** *Star* 3 Aug. 1/6 Praiseworthy zeal for a feeless theatre.

feeling ('fiːlɪŋ), *vbl. sb.* [f. FEEL *v.* + -ING[1].]

1. a. The action of the vb. FEEL in various senses; an instance of the same. Chiefly *gerundial.*

c **1400** *Lanfranc's Cirurg.* 140 In þis ben yvel signes.. crampe to schite wiþoute felynge & unmovablete of alle þe membres. **1611** BIBLE *Eph.* iv. 19 Who being past feeling haue giuen themselues ouer vnto lasciuiousnesse. **1791** BOSWELL *Johnson* an. 1752, Love is not a subject of reasoning, but of feeling. **1805** *Med. Jrnl.* XIV. 14 From the first feeling of a febrile attack. **1833** *Regul. Instr. Cavalry* (1844) 44 The horse must be kept attentive by a light feeling of the bridle.

attrib. **1754** A. MURPHY *Gray's Inn Jrnl.* No. 66 These, in their Feeling-hours of Distress, are reported to have reproached themselves with their Folly.

†**b.** *in (the) feeling:* = 'to the feel' (see FEEL *sb.* 3). *Obs.*

c **1400** *Lanfranc's Cirurg.* 305 Whanne it is not hoot in felinge. **1577** B. GOOGE *Heresbach's Husb.* III. (1586) 128 His hide not hard, or stubborne in feeling. **1662** J. DAVIES tr. *Mandelslo's Trav.* 155 It is of a reddish colour, as smooth, and slippery in the feeling as soap. **1669** STURMY *Mariner's Mag.* v. xii. 65 The harder the Corns of Powder are in feeling, by so much the better it is.

c. *attrib.* (Cf. FEEL *v.* 5.)

a **1849** SIR R. WILSON *Life* (1862) I. ii. 67 So soon as the Austrian Hussars had fired with their skirmishers a few feeling shot.

2. a. The faculty or power by which one feels (in sense 6 of the vb.); the 'sense of touch' in the looser acceptation of the term, in which it includes all physical sensibility not referable to the special senses of sight, hearing, taste, and smell.

c **1175** *Lamb. Hom.* 75 Hore blawing, hore smelling, heore feling wes al iattret. *c* **1230** *Hali Meid.* 13 Hire fif wittes, sihðe & herinege smecchunge & smealunge & euch limes felunge. *c* **1340** *Cursor M.* 17018 (Fairf.) Heryng, speche, sight, smellyng & felyng are wyttes v. **1398** TREVISA *Barth. De P.R.* III. ix. (1495) 55 The spyryte of felynge is shedde in to all the body. **1535** COVERDALE *2 Kings* iv. 31 There was nether voyce ner felynge. **1601** HOLLAND *Pliny* x. lxxi. 306 There is not a living creature..but hath the sence of feeling, although it have none else. **1669** A. BROWNE *Ars Pict.* (1675) 65 Finally by the feeling, we touch cold and hot, moist and dry. **1712** ADDISON *Spect.* No. 411 ¶1 The Sense of Feeling can indeed give us a Notion of..Shape. **1727** A. HAMILTON *New Acc. E. Ind.* II. xli. 109 The Elephant would find out the Gold among the Lead, by the nice Feeling of his Proboscis. **1828** STARK *Elem. Nat. Hist.* I. 30 A hoof.. blunts the feeling, and renders the foot incapable of seizing. **1871** R. ELLIS *Catullus* lxiv. 189 Yet from grief-worn limbs shall feeling wholly depart not.

b. A physical sensation or perception through the sense of touch or the general sensibility of the body.

c **1380** WYCLIF *Serm.* Sel. Wks. II. 10 Wiþ þis felyng of þis womman God ȝaf hir witt to prophecie þus. **1614** RALEIGH *Hist. World* iii. §7. 45 The ayre is so thinne, that it is not sufficient to beare vp the body of a bird hauing therein no feeling of her wings. **1805** *Med. Jrnl.* XIV. 242 It is often difficult..to describe on paper every feeling and appearance we notice. **1851** CARPENTER *Man. Phys.* (ed. 2) 572 A feeling of some of the corporeal changes taking place within themselves. **1884** tr. *Lotze's Metaph.* 524 That feeling which instructs us respecting the position, the movement, and the amount of exertion of our limbs.

†**3.** Passive experience; sensible proof; knowledge of an object through having felt its effects.

1526 TINDALE *Rom.* v. 4 Pacience bryngeth felynge, felynge bryngeth hope. **1630** *R. Johnson's Kingd. & Commw.* 100 Spaine both knowes us, and hath of late had some feeling of us.

4. a. The condition of being emotionally affected; an instance of this; an emotion. Often specialized by *of* with *fear, hope,* etc.

c **1400** *Test. Love* I. (1532) 327/1 Al my passyons and felynges weren loste. **1600** J. PORY tr. *Leo's Africa* II. 392 The which with great feeling, and contentment having understood..he instituted a Synod. **1632** J. HAYWARD tr. *Biondi's Eromena* 28 He felt in his heart..a..conceit or feeling of feare. **1639** tr. *Du Bosq's Compl. Woman* II. 13 Separation is so often made without any feeling. **1678** BUTLER *Hud.* III. ii. 1685 Fear that keeps all Feeling out As lesser pains are by the Gout. **1814** SCOTT *Wav.* lxi, Feelings more easily conceived than described. **1839** T. BEALE *Sperm Whale* 281 From that moment a feeling of hopelessness ran through us. **1856** FROUDE *Hist. Eng.* (1858) I. v. 463 All classes..were agreed in one common feeling of displeasure. **1877** E. R. CONDER *Bas. Faith* i. 13 Religious feelings differ from other feelings by their nature and by their object.

b. *pl.* in collective sense. Emotions, susceptibilities, sympathies.

1771 MRS. GRIFFITH tr. *Viaud's Shipwreck* 4 They need none of these heightenings to interest the feelings of my friend. **1791** MRS. RADCLIFFE *Rom. Forest* x, She tried to command her feelings so as to avoid disturbing the family. **1804** NELSON *Lett.* (1814) II. 57 Do not hurt my feelings by telling me that I neglect any opportunity. **1828** J. W. CROKER *C. Papers* (1884) I. xiii. 404 All my time being employed in assuaging what gentlemen call their feelings. **1850** MRS. STOWE *Uncle Tom's C.* vii, Both saw the absolute necessity of putting a constraint on their feelings.

5. Capacity or readiness to feel; susceptibility to the higher and more refined emotions; *esp.* sensibility or tenderness for the sufferings of others. *good feeling*: kindly and equitable spirit.

1588 SHAKS. *L.L.L.* IV. ii. 80 We thankfull should be Which we of taste and feeling are, for those parts that doe fructifie in vs more then he. **1600** E. BLOUNT tr. *Conestaggio* 44 Who if he had any feeling of a man, should [etc.]. **1622** BACON *Hen. VII* 33 Their king..out of a Princely feeling, was sparing, and compassionate towards his Subjects. **1731** SWIFT *Let. to Gay* 10 Sept., She has..not one grain of Feeling. **1752** HUME *Ess. & Treat.* (1777) I. 4 The delicacy of his feeling makes him sensibly touched. **1796** JANE AUSTEN *Sense & Sens.* xv. (1852) 63 Is he not a man of honour and feeling? **1802** MAR. EDGEWORTH *Moral T.* (1816) I. xvii. 142 He thinks I have no feeling. **1848** MACAULAY *Hist. Eng.* II. 89 The Church of England was saved from this outrage by the good sense and good feeling of the pope. **1849** RUSKIN *Sev. Lamps* ii. §19. 49 A woman of feeling would not wear false jewels.

6. Pleasurable or painful consciousness, emotional appreciation or sense (*of* one's own condition or some external fact).

c **1400** *Rom. Rose* 6449 Who so hath in his felyng The consequence of such shryvyng. **1605** SHAKS. *Lear* IV. vi. 287, I..haue ingenious feeling Of my huge Sorrowes. **1638** BAKER tr. *Balzac's Lett.* I. 69 The feeling I have of the courtesies received from him. **1683** D. A. *Art Converse* 56 You would easily be wrought into some feeling of your folly in this point. **1705** STANHOPE *Paraphr.* II. 296 They have already sufficient feeling of their disease. **1814** D'ISRAELI *Quarrels Auth.* (1867) 379 He was..too conscious of his superiority to betray a feeling of injury. **1828** SCOTT *F.M. Perth* ii, To encourage with a feeling of safety those whom [etc.]. **1874** MICKLETHWAITE *Mod. Par. Churches* 30 The feeling of perfect equality inside the church.

7. a. What one feels in regard to something; emotional attitude or opinion, sentiment. †In early use (cf. FEEL *v.* 15 a): Opinion.

c **1449** PECOCK *Repr.* 87 The disturblaunce and dyuerse feelingis had among ȝou silf now in Ynglond. *c* **1450** tr. *De Imitatione* I. ix, Wherfore truste not to muche in thin ovne felyng, but desire gladly to here oþir mennys felinges. **1760** GOLDSM. *Cit. W.* xxxviii, If we survey a king not only opposing his own feelings, but reluctantly refusing those he regards. **1771** MRS. GRIFFITH tr. *Viaud's Shipwreck* 236, I communicated my thoughts and feelings to Mr. Wright. **1828** D'ISRAELI *Chas. I,* I. v. 120 The feelings of the Romanists were sadly put to the test by a circumstance which now occurred. *Ibid.* II. xi. 287 The feelings of two ages attest the greatness of Hampden's name. **1863** MRS. CARLYLE *Lett.* III. 186 You know my feelings about religious excitement-ecstatics. **1874** GREEN *Short Hist.* viii. §10. 577 Cromwell bowed to the feeling of the nation. **1875** JOWETT *Plato* (ed. 2) V. 7 They have the feelings of old men about youth.

b. *transf.* Of a language: Instinctive preferences of expression.

1875 JOWETT *Plato* (ed. 2) I. p. xv, The feeling of the modern language is more opposed to tautology.

c. In commercial use, *feeling* (*of the market*): the degree of readiness to buy prevailing amongst traders.

1888 *Daily News* 11 July 2/7 An improved feeling is also perceptible in ropes.

8. In objective sense: The quality or condition which is felt to belong to anything; the impression produced by it upon a person.

1593 SHAKS. *Rich. II,* I. iii. 301 The apprehension of the good, Giues but the greater feeling to the worse. **1884** W. C. SMITH *Kildrostan* 45 He nigh lost his wits ere morning..So weird-like was the feeling of the place.

9. *Psychol.* **a.** By some writers (*e.g.* Brown, J. Mill, J. S. Mill) used for 'a fact or state of consciousness'. **b.** By others as a generic term comprising sensation, desire, and emotion, but excluding perception and thought. **c.** After Kant's use of *gefühl,* restricted to the element of pleasure or pain in any mental state. **d.** An intuitive cognition or belief neither requiring nor admitting of proof.

1739 HUME *Treatise* I. IV. §4 I. 513 Tho' bodies are felt by means of their solidity, yet the feeling is a quite different

thing from the solidity. *c* **1810** BROWN *Lect. Philos.* xi. (1838) 71 Consciousness.. is only a general term for all our feelings, of whatever species these may be,—sensations, thoughts, desires;—in short, all those states or affections of mind in which the phenomena of mind consist. *Ibid.* xxvi. (1838) 166/2 The feelings of extension, resistance, joy, sorrow, fragrance, colour, hope, fear, heat, cold, admiration, resentment. **1836–7** HAMILTON *Lect. Metaph.* (1859) I. xi. 186 This division of the phænomena of mind into the three great classes of the Cognitive faculties,—the Feelings, or capacities of Pleasure and Pain,—and the Exertive or Conative Powers.. was first promulgated by Kant. *Ibid.* II. xli. 492 The first grand distribution of our feelings will, therefore, be into the Sensations,—that is, the Sensitive or External Feelings; and into the Sentiments,—that is, the Mental or Internal Feelings. **1841–2** —— in *Reid's Wks.* 760 Feeling is a term preferable to Consciousness.. in so far as the latter does not mark so well the simplicity, ultimacy, and incomprehensibility of our original apprehensions. **1846** MILL *Logic* I. iii. §3. 66 Feeling, in the proper sense of the term, is a genus, of which Sensation, Emotion, and Thought, are subordinate species. **1855** BAIN *Senses & Int.* I. i. §3 The presence of Feeling is the foremost.. mark of mind. **1871** TYNDALL *Fragm. Sc.* (1879) II. xv. 375 Feeling appeared in the world before knowledge. **1875** JOWETT *Plato* (ed. 2) IV. 14 Feeling is not opposed to knowledge, and in all consciousness there is an element of both. **1892** SULLY *The Human Mind* iv. I. 64 The term feeling.. in a stricter sense is confined to those modes of consciousness which are in a peculiar sense affections of the subject, and which do not, in the same direct way as our thoughts and volitions, involve a clear reference to objects. *Ibid.* xiii. II. 1 We include under the head of feeling all psychical states or phenomena so far as they have the element or aspect of the agreeable and disagreeable.

e. Const. *in, into, out.*

1926 H. J. LASKI *Let.* 2 May (1953) II. 838 The acute pleasure that the feeling-out of other minds gives one. **1933** H. READ *Art Now* I. 49 No mere fellow-feeling, or feeling *with*, but rather a form of imaginative identification of the self with the object, a feeling *into*. **1949** KOESTLER *Insight & Outlook* xxvi. 359 This feeling-in process, or empathy, is.. based on the projection of part of our own personality into the shell of the other.

10. In Fine Art; cf. senses 4–6. **a.** *Painting.* (see quot. 1854). **b.** *Archit.* The general tone of a building or style of architecture; the impression produced on a spectator.

1854 FAIRHOLT *Dict. Terms Art, Feeling*, that visible quality in a work of Art which forcibly depicts the mental emotion of the painter, or which exhibits his perfect mastery over the materials of Art. **1859** JEPHSON *Brittany* v. 52 A favourable example of Renaissance, retaining as it does much Gothic feeling. **1874** MICKLETHWAITE *Mod. Par. Churches* 10 If the whole feeling of a building leads up to one point.

c. Of a musical performer: Sympathetic appreciation of the emotional purport of a composition, manifested in the manner of rendering.

1824 BYRON *Juan* XVI. xli, The circle.. applauds.. the tones, the feeling, and the execution.

11. *attrib.* and *Comb.*: (sense 9), esp. after G. compounds of *gefühl*, e.g. *gefühlston* (Wundt).

1892 SULLY *The Human Mind* iv. I. 8 The proposition that feeling as such has no quality (apart from the feeling-quality itself, agreeableness, disagreeableness) is held by most psychologists. **1892** *Rep. 2nd Internat. Congr. Exper. Psychol.* 34 The feeling-tone of belief appeared.. completely neutral, except so far as the subject-matter of belief caused it to have a pleasureable or painful quality. **1894** D. IRONS in *Mind* III. 93 Under feeling should be included on the one hand pleasure and pain, and on the other that feeling towards the object, which for the present we may call feeling attitude. The term is not unexceptionable, but is used for convenience instead of some such formula as 'feeling in relation to'. **1901** E. B. TITCHENER *Exper. Psychol.* I. I. ii. 54 Likeness may mean 'likeness of *feeling-effect*'. **1906** S. S. LAURIE *Synthetica* I. 136 This entitative feeling-potency does not contain the 'modes' of sense. **1909** W. M. URBAN *Valuation* ii. 37 Feeling or feeling-disposition is always presupposed by desire. **1912** [see AMBIVALENCE, -ENCY]. **1919** M. K. BRADBY *Psycho-Analysis* 58 Certain unconscious factors.. give the complex its peculiar feeling-tone. *Ibid.* 150 A woman who heard the first maroon announcing the Armistice on November 11th, 1918, responded with an instantaneous feeling-thought. **1920** T. P. NUNN *Education* 125 Feeling-spread is almost wholly biological imitation. *Ibid.* 134 Pugnacity is an example of the instincts in which the feeling-element is a definite emotion. **1937** *Discovery* July 216/2 The feeling-values of purple and violet are 'uncertain'. **1960** C. DAY LEWIS *Buried Day* iii. 56, I all unwittingly responded with the feeling-tone of a woman.

feeling (ˈfiːlɪŋ), *ppl. a.* [f. as prec. + -ING^{2}.] That feels.

1. a. That is the subject of sensation; sentient. **b.** Capable of sensation; sensitive.

c **1400** *Lanfranc's Cirurg.* (MS. A) 174 In þe heed þerof is fleisch þat is felynge. *c* **1430** *Hymns Virg.* (1867) 19 Wiþ beestis, feelinge lijf haue we. **1548–77** VICARY *Anat.* iv. (1888) 31 Seuen payre of sensatiue or feeling senews. **1602** CAREW *Cornwall* 6 a, Then passe on to those things, of growing, and feeling life, which upon her face doe relieue themselues. **1867** M. ARNOLD *Youth & Calm* Poems 1877 I. 24 For feeling nerves and living breath.

transf. **1680** OTWAY *Orphan* III. vii, The feeling Ayr's at rest.

2. Affected by emotion; accessible to emotion; sympathetic, compassionate.

1618 E. ELTON *Rom.* vii. (1622) 494 Let them with feeling hearts magnifie the Name of the Lord. **1639** *Bury Wills* (1850) 179, I haue bene, am, and ever shalbee, a feeleing member. **1772** *Ann. Reg.* 194/2 The whole demeanor.. did honour to them as feeling men, and peaceable citizens. **1854** J. S. C. ABBOTT *Napoleon* (1855) I. xiv. 243 Bonaparte, apart from politics, was feeling, kind, and accessible to pity.

b. Of language, manner, etc.: Indicating emotion or sensibility.

a **1586** SIDNEY *Arcadia* Wks. (Grosart) II. 61 Thy wailing words do much my spirit moue, They uttered are in such a feeling fashion. **1590** SPENSER *F.Q.* III. ii. 15 His feeling wordes her feeble sence much pleased. **1737** *Hist. Clorana* 77 This discourse was too feeling for Bellmont to bear much longer. **1799** SHERIDAN *Pizarro* IV. i, A feeling boldness in those eyes assures me that [etc.]. **1880** MRS. RIDDELL *Myst. Palace Gard.* xiv. (1881) 135 He could not have used more feeling language.

3. In quasi-passive sense: That is deeply or sensibly felt or realized, heart-felt, acute, vivid.

1530 TINDALE *Answ. More* Wks. (1573) 250/1 God hath.. geuen them a feeling faith of the mercy that is in Christ Jesu. **1556** J. HEYWOOD *Spider & F.* liii. 31 It was to him, a feeling greefe of grudge. **1605** SHAKS. *Lear* IV. vi. 226. **1632** J. HAYWARD tr. *Biondi's Eromena* 150 Knowing now by a feeling experience, her fathers reasons to be true. **1706** CIBBER *Perolla* 1, It is a feeling Pleasure With such Excesses to afflict thy Soul. **1721** SOUTHERNE *Oroon.* V. iv, I had a feeling [ed. 1696 living] sense Of all your royal favours.

feelingful (ˈfiːlɪŋfʊl), *a.* [f. FEELING *vbl. sb.* + -FUL.] Full of feeling.

1907 R. BOUGHTON *Bach* i. 6 Composers of Passions—human and feelingful if crude and naïve. **1943** H. READ *Educ. through Art* v. xvi. 147 Decoration.. implies a certain compromise between means and end, the 'feelingful' adaptation of colour and design to a given form or space.

feelingless (ˈfiːlɪŋlɪs), *a.* [f. FEELING *vbl. sb.* + -LESS.] Without feeling; devoid of feeling.

1821 *Blackw. Mag.* VIII. 622 Of savage Windram, feelingless and fierce. **1860** RUSKIN *Mod. Paint.* V. 303 For some time his [Turner's] work is, apparently, feelingless. **1876** H. SPENCER *Princ. Sociol.* (1877) I. 479 Feelingless units and units which monopolize feeling.

Hence **ˈfeelinglessly** *adv.*

1856 RUSKIN *Mod. Paint.* III. IV. xii. §15 Such expressions are not ignorantly and feelinglessly caught up.

feelingly (ˈfiːlɪŋlɪ), *adv.* [f. FEELING *ppl. a.* + -LY^{2}.]

†**1.** Consciously. *Obs.*

c **1440** HYLTON *Scala Perf.* (W. de W. 1494) II. iii, All chosen Soules.. hathe trouthe in cryste.. openly and felyngly as.. wyse men haue, or elles generally as chyldren haue.

†**2.** With just perception, understandingly, sensibly; appropriately, to the purpose. *Obs.*

1382 WYCLIF *Ecclus.* xiii. 27 He spac felendely [L. *sensate*] 'or wisely' weel. *c* **1386** CHAUCER *Knt.'s T.* 1345 Who most felyngly speketh of love. **1555** WATREMAN *Fardle Facions* App. 306 Sensibly to giue the meaninge of those infinite threasoures with suche wordes as falle moste felinglie for them. **1601** SHAKS. *Twel. N.* II. iii. 172 He shall finde himselfe most feelingly personated. **1630** *R. Johnson's Kingd. & Commw.* 628 The ancient exprobration of the Britons against the Romans.. cannot more feelingly be applied than unto these Indian Spaniards. **1646** S. PAGE in Spurgeon *Treas. Dav.* Ps. li. 8 The pain of the affliction exprest so feelingly in the breaking of bones.

3. With emotion; in a manner manifesting emotion.

1593 SHAKS. *Lucr.* 1492 Here feelingly she weeps Troys painted woes. *a* **1679** HOBBES *Rhet.* III. vii. (1681) 108 By speaking Feelingly; that is, with such Passion as is fit for the matter he is in. **1713** STEELE *Guardian* I. No. 44 ¶5 The whole assembly seemed to condole with me very feelingly. **1807** G. CHALMERS *Caledonia* I. III. vii. 381 The bard speaks feelingly of the wretchedness of his age. **1839** YEOWELL *Anc. Brit. Ch.* Pref. (1847) 5 He feelingly deplores the miserable state of his country.

4. By or from actual personal feeling, knowledge, or experience.

a **1534** MORE *De Quat. Noviss.* Wks. 76/2 Which if we.. so feelyngly perceyued as we myght [etc.]. *a* **1618** RALEIGH *Advice of Son* in *Rem.* (1661) 118 In your Soul shall you feelingly find these terrible fears. **1834** SOUTHEY *Doctor* xi. (1862) 30 No man knows the value of time more feelingly than I do. **1885** J. BONAR *Malthus* I. i. 23 He wrote feelingly, as he had the malady [toothache] at the time of writing.

†**5.** Sensitively. *Obs.*

1796 MORSE *Amer. Geog.* I. 319 A people feelingly alive to every thing that could affect the rights for which they had been contending. **1806** METCALFE in Owen *Wellesley's Desp.* 808, I would wish to see our government feelingly alive to points of honor. **1806** W. TAYLOR in Robberds *Mem.* II. 125 You seemed to me.. to shiver in the breeze too feelingly.

6. In such a manner as to be felt or to leave an impression behind.

1413 LYDG. *Pylgr. Sowle* IV. xxvi. (1483) 72 Also I may seye more felyngly to thyne experyence as seynt austyn techeth. **1534** MORE *On the Passion* Wks. 1313/1 Thoughe it bee.. ethe inoughe for any manne to saye the worde.. yet is it harde for many a man to let it fal felyngly, and sincke downe depe into his hert. **1600** SHAKS. *A.Y.L.* II. i. 11 These are counsellors That feelingly perswade me what I am. *a* **1657** R. LOVEDAY *Lett.* (1663) 69 J. W.'s sicknesse.. does affect me as feelingly as can be requir'd from an unbiass'd friendship. **1853** KANE *Grinnell Exp.* xxviii. (1856) 231 But a breeze.. never failed to persuade us, and that feelingly, that the mercury was honest.

feelingness (ˈfiːlɪŋnɪs). [f. FEELING *ppl. a.* + -NESS.] Emotional quality or character.

1870 G. MEREDITH *Lett.* (1912) I. 216 The feelingness of your letter of Mickleham was much felt there. **1901** F. H. BURNETT *Making of Marchioness* II. vi, 'I do *love* him so,' she whispered hysterically. 'I do so *love* him, and I shall so *miss* him!' with the italicised feelingness of old.

feelless (ˈfiːllɪs), *a. Sc. rare.* [f. FEEL *sb.* + -LESS.] Without feel or feeling, insensible.

1820 *Marmaiden of Clyde* xxi. in *Edin. Mag.* May 423, I.. feelless lay, while the laidlie droich Perform'd his lord's commands.

†**ˈfeelsome,** *a. Obs. rare.* [f. FEEL + -SOME.] Attractive to the feeling or sense; in quot., = tasty.

c **1440** *York Myst.* xlvi. 136 Haile! floure fresshe florisshed þi frewte is full felesome.

feelthy (ˈfiːlθɪ), *a. slang.* [Jocular imitation of foreign pronunc. of FILTHY *a.*] Obscene.

1933 E. A. ROBERTSON *Ordinary Families* vi. 112 Buy a feelthy peecture, lady? **1935** G. GORER *Africa Dances* III. i. 193 Little bronze figures of an obscenity which resembles feelthy postcards. **1962** *Spectator* 11 May 622/2 Tiny ant-like creatures go about their feelthy business. **1963** B. S. JOHNSON *Travelling People* iv. 68 Maurie has a great collection of feelthy books down here—including a first edition of Cleland's *Fanny Hill, or the Memoirs of a Woman of Pleasure.*

feely (ˈfiːlɪ). Usu. in *pl.* feelies. [f. FEEL *v.* + -Y^{6}.] A (hypothetical) talking film augmented by tactual effects.

1931 [see EGALITARIAN *a.*]. **1932** A. HUXLEY *Brave New World* iii. 39 Going to the Feelies this evening, Henry?.. I hear the new one at the Alhambra is first-rate... The most amazing tactual effects. *Ibid.* xi. 197 Take hold of those metal knobs on the arms of your chair... Otherwise you won't get any of the feely effects. **1964** *Discovery* Oct. 22/1 We shall certainly need to be most cautious if techniques develop—to colour, three dimensions, or even to the 'smellies' and 'feelies'.

feem(e, var. of FEME, *Obs.*, woman.

†**ˈfeeman.** *Obs.* Also **feman.** [f. FEE *sb.*^{2} + MAN *sb.*^{1}]. A vassal.

1517 *Will of Grigge* (Somerset Ho.), One of the Feemen wᵗ our soveraigne Lordᵉ the Kyng.

Hence **ˈfeemanly,** as befits a vassal. **feemanship,** the state or condition of a vassal.

1509 in Walbran *Mem. Fountains Abbey* (Surtees Soc.) 233 And also he shall kepe upon the saide graunge, trewly and femanlye, lx kye.. His office or service of husbandry and femanshipe.

feen, feend(e, obs. ff. FEN, FIEND.

feeoffee: see FEOFFEE.

feer (fiːr) *sb.*^{1} Only ME. and *Sc.* Forms: 3 feor, 8– *Sc.* fiar, fier, feer. [ME. *feor* a. OF. *feor, feur, fuer* fixed price, standard: L. *forum* (in class. L. market).]

†**1.** A price. *Obs.*

a **1225** *Ancr. R.* 398 Sete feor o ðine luue. *a* **1240** *Wohunge* in *Cott. Hom.* 287 ȝif þat i mi luue bede for to selle and setle feor þer upon swa hehe swa ich eauer wile. *c* **1320** *Cast. Love* 1091 ȝif þou wilt him bugge to his feore.

2. *Sc.* See quot. and FIARS.

18.. JAMIESON, *Fier, Feer,* a standard of any kind. Yarn is said to be spun *by*, i.e. beyond, *the fier*, when it is drawn smaller than the proper thickness.

†**ˈfeer,** *sb.*^{2} *Obs. rare.* See also FIAR. [f. FEE *v.* + -ER^{1}.] One who fees or gives a fee to another.

1583 STUBBES *Anat. Abus.* II. (1882) 34 They are.. in fee with the Drapers, that if a man come to them to desire them to helpe them to buy a piece of cloth.. they will straightway conduct them to their feer.

feer (ˈfɪə(r)), *sb.*^{3} *Mining.* [f. FEE *v.*^{2} + -ER^{1}.] One who fees or loads up the coal.

1883 GRESLEY *Gloss. Coal Mining, Feer.*

†**feer, fere,** *a. Obs. rare.* [a. OF. *fer, fier* (mod.Fr. *fier.*) = Pr. *fer*, It. and Sp. *fiero*:—L. *fer-us*: see FIERCE.] Bold, fierce; proud.

c **1375** *Sc. Leg. Saints, Eufemia* 141 þe Juge fel & fere. —— *Tecla* 217 Syne come a lyone fel & fere. *c* **1380** *Sir Ferumb.* 329 A knyȝt ful feer. *Ibid.* 414 Roland ys.. so coraious & so fere. *c* **1450** *Guy Warw.* (C.) 1428 He was a bolde man and a fere.

feer (fiːr, fɪə(r)), *v.* Forms: 5 fere, 8–9 feer, 9 *Sc.* feir. [Perh. (as suggested by Jamieson) repr. OE. *fyrian* to make a furrow (:—**furhjan*), f. *furh* FURROW *sb.*; for the phonology cf. *beir, beere* as variants of BIRR *sb.*]

'To mark off the breadth of every ridge (of land) for ploughing, by drawing a furrow on each side of the space allotted for it' (Jam.).

c **1400** *York Manual* (Surtees) 224* Yee shale praye for all lande tilland and lee ferand. **1862** J. WILSON *Farming* vi. 206 This operation—called in Scotland feiring the land—is usually entrusted to the most skilful ploughman on each farm. **1881** *Leicestersh. Gloss.* s.v., To feer land, is to set it out as it is intended to be ploughed.

feer(e, obs. form of FEAR.

feer(e, var. of FERE *sb.*, *Obs.* companion.

féerie (ˈfeəri, ˈfeɪəri). Also **féery, feërie.** [F. *féerie*, f. *fée* fairy; see FAIRY *sb.*] A spectacular theatrical production involving the representation of fairy scenes and characters.

1878 *Lloyd's Weekly* 19 May 7/2 A magnificent *féerie*, in which five Nubian lions are announced as about to make their *début*. **1886** *Athenæum* 24 July 116/3 M. Victorien

Sardou is at work on a *féerie*, or rather a piece for children, intended for the Porte-Saint-Martin. **1895** *Daily News* 5 Feb. 5/4 It is not strictly an opera, but is described as a dramatic feërie, entitled 'The Royal Infants'.

'feering, *vbl. sb.* [f. FEER *v.* + -ING¹.] The action of the vb. FEER; also *attrib.*

1799 J. ROBERTSON *Agric. Perth* 248 The feering of a gathered ridge. **1862** J. WILSON *Farming* vi. 206 This feiring is only required when a process of fallowing..has obliterated the former ridges. *Ibid.*, The ploughman.. erects his three or more feiring poles perfectly in line, at a distance from the fence equal to half the width of the ridges or spaces in which it is proposed to plough the field.

b. *concr.* One of the rectangular spaces of land between the furrows; a land.

1846 J. BAXTER *Libr. Pract. Agric.* (ed. 4) I. 257 Spaces for ploughing, called feerings, of generally thirty yards in width are marked off. **1851** *Jrnl. R. Agric. Soc.* XII. I. 125 In Scotland the land is ploughed.. in broad feirings of various dimensions. **1879** MISS JACKSON *Shropsh. Word-bk.*, *Feerings*, spaces of ploughed land from eight to more yards in width.

†**'feerness.** *Obs. rare.* [f. FEER *a.* + -NESS.] Boldness, pride.

1475 *Bk. Noblesse* 20 For now it is tyme to clothe you.. with the cotes of armes of youre auncien feernesse.

†**'feeror.** *Obs.* In 8 fearer, -or. [aphet. f. of AFFEEROR.] = AFFEEROR.

1711 W. STORR in *Yorksh. Archæol. Jrnl.* VII. 55 Fines are assessed by the steward..assisted by two..'fearers' or 'fearors'.

feers, obs. form of FIERCE *a.*

feerth(e, obs. form of FOURTH.

†**'feery-fary.** *Obs. Sc.* Forms: 6 fery fary, fe(i)rie farye, fiery fairy, 7 feery fary, 8 fearie-fairy. [reduplicated form of FARY.] 'Bustle, confusion' (Jam.).

1535 STEWART *Cron. Scot.* III. 109 The ferie farye..Wes maid that tyme at mariage of our king. **1597** MONTGOMERIE *Cherrie & Slae* 252 Quha reft me, and left me In sik a feirie-farye. **1641** R. BAILLIE *Jrnl. & Lett.* (1775) I. xxviii. 285 Chamber and table discourse, for argument, flum-flams, and fearie-fairies, could not be treasons. *a* **1724** *Battle of Harlaw* ii. in *Evergreen* (1761) I. 78 All Folks war in a fiery fairy.

,fee-'simple. *Law.* [a. AF. *fee-simple* (Littleton); see FEE *sb.*² and SIMPLE; in Anglo-Lat. *feodum simplex* or *purum*, in AF. *fee pur*. The combination is not found in continental use; it seems to have been intended to denote a 'fee' in the unqualified sense of the word, as opposed to a FEE-TAIL.]

An estate in land, etc. belonging to the owner and his heirs for ever, without limitation to any particular class of heirs. ***in fee-simple***: in absolute possession.

1463 *Bury Wills* (1850) 31 The seid lond to remayne to me infysympill. **1523** FITZHERB. *Surv.* 12 b, Tenauntes in fee symple. **1577** NORTHBROOKE *Dicing* (1843) 115 It causeth manie of them..to bring their fee simple into fee single. **1593** SHAKS. *2 Hen. VI*, IV. x. 27 Heere's the Lord of the soile come to seize me for a stray, for entering his Fee-simple without leaue. **1667** PEPYS *Diary* (1879) IV. 260 Unless we could buy the fee-simple of it. **1767** BLACKSTONE *Comm.* II. 104 Tenant in fee-simple..is he that hath lands, tenements, or hereditaments, to hold to him and his heirs for ever. **1849** BRIGHT *Sp. Burden on Land* 15 Mar., A rise in the value of the fee-simple of an acre.

transf. and *fig.* **1601** SHAKS. *All's Well* IV. iii. 311 He will sell the fee-simple of his saluation. **1621** BURTON *Anat. Mel.* III. iv. I. iii. (1651) 661 They are the true heirs, have the Feesimple of heaven by a peculiar donation. **1781** COWPER *Conversation* 590 Is sparkling wit.. The fixed fee-simple of the vain and light? **1880** MRS. LYNN LINTON *Rebel of Family* I. iv, Here were four women, of any one of whom he had the fee simple.

b. *attrib.* (*lit.* and *fig.*) as ***fee-simple-blood, -estate, -ground, -land, -purchase, -wits.***

1463 *Bury Wills* (1850) 31 Fysympil grownd. **1607** HEYWOOD *Fayre Mayde* Wks. 1874 II. 47 Their own feesimple wits. **1639** DRUMM. OF HAWTH. *Challenge Knts. Err.* Wks. (1711) 233 We of hereditary and fee-simple blood. **1710** *Lond. Gaz.* No. 4723/3 A Fee Simple Estate..inclosed with Quick Fences. **1807** VANCOUVER *Agric. Devon* (1813) 308 Fee-simple purchase of 140 acres.

feet, pl. of FOOT.

,fee-'tail. *Law.* [a. AF. *fee tailé* (the final *é* being dropped as in some other legal words) = Anglo-L. *feudum talliatum*; the second word is the pa. pple. of OF. *taillier* (mod.F. *tailler*) lit. 'to cut', whence, to fix precisely, limit.]

An estate of inheritance entailed or limited to some particular class of heirs of the person to whom it is granted; a limited fee. ***fee-tail expectant***: see EXPECTANT *a.* 3.

[**1294** *Year-bk. 21–2 Edw. I* (Rolls) 365 Feodum talliatum. *Ibid.* 641 La ou home feffe un autre en fee pur e nent de fee tayle.] **1495** *Act 11 Hen. VII*, c. 9 §2 Londes..not being his owne enheritaunce..in fe taille. **1602** *2nd Pt. Return fr. Pernass.* IV. ii. (Arb.) 52 Nay thats plaine in Littleton, for if that fee-simple, and the fee taile be put together, it is called hotch-potch. *a* **1618** RALEIGH in Gutch *Coll. Cur.* I. 78 In his demesn, as of fee-tail. **1628** COKE *On Litt.* 27 b, Tenant in Fee Tayle. **1741** T. ROBINSON *Gavelkind* v. 78 In Fee or Fee-Tail expectant on an Estate for Life or in Tail. **1817** W. SELWYN *Law Nisi Prius* (ed. 4) II. 1115 Whether he had an estate in fee, fee-tail, or for life. **1831–2** *Act 2–3 Will. IV*, c. 80 §3 in *Oxf. & Camb. Enactm.* 161 Tenants in fee tail.

feetless ('fiːtlɪs), *a.* [f. *feet*, pl. of FOOT + -LESS.] Without feet. Cf. FOOTLESS.

1605 CAMDEN *Rem.* (1870) 231 Three feetless Birds. **1639** FULLER *Holy War* IV. xvi. 196 Mangled, headlesse, handlesse, feetlesse corpses. **1656** J. SERGEANT tr. *T. White's Peripat. Inst.* 97 Something like this is the creeping of feetlesse Creatures.

feetly, obs. form of FEATLY.

feeze (fiːz), *sb.* Forms: 4 veze, 6 feas(e, 6–7 feese, 7 feaze, 7– feeze, 9 *U.S.* pheese, -ze. [f. FEEZE *v.*¹]

1. A rush, impetus; hence, a violent impact. Also, a rub. Now *dial.* and *U.S.*

1386 CHAUCER *Knt.'s T.* 1127 And there out came a rage and such a veze, That it made al the gate for to rese. **1592** WYRLEY *Armorie* 50 They light vpon him..and beare him downe with mightie feas. **1603** KNOLLES *Hist. Turkes* (1621) 878 Both their [galleys] beakes were with the feaze broken off. **1847** MATHER in *Whistlebinkie* (1890) II. 165 Wi' a lick o' sweet oil an' a feeze o' her hand. **1865** LOWELL *Lett.* (1894) I. 349 Even the locust's cry is no longer a mere impertinent feeze of sound.

†**b.** ***to fetch or take (one's) feeze***: to take a short run before leaping. ***to take one's full feeze***: to start at full speed. *Obs.*

1571 CAMPION *Hist. Irel.* II. ix. (1633) 120 Advising you though you have fetched your feaze, yet to look well ere you leape over. **1580** BARET *Alv.* R 41 To leape, taking his race, or fetching his feese, *ex procursu salire*. **1600** HOLLAND *Livy* I. lxv. (1609) 87 b, They [the Roman soldiers] tooke their full feese, and ran up the hill. **1675** T. TULLY *Let. Baxter* 19 If a man do but goe back a little to take his feeze, he may easily jump over it.

2. *U.S.* chiefly *colloq.* A state of alarm or perturbation.

1846 WORCESTER, *Pheese*, a fit of fretfulness. **1855** LOWELL *Let.* in *Atlantic Monthly* Dec. (1892) 749/2 So I am in a feeze half the time. *a* **1865** HALIBURTON (Cent. Dict.), When a man's in a feese, there's no more sleep that hitch.

feeze (fiːz), *v.*¹ *Obs.* exc. *dial.* Forms: 1 fésian, 3–6 fese(n, -yn, 3 *south.* vesen, 5, 7 feese, -ze, (6 pheeze, 7 feize, pheese), 7 *south.* veeze, veize, veze, 6, 9 fease, *south.* vease, 6–9 feaze. [OE. *fésian* (? also *fésan*), *fýsian* to drive, corresponds to ON. **feysa* (mod.Norwegian *föysa*, Sw. *fösa*), app.:—**fausjōjan*, *fausjan*. It is possible that this word and ON. *fiúka*, *feyka*, of similar meaning, are from a Teut. root *feu*, *fau*, differentiated by *s* and *k* (pre-Teut. *g*) suffixes.

Totally unconnected with OE. *fýsan* (:—**funsjan*) to hurry, which survived into early ME. as *fusen* (y): see FUSE *v.*¹]

†**1.** *trans.* To drive; to drive off or away; to make (one) run, put to flight; to frighten away. Often with *away*. Also ***to feeze about***. *Obs.*

c **890** *Laws Edward & Guthrum* xi, Ðonne fysie hi man of earde. **1014** WULFSTAN *Hom.* (1883) xxxiii. 162 Ðæt oft on ʒefeohte an fesep tyne. *a* **1300** *Signa ante Judicium* 172 in *E.E.P.* (1862) 12 Al þe fentis sal.. be ifesid in to helle. **1387** TREVISA *Higden* (Rolls) I. 339 Powder of erþe of þat lond i-sowe in oþer londes vseþ [*v.r.* veseþ] awey wormes. *c* **1400** *Beryn* Prol. 351 Shal I com þen, Cristian, & fese a-wey þe Cat? **1548** UDALL, etc. *Erasm. Par. Luke* viii. 29 He should bee drieuen and feased of the deiuill into deserte places. **1577–87** HOLINSHED *Chron.* II. 10/2 They feazed awaie the Irish. **1583** STANYHURST *Æneis* I. (Arb.) 31 Lyke bees.. Feaze away the droane bees with sting, from maunger, or hiuecot. **1689** C. MATHER *Mem. Providences* 62 A Devil would..make her laugh to see how he feaz'd 'em about.

b. To impel.

1610 *Mirr. Mag., Sir N. Burdet* xvi. 480 Those eager impes whom food-want feaz'd to fight amaine.

2. To frighten, put into a state of alarm.

c **1440** CAPGRAVE *Life St. Kath.* v. 611 Bete hir weel, right for hir blaspheme, To fese hem alle that troste in hir doctryne. **1460** *Christ's Compl.* 471 in *Pol. Rel. & L. Poems* (1866) 198 Ful foule schulde þi foos be fesid If þou myʒte ouer hem as y ouer þee may. **1887** *Kent Gloss.*, *Fease*, to fret, worry.

3. The threat 'I'll feeze you' seems to have given rise to the following senses: **a.** *vaguely*, To 'do for', 'settle the business of' (a person). **b.** To beat, flog.

a. 1596 SHAKS. *Tam. Shr.* Induct. i. 1 Ile pheeze you infaith. **1613** BEAUM. & FL. *Coxcomb* I. vi, I'll feese you. **1620** FLETCHER *Chances* II. i, H'as giv'n me my *quietus est*: I felt him In my small guts: I'me sure h'as feez'd me.

b. 1610 B. JONSON *Alch.* v. v, Come, will you quarrel? I will feize you, sirrah. **1631** MASSINGER *Emperor East* IV. ii, *Countryman.* Zookers! Had I one of you zingle, with this twig I would so veeze you! **1674** J. W[RIGHT] *Mock-Thyestes* 101 Your Toby I'le so feaze with this Rod..That [etc.].

feeze (fiːz), *v.*² *dial.*

1. *trans.* To twist or turn with a screw-like motion; to screw. Also with *off*, *on*, *up*.

1806 A. DOUGLAS *Poems* 43, I downa feeze my fiddle-string. **1813** W. LESLIE *View Nairn* Gloss., *Feeze*, to turn a screw nail.

b. *fig.* To insinuate.

1813 W. LESLIE *View Nairn* Gloss., *Feeze*, to insinuate into unmerited confidence or favour. **1824** JAMIESON s.v., One feezes himself into the good graces of another.

2. *intr.* for *refl.* To wind in and out; to hang off and on.

17.. in Ritson *Scot. Songs* (1794) I. 287 My ewie never play'd the like But fees'd [*printed* tees'd] about the barn-yard wa'.

feff, feffment: see FEOFF.

feg(e, fegg, Sc. and north. forms of FIG.

fegary (fɪ'gɛərɪ). *dial.* and *colloq.* Also 7 fagarie, -ary, 7–8 figary, (7 figuary), 8 fleegerie, 9 fee-, fleegary. [A corruption of VAGARY.]

1. A vagary, prank, freak; a whim, eccentricity.

1600 DEKKER *Fortunatus* Wks. 1873 I. 116 Your body is little mended by your fetching fegaries. **1625** SHIRLEY *Love-tricks* III. v, I have a great desire to be taught some of your figaries. **1659** *Lady Alimony* II. i. in Hazl. *Dodsley* XIV. 289, I know all their fagaries to a hair. **1663** *Flagellum, or O. Cromwell* (1672) 60 Caprichio's of Biennial Parliaments and the like Figaries. **1748** RICHARDSON *Clarissa* (1811) V. 183 The world must stand still for their figaries.

2. Gewgaws, trifles; fineries in dress.

1724 RAMSAY *Love inviting Reason* iii, Dinna prefer your fleegeries to me. **1808** MAYNE *Siller Gun* 56 iii. 2 Grave dames in a' their nice feegaries. **1823** TENNANT *Card. Beaton* I. iii, As braw a hizzie, wi' her fardingales and her fleegaries, as ony.

Hence **fe'gary** (also *flagary*), *v. intr.*, to busy oneself about trifles in dress.

1821 H. DUNCAN *Young S. Country Weaver* (ed. 2) 45 Did I come hame..to stan' and look at your flagarying there?

fegs (fɛgz). *Obs.* exc. *Sc.* and *dial.* Forms: 6–7 feckins, 6–8 fackins, 7–8 faikine, 8 feggings, 9 faikins, 7 fac, feck, 7–9 facks, 8–9 fags, 9 faags, faiks, feck(s, faix, 8– fegs. [The forms here collected are distortions of FAY *sb.*¹, FAITH, perh. with suffix -KIN(S, frequent in such trivial quasi-oaths; cf. *bodykins*, *by'rlakin*.]

1. As an (unmeaning) sb. in exclamatory phrases expressing asseveration or astonishment. See also I'FEGS.

1598 B. JONSON *Ev. Man in Hum.* I. iii, By my fackins. **1600** HEYWOOD *1 Edw. I*, III. i, No, by my feckins! **1610** B. JONSON *Alch.* I. ii, How! Sweare by your fac? *a* **1627** MIDDLETON *Quiet Life* II. ii, By my facks, sir. **16..** *Robin Hood & Q. Kath.* 90 in Furniv. *Percy Folio* I. 42 By faikine of my body. *a* **1654** WEBSTER & ROWLEY *Cure for Cuckold* IV. iii, By my feck. **1726** VANBRUGH *Journ. Lond.* III. i, No, by good feggings. **1768** BEATTIE *To Mr. A. Ross* v, O' my fegs. **1880** JAMIESON s.v., My faiks! **1884** *Chester Gloss.*, *Good Fecks!*

2. As simple asseverative.

1638 BROME *Antipodes* v. iv. Wks. 1873 III. 322 Nay facks I am not jealous. **1790** A. WILSON *To W. Mitchell* Poet. Wks. (1846) 113 Fegs. **1804** ANDERSON *Cumbrld. Ball.* 104 Sae faikins we mun hev a sweat. **1863** *Tyneside Songs* 86 Faix they've got a warnin'. **1875** *Sussex Gloss.*, Why! you are smart, fegs! **1891** BARRIE *Little Minister* II. 191 Na, faags! it was waur than that.

fegue, obs. form of FEAGUE.

Fehling ('feɪlɪŋ). The name of Hermann von *Fehling* (1812–1885), German chemist, used *attrib.* or in the possessive to designate an alkaline solution of cupric sulphate and Rochelle salt used in sugar analysis; also *ellipt.* Hence ***Fehling('s) reaction, test.***

1873 *Jrnl. Chem. Soc.* XI. 265 The crystals, which are permanent in the air, neither hygroscopic nor efflorescent, are recommended by the author for the titration of Fehling's solution. **1887** *Encycl. Brit.* XXII. 624/1 Every c.c. of Fehling solution oxidises about 5 milli-grams..of dextrose. **1909** *Cent. Dict.* Suppl. 464/3 Fehling's reagent, test. **1946** *Nature* 31 Aug. 295/2 The distillate slightly reduced Fehling's solution. **1954** *Thorpe's Dict. Appl. Chem.* (ed. 4) XI. 203/2 Soxhlet's Fehling solution in excess is boiled with sugar solution. *Ibid.* 205/2 Into a flask of 300–400 ml. capacity, measure 10 ml. or 25 ml. of Fehling. **1960** A. E. BENDER *Dict. Nutrition* 48/2 *Fehling's test*, for reducing substances, mostly used to distinguish reducing from non-reducing sugars.

fei ('feɪiː). [Tahitian vernacular name of the plant and fruit.] A type of plantain, *Musa fehi*, native of Tahiti and New Caledonia.

1829 W. ELLIS *Polynesian Researches* I. xiii. 374 In several of these islands, the *fei* is the principal support of the inhabitants. The plantain is a fruit that is always acceptable. **1894** STEVENSON & OSBOURNE *Ebb-Tide* I. ii, Five Kanakas ..were squatted round a basin of fried feis. **1926** *Univ. Calif. Pub. Bot.* XII. 156 The Fe'i are of the greatest interest ethnobotanically. **1959** TINDALE & LINDSAY *Rangatira* i. 13 The big red-gold fei plantains grew sparsely on the slopes of the central mountain.

feid, obs. Sc. form of FEUD *sb.*¹, enmity.

feie(n, feier, obs. forms of FAY *v.*¹, FAIR.

feigh (feːx), *int. Sc.* An expression of disgust or abomination. Cf. FAUGH, FIE.

1715 RAMSAY *Christ's Kirk Gr.* II. vi, Ye stink o' leeks, O feigh!

feigh, var. of FAY *v.*²

†**feign,** *sb. Obs. rare*⁻¹. [f. next vb.] The action of feigning; pretence, deceit. In phrase, ***without feign.***

c **1320** *Cast. Love* 1482 Another that come fro hevyn, with-out feyn.

feign (feɪn), *v.* Forms: 3–7 feigne, feine, -yne, 6 feygne, (3 feinyhe, 5 feyn-yn), 3–5 fene, (4 feny),

4–7 fain(e, -yn(e, (6 feane), 6–7 faigne (6 faynd), 6– feign. *Sc.* 4 fenyhe, 5 fenȝe, fenye, 6 feinȝie, feinȝie, feynȝe (*printed* feynze), 7 fane. Also 4 i-feyn. [ME. *feinen*, *feignen*, ad. OF. *feindre* (pr. pple. *feign-ant*):—Lat. *fingĕre* to form, mould, feign, whence FICTION, FIGMENT. Cf. Pr. *fenher*, *finher*, Sp., Pg. *fingir*, It. *fingere*.]

I. 1. *trans.* In material sense: To fashion, form, shape. *Obs.* exc. as nonce-use after Lat.

a **1300** *E.E. Psalter* xciii. [xciv.] 9 Þat feinyhes egh, noght sees with-al? **1877** L. MORRIS *Epic Hades* I. 71 A dull fretful child Crushes its toys and knows not with what skill Those feeble forms are feigned.

II. To fashion fictitiously or deceptively.

2. To invent (a story, excuse, accusation); to forge (a document).

a **1300** *Cursor M.* 22007 (Cott.) Nathing sal I fene yow neu. **1297** R. GLOUC. (1724) 421 Somme feynede a delay. **1393** GOWER *Conf.* III. 175 Thou hast feigned This tale. **1430–50** tr. *Higden* (Rolls) II. 373 Somme fables be feynede for cause of delectation. **1534** CRANMER in Ellis *Orig. Lett.* Ser. III. II. 317 All that ever she said was fayned of her owne ymagynacion. **1655** FULLER *Ch. Hist.* I. iii. §7 As I find little, so I will feign nothing. **1736** BUTLER *Anal.* I. II. vii. 265 There is nothing in the Characters, which would raise a Thought of their being feigned. **1790** PALEY *Horæ Paul.* Rom. ii. 19 Shall we say that the author..feigned this anecdote of St. Paul? **1862** LD. BROUGHAM *Brit. Const.* x. 128 Fables, feigned by the superstition..of the people.

†**b.** *to feign* (a slander, fault) *upon*, *against*: to allege falsely against, attribute falsely to. *Obs.*

1535 JOYE *Apol. Tindale* 1 Sclaunders fayned upon me. *c* **1615** *Lives Women Saints* 31 She fayned her owne falte on the chaste yong prince. **1654** tr. *Martinius' Conq. China* 205 Having feigned many crimes against the Priests.

†**c.** To invent, 'coin' (a word). *Obs.*

1607 TOPSELL *Four-f. Beasts* (1673) 413 In Germany they call it 'Pile' and 'Zisel'; and of this German word was the Latine 'Citellus' feigned. *Ibid.* 101 [see FEIGNED *ppl. a.* 2].

†**d.** To contrive (a deception). *Obs.*

1690 W. WALKER *Idiomat. Anglo-Lat.* 170 They fain a wile..among themselves.

3. To relate or represent in fiction; to fable. Const. with simple complement, with *obj.* and *inf.*, or with sentence as *obj.* Now *rare*.

1413 LYDG. *Pilgr. Sowle* v. viii. (1483) 99 Orpheus was so swete an harpoure as the clerkes feynen that [etc.]. *a* **1569** KINGESMYLL *Godly Advise* (1580) 15 The Poets..fained there were iii She Goddesses in contention for their beautie. **1585** JAS. I *Ess. Poesie* (Arb.) 75 Harpyes..whome the Poets feynzeis to represent theuis. **1598** BARCKLEY *Felic. Man* II. (1603) 118 Diogenes is fained to see the rich King Crœsus among the dead. **1642** FULLER *Holy & Prof. St.* II. viii. 77 Well did the Poets feigne Pallas Patronesse of arts and armes. *c* **1645** HOWELL *Lett.* II. 34 They faind a Post to come puffing upon the stage. **1667** MILTON *P.L.* XI. 627 Things.. worse Than Fables yet have feign'd. **1727** DE FOE *Syst. Magic* I. ii. (1840) 41 Atlas..is feigned by the ancients to carry the world upon his shoulders. **1770** LANGHORNE *Plutarch* (1879) I. 65/2 The poets feign of Hercules, that only with a club and lion's skin he travelled over the world. **1816** J. WILSON *City of Plague* III. i. 343 Drest is she all in white, as Poets feign The angel Innocence.

†**b.** *absol.* and *intr.* To make fictitious statements; to indulge in fiction. *Obs.*

c **1384** CHAUCER *H. Fame* III. 388 Oon seyde that Omere made lyes, Feyninge in his poetryes. *c* **1400** *Destr. Troy* 419 Ouyd..feynit in his fablis. **1570** B. GOOGE *Pop. Kingd.* I. 15 Nor vnaduisedly we speake, nor rashly thereof fayne. **1605** B. JONSON *Volpone* II. i, He that should write But such a fellow, should be thought to faine Extremely. **1636** R. JAMES *Iter Lanc.* (1845) 4 If storyes do not faine.

4. (More fully, †*to feign to oneself*.) To conjure up (delusive representations); to picture to oneself, imagine (what is unreal). Now *rare*.

1377 LANGL. *P. Pl.* B. Prol. 36 Somme..Feynen hem fantasies. **1525** TINDALE *Matt.* ix. 15 *marg.-note*, They fain themself no pain. **1578** TIMME *Caluine on Gen.*, Cain.. feigned to himself so many enemies, as there were men in the world. **1608** BP. HALL *Char. Virtues & V.*, Either there are bugs, or he faineth them. **1635** R. N. *Camden's Hist. Eliz.* I. 32 Some..feigned unto themselves vain dreames. **1674** OWEN *Holy Spirit* (1693) 200 Men have but deceived themselves..when they have feigned a Glory and a Beauty of the Church in other things. **1886** GURNEY *Phantasms of Living* I. 499 A sane..mind..can feign voices where there is silence.

†**b.** To imagine, believe erroneously and arbitrarily. Const. with *obj.* and *inf.*, or object clause.

1557 *Tottell's Misc.* (Arb.) 227 The soules..Are not in such a place, As foolish folke do faine. **1596** SPENSER *F.Q.* VI. xii. 19 Art thou yet alive, whom dead I long did faine? **1604** E. G. *D'Acosta's Hist. Indies* III. vi. 137 We faine, that some Angell and intellectuall Spirite dooth walk with the Comet. **1662** STILLINGFL. *Orig. Sacr.* I. iv. §11 The Straights, where they fained Hercules his pillars to be. **1728** NEWTON *Chronol. Amended* 29 The ancients..feigned that this Island ..had been as big as all Europe.

c. To assume fictitiously for purposes of calculation. *arch.* or *Obs.*

1688 M. PRIOR *Ode Ex. iii.* 14 vi, And he too..Studies new Lines, and other Circles feigns. **1812** WOODHOUSE *Astron.* i. 3 The bounding line of the horizon is feigned to be a circle. *Ibid.* x. 77 It becomes necessary then, to feign an observer in the center of the earth.

5. *trans.* To assert or maintain fictitiously; to allege, make out, pretend. Const. †with simple *obj.* or complement (rare), with *obj.* and *inf.*, or with sentence as *obj.*

a **1300** *E.E. Psalter* xciii. [xciv.] 20 Whor sete of wicknes sal cleve to þe, Þate feinyhes swinke in bode to be? *c* **1385** CHAUCER *L.G.W.* 932 *Dido*, Feyning the hors y-offred to Minerve. **1387** TREVISA *Higden* (Rolls) VII. 61 Þe kyng.. wolde..feyne trespas for to byneme hem [Englisshe] here money. **1541** BARNES *Wks.* (1573) 189/1 To faine God to bee displeased with your king. **1548** HALL *Chron.* 232 b, Fayning that he was thycke of hearyng. **1554** LATIMER in Strype *Eccl. Mem.* III. App. xxxiv. 90 That which is fayned of many, I for my Parte, take it but for a Papistical Invention. **1583** STANYHURST *Aeneis* II. (Arb.) 61 The right valeant (whose soon thou art [*printed* thwart] feigned) Achilles. **1840** DICKENS *Old C. Shop* xviii, And feigning that his doing so was needful to the welfare of the cookery. **1863** DRAPER *Intell. Devel. Europe* i. 4 [Man] has been feigned.. to possess another immaterial principle.

†**6.** To put a false appearance upon; to disguise, dissemble, conceal. *Obs.*

1393 GOWER *Conf.* III. 208 She hath her..body feigned. *c* **1400** *Destr. Troy* 34 Poeyetis..With ffablis and falshed fayned þere speche. *Ibid.* 253 The ffalshed he faynit vnder faire wordes. *c* **1500** *Lancelot* 2397 The lady fayndit..The lowe quhich long hath ben In to her thocht. **1590** SPENSER *F.Q.* II. iii. 20 Both doe strive their fearefulnesse to faine.

†**7.** *refl.* **a.** To disguise one's sentiments, practise dissimulation, dissemble. Also *intr.* for *refl.* *Obs.*

c **1290** *S. Eng. Leg.* I. 186, *Vincent* 49 Þov feinest þe. **1297** R. GLOUC. (Rolls) 2376 Naþeles he fenede him, þat me vnder ȝete it noȝt. **13..** *Leg. Rood* (1871) 85 All for noght þou feynes þe. **1382** WYCLIF *Ecclus.* xxiii. 13 If he shul feyne [*si dissimulaverit*] he shal trespasen double. *c* **1450** *Merlin* 14 When she it sough, she fayned her. **1523** LD. BERNERS *Froiss.* I. vii. 6 It was counsailed to the kyng..hym selfe to fayne. **1559** *Mirr. Mag.*, *Mortimers* xix, Bid them beware their enmies when they faine.

†**b.** To assume a deceptive bearing. *Obs.*

c **1470** HENRY *Wallace* VI. 208 Quhen Wallace feld thar curage was so small, He fenȝeit him for to comfort thaim all. **1526** *Pilgr. Perf.* (W. de W. 1531) 96 Fayne thy self to appere outwardly more perfyte..than thou art.

8. *trans.* To make a show of, put on an appearance of, put on, pretend, simulate, sham; †to pretend to utter (words).

c **1340** HAMPOLE *Prose Tr.* 10 Ypocrittes..feyne gud dede with-owttene. **1375** BARBOUR *Bruce* I. 344 To fenyhe foly quhile is wyt. **1387** TREVISA *Higden* (Rolls) VII. 85 Duke Edrik..feynynge a vomet..seide þat he was seek. **1393** GOWER *Conf.* I. 181 She feigned wordes in his ere. *c* **1400** *Destr. Troy* 3597 Fayne euer feire chere. **1598** R. T[OFTE] *Months Minde* G v, All was fained, 'twas not from the hart. **1602** MARSTON *Antonio's Rev.* v. iii. Wks. 1856 I. 134 Each man straines To faine a jocund eye. **1741** MIDDLETON *Cicero* I. v. 385 Escaped death, onely by feigning it. **1791** BOSWELL *Johnson* (1816) IV. 437 The serenity that is not felt, it can be no virtue to feign. *a* **1839** PRAED *Poems* (1864) II. 162 The agony Which others feel or feign. **1856** KANE *Arct. Expl.* II. vi. 72 They are both feigning sickness this morning.

b. *absol.* To practise simulation.

1612 T. TAYLOR *Comm. Titus* i. 2 He seemeth to faine, by vttering things clean contrary to his mind. **1671** MILTON *P.R.* I. 474 It may stand him more in stead to..feign. **1724** RAMSAY *Tea-t. Misc.* (1733) I. 99 Tho' she be fair I will not fenzie. *a* **1774** GOLDSM. *Madrigal* 3 Wks. (Globe) 691 Myra, too sincere for feigning. **1849** C. BRONTE *Shirley* xiii, She cannot feign; she scorns hypocrisy.

9. With *refl. pron.* as obj. followed by simple complement, †*as*, or *to be*: To make oneself appear, put on an appearance of being. †Formerly in wider use, with the refl. obj. followed by *inf.*, *that*, *as that*.

1297 R. GLOUC. (1724) 336 He feynede hym somdel syk. **1340** HAMPOLE *Pr. Consc.* 4233 He sal hym feyn first als haly. *c* **1386** CHAUCER *Merch. T.* 706 Sche feyned hir as that sche moste goon. **1387** TREVISA *Higden* (Rolls) VII. 59 A wel false traytour..þat couþe wel feyne hym self trewe frende. **1393** LANGL. *P. Pl.* C. IX. 128 Tho..feynede hem blynde. *c* **1400** MAUNDEV. (Roxb.) xv. 66 A mysdoer..þat..thurgh his enchauntementz feyned him ane aungell. **1483** CAXTON *Gold. Leg.* 97/1 She fayned her alleway to be seke. **1568** GRAFTON *Chron.* II. 204 The Queene..did feyne her selfe that shee would go on pilgrimage. **1611** BIBLE *2 Sam.* xiv. 2 Faine thy selfe to be a mourner. **1726** DE FOE *Hist. Devil* I. xi. (1840) 164 Satan made David feign himself mad. **1859** SMILES *Self-Help* iii. 53 To..reconcile myself to it..is more manly than to feign myself above it.

b. *intr.* To pretend, make oneself appear. Const. *to* with *inf.* †Formerly with the same constructions as the refl. use above.

c **1400** MAUNDEV. (Roxb.) iii. 10 He made signe of etyng and feyned as he had etyn. *c* **1450** *St. Cuthbert* (Surtees) 6344 He feynd als he þe toumbe walde kys. **1563–87** FOXE *A. & M.* (1684) II. 79/1 He that hath no Faith, and yet faineth or pretendeth to haue. **1590** SPENSER *F.Q.* II. i. 9 Feigning ..in every limb to quake Through inward feare. **1632** J. HAYWARD tr. *Biondi's Eromena* 6 Fayning to goe recreate himselfe..gave order publikly. **1778** HAN. MORE *Florio* II. 185 Yet feigned to praise the gothic treat. **1784** *Unfort. Sensibility* II. 47, I have sometimes feigned sick, when I had no other succedaneum for avoiding their parties. **1843** EMERSON *Carlyle* Wks. (Bohn) III. 312 Such an appeal to the conscience..as cannot be..feigned to be forgotten. **1865** DICKENS *Mut. Fr.* II. xvi, Tremlow feigns to compare the portrait.

10. To counterfeit, imitate deceptively (*esp.* a voice, handwriting).

1484 CAXTON *Æsop* II. ix, The wulf..faynynge the gotes voyce sayd. **1590** SPENSER *F.Q.* I. vii. 1 Truth, whose shape she [deceipt] well can faine. **1797** MRS. RADCLIFFE *Italian* IV, It was not difficult to disguise or to feign a voice. **1847** EMERSON *Poems* (1857) 213 Feigning dwarfs, they crouch and creep.

†**b.** To adulterate. *Obs. rare.*

1398 TREVISA *Barth. De P.R.* XVII. v. (1495) 606 The tree of aloes is feyned [*sophisticatum*] wyth a tree that is lyke therto in weyght & in knottes. **1614** T. ADAMS *Devills Banquet* 324 Sometimes they faine it [this Balme] with water.

†**c.** To pass off (a thing) *for* something else. **1393** GOWER *Conf.* I. 17 Lo, how they feignen chalk for chese.

†**11.** To pretend to make (a pass) or to deal (a blow); also *absol.* to make a feint. *Obs.*

c **1386** CHAUCER *Knt.'s T.* 1757 He feyneth on his foot with a tronchoun. **1470–85** MALORY *Arthur* x. xix, Some whyle they fayned, some whyle they strake as wyld men. **1632** J. HAYWARD tr. *Biondi's Eromena* 3 Making with his point towards the others face, and faining a passage..The Prince ..fained at him divers foynes.

†**12.** *Music.* **a.** To sing softly, hum an air. **b.** To sing with due regard to the 'accidentals', which the old notation did not indicate. [See *Musica ficta* in Grove *Dict. Mus.*; cf. also F. *par feinte* 'by the alteration of a semitone'.] *Obs.*

c **1440** *Promp. Parv.* 153/1 Feynyn yn syngynge, or synge lowe. **1526** *Pilgr. Perf.* (W. de W. 1531) 158 b, Not.. feynynge, but with a full brest & hole voyce. *a* **1529** SKELTON *Comely Coystrowne* 53 He techyth them..to solf & to fayne. —— *Bowge of Courte* 233 His throte was clere, and lustely coude fayne. **1530** PALSGR. 548/1 We maye nat synge out..but lette us fayne this songe. **1553** T. WILSON *Rhet.* 72 He feyneth to the lute marveilouse swetely.

†**III. 13.** [After OF. *feindre*, *se feindre*.] *intr.* and *refl.* To avoid one's duty by false pretences; to shirk, flinch, hang back. Also with *inf.*: To be reluctant or afraid *to* do something; to avoid, shirk (doing). *Obs.*

c **1300** *K. Alis.* 5884 Perdicas feyned noughth, For als a wode lyoun he faughth. *c* **1369** CHAUCER *Dethe Blaunche* 317 Noon of hem..feyned To singe. ? *a* **1400** *Morte Arth.* 1734 Feyne ȝow noghte feyntly..Bot luke ȝe fyghte faythe-fully. *c* **1400** *Rom. Rose* 1797 Never this archer wolde feyne To shete at me. *Ibid.* 2996 If I may helpe you in ought, I shall not faine. **14..** LYDG. *Temple of Glas* 996 She me constreyned..To ȝoure seruise, & neuer forto feyne. *c* **1430** *Syr Gener.* (Roxb.) 4721 Ye se me feyne neuer a dele. *c* **1460** *Towneley Myst.* (Surtees) 172 On both parties thus I play, and fenys me to ordan The right. **1523–5** LD. BERNERS *Froiss.* I. cccxiii. 194 b, There they made a great assaut. The Englysshmen fayned nat. **1535** STEWART *Cron. Scot.* I. 566 Exhortand thame..for na fray to feinȝie nor to fle.

†**b.** *trans.* To shirk, avoid fulfilling (a command); to 'shuffle out of' (one's word). *Obs.*

c **1300** *Beket* 42 Gilbert..feignede his word her and ther: and ne grantede noȝt. *c* **1386** CHAUCER *Clerk's T.* 473 Lordes hestes mow not ben i-feynit.

feigned (feɪnd), *ppl. a.* Also 5 feynit, *Sc.* 6 feinyeat, fenȝeid, -it, fei-, feynȝeit, feinȝed, feinyet. [f. prec. + -ED[1].]

†**1.** Fashioned, formed, shaped. *Obs.*

c **1400** *Apol. Loll.* 85 His feynar haþ hopid in his feynid þingis.

2. Fictitiously invented or devised. Also, related in fiction, fabled. *Obs.* or *arch.*

c **1374** CHAUCER *Compl. Mars.* 173 This is no feyned mater that I telle. *c* **1450** HENRYSON *Mor. Fab.* 3 Feinzed Fables. **1552** *Bk. Com. Prayer* Communion, Feyned excuses. *a* **1572** KNOX *Hist. Ref.* Wks. 1846 I. 74 Quhilk reportis ar all.. fenzeit, and untrew. **1607** TOPSELL *Four-f. Beasts* (1673) 101 A peculiar voyce which the French call by a feigned word, 'Reere'. **1623** LISLE *Ælfric on O. & N. Test.* Pref. ¶4 The faigned games of Homer and Virgil. **1670** TENISON (*title*), Creed of Mr. Hobbes Examined, in a feigned conference between Him and a Student of Divinity. **1728** NEWTON *Chronol. Amended* Introd. 6 The Priests..had filled up the interval with feigned Kings. **1820** HAZLITT *Lect. Dram. Lit.* 19 To be found in history, whether actual or feigned.

†**b.** Contrived for deception. *Obs.*

c **1440** *Promp. Parv.* 153/1 Feynyd sleythe of falshede.

†**3.** Fictitiously or arbitrarily supposed; imaginary. *feigned price*: = 'fancy price'. *Obs.*

1526 *Pilgr. Perf.* (W. de W. 1531) 276 Aboue the necessite of nature they wyll haue theyr feyned necessaryes. **1607–12** BACON *Ess. Riches* (Arb.) 232 What fayned prices are set vpponn litle stones. **1726** tr. *Gregory's Astronomy* I. 319 As many Degrees of the feigned Equator.

4. Of attributes, actions, diseases, etc.: Simulated, counterfeited, pretended, sham.

1413 LYDG. *Pilgr. Sowle* IV. xxx. (1483) 80 Another thynge is a veray hede and another a feyned hede. **1483** CAXTON *G. de la Tour* L v b, They gyue out of theyr brestes grete and fayned syghes. *a* **1577** GASCOIGNE *Wks.* (1587) 106 All her guiles she hid With fained teares. **1609** SKENE *Reg. Maj.*, *Stat. Robert I*, 33 Inquisition salbe taken, gif that be done be fenzeid furie, or not. **1642** R. CARPENTER *Experience* III. v. 108 We must be..carefull that these Acts in their exercise, be true..not faigned and superficiall. **1709** STEELE *Tatler* No. 1 ¶6 Personating Feigned Sorrows. **1776** GIBBON *Decl. & F.* I. 414 Their mutual fears produced..a feigned reconciliation. **1803** *Med. Jrnl.* IX. 72 Feigned and Concealed Diseases. **1848** MACAULAY *Hist. Eng.* II. 163 Mortal enemies..came every day to pay their feigned civilities.

†**b.** Prefixed to personal designations: That is such only in pretence; pretended. *Obs.*

c **1386** CHAUCER *Melib.* ¶289 Youre trewe freendes and youre feyned counseillours. **1548** HALL *Chron.* 211 A fained, false and a coloured frende. **1550** CROWLEY *Inform. & Petit.* 175 Wee are but fayned Christians, we beare the name onely. **1647** N. BACON *Disc. Govt. Eng.* I. iv. 16 Fained Friends, becoming unfained Foes.

†**c.** Of things: Counterfeit, spurious, sham.

1665 SIR T. HERBERT *Trav.* (1677) 223 Mosques..are in their Cupolaes curiously ceruleated with a feigned Turquoise. **1703** MAUNDRELL *Journ. Jerus.* (1732) 74 Took down the feigned Body from the Cross.

d. Of a name, etc.: Assumed, fictitious. Of a voice, handwriting, etc.: Disguised.

1559 W. CUNNINGHAM *Cosmogr. Glasse* A vj b, I have reduced it into the forme of a Dialoge: the names of the personages indede fained [etc.]. **1596** SPENSER *F.Q.* IV. i. 7

To hide her fained sex. **1675** MARVELL *Corr.* ccxliii. Wks. 1872–5 II. 457, I cannot tell whether it be a true or a fained name. **1762** J. BROWN *Poetry & Mus.* vii. (1763) 141 The Poets..represent real Characters under feigned names. **1777** SHERIDAN *Sch. Scand.* I. i, I copied them..in a feigned hand. **1837** LYTTON *E. Maltrav.* 29 The feigned address he had previously assumed.

†**5.** *Mus.* **a.** (see FEIGN *v.* 12 b.) **b.** = FALSETTO 3. *Obs.*

1609 DOULAND *Ornith. Microl.* 24 The fained Scale exceedes the others both in height and depth. For it addeth a Ditone vnder *Vt* base, because it sings *fa* in *A*, and it riseth aboue *eela* by two degrees, for in it it sounds *fa*. *Ibid.*, Fained Musicke is..a Song made beyond the regular Compasse of the Scales. Or, it is a Song, which is full of Coniunctions [i.e. accidental flats]. **1674** PLAYFORD *Skill Mus.* I. xi. 43 Increasing of the Voice in the Treble Part..in Feigned Voices, doth oftentimes become harsh.

6. *Law.* (See quots.)

1483 *Act 1 Rich. III*, c. 6 §1 Feyned playntes. **1542–3** *Act 34–5 Hen. VIII*, c. 4 The aforesaide false and fayned recouere. **1592** WEST *1st Pt. Symbol.* §5 G, The feined consent is by Lawe for some fact, when the consent of both parties appeareth not, and yet inasmuch as the fact is done, they are by Law both feined and deemed to consent. *a* **1709** ATKYNS *Parl. & Pol. Tracts* (1734) 317 The feigned Action ..the Lord Chief Justice seems to justify. **1768** BLACKSTONE *Comm.* III. III. xxvii. 452 As no jury can be summoned to attend this court [Equity], the fact is.. directed to be tried ..upon a feigned issue. For (in order to..have the point in dispute..put in issue) an action is feigned to be brought. **1818** CRUISE *Digest* (ed. 2) V. 519 Any such feigned recovery.

7. *Mil.* = FALSE *a.* 14.

1598 BARRET *Theor. Warres* III. i. 35 Fained skirmishes. **1783** WATSON *Philip III* (1839) 69 A third detachment was sent to make a feigned attack in another quarter. **1876** VOYLE *Milit. Dict.* 135/1 A feigned assault..for the purpose of diverting the enemy from the real point of attack.

†**8.** Of persons, their manner, faces, etc.: Made up to a certain appearance, got up for a purpose; hence, deceitful, insincere. *Obs.*

c **1374** CHAUCER *Anel. & Arc.* 97 He was fals, his was but feyned chere. *c* **1386** —— *Man of Law's T.* 264 O feyned womman, alle that may confounde Vertu and innocence..Is bred in the. **1393** GOWER *Conf.* III. 158 They..by fallas Of feigned wordis make him wene, That black is white. **1530** LYNDESAY *Test. Papyngo* 195 Hauyng sic traist in to thy [Fortune's] fenȝeit face. **1535** COVERDALE *Ps.* xvi[i]. 1 My prayer, that goeth not out of a fayned mouth [**1611** *Ibid.* Fained lips]. **1536** STARKEY *Let. to Cromwell* in *England* (1878) p. xli, You schal neuer fynd me faynyd man. *a* **1605** MONTGOMERIE *Descr. Vane Lovers* 46 Vhar thou finds tham faynd refrane. **1654** tr. *Scudery's Curia Pol.* 124 Amurath.. in a fained manner..seemed inclinable to offer me the Crown.

feignedly (ˈfeɪnɪdlɪ), *adv.* [f. prec. + -LY².] In a feigned manner.

1. Pretendedly, not really; deceitfully.

1535 COVERDALE *Dan.* xi. 34 Many shal cleue vnto them faynedly. **1602** WARNER *Alb. Eng.* x. lx. (1612) 264 Yeat better plainely to reproue than fainedly to kisse. **1700** TYRRELL *Hist. Eng.* II. 723 Others, tho' feignedly, adher'd to him. **1882–3** SCHAFF *Encycl. Relig. Knowl.* III. 1938 The conversion was not with the whole heart, but feignedly.

2. *Law.* By a fiction; fictitiously.

1592 WEST *1st Pt. Symbol.* §11 C, Consent is sometimes used in deede and sometimes fainedly as in law.

feignedness (ˈfeɪnɪdnɪs). [f. as prec. + -NESS.] The quality or state of being feigned; †deceitfulness; insincerity.

1435 MISYN *Fire of Love* 58 With-oute cessyng to Ioy of godis sight, all fenydnes put bak. **1535** COVERDALE *Ecclus.* i. 30 Thy hert is full of faynednes and disceate. **1587** J. HARMAR *Beza's Serm.* iii. 39 The church is not the school of fainednesse. **1683** WILKINSON in *Mem. J. Story Revived* 7 He..greatly abhorred Feignedness. **1711** SHAFTESB. *Charac.* (1737) II. II. ii. 162 A certain Subtlety and Feignedness of Carriage.

feigner (ˈfeɪnə(r)). [f. FEIGN *v.* + -ER¹.] One who or that which feigns, in various senses of the vb.; †a fashioner, constructor, inventor; the contriver of a fiction (*obs.*); a simulator, pretender, counterfeiter.

1382 WYCLIF *Deut.* xiii. 5 That prophete or feyner of swevenes shal be slayn. *c* **1400** *Apol. Loll.* 85 Wat profitiþ a grauen þing? for his feynar haþ hopid in his feynid þingis. **1488** CAXTON *Chast. Goddes Chyld.* 28 In goddes sighte they ben very fyctifs feyners. **1535** STEWART *Cron. Scot.* III. 276 Ane freir..flatterar and fenȝear. **1591** SYLVESTER *Du Bartas* I. v. 715 The greene Parrat, fainer of our Words. **1598** *Ibid.* II. ii. II. *Babylon* 614 The fluent fainer of Orlandos error. **1636** B. JONSON *Discov.* Wks. (Rtldg.) 761/2 A poet is..a maker or a fainer: his art, an art of imitation, or faining. **1678** CUDWORTH *Intell. Syst.* 693 This Notion..was from the first Feigner or Inventor of it, propagated all along and conveyed down, by Oral Tradition. **1827** *Examiner* 50/2 Either Farmers are dreadful feigners, or their present endurance cannot last long. **1863** HOLME LEE *A. Warleigh's Fort.* III. 104 She was a bad feigner.

feigning (ˈfeɪnɪŋ), *vbl. sb.* [f. as prec. + -ING¹.]

1. The action of the vb. FEIGN in various senses; an instance of this. ***without*** **(†*but*)** ***feigning***: unfeignedly, sincerely.

1375 BARBOUR *Bruce* I. 74 He suld swer that, but fenȝeyng, He suld that arbytre disclar. *c* **1380** WYCLIF *Sel. Wks.* III. 341 He was clepid þe pope..aftirward camen oþer names bi feynyng of ypocritis. *c* **1385** CHAUCER *L.G.W.* *1556 Hypsip. & Medea*, With feynynge, & with every subtyl dede. *c* **1460** *Towneley Myst.* (Surtees) 209 Tryp on thi tose, without any fenyng. **1490** CAXTON *Eneydos* xvi. 65 That yf it were aperceyued..men shold wene that it were a manere of a feynynge. **1568** GRAFTON *Chron.* II. 186 Craftie and imagined faynings. **1601** SHAKS. *Twel. N.* III. i. 110 'Twas neuer merry world, Since lowly feigning was call'd complement. **1636** B. JONSON *Discov.* Wks. (Rtldg.) 761/2 His [the Poet's] Art [is] an Art of imitation, or faining. **1789** MRS. PIOZZI *Journ. France* I. 91 The Lombards..please you without feigning. **1875** JOWETT *Plato* (ed. 2) III. 143 Poets are also the representatives of falsehood and feigning.

†**b.** ***feigning of person***: personification. *rare.*

1561 DAUS tr. *Bullinger on Apoc.* (1573) 283 S. John by a fayning of person sayth, from whose face fledde away both heauen and earth.

†**2.** quasi-*concr.* A creation or production (of the mind); an assumption, fiction, fable. *Obs.*

1388 WYCLIF *Jer.* I. 38 The lond..hath glorie in false feynyngis. *c* **1430** LYDG. *Bochas* I. iv. (1544) 6 b, Of poetes the feigning to unfold. **1563–87** FOXE *A. & M.* (1596) 141/2 The like fainings and monstrous miracles. **1614** RALEIGH *Hist. World* II. 350 All which fainings..Josephus and Tertullian have sufficiently answered. **1627** SPEED *England* xxv. §3 Poets in their faynings will haue the Nymphs residence in shady greene groues.

feigning (ˈfeɪnɪŋ), *ppl. a.* [f. as prec. + -ING².] That feigns.

†**1.** Given to inventing; imaginative. *Obs.*

1483 *Cath. Angl.* 125/1 Feynynge, *ficticiosus*. **1600** SHAKS. *A.Y.L.* III. iii. 20 The truest poetrie is the most faining.

2. Dissembling, deceitful.

c **1400** *Destr. Troy* 966 He..welcomed hom all With a faynyng fare vnder faire chere. *a* **1569** KINGESMYLL *Man's Est.* i. (1580) 8 Those fainyng folke. **1590** SHAKS. *Mids. N.* I. i. 31 Verses of faining loue. **1701** ROWE *Amb. Step-Moth.* IV. iii. 2002 Suspect this feigning Boy.

†**3.** Shirking, cowardly. *Obs.* Cf. FEIGN *v.* 13.

c **1400** *Destr. Troy* 4576 þis fenyond fare is forthoryng to hom, To assemble..souldiors ynogh.

†**4.** Of the voice: see FEIGN *v.* 12. *Obs.*

1590 SHAKS. *Mids. N.* I. i. 31 Thou hast by Moone-light at her window sung, With faining voice.

5. quasi-*adv.* Pretendedly, seemingly.

1620 QUARLES *Jonah* (1638) 11 How faining deafe is he?

Hence **ˈfeigningly** *adv.*, in a feigning manner; artfully, dissemblingly.

1387 TREVISA *Higden* (Rolls) II. 375 þe ordre of tellynge of þe þing..is feynyngliche i-tolde. *c* **1422** HOCCLEVE *Learn to Die* 359 Whethir he verraily or feynyngly Repente. *c* **1500** *Melusine* 28 All this said she feynyngly to thende that the other shuld nat perceyue to what thinge she tended. **1561** T. HOBY tr. *Castiglione's Courtyer* Zz iij b, To sett out her beawtye..as feininglye as she can. **1605** STOW *Ann. West Saxons* an. 1011 Peace..to the which they feininglie assented. **1650** S. CLARKE *Eccl. Hist.* (1654) 542 The King feigningly complained that since the death of Cromwel, England was much troubled with hereticall factions.

feijoa (feɪˈdʒəʊə, fiː-, feɪˈjəʊə), [mod.L. (O. Berg 1858 in *Linnæa* XXIX. 258), f. the name of J. da Silva *Feijo*, 19th-century Spanish naturalist.] An evergreen shrub or small tree of the genus so named, which is native to South America and belongs to the family Myrtaceæ; also, the fruit of this tree.

1898 *Curtis's Bot. Mag.* CXXIV. Tab. 7620 *Feijoa* was discovered by the late Fr. Sellow of Potsdam, who, in 1819, accompanied Prince Neuwied in his journey to Brasil... Over and above the beauty of the foliage and flower of the plant, it is remarkable for the rich aromatic odour and flavour of its guava-like fruit. **1920** W. POPENOE *Man. Tropical & Subtropical Fruits* ix. 294 In its native country the feijoa is scarcely known as a cultivated plant. **1958** *N.Z. Listener* 18 Apr. 23/1 Feijoas or Salad Plant... To eat feijoas, scoop out the centre with a spoon similar to the passion fruit method.

feil, var. form of FELE *a.*, much.

feil-beg: see FILIBEG.

feild(e, obs. forms of FIELD.

feile, fein, obs. forms of FAIL, FAIN, VEIN.

†**feind, feint.** *Obs. rare.* [Of obscure origin; it can hardly be a var. of FIEND; a subst. use of FEIGNED, FEINT *adjs.*?] ? A phantom, goblin.

1658–9 *Burton's Diary* (1828) IV. 64 Those feints, which come nearest the shape of man, are most ugly and dangerous. **1703** T. N. *City & C. Purchaser* 7 There are really no such standing Species of Animals, and Vegetables [as fauns, mermaids, etc.] in Nature, tho' the belief of such feinds hath been propagated by Orators.

feind(e, obs. forms of FIEND.

feindill, error for *seindill*, SENDLE.

1560 ROLLAND *Crt. Venus* Prol. 31 The last..is callit Melancoly..Heuie heidit, and feindill in game or glew.

Feinne (ˈfeɪŋə), *sb. pl.* Also Fein. [Ir. *feinne*, pl. of FIAN(N.] The soldiers of the ancient Irish militia. Cf. FENIAN and FIAN(N.

1782 *Gentl. Mag.* LII. 570/2 The songs relating to the Feinne, and their Chieftain, Fion-mac-Coul. *Ibid.* 571/1 The whole host of the Feinne, or Fingalians. **1872** J. F. CAMPBELL *Leabhar na Feinne* 33 Fionn and the Feinne were the successors of Cumhal and Cuchullin. **1891** *Youthful Exploits of Fionn* 96 A company of the old Feinne. **1891** A. MACDOUGALL *Folk & Hero Tales* 35 The Fein looked at each other.

feint (feɪnt), *sb.* [a. Fr. *feinte* (= Pr. *fenha*, *fencha*, OSp. and It. *finta*), abstr. noun, f. *feindre* to FEIGN.]

1. A feigned or false attack. Also in phrases ***in feint, to make a feint.***

a. *Fencing* and *Boxing*. A blow, cut, or thrust aimed at a part other than that which is the real object of attack.

[**1600** O. E. *Repl. to Libel* I. iii. 67 A finta, or fained shew of a downe right blow.] **1684** R. H. *School Recreat.* 63 To take..a Feint on this Guard will signifie little or nothing. **1706** in PHILLIPS (ed. Kersey). **1730–6** in BAILEY (folio). **1817** SCOTT *Rob Roy* xxv, He exhausted every feint and stratagem proper to the science of defence. **1825** WATERTON *Wand. S. Amer.* III. iii. 251, I made a feint to cut them down. **1872** BAKER *Nile Tribut.* viii. 117 A feint at the head causes them to raise the shield. **1879** FARRAR *St. Paul* II. 73 He aimed straight blows, and not in feint, at the enemy.

b. *Mil.* A movement made with the object of deceiving an enemy as to a general's real plans.

1683 TEMPLE *Mem.* Wks. 1731 I. 458 Friburg had been taken by a Feint of the Duke. **1701** *Lond. Gaz.* No. 3713/1 Some troops were ordered to make a Feint. **1783** WATSON *Philip III* (1793) II. v. 108 By making a feint of storming which he hoped to save Vercelli. **1809** WELLINGTON in Gurw. *Desp.* V. 30 These movements are intended only as a feint. **1868** G. DUFF *Pol. Surv.* 65 She..may make an attack on India by way of feint.

2. *transf.* and *fig.* An assumed appearance; a pretence, stratagem.

1679 SIR C. LYTTELTON in *Hatton Corr.* (1878) 206 All this is but a feint. **1740** SOMERVILLE *Hobbinol* II. 410 A Feint he made With well dissembled Guile. **1754** SHERLOCK *Disc.* (1759) I. ix. 265 This Objection is not a mere Feint. **1832** LANDER *Adv. Niger* I. iv. 182 We imagine that it is only a feint of Mausolah to detain us. **1851** GALLENGA *Italy* 49 That protest..would have been merely a feint. **1852** DICKENS *Christmas Bks., Haunted Man.* (C. D. ed.) 206 Mr. Williams..made a feint of accidentally knocking the table with a decanter.

b. *Rhetoric.* (See quot.)

1730–6 BAILEY (folio), *Feint*, a figure whereby the orator touches on something, in making a show of passing it over in silence.

†**3.** *Music.* (See quot.) [So formerly Fr. *feinte*.]

1730–6 BAILEY (folio), *Feint*, sb. (in Musick) a semi-tone, the same that is called Diesis. **1823** in CRABB.

feint (feɪnt), *a.* [a. Fr. *feint*, pa. pple. of *feindre* to FEIGN.] **1.** Feigned, false, or counterfeit; sham; = FAINT *a.* 1. Now *rare.*

c **1340** *Cursor M.* 19535 (Trin.) þerfore toke he bapteme feynt [*v.r.* faint]. *c* **1400** *Rom. Rose* 433 She gan..To make many a feynt praiere To God. *c* **1698** LOCKE *Cond. Underst.* §33 Dressed up into any faint appearance of it. **1702** *Lond. Gaz.* No. 3835/2 The Major..made a feint Retreat. **1704** *Ibid.* No. 3986/2 Amusing the French with..feint Marches. **1855** THACKERAY *Newcomes* II. 90 We wear feint smiles over our tears and deceive our children.

2. In commercial use, the usual spelling of FAINT *a.* 5 c; freq. quasi-*adv.*

1859 *Stationers' Hand-bk.* (ed. 2) 72 Feint only, the term for a book having merely feint blue lines across the page from left to right. **1895** *Army & Navy Co-op. Soc. Price List* 15 Sept. 525 Foolscap Paper—Ruled with Money Columns and Feint Lines. **1930** *Publishers' Circ.* 13 Sept. 321/2 The actual book itself should be of foolscap size, ruled feint.

feint, *v.* Also 6 faint. [In sense 1 f. F. *feint*, pa. pple. of *feindre* to FEIGN; see the variant FAINT *v.* In sense 2 f. FEINT *sb.*]

†**1.** To deceive. *Obs.*

1320 [see FEINTING].

2. *Mil.*, *Boxing* and *Fencing*. **a.** *intr.* To make a feint or sham attack. Const. *at*, *on*, *upon*. **b.** *trans.* To make a feint upon. *rare.* **c.** To pretend to make (a pass or cut).

1833 *Regul. Instr. Cavalry* I. 130 Feint cut 'Two'; and shift leg to 'First Position'. *Ibid.* I. 149 Feint 'Third Point' under, and deliver 'Second Point' over the arm. **1854** BADHAM *Halieut.* 419 He watched them..as they feinted, skirmished, or made onslaught. **1857** HUGHES *Tom Brown* II. iii, Feint him—use your legs! draw him out. **1880** L. WALLACE *Ben-Hur* 381 Ben-Hur feinted with his right hand. **1890** *Sat. Rev.* 6 Sept. 296/2 He feinted at his enemy's toes.

Hence **ˈfeinting** *vbl. sb.*, in senses of the vb.; also *attrib.*, and *ppl. a.*

c **1314** *Guy Warw.* (A.) 444 Erl Jonas..Loke wiþ him be no feynting. **1579** LYLY *Euphues* (Arb.) 110 They flutter them-selues with a fainting farewell, deferring euer vntil to morrow. **1684** R. H. *School Recreat.* 71 Feinting or Falsifying. Of these there are several Kinds. **1858** O. W. HOLMES *Aut. Breakf.-t.* (1865) 68 Feinting, dodging, stopping, hitting, countering. **1871** *Daily News* 24 July, It was obvious that force had been thus disposed for feinting purposes.

feintise, var. of FAINTISE.

feints, var. of FAINTS.

feinye, -yie, obs. Sc. forms of FEIGN.

†**feir.** *Obs. Sc.* Also 4–6 fere, 5, 7 feare, 6 fier. [aphet. f. EFFEIR.] Appearance, demeanour, look, show; = *affere* (AFFAIR 6), EFFEIR *sb.* 2.

c **1440** *Gaw. & Gol.* xiii, He wes ladlike of lait, and light of his fere. *c* **1470** HENRY *Wallace* IX. 101 Tell me his feyr, and how I sall him knaw. *c* **1500** *Felon Sowe Rokeby* in Whitaker *Hist. Craven* (1805) 418 Scho rase up with a felon fere. **1528** LYNDESAY *Dream* 447 Quha wald behauld his countynance and feir, Mycht call hym, weill, the god of men of weir.

b. ***in feir of war***: in martial array.

1449 *Sc. Acts Jas. II* (1597) §25 Gif onie man..risis in feire of weir against him [the King]. **1550** LYNDESAY *Sqr. Meldrum* 1231 Thrie scoir..Accowterit weill in feir of weir. *c* **1565** LINDESAY (Pitscottie) *Chron. Scot.* (1728) 215 The

Queen made proclamation..that all men should be at her in Fier of War.

c. *pl.* Gestures, ways, 'points' of a person's exterior.

c **1375** BARBOUR *Troy-bk.* II. 2501 He kend him be his feris. *Ibid.* II. 3003 With brokine speche and with waik feris. **1513** DOUGLAS *Æneis* III. ix. 14 Bot he was Greik be all his vthir feris. *a* **1548** *Thrie Priests of Peblis* in Pinkerton *Scot. Poems* (1792) I. 19 He feinyeit him ane fule, fond in his feris.

feir, var. FERE *v. Obs.* to appertain, be proper.

feir, obs. and Sc. form of FEAR.

feird, obs. Sc. var. of FOURTH.

†**'feirie**, *a. Sc. Obs.* Also 5, 6 fery, 7, 8 feerie. [? repr. OE. **férig*, f. *fór* action of going (see FORE *sb.*) + *-ig*, -Y[1]: cf. the synonymous FERE *a.*] Fit to travel; hence nimble, vigorous. Const. *of*.

c **1425** WYNTOUN *Cron.* IX. ix. 10 His eldare Swne Wes noucht fery. **1513** DOUGLAS *Æneis* VI. v. 20 Als fery and als swipper as a page. *a* **1548** *Thrie Priests of Peblis* in Pinkerton *Scot. Poems* (1792) I. 18 The king was..Ane feirie man on fute. **17..** in Watson *Collect.* I. (1706) 59 Of foot he is not feerie. **1794** BURNS *Deuk's Dang O'er My Daddy*, O haud your tongue, my feirie auld wife.

b. quasi-*adv.* Cleverly, actively.

1810 in Cromek *Rem. Nithsdale & Annandale Song* (1880) 54 An feerie can cross it in two braid cockle shells.

Hence **'feirily** *adv.*, nimbly, actively.

1550 LYNDESAY *Sqr. Meldrum* 475 Quhen thay saw him sa feirelie Loup on his Hors. **1552** —— *Dreme* 12 Sumtyme in dansing, feiralie I flang. **1763** W. THOM *Donaldsoniad*, Wks. (1799) 368 It wad be better if it was a' dun bi ane that cou'd gae throw it feerily and cannily.

feirschipe, var. of FAIRSHIP.

feis (fɛʃ, feɪʃ). Pl. feiseanna. Also fes(s. [a. Ir. *feis*, *fess* meeting, assembly.]

1. An assembly of kings, chiefs, etc., being a kind of early Celtic parliament.

1792 *Encycl. Brit.* IX. 313/1 Ollam Fodla..erected a grand seminary of learning, and instituted the *Fes*, or triennial convention of provincial kings, priests, and poets, at Feamor or Tarah in Meath. **1880** *Ibid.* XIII. 250/2 He summoned a convention (*feis* or *fess*)..to assemble at Druimceta. **1898** J. HERON *Celtic Ch.* i. 19 The *Feis* was an assembly of all the kings, chiefs, ollamhs, and other leading men, and lasted for seven days. **1905** *Daily Chron.* 15 June 3/1 The whole scheme of [old Irish] national life turned on central feiseanna—social, legislative, and literary functions.

2. An Irish or Scottish festival of the arts, resembling the Welsh Eisteddfod.

1896 *Daily News* 2 Oct. 5/2 The 'Feis' extending over four days. **1896** *Westm. Gaz.* 3 Oct. 8/1 The *Feis* is announced to take place next May. **1910** *Daily Chron.* 3 Jan. 3/4 In her incidental reference to latter-day Feiseanna. **1916** *N. & Q.* 12th Ser. II. 71 The feis portions of local shows. **1938** L. MACNEICE *I crossed Minch* xii. 162 The school-kids recited her songs at the local Feis. **1955** *Times* 25 July 6/4 A similar ban was imposed last year and prevented the holding of a procession in the town [*sc.* Newtown Butler] in connexion with an annual Roman Catholic feis (festival).

feist, var. FIST *sb.*[2]

feisty ('faɪstɪ), *a. U.S. slang* (orig. *dial.*). [f. *feist* = FIST *sb.*[2] 3 + -Y[1].] Aggressive, excitable, touchy.

1896, etc. in Wentworth *Amer. Dial. Dict.* s.v. Ficety, etc. **1913** H. KEPHART *Our Southern Highlanders* 94 Feisty means when a feller's allers wigglin' about, wantin' ever'body to see him, like a kid when the preacher comes. **1926** E. M. ROBERTS *Time of Man* 152 That-there feisty bay mare jumped straight upwards and broke the tongue outen the plow. **1965** 'D. SHANNON' *Death-bringers* (1966) xiii. 162 Luther gets a little feisty after a few drinks, and he began to argue with him. **1968** J. POTTS *Trash Stealer* xiii. 148 He couldn't shake her loose—she hung on to his arm, feisty as a terrier.

feit, obs. form of FEAT.

feitergrasse, var. of *faitour's grass* obs.: see FAITOUR 2.

feith, feizable, obs. ff. FAITH, FEASIBLE.

feitisso: see FETISH.

fel, obs. var. of FELL.

fela, obs. form of FELLOW.

felafel (fɛ'lɑːfəl). Also falafel, filafil. [ad. Arab. *falāfil*.] (See quot. 1951.)

1951 *Commentary* (N.Y.) XI. 269 *Falafel*: sharp peppers and fried dried pea balls sandwiched in a flat roll called a *pitah*. *Falafel* is a standard meal around some urban and most interurban bus stops, where one spends a good part of one's life. **1955** P. SMOUHA *Middle Eastern Cooking* 74 Filafil ..Broad beans..garlic..onion..oil... Form mixture.. into balls..and fry them. **1962** A. RAMATI *Israel Today* 299 *Falafel*, spiced fried balls of chick peas and hot pepper, soaked in a relish and chilisauce. Usually served in bread. **1963** J. COMAY *Introd. Israel* xiv. 247 *Felafel*. (Bought off a stand in a street) is made of a highly spiced mixture of deep-fried balls of ground chickpea, small peppers, and pickled cucumbers, served hot between halves of peeta. It can be ordered hot (pepper hot) or mild. **1968** C. RODEN *Bk. Middle Eastern Food* 38 Falafel..is one of Egypt's national dishes. **1968** P. DURST *Badge of Infamy* i. 4 A Christian Arab sold cold drinks and *felafel* in an envelope of bread. **1970** *Guardian* 8 Oct. 13/2 You can now eat a bag of felafel—hot bean fritters—as you wander round the streets of Amman.

felanders, obs. form of FILANDERS.

fe'lapton. *Logic.* A mnemonic word representing the fourth mood in the third figure of syllogisms, in which the major premiss is a universal negative, the minor premiss a universal affirmative, and the conclusion a particular negative.

1551 T. WILSON *Logike* H ij a, *Fe.* No vertue should be eschued. *Lap.* All vertue hath her wo with her. *Ton.* Therfore some wo shoulde not be eschued. **1741** CHAMBERS *Cycl.*, *Felapton.* **1827** WHATELY *Logic* ii. (ed. 2) 98 Felapton. **1871** tr. *Taine's Hist. Eng. Lit.* (1873) I. 135 They still set their Barbara and Felapton, but only in the way of routine.

felau, feld(e, obs. ff. FELLOW, FIELD.

‖**feldgrau** ('fɛltgraʊ). [G.] Field-grey; hence, a German soldier in a uniform of this colour.

1934 in WEBSTER. **1945** R. HARGREAVES *Enemy at Gate* 296 The *feldgraus* crept into the labyrinth of streets. **1946** H. NICOLSON *Diary* 30 Apr. (1968) III. 58 Keitel, in *feldgrau* uniform stripped of all badges..looks trim, tough. **1958** H. WILLIAMSON *Love & Loveless* xvii. 294 Although the Germans in *feld-grau* were men, too, there was no feeling from them. **1960** S. BECKER tr. *Schwarz-Bart's Last of Just* (1961) VIII. 388 The Feldgrau buses deposited fifteen hundred orphans in the..snow-covered roll-call ground.

feldifair, -fare, obs. forms of FIELDFARE.

‖**feldscher** ('fɛldʃə(r)). Also feldschar, feldsher. [Russ. *fél'dsher*, ad. G. *feldscher* field surgeon.] In Russia, a person with practical training in medicine and surgery, but without professional medical qualifications; a physician's or surgeon's assistant; a local medical auxiliary.

1877 D. M. WALLACE *Russia* I. v. 104 There is not exactly a doctor, but there is a Feldsher in the village. **1916** H. S. WALPOLE *Dark Forest* I. iv, Like an old feldschar in my village who hates our village Pope. **1925** *Contemp. Rev.* June 752 In Russia the place of doctor or nurse is often filled by a 'feldscher' or half-trained doctor only. **1937** H. E. SIGERIST *Socialized Med. in Soviet Union* iii. 139 All European armies used to have surgeons who had not been trained in universities... During the nineteenth century most..replaced the feldshers with army surgeons of academic standing... The Russian army preserved the feldsher. He practised not only in the army but also among civilians... Many rural medical stations were headed by feldshers. **1957** H. BOWER *Short Guide Soviet Life* 58 There are also 600 schools for training nurses, *feldshers* (auxiliary nurses) and midwives.

feldspar, felspar ('fɛldspɑː(r), 'fɛlspɑː(r)). *Min.* Forms: α. 8 feldspat(h, feltspat. β. 8 fieldspar, 8– feldspar. γ. 8–9 felspar. [The forms *feldspat(h*, *feltspat* are adoptions (the latter through Sw.) of Ger. *feldspat(h*, f. *feld* FIELD + *spat(h* spar. Almost contemporaneously appear the wholly or partially translated forms *field-*, *feldspar*. The corrupt spelling *felspar* was introduced by Kirwan on the ground of a supposed derivation from *fels*, and is still more common than the correct form.]

A name given to a group of minerals, usually white or flesh-red in colour, occurring in crystals or in crystalline masses. They consist of a silicate of alumina with soda, potash, lime, etc.

1757 E. M. COSTA *Nat. Hist. Fossils* 287 The opaque quartz or feldspath. **1772** tr. *Cronstedt's Min.* App. 8 If the characters of this field-spar are accurately examined. **1776** G. EDWARDS *Fossilology* 54 A black felt-spat..found in Sweden. **1784** KIRWAN *Elem. Min.* 102 Sandstone mixed with mica and feltspar. **1785** J. HUTTON *Th. Earth* in *Trans. R. Soc. Edin.* I. 229 Strata consolidated by feld-spar. **1792** *Phil. Trans.* LXXXII. 30 D. Hoffman discovered that red blende and feldspat were luminous when pieces of either were rubbed together. **1794** KIRWAN *Min.* I. 317 *note*, This name seems to me derived from *fels*, a rock..hence I write it thus, felspar. **1835** SIR J. C. ROSS *Narr. 2nd Voy.* xxix. 406 Large crystals of felspar. **1860** MAURY *Phys. Geog. Sea* x. §494. 272 Granite is generally composed of feldspar, mica, and quartz.

attrib. **1807** T. THOMSON *Chem.* (ed. 3) II. 501 The felspar glaze does not melt at the heat requisite for fusing the colours. **1830** LYELL *Princ. Geol.* I. 263 Traversed in all directions by veins of felspar porphyry. **1862** DANA *Man. Geol.* §85. 80 *Feldspar-Euphotide*..consisting of a minutely-granular feldspathic base with disseminated diallage or smaragdite. **1872** W. S. SYMONDS *Rec. Rocks* iv. 113 Criccieth Castle stands on a felspar rock.

Hence **'feldsparic** *a*, resembling feldspar; = FELDSPATHIC. **'feldsparite** = FELDSPAR. **'feldsparry** *a.*, containing feldspar.

1811 PINKERTON *Petral.* I. 157 Hardness, of course felsparic. **1832** BOASE *Geol. Cornwall* 211 Felsparite or Felspar-Rock. **1852** TH. ROSS tr. *Humboldt's Trav.* I. ii. 98 The feldsparry lavas of the Peak.

feldspathic, felspathic (fɛld-, fɛl'spæθɪk), *a.* [f. *fel(d)spath* (see prec.) + -IC.] Of the nature of or containing feldspar.

1832 LYELL *Princ. Geol.* II. 295 The decomposition of felspathic lavas. **1845** DARWIN *Voy. Nat.* xxi. (1873) 486 Feldspathic rocks have produced a clayey soil. **1879** J. J. YOUNG *Ceram. Art* 56 Artificial porcelain may be made from ..felspathic clay.

feldspathoid, felspathoid ('fɛldspəθɔɪd, 'fɛlspəθɔɪd). *Min.* [f. *fel(d)spath* (see FELDSPAR, FELSPAR) + -OID.] Any of a group of minerals chemically similar to the feldspars, but containing less silica. Hence ˌ**fel(d)spa'thoidal** *a.*

1896 J. F. KEMP *Handbk. Rocks* i. 6 (*heading*) *Feldspathoids.* With the feldspars are placed two other important and closely related minerals, nepheline and leucite. *Ibid.*, The feldspars, together with the feldspathoids nepheline and leucite, are the most important of the rock-making minerals in their relations to the classification of rocks. **1910** *Bull. Geol. Soc. Amer.* XXI. 87 Monzonite may not be rich in alkalies nor carry any feldspathoid. **1912** [see FELSIC *a.*]. **1930** *Geol. Mag.* LXVII. 416 The hypothesis of the origin of felspathoidal rocks by reaction between magma and limestone. **1959** C. S. HURLBUT *Dana's Man. Mineral.* (ed. 17) 500 The feldspathoids are chemically similar to the feldspars, in that they are aluminosilicates of chiefly potassium, sodium, and calcium but with minor amounts of other ions. **1968** *Mineral. Abstr.* XIX. 234 Carbonate-rich feldspathoidal rocks from Nsala vent.

ˌ**fel(d)spa'those**, *a.* [+ -OSE.] = FELDSPATHIC, FELSPATHIC *a.*

1811 PINKERTON *Petral.* II. 448 It contains many felspathose points. **1879** DANA *Man. Geol.* (ed. 3) 74 *Feldspathose.*

feldyfar, dial. form of FIELDFARE.

†**fele**, *adv.* (quasi-*sb.*) and *a. Obs.* Forms: α. 1–2 fela, feola, *north.* feolu, feolo, 2–4 feole, (3 feola, fole), 3–4 fale, 3–6 feil(l(e, 4–5 feel(e, 4–6 fel(e, fell(e. β. (2 veale), 3 vale, (væle, veole), 3–4 vele. *Compar.* 4 feler, 5 felire. [OE. *feolo*, *feolu* (Mercian and Northumb.), *feola*, *fela* (WSax.) are respectively the accus. and the oblique case neuter (used adverbially, and hence as quasi-sb.) of a Com. Teut. adj., of which the other Teut. langs. have in their early forms only the accus. neut. as adv. and quasi-sb.: OFris. *felo*, OS. *filo*, *filu* (Du. *veel*), OHG. *filu*, *filo* (MHG. *vil*, *vile*, mod.Ger. *viel*, the latter also inflected as adj.), ON. *fiǫl* (chiefly in comb.), Goth. *filu*:—pre- Teut. **felu*:—OTeut. **pélu* (with ablaut-var. **polú*) much; cf. Skr. *purú*, Gr. πολύς, OIr. *il*.]

A. *adv.*

1. To a great extent or degree, much. Also in *so*, *too fele*.

Beowulf 1379 þær þu findan miht fela-synnigne secᵹ. *c* **950** *Lindisf. Gosp.* Luke vii. 47 Forðon lufade feolo. *c* **1000** *Wife's Compl.* 26 (Gr.) Sceal ic..mines fela leofan fæhðu dreogan. *a* **1250** *Prov. Ælfred* 196 in *O.E. Misc.* (1872) 114 Ne ilef þu nouht to fele uppe þe see. *a* **1300** *Cursor M.* 8991 (Cott.) Thoru wimmen þat he luued sa fele. *c* **1300** *Havelok* 2442 He bounden him so fele sore. *c* **1400** *Destr. Troy* 1884 Syn þe fre is so faire, & so fele vertus. *c* **1470** HENRY *Wallace* I. 56 Fell awfull in effer. **1598** HAKLUYT *Voy.* I. 192 The Beere, That they drinken feele too good chepe.

2. quasi-*sb.* Much, a great number or quantity. Chiefly with partitive genitive. Often qualified by *how*, *like*, *so*, *too*.

After the OE. period this use is seldom distinguishable from the adj.; later instances are placed here only when their grammatical character is evidenced by inflexion of the following sb.

Beowulf 1060 Fela sceal ᵹebidan leofes and laðes. *c* **825** *Vesp. Psalter* lxv[i]. 16 Ic seg[c]o eow alle ða ondredað dryhten hu feolu dyde sawle minre. *a* **900** *Charter* in *O.E. Texts* (1885) 444, & swae feola sufla. *c* **1000** *Ags. Gosp.* Matt. xxvi. 19 Fela ic hæbbe ᵹeþolod todæᵹ þurh ᵹesyhðe for hym. *c* **1000** *Sax. Leechd.* II. 208 Ne forlæt þu þæs blodes to fela on ænne siþ. *c* **1175** *Lamb. Hom.* 9 Monie and feole oðre godene werke. *a* **1300** *Sinners Beware* 87 in *O.E. Misc.* 75 Sunnen seouene þat bringeþ vt of heouene Swiþe vele manne.

B. *adj.* (Indeclinable; but as the word after 11th c. was used all but exclusively of multitude, not of quantity, the final *e* was prob. felt in ME. as a pl. ending. A solitary instance of *felen* dat. pl. occurs in the Ayenbite.)

1. With *sb.* in *pl.* Many. Often preceded by *as*, *how*, *so*; also in *many and fele*.

O.E. Chron. an. 963 (Laud MS.) Se biscop..bohte þa feola cotlif æt se king. *Ibid.* an. 1124 Fela soðfeste men sæidon [etc.]. *c* **1175** *Lamb. Hom.* 117 Fela stuntnesse beoð. **1297** R. GLOUC. (Rolls) 3067 Suche stones, so grete & so uale. *a* **1300** *Cursor M.* 18268 (Cott.) Hu fele pines ai sal þou fele. *c* **1305** *Land Cokayne* 95 þer beþ briddes mani and fale. **1340** *Ayenb.* 5 þou ne sselt habbe uele godes. **1382** WYCLIF *Gen.* xxiv. 22 As feel arm serclis. *c* **1420** *Chron. Vilod.* 586 Sekemen come þedur mony and ffele. *c* **1425** *Seven Sag.* (P.) 1110 He..hadde..of the quene many gyftis fele. *c* **1500** *Lancelot* 768 Galiot haith chargit hyme to tak Als fell folk. **1513** DOUGLAS *Æneis* I. i. 83 Sa fele ȝeris. **1598** HAKLUYT *Voy.* I. 201 So fele shippes this yeere there ware, That moch losse for vnfreyght they bare.

b. With *sb.* in *sing.* Much.

a **1300** *Cursor M.* 4050 (Cott.) þat..sufferd sa fele peril. *c* **1400** *Ywaine & Gaw.* 1392 That so fele folk led obowt. *c* **1440** *Generydes* 6701 With kysseng fele. **1535** STEWART *Cron. Scot.* II. 54 Feill folk als out of Germania.

2. In predicative use: Much, many, numerous. Also in compar.: More in number, more numerous.

a **1300** *Cursor M.* 14079 (Cott.) þe folk him foluand was ful fell. *c* **1340** *Gaw. & Gr. Knt.* 1391, I wowche hit saf fynly, þaȝ feler hit were. **1340–70** *Alex. & Dind.* 528 So fale folewen þe folk. *c* **1400** *Destr. Troy* 4869 þai are feler of folke. *a* **1400–50** *Alexander* 2084 A pake out of nounbre, Felire þan his folke be full fyue thousand.

3. *absol.* in *pl.* Many persons.

c **1175** *Lamb. Hom.* 107 He mei findan fele þe beoð bet iþoȝen and istoȝen þene he. *c* **1200** ORMIN 7640 Fele shulenn

fallenn & fele shulenn risenn upp. *a* **1300** *Cursor M.* 8495 (Cott.) þis writte wit fele was red and sene. **1340** *Ayenb.* 102 God, þet..yefþ more bleþeliche..to uelen þanne to onen allone. **1375** BARBOUR *Bruce* XVI. 641 In sum bargis sa feill can ga..That thai ourtummyllit. *c* **1450** *Bk. Curtasye* 522 in *Babees Bk.* (1868) 316 Few ar trew, but fele ar fals.

b. quasi-*sb.* Many *of.* Cf. A. 2.

a **1300** *Cursor M.* 7012 (Cott.) Fourti thusand of israel, O beniamin negh als fel. *c* **1394** *P. Pl. Crede* 547 Fele of þise poyntes. *a* **1455** HOLLAND *Howlat* 522 Feile of the fals folk, that fled of befor.

4. In comb. with sb., forming an adj., as ***fele-kyn***, of many kinds, various; or an adv., as ***fele-sith***, ***-syss***, ***feltymes*** many times, often. Also FELEFOLD.

c **1200** ORMIN 3573 Hire sune wass himm lic O fele kinne wise. [*c* **1205** LAY. 1717 On feole kunne wisen.] *a* **1300** *Cursor M.* 28380 (Cott.) Oure fele-sith haf i ben to spend þe gode wit skil þat godd me send. **13..** *E.E. Allit. P.* B. 1483 Of mony kyndes, of fele-kyn hues. **1375** BARBOUR *Bruce* III. 651 Felesyss, quhen thou art away. *Ibid.* xx. 225 That ȝhe haf done till me feill siss. **1382** WYCLIF *Ecclus.* xx. 18 Hou ofte sithes and hou fele shul thei scorne hym? *c* **1400** *Destr. Troy* 3014 Of hir fairehede feltymes hade þe freike herd.

†**fele**, *a.*[2] *Obs.* Also 3 felle, 4 fale, feele, fel, 5 fall. See also FIEL. [OE. *fǽle*, corresp. to OHG. *feili* purchasable (mod.G. *feil*).] **a.** In OE.: One's own; dear, faithful, good. **b.** In ME.: Proper, of the right sort, good.

c **1000** *Ags. Ps.* (Gr.) lxxviii. [lxxix.] 1 þin fæle hus. *Ibid.* cxviii. [cxix.] 105 þæt is fæle blæcern minum fotum. *a* **1250** *Owl & Night.* 1376 Ah schaltu, wrecche, luve tele..vich luve is fele, Bi-tweone wepmon and wimmane? **1387** TREVISA *Higden* (Rolls) I. 399 As þei God..Made þat lond so feele To be celer of al heele. *a* **1400** *Sir Perc.* 729 Thou art fele, That thou ne wille away stele.

fele, obs. form of FILE *v.*[2]

†**'felefold**, *a.* (*adv.*). *Obs.* [f. FELE *a.*[1] + FOLD.] = MANIFOLD. Also *absol.* in ***by felefold***: by a great deal, many times over.

c **1000** *Ags. Ps.* (Spelm.) xxxv[i]. 6 Domas ðine neowelnys micellu oððe felefeald. *c* **1175** *Lamb. Hom.* 135 Alswa of ane sede cumeð fele folde weste. *c* **1205** LAY. 4249 Beoð on beoken feole feld bisnen. *a* **1225** *Ancr. R.* 180 Boðe [temptaciuns] beoð feoleuold. *c* **1340** *Gaw. & Gr. Knt.* 1545 Hit were a fole fele-folde. *c* **1374** CHAUCER *Boeth.* II. i. 30, I vnderstonde þe felefolde colour & deceites of þilke merueillous monstre fortune. **1377** LANGL. *P. Pl.* B. XIII. 320 It was fouler bi felefold þan it firste semed.

b. As *adv.* In manifold ways.

1340 *Ayenb.* 212 Naȝt wordes afaited and y-sliked ueleuold.

Hence †**'felefold** *v. Obs.*, to increase, multiply. **a.** *trans.* **b.** *intr.* for *refl.*

a **1300** *E.E. Psalter* iii. 2 Hou fele-folded are þai, þat droves me to do me wa. *Ibid.* xi. 9 [xii. 8] Men sones fele-faldes tou. *Ibid.* cxxxviii[-ix]. 18 Over se-sand fele-falde sal þai.

felenous(e, obs. form of FELONOUS.

felet, obs. form of FILLET.

felewote, obs. form of VELVET.

felf, obs. and dial. var. of FELLOE, FELLY.

felfar, obs. form of FIELDFARE.

felghe, obs. form of FELLOE, FELLY.

‖**Félibre** (felibr). [F. *félibre*, a. Prov. *felibre* any one of the teachers in the temple to whom Jesus put questions as a child (Luke 2: 46), prob. (Bloch & von Wartburg) f. Low Latin *fellibris*, var. of *fellebris* nursling (of the Muses), f. L. *fellāre* to suck.] A word used by F. Mistral (1830–1914) to designate a member of the brotherhood which was founded in 1854 by seven Provençal writers for the maintenance and purification of Provençal as a literary language, and also for the promotion of the artistic interests of the South of France. Also as *adj.*

1876 G. MEREDITH *Let.* 6 Oct. (1970) I. 527 As to the song, my wife worked at it Trojanly and I, as it were a drum accompaniment, thumped out the Félibre lingo. **1892** *Ibid.* 13 Dec. II. 1112 Wyse was an enthusiastic félibre, and published Provençal verses. **1902** *Encycl. Brit.* XXXII. 44/1 Greatest of them all, the true and acknowledged forerunner of the *félibres*, Jacques Jasmin (1798–1864), the hairdresser of Agen. *Ibid.* 45/1 The *félibres* are in no sense of the word the direct successors of the troubadours. **1904** *Westm. Gaz.* 27 May 12/2 The Félibres, who have just been celebrating their jubilee. **1964** *Archivum Linguisticum* 38 Roumanille, however, finally succeeded in persuading his fellow *félibres* to adopt the phonetic system.

Hence **Fé'librian** *a.*, relating to the Félibres, or to the Provençal literature produced by them; **Félibrism** ('feɪlɪbrɪz(ə)m), the movement instituted by the Félibres; the principles underlying that movement.

1908 *Daily Chron.* 16 Jan. 4/4 He plunged into the centre of things Félibrian. **1911** *Daily News* 11 Mar. 6/4 The literary output of Félibrism has been mainly poetic.

‖**Félibrige** (felibriʒ). [F. *Félibrige*, ad. Prov. *Felibrige*, f. *felibre*: see prec.] The name of the literary school formed by the Félibres.

1902 *Encycl. Brit.* XXXII. 44/2 The most widely read of the *Félibrige* publications is the *Armana Prouvençau*, which ..contains much of the best work of the school. **1907** *Daily Chron.* 14 Nov. 3/3 Two other pioneers of the 'Félibrige' movement, Roumanille and Mathieu. **1927** *Observer* 18 Sept. 12 The Félibrige is the association..whose object is to keep alive the traditions and the language of Provence. **1964** *Archivum Linguisticum* 38 The Félibrige, therefore, outside Provence, has no common literary language.

felicide ('fiːlɪsaɪd). [f. L. *fēli-*, *fēles* cat + -CIDE 2.] The action of killing a cat, cat-slaying.

1832 SOUTHEY *Corresp. with C. Bowles* (1881) 259 Those repeated acts of felicide. **1836** *Tait's Mag.* III. 568 He hurled it, with premeditated felicide, in the direction of his supreme abomination. **1868** *Morn. Star* 25 Jan., One poor woman..confessed to having committed an act of felicide.

felicific (fiːlɪ'sɪfɪk), *a. Ethics.* [ad. L. *fēlīcificus*, f. *fēlīci-*, *fēlix* happy + *-ficus* making: see -FIC.] Making or tending to make happy; productive of happiness.

1865 J. GROTE *Moral Ideas* x. (1876) 205 Concentrate your felicific effort where..none of it will be lost. **1874** SIDGWICK *Meth. Ethics* xiv. 373 Its felicific tendency is not at first apparent. **1877** J. SULLY *Pessimism* 164 Knowledge of the real felicific value of life.

felicificability (fiːlɪˌsɪfɪkə'bɪlɪtɪ). [f. **felicificable* (f. prec. + -ABLE): see *-bility*, -ITY.]

1865 J. GROTE *Moral Ideas* ii. 33 Felicificability or capacity for happiness.

felicificative (fiːlɪ'sɪfɪkətɪv). [f. as if L. **fēlīcifi'c-āre* (see next) + -ATIVE.] Tending to make happy. Hence **feli'cificativeness**, tendency to make happy or produce happiness.

1865 J. GROTE *Moral Ideas* ii. (1876) The original egence of God..is in another word felicificativeness.

†**fe'licify**, *v. Obs. rare.* [f. as if ad. L. **fēlīcificāre*, L. *fēlīci-*, *fēlix* + *-ficāre*: see -FY.] *trans.* To render happy; also *absol.*

1683 E. HOOKER *Pref. Ep. Pordage's Mystic Div.* 92 Whom ..the allwise..and most mercifull God mai..sanctifi, tranquillifi and felicifi. **1698** *Whole Art of Knowledge* I. §31. 23 The temper of true government most felicifies and perpetuates it.

†**fe'licious**, *a. Obs.* Also in 5 felecyows. [f. L. *fēlīci-*, *fēlix* + -OUS.] **a.** Happy, joyous. **b.** Fortunate, prosperous.

c **1485** *Digby Myst.* (1882) III. 947 Of felachyp most felecyows. **1599** A. M. tr. *Gabelhouer's Bk. Physicke* 110/1 His brethren..have..experimentede the same, with felicious event. *a* **1635** NAUNTON *Fragm. Reg.* (Arb.) 16 In all which [warres] she was felicious [**1735** felicitous] and victorious. **1654** COKAINE *Dianea* IV. 352 These words..were attended by a felicious shout.

†**fe'licitate**, *pa. pple. Obs.* [ad. L. *fēlīcitātus*, pa. pple. of *fēlīcitāre*: see next.] Made happy.

1605 SHAKS. *Lear* I. i. 77, I am alone felicitate In your deere Highnesse loue.

felicitate (fɪ'lɪsɪteɪt), *v.* [f. ppl. stem of L. *fēlīcitāre* to make happy, f. *fēlīci-*, *fēlix* happy.]

1. *trans.* To render or make happy; also *absol.* Now *rare*; see FELICITATED *ppl. a.*

1628 WITHER *Brit. Rememb.* III. 261 Of themselves, nor paines, nor pleasures can Felicitate. **1668** DRYDEN *Evening's Love* V. i, Since I cannot make myself happy, I will have the glory to felicitate another. **1741** WATTS *Improv. Mind* I. xvii. 254 A glorious Entertainment..would..felicitate his Spirit, if [etc.]. **1792** A. BELL in Southey's *Life* (1844) I. 436 Your occupations..have a tendency to..felicitate our days. **1825** T. BARBER *Serm. Import. Relig. Nat. Educ.* 40 It settles, composes, and felicitates the soul. **1856** J. MACNAUGHT *Doctr. Inspiration* (1857) 193 It has felicitated the death of all who have learned in it to talk with God.

†**b.** To render prosperous. *Obs.*

1634 SIR T. HERBERT *Trav.* (1638) 92 A citty in Bengala and felicitated by Ganges. **1646** SIR T. BROWNE *Pseud. Ep.* VI. vii. 307 The Sunne's..influence is conceived..to felicitate India more then any after.

2. To reckon or pronounce happy or fortunate; to congratulate. Now only with obj. a person. Const. *on*, *upon*.

1634 SIR T. HERBERT *Trav.* (1838) 182 A glorious miser fælicitating his death, so it be in contemplation of his rich idolatry. **1646** SIR T. BROWNE *Pseud. Ep.* IV. ix. 201 Speeches, felicitating the good, or deprecating the evil to follow. **1715** *Wodrow Corr.* (1843) II. 77 This comes to felicitate you upon your wife's safe delivery. **1812** D'ISRAELI *Calam. Auth.* (1867) 215 A great poet felicitated himself that poetry was not the business of his life. **1855** MACAULAY *Hist. Eng.* III. 645 The enemies of France..eagerly felicitated one another. **1873** SYMONDS *Grk. Poets* vi. 175 The victor might be felicitated on his good fortune.

†**3. a.** *trans.* To offer congratulations on (something). **b.** *intr.* To join in congratulations *with*.

1684 J. PETER *Siege Vienna* 104 Of other Princes..there were great numbers that came to felicitate his Majesties happy return. **1799** NELSON in Nicolas *Disp.* III. 447, I felicitate with you on the happy success of the allied Arms.

Hence **fe'licitated** *ppl a.*, **fe'licitating** *ppl. a.*

1755 AMORY *Mem.* (1769) I. 280 It commands us to acquire a felicitating temper, and to communicate happiness adequate to our power. **1772** JOHNSON 27 Mar. in *Boswell*, The happiness of an unembodied spirit will consist..in the possession of felicitating ideas. **1806** A. KNOX *Rem.* I. 21 This felicitating influence of our divine religion. **1890** tr. *Pfleiderer's Developm. Theology* II. ii. 118 A life of invigorated and felicitated God-consciousness.

felicitation (fɪˌlɪsɪ'teɪʃən). [noun of action f. prec.: see -ATION. Cf. F. *félicitation*.] The action of congratulating; an instance of the same; a congratulatory speech or message. Also *attrib.*

1709 *Lond. Gaz.* No. 4571/2 The..Empress came..to make her the Compliments of Fælicitation. **1790** BURKE *Fr. Rev.* 103 A felicitation on the present new year. **1801** T. JEFFERSON *Writ.* (1830) III. 464, I thank [you] for your kind felicitations on my election. **1817** BP. R. WATSON *Anecd.* I. 108, I did not..break in upon you, either with my acknowledgments or felicitations. **1860** W. COLLINS *Wom. White* II. vi. 211 Pray present my best respects and felicitations. **1882** *Times* 4 Mar. 5 A number of felicitation cards have been left.

felicitator (fɪ'lɪsɪteɪtə(r)). [agent-n. f. as prec.] One who offers congratulations.

1890 *Times* 2 Jan. 3/1 A compliment which his Majesty.. paid to none other of his felicitators.

felicitous (fɪ'lɪsɪtəs), *a.* [f. FELICITY + -OUS.] Characterized by felicity.

1. a. Indicative of or marked by extreme happiness; blissful. *rare.*

1824 DIBDIN *Libr. Comp.* 606, I am well aware of that felicitous palpitation of heart. **1886** RUSKIN *Præterita* I. i. 29 In the refinement of their highly educated..benevolent, and felicitous lives.

†**b.** Fortunate, prosperous, successful. *Obs.*

1735 [see FELICIOUS].

2. Of an action, expression, manner, etc.: Admirably suited to the occasion; strikingly apt or appropriate.

1789 P. STUART *Let. to Burns* 5 Aug., His manner was so felicitous, that he enraptured every person around him. **1802** PALEY *Nat. Theol.* xxvi. (1803) 519 A felicitous adaptation of the organ to the object. **1839** CARLYLE *Chartism* (1858) 3 A Reform Ministry has 'put down.. Chartism' in the most felicitous effectual manner. **1848** W. H. BARTLETT *Egypt to Pal.* xxvii. (1879) 528 We esteemed it a felicitous rounding off of our journey. **1866** FELTON *Anc. & Mod. Gr.* II. x. 190 This striking essay..abounds in.. felicitous comparisons. **1878** R. W. DALE *Lect. Preach.* v. 120 A felicitous illustration.

b. Of persons: Happy or pleasantly apt in expression, manner, or style.

1831 LAMB *Elia* Ser. I. *Old Benchers I.T.*, Felicitous in jests upon his own figure. **1824** DIBDIN *Libr. Comp.* 765 The witty, the felicitous, the inimitable Fontaine. **1841** W. SPALDING *Italy & It. Isl.* II. 389 He is..sometimes singularly felicitous, in striking out insulated views.

Hence **fe'licitousness**, the quality or state of being felicitous.

1727 in BAILEY vol. II.; and in mod. Dicts.

felicitously (fɪ'lɪsɪtəslɪ), *adv.* [f. as prec. + -LY[2].] In a felicitous manner.

1. Happily, prosperously, successfully.

1539 CROMWELL in Burnet *Hist. Ref.* (1679) I. III. xvii. 196, I..shall pray..that..your most dear Son, may succeed you to Reign long, prosperously, and felicitously.

2. In an admirably fitting manner; with striking appropriateness or grace.

1828 MISS MITFORD *Village* Ser. III. (1863) 70 Never had painter more felicitously realized his conception. **1832** J. J. PARK *Dogmas of Constit.* Pref. 17 Sciences..felicitously denominated by the French authors, 'les sciences d'observation'. **1863** A. B. GROSART *Small Sins* (ed. 2) 77, I emphasise the word 'spoil'..it is exquisitely and felicitously descriptive. **1893** *Publishers' Circular* 3 June 623/1 Cruikshank's..designs..felicitously render the grotesque ..character of the tales.

felicity (fɪ'lɪsɪtɪ). Forms: 4–6 feli-, felycite(e, -yte, 6–7 felicitie, -ye, (6 *Sc.* felyscitie, -syte), 5– felicity. [a. OF. *felicité* (Fr. *félicité*), ad. L. *fēlīcitātem*, f. *fēlix* happy.]

1. The state of being happy; happiness (in mod. use with stronger sense, intense happiness, bliss); a particular instance or kind of this.

c **1386** CHAUCER *Clerk's T.* 53 We mighten live in more felicitee. **1441** *Pol. Poems* (Rolls) II. 206, I felle ffrom alle felycyté. **1552** LYNDESAY *Monarche* 5093 Fairweill all vaine felyscitie! **1602** SHAKS. *Ham.* v. ii. 358 Absent thee from felicitie awhile. **1651** LD. DIGBY, etc. *Lett. conc. Relig.* I. 2, I aspire yet to a farr greater felicity. **1722** WOLLASTON *Relig. Nat.* ix. 217 The injoyment of an humble..expectation of felicity hereafter. **1794** MRS. RADCLIFFE *Myst. Udolpho* i, Conjugal felicity and parental duties divided his attention. **1807** *Med. Jrnl.* XVII. 541 Sincerely wishing you every felicity. **1839** HALLAM *Hist. Lit.* (1855) III. 118 Felicity.. consists not in having prospered but in prospering.

Comb. **1799** R. WARNER *Walk* (1800) 83 Those felicity hunters, the teazing insects of fashion.

†**b.** Phrases: ***to have, take felicity in*** or ***to*** with *inf.*: to take delight or pleasure in or to. ***to place, set one's felicity in***: to find one's chief delight in.

1542 UDALL in *Lett. Lit. Men* (Camden) 6 Settying his moste delite and felicitee in the veray infamie of the same. **1596** SPENSER *State Irel.* Wks. (1862) 517/1 The..Northern Nations..tooke no felicity in that countrey. **1622** R. HAWKINS *Voy. S. Sea* (1847) 153 A man known to put his felicitie in that vice. **1691** HARTCLIFFE *Virtues* 7 The more polite..sort of Men place their Felicity in Honours. **1758** JORTIN *Erasmus* I. 175 He took a felicity to set out sundry Commentaries upon the Fathers works.

2. That which causes or promotes happiness; a source of happiness, a blessing.

c **1385** CHAUCER *L.G.W.* 2588 *Hypermnestra*, This thought her was felicité. **1490** CAXTON *Eneydos* xxvii. 105 O felycyte meruelleouse wherof I shulde be well happy. **1597** MORLEY *Introd. Mus.* 182 His coine..is his only hope and felicitie. **1634** W. TIRWHYT *Balzac's Lett.* 159 The happinesse of your Family..is a publick Felicity. *a* **1661** FULLER *Worthies* (1840) I. 211 God bestoweth personal felicities on some far above the proportion of others. **1734** tr. *Rollin's Anc. Hist.* (1827) Pref. 27 A woman who formed his felicity. **1874** MAURICE *Friendship Bks.* viii. 221 He also had many felicities he was thankful for.

3. Prosperity; good fortune, success. Now *rare*.

1393 GOWER *Conf.* III. 118 He hath of proprete Good spede and great felicite. **1494** FABYAN *Chron.* VII. 550 It is not possyble for that Kyngedome to stande in felycite. **1533** BELLENDEN *Livy* II. (1822) 171 The Faderis..faucht with grete felicite aganis the Volschis. **1652–62** HEYLIN *Cosmogr.* III. (1673) 7/1 He was..vanquished by the valour and felicity of L. Sylla. **1738** NEAL *Hist. Purit.* IV. 274 The old Clergy..were intoxicated with their new felicity. **1780** HARRIS *Philol. Enq.* Wks. (1841) 464 Athens..enjoyed more than all others the general felicity. **1865** CARLYLE *Fredk. Gt.* V. xv. i. 271 This General's strategic felicity and his domestic were fatally cut-down.

†**b.** *pl.* Prosperous circumstances; successful enterprises; successes.

1625 BACON *Ess. Adversity* (Arb.) 505 Describing the Afflictions of Iob, then the Felicities of Salomon. **1694** FALLE *Jersey* i. 29 The Spaniards: Whose aims..were defeated by the Felicities of that Queen. *a* **1731** ATTERBURY (J.), The felicities of her wonderful reign may be complete.

c. A stroke of fortune; a fortunate trait (in an individual).

1761 HUME *Hist. Eng.* III. lxi. 326 The easy subduing of this insurrection..was a singular felicity to the protector. **1779–81** JOHNSON *L.P.*, *Pope* Wks. IV. 6 It was the felicity of Pope to rate himself at his real value. **1861** TULLOCH *Eng. Purit.* ii. 284 It was the felicity of Cromwell to detect this gift of government.

d. Singular fortunateness (of an occurrence). Cf. 4.

1809–10 COLERIDGE *Friend* (1865) 157 By a rare felicity of accident.

4. A happy faculty in art or speech; admirable appropriateness or grace of invention or expression.

1605 BACON *Adv. Learn.* I. Ded. §2 Your Maiesties manner of speech is indeed..full of facilitie, and felicitie. **1727** POPE, etc. *Art of Sinking* 82 Many painters..have with felicity copied a small-pox. **1833** LAMB *Elia* Ser. II. *Pop. Fallacies* (1865) 411 We must pronounce [this pun] a monument of curious felicity. **1873** SYMONDS *Grk. Poets* x. 336 Moschus is remarkable for occasional felicities of language. **1876** J. H. NEWMAN *Hist. Sk.* I. II. xii. 295 A style, which adapts itself with singular felicity to every class of subjects.

b. A happy inspiration, an admirably well-chosen expression.

1665 J. SPENCER *Vulg. Prophecies* 74 The extempore felicities of the Orators of those times. **1779–81** JOHNSON *L.P.*, *Denham* Wks. II. 78 Those felicities which cannot be produced at will by wit and labour. **1870** LOWELL *Among my Bks.* Ser. I. (1873) 176 It is from such felicities that the rhetoricians deduce..their statutes.

†**5.** Of a planet: A favourable aspect. *Obs.*

c **1391** CHAUCER *Astrol.* II. §4 Thei haue a fortunat planete in hir assendent & ȝit in his felicite. **1393** GOWER *Conf.* III. 116 And upon such felicite Stant Jupiter in his degre.

felid (ˈfiːlɪd). [ad. mod.L. *fēlid-æ*, f. *fēles* cat.] One of the *Felidæ* or cat-tribe.

feliform (ˈfiːlɪfɔːm). [f. L. *fēli-*, *fēles* cat + -FORM.] Having the form of a cat.

feline (ˈfiːlaɪn, -lɪn), *a.* and *sb.* [ad. L. *fēlīn-us*, f. *fēles* cat.]

A. *adj.* **a.** Of or pertaining to cats or their species, cat-like in form or structure. **b.** Resembling a cat in any respect, cat-like in character or quality.

a. **1681** GREW *Musæum Reg. Soc.* 16 From which [the Bevir] he [the Otter] differs..in his Tail, which is feline, or a long Taper. **1833** SIR C. BELL *Hand* (1834) 149 The feline quadrupeds. **1850** LYELL *2nd Visit U.S.* II. 335 The feline tribe and the foxes. **1876** C. M. DAVIES *Unorth. Lond.* 159 Fanaticism has within it a more than feline tenacity of life.

b. **1843** LYTTON *Last Bar.* I. i, The feline care with which he stepped aside from any patches of mire. **1851** H. MELVILLE *Whale* xli. 204 Human madness is oftentimes a..most feline thing.

B. *sb.* An animal of the cat tribe.

1861 WOOD *Illustr. Nat. Hist.* I. 196 The large savage feline that ranges the waste lands. **1889** *Pall Mall G.* 14 Oct. 3/3 The eyes are..as bright as a feline's in the dark.

Hence **ˈfelinely** *adv.*, in a feline manner; **ˈfelineness**, the state of being feline.

1848 LYTTON *Harold* VII. iv, The rings through which scratched so felinely the paw of..Griffin. **1865** CARLYLE *Fredk. Gt.* V. XIV. v. 202 Noailles has us in a perfect mouse-trap, *souricière* as he felinely calls it. **1893** *National Observer* 25 Mar. 467/2 His gait was felinely nimble.

felinity (fɪˈlɪnɪtɪ). [f. prec. + -ITY.] The quality of being feline; a cat-like disposition; the typical qualities of the cat-tribe.

1855 'M. HARLAND' *Hidden Path* xxviii. 270 This idiosyncrasy of his felinity tormented Bella more than ever. **1882** F. W. HARPER in *Spectator* 30 Dec. 1682 Felinity, at least the highest part of it, is included in humanity.

feliole, var. of FILIOLE *Obs.*

felk, var. of FELLOE, FELLY.

fell (fɛl), *sb.*[1] Forms: 1 fel(l, 2–7 fel, 3–6 felle, 2– fell. Also 3–4 **vel**, **velle**. [Com. Teut.: OE. *fel*, *fell* str. neut., OFris. *fel*, OS. *fel* (Du. *vel*), OHG. *fel* (MHG. *vel*, mod.Ger. *fell*), ON. (*ber-*) *fiall*, Goth. (*þruts-*) *fill* n.:—OTeut. **fello*(*m*:— pre-Teut. **pello-*:—**pelno-*, cognate with Gr. πέλλα, Lat. *pellis* skin; a derivative from the same root is FILM.]

1. The skin or hide of an animal: **a.** with the hair, wool, etc.

Beowulf 2088 (Gr.) Sio wæs orþoncum eall ȝeȝyrwed.. dracan fellum. *c* **1000** *Sax. Leechd.* II. 334 Nim mereswines fel. *a* **1175** *Cott. Hom.* 225 God ham ȝeworhta þa reaf of fellan and hi were mid þan fellen ȝescridde. *c* **1220** *Bestiary* 135 For his fel he [neddre] ðer leteð. **1340** *Ayenb.* 210 Zuych difference ase þer is be-tuene..þe uelle and þe beste. **1399** LANGL. *Rich. Redeles* III. 24 The herte..ffedith him on þe venym, his ffelle to anewe. *a* **1400–50** *Alexander* 5083 Sum fellis of fischis. *c* **1483** CAXTON *Vocab.* 9 b, Of shepes fellis. **1551** ROBINSON tr. *More's Utop.* (Arb.) 98 They carie furth ..purple died felles. **1612** DRAYTON *Poly-olb.* vii. 104 Her Wooll whose Staple doth excell..the golden Phrygian Fell. **1757** DYER *Fleece* (1807) 68 In loose locks of fells she most delights. **1831** CARLYLE *Sart. Res.* I. viii. 37 The Horse I ride has his own whole fell. **1870** MORRIS *Earthly Par.* III. IV. 6 A lion's skin..So wrought with gold that the fell showed but dim Betwixt the threads.

†**b.** as distinguished from the hair, etc. *Obs.*

a **1225** *Ancr. R.* 418 Uelles wel i-tauwed. **1436** *Pol. Poems* (Rolls) II. 168 Of Scotlonde the commoditees Ar ffelles, hydes, and of wolle the ffleesse. **1581** W. STAFFORD *Exam. Compl.* ii. (1876) 51 Of our felles they make Spanish skins, Gloues, and Girdels. **1615** T. ADAMS *Lycanthropy* 20 His fell good, his fleece good, his flesh good. **1719** D'URFEY *Pills* V. 294 Wool, New pull d from tanned Fells.

c. *Proverbs.*

1548 HALL *Chron.* (1809) 106 The old Proverbe..which saieth 'If Shepe ronne wilfully emongest Wolves they shall lese ether Life or Fell.' **1579** GOSSON *Sch. Abuse* (Arb.) 20 The woolf iettes in weathers felles.

2. Said of the human skin, rarely of the skin covering an organ of the body. Often in phr. ***flesh and fell***: see FLESH. Now only as *transf.* from 1.

c **1000** *Juliana* 591 (Gr.) Næs..ne feax ne fel fyre ȝemæled. *c* **1200** ORMIN 8591, I fell & flæsh wiþþuten dæþ. *a* **1300** *Sarmun* vi. in *E.E.P.* (1862) 2 þi velle þat is wiþ-oute. **1387** TREVISA *Higden* (Rolls) VI. 247 An evel þat was bytwene vel and flesche. *c* **1450** *St. Cuthbert* (Surtees) 6076 In synnes, in Ioyntes, in fell, and flessh. **1561** HOLLYBUSH *Hom. Apoth.* 19 b, The celles or felles that enuiron the harte. **1606** HOLLAND *Sueton.* 239 That kind of dropsy wherein water runneth between the fell and the flesh. **1831** CARLYLE *Sart. Res.* (1858) 23 The rest of his body sheeted in its thick natural fell. **1890** H. M. STANLEY in *Times* 6 May, A light brown fell stood out very clearly.

fig. *a* **1225** *Ancr. R.* 120 Nis þer, þeonne, bute vorworpen sone þet ruwe vel abute þe heorte.

†**b.** 'The flesh immediately under the skin' (Burns *Gloss.*). *Obs.*

1559 *Mirr. Mag.*, *Dk. Gloucester* xiii, She haply with her nayles may claw hym to the fell. **1567** TURBERV. *Epitaphes, etc.* 108 b, Augmenting still his secret sore by piercing fell and skin. **1786** BURNS *Ordination* xii. 5 See, how she peels the skin an' fell As ane were peelin onions!

3. A covering of hair, wool, etc., *esp.* when thick and matted; a fleece. Often in phr. ***a fell of hair***, a head or shock of hair.

1600 SHAKS. *A.Y.L.* III. ii. 55 We are still handling our Ewes and their Fels you know are greasie. **1605** —— *Macb.* v. v. 11 My Fell of haire Would at a dismall Treatise rowze, and stirre As life were in't. *c* **1640** J. SMYTH *Lives Berkeleys* (1883) I. 162 A Sheepskyn accordinge to the growth of the fell. **1842** N. A. WOODS *Tour Canada* 14 Their flat Tartar features half hidden under a fell of coarse, unkempt hair. **1844** LOWELL *Columbus*, The surly fell of Ocean's bristled neck! **1872** LOWELL *Dante* Prose Wks. 1800 IV. 204 *note*, Reason (Virgil) first carries him down by clinging to the fell of Satan.

4. *attrib.* and *Comb.*, as *fell-rot* (Sc.), *-ware*, *-wound*. Also **fell-ill** *Sc.* (see quot.); **fell-poake** *Sc.*, waste clippings or parings resulting from the preparation of skins (used for manure); **fell-wool** (see quot. 1888), and FELL-MONGER.

1798 R. DOUGLAS *Agric. Roxb.* 149 Aged cattle..are liable to be hide bound, a disease known here..by the name of the *fell-ill. *a* **1803** J. GRETTON in *A. Hunter's Georg. Ess.* (1803) III. 139 Get your *fell-poake on your head-land by the latter end of October. **1799** *Ess. Highland Soc.* III. 465 Many different kinds of rot..as the..*fell-rot, the bone-rot and other rots. **1399** LANGL. *Rich. Redeles* III. 150 Ffurris of ffoyne and oþer *ffelle-ware. **1552** *Act 5–6 Edw. VI*, c. 6 §1 Mingling *Fell-wool and Lambs-wool..with Fleece-wool. **1677** PLOT *Oxfordsh.* 278 This Fell wool they separate into five or six sorts. **1888** ELWORTHY *W. Somerset Word-bk.*, *Fell-wool*, the wool pulled from sheep-skins in distinction from the fleece wool shorn from the living animal. **1382** WYCLIF *Lev.* xiii. 19 In the place of the bocche aperith a *fel wounde [Lat. *cicatrix*]. **1382** —— *Jer.* xxx. 17 Y schal helen parfitly thi felle wounde to thee.

fell (fɛl), *sb.*[2] Also 4–5 felle, 4–7 fel. [a. ON. *fiall* (Sw. *fiäll*, Da. (*fjeld*) mountain, perh.:—OTeut. **felzo*(*m*, related by ablaut to **faliso-*, OHG. *felis*, mod.G. *fels* rock.]

1. A hill, mountain. Obs. exc. in proper names of hills in the north-west of England, as Bowfell, Scawfell, etc.

a **1300** *Cursor M.* 6461 (Cott.) Moyses went vp-on þat fell, and fourti dais can þer-on duell. *Ibid.* 22534 (Cott.) Þe dals up-rise, þe fells dun fall. *c* **1400** MAUNDEV. (Roxb.) xiv. 64 Thurgh þe straytes of mountaynes and felles. *c* **1470** HARDING *Chron.* CIII. vii, His graue is yet..vpon the fell. **1535** STEWART *Cron. Scot.* III. 435 With clarions.. Quhomeof the sound did found attouir the fell. **1610** HOLLAND *Camden's Brit.* I. 755 High topped hilles and huge fels standing thicke together.

2. a. A wild, elevated stretch of waste or pasture land; a moorland ridge, down. Now chiefly in the north of England and parts of Scotland. Formerly often in phr. ***frith*** (***firth***) ***and fell***: see FRITH.

a **1300** *Cursor M.* 7697 (Cott.) In frith and fell, Saul soght dauid for to quell. *c* **1420** *Anturs of Arth.* iv, Thay questun, thay quellun By frythun, by fellun. **1486** *Bk. St. Albans* E j a, Wheresoeuer ye fare by fryth or by fell. **1549** *Compl. Scot.* vi. 66 The laif of ther fat flokkis follouit on the fellis. **1562** TURNER *Herbal* II. 57 a, Feniculum..groweth in..wild mores, called felles. **1612** DRAYTON *Poly-olb.* xvii, The Syluans that..did dwell, Both in the tufty Frith, and in the mossy Fell. **1769** GRAY *Lett.* Wks. 1836 IV. 145 Greystock town and castle..lie only 3 miles (over the Fells) from Ulzwater. **1867** JEAN INGELOW *Gladys* 169 With fell and precipice, It ran down steeply to the water's brink. **1872** JENKINSON *Guide Eng. Lakes* (1879) 121 The fell is ascended by the side of a ravine. **1880** MISS BROUGHTON *Sec. Th.* III. i, Fells and becks, whose cool memory has often come back ..to her.

¶**b.** In 16–17th c. understood to mean: A marsh, fen.

1514 FITZHERB. *Just. Peas* (1538) 115 Lowe grounds for medowes, felles, fennes. **1583** STANYHURST *Æneis* I. (Arb.) 23 Throgh fels and trenches thee chase thee coompanye tracked. **1611** SPEED *Theat. Gt. Brit.* Pref., Her Fels and Fens so replenished with wilde foule. **1612** DRAYTON *Poly-olb.* iii. 42 Ye..be grac't With floods or marshie fels.

c. *Sc.* 'A field pretty level on the side or top of a hill' (Burns *Glossary* in *Poems* 1787).

1794 BURNS *Now Westlin Winds* ii, The partridge loves the fruitful fells; The plover loves the mountains.

3. *attrib*, as in ***fell-berry***, ***-farm***, ***-foot***, ***-gate***, ***-head***, ***-land*** (hence ***-lander***), ***-mouse***, ***-mutton***, ***-range***, ***-ridge***, ***-sheep***, ***-side***, ***-top***, ***-walker***, ***-walking***; **fell-bloom**, the flower of Bird's-foot Trefoil, *Lotus corniculatus* (Jam.); **fell-field** (see quot. 1916); **fell hound**, a variety of foxhound bred for hunting in hill-country; **fell-thrush**, the missel-thrush.

1884 *Pall Mall G.* 16 July 4/2 We make wonderfully good *fell-berry puddings. **1908** W. G. COLLINGWOOD *Scand. Brit.* II. ii. 180 In Cumberland..on *fell farms. **1951** M. LLOYD (*title*) Fell Farm Holiday. **1916** B. D. JACKSON *Gloss. Bot. Terms* (ed. 3) 144 **Fell-fields*, districts of dwarf, scattered plants, chiefly Cryptogams. **1959** A. H. MCLINTOCK *Descr. Atlas N.Z.* 28 Subalpine scrub and fellfield in more elevated situations. **1761** in *Wesley's Jrnl.* 18 Apr. (1827) III. 49 'Take the galloway, and guide them to the *Fell foot'. **1867** SMYTH *Sailor's Word-bk.*, **Fell-head*, the top of a mountain not distinguished by a peak. **1920** R. CLAPHAM *Foxhunting on Lakeland Fells* iii. 51 A *fell hound should stand under, rather than over, 22½ inches. **1948** C. E. LLOYD in B. Vesey-Fitzgerald *Bk. Dog* II. 452 The Royal Fell Hound Show has done a lot not only to improve the breed but also to promote interest and goodwill. **1890** *Westmoreland Gaz.* 8 Nov. 4/3, 2,640 Acres of *Fell Land. **1774** T. WEST *Antiq. Furness* p. xlv, The *fellanders of Furness. **1874** DASENT *Tales fr. Fjeld* 332 There was no end to the *fell-mouse's greediness. **1769** GRAY *Lett.* Wks. 1836 IV. 158 *Fell-mutton is now in season. **1863** *Spring Lapl.* 55 The great dividing *fell-range between Norway and Sweden. **1886** *Pall Mall G.* 6 Aug. 5/2 The ptarmigan ..soaring over the *fell-ridge with a low chuckle. *Ibid.* 9 Aug. 4/1 The *fell sheep suffered severely. **1862** T. SHORTER in *Weldon's Register* Aug. 24 His early *fell-side neighbours. **1872** JENKINSON *Guide Eng. Lakes* (1879) 322 A point on the fellside is reached where are two paths. **1879** *Cumbrld. Gloss.* Suppl., **Fell thrush*. **1886** *Pall Mall G.* 6 Aug. 5/2 That *fell top appeared to be uninhabited by any more [ptarmigan]. **1957** CLARK & PYATT *Mountaineering in Brit.* i. 24 Jackson.. was a persistent *fell-walker and scrambler. **1956** C. EVANS *On Climbing* i. 13 It is as common to start by being taken up a climb as by *fell-walking.

†**fell**, *sb.*[3] *Obs. rare*⁻¹. [a. L. *fell-*, *fel* gall.] Gall, bitterness; hence, animosity, rancour.

1590 SPENSER *F.Q.* III. xi. 2 Untroubled of vile feare or bitter fell.

fell (fɛl), *sb.*[4] [f. FELL *v.*; in some senses perh. repr. OE. *fiell*: see FALL *sb.*]

1. The action of the vb. FELL in various senses.

a. A knockdown blow.

1877 *Holderness Gloss.* s.v., 'If thoo disn't 'mind ah sal be givin tha a fell inoo.'

b. A cutting down of timber; *concr.* the timber cut down at one season; = FALL *sb.*[1] 14.

165. CROMWELL in Carlyle *Lett. & Sp.* (1871) I. 280 Ordinary fells. **1663** PEPYS *Diary* 11 Dec., When a fell is made, they leave here and there a grown tree. **1727** BRADLEY *Fam. Dict.* s.v. *Coppice*, Leave young Trees enough, you may take down the worst at the next Fell. **1767** A. YOUNG *Farmer's Lett. People* 156 A small fell will amount to..thirty pounds. **1888** RIDER HAGGARD *Col. Quaritch* I. x, The trees were gone..'Cut down this spring fell'.

c. The sewing down (a fold, etc.) level with the cloth (see FELL *v.* 6); *concr.* a 'felled' seam.

1874 KNIGHT *Dict. Mech.*, *Fell*..a form of hem in which one edge is folded over the other and sewed down; or in which one edge is left projecting and is sewed down over the previous seam. **1885** BRIETZCKE & ROOPER *Plain Needlewk.* 29 The fell..means, hemming neatly the turned down edge on to the material itself. **1885** MRS. CROLY *Man. Needlework* 9 Hem, fell, gather and buttonhole.

d. A 'fall' of lambs. *Obs.* exc. *dial.*

1625 B. JONSON *Pan's Anniversary*, So shall the first of all our fells be thine. **1823** in MOOR *Suffolk Words*.

2. 'The line of termination of a web in the process of weaving, formed by the last weft-thread driven up by the lay; the line to which the warp is at any instant wefted' (Ogilvie).

1874 in KNIGHT *Dict. Mech.* s.v. **1882** in CAULFEILD *Dict. Needlewk.* s.v. *Felling*.

3. *Comb*, as ***fell wood***, timber ready to be felled; fellable wood.

1736 NEAL *Hist. Purit.* III. 21 The Londoners were distressed..for coals, which obliged them to have recourse to the..cutting down all fell wood on the estates of Delinquents.

fell (fɛl), *sb.*[5] *Mining*. **a.** Lead ore in its rough state. Cf. BOUSE *sb.*[2] **b.** Lead ore siftings.

1653 MANLOVE *Lead-mines* 266 Fell, Bous and Knock-barke. **1851** [see BOUSE *sb.*[2]]. **1874** KNIGHT *Dict. Mech.*, *Fell*..the finer portions of lead ore which fall through the meshes of the sieve when the ore is sorted by sifting.

Fell (fɛl), *sb.*[6] Name of John *Fell* (1625–86), dean of Christ Church and bishop of Oxford, designating the founts of type and matrices procured by him for the Oxford University Press, the use of which has been revived in recent years.

1900 H. HART *Cent. Oxf. Typogr.* p. ix, All doubts and conjectures as to where most of the Fell types were purchased may..now be regarded as disposed of. **1922** D. B. UPDIKE *Printing Types* II. 199 Caslon and Fell revivals. **1960** G. A. GLAISTER *Gloss. Bk.* 134/2 *Fell types*, the type-face purchased by Doctor John Fell for the Oxford University Press, *c.* 1672. They were cut by Dirck and Bartholomew Voskens of Amsterdam and were a source of inspiration to English type-designers of the time. They are in use today at the Clarendon Press, having been revived in 1876 by C. H. O. Daniel. **1966** H. WILLIAMSON *Methods Bk. Design* (ed. 2) xi. 152 The larger Fell founts..have a bold irregularity which makes most founts now in use look prim.

fell (fɛl), *a.* and *adv.* Forms: 3–5 felle, 3–6 fel(e, 3– fell. [a. OF. *fel* = Pr. *fel*, It. *fello* fierce, cruel, savage:—popular Lat. *fellō*, nom. of *fellōn-em* sb.: see FELON.] **A.** *adj.*

1. Of animals and men, their actions and attributes: Fierce, savage; cruel, ruthless; dreadful, terrible. Also in ***cruel and fell, fierce and fell.*** Now only *poet.* or *rhetorical*.

a **1300** *Cursor M.* 3974 (Cott.) Esau..was fel and wald noght spare. *Ibid.* 20935 (Cott.) [P]Aul..bicome..schep o wolf, and mek of fell. **1340** *Ayenb.* 61 Þe felliste best þet me clepeþ hyane. *c* **1350** *Will. Palerne* 3614 Þo bi-gan þat batayle..Feller saw neuer frek from Adam to þis time. *c* **1400** MAUNDEV. (Roxb.) xi. 44 Herode was a full wikkid man and a fell. *c* **1450** *Gesta Rom.* xxxi. 115 (Add. MS.) By a felle lyon thou shalt lose thi lyf. *c* **1470** HENRY *Wallace* I. 109 Quhen fechtyng was fellast. **1483** CAXTON *G. de la Tour* x. 14 Alle proude hertys that be felle. **1553** BRENDE *Q. Curtius* S vij, He beheld them with a fell countenaunce and rose up to have stricken at them. **1622** DEKKER *Virg. Martir* I. Wks. 1873 IV. 10 My fell hate. **1634** MILTON *Comus* 257 Fell Charybdis murmured soft applause. **1653** H. COGAN tr. *Pinto's Trav.* xxii. 78 Such fell and cruel people, as the Chineses were. **1688** R. HOLME *Armoury* II. 184/2 The..Ban-dog..is fierce, is fell, is stout, is strong. **1748** RICHARDSON *Clarissa* (1811) I. xxxiii. 238, 'I will risque all consequences' said the fell wretch. **1812** BYRON *Ch. Har.* I. xv, And earth from fellest foemen purge. **1813** SCOTT *Rokeby* IV. xxvi, His fell design. **1847** EMERSON *Poems, Dæmonic Love* Wks. (Bohn) I. 465 Even the fell Furies are appeased. **1864** BURTON *Scot Abr.* I. iii. 118 With all the fell ferocity of men falling on their bitterest feudal enemy. **1877** C. GEIKIE *Christ* xxiii. (1879) 255 The soul..drawn down to earth by a fell necessity.

2. Of things, *esp.* of natural agents, weapons, disease, suffering, etc.: Keen, piercing, intensely painful or destructive. Of poison: Deadly. Still *dial.* in colloquial use; in literature only *poet.* and *rhetorical*: Dire, appallingly cruel or destructive.

13.. *E.E. Allit. P.* B. 421 [The Ark] Flote forthe with the flyt of þe felle wyndez. *Ibid.* B. 954 Felle flaunkes of fyr. *a* **1330** *Otuel* 59 Oliuer..bar a spere kene & fel. **1377** LANGL. *P. Pl.* B. XVI. 31 Þe flesshe is a fel wynde. *c* **1440** *York Myst.* xiv. 72 Þe fellest freese þat euer I felyd. *c* **1440** *Bone Flor.* 1973 Hys sekeness was so felle. *c* **1475** *Rauf Coilȝear* 74 The wedderis ar sa fell, that fallis on the feild. **1559** W. CUNNINGHAM *Cosmogr. Glasse* 66 Like as the Zones..the middest of them all men eschew, the burning is so fell. **1567** TURBERV. *Epitaphes, etc.* (1837) 386 Small arrowis, cruel heads, that fel and forked be. **1663** BUTLER *Hud.* I. ii. 803 To guard its Leader from fell bane. **1729** T. COOKE *Tales, Proposals, etc.* 139 With the fellest Venom swells his Veins. **1742** GRAY *To Adversity* v, Despair, and fell Disease, and ghastly Poverty. **1757** SMOLLETT *Reprisal* Epil., Such fell seas of trouble. **1787** BURNS *Winter Night* i, Biting Boreas, fell and doure. **1831** CARLYLE *Misc.* (1857) II. 309 Common ashes are solemnly labelled as fell poison. **1867** G. MACDONALD *Poems* 194 Hunger fell is joined with frost.

b. of an incident, portion of time, etc.

c **1340** *Cursor M.* 22428 (Fairf.) Þe cruel dais & felle be-for domis-dai þai salle be sene. *c* **1425** WYNTOUN *Cron.* VII. ii. 53 For drede of fellare chawns Sum of þaim þan fled in Frawns. *c* **1470** HENRY *Wallace* IV. 110 Bot fell tithings was brocht Persie beforn. **1557** *Tottell's Misc.*, *Golden Meane* (1870) 256 Of lofty ruing towers the fals the feller be. **1799** SHERIDAN *Pizarro* III. ii, The last and fellest peril of thy life. **1821** JOANNA BAILLIE *Met. Leg.*, *Columb.* xlv, The injured Hero's fellest hour.

c. *Sc.* With reference to taste: Keen, pungent.

1786 BURNS *Cotter's Saturd. Nt.* 96 The dame brings forth ..her weel-hain'd kebbuck, fell.

†3. Hot, angry, enraged, virulent. *Obs.*

1382 WYCLIF *Ecclus.* xxiii. 22 A fel soule as fyr brennende shal not be quenchid. *a* **1450** *Knt. de la Tour* (1868) 86 Amon was right fel and wrothe. **1558** BP. WATSON *Sev. Sacram.* xxix. 186 The manne ought not to be bitter and fell agaynste his wyfe in vsing brawlinges. **1590** SHAKS. *Mids. N.* II. i. 20 Oberon is passing fell and wrath.

4. Full of spirit, sturdy, doughty. *Obs.* exc. *dial.*

c **1330** R. BRUNNE *Chron.* (1810) 125 Þe burgeis were fulle felle. *c* **1400** *Destr. Troy* 129 A faire man of feturs, & fellist in armys. **1475** *Bk. Noblesse* 64 To make the Romains more egir and fellir in that bataile. **1522** *World & Child* in Hazl. *Dodsley* I. 252 So fell a fighter in a field was there never y-found. **1593** DRAYTON *Eclogues* IV. 122 Fell was he and eager bent In Battaile. **1815** SCOTT *Guy M.* xxii, A fell chield at the vermin. **1876** *Whitby Gloss.* s.v., 'I wasn't i' fell order', not in able condition.

b. Const. *for, on*, †*to*: In earnest, eager; bent or intent *upon*. *Obs.* exc. *dial.*

1666 PEPYS *Diary* 15 Jan., I am so fell to my business that I..will not go. **1876** *Whitby Gloss.* s.v., 'Thoo's mair fell for thy dinner than rife for a race.' **1888** RIDER HAGGARD *Col. Quaritch* xxviii, I am rarely fell on seeing them and having a holiday look round Lunnon.

†5. Shrewd; clever, cunning. *Obs.*

c **1275** LAY. 5302 Mid hire felle [*c* **1205** præt] wrenches. **1382** WYCLIF *Prov.* xii. 16 Who forsothe the dissymulith wrongus is fel. *c* **1400** *Beryn* 1853 Evandir was his name, that sottill was and fell. *c* **1475** *Partenay* 1237 Till thay wer growyn ryght large, wyse, and fell. **1561** RANDOLPH *Let.* 7 Dec. in Keith *Hist. Ch. & St. Scot.* (1734) I. 205 Liddington hath a crafty Head and fell Tongue. **1725** RAMSAY *Gent. Sheph.* III. ii, The fellest fortune-teller e'er was seen.

6. In weakened sense: Exceedingly great, huge, mighty. *Obs.* exc. *Sc.*

1515 *Scot. Field* 44 There they fell, at the first shotte Many a fell fothir. **1586** FERNE *Blaz. Gentrie* 22 This Harrat hath spent a fell time in bussing like a preacher. **1889** J. M. BARRIE *Window in Thrums* xiv. 131 'It had a fell lot o' brass aboot it.'

†7. quasi-*sb.* The *adj.* used *absol. Obs.*

a **1300** *Cursor M.* 1124 (Cott.), 'Caym ware es þi broiþer abell?' 'I wat neuer,' said he, þat fell. *c* **1340** *Gaw. & Gr. Knt.* 1565 Þer þe felle bydez.

8. *Comb.*, as ***fell-like*** adj. (*dial.*)

1854 *Phemie Millar* VII. 179 She did think it was a fell like thing that any one..should be thinking of nonsense.

B. *adv.*

1. In a 'fell' manner; †cruelly, fiercely (*obs.*); eagerly, vigorously, excessively (*obs.* exc. *dial.*).

a **1300** *Cursor M.* 23997 (Cott.) Quen i sagh þaa juus snell, Rise again mi sun sua fell, ful wanles wex i þan. *c* **1320** *Sir Tristr.* 97 He..Was wounded in þat fiȝt Ful felle. **13..** *E.E. Allit. P.* B. 1040 þat fel fretes þe flesch & festred bones. *c* **1470** HARDING *Chron.* CXCVII. v, He chastised theim no feller as was sene. **1597** MONTGOMERIE *Misc. Poems* xxii. 10 'Fell peart,' quod Cupid, 'thou appeirs.' **1832–53** *Whistle-binkie* (Sc. Songs) Ser. III. 114 Our Sawnies and Maggies..At e'en blythe will dance, yet work fell the neist morn. **1863** MORTON *Cycl. Agric.* (E.D.S.), A plough goes too fell when going deeper than is wished. **1876** *Whitby Gloss.*, He eats his meat varry fell. **1889** J. M. BARRIE *Window in Thrums* xvi. 148 She was 'complaining fell (considerably) about her back the day'.

2. *Comb.* with ppl. adjs.

1587 *Misfort. Arthur* I. ii. in Hazl. *Dodsley* IV. 268 Cast off this..fell-disposed mind. **1593** SHAKS. *2 Hen. VI*, v. i. 146 These fell-lurking Curres. **1795** *Fate Sedley* II. 62 Goaded by the fell pointed spear. **1876** *Whitby Gloss.* s.v., *Fell-bred*, of a vicious kind.

fell (fɛl), *v.* *Pa. t.* and *pa. pple.* felled (fɛld). Forms: 1 fellan, fyllan, *Northumb.* fællan, 2–5 felle(n, (5 fellyn), 4–6 fel, 3– fell. [OE. *fellan, fiellan, fyllan* = OFris. *falla, fella*, OS. *fellian* (Du. *vellen*), OHG. *fellen* (MHG. *vellen*, mod.Ger. *fällen*), ON. *fella* (Da. *fælde*, Sw. *fälla*):—OTeut. **falljan*, causative of **fall-an* FALL *v.*]

trans. To cause to fall.

1. To cut, knock, or strike down (a man or animal). †Also, to bring down (with a missile). Often with *down, to the ground*, etc.

c **1000** *Ags. Ps.* (Thorpe) cxxxviii. 16 [cxxxix. 19] Ʒif þu syððan wylt þa firenfullan fyllan mid deaðe. *a* **1325** *Prose Psalter* cv[i] 26 He feld hem doun in wildernesse. *a* **1330** *Otuel* 60 Anwe of Nubie..felde Oliuer to grounde. **1375** BARBOUR *Bruce* XII. 524 Mon worthy men..wes fellit in that ficht. *a* **1400** *Cov. Myst.* (1841) 65 Opyn in the fielde the fend he shal felle. *c* **1489** CAXTON *Sonnes of Aymon* xii. 288, I felde hym doun ded afore me to therthe. *c* **1500** *Lancelot* 3299 Sum in the feld fellit is in swon. **1600** HOLLAND *Livy* XXIII. 490 Most of them were felled and strucken stark dead. **1671** NARBOROUGH *Jrnl.* in *Acc. Sev. Late Voy.* I. (1694) 168 A great White Bear..which he shot at, and fell'd her down. **1698** FRYER *Acc. E. India & P.* 41 On the top of a withered Stump sate perching a Chamelion..I caused a Black..to fell him with an Earthen Pellet. **1702** POPE *Wife of Bath* 416, I, with one buffet fell'd him on the floor. **1843** LEVER *J. Hinton* xxix, Straight between the eyes the weapon struck me, and felled me to the ground. **1852** R. F. BURTON *Falconry in Vall. of Indus* v. 60 If two [hawks] are flown they are certain to fell the game. **1855** SMEDLEY *H. Coverdale* li, With one blow of this [fist] I believe I could fell an ox.

absol. *c* **1400** *Melayne* 266 Thay felde faste of oure chevalrye. **1535** STEWART *Cron. Scot.* (1858) I. 332 Bot still thai stude durst nother fell nor fle. **1542–5** BRINKLOW *Lament.* (1874) 86 When he striketh, he felleth to the grounde.

†**b.** ***to fell along***: to lay (a man) at full length.

1665 DRYDEN *Indian Emp.* II. ii, I fell'd along a Man of bearded Face. **1668** —— *Evening's Love* v. i, A huge giant seized my torch, and felled me along.

†**c.** To kill. *Obs.*

a **1300** *Cursor M.* 22903 (Cott.) An hungre leon..þis wolf ..feld ant ete him al. **1362** LANGL. *P. Pl.* A. XII. 65, I shal felle þat freke in a fewe dayes! *a* **1400–50** *Alexander* 3011 (Dublin MS.) Full fele fleys may nott felle bott a few wasspez. **1681** COLVIL *Whigs Supplic.* (1751) 58 They felled all our hens and cocks.

d. Of a disease, hunger, etc.: To lay low, lay prostrate; †to kill. *Obs.* exc. *dial.*

c **900** *Bæda's Hist.* IV. xvii. [xiii.] (1891) 302 Heo mid arleasre cwale fylde wæron. *c* **1200** *Trin. Coll. Hom.* 177 Þenne hit þat tuderinde wiðleoð and cumeð coðe oðer qualm and michel þerof felleð. *a* **1605** MONTGOMERIE *Flyting w. Polwart* 305 The fersie, the falling-euill, that fels many freikes. **1665** BOYLE *Occas. Refl.* II. iii. (1845) 106 Feavers burn us..Epilepsies fell us, Colicks tear us. **1855** ROBINSON *Whitby Gloss.*, 'Felled with his ailment', prostrate with sickness.

†**e.** *fig.* To cast down, defeat, ruin, humiliate. *Obs.* Also *dial.* of anything startling: To 'knock (one) down'.

c **1000** *Ags. Ps.* (Thorpe) lxxiii. 22 [lxxiv. 23] Fyll þa ofer hydigan. *a* **1340** HAMPOLE *Psalter* cxxii. 1 Ill luf fellis us doun in til the erth. **1535** COVERDALE *Isa.* x. 33 He shal..fel the hie mynded. **1602** MARSTON *Antonio's Rev.* IV. i, Starke feld with brusing stroke of chance. **1855** MRS. GASKELL *North & S.* xxxvi, 'I'm welly felled wi' seeing him.'

2. To cut down (a tree). Also, † ***to fell down***.

a **1000** *Riddles* ii. 9 (Gr.) Ic..beamas fylle. *a* **1300** *Cursor M.* 12395 (Cott.) He him suld sli timber fell. ? *a* **1400** *Morte Arth.* 1247 He fellez forestez fele. **1520** *Caxton's Chron. Eng.* II. 11 b/2 Brute caused to fell downe woddes. **1545** BRINKLOW *Compl.* xxiii. (1874) 58 Ye must fell down to the ground those rotten postys, the bisshops. **1577** B. GOOGE *Heresbach's Husb.* II. (1586) 105 b, The chesnut may bee felde every seventh yeere. **1667** MILTON *P.L.* VI. 575 Oak or Firr With branches lopt in Wood or Mountain fell'd. **1725** DE FOE *Voy. round World* (1840) 340 They found three trees ..and they..felled and shaped them. **1869** LECKY *Europ. Mor.* II. i. 195 Gigantic forests were felled.

absol. **1847** MARRYAT *Childr. N. Forest* xiii, They went out to fell at a cluster of small spruce fir about a mile off.

†3. To break down, overthrow, knock down (a building, construction, or erection of any kind).

a **1000** *Crist* 486 (Gr.) Hergas fyllað. *Ibid.* 709 (Gr.) þa synsceaðan..godes tempel..fyldon. *a* **1000** *Cross* 73 (Gr.) þa us man fyllan ongan ealle to eorðan. *c* **1290** *S. Eng. Leg.* I. 366/43 Þe prince for wrathþe of his [seint Iacob's] prechingue þe laddre a-doun gan felle. **1297** R. GLOUC. (1724) 526 A wynd..So grete yt com, þat yt yelde mony hous adoun. *c* **1430** *Syr Gener.* (Roxb.) 4002 Amalek he smote on the crovn That twoo quarters he feld a-doun Of his helme. **1467** *Mann. & Househ. Exp.* 172 The walls of the salte howses..shal be felled or it be long. **1607** TOPSELL *Serpents* (1658) 785 The..web..if one throw or cast dust upon it..will rather be distended and stretched, then either undone, broken, or felled down.

†**b.** To knock (fruit or leaves) off a tree. *Obs.*

1393 LANGL. *P. Pl.* C. XIX. 128 That elde felde efte þat frut. *c* **1400** *Rom. Rose* 911 Nyghtyngales..The leeves felden as they flyen.

†4. To cause to stumble; to trip up; in quot. *fig. Obs.*

c **975** *Rushw. Gosp.* Matt. v. 29 Gif þanne þin eȝe þæt swiþre fælle þec ahloca hit & awerp from ðe. **1377** LANGL. *P. Pl.* B. III. 126 Ʒowre fadre she felled þorw fals biheste.

†5. Without the notion of suddenness or violence: To bring or let down, lower, abate. *Obs.*

a **1300** *Cursor M.* 1480 (Cott.) Þan sal þai fel þat fals strijf. *Ibid.* 3376 (Cott.) Þe mikel luue o rebecca þan feld þe soru o dame sarra. **1303** R. BRUNNE *Handl. Synne* 890 Y shal ȝow telle What shal best þys tempest felle. *c* **1330** —— *Chron.* (1810) 48 Þe burgeis of London..said þei suld fond to felle Knoutes pride. *c* **1400** *Test. Love* I. (1560) 275 b/1 My blisse and my mirth arn felde. *c* **1430** *Syr Gener.* (Roxb.) 2712 His hote loue I shal fell. **14..** *How Goode Wif Taught hir Daughter* 25 in Hazl. *E.P.P.* 49 Ne goe thou noght to tauerne thi wurchipe to felle. *c* **1460** *Towneley Myst.* (Surtees) 177 To felle alle fowlle defame. *c* **1620** A. HUME *Brit. Tongue* (1865) 22 The Circumflex accent both liftes and felles the syllab that it possesseth.

6. To stitch down (the wider of the two edges left projecting by a seam) so that it lies flat over the other edge and leaves a smooth surface on the under-side of the seam. Also, ***to fell a seam***.

[Etymological identity with the other senses is not certain; but the general sense 'cause to fall' appears applicable.]

1758 FRANKLIN *Let.* Wks. 1887 III. 7 It is to be sewed together, the edges being first felled down. **1842** BARHAM *Ingol. Leg.*, *Aunt Fanny*, Each..began working..'Felling the Seams', and 'whipping the Frill'. **1887** *Spons' Househ. Managem.*, *Workroom* 891 Fell down the turnings, or only overcast them. **1892** *Weldon's Ladies' Jrnl.* Oct. 73 This opening is turned in once on the wrong side, over which is felled a piece of binding.

absol. **1862** M. T. MORRALL *Needle-making* 41 I'm teaching little Mary to gather and to fell.

Hence **'felling** *ppl. a.*

1597 DANIEL *Civ. Wars* III. lxxv, Now wardes a felling blow, now strikes again.

fella, fellah, representing an affected or vulgar pronunciation of FELLOW *sb.* 9: see FELLER[2].

1864 J. S. LE FANU *Uncle Silas* II. xiii. 203, I did see two horses yoked to a shay, and a fellah a pullin' a box up o' top. **1909** A. HUXLEY *Let.* 2 Apr. (1969) 30 There is to be an huge auction of all the appurtenances of the leaving fellahs. **1912** A. CONAN DOYLE *Lost World* vi. 84 Young fellah my lad. **1920** 'SAPPER' *Bull-Dog Drummond* i. 38 'An engaging fellah,' said Hugh. 'What particular form of crime does he favour?' **1933** *Times Lit. Suppl.* 9 Nov. 777/2 We feel that, stout fellah though Furness..is, he would look rather nice at the end of a rope. **1934** W. HOLTBY *Truth is not Sober* 76 Among the things a Fella does, correct grammar is not necessarily included. **1949** E. HYAMS *Not in our Stars* 73 Well, young fella-me-lad. **1952** E. WILSON *Equations of*

Love 177 Seemed a nice fella. **1968** R. CLAPPERTON *No News on Monday* viii. 99 The fellah took that opportunity.

fellable (ˈfɛləb(ə)l), *a.* [f. FELL *v.* + -ABLE.] That may be felled; fit or ready to be cut down.

1581 *Act 23 Eliz.* c. 5 Preamb., Fellable Woods serving for Fewel. **1711** *Lond. Gaz.* No. 4837/3 A good Quantity of Timber, great part of it fellable. **1726** *Dict. Rust.* s.v. *Tiller*, A little Tree left to grow till it be fellable. **1830** MRS. BRAY *Fitz of F.* xii. (1884) 102 These woods cannot possibly be considered under the clause of *cædua sylva*, fellable wood.

fellage (ˈfɛlɪdʒ). *rare.* [f. as prec. + -AGE.] The action or process of felling or cutting down.

1839 BAILEY *Festus* (1848) 4/2 Why score the young green bole For fellage?

‖**fellagha** (fɛˈlɑːgə). [ad. colloq. Arab. *fəllāga*, pl. of *fəllāg* bandit, robber.] A guerrilla soldier of a nationalist movement in Algeria and Tunisia when the two countries were under French control. Also as *pl.* and *attrib.*

1954 *Time* 5 July 24 The *fellagha*, rising up in Tunisia's rich but savage hinterland, so far number about 400 fighters. **1955** *Ann. Reg. 1954* 202 The French and Tunisian Governments appealed to the *fellaghas*, promising an amnesty. **1955** *Times* 19 May 14/4 The *fellagha* activities last autumn [in Tunisia]. **1958** *Listener* 18 Sept. 433/2 When the *fellagha* say independence, they mean the end of bad times [in Algeria].

fellah (ˈfɛlə). *Pl.* fellaheen, fellahs; fellahin (now the usual form). [a. Arab. *fellāḥ* husbandman, f. *falaḥa* to till the soil.] A peasant in Arabic-speaking countries; in Eng. applied *esp.* to those of Egypt. Also *fig.*

1743 POCOCKE *Descr. East* I. 177 The Mahometan inhabitants of Egypt are either original natives, in the villages call'd Filaws, or they are of the Arab race. **1802** *Ann. Reg.* 742 The Fellahs.. are the farmers and husbandmen of the country. **1856** STANLEY *Sinai & Pal.* i. (1858) 22 *note*, 'Fellah' and 'Fellahîn' the inhabitants of villages and cultivated ground. **1877** A. B. EDWARDS *Up Nile* xxii. 714 Farther on, the brown Fellaheen.. are cutting clover. **1912** [see BEDU]. **1932** *Times Lit. Suppl.* 11 Feb. 86/3 Cities and civilization dying of inanition after eating up the best of the rural population and leaving only the fellahin type. **1947** S. BELLOW *Victim* i. 3 The people.., barbaric fellahin among the stupendous monuments of their mystery.

fellatio (fɛˈleɪʃɪəʊ, fɛˈlɑːtɪəʊ). Also **fellation.** [mod.L., f. *fellātus*, pa. pple. of L. *fellāre* to suck.] A sexual act in which the partner's penis is sucked or licked. Hence **feˈllator**, *fem.* **feˈllatrix**, the partner who performs such an act. Also **feˈllatory** *a.*, of or relating to fellatio; (as a back-formation) **fellate** (fɛˈleɪt) *v.*, to practise fellatio on.

1887 L. C. SMITHERS tr. *Forberg's Man. Classical Erotology* iii. 72 The verge, introduced into the mouth, wants to be tickled either by the lips or the tongue, and sucked; the party who does this service to the penis is a fellator or sucker. *Ibid.* 73 This fellatrix seems to have borne the name of Labda. *Ibid.* 97 With regard to the subject of fellation, we must not pass over in silence the raven, whom our constant authority (Martial XIV. 74) calls a fellator. **1888** tr. *Priapeia* 142 The patient (fellator or sucker) provokes the orgasm by the manipulation of his (or her) lips and tongue on the agent's member. *Ibid.* 159 Martial directs many epigrams against fellators. *Ibid.* (index) 232 Fellation. **1897** H. ELLIS *Stud. Psychol. Sex* I. v. 118 Taking the twenty-four inverted men.. I find that three.. have never had any physical relationship with their own sex... In two or three cases *fellatio* is the form preferred. **1901** A. ALLINSON tr. *J. Rosenbaum's Plague of Lust* II. xxii. 29 *Fellator* and *fellatrix* .. were liable to suffer from ulcers of the throat. *Ibid.* 31 Yet another consequence of fellation was pain in the mouth. **1916** A. A. BRILL tr. *Freud's Leonardo da Vinci* ii. 39 The situation contained in the phantasy.. corresponds to the idea of fellatio, a sexual act in which the member is placed into the mouth of the other person. **1955** *Psychiatr. Q.* XXIX. 222 She had cunnilinctual and fellatory relationships with him. **1964** S. BELLOW *Herzog* 229 Someone must have told him that fellatio was the path to truth and honour. **1968** *New Amer. Rev.* II. 159 She makes various attempts through the film to rouse him (including the clearest suggestion of fellation that I have seen in an American picture.) **1968** J. UPDIKE *Couples* (1969) v. 482 Lazily she fellated him while he combed her lovely hair. **1969** G. LEGMAN *Rationale of Dirty Joke* viii. 552 An old roué marries an innocent virgin, but being impotent he teaches her to fellate him. **1969** *New Society* 1 May 664/1 The man had just submitted to fellatio on the part of a second man.

felle, obs. form of FALL *sb.*², trap.

felled (fɛld), *ppl. a.*¹ [f. FELL *v.* + -ED¹.]

1. Of timber: That has been cut down.

1820 D. WORDSWORTH *Tour Continent* 11 Aug. in *Jrnls.* (1941) II. 126 The first signs of occupancy and labour we had noticed in our descent were *felled* trees. **1844** H. H. WILSON *Brit. India* III. 123 A thick abatis of felled trees and brushwood. **1865** LIVINGSTONE *Zambesi* 546 The felled wood was gathered into heaps. **1870** MORRIS *Earthly Par.* III. IV. 369 On a felled oaken tree We sat.

2. Of a seam: Sewn down so as to be level with the material.

1885 BRIETZCKE & ROOPER *Plain Needlewk.* 29 A felled seam, when finished, must lie perfectly flat on both sides.

felled (fɛld), *ppl. a.*² [f. FELL *sb.*¹ + -ED².] Having a fell. Chiefly in comb., as ***full-felled***, ***white-felled*** adjs.

1618 CHAPMAN *Hesiod* I. 364 Full-fell'd sheep are shorn with festivals. **1867** MORRIS *Jason* XVI. 384 Lands where dwells the sluggish white-felled bear. **1952** DYLAN THOMAS *Coll. Poems* p. ix, O kingdom of neighbours, finned Felled and quilled, flash to my patch.

†**felleous** (ˈfɛlɪəs), *a. Obs.* [f. L. *felle-us* (f. *fel* gall) + -OUS.] = BILIARY.

1684 tr. *Bonet's Merc. Compit.* VI. 232 When the felleous humour.. is voided upwards. *Ibid.* XIX. 689 The felleous Ferment. **1884** in *Syd. Soc. Lex.*

feller¹ (ˈfɛlə(r)). [f. FELL *v.* + -ER¹.] One who or that which fells.

1. One who knocks down (a person). *lit.* and *fig.*

a **1400** *Covt. Myst.* (Shaks. Soc.) 159 Heyl! ffellere of the fende! *c* **1611** CHAPMAN *Iliad* XV. 475 Whose fall when Meges view'd, He let fly at his feller's life.

2. One who cuts down (timber); a wood-cutter.

1466 *Mann. & Househ. Exp.* 346 Item, to ij. fellers of tymbre.. viij. d. **1553** *Act 7 Edw. VI*, c. 7 §1 The Penalty.. dependeth.. not upon the.. Feller of the same [Fuel]. **1650** T. B. *Worcester's Apoph.* 80 The hatchet of one of the fellers chanc'd to strike out a chip. **17..** ELIZ. CARTER *Lett.* (1808) 410 The Hamadryads.. will scream in the ears of the feller till he drops his axe. **1790** BURNS *Ep. to R. Graham* xiii, The rooted oaks would fly, Before th' approaching fellers. **1859** R. F. BURTON *Centr. Afr.* in *Jrnl. Geog. Soc.* XXIX, Trees .. against which no feller has come up. [After *Isa.* xiv. 8.]

3. An attachment to a sewing machine for 'felling' (see FELL *v* 6).

1874 in KNIGHT *Dict. Mech.*

4. One who sews in various trades.

1894 *N. Brit. Daily Mail* 5 Sept. 4 The wages of the fellers, whether on day work or on piece work, ranged from 1s 6d to 2s 6d. **1921** *Dict. Occup. Terms* (1927) §404 *Finisher*, tailor's finisher; feller; sews by hand, sleeve linings, vest arm holes. *Ibid.* §411 *Feller*, sews seams of gloves with a particular kind of felling stitch on treadle machine.

feller² (ˈfɛlə(r)). Vulgar or affected (cf. FELLA) form of FELLOW *sb.* 9. Also in jocular phr. ***young feller-me-*** (or ***my-***)***lad***, orig. used vocatively with an implication of disapproval or reproof; hence as compound sb. designating a young man of a frivolous or irresponsible character; also (occas.) of women.

1825 J. NEAL *Bro. Jonathan* I. i. 12 A lawyer.. put Peters down for 'a confounded smart feller'. **1849** THACKERAY *Pendennis* I. xxvi. 252 Mr. Pynsent, you're a good feller. **1880** *Punch* 20 Nov. 234 Why, there was an Actor, by Jingo! and a scientific chap, and an artist feller. **1897** KIPLING *Capt. Cour.* 17 You've nigh slep' the clock around, young feller. **1909** WODEHOUSE *Swoop!* vi. 86 Not so much of your eight hundred and seventy-five, young feller me lad. **1913** L. A. HARKER *Ffolliots of Redmarley* xxiv. 321, I beheld Miss Bax seemingly in difficulties with two young feller-me-lads, who evidently had no intention of going on. **1930** D. H. LAWRENCE *Nettles* 23 She's a marv'lous, delicious, high-spirited feller. **1939** J. CARY *Mr. Johnson* 154 All right, you remember that, young fellermelad. **1946** K. TENNANT *Lost Haven* (1947) i. 17 A feller that's just risen from his bed of 'flu. **1971** *Petticoat* 17 July 2/2 If we did walk into a pub alone and not one feller blinked an eyelid we'd probably think there was something wrong with us.

fell-fare, var. of FIELDFARE.

†ˈ**fellhead.** *Obs. rare.* In 4 felhede. [f. FELL *a.* + -HEAD.] = FELLNESS.

1340 *Ayenb.* 29 Þe felhede of herte huerof comeþ vale boȝ s. *Ibid.* 159 Loue: a-ye enuye. Mildnesse: a-ye fel-hede.

fellic (ˈfɛlɪk), *a.* [f. L. *fell-*, *fel* gall + -IC.] Only in *fellic acid* (see quot. 1889).

1884 *Syd. Soc. Lex.*, *Fellic acid*, same as *Fellinic acid*. **1889** MUIR & MORLEY *Watts' Dict. Chem.* II. 537 *Fellic acid* $C_{23}H_{40}O_4$ [120°], an acid said to accompany cholic acid in human bile.

†ˈ**fellicate**, *v. Obs.*⁻⁰ [f. late L. *fellicāt-*, ppl. stem of *fellicāre*, f. L. *fellāre* to suck.] *trans.* To suck.

1623-6 in COCKERAM.

felliducous (ˈfɛlɪˌdjuːkəs), *a.* [f. late L. *fellidūc-us* (f. L. *fel* gall, bile + *dūc-ĕre* to lead) + -OUS.] (See quot.)

1884 *Syd. Soc. Lex.*, *Felliducous*, term applied to remedies inducing a flow of bile; cholagogue.

fellifluous (fɛˈlɪfluːəs), *a.* [f. late L. *felliflu-us* (f. *fel* gall + *fluĕre* to flow) + -OUS.] Flowing with gall.

1656-81 in BLOUNT *Glossogr.* **1721-1800** in BAILEY. **1884** in *Syd. Soc. Lex.*

felling (ˈfɛlɪŋ), *vbl. sb.* [f. FELL *v.* + -ING¹.]

1. a. The action or an act of cutting down (timber); *concr.* the quantity cut down. In quot. 1654 gerundially with omission of *in.*

1543 *Act 35 Hen. VIII*, c. 17 §1 Such Standils.. as have been left there standing at any the felling of the same Coppice Woods. **1624** CAPT. SMITH *Virginia* v. 194 The felling of marked trees appointed for bounds. **1651** R. CHILD in *Hartlib's Legacy* (1655) 47 They every felling cut down the standers, which they left the felling before. **1654** EVELYN *Mem.* (1857) I. 302 Saw my Lord Craven's house.. now in ruins, his goodly woods felling by the rebels. **1663** GERBIER *Counsel* 109 No other cost but felling and lading. **1884** SIR E. FRY in *Law Reports* 28 Ch. Div. 231 They have treated the.. fellings of larch trees as income to be paid to the tenant.

†**b.** ?*concr.* A clearing. *Obs.* (If this be the sense, the word in quot. is due to misinterpretation of *fell* = mountain, in an earlier text.)

a **1300** *Cursor M.* 2832 (Gött.) Make ȝe in þe plain na duelling, Til ȝe bi comen to ȝone felling.

†**2.** *Sc.* 'Lowering, down-bringing; abatement, deduction' (Jam. *Supp.*). *Obs.* Cf. FELL *v.* 5.

c **1300** *Stat. Gilde* xxviii. in *Anc. Laws Burghs Scot.* 77 Pacabit mercatori a quo predicta emerat secundum forum prius factum sine felling uel herlebreking.

3. (See FELL *v.* 6.)

1841 LADY WILTON *Art of Needlework* (ed. 3) xx. 317 There are.. hemming—felling—and basting. **1875** *Plain Needlework* 11 Here are taught hemming.. felling, and fixing.

4. *attrib.* and *Comb.*, as ***felling-axe***, ***-machine***, ***-saw***, ***-time***; **felling-bird**, the Wryneck (*Yunx torquilla*).

1486 *Nottingham Rec.* III. 244 For a grete fellyng axe. **1549** *Privy Council Acts* ii. (1890) 350 Felling axes, *l*: hatchetes, *l*. *Ibid.* 349 Felling axes, iiij dousen. **1669** WORLIDGE *Syst. Agric.* (1681) 109 The best way is at felling-time to new cut them. **1691** *Lond. Gaz.* No. 2675/3, 20 Men with Felling Axes. **1874** KNIGHT *Dict. Mech.*, *Felling-saw*. **1877** *N. W. Linc. Gloss.*, *Felling axe*, an axe with a long and narrow head used for felling trees. **1883** *Hampsh. Gloss.*, *Felling-bird*.. its note being first heard about the time.. when oaks are felled.

fellinic (fɛˈlɪnɪk), *a. Chem.* [f. L. *fell-*, *fel* gall + -IN + -IC.] *fellinic acid*: **a.** see quot. 1884; **b.** see quot. 1887.

1845 G. E. DAY tr. *Simon's Anim. Chem.* I. 48 Cholinic and fellinic acids are associated in the alcoholic solution. **1884** *Syd. Soc. Lex.*, *Fellinic acid* $C_{50}H_{36}O_{64}HO$, an acid obtained, according to Berzelius, by treating bile with hydrochloric acid. **1887** *Lancet* 31 Dec. 1319/2 A new acid .. has been discovered by Schotten in human bile, and named fellinic acid.

†ˈ**fellish**, *a.*¹ *Obs. rare.* [f. FELL *sb.*² + -ISH.] Pertaining to or resembling a fell.

1570 LEVINS *Manip.* 145 Fellish, *montanus.*

†ˈ**fellish**, *a.*² *Obs. rare.* [f. FELL *a.* + -ISH.] Somewhat fell or fierce.

c **1650** BRATHWAIT *Barnabees Jrnl.* (1818) 121 Never was wild boare more fellish.

ˈ**fellˌmonger.** [f. FELL *sb.*¹ + MONGER.] A dealer in skins or hides of animals, *esp.* sheep-skins. In modern use restricted to an operative who works skins.

1530 PALSGR. 219/2 Felmongar, *megissier.* **1681** OTWAY *Soldier's Fort.* IV. i, A frouzy Fellmonger. **1745** *De Foe's Eng. Tradesman* II. xlvii. 188 The wool being taken from the skin by the fellmonger. **1834** *Brit. Husb.* I. 423 Fell-mongers' poake.. is the waste arising from the preparation of skins. **1845** DODD *Brit. Manuf.* V. 195 There are in Bermondsey several manufacturers called fellmongers, whose business it is to bring sheep-skins into a certain state of preparation before the leather-dresser commences his operations thereon. **1869** BLACKMORE *Lorna D.* ii, Shopkeepers' sons, young grocers, fellmongers, &c. **1921** *Dict. Occup. Terms* (1927) §338 *Fellmonger*, general term for any person employed in fellmongery trade, e.g. washing sheep skins, painting pelt side of skins with chemicals to facilitate subsequent pulling [etc.]. **1960** *New Scientist* 9 June 1496/1 (Advt.), A machine for fellmongers who prepare woolled sheepskins.

Hence ˈ**fellmongered** *a.*, ˈ**fellmongering** *vbl. sb.*; ˈ**fellˌmongery**, the craft or calling of a fellmonger; in quot. *attrib.*

1759 B. MARTIN *Nat. Hist. Eng.* I. 393 Likewise a good Trade in the Felmongery Business. **1895** *Australas. Pastoralists' Rev.* 15 Aug. 284 The very large quantity of fellmongered wool sold in Sydney. **1897** *Daily News* 7 Oct. 2/2 Fellmongering and leather dressing premises.

fellness (ˈfɛlnɪs). [f. FELL *a.* + -NESS.] The quality of being 'fell': see senses of the adj.

1. Fierceness, harshness, cruelty; †sternness, severity. Now (exc. in north. dial.) only *poet.* and *rhetorical*: Appalling cruelty, malignity, or destructive effect.

c **1380** WYCLIF *Serm.* Sel. Wks. I. 55 Oþir servantis.. tellen to God þis felnes and preien him of venjance. **1387** TREVISA *Higden* (Rolls) VII. 151 [Gregory VI] a man of religioun and felnes [Lat. *severitatis*]. *a* **1400** *Relig. Pieces fr. Thornton MS.* (1867) 27 Þis worde Gaste sowunes sumwhate into fellenes. *c* **1440** *Gesta Rom.* xci. 417 (Add. MS.) In a grete felnesse and angre he sente messyngers for the foxe. **1587** *Misfortunes Arthur* IV. ii. in Hazl. *Dodsley* IV. 323 No fear nor fellness fail'd on either side. **1678** R. L'ESTRANGE *Seneca's Mor.* (1702) 297 There is a Ghastly kind of Felness in the Aspect of a Mad Dog. **1719** YOUNG *Busiris* I. i, Such was the fellness of his boiling rage. **1814** CARY *Dante* (Chandos ed.) 125 Look how that beast to felness hath relaps'd From having lost correction of the spur. **1865** CARLYLE *Fredk. Gt.* VI. xv. xiii. 98 A fellness of humour against Friedrich.

b. Keenness, fierceness (of wind, etc.); angry painfulness. *Obs.* exc. *dial.*

c **1374** CHAUCER *Boeth.* I. vi. 25 Þe felnesse of the wynde. **1642** ROGERS *Naaman* 466 If that [the felon upon the hand] were out the felnesse would cease.

†**2.** Shrewdness, wisdom. *Obs.*

1382 WYCLIF *Job* v. 13 That caccheth wise men in ther felnesse. **1382** —— *Prov.* i. 4 That felnesse be ȝeue to litle childer.

felloe ('fɛləʊ), **felly** ('fɛlɪ). Forms: α. 1 **felᵹ**, (*pl.* **felᵹa**), 4 **feleyȝhe**, 5 **felghe**. β. 5 **felwe**, **felow(e**, 6 **fallow**, 6–7 **fellow**, 6 **felloe**. γ. 3–5 **fely**, **vely**, (*pl.* 3 **velien**, **-on**), 6–8 *Sc.* **filly**, 7 **fally**, 7–8 **fellee**, 8 **felley**, 6– **felly**. δ. 7 **fellff**, **felfe**, 9 *dial.* **felf**, **felve**, **felk**, 7–8 **fell**. [OE. *felᵹ* str. fem. corresponds to MDu., Du. *velge*, OHG. *felga* (mod.Ger. *felge*). Possibly cognate with OTeut. **felhan* (see FELE *v.*), in the sense 'to fit together' (recorded for the OHG. *felahan*).

The diversity of forms is due to the varying pronunciation of the OE. ᵹ, depending on the nature of the sound which followed it in the inflected cases. In the plural *felᵹa* it was the voiced guttural spirant, which in late ME. developed into *w*, producing the β forms. In the dative *felᵹe* it was the voiced palatal spirant, and this very early became vocalized as (ɪ), whence the γ forms. The δ forms are due to the normal unvoicing of the ᵹ where it was final, viz. in the nom. and accus. sing.; the resulting sound (x) eventually developed into (f), as in *laugh*, *enough*, etc.; in some dialects, however, it became (k), and in others was dropped. (With the forms *felf*, *felk*, cf. the Derbyshire place-name now variously spelt *Belph*, *Belk*, but in 13th c. *Belgh*.) In England the forms *felloe*, *felly* seem to be equally in good use; in the U.S. *felly* appears to be preferred.]

The exterior rim, or a part of the rim, of a wheel, supported by the spokes. In *pl.* the curved pieces of wood which, joined together, form the circular rim of a wheel.

α. *c* **888** K. ÆLFRED *Boeth.* xxix. §7 Ælces spacan biþ oþer ende fæst on þære nafe, oþer on ðære felᵹe. *c* **1000** ÆLFRIC *Gloss.* in Wr.-Wülcker 106 *Cantus*, felga. ?*a* **1400** *Morte Arth.* 3309 He fongede faste one þe feleyghes. **1485** *Inv.* in *Ripon Ch. Acts* 373 Decem gang de felghes.

β. **14..** *Nom.* in Wr.-Wülcker 727 *Hec cantus*, a felowe. **1411** *Nottingham Rec.* II. 86, xj. felowes, vd. *c* **1440** *Promp. Parv.* 154/2 Felwe of a qwele..*cantus*. **1552** HULOET, Fallowes or straikes of a carte. **1572** *Wills & Inv. N.C.* (Surtees) I. 349 Fellowes for wheles vs. **1611** COTGR., *Iantes*, the fellowes of a wheele. **1688** R. HOLME *Armoury* III. 327/2, I find..a Felloe, and two Spokes fixed to a peece of a Nave. **1731** BEIGHTON in *Phil. Trans.* XXXVII. 5 Four Rings, or Sets of Felloes. **1837** CARLYLE *Fr. Rev.* (1872) I. v. vi. 166 Never over nave or felloe did thy axe strike such a stroke. **1863** WHYTE MELVILLE *Gladiators* I. 14 The very spokes and felloes of the wheels were carved in patterns.

γ. *a* **1225** *Juliana* 56 þurh spiten hit al spaken ant uelien. **1382** WYCLIF *1 Kings* vii. 33 The spokys and the felijs and the naue. **14..** *Metr. Voc.* in Wr.-Wülcker 628 Vely, *canti.* **1523** FITZHERB. *Husb.* §5 Nathes, spokes, fellyes, and dowles. **1602** SHAKS. *Ham.* II. ii. 517 Breake all the Spokes and Fallies from her wheele. **1621** G. SANDYS *Ovid's Met.* II. (1626) 24 On siluer Spokes the golden Fellies rol'd. **1745** *Beverley Beck Act* ii. 4 Wheels..shall be made to contain the full breadth of nine inches in the felley. **1773** FRANKLIN *Lett.* Wks. 1840 VI. 383 The new art of making carriage wheels, the fellies of one piece. **1880** L. WALLACE *Ben-Hur* 209 Bronze tires held the fellies, which were of shining ebony.

δ. **1598** CHAPMAN *Iliad* IV. 525 The Fell'ffs or out-parts of a wheele. *Ibid.* v. 732 The Axle-tree was steele The Felffes incorruptible gold. **1641** BEST *Farm. Bks.* (Surtees) 35 To ..see that the axle-trees and felfes of the waines bee sownde and firme. **1681** W. ROBERTSON *Phraseol. Gen.* (1693) 600 The fells or streaks of a cart, *radii.* **1799** G. SMITH *Laboratory* I. 27 The nave..in which the joiners glue the spokes, according to the number of the fells. **1877** *N. W. Linc. Gloss.*, *Felfs.* **1888** *Sheffield Gloss.*, *Felk.*

b. *attrib.* and *Comb.*, as ***felly-timber***. In names of machines or implements used in making fellies, as ***felly-auger***, ***-dresser***. Also **felly-coupling**.

1874 KNIGHT *Dict. Mech.*, **Felly-auger*, a hollow auger for fashioning the round tenon on the end of a spoke. *Ibid.*, **Felly-coupling*, a box for enclosing the adjacent ends of fellies in the rim of a wheel. *Ibid.*, **Felly-dresser*, a machine for dressing the edges of fellies. **1649** BLITHE *Eng. Improv. Impr.* (1652) 167 Good for *felly-timber also.

fellon(e, obs. forms of FELON.

fello-plastic, var. f. of PHELLOPLASTIC.
1802 W. TAYLOR in *Memoir* I. 416.

fellow ('fɛləʊ), *sb.* Forms: 1 **féolaᵹa**, 3–4 **felaȝe**, **felau**, (3 **felawȝe**, **fe-**, **feolah(e**, **feolawe**, 4 **felauh**, *south.* **velaȝe**, 5 **felay**, **-loy**, **-loȝe**), 3–5 **felagh(e**, (3 *south.* **velaghe**), 3–5 **fala**, 4–5 **fela**, 3–6 **felaw(e**, 4–6 **felow(e**, (5–6 **fel(l)o**, 7 **feloe**), 6–7 **fellowe**, 6– **fellow**. Also *Sc.* 4–9 **fallow**, (5 **fallowe**, 6 **falow**); and in renderings of dialectal and vulgar speech, 9 **fally**, **felly**, **fellaw**, **feller**. [Late OE. *féolaᵹa* wk. masc., a. ON. *félage*, f. *fé* = OE. *feoh* property, money (FEE *sb.*[1]) + *lag-* (in ON. *leggja*, OE. *lęcᵹan*:—OTeut. **lagjan*) to LAY. The primary sense is 'one who lays down money in a joint undertaking with others'; the related ON. *félag* str. neut. is 'a laying together of money', a business partnership, hence a partnership or society generally. Cf. Da. *fælle* comrade, also *fælles* (:—ON. *félags*, gen. of *félag*) common.]

I. As simple *sb.*

†**1. a.** One who shares with another in a possession, official dignity, or in the performance of any work; a partner, colleague, co-worker. Also, one united with another in a covenant for common ends; an ally. *Obs.*

1016 *O.E. Chron.* (Cott. Tib. B iv), Beᵹen þa cyningas [Eadmund and Cnut]..wurdon feolaᵹan & wedbroðra..& feng þa Eadmund cyng to West Sexan & Cnut to þam norðdæle. *c* **1250** *Gen. & Ex.* 1761 Min mog, min neue, and felaȝe. *a* **1300** *Cursor M.* 7648 (Cott.) Ionathas, To dauid tru felau..was. **1389** in *Eng. Gilds* (1870) 30 Y alderman & his felas. *c* **1440** *Promp. Parv.* 153/2 Fela, or felow yn offyce, *collega.* *c* **1466** SIR J. PASTON in *Lett.* No. 566 II. 295, I wolde nat that myn oncle William scholde cawse hym to take on hym as hys felawe. **1534** WHITINTON *Tullyes Offices* I. (1540) 65 Pericles..had a felowe in offyce in his Mayraltie. **1546** in W. H. Turner *Select. Rec. Oxford* 226 Item, to Peter the sawyer and his felowe, for sawyng the tables. **1577** HANMER *Anc. Eccl. Hist.* (1619) 177 Friends and fellowes of the Romans. **1626** BACON *Sylva* §294 Time and Heat are Fellows in many Effects.

†**b.** In a bad sense: An accomplice. *Obs.* exc. as contextual use of 2.

c **1340** *Cursor M.* 18416 (Trin.) Iewes me honged ihesu bi syde Me & my felowe. **1382** WYCLIF *Isa.* i. 23 Thi princes ..felawes of theues. *c* **1440** *Promp. Parv.* 154/1 Felowys, y-knytte to-gedyr in wykydnesse, *complices.* *c* **1500** *Nut-Brown Maid* 134 It were a curssed dede; To be felow with an out-lawe. *a* **1533** FRITH *Disput. Purgatorye* D iij, The bodye was felowe & pertener with the soule in commyttynge the cryme. **1579** TOMSON *Calvin's Serm. Tim.* 911/1 We thinke we are quit and innocent, if wee bee able to say, wee are not the first, and wee haue a great sort of fellowes. **1828** SCOTT *F.M. Perth* xxi, Rothsay and his fellows..were in the street in mask. **1848** MACAULAY *Hist. Eng.* II. 116 His fellows rescued him and beat the hangman.

†**c.** A partaker, sharer *of*. *Obs.*

1382 WYCLIF *Ecclus.* vi. 10 A frend, felawe of the bord [**1388** felowe of table]. *c* **1385** CHAUCER *L.G.W.* 895 *Thisbe*, I wol be felawe & cause eek of thy deeth. *c* **1400** *Apol. Loll.* 49 þis is..to wylen to mak God felow of þis violence. **1545** *Primer Hen. VIII* (1546) 68 Felow of Thy Fathers light. **1611** SHAKS. *Wint. T.* III. ii. 39 Behold me, A Fellow of the Royall Bed. **1667** MILTON *P.L.* I. 606 The fellows of his crime.

2. a. In vaguer use: One that is associated with another in habitual or temporary companionship; a companion, associate, comrade. Now *rare* exc. in *pl.*, or with const. *in*.

c **1200** *Vices & Virtues* (1888) 139 He lið fram alle hise felawȝes. *c* **1350** *Will. Palerne* 4888 þemperour & he.. felawes hade beene. **1387** TREVISA *Higden* (Rolls) V. 397 Austyn com..wiþ fourty felawes. *c* **1440** *Promp. Parv.* 154/1 Felow yn walkynge by þe way, *comes.* **1526** *Pilgr. Perf.* (W. de W. 1531) 163 b, Pryuate prayer that they saye by themselfe, or with a felowe. **1611** BIBLE *Jonah* i. 7 They said euery one to his fellow; Come, and let vs cast lots. **1641** J. JACKSON *True Evang. T.* I. 32 Felicitas with her seven Sons, were..fellowes in martyrdome. **1653** H. COGAN tr. *Pinto's Trav.* iv. 8 Brave men, their fellows in arms. **1725** DE FOE *Voy. round World* (1840) 64 They, being separated from their fellows, were obliged to fly. **1797** LAMB *Lett.* (1888) I. 75 A friend should never be reduced to beg an alms of his fellow. **1874** MORLEY *Compromise* (1885) 111 The little circle of his fellows which constitutes the world of a man.

Proverb. *c* **1590** MARLOWE *Faust.* ii. Wks. (Rtldg.) 82/1 Ask my fellow if I be a thief. **1610** A. COOKE *Pope Joan* in *Harl. Misc.* (Malh.) IV. 40. **1678** BUNYAN *Pilgr.* I. 201.

†**b.** Less frequently said of women. *Obs.*

c **1330** *Florice & Bl.* 509 (1857) Clarice..said to Blaunche-flour Felawe knouestou thou ought this flour. *c* **1340** *Cursor M.* 8607 (Fairf.) To hir felaw ho putt þat barne þat hir-self had for-farne. **14..** *Prose Legends* in *Anglia* VIII. 194 She wente wiþ confessours hir felowes, þat were wymen. **1598** YONG *Diana* 301 The Nymphes our fellowes. **1611** BIBLE *Judg.* xi. 37 She said..Let me alone two moneths, that I may goe vp and downe vpon the mountaines ..I, and my fellowes [1885 (Revised) companions].

†**c.** *fig.*

a **1300** *Cursor M.* 29051 (Cott.) Fasting agh..To haf foluand þir four felaus, Fredom, gladdeschipe, houe, and time. *c* **1320** *Cast. Love* 508 Wysdam is not worth an hawe But Pes therwyth be felawe. *c* **1400** *Destr. Troy* 4842 Who so frend is & felow to þat foule vise. **1548** HALL *Chron.* 8 Good hope..is the best felowe and companion. **1577** B. GOOGE *Heresbach's Husb.* I. (1586) 12 Order is a jolly felowe.

†**d.** of animals. *Obs.*

c **1300** *St. Brandan* 213 The fowel..to his felawes wende. *c* **1340** *Gaw. & Gr. Knt.* 1702 A kenet kryes þerof, þe hunt on hym calles, His felaȝes fallen hym to. **1577** B. GOOGE *Heresbach's Husb.* IV. (1586) 161 Those..eate up either their owne Egges or their fellowes. **1692** R. L'ESTRANGE *Fables* cccxxx, A Certain Shepherd had One Favourite Dog..and took more Care of him..then of any of his Fellows.

e. of things.

c **1420** *Pallad. on Husb.* III. 553 In delues breef this cannes eyon doo, And iche half a foote his felawe froo. **1697** DRYDEN *Virgil* Postcript, If the last þneid shine amongst its fellows. **1725** POPE *Odyss.* III. 383 Five tall barks the winds and waters tost Far from their fellows. **1871** FREEMAN *Norm. Conq.* (1876) IV. xviii. 201 A height of less elevation than some of its fellows.

3. a. ***good*** or ***jolly fellow***: an agreeable or pleasant companion; usually, one who is fond of feasting and good company, a convivialist; = 'boon companion'; *spec.* of a woman. In *pl.* a set of jolly or sociable companions. †***to be playing the good fellow***: to be enjoying oneself in gay company.

c **1305** *Pilate* 34 in *E.E.P.* (1862) 112 For þat on was god and þat oþer schrewe: gode felawes neuere hi nere. *c* **1386** CHAUCER *Prol.* 395 He was a good felawe. *c* **1450** *Merlin* 318 Thei wente to sitte doune alle v togeder as goode felowes and trewe. **1535** COVERDALE *Ecclus.* xiii. 6 He shal be a good felowe with thee. **1570** BUCHANAN *Ane Admonitioun* Wks. (1892) 24 Ministeris gettis all and leavis na thing to gude fallowis. **1640** BASTWICK *Lord Bps.* vii. G b, They fill themselves with strong drinke, and are good Fellows. **1667** PEPYS *Diary* 14 Oct., I suppose he is playing the good fellow in the town. **1813** L. HUNT in *Examiner* 15 Feb. 98/2 A *Raic* ..we should interpret by the phrase Jolly Fellow. **1840** DICKENS *Old C. Shop* xxxvi. 298 Nay, he [*sc.* Mr. Swiveller] would sometimes reward her [*sc.* Miss Brass] with a hearty slap on the back, and protest that she was a devilish good fellow. **1870** EMERSON *Soc. & Solit.* Wks. (Bohn) III. 2 Good fellows, fond of dancing, port, and clubs. **1876** A. TROLLOPE *Prime Minister* II. xvii. 281 There was a feeling abroad that 'Glencora' was a 'good sort of fellow' and ought to be supported. **1884** W. C. SMITH *Kildrostan* 62 Sick of clubs and jolly fellows. **1928** E. A. ROBERTSON *Cullum* x. 185 'My darling fellow,' started one [letter], 'That's the only title I can find with which to pay homage to your male companionableness... You are the only woman I've ever known who will argue..on an abstract question.' **1942** P. ABRAHAMS *Dark Testament* II. iii. 111 He's lucky and you're a fine fellow. You girls were right to call each other 'fellow'.

†**b.** ***good fellow***: a docile, manageable or tractable person or thing. *Obs.*

1576 TURBERV. *Venerie* 101 When..you perceyve she beginnes to bee muche better fellowe..and that shee seemeth to beginne to be reclaymed. **1577** B. GOOGE *Heresbach's Husb.* I. 31 The Oate is not daungerous in the choyse of his grounde, but groweth lyke a good fellowe in euery place. *Ibid.* III. 128 Whiche wyll make him [a steere] in three dayes, as good a fellowe as you woulde wishe him to be. **1639** LADY DENTON in *Verney Papers* (1853) 274 The childe was feloe good a nofe in my house.

c. ***fellow well-met***: a boon companion. ***to be (hail) fellow well met***: to be on terms of free and easy companionship *with* (a person).

1581 PETTIE *Guazzo's Civ. Conv.* III. (1586) 171 Being as you say haile fellow well met with his servant. **1858** GEN. P. THOMPSON *Audi Alt.* I. xxxvi. 137 The High Church Tory ..offers..to be fellow well met with any of them. **1885** W. J. FITZPATRICK *Life of T. N. Burke* I. 308 The best fellow-well-met in the world.

4. The complementary individual of a pair; the mate, 'marrow'.

a. Of a person: The consort, spouse, husband or wife. Also of animals. Now *colloq.* and *dial.*

a **1300** *Cursor M.* 9405 (Cott.) He wroght a felau of his ban Till adam. *c* **1460** *Towneley Myst.* (Surtees) 6 Eve, my felow, how thynk the this? **1538** in Pitcairn *Crim. Trials Scot.* I. 251* His [the King's] derrest fallow the Quene. *a* **1592** H. SMITH *Serm.* (1631) 16 It is good for man to haue a fellow. **1601** HOLLAND *Pliny* I. 224 When they be but heifers of one yeare..they are let go to the fellow and breed. **1610** SHAKS. *Temp.* III. i. 84, I am your wife, if you will marrie me..to be your fellow, You may denie me; but I'll be your seruant. **1966** F. SHAW et al. *Lern Yerself Scouse* 39 It's fer my feller's carryin-out. It is for my husband's packed lunch.

b. That which makes a pair with something else: a counterpart, match.

1599 SHAKS. *Hen. V*, IV. viii. 42 Giue me thy Gloue Souldier; Looke, heere is the fellow of it. **1623** SIR R. BOYLE *Diary* (1886) II. 85, I gaue Sir Wm parsons Lady a fair bay coach gelding and am to send her a fellow to him. **1711** ADDISON *Spect.* No. 86 ¶6 In..such Cases the Soul and the Body do not seem to be Fellows. **1719** DE FOE *Crusoe* (1840) I. iii. 53 Two shoes that were not fellows. **1856** KANE *Arct. Expl.* I. xxxi. 430, I ran..throwing off first one mitten and then its fellow to avoid pursuit. **1874** CARPENTER *Ment. Phys.* I. ii. §68 While one leg was convulsed, its fellow remained quiet.

c. That which matches or resembles another; the like.

1605 SHAKS. *Macb.* II. iii. 68 *Macb.* 'Twas a rough Night. *Len.* My young remembrance cannot paralell A fellow to it. **1668** R. L'ESTRANGE *Vis. Quev.* (1708) 310 So terrible an Uproar, and Disorder in Hell, that..the oldest Devil never knew the Fellow of it. **1741** RICHARDSON *Pamela* (1824) I. xxix. 46 Four other shifts, one the fellow to that I have on. **1871** FREEMAN *Norm. Conq.* (1876) IV. xviii. 240 His march must..have been the fellow of the great march which carried Harold from London to Stamfordbridge. **1884** J. PAYNE *1001 Nights* IX. 101 The watch, whose fashion also is of my own invention, nor is there the fellow of it in Bassora.

d. quasi-*adj.* An equivalent *to*: a match with.

1607 TOURNEUR *Rev. Trag.* I. i, Had his estate beene fellow to his mind. ? **1674** LADY CHAWORTH in *Hist. MSS. Comm.* 12th Rep. App. v. 27 A very old perspective almost fellow to that you have. **1858** BUSHNELL *Serm. New Life* 33 They..have nothing fellow to God in their substance.

5. One who shares with another in any attribute; one belonging to the same class:

a. in position or rank: An equal, peer. Now chiefly *pl.*

c **1230** *Hali Meid.* 19 Engles hwas felahes ha beoð. *a* **1300** *Cursor M.* 22778 (Cott.) þir men sal be þan his felaghes. *a* **1340** HAMPOLE *Psalter* xxi. 21 Proude men þat raises þaim up singulerly & suffers na felaghis. **1456** *How Wise Man taught Son* 132 in Hazl. *E.P.P.* I. 175 Thy wyfe..Thof sche be servant in degre, In som degre sche felaw ys. **1529** in Fiddes *Wolsey* II. (1726) 173 He us'd himself more like a Fellow to your Highness than like a subject. **1580** *Godly Admonition* in *Liturg. Serv. Q. Eliz.* (Parker Soc.) 573 Servants are become..fellows with masters. **1600** FAIRFAX tr. Tasso *Godfrey of Bulloigne* I. xii, His fellowes late, shall be his subjects now. **1721–1800** in BAILEY.

b. in ability, qualities or value: A 'match'.

1428 *Sc. Act 22 Jas. I*, 1 Mar. (Record ed. II. 15/1), Of their rentis, ilk punde sal be vtheris fallowe to the contribution of þe said Costes. *c* **1450** HOLLAND *Howlat* 913 So fair is my fetherem I haf no falowe. **1551** ROBINSON tr. *More's Utop.* I. (Arb.) 28 In reasonynge, and debatyng of matters..he hadde few fellowes. **1583** HOLLYBAND *Campo di Fior* 53 Varro..amongest the learned maisters of this schoole hath no fellows. **1687** T. BROWN *Saints in Uproar* Wks. 1730 I. 73 St. Longinus and St. Amphibalus..have not their fellows in the almanack. **1738** SWIFT *Directions to Servants*, Feeling has no fellow. **1751** SMOLLETT *Per. Pic.* (1870) I. xii. 57 Mr. Jennings is gone, and Mr. Keypstick will never meet with his fellow. **1892** *Nation* (N.Y.) 8 Dec. 435/1 The strange poetic nature..has had no fellow unless in Rembrandt.

c. in kind: One's fellow-man, 'neighbour'; also of things: Another of the sort.

1477 EARL RIVERS (Caxton) *Dictes* 11 Wyl noon of you do to your felowe otherwyse than ye wolde be don to. **1651** HOBBES *Leviath.* II. xvii. 87 Irrational creatures..as long as they be at ease..are not offended with their fellowes. **1764**

GOLDSM. *Trav.* 62 Some spot..Where my worn soul..May gather bliss to see my fellows blest. **1818** BYRON *Mazeppa* iii, Danger levels man and brute, And all are fellows in their need. **1868** FREEMAN *Norm. Conq.* (1877) II. viii. 241 There was no acknowledged legal right in churl..to make open war upon his fellow.

d. A contemporary. Chiefly *pl.*

1874 GREEN *Short Hist.* vii. §7. 425 Shakspere had now passed far beyond his fellows. **1886** SWINBURNE *Middleton* in *19th Cent.* Jan. 138 Fellows and followers of Shakespeare.

6. One of a company or party whose interests are common; a member.

c **1386** CHAUCER *Reeve's T.* 191 Men woln us foles calle, Bathe the wardeyn, and eek our felaws alle. *c* **1450** *Merlin* 171 A felowe of the rounde table. *c* **1450** *Robin Hoode & Monk* lxxx. in Child *Ballads* (1888) v. cxix. 100/2, 'I make þe maister', seid Robyn Hode..'Nay..lat me be a felow', seid Litull John. **1481** CAXTON *Myrr.* I. v. 22 He recorded their resons heeryng alle the felawys. **1547–64** BAULDWIN *Mor. Philos.* (Palfr.) 120 One vicious fellow destroyeth a whole companie. **1592** WEST *1st Pt. Symbol.* §27 B, The generall societie of goodes..extendeth to all thinges of the partners or fellowes. **1871** R. ELLIS *Catullus* lxii. 32 Sisters, Hesper a fellow of our bright company.

7. In college and university use:

a. *orig.* The name (corresponding to the Latin *socius*) given to the incorporated members of a college or collegiate foundation (whether in a University or otherwise: see COLLEGE 4); one of the company or corporation who, with their head, constitute a 'college'; e.g. 'the Provost and Fellows of Chelsea College, of Eton College, or King's College, Cambridge'; 'the Warden and Fellows of All Souls, Oxford'.

In colleges chiefly devoted to the purposes of study and education, the Fellows were, in early usage, often included under the term *scholars*; the latter term is, in later use, mostly restricted to junior members of the foundation, who are still under tuition, the term *fellow* being applied to the Senior Scholars, who have graduated, or otherwise passed out of the stage of tutelage. In those colleges that have become educational institutions, undertaking the school or university teaching of youths not on the foundation, the Fellows consist of those graduate members who have been co-opted upon the foundation with emoluments from its corporate revenue, and who constitute with their Head (usually elected by themselves from their own number) the governing body of the institution. Most colleges of this class have now also *Honorary Fellows*, who receive no emoluments, and have no share in the government. When a distinguished scholar vacates a fellowship, he or she is often elected an honorary fellow.

c **1449** PECOCK *Repr.* III. xviii. 401 That the maister and the felawis kepe the statutis of the collegis. **1511–2** *Act 3 Hen. VIII*, c. 22 §5 Any..persone being fellowe or scoler of any of the said Colleges. **1644** HUNTON *Vind. Treat. Monarchy* v. 41 In the Colledges, the Fellowes have an effectuall, and more then morall limiting Power. **1691** WOOD *Ath. Oxon.* I. 17 Thomas Lynacre..was chosen Fellow of Allsouls Coll. in 1484. *a* **1704** T. BROWN *Table Talk* in *Coll. of Poems* 124 Nothing is so Imperious, as a Fellow of a Colledge upon his own Dunghil. **1843** COLERIDGE in Stanley *Arnold's Life & Corr.* (1844) I. i. 9 Twenty fellows and twenty scholars, with four exhibitioners, form the foundation [of Corpus]. **1886** LAURIE *Lect. Rise Univ.* xiii. 247 It was thus a college composed solely of 'Fellows'. **1899** *Westm. Gaz.* 24 Nov. 10/1 A lady 'research' Fellow already exists in Wales. **1921** *Oxf. Univ. Cal.*, Somerville College... Lady Carlisle Fellow. **1971** *Ibid.* 275 A supplemental charter and new statutes were granted by which the Principal and Fellows [of St. Hilda's College] became the Governing Body.

b. On the analogy of the preceding use, the designation 'Fellows' is now applied, in some universities, to the holders of certain stipendiary positions (called 'Fellowships') tenable by elected graduates for a limited number of years, on condition of pursuing some specified branch of study.

The Radcliffe and the Craven Travelling Fellowships are the only examples in the ancient English Universities. Fellowships in this sense have been founded in the Scottish Universities, in the University of Durham and the Victoria University; and in some universities and colleges in the U.S.

1888 *Histor. Reg. Univ. Oxf.* 110 Every Fellow is required to spend at least eight months of each year of his tenure of the [Craven] Fellowship abroad. *Ibid.* 112 The first two Fellows were elected [to Radcliffe's Travelling Fellowships] in July 1715. **1892–3** *Edin. Univ. Cal.* 537 Scholars, Bursars, or Fellows must apply to the Convener of the Science Degrees Committee.

c. In some of the younger British universities and colleges, and in some of those in the U.S., the 'Fellows' are the members of the governing or administrative body; in others the title is merely honorary, conferred as a special distinction on a limited number of graduates. Cf. sense 8.

1837 *Charter Univ. Lond.*, The Chancellor, Vice-Chancellor, and Fellows..shall constitute the Senate of the said University.

8. a. The title given in various learned societies, either to all their members (as in the Royal Society, the Society of Antiquaries), or to a specially privileged class among them.

In the case of the Royal Society, the official Latin equivalent is *sodalis*.

1664 *(title)*, A List of the Fellows of the Royal Society. **1709** STEELE *Tatler* No. 15 ¶2 A Fellow of the Royal Society, who had writ upon Cold Baths. **1801** *Med. Jrnl.* V. 314 A Fellow, that is, any Member who resides within seven miles of London. **1886** *Act 49–50 Vict.* c. 48 §6 A fellow of a college of physicians.

†**b.** A bencher of an Inn of Court. *Obs.*

1536 WRIOTHESLEY *Chron.* (1875) I. 57 An atturney of the lawe and felowe of Graies Inne.

†**c.** *Fellow of the (order of the) Garter* = Knight of the Order of the Garter. *Obs.*

1475 *Bk. Noblesse* 46 The full noble knight, a felow of the Garter, ser Johan Chaundos. **1584** POWEL *Lloyd's Cambria* 397 Chosen to be Fellowe of the order of the Garter.

9. A familiar synonym for: Man, male person. (Cf. COMPANION 5, and F. *compagnon*.)

a. with qualifying adj., as *good, bad, brave, clever, foolish, old, young*, etc., and in phrases like *what a fellow*, etc. (Cf. 3, from which this use was app. a development). *poor fellow*: often used exclamatorily as an expression of pity. *stout fellow* [STOUT *a.* and *adv.* A. *adj.* 3].

c **1440** *York Myst.* xvii. 31, I hope I haue her felaws fonde. **1549** LATIMER *Ploughers* (Arb.) 29 Moyses was a wonderful felowe, and dyd his dutie being a maried man. **1570–6** LAMBARDE *Peramb. Kent* (1826) 280 This our good fellow was not so cunning (belike) as Dionysius was. **1577** B. GOOGE *Heresbach's Husb.* II. 105 Vitruuius an excellent fellowe in building. **1607** SHAKS. *Timon* I. i. 229 Thou hast fegin'd him a worthy Fellow. **1642** ROGERS *Naaman* 108 Precise preachers and zealous fellowes. **1711** STEELE *Spect.* No. 48 ¶4, I am an old Fellow, and extremely troubled with the Gout. **1749** FIELDING *Tom Jones* XI. vii, You don't know what a devil of a fellow he is. **1752** HUME *Ess. & Treat.* (1777) II. 313 A good-natured, sensible fellow. **1811** COMBE *Devil upon Two Sticks* (1817) VI. 40 A most pleasant fellow of a clergyman. **1857** MRS. CARLYLE *Lett.* II. 330 He looked dreadfully weak still, poor fellow! **1915** KIPLING *Debits & Credits* (1927) 31, I lay behind this stout fellow and saw him well into the open. **1919** J. BUCHAN *Mr Standfast* ix. 170 You're going to be a stout fellow and start in two hours' time. And you're going to take me with you. **1922** —— *Huntingtower* iv. 76 'I got inside the House.' 'Stout fellow,' said Heritage. **1970** *Guardian* 6 Apr. 11/1 The stout fella tradition of never striking against the public interest.

b. used in familiar address in phrases, *my dear fellow*, *my good fellow* (the latter now implying a tone of remonstrance or censure), *old fellow*. *young fellow-me-*(or *my-*)*lad*: see FELLER² and FELLA.

1836 MARRYAT *Midsh. Easy* xxii, I'll tell you how it is, my dear fellow. **1926** E. F. SPANNER *Navigators* 36 This young fellow-me-lad seems to have spent ten minutes or so diving in and out among the wreckage. **1929** W. DEEPING *Roper's Row* iv. §1 There were young fellow-my-lads who began to take notice.

c. In some dialects, and in unceremonious colloquial speech (*esp.* among young men), used without adj. as the ordinary equivalent for 'man'. *a fellow*: often = 'one', 'anybody', vaguely indicating the speaker himself.

1861 HUGHES *Tom Brown at Oxf.* ix, They don't deny themselves the pleasure of looking at a fellow as if he were a Turk. **1865** H. KINGSLEY *Hillyars & B.* xii, The names of the fellows who got bailed up by young Hillyar.

d. applied by schoolboys to themselves and each other.

(Possibly orig. a use of sense 6; not now so apprehended.)
c **1838** in Stanley *Arnold* I. 157 'He calls us fellows', was the astonished expression of the boys when..they heard him speak of them by the familiar name in use among themselves. **1844** J. T. HEWLETT *Parsons & W.* xv, One of our 'old fellows', as we used to call those who had left school. *Mod.* After morning school some of our fellows went for a spin.

e. jocularly applied to an animal or a thing.

1816 SCOTT *Antiq.* xxi, The red cock's..been roasting, puir fallow, in this dark hole. **1828** —— *F.M. Perth* ii, This fellow (laying his hand on his purse)..was somewhat lank and low in condition.

10. †**a.** Used as the customary title of address to a servant or other person of humble station. *Obs.*

In 14th c. it implied polite condescension, = 'comrade', 'my friend' (cf. mod.F. *mon ami* similarly used). In Shakspere's time this notion had disappeared, but the word when addressed to a servant does not seem to have necessarily implied haughtiness or contempt, though its application to one not greatly inferior was a gross insult (cf. c).

c **1350** *Will. Palerne* 275 þemperour..clepud to him þe couherde & curteysly seide; now telle me, felawe..sei þou euer þemperour? *c* **1477** CAXTON *Jason* 23 Vaissale or felawe [orig. *vassal*] thou hast done me now the most grettest dishonour. **15..** *King & Hermit* 328 in Hazl. *E.P.P.* I. 25 Unto the knave seyd the frere Ffelow, go wyȝtly here. **1588** SHAKS. *L.L.L.* IV. i. 103 Thou fellow, a word. Who gaue thee this Letter? **1594** —— *Rich. III*, III. ii. 108 Gramercie fellow: there, drinke that for me.

†**b.** One of the common people. *Obs.*

c **1430** *Freemasonry* 99 Of lord ny felow, whether he be, Of hem thou take no maner of fe. **1483** CAXTON *G. de la Tour* L iv b, Of lordes and of felawes.

c. *contemptuously.* A person of no esteem or worth.

c **1440** *York Myst.* xxiv. 3 þis felowe..we with folye fande. **1535** COVERDALE *Micah* ii. 12 A fleshly felowe and a preacher of lyes. *c* **1570** *Sempill Ballates* x. (1872) 54 This..fallow of na kin..Begouth to reule. **1594** SHAKS. *Rich. III*, v. iii. 325 A paltry Fellow, Long kept in Britaine at our Mothers cost, A Milke-sop. *c* **1660** SOUTH *Serm. John* vii. 17 Serm. 1715 I. 229 Fellows that set up for Messias's. **1734** POPE *Ess. Man* IV. 203 Worth makes the man, the want of it the fellow. **1749** FIELDING *Tom Jones* XVII. ii, You..have so disdainfully called him fellow. *a* **1776** *Lizie Wan* vii. in Child *Ballads* II. li. (1884) 448/2, I see by thy ill colour Some fallow's deed thou hast done. **1826** DISRAELI *Viv. Grey* v. xiii, This is some vile conspiracy of your own, fellow. **1837** DICKENS *Pickw.* xv, 'Sir', said Mr. Tupman, 'you're a fellow'. **1884** PAE *Eustace* 68 'The fellow's drunk', ejaculated Randolph.

d. A Negro. *U.S. Obs.*

1753 in *New Jersey Archives* (1897) 1st Ser. XIX. 270 Run away..a Mulatto Fellow named Anthony... Whoever takes up said Fellow..shall have Three Pounds Reward. **1860** BARTLETT *Dict. Amer.* (ed. 3) 144 *Fellow or Black Fellow*, a black man. Southern.

II. *attrib.* and *Comb.*

11. *appositively* (quasi-*adj.*). Prefixed to sbs., forming an unlimited number of quasi-compounds (in which the use of the hyphen is optional). Equivalent to the earlier EVEN- *Comb.* 2, and to CO-, JOINT *a.*

No instances of this use are found in our material earlier than Tindale and Coverdale 1534–5; *felow-bacheler* is printed in Gower *Conf.* III. 292, but the best MSS. have *felon* or *feloun*; Palsgrave 1530 has *felow man, woman*, but here the second word is only added for distinction. Cf. quot. *c*1400 in a.

a. Denoting a person or thing that agrees with another in belonging to the designated class, as in *fellow-angel, -apostle, -being, -bishop, -Christian, -fault, -man, -planet, -sinner, -worm*; FELLOW-CREATURE.

1625 QUARLES *Fun. Eleg.* vii, It sigh'd..To be..enthron'd Among his *fellow Angells. **1647** SANDERSON *Serm.* II. 218 He taught Judas to be so much wiser..than his *fellow-apostles. **1810** J. CONDER *Reverie* in *Associate Minstrels* 9* Can I trust a *fellow-being? **1864** BURTON *Scot Abr.* I. iii. 149 A fat philosopher..totally innocent of the death of a fellow-being. [*c* **1400** *Apol. Loll.* 59 Bernard seiþ to pope Eugeni, þi *felawis bischops lere þei at þe to haue, etc.] **1565** JEWEL *Repl. Harding* (1611) 176 The true Councels, which we haue receiued from our holy fellow-bishop Cyrillus of Alexandria. **1642** MILTON *Apol. Smect.* Wks. (1847) 82/2 To proclaim a croisade against his *fellow-christian. **1853** LANDOR *Last Fruit* 131 A fellow Christian..enjoying a secret pleasure in saying unpleasant things. **1600** SHAKS. *A.Y.L.* III. ii. 373 Euerie one fault seeming monstrous til his *fellow-fault came to match it. **1756** FRANKLIN *Let.* Wks. 1887 II. 460 These kindnesses from men I can only..return on their *fellow-men. **1813** BYRON *Giaour* 329 On desert sands 'twere joy to scan The rudest steps of fellow man. **1684** T. BURNET *Th. Earth* I. 194 The earth with the rest of its *fellow-planets. **1732** BERKELEY *Alciphr.* VI. §16 Man..is himself a *fellow-sinner with them. **1860** HOOK *Lives Abps.* (1869) II. ii. 111 We have to labour among our fellow-sinners. **1689** C. MATHER *Mem. Prov.* 24 The Devils are seldome able to hurt us..without a Commission from some of our *fellow-worms. **1719** WATTS *Hymns* II. xlvi, Worms were never rais'd so high Above their meanest fellow-worm.

b. Denoting a person or (occasionally) a thing that is associated with another in companionship or co-operation in what the sb. implies, as *fellow-boarder, -captive, -cause, -clerk, -communicant, -conspirator, -emigrant, -guest, -labourer, -lodger, -passenger, -prisoner, -student, -sufferer, -worker, -workman.* Also FELLOW-SOLDIER, FELLOW-TRAVELLER.

1871 MOTLEY *Corr.* (1889) II. x. 325 He is a *fellow-boarder with your son. *a* **1569** KINGESMYLL *Confl. Satan* (1578) 36 Hee is a *fellow-captive with Paul. **1749** JOHNSON *Irene* I. i, A galley lies Mann'd with the bravest of our fellow-captives. **1821** BYRON *Juan* IV. lxxx, He saw some fellow captives. **1581** W. CLARKE in *Confer.* IV. (1584) Ffiv b, It should bee a *fellowe cause in our iustification with Christes righteousnes. **1886** T. HOPKINS *'Twixt Love & Duty* xii, He did not grudge a holiday to his *fellow-clerks. **1670** *Devout Commun.* (1688) 122 Interceding with him for..our *fellow-communicants. **1899** 'MARK TWAIN' *Man corrupted Hadl.* (1900) 160 He shall deceive his fellow-conspirators. **1936** *Discovery* Oct. 321/2 All the members of this pact wore a black pin as a sign to fellow-conspirators. **1848** MACAULAY *Hist. Eng.* I. 534 He..found among his *fellow emigrants men ready to listen to his evil counsels. **1591** PERCIVALL *Sp. Dict.*, *Comensal*, a *fellow guest. **1709** SHAFTESB. *Moralists* II. §2. 71, I..being so violently decry'd by my two Fellow Guests. **1625** USSHER *Answ. Jesuit* 31 The word of God..was both by themselves and others of their *fellow-labourers delivered by word of mouth. *a* **1704** T. BROWN *Quakers Serm.* Wks. 1730 I. 105 Our dear brother and fellow-labourer hath gone a little astray. **1832** MISS MITFORD *Village* Ser. v. (1863) 318 Men..persuading their fellow-labourers to join them at every farm they visited. **1678** DRYDEN *Limberham* II. Wks. (1883) VI. 49 This is Mr. Woodall, your new *fellow-lodger. **1755** SMOLLETT *Quix.* (1803) II. 193 His fellow-lodgers were persons of rank. **1879** HOWELLS *L. Aroostook* I. vi, One never can know what one's *fellow-passengers are going to be. **1611** BIBLE *Rom.* xvi. 7 Andronicus and Iunia my kinsmen and my *fellow prisoners. **1725** DE FOE *Voy. round World* (1840) 61 He thought his two fellow-prisoners might be trusted. **1875** TENNYSON *Q. Mary* I. iv, The two were fellow-prisoners..in yon accursed Tower. **1602** SHAKS. *Ham.* I. ii. 177, I pray thee, doe not mock me, *fellowstudent. **1712** STEELE *Spect.* No. 526 ¶3 Fellow-templars, fellow-students. **1860** TYNDALL *Glac.* I. xxv. 186 A former fellow student. **1687** DRYDEN *Hind & P.* I. 563 Her friend and *fellow-suff'rer in the plot. **1762–71** H. WALPOLE *Vertue's Anecd. Paint.* (1786) III. 182 He..bequeathed most of what he had to his fellow-sufferers. **1611** BIBLE *Col.* iv. 11 These..are my *fellowworkers vnto the kingdome of God. **1660** JER. TAYLOR *Worthy Commun.* Introd. 7 Fellow-workers with God in the laboratories of salvation. **1951** R. FIRTH *Elem. Social Organiz.* i. 23 According to his fears or his politics, he may interpret this as a symbol of anger or of solidarity among fellow-workers. **1961** NEW ENGLISH BIBLE *Philemon* 1 From Paul..to Philemon our dear friend and fellow-worker. **1535** COVERDALE *Acts* xix. 25 The *feloweworkmen of the same occupacion. **1646** H. LAWRENCE *Comm. Angells* 24 Angells..whom hee vouchsafeth to use as fellow-workemen with himselfe. **1875** JOWETT *Plato* (ed. 2) I. 141 He and his fellow-workmen have taught them.

c. (with sb. of relative signification.) Denoting a person or thing that stands in the designated relation to the same object as another, as in *fellow-burgess*, *-burgher*, *-disciple*, *-member*, *-servant*, *-townsman*, *-tribesman*; †**fellow-brother**, a member of the same brotherhood; **fellow-collegian**, † **-collegiate**, a member of the same college; **fellow-craftsman**, one of the same craft; **fellow-subject**, a subject of the same sovereign. Also FELLOW-CITIZEN, -COUNTRYMAN, -HEIR.

a **1575** ABP. PARKER *Corr.* 425 To..give some testimony of my *fellow-brothers. **1638** SANDERSON *Serm.* II. 115 We ought..so to behave our selves in the house of God..as becometh fellow-brethren. **1638** DRUMM. OF HAWTH. *Irene* Wks. (1711) 164 To..wander amongst..his slaughter'd acquaintances and *fellow-burgesses. **1835** W. IRVING *Tour Prairies* xxxii, The atrocious murders of their *fellow-burghers. **1791** BOSWELL *Johnson* an. 1729, I do not find that he formed any close intimacies with his *fellow-collegians. **1667–9** BUTLER *Rem.* (1759) II. 318 He..talks of authors as familiarly as his *fellow-collegiates. **1836** H. ROGERS *J. Howe* vi. (1863) 160 He had been an intimate friend and fellow-collegiate of Stowe's. **1856** R. A. VAUGHAN *Mystics* (1860) II. 65 The..youth shrank from the..riotous companionship of his *fellow-craftsmen. **1611** BIBLE *John* xi. 16 Then said Thomas..vnto his *fellowe disciples, Let us also go. **1852** H. ROGERS *Ecl. Faith* (1853) 17 [He] has almost battered out the brains of a fellow disciple. **1640** SANDERSON *Serm.* 148 Though they be our *fellow-members, yet have we little fellow-feeling of their griefs. **1863** A. B. GROSART *Small Sins* (ed. 2) 48 A divided heart toward some fellow-member. **1534** TINDALE *Col.* iv. 7 Tichicos..which is a..*feloweservaunt in the Lorde. **1591** SHAKS. *Two Gent.* II. iv. 105. **1667** MILTON *P.L.* VIII. 225 Nor less think wee in Heav'n of thee on Earth Than of our fellow servant. **1713** STEELE *Englishman* No. 1. 9 He treats us Senators like his Fellow-Servants. **1648** SYMMONS *Vind. Chas. I* 40 His poor people..are most mercilesly butchered..by their *fellow-subjects. **1711** ADDISON *Spect.* No. 125 ¶8 We should not..regard our Fellow-Subjects as Whigs or Tories. **1876** BANCROFT *Hist. U.S.* III. xi. 451 That from Rhode Island..claimed..equal rights with their fellow-subjects in Great Britain. **1846** LANDOR *Imag. Conv.* I. 237/1 Valour in a *fellow-townsman is the exciter of our praise. **1853** HICKIE tr. *Aristoph.* (1872) II. 422 Call your *fellow-tribesmen to your aid. **1867** O. W. HOLMES *Guardian Angel* xiii. (1891) 158 His descriptions of the future which was in store for the great bulk of his..*fellow-worldsmen.

d. Sometimes prefixed pleonastically to sbs. which themselves imply companionship or participation. Now *rare*.

1552 HULOET, Fellow-companion, *comes*. **1603** SHAKS. *Meas. for M.* IV. ii. 19, I would bee glad to receiue some instruction from my fellow partner. **1649** DRUMM. OF HAWTH. *Hist. Jas. III* Wks. (1711) 47 He had only for his fellow-companions astrologers and sooth-sayers. **1760** STERNE *Serm.* (1773) I. 127 She looked upon him as a fellow-partner. **1858** HAWTHORNE *Fr. & It. Jrnls.* (1883) 63 Seeing in England more of my fellow-compatriots than ever before.

12. rarely *attrib.* with the sense: Equal, befitting an equal.

1638 FORD *Fancies* IV. ii, The great duke..would lift up my head to fellow-pomp amongst his nobles.

13. *Comb.* with vbl. sbs., agent-nouns, and pples., imitating L. words with *co(m-*, *con-*. Only in a few words originating in 16–17th c., as †**fellow-bordering** *ppl. a.* (= L. *confinis*), conterminous, neighbouring; **fellow-helper** (= L. *coadjutor*), one who helps in the way of co-operation; †**fellow-inspired**, endowed with a like gift of inspiration; †**fellow-knower** (= L. *conscius* sb.), one who is privy to (a secret); so †*fellow-knowing* ppl. a.; †**fellow-yoked** pple., mutually yoked. Also FELLOW-FEELING.

a **1628** F. GREVILLE *Sidney* (1652) 28 [This Emperor]..got credit with his *fellow-bordering Princes. **1535** COVERDALE 1 *Esdras* vii. 1 The other landlordes with their companyons..were *fellow helpers with the olde rulers of the Iewes. **1611** BIBLE 2 *Cor.* viii. 23 He is my partner and fellow helper. **1685** H. MORE *Illustr.* 342 This Angel and John..were *fellow-inspired Souls..both endued with the Spirit of Prophecy. **1662** J. CHANDLER *Van Helmont's Oriat.* 103 Not that I am..a *fellow-knower of, or a searcher into divine Counsel. *Ibid.* 88 The same God might be a conscious or *fellow-knowing revenger..of our sin. **1620** MIDDLETON & ROWLEY *World Tost at Tennis* 571 Wks. 1886 VII. 177 I'll not be *fellow-yok'd with death.

fellow ('fɛləʊ), *v.* Forms: 4 *felaghe*, *south.* *velaȝe*, 4–6 *felow*, 5 *felewe*, 6 *Sc.* *fallow*, 6– *fellow*. [f. prec. sb.]

†**1.** *trans.* To conjoin, associate (a person or thing) in partnership or companionship *with*, *to* (another). *Obs.*

a **1340** HAMPOLE *Psalter* v. 11 Wham swa þai may felaghe wiþ þaim. **1340** *Ayenb.* 101 þou him uelaȝest mid þe huanne þou zayst: 'yef ous' and ne zayst naȝt 'yef me'. *c* **1410** LOVE *Bonavent. Mirr.* lvi. (Gibbs MS.) 110 He ioyneþ and feleweþ hym to hem homely. **1450–1530** *Myrr. our Ladye* 146 That..they may..deserue to be felowed to thy chosen. *a* **1577** SIR T. SMITH *Commw. Eng.* xi. (1589) 13 A man..is..desirous to fellow himselfe to another, and so to liue in couple. **1589** T. L. *Advt. Q. Eliz.* (1651) 47 Who being fellowed in glory with the highest. **1594** CAREW *Tasso* (1881) 96 Blush of scorne fellowd with that of shame.

b. To put on a level *with*; to make, or represent as, an equal or match *to*.

1450–1530 *Myrr. our Ladye* 251 O moder of lyfe, whiche by thyne obedience ys mekely felowed vnto vs. **1500–20** DUNBAR *Thistle & Rose* xx, Lat no nettill vyle..Hir fallow to the gudly flour-de-lyce. **1648** BP. HALL *Select Thoughts* §100 Who..called every wolf his brother..fellowing himself with every thing that had life. **1884** W. H. WARD in *Century Mag.* XXVII. 820 It is this quality..which fellows him..with Milton.

†**2. a.** To be a fellow to; to accompany, be associated with. **b.** To be a partner or sharer in.

1434 MISYN *Mending of Life* 119 So þat it be not greuus to an [vn]profetabyll seruand to felo his lorde. **1593** Q. ELIZ. *Boethius* 6 Easing thy Labor with felowing of thi paine. **1611** SHAKS. *Wint. T.* I. ii. 142 Affection..With what's vnreall thou coactiue art, And fellow'st nothing. **1614** SYLVESTER *Little Bartas* 454 All Delights of Earth have ever been Fellow'd or follow'd by some tragick Teen. **1639** FULLER *Holy War* i. (1647) 8 The conquer'd fellow for the most part the religion of the conquerors.

3. To produce a fellow to; to equal, match.

1656 HEYLIN *Surv. France* 74 It will be a palace..not fellowed in Europe. **1716** CIBBER *Love makes Man* III. iii, It's impossible to fellow it, but in Paris. **1862** LADY MORGAN *Mem.* II. 469, I have at this moment, perfuming my rooms, twelve Hyacinths..fellow me that in your garden!

†**b.** To arrange in pairs; to pair. *Obs.*

1654 [see FELLOWED *ppl. a.*]. **1751** R. PALTOCK *P. Wilkins* xlvi. (1883) 137/2, I here found..so many shoes, as when I had fellowed them, served me as long as I stayed.

4. *nonce-use.* To address as 'fellow'.

1752 FIELDING *Amelia* VIII. vi, 'Don't fellow me'.

Hence †'**fellowed** *ppl. a.*, joined together in pairs.

1654 WHITLOCK *Zootomia* 115 He can teach..whether the Kidneyes be fellowed or single, and how many Hearts most Men have. **1698** T. MOLYNEUX in *Phil. Trans.* XX. 216 Naturally fellow'd in Pairs. **1775** in ASH.

†'**fellowable**, *a.* *Obs.* *rare*$^{-1}$. In 5 feleable. [f. FELLOW *v.* or *sb.* + -ABLE.] Agreeable as a fellow or companion; sociable.

c **1440** *Promp. Parv.* 154/1 Feleable, *socialis*.

ˌ**fellow-'citizen.** [FELLOW *sb.* 11 c.] A citizen of the same city or polity as another.

1578 *Chr. Prayers* in *Priv. Prayers* (1851) 448 The angels, and holy souls of men, are most blessed fellow-citizens. **1611** BIBLE *Eph.* ii. 19 Yee are..fellow citizens with the Saints. *a* **1704** T. BROWN *Pleas. Epist.* Wks. 1730 I. 109 This may serve, fellow-citizens, to give you some idea of the man. **1752** HUME *Ess. & Treat.* (1777) I. 348 A single man can scarcely be industrious, where all his fellow-citizens are idle. **1873** H. SPENCER *Stud. Sociol.* vi. 387 He is partially coerced into..co-operation with his fellow citizens.

Hence ˌ**fellow-'citizenship.**

1796 MORSE *Amer. Geog.* II. 323 The city of Neuchatel has also a strict alliance of fellowcitizenship with Berne. **1858** J. MARTINEAU *Stud. Chr.* 311 The 'Fraternity'..aims to neutralize by fellow-citizenship the diversities..of nature.

ˌ**fellow-'commoner.** [In senses 1 and 3, see FELLOW *sb.* 11 b; in sense 2, see FELLOW *sb.* 7 a.]

†**1.** A joint-partaker of anything along with others; *esp.* one who eats at the same table or shares in a common meal: see COMMONER *sb.* 5, 6.

1591 FLORIO *Sec. Fruites* 87 We haue been..fellowe commoners at the vniuersitie. **1607** TOPSELL *Four-f. Beasts* Pref., They were ordained..to be Fellow-commoners with Man. **1642** FULLER *Holy & Prof. St.* IV. xvii. 328 Their Generall was Fellow-commoner with them.

2. A privileged class of undergraduates in certain colleges of Oxford and Cambridge, and at Trinity College, Dublin. See COMMONER 6.

So called from having the privilege of dining at the Fellows' table, being thus 'commoners with the Fellows'. 'At Oxford the existence of a higher grade of undergraduates (in some colleges called 'fellow-commoners', in the majority 'gentlemen commoners') is still recognized by the University Statutes, but the only house that has fellow-commoners on its books is Worcester College. At Cambridge, there were formerly fellow-commoners at most colleges, but the status is now nearly obsolete' (N.E.D., 1895).

1637 EVELYN *Diary* 10 May, The Fellow Com'uners in Balliol were no more exempt from Exercise than the meanest scholars there. **1664** PEPYS *Diary* (1879) III. 48 Sir John Skeffington, whom I knew at Magdalen College, a fellow-commoner. **1758** JOHNSON *Idler* No. 33 ¶9 Did not fall asleep till ten, a young fellow-commoner being very noisy over my head. **1811** BYRON *Th. Present State Greece* Wks. (1846) 766/2 He is..better educated than a fellow-commoner of most colleges. **1848** THACKERAY *Bk. Snobs* xiii, The lads with gold and silver lace are sons of rich gentlemen, and called Fellow Commoners: they are privileged to feed better than the pensioners, and to have wine with their victuals. **1893** *Dublin Univ. Cal.* 15 Fellow-Commoners..have the privilege of dining at the Fellows' Table.

b. *Camb. Univ. slang.* (See quots.) ? *Obs.*

1785 GROSE *Dict. Vulg. Tongue*, Fellow commoner, an empty bottle, so called at the University at Cambridge, where fellow commoners are not in general considered as over full of learning. **1794** *Gentl. Mag.* Dec. 1084/2 A bottle decanted was..denominated a fellow commoner.

3. One who has a right of common with others.

1690 LOCKE *Gov.* II. v. §32 He cannot inclose, without the Consent of all his Fellow-Commoners, all Mankind.

ˌ**fellow-'countryman.** [FELLOW *sb.* 11 c.] One belonging to the same country with another; a compatriot.

1583 STOCKER *Hist. Civ. Warres Low C.* I. 111 They..keepe their faith..with their fellow countrie men. **1639** FULLER *Holy War* IV. xvi. 196 The..corpses of their fellow-countreymen. **1793** W. ROBERTS *Looker-on* (1794) III. 202 A fellow-countryman from Scotland. **1812** BYRON *Ch. Har.* II. lxvi, When..fellow-countrymen [would] have stood aloof. **1877** BLACK *Green Past.* iii. (1878) 22 The cry of our fellow-countrymen in prison.

ˌ**fellow-'creature.** [FELLOW *sb.* 11 a, c.] A production of the same Creator; now applied only to human beings and (less frequently) animals.

a **1648** LD. HERBERT *Life* (1886) 57 All herbs and plants, being our fellow-creatures. **1682** OTWAY *Venice Preserved* I. i, A..villain: To see the sufferings of my fellow-creatures, And own myself a man. **1729** BUTLER *Serm.* Wks. 1874 II. 51 A good man is friendly to his fellow-creatures, and a lover of mankind. **1809–10** COLERIDGE *Friend* (1865) 61 Virtue would not be virtue, could it be given by one fellow-creature to another. **1878** BROWNING *La Saisiaz* 48 Yon worm, man's fellow-creature.

†'**fellower.** *Obs.* *rare*$^{-1}$. [f. FELLOW *v.* + -ER[1].] That which accompanies.

1652 COLLINGES *Caveat for Prof.* iv. (1653) 21 The Gentle-man calls it and its fellowers *Reasons*.

'**fellowess.** *rare.* [f. FELLOW *sb.* + -ESS.] A female 'fellow'. Cf. FELLOW 9, 10.

1748 RICHARDSON *Clarissa* (1811) III. xix. 117 Who can have patience with such fellows and fellowesses? **1796** MAD. D'ARBLAY *Camilla* V. IX. iv, Your bachelor uncles, and maiden aunts, are the most tantalizing fellows and fellowesses in the creation. **1935** S. DESMOND *Afr. Log* I. 256 Good fellows and fellowesses all.

†'**fellow-'feel,** *v.* *Obs.* [Back-formation from FELLOW-FEELING.]

1. *intr.* To share the feelings of others; to feel in common, sympathize *with*.

1612 T. TAYLOR *Comm. Titus* ii. 8 They partake and fellow-feele in the afflictions of the Gospel. **1641** W. HOOKE *New Eng. Teares* 5 It is the part of one member to fellow-feele with another.

2. *trans.* To share the feeling of; to sympathize with (another's suffering). *rare*; there are several examples in the author quoted.

1642 ROGERS *Naaman* 319 Not to leave them to themselves, but to fellow-feele their affliction.

Hence ˌ**fellow-'feeler**, a sympathizer; ˌ**fellow-'feeling** *a.*, sympathetic.

1611 BEAUM. & FL. *Kt. Burn. Pestle* III. v, Am I not your fellow-feeler..in all our miseries? **1622** S. WARD *Life Faith* (1627) 84 A..fellow-feeling elder brother. **1677** GILPIN *Dæmonol.* (1867) 223 To bear one another's burdens..shews us to be fellow-feeling members of the same body. **1708** *Brit. Apollo* No. 87. 1/2 A fellow-feeling Tenderness.

ˌ**fellow-'feeling,** *vbl. sb.* [See FELLOW *sb.* 13; a rendering of L. *compassio*, Gr. συμπάθεια SYMPATHY.]

1. Participation in the feelings of others; sympathy.

1613 R. C. *Table Alph.* (ed. 3) *Compassion*, pittie, fellow-feeling. **1623** ROWLANDSON *God's Bless.* 62 Men of other callings should have a fellow-feeling of those miseries. **1690** EARL MELFORT in *Ellis' Orig. Lett.* Ser. II. No. 384 IV. 190 There is not such a thing as fellow-feeling (the presbyterian word). *a* **1716** BLACKALL *Wks.* (1723) I. 70 Mercy, properly speaking, is an Affection of the Mind..'tis a fellow-feeling of another's Sufferings. **1818** HAZLITT *Eng. Poets* ii. (1870) 52 Inanimate objects..have a fellow-feeling in the interest of the story. **1857** W. COLLINS *Dead Secret* II. i. (1861) 37, I have a fellow-feeling for others who are like me.

2. Sense of community of interest.

1712 ARBUTHNOT *John Bull* I. x, Even your milk woman and your nursery maid have a fellow-feeling. **1755** JOHNSON, *Fellow-feeling*, combination, joint interest; commonly in an ill sense. [This is no longer correct.] **1809** BYRON *Bards & Rev.* xiv, A fellow-feeling makes us wond'rous kind.

ˌ**fellow-'heir.** A partner in an inheritance; a joint heir.

1585 ABP. SANDYS *Serm.* (1841) 204 We are made..fellow-heirs with Christ of God's kingdom. **1611** BIBLE *Eph.* iii. 6 The Gentiles should be fellowheires. **1675** BROOKS *Gold. Key* Wks. 1867 V. 551 Suffering saints and you are fellow-heirs. **1869** W. P. MACKAY *Grace & Truth* (1875) 68 Christians are fellow-heirs with Christ.

Hence ˌ**fellow-'heirship.**

1869 GOULBURN *Purs. Holiness* i. 5 The truth of the Gentiles' fellow-heirship.

fellowless ('fɛləʊlɪs), *a.* [f. FELLOW *sb.* + -LESS.] Without a fellow.

1. †Without a companion; alone, solitary (*obs.*). Of one of a pair: Without the fellow.

a **1420** HOCCLEVE *De Reg. Princ.* 8, I say; yf thow go felaweles, Alle solitarie. **1887** *Sat. Rev.* 5 Feb. 196 A fellowless glove.

2. *poet.* Without a peer or equal; matchless.

1580 SIDNEY *Arcadia* (1622) 417 The fellowlesse Philoclea. **1598** CHAPMAN *Iliad* II. 434 Hypothebs, whose well-built walls are rare and fellowless. *c* **1611** *Ibid.* XII. 108 Both these Were best of all men but himself, but he was fellowless. **1863** W. LANCASTER *Præterita* 43 Thinking on..the archer hand Once fellowless in Hellas.

†'**fellowlike,** *a.* and *adv.* *Obs.* [f. as prec. + -LIKE.] **A.** *adj.* Like a fellow.

a. Like a companion or mate; on a level; on the same footing; similar. Const. *with*.

1526 *Pilgr. Perf.* (W. de W. 1531) 63 b, To..make hym equall or felowe lyke, with kynges. **1596** BP. W. BARLOW *Three Serm.* i. 16 These two are such fellowlike companions. **1928** T. HARDY *Coll. Poems* 5 Change and Chancefulness..wrought us fellow-like.

b. Companionable, sociable; sympathetic.

1580 HOLLYBAND *Treas. Fr. Tong*, A fellowlike man. *a* **1603** T. CARTWRIGHT *Confut. Rhem. N.T.* (1618) 79 Hee ioyned himselfe..in fellowship and fellowlike communion

with him. *a* **1633** LENNARD tr. *Charron's Wisd.* I. xxxii, We sigh..and with a fellow-like feeling pity their miseries.

B. *adv.* **a.** Like one's fellows, on the same footing or level; in like manner, similarly.

c **1530** LD. BERNERS *Arth. Lyt. Bryt.* (1814) 113 He was named felawlyke to Bucyfal. *a* **1569** KINGESMYLL *Confl. Satan* (1578) 36 Hee is a felowe captive with Paul, and shall be felowelike ransomed with Paul.

b. Like a fellow, companion, or equal; sociably.

1580 SIDNEY *Arcadia* (1622) 399 He..fellow-like let his dominion slide. **1609** BIBLE (Douay) *Ecclus.* xiii. 14 Stay not to speake felowlike with him. *a* **1628** F. GREVILLE *Sidney* (1652) 24 He so fellow-like encompassed with them. **1678** in LITTLETON *Lat. Dict.*

c. ? Like a 'fellow' or person of little worth.

1632 SANDERSON *Serm.* (1637) 611 Servants..that will work hard..so long as their master's eye is upon them, but when his back is turned can be content to goe on fayre and softly and fellow-like.

'fellowly, *a.* and *adv.* [f. as prec. + -LY.]

A. *adj.* Like or pertaining to a fellow.

1. Pertaining to or befitting comrades or friendly associates; social. More recently revived in *poet.* and *rhet.* use.

a **1225** *Ancr. R.* 276 Prudes salue is edmodnesse: ondes salue, feolauliche luue. **1435** MISYN *Fire of Love* II. iv. 77 Þat of felaly song of charite my substans I myȝt ransake. **1450–1530** *Myrr. our Ladye* 329 Vertues & blyssed seraphyn synge togither with felowly ioy. **1578** BANISTER *Hist. Man* Pref. 5 To..the Maister, Wardens..and fellowly Fraternitie of Chirurgians. **1883** G. MEREDITH *Joy of Earth* 11 Love it [*sc.* the light] so you could accost Fellowly a livid ghost. **1898** T. HARDY *Wessex Poems* 1 Change and chancefulness in my flowering youthtime, Set me sun by sun near to one unchosen; Wrought us fellowly, and despite divergence, Friends interblent us. **1903** *Trawl* May 3 The fellowly enfolding of the night. **1918** W. J. JUPP *Wayfarings* viii. 93 The revealings of a spirit fellowly and accordant with his own.

2. Companionable, sociable, sympathetic.

a **1440** *Found. St. Bartholomew's* 3 Thiswyse to kyng and grete men..famylier and felowly he was. *c* **1500** *Yng. Childr. Bk.* 94 in *Babees Bk.* 21 Ete & drinke, & be feleyly. **1573** G. HARVEY *Letter-bk.* (Camden) 4 After dinner..I continuid as long as ani, and was as fellowli as the best. **1610** SHAKS. *Temp.* v. i. 64 Mine eyes ev'n sociable to the shew of thine Fall fellowly drops. **1688** BUNYAN *Jerus. Sinn. Saved* (1886) 112 Why not fellowly with our carnal neighbours? **1887** *Kentish Gloss.*, *Fellowly*, familiar, free.

B. *adv.* In a manner like a fellow or equal; on equal terms; sociably; hence, familiarly.

a **1225** *Ancr. R.* 38 Delen in his pinen veolauliche on eorðe. **1435** MISYN *Fire of Love* 92 To-gidyr beand & acordand be kyndely stirryng felaly þa ar glad. **1582** BENTLEY *Mon. Matrones* III. 305 Then seeing more felowlie the glorie of the Lord, we shall be transformed into the same image. *a* **1631** DONNE *Serm.* ix. 92 To behave themselves fellowly and frowardly towards Great Persons.

†**'fellowred.** *Obs.* Forms: 3 felau-, feolau-, *south.* velau-, veolaured(d)en, 3–4 felau-, felared(e, 4 *south.* velaȝrede, 4–5 felawrede, -dyn, 5 felow(e)red(d)e. [f. FELLOW + OE. *-rǽden* condition: see -RED.]

1. The condition or state of being fellows or companions; companionship, company, fellowship, society. *to bear* (*a person*) *fellowred*: to bear him company.

a **1225** *Ancr. R.* 106 Uorto beren him ueolauredden [*v.r.* feorreden]. *c* **1250** *Old Kent. Serm.* in *O.E. Misc.* (1872) 31 Se [lepre] liest þe felarede of oþer men. **1340** *Ayenb.* 16 Prede brek uerst uelaȝrede and ordre.

b. *for fellowred*: for comradeship's sake.

a **1300** *Cursor M.* 20380 (Cott.) Qui wepes tu sua..For felaured now sai þou me. **1340** *Ayenb.* 38 Þe þyeues be uelaȝrede byeþ þo þet parteþ of þe þyefþe oþer uor uelaȝrede oþer by yefþe oþer be begginge.

2. Intercourse, *esp.* spiritual; = COMMUNION 2 b.

a **1300** *Cursor M.* 27975 (Cott.) Þoru þis gilt es þat felaureden spilt þat tuix crist and vs suld be. **1340** *Ayenb.* 14 'Þe mennesse of halȝen' þet is to zigge þe uelaȝrede of alle þe halȝen. *a* **1400** *Relig. Pieces fr. Thornton MS.* (1867) 3 That es comonynge and felawrede of all cristene.

3. Sexual intercourse.

c **1250** *Old Kent. Serm.* in *O.E. Misc.* (1872) 31 Wyman deseiurd fram mannes felarede. **13..** *MS. Harl.* 1701. 11 (Halliw.) But thou dedyst no foly dede, That ys fleshly felaurede. **1340** *Ayenb.* 9 Þou ne sselt naȝt wylni uelaȝrede ulesslich wyþ oþre manne wyf.

4. A company of fellows or comrades.

c **1326** *Coer de L.* 3137 Blythe was the Crystene felawrede, Off Kyng Richard. **1340** *Ayenb.* 16 He vil uram heuene and becom dyeuel, and he and al his uelaȝrede. *c* **1430** *Syr Gener.* (Roxb.) 3586 He had a grete felowrede. *c* **1430** *Hymns Virg.* (1867) 121 Seynt peter, noþer his felow-redde, Dar nott speke a word.

fellowship ('fɛləʊʃɪp), *sb.* [f. FELLOW *sb.* + -SHIP.] Primarily, the condition or quality of being a FELLOW, in various senses.

1. †**a.** Partnership; membership of a society. Also, in political sense, alliance. *Obs.*

1382 WYCLIF *1 Macc.* viii. 17 He sente hem to Rome, for to ordeyne with hem frendship and felawship. **1592** WEST *1st Pt. Symbol.* §26 C, There may be partnership or fellowship amongst the persons contracting. **1602** SHAKS. *Ham.* III. ii. 289 Would not this Sir..get me a Fellowship in a crie of Players. **1623** BINGHAM *Xenophon* 87 They would enter into fellowship of warre with the Grecians.

b. Participation, sharing (in an action, condition, etc.); 'something in common', community of interest, sentiment, nature, etc.

a **1240** *Ureisun* in *Cott. Hom.* 185 Ich nabbe no mong, ne felawscipe, ne priuete, wiþ þe world. **1382** WYCLIF *2 Cor.* vi. 14 What felowschip of liȝt to derkenessis? **1535** COVERDALE *Acts* i. 17 He..had opteyned the felashippe of this mynistracion. **1671** MILTON *P.R.* I. 401, I feel by proof That fellowship in pain divides not smart. **1714** SWIFT *Epist. Corr.* Wks. 1841 II. 529, I congratulate with England for joining with us here in the fellowship of slavery. **1869** W. P. MACKAY *Grace & Truth* (1875) 244 Christians can have fellowship with Christ..as the rejected of earth.

2. Companionship, company, society; an instance of this. Also, *to bear* (*a person*) *fellowship*; *to have, hold,* †*fall in, fellowship with* (*a person*).

c **1200** *Vices & Virtues* (1888) 41 Ðas ȝewerȝede gaste[s] felauscipe fram e[u]wȝ driuen. *a* **1225** *Ancr. R.* 160 Vor þi fleih sein Johan þe feolauschipe of fule men. *a* **1300** *Cursor M.* 12568 (Cott.) All þai felascip him bar. *a* **1340** HAMPOLE *Psalter* vi. 7, I dwelled lange in synn & in felaghschip of ill men. **1393** LANGL. *P. Pl.* C. IV. 155 For hue ys fayne of þy felaushep. **1449** ? M. PASTON in *Paston Lett.* I. 83 Purry felle in felaschepe with Willyum Hasard at Querles. *c* **1450** *Merlin* 218 The feliship of so worthi men is not to be refused. **1484** CAXTON *Æsop* I. vi, The poure ought not to hold felauship with the myghty. **1535** COVERDALE *Wisd.* viii. 16 Hir felawshipe hath no tediousnesse. **1607** SHAKS. *Cor.* v. iii. 175 He..kneeles, and holds vp hands for fellowship. **1690** LOCKE *Hum. Und.* III. i. §1 A necessity to have fellowship with those of his own kind. **1814** CARY *Dante's Parad.* VIII. 121 Were it worse for man, If he lived not in fellowship on earth? **1855** MACAULAY *Hist. Eng.* III. 404 The least respectable members of that party renounced fellowship with him.

transf. **1578** BANISTER *Hist. Man* v. 70 The fift veyne, being not depriued of the felowshyp of an Arterie.

†**b.** *collect.* Habitual companions; = COMPANY 4 b. *Obs.*

14.. *Tundale's Vis.* 183 This his thi felyschyp thou caytyff That thou chase to the in thi lyffe. **1548** FORREST *Pleas. Poesye* 90 They shull pluck too their societee, Feloshippe that neuer will after goode bee.

†**3.** Communication, dealing, intercourse. *Obs.*

1555 WATREMAN *Fardle Facions* II. ix. 202 As he iudgeth theim..by his eye..without further trade or feloweshippe betwixte theim. **1613** SHAKS. *Hen. VIII*, III. i. 121, I am old my Lords, And all the Fellowship I hold now with him Is onely my Obedience.

b. Mutual intercourse, *esp.* spiritual; intimate personal converse; = COMMUNION 2 a, b, c.

a **1300** *Cursor M.* 10401 (Cott.) Þir hundreth scepe..Bitakens felascip, i-wiss, Of halus hei in heuen bliss. *c* **1380** WYCLIF *Sel. Wks.* III. 422 [Þei] were translate to felowschippe and dwellyng wiþ Gods. *a* **1400** *Cov. Myst.* (1841) 16 Than Cryst them ovyrtok..And walkyd in felachep fforth with hem too. **1535** STEWART *Cron. Scot.* II. 144 But fallowschip of ony bot thame sell. **1611** BIBLE *Transl. Pref.* 3 The end and reward of the studie [of Scripture being] fellowship with the Saints. **1746–7** HERVEY *Medit.* (1818) 12 Who admits us to a fellowship with himself. **1871** MACDUFF *Mem. Patmos* ii. 23 Since John had last held visible fellowship with his Redeemer.

†**c.** Sexual intercourse. More fully *fleshly fellowship*. *Obs.*

13.. *E.E. Allit. P.* B. 271 Þe fende..fallen in felaȝschyp with hem on folken wyse. *c* **1400** MAUNDEV. (Roxb.) xvii. 77 When þai will hafe felischepe of men. *c* **1450** *Merlin* 7 We be made..to haue counfort and ioye of mannes felishep. **1450–1530** *Myrr. our Ladye* 191 He fledde the flesshely felyshyp of hys wyfe.

4. = COMMUNION 3. *to give the right hand of fellowship* (after Gal. ii. 9): to acknowledge a person as entitled to communion; also *transf.*

In several Protestant denominations, a literal giving 'the right hand of fellowship' by some representative person is part of the ceremony of admitting a person to church-membership, and of the ordination or induction of a minister.

1382 WYCLIF *Gal.* ii. 9 James and Cephas..and John ..ȝauen to me and Barnabas the riȝt hondis of felowschip. **1539** CRANMER *ibid.*, Ryght handes of that felouschippe. **1611** BIBLE *ibid.*, Right handes of fellowship. *a* **1649** WINTHROP *New Eng.* (1853) I. 215 The elder desired of the churches that..they would give them the right hand of fellowship. **1661** BRAMHALL *Just Vind.* i. 3 They haue separated them-selues..from the fellowship of their own Sisters. **1809–10** COLERIDGE *Friend* (1865) 57, I will honour and hold forth the right hand of fellowship to every individual who, etc. **1875** JOWETT *Plato* (ed. 2) III. 64 He shall receive the right hand of fellowship.

5. The spirit of comradeship; friendliness. *good fellowship* (parasynthetically): the temper and disposition of a 'good fellow'. So, *bad fellowship*. †*of fellowship*: out of friendly feeling.

c **1370** CHAUCER *Troylus* II. 157 He..wher hym lyst, best felawship can To such as hym thinkith able to thrive. **1462** *Paston Lett.* No. 445 II. 95 Hertely thankyng you..of the felyshipp that my cosyn your sonne shewid unto me. **1463** *Bury Wills* (Camden) 36 My beedys of jeet..for rememberaunce of old good felashipp. **1570** NORTH *Doni's Mor. Philos.* II. (1888) 117 First of fellowship heare me but foure wordes. **1604** JAS. I. *Counterbl.* (Arb.) 111 It is become ..a point of good fellowship. **1670** MAYNWARING *Vita Sana* vi. 67 Drink for necessity, not for bad fellowship. **1818** SHELLEY *Rosalind & Helen* 121 The birds..with fearless fellowship..round him wheel. **1837** W. IRVING *Capt. Bonneville* II. 86 The rival companies..prosecuted their journey in great good fellowship. **1863** GEO. ELIOT *Romola* (1880) I. 2 There must still be fellowship..for him among the inheritors of his birthplace.

†**b.** *collect. good fellowship* = 'good fellows'.

1647 CLARENDON *Hist. Reb.* VII. (1703) II. 225 Wilmot.. was..much belov'd by all the good fellowship of the Army.

6. A body of fellows or equals; a company. Now *rare* (*arch.*).

c **1290** *S. Eng. Leg.* I. 27/23 A felauȝschipe of quoynte Men. *a* **1300** *Cursor M.* 14249 (Cott.) Jesus..was cummen ..Wit his felauscip þat he ledd. *c* **1350** *Will. Palerne* 1317 But feiþli his felachipe forþ wiþ him he hadde. *c* **1386** CHAUCER *Prol.* 32, I was of hir felawschipe anon. *c* **1400** MAUNDEV. (Roxb.) ix. 34 Iosue and Caleph and þaire felyschepe come first. **1471** SIR J. PASTON in *Lett.* No. 675 III. 15 Sir Thomas Fulfforthe is goon owt off Sceyntewarye and a gret ffelaschyp ffettchyd hym. **1535** COVERDALE *Isa.* xliv. 10 Beholde all the felashippe of them must be brought to confucion. **1549** *Bk. Com. Prayer, Te Deum*, The goodly felowship [L. *numerus*] of the Prophetes. **1640** YORKE *Union Hon.* 27 With his sonne the young Prince of Wales, and a very noble fellowship. **1742** BAILEY, *Fellowship*, a Company. **1879** BUTCHER & LANG *Odyssey* 160 He went on his way and with him two and twenty of my fellowship.

transf. **1827** SCOTT *Jrnl.* (1890) I. 383, I am sorry when I think of the goodly fellowship of vessels which are now scattered on the ocean.

†**b.** A body of armed men. *Obs.*

c **1380** *Sir Ferumb.* 5313 A..takeþ til hym scheld & sperre ..Oþer felaschip ne takeþ he non. **1467** MARG. PASTON in *Lett.* No. 576 II. 308 He..sendyth dayly aspies to understand what felesshep kepe the place. *c* **1500** *Three Kings' Sons* 97 Therfore toke he his feliship, &..went to releef his first company.

†**c.** The crew of a vessel. *Obs.*

1466 *Mann. & Househ. Exp.* 169 My lorde..ȝafe..to the felschepe of the Kervel. **1513** DOUGLAS *Æneis* I. vi. 158 Thi schippis and fallowschip on the samyn wise.

d. In the Eucharistic service, the words *cum omni militia cælestis exercitus* have from an early date been rendered 'with all the holy fellowship of heaven'; possibly with some allusion to 6 b.

1389 in *Eng. Gilds* (1870) 116 In honʳ of ihesu crist..and al the holy felichipe of heuen. *c* **1450** *Bidding Prayer* iii. in *Lay Folks Mass Bk.* 71 All þe feir falychyp þat is in heuen. **1583** STANYHURST *Æneis* III. (Arb.) 90 Al the heunly feloship from the earth such a monster abandon.

†**e.** An ordinary meal or entertainment for a company or household. *Obs.*

1494 *Househ. Ord.* 121 As for the Shrove Thursday at night there longeth none estate to be kepte, but onely a fellowshippe.

7. A guild, corporation, company. Now *rare*. *fellowship of porters*: see 11 b.

1515 SIR R. JERNEGAN in Strype *Eccl. Mem.* I. App. vii. 13 The same passport may be sent..to the Master of the fellowship. **1523** *Act 14–15 Hen. VIII*, c. 2 All wardens and maisters of felowshyppes of all and euery such handie craftes. **1560** *Grant of City of Lond.* 1 Feb. in Entick *London* (1766) IV. 228 Being freemen of this city in the fellowship of the stationers. **1622** MISSELDEN *Free Trade* (ed. 2) 74 That..fellowship of the Merchants Adventurers of England. **1692** *Lond. Gaz.* No. 2799/4 Mr. Thomas Johnson Clerk to the Fellowship of Carmen. **1740** in Hanway *Trav.* (1762) I. I. ix. 43 Any subject..hath a right to be made free of the said fellowship. **1819** E. MACKENZIE *Hist. Newcastle* (1827) 706 *note*, Waits, or Musicians, were an ancient fellowship.

transf. *a* **1626** BP. ANDREWES *Serm.* (1661) 700 A fellowship or Society, which is called the fellowship or corporation of the Gospell.

†**b.** *collect.* The members of a corporation or guild. *Obs.*

c **1440** *Gesta Rom.* xi. 35 (Add. MS.) His felishipp put out his eyen. **1513** *Act 5 Hen. VIII*, c. 6 The Wardens and felisshippe of the crafte..of Surgeons enfraunchesid in the Citie of London. **1571** in W. H. Turner *Select. Rec. Oxford* 335 The Master Wardens..and Fellowship of the sayde occupation. **1649** *Lawfulnesse Present Govt.* 9 The Mayor of London and his Fellowship received him.

c. In wider sense: An association or union of any kind; also a brotherhood, fraternity.

1541 BARNES *Wks.* (1573) 246/1 Wee beleeue..that holy church is a communion or felowshyp of holy men. **1683** in *Faithful Contendings* (1780) 59 It was desired that every one of the fellowships that sends Commissioners..would be conscientious in choosing of them. **1775** JOHNSON *West. Islands* Wks. X. 424 Land is sometimes leased to a small fellowship. **1847** MRS. A. KERR *Hist. Servia* x. 191 The peaceful fellowships in villages..had also the right. **1861** MILL *Utilit.* v. 90 A person's fitness to exist as one of the fellowship of human beings. **1883** O. B. FROTHINGHAM in Schaff *Encycl. Relig. Knowl.* 2381 The public..gave to the little fellowship the name of the 'Transcendental Club'. **1889** *Lux Mundi* iv. (1890) 178 Building up a new cosmopolitan fellowship.

8. The position or dignity, or the emoluments, of a 'fellow' in a college, university, learned society, etc.

1536 *Act 27 Hen. VIII*, c. 42 §1 in *Oxf. & Camb. Enactm.* 13 The said..Chauntries, free Chapelle Felowshippes, Scolershippes. **1631** T. POWELL *Tom All Trades* 148 In some Colledges the Fellowship follows the Schollership. *a* **1674** CLARENDON *Hist. Reb.* x. (1704) III. 56 They placed ..such other of the same leven in the Fellowships. **1868** *Med. Jrnl.* XIX. 271 He had it in contemplation..to offer himself a candidate for a fellowship in the London College of Physicians. **1868** M. PATTISON *Academ. Org.* iv. 57 The proposal to commute fellowships into scholarships.

†**b.** *collect.* The body of 'fellows' in a college or university; the society constituted by the 'fellows'. *Obs.*

1480 *Bury Wills* (1850) 58 The seid maistʳ, presedent, or reuler, and phelaschep of the seid collage. **1567** in Gutch *Coll. Cur.* II. 278 The said Richard Barber..shall call the whole fellowship then present within the College together. **1710** HEARNE *Collect.* (Oxf. Hist. Soc.) III. 53 Any one that ever entered that Fellowship. **1796** MORSE *Amer. Geog.* I. 437 Adjudging and conferring degrees, which exclusively belongs to the fellowship as a learned faculty.

9. *Arith.* The process by which a partner's share of gain or loss is determined in proportion to his share of the capital.

1561 RECORDE *Gr. Artes* Yj, Thus you are.. sufficiently instructed in the rule of felowship. **1594** BLUNDEVIL *Exerc.* I. xii. (ed. 7) 36 This is to be wrought according to the Rule of fellowship. **1661** HODDER *Arithmetick* 148 The Rule of Fellowship without time. **1695** ALINGHAM *Geom. Epit.* 66 This *Theo.* helps to demonstrate the Rule of Fellowship. **1806** HUTTON *Course Math.* I. 120 Fellowship is either Single or Double. **1859** BARN. SMITH *Arith. & Algebra* (ed. 6) 508 Fellowship or Partnership.

10. *pl.* Short for *fellowship-porters.* (See 11 b.)

1865 DICKENS *Mut. Fr.* I. vi, The Fellowships don't want you at all.

11. *attrib.* and *Comb.*, (sense 7) as ***fellowship-merchant***; (sense 8) as ***fellowship-examination, -honour***; also, **fellowship-meeting**, an association formed for the purpose of religious converse.

1866 MRS. GASKELL *Wives & Dau.* I. 307, I shall be going up for my *fellowship examination. **1893** *Daily News* 7 July 11/3 The only American woman, holding the *fellowship honour of the Royal Geographical Society. **1679** J. FINLAY IN *Cloud of Witnesses* (1810) 185, I bear my testimony to the *fellowship meetings of the Lord's people. **1806** FORSYTH *Beauties Scot.* III. 176 All the fellowship-meetings of the parish of Cambuslang assembled. **1485** *Act 1 Hen. VII*, c. 3 §1 No proteccion be.. allowed in the Courte before the .. *Felishipp merchauntes of the Staple at Calais.

b. fellowship porter, a member of the 'fellowship' of the Porters of Billingsgate, a guild having certain monopolies in the City of London; see quots.

There was also a Guild of Fellowship Porters in Edinburgh, who joined the Trone-men in 1694 (Walford *Hist. Gilds* 87).

1620 *Draft Act Common Council* 5 Oct. in *Acts & Rep. Com. Council* (Guildhall Lib.) No. 4 That the Company and ffellowship of Porters of Billingsgate.. shall.. continue to be from henceforth one Company or Brotherhood. **1681** DELAUNE *State of London* 341 The Porters of London are of two sorts. 1. Ticket Porters.. 2. Fellowship Porters. To these belong the.. landing, housing, carrying or recarrying all measurable Goods, as Corn, Salt, Coals, &c. **1854** *Rep. Parl. Comm. Corporation of London* 23 The Fellowship of Porters, which exists as a separate body, created by an Act of Common Council. No person can be admitted as a Fellow of this body who is not free of the City of London. **1890** *Daily News* 18 July 7/2 The complainant is a fellowship porter.

fellowship ('fɛləʊʃɪp), *v.* [f. prec. sb.]

†**1.** *trans.* To unite in fellowship; to connect or associate (a person or thing) *with* or *to* another; *refl.* to enter into companionship. *Obs.*

c **1374** CHAUCER *Boeth.* II. vi. 53 Contrarious þinges ne ben not wont to ben yfelawshiped togidres. **1382** WYCLIF *Gen.* xxvi. 7 She was to hym felowshipte thur3 mariage. *c* **1440** *Secrees* 182 Twoo men þat felawschipped hem to gedre in a way. **1491** CAXTON *Vitas Patr.* (W. de W. 1495) I. xlix. 98 a/1 They can not be compatyble ne felyshypped wyth the other. **1561** T. HOBY tr. *Castiglione's Courtyer* Yy iv b, To felowship him self.. with men of the best sort.

†**2.** To accompany. *Obs.*

c **1374** CHAUCER *Boeth.* IV. iii. 121 Grete peyne felawshipeþ and folweþ hem. **1483** CAXTON *Gold. Leg.* 405/1, I shal yet felawship the unto the gate.

3. To admit to fellowship, enter into fellowship with. Now only in religious use.

c **1440** *Gesta Rom.* xxxiv. 135 (Harl. MS.) Then pes seynge hir sistris alle in acorde.. she turnid ayene.. then pes was felashipid among hem. *a* **1860** *Eclectic Rev.* (Worcester), Whom he had openly fellowshipped. **1882** A. MAHAN *Autobiog.* xi. 242 A charity which fellowshipped anything.

4. *intr.* To join in fellowship; to associate *with.* Now only in religious use, and chiefly U.S.

c **1410** LOVE *Bonavent. Mirr.* lvi. (Gibbs MS.) Oure lorde Jesu came.. and felischippede with hem. **1472** in *Surtees Misc.* (1890) 26 Derrick his lepere, & his not abyll to felychep emange the pepell. **1561** T. HOBY *Castiglione's Courtyer* A iij b, Like maye fellowship.. with his like. **1883-4** J. G. BUTLER *Bible-Work* II. 109 He [Peter] fellowshipped freely with Gentile believers. **1886** *Chr. Life* 1 May, He never fellowshipped with any of our churches.

Hence **'fellowshipping** *vbl. sb.*, the action of forming a fellowship; in quot. *concr.* as the alleged proper term for a company of yeomen.

1486 *Bk. St. Albans* F vj a, A ffelishippyng of yomen.

,fellow-'soldier. One who fights under the same standard as another; a companion-in-arms.

1526-34 TINDALE *Phil.* ii. 25 Epaphroditus.. my.. felowe soudier. **1593** SHAKS. 3 *Hen. VI*, IV. vii. 70 Come, fellow Souldior, make thou proclamation. **1777** W. ROBERTSON *Hist. Amer.* (1783) II. 244 To avoid the imputation of cowardice from their fellow-soldiers. **1882** J. TAYLOR *Sc. Covenanters* 161 He met with his former fellow-soldier.

,fellow-'traveller. [FELLOW *sb.* 11 b.] **1.** One who travels along with another.

1611 T. CORYAT *Crudities* (Epist. Dedic.), Often disswaded by some of my fellow trauellers from gathering any Obseruations at all till I came into Italie. **1665** SIR T. HERBERT *Trav.* 125 Elpenor his fellow-traveller being dead. **1711** ADDISON *Spect.* No. 58 ¶12 The Impatience of my Friends and Fellow-Travellers. **1829** LYTTON *Devereux* IV. viii, My veteran fellow-traveller took leave of me. **1814** WORDSWORTH *Excursion* II. 55 My Fellow Traveller said with earnest voice, As if the thought were but a moment old, That I must yield myself without reserve. **1850** —— *Prelude* VI. 161 The brook and road Were fellow-travellers in this gloomy strait.

2. *transf.* One who sympathizes with the Communist movement without actually being a party member. Also in extended uses.

The equiv. Russ. *popútchik* (Trotsky) was used of non-communist writers sympathizing with the Revolution.

1936 *Nation* (N.Y.) 24 Oct. 471/1 The new phenomenon is the fellow-traveler. The term has a Russian background and means someone who does not accept all your aims but has enough in common with you to accompany you in a comradely fashion part of the way. In this campaign both Mr. Landon and Mr. Roosevelt have acquired fellow-travelers. **1941** AUDEN *New Year Let.* II. 39 A liberal fellow traveller ran With sansculotte and Jacobin Nor guessed what circles he was in. **1942** E. WAUGH *Put out More Flags* ii. 131 'I was never a party member.' 'Party?' 'Communist party. I was what they call in their horrible jargon, a fellow traveller.' **1946** [see CRYPTO]. **1952** A. WILSON *Hemlock & After* 147 Bernard, if not a fellow-traveller, was certainly the perfect material for Communist propaganda. **1957** S. JAMESON *Cup of Tea for Mr. Thorgill* vi. 48 He was also, quite openly, a fellow-traveller, going faithfully through all the rites: adoration of Russia, reverence for that fabled Beast, *the proletariat.* **1964** C. CHAPLIN *Autobiogr.* xxix. 491 They were carrying signs that read: 'Chaplin's a fellow traveller.' **1969** L. WOOLF *Journey not Arrival Matters* iii. 139 He was distinctly a Fellow Traveller, and may, for all I knew, have been a member of the Communist Party.

Hence (as a back-formation) **fellow-travel** *v. intr.*, to be a fellow-traveller; *trans.*, to support (the Communist movement) as a fellow-traveller; freq. as **fellow-travelling** *vbl. sb.* and *ppl. a.*

1858 (*title*) Fellow travelling; or, The experience of life. **1941** *Time* 31 Mar. 42 The Communist fellow-traveling American Peace Mobilization. *Ibid.* 30 June 42 His fellow-traveling had done him no good with the brass hats. **1948** *Ann. Reg.* *1947* 240 Those [of the Left] who.. would have no taint of 'fellow-travelling', broke with Mr. Wallace. **1949** *Life* 4 Apr. 39/1 Its host was the U.S.'s own National Council of Arts, Sciences and Professions, dominated by intellectuals who fellow-travel the Communist line. **1963** *Observer* 18 Aug. 20/8 The Germans who fellow-travelled with Hitler in the 1930s were guilty of a gross dereliction of national duty. **1964** 'W. HAGGARD' *Anatagonists* iii. 29 The high rich Left.. [would] talk and they'd fellow-travel but they'd never know the passion.

†**'felly**, *a. Obs.* [f. FELL *a.* + -LY[1].] = FELL.

1401 *Pol. Poems* (Rolls) II. 17 The felliest folke that ever Antichrist found. **1749** *Exile's Lament.* in *Jacobite Songs & Ballads* (1887) 263 Driven by fortune's felly spite.

felly ('fɛlɪ), *adv.* Forms: 3 fellik, 4 fellely, 4-5 fellich(e, (4 fell liche, fellyche), 4-6 felli(e, (6 fellye), 4- felly. *Compar.* 4 fellaker. [f. FELL *a.* + -LY[2].] In a fell manner.

1. Fiercely, cruelly, harshly; with deadly malignity or destructive effect.

a **1300** *Cursor M.* 4143 (Cott.) Ful fellik þai a-gain answard, 'Quar-for suld we of oght be ferd?' *a* **1340** HAMPOLE *Psalter* lxxvii. 53 Temptacioun þat felly smytes þe hertes of foles. **1340** *Ayenb.* 174 þe more he him smit þe more fellaker: huanne he him yziȝþ onlosti and sleauuol. *c* **1440** *Gaw. & Gol.* 576 The feght sa felly thai fang. **1481** CAXTON *Reynard* (Arb.) 89 The kyng hier saith so felly, that my fadre nor I dyde hym neuer good. **1555** WATREMAN *Fardle Facions* II. viii. 179 The more thei haue, the fellier gnaweth their longing. **1566** DRANT *Horace' Sat.* II. iii, With feuer quartayne, felly toste. **1567** H. MORE *Song of Soul* I. II. xxvii, The hearts do ne're agree But felly one another do upbray. **1748** THOMSON *Cast. Indol.* II. xliii, He sat him felly down and gnaw'd his bitter nail. **1802** G. COLMAN *Br. Grins, Knt. & Friar* I. liii, In the Field, where late he fought so felly. **1811** SCOTT *Don Roderick* li, Never hath the harp of minstrel rung Of faith so felly proved, so firmly true! **1866** READE *Griffith Gaunt* xxv, He tore the purse out of Leonard's hand: then seized him felly by the throat.

b. †Bitterly, keenly; terribly (*obs.*); hence *dial.* exceedingly.

1375 BARBOUR *Bruce* x. 479 He wes Woundit so felly in the face, That he wes dredand of his lif. *Ibid.* XVI. 217 Thai war so felly fleyit thar That [etc.]. *a* **1400-50** *Alexander* 3647 Oure mody kyng of Messedone.. Seis þaim faile so ethfully and felly was greued. **1583** STANYHURST *Aeneis* II. (Arb.) 58 They clymb, in lefthand, with shieldes, tools felye rebating. **1807** J. STAGG *Poems* 37 They ran.. Till a' war felly spent.

†**2.** Craftily, cunningly, artfully. *Obs.*

1382 WYCLIF *Josh.* ix. 4 Thei that dwelten in Gabaon.. fellich thenkynge, token to hem meetis [etc.]. **1387** TREVISA *Higden* (Rolls) II. 317 þerfore he byþouȝt hym felliche and gilefulliche to bere a doun þe children of Israel. *c* **1400** *Beryn* 311 With half a sclepy eye pourid fellich vndir hir hood. **1450-1530** *Myrr. our Ladye* 44 The more effectuall.. that prayer is.. the more felly.. laboureth the malycyous enemy to lette it.

felly ('fɛlɪ), *v. dial.* [variant of FALLOW *v.*[2]]

1788 W. MARSHALL *Yorksh.* Gloss., *Felly*, to break up a fallow. **1876** *Whitby Gloss.*, *Felly*, to break up the fallow ground, to plough up the stubble before sowing the crop.

felly, alternative form of FELLOE.

‖**felo-de-se** (,fɛləʊ diː 'siː) Pl. felones-, felos-de-se. [Anglo-Lat. *felō* FELON, *dē sē* of himself.]

1. One who 'deliberately puts an end to his own existence, or commits any unlawful malicious act, the consequence of which is his own death' (Blackstone).

[*c* **1250** BRACTON III. II. xxxi, Eodem modo quo quis feloniam facere possit interficiendo alium, ita feloniam facere possit interficiendo seipsum, quæ quidem felonia dicitur fieri de seipso.] **1651** G. W. tr. *Cowel's Inst.* 124 He that murders himself, is by us termed *Felo de se.* **1689** HICKERINGILL *Modest Inq.* iv. 30 How desperately they stabb themselves, and are *Felones de se.* **1814** BYRON in Moore *Life* (1875) 421 That 'felo de se' who.. Walk'd out of his depth and was lost in a calm sea. **1874** G. W. DASENT *Half a Life* I. 85 Dick.. pronounced him.. to be, in fact, felo de se.

b. *fig.*

1678 *Lively Orac.* iii. 40 Making their Natures a kind of *felo de se* to prompt the destroying itself. **1704** E. WARD *Dissenting Hypocrite* 34 That Church is Moderate and Easy T' excess, which would be Felo de se. **1749** FIELDING *Tom Jones* VIII. xiv, That Protestants.. should be.. such Felos de se, I cannot believe it. **1767** BLACKSTONE *Comm.* II. 31 This *modus* is *felo de se* and destroys itself. **1840** DE QUINCEY *Style* Wks. 1862 X. 164 A man who [etc.].. would be a madman and a felo-de-se, as respected his reliance upon that doctrine.

attrib. **1826** *Edin. Rev.* XLV. 171 This felo de se system.

c. In etymological nonce-use (see quot.).

1670 CLARENDON *Ess.* Tracts (1727) 198 He is literally *felo de se*, who deprives and robs himself of that which no body but himself can rob him of.

2. A case to which the verdict 'felo de se' is appropriate; self-murder, suicide.

1771 E. LONG *Trial of Dog 'Porter'* in Hone *Every-day Bk.* II. 205 Your worships should incline to deem it a *felo de se.* **1840** HOOD *Up the Rhine* 202 Werther, who brought *felo-de-se* into vogue. **1883** S. C. HALL *Retrospect* I. 45 The 'crowner's quest' had pronounced the wretched creature guilty of felo-de-se.

felon ('fɛlən), *a.* and *sb.*[1] Forms: α. 3-5 feloun(e, -un(e, 4-6 felown(e, *Sc.* felloun(e, 5 felone, (feleyn), 6-8 fellon(e, 3- felon. β. (in adj. only) 4-5 felo(u)ns; cf. *felunsly* s.v. FELONLY. [a. OF. *felon* adj. and sb. = Pr. *felon, felhon, fellon* adj., Sp. *fellon*, It. *fellone* adj. and sb.:—vulgar L. **fellōn-em.* From its formation, the word must have been originally a sb., *fel* (:—*'fello*), whence FELL *a.*, being the subj. case, and *felon* (:—*fe'llōn-*) the obj. case; but so far as documentary evidence goes, both forms were indiscriminately used in OF. as adj., and the recorded subst. use of the latter is derivative. The curious Eng. form *felouns* adj. may perh. be due (like *fiers* FIERCE) to the *-s* of the nom. case in OF. (in this instance a product of analogy).

The ultimate etymology is uncertain. Of the many conjectures proposed the most probable is that *fellōne-m* is a derivative of L. *fell-, fel* gall, the original sense being 'one who, or something which, is full of bitterness' (or 'venom', the two notions, as many linguistic facts show, being closely associated in the popular mind). In support of this view it may be pointed out that the sb. has had the senses of 'an envenomed sore' and 'cholera' (see FELON *sb.*[2]); moreover, this etymology accounts perfectly for the strangely divergent senses which the adj. has in the Rom. langs.: 'wicked', 'angry', 'brave', 'melancholy, sad' (It. *fellone*), 'intensely painful'. Of the other suggestions that have been made the most plausible is perhaps that of Prof. R. Atkinson of Dublin, that *fello* was originally a term of obscene abuse, f. L. *fellāre* as used in a peculiar sense by Martial and Catullus. Some scholars think that *fello* is from OHG. **fillo*, an unrecorded derivative of *fillen* to scourge (cf. med.L. *fillo* rascal); others have sought to connect it with the obscure second element in the OE. words *wælfel* (from *wæl* carnage; occurring only once, as an epithet of the raven) and *ælfæle, ealfelo* (usually supposed to be from *eal* all; only twice, as an epithet of *áttor* poison). The mod.Da. *fæl* horrible, disgusting, has also been compared; the MDu. *fel* is adopted from Fr. The Celtic words often cited are out of the question; the OF. word cannot have come from Wales or Ireland, and Gaulish appears not to have possessed the sound *f*; the Welsh *ff* and the Irish *f* do not correspond etymologically.]

A. *adj.*

1. Of persons and animals, their actions, feelings, etc.: Cruel, fierce, terrible; wicked, base. Now *poet.*

a **1300** *Cursor M.* 1160 (Cott.) Quen felauscipe.. Mought te drau fra felon dede. *Ibid.* 5896 (Cott.) It become a worme felon. **1375** BARBOUR *Bruce* I. 47 Enwy, that is sa feloune. *c* **1489** CAXTON *Blanchardyn* liii. 205 So bigan they to smyte amonge their felon enmyes. **1513** DOUGLAS *Æneis* XIII. i. 95 Hys felloun fa is kyllit thus. **1549** *Compl. Scot.* Prol. 14 Fechtand be fellone forse. ? *a* **1550** *Freiris of Berwik* 553 in *Dunbar's Poems* (1893) 303 With that Symone a felloun flap lait fle. **1575** J. STILL *Gamm. Gurton* I. iii. in Hazl. *Dodsley* III. 179 Perchance some felon spirit may haunt our house indeed. **1687** DRYDEN *Hind & P.* III. 1170 Courtesies.. No gratitude in felon minds beget. **1725** POPE *Odyss.* IX. 712 Vain shews of love to veil his felon hate. **1735** THOMSON *Liberty* IV. 1189 The felon undermining Hand Of dark Corruption. **1813** BYRON *Giaour* 677 The steel Which taught the felon heart to feel. **1855** SINGLETON *Virgil* I. 33 Both gods and stars the mother felon calls.

β. *c* **1340** *Cursor M.* 9973 (Trin.) Mary mayden.. stondeþ for shelde & targe aȝeines alle oure felouns foo. *c* **1440** *York Myst.* xi. 39 Tho felons folke [Jewes] Sir, first was fonn In kyng Pharo ȝoure fadyr dayse. *a* **1450** *Knt. de la Tour* 14 Curtesye.. aught to refraine felons proude herte of man and woman.

b. *transf.* Of things and places: Savage, wild; (of weapons) murderous.

c **1320** *Sir Tristr.* 1446 Wiþ a spere feloun He smot him in þe side. *c* **1450** *Merlin* 269 It semed by her armes that thei were come from felon place. **1513** DOUGLAS *Æneis* IV. x. 19 And felloun stormis of ire gan hir to schaik. **1566** DRANT *Horace' Sat.* vii. D vj b, The fellone tongue of Rupilie. **1637** MILTON *Lycidas* 91 He asked.. the felon winds, What hard mishap had doomed this gentle swain? **1781** COWPER *Truth* 445 Often unbelief.. Flies to the tempting pool, or felon knife. *c* **1800** K. WHITE *Lett.* (1837) 204 To snatch the victim from thy felon wave. **1814** SCOTT *Massacre Glencoe* 26 The hand that mingled in the meal, At midnight drew the felon steel.

†**c.** Angry, sullen. *Obs.*

c 1374 CHAUCER *Troylus* v. 199 With felon [It. *fellone*] look and face dispitouse. 1567 DRANT *Horace' Epist.* II. 63 Like a woolfe..Incensd, with fellon fasting face.

†2. Brave, courageous, sturdy. *Obs.*

1375 BARBOUR *Bruce* VIII. 454 He wes bath ȝoung, stout, and felloun. 1596 DALRYMPLE tr. *Leslie's Hist. Scot.* II. (1887) 131 Fergus..is namet first King of Scottis..for his fellowne fortitude.

†3. 'Terribly' great, 'tremendous', huge. *Sc. Obs.*

c 1450 HENRYSON *Mor. Fab.* 74 The man..was in an felloun fray. 1513 DOUGLAS *Æneis* v. iii. 30 The busteus barge, yclepit Chimera Gyas with felloun fard furth brocht alswa. 1536 BELLENDEN *Cron. Scot.* (1821) I. p. xxxvii, With ane fellon stoure. *c* 1570 *Sat. Poems Reform.* xx. 25 In felloun feir at me thay speir. *a* 1605 POLWART *Flyting w. Montgomerie* 208 Fore store of lambes and lang-tailde wedders..In fellon flockes.

†4. With sense derived from the sb.: Feloniously acquired, stolen. *Obs. rare*$^{-1}$.

1631 FULLER *David's Hainous Sinne* xix. (D.), Whose greedy pawes with fellon goods were found.

B. *sb.*[1]

†1. A vile or wicked person, a villain, wretch, monster. Sometimes applied to the Devil or an evil spirit. *Obs.*

a 1300 *Cursor M.* 11481 (Gött.) Herodes, þat fals feloune. *Ibid.* 12982 (Gött.) 'Ne seis þu noght', said þe felune. 1340 *Ayenb.* 29 Þe uour werreres þet þe feloun hep. *a* 1400 *Octouian* 943 He..bad hym fynd a champioun To feyght with that foule feloun. 1485 CAXTON *Chas. Gt.* 100 The frenssh men ben moche felons. 1594 CAREW *Tasso* (1881) 27 This fellon then his made rage tempereth. 1697 DRYDEN *Virg. Æneid* VI. 804 He, the King of Heav'n..Down to the deep Abyss the flaming Felon strook. 1814 SCOTT *Ld. of Isles* III. xxiv, Yet sunk the felon's moody ire Before Lord Ronald's glance of fire.

†2. In good sense: A brave man, a warrior. *Obs. rare.*

a 1400-50 *Alexander* 819* Fers felons with hym fangez & florens enowe.

3. *Law.* One who has committed felony.

1297 R. GLOUC. (Rolls) 9668 Al þat þe felon hath, þe kinges it is. 1393 LANGL. *P. Pl.* C. XI. 240 Þauh þe fader be a frankelayne and for a felon be hanged. *c* 1460 *Play Sacram.* 505 Hold prestly [?] on thys feleyn & faste bynd him to a poste. 1467 in *Eng. Gilds* (1870) 389 Mansleers, ffelons, Outlawes. 1526 *Pilgr. Perf.* (W. de W. 1531) 301 They dyd leade the bounden as they do theues or felons. 1575 *Nottingham Rec.* IV. 158 Ralfe the felon that brake Maister Askewe house. 1592 SHAKS. *Rom. & Jul.* v. iii. 69, I do.. apprehend thee for a Fellon here. 1683 *Col. Rec. Pennsylv.* I. 72 It was proposed that no fellons be brought into this Contrey. 1728 POPE *Dunc.* I. 281 With less reading than makes felons scape. 1796 BURKE *Regic. Peace* Wks. 1842 II. 318 A gang of felons and murderers. 1818 CRUISE *Digest* (ed. 2) III. 267 Pursued with hue and cry as a felon. 1878 EMERSON *Misc. Papers, Fort. Republic* Wks. (Bohn) III. 398 The felon is the logical extreme of the epicure and coxcomb.

transf. 1735 SOMERVILLE *Chase* III. 168 Each sounding Horn proclaims the Felon [a Fox] dead. 1768-74 TUCKER *Lt. Nat.* (1852) I. 26 All this we ascribe to Roger, for we say he brought down the felon [a hawk].

†b. *felon-de-se, felon of oneself*: = FELO-DE-SE.

1648 BP. HALL *Sel. Thoughts* §34 Nothing is more odious amongst men than for a man to be a felon of himself. 1655 FULLER *Ch. Hist.* v. i. §3 A stake is..the monument generally erected for Felons de Se. 1678 MARVELL *Growth Popery* Wks. 1875 IV. 322 If a House [of Parliament] shall once be felon of itself and stop its own breath.

†4. = FELONY 1, 2. *Obs.*

c 1325 *Cursor M.* 22861 (Edin.) Þoru þair feloun and þair sine. *c* 1340 *Ibid.* 13244 (Fairf.) To þe Iewes fulle of feloun til ham he made his sarmoun.

5. *attrib.* and *Comb.*, as *felon-bushranger, felon-worshipper*; **felon-setter** (*Anglo-Irish*), a thief-taker. Also **felon-setting** *vbl. sb.* (see quots.).

1859 CORNWALLIS *New World* I. 99 A country infested with *felon bushrangers of the most desperate character. 1864 *People* (Dublin) Feb., The Irish people believe that Mr. Sullivan has more than once acted the part of a *felon-setter. 1890 *Pall Mall G.* 20 Sept. 4/3 The *felon-setting policy in which they have been engaged for a long time past. 1922 JOYCE *Ulysses* 626 Refuse to have anything to do with them..and their felonsetting. 1970 *Guardian* 6 June 11/7 Felon setting is a peculiarly Irish term, which recalls a deep and ancient hatred of the informer, a central figure in Irish history. It is felon setting to whisper to the Guards or the Special Branch about what the boys are up to. To some, apparently, it was felon setting for Jack Lynch to pass the documents in the arms affair to the Attorney-General. 1857 *Sat. Rev.* III. 272/1 There appear to be three great classes of *felon-worshippers.

felon ('fɛlən), *sb.*[2] Also fellon. [Perh. a. OF. **felon*; a 16th c. quot. in Godef. s.v. has *felons* app. corresponding to *ulceribus* in the L. original; but the translation is loose, and the word may mean 'cholera', as in Cotgr.; cf. quot. *c* 1116 below. The sense is consistent with derivation from L. *fell-, fel* gall; see FELON *a.* and *sb.*[1]]

1. A small abscess or boil, an inflamed sore.

[?*c* 1116 RADULPHUS *Ep. ad Elyenses* in *Acta SS.* V. (1867) 468 Morbus, quem vulgo fellonem nuncupant, felle suo viroso me miserum graviter occupavit. (The disease, described in absurdly bombastic terms, seems to have been a scrofulous swelling of the neck.)] 1340 HAMPOLE *Pr. Consc.* 2995 Kylles and felouns and apostyms. 14.. *Lat. Eng. Voc.* in Wr.-Wülcker 564 Antrax, the felon. 14.. *Pict. Voc.* ibid. 791 *Hec Antrax*, a felun, bleyn. *c* 1440 *Promp. Parv.* 154/2 Felone, soore, *antrax.* 1547 BOORDE *Brev. Health* xxiv. 15 b. In Englyshe it is named a Felon, and is lyke a Carbocle. 1689 MOYLE *Sea Chyrurg.* II. xxv. 80 To ripen these Boyles and Felons apply this Cataplasme. 1740 BERKELEY *Let.* Wks. 1871 IV. 263 What you call a felon is called in the books a phlegmon. 1826 J. WILLIAMS *Last Legacy* 11 Felons..or any such tumor on the hands or feet or elsewhere. 1880 *E. Cornwall Gloss., Fellon*, inflammation.

b. *esp.* A whitlow under or near the nail of a finger or toe.

1578 LYTE *Dodoens* VI. lxix. 747 The felons or noughtie sores which rise about the toppes of toes and fingers. 1667 SIR W. WILLOUGHBY in *Lauderdale Papers* (1885) II. xx. 28, I am trubled..wth an effeminate desease called a ffellon on my fore finger. 1746 HOWELL in *Phil. Trans.* XLIV. 228 The Fellon, or worst kind of Whitflow. 1874 HARDY *Madding Crowd* xxxii, He's had that felon upon his finger.

2. With reference to animals: **a.** in prec. sense, **b.** (see quot. 1855).

c 1450 *Bk. Hawkyng* in *Rel. Ant.* I. 301 A wykked felone is swolle of such maner coverte that no man may it hele, that the hawke schal not dye. 1595 MARKHAM *Bk. St. Albans* I. 23 If your hawke haue a felon swolne on her. 1748 tr. *Vegetius' Distemp. Horses* 62 He will have Fellons or small Biles in his Back. 1842 C. W. JOHNSON *Farmer's Encycl., Felon*..In farriery, a term for a sort of inflammation in animals, similar to that of whitlow in the human subject. 1855 ROBINSON *Whitby Gloss., Fellon*, the soreness of a cow's skin from cold or checked perspiration.

3. *attrib.* In various names of plants, herbs, etc., as **felon-berry** (see quot. 1715); **felon-grass** (*a*) *Imperatoria Ostruthium* (? miscalled 'angelica' in quot. 1824); (*b*) *Helleborus niger*; (*c*) *Geranium Robertianum*; **felon-herb** (see quot. 1878); **felon-weed**, *Senecio Jacobæa*; **felon-wood**, (*a*) *Solanum Dulcamara*; (*b*) *Imperatoria Ostruthium*; **felon-wort** (see quot. 1878).

a 1715 BUDDLE *MS.* in Britten & Holland *Plant-n.*, *Fellon-berry, *Bryonia dioica.* 1824-80 JAMIESON, *Fellin-grass, the plant called Angelica. 1878 BRITTEN & HOLLAND *Plant-n., Fellon Grass. Ibid.*, *Fellon-herb, (1) *Artemisia vulgaris*..(2) *Hieracium Pilosella.* 1579 LANGHAM *Gard. Health* (1633) 577 It healeth felons..It is called *fellon-weede. 1878 BRITTEN & HOLLAND *Plant-n., Fellon-weed.* 1861 MISS PRATT *Flower. Pl.* IV. 70 (Woody Nightshade or Bittersweet)..The plant is in some places called *Felon-wood. 1878 BRITTEN & HOLLAND *Plant-n., Fellon-wood.* 1706 PHILLIPS (ed. Kersey), *Felon-wort, an Herb. 1878 BRITTEN & HOLLAND *Plant-n., Fellon-wort*, (1) *Solanum Dulcamara*..(2) *Chelidonium majus*..(3) *Imperatoria Ostruthium*..(4) *Geranium Robertianum.*

feloness ('fɛlənɪs). *rare.* [f. FELON *sb.*[1] + -ESS.] A female felon.

1845 BROWNING *Flight Duchess*, His mother's yellowness ..When she heard what she called the flight of the feloness.

†**fe'lonian**, *sb. Obs. rare*$^{-1}$. [f. FELON-Y + -IAN.] = FELON.

1594 ? GREENE *Selimus* Wks. XIV. 266 These are some felonians, that seeke to rob me.

felonious (fɛ'ləʊnɪəs), *a.* [f. FELONY + -OUS.]

1. Wicked, atrociously criminal. Cf. FELON *a.*, FELONOUS. Now chiefly *poet.*

1575 J. STILL *Gamm. Gurton* III. iii. in Hazl. *Dodsley* III. 219 Diccons devil..Of Cat and Chat, and Doctor Rat, a felonious tale did tell. 1593 SHAKS. *2 Hen. VI*, III. i. 129 Vnlesse it were a bloody Murtherer, Or foule felonious Theefe. 1599 *Warn. Faire Wom.* II. 1206 How sayest thou to these fellonious murders, art thou guilty or not guilty? 1601 HOLLAND *Pliny* II. 12 The wicked rable..committed such fellonious outrages, as [etc.]. 1651 SIR H. WOTTON in Ellis *Orig. Lett.* Ser. I. III. 254 *note*, That felonious conception. *c* 1750 SHENSTONE *Elegies* vii. 63 Does not felonious Envy bar the road? 1827 POLLOK *Course T.* IX. 204 With most felonious aim.

2. *Law.* Of or pertaining to felony; of the nature of felony. Hence, in popular lang. of an act or purpose: Thievish.

1634 MILTON *Comus* 196 O thievish night! Why should'st thou, but for some felonious end, In thy dark lantern thus close up the stars? 1769 BLACKSTONE *Comm.* IV. 188 Felonious homicide..the killing of a human creature.. without justification or excuse. *Ibid.* IV. 227 Such breaking and entry must be with a felonious intent. *c* 1780 ERSKINE *Sp. Trial Lord G. Gordon* (1810) I. 82 A felonious riot. 1812 SIR H. DAVY *Chem. Philos.* 14 An act was passed..making them felonious. 1869 *Pall Mall G.* 5 Oct. 7 Condemning the appropriation of tenants' improvements as 'felonious'.

b. Of a person: That has committed felony.

1857 *Sat. Rev.* III. 271/2 He sees no longer the respectable..Mr. Redpath, but only the felonious clerk.

Hence **fe'loniousness**, the quality or state of being felonious.

1727 in BAILEY vol. II. 1886 *Pall Mall G.* 6 Aug. 4/1 A young man..does not forge a cheque for a paltry £20 in a mere access of playful feloniousness.

feloniously (fɛ'ləʊnɪəslɪ), *adv.* [f. FELONIUS *a.* + -LY[2].] In a felonious manner.

1495 *Act 11 Hen. VII*, c. 59 Preamb., Evyll disposed persones..intendyng..feloniously to have broken the hous of your seid Subget. 1548 HALL *Chron.* Hen. VIII, an. 6 55 b, [They] of their set malice, then, & their, felonyously kylled & murthered the sayde Richard Hun. 1720 *Proc. in Old Bailey* 7 Dec., Feloniously stealing 27 pound weight of Sugar. 1844 WILLIAMS *Real Prop.* (1877) 1 No man, be he ever so feloniously disposed, can run away with an acre of land. 1874 MOTLEY *Barneveld* II. xiv. 128 The Cloister Church had been..surreptitiously and feloniously seized.

†'**felonish**, *a. Obs. rare*$^{-1}$. [f. FELON + -ISH.] = FELON *a.* 1.

1530 PALSGR. 312/2 Fell or felonysshe, *felonneux.*

†'**felonly**, *adv. Obs.* [f. FELON *a.* + -LY[2].] In a 'felon' manner, wickedly; fiercely, bitterly, cruelly, severely, also in weaker sense, grievously.

a 1300 *Cursor M.* 12286 (Cott.) Yur sun urs nu feld wit strijf And felunsli him broght o lijf. 1303 R. BRUNNE *Handl. Synne* 1358 Who so demyþ felunsly..He shal no mercy haue. *Ibid.* 1441 A man..þat felunlyche dyde euere wrong. *c* 1330 — *Chron. Wace* (Rolls) 3028 Þe felonloker þey hem abated. *c* 1475 *Rauf Coilȝear* 18 Sa feirslie fra the Firmament, sa fellounlie it fure. 1533 BELLENDEN *Livy* v. (1822) 473 The Gaulis als war fellony [*read* fellonly] invadit be pestilence. 1581 MULCASTER *Positions* xxxvii. (1887) 166 Ouerflowing number..doth festure fellonly..with most rebellious enterprises.

†'**felonment**, *adv. Obs. rare.* [a. Of. *felonement*, f. *felon* FELON *a.* + *-ment* advb. suffix.] Fiercely, feloniously.

c 1470 HARDING *Chron.* CLII. ii, Surmittyng hym of robbery felonoment. *Ibid.* CCX. vi, Some gaue hym batayle full felonement.

†'**felonous**, *a. Obs.* Also 4-5 felonnous, (4 felen-, 5 fellenouse). [f. FELON + -OUS.] Of the nature of a felon; like a felon.

1. Wicked, evil, mischievous.

c 1374 CHAUCER *Boeth.* I. iv. 18 Swiche þinges as euery felonous man haþ conceyued in hys þouȝt aȝeins innocent. *c* 1400 MAUNDEV. (1839) vi. 65 Thei ben right felonouse & foule. 1483 CAXTON *Gold. Leg.* 367/1 A ryght felonnous deuylle. 1533-4 *Act 25 Hen. VIII*, c. 3 §1 Felony and felonous stealynge of the same goodes. 1591 SPENSER *Virgil's Gnat* 295 He spide his foe with felonous intent. 1594 *First Pt. Contention* (1843) 35 A murtherer or foule felonous theefe.

2. Fierce, cruel, violent. Also, bold, sturdy.

c 1386 CHAUCER *Pars. T.* ¶364 Whan that meinie is felonous and damageous to the peple by hardinesse of high lordeship. *c* 1400 MAUNDEV. (1839) xxviii. 291 He is a full felonous Best. *c* 1477 CAXTON *Jason* 23 A tyrant felonnous. 1523 LD. BERNERS *Froiss.* I. ccclxxxiv. 648 He..answered them with a felonous regarde. 1596 SPENSER *F.Q.* IV. x. 33 He..bit his lip for felonous despight.

3. Thievish. *rare*$^{-0}$.

1570 LEVINS *Manip.* 225 Felonouse, *furax.*

Hence '**felonously** *adv.*

1436 *Rolls Parlt.* IV. 498 Þe said William felonousely and flesshly knewe and ravysshed þe said Isabell. 1525 LD. BERNERS *Froiss.* II. xciiii. [xc.] 281 They sayd it was falsely and felonously done. 1532-3 *Act 24 Hen. VIII*, c. 5 If any euyl disposed person..do attempt felonouslye to robbe.. any person.

felonry ('fɛlənrɪ). [f. FELON + -RY.] The whole body or class of felons. Originally applied to the convict population of Australia.

1837 J. MUDIE *Felonry N.S. Wales* Introd. 6 The author has ventured to coin the word *felonry* as the appellative of an order or class of persons in New South Wales. 1850 CARLYLE *Latter-d. Pamph.* ii. 23 Interesting White Felonry who are not idle, but have enlisted into the Devil's regiments of the line. 1858 T. MCCOMBIE *Hist. Victoria* xv. 224 The inundation of the Australian colonies with British felonry.

felony ('fɛlənɪ), *sb.*[1] Forms: 3 feluni(e, felonnie, (felun(n)e, -i, 4 felunnye), 3-5 felonny(e, 3-7 feloni(e, -ye, 4 felone, -ounie, -y, -owny, 6-7 fellony, 3- felony. [ad. Fr. *felonie* = Pr. *fellonia, felnia, feunia*, Sp. *felonia*, It. *fellonia*:—Com. Romanic **fello'nia*, f. *fellone* FELON; see -Y.]

†1. **a.** Villany, wickedness, baseness. *Obs.*

c 1290 *S. Eng. Leg.* I. 31/75 Ake ȝut for al is felonie, ne bi-lefde ore louerd nouȝt þat [etc.]. *c* 1320 *Seuyn Sag.* (W.) 1003 With gret felonie and with wouhgh. 1393 GOWER *Conf.* II. 317, I shall..tellen hem thy felonie. *c* 1489 CAXTON *Sonnes of Aymon* xxiii. 496 He hathe well shewed atte this tyme a grete parte of his grete felony.

†**b.** Anger, wrath. *Obs.* After OF. in which it is very common.

c 1290 *S. Eng. Leg.* I. 62/299 For ore louerd euenede himsulf to a tomb..And for it is with-oute felonie, and milde ase ihesu crist. 1375 BARBOUR *Bruce* I. 440 Fra his presence went in hy, For he dred sayr his felouny. 1485 CAXTON *Paris & V.* (1868) 38 Sodeynly the doulphyn was moeued in grete felonnye. 1513 DOUGLAS *Æneis* x. viii. 100 Turnus smyttin full of fellony. 1523 LD. BERNERS *Froiss.* I. cccxxvi. 510 So moche rose the felony of the romayns yt suche as were next to ye conclaue..brake vp the dore of the conclaue.

†**c.** Daring, recklessness. *Obs.*

1485 CAXTON *Chas. Gt.* 109 The admyrall bygan to lawhe for felonnye.

†2. Guile, deceit, treachery, perfidy. *Obs.*

1297 R. GLOUC. (Rolls) 1446 He biþoȝte him of felonie. *c* 1325 *Coer de L.* 4047 The Sarezynes, for felounie, Soone senten out a spie, That hadde be Crystene in hys youthe. *c* 1400 *Beryn* 1169 She hid so hir felony, & spak so in covert. *c* 1477 CAXTON *Jason* 78 He ansuerde to him with a mouthe ful of felonnye that [etc.]. *a* 1533 LD. BERNERS *Huon* ii. 4 Whan by hys felony he slew Baudouyn.

†3. A crime, misdeed, sin. *Obs.*

a 1300 *Cursor M.* 16852 (Gött.) Ioseph..of arimathie, Ne grantted neuer wid will ne werk, to þaire gret felune. 13.. *E.E. Allit. P.* B. 205 Þe fyrste felonye þ e falce fende wroȝt. *c* 1400 *Prymer* 63 Schewe to me my felonyes & trespassis! 1523 LD. BERNERS *Froiss.* I. vii. 5 She..lamentably recounted to hym all the felonyes and iniuries done to her.

4. *Law.* **a.** (Feudal Law.) An act on the part of a vassal which involved the forfeiture of his fee.

[1292 BRITTON I. vi. §3 Volums, que lour terres alienez puis lour felonies fetes soint eschetes as seignurages des feez.] *c* 1330 R. BRUNNE *Chron.* (1810) 207 Somond haf þei Jon, to Philip courte him dede, To tak his Jugement of þat felonie [MS. *felonse*; rime-word *Bretaynie*]. 1480 CAXTON

Cron. Eng. cxciii. 169 Or els the man..shold be falsely endyted of forest or of felonye. **1846** McCulloch *Acc. Brit. Empire* (1854) II. 471 The term felony..seems..to have originally signified the act or offence by which an estate or fief was forfeited and escheated to the lord.

b. (Common and Statute Law.) Formerly the general name for a class of crimes which may loosely be said to be regarded by the law as of a graver character than those called misdemeanours. No longer differentiated from misdemeanour (see quot. 1967).

The class comprises those offences the penalty of which formerly included forfeiture of lands and goods, and corruption of blood, together with others that have been added to the list by statute. (But see quot. 1883.) Properly including *treason*, but often used in opposition to it.

[**1292** Britton I. ii. §10 Si la felonie eyt esté fete hors de mesoun.] **1303** R. Brunne *Handl. Synne* 1310 Sle no man wyþ þyn honde Wyþ outyn iustyce, for felonye. **1472** in *Surtees Misc.* (1890) 24 Thomas Dransfeld is a theef and has knowelach felony. **1531** *Dial. on Laws Eng.* I. viii. (1638) 18 If a man steal goods to the value of twelve pence or above, it is felony. **1553** T. Wilson *Rhet.* 64 b, I have accused this man of felonie because he tooke my pursse by the high waie side. **1621** Elsing *Debates Ho. Lords* (Camden) 113 Wemen convicted of small felonyes. *a* **1633** Austin *Medit.* (1635) 191 His [St. John Baptist's] Imprisonment..was neither for Felony, nor Treason, but for being witnesse to the Truth. **1727** De Foe *Syst. Magic* I. iii. (1840) 84 He committed a felony even with his fetters on. **1769** Blackstone *Comm.* IV. 94 Felony..comprizes every species of crime, which occasioned at common law the forfeiture of lands or goods. **1773** Brydone *Sicily* vi. (1809) 67 Happy it is that poetical theft is no felony. **1774** Goldsm. *Nat. Hist.* (1776) V. 118 It was made felony in the reign of Edward the Third to steal a hawk. **1838** Dickens *Nich. Nick.* i, All means short of felony. **1856** Emerson *Eng. Traits, Wealth* Wks. (Bohn) II. 73 The rights of property nothing but felony and treason can override. **1883** J. F. Stephen *Hist. Criminal Law* II. 192 It is usually said that felony means a crime which involved the punishment of forfeiture, but this definition would be too large, for it would include misprision of treason, which is a misdemeanour. **1967** *Act Eliz. II* c. 58 Criminal Law Act. An Act to amend the law of England and Wales by abolishing the division of crimes into felonies and misdemeanours.

transf. **1831** Brewster *Newton* (1855) II. xv. 43 Such intellectual felony. **1859** Smiles *Self-Help* x. (1860) 22 The acquisition of knowledge may protect a man against the meaner felonies of life.

c. *felony-de-se*: an action or instance in which a person is 'felo-de-se'. Cf. felo-de-se 2.

1822 Byron *Vis. Judg.* xciv, Quite a poetic felony 'de se.' **1835** Hood *Dead Robbery* i, P'rhaps, of all the felonies de se ..Two-thirds have been through want of *l. s. d.*!

†**'felony**, *sb.*[2] *Obs. rare*$^{-1}$. [a. F. *felonie* (16th c.), f. *felon* of same meaning (see Cotgr.).] Cholera.

1578 Lyte *Dodoens* II. lxxiv. 246 The cholerique passion otherwise called the felonie [Fr. *la colerique passion aultrement dicte felonie*], that is, when one doth vomit continually.

†**'felony**, *v. Obs. rare*$^{-1}$. [f. felony *sb.*[1]] *trans.* ? To perpetrate feloniously.

1502 *Ord. Crysten Men* (W. de W. 1506) IV. xxi. 250 All domages and oppressyons the whiche by defaute of correccyon ben felonyed.

†**feloure**. *Obs.* Also 4 feylour, foler. [a. OF. *fueilleure, -ure*, f. *fueil* leaf.] Foliage.

13.. *E.E. Allit. P.* B. 1410 Foles in foler flakerande bitwene. *a* **1400-50** *Alexander* 4821 Cald was þe maste, Quare-of þe feloure & þe frute as fygis it sawourd. *Ibid.* 5004 Þe lind of þe liȝt son louely clethid, With feylour as of fine gold.

felsen, var. of filsen *v. Obs.*

‖**felsenmeer** ('fɛlzənmɪə(r)). *Physical Geogr.* Pl. felsenmeere. [G., lit. rock-sea.] An expanse of angular frost-riven rocks which may develop on flat terrain in arctic and alpine climates; a boulder field.

1905 *Jrnl. Geol.* XIII. 121 The lack of a commonly used English equivalent for the German word *Felsenmeer*. *Ibid.*, The development of the *Felsenmeer* means a vast increase of rock surface on which frost, changes of temperature, and all the other chief methods of weathering..can act. **1954** W. D. Thornbury *Princ. Geomorphol.* v. 69 It is common to find at high altitudes accumulations of riven rocks known as *felsenmeere*. These boulder fields attest to the rapidity of the weathering processes at high altitudes. **1963** A. N. Strahler *Earth Sciences* xxv. 455 The ground may be covered with large angular blocks of fresh rock in an accumulation known as a felsenmeer (literally, a rock sea), or boulder field.

felsic ('fɛlsɪk), *a. Min.* [f. fe(ldspar + l*enad* (= feldspathoid) + s(ilica + -ic.] Of or pertaining to such light-coloured minerals as the feldspars, the feldspathoids, quartz, and muscovite, or to rocks containing a high proportion of these or similar minerals.

1912 W. Cross et al. in *Jrnl. Geol.* XX. 561 We suggest the term *felsic* for the group of modal feldspars, feldspathoids, and quartz. **1965** G. J. Williams *Econ. Geol. N.Z.* iv. 38/1 The host-rock is a splintery siliceous bluish-grey slate with some micaceous, talcose and felsic facies.

felsite ('fɛlsaɪt). *Min.* [f. *fels* (in *felspar* feldspar) + -ite.

The name was given by Kirwan himself (not by Widenmann as his language might seem to imply), and its form is due to his erroneous explanation of *feldspath* (see feldspar).]

= felstone.

1794 Kirwan *Min.* I. 326 Felsite, or compact Felspar of Widenmann. **1804** *Edin. Rev.* III. 310 Kirwan..has called a substance in question Felsite, and not compact fieldstone. **1868** Dana *Min.* §315 (1880) 352 Felsite..constitutes the base of albite porphyry. **1882** W. J. Harrison in *Knowledge* 6 Oct. 305 A cream-coloured felsite.

attrib., as in *felsite porphyry* (see quot.).

1877 Le Conte *Elem. Geol.* II. (1879) 206 Felsite porphyry ..consists of a grayish or reddish feldspathic mass, containing large crystals of lighter colored and purer feldspar.

Hence **fel'sitic** *a.*, consisting of or containing felsite or felstone.

1879 Prof. Hughes in *Q. Jrnl. Geol. Soc.* XXXV. 682 The Felsitic series, consisting chiefly of quartz felsites and probably also of volcanic origin. **1880** Rudler in *Encycl. Brit.* (ed. 9) XI. 49 Crystals of orthoclase disseminated through a felsitic matrix. In these veins the granite is apt to ..become either fine-grained or felsitic.

felso'banyite. *Min.* [f. (by Haidinger 1852) *Felsobany-a* in Hungary, near which it is found + -ite.] An orthorhombic sulphate of aluminium found in white or yellowish concretions. Also called *Gibbsite*.

1856 C. U. Shepard *Min.* 399 *Felsobanyte*, In six-sided folia, with two angles of 112°. **1863-72** Watts *Dict. Chem.* II. 838 *Gibbsite*..Native trihydrate of aluminium, called also *Felsobanyite*. **1868** Dana *Min.* §695 (1880) 662.

felspar, felspath-: see felds-.

felstone ('fɛlstəʊn). *Min.* [ad. Ger. *felsstein*, f. *fels* rock + *stein* stone. By early German mineralogists used vaguely for amorphous rocks; association with felsite has given it a more restricted meaning.] (See quot. 1865.)

1858 Geikie *Hist. Boulder* xii. 240 Traps..consisting..of felspar, whence they are known as felstones. **1865** Page *Handbk. Geol. Terms* (ed. 2), *Felstone*, the term now generally employed by geologists to designate compact felspar which occurs in amorphous rock-masses..The term Felsite was at one time employed for the same purpose, but is now all but obsolete. **1875** Croll *Climate & T.* xxvii. 440 The top of the hill is composed of a compact porphyritic felstone.

attrib. **1882** J. Hardy in *Proc. Berw. Nat. Club* IX. 466 A very perfect felstone celt.

felt (fɛlt), *sb.*[1] Also 4 feltte, 5 feelte, 6 (fealt,) felte, fylt. [OE. *felt* = MDu. and Du. *vilt*, OHG. *filz* (MHG. *vilz*, mod.G. *filz*), Sw. and Da. *filt*:—OTeut. **felto-z-*, *filtiz-*:—pre-Teut. **peldos-*, *-es-*. Kluge compares OSlav. *plŭstĭ* of same meaning.

From the WGer. **filtir*:—OTeut. **filtiz* comes the med.L. *filtrum* filter.]

1. A kind of cloth or stuff made of wool, or of wool and fur or hair, fulled or wrought into a compact substance by rolling and pressure, with lees or size. Also *pl.*

c **1000** Ælfric *Gloss.* in Wr.-Wülcker 120 *Centrum, uel filtrum*, felt. *c* **1440** *Promp. Parv.* 154/2 Feelte or quylte, *filtrum*. *c* **1450** *J. de Garlande* in Wright *Voc.* 124 Capellarii faciunt capella (hattys) de fultro (feltte). **1555** Eden *Decades* 281 Clokes made of whyte feltes. **1613** Purchas *Pilgrimage* IV. xiii. (1614) 411 They have also Idolls of Felt. **1675** Ogilby *Brit.* 66 Their Trade is in making Serges and Felts. **1801** Wolcott (P. Pindar) *Tears & Smiles* Wks. 1812 V. 58 Mute Silence with her feet in felt, Did stalk from vale to vale. **1848** Dickens *Dombey* xviii, After dark there come some visitors, with shoes of felt. **1892** *Daily News* 18 May 2/7 A fair trade is passing in..felts.

2. a. A piece of this material, something made of felt. †In early use: A filter made of felt or cloth.

1527 Andrew *Brunswyke's Distyll. Waters* A j b, The first without coste is done thrughe a thre cornered fylt named per filtri distillacionem. **1544** Phaer *Regim. Lyfe* (1553) G vij a, Take a great sponge or els a felt of a hat, and stiepe it in wine. *c* **1550** Lloyd *Treas. Health* (1585) Ij, A felte of heare or cloth. **1612** Woodall *Surg. Mate* Wks. (1653) 253 Filtrum, a felt. This filtring with a felt, is a kind of preparation of medicines liquid. **1708** Motteux *Rabelais* IV. xxxi. (1737) 128 His Throat, like a Felt to distil Hippocras. **1753** Hanway *Trav.* (1762) I. III. xxxiv. 155 On the sides of the room are felts about a yard broad. **1853** M. Arnold *Sohrab & Rustum* 27 The old man sleeping on the bed Of rugs and felts.

b. *esp.* A felt hat.

c **1450** *Merlin* 279 And on his heede a felt. **1552** *Act 5-6 Edw. VI*, c. 24 §2 They that shall so make or work any such Felts or Hats. **1587** Turberv. *Epit. & Sonn.* (1837) 386 The Cassocke beares his fealt, to force away the raine. **1621** G. Sandys *Ovid's Met.* I. (1626) 18 He wings his heeles, puts on his Felt, and takes His drowsie Rod. **1745** *De Foe's Eng. Tradesman* xxvi. (1841) I. 263 The hat is a felt from Leicester. **1812** H. & J. Smith *Rej. Addr., Theatre* (1852) 166 The youth with joy unfeign'd Regained the felt, and felt what he regained. **1892** *Pall Mall G.* 18 Aug. 1/2 There is no very striking novelty in felts.

†**c.** *transf.* A hat made of any other material.

1610 B. Jonson *Alch.* I. i, A felt of rugg. **1634** Sir T. Herbert *Trav.* (1638) 338 Others weare high caps or felts made of fine twigs.

d. A piece of woven cloth with a felted nap used in paper-making.

1752 Chambers *Cycl.* II. s.v. Paper, The coucher, who couches it upon a felt laid on a plank, and lays another felt on it. **1839** Ure *Dict. Arts* 927 Felts and paper are alternately stratified, till a heap of six or eight quires is formed. **1957** *Encycl. Brit.* XVII. 236/1 Some machines are provided with an endless felt which presses against the wire to pick off the paper and carry it through the first press.

3. A thickly matted mass of hair or other fibrous substance; hence, a provincial name for the creeping wheat-grass or couch-grass (*Triticum repens*).

13.. *E.E. Allit. P.* B. 1689 Faxe fyltered & felt flosed hym vmbe. **1794** *Statist. Acc. Scot.* XI. 374 The creeping wheat-grass, known by the vulgar name of felt or pirl-grass. **1866** Gregor *Dial. Banff*, 'The lan's a' ae felt of weeds.' 'That steer hiz a richt felt o' hair.'

4. *attrib.* and *Comb.* **a.** attrib. in sense 'concerned with felt', as *felt-branch*; 'suitable for felting', as *felt-wool*; 'made of felt', as *felt-cap, -cape, -carpet, -carpeting, -cloak, -cloth, -hat, -mantle*; also *felt-like* adj. **b.** objective, as *felt-maker, -making, -monger, -roller, -washer*. **c.** instrumental, as *felt-lined, -shod*.

1883 *Daily News* 17 Sept. 2/3 Quietness still prevails in the *felt branches. **1886** Sheldon tr. *Flaubert's Salammbo* 8 Little, conical-shaped, black *felt caps. **1865** Kingsley *Herew.* iv, They adopted plaid trousers and *felt capes. **1874** Knight *Dict. Mech.*, **Felt-carpet*. **1881** *Every Man his own Mechanic* §798. 366 A piece of *felt carpeting. **1599** Hakluyt *Voy.* II. 162 *Felt clokes. **1882** in Ogilvie (Annandale), **Felt-cloth*. **1457** in Rogers *Agric. & Prices* III. 555/3, 1 *felt hat, -/10. **1703** T. N. *City & C. Purchaser* 190, 2 pieces of an old Felt-hat. **1865** Kingsley *Herew.* xiii, He had a broad felt hat and long boots. **1611** Cotgr., *Feustre* ..the thicke hairen and *felt-like stuffe vsed by Sadlers for stuffing. **1893** *Daily News* 6 Mar. 7/4 In *felt-lined cases. **1562** *Act 5 Eliz.* c. 4 §3 Hatmakers or *Feltmakers. **1641** Sir E. Dering *Sp. on Relig.* xiv. 64 Braziers, Feltmakers, doe climbe our..Pulpits. **1879** C. Dickens *Dict. Lond.* 70/3 *City Companies*..Feltmakers. **1665-6** Pepys *Diary* (1879) III. 386 The trade of *felt-making. **1844** J. Rennie *Bird Archit.* 202 Felt-making Birds. **1583** Hollyband *Campo di Fior* 381 Bring me my long *felt mantell. **1630** J. Taylor (Water P.) *Pastoral* Wks. III. 58/1 Felmongers, Leather sellers, *Feltmongers, Taylors, and an infinite number of other Trades and Functions. **1874** Knight *Dict. Mech.*, *Felt* 2.. appurtenances of the felt are known as *felt-washers, *felt-rollers, etc. **1844** I. Williams *Baptistery* xxiii. 240 Where silence..With *felt-shod footsteps softly went. **1607** Topsell *Four-f. Beasts* 626 And the wooll thereof..is called Feltriolana, *Felt-wooll. **1705** *Lond. Gaz.* No. 4184/4, 302 Bags of Cloth wash'd and unwash'd Spanish Felt Wooll.

d. Special combs., as **felt-grain** (see quot. 1874); †**felt-lock**, ? a matted forelock; **felt-side**, the upper surface of a sheet of machine-made paper (see sense 2d, quot. 1957); **felt(-tip, -tipped) pen**, a pen with a felt point, used for labelling, etc.; also *ellipt.* as **felt-tip**; so **felt-tip** *v. trans.*, to write (something) using a felt-tipped pen; **felt-work**, a structure resembling felt.

1703 T. N. *City & C. Purchaser* 187 **Felt-grain*..is that Grain which is seen to run round in Rings at the end of a Tree. **1874** Knight *Dict. Mech.*, *Felt-grain*..the grain of wood whose direction is from the pith to the bark; the direction of the medullary rays in oak and some other timber. **1631** Shirley *Mart. Souldier* IV. iii. in Bullen *O. Pl.* I. 236 Her haire..curles like a witches *feltlocks. **1650** Bulwer *Anthropomet.* 53 For which cause they [the Irish] nourish long Fealt-locks hanging down to their shoulders. **1957** *Stationery Trade Ref. Bk.* 33/2 Cushman & Denison Co. Ltd... Manufacturers of *felt tip pens and inks. **1964** *Trademark Register 1963* (U.S.) 268 *Yankee-Doodle*. Zip-Mark Corp...felt-tipped pens. **1965** *Ibid. 1964* 230 *Felt-riter*. Time Saving Specialities..felt marking pens. **1966** *Guardian* 3 Jan. 2/5 The secret bards [*sc.* graffiti-writers] have taken to felt-tipped pens. **1966** D. Francis *Flying Finish* x. 127 Mike..was already writing names on disposable cups with a red felt pen. **1967** T. Baird *Finding Out* x. 87 He charted a course with a felt-tipped marking pen. **1969** *Soviet Weekly* 6 Sept. 2 Anyhow, I got the job of buying all the things that did not require his personal attendance—notebooks, ball-points, feltpens, [etc.]. **1973** *Daily Tel.* 8 May 18/7 Of the six obscenities 'felt-tipped' on the seat, three were spelt correctly. **1975** *Language for Life* (Dept. Educ. & Sci.) xi. 185 There should be plenty of suitable tools: soft pencils, crayons, and felt-tips. **1978** *Times Lit. Suppl.* 1 Dec. 1392/2 Others are hastily scrawled in blunt pencil,..or a child's mauve felt tip. **1984** *Times* 30 Oct. 10/1 We took the measure..to prevent the irresponsible few from felt-tipping record requests on the paving stones. **1959** R. Hostettler et al. *Techn. Terms Printing Ind.* (ed. 3) 75 (*caption*) Felt side; top side. **1844** J. Rennie *Bird Archit.* 209 Several species of birds which construct nests of *felt-work in Southern Africa.

†**felt**, *sb.*[2] *Sc. Obs.* = calculus 1. Also *attrib.* in *felt-gravel*.

c **1520** A. Myln *Vitæ Dunkeld. eccl. episcop.* (Bann. Clb.) 47 Calculo (quem lie felt vulgo dicebant) depressus. *a* **1605** Montgomerie *Flyting w. Polwart* 313 The frencie, the fluxes, the fyke, and the felt. *a* **1639** Spottiswood *Hist. Ch. Scot.* (1655) 101 He was tormented with the Felt gravel.

felt (fɛlt), *sb.*[3] *dial.* See quots.

1881 *Leicestersh. Gloss.*, *Felt*, the fieldfare. **1885** Swainson *Prov. Names Brit. Birds* 2 Missel Thrush..Big Felt (Ireland).

felt (fɛlt), *sb.*[4] *dial.* [? a confusion of fell *sb.*[1], felt *sb.*[1], pelt *sb.*] A skin or hide.

1708 Mortimer *Husb.* (ed. 2) 179 To know whether they [sheep] are sound or not, see that..the Felt [be] loose. **1783** Ainsworth *Lat. Dict.* (Morell) 11, *Exuviæ*..(3) The skin, felt, or hide, of a beast, taken from the flesh. **1888** Elworthy *W. Somerset Word-bk.*, *Felt*..raw hide; dried untanned skin of any animal.

felt (fɛlt), *ppl. a.* [pa. pple. of FEEL *v.*] In various senses of the vb. FEEL.

1581 MULCASTER *Positions* xxx. (1887) 113 Where no sensible let is, no felt feeblenesse. **1640** BP. HALL *Chr. Moder.* 23/1 Sorrow is for present and felt evils. **1833** CHALMERS *Const. Man* (1835) I. i. 109 Armed with the felt authority of a master. **1850** McCOSH *Div. Govt.* I. ii. (1874) 41 Man is in felt contact nowhere with the Creator. **1885** NICOLSON *Mem. Adam Black* Pref. 5 One of the 'felt wants' of our time.

felt (fɛlt), *v.* [f. FELT *sb.*[1]]

1. *trans.* To make into felt; to bring into a consistence like that of felt; to mat or press together. Also, *to felt together.*

1513 [see *ppl. a.*]. **1601** HOLLAND *Pliny* XI. xxiii, They fal to beat, to felt, and thicken it close with their feet. **1609** —— *Amm. Marcell.* XVII. vii. 89 The sides thereof, hard baked or felted together. **1677** HALE *Prim. Orig. Man.* II. iv. 157 One Man [*printed* Men] felts it into a Hat. **1805** LUCCOCK *Nat. Wool* 164 So little is known of the proceedings of nature in the operation of felting. **1835** URE *Philos. Manuf.* 153 Too great a velocity in these parts would be apt to knot and felt the wool. **1861** HULME tr. *Moquin-Tandon* II. III. 68 The hairs become felted together in balls. **1862** C. A. JOHNS *Brit. Birds* (1874) 73 A compact nest of moss, felted so as to be impervious to water. **1874** COOKE *Fungi* 75 The fertile threads are either free or only slightly felted. **1879** *Cassell's Techn. Educ.* IV. 342/1 The cloth is felted, that is, the fibres of the wool..interlock or hook into each other.

b. To make of felt.

1325, 1513, 1854 [see *ppl. a.*].

2. *intr.* for *refl.* To form into felt-like masses, to become matted together.

1791 HAMILTON *Berthollet's Dyeing* I. I. II. i. 129 The disposition to felting which the hair of animals generally possesses. **1805** LUCCOCK *Nat. Wool* 135 The tendency of the coat to felt upon the back of the sheep is a very curious property of wool. **1879** *Encycl. Brit.* (ed. 9) IX. 68/2 Unwashed wool, being coated with the natural grease does not felt. **1881** MIVART *Cat* 23 True hair..has not the property of 'felting', because its surface is smooth.

3. *trans.* To cover with felt.

1883 *Daily News* 17 Sept. 3/2 The roof of one of the huts has just been newly felted. *Mod.* The cylinder of that steam-engine should be felted.

Hence **'felted** *ppl. a.*

c **1325** *Poem Times Edw. II* 145 in *Pol. Songs* (Camden) 330 Hi weren sockes in here shon, and felted botes above. **1513** DOUGLAS *Æneis* VI. v. 11 Lyart feltat tatis. **1603** HOLLAND *Plutarch's Mor., Opin. of Phil.* xxv. 824 The Moone is a thicke, compact, and felted cloud. **1831** CARLYLE *Sart. Res.* (1858) 35 Thy impenetrable, felted or woven, case of wool. **1847** ANSTED *Anc. World* xiii. 319 A curly felted mane at the fore part of the body. **1854** MARION HARLAND *Alone* xxv, A pair of felted slippers. **1878** HUXLEY *Physiogr.* 233 Muddy matter..helps to consolidate the felted mass.

felt(e, obs. form of FIELD.

†**'felter,** *sb.*[1] *Obs. rare.* [f. FELTER *v.*]

1. Felting or tangle; = FELTERING *vbl. sb.*

1615 MARKHAM *Eng. Housew.* II. v. (1668) 125 If you find any hard knot or other felter in the Wooll.

2. A kind of worm or maggot found in the skins of cattle. More fully *felter-worm*. [Perh. a distinct word.]

1617 MARKHAM *Caval.* VII. 85 To kill the Warble or Felter, bathe your horse..with burnt Sacke and vinegar mixt together. **1639** T. DE GRAY *Compl. Horsem.* 38 This is most profitable for..the felter-worme.

felter ('fɛltə(r)), *sb.*[2] [f. FELT *v.* + -ER[1].]

1. One who makes or works with felt.

1605 SYLVESTER *Du Bartas*, Colonies 677 (Grosart) I. 151 Brewers, Bakers, Cutlers, Felters. **1720** *Stow's Surv.* (ed. Strype 1754) II. v. xv. 326/1 Those Spanish wools for Felters were not Fleece wools.

2. A bird which makes a felt-like nest.

1880 *Libr. Univ. Knowl.* X. 496 The subjects of his treatment include..weavers, tailors, felters.

†**felter** ('fɛltə(r)), *v. Obs.* exc. *dial.* Also 4 **fylter,** 5 **filter,** 6 **feltir,** 8 **falter;** and see FEWTER. [ad. OF. *feltrer*, f. *feltre* felt = It. *feltro*:—med.L. *filtrum*: see FILTER *sb.* Cf. It. *feltrare*.]

1. *trans.* To tangle (hair, etc.); to mat together. Also, *to felter together.*

13.. *E.E. Allit. P.* B. 1689 Faxe fyltered. ?*a* **1400** *Morte Arth.* 1078 His fax and foretoppe Was filterede to-geders. *c* **1460** *Towneley Myst.* 85 With a hede lyke a clowde felterd his here. **1549** *Compl. Scot.* vii. 68 Hyr hayr..vas feltrit & trachlit out of ordour. **1598** TOFTE *Alba* (1880) 40 Phoebus no more doth combe his tresses faire, But careles lets them feltred hang in th' aire. **1615** MARKHAM *Eng. Housew.* II. v. (1668) 123 So divide the wooll, as not any part thereof may be feltred or close together. **1641** BEST *Farm. Bks.* (Surtees) 57 They [pea roots] pull the best when they are the most feltered togeather. **1876** *Mid-Yorks. Gloss.*, *Felter*, to clot.

†**b.** *intr.* To make a felted or matted surface.

1621 MARKHAM *Prev. Hunger* (1655) 158 Bird-lyme..doth so stick and felter vpon the same [feathers], that it is almost in no wise to be taken away.

2. *trans.* To entangle or catch as in a net. Of a garment: To cling about, encumber. Cf. FALTER *v.*[2]

1567 *Sat. Poems Reform.* iv. 129 Quhair Venus anis geltis ..Sic sylit subiectis felterit in hir snair, Wisdome is exilit. **1596** DALRYMPLE tr. *Leslie's Hist. Scot.* (1888) I. 09 Quhen now in wardlie effairis thay war sa feltired. **1597** JAMES I *Demonol.* III. Wks. (1616) 129 That hee may thereby have them feltred the sikerer in his snares. **1768** ROSS *Helenore* I. 57 An' Lindy's coat ay feltring her aboon. **1876** *Whitby Gloss.*, *Felter'd*, entangled; stunned or confused.

†**3.** *intr.* **a.** To be huddled together. **b.** To mingle in carnal intercourse. **c.** To join in strife; also, *to felter together.*

13.. *E.E. Allit. P.* B. 224 Fylter fenden folk forty dayez lencþe. *Ibid.* B. 696, & fylter folyly in fere, on femmalez wyse. *Ibid.* B. 1191 þay feȝt & þay fende of, & fylter togeder. *c* **1340** *Gaw. & Gr. Knt.* 986, I schal fonde, bi my fayth, to fylter wyth þe best.

†**4.** *trans.* = FILTER *v. Obs.*

1563 HYLL *Art Garden.* (1593) 152 They may so drop continually water on them in the forme of feltring. **1610** B. JONSON *Alch.* II. iii, Let the water in Glasse E be feltred.

Hence **'feltering** *vbl. sb.*, the action of the vb. FELTER. In quot. *concr.* a matted lock.

1615 MARKHAM *Eng. Housew.* II. v. (1668) 123 She shall cut away all the course locks, pitch, brands, tard locks, and other felterings.

†**'feltered,** *ppl. a. Obs.* [f. prec. + -ED[1].]

1. In various senses of the vb.

?*a* **1400** *Morte Arth.* 2149 Ffacez fetteled unfaire in filterede lakes. **1567** TURBERV. *Ovid's Epist.* 16 b, Heavy helmet on thy head and feltred lockes to beare. **1581** MULCASTER *Positions* xxxix. (1887) 211 [Her hair is] a feltryd borough for white footed beastes. **1600** FAIRFAX *Tasso* IV. vii. 56 His feltred lockes. **1787** GROSE *Prov. Gloss.*, *Falter'd*, revelled, dishevelled.

2. Having matted hair or wool.

c **1460** *Emare* 540 A fowll feltred fende. **1598** CHAPMAN *Iliad* III. 219 Like a well-grown bell-wether, or feltred ram.

b. *filthy-feltered*: matted or clogged with filth.

1581 NUCE *Seneca's Octavia* I. iv, Griesly Plutos filthie feltred denne.

felteric ('fɛlt(ə)rɪk). Also 7–9 **feltric(k,** *pl.* **feltrics.** A disorder of horses (see quot. 1876).

1639 T. DE GRAY *Compl. Horsem.* 38 Swelling under the belly, which is a disease called the feltrick. **1798** R. PARKINSON *Exper. Farmer* I. 279 Some get what is called the felteric. **1876** *Whitby Gloss.*, *Feltrics*, knotty enlargements beneath the hair and skin of horses.

felting ('fɛltɪŋ), *vbl. sb.* [f. FELT *v.* + -ING[1].]

1. a. The action or process of making felt.

1686 PLOT *Staffordsh.* 109 Beside Wool, for..Felting. **1806** W. TAYLOR in *Ann. Rev.* IV. 772 Felting is a much simpler process than weaving. **1844** J. RENNIE *Bird Archit.* 207 The goldfinch is more neat in the execution of its felting than the chaffinch. **1870** YEATS *Nat. Hist. Comm.* 261 Felting is a process by which the different kinds of hair and wool are interlaced or intertwined.

b. Of the hair (see quot. 1848).

1848 DUNGLISON *Dict. Med. Sci.* (ed. 7), *Felting*,..a term applied to the hair when inextricably interlaced, as occurs occasionally in women from inattention. **1864** W. T. FOX *Class. Skin Dis.* 75 Canities, Felting. **1966** J. S. COX *Illustr. Dict. Hairdressing* 57/1 *Felting*, the matting or entangling by movement and pressure of hair into a hair mouse.

c. Of woollen fibres and paper: matting and shrinking.

1884 W. S. B. MACLAREN *Spinning* iv. 58 By this rough arrangement of the fibres they..lap round each other more firmly in the felting; because as wool shrinks in the process, a fibre which is wrapped round several others will get a firmer grip. **1905** GOODCHILD & TWENEY *Technol. & Sci. Dict.* 496/2 The wet web then passes through press rolls to ensure perfect felting and even thickness. **1920** CROSS & BEVAN *Paper Making* (ed. 5) ii. 86 The degree in which felting takes place will depend..upon the form or microscopic peculiarities of the fibres. **1960** *Which?* Apr. 91/1 Rubbing the material by hand, in a washing machine, or in a tumbler drier when wet (or even just damp) may cause felting. **1970** *Nature* 14 Feb. 634/2 Felting is the progressive fibre entanglement in wool resulting from mechanical agitation, particularly in the presence of water.

2. *concr.* Felted cloth.

1849 *Florist* 32 A paper-manufacturer presented us with some felting. **1891** *Pall Mall G.* 22 Oct. 2/2 Protected from the intense cold..by double windows and felting.

3. *attrib.*

1805 LUCCOCK *Nat. Wool* 34 Such a valuable property in wool as the felting quality. **1842** PRICHARD *Nat. Hist. Man* 101 The felting quality of wool is owing to the rough nature of the surface of its filaments. **1859** SALA *Gas-light & D.* 98 A felting comb with all the back teeth knocked out.

feltness ('fɛltnɪs). [f. FELT *ppl. a.* + -NESS.] The quality or state of being felt.

1884 *Mind* IX. 1 The immediate feltness of a mental state. **1891** E. BELFORT BAX *Outlooks from New Standp.* iii. 185 Its whatness, its quality, is but the 'feltness' of the second moment of the synthesis.

†**feltrike.** *Obs.*—[0] [Of obscure formation; prob. a corruption of the L. name *fel terræ* 'gall of the earth', given to the plant on account of its bitterness and perhaps also its yellow colour.] = *earth-gall*; prob. the Yellow Centaury (*Chlora perfoliata*).

The name *earth-gall* appears to have been sometimes applied also to the Lesser Centaury (*Erythræa Centaureum*), and perhaps to other gentianaceous plants.

[*c* **1000** *Sax. Leechd.* II. 126 Wiþ asleȝenum lice, brom; feltere; ȝearwe; hofe.] *c* **1440** *Promp. Parv.* 154/2 Feltryke, herbe, *fistra, fel terre, centaurea.* **1530** PALSGR. 219/2 Feltryke an herbe.

feltwort ('fɛltwɜːt). *Bot.* [OE. *feltwyrt*, f. FELT *sb.* + *wyrt*, WORT.] A name given to the Mullein (*Verbascum Thapsus*).

c **1000** *Sax. Leechd.* I. 174 Ðeos wyrt þe man uerbascum, & oðrum naman feltwyrt nemneð. **14..** *Lat.-Eng Voc.* in Wr.-Wülcker 564 *Annodoma*, feltwort. **1878–86** BRITTEN & HOLLAND *Plant-n.*, *Feltwort.*

felty ('fɛltɪ), *a.* [f. FELT *sb.* + -Y[1].] Somewhat resembling felt, felt-like. Also in comb. *felty-looking* adj.

1846 C. SPENCE in *Harp of Perthshire* (1893) 130 High on thy crest The wagtail builds her felty nest. **1847–9** TODD *Cycl. Anat.* IV. 84/1 A felty-looking mass. **1885** H. O. FORBES *Nat. Wand. E. Archip.* 94 Its perianth densely covered with a felty mass of white wool.

feltyfare, -flier, dial. forms of FIELDFARE.

1839 MACGILLIVRAY *Hist. Brit. Birds* II. 105 *Turdus pilaris*, the chestnut-backed Thrush, or Fieldfare.. Feltyfare, Feldyfar, Feltyflier, Grey Thrush.

felucca (fɛ'lʌkə). Forms: 7 **fal-, feluke, -uque, feleucca, filucca,** 7–8 **falucca,** (7 **falluca, -ocque**), 7 **phalucco,** 8 **felouca,** 8–9 **-uca,** 9 **felouk, -ucco,** 7– **felucca.** [a. It. *felu(c)ca*, Fr. *felouque*, Sp. *faluca*, Pg. *falua*, mod.Arab. *falūkah*, also *fulaikah*.

Devic considers it to be of Arabic formation, cognate with Arab. *fulk* ship, f. root *falaka* to be round.]

A small vessel propelled by oars or lateen sails, or both, used, chiefly in the Mediterranean, for coasting voyages.

1628 DIGBY *Voy. Medit.*, I sent out my pinnace and a falluca. **1655** *Theophania* 2 The chief Lord of the place.. entred into a Fallocque that waited for him. **1662** J. BARGRAVE *Pope Alex. VII* (1867) 38 Brancaccio..fled in a felucca [a boat about as big as a Gravesend barge, J.B.] towards Rome. **1728** MORGAN *Algiers* II. iv. 279 The Felucca..landed them privately at Cape Zafran. **1769** FALCONER *Dict. Marine* (1789) F iv b, A felucca is a strong passage-boat used in the Mediterranean, with from ten to sixteen banks of oars. **1799** NELSON *Lett.* (1814) II. 194, I have been with Acton to get a felucca, to send Ball's dispatch to you. **1879** LADY BRASSEY *Sunsh. & Storm* (1880) 19 Some officers had started at night in a felucca.

Hence **fe'lucca** *v.*, to put on board a felucca.

1728 DE FOE *Mem. Capt. G. Carleton* (1841) 30 He again felucca'd himself, and they saw him no more till [etc.].

felwet, obs. form of VELVET.

felwort ('fɛlwɜːt). [OE. *feldwyrt*, f. *feld* field + *wyrt* root.] **a.** *Gentiana lutea*, and other species of gentian. **b.** *Swertia perennis.*

c **1000** *Sax. Leechd.* I. 110 Ðeos wyrt þe man ȝentianam & oðrum naman feld-wyrt nemneþ. **1516** *Grete Herball* lxxxvi. Lvb, *De gentiane*, felwort or baldymony. **1578** LYTE *Dodoens* III. xii. 332 Gentian is called..in English Felworte. **1641** FRENCH *Distill.* ii. (1651) 46 Take of..the leaves of Felwort. **1756** WATSON in *Phil. Trans.* XLIX. 820 Dwarf Autumnal Gentian, or Fellwort. **1878–86** BRITTEN & HOLLAND *Plant-n.*, *Felwort, Gentiana Amarella*..and other species of gentian.

b. 1820 T. GREEN *Univ. Herb.* II. 640 *Swertia Perennis*, Marsh Swertia or Felwort.

female ('fiːmeɪl), *a.* and *sb.* Forms: 4–6 **femelle,** (4 **femmale, -el**), 5–6 **femelle,** (6 **faemale**), 5–7 **femal(l(e,** *Sc.* **famell,** (7 **foemal**), 4– **female.** [ME. *femelle* (14th c.), a. OF. *femelle* sb. fem. (= Pr. *femela*):—L. *fēmella*, dim. of *fēmina* woman.

In class. L. *femella* occurs only with the sense 'little woman'; but in popular Lat. it appears to have been used, like the equivalent mod.Ger. *weibchen*, to denote the female of any of the lower animals, and hence as a designation of the sex in general; cf. *masculus*, lit. 'little man', but used already in class. Lat. both as sb. and adj. = 'male'. The Fr. word has always been chiefly a sb. (though a few instances occur of OF. and Pr. *femel*, med.L. *femellus* adj.); but from the earliest times it was often used in apposition with an epicene sb., thus becoming a quasi-adj., and in modern Fr. it is to some extent used as a genuine adj. (the form *femelle* serving for both grammatical genders). In Eng., on the other hand, the adjectival use is by far the more prominent: the feeling of the mod. lang. apprehends the sb. as an absolute use of the adj. In 14th c. the ending was confused with the adjectival suffix *-el, -al*; the present form *female* arises from association with *male*, with which it rimes in Barbour *c* 1375.]

A. *adj.*

I. Belonging to the sex which bears offspring.

1. a. of human beings. In *Law*: *heir, line female.* Also predicatively.

1382 WYCLIF *Gen.* i. 27 God made of nouȝt man to the ymage and his lickenes..maal and femaal he made hem of nouȝt. **14..** *Black Bk. of Admiralty* II. 121 Heyres female. *c* **1425** WYNTOUN *Cron.* IV. xix. 34 He sulde be Kyng of all þe hale Ðat cummyn was be Lyne female. *c* **1440** *Promp. Parv.* 154/2 Femelle, *feminius.* **1594** BARNFIELD *Compl. Chastitie* iv, Euerie faemale creature. **1609** SKENE *Reg. Maj.* 59 Lands halden be frie Soccage, quhen heires male and famell baith persews. **1634** SIR T. HERBERT *Trav.* 115 Twelue female beauties. **1671** MILTON *Samson* 711 Who is this, what thing of Sea or Land? Femal of sex it seems. **1818** CRUISE *Digest* (ed. 2) IV. 394 The word issue equally comprehends male and female children. **1828** SCOTT *F.M. Perth* xxx, His female vassals. **1841** LANE *Arab. Nts.* i. *note*, White female slaves are kept by many men.

b. of animals; often = *she-*.

1388 WYCLIF *Hos.* xiii. 8 As a femal bere, whanne the whelps ben rauyschid. *a* **1400** *Octouian* 310 A female ape. **1486** *Bk. St. Albans* E iij a, Other while he is male..And other while female and kyndelis by kynde. *a* **1500** *Colkelbie Sow* 850 Twenty four chikkynis of thame scho hes, Twelf maill and twell famell be croniculis cleir. **1552** HULOET, Female dragon, *dracena.* **1667** MILTON *P.L.* VII. 490 The Femal Bee, that feeds her Husband Drone. **1774** GOLDSM. *Nat. Hist.* (1776) VII. 298 He enclosed a female scorpion.. in a glass vessel. **1870** PENNELL *Mod. Pract. Angler* 148 A female Salmon.

absol. *c* **1320** *Seuyn Sag.* (W.) 3716 Ye se..How a rauen sittes and cries allane..It es the femal of the thre. **1393** GOWER *Conf.* II. 45 She sigh the bestes in her kinde..The male go with the femele. **1861** CHAILLU *Equat. Afr.* xx. (ed.

2) 355 In both male and female the hair is found worn off the back.

2. *transf.* of plants, trees: **a.** When the sex is attributed only from some accident of habit, colour, etc.; sometimes after L. *femina. spec. female fern* = LADY-FERN.

1548 TURNER *Names of Herbes* (1881) 12 The male [pympernel] hath a crimsin floure, and the female hath a blewe floure. **1551** —— *Herbal* I. (1568) C iij b, Pympernell is of .ij. kyndes: it that hath the blewe floure, is called the female. **1577** B. GOOGE *Heresbach's Husb.* II. (1586) 102 b, The female Elmes.. have no seede. **1578** LYTE *Dodoens* III. lx. 400 Two kindes of Fernes.. the male and female. *Ibid.* VI. li. 726 The wilde Cornell tree, is called.. in Latin, *Cornus fœmina*: in Englishe, the female Cornel tree. **1590** SHAKS. *Mids. N.* IV. i. 48 The female Iuy so Enrings the barky fingers of the Elme. **1597** GERARDE *Herball* II. ccccxlix. 969 *Filix fœmina.* Female Ferne or brakes. *Ibid.* 970 In English Brake, common Ferne, and Female Ferne. **1726** LEONI *Alberti's Archit.* I. 27 a, The female Larch Tree.. is almost of the Colour of Honey. **1728** R. BRADLEY *Bot. Dict.* I. s.v. *Filix.* The sharp pointed Female Fern hath the mains Stalks about a Foot long. **1788** RUSSELL in *Phil. Trans.* LXXX. 275 The Female Bamboo.. is distinguished by the largeness of its cavity from the male. **1846** ELLIS *Elgin Marb.* I. 105 The female myrtle. **1870** KINGSLEY in *Gd. Words* 210/1 A male and female papaw, their stems some fifteen feet high. **1878–86** BRITTEN & HOLLAND *Plant-n.* 178 Female Hems. 'Wild hemp.' **1879** PRIOR *Plant-n.* 78 Female-fern, of old writers, not the species now called Lady-fern, but the brake. **1908** E. STEP *Wayside & Woodland Ferns* 45 The ancients had their Male and Female-ferns, their *Filix-mas* and *Filix-fœmina.*

b. *esp.* in *female hemp* = *fimble-hemp*: see FIMBLE *sb.*

1523, 1877 [see CARL HEMP 1]. **1577** [see CARL HEMP 2].

c. Of the parts of a plant: Fruit-bearing; resulting in a new individual.

1791 *Gentl. Mag.* 2/2 The ear.. is the female part [of maize]. **1846** J. BAXTER *Libr. Pract. Agric.* (ed. 4) I. 118 The stamen.. is called.. the *male* part: the pistil, being the recipient, is called the *female.* **1882** VINES *Sachs' Bot.* 897 The female cell or oosphere.

d. Of a blossom or flower: Having a pistil and no stamens; pistillate; fruit-bearing.

1796 WITHERING *Brit. Plants* (ed. 3) I. 188 In the Ribes alpinum, the male and female flowers are sometimes found on different plants. **1880** GRAY *Struct. Bot.* vi. §3. 191 Flowers are.. Female, when the pistils are present and the stamens absent. **1882** *The Garden* 11 Mar. 169/3 Little red-tipped female blossoms give promise of a good crop.

II. Of or pertaining to those of this sex.

3. Composed or consisting of women, or of female animals or plants.

1552 HULOET, Female, of the feminine sorte. **1631** WIDDOWES *Nat. Philos.* (ed. 2) 49 There be sexes of hearbes.. namely, the Male or Female. **1659** HAMMOND *On Ps.* lxviii. 11 Annot. 333 All the femal quire.. solemnly came out. **1667** MILTON *P.L.* XI. 610 That fair female Troop.. that seemd Of Goddesses. **1697** DRYDEN *Virg. Georg.* IV. 795 Heifars from his Female Store he took. **1710–11** *Swift's Lett.* (1767) III. 111 They keep as good female company as I do male. **1772** *Ann. Reg.* 261 An use of the term *female sex*.. not altogether justified by usage.

4. a. Of or pertaining to a woman or women.

1635 A. STAFFORD (*title*), The Femall Glory: or, the Life.. of our blessed Lady. **1700** DRYDEN *Ovid's Metam.* xii. 809 By a Female Hand.. He was to die. **1712–4** POPE *Rape Lock* IV. 83 There she collects the force of female lungs. **1779–81** JOHNSON *L.P., Pope* Wks. IV. 123 The whole detail of a female-day. **1812** BYRON *Ch. Har.* I. lxviii, Nor shrinks the female eye. **1823** F. CLISSOLD *Ascent of Mont Blanc* 22 *note*, Female intrepidity may finally surmount danger. **1868** CRACROFT *Ess.* II. 277 All this comes of a female instead of a masculine education.

b. Engaged in or exercised by women.

a **1690** RUSHW. *Hist. Coll.* (1721) V. 358 Serjeant Francis, and one Mr. Pulford were committed for encouraging this Female Riot. **1762** J. BROWN *Poetry & Mus.* x. (1763) 180 Miriam.. led the female Dance and Choir. **1776** GIBBON *Decl. & F.* I. 153 A female reign would have appeared an inexpiable prodigy. **1884** *Chr. World* 19 June 453/1 Female suffrage was.. contrary to the manifest order of nature.

5. Peculiar to or characteristic of womankind.

1632 LITHGOW *Trav.* III. 83, I.. clothed him in a female habite. **1667** MILTON *P.L.* IX. 999 Fondly overcome with Femal charm. **1717** LADY M. W. MONTAGUE *Lett.* II. xlvii. 39 A true female spirit of contradiction. **1732** ARBUTHNOT *Rules of Diet* 258 Chesnuts are good in Female Weaknesses. **1855** THACKERAY *Newcomes* II. 210 'My-dearesting' each other with.. female fervour. **1863** *Sat. Rev.* 385 These letters.. Johnsonian in aim, and intensely female—we do not mean feminine—in style.

†**6.** Womanish; effeminate; weakly. *Obs.*

1593 SHAKS. *Rich. II*, III. ii. 114 Boyes.. clap their female ioints In stiffe vnwieldie Armes. **1594** MARLOWE & NASHE *Dido* IV. iii, I may not dure this female drudgery. **1632** LITHGOW *Trav.* II. 65, I have heard them often demaund the English.. what they did with such Leprous stuffe [Zante currants].. A question.. worthy of such a female Traffike. **1676** DRYDEN *Aureng-Zebe* IV. Wks. (1883) V. 263, I smile at what your female fear foresees. **1725** POPE *Odyss.* I. 469 Your female discord end, Ye deedless boasters! **1771** GOLDSM. *Hist. Eng.* II. 227 The king remained in his tent, awaiting the issue of the combat with female doubts and apprehensions.

III. Applied to various material and immaterial things, denoting simplicity, inferiority, weakness or the like.

†**7. a.** Simple; plain, undisguised. **b.** Inferior.

1601 B. JONSON *Poetaster* IV. i, To tell you the femall truth (which is the simple truth) ladies. **1649** BLITHE *Eng. Improv. Impr.* (1653) 48 Where there can be a Male-Improvement offer not to the Common-Wealth a Female.

8. Said of the inner layer of horn on a horse's foot, or of bark on a tree.

1639 T. DE GRAY *Compl. Horsem.* 72 If the foot be bruised with the shoo, or that the femall horn be hurt. **1884** BOWER & SCOTT *De Bary's Phaner.* 557 The.. superficially-formed layer (called the male) is removed from the stem.. a new periderm appears.. This periderm grows quicker than the external male cork, and is used technically as 'female cork'.

9. Said of precious stones, on account of paleness or other accident of colour. Cf. 2 a.

c **1400** MAUNDEV. (1839) xiv. 158 Thei [the dyamandes] growen to gedre, male and femele. **1601** HOLLAND *Pliny* XXXVI. xvi. 587 That [loadstone] of Troas is blacke, and of the female sex, in which regard it is not of that vertue that others be. *Ibid.* XXXVII. vii. 617 The female Sandastres.. carrie not such an ardent shew of fire. **1865** EMANUEL *Diamonds* 112 The ancients called sapphires male and female.. the pale blue, approaching the white, [was] the female.

†**10. a.** *female rime*: = *feminine rime*; see FEMININE.

1581 SIDNEY *Apol. Poetrie* (Arb.) 71 Ryme.. in the last silable, by the French named the Masculine ryme.. in the next to the last, which the French call the Female. **1666** DRYDEN *Ann. Mirab.* To Sir R. Howard, The Female Rhymes.. are still in use amongst other nations. **1685** —— *Albion & Albanus Pref.* Wks. (1883) VII. 234 Our scarcity of female rhymes.

b. *Mus. female cadence, -close* (see quot. 1954). Cf. FEMININE *a.* 6 b, quot. 1844.

1928 E. BLOM *Limit. Mus.* 85 Mendelssohn uses female closes to excess. **1954** *Grove's Dict. Mus.* (ed. 5) III. 60/2 *Female, feminine cadence*, a cadence in which the concluding chord falls on the weak beat of the bar.

IV. 11. a. A distinctive term for that part of an instrument or contrivance which is adapted to receive the corresponding or male part.

a **1856** H. MILLER *Paper* in *O.R. Sandst.* (1874) 342 The male half of the hinge belongs to the head, and the female half to the jaw. **1889** *Mayne's Med. Voc., Female*.. the part of a double-limbed instrument which receives the male or corresponding part.

b. (See quot.)

1688 R. HOLME *Armoury* III. xii. 433/1 There is no difference between the male and female Trepan, but for the Pin in the middle which the female wants.

c. '*female gauge*, an internal or bored gauge' (Lockwood 1888); '*female joint*, the socket or faucet-piece of a spigot-and-faucet joint' (Ogilv.); *female screw, socket*, a circular hole or socket having a spiral thread adapted to receive the thread of the male screw.

1669 BOYLE *Contn. New Exp.* II. (1682) 11 A Female Screw, to receive the Male-screw of the Stop-cock. **1703** MOXON *Mech. Exerc.* 106 Two Male Screws fitted into two Female Screws. **1839** G. BIRD *Nat. Philos.* 72 The female screw.. must be of such a size as to admit the projecting thread of the.. male screw. **1870** *Eng. Mech.* 18 Mar. 653/1 A screw working in a female socket.

B. *sb.*

1. A female animal: **a.** of lower animals. Often in *his female*: his mate.

1377 LANGL. *P. Pl.* B. XI. 331 In euenynges also ȝe[de] males fro femeles. **1481** CAXTON *Myrr.* II. xiv. 97 Byrdes that ben femalles may not abyde there. **1553** EDEN *Treat. Newe Ind.* (Arb.) 15 The females [elephants] are of greater fiercenesse then the males. **1585** J. B. tr. *Viret's Sch. Beastes* D iv, This bird [Halcion] loveth singularly his femal. **1697** DRYDEN *Virg. Georg.* III. 416 The Wars the spotted Linx's make With their fierce Rivals, for the Female's sake. **1769** J. WALLIS *Nat. Hist. Northumb.* I. xii. 410 A female, with a calf at her foot, is not to be approached without danger. **1847** MARRYAT *Childr. N. Forest* iv, The stag.. was.. acting as a sentinel for the females. **1881** LUBBOCK *Ants, Bees & Wasps* 8 The abdomen of the females sometimes increases in size.

b. generally, including the human species.

c **1386** CHAUCER *Wife's Prol.* 122 To knowe a femel fro a male. *c* **1440** *Promp. Parv.* 154/2 Femel, no male, *femella.* **1540** HYRDE tr. *Vives' Instr. Chr. Wom.* II. ii. vj b, As sone as the man lokedde upon the femalle of his kynde, he beganne to loue her aboue all thynges. **1590** SHAKS. *Com. Err.* II. i. 24 Man.. Are masters to their females, and their Lords. **1615** CROOKE *Body of Man* 272 The Female generateth in her selfe, the Male not in himselfe but in the Female. **1800** *Med. Jrnl.* IV. 320 The female of every animal in a state of parturition is possessed of a placenta, or substance analogous thereto. **1851** CARPENTER *Man. Phys.* (ed. 2) 503 Conception and Parturition, in the Human female.

2. A female person; a woman or girl.

a. In express or consciously implied antithesis with *male*; *esp.* one of the female individuals in any class or enumeration comprising persons of both sexes.

c **1315** SHOREHAM 44 Me schel the mannes lenden anelye, The navele of the femele. **1375** BARBOUR *Bruce* I. 59 Ther mycht succed na female. **1535** STEWART *Cron. Scot.* III. 139 Of king Williame the successioun did faill.. bayth of famell and maill. **1649** BP. HALL *Cases Consc.* IV. v. 436 If the like exorbitancies of the other sexe were not meant to be comprehended, females should be lawlesse, and the law imperfect. **1652** GAULE *Magastrom.* 243 Saturne did onely eate up his male children, not his females. **1818** CRUISE *Digest* (ed. 2) III. 355 The females.. incapable of performing any military service. **1861** MAINE *Anc. Law* 159 The Danish and Swedish laws, harsh.. to all females.

b. As a mere synonym for 'woman'. Freq. in phr. *the female of the species.*

The simple use is now commonly avoided by good writers, exc. with contemptuous implication.

c **1380** WYCLIF *Sel. Wks.* II. 408 Two femalis shulen be grynding at a queerne. *c* **1460** *Towneley Myst.* (Surtees) 311 Of femellys a quantite here fynde I parte. **1590** SHAKS. *Mids. N.* III. ii. 441 Cupid is a knauish lad Thus to make poore females mad. **1632** LITHGOW *Trav.* x. 478 Females have extreames, and two we see, Eyther too wicked, or too good they be. **1713** STEELE *Guardian* No. 45 ¶1, I would strictly recommend to any young females not to dally with men [etc.]. **1773** WILKES *Corr.* (1805) IV. 141 Just putting on my hat, to attend the females to church. **1801** STRUTT *Sports & Past.* IV. i. 263 Dancing.. an essential part of a young female's education. **1849** E. E. NAPIER *Excurs. S. Africa* I. 112 The 'Totty' of the present day: and his female, (for the creature can scarcely be dignified by the name of woman). **1865** J. G. BERTRAM *Harvest of Sea* (1873) 193 This is performed by females, hundreds of whom annually find well-paid occupation at the gutting-troughs. **1889** *Pall Mall G.* 10 Aug. 7/2 They are no ladies. The only word good enough for them is the word of opprobrium—females. **1911** KIPLING in *Morning Post* 20 Oct. 7/3 (*title*) The female of the species. **1922** WODEHOUSE *Clicking of Cuthbert* ix. 220 The Bingley-Perkins combination, owing to some inspired work by the female of the species, managed to keep their lead. **1940** H. G. WELLS *Babes in Darkling Wood* II. i. 144 The female of the species.. by the age of fifteen has a clearer sense of reality in these things than most men have to the doddering end of their days. **1961** J. MACLAREN-ROSS *Doomsday Book* II. iii. 128 The female of the species first —take hold of her arm, George.

3. *attrib.*, as *female-bar, -determiner, -determining, -foe*; **female-bane**, transl. of Gr. θηλυφόνον aconite. lit. 'a thing deadly to females'; **female circumcision** = CLITORIDECTOMY; **female impersonation**, the personating of a female by a male on the stage; hence **female (im)personator**; **female pill**, any preparation intended as an abortifacient.

1599 SHAKS. *Hen. V*, I. ii. 42 Pharamond The founder of this Law, and Female Barre. **1601** HOLLAND *Pliny* II. 271 Others, for the reason before shewed, call it [Aconite] Theliphonon [*marg.* Femalbane]. *c* **1645** HOWELL *Lett.* (1753) 445 A thousand such instances are not able to make me a misogenes, a female foe. [**1837** *Penny Cycl.* VII. 197/1 An account of what he calls the circumcision of females.. by some of the African tribes is given by Bosman in his 'Description of the Coast of Guinea'.] **1875** *Porcupine* 2 Jan. 635/3 Eugene, still *facile princeps* in female impersonation and falsetto. **1894** HARDY in *Harper's Mag.* XXIX. Dec. 74/1 Physician Vilbert's golden ointment, life-drops, and female pills. **1897** *Sears, Roebuck Catal.* 27/1 *Female Pills*... If the very complete directions.. will be followed closely, all will be well... With useful information and instructions to ladies concerning their troubles. **1905** *Lancet* 18 Nov. 1497/1 Madame Hipolite's world-renowned Female Pills, the safest and surest. **1909** J. R. WARE *Passing Eng.* 129/1 *Female personator*.. the performer is a male who impersonates female appearance, singing, and dancing. **1931** J. S. HUXLEY *What dare I Think* i. 13 Sex is determined at conception by.. male-determining and female-determining [cells], of which the female determiners are a little the bigger. **1931** E. WAUGH *Remote People* 209 The rite of female circumcision.. is one of the battlegrounds between missionaries and anthropologists. **1956** H. E. LAMBERT *Kikuyu Soc. & Polit. Inst.* vii. 143 An order limiting the operation of 'female circumcision' to an incision of sufficient depth and extent for the removal of the glans clitoridis only. (Passed in 1932.) **1957** *New Biol.* XXIII. 23 The barred horizontal line represents the threshold between male-determining and female-determining concentration zones. **1958** M. KELLY *Christmas Egg* I. 9 A shop.. advertising that a long-dead proprietor had been 'Agent for Female Pills, by the King's Letters Patent 1743'. **1963** A. HERON *Towards Quaker View of Sex* 68 Some [transvestites] go on the stage as female impersonators. **1967** *Listener* 5 Jan. 35/2 Leo McKern's unexpected female impersonation as the Duchess. **1970** *Guardian* 16 Sept. 11/6 Female circumcision.. is the crude severing or scarring of the clitoral area in girls approaching puberty.

'femalely, *adv.* So as to suit a female; in a female way.

1867 MISS BROUGHTON *Cometh up as a Flower* xviii, Before the door.. stand many horses, malely and femalely saddled. **1966** B. GLEMSER *Dear Hungarian Friend* ii. 29 She was emphatically a girl, most femalely female.

'femaleness. 1. The character or qualities of a female.

1892 W. W. PEYTON *Memor. Jesus* iv. 94 In maleness and femaleness there is a likeness to the divine nature. **1955** E. HYAMS *Slaughterhouse Informer* 6 She gave out.. a kind of essence of lusty femaleness.

2. *Biol.* The quality of being female.

1889 GEDDES & THOMSON *Evol. Sex* iii. 92 After maleness and femaleness have been partly established. **1894** H. DRUMMOND *Ascent of Man* vii. 315 That this division into maleness and femaleness should run between almost every two of every plant and every animal in existence, must have implications of a quite exceptional kind. *Ibid.* 323 What exactly maleness is, and what femaleness, has been one of the problems of the world. **1902** *Encycl. Brit.* XXXII. 210/1 That maleness and femaleness may be regarded as expressing metabolic alternatives open to the germ-cell in its development. **1930** G. R. DE BEER *Embryol. & Evol.* iii. 22 The various organs and parts of the body do not all switch over from maleness to femaleness together. **1949** M. MEAD *Male & Female* i. 3 How are men and women to think about their maleness and their femaleness in this twentieth century. **1963** A. HERON *Towards Quaker View of Sex* iii. 32 A friendship.. between two women in whom femaleness predominates.

†**'femalism.** *Obs. rare*⁻¹. [f. FEMALE + -ISM.] = prec. In quot., curiosity.

1779 *Sylph* I. 207 But femaleism prevailed, and I examined the contents.

†**femalist.** *Obs. rare*⁻¹. [f. FEMALE + -IST.] One devoted to the female sex.

1613 MARSTON *Insatiate Countess* IV. iii. 54 Beauty can.. make him [War] smile upon delightful Peace, Courting her smoothly as a femalist.

femality (fɪˈmælɪtɪ). Somewhat *humorous*. [f. FEMALE *sb.* + -ITY. Cf. OF. *femelete*.]

1. Female nature or characteristics.

1754 RICHARDSON *Grandison* (1781) VI. xxii. 117, I was afraid of your *Femality*, when you came face to face. **1773** *Lady's Mag.* IV. 3 My femality, or in other words, my curiosity was greater. **1844** MARG. FULLER *Wom. 19th C.* (1862) 115 Feminine element spoken of as Femality.

b. *pl.* Samples of female character, females.

c **1801** T. SELWYN *Warning to Batchelors* ii. (MS.), Knights of the chace To be hunted yourselves were a pitiful case; Suspect these femalities.

2. Effeminacy, unmanliness.

? **16..** *Songs Lond. Prentices* (Percy) 68 Disband feamality, let courage be your portion.

femalize (ˈfiːməlaɪz), *v.* [f. FEMALE *a.* + -IZE.]

† **1.** *intr.* To become effeminate or unmanly. *Obs.*

1674 T. DUFFETT *Sp. Rogue* 11, Men are so Femaliz'd, so idle grown, They court the Coy, and slight what may be won.

2. *trans.* To give a feminine designation or ending to. [See quots. for *ppl. a.*]

Hence **ˈfemalized** *ppl. a.*

1709 SHAFTESB. *Freedom of Wit & Humour* (1711) I. III. §I. 105 note, When they consider.. the very Formation of the word *Κοινονοημοσύνη* upon the Model of the other femaliz'd Virtues, the *Εὐγνωμοσύνη, Σωφροσύνη, Δικαιοσύνη*, ect., they will no longer hesitate on this Interpretation. **1887** *N. & Q.* 7th Ser. III. 95 The following femalized Christian names: Alexandrina, Andrewina.. and Williamina.

femay, var. of FUMAY, *Obs.*

femble, var. of FIMBLE.

feme (fɛm). Also 6 feeme, 6–7 fem, 8–9 femme. [a. OF. *feme*, Fr. *femme* woman, wife.]

1. *Law.* (Chiefly conjoined with *baron*.) Wife.

(The technical spelling is *feme*; but in non-professional use the mod.F. form has often been adopted. So also in *feme-covert*: see below.)

[**1292**], **1594**, **1611** [see BARON *sb.* 5]. *a* **1626** BACON *Max. & Uses Com. Law* i. (1636) 2 The feme is entitled to dower. **1714** SCROGGS *Courts-leet* (ed. 3) 161 If a Feme Copyholder for Life takes Husband, who commits a Waste, this shall bind the Wife. [**1813** BYRON in Moore *Life* (1847) 217 Divorce ruins the poor *femme*.] **1818** CRUISE *Digest* (ed. 2) II. 334 The feme died leaving issue; then the baron died. **1873** DIXON *Two Queens* II. IX. viii. 142 An ancient custom of the land described the man and wife as baron and feme.

† **2.** In 16th c. often used (in verse and somewhat playfully) for: Woman. *Obs.*

1567 TURBERV. *Ovid's Epist.* 76 So bolde Away to have a Greekish feme purloynde. **1577** T. KENDALL *Flowers of Epigrammes* 58 Three ills that mischefe men.. the Fem, the Flud, the Fire. **1594** WILLOBIE *Avisa* (1880) 15 Nature hath begot Of Fleeting Feemes, such fickle store. **1653** H. WHISTLER *Upshot Inf. Baptisme* i. 6 The Fem was concerned as (in desire) one.

feme covert (fɛm ˈkʌvət) *Law.* [a. AF. *feme covert* a woman 'covered' (= mod.F. *couverte*), i.e. under protection.] **a.** A woman under cover or protection of her husband; a married woman. (Cf. FEME and COVERT *a.* 4.)

[**1528** PERKINS *Prof. Bk.* (1532) 2 *marg.*, Graunt de feme couert est void.] **1602** FULBECKE *1st Pt. Parall.* 4 A feme couert cannot make a contract. **1668** R. L'ESTRANGE *Vis. Quev.* (1708) 70 My poor wife.. being a Feme-Coverte, not an Officer durst come near her. **1743** FIELDING *Wedding-Day* IV. v, Do you know, sir, that this lady is a femme couverte? **1818** CRUISE *Digest* (ed. 2) I. 111 On petition of.. femes covert. **1858** LD. ST. LEONARDS *Handy-bk. Prop. Law* xxv. 189 An infant, lunatic, *feme covert*, or [etc.].

b. *humorously*: Wife.

1678 BUTLER *Hud.* III. I. 862 Those.. femme couerts to all mankind.

femenine, obs. form of FEMININE.

femerell (ˈfɛmərɪl). Forms: 5 fomerel(l, fumrell, 5–6 fymrel(le, fumerill, 6 fymerelle, fomeril, fum(m)erel(l, 5– femerell. [ad. OF. *fumeraille* altered form of *fumerole* = It. *fumaruolo*:—L. *fūmāriolum*, dim. of *fūmārium*, f. *fūmus* smoke.]

'A lantern, louvre, or covering placed on the roof of a kitchen, hall, etc. for the purpose of ventilation or the escape of smoke' (Weale, 1849).

c **1440** *Promp. Parv.* 169/2 Fomerel of an halle, *fumarium*. *Ibid.* 182/2 Fumrell of an hows, *fumarium*. **1446** *Churchw. Acc. Yatton* (Som. Rec. Soc.) 84 It. payd to Welyam Stonhowse for settyng in of to femerell in the stepyl, xd. **1500** *Ortus Voc.* Pviij, *Fumerale*, a fumerill. **1511** *Nottingham Rec.* III. 335 Ye fymerelle of ye chymney. **16..** *Jrnl. Bk. Expences* in Gutch *Coll. Cur.* (1781) I. 204 Spent about the Femerell of the New Kitchin.. xviiis. viiid. **1885** LAW *Hampton Court* I. xiii. 174 The inside of the femerell was as richly decorated as the rest of the roof.

feme-sole (ˈfɛmsəʊl) *Law.* [a. AF. *feme soul(e* a woman alone.] **a.** A woman who has not the protection of a husband; an unmarried woman, a spinster; a widow. **b.** A married woman who with respect to property is as independent of her husband as if she were unmarried.

Also *attrib.*, as ***feme-sole merchant, trader***, a married woman who uses a trade alone, or without her husband (Webster).

[**1528** PERKINS *Prof. Bk.* (1532) 2 Mes si feme soule soit executrix. *Ibid.* 2 b, Si feme soul.. fist fait del graunt.] **1642** *Ibid.* (*transl. of prec.*) i. §20 If.. the wife as a feme sole.. grant a rent. **1714** SCROGGS *Courts-leet* (ed. 3) 90 If the Cattle of a Feme-sole be taken, and afterwards she marry. **1845** LD. CAMPBELL *Chancellors* (1857) I. vii. 121 The Queen Consort.. being privileged as a feme sole. **1858** LD. ST. LEONARDS *Handy-bk. Prop. Law* xii. 73 She becomes, after the judicial separation.. a *feme sole*, a single woman, with respect to property.

femetorie, obs. form of FUMITORY.

femic (ˈfɛmɪk), *a.* *Petrogr.* [See quot. 1902.] Of or pertaining to one of the two primary categories erected by Cross, Iddings, Pirsson, and Washington to classify the igneous rocks, and broadly including the non-aluminous ferromagnesian rocks (see also quots.).

1902 W. CROSS et al. in *Jrnl. Geol.* X. 573 To express concisely the two groups of standard minerals and their chemical characters in part, the words *sal* and *fem* have been adopted... *Fem* indicates Group II, since its minerals are dominantly *ferromagnesian*. As adjectives to express these ideas the words *salic* and *femic* will be used. **1912** *Ibid.* XX. 560 Some petrographers have fancied the terms salic and femic as short words, which they wish to apply to modal quartz, feldspar, and felspathoid minerals in one case, and to all modal ferromagnesian minerals in the other. These terms have also been applied to major rock groups. Such applications are not proper uses of these terms. **1920** A. H. FAY *Gloss. Mining & Mineral Ind.* 264/2 *Femic*... Often but incorrectly used in place of Mafic or Subsilicic. **1932** F. F. GROUT *Petrography* II. 46 The terms 'salic' and 'femic' refer to calculated *molecules*, not actual minerals, and should be used only in connection with chemical composition. **1939** A. JOHANNSEN *Descr. Petrogr.* (ed. 2) I. viii. 86 *Femic* does not mean 'ferromagnesian'. **1966** *Mineral. Abstr.* XVII. 704 The problems of the determination of the amounts of femic minerals are discussed.

femicide[1] (ˈfɛmɪsaɪd). [f. FEME + -(I)CIDE: see -CIDE 1.] One who kills a woman.

1828 R. MACNISH (*title*), Confessions of an unexecuted Femicide.

femicide[2] (ˈfɛmɪsaɪd). [f. FEME + -(I)CIDE: see -CIDE 2] The killing of a woman.

1801 *Satirical View Lond.* 60 This species of delinquency may be denominated *femicide*. **1848** WHARTON *Law Lex.*, *Femicide*, the killing of a woman.

femina (ˈfɛmɪnə). *S. Afr.* Usu. in pl. feminas, femina. The long feathers from the wing-tips of a female ostrich.

1881 A. DOUGLASS *Ostrich Farm. S. Afr.* xiii. 84 To show all the whites together, and then the feminas. **1896** R. WALLACE *Farm. Industr. Cape Col.* xi. 235 White and Light Femina were very firm. Dark Femina, 5s. and 10s. per lb. higher.

feminacy (ˈfɛmɪnəsɪ). [f. L. *fēmin-a* + -ACY, after EFFEMINACY.] Female nature, femality.

1847 LYTTON *Lucretia* (1853) 37 The face took from the figure the charm of feminacy.

feminal (ˈfɛmɪnəl), *a.* Also 4 femynalle. [a. OF. *feminal* = Pr. *feminal*, f. Lat. type **fēminālis*, f. *fēmina* woman.] † **1.** Of or pertaining to a female or woman; female. *Obs.*

1398 TREVISA *Barth. De P.R.* XVII. cxli. (1495) 698 Rewe is yeuen ayenst femynalle fluxe. **17..** WEST *On Abuse Travelling* xlvi. in *Dodsl.* (1748) II. 82 For wealth, or fame, or honor feminal.

2. = FEMININE *a.* 4.

1907 *Ladies' Field* 10 Aug. 357/1 Combine the perfection of physical strength with the highest type of feminal beauty. **1922** H. M. BARCYNSKA *Webs* xxv. 207 In her emotional tumult, sheerly feminal, she believed every word she said.

feminality (fɛmɪˈnælɪtɪ). [f. prec. + -ITY.]

1. The quality or condition of a female; female nature. Now *rare*.

1646 SIR T. BROWN *Pseud. Ep.* III. xvii. 148 If in the minority of naturall vigor, the parts of feminality take place. **1702** FARQUHAR *Inconstant* IV. ii, Not half so much as devoting 'em [a beautiful face and person] to a pretty fellow. If our feminality had no business in this world, why was it sent hither? **1883** MRS. LYNN LINTON *Social Ess.* II. 10 Thinking.. womanhood a mistake in exact proportion to its feminality.

2. *pl.* only *concr.* or quasi-*concr.* **a.** The personality of a woman; a female person. **b.** A female trait or peculiarity. **c.** Something that women delight in; a knick-knack.

1825 *New Monthly Mag.* XIV. 262 Ladies are not permitted to advance their feminalities beyond so chaste a threshold. **1834** *Tait's Mag.* I. 204 Certain feminalities.. peep through every page. **1840** MRS. TROLLOPE in *New Monthly Mag.* LX. 199 All these pretty 'feminalities'.

† **ˈfeminary**, *a.* *Obs.* [f. L. *fēmin-a* + -ARY.] Womanish.

1630 LENNARD tr. *Charron's Wisd.* II. iii. §13. 277 A feminarie, sottish calmeness, and vitious facilitie.

† **ˈfeminate**, *a.* *Obs. rare.* [ad. L. *fēmināt-us*, f. *fēmina* woman.] **a.** Resembling a woman; effeminate. **b.** Female, feminine.

a **1533** LD. BERNERS *Gold. Bk. M. Aurel.* (1546) Ll, With halfe a berde, as a feminate man. **1557** NORTH tr. *Gueuara's Diall of Princes* 82 a/1 Money doth not only breake the feminate and tender hartes, but also the hard and craggy rockes. **1633** FORD *Broken H.* V. iii, A nation warlike.. cannot brook A feminate authority.

Hence † **ˈfeminately** *adv.* *Obs.*

1598 FLORIO, *Inzazzeare*, to goe walking wantony, idly or feminatlie vp and downe the streetes.

† **ˈfemine**, *a.* *Obs.* Also 5 femyn(e. [Contracted f. FEMININE.] = FEMININE *a.*

1530 PALSGR. 156 All the feestes of the yere be of the femyne gendre. **1564** GOLDING *Justine* 17 b, In Xerxes was to be sene a kind of femine fearfulnesse. **1610** *Mirr. Mag.*, *Lady Ebbe* xv, To do the like against the Femine kind.

femineity (fɛmɪˈniːɪtɪ). [f. L. *fēmine-us* womanish (f. *fēmina*) + -ITY.] The quality or nature of the female sex; womanliness; womanishness.

1820 COLERIDGE *Lett., Convers., etc.* I. 72 The very essence of femineity seems to speak in the.. true and touching words. *Ibid.* II. 228 Of all men I ever knew Wordsworth has the least femineity in his mind. **1858** O. W. HOLMES *Aut. Breakf.-t.* (1883) 188 It had so much *woman* in it,—*muliebrity*, as well as *femineity*.

feminicide (fɪˈmɪnɪsaɪd). *rare.* [f. L. *fēmina* + -(I)CIDE 2.] = FEMICIDE[2].

1833 *Blackw. Mag.* XXXIII. 545 Our transcendent powers of cold-blooded feminicide.

femiˈnicity. [f. L. *fēmin-a*, after *rusticity*.] The quality or condition of a woman; womanliness.

1843 *Fraser's Mag.* XXVII. 226 Beautiful are both these women in their graceful feminicity.

feminie (ˈfɛmɪnɪ). *arch.* Also 5 femyne, femynye, 6 femynie. [a. OF. *feminie*, f. L. *fēmina* woman.] Womankind; a 'set' of women, *esp.* the Amazons; also the country of the Amazons.

c **1386** CHAUCER *Knt.'s T.* 8 He conquered all the regne of Feminie. *c* **1400** *Destr. Troy* 6669 The qwene of femyne þat freike so faithfully louyt. *c* **1430** *Pilgr. Lyf Manhode* II. xcix. (1869) 111, I wot neuere whether i be in femynye, ther wommen hauen the lordship. **1561** *Schole-house of Women* 9 in Hazl. *E.P.P.* IV. 106 A foole of late contrived a boke, And all in praise of the femynie. **1692** COLES, *Feminie*, the women's country. **1822** BYRON *Werner* IV. i, You bid me.. look into The eyes of feminie. **1834** *Fraser's Mag.* IX. 639 The dingy feminie who cry their brooms. **1836** M. J. CHAPMAN *ibid.* XIV. 22 At the good deeds of feminie let no man.. Sneer idly.

† **ˈfeminile**, *a.* *Obs.*[—1] [f. L. *fēmin-a* + -ILE; cf. It. *femminile*.] Peculiar to a woman; feminine.

1650 BULWER *Anthropomet.* iii. 64 This forehead is also called a great forehead, if it be compared with a feminile forehead.

feminility (fɛmɪˈnɪlɪtɪ). [f. prec. + -ITY.] The character or disposition peculiar to a woman; womanliness, womanishness. Also quasi-*concr.*

1838 *Fraser's Mag.* XVIII. 89 True feminility is oftener found contemplating the exquisite points of some soul-subduing picture. **1890** H. ELLIS *Criminal* iii. 53 The corresponding character (feminility) is not found so often.

feminine (ˈfɛmɪnɪn), *a.* and *sb.* Forms: 4–6 femynyne, 5–6 femenine, -yn(e, 5 femynyng, 6 feminin, -yne, (*Sc.* famenene), 7–8 fœminine, 4– feminine. [a. OF. and Fr. *feminin, -ine*, ad. L. *fēminīnus*, f. *fēmina* woman.]

A. *adj.* **1. a.** Of persons or animals: Belonging to the female sex; female. Now *rare*.

c **1384** CHAUCER *H. Fame* III. 275, I sawe perpetually ystalled A feminyne creature. **1393** GOWER *Conf.* II. 313 The preie, which is feminine. *c* **1470** HARDING *Chron.* 279 Edmond.. None issue had neither male ne feminine. *c* **1500** *Melusine* 369 And now for a serpent of femenyne nature ye shake for fere. **1532** MORE *Confut. Tindale* Wks. 434/2, I had as leue he bare them both a bare charitie, as with ye frayle feminyne sexe fall to farre in loue. **1588** SHAKS. *L.L.L.* IV. ii 83 But.. a soule Feminine saluteth vs. **1613** PURCHAS *Pilgrimage* (1625) 319 Of which Manly fœminine people [Amazons] ancient authors disagree. **1667** MILTON *P.L.* I. 423 Those Male, These Feminine.

b. *humorously*.

1860 O. W. HOLMES *Elsie V.* (1887) 106 A side of feminine beef was.. obtained.

2. In same sense, of objects to which sex is attributed, or which have feminine names, *esp.* one of the heavenly bodies.

1601 HOLLAND *Pliny* I. 44 They say that the Moone is a planet Fœminine. **1633** T. ADAMS *Exp. 2 Peter* ii. 10 Under her conduct and standard marcheth the whole feminine army, envy, avarice, pride, &c. **1653** H. MORE *Conject. Cabbal.* (1713) 83 Five is acknowledged.. to be Male and Female, consisting of Three and Two, the two first Masculine and Feminine numbers. *a* **1658** CLEVELAND *Hermaphr.* 6 Wks. 1687. 19 We chastise the God of Wine With Water that is Feminine. **1751** HARRIS *Hermes* Wks. 1841. 130 The earth.. is universally feminine. **1839** BAILEY *Festus* (1854) 121 Ye juried stars.. Henceforth ye shine in vain to man: Earthy, or moist, or feminine, or fixed.

3. Of or pertaining to a woman, or to women; consisting of women; carried on by women.

c **1489** CAXTON *Blanchardyn* xlix. 189 She lefte asyde her femenyne wyll. *c* **1500** *Melusine* 322 How be it dyuers haue sith sen her in femenyn figure. *Ibid.* 354 Which cryed with a femenyne voys. **1583** STANYHURST *Æneis* I. (Arb.) 36 Or wyl you soiourne in this my feminin empyre? **1642** FULLER *Holy & Prof. St.* I. ii. 31 Take notice of some principall of the orders she made in those feminine Academies. **1649** MILTON *Eikon.* vii. (1851) 388 Govern'd and overswaid at home under a Feminine usurpation. **1844** DISRAELI *Coningsby* III. iii, Feminine society. **1865** MISS BRADDON *Only a Clod* xxxviii, They were growing too serious for feminine discussion or friendly sympathy. **1876** —— *J. Haggard's Dau.* I. 9 The feminine element in the business was supplied by his maiden sister.

4. a. Characteristic of, peculiar or proper to women; womanlike, womanly.

14.. *Epiph.* in *Tundale's Vis.* 113 Sche answered most femynyne of chere Full prudently to euery questyon. *c* **1440** *Promp. Parv.* 154/2 Femynyne, or woman lyke, *muliebris*. **1555** EDEN *Decades* 340 Of complexion feminine and flegmatike in comparison to gold. **1601** HOLLAND *Pliny* II. 219 To such as be of a fœminine and delicate bodie. **1667** MILTON *P.L.* IX. 458 Her [Eve's] Heav'nly forme Angelic, but more soft, and Feminine. **1751** JOHNSON *Rambler* No. 149 ⁋ 11 My sister..the young ladies are hourly tormenting by every art of feminine persecution. **1835** LYTTON *Rienzi* I. i, There was something almost feminine in the tender deference with which he appeared to listen. **1873** LOWELL *Among my Bks.* Ser. II. 23 The most virile of poets cannot be adequately rendered in the most feminine of languages.

†**b.** Such as a woman is capable of. *Obs.*

1672 SIR T. BROWNE *Let. to Friend* xix, Some dreams I confess may admit of easie and feminine exposition.

5. Depreciatively: Womanish, effeminate. ? *Obs.*

c **1430** LYDG. *Bochas* II. xiv. (1554) 53 b, Last of eche one was Sardanapall, Most feminine of condicion. **1548** HALL *Chron.* 18 Rebukyng their timerous heartes, and Feminine audacitie. **1614** RALEIGH *Hist. World* I. II. i. §1. 217 Ninias being esteemed no man of warre at all, but altogether feminine. **1647** CLARENDON *Hist. Reb.* I. (1702) I. 41 He was of so unhappy a feminine temper, that he was always in a terrible fright. **1651** HOBBES *Leviath.* II. xxi. 112 Not onely to women, but also to men of feminine courage.

6. a. *Gram.* Of the gender to which appellations of females belong. Of a termination: Proper to this gender. †Of a connected sentence: Consisting of words of this gender.

c **1400** *Test. Love* II. (1560) 282/2 So speak I in feminine gendre in general. **1632** LITHGOW *Trav.* x. 472 Spewing forth also this Fœminine Latine: *Nam mansueta et misericordiosa est Ecclesia, O Ecclesia Romana!* **1774** J. BRYANT *Mythol.* II. 41 Cora..was..a fœminine title of the Sun. **1821** R. TURNER *Arts & Sc.* (ed. 18) 55 Most feminine nouns end in ת or ה. **1845** STODDART *Encycl. Metrop.* I. 30/1 Every noun denoting a female animal is feminine.

b. *Prosody.* ***feminine rime***: in French versification, one ending in a 'mute *e*' (so called because the mute *e* is used as a feminine suffix); hence in wider sense, a rime of two syllables of which the second is unstressed. So ***feminine ending, termination*** (of a line of verse or musical phrase); ***feminine cæsura***, one which does not immediately follow the ictus. ***the*** e ***feminine***: the French '*e* mute', and the similar sound in ME. (dropped in the later language).

1603 S. DANIEL *Defence Rhyme* sig. H3ʳ, Two feminine nūbers (or Trochees, if so you wil call them). **1775** TYRWHITT *Chaucer's Wks.* Pref. Ess. III. §16 Nothing will be ..of such..use for supplying the deficiencies of Chaucer's metre, as the pronunciation of the *e* feminine. **1837–9** HALLAM *Hist. Lit.* I. i. I. §34. 31 The Alexandrine..had generally a feminine termination. **1844** BICK & FELTON tr. *Munk's Metres* 27 The former close, because it terminates in a thesis, and is on that account, less forcible, is called feminine, the latter, masculine. **1870** LOWELL *Study Wind.* (1886) 247 Of feminine rhymes we find..*famë, justicë.* **1880** SWINBURNE *Stud. Shaks.* ii. (ed. 2) 92 Verses with a double ending—which in English verse at least are not in themselves feminine. **1893** E. PROUT *Mus. Form* ii. 9 What is termed by prosodists a 'feminine ending'—that is, the ending of a verse (in musical language, of a 'phrase') on an unaccented note following the accented note on which the actual cadence mostly occurs. **1955** J. A. WESTRUP in H. van Thal *Fanfare for E. Newman* xiii. 188 The feminine endings in the melody are similar to those found in early eighteenth-century instrumental music.

B. *sb.*

1. The adj. used absolutely.

†**a.** *gen.* She that is, or they that are feminine; woman, women. *Obs.*

c **1440** *Songs & Carols 15th C.* (Percy) 65 Not only in Englond, but of every nacion, The femynyng wyl presume men forto gyd. *a* **1605** MONTGOMERIE *Poems* (S.T.S.) lii. 25 The facultie of famenene is so, Vnto thair freind to be his fo. **1667** MILTON *P.L.* x. 893 Not fill the World at once With men as Angels without Feminine.

b. With defining word: The feminine element in human nature. ***the eternal feminine*** as a literal rendering of G. *das ewig-weibliche* (Goethe).

1892 *Pall Mall G.* 16 June 3/1 The volumes..display the above-noted characteristics of the eternal feminine in its singing moods. **1898** *Daily News* 5 Sept. 6/2 The Eternal Feminine played a larger part in Oxford social life in the earlier part of the eighteenth century than she has since done. **1912** W. J. LOCKE *Aristide Pujol* ix, His quest being little Jean and not the eternal feminine.

c. A person, rarely an animal, that is feminine; a female, a woman. Now only *humorously*.

1513 BRADSHAW *St. Werburge* I. 2021 Doctryne Fer aboue the age of so yonge a femynyne. **1599** HAKLUYT *Voy.* II. I. 235 When..the Eliphant is so entangled, they guide the feminines towards the Pallace. **1606** DAY *Ile of Guls* II. v, Sweete Femenine, clip off the taile of thy discourse with the sissars of attention. **1665** GLANVILL *Sceps. Sci.* xv. 87 While all things are judg'd according to their suitableness..to the fond Feminine. **1774** J. BRYANT *Mythol.* I. 202 The Deity.. was represented as a feminine. **1887** *Graphic* 15 Jan. 67/1 We are two lone feminines.

2. *Gram.* A word of the feminine gender.

1607 TOPSELL *Four-f. Beasts* 114 They call it Zebi, and the feminin herof Zebiah. **1612** BRINSLEY *Pos. Parts* (1669) 105 These feminines want the singular number; *exuviæ, phaleræ.* **1612** —— *Lud. Lit.* 128 In wordes of three terminations, the first is the Masculine, the second the Feminine, the third is the Neuter. **1706** A. BEDFORD *Temple Mus.* vii. 117 All Fœminines of the Singular Number, do end in ה. **1774** J. BRYANT *Mythol.* I. 55 Eliza..It was made a feminine in aftertimes. **1885** MASON *Engl. Gram.* 25 Seamstress and songstress are double feminines.

† **'feminine,** *v. Obs.* [f. prec.] *trans.* To make feminine; to weaken, effeminate.

1583 STUBBES *Anat. Abus.* I. (1879) 170 Musicke..dooth rather femenine the minde.

femininely ('fɛmɪnɪnlɪ), *adv.* [f. as prec. + -LY².] In a feminine manner, like a woman; womanishly. Also, in the feminine gender.

1649 ROBERTS *Clavis Bibl.* 365 Nor as any peculiar Dialect of this tongue, using this word sometimes femininely. **1814** BYRON *Lara* I. xxvii, So femininely white [that hand] might bespeak Another sex. **1821** —— *Juan* v. lxxx, Now being femininely all arrayed..He look'd in almost all respects a maid. **1859** TENNYSON *Enid* 1124 Femininely fair and dissolutely pale.

feminineness ('fɛmɪnɪnnɪs). [f. as prec. + -NESS.] The state or quality of being feminine; womanliness.

1849 THOREAU *Week on Concord* 392 It was such a feminineness..as is rarest to find in woman. **1859** *Times* 23 Nov. 8/4 Buoncompagni..is gentle even to feminineness. **1890** *Blackw. Mag.* CXLVII. 258/2 Without derogating from her feminineness.

'femininism. [f. as prec. + -ISM.]

1. The state of being feminine.

1846 in WORCESTER (citing *Phren. Jrnl.*), and in mod. Dicts.

2. A feminine or woman's word or expression.

1892 F. HALL in *Nation* 13 Oct. 282/3 The locution [*very pleased*] has been, all along, in the main a femininism.

femi'ninitude. *nonce-wd.* [f. FEMININ-E + -(I)TUDE.] The characteristic quality of feminine persons; womanishness.

1878 J. THOMSON *Plenipotent Key* 19 The spite is but his [Froude's] femininitude.

femininity (fɛmɪ'nɪnɪtɪ). [ME. *femininite*, f. as prec. + -ITY. Cf. Fr. *femininité.*]

1. Feminine quality; the characteristic quality or assemblage of qualities pertaining to the female sex, womanliness; in early use also, female nature.

c **1386** CHAUCER *Man of Law's T.* 262 O serpent under femynynytee. **14..** LYDG. *Temple of Glas* 1045 Hir face, of femyny[ni]te: Thuruȝ honest drede abaisshed so was she. *c* **1430** *Compleynt* 326 ibid. App. 63 In whame yche vertue is at rest..Prudence and femynynytee. **1835** *Blackw. Mag.* XXXVII. 230 She was all that my most romantic dreams had fancied of femininity. **1893** *Westm. Gaz.* 22 Feb. 4/2 What she [the American woman] conspicuously lacks, on the other hand, is essential femininity.

concr. *a* **1876** G. DAWSON *Biog. Lect.* (1886) 194 A perfect femininity of architecture, the Venus of Gothic creation.

2. In depreciative sense: Womanishness.

1863 E. L. SWIFTE in *N. & Q.* 3rd Ser. IV. 264 A certain femininity, which our *patresfamilias* call changeableness. **1879** T. P. O'CONNOR *Beaconsfield* 136 Features delicate almost to femininity. **1855** *Manch. Exam.* 22 July 3/1 The femininity of Fénelon's nature.

3. In applied senses: **a.** The fact of being a female. **b.** Feminine peculiarity (in shape).

1867 *Morn. Star* 26 Nov., There is no doubt of her femininity, though her counterfeit of a man is..perfect. **1891** *Pall Mall G.* 2 June 2/1 A part for which the exuberant femininity of her physique obviously disqualifies her.

4. *concr.* Women in general; womankind.

1865 *Daily Tel.* 12 Apr. 7 Crinoline..has..enlightened us respecting the not faultless ankles of femininity. **1878** MRS. RIDDELL *Mother's Darl.* II. xv. 134 She had changed..into a tenderer and softened specimen of femininity.

'femininize, *v. rare*⁻¹. [f. FEMININE + -IZE.] *trans.* To make (a word) feminine, to give a feminine form to.

1868 F. HALL *Benares* 8 The name of King Champa, femininized, became that of the metropolis of Anga, Champâ.

feminism ('fɛmɪnɪz(ə)m). [f. L. *fēmin-a* + -ISM.] **1.** The qualities of females.

1851 in OGILVIE.

2. [After F. *féminisme.*] Advocacy of the rights of women (based on the theory of equality of the sexes). (Cf. WOMANISM.)

1895 *Athenæum* 27 Apr. 533/2 Her intellectual evolution and her coquettings with the doctrines of 'feminism' are traced with real humour. **1908** *Daily Chron.* 7 May 4/7 In Germany feminism is openly Socialistic. **1909** *Ibid.* 29 May 4/4 Suffragists, suffragettes, and all the other phases in the crescendo of feminism.

3. *Path.* The development of female secondary sexual characteristics in a male.

1882 *Syd. Soc. Lex.* II, *Feminism*, the qualities of a female. Also Lorain's term for the arrest of development of the male towards the age of puberty, which gives to it somewhat of the attributes of the female. **1945** H. BURROWS *Biol. Actions Sex Hormones* xxiii. 453 The symptoms of adrenal virilism and feminism are caused by an excessive production of androgen or oestrogen by the adrenal.

feminist ('fɛmɪnɪst), *a.* and *sb.* Also **'femininist.** [ad. F. *féministe*, f. L. *fēmina* woman: see -IST.]

A. *adj.* Of or pertaining to feminism, or to women. **B.** *sb.* An advocate of feminism.

1894 *Daily News* 12 Oct. 5/5 What our Paris Correspondent describes as a 'Feminist' group is being formed in the French Chamber of Deputies. **1895** *Critic* 2 Feb. 90/2 The writer depicts Ford as the deepest 'femininist' in the Shakespearian constellation. **1898** *Daily Chron.* 15 Oct. 5/1 The lady Parliamentary reporter is the latest development of the feminist movement in New Zealand. **1904** *Athenæum* 26 Nov. 730/2 There have been feminists who claimed George Eliot as the rival of Thackeray. **1920** W. J. LOCKE *House of Baltazar* v. 56 We're out of this feminist hurly-burly. **1930** *Manch. Guardian* 15 Sept. 7/7 Feminists are rare birds in Russia.

Hence **femi'nistic, femini'nistic** *adjs.*

1902 M. BEERBOHM *Around Theatres* (1924) I. 365 Ibsen's femininistic propaganda. **1908** *Westm. Gaz.* 11 Sept. 6/3 Some thinkers in Hungary anticipate feministic developments even in Turkey. **1912** *Englishwoman* Mar. 261 This society is only feministic in so far as it strives to give women better opportunities.

feminity (fɪ'mɪnɪtɪ). [ME. *feminite*, a. OF. *feminité*, f. Lat. type **fēminitas*, f. *fēmina* woman.]

1. = FEMININITY 1.

1386 CHAUCER *Man of Law's T.* 262 (Lansd. 360), O serpent vnder femenyte. *c* **1470** HARDING *Chron.* Proem xiv, The thyrde sonne..wedded dame Blaunch, ful of feminytee. *c* **1485** *Digby Myst.* (1882) III. 71 Here is mary, ful fayr and ful of femynyte. **14..** *Pol. Rel. & L. Poems* (1866) 43 Goodnes, the Rote of all vertve Which Rotide is in youre femynite. **1595** SPENSER *Col. Clout* 515 She is the.. mirrhor of feminitie. **1854** MARION HARLAND *Alone* iv, She laughed at the ludicrous repetition of feminity in the second line. **1868** BROWNING *Ring & Bk.* IX. 299 Put forth each charm And proper floweret of feminity.

2. = FEMININITY 2.

1669 H. MORE *Exp. 7 Epist.* vi. 83 There being all these symptoms of Feminity in the Church of Rome. **1890** J. FORSTER in *Academy* 23 Aug. 149/2 There is..a decided note of feminity in his genius; a want of manly strength.

3. = FEMININITY 4; also a band of women.

† ***queen of feminity***: queen of the Amazons.

c **1430** LYDG. *Bochas* I. viii. (1544) 14 a, Theseus.. Weddid Apolita..The hardy quene of femynitie. **1513** BRADSHAW *St. Werburge* I. 1633 Nexte in ordre..Was our blessed lady, floure of femynyte. **1813** HOGG *Queen's Wake* 171, I haif watchit..Quhairevir blumis femenitye. **1816** SCOTT *Antiq.* xxii, I tell thee, Mary, Hector's understanding, and far more that of feminity, is inadequate to comprehend the extent of the loss. **1872** BROWNING *Fifine* xxi, Provided..this feminity be followed By..Fifine!

feminivorous (fɛmɪ'nɪvərəs), *a. rare*⁻¹. [f. L. *fēmin-a* woman + -*(i)vor-us* devouring + -OUS.] That eats the flesh of women.

1820 *Examiner* No. 644. 523/1 Our feminivorous bride-groom however is somewhat inconsistently represented.

feminization (ˌfɛmɪnaɪ'zeɪʃən). [f. next + -ATION.] **1. a.** The action of making feminine. **b.** The giving of a feminine inflexion to a word.

1844 *Blackw. Mag.* LV. 510 There is a sweetness, a softness, and feminization of tone, in the lower passages. **1886** H. JAMES *Bostonians* III. II. xxxiv. 52 'To save it [the sex] from what?' she asked. 'From the most damnable feminisation!' **1891** MISS DOWIE *Girl in Karp.* 115 Their [Poles'] careless and light-hearted feminisation of a verb. **1960** *20th Cent.* May 401 The process of softening in the worker. I should..call it his feminization.

2. *Biol.* The assumption of female sexual characteristics (by a male animal or plant); the occurrence of female sexual characteristics in a person who is genetically male.

1922 F. H. A. MARSHALL *Physiology of Reproduction* (ed. 2) xv. 697 (*caption*) Feminisation of guinea-pig... The animals are arranged in the following order:—Normal male, two feminised brothers, castrated brother. **1957** *New Biol.* XXIII. 16 The time of transition to female flower formation provides a convenient index of the 'feminization' of the plant. **1959** *Lancet* 17 Oct. 592/1 Apparent females with testicular feminisation are sex-reversed males. **1970** *Sci. Jrnl.* June 50/1 However in rare cases, known as testicular feminization, the male organs do not develop although the foetus has testes and a male genetic constitution.

feminize ('fɛmɪnaɪz), *v.* [f. L. *fēmin-a* + -IZE. Cf. Fr. *féminiser.*]

1. a. *trans.* To make feminine or womanish; to give a feminine cast to (a description). **b.** *intr.* To become or grow feminine.

1652, 1653 [see FEMINIZED]. **1776** 'COURTNEY MELMOTH' [S. T. Pratt] *Pupil of Pleas.* II. 98 It only served the more to feminize..and to recommend her to the spectator. **1790** MRS. A. M. JOHNSON *Monmouth* I. 175 Let not an idea of her feminize a soul that should now burn but for glory and a crown. **1841** J. T. HEWLETT *Parish Clerk* III. 81 Feminize this description..and you see Harriette. **1866** *Ch. Times* 6 Jan. 2/3 Any more than a boy is feminized by learning music. **1892** *Nation* 21 July 45/2 May it not be said that he feminized him too much?

b. **1852** *Blackw. Mag.* LXXI. 85 The women..would make those present look very small..but that they are feminising.

2. *trans. Biol.* To induce female sexual characteristics in.

1922 [see FEMINIZATION 2]. **1924** G. R. DE BEER *Growth* ix. 62 By grafting a male gland into a female the latter can be masculinized, and a male can be feminized by the converse graft. **1962** D. J. B. ASHLEY *Human Intersex* iv. 60 Parabiosis experiments on primitive vertebrates showed inversion of sex in either direction, males were feminized and females masculinized.

Hence **'feminized** *ppl. a.*, **'feminizing** *vbl. sb.* and *ppl. a.*

1652 WRIGHT tr. *Camus' Nature's Paradox* 113 Her vigorous exertion made them incline to the thought of her

beeing a Male Feminiz'd. **1653** H. MORE *Conject. Cabbal.* 45 The Serpent said to the feminized Adam. **1867** *Ch. Times* 6 July 236/4 The feminizing of the clerical mind is one of.. many.. evils. **1890** *Harper's Mag.* July 320/1 The husband, if he has become sufficiently.. feminized, may go to the House. **1962** D. J. B. ASHLEY *Human Intersex* v. 75 Tumours of the adrenal cortex which secreted feminizing hormones.

femino- ('fɛmɪnəʊ), used as combining form (see -O) of L. *fēmina* woman, in sense 'female'. **feminophobia**, fear of women (see quot. 1960); *nonce-wd.*

1884 [see MASCULO-]. **1960** KOESTLER *Lotus & Robot* II. viii. 213 One would have to coin the term feminophobia—the behaviour of shy young men in the presence of members of the opposite sex.

feminoid ('fɛmɪnɔɪd), *a.* [f. L. *fēmin-a* woman + -OID.] Feminine (but not female); of female form or appearance.

1923 J. S. HUXLEY *Ess. Biologist* iv. 145 The 'feminoid' man shows the reverse tendency. **1932** *Times Lit. Suppl.* 18 Aug. 583/2 Man after infancy has a 'feminoid' phase. **1964** L. MARTIN *Clinical Endocrinol.* (ed. 4) vi. 215 Feminoid external genitalia.

femishing: see FUMISHING *Obs.*

‖**femme** (fam). [Fr.] **1.** Woman, wife. *rare.* In the *U.S. colloq.* (with pronunc. (fɛm)), girl. Also, a lesbian who adopts a passive, feminine role (opp. BUTCH *sb.*[1]).

1814 BYRON *Jrnl.* 16 Jan. (1875) 361 Divorce ruins the poor *femme.* **1928** J. P. MCEVOY *Showgirl* iv. 52 Eight femmes and a pair of male hoofers take up the burden when she is off. **1936** *Nat. Geogr. Mag.* LXIX. 778/2 West Point slang... A young lady is a 'femme' or 'fem'. **1944** [see BRUSH *v.*[2] 5 b]. **1961** W. BROWN *Bedeviled* 71 A step upward on the social ladder are the female transvestites and their '*femmes*' who congregate in the 'gay' bars of Greenwich Village. **1966** [see BUTCH *sb.*[1]].

2. In Fr. combinations. **femme de ménage** (fam də menaʒ), a charwoman, or domestic help; **femme du monde** (fam dy mɔ̃d), a woman of the world; **femme fatale** (fam fatal), a dangerously attractive woman; **femme incomprise** (fam ɛ̃kɔ̃priz), a woman who is misunderstood or not truly appreciated.

1849 THACKERAY *Pendennis* I. xxiii. 217 Miss Amory is a *femme incomprise.* **1870** MRS. OGIER WARD *Jrnl.* 16 Nov. in *Outside Paris* (1871) 41 To cook for them.. I am obliged to hire a femme de menage. **1885** A. EDWARDS *Girton Girl* II. iii. 35 Poor Linda must practise many a humiliating economy in her lot of femme incomprise. **1894** W. JAMES *Let.* 24 Jan. in R. B. Perry *Tht. & Char. W. James* (1935) II. 188 His wife was a *femme du monde*, however, and fully made up for his lack of conversation. *c* **1903** WYNDHAM LEWIS *Let.* (1963) 10 At this studio there is a femme de menage that does your room. **1912** G. B. SHAW *Let.* 19 Aug. (1952) 39 Here I saw a *Femme Fatale* who was a fine figure of a woman. **1913** D. H. LAWRENCE *Sons & Lovers* xii. 318 The dormant woman was the *femme incomprise.* **1919** C. MACKENZIE *Sylvia & Michael* iii. 71 If she did not know what Eliane was, she might easily have mistaken her for a *femme du monde* like herself. **1924** Femme fatale [see BLAH *sb.*]. **1936** E. H. W. MEYERSTEIN *Let.* 7 Jan. (1959) 180 As if these gay twitterers, like the eternal femme incomprise, refused to impart the secrets of their being to any! **1938** *Times Lit. Suppl.* 28 May 371/1 A pretty *femme fatale* who lost her head. **1944** W. S. MAUGHAM *Razor's Edge* i. 36 There's no better education for a young man than to become the lover of a woman of a certain age and.. if she's.. a *femme du monde*.. it would immediately give him a situation in Paris. **1954** M. F. RODELL *Mystery Fiction* ix. 56 Whirling in a high-powered car from Monte Carlo to Cap d'Antibes on the trail of an exotically beautiful *femme fatale.* **1955** E. POUND *Section: Rock-Drill* lxxxvi. 26 'Le prussien c'est un chic homme.' Said the aged femme de ménage with four teeth out.

‖**femme de chambre** (fam də ʃɑ̃br). [Fr.]

1. A lady's maid.

1762 STERNE *Let.* 12 Aug., I have got a.. decent *femme de chambre*, and a good-looking *laquais.* **1824** MEDWIN *Convers. Byron* (1832) I. 48 Fletcher's.. wife.. was at that time *femme de chambre* to Lady Byron. **1849** THACKERAY *Pendennis* lvii. (1885) 564 Martha.. as *femme de chambre*, accompanied her young mistress.

2. A chambermaid.

a **1828** D. WORDSWORTH *Tour Continent* in *Jrnls.* (1941) II. 10 Pretty *Femme de chambre*.. her keys by her side. **1890** *Eng. Illust. Mag.* Christmas No. 272 The crisp and beaming *femmes de chambre* of our neighbours across the Channel.

femoral ('fɛmərəl), *a.* and *sb.* [f. L. *femor-*, *femur* thigh + -AL[1].]

A. *adj.* Of or pertaining to the femur or thigh. Chiefly *Anat.*, as *femoral artery, bone*, etc.

1782 S. SHARP *Surgery* Intr. (ed. 10) 50 The largest crooked needle.. should be used.. in taking up the.. femoral.. arteries in amputation. **1800** *Med. Jrnl.* IV. 333 The phænomena which occurred in a case of deep-seated femoral hernia. **1821** SCOTT *Kenilw.* xxx, Flibbertigibbet.. thrust a pin into the rear of the short femoral garment. **1840** HOOD *Kilmansegg, Her Accident* xx, The femoral bone of her dexter leg. **1872** F. G. THOMAS *Dis. Women* 636 They may enter the femoral, umbilical and ischiatic openings.

B. *sb.* = *femoral artery.*

1859 TODD *Cycl. Anat.* V. 542/1 In the Sloth.. the brachials and femorals are split up. **1881** MIVART *Cat* 213 The femoral gives off a large branch called the deep femoral.

†'**femorals**, *sb. pl. Obs.* In 7 femoralles. [a. OF. *femoralles* = late L. *femorālia*, f. *femor-*, *femur* thigh.] Clothing for the thighs; breeches.

1609 BIBLE (Douay) *Lev.* vi. 10 The priest shal be revested with the tunike and the linnen femoralles.

femoro- ('fɛmərəʊ), used as combining form (see -O) of FEMUR = pertaining to the femur; also = FEMORAL *a.*

1839 HOOPER *Med. Dict.* (ed. 7) 624/1 Femorocele. **1872** G. M. HUMPHRY *Obs. Myol.* 22 This femoro-fibular muscle appears to represent the short or femoral origin of the biceps. **1897** *Brit. Jrnl. Dermatol.* IX. 146 In the groins, and about the pubes, penis, and femoro-scrotal folds the scar is seen to be breaking down. **1898** [see AUTOTOMY]. **1900** DORLAND *Med. Dict.* 254/1 *Femorocele*, femoral hernia. **1962** *Lancet* 8 Dec. 1195/1 Femoropopliteal arterial bypass was advised.

femto- ('fɛmtəʊ), *prefix.* [ad. Da., Norw. *femten* fifteen + -O.] Prefixed to the names of units in metric systems to form the names of units 10^{15} times smaller.

1961 *Symbols, Units & Nomencl. Physics* (Internat. Union Pure & Appl. Physics) 5 (*heading*) The following prefixes should be used to indicate decimal fractions or multiples of a unit... Femto. **1963** *Nature* 16 Mar. 1056/1 The International Committee [on Weights and Measures].. adopted two new prefixes for denoting sub-multiples of units. They are: femto, 10^{-15}, symbol 'f'.

femur ('fiːmə(r)). Pl. femurs ('fiːməz), femora ('fɛmərə). [a. L. *femur* thigh.]

1. *Anat.* The thigh bone in man and other vertebrata.

1799 in *Med. Jrnl.* II. 482 The femur.. was found in blackish fragments. **1830** R. KNOX *Béclard's Anat.* §615 A case of false joint in consequence of the fracture of the neck of the femur. **1869** GILLMORE *Reptiles & Birds* i. 12 The femur, or thigh, is much lengthened and slightly curved. **1872** NICHOLSON *Palæont.* 314 The thigh-bone or femur, corresponding with the humerus in the fore-limb.

2. *Entom.* The corresponding part in an insect; the third articulation of the foot.

1834 MCMURTRIE *Cuvier's Anim. Kingd.* 327 The ambulatory organs of locomotion consist of.. a femur, etc. **1875** W. HOUGHTON *Sk. Brit. Insects* 128 In some genera the femur of the hind legs is enormously swollen.

3. *Arch.* 'The space between the channels [of the Triglyph]' (Gwilt).

1563 SHUTE *Archit.* D j b, The pillor shalbe garnished with Canalicoli.. and the fifth parte is for Striæ, which are also called Femora.

fen (fɛn), *sb.*[1] Forms: α. 1 fen(n, 3–7 fenn(e, (4 feen, 6 finne, fene), 2– fen. β. 2 ven, 2–4 venn(e. [OE. *fen*, *fenn* neut., masc. = OFris. *fenne*, *fene* masc. (MDu., MLG. *venne*, Du. *ven* fem., Du. *veen* neut.) water-meadow, bog, OHG. *fenna* fem., *fenni* neut. (Ger. *fenne* neut., *fehn* fem.) marsh, ON. *fen* neut., quagmire, Goth. *fani* neut., mud:—OTeut. **fanjo(m* (*-jo-z*, *-jâ*).]

1. a. Low land covered wholly or partially with shallow water, or subject to frequent inundations; a tract of such land, a marsh.

Beowulf 104 (Gr.) Se þe moras heold fen and fæsten. *c* **888** K. ÆLFRED *Boeth.* xviii. §2, & eall þæt his fennas & moras ʒenumen habbað. *c* **1205** LAY. 18113 He.. drof Irisce men ʒeond wateres and ʒeond fenes. **1297** R. GLOUC. (Rolls) 146 Grantebrigge & hontendone mest plente of dep ven. *c* **1325** *King of Almaigne* in *Pol. Songs* (Camden) 70 He hath robbed Engelond, the mores ant th[e] fenne. *c* **1440** *York Myst.* vii. 126 They will slee me, be ffenne or ffrith. **1523** SKELTON *Garl. Laurel* 1321 In Lerna, the Grekis fen. **1600** HAKLUYT *Voy.* (1810) III. 584 Mexico, which is seated in a great fen. **1727–46** THOMSON *Summer* 1028 The joyless sun.. draws the copious steam from swampy fens. **1808** J. BARLOW *Columb.* IV. 593 Win from the waters every stagnant fen. **1883** STEVENSON *Treas. Isl.* III. xiv. (1886) 111 The margin of the broad, reedy fen.

fig. **1676** MARVELL *Mr. Smirke* 36 He did.. cut Poe-dike to let in a Flood of all Heresies, upon the Fenns of Christianity. **1802** WORDSW. '*Milton! thou should'st be living*', England hath need of thee; she is a fen Of stagnant waters. **1866** ALGER *Solit. Nat. & Man* III. 129 The hot fen of emulation and vice.

b. esp. † *the fen* (obs.), *the fens*: certain low-lying districts in Cambridgeshire, Lincolnshire, and some adjoining counties.

905 *O.E. Chron.* an. 905 Eall oð ða fennas norð. *c* **1540** *Pilgr. Tale* 1 in *Thynne's Animadv.* (1875) App. I. 77 In lincolneshyr, fast by the fene, ther stant a hows. **1631** *Star Chamb. Cases* (Camden) 59 Divers lands and wast grounds called the Fennes. **1770** GRAY in *Corr. N. Nicholls* (1843) 115 Two hundred thousand acres are drowned in the Fens here. **1809** *Med. Jrnl.* XXI. 92 A short visit to the Fens of Cambridgeshire. **1890** *Murray's Handbk. Lincolnshire* 4 Large flocks of geese are still kept in the Fens about Spalding.

†**2.** Mud, clay, dirt, mire, filth. Also, excrement.

c **897** K. ÆLFRED *Gregory's Past.* xvi. 104 He underfehð ðæt fenn ðara ðweandra. *c* **1000** ÆLFRIC *Gloss.* in Wr.-Wülcker 147 *Limus, lutum*, fenn. *c* **1175** *Lamb. Hom.* 47 Ieremie.. stod.. in þe uenne up to his muðe. *c* **1250** *Gen. & Ex.* 490 Or or flum noe spredde his fen. **1340** HAMPOLE *Pr. Consc.* 655 Of þe comes mykel foul thyng, Als fen, and uryn and spyttyng. *c* **1380** WYCLIF *Wks.* (1880) 62 To.. baþe hem in lustis as swyn in feen. **1460** *Lybeaus Disc.* 1500 Bothe maydenes, and garssoun, Fowyll fen schull on the throwe. **1513** DOUGLAS *Æneis* III. iv. 17 The vile belleis of thai cursit schrewis Aboundis of fen maist abhominable. **1535** STEWART *Cron. Scot.* III. 440 The loving in ane mannis mouth, Maid of him self, stinkis lyke ony fen Into the eiris of all vther men.

fig. **1387** TREVISA *Higden* (Rolls) I. 17 Virgile souʒt gold of wit and wisdom in the fen of Ennii þe poete.

3. *slang.* (see quots.) ? *Obs.*

a **1700** B. E. *Dict. Cant. Crew, Fag the Fen*, drub the Whore. **1725** *New Cant. Dict.*, *Fen*, a Strumpet, or Bawd, a common Prostitute.

4. *attrib.* and *Comb.* **a.** simple attributive, as ***fen bank, -boat, -boot, -country, -duck, -dyke, -earth, -fowl, -frog, -grass, -land*** (whence ***fenlander***), ***-river, -rush, -skate, -skater, -skating, -soil.*** **b.** objective, as ***fen-affecter, -dweller, -farmer, -farming, -paring.*** **c.** originative, as ***fen-born, -bred, -sucked*** adjs.

1616 CHAPMAN *Batrachom.* 17 The farre-fam'de *Fen-affecter. **1691** RAY *Creation* II. (1692) 73 The *Fenbanks in the Isle of Ely. **1890** *Daily News* 12 June 6/2 A fen-bank about six miles from Peterborough. **1766** PENNANT *Zool.* (1769) III. 272 One of the little *fen boats. **1805** *Edin. Rev.* V. 401 The hard seam of his *fen-boot. **1641** MILTON *Ch. Govt.* II. 63 That *fenborn serpent. **1871** SWINBURNE *Songs bef. Sunrise, Eve of Revolution* 296 These fen-born fires. **1597** DRAYTON *Mortimeriados* 116 The *fen-bred vapours. **1830** T. ALLEN *Hist. Lincolnsh.* I. iii. 65 Other rivers of the *Fen Country. **1867** FREEMAN *Norm. Conq.* (1876) I. vi. 441 The great religious houses of the fen country. **1620** VENNER *Via Recta* iii. 65 The *Fenducke, or Moore-hen. **1610** *Fen-dweller [see FEN-MAN]. **1647** FULLER *Good Th. in Worse T.* (1841) 84 Strange that those fen-dwellers should approach the fiery region. **1878** MILLER & SKERTCHLEY *Fenland* xiii. 416 The spleen of fen-dwellers is often enlarged. *c* **1710** C. FIENNES *Diary* (1888) 127 Ye *ffendiks.. are deep ditches wth draines. *a* **1728** WOODWARD *Fossils* (1729) I. 205 The surface is of Black *Fen Earth. **1891** A. J. FOSTER *The Ouse* 196 The *fen-farmers still gather in its market-place on Thursdays. **1852** CLARKE *Fen Sketches* 262 The unexampled improvements which have taken place in *Fen-farming. **1865** KINGSLEY *Herew.* xxi, Listen ye *fen-frogs all. **1844** HARDY in *Proc. Berw. Nat. Club* II. 108 A covering of *Fen-grasses. *a* **1000** *Guthlac* (1848) 50 He þurh þa *fenland reow. **1070** *O.E. Chron.* an. 1070 þet Englisce folc of eall þa feon landes comen to heom. **1855** LONGF. *Hiaw.* Introd. 30 In the moorlands and the fen-lands. *a* **1661** FULLER *Worthies* (1811) II. 21 *Apud Girvios*; that is, amongst the *Fenlanders. **1797** A. YOUNG *Agric. of Suffolk* 161 A very complete and effective tool, called a *fen-paring plough, the furrow of which is burnt. **1546** LANGLEY *Pol. Verg. De Invent.* II. vii. 45 a, A kind of *fen-rishes yt grew in the marish groundes of Egipt. **1892** *Badminton Libr., Skating* vii. 268 A standard type of *Fen skates. **1882** N. & A. GOODMAN (*title*), Handbook of *Fen skating. **1846** J. BAXTER *Libr. Pract. Agric.* (ed. 4) I. 375 Light *fen soils. **1605** SHAKS. *Lear* II. iv. 169 You *Fen-suck'd Fogges.

d. In various plant-names, etc.: as, **fen-berry**, the cranberry (*Vaccinium Oxycoccus*); **fen-cress** = WATERCRESS (*Nasturtium officinale*); †**fen-down** = COTTON-GRASS; **fen grapes** = *fenberry*; **fen lentil**, water lentils (*Lemna minor*); **fen-rue** (see quot.); †**fen whort** = *fen-berry.*

1578 LYTE *Dodoens* VI. xi. 671 Those which the Germaynes doo call Veenbesien, that is to say Marsh or *Fen-berries. **1678** LITTLETON *Lat. Dict.* s.v., *Fen-berries.* **1863** PRIOR *Plant-n.* (1879) 77 *Fen-berry*, from its growing in fens, the cranberry. *c* **1000** *Sax. Leechd.* II. 18 Wiþ heafod wærce, ʒenim.. *fencersan. **1818** TODD, *Fen-cress.* **1495** *Act 11 Hen. VII*, c. 19 With no scalded fethers nor *fen downe nor none other unlawful and corrupt stuffes. **1720** STRYPE *Stow's Surv.* (1754) II. 317/2 They.. bought Fen Down.. for an Half penny a Pound, and sold the same among Feathers for 6d. a Pound. **1597** GERARDE *Herbal* III. clxvi. 1367 Moszbeeren, Veenbesien; that is to saie *Fen grapes or Fen berries. **1878–86** BRITTEN & HOLLAND *Plant-n.*, Fen Grapes, *Vaccinium Oxycoccus* L. **1601** HOLLAND *Pliny* I. 378 After the manner of *Fen-lentils or Duckes meat. **1863** PRIOR *Plant-n.* (1879) 77 **Fen-Rue*, from its divided rue-like leaves and place of growth. *Thalictrum flavum* L. **1578** LYTE *Dodoens* VI. xi. 671 Marrishe or *Fen Whortes grow.. in low, moyst places.

5. Special comb. †**fen-canopy** (see quot.); **fen-cock** (see quot.); **fen-cricket**, the mole cricket (*Gryllotalpa vulgaris*); **fen-fever**, a malarious fever; **fen-fire** = IGNIS FATUUS, a will of the wisp; **fen-goose**, usually the Grey-Lag Goose (*Anser cinereus*); **fen-nightingale** (see quot.); **fen-oak** (see quot.); **fen-pole**, a jumping pole for crossing ditches, etc.; **fen-reeve**, an officer having charge of fen lands; **fen-runners**, a kind of skates suitable for fen-skating; **fen-shake**, the ague; **fen-slodger**, a name given to the Fen-men; **fen-thrush** (see quot.); **fen wainscot (moth)**, a moth, *Arenostola phragmitidis*, found in marshy places. Also FEN-HOOD, FEN-MAN.

1658 ROWLAND *Moufet's Theat. Ins.* 957 Our Countreymen that live about the Fens have invented a ..*Fen-canopy.. made of.. Cowes dung.. with the smell and juice whereof the Gnats being very much taken.. let them sleep quietly in their beds. **1880** *W. Cornwall Gloss.*, **Fencock*, the water-rail. **1678** LITTLETON *Lat. Dict.*, A *Fen-cricket, *gryllotalpa.* **1753** CHAMBERS *Cycl. Supp.*, *Fen-cricket*, a name given by some people to the gryllotalpa. **1772** J. LIND (*title*), A Treatise on the Putrid and Remitting *Fen Fever. **1814–5** SHELLEY '*The cold earth*' iii, As a *fenfire's beam on a sluggish stream, Gleams dimly. **18..** SWINBURNE *Athens*, Mocked as whom the fen-fire leads. **1606** SYLVESTER *Du Bartas* II. iv. II. *Magnif.* 426 The wilde *Fen-goose. **1766** PENNANT *Zool.* (1776. 4°) II. 482 Grey Lag, the Fen-Goose of Lister. **1885** SWAINSON *Prov. Names Birds* 147 Fen, or Marsh, goose. *a* **1825** FORBY *Voc. E. Anglia*, **Fen-nightingale*, a frog. **1868** W. H. WHEELER *Fens S. Lincolnsh.* 69 Nor must the mention of the fen nightingales or frogs be omitted. **1886** *S.W. Linc. Gloss.*, **Fen-oaks*, willows. **1844** *Camp of Refuge* I. 10 It was a *fen-pole, such.. as our fenners yet use. **1865** W. WHITE *E. Eng.*

II. 172 The common lands are under the charge of '*fen-reeves'. **1873** KINGSLEY *Plays & Puritans* 76 How merrily their long *fen-runners whistled along the ice-lane. **1794** G. ADAMS *Nat. & Exp. Philos.* I. ix. 350 What they [imported Irish reapers] call the *fen-shake. **1856** P. THOMPSON *Hist. Boston* 644 The Fenmen..were a century later known as Slodgers or *Fen-Slodgers. **1893** BARING GOULD *Cheap Jack Zita* I. 57 Sons or grandsons of half-wild fen-slodgers. **1654** in *East Anglian* (1871) IV. 14 They have chosen John Kent to be *ffenn Reeve for the parish of Gillingham All Sts. **1910** H. M. DOUGHTY *Chron. Theberton* xv. 209 Fen reeves had been elected every year by 'town meeting'. **1854** BAKER *Gloss. Northampton* I. 226 **Fen-thrush*, the missel-thrush, *Turdus viscivorus*. **1885** SWAINSON *Prov. Names Birds* 2 Missel Thrush (*Turdus viscivorus*)..Fen Thrush (Northants). **1860** H. N. HUMPHREYS *Genera Brit. Moths* I. 67 The *Fen Wainscot..has the anterior wings rather bluntly lanceolate. **1951** COLYER & HAMMOND *Flies Brit. Isles* xx. 251 One [*sc.* a larva of *Cnemopogon apicalis*] has been recorded from a caterpillar of the Fen Wainscot Moth.

fen (fɛn), *sb.*² *dial.* [OE. *fyne* mildew; the mod. form (with *e* for OE. *y*) is Kentish; cf. FENNY *a.*², VINEWED.] A mould or parasitical fungus that attacks the hop-plant.

1731 S. HALES *Stat. Ess.* I. 33 Hops were all infected with mold or fen. **1805** R. W. DICKSON *Pract. Agric.* (1807) II. 249 The mould or fen mostly occurs at a somewhat later period. **1842** JOHNSON *Farmer's Encycl.*, *Fen*, the name of a distemper to which hops are subject. It consists of a quick-growing mould or moss.

‖**fen**, *sb.*³ [*fen*, in L. version of Avicenna, ad. Arab. *fann* species, class.] A section in Avicenna's Canon.

c **1386** CHAUCER *Pard. T.* 562, I suppose that Avycen Wrot never in canoun, ne in non fen Mo wonder sorwes. **1541** R. COPLAND *Guydon's Quest. Chirurg.* Q iij, Sayth Auycen in his fyrste fen of the fyrste boke of his Canon.

†**fen**, *v.*¹ *Obs. rare.* [? f. OF. *fien* dung (see FIENTS); but cf. FEN *sb.*¹ 2.

The word occurs several times on the page, always in the form *fenon* (inf. and 3 pers. pl.).]

intr. Of certain animals: To void dung.

1486 *Bk. St. Albans* F ij a, All bestis that bere talow and stonde vpright Femayen when thay do so say as I the kenne And all oder fenon that rowken downe thenne.

fen (fɛn), *v.*² Also fain. [Usually taken to be a corruption of FEND *v.*] *trans.* To forbid. Only in '*Fen* (*larks*, etc.)!', a prohibitory exclamation, used chiefly by boys at marbles, etc., in order to balk, bar, or prevent some action on the part of another.

1823 MOOR *Suffolk Words* 125 Fen slips over again. **1852** DICKENS *Bleak Ho.* xvi, 'I'm fly', says Jo. 'But fen larks, you know! Stow hooking it'. **1864** BARTLETT *Dict. Amer.*, 'Fen play', I forbid you to play. **1888** *Berksh. Gloss.* s.v. *Ven*, If one player says 'ven knuckledown' this means that his opponent must shoot his marble without resting his hand on the ground.

†'**fenage.** *rare*⁻¹. [a. OF. *fenage*, f. *fener* to make hay:—late L. *fænāre*, f. L. *fænum* hay.] Hay crop.

1610 W. FOLKINGHAM *Art of Survey* I. x. 25 The sowing of the seede of Trefoyle..doth much inrich Meddowes..both in Forrage and Fenage.

fenaunce, obs. form of FINANCE.

†'**fenbrede.** *Obs. rare.* [perh. f. FEN *sb.*¹ + BRED, board.] = Mould-board.

1523 FITZHERB. *Husb.* §3 The fenbrede is a thyn borde, pynned or nayled..to the lyft syde of the shethe in the ferther ende, and to the ploughe tayle in the hynder ende.

fence, *sb.* Also 4 fens, 6 fenst. [aphet. f. of DEFENCE.]

†**1. a.** The action of defending; = DEFENCE. Also, the attitude of self-defence; in ***to stand at fence***.

c **1330** R. BRUNNE *Chron. Wace* (Rolls) 8638 þen Octa studied in his þought: To stonde to fens auailled nought. **1375** BARBOUR *Bruce* xx. 384 That for default of fenss so was To-fruschit in-to placis ser. *c* **1430** *Syr Tryam.* 551 He stode at fence ageyne them. *a* **1400-50** *Alexander* 4753 For nouthire fondis he to flee ne na fens made. *c* **1500** *Felon Sowe Rokeby* in Whitaker *Craven* (1878) 569 Yet, for the fence that he colde make, Scho strake yt fro his hande.

†**b.** ***cap of fence***: see CAP *sb.* 4. ***coat of fence***: see COAT *sb.* 5. So ***doublet of fence***: see DOUBLET. ***house of fence***: a fortified house. ***man of fence***: a defender. *Obs.*

c **1425** WYNTOUN *Cron.* IX. xxi. 12 Ðe Hous of fens of Dalwolsy. **1463** *Mann. & Househ. Exp.* (1841) 158 Ffusten ..ffor to make doblettys off ffence. *c* **1470** HENRY *Wallace* v. 1095 No man of fens is left that house within. **1488** *Will of Sharnebourne* (Somerset Ho.), Doblette of fence. **1514** *Will of R. Peke of Wkd.* 4 June, All my cottes of fense of manse body. **1555** *Reg. Gild Corp. Christi York* (Surtees) 202 My coote of fenst, and steele cappe. **1664** *Flodden F.* I. 5 Each house of fence to fortify.

2. a. The action, practice, or art of fencing, or use of the sword. ***to make fence***: to assume a fencing attitude. Also, ***master, teacher of fence***.

1533 UDALL *Flowres Latine Speaking* (1560) 133 *Disciplina gladiatoria*, is..the waie of trainyng men in..the schooles that maisters of fence keepe. **1535** in W. H. Turner *Select. Rec. Oxford* 131 Dennys, a poore scholler and a teacher of fence. **1599** SHAKS. *Much Ado* v. i. 75 Ile proue it on his body..Despight his nice fence. **1651** HOBBES *Leviath.* I. v. 22 Trusting to the false rules of a master of Fence. **1828** SCOTT *F.M. Perth* iv, A man must know his fence, or have a short lease of his life. **1831** *Examiner* 17/2 He will point his sword at shadows, and make fence at your cat. **1855** MACAULAY *Hist. Eng.* IV. 459 A man of..consummate skill in fence. **1863** MRS. C. CLARKE *Shaks. Char.* iii. 87 Osric..comes to announce..the wager at fence with Laertes.

b. *transf.*

1634 MILTON *Comus* 790 Enjoy your..gay rhetoric, That hath so well been taught her dazzling fence. **1862** MERIVALE *Rom. Emp.* (1865) V. xliv. 254 Fence of tongue was the weapon with which they were to maintain..their honour. **1871** BLACKIE *Four Phases* i. 79 The Sophists were cunning masters of fence. **1883** *Contemp. Rev.* June 871 That shrewd critic and experienced professor of Parliamentary fence.

†**3.** Means or method of defence; protection, security. *Obs.*

c **1440** *Promp. Parv.* 155/1 Fence, defence fro enmyes, *proteccio, defensio.* **1565** JEWEL *Repl. Harding* 550 It is thought to be the surest fence, & strongest warde for that Religion, that they should be keapte stil in ignorance. **1627** MAY *Lucan* II. 408 His choisest buildings were but fence for cold. **1691** T. H[ALE] *Acc. New Invent.* 39 To deliver up his Majesty's Ships to the..Worm..wholly unprovided of any Fence against them. **1745** *De Foe's Eng. Tradesman* (1841) I. ix. 67 Employment is said to be the best fence against temptation. **1756** NUGENT *Montesquieu's Spir. Laws* (1758) I. XII. ii. 261 The subject has no fence to secure his innocence.

Proverb. **1674** N. FAIRFAX *Bulk & Selv.* 98, I dare be bold to say, 'Tis such a flail as there can ne're be fence for. **1730** SWIFT *Poems, On Stephen Duck* 115 The Proverb says; No Fence against a Flail.

4. *concr.* That which serves as a defence.

†**a.** Of persons: A bulwark, defence. *Obs.*

c **1400** *Destr. Troy* 7363 He was fully the fens..Of all the tulkes of Troy. **1552** *Godly Prayers* in *Liturg. Serv. Q. Eliz.* (1847) 248 O Lord Jesus Christ, the only stay and fence of our mortal state.

b. Of things: A defence, bulwark. *arch.* (now with mixture of sense 5).

c **1440** *Promp. Parv.* 155/1 Fence, or defence of closynge (clothynge, P.). **1548** UDALL, etc. *Erasm. Par. Luke* x. 4, I send you forth naked, wythout weapon or fense. **1671** GREW *Anat. Plants* (1682) I. ii. 17 The Skin is the Fence of the Cortical Body. **1697** DRYDEN *Virg. Georg.* II. 483 A hilly Heap of Stones above to lay, And press the Plants with Sherds of Potters Clay. This Fence against immod'rate Rain they found. **1700** S. L. tr. *Fryke's Voy. E. Ind.* 183 [The river] is a mighty Fence to the City Odia. **1727** SWIFT *Gulliver* IV. iv. 278 My whole body wanted a fence against heat and cold. **1814** SCOTT *Ld. of Isles* III. xix, Deer-hides o'er them cast, Made a rude fence against the blast. **1838** THIRLWALL *Greece* II. 278 They hastily formed a high fence out of the wrecks round the fleet.

fig. **1732** LEDIARD *Sethos* II, Strangers would not believe there was a sufficient fence against crimes. **1860** PUSEY *Min. Proph.* 311 They sin, who first remove the skin..or outward tender fences of God's graces.

†**c.** *spec.* The tusk of an elephant (= Fr. *défense*). Also, the involucre of a flower. *Obs.*

1727 *Philip Quarll* 219 The Fences of an Elephant, and the Tusks of a wild Boar. **1776** WITHERING *Brit. Plants* (1796) II. 171 Involucrum, or fence, 2 leafits..to each floret.

5. a. An enclosure or barrier (*e.g.* a hedge, wall, railing, palisade, etc.) along the boundary of a field, park, yard or any place which it is desired to defend from intruders. ***sunk fence***: one placed along the bottom of a depression in the ground; sometimes applied to a ditch. Often preceded by a qualifying word, as: *gun-*, *pale-*, *quick-*, *ring-*, *snake-*, *wire-*, etc. *fence*, for which see those words.

1512 *Nottingham Rec.* III. 340 Owre fense be twixe our medo and Wilforth Pastur. **1570** LEVINS *Manip.* 63/16 A Fence, *vallum.* **1611** BIBLE *Ps.* lxii. 3 As a bowing wall shall ye be, and as a tottering fence. **1697** DRYDEN *Æneid* IX. 457 The famished lion..O'erleaps the fences of the nightly fold. **1711** ADDISON *Spect.* No 56 ⁋3 This huge Thicket of Thorns and Brakes was designed as a kind of Fence or quick-set Hedge. **1767** A. YOUNG *Farmer's Lett. People* 62 They..keep their fences in admirable repair. **1786** GILPIN *Obs. Pict. Beauty Cumbrld.* I. 136 The lake performing the office of a sunk fence. **1832** *Act 2-3 Will. IV*, c. 64 Sched. O. 1648 That point in a stone fence which is immediately opposite a..pool. **1832** HT. MARTINEAU *Ireland* i. 2 A turf bank, was the best kind of fence used. **1891** EDGE in *Law Times* XC. 395/1 An ordinary fence, consisting of a ditch and a bank.

b. *transf.* and *fig.*

1639 FULLER *Holy War* I. iii. (1840) 4 When the fence of order was broken. **1691** HARTCLIFFE *Virtues* 105 Those who have broken through all the Fences of Law. **1712-4** POPE *Rape Lock* II. 119 Oft have we known that seven-fold fence [petticoats] to fail. **1761-2** HUME *Hist. Eng.* (1806) V. lxx. 250 To throw down all fences of the constitution. **1820** LAMB *Elia* Ser. I. *Christ's Hosp.*, Breaking down the strong fences of shame, and awkwardness.

c. Phrases: chiefly U.S. (***to stand*** or ***sit***) ***on*** or ***upon the fence***: (to be) undecided in opinion, or neutral in action. (***to be***) ***on a person's, the other side of the fence***: (to be) on his side, on the side opposed to him. ***to descend on the right side of the fence***: to take the side of the winner. ***to mend*** (or ***look after***) ***one's fences***, of a member of Congress: to renew contact with the electors; also, by extension, to make one's peace (with a person). ***to put one's horse at a fence***: to spur him on to leap it. ***to rush one's fences***, to act precipitately. ***to make a Virginia fence***: 'to walk like a drunken man' (Lowell *Biglow Papers* Introd.). ***over the fence*** (Austral. and N.Z. colloq.), see quot. 1941.

1745 FRANKLIN *Drinker's Dict.* Wks. 1887 II. 26 He makes a Virginia Fence. **1828** *Richmond Whig* 13 Aug. 1/5 (Th.), There are certain Administration Editors, Editors for a long time on the fence, who occasionally undertake..to sit as censors upon their fatigued and dusty brethren. **1829** R. C. SANDS *Writings* (1834) II. 160 Mr. Spratt..was 'on the fence'; where, like a wise man, he determined to sit, until he had made up his mind on which side to get off. **1830** *Annals of Cleveland* No. 316, Now all would-but-dare-not-be-politicians who insist in sitting on the fence, will be amerced a penalty for the same. **1848** LOWELL *Biglow P.* Poems 1890 II. 82 A man represents Not the fellers that sent him, but them on the fence. **1862** *Ibid.* 287, I mean a kin' o' hangin' roun' an' settin' on the fence. **1852** MRS. STOWE *Uncle Tom's C.* vi, It's allers best to stand missis's side the fence. **1863** HOLLAND *Lett. Joneses* v. 80 Any man who would stand upon the fence. **1868** J. T. TROWBRIDGE *Three Scouts* in *Beeton's Boys' Ann.* Suppl. i. 4, I judge your sympathies are more on t'other side of the secession fence than on ours. **1887** A. LANG *Myth, Ritual & Relig.* II. 350 Mr. Morgan..puts his hobby at its highest fence. **1888** *Congress. Rec.* 16 Aug. 7646/1 [They] are at home seeking renomination or looking after their fences. **1889** BARRÈRE & LELAND *Dict. Slang, Mend fences, to* (American), to mend or repair fences for a man is to attend to his interests. **1891** SALISBURY in *Guardian* 28 Jan. 158/2 They gently descended on the right side of the fence. **1906** *Forum* Apr. 444 An early adjournment of the session is deemed essential in order that the members may go home to mend their fences, as the saying is. **1917** A. HUXLEY *Let.* 3 Aug. (1969) 132 As Dean Inge said early in this war, 'God is sitting on the fence and it is perfectly uncertain on which side He will come down.' **1918** *Chrons. N.Z.E.F.* 19 July 276/1 'It's over the blooming fence,' he announced... 'These..bounds. First they put Paris Plage out of bounds.' **1922** G. FRANKAU *Love Story A. Brunton* i. 16 Aliette was not the type of woman who liked rushing her fences, either mentally or on horseback. **1925** A. HUXLEY *Let.* 16 Sept. (1969) 253 We shall be looking at things mostly from the Indian side of the fence. **1927** *Daily Express* 8 Sept. 2/4 The French delegation, which has hitherto been sitting on the fence, has suddenly become exceedingly active. **1937** 'G. ORWELL' *Road to Wigan Pier* xii. 243 The fence on which the literary gent sits..is now pinching his bottom intolerably. **1941** BAKER *Dict. Austral. Slang* 28 *Over the fence*, unreasonable, beyond the pale of common-sense or justice. **1949** N. BALCHIN *Sort of Traitors* iv. 81 You fight all your life for something and then before you know where you are you're on the other side of the fence fighting against it. **1959** *Spectator* 21 Aug. 213/3 It is a pity we have not mended our fences with Colonel Nasser. **1966** *Times* 11 May 13/1 There are still fences to be mended and fingers to be kept in pies. *Ibid.* 13 May 1/7 Britain would not let slip any opportunity in this matter, but there was no question of precipitate action or rushing fences. **1970** 'W. HAGGARD' *Hardliners* viii. 85 It was a thousand pities that Bull's predecessor had been so stupid... There were fences to be mended here and Albert Bull intended to mend them.

6. Technical uses.

a. A guard, guide, or gauge designed to regulate the movements of a tool or machine.

1703 MOXON *Mech. Exerc.* 72 The Fence of the Plow [a grooving-plane] is set to that Distance off the Iron-Plate of the Plow, that you intend the Groove shall lie off the edge of the Board. *Ibid.* 79 The Handle should on either side become a Fence to the Tongue. *Ibid.* 90 These Nails are..to serve for Fences to set, and fit each piece into its proper place. **1823** P. NICHOLSON *Pract. Build.* 222 Fence of a Plane.—A guard, which obliges it to work to a certain horizontal breadth from the arris. **1872** J. RICHARDS *Wood-working Machinery* 185 A long strip or fence passing behind as well as in front of the saw.

b. (See quots.)

1867 SMYTH *Sailor's Word-bk.*, *Fence*, the arm of the hammer-spring of a gun-lock. **1874** KNIGHT *Dict. Mech.* I. 1835/2 *Fence* (locks), an arm or protection which enters the gates of the tumblers when they are adjusted in proper position and coincidence.

c. A ferrule. *rare.*

1862 BORROW *Wild Wales* I. 231 A thin polished black stick..at the end was a brass fence.

7. A state of prohibition. *rare* exc. *attrib.*; cf. *fence-date*, *-month*, *-season*, *-time* in 11.

1874 STUBBS *Const. Hist.* I. xii. 537 [By the Great Charter] all rivers placed in fence [L. *in defenso*] are thrown open.

8. *Thieves' slang.* **a.** A receiver of stolen goods.

a **1700** in B. E. *Dict. Cant. Crew.* **1708** J. HALL *Mem.*, The fence and he are like the devil and the doctor. **1812** *Sporting Mag.* XXXIX. 209 Habberfield..was considered the safest fence about town. **1838** DICKENS *O. Twist* xiii, Ill-treating the boys, you..in-sa-ti-a-ble old fence.

b. A receiving house for stolen goods.

1847 *Illust. Lond. News* 22 May 232 The keeper of the 'fence' loves to set up in business there. **1848** *Punch* XIV. 149 Let M. Galignani rejoice; and let his Bibliothèque..still remain the greatest literary 'fence' in Europe. **1863** W. B. JERROLD *Sign. Distress* iii. 26 The slums of London—the fences and padding-kens.

9. *Sc. Law.* [from the vb.] The action of fencing in various senses. Cf. FENCE *v.* 8.

1541 *Burgh Rec. Prestwick* 2 June (1834) 57 For þe losen of ane fens maid be þe said Allexr. apoun ane wob of Jonat Hunter. *c* **1575** BALFOUR *Practicks* 273 The affirmatioun and fence of the court, that na man tak speach upon hand..except the persewar and defender.

10. *attrib.* and *Comb.* General relations: **a.** appositive (sense 5), as ***fence-wall***. **b.** attributive (sense 2), as ***fence-school***; (sense 4 b), as †***fence-fabric***; (sense 5), as ***fence-post***. **c.** objective (sense 5) ***fence-breaker***, ***-breaking***.

1878 E. S. ELWELL *Boy Colonists* 218 He knew [where] Geddes' old horse, our old friend the *fence-breaker, was feeding. **1900** *Westm. Gaz.* 8 June 4/3, I hope the *fence-breaking will be omitted from the programme. **1609** HOLLAND *Amm. Marcell.* XXIX. ix. 253 The *Fence-fabrickes and all devices else requisite for a siege, were in readinesse. **1792** *Trans. Soc. Promotion Agric., Arts & Manuf.* (U.S.) I. 26 Ship-trunnels, *fence-posts, mill-cogs and fire-wood. **1853** B. F. TAYLOR *Jan. & June* (1871) 13

Life . . laid away in 'Patent Burial Cases' and fastened to rails and fence-posts. **1874** KNIGHT *Dict. Mech.* I. 836/1 A device . . used for driving fence-posts. **1885** H. C. MCCOOK *Tenants of Old Farm* 196, I was standing by a fence-post. **1598** BARRET *Theor. Warres* I. i. 7 As one that vseth often the *Fence-schooles. **1642** FULLER *Holy & Prof. St.* IV. x. 285 He was diligent in . . beating down . . the Manicheans, in whose Fence-school he was formerly brought up. **1823** P. NICHOLSON *Pract. Build.* 338 *Fence-Wall—A wall used to prevent the encroachment of men or animals.

11. Special comb.: **fence-arbour**, a piece in a combination lock which connects the spindle and the tumblers; **fence corner** *U.S.*, (*a*) one of the four corners of a fenced enclosure; (*b*) one of the many angles made by a zig-zag rail fence; also *attrib.*; **fence-guards** (see quot.); **fence-jack** (see quot.); **fence-line**, (*a*) = FENCE *sb.* 5; (*b*) the straight strip of land on which a fence is to be erected; **fence-lizard** (see quot.); **fence-man**, a gladiator; *U.S.*, one who practises 'sitting on the fence', who avoids taking a side in an issue; **fence-month**, (*a*) originally the time of fawning for deer, a period of about 30 days at the end of June and beginning of July, during which hunting was forbidden; (*b*) more broadly: the close season for fishing, etc., during the time of breeding, not always being restricted to one month; **fence-play**, † (*a*) a gladiatorial combat; (*b*) *transf.* discussion; **fence-rail** *U.S.*, a long, rough rail for fencing, split from a small log; **ˈfence-ˌrider** *U.S.* (see quot. 1920); also *fig.* = *fence-man*; **fence-riding** *U.S.*, 'sitting on the fence'; avoidance of committing oneself to one or other of two contrary policies; †**fence-roof**, a roof for defence = L. *testudo*; **fence-row** *U.S.*, a fence with the row of shrubs and other vegetation which frequently grows up under its protection; **fence-season**, **fence-time**, a close season or time for fish, swans, etc. (see *fence-month*); **fence-shop**, a shop at which stolen goods are sold; **fence-sitter**, one who 'sits on the fence'; **fence-sitting**, the action of 'sitting on the fence'; also *attrib.*; **fence-viewer**, (*U.S.*) an officer whose duty it is to see to the erection and maintenance of boundary and highway fences.

1902 *Encycl. Brit.* XXXII. 360/1 A balanced *fence arbour. **1832** J. P. KENNEDY *Swallow Barn* I. xi. 153 He slowly went to the *fence corner, and untied his horse. **1846** J. J. HOOPER *Adv. Simon Suggs* i. 14 Simon and Bill were in a fence corner very earnestly engaged at 'seven up'. **1855** *Knickerbocker* XLV. 197 Posting himself at night in a fence-corner, he saw her at one end of a hollow log. **1874** E. EGGLESTON *Circuit Rider* xxviii. 272 Patty climbed upon a fence-corner. **1876** *Daily News* 5 Oct. 6/1 He sallies from his siesta in a fence corner. **1901** S. E. WHITE *Claim Jumpers* iv. 64 It was . . not as large as a good-sized rat, quite smaller than our own fence-corner chipmunks of the East. **1883** W. S. GRESLEY *Gloss. Coal Mining*, **Fence-guards*, rails fixed round the mouth of a pit-shaft, to keep people and things from falling in. **1874** KNIGHT *Dict. Mech.* I. 836/1 **Fence-jack*, a lever jack adapted for lifting the corner or lock of a worm-fence in order to lay in a new bottom-rail. **1858** J. A. WARDER *Hedges & Evergreens* ii. 38 Its cheapness . . demands its . . adoption where *fence-lines are to be permanent. **1950** *N.Z. Jrnl. Agric.* Apr. 336/3 To aid adoption . . [of orphan lambs] the [foster-parent] ewes have to be tied to a fenceline. **1961** B. CRUMP *Hang On a Minute* 120 They still had to clear the fence line, lay out the material and erect nearly four miles of boundary fence. **1963** N. HILLIARD *Piece of Land* 106 He'd just as soon sleep in a tent along the fence-line. **1889** *Century Dict.*, **Fence-lizard*, the common small lizard or swift of the United States. **1553** GRIMALDE *Cicero's Offices* II. (1558) 98 With hired *fencemen he suppressed all Publius Clodius attempts. **1580** HOLLYBAND *Treas. Fr. Tong, Gladiateur* . . a maister of Fence, a fence man. **1828** *Ohio State Jrnl.* 30 Jan. 3/5 It would be well perhaps for him to inform the public as to their politics. How many neutrals, fencemen &c. **1848** *N.Y. Herald* 14 Oct. (Bartlett 1859), All the fence-men, all the doubters, all the seekers after majorities, will now bustle up. **1889** FARMER *Americanisms* s.v. *Fence*, The possessors of highly developed bumps of caution are called *fence men*; they run with the hare and hunt with the hounds, an operation which receives the equally descriptive name of *fence-riding*. **1594** CROMPTON *Jurisdiction* 197 *Fence moneth is alwaies xv daies afore Midsomer and xv daies after. **1766** PENNANT *Zool.* (1769) III. 245 There is no law for preserving the fish in it during the fence months. **1855** DORAN *Queens Eng. Ho. Hanover* II. vii. 117 The bucks were denied, and he himself once shut out, on pretence it was fence month. **1580** NORTH *Plutarch* (1676) 434 Games . . Wrestlings, and *Fence-playes. **1878** BROWNING *La Saisiaz* 25 Passing lightly in review . . a certain fence-play-strife. **1733** W. BYRD *Journey to Eden* 27 Sept. in *Westover MSS.* (1841) 110 We found the land . . very thin of trees, and those that were standing fit for little but fuel and *fence-rails. **1814** J. TAYLOR *Arator* (ed. 2) 177 Small common fence rails . . make folds with less labour . . than any I have ever tried. **1853** J. G. BALDWIN *Flush Times Alabama* 110 Buck Jones . . seized a fence rail, grasped it in both hands, and . . hurled the same. **1945** *Reader's Digest* Jan. 53/2 He hewed out 300 fence rails, ten feet long. **1834** 'J. DOWNING' *Life A. Jackson* 91 The *fence riders now took courage and jumpt clean off. **1909** R. A. WASON *Happy Hawkins* 207, I met the foreman o' the E.Z. outfit ridin' into town to see if he couldn't pick up a fence-rider. **1920** J. M. HUNTER *Trail Drivers of Texas* 298 The fence rider, also called the 'line rider', is employed to ride fences and repair them. *a* **1859** *N.Y. Mirror* (Bartlett), The dividing line . . admits of no *fence-riding; the candidate must be on one side or the other. **1868** *Congress. Globe* 17 July (De Vere), This question is one of clear right and wrong, and there can be no fence-riding, when the rights of four millions of men are at stake. **1889** Fence-riding [see *fence-man*]. **1609** HOLLAND *Amm. Marcell.* XXIX. xiv. 372 The Romans . . fitted their shields close one to another in manner of a *fence-roufe. **1842** *Amer. Pioneer* I. 43, I was alone, clearing out a *fence row, about a quarter of a mile from the house. **1855** *Trans. Mich. Agric. Soc.* VI. 144 The fence rows were free from weeds and bushes. **1901** N. L. BRITTON *Man. Flora N. States* 952 Along fence-rows in partial shade. **1948** *Country Gentleman* May 175/2 He had cut the fence rows from the board fence. **1880** *Times* 21 Dec. 6/4 To stop . . the alleged traffic of salmon during the 'close' or '*fence' season. **1789** G. PARKER *Life's Painter* xv. 153 In Field-lane, where the handkerchiefs are carried, there are a number of shops called *Fence-shops, where you may buy any number. **1905** *Westm. Gaz.* 8 July 1/2 *Fence-sitters . . are to be shaken out. **1949** J. R. COLE *It was so Late* 12 Why don't you make up your mind—you fence sitter! **1960** *Spectator* 7 Oct. 507 One of the Labour Party's most accomplished fence-sitters. **1904** *Westm. Gaz.* 11 Feb. 1/3 This situation will . . be prolonged until the *fence-sitting Unionists . . come down on one side or the other. **1905** *Ibid.* 5 Mar. 1/2 It is very well to . . denounce Mr. Balfour for timidity and fence-sitting. **1956** *Essays in Criticism* VI. 95 One would have welcomed . . less academic fence-sitting. **1959** *Times Lit. Suppl.* 29 May 322/4 The seminar-paper tends to provide . . a fence-sitting indecision. **1546** *Plumpton Corr.* 251 Ye shall come no time wrong, *fence-time then other. **1584** in Binnell *Descr. Thames* (1758) 63 Fence . . Times, in which these Fishes are not to be taken. **1661** in *Rec. Early Hist. Boston* (1880) IV. 109 *Fence viewers: for the necke of land, Richard Withington, [etc.]. **1880** *Scribner's Monthly* Feb. 504 A hare . . or . . a brown wood wren. . . These are the fence viewers of the wood lot. **1886** *J. Hopkins' Univ. Stud.* IV. 20 In 1647, fence viewers were appointed, by whom . . every new building had to be approved.

fence (fɛns), *v.* Also 5–6 **fens(e**. [f. the sb.]

1. *intr.* **a.** To practise the use of the foil or sword. **b.** To use the sword scientifically either for offence or defence.

1598 SHAKS. *Merry W.* II. iii. 14 Alas sir, I cannot fence. **1684** R. H. *School Recreat.* 57 Defending your self from the Thrusts or Blows of those you Fence with. **1737** FIELDING *Hist. Reg.* III. Wks. 1882 X. 225, I do a warrior! I never learnt to fence. **1779** SHERIDAN *Critic* III. Wks. 1873 II. 181 Captain, thou hast fenced well! **1829** LYTTON *Disowned* 147, I hope you both fence and shoot well.

c. *transf.* of animals.

1697 DRYDEN *Virg. Georg.* III. 343 The bellowing Rivals . . fence, they push, and pushing loudly roar.

d. *fig.* Frequently of a witness: ***to fence with*** (rarely trans. ***to fence***), to parry, try to evade (a question).

1665 BOYLE *Occas. Refl.* III. vi. (1845) 158 He rather fences with sin. **1677** YARRANTON *Eng. Improv.* 9 The Friends . . fence to get all the Estate. **1855** MOTLEY *Dutch Rep.* (1864) I. 151 For several months . . diplomatists fenced among themselves. **1865** CARLYLE *Fredk. Gt.* VI. xx. iii. 47 Seldom in the Arena of this Universe did a Son of Adam fence better for himself. **1880** KINGLAKE *Crimea* VI. v. 175 The gallant French . . could only fence with an evil so great. **1887** JESSOPP *Arcady* vi. 181 The question he seemed disposed to fence with. **1890** *Standard* 22 Feb. 5/2 The Chairman . . ought . . to be able to overcome the tendency to 'fence' awkward questions.

2. *trans.* (Const. *against*, *from*.) To screen, shield, protect: **a.** the body, or a part of it.

1549 OLDE *Erasm. Par. 2 Cor.* vi. 7 On euery syde surely fensed with the armoure of iustice. **1581** MULCASTER *Positions* xxvii. (1887) 106 The arme in this [arm ball] is fensed with a wooden brace. **1586** A. DAY *Eng. Secretary* (1625) 139 His pined corps, whom furres must fence from the least blast of cold. **1611** BIBLE *2 Sam.* xxiii. 7 The man . . must be fenced with yron. **1650** FULLER *Pisgah* I. v. 11 All fishes in armour fenced with shels. **1691** RAY *Creation* II. (1704) 378 The extremities of their Toes were fenc'd with Hoofs. **1826** MISS MITFORD *Village* Ser. II. (1863) 249 Running down the street with an umbrella . . to fence their lodger . . from the . . shower. **1876** BLACKMORE *Cripps* v. (1877) 27 With one hand fencing her forehead.

b. a building, locality, *esp.* from weather or wind.

1577 B. GOOGE *Heresbach's Husb.* I. (1586) 12 b, I lay my corne upon a fayre floore, closely fenced and seeled against Mise. **1600** HAKLUYT *Voy.* (1810) III. 360 We rode at anker in a place well fenced from the wind. **1650** FULLER *Pisgah* II. 60 [Jordan] is fenced by its own breadth and depth against all Passengers. **1705** ADDISON *Italy* 7 A spacious Harbour . . Fenc'd to the West. **1756–7** tr. *Keysler's Trav.* (1760) IV. 5 This city is fenced from the violence of the waves by several small islands. **1810** SCOTT *Lady of L.* I. xxvi, Moss . . and leaves combined To fence each crevice from the wind. **1841** JAMES *Brigand* ii, The kitchen was well fenced from the wind and rain.

c. *gen.* in material or immaterial sense.

c **1510** MORE *Picus* Wks. 8/1 Fensyng my selfe with the crucifixe. **1553** T. WILSON *Rhet.* 57 Every creature livyng should fense it self against outward violence. **1593** SHAKS. *3 Hen. VI*, II. vi. 75 Where's Captaine Margaret, to fence you now? **1602** FULBECKE *Pandectes* 16 By the continuall practise of nations . . the right of Primogeniture . . is fenced, supported and defended. **1639** FULLER *Holy War* III. iii. (1840) 119 Fencing his former villanies by committing new ones. **1681–6** J. SCOTT *Chr. Life* (1747) III. 378 Another of those Ministries . . is to fence . . its Peace. **1692** tr. *Milton's Def. Pop.* Wks. 1738 I. 460 We may fence ourselves against the latter [open enemies]. **1850** BLACKIE *Æschylus* II. 160 Fence every gate with valiant-hearted men. **1884** TENNYSON *Becket* 143 He fenced his royal promise with an *if*.

†**3.** *trans.* To equip for defence. *Obs.*

1599 HAKLUYT *Voy.* II. I. 131 A ship . . well fensed with munitions.

†**4.** *intr.* To set up a defence *against*; to provide protection *against*. *Obs.*

1676 TEMPLE *Let. to Sir E. Dearing* Wks. 1731 II. 357, I made use of this Circumstance to fence against this Resolution of the States. **1691** RAY *Creation* I. (1692) 140 Feathers very thick set upon their Breasts . . to fence against the cold of the water. **1702** A. CHARLETT in *Pepys' Diary* VI. 246 The relapse of which I must fence against. **1709** SWIFT *Adv. Relig.* Wks. (1778) II. 82 The common prudence of mankind . . is in no sort able to fence against them. **1759** STERNE *Tr. Shandy* I. Ded. Epist., I live in a constant endeavour to fence against the infirmities of ill health.

5. *trans.* To keep out, ward off, repel. Said both of persons and things. Also ***to fence off***, ***out***. Often with mixture of sense 6. *arch.*

a **1592** GREENE *Poems, Shepherd's Ode* 66 A cloak of grey fenc'd the rain. **1639** FULLER *Holy War* I. ix. 14 The Bosporus was too narrow a ditch . . to fense the Pagans out of West Christendome. **1643** BURROUGHES *Exp. Hosea* viii. (1652) 285 They fenced off thy word as with a shield. *c* **1710** C. FIENNES *Diary* (1888) 130 These high banks are made to . . ffence out yᵉ water. **1725** DE FOE *Voy. round World* (1840) 327 They had . . no bows to fence off the waves. **1742** SHENSTONE *Schoolmistr.* 65 A russet kirtle fenc'd the nipping air. **1785** PALEY *Moral Phil.* (1818) II. 342 Government is well warranted in fencing out the whole sect from situations of trust and power. **1816** SCOTT *Old Mort.* xix, A cup of sack shall fence the cold.

6. *trans.* To surround with or as with a fence (see FENCE *sb.* 4, 5); to enclose, fortify, protect.

1435 *Nottingham Rec.* II. 355 Thay to fens it [Est Croft] ham selfe at thayre awne coste. **1494** FABYAN *Chron.* VII. 466 Yᵉ Englysshe hoste . . was myghtely fensyd with wood and tryes. **1535** COVERDALE *Ezek.* xxxvi. 35 The . . broken downe cities, are now stronge and fensed agayne. **1583** STANYHURST *Æneis* II. (Arb.) 54 Whate forte were best to be fenced? **1611** BIBLE *Isa.* v. 2 Hee fenced it, and gathered out the stones thereof. **1631** T. MAY tr. *Barclay's Mirrour of Mindes* ii. 39 The lands of priuate men . . were fenced with ditches. **1650** FULLER *Pisgah* III. ii. 317 The roofs were flat and fenced with battlements. **1719** DE FOE *Crusoe* (1840) I. x. 173 Well fenced either with hedge or pale. **1793** *Trans. Soc. Encourag. Arts* IV. 4 Which are all fenced with a good stone wall. **1832** LYTTON *Eugene A.* I. i. 3 The greater part of them fenced also from the un-frequented road a little spot.

absol. **1892** *Midland News* 4 Mar. 6 We must fence more, and we shall be . . independent of herds.

fig. **1683** BURNET tr. *More's Utopia* (1685) 110 The Minds of the Utopians, when fenced with a Love for Learning. **1763–5** CHURCHILL *Poems, Conference*, Thy writings so well fenc'd in Law. **1841** MYERS *Cath. Th.* IV. §26. 306 The Jews were . . fenced against communion with them. **1843** H. ROGERS *Ess.* (1860) III. 46 Vincentius . . takes care . . to fence his proposition with . . limitations. **1870** EMERSON *Soc. & Solit., Bks.* Wks. (Bohn) III. 77 The men themselves were . . fenced by etiquette.

b. with *about*, *in*, *round*, *up*. ***to fence off***: to keep off by a fence. Also *absol.*

1535 COVERDALE *2 Chron.* xiv. 7 Let vs buylde vp these cities, and fense them rounde aboute with walles. **1611** BIBLE *Job* xix. 8 Hee hath fenced vp my way. **1615** G. SANDYS *Trav.* 100 Which makes the countrey people to fence in those places. **1667** MILTON *P.L.* IV. 697 On either side Acanthus . . Fenc'd up the verdant wall. **1697** DAMPIER *Voy.* I. viii. 222 These leaves are fenced round with strong Prickles above an inch long. **1713** STEELE *Englishman* No. 3. 15 His Property is fenced about with Laws and Privileges. **1822** 'B. CORNWALL' *Poems, Let. Boccaccio* v, Her dwelling was Fenced round by trees. **1869** R. B. SMYTH *Goldfields of Victoria* 610 *Fencing in a Claim*, making a drive round the boundaries of an alluvial claim to secure the wash-dirt. **1877** E. R. CONDER *Bas. Faith* viii. 349 It will be difficult to fence in securely on the side of Pantheism.

c. To part off by a fence or fences. In quot. *fig.*

1881 C. DE KAY *Vision of Nimrod* ii. 9 Nation I fenced from nation.

†**d.** Of a thing: To serve as a fence for. *Obs.*

1523 FITZHERB. *Husb.* §125 Yf it [thy dyche] be .v. fote brode [t]han it wolde . . fence it selfe & the lower hedge wyll serue.

7. *intr.* Of a horse: To leap a fence.

1884 A. WATSON in *Longm. Mag.* III. 611 What he lacks in speed is . . compensated for by the cleverness with which he fences. **1891** *Field* 7 Mar. 338/1 Harlequin and Fast Day went to the front . . the way they fenced was a treat to see.

8. *trans.* (*Sc. Law.*) **a.** To open the proceedings of (the Parliament or a Court of Law) by the use of a form of words forbidding persons to interrupt or obstruct the proceedings unnecessarily.

1513–75 *Diurn. Occurrents* (Bannatyne Club) 214 He post to William Pikis hous . . and thair fensit the Parliament. *c* **1565** LINDESAY (Pitscottie) *Chron. Scot.* (1728) 199 The Queen . . stayed till the Parliament was fenced. **1609** SKENE *Reg. Maj.* 158 The Court sould be fensed. **1637** RUTHERFORD *Lett.* (1862) I. 198, I know not if this court kept within my soul be fenced in Christ's name. **1663** SPALDING *Troub. Chas. I* (1792) I. 191 The parliament is fenced. **1818** SCOTT *Hrt. Midl.* xxi, 'They wunna fence the court.'

b. To prohibit by law, edict, or proclamation.

1596 *Burgh Rec. Glasgow* 6 Aug. (1876) I. 180 Bot to fens the same fra doing thairof.

c. To poind or arrest for debt.

1570 *Burgh Rec. Prestwick* 20 Nov. (1834) 72 For this geyr . . quhilk was fencet in his hand be Jhone Ondirwood officer.

†**d.** Hence, ***to fence a band***: to make a league (L. *ferīre fœdus*). *Obs. rare*$^{-1}$.

1533 BELLENDEN *Livy* I. (1822) 41 Commandis you me to fens ane band with the Fader-Patrate of Albane pepill?

9. In the Scottish Presbyterian Churches: ***to fence the tables***: to deliver an exhortation calculated to deter unworthy persons from communicating.

1709 W. STEWART (of Pardovan) *Worship Ch. Scotl.* II. iv. 140 He fenceth and openeth the Tables. **1833** *Fraser's Mag.* VIII. 406 The objurgation, or fencing the tables, was concluded. **1879** JAMIESON *Scot. Dict.* s.v. *Bicker-raid*, A clergyman in fencing the tables at a sacrament, debarred all who had been guilty of [etc.]. **1882** [see DEBARRATION].

10. To close for hunting or fishing (a forest, river, etc.).

1767 BLACKSTONE *Comm.* II. 39 The rivers that were fenced..were directed to be laid open.

†**11.** To keep in position by a gauge or guide. Cf. FENCE *sb.* 6 a. *Obs.*

1703 MOXON *Mech. Exerc.* 90 Should you not thus Fence them..one piece being never so little out of its due Position, would drive the next piece more out.

12. *slang.* **a.** To purchase or sell with guilty knowledge (stolen goods). Also *absol.*

1610 ROWLANDS *Martin Mark-all* Cij/2 To fence property [*printed* properly], to sell anything that is stolne. **1789** G. PARKER *Life's Painter* 153 Fenced is disposing of anything stolen for a quarter of the value. **1819** J. H. VAUX *Mem.* I. xii. 141 He knew where to fence the book. **1840** MARRYAT *Poor Jack* xviii, Does old Nanny fence?

b. To spend or lay out (money).

a **1700** B. E. *Dict. Cant. Crew, Fence*, to Spend or Lay out. *Fence his Hog*, to Spend his Shilling. **1725** in *New Cant. Dict.*

fenced (fɛnst), *ppl. a.* [f. prec. + -ED[1].] In various senses of the vb. **a.** Furnished with defences, fortified. Now only in Biblical phraseology. **b.** Provided with a hedge or rail, railed off, enclosed. *lit.* and *fig.* Also *fenced in.* **c.** *Sc. Law.* Poinded; see FENCE *v.* 8 c.

c **1440** *Promp. Parv.* 155/1 Fencyd, or defencyd, *defensus, munitus, defensatus.* **1535** COVERDALE *Judith* iii. 6 Holofernes ..conquered all stronge fensed cities. **1600** FAIRFAX *Tasso* II. lxxv, In fensed towres bestowed is their graine. **1611** BIBLE *2 Kings* xvii. 9 They built them high places..from the tower of the watchmen, to the fenced city. **1637** RUTHERFORD *Lett.* (1862) I. 207 Fenced goods that ye cannot intromit with. **1746–7** HERVEY *Medit.* (1818) 203, I might have beheld our fenced cities encompassed with armies. **1853** MARSDEN *Early Purit.* 77 The fenced enclosures of a university. **1853** MAURICE *Proph. & Kings* xii. 198 He speaks..of its villages and fenced cities. **1957** *New Yorker* 29 June 64/3 An enormous, fenced-in storage area piled high with crates and packages. **1960** *Farmer & Stockbreeder* 1 Mar. Suppl. 1 He..pushed the pair of us into a..fenced-in yard.

fenceful (ˈfɛnsfʊl), *a.* [f. FENCE *sb.* + -FUL.] Affording defence; protecting or shielding.

1616 CHAPMAN *Batrachom.* (1858) 8 Their fenceful bucklers were The middle rounds of can' sticks. **1729** SAVAGE *Wanderer* I. 194 [He] firms the conquest with his fenceful mound. **1751** G. WEST *Education* xlviii, High o'er his Head he held his fenceful Shield.

fenceless (ˈfɛnslɪs), *a.* [f. as prec. + -LESS.]

1. a. Without an enclosure or hedge; unenclosed, open.

1587 TURBERV. *Epit. & Sonnets* (1837) 397 As plant shall proove upon the fencelesse land. **1649** ROBERTS *Clavis Bibl.* 432 Utterly to lay this vineyard waste, fencelesse, fruitlesse. **1770** GOLDSM. *Des. Vill.* 307 Those fenceless fields the sons of wealth divide. **1887** R. MEEKER in *Harper's Mag.* Apr. 725/2 The fenceless, treeless landscape of the steppe.

b. Without a fortification; unfortified.

1740 C. PITT *Æneid* XII. 789 Before him..the fenceless city lay. *a* **1873** LYTTON *Pausanias* IV. vi. (1878) 509 The fenceless villages of Sparta.

2. Without means of defence; defenceless.

1594 CAREW *Tasso* (1881) 60 Fencelesse my brest, why stay you it to cleaue? **1667** MILTON *P.L.* x. 303 The Wall Immoveable of this now fenceless world. *c* **1750** SHENSTONE *Love & Hon.* Wks. (1764) I. 327 On my fenceless head it's phial'd wrath May fate exhaust. **1813** SCOTT *Rokeby* I. xvi, O'er my friend my cloak I threw, And fenceless faced the deadly dew. **1850** BLACKIE *Æschylus* II. 254 The Greeks Our fenceless chiefs..Mowed down.

absol. **1887** *Century Mag.* July 334 Look what arms the fenceless wield, Frailest things have frailty's shield!

Hence ˈ**fencelessness**, †lack of skill in fence (*obs.*); the condition of not being protected by a fence.

1656 TRAPP *Comm. Matt.* vii. 3 A general doctrine, not applied, is as a sword without an edge, not in itself, but to us, through our singular fencelessness. **1856** RUSKIN *Mod. Paint.* III. IV. xiv. §34 The fencelessness..of the free virtue lead[s] to the loving..order of eternal happiness.

fencelet (ˈfɛnslɪt). *rare.* [f. FENCE *sb.* + -LET.] A small fence or hedge.

1892 *Field* 19 Mar. 396/1 A sort of second fencelet planted on the edge of the dyke.

fencer (ˈfɛnsə(r)). [f. FENCE *v.* + -ER[1].]

1. One who fences. **a.** One who fights, or practises fencing with a foil or sword; a swordsman.

1581 PETTIE *Guazzo's Civ. Conv.* I. (1586) 37 b, A fencer, who making at his enimies head, striketh him on the legge. **1599** SHAKS. *Much Ado* v. ii. 13 As blunt as the Fencers foiles. **1649** BP. HALL *Cases Consc.* II. ii. 109 Whether of the two is the better Fencer. **1712** STEELE *Spect.* No. 422 ¶6 They do not thrust with the Skill of Fencers. **1809** ROLAND *Fencing* 39 There has been, even by good Fencers, some controversy respecting this parade. **1829** LYTTON *Devereux* I. iv, You are the best fencer in the school.

†**b.** One who fences in public shows; a hired or professional swordsman. *Obs.*

1572 *Act 14 Eliz.* c. 5 §5 All Fencers..Comon Players in Enterludes, & minstrels, not belonging to any Baron. **1583** FLEETWOOD in Ellis *Orig. Lett.* I. II. 292 One Dwelles, a fenser nere Cicell howse. **1601** SHAKS. *Twel. N.* III. iv. 307 He has bin Fencer to the Sophy. **1603** KNOLLES *Hist. Turks* (1638) 158 He..appointed certaine Ruffians and Fencers to watch her house.

†**c.** A gladiator. Also *fencer at the sharp. Obs.*

1587 GOLDING *De Mornay* xxiii. 349 They had not made their wonted shewes of Fensers. **1632** LE GRYS tr. *Velleius Paterc.* 225 Most magnificent shewes of fencers at the sharpe. **1637** R. HUMPHREY tr. *St. Ambrose* I. 137 The clamour of gamesters, the slaughter of fensers. **1693** CONGREVE *Juvenal* xi. 15 A man..Able for arms..'Mongst common Fencers, Practices the Trade, That End debasing, for which Arms were made.

d. *fig.*

a **1680** BUTLER *Rem.* (1759) II. 206 A Quibbler..is a Fencer of Language. *a* **1715** BURNET *Own Time* (1766) I. 254 Here were a couple of fencers engaged in disputes.

2. Chiefly *Austr.* and *N.Z.* One employed in putting up fences.

1881 MRS. C. PRAED *Policy & P.* I. 241 'Where is father?' ..'In the office settling with the fencers.' **1881** *Instr. Census Clerks* (1885) 98 s.v. *General labourer*, Fencer. **1892** *Pall Mall G.* 7 June 7/1 This shuts Kanakas out from the business of..sawyers, splitters, fencers. **1921** H. GUTHRIE-SMITH *Tutira* xxxviii. 382 Owners and employees had worked shoulder to shoulder as..butchers, fencers, bullock-punchers. **1950** *N.Z. Jrnl. Agric.* Oct. 356/2 Two fencers are kept in steady work at Glenaray [sheep station, Southland].

3. A horse that jumps fences. Chiefly with prefixed adj., as a *good, bold,* etc. *fencer.*

1852 R. S. SURTEES *Sponge's Sp. Tour* xliv. 249 Don't know that I ever rode a better fencer. **1876** *World* No. 120. 12 Few areas..require a bigger or bolder fencer.

4. *slang.* (See quots.)

a **1700** B. E. *Dict. Cant. Crew, Queere-cole-fencer*, a Receiver and putter off [of] false Money. *c* **1700** *Street Robberies Consider'd*, Fencer, receiver of stolen goods.

5. *Comb.*, as ***fencer-like*** adj.; †**fencer-month** = *fence-month.*

1660 FISHER *Rustick's Alarm* Wks. (1679) 208 Ye glory in your Fencer-like Faculties of Disputing. *a* **1700** B. E. *Dict. Cant. Crew, Season of Beasts*, a Hart or Buck begins at the end of Fencer-Month.

Hence ˈ**fenceress** [+ -ESS], a female fencer.

a **1661** HOLYDAY *Juvenal* 93 What young face Caught Hippia thus? for which she chose disgrace, To be instil'd the fenceress!

fenchane (ˈfɛntʃeɪn). *Chem.* [f. FENCH(ONE + -ANE.] A liquid that is chemically a saturated bicyclic hydrocarbon of the terpene series, $C_{10}H_{18}$, and may be considered the parent compound of a series including the fenchenes and fenchone; also applied to some related isomers of this (see quots. 1949).

1907 *Jrnl. Chem. Soc.* XCII. I. 24 The close relationship of camphane and fenchane. **1949** SIMONSEN & OWEN *Terpenes* (ed. 2) II. vi. 528 By the catalytic hydrogenation of α-fenchene..Zelinski [1904] prepared a saturated hydrocarbon, $C_{10}H_{18}$, to which he gave the name fenchane. .. In 1911 Wolff and Kishner prepared from fenchonehydrazone an isomeric hydrocarbon having completely different properties... This hydrocarbon was designated fenchane, whilst for Zelinski's hydrocarbon the name *iso*bornylane was adopted. [*Note*] *iso*Bornylane is also termed α-fenchane. *Ibid.* 530 On reduction..it [*sc. iso*bornylol] does not give *iso*bornylane, but a hydrocarbon ..termed β-fenchane. **1953** EASTMAN & NOLLER in H. Gilman *Org. Chem.* IV. vii. 656 The most important naturally occurring terpene having the fenchane carbon skeleton is fenchone.

†**fenche.** *Obs.* Some part of the carcase of a deer.

c **1560** J. LACY *Wyl Bucke his Testament* a iij, The fenche rostid and yᵉ filet, and noumbels rosted.

fenchene (ˈfɛntʃiːn). *Chem.* [ad. G. *fenchen* (O. Wallach 1891, in *Ann. der Chem.* CCLXIII. 151), f. *fenchel* fennel: see -ENE.] Any of several isomeric unsaturated terpenes, $C_{10}H_{16}$, that are related to fenchane and are isolated as oily liquids.

1891 *Jrnl. Chem. Soc.* LX. II. 1083 Fenchone, on reduction, yields fenchyl alcohol, and from this one obtains fenchyl chloride and fenchene. **1941** *Thorpe's Dict. Appl. Chem.* (ed. 4) V. 5/2 *cyclo*Fenchene..is present in the mixture of fenchenes prepared by any of the general methods.

fenchone (ˈfɛntʃəʊn). *Chem.* [ad. G. *fenchon* (O. Wallach 1891, in *Ann. der Chem.* CCLXIII. 129), f. G. *fenchel* fennel: see -ONE.] An oily liquid with a camphor-like smell which occurs naturally in two enantiomorphic forms in various essential oils (as fennel oil and thuja oil) and is chemically a bicyclic ketone, $C_{10}H_{16}O$, of the terpene series.

1891 *Jrnl. Chem. Soc.* LX. II. 1082 In many fennel oils a liquid, camphor-like substance occurs. This compound is called fenchone, and is isomeric with camphor. **1932** J. L. SIMONSEN *Terpenes* II. I. vi. 569 Fenchone is distinguished from other dicyclic ketones by its low boiling-point. **1949** E. GUENTHER *Essential Oils* II. 420 Fenchone serves mainly as an odor adjunct in room sprays and bath preparations of pine character. **1953** [see FENCHANE]. **1955** *Jrnl. Indian Chem. Soc.* XXXII. 228 The essential oil of *Brunella vulgaris*, Linn has been found to consist mainly of *d*-camphor and *d*-fenchone.

fencible (ˈfɛnsɪb(ə)l), *a.* and *sb.* Forms: 4–6 fensable, 5–6 fensabil(e, 5–7 fensible, (6 -ibill), 7– fencible. [Short for *defensable*, DEFENSIBLE.]

A. *adj.*

1. Of a person: Capable of making defence; fit and liable to be called on for defensive military service. Chiefly *Sc.*

c **1325** *Coer de L.* 3296 For we have herinne Syxty thousand men fensable. *c* **1475** *Rauf Coilȝear* 329 One thousand..of fensabill men. **1535** STEWART *Cron. Scot.* II. 475 All other men commandit for to tak..That fensabill war. **1637–50** ROW *Hist. Kirk.* (1842) 519 The toune of Aberdeen wes charged, that all fensible persons appeare in their arms. **1693** E. HALLEY in *Phil. Trans.* XVII. 601 The whole Force this City can raise of Fencible Men, as the Scotch call them, is about 9000. **1756** *Ibid.* XLIX. 880 There can be no increase at all of our fencible men. **1820** SCOTT *Monast.* xxxiv, Where is the roll of fencible men liable to do suit and service to the Halidome? **1837** CARLYLE *Fr. Rev.* I. v. iv, Let fencible men..keep watch and ward.

2. Of arms and armour: Capable of being used for defence. *Sc.*

a **1572** KNOX *Hist. Ref.* Wks. 1846 I. 87 The soldeouris caist from thame thaire pickis..and utheris weaponis fensable. **15..** *Aberdeen Reg.* V. 20 (Jam.) To consider.. euery nychtbour quhay hes fensabil geir & vappynnis.

3. Of a fortress, town, etc.: Capable of being defended; strong, well-fortified.

1590 SPENSER *F.Q.* III. x. 10 No fort so fensible..But that continuall battery will rive. **1599** HAKLUYT *Voy.* II. 132 A roade..made very fensible with strong walls. **1632** LITHGOW *Trav.* VI. 299 Houses, being Walled and fensible against the Arabs. *a* **1682** SIR J. TURNER *Mem., Battle of Preston*, Baillie had..lodged the foot..among very fencible enclosures. **1820** SCOTT *Monast.* ix, This old tower of thine is fencible enough.

b. *transf.* of a building: That is in good repair.

1417 *Surtees Misc.* (1890) 13 þat the foresayd Thomas make hys pryve fensilble als it awe to be.

4. Such as will serve as a fence or enclosure.

1799 J. ROBERTSON *Agric. Perth* 84 All fences..must be left..in a fencible condition.

5. The sb. used *attrib.*: Belonging to the corps called *Fencibles.*

1795 *Hist. Europe* in *Ann. Reg.* (1796) 50/2 The expences accompanying the fencible cavalry. **1804** WELLINGTON in Gurw. *Desp.* II. 642 To station the fencible battalion at Surat. **1844** *Regul. & Ord. Army* 4 Officers of Fencible and Militia Regiments rank together.

B. *sb.* A soldier liable only for defensive service at home. Also, ***land-, river-, sea-fencible.***

1796 *Sporting Mag.* VII. 279 A military hero, whom the.. tactics of the day denominate a fencible. **1803** G. ROSE *Diaries* (1860) II. 57 Captain Essington, commanding the Sea Fencibles at Dover. **1806** A. DUNCAN *Nelson's Fun.* 12 The river fencibles were stationed close to the entrance. **1816** SCOTT *Antiq.* xlv, 'A' the sea fencibles, and the land fencibles..are on fit.' **1837** LOCKHART *Scott* (1839) I. 305 Captain in the Perthshire Fencibles. **1839** J. STEVENSON *Justiciary Garland* 75 A fencible I'll guard at home.

†**fencibly,** *adv. Obs.* [f. prec. adj. + -LY[2].] So as to be capable of being defended.

1523 LD. BERNERS *Froiss.* I. ccix. 250 A square toure thick walled, and fensably furnysshed for the warre.

fencing (ˈfɛnsɪŋ), *vbl. sb.* [f. FENCE *v.* + -ING[1].] The action of the vb. FENCE.

1. The action or art of using the sword scientifically as a weapon of offence or defence; the practice of this art with a blunted sword, foil, or stick.

1581 MULCASTER *Positions* xviii. (1887) 79 Concerning fensing, or skill how to handle the weapon. **1642** FULLER *Holy & Prof. St.* III. xiii. 185 Fencing is warre without anger. *a* **1735** ARBUTHNOT & POPE *Martin Scrib.* vii. in *Pope's Wks.* (1741) II. 26 These..could no more be learned alone than Fencing or Cudgel-playing. **1829** LYTTON *Devereux* I. iv, Fencing is an accomplishment in which Gerald is very nearly my equal.

fig. **1608** SHAKS. *Per.* IV. vi. 62 'Pray you, without any more virginal fencing. **1687** DRYDEN *Hind. & P.* II. 33 After long fencing push'd against a wall, Your salvo comes, that he's not there at all. **1849** HELPS *Friends in C.* (1854) II. 9 There is skilful fencing even in your talk. **1876** FREEMAN *Norm. Conq.* V. xxiii. 117 A piece of diplomatic fencing.

¶ In wider sense: (see quot.).

1692 O. WALKER *Histor. Illustr.* 158 Fencing, Pugilatus, was fighting with Fists.

2. The action of protecting, or of setting up a defence *against* (evil). †Also quasi-*concr.*, means of defence (*obs.*).

1489 CAXTON *Faytes of A.* I. x. 27 In sawtyng or fensyng of a forteresse a slynge is good. *a* **1661** FULLER *Worthies* (1840) I. ii. 4 Providence having given men hands..all clothing and fencing is..bestowed upon him. **1668** CULPEPPER & COLE *Barthol. Anat.* II. i. 88 The more noble parts require great fencing. **1761** HUME *Hist. Eng.* II. xxxvii. 308 The fencing against the pains and infirmities under which he laboured occupied a great part of his time.

3. The action of putting up fences or enclosing with a fence or protection; also *fencing in.*

1628 BP. HALL *Serm.* Wks. 1634 II. 311 All this provision of..Fencing, Stoning, Planting, were nothing without a continuall over-sight. **1719** DE FOE *Crusoe* (1840) I. xvi. 274, I went on with my..planting and fencing. **1817–8** COBBETT *Resid. U.S.* (1822) 107 Fencing..presses itself upon the attention of the..Farmer. **1892** LOCKWOOD *Dict. Mech. Engin.*, Fencing In.—The enclosure of machinery.. Fencing in is compulsory.

b. *concr.* An enclosure or railing; fences collectively; sometimes preceded by some qualifying word, as ***rail-, stone-, wire-fencing.*** Also the materials of fences for farms (*U.S.*).

c **1585** R. BROWNE *Answ. Cartwright* 44 Let [him]..shewe ..an orcharde..without..some safe inclosing or fencing. **1857** RUSKIN *Elem. Drawing* 326 A decayed fragment or two of fencing fill the gaps in the bank. **1881** *Encycl. Brit.* (ed. 9) XII. 190/1 For..Sussex, where..the fencing for the most part [is] what is called cramped.

4. The action of leaping a fence.

1827 *Sporting Mag.* XX. 203 With our first fox we had some very severe fencing. **1861** WHYTE-MELVILLE *Mkt. Harborough* 275 When hounds run best pace, horses have not wind for extraordinary exertions in the matter of fencing.

5. *Sc.* The opening of a Parliament or Court of Justice with the prescribed formula denouncing penalties against disturbers. Cf. FENCE *v.* 8.

1708 *Proclam.* in *Lond. Gaz.* No. 4464/4 Our Proclamation to be..read in Open Court immediately after Fencing thereof. **1752** J. LOUTHIAN *Form of Process* (ed. 2) 232 That ye..be present at the said Justice-court, before the down-sitting and fencing thereof.

6. *slang.* The action or habit of receiving or dealing in stolen goods.

1851 MAYHEW *Lond. Labour* I. 255 Their 'fencing'..does not extend to any plate. **1880** *Standard* 12 Apr. 5/2 Receiving stolen property, or 'fencing'..is largely practised in London.

7. *attrib.* and *Comb.*, (sense 1), as ***fencing-foils***, ***-grace***, ***-hall***, ***-master***, ***-match***, ***-room***, ***-school***, ***-skill***, etc.; (sense 3), as ***fencing-branch***, ***-gear***, ***post***, ***-wire***; also, **fencing-cully**, a receiver and storer of stolen goods; **fencing-gauge** (see quot.); **fencing-ken** or **-repository**, a storing place for stolen goods; **fencing-machine**, a machine for shaping, fitting and finishing posts, rails, etc. for fences (*Cent. Dict.*); **fencing-nail** (see quot.).

1669 WORLIDGE *Syst. Agric.* (1681) 101 The Black-Thorn [etc.]..yield a very good *Fencing-branch. *a* **1700** B. E. *Dict. Cant. Crew*, **Fencing Cully*, a Broker, or Receiver of Stolen goods. **1829** LYTTON *Devereux* II. i, A table was covered with books, a couple of *fencing-foils..and..letters. **1874** KNIGHT *Dict. Mech.* I. 836/1 **Fencing-gage*, an implement to space and hold boards against a post while nailing them. *a* **1950** L. SKUTHORPE in *Austral. Short Stories* (1951) 132 Get the *fencing-gear, lads, and put that fence up again. **1597** SHAKS. *2 Hen. IV*, II. i. 206 This is the right *Fencing grace..tap for tap, and so part faire. **1601** HOLLAND *Pliny* I. 434 Our common *fencing-halls, and places of publick exercises. *a* **1700** B. E. *Dict. Cant. Crew*, **Fencing-ken*, the Magazine..where Stolen goods are secured. *a* **1648** LD. HERBERT *Life* (1870) 34 The good *fencing-masters..present a foyle or fleuret to their scholars. **1779** SHERIDAN *Critic* II. ii, As smart as hits in a *fencing-match. **1874** KNIGHT *Dict. Mech.* I. 836/1 **Fencing-nail*, a heavy nail of its class adapted for fastening on fencing-boards. **1877** H. C. HODGE *Arizona* 59 The forests of juniper will furnish large quantities of the most durable railroad ties, *fencing posts. **1950** *N.Z. Jrnl. Agric.* Mar. 233/1 Pre-cast [concrete] products such as blocks and fencing posts. **1812** *Sporting Mag.* XXXIX. 209 A convenient *fencing repository. **1897** *Outing* (U.S.) XXX. 200/1 The contest was held March 20th in the *fencing-room of the New York Athletic Club. **1637** NABBES *Microcosm.* I, I was bred up in Mars his *Fencing-schoole. **1712** BUDGELL *Spect.* No. 539 ¶1 Like him who comes into a fencing-school to pick a quarrel. **1878** *Rep. Indian Affairs* (U.S.) 35, I suggested that *fencing-wire be supplied. **1908** *Westm. Gaz.* 11 June 2/1 The fencing-wire trade. **1936** A. RUSSELL *Gone Nomad* vi. 45, I had unloosed the wrong tie rope, thereby dropping a coil of fencing wire on Brown's toes.

fend (fɛnd), *sb.* *Sc.* and *dial.* [f. next vb.]

1. A shift or effort which one makes for oneself. ***to make a fend***: to make a venture.

a **1724** *Borrowstoun Mous* in Ramsay *Evergreen* I. 144 Scho maid an easy Fen. **1794** BURNS *Tam Glen* ii, I'm thinking, wi' sic a braw fallow, In poortith I might mak a fen'. *a* **1810** TANNAHILL *Poems* (1846) 25, I think, through life I'll make a canny fen', Wi hurcheon Nancy. **1824** SCOTT *St. Ronan's* xx, Out I wad be, and out John Bowler gat me, but wi' nae sma fight and fend. **1855** ROBINSON *Whitby Gloss.*, 'They make a good fend for a living.' **1877** *Holderness Gloss.*, 'He disn't seem to mak a bit o' fend.'

2. Activity in making shifts for oneself, energy.

1788 MARSHALL *Yorksh. Gloss.*, *Fend*, activity, management, assiduity, prowess. **1876** *Whitby Gloss.*

3. Provisions, fare.

1804 TARRAS *Poems* 54 Nae sumptuous fend, but hamely food.

†**4.** *Naut.* = FENDER *sb.* *Obs.*

1658 PHILLIPS, *Fends*, things hung over a Ships side to keep another Ship from rubbing against it.

5. *Comb.*, as **fend-bolt** (*Naut.*) = FENDER *sb.* 2 b; **fend-full** *a.* *Sc.*, full of shifts or expedients.

1678 PHILLIPS, *Fenders*, pieces of old Cables [etc.]..hung over a Ships side..called also *Fend-bolts. **1867** SMYTH *Sailor's Word-bk.*, *Fend* or *Fender Bolts*, made with long and thick heads, struck into the outermost bends or wales of a ship, to save her sides from hurts and bruises. **1820** *Blackw. Mag.* Dec. 321 Else yere grown less *fendfou than I ever saw ye.

fend (fɛnd), *v.* Also 4–6 fende, (4 fenden), 7–8 *Sc.*, 9 *dial.* fain, fen. [Shortened from DEFEND.]

1. *trans.* = DEFEND *v.* Now *arch.* or *poet.*

a **1300** *Cursor M.* 28851 (Cott.) Almus..feddes his saul fra þe fend. *c* **1330** R. BRUNNE *Chron.* (1810) 195 He com right son, Normundie to fende. **1393** LANGL. *P. Pl.* C. XXII. 46 He..fendede hem fro foule vueles. *c* **1400** *Lanfranc's Cirurg.* 13 If þat we kunne fende him fro a fevere. *c* **1470** HENRY *Wallace* IV. 615 Wallace in ire a burly brand can draw..To fende his men with his deyr worthi hand. **1503** DUNBAR *Thistle & Rose* 133 And said, 'In feild go furth and fend the laif'. **1568** FULWELL *Like Will to Like* in Hazl. *Dodsley* III. 322 Fend your heads, sirs, for I will to it more once. **1647** H. MORE *Song of Soul* I. I. xxvii, O heavenly Salems sons! you fend the right. *a* **1774** FERGUSSON *Poems* (1789) II. 32 My trees..Shall fend ye frae ilk blast o' wind. **1845** W. E. FRYE tr. *Oehlenschl. Gods* 83, I only sought my realm to fend By wizard spell and mystic song. **1863** EMERSON *Boston Hymn* 16 Freedom..shall..fend you with his wing.

b. *refl.* and *intr.* for *refl.*

c **1330** R. BRUNNE *Chron.* (1810) 216 þo þat þer purueiance of Oxenford not held, With scheld & with lance fend him in þe feld. *c* **1400** *Destr. Troy* 10142 The freike with a fauchon fendit hym well. **1573** *Satir. Poems Reform.* xl. 196 How he suld fend from furie and thair fead. **1724** R. FALCONER *Voy.* (1769) 101 What will come, will come, and there's no fending against it. **1837** R. NICOLL *Poems* (1842) 17 To fend against the winter cauld The heather we will pu'. **1864** SIR J. K. JAMES *Tasso* (1865) II. XIV. xxiv, An agent prompt to fend and to attack. **1865** S. EVANS *Bro. Fabian* 49 Goodman true, wouldst fend thyself From witchcraft and midnight elf?

2. *intr.* ***to fend and prove***: to argue, wrangle.

1575 LANEHAM *Let.* (1871) 17 Thus, with fending & prooving, with plucking & tugging. *c* **1698** LOCKE *Cond. Underst.* xxxi, Being able to fend and prove with them. **1702** VANBRUGH *False Friend* I, Instead of fending and proving with his mistress, he should come to..a..parrying and thrusting with you. **1721** STRYPE *Eccl. Mem.* II. xxviii. 478 That delighted not in fending and proving. **1855** ROBINSON *Whitby Gloss.*, *Fending and Proving*, arguing and defending. **1877** *N.W. Linc. Gloss.*, After fendin' an' provin' about summats.

3. To ward or keep off, turn aside, keep out or at a distance. Also, ***to fend back***.

c **1572** GASCOIGNE *Fruites Warre* (1831) 217 So might we..fend our foes with blowes of English blade. **1697** DRYDEN *Virg. Georg.* III. 466 With Fern beneath, to fend the bitter Cold. **1712** MRS. CENTLIVRE *Perplexed Lovers* I. i, You shall not want a friend to fend that blow! **1787** BURNS *Holy Fair* 73 Here stands a shed to fend the show'rs. **1804** TARRAS *Poems* 22 To..fend the heat o' simmer blinter. **1823** CRABB *Technol. Dict.*, 'Fend the boat', prevent it striking against any thing. **1860** MAURY *Phys. Geog. Sea* ii. §143 Warm water..in contact with a cold non-conducting cushion of cold water to fend it from the bottom. **1876** BLACKMORE *Cripps* ii. (1877) 12 Fending the twigs from her eyes and bonnet. **1877** KINGLAKE *Crimea* VI. vi. 364 It enabled him to fend back the masses confronting him.

b. esp. with *off*.

a **1400–50** *Alexander* 1031 þar a cite he assailes..Bot wees wiȝtly with-in þe wallis ascendid, Freschly fendid of & fersly with-stude. *c* **1570** *Marr. Wit & Science* IV. i. in Hazl. *Dodsley* II. 364 To fend and keep him off awhile, until his rage be out. **1669** PENN *No Cross* xx. §23 Do you think that Words will fend off the Blows of Eternal Vengeance? **1816** SCOTT *Antiq.* xxxvii, 'Ye had aye a good roof ower your head to fend aff the weather.' **1861** HUGHES *Tom Brown at Oxf.* xiii. (1889) 127 Catch hold of the long boat-hook, and fend her [the boat] off. **1865** LIVINGSTONE *Zambesi* xxiv. 481 A spoonful in hot water..to fend off a chill and fever.

absol. **13..** *E.E. Allit. P.* B. 1191 þay feȝt & þay fende of, & fylter togeder. **1864** E. SARGENT *Peculiar* III. 125 The man of nerve looks boldly at the danger and fends off accordingly.

4. *intr.* To make an effort, strive or try to do something; to make a shift; to take precautions *against*. *Sc.* and *dial.*

15.. in Sibbald *Chron. Scot. Poetry* II. 46 Few for falsett now may fend. *c* **1680** [F. SEMPILL] *Banishm. Poverty* in Watson *Collect.* I. 13 Then I knew no way how to fen. **1712** MRS. CENTLIVRE *Perplexed Lovers* IV, We must fend against that. **1788** MARSHALL *Yorksh. Gloss.*, *Fend*, to strive as for a livelihood. **1794** BURNS *Gane is the day*, Semple-folk maun fecht and fen. **1859** GEO. ELIOT *A. Bede* (ed. 4) I. 45 I'd make a shift, and fend indoor and out, to give you more liberty. **1865** E. WAUGH *Lanc. Songs*, God bless him that fends for his livin', An' houds up his yed through it o'!

b. ***to fend for***: to make shift for, look after, provide for. So in ***to fend for oneself***. Chiefly *dial.* or *colloq.*

1629 JACKSON *Treat. Div. Essence* II. Wks. 1673 II. 139 They do not..direct their brood in their motions, but leave them to fend for themselves. **1660** H. MORE *Myst. Godl.* To Rdr. 24 They are such as..fend for themselves as well as they may. **1785** HUTTON *Bran New Wark* 468 When the awner will not fend for his sell. **1787** GROSE *Prov. Gloss.*, I ha twa bairns to fend for. **1818** SCOTT *Hrt. Midl.* xx, 'Ane wad hae carried me through the warld, and friended me, and fended for me.' **1859** GEO. ELIOT *A. Bede* 94 'Lads as could fend for their sens.'

c. = FARE *v.*[1] 7. *dial.*

1781 HUTTON *Tour to Caves* Gloss., *How fend you*, how fare you? **1790** MRS. WHEELER *Westmld. Dial.* (1821) 113 I'd kna haw they fend all. **1794** BURNS *Carle of Kellyburn Braes* ii, He met wi' the devil; says, 'How do you fen?' **1872** BLACK *Adv. Phaeton* 23 'How fens tee, Jeck? gaily?'

5. *trans.* = *to fend for* (4 b). Hence, to provide sustenance for, support, maintain. Chiefly *Sc.* and *dial.*

1637 RUTHERFORD *Lett.* (1862) I. 223 Fend thyself, I will hold my grips of thee no longer. **1674** RAY *N.C. Words*, To *Fend*; to shift for. *a* **1774** FERGUSSON *Poems*, *Rising of Session* 18 Hain'd mu'ter hauds the mill at ease And fends the Miller. **1787** BURNS *Death of Mailie* 32 Gie them guid cow-milk their fill, Till they be fit to fend themsel. **1816** SCOTT *Old Mort.* v, 'They are puirly armed, and warse fended wi' victual.'

†**6.** To forbid. *Obs.* exc. *dial.* Cf. FEN *v.*

c **1460** *Towneley Myst.* (Surtees) 9, I fend, Godes forbot, that ever thou thrife. **1888** ELWORTHY *W. Somerset Word-bk.*, Ee fain un vrum gwain pun eez graewn.

Hence **'fended** *ppl. a.*, **'fending** *ppl. a.*

1867 EMERSON *May-Day, etc.* Wks. (Bohn) III. 423 This Oreads' fended Paradise. **1883** *Almondbury Gloss.*, *Fending*..industrious.

fend(e, obs. form of FIEND.

fendable ('fɛndəb(ə)l), *a.* *dial.* Also fendible. [f. FEND *v.* + -ABLE.] Capable of fending or shifting for oneself.

1674 RAY *N.C. Words* 18 *Fendable*, one that can shift for himself. **1855** ROBINSON *Whitby Gloss.*, 'A brave fendable body in a family', a famous household manager. **1869** *Lonsdale Gloss.*, 'She's a gay fendible body.'

Fendant (fɑ̃dɑ̃). [Swiss-Fr., the name of a grape.] A dry white wine produced in south-western Switzerland.

1911 *Encycl. Brit.* XXVI. 242/1 Among the best Swiss wines are those of..Muscat, Fendant and Vin du Glacier (all in the Valais). [**1926** P. M. SHAND *Bk. Wine* vii. 213 The generic name of the Vallais wines is that of their informing grape, Fendant de Sion or Fendant de Vallais.] **1962** *Economist* 29 Dec. 1283/1 Fendant served in tumblers in the lesser taverns can be quite sharp and unrewarding. **1970** P. MOYES *Who saw her Die?* xvii. 218 Their tiredness fell away miraculously under the benign influence of..a flask of Fendant.

fender ('fɛndə(r)), *sb.* [f. FEND *v.* + -ER.]

1. = DEFENDER. *Obs.* exc. *dial.*

a **1400–50** *Alexander* 1839 þe fendere of grece. *c* **1440** *Promp. Parv.* 155 Fendowre, or defendowre. **1678** *Four for a Penny* 3 He [a Pawnbroker] is..the Common Fender of all Bulkers and Shoplifts in the Town. **1876** *Whitby Gloss.*, *Fender*, a defender in all senses.

2. Something that serves to fend or keep off something else: **a.** in gen. sense.

1615 E. S. *Britains Buss* in Arb. *Garner* III. 627 Fenders or long poles. **1825** *Ann. Reg.* 247* This bone constitutes a fin, or fender. **1841** CATLIN *N. Amer. Ind.* (1844) I. iv. 32 Protected with the shield or arrow fender. **1864** SALA in *Daily Tel.* 29 July, The coal bunkers..in a state of repletion are the best kind of 'fenders' for the protection of the boilers from shot and shell. **1882** BUCKLAND *Notes & Jottings* 159 The loose feathers of the neck forming a fender to the shoulder of the wing. **1893** *Temple Bar Mag.* XCVIII. 468 The fenders..the tiaras of the chaperones.

b. *Naut.* A piece of old cable, or other yielding material, hung over a vessel's side to preserve it from chafing or collision with a wharf or with other vessels. Also (see quot. 1850).

1626 CAPT. SMITH *Accid. Yng. Seamen* 16 They serue for Iunkes, fenders and braded plackets for brests of defence. **1627** —— *Seaman's Gram.* vii. 30 Fenders are peeces of old Hawsers called Iunkes hung ouer the ship sides to keepe them from brusing. **1821** A. FISHER *Jrnl. Arctic Reg.* 34 We were obliged to put fenders of junk over the ship's side to prevent her from being damaged by the ice. *c* **1850** *Rudim. Navig.* (Weale) 117 *Fenders*, two pieces of oak plank fayed edgewise, perpendicularly, against the top-sides abreast the main hatchway, to prevent the sides of the ship from being rubbed by the hoisting of anything on board. **1885** RUNCIMAN *Skippers & Sh.* 212 A sailor slipped a cork fender over the side.

c. A large piece of timber placed as a guard in front of any structure, *esp.* a pier, dock-wall, etc. Also *fender-pile* (see 7).

1739 LABELYE *Short Acc. Piers Westm. Bridge* 19 The Use of these Fenders..was to secure the Works from the Approach of Barges. **1838** SIMMS *Public Wks. Gt. Brit.* ii. 7 The wing walls..of the lock are defended by detached guards or fenders of timber. **1856** in BREES *Terms Archit. etc.* **1892** *Daily News* 27 Oct. 2/6 The wheel of his van struck a fender immediately outside some hoarding.

d. In various other technical uses (see quots.).

1874 KNIGHT *Dict. Mech.*, *Fender*, an attachment to a cultivator-plow to keep clods from rolling on to the young corn. [Also,] A rub-plate on the bed of a wagon or carriage to take the rub of the wheel when the vehicle is turning short. **1884** *Ibid.* Suppl., *Fender*, a screen against a carriage or car-step to keep dirt or mud from being thrown upon it by the wheels. A fender board.

e. See quot. Cf. FENCE 4 c.

1894 M. GRANT in *Cent. Mag.* XLVII. 352/2 The double fenders or brow-antlers [of the moose] do the most damage.

f. A mudguard over a wheel of a motor vehicle. *N. Amer.*

1919 S. LEWIS *Free Air* 103 Claire..had enjoyed the sight of their duffle-bags stuck up between the sleek fenders and the hood. **1928** *Punch* 25 Apr. p. xxx/3 (Advt.), Fender guards to match for rear. **1932** E. WILSON *Devil take Hindmost* viii. 47 A thousand-ton electric shear..reduces chassis, springs, wheels, fenders and all to a junk fodder of iron spines. **1960** *Times* 14 Sept. 12/6 When we hired a car in California we found that a car..bristles with surprises. You scrape the fender. **1963** H. GARNER in R. Weaver *Canad. Short Stories* 2nd Ser. (1968) 41 There was no sign of a flat tire, but its left front fender was loose.

3. a. A metal frame placed in front of a fire to keep falling coals from rolling out into the room.

1688 MIEGE *Fr. Dict.*, *Fender*. **1710** SWIFT *Jrnl. to Stella* 24 Dec., Only a mouse within the fender to warm himself. **1765** LAYARD in *Phil. Trans.* LVI. 17 An iron fender. **1834** MRS. CARLYLE *Lett.* I. 11 She actually borrowed one of the brass fenders. **1861** DICKENS *Gt. Expect.* xxx, Sitting with our feet on the fender.

b. A fire-guard. ? *U.S.*

1874 in KNIGHT *Dict. Mech.*

c. *Building.* 'A dwarf wall in the basement of a house, built up to carry the front hearth of a fireplace' (Gwilt).

4. A sluice-gate. Sometimes applied to the whole sluice.

1847 C. G. ADDISON *Law of Contracts* II. i. §i. (1883) 248 A sliding fender used to prevent the escape of water from a mill-stream. **1868** *Law Reports* Q. Bench Div. III. 289 In that part of the dam..is placed a fender or set of fenders. **1884** *Daily News* 23 July 5/2 The paddler of a canoe got sucked under a fender into a swift stream.

5. A device made of rushes, leaves, or plaited paper, with which seals were sometimes encircled to secure them from injury.

1864 BOUTELL *Heraldry Hist. & Pop.* xxiv. §1 (ed. 3) 399 'Fenders' of this kind have been found attached to seals as early as 1380. **1891** J. P. EARWAKER in *Proc. Soc. Antiq.* 19 Feb. 255 The seal is..protected by a twisted rush fender.

6. (See quot.) ? *Obs.*

1682 J. COLLINS *Salt & Fishery* 14 [Crude sea-salt is] carried in wicker Baskets or Fenders to Brine Wells.

7. *attrib.* and *Comb.*, as ***fender-maker***; **fender-beam**, (*a*) (see quot. 1874); (*b*) = *fender-stop*; **fender-bender** *slang* (chiefly *U.S.*), a (usu. minor) motor accident; **fender-board** (see quot. 1884 in sense 2 d); **fender-bolt** *Naut.*, (*a*) (see quot. 1867); (*b*) a bolt by which a fender is attached to a ship, etc.; **fender-pile** = FENDER *sb.* 2 c; **fender-post** (see quot.); **fender-stool**, a kind of long footstool usually placed close to the fender; **fender-stop** (see quot.); **fender wall** = FENDER 3 c.

1874 KNIGHT *Dict. Mech.*, **Fender-beam* 1. The horizontal beam into which the posts of a saw-mill gate are framed at top. 2. The inclined advance piece of an ice-breaker. 3. A beam suspended over a vessel's side to ward off ice and preserve the planking and sheathing of the vessel. **1966** *Time* 14 Oct. 39/2 To the TV reporter, his producer is a man who dotes on '*fender-bender footage': auto crashes, fires, demonstrations, fights. **1975** *Guardian Weekly* 16 Nov. 20 It would be hard to top the hassle of a Moscow fender-bender. **1981** PLATE & DARVI *Secret Police* i. 2 A fender-bender at a busy intersection. **1678** A. LITTLETON *Lat. Dict.* s.v., **Fender-bolts*. **1769** FALCONER *Dict. Marine* (1789) G b, Fender-bolts.. driven into the wales, stem, or sides of.. small vessels.. to defend their timber-work. **1867** SMYTH *Sailor's Word-bk.*, *Fender Bolts*. **1891** *Daily News* 26 Jan. 2/5 The season has been a busy one for *fender and fire-iron makers. **1739** LABELYE *Short Acc. Piers Westm. Bridge* 36 The *Fender-piles which guarded the North-point of this Pier. **1793** SMEATON *Edystone L.* §224 Fixing the Fender Piles on the east side of the rock. **1867** SMYTH *Sailor's Word-bk.*, *Fender-piles*. **1874** KNIGHT *Dict. Mech.*, **Fender-post*, one of the guiding stanchions of a saw-gate. **1870** MISS BROUGHTON *Red as Rose* I. 260 Let me put you down in the raffle for a *fender-stool. **1856** BREES *Terms Archit. etc.*, **Fender Stop*, the beams fixed at the extremity of a line of rails.. to stop the carriages and prevent their running off. **1894** J. P. ALLEN *Pract. Building Constr.* ii. 28 *Fender walls are those built round fireplaces to carry the hearth-stones and take the ends of the joists, which would otherwise have to be trimmed. **1924** W. M. F. PETRIE *Relig. Life Anc. Egypt* 124 Successive coatings of wall, and fender walls before the doorway.

fender (ˈfɛndə(r)), *v.* [f. prec. sb.] To provide with a fender or fenders.

Mod. (*techn.*). Specifications for fendering the river banks.

fendered, *a.* [f. FENDER *sb.* + -ED[2].] Provided with a fender or fenders.

1795 R. DODD *Rep. Improv. Hartlepool* 8 This pier.. well fendered, piled, &c. **1927** *Blackw. Mag.* Sept. 368/2 The tug thrust her fendered nose against the timbers.

fenderless (ˈfɛndəlɪs), *a.* [f. FENDER *sb.* + -LESS.] Having no fender.

1878 *Daily News* 2 Jan., The fenderless grate. **1880** *Ibid.* 15 Oct., House after house.. fenderless, without fire-irons.

fendillate (ˈfɛndɪleɪt), *v.* *Min. rare.* [f. F. *fendill-er* (dim. of *fendre*:—L. *findĕre* to split) + -ATE[3].] *trans.* To crack with many small fissures. Hence **ˈfendillated** *ppl. a.*; **fendiˈllation**, fendillated condition.

1853 TH. ROSS *Humboldt's Trav.* III. xxix. 168 This rock is much fendillated. *Ibid.* III. xxxii. 401 Fendillated crystals of pyroxene and mesotype. *Ibid.* 402 These, by their fendillation and open crevices, seem to establish that permanent communication between the surface of the soil and the interior of the globe.

fending (ˈfɛndɪŋ), *vbl. sb.* [f. FEND *v.* + -ING[1].]

1. The action of the vb. FEND; an instance of this; *esp.* in ***fending and proving*** (cf. FEND *v.* 2).

1583 RICH *Phylotus & Emelia* (1835) 31 After greate fendyng and prouyng had in the matter. **1655** FULLER *Ch. Hist.* VIII. iii. §9 Much fending, and proving there was betwixt them. **1751** JOHNSON *Rambler* No. 95 ¶2 The whole discipline of fending and proving. **1771** *Contemplative Man* ii. 10 There's no fending against Wind and Water. **1824** T. JEFFERSON *Writ.* (1830) IV. 407 With fendings and provings of personal slanders.

2. *Sc.* Provision.

1816 SCOTT *Antiq.* xi, 'That hae stouth and routh, and fire and fending, and meat and claith.'

fend-off (ˈfɛndɒf), *sb.* [f. FEND *v.* + OFF.] The action of fending off; hence *concr.* something that fends off. Also *attrib.*

1830 *Examiner* 177/2 A Committee.. is the fend-off to importunity, and the contrivance for obtaining time. **1883** GRESLEY *Coal Mining Gloss.*, *Fend off bob*, a beam hinged at one end and having a free reciprocating motion fixed at a bend in a shaft.. to guide the pump rods passing round the bend. **1880** *Antrim & Down Gloss.*, *Fend off post*, a post set in the ground to protect an object from injury by carts, etc., coming in contact with it.

ˈfendy, *a. dial.* [f. FEND *v.* + -Y[1].] (See quots.)

1782 SIR J. SINCLAIR *Observ. Sc. Dial.* 101 *Fendy*. Dexterous at finding out expedients. **1814** SCOTT *Wav.* xviii, Alice.. he said, was both canny and fendy. **1851** *Cumbrld. Gloss.*, *Fendy*, thrifty, managing. **1863** J. BROWN *Horæ Subs.* (1882) 90 A fendy wife. **1870** DR. BARBER *Forness Folk* 32 She's a gay fendy, lile body.

fene, obs. form of FEIGN.

†**fenerate**, *v.* *Obs.*—[0] [f. L. *fænerāt-* ppl. stem of *fæner-āre*, f. **fæner-* var. of *fænor-*, *fænus* interest: see -ATE.] *trans.* To lend on interest.

1623-6 COCKERAM, *Fænerate*, to put money to vsurie.

†**feneˈration.** *Obs.* [ad. L. *fænerātiōn-em*, n. of action f. *fænerāre*: see FENERATE *v.*] The action or practice of lending on interest; usury.

1598 BARCKLEY *Felic. Man* v. (1603) 549 True love.. hath respect only to his friends necessitie, without merchandize or feneration. **1612-5** BP. HALL *Contempl. N.T.* IV. iii, Giving to the poor is feneration to God: the greater bank, the more interest. **1650** SIR T. BROWNE *Pseud. Ep.* (ed. 2) 120 What vices therein it [the hare] figured; that is.. feneration or usury from its fecundity. **1721** in BAILEY. **1798** H. T. COLEBROOKE tr. *Digest of Hindu Law* (1801) I. 7 Feneration at the rate of an eightieth part by the month.

b. Interest on money lent.

In some mod. Dicts.

feneraˈtitious, *a.* *Obs.*—[0] [f. L. *fænerātīci-us* (f. *fænerāre*) + -OUS.] 'Taken or given to usury, or pertaining thereto' (Blount *Glossogr.* 1656–81).

†**ˈfenerator.** *Obs. rare*—[1]. [a. L. *fænerātor*, agent-n. f. *fænerāre*: see FENERATE and -OR.] A money-lender, usurer.

1447 BOKENHAM *Seyntys* (Roxb.) 158 Two detours quoth cryst to oon feneratour Were whylom Symund in a cuntre.

feneraˈtorial, *a. rare*—[1]. [f. L. *fænerātōri-us* (f. *fænerātor*) + -AL[1].] Pertaining to usury.

1793 J. BERESFORD in *Looker-on* No. 79 The magic of the foeneratorial rod was not wanting for the purposes of converting his watches into wealth.

fenestella (fɛnɪˈstɛlə). [a. L. *fenestella*, dim. of *fenestra* window.]

1. *Arch.* **a.** A small window-like niche in the wall on the south side of the altar, containing the piscina and often the credence.

1797 *Gentl. Mag.* LXVII. II. 649 A fenestella in the South wall of the chancel. **1839** STONEHOUSE *Axholme* 226 The fenestella, or small niche, contained a vessel, bason, or piscina, for washing the hands. **1843** *Ecclesiologist* II. 56 A Fenestella with Credence-shelf.

b. A small window.

1848 B. WEBB *Continent. Eccles.* 57 The dwarf-wall is pierced by a broad fenestella with a trefoliated head. **1849** WEALE *Dict. Terms* 183/1 *Fenestella*.. a little window.

2. *Zool.* (See quots.)

1849 MURCHISON *Siluria* ix. (1867) 188 The species [of Lower Silurian Zoophytes] with a net-like form, Fenestella and Retepora. *Ibid.* x. (1867) 217 The beautiful little cup-shaped Fenestella of the Wenlock limestone. **1879** ROSSITER *Dict. Sci. Terms*, *Fenestella*, a polyzoon; known by many fossil remains in Devonian limestones and other rocks.

fenestellid (fɛnɪˈstɛlɪd). *Palæont.* [f. L. *fenestell-a* + -ID.] One of the *Fenestellidæ*, a family of palæozoic polyzoans.

1882 *Athenæum* 24 June 798/3 A new Spiral Fenestellid from the Upper Silurian Beds of Ohio.

†**ˈfenester.** *Obs.* Forms: 3–5 fenestre, 6 fenester. [a. OF. *fenestre* (Fr. *fenêtre*):—L. *fenestra*: see next.] A window.

c **1290** *S. Eng. Leg.* I. 229/337 Þo cam þare-in a fuyri arewe at a fenestre a-non. *a* **1300** *Land Cokayne* 114 in *E.E.P.* (1862) 159 All þe fenestres þat beþ of glasse. **1393** LANGL. *P. Pl.* C. XXI. 13 Then was faith in a fenestre and cryde. *a* **1400** in *Eng. Gilds* (1870) 362 By leue of þe baylyues.. nyme þe dores & þe fenestres. **1483** CAXTON *Gold. Leg.* 370/4 Thyse thre fenestres or wyndowes betokene clerely the fader the sone and the holy ghoost. **1510-20** *Compl. too late maryed* (1862) 7 Breke I dyd dores and fenesters. **1513** DOUGLAS *Æneis* XII. Prol. 169 Cleir fenystaris of glas. **1548** HALL *Chron.* (1809) 605 In the Fenestres and wyndowes were images resemblynge men of warre.

‖**fenestra** (fɪˈnɛstrə). Pl. fenestræ. [L. *fenestra* window, f. root of Gr. φαίνειν to show.] A small hole or transparent spot resembling a hole.

1. *Anat.* A small hole or opening in a bone, etc.; *esp.* applied to the two openings on the inner wall of the tympanum of the ear, ***fenestra ovalis, rotunda*** (see quot. 1884).

1844 HOBLYN *Dict. Med. Terms* 121/1 *Fenestra ovalis* and *rotunda*.. the oval and round apertures of the internal ear. **1854** OWEN *Skel. & Teeth* (1855) 33 The alisphenoids, form the anterior half of the fenestra ovalis. **1870** ROLLESTON *Anim. Life* 7 An interorbital fenestra. **1877** HUXLEY *Anat. Inv. Anim.* vii. 400 An oval fenestra, covered only by a thin and transparent portion of the integument. **1884** BARR *Dis. Ear* III. i. 260 The fenestra ovalis or opening into the vestibule and the fenestra rotunda or opening into the cochlea. The fenestra ovalis is in the upper and back part of the inner wall.. at the bottom of a recess.. The fenestra rotunda.. is also situated at the bottom of a recess in the bone.

2. *Zool.* (See quot.)

1881 VINES in *Nature* No. 620. 463 Fenestræ.. openings [in the zoarium].. connected by the general substance of the zoarium.

3. *Bot.* See quot. Also 'an opening through a membrane' (*Treas. Bot.* 1866).

1828 STARK *Elem. Nat. Hist.* II. 459 The part at which the seed has separated from the ovary is indicated by a small mark or scar, called *fenestra*.

4. *Surg.* **a.** A perforation in a surgical instrument other than in the handle.

In quot. 1963 *fenestra* has apparently been taken as a plural form.

1876 DUNGLISON *Dict. Med. Sci.* (rev. ed.) 411/2 The term *fenestra* is also applied to the open space in the blades of a forceps. **1899** C. TRUAX *Mechanics of Surgery* xxiii. 479 The sac wall, when held in this forceps, will protrude through the fenestræ of the blades, whose sharply serrated edges insure a firm grasp. **1963** MITCHELL-HEGGS & DREW *Instruments of Surgery* i. 46 Charnley's dissecting forceps is designed in addition to grip suture material firmly when tying knots... The suture is trapped in the fenestrum by the block projection on the opposing jaw.

b. An opening in a dressing, plaster, etc., for access or the relief of pressure.

1876 C. H. LEONARD *Man. Bandaging* x. 116 It would be well to coat the margins of the fenestrae.. with parrafin [*sic*], so as to prevent the absorbtion [*sic*]of the fluids by the dressing. **1914** E. L. ELIASON *Pract. Bandaging* v. 109 The gauze dressing over the wound should be the size and shape of the desired fenestra or window.

c. A hole cut by a surgeon in any structure of the body.

1941 *Surg. Gynec. & Obstet.* LXXII. 472 This surgically made fenestra remains open. **1958** F. B. KORKIS *Rec. Adv. Oto-Laryngol.* (ed. 3) iv. 59 Closure of the newly made fenestra.. is not as frequent as it was in the early days of the operation.

†**feˈnestral**, *sb. Obs.* Also 5 fenestralle, 6 fenestrall. [a. OF. *fenestral*, f. *fenestre*: see FENESTER.] A window-frame or lattice, often fitted with cloth or paper as a substitute for crystal or glass; a window. Rarely of the filling in of the frame: A window-pane.

[**1291** *Accts. Exors. Q. Eleanor* in *Househ. Exps.* (Roxb.) 135 Pro canabo ad fenestrallas.. iij d.] **1399** *Mem. Ripon* (Surtees) III. 129 Et in j parva serura emp. pro j fenestrall infra capellam Beatæ Mariæ, 2½*d*. **1430** LYDG. *Chron. Troy* II. xi, All the windowes and eche fenestrall Wrought were of beryle & of cleare crystall. *c* **1430** —— *Min. Poems* (Percy Soc.) 203 To lite what shuld hire baggys been, Whoos fenestralle were hard to glase. **1519** HORMAN *Vulg.* 242 Paper or lyn clothe straked a crosse with losyngz: make fenestrals in stede of glasen wyndowes. **1523** SKELTON *Garl. Laurel* 1387 The fenestrall, Glittryng and glistryng and gloriously glasid. **1530** PALSGR. 219/2 Fenestrall, *chassis de toille, ou de paupier*. [**1851** TURNER *Dom. Archit.* II. i. 13 The windows were usually fitted with.. lattices or fenestrals.]

transf. *c* **1430** *Pilgr. Lyf Manhode* II. xlii. (1869) 92 Thou shuldest not weene that the soule haue neede of these eyen.. For bifore and bihynde, with oute bodelych fenestralle, he seeth his gostlich good.

fenestral (fɪˈnɛstrəl), *a.* [ad. L. *fenestrāl-is*, f. *fenestra*; see FENESTRA.]

1. Of or pertaining to a window.

1674-81 in BLOUNT *Glossogr.* **1691** WOOD *Ath. Oxon.* II. 699 Collections of monumental and fenestral inscriptions. **1696-9** BP. W. NICOLSON *Eng. Hist. Libr.* II. 145 Anth. Wood Collected the.. Fenestral Inscriptions.. in the County of Oxford. **1776** R. GRAVES *Euphrosyne* I. iv, On almost every occasion of human life.. Fenestral, Parietal, and what not.

2. *Anat.* and *Surg.* 'Having small openings like windows' (Wagstaffe). ***fenestral bandage***, 'a bandage, compress, or plaster with small perforations or openings to facilitate discharge' (Dunglison). Cf. FENESTRATE *v.*

3. *Biol.* **a.** Of, pertaining to, or of the nature of a fenestra. **b.** Furnished with fenestræ.

1865 GOSSE *Land & Sea* (1874) 156 Pseudopodia that project through the fenestral apertures.

fenestrate (fɪˈnɛstrət), *a.* [ad. L. *fenestrāt-us*, pa. pple. of *fenestrāre*, f. FENESTRA.]

1. Having small perforations or openings like a window. Chiefly *Bot.* and *Zool.*

1835 LINDLEY *Introd. Bot.* (1848) II. 21 The.. phragma has a slit in its centre, and is said to be *fenestrate*. **1846** DANA *Zooph.* (1848) 514 Parietes fenestrate. **1860** BALFOUR *Man. Bot.* §555 The replum.. sometimes exhibits perforations, becoming fenestrate. **1874** M. COOKE *Fungi* 132 The sporidia in Hysterium proper are.. sometimes fenestrate.

2. *Entom.* = FENESTRATED 3.

1842 in BRANDE.

fenestrate (fɪˈnɛstreɪt), *v. rare.* [f. L. *fenestrāt-* ppl. stem of *fenestrāre* (f. FENESTRA); see -ATE.] *trans.* To furnish (a bandage) with small holes or openings.

1887 *Lancet* 24 Sept. 604/1 Harelip strapping.. is fenestrated, and cut into strips.

fenestrated (fɪˈnɛstreɪtɪd), *ppl. a.* [f. L. *fenestrāt-us* (see prec.) + -ED[1].]

1. *Arch.* Furnished with windows.

1849 WEALE *Dict. Terms* 183/2 Astylar and fenestrated ought.. to be merely convertible terms; but as they are not [etc.]. In mod. Dicts.

2. a. In scientific use: Pierced with a hole or with holes; perforated. ***fenestrated membrane*** (Anat.): that form of the elastic tissue of the middle or contractile coat of the arteries, in which it presents a homogeneous membrane the meshes of which appear as simple perforations' (Hoblyn, 1868).

1849-52 TODD *Cycl. Anat.* IV. 1370/1 Fenestrated membrane. **1865** GOSSE *Land & Sea* 156 The shells [of Polycystina] are siliceous.. Their walls beautifully fenestrated with large angular or circular perforations. **1878** BELL *Gegenbauer's Comp. Anat.* 476 The coracoid.. is not unfrequently fenestrated. **1886** GUILLEMARD *Cruise of Marchesa* II. 188 Fleshy, fenestrated leaves.

b. Of a surgical instrument: having one or more fenestræ.

1881 *Trans. Obstet. Soc. Lond.* XXII. 46 These forceps, fenestrated longitudinally. **1915** A. MACLENNAN *Surgical Materials* VI. 210 (*caption*) Common type of clamp, with milled and fenestrated blades. **1963** MITCHELL-HEGGS & DREW *Instruments of Surgery* i. 55 Everett's pile forceps..

have a pair of fenestrated, grooved blades to accommodate the tissue of the haemorrhoid or 'pile'.

3. *Entom.* Having transparent spots.

1826 KIRBY & SP. *Entomol.* (1828) III. xxxii. 301 The male Locustæ have a fenestrated ocellus.

fenestration (fɛnɪˈstreɪʃən). [n. of action f. L. *fenestrāre*: see FENESTRATE *v.*]

1. The arrangement of windows in a building.

1846 *Civ. Eng. & Archit. Jrnl.* IX. 293 The fenestration of Soane's building was praiseworthy. **1879** SIR G. G. SCOTT *Lect. Archit.* I. 159, I see no difference of principle in the fenestration of the Early French and the Early English Pointed styles.

2. *Anat.* **a.** The process of becoming perforated; the formation of small holes. **b.** The condition of being fenestrated or perforated.

1870 ROLLESTON *Anim. Life* 150 Reduced by extreme fenestration to mere series of filaments. **1881** MIVART *Cat* 329 Fenestration—denoting that a solid structure has dissolved itself at one spot or more, so as to give rise to an aperture perforating it.

3. *Surg.* An opening made surgically to provide a passage through an anatomical structure; *esp.* the operation of cutting such an opening into the labyrinth of the ear to restore hearing in cases of otosclerosis.

1935 R. S. STEVENSON *Rec. Adv. Laryngol. & Otol.* v. 80 (*caption*) Fenestration of thyroid cartilage: Ledoux's method. **1937** *Bull. N.Y. Acad. Med.* XIII. 675 (*heading*) Operations based on fenestration of the labyrinth. **1949** G. M. COATES in F. Christopher *Textbk. Surg.* (ed. 5) xviii. 771 The theoretical basis of the fenestration operation is that by producing a new window into the internal ear..the impeded fenestra ovale is by-passed and sound impulses are again projected to the fluids of the internal ear and the cochlea. **1958** F. B. KORKIS *Rec. Adv. Oto-Laryngol.* (ed. 3) iv. 59 The operation of fenestration itself is being challenged..on account of the introduction of a less radical procedure—mobilization of the stapes.

†**fene'strelle.** *Obs. rare.* [a. OF. *fenestrelle*, dim. of *fenestre*: see FENESTER.] A small window.

c **1420** *Pallad. on Husb.* I. 534 A toure with plaine and whited walles, And fenestrelles iiii. *Ibid.* 545 In every fenestrell [sic *MS.*; *printed* -tell].

fenestriform (fɪˈnɛstrɪfɔːm), *a. rare*⁻¹. [f. L. *fenestra* window + -(I)FORM.] Window-shaped.

1860 *Ecclesiologist* XXI. 359 The most westernly [bay]..carries outside fenestriform panelling.

fenestrule (fɪˈnɛstruːl). *Zool.* [ad. L. *fenestrula*, dim. of FENESTRA.] (See quot. 1881.)

1872 NICHOLSON *Palæont.* 196 The branches of the cœnœcium unite with one another in such a manner as to form ovate interspaces or 'fenestrules'. **1881** *Nature* 15 Sept. 463/1 Fenestrules.—The square, oblong, or partially rounded openings in the zoarium—connected by non-cellular dissepiments—of Fenestella, Polypora, and species allied to these.

†**fenfield man.** *Obs.* (See quot.)

c **1630** RISDON *Surv. Devon* §215 (1810) 223 There are certain tenants dwelling in and about the moor, which are called *Fenfield Men*, in ancient times *Fengfield*, and these be the king's special tenants, pay him yearly rent..They may winter in the..forest so much cattle as they can keep, so that it be by day.

†**feng**, *sb. Obs.* Also 3 *south. dial.* **veng.** [OE. *fęng* str. masc. = OFris. *feng* ON. *fengr*.:—OTeut. **fangjo-z*, f. root of **fanhan*, OE. *fón*: see FANG *v.*¹] **a.** = FANG *sb.* 1. **b.** = FANG *sb.* 2.

c **1175** *Lamb. Hom.* 39 Leteð eower stale and eower reaflac for nis þer nan feng on. *c* **1205** LAY. 1773 Swa heo ferden to heora scipa mid allen heora uenge. *Ibid.* 8610 We scullen ..ȝemen þes fehtes & nawiht þes fenges. *a* **1250** *Owl & Night.* 1285 At eche fenge Thu fallest mid thine ahene swenge.

fengite: see PHENGITE. *Min.*

‖**feng-shui** (ˈfʌŋʃuːɪ). Also 8 fong-choui. [Chinese, f. *feng* wind + *shui* water.] In Chinese mythology, a system of spirit influences, good and evil, which inhabit the natural features of landscapes; hence, a kind of geomancy for dealing with these influences in determining sites for houses and graves. Also in extended use.

1797 *Encycl. Brit.* IV. 679/1 The greater part of the Chinese are of the opinion that all the happiness and misfortunes of life depend upon the *fong-choui*. **1883** *Ibid.* XV. 204/1 The *feng-shui*, or 'wind-and-water' magic, is a system the practitioners of which regulate the building of houses and tombs by their local aspects. **1906** W. DE MORGAN *Joseph Vance* xxvii. 252, I think what the Chinese call the Feng-Shui of the sofa-back had a good deal to answer for. *a* **1936** KIPLING *Something of Myself* (1937) vii. 178 We entered and felt her Spirit—her Feng Shui—to be good. **1967** 'A. CORDELL' *Bright Cantonese* xi. 123, I climbed to the grave of my mother, which was fine for *Feng Shui* with its wind and water.

Fengu: see FINGO.

'**fen-hood.** *nonce-wd.* Fens collectively.

1834 *New Monthly Mag.* XLI. 324 A place ensconced in fenhood.

Fenian (ˈfiːnɪən), *sb.* and *a.* [f. OIr. *féne* 'one of the names of the ancient population of Ireland' (Windisch), confused in modern times with *fíann* fem. collect., the name of a body of warriors who are said to have been the defenders of Ireland in the time of Finn and other legendary Irish kings.]

A. *sb.*

1. (See quot. 1879.) *Obs.* exc. *Hist.*

1816 SCOTT *Antiq.* xxx, [A pretended translation from Ossian] Do you compare your psalms To the tales of the bare-armed Fenians? **1861** E. O'CURRY *Lect. MS. Materials Anc. Ir. Hist.* 302 Goll Mac Morna, the great chief of the Connacht Fenians. **1879** *Encycl. Brit.* IX. 75/1 According to popular tradition the Fians, or Fenians were mercenary tribes acting as a permanent military force for the support of the Ard Rig, or king of Eire.

2. One of an organization or 'brotherhood' formed among the Irish in the United States of America for promoting and assisting revolutionary movements, and for the overthrow of the English government in Ireland.

1864 *Leeds Mercury* 11 Mar., The men known under the general name of Fenians..are regarded with no friendly eye by the Roman Catholic clergy in Ireland and America. **1865** *Sat. Rev.* 4 Mar. 240 Rebels (of late called Fenians). **1880** MᶜCARTHY *Own Times* IV. liii. 139 Several Fenians were taken and shot.

B. *adj.*

1. Of or pertaining to the Fenians (FENIAN *sb.* 1).

1861 E. O'CURRY *Lect. MS. Materials Anc. Ir. Hist.* 299 The Fenian Poems, many of which are attributed to Oisin and Fergus. **1862** W. F. SKENE in *Bk. of Lismore* Introd. 80 Districts in which the Fenian names enter most largely into the topography of the Highlands.

2. Of or pertaining to the Fenians (*sb.* 2) or to Fenianism. ***Fenian Brotherhood*** (see quot. 1890).

1865 *Ann. Reg.* 172 The new conspiracy commonly known by the name of 'Fenian'. *Ibid.* 175 A..secret society called the Fenian Brotherhood. **1890** C. L. NORTON *Polit. Americanisms* 43 As generally understood in America, the 'Fenian Brotherhood' is a league pledged to the liberation of Ireland.

Fenianism (ˈfiːnɪənɪz(ə)m). [f. prec. + -ISM.] The principles, purposes and methods of the Fenians.

1866 *Spectator* 1 Dec. 1329 The revival of Fenianism is as formidable as its outbreak. **1870** LOWELL *Among my Bks.* Ser. I. (1873) 131 The..invisible omnipresence of Fenianism. **1880** MᶜCARTHY *Own Times* IV. liii. 147 Their deaths did not discourage the spirit of Fenianism.

†**fenicu'laceous,** *a. Obs. rare*⁻¹. [f. L. *fæniculum* fennel + -ACEOUS.] Resembling fennel.

1657 TOMLINSON *Renou's Disp.* 240 Wilde Parsnip..its stalk and muscary being feniculaceous.

fenix, obs. form of PHŒNIX.

†**fenk,** *v. Obs.* In 4 fenke, venke. [ad. OF. *vencre* (mod.F. *vaincre*):—L. *vincĕre*.] *trans.* To vanquish; conquer. Also *absol.*

c **1320** *Seuyn Sag.* (W.) 2024 Ouercomen, venkud, and bitraid. **1340–70** *Alisaunder* 323 Philip fenkes in fyght. **1340–70** *Alex. & Dind.* 339 Haddest þou fenked þe fon..þat in þi flech dwellen.

fenks (fɛnks), *pl.* Also **finks.** The fibrous parts of the blubber of a whale, which contain the oil; the refuse of the blubber when melted. Also in *Comb.*, as ***fenk(s)-back***: see quot.

1820 SCORESBY *Acc. Arctic Reg.* II. 399 A 'fenk-back' or depository for the refuse of the blubber. *Ibid.* II. 434 The fenks..form an excellent manure. **1836** *Uncle Philip's Convers. Whale Fishery* 232 The men..stir the blubber with poles..to prevent the fenks from sticking to the sides. **1876** *Whitby Gloss., Finks.*

†**fen-lich,** *a.* and *adv.* [OE. *fenlic*, f. FEN *sb.*¹ + *-lic*, -LY¹; the mod. form would be **fenly*.] Fenny, dirty, marshy, miry. Hence '**fenliche** *adv.*, filthily.

c **1000** ÆLFRIC *Gram.* ix. (Z.) 45 *Paluster*, fenlic. *c* **1000** *St. Guthlac* (1848) 22 Betwyx þa fenlican ȝewrido þæs widgillan westenes, þæt he ana ongan eardian. *a* **1225** *Ancr. R.* 206 Hwo se nule iðe muchele fulðe uenliche uallen. *a* **1240** *Ureisun* in *Cott. Hom.* 202 Ich ham wið hore horie fenliche ifuled.

'**fen-like,** *a.* Resembling a fen, marshy.

1561 DAUS tr. *Bullinger on Apoc.* (1573) 225 b, Altogether froggelyke and fenlyke. **1660** HOWELL *Lexicon*, Fennie, fen-like, *marescageux, palustre.*

'**fen-man.** An inhabitant of the fens.

1610 HOLLAND *Camden's Brit.* 491 Girvij that is, as some interpret it, Fen-men or Fen-dwellers. **1611** COTGR. s.v. *Boeuf*, As our fenne-men [say], rather catch a ducke than feed an Oxe. **1626** BACON *Sylva* §600 The Fen-men hold that the Sewers must be kept. **1766** PENNANT *Zool.* (1776) I. 254 Stares..do great damage to the fen men by roosting on the reeds. **1856** P. THOMPSON *Hist. Boston* 644 The fen-men ..were, a century later, known as the Slodgers, or Fen-Slodgers. **1865** KINGSLEY *Herew.* Prel. 19 After the snow would come the fenman's yearly holiday.

Fenn (fɛn). The name of Charles Fenn (1840–1925), English entomologist, used in **Fenn's wainscot**, a moth, *Arenostola brevilinea*, first described by him in 1864.

[**1869** E. NEWMAN *Illustr. Nat. Hist. Brit. Moths* 271/2 Fenn's Nonagria.] **1907** R. SOUTH *Moths Brit. Isl.* I. 308 Fenn's Wainscot (*Leucania brevilinea*). **1955** E. B. FORD *Moths* x. 136 The Flame Wainscot, *Senta flammea* Curtis, and Fenn's Wainscot, *Arenostola brevilinea* Fenn, would often be searched for in vain.

†'**fenne.** *Obs. rare*⁻¹. ? A dragon.

1567 TURBERV. tr. *Ovid's Ep.* vi. 25 And that the waker Fenne the golden spoyle did keepe.

‖**fennec** (ˈfɛnɪk). *Zool.* Also fennic. [Arab. *fenek*, a name vaguely applied to various fur-bearing animals.] The name of an animal (*Canis zerda*) found in Africa, resembling a small fox, but having very long ears.

1790 BRUCE *Trav.* V. 135 After leaving Algiers I met with another fennec at Tunis. **1848** CRAIG, *Fennic.* *c* **1850** *Nat. Encycl.* I. 264 Various species of foxes and fox-like animals, among which we may notice the fennec. **1888** *Riverside Nat. Hist.* V. 412 The Fennec is a pretty little animal, ranging over a large part of Africa.

fennel (ˈfɛnəl). Forms: 1 finugl, finul(e, fenol, finol, 3, 5 fenyl(le, (4 fynel, 5, 7 fenil, 6 foenall), 4–7 fenel(l(e, 6–7 fennell, 7– fennel. See also FINKLE. [OE. *finugl, finule* wk. fem., *fenol, finul* masc., ad. popular L. *fēnuclum, fēnoclum* (substituted for class. L. *fæniculum*, dim. of *fænum* hay); from the same form come OF. *fenoil* (mod.F. *fenouil*), Pr. *fenolh*, It. *finocchio*, Sp. *hinojo*.]

1. A fragrant perennial umbellifer (*Fæniculum vulgare*) having yellow flowers, cultivated chiefly for its use in sauces eaten with salmon, etc.

a **700** *Epinal Gloss.* 451 *Finiculus*, finugl. *c* **1000** ÆLFRIC *Gloss.* in Wr.-Wülcker 322 *Feniculum*, fenol. *a* **1310** in Wright *Lyric P.* xiii. 44 The fenyl ant the fille. **1393** GOWER *Conf.* III. 129 His herbe..The vertuous fenel. **1486** *Bk. St. Albans* B iv b, Wassh the flesh..in yᵉ Juce of fenell. **1533** ELYOT *Cast. Helthe* (1539) 41 a, Wyne..wherin the rootes of persely or fenel be stieped. **1538** TURNER *Libellus*, Foenell, *Feniculum.* **1602** SHAKS. *Ham.* IV. v. 180 There's Fennell for you. **1667** MILTON *P.L.* IX. 581 A savorie odour..more pleas'd my sense Than smell of sweetest Fenel. **1732** ARBUTHNOT *Rules of Diet* 260 Fennel..contains a subtil Spice. **1770** GOLDSM. *Des. Vill.* 234 With aspen boughs, and flowers and fennel gay. **1796** MRS. GLASSE *Cookery* xviii. 291 Garnish with fennel and parsley. **1841–6** LONGF. *Goblet of Life* v, The fennel with its yellow flowers. **1879** BROWNING *Pheidippides* 82 This herbage I bear—Fennel, whatever it bode.

b. With qualifying words indicating different species; *esp.* **Indian fennel**, *Fæniculum Panmorium*, an annual variety of *F. vulgare* employed in India in curries and for medicinal purposes. **sweet fennel**, *Fæniculum dulce* or *officinale*, grown in kitchen-gardens for the sake of its leaves.

1796 C. MARSHALL *Garden.* xvi. (1813) 267 Sweet fennel is an annual, cultivated for its seeds in medicine. **1811** A. T. THOMSON *Lond. Disp.* (1818) 34 The root of..the common fennel, and the seed of..the sweet fennel, are officinal.

2. Popularly applied to plants resembling the preceding, as **dog** or **dog's fennel**, *Anthemis Cotula*; **hog's fennel**, *Peucedanum officinale*; **horse fennel**, *Seseli Hippomarathrum*; **sea fennel**, *Crithmum maritimum*; **sow fennel** = *hog's f.*; **water fennel**, *Callitriche verna.*

1523 FITZHERB. *Husb.* §20 Doggefenell..in the commynge vp is lyke fenell, and beareth many white floures. **1688** R. HOLME *Armoury* II. 73/1 The dog Fennel hath small deep dark leaves. **1712** tr. *Pomet's Hist. Drugs* I. 7 Another kind of Fennel..bears the Name of Sea-Fennel. **1863** PRIOR *Plant-n.* (1879) 77 Dog's Fennel.

b. fennel-flower, a herb of the genus *Nigella*. Also with distinguishing epithets, as ***common, Spanish, small, wild fennel-flower.***

1863 PRIOR *Plant-n.* (1879) 77 Fennel-Flower, from its fennel-like finely divided leaves. **1868** HEREMAN *Paxton's Bot. Dict.* 392/2 The species of Fennel-flower are curious and ornamental.

c. fennel-giant (*Ferula communis*), a plant of the genus *Ferula*; also with distinguishing epithets, as *broad-leaved, furrowed, knotted*, etc. = *giant-fennel.*

1578 LYTE *Dodoens* II. lxxxix. 269 The seconde kinde is called..wilde Fenell, and great Fenell: and of some Fenell Giant. **1591** SYLVESTER *Du Bartas* I. iii. (1641) 27/2 Th' Hearb Sagapen [*side note* Fenelgyant] serves the slowe Asse for meat. **1654** GATAKER *Disc. Apol.* 70 A Ferula, or Fennel-giant, as some term it. **1794** MARTYN *Rousseau's Bot.* xxii. 237 It [Ferula] is so lofty and large a plant as to have acquired the name of Fennel Giant. **1848** in CRAIG.

3. As an emblem of flattery.

1584 LYLY *Sappho* II. iv, Fancy is a worme, that feedeth first upon fenell. **1592** GREENE *Upst. Courtier* (1871) 2 Womans weeds, fennel I mean for flatterers. **1634** *Phyala Lachrymarum* (Nares), Nor fennell-finkle bring for flattery.

4. *attrib.* and *Comb.*, as ***fennel-plant, -root, -seed, stalk; fennel-like, -rubbed*** adjs.: also †**fennel apple**, the name of a variety of apple; **fennel oil**, 'the oil of common fennel containing anethol and a terpene' (Watts); **fennel water**, a spirituous liquor prepared from fennel seed, = FENOUILLETTE.

1664 EVELYN *Kal. Hort.* (1729) 225 Apples..*Fennel Apple. **1721** in BAILEY. **1855** SINGLETON *Virgil* I. 65 Blooming *fennel-plants And giant lilies tossing to and fro. **1642** MILTON *Apol. Smect.* (1851) 288 To see clearer then any *fenell rub'd Serpent. *c* **1000** *Sax. Leechd.* III. 28 *Finol sæd..gnid to duste. **1362** LANGL. *P. Pl.* A. v. 156, I haue.. A Ferþing-worþ of Fenel-seed for þis Fastyng dayes. **1626** BACON *Sylva* §528 Take Earth made with Marjoram.. bruised, or stamped, and set in it Fennell-Seed. **1691** RAY *Creation* I. 75 You can by no Culture..extend a *Fennel Stalk to the stature and bigness of an Oak. **1757** A. COOPER *Distiller* II. v. (1760) 126 Simple Waters now commonly made are..Cinamon-water, *Fennel-water, etc. **1879** *Encycl. Brit.* (ed. 9) IX. 76/1 The fruits..are used for the preparation of oil of fennel and fennel water.

fenner ('fɛnə(r)). [f. FEN *sb.*[1] + -ER[1]] = FENMAN.

1844 [see FEN *sb.*[1] 5]. **1900** *Daily Express* 26 June 4/5 When we poor fenners skate the ice. **1940** F. KITCHEN *Brother to Ox* vi. 98 You could pick out the Lincolnshire 'fenners' by their fancy for bright blue cords.

†'**fennilich**, *a. Obs.* [f. FENNY + *-lich*, -LY[1].] Dirty, filthy, miry.

a **1225** *St. Marher.* 15 Fule ant fenniliche i fleschliche fulthen. *c* **1230** *Hali Meid.* 11 Into fulðe fenniliche akasteð se monie.

†'**fennin, fenny.** *Obs.* [Corruption of Ger. *pfenni(n)g*.] English names for the German coin *pfennig*, now (1895) worth about a tenth of a penny.

1611 CORYAT *Crudities* 465 Tinne money called fennies. **1756** NUGENT *Gr. Tour* II. 61 In most of the king of Prussia's dominions, the moneys are expressed by crowns..grosses, and fennins.

fennish ('fɛnɪʃ), *a.* [f. FEN *sb.*[1] + -ISH.]

1. = FENNY *a.*[1] 1.

1577 B. GOOGE *Heresbach's Husb.* I. (1586) 24 The land it selfe is..called.. fennishe, where the water still continues. **1602** FULBECKE *2nd Pt. Parall.* 54 To turne..fennish ground into firme ground. **1661** LOVELL *Hist. Anim. & Min.* 145 In Fennish and watery places. **1727** in BAILEY vol. II.

2. Belonging to or produced from a fen. Also of a bird: Inhabiting the fen.

1574 WHITGIFT *Def. Aunsw.* iii. §30. 378 All the Fennishe waters in a whole Countrey. **1600** *Maides Metam.* II. in Bullen *O. Pl.* I. 120 Where fennish fogges and vapours do abound. **1661** LOVELL *Hist. Anim. & Min.* Introd. 4 Tit-mouse, great fennish. **1851** *College Life time Jas. I*, 63 Symonds fell a victim to the fennish malaria.

3. Savouring of the fen; muddy.

1661 J. CHILDREY *Brit. Bacon* 88 The Stews..were made to feed Pikes and Tenches fat, and to scour them from their muddy Fennish taste.

Fennoscandia (fɛnəʊ'skændɪə). *Geol.* Also Fenno-Scandia, Fennoskandia. [ad. G. *fennoskandisch* adj. (W. Ramsay 1904, in *Fennia* XXI. VII. 44), f. L. *Fenn-i* the Finns + -O: see SCANDIAN *a.*] An ancient land mass in north-western Europe comprising most of Scandinavia and Finland and parts of the Soviet Union west of the White Sea. Also in extended use, Scandinavia and Finland as a political unit. Hence **Fenno'scandian, ˌFennoscandi'navian** *adjs.*

1907 tr. J. J. SEDERHOLM in *Bull. Commission Géol. de Finlande* V. XXIII. 91 The earnest discussion among Fenno-Scandian geologists,..concerning the origin of the gneissose rocks. *Ibid.* 92 Pre-Cambrian sedimentary formations have been traced through the whole eastern part of Fenno-Scandia. **1910** *Encycl. Brit.* XII. 59/2 Fennoscandia (the name for Scandinavia with Finland as a single geological region). **1944** *Proc. Geol. Assoc.* LV. 61 (*heading*) The Fennoskandian contributions. **1956** L. U. DE SITTER *Struct. Geol.* xxv. 367 Pre-Cambrian rocks of Fennoskandia and Greenland. **1962** E. W SPENCER *Basic Concepts Physical Geol.* xii. 212 In such areas as the Canadian Shield and the Fennoscandinavian Shield the surface is rising at measurable rates. **1966** *Times* 3 Feb. 13/2 President Kekkonen's proposals for a neutral 'Fenno-Scandia', to include not only Finland and Sweden but also Norway and perhaps Denmark if they were prepared to leave Nato.

fenny ('fɛnɪ), *a.*[1] [OE. *fenniȝ*, f. *fenn* FEN.]

1. Of the nature of, or characterized by, fen; boggy, swampy.

c **1000** ÆLFRIC *Gloss.* in Wr.-Wülcker 147 *Uliginosus ager*, fenniȝ æcer. *c* **1420** *Pallad. on Husb.* II. 22 The fenny feeld it is not forto plowe. *a* **1440** *Found. St. Bartholomew's* 12 Right vncleene it was and as a maryce dunge and fenny with water. **1553** EDEN *Treat. Newe Ind.* (Arb.) 19 They are.. engendered..in fennie & marrishe groundes. **1624** CAPT. SMITH *Virginia* IV. 162 Large Fenny vnwholsome Marshes. **1712** STEELE *Spect.* No. 406 ¶4 They journey through the fenny Moors. **1805** LUCCOCK *Nat. Wool* 186 Almost the only animal of the kind known through the fenny district. **1858** BUSHNELL *Nat. & Supernat.* vi. (1864) 192 Muddy rivers, with their fenny shores, tenanted by hideous alligators.

2. Inhabiting, growing, or produced in a fen. Now only of plants.

1543 TRAHERON *Vigo's Chirurg.* II. ix. 42 He must abstaine also from maryshe fyshes and fennie, and drye..oystres. **1545** ASCHAM *Toxoph.* (Arb.) 128 A fennye goose. **1587** HARRISON *England* II. xxii. (1877) I. 343 Fennie bote, broome, turffe, [etc.]..will be good merchandize euen in the citie of London. **1605** SHAKS. *Macb.* IV. i. 12 Fillet of a Fenny Snake, In the Cauldron boyle and bake. **1607** TOPSELL *Serpents* (1608) 705 Dragons..fenny, and living in the marishes. *c* **1629** LAYTON *Synos Plea* Ep. Ded., Fenny-Bitters in their hollowe canne make a terrible noyse. **1660** LOVELL *Hist. Anim. & Min.* 181 They are a fenny fowl. *a* **1721** PRIOR *Solomon* I. 324 In the troubl'd Stream and fenny Brake. **1818** KEATS *Endym.* I. 80 Winding through palmy fern, and rushes fenny. **1822** HOOD *Lycus*, Like a long silver rivulet under The long fenny grass.

†**3.** Muddy, dirty. Also *fig. Obs.*

c **897** K. ÆLFRED *Gregory's Past.* xiii. 74 Gif sio [hond].. bið..fenneȝu. **13..** *E.E. Allit. P.* B. 1113 Þaȝ þou be man fenny, & al to-marred in myre..þou may schyne þurȝ schryfte. *a* **1340** HAMPOLE *Psalter* lxxvii. 50 Vayn ianglynge þat is in fenny wittes. **1635** QUARLES *Embl.* II. xiv. (1718) 118 What fenny trash maintains the smoth'ring fires Of his desires!

4. *Comb.*, **fenny-seated** *a.*, situated in a fen; †**fenny-stones**, a kind of Orchis.

1631 WEEVER *Anc. Fun. Mon.* 58 That famous fenny-seated Monastery. **1597** GERARDE *Herbal* I. cv. 174 Of Fennie stones. **1678** PHILLIPS, *Fenny-stones*, a plant somewhat of the nature and kind of the Cynos Orchis or Dog-stones. **1721–1800** BAILEY, *Fenny-stones*.

'**fenny**, *a.*[2] *Obs.* exc. *dial.* Also 1 fyniȝ, 8 vinny. [OE. *fyniȝ*, f. *fyne*, FEN *sb.*[2] mould. Cf. FINEW.] Spoiled with damp, mouldy, musty.

c **1000** ÆLFRIC *Josh.* ix. 5 Finnie hlafas. **1573** TUSSER *Husb.* xxxv. (1878) 83 More fennie the laier the better his lust, more apt to beare hops when it crumbles like dust. **1674** RAY *S. & E.C. Words* 65 Fenny cheese, mouldy cheese, Kent. **1736** LEWIS *Thanet Gloss.*, *Fenny*, rotten, mouldy cheese 'vinny cheese'. *c* **1860** *Kentish dial.*, 'This bread is fenny ma'am, all through lying in that damp place.'

fennyxe, obs. form of PHŒNIX.

feno(c)chio, obs. f. FINOCHIO, sweet fennel.

fenoe, fenoed, var. of FINEW, FINEWED, *Obs.*

†'**fenory.** *Obs. rare*[−1]. [f. L. *fænor-*, *fænus* interest + -Y[3].] Interest of money.

1572 T. WILSON *Usurye* 85 b, Usurye or fenorye is a gayne demaunded aboue yᵉ principal.

†**fenouil.** [in F. *fenouillet*, f. *fenouil* FENNEL.] = *fennel apple*; see FENNEL 4.

1664 EVELYN *Kal. Hort.* (1729) 207 Apples..John-Apples, Robillard, Red Fennouil.

†**fenoui'llette.** Also 8 fenouillet(e. [a. F. *fenouillette*, f. *fenouil* FENNEL.] Fennel water.

1706 *Lond. Gaz.* No. 4280/4 French Wines, most Clarets, Prunes, Brandy, and Fenouillete. **1715** *Dr. Swift's Real Diary* 5 (D.) He's a silly fellow. Went home to take some fenouillet I was so sick of him. **1758** J. S. *Le Dran's Observ. Surg.* (1771) 282, I..found a scent of Fenouillette.

fenow(e, -ed, var. of FINEW, FINEWED, *Obs.*

fensabill, -bly, obs. ff. FENCIBLE, FENCIBLY.

†'**fensive**, *a. Obs.* [Shortened form of DEFENSIVE.] = DEFENSIVE.

1583 STANYHURST *Æneis* II. (Arb.) 53 Fensiue seruice. **1595** BARNFIELD *Sonn.* i, Skin, the bodies fensiue wall. **1602** WARNER *Alb. Eng.* 15 The Troyans..seeke to retire into their fensive towne. **1621** QUARLES *Div. Poems, Esther* (1717) 157 The Hills His fensive Bulwarks are.

fenster ('fɛnstə(r)). *Geol.* [G., lit. window.] An opening or 'window' eroded through an older stratum in a region of overfolding or overthrusting, exposing a younger stratum beneath.

1925 *Bull. Virginia Geol. Surv.* xxv. 45 Occurrences, where the erosion of the older, overlying rocks has exposed the younger or underlying rocks, have generally been called fensters. **1933** W. H. BUCHER *Deform. Earth's Crust* vii. 176 This is beautifully shown on the map by the 'embayments' and 'fensters' of Palaeozoic formations. **1939** A. K. LOBECK *Geomorphol.* xvii. 605 So called windows or fensters are produced by the erosion of plateau areas, so that the youngest strata of an under-lying nappe are exposed at the bottom of the valley thus formed. **1954** W. D. THORNBURY *Princ. Geomorphol.* x. 273 In the early stages of dissection of a nappe, erosion may penetrate the overthrust mass and locally expose patches of the younger rocks below it. Such exposures are called fensters or windows.

†'**fensure.** *Obs.* Also 6 feanser. [f. *fens*, obs. f. FENCE *v.* + -URE.] A fence.

1552 HULOET, Fence or fensure, *vallum. a* **1700** *Lord of Lorn* in *Roxb. Ball.* (1874) II. 352 The Lady is a hunting gone over feanser that is so high.

fent (fɛnt), *sb.* Also 5 vent, 5–7 fente, 7 fenth. [ad. Fr. *fente*, f. *fendre*:—L. *findĕre* to split.]

1. A short slit or opening in a robe, *esp.* the opening at the throat, usually closed by a brooch, trimmed with fur, etc. Also a placket or placket-hole. Now chiefly *dial.*

c **1430** *Syr Gener.* (Roxb.) 5941 The stroke vndre the fent, Queyntly al a-side it went. *c* **1440** *Promp. Parv.* 156 Fente of a clothe, *fibulatorium. c* **1450** HENRYSON *Mor. Fab.* 55 Flours fair furred on euerie fent. **1459** *Wardrobe Sir T. Fastolf* in *Archæologia* XXI. 253, i jakket of red felwet, the ventis bounde with red lether. *a* **1500** *Assembly of Ladies*, The coller and the vent..With greate perles..were couched al after one worching. **1502** *Privy Purse Exp. Eliz. of York* (1830) 69 Item for a nayle of sarcenet for fentes for the same gowne iiijd. **1530** PALSGR. 219/2 Fent of a gowne, *fente.* **1611** COTGR., *La fente d'une chemise*, the fent of a shirt. **1652** URQUHART *Jewel* Wks. (1834) 241 A cloth of gold petticoat, in the anterior fente whereof was an asteristick ouch. **1814** *Law Case* (Jam.), He put his hand..into the fent of her petticoat.

2. †**a.** A crack in the skin (*obs.*); **b.** (see quot. 1776); c. an opening or rift in the ground.

1597 LOWE *Chirurg.* (1634) 188 Clifts or Fenths in the Eares or Nose. **1776** DA COSTA *Conch.* 243 The fent (Rima) is the opening of the Shells on the Slopes. **1878** LADY HERBERT tr. *Hübner's Ramble* II. ii. 244 A ravine, or rather a deep fent in the soil.

3. *dial.* The binding of any part of the dress.

1847 in HALLIWELL. **1877** *N.W. Linc. Gloss.*, *Fent*, the binding of a woman's dress.

4. A remnant (of cloth).

1844 S. BAMFORD *Pass. Life Radical* ix. 60 Her outer garments were of very homely material, being seemingly cotton fents dyed blue. **1855** ROBINSON *Whitby Gloss.*, *Fents* ..remnants of cloth in varieties. **1860** O'NEILL *Chem. Calico-Printing* 312 If a fent mordanted for black and purple be dipped in hot caustic soda, it will [etc.]. **1865** B. BRIERLEY *Irkdale* I. 156 A couple of fents of his own weaving.

5. *attrib.*, (sense 4) as ***fent-dealer, -merchant.***

1884 *Manch. Exam.* 18 Sept. 5/3 Mr. M...started in business as a fent and general merchant. **1892** SIMMONDS *Trade Dict.* Sup., *Fent-Dealer*, a piece broker, a retailer of remnants of cloth.

†**fent**, *v. Obs. rare*[−1]. [f. prec. sb.] *trans.* ? To make slits in.

1589 *Nottingham Rec.* IV. 277 For fentinge tenne moryons ijs. iijd.

fent, -ly, obs. and dial. ff. FAINT *sb.*, FAINTLY.

fenugreek ('fɛnju:gri:k). Forms: 1 fenogrecum, 4–5 fene-, feyngrek, (4 feiny greke), 6 fene-, feny-greke, fen(e)-, fenigreek(e, (6 fenecryck, 7 fœnegreeke), 6–7 feni-, feny-, fenugrec(k, (8 fenegry), 7 fenu-Greek, 9 fœnugreek, 7– fenugreek. [OE. *fenogræcum*, L. *fænugræcum* for *fænum Græcum* Greek hay, the name given by the Romans (see quot. 1861). The ME. and later forms are ad. Fr. *fenugrec* = Pr. *fenugrec*, *fengrec*.]

1. A leguminous plant (*Trigonella Fœnum Græcum*) cultivated for its seeds, which are used by farriers.

c **1000** *Sax. Leechd.* II. 181 Wiþ sarum maȝan eft ȝedo on wearmne ele þa wyrt þe hatte fenogrecum. **13..** *Med. Receipt* in *Rel. Ant.* I. 51 Tak..feinygreke..and farse the catte. *c* **1420** *Pallad. on Husb.* II. 43 Ffeyngrek..is to be sowe ..in this Janes ende. **1562** TURNER *Herbal* II. 5 a, The flour or meale of Fenegreke. **1631** MARKHAM *Cheap Husb.* I. Table Hard Words, *Fenugreek* is an Herb which hath a long slender trailing stalk. **1708** W. KING *Cookery* ix, The herb *fenugreek*, with pickles, oil, and wine, was a Roman dainty. **1861** MISS PRATT *Flower. Pl.* II. 97 *Fenugreek*..so called by the Romans from their having adopted..the practice of cutting and drying it for fodder. **1877** ERICHSEN *Surg.* I. 15 The patient should be roused by the use of vinegar or fenugreek.

2. *attrib.*, as ***fenugreek-flower, -seed.***

1614 MARKHAM *Cheap Husb.* I. v. (1668) 41 Take..of Fenugreek-seed one ounce. **1643** J. STEER tr. *Exp. Chyrurg.* vi. 25 A Decoction of Fœnegreeke or Melelot flowers. **1791** HAMILTON *Berthollet's Dyeing* II. II. III. ii. 136 One dram of fenugreek seed. **1853** SOYER *Pantroph.* 144 Cook it in a saucepan with..fenugreek seed.

fenum, obs. f. FŒNUM, dial. f. of VENOM.

feny(ne, obs. form of FEIGN.

fenyce, obs. form of PHŒNIX.

†'**fenyent**, *a. Sc. Obs. rare.* [a. OF. *feignant*.] = FAINEANT *attrib.*

1444 *Sc. Acts* 19 Jan. (*title*), Act for the way-putting of Fenyent Fules.

fenyhe, -ye, -yie, obs. Sc. forms of FEIGN.

fenysh, obs. form of FINISH.

feo, obs. form of FEE *sb.*[1] and [2].

feoble, obs. form of FEEBLE.

feod(e, obs. forms of FEUD *sb.*[1] and [2].

feodary, feodatory: see FEU-.

feoff, var. form of FIEF *sb.*

feoff (fɛf), *v.* Forms: 3 feoffen, 3–7 feff, 6–7 feoffe, (feofe, feoffee), 4–7 feoff, (9 *dial.* feft). *Pa. t.* and *pa. pple.* feoffed; also 5–6 feft(e, 7 feoft. See also FIEF *v.* [Early ME. *feoffen*, ad. AF. *feoffer*, OF. *fieuffer*, *fieffer*, f. *fieu*, *fief*: see FEE *sb.*[2], FIEF *sb.*]

1. *Law. trans.* To put in legal possession (properly confined to freehold interests in corporeal hereditaments; formerly sometimes inaccurately used of leasehold); = ENFEOFF *v.* 1. ? *Obs.*

c **1290** *S. Eng. Leg.* I. 463/33 To feoffen heore children þare-wiz echon. **1297** R. GLOUC. (Rolls) 7585 Men of religion of normandie..He feffede here mid londes. *c* **1330** R. BRUNNE *Chron.* (1810) 35 Þe abbey of Rumeye he feffed richely With rentes. *c* **1375** *Sc. Leg. Saints, Justina* 648 Þe bischope gert þane a nunry make & feffit for Justinis sake. *c* **1386** CHAUCER *Merch. T.* 454 Every script and bond, By which that sche was feoffed in his lond. **1415** *E.E. Wills* (1882) 24 The londes rentes that ȝe bun feoffed In. *c* **1425** WYNTOUN *Cron.* v. x. 347 He fefte þe kyrk..Wytht gret fe fayre and fre Franchys. *c* **1430** *How Wise Mon tauȝt Son* 96 in *Babees Bk.* (1868) 51 For ritchesse take hir neuere þe more þouȝ sche wolde þee boþe feffe & ceese. **1520** *Caxton's Chron. Eng.* v. 49 b/2 Whan Arthur had thus his knyghtes feoffed. **1573** TUSSER *Husb.* cxiii. (1878) 213 Gentrie standes, not all by landes, Nor all so feft. **1620** BP. HALL

Hon. Mar. Clergie II. §8 Anastatius..feoffed in some Temporalties which hee would rather die than not leave to his issue.

b. ***to feoff*** (one person) ***to the use of*** (another): to invest with the legal estate, subject to an obligation to allow the use to (the other person).

Until 1535 this proceeding was very commonly resorted to to evade the burdens incident to ownership of land. The Statute of Uses passed in that year provided that in all cases of feoffment to uses the *cestui que use* should have the legal estate.

1491 *Act 7 Hen. VII*, c. 20 §7 Persones feoffed or seased to thuse of theym.

†**c.** *fig. Obs.*

c **1330** R. BRUNNE *Chron.* (1810) 239 Men gyf God þe lest, þe feffe him with a ferþing. *c* **1350** *Will. Palerne* 193 Til alle his felawes were ferst feffed to here paie. *c* **1374** CHAUCER *Boeth.* II. iii. 38 þo feffedest þou fortune wiþ glosynge wordes. *c* **1450** *Crt. of Love* 932 Nay God forbid to feffe you so with grace. *c* **1460** *Towneley Myst.* (Surtees) 115 Ye two are welle feft, sam in a stede. *a* **1656** BP. HALL *Rem. Wks.* (1660) 154 That we may be feoffed in that blessed inheritance.

d. †In wider sense: To present (a person) *with* anything (*obs.*). Also *dial.* (see quot. 1855).

1377 LANGL. *P. Pl.* B. II. 146 And feffe false-witnes with floreines ynowe. *c* **1450** *Merlin* 374 The kynge hym feffed with his right glove. **1855** ROBINSON *Whitby Gloss.*, *Fefted*, legally secured with a maintenance. 'He fefted his wife on so much a year.'

†**2.** To confer (a heritable possession) *upon*. Chiefly *fig. Obs.*

1571 GOLDING *Calvin on Ps.* lxxiii. 7 God feoffeth abundance of all good thinges upon them. **1592** WARNER *Alb. Eng.* VII. xxxv. (1612) 169 Those Stiles..were strange, but thay Did feofe them on the base-borne Muffe. **1612–5** BP. HALL *Contempl.*, *O.T.* x. vi, He makes his son his priest, and feoffees that sinne upon his sonne which he received from his mother. **1649** —— *Cases Consc.* III. i. (1654) 169 Feoffing a supernaturall vertue upon drugges.

feoffee (fɛ'fiː). *Law.* Forms: 5–6 feffee, 5 fefee, -i(e, 5–7 feoffe, 5–8 feofe(e, 7 feofy, 9 feeoffe(e, 6– feoffee. [ad. AF. *feoffé*, pa. pple. of *feoffer*: see prec.]

1. The person to whom a freehold estate in land is conveyed by a feoffment.

1542–3 *Act 34–5 Hen. VIII*, c. 5 §17 The donees, feoffes, lessees, and deuisees therof. **1660** BOND *Scut. Reg.* 92 The Feoffee his title is only from the Feoffor. **1818** CRUISE *Digest* (ed. 2) IV. 427 In this case..the feoffee hath an estate upon condition. **1876** DIGBY *Real Prop.* i. 49 The grantor is called the feoffor, the grantee the feoffee.

2. *spec.* **a.** (More fully ***feoffee in*** or ***of trust***.) A trustee invested with a freehold estate in land. Now chiefly applied in *pl.* to certain boards of elected or nominated trustees holding land for charitable or other public purposes. Also in ***feoffee to uses***: see FEOFF *v.* 1 b.

[**1275** *Stat. Westm.* I. 3 *Edw. I*, c. 48 Et si lenfaunt seit aloingne ou destourbe par le gardein ou par le feoffe ou par autre par quei il ne puisse sasise suire.] **1411** *E.E. Wills* (1882) 19 Tenementes..stondynge in feffies handes. **1491** *Act 7 Hen. VII*, c. 2 §5 They and their feoffes to the use of every of theym. **1593** NORDEN *Spec. Brit.*, *M'sex.* I. 22 The schole is in the disposition of sixe governors or feffees. **1596** SPENSER *State Irel.* (1633) 19 Desmond..conveyed secretly all his lands to Feoffees of trust. **1631** T. POWELL *Tom all Trades* 145 In the gift of the Executor, Heire, or Feofee of such Donor. **1647** DIGGES *Unlawf. Taking Arms* ii. 21 As children who have lost a father, and whose fortunes by his care are left to Feoffees in trust. **1655** *Gouge's Comm. Heb.*, *Life*, He was chosen a Trustee or Feofy. **1680** EVELYN *Diary* (1827) III. 26 A meeting of the feoffees of the poore of our parish. **1735** H. GRESWOLD *Let. to Walmesley* in Boswell *Johnson* an. 1736, It takeing up some time to informe the feoffees [of the school] of the contents thereof. **1861** W. S. PERRY *Hist. Ch. Eng.* I. xii. 417 The attempt which the Puritans were..making to strengthen their party, by means of a Corporation of Feoffees to buy up impropriations.

fig. **1655** GURNALL *Chr. in Arm.* xl. (1669) 392/1 Art thou not God's feoffee in trust to take care of their souls?

†**b.** (More fully ***feoffee in mortgage***.) A mortgagee. *Obs.*

1590 SWINBURNE *Testaments* 93 In this case..the feoffee could not deuise the corne growing vpon the said lande. **1628** COKE *On Litt.* 209 b, The Feoffee in morgage.

Hence **'feoffeeship**, the office of a feoffee.

1652 GAULE *Magastrom.* 239 Whether you shall waxe rich by..offices, places, executorship, feoffeship, &c.

feoffment ('fɛfmənt). *Law.* Forms: 4–6, 9 *dial.* feff(e)ment, (5 feefe-, fef(e)ment), feoffament, 5, 9 *dial.* feftment, 6–7 feoffe-, feof(e)ment, 6– feoffment. [a. AF. *feoffement*; see FEOFF *v.* and -MENT.]

1. The action of investing a person with a fief or fee. In technical lang. applied *esp.* to the particular mode of conveyance (originally the only one used, but now almost obsolete) in which a person is invested with a freehold estate in lands by livery of seisin (at common law generally but not necessarily evidenced by a deed, which however is now required by statute).

c **1330** R. BRUNNE *Chron.* (1810) 254 Edward..salle gyue Philip þe Kyng Alle holy Gascoyn..After þe forty dayes of þat feffement, Philip..salle gyue [etc.]. **1439** *E.E. Wills* (1882) 118 By wey of graunt or feeffement. **1440** *Promp. Parv.* 153 Fefement, *feofamentum*. **1465** *Mann. & Househ. Exp.* 475 Item, to go throw wyth the feffement of my lordes of Norffolke. **1531** *Dial. on Laws Eng.* I. xxi. (1638) 39 He that hath the estate, may lawfully..make a feoffement thereof. **1660** R. COKE *Power & Subj.* 25 Feoffment..is the most ancient and necessary Conveyance which is used by the Common Law. **1767** BLACKSTONE *Comm.* II. II. xx. 311 By the mere words of the deed the feoffment is by no means perfected. **1875** POSTE *Gaius* II. Comm. (ed. 2) 172 The essence of a feoffment is livery of seisin.

b. *spec.* (more fully) ***feoffment in, of, upon, trust; feoffment to uses***: see FEOFF *v.* 1 b.

1489 *Plumpton Corr.* 70 A feoffament of trust indented made by your mastership unto me. **1490** *Ibid.* 97 William Plompton..shewed to me a copy of astate & feftment, mad by my master..to certaine feofes, to his beofe [= to his own use] of lands..for terme of his lyfe. **1538** LELAND *Itin.* IV. 14 To whom he left his Land in Feoment withowt Declaration of Wylle to any use. **1552** HULOET, Feofment of trust, *fidei commissum*. **1606** HOLLAND *Sueton.* §23. 165 The iurisdiction as touching feofments upon trust. **1695** KENNETT *Par. Antiq.* (1818) II. 58 This feoffment was judicially suppressed..Feb. 13, 1633. **1827** HALLAM *Const. Hist.* (1876) I. vi. 344 The practice of feoffments to uses.

c. *dial.* An endowment.

1561 *Richmond. Wills* (Surtees) 151, I will that all suche feoffaments and annuities as I have made unto Symonde.. Askwithe shall stand according to th' effecte of my graunte thereof maide. **1855** ROBINSON *Whitby Gloss.*, *Feftments*, portions of property belonging to an endowment.

d. ***deed of feoffment***: The instrument or deed by which corporeal hereditaments are conveyed.

1545–6 in *Eng. Gilds* (1870) 252 Hys dede of feoffement. **1616** B. JONSON *Devil an Ass* IV. iii, He..ha's caused A deed of feoffment..To be drawne yonder. **1765** BLACKSTONE *Comm.* I. 79 By the custom of gavelkind, an infant of fifteen years may by one species of conveyance (called a deed of feoffment) convey away his lands in fee simple. **1876** BANCROFT *Hist. U.S.* II. xxiv. 111 The lower province was granted by two deeds of feoffment.

†**2.** = 1 d. *Obs.*

1377 LANGL. *P. Pl.* B. II. 72 Symonye and cyuile.. vnfoldeth þe feffement. **14..** *Plumpton Corr.* 46 My nephew ..shewed to me a wyll made upon a feftment. **1672** PETTY *Pol. Anat.* (1691) 7 Forg'd Feofments.

3. The fief conferred.

c **1330** R. BRUNNE *Chron.* (1810) 249 Fo [*v.r.* To] wild þe feffementes ald & þei granted þertille.

feoffor, feoffer ('fɛfər). *Law.* Forms: 5 feffer, (6 -or), -our(e, fefowre, 6 feofer, -ffour, 7 -ffeer, 5– feoffor, 6– feoffer. [ad. AF. *feoffour*, f. *feoffer* FEOFF *v.*]

1. One who makes a feoffment to another. Rarely *Hist.* in feudal sense: One who invests another with a fief.

1440 *Promp. Parv.* 153 Fefowre, *feofatus*. **1483** *Act 1 Rich. III*, c. 1 The Sellers, Feoffors, Donors, or Granters. **1594** WEST *2nd Pt. Symbol, Chancerie* §37 The feoffor..may reenter and have hys land again. **1613** SIR H. FINCH *Law* (1636) 133 A good Liuery of seisin if the other enter in the feoffors life time. **1767** BLACKSTONE *Comm.* II. II. xx. 311 Unless the feoffor..hath given it a longer continuance. **1865** NICHOLS *Britton* II. 6 The first feoffor or the lord of the most ancient fee has a better right. **1888** *Eng. Hist. Rev.* III. 41 Can a feoffer dispose of a fief without the written consent of his feodary?

¶**2.** Formerly often misused for FEOFFEE.

1426 *E.E. Wills* (1882) 71, I praye my feffours þat þay wolde enfeffe Philippe Dene on .vj. marces of rente. **1535** J. ATWELL in *Wells Wills* (1890) 82 My feoffers of all my lands in Bromfelde. **1603** H. CROSSE *Vertues Commw.* (1878) 91 Hee is a bayliffe, steward, and Feoffer in trust.

†**feofydye.** *Obs.* = Feoffment in trust (Anglo-L. *feoffamentum fidei*; ? abbreviated *feoff. fidei*).

1544–5 J. MERE *Let.* in *Abp. Parker's Corr.* (Parker Soc.) 18, I would most heartily desire you..to know who receiveth the feofydye of West Walton in Marshlands.

feoh, obs. form of FEE *sb.*[1]

feole, variant form of FELE *a.* and *adv.*

feon, feond, obs. forms of PHEON, FIEND.

feood, obs. form of FEUD *sb.*[1]

†**fer**, *v.* App. meaningless: see context of quot. 1599, of which the phrase in 1611 is prob. an echo.

1599 SHAKS. *Hen. V*, IV. iv. 29 *Boy.* He sayes his Name is M. Fer. *Pist.* M. Fer: Ile fer him, and firke him, and ferret him. **1611** BARREY *Ram Alley* II. i, I..could haue ferd and ferkt y'away a wench As soone as eare a man a liue.

fer, obs. form of FAR; FEAR *sb.*[1]; FIRE.

fera, var. FERRA.

feracious (fə'reɪʃəs), *a.* [f. L. *ferāci-*, *ferāx* (f. *fer-re* to bear) + -OUS.] Bearing abundantly; fruitful, prolific.

1637 POCKLINGTON *Altare Chr.* 148 This feracious and pregnant Plebiscite. **1657** TOMLINSON *Renou's Disp.* 303 Which being very feracious would surrept all aliment from their wheat. **1735** THOMSON *Liberty* III. 363 Like an oak, Nurs'd on feracious Algidum. **1843** CARLYLE *Past & Pr.* (1858) 139 A world so feracious, teeming with endless results.

feracity (fə'ræsɪtɪ). *rare.* [ad. L. *ferācitāt-em*, noun of quality f. *ferāx*: see prec. and -ACITY.] The quality of being feracious; fruitfulness, productiveness. † Of a person: The profit he makes.

c **1420** *Pallad. on Husb.* XII. 68 [The olive] wagged with wynde of feracitee. **1448** *MS. Records Grocers Company, Facsimile Copy* 292 That eny seche brocour..Shulde be contributory to the werkes of the place. Euery Brocour after his feraucite. **1650** ELDERFIELD *Tythes* 134 The earth, cursed..into a..natural feracity of briars and thorns. **1793** BEATTIE *Moral Sc.* IV. i. §3. 517 Such writers, instead of brittle, would say fragile, instead of fruitfulness, feracity. **1822** MRS. E. NATHAN *Langreath* III. 290 The lack of feracity arising from the lower orders becoming desidiose.

‖**feræ naturæ** ('fɪəriː næ'tʃʊəriː, 'fɛraɪ næ'tjuːraɪ). [L., = belonging to the wild part of nature.] Animals living in a wild state, undomesticated animals. Also as quasi-*adj.* and *fig.*

a **1661** FULLER *Worthies* (1662) II. 21 Such who object that *heads of Stagges* had been more proper for her, the *Goddesse of the Game*, may first satisfie us, Whether any Creatures *feræ Naturæ* (as which they could not certainly compass at all seasons) were usually offered for Sacrifices. **1668** DRYDEN *Even. Love* (1671) IV. sig. H3, Women are not compris'd in our Laws of friend-ship: they are *feræ naturæ*. **1873** C. M. YONGE *Pillars of House* IV. xxxv. 5 He evidently viewed himself as the Underwood who alone could do his duty by the *feræ naturæ* of the estate. **1897** E. A. BARTLETT *Battlefields of Thessaly* xiii. 302 The weapons had been fairly purchased by us from the Arnauts, who had found them abandoned, in fact as *feræ naturæ*. **1959** JOWITT *Dict. Eng. Law* I. 120 At common law animals *feræ naturæ* which are fit for human food are the subject of larceny if they either are in confinement or have actually been tamed; but at common law there can be no larceny of such animals as a lion or a gorilla, even though they are tame or kept in confinement.

Feraghan ('fɛrəgɑːn). [Pers., f. *Fergana*, *Ferghana*, name of a region in Soviet central Asia.] A costly rug made in Persia, usu. of cotton.

1929 *Encycl. Brit.* XIX. 624 Feraghan. A type much prized in the East. The best, usually small, are finely woven with a short pile. They have the Ghiordes knot, a cotton pile, and two lines of weft. The colouring is soft, and evenly toned patterns like the herati are common. **1931** A. U. DILLEY *Oriental Rugs & Carpets* iv. 124 Except for a small number woven in medallion pattern upon a plain field, the Feraghans were produced in all-over design. **1960** H. HAYWARD *Antique Coll.* 117/1 *Feraghan carpets*, Persian carpets woven with a Sehna knot, which..vary slightly in the treatment of the traditional Herat design.

feral ('fɪərəl), *a.*[1] [ad. L. *fērāl-is* of or pertaining to funeral rites or to the dead.]

1. Of a deadly nature; deadly, fatal.

1621 BURTON *Anat. Mel.* I. i. II. xi. (1651) 30 Thence come ..vitious habits..feral diseases. **1652** GAULE *Magastrom.* 303 Cæsar himselfe had noted, that the Ides of March would be ferall to him. **1773** J. ROSS *Fratricide* (MS.) II. 298 The feral tempter..Stalks noiseless round him.

b. *Astrol.* (See quots.)

The astrologers identified this with FERAL *a.*[2]

1647 LILLY *Chr. Astrol.* xvi. 89 Feral Signes are ♌ [Leo] and last part of ♐ [Sagittarius]. *Ibid.* clvi. 648 ♂ in the seventh in ferall signes, argues death by Distraction. **1658–1706** PHILLIPS, *Feral Signs* are Leo and the last part of Sagittarius, so call'd, not only upon Account of the representing the Figure of wild Beasts, but also [etc.]. **1819** J. WILSON *Dict. Astrol.*, The ☽ is also said to be feral, when she is void of course, having separated from a planet, and applying to no other.

2. Of or pertaining to the dead; funereal, gloomy.

1640 GAUDEN *Love Truth* (1641) 26 Those Owles, and Bats, and ferall Birds that love Darknesse. **1648** *Eikon Bas.* 134 Such a degree of splendour, as those ferall birds shall be grieved to behold. **1678** H. VAUGHAN *Thalia Rediv.* (1858) 246 A night, where..feral fires appear instead of stars. **1705** BERKELEY *Cave Dunmore* Wks. 1871 IV. 504 Ravens, screech-owls, and such like feral birds. **1785** HEADLEY *Ruins Broomholm Priory* 14 in *Fugitive Pieces* 4 Oft the Bird of Night Lengthens her feral note. **1881** PALGRAVE *Visions of Eng.* 302 In feral order slow, The slaughter-barges go.

feral ('fɪərəl, 'fɛrəl), *a.*[2] [f. L. *fer-a* wild beast + -AL[1].]

1. Of an animal: Wild, untamed. Of a plant, also (*rarely*), of ground: Uncultivated.

Now often applied to animals or plants that have lapsed into a wild from a domesticated condition.

1659 D. PELL *Impr. Sea* 213 It is impossible to reduce this feral creature. **1859** DARWIN *Orig. Spec.* i. (1878) 18 The dovecot pigeon..has become feral in several places. **1875** LYELL *Princ. Geol.* II. III. xxxv. 281 Domesticated animals allowed to run wild or become 'feral'. **1877** COUES & ALLEN *N. Amer. Rod.* 200 A corresponding variability is as normal to some purely feral animals as to the semi-domesticated species. **1882** W. T. T. DYER in *Nature* XXV. 390 The Jardin des Plantes deals not merely with plants in their feral, but also in their cultivated state. **1882** GEIKIE *Geol. Sketches* 377 The feral ground, or territory left in a state of nature and given up to game, lies mostly upon rocks.

2. Of, pertaining to, or resembling a wild beast; brutal, savage.

1604 T. WRIGHT *Passions* v. 268 Some..arrive at a certayne ferall or savage brutishnesse. **1659** D. PELL *Impr. Sea* 299 That feral and savage kinde of people which are.. of a Cannibal..nature. *Ibid.* 368 Against the Spaniard, and the rest of our feral, and remote Antagonists. **1838** *Blackw. Mag.* XLIII. 789 A..more potent charm..which converts the *feral* into the *human* being. **1847** GILFILLAN in *Tait's Mag.* XIV. 622 It is not the feral or fiendish element in human nature.

3. Used as *sb.*: A wild-beast. *Obs. rare.*

1639 G. DANIEL *Ecclus.* xiii. 61 What [alliance] 'twixt those ferals of Societie, Hiena and the Dog?

Hence **fe'rality**, the state of being feral.

1885 STALLYBRASS tr. *Hehn's Wand. Plants & Anim.* 21 There often sets in..a period of ferality, when the land presents the appearance..of being exhausted by culture.

Ibid. 39 The freedom in which young horses were bred must have frequently led to complete ferality.

Ferangi: see FERINGHEE.

‖**ferash** (fɛˈrɑːʃ). *Anglo-Ind.* Also 7 **farras, frass**, 9- **farrash**. [Urdū from Arab. *farrāsh*, f. *farasha* to spread.] 'A menial servant whose proper business is to spread carpets, pitch tents, etc., and do similar domestic work. In more common use in India two centuries ago than now' (Yule).

1600 J. PORY tr. *Leo's Africa* II. 321 Other officers called Farrasin, that is..chamberlaines. **1698** FRYER *Acc. E. India & P.* 67 Where live the Frasses, or Porters also. **1824** *Hajji Baba* I. 59, I am a ferash, (a carpet spreader) said he. **1873** H. BLOCHMANN tr. *Abu al Fazl ibn Mubarak's Ain I Akbari* I. xvi. 47 Besides, there are employed a thousand Farráshes, natives of I'rán, Túrán, and Hindustan. **1876** A. ARNOLD in *Contemp. Rev.* June 31 The governor..kindly sent ten ferashes, or servants, to conduct us. **1894** *Safar Nameh Persian Pict.* 162 It belonged to the Shah's farrash. **1965** B. SWEET-ESCOTT *Baker St. Irregular* iii. 80 Nobody seemed surprised at Ankara when the bags were handed over to the embassy's *farrash* at the station by me and not by my friend at Tripoli.

ferbam (ˈfɜːbæm). *Chem.* [f. *fer*ric dimethyldithiocar*bam*ate, the systematic name.] A black powder used as a fungicide, esp. in the control of rust diseases of plants; $[(CH_3)_2N{\cdot}CS{\cdot}S{\cdot}]_3Fe$.

1950 *Phytopathology* XL. 118 The Subcommittee on Fungicide Nomenclature of The American Phytopathological Society, cooperating with the Interdepartmental Committee on Pest Control, has selected common names for five commercially-available fungicidal chemicals which are useful in the control of various destructive plant diseases... The coined common names and designations are: *Ferbam* for the fungicidal chemical, ferric dimethyl dithiocarbamate. **1956** *Dict. Gardening* (*R.H.S.*) Suppl. 216/1 Ferbam is commonly used in the U.S.A. to control apple scab and apple rust. **1960** *Times Rev. Industry* Sept. 7/2 One group of fungicides, with names suggestive of Old Testament prophets—nabam, thiram, ferbam, ziram and zineb—can all impart a foreign flavour into the fruits to which they are applied. **1967** S. E. A. McCALLAN in D. C. Torgeson *Fungicides* I. i. 14 In comparison with the older recommendations of 12–16 lb of sulfur per 100 gal of spray..the use of ferbam at 1½ lb/100 gal seemed strikingly effective.

ferberite (ˈfɜːrbəraɪt). *Min.* [f. *Ferber* name of two celebrated mineralogists + -ITE.]

†**1.** A proposed name (after J. J. Ferber) for a variety of gneiss. *Obs.*

1811 PINKERTON *Petral.* I. 216 The other may be called Ferberite, an honour due to Ferber.

2. A variety of wolfram from Southern Spain (named by Liebe after R. Ferber 1863).

1868 DANA *Min.* 604 Ferberite..on charcoal fuses easily to a magnetic globule.

†**ˈferblet**, *a. Obs.* [Perh. for **forblet*, pa. pple. of **forblete* to make soft, f. *blete* soft.] ? Effeminate.

a **1300** *Fragm. Pop. Sc.* (Wright) 275 A slouȝ wrecche and ferblet, fast and loth to ȝeve his god. *Ibid.* 280 Debonere ferblet, and lute luste to swynke.

fercest, -cost, var. forms of FARCOST, *Obs.*

†**ˈfercule.** *Obs. rare.* [ad. L. *fercul-um*, f. *ferre* to bear.] A frame, barrow, bier.

1606 HOLLAND *Sueton.* 131 He conveighed them within two Fercules (or frames)..into the Mausoleum.

†**ferd**, *sb.*[1] *Obs.* Forms: 1 fyrd, 2–4 ferde, (3 verde, 2 ferede), 3–5 ferd, (3 færd, feord), 5 furde, furthe. See also FARD *sb.* [OE. *ferd, fierd, fyrd* str. fem. = OFris. *ferd*, OS. *fard* (MDu. *vaert*, Du. *vaard, vaart*), OHG. *fart* (MHG. *vart*, Ger. *fahrt*), ON. *ferð* (Da. and Sw. *fard*):—OTeut. **farti-z* (:—pre-Teut. **porti-s*), f. root *far-* (Aryan *por-*) to go, FARE *v.*[1]]

1. A military expedition. OE. only.

a **1000** *Byrhtnoth* 221 (Gr.) þæt ic of þisse fyrde feran wille. *c* **1000** *Ags. Ps.* (Thorpe) xliii. 11 [xliv. 9] þeah þu..mid us ne fare on fyrd.

b. *in ferd*: in warlike array.

c **1330** R. BRUNNE *Chron.* (1810) 163 With þe wille I go als felawes in ferd.

2. An army, host.

823 *O.E. Chron.* an. 823 þa sende he Æþelwulf his sunu of þære fierde. **1154** *Ibid.* an. 1140 Te king ferde agenes him mid micel mare ferd. *c* **1205** LAY. 4152 He somenede færd swulc nes næuere ær on erde. *a* **1225** *Ancr. R.* 250 Ter men uihteð in þeos stronge uerdes. *a* **1250** *Owl & Night.* 1668 Havestu..ibanned ferde. *c* **1300** *Havelok* 2384 Robert..was of al þe ferd Mayster. *c* **1330** *Assump. Virg.* 116 He schal sende after þee Of heuene ferde moche plente. *c* **1350** *Will. Palerne* 386 þemperour..on his blonk rides..til he fond al his fre ferd.

3. A band, company, troop; a great number.

1297 R. GLOUC. (Rolls) 7920 A uerde þer was binorþe þat robbede al so uaste. *c* **1350** *Will. Palerne* 5326 þe fairest ferde of folk þat euer bi-fore was seie. *a* **1400–50** *Alexander* 5577 Ferly ferd of his folke was in þe fild strangild. *c* **1400** *Destr. Troy* 4094 With fyfty [shippes] in a furthe. *c* **1420** *Anturs of Arth.* xv. (Bannatyne Club) 103 þere folowes me a ferde of fendis full fell.

4. *Comb.* in early law terms, **ferd-fare** (see quot. 1641); **ferd-wite** (see quots.).

c **1020** *Secular Laws Cnut* §66 Gif hwa burh-bote oþþe bricȝbote oþþ e fyrd-fare forsille. *c* **1250** *Gloss. Law Terms* in *Rel. Ant.* I. 33 Ferdware, *quite de aler en ost.* **1641** *Termes de la Ley* 160 *Ferdfare* is to be quit from going to warre. *c* **1020** *Secular Laws Cnut* §12 Fyrd-wite. *c* **1250** *Gloss. Law Terms* in *Rel. Ant.* I. 33 Ferdwite, *quite de murance de ost.* **1641** *Termes de la Ley* 160 *Ferdwit.* **1684–1701** COWELL *Law Dict.*, *Ferdwit*, quit of murder committed in the army; also a fine imposed on persons for not going forth in a military expedition.

†**ferd**, *sb.*[2] *Obs.* Forms: 4–5 feerd, ferd(e. [subst. use of *ferd*, FEARED *ppl. a.*] Fear, terror. Chiefly in phrase ***for ferd***. Const. with *inf.* or with subord. clause introduced by *lest* or *that*.

a **1300** *Cursor M.* 3651 (Cott.) For ferde atte he mistraw, þou salle say þou art esau. **13..** *E.E. Allit. P.* C. 215 þenne such a ferde on hem fel. *c* **1330** R. BRUNNE *Chron.* (1810) 88 Malcolme..fled for ferd. *c* **1384** CHAUCER *H. Fame* II. 442 He for ferde lost hys wyt. *c* **1420** *Pallad. on Husb.* IV. 160 For ferde of sonne On hem let inne. *a* **1450** *Knt. de la Tour* 36 Loke that ye have ever a frende..by you, for ferde. *c* **1460** *Towneley Myst.* (Surtees) 40 It gars me quake for ferd to dee.

ferd, var. form of FARD *sb.*[1] *Sc. Obs.*

ferd, obs. form of FEARED *ppl. a.*

ferd, obs. form of FOURTH.

†**ˈferdegew.** ? A vulgarism for FARTHINGALE.

a **1553** UDALL *Royster D.* II. iii. (Arb.) 35 We shall go in our frenche hoodes euery day; In our silk cassocks..In our tricke ferdegews, and billiments of golde.

‖**fer-de-lance** (fɛr də lɑ̃s, fɛə də lɑːns, læns). [Fr. = head of a lance (*fer* lit. 'iron').]

1. *Her.* A lance-head used as a charge.

1892 WOODWARD & BURNETT *Heraldry* II. 731 *Fer-de-lance*, sometimes pointed, sometimes blunt.

2. (See quots.)

1880 *Cassell's Nat. Hist.* IV. 319 The Yellow Viper of Martinique (*Bothrops lanceolatus*) called Fer-de-Lance there. **1888** *Riverside Nat. Hist.* III. 396 The genus *Trigonocephalus* includes the most venomous animal of the western hemisphere, the celebrated fer-de-lance, *T. lanceolatus*, of Brazil.

‖**fer-de-moline** (fɛə də ˈmɒliːn). *Her.* [a. F. *fer de moulin* 'iron of a mill'.] (See quots.)

1741 CHAMBERS *Cycl.*, *Fer de Moulin*..is a bearing in heraldry; supposed to represent the iron-ink, or ink of a mill, which sustains the moving mill-stone. **1864** BOUTELL *Heraldry Hist. & Pop.* xvii. §2. 270 The fer-de-moline or.

ferder, obs. form of FURTHER *v.*

†**ˈferdful.** *Obs.* Forms: 4–5 ferdful(l, feerdful, (4 fertful), 5 ferdefull, ferdfulle. [f. FERD *sb.*[2] + -FUL.]

1. *objectively.* Inspiring fear; awsome, dreadful; = FEARFUL I.

c **1380** WYCLIF *Sel. Wks.* III. 21 Who is þee liik in stalworþnes, Lord?..feerdful and preisable and doinge wondris? **1388** —— *Dan.* ii. 31 The loking therof [the ymage] was ferdful. **1414** BRAMPTON *Penit. Ps.* xl. (Percy Soc.) 16 Lord!..Thi ferdefull face whan I schal se. **1488** CAXTON *Chast. Goddes Chyld.* 89 It was..ferdfull to Peter for to be wyth cryst in his cruel persecucyon.

2. *subjectively.* Full of fear; timorous. Also, Cautious through fear (of offending); wary. Cf. FEARFUL 3.

1382 WYCLIF *Prov.* xxviii. 14 Blisful the man that euermore is ferdful. **1398** TREVISA *Barth. De P.R.* v. xxxvi. (1495) 151 The man is beraft boldenes and hardenes and is fertful. **14..** HOCCLEVE *Ad beatam Virginem* 47 Hir ferdful shame, hir shende wole. *c* **1489** CAXTON *Sonnes of Aymon* ix. 249 Now shew ye well that ye be ferdfull. *a* **1502** in Arnolde *Chron.* (1811) 264, I knowe myself so ferdful for defaute of comyng.

Hence **ˈferdfulness** = FEARFULNESS.

1388 WYCLIF *Ezek.* xxxii. 23 Alle..fallynge doun bi swerd, whiche ȝauen sum tyme her ferdfulnesse in the lond of lyuinge men. **1398** TREVISA *Barth. De P.R.* VIII. i. (1495) 296 The worlde is place..of ferdfulnes and of shame. **14..** *Prose Legends* in *Anglia* VIII. 143 [The fiend] caste hir downe in to dispayre by ferdefulnesse.

†**ˈferding.** *Obs.* Also 1 fyrdung, 4 fardung. [OE. *fyrdung*, f. *fyrdian* to go on an expedition, f. *fyrd*, FERD *sb.*[1]] A military expedition; an army.

c **1000** *Laws Ethelred* V. 26 Beo man ȝeorne..ymbe fyrdunga. *c* **1020** *Secular Laws Cnut* §79 And se man þe on þam fyrdunge ætforan his hlaforde fealle. *c* **1200** *Trin. Coll. Hom.* 189 Mannes liflode buuen eorðe is fardung. *c* **1250** *Gen. & Ex.* 842 On-kumen was cadalamor, king of elam, wið ferding stor.

†**ˈferdlac.** *Obs.* In 4 ferdlayk. [f. *ferd*, FEARED *ppl. a.*: see -LOCK.] A state of fear, terror.

1340 HAMPOLE *Pr. Consc.* 2915 Ne he for ferdelayk is witte shuld lese. *Ibid.* 6427 þe synful þar [in helle] sal fele, þai suld in grete ferdlayk be broght.

†**ˈferdly**, *a. Obs. rare*⁻¹. [f. FERD *sb.*[2] + -LY[1].] Fearful, frightful.

1440 in *Pol. Rel. & L. Poems* (1866) 216 Nad I ben babtyzyd in water and salt, This ferdly fester wolde neuer me froo.

ferdness, obs. form of FEAREDNESS.

ˈferdship. *Obs.* [f. *ferd*, FEARED *ppl. a.* + -SHIP.] Terror.

a **1400–50** *Alexander* 988 And letis all ferdschip at flee.

†**ˈferdy**, *a. Obs. rare*⁻¹. [f. FERD *sb.*[2] + -Y[1].] Fearful, timid.

c **1340** *Cursor M.* 17685 (Trin.) He seide Joseph be not ferdy.

fere, *sb.*[1] *Obs.* exc. *arch.* Forms: α. 1 *Northumb.* fœra, 2–9 fere, 3 *south.* vere, 3–6 fer, 3, 6–8 *Sc.* feir, (5 feyr), 4–8 feare, 4–9 feer(e. β. 6–8 phear(e, pheer(e, 7 phere. [ME. *fere*, ONorthumb. *fœra*, aphetic f. OE. *ȝeféra* (Y-FERE):—pre-Eng. **ȝifōrjon-*, f. *gi-* (Y-) together + **fōrâ* going, way, f. ablaut-root of *faran*.]

1. A companion, comrade, mate, partner; whether male or female; †rarely in comb. with a sb., as *meat-*, *play-*, *school-*, *sucking-fere*: see those words.

c **975** *Rushw. Gosp.* Matt. xxiii. 30 Ne wærun we foeran eora in blodgyte uitgana. *c* **1205** LAY. 26135 Howel..nom al his feren and ferde to þan munte. *a* **1225** *Ancr. R.* 86 þu hauest monie ueren. *a* **1300** *Cursor M.* 8607 (Cott.) Fra hir fere sco stall hir barn. **1375** BARBOUR *Bruce* VI. 70 Till hunt hym owt off the land..as he war..a theyff, or theyffs fer. **1393** LANGL. *P. Pl.* C. XVIII. 19 Peter..and hus fere Andreu. *c* **1420** *Sir Amadace* (Camden) lviii, 'Is he comun' he sayd, 'my nowun true fere?' **1535** STEWART *Cron. Scot.* II. 600 Few feiris with him that tyme he hed. *a* **1572** GASCOIGNE *Arraignm. of Lover*, A quest, Of whom was falshoode formoste feere. **1575** *Appius & Virginia* in Hazl. *Dodsley* IV. 113 My sovereign lord and friendly pheer. **1627** DRAYTON *Agincourt* 100 Englands valient Infantry his Pheres. *a* **1775** *'Hobie Noble'* vii. in Child *Ballads* clxxxix. (1890) 2/1 My feiries five! **1830** TENNYSON *Poems* 40 The lamb..raceth freely with his fere. **1867** JEAN INGELOW *Story Doom* v. 58 [She] went forth With fair and flattering words, among her feres. **1880** WEBB *Goethe's Faust* 24 Mine ancient fere, be merry!

b. in phrases: ***to choose, have, love, take to*** or ***unto*** (***one's***) ***fere***.

c **1200** *Trin. Coll. Hom.* 11 Elch man haueð to fere on engel of heuene. *a* **1250** *Prov. Ælfred* 222 in *O.E. Misc.* 116 Ne may he for-vare þe hyne haueþ to vere. *c* **1300** *Cursor M.* 4450 (Gott.) Bot þe mayster iaoler To ioseph taght þaim vnto fere. *c* **1320** *Cast. Love* 483 He ne louede [me] neuere to fere, þat Merci my suster nul not here. *c* **1420** *Chron. Vilod.* 498 Whom shall y haue now to my ffer? *c* **1440** *Partonope* 129 Ye haue chose me to youre feere.

c. of inanimate things.

1593 SOUTHWELL *St. Peter's Compl.* To Rdr., Licence my single penne to seeke a pheere. **1595** —— *Poems, David's Peccavi* i, Feares now are my pheares.

2. A consort; spouse; a husband or wife; †rarely ***nuptial***, ***wedded fere***. Also in phrases, ***to give, have, marry, take, wed to one's fere***.

c **1175** *Lamb. Hom.* 93 Me buried heo [Sapphira] mid hire fere. *a* **1300** *Cursor M.* 26692 Adam..and eue his fere. *c* **1330** *Arth. & Merl.* 481 Fortiger for loue fin Hir tok to fere and to wiue. ? *a* **1400** *Chester Pl.* (Shaks. Soc.) 208 With another then her feare We founde her doe amisse. *c* **1430** *Hymns Virg.* (1867) 105 þou shalt not desire þi neiȝboris feere. *c* **1450** LONELICH *Grail* lv. 212 To ȝowre owne brothir ..My dowhter I schal ȝeven to his fere. *c* **1550** *Adam Bell* in Ritson *Anc. Pop. P.* (1791) 6 Two of them were single men, The third had a wedded fere. *c* **1611** CHAPMAN *Iliad* XVIII. 339 The nuptial fere Of famous Vulcan. **1612** *Two Noble Kinsmen* v. ii, This anatomy Had by this young fair pheer a boy. *a* **1765** *Sir Cawline* ii. in Child *Ballads* (1885) III. lxi. 58/1 Knights and lordes they woed her both, Trusted to haue beene her feere. **1798** COLERIDGE *Anc. Mar.* 111, Are these two all..That woman and her fleshless Pheere? **1871** B. TAYLOR *Faust* (1875) II. III. i. 187 Paris..Took thee, the widow, as his fere.

b. Of animals: Mate.

a **1547** SURREY in *Tottell's Misc.* (Arb.) 218 Eche beast can chose hys fere according to his minde. **1589** GREENE *Poems, Melicertus' Madrigal* i, No turtle without fere. **1591** SYLVESTER *Du Bartas* I. v. (1605) 152 If the Fisher haue surpriz'd her [the Mullet's] Pheere..She followeth. **1603** DRAYTON *Odes* iii. 33 Each little Bird..Doth chuse her loved Pheere.

3. An equal. **a.** Of a person: Peer; also in phrase, ***without*** (***peer or***) ***fere***. **b.** Of a thing: in phrase, ***fere for fere*** (Sc.), every way equal.

13.. *E.E. Allit. P.* A. 1149 Among her ferez þat watz so quyt! *c* **1340** *Cursor M.* 5144 (Trin.) Ar þei no knyȝtis ny knyȝtis fere. **1548** HALL *Chron.* 181 b, Thynkyng hymself a kyng, without either peere or fere. **15..** *Knt. of Curtesy* 460 A, noble Knight, withouten fere! **1636** JAMES *Iter Lanc.* (1845) 4 Fairies..of their feres good housewife praises winne. **1768** ROSS *Helenore* I. 11 For joining hands the just were feer for feer.

†**fere**, *sb.*[2] *Obs.* Forms: α. 3 fer, 3–7 fere, (4 *south.* vere), 5 *Sc.* feir, 4–7 feare. [aphetic f. OE. *ȝefér* neut. (:—**ȝifōrjo(m)*, f. as prec.]

1. Companionship; chiefly *concr.* a body of companions, company, party.

a **1300** *Cursor M.* 20419 (Cott.) Lokes..þat na man of our fer bi-fore his mak latli chere. *c* **1325** *Ibid.* 24947 (Edin.) Wit al þair farnet and þair fer þai com to land. *c* **1340** *Ibid.* 23208 (Trin.) Crist let vs neuer be in þat fere. *c* **1400** *Destr. Troy* 1132 With all the fere þat hym folowes.

2. In phrase **in fere, i fere** (often written as one word, and spelt *y-*): in company, together; in common. ***al in fere***: all together, altogether.

c **1205** LAY. 27435 Twein kinges þere æuere ifere. *a* **1300** *Signa ante Jud.* 117 in *E.E.P.* (1862) 11 Al þe see sal draw ifere. *c* **1374** CHAUCER *Troylus* II. 1217 She lykyd al infere, His persone, his aray, his loke, his chere. *c* **1400** *Sowdone Bab.* 119 Shippes shene, vij hundred were gadered al in fere. **1480** CAXTON *Chron. Eng.* iv. 9 Gogmagog and corin undertake for to wrastlyn y fere. **1513** DOUGLAS *Æneis* x. v. 15 All sammyn swam thai, hand in hand yfeir. **1563** *Mirr. Mag., Induct.* lxxiv, Sighes and teares, sobs, shrykes, and all y fere. **1613** W. BROWNE *Sheph. Pipe* Wks. 1772 III. 11 All th'eritage which..he me left, all in feere Leave I thee. **1748** THOMSON *Cast. Indol.* II. xxxv, Much they moraliz'd as thus yfere they yode.

¶**b.** G. Douglas uses the pl. form in rime-words.

1513 DOUGLAS *Æneis* I. Pref. 251 All inferis. *Ibid.* II. viii. 90 All infeiris. *Ibid.* x. vii. 628 All yferis.

†**fere**, *sb.*³ *Obs.* [a. ON. *fǿri*:—neut. of OTeut. **fôrjo-* FERE *a.*] Ability, power; health.

c **1200** ORMIN 1251 A33 affterr þine fere. *c* **1340** *Cursor M.* 3829 (Fairf.) He was in gode fere, hale and sounde.

†**fere**, *a. Obs.* (after 15th c. only *Sc.*) Forms: 2–9 fere, 3–5 fer, (3 feore, 4 feere). *Sc.* 4–6 feir, 8–9 fier, (9 fear). [a. ON. *fǿrr* (or possibly repr. OE. **fére*) = OFris. *fére*:—OTeut. type **fôrjo-*, f. **fôrâ* (OE. *fór*, ME. FORE *sb.*) going, way, f. *faran* FARE *v.*¹]

Able to go, in health; hence *gen.* able, strong; sound, 'whole'. Also in phrase ***whole and fere***.

c **1175** *Lamb. Hom.* 25 Hal and fere and strong and stelewurðe. *c* **1205** LAY. 17618 3if ich mai beon feore, ich þe cumen after sone. *c* **1300** *Cursor M.* 3829 (Cott.) He es bath hail and fere. **1375** BARBOUR *Bruce* VI. 315 Thai thar lord fand haill and feir. *a* **1400–50** *Alexander* 4282 As fresche & as fere a[s] fisch quen he plays. *c* **1440** *Bone Flor.* 2006 The holy nonne..makyth the syke thus fere. **1536** BELLENDEN *Cron. Scot.* (1821) I. p. li, Thay come haill and feir in thair bodyis to extreme age. **1784** BURNS *Ep. to Davie* ii, We're fit to win our daily bread, As lang's we're hale and fier. **1806** A. DOUGLAS *Poems* 22 There's Jenny, comely, fier, an tight. **1816** SCOTT *Antiq.* xxvii, 'I trust to find ye baith haill and fere.'

absol. a **1300** *Cursor M.* 20119 (Cott.) To fere and seke ai did scho bote.

†**fere**, *v.*¹ *Obs.* Forms: *Inf.* 1–2 féran (1 *Northumb.* fœran), 2 feren, (fearen), 3 færen, *south.* væren. *Pa. t.* 1 fér(e)de, 2–5 ferd(e, 4 *south.* verde, (2 feorde, foerde, 3 færde), 3–5 farde, 3–4 furde. [OE. *féran* wk. vb., corresp. to OFris. *fêra*, OS. *fôrian* (Du. *voeren*) to carry, OHG. *fuoren* (MHG. *vüeren*, mod.G. *führen* to lead), ON. *fǿra* (Sw. *föra*, Da. *føre*) to bring:—OTeut. **fôrjan*, f. **fôra* (OE. *fôr*, FORE *sb.* way), f. ablaut-root of *faran*, FARE *v.*¹

The OE. verb, unlike all the equivalent forms in other Teut. langs., was intransitive, having the sense 'to take a journey, march, travel'. The difference in meaning between *faran* and *féran* even in OE. is hardly perceptible, and in ME. it wholly vanishes, *fare* being more and more restricted to the present-stem and *fere* to the pa. t. and pa. pple. See the remarks s.v. FARE *v.*¹]

1. *intr.* To travel, journey, go; = FARE *v.*¹ 1, 2.

Beowulf 301 Gewiton him þa feran. *c* **950** *Lindisf. Gosp.* John iv. 3 Forleort iudeam & foerde eftersona in ðær mægð. *c* **1175** *Lamb. Hom.* 3 Redliche heo eou leted fere þer-mid. *c* **1205** LAY. 4471 His cnihtes mid him seoluen to þare sæ færden. *a* **1225** *Leg. Kath.* 5 Ah Constentin ferde..into Fronc londe. *a* **1300** *Cursor M.* 3958 (Cott.) Ful wrathli gains him he ferd. *c* **1330** R. BRUNNE *Chron.* (1810) 124 Þer schip ferd on the flode. *a* **1400–50** *Alexander* 5549 Sum ferd all on foure feete. *c* **1420** *Sir Amadace* (Camden) xxxvii, Thro the forest as he ferd.

2. To proceed, go on, behave; = FARE *v.*¹ 4; to deal *with*.

1154 *O.E. Chron.* (Laud MS.) an. 1132 þa wiste þe king ð[at] he feorde mid suicdom. *c* **1175** *Lamb. Hom.* 103 þenne mon..mid fikenunge fearð. *a* **1300** *Cursor M.* 5719 (Cott.) þat folk sua wit þam ferd. *c* **1300** *Beket* 2076 And furde as men that wode were. **1377** LANGL. *P. Pl.* B. XI. 410 Ri3t so ferde resoun bi the. *c* **1440** *Generydes* 4786 As a man beside hem self he farde. **1450** *Paston. Lett.* No. 93 I. 125 Oon of the lewdeste of the shippe badde hym ley down hys hedde and he shoulde be fair ferd wyth. *c* **1450** LONELICH *Grail* xlix. 123 Thus with Iosephe ferden they there wel falsly. **1483** CAXTON *G. de la Tour* xix. 218 The fairer that she is ferde with, the more ferdfulle she shulde be to displese.

b. To take place, happen; = FARE *v.*¹ 6.

1297 R. GLOUC. (1724) 538 So it ferde ouer al. *c* **1300** *Beket* 2143 As hit bi oure Louerd furde. *c* **1350** *Will. Palerne* 1921 Cairende ouer cuntreis as here cas ferde. *c* **1440** *Boctus, Laud MS.* 559. 3 b, Hee was wrothe that hit soo ferde.

3. = FARE *v.*¹ 7, 8.

a **1300** *Cursor M.* 2850 (Cott.) Hir langed to see how þai fard. *c* **1340** *Ibid.* 23162 (Trin.) For 3ou ferde I neuer þe bet. *c* **1350** *Will. Palerne* 1497 He went wi3tli to william to wite how he ferde. *c* **1400** *Rom. Rose* 499, I my silf so mery ferde. *c* **1420** *Chron. Vilod.* 540 þat blessed virgyne hurre dou3ter ry3t well ferde. *c* **1477** CAXTON *Jason* 18 She..demanded him how he..ferde.

4. Combined with advbs.: = FARE *v.*¹ III.

Beowulf 1632 Ferdon forð þonon. *c* **900** *Bæda's Hist.* I. viii. (1890) 42 Ferde he [Constantinus] forð on Breotone. *a* **1300** *Cursor M.* 11731 (Cott.) Forth þai ferd þair wai. *c* **1350** *Will. Palerne* 30 It..ferde fast aboute floures to gadere. **1352** MINOT *Poems* iv. 19 Furth he ferd into France. *a* **1400–50** *Alexander* 813 (Dublin MS.) Forth with eufestyus he ferd.

†**fere**, *v.*² *Obs.* Also 3 feir. [aphet. form of AFFEIR, EFFEIR.] *intr.* To fall by right, appertain, become, be proper or meet. Const. with *dat.*; also *for, till, to.* Chiefly *impers.*

a **1300** *Cursor M.* 21444 (Cott.) þou sal haf broþer al þat þe fers. *a* **1300** *E.E. Psalter* lxiv. 2 [lxv. 1] þe feres loft-sang, God, on-on, For to have in Syon. *c* **1375** *Sc. Leg. Saints, Thomas* 211 Richt wele it feris þe Seruand to kingis fore to be. *a* **1455** *Houlate* xxvii, The Papis armes at poynt to blason and beir As feris for a persewant. **1513** DOUGLAS *Æneis* I. vi. 54 Honour..quhilk feris me nocht to haue.

†**fere**, *v.*³ *Obs.* Also 7 feare. [f. FERE *sb.*¹] **a.** To be a companion to; accompany. **b.** To make companions of; unite. **c.** To provide with a consort; to mate.

c **1400** *Rom. Rose* 5281 If bothe the hertis Love hath fered, Joy and woo they shulle departe. *c* **1440** *Bone Flor.* 2086 Allas that we came here, Thys false traytur for to fere. **1632** *Womens Rights* 328, I..am like neuer to be feared, vnlesse some widdow be moued with compassion towards mee.

fere: see FEER *a.*, fierce.

fere, obs. form of FAR, FEAR, FEER, FERRY *v.*, FIRE.

fere, var. of FEIR, *Obs. Sc.*, appearance.

fered, obs. form of FEARED *ppl. a.*

†**ferelay.** *Obs.* [? a. ON. *ferju-leiga*, f. *ferja* ferry + *leiga* toll.] ? Passage-money.

1547 *Nottingham Rec.* IV. 90 Item the ferelaye ij d. **1578** *Ibid.* IV. 178 Payd for the sawgers ferelay viij d.

feretory ('fɛrɪtərɪ). Forms: 4–5 fertre, (5 fiertre, feretre, fe(e)rtir, -yr, fertur(e, feratour), 5–6 fertour, feretorye, (6 fer(t)ter, fereture, -tery, fer(r)etorie, 8–9 fer(r)etry, 8– feretory. [The current form is a perversion (by assimilation to various names of objects used in ritual) of ME. *fertre*, a. OF. *fiertre*:—L. *feretrum*, ad. Gr. φέρετρον, f. φέρειν to bear.]

1. A portable or stationary shrine, often made of or adorned with costly materials, in which were deposited the remains or relics of saints; a tomb.

c **1330** R. BRUNNE *Chron.* (1810) 36 He tok vp the bones, In a fertre tham laid. *c* **1375** *Sc. Leg. Saints, Clement* 919 Quhene þe pupule come to se His fertyre & til hyme pray. **1483** CAXTON *Gold. Leg.* 156/4 His bones there leyde in a worshypful fiertre or shryne. **1535** STEWART *Cron. Scot.* III. 92 Of Sanct Thomas translatit wer the bonis Intill ane ferter ..fra his graif. **1593** *Rites & Mon. Ch. Durh.* (Surtees) 58 A most sumptuous..shrine above the High Alter, called the Fereture. **1709** HEARNE *Collect.* (Oxf. Hist. Soc.) II. 261 Reliques belonging to St. Cuthbert's Feretory. **1762** H. WALPOLE *Vertue's Anecd. Paint.* (1765) I. i. 19 Porphyry stones for Edward the Confessor's feretory. **1844** LINGARD *Anglo-Sax. Ch.* (1845) II. ix. 80 The coffin was then brought from the feretory. **1863** SIR G. G. SCOTT *Glean. Westm. Abb.* (ed. 2) 130 The golden feretory..was placed above the marble and mosaic base.

2. In etymological sense: A bier.

c **1400** MAUNDEV. (1839) xxi. 225 Thei setten hem upon a blak Fertre. **1458** *Will of Duchess Exeter* (Somerset Ho.), I ..forbede..any..solempne Hers or Ferture. **1513** DOUGLAS *Æneis* VI. xv. 68 How mony fertyris..Sall thow behald. *a* **1572** KNOX *Hist. Ref.* Wks. (1846) I. 259 A barrow, called there fertory. **1848** B. WEBB *Continent. Eccles.* 16 A relic of the patron saint was exposed on a feretry in the nave.

3. A small room or chapel attached to an abbey or a church, in which shrines were deposited.

1449 *Will Sir W. Bruges* in *Illust. Mann. & Exps.* (1797) 133 In the middle of the feretorye a gret round blak corver. **1480** CAXTON *Chron. Eng.* cclxi, The feratour of the abbey of Westmestre. **1593** *Rites & Mon. Ch. Durh.* (Surtees) 6 The shrine of the holy and blessed man Saint Cuthbert within the Feretory. **1727** DART *Canterb. Cathedr.* 33 The lesser Armary..contain'd nothing but the Body of St. Blaise, being rather a Feretry than Store-room. **1860** HOOK *Lives Abps.* I. vii. 382 He [Odo] was taken up in his leaden coffin, and placed in the feretry of S. Dunstan.

4. *attrib.*, as ***feretory-aisle***.

1489 *Churchw. Acc. St. Margaret's, Westminster* (Nichols 1797) 3 Lady Jakes for her grave in the feretre isle 7*s.* 4*d.* **1853** ROCK *Ch. of Fathers* III. x. 409 The feretory aisle.

†'**feretrar.** *Obs. rare*⁻¹. In 5 ffertrer. [ad. med.L. *feretrāri-us*, f. *feretrum*: see FERETORY and -ARY.] The custodian of the shrines.

1463 *Bury Wills* (1850) 35 Wher..the ffertrerys..fynde a place moost convenient. **1828** RAINE *St. Cuthbert* 113 The Latin name of this officer was Feretrarius, which I translate *Feretrar*, or *Shrine Keeper*.

‖'**feretrum.** [L. *feretrum*: see FERETORY.] = FERETORY 1.

1536 in *Antiq. Sarisb.* (1771) 192 A Feretrum, silver and gilt, with four pillars and one steeple. **1878** MACKINTOSH *Hist. Civilization Scot.* I. xi. 496 The feretrum, the shrine in which the..remains of the Saint were supposed to be kept.

'**fer-flax.** [f. F. *fer* iron + FLAX.] (See quot.)

1889 *Daily News* 10 May 2/7 A material known as fer-flax, composed of iron and vegetable fibre shreds.

ferforth, obs. form of FAR-FORTH.

ferganite (fɜː'gɑːnaɪt, 'fɜːgənaɪt). *Min.* Also ferghanite. [ad. Russ. *ferganit* (I. A. Antipov 1908, in *Górnyi Zhurnál* LXXXIV. IV. 259), f. *Ferg(h)an-a* (see FERAGHAN): see -ITE¹.] A hydrated vanadate of uranium.

1910 *Mineral. Mag.* XV. 421 Ferganite. **1925** *Ibid.* XX. 294 It has already been suggested by K. A. Nenadkevich that ferganite is identical with tyuyamunite... On the other hand, ferganite may represent a leached or weathered product of tyuyamunite. **1958** E. W. HEINRICH *Mineral. & Geol. Radioact. Raw Materials* ii. 106 Ferghanite. Supposedly $U_3(VO_4)_2 \cdot 6H_2O$.

fergusonite ('fɜːgəsənaɪt). *Min.* [named after *Ferguson* (of Raith); see -ITE.] 'A metaniobate (and tantalate) of yttrium with erbium, cerium, uranium, iron, calcium, etc.' (Dana).

1827 *Trans. Roy. Soc. Edinb.* X. II. 271 Fergusonite, a new mineral species. **1873** WATTS *Fownes' Chem.* 376 It has since been found in fergusonite.

‖**feria** ('fɪərɪə). *Eccl.* [L. *fēria* holiday (see FAIR *sb.*), in late L. used with prefixed ordinal for 'day of the week'; thus *secunda feria* = Monday; but Sunday (*Dominicus*, *Dominica*) and Saturday (*Sabbatum*) were usually spoken of by their names.

In Portuguese *segunda*, *terça*, etc. *feira* are still the current names of the days of the week.]

1. A day of the week; a weekday, *esp.* an ordinary weekday as opposed to a festival. ***greater feria***: a particular day of a certain week, that has an office or commemoration proper to it, as Ash Wednesday, Monday in Rogation Week, etc.

1853 CDL. WISEMAN *Ess.* III. 76 *note*, The Sundays and ferias of Lent and Advent. **1866** F. G. LEE *Direct. Angl.* (ed. 3) 354 *Feria*, a week day on which no holiday falls. **1883** BLACK in *Encycl. Brit.* (ed. 9) XVI. 510/2 It [the Roman missal] contains the proper introit, collect..for the festivals and ferias connected with the ecclesiastical seasons.

2. [Sp.] = FAIR *sb.*¹ 1.

1844 J. GREGG *Commerce Prairies* II. 85 At certain seasons of the year, there are held regular *ferias*, at which people assemble in great numbers, as well of sellers as of purchasers. [**1846** R. FORD *Gatherings from Spain* v. 43 The Spanish term *Feria* signifies at once a religious function, a holiday, and a fair.] **1932** E. HEMINGWAY *Death in Afternoon* iv. 41 The local fairs of ferias, which usually commence on the Saint's day of the town. **1939** SPENDER & GILI tr. *Lorca's Poems* 123 How dazzling in the feria! **1957** A. MACNAB *Bulls of Iberia* iv. 43 In provincial *ferias*, the unboxing of the bulls ..is an event worth seeing.

ferial ('fɪərɪəl), *a.* and *sb.* [a. Fr. *férial*, ad. med.L. *fēriālis*, f. *fēria*: see prec.] **A.** *adj.*

1. Pertaining to the days of the week, or to a week-day as distinguished from a festival.

1387 TREVISA *Higden* (Rolls) VI. 293 Alcuinus..ordeyned here orisouns and office of masse for ferial days [*per ferias*]. *c* **1450** tr. *De Imitatione* I. xix. 23 Somme are more sauory in festiuale days, and somme in feriall. **1494** FABYAN v. lxxxiii. 60 The thirde Feryall daye in the weke they named Wodnesday. **1503** *Kalender Sheph.* (1506) A v, The letters feryals of this Kalender. **1542** BOORDE *Dyetary* vii. (1870) 243 Serve God the holy dayes..more dylygentler than to do theyr worke the feryall dayes. **1563–87** FOXE *A. & M.* (1684) II. 326 The commemmoration of Thomas Becket..shall be ..omitted & instead thereof the ferial service used. **1858** FABER *Life Xavier* 65 In the afternoons of ferial days he visited the prisons. **1882–3** SCHAFF *Encycl. Relig. Knowl.* 1956 The distinction between the festival and the simpler ferial manner in the Gregorian style of church-music.

2. Pertaining to a holiday.

c **1500** *For to serve a Lord* vi. in *Babees Bk.* (1868) 372 In feriall tyme serve chese shraped with sugur. **1549** *Banff Council Rec.* in Cramond *Ann. Banff* (1891) I. 25 Inhebitis all utheris to sell ony flysche upon feriall or holy day. **1860** MRS. BYRNE *Undercurrents Overlooked* I. 75 Admiral Mackau..ordered that all works in the navy should be suspended on ferial days.

3. *Sc. Law.* ***ferial day, time***: in which the law-courts were closed, and legal process was invalid.

1471 *Act Audit.* (1839) 16 The last court..was within feryale tyme. **1478** *Act Dom. Conc.* (1839) 16/1 Thai gert it [a brief of inquest] be serwit in hervist, quhilk is feriale tyme & forbiddin of the law. **1538** *St. Papers Hen. VIII*, I. 396 Every day in the next weeke shalbe feriall, except Fryday and Saterday. **1637** *Let.* in *Biblioth. Regia* 140 Since..the rising of his Majesties Council in this ferial time.

¶**4.** = FERAL *a.*¹

1528 *Impeachm. Wolsey* in Furniv. *Ball.* I. 359 Antropose commyth..þᵉ to Areste with hys feryall Mase.

B. *sb.* A week day not a feast or festival.

1877 J. D. CHAMBERS *Divine Worship* 84 Sundays as well as Ferials differed in Order, Dignity, and Precedence.

feriate ('fɪərɪə(ɪ)t), *a.* and *sb. Sc.* [ad. L. *fēriātus*, pa. pple. of *fēriārī* (see FERIE *v.*), f. *fēria*.]

A. *adj.* Of or belonging to a (legal) vacation.

c **1450** HENRYSON *Tale of Dog* 54 The tyme is feriate, Quhairfoir no Juge suld sit in Consistorie. **1637** *Acts Sed.* 29 July, Comprending herein all vacant and feriat tymes. **1825** LD. COCKBURN *Mem.* ii. 134 He groaned over the gradual disappearance of the *Feriat* days of periodical festivity.

B. *sb.* Vacation, holiday.

1727 *Banff Burgh Rec.* in Cramond *Ann. Banff* (1843) II. 182 The Council allow the Grammer schollars feriot and waccancie from the date hereof to the 20th Janry.

†**feri'ation.** *Obs.* [n. of action f. L. *fēriārī*: see prec.] Holiday keeping; cessation of work.

1612–15 BP. HALL *Contempl.*, *N.T.* IV. xi, Here was not a mere feriation but a feasting. **1646** SIR T. BROWNE *Pseud. Ep.* IV. xiii. 222 As though there were any feriation in nature. **1822** MRS. E. NATHAN *Langreath* III. 291 [A pedantic speaker says:] No act of feriation marks the cheerful cornfield.

ferid, -it, obs. forms of FEARED *ppl. a.*

‖**feridgi** (fə'rɪdʒiː). Also 8 ferigee, ferijee. [Turk. *fèrājé*, vulgarly *fèrèjé*.] (See quots.)

1717 LADY M. W. MONTAGU *Let.* 1 Apr. (1825) 153 Their shapes are also wholly concealed, by a thing they call a ferigee. **1743** R. POCOCKE *Descr. East.* I. IV. v. 189 The dress of ceremony of the Turks, call'd the Ferijee, made like a night-gown. **1883** E. O'DONOVAN *Merv* vi, A mantle of calico which shrouds her from head to heel, and is here styled the *feridgi*.

†'**ferie**, *sb. Obs.* [a. OF. *ferie*, ad. L. *fēria*.]

1. A festival, holiday. Also *attrib.*

1377 LANGL. *P. Pl.* B. XIII. 415 Vch day is haliday with hym or an heigh ferye. **14..** *Circumcision* in *Tundale's Vis.* (1843) 85 Thys hee ferye That called is the circunsision. **1538** BALE *Thre Lawes* 821 Sondayes & other feryes. **1548** W. THOMAS *Ital. Gram.* (1567), *Feria*, the ferrie daies noted and obserued by the cleargie. **1616** BULLOKAR, *Ferie*, a holiday.

2. = FERIA.

c **1380** WYCLIF *Serm.* Sel. Wks. II. 57 How þe Sabot shulde be turnide fro Satirdaie to þe first ferie. **1387** TREVISA *Higden* (Rolls) VII. 81 þe next fery after the feste of All Halwes. *c* **1420** *Chron. Vilod.* 151 þe secunde ffery þ^t^ þay be gon to wyrche. **1563** GRAFTON *Chron.* II. 61 Because it was Sunday, nothing was doone. So the day after, which was the second fery, the archebishop [Becket] was cited to apere. **1588** A. KING tr. *Canisius' Catech.* 109 Euerie fourt ferie (called wenesday).

† **'ferie**, *v. Obs.* Also 6 **fery**. [ad. L. *fēriārī*, f. *fēria* holiday.] *intr.* To keep holiday.

1496 *Dives & Paup.* (W. de W.) III. ii. 136/2 Euery daye we be bounde to ferie & to rest from synne. **1548** HOOPER *Ten Commandm.* 115 To abuse the sabbothe..is as mouche as to fery unto god, and work to the deuill.

† **'ferient**, *a. Obs.*$^{-0}$ [ad. L. *ferient-em*, pr. pple. of *ferīre* to strike.] 'Striking, hitting, or knocking' (Blount *Glossogr.* 1656–81).

feriler, var. form of FERULAR.

† **ferine**, *sb. Sc. Obs. rare*$^{-1}$. [ad. Fr. *farine* FARINA.] Meal.

1538 *Aberd. Reg.* V. 16 (Jam.) Sewin bollis ferine.

ferine ('fɪəraɪn), *a.* and *sb.* [ad. L. *ferīn-us*, f. *fera* wild beast. Cf. Fr. *férin* (sense 3).]

A. *adj.* **1.** Of or pertaining to, or of the nature of, a wild animal, or wild animals.

1678 CUDWORTH *Intell. Syst.* 865 Transmigration of Humane Souls there into Ferine Bodies. **1708** MOTTEUX *Rabelais* (1737) V. 230 Some in ferine Venation take Delight. **1749** FIELDING *Tom Jones* v. xi, That gentle daliance, which..passes between lovers of the ferine kind. **1871** BLACKIE *Four Phases* i. 16 Dogs and cocks..and other ferine combatants.

b. Wild, untamed.

1677 HALE *Prim. Orig. Man.* II. vii. 202 The only difficulty ..is touching those ferine..and untamable Beasts. **1713** DERHAM *Phys. Theol.* IV. x. 178 Such as are of a Ferine, not a Domestick Nature. **1728** MORGAN *Algiers* I. Pref. 6 Instinct..like that of the ferine Animals.

2. Of human beings, their actions and attributes: Bestial, beast-like.

1640 BP. REYNOLDS *Passions* xvi. 165 Brutish and unnaturall Desires, which the Philosopher calleth *ferine*. **1678** NORRIS *Coll. Misc.* (1699) 305 A man to..suffer the ferine and brutish part to get the Ascendant over that which is Rational and Divine. **1786** tr. *Swedenborg's Chr. Relig.* §588 A man..from his inherent ferine nature would plunder and massacre. **1822** SOUTHEY in *Q. Rev.* XXVI. 294 It was necessary to become as ferine as themselves.

absol. **1846** LANDOR *Imag. Conv.* II. 218 There are certain colours also of the mind lively enough to excite choler at a distance in the silly and ferine.

3. Of a disease: Malignant. *rare.*

1666 G. HARVEY *Morb. Angl.* x. 103 Thus a ferin Catarrh happens, which through it's corrosive quality oft Ulcerates the Lungs. **1884** in *Syd. Soc. Lex.*

B. *sb.* A wild beast.

In mod. Dicts.

Hence **'ferinely** *adv.*, **'ferineness**.

1677 HALE *Prim. Orig. Man.* II. vii. 197 A conversation with those..would easily assimilate..the next Generation to Barbarism and Ferineness. **1847** CRAIG, *Ferinely*.

† **'fering(e**, *adv. Obs.* [OE. *fǽringa, fǽrunga* (= OS. *fârungo*, OHG. *fâringa*), f. *fǽr*: see FEAR *sb.*[1]] Suddenly. After 12th c. only with genitival *s*, used quasi-*adj.* in *feringes dede*, sudden death.

c **1000** *Ags. Gosp.* Luke ii. 13 And þa wæs færinga [*c* **1160** *Hatton Gosp.* Luke ii. 13 færinge] geworden mid þam engle mycelnes heofonlices werydes. *c* **1180** *Rood-Tree* (1894) 26/12 þa feringæ wearð heo bæften al on brune. *a* **1300** *Cursor M.* 7835 (Cott.) Qua lais hand in feloni O king..O ferings ded..He dei. *c* **1330** R. BRUNNE *Chron.* (1810) 185 þis ȝere falle him þe ferynges dede.

Hence † **'feringly** *adv.*, suddenly.

a **1300** *E.E. Psalter* lxiii[i]. 4 Ferinkli schote him sal þai swa. *Ibid.* lxxii[i]. 19 Ferinkli..Waned þai.

Feringhee (fə'rɪŋgiː). Forms: 6 **firingi**, 7 **fringe**, **frangee**, 8 **fe-**, **firingy**, 9 **faringee**, **ferenghi**, **feringhee**; **ferangi**. [An oriental adoption of FRANK, with Arab. ethnic suffix *-i*; in Arab. *faranjī*, in Pers. *farangī*.]

Formerly, the ordinary Indian term for a European; in 19th c. applied esp. to the Indian-born Portuguese, and contemptuously to other Europeans.

1634 SIR T. HERBERT *Trav.* 171 A Christian. Frangee. **1638** W. BRUTON in *Hakluyt's Voy.* (1807) V. 52 The Portugals which they call by the name of Fringes. **1755** HOLWELL in J. Long *Select. Rec. Govt.* (1869) 59 (Yule) By Feringy I mean all the black mustee Portugese Christians residing in the settlement. **1774** BOGLE in Markham *Tibet* (1876) 176 Everybody was afraid of the Fringies. *c* **1813** MRS. SHERWOOD *Ayah & Lady* Gloss., *Feringhees*, Franks. A name given generally to Europeans in India, and to the descendants of the Portuguese, who first settled in India: these are called Black Feringhees, being remarkably dark. **1834** CAUNTER *Orient. Ann.* v. 60 The unhallowed feet of faringees or Christians. **1866** A. LYALL *Old Pindaree* iii, in *Verses written in India* (1889) 2 There goes my lord the Feringhee, who talks so civil and bland. **1919** W. H. DOWNING *Digger Dial.* 57 *Ferangi*, European. **1936** F. STARK *S. Gates Arabia* xv. 162 No Ferangi goes without a servant.

ferio ('fɛrɪəʊ). *Logic.* A mnemonic word designating the fourth mood of the first figure of syllogisms (see quot. 1551).

1551 T. WILSON *Logike* G vij b, In Ferio, the first must be a negatiue vniuersall, the second an affirmatiue particular, the third a negatiue particular. **1589** *Pappe w. Hatchet* (1844) 38 They bee all in celarent, and dare not shewe their heads, for wee will answere them in ferio and cut their combes. **1702** FARQUHAR *Inconstant* II. i. Wks. (1892) I. 351 Nursed up with Barbara, Celarunt, Darii, Ferio, Baralipton. **1864** BOWEN *Logic* vii. 199 These [Moods] are named Barbara, Celarent, Darii, and Ferio.

ferison (fɛ'raɪsɒn). *Logic.* Also 6 **pheryson**. A mnemonic word representing the sixth mood of the third figure of syllogisms (quantitatively similar to Ferio, but differing in the position of the middle term).

1509 BARCLAY *Shyppe of Folys* (1874) I. 144 Another comyth in with bocardo and pheryson. **1741** CHAMBERS *Cycl.* s.v. *Mood*, Ferison. **1864** BOWEN *Logic* vii. 200.

ferity ('fɛrɪtɪ). Also (6 **feritee**), 7 **feritie**. [ad. L. *feritāt-em*, f. *ferus* wild; see -ITY.]

1. The quality or state of being wild or savage; brutishness, wildness; hence, ferocity.

c **1534** tr. *Pol. Verg. Eng. Hist.* (Camden) I. 109 The rude raginge of the frenetick Scotts..encresed with more beastlie feritee. **1682** SPRAT *Serm. bef. Artillery Co.* 15 Is it not brutish Ferity rather than manly boldness. **1774** J. BRYANT *Mythol.* II. 363 The lion ramped: the pard sported..none of them betrayed any ferity. **1883** J. BURROUGHS in *Century Mag.* XXVII. 111 Even in rugged Scotland, nature is..a good way short of the ferity of the moose.

b. Of a plant, etc.: Wildness, uncultivated condition.

1664 EVELYN *Sylva* (1776) 648 The Suckers..forgetting the Ferity of their Nature. **1713** DERHAM *Phys. Theol.* II. vi. 55 So many Plants..are very noxious; some by their Ferity, and others by their poisonous Nature.

2. Savage or barbarous condition; †a form or instance of this.

1646 SIR T. BROWNE *Pseud. Ep.* VII. xix. 384 Though the blindnesse of some ferities have savaged on the dead..yet had they therein no designe upon the soule. **1652–62** HEYLIN *Cosmogr.* II. (1682) 204 The Ferity and barbarous condition of the first Inhabitants. **1705** STANHOPE *Paraphr.* I. 415 The ancient Rudeness and Ferity of our Country. **1848** HERBERT in *Todd's Nennius* p. xcix, A population of the extremest ferity.

† **3.** Barbarity, barbarous or savage cruelty or inhumanity. *Obs.*

1614 RALEIGH *Hist. World* v. ii. §2. 584 The true nature of tyranny..is none other than Ferity. **1658** SIR T. BROWNE *Hydriot.* iii. 45 To burn the bones of the King of Edom for Lyme, seems no irrationall ferity. **1718** PRIDEAUX *Connection* II. I. 19 Fearing the brutal ferity of his Son.

ferk, var. of FIRK *sb.* and *v.*

† **'ferlac.** *Obs.* Also 3 **farlac**, **fearlac**. [f. FEAR *sb.*[1]: see -LOCK.] Fear, terror.

a **1225** *Ancr. R.* 306 Kume uorð þer efter ferlac, þuruh þe demares heste. *a* **1225** *St. Marher.* 16 Swuch farlac ich fele. *c* **1320** *Cast. Love* 672 In þe mere he stont bi-twene two, Ne haþ he ferlak for no fo.

ferle, obs. var of FERULE.

1559 *Mirr. Mag., Mortimer* ix, The one of knighthoode bare the ferle.

† **'ferliful**, *a. Sc.* and *north. dial. Obs.* [f. FERLY *sb.* + -FUL.] Fearful, wonderful.

a **1300** *Cursor M.* 9314 (Cott.) Man sal him clep wit nams sere, 'Ferliful' and 'conseiler'. **1375** BARBOUR *Bruce* XII. 453 The mast ferlifull sycht That euir I saw. *c* **1475** *Rauf Coilȝear* 2 Thair fell ane ferlyfull flan within thay fellis wide.

quasi-*adv.* **1508** DUNBAR *Tua Mariit Wemen* 26 Off ferliful fyne favour war thair faceis meik.

Hence **'ferlifully** *adv.*, fearfully, wonderfully.

c **1425** WYNTOUN *Cron.* VIII. xxxiv. 63 Swa deyd þat knycht ferlyfully.

† **'ferlily**, *adv. Obs.* [f. as prec. + -LY[2].] Wonderfully, extraordinarily.

a **1300** *Cursor M.* 11424 (Cott.) þe stern went forth-wit þat þam ledd, And ferlilic þan war þai fedd. **13..** *E.E. Allit. P.* B. 962 For when þat þe helle herde þe houndez of heuen He watz ferlyly fayn.

† **'ferling.** *Obs.* exc. *Hist.* [OE. *féorðling*, f. *féorð-a* FOURTH + -LING.] = FARTHING.

1. As a coin: The fourth part of a penny.

c **1000** *Ags. Gosp.* Luke xxi. 2 þa ȝeseah he sume earme wydewan bringan tweȝen feorð-lingas. *a* **1300** *Agst. King of Almaigne* 10 in *Pol. Songs* (Camden) 69 Richard..spende al is tresour opon swyvyng; Haveth he nout of Walingford o ferlyng. **1605** CAMDEN *Rem.* (1636) 125 Two Easterlings & one ferling. **1707** FLEETWOOD *Chron. Prec.* (1745) 40 Ferling ..is a Farthing or the 4th Part of a Sterling.

2. (See quot.)

1610 HOLLAND *Camden's Brit.* I. 497 There were in this Borrough foure Ferlings, that is quarters or wards.

3. The fourth part **a.** of an acre; **b.** of a hide.

1695 KENNETT *Par. Antiq.* Gloss. s.v. *Furendellus*, A fardingel, farundel or ferling of land, i.e. the fourth part of an acre. **1846** G. OLIVER *Monast. Exon.* 321 *note*, The ferling was, perhaps, thirty acres.

† **ferlins.**

1714 *Fr. Bk. of Rates* 69 Ferlins-Stuffs.

ferlot, var. of FIRLOT.

ferly ('fɜːlɪ), *a.* and *sb.* Forms: 1 **fǽrlic**, 3 **fæ(i)rlich**, **feorlic(h**, 4 **-lych**, *south.* **veorlich**, 3–4 **ferlic(h**, **-lik(e**, **-lych**, 3–5 **ferli**, (4 **feerli**, **furley**, 6 **ferrely**, 8 **ferley**), 3 **farli(k**, 5–9 **farley**, **-ly**, 5–6 **fear(e)ly**, 3 **ferly**. [OE. *fǽrlic* sudden, f. *fǽr* (see FEAR) + *lic*, -LY[1]. Cf. MDu. *vêrlich* (Du. *gevaarlijk*), MHG. *vǽrlich* (Ger. *gefährlich*), ON. *fárligr* (Dan., Sw. *farlig*) dangerous.]

† **A.** *adj. Obs.*

1. Sudden, unexpected.

c **893** K. ÆLFRED *Oros.* IV. v. §1, & him þær becom swa færlic yfel þæt [etc]. *c* **1000** ÆLFRIC *Gloss.* in Wr.-Wülcker 175 *Imber*, færlic ren. *c* **1200** *Trin. Coll. Hom.* 61 Gif he þurh ferliche deð saule fro þe lichame deleð. *c* **1275** *Long Life* 15 in *O.E. Misc.* (1872) 157 Fox and ferlych is his [deþes] wrench. *a* **1300** *Cursor M.* 3984 (Cott.) þat ferli flode. **1382** WYCLIF *Prov.* i. 27 Whan shal falle feerli [*repentina*] wrecchidnesse.

2. Dreadful, frightful, terrible.

c **1205** LAY. 25553 Feorlic wes þat sweouen, þene king hit auerde. *a* **1225** *St. Marher.* 23 Ich iseh hwer ha faht wið þe feorliche feont. *c* **1330** R. BRUNNE *Chron.* (1810) 305 To se it was ferlike. **1460** *Pol. Poems* (Rolls) II. 252 Furres of ferly bestes. *a* **1577** GASCOIGNE *Wks.* (1587) 164 A fearly chaunce: whereon alone to thinke My hande now quakis.

3. Strange, wonderful, wondrous, marvellous.

a **1225** *Ancr. R.* 112 þet nes non veorlich wunder. *a* **1300** *Cursor M.* 10863 (Cott.) He sal be of ful farli fame. *c* **1386** CHAUCER *Reeve's T.* 253 Wha herkned ever swilk a ferly thing? *c* **1450** *St. Cuthbert* (Surtees) 4274 þus fell þis ferly thing. **1549–62** STERNHOLD & H. *Audi Israel*, Attend, my people, and give eare, Of fearely things I will thee tell. *a* **1650** *Eger & Grine* 974 in Furniv. *Percy Folio* I. 384 His steed was of a furley kinde.

b. Wonderfully great.

a **1300** *Cursor M.* 12080 (Gött.) A maister was þar selcuth kene, At iesu was him ferli tene. *a* **1400–50** *Alexander* 5577 Ferly ferd of his folke was in þe fild strangild.

B. *sb.* Now chiefly *Sc.* and *dial.*

1. Something wonderful, a marvel, wonder. ***no ferly***: no wonder. ***what ferly***: what wonder.

c **1205** LAY. 5381 Heom þuhte muchel ferlich. *a* **1300** *Cursor. M.* 11 (Gött.) Of ferlijs þat his knightes fell. **1340** HAMPOLE *Pr. Consc.* 2955 If he þan haf drede, it es na ferly. *c* **1350** *Will. Palerne* 3280 Moche folk him folwed þat ferli to bi-hold. *c* **1450** *St. Cuthbert* (Surtees) 1023 Here a ferly þat befell. **1535** STEWART *Cron. Scot.* II. 271 As for farleis richt few thairin he saw. *a* **1605** MONTGOMERIE *Devotional Poems* vi. 45 Vhat ferly, freind, thoght thou be fleyd To go befor so grit a Iudge. **1646** G. DANIEL *Poems* Wks. 1878 I. 57 To let the world know of some Death Or novel ffarley. *c* **1720** *Bewick & Graham* xxvi. in Child *Ballads* VII. ccxi. 147/1 To see what farleys he coud see. **1780** J. MAYNE *Siller Gun* I. (1808) 117 The ferly is..They walk'd sae sicker! **1785** BURNS *To J. Smith* 164 Nae ferly tho' ye do despise The hairum-scairum, ramstam boys. **1790** MRS. WHEELER *Westmld. Dial.* (1821) 98 What saw yee else; onny new farly? **1868** G. MACDONALD *R. Falconer* I. 12 'I'm no sic ferlie that onybody needs be frichtit at me.' **1935** C. DAY LEWIS *Time to Dance* 23 Those ferlies you'll not behold Till the guardians of that valley have crossed Your hand with fairy gold. **1962** DAVIS & WRENN *Eng. & Medieval Studies* 225 But for anthropology 'we' should have taken the ferlies in medieval romance like trivial excitements in a boy's blood. *Ibid.* 227 The idea that ferlies are Jungian outcroppings from the collective unconscious.

2. Wonder, astonishment.

a **1300** *Floriz & Bl.* 456 þo nuste Floriz what to rede For þe ferlich þat he hadde. **13..** *E.E. Allit. P.* A. 1085, I stod as stylle as dased quayle, For ferly of þat freuch [*printed* french] figure. **1393** LANGL. *P. Pl.* C. XII. 228 Litel ferly ich haue. *c* **1475** *Rauf Coilȝear* 903 Now haue I ferlie, gif I fauour the ocht.

† **'ferly**, *adv. Obs.* Forms: 1 **fǽrlíce**, **ferlice**, 2–4 **fer-**, **færliche**, (3 **fær-** **ferlike**), 3–4 *south.* **veor-**, **verliche**, **-lych**, 3–6 **far-**, **ferli(e**, **-ly**, 4 **feerlich**, **-li**, **-ly**, (5 **fairlie**), 3– **ferly**. [OE. *fǽrlíce*: see FERLY *a.* and -LY[2].]

1. Suddenly, unexpectedly.

c **1000** *Ags. Gosp.* Luke ix. 39, & he færlice hrymð. *c* **1175** *Lamb. Hom.* 89 On þisse deie..com ferliche muchel swei of heofne. *c* **1200** ORMIN 665 ȝiff þatt itt ohht færlike seþ þe wlite off englekinde. **1297** R. GLOUC. (1724) 299 Somme deyde verlych as hii vp ryȝt stode. **1340** *Ayenb.* 130 Ase uayr weder went in-to rene and uerliche makeþ his blench. **1382** WYCLIF *Josh.* x. 9 Josue felle on hem feerlich. *c* **1440** *Generydes* 5815 Eche vppon other ferly on they sett. *c* **1475** *Rauf Coilȝear* 176 In feir fairlie he foundis..Quhair the Coilȝear bad, sa braithlie he beird.

2. Dreadfully, frightfully, terribly.

13.. *E.E. Allit. P.* B. 960 Al bi-rolled wyth þe rayn, rostted & brenned, & ferly flayed þat folk þat in þose fees lenged. *c* **1330** R. BRUNNE *Chron.* (1810) 18 He felt him heuy & ferly seke.

3. Wonderfully, marvellously, extraordinarily.

a **1225** *Ancr. R.* 148 A ueorlich god word þet te holi Job seide. *c* **1250** *Gen. & Ex.* 2799 Ic sal werken ferlike strong. *a* **1300** *Cursor M.* 4263 (Cott.) Ioseph was farli fair in face. *c* **1350** *Will. Palerne* 3238 þe horse..gan fare wiþ his fet & ferliche neiȝede. *c* **1450** HENRYSON *Mor. Fab.* 52 Flowres ferly sweete. *c* **1460** *Towneley Myst.* (Surtees) 49, I wille you telle Tythynges farly goode. **1535** STEWART *Cron. Scot.* (1858) I. 42 Thocht tha war ȝoung, ȝit tha wer farlie fair.

ferly ('fɜːlɪ), *v. Obs.* exc. *Sc.* Forms: 4 **ferli**, 4–8 **ferlie**, (9 **ferley**), 4–6 **farley**, **-lie**, **-lye**, 5– **ferly**. [f. FERLY *a.*] **1.** *intr.* To wonder.

1375 BARBOUR *Bruce* VI. 323 Thai..Farlyit, and ȝarnyt hym to se. *a* **1400–50** *Alexander* 4761 Quen he had ferlied his fill. *c* **1500** *Lancelot* 3117 That euery wight ferleit of his deid. **1513** DOUGLAS *Æneis* x. Prol. 86 Frend ferly not. **1597** MONTGOMERIE *Cherrie & Slae* 846 Nane ferlies mair than fulis. **1725** RAMSAY *Gent. Sheph.* II. iv, *Peggy.* They'll wonder what can make us stay. *Patie.* And let them ferly.

1786 BURNS *Twa Dogs* 122 They'll.. tell what new taxation's comin, An' ferlie at the folk in Lon'on. *c* **1826** HOGG *Meg o' Marley* 20 Wks. 1840 V. 97 He.. sits down but to ferly.

b. quasi-*trans.* with sentence as *obj.*

c **1400** *Melayne* 1474 Thay ferlyde why he fewterde his spere. **1500–20** DUNBAR *Fenȝeit Freir* 63 All fowill ferleit quhat he sowld be. **1801** R. GILL *Tint Quey* in Chambers *Pop. Hum. Scot. Poems* (1862) 178 Ilk ane ferlied nae a wee, What luckless gate the chiel could be.

2. *trans.* To amaze, astonish. Only *impers.* and in *passive.*

a **1300** *Cursor M.* 17361 (Gött.) Ful ferlid all þan war þai. *c* **1400** *Melayne* 552 Me ferlys of thy fure. *a* **1400–50** *Alexander* 4991 þe wale kyng.. Was in þe figure of hire fourme noȝt ferlied a littell. *c* **1450** *St. Cuthbert* (Surtees) 2405 Na man be ferlyd, Bede biddes.

†**ferm**, *v. Obs.* Also 4 ferme, -ye. [a. OF. *ferme-r*:—L. *firmāre* to make fast, f. *firm-us* firm.]

1. *trans.* To establish, make firm.

c **1330** R. BRUNNE *Chron. Wace* (Rolls) 15507 Wyues þey toke, þer loues to ferme Two sones had þey at o terme. **1377** LANGL. *P. Pl.* B. x. 74 þat folke is nouȝte fermed in þe feith. *c* **1380** *Sir Ferumb.* 2113 þay.. cussede i-same an haste, To fermye loue by-twene hem. **1513** DOUGLAS *Æneis* x. v. 174 Or thai thar fute steppis ferm and tak array.

2. To shut up, blockade.

1513 DOUGLAS *Æneis* x. v. 181 He suld nocht from the sege vprais, Bot still remane to ferm and clos the toun. **1655** J. JENNINGS tr. *Elise* 2 As a Neptune ferming the winds of sedition in their gale.

3. = AFFIRM *v.*

a **1455** HOLLAND *Houlate* xli, Thus in defence of the faith as fermes ynewe.. The douchty Douglas is dede.

fermacy, obs. form of PHARMACY.

fermage, ferm(e, etc., var. of FARMAGE, FARM, etc.

fermail (ˈfɜːmeɪl). *Antiq.* and *Her.* Also 5 fermayll(e, 6 fermaulx, 7 fermaile, -ale, -ault. [a. OF. *fermaille* a clasp:—med.L. *firmāculum*, f. *firmāre* to fix.] A buckle or clasp; a setting.

1480 CAXTON *Ovid's Met.* x. iv, A fermayll of gemes plesaunt. **1483** —— *G. de la Tour* M iij, To wynne suche ouches or fermaylles. **1572** BOSSEWELL *Armorie* II. 38 b, One fermaulx lozengie. **1610** GUILLIM *Heraldry* IV. xv. (1660) 344 He beareth.. on a chief.. as many fermailes or buckles. **1688** R. HOLME *Armoury* III. 304/2 Buckles are called Fermales or Fermaults. **1865** *Athenæum* No. 1954. 494/2 A Charact Fermail of the fourteenth century. **1877** LL. JEWITT *Half-hrs. Eng. Antiq.* 126 A circular object.. intended for a mirror, or for a circular brooch or fermail.

fermance, var. of FIRMANCE.

Fermat (ˈfɛrma). The name of Pierre de *Fermat* (1601–65), French mathematician, used attrib. or in the possessive to designate certain results and concepts introduced by him, as ***Fermat's last theorem***, a famous unproved theorem (of which Fermat said he had 'a truly wonderful proof'), viz. that if *n* is an integer greater than 2, $x^n + y^n = z^n$ has no positive integral solutions; ***Fermat's law*** = *Fermat's principle*; ***Fermat('s) number***, a number of the form $2^{2^n} + 1$, where *n* is a positive integer; ***Fermat's principle***, the principle that the path taken by a ray of light between any two points is such that the integral along it of the refractive index of the medium has a stationary value; ***Fermat's theorem***, (*a*) that if *p* is a prime number and *a* an integer not divisible by *p*, then $a^{p-1} - 1$ is divisible by *p*; (*b*) = *Fermat's last theorem*. Also **Fermatian** (fɜːˈmeɪʃən), *a.* and *sb.* (*rare*).

1811 P. BARLOW *Elem. Invest. Theory of Numbers* ii. 48 [This] leads us at once to the demonstration of one of Fermat's theorems, that he considered as one of his principal numerical propositions. **1839** *Phil. Mag.* 3rd Ser. XIV. 48 Horner's extension of Fermat's theorem suggested this extension of Sir John Wilson's to me. **1845** *Ibid.* XXVII. 286 (*heading*) Proof of Fermat's Undemonstrated Theorem, that $x^n + y^n = z^n$ is only possible in whole numbers when $n = 1$ or 2. **1865** BRANDE & COX *Dict. Sci., Lit. & Art* I. 879/1 Another theorem, distinguished as Fermat's last Theorem, has obtained great celebrity on account of the numerous attempts that have been made to demonstrate it. **1884** A. DANIELL *Text-bk. Physics* v. 125 Fermat's Law. **1887** J. J. SYLVESTER in *Nature* 15 Dec. 153, I have found it useful to denote $p^i - 1$ when *p* and *i* are left general as the Fermatian function, and when *p* and *i* have specific values as the *i*th Fermatian of *p*. **1888** *Encycl. Brit.* XXIV. 424/1 It follows that the course of a ray is that for which the time.. is a minimum. This is Fermat's principle of least time. **1906** *Bull. Amer. Math. Soc.* XII. 449 Fermat's numbers.. are known to be prime for $n = 0, 1, 2, 3, 4$, and composite for $n = 5, 6, 7, 9, 11, 12, 18, 23, 36, 38$. **1948** O. ORE *Number Theory* viii. 204 This is the famous Fermat's theorem, sometimes called Fermat's last theorem, on which the most prominent mathematicians have tried their skill ever since its announcement three hundred years ago. **1959** BORN & WOLF *Princ. Optics* 737 The laws of geometrical optics may be derived from Fermat's principle. **1966** OGILVY & ANDERSON *Excurs. Number Theory* iii. 36 The higher Fermat numbers have been the subject of prolonged study.

‖**fermata** (fəˈmɑːtə). *Mus.* Pl. fermatas, fermate. [It.] A pause of unspecified length; the sign indicating such a pause.

[**1842** J. F. WARNER *Univ. Dict. Mus. Terms* p. xxxviii/2 *Fermata* is the Italian name for what we call a *hold*.] **1876** STAINER & BARRETT *Dict. Mus. Terms* 165/1 Fermata (*It.*), a pause (from *fermare*, to stay, or stop). **1889** *Cent. Dict.*, *Fermata*,.. A pause in the accompaniment to give room for an extended cadenza by the soloist. **1955** AUDEN *Shield of Achilles* ii. 43 In timeless fermatas of awe and delight. **1962** *Times* 6 Apr. 17/6 Tempo-changes were ungainly and dramatic fermate ill-judged. **1969** *Daily Tel.* 18 Jan. 17/5 At the same time the fermatas, traditionally signposts inviting improvised insertions, grow scarcer.

†**ferme.** *Cant. Obs.* A hole.

1620 DEKKER *Villanies Discovered* xvii. P ij, A short staffe.. having in the Nab or head of it, a Ferme (that is to say a hole). **1688** R. HOLME *Armory* III. iii. 168 *Ferme*, Hole, Cave, or hiding place. **1725** in *New Cant. Dict.*

ferment, var. of FERRAMENT, *Obs.*

ferment (ˈfɜːmənt), *sb.* Also 6 fermente, 7 firment. [a. Fr. *ferment*, ad. L. *fermentum*, f. root of *ferv-ēre* to boil.]

1. a. *orig.* Leaven or yeast. Hence *gen.* an agent which causes fermentation (see FERMENTATION 1).

Modern chemists recognize two classes of ferments: ***organized ferments***, which are living vegetable organisms, as the yeast plant and other microscopic fungi; and ***unorganized*** or ***chemical ferments***, which are certain compounds of organic origin, as *diastase*, *pepsin*, etc. (now replaced in scientific use by *enzyme*).

c **1420** *Pallad. on Husb.* XI. 524 Use this ferment For musty brede. **1683** ROBINSON in *Ray's Corr.* (1848) 138 The venom.. may chiefly consist in a subtle acid ferment. **1774** J. BRYANT *Mythol.* II. 59 He taught the nations the use of ferment. **1807** *Med. Jrnl.* XVII. 198 Hence he concludes, that albumen.. is the true ferment. **1871** TYNDALL *Fragm. Sc.* (1879) I. v. 138 Pasteur.. proved the real 'ferments'.. to be organised beings. **1890** *Jrnl. Chem. Soc.* LVII. 530 The expression *ferment* is more frequently than not employed as the equivalent of *unorganised ferment*... Several words have been coined in place of unorganised ferment, notably *zymase* and *enzyme*. **1945** E. B. FORD *Butterflies* iii. 58 It [*sc.* melanin] is produced by the oxidation of.. 'tyrosin' (an amino-acid), through the action of a ferment, 'tyrosinase'.

fig. **1643** SIR T. BROWNE *Relig. Med.* I. §267 The.. ferment of all.. Religious actions, is Wisedome. **1690** LOCKE *Govt.* II. xix. (Rtldg.) 224 This hypothesis lays a ferment for frequent rebellion. **1722** WOLLASTON *Relig. Nat.* ix. 173 Gentle ferments working in our breasts. **1877** TYNDALL in *Daily News* 2 Oct. 2/5 A ferment long confined to individuals, but which may.. become the leaven of the race.

†**b.** *spec.* in *Alchemy* (cf. FERMENTATION 1 b); sometimes applied to the 'philosopher's stone'. Also in cosmological speculations (see quot. 1677).

1471 RIPLEY *Comp. Alch.* IX. in Ashm. (1652) 175 Ferment whych Leven we call. **1610** B. JONSON *Alch.* II. ii, The red ferment Has done his office. **1677** *Phil. Trans.* XII. 884 By *Ferments* he means the aforesaid Principles, (or Seminal sparks hidden in matter) actually put into motion, and by the variety of that motion producing the variety of bodies. **1677** HALE *Prim. Orig. Man.* II. vii. 193 Those Shells arise *de novo*, not barely from the Plastick power of the Earth.. but from certain Seminal Ferments brought thither.

2. = FERMENTATION 1.

1605 TIMME *Quersit.* I. vii. 28 The more strong the wine shal be, the more sharpe the ferment of the vineger. **1695** BLACKMORE *Pr. Arth.* II. 75 He through the Mass a mighty Ferment spread. **1707** FLOYER *Physic. Pulse-Watch* 208 Abating the Ferment and Quantity of Humours. **1725** BRADLEY *Fam. Dict.* s.v. *Quinquina*, Stopping the Ferment of Intermitting Fevers. **1744** BERKELEY *Siris* §111 The first ferment of new wine.

3. *fig.* Agitation, excitement, tumult; = FERMENTATION 2.

1672 MARVELL *Reh. Transp.* I. 33 The Ecclesiastical Rigours here were in the highest ferment. **1681** DRYDEN *Abs. & Achit.* 140 Several Factions from this first Ferment, Work up to Foam, and threat the Government. **1781** GIBBON *Decl. & F.* xxx. III. 88 The minister.. attempted to allay the general ferment. **1829** I. TAYLOR *Enthus.* ix. 240 A ferment of sinister feelings. **1848** MACAULAY *Hist. Eng.* II. 20 The foreign embassies were all in a ferment.

4. *attrib.* and *Comb.*

1863 H. WATTS *Dict. Chem.* II. 634 Ferment-oils.. are volatile oils, produced by the fermentation of various plants, not originally contained therein, and essentially different from the oils which are extracted from unfermented plants by distillation with water. **1886** *Encycl. Brit.* XXI. 400/2 In 1870 Pasteur had proved that a disease of silkworms was due to a ferment-organism of the nature of a Schizomycete. **1898** H. MANDERS (*title*) The ferment treatment of cancer and tuberculosis.

ferment (fəˈmɛnt), *v.* [a. F. *fermenter*, ad. L. *fermentāre*, f. *fermentum* leaven: see prec. sb.]

1. *intr.* Of material substances (in early use primarily of dough or saccharine fluids): To undergo the action of a ferment; to suffer fermentation; to 'work'. (The precise meaning has varied with that of the sbs. FERMENT, FERMENTATION.)

1398 TREVISA *Barth. De P.R.* XVII. lxviii. (1495) 644 Soure dough hyghte fermentum, for it makyth paast ferment and maketh it also aryse [*excrescere et fervere facit pastam*]. **1663** COWLEY *Verses, To Royal Society* iv, All their juyce did.. Ferment into a.. refreshing Wine. **1665** HOOKE *Microgr.* 190 Flies swarming, about any piece of flesh that does begin a little to ferment. **1697** DRYDEN *Virg. Georg.* IV. 436 The tainted Blood.. Begins to boyl, and thro' the Bones ferment. **1707** *Curios. in Husb. & Gard.* 66 These mineral Substances.. ferment, rise up in Vapours and Steams. **1791** BEDDOES in *Phil. Trans.* LXXXI. 174 As it approaches more and more towards nature [malleable iron] it adheres less; and when the tools come clear up out of the mass, he judges it to be fermented enough [cf. FERMENTATION 1 d]. **1813** SIR H. DAVY *Agric. Chem.* (1814) 6 Dung which has fermented. **1838** T. THOMSON *Chem. Org. Bodies* 370 The blue precipitate.. is removed into a copper boiler till it assumes the appearance of effervescing, or till it ferments. **1842** A. COMBE *Physiol. Digestion* (ed. 4) 290 We allow bread to ferment.

b. *fig.*

1671 MILTON *Samson* 619 My griefs.. ferment and rage. **1771** JOHNSON *Lett. to Mrs. Thrale* 3 July, These reflections fermented in my mind. **1781** GIBBON *Decl. & F.* III. lxvii. 686 Fanaticism fermented in anarchy. **1856** FROUDE *Hist. Eng.* (1885) I. i. 65 The northern counties were fermenting in a half-suppressed rebellion. **1879** O. W. HOLMES *Motley* ii. 10 His mind was doubtless fermenting with projects.

2. *trans.* To subject to fermentation; to cause fermentation in.

1672–3 GREW *Anat. Roots* II. §18 (1682) 83 The Sap.. is.. fermented therein. **1815** J. SMITH *Panorama Sc. & Art* II. 502 Liquors are fermented for the use of the table. **1830** M. DONOVAN *Dom. Econ.* I. 373 The yest, made use of in the process of fermenting the dough. **1834** *Brit. Husb.* I. 272 There was as much moisture as was necessary to ferment the straw.

fig. **1759** R. HURD *Dial.* i. *Sincerity in Commerce* 29 Fanaticism.. fermented with the leaven of earthly avarice. **1791–1823** D'ISRAELI *Cur. Lit.* (1866) 459/1 His vast.. curiosity fermenting his immense book-knowledge.

3. *transf.* and *fig.* To work up into a ferment or agitation; to excite, stir up.

1667 *Decay Chr. Piety* ix. §5 When bitter zeal was once fermented. **1704** POPE *Windsor For.* 93 Ye vig'rous swains, while youth ferments your blood. **1712** BLACKMORE *Creation*, Fierce winds.. with their furious breath ferment the deep. **1837** DICKENS *Pickw.* x, Ladies who are endeavouring to ferment themselves into hysterics. **1852** MRS. JAMESON *Leg. Madonna* Introd. (1857) 25 A mere contemplative enthusiasm.. fermented into life and form. **1856** EMERSON *Eng. Traits, Religion* Wks. (Bohn) II. 96 The Christianity which fermented Europe.

b. To exacerbate; to foment, inflame.

1660 in Picton *L'pool Munic. Rec.* (1883) I. 306 Findinge.. the same disputes.. fermented.. against the merchants. *a* **1704** T. BROWN *Eng. Satire* Wks. 1730 I. 28 He fermented the passions of the vicious. **1764** FOOTE *Mayor of G.* II. Wks. 1799 I. 186 To.. ferment a difference between husband and wife. **1868** *Times* 21 Jan., To shew him fermenting the Garibaldian movements.

fermentable (fəˈmɛntəb(ə)l), *a.* [f. FERMENT *v.* + -ABLE.]

1. Capable of being fermented.

1731–7 MILLER *Gard. Dict.* s.v. *Wine*, Fermentable Bodies. **1795** BURKE *Corr.* (1844) IV. 271 This fermentable sap portends the dry-rot. **1850** DAUBENY *Atom. Th.* x. (ed. 2) 347 The cells which contain the saccharine and other fermentable matters. **1869** E. A. PARKES *Pract. Hygiene* (ed. 3) 96 Organic fermentable liquids change very slowly.

fig. **1732** *Hist. Litteraria* IV. 22 He proceeds to range fermentable Subjects into Classes. **1840** MILL *Ess.* (1859) II. 408 The.. fermentable elements of French society.

2. Capable of causing fermentation. *rare.*

1846 J. BAXTER *Libr. Pract. Agric.* (ed. 4) I. 133 The fermented liquor must be separated as much as possible from the yeast or fermentable matter.

Hence ˌ**fermentaˈbility**, the quality of being fermentable.

1788 *Projects* in *Ann. Reg.* 85 Newman.. was unwilling to admit of the fermentability of milk. **1912** A. C. CHAPMAN *Brewing* iv. 55 A wort having just the degree of fermentability required.

†**fermenˈtaceous**, *a. Obs.* [f. FERMENT *sb.* + -ACEOUS.] Having the properties of a ferment.

1662 J. CHANDLER *Van Helmont's Oriat.* 140 Fermentaceous Odour dwells every where. **1682** T. GIBSON *Anat.* (1697) 41 Hunger is caused from fermentaceous particles.

ferˈmental, *a.* [f. FERMENT *sb.* + -AL[1].] Of, pertaining to, or of the nature of, a ferment or fermentation.

1650 SIR T. BROWNE *Pseud. Ep.* II. vii. 783 Cucumbers.. may also debiliate the.. fermentall faculty of the stomack. **1676** NEWTON in Rigaud *Corr. Sci. Men* (1841) II. 389 The frame of nature may be nothing but ether condensed by a fermental principle. **1694** WESTMACOTT *Script. Herb.* (1695) 152 Intense cold.. prevents their Fruit-bearing by suspending the fermental action of the Principles. **1753** CHAMBERS *Cycl. Suppl.* s.v. *Zymology*, The fermental principles of acid and sulphur connatural to that oil [*sc.* oil of vitriol]. **1922** *Glasgow Herald* 21 Aug. 7 Sugar or any other kind of fermental food.

fermentarian (fɜːmənˈtɛərɪən). *Eccl. Hist.* [f. L. *fermentāri-us* (f. *fermentum*: see FERMENT *sb.*) + -AN.] A name applied in reproach by Latin Christians to those of the Greek church, as using fermented bread in the Eucharist.

1775 in ASH.

†**fermenˈtarious**, *a. Obs.*—[0] [f. L. *fermentāri-us* (f. *fermentum*: see FERMENT *sb.*) + -OUS.] Made of leaven; belonging to fermentation.

1656–81 in BLOUNT *Glossogr.* **1775** in ASH.

†**ˈfermentate**, *v. Obs.* [f. L. *fermentāt-* ppl. stem of *fermentāre*, to ferment.] *trans.* To cause to ferment; to leaven.

1599 A. M. tr. *Gabelhouer's Bk. Physicke* 208/2, Rye meale to be fermentatede with sower leaven. **1615** CROOKE *Body of*

Man 218 A certaine paste should..bee fermentated..into the form of a man. **1657** TOMLINSON *Renou's Disp.* 105 The conditure is excellently fermentated.

fig. *a* **1670** HACKET *Abp. Williams* II. 179 The largest part of the Lords were fermentated with an Anti-episcopal Sourness.

absol. **1656** BEN ISRAEL *Vind. Jud.* in *Phenix* (1708) II. 394 Every confection ought to be so pure as not to admit of..any thing that may fermentate.

Hence **'fermentated** *ppl. a.*

1656–81 in BLOUNT *Glossogr.* **1676–1717** in COLES. **1860** in WORCESTER (citing BACON).

fermentation (fɜːmən'teɪʃən). [ad. L. *fermentātiōn-em*, n. of action f. *ferment-āre* to FERMENT.] The action or process of fermenting.

1. A process of the nature of that resulting from the operation of leaven on dough or on saccharine liquids.

The features superficially recognizable in the process in these instances are an effervescence or internal commotion, with evolution of heat, in the substance operated on, and a resulting alteration of its properties. Before the rise of modern chemistry, the term was applied to all chemical changes exhibiting these characters; in Alchemy, it was the name of an internal change supposed to be produced in metals by a 'ferment', operating after the manner of leaven. In modern science the name is restricted to a definite class of chemical changes peculiar to organic compounds, and produced in them by the stimulus of a 'ferment' (see FERMENT *sb.* 1); the various kinds of fermentation are distinguished by qualifying adjs., as *acetous, alcoholic, butyric, lactic, putrefactive*, etc. (see those words). In popular language the term is no longer applied to other kinds of change than those which it denotes in scientific use, but it usually conveys the notion of a sensible effervescence or 'working', which is not involved in the chemical sense.

a. in applications covered by the modern scientific sense.

1601 HOLLAND *Pliny* XXIII. vii. II. 170 Some used to put thereunto [the juice out of mulberries] myrrhe and cypresse, setting all to frie and take their fermentation in the sun. *a* **1682** SIR T. BROWNE *Tracts* (1684) 26 Made by hindring and keeping the must from fermentation or working. **1718** QUINCY *Compl. Disp.* 8 The second is the inflammable Spirit of Vegetable, and what is procured by the help of Fermentation. **1796** C. MARSHALL *Garden.* xiii. (1813) 179 The dung of animals..is put together for fermentation. **1842** A. COMBE *Physiol. Digestion* (ed. 4) 110 Others.. contended, that chymification results from simple fermentation of the alimentary mass. **1874** M. COOKE *Fungi* 3 These cells are capable of producing fermentation in certain liquids.

†**b.** in *Alchemy*. *Obs.*

c **1386** CHAUCER *Can. Yeom. Prol. & T.* 264 Oure cementynge and fermentacioun. **1471** RIPLEY *Comp. Alch.* IX. in Ashm. (1652) 173 Trew Fermentacyon few Workers do understond. **1599** THYNNE *Animadv.* (1875) 32 Fermentacione ys a peculier terme of Alchymye. **1610** B. JONSON *Alch.* I. i, Because o' your fermentation, and cibation.

†**c.** in various other vague applications. *Obs.*

a **1661** FULLER *Worthies* (1840) III. 91 Others impute the heat..to the fermentation of several minerals. **1671** GREW *Anat. Plants* I. i. §30 (1682) 6 The General Cause of the growth of a..Seed, is Fermentation. **1678** *State Trials, Earl of Pembroke* (1810) 1341 Claret, and..small-beer..set the blood upon a fermentation. **1707** *Curios. in Husb. & Gard.* 67 An acid Salt mingles it self with an Alkali: from which Mixture results a Fermentation, and very sensible Heat. **1728–46** THOMSON *Spring* 569 The torpid sap..in fluent dance, And lively fermentation, mounting. **1794** SULIVAN *View Nat.* I. 69 As soon as our continents were thus delivered from the waters, the fermentations..ceased.

†**d.** *Iron-smelting*: see quot. *Obs.*

1791 BEDDOES in *Phil. Trans.* LXXXI. 174 The hottest part of the mass begins to heave and swell..The workman calls this appearance fermentation.

2. *fig.* The state of being excited by emotion or passion; agitation, excitement, working. Sometimes (with more complete metaphor): A state of agitation tending to bring about a purer, more wholesome, or more stable condition of things.

c **1660** J. GIBBON in Spurgeon *Treas. Dav.* cxix. 9 A young man..in the highest fermentation of his youthful lusts. **1682** EARL ANGLESEY *State Govt.* in Somers *Tracts* II. 196 Predicting..the happy, future State of our Country; and that the then Fermentation would be perfective to it. **1752** HUME *Ess. & Treat.* (1777) I. 288 The minds of men being once..put into a fermentation. **1845** S. AUSTIN *Ranke's Hist. Ref.* II. 161 Whether in such a state of fermentation, they would wait patiently. **1859** MILL *Liberty* ii. 61 In the intellectual fermentation of Germany, etc.

fermentatious (fɜːmɛn'teɪʃəs), *a.* [f. FERMENTATION: see -OUS.] Of a disease: That is produced by some morbific principle or organism acting on the system like a ferment.

1888 *Scott. Leader* 6 Dec. 5 The vast increase they show in deaths from other 'zymotic' (or 'fermentatious') diseases.

fermentative (fə'mɛntətɪv), *a.* [f. L. *fermentāt-* ppl. stem of *fermentāre* + -IVE. Cf. Fr. *fermentatif.*]

1. Of, pertaining to, or of the nature of fermentation; developed by fermentation.

1665 HOOKE *Microgr.* 122 Vegetation, which is set a moving by the putrifactive and fermentative heat. **1693** BLANCARD *Phys. Dict.* 205/2 Some filthy and fermentative Matter. **1757** A. COOPER *Distiller* I. ii. (1760) 10 The succeeding Separation or fermentative Motion, is a very different Thing. **1850** DAUBENY *Atom. Th.* x. (ed. 2) 350 Watching it during the continuance of the fermentative process. **1869** E. A. PARKES *Pract. Hygiene* (ed. 5) 20 The organic matter may..commence to undergo fermentative changes.

2. Tending to cause or undergo fermentation.

1661 CHILDREY *Brit. Bacon.* 43, I doubt whether either of them hath any thing of a fermentative power in them. **1671** GREW *Anat. Plants* I. i. §31 (1682) 7 Beer, or any other Fermentative Liquor. **1748** HARTLEY *Observ. Man* I. i. 46 The fermentative Disposition of the fresh Chyle. **1876** FOSTER *Phys.* II. i. 219 The fermentative activity of yeast.

Hence **fer'mentatively** *adv.*, and **fer'mentativeness**.

1684 TYSON *Hist. R. Soc.* iv. 172 (T.) The white of the egg he concluded, from its fermentativeness, to be impregnated with air. **1890** WEBSTER, *Fermentatively*.

fermentatory (fə'mɛntətərɪ), *a.* [f. Lat. type **fermentātōrius*, f. *fermentāre* to ferment.] = FERMENTATIVE 1.

1765 BROWNRIGG in *Phil. Trans.* LV. 227 Liquors, which ..by their fermentatory motion, generate more air than they can imbibe. **1770** *Monthly Rev.* 302 A fermentatory process is carried on in the stomach.

fermented (fə'mɛntɪd), *ppl. a.* [f. FERMENT *v.* + -ED[1].] Of a liquor: That has been through the process of fermentation. Of bread: Leavened.

1555 EDEN *Decades* 258 Fermented breade dipte in a sponefull of wyne. **1646** SIR T. BROWNE *Pseud. Ep.* II. iv. 82 From the distillation of fermented urine..ariseth an Aqua vitæ. **1732** ARBUTHNOT *Rules of Diet* 261 All fermented Spirits, the [stimulating] Effects of which are very sudden. **1813** SIR H. DAVY *Agric. Chem.* (1814) 136 The spirits distilled from different fermented liquors differ in their flavour.

fermenter, fermentor (fə'mɛntə(r)). [f. FERMENT *v.* + -ER[1].] **a.** A vessel in which fermentation occurs. **b.** An organism that causes fermentation.

1918 *Jrnl. Med. Res.* XXXIX. 34 The presence of these slow lactose fermenters in the material examined presented a serious problem. **1925** *Jrnl. Biol. Chem* LXII. 790 This solution..and sufficient water to make 30 liters, were placed in a cylindrical stoneware crock which served as a 'fermenter'. **1944** *Chem. & Engin. News* 25 Apr. 592/1 The production of penicillin in vat fermenters. **1947** *Jrnl. Bacteriol.* LIV. 689 This fermentor has an operating capacity of 500 to 2,000 ml. **1949** E. CHAIN in H. W. Florey et al. *Antibiotics* xvii. 709 The fermenters used in penicillin-manufacturing plants are made from good-quality mild steel or stainless steel. **1959** *Appl. Microbiol.* VII. 238/1 Four fermentations..were made in 5-gal agitated fermentors. **1967** *Biol. Abstr.* XLVIII. 7290/2 B-alanine in conjunction with KNO_3 incorporated into a primary isolation medium, is a vital ingredient in differentiating the genus *Proteus* from other non-lactose fermenters.

fermentescible (ˌfɜːmən'tɛsɪb(ə)l), *a.* Also (*erron.*) -iscible. [f. FERMENT *v.* + *-escible* (see -ESCE and -IBLE).] **a.** Having the power to cause fermentation. **b.** Capable of being fermented.

1684 tr. *Bonet's Merc. Compit.* xix. 730 Fermentiscible and often bilious Humours bred of..Meat corrupted. **1807** *Med. Jrnl.* XXII. 198 The albumen..was so altered.. without having lost its fermentescible action. **1814** *Edin. Rev.* XXIII. 129 To excite fermentation in a fermentiscible fluid. **1865** *Reader* No. 117. 346/3 Fermentescible liquids.

fer'menting, *vbl. sb.* [f. as prec. + -ING[1].] The action of the vb. FERMENT; also *attrib.*

1471 RIPLEY *Comp. Alch.* IX. in Ashm. (1652) 173 Fermentyng in dyvers maners is don. **1831** CARLYLE *Sart. Res.* (1858) 13 What a Fermenting-vat lies simmering and hid! **1846** J. BAXTER *Libr. Pract. Agric.* (ed. 4) II. 415 Twenty gallons in each fermenting tub. **1856** KANE *Arct. Expl.* II. xi. 37 My..study-lamp is now fixed under a barrel to..raise a fermenting temperature.

fermenting (fə'mɛntɪŋ), *ppl. a.* [f. as prec. + -ING[2].] That ferments; in senses of the verb.

1697 DRYDEN *Virg. Georg.* II. 10 When with fermenting Juice the Vat o'erflows. **1705** ADDISON *Campaign* 108 Their Courage dwells not in a troubl'd Flood Of mounting Spirits, and fermenting Blood. **1816** J. SCOTT *Vis. Paris* Pref. (ed. 5) 4 The fermenting mischief burst forth. **1872** TAUNT *Map of Thames* 15 The bung flies upwards from the fermenting beer.

fermentitious (ˌfɜːmən'tɪʃəs), *a.* [f. assumed L. **fermentīci-us* (f. *fermentum* FERMENT *sb.*) + -OUS.] Of a fermenting or effervescent nature.

1807 A. KNOX *Let. Butterworth* Rem. (1834) I. 67 It can deceive us by no fermentitious feeling. **1820** —— *Let. H. More* Rem. (1837) III. 464 Mr. Southey..seems to take.. pleasure in shewing off the annoying spectacles of fermentitious religion.

fermentive (fə'mɛntɪv), *a.* [f. FERMENT *sb.* or *v.* + -IVE.] Tending to produce fermentation.

1672 *Phil. Trans.* VII. 4030 Seeds, which by the vertue of their fermentive Odours perform these transmutations upon Matter. **1674** R. GODFREY *Inj. & Ab. Physic* 2 Were not Diseases themselves..in a manner poysonous and Fermentive. **1888** *Athenæum* 25 Feb. 247/3 The fermentive organism is..absolutely essential to the setting up of destructive rotting.

fig. **1656** *Artif. Handsom.* 104 Which is as strong a leaven to puffe the mind, as any thing, and no lesse fermentive when naturall, than when artificiall.

‖**fermentum** (fə'mɛntəm). [med.L. use of L. *fermentum* yeast, FERMENT *sb.*] In the church in Rome from at least the fifth century, a portion of the eucharistic oblation sent from the Papal Mass to a presbyter about to celebrate the eucharist in one of the neighbouring churches.

1719 J. BINGHAM *Origines Ecclesiasticæ* VI. xv. ii. 610 The Ancients.. many Times spake of leavened Bread, and sometimes the Eucharist is called Fermentum, Leaven, upon that Account. *Ibid.* 611 As appears from..a Letter of Pope Innocent, where he says, it was the Custom at Rome to consecrate the Fermentum, that is, the Eucharist, in the Mother Church, and send it thence on the Lord's Day to the Presbyters in the Tituli or lesser Churches. **1884** ADDIS & ARNOLD *Cath. Dict.* s.v. *Reservation*, A supposed decretal of Pope Innocent to Decentius proves that the Bishop of Rome sent the *fermentum* or consecrated host 'per titulos'—*i.e.* to the chief churches of the city. **1937** FORTESCUE & THURSTON *Mass* ix. 368 It is clear really that the fermentum was the Holy Eucharist... As the Sancta were a symbol of the identity of the sacrifice from one Mass to another, so was the fermentum a sign of union between the bishop and his clergy. **1957** *Oxf. Dict. Chr. Church* 500/1 *Fermentum*, in Rome (5th cent.), the fragments of the Bread of the Eucharist sent on Sundays from the Papal Mass to the presbyters in the parish churches (*tituli*) to typify the unity of the faithful in Christ.

†**'fermerer**[1]. *Obs.* [f. FERMERY + -ER[1].] The superintendent of a (monastic) infirmary. Cf. ENFERMER.

c **1386** CHAUCER *Sompn. T.* 151 So did our sextein, and our fermerere, That han ben trewe feeres fifty yere. **1483** *Cath. Angl.* 127/2 A Fermerer, *jnfirmarius*.

†**'fermerer**[2]. *Sc. Obs.* Forms: 6 fermorar, 7 fermarer, -orer. [f. *fermer*, FARMER[2] + -ER[1].] = FARMER *sb.*[2] 2 and 3.

a **1572** KNOX *Hist. Ref.* IV. (1632) 298 Thair Factours and Fermorars. **1609** SKENE *Reg. Maj., Stat. David II*, 43 Fermorers borne of husband men..may not ficht for the libertie of their predicessours. *Ibid.* Table 79 *Fermarer*, or tenent to any man.

'fermery, 'farmery. *Obs.* exc. *Hist.* Forms: α. 4–6 fermerie, -y(e, 4–7 fermori(e, -y(e, 5 fermary(e, 7 *Hist.* fermarie, firmorie, firmary. β. 6 farmarie, -erye, -ory, 7 farmary, 6– farmery. [aphet. f. OF. *enfermerie*, ad. med L. *infirmāria*: see INFIRMARY.] = INFIRMARY; chiefly, the infirmary of a monastery.

1377 LANGL. *P. Pl.* B. XIII. 108 If ȝe fare so in ȝowre fermorie. *c* **1394** *P. Pl. Crede* 212 Fermery and fraitur with fele mo houses. *c* **1430** *Pilgr. Lyf Manhode* IV. lx. (1869) 205, I wole lede þee with me..in to þe fermerye to reste. *c* **1550** BALE *K. Johan* 82 Gett thee to the farmerye. **1593** *Rites & Mon. Ch. Durh.* (Surtees) 44 A chamber called the Dead Mane's Chamber in the said Farmery. **1611** SPEED *Hist. Gt. Brit.* IX. viii. §62 The rehearsall..of his dying in the Firmary. **1626** SPELMAN *Gloss., Firmarium al. Fermarium*, Angl. a fermarie. **1655** FULLER *Ch. Hist.* VI. ii. 287 Infirmarium or the firmorie. **1891** W. H. ST. J. HOPE in Venables *Chron. de Parco Lude* Introd. 55 Of the farmery (*infirmitorium*)..very little has been made out.

attrib. *a* **1490** BOTONER *Itin.* (Nasmith 1778) 83 The fermarye chyrch continet in longitudine 34 virgas.

fermete, var. of FIRMITY, *Obs.*

Fermi ('fɜːmɪ). [The name of Enrico *Fermi* (1901–54), Italian-born physicist.] **1.** Used attrib. to designate certain principles and concepts arising out of Fermi's work, as ***Fermi* (*coupling*) *constant*, *effect*, *energy*, *gas*, *interaction*, *level*, *liquid*, *sea***; also ***Fermi distribution*, *statistics*** (see FERMI-DIRAC); **Fermi surface**, a surface in momentum space representing the maximum energy, at absolute zero, of the electrons in a crystal with respect to their direction of motion.

1927 *Sci. Abstr.* A. XXX. 741 The Fermi statistics were developed for the electronic gas. **1933** SLATER & FRANK *Introd. Theoret. Physics* xli. 540 In Fig. 83..we plot the potential in which the electrons may be assumed to move. This is constant..throughout the metal, and the horizontal lines symbolize the Fermi levels, filled with electrons at the absolute zero. **1934** *Chem. Abstr.* XXVIII. 7148 (*heading*) The Fermi effect in aluminium. **1936** MOTT & SNEDDON *Theory of Properties of Metals & Alloys* ii. 53 The *mean* kinetic energy of the electrons will be called the 'mean Fermi energy'. **1937** *Chem. Abstr.* XXXI. 3777/1 (*heading*) Theoretical significance of the Fermi constant. **1951** *Nuovo Cimento* VIII. 749 A universal Fermi interaction (that is, a direct interaction with a unique coupling constant among any four of the five particles of spin ½, [etc.]). **1952** *Proc. R. Soc.* A. CCXV. 491 For the group I metals, copper, silver and gold, distortion of the Fermi surface should be small. **1953** E. SEGRÈ *Exper. Nucl. Physics* II. VI. 144 The simplest of the nuclear models, that of the Fermi gas of non-interacting nucleons contained in a well of assigned diameter and depth. **1955** H. B. G. CASIMIR in W. Pauli *Niels Bohr* 119 If the behaviour of the electrons can be described by a Fermi distribution of single electron wave functions, then at the absolute zero all levels up to a certain energy ϵ_0 will be occupied. **1955** *Rev. Mod. Physics* July 252/2 The introduction of the Fermi sea of electrons to rescue the relativistic theory of the electron. **1966** E. J. KONOPINSKI *Theory Beta Radioactivity* iv. 103 A 'Fermi coupling constant', *g*, has been introduced here... It will measure the strength of the *β*-interaction. **1966** *New Scientist* 20 Jan. 155/1 An attempt to draw an analogy between the behaviour of liquid helium-3 at low temperatures and electrons in metals—which constitute what is called a Fermi liquid. **1970** *McGraw-Hill Yearbk. Sci. & Technol.* 187/1 The electronic properties of metals and degenerate semiconductors are largely determined by the behavior of electrons at and near the Fermi surface.

2. (With lower-case initial.) A unit of length used in nuclear physics, equal to 10^{-15} m.

1956 R. HOFSTADTER in *Rev. Mod. Physics* XXVIII. 214/2 Henceforth, we shall measure all distances in terms of 10^{-13} cm as a unit and shall call this unit the fermi. For example, this formula puts the edge of the nuclear sphere of gold at a distance of 8·45 fermis from the center of the nucleus. **1965** C. M. H. SMITH *Textbk. Nucl. Physics* ix. 263 Nuclear radii are approximately given by the formula $r = 1{\cdot}20\,A^{\frac{1}{3}}$ fermi. **1971** *Sci. Amer.* July 101/3 The characteristic distance for a rho-nucleon interaction to occur in nuclear matter..is about three fermis.

Fermi-Dirac (ˌfɜːmɪdɪˈræk). The names of Enrico *Fermi* (see prec.) and P. A. M. *Dirac* (b. 1902), English physicist, used to designate certain results and concepts in physics arising out of their work, as **Fermi-Dirac distribution (function)**, a distribution function of the number of particles in a system of fermions that have a given energy; **Fermi-Dirac statistics**, a type of quantum statistics used to describe systems of identical particles that have wave-functions that are antisymmetric with respect to an interchange of co-ordinates of any two particles.

[**1927** *Proc. R. Soc.* A. CXIII. 433 It has..seemed worth while to reopen the discussion by examining..a quite general form of statistical mechanics of which the classical form and Einstein's and Fermi-Dirac's are special cases.] **1928** *Proc. Physical Soc.* XL. 329 Degeneracy in the Fermi-Dirac statistics occurs when λ is large and negative. **1931** [see EINSTEIN-BOSE]. **1933** HARNWELL & LIVINGGOOD *Exper. Atomic Physics* vi. 192 The distribution function.. which is known as the Fermi-Dirac distribution. **1957** *Encycl. Brit.* VIII. 218/2 The electrons in the metal obey the so-called 'Fermi-Dirac statistics', which means that they have only a very small specific heat. **1968** C. G. KUPER *Introd. Theory Superconductivity* ii. 33 Then the distribution function for quasiparticles will be the normal Fermi-Dirac distribution $f(E) = \{1 + \exp(\beta E)\}^{-1}$, where $\beta = 1/kT$.

† **ˈfermillet.** *Obs.* Also 6 formelet. [a. OF. *fermillet*, *fermaillet*, dim. of *fermail* FERMAIL.] An ornamental clasp, buckle, or setting.

c **1475** *Partenay* 1082 A formelet, of gret ualure beyng, With presious stonis gernesshed that thyng. **1633** J. DONE tr. *Aristeas' Hist. Septuagint* 49 Those Stones were sustayned..by Buckles and Fermillets of Gold for more firmnesse.

fermion (ˈfɜːmɪɒn). [f. the name of E. *Fermi* (see FERMI) + -ON.] A particle that obeys the Fermi-Dirac statistics. Cf. BOSON.

1947 P. A. M. DIRAC *Princ. Quantum Mech.* (ed. 3) ix. 210 It leads to a special statistics, which was first studied by Fermi, so we shall call particles for which only antisymmetrical states occur in nature *fermions*. **1953, 1955** [see BOSON]. **1963** *New Scientist* 1 Aug. 255/1 Only one fermion can exist in a particular state at any given time. **1968** M. S. LIVINGSTON *Particle Physics* iii. 59 It is found experimentally that electrons, protons, and neutrons are all fermions and that they have intrinsic spin $s = \frac{1}{2}(h/2\pi)$.

† **ˈfermison.** *Obs.* Forms: 4 fermyson, -soun, 5 fermeson. [a. AF. *fermyson*, OF. *fermeyson*, *fermoyson*:—L. *firmātiōn-em*, n. of action f. *firmāre*, in med.L. to close (F. *fermer*).]

1. A close-time for the male deer. *attrib.*

[**1248** *Foot of Fines* (Record Office), co. Stafford, Quod Hugo et heredes sui..quolibet anno possint capere in predicto parco unam damam in fermisona inter festum Sancti Martini et Purificationem Beatæ Mariæ et unum damum in pinguedine inter festum Sanctæ Crucis in Mayo et festum Sanctæ Crucis in Septembri. *c* **1325** *Gloss. W. de Biblesw.* in Wright *Voc.* 174 Assez par my la mesoun De treste du fermeyson [*Eng. Gloss.* taken of gres tyme].] *c* **1340** *Gaw. & Gr. Knt.* 1156 þe fre lorde hade de-fende in fermysoun tyme þat þer schulde no mon mene to þe male dere. ? *a* **1400** *Morte Arth.* 180 Fflesch fluriste of fermysone.

2. A place where deer were kept.

c **1420** *Anturs of Arth.* (Camden) i, By fermesones by frythys, and felles.

fermium (ˈfɜːmɪəm). *Chem.* [f. the name of E. *Fermi* (see FERMI) + -IUM.] An artificially produced radioactive element, atomic number 100. Symbol Fm.

1955 A. GHIORSO et al. in *Physical Rev.* 1 Aug. 1049/1 We suggest for the element with the atomic number 99 the name einsteinium (symbol E) after Albert Einstein, and for the element with atomic number 100 the name fermium (symbol Fm), after Enrico Fermi. **1957** KATZ & SEABORG *Chem. Actinide Elements* x. 403 In all respects fermium in aqueous solutions behaves as a tripositive ion. **1966** *New Scientist* 23 June 774/1 Fermium-257, hitherto the heaviest material ever created by man.

fermorite (ˈfɜːməraɪt). *Min.* [f. name of Sir Lewis *Fermor* (1880–1954), of the Geological Survey of India: see -ITE[1].] An arsenate and phosphate of calcium and strontium in the apatite group.

1910 PRIOR & SMITH in *Nature* 23 June 513/1 The name fermorite, after Dr. L. L. Fermor, of the Geological Survey of India,..is proposed for this analogue. **1938** *Amer. Mineralogist* XXIII. 11 Fermorite is an example of the substitution of Sr for Ca but this mineral also shows an appreciable substitution of As for P. **1959** [see ELLESTADITE].

† **fern,** *a.* and *adv. Obs.* Forms: 1 fyrn, 3 fer(r)en, (furne), 3 *Layamon* v(e)orne, 4–5 fern, (4 feorn, 6 farne). Also (as *adv.* and in *Comb.*) with prefix, 1 ȝefyrn, 2 ȝefern, 3 ifurn, ivurn, ifeorn, iv(e)orn, 4 yfern. [Perh. repr. two different but synonymous formations (from different ablaut-grades of the same root). The OE. *fyrn* with *y* from *u*, an *-i* stem that has passed into the *-o* declension, seems to be a peculiarly Eng. formation (perh. in origin a sb., as the form with prefixed *ȝe* may suggest), cognate with OS. *furn*, *forn* adv. formerly (also in comb. *an furndagon* = OE. *on fyrndaȝum*), OHG. *forn* (MHG. *vorn*) formerly, ON. *forn* adj. ancient (Sw. *forn*). The sense 'of last year', though not recorded before the ME. period, seems to point to an OE. **fierne*, which would correspond to OS. *fern* past (of years), OHG. *firni* old (MHG. *virne* old, *verne* adv. last year, mod.Ger. *firne* old, of last year), Goth. *fairneis* old:—OTeut. **fernjo-*, cognate with Lith. *pernai* adv., last year.]

A. *adj.*

1. Of time: Former, ancient, of old.

After 15th c. only in phrase *old fern days* or *years*; cf. 3 and FERNYEAR.

a **1000** *Riddles* lxxxi. 9 (Gr.) Fyrn forð-ȝesceaft. *c* **1275** LAY. 24795 Julius..þat in vorne daȝe bi-wan hit mid fihte. *c* **1300** *K. Alis.* 6356 Feorne men..Clepeth heom Agofagy. *a* **1400** *Octouian* 477 Hyt ys well fern men seyden so. **1529, 1562** [see FERNYEAR A. 1]. **1571** BP. LESLEY *Title Success.* II. 6 b, I might here fetche foorth olde farne dayes.

2. *fern year*: last year: see FERNYEAR.

3. *Comb.* **fern-days**, days of old.

a **1000** *Andreas* 753 (Gr.) þis is se ilca ealwalda god þone on fyrndagum fæderas cuðon. *c* **1205** LAY. 27118 þat Merlin i furn daȝen seide.

B. *adv.* Long ago, of old, formerly, a long time.

α. *a* **1000** *Guthlac* 841 (Gr.) þone bitran drync þone Eve fyrn Adame geaf. *c* **1200** *Trin. Coll. Hom.* 59 Feren it is þat we and ure heldrene habbeð ben turnd fro him. *Ibid.* 161 Hit is ferren atleien holie tiðe. **1377** LANGL. *P. Pl.* B. xv. 226 It is ferne [*v.r.* fern] agoo in seynt Fraunceys tyme. *c* **1386** CHAUCER *Sqr.'s T.* 248 For they han knowen it so fern. *c* **1422** HOCCLEVE *Jereslaus's Wife* 199 It is ago fern syn I spak yow to Of loue.

β. *c* **1000** *Wulfstan* (Napier) xviii. 104 Eala, ȝefyrn is, þæt ðurh deofol fela þinga misfor. *c* **1205** LAY. 24017 þa iuurn here stoden. *a* **1250** *Owl & Night.* 1306 Heo were ifurn of prestes muþe Amansed. *c* **1275** in *O.E. Misc.* (1872) 193 Ifurn ich habbe isunehed mid worke and mid worde. *c* **1380** *Sir Ferumb.* 3207 Wel y-fern þay holpe ous nouȝt.

fern (fɜːn), *sb.*[1] Forms: 1 fearn, 3 *south.* værne, 4–7 ferne, 6–7 fearn(e, (6 *Sc.* farne, 7 fyrne, 9 *dial.* fearn), 7 ferron, 6– fern. [OE. *fearn* str. neut. = MDu. *væren* (Du. *varen*), OHG. *farn*, *farm* (MHG. *varn*, *varm*, mod.Ger. *farn*) neut. and masc. (not recorded in ON., but cf. Sw. dial. *fänne* :—ON. **ferne*):—OTeut. **farno-*:—OAryan **porno-*, whence Skr. *parna* neut., wing, feather, leaf. The primitive meaning of the word is doubtless 'feather'; for the transferred application cf. Gr. πτερόν feather, πτερίς fern.]

1. One of a large group of vascular cryptogamous plants constituting the N.O. *Filices*; a single plant or frond of the same; also *collect.* in *sing.*

flowering or **royal fern**: *Osmunda regalis*; see OSMUND. **hard fern** = *Blechnum*. **lady-fern** = *Athyrium filix femina*. **male fern** = *Lastrea filix-mas*. **prickly fern** = *Polystichum aculeatum*.

For *bladder-*, *buckler-*, *hare-foot-*, *holly-*, *maidenhair-*, *tree-*, etc. *fern*, see those words.

a **800** *Corpus Gloss.*, *Filix*, fearn. *c* **888** K. ÆLFRED *Boeth.* xxiii. §1 Atio ærest of þa þornas & þa fyrsas & þæt fearn. *c* **1205** LAY. 12817, I wude i wilderne inne hæðe & inne uærne. *c* **1330** *Arth. & Merl.* 8875 No gaf he ther of nought a ferne. *c* **1386** CHAUCER *Sqr.'s T.* 247 Yit is glas nought like aisschen of ferne. *c* **1400** MAUNDEV. (1839) xxxi. 307 Tentes, made of black Ferne. **1477** NORTON *Ord. Alch.* vi. in Ashm. (1652) 95 Of Ashes of Ferne. **1523** FITZHERB. *Surv.* 6 b, Brome, gorse, fyrs, braken, ferne. **1621** SIR R. BOYLE in *Lismore Pap.* (1886) II. 16 He is to vse ffyrnes and heath, but not wood to brew withal. **1639** T. DE GRAY *Compl. Horseman* 319 Take the root of male brake or fearn. **1771** SMOLLETT *Humph. Cl.* (1815) 259 A brown desert..that produces nothing but heath and fern. **1814** SCOTT *Ld. of Isles* v. xix, The tall fern obscured the lawn. **1842** TENNYSON *Talking Oak* 201 Hidden deep in fern.

2. a. *attrib.* and *Comb.*: simple attrib., as *fern-ashes*, *-bracken*, *-bug*, *-bush*, *-covert*, *-faggot*, *-frond*, *-harvest*, *-leaf*, *-moth* (also *ellipt.*), *-plant*, *-root*, *-spore*, *-stalk*, *-stem*, *-tuft*, *-weevil*; objective, as *fern-gatherer*, *-grower*, *-lover*, *-thief*; instrumental and parasynthetic, as *fern-clad*, *-crowned*, *-fringed*, *-leaved*, *-thatched* adjs.; similative, as *fern-like* adj.

c **1386** CHAUCER *Sqr.'s T.* 246 To maken of *fern asshen glas. **1745** *Beverley Beck Act* ii. 2 Every quarter of fern ashes. **1959** SOUTHWOOD & LESTON *Land & Water Bugs* viii. 203 *Bryocoris pteridis*,..*fernbug. Widely distributed in the British Isles this bug feeds on ferns. **1567** JEWEL *Def. Apol.* II. 255 In like order of reason he might haue saide it is not a *fearn bushe. **1580** LYLY *Euphues* (Arb.) 319 It is a blynde Goose that knoweth not a Foxe from a Fearne-bush. **1841** LEVER *C. O'Malley* cviii, An apparently endless succession of *fern-clad hills. **1859** G. MEREDITH *R. Feverel* xxi, A pine overlooking the *fern-covert. **1612** DRAYTON *Poly-olb.* xvii. 23 The *Fearne-crown'd Flood. **1703** T. N. *City & C. Purchaser* 47 Heath, Brake, or *Fern Faggots. **1842** FABER *Styrian Lake* 131 The *fern-fringed wall. **1879** *Encycl. Brit.* IX. 101/1 Columna in 1648 compared the *fern frond to butcher's broom. **1886** HALL CAINE *Son of Hagar* III. xi, I'm a *fern-gatherer. **1864** T. MOORE *Brit. Ferns* 15 The amateur *Ferngrower. **1855** MRS. GASKELL *North & S.* ii, The *Fern-harvest was over. **1688** R. HOLME *Armoury* II. iv. 60/2 He beareth Argent, a *Fern leaf, Vert. **1937** *Burlington Mag.* Aug. 89/2 Fragments of these Fern Leaf Jars. **1840** MRS. NORTON *Dream* 82 *Fern-leaved Mimosa. **1650** How *Phytologia Brit.* 77 *Muscus filicinus* Park. *Fernlike Mosse. **1884** BOWER & SCOTT *De Bary's Phaner.* 179 In..Fern-like plants tubes are found. **1865** N. BELLAIRS *Hardy Ferns* x. 112, I did what I advise other *Fern-lovers to do. **1909** *Daily Chron.* 11 Feb. 3/3 Fern lovers throughout the kingdom are waging a war with the fern grubber. **1908** R. SOUTH *Moths Brit. Is.* II. 257 (*heading*) The *Fern (*Phibalapteryx* (*Coenocalpe*) *tersata*). **1958** W. J. STOKOE *Caterp. Brit. Moths* (rev. ed.) II. 155 (*heading*) The Fern Moth. *Horisme tersata*. **1882** VINES *Sach's Bot.* 225 Gulbs from which *Fern-plants are directly developed. **1480** CAXTON *Chron. Eng.* ccli. 322 Poure peple made hem brede of *fern rotes. **1753** CHAMBERS *Cycl. Supp.*, *Fern-root* was frequently prescribed by the antients in diet-drinks, for removing obstructions. **1589** R. HARVEY *Pl. Perc.* 13, I thinke the mad slaue, hath tasted on a *ferne-stalke, that he walkes so invisible. **1884** BOWER & SCOTT *De Bary's Phaner.* 289 A number of *Fern-stems with leaves in many rows. **1614** SYLVESTER *Bethulia's Rescue* III. 29 Their *Fern-thatcht Towns. **1888** *Athenæum* 21 July 105/2 Some *fern thieves were captured. *a* **1835** MRS. HEMANS *Poems, Hour of Romance*, Under the *fern-tufts. **1959** E. F. LINSSEN *Beetles Brit. Is.* II. 206 The Australian *Fern Weevils..one of these, *Syagrius intrudens*..has been introduced into our islands.

b. Special comb.: **fern-allies**, plants of a nature allied to that of ferns; **fern-bird** *N.Z.*, a bird of the genus *Bowdleria*; **fern-bracken** = BRACKEN (Britten & H.); **fern-brake**, (*a*) = prec.; (*b*) a thicket of fern; † **fern-bud**, a kind of fern-fly, used by anglers; **fern-chafer**, a beetle (*Scarabæus* or *Amphimalla solstitialis*); **fern-crushing** *N.Z.* (see quot. 1947); so **fern-crusher**; also *fern-crushed a.*; **fern-cup**, the cup-like form of the fern just after coming through the ground; **fern-fly**, a fly frequenting fern; **fern-gale**, the Sweet Fern (*Myrica Comptonia*); **fern-grinding** *N.Z.*, = *fern-crushing*; **fern-house**, a conservatory in which ferns are grown; **fern-land**, (*a*) land covered with fern *N.Z.*; (*b*) a name applied, esp. by Australians, to New Zealand; **Fernleaf** (see quots.); **fern-moss**, a genus of mosses, *Fissidens*; **fern-oil** (see quot.); † **fern-sitter**, a name given to the hare; **fern-tree** = *tree-fern*; **fern-web**, a beetle (*Scarabæus* or *Melorontha horticola*). Also FERN-OWL, -SEED.

1879 *Encycl. Brit.* IX. 100/2 Groups..often spoken of.. as *Fern-allies. **1882** W. L. BULLER *Man. Birds N.Z.* 17 *Sphenocacus punctatus*. Quoy and Gaim. *Fern-bird. Utick. Matata. **1888** Fern-bird [see *swamp sparrow* (b)]. **1963** *Weekly News* (Auckland) 26 June 31 Fern-birds habitually nest among the raupo reeds. **1611** CHAPMAN *May Day* Plays 1873 II. 352 A bath of *fernebraks for your fustie bodie. **1622** FLETCHER *Beggar's Bush* v. i, Your breech is safe enough: the wolf's a fern-brake. **1760** *Walton & Cotton's Angler* App. (1760) 121 **Fern-Bud*, this fly is got on Fern. **1774** G. WHITE *Selborne* lx. 103 The appearance..of the *fern-chafer. **1816** KIRBY & SP. *Entomol.* xvi. (1828) II. 5. Of this nature seems to be that of the cockchafer and fern-chafer. **1891** R. WALLACE *Rural Econ. Austral. & N.Z.* xv. 231 In the New Zealand climate *fern-crushed pasture-land of good and medium quality will support one to three sheep per acre. **1916** *N.Z. Jrnl. Agric.* 20 June 435 Cattle are often looked upon as more efficient fern-crushers than are sheep on land suitable for cattle. **1891** R. WALLACE *Rural Econ. Austral. & N.Z.* xv. 230 **Fern crushing*. Of the fern country, that upon a limestone formation is the best and the least expensive to break in. **1947** A. CLARK in H. Belshaw *N.Z.* ii. 40 Hence beef-cattle are used for 'fern-crushing', that is, for keeping in check the undesirable second growth of bracken fern over large areas of the North Island hills. **1888** *Pall Mall G.* 4 July 5/1 In their nightly gambols through my garden they too often destroy..my choicest *fern-cups. **1676** COTTON *Angler* II. 330 The *Fern-fly..is of the colour of Fern or Bracken. **1686** PLOT *Staffordsh.* 233 The Fern-Flyes..feed on the young corn and grass, and hinder their growth. **1867** F. FRANCIS *Angling* vi. (1880) 230 The Fern Fly..known to children..as, 'Soldiers and Sailors'. **1921** H. GUTHRIE-SMITH *Tutira* xvii. 134 The operation known..as 'fern-crushing' or '*fern-grinding'. **1847** J. PAGET *Mem. & Lett.* 15 Sept. (1901) 157 You who occasionally see green fields cannot imagine the refreshment of my *fern-house. **1851** *Gardeners' Chron.* 27 Dec. 823/2 We entertain no doubt about cold Fern houses becoming in time as common as greenhouses. **1891** L. T. MEADE *Sweet Girl Graduate* x. 89 I'll take you into our fern-house... We have got such exquisite maidenhairs. **1943** K. TENNANT *Ride on Stranger* (1968) viii. 82 He had plenty of time to..tend the ferns in a dirty little fernhouse. **1843** *N.Z. Company Rep.* (1844) I Dec. XIV. 121 The facilities, however, which *fern land offers, compared with bush or flax land, has induced a large proportion of the settlers to prefer it for their first operation. **1933** *Bulletin* (Sydney) 13 Sept. 10/2 Willeby has written nothing with the slightest flavour of Fernland. **1916** *Chrons. N.Z.E.F.* 15 Nov. 127/1 Call them 'Over-seas soldiers' or 'Down-under' men,..Call them 'Corn-stalks' or '*Fernleaves'—all out for a fight—But don't call them Anzacs, for that isn't right. **1925** FRASER & GIBBONS *Soldier & Sailor Words* 93 *Fernleaves*, a familiar term for the New Zealanders. (From the New Zealand badge.) **1698** J. PETIVER in *Phil. Trans.* XX. 398 Our common *Fern Moss. **1868** TRIPP *Brit. Mosses* 181 Marsh Fern Moss..Rock Fern Moss. **1753** CHAMBERS *Cycl. Supp.*, **Fern-oil* in pottery, a name given..to a sort of varnish, which the Chinese use in their porcelain manufactories. It is also called lime-oil.

a **1325** *Names of Hare* in *Rel. Ant.* I. 134 The hare The liȝtt-fot, the *fernsittere. **1827** HELLYER in Bischoff *Van Diemen's Land* (1852) 166 *Fern trees twenty feet in height. **1884** BOLDREWOOD *Melb. Mem.* xx. 147 Picnics to fern-tree gullies..were successfully carried out. **1796** W. MARSHALL *W. Devon. Gloss.*, *Fern-web. **1869** BLACKMORE *Lorna D.* vii. (ed. 12) 37 With a hook and a bit of worm on it, or a fern-web.

Hence **ferned** *ppl. a.*, fern-grown; **'fernist**, one who cultivates or takes an interest in ferns; **'fernless** *a.*, devoid of ferns.

1845 HIRST *Poems* 155, I tread on ferned and laurelled hills. **1865** *Athenæum* No. 1959. 648/3 The fernist of meanest capacity. **1888** —— 21 July 105/2 Fairlight Glen, once the loveliest spot on the southern coast, now almost fernless. **1893** T. E. BROWN *Old John, etc.* 177 Rose plot, Fringed pool, Ferned grot.

† **fern**, *sb.*[2] *Obs.* [perh. repr. OE. *firen*, ON. *firn* pl., orig. a crime, monstrous thing; for the sense cf. mod.Icel. *firní* 'a great deal, a lot' (Vigf.).] A huge quantity or number.

a **1300** *Cursor M.* 3998 (Cott.) O þis gret aght þou has me lent I sal gret fern be-for me sent. *c* **1325** *Metr. Hom.* 126 A lazer..Com and asked Crist his hele, Bifor that fern of folc sa fele.

fern, *sb.*[3] *Obs.* exc. *dial.* Also 4, 6 verne, 7 fearne. [ME. *verne*, perh. f. VIRON to go round, a. F. *vironner*, f. *viron* circuit.] A windlass.

[*a* **1327** *Acc. Works Westm. Palace* in *Promp. Parv.* 510 *note*, Gynes voc' fernes. **1328** *Ibid.*, Circa facturam cujusdam verne sive ingenii.] **1546** LANGLEY *Pol. Verg. De Invent.* II. vii. 47b, Cranes or Vernes to winde up great Weightes. **1574** *Nottingham Rec.* IV. 155 The vse of a ferne to lode the tymber wyth. **1611** COTGR., *Moulinet à brassières*, the barrell of a windlasse or fearne. *Ibid.*, *Chevie*, the engine called by architects, etc. a fearne. **1847–78** HALLIWELL, *Fearn*, a windlass. *Linc.*

fern (fɜːn), *v.* [f. FERN *sb.*[1]]

1. *trans.* To cover with fern.

c **1420** *Pallad. on Husb.* I. 338 The mapul, ooke and assche endureth longe In floryng yf thou ferne it welle. **1862** *Macm. Mag.* Sept. 426 How was it [island] lichened and mossed, ferned and heathed?

2. *intr.* To feed upon fern. ? *Obs.*

1576 TURBERV. *Venerie* 153 When he feedeth on fearne or rootes, then it is called rowting or fearning. **1688** R. HOLME *Armoury* II. 135/2 For the Feeding..if..Boar and Swine..be in open Grounds, on Heaths..they are Fearning.

fernambu(c)k, etc., obs. varr. PERNAMBUCO.

fernery ('fɜːnərɪ). [f. FERN *sb.*[1] + -ERY.] A place or a glass-case where ferns are grown.

1840 E. NEWMAN *Brit. Ferns* Introd. (1844) 11 A fernery ..should possess..a pure atmosphere. **1863** BATES *Nat. Amazon* I. 70 The whole forest glade formed a vast fernery. **1865** N. BELLAIRS *Hardy Ferns* v. 48, I had a Fernery made for my spoils. *Ibid.* v. 58 Nothing but Ferns should be planted in a Fernery. **1895** E. J. LOWE *Fern Growing* 159 For bog Ferns, a low part of the Fernery well flooded twice a day will be a good substitution for a marsh. **1969** *Sydney Morning Herald* 24 May 48/10 (Advt.), Large fibro-tiled Home, 3 bedrooms,..toolshed, fernery, garage.

fernicle, var. of VERNICLE, *Obs.*

† **fern-osmund.** *Obs. rare*[−1]. [f. FERN *sb.*[1] + OSMUND.] The Royal Fern, *Osmunda regalis*.

1614 MARKHAM *Cheap Husb.* Table of Hard Words, *Ferne Osmund* is an hearbe of some called *Water-Ferne*, hath a trianguler stalke..and it growes in Boggs. *Ibid.* I. lxvi. 39. [Some later editions have the misprinted form *fernsmund*, which has been copied into mod. Dicts.]

'fern-owl. [f. FERN *sb.*[1] + OWL.] **a.** The Nightjar or Goatsucker, *Caprimulgus europæus*; **b.** the Short-eared owl, *Asio brachyotus*.

a. 1678 RAY *Willughby's Ornith.* II. iii. §1. 107 The Fern-owl..or Goat-sucker, *Caprimulgus*. **1793** G. WHITE *Selborne* (1853) II. xxx. 246 Not long after a fern owl was procured. **1832–5** E. JESSE *Glean. Nat. Hist.* (1843) 221 The fern-owl, or night-jar. **1870** MORRIS *Earthly Par.* II. III. 44 'Midst bittern's boom and fern-owl's cry.

b. 1885 SWAINSON *Prov. Names Brit. Birds* 129 Short-eared owl..Fern-Owl (Ireland).

'fern-seed. The 'seed' of the fern. Before the mode of reproduction of ferns was understood, they were popularly supposed to produce an invisible seed, which was capable of communicating its invisibility to any person who possessed it.

1596 SHAKS. *1 Hen. IV*, II. i. 96 We haue the receit of Fern-seede, we walke inuisible. **1630** B. JONSON *New Inn* I. Wks. (Rtldg.) 411/1, I had No med'cine, sir, to go invisible; No fern-seed in my pocket. **1756** SMART *Horat. Canons Friendsh.* 76 Ask thy heart, if Custom..Hath sown no undiscover'd fern-seed there. **1815** SCOTT *Guy Mann.* xlv, 'They say she has gathered the fern-seed and can gang ony gate she likes.' **1859** SALA *Tw. round Clock* (1861) 266 We.. are in the receipt of fern-seed, and can walk invisible.

fernshaw ('fɜːnʃɔː). [f. FERN + SHAW.] A brake or thicket of fern.

1845 BROWNING *Flight of Duchess* xiii, Some story or other Of hill or dale, oakwood or fernshaw.

fernticle ('fɜːntɪk(ə)l). *Obs.* exc. *dial.* Also 5 **farntikylle, ferntykll e, 6 fayrntikle, 9 fantic(k)le, farntic(k)le,** *Sc.* **fairnitickle.** 'A freckle on the skin, resembling the seed of fern' (W.).

1483 *Cath. Angl.* 123/1 A Farntikylle, *lenticula*. *Ibid.* 128/1 A Ferntykylle, *cesia*. **1551** TURNER *Herbal* I. (1568) P iij a, Rocket..taketh away frekles or fayrntikles with vinegre. **1876** *Whitby Gloss.*, *Farnticles*..the brown 'pin point pops' clustered in the complexion.

Hence **'fernticled** *ppl. a.*, freckled.

1483 *Cath. Angl.* 123/1 Farntykylde, *lentiginosus*. **1719** D'URFEY *Pills* VI. 351 Pluggy fac'd Wat..And..farnicled Huggy. **1880** *Antrim & Down Gloss.*, *Farn-tickled*.

ferny ('fɜːnɪ), *a.* [f. FERN *sb.*[1] + -Y[1].]

1. Abounding in fern, overgrown with fern.

1523 FITZHERB. *Husb.* §50 That sycknes is moste commonly on..ferny grounde. **1667** *Phil. Trans.* II. 525 The Surface thereof..is Heathy, Ferny and Furzy. *a* **1722** LISLE *Husb.* (1752) 4 A red, sandy, ferny ground. **1808** SCOTT *Marm.* IV. xv, The wild buck bells from ferny brake. **1860** DONALDSON *Bush Lays* 87 The flat ferny wastes all lie sleeping.

2. Of or pertaining to fern, consisting of fern.

1710 PHILLIPS *Pastorals* vi. 29 When Locusts in the Fearny Bushes cry. *a* **1717** PARNELL *Flies* 72 Your ferny shade forsakes the vale. **1804** J. GRAHAME *Sabbath* (1808) 67 Woodless its banks but green with ferny leaves. **1884** *Bazaar* 10 Dec. 621/5 A..gorsy, ferny growth.

3. Of a fern-like nature, resembling fern.

1791 E. DARWIN *Bot. Gard.* I. 76 Ferny foliage. **1870** J. RHOADES *Poems* 131 Every pane is hoar with ferny rime.

† **'fernyear, fern year,** *sb.* and *adv.* *Obs.* Forms: α. 1 fyrnȝéar, 4 fernȝere, -yere, (5 ferner), 5, 8, 9 fernyear, 9 *Sc.* foirnyear. β. 3 ivurnȝer. [OE. *fyrnȝéar*: see FERN *a.* and YEAR[1]. From 14th c. often as two words, the adj. being inflected in ME.] **A.** *sb.*

1. A past year.

c **1000** *Gnomic Vers.* (Cott.) 12 (Gr.) Fyrnȝearum frod. *c* **1205** LAY. 25139, I þan iuurn ȝere. **1377** LANGL. *P. Pl.* B. XII. 5 How fele fernȝeres are faren and so fewe to come. **1481** CAXTON *Reynard* (Arb.) 32 Yf myn aunte..bethought her wel of olde ferners she wolde not suffre that I shold haue ony harme. **1529** MORE *Supplic. Soulys* Wks. 296/1 Old farne yeres. **1562** J. HEYWOOD *Prov. & Epigr.* (1867) 4 Ye regarde ..good prouerbes of olde ferne yeeres.

2. Last year, 'yester-year'. [Cf. mod.Ger. *firnewein* wine of last year.]

¶Skinner took Chaucer's *ferne yere* to mean February! Hence in COLES 1692–1732.

c **1374** CHAUCER *Troylus* v. 1176 Farwel al the snowgh of ferne yere! **1406** HOCCLEVE *La Male Regle* 423, I dar nat speke a word of ferne yeer. **15..** *Sir Egeir* (1711) 19 He.. then told him a fern-years tale. **1737** RAMSAY *Scot. Prov.* xviii. 14 If I live anither year, I'll ca' this year fern-year.

B. *adv.* **a.** In past years. [Cf. OE. *fyrnȝéara*, where the second element = YORE *adv.*] **b.** In the course of last year.

[*c* **1000** *Ags. Ps.* (Thorpe) xciv. 9 [xcv. 8] Swa on grimnesse, fyrn-ȝeara dydan.] **1377** LANGL. *P. Pl.* B. v. 440 The kyndenesse þat myne euene-cristene kidde me fernyere. **1786** *Harvest Rig* in Chambers *Pop. Poems Scot.* (1862) 62 They'll..reckon up what time fernyear The kirn was held. **1806** J. NICOL *Poems* II. 3 (Jam.) He, fairnyear, 'gainst the en'mie's power, Wi a choice gang had wander'd.

† **fe'roce,** *a.* *Obs. rare.*[−1] [ad. L. *ferōce-m*, *ferox*.] = FEROCIOUS *a.*

1641 J. JACKSON *True Evang. T.* I. 70 Feroce and belluine men [shal cohabit] with the meek and placable.

† **fe'rocient,** *a.* *Obs.* [ad. L. *ferōcient-em*, pr. pple. of *ferōcīre*, f. *ferox* fierce.] Raging ferociously.

1654 H. L'ESTRANGE *Chas. I* (1655) 94 So ferocient it [fire] was, as the Ambassadour..hardly..escaped. **1655–62** H. MORE *Antid. Atheism* (1662) 182 [Apostate spirits] that are more ferocient. **1684** tr. *Bonet's Merc. Compit.* VI. 176 Vitriolate Acidity..able to..coagulate the ferocient Spirits.

ferocify (fə'rɒsɪfaɪ), *v.* [f. L. *ferōci-* stem of *ferox* + -FY.] *trans.* To make ferocious or fierce.

1855 in Ogilvie Supp.

ferocious (fə'rəʊʃəs), *a.* [f. L. *ferōci-*, *ferox* fierce, ferocious + -OUS.]

1. Of animals or persons, their dispositions or actions: Fierce, savage; savagely cruel or destructive.

1646 SIR T. BROWNE *Pseud. Ep.* III. xvi. 144 The Lyon a ..ferocious animall hath young ones but seldome. **1791** BOSWELL *Johnson* (1816) III. 87 He was by no means of that ferocious..character. **1794** SULLIVAN *View Nat.* I. 188 The most..ferocious beasts are alarmed by it. **1828** SCOTT *F.M. Perth* xxiii, One whom they had been taught to consider as a ferocious..libertine. *a* **1853** ROBERTSON *Lect.* ii. (1858) 76, I cannot see anything manly in that ferocious struggle. **1886** SHELDON tr. *Flaubert's Salammbo* 1 And pits for ferocious animals.

Comb. **1849** JAMES *Woodman* ii, Is he a ferocious-looking man?

2. Indicating or characterized by ferocity.

1728 POPE *Dunc.* II. 328 Slow rose a form..shaking..And each ferocious feature grim with ooze. **1826** KIRBY & SP. *Entomol.* xlvii. (1828) IV. 418 Their prominent or ferocious eyes.

Hence **fe'rociously** *adv.* **fe'rociousness.**

1766 FORDYCE *Serm. Yng. Wom.* (1767) II. xiii. 223 Roughness, and even ferociousness, in a man, we often overlook. **1775** MRS. HARRIS in *Priv. Lett. Ld. Malmesbury* I. 303 He [Dr. Johnson] feeds nastily and ferociously. **1818** HALLAM *Mid. Ages* (1872) I. 52 The respect which was felt ..mitigated in all the rancour and ferociousness of hostility. **1856** KANE *Arct. Expl.* I. xxix. 394 They [rats] gnawed her feet and nails so ferociously that we drew her up yelping. **1867** MISS BRADDON *Aur. Floyd* i. 10 They hate me so ferociously.

† **fe'rocitate,** *v.* *Obs.* [f. FEROCITY + -ATE.] *trans.* To make ferocious; to taint with fierceness.

1666 G. HARVEY *Morb. Angl.* iv. 49 The salin..is apt to ferocitate and irritate the spirits.

ferocity (fə'rɒsɪtɪ). [ad. Fr. *férocité*, ad. L. *ferōcitāt-em*, f. *ferox* FEROCIOUS.] The quality or state of being ferocious; habitual fierceness or savageness; an instance of the same.

1606 WARNER *Alb. Eng.* XIV. lxxxvi. (1612) 355 With such perseuerant hatred and ferocitie. **1749** FIELDING *Tom Jones* II. iv, Grimalkin..degenerates not in ferosity from the elder branches of her house. **1793** BURKE *Policy of Allies* Wks. 1842 I. 594 Such their ferocity..that no engagement would hold with them for three months. **1831** CARLYLE *Misc.* (1857) II. 213 These ferocities and Sibylline frenzies. **1851** RUSKIN *Mod. Paint.* II. III. I. xiv. §28 It [fear] is always joined with ferocity.

ferocize (fə'rəʊsaɪz), *v. rare*[−1]. [f. L. *ferōc-em* + -IZE.] *trans.* To make ferocious.

1816 W. TAYLOR in *Monthly Rev.* LXXXI. 537 That hatred of war which..ferocizes man.

Feroese, var. FAROESE.

† **'ferous,** *a.* *Obs. rare.*[−1] [f. L. *fer-us* wild + -OUS.] Wild, savage.

1653 A. WILSON *Jas. I.* 75 To chace away those ferous, and indomitable Creatures.

-ferous, in actual use always **-iferous** ('ɪfərəs), an adjectival suffix f. L. *-fer* producing (f. *ferre* to bear) + -OUS. In Lat. the suffix *-fer* was always preceded by *ĭ*, either belonging to the stem as in *pestifer*, substituted for the stem-vowel as in *sensifer*, or inserted as a connecting vowel as in *ærifer*; so that the suffix practically appears in Lat. as *-ifer*, and in Eng. as *-iferous*. In Eng. it appeared first in words taken from Lat., either directly or through Fr. adaptations in *-fère*, as in *auriferous*, *bacciferous*, *biferous*, *cruciferous*, *frugiferous*, *glandiferous*, *lactiferous*, *metalliferous*, *odoriferous*, *pomiferous*, *rosiferous*, *soporiferous*, *thuriferous*, *vociferous*. On the analogy thus established *-iferous* became a living English suffix, capable of combining with any Latin stem, and forms an unlimited number of derivatives, *esp.* in Natural History, as *acidiferous*, *argentiferous*, *carboniferous*, *cocciferous*, *fossiliferous*, *lucriferous*, *sanguiferous*, *umbelliferous*.

ferow, obs. form of FARROW *a.*

ferox ('fɛrɒks). [a. L. (*salmo*) *ferox* lit. 'fierce salmon', the scientific name.] A fish (*Salmo ferox*), the great Lake Trout.

1867 F. FRANCIS *Angling* xi. (1880) 403 Lough Melvin.. contains salmon grilse, charr, ferox. **1884** M. G. WATKINS in *Longm. Mag.* June 176 Every now and then we had a ferox for dinner.

ferozone ('fɛrəʊzəʊn). Also ferro-. [Formerly a proprietary name, app. arbitrarily formed.] A mineral substance containing ferrous sulphate and other metal salts formerly used as a precipitant in the treatment of sewage.

1888 *Brit. Pat.* 11,663 8 *Treatment of Sewage*... Use corresponding sized pieces of basic-cinder or slag the refuse of steel works or ferozone or gypsum..or other porous and water purifying material. **1898** [see POLARITE]. **1910** MAXWELL & BROWN *Encycl. Municip. & Sanit. Engin.* 164/1 The object of 'ferozone' is to act as a precipitant and to assist in the disinfection and deodorisation of the sewage and sludge. **1927** T. H. P. VEAL *Disposal of Sewage* v. 66 Alumino-ferric and ferrozone are more expensive than lime but are more easily applied.

ferr(e, obs. form of FAR *sb.*, *a.*, and *v.*

‖ **ferra** ('fɛrə). Also fera, and in Fr. form féra. [Local It.] A species of whitefish, *Coregonus fera*, of the family Salmonidæ, found in the Swiss lakes and Lake Como.

1807 [see POLLAN]. **1879** *Encycl. Brit.* X. 152/1 The Lake of Geneva is not so rich in fish as many of the smaller lakes of Switzerland... The 'fera' (*Coregonus fera*) is economically the most important species. **1925** *Glasgow Herald* 5 Aug. 8 The 'ferra' of Lake Geneva. **1930** A. BENNETT *Imperial Palace* xl. 286 My Feras have arrived. **1966** P. V. PRICE *France* 307 The mountain lakes and streams yield fine fish, of which three..are unlikely to be found elsewhere—the *féra*, *lavaret* and *omble chevalier*; all are types of salmon, but the last looks more like a trout.

ferrade, var. of FERRED *Obs.*

ferrage, obs. form of FERRIAGE.

ferrall, obs. form of FERULE.

† **'ferrament.** *Obs.* Forms: 5 ferremen(t, 5–7 ferrament, (ferment). [a. OF. *ferrement*, ad. L. *ferrāment-um* implement of iron, after which the word was refashioned. Cf. FARREMENT.] In *pl.*

Articles of iron; iron instruments or tools; irons, shackles; iron fittings, ironwork.

a **1440** *Found. St. Bartholomew's* 37 Hym-self so chargid with ferramentys and Iryns. **1446** *Yatton Churchw. Acc.* (Somerset Rec. Soc.) 84 It. payd for ferments to the stepyl wyndows..vii^s. x^d. **1474** CAXTON *Chesse* III. v. (1860) G vj, The fferremens and Instrumentis that hangen on the gurdel. **1489** —— *Faytes of A.* II. xxiii. 137 Cartes with ferrementes for to carie the roddes for the engins. *Ibid.* II. xxxv. 153 With grete mastes armed aboue wyth sharp ferrementes. **1597** LOWE *Chirurg.* I. ii. (1634) 9 How many kinds of ferraments ought the Chyrurgion..to carry. *c* **1640** J. SMYTH *Lives Berkeleys* (1883) II. 66 The ferments of iron in the windows. **1660** *Charac. Italy* 34 Their Bergamasque..a poor..Crablouse..cloyster'd up within these ferraments..hath not room to breath.

ferrandin, var. of FARANDINE, *Obs.*

† **ferrane, ferranea.** *Obs.* See quots.

1812 SIR H. DAVY *Chem. Philos.* 388 There are 2 compounds of iron and chlorine..one..formed by burning iron wire in the gas..I have called it *Ferranea*..The other..is a dark gray opaque substance..and..may be named *ferrane*.

Ferranti (fə'ræntɪ). The name of S. Z. de *Ferranti* (1864–1930), English electrical engineer, used attrib. to designate certain apparatus invented by him, and a phenomenon first observed in connection with the high-voltage cables designed by him.

1893 T. O'C. SLOANE *Stand. Electr. Dict.* 251 *Ferranti effect*, an effect as yet not definitely explained, observed in the mains of the Deptford, Eng., alternating current plant. **1893** M. H. KILGOUR et al. *Electr. Distrib.* xi. 387 The Ferranti mains are made with a very large margin of safety. **1902** *Encycl. Brit.* XXXIII. 424 The Ferranti rectifier is much employed for rectifying alternating current for arc lighting purposes. **1940** *Chambers's Techn. Dict.* 328/1 *Ferranti effect*, the rise in voltage which takes place at the end of a long transmission line when the load is thrown off. **1942** MEARES & NEALE *Electr. Engin. Pract.* (ed. 5) II. xvii. 94 The Ferranti rectifier consists of a synchronous motor driving a commutator, alternate segments of which are connected to slip rings on the same shaft. **1946** P. J. SELGIN *Electr. Transmission* v. 107 Any value higher than this will result in the Ferranti effect, the line acting in this respect as a step-up transformer.

† **Fe'rrara.** *Obs. rare*$^{-1}$. A broadsword; more fully, an 'Andrea Ferrara'. Cf. ANDREW I.

1762 CHURCHILL *Poems, Proph. Famine*, There saw I..the Ferrara..Unwilling grace the aukward victor's side. **1785** GROSE *Dict. Vulg. Tongue* s.v. *Ferrara*, An Andrea Ferrara has become the common name for the glaymore, or highland broad-sword.

Ferrarese (fɛrə'riːz), *sb.* and *a.* [a. It. *ferrarese*, f. *Ferrara* the name of a city in Italy + -ESE.] **A.** *sb.* (*pl.*) The Ferrarese people. (Formerly also pl. *Ferareses.*) **B.** *adj.* Of or pertaining to Ferrara.

1573 GASCOIGNE *Supposes* II. ii. 19 These Ferareses be as craftie as the deuill of hell. *Ibid.*, They are Ferareses all. **1881** *Encycl. Brit.* XII. 535/2 Messrs J. and H. Gwynne constructed some pumps for draining the Ferrarese Marshes. **1930** E. POUND *XXX Cantos* xxiv. 111 To breed in Ferrara among thin-legged Ferrarese. **1932** *Times Lit. Suppl.* 25 Feb. 127/1 The Ferrarese school was itself derivative. **1949** E. POUND *Pisan Cantos* lxxvii. 61 In flat Ferrarese country.

† **'ferrary.** *Obs.* [ad. L. (*ars*) *ferrāria*; but cf. FERRURIE.] The smith's art; iron-working.

1609 HEYWOOD *Brit. Troy* XIII. xxxvii, Vulcan works in heauenly Ferrarie. *c* **1611** CHAPMAN *Iliad* XIV. 141 The God of ferrary.

ferrate ('fɛreɪt). *Chem.* [f. L. *ferr-um* iron + -ATE[4].] A salt of ferric acid.

1854 J. SCOFFERN in *Orr's Circ. Sc.* Chem. 439 A solution of ferrate of potash is obtained. **1873** WATTS *Fownes' Chem.* (ed. 11) 455 A class of salts called ferrates.

ferrateen. *rare*$^{-1}$. Cf. FERRETING *sb.*

1821 SCOTT *Kenilw.* xxiv, Thou false man of frail cambric and ferrateen.

ferratin ('fɛrətɪn). *Biochem.* [f. L. *ferrāt-us* containing iron + -IN[1].] A substance formerly supposed to be an iron-containing protein that occurs esp. in the liver (see quot. 1946).

1893 O. SCHMIEDEBERG in *Practitioner* Dec. 427, I have now..succeeded..in isolating it in an unmixed condition from pig's liver. It contains, on the average, 6 per cent. of iron, and may briefly be referred to as Ferratin. *Ibid.*, Ferratin is the only combination of iron which is ingested with food, and which is found stored up in the tissues as a reserve-material for the formation of blood. **1909** *Chem. Abstr.* III. 2008 Schmiedeberg prepared 'ferratin' and called it a 'ferrialbuminic acid' of 6% Fe content... The compd. is not a 'ferri-albuminic acid' but is a Fe-containing nucleo-protein. **1930** *Proc. Soc. Exper. Biol. & Med.* XXVIII. 294 The serum of a rabbit treated with sheep ferratin gave precipitin reactions with beef, hog and sheep ferratins..but not with any of the corresponding sera. **1946** *Chem. Rev.* XXXVIII. 381 According to Schmiedeberg..the iron was attached to a protein and this compound, which he called Ferratin, was present in spleen, liver, and marrow...(Today we know that this compound was a mixture of denatured ferritin and denatured proteins.)

† **ferraunt**, *a. Obs.* Also 4 farant, fera(w)nt, feraunte. [a. OF. *ferrant*, f. *fer*:—L. *ferrum* iron.] Of a horse: Iron-grey. Also *absol.*

c **1300** *K. Alis.* 3460 With him cam mony stede farant. ? *a* **1400** *Morte Arth.* 2140 Ffewters in freely one fferaunte stedes. *Ibid.* 2451 One ferawnt stedes. *a* **1440** *Sir Degrev.* 371 On a sted fferraunt.

ferray, obs. form of FORAY.

ferrazite ('fɛrəzaɪt). *Min.* [f. name of J. B. de Araujo *Ferraz*, of the Geological Survey of Brazil: see -ITE[1].] A hydrated phosphate of lead, barium, and aluminium.

1919 LEE & DE MORAES in *Amer. Jrnl. Sci.* XLVIII. 354 We feel justified in claiming novelty for the mineral, and suggest for it the name of *Ferrazite*. **1951** C. PALACHE et al. *Dana's Syst. Min.* (ed. 7) II. 832 *Ferrazite*... Found as discoidal pebbles (favas) of granular structure in the diamond sands of the Diamantina district, Minas Geraes, Brazil.

† **ferre.** *Falconry. Obs.*

[**1486** *Bk. St. Albans* D j b, Iff yowre hawke nym the fowle at the fer side of the Ryuer..from you Then she sleeth the fowle at the fer Jutty and if she slee it uppon that side that ye ben on..ye shall say she hath sleen the fowle at the Jutty ferry.] **1602** HEYWOOD *Woman Killed* Wks. 1874 II. 99 Your's [*i.e.* your hawk] missed her at the ferre.

† **'ferreal.** *Obs. rare*$^{-1}$. [f. L. *ferre-us* (f. *ferrum* iron) + -AL[1].] Of or pertaining to iron.

1599 A. M. tr. *Gabelhouer's Bk. Physicke* 379/2 [Recipe for] the ferreall poudre, called *Crocus Martis*.

ferrean ('fɛrɪən), *a. rare.* [f. as prec. + -AN.] = FERREOUS 2.

1656–81 BLOUNT *Glossogr.*, *Ferrean*, iron-like; hard-hearted, cruel. **1828** SOUTHEY *Gridiron* vi. in *Life* (1850) V. 364 From the air The ferrean atoms came. [In some mod. Dicts.]

† **'ferred, 'ferhede.** *Obs.* Forms: α. (1 ȝeférræden), 3 ferræden, færeden, fer(r)eden, 3–4 ferede, ferred(e, (4 ferrade). β. 3 fer-, verhede. [aphetic f. OE. *ȝeférræden*, f. *ȝeféra* FERE *sb.*[1] + *rǣden* condition: see -RED. As in other similar compounds of sbs. ending in *-r*, the suffix *-red* was in 13th c. replaced by *-hede* (see -HEAD).] Companionship, society, fellowship; a company.

α. *c* **1200** *Trin. Coll. Hom.* 23 Ich ileue þat halgan..habben ferrede on alle holinesse. *c* **1205** LAY. 6020 Heo gunnen senden of Romanisce ende feower ferrædene. *a* **1225** *Leg. Kath.* 703 Tu schalt..beon þenne underfon i þe feire ferreden & i þe murie of meidnes. *c* **1314** *Guy Warw.* (A.) 1354 Leuer ous were heron be ded, Than thou wer ded in our ferred. *c* **1325** *Coer de L.* 2278 Him followed ful great ferrede. *c* **1330** *Arth. & Merl.* (Kölb.) 3528 With gret ferrade [*rime-wd.* made]. *c* **1380** *Sir Ferumb.* 2060 þou art now..among þes fair ferede.

β. **1297** R. GLOUC. (Rolls) 2917 He wende in þis verhede [*v.r.* ferhede] Toward bataile. *c* **1300** *K. Alis.* 3060 The riche king of Mede, Hadde never suche ferhede. *c* **1325** *Coer de L.* 1920 Him followed ful great ferhede.

ferredoxin (fɛrɪ'dɒksɪn). *Biochem.* [f. *fer* (repr. L. *ferrum* iron) + REDOX + -IN[1].] Any of certain iron-containing proteins of low redox potential which participate in intracellular electron-transfer processes.

1962 L. E. MORTENSON et al. in *Biochem. & Biophys. Res. Comm.* VII. 448 An electron-transferring protein that links hydrogenase with a variety of electron donors or acceptors has been obtained from *Clostridium pasteurianum*... The new factor, which at the present stage contains iron but no detectable heme or flavin, has been named 'ferredoxin'. **1966** *Structure & Bonding* I. 112 Ferredoxin is found in representatives of all major groups or organisms except animals. *Ibid.* 121 The bacterial ferredoxins, in general, are similar to each other in amino acid content, but differ in detail. **1970** *New Scientist* 9 July 65/2 The class of molecules known as ferredoxins..may have up to ten iron atoms per molecule.

ferrekyn, obs. Sc. form of FIRKIN.

ferrel(l, obs. form of FERRULE *v.*

'ferrell. *dial.* See quot.

1861 *Jrnl. R. Agric. Soc.* XXII. II. 248 There occur in spots blocks of concrete, cemented gravel, clay, and iron, *Hamptonicè*, 'verrells' or 'ferrells'. **1883** *Hampsh. Gloss.* 104 *Ferrol*, an indurated lump of gravel, sand, and iron. These ferrols frequently occur in the heath-lands of North Hampshire.

† **'ferren**, *adv.* and *a. Obs.* Forms: 1 feorran, feorran(n)e, feorrene, 2–4 ferren(e, (3 feren, verren, 4 ferynne, furrene), 3 feorre(n, 3–5 ferne, 6 farren. Also (after preps. *of, on*) ferrom(e, ferrum; see A-FERROM. [OE. *feorran, feorrane, feorrene*, corresp. to OS. *ferrana, ferran*, OHG. *ferrana, -no*, f. OTeut. **ferr-* FAR *adv.* The adj. appears first in 12th c.; its development from the adv. is paralleled in the mod.G. *fern*.] **A.** *adv.*

1. From far, from a distance.

Beowulf 839 (Gr.) Feorran and nean. *a* **1000** *Cædmon's Gen.* 1836 (Gr.) Uncer tweȝa feorren cumenra. *c* **1000** *Elene* 993 (Gr.) Feorran ȝeferede. *a* **1225** *Ancr. R.* 70 3if eni god mon is feorrene ikumen. *a* **1250** *Owl & Night.* 1320 Hwat canstu..of storre, Bute that thu bi-haitest hi feorre?

2. Afar, far away, at or to a distance.

c **888** K. ÆLFRED *Boeth.* xxxix. §5 Ða onȝon he sprecan swiðe feorran ymbuton. *c* **1000** *Ags. Gosp.* Matt. xxvi. 58 Petrus hym fylide feorrane. *c* **1205** LAY. 25733 þa iseȝen heo nawiht feorren a muchel fur smokien. *a* **1225** *Juliana* 71 þa..belial þat ha hefde ibeaten feorren to bihinden. *c* **1250** *Gen. & Ex.* 2601 Maria dowter ful feren stod. *c* **1315** SHOREHAM 137 The sonne and monne and many sterren By easte arysethe swythe ferren.

3. Preceded by prep.; *of, on* (*o*), *from ferren* (*ferrom*): from or at a distance; see A-FERROM.

a **1240** *Sawles Warde* in *Cott. Hom.* 249 A sonde..of feorren icumen. *a* **1300** *Cursor M.* 11744 (Gött.) þai lokid þaim on ferrom fra. *Ibid.* 27372 (Cott.) O ferrum for to spi. *c* **1300** *Havelok* 1864 Gleyues schoten him fro ferne. **1352** MINOT *Poems* vii. 89 He saw þe toun o-ferrum bren. *c* **1400** MAUNDEV. (Roxb.) xvi. 72 þe whilk men may see on ferrum. *a* **1400–50** *Alexander* 5520 In hokis of iren Flesch on ferrom þaim fra. *c* **1470** HARDING *Chron.* VI. iii. 5 Shyppes came..Fro ferrome sene.

B. *adj.* Distant, far, remote.

c **1160** *Hatton Gosp.* Luke xix. 12 Sum æthelboren man ferde on ferren [*c* **1000** *Corpus* fyrlen] land. *c* **1205** LAY. 3331 ȝef ferrene kinges hiherde þa tidinde. *c* **1250** *O. Kent Serm.* in *O.E. Misc.* (1871) 27 þo þrie kinges of hepenesse þet comen fram verrene londes ure louerd to seche. *c* **1305** *S. Kather.* 20 in *E.E.P.* (1862) 90 So moche folc of furrene lond. *c* **1374** CHAUCER *Boeth.* II. vii. 60 Al þouȝ [þat] renoune y-spradde passynge to ferne poeples goþ by dyuerse tonges. *c* **1386** —— *Prol.* 14 Thanne longen folk to goon on pilgrimages..To ferne halwes. *c* **1420** *Chron. Vilod.* 745 þere come foure clerkes to Wyltone from ferne lond. **1548** GEST *Pr. Masse* 126 In farren contreis.

ferreous ('fɛrɪəs), *a.* [f. L. *ferre-us* (f. *ferrum* iron) + -OUS.]

1. Of or pertaining to iron; consisting of or containing iron.

1646 SIR T. BROWNE *Pseud. Ep.* II. iii. 67 Veyned..with a few magneticall and ferreous lines. *Ibid.* (ed. 1) 69 It carried away all ferreous and earthy parts. **1842–3** GROVE *Corr. Phys. Forces* (1874) 129 A magnet being itself moved will move other ferreous bodies.

2. Hard as iron; iron-like. *rare.*

1822 *Blackw. Mag.* XII. 280 Nothing too tough and ferreous for their digestion.

3. *Entom.* 'Of a metallic-grey hue, like that of polished iron' (*Cent. Dict.*).

ferrer[1] ('fɛrə(r)). *Obs.* exc. *dial.* [ad. OF. *ferriere*: see BARREL-FERRER.] **a.** = BARREL-FERRER. **b.** (See quot. 1877).

a **1483** *Liber Niger* in *Househ. Ord.* 75 Ther sergeaunt [of the cellar] hathe in keepinge..ferrers and portatives. **1877** *N.W. Linc. Gloss.*, *Ferrer*, a cask having iron hoops.

† **'ferrer**[2], **'ferrour.** *Obs.* Forms: 4–8 ferrer, 4–5 ferour, 5–6 ferror, -our(e, 6 farrour, (5 ferere, -owre, ferrur, 6 farrer, ferrar). [a. OF. *ferreor*, *ferour* (Fr. *ferreur*) = Sp. *herrador*, It. *ferratore*:—med.L. *ferrātōr-em*, agent-n. f. *ferrāre* to shoe horses, f. *ferrum* iron, in med.L. horseshoe: see FARRIER.]

1. A worker in iron; a smith.

c **1380** WYCLIF *Serm.* Sel. Wks. I. 407 God is a ferour and he is Goddis instrument. *c* **1400** *Destr. Troy* 1593 Fferrers, flechours, fele men of crafte. **14..** *Nominale* in Wr.-Wülcker 686 *Hic farrator*, a ferrur. *c* **1440** *Promp. Parv.* 157/2 Ferrowre, smythe, *ferrarius*. **1583** GOLDING *Calvin on Deut.* cxxxvii. 845 The Farrour or locksmith hath an anuel. **1609** HOLLAND *Amm. Marcell.* XIV. xi. 28 Andriscus..she taught the Ferrars craft for to get his living.

2. = FARRIER I.

1426 *E.E. Wills* (1882) 76, I make myn executours..Iohn Carpinter, comoun clerk, & Iohn Spore, ferroure. *c* **1515** *Cocke Lorell's B.* (Percy Soc.) 9 Brydel bytters, blacke smythes, and ferrars. **1552** HULOET, Ferroure, horseleche, or smythe whyche cureth horses, *veterinarius medicus*. **1601** HOLLAND *Pliny* II. 480 Poppæa..was knowne to cause her Ferrers ordinarily to shooe her coach-horses..with cleane gold. **1798** *Sporting Mag.* XII. 21 Encouraged by the nobility..as riding-masters or ferrers.

3. With sb. prefixed as *sergeant-, valet-, yeoman-ferrer*: An official who had care of the horses in a large household.

1455 *Househ. Ord.* 23 In th' office of the Stable—1 Sergeant Ferrour—1 Yoman Ferrour. *a* **1512** FABYAN *Chron.* VII. 686 A tall yoman, somtyme sergeaunt ferrour to the kyng. **1541** *Act 33 Hen. VIII*, c. 12 §16 The serieant or chief ferrour..shall..bringe with him the serynge yrons. **1601** F. TATE *Househ. Ord. Edw. II*, §56 (1876) 44 He shal haue a vallet ferrour under him to shue the horses.

ferret ('fɛrɪt), *sb.*[1] Forms: 4 fyrette, 5 for-, feret(te, 5–7 firret(te, 7 ferrit, 6– ferret. [a. OF. (?**firet*), *fuiret*, *furet* (mod.F. *furet*) = It. *furetto*, dim. of the Com. Rom. word which appears in OF. as *firon*, *fuiron* (:—L. type **fūriōn-em*), *furon* = Pr. *furon*, Cat. *furó*, Sp. *huron* (earlier *furon*), Pg. *furão*:—late L. *fūrōn-em*, recorded in 7th c. by Isidore *Etym.* XII. ii. §39; usually identified with late L. *fūrōn-em* robber (f. L. *fūr* thief; common in the Langobardic laws), whence It. *furone* robber.

The F. dim. was adopted as MDu. *foret, furet, fret*, mod.Du. *fret*, mod.G. *frett, frettchen*; the OF. *furon* appears in early mod.Du. *veure*, Westphal. *vürn*, denoting the same or a similar animal.]

1. a. A half-tamed variety of the common polecat (*Putorius fœtidus*), kept for the purpose of driving rabbits from their burrows, destroying rats, etc.

1398 TREVISA *Barth. De P.R.* XVIII. lxxv. (1495) 829 A fyrette hyghte Migale and is a lytyll beest as it were a wesel. *c* **1440** *Promp. Parv.* 171/2 Forette, or ferette, lytyll beste. ? *a* **1500** *Chester Pl.* (Shaks. Soc.) I. 51 Heare are beares.. squirelles, and firrette. **1581** LAMBARDE *Eiren.* IV. iv. (1588) 444 If any.. Labourer have used firrets.. to take or destroy Deere. **1616** SURFL. & MARKH. *Country Farme* 647 Good hunters will neuer put their ferret into any earth, whose mouth they see stopt. **1647** H. MORE *Song of Soul* I. II. lxxxv, Strait Graculo with eyes as fierce as Ferrit Reply'd. **1766** PENNANT *Zool.* (1768) I. 78 Warreners assert that the Polecat will mix with the ferret. **1844** *Penny Cycl.* XXVII. 167/1 Ferrets should not be fed before they are taken to the warren. **1879** *Encycl. Brit.* (ed. 9) IX. 109/1 The ferret is peculiarly intolerant of cold.

b. *transf.* and *fig.*

1626 L. OWEN *Spec. Jesuit.* (1629) 66 These Ferrets (or if you will Iesuites). **1641** MILTON *Reform.* I. (1851) 31 Many of those that pretend to be great Rabbies in these studies.. have bin but the Ferrets and Moushunts of an Index. **1856** BOKER *Poems* (1857) II. 25 A cunning ferret after doubtful phrases. **1891** *Daily News* 19 June 7/3 He engaged him as a kind of ferret or detective. **1946** BRICKHILL & NORTON *Escape to Danger* xv. 140 Night and day.. German security guards patrolled and snooped... These guards were known by us as 'ferrets'. **1960** *Times* 2 Dec. 17/2 A more recent approach starts from a device known as a 'ferret' which operates in the mains themselves. Its ordinary use is in cleaning out mains and it consists of an arrangement of water-propelled cleaning brushes.

2. *slang.* **a.** A dunning tradesman (see quot. 1700). ? *Obs.* **b.** (See quot. 1889.) †**c.** A pawnbroker (Bailey 1736). *Obs.*

a **1700** B. E. *Dict. Cant. Crew, Ferret*, a Tradesman that sells Goods to young Unthrifts, upon Trust at excessive Rates, and then continually duns them for the debt. **1725** in *New Cant. Dict.* **1889** BARRÈRE & LELAND *Slang Dict., Ferret*, a young thief who gets into a coal barge and throws coal over the side to his confederates.

3. *attrib.* and *Comb.*: simple attrib., as ***ferret-eye***; parasynthetic and similative, as ***ferret-eyed, -faced, -like*** adjs. Also †**ferret-claw** v., *fig.* to scratch, claw like a ferret; to strip bare; **ferret-eye**, 'the spur-winged goose, so called from the red circle around the eyes' (Webster 1890).

1591 GREENE *Disc. Coosnage*, So *ferret-claw him at cards that they leave him as bare of money, as an ape of a taile. *c* **1620** FLETCHER *Wom. Pleased* III. iv, H'as light legs else I had so ferret-claw'd him. *a* **1586** SIDNEY (J.), Having threatning.. in her *ferret eyes. **1601** SHAKS. *Jul. C.* I. ii. 186 Cicero Lookes with.. Ferret.. eyes. **1781** BENTHAM *Wks.* (1838–43) X. 104 A hook nose and ferret eyes. **1837** MARRYAT *Snarleyyow* (ed. 2) III. iii. 36 Vanslyperken, whose.. small ferret-eyes, and downcast look, were certainly not in his favour. *a* **1700** B. E. *Dict. Cant. Crew*, **Ferret-eyed*: or Eyes as red as a Ferret. **1850** EB. ELLIOTT *More Verse & Prose* I. 18 Cried To prayerless Want, his plunderer ferret-eyed. **1870** L'ESTRANGE *Miss Mitford* I. v. 156 They are really ferret-eyed this morning. **1840** BARHAM *Ingol. Leg., Spectre of Tapp.*, A little *ferret-faced woman. **1801** *Monthly Mirror* June 421 The contour of the face is what is called **ferret-like*. **1843** JAMES *Forest Days* ii, A shrewd merry, ferret-like face.

ferret ('fɛrɪt), *sb.*[2] Forms: 6 foret, 7 ferrit, 7– ferret. See also FLORET. [Usually believed to be ad. It. *fioretti* floss-silk (rendered 'ferret silk' by Florio: see quot. 1598), pl. of *fioretto*, dim. of *fiore* flower; the corresponding F. *fleuret* has senses answering to both those explained below.]

†**1.** attrib. ***ferret-silk*** = floss silk. *Obs.*

1576 GASCOIGNE *Steele Gl.* (Arb.) 80 When perchmentiers [*i.e.* makers of trimmings, F. *passementiers*] put in no ferret Silke. **1598** FLORIO, *Fioretti*.. a kind of course silke called foret or ferret silke. **1612** *Sc. Bk. Customs* in *Halyburton's Ledger* (1867) 326 Filosell or ferrett silk the pound viii li.

2. A stout tape most commonly made of cotton, but also of silk; then known as Italian ferret. ***green-ferret***, fig. of officialism (cf. *red-tape*). Also *attrib.*, as ***ferret-ribbon, -ribboning***.

1649 *Gild Law* in Mackenzie *Newcastle* II. 666 *note*, They shall wear no show strings better than ferret.. ribbin. **1668** DRYDEN *Evening's Love* IV. iii, There's your ferret-ribboning for garters. **1697** *Lond. Gaz.* No. 3331/4 Leather Breeches, tied at the Knees with green Ferrit. **1715** *Ibid.* No. 5327/2 The working of Galloons, Ribbons, Ferret, &c. by Mills. **1783** W. F. MARTYN *Geog. Mag.* II. 268 The inhabitants [of Amiens] carry on a manufacture of ferrets. **1812** H. & J. SMITH *Rej. Addr.* (1839) 54 Red wax and green ferret Are fixed at the foot of the deeds. **1826** MISS MITFORD *Village* Ser. II. (1863) 426 The bobbin, the ferret, shirt-buttons, shoe-strings? **1836** in Mrs. Papendiek *Crt. Q. Charlotte* (1887) II. 257 The venetian blinds I had new strung at home with silk ferret. **1852** DICKENS *Bleak Ho.* x, Mr. Snagsby has dealt in.. red tape and green ferret.

†'**ferret**, *sb.*[3] *rare*[−1]. *Glass-making.* [a. Fr. *ferret, féret*, dim. of *fer* iron.] See quot.

1662 MERRETT tr. *Neri's Art of Glass* 364 *Ferrets* are the Irons wherewith they try whether the Metall be fit to work, as also those Irons which make the Ring at the mouth of Glass Bottles. **1753** in CHAMBERS *Suppl.* Hence in mod. Dicts. **1874** in KNIGHT.

ferret ('fɛrɪt), *v.* [f. FERRET *sb.*[1]; cf. F. *fureter* (16th c. in Littré), which may be the source.]

1. *intr.* To hunt with ferrets.

c **1450** LYDG. in *Pol. Rel. & L. Poems* (1866) 26 With hem that fyrretyth robbe conynghertys. **1576, 1673, 1879** [see FERRETING *vbl. sb.*[1]].

b. *trans.* To hunt over (ground) with a ferret; to clear out by means of a ferret.

a **1483** *Liber Niger* in *Househ. Ord.* 66 To geve any servaunts occasion to furett.. any mannys warreynes. **1879** JEFFERIES *Wild Life in S.C.* 214 Even if the burrows be ferreted, in a few weeks this great hole shows signs of fresh inhabitants. *Ibid.* 248 In ferreting this place.

2. *trans.* To take (rabbits, etc.) with ferrets. Also, to drive forth by means of a ferret.

1577–87 HOLINSHED *Chron.* III. 893/2 Some fell to drinking, some to ferretting of other mens conies. **1579** GOSSON *Sch. Abuse* (Arb.) 35 These prettie Rabbets very cunningly ferretted from their borrowes. *a* **1700** B. E. *Dict. Cant. Crew, Ferreted*, hunted as Conies. **1724** SWIFT *Wood's Execution* Wks. 1738 IV. 234 *Rabbet-catcher*, I'll ferret him. **1884** *York Herald* 26 Aug. 6/2 The tenants.. have permission to ferret and dig rabbits.

3. Of actions resembling a ferret's.

a. To hunt after; to worry. Also with *about*.

1599 SHAKS. *Hen. V*, IV. iv. 30 Ile fer him, and firke him, and ferret him. **1605** *Old King Leir* in Nichols *Six Old Plays* (1779) 461 I'll ferret you ere night for that word. **1663** BUTLER *Hud.* I. iii. 236 And.. vow'd He'd ferret him, lurk where he wou'd. **1713** STEELE *Guardian* No. 132 ⁋4 She does so ferrit them about.. that they.. give her immediate warning. **1810** LAMB *Let. to Manning* (1888) I. 115 He ferrets me day and night to do something.

b. To drive *from, off, out of* (a place). Also, ***to ferret about, away, forth, out***.

1601 DEACON & WALKER *Spirits & Divels* 287 You are almost quite ferreted foorth from all your starting holes. **1607** TOPSELL *Four-f. Beasts* (1658) 177 With Terriar Dogs they ferret him out of his den again. **1655** GURNALL *Chr. in Arm.* iv. (1669) 193/2 Speak.. did the Lord ever ferret thee out of this burrow? *a* **1679** EARL ORRERY *Guzman* III I'll ferret him away. **1683** WYCHERLEY *Country Wife* IV. iii, I'll ferret her out to you presently. **1691** WOOD *Ath. Oxon.* II. 124 Dr. Laud.. sifted and ferreted him about from one hole to another. **1727** A. HAMILTON *New Acc. E. Ind.* I. viii. 86 They.. took Counsel to ferret them off their Island. **1824** W. IRVING *T. Trav.* II. 241 Measures were accordingly taken.. to ferret this vermin brood out of the colonies.

c. *intr.* To rummage, search about; †to be restless, worry; also, ***to ferret up and down***.

1580 NORTH *Plutarch* (1676) 963 Souldiers, who went ferriting up and down in his House. **1624** GEE *Foot out of Snare* 52 Making him [a duiell] ferret vp and downe, from tongue to toe. **1693** SOUTHERNE *Maid's last Prayer* II. ii, You must be.. ferreting in my Borough. **1792** A. YOUNG *Trav. France* 201 Ferret among the booksellers and find more tracts.. upon agriculture than I expected. **1806–7** J. BERESFORD *Miseries Hum. Life* xx. (1826) 276 How would these conjurors ferret and sweat, To see us pair off. **1891** E. GOSSE *Gossip in Library* xii. 150 He has to ferret among the pawnbrokers for scraps of finery.

d. *trans.* To search (a place); also, to question (a person) searchingly. *rare.*

1583 STANYHURST *Æneis* I. (Arb.) 27 Æneas.. vpgot, too ferret al vncooth Nouks of strang country. **1607** SYLVESTER *Du Bartas* II. iv. Magnificence 198 Ferret all Corners of this neather Ball. **1647** WHARTON *Wks.* (1683) 277, I have proposed.. to ferret the poor Quack in point of Art.

e. To burrow (a passage). *rare.*

1583 STANYHURST *Æneis* III. (Arb.) 93 Alpheus.. this passadge ferreted.

4. ***to ferret out, up***: To search out, discover, bring to light.

1577–87 HOLINSHED *Chron.* II. 36/2 That he were able to ferret out such.. brats. **1581** J. BELL *Haddon's Answ. Osor.* 122b, Let us now fyrritte out the other, and see what vermine it is. *a* **1643** W. CARTWRIGHT *Ordinary* V. iv, Let's in, and ferret out these cheating rake-hells. **1775** WESLEY *Wks.* (1872) XII. 324 Rather ferret them out, and drag them into open day. **1847** ALB. SMITH *Chr. Tadpole* xxxix. (1879) 330 She had been out in the village, and ferretted up all the guides. **1852** DICKENS *Bleak Ho.* ix, I have ferreted out evidence, got up cases.

5. *slang.* To cheat.

a **1700** B. E. *Dict. Cant. Crew, Ferreted*, cheated.

ferreter ('fɛrɪtə(r)). [f. prec. + -ER[1].] **a.** One who searches for rabbits, etc. with a ferret. **b.** One who searches minutely; a rummager. Also with *out*.

a. 1601 F. TATE *Househ. Ord. Edw. II*, §58 (1876) 45 A ferretter, who shal have ij ferretes and a boy to help him. *a* **1652** BROME *City Wit* I. Wks. 1873 I. 288, I have heard my Mother say his Father was a Ferretter. **1878** JEFFERIES *Gamekeeper at H.* 33 Assistants, who act as beaters, ferreters, etc. **1887** W. RYE *Norfolk Broads* 13 The Poet found it [rabbit] in the ferreter's bag.

b. 1611 COTGR., *Fureteur*, a ferreter, searcher. **1857** PLANCHÉ *Fairy Tales* 261 Monkeys are always great ferreters by profession. **1863** *Scotsman* 7 May, Croker.. that indefatigable ferreter out of mistakes.

ferreting ('fɛrɪtɪŋ), *vbl. sb.* [f. as prec. + -ING[1].] The action of the verb in various senses. **a.** The action of taking rabbits, etc. with a ferret. **b.** The action or process of searching minutely.

1576 TURBERV. *Venerie* 180, I accumpte ferrettyng one of the coldest.. chases that can be followed. **1673** *News from Channel* in Ansted *Channel Isl.* I. iv. (1862) 89 Whither we commonly go a ferreting. **1859** HELPS *Friends in C.* Ser. II. I. v. 201 Notwithstanding all the ferreting that has gone on, we know.. little of Shakespeare's life. **1879** JEFFERIES *Wild Life in S. Co.* 136 The guns are laid aside, though some ferreting is still going on.

ferreting ('fɛrɪtɪŋ), *sb.* [f. FERRET *sb.*[2] + -ING[1].] = FERRET *sb.*[2]

1670 *Overseer's Acc. Holy Cross, Canterb.*, Tape and Fereting for Bullocks girle. *a* **1754** S. GALE in *Bibl. Topog. Brit.* III. 21 Waistcoats.. edged and trimmed with black ribbands or ferreting. **1845** MRS. S. C. HALL *Whiteboy* iv. 27 A.. straw hat, with a piece of black coarse ferretting dangling from it.

ferretto (fɛ'rɛtəʊ). Also feretto. [a. It. *ferretto (di Spagna)*, dim. of *ferro* iron:—L. *ferrum*.] Copper calcined with brimstone or white vitriol, used to colour glass.

1662 MERRETT tr. *Neri's Art of Glass* 29 To make Ferretto is nothing but a simple Calcination of Copper. **1753** CHAMBERS *Cycl. Supp., Feretto*, a substance which serves to colour glass. **1799** G. SMITH *Laboratory* I. 123 Feretto of Spain, is thus prepared.

ferrety ('fɛrɪtɪ), *a.* [f. FERRET *sb.*[1] + -Y[1].] Resembling a ferret or a ferret's.

1801 *Med. Jrnl.* V. 15 Indicated by a flushed countenance, ferrety eye. **1876** J. WEISS *Wit, Hum. & Shaks.* ii. 54 There is nothing more feretty than your cynic. **1877** BLACK *Green Past.* xi, The man.. looked at Balfour with a pair of keen and ferrety eyes. **1883** G. H. BOUGHTON in *Harper's Mag.* Mar. 528/1 Jacob translated for the ferrety old dame.

ferri- ('fɛrɪ), formerly **ferrid-**, used in Organic Chemistry in the names of certain compounds to indicate the presence of iron in the 'ferric' state (cf. FERRO-, the corresponding prefix used when the iron is in the 'ferrous' state). **ferricyan'hydric** or **ferricy'anic acid**, an acid, H_4FeCy_6, procured from various ferricyanides, and crystallizing in lustrous brownish-green needles. **ferri'cyanide**, a salt of ferricyanhydric acid, e.g. ***potassium ferricyanide***, red prussiate of potash; ***ferrous ferricyanide***, Turnbull's blue. **ferricy'anogen**, the hypothetical radical $FeCy_2$ supposed to exist in ferricyanhydric acid.

1845 G. E. DAY tr. *Simon's Anim. Chem.* I. 16 Ferrocyanide and ferridcyanide of potassium. **1848** CRAIG, *Ferridcyanogen.* **1854** J. SCOFFERN in *Orr's Circ. Sc.* Chem. 443 A.. hydracid, *ferrosesquicyanic acid*, or *ferridcyanic acid.* **1869** ROSCOE *Elem. Chem.* 377 Ferricyanic Acid. **1878** KINGZETT *Anim. Chem.* 379 Potassic ferro- and ferri-cyanide.

ferriage ('fɛrɪɪdʒ). Also 5 fery-, feriage, 6 ferrage, 9 ferryage. [f. FERRY *sb.* and *v.* + -AGE.]

1. The action or business of ferrying a person or thing over a stream or other water; conveyance over a ferry.

c **1450** *Merlin* 606 We requere feriage for oure horse at this forde. **1464** *Mann. & Househ. Exp.* 241 To pay ffor my ladyis fferyage att the ffery. **1678–96** in PHILLIPS. **1691** T. H[ALE] *Acc. New Invent.* p. xcv, The right of the Ferriage over all Rivers between the first Bridges and the Sea is a Perquisite of Admiralty. **1835** W. IRVING *Tour Prairies* xii, This Indian mode of ferriage. **1880** MISS BIRD *Japan* II. 268 We were detained.. waiting ferriage.

2. The fare or price paid for the use of a ferry.

c **1440** *Promp. Parv.* 156/2 Feryage, *feriagium.* **1573** ABP. PARKER *Let.* in *Corr.* (1858) 455 Journeying, ferriage, carriage.. &c. **1599** MINSHEU *Sp. Dict., Fletadór*, one that payeth ferriage, or passage money. **1735** *Col. Rec. Pennsylv.* IV. 22 An Act for ascertaining the Rates of Ferriages to be taken at divers Ferries. **1761** FRANKLIN *Let.* Wks. 1887 III. 145 They were by law to receive no ferriage of him. **1807** W. IRVING *Salmag.* (1824) 58 Ferryage nine-pence. **1859** R. F. BURTON *Centr. Afr.* in *Jrnl. Geog. Soc.* XXIX. 194 Settling ferriage with the.. Lord of the Ferry.

ferrian ('fɛrɪən), *a. Min.* [f. L. *ferr-um* iron + -IAN.] Of a mineral: having a (small) proportion of a constituent element replaced by ferric iron.

1930 [see FERROAN *a.*]. **1954** *Thorpe's Dict. Appl. Chem.* (ed. 4) XI. 883/1 Ferrian wad contains an increasing proportion of ferric oxide, and grades into goethite or limonite. **1959** W. H. DENNEN *Princ. Mineral.* vii. 271 Chemical varieties [of cassiterite]: Ferrian, tantalian (ainalite).

ferriar, -er, obs. forms of FARRIER.

ferric ('fɛrɪk), *a.* [f. L. *ferr-um* iron + -IC. Cf. F. *ferrique*.]

1. Of, pertaining to, or extracted from iron.

1799 SIR H. DAVY in Beddoes *Contrib. to Phys. & Med. Knowl.* (1799) 184 The argentic and ferric phosoxyds. **1852** JOUBERT in *Jrnl. Soc. Arts* 26 Nov., A ferric solution should be employed. **1885** S. TROMHOLT *Aurora Borealis* I. 285 The Aurora Borealis should be produced by the earth's entering into clouds of ferric dust.

2. *Chem.* applied to compounds in which iron exists in its higher degree of valency, as ***ferric acid***, a hypothetical acid H_2FeO, assumed to exist in the salts called ferrates; ***ferric bromide*** $FeBr_3$; ***ferric chloride*** $FeCl_3$; ***ferric fluoride*** FeF_3; ***ferric oxide*** Fe_2O_3; ***ferric sulphide*** Fe_2S_3. Also *ferric state*: see quot. 1881.

1853 W. GREGORY *Inorg. Chem.* (ed. 3) 214 Ferric Acid.. corresponding to manganic acid, is also unknown in the separate state. **1881** *Times* Jan. 3/6 The metal [iron] itself when in the ferric state, or state of highest combining power. **1882** GEIKIE *Text-bk. Geol.* II. II. §6. 174 Precipitates, consisting.. partly of the hydrated ferric oxide.

†'**ferrical**, *a. Obs.* [f. as FERRIC + -AL[1].] Of or pertaining to iron.

1612 STURTEVANT *Metallica* x. 72 The permanent.. instruments, and meanes which make up the Ferricall Furnace. *Ibid.* xi. 78 Iron furnaces.. may be much reformed.. with small charges, hauing our Ferricall inuention suited to them.

†**ferri'calcite.** *Min. Obs.* [f. L. *ferri-*, comb. form of *ferrum* iron + *calc-* CALX + -ITE.] An older name for CERITE, formerly supposed erroneously to be a 'calx' or oxide of iron.

1794 KIRWAN *Min.* I. 110 Species mixed with a notable proportion of iron, *ferricalcites.*

ferricrete ('fɛrɪkriːt). *Geol.* [f. FERRI- + CON)CRETE *sb.*, after CALCRETE.] Any breccia, conglomerate, or soil zone consisting of soil or other fragmentary material cemented by iron compounds.

1902 G. W. LAMPLUGH in *Geol. Mag.* 4th Ser. IX. 575, I have the hardihood to suggest..'ferricrete' when the binding substance is an iron-oxide. **1949** *Proc. Prehist. Soc.* XV. 48 Single beads of ferricrete grit, bone and kankar were also found. **1955** *Antiquity* XXIX. 206 The site is transversed by ferricrete ridges, marking a preceding wetter period, and this ferricrete postdates the 20–25 ft. beach. **1959** [see CALCRETE]. **1968** R. W. FAIRBRIDGE *Encycl. Geomorphol.* 554 Ferruginous sand-stone tends to develop a very remarkable ferricrete induration along its normal joint planes.

ferrie, obs. Sc. form of FARROW *v.*

ferrier ('fɛrɪə(r)). Also 5–7 *Sc.* **feryare, ferrear, -iour,** 8, 9 **ferryer.** [f. FERRY *v.* + -ER[1].]

1. = FERRYMAN.

c **1440** *Promp. Parv.* 156/2 Feryare, *pormeus.* **1513** DOUGLAS *Æneis* VI. v. 8 Thir riueris..kepit war By ane Charon, a grislie ferriar. **1605** STOW *Ann.* 250 The ferrier and his wife deceesing, left the same ferrie to their daughter. **1752** J. B. MACCOLL in *Scots Mag.* Aug. (1753) 400/1 He met Archibald Macinish ferrier. **1860** *All Year Round* No. 55. 119 The ghosts..have..become..ferriers. **1871** BROWNING *Balaust.* (1881) 45 The ferryer of the dead, Charon..Calls me.

2. *dial.* (See quot.)

1886 *Chesh. Gloss.*, *Ferrier*, salt-mining term; one who ferries or conveys the rock salt from the workings to the shaft.

ferriferous (fɛ'rɪfərəs), *a.* [f. L. *ferr-um* + -(I)FEROUS.] Producing or yielding iron; ***ferriferous rock***, a rock containing iron ore.

1811 PINKERTON *Petral.* I. 486 This excellent mineralogist suspects [it] to be ferriferous carbonate of lime. **1871** *Proc. Amer. Phil. Soc.* XII. 137 The fireclay under the ferriferous coal. **1883** *Anthropological Jrnl.* 322 Black heaps are more or less common in connection with certain ferriferous rocks.

†**fe'rrific**, *a. Obs.* [f. L. *ferr-um* iron + *-fic-us* making: see -FIC.] Iron-making; iron-producing.

1671 *Phil. Trans.* VI. 2235 The *Ferrifick* (if we may be allow'd to frame such a word) or the Iron-making Principle. Hence **1753** in CHAMBERS *Cycl. Supp.*

†**'ferrilite.** *Min. Obs.* [f. L. *ferr-um* + -(I)LITE.] = ROWLEY RAG.

1799 KIRWAN *Geol. Ess.* 200 Again 50 Silex 30 Argil 15 Calx 5 Iron should I imagine give wacken..and if the calx be eliminated, and in its place, iron substituted, ferrilite will result. **1804** WATT in *Phil. Trans.* XCIV. 281 *note*, Mr. Kirwan states the specific gravity of rowley rag, which he calls *ferrilite*, at 2.748.

ferrimagnetism (fɛrɪ'mægnɪtɪz(ə)m). [ad. F. *ferrimagnétism-e* (L. Néel 1948, in *Ann. de Physique* III. 146), f. FERRI- taken as an altered form of FERRO-) + MAGNETISM.] A type of magnetism which is macroscopically similar to ordinary ferromagnetism but which is attributed to the non-parallel (esp. antiparallel) alignment of neighbouring atoms or ions having unequal magnetic moments.

1948 *Physics Abstr.* LI. 336/1 In some cases (ferrimagnetism) the substance behaves at a low temperature like a ferromagnetic, but..the saturation magnetization at 0°K is much less than that corresponding to complete parallelism of all the spins. **1966** [see FERROMAGNETISM].

Hence **ferri'magnet**, a ferrimagnetic solid; **ferrimag'netic** *a.* and *sb.*, (a substance) possessing the properties of **ferrimagnetism.**

1950 *Physics Abstr.* LIII. 756/2 It is shown that the ferrites (ferrimagnetics) are a special case of antiferromagnetism. **1951** L. F. BATES *Mod. Magnetism* (ed. 3) viii. 322 The ferrites are ferrimagnetic substances which obey the general chemical formula Fe_2O_3MO, where M is a bivalent metal. **1955** *Amer. Jrnl. Physics* XXIII. 357/2 In a ferrimagnetic material..the complete magnetic structure contains more than one kind of magnetic ion, or more than one kind of crystallographic site. **1963** J. K. STANLEY *Electr. & Magn. Prop. Metals* v. 218 Ferrimagnets are much weaker than ferromagnets. **1966** PHILLIPS & WILLIAMS *Inorg. Chem.* II. xxviii. 421 Many of these compounds, e.g. $MgFe_2O_4$, show some magnetism despite the aligning of Fe^{3+} spins and they have been called ferrimagnetics. **1968** *Jrnl. Applied Physics* XXXIX. 903/1 If a ferrimagnet is submitted to an external increasing magnetic field individual sublattice rotations start to occur at some threshold field.

Ferris ('fɛrɪs). The name of G. W. G. *Ferris* (1859–96), American engineer, used attrib. to designate a fairground machine, the ***Ferris wheel*** (see quot. 1897), invented and first erected by him. Also *fig.*

1893 *Sci. Amer.* 9 Sept. 169/1 The World's Columbian Exposition—A view from the Ferris wheel. **1897** R. JOHNSON *Hist. World's Columb. Expos.* I. 77 The feature at the Exposition that corresponded in its character with the Eiffel Tower at the Paris Exposition of 1889 was the Ferris Wheel—an enormous wheel two hundred and fifty feet in diameter, projected into the air, hung upon supports of steel framework by an axle thirty-two inches in diameter, forty-five feet long, and weighing fifty-six tons... On the periphery of the wheel were hung thirty-six passenger cars, each with a seating capacity of forty to sixty persons. **1927** *Blackw. Mag.* Sept. 358/2 Two ferris wheels squeaked like pigs in agony. **1947** AUDEN *Age of Anxiety* VI. 136 Fortune's Ferris-wheel. *a* **1963** L. MACNEICE *Astrol.* (1964) iv. 120 It was Ptolemy who invented what Arthur Koestler has called 'the ferris-wheel universe'. **1969** AUDEN *City without Walls* 91 As passive objects, packed tightly together On Roller-Coaster or Ferris-Wheel, mortals Taste in their solid flesh the volitional joys of a seraph.

ferrite ('fɛraɪt). [f. L. *ferr-um* iron + -ITE.]

1. *Min.* **a.** 'A name proposed by Vogelsang for the amorphous hydroxide of iron, which in red or yellow particles plays an important part in many rocks, and whose composition is as yet undetermined' (Dana *Min.* 1875 App. 11.).

1879 RUTLEY *Stud. Rocks* x. 167 Ferrite is amorphous red, brown, or yellow earthy matter.

b. 'An alteration product of chrysolite in the doleryte between Gleniffar and Boyleston near Glasgow, Scotland' (Dana *Min.* (1892) 455).

2. Any compound that can be regarded as being formed from ferric oxide and a basic oxide or from ferric hydroxide and a base; *esp.* any of the compounds with the formula MFe_2O_4 (where M is a bivalent metal ion or a stoicheiometrically equivalent mixture of such ions), many of which have magnetic properties and a low electrical conductivity that make them suitable for use in high-frequency electrical components.

1851 H. WATTS tr. *Gmelin's Hand-bk. Chem.* V. 271 Ferrite of Soda.—78 pts. (1 At.) of ferric oxide mixed with excess of ignited carbonate of soda..form a difficultly fusible mixture. **1897** ROSCOE & SCHORLEMMER *Treat. Chem.* (ed. 3) II. 998 Ferric oxide combines with several basic monoxides to form compounds known as ferrites. **1921** J. R. PARTINGTON *Text-bk. Inorg. Chem.* xlviii. 987 With very strong bases unstable ferrites, *e.g.*, $Na_2Fe_2O_4$, are formed. **1936** *Physica* III. 463 The 'ferrites'..can be made by thoroughly mixing the finely divided oxide components in powder form, pressing it into a bar and heating the latter for a long time. **1950** *Proc. Inst. Electr. Engineers* XCVII. II. 238/1 Not all the ferrites are markedly magnetic, zinc and cadmium ferrites being notable exceptions. **1950** N. V. SIDGWICK *Chem. Elements* II. 1353 A variety of more complicated ferrites, with more than one Fe_2O_3 to each M'_2O or (more often) $M''O$, are known. **1955** *Sci. Amer.* Jan. 68/1 The ferrites and the pressed-powder magnets..are now attracting a great deal of attention. **1958** N. CUSACK *Electr. & Magn. Prop. Solids* xv. 350 The natural mineral ferrous ferrite is called magnetite and is the original lodestone.

3. *Metallurgy.* A soft allotrope of pure iron which has a body-centred cubic crystal structure and is stable below 910°C (*alpha iron*) and above 1403°C (*delta ferrite*, *delta iron*); also, a solid solution based on this allotrope, occurring in low-carbon iron alloys as an almost carbon-free constituent.

1888 H. M. HOWE *Metallurgy of Steel* in *Engin. & Mining Jrnl.* 18 Aug. 132 Minerals which compose iron. Name suggested here. Ferrite. Nearly pure iron. **1889, 1900** [see PEARLITE]. **1923** GLAZEBROOK *Dict. Appl. Physics* V. 328/2 In commercial iron and steel the ferrite is not pure, but contains dissolved substances, of which the chief are silicon, phosphorus, and manganese. **1957** [see ALPHA 3d]. **1958** *Jrnl. Iron & Steel Inst.* CXC. 92/2 The ferrites studied..were seven of the Mn–Zn..and two of the Co–Zn type with low Curie points.

4. *attrib.* and *Comb.* (in sense 2), esp. ***ferrite core*** (CORE *sb.*[1] 10, 10b).

1949 *RCA Rev.* Sept. 392 It is easy to obtain a Q of the order of 50 when using a partially saturated ferrite core. *Ibid.* 387 The use of ferrite-cored coils permits the use of exciter frequencies up to a few megacycles. **1954** E. MOLLOY *Radio & Telev. Engin. Ref. Bk.* xiv. 19 The small size of the ferrite-rod aerial makes it suitable for very small receivers. **1964** *Ann. N.Y. Acad. Sci.* CXV. 654 The LINC is a small stored-program digital computer which uses transistor circuitry and a random-access ferrite-core memory. **1965** *New Scientist* 6 May 368/1 The main interest in the wide range of synthetic ferrite crystalline compounds, fashioned by techniques familiar to the ceramics industry, has lain in their widespread use as small components in the telecommunications and electronics industries. **1970** *Nature* 12 Dec. 1039/1 The access time for the present ferrite core store is about 0·5 μs.

ferritic (fə'rɪtɪk), *a.* [f. FERRIT(E + -IC.] Containing, composed of, or characteristic of ferrite (FERRITE 3).

1927 *Amer. Inst. Mining & Metall. Engineers Techn. Bull.* No 14, 19 Farther away from the pipe the martensitic structure..is broken up by grains of distinctly ferritic appearance. **1934** *Jrnl. Iron & Steel Inst.* CXXX. II. 192 The hardness diminishes as the structure of these irons becomes more ferritic. **1958** *Times Rev. Industry* Feb. 40/1 Small additions of about 0·03 per cent. of boron have also been made to some of the heat-resisting ferritic stainless steels. **1961** *Metals Handbk.* (Amer. Soc. Metals) (ed. 8) I. 408/2 The terms martensitic, ferritic, austenitic, and precipitation hardening are used only in an unprecise qualitative sense, to differentiate classes of steels on the basis of their behavior during heat treatment.

ferritin ('fɛrɪtɪn). *Biochem.* [a. Czech *ferritin* (V. Laufberger 1934, in *Biologické Listy* XIX. 77), f. FERRI- after FERRATIN.] A water-soluble crystalline protein containing ferric iron that occurs in many animals, esp. in the liver and spleen, and is involved in the storage of iron by the body.

1937 *Chem. Abstr.* XXXI. 3979 Ferritin obtained from horse spleen contained 21% of trivalent Fe, combined with albumin. **1951** A. GROLLMAN *Pharmacol. & Therapeutics* xxxi. 716 The iron..taken up from the gastro-intestinal tract is combined with protein (as ferritin) in the mucosa and released in response to the demands of the body. **1957** *New Biol.* XXIII. 80 The rapid synthesis of the iron-containing protein, ferritin, in the livers of rats following the injection of large doses of 'soluble' iron. **1962** *New Scientist* 21 June 658/2 Biologically active iron compounds such as transferrin, ferritin, and haemosiderin.

ferrivorous (fə'rɪvərəs), *a. nonce-wd.* [f. L. *ferr-um* iron + *-(i)vor-us* + -OUS.] Feeding on iron.

1834 SOUTHEY *Doctor* cxxviii, This poor creature was really ferrivorous.

ferro- (fɛrəʊ).

1. **a.** Used as combining form of L. *ferrum* iron, chiefly *Min.* in the names of species containing iron, as **ferro-calcite**, a variety of calcite which contains carbonate of iron and turns brown on exposure (Dana 1868); **ferro-cobaltine, ferro-cobaltite,** compounds of iron and cobalt; †**ferro-columbite**, a synonym of tantalite, columbic and tantalic acid being mistaken for each other (Shepard 1844); ˌ**ferromag'nesian** *a.* [-AN], containing iron and magnesium; **ferromanganese**, see quots.; **ferrotellurite**, a tellurite of iron formed as microscopic yellow crystals on quartz; **ferro-tungsten**, iron containing a certain percentage of tungsten.

1868 DANA *Min.* 678 *Ferrocalcite. Ibid.* 72 *Ferrocobaltite.* **1844** SHEPARD *Min.* 154 *Ferrocolumbite.* **1881** *Encycl. Brit.* XIII. 352/1 The richer manganeisens (containing 15 per cent. and upward of manganese)..the term 'ferro-manganese' being applied to these products. **1877** *Amer. Jrnl. Sc.* Ser. III. XIV. 424 *Ferro-tellurite*, a crystalline coating on quartz. **1881** *Encycl. Brit.* XIII. 352/1 Biermann of Hanover has prepared ferro-tungsten containing from 20 to 50 per cent. of tungsten and a few parts per cent. of manganese. **1902** H. A. MIERS *Mineralogy* 471 Biotite (Ferro-magnesian Mica). **1944** A. HOLMES *Princ. Physical Geol.* iv. 42 Rocks in which olivine is the most abundant mineral (generally in association with other ferro-magnesian minerals) are called peridotite. **1970** *Nature* 6 June 927/1 The lunar rocks..contain large amounts of ferromagnesian minerals.

b. *Metallurgy.* In names of ferro-alloys with the meaning 'iron and', as ***ferro-aluminium***, ***ferrochrome*** (= next), ***ferrochromium***, ***ferromanganese***, ***ferromolybdenum***, ***ferro-silicon***, ***ferrotitanium***, ***ferrotungsten***, ***ferro-vanadium***. Also **ferro-alloy**, a crude alloy of iron with one or more other elements, esp. metals, used as a means of introducing them into steel, etc.

1905 *Electr. Rev.* 31 Mar. 517/2 The production of special steels and ferro-alloys. **1928** KINGZETT *Chem. Encycl.* (ed. 4) 395 Ferro-alloys are used in the steel industry to remove oxygen and nitrogen from molten steel, or to introduce into the steel a small proportion of the metal. **1960** *Times* 31 May (S. Afr. Suppl.) p. iv/4 The ferro-alloys used by the Union's iron and steel industry. **1888** *Chem. News* 6 July 11/2, I have applied this method to all the grades of ferro-aluminium that we manufacture, varying from 1 to 19 per cent Al. **1953** CASE & VAN HORN *Aluminium in Iron & Steel* i. 14 Ferroaluminium is an alloy of Fe and 40–50% Al. **1878** *Jrnl. Chem. Soc.* XXXIV. 772 The discovery of chrome-steel and ferrochrome by Berthier in 1821. **1958** *Times Rev. Industry* Mar. 47/3 Special steelmakers are in a dilemma about carbon-free ferro-chrome, one of the basic raw materials of special alloy steels. **1894** *Jrnl. Chem. Soc.* LXVI. II. 452 The crystals from chrome steel are smaller than those from ferrochromium. **1966** *McGraw-Hill Encycl. Sci. & Technol.* III. 104/1 Chromium is produced in the form of an iron alloy, ferro-chromium, by the reduction of chromite ores..in the electric furnace. **1864** O. E. PRIEGER *Brit. Pat.* 1366 2 June 3 My Invention consists in the production and manufacture of ferro-manganese, that is to say, the combination of metallic manganese with iron in various proportions. *Ibid.* 5 Ferro-manganese is a perfectly metallic substance, hitherto unknown, and containing solely manganese metal and iron with traces of carbon. **1881** Ferromanganese [see FERRO- 1]. **1967** A. H. COTTRELL *Introd. Metallurgy* xi. 132 The problem was solved in 1857 by Robert Mushet, who deoxidized the steel by adding a little manganese to it, in the form of ferro-manganese or spiegeleisen..before casting. **1902** *Jrnl. Soc. Chem. Industry* 30 June 832/1 (*heading*) The volumetric determination of molybdenum in molybdenum steel and ferro-molybdenum. **1963** W. H. DENNIS *Metallurgy Ferrous Metals* viii. 133 Ferro-molybdenum is added to steel chiefly to improve hardness and increase toughness. **1882** *Jrnl. Chem. Soc.* XLII. 118 (*heading*) Ferro-silicon. **1965** G. J. WILLIAMS *Econ. Geol. N.Z.* xvi. 262/2 A source of pure silica is of course fundamental for the manufacture of ferro-silicon. **1893** *Jrnl. Chem. Soc.* LXIV. II. 97 Ferrotitanium can only be dissolved by fusion with sodium hydrogen sulphate and treatment with cold water. **1953** AITCHISON & PUMPHREY *Engineering Steels* xii. 503 If the steel is to be cast into greensand moulds..special deoxidisers, such as aluminium or ferro-titanium, should always be added to the ladle. **1881** Ferrotungsten [see FERRO- 1]. **1955** KIRK & OTHMER *Encycl. Chem. Technol.* XIV. 359 In recent years..there has been a general trend toward the use of high-purity tungsten concentrates..instead of the ferroalloy by the steel industry due to the disadvantages of high-melting ferrotungsten. **1904** *Jrnl. Chem. Soc.* LXXXVI. II. 824 Ferrovanadium, containing 33 per cent. of vanadium, is made by igniting in the electric furnace the precipitate obtained by mixing sodium vanadate, iron sulphate, and sodium carbonate.

1956 W. D. HARGREAVES in D. L. Linton *Sheffield* 280 The city therefore uses quite large tonnages of pig-iron and of alloying metals, either in the pure form or as alloys such as ferro-chrome, ferro-vanadium, [etc.].

c. Used in a general sense to signify some connection with iron, as **ˌferrobac'terium** = *iron bacterium*; **ferro-ce'ment** [ad. It. *ferrocemento* (P. L. Nervi 1951, in *Ingegnere* XXV. 17)], a construction material made from cement mortar in the form of thin slabs reinforced with a meshwork of steel rods or wires; **fe'rrometer** [a. G. *ferrometer*], a type of instrument for determining the magnetic properties of a ferromagnetic material; **ferro-'resonance** *Electr.*, a type of resonance in which periodic saturation of an iron-cored inductance produces non-sinusoidal oscillations in a circuit; so **ferro-'resonant** *a.*; **ferrospi'nel** [*ferro-* in FERROMAGNETIC *a.* and *sb.*], a ferromagnetic substance having a spinel structure (as some synthetic ferrites). Also FERRO-CONCRETE.

1900 B. D. JACKSON *Gloss. Bot. Terms* 100/1 *Ferro-bacteria*, bacteria which oxidize ferrous to ferric salts. **1963** D. W. & E. E. HUMPHRIES tr. *Termier's Erosion & Sedimentation* vi. 143 It is known that the ferrobacteria can precipitate hydrated iron oxide, accompanied by alumina. **1956** tr. P. L. Nervi in *C & CA Library Translation No. 60* 1 It may be of interest to give an account..of a new material which, from its composition and method of construction, I propose calling 'ferro-cement'. **1963** *Engineering* 8 Feb. 232/1 Several ships were built during and after the Second World War in Italy from ferro-cement, as distinct from others built elsewhere from reinforced concrete. **1965** W. H. TAYLOR *Concrete Technol. & Pract.* xxxv. 553 Many spatial frames erected with ferro-cement include the 312-ft span corrugated vault of the Turin exhibition hall in Italy. **1935** *Sci. Abstr.* B. XXXVIII. 272 A description of the extension of the use of the ferrometer to the delineation of hysteresis loops. **1951** R. M. BOZORTH *Ferromagnetism* xix. 854 (*caption*) Basic circuit of the ferrometer, for determining current-voltage characteristics of a material, using a phase-shifter and rectifier. **1924** S. R. ROGET *Dict. Electr. Terms* 88 *Ferro-resonance*, the peculiar condition of resonance which can be produced in armoured cables when the iron sheathing causes a variation of the inductance according to the current. **1956** T. E. IVALL *Electronic Computers* viii. 103 Ferro-resonance is the condition which exists when a saturable inductor and a capacitor resonate so that the increased current at resonance keeps the inductor core saturated. **1949** *Electronic Engin.* XXI. 138 (*caption*) 5 watt ferro-resonant converter..which reduces the 50 c/s mains frequency to $16\frac{2}{3}$ c/s. **1950** R. L. HARVEY et al. in *RCA Rev.* Sept. 321 Ferrospinels are unique crystalline materials of spinel structure which are formed at high temperatures by solid-phase reaction of iron oxide and one or more of certain other metal oxides. [*Note*] The coined word *ferrospinel* is used to denote a *ferro*magnetic spinel... Ferrospinels are sometimes called 'ferrites'. **1953** F. LANGFORD-SMITH *Radio Designer's Handbk.* (ed. 4) xi. 459 Ferrospinels are being used increasingly in electronic equipment operating in the frequency range of 10 to 5000 Kc/s.

2. *Chem.* Originally used with the general sense 'containing iron'; but now applied to designate 'ferrous' as opposed to 'ferric' compounds of iron: cf. FERRI-. †**ferro'cyanate** = *ferrocyanide* (the distinction in quot. 1810–26 belongs to an obsolete theory of the structure of acids and salts). **ferrocyan'hydric** or **ferrocy'anic acid**, a tetrabasic acid, H_4FeCy_2, forming a white crystalline powder. **ferro'cyanide**, a salt of ferrocyanhydric acid, as ***potassium ferrocyanide***, popularly yellow prussiate of potash. **ferrocy'anogen**, the hypothetical radical $FeCy_2$ supposed to exist in ferrocyanides. **ferro'prussiate** = *ferrocyanide* (see 3). †**ferro'prussic acid** = *ferrocyanhydric acid.*

1810–26 HENRY *Elem. Chem.* (1826) I. 461 The salt called triple prussiate (ferro-cyanate) of baryta. **1819** CHILDREN *Chem. Anal.* 327 *Ferrocyanic Acid*: we are indebted to Mr. Porrett for the first correct ideas of this acid. **1810–26** HENRY *Elem. Chem.* (1826) I. 463 The compound obtained is, therefore, no longer a prussiate or ferro-cyanate, but a *ferro-cyanide*. **1842** GROVE *Corr. Phys. Forces* 51 This is washed with an acid, which then gives with ferro-cyanide of potassium, the prussian blue precipitate. **1869** ROSCOE *Elem. Chem.* 377 By acting with potassium amalgam on an aqueous solution the ferricyanide is converted into ferro-cyanide. **1850** DAUBENY *Atom. Th.* vii. (ed. 2) 215 Cy 1 + iron 1 forms ferrocyanogen. **1876** MELDOLA in *Encycl. Brit.* V. 555/1 The group $FeCy_6$ is regarded as an acid radicle (ferrocyanogen), and a large number of its salts (ferro-cyanides) are known.

3. *Photogr.* **ferro-'gallic** *a.*, designating a photocopying process in which paper is sensitized with a solution containing ferric salts and developed in gallic acid; also, the paper so sensitized; **ferro-'prussiate**, used *attrib.* to designate a process for making blueprints in which paper is sensitized with a solution of potassium ferricyanide and ferric ammonium citrate and developed in water, and also the paper so sensitized.

1902 *Encycl. Brit.* XXXI. 703/2 For architects and engineers, cyanotype and ferro-gallic papers are prepared in rolls of considerable width for the direct reproduction of tracings and drawings, as blue or black prints by these methods. **1918** *Photo-Miniature* Mar. Gloss., *Ferro-gallic process*, for copying plans giving black lines on white ground. **1957** SOUTHWORTH & BENTLEY *Photogr. Chemicals & Chemistry* (ed. 3) 91 *Gallic acid*... Its formation of a blue-black ink-like compound with ferric salts is made use of in the ferro-gallic black-line modification of the blue-print process, gallic acid being employed as developer. **1887** S. K. BURTON *Pract. Guide Photogr. & Photo-Mech. Printing* II. 103 (*heading*) Marion's Ferro-Prussiate, or Blue Process. *Ibid.*, Of all the various methods for reproducing Drawing, Marion's Ferro-Prussiate Process is still the simplest and most practical. *Ibid.* 105 In the course of printing, the Ferro-Prussiate Paper assumes various tints. **1911** *Encycl. Brit.* XXVI. 93/2 The earliest discovered process [of photo copying], the ferroprussiate, is still the one most largely used. **1953** KIRK & OTHMER *Encycl. Chem. Technol.* XI. 146 The common negative blueprint or ferroprussiate process was discovered by Sir John Herschel in 1842, and has undergone only slight modification.

ferroan ('fɛrəʊən, fə'rəʊən), *a.* *Min.* [f. L. *ferrum* iron + -OAN.] Of a mineral: having a (small) proportion of a constituent element replaced by ferrous iron.

1930 W. T. SCHALLER in *Amer. Mineralogist* XV. 571 Iron —ferroan, ferrian. **1944** C. PALACHE et al. *Dana's Syst. Min.* (ed. 7) I. 637 Some fibrous brucite is reported to be highly ferroan, but this may be owing to admixed magnetite. **1965** G. J. WILLIAMS *Econ. Geol. N.Z.* xi. 167/2 The occurrence of camptonites, vogesites and monchiquite with abundant ferroan dolomite.

ferrocene ('fɛrəʊsiːn). *Chem.* [f. FERRO- + cyclopentadi*ene*.] An orange crystalline compound, $Fe(C_5H_5)_2$, a molecule of which consists of an iron atom symmetrically situated between two parallel, superimposed hydrocarbon rings of aromatic character.

1952 R. B. WOODWARD et al. in *Jrnl. Amer. Chem. Soc.* LXXIV. 3458 We now wish to record experiments which demonstrate typically aromatic properties of this unique iron compound, for which we propose the name *ferrocene*. **1957** *Jrnl. Chem. Educ.* XXXIV. 271/1 Ferrocene has demonstrated significant antiknock properties in fuels for spark ignition engines. **1963** J. H. HARWOOD *Industr. Applic. Organometallic Compounds* 183 Derivatives of ferrocene are effective ultra-violet absorbers for space-ship coatings. **1965** *New Scientist* 2 Dec. 658 (*caption*) Dicyclopentadienyl iron, or ferrocene, the first member of a new class of organometallic compounds.

ferro-concrete (ˌfɛrəʊ'kɒnkriːt). [FERRO-.] = *armoured* CONCRETE or REINFORCED CONCRETE. Also as *adj.*, composed or constructed of ferro-concrete.

1900 G. L. MOUCHEL *Brit. Pat. 8831*, This invention relates to building blocks, caissons, piers,..and analogous structures, and it has for its object to employ in the manufacture, construction, or erection of such structures suitable forms of 'ferro-concrete' *i.e.* concrete having embedded in it a strengthening metal skeleton or framework. **1907** [see CONCRETE *sb.* 3]. **1914** *Scotsman* 12 Oct. 8/7 The tall white ferro-concrete telegraph posts lining many of the main roads. **1928** *Oxf. Poetry* 42 Fierce ferro-concrete blares, On Woolworth, on! **1957** *London Mag.* Feb. 73 As a result their poems are integrated constructions that look like towers of ferro-concrete.

ferroelectric (ˌfɛrəʊɪ'lɛktrɪk), *a.* and *sb.* [f. ELECTRIC *a.* and *sb.*, after *ferromagnetic*.]

A. *adj.* **a.** Of a body or substance: having the property that a permanent electric polarization can be induced or reversed by the application of an electric field; exhibiting hysteresis between displacement and an applied electric field. **b.** Of or pertaining to ferroelectricity.

1935 H. MUELLER in *Physical Rev.* 2nd Ser. XLVII. 180 The dielectric properties of Rochelle salt..are analogous to the ferromagnetic properties near the Curie point. This fact justifies the use of Eq. (7) for the 'ferro-electric' temperature range. **1940** *Ibid.* LVII. 829/2 It neglects the large piezoelectric effects which occur in all ferroelectric crystals. **1955** *Sci. Amer.* June 96/2 The material used in the experimental ferroelectric memory systems is barium titanate.

B. *sb.* A ferroelectric body or substance.

1946 *Nature* 15 June 808/1 As distinct from other known ferro-electrics, barium titanate does not contain hydrogen. **1958** *Electronic Engin.* XXX. 678 The application of a polarizing field will switch the ferro-electric to one or other of its stable states. **1970** J. GRINDLAY *Introd. Phenomenol. Theory Ferroelectr.* i. 1 Many ferroelectrics possess a spontaneous dipole moment only in certain temperature ranges.

ferroe'lectrically, *adv.* [f. prec. + -AL + -LY².] In a ferroelectric way.

1954 C. ZWIKKER *Physical Prop. Solid Materials* xii. 216 Rochelle salt..also has a lower Curie point (−20°C) below which the material behaves non-ferroelectrically. **1971** *Nature* 25 June 542/2 Lattice vibrations in ionic crystals which order ferroelectrically..are reviewed.

ferroelectricity (ˌfɛrəʊɪlɛk'trɪsɪtɪ). [f. as prec. + -ITY.] The quality of being ferroelectric; the phenomena exhibited by ferroelectric substances.

1946 *Industr. & Engin. Chem.* XXXVIII. 1108/2 This distinguishes barium titanate from potassium dihydrogen phosphate.., where the dielectric anomalies and dielectric saturation (ferroelectricity) are accompanied by pronounced λ-points. **1950** *Physical Rev.* 2nd Ser. LXXVIII. 748 Even a relatively small ionic polarizability for the Ti ions will be enough to lead to ferroelectricity. **1967** B. T. MATTHIAS in E. F. Weller *Ferroelectricity* 182 Ferroelectricity..really has very little or nothing in common with iron and magnetic forces.

ferromagnet (fɛrəʊ'mægnɪt). [Back-formation from next, after *magnet* and *magnetic*.] A ferromagnetic body or substance.

1941 *Physical Rev.* 2nd Ser. LX. 252 (*heading*) Statistics of the two-dimensional ferromagnet. *Ibid.* 252/2 The present paper is an attempt to gain sound statistical information about some model of a ferromagnet. **1949** *Ibid.* LXXVI. 1195/2 In a single-domain ferromagnet, the bound surface charge creates a depolarizing field. **1968** R. A. LEVY *Princ. Solid State Physics* v. 237 Macroscopically a ferromagnet often appears not to have any spontaneous magnetization, because the domain magnetizations are randomly oriented and thereby cancel one another.

ferromagnetic (ˌfɛrəʊmæg'nɛtɪk), *a.* and *sb.* [f. FERRO- + MAGNETIC *a.* and *sb.*] **A.** *adj.* †**1.** Used synonymously with PARAMAGNETIC *a.*: having a positive magnetic susceptibility. *Obs.*

1850 W. THOMSON in *Phil. Mag.* 3rd Ser. XXXVII. 250 It appears to me very probable that this assumption is correct for all known diamagnetic substances, and for homogeneous feebly ferromagnetic substances. *Ibid.* 253 A homogeneous feebly ferromagnetic substance, containing no iron. **1872–5** CLIFFORD *Lect.* (1879) I. 241 Faraday gives reasons for believing that all bodies are either ferromagnetic or diamagnetic. **1881** MAXWELL *Electr. & Magn.* II. 46 When the magnetization is in the same direction as the magnetic force..the substance is called Paramagnetic, Ferromagnetic, or more simply Magnetic. **1880** J. E. H. GORDON *Physical Treat. Electr. & Magn.* II. xxxi. 14 Iron and similar bodies which are attracted by the magnet are called Ferro-magnetic, or sometimes Para-magnetic bodies. Substances which are repelled are called Diamagnetic. **1886** *Phil. Trans. R. Soc.* CLXXVI. 468 Most bodies are either very slightly ferro-magnetic or very slightly diamagnetic. On the other hand iron, nickel, and cobalt are enormously magnetic.

2. a. Of a body or substance: having a large, variable magnetic permeability and exhibiting hysteresis. **b.** Characteristic of or pertaining to ferromagnetism.

The distinction between ferromagnetic and paramagnetic substances was first emphasized by P. Curie (*Ann. de Chim. et de Phys.* (1895) 7me Sér. V. 289).

1896 E. ATKINSON tr. *H. du Bois's Magn. Circuit* i. 9 By many authors the terms 'ferromagnetic' and 'para-magnetic' are used pretty indiscriminately. For the present it may be as well to keep the two groups separate. **1929** W. PEDDIE *Molec. Magn.* iv. 57 Ferromagnetic substances become paramagnetic at sufficiently high temperature. **1951** L. F. BATES *Mod. Magn.* (ed. 3) viii. 322 The ferrites are ferrimagnetic substances... They are all ferromagnetic at room temperatures, except zinc ferrite, which is paramagnetic, and cadmium ferrite which is sometimes paramagnetic and sometimes ferro-magnetic. **1962** K. J. STANDLEY *Oxide Magn. Materials* i. 2 One may regard each sub-lattice [of a ferrimagnetic material] as ferromagnetic. **1965** A. H. MORRISH *Physical Princ. Magn.* i. 4 If the atomic moments are aligned parallel, the substance is said to be ferromagnetic.

B. *sb.* A ferromagnetic body or substance.

1850 *Phil. Mag.* 3rd Ser. XXXVII. 253 A small ball of this body would, when acted upon by a feeble magnetizing force, become on the whole magnetized like a ferromagnetic, and would be urged from places of weaker towards places of stronger force. **1914** POYNTING & THOMSON *Text-bk. Physics* xvi. 207 Though Faraday only used the two classes, paramagnetics and diamagnetics, and to one or other of these referred all bodies, it is usual now to separate out the three metals iron, nickel, and cobalt, and to these may probably be added manganese, and to class them as Ferromagnetics. **1962** *Times* 12 Oct. 2/6 Studies of paramagnetics and ferro-magnetics.

ferromagnetism (fɛrəʊ'mægnɪtɪz(ə)m). [f. FERRO- + MAGNETISM.

Gregory's use of *ferromagnetism* was independent of Thomson's use of *ferromagnetic*; in the preface to his *Lett. Anim. Magnetism* (1851) Gregory states that it resulted from his mishearing the (then new) word *paramagnetism*.]

The quality of being ferromagnetic; the phenomena exhibited by ferromagnetic materials. (Broadly including ferrimagnetism but in some contexts contrasted with it.)

1851 W. GREGORY *Lett. Anim. Magnet.* Pref. 15 Heat, light, electricity and ferro-magnetism. *Ibid.* Pref. 16, I understand by Ferro-magnetism almost the same as Dr. Faraday does by Para-magnetism; and I use the term in contradistinction to Vital or Animal Magnetism. **1930** E. C. STONER *Magnetism* iv. 74 Ferromagnetism is to be attributed to the spin moments of the electrons in the atoms and ions, and not to the spin moments of free electrons, which normally should give rise only to a small paramagnetism. **1957** *Encycl. Brit.* IX. 186/1 Ferro-magnetism is the kind of magnetism associated with iron, cobalt and nickel and some alloys. **1966** *McGraw-Hill Encycl. Sci. & Technol.* V. 229/1 Some materials exhibit a special form of ferromagnetism below the Curie temperature called ferrimagnetism.

‖**ferronerie, ferronnerie** (fɛrɔnri). [Fr. *ferronnerie* ironwork, wrought iron.] (See quot. 1960.)

1925 B. RACKHAM tr. *Hannover's Pottery* I. iv. 281 Thus certain large basins and plateaux (often in 'broken' shapes), with scenes of pastoral gallantry within borders of rococo ornament or *décor ferronerie*, are painted in colours of the Guillibaud class. **1934** *Burlington Mag.* Apr. 170/2 To the Italian velvet designs imitated by Turkish weavers can be added one of the 'ferronerie' type. **1944** *Ibid.* Nov. 284/1 A remarkable polychrome type with *ferronerie* decoration done under Netherlandish influence. **1960** R. G. HAGGAR *Conc. Encycl. Cont. Pott. & Porc.* 172/1 *A ferronnerie*, ornament consisting of arabesques, scrolls and volutes resembling or imitating ironwork, characteristic of the Antwerp maiolica painters of the sixteenth century and originating with them.

‖**ferronière, ferronnière** (fɛrɔnjɛr). [Fr. *ferronière*, a frontlet; a coronet worn on the forehead: after Leonardo da Vinci's portrait *La Belle Ferronnière*.] (See quot. 1960.)

1840 THACKERAY in *Fraser's Mag.* June 681/2 The sisters ..with pink scarfs..and brass *ferronières*..were voted very charming. **1908** H. C. SMITH *Jewellery* xx. 172 This head ornament is known as the *ferronière*. **1960** H. HAYWARD *Antique Coll.* 117/1 *Ferronière*, a chain worn as an ornament encircling the head with a jewel in the centre.

ferroso- (fɛˈrəʊsəʊ), *Chem.*, combining form of mod.L. *ferrōsus* FERROUS. Only in *ferroso-ferric oxide* (see quots.).

1853 R. HUNT *Man. Photography* 55 That peculiar intermediate oxide to which the name of *Ferroso-ferric* has been given by Berzelius. **1870** J. T. SPRAGUE in *Eng. Mech.* 11 Mar. 621/3 A natural substance, Ferrosoferric Oxide Fe_3O_4..known as the loadstone.

ferrotype (ˈfɛrətaɪp). [f. FERRO- + TYPE.]

1. 'A term applied by Mr. Robert Hunt, the discoverer, to some photographic processes in which the salts of iron are the principal agents' (Ogilv.).

1844 R. HUNT in *14th Rep. Brit. Assoc.* (1845) II. 36 On the Ferrotype, and the Property of Sulphate of Iron in developing Photographic Images. **1845** *Athenæum* 22 Feb. 203 The Energiatype, or, as the discoverer now names the process, the Ferrotype.

2. A process by which positive photographs are taken on thin iron plates; a photograph so taken. Also *attrib.*, as ***ferrotype plate, process.***

1879 G. PRESCOTT *Sp. Telephone* 89 The ferrotype plate used by photographers. **1880** *Times* 5 Oct. 6/6 Ferrotypes.. so called from being done on thin iron instead of glass.

b. = *ferrotype plate*.

1879 G. PRESCOTT *Sp. Telephone* 274 Two small blocks of wood..one perforated for the mouth-piece and holding a ferrotype.

Hence **ˈferrotyper**, one who takes photographs by the ferrotype process.

ferrour: see FERRER.

ferrous (ˈfɛrəs), *a. Chem.* [f. L. *ferr-um* iron + -OUS.] **1.** A term applied to compounds in which iron combines as a divalent, e.g. ***ferrous oxide***, FeO, also called *iron protoxide*. Also, characteristic of ferrous compounds; of or pertaining to iron in its bivalent state; applied to iron in that state.

c **1865** G. GORE in *Circ. Sc.* I. 199/2 Ferrous sulphate (protosulphate of iron). **1873** J. P. COOKE *New Chem.* 173 Ferrous and ferric sulphates..correspond to ferrous and ferric oxides. **1876** HARLEY *Mat. Med.* 204 Iron forms with chlorine..Ferrous chloride. **1878** W. ABNEY *Treat. Photogr.* iv. 30 The action of light on all ferric salts, *under certain conditions*, is to reduce them to the ferrous state. **1940** R. L. HADEN *Princ. Hematol.* (ed. 2) iv. 53 The iron attached to the hematin is in the ferrous form. **1950** *Science News* XV. 100 Its absorption bands are visible only when the iron which is in its molecule is in the reduced or ferrous state. **1962** P. J. & B. DURRANT *Introd. Adv. Inorg. Chem.* xxiv. 1023 The oxides and sulphides of iron are giant molecule compounds in which either the ferrous or the ferric ion is present. *Ibid.* 1025 Compounds of ferrous iron.

2. Containing iron in significant quantities; of or pertaining to iron.

1887 *Proc. R. Soc.* XLII. 202 There was but little space, outside the section of the iron, enclosed by the coil; and the small amount of magnetic induction in this non-ferrous space was allowed for. **1915** IBBOTSON & AITCHISON *Anal. Non-Ferrous Alloys* p. v, The chemistry of the ferrous alloys. **1954** J. L. BRAY *Ferrous Process Metallurgy* i. 1 For the manufacture of ferrous alloys, large quantities of iron ore.. are required.

ferrozone: see FEROZONE.

ferruginate (fəˈruːdʒɪneɪt), *v.* [f. L. *ferrūgin-*, *ferrūgō* + -ATE³.] To give to (anything) the colour or properties of the rust of iron. Hence **feˈrruginated** *ppl. a.*, in mod. Dicts.

ferrugineous (fɛruːˈdʒɪnɪəs), *a.* [f. L. *ferrūgine-us* (f. *ferrūgin-em* iron rust) + -OUS.] = FERRUGINOUS in all senses.

1663 BULLOKAR, *Ferrugineous*, rusty, of an iron color. **1671** J. WEBSTER *Metallogr.* xxviii. 350 It [Loadstone] is a hard Stone, ferrugineous, or irony. **1691** RAY *Creation* (1714) 87 Hence they [waters] are cold, hot..ferrugineous, etc. **1750** G. HUGHES *Barbadoes* II. 55 Stones..containing, by their dusky ferrugineous Colour, probably much Iron. **1859** FARRAR *J. Home* 108 Black as the ferrugineous ferry-boat of Charon. **1882** *Garden* 1 Apr. 212/1 The leaves..are very ferrugineous beneath.

ferruginous (fəˈruːdʒɪnəs), *a.* [f. L. *ferrūgin-*, *ferrūgō* iron rust (f. *ferrum* iron) + -OUS. Cf. F. *ferrugineux*.

The use 1 b, which exists also in Fr., is due to the word being referred directly to the L. *ferrum*, as if its formation were analogous to that of *oleaginous*, etc.]

1. a. Originally: Of or pertaining to, of the nature of, iron rust; containing iron rust (said *esp.* of mineral springs, earths, etc.). **b.** Now commonly: Of the nature of iron as a chemical element; containing iron as a constituent.

a **1661** FULLER *Worthies, Bristol* III. 34 The Water thereof runneth through some Mineral of Iron, as appeareth by the rusty ferruginous taste. **1684** BOYLE *Mineral Waters* Wks. 1772 IV. 798 Mineral waters, especially ferruginous ones. **1792** A. YOUNG *Trav. France* 290 Franche Compté abounds with red ferruginous loams. **1807** T. THOMSON *Chem.* (ed. 3) II. 342 Ferruginous prussiate of potash. **1816** W. SMITH *Strata Ident.* 12 Concreted by a ferruginous cement. **1834** MRS. SOMERVILLE *Connex. Phys. Sc.* xxx. (1849) 352 A ferruginous body acquires polarity. **1871** BLACKIE *Four Phases* i. 122 The variations of the magnetic needle near ferruginous rocks. **1871** *Daily News* 21 Sept., A very insignificant ferruginous spring was the only one they came across.

2. Resembling iron-rust in colour; reddish brown.

1656–81 BLOUNT *Glossogr.*, *Ferruginous*..of the colour of rusty iron. **1766** PENNANT *Zool.* (1768) I. 104 The whole upper part of the body is of a ferruginous color. **1789** MILLS in *Phil. Trans.* LXXX. 93 The water..tinges the sides of a ferruginous hue. **1870** HOOKER *Stud. Flora* 462 Root-stock ..clothed with broad ferruginous scales.

b. In the names of animals, plants or minerals.

1847 CRAIG, *Ferruginous opal*, or Jasper opal. **1861** MISS PRATT *Flower Pl.* V. 95 Ferruginous Sallow. **1876** SMILES *Sc. Natur.* xv. (ed. 4) 259 The Ferruginous..and the Eider duck visit the lock occasionally.

Hence, **feˈrruginousness**.

1727 in BAILEY vol. II.

ferrular, -ule, var. ff. of FERULAR, -ULE.

ferrule (ˈfɛrəl), *sb.* Forms: 5 vyrell, 7–8 verrel, -il(l, 7–9 ferrel, -il, (7 ferrell), 8–9 ferule, 8– ferrule, 9 ferrol. [transformed (as if dim. of L. *ferrum*) from the older *vyroll*, VERREL, VIRL, ad. OF. *virelle*, *virol* (Fr. *virole*), med.L. *virola*:—L. *viriola*, dim. of *viriæ*, pl. bracelets.]

1. A ring or cap of metal put round the end of a stick, tube, etc. to strengthen it, or prevent splitting and wearing.

1611 COTGR., *Cartibes d'vn moulinet*, the ferrels, or bands of yron whereby the ends of a windlesse are strengthened. **1685** *Lond. Gaz.* No. 2054/4 A Joynt Cane, wrought with a Gold Head on it, and a Brass Ferril. **1709** F. HAUKSBEE *Phys.-Mech. Exp.* v. (1719) 104, I took a fine Glass Tube.. The upper Orifice had a Ferrel..cemented on it. **1715** KERSEY, *Verrel* or *Verril*, a little Brass or Iron ring, at the small end of a Cane, or Handle of a Tool, etc. **1794** W. FELTON *Carriages* (1801) I. 222 The dragstaff..is made of strong ash, with iron ferrules on the ends. **1820** L. HUNT *Indicator* No. 33 (1822) I. 257 Instead of the brass ferrel poking in the mud. **1838** DICKENS *Nich. Nick.* xxv, Producing a fat green cotton one [umbrella] with a battered ferrule. **1844** *Regul. & Ord. Army* 10 The Lance of the Standards and Guidons to be nine feet long (spear and ferrel included). [So in **1860**; the word is not used in recent editions.]

attrib. **1799** *Spirit Pub. Journals* (1800) III. 209 Taking especial care that the ferule end..be sufficiently dirty.

2. a. A ring or band, usually either giving additional strength or holding the parts of anything together.

1632 SHERWOOD, Verrill, or iron band for a woodden toole, *virole*. **1708** *Brit. Apollo* No. 117. 4/2 Dropt..a Cane ..with a Silver Ferril. **1726** DESAGULIERS in *Phil. Trans.* XXXIV. 79, I fix'd a Leaden Pipe..of 2 Inches in the Bore, by means of 3 Ferrels, or short Communication-Pipes. **1730** SAVERY *ibid.* XXXVI. 298 The Glass Concave was fixed in the great End of a thin Brass Ferule. **1773** *Ibid.* LXIII. 418, I cover this part of the tube with a brass verrel. **1832** BABBAGE *Econ. Manuf.* i. (ed. 3) 10 A glazier's apprentice, when using a diamond set in a conical ferrule. **1833** LOUDON *Encycl. Archit.* 750 Ferrol, in plumbing, is a brass tube soldered to the lead pipe at one end, and then driven into the main water-pipe. **1855** HOLDEN *Hum. Osteol.* (1878) 37 A broad and thick ferule of cartilage. **1859** GULLICK & TIMBS *Paint.* 296 Flat brushes, in German-silver ferules. **1867** J. HOGG *Microsc.* I. i. 7 A handle of ebony..is attached by a brass ferrule and two screws. **1904** GOODCHILD & TWENEY *Technol. & Sci. Dict.* 219/2 *Ferrule*, a small pulley used for rotating drills, or pieces of work that have to be turned or otherwise operated on. **1940** *Chambers's Techn. Dict.* 328/2 *Ferrule*, a slotted metal tube into the ends of which the conductors of a joint are inserted.

b. (See quot.)

1899 C. K. PAUL *Memories* viii. 249 '*Ferrule* of a book', means the corner. 'Do you mean that one with the yellow *ferrule*.'

3. (*Steam-engine.*) 'A bushing for expanding the end of a flue' (Webster).

4. The frame of a slate.

1847–78 in HALLIWELL.

5. *Naut.*

1823 CRABB, *Ferrule*, a small iron hook fixed on the extremity of the yards, boom, etc.

ferrule, ferrel (ˈfɛrəl), *v.* Also 5 vyrell, 7– ferrel(l, 8 ferril. [f. prec.] *trans.* To fit or furnish with a ferrule.

1496 *Bk. St. Albans, Fishing* 8 Thenne vyrell the staffe at bothe endes wyth longe hopis of yron. **1670** NARBOROUGH *Jrnl.* in *Acc. Sev. Late Voy.* I. (1694) 89 The Staves..were headed and ferrelled with Silver. **1712** J. JAMES tr. *Le Blond's Gardening* 196 Wooden Pipes..are ferriled and girdled with Iron. **1787** BEST *Angling* (ed. 2) 10 If you ferrel it [the rod], observe that they [pieces] fit. **1870** THORNBURY *Old Stories Re-told* 247 To ferrule the pikes.

ˈferruled (ˈfɛrəld), *ppl. a.* [f. as prec. + -ED².] Provided with a ferrule.

1867 F. FRANCIS *Angling* ix. (1880) 318 A spliced rod is very little heavier than a ferruled one two feet shorter. **1884** *Pall Mall G.* 23 Feb. 2/2 The feruled ends of dripping umbrellas. **1893** *Westm. Gaz.* 20 Mar. 8/3 Ferruled tubes having been put in, she [the *Vulcan* torpedo-depôt-ship] has now realised the original expectations.

ferruminate (fəˈruːmɪneɪt), *v. Obs.* or *arch.* [f. L. *ferrūmināt-*, ppl. stem of *ferrūmināre* to cement, f. *ferrūmen* cement, f. *ferrum* iron.] *trans.* To cement, solder, unite.

1623 in COCKERAM. *a* **1641** BP. R. MOUNTAGU *Acts & Mon.* (1642) 281 A course directly tending to break asunder that which he intended to ferruminate and to foment. **1650** CHARLETON *Paradoxes* Prol. 23 The Terrestriall Atomes are fixed, coagmentated, and ferruminated into a solid Concretion. **1657** TOMLINSON *Renou's Disp.* 399* The flave [Boras] is best for ferruminating gold.

fig. **1819** COLERIDGE *Lit. Rem.* (1836) II. 275 Other passages ferruminated by Jonson from Seneca's tragedies.

ferrumination (fəˌruːmɪˈneɪʃən). *Obs.* or *arch.* [ad. L. *ferrūminātiōn-em*, n. of action f. *ferrūmināre*; see prec.] The action of cementing together.

1612 WOODALL *Surg. Mate* Wks. (1653) 271 *Ferrumination* is the joyning together of a fracture in one and the same Metal..by a Mineral flux. **1657** TOMLINSON *Renou's Disp.* 124 It helps the ferrumination of broken bones.

fig. **1817** COLERIDGE *Biog. Lit.* 10, I mention this by way of elucidating one of the most ordinary processes in the ferrumination of these centos.

ferrup (ˈfɛrʌp). *Obs.* exc. *dial.* Used in exclamations, † ***what a ferrup, what the ferrups*** (= 'what the deuce'), ***by the ferrups.***

1679 DRYDEN *Tr. & Cr.* III. ii, Put up, and vanish; they are coming out: What a ferrup, will you play when the dance is done? *c* **1860** STATON *Rays fro' th' Loomenary* 38 Nay by the ferrups. **1865** MISS LAHEE *Betty o' Yeps Tale* (1870) 20 Whoy, what the ferrups don yo myen?

ferrur, var. of FERRER *Obs.*

† **ˈferrure.** *Obs.*—⁰ [a. Fr. *ferrure*, f. *ferrer* to shoe (horses):—L. *ferrāre*, f. *ferrum* iron.] Horse-shoeing, farriery.

1692–1732 in COLES. **1775** in ASH.

† **ˈferrurie.** *Obs. rare.* Also ferrurye. [f. *ferrour*, FERRER + -Y³.] = FARRIERY.

1601 F. TATE *Househ. Ord. Edw. II* §56 (1876) 42 A vallet carnauer that hath knoledge in marshausy & ferrurie.

ferry (ˈfɛrɪ), *sb.*¹ Forms: 5 ferrye, 5–6 fery(e, 6 ferrie, 5– ferry. [f. the vb.; its late appearance seems to exclude the supposition that it is a. ON. *ferja* of equivalent formation. Cf. Du. *veer*, MHG. *vere*, *ver*, mod.G. *fähre* in same sense.]

† **1.** A passage or crossing. *Obs.*

c **1425** WYNTOUN *Cron.* VIII. xl. 143 At þe Ferry of þe Hill þai mete.

2. *esp.* A passage or place where boats pass over a river, etc. to transport passengers and goods.

c **1440** *Promp. Parv.* 156/2 Fery over a watyr. *c* **1470** HENRY *Wallace* I. 285 Besyd Landoris the ferrye our thai past. **1535** COVERDALE *Judg.* iii. 28 They folowed him, & wanne yᵉ ferye of Iordane. **1538** LELAND *Itin.* I. 31 There be 4..Placis namid as ferys apon the Water of Lindis. **1611** CORYAT *Crudities* 20 The ferry where we were transported into the Ile of France. **1775** WYNDHAM *Tour Wales* 42 Just above the ferry is the seat of Mr. Vernon. **1825** J. NEAL *Bro. Jonathan* II. 95 We blow..when we come nigh the taverns ..or post offices, or ferries.

3. a. Provision for the conveyance of passengers, etc. by boat from one shore to the other.

c **1489** CAXTON *Blanchardyn* viii. 33 The knight of the Ferry attended to receiue him. **1700** *Mod. Law Reports* III. 294 The Defendant had petitioned the king to destroy the Ferry. **1847** MRS. A. KERR *Hist. Servia* x. 193 Not to interfere with the ferry of Poscharewaz. **1892** GARDINER *Student's Hist. Eng.* 20 A ferry was established where London Bridge now stands.

fig. **1850** CARLYLE *Latter-d. Pamph.* v. 32 We have all of us our ferries in this world.

b. = FERRY-BOAT.

1590 SPENSER *F.Q.* II. vi. 19 She soon to hand Her ferry brought. **1596** SHAKS. *Merch. V.* III. iv. 53 Bring them I pray thee..to the common Ferrie Which trades to Venice. **1701** *Lond. Gaz.* No. 3722/1 The French had sunk divers Ferries and other Boats in the River. **1798** R. P. *Tour in Wales* 24 (MS.) We here engaged a ferry over the Wye. **1951** *Oxf. Jun. Encycl.* IV. 147 (*caption*) Dover-Dunkirk train-ferry in Dover docks. The opening through which the trains run on to the ferry can be seen on the left. **1961** F. H. BURGESS *Dict. Sailing* 85 *Ferry*,..any boat employed in ferrying goods and passengers.

c. Used allusively with reference to Charon's ferry (see CHARON); ***to take the ferry***: to die.

1895 G. MEREDITH *Amaz. Marr.* xxviii, The Lethean ferry-boatload. **1928** GALSWORTHY *Swan Song* III. vi. 266 What are you going to do with your pictures when you take the ferry? Leave them to the nation?

d. Used jocularly to describe the passage between England and New York, Australia, or New Zealand.

1902 C. HYNE *Mr. Horrocks Purser* 57 They see funny things on the Atlantic ferry which rich young men get mixed up in. **1907** *Daily Chron.* 11 June 10/4 Nearly all the Australian States are now offering assisted passages to selected immigrants... Why should not the Imperial Government take a hand in this, and in certain cases contribute the other £6, and thus realise the 'free ferry'? **1930** C. E. LEE (*title*) The Blue Riband: the romance of the Atlantic ferry.

e. Of aircraft: a flight for carrying goods or persons from one place to another, esp. one of a

series of flights on a regular course; also applied to the aircraft itself. Of spacecraft: a module that can be separated from the main craft, e.g. for the final descent to the surface of the moon; so *ferry rocket*. Freq. *attrib.* and *Comb.*

1917 *Flying* 28 Nov. 296/1 Should you chance to live in eastern or south eastern counties you may see them going over..flown by ferry pilots. **1933** *Meccano Mag.* Nov. 845/3 If a machine is intended purely for joy riding and short ferry services, arrangement can be made for an eight-seater to be provided. **1939** *Flying* 1 July 4/1 Applications are being invited from those wishing to take part in these long-distance ferry flights. **1939** *Flight* 9 Nov. 373/1 The chances that an enemy machine might masquerade as a ferry are very small. *Ibid.* 373/2 The senior pilots of a ferry unit must remember the layout, characteristics, and fuel systems of as many as ten or a dozen machines. **1940** *Ibid.* 28 Mar. 282/1 Groups were attached to the two Service ferry pools and these groups worked happily. *Ibid.*, Those experts in all-type ferry flying, the R.A.F. pilots. **1942** *Times Weekly* 9 Sept. 9/1 Filling petrol tanks of United States ferry planes at airports newly laid out in jungles or deserts. **1943** *Jane's All World's Aircraft, 1942* 29a/2 In June, 1941, the R.A.F. formed the Ferry Command to take charge of all trans-Atlantic deliveries by air. *Ibid.* 30a/1 The West African ferry route to the Middle East is also used by the communications aircraft on the United Nations. **1943** *Times Weekly* 19 May 8/2 A pool of ferry pilots..flew aircraft of all types right across Africa to Khartoum and Cairo. **1951** A. C. Clarke *Exploration Space* 78 At the end of these manœuvres, which would occupy only a few hours, it would be back in a stable, circular orbit waiting to be refuelled and serviced, and the crew could be taken down to Earth by one of the winged 'ferry' rockets. **1960** F. Gaynor *Dict. Aerospace* 90 *Ferry rocket*, the final step of the planned piloted space vehicle, designed for transporting personnel between earth and the terminal orbit. **1969** *Times* 3 June Suppl. p. iii/8 The two-stage module—the disposable landing ferry that takes the astronauts from their circling space-craft to the lunar surface—is at the heart of the American plans to land two men on the moon this summer.

4. *Law.* The right of ferrying men and animals across a river, etc., and of levying toll for so doing.

1721 *Termes de la Ley* 344 *Ferry*, is a Liberty by Prescription, or the Kings Grant. **1708** Shower *Reports* 257 If a Ferry were granted at this Day, he that accepts such Grant, is bound to keep a Boat for the Publick Good. **1843** Meeson & Welsby *Exchequer Reports* X. 161 The defendants..were possessed of a certain ferry across..the River Mersey. **1862** *Law Reports* XXXI. Common Pl. 247 The plaintiffs are the lessees of an ancient ferry.

5. *attrib.* and *Comb.* **a.** Chiefly attributive, as ***ferry-boy, -craft, -place, -pole, -receipts, -service, -warden, -way.***

1812 *Examiner* 21 Dec. 816/2 James Dean, a *ferry-boy. *c* **1470** Henry *Wallace* ix. 1306 For *fery craft na fraucht he thocht to crawe. *c* **1440** *Promp. Parv.* 156/2 *Fery place. **1665** Pepys *Diary* (1879) III. 193 Mr. Carteret and I to the ferry-place at Greenwich. **1806** *Sporting Mag.* XXVII. 173 The ferry-place at Portsea. *a* **1661** Holyday *Juvenal* 23 There are..A *ferry-poal, and frogs in Stygian waves. **1858** J. B. Norton *Topics* 186 The surplus *ferry receipts..are..given up by the State. **1892** *Pall Mall G.* 23 Feb. 3/3 It is proposed to build a pier here, and..to establish a *ferry service. **1576** *Act 18 Eliz.* c. 10 §10 The said *Ferry-warden. **1884** *Harper's Mag.* Oct. 809/1 The town voted to discontinue the *ferryway and the ferry.

b. Special comb., as **ferry-bridge** (see quot.); **ferry-flat**, *U.S.* a flat boat used for crossing (and sometimes descending) rivers; **ferry-house**, the residence of a ferry-man, also *attrib.*; †**ferry-look** (see quot.); **ferry-louper**, one who has crossed from the mainland, *Orkn.*; **ferry-master**, *U.S.* a person in charge of a ferry; also, one who collects the tolls at a ferry (*Cent. Dict.*); **ferry-nab** (see quot.); **ferry-railway** (see quot.). Also ferry-boat, ferryman.

1874 Knight *Dict. Mech.*, **Ferry-bridge*, a form of ferry-boat in which the railway-train moves on to the elevated deck, is transported across the water and then lands upon the other side. **1828** Flint *Mississippi Valley* I. 230 The *ferry flat is a scow-boat. **1838** Dickens *O. Twist* xxi, There was a light in the *ferry-house window. **1862** H. Marryat *Year in Sweden* II. 329 A ferryhouse stretches out like a sickle in the blue sea. **1769** *De Foe's Tour Gt. Brit.* I. 153 [The keeper of this ferry has the right] to dredge for Oysters within the compass of his *Ferry-look which extends..60 Fathoms, on each Side of the Castle. **1868** D. Gorrie *Summ. & Wint. Orkneys* iv. 143 This misguided man was a *ferry-louper. **1883** *All Year Round* 19 May 465 Shouts [came] for a boat, as if from the *ferry-nab, or point, on the other side. **1847** Knight *Dict. Mech.*, **Ferry-railway*, one whose track is on the bottom of the watercourse and whose carriage has an elevated deck which supports the train.

†**'ferry**, *sb.*² *Cookery. Obs.* [Etymology unknown; OF. had 'pain *feré*', explained by Godef. as 'bread *for a festival*'.] More fully, ***caudle ferry***: A kind of spiced drink made with wine and eggs. Also app. some kind of sauce.

?*c* **1390** *Form Cury* xli. 27 *Cawdel ferry*. Take floer of Payndemayn and gode wyne, etc. *c* **1475** *Noble Bk. Cookry* (1882) 32 *Cawdelle ferry*. Tak clene yolks of egge welle betene, etc. **1504** in Leland *Collect.* VI. 21 Carpe in ferry.

ferry ('fɛrɪ), *v.* Forms: 1 ferian, feriȝ(e)an, 2–3 ferien, 4–5 fery, fere, 6 ferrie, 6– ferry. Also 3–4 verie(n, (5 veryen). [OE. *fęrian* = OHG. *feren*, ON. *ferja*, Goth. *farjan*:—OTeut. **farjan*, f. *far-ᵒᵐ*: see fare *sb.*]

1. *trans.* To carry, convey, transport, take from one place to another.

Beowulf 333 (Gr.) Hwanon feriȝeað ȝe fætte scyldas? *a* **1000** *Elene* 108 (Gr.) Heht..wiȝend..þæt haliȝe treo him beforan ferian. *c* **1175** *Lamb. Hom.* 111 ȝif he ȝeher-godne mon fereð to buriene. *c* **1205** Lay. 10559 He uerde forð in sæ uereden hine vðen. *a* **1300** *Seven Sins* 42 in *E.E.P.* (1862) 19 Þe fend him deriiþ. and is soul to helle he feriiþ. **13..** *E.E. Allit. P.* B. 1790 Þe kyng..watz kaȝt by þe heles, Feryed out bi þe fete. **1583** Stubbes *Anat. Abus.* ii. (1882) 82 We..ferrie it to the deuil. **1970** H. Waugh *Finish me Off* (1971) 163 Then we warn the doormen and the super on her building that it wouldn't look good for them to ferry customers to her apartment.

2. a. *esp.* To transport or convey over water (now only over a stream, canal, etc., formerly also over the sea) in a boat or ship, etc. Often *to ferry* (a person, etc.) ***over*** or ***across***.

a **1000** *Andreas* 293 (Gr.) We þe..willað feriȝan freolice ofer fisces bæð. *a* **1000** *Riddles* xv. 7 (Gr.) Mec..mere-hengest fereð ofer flodas. **1587** F. James in Hearne *Collect.* (Oxf. Hist. Soc.) I. 199 For ferrienge oure horses..from Lambeth..6*d*. **1602** Fulbecke *2nd Pt. Parall.* 21 In this case without ferrying ouer the horse there was nothing due vnto the bargeman. **1609** Heywood *Brit. Troy* v. xi. 6 Charon is tyr'd, with ferring soules to hell. **1701** *Lond. Gaz.* No. 3722/2 Before night almost half of them were ferried over. **1784** Cowper *Task* ii. 38 They themselves once ferried o'er the wave..are emancipate and loosed. **1822** Hazlitt *Table-t.* II. iii. 45 A girl who had ferried me over the Severn. **1877** Miss Yonge *Cameos* IV. i. 15 He was ferried to the French bank.

absol. **1457** *Nottingham Rec.* II. 365 Peid to Tomas Smyth, for fereyng v. days at yᵉ Bryges. **1843** Marryat *M. Violet* xliv, The owner of a ferry..ferries only when he chooses.

b. To work (a boat, etc.) *across* or *over*.

1771 Mrs. Griffith tr. *Viaud's Shipwreck* 92 The rotten canoe, that he had however contrived to ferry over. **1854** J. S. C. Abbott *Napoleon* (1855) II. xv. 281 He promised a napoleon to every boat which was ferried across.

c. Of a vessel: To serve as a ferry-boat over.

1872 W. F. Butler *Great Lone Land* iv. (1875) 55 A steamer ferries the broad swift-running stream.

d. To fly (an aircraft), or to transport by air, from one place to another, esp. on some regular route, as from a factory to an airfield.

1921 *Flight* XIII. 620/2 Both the Aircraft Disposal Company, and the Bristol people, are having difficulty in finding pilots to ferry these machines across to Spain. *Ibid.* 662/2 He is..'ferrying' machines from Liverpool to Croydon. **1932** R. Mahachek *Airplane Pilot's Man.* 353 *Ferrying*, delivering an airplane to another point by flying it. **1940** *Flight* 28 Mar. 282/1 Women pilots..were..attached to a certain factory for the ferrying of trainers. **1943** *Times Weekly* 19 May 8/2 Gradually the ferrying route came into operation. **1958** *Daily Mail* 18 July 1/1 Israel's permission to ferry troop-carriers through her air-space was not at first fully cleared.

3. a. *intr.* for *refl.* To convey oneself, go; now only, to pass over water in a boat or by a ferry. Of a boat: To pass to and fro.

a **1000** *Byrhtnoth* 179 (Gr.) Þæt min sawul to þe siðian mote..mid friðe ferian. *c* **1380** Wyclif *Serm.* Sel. Wks. II. 178 Crist seide to hem verie we over þe water. *c* **1450** Lonelich *Grail* l. 176 In to here schippe forto take him, forto veryen ouer that lake. **1589** Greene *Menaphon* (Arb.) 30 She sayling to Styx, thow ferriest ouer to Phlegeton. **1600** Holland *Livy* v. i. (1609) 1383 *note*, They that would goe to it, used to ferry over in small punts or whirries. **1630** *R. Johnson's Kingd. & Commw.* 631 Upon these waters doe ferry fiftie thousand Boats..to serve the use of the Citie. **1787** Burns *Verse*, When death's dark stream I ferry o'er. **1833** Lamb *Elia* (1860) 267 It irks me to think that..thou shouldst ferry over..in crazy Stygian wherry. **1836** T. Hook *G. Gurney* III. 333, I intended to remain until the weather cleared before I ferried back. **1887** L. Oliphant *Episodes* 72, I ferried across it.

†**b.** *fig.* *to ferry over*: to pass over, pretermit.

1477 J. Paston in *Paston Lett.* No. 787 III. 175, I may not wryght longe, wherffor I ffery over all thyngs tyll I may awayte on you my selff.

ferryable ('fɛrɪəb(ə)l), *a.* [f. prec. + -able.] Of a water: That may be crossed in a ferry-boat.

1888 *Blackw. Mag.* Aug. 242 A place..on the Indus, where it is fordable or ferryable.

ferryage, ferryer: see ferriage, ferrier.

'ferry-boat. [f. ferry *sb.* + boat *sb.*] A boat used for conveying passengers, etc. across a ferry.

c **1440** *Promp. Parv.* 156/2 Feryboot, *portemia*. **1458** *Nottingham Rec.* II. 220, vs. viijd. receptis de proficuis de ferybotes de tempore. **1580** Baret *Alv.* B. 895 A ferry boate to cary ouer horses. **1644** Evelyn *Mem.* (1819) I. 123 The Tiber..I crossed in a ferry-boate. **1725** De Foe *Voy. round World* (1840) 322 One large float with sides to it, like a punt or ferry boat. **1811** Wellington in Gurw. *Desp.* VII. 418, I shall pay the proprietor of the ferry boats any reasonable sum for the time. **1858** W. Ellis *Visits Madagascar* viii. 215 A windlass for the large ferry-boat.

ferrying ('fɛrɪɪŋ), *vbl. sb.* [f. ferry *v.* + -ing¹.] The action of the vb. ferry; an instance of the same. Also *attrib.*, as *ferrying-fee, station.*

1873 A. W. Ward tr. *Curtius' Hist. Greece* I. ii. ii. 311 The 'Parali' lived by..ferrying..and fishing. **1879** J. Todhunter *Alcestis* 47 Methought I waited..For Charon's dismal ferrying. **1887** *Pall Mall G.* 8 Mar. 4/2 The..fisher-folk..would practically be deprived of the ferrying-fees between the steamers and the grotto. **1873** A. W. Ward tr. *Curtius' Hist. Greece* I. ii. i. 271 A mere ferrying station.

ferrying ('fɛrɪɪŋ), *ppl. a.* [f. as prec. + -ing².] That ferries.

a **1683** Oldham *Poet. Wks.* (1686) 55 Ferrying Cowls Religious Pilgrims bore, O'er waves without the help of Sail, or Oar.

'ferryman. [f. ferry *sb.* + man.] One who keeps or looks after a ferry.

1464 *Mann. & Househ. Exp.* 162, [I] payd to the ferry-manes wyffe..xij. *d*. **1559** *Mirr. Mag.*, *Dk. Clarence* xxxiv, As wise as Goose the fery man. **1615** G. Sandys *Trav.* 134 Charon grim Ferri-man, these streames doth guard. **1753** Hanway *Trav.* (1762) I. ii. xii. 55 The ferry-man began to be insolent. **1833** Ht. Martineau *Tale of Tyne* i. 1 He was a pretty ferryman to let a passenger stand calling for his boat. **1878** B. Taylor *Deukalion* i. iv. 35 The ancient ferryman of Hades.

attrib. **1801** M. G. Lewis in *Tales of Wond.* I. No. i. 7 The ferryman-fiend.

†**fers.** *Chess. Obs.* Also 5 fiers, 6 ferse, 7 feers. [a. OF. *fierce, fierche, fierge* (in med.L. *fercia, farzia*), ad. (ultimately) Pers. *ferzēn*, Arab. *firzān*, also *ferz*. The Pers. word means 'wise man', 'counsellor'.]

1. The piece now known as the queen.

c **1369** Chaucer *Dethe Blaunche* 654 She stal on me and took my fers And whan I saw my fers aweye Alas! I couthe no lenger pleye. *a* **1547** Surrey in *Tottell's Misc.* (Arb.) 21 And when your ferse is had, And all your warre is done. **1663–76** Bullokar, *Fers*, the Queen at Chess-play.

2. A pawn which has passed to the eighth square (see quot.).

1474 Caxton *Chesse* iv. vii. (1860) L iv, He may not goo on neyther side til he hath been in the fardest ligne of theschequer, & that he hath taken the nature of the draughtes of the quene; & than he is a fiers.

3. ***the ferses twelve***: according to Prof. Skeat, all the men exc. the king (the bishops, knights, and rooks, being counted as one each).

c **1369** Chaucer *Dethe Blaunche* 723 Thogh ye had lost the ferses twelve. [**1671** Skinner, *Fers, Feers, Feerses*, men at Chess. **1692–1732** in Coles.]

fers, obs. f. farce *v.*, fierce *a.*, furze, verse.

†**ferse**, *v. Obs.* Forms: 1 feorsian, fyrsian, 3 fersien, firsin, fursen, *Orm.* ferrsenn. [OE. *feorsian, fyrsian*, f. *feor*, far.] *trans.* To remove, put at a distance; hence, to forsake; with *refl. pron.* as *obj.* to withdraw, go away.

c **1000** *Ags. Ps.* (Lamb.) lxxii[i]. 27 (Toller) Ða ðe fyrsiaþ hiȝ fram ðe. *c* **1200** *Trin. Coll. Hom.* 205 Fersien hit fro him swo þat he it nabbe. *c* **1200** Ormin 19663 Nohht ne birrþ þe ferrsenn þe Ne flen fra þeȝȝm off tune. *a* **1225** *Ancr. R.* 76 He furseð him awei urommard ure stefne. *a* **1225** *Juliana* 16 Ne schal me firsin him from nowðer deouel ne mon.

fersie, obs. Sc. form of farcy.

1598 D. Fergusson *Scot. Prov.* (1785) 12 Fire is good for the fersie. *a* **1605** Montgomerie *Flyting w. Polwart* 305 The fersie, the falling-euill, that fels manie freikes.

ferte, var. of fart *sb.* 2.

1565–73 Cooper *Thesaurus, Scriblita*, a delicate meate of paste stuffed and wounded like a rope: a ferte of Portugall.

†**'fertee.** *Obs.*⁻¹ [a. OF. *ferté* = Pr. *fiertat, fertat*:—L. *feritāt-em*, f. *ferus* fierce.] Fierceness.

c **1380** *Sir Ferumb.* 664 Firumbras þe heþene kyng was a man of gret fertee.

'ferter, *v. Obs.* [f. ME. *fertre* shrine: see feretory.] *trans.* To put in a shrine, enshrine.

c **1325** *Metr. Hom.* 143 He..bar thir bannes menskelye And fertered thaim at a nunrye. *c* **1450** *St. Cuthbert* (Surtees) 6995 And þare he fertird þaim [banes] in hy.

ferth, obs. form of fourth.

ferther, obs. form of further.

fertigation (fɜːtɪ'geɪʃən). orig. *U.S.* [Blend of fertilizer and irrigation.] A method of plant fertilization in which liquid fertilizer is added to the water in an irrigation system.

1967 *Farm Q.* XXII. 60/1 Fertigation, as some call it, began in the West when farmers started bubbling anhydrous ammonia into irrigation ditches. **1971** *Fertilizer Solutions* XV. 38/1 Overhead sprinkler fertigation lends itself well to increment feeding, that is, balanced fertilizing through each cycle of the system. **1983** *Economist* 25 June 73/4 The latest refinement of drip irrigation is called 'fertigation': liquid fertiliser is added to the irrigation water and thus fed directly to the plant.

†**'fertilage.** *Obs.* [f. fertile + -age.] The action or process of fertilizing.

1610 W. Folkingham *Art of Survey* i. viii. 15 Fertilage consists in the enriching of the Soyle. **1688** R. Holme *Armoury* iii. 333/2 Fertilage is an enriching of Soil.

fertile ('fɜːtɪl, -taɪl), *a.* Forms: 5–6 fertyl(e, -yll, 7–8 fertil(l, (6 fartyll, 6–7 firtile, -ill, 7 furtill, fertle), 5– fertile. [a. OF. *fertil* (Fr. *fertile* = Pr. *fertil*), ad. L. *fertilis*, f. *ferre* to bear.]

1. Bearing or producing in abundance; fruitful, prolific. Const. *of, in*, rarely †*to*.

a. *lit.* of the soil, a district or region, rarely of animals.

c **1460** Fortescue *Abs. & Lim. Mon.* iii, Dwellyn thai in on the most fertile reaume of the worlde. **1484** Caxton

Æsop v. viii, This yere shalle be the..moost fertyle of alle maner of corne. **1581** SIDNEY *Apol. Poetrie* (Arb.) 62 The firtilest ground must bee manured. **1624** CAPT. SMITH *Virginia* III. xi. 87 The ground was..exceeding furtill. **1785** SARAH FIELDING *Ophelia* II. ix, A soil..not..fertile of any thing but weeds. **1832** HT. MARTINEAU *Life in Wilds* i. 3 The plains..are fertile in native plants. **1853** C. BRONTE *Villette* xv, These September suns shone..on fertile plains.

b. *transf.* and *fig.*

1481 CAXTON *Myrr.* II. iv. 68 It [Probane, Ceylon] is moche plenteuous of gold and syluer and moche fertyle of other thynges. **1603** DRAYTON *Odes* ii. 43 That Spray to fame so fertle, The Louer-crowning Mirtle. **1730** A. GORDON *Maffei's Amphith.* 23 Augustus..being of a fertile and jovial Disposition. **1791** *Gentl. Mag.* 26/2 The offspring of his fertile imagination. **1819** T. JEFFERSON *Autobiog.* Wks. 1859 I. 121 He was..fertile in resources. **1848** MACAULAY *Hist. Eng.* I. 216 One family, singularly fertile of great men. **1869** FREEMAN *Norm. Conq.* (1876) III. xiv. 335 England was ..a land fertile in warriors.

c. *fertile crescent* (see quot. 1914).

1914 J. H. BREASTED in Breasted & Robinson *Outl. Europ. Hist.* I. iii. 56 This fertile crescent is approximately a semicircle..with one wing stretching along the eastern shores of the Mediterranean, the other reaching out to the Persian Gulf. *Ibid.* 57 This great semicircle, for lack of a name, may be called the fertile crescent. **1945** AUDEN *Coll. Poetry* 343 The earth debates: the Fertile Crescent argues. **1950** H. L. LORIMER *Homer & Monuments* ii. 83 The tip of the 'fertile crescent', whence a main trade route leads into the interior. **1958** *Spectator* 7 Feb. 159/2 The rulers of Syria ..had no wish so soon afterwards to be engulfed within the Fertile Crescent scheme then being mooted. **1970** *Guardian* 10 Sept. 15/2 There's an old fable told in the lands of the Fertile Crescent.

d. *Nuclear Physics.* Capable of being transformed into a fissile isotope by the capture of a neutron.

1949 *Nucleonics* Dec. 41/2 The concentration of the new fissionable material builds up within the fertile material. **1963** PETERSON & WYMER *Chem. Nuclear Technol.* i. 3 This type of reactor contains fertile material, either U^{238} or thorium, which is converted to fuel by neutrons in excess of those needed to maintain the fission process.

2. Causing or tending to promote fertility.

1597 BP. HALL *Sat.* I. ii, The coole streame that tooke his endles name, From out the fertile hoofe of winged steed. **1621** BURTON *Anat. Mel.* II. ii. III. 248 The Brise..most pleasant and fertile. **1657** AUSTEN *Fruit Trees* I. 71 Lay Pigeons dung..(or the like stuffe, that is very hot, and fertill) to the roots. **1847** EMERSON *Poems*, Wks. (Bohn) I. 485 They thank the spring-flood for its fertile slime.

fig. **1596** SHAKS. *2 Hen. IV*, IV. iii. 131 With..good store of Fertile Sherris.

†**3.** Copiously produced, abundant. *Obs.*

1601 SHAKS. *Twel. N.* I. v. 274 *Ol.* How does he loue me? *Vio.* With adorations, fertill teares. **1667** MILTON *P.L.* IX. 801 Shall..the fertil burden ease Of thy full branches.

4. *Comb.* **fertile-brained** *a.* = *fertile-headed* (*b*); **fertile-fresh** *a.*, having luxuriant foliage; **fertile-headed** *a.*, (*a*) many headed; (*b*) rich in expedients.

1598 SHAKS. *Merry W.* v. v. 72 Greene let it be, More fertile-fresh then all the Field to see. **1632** MASSINGER & FIELD *Fatal Dowry* I. i, Cerberus..loud and fertile-headed. **1754** J. SHEBBEARE *Matrimony* (1766) I. 230 The fertile-headed Woman..whipt a ten-peck Bag over her Gallant's Head. **1894** H. NISBET *Bush Girl's Romance* 275 It seemed to be all plain enough sailing to this fertile-brained.. sybarite.

Hence †'**fertile** *v. Obs.*⁻¹ = FERTILIZE *v.*; '**fertilely** *adv.*; '**fertileness** *rare* = FERTILITY.

1580 SIDNEY *Arcadia* (1622) 155 Who..could not but fertilly requite his fathers fatherly education. **1581** —— *Apol. Poetrie* (Arb.) 19 The fertilnes of the Italian wit. **1613** MARKHAM *Eng. Husb.* II. I. v. (1635) 27 According to the fertilenesse of the soyle in which they grow. **1627–47** FELTHAM *Resolves* I. lxxxi. 252 He that hopes too much shall coozen himself at last; especially if his industry goes not along to fertile it. **1661–6** WOOD *City of Oxford* (Oxf. Hist. Soc.) I. 395 The meedes adjoyning are fertilly soyled.

†'**fertilent**, *a. Sc. Obs.*⁻¹ [f. prec. after analogy of *opulent, pestilent.*] Abundant, plentiful.

1535 STEWART *Cron. Scot.* II. 553 Palȝeonis..Quhilk furneist war rycht riche and fertilent, With gold and siluer.

†**fer'tilitate**, *v. Obs.* [f. next, after *debilitate.*] *trans.* To render fertile, fertilize.

1634 SIR T. HERBERT *Trav.* (1638) 193 A sweet rivolet playes..through the Towne, fertilitating the..Gardens. **1650** SIR T. BROWNE *Pseud. Ep.* III. xxviii. (ed. 2) 151 A Cock will in one day fertilitate the whole..cluster of egges.

Hence †**fer'tilitating** *ppl. a.*

1646 SIR T. BROWNE *Pseud. Ep.* VII. vii. 352 From whence ..wee cannot inferre a fertilitating [*printed* fertiliating; corrected in ed. **1658**] condition or property of fecundation.

fertility (fə'tɪlɪtɪ). Forms: 5 fertylyte, 6–8 fertilitie, -illity(e, (fortylite), 6– **fertility**. [a. Fr. *fertilité*, ad. L. *fertilitāt-em*, f. *fertilis* FERTILE.] The quality of being fertile; fecundity, fruitfulness, productiveness.

a. *lit.* of the soil, a region, etc.; also of plants and animals.

1490 CAXTON *Eneydos* xxv. 92 The troienne folke multyplied..in grete quantite..for the fertylyte of the grounde. **1538** STARKEY *England* I. i. 12 Maruelous culture and Fortylite. *c* **1610–15** *Women Saints* (1886) 189 The first fruite of our mothers fertilitie. **1818** BYRON *Ch. Har.* IV. xxvi, Thy waste More rich than other climes' fertility. **1859** DARWIN *Orig. Spec.* iv. (1873) 75 The fertility of this clover absolutely depends on bees visiting the flowers.

b. *transf.* and *fig.*

1615 G. SANDYS *Trav.* 103 Such iarres proceeded from their fertility of Gods, differing in each seuerall iurisdiction. **1666** DRYDEN *Ann. Mirab.* Let. to Sir R. Howard, The quickness of the Imagination is seen in the invention; the fertility in the Fancy. **1750** JOHNSON *Rambler* No. 75 ¶4, I found some..fertility of fancy. **1802** PLAYFAIR *Illustr. Hutton. Th.* 495 All the fertility of his invention. **1848** MACAULAY *Hist. Eng.* II. 637 Halifax..in fertility of thought..had no rival. **1878** BOSW. SMITH *Carthage* 136 Himilco..was a man..of fertility of resource.

c. *pl.* Productive powers.

1626–7 LD. FALKLAND in *Abp. Ussher's Lett.* (1686) 379 A general..valluation of the different Fertilities. **1708** SWIFT *Sacram. Test.* Wks. (1778) IV. 219 The fertilities of the soil. **1868** ROGERS *Pol. Econ.* xii. (1876) 164 Ground-rent..is a payment made for a particular site because it has certain conveniences, productive powers, or..fertilities, which another site..would not possess.

d. Distinguished from *fecundity* (see FECUND, FECUNDITY).

1866–1936 [see FECUNDITY]. **1938** E. CHARLES in L. Hogben *Political Arith.* xi. 73 (*heading*) The effect of present trends in fertility and mortality upon the future population of Great Britain and upon its age composition. **1964** [see FECUNDITY].

e. *attrib.* and *Comb.*

1913 E. N. FALLAIZE in J. Hastings *Encycl. Relig. & Ethics* VI. 523 (*heading*) Fertility charms. **1932** R. KNOX *Broadcast Minds* vi. 141 Presenting..the Resurrection as one among a series of fertility-legends. **1933** E. K. CHAMBERS *Eng. Folk-Play* 223 He [*sc.* Dionysus] remains primarily a fertility-god, with the bull, and perhaps the goat, and the *phallus* as his attributes. **1933** R. TUVE *Seasons & Months* i. 40 Whatever remnants of fertility cult lie behind such English folk customs as..'Rogation Day'. **1942** *Burlington Mag.* Apr. 98/2 Being used to ecstatic fertility-rites, the more dogmatic and controlled calendar-rites could not catch their emotions. **1952** GERTH & MARTINDALE tr. *Weber's Anc. Judaism* xi. 279 The prophets declaimed against the rural orgiasticism of the fertility cults. **1952** P. HUGHES *Witchcraft* x. 128 The crescendo of the fertility dance. **1956** D. H. WILLSON *King James VI. & I.* vii. 104 The witch cult in Scotland was derived in part from ancient heathen practice..in which the ritual consisted largely of fertility rites. **1962** [see AMORAL *a.*]. **1964** *Punch* 11 Mar. 394/3 Most large hospitals are now equipped with fertility clinics. **1965** *Ibid.* 25 Aug. 270/2 First the pill, now fertility drugs—what's that but a return to *stop go?* **1968** *Daily Tel.* 12 Nov. 1/6 Mrs. Pennington..has been taking the fertility drug gonadotrophin, the same drug taken by Mrs. Sheila Thorns who gave birth to sextuplets.

fertilizable ('fɜːtɪˌlaɪzəb(ə)l), *a.* Also **-isable**. [f. FERTILIZE + -ABLE. Cf. F. *fertilisable.*]

a. Of land, etc.: Capable of being fertilized. **b.** Of the female, or an ovum: Susceptible of impregnation.

1832 R. MUDIE *Bot. Annual* 140 The ovary is the.. important part of the fertilizable organ. **1877** HUXLEY *Anat. Inv. Anim.* vii. 446 The perfect fertilisable female. **1880** BURTON *Reign Q. Anne* III. xviii. 197 Unfertile but fertilisable clay.

fertilization (ˌfɜːtɪlaɪ'zeɪʃən). Also **-isation**. [n. of action f. as prec. + -ATION; cf. F. *fertilisation.*] **1. a.** The action or process of rendering fertile.

1863 J. G. MURPHY *Comm. Gen.* xii. 11 The two sides of the Nile, its fertilization by a natural cause.

b. *spec. Biol.* Fecundation; see FERTILIZE 2.

1857 WHEWELL *Hist. Induct. Sc.* III. 223 The fertilization of the date-palms. **1862** DARWIN *Fertil. Orchids* i. 33 These species..require the aid of insects for their fertilization. **1882** VINES *Sachs' Bot.* 525 The first manifest result of fertilisation in the oospore is the division of its nucleus.

c. *fig.*

1922 H. CRANE *Let.* 7 Nov. (1965) 104 This wholesale 'fertilization' of America by such half-baked people as the Algonquin gang. **1933** E. K. CHAMBERS *Eng. Folk-Play* 11 An extreme case of fertilization from a distance is at Icomb in Gloucestershire, where a second act must have been added from a Scottish source. **1957** E. SITWELL *Coll. Poems* 423 The fertilisation of his singing breath.

2. *attrib.* **fertilization tube** *Mycology*, a tube-like outgrowth of the antheridium in certain phycomycetous fungi which penetrates the oogonium and forms a passage for a male nucleus to reach an egg.

1887 H. E. F. GARNSEY tr. *De Bary's Fungi* v. 134 When the oosphere has been formed in the oogonium, the antheridium sends a delicate cylindrical or conical tube-like process, the fertilisation-tube, from the part of its surface which is in contact with the oogonium into the interior of the latter. **1930** H. M. FITZPATRICK *Lower Fungi* vii. 153 As soon as the oospheres are differentiated the antheridia form delicate fertilization tubes. **1970** J. WEBSTER *Introd. Fungi* 72 Fertilisation is accomplished by the penetration of fertilisation tubes into the eggs.

Hence ˌ**fertili'zational** *a.*, of or pertaining to fertilization.

1888 J. T. GULICK in *Linn. Soc. Jrnl.* XX. 233, I venture to call this principle Fertilizational Segregation.

fertilize ('fɜːtɪlaɪz), *v.* [f. FERTILE + -IZE.]

1. *trans.* To make fertile; to enrich (the soil).

1648 W. MOUNTAGUE *Devout Ess.* I. xi. §1. 128 Our earth needs no rain to fall upon it..to fertilize it. **1760** DERRICK *Lett.* (1767) I. 97 He..fertilised bogs, and cultivated barren sands. **1860** MOTLEY *Netherl.* (1868) I. i. 8 Three great rivers which had fertilized happier portions of Europe.

b. *gen.* To render productive. *lit.* and *fig.*

1828 MACKINTOSH *Sp. Ho. Comm.* 2 May Wks. 1846 III. 487 The members of the Legislature..attempted to exclude all the industry..of other countries from flowing in to enrich and fertilise their shores. **1866** LIDDON *Bampt. Lect.* v. (1875) 225 Intense religious conviction fertilizes intellect. **1868** PEARD *Water-Farm.* ii. 11 Can nothing be done to fertilise the vast majority of our streams?

2. *Biol.* To make (an ovum, an oospore, a female individual or organ) fruitful by the introduction of the male element; to fecundate.

Chiefly *Bot.*; in Zoology common with reference to ova, but otherwise rare.

1859 DARWIN *Orig. Spec.* iv. (1873) 79, I have not found a single terrestrial animal which can fertilize itself. **1861** DELAMER *Fl. Gard.* 145 If..the Moss Rose..is fertilized with Rosa Gallica, interesting hybrids are the result. **1879** LUBBOCK *Sci. Lect.* i. 8 It is a great advantage..that the flower should be fertilised by pollen from a different stock.

Hence '**fertilized** *ppl. a.* '**fertilizing** *vbl. sb.*, also *attrib.* '**fertilizing** *ppl. a.*

1651 R. CHILD in *Hartlib's Legacy* (1655) 34 In other places they have a like fertilizing fatnesse. **1655** In *Hartlib's Legacy* 193 A rich earth for Compost worth twenty shillings a load at the least for the fertilizing of land. **1807** CRABBE *Par. Reg.* III. 275 Fertilizing showers. **1849** J. F. W. JOHNSTON *Exper. Agric.* vii. 118 Gypsum has a remarkably fertilising effect when applied to certain crops on certain soils. **1868** PEARD *Water-Farm.* v. 54 A tiny fish creeps from each fertilised egg. **1884** *Athenæum* 12 Jan. 49/3 The author attributes the supply of fertilizing mud in Egypt to the White Nile.

fertilizer ('fɜːtɪlaɪzə(r)). [f. prec. + -ER¹.]

1. One who or that which fertilizes (land).

a **1661** FULLER *Worthies, Kent* II. (1662) 57 Saint-foime, or Holy-hay..being found to be a great Fertilizer of Barren-ground. **1794** SULLIVAN *View Nat.* I. 377 The agency of snow as a fertilizer. **1815** W. TAYLOR in *Monthly Mag.* XXXVIII. 500 The torrent, now the fertilizer, now the ravager of districts. **1872** SPURGEON *Treas. Dav.* Ps. lxv. 11 The march of Jehovah, the Fertiliser, may be traced by the abundance which he creates.

b. said *esp.* of manures.

1846 J. BAXTER *Libr. Pract. Agric.* (ed. 4) II. 61 Nitrate of potash..when employed as a fertilizer, is generally sown by hand.

attrib. **1893** *Act 56 & 57 Vict.* c. 56 (*title*) The Fertilisers and Feeding Stuffs Act.

2. An agent of fertilization in plants.

1844 DARWIN in *Life & Lett.* (1887) II. 30 Flies are good fertilizers. **1880** A. R. WALLACE *Isl. Life* 473 Suitable fertilisers and other favourable conditions.

fertilizin (fɜː'tɪlɪzɪn, fɜːtɪ'laɪzɪn). *Zool.* Also **fertilisin**. [f. FERTILIZ(E *v.* + -IN¹.] Any of a class of substances released into the surrounding water by the eggs of some aquatic animals and agglutinating sperm, usually only that of the same species.

1919 F. R. LILLIE *Probl. Fertilization* i. 27 The fertilizable condition of the egg depends upon the presence of a specific substance... This substance may therefore be called the fertilizing substance, or fertilizin... It is..a colloidal substance,..exhibiting some of the properties of a ferment. **1940** *Chambers's Techn. Dict.* 328/2 *Fertilisin*, a substance which is present in the cortex of an ovum and assists in the activation of the ovum. **1960** L. PICKEN *Organization of Cells* viii. 339 Even among echinoids, however, agglutination is not universal, though there is reason to suppose that a fertilizin is none the less secreted.

fertlet, obs. var. of FIRLOT.

ferula ('fɛr(j)ʊlə). [a. L. *ferula* giant fennel, a rod.]

1. *Bot.* A genus of plants; the giant fennel.

1398 TREVISA *Barth. De P.R.* XVII. lxxi. (1495) 645 Ferula is an herbe. **1562** TURNER *Herbal* II. 1 b, The nature of Ferula is the sorest enemie that can be to Lampreys. **1693** SIR T. P. BLOUNT *Nat. Hist.* 465 Vossius..affirms them to be Arborescent Ferula's. **1811** A. T. THOMSON *Lond. Disp.* (1818) 175 This species of ferula is a native of..Persia. **1868** MRS. H. L. EVANS *Wint. in Algeria* 25 The beautiful feathery leaf of the ferula.

2. From the use of the fennel-stalk in Roman times: A cane, rod, or other instrument of punishment, *esp.* a flat piece of wood (see FERULE 2 quot. 1825); *fig.* school discipline.

1580 NORTH *Plutarch* (1676) 612 Many..do put forth their hands to be stricken..with the ferula. **1612** BRINSLEY *Lud. Lit.* xix. (1627) 215, I have laboured and striven by ferula, and all meanes of severity. **1712** E. COOKE *Voy. S. Sea* 123 We..had Ferula's made to punish Swearing. **1840** *P. Parley's Ann.* 316 They had never known the infliction of chastisement from either cane or ferula. **1851** CARLYLE *Sterling* I. iv. (1872) 27 His ever-changing course..which was passed so nomadically under ferulas of various colour.

3. *Surg.* A long splint.

1688 R. HOLME *Armoury* III. 444. **1884** in *Syd. Soc. Lex.*

ferulaceous (fɛr(j)uː'leɪʃəs), *a.* [f. L. *ferulāce-us* (f. *ferul-a* giant fennel) + -OUS: see -ACEOUS.] Resembling the ferula; having a stalk like a ferula.

1657 *Phys. Dict.*, *Ferulaceous*, like the herb ferula. **1691** RAY *Creation* I. (1692) 194 These [Fountain] Trees are of the Ferulaceous kind. **1755** PORTER in *Phil. Trans.* XLIX. 253 The asa fœtida is drawn from a ferulaceous plant.

feru'laic, '**ferulic**, *a. Chem.* [f. FERULA + -IC.] In *ferul(a)ic acid*: see quot.

1876 HARLEY *Mat. Med.* 598 The resin [Assafœtida].. contains ferulaic acid, $C_{10}H_{10}O_4$, which forms iridescent prisms. **1879** WATTS *Dict. Chem.* 3rd Suppl., *Ferulic acid.*

†'**ferular.** *Obs.* Also 7 ferrular, feriler, -uler. [ad. L. *ferulār-is* of or belonging to the giant fennel.] = FERULA 2.

1594 O. B. *Quest. Profitable Concernings* K iv a, A Feruler to admonish them with. **1600** ABP. ABBOT *Exp. Jonah* 364 The wicked are the worse when they are under the ferular. **1644** MILTON *Areop.* 20 What advantage is it to be a man..

if we have only scapt the ferular, to come under the fescu of an Imprimatur? **1688** R. HOLME *Armoury* III. 312/1 The Ferrular is an Instrument used by School-Masters to correct their Scholars. **1706** in PHILLIPS (ed. Kersey). **1775** in ASH.

ferule (ˈfɛrjuːl), *sb.* Also 6 ferrall, 6–7 ferul(l. [ad. L. *ferul-a*: see FERULA.]

1. = FERULA 1. Also a plant or stalk of it.

c **1420** *Pallad. on Husb.* I. 1049 Take ferules eke or saly twigges take. **1589** FLEMING *Bucol. Virg.* x. 30 Syluanus.. came.. Shaking his flouring feruls. **1620** BRINSLEY *Virg. Eclog.* 95 The ferule is a.. big herbe like vnto fennel giant.

2. = FERULA 2.

1599 BP. HALL *Sat.* IV. i. 169 My rimes relish of the ferule still. **1636** B. JONSON *Discov.* (1641) 115 From the rodde, or ferule, I would have them free. *a* **1656** BP. HALL *Rem. Wks.* (1660) 304 Whilst he was under the ferule. **1825** HONE *Every-day Bk.* I. 967 The ferule.. was a sort of flat ruler, widened at the inflicting end into a shape resembling a pear .. with a.. hole in the middle, to raise blisters. **1850** W. IRVING *Goldsmith* i. 23 He resumed the ferule. **1875** FARRAR *Seekers* I. ii. 24 To learn at the point of the ferule—trash.

3. *attrib.* and *Comb.*, as †*ferule-rod*; †**ferule-fingered** *a.*, whose fingers are liable to the ferule.

1528 *Impeachm. Wolsey* 192 in Furnivall *Ball.* I. 358 Be ware of the Ferrall Rodde! **1620** BP. HALL *Hon. Mar. Clergy* 127 Those ancient ferule-fingred Boy-Popes.

ferule, var. of FERRULE *sb.* and *v.*

ferule (ˈfɛrjuːl), *v.* Also 6 ferrule. [f. prec.] *trans.* To beat, strike, with a ferule.

1579 GOSSON *Sch. Abuse* (Arb.) 24, I shoulde.. bee Ferruled for my faulte. **1873** CHANNING in Salt *Thoreau* (1890) 26 So he did.. by feruling six of his pupils. **1878** MRS. STOWE *Poganuc P.* xiv. 121 To ferule.. disorderly scholars.

feruler, var. of FERULAR.

†ˈ**fervefy**, *v. Obs. rare.* [ad. L. *fervefacĕre*, f. *fervēre* to boil: see -FY.] *trans.* To make boiling hot. Hence ˈ**fervefied** *ppl. a.*

1599 A. M. tr. *Gabelhouer's Bk. Physicke* 27/2 Cause then your Armes.. with a fervefyede clothe to be.. rubbed. *Ibid.* 65/2 Take a Horseshoe, and fervefye the same. **1657** TOMLINSON *Renou's Disp.* 159* To fervefy or decoct.

†ˈ**fervence.** *Obs.* Also 5 farvence, vervens. [a. OF. *fervence*, as if ad. L. **ferventia*, f. *ferventem*: see FERVENT and -ENCE.]

1. Boiling or glowing heat. Also, Violent ebullition, fermentation.

14.. LYDG. *Temple of Glas* 356 For þouȝe I brenne with feruence and with hete, Wiþ-in myn hert I mot complein of cold. *c* **1420** *Pallad. on Husb.* XI. 441 Of fynest must in oon metrete Or it be atte the state of his fervence. **1432–50** tr. *Higden* (Rolls) I. 429 An holy welle, whiche is of so grete feruence that hit castethe owte thynges caste in to hit. *a* **1634** CHAPMAN *Revenge for Honour* Plays 1873 III. 332 Rays lascivious.. ingender by too piercing fervence intemperate.. heats.

2. *fig.* Warmth of the emotions, intensity of feeling or desire, fervency.

c **1430** LYDG. *Black Knt.* xxx, If that any now be in this place, That fele in love brenning of fervence.. Lat him of routh lay to audience. *c* **1485** *Digby Myst.* (1882) III. 1093 þey woll with veruens of love me seke. *a* **1529** SKELTON *Pr. to H. Ghost* 1 O firy feruence, inflamed with all grace. *a* **1538** HEN. VIII *Let. to A. Boleyn* in *Select. Harl. Misc.* (1793) 147, I think.. my fervence of love causeth it. **1591** *Troub. Raigne K. John* II. (1611) 84 Zeale.. Spurs them on with feruence to this shrine.

fervency (ˈfɜːvənsɪ). Also 5 farvence, 6–7 fervencie. [f. as prec.: see -ENCY.]

1. The state or quality of being fervent; glowing or burning heat, intensity of heat. Now *rare.*

1598 CHAPMAN *Iliad* VI. 185 Flames of deadly fervency flew from her breath and eyes. **1633** P. FLETCHER *Pisc. Ecl.* I. 2 About his head a rocky canopie.. Rebutting Phœbus parching fervencie. **1879** G. MEREDITH *Egoist* III. x. 214 It is the sole star which.. preserves an indomitable fervency.

†**b.** Of cold: Intensity, severity. *Obs.*

1615 CHAPMAN *Odyss.* XIV. 693 The fervency Of that sharp night would kill me.

2. *fig.* 'Heat of mind', intensity of feeling or desire, warmth of devotion, zeal, ardour, eagerness; †an instance of the same.

1554 KNOX *Faythf. Admon.* D vj b, Peter in a feruencie first left his bote. **1600** E. BLOUNT tr. *Conestaggio* 6 They continued their new navigation, with greater fervencie. **1672–5** COMBER *Comp. Temple* (1702) 368 The Motives that ought to excite our Fervency. **1734** WATTS *Relig. Juv.* (1789) 216 He drew some practical inferences.. with some degree of fervency. **1824** SOUTHEY *Bk. of Ch.* (1841) 173 The prayer which was preferred with increased fervency at a martyr's grave. **1865** KINGSLEY *Herew.* xv, She would never have known the fervency of your love.

fervent (ˈfɜːvənt), *a.* Forms: 4–6 **feruente, vervente,** (5 **ferfent, furvaunte,** 6 **farvente, fervant**), 4– **fervent.** [a. F. *fervent*, ad. L. *fervent-em, fervens*, pr. pple. of *fervēre* to boil, glow.]

1. Hot, burning, glowing, boiling.

a **1400–50** *Alexander* 3871 Flawmes feruent as fyre. *c* **1400** *Lanfranc's Cirurg.* 311 In þis caas we mowen use hoot fervent oile. **1514** BARCLAY *Cyt. & Uplondyshm.* (Percy Soc.) p. lxix, The Sunne is not fervent. **1572** J. JONES *Bathes of Bath* II. 10 Actuall fyre, working upon the water itself cannot put into it a greater degree of heat, then the degree of fervent heate. **1611** BIBLE *2 Pet.* iii. 10 The Elements shall melt with feruent heat. **1704** J. PITTS *Acc. Mohometans* 56, I have seen many.. to work all day.. in the most fervent Harvest time. **1849** MRS. SOMERVILLE *Connect. Phys. Sc.* xxvii. 300 The short but fervent summers at the polar regions. **1874** S. COX *Pilgr. Ps.* vii. 147 A fervent waste in which it is lost.

fig. **1529** MORE *Dyaloge* I. Wks. 119/2 Let them all.. lerne that god deliteth to se the feruent hete of yᵉ hartis deuocion boile out by yᵉ body.

†**b.** In mediæval pharmacy, of drugs: = HOT.

1398 TREVISA *Barth. De P.R.* XIX. lxxvii. (1495) 908 Some thynges that drawyth laxeth also and be feruent as Scamonea. **1578** LYTE *Dodoens* II. xxx. 187 The common Camomill.. is not so fervent as the Romaine Camomill, but more pleasant.

†**c.** Of cold: Intense, severe. *Obs.*

1448 R. FOX *Chron.* (Camden) 116 Hit was a fervent coolde weder. **1473** WARKW. *Chron.* (Camden) 3 Ther was one fervent froste thrugh Englande. **1535** STEWART *Cron. Scot.* II. 337 The fervent frost so bitter wes. **1634** HARINGTON *Salernes Regim.* 182 A fervent cold Countrey.

2. Of persons, their passions, dispositions, or actions: Ardent, intensely earnest. From 17th c. almost exclusively with reference to love or hatred, zeal, devotion or aspiration.

c **1400** *Destr. Troy* 2154 Than was Priam.. more feruent to fight. **14..** *Why I Can't be a Nun* 7 in *E.E.P.* (1862) 138 They were as ferfent as ony fyre To execute her lordys byddyng. **1534** TINDALE *1 Pet.* iv. 8 Above all thinges haue fervent love amonge you. **1561** DAUS tr. *Bullinger on Apoc.* (1573) 25 b, We of this Church who haue bene feruenter xxx. yeares ago than we be at this day. **1591** SPENSER *Gnat* 296 He spide his foe with.. feruent eyes to his destruction bent. **1673** *Lady's Call.* II. §1 ¶23. 65 By the ferventest praiers implore.. God. **1738** WESLEY *Ps.* xiii. 8 My Heart in fervent Wishes burns. **1768–74** TUCKER *Lt. Nat.* (1852) II. 215 It proves the glow of his kindness the ferventer. **1856** MRS. BROWNING *Aur. Leigh* I. 944 Many fervent souls strike rhyme on rhyme.

b. Of conflict, uproar, formerly also of pestilence, a wild beast, etc.: Hot, fierce, raging. Now *rare.*

1465 MARG. PASTON in *Lett.* No. 523 II. 226 The pestylens is so fervent in Norwych that [etc.]. **1494** FABYAN *Chron.* IV. lxvii. 46 Whiche persecucion.. was so sharpe & feruent, that [etc.]. **1551** ROBINSON tr. *More's Utop.* (Arb.) 139 When the battel is.. most fierce and fervent. **1607** TOPSELL *Four-f. Beasts* (1658) 543 There appeared unto them a Boar.. having fire-burning eyes, a despiteful look.. and every way fervent. **1814** WORDSW. *White Doe of Ryl.* I. 43 A moment ends the fervent din.

†ˈ**fervent**, *v. Obs.*$^{-0}$ [f. prec.] *trans.* To utter fervently. Hence **fervented** *ppl. a.*

a **1626** W. SCLATER *Serm. Exper.* (1638) 68 Their.. fervented supplication to have life prorogued.

fervently (ˈfɜːvəntlɪ), *adv.* [f. FERVENT *a.* + -LY.] In a fervent manner.

†**1.** Burningly, intensely, severely. *Obs.*

1480 CAXTON *Chron. Eng.* ccxliii. 293 He myght not wel endure no whyle so feruently he was take. **1561** HOLLYBUSH *Hom. Apoth.* 27 a, He that hath the jaundis so fervently and sore. **1627** HAKEWILL *Apol.* II. vii. §1. 110 It continued so feruently hot.

2. With warmth of feeling; ardently, earnestly, hotly, passionately. Now *rare* exc. in expressions of love, desire, prayer, etc.

c **1374** CHAUCER *Troylus* IV. 1356 The whiche frendes feruentliche hym preye To senden efter more. **1494** FABYAN *Chron.* V. cxiii. 86 Chilperich heryng of the.. takynge of his sone, was.. more feruently amouyd. **1568** GRAFTON *Chron.* II. 27 The king.. pursued them more fervently then circumspectly. **1611** BIBLE *Col.* iv. 12 Alwaies labouring feruently for you in praiers. **1749** FIELDING *Tom Jones* III. 94 Mrs. Fitzpatrick then renewed her proposal and very fervently recommended it. **1794** SULLIVAN *View Nat.* I. 9 Most fervently do I love my God, my king. **1825** T. JEFFERSON *Autobiog.* Wks. (1859) I. 83, I had fervently pressed the Treasury board to replenish this particular deposit. **1848** C. BRONTË *J. Eyre* (1873) 3, I wished fervently he might not discover my hiding-place. **1874** STUBBS *Const. Hist.* (1875) III. xviii. 31 Henry.. was fervently orthodox.

ferventness (ˈfɜːvəntnɪs). Now *rare.* [f. FERVENT + -NESS.] The quality of being fervent.

1. Boiling, burning, or glowing heat; = FERVOUR 1.

1398 TREVISA *Barth. De P.R.* X. ix. (1495) 379 Smalle asshes.. slakyth.. the feruentnes of the cole. **1533** ELYOT *Cast. Helthe* (1541) 73 a, It [melancholy] may not be so littell, that the bloud and spirites in their ferventnes, be as it were unbridlyd. **1586** BRIGHT *Melanch.* xxvii. 153 Although it [water] be hote, yet inferiour in degree to the heate of feruentnes. **1600** F. WALKER *Sp. Mandeville* 46 b, The great feruentnes of the hot starres.

2. Ardour, eagerness, vigour, zeal; also an instance of the same; = FERVOUR 2.

c **1430** *Wyclif's Num.* xxv. 11 [MS. S], Y my silf schulde not do awai the sones of Israel in my greet hete [feruentnesse of veniaunce]. **1477** EARL RIVERS (Caxton) *Dictes* 133 Whyche wil not be wele.. stered for the feruentnesse of the same tempest. **1528** TINDALE *Parab. Mammon* Wks. I. 84 Christ here teacheth Simon by the ferventnesse of love. **1611** SPEED *Hist. Gt. Brit.* IX. viii. (1632) 581 The Archbishops feruentnesse in using such eager perswasions. **1631** *Celestina* III. 40 His.. ferventnesse of affection is sufficient to marre him. **1727** BAILEY vol. II, *Ferventness.*

fervescent (fəˈvɛsənt), *a.* [ad. L. *fervēscent-em*, pr. pple. of *fervēscĕre*, inceptive verb f. *fervēre* to be hot.] Growing hot.

1683 SALMON *Doron Med.* I. 162 Fixing the fervescent and corrosive Humors. **1730–6** in BAILEY (folio). **1775** in ASH.

fervid (ˈfɜːvɪd), *a.* Also 7 fervide. [ad. L. *fervid-us* burning, vehement, f. *fervēre* to glow.]

1. Burning, glowing, hot. Now *poet.* or *rhetorical.*

1599 A. M. tr. *Gabelhouer's Bk. Physicke* 6/2 Let it stand a day or two in som fervide place. **1667** MILTON *P.L.* V. 301 The mounted Sun Shot down direct his fervid Raies. **1718** POPE *Iliad* XVI. 939 Sol had driven His fervid orb through half the vault of heaven. **1794** SULLIVAN *View Nat.* II. 55 The more fervid the lightning, the more animated they appear. **1833** N. ARNOTT *Physics* (ed. 5) II. 62 His attention was soon recalled to the fervid land of the sun. **1851** THACKERAY *Eng. Hum.* ii. (1858) 59 To hang on in the dust behind the fervid wheels of the parliamentary chariot.

transf. **1865** SWINBURNE *Poems & Ball.*, *Hendecasyllables* 5 Flame as fierce as the fervid eyes of lions. **1871** M. COLLINS *Mrq. & Merch.* II. iii. 61 The Christmas night had been fervid.. There had been a dinner.

2. *fig.* Glowing, intensely impassioned.

1656–81 BLOUNT *Glossogr.*, *Fervid*, fierce, vehement. *a* **1717** PARNELL *Happy Man* 16 The fervid wishes, holy fires, Which thus a melted heart refine. **1779–81** JOHNSON *L.P.* Wks. 1816 X. 122 He is warm rather than fervid. **1828** CARLYLE *Misc.* (1857) I. 211 Of Burns's fervid affection.. we have spoken already. **1838** DICKENS *Nich. Nick.* xxvii, It is your.. fervid imagination, which throws you into a glow of genius and excitement. **1855** MACAULAY *Hist. Eng.* IV. 335 The fervid loyalty with which Charles had been welcomed back to Dover. **1872** BLACKIE *Lays Highl.* 155 Without the call of fervid preacher.

Hence **ferˈvidity** [+ -ITY]: (*a*) Intense heat. (*b*) Passion, zeal (J.). ˈ**fervidly** *adv.*, in a fervid manner; earnestly. ˈ**fervidness**, the state or quality of being fervid.

1692 BENTLEY *Boyle Lect.* Serm. vi. 188 A kind of injury done to him by the fervidness of St. Peter. **1727** BAILEY vol. II, *Fervidity*. **1775** ASH, *Fervidity*, heat. **1847** CRAIG, *Fervidly*, very hotly, with glowing warmth. **1872** GEO. ELIOT *Middlem.* i, A young lady.. knelt down.. by the side of a sick labourer and prayed fervidly.

fervol, obs. form of FEARFUL.

ˈ**fervorous**, *a. rare.* Also 7 -erous. [f. next + -OUS.] Full of fervour; ardent, warm.

1602 T. FITZHERBERT *Apol.* 36 b, As.. feruerous in the loue of God, as they are.. fyry in sensual appetyt. **1658** SLINGSBY *Diary* (1836) 203 Faithful and fervorous Professors. **1669** WOODHEAD *St. Teresa* I. xv. 94 They had a mind to cool the fervorous employment of the Will. **1920** H. BEGBIE *Life Wm. Booth.* I. ii. 31 A young lover, after parting from his sweetheart late one night, was in so fervorous a mood of happiness that.. he threw his stick into the air.

fervour, fervor (ˈfɜːvə(r)). Also 6 fervoure, 7 ferver. [ME. *fervor, -our*, a. OF. *fervor, -our* (mod.F. *ferveur*) = Pr. and Sp. *fervor*, It. *fervore*, ad. L. *fervōre-m*, f. *fervēre* to be hot. For use of *fervour* or *fervor* see FAVOUR.]

1. Glowing condition, intense heat.

c **1440** HYLTON *Scala Perf.* (W. de W. 1494) II. xxxiv, They.. panten soo strongly that they brast into bodily feruours. **1529** MORE *Dyaloge* I. Wks. 1164/2 These prayers .. of his holye Martirs, in the feruoure of theyr torment. **1625** PURCHAS *Pilgrims* II. 1317 A number of Lamps which .. yeelds vnto the roome an immoderate feruor. **1725** POPE *Odyss.* X. 184 Some power divine.. Sent a tall stag.. To cool his fervour in the chrystal flood. **1794** MRS. PIOZZI *Synon.* I. 207 Such effects follow naturally the fervour of an African climate. **1813** SHELLEY *Q. Mab* viii. 71 Those deserts.. whose.. fervors scarce allowed A bird to live. **1891** SIR R. BALL in *Melbourne Argus* 16 May, The moon was also doubtless in a condition of equal fervour.

†**b.** Of water: Boiling, seething. *Obs.*

a **1440** *Found. St. Bartholomew's* 43 The swellynge [sea], yn his feruor.. leift vp hym-self. **1656** tr. *Hobbes' Elem. Philos.* (1839) 324 All fervour or seething is not caused by fire.

2. Warmth or glow of feeling, passion, vehemence, intense zeal; an instance of the same.

1340 HAMPOLE *Pr. Consc.* 250 Fervor of thoght. **1382** WYCLIF *John* ii. 17 The feruour of loue of thin hous hath etun me. **1483** CAXTON *Gold. Leg.* 363 b/1 She.. had more feruour of deuocion. **1531** *Dial. on Laws Eng.* II. liii. (1638) 160 A veniall sinne.. letteth the fervour thereof [charity]. **1638** BAKER tr. *Balzac's Lett.* II. 30 Such fervour is as well beseeming fresh souldiers as young Fryers. **1732** LAW *Serious C.* xiv. (ed. 2) 240 And begin to know what Saints.. have meant by fervours of devotion. **1830** D'ISRAELI *Chas. I* III. ix. 196 The fervour of loyalty vied with the pride of magnificence. **1882** A. W. WARD *Dickens* iii. 50 A fervour unique even in the history of American enthusiasms.

fery, obs. form of FARROW *v.*

1337 in *Liber Pluscardensis* IX. xxxvi, Isal ger thi sow fery agayn hir wil.

feryage, obs. form of FERRIAGE.

fesande, obs. form of PHEASANT.

fesapo. *Logic.* A mnemonic word representing the fourth mood of the fourth figure of syllogisms, in which the major premiss is a universal negative, the minor premiss a universal affirmative, and the conclusion a particular negative; the middle term being subject of the major and predicate of the minor premiss.

1827 WHATELY *Logic* ii. (ed. 2) 98 Fesapo. **1864** BOWEN *Logic* vii. 200.

fesaun(t, -awnt, obs. forms of PHEASANT.

Fescennine (ˈfɛsəˌnaɪn), *a.* and *sb.* [ad. L. *Fescennin-us* pertaining to *Fescennia* in Etruria, famous for a sort of jeering dialogues in verse.]

A. *adj.* esp. in *Fescennine verses.* Pertaining to or characteristic of Fescennia; usually in a bad sense, licentious, obscene, scurrilous.

1601 HOLLAND *Pliny* I. 443 Wanton Fescennine ceremonies. *a* 1637 B. JONSON *Underwoods* (1640) 243 We.. dare not aske our wish in Language fescennine. 1726 AMHERST *Terræ Fil.* i. (ed. 3) 1 A merry oration in the fescennine manner. 1815 SCOTT *Guy M.* xxxvi, To repeat a certain number of Fescennine verses. 1873 SYMONDS *Grk. Poets* viii. 252 A rude Fescennine license.

†**B.** *sb.* A song or verses of a licentious or scurrilous character. *Obs.*

1621–51 BURTON *Anat. Mel.* III. i. I. i. 409 Menander.. did.. write Fescennines, Attellanes, and lascivious songs. 1660 JER. TAYLOR *Duct. Dubit.* II. iii. rule 5 §1, I haue seene parts of Virgil changed into impure fescennines.

fescue (ˈfɛskjuː), *sb.* Forms: 4–6 festu(e, (6 -ew, -ure, -we, 7 -er), 6 fe(e)skew, 7 fes(t)kue, 8 fescu, 8–9 fesque, 9 *dial.* vester, 6– fescue. [a. OF. *festu* (Fr. *fétu*) a straw:—popular L. **festūcum* = class. L. *festūca.* Cf. Pr. *festuc* masc., *festuca, festuga* fem., It. *festuco* masc., *festuca* fem.]

†**1.** A straw, rush, twig; a small piece of straw, a mote in the eye (with ref. to Matt. vii. 3). Hence, a thing of little importance. *Obs.*

1377 LANGL. *P. Pl.* B. x. 278 Þe beem lithe in ȝowre eyghen, And þe festu is fallen for ȝoure defaute, In alle manere men. 1382 WYCLIF *Matt.* vii. 3 What seest thou a festu, or a litil mote, in the eiȝe of thi brother. *c* 1440 *Promp. Parv.* 163/1 Fyschelle of fyschew, or festu, *festuca.* 1483 CAXTON *Gold. Leg.* 400 b/1 He demaunded hym of the festue and of the beme. 1592 G. HARVEY *Pierce's Super.* 54 A pretty feate for amber, to iuggle chaffe, festues or the like weighty burdens. 1610 HOLLAND *Camden's Brit.* I. 720 Thin strawes and fescues small.

2. A small stick, pin, etc. used for pointing out the letters to children learning to read; a pointer.

1513 *MS. Acc. St. John's Hosp., Canterb.*, Payd for iiij festewys iijd. 1533 MORE *Answ. Poysoned Bk.* Wks. 1102/1, I shall.. lay it afore him agayn, and sette him to it with a festue, that he shall not say but he saw it. 1589 NASHE *Martins Months Minde* 7 Though their fescue euen then pointed at Capitall letters. 1612 *Two Noble K.* II. ii, Ay, do but put A feskve in her fist. 1714 GAY *What d'ye call it* I. i. 8, I.. Taught him his Catechism, the Fescue held. 1762 FOOTE *Orator* I. Wks. 1799 I. 197 The fescues and fasces, which have been.. consigned to one, or more matron in every village. 1825 J. JENNINGS *Dial. W. Eng.* Gloss. 81 *Vester*.. a fescue. 1876 BROWNING *Pacchiarotto* 19 Play schoolmaster, point as with fescue.

fig. 1644 [see FERULAR]. 1648 EARL WESTMRLD. *Otia Sacra* (1879) 53 As Appetite, Not Reasons Fescue shall direct.

†**3.** *transf.* (*nonce-uses.*) **a.** The shadow on a sundial. **b.** A plectrum for use with the harp or lyre.

1607 W[ENTWORTH] S[MITH] *Puritaine* IV. 47 The feskewe of the Diall is vpon the Chrisse-crosse of Noone. 1616 CHAPMAN *Homer's Hymn to Apollo* 288 And with thy golden fescue play'dst upon Thy hollow harp.

4. More fully *fescue-grass*: A genus (*Festuca*) of grasses. ***hard, sheep's, meadow fescue***: translations of the botanical names of species, *F. duriuscula, ovina, pratensis.* Also ***Chewings fescue*** [f. the name of Charles Chewings (1859–1937)], a New Zealand pasture and lawn grass, *Festuca rubra* subsp. *commutata.*

1762 W. HUDSON *Flor. Angl.* Index, Fescue-grass, hard, meadow, sheep's, tall. 1794 MARTYN *Rousseau's Bot.* xiii. 138 *Sheeps fescue* is a well known grass, always to be found in sheep commons. *Ibid.* 139 *Meadow Fescue*, one of the best grasses for cultivation, has a culm for two feet high. 1796 MORSE *Amer. Geog.* I. 187 Fesque grass (Festuco) many species. 1813 SIR H. DAVY *Agric. Chem.* viii. (1814) 362 Tall fescue grass stands highest. 1854 HOOKER *Himal. Jrnls.* II. xxiv. 176 Short sedges and fescue-grass. 1855 MORTON *Cycl. Agric.* 863/2 s.v. *Festuca*, The hard fescue. 1864 TENNYSON *Aylmer's F.* 530 Sweeping the frothfly from the fescue. 1917 S. F. ARMSTRONG *Brit. Grasses* viii. 152 Seeds of Chewing's Fescue should have a purity of 90 to 95 per cent. 1925 *N.Z. Jrnl. Agric.* XXXI. 357 Mr. Chewings harvested the fescue-field and marketed the seed, presumably as 'Chewings's fescue'. This would be about the year 1885. 1954 C. E. HUBBARD *Grasses* 115 The name 'Chewings Fescue' is from a Mr. Chewings who first sold its seed in New Zealand.

†**fescue,** *v. Obs.* [f. prec. sb.] *trans.* To direct or assist in reading with a fescue.

1641 MILTON *Animadv.* (1851) 201 Fescu'd to a formal injunction of his rote-lesson. 1714 MANDEVILLE *Fab. Bees* II. (1733) 9 They.. want more Fescuing and a broader Explanation. *a* 1749 PHILIPS *Odes* (1807) 83 Fescu'd now perhaps in spelling.

fese, fesels, var. of FEEZE *v.*, FASELS, *Obs.*

fesician, fesike, obs. ff. PHYSICIAN, PHYSIC.

fesion, obs. form of PHEASANT.

†**fess,** *sb. Obs.*

1716 *Lond. Gaz.* No. 5439/4 A black Mare.. With a Fess Tail, lately dock'd.

fess, 'fess, *v.* orig. *U.S.* Aphetic for CONFESS *v.* Freq. with *up.*

1840 *Knickerbocker* XVI. 112 It would be a sad thing to die here all alone in the woods with a lie in your mouth; so 'fess clean. 1868 L. M. ALCOTT *Little Women* (1871) ix. 114, I shall tell them myself, all about it, and "fess" to mother how silly I've been. 1876 C. M. YONGE *Three Brides* ii. 26 'Come 'fess, Julius,' said she... "Fess and make it up.' 1930 *Randolph* (W. Va.) *Enterprise* 20 Nov. 1/1 The joke is on him and he may as well 'Fess up' to it. 1941 R. A. HEINLEIN *Menace from Earth* (1966) 75 If I had told you that you were going back to meet yourself face to face, would you have believed me? Come now, 'fess up. 1947 N. MARSH *Final Curtain* xiv. 214 I've come to 'fess up', like a good boy.

fesse[1] (fɛs). *Her.* Also 6 fece. [a. OF. *fesse*:—L. *fascia* band; mod.F. has *fasce* ad. L.]

1. An ordinary formed by two horizontal lines drawn across the middle of the field, and usually containing between them one third of the escutcheon.

1486 *Bk. St. Albans Her.* b ij, All the bastardis of all cotarmuris shall bere a fesse. *c* 1500 in *Q. Eliz. Acad.* (1869) 98 Pales, bendis, feces cheveronis. 1562 LEIGH *Armorie* 113 b, The fielde Argent, a Fesse, Azure. 1688 R. HOLME *Armoury* I. iii. 34/1 Fesse, Gules. 1763 *Brit. Mag.* IV. 238 Argent, on a fess, azure, three lozenges, or. 1872 RUSKIN *Eagle's N.* §235 The Fesse, a horizontal bar across the middle of the shield, represents the knight's girdle.

b. *in fesse* (see quot. 1889). ***party per fesse***: (of the shield) divided by a horizontal line through the middle.

1572 BOSSEWELL *Armorie* II. 54 He beareth d'Argente, fiue Fusilles in Fesse Gules. 1705 HEARNE *Collect.* 12 Dec., A Book Expansed in Fesse. 1830 ROBSON *Brit. Herald.* III. Gloss., *Fesseways* or *in fesse.* 1889 ELVIN *Dict. Herald.* 60 *In Fesse*, a term to express the position of charges when they occupy the position assigned to that ordinary.

2. *attrib.* and *Comb.*, as *fesse-line*; **fesse-point,** the exact centre of the escutcheon; †**fesse-target** (see quot. 1889). Also **fesse-ways, fesse-wise** *adv.* = *in fesse* (see FESSE 1 b).

1775 ASH, **Fesse line*, the line that constitutes the fesse. 1562 LEIGH *Armorie* 42 a, The *Fesse poynt. 1864 BOUTELL *Heraldry Hist. & Pop.* v. 23 The heraldic Cross.. is produced by the meeting of two vertical with two horizontal lines, about the Fesse point. 1586 FERNE *Blaz. Gentrie* 206 Adding to the same a *fesse Target, or scutcheon of pretence. 1889 ELVIN *Dict. Herald.* 60 *Fesse-Target*, an old term for Escutcheon of Pretence. 1725 COATS *Dict. Herald.* (ed. 2) 144 **Fesse-ways* or in Fesse denotes things born after the Manner of a Fesse. 1830 [see 1 b]. 1775 ASH, **Fesse-wise.* 1864 BOUTELL *Heraldry Hist. & Pop.* xxi. §11 (ed. 3) 369 Two buckles, their tongues fesse-wise.

fesse[2]. *Obs.* exc. *dial.* A pale blue colour.

1577–87 HARRISON *England* III. viii, The floure [of the Saffron Crocus] beginneth to appeere of a whitish blew fesse, or skie colour. 1847–78 HALLIWELL, *Fess*.. a light blue colour. *Somerset.*

fessel, obs. form of VESSEL.

†**ˈfessely,** *a. Her. Obs.* [f. FESSE *sb.* + -LY[1].] = Party per fesse; see FESSE 1 b.

1486 *Bk. St. Albans, Her.* B iij b, *Fyesly* is called in armys iij manere weys, *fesy* bagy, *fesy* target, and *fesy* generall. 1889 ELVIN *Dict. Herald.* 60 *Fessely*, party per fesse.

†**fessey,** *a. Her.* Also 5 fesy. [f. FESSE + -Y.] Of a coat of arms: Containing a fesse.

1486 [see FESSELY]. 1586 FERNE *Blaz. Gentrie* 180 This Scutcheon following is also a fessey Armes.

fessin, Sc. form of FASTEN *v.*

1552 ABP. HAMILTOUN *Catech.* (1884) 77 Samekil is the lufe of God and our nychbour fessinit and linkit togiddir.

†**ˈfessitude.** *Obs. rare*[−0]. [as if ad. L. **fessitūd-ō*, f. *fessus* wearied.] Weariness, fatigue.

1656–81 in BLOUNT *Glossogr.* 1721–1800 in BAILEY.

†**ˈfessive,** *a. Obs. rare*[−1]. [f. L. *fess-us* wearied + -IVE.] Wearied, fatigued.

a 1774 FERGUSSON *Poems, Saturday's Exp.* 136 So we, with fessive joints and lingering pace, Moved slowly on.

fessoun, obs. Sc. form of FASHION.

1508 DUNBAR *Twa Mariit Wemen* 189 He has a forme without force and fessoun.

fest (fɛst). *U.S.* [a. G. *fest* festival.] With qualifying word, as GABFEST, *hen fest, talk fest,* etc., denoting a festival or special occasion.

1865 *Harper's Weekly* 5 Aug. 490/2 Arrangements were made for the Saengerfest. 1889 *Kansas Times & Star* 24 June, Bob Ricketts won the gold medal at the shooting fest of the Kansas City Gun Club Saturday. 1910 *Chicago Daily Maroon* 10 June 1/2 After the roll call a 'talk fest' was indulged in by some of the old timers. 1924 [see BULL *sb.*[4] 3 b]. 1945 A. J. LIEBLING in *Best Amer. Short Stories* (1946) 275 He explained that a rat fest was a 'rat race, but all bollixed up'. 1952 M. STEEN *Phoenix Rising* iv. 86 Some kind of a liquor-fest in an off-colour bar. 1963 M. MCCARTHY *Group* i. 23 She.. loved.. a good hen fest. 1970 *Guardian* 26 Sept. 11/2 'Cinema City', the Round House's filmfest, ended with an open forum.

fest, fest-, obs. ff. FAST, FAST-, FEAST, FIST.

‖**festa** (ˈfɛsta). [It. *festa*:—L. *festa* (see FEAST *sb.*).] A feast, festival, holy day; also *attrib.*

1818 SHELLEY *Lett.* Pr. Wks. 1888 II. 242 The day on which I visited it, was festa. 1868 BROWNING *Ring & Bk.* VII. 966 Sure that to-morrow would be festa-day. 1886 RUSKIN *Præterita* I. 391 The day it came home was a festa.

festal (ˈfɛstəl), *a.* and *sb.* [a. OF. *festal, festel,* f. L. *fest-um*: see FEAST and -AL[1].] **A.** *adj.*

1. Of or pertaining to a feast or festivity.

1479 in *Eng. Gilds* (1870) 414 The festall daie of Seynt Mighell Tharchangell. 1740 SOMERVILLE *Hobbinol* II. (1749) 139 Blind British Bards.. on festal Days Shall chant this mournful Tale. 1838 THIRLWALL *Greece* II. xi. 67 She presented herself in her festal dress. 1847 DE QUINCEY *Sp. Mil. Nun* viii. (1853) 16 A place.. radiant with festal pleasures.

b. Of a person: Keeping holiday. Of a place: Given up to feasting or festivity.

1798 SOTHEBY tr. *Wieland's Oberon* (1826) I. 15 At Bourdeaux' festal town. 1801 SOUTHEY *Thalaba* VI. xxviii, From tents of revelry, From festal bowers, to solitude he ran. 1863 HAWTHORNE *Our Old Home* 251 The aspect of Greenwich park, with all those festal people wandering through it.

2. Befitting a feast; hence, gay, joyous.

1749 CHESTERF. *Lett.* II. ccxii. 311 No warmth of festal mirth. 1847 EMERSON *Repr. Men, Shaks.* Wks. (Bohn) I. 364 He touches nothing that does not borrow health and longevity from his festal style. 1858 DE QUINCEY *Autobiog. Sk.* Wks. I. 200 The ball-room wore an elegant and festal air.

b. quasi-*adv.*

1747 COLLINS *Passions* 87 Amid the festal sounding shades.

B. *sb.* A feast, festivity, merry-making.

1818 SHELLEY *Rev. Islam* v. lvi, Gore Or poison none this festal did pollute. 1871 B. TAYLOR *Faust* (1875) II. II. iii. 140 Off to the cheerful festals of the Sea!

Hence **ˈfestally** *adv.*, in a festal manner.

1852 G. W. CURTIS *Wanderer in Syria* 279 The way could not have been more festally adorned. 1883 STEVENSON *Silverado Sq.* (1886) 5 The chapel bell.. sounded most festally that sunny Sunday.

†**ˈfestel.** *Obs. rare.* Also 5 festylle. [f. *fest*, var. of FAST *v.* + -EL.] Something that makes fast.

a 1300 *E.E. Psalter* cxlix. 8. 1483 *Cath. Angl.* 128/2 A Festylle, *firmatorium.*

festement, obs. form of VESTMENT.

†**ˈfestenance, festynens.** *Obs. Sc.* [f. FASTEN *v.* + -ANCE.] Confinement, durance.

1425 *Sc. Acts Jas. I* (1814) II. 11/2 The schiref sal ger.. kep þaim in festynance. 1533 BELLENDEN *Livy* III. (1822) 225, I wil kepe him in festynens.

fester (ˈfɛstə(r)), *sb.* Forms: 4–6 festre, festure, (5 festyre), 4– fester. [a. OF. *festre* (for the change in termination from *-le* to *-re* cf. Fr. *chapitre, épître*: see CHAPITLE, EPISTLE) = Pr., Sp., It. *fistola*:—L. *fistula*: see FISTULA.]

1. In early use = FISTULA; subsequently, a rankling sore, an ulcer. In mod. use: 'A superficial suppuration resulting from irritation of the skin' (Quain *Dict. Med.* 1882).

a 1300 *Cursor M.* 11824 (Cott.) Þe fester thrild his bodi thurgh. 1398 TREVISA *Barth. De P.R.* VII. lix. (1495) 275 To the Canker and Festure [orig. *fistulam*]. *Ibid.* XVII. xiv, Festre. *c* 1400 *Lanfranc's Cirurg.* 89 Festre.. haþ wiþinne him a calose hardnesse al aboute as it were a goos penne or ellis a kane. *Ibid.* 292 Þis hole is clepid a festre of þe ers. 1547 BOORDE *Brev. Health* xxv. 15 b, The pyles or Emerodes, Fystles, and Festures. 1607 TOPSELL *Four-f. Beasts* (1658) 501 Sheeps wool.. mingled with Hony is very medicinable for old sores or festers.

fig. 1834 LYTTON *Pompeii* IV. ii, Thus, in the rankling festers of the mind, our art is.. to divert.. the pain.

†**2.** A cicatrice, scar. *Obs.*

14.. *Nom.* in Wr.-Wülcker 708 *Hec cicatrix*, a festyre. 1483 *Cath. Angl.* 128/2 A Fester, *cicatrix.* 1541 R. COPLAND *Galyen's Terapeutyke* 2 H j b, Yf ye wyl bryng yᵉ vlcere to a festre.

3. [from the vb.] The action or process of causing a fester; = FESTERING *vbl. sb.*

1860 I. TAYLOR *Ultimate Civilization* 117 Used to the fester of the chain upon their necks.

fester (ˈfɛstə(r)), *v.* Forms: 5 fe(e)stryn, (feestern), (5 festur, feyster), 5–6 festyr, (6 feaster), 4– fester. [f. prec. sb.; OF. had *festrir* in similar senses.]

1. *intr.* Of a wound or sore: To become a fester, to gather or generate pus or matter, to ulcerate.

1377 LANGL. *P. Pl.* B. XVII. 92 So festred ben his woundis. 1414 BRAMPTON *Penit. Ps.* xxxv. (Percy Soc.) 18 My woundes festryn and rotyn with inne. 1530 PALSGR. 548/2 Though this wounde be closed above, yet it feastreth byneth and is full of mater. 1635 R. BOLTON *Comf. Affl. Consc.* xvi. 315 Draw a skinne onely over the spirituall wound whereby it festers and rankles underneath more dangerously. 1747 WESLEY *Prim. Physic* (1762) 92 A Prick or cut that festers. 1862 MERIVALE *Rom. Emp.* V. xliii. 205 The wound festered in silence and concealment.

b. Of poison, an imbedded arrow, a disease: To envenom the surrounding parts progressively; to rankle. Hence *fig.* of resentment, grief, etc.

1589 R. HARVEY *Pl. Perc.* (1860) 18 His owne poison would haue festered in his owne flesh. *a* 1639 WOTTON in *Reliq.* (1651) 112 There had been ancient quarrels.. which might perhaps lye festering in his breast. 1695 BLACKMORE *Pr. Arth.* III. 489 Th' Almighty's Arrows Fester in their Heart. 1781 J. MOORE *View Soc. It.* (1790) I. xii. 132 A strong resentment.. festered in the breasts of some individuals. 1869 LECKY *Europ. Mor.* II. v. 301 An appalling amount of moral evil is festering uncontrolled. 1871 FREEMAN *Norm. Conq.* (1876) IV. xviii. 119 The troubles of Saxony.. if they had not yet broken forth, were already festering in silence. 1874 GREEN *Short Hist.* iii. §6. 145 Fever or plague.. festered in the wretched hovels.

c. *to fester into*: to become or pass into by festering, *lit.* and *fig.*

c **1420** *Pallad. on Husb.* XI. 49 But kytte not to nygh, lest thai..feestern into a wounde. **1777** BURKE *Let. Sheriffs of Bristol* Wks. III. 141 Smitten pride smarting from its wounds, festers into new rancour. **1790** —— *Fr. Rev.* 212, I must bear with infirmities until they fester into crimes.

2. To putrefy, rot; to become pestiferous or loathsome by corruption.

1540 TAVERNER *Epist. Ester daye, Postil,* The leven of malice roted & festred in us. **1599** SHAKS. *Hen. V,* IV. iii. 28 These fields: where (wretches) their poore bodies Must lye and fester. *c* **1600** —— *Sonn.* xciv, Lillies that fester smell far worse then weedes. **1628** PRYNNE *Cens. Cozens* 70 Their sickly Soules fester, rot and pine away. *c* **1820** S. ROGERS *Italy, Lake of Geneva* 33 Ere long to die..And fester with the vilest. **1883** *Century Mag.* June 218/1 The slimy old moat that once festered under the palisade wall.

3. *trans.* To cause festering in (*lit.* and *fig.*); to allow (malice) to rankle.

1579 LYLY *Euphues* (Arb.) 47 All which humors are by so much the more easier to be purged, by how much the lesse they haue festred the sinewes. **1602** MARSTON *Antonio's Rev.* I. i, I..festred rankling malice in my breast. **1697** CONGREVE *Mourn. Bride* III. vi, Remorseless chains.. festring thy limbs With rankling rust. **1706** ESTCOURT *Fair Examp.* v. i, Take heed, lest your ungentle Hand shou'd fester what you mean to heal. **1818** MRS. SHELLEY *Frankenst.* vi. (1865) 89 That will heal instead of festering, the wounds of our minds. **1850** MRS. BROWNING *Prom. Bound* Poems I. 148 A terror strikes through me, And festers my soul.

absol. *a* **1592** GREENE *Orpharion* Wks. (Grosart) XII. 16 Giuing them one day an incarnatiue to heale, and the next day, a contrary medicine to fester.

†**4.** = CICATRIZE 1. *Obs.*

c **1440** *Bone Flor.* 1945 The leche had helyd hyt ovyr tyte, And hyt was festurd wythowte delyte. **1541** R. COPLAND *Galyen's Terapeutyke* F iv b, Lykewyse in the vlceres.. that yᵗ is egal to be festred [Lat. Galen *Methodi Med.* IV. v, Quod æquabile est, cicatrice induci].

festered (ˈfɛstəd), *ppl. a.* [f. FESTER *v.*¹ + -ED¹.] In senses of the vb.; *lit.* and *fig.*

1430 LYDG. *Chron. Troy* II. xii, Newe made festred sores. **1526** *Pilgr. Perf.* (W. de W. 1531) 254 b, Vnto the openynge of the foresayd closed and festred woundes. *a* **1533** FRITH *Another Bk. agst. Rastell* (1829) 220 My youth hath disclosed their festered ignorance. **1602** FULBECKE *1st Pt. Parall.* 15 Else the secrete fault was some festered and inueterate disease. **1671** MILTON *Samson* 186 Apt words.. are as balm to fester'd wounds.

festering (ˈfɛstərɪŋ), *vbl. sb.* [f. as prec. + -ING¹.] The action of the vb. FESTER; an instance of this. Also *concr.* a fester.

c **1440** *Promp. Parv.* 158/2 Feestrynge of wowndys, *cicatricatio.* **1541** R. COPLAND *Galyen's Terapeutyke* 2 F j, Vlceres that come nat to festring. **1608–11** BP. HALL *Medit. & Vowes* II. §4 What can ensue, but a festering of the part? **1804** *Med. Jrnl.* XII. 98 It appears more like a common festering produced by a thorn.

festering (ˈfɛstərɪŋ), *ppl. a.* [f. as prec. + -ING².] That festers, in senses of the vb.

1596 SPENSER *F.Q.* VI. vi. 5 Inward corruption and infected sin..And festering sore, did rankle yet within. **1654** E. JOHNSON *Wond. wrkg. Provid.* iii. 5 Lest from their festering Teeth a Gangrin grow. **1704** J. TRAPP *Abra-Mule* IV. i. 1707 My festring sorrows smart. **1843** CARLYLE *Past. & Pr.* (1858) 224 Draining off the sour festering water. **1884** BIBLE (R.V.) *Isa.* i. 6 Wounds, and bruises, and festering sores.

festerment (ˈfɛstəmənt). [f. FESTER *v.* + -MENT.] **a.** The process or state of festering. In quots. *fig.* **b.** *dial.* A rotting mass.

1833 CHALMERS *Const. Man* (1834) II. vii. 5 The brooding fountain of so many..festerments. **1845** *North Brit. Rev.* II. 488 The population..have been thrown..into the festerment of an universal discontent. **1884** *Chesh. Gloss.* s.v., A festerment o' weeds.

festerous (ˈfɛstərəs), *a. rare.* [f. as prec. + -OUS.] In a festering condition.

1854 SYD. DOBELL *Balder* ix. 46 His branchless trunk Rose festerous through the morning.

†ˈ**festial**, *sb. Obs.* [ad. med.L. *festiālis* (perh. error for *festīvālis*), in many MSS. of the original work translated by Caxton.] = FESTIVAL *sb.* 2.

1483 CAXTON *Liber Fest.* Prol., I will and pray that it be called a Festial [ed. **1491** festiuall]. **1725** HEARNE *R. Brunne* Pref. §xvii, An excellent MS. of the Book called Festival or Festial.

†ˈ**festial**, *a. Obs. rare*⁻¹. [f. L. *festum* (see FEAST *sb.*) + -(I)AL.] Pertaining to a feast.

1737 WATERLAND *Eucharist* 461 The Feast and the Covenant were..one federal feasting, or festial covenanting.

†**festier**. *Obs. rare.* Also festerie. [a. F. *festiere* (Cotgr.), *festier* (15th c.) ridge-tile, f. OF. *fest* (mod.F. *faîte*) ridge of a roof.] = FASTIGIUM 2.

1601 HOLLAND *Pliny* II. 552 The images wherwith the festeries & lovers of the said church stood adorned. *Ibid.* 553 The festiers and lanterns of temples.

festike, var. of FISTIC, pistachio nut.

festilogy (fɛˈstɪlədʒɪ). *Eccl. Antiq.* Also festology. [ad. med.L. *festilogium*, f. L. *festum* feast, after *martilogium* corrupt form of *martyrologium*; the word was a translation of Middle Irish *félire.*] A treatise on ecclesiastical festivals.

1845 PETRIE *Round Towers* 355 In the Festilogy of Ængus this Constantine is set down as *Rex Rathenīæ.* **1864** BP. FORBES in *Liber Eccl. Terrenarii de Arbuthnott* Pref. 73 Some allusions in the Irish Festologies. **1867** tr. *De Montalembert's Monks of West* III. 293 Under the name of *sanctilogy* or *festilogy*..this circle of biographies was the spiritual reading of the monks. **1882** R. C. MACLAGAN *Scot. Myths* 148 The Festology of Angus.

festin, obs. form of FESTOON.

‖**festina lente** (ˈfɛstɪnə ˈlɛntɪ), *phr.* [L. (Suet. *Aug.* 25) *festīnā*, imper. of *festīnāre* to hasten + *lentē* slowly.] Make haste slowly. Also as quasi-*sb.* (Cf. HASTE *sb.*)

1590 LODGE *Rosalynde* (1592) sig. O2ʳ, *Festina lenter* [*sic*], especially in loue. **1633** T. ADAMS *Exp. 2 Pet.* II. 1272 *Festina lentè*: which is the golden meane betweene those two extremes, of Sluggishnesse, and Precipitancy. **1749** FIELDING *Tom Jones* III. VIII. iv. 169 *Festina lentè* is a Proverb which I learnt long before I ever touched a Razor. **1864** R. BROWNING *Dramatis Personae* 167 He stops me—'*Festina lentè!*' **1893** C. M. YONGE *Girl's Little Book* 43 Be not too quick to do things well. 'Festina Lente.' **1927** W. CATHER *Death comes for Archbishop* I. iii. 38 There is enough to do here. *Festina lente.* I have made a resolve not to go more than three days' journey..for one year. **1932** SPENDER & ASQUITH *Life H.H. Asquith* II. xxxvii. 101 The *festina lente* of his method, which sometimes laid him open to reproach.

†ˈ**festinance**. *Obs. rare*⁻⁰. [a. OF. *festinance*, ad. L. *festinantia*, n. of state f. *festinant-em*, pr. pple. of *festīnāre* to hasten.] Haste, speed.

1730–6 in BAILEY (folio). **1775** in ASH.

†ˈ**festinancy**. *Obs. rare*⁻¹. [ad. L. *festīnantia*: see prec. and -ANCY.] Haste, hurry.

1660 BURNEY *Κέρδ. Δῶρον* Ep. Ded., Sermons..which.. come without festinancie to the Presse.

ˈ**festinate**, *a. Obs.* exc. *arch.* [ad. L. *festīnāt-us*, pa. pple. of *festīnāre*: see next.] Hasty, hurried.

1605 SHAKS. *Lear* III. vii. 10 Aduice the Duke where you are going, to a most festinate [*pr.* festiuate] preparation. **1822** MRS. E. NATHAN *Langreath* III. 292 [A pedantic speaker says:] Let me not be too festinate in hoping [etc.].

Hence ˈ**festinately** *adv.*, hastily, speedily.

1588 SHAKS. *L.L.L.* III. i. 6 Bring him festinatly hither. **1886** G. B. SHAW *Let.* 11 Sept. (1965) 160 Festinately yrs GBS. **1923** *Glasgow Herald* 13 Dec. 4 Others have said, also too festinately, that Dr. Whyte owed his power to his interest in literature.

festinate (ˈfɛstɪneɪt), *v.* [f. ppl. stem of L. *festīnāre* to hasten.] †**a.** *intr.* To hasten, make haste (*obs. rare*⁻¹). **b.** *trans.* To hasten, accelerate.

a. **1652** F. KIRKMAN *Clerio & Lozia* 128 This fair Princess festinated rather to see her servant, than those.

b. **1812** SHELLEY *Let. to Ld. Ellenborough* Prose Wks. 1888 II. 383, I warn you against festinating that period. **1812** —— *Let.* in Hogg *Life* (1858) II. iii. 100 It is possible to festinate, or retard, the progress of human perfectibility.

festination (fɛstɪˈneɪʃən). [ad. L. *festīnātiōn-em*, f. *festīnāre*: see FESTINATE *v.*] The action of the vb. FESTINATE; haste, speed. *Obs.* or *arch.*

1540–1 ELYOT *Image Govt.* (1556) 86 To come..to Rome at his leisure, without festinacion or travayle. **1613–18** DANIEL *Coll. Hist. Eng.* (1626) 173 The solemnity with much festination, and little reuerence is performed. **1661** K. W. *Conf. Charac., Colledge Butler* (1860) 71 He's a.. Cervus in his speed and festination. **1721–1800** in BAILEY. **1822** T. TAYLOR *Apuleius* VIII. 177 The temerity of a blind festination.

b. *spec.* (*Path.*) Involuntary hurrying in walking, as observed in some nervous diseases.

1878 A. HAMILTON *Nerv. Dis.* 407 Any attempt at locomotion is attended by what has been called 'festination'.

†**fe'stin(e)**. *Obs.* [variously ad. Sp. or Fr. *festin* and It. *festino*: see next.] = next.

1520 SIR R. WINGFIELD in *St. Papers Hen. VIII,* VI. 55 By reason of the festyne kept the Sondaye at nyght. **1670–98** LASSELS *Voy. Italy* I. 137, I saw divers palaces of Noblemen upon occasion of their Festine. **1738** [G. SMITH] *Curious Relations* I. iv. 526 As the Festine would not allow to see him that Day, he sent him Word, that he was welcome to his Court. **1819** *Metropolis* II. 85 Not to mention the splendid festins of our noblesse.

†**festino**¹ (fɛˈstiːnəʊ). *Obs.* [a. It. *festino*, dim. of *festa* FEAST *sb.* Hence Fr. and Sp. *festin*: see prec.] An entertainment or feast.

1741 H. WALPOLE *Lett. H. Mann* (1834) I. iii. 9 How excessively obliging to go to Madame Grifoni's festino. **1766** STERNE *Let.* 5 Feb. Wks. (1872) 419/1 Nothing but operas..festinoes and masquerades. **1865** LESLIE & TAYLOR *Sir J. Reynolds* II. vi. 100 The balls and festinos.

attrib. **1778** SHERIDAN *Camp* II. iii, With festino tents and opera pavilions.

festino² (fɛˈstaɪnəʊ). *Logic.* A mnemonic word, representing the third mood of the second figure of syllogisms, in which the major premiss is a universal negative, the minor premiss a particular affirmative, and the conclusion a particular negative; the middle term being the predicate of both premisses.

1551 T. WILSON *Logike* H j b, *Fes.* No true diuine contemneth philosophie. *Ti.* Some Englishe preachers contemne philosophie. *No.* Ergo some Englishe preachers are no true diuines. **1837–8** SIR W. HAMILTON *Logic* xxii. I. 437 Festino, in the second figure, is thus only Ferio in the first, with its sumption converted. **1893** W. MINTO *Logic* 178 Thus Festino is reduced to Ferio.

†ˈ**festiso**. *Obs. rare*⁻¹. [var. of *fetisso*: see FETISH.] A fetish.

1680 MORDEN *Geog. Rect.* (1685) 487 Keeping their Festisoes day or Sabbath on the Thursday.

festival (ˈfɛstɪvəl), *a.* and *sb.* Forms: 4 festivale, 5–7 festi-, festyval(l(e, (7 feastival, festifal), 4, 6– festival. [a. OF. *festival, -vel*, ad. med.Lat. *festīvālis*, f. L. *festivus* (see FESTIVE).]

A. *adj.*

1. Of or pertaining to a feast, befitting a feast-day.

Now apprehended as the sb. used *attrib.*; hence no longer in predicative use.

13.. *E.E. Allit. P.* B. 136 Ne no festiual frok. **1483** *Cath. Angl.* 128/2 Festivalle, *celeber.* **1545** JOYE *Exp. Dan.* vii. 108/2 How many festiuall hygh dayes to worship saints haue thei made themselues. *c* **1568** FULKE *Answ. Chr. Prot.* (1577) 23 Such dayes are festiuall to those Saincts, that [etc.]. **1595** SHAKS. *John* III. i. 76 This blessed day, Euer in France shall be kept festiuall. **1659** HAMMOND *On Ps.* xxiii. 5 Thou entertainest me with wine and oyle in the most festival manner. **1774** WARTON *Hist. Eng. Poetry* iii. 112 Sung to the harp by the poets of Provence at festival solemnities. **1847** GROTE *Greece* II. xlviii. (1862) IV. 216 Knowing no other festival recreation. **1884** BIBLE (R.V.) *Isa.* iii. 22 The festival robes and the mantles.

†**2.** Glad, joyful, merry. *Obs.*

1592 R. D. *Hypnerotomachia* 97 The aierie Teda beloved of the mountains, Celebrated and preserved for the festivall Oreades. **1651** JER. TAYLOR *Holy Living* (1727) 220 Our most festival and freeer joys. *c* **1686** *Roxb. Ball.* II. 138 My Festival Fellows was Roisterous Boys.

B. *sb.*

1. a. A time of festive celebration, a festal day. Also occasionally, a festive celebration, merry-making. Also, ***to hold, keep, make, proclaim festival. harvest festival***: see HARVEST.

1589 WARNER *Alb. Eng.* VI. xxxi. (1612) 152 There was I, unseene of them, the Festifal to see. **1591** SHAKS. *1 Hen. VI,* I. vi. 26 Her Ashes..shall be at high Festiuals Before the Kings and Queenes of France. **1653** HOLCROFT *Procopius* I. 22 Those storms..which happened about that feastival. **1671** MILTON *Samson* 1598 The morning trumpets festival proclam'd Through each high street. **1726** AYLIFFE *Parergon* 472 These Holidays or Saints-Days..were in the ancient Church called *Festivals.* **1801** SOUTHEY *Thalaba* I. xxxviii, Here to repair, and hold high festival. **1820** W. IRVING *Sketch Bk.* II. 30 Of all the old festivals, that of Christmas awakens the..most heartfelt associations. **1822** K. DIGBY *Broadst. Hon.* (1846) II. *Tancredus* 89 St. George ..his festival was celebrated as early as the time of Constantine. **1832** HT. MARTINEAU *Life in Wilds* ix. 109 Children always ready to make a festival.

b. A musical performance or series of performances at recurring periods, mostly of three years, e.g. the *Handel Festival*, the *Birmingham* and *Norwich Festivals* (see Grove *Dict. Mus.* s.v. *Festivals*). Also applied to a series of films, theatrical performances, etc.

1857 MRS. GASKELL *Let.* Aug. (1966) 466 M. & Mme Mohl..come here, after the Worcester Festival. **1864** *Chambers's Jrnl.* Shaks. Tercentenary No. 2/1 At the present moment, when a grand Tercentenary Festival of the birth of Shakespeare is about to be celebrated at his native place. **1877** G. B. SHAW *How to become Mus. Critic* (1960) 20 The forthcoming Wagner Festival at the Albert Hall. *Ibid.* 32 The aims of the Festival-givers necessarily are, firstly, commercial; secondly, phenomenal; and, lastly, artistic. **1909** *Englishwoman* Apr. 298, I am convinced that there is enough appreciation of Wagner in England to build a modest festival theatre. **1926** *Publishers' Weekly* 1 May 1474/2 The annual Shakespeare festival at Stratford-on-Avon. **1930** *Times Lit. Suppl.* 551/3 A festival production of *The Pretenders.* **1951** [see *film festival* s.v. FILM *sb.* 7 c]. **1959** *Times* 28 Aug. 11/4 The returned festival-goer can.. compare his notes with Burney's. **1970** G. SPANIER *And now it's Sables* 133 Every summer in Paris we have an International Theatre Festival.

†**2.** The name given to a book in use before the Reformation, containing an exhortation for every festival-day, and frequently illustrative narratives.

1491 [see FESTIAL *sb.*] **1508** (*title*), The Festyuall, or Sermons on Sundays and Holidaies. **1610** A. COOKE *Pope Joan* in *Harl. Misc.* (Malh.) IV. 77 Or, if..you dare not read the scriptures, read your legends and festivals.

3. = FAIR *sb.*¹ 1 c. *U.S.*

1869 'MARK TWAIN' *Innoc. Abr.* 602 Ladies' Festivals where they were importuned to buy by bevies of lovely young ladies. **1944** *Greeley* (Colo.) *Daily Tribune* 21 Sept. 3/3 The annual mission festival, conducted by the Zion Evangelical Lutheran church Sunday.

festival-day. [f. FESTIVAL *a.* or *sb.* + DAY.] The day on which a festival is held or kept.

1389 in *Eng. Gilds* (1870) 45 On candelle..brennend euery festiuale dai thorow-out þe yere. **1489** CAXTON *Faytes of A.* IV. xiv. 270 The festyual dayes be ordeyned for to serue god onely. **1582** N. T. (Rhem.) *John* vii. 2 The festival day of the Iewes, Scenopégia, was at hand. **1623** COCKERAM, *Vigill,* the eue or day before a festiuall day. **1844** DICKENS *Chuzzlewit* xxxiv. (1890) 431 'If the biler of this vessel was toe bust, sir..this would be a festival day in the calendar of despotism.'

†ˈ**festivally**, *adv. Obs.* [f. FESTIVAL *a.* + -LY².] **a.** Joyously, gaily. **b.** In a festival or holiday manner, like a festival.

c 1374 CHAUCER *Boeth.* II. vii. 59 How a man scorned festiualy and myrily swiche vanite. *c* 1450 *Mirour Saluacioun* 3818 Til his hovse he broght it with alle his myght festivaly. 1483 *Cath. Angl.* 128/2 Festyually, *festiue, solenniter.* 1612 BREREWOOD *Lang. & Relig.* xv. 156 They [Grecians] solemnize Saturday..festivally. 1625 K. LONG tr. *Barclay's Argenis* III. iii. 155 With thee Peace festivally clad is come. 1662 GUNNING *Lent Fast* 37 We [Christians] as festivally remembered Jesus Christ our true Passeover.

festive (ˈfɛstɪv), *a.* [ad. L. *festīv-us*, f. *festum*: see FEAST and -IVE. Cf. F. *festif.*]

1. Of or pertaining to a feast; such as befits a feast.

1651 SHERBURNE tr. *Martial's Epigr.* II. xli, All festive jollities forbear. 1744 THOMSON *Summer* 400 The glad Circle..yield their Souls To festive Mirth. 1791 BURKE *Th. French Affairs* Wks. 1842 I. 578 The appointment of festive anniversaries. 1829 LYTTON *Disowned* 56 The anointed ones were in purple and festive pomp. *a* 1839 PRAED *Poems* (1864) II. 108 Around the festive board. 1869 BOUTELL *Arms & Arm.* ii. 36 The Grecian festive games. 1888 MISS A. K. GREEN *Behind Closed Doors* iv, A festive scene burst upon them.

b. Mirthful, joyous, glad, cheerful.

1774 WARTON *Hist. Eng. Poetry* I. II. 4/1 His vein was chiefly festive and satirical. 1826 DISRAELI *Viv. Grey* v. xi, Her air was not festive, she seemed abstracted and disturbed. 1862 STANLEY *Jew. Ch.* (1877) I. v. 104 The festive character which ran through the whole transaction.

2. Of persons: Employed in, or fond of feasting; convivial, jovial. Of a place or season: Appropriated or devoted to feasting.

the festive season: spec. = 'Christmas-tide'.

1735 NIXON *To W. Somervile* in Somervile *Chase*, The festive Night awakes th' harmonious Lay. 1770 GOLDSM. *Des. Vill.* 226 The parlour splendours of that festive place. 1801 SOUTHEY *Thalaba* VI, On silken carpets sate the festive train. 1848 MACAULAY *Hist. Eng.* I. 353 The new magistrates..belonged to a more festive party. 1857 WILLMOTT *Pleas. Lit.* xxi. 130 A short review of his friend's festive evenings.

Hence **ˈfestively** *adv.*, in a festive manner.

1806 WORDSW. '*Where lies the Land*', Festively she [a ship] puts forth in trim array. 1883 *Pall Mall G.* 20 Nov. 5/1 After studying his pages one may..keep festively the birthdays of Fräulein Goethe's acquaintances.

festivity (fɛˈstɪvɪtɪ). Forms: 4-6 **festivite**, (5 **festyvyte**, 6 **feastivitie**), 7 **festivitie**, 7- **festivity**. [a. OF. *festivité*, ad. L. *festīvitāt-em*, f. *festīvus* festive.]

1. †**a.** Festive quality, condition, or nature; fitness for occasions of rejoicing; mirthfulness, cheerful urbanity; also (of writing, etc.), agreeable elegance.

1613 R. C. *Table Alph.* (ed. 3), *Festiuitie*, mirth, pleasantnesse. 1622 S. WARD *Life of Faith in Death* (1627) 108 Soules..adorned with white Robes, that is..glorified with perfect righteousnesse, puritie..and festiuitie. 1657 W. RAND tr. *Gassendi's Life of Peiresc* II. 274 Your.. Urbanity and pleasant jesting has not bin by me answered and recompensed with like festivity. *a* 1661 FULLER *Worthies* (1840) II. 517 The festivity of his poems. 1681 H. MORE *Expos. Dan.* 286 The contrivance of the Prophetick Parable is of admirable elegancy and festivity.

b. Rejoicing, mirth, gaiety, such as befits a feast.

1756-7 tr. *Keysler's Trav.* (1760) II. 139 The vintage is a time of general festivity. 1801 SOUTHEY *Thalaba* VI. xxiv, The music of festivity. 1832 G. DOWNES *Lett. Cont. Countries* 240 The old man..was honoured with a sort of triumph, succeeded by general festivity. 1884 RITA *Vivienne* v. iii, There were laughter and mirth and festivity in the air.

2. A festive celebration, an occasion of feasting or rejoicing. In *pl.* Festive proceedings.

1387 TREVISA *Higden* (Rolls) VII. 119 It byfel in a festivite þat..o knyght offred nouȝt. 1436 *Pol. Poems* (Rolls) II. 197 At his grete festivite Kynges and yerles..were there presente. 1579 FULKE *Refut. Rastel* 798 That our feastiuitie may be made in remembraunce of the reste. 1624 GATAKER *Transubst.* 94 In his Easter-day Sermon turning his Speech to the Festivity itselfe. 1678 SOUTH *Serm.* II. x. 356 There happening a great and solemn festivity..he [David] condescends,..to beg of a rich..man some small repast. 1679 BURNET *Hist. Ref.* III. 244 The King..ordered..the office for his [Becket's] festivity to be dasht out of all Breviaries. 1837 DICKENS *Pickw.* ii, Tupman again expressed an earnest wish to be present at the festivity. 1848 LYTTON *Harold* VI. i, Several persons bustling into London to share in the festivities of the day. 1861 M. PATTISON *Ess.* (1889) I. 45 The Great Hall, serving..as a banqueting-room for the oft-recurring festivities.

festivous (ˈfɛstɪvəs), *a.* [f. L. *festīv-us*, f. *festum* a feast + -OUS.] = FESTIVE in all senses.

The older pronunc. was (fɛsˈtaɪvəs).

1654 GAYTON *Pleas. Notes*, page-heading, Festivovs Notes Vpon Don Quixot. 1654 J. SPEED *Verses, ibid.* **1 b, A magick circle of Festivous wit. 1665 MANLEY *Grotius' Low C. Warres* 685 Superabundant and festivous Gratulations. 1782 W. F. MARTYN *Geog. Mag.* I. 67 The Georgians..on festivious occasions indulge in the most unbounded excess. 1829 SCOTT *Anne of G.* xxx, Some pretty pageant or festivous mummery. 1865 *Spectator* 21 Jan. 70 Thanksgiving Day..is not regarded as a festival, and not very festivous.

festology: see FESTILOGY.

festoon (fɛˈstuːn), *sb.* Also 7 **festin**, 8 **feston**. [ad. Fr. *feston* (= Sp. *feston*, Pg. *festão*), ad. It. *festone*; believed to be f. *festa* FEAST *sb.*; the etymological sense would thus be 'decoration for a feast'.]

1. a. A chain or garland of flowers, leaves, etc., suspended in a curved form between two points.

1686 AGLIONBY *Painting Illust.* Expl. of Terms, *Festoon*, is an Ornament of Flowers, employed in Borders and Decorations. *a* 1732 GAY *Story of Arachne* 209 Festoons of flow'rs inwove with ivy shine. 1754 MRS. DELANY *Let. to Mrs. Dewes* 6 July, I have not yet got shells large enough for the festoons. 1792 A. YOUNG *Trav. France* 22 Here..see.. vines, trained in festoons, from tree to tree. 1820 W. IRVING *Sketch Bk.* II. 368 Strings of dried apples and peaches hang in gay festoons along the walls. 1852 D. G. MITCHELL *Batte Summer* 204 A rich festoon of nine banners. 1856 KANE *Arct. Expl.* I. x. 106 Steaks of salt junk..are..soaked in festoons under the ice.

b. *transf.* Something hanging in this shape.

1841-44 EMERSON *Ess.*, *Heroism* Wks. (Bohn) I. 102 Thunderclouds are Jove's festoons. 1870 E. PEACOCK *Ralf Skirl.* II. 8 Large festoons of blue and white ribbon. 1887 RUSKIN *Præterita* II. 398 The curved rock from which the waterfall leaps into its calm festoons.

2. *Archit.* A carved or moulded ornament representing this. ***festoon and tassel border***, in *pottery*: a band representing alternately festoons and a hanging or drooping ornament.

1676 COLES, *Festoon.* 1682 WHELER *Journ. Greece* v. 394 We saw..an Altar or Pedestal for a Statue, with Festins carv'd about it. 1692 SETTLE *Triumphs Lond.*, An Arch, on which is erected the King's-Arms in a most noble Shield, with Festoons of Silver on each side. 1762-71 H. WALPOLE *Vertue's Anecd. Paint.* (1786) III. 291 It represents Flora.. and boys in alto-relievo supporting festoons. 1875 FORTNUM *Majolica* x. 88 On which are represented..festoons of fruit. 1879 H. PHILLIPS *Notes Coins* 10 The puteal which this coin presents has on each side a lyre suspended by a festoon.

3. *Ornith.* A lobe on the cutting edge of a hawk's beak.

1855 DALLAS *Nat. Hist.* II. 360 The True or Noble Falcons, which are distinguished..by..a slight festoon or sinuosity on the lateral margins of the upper mandible.

4. Collector's name of a moth.

1819 G. SAMOUELLE *Entomol. Compend.* 432 *Apoda Testudo*, the Festoon.

5. *attrib.* and *Comb.*, as ***festoon-curtain***, ***-vineyard***, ***-work***; ***festoon-like***, adj. ***festoon-lighting*** (see quot.).

1794 W. FELTON *Carriages* (1801) II. 17 To a set of *festoon Curtains for a Coach. 1931 ROGET *Dict. Electr. Terms* (ed. 2) 120/2 **Festoon lighting*, lighting by incandescent lamps arranged at regular intervals in special holders, along a flexible cable. 1870 ROLLESTON *Anim. Life* 32 In several *festoon-like coils. 1717 BERKELEY *Jrnl. Tour Italy* 9 June, *Festoon vineyards right and left. 1893 HUXLEY in *Westm. Gaz.* 29 Dec. 4/3, I was not over-burdened with love for such dialectic *festoon-work.

festoon (fɛˈstuːn), *v.* [f. prec.; Fr. has *festonner.*]

†**1.** *intr.* To hang in festoons. *Obs.*

1789 MRS. PIOZZI *Journ. France* I. 236 With vines richly festooning up and down them.

2. *trans.* To adorn with or as with festoons.

1800 MOORE *Anacreon* xlvi. 18 Clusters ripe festoon the vine. 1841 EMERSON *Nat., Meth. Nat.* Wks. (Bohn) II. 224 Vegetable life, which..festoons the globe with a garland of grasses and vines. 1870 DISRAELI *Lothair* lxvi. 349 The arcades were festooned.

3. To form into festoons; to hang up in or like festoons. Also with *up.*

1801 GABRIELLI *Myst. Husb.* I. 267 The curtains..were festooned up with gold and silver cord. 1811 W. TAYLOR in Robberds *Mem.* II. 350 We should gladly have festooned for you the last garlands of our hospitality. 1859 JEPHSON *Brittany* ii. 19 Curtains, which were tastefully festooned in graceful folds. 1872 C. KING *Mountain. Sierra Nev.* xiv. 286 Vigilance Committees..quickly began to festoon their ..fellow-men from tree to tree.

4. To connect by festoons.

1832 TENNYSON *Dream Fair Women* 70 Growths of jasmine turn Their humid arms festooning tree to tree.

Hence **feˈstooned** *ppl. a.*; **feˈstooning** *vbl. sb.* and *ppl. a.*

1811 PINKERTON *Petral.* II. 84 Their undulating and festooned form. 1860 TYNDALL *Glac.* I. xxvii. 205 A festooned curtain formed entirely of minute ice crystals. 1876 'MARK TWAIN' *Tom Sawyer* xiii. 118 Foliage and festooning vines. 1884 *Syd. Soc. Lex.*, *Festooned-rings*, the tendinous rings of the auriculo-ventricular and arterial openings in the heart.

festoonery (fɛˈstuːnərɪ). [f. as prec. + -ERY.] *collect.* A group of objects arranged in festoons; a festoon-like arrangement.

1836 *Blackw. Mag.* XXXIX. 352 Everything in them so bent..as if conscious of..their festoonery of silver. 1864 HAWTHORNE *Grimshawe* viii. (1891) 91 The singular aspect of the room..the spider festoonery, and other strange accompaniments. 1881 MAYNE REID *Free Lances* I. v. 57 The drooping festoonery of the trees.

festoony (fɛˈstuːnɪ), *a. rare.* [f. FESTOON *sb.* + -Y[1].] Of, pertaining to, or resembling a festoon; in quot. of a person: Making festoon-like movements.

1864 WEBSTER quoting Sir J. Herschel. 1884 BARING-GOULD *Mehalah* xxi. 287 The close [of her round] saw her thick of speech, leery of eye, festoony of walk.

festraw, var. form of FEASETRAW, fescue.

†**ˈfestry**, *a. Obs.* [f. FESTER *sb.* + -Y[1].] Full of festers, festering.

c 1400 *Lanfranc's Cirurg.* 341 A good oynement for to make clene ulcera þat ben hori & festri & polipum. 1565 JEWEL *Def. Apol.* (1611) 547 Somewhat to salue a festry matter, ye tel vs a long tedious tale.

‖**Festschrift, festschrift** (ˈfɛst-ʃrɪft). Pl **-en**, **-s**. [G., lit. 'festival-writing'.] A collection of writings forming a volume presented to a scholar or savant on the occasion of his attaining a certain age or period in his career.

1898 *Bull. Amer. Math. Soc.* IV. 228 Stated by Kronecker in the Festschrift but without proof, its demonstration is a signal achievement of Minkowski. 1901 *Eng. Misc. Furnivall* 491 An English Miscellany or 'Festschrift' in Dr. Furnivall's honour. 1931 *Periodical* June 100 Dr. Cowley.. contributed to the Sir Arthur Evans and the Reginald Lane Poole *festschrifts.* 1931 *Times Lit. Suppl.* 1 Oct. 757/3 Lectures, collected papers and *Festschriften.* 1943 *Mind* LII. 370 This volume, a *Festschrift* presented to M. Maritain on his sixtieth birthday, comprises some twenty papers written by American admirers of his writings. 1961 *Times* 5 Oct. 17/3 The 22..historians..who pay tribute to Dr. Gooch in this bumper *Festschrift.* 1967 [see *birthday book* s.v. BIRTHDAY 3]. 1969 *Nature* 1 Nov. 400/1 The mythology of molecular biology and the festschrift.. celebrating Delbrück's sixtieth birthday in 1966, abound with stories of Delbrück's insistence on rigorous evidence for any claim. 1971 *Ibid.* 11 June 399/1 *Festschriften* are for men who have put their stamp on some branch of enquiry during a certain period of time.

†**ˈfestual**, *a. Obs.* [f. L. *festum* FEAST + -UAL, after *spiritual*, etc.] Festival, festal.

1500-20 DUNBAR *Poems* ix. 83 To keipe the festuall and the fasting day. 1513 DOUGLAS *Æneis* IV. viii. 107 With.. festuall burgeonis arrayit. 1546 LANGLEY *Pol. Verg. De Invent.* II. iv. 42 a, Their festuall dayes. 1616 SIR W. ALEXANDER *Poem* in *Drummond's Wks.* (1711) 150 Happy Day, to which..(the consecrated) Festual Pomp is due. 1637 GILLESPIE *Eng. Pop. Cerem.* III. ii. 22 It is not necessary to keep any festuall day. 1864 J. A. SYMONDS *Let.* 23 Jan. (1967) I. 437 A sound of tragic pipe & festual sonorous verse & rapt oration in the porches of the gods.

†**festuˈcaceous**, *a. Obs. rare.* [f. L. *festūc-a* stalk + -ACEOUS.] Stalk-like.

1657 TOMLINSON *Renou's Disp.* 361 It emitts from one root many..festucaceous surcles.

†**feˈstuceous**, *a. Obs. rare.* [f. as prec. + -EOUS.] Like a straw.

1658 J. ROBINSON *Eudoxa* II. 123 Electrick bodies, drawing up festuceous fragments.

festucine (ˈfɛstjʊsaɪn), *a.* [f. as prec. + -INE.]

a. Straw-coloured. **b.** (See quot. 1823.)

1646 SIR T. BROWNE *Pseud. Ep.* v. iii. 237 Herein may be discovered a little insect of a festucine or pale green, resembling in all parts a Locust, or what we call a Grashopper. 1823 CRABB *Technol. Dict.*, *Festucine* (Min.), an epithet for a shivery or splintery fracture. 1874 M. COLLINS *Transmigr.* III. i. 3 Her turquoise eyes suited her festucine hair.

†**ˈfestucous**, *a. Obs.* [f. as prec. + -OUS.]

a. Straw-like. **b.** (See quot. 1656; ? a mistake.)

1646 SIR T. BROWNE *Pseud. Ep.* II. iv. 81 If we speake of strawes or festucous divisions lightly drawen over with oyle. 1656-81 BLOUNT *Glossogr.*, *Festucous*, belonging to a young tender sprig or stalk of a tree or herb from the root upward.

†**ˈfesty**, *v. Obs.* [ad. OF. *festi-er*, *festeier*:—vulgar L. **festicare*, f. *festum* FEAST *sb.*] = FEAST *v.* in various senses.

1382 WYCLIF *Wisd.* viii. 9, I purposide this to bringe to me, to festeye with me. *c* 1386 CHAUCER *Sqr.'s T.* 337 This Cambuscan his lordes festeying, Til that wel nigh the day began to spring. 1483 CAXTON *G. de la Tour* E b, [They] festyed and chyered their fader. 1490 —— *Eneydos* xvi. 63 Mercuryus drewe thyderwarde for to festye the savd athlas. *c* 1500 *Melusine* 49 They all shalbe..wel festyed bothe of delycyous meetes and drynkes.

†**ˈfestyfull**, *a. Obs.* [Altered form of FESTIVAL; cf. FEASTFUL.] = FESTIVAL *a.*

c 1400 MAUNDEV. (1839) xix. 208 To theise ydoles þei ȝeuen to ete at grete festyfull dayes. 1586 SIR E. HOBY *Pol. Disc. Truth* xi. 41 The festifull dayes, which many dedicate to Bacchus and Venus.

†**fet**, *v. Obs.* exc. *dial.* Forms: 1 **fetian**, **fetiȝ(e)an**, 3-6 **fett(e**, **fete**, 3 *south.* **vette**, 3-5 **fott(e**, **fot(e**, 4-5 **fatte**, (4 **fat**, 5 **fautt**, **feytte**), 3-7 **fet**, 9 *dial.* **fot**. *Pa. t.* 1 **fetode**, 1-6 **fette**, 2 **fætte**, **fatte**, **featte**, *south.* **vatte**, **vætte**, **vette**, 3-4 **fotte**, 4-7 **fet**. *Pa. pple.* 1 **fetod**, **feotod**, 4-6 **fett(e**, 3-5 **fott**, 4-5 **fotte**, 4 **fate**, 6 **fatt**, 4-7, 9 *dial.* **fet**. [OE. *fetian* (also *ȝefetian*), a verb app. of the Teut. *-êjan* class. Its affinities are obscure; possibly it is related by ablaut to OE. *fæt* step, *fæt* vessel, OHG. *faȥȥôn* (MHG. *vaȥȥen*, mod.G. *fassen*) to grasp, seize. See FETCH *v.*

After the OE. period chiefly used in the pa. t. and pa. pple.; hence the normal form *fete* of the present-stem was from an early date commonly replaced by *fet*, *fett(e*, by assimilation to the more frequent forms.]

A synonym of FETCH in various senses.

1. = FETCH *v.* I.

a. with obj. a person; = FETCH *v.* 1 a.

Beowulf 2625 Wæs to bure Beowulf fetod. *a* 1000 *Cædmon's Gen.* 2666 (Gr.) He..heht him fetiȝean to sprecan sine. *c* 1200 *Trin. Coll. Hom.* 61 Ure louerd ihesu criste fette adam ut of helle. 1297 R. GLOUC. (Rolls) 9218 Þe bissop vette Alisandre of lincolne. *a* 1300 *Cursor M.* 14965 (Gött.) Gas fet hir me. *c* 1314 *Guy Warw.* (A.) 4872 Fete hir to me. *c* 1325 *Coer de L.* 105 The kyng..bad That his doughter were forth fette. *c* 1386 CHAUCER *Sompn. T.* 451 Forth he

goth..And fat his felaw. *c* **1420** *Chron. Vilod.* 1931 Hurre soule was fate to heuene wᵗ angels fre. *c* **1440** *York Myst.* xx. 226 Go furthe and fette youre sone. **1519** *Four Elem.* in Hazl. *Dodsley* I. 43, I will go fet hither a company. **1548** HALL *Chron.* (1809) 665 A farre frend is not sone fet. **1568** GRAFTON *Chron.* II. 194 The sayd Piers was fet home againe. **1611** BIBLE *2 Sam.* xi. 27 Dauid sent, and fet her to his house. **1613** WITHER *Abuses Stript* II. i. Juven. (1633) 127 Till death doth fet yee.

b. with a thing as obj.; = FETCH *v.* 1 b.

c **1250** *Gen. & Ex.* 2744 He comen water to feten. **1297** R. GLOUC. (Rolls) 3073 Geans wule vette þulke stones vor medicine. *a* **1300** *Cursor M.* 12310 (Gött.) Water fra þe welle to fott. *c* **1374** CHAUCER *Troylus* v. 852 The wyn men forth hym fette. *c* **1400** MAUNDEV. (1839) iv. 32 Men comen fro fer ..for to fetten of that gravelle. *c* **1440** *Gesta Rom.* lxv. 282 (Harl. MS.) He went home, and fette a long rope. **1521** *Bury Wills* (1850) 124 For fettyng hom of lede..from Berwill xvjd. *a* **1553** UDALL *Royster D.* IV. viii. (Arb.) 76 Shall I go fet our goose? **1560** BECON *New Catech.* Wks. 1844 II. 304 Jehu..caused..all the images to be fet out of the temple of Baal. **1577** tr. *Bullinger's Decades* (1592) 287 Let a little water be fett. **1628** WITHER *Brit. Rememb.* I. 349 Nought But what was fet farre off. **1865** HARLAND *Lanc. Lyrics* 76 He said he'd fot it every neet. **1876** *Oxfordsh. Gloss.* s.v. *Fet*, I ha' bin an' fot a bit a coal.

2. = FETCH *v.* 2.

a **1000** *Prov.* (Kemble) 61 (Bosw.) Ælc ydel fet unhælo. **1387** TREVISA *Higden* (Rolls) I. 173 þei..fette to hem grete strengþe. *c* **1420** *Pallad. on Husb.* IV. 192 Therof [water] uppe wol be fette By rootes. **1559** *Ludlow Churchw. Acc.* (Camden) 94 For my charges goinge to Herforde fatt be a sitacion. **1602** WARNER *Alb. Eng.* IX. li. (1612) 230 This Spanish Inquisition is a Trappe, so slyelie set, as into it Wise, Godly, Rich, by Blanchers bace are fet.

3. = FETCH *v.* 5.

c **1175** *Lamb. Hom.* 83 He uatte þet he nes and nawiht ne lefde of þet he wes. *c* **1205** LAY. 29673 Moni mon þer uætte hele. *a* **1225** *Leg. Kath.* 2499, I þe munt of Synai þer Moyses fatte þe lahe at ure lauerd. *c* **1275** LAY. 6460 þe king.. toward þan deore þare he deaþ featte. *c* **1340** *Gaw. & Gr. Knt.* 451 To þe grene chapel þou chose, I charge þe to fotte, Such a dunt as þou hatz dalt. *c* **1420** *Chron. Vilod.* 2346 Crokette & maymotte fatton þere hurre hele. **1432–50** tr. *Higden* (Rolls) I. 319 þere [Colchos] Iason fette þe golden flees. *a* **1450** in *Eng. Gilds* (1870) 447 At qwat place the bretheren..shul fetten her wax. *c* **1460** *Towneley Myst.* 17 Thus am I comen bofettes to fott.

4. = FETCH *v.* 6, 6 b, c.

a **1300** *Cursor M.* 36 (Cott.) He fettes fro þe rote his kynd. **1393** GOWER *Conf.* I. 44 Wherof the worlde ensample fette May after this. *c* **1430** LYDG. *Min. Poems* (Percy Soc.) 20 To se their kyng..From two trewes trewly fet the lyne. **1526** *Pilgr. Perf.* (W. de W. 1531) 206 b, Thou shalt..fette..thy confort of his blessed deth and passion. **1547** J. HARRISON *Exhort. Scottes* 212 To fet our examples not out of straunge countreys. **1588** FRAUNCE *Lawiers Log.* I. i. 4 b, An argument is either inhærent or fet elsewhere.

5. = FETCH *v.* 7.

1556 J. HEYWOOD *Spider & F.* xiii. 1 The flie..fet such a persing sigh. **1642** H. MORE *Song of Soul* I. III. lxvii, These two old ones their last gasp had fet.

6. = FETCH *v.* 9.

1297 R. GLOUC. (1724) 437, & verrore her wey uette To þe kynges owe ost of France. *c* **1425** *Seven Sag.* (Percy Soc.) 957 The bore..bygan tothes to wette, And to the tre byre he fette. **1470–85** MALORY *Arthur* X. ii, He..fette his cours.. hurlynge vpon sir palomydes. **1583** GOLDING *Calvin on Deut.* xi. 61 After the people had fet a windlasse and trayled about the mountaine Seir. **1651** *Fuller's Abel Rediv., Tailor* 177 He leap't, and fet a frisk, or two.

7. = FETCH *v.* 10 a.

a **1547** SURREY *Aeneid* II. 35 They..with that winde had fet the land of Grece. **1563** *Mirr. Mag.* Induct. lxxi, In a while we fet the shore.

8. Idiomatically combined with advbs.: see FETCH *v.* II. ***to fet again***: to restore to consciousness. ***to fet in***: to take in a supply of. ***to fet off***: to 'pick off', kill.

a **1553** UDALL *Royster D.* III. iii. (Arb.) 46, I will rubbe your temples, and fette you againe. **1602** SIR H. DOCKWRA *Let.* in Moryson *Itin.* II. III. i. 259, I..fet in turffe..for fewell. **1603** KNOLLES *Hist. Turks* (1621) 416 None..could stirre within shot, but he was forthwith fet off. *Ibid.* 582 In danger to be fet off with shot. **1635** N. R. *Camden's Hist. Eliz.* III. xxviii. 285 Cuba..where they fet in fresh..water.

fet, obs. form of FAT.

fetal, var. FŒTAL *a.*

fetch (fɛtʃ), *sb.*¹ [f. FETCH *v.*]

1. a. The action of fetching, bringing from a distance, or reaching after; *lit.* and *fig.*; a long stretch, a far-reaching effort. Also *to take a fetch.*

1549 CHALONER *Erasmus on Folly* N iij a, To the ende he myght shew his learnyng to the people..he toke a new fetche in his mattier. *c* **1555** HARPSFIELD *Divorce Hen. VIII* (1878) 88 With all their fine long fetches and..arguments. **1612** SHELTON *Quix.* I. I. viii. 52 Nor did he hold the Fetch of Adventures to be a Labour. **1662** GLANVILL *Lux Orient.* viii. (1682) 61 There being vast fetches in the divine wisdom which we comprehend not. **1681** —— *Sadducismus* II. (1726) 450 Certainly Wit is not..a Wild fetch. **1692** BP. PATRICK *Answ. to Touchstone* 74 From that which follows, there is a wonderful fetch. **1831** E. IRVING *Expos. Rev.* I. 354 Deep fetches from the secrets of God. **1855** BAIN *Senses & Int.* III. ii. §14 We can..leap from one species..to the remotest fetches. **1881** SHAIRP *Asp. Poetry* ii. 59 What but a great fetch of imaginative power? **1938** J. H. MCCULLOCH *Sheep Dogs* iv. 35 (*heading*) Course: [for qualifying trials].. Gathering—400 yards. In outrun, dog may be directed on either side. Straight fetch through gate set midway. **1946** F. D. DAVISON *Dusty* xi. 117 The trial had four phases..the fetch, when he [*sc.* the dog] brought them [*sc.* the sheep] down the length of the course to where his owner waited [etc.].

†**b.** A 'sweep', sweeping movement. *Obs.*

1617 HALL *Quo Vadis* Wks. §16. 59 So haue we seene an Hauke..after many carelesse..fetches, to towre vp vnto the prey intended. *a* **1625** FLETCHER *Nice Valour* IV. i, Gave his cuffe With such a fetch and reach of gentrie. *a* **1654** SELDEN *Table-t.* (Arb.) 90 Some mathematicians..could with one fetch of their Pen make an exact Circle.

2. A contrivance, dodge, stratagem, trick; also, ***a fetch of law, policy, state***, and ***to cast a fetch.***

c **1530** REDFORDE *Play Wit & Sc.* (1848) 8 Beware the fechys Of Tediousnes. **1549–62** STERNHOLD & H. *Ps.* xli. 7 And cast their fetches how to trap me with some mortall harme. **1575** GRINDAL *Let. to Burleigh* Wks. (1843) 352 By lease or any other fetch of law. **1635** N. R. *Camden's Hist. Eliz.* III. 355 The crafty fetches of the wilie Prince of Orange. *a* **1677** BARROW *Serm.* (1683) II. ix. 135 No struglings of might, no fetches of policy. **1718** *Freethinker* No. 49. 355, I know the Sex too well, not to understand.. their Termegant Fetches. **1745** P. THOMAS *Jrnl. Anson's Voy.* 267 This might be another of their politick Fetches. **1762** FOOTE *Liar* II. Wks. 1799 I. 300 A mere fetch to favour his retreat. **1848** LOWELL *Fable for Critics* Poet. Wks. (1879) 135 A fetch, I must say, most transparent and flat. **1858** BUSHNELL *Nat. & Supernat.* xi. (1864) 365 It is no ingenious fetches of argument that we want.

3. *Naut.* **a.** An act of tacking. **b.** (See quots.) More generally, the expanse of water over which the wind blows before it reaches the point of observation (on the water or at the water's edge); the distance that waves can travel continuously without obstruction.

a. **1555** EDEN *Decades* 231 They remayned..abowte that cape with many fetches compassyng the wynd. **1698** FRYER *Acc. E. India & P.* 51 After several Fetches to and again, at last they were within Call of us.

b. **1867** SMYTH *Sailor's Word-bk.*, *Fetch* of a bay or gulf, the whole stretch from head to head or point to point. **1880** T. STEVENSON in *Encycl. Brit.* XI. 456/2 The line of greatest fetch or reach of open sea. **1882** *Ibid.* XIV. 615/1 What is wanted is to ascertain in such shorter seas the height of waves in relation to the length of 'fetch' in which they are generated. **1934** *Geogr. Jrnl.* LXXXIV. 272 The fetch must of course be sufficient; a moderate gale would develop on Lake Superior a wave of only half the height that it would have if in the open Atlantic Ocean. **1950** P. H. KUENEN *Marine Geol.* i. 76 In the Mediterranean, where the length of fetch is restricted, the highest waves reported are 4 to 5 m. **1965** H. J. MCLELLAN *Elem. Physical Oceanogr.* xiv. 99/1 Some quite sophisticated methods have been developed for the prediction of wind wave conditions based on the variables Fetch, Duration, and Wind Speed.

4. *dial.* **a.** An indrawn breath, a sigh. **b.** A difficulty in breathing.

1832 W. STEPHENSON *Gateshead Local Poems* 18 Peggy said, and gave a fetch, 'Then I'll go and attend him'. **1876** *Whitby Gloss.* s.v., 'I have a fetch and a catch', a stitch in the side. **1878** *Cumbrld. Gloss.*, *Fetch*, an indrawn breath.

5. *nonce-use.* A decoy-bird.

1624 MASSINGER *Parl. Love* IV. iii, This fellow..looks as if he were her call, her fetch.

†**6.** with adv. ***fetch-about***: a roundabout phrase, a circumlocution. Cf. FETCH *v.* 11. *Obs.*

1540 COVERDALE *Fruitf. Less.* Pref. Wks. 1844 I. 207 Though the grace of the Holy Ghost use not long fetches about. **1587** GOLDING *De Mornay* vi. 82 After many florishes and fetches about.

fetch (fɛtʃ), *sb.*² [Of obscure origin.

Although Grose in our first quot. assigns the word to the north of England, there seems to be no other evidence that the simple sb. was ever in popular use elsewhere than in Ireland. The supposition that it is shortened from FETCH-LIFE, or some equivalent compound of the vb.-stem, would plausibly account for the sense. On the other hand, it may be noted that the Corpus Glossary *a* 800 has '*Faecce* maere'. As *fæcce* seems to admit of no explanation as a Lat. word, it may be conjectured to be OE., and the source of the present sb.; in the archetype followed *fæcce* and *mære* (nightmare) may have been given as alternative English glosses on some Lat. word, and the compiler may have mistaken the former for a Lat. lemma.]

1. The apparition, double, or wraith of a living person; see quot. 1825.

1787 GROSE *Prov. Gloss.*, *Fetch*, the apparition of a person living. N[orth Country]. **1825** J. BANIM *Tales O'Hara Fam.*, *The Fetches*, In Ireland, 'a fetch' is the supernatural facsimile of some individual, which comes to ensure to its original a happy longevity, or immediate dissolution; if seen in the morning, the one event is predicted; if in the evening, the other. **1830** SCOTT *Demonol.* vi. 177 His..fetch or wraith, or double-ganger. **1862** MARY LEADBEATER *Ann. Ballitore* I. vi. 188 She believed she had seen his fetch as a forerunner of his death. **1871** TYLOR *Prim. Cult.* I. 408 The Earl of Cornwall met the fetch of his friend William Rufus.

fig. **1839** *New Monthly Mag.* LV. 342 Presentiment is the Fetch of danger.

2. ? *Comb.* **fetch-like** = sense 1.

1841 S. C. HALL *Irel.* I. 13 Seeing his fetch-like before me.

†**fetch**, *sb.*³ *Naut. Obs.* var. or perversion of FISH *sb.*²

1670 NARBOROUGH *Jrnl.* in *Acc. Sev. Late Voy.* I. (1711) 113, I was much afraid that I should lose my Main-mast, it fetched such Way, and broke the Spikes that fastned the Fetches with working.

fetch, obs. form of VETCH.

fetch (fɛtʃ), *v.* Forms: 1 feccan, fæccan, 2 feccean, 2–4 fec(c)hen, 3 *Orm.* fecchenn, 3–5 fechchen, *south.* vechchen, (3 fæchen, fechin, 4 fec(c)hyn, 5 fetchyn), 4–6 fec(c)he, *south.* vecche, 4–5 fech, foc(c)he, 5–6 fac(c)h(e, *south.* vacche, (4 fochche), 3–6 fetche(n, fatche, (5 fotche), 9 *dial.* fatch, vetch, *Sc.* fesh, 6– fetch. *Pa. t.* 3 fæhte, 5 feight(e, 8 fought, *Sc.* fush, 6– fetched. [OE. *fecc(e)an*; according to Platt (*Anglia* VI.) and Sievers an altered form of *fetian* (see FET *v.*), the originally syllabic *i* having, it is supposed, become consonantal, and the resulting combination (tj) having developed into the closely resembling sound expressed by *cc*, i.e. either the geminated palatal stop, or something between this and its mod. representative (tʃ). Cf. OE. *orceard* orchard from *ort-ʒeard*.

Although no other instance is known in which the change of *ti* into *cc* (= tʃ) has occurred, the correctness of the explanation is strongly supported by the fact that in OE. the forms with *cc* are confined to those parts of the vb. in which the regular conjugation of *fetian* has an *i*. Thus *fetian, fetie, fetiað* gave place to *feccan, fecce, feccað*, but *feta, fetast, fetað* remained unchanged.]

I. 1. *trans.* To go in quest of, and convey or conduct back. The first part of the notion is often additionally expressed by *go* or *come*.

a. with obj. a person or animal.

c **1000** ÆLFRIC *Gen.* xlii. 34 þæt ʒe þisne eowerne broþur feccon. *a* **1123** *O.E. Chron.* an. 1121 He his dohter let feccean. *c* **1200** *Trin. Coll. Hom.* 75 Wanne þu lest wenst deað cumeð to fecchende þe. *a* **1225** *Ancr. R.* 368 He wule.. uechchen hire allunge to him to glorie buten ende. ? *a* **1400** *Chester Pl.* (Shaks. Soc.) I. 199 Goe fourthe, Joseph..And fatche our sonne. *c* **1420** *Chron. Vilod.* 732 þey wolden þᵗ theffe ouʒt fache. **1535** COVERDALE *1 Sam.* xvii. 31 Saul.. caused him [Dauid] be fetched. **1588** SHAKS. *Tit. A.* II. iii. 53 Ile goe fetch thy sonnes To backe thy quarrell. **1600** —— *A.Y.L.* III. iii. 1, I wil fetch vp your Goates. **1632** J. HAYWARD tr. *Biondi's Eromena* 104 The Frigat..went to fetch her aboord. **1747** HOADLEY *Susp. Husb.* I. i, The Devil fetch me, Child, you look'd so prettily, that [etc.]. **1771** FRANKLIN *Autobiog.* Wks. 1840 I. 30 There were some small boats and we called to them to fetch us. **1845** E. HOLMES *Mozart* 17 We are everywhere fetched..in the carriages of the nobility. **1845** S. AUSTIN *Ranke's Hist. Ref.* II. 83 His hearers..went armed to fetch him.

b. with obj. a thing.

c **1000** *Ags. Gosp.* Matt. xxiv. 17 Ne ga he nyðyr þat he æniʒ þing on his huse fecce. *c* **1200** ORMIN 8633 He badd tatt ʒho shollde himm þa an litell water fecchenn. *c* **1205** LAY. 17305 Brutes..comen..to fæchen þa stanes. *c* **1250** *Gen. & Ex.* 2889 Hem-seluen he fetchden ðe chaf. *c* **1340** *Cursor M.* 8716 (Fairf.) He bad ga focche his brande. *c* **1385** CHAUCER *L.G.W.* 1347 *Dido*, And bad hire norice..gon To fechyn fyr. *c* **1400** *Destr. Troy* 4099 Poterhas & Protesselon.. fecchid out of Philace..fyfte shippes. *c* **1460** *Towneley Myst.* 199 A stoylle Go fotche us. *c* **1511** *1st Eng. Bk. Amer.* (Arb.) Introd. 27 They can goen vnder the water & feche so the fysshes out of the water. **1546** *Ludlow Churchw. Acc.* (Camden) 26 A horse to fache the rope. **1610** SHAKS. *Temp.* IV. i. 213, I will fetch off my bottle. **1632** LITHGOW *Trav.* x. 477 Goe fetch me Wine. **1697** DAMPIER *Voy.* I. xv. 412 Our Guide made..signs for us to fetch..some of our meat. **1722** DE FOE *Moll Flanders* (1840) 46 Step and fetch my flute. **1809** KENDALL *Trav.* II. xlvii. 150 He had then gone home ..to fetch a knife. **1837** DICKENS *Pickw.* ii, The first cab had been fetched from the public-house.

†**c.** To steal. *Obs.*

1377 LANGL. *P. Pl.* B. IV. 51 Bothe my gees & my grys his gadelynges feccheth. **1622** FLETCHER *Beggar's Bush* V. i, What's the action we are for now? ha?..The fetching of a back of clothes or so.

d. ***to fetch and carry***: *lit.* chiefly of dogs (cf. CARRY 2); *fig.* to run backwards and forwards with news, tales, etc. Hence ***fetch-and-carry*** sb., the action of fetching and carrying; one who fetches and carries, a subservient person; also as *adj.*, tale-bearing.

1591 SHAKS. *Two Gent.* III. i. 274 Her Masters-maid.. hath more qualities then a Water-Spaniell..Imprimis, Shee can fetch and carry. **1696** *Lond. Gaz.* No. 3229/4 A brown Gelding..will fetch and carry like a Dog. **1770** FOOTE *Lame Lover* II. Wks. 1799 II. 80 Miss is so fond of fetching and carrying. **1774** GOLDSM. *Nat. Hist.* (1776) V. 226 A raven.. may be taught to fetch and carry like a spaniel. **1787** W. COWPER *Let.* 24 Dec. (1904) III. 198, I gave him [*sc.* a dog] a lesson in the science of fetch and carry. **1818** SCOTT *Hrt. Midl.* xlix, That fetch-and-carry tell-tale. **1838** J. P. KENNEDY *Rob of Bowl* I. 43 Come and go as you list—none of your fetch and carry. **1871** B. TAYLOR *Faust* (1875) I. xii. 145 As if nobody had nothing to fetch and carry, But spying all the doings of one's neighbor. **1905** D. G. PHILLIPS *Plum Tree* 284 He is the fetch-and-carry of an impudent and cowardly crowd in Wall Street. *c* **1926** 'MIXER' *Transport Workers' Song Bk.* 35 He's a..sort of fetch-and-carry For the comic 'Welfare League'.

2. a. To cause to come, as by a summons or constraining force; to succeed in bringing; to draw forth, elicit (*e.g.* blood, tears, etc.). Now *rare.*

c **1374** CHAUCER *Anel. & Arc.* 341 To your routh, and to your trouth I crye, But well away, to ferre been they to fetch. **1552** HULOET, Fetche by callinge, *accerso.* **1553** BALE *Vocacyon* in *Harl. Misc.* (Malh.) I. 348 They can fetch their frendes sowles from flaminge purgatory. **1580** SIDNEY *Arcadia* IV. (1590) 427 Shee..with a pitiful cry fetched his eyes unto her. **1596** SHAKS. *Tam. Shr.* Induct. ii. 48 Thy hounds shall..fetch shrill ecchoes from the hollow earth. **1621** BP. HALL *Heaven upon Earth* §4 An vnwonted extremitie of the blow shall fetch blood of the soule. **1622** SPARROW *Bk. Com. Prayer* (1661) 119 A new Star..fetcht the Sages of the East to..worship him. **1691** RAY *Creation* (1714) 228 The infant after divers times drawing fetch'd some milk. **1697** DAMPIER *Voy.* I. xvi. 442 The way of fetching Fire out of Wood. **1733** POPE *Ess. Man* III. 222 Fetch th' aerial eagle to the ground. **1821** CLARE *Vill. Minstr.* I. 25 Sympathy would fetch the tear From each young list'ner. **1862** THACKERAY *Four Georges* ii, The great bell fetches us into a parlor.

b. To make (the butter) 'come' by churning.

1853 *Jrnl. R. Agric. Soc.* XIV. I. 74 The old barrel-churn ..will fetch it [butter] in cold weather in a quarter of an hour. **1844** W. BARNES *Poems Rural Life, Dorset Dial., A Witch* 21 Tha cooden vetch the butter in the churn.

c. ***to fetch the water***, and (hence) ***to fetch the pump***: to obtain a flow of water by 'priming'.

1769 FALCONER *Dict. Marine* (1789), *Charger la pompe*, to fetch the pump. *c* **1790** IMISON *Sch. Art* I. 170 Water is commonly poured thereon down the pipe, vulgarly called fetching the water. **1867** SMYTH *Sailor's Word-bk., Fetching the pump.*

†**d.** To restore to consciousness; = 12 b. *Obs.*

1621 LADY M. WROTH *Urania* 493 She..then fainted againe, and againe they fetched her. **1728** GAY *Begg. Op.* I. viii, Give her another Glass..This, you see, fetches her. **1744** *Much Ado* in *S. Fielding's Lett. D. Simple* (1752) II. 185 She is coming, Madam, to herself—I believe we have fetched her.

3. Of a commodity: To 'bring in', realize, sell for (a certain price). †Also *rarely* of money: To purchase, procure (commodities).

1605 BACON *Adv. Learn.* II. 48 b, As money will fetch all other commodities, so this knowledge is that which should purchase all the rest. **1695** LOCKE *Further Consid. Value of Money* (ed. 2) 103 During such a state, Silver in the Coin will never fetch as much as the Silver in Bullion. **1752** FOOTE *Taste* I. 3 The Guido, what did that fetch? **1832** HT. MARTINEAU *Homes Abroad* iv. 57 His land..fetched 15*s*. an acre. **1878** BOSW. SMITH *Carthage* 358 Wretched creatures ..exposed for what little they could fetch in the Roman Forum.

4. To move to interest, admiration, or goodwill by some happy contrivance or telling feature; to attract irresistibly. Also *absol.* to 'take', attract, be telling or effective. Now *colloq.* or *slang.*

1605 B. JONSON *Volpone* I. ii, I apprehend What thoughts he has..That this would fetch you. **1607** DEKKER *Westw. Hoe!* II. ii, *Earl.* Ha! *Bird.* O, I thought I should fetch you. **1708** MRS. CENTLIVRE *Busie Body* I. i. Wks. 1872 II. 64 If thou'rt in Love with two hundred, Gold will fetch 'em. **1819** L. HUNT *Indicator* No. 2 (1822) I. 10 A venerable piece of earthenware..will fetch his imagination more than ever it fetched potter. **1882** BESANT *All Sorts* xxx, You shall..come on dressed in a pink costoom, which generally fetches at an entertainment. **1886** J. K. JEROME *Idle Thoughts* (1889) 109 To say that the child has got its father's nose..fetches the parents. **1931** A. HUXLEY *Let.* 25 Sept. (1969) 355 Another sign of his cleverness was the exploiting of the psycho-analytical rigmarole, which will fetch 100's of earnest imbeciles. **1957** R. HOGGART *Auden* 36 Jazz enthusiasts say that a solo performer 'fetches' them.

†**5. a.** To go and receive; to obtain, get (an object of pursuit); to 'come by' (one's death). *Obs.*

a **1200** *Moral Ode* 222 Ich elches worldes wele þer me mahte feche. *c* **1200** *Trin. Coll. Hom.* 187 Manie mannisshe folgeden ure drihte..sume to fechen at him here hele. *c* **1205** LAY. 6460 þiðerward wende þe king..to-ward þon deore þer he dæð fæhte [*c* **1275** featte]. *c* **1340** *Gaw. & Gr. Knt.* 396 þou schal seche me þi-self..& foch þe such wages As þou deles me to day. **1377** LANGL. *P. Pl.* B. IX. 169 If þe deuel help To folwen after þe [Dunmow] flicche, fecche þei it neuere. **1489–90** *Plumpton Corr.* (1839) 91 Fech your pardon and my ladyes. *a* **1555** LATIMER *Serm. & Rem.* (1845) 179 Christ sent this man unto the priest to fetch there his absolution. **1656** WALLER *Panegyric to Cromwell* iv, The seat of empire, where the Irish come..to fetch their doom.

b. *colloq.* To obtain, 'take out' (a court summons, etc.) against a person. Also ***to fetch law of***: to bring an action against.

1832 *Examiner* 412/2 They were better pleased at what they had done than if they had 'fetched law' of him.

c. *Cricket.* To score (a certain number of runs). ? *Obs.*

1735 in H. T. Waghorn *Cricket Scores* (1899) 11 The Londoners went in first and fetched 95. *c* **1806** in *Daily Chron.* (1906) 12 July 4/7 'On Thursday' (a hundred years ago)..'Hambledon fetched 144 and Winchester 107 runs.' **1906** A. E. KNIGHT *Compl. Cricketer* 345 *Fetch* is an almost obsolete word for 'score'.

6. a. To draw, derive, 'borrow' from a source, *esp.* from one more or less remote. Const. *from* or *out of.* Now *rare.*

1552 HULOET, Fetche out of boke, *depromere.* *a* **1568** ASCHAM *Scholem.* I. (Arb.) 72 Italie now, is not..so fitte a place..for yong men..to fetch either wisedome or honestie from thence. **1591** G. FLETCHER *Russe Commw.* (Hakluyt Soc.) 8 The right [river] Ocka..fetcheth his head from the borders of the Chrim. **1604** SHAKS. *Oth.* I. ii. 21, I fetch my life and being, From Men of Royall Seige. **1631** WEEVER *Anc. Fun. Mon.* 277 A..fashion..fetched from the French. **1651** R. CHILD in *Hartlib's Legacy* (1655) 11, I desire not to fetch Causes afar off, and to tell you of the sad Conjunctions of Mars and Saturn. **1655** CULPEPPER *Riverius* XIII. i. 363 The Cure of this Disease..you must fetch..from the Chapter treating thereof. **1712** ADDISON *Spect.* No. 321 ¶13 He fetched this beautiful Circumstance from the Iliad. **1806–7** J. BERESFORD *Miseries Hum. Life* (1826) v. Concl., To fetch a parallel case out of Roman history. **1871** R. H. HUTTON *Ess.* (1877) I. 37 A so-called 'equivalent' for concrete fact..has..been fetched out of actual existence.

†**b.** To derive as from a cause or origin; to infer (an argument, conclusion). *Obs.*

1567 MAPLET *Gr. Forest* 27 The thirde difference is fetched from their tast or sauor. **1625** BURGES *Pers. Tithes* 2 Nor to fetch any Argument from that Tenet to proue the point in hand. **1662** STILLINGFL. *Orig. Sacr.* I. iii. §3 That they were the more Eastern Chaldæans..Scaliger..fetcheth from the signification of the word. **1668** CULPEPPER & COLE *Barthol. Anat.* I. ix. 20 From the indignation [of the Pylorus] he fetches the cause of the Palsie. **1691** RAY *Creation* (1701) 251 Some fetch an Argument of Providence from the variety of Lineaments in the Faces of Men.

†**c.** To deduce (the origin of); to derive (a pedigree, etc.). ***to fetch far*** or ***higher***: to find a distant or higher origin for. Also *absol. Obs.*

1553 BALE *Vocacyon* in *Harl. Misc.* (Malh.) I. 355 To fatch this thinge from the first foundacion. **1577** B. GOOGE *Heresbach's Husb.* I. (1586) 4 b, As farre as I can fetche my petigree, all my Auncestours were occupiers of husbandry. **1581** PETTIE *Guazzo's Civ. Conv.* II. (1586) 99 b, By the example of Lysimachus..Yea, and without fetching so farre, wee see [etc.]. **1635** N. R. *Camden's Hist. Eliz.* II. 113 Touching this Rebellion (to fetch the matter a little higher). **1662** STILLINGFL. *Orig. Sacr.* I. i. §11 Many great Families ..fetched their pedegree from the Gods.

†**d.** To derive (a word) etymologically. *Obs.*

1605 R. CAREW in *Lett. Lit. Men* (Camden) 100 Some [words] are directlie fetched from the latine. **1605** CAMDEN *Rem.* (1637) 75, I rather would fetch *Hoel* from *Hælius.* **1680** MORDEN *Geog. Rect.* (1685) 43 The more Iudicious fetch their Name from the Name given by Mela, Sinus Codanus.

7. a. To draw, get, take (breath, †a breathing); now *rare.* Hence by extension, To heave (a sigh); to utter (a groan, scream); to drain (a draught).

1552 HULOET, Fetche breath or winde, *prospiro.* **1565** COOPER *Thesaurus, Asthma,* a disease, when..a man can hardely fetch his breathe. **1580** SIDNEY *Arcadia* III. (1590) 276 Damœtas..had fetched many a sower breathed sigh. **1607** TOPSELL *Four-f. Beasts* (1658) 293 The Horse will.. fetch his breath short. **1632** J. HAYWARD tr. *Biondi's Eromena* 106 The sicke woman..(fetching a deepe sigh) return'd her this answer. **1691** G. EMILIANNE *Observations* 248 They drink in good earnest, and fetch the greatest Draughts they can. **1707** J. STEVENS tr. *Quevedo's Com. Wks.* (1709) 53 Fetching such dreadful Groans. **1735** LD. G. LYTTELTON *Lett. fr. a Persian* (1744) 132 She fetched a Scream. **1748** J. MASON *Elocut.* 24 You are not to fetch your Breath..till you come to the Period. **1802** T. BEDDOES *Hygëia* vii. 62 The child..was still fetching deep sobs. **1840** DICKENS *Barn. Rudge* xxi, 'Very good', said Mr. Tappertit, fetching a long breath. **1875** HOWELLS *Foregone Concl.* 145 The young girl..fetched a long sigh.

b. *absol.* (See quot.)

1855 ROBINSON *Whitby Gloss., To Fetch,* painfully to draw in the breath.

8. a. To deal, strike (a blow); to make (a stroke). Now chiefly *colloq.* † ***to fetch a fetch***: to try a stratagem.

13.. *E.E. Allit. P.* A. 1157 No-þyng myȝt me dere To fech me bur & take me halte. **1559** *Mirr. Mag., Jas. I Scotl.* iii, He false traytour..To get the crowne, began to fetch a fetch. **1611** BIBLE *Deut.* xix. 5 His hand fetcheth a stroke with the axe. **1664** E. BUSHNELL *Compl. Shipwright* 68 To fetch a stroake with the Oares. **1678** BUNYAN *Pilgr.* I. 72 Apollyon was fetching of his last blow. **1865** *Punch* XLIX. 228 Fetch 'im [a donkey] a good whack 'ith your rumbereller! **1888** *Sheffield Gloss.* s.v., I'll fetch thee a nope [knock].

b. Hence, To 'have at', reach, strike (a person).

1556 J. HEYWOOD *Spider & F.* lvii. Bbj b, Vew yonder copweb castell..Behold..How thordinance lieth: flies fer and nere to fach. **1608** SHAKS. *Per.* II. i. 17 I'll fetch thee with a wannion. **1625** BACON *Ess., Vicissitude* (Arb.) 575 The Conditions of Weapons, and their Improuement are; First, the Fetching a farre of. **1869** 'MARK TWAIN' *Innoc. Abr.* 37, I could throw a rock here without hitting a captain... You'd fetch the captain of the watch, maybe. **1870** —— *Curious Republic Gondour* (1919) 45 And fetch me with the butt-end of the gun.

9. a. To make or perform (a movement); to take (a walk, run, leap, etc.). Of a river: To make (a turn, winding, etc.). *Obs.* exc. *arch.*

1530 PALSGR. 548/2, I fetche a gambolde or a fryske in daunsyng. **1596** SHAKS. *Merch. V.* V. i. 73 Colts, Fetching mad bounds. **1601** HOLLAND *Pliny* I. 108 The riuer.. fetcheth such windings to and fro. **1611** BEAUM. & FL. *Maid's Trag.* III. i, She..did fetch so still a sleep. **1632** LITHGOW *Trav.* v. 205, I would often fetch a walke, to stretch my legs. **1669** DRYDEN *Tyrannic Love* IV. ii, Some faint Pilgrim..resolv'd to fetch his leap..Runs to the Bank. **1700** CONGREVE *Way of World* IV. iv, If so be that I might not be troublesome, I would have fought a walk with you. **1758** MRS. DELANY *Autobiog.* (1861) III. 508 According to the country phrase, yesterday Sally and I 'fetched a charming walk'. **1759** B. MARTIN *Nat. Hist. Eng.* I. 213 The River fetches a large Winding. **1762** STERNE *Tr. Shandy* V. xxix, Suddenly..he fetched a gambol upon one foot. **1795** *Jemima* I. 105 They are all..gone to fetch an airing. **1829** SOUTHEY *Corr. with C. Bowles* (1881) 181, I shall..in vulgar English, fetch a walk. **1859** THACKERAY *Virgin.* (1879) I. 364 Mr. Warrington..was gone to fetch a walk in the moonlight. *a* **1910** 'MARK TWAIN' *Autobiogr.* (1924) I. 237 A brook that never goes straight for a minute..sometimes fetching a horse-shoe three quarters of a mile around.

b. Phrases. † ***to fetch one's birr, course, feeze*** (see BIRR *sb.* 2, COURSE *sb.* 11, FEEZE *sb.* 1 b); ***to fetch a circuit***: see CIRCUIT *sb.* 3 d; ***to fetch a compass***: see COMPASS *sb.* 11 d; ***to fetch the farm***: see FARM *sb.*[2] 8.

1535 [see COMPASS *sb.* 11 d]. **1547** J. HARRISON *Exhort. Scottes* 213 As one that intendeth to make a greate lepe, I muste..ronne back to fetche my course. **1547, 1551** [see CIRCUIT *sb.* 3 d]. **1552** HULOET, Fetche a compasse in speakinge, *ambagio.* **1621** BURTON *Anat. Mel.* II. ii. 111, A long-winged hawk..mounts aloft and..fetcheth many a circuit in the air. **1653** MILTON *Hirelings* Wks. (1851) 384 Train'd up..by the Scripture..without fetching the compass of other Arts and Sciences. **1722** DE FOE *Plague* (1754) 147 Leaving Stepney, they fetched a long Compass. *Ibid.* 16 My Brother..fetch'd a Round farther into Buckinghamshire. **1814** SCOTT *Wav.* lxii, He fetched a large circuit..avoiding the hamlet. **1837**, *a* **1847** [see COMPASS *sb.* 11 d]. **1859** TENNENT *Ceylon* II. VIII. iv. 350 It is..necessary to fetch a circuit of many miles. **1883** *Century Mag.* XXVI. 907/1 He had fetched a compass of the whole [isle].

10. *Naut.* (see also branch II). **a.** To arrive at, come to, reach; to come up with (a vessel).

1556 W. TOWRSON in Hakluyt *Voy.* (1589) 98 It was the 14 day of October before we could fetch Dartmouth. **1693** *Lond. Gaz.* No. 2888/3 After the Enemy had fetched them [ships]. **1748** *Anson's Voy.* II. ii. 129 The Gloucester..spent a month in her endeavours to fetch the bay. **1795** NELSON in Nicolas *Disp.* (1845) II. 13 We could have fetched the Sans Culotte. **1835** MARRYAT *Jac. Faithf.* viii, You'll not fetch the bridges this tide. **1880** MRS. PARR *Adam & Eve* v. 69 A poor nigger-black, who never fetched the shore alive.

transf. and *fig.* **1637** RUTHERFORD *Lett.* (1862) I. 212, I know that..ye intend to fetch heaven..and to take it with the wind on your face. **1667** MILTON *P.L.* VIII. 137 If Earth industrious of her self fetch Day Travelling East. **1898** H. S. CANFIELD *Maid of Frontier* 178 We fetched Chisolm's house just a little before sundown. **1930** T. E. LAWRENCE *Let.* 25 Feb. (1938) 682 Now-a-days I'm lucky to fetch London once in three months.

b. To get into (the wake of a vessel); to get into the course or current of (the wind). ? *Obs.*

1630 *R. Johnson's Kingd. & Commw.* 239 Outward they touch to take in fresh water, and fetch the wind. **1669** STURMY *Mariner's Mag.* I. 19 The Chase is about, come fetch her wack. **1671** R. BOHUN *Wind* 90 They should make a circuit without the Tropicks, to fetch their Western Winds. **1748** *Anson's Voy.* III. viii. 377 Little more than a league distant from the galeon, and could fetch her wake.

c. ***to fetch headway*** or ***sternway***: 'said of a vessel gathering motion ahead or astern' (Adm. Smyth).

d. ***to fetch way***: to move or shift (from the proper place); to break loose. Cf. 13.

1670 NARBOROUGH *Jrnl.* in *Acc. Sev. Late Voy.* I. (1711) 113 My Main-mast..fetched such Way. **1769** FALCONER *Dict. Marine* (1789), The mast fetches way. **1800** *Naval Chron.* IV. 55 A shot has fetched way in the gun. **1840** MARRYAT *Poor Jack* xxiii, The upper part of the cargo fetched way a little, for it was loosely stowed. **1867** SMYTH *Sailor's Word-bk., To fetch way*: said of a gun or anything which escapes from its place by the vessel's motion at sea.

e. *intr.* To take a course; to reach a specified position, bring one's vessel up.

1586 MARLOWE *1st Pt. Tamburl.* III. iii. 256 The Persian fleet and men of war..Have fetched about the Indian continent. **1669** NARBOROUGH *Jrnl.* in *Acc. Sev. Late Voy.* I. (1711) 8 Two points of land by which a man may fetch into any part of the Bay. **1772–84** COOK *Voy.* (1790) V. 1811 We stood over to Cape Elizabeth, under which we fetched at about five in the afternoon. **1836** MARRYAT *Midsh. Easy* xiii, He..tacked in shore, and fetched well to windward of the low point. **1839** —— *Phant. Ship* xix, The *Dort*..tacked, and fetched alongside of the frigate. **1883** J. D. J. KELLY in *Harper's Mag.* Aug. 447/2 A boat..with ability to fetch to windward.

†**f.** ***to fetch of, upon***: to gain upon. *Obs.*

1659 D. PELL *Impr. Sea* 312 Our ships..fetching abundantly of them. **1693** *Lond. Gaz.* No. 2888/2 The Admiral..of the Blue..fetching very fast upon us.

II. Idiomatically combined with advs. (For non-specialized comb., see the simple senses and the advs.)

†**11. fetch about. a.** *trans.* In sense 9, 9 b, ***to fetch about a compass, to fetch a way about.*** Hence with ellipsis of object: To take a roundabout course or method. †Also *refl.* in same sense.

1551 ROBINSON *More's Utop.* II. (Arb.) 72 Which fetcheth about a circuite or compasse of v.c. miles. *c* **1585** R. BROWNE *Answ. Cartwright* 6 What neede hee haue fetched about and made suche adoo. **1595** SHAKS. *John* IV. ii. 24 Like a shifted winde vnto a saile, It makes the course of thoughts to fetch about. **1607** TOURNEUR *Rev. Trag.* IV. i, You fetch about well, but lets talke in present. **1625** BACON *Ess., Cunning* (Arb.) 441 It is strange, how..farre about they will fetch. **1650** W. BROUGH *Sacr. Princ.* (1659) 551 Tacking and fetching yourselves about as the wind serves. **1825** MRS. SHERWOOD *Young Forester* in *Houlston Tracts* I. II. 5 Fetching a way about, in order that his brothers might not trace his steps.

b. To swing round (the arm, a weapon) so as to gather impetus for a stroke. Also *intr.* for *refl.*

1609 BIBLE (Douay) *1 Kings* xvii. 49 Fetching it [the sling] about [he] stroke the Philistian in the forehead. **1674** N. FAIRFAX *Bulk & Selv.* 122 To gather strength enough (as the arm does by fetching about).

†**c.** To contrive, devise, plan. *Obs.*

1611 BIBLE *2 Sam.* xiv. 20 To fetch about this forme of speech. **1667** H. MORE *Div. Dial.* I. xxvii. (1713) 56 This is cunningly fetch'd about.

12. fetch again. †**a.** *trans.* To take or get back; to recoup, make good. *Obs.*

1535 COVERDALE *2 Sam.* viii. 3 He wente to fetch his power agayne. **1614** BP. HALL *Recoll. Treat.* 917 When God had fetcht againe all the life which he had given. **1617** HIERON *Wks.* (1619–20) II. 251 To fetch againe those losses which he hath receyued.

†**b.** To revive, restore to consciousness. *Obs.*

1601 BP. W. BARLOW *Serm. Paules Crosse* 49 To fetch her againe. **1626** BACON *Sylva* §694 (1627) 174 For smells, wee see their great and sudden Effect in fetching Men again, when they swoune. **1669** BUNYAN *Holy Citie* 252 Revivings, that, (like Aquavitæ) do fetch again, and chear up the soul.

13. fetch away. *intr.* To move or shift from its proper place; to get loose. Cf. 10 d.

1769 FALCONER *Dict. Marine* (1789), *Chock,* a..wedge used to confine a cask..to prevent it from fetching away when the ship is in motion. **1808** *Sporting Mag.* XXX. 123 We fetch away, and are tossed to the farthest side of the cabin. **1853** KANE *Grinnell Exp.* xx. (1856) 152 Even anchors and quarter-boats, have 'fetched away'. **1890** W. C. RUSSELL *Ocean Trag.* II. xxi. 182 Every..article on the breakfast table fetching away with a hideous crash.

14. fetch down. *trans.* = *bring down* (BRING *v.* 18), but more colloquial and expressive of

vigorous action. **a.** To bring to the ground by a shot or a blow. **b.** To force down (prices, etc.).

1705 BOSMAN *Guinea* (1721) 298 This vast Number of Shot..were not sufficient to fetch him [Elephant] down. **1726** *Adv. Capt. R. Boyle* 155, I levell'd all at Hamet, and.. had the good Fortune to fetch him down. **1801** WINDHAM *Sp.* (1812) II. 30 There were but few whom they were able to fetch down at a blow. **1841** R. B. PEAKE *Court & City* I. iii, The late war has fetched down the price of women. **1879** R. H. ELLIOT *Written on Foreheads* I. 7 Fetching down the young rooks from the tree tops.

15. fetch in. †**a.** *trans.* To gain for an adherent. *Obs.*

1614 BP. HALL *Recoll. Treat.* 248 All the powers and craft of hell cannot fetch him in for a customer to evill. **1647–8** COTTERELL *Davila's Hist. Fr.* (1678) 13 Like artifices were used to fetch in the rest.

†**b.** To close in upon, surround; to enclose, take in. Also to include (in one's voyage).

1563 GOLDING *Cæsar* (1565) 68 They fetched in on euery syde and slew those that stoode in good hope..of wynning theyr Campe. **1594** BLUNDEVIL *Exerc.* V. (ed. 7) 565 He.. turning to the South, did fetch in all the Sea-Coasts untill he came to Capo Razo. **1670–98** LASSELS *Voy. Italy* I. 65 A cage of Iron..so high that it fetcheth in a world of Laurel.

†**c.** To 'take in'; cheat. *Obs.*

1592 GREENE *Upst. Courtier* in *Harl. Misc.* (Malh.) II. 242 They were all fethered of one winge to fetch in young gentlemen. **1612** ROWLANDS *More Knaues Yet?* 33 Who will be drawne at Dice and Cards to play..And be fetch'd in for all that's in his purse?

16. fetch off. †**a.** To bring out of a difficulty; to deliver, rescue. Cf. *bring off.* *Obs.*

1648 JENKYN *Blind Guide* i. 16 This hereticall and rediculous soul fetcheth off himself thus. **1650** R. STAPYLTON *Strada's Low-C. Warres* III. 62 The whole Market-place..strove to fetch off the prisoners.

†**b.** To 'do' or 'do for'; to get the better of; to make an end of. *Obs.*

1597 SHAKS. *2 Hen. IV*, III. ii. 324 As I returne, I will fetch off these Iustices. **1613** *Notorious Cousnages of J. & A. West* vi, She hath fetcht off Usurers and Misers, as finely as they fetch off young heires. **1618** in Gutch *Coll. Cur.* II. 423 My Lord of Essex was fetcht off by a trick. **1633** BP. HALL *Occas. Medit.* lxxvii. 190 What fine devises..to fetch off lives. **1653** H. MORE *Antid. Ath.* III. xi. (1712) 122 We may add a third [Question], which may haply fetch off the other two.

†**c.** To drain, drink off (a draught). Cf. 7. *Obs.*

1657 W. RAND tr. *Gassendi's Life of Peiresc* II. 99 He fetcht off the Lusty Bowle of wine. *Ibid.* II. 137 Novellius Torquatus..is reported to have fetcht off at one draught.. three Congii or Roman Gallons of wine.

17. fetch out. To draw forth; to bring into clearness; to develop and display.

1644 MILTON *Educ.*, These ways..if there were any Secret excellence among them would fetch it out. **1711** ADDISON *Spect.* No. 215 ¶1 Marble..shews none of its inherent Beauties, till the Skill of the Polisher fetches out the Colours. **1847** L. HUNT *Jar Honey* x. (1848) 134 It fetches out..the most beautiful strength of the human heart.

18. fetch over. †**a.** *trans.* To succeed in delivering (a blow). *Obs.*

a **1640** J. BALL *Answ. to Can* I. (1642) 119 He might fetch over a sure blow upon us.

†**b.** To get the better of. *Obs.*

c **1600** DAY *Begg. Bednall Gr.* II. ii. (1881) 35 'Tis he that I fetch'd over for the sattin suite and left him in pawn for the reckoning. **1680** R. L'ESTRANGE *Colloq. Erasm.* 199 They have fetch'd me over many and many a time.

†**c.** To go over; to repeat. *Obs.*

1642 ROGERS *Naaman* 606 What might be the cause why Isaac fetcht over the blessing the second time.

19. fetch round (or **around**). *intr.* To recover, to regain consciousness. Also *trans.*

1870 G. MEREDITH *Let.* ? Sept. (1970) I. 426 This salt-water fetches me round, Tuck. It's the next best to mountain air. **1874** HARDY *Far fr. Madding Crowd* I. ii. 21, I do hope Daisy [*sc.* a cow] will fetch round again now. **1889** 'MARK TWAIN' *Connecticut Yankee* 135 You feel strange, like somebody that has been struck by lightning and hasn't quite fetched around yet, and can't just get his bearings.

20. fetch through. *intr.* To win through.

1912 R. F. SCOTT *Jrnl.* 16–17 Mar. in *Last Exped.* (1913) I. 593 Though we constantly talk of fetching through, I don't think any one of us believes it in his heart.

21. fetch up. †**a.** *trans.* To bring to a higher level or position; to elevate, raise. *Obs.*

1606 SHAKS. *Ant. & Cl.* IV. xv. 35 The strong wing'd Mercury should fetch thee vp, And set thee by Ioves side. **1607–12** BACON *Ess., Seeming Wise* (Arb.) 216 Hee fetched one of his browes vp to his forehead. **1705** ADDISON *Italy* (J.), Any of those arts..may be fetched up to its perfection in ten..years. **1711** —— *Spect.* No. 119 ¶3 They have.. fetched themselves up to the Fashion of the polite World.

b. To vomit. Also of a medicine, etc.: To promote expectoration of. Cf. *bring up.*

1599 H. BUTTES *Dyets drie Dinner* N iij b, Butter.. fetcheth up fleame cloddered about the breast and lungs. **1622** MASSINGER *Virg. Mart.* V. i, Fetch up What thou hast swallowed.

c. To recall (to the mind); to bring to light.

1614 BP. HALL *Recoll. Treat.* 454 To fetch up olde wordes from forgetfulnesse. **1817** CHALMERS *Astron. Disc.* iv. (1852) 93 The knowledge..he cannot fetch up himself from the obscurity of this wondrous..scene.

†**d.** To rouse or stir up (a horse). *Obs.*

1565 COOPER *Thesaurus* s.v. *Equus*, To fetch vp with the spurre. **1573** in BARET *Alv.* F 401.

†**e.** To overthrow, 'trip up'. *Obs.*

1615 T. ADAMS *Spir. Nauig.* 43 The strongest Sampson has been fetched up by this wrastler.

f. To make up (lee way, lost ground, time, etc.).

1665 J. WILSON *Projectors* I. Dram. Wks. (1874) 227, I shall have the custody of the parish stock. If that will serve you, command it; we shall be able, I hope, to fetch it up again before my time be out. **1709** STANHOPE *Paraphr.* IV. 122 Penitents..will..fetch up the Time they have lost. **1741** RICHARDSON *Pamela* (1824) I. 122 Mrs. Jewkes lies snoring in bed, fetching up her last night's disturbance. **1794** T. JEFFERSON *Writ.* (1859) IV. 112 The time is coming when we shall fetch up the lee-way of our vessel. **1825** *Thomas Brown* in *Houlston Tracts* I. xvi. 3 Thomas did not mind playing a day or two in the week, for..he knew he could easily fetch it up again. **1846** *Jrnl. R. Agric. Soc.* VII. II. 686 [They] have much lee way to fetch up.

†**g.** To come up with, overtake. *Obs.*

a **1622** R. HAWKINS *Voy. S. Sea* (1847) 179 Being out of hope to fetch up this shippe. **1669** STURMY *Mariner's Mag.* I. 14 The Moon must go longer 2 days..before she can fetch up the Sun, to come into Conjunction with her. **1692** R. L'ESTRANGE *Fables* cxxxiii, Says he [the Hare], I can fetch up the Tortoise when I please. **1751** PALTOCK *P. Wilkins* I. v. 45 We fetched her up, and..fired a shot.

h. *Naut.* To come or get to (a place); to reach; to come in sight of; (also *to fetch up the sight of*) to sail along. ? *Obs.*

1556 W. TOWRSON in Hakluyt *Voy.* (1589) 108 It is hard to fetch upp a towne here if a shippe ouer shoote it. **1632** LITHGOW *Trav.* III. 96 As we fetched up the sight of Nicasia. *Ibid.* V. 181 We fetched up the coast of Cylicia. *Ibid.* IX. 398 We fetched up the little Ile of Strombolo.

i. *intr.* for *refl.* To come to a stand; to 'pull up'; to stop. Also *trans.*

1838 J. C. NEAL *Charcoal Sks.* 96, I was soon fetch'd up in the victualling line—and I busted for the benefit of my creditors. **1848** BARTLETT *Dict. Amer.*, *To fetch up*, to stop suddenly... We often hear the phrase 'He fetched up all standing' that is, he made a sudden halt. It is a nautical vulgarism. **1858** HAWTHORNE *Fr. & It. Jrnls.* V. 705 When in quest of any particular point, are likely enough to fetch up at some other. **1859** 'N. HOGG' *Poet. Lett.* (1865) 44 Wul tha nex thing thay dood was ta holler out 'Dress!'.. Wat thay main'd wis ta vetch up a little bit zmurt. **1883** W. WHITMAN *Specimen Days* 139, I made quite a western journey, fetching up at Denver, Colorado. **1890** G. W. PERRIE *Buckskin Mose* ii. 25 Waukegan was designated as the place where he might probably fetch up. **1898** E. N. WESTCOTT *David Harum* 175, I..walked alongside the el'phant..till they fetched up inside the tent. **1902** *Chambers's Jrnl.* Mar. 186/2 Before he could more than grab at the rein lying loosely on the pommel, the filly 'fetched up' against a dead box-tree, hard as cast-iron. **1906** *Springfield Weekly Republ.* 11 Oct. 1 If he tries often enough he may fetch up in Congress. **1956** A. L. ROWSE *Early Churchills* xviii. 391 Some of her business correspondence..has fetched up on the other side of the Atlantic. **1971** *Listener* 8 Apr. 449/3, I grew used to bummelling around the Bond Street dealers and fetching up for tea at the National Gallery or the Tate.

j. To bring up, rear, or train (children.) *U.S.*

1841 *Knickerbocker* XVII. 156 Harry Cott says he was 'fetched up' on Long-Island. **1869** MRS. STOWE *Oldtown Folks* xx. 237, I was fetchin' on her up to work for her livin' as I was fetched up. **1890** S. O. JEWETT *Strangers & Wayfarers* 205 We've gone and fetched ye up the best we could.

fetch-, the vb.-stem in *comb.* with adv., as **fetch-after**, see quot. 1888; with *sb.* as *obj.*; †**fetch-fire** *attrib.*; **fetch-water**, a water-carrier.

1598 CHAPMAN *Iliad* VI. 495 But spin the Greek wives' webs of task, and their fetch-water be. **1784** *Unfortunate Sensibility* II. 10 In a country-town a much less change would have been a sufficient topic for a fetch-fire gossip, or a bake-house conversation. **1888** *Lancet* 30 June 1308 The forms of caterpillar known..popularly..as 'fetch-afters', from their mode of progression.

fetch-candle. = FETCH-LIGHT.

1852 H. WEDGWOOD in *N. & Q.* 1st Ser. VI. 17 The superstition..in Pembrokeshire appears in the shape of the fetch-candle. (In mod. Dicts.)

fetched (fɛtʃt), *ppl. a.* [f. FETCH *v.* + -ED¹.] Only in combs., as DEEP-FETCHED, FAR-FETCHED.

fetcher (ˈfɛtʃə(r)). [f. FETCH *v.* + -ER¹.]

1. One who or that which fetches, in various senses of the verb. Also in phrase *fetcher and carrier*, and in comb., as *water-fetcher*, etc.

1552 HULOET, Fetcher of water. *Aquarius.* **1580** HOLLYBAND *Treas. Fr. Tong, Faiseur de soubresaults*, a fetcher of gamboldes, a tumbler. **1601** WEEVER *Mirr. Mart.* B vij, The fetcher of Euridice from hell. **1751** GRAY *Wks.* (1825) II. 161 You will take me for a mere poet and a fetcher and carrier of sing-song. *a* **1863** THACKERAY *Mr. & Mrs. Berry* ii, The poor fellow has been employed..in the same office of fetcher and carrier. **1877** KINGLAKE *Crimea* VI. vi. 97 The wood and the water fetchers went out.

†**b.** *spec.* (see quot. 1890). *Obs.*

1890 P. H. BROWN *George Buchanan* ii. 27 Lads proceeding to Cambridge from the remoter districts went in a body under a 'fetcher'. **1892** *Q. Rev.* Jan. 24 The students ..were collected by 'fetchers' brought to Oxford, &c.

2. With advbs., as *fetcher in.*

1611 CHAPMAN *Iliad* I. 167 Of fight (the fetcher in of this) My hands haue most share. **1660** HOWELL, Fetcher in, *ameneur.*

fetching (ˈfɛtʃɪŋ), *vbl. sb.* [f. FETCH *v.* + -ING¹.]

1. The action of the vb. FETCH in various senses. †*fetching of boards*: = tacking: see BOARD *sb.* 15.

c **1374** CHAUCER *Troylus* V. 890 Swich wreche on hem, for fecchyng of Eleyne, Ther shal ben take. **1464** *Nottingham Rec.* II. 377 For fecchyng of money at Retforde by ij tymes. **1581** MULCASTER *Positions* xx. (1887) 84 To procure easie fetching of ones breath, it is verie soueraine. **1622** MABBE tr. *Aleman's Guzman d'Alf.* I. III. v. 216 Let me liue..in a spacious Countrey..where there is few fetching of boords. **1672** PETTY *Pol. Anat.* (1691) 76 Fuel costs nothing but fetching. **1727** DE FOE *Syst. Magic* V. iii. 89 To give them Job's goods merely for fetching. **1882** MISS BRADDON *Mt. Royal* I. ii. 57, I hate such fetching and carrying. **1884** H. M. LEATHES *Notes Nat. Hist.* 110 Their [dogs'] natural propensities for hunting, watching, and fetching.

2. With *again*, *up*, etc.: see adv. combs. of verb.

1513 MORE in Grafton *Chron.* II. 770 The fetching forth of this noble man to his honour and welth. **1617** HIERON *Wks.* II. 252 The reuiuing and fetching againe of a decayed Christian! **1633** BP. HALL *Occas. Medit.* (1851) 205 The fetching up my soul from this vale of misery and tears. **1673** PENN *Chr. a Quaker* xxii. 588 It is not Fetching in this Thought..that gives Right Peace.

fetching (ˈfɛtʃɪŋ), *ppl. a.* [f. FETCH *v.* + -ING².]

†**1.** That contrives, plans, schemes; crafty, designing. *Obs.*

1581 PETTIE *Guazzo's Civ. Conv.* II. (1586) 97 b, Such fetching heads..consume themselves in a manner awaie, in devising new kindes of extortion. **1583** FOXE *A. & M.* (ed. 4) 575/1 What cannot the fetchyng practise of the Romish Prelates bring about?

2. Alluring, fascinating, pleasing, 'taking'.

1880 MRS. FORRESTER *Roy & V.* I. 284 There is nothing ..so fetching as a beautiful voice. **1881** MISS BRADDON *Asph.* xxvii. 297 'What a fetching get-up,' said Edgar. **1891** *Athenæum* 21 Nov. 685/2 The imitation from Wordsworth is particularly 'fetching'.

Hence ˈ**fetchingly** *adv.*

1889 *Cath. News* 3 Aug. 5/1 She was fetchingly attired.

†**fetch-life.** *Obs. rare*⁻¹. In quot. -liefe. [? f. FETCH *vb.* + LIFE.] ? A messenger sent to 'fetch' the soul of a dying person.

1583 STANYHURST *Æneis* IV. 486 (Arb.) 111 On thee turrets the skrich howle, lyke fetchliefe ysetled, Her burial roundel doth ruck.

fetch-light. [Of uncertain formation; perh. f. FETCH *sb.*², if that be an old word. But it may be f. FETCH *v.*, as the 'corpse-candle' is supposed to be a light sent to 'fetch' the doomed person.]

A name given (app. in South Wales) to the 'corpse-candle' (Welsh *canwyll corff*), a spectral light supposed to be seen before a person's death travelling from his house to his grave.

1692 *Athenian Mercury* VI. vi. 1/1 Before the Death of any person in the Family, there is an Appearance vulgarly called a Fetch-light.

fetchling, var. of VETCHLING.

1651 R. CHILD in *Hartlib's Legacy* (1755) 1 Saint Foine, called by Parkinson..Medick Fetchling.

ˈ**fetch-up**, *sb.* [f. vbl. phr. *fetch up*, FETCH *v.* 21 i.] A coming to a stand-still; stopping.

1866 A. D. WHITNEY *L. Goldthwaite* x, It isn't the fall that hurts,—it's the fetch-up. **1927** *Harper's Mag.* Nov. 82 They had both been born in this house, but India had been born longer ago than Flagg, so his fetch-up was the sharper.

fête (‖fɛt, feɪt), *sb.* [a. F. *fête*: see FEAST *sb.*]

1. a. A festival, an entertainment on a large scale.

1754 H. WALPOLE *Lett.* (1857) II. 308 The great fête at St. Cloud. **1779** SHERIDAN *Critic* III. Wks. 1873 II. 184, I suppose Thames..to compliment Britannia with a fête in honour of the victory. **1818** BYRON *Mazeppa* iv, He gave prodigious fêtes. *a* **1839** PRAED *Poems* (1864) I. 212 Titled dames gave fêtes upon the water. **1849** THACKERAY *Pendennis* i, The guests at my Lord So-and-so's fête.

b. A bazaar-like function designed to raise money for some charitable purpose.

1893 YONGE & COLERIDGE *Strolling Players* v. 37 We can act at Primrose *fêtes*, and do good in that way. **1894** W. PATER *Let.* 19 June (1970) 268 Sincere congratulations on the success of the Fête. **1962** H. THURSTON *Where is thy Sting?* iii. 32 The delivery of some jumble for the church fête.

2. The festival of the saint after whom a person is named; in Roman Catholic countries observed as the birthday is in England.

1805 C. WILMOT *Let.* 7 Dec. in *Russ. Jrnls.* (1934) II. 207 The Princess & I being Names sakes she was resolved this Fête should be double celebrated, & therefore the eve of the day a solemn Mass was held. **1840** THACKERAY *Paris Sk.-bk.* (1869) 143 It is the fête of little Jacob yonder, whose brothers and sisters have all come from their schools to dance at his birthday. **1877** [see 3].

3. *attrib.*, as *fête-day*; also **fête-contractor**, one who contracts to provide a fête or entertainment.

1817 J. SCOTT *Paris Revisit.* (ed. 4) 270 The towns of France have all their particular fête days. **1877** J. T. FIELDS *Underbrush* (1881) 224 A Councillor of the Parliament, sent her on her fête-day, a bouquet. **1885** MABEL COLLINS *Prettiest Woman* viii, Life was like one long fête day. **1886** *York Herald* 7 Aug. 2/5 Public caterer, decorator, and fete contractor.

Hence ˈ**fêteless** *a.*, having no fête.

1861 CUNNINGHAM *Wheat & Tares* 50 The poor fêteless children haunted him.

fête (feɪt), *v.* [ad. F. *fêter*, f. *fête*: see prec.] *trans.* To entertain (a person) at a fête; to feast; also, to give a fête in honour of, commemorate (some event, etc.) by a fête.

1819 *Edin. Rev.* XXXII. 221 He was in general too fond of flattering and 'feteing' his master. *a* **1845** BARHAM *Ingol. Leg., Hermann*, The murder thus out, Hermann's fêted and thanked. **1849** THACKERAY *Pendennis* lxvi, The..two footmen..intoxicated the page at a wine-shop, to fête Laura's recovery. **1879** HUXLEY *Hume* 36 Great nobles fêted

him. **1892** *Nation* (N.Y.) 29 Sept. 239/2 The Government.. judging..that the anniversary of the invasion of the Tuileries by the people..ought not to be fêted.

Hence ˈ**fêted** *ppl. a.*

1828 Disraeli *Voy. Capt. Popanilla* xiii. 158 A habit quite refreshing to fêted characters. **1852** Mrs. Smythies *Bride Elect* xxxiii, Fair and fêted guest as she was!

fete, obs. form of feat.

‖**fête-champêtre.** [Fr.; f. *fête* (see fête *sb.*) + *champêtre* rural:—L. *campestrem*, f. *campus* a field.] An outdoor entertainment, a rural festival.

1774 H. Walpole *Lett. H. Mann* (1857) VI. 88 He gives her a most splendid entertainment..and calls it a fête champêtre. **1800** Mar. Edgeworth *Belinda* xi, He began to talk of the last fête champêtre at Frogmore. **1884** S. Dowell *Taxes in Eng.* III. 281 The battue system developed into the sort of fête champêtre, with hot lunch, champagne, and liveried attendants.

feteesh, obs. form of fetish.

‖**fête galante.** [Fr.; f. *fête* (see fête *sb.*) + *galante*, fem. of *galant* gay, elegant.] A fête-champêtre, esp. of the type depicted by Watteau.

[**1869** P. Verlaine (*title*) Fêtes galantes.] **1912** W. Deeping *Sincerity* xxxvi. 268 Those stretches of grass.. dreamed of for *fêtes galantes.* **1925** *Oxf. Poetry* 7 The Watteau *fêtes galantes.* **1955** *Times* 16 July 8/4 The older masters in this collection included a pair of charming *fête galante* subjects, *The Swing* and *The Dance*, by Jean-Baptiste Pater.

fetel(es, var. fetles, ME., vessel.

fetessor, obs. form of fetisher.

fetfa, var. of fetwa.

fether(e, obs. form of feather.

†ˈ**fetherfooted.** *Obs. rare*$^{-1}$. [f. OE. **fiðer*- comb. form of *féower*, four. Cf. OE. *fiðerfót*, *-féte* in same sense.] Fourfooted.

c **1175** *Lamb. Hom.* 43 Innan þan ilke sea weren unaneomned deor summe feðer fotetd, summe al bute fet.

†ˈ**fethok.** *Sc. Obs. rare*$^{-1}$. [A variant form of fitchew.] A polecat.

1424 *Sc. Acts Jas. I* (1814) II. 6 And for x fulmartis skynnis, called fethokis, viij*d.*

†ˈ**fethre**, *v. Obs.* In 3 *south.* **veð(ð)re.** [repr. OE. **féðran*, f. *fóðer* a load: see fother.] *trans.* To load.

a **1225** *Ancr. R.* 140 Louerd..þu hauest imaked uoðer to heui uorte ueðren mide þe soule. *Ibid.* 204 Uor hit is iueððred þet is, icharged.

fetial, fecial (ˈfiːʃəl), *a.* and *sb.* [ad. L. *fetiālis* (erroneously *fec-*): of unknown origin.]

A. *adj.* Of or pertaining to the *fetiales* (see B.); hence, heraldic, ambassadorial. *fetial law*: the Roman law relating to declarations of war and treaties of peace.

1553 Grimalde *Cicero's Offices* I. (1558) 16 The feciall lawe of the people of Rome. **1684** tr. *Agrippa's Van. Arts* lxxxi. 279 Every Servile and Mechanick-fellow, fecial Messengers, and Caduceators. **1826** Kent *Comm.* 6 The fecial law relating to declarations of war. **1839** W. O. Manning *Law Nations* IV. vi. (1875) 196 The Romans, whose fecial college, etc. **1866** *Cornh. Mag.* Nov. 631 The members of the Fetial profession.

B. *sb.* One of the *fetiales*, a Roman college of priests, who fulfilled the function of heralds, and performed the rites connected with the declaration of war and the conclusion of peace.

1533 Bellenden *Livy* I. (1822) 41 'Deliver to me,' said the Feciall, 'the herbe.' **1602** Segar *Hon. Mil. & Civ.* I. iii. 4 It was not lawfull for..any Souldier to take Armes, untill the Fæcials had so commanded or allowed. **1835** Thirlwall *Greece* I. 173 It does not appear that they were employed, like the Italian Fetials, to make formal declarations of war. **1875** Merivale *Gen. Hist. Rome* xiii. (1877) 76 Striking the fecial a blow.

feticide: see fœ-.

fetid, fœtid (ˈfɛtɪd, ˈfiːtɪd), *a.* and *sb.* Forms: 6 foetide, (7 fetode, 8 fætid), 7- fetid, fœtid. [ad. L. *fētid-us* (often incorrectly written *fœtidus*), f. *fētēre* to have an offensive smell.]

A. *adj.* Having an offensive smell; stinking.

1599 A. M. tr. *Gabelhouer's Bk. Physicke* 159/2 It maketh to blister both handes, & feet, out of which issueth foetide, and stinckinge water. **1661** Lovell *Hist. Anim. & Min.* 157 Heron, the flesh is better..though some count it fœtid. **1732** Arbuthnot *Rules of Diet* 362 Animal Humours, by Heat, stink and grow foetid. **1775** Adair *Amer. Ind.* 209 A kind of wild sheep..which are of so faetid a smell. **1851** Mayne Reid *Scalp Hunt.* v. 41 They [buzzard vultures] tore out the eyes of the quarry with their fetid beaks. **1879** Green *Read. Eng. Hist.* xxi. 107 Sent up their fetid odours, rank with fever.

fig. **1805** Foster *Ess.* I. vii. 109 The foetid heroes of the Dunciad. **1810** Bentham *Packing* (1821) 205 Any such fœtid mass of dead letter, as the labyrinth composed of the books of practice. **1874** Stubbs *Const. Hist.* (1875) III. xviii. 77 The fetid atmosphere of a court.

b. *fetid gum* (see quot.); *fetid pill*, a pill containing Asafœtida.

1789 W. Buchan *Dom. Med.* (1790) 299 The patient may ..take..fœtid pills every six hours. **1858** Carpenter *Veg. Phys.* §593 Fœtid gums are of the nature of Gum-resins.. and are distinguished by their powerfully disagreeable odour. Those most in use are Assafœtida and Galbanum.

†**B.** *sb. pl.* Fetid drugs. *Obs.*

1707 Floyer *Physic. Pulse-Watch* 333 Drawer of Fætids. **1710** T. Fuller *Pharm. Extemp.* 394, I know that Fætids will repress Vapours in Women. **1748** Hartley *Observ. Man.* I. ii. 183 The Smell of those Fetids which revive.

Hence **feˈtidity** [+ -ity], the quality or state of being fetid; a fetid nature or condition; foulness, ill savour, offensiveness. ˈ**fetidly** *adv.*, in a fetid condition or manner; offensively. ˈ**fetidness** = fetidity. Also *concr.* something fetid.

1704 R. Brown tr. *Plutarch's Morals* III. 465 Salts with the Sea-water..colliquating whatever is foreign and superfluous, suffer no fetidness or putrefaction to breed. **1831** J. Davies *Manual Mat. Med.* 283 Of a penetrating smell, and remarkable for its fetidity. **1860** Pusey *Min. Proph.* 124 What an image..of the fetidness of sin. **1869** *Daily News* 5 Jan., Often foully dirty and so fœtidly uncomfortable..the Marylebone cells call strongly for reformation.

†**fetida.** *Obs. rare.* [short for asafœtida.]

1599 Hakluyt *Voy.* II. I. 218 There goeth out of Chaul.. great store of Fetida. **1736** Bailey *Housh. Dict.* 250 Let the person..take cocea pills or foetida.

fetiferous: see fœ-.

fetir, obs. form of feature.

fetis(e, var. of featous *a. Obs.*

fetish (ˈfɛtɪʃ, ˈfiːtɪʃ), *sb.* Forms: 7-8 fetisso, (8 feitisso), (7 fateish, 9 feteesh, -tisch, -tishe, -tiss), 8- fetich(e, fetish. [a. F. *fétiche*, ad. Pg. *feitiço* sb. charm, sorcery (from which the earliest Eng. forms are directly adopted) = Sp. *hechizo* in same sense; a subst. use of *feitiço* adj. 'made by art, artificial, skilfully contrived' = Sp. *hechizo*, It. *fattizio*, OF. *faitis* (see featous):—L. *facticius* factitious.]

1. a. Originally, any of the objects used by the Negroes of the Guinea coast and the neighbouring regions as amulets or means of enchantment, or regarded by them with superstitious dread. **b.** By writers on anthropology (following C. de Brosses, *Le Culte des Dieux Fétiches*, 1760) used in wider sense: An inanimate object worshipped by savages on account of its supposed inherent magical powers, or as being animated by a spirit.

A *fetish* (in sense 1 b) differs from an *idol* in that it is worshipped in its own character, not as the image, symbol, or occasional residence of a deity.

1613 Purchas *Pilgrimage* VI. xv. (1614) 651 Hereon were set many strawen Rings called *Fatissos* or *Gods.* **1696** Ovington *Voy. Suratt* 67 They [these Africans] travel nowhere without their Fateish about them. **1723** J. Atkins *Voy. Guinea* (1735) 102 There is also at Cabo Corso, a publick Fetish, the Guardian of them all; and that is the Rock Tabra. **1746** J. Barbot *Descr. Guinea* 230 The..gold is..cast into sundry shapes and sizes, which some there call Fetissos, signifying in Portuguese charms. **1761** *Brit. Mag.* II. 294 The chief fetiche is the snake. **1803** T. Winterbottom *Sierra Leone* I. vii. 123 The gree-gree, or fetish, hung round their neck. *Ibid.* I. xiv. 228 Idols. These are called Fe-teesh. **1809-10** Coleridge *Friend* (1837) III. 84 As well might the poor African prepare for himself a fetisch by plucking out the eyes of the eagle. **1851-9** Prichard in *Man. Sci. Enq.* 265 Others..worship fetiches or visible objects in which they suppose some magical or supernatural power to be concealed. **1865** Livingstone *Zambesi* xxv. 523 A greegree or fetish is thrown away as useless when the consecrating nostrum is discovered to be inoperative. **1879** *Encycl. Brit.* IX. 118 If the wishes of the worshipper be not granted..the fetich..is kicked, stamped on, dragged through the mud.

c. *fig.* Something irrationally reverenced.

1837 Emerson *Addr. Amer. Schol.* Wks. (Bohn) II. 183 Some fetish of a government..is cried up by half mankind. **1867** Goldw. Smith *Three Eng. Statesmen* (1882) 192 He was a worshipper of Constitutional Monarchy. It was his fetish. **1870** Lowell *Among my Bks.* Ser. I. (1873) 140 Public opinion, the fetish even of the nineteenth century.

d. *Psychol.* An object, a non-sexual part of the body, or a particular action which abnormally serves as the stimulus to, or the end in itself of, sexual desire.

1901 E. Morselli in Baldwin *Dict. Philos.* I. 380/2 In certain perversions of the sexual instinct, the person, part of the body, or particular object belonging to the person by whom the impulse is excited, is called the fetich of the patient. **1954** Dorcus & Shaffer *Textbk. Abnormal Psychol.* (ed. 4) vii. 262 It is only when the fetish assumes the proportion that it inhibits the usual processes of the amatory desire that it belongs in the latter [abnormal] category. **1963** A. Heron *Towards Quaker View of Sex* 71 *Fetish*, some object to which special sexual significance is attached.

†**2.** In representations of Negro language: Incantation, worship; a magical or religious rite or observance; an oath. *Obs.*

1705 Bosman *Guinea* x. (1721) 123 They cry out, Let us make Fetiche; by which they express as much, as let us perform our Religious Worship. *Ibid.*, If they are injured by another, they make Fetiche to destroy him. **1727** W. Snelgrave *Acc. Guinea* (1734) 22 The Lord of the Place had taken his Fetiche or Oath. *Ibid.* 59 They have all their particular Fetiches..Some are to eat no Sheep, others no Goats. **1802** Mar. Edgeworth *Grateful Negro* (1832) 245 *note*, An old Koromantyn negro..administered the fetish, or solemn oath. **1828** G. W. Bridges *Ann. Jamaica* II. xix. 404 To take a fetiche is to take an oath, and to make a fetiche is to render worship.

†**3.** (See quot.) *Obs.*

1705 Bosman *Guinea* vi. (1721) 65 Gold..mixed with Fetiche's, which are a sort of artificial Gold composed of several Ingredients.

4. *attrib.* and *Comb.* **a.** simple attrib., as *fetish-bird*, *-ceremony*, *-day*, *-gold*, *-house*, *object*, *-priest*, *-word*, *-worship.* **b.** objective, as *fetish-monger*, *-worshipper*, *-worshipping*; also **fetish-man, -woman**, (*a*) one who claims to have communion with and power over fetishes, a fetish-priest; (*b*) a fetish-worshipper.

1924 R. M. Ogden tr. *Koffka's Growth of Mind* vi. 347 If a white man shoots an invulnerable *fetish-bird, this does not destroy the bird's invulnerability in their eyes. **1613** Purchas *Pilgrimage* VI. xv. (1614) 649 Causing her to eat salt with divers *Fetisso ceremonies hereafter mentioned. **1819** Bowdich *Miss. to Ashantee* II. iv. 266 In Ashantee there is not a common *fetish day. **1723** J. Atkins *Voy. Guinea* (1735) 183 The *Fetish-Gold is that which the Negroes cast into various Shapes and wear as Ornaments. **1819** Bowdich *Miss. to Ashantee* II. iii. 254 The gold..deposited with their bones in the *fetish house..is sacred. **1723** J. Atkins *Voy. Guinea* (1735) 101 The Cunning of the *Fetish-Man (or Priest). **1836** Marryat *Midsh. Easy* 9 He..went away in wrath to the fetishman, and..asked for a fetish against his rival. **1889** *Dublin Rev.* Jan. 134 A rude tribe of fetishmen and idol-worshippers. **1888** *Scott. Leader* 9 Oct. 4 The innate separatism of the Unionist *fetishmonger stands confessed. **1914** W. McDougall *Introd. Soc. Psychol.* Suppl. ii. 407 If woman were by nature nothing more for man than an object capable of stimulating his 'erogenous zones'..she would be merely the chief of many '*fetish objects'. **1958** *Spectator* 1 Aug. 168/3 His favourite teddy or toy or whatever is his 'fetish object' should, of course, go with him. **1877** tr. *Tiele's Hist. Relig.* 10 The power possessed by the..*fetish priests is by no means small. **1723** J. Atkins *Voy. Guinea* (1735) 104 At Accra they have *Fetish-Women..who pretend Divination. **1870** Lubbock *Orig. Civiliz.* i. (1875) 22 The Fetish women in Dahomey. *a* **1930** D. H. Lawrence *Phoenix* (1936) 396 To most of us today it [*sc.* 'God'] is a *fetish-word. **1807** W. Taylor in *Monthly Mag.* XXIII. 539 The Veneration for the Lares was originally a *Fetiche-worship. **1860** Tristram *Gt. Sahara* i. 16 Traces of fetish worship in Algiers. **1857** *Sat. Rev.* III. 345/2 Miserable *fetish-worshippers. **1860** W. G. Clark *Vac. Tour* 54 One must go among *fetish-worshipping savages.

Hence ˈ**fetishized** *a.*

1889 P. T. Forsyth *Religion in Recent Art* 184 The Christian faith, not parched..or fetishised, but pervaded.. with the solemn human soul. **1962** *Listener* 22 Mar. 512/2 Lukács's description of existentialism as a 'permanent carnival of fetishized inwardness' touched a raw nerve.

†ˈ**fetish**, *v. Obs.* [f. prec.] **a.** *trans.* To provide or adorn with a fetish: see fetish *sb.* 1. **b.** *intr.* for *refl.* To adorn oneself, dress up.

1723 J. Atkins *Voy. Guinea* (1735) 61 The Women are fondest of what they call Fetishing, setting themselves out to attract the good Graces of the Men. *Ibid.* 73 The Natives are ..better fetished than their Neighbours. *Ibid.* 88 The Women fetish with a coarse Paint of Earth on their Faces. *Ibid.* 95 She..being always barefoot and fetished with Chains and Gobbets of Gold, at her Ancles.

fetisheer, fetisher (fɛtɪˈʃɪə(r), ˈfɛtɪʃə(r)). Forms: 7 fetissero, (7 fetessor, 9 fetisser), 8 feticheer, -er, (9 fetisheer), 7- fetisher. [ad. Pg. *feiticeiro*, f. *feitiço*: see fetish *sb.*; influenced in the later forms by Fr. *fétiche* or Eng. *fetish.*]

1. A charmer, sorcerer, 'medicine-man'; a priest.

1613 Purchas *Pilgrimage* VI. xv. (1614) 653 A certaine water offered them to drinke by the Fetissero. **1687** J. Hillier in *Phil. Trans.* (1697) XIX. 687 The Fetishers had done all they could to save his [the King of Feton's] Life. **1783** W. F. Martyn *Geog. Mag.* I. 676 Each feticheer or priest, has a fetiche of his own. **1844** Ld. Brougham *A. Lunel* II. ix. 237 The Fetisser or priest now muttered over the board certain incantations. **1864** *Sat. Rev.* XVIII. 458/1 The priests or fetisheers are all-powerful in Dahome.

2. = fetish *sb.* 1.

1665 Sir T. Herbert *Trav.* (1677) 9 Mokisses, fetessors, deformed Idols being indeared amongst them. **1699** Dampier *Voy.* II. II. iv. 105 The Natives call him..and say he [Hippopotamus] is Fetissero, which is a kind of God.

Hence **fetiˈsheeress**, a female fetisheer.

1864 R. F. Burton *Dahome* II. 155 A quarter of the female population in Dahome may be fetisheeresses.

fetishic (ˈfɛtɪʃɪk), *a.* [f. fetish *sb.* + -ic.] Characterized by adoration of a fetish.

1883 *Academy* No. 562. 100 Snake-worship was..one of the commonest forms of fetishic religion.

fetishism (ˈfɛtɪʃɪz(ə)m). Also **fetichism.** [f. fetish + -ism. Cf. Fr. *fétichisme.*]

1. a. The worship of fetishes; an instance of this; the superstition of which this is the characteristic feature.

1801 W. Taylor in *Monthly Mag.* II. 646 He detects everywhere fetishism or the worship of tools. **1846** Grote *Greece* I. xvi. I. 462 An original fetichism in which particular objects had themselves been supposed to be endued with life. **1853** Kingsley *Hypatia* xxx. 382 Dabbling in magic, astrology, and barbarian fetichisms.

b. *Econ.* (See *commodity fetishism.*)

2. *Psychol.* A perversion of the sexual instinct, often resulting from earlier repression, whereby sexual desire is stimulated by, or has as its goal,

some kind of inanimate object (often shoes, rubber, or underclothes), or a particular non-sexual part of the body (feet, hair, etc.), or the performance of certain non-sexual actions.
1897 H. ELLIS *Stud. Psychol. Sex* I. vi. 129 The view that sexual inversion is..explained by..early association.. seems to be supported by what we know of erotic fetishism, by which a woman's hair, or foot, or even clothing, becomes the focus of a man's sexual aspirations. **1954** DORCUS & SHAFFER *Textbk. Abnormal Psychol.* (ed. 4) vii. 262 Fetishism is considered by some theorists to be a defense against fear of being rejected by a member of the opposite sex, hence the substitution of an object that cannot reject or a part of the body against which there is no prohibition. **1963** A. HERON *Towards Quaker View of Sex* 66 Fetishism involves the focussing of sexual attention upon an object or upon one part of the loved-one, instead of upon the whole person.

fetishist ('fɛtɪʃɪst). Also fetichist. [f. as prec. + -IST. Cf. Fr. *fétichiste*.]
1. One who worships a fetish.
1845 O. BROWNSON *Wks.* VI. 384 As well might we charge the people of Massachusetts with being fetichists. **1865** MILL in *Westm. Rev.* XXVIII. 35 The Fetishist thinks.. that his Fetish is alive. **1870** LUBBOCK *Orig. Civiliz.* i. 4 These races were Fetichists before they became Buddist. **1897** H. ELLIS *Stud. Psychol. Sex* I. vi. 130 There is reason to believe that the erotic fetichist usually displays the further congenital element of hereditary neurosis. **1906** *Ibid.* V. ii. 15 Casanova, an acute student and lover of women who was in no degree a foot fetichist, remarks that all men who share his interest in women are attracted by their feet. **1954** I. MURDOCH *Under Net* xv. 219, I am not a fetishist and I would rather hold a woman any day than her shoes. **1956** [see AVERSION 7]. **1965** G. MELLY *Owning-Up* vi. 69 A large collie dog called Shaun..was a coat fetishist, and could often be surprised rogering the mackintoshes in the hall. **1968** B. SPACKS *Sophomore* 19 'Oh', he said, 'the *brassiere*! I'm just'—he laughed dryly—'a clothes fetishist, that's all.'
2. quasi-*adj.* = FETISHISTIC.
1859 R. F. BURTON *Centr. Afr.* in *Jrnl. Geog. Soc.* XXIX. 339 The faith of ancient Egypt..was essentially fetissist. **1861** GOLDW. SMITH *Lect. Doctr. Progress* 6 The negro and fetichist populations of Africa.

fetishistic (fɛtɪ'ʃɪstɪk), *a.* Also fetichistic. [f. prec. + -IC.] Of, pertaining to, characterized by, or resembling fetishism.
1867 LEWES *Hist. Philos.* I. p. xlii, Suppose one of the travellers to be..still in the fetichistic stage. **1868** FISKE in *Fortn. Rev.* IV. 295 It is the primitive fetichistic habit of thought. **1877** E. R. CONDER *Bas. Faith* i. 5 Some germs of fetishistic religion.
Hence **feti'shistically**, *adv.*, in a fetishistic manner or spirit.
1951 C. BERG *Unconscious Significance of Hair* vii. 61 This matter of the genital organ and its concealment by drawers or figleaf—or fetishistically by hair.

fetishry ('fɛtɪʃrɪ). [f. FETISH *sb.* + -RY.] *collect.* Objects regarded as fetishes; an example or specimen of these.
1885 D. C. MURRAY *Rainbow Gold* I. II. vi. 76 The black man passes the bit of rag or broken stick or other fetishry.

fetisly, -liche, var. ff. of FEATOUSLY.

†**fetissan**, *a. Obs. rare*⁻¹. [f. *fetiss*, FETISH + -AN.] Of the nature of a fetish; fetish-like.
1613 PURCHAS *Pilgrimage* VI. xv. (1614) 652 If this Fetissan portion did not pacifie their angrie moode, by daily presents of meat and drinke.

fetisso, fetissero, obs. ff. FETISH, FETISHER.

†'**fetles.** *Obs.* Forms: α. 1 fætels, fétels, *Orm.* fetless, *south.* vetles, 3 fet(e)les. β. *north. dial.* 3–4 fetel, -il. [OE. *fætels* str. masc., perh. related by ablaut to *fæt*, FAT *sb.*, VAT. In northern ME. the final *s* disappeared, as in mod. *burial* from *buriels*.] A vessel or receptacle; a bag, cask, sack. In religious lang. used *fig.* = 'vessel'.
α. *c* **893** K. ÆLFRED *Oros.* I. i. §21 Twegen fætels full ealaþ oððe wæteres. *c* **1000** *Sax. Leechd.* III. 16 Do..on swylc fætels swylc ðu wille. *c* **1200** ORMIN 14450 þe firrste fetless wass Brerdfull off waterr filledd. *a* **1225** *Ancr. R.* 164 þis bruchele uetles, þet is wummone vleschs. *a* **1225** *Juliana* 18 Ower mix mawmex þat beoð þes feondes fetles. *c* **1250** *Gen. & Ex.* 561 Ðat arche was a feteles good. *c* **1300** *St. Margarete* 207 He..in a strong vetles ous broȝte: & in a put ous caste.
β. *a* **1300** *Cursor M.* 20932 (Cott.) Of chesing fetil wroght he was. *c* **1325** *Metr. Hom.* 140 Len me sum fetel tharto, Quarin I mai thin almous do. *c* **1340** *Cursor M.* 21623 (Edin.) A fetil that it war noȝte tinte [was] set vndir that licur for to hinte.

fetlock ('fɛtlɒk), *sb.* Forms: 4 feetlakk, 4–5 fet(e)lak, 5 fytlo(c)k, (7 fitlock), 6, 8, 9 foot(e)lock, (6 fotelocke), 6 fete-, 7 feetlock, 6– fetlock. [ME. *fetlak, fytlok*, corresponding to MHG. *fiȥlach, visȥlach* (mod.Ger. *fiszloch*); the formation is obscure; connexion with Ger. *fessel* pastern has been suggested. The word was early interpreted as f. FOOT *sb.* + LOCK (of hair), and this notion has influenced the spelling of some of the forms. Sense 2 is due to confusion with FETTERLOCK.]
1. That part of a horse's leg where the tuft of hair grows behind the pastern-joint; the tuft itself.
c **1325** *Coer de L.* 5816 Up to the feetlakkes in blood. *c* **1330** *Arth. & Merl.* (Kölbing) 5892 To þe fitlokes in þe blod. *a* **1400–50** *Alexander* 2049 þat foles ferd in þe flosches to þe fetelakis. **1470–85** MALORY *Arthur* I. xvii, Her horses went in blood up to the fytlokys. **1592** SHAKS. *Ven. & Ad.* 295 Fetlocks shag, and long. **1596** BP. W. BARLOW *Three Serm.* i. 21 Falling to the ground they laie so thick, that they couered the horse footelockes. **1621** G. SANDYS *Ovid's Met.* IV. (1626) 82 Where Titan's panting steeds..bathe their fierie feet-locks in the Deepe. **1697** DRYDEN *Æneid* v. 739 White were the fetlocks of his feet. **1796** MORSE *Amer. Geog.* I. 397 This wilderness, where the horse sinks to his fetlocks at every step. **1837** W. IRVING *Capt. Bonneville* I. 47 The horses were often to the fetlock. **1880** BROWNING *Dram. Idylls, Muléykeh* 36 Her fetlock is foam-splashed too.
b. *transf.* of a human being.
1645 Z. BOYD *Holy Songs* in *Zion's Flowers* (1855) App. 12/2 These..dance and leap..With nimble fet-locks.
2. An apparatus fixed on the leg of a horse to prevent running away; = FETTERLOCK.
1695 MOTTEUX *St. Olon's Morocco* 171 Each Horse..is only fasten'd to a Stake and Fetlocks. **1828–40** BERRY *Encycl. Herald.* I, *Fetterlock* or *Fetlock*, a horse fetlock. **1856** [see 3]. **1889** in ELVIN *Dict. Heraldry*.
3. *attrib.* and *Comb.*, as *fetlock-chain, -hair, -joint*; **fetlock-boot** (see quot.); **fetlock-deep** *a.* (*adv.*), so as to cover the fetlocks.
1874 KNIGHT *Dict. Mech.*, *Fetlock-boot..a protection for the fetlock and pastern of a horse. **1856** WHITTIER *Old Burying Ground* 19 The farm-horse drags his *fetlock chain. **1599** SHAKS. *Hen. V*, IV. vii. 82 Wounded steeds Fret *fetlocke deepe in gore. **1865** KINGSLEY *Herew.* vi, He reined up his horse, fetlock deep in water. *c* **1720** GIBSON *Farrier's Guide* I. vi. (1738) 94 Whereon the *Footlock hair does grow. **1725** BRADLEY *Fam. Dict.* II. s.v. *Parts Horse's Body*, The Pastern or *Footlock Joint. **1843** YOUATT *Horse* xvi. 349 A serious affection of the fetlock-joint.

fetlocked ('fɛtlɒkt), *a.* [f. FETLOCK *sb.* + -ED².]
a. Having a fetlock. **b.** Hobbled or fastened by the fetlock; hence, hampered, shackled.
1725 PATTISON in *Prior's Poems* (1733) III. xli, The Careless Husband and the Peevish wife; The Troubles of the Fetlock'd-Couple shew. **1870** LOWELL *Among my Bks.* Ser. I. (1873) 157 A language..not yet fetlocked by dictionary and grammar mongers.

fetor, fœtor ('fi:tɔ:(r)). Forms: (5 fetoure), 7–9 fætor, 6– fetor, fœtor. [a. L. *fētor* (incorrectly *fœtor*), f. *fētēre*: see FETID.] An offensive smell; a stench.
c **1450** *Mirour Saluacioun* 416 Filles a man at eende with rotynnesse and fetoure. **1535** STEWART *Cron. Scot.* II. 313 His dolour did incres, With foull fetor that wes intollerabill. **1646** SIR T. BROWNE *Pseud. Ep.* IV. x. 201 The Fætor whereof may discover it self by sweat and urine. **1759** *Phil. Trans.* LI. 275 The fetor of these waters is not owing to mere stagnation. **1851** H. D. WOLFF *Pictures Spanish Life* (1853) 179 The fœtor of coke and oil will drown the perfume of the lily and the rose. **1856** KANE *Arct. Expl.* I. xix. 235 This flesh..of the female seal..has not the fetor of her mate's.

‖**fetta** ('fɛtə). Also feta. [mod. Gr. *φέτα*.] A white, salty, ewe's-milk cheese made in Greece.
1956 A. SIMON *Cheeses of World* 139 *Feta*..is usually made from ewe's milk but occasionally from goat's milk. **1963** *Spectator* 12 July 65 There was another cheese too, that strange white one which comes in soft slabs from all countries of the Eastern Mediterranean; it is called *fetta*. **1970** *Times* 29 Apr. 18/4 Most refreshing is the salad to which fetta, the sharp white sheep's cheese (made as in Greece) is added. **1971** *Sunday Times* (Colour Suppl.) 28 Mar. 39/4 Fetta eaten with bread and olives is a favourite Greek snack and some Greeks like to start the day with Fetta, bread and jam.

‖**fettbol, -bole** ('fɛtbəʊl). *Min.* [Ger. *fettbol* (Freiesleben 1831), f. *fett* FAT *sb.*¹ + *bol* BOLE.] A variety of CHLOROPAL.
1835 C. U. SHEPARD *Min.* II. 207 Fettbole. Massive; composition impalpable. **1868** DANA *Min.* 461 *Fettbol* has a liver-brown color, a slightly greasy lustre.

fett(e), obs. form of FAT, FEAT.

fetter ('fɛtə(r)), *sb.* Forms: 1 feotor, feter, fetor, 3–7 feter, 4 fet(t)re, *south.* vetre, (5 feder, fettir, -our, -yr, fetur, -yr, 6 fetrer, fettar), 6– fetter. [OE. *feter* fem., cogn. with OS. *feteros* pl. m. (Du. *veter* m. lace), OHG. *feȥȥera*, MHG. *veȥȥer* (early mod.Ger. *fesser*) fem., ON. *fioturr* m. (Sw. *fjättrar* pl.):—OTeut. **feterâ, -ro-z*, f. *fet-* (:—OAryan *ped-*) ablaut-form of *fôt* FOOT. Cf. L. *pedica*, Gr. *πέδη* of identical meaning and root.]
1. A chain or shackle for the feet of a human being or animal; hence *gen.* a bond, shackle. (rare in *sing.*)
c **800** *Corpus Gl.*, *Pedo, vel paturum*, feotor. *c* **950** *Lindisf. Gosp.* Mark v. 4 Forðon oftust mið feotrum..gebunden wæs. *c* **1000** *Ags. Ps.* lxxviii. 11 On feterum fæste. *c* **1290** *S. Eng. Leg.* I. 107/20 Ake euere he hadde ane peire feteres. **13..** *E.E. Allit. P.* B. 1255 Festned fettres to her fete under fole wombes. *c* **1380** *Sir Ferumb.* 1313 Of al hure chaynes he haþ him raft; & ek hure vetres oundo. *c* **1430** *Syr Gener.* (Roxb.) 2741 A pare of fetures on him fest. *c* **1489** CAXTON *Sonnes of Aymon* xvi. 370 His feters that were on his fete. *a* **1541** WYATT in *Tottell's Misc.* (Arb.) 82 Clinkyng of fetrers would such Musick craue. **1652** ASHMOLE *Theat. Chem.* 216 Ryngyng of Feteris maketh no mere sown. **1794** BURKE *Sp. W. Hastings*, They..loaded their limbs with fetters. **1876** HUMPHREYS *Coin Coll. Man.* ix. 107 Antony presented Artavasdes..to Cleopatra in golden fetters.
b. *pl.* = Captivity.
1704 ADDISON *Poems, Campaign*, Those who 'scape the fetters and the sword. *a* **1839** PRAED *Poems* (1864) I. 210, I ..thought that freedom was as sweet as fetters.
2. *transf.* and *fig.* Anything that confines, impedes, or restrains; a check, restraint.
c **1000** *Wanderer* 21 (Gr.) Ic modsefan minne sceolde.. feterum sælan. **1560** ROLLAND *Crt. Venus* I. 866 Deliuering it..To the beirar agane..But falt or fetter. **1602** SHAKS. *Ham.* III. iii. 25 We will Fetters put vpon this feare. **1676** DRYDEN *Aurengz.* Prol. 9 Passion's too fierce to be in Fetters bound. **1781** COWPER *Hope* 449 The sacred book..Bound in the fetters of an unknown tongue. **1818** CRUISE *Digest* (ed. 2) IV. 530 The Court of Chancery will not loose the fetters he has put upon himself. **1851** ROBERTSON *Serm.* I. xviii. (1866) 305 He who puts fetters on the mind. **1871** FREEMAN *Norm. Conq.* (1876) IV. xvii. 66 Fortresses, which became in truth the fetters of England.

fetter ('fɛtə(r)), *v.*¹ Forms: 4–6 feter(e, fet(t)re, (5 fedre, -dyr, fether, fet(t)yr, fetur), 6– fetter. [f. prec. sb.; cf. OFris. *fitera*, OHG. (*ka-*) *feȥarôn*, ON. *fiotra*.]
1. *trans.* To bind with or as with fetters; to chain, fasten, shackle.
c **1300** *Havelok* 2758 He..dide him binde and fetere wel With gode feteres al of stel. *c* **1386** CHAUCER *Knt.'s T.* 371 Elles had I dweld..I-fetered in his prisoun for evere moo. *c* **1420** *Chron. Vilod.* 942 He hadde y ffedryde to gedur his leygus two. *c* **1489** CAXTON *Sonnes of Aymon* xvi. 369 He made to be broughte a grete payre of yrens, and fetred hym wyth theym. **1535** STEWART *Cron.*, The king..in presoun strang, Fetrit richt fast. **1647** WARD *Simp. Cobler* 54 Is *Majestas Imperii* growne so kickish, that it cannot stand quiet..unlesse it be fettered? **1791** MRS. RADCLIFFE *Rom. Forest* xii, See that he is strongly fettered. **1835** W. IRVING *Tour Prairies* 276, I now fettered my horse to prevent his straying. **1847** GROTE *Greece* (1862) III. xxxi. 145 The actual chains in which the prisoners had been fettered.
b. *transf.* and *fig.* To impose restraint upon; to confine, impede, restrain. Also with *down*.
1526 *Pilgr. Perf.* (W. de W. 1531) 172 Synne, in the whiche we be wrapped and fettered. *a* **1586** SIDNEY *Arcad.* II. xxii. 200 Nether her woorthinesse..nor his owne suffering for her..could fetter his ficklenes. **1633** P. FLETCHER *Poet. Misc.* 79 Fond man, that thinks such fire and aire to fetter. **1681** TEMPLE *Mem.* III. Wks. 1731 I. 359, I never could..endure to be fetter'd in Business. **1711** STEELE *Spect.* No. 20 ¶4 The generality of the World are fettered by Rules. **1756** C. LUCAS *Ess. Waters* II. 142 All the other mills ..have their wheels fettered with icy chains. **1788** PRIESTLEY *Lect. Hist.* v. lxv. 521 The best faculties..may be sunk and fettered by superstition. **1837** J. H. NEWMAN *Par. Serm.* (ed. 2) III. xxv. 420 Can any..human doctrine fetter down our hearts? **1844** STANLEY *Arnold* (1858) I. v. 207 The surest way to fetter our own progress.
†**2.** To bind (a wheel) with a tire. *Obs.*
1523 FITZHERB. *Husb.* §5 The wheles..muste be well fettred with wood or yren.

†'**fetter**, *v.*² *Obs.*⁻¹ [? f. **fetter*, corruption of FAITOUR.] *trans.* See quot.
1587 MASCALL *Govt. Cattle* (1653) 25 Also there be many men that fetter them, which is, to cut the dew-lap before on the brisket.

fetter, obs. form of FEATURE.

fettered ('fɛtəd), *ppl. a.* [f. FETTER *v.* + -ED¹.]
1. Bound with fetters or chains.
a **1325** *Prose Psalter* ci[i]. 21 He herd þe waie-mentynges of þe fettered. **1556** J. HEYWOOD *Spider & F.* ii. B j b, The fettred flie. **1602** MARSTON *Antonio's Rev.* III. ii. Wks. 1856 I. 107 May I be fetter'd slave to coward Chaunce. **1696** *Lond. Gaz.* No. 3214/4 Two black Geldings, the one..side fettered. **1814** BYRON *Corsair* III. ix, He, fast as fetter'd limbs allow, pursued. **1880** MISS BRADDON *Just as I am* vi, His fettered wrists hanging in front of him.
b. *fig.* Hampered by disadvantageous conditions.
1856 OLMSTED *Slave States* 140 It is the old, fettered, barbarian labor-system.
2. (See quot.)
1884 *Syd. Soc. Lex.*, *Fettered*, in *Biol.*, applied to the limbs of animals when, by their retention within the integuments, or by their backward stretched position, they are unfit for walking.
Hence '**fetteredness**, the state of being fettered.
1656 W. MONTAGUE *Accompl. Wom.* 112 Gracefulness is ..averse to this slavery and fetterednesse.

fetterer ('fɛtərə(r)). [f. FETTER *v.* + -ER¹.] One who fastens fetters on (a person). *lit.* and *fig.*
1611 COTGR., *Entraveur*, a fetterer, a shackler. **1846** LANDOR *Imag. Conv.* I. 75 Which was the fetterer?

fetterfoe, obs. var. FEATHERFEW, feverfew.
? *a* **1500** *Chester Pl.* (Shaks. Soc.) I. 120 Here be more erbes..Fynter fanter and ffetter foe.

fettering ('fɛtərɪŋ), *vbl. sb.* [f. FETTER *v.*¹ + -ING¹.] The action of binding with fetters.
a **1623** GOSSON in Spurgeon *Treas. Dav.* Ps. cxlix. 8 If he once fall to fettering of princes..no flesh shall be able to knock off their bolts again. **1873** BURTON *Hist. Scot.* V. lix. 332 The Perth citizen's familiar way of treating the fettering of a Highlander. **1874** H. R. REYNOLDS *John Bapt.* ii. 98 That sign shall be..the fettering of such unwilling tongue.
attrib. **1812** *Examiner* 28 Sept. 621/2 The old man was.. pushed forward to the fettering block.

fetterless ('fɛtəlɪs), *a.* [f. FETTER *sb.* and *v.* + -LESS.] Without fetters; unfettered; that cannot be fettered. *lit.* and *fig.*
1604 MARSTON *Malcontent* I. iii, A tongue As fetterlesse as is an emperours. **1804** MOORE *To Boston Frigate* 9 Though man have the wings of the fetterless wind. **1816** J. GILCHRIST *Philos. Etym.* 202, I would rather see them as

wild, lawless and fetterless as the bold Arab. **1892** M. FIELD *Sight & Song* 40 Fetterless her ample form.

fetterlock ('fɛtəlɒk). Also 5 feter-, -ir-, -yr-, 6 fether-, 7 feawter-, fewter-. [f. FETTER *sb.* + LOCK; in sense 1 a corruption of FETLOCK.]

1. = FETLOCK 1. Also used *attrib.*

1587 MASCALL *Govt. Cattle* (1627) 135 They clippe away all the hayre sauing the fetherlocke. **1617** MARKHAM *Caval.* II. 9 His ioyntes beneath his knees great, with long feawter lockes. **1678** *Lond. Gaz.* No. 1338/4 A grey Mare..charm'd upon the 4 fetter-lock joints. **1688** R. HOLME *Armoury* II. 154/1 The Fewter-lock. **1716** *Lond. Gaz.* No. 5470/4 The Fetter-Locks behind bigger than the other. **1841** CATLIN *N. Amer. Ind.* (1844) II. xlv. 85 Our horses' feet were sinking at every step above their fetterlocks.

b. *transf.* of a human being.

1664 BUTLER *Hud.* II. i. 91 To set at large his Fetter-locks.

2. An apparatus fixed to the foot of a horse, to prevent his running away.

c **1440** *Promp. Parv.* 159/1 Fetyrlokke, *sera compeditalis.* **1530** PALSGR. 220/1 Fetterlocke, *serrure a goujons.* **1610** HOLLAND *Camden's Brit.* I. 510 The forme of the Keepe.. built like a fetter-lock.

fig. **1841** JAMES *Brigand* xxi, Despotic suspicion had not invented the fetter-lock of passports.

b. The same represented on a badge, shield, etc. Also a jewel of the same form.

It is figured as a cylinder to which a chain or steel band is attached in the form of a D, one end being permanently fixed and the other secured by a lock.

1463 *Bury Wills* (1850) 37 A litil fetirlok of gold with a lace of perle and smal bedys therto of blak. *c* **1465** *Pol. Rel. & L. Poems* (1866) 2 An F. for þe feterlock þat is of grete substance. **1605** CAMDEN *Rem.* (1637) 346 King Edward.. bare his white Rose, the fetterlocke before specified. **1646** BUCK *Rich. III*, IV. 115 The device was, A Faulcon encompassed with a Fetter-lock. **1820** SCOTT *Ivanhoe* xxix, A fetterlock, and a shacklebolt on a field-sable.

†'**fettery**, *a.* *Obs.*⁻¹ [f. FETTER *sb.* + -Y¹.] Of the nature of fetters; binding, constraining.

1654 GAYTON *Pleas. Notes* III. viii. 123 The fettery Hand-Cuffs of Gines Passamont.

fettle ('fɛt(ə)l), *sb.*¹ *Obs.* exc. *Sc.* and *dial.* [OE. *fetel* = OHG. *fezzil* (MHG. *vezzil*, Ger. *fessel*) chain, band, ON. *fetill* bandage, strap:—OTeut. **fatilo-z*, f. root *fat-* to hold.] **a.** In OE. A girdle, belt. **b.** A bandage. **c.** A handle in the side of a large basket, etc. Also *attrib.*, as ***fettle strap.***

c **888** K. ÆLFRED *Boeth.* xxxvii. §1 Mid fetlum & mid ȝyldenum hylt sweordum. *a* **1000** *Boeth. Metr.* xxv. 19 Sweordum & fetelum. **1599** A. M. tr. *Gabelhouer's Bk. Physicke* 306/2 We must rowle the same [a wound] with narrowe rowles, or with Fetles, accordinge to the constitution of the disease. **1812** J. HENDERSON *Agric. Surv. Caithn.* 69 Each cassie has a fettle or handle in each side. **1847–78** HALLIWELL, *Fettel*, a cord used to a pannier. **1877** *N.W. Linc. Gloss.*, *Fettle-strap*, the strap which sustains a pannier.

fettle ('fɛt(ə)l), *sb.*² [f. next vb.]

1. Condition, state, trim; in phr. *(to be) in (good, high,* etc.) *fettle.* Also in *pl.* the points, 'ins and outs' (of anything); but this may belong to FETTLE *sb.*¹

c **1750** J. COLLIER (Tim Bobbin) *Lanc. Dialect.* Gloss., *Fettle*, dress, case, condition. **1768** ROSS *Helenore* 23 Her tongue for fear tint fettle in her cheek. **1804** R. ANDERSON *Cumbrld. Ball.* 90 We were young, and beath i' fettle. **1829** J. R. BEST *Pers. & Lit. Mem.* 365 A critic, who knows what the north-countryman calls the fettles of the business, may suspect an equivocation. **1850** *Tales Kirkb.* Ser. II. 270 I'm in terrible poor fettle with the toothache. **1857** E. WAUGH *Lanc. Life*, A Shetland pony in good fettle. **1859** O. W. HOLMES *Prof. Breakf.-t.* xii. (1891) 313 The young man John is..'in fustrate fettle'. **1890** W. BEATTY-KINGSTON in *Fortn. Rev.* May 729 It would..be surprising were they not in fine fettle.

2. The material used for 'fettling' a furnace.

1894 *Harper's Mag.* Feb. 420/2 The molten metal is thoroughly stirred or 'rabbled' to make it uniform and secure the incorporation of the 'fettle'.

fettle ('fɛt(ə)l), *v.* Forms: 4–6 fettel, 4–7 fetle, (5 fettil, fetyl), 5–6 fetel(e, 9 *dial.* fottle, 4– fettle. [Possibly f. OE. *fetel*, FETTLE *sb.*¹; the primary sense would then be 'to gird up'.]

1. *trans.* To make ready, put in order, arrange. Now only *dial.* to put to rights, 'tidy up', scour; also, to groom (a horse), attend to (cattle).

13.. *E.E. Allit. P.* B. 585 He þat fetly in face fettled alle eres. *Ibid.* C. 38 In þe tyxte þere þyse two arn on teme layde, Hit arn fettled in on forme. *c* **1340** *Gaw. & Gr. Knt.* 656 Now alle þese fyue syþez, forsoþe, were fetled on þis knyȝt. *a* **1400–50** *Alexander* 626 And faste by his enfourme was fettild his place. **1561** *Schole-house of Women* 571 in Hazl. *E.P.P.* IV. 127 Our fily is fetled unto the saddle. **1787** GROSE *Provinc. Gloss.*, *To fettle th' tits*, to dress the horses. **1849** A. BRONTE *Agnes Grey* (1858) 360, I..fettled up th' fireplace a bit. **1864** T. CLARKE in *Kendal Mercury* 30 Jan., Woif hed fottled him a noice loil poi i' thoon. **1880** *Dorothy* 46, I can ..Fettle both horses and cows.

b. *techn.* To line (a puddling furnace, etc.); to scour (rough castings).

1881 C. R. A. WRIGHT in *Encycl. Brit.* (ed. 9) XIII. 324/1 In fettling the furnace either oxide of iron bricks moulded to fit the furnace are built in, or, etc. **1884** *Imp. & Mach. Rev.* 1 Dec. 6716/2 A castings-cleaner, capable of holding a ton of rough castings and fettling them in an hour.

c. To 'do for' (a person), to beat.

1863 KINGSLEY *Water-bab.* 322 Tom offered to..fettle him over the head with a brick. **1884** *Cheshire Gloss.* s.v., A mother will threaten her child 'I'll fettle thee'.

d. To mull (ale or porter); see FETTLED below.

†**2.** *refl.* and *intr.* for *refl.* To get (oneself) ready; to prepare; to address oneself to battle. *Obs.* exc. *dial.* (see quot. 1855).

13.. *E.E. Allit. P.* C. 435 On a felde he fettelez hym to bide. *c* **1425** WYNTOUN *Cron.* VIII. xvi. 197 The Scottis.. Tuk the feld, and manlykly Fetlyt wyth thare fais in fycht. **1515** *Scot. Field* 304 in Furniv. *Percy Folio* I. 227 He fettlen them to sowpe..on a banke. **1597–8** BP. HALL *Sat.* IV. vi. 43 He..sels his teeme and fetleth to the warre. **1600** HOLLAND *Livy* XXI. xvi. (1609) 402 They rather trembled..than fetled themselves to consultation. **1674** RAY *N.C. Words*, *Fettle*, to set or go about any thing. **1855** ROBINSON *Whitby Gloss.*, 'We are just fettling for off.'

b. To busy oneself; to fuss.

1745 SWIFT *Direct. Servants* iii, Pretend to fettle about the Room. **1858** CARLYLE *Fredk. Gt.* (1865) II. VII. vii. 325 He is getting his saddle altered: fettling about this and that.

Hence '**fettled** *ppl. a.*, in senses of the vb.

c **1460** *Towneley Myst.* 309 Ylle fetyld. **1861** *Temple Bar Mag.* I. 420 A pint of fettled porter. **1863** MISS BRADDON *J. Marchmont* I. 95 A mug of fettled beer. **1884** *Cheshire Gloss.*, *Fettled Ale*, ale mulled with ginger and sugar.

fettler ('fɛtlə(r)). *dial.* and *techn.* [f. FETTLE *v.* + -ER¹.] One who 'fettles'; *spec.* in various trades.

1871 *Daily News* 18 Aug., The cloth finishers, dressers, fettlers, and willeyers, are taking steps to obtain a general advance. **1881** *Instr. Census Clerks* (1885) 87 *Railway labourer, navvy,*..fettler. **1883** *Almondbury & Huddersf. Gloss.*, *Fettler*, one who cleans up; especially one whose business it is to clean machinery, engines, &c. **1884** *Cheshire Gloss.*, *Fettler*, one who sharpens the knives of the fustian cutters. **1892** *Labour Commission* Gloss., *Fettler*, the person who cleans out the fudd and dirt that accumulates in the cards of the scribbler and condenser. **1900** H. LAWSON *On Track* 44 The inspector hurried to his horse, and cantered off along the line in the direction of the fettlers' camp. **1962** MARSHALL & DRYSDALE *Journey among Men* 188 Twenty miles along the line we met four fettlers on a motor-driven trolley. **1964** *People* (Austral.) 16 Dec. 45/4 Nowadays, I am a railway fettler.

fettling ('fɛtlɪŋ), *vbl. sb.* [f. FETTLE *v.* + -ING¹.]

1. a. The action of the verb FETTLE in various senses; an instance of this.

1847 A. BRONTE *Agnes Grey* xi. 168 I'd no heart to sweeping an' fettling, an' washing pots. **1859** 'T. TREDDLEHOYLE' *Bairnsla Foaks' Ann.* Feb. [10] Two owd worthies there thowt it a nice chonce to gie it a good fetlin aht. **1865** CARLYLE *Fredk. Gt.* IX. XX. ii. 18 Friedrich calculated there would be very considerable fettling and haggling. **1869** *Lonsdale Gloss.*, 'I gev him a good fettling.' **1958** *New Scientist* 13 Nov. 1269/2 When the carding engine is restarted after this 'fettling' [*sc.* removal of dirt] a lot of the fibres fed in go at first to replace the dirt and fibres just removed. **1960** H. POWELL *Beginner's Bk. Pottery* II. 63 *Fettling*, trimming cast models when mould joints leave lines of clay. **1960** R. LISTER *Dec. Cast Iron-work* 227 *Fettling brush*, a wire brush used in fettling. *Ibid.*, *Fettling hole*, in a cupola, the aperture through which the debris may be removed after a melt. *Ibid.* ii. 55 The castings are removed from the sand moulds in a knockout... From here they are taken to the fettling shop and subjected to a series of cleaning processes.

b. *spec.* The action of lining a puddling furnace; hence, the materials used for this. Also *attrib.*

1864 PERCY *Iron & Steel* 669 Iron puddled with limestone fettling is always rotten. **1872** *Daily News* 7 Oct. 6 His judgment..was against Sunday fettling. **1890** *Iron & Steel Trades Jrnl.* 4 Jan. 20/2 Sales of cokes and fettling minerals are recorded in large quantities.

‖**fettstein** ('fɛtstaɪn). *Min.* [Ger. *fettstein* (Werner 1808), f. *fett* fat + *stein* stone.] = ELÆOLITE.

1815 W. PHILLIPS *Outl. Min. Geol.* (1818) 32 The fettstein consists of 44 silex, 34 alumine, 4 oxide of iron, a small portion of lime, and 16 parts of soda and potash. **1859** PAGE *Geol. Terms* s.v.

‖**fettuccine** (fettut'tʃine). [It., pl. of *fettuccina*, dim. of *fetta* slice, ribbon.] An Italian pasta made in strips or ribbons.

1922 S. LEWIS *Babbitt* xv. 196 A little *trattoria*..where you get the best *fettuccine* in the world. **1962** *Sunday Express* 18 Feb. 22/5 The Italians..are justly proud of their Ferraris, their *fettuccine*, their females. **1964** *Guardian* 22 May 8/5 *Fettuccine*, long wide noodles with egg.

feture, fetus: see FŒTURE, FŒTUS.

‖**fetwa** ('fɛtwɑ). Forms: 7–9 fetfa, 8 fetva, 9 fethwa, fetwa. [Arab. *fetwa* (pronounced by the Turks *fetfa*), f. *fatā*, in 4th conj. to instruct by a legal decision (pr. pple. *muftī* MUFTI).] A decision given (usually in writing) by a Mufti or other Moslem juridical authority.

1625 PURCHAS *Pilgrims* II. ix. 1608 Fetfa's that is, Declarations, or Iudgements of the Muftee. **1704** J. TRAPP *Abra-Mulé* v. i. 2000 In less than half an hour, The black deposing Fetfa will be sign'd. **1802** *Paris as it was* II. lxviii. 334 A fetfa or diploma of the Grand Signior. **1836** LANE *Mod. Egypt* I. 134 The Náib..desires the plaintiff to procure a fet'wa (or judicial decision) from the Moof'tee. **1882** *Times* 5 Apr. 9/4 The fetwa from the great Mahomedan Academy will be awaited with curiosity.

feu (fjuː), *sb.* *Sc. Law.* Forms: 5–8 few, 6– feu. [a. OF. *feu, fieu, fiu*; see the variant FEE *sb.*²]

1. = FEE *sb.*² 1; also, a tract of land held in fee. (Used by modern Scottish jurists indiscriminately with *fee* as a rendering of med.L. *feudum.*)

1609 SKENE *Reg. Maj.* Table, s.v., Gif the vassall committis ane trespas aganis his overlord: he tines his few halden of him. *lib.* 2. *c.* 63, 4. [The word is not in the text, which renders *feudum* by 'lands'.] **1754** ERSKINE *Princ. Sc. Law* (1809) 136 Allodial goods are opposed to feus. *a* **1768** —— *Instit. Sc. Law* (1773) I. 209 When mention is made of a feu or subfeu, we are not necessarily to understand a grant of lands holden in feu-farm, but a feudal grant in general.. unless where the subject treated of naturally confines it to a feu-holding.

2. A feudal tenure of land in which the vassal, in place of military service, makes a return of grain or money (opposed to WARD or military holding and BLANCH or holding at a nominal rent); a grant of lands on these conditions; in mod. use, a perpetual lease for a fixed rent (= FEU-FARM). Phrases: ***in, upon feu***: subject to such payments or performance of duties; also ***to hold feu, set into feu.***

1497 *Ld. Treas. Acc. Scot.* I. 315, I resauit fra the Lard of Teling..of the releif of few and blanchferme of the entre of Johne Lord Glammys, thretj thre lib. **1535** LYNDESAY *Satyre* 2685 Set into few ȝour temporall lands. **1570** *Satir. Poems Reform.* xxiii. 30 Thocht thair was sum that tuik thy rowmis in few. **1720** *Lond. Gaz.* No. 5866/3 A small Part holding Few of the Earl of Strathmore. **1759** ROBERTSON *Hist. Scot.* (1817) II. III. 74 By granting feus, and perpetual leases of lands. **1826** SCOTT *Provinc. Antiq.* II. 110 A grant for disposing of it, in feu. **1892** GLADSTONE in *Daily News* 25 Mar. 3/4 To hold land upon feu from the landlord.

b. A piece of land held 'in feu'; a holding.

1791 NEWTE *Tour Eng. & Scot.* 375 A small piece, or feu of ground in Fifeshire. **1820** SCOTT *Monast.* i, The vassals of the church..were permitted in comparative quiet to possess their farms and feus. **1864** A. MᶜKAY *Hist. Kilmarnock* 313 On the other side some feus were unoccupied.

3. *attrib.* and *Comb.*; simple attrib., as ***feu-grant, -parchment, -rent, -system***; special comb., as **feu-annual** (see quot. 1710), hence *-annualer*; **feu-charter** = next; **feu-contract**, the contract regulating the giving out of land in feu, between the superior and vassal; **feu-duty**, the annual rent paid by a vassal to his superior for tenure of lands; **feu-holding**, a tenure of lands in feu; **feu-right**, the right of holding (land, etc.) in feu.

1597 SKENE *De Verb. Sign.* s.v. *Annuell*, In the Actes of Parliament maid be Queene Marie 4 Parlia. 29. Maij c. 10 mention is maid of ground annuell, *few annuell and top annuell, quhairof I..am incertaine quhat they do signifie. **1710** J. DUNDAS *View Feud. Law* Gloss. 127 *Few-annuals*, that which is due by the *Reddendo* of the Property of the Ground, before the House was built within Burgh. **1551** *Sc. Acts Q. Mary* (1597) §10. 134b, The *few annuellaris. *a* **1768** ERSKINE *Instit. Sc. Law* (1773) I. 207 The word *feu-charter is never made use of but to denote the special tenure by feu-farm. **1832** AUSTIN *Jurispr.* (1879) II. lii. 879 The *feu-contract is in the nature of a perpetual lease and is in Scotland the usual mode of letting land for building purposes. **1597** *Sc. Acts Jas. VI*, §246 Incase it sal happen ..ony vassall or fewar..to failzie in making of payment of his *few dewtie. **1854** H. MILLER *Sch. & Schm.* xvi. (1857) 356 Paying a large arrear of feu-duty. *a* **1768** ERSKINE *Instit. Sc. Law* (1773) I. 222 The vassal's loss of his *feu-grant. **1748** *De Foe's Tour Gt. Brit.* IV. 39 Converted into Blanch and *Feu holdings. **1873** BURTON *Hist. Scot.* V. lxiv. 444 Some of the beneficial interests thus conveyed were mere leases, others were feu-holdings. **1825** SCOTT *Fam. Lett.* 12 Oct. (1894) II. 353 A grim old Antiquary..all *feu-parchment, snuff, and..whisky toddy. **1866** MISS MULOCK *Noble Life* xv. 267 Houses..the *feu-rents of which made the estate..more valuable every year. **1774** *Petit.* in MᶜKay *Hist. Kilmarnock* App. iii. 305 The reddendo of this *feu-right is £7 Scots yearly. **1891** *Labour Commission* Gloss., The *feu system is a custom (in use in Scotland) under which a piece of land is purchased by a perpetual yearly payment.

feu (fjuː), *v.* [f. FEU *sb.*] *trans.* To grant (land) upon feu. Also to ***feu off, out.***

1717 DE FOE *Mem. Ch. Scot.* II. 23 Temporalities feu'd to themselves. **1799** J. ROBERTSON *Agric. Perth* 59 He had recourse to wadsetts; or feued off a part of his property at a quit-rent. **1854** H. MILLER *Sch. & Schm.* xiv. (1857) 301 A little bit of ground, which he had failed in getting feued out for buildings. **1866** MISS MULOCK *Noble Life* vii. 109 To find out the exact extent and divisions of his property, and to whom it was feued.

‖**feu** (fø), *a.* [Fr., deceased.] = LATE *a.*¹ 5.

1813 J. AUSTEN *Let.* 3 Nov. (1932) II. 366 The Bru of feu the Archbishop says she cannot pay for it immediately. **1868** C. M. YONGE *Chaplet Pearls* II. xliii. 252 Discoursing..on *feu* M. l'Amiral's saying. **1912** A. LANG *Shakes., Bacon & Gt. Unknown* v. 113 Mr. Reed, a Baconian of whom Mr. Collins wrote in terms worthy of *feu* Mr. Bludyer.

†'**feuage.** *Obs. rare.* [a. OF. *feuage, fouage*, f. *feu* fire.] (See quots.)

1618 DANIEL *Coll. Hist. Eng.* 214 The Prince of Wales.. imposing a new taxation upon the Gascoignes, of Feuage or Chymney mony..discontented the people. **1706** PHILLIPS (ed. Kersey), *Fuage* or *Focage*, Hearth-money, an Imposition of Twelve-pence for every Fire-hearth.

feuar ('fjuːə(r)). *Sc.* Forms: 6 fear, fewar, 7 fier, 8 feuer, 9 feur, 7– fewar. See FIAR. [f. FEU *sb.* + -AR.] One who holds land upon feu.

1513–75 *Diurn. Occurrents* (1833) 237 Alexander Stewart fear of Garuleis. **1597** *Sc. Acts Jas. VI*, §246 Ony vassal or fewar, haldand landes in few-ferme. **1637–50** ROW *Hist. Kirk* (1842) 105 The fier of Fintray. **1753** *Scots Mag.* Feb.

86/2 Except of feuer of 31*l*. Scots of valued rent. **1843** Scott *Monast.* I. *note*, Descendants of such feuars..are still to be found in possession of their family inheritances. **1876** Grant *Burgh Sch. Scotl.* II. ii. 109 Neighbouring feuars and proprietors.

feud (fjuːd), *sb.*[1] Forms: α. (after the early 14th c. almost exclusively *Sc.*) 3–6 **fede**, 4 **fed**, (6 **fade**), 6–7 **fead**, **feed(e**, 4–8 **feid(e**. β. 6 **food(e**, **feood**, **fude**, 6–7 **fuid(e**, 6–8 **fewd(e**, 7 **feaud**, **feode**, **feude**, 7– **feud**. [The northern ME. *fede* is a. OF. *fede*, *feide*, *faide* (the phrase *fede mortel* = 'deadly feud' is recorded from 13th c.), ad. OHG. *fêhida* (whence MHG. *vêhede*, *vêde*, mod.G. *fehde*) = OE. *fǽhþ(u* enmity:—OTeut. **faihiþâ* str. fem., noun of quality or state f. **faiho-* adj.: see FOE. In 14–15th c. the word occurs only in Sc. writers, the form being always *fede*, *feide*, or something phonetically equivalent. In the 16th c. it was adopted in England (being often expressly spoken of as a northern word), with an unexplained change of form, as *food(e*, *feood*, *fuid*, *fewd*, whence in 17th c. the form now current. The ordinary statement that the change of form was due to the influence of FEUD *sb.*[2] is obviously incorrect; FEUD *sb.*[2] is not recorded in our material until half a century after the appearance of the forms *foode*, *fewd*, and would not account for them even if it were proved to have existed earlier; moreover, even in the 17th c. it was merely a rare technical word used by writers on the 'feudal system', and its sense is too remote from that of the northern *feide* for the assumed influence to have operated.

A plausible supposition is that there was an OE. **féod* str. fem. (f. *féoȝan* to hate) corresponding to Goth. *fijaþwa* as *fréod* friendship to Goth. *frijaþwa*. This would in ME. normally become *fede*, coalescing with the Rom. word of similar sound and meaning; but there may have been a northern Eng. dialect in which the word was pronounced with a 'rising' diphthong cf. mod.Eng. *four* from OE. *féower*), and from which the β forms were adopted. In 17th c. the word was occasionally altered into FOEHOOD.]

†**1.** Active hatred or enmity, hostility, ill-will.

α. [*Beowulf* 109 Ne ȝefeah he þære fæhðe.] *a* **1300** *Cursor M.* 27455 (Cott.) He haldes wreth in hert and fede. *c* **1375** *Sc. Leg. Saints, Margarete* 476 For þare vertu fed haf I. *c* **1470** Henry *Wallace* I. 354 A mar quiet sted, Quhar Wilȝham mycht be bettir fra thair fede. *c* **1475** *Rauf Coilȝear* 969 His wyfe wuld he nocht forȝet, for dout of Goddis feid. **1556** Lauder *Tractate* 11 Nother to spair, for lufe nor fede, To do dew Iustice to the dede. **1570** Levins *Manip.* 205/34 *Feade*, odium. **1596** Dalrymple tr. *Leslie's Hist. Scot.* 92 The fade and inimitie borne towards thair parents. **1787** Burns *Tam Samson's Elegy* x, Till coward death behind him jumpit, Wi deadly feide.

β. **1566** Painter *Pal. Pleas.* I. 1 Two..cities..bare eche other..deadlye foode. **1596** Spenser *F.Q.* IV. i. 26 Deadly feood. **1598** Florio, *Aizza*, anger, fude, moode. **1631** Gouge *God's Arrows* iii. §3. 187 This immortall fewde against worshippers of the true God. **1705** *Dyet of Poland* 4 A Vice which rankles up to Fewd.

b. *Sc.* Used in contradistinction to *favour*.

α. **1530** Lyndesay *Test. Papyngo* 622 The veritie..thay sulde declare, Without regarde to fauour or to fede. **1560** Rolland *Seven Sages* (1837) 1 Thay tuke na cure of na manis fauour nor feid. **1609** Skene *Reg. Maj.* 137 For feed or favour of anie man. **1637–50** Row *Hist. Kirk* (1842) 446 Thus have I..spoken nothing..but the trueth, and that impartiallie, without fead or favour to any.

β. **1843** Carlyle *Past & Pr.* (1858) 145 Decided without feud or favour.

2. A state of bitter and lasting mutual hostility. (From 16th c. often with allusion to 3.) Phrases: *to be at* (*deadly*) *feud*, †*to have* (*a person*) *at feud*.

α. *c* **1425** Wyntoun *Cron.* VII. ix. 529 In þare ire Of awld Fede, and gret dyscord. **1535** Stewart *Cron. Scot.* II. 201 Syne sueir on bell and buik, That euerie on to vther sould be trew In tyme to cum for ald feid or for new. *a* **1775** *Hobie Noble* ix. in Child *Ballads* (1890) VII. clxxxix. 2/2 The land-sergeant has me at feid.

β. **1583** Golding *Calvin on Deut.* iv. 21 Hee will alwayis bee at deadly foode with mee. **1601** Holland *Pliny* x. lxxiv. 308 Crowes and Owles are at mortall feaud one with another. **1611** Bible *Transl. Pref.* 10 His Queene and his..heire were at deadly fuide with him. **1614** Bp. Hall *Recoll. Treat.* 603 Of which sort there are divers at this day..at deadly feode with the other Jewes. *c* **1661** *Argyle's Will* in *Harl. Misc.* (1746) VIII. 30/2 He [Argyle] was at Feud with all his Superiors in Scotland. *a* **1715** Burnet *Own Time* (1766) I. 6 Seeds of lasting feuds and animosities. **1847** Grote *Greece* II. xlvii. (1862) IV. 189 Their ancient feud against Korkyra. **1871** Freeman *Norm. Conq.* (1876) IV. xvii. 77 A partizan of Tostig would naturally be at feud with Oswulf.

3. A state of perpetual hostility between two families, tribes, or individuals, marked by murderous assaults in revenge for some previous insult or injury. More fully *deadly feud*. Cf. VENDETTA. Phrases as in 2.

α. **1582–8** *Hist. James VI* (1804) 225 That nathing done..be comptit as deadlie fead in judgement. **1599** Jas. I *Βασιλ. Δωρον* (1603) 47 Rest not, until yee roote out these barbarous feides. **1609** Skene *Reg. Maj.* 46 For the mainteining of weir (or deadlie fead) quhilk he hes with ane other. *a* **1657** Sir J. Balfour *Ann. Scot.* (1824–5) II. 68 His Maiesties sentence and decreitt being read concerning all feeds and matters of blood betuix the Hayes and Gordons.

β. **1568** Lambarde *Ἀρχαιονομία* B iij, Capitales inimicitiæ, Saxonicè fœþh [*sic*], nomen..a borealibus Anglis hac nostra memoria vsurpatum. Illi vero dictione non ita multum a priori dissidente, *fewd*, et *Deadly fewd* appellant. **1601** *Act 43 Eliz.* c. 13 Whosoever shall..take any of her Majestie's Subjects..or make a praye or spoile of his Persone or Goodes, upon deadlie feude or otherwise. **1613** Purchas *Pilgrimage* VI. xi. 525 Mutuall feuds and battels betwixt their seuerall Tribes and kindreds. **1797** Tomlins *Law Dict.*, *Deadly feud* is a profession of an irreconcileable hatred, till a person is revenged even by the death of his enemy. **1814** Scott *Ld. of Isles* III. iv, Until these feuds so fierce and fell The Abbot reconciles. **1845** H. H. Wilson *Brit. India* I. I. vi. 317 A tribe which was at deadly feud with the Joasmis. **1868** Freeman *Norm. Conq.* (1876) II. vii. 108 Carrying out an ancestral deadly feud.

†**4.** A murderous conspiracy. *Obs. rare*[−1].

So OF. *feide*. This is our only southern instance of the word before 16th c.

c **1300** *K. Alis.* 96 Kyng Phelippe, of gret thede, Maister was of that feide.

5. A quarrel, contention, bickering.

α. *c* **1565** Lindesay (Pitscottie) *Chron. Scot.* (1728) 6 If it shall chance us to continue any further in this fead it shall redound to his advantage.

β. **1662** Stillingfl. *Orig. Sacr.* I. vi. §1 We see how small a matter will beget a feud between learned men. **1732** Berkeley *Alciphr.* v. §17 The perpetual feuds between the patricians and plebeians. **1754** Richardson *Grandison* (1781) IV. iv. 23 We were in the midst of a feud when you arrived. **1835** Thirlwall *Greece* I. vii. 279 The domestic feuds which agitated the family of Temenus. **1841** D'Israeli *Amen. Lit.* (1867) 53 The hero had come not to seek feud, nor to provoke insult.

6. *attrib.*, as *feud-foe*. Also, **feud-bote**, *Hist.* [ad. OE. *fǽhþ-bót*], a recompense for engaging in a feud, a compensation for homicide.

[*c* **1000** *Laws Ethelred* ix. §25 And ne þearf ænig mynster-munuc ahwar mid rihte fæhð-bote biddan ne fæhð-bote betan.] **1681** Blount *Glossogr.*, *Feud-boote*. **1706** Phillips (ed. Kersey), *Feud-bote*. **1721–1800** in Bailey. **1640** *King & North. Man* 343 in Hazl. *E.P.P.* IV. 306 If that I doe ever meete with your fewd foes, Ise sweare by this staffe that their hide I won bang.

feud, feod (fjuːd), *sb.*[2] [ad. med.L. *feudum*, *feodum*: see FEE *sb.*[2]]

1. = FEE *sb.*[2] 1.

1614 Selden *Titles Hon.* 61, I might with casting about, frame the nature of Feuds, or Patronage. **1708** *Termes de la Ley* 336 Feod is a right which the Vassal hath in Land. **1818** Cruise *Digest* (ed. 2) III. 151 The Conqueror conferred the estates..on his principal followers as strict feuds. **1872** E. W. Robertson *Hist. Ess.* 256 The Benefice began to be converted into the hereditary Feud.

2. = FEE *sb.*[2] 3.

1806 A. Duncan *Nelson* 117 His Majesty conferred on him the title of Duke of Bronte, annexing to it the feud of that name. **1825** T. Jefferson *Autobiog.* Wks. 1859 I. 91 Residing constantly on their patrimonial feuds. **1865** Maffei *Brigand Life* II. 271 The old papal feud of Beneventum.

feud (fjuːd), *v.* [f. FEUD[1].] *intr.* To conduct a feud. Hence **'feuding** *ppl. a.* and *vbl. sb.*

1673 P. Walsh *Advocate of Conscience Liberty* ii. 24 Resolved in all meetings to feud about the Rom. Religion. **1900** in *Eng. Dial. Dict.* **1910** 'O. Henry' *Whirligigs* (1916) x. 104, I was told that the Durkees and Tatums had been feuding for years. **1938** *Amer. Speech* XIII. 195 Feuding. **1952** *Economist* 24 May 517 Two sets of feuding delegates, each demanding to be recognized. **1952** *History Today* July 451 (*title*) A Background to feuding: the vendetta in Kentucky. *Ibid.* 452/2 The figure of the feuding hillman..is a phenomenon of modern America rather than of pioneer times. **1955** P. M. Kendall *Richard Third* I. i. 32 Such was the feuding among the nobles that if one Lord espoused York's cause, another instantly upheld the Queen. **1959** *Birmingham Mail* 5 Feb. 3/8 There's more feuding at the factory.

feudal ('fjuːdəl), *a.*[1] and *sb.* Forms: 7 **feudall**, 7–9 **feodal**, (8 *Sc.* **fewdal**), 7– **feudal**. [ad. med.L. *feudālis*, *feodālis*, f. *feud-um*, *feod-um*, FEUD *sb.*[2] Cf. F. *féodal*.]

A. *adj.*

1. Of or pertaining to a feud or fief; of the nature of a feud or fief.

1614 Selden *Titles Hon.* 188 Neither did the Prouinces make them otherwise then Personal. For they were not annext to them as Feudall. *a* **1677** Hale *Com. Law Eng.* ix. 183 Wales, that was not alwayes the Feudal Territory of..England. **1710** J. Dundas *View Feudal Law* xii. 47 The Money got for a Few is moveable..not Fewdal, for it does not succeed in place of the Few. **1861** Kemp *Comm.* (1873) III. liii. 497 The conversion of allodial into feudal estates.

b. *Her.* (See quot.)

1847 *Gloss. Heraldry*, *Arms of Succession*, otherwise called *feudal arms*, are those borne by the possessors of certain lordships or estates.

2. Of or pertaining to the holding of land in feud.

1639 Spelman *Feuds & Tenures* xxiii. 38 There was no..intervenient Lord to claim them by any feodal Tenure. **1767** Blackstone *Comm.* II. 39 In all countries where the feodal polity has prevailed. **1781** Gibbon *Decl. & F.* II. 48 The first rudiments of the feudal tenures. **1873** H. Spencer *Stud. Sociol.* v. 103 The feudal arrangement of attachment to the soil.

b. ***feudal system***: the system of polity which prevailed in Europe during the Middle Ages, and which was based on the relation of superior and vassal arising out of the holding of lands in feud.

1776 Adam Smith *W.N.* (1869) I. I. xi. 251 Poland, where the feudal system still continues to take place. **1875** Kingsley *Herew.* ix, The feudal system never took root in their soil.

3. Of or pertaining to the feudal system; existing or such as existed under that system. ***feudal lawyer***: one learned in feudal law. ***feudal writers***: those who treat of the feudal system.

1665 *Surv. Aff. Netherl.* 32 By the Feodall (*printed* Feodau) Law that King, their Lord, had forfeited his Right to his Fee. **1765** Blackstone *Comm.* I. 241 According to the known distribution of the feodal writers. **1807** Crabbe *Par. Reg.* II. 206 Like them, in feudal days their valiant lords. **1816** Scott *Old Mort.* ii, Those feudal institutions which united the vassal to the liege lord, and both to the Crown. **1840** T. A. Trollope *Summ. in Brittany* II. 106 The ruins of two ancient feodal castles. **1886** Stubbs *Med. & Mod. Hist.* 64 It is time..that we had a feudal map of England.

b. ***feudal vassal, lord***, etc.: one holding that position in the sense implied in the feudal system.

1639 Spelman *Feuds & Tenures* ii. 4 Their Feudal Vassals..enjoyed their Feuds..from year to year at the pleasure of their Lords. **1839** W. Chambers *Tour Holland* 65/1 Otho, the feudal proprietor of this stronghold. **1856** Froude *Hist. Eng.* (1858) I. i. 18 That loyalty with which the people followed the standard..of their feudal superiors.

c. Occasionally of persons or their opinions: Adhering to the principles of the feudal system.

1876 Freeman *Norm. Conq.* V. xxiv. 463 Lawyers..would naturally look at everything with feudal eyes. **1883** Ouida *Wanda* I. 89 We are very feudal still.

†**B.** *sb. pl.* Feudal privileges. *Obs. rare.*

1625 F. Markham *Bk. Hon.* II. iv. §5 All sorts..shall enjoy their Feodalls and Rights, to which they are truely borne.

Hence **'feudally** *adv.*, in a feudal manner or spirit; under feudal conditions.

1839 Hallam *Hist. Lit.* ii. II. §44 The Pope..cannot depose these princes..unless they are feudally his vassals. **1850** Mazzini *Royalty & Repub.* 158 Abjectly..trembling before the people when it arose..yet feudally insolent when the lion was quieted again. **1873** Miss Broughton *Nancy* II. 184 A very aged, ignorant, and feudally loyal couple.

feudal ('fjuːdəl), *a.*[2] *rare.* [f. FEUD *sb.*[1] + -AL[1].] Of or pertaining to a (deadly) feud.

1805 Scott *Last Minstr.* I. viii, The havoc of the feudal war. *Ibid.* III. iv, The foemen's feudal hate.

feudalism ('fjuːdəlɪz(ə)m). [f. FEUDAL *a.*[1] + -ISM.] The feudal system, or its principles.

1839 Keightley *Hist. Eng.* I. 82 The peculiar usages of feudalism. **1861** Wright *Ess. Archæol.* II. xiv. 39 Feudalism had originated in France. **1867** Freeman *Norm. Conq.* (1876) I. iii. 91 There was no systematic feudalism, but the elements of feudalism were there. **1875** Maine *Hist. Inst.* vi. 154 Feudalism had grown up from two great sources, the Benefice and the practice of Commendation.

feudalist ('fjuːdəlɪst). [f. as prec. + -IST.]

1. a. A representative of the feudal system.

1822 *Blackw. Mag.* XII. 268 The Castle [of Edinburgh], the architectural chieftain of those grey and rugged feudalists below. **1831** *Crayons from Commons* 28 To make each Border feudalist rejoice.

b. An adherent or supporter of the feudal system.

1870 *Daily News* 6 Sept. 4 Those wretched feudalists [the Prussians]. **1874** Maurice *Friendship Bks.* v. 149 That kind of civilization which I said the feudalists could not give. **1888** *Truth* 19 July 98/1 The Emperor is far more of a feudalist than the Prince [Bismarck].

2. One learned in feudal law; = FEUDIST.

feudalistic (fjuːdə'lɪstɪk), *a.* [f. prec. + -IC.] Of the nature of feudalism; inclined to feudalism.

1882–3 Schaff *Encycl. Relig. Knowl.* III. 1719 The new mediæval forms, hierarchical and feudalistic. **1886** A. M. Elliott in *Amer. Jrnl. Philol.* July VII. 152 The main tenor of his life was feudalistic.

feudality (fjuː'dælɪtɪ). [ad. F. *feudalité* (Cotgr.), *feodalité*, f. *feudal* (Cotgr.), *feodal*: see FEUDAL *a.*[1] and -ITY.]

1. The quality or state of being feudal; the principles and practice of the feudal system.

1790 Burke *Fr. Rev.* Wks. V. 395 The leaders teach the people to abhor and reject all feodality as the barbarism of tyranny. **1827** Hallam *Const. Hist.* (1876) I. i. 7 [The holding of Assizes] had a powerful tendency..to check the influence of feudality and clanship. **1845** Mill *Ess.* II. 265 The very essence of feudality was..the fusion of property and sovereignty. **1858** Buckle *Civiliz.* (1869) II. ii. 111 There followed that struggle between feudality and the church. **1877** Miss Yonge *Cameos* IV. iii. 36 The many means of raising money that feudality afforded.

b. *pl.* Feudal principles.

1814 *Witness* I. iii, It was a breach in your feudalities To change the place.

2. A feudal regime or system; a feudal-like power; a feudal holding, a fief.

1800 Coleridge *Piccolom.* II. viii, All the great Bohemian feodalities. **1821** *Examiner* 237/2 Capital in Great Britain has become a feudality. **1840** Carlyle *Heroes* (1858) 366 He..strove to connect himself with..the old false Feudalities which he once saw clearly to be false. **1844** H. H. Wilson *Brit. India* I. 203 A principle recognised throughout the feudality of India.

†**3.** (See quot.) *Obs.*[−0]

1701 Kennet *Cowel's Law Dict.*, *Feodalitas*, Feodality or Fidelity paid to the Lord by his feodal tenant. Hence **1797** Tomlins *Law Dict.*, *Feodality*, fealty. **1847** in Craig.

feudalization (ˌfjuːdəlaɪ'zeɪʃən). [f. next + -ATION.] The action of the vb. FEUDALIZE; the

reduction (of a country) under the feudal system.

1862 LD. BROUGHAM *Brit. Const.* xi. 147 William had.. completed the feudalization of the whole Kingdom. **1874** STUBBS *Const. Hist.* (1875) I. xi. 360 The tendency towards feudalisation of the governmental machinery. **1876** FREEMAN *Norm. Conq.* V. xxiv. 460 The feudalization of Europe.

feudalize ('fju:dəlaɪz), *v.* [f. FEUDAL *a.*^{1} + -IZE.] *trans.* To make feudal, bring under the feudal system, impart a feudal character to; to convert (lands) into feudal holdings. Also, to reduce (persons) to the condition of feudal dependants.

1828 *Examiner* 147/1 Could human beings be stultified and feudalized, like the peasantry in days of yore, into something a very little beyond the clods they trod upon. **1862** LD. BROUGHAM *Brit. Const.* iii. 42 Allodial property was daily diminished in amount by proprietors feudalizing it. **1868** MILMAN *St. Paul's* ii. 15 The Norman Conquest feudalised the Church..of England.

Hence '**feudalized** *ppl. a.*; '**feudalizing** *vbl. sb.*

1851 OGILVIE, *Feudalizing*, reducing to a feudal form. **1852** LD. COCKBURN *Jeffrey* I. 365 Its strongly feudalised condition. **1867** FREEMAN *Norm. Conq.* (1876) I. iv. 252 The feudalizing process went on vigorously. **1875** MAINE *Hist. Inst.* iii. 91 This is no doubt true of feudalised countries.

‖**feu d'artifice** (fø dartifis). [Fr., lit. 'fire of artifice'.] Fireworks (sense 4 c). Also *transf.*

1699 M. LISTER *Journey to Paris* (ed. 3) 180 The Cardinal of Furstenbourgh..closed the public Rejoicings for the conclusion of the Peace with the last *Feu d'Artifice*. **1818** E. BLAQUIÈRE tr. *Pananti's Narr. Res. Algiers* ii. 59 The many salutes..reminded me that there are *feux d'artifice*, as well as *feux de joie*. **1834** M. EDGEWORTH *Helen* I. xv. 312 'Well, fireworks, if you will,' said Lady Davenant,..'it's all *feu d'artifice* after all.' **1916** G. SAINTSBURY *Peace Augustans* viii. 286 As a sort of poetical *feu d'artifice* the things are fine.

'**feudary**, '**feodary**, *sb.* and *a.* *Obs.* exc. *arch.* Forms: 4–9 **feodary**, 5–7 **-ie**, (5 **feudory**, 6 **feodarry**), 6–7 **feudary**, (7 **-ie**), (7 **feodar, feadary, fæd-, foedery**). [ad. med.L. *feodāri-us*, f. *feodum, feudum*: see FEUD *sb.*^{2} and -ARY.]

A. *sb.*

1. One who holds lands of an overlord on condition of homage and service; a feudal tenant, a vassal.

1387 TREVISA *Higden* (Rolls) VIII. 191 So þat after þat tyme he [John] and his heires schulde be feodaries to þe chirche of Rome. **1494** FABYAN *Chron.* VII. 319 To holde it euer after..as feodaries of yᵉ pope. **1568** GRAFTON *Chron.* II. 222 The King of Scottes bound himselfe and them to be Feodaries to the Crowne of England. **1613–18** DANIEL *Coll. Hist. Eng.* (1626) 134 He seemed absolutely the Popes Feudary. **1631** MASSINGER *Beleeve as you list* II. ii, Our confœderates and freindes Founde it as firme as fate, and seaventeene Kinges, Our fædaries. **1650** FULLER *Pisgah* I. ii. 5 Accepted of the Jewish King to be honourary feodaries unto him. **1836** M. J. CHAPMAN in *Fraser's Mag.* XIV. 26 Earth..shall to the despot homage yield, All power and all dominion shall be his By thee, his feodary.

b. A subject, dependant, retainer, servant.

1620 FORD *Line of Life* Ded., The sacrifice is a thriftie loue ..and the Presentor a feodarie to such as are maisters..of their..owne affections. *a* **1656** USSHER *Ann.* VI. (1658) 459 The Senate was ready to do him all friendly offices, provided, that he became their feadary. **1871** R. ELLIS *Catullus* lxiii. 68 O am I to live the god's slave? feodary be to Cybele?

†**2.** An officer of the ancient Court of Wards (see quot. 1641). *Obs.*

1495 *Act 11 Hen. VII*, c. 32 Preamb., The Office of Feodarie in the Countie of Essex. **1540** *Act 32 Hen. VIII*, c. 46 Al surveiors and feodaries, that shalbe appoyncted by ..the said court. *c* **1630** RISDON *Surv. Devon* (1714) II. 77 It became Mr. Eveleigh's Feodary of his County. **1641** *Termes de la Ley* 160 Feodary is an Office in the Court of Wards, appointed to..receive all the rents of the Wards lands within his circuit, etc. **1736** CARTE *Ormonde* II. 249 The inquisitions post mortem taken by escheators and feodaries.

¶**3.** A confederate. (See FEDARIE.)

B. *adj.* Feudally subject. Const. *to.*

1577–87 HOLINSHED *Chron.* III. 1166/1 His kingdome made feodarie to Rome. **1648** MILTON *Observ. Art. Peace* Wks. 1738 I. 351 A whole Feudary Kingdom. **1651** G. W. tr. *Cowel's Inst.* 74 A Subject..himself is either mediately or immediately Feodary to the King. **1655** FULLER *Ch. Hist.* III. iv. §16 Iohn..being..not free, but feodary.

†'**feudatary**, *a.* and *sb.* *Obs.* Forms: (6 **feudotarie**, 7 **feodatary, -otary, feudataire, -arie, foeditary, -otarie**), 7–9 **feudatary**. [ad. med.L. *feudātāri-us*, f. *feudāt-* ppl. stem of *feudāre* to enfeoff, f. *feudum*: see FEUD *sb.*^{2} and -ARY. Cf. Fr. *feudataire.*]

A. *adj.* = FEUDATORY A. 1.

1614 SELDEN *Titles Hon.* 211 Such as are mongst vs feudatarie marquesses. **1635** PAGITT *Christianogr.* 65 Prusland..whose Duke is Feodotary to the Duke of Poland. **1674** *Ch. & Court of Rome* 19 Soveraign Princes are not here meant, but onely Feudatary.

B. *sb.*

1. = FEUDATORY B. 1.

1586 FERNE *Blaz. Gentrie* 141 There is also a King, and he a homager, or feudotarie to the estate and Maiestie of another King, as to his superior lord. **1614** SELDEN *Titles Hon.* 29 Now it acknowledges no superior. But so many as ..do, as feudataries to other Princes, are excluded. **1676** R. DIXON *Two Test.* VII. 489 The Unfaithful are the Devils Feudataries. **1708** J. CHAMBERLAYNE *St. Gt. Brit.* I. III. iii. (1743) 164 All the Lords of England..are feudataries to the King. **1818** HALLAM *Mid. Ages* (1872) I. 31 The perfect integrity of Louis..accustomed even the most jealous feudataries to look upon him as their judge.

2. = FEUDARY B. 2.

1607 in COWELL *Interpr.*,

feuda'torial, *a.* [f. next + -AL^{1}.] = FEUDAL.

1789 MRS. PIOZZI *Journ. France* I. 126 A settled system of feudatorial life.

feudatory ('fju:dətərɪ), *a.* and *sb.* Also 7 **feodatory.** [ad. L. type *feudātōri-us, f. med.L. *feudāre* to enfeoff, f. *feudum*: see FEUD *sb.*^{2} and -ORY.]

A. *adj.*

1. a. Of a person: Owing feudal allegiance to another; subject. **b.** Of a kingdom, etc.: Under the overlordship of an outside sovereign. Const. *to.*

a. 1592 BACON *Observ. Libel* Wks. 1753 I. 519 Any beneficiary or feodatory king. **1680** MORDEN *Geog. Rect.* (1685) 217 He is Feudatory to the Pope. **1796** MORSE *Amer. Geog.* II. 219 Low or feudatory nobility. **1828** TYTLER *Hist. Scot.* (1864) I. 9 The petty chiefs..had for a long period been feudatory to the Norwegian crown.

b. 1759 ROBERTSON *Hist. Scot.* (1802) I. I. 207 If the one crown had been considered..as feudatory to the other. **1884** *Manch. Exam.* 12 Sept. 5/1 The armies kept up by the feudatory states. **1890** *Daily News* 30 Dec. 5/6 Feudatory India.

2. Of or pertaining to vassals or retainers.

1861 LYTTON & FANE *Tannhäuser* 23 From..all the feudatory festivals, Men miss'd Tannhäuser.

B. *sb.*

1. One who holds his lands by feudal tenure; a feudal vassal.

1765 BLACKSTONE *Comm.* I. II. iv. 45 The feudatory could not aliene or dispose of his feud. **1814** SCOTT *Chivalry* (1874) 49 The barons or great feudatories of the crown. **1843** PRESCOTT *Mexico* IV. v. (1864) 236 The Indian Monarch had declared himself the feudatory of the Spanish. *transf.* **1825** BENTHAM *Indicat. Ld. Eldon* 10 Court, sitting as yet in public, cannot convert itself into a sinecurist: this accommodation it cannot afford to any but its feudatories.

2. A feud, fief, or fee; a dependent lordship.

1644 EVELYN *Diary* 22 Nov., The kingdomes of Naples and Sicily, pretended feudatorys to the Pope. **1680** MORDEN *Geog. Rect.* (1685) 110 Lorrain..the Duke whereof is a Prince of the Empire, and the Country was reckoned a Feodatory thereof. **1783** W. F. MARTYN *Geog. Mag.* I. 424 A feudatory of Thibet. **1873** LOWELL *Among my Bks.* Ser. II. 104 If he made the gift, the pope should hold it as a feudatory of the Empire.

feudee (fju:'di:). *rare*$^{-1}$. [f. FEUD *sb.*^{1} + -EE.] One to whom a feud has been granted; a tenant.

1875 J. FISHER *Landholding in England* IV. 38 The feudee only became tenant for life.

‖**feu de joie** (fø də ʒwa). Also pl. feux de joie. [Fr.; *lit.* 'fire of joy'.]

†**1.** A bonfire; also *fig.* *Obs.*

1609 BP. W. BARLOW *Answ. Nameless Cath.* 11 The Iesuites..would..haue been pleasant Spectators thereof, as at a Feu-de-ioy. **1771** MRS. GRIFFITH tr. *Viaud's Shipwreck* 159 To illuminate our feux de joye. [**1888** J. PAYN *Myst. Mirbridge* vii, The news that the Home Farm was on fire, which he announced as though it were a feu de joie.]

2. (See quot. 1867.)

1728 G. CARLETON *Mem. Eng. Officer* 35 Sunday the 17th Day of August, the Army was drawn out, as most others as well as my self apprehended, in order to a *feux de Joye*. **1801** *Sporting Mag.* XIX. 146 They had fired a feu-de-joye opposite their Major's house. **1867** SMYTH *Sailor's Word-bk.*, *Feu-de-joie*, a salute fired by musketry on occasions of public rejoicing, so that it should pass from man to man rapidly and steadily down one rank and up the other, giving one long continuous sound. **1958** P. KEMP *No Colours or Crest* viii. 174 A sudden fusillade of shots brought us to our feet..; it proved to be a wedding in the village, which the guests were celebrating in traditional style with a *feu-de-joie*.

3. *transf.* and *fig.*

1658 J. ROBINSON *Eudoxa* i. 10 Unexpected calamities will quench the feudejoy of a long fore-set gratulation. **1804** T. G. FESSENDEN *Orig. Poems* 43 Then his heart, with rapture dancing, Kindled to a feu-de-joye. **1935** *Punch* 6 Nov. 526/1, I sent on as next turn the Mystery *Feu de Joie* [*sc.* a firework]. **1963** *Times Lit. Suppl.* 18 Jan. 44/2 But the book remains a *feu de joie*.

†**feudigrapher.** *Obs.* [f. med.L. *feudum* (see FEUD *sb.*^{2}) + -GRAPH + -ER^{1}.] (See quot. 1688.)

1610 W. FOLKINGHAM *Art of Survey* To Rdr. 3 It behoues an honest and faithfull Feudigrapher..to approue himselfe an intelligent and diligent Improuer. **1688** R. HOLME *Armoury* III. 138/2 Feudigrapher is a Surveyor of Farmes and Freehold Lands.

feudist ('fju:dɪst). Also 7 **feodist, pheudist.** [f. FEUD *sb.*^{2} + -IST. Cf. F. *feudiste.*]

1. A writer or authority on feuds, one versed in feudal law. Also *attrib.*

1607 COWELL *Interpr.*, *Fealtie*, This oath..is vsed among the feudists. **1610** W. FOLKINGHAM *Art of Survey* III. ii. 67 Many Feudists doe holde that Feudatarius hath not an entire property in his Fee. **1639** SPELMAN *Feuds & Tenures* xxiii. 37 The Feodists therefore call them *Caduca*. *a* **1682** SIR T. BROWNE *Tracts* viii. (1684) 150 The Feudist term *Ligeus a Ligando*. **1767** BLACKSTONE *Comm.* II. 50 The oath of fealty, which made in the sense of the feudists every man that took it a tenant or vassal. **1845** STEPHEN *Laws Eng.* I. 185 *Allodium*, the name by which the feudists abroad distinguished such estates of the subject as were not holden of any superior.

†**2. a.** The holder of a feud or estate. **b.** One living under the feudal system. *Obs.*

1610 W. FOLKINGHAM *Art of Survey* IV. i. 80 All..Rents, Seruices, Issues, and profits accrewing and renewing to the Feudist or Possident. **1767** BLACKSTONE *Comm.* II. xiv. 215 The Greeks, the Romans..and even originally the feudists, divided the lands equally.

3. A person who has a feud with another. *U.S.*

1901 *Munsey's Mag.* XXV. 614/1 To speak of his feud to a feudist is a serious breach of the mountain etiquette. **1909** 'O. HENRY' *Roads of Destiny* viii. 130 The punchers from that ranch were more relentless and vengeful than Kentucky feudists. **1922** *Daily Mail* 13 Dec. 9 Neighbours, formerly the best of friends, are now virtually feudists. **1927** A. NEVINS *Emergence Mod. America* 252 A gang of horse thieves and outlaws; moonshiners, hunters and feudists. **1948** *Sat. Even. Post* 16 Oct. 38/1 Indian fighters, trail drivers, fence cutters, feudists, monumental liars.

†**feu'distical**, *a.* *Obs. rare.* [f. prec. + -IC + -AL^{1}.] = FEUDAL.

a **1618** RALEIGH in Gutch *Coll. Cur.* I. 72 The civil, or feudistical laws.

feu-farm ('fju:fa:m). *Sc. Law.* [ad. OF. *feuferme*: see FEE-FARM.]

1. That kind of tenure by which land is held of a superior on payment of a certain yearly rent. Also, *to hold, let, set in feu-farm.* Cf. FEE-FARM 1.

14.. *Burgh Laws* xcv. (*Sc. Stat.* I), Of landys lattin till feuferme in burgh. **1457** *Sc. Acts Jas. II* (1597) §72 Vpon setting of few-ferme of his awin land. **1473–4** *Ld. Treas. Acc. Scot.* I. 3 Componit for the fewferme of Johne of Sollaris for the grene ȝardis besyde Strivueline, composicio xx li. **1564** *Sc. Acts Q. Mary* (1597) §88 Confirmation to be obteined vpon infeftmentes of few-ferme of the Kirk-landes. **1597** *Sc. Acts Jas. VI* §246 Ony vassall or fewar, haldand landes in few-ferme. *a* **1768** ERSKINE *Instit. Sc. Law* (1773) I. 209 A grant of lands holden in feu-farm. **1872** E. W. ROBERTSON *Hist. Ess.* 138 It was not allowable..for the tenants in 'Ward and Blench' to sublet their lands in feu-farm.

2. The annual duty or rent paid to a superior by his vassal for tenure of lands.

1582–8 *Hist. Jas. VI* (1804) 224 The rentis, few fermes, and mealls of the lands of Pendreith.

'**feu-farmer.** *Sc. Law.* [ad. OF. *feufermier*: see FEE-FARMER.] = FEE-FARMER.

1609 SKENE *Reg. Maj.* 32 The fewfermer thereafter constrained by necessitie, is compelled to sell the lands.

‖**feu follet** (fø fɔlɛ). [Fr., lit. 'frolicsome fire'.] Ignis fatuus.

1832 J. S. MILL *Let.* 17 July (1910) I. 32 It is possible our light may be nothing but a *feu follet*. **1967** *Times* 7 Sept. 7/5 He [*sc.* Flaubert] pursued what one must surely regard as the *feu follet* of 'pure form'.

feuge, obs. form of FUGUE. *Mus.*

‖**feuillage.** *Obs. rare.* [F. *feuillage*, f. *feuille*: see FEUILLE.] Foliage.

1714 JERVAS *Let. to Pope* 20 Aug. in *Pope's Lett.* (1737) 107, I..inclose the out-line..that you may determine whether you would have it..reduced to make room for feuillage or laurel round the oval. **1858** SIMMONDS *Dict. Trade*, *Feuillage* (French), foliage; a row of leaves, branched-work.

‖**feuillantine.** *Obs.* [F.; prob. from the *Feuillantines*, a congregation of nuns.] (See quot.)

1706 PHILLIPS (ed. Kersey), *Feuillantins*..small Tarts.. filled with Sweat-meats. **1725** BRADLEY *Fam. Dict.* s.v. *Tarts*, It may be garnish'd with Fevillantines or small Fleurons of all sorts of Fruits.

feuille (fœj). [a. F. *feuille* leaf.] †**a.** A thin plate; a leaf (*obs.*). **b.** The name of a colour: see quot.

1662 PETTY *Taxes* 35 If bullion be..beaten into feuilles. **1883** *Cassell's Fam. Mag.* Nov. 755/2 A very light green, known as Feuille.

‖**feuillemorte** (fœjmɔrt), *a.* More commonly in anglicized and corrupted forms: see FILEMOT. [Fr.; *lit.* 'dead leaf'.] Of the colour of a dead or faded leaf, brown or yellowish brown.

1690 LOCKE *Hum. Und.* III. xi. (ed. 3) 294 To make a Country-man understand what Feuillemorte Colour signifies. **1876** OUIDA *Winter City* ii. 22 She had feuille morte velvet slashed with the palest of ambers.

b. *Comb.*, as *feuillemorte-coloured* adj.

1840 H. AINSWORTH *Tower of London* ix, An ample feuillemorte coloured cloak.

†**feuillet**^{1}. *Obs.* Also 8 **feuillette.** [a. F. *feuillette*:—med.L. *folietta* a measure of wine.] A half-hogshead.

1711 *Lond. Gaz.* No. 4989/3, 44 Feuillettes, or half-hogsheads of Burgundy. **1794** BURKE *Corr.* (1844) IV. 243 Four feuillets of the best Burgundy.

‖**feuillet**^{2} (fœjɛ). *Diamond-cutting.* [F. *feuillet*, dim. of *feuille* (see FEUILLE).] (See quot.)

1874 KNIGHT *Dict. Mech.*, *Feuillets*..the projecting points of the triangular facets in a rose-cut diamond, whose bases join those of the triangles of the central pyramid.

feuilleton (fœjətɔ̃). [a. F. *feuilleton*, f. *feuillet*, dim. of *feuille* leaf.] In French newspapers (or others in which the French custom is followed), a portion of one or more pages (at the bottom) marked off from the rest of the page by a rule,

and appropriated to light literature, criticism, etc.; an article or work printed in the feuilleton.

1845 *Athenæum* 11 Jan. 42 The tendency of the newspaper feuilleton, in France, to absorb the entire literature of the day. **1861** *Sat. Rev.* 16 Dec. 621 The *Causeries de Quinzaine* have the usual merits of French feuilletons. **1863** *Macm. Mag.* Mar. 394 Most of the journals [Russian] are furnished with a *feuilleton* in the shape of a romance. **1887** *Pall Mall G.* 18 July 2/2 The *Siècle* published feuilletons daily on literature, history, fine art, science, and fiction. **1892** *Nation* 16 June 452/3 He writes a feuilleton on current musical topics for the Vienna *Neue Freie Presse*.

Hence **'feuilletonism**, aptitude for writing feuilletons; **'feuilletonist**, a writer of feuilletons; also ‖**feuilletoniste** (-ist); **feuilleto'nistic** *a.*, characteristic of or suitable for a feuilletonist.

1840 *Blackw. Mag.* XLVIII. 524 The number of young *feuilletonists*.. is now very considerable in France. **1843** *Ibid.* LIV. 674 The *feuilletonists*, or short story-tellers. **1876** *Times* 15 May 5/3 The extremest type of eccentricity imagined of Englishmen by French *feuilletonistes*. **1885** C. Lowe *Bismarck* II. x. 42 The Count.. worried his Chief with what the latter called 'feuilletonistic' remarks about the difficulties of his social.. position in Paris. **1888** Tyrrell in *Fortn. Rev.* Jan. 59 If men refrained from dignifying.. feuilletonism.. with the name of scholarship. **1916** A. Huxley *Let.* 29 Sept. (1969) 114 They wish to provide the industrious feuilletoniste with the materials for his hideous business. **1960** Auden *Homage to Clio* 47 Autobiographers are just like other historians: some are Whigs, some Tories, .. some Feuilletonistes, etc.

feuing ('fju:ɪŋ), *vbl. sb. Sc.* The action of feu *v.*

1596 in J. Melville *Diary* (1842) 336 Fewing of the saids Teinds,.. and fewing of the saids gleibs. **1844** J. Ballantine *Miller of Deanhaugh* xx. 306 His brother, Lawyer Cauldwell, and he have been speculating largely in feuing and building. **1893** Duke of Argyll *Unseen Found. Soc.* xvii. 536 No exclusive or preferential right of leasing, or of purchasing, or of feuing, had ever been conceded to local bodies. **1909** *Westm. Gaz.* 7 Aug. 2/1 The Scottish feuing method. **1937** E. Percy *John Knox* xiii. 219 Scotland evolved.. the 'feuing' of land to hereditary tenants.. In the hands of the Church it became the rake's road to dilapidation.

Feulgen ('fɔɪlgən). *Cytology.* The name of R. J. *Feulgen* (1884–1955), German biochemist, used attrib. or occas. in the possessive to denote the methods and materials he used, and the reaction involved, in preferentially staining cell organelles containing DNA, esp. chromosomes; so *Feulgen reaction, solution, stain* (also as vb.), *test*, etc. Also in related phrases as *Feulgen-positive, -negative*, respectively staining, or not staining, by his technique. Also *absol.*

1928 R. J. Ludford in *Proc. R. Soc.* B. CII. 402 By Feulgen reaction no chromatin can be detected in either the oxyphil or basophil staining nucleoli. **1929** McClung & Heuser in C. E. McClung *Handbk. Microscop. Techn.* xi. 483 (*heading*) Feulgen's Stain.. Recently Feulgen has presented a method which he considers capable of indicating chromatin by a specific reaction. **1941** *Bot. Rev.* VII. 442 A long list of Feulgen tests.. shows that there are many plant nuclei that give a negative reaction, as well as those that are positive. *Ibid.* 443 There are no indications what the chromosome nucleic acids may be in the plants that react Feulgen-negative. **1952** J. D. White in G. H. Bourne *Cytol. & Cell Physiol.* (ed. 2) v. 192 It has been generally believed that the Feulgen reaction (staining with leuco-basic fuchsin after hydrolysis) is specific for desoxyribose nucleic acid. **1954** *Nature* 1 May 828/2 In mature pollen grains.. the generative nucleus is Feulgen-positive while the vegetative nucleus gives a negative reaction. **1956** *Nature* 11 Feb. 272/1 Weakly Feulgen-staining segments. **1965** A. K. & A. Sharma *Chromosome Techniques* v. 116 Feulgen solution or, more precisely, fuchsin sulphurous acid is prepared from the dye, basic fuchsin. **1968** *Brit. Med. Bull.* XXIV. 260/2 Specimens stained with dyes such as orcein and Feulgen.

†**feute, fewte.** *Obs.* Forms: 4 feute, (foute, fuyt), 5 feaute, fewte, (fute). [ad. OF. *fuite* 'voies du cerf qui fuit' (Littré), f. *fuir*:—L. *fugĕre* to flee. Cf. fewe, fuse.] The traces or track (of an animal).

c **1340** *Gaw. & Gr. Knt.* 1425 Þe howndez.. fellen as fast to þe fuyt. *c* **1350** *Will. Palerne* 33 Þe.. hound.. Feld foute of þe child. *Ibid.* 2189 Whan þe houndes hadde feute of þe hende best. *c* **1440** *Promp. Parv.* 159 Fewte, *vestigium*. **1470–85** Malory *Arthur* vi. xiv, He saw a black brachet sekyng.. as it had ben in the feaute of an hurt dere.

feuter, feutered, obs. forms of feature, -ed.

feuter, feuterer: see fewt-.

fever ('fi:və(r)), *sb.*[1] Forms: 1 féfer, -or, 2 feofer, (3 fefre), 3–5 fevere, (4 feavor), 4–5 fevre, fyver(e, 5 febre, (fevire, -oure, fewer), 6–8 feaver, 7 feavour, (feevor, 7–8 fevour), 3– fever. [OE. *féfor* str. masc., ad. L. *febris* fem., whence OF. *fievre* (mod.F. *fièvre*), Pr., Pg. *febre*, Sp. *fiebre*, It. *febbre*; adopted independently in the Teut. langs.; OHG. *fiebar* (MHG. *vieber*, mod.G. *fieber*) neut., Sw. *feber*, Da. *fever* (not in Du.).

The etymology of *febris* is obscure. Brugmann (*Grundriss* II. 92) regards it as a reduplicate formation (:—pre-Latin **bhe-bhr-*) on the root which appears in Skr. *bhur-* to be restless.]

1. *Pathol.* **a.** A morbid condition of the system, characterized by undue elevation of the temperature, and excessive change and destruction of the tissues; an instance of this. **b.** The generic name of a group of diseases agreeing in the above general characteristics, each of which is specially designated by some distinctive appellation, as *intermittent, puerperal, scarlet, typhoid, yellow*, etc. *fever*, for which see under the defining word.

c **1000** *Sax. Leechd.* I. 148 Gif him fefer derige. *c* **1000** *Ags. Gosp.* Matt. viii. 15, & he æthran hyre hand, & se fefor [*c* **1160** *Hatton G.* feofer] hiȝ forlet. *a* **1225** *Ancr. R.* 112 Þet was oðe fefre. *a* **1300** *Cursor M.* 20963 (Cott.) Man þat in feuer was vnfer. **1387** Trevisa *Higden* (Rolls) I. 333 Men of þat lond haueþ no feuere. *a* **1400–50** *Alexander* 2546 Þat he was fallen in a feuire. **1494** Fabyan *Chron.* vi. clxv. 160 The Emperoure Charlys remouyd to the Cytie of Mantue, where he was grudgyd with a feuoure. **1547** Boorde *Brev. Health* cxxxv. (1557) 49 b, A Feuer is an vnnaturall heate grounded in the hearte and lyuer. **1598** B. Jonson *Ev. Man in Hum.* ii. iii, I will once more striue.. to.. shake the feaver off. **1614** Markham *Cheap Husb.* i. viii. (1668) 48 Feavers of all sorts as the Quotidian [etc.]. **1678** *Hatton Corr.* (1878) 169 Have a care of coming neare those that have the feavour. **1781** Gibbon *Decl. & F.* II. 134 *foot-n.*, She.. died of a fever on the road. **1840** Dickens *Barn. Rudge* v, The fever has left him. **1856** Emerson *Eng. Traits, Char.* Wks. (Bohn) II. 57 His [an Englishman's] hilarity is like an attack of fever.

†**c.** *fever ague* [ad. OF. *fievre ague*, lit. 'acute fever']: = ague (*obs.*). *fever lent* [ad. OF. *fievre lente*]: a slow fever (*obs.*). *fever and ague* = malaria. (*obs.* exc. *U.S.*)

1338 R. Brunne *Chron.* (Rolls) 15729 Þe ffeuere agu ful sore hym hatte. **1398** Trevisa *Barth. De P.R.* xvii. cxxxvi. (1495) 692 Oleum rosaceum helpyth ayenst.. fyre agu. *c* **1400** in *Rel. Ant.* I. 54 For the fever lente: quha that has the fever agu, that men calles lente evell, if the sekeman heved werkes that he may noght slepp, tak [etc.]. *c* **1440** *Promp. Parv.* 163 *Fyvere agu*, querquera. **1658** J. Hull *Diaries* Aug. (1857) 184 Much sickness in the southern colonies,—fevers and agues, of which many died. **1676** S. Sewall *Diary* (1878) I. 22 Told.. of the death of Goodman Titcomb.. after about a fort-night sickness of the Fever and Ague. **1743** in Ellis *Mod. Husb.* II. i. 46, I have lately been very ill of a Fever and Ague. **1846** *Knickerbocker* XXVII. 55 Fever-and-ague riots among the ditches and green ponds. *a* **1874** R. Glisan *Jrnl. Army Life* (1874) xxxi. 444 They would be prostrated with the various forms of malarious fever—such as fever and ague. **1904** Capt. R. E. Lee *Recoll. & Lett. Gen. R. E. Lee* xx. 364 To keep him free from fever-and-ague, my brother dosed him freely with cholagogue.

d. *artificial fever*: a fever which is induced, for therapeutic reasons.

1924 *Jrnl. Mental Sci.* LXX. 88 Malaria therapy in general paralysis is justified;.. the artificial fever induced is easily, promptly and effectively controlled. **1935** *Discovery* Aug. 226/1 For the general production of artificial fever such longer wave-lengths may be used.

†**2.** In *pl.* with singular sense. *Obs.*

c **1000** *Ags. Gosp.* Luke iv. 38 Ða wæs simones sweȝer ȝeswenced on mycelum feferum [*c* **1160** *Hatton G.* feofren]. **1382** Wyclif *Matt.* viii. 14 He say his wyues moder liggynge and shakun with feueris. *c* **1450** *St. Cuthbert* (Surtees) 5583 Þar was a clerk.. þat þe feuers had. **1491** Caxton *Vitas Patr.* (W. de W. 1495) i. xl. 60 a/1 She hadde the febres or asces. *a* **1605** Montgomerie *Flyting* 314 The feavers, the fearcie, with the speinȝie flees.

3. A state of intense nervous excitement, agitation, heat; an instance of this.

1586 T. B. *La Primaud. Fr. Acad.* i. 666 There are.. two causes intermingled, which breede this franticke feaver of our France. **1606** Shaks. *Tr. & Cr.* i. iii. 133 An enuious Feauer Of pale and bloodlesse Emulation. **1649** Jer. Taylor *Gt. Exemp.* ii. Ad Ser. xii. 57 The spirits leap out from their cells of austerity and sobriety, and are warmed into feavers and wildnesses. **1737** Pope *Hor. Epist.* i. i. 58 This Fever of the soul. **1779** Mad. D'Arblay *Diary* Feb., Both she and Miss S. S. were in fevers.. from apprehension. **1814** Sir R. Wilson *Diary* II. 353 The fever excited by the news from France has not yet been allayed. **1842** J. H. Newman *Par. Serm.* (ed. 2) V. viii. 120 A mode of life free from.. fever of mind. **1873** Black *Pr. Thule* v. 75 A fever of anticipation.. seemed to stir in his blood. **1883** E. Pennell-Elmhirst *Cream Leicestersh.* 424 A fine fox set the field in a fever.

4. *attrib.* and *Comb.* **a.** simple attrib., as *fever-bale, -dream, -fire, -fit, -glow, -grass, -hospital, -life, -nest, -patient, -pitch, -spasm, -thirst, -vomit, -ward*; *fever-like* adj. and adv. **b.** objective, as *fever-cooling, -destroying* adjs. **c.** instrumental, as *fever-cracking, -haunted, -maddened, -parched, -shaken, -sick, -smitten, -stricken, -troubled, -weakened* adjs.

1844 Mrs. Browning *Bertha* ix, I lose that *fever-bale And my thoughts grow calm again. **1727–46** Thomson *Summer* 668 The spreading tamarind.. shakes.. its *fever-cooling fruit. **1861** Mrs. Norton *Lady La G.* iv. 331 Nor fresh cooling drinks To woo the *fever-cracking lip. **1884** *Syd. Soc. Lex.*, **Fever-destroying tree*, the *Eucalyptus globulus*. **1834** Mrs. Hemans *Eng. Martyrs* i. 2 The cavern of the prisoner's *fever-dream. **1898** T. Watts-Dunton *Aylwin* xii. 329 The *fever-fires in my brain. **1681** Temple *Mem.* iii. Wks. 1731 I. 343 Being free of any Return of his *Fever Fits. **1830** Scott *Demonol.* i. 39 A sudden and temporary fever-fit. **1842** Emerson *Lect., Transcendentalist* Wks. (Bohn) II. 289, I wish to exchange.. this *fever-glow for a benign climate. **1893** C. Sullivan *Jamaica Cookery Bk.* 112 *Fever grass is a fragrant smelling lemony grass; it is excellent in fever just boiled and sweetened. **1930** R. Macaulay *Staying with Relations* ix. 127 The fever grass, that one eats to cure malaria. **1864** Kingsley *Rom. & Teut.* i. (1875) 13 Nothing was left save *fever-haunted plains. **1822** J. M. Good *Study Med.* II. 194 The inestimable advantage of such establishments as *Fever Houses or Infirmaries in all populous towns,.. superintended by the active humanity and established talents which are so conspicuous in the Fever Hospital of this metropolis. **1964** G. L. Cohen *What's Wrong with Hospitals?* iv. 73 Laymen still shrink from entering a 'fever hospital': the very name evokes plague and pox. **1877** Gen. Gordon in *Pall Mall G.* 4 Mar. (1884) 11/1 It is a *fever life I lead. *a* **1577** Gascoigne *Wks.* (1587) 5 And *feverlike I feede my fancie still With such repast as most empaires my health. **1612** Drayton *Poly-olb.* vii. Argt., When the Higre takes her, How fever-like the sickness shakes her. **1884** *Syd. Soc. Lex.*, **Fever-nests*, localities where.. fever is generated. **1802** *Med. Jrnl.* VIII. 562 The reception of *fever patients. **1683** Chalkhill *Thealma & Cl.* 26 Like a distempered Body *Fever-shaken. **1599** Peele *David & Bethsabe* Wks. (Rtldg.) 466/1 Lie down upon thy bed Feigning thee *fever-sick and ill-at-ease. **1884** *Syd. Soc. Lex.*, *Feversick*. **1884** *Pall Mall G.* 23 Feb. 4 Vera Cruz, that.. *fever-smitten port. **1863** W. Phillips *Speeches* vi. 152 Of which revolution is the *fever-spasm. **1818** Shelley *Marenghi* viii, The *fever-stricken serf. *a* **1835** Mrs. Hemans *Ancestral Song* 77 All the *fever-thirst is still'd. **1836** J. H. Newman in *Lyra Apost.* (1849) 87 That *fever-troubled state. **1671** Salmon *Syn. Med.* iii. lxxxii. 713 If there be *Feaver vomit. **1802** *Med. Jrnl.* VIII. 562 By converting these *fever-wards.. to the purpose of a general house of recovery for all infectious fever which might occur in the town. **1597** Shaks. *2 Hen. IV*, i. i. 140 The Wretch, whose *Feauer-weakned ioynts, Like strengthlesse Hindges, buckle vnder life. **1904** *Daily Chron.* 29 Dec. 4/4 Fever-parched lips. **1962** L. Deighton *Ipcress File* xxxi. 200 The tape recordings.. must have worked everyone up to fever pitch.

5. Special comb.: **fever-bark**, bark useful in cases of fever; **fever-blister** (see quot.); **fever-bush** (see quot. 1884); **fever-chart**, a chart recording the course of fever in a patient; also *fig.*; **fever-fly**, the *Dilophus vulgaris*; **fever-heat**, the high temperature of the body in fever (on some thermometers marked at 112° F.), also *fig.*; †**fever-hectic**, = *hectic fever* (see hectic); **fever-nut**, the seeds of *Cæsalpina Bonducella*; **fever-powder**, a remedy for fever; **fever-root** (see quot. 1884), also *fever and ague root*; **fever-sore** (see quot.); **fever therapy**, the treatment of disease by induced fever (see 1 d); **fever-trap**, a place where one is liable to be caught by fever; **fever-tree, -twig** (see quots.); **fever-weed**, a plant of the genus *Eryngium*; **fever-wood** (see quot.); **fever-wort**, (*a*) (see quot.); (*b*) a plant of the genus *Eupatorium* (Worc.). Also fever-lurden.

1659 *Fever bark [see Jesuit *sb.* 4 c]. **1830** Lindley *Nat. Syst. Bot.* 205 A kind of fever bark is obtained.. from Rondeletia febrifuga. **1920** H. G. Greenish *Text-bk. Mat. Med.* (ed. 3) vii. 268 The latter bark [of *Alstonia constricta*] is also known as Australian fever bark. **1884** *Syd. Soc. Lex.*, **Fever blister*, the herpes of the lips which occurs frequently in feverish or catarrhal disturbances of the body. **1792** J. Belknap *Hist. New-Hampsh.* III. 97 The Spice-wood (*Laurus benzoin*) or.. *Feverbush, is.. common in New-Hampshire. **1884** *Syd. Soc. Lex.*, *Feverbush*, the *Benzoin odoriferum* and also the *Prinos verticillatus*. **1940** T. S. Eliot *East Coker* iv. 12 The sharp compassion of the healer's art Resolving the enigma of the *fever chart. **1958** *Spectator* 17 Jan. 71/3 A sort of dossier or fever-chart of the controversy which raged intermittently.. for several months. **1889** Miss E. A. Ormerod *Injurious Insects* (1890) 129 *Fever Fly. **1838** Prescott *Ferd. & Is.* ii. vi. (1849) II. 367 Ximenes whose zeal had mounted up to *fever heat.. was not to be cooled by any opposition. **1889** Jessopp *Coming of Friars* vii. 309 The feeling of the country was approaching fever heat. **1607** Topsell *Serpents* (1653) 725 For *Fever-hecticks they prepare them thus. **1795** R. Anderson *Life Johnson* 14 He had for his school-fellows Dr. James, inventor of the *fever-powder, Mr. Lowe, [etc.]. **1853** Dunglison *Med. Dict.* (ed. 9), **Fever-root*. **1884** *Syd. Soc. Lex.*, *Fever-root*, the *Pterospora andromedea*: also the *Triosteum perfoliatum*. **1676** T. Glover in *Phil. Trans.* XI. 630 The English call it the *Fever and Ague-root. **1860** Worcester, **Fever-sore*, the common name of a species of caries or necrosis. **1924** *Jrnl. Mental Sci.* LXX. 89 Three cases were of undoubted general paralysis which had as yet not been subjected to any form of *fever therapy. **1944** E. C. Pearce *Fevers & Fever Nursing* (ed. 6) xvii. 294 Fever therapy is employed in the later stages of chronic syphilis. **1891** C. Creighton *Hist. Epidemics* 589 More recent visitors.. have remarked upon their towns and villages as *fever-traps. **1876** *Forest & Stream* 13 July 375/3 The large tribe of the Eucalyptus (honey or *fever trees). **1884** *Syd. Soc. Lex.*, *Fever tree*, the *Pinckneya pubens*. *Ibid.*, **Fever twig*, the *Celastrus scandens*. **1855** H. Clarke *Dict.*, **Fever-weed*, an *eryngium*. **1884** *Syd. Soc. Lex.*, **Fever wood*, the *Benzoin odoriferum*. **1611** Cotgr., *Sacotin*, *feauerwort. **1836** Loudon *Encycl. Plants* 170 *Triosteum*, feverwort.

†**'fever**, *sb.*[2] *Obs.*[−1] [ad. OF. *fevere, fevre, febvre, fabre* = Pr. *fabre*, It. *fabbro*, OSp. *fabro*:—L. *fabr-um, faber*.] A smith.

1415 *York Myst.* Introd. 22 Feuers, Couureours [etc.].

fever ('fi:və(r)), *v.* [f. fever *sb.*[1]]

1. *trans.* To put or throw into a fever; *lit.* and *fig.* Also, † *to fever* (one) *into*.

1606 Shaks. *Ant. & Cl.* iii. xiii. 138 The white hand of a Lady Feauer thee. **1624** Heywood *Gunaik.* ix. 430 His words.. feavered her all over. **1689** Rycaut *Hist. Turks* II. 189 His passion feavered him into a desperate sickness. **1748** Thomson *Cast. Indol.* ii. 265 To his licentious wish each must be blest, With joy be fevered. **1820** Keats *Isabel* vi, The ruddy tide.. Fever'd his high conceit of such a bride. *a* **1853** Robertson *Serm.* Ser. iii. xx. 262 A heart which sin has fevered. **1862** T. A. Trollope *Marietta* I. xvi, Tending.. to wear out and fever her body.

2. *intr.* To become feverish, to be seized with a fever. Also (*nonce-use*) of the eyes, *to fever out*: to start out with fever or excitement.

1754-64 SMELLIE *Midwif.* III. 380 She fevered and died. **1791** NEWTE *Tour Eng. & Scotl.* 171 He never fevered with the fracture, and very soon recovered. **1820** KEATS *Hyperion* I. 138 This passion..made..His eyes to fever out, his voice to cease. **1827** SCOTT *Jrnl.* 5 Jan., I waked..for five or six hours I think, then fevered a little.

fig. **1814** BYRON *Lara* I. xxvi, A hectic tint of secret care That for a burning moment fever'd there. **1818** BYRON *Ch. Har.* IV. cxxii, Of its own beauty is the mind diseased, And fevers into false creation. **1834** DISRAELI *Rev. Epick* III. vii, That eager blood That in old days..So oft hath fevered o'er victorious dreams.

Hence **ˈfevering** *ppl. a.*

1794 J. WILLIAMS *Crying Ep.* 70 That high day of fevering youth. **1892** W. B. SCOTT *Autob.* I. ix. 98 At this moment of fevering unrest.

†ˈfeverable, *a. Obs.*$^{-1}$ [f. FEVER *sb.* or *v.* + -ABLE.] Affecting with fever; fever-like.

1568 G. SKEYNE *Descr. Pest* Aiij, Ane feuerable infectioun, maist cruelle.

fevered (ˈfiːvəd), *ppl. a.* [f. as prec. + -ED.] **a.** Of the body: Affected with fever, extremely heated. **b.** Of the mind: Excited, over-wrought.

1628 FELTHAM *Resolves* II. lxxxiv. 241 A feavered Body; a boyling Stomacke. *a* **1653** G. DANIEL *Idyll* ii. 45 For Feavered Minds, who..find noe Ease. **1697** DRYDEN *Virg. Æneid* IV, Her blood all fever'd. **1801** SOUTHEY *Thalaba* V. i, He lifted his fever'd face to heaven. **1843** J. MARTINEAU *Chr. Life* (1867) 148 A gale from heaven fanned his fevered brow. **1850** MRS. JAMESON *Leg. Monast. Ord.* (1863) 228 Her attempt to guide or crush the..fevered spirits of the time. **1865** MRS. CARLYLE *Lett.* III. 283 It is such a pity to arrive at home entirely fevered.

feverel, var. of FEBRUARY.

†ˈfeveress. *Obs.*$^{-1}$ [f. FEVER *sb.* + -ESS^{2}.] Feverishness; fever.

1398 TREVISA *Barth. De P.R.* XVII. cxvi. (1495) 680 In them is moche superfluyte of watry moysture..that is matere of longe durynge feueresse.

feveret (ˈfiːvərɪt). Also 8 **feverette.** [f. as prec. + -ET^{1}.] A slight fever.

1712 THORESBY *Diary* II. 149 This new distemper..by physicians called a Feveret. **1769** *St. James' Chron.* 3-5 Aug. 4/2 You will certainly throw yourself into a violent Fever, or at least a Feveret. **1796** C. BURNEY *Mem. Metastasio* II. 129 Your most welcome letter found me struggling with a catarrh and feverette. **1863** T. THOMPSON *Ann. Influenza* 59 Throughout the whole course of this feveret, the patients expectorate largely.

fig. **1836** T. HOOK *G. Gurney* II. 211 They kept me in a perpetual feveret.

feverfew (ˈfiːvəfjuː, ˈfɛv-). Forms: 1 **féferfuȝe, -fuȝie,** 5 **fevyrfue,** 6 **-fewe, fewerfew,** 7 **feverfue, feaverfew,** *Sc.* **feverfoylie,** 5- **feverfew.** See also FEATHERFEW, FETTERFOE. [OE. *féferfuȝe, -fuȝie,* ad. late L. *febrifuga,* L. *febrifugia,* f. L. *febri-* (*febris*) fever + *fug-āre* to drive away.

The mod. form cannot directly descend from the OE.; its source is the AF. **fevrefue* (*fewerfue c* 1265 in Wr.-Wülck. 556), which normally represents the Lat. Under FEATHERFEW (a corruption suggested by the 'feather-like' appearance of the leaves) will be found forms in *-foy* (:—OE. *-fuȝie*), which in some dialects has been corrupted into *-foil.* The name *feather-foil* has by botanical writers been applied to another 'feather-leaved' plant: see FEATHER *sb.* 19.]

a. The plant *Pyrethrum Parthenium.* **b.** *dial.* The *Erythræa Centaurium.*

c **1000** ÆLFRIC *Gloss.* in Wr.-Wülcker 134 *Febrefugia*.. feferfuge. *c* **1000** *Sax. Leechd.* I. 134 Curmelle feferfuge. *c* **1425** *Eng. Voc.* in Wr.-Wülcker 645 *Hec febrifuga,* fevyrfew. **1562** TURNER *Herbal* II. 79 b, The new writers hold.. that feuerfew is better for weomen. **1579** LANGHAM *Gard. Health* (1633) 234 Feuerfue comforteth the stomacke, and is good for the feuer quotidian. **1673** WEDDERBURN *Voc.* 18 (Jam.) *Matricaria,* feverfoylie. **1741** *Compl. Fam. Piece* I. iv. 258 Feverfew, Catmint, Pennyroyal, each 3 Handfuls. **1861** MISS PRATT *Flower. Pl.* III. 314 Common Fever-few.

feverish (ˈfiːvərɪʃ), *a.* [f. FEVER *sb.* + -ISH.] **1. a.** Having the symptoms constituting fever (see FEVER *sb.* 1 a). **†b.** Ill of a fever (*obs.*).

1647 COWLEY *Mistress, Cure* ii, Drink which feaverish men desire. **1680** BURNET *Rochester* 70 A Feaverish Man cannot judge of Tasts. **1701** PENN in *Pa. Hist. Soc. Mem.* IX. 47, [I] have had a restless, feverish night. **1779** JOHNSON *Life Ascham* Wks. IV. 635 He was for some years hectically feverish. **1796** JANE AUSTEN *Sense & Sens.* (1849) 228 Though heavy and feverish..a good night's rest was to cure her.

2. *fig.* Excited, fitful, restless, now hot now cold.

1634 MILTON *Comus* 8 Men..Strive to keep up a frail and feverish being. **1670** BAXTER *Cure Ch. Div.* 174 To turn the native heat of Religion into a feavourish outside zeal about words. **1752** HUME *Ess. & Treat.* (1777) I. 165 This feverish uncertainty..in Human conduct seems unavoidable. **1855** MACAULAY *Hist. Eng.* III. 228 A few hours of feverish joy were followed by weeks of misery.

3. †a. Pertaining to fever. ***feverish matter***: the impurity in the blood supposed to give rise to fever (*obs.*). **b.** Of the nature of fever; resembling fever or its symptoms.

1398 TREVISA *Barth. De P.R.* VII. xliii. (1495) 256 Rysynge and stondynge of heere..comith in the bodi of feuerysshe matere. **1651** BIGGS *New Disp.* ¶230 The feavorish matter doth not swim in the blood. **1680** WOOD *Life* (Oxf. Hist. Soc.) II. 497 This month..is an odde feaverish sickness dominant. **1695** BLACKMORE *Pr. Arth.* I. 575 Her Feaverish Thirst drinks down a Sea of Blood. **1732** ARBUTHNOT *Rules of Diet* 324 The Regimen..in the Article of Feverish Rigors. **1802** *Med. Jrnl.* VIII. 428 Its effects in abating the feverish exacerbations are so considerable. **1810** SCOTT *Lady of L.* II. xxxii, In feverish flood, One instant rushed the throbbing blood.

4. Of climate, food, etc.: Apt to cause fever. Of a country: Infested by fever.

1669 NARBOROUGH *Jrnl.* in *Acc. Sev. Late Voy.* I. (1694) 14 A Fish larger than a Bonetto, but..feaverish Diet. **1803** W. TAYLOR in *Ann. Rev.* I. 315 The feverish shore of St. Domingo. **1879** SIR G. CAMPBELL *White & Black* 253 Tracts which are exceedingly feverish in summer. **1885** G. S. FORBES *Wild Life in Canara* 34 The climate of Soopah was occasionally very feverish for Hindoos.

feverishly (ˈfiːvərɪʃlɪ), *adv.* [f. prec. + -LY^{2}.] In a feverish manner: **†a.** *lit.* With the symptoms of fever (*obs.*). **b.** *fig.* As if under the influence of fever; excitedly, fitfully, nervously, restlessly.

1647 R. STAPYLTON *Juvenal* 227 If they..find..Gallita feaverishly inclin'd, They post up prayers. **1684** tr. *Bonet's Merc. Compit.* XVI. 575 The Blood fermenting Feverishly through excess of Sulphur. **1833** LAMB *Elia* (1860) 396 Feverishly looking for this night's repetition of the folly. **1852** MRS. STOWE *Uncle Tom's C.* xxi, He watched Eva feverishly day by day. **1893** *Daily News* 29 June 6/4 In spite of a slight rally the closing was feverishly weak.

feverishness (ˈfiːvərɪʃnɪs). [f. as prec. + -NESS.] The state or condition of being feverish; an instance of the same. *lit.* and *fig.*

1662 R. MATHEW *Unl. Alch.* §76. 97 It is to their great benefit, in taking off from them..feverishness. **1709** LD. SHAFTESBURY *Charact.* (1711) II. 129 Satiety..and Feverishness of Desire, attend those who passionately study Pleasure. **1764** ELIZ. CARTER *Let.* Jan. (1809) III. 237 Lord Lyttelton has a slight feverishness. **1860-1** FLO. NIGHTINGALE *Nursing* 55 Feverishness is generally supposed to be a symptom of fever—in nine cases out of ten it is a symptom of bedding.

ˈfeverite. *nonce-wd.* One who is ill of a fever.

1800 LAMB *Lett.* (1888) I. 143, I have..obtained two young hands to supply the loss of the feverites.

feverless (ˈfiːvəlɪs). [f. FEVER *sb.* + -LESS.] Without fever, devoid of heat.

1819 KEATS in W. M. Rossetti *Life* 161 Claret..fills one's mouth with a gushing freshness—then goes down cool and feverless.

†ˈfever-ˈlurden. [f. FEVER *sb.* + LURDAN (imitating medical names of fevers). Said to survive *dial.* as *fever-lurgan, -lurgy, -largie.*] The disease of laziness.

c **1500** *Blowbol's Test.* 75 in Hazl. *E.P.P.* I. 93, I trow he was infecte certeyn With the faitour, or the fever lordeyn. **1547** BOORDE *Brev. Health* cli. (1557) 55, I had almoste forgotten the feuer lurden, with the whiche manye..yonge persons bee sore infected nowe a dayes. **1636** HEYLIN *Sabbath* II. 149 They have a feaver-lurdane, and they cannot stirre. **1808** JAMIESON *Fever-largie,* expl. 'Two stomachs to eat, and none to work'; county unknown.

†ˈfeverly, *a. Obs.*$^{-1}$ [f. as prec. + -LY^{1}.] = FEVERISH 3.

1477 NORTON *Ord. Alch.* v. in Ashm. (1652) 62 Feaverly heate maketh no digestion. **1847** CRAIG *Feverly,* like a fever.

feverous (ˈfiːvərəs), *a.* [f. as prec. + -OUS.] **†1.** Ill of fever; affected by fever; = FEVERISH 1.

1398 TREVISA *Barth. De P.R.* XVII. xcix. (1495) 665 Swete pomegarnades easith..feuerous men. *c* **1400** *Lanfranc's Cirurg.* 222 It wole make a man yvel disposed & feverous. **1620** VENNER *Via Recta* ii. 24 They are lesse hurtfull, for such as are feuorous, then other wines are. **1796** COLERIDGE *Dest. Nations* Poems I. 206 Cool drops on a feverous cheek.

transf. and *fig.* **1800** HURDIS *Fav. Village* 101 The fev'rous kettle with internal evil..totters on the bars. **1820** KEATS *Eve St. Agnes* x, A hundred swords Will storm his heart, Love's fev'rous citadel.

2. *fig.* = FEVERISH 2.

1603 SHAKS. *Meas. for M.* III. i. 75, I do feare thee Claudio ..Least thou a feauorous life shouldst entertaine. **1649** MILTON *Eikon.* xv. (1851) 450 The feverous rage of Tyrannizing. **1749** SMOLLETT *Regicide* v. i, Whose fev'rous life..feels the incessant throb Of ghastly paine! **1817** COLERIDGE *Biog. Lit.* I. ix. 139 His intellectual powers were never stimulated into fev'rous energy. **1865** RUSKIN *Sesame* p. xv, Feverous haste..has become the law of their being.

3. Of, pertaining to, of the nature of, or characteristic of a fever; = FEVERISH 3.

1393 GOWER *Conf.* II. 147 This feverous malady. **1503** HAWES *Examp. Virt.* xii. 237 Exylynge the feuerous frosty coldnes. **1576** BAKER *Jewell of Health* 4 a, The..feverous burning of the Heart. **1645** BP. HALL *Remedy Discontents* 53 They finde themselves overtaken vvith feverous distempers. **1796-7** COLERIDGE *Poems* (1862) 30 A dreamy pang in morning's feverous doze. **1820** KEATS *Isabel* xliv, What feverous hectic flame Burns in thee, child? **1864** TENNYSON *En. Ard.* 230 A night of feverous wakefulness.

4. Apt to cause fever.

1626 BACON *Sylva* §786 Southern-Winds..without Rain, do cause a Fevorous disposition of the Year. **1827** H. COLERIDGE *On Infancy* in *Lit. World* 21 Mar. (1890) The feverous summer's beam alike she dreads. **1850** KINGSLEY *Alt. Locke* xli, Hark! from..Feverous alley..Swells the wail of Englishmen. **1890** *Longman's Mag.* July 284 He was glad ..to retire from the feverous autumn.

Hence **ˈfeverously** *adv.*

a **1631** DONNE *Poems* (1650) 77 A malady Desperately hot, or changing feverously. **1829** *Anniversary, The Poet* 249 He, who..feverously grasps at a splendid loss. **1879** G. MACDONALD *P. Faber* III. i. 4 Either she would talk feverously, or sit in the gloomiest silence.

†ˈfevery, *a. Obs.* [f. as prec. + -Y^{1}.] Affected by fever; feverish.

1611 B. JONSON *Catiline* III. ii, And all thy body feuery. ? **1612** CHAPMAN *To Live with Little* Wks. 1875. 158 A fevery man's thirst.

few (fjuː), *a.* Forms: 1 **féawe, féawa, féa,** 2 **fæu,** 2-3 **feawe,** *Orm.* **fæwe,** 4 *south.* **veawe,** (3 **feaue**), 3-6 **fewe,** 3-4 *south.* **vewe,** 3-5 **feu(e,** (3 **feuwe, fawe,** *south.* **vawe, fowe,** 6 **feowe**), 3 **fa,** 3-5 **fo(e, fon(e,** (3 **foun, fune,** 5 **fewne, foyn(e**), 4- **few.** *compar.* 4 **fewere,** *Sc.* **fewar, foner,** 6- **fewer.** *superl.* 5 **fewis(t,** 6- **fewest.** [Common Teut.: OE. *féawe* pl. (usually *féawa* on the analogy of the adverbial *fela,* FELE many), contracted *féa,* corresp. to OFris. *fê* (very rare), OS. *fâh,* OHG. *fao, fô,* pl. *fôhe,* ON. *fá-r* (Sw. *få,* Da. *foa*), Goth. *fawai* pl.; repr. OTeut. **fawo-*, cognate with L. *pau-cus,* Gr. παῦ-ρος of same meaning, L. *paullus* little (:—**pau-r-los*), *pau-per* poor, and perh. with Gr. παύειν to stop.

The equivalent words in OHG. and ON., and the synonymous cognates in Gr. and Lat., were occasionally used in sing. with the senses 'rare', 'not numerous', 'small in quantity'. In OE. the sing. is not recorded, unless *féa* with partitive genitive (as in *féa worda*) may sometimes be neut. absol.; cf. similar use of ON. *fátt,* Fr. *un peu de.* The use of *féa* as adv. 'little, not much' is another survival of the prehistoric use of the sing. The word is not found in the extant remains of ONorthumbrian. The ME. forms *fa* (northern), *fo* (northern and north midland) have the appearance of being from ON.; the forms *fon(e, foun, fewne,* etc. seem to have arisen from the addition of *n* as a plural suffix, but the *n* remains in the comparative *foner.*]

1. Not many; amounting to a small number. Often preceded by *but, †full, so, too, very, †well.*

Without prefixed word, *few* usually implies antithesis with 'many', while in *a few, some few* the antithesis is with 'none at all'. Cf. 'few, or perhaps none', 'a few, or perhaps many'.

a. qualifying a plural sb. expressed or to be supplied from context.

c **900** *Bæda's Hist.* I. xvi. [xxix.] (1890) 88 þætte her wære micel rip onweard & fea worhton. **1154** *O.E. Chron.* (Laud MS.) an. 1138 Mid fæu men. *c* **1200** *Vices & Virtues* (1888) 25 Ðis understandeþ auer to feawe saules. *c* **1275** LAY. 26669 [Hii] leope to þan Bruttus and feue hii þar nemen. *a* **1300** *Cursor M.* 27864 (Cott.) þar es sinnes foun..wers for to mend. **1340** HAMPOLE *Pr. Consc.* 764 Fone men may now fourty yhere pas, And foner fifty. *c* **1400** MAUNDEV. (Roxb.) vii. 24 In Egipte er bot fewe castelles. *c* **1420** *Sir Amadace* (Camden) lxx, Ther is ladis now in lond fulle foe That wold haue seruut hor lord soe. *c* **1440** *York Myst.* xxi. 72 With wordes fewne. **1526** *Pilgr. Perf.* (W. de W. 1531) 123 b, The gyfte of prerogatyue called discrecyon..is but in fewe persones. **1596** SHAKS. *1 Hen. IV,* II. iv. 111 That euer this Fellow should haue fewer words then a Parret. **1599** —— *Much Ado* I. i. 7 How many Gentlemen haue you lost? But few. **1611** BIBLE *Job* xiv. 1 Man that is borne of a woman, is of few dayes. **1734** BERKELEY *Hylas & P.* (ed. 3) II. Wks. 1871 I. 306 Few men think, yet all have opinions. **1751** ORRERY *Remarks on Swift,* Guilty in so few sentences of so many solecisms. **1762-71** H. WALPOLE *Vertue's Anecd. Paint.* (1786) III. 47 No fewer than twenty-eight views. **1845** BUDD *Dis. Liver* 280 Among the numbers of bodies that I examined..very few..had gall-stones. **1870** E. PEACOCK *Ralf Skirl.* II. 189 A man of few words.

b. *absol.* = *few persons.*

Beowulf 1412 (Gr.) He feara sum beforan gengde. *c* **975** *Rushw. Gosp.* Matt. xx. 16 Moniȝe forþon sindun ȝecæȝed & feawe soðlice ȝecoren. *c* **1000** *Ags. Gosp.* ibid., And feawa ȝecorene. *a* **1225** *Leg. Kath.* 950 For nis him no derure for to adweschen feole þen fewe. *a* **1300** *Cursor M.* 8496 (Cott.) Fa it wist quat it wald mene. *c* **1340** *Ibid.* 19495 (Trin.) Of fewere þen of þre may no bisshop sacred be. *c* **1430** *Syr Tryam.* 540 Fewe for hym wepyth. **1484** CAXTON *Fables of Alfonce* (1889) 1 Many one ben frendes of wordes only, but fewe ben in fayth or dede. **1548** HALL *Chron.* 161 Many sought for him, but few espied hym. **1653** HOLCROFT *Procopius* I. 8 The Enemy..entring the Town by few at a time. **1774** GOLDSM. *Nat. Hist.* (1776) V. 47 That curiosity very few have an opportunity of gratifying. **1821** SHELLEY *Hellas* 184 Few dare, and few who dare Win the desired communion.

c. followed by partitive genitive, and later by *of.*

Beowulf 2662 (Gr.) Fea worda cwæð. **918** *O.E. Chron.* an. 918 Hira feawa on weȝ comon. *c* **1000** *Ags. Gosp.* Matt. ix. 37 Witodlice micel rip ys, and feawa wyrhtyna. **1297** R. GLOUC. (1724) 402 þere of scapede vewe alyue. *c* **1330** R. BRUNNE *Chron.* (1725) 242 He went to play a wile with fo of his banere. **1526** *Pilgr. Perf.* (W. de W. 1531) 14 Fewe of them..miscaryed. **1611** BIBLE *Deut.* vii. 7 Ye were the fewest of all people. **1848** MACAULAY *Hist. Eng.* I. 445 Few of the members of the late cabinet had any reason to expect his favour. **1875** HELPS *Es., Aids Contentment* 11 How few of your fellow-creatures can have the opportunity.

d. predicatively, freq. in phr. ***few and far between.***

c **825** *Vesp. Psalter* cvii. 39 Fea ȝewordne sindun. *c* **1000** *Ags. Ps.* cviii[i]. 8 Sien dæȝas his fea. *a* **1300** *E.E. Psalter* cvi[i]. 39 þai ere fone made. *a* **1300** *Cursor M.* 8599 (Cott.) þair clathes was sa gnede and fa. **1483** *Cath. Angl.* 129/2 To be Fewe, *rarere.* **1594** HOOKER *Eccl. Pol.* I. (1676) 71 It behoveth our words to be wary and few. **1668** R. VERNEY *Let.* c July in *Mem. Verney Fam.* (1899) IV. iii. 89 Hedges are few and far between. **1711** ADDISON *Spect.* No. 93 ¶1 We are always complaining our Days are few. **1764** GOLDSM. *Trav.* 212 If few their wants, their pleasures are but few. **1799** T. CAMPBELL *Pleasures of Hope* II. 375 What though my wingèd hours of bliss have been, Like angel-visits, few and far between? **1848** MACAULAY *Hist. Eng.* II. 441 The gunmakers of Utrecht were found too few to execute the orders. **1863** LYELL *Antiq. Man* 4 They may be fewer in number than was supposed. **1865** J. C. WILCOCKS

Sea Fisherman (1875) 163 The weed becomes very troublesome, and the fish consequently few and far between. **1965** *Listener* 20 May 759/3 Repair garages which are equally few and far between.

e. ***some few***: an inconsiderable number of. Also *ellipt.*, *absol.*, and followed by *of*.

1593 SHAKS. *Rich. II*, III. iii. 4 The king..lately landed With some few priuate friends. **1621** BP. MOUNTAGU *Diatribæ* 526 Vnlesse 'some few' and 'many' in your language be all one. **1684** J. LACY *Sir H. Buffoon* v. 111 Dram. Wks. (1875) 294 *Jud.* He is the first subject that ever made himself a Knight. *Her.* Not by some few, my lord. **1747** S. FIELDING *Lett. David Simple* (1752) II. 158 Some few women. *Mod.* Some few of the survivors are still living.

f. ***the few***: a specified company small in number; often with qualifying adj. Now often = 'the minority'; opposed to *the many*.

1549 COVERDALE *Erasm. Par. 2 Cor.* vi. 17 They are but fewe, but onles ye auoyde the same fewes companie. **1676** MARVELL *Mr. Smirke* 28 A Few of the Few..have been carrying on a constant Conspiracy. **1697** DRYDEN *Virg. Æneid* IX. 244 The wakeful few, the fuming Flaggon ply. **1777** PRIESTLEY *Matt. & Spir.* (1782) I. Pref. 10 The favour of the few may silence the clamour of the many. **1875** JOWETT *Plato* (ed. 2) III. 183 A life not for the many, but for the few.

†**g.** ellipt. ***in few*** = in few words; in short. Also, *to speak few* (= L. *pauca loqui*). *Obs.*

1526 *Pilgr. Perf.* (W. de W. 1531) 246 b, Be euer doynge well, & speke but fewe. **1565** JEWEL *Def. Apol.* (1611) 116 To say al in few, they refused the name. **1597** SHAKS. *2 Hen. IV*, I. i. 112 In few; his death..tooke fire and heate away. **1611** B. JONSON *Catiline* III. ii, I'll..end in few. **1667** MILTON *P.L.* x. 157 He thus to Eve in few: Say Woman, what is this which thou hast done? **1725** POPE *Odyss.* I. 476 The firm resolve I here in few disclose. **1742** YOUNG *Nt. Th.* ix. 533 In few, to close the whole, The moral muse has shadow'd out a sketch. **1848** J. A. CARLYLE tr. *Dante's Inferno* (1849) 71 Who shall tell in few the many fresh pains and travails that I saw?

h. ***at (the) fewest***: at the lowest estimate of number.

a **1400–50** *Alexander* 3599 Of sithid chariotis him sued.. At þe fewist, as I find a fouretene thousand. *Ibid.* 3738 Of females at þe fewis foure & xx^ti Mille.

2. Like the cardinal numerals, *few* may be used to form with a plural sb. a virtual collective noun, preceded by *a*, *every*, or (rarely) *that*, but construed with plural verb. (Cf. ME. *an five mile*, *an fourti ȝer*; and see EVERY 1 e.)

a. ***a few***: a small number of. ***not a few***: many.

1297 R. GLOUC. (1724) 18 þe kyng with a fewe men hymself flew at þe laste. *c* **1386** CHAUCER *Prol.* 641 A fewe termes coude he. *c* **1400** *Rom. Rose* 5988 He shall in a fewe stoundes Lese all his markes. **1550** SIR R. MORYSINE *Let.* 17 Dec. in Tytler *Edw. VI*, I. 345 I pray you let me now and then have a few lines from you. **1611** SHAKS. *Cymb.* IV. ii. 283 Heere's a few Flowres. **1744** BERKELEY *Siris* §82 The..constant use of tar-water for a few weeks. **1796** H. HUNTER tr. *St.-Pierre's Stud. Nat.* (1799) II. 474, I will deliver my thoughts..in a few words. **1848** W. H. BARTLETT *Egypt to Pal.* x. (1879) 220 One rock a few feet square.

b. with ellipsis of sb. Often followed by *of*. Also *absol.* a few persons; occas. with an adj., as *a faithful*, *select*, etc. *few*, in which it approaches the nature of a sb. †*a fewer*: a smaller number *of*.

a **1300** *Cursor M.* 19782 (Cott.) He badd þa men be all vtedon, þat in þat hus left bot a fon. *c* **1380** *Sir Ferumb.* 953 Al þe feldes þo wern y-fuld of dede men on þe grounde, Saue an vewe þat leye & ȝulde. *a* **1400–50** *Alexander* 2061 Fra his faes with a fewe þe filde to de-voide. *c* **1460** *Towneley Myst.* (Surtees) 105, I shall say thertylle of good wordes a foyne. **1547** LATIMER *Serm. & Rem.* (1845) 426 Of which sort we have a fewer amongst us than I would. **1601** SHAKS. *All's Well* I. i. 73 Loue all, trust a few, Doe wrong to none. **1719** DE FOE *Crusoe* (1882) 540 Thieves, of which, it seems there were not a few. **1723** POPE *Let. to Swift* 12 Jan., To pass my days with you, and a few such as you. *a* **1745** SWIFT *Wks.* 1778 VI. 358 Party is the madness of many, for the gain of a few. **1801** SOUTHEY *Thalaba* I. xliii, A faithful few Prest through the throng to join him. **1871** MORLEY *Voltaire* (1886) 2 A level which had..been reached only by a few. **1872** HARDWICK *Trad. Lanc.* 175 A select few of tried old friends.

c. ***that few***: rarely used for *those few*.

1854 TENNYSON *To F. D. Maurice* 5 That honest few Who give the Fiend himself his due. **1861** PRESIDENT LINCOLN *Message to Congress* 3 Dec., A few men own capital, and that few avoid labour themselves.

d. ***a good few***: a fair number (*of*); (*dial.* and *colloq.*). ***quite a few*** (U.S.): a considerable number.

1828 D. M. MOIR *Mansie Wauch* vii. 58 We collected a good few friends to a tea-drinking. **1863** MRS. TOOGOOD *Yorksh. Dial.*, There were a good few apples on it. **1864** CARLYLE *Fredk. Gt.* IV. 122 Of cannon a good few. **1865** *Ibid.* V. XIX. v. 499 A good few sorrows. **1865** J. G. BERTRAM *Harvest of Sea* (1873) 85 As soon as they are able to eat—which is not for a good few days. **1883** P. ROBINSON in *Harper's Mag.* Oct. 706/1 There's quite a few about among the rocks.

e. ***every few*** (***hours, miles***, etc.): every series or group of a few; chiefly in advb. phrases.

f. ***to have a few*** (***in***): to have or to have had several alcoholic drinks. *colloq.*

1946 F. SARGESON *That Summer* 132 He had a good few in certainly, and so had Maggie, but they weren't all that tight. **1947** 'A. P. GASKELL' *Big Game* 88 They'll probably have a few in by this time too, and boy, would I like to be the same. **1960** M. SPARK *Ballad of Peckham Rye* vii. 150 'Nelly's had a few,' Humphrey said.. 'She's a bit shaky on the pins tonight.' **1968** K. WEATHERLY *Roo Shooter* 2/3 The shooter walked fifteen or twenty miles carrying his swag, had a few at the pub, then found somewhere to roll his bluey.

g. ***the Few*** [an allusion to a speech of Sir Winston Churchill: see quot. 1940], an informal title of respect for the R.A.F. pilots who took part in the Battle of Britain.

[**1940** W. S. CHURCHILL *Into Battle* (1941) 259 Never in the field of human conflict was so much owed by so many to so few.] **1941** *Illustr. London News* 19 Apr. 518/1 In the above series of portraits,..the artist..shows characteristic types of those few to whom 'so many owe so much'. **1960** B. ROBERTSON *Spitfire* viii. 34/2 (*caption*) One of the 'few'. A fighter pilot rigged for battle. **1963** D. IRVING *Destruction of Dresden* I. i. 26 On the 18th [July 1940] the Few brought down 71 enemy planes. **1978** *Jrnl. R. Soc. Arts* CXXVI. 25/2 The scientists.., together with the Few, had saved Britain in 1940 when everything appeared lost.

†**3.** Of a company or number: Small. So of a leader, ***to be few in number***. *Obs.*

1460 *Paston Lett.* No. 357 I. 526 The Duc of Excestre and other, with a few mayne. **1475** *Bk. Noblesse*, He saw so few a companie of the Romains. **1531** ELYOT *Gov.* I. xviii, A few nombre of houndes. *c* **1565** LINDESAY (Pitscottie) *Chron. Scot.* (1728) 120 The earl of Angus was come..and but a few number with him. *c* **1610** SIR J. MELVIL *Mem.* (1735) 13 He ..did ride to the Parties himself with a few company. **1611** BIBLE *Gen.* xxxiv. 30, I being few in number. **1711** SWIFT *Let.* 19 July, There was a drawing-room to-day..but so few company, that [etc.]. **1828** C. WORDSWORTH *Charles I, Author of Icôn Basilikè* 133 Their number assuredly has not been few.

4. Of quantity: Not much. ***a few***: a little.

a. qualifying a sb. in sing. *Obs.* exc. *dial.* in *a few broth*, *gruel*, *porridge*.

[Possibly a survival of the use of the sing. of the adj. as in ON.; but the sbs. to which it is now prefixed are treated in dialects as plural, and referred to with pl. pronoun.]

1362 LANGL. *P. Pl.* A. VII. 269 A fewe Cruddes and Craym. **1550** LEVER *Serm.* (Arb.) 122 Hauyng a fewe porage made of the brothe of the same byefe. **1607** TOPSELL *Four-f. Beasts* (1658) 199 Broath..to sup now and then a few. **1641** BEST *Farm. Bks.* (Surtees) 68 A pecke..of malte and some few honey. **1803** S. PEGGE *Anecd. Eng. Lang.* xvi. (1844) 181 'Stay a few while,' a Londoner says. **1825** BROCKETT *N.C. Words* 73 A 'little few broth'. **1881** *Leicestersh. Gloss.*, 'Av' a few moor broth..thee're very good to-dee!'

b. absol. ***a few***. Used *colloq.* or *slang* in ironical sense, = 'a good bit'; also *adverbially*. Also, ***not a few***: considerably.

[Perh. orig. a comic Gallicism, after Fr. *un peu*.]

1761 A. MURPHY *Citizen* II. i, I..throw my eyes about a few. **1778** SUSAN BURNEY *Let.* in *Mad. D'Arblay's Early Diary* July, Your letter which diverted him not a few. **1807** W. IRVING *Salmag.* (1824) 199 He was determined to astonish the natives a few! **1837–40** HALIBURTON *Clockm.* (1862) 177 You must lie a few to put 'em off well. **1855** SMEDLEY *H. Coverdale* v. 26 'Can you sit a leap?' 'I believe you, rayther, just a very few.' **1857** KINGSLEY *Two Y. Ago* III. vii, If one man in a town has pluck and money, he may do it. It'll cost him a few. **1865** LOWELL *Lett.* (1894) I. 347, I am..a little few (*un petit peu*) vexed. *a* **1953** H. BELLOC *Coll. Poems* (1958) 136 When Mr Rhys shall hear that you Are in the hands of the police It will disturb him not a few.

5. *Comb.*, parasynthetic, as ***few-acred***, ***-celled***, ***-flowered***, ***-layered***, ***-seeded***, ***-whorled***.

1847 LONGF. *Ev.* II. ii. 9 *Few-acred farmers. **1875** DAWSON *Dawn of Life* vi. 139 *Few-celled germs. **1776** WITHERING *Brit. Plants* (1796) II. 138 *Few-flowered. **1861** MISS PRATT *Flower. Pl.* VI. 25 Few-flowered Sedge. Spikelet of from four to six flowers, the two upper barren. **1884** BOWER & SCOTT *De Bary's Phaner. & Ferns* 518 Narrow one- or *few-layered bands. **1830** LINDLEY *Nat. Syst. Bot.* 175 *Few-seeded fruit. **1851** WOODWARD *Mollusca* 83 Shell involute..*few-whirled.

fewd(e, obs. form of FEUD *sb.*¹

†**fewe.** *Obs. rare*⁻¹. [? a. OF. *fuie*:—L. *fuga* flight; cf. FEUTE. The synonym FUSE seems to have arisen from the plural of this word; otherwise a misprint for *fewte* might be suspected.] = FEUTE *sb.*

1525 LD. BERNERS *Froiss.* II. xxvii. 32 b, He was ryght desyrous to folowe his pray, and folowed the fewe of the hart.

fewel, obs. form of FUEL.

fewer, fewle, obs. forms of FEVER, FOWL.

†**fewmand**, *v.* *Obs.*⁻¹ [Belongs to the imaginary Sherwood dialect of the piece; cf. FUMISH.] *trans.* To foul, to soil.

1637 B. JONSON *Sad Sheph.* II. ii, They [a young badger and a ferret] fewmand all the claithes.

fewmets, fewmishing: see FU-.

fewness ('fjuːnɪs). [f. FEW + -NESS.] The quality or fact of being few.

1. Scantiness in number; paucity, small number.

c **900** *Bæda's Hist.* III. xv. [xxi.] (1891) 222 Seo feanis nedde þara sacerda þætte aan biscop sceolde beon ofer tuu folc. *c* **1000** *Ags. Ps.* ci[i]. 24 Feanisse deȝa minra seȝe me. *a* **1300** *E.E. Psalter*, *ibid.*, Feunesse of mi daies. **1382** WYCLIF *ibid.*, Fewenesse of my daȝis. **1482** *Monk of Evesham* (Arb.) 89 The fewnes of spyrytuall men. **1535** STEWART *Cron. Scot.* I. 387 For feuenes thai did fle. **1611** SPEED *Hist. Gt. Brit.* VII. xxxvi. (1632) 385 Seeing the fewnes of their pursuers. **1709** HEARNE *Collect.* (Oxf. Hist. Soc.) II. 282 Spoke in vain because of the fewness of Auditors. **1859** JEPHSON *Brittany* ii. 9, I congratulated myself..on the fewness of the things which I possessed.

†**b.** ***fewness and truth***: in few words and truly. *Obs.*

1603 SHAKS. *Meas. for M.* I. iv. 39 Fewnes, and truth; tis thus, Your brother, and his louer haue embrac'd.

2. Scantiness in amount; small quantity. *rare.*

1861 DARWIN in *Life & Lett.* (1887) III. 265 The pollen, so important from its fewness. **1884** TENNYSON *Becket* III. iii, Doth not the fewness of anything make the fulness of it in estimation?

fewsty, obs. form of FUSTY.

fewt(e(e, fewthe, -tye, obs. ff. of FEALTY.

fewte, var. form of FEUTE, *Obs.*

†**'fewter**, *sb.* *Obs.* Forms: 4 feuter, (fewtyre), 5 fewter, -tir(e, -tre. [a. OF. *feutre*, *fautre* (:—late L. *filtrum*: see FELT, FILTER), lit. 'felt', hence a felt-lined socket for a spear.]

The rest or support for a lance or spear attached to the saddle of a knight or man-at-arms.

c **1350** *Will. Palerne* 3437 Wiþ spere festened in feuter. ? *a* **1400** *Morte Arth.* 1366 A faire floreschte spere in fewtyre he castes. *c* **1450** *Merlin* 127 Gripynge his spere in the fewtre. *c* **1470** HENRY *Wallace* III. 168 Thair cheyff chyftan ..In fewtir kest a fellone aspre sper. **1470–85** MALORY *Arthur* VI. ii, Syre Ector..in fewter cast his spere and smote the other knyghte a grete buffet.

†**'fewter**, *v.*¹ *Obs.* [f. prec. sb.] *trans.* To put (a spear) into the 'fewter' or rest.

c **1400** *Melayne* 1474 Thay ferlyde why he fewterde his spere. **1470–85** MALORY *Arthur* VI. vi, And thenne they fewtryd their sperys. **1557** *K. Arthur* (Copland) v. ix, Whan syr Gawayn espyed this gaye knyght he fewtred hys spere and rode strayght unto hym. **1596** SPENSER *F.Q.* IV. vi. 10 He his threatfull speare Gan fewter.

†**'fewter**, *v.*² *Obs.* Also FELTER. [ad. OF. *feutrer* to make into felt.] **a.** *trans.* To pack or set (men) close together. **b.** *intr.* for *refl.* To close in battle, come to close quarters.

? *a* **1400** *Morte Arth.* 1711 Ffifty thosandez of folke..are fewteride on frounte undyr ȝone fre-bowes. **1513** DOUGLAS *Æneis* x. vi. 166 Thai fewtyr fut to fut and man to man.

†**'fewterer.** *Obs.* Forms: α. 4–5 **vewter.** β. 6–8 feuterer, futerer, pheu-, phewterer, 6– fewterer. [ME. *vewter* and early mod.E. *fewterer* appear to be corrupted adoptions of AF. *veutrier* (= Anglo-Lat. *veltrarius*) in same sense, f. OF. *veutre*, *vautre*, *veltre* (later F. *vautre*) = Pr. *veltre*, It. *veltro*:—popular L. **veltrum*, corruption of L. *vertragum* (nom. *-us*) greyhound, a Gaulish word, f. Celtic *ver-* intensive prefix + root *trag-* to run.]

A keeper of greyhounds. Also in a wider sense, an attendant. Also with defining word prefixed; as ***fox-***, ***yeoman-fewterer***.

c **1340** *Gaw. & Gr. Knt.* 1146 To trystors vewters ȝod. *c* **1450** *Bk. Curtasye* 631 in *Babees Bk.* (1868) 320 Þo vewter, two cast of brede he tase, Two lesshe of grehoundes yf þat he hase. **1545** JOYE *Exp. Dan.* iii. E v b, These pharisaicall foxe fewterers. **1599** B. JONSON *Ev. Man out of Hum.* II. iii, And perhaps stumble upon a yeoman pheuterer, as I doe now. *a* **1625** FLETCHER *Woman's Prize* II, ii, A dry nurse to his coughs, a fewterer To such a nasty fellow. **1691** BLOUNT *Law Dict.* s.v. *Vautrier*, Hence our corrupted word Feuterer, for a Dog-keeper. **1741** *Compl. Fam.-Piece* II. i. 312 He that is chosen Fewterer, or that lets loose the Greyhounds. **1801** *Sporting Mag.* XVIII. 100 Feuterer, a dog-keeper.

fewterlock, dial. form of FETTERLOCK.

fewtir(e, var. of FEWTER, *Obs.*

†**'fewtrer.** *Obs. rare*⁻¹. [a. OF. *feutrier*, f. *feutre* felt.] A felt-maker, a worker in felt.

14.. *Lat.-Eng. Voc.* in Wr.-Wülcker 582 *Fedorarius* [? read *foderarius*], a fewtrer.

fewtrils ('fjuːtrɪlz), *sb. pl.* *dial.* Little things, trifles. Cf. FATTRELS.

c **1750** J. COLLIER (Tim Bobbin) *Lanc. Dial.* Gloss., *Fewtrils*, little things. **1854** DICKENS *Hard T.* I. xi, 'I ha' gotten decent fewtrils about me agen.' **1857** J. SCHOLES *Jaunt to see Queen* 28 (Lanc. Gloss.) Peg had hur hoppet ov hur arm wi her odd fewtrils.

†**'fewty.** *Obs. Sc.* In 6 fewtie. [f. FEW + -TY.] The condition of being few; scarcity.

1596 DALRYMPLE tr. *Leslie's Hist. Scot.* (1885) 59 The raritie and fewtie or scant of sum of thame.

†**fex.** *Obs. rare*⁻¹. [ad. L. *fæx*. Cf. FÆCES.] Sediment, waste, excrement.

1545 RAYNOLD *Byrth Mankynde* (1564) 73 b, A watery substance, thicke like bryne, or other fex mixed with water.

fex, var. of FAX *sb.*¹, *Obs.*, hair.

fey (feɪ), *a.* Formerly chiefly *Sc.* Forms: 1 fǽȝe, 3 fæiȝe, *south.* væiȝe, vaiȝe, fæie, *south.* væie, faie, 3–4 feie, *south.* veie, feye, 4 feiȝe, *south.* veiȝe, fei, 4–5 fay, (8 fie), 4– fey. [Common Teut.; OE. *fǽȝe* = OS. *fêgi* (MDu. *vêge*, Du. *veeg*), OHG. *feigi* (MHG. *veige* in same sense, also timid, cowardly, mod.G. *feige* cowardly), ON.

feigr:—OTeut. **faigjo-*; the ulterior etymology is uncertain: see Kluge and Franck.]

1. Fated to die, doomed to death; also, at the point of death; dying. In literary use now *arch.* Still in popular use in Scotland: see quot. 1861.

Beowulf 1568 (Gr.) Bil eal þurhwod fæȝne flæschoman. *Ibid.* 2141 Næs ic fæȝe þa ȝyt. *a* **1000** *Byrhtnoth* 119 (Gr.) Æt fotum feoll fæȝe cempa. *c* **1205** LAY. 517 Heo weren summe faie [*c* **1275** veie]. **1393** LANGL. *P. Pl.* C. XVI. 2 As a frek þat feye were forth gan ich walke. *c* **1450** HENRYSON *Mor. Fab.* 58 Death on the fayest fall. *c* **1470** HENRY *Wallace* IV. 92 Fey on the feld he has him left for deid. **1535** STEWART *Cron. Scot.* II. 378 Throw misgyding, or than the man wes fey. **17..** *Jock o' the Side* xxx. in Scott *Minstr. Scotr. Bord.* (1869) 103 There'l nae man die but him that's fie. **1790** BURNS *Sheriffmuir* ii, Thro' they dash'd, and hew'd, and smash'd, Till fey men died awa, man. **1828** SCOTT *F.M. Perth* xvi, Man! art thou fey! **1861** RAMSAY *Remin.* Ser. II. 75 When a person does anything that is contrary to his habits or dispositions it is common..to say, 'I wish the bodie be na fey'; that is, that this unwonted act may not be a prelude to his death. **1882** A. LANG *Helen of Troy* VI. xvi, O'er strange meat they revell'd like folk fey.

absol. a **1000** *Andreas* 1532 (Gr.) Fæȝe swulton..on ȝeofene. *c* **1205** LAY. 31227 Feollen þa uaiȝe. *a* **1250** *Prov. Ælfred* 170 in *O.E. Misc.* 112 For nys no wrt..þat euer mvwe þas feye furþ vp-holde. **1799** A. JOHNSTON in *Statist. Acc. Scotl.* XXI. 148 The Fye gave due warning by certain signs of approaching mortality. *Ibid.* 149 [Superstition having diminished,] the Fye has withdrawn his warning, and the elf his arrows. [In Hone's *Every-day Bk.* II. 1019, followed by many later writers, *fye* in quots. 1799 is taken as a synonym of FETCH. This seems to be a mistake.]

†**2.** Leading to or presaging death; deadly, fatal. *Obs.*

c **1470** HENRY *Wallace* IX. 1342 Full fey was maid that rout. **1513** DOUGLAS *Æneis* X. Prol. 124 Bittyr was that frute for his ofspring and fey. **1799** *Statist. Acc. Scot.* XXI. 150 What Fye token do ye see about me?

†**3.** Accursed, unfortunate, unlucky. *Obs.*

a **1000** *Crist* 1534 (Gr.) On þæt deope dæl..ȝefeallað.. synfulra here..fæȝe gæstas. **1340-70** *Alisaunder* 397 For ðis feye folk ðer so fouli was harmed. **1513** DOUGLAS *Æneis* III. ix. 48 And of the company of fey Vlixes.

†**4.** Feeble, timid; sickly, weak. *Obs.*

a **1000** *Guthlac* 281 (Gr.) Nis min breostsefa forht ne fæȝe. *c* **1350** *Med. MS.* in *Archæol.* XXX. 376 Parwynke..beryth blo flour, His stalkys arn..feynt & feye. *c* **1420** *Avow. Arth.* iv, Feye folke will he fere. **1513** DOUGLAS *Æneis* XII. v. 41 That now, thus sleuthfully, sa fant and fey Huvis still on thir feldis.

5. Disordered in mind like one about to die; possessing or displaying magical, fairylike, or unearthly qualities. Now freq. used ironically, in sense 'affected, whimsy'.

1823 J. GALT *Entail* I. viii. 62 Surely the man's fey about his entails and his properties. **1856** J. BALLANTINE *Poems* 207 Wad ye rax his craig, When our daughter is fey for a man? **1921** M. CORELLI *Secret Power* iii. 34 'But I was "fey" from my birth—.' 'What is *fey*?' interrupted Miss Herbert. .. 'It's just everything that everybody else is *not*'—Morgana replied—"Fey" people are magic people; they see what no one else sees,—they hear voices that no one else hears—voices that whisper secrets and tell of wonders as yet undiscovered.' **1930** 'E. QUEEN' *French Powder Myst.* xxx. 251 'Have you gone fey?' gasped the Inspector. 'Like a fox,' said Ellery. **1930** J. DOUGLAS *Down Shoe Lane* 289 They become fey and fond. **1937** H. G. WELLS *Star Begotten* iii. 66 Are there people—what shall I call them?—*fey* people about? People as sane as you and I and yet strange? **1938** —— *Apropos of Dolores* vi. 293 One of these toy trains of theirs seemed to come out of the ground beside us... They [*sc.* the passengers] seemed indeed to be inhabitants of some different, some elfin world... She was all agog to see that fey train once more. **1952** C. DAY LEWIS tr. *Virgil's Aeneid* VI. 119 Her fey heart swelled in ecstasy. **1955** E. COXHEAD *Figure in Mist* ii. 63 A gaze that was not at all fey, but.. remarkably shrewd. **1959** *Listener* 4 June 998/1 Sensible elder daughter, and fey younger daughter. **1969** D. BURNHAM *Through Dooms of Love* 219 Now your wife would be perfect for the part; she's got that fey look as though she's had breakfast with a leprechaun.

Hence **'feydom**, the state of being 'fey'; **'feyly** *adv.*

1823 GALT *Entail* I. 156 'I would hae thought the half o't an unco almous frae you. I hope it's no a fedam afore death.' **1959** *Times* 6 Mar. 14/5 She feyly resumes the gestures of a Spanish dancer in return to her past on the music halls. **1964** 'W. HAGGARD' *Antagonists* i. 13 A light from a feyly gothic window.

fey, var. of FAY *sb.*[1] *Obs.* faith.

fey, obs. form of FAY *v.*[2], FEE *sb.*[2], FOE.

feyde, feyer, obs. forms of FEED, FAR.

feyffe, obs. form of FIVE.

feygne, feynze, feynyn, obs. ff. FEIGN *v.*

feylour, var. of FELOURE, *Obs.*

feyn(e(n, obs. forms of FAIN, FEIGN.

feynd, feynt, obs. and Sc. forms of FIEND.

feyness ('feɪnɪs). [f. FEY *a.* + -NESS.] The state or quality of being fey.

1873 J. BROWN *Round Table Club* 254 She wis a bonnie lassie—ower bonnie tae live lang. There wis a feyness aboot her. **1926** *Spectator* 9 Oct. 568/1 That queer, elusive 'feyness'..of Miss Fay Compton. **1927** K. MACLEOD *Road to Isles* i. 27 There is also in it a whole storm of rapture, perhaps of feyness. Gladness must come to its own some time. **1930** *Time & Tide* 24 May 677 That ethereal physique and effect of feyness which has helped her to so many of her successes. **1963** *Listener* 21 Mar. 529/2, I find it difficult to reconcile the authorship of the flip, alert opening scenes with the awful feyness of what followed. **1968** R. V. BESTE *Repeat Instructions* xxiv. 271 There was no trace of feyness in the grim, drawn lines of his face.

feynt(e, feyre, obs. forms of FAINT, FEAR *v.*

feysaunte, obs. form of PHEASANT.

feyt, obs. form of FIGHT.

feythhed. *Obs.* [f. OE. *fǽhþ* enmity + *-hed*, -HEAD.] Hostility.

1297 R. GLOUC. (Rolls) App. G 59 Cloten..his foredene [*v.r.* feythhed] for howede.

feytous, var. of FEATOUS *a. Obs.*

fez (fɛz). [a. (? through F. *fez*) Turk. *fes*, *fês*; the name of the town *Fez* (in Morocco) is spelt in the same way, and it is alleged that the *fez* is so called from the town, where formerly it was chiefly manufactured.]

A skull-cap formerly of wool, now of felt, of a dull crimson colour, in the form of a truncated cone, ornamented with a long black tassel; formerly the national head-dress of the Turks.

1802-3 tr. *Pallas' Trav.* (1812) II. 347 The clergy and the aged wear under it [a high cap] the Fez, or a red, woven calotte. **1851** LAYARD *Pop. Acc. Discov. Nineveh* viii. 196 Round his fez..endless folds of white linen. **1863** SPEKE *Discov. Nile* 261, I gave each of my men a fez cap. **1884** J. T. BENT in *Macm. Mag.* Oct. 426/2 The island sailors with their blue baggy trousers, red fezes, and bare legs.

Hence **fezzed** *ppl. a.*, furnished with or wearing a fez. Also **'fezzy** *a.*, *nonce-wd.*, in same sense.

1864 J. A. GRANT *Walk across Africa* xiii. 324 Well-dressed men, 'fezzed' or turbaned. **1876** G. MEREDITH *Beauch. Career* I. iv. 63 The fezzy defenders of the border fortress. **1891** *New Review* Dec. 517 Fezzed officials. **1959** *Encounter* Oct. 4/2 A Sick Man or two prettily fezzed in the foreground. **1971** G. HOUSEHOLD *Doom's Caravan* iii. 103 A decrepit baggage camel..waiting for some fezzed fool to sit on its back and be photographed.

fezen, fezzan, dial. forms of PHEASANT.

†**'fiable, 'feable**, *a. Obs.* [a. OF. *fiable*, *feable*, faithful, confident, f. *fier* to trust.] Faithful; in quot. quasi-*sb.*

1483 CAXTON *Gold. Leg.* 437/2 Fader wylte thou receyue thys hoostye..for al the fyables of god that are or lyue.

Hence **'feably** *adv.*, confidently.

c **1490** CAXTON *Blanchardyn* (E.E.T.S.) 128 Seeng þat feabli he myght speke without doubte or fear.

‖**fiacre** (fjakr). [F. *fiacre*; it is said that the vehicles first so called belonged to an innkeeper (in 1648) who lived at the sign of St. *Fiacre* (De Broc *Anc. Régime* II. 188).] A small four-wheeled carriage for hire, a hackney-coach, a French cab.

1699 M. LISTER *Journ. Paris* xii, They are most, even Fiacres or Hackneys, hung with Double Springs. **1741** tr. *D'Argens' Chinese Lett.* i. 5 This miserable Vehicle, which the French call a Fiacre (i.e. a Hackney-Coach). **1826** LONGF. in *Life* (1891) I. vii. 81 Cabriolets, fiacres, and carriages of all kinds. **1885** R. BUCHANAN *Annan Water* xxvii, Hailing a fiacre, he jumped in.

fialle, obs. form of PHIAL.

†**fiançailles**, *sb. pl. Obs.* In 5 **fyansialles**, 7 **fiancialles, fiansals.** [a. F. *fiançailles* sb. pl., a betrothal, f. *fiancer* to betroth.] A betrothal.

c **1477** CAXTON *Jason* 127 During the fyansialles and trouthplightyng of Iason and Creusa. **1625** J. CHAMBERLAIN *Let.* 6 May in *Crt. & Times Chas. I* (1848) I. 18 The fiancialles were performed on Thursday. **1655** DIGGES *Compl. Ambass.* 183 Might she with a good Conscience substitute a Papist for her sons Proctor for the Fiansals.

†**'fiance**, *sb. Obs.* Forms: 4-5 **fiaunce**, 5-6 **fyaunce**, (5 **fyence**), 6 **fiance.** [a. OF. *fiance* f. *fier* to trust.]

1. Confidence, trust.

1340 *Ayenb.* 164 þe uerste poynte of prowesse hi clepieþ magnanimitie. þe oþer fiaunce. *c* **1400** *Rom. Rose* 5484 In whom no man shulde affye, Nor in hir yeftis have fiaunce. *c* **1440** *Generyaes* 5610 In whom suerly is all her fyence. *a* **1555** PHILPOT tr. *Curio's Def.* in *Exam. & Writ.* (Parker Soc.) 348 They admonish me that I neither give any fiance to thee.

2. A promise, word of honour.

1470-85 MALORY *Arthur* I. iii, Syre Ector..made fyaunce to the kyng for to nourisshe the child lyke as the Kynge desyred. **1592** WYRLEY *Armorie* 70 From his gag'd fiaunce cleere I set him free.

†**'fiance**, *v. Obs.* [f. F. *fiancer*, f. *fiance* a promise; see prec.]

1. *trans.* **a.** = AFFIANCE *v.* 2. **b.** To give one's troth to; to take as one's betrothed.

a **1450** *Knt. de la Tour* lxxvii. 99 He wold graunte and fyaunce her to a man whiche was a paynym. **1560** DAUS tr. *Sleidane's Comm.* 433 a, The Duke of Florence had fiaunced his daughter to Ascanio the Byshop of Romes nephewe. **1613-8** DANIEL *Coll. Hist. Eng.* (1626) 29 Harold was fyanced to..the Duke's daughter.

b. 1483 CAXTON *Gold. Leg.* 119 b/2 Another louer..hath fyanced me by his fayth. *a* **1533** LD. BERNERS *Huon* xviii. 50 To fyaunce and to kys thre tymes the fayre Esclaramonde. **1587** HARMAR tr. *Beza's Serm.* i. 9 He hath..fianced & betrothed to himself his church.

2. To make to promise, put upon one's parole.

1592 WYRLEY *Armorie* 74 Rich prisoners were woon and fienced Vpon their faiths.

‖**fiancé** *masc.*, **fiancée** *fem.* (fi:'ɑ̃:seɪ). [F. *fiancé*, *fiancée*, pa. pple. f. *fiancer* to betroth.] A betrothed person.

1853 LD. HOUGHTON in *Life* (1891) I. xi. 490 Nobody much here except Clough and his *fiancée*, a clever-looking girl. **1864** *London Society* VI. 58 The bride elect, the *fiancé*, the trousseau..she took under her most special charge. **1885** *Graphic* 3 Jan. 10/2 The *fiancé*, Prince Henry. **1890** BESANT *Demoniac* ii. 26 He would not trust himself to see his *fiancée*, Elinor Thanet.

fianchetto (fjan'tʃɛtto, fɪən'tʃɛtəʊ). *Chess.* [It., dim. of *fianco* FLANK *sb.*[1]] The development of a bishop by moving it one square to a long diagonal of the board. Hence **fianchetto** *v. trans.*, to develop (a bishop) in this way; also **fian'chettoed** *ppl. a.*

1848 H. STAUNTON *Chess-Player's Handbk.* 379 The Fianchetto. White: I. P to K's 4th. Black: I. P to Q Kt's 3rd. Black's present move, which the Italians call 'Il Fianchetto di Donna'..may be made by the second player without harm. **1927** *Brit. Chess Mag.* XLVII. 168 If intending to fianchetto his Bishop it would have been better to begin the preparation on the 4th move. **1957** L. BARDEN *Guide to Chess Openings* 69 Black's fianchettoed Bishop. **1969** A. GLYN *Dragon Variation* i. 9 Mrs. Oppenheimer decided to fianchetto her white-square Bishop and moved her Queen's Knight's Pawn to Knight 3. *Ibid.*, She decided to complete the fianchetto of her Bishop, and played Bishop to Knight 2, defending her Knight and commanding the long white diagonal.

Fian(n) (fi:n). [Irish *fian*, pl. *fianna* orig. 'band of hunters'. The form *fiann* is a back-formation from the plural.] **1.** A legendary Irish warrior, one of the soldiers of Fionn mac Cumhail; = FENIAN *sb.* 1.

1787 M. YOUNG (*title*) Ancient Gælic poems respecting the race of the Fians, collected in the Highlands of Scotland in the years 1784-1786. **1879** [see FENIAN *sb.* 1]. **1891** J. G. CAMPBELL *Fians* p. xii, The Fian heroes are to this day prominent in proverbs and riddles. **1909** D. A. MACKENZIE *Elves & Heroes* p. ix, The Ossianic or Fian Cycle. **1932** *Irish Free State Official Handbk.* iv. 45 About the same time [*sc.* end of 3rd cent.] we trace the establishment in Ireland of permanent military forces, the Fiana, adopted, no doubt, in imitation of the Roman military organisation. **1967** D. EDWARDS-REES *Ireland's Story* ii. 13 In the third century A.D. Cormac the High King had a standing force of professional warriors called the *Fianna*.

2. *Fianna Fáil* ('fi:ənə fɔɪl). [Ir. *fianna* pl. (see sense 1) + *fál* (see below).] An Irish political organization and party which was founded in 1926 and entered the Dail Eireann in 1927.

Irish *Fáil* is the genitive of *fál* 'defensive fortification', and is cognate with L. *vallum* WALL *sb.*[1] It was applied to the rampart of mountains surrounding the central plain of Ireland, so that *Inis Fáil* 'island of the rampart' came to mean 'Ireland'. The phr. *Fianna Fáil* was used in 15th-cent. poetry in the neutral sense 'people of Ireland.' The founders of the Fianna Fáil party, however, interpreted the phr. as meaning 'soldiers of destiny'. (A. J. Bliss.)

1927 *Observer* 27 Mar. 20/2 Fianna Fail—Mr De Valera's Republicans. **1933** [see ALL-OVER *adj. phr.* 3]. **1958** *Listener* 9 Oct. 571/2 Fianna Fail is trying to get rid of Proportional Representation. **1971** *Times* 18 Aug. 2/3 Pressure inside the ruling Fianna Fail Party for stronger action on Northern Ireland.

fiansals, obs. form of FIANÇAILLES.

fiant ('faɪənt). Also 6 **fiaunt, fyaunte.** [L. *fiant* (3rd pers. pl. pres. subj. of *fierī*: see FIAT), in the formula *fiant literæ patentes*, 'let letters patent be made out', with which these documents formerly commenced.]

A warrant addressed to the Irish Chancery for a grant under the Great Seal. By Spenser used *transf.*

1534 SKEFFYNGTON in *St. Papers Hen. VIII*, II. 193 There be serteyne fyauntes made, to be put up to the Kynges Highnes, for officis in Ireland. **1591** SPENSER *M. Hubberd* 1144 Through his hand alone must passe the Fiaunt. **1614** in *Cal. State Papers, Ireland* 7 Dec. 530 Warrant to draw forth a fiant of pardon unto Connor Roe Magwire, Esq. **1875** *Seventh Rep. Deputy Keeper Records Irel.* 27 The 'Fiants'..extend from the 12th year of Henry VIII to the present time.

†**'fiants**, *sb. Obs.* Forms: 6-7 **feance(s, fya(u)nts**, 7-8 **fiant(e)s**, 8 **fuants.** [a. OF. *fient* masc., *fiente* fem. dung (repr. popular L. types **femitum*, *-a*, f. **femus*, L. *fimus* dung), also *fiens*, pl. of *fien*, repr. L. *fimum.* The specialization of sense seems to be Eng.] The dung of certain animals, e.g. the badger, fox, etc. (see quots.).

1576 TURBERV. *Venerie* 184 The Badgerd pigges at comming out of the earth do commonly..cast their fyaunts. **1630** J. TAYLOR (Water P.) *Wks.* I. 93/1 A Deeres Fewmets, a Bore or a Beares Leasses, a Hare or Conneys Crottoyes, a Fox or a Badgers Feance. **1727** BRADLEY *Fam. Dict.* s.v. *Badger*, One of them casts his Fiants long, like a Fox. **1741** *Compl. Fam. Piece* II. i. 297 The Hog-Badgers..use to cast their Fiants or Dung in a small Hole.

Hence †**'fiant** *v.*, of an animal: to cast its excrements; to dung. *Obs.*

1576 Turberv. *Venerie* 184 They fyaunt within it [a hole] and hide it.

fiar ('fiːə(r)), *sb. Sc.* Also 6, 8 fear and see FEUAR. [? f. FEE *sb.*^{2} + -AR, -ER.] The owner of the fee-simple of a property, as opposed to the life-renter. ***conjunct fiar*** (see quot. 1597).

1597 Skene *De Verb. Sign.* s.v. *Feodum*, In this case the husband is proprietar and the wife is conjunct fear or liferentar. 1646 *Sc. Acts Chas. I* (1819) VI. 204 If the partie Delinquent be.. a Fiar, or hes any estate contracted to him. 1734 R. Keith *Hist. Ch. Scot.* 50 *note*, The Persons contained in the Summons were these viz. Norman Leslie, Fear of Rothes, &c. 1815 Scott *Guy M.* xxxvii, The old lady was certainly absolute fiar. 1832 Austin *Jurispr.* (1879) II. l. 858 The fiar (i.e. dominus or reversioner) may enter and work them. 1883 Ld. R. Clark in *Law Reports* 9 App. Cases 315/1 The trust purposes fail, so that the truster is the fiar of the trust estate.

fiard, fjard (fjɑːd). Also fjärd. [a. Sw. *fjärd* bay, area of water between mainland and islands, cogn. with FIORD.] An arm of the sea similar to a fiord but having a broader and more irregular shape and occurring on coasts of lower relief.

1904 A. Knox *Gloss. Geogr. & Topogr. Terms* 116 Fjärd (*Sw.*), frith or long narrow inlet, bay. 1913 J. W. Gregory *Nature & Origin Fiords* iii. 67 The essential difference between fiords and fiards is that the latter occur in coasts where the land is low. 1934 M. R. Shackleton *Europe* xv. 204 Other sea lochs.. with lower banks have been termed 'fjards', such as those occurring on the southern coast of Norway. 1940 C. M. Rice *Dict. Geol. Terms* 135/2 Fiards are shorter and shallower than fiords... Norway is a fiord country, while Sweden has few fiords but many fiards. 1965 F. J. Monkhouse *Princ. Phys. Geogr.* 325 Around the low-lying coasts of southern Sweden are numerous indentations to which are given the name of *fjärd*... Apart from their lower shores and surroundings they are broader and less regular than fjords.

fiars ('fiərz), *pl. Sc.* [Pl. of *fier*, FEER a standard.] The prices, annually fixed, of the different kinds of grain. Also more fully ***fiar(s prices***, and ***sheriff-fiars***. ***fiars-court***, the court at which the prices are fixed.

1723 *Acts Sederunt* 21 Dec. (1790) 278 Act declaring and appointing the Manner of striking the Sheriff-fiars. *Ibid.*, That there is a general complaint, That the said fiars are struck.. without due care. *Ibid.* 279 Determining and fixing the fiar-prices. 1835 *Act 5–6 Will. IV*, c. 63 §16 The Fiar Prices of all Grain in every County shall be struck by the Imperial Quarter. 1861 W. Bell *Dict. Law Scot.* s.v., The prices fixed by the opinion of the jury and sanctioned by the judge are termed the fiars of that year. 1887 *Scotsman* 8 Mar., At a Fiars Court for the county of Renfrew held.. in Paisley, the prices of the season's crops were struck.

fiasco (fiː'æskəʊ). [a. (in sense 2 through F.) It. *fiasco* (see FLASK) lit. 'a flask, bottle'.

The fig. use of the phrase *far fiasco* (lit. 'to make a bottle') in the sense 'to break down or fail in a performance' is of obscure origin; Italian etymologists have proposed various guesses, and alleged incidents in Italian theatrical history are related to account for it.]

‖ 1. A bottle, flask.

1887 *Athenæum* 12 Nov. 635/3 A fiasco of good Chianti could be had for a paul.

2. A failure or break-down in a dramatic or musical performance. Also in a general sense: An ignominious failure, a 'mull'.

1855 Ld. Lonsdale in *Croker Papers* (1884) III. xxix. 325 Derby has made what the theatrical people call a *fiasco*. 1868 M. Pattison *Academ. Org.* vii. 329 We have lately had some rude reminders.. in the fiasco of our railway system, &c. 1879 Farrar *St. Paul* II. 347 They would take care that he should cause no second fiasco by turning their theologic jealousies against each other.

fiat ('faɪæt). [a. L. *fiat* 'let it be done', 'let there be made', 3rd pers. sing. pres. subj. of *fierī*, used as passive of *facĕre* to do, make.]

1. *orig.* The word 'fiat' itself, or a formula containing it, by which a competent authority gave his sanction to a proposed arrangement, to the performance of a request, etc. Hence, an authoritative sanction, an authorization. †***fiat in bankruptcy***: see quot. 1848.

[Compare the following examples in med.L.: Ita fiat ut ego Chlodoveus volui (*Grant by Clovis* in Mabillon *De Re Diplomatica* vi. li. (1681) 463). Signaturæ autem Papales expediuntur ab ipsa sanctitate per Fiat simplex, vel per Fiat geminatum, vel per Fiat proprio motu, vel per Fiat, ut petitur (*Compend. Benefic. Expos.* in Du Cange s.v.).]

1636 Sanderson *Serm.* II. 60 Unless the Lord be pleased to set His fiat unto it, and to confirm it with His royal assent. 1647 N. Bacon *Disc. Govt. Eng.* i. Concl. (1739) 201 Nothing can be concluded without the King's Fiat. *a* 1670 Hacket *Abp. Williams* i. §101. 90 That all the Lecturers.. be Licenced.. with a Fiat from the Lord Arch-Bishop of Canterbury. 1768 *Priv. Lett. Ld. Malmesbury* I. 157 Mr. Wilkes not being in custody, the Attorney-General has refused his fiat to the writ of error which he wishes to sue out. 1834 Lytton *Pompeii* iv. ix, I tell thee I have the fiat of the prætor. 1848 Wharton *Law Lex.*, *Fiat in Bankruptcy*, the authority of the Lord Chancellor to a commissioner of bankrupts, authorising him to proceed in the bankruptcy of a trader mentioned therein. 1865 Carlyle *Fredk. Gt.* VI. xvi. i. 132 The decisive fiat was given: 'Yes; start on it, in God's name!'

b. *gen.* An authoritative pronouncement, decree, command, order.

a 1750 A. Hill *Wedding Day* Wks. 1753 III. 173 Our hands, at length, the unchanging fiat bound. 1810 Shelley *Zastrozzi* xvii, Still Zastrozzi stood unmoved, and fearlessly awaited the fiat of his destiny. 1874 Stubbs *Const. Hist.* II. xvii. 570 To determine by the fiat of the king alone the course of national policy. 1883 J. Hawthorne *Dust* I. 44 Whose fiat in matters of fashion was law.

2. With reference to '*fiat lux*' (let there be light) Gen. i. 3 in the Vulgate: A command having for its object the creation, formation, or construction of something.

a 1631 Donne *Storm* 70 So that we (except God say Another 'Fiat') shall haue noe more day. 1710 Berkeley *Princ. Hum. Knowl.* §60 If it be a Spirit that immediately produces every effect by a *fiat* or act of his will. 1779 T. Jefferson *Corr.* Wks. 1859 I. 215 Put into movement.. by the fiat of a comprehensive mind. 1871 Tyndall *Fragm. Sc.* (1879) I. i. 6 Was space furnished at once, by the fiat of Omnipotence, with these burning orbs? 1872 Yeats *Growth Comm.* 358 St. Petersburg.. sprang into existence by the fiat of royal will.

3. *attrib.*, as ***fiat-power***; **fiat-money**, *U.S.* money (such as an inconvertible paper currency) which is made legal tender by a 'fiat' of the government, without having an intrinsic or promissory value equal to its nominal value.

1880 E. Kirke *Garfield* 30 We shall still hear echoes of the old conflict, such as.. the virtues of 'fiat-money'. 1887 A. Johnston in *New Princeton Rev.* IV. 176 The verdict of approval, however, has usually taken a form which implies a certain fiat power in the Convention. 1888 Bryce *Amer. Commw.* II. iii. lvi. 369 *note*, Greenbacks, or so-called 'fiat money'.

fiat ('faɪæt), *v.* [f. prec.] *trans.* To attach a 'fiat' to; to sanction.

1831 *Fraser's Mag.* IV. 246 Their adjudication is all but fiated when they go out of office. 1863 Le Fanu *House by Churchyard* (ed. 2) I. 7 My uncle fiated the sexton's presentment, and the work commenced forthwith. 1871 *Times* 25 Feb., Mr. Justice Fitzgerald to-day fiated a presentment for 500*l.* to the family of M'Mahon.

fiat lux ('faɪæt lʌks). [L., = let there be light.] Used allusively with reference to Gen. i. 3.

a 1680 S. Charnock *Disc. Knowl. God* in *Wks.* (1684) II. 405 The new Creation as well as the old begins with a *Fiat lux*. 1905 *Daily Chron.* 21 Apr. 3/1 The death-knell of tyranny in these islands, a *fiat-lux* in the history of the Western hemisphere.

fiaunt, obs. var. of FIANT.

fib (fɪb), *sb.*^{1} *colloq.* Also 8 phibb. [Of obscure origin; possibly shortened from FIBLE-FABLE.]

1. A venial or trivial falsehood; often used as a jocular euphemism for 'a lie'.

1611 Cotgr., *Bourde*, a ieast, fib, tale of a tub. 1726 De Foe *Hist. Devil* ii. iv. (1840) 221, I think it is a fib. 1773 Goldsm. *Stoops to Conq.* iii, Ask me no questions, and I'll tell you no fibs. 1826 Scott *Woodst.* x, A fib never failed a fanatic. 1842 Thackeray *Fitz-Boodle's Prof.* i, He must not.. tell fibs about himself or them. 1875 H. James *R. Hudson* ii. 48 No one.. was used to offering hollow welcomes or telling polite fibs.

2. One who tells 'fibs'; a fibber, a liar.

1568 *Hist. Jacob & Esau* v. vi. in Hazl. *Dodsley* II. 254 What sayest thou, thou fib? 1861 H. Kingsley *Ravenshoe* III. ix. 140 'Oh! you dreadful fib', said Flora.

fib (fɪb), *sb.*^{2} [f. FIB *v.*^{2}] A blow.

1814 *Sporting Mag.* XLIV. 111 A fib.. which he gave the Black under the left ribs.

fib (fɪb), *v.*^{1} Also 7 fibb, 8 phib. [f. FIB *sb.*] *intr.* To tell a fib; to lie.

1690 Dryden *Amphitryon* iv. i, I do not say he lyes neither: no, I am too well bred for that: but his Lordship fibbs most abominably. 1712 Arbuthnot *John Bull* iv. iv, Any particular mark.. whereby one may know when you fib. *a* 1839 Praed *Poems* (1864) II. 8 Both were very apt to fib! 1863 A. Smith *Dreamthorp* 11 Could I have fibbed.. Could I have betrayed a comrade?

¶ Webster 1864 cites De Quincey for a transitive use, 'To tell a fib to'; see quot. 1830 s.v. FIB *v.*^{2}

Hence '**fibbing** *vbl. sb.*, the action of the vb., an instance of this; '**fibbing** *ppl. a.*

1749 Fielding *Tom Jones* xiii. xii, At the expence of a little fibbing. 1820 Lamb *Final Mem.* iii. To Miss Hutchinson 255, I shall certainly go to the naughty man some day for my fibbings. 1879 G. Meredith *Egoist* xxviii, No one could doubt his talent for elegant fibbing.

fib (fɪb), *v.*^{2} *slang. trans.* To strike or beat, to deliver blows in quick succession upon, as in pugilism. ***to fib about***: to knock about. Also *absol.* or *intr.*

1665 R. Head *Eng. Rogue* iv. 32 *Fib*, to beat. 1692 Coles, *Fib*, to beat. 1785 Grose *Dict. Vulg. Tongue* s.v. *Fib*, Fib the cove's quarron in the rumpad for the lour in his bung, beat the fellow in the highway for the money in his purse. 1808 *Sporting Mag.* XXXII. 77 Gully.. fibbed him and kept him from falling. 1812 *Ibid.* XXXIX. 19 Crib.. fibbed until Molineux fell. 1831 *Mirror* XVII. 247/1 If two men choose to stand up and fib each other about.. why let them do it. 1865 G. F. Berkeley *My Life* I. 311, I fibbed at half-a-dozen waistcoats and faces with all my might and main. *fig.* 1811 Southey *Lett.* (1856) II. 236 As you will see in the 'Quarterly', where I have fibbed the 'Edinburgh' (as in the 'fancy' say) most completely. 1830 De Quincey *Bentley* Wks. VII. 90 Here, again, Bentley got Bishop Greene under his arm, and 'fibbed' him cruelly.

Hence '**fibbing** *vbl. sb.*, the action of the vb., an instance of this. Also *attrib.*

1812 J. H. Vaux *Flash Dict.*, *Fibbing-gloak*, a pugilist; *fibbing-match*, a boxing-match. 1814 *Sporting Mag.* XLIV. 72 Oliver got at the fibbing system. 1816 *Times* 25 Jan., Explain the terms.. fibbing—cross buttock.. bang up—and —prime. 1840 Barham *Ingol. Leg.*, *Bagman's Dog*, Muses More skill'd than my meek one in fibbings and bruises.

fibber ('fɪbə(r)). [f. FIB *v.*^{1} + -ER^1.] One who fibs or tells fibs; a petty liar.

1723 Dyche *Dict.*, *Fibber*. 1746 *Brit. Mag.* 381 Molly.. was received as a great Fibber. 1798 W. Taylor in *Monthly Rev.* XXVI. 533 At length then, you fibber, you are return'd. 1882 Payn *For Cash only* xxvi, For one's lover to be a fibber is bad enough.

fibbery ('fɪbərɪ). [f. prec. + -Y.] The practice of a fibber; falsehood, lying.

1857 'Ducange Anglicus' *Vulg. Tongue* 42 'The Leary Man' 6 And if you come to fibbery, You must mug one or two. 1870 *Standard* 12 Dec., An official report, full of delicate fibbery, was placarded to reassure the public.

† '**fiberkie**. *Sc. Obs. rare.* [f. *fiber*, FIBRE + *-kie*, Sc. dim. suffix.] A small fibre; a fibril.

1668 Culpepper & Cole *Barthol. Anat.* ii. iii. 91 The Pericardium.. is firmly fastned.. by little smal Fiberkies.

† **fibicches**, *pl. Obs. rare.* In 4 febicchis, fybicches. ? Contrivances, cheating tricks.

1362 Langl. *P. Pl.* A. xi. 156 ȝet arn þere febicchis of Forellis of mony mennes wittes. 1377 *Ibid.* B. x. 211 ȝet ar þere fybicches in forceres of fele mennes makynge.

'**fible-'fable**. *Obs.* exc. *dial.* Also 6 fybble-fable. [reduplication of FABLE.] Nonsense.

1581 J. Bell *Haddon's Answ. Osor.* 407 The most fybble-fable y^t ever could be imagined. 1847 Halliwell, *Fible-fable*, nonsense.

† '**fibling**, *ppl. a.* ? *nonce-wd.* [as if pr. pple. of *fibble v., f. FIB *sb.*^{1} or *v*^{1}.] Addicted to telling little fibs.

1681 Hickeringill *Vind. Naked Truth* ii. 36 A fibling, quibbling, fribling, fumbling Arch-Deacon.

Fibonacci (fiːbəʊ'nɑːtʃɪ, -æ-). The name of Leonardo *Fibonacci*, also called Leonardo Pisano (*fl.* 1200), Tuscan mathematician, used *attrib.* or in the possessive, esp. in ***Fibonacci('s) numbers***, the numbers 1, 1, 2, 3, 5, 8, . ., where every number after the first two is the sum of the two preceding numbers (0 is sometimes included as the first term); ***Fibonacci('s) sequence, series***, the series of Fibonacci numbers, or any similar series in which each term is an integer equal to the sum of the two preceding terms.

1891 *Cent. Dict.* VII. 5509/2 *Fibonacci's series*, the phyllotactic succession of numbers: 0, 1, 1, 2, 3, 5, . . etc. 1901 *Ann. Bot.* XV. 481 This series of fractional expressions, which involves the utilization of the Fibonacci ratio series 2, 3, 5, 8, 13, &c., has thus proved for over sixty years the ground-work of all theories of phyllotaxis. 1914 T. A. Cook *Curves of Life* v. 88 The fact that these Fibonacci numbers dominated leaf-arrangements in the case of higher plants was first established by the German botanists, Schimper and Braun (1830). 1929 *Mind* XXXVIII. 54 The side of the decagon.. may be read off at once to any required degree of accuracy from our table of the Sectio Divina or Golden Mean, or in other words from our Fibonacci series. 1938 Hardy & Wright *Introd. Theory of Numbers* x. 147 The series (U_n) or 1, 1, 2, 3, 5, [etc.].. is usually called Fibonacci's series. 1939 W. W. R. Ball *Math. Recreations & Ess.* (ed. 11) ii. 57 The ratios of alternate Fibonacci numbers are said to measure the fraction of a turn between successive leaves on the stalk of a plant: $\frac{1}{2}$ for grasses, $\frac{1}{3}$ for sedges, $\frac{2}{5}$ for the apple, cherry, etc., $\frac{3}{8}$ for the common plantain, . . and so on. 1961 H. S. M. Coxeter *Introd. Geom.* xi. 172 Fibonacci numbers as large as $f_{10} = 55, f_{11} = 89, f_{12} = 144$ arise as the numbers of visible spirals in certain varieties of sunflower. 1964 *Fibonacci Q.* Feb. 34 The only Fibonacci sequence having all primes as divisors [of] one or other of its terms is the one Fibonacci sequence with a zero element, namely: 0, 1, 1, 2, 3, 5, 8, 13, . . . 1970 *Daily Tel.* 27 June 7, I do not for a moment believe that the musical sense can be traced back to the employment.. of numbers from the Fibonacci series (1, 1, 2, 3, 5, 8, 13 and so on), with their ever closer approximation to the golden section.

‖ **fibra**. *Obs.* Pl. fibræ, fibra's. [L. *fibra* FIBRE.] A fibre, filament.

1641 Wilkins *Math. Magick* i. v. (1648) 29 There are besides divers fibræ or hairy substances. 1657 M. Lawrence *Use & Practice of Faith* 15 The youngest plants thrust their fibra's into the earth. *a* 1661 Fuller *Worthies* i. 330 The many fibræ appendant to the root thereof. 1775 Ash, *Fibra*.

† '**fibrate**, *v. Obs.*$^{-0}$ [f. L. *fibr-a* + -ATE^3.] *trans.* To supply (something) with fibres or filaments. Hence '**fibrated** *ppl. a.*

1681 tr. *Willis' Rem. Med. Wks.* Vocab., Fibrated, that has small and hairy strings.

fibre ('faɪbə(r)), *sb.* Forms: 4 fybre, 7 fiuer, fiver, 7, 9 fiber, 9 fifer (*dial.*), 7– fibre. [a. F. *fibre* (= Sp., Pg., It. *fibra*), ad. L. *fibra*, of uncertain origin; variously referred by etymologists to L. roots *fid-* (as in *findĕre* to split) and *fis-* or *fi-* (as in *filum* thread). The spelling *fiber* is common in the U.S., but is now rare in England.]

† 1. After Latin usage: a. A lobe or portion of the liver. b. *pl.* The entrails. *Obs.*

1398 Trevisa *Barth. De P.R.* v. xxxix. (1495) 153 The endes of the lyuer hyght fybre for they.. beclepyth the stomake. 1598 Grenewey *Tacitus' Ann.* xiv. x, They.. aske

counsell of their gods by the aspect of mans intrales and fibres. **1601** HOLLAND *Pliny* I. 342 The lobes or fibres in the smal Liuers of certaine Mice.

2. *Phys.* One of a number of thread-like bodies or filaments, that enter into the composition of animal (muscular, nervous, etc.) and vegetable tissue. **a.** in animals. ***fibres of Corti***: see CORTIAN *a.*

1607 TOPSELL *Four-f. Beasts* (1658) 99 His blood..hath no Fibres or small veins in it. **1621** G. SANDYS *Ovid's Met.* VI. (1626) 113 The threds Of life, his fiuers, wrathfull Delius shreds. **1646** SIR T. BROWNE *Pseud. Ep.* III. xv. 142 Wormes ..whose bodies consist of round and annulary fibers. **1664** POWER *Exp. Philos.* I. 5 Her wings look like a Sea-fan with black thick ribs or fibers, dispers'd..through them. **1704** F. FULLER *Med. Gymn.* (1711) 33 The Fibre it self strengthens by Use. **1793** HOLCROFT *Lavater's Physiog.* xx. 98 In cold countries the fibres of the tongue must be less flexible. **1808** A. PARSONS *Trav.* i. 7 The natives eat the myrtle berries as an astringent; their fibres being rendered extremely lax by the climate. **1855** BAIN *Senses & Int.* I. ii. §4 The optic nerve ..might contain as many as a million of fibres. **1888** J. MARTINEAU *Study Relig.* I. II. i. 305 Its two thousand fibres of Corti stretched.

fig. *a* **1634** CHAPMAN (W.), Yet had no fibres in him, nor no force. **1638** W. GRANT in *G. Sandys' Paraphr. Div. Poems* Pref. Verse, Truth..so sweetely strikes Upon the Cords, and Fivers of the Heart. **1742** YOUNG *Nt. Th.* v. 1059 The tender tyes, Close-twisted with the fibres of the heart! **1831** CARLYLE *Misc.* (1857) II. 329 Every fibre of him is Philistine. **1847** EMERSON *Poems, Monadnoc* Wks. (Bohn) I. 435 And of the fibre..Whose throbs are love. *a* **1853** ROBERTSON *Addr.* ii. (1858) 55 They are bound up in every fibre of my being.

b. in plants; esp. an elongated cell that lacks protoplasm, has thick walls and tapering ends, and serves to strengthen plant tissue.

1663 COWLEY *Ode Dr. Harvey* i, No smallest Fibres of a Plant..His passage after her withstood. **1676** HALE *Contempl.* I. 254 A Worm..gnaws asunder the Roots and Fibres of it. **1703** POPE *Vertumnus* 16 The thirsty plants.. feed their fibres with reviving dew. **1791** HAMILTON *Berthollet's Dyeing* I. I. I. iii. 52 The vascular fibres of the bark. **1838** T. THOMSON *Chem. Org. Bodies* II. v. 984 There is..an attraction between vegetable fibres and watery liquids. **1857** A. HENFREY *Elem. Bot.* 513 Prosenchyma is composed of cells elongated greatly in one direction, and attenuated to a more or less acute point at each end, forming what is called a fibre. **1865** LUBBOCK *Preh. Times* xiii. (1869) 462 They also used the fibres of the cocoa nut for making threads. **1919** F. O. BOWER *Bot. Living Plant* ii. 28 The old name *parenchyma* is kept for a tissue of roughly spherical or oblong cells with square ends, while long thick-walled cells with pointed ends are called *fibres*. **1965** BELL & COOMBE tr. *Strasburger's Textbk. Bot.* (new ed.) 107 Within the limit of elasticity, the load-bearing capacity of sclerenchyma fibres taken from the living plant is, generally speaking, equal to that of the best wrought iron.

3. One of the thread-like filaments of organic structure which form a textile or other material substance; also *transf.* of inorganic substances.

1827 FARADAY *Chem. Manip.* ii. 49 A silk fibre. **1832** BABBAGE *Econ. Manuf.* iv. (ed. 3) 32 Twisting the fibres of wool by the fingers would be a most tedious operation. **1832** G. R. PORTER *Porcelain & Gl.* 282 Delicate..fibres of glass joined with the greatest nicety. **1878** HUXLEY *Physiogr.* 193 A very liquid lava may be caught by the wind, and drawn out into delicate fibres.

4. *collect.* **a.** A substance consisting of fibres, whether animal or vegetable. Also, Fibrous structure.

1810 HENRY *Elem. Chem.* (1826) II. 273 The woody fibre ..does not undergo any change. **1831** R. KNOX *Cloquet's Anat.* 7 *Nervous fibre*: this is the peculiar substance of which the brain and nerves are composed. **1847** EMERSON *Repr. Men, Montaigne* Wks. (Bohn) I. 349 He has contrived to get so much bone and fibre as he wants. **1854** H. MILLER *Footpr. Creat.* x. (1874) 183 *note*, Pieces of coal which exhibit the ligneous fibre. **1858** CARPENTER *Veg. Phys.* §42 Even these primary tissues may be regarded as consisting of other parts still more simple,—namely, membrane and fibre.

b. *fig.*

1855 BAIN *Senses & Int.* III. iv. §17 A man of the political fibre. **1872** BAGEHOT *Physics & Pol.* (1876) 47 There is an improvement in our fibre—moral, if not physical. **1885** *Century Mag.* XXX. 398/1 This love of fierce and cruel sport was in the fiber.

c. A structure characteristic of wrought metal in which there is a directional alignment or elongation of crystals or inclusions.

1855 W. TRURAN *Iron Manuf. Gt. Brit.* XVIII. 161 If the several layers [of metal] are thin and cross each other, the tendency of one layer to develope fibre is neutralized by the opposite tendency of the other. **1928** WILLIAMS & HOMERBERG *Princ. Metallogr.* (ed. 2) vi. 200 A study of fiber in steel is of great importance..in the manufacture of such articles as crankshafts, gears, and other forgings. **1966** *McGraw-Hill Encycl. Sci. & Technol.* VIII. 286/2 Hot-working processes, such as forging, align the inclusions (fiber structure).

5. *esp.* A fibrous substance fit for use in textile fabrics.

1870 YEATS *Nat. Hist. Comm.* 70 Vegetable fibres find India their most prolific home. **1875** D. KAY in *Encycl. Brit.* (ed. 9) I. 565/1 The most important fibre is the crin vegetal ..produced from the dwarf palm. **1879** J. PATON *Ibid.* IX. 131/2 *Textile Fibres*..include all substances capable of being spun, woven, or felted. **1892** K. TYNAN in *Speaker* 3 Sept. 290/1 [The roses] were swathed in cocoanut fibre and sacking.

6. A subdivision of a root, a small root or rootlet; occas. of a twig.

1656–81 BLOUNT *Glossogr.*, *Fibers*, the smal threads, or hair-like strings of roots. **1694** *Acc. Sev. Late Voy.* II. 56 The Root consists of many small Fibers. **1787** WINTER *Syst. Husb.* 153 Their numerous fibres or lateral roots will extend themselves horizontally. **1807** J. E. SMITH *Phys. Bot.* 105 After they [plants] have begun to throw out new fibres, it is more or less dangerous..to remove them. **1810** SCOTT *Lady of L.* I. xxv, Where weeping birch and willow round With their long fibres swept the ground. **1821** SHELLEY *Prometh. Unb.* I. 154 To the last fibre of the loftiest tree. **1840** SPURDENS *Suppl. Voc. E. Anglia*, *Fifers*..fibrous roots.

fig. *a* **1679** T. GOODWIN *Wks.* (1697) IV. II. 65 To apply Christ, is..to strike forth a Sprig or Fibre from every Faculty into him. **1869** GOULBURN *Purs. Holiness* vii. 55 Whatever fibres there are in our nature by which we cling and cleave to those around us. **1879** FARRAR *St. Paul* (1883) 177 A man who had tried..to extirpate the very fibres of the church.

†**7.** In Kepler's system of celestial physics: see quot. *Obs.*

[**1618** KEPLER *Epit. Astron. Copernic.* v. (1635) 643 Posuimus, in cuiuslibet planetæ corpore duplices inesse fibras..fibræ latitudinis fere quidem in parallelo situ manent toto circuitu.] **1715** tr. *Gregory's Astron.* I. I. lxviii. 139 [The Planet] will come nearer to the Sun, till the Right lines drawn according to the direction of this part (that is, the Fibres along which this attractive Virtue is propagated from the Sun)..are no more inclined to the Sun. *Ibid.* lxix. 143 In each Planet there are Fibres (which he calls from their Office, the Fibres of Latitude).

8. *attrib.* and *Comb.*, as ***fibre-cultivation, -dresser, -form, -machine, -mute, needle***; ***fibre-dressing, -forming, -yielding*** adjs.; also **fibre-basket** (see quot.); **fibre-board, fibreboard,** (a piece of) board made from compressed cellulosic fibrous material (as wood pulp); **fibre-cell** (see quot. 1884); **fibre-faced** *a.*, (*a*) *U.S.* (paper) having a surface composed of visible fibres; (*b*) having a facing or coat of fibre; **fibre-gun** (see quot.); **fibre optics**, the study and application of the transmission of images by means of total internal reflection through fibres of glass or other transparent solids; so ***fibre-optic*** adj.; **fibre plant**, any plant that produces a fibre of commercial value; **fibre-saturation point**, in the drying of timber, the point at which the cell cavities have lost all their moisture but none has been removed from the cell walls, corresponding in most woods to a moisture content of about 30 per cent of the dry weight; **fibre-stitch** (see quots.); **fibre stress**, the local longitudinal stress in a body at a point in, or along a line through, a cross-section over which the stress is not uniform; **fibre-tip(ped)** *a.*, of a pen: having a tip made of tightly-packed capillary fibres which hold the ink; cf. *felt(-tip, -tipped) pen* s.v. FELT *sb.*[1] 4 d; also *ellipt.* as **fibre tip**; **fibre-tracheid** *Bot.*, a fibre-like tracheid that typically has a thick wall, tapering ends, and bordered pits with slit-like apertures; **fibre tract** [TRACT *sb.*[3] 3 b (*a*)], a bundle of nerve-fibres, esp. one in which the fibres have a common origin, termination, and function.

1884 *Syd. Soc. Lex.*, **Fibre-basket*, Schultze's term for the sustentacular tissue of the retina. **1897** *Sears, Roebuck Catal.* 616/2 Lunch boxes... Well made of compressed *fibre board. **1916** *Bull. U.S. Dept. Agric. No. 322* 17 It would seem that tow would be a more desirable as well as a more profitable raw material than straw for the fiber-board manufacturer. **1950** C. C. HANDISYDE *Building Materials* xix. 263 Fibreboards should be unpacked and stacked on a clean dry surface. **1970** *Nature* 9 May 489/1 The chief problem with making fibre board from bagasse is that vast amounts of dust are created when the material is pulped. **1878** BELL *Gegenbauer's Comp. Anat.* 31 The..contractile *fibre-cells constitute the first form. **1884** *Syd. Soc. Lex.*, *Fibre-cell*, Kölliker's term for the fusiform, nucleated, cellular structures which form the involuntary muscles. **1892** *Pall Mall G.* 21 July 7/1 The progress made in *fibre cultivation in the colony. **1904** *Daily Chron.* 9 Dec. 7/3 A younger brother, who was employed at a horse-hair and *fibre dressers. **1919** *Brit. Manufacturer* Nov. 25/1 Passing on to more specialised agricultural appliances, we find great attention paid to *fibre-dressing machinery, especially in the Yorkshire and Lancashire districts. *a* **1884** KNIGHT *Dict. Mech.* Suppl. 332/2 **Fiber-faced paper*, a means of security against the restoration of the surface of check or draft-paper after it has been tampered with. It consists in imbedding in the pulp..a layer of fibers, the outer ends of which are then raised in the form of a nap, [etc.]. **1922** *Times* 20 June 8/5 At right angles to this disc is a fibre-faced wheel which is mounted on a castellated shaft, along which it can be slid by means of the 'gear' lever. **1946** *Nature* 19 Oct. 553/2 Alginic acid yarn can be acetylated without loss of *fibre-form. *Ibid.* 28 Dec. 930/1 A new *fibre-forming polymer..to which the name 'Terylene' has been provisionally assigned. **1874** KNIGHT *Dict. Mech.*, **Fiber-gun*, a device for disintegrating vegetable fiber. **1887** *Pall Mall G.* 6 May 12/1 A few leaves ..were recently passed through Death's *fibre machine. **1946** A. L. BACHARACH *Brit. Mus.* vii. 107 The trumpets should use *fibre mutes (now in general use, but then confined to jazz bands) instead of the old pear-shaped brass ones. **1913** *Talking Machine News & Jrnl. Amusements* Feb. 147/2, I should advise 'Troubled' to try the *Fibre needles advertised in this paper. **1929** WILSON & WEBB *Mod. Gramophones* 153 A fibre needle, in a sound-box specially made for it. **1961** *Flight* LXXIX. 728/1 Windows in the passenger cabin..may be augmented by closed-circuit television or '*fibre optic' devices. **1965** *Amer. Jrnl. Cardiol.* XV. 672/1 The fiberoptic system depends upon the efficient transmission of light lengthwise along glass fibers, each of which has a core of high refractive index and a sheath of low refractive index. **1956** *Times* 3 Dec. 59/1 If one beam of light can be transmitted along a glass tube, why not transmit detailed images along the same path?.. Dr. Narinder Singh Kapany, 30, has succeeded by applying a technique he refers to as '*fiber optics'. *Ibid.*, Fiber optics derives its name from its use of hair-thin strands of optical glass as light carriers. **1957** N. S. KAPANY in *Jrnl. Optical Soc. Amer.* XLVII. 117 (*heading*) An introduction to fiber optics. **1961** *Engineering* 4 Aug. 134/1 Fibre optics grew out of a need to look round corners, e.g. into complex castings or inside the kidney of a living person. **1970** *Times Lit. Suppl.* 23 July 817/1 The action of the vocal cords during speech can be observed.. through a flexible fiber-optics tube which is inserted through the nose so that its end hangs above the vocal cords. **1887** C. A. MOLONEY *Sk. Forestry W. Afr.* 277 'Buaze' *fibre plant of the Zambesi (*Securidaca longipedunculata*). **1957** *Encycl. Brit.* VII. 939/1 The fibre plant *Carludovica palmata* (not a palm), used for making Panama hats. **1930** *Forestry* IV. 34 The loss of the free moisture marks the first stage in drying at any point in the wood, and it is not until this moisture has all gone and the stage known as 'the *fibre saturation point' is reached, that the cell-walls begin to dry. **1882** CAULFEILD & SAWARD *Dict. Needlework*, **Fibre stitch*, a stitch used in Honiton and other Pillow Laces to make open leaves, with a fibre running down their centres. **1957** M. B. PICKEN *Fashion Dict.* 129 *Fiber-stitch*, stitch used in bobbin lace. **1905** A. H. HELLER *Stresses in Structures* vii. 91 The maximum unit *fiber stress (working stress). **1931** G. A. GARRATT *Mech. Prop. Wood* IV. 200 In large beams the weight should be taken into account in calculating the fiber stress. **1952** *Special Rep. Iron & Steel Inst.* XLIII. iv. 171/2 The maximum fibre stress in bending may be distinctly less than that based on an elastic state of distribution. [**1965** *Geyer's Dealer Topics* July 54/2 Fine point marking pen has acrylic fiber-tip.] **1969** *Encycl. Amer.* XV. 180/1 The greatest progress in the development of writing inks has taken place since the 1940's..due to the development..of.. the ball-point pen, the felt-tip marker, and the *fiber-tip pen. **1971** *Sunday Times* 31 Oct. 17/3 Ball-points, fibre-tips and fountain pens all freeze up, as does the hand that tries to push them in sub-zero conditions. **1976** *Electr. Australia* Apr. 75/1 A Nestler B5 pen generally gives more control than is possible with brushes or fibre tips. **1983** *Austral. Microcomputer Mag.* Sept. 89/4 Wet ink drawing pens, felt-tip markers and fibre-tip pens may be used. **1974** *Encycl. Brit. Macropædia* XIX. 1046/1 A Japanese-made *fibre-tipped pen found great success in the Japanese and U.S. markets beginning in 1964. **1985** *Observer* (Colour Suppl.) 10 Mar. 31/1 There is an overwhelming choice of felt and fibre tipped pens on the market. **1898** H. C. PORTER tr. *Strasburger's Text-bk. Bot.* 129 In Oaks, Beeches, and in the *Rosiflorae* wood fibres are absent, and the necessary rigidity is provided for by *fibre tracheids. **1953** K. ESAU *Plant Anat.* x. 204 Wall thickness and particularly the nature of pitting are used to differentiate between the two main categories of wood fibers, fiber-tracheids and libriform fibers. **1904** *Brit. Jrnl. Psychol.* I. 53 *Fibre-tracts from corresponding halves of the retinae both go to the occipital region of one and the same hemisphere. **1959** *Chambers's Encycl.* IX. 771/2 The medulla oblongata contains nerve cells and fibre tracts associated with certain of the cranial nerves. **1908** R. W. SINDALL *Manuf. Paper* ii. 40 A large and important genus of *fibre-yielding plants.

fibre ('faɪbə(r)), *v. rare.* [f. prec. sb.] *intr.* Of plants: To form or throw out fibres.

1869 *Daily News* 6 Feb., The plant is sufficiently strong, with ample room to fibre as prodigally as it likes.

fibred ('faɪbəd), *ppl. a.* [f. FIBRE *sb.* + -ED[2].] Furnished with fibres; chiefly in comb., as ***finely-fibred, three-fibred***, etc. Also *fig.*

1776 WITHERING *Brit. Plants* (1796) II. 14 Serpyllifolia.. leaves..3-fibred. **1844** MRS. BROWNING *Lost Bower* xxiv, The wild hop fibred closely.

fig. **1869** BUSHNELL *Wom. Suffrage* viii. 177 They have a nature fibred and feathered for the highest inspirations. **1874** BLACKIE *Self-Cult.* 67 Some of the kindliest and most finely-fibred affections.

'fibreglass, 'fibre(-)glass. Also Fiberglas [U.S. proprietary term.] Any material consisting of very thin glass filaments made into a textile or paper, or embedded in plastic or other substances for use as a construction or insulating material; also, glass in the form of filaments suitable for such uses. Freq. *attrib.*; also *Comb.*

1937 *Amer. Dyestuff Reporter* XXVI. P182 (*heading*) 'Fiberglas' products. *Ibid.*, There are many types of Fiberglas fibers. They vary in diameter according to their use. **1938** *Ceramic Age* XXXI. 9/1 Owens-Illinois Fiberglas, the trade-mark of the material discussed in this paper, already has become a modern, commercial raw material..in the textile industry. **1941** *Flight* 6 Feb. 113/2 A fabric made of 'fibre glass' for wing covering. **1951** *Good Housek. Home Encycl.* 135/1 A quilt of fibre glass between the bedroom ceiling and the roof gives protection against cold. **1956** 'N. SHUTE' *Beyond Black Stump* i. 14 The new styles in outboard motors and fibreglass boats. **1960** *Spectator* 22 July 133/1 As light and fast and manœuvrable as a fibre-glass racing car. **1964** G. SLAYTER in O. A. Battista *Synthetic Fibers in Papermaking* v. 103 When impregnated with suitable oils or resins, Fiberglas papers have excellent dielectric strength. **1969** *Jane's Freight Containers 1968–69* 464/1 A fibreglass-resin patch is all that is needed to plug puncture holes.

fibreless ('faɪbəlɪs), *a.* [f. FIBRE + -LESS.] Without fibres or fibre; without strength, nerveless.

1864 *Sat. Rev.* 21 May, More nerveless and fibreless than a screeching sopranello in the Papal choir. **1884** *L'pool Mercury* 3 Mar. 5/3 The fibreless Liberals who went into alliance with them.

fibrement ('faɪbəmənt). *rare.* [f. FIBRE + -MENT.] The process of making fibre or flesh.

1876 LANIER *Poems, Clover* 118 The pasture is God's pasture; systems strange Of food and fiberment he hath.

fibrescope (ˈfaɪbəskəʊp). Also **fiberscope**. [f. FIBRE *sb.* + -SCOPE.] A fibre-optic device used to view inaccessible internal structure, esp. in medicine to examine passages in the body.

1954 HOPKINS & KAPANY in *Nature* 2 Jan. 39/2 An optical unit has been devised which will convey optical images along a flexible axis. The unit comprises a bundle of fibres of glass, or other transparent material, and it therefore appears appropriate to introduce the term 'fibrescope' to denote it. **1961** *Lancet* 20 May 1074/1 The fiberscope superficially resembles a conventional gastro-scope... The shaft of the instrument contains the glass fibre bundle which transmits the image to the eye-piece and is completely flexible throughout its entire length. **1961** *New Scientist* 1 June 494 A new device for viewing the lower part of the gullet, stomach, duodenum and a foot of the small intestine . . known as the fiberscope.

fibrid (ˈfaɪbrɪd). [f. FIBR(E + -ID.] A synthetic polymer material, used principally for bonding synthetic fibres, esp. in *Paper-making*.

1960 *New Scientist* 10 Nov. 1234/3 The fibrid . . developed by the Du Pont organization in the United States. Fibrids . . may be derived from polyamides (nylon), polyesters (like Terylene) or acrylic compounds such as Orlon. **1964** D. G. BANNERMANN in O. A. Battista *Synthetic Fibers in Papermaking* iv. 92 Papers of 100% Dacron polyester fiber bonded with polyester fibrid 201 retain 91% of their dry strength when wet at room temperature.

fibriform (ˈfaɪbrɪfɔːm), *a.* [f. FIBRE + -(I)FORM.] Having the form of a fibre or fibres; fibre-like.

1846 DANA *Zooph.* (1848) 700 Coralla calcareous, consisting of fibriform tubes. **1884** BOWER & SCOTT *De Bary's Phaner. & Ferns* 497 They then always belong to the 'fibriform' category, resembling woody fibres in shape.

fibril (ˈfaɪbrɪl). [ad. mod.L. *fibrilla*: see next. Cf. Fr. *fibrille.*] A small fibre.

1. a. *Phys.* The subdivision of a fibre (see FIBRE 2 a) in a nerve, muscle, etc., and in vegetable fibres and man-made fibres.

1681 tr. *Willis' Rem. Med. Wks.* Vocab., *Fibrils*, little small strings of fibres, or of the nerves or veins. **1713** CHESELDEN *Anat.* III. xv. (1726) 247 The nervous fibrils probably do not communicate. **1794** G. ADAMS *Nat. & Exp. Philos.* II. xvii. 286 The corresponding fibrils of the two retinas. **1805** CARLISLE in *Phil. Trans.* XCVI. 8 Three large superficial nerves . . give off fibrils at right angles. **1855** H. SPENCER *Princ. Psychol.* (1872) I. I. iii. 53 An extremely delicate fibril less than $\frac{1}{100}$ of an inch in length.

b. Any thread-like molecular formation such as occurs in some colloidal systems and proteins.

1931 S. S. KISTLER in *Colloid Symposium Monograph* 63 The greater strength of the gel after it has been converted to an aerogel is doubtless due to dehydration of the fibrils. **1944** *Jrnl. Amer. Chem. Soc.* LXVI. 663/1 Electron micrographs of this material [*sc.* insulin hydro-chloride] reveal the presence of uniform fibrils several microns in length, having uniform widths of approximately 200 A (an asymmetry well above 100). **1944** E. HEUSER *Chem. Cellulose* ii. 16 Seifriz and Hock separated wood pulp fibers into fibrils, 1·4 μ thick. **1948** SCHMIDT & MARLIES *Princ. High-Polymer Theory & Pract.* xi. 468 Rayons having a high order of crystallite orientation separate into fibrils under the action of appropriate chemical agents. **1959** [see FIBRILLAR *a.*]. **1968** A. WHITE et al. *Princ. Biochem.* (ed. 4) xxxviii. 874 Hydrogen and electrostatic bonds are responsible for the end-to-end alignment which results in fibrils many times longer than the tropocollagen molecule.

2. *Bot.* The ultimate subdivision of a root.

1664 EVELYN *Sylva* (1776) 51 Theophrastus gives us great caution . . to preserve the roots and especially the earth adhering to the smallest Fibrils. **1835** LINDLEY *Introd. Bot.* (1848) I. 237 The minute subdivisions [of the root] have been . . called radicles . . others name them fibrils. **1860** OLIVER *Less. Bot.* (1873) 11 A Root . . gives off fibrils irregularly.

3. Something resembling a small fibre.

1876 GEO. ELIOT *Dan. Der.* III. xx, Her dark hair curling in fresh fibrils as it gradually dried.

fibrilla (faɪˈbrɪlə). Pl. **fibrillæ** (faɪˈbrɪliː). [mod. L. *fibrilla*, dim. of L. *fibra* FIBRE.] = prec.

1665–6 *Phil. Trans.* I. 317 A Nerve, or a Fibrilla related to it is touch'd. *a* **1754** MEAD *Wks.* (1762) II. 535 Rays of light, falling on the small arteries, instead of the nervous fibrillæ. **1757** WATSON *Chem. Ess.* IV. 120 Fibrillæ of feathers. **1854** J. HOGG *Microsc.* I. iii. 112 The most delicate of the elementary tissues of animals, such as . . the ultimate fibrillæ of muscles. **1872** HUXLEY *Phys.* ix. 222 If the fibrillæ of the optic nerve are capable of being affected by light.

fibrillar (ˈfaɪbrɪlə(r)), *a.* [f. prec. + -AR.] Of, pertaining to, of the nature of, or characteristic of a fibrilla or fibrillæ.

1847–9 TODD *Cycl. Anat.* IV. 119/2 Fibrillar substance occurs in Growths in many varieties of form. **1859** CARPENTER *Anim. Phys.* i. (1872) 33 The coagulum or clot being distinguished from that of albumen . . by the fibrillar arrangement of its particles. **1935** *Chem. Abstr.* XXIX. 2049/2 In certain circumstances the separation of fibrils can be observed; it is probable, therefore, that the 'amorphous' coagula are also fibrillar. **1948** GLASSTONE *Physical Chem.* (ed. 2) xiv. 1263 A modification of the fibrillar theory is that the gel consists of a three-dimensional network, formed by linking and cross-linking of molecular chains. **1959** *New Scientist* 5 Mar. 511/3 The crystal structure . . continues . . in fibrillar form, although the particular molecules of which a fibril is composed are continually changing.

fibrillary (ˈfaɪbrɪlərɪ), *a.* [f. FIBRILLA + -ARY.]

1. = FIBRILLAR.

1788 tr. *Swedenborg's Wisd. Angels* §365 The . . fibrillary Substance begins and proceeds thence every where.

2. Exhibiting fibrillation (sense 1 b).

1875 H. C. WOOD *Therap.* (1879) 312 When the poison is applied . . fibrillary contractions . . are induced in the muscles. **1911** *Jrnl. Physiol.* XLII. p. vii, The heart passed into a state of fibrillary contraction. **1968** LUISADA & SAINANI *Primer of Cardiac Diagnosis* xiii. 91 The fibrillary contractions of the atrium are small and not co-ordinated.

fibrillate (ˈfaɪbrɪlət), *a.* [f. FIBRILLA + -ATE[2].] = FIBRILLATED.

1884 tr. *De Bary's Fungi* I. ii. §13. 57 In large compound sporophores the surface of sections or broken pieces may often appear fibrillate even to the naked eye.

fibrillate (ˈfaɪbrɪleɪt), *v.* [f. FIBRILLA + -ATE[3].]

1. *intr.* Of the blood: To turn into fibrillæ; to form fibrils or fibres.

1839–47 TODD *Cycl. Anat.* III. 746/2 Place a drop of the colourless liquor sanguinis, before it fibrillates, on each of the large slips. **1854** JONES & SIEV. *Pathol. Anat.* ii. 29 It appears as an homogeneo-granular blastema . . with more or less marked tendency to fibrillate or form actual fibres.

2. *intr.* Of muscle: to undergo fibrillation (sense 1 b).

1910 T. LEWIS in *Heart* I. 335 These variations are generated in the auricle and . . are only present when the auricle fibrillates. **1960** *Brit. Med. Jrnl.* 7 May 1381/1 Atria which were fibrillating at 37°C. ceased to fibrillate when the temperature was reduced to 27°C.

3. a. *trans.* To break down or split into fibrils or filaments (see FIBRILLATION 2).

1929 CLAPPERTON & HENDERSON *Mod. Paper-Making* vi. 84 If our beater bars are too sharp we have great difficulty in fibrillating the fibres; instead we may cut them. **1958** *Times Rev. Industry* May 17/2 The suspended pulp is then refined in two stages, chiefly to remove lumps and to fibrillate the individual cellulose fibres. **1969** *Sci. Jrnl.* Nov. 23/3 When a 0·05 mm thick film of polyethylene was fibrillated it was found that string could be produced at nearly 30 metres/minute.

b. *intr.* Of a fibre: to split up into fibrils.

1942 J. GRANT *Lab. Handbk. Pulp & Paper Manuf.* v. 104 Esparto will not hydrate or fibrillate to any significant extent, although . . it may be cut. **1952** J. P. CASEY *Pulp & Paper* I. vi. 339 Softwood fibers tend to fibrillate to a greater extent than hardwood fibers.

Hence **ˈfibrillating** *ppl. a.*

1854 JONES & SIEV. *Pathol. Anat.* ii. 30 A thin layer of . . fibrillating material . . unites and holds together the divided surfaces. **1875** H. WALTON *Dis. Eye* p. xxii, Its circumference is dark and fibrillating.

fibrillated (ˈfaɪbrɪleɪtɪd), *ppl. a.* [f. prec. + -ED[1].] **a.** Arranged in fibrils; having a fibrillar structure.

1847–9 TODD *Cycl. Anat.* IV. 138/2 Simple condensation of the original fibrillated fibrin. **1851** CARPENTER *Man. Phys.* (ed. 2) 319 The fibrillated network forming the buffy coat undergoes the slow contraction. **1877** HUXLEY *Anat. Inv. Anim.* ii. 104 A . . cortical layer, fibrillated in a direction perpendicular to the surface.

b. Having been split up into fibrils by fibrillation.

1929 CLAPPERTON & HENDERSON *Mod. Paper-Making* vi. 83 The strength is caused by the fibres being 'fibrillated', and this, we think, should be the proper word to describe the condition. *Ibid.* 85 All the extra surfaces of the fibrillated fibres retain some surface water. **1951** A. B. GREEN in J. N. Stephenson *Pulp & Paper Manuf.* II. iii. 189 When fibrils become loosened from the original fiber, the fiber appears under the microscope as broomed, or partially fibrillated.

fibrillation (faɪbrɪˈleɪʃən). [f. as prec.; see -ATION.] **1. a.** The process of becoming fibrillated; the state or condition of being fibrillated; an arrangement into fibrils; also *concr.* a fibrillated mass.

1839–47 TODD *Cycl. Anat.* III. 743/2 But in the ordinary fibrin of the blood, the fibrillation is less distinct. **1845** TODD & BOWMAN *Phys. Anat.* I. 227 A nerve . . presents itself as a pale cord with a longitudinal fibrillation. **1861** T. GRAHAM *Pract. Med.* 22 The coagulation or fibrillation of the fibrine. **1875** H. WALTON *Dis. Eye* p. xxii, From this fibrillation the posterior set of fibres pass.

b. A quivering movement in the fibrils of a muscle or nerve, esp. the muscles of the heart.

1882 QUAIN *Med. Dict.*, *Fibrillation, muscular*, a localised quivering or flickering of muscular fibres. **1906** CUSHNY & EDMUNDS in W. Bulloch *Stud. Path.* 95 (*title*) Paroxysmal irregularity of the heart and auricular fibrillation. **1930** *Q. Jrnl. Med.* XXIII. 309 Certain obvious consequences of fibrillation of the auricle, such as the lowered efficiency of the ventricle. **1965** W. I. GEFTER et al. *Synopsis Cardiol.* xv. 395 Ventricular fibrillation is usually a terminal event.

2. The process of splitting into fibrils or thin filaments; esp. in *Paper-making*, the beating of vegetable fibres so that they are (partially) separated into their component fibrils.

1929 CLAPPERTON & HENDERSON *Mod. Paper-Making* vi. 76 In beating such stock as esparto and wood, very little fibrillation is necessary. **1952** L. G. COTTRALL *Introd. Stuff Prep.* ix. 72 By means of wide blunt bars made of suitable material we can effect the fibrillation of the fibres with a minimum of cutting. **1969** *Sci. Jrnl.* Nov. 23/3 Fibrillation technique for making string from plastics films has recently become very popular.

fibrilliferous (faɪbrɪˈlɪfərəs), *a.* [f. as next + -(I)FEROUS.] Bearing or provided with fibrils.

In some mod. Dicts.

fibrilliform (faɪˈbrɪlɪfɔːm), *a.* [f. FIBRILLA + -(I)FORM.] Having the form of a fibril or fibrils.

1847–9 TODD *Cycl. Anat.* IV. 398/1 The fibrilliform fronds of the fresh-water algæ. **1870** BENTLEY *Bot.* 37 Inextricably interwoven . . so as to form a loose fibrilliform tissue.

fibrillose (ˌfaɪbrɪˈləʊs), *a.* Also **fibrilose**. [f. as prec. + -OSE.] **a.** Covered or supplied with fibrils; composed of fibrils. **b.** Marked with fine lines as if composed of fine fibrils; finely striate.

1829 LOUDON *Encycl. Plants* 1099 *Fibrillose*, covered with little strings or fibres. **1846** *Proc. Berw. Nat. Club* II. 175 The . . stalk . . is pale, a very little fibrilose. **1866** BERKELEY in *Intell. Observ.* No. 50. 95 Pileus silky or fibrillose.

fibriˈlloso-, comb. form of prec.; only in **fibriˌlloso-ˈstriate** *a.* [+ -STRIATE], = FIBRILLOSE b.

1846 BERKELEY in *Proc. Berw. Nat. Club* II. 190 Cup . . minutely fibrilloso-striate.

†ˈfibrillous, *a. Obs.* [f. FIBRILLA + -OUS.] **a.** Full of fibrils; composed of fibrils. **b.** Of or pertaining to a fibril.

1737 D. BAYNE *Nerves* 14 Hence arise those uneasy Sensations, Pains, fibrillous Spasms, &c. **1746** ARDERON in *Phil. Trans.* XLIV. 427 Its little fibrillous Fins are always in Motion. **1748** *Ibid.* XLV. 322 The Distemper still gained Ground; and . . a fine fibrillous Substance grew out from it. **1765** STERNE *Tr. Shandy* VII. xxxi, The brain being tender and fibrillous.

fibrin (ˈfaɪbrɪn). Formerly also **fibrine**, and in L. form **fibrina**. [f. FIBRE + -IN.] **1. a.** Orig., an albuminoid or protein compound substance found in animal matter; coagulable lymph. In modern use, an insoluble protein, formed from fibrinogen during blood clotting, which polymerizes to give the network of the clot.

1800 *Phil. Trans.* XC. 375 The substance called fibrin by the chemists. **1802** *Med. Jrnl.* VIII. 297 A disposition to the formation of Fibrina. **1804** W. NICHOLSON tr. *A. F. Fourcroy's Gen. Syst. Chem. Knowl.* IX. 214 (*heading*) Of the fibrous Part of the Blood, or of the Fibrine. **1813** SIR H. DAVY *Agric. Chem.* vi. (1814) 275 Fibrine constitutes the basis of the muscular fibre of animals. **1842** A. COMBE *Physiol. Digest.* (ed. 4) 292 Fibrin is that whitish and tenacious mass which constitutes the solid part of coagulated blood. **1845** *London Med. Gaz.* 3rd Ser. I. 618/2 The washed clot is the substance which is usually, but very erroneously, named the *fibrin of the blood*. **1869** ROSCOE *Elem. Chem.* 434 The fibrin of flesh appears to differ from that of blood. **1927** R. J. S. MCDOWALL *Clin. Physiol.* xv. 147 Fibrinogen, which is converted into the fibrin of the clot. **1961** R. G. MACFARLANE in Macfarlane & Robb-Smith *Functions of Blood* vii. 322 During the clotting of fibrinogen, the products are fibrin, which is a polymer formed by union of major residues of the fibrinogen molecules, and fibrinopeptide. **1970** *Nature* 14 Nov. 669 The conversion of fibrinogen to fibrin . . is the last stage of the complex process of blood coagulation.

b. A similar substance in vegetable matter.

1819 J. E. CHILDREN *Chem. Anal.* 293 Vegetable fibrin was obtained by Vauquelin from the juice of the papaw tree. **1856** *Farmer's Mag.* Jan. 2 We give him beans, which abound in fibrine. **1858** CARPENTER *Veg. Phys.* §32 Gluten, fibrin, albumen, caseine, etc., form the basis of all vegetable . . tissues.

2. *Comb.*, as **†fibrin-ferment** [a. G. *fibrinferment* (A. Schmidt 1872, in *Arch f. ges. Physiol.* VI. 447)], = THROMBIN *Obs.*; **fibrin film**, a thin sheet of fibrin mixed with a plasticizing agent and used mainly in neurosurgery and to treat burns; **fibrin foam**, a spongy preparation of fibrin used as a hæmostatic in surgery; **fibrin-peptone** (see quot.).

1876 *Jrnl. Chem. Soc.* I. 945 The author [*sc.* Alex Schmidt] proceeds to show . . that fibrin-ferment is not a body pre-existing in the blood, which was originally in the red blood corpuscles, and only after its exit from the body passed over into the plasma. **1898**, **1900** Fibrin ferment [see THROMBIN]. **1923** A. W. FULLER *Anæmia* i. 8 The blood-plasma is the fluid medium containing . . fibrin-ferment, for coagulation purposes. **1951** A. GROLLMAN *Pharmacol. & Therapeutics* xxviii. 633 Fibrin foam . . is an effective hemostatic agent and may be left *in situ*. It has replaced the fibrin ferments and thromboplastic substances used previously for this purpose. **1944** FERRY & MORRISON in *Jrnl. Clin. Invest.* XXIII. 566 We shall describe these clots, as well as two kinds of derived products—the fibrin films and fibrinogen plastics—which we have developed from the same proteins. **1968** M. GERENDÁS in K. Laki *Fibrinogen* xiii. 294 In essence, fibrin film is a condensed fibrin clot in which the strands are more or less oriented. The film can be stretched and is elastic. **1944** *Jrnl. Neurosurg.* I. 23 A spongy substance, which has been designated as 'fibrin foam'. **1963** *Brit. Pharm. Codex* 955 Human Fibrin Foam is a dry artificial sponge of human fibrin. It is prepared by clotting with human thrombin a foam of a solution of human fibrinogen... Human fibrin foam is used . . as a hæmostatic agent in surgery. **1884** *Syd. Soc. Lex.*, *Fibrin-peptone*, the peptone resulting from the digestion in gastric juice of fibrine.

fibrination (faɪbrɪˈneɪʃən). [f. FIBRIN + -ATION.] The action or process of adding fibrin to the blood.

1884 in *Syd. Soc. Lex.*

fibrine (ˈfaɪbraɪn), *a.* [f. FIBRE + -INE[1].] Having the appearance of fibres; fibre-like.

1881 W. C. RUSSELL *Ocean Free Lance* II. 248 Fires . . shot out . . in fibrine forms like the wreathing of innumerable tendrils of plants.

fibrino- (ˈfaɪbrɪnəʊ), used as a comb. form of FIBRIN, chiefly *Phys.*, as **ˌfibrino-alˈbuminous**

a., consisting of fibrin and albumen; **ˈfibrinogen** [+ -GEN], a soluble protein occurring in blood plasma, the precursor of fibrin; **ˌfibrino-geˈnetic, ˌfibrino-ˈgenic** [see -GENIC], **fibriˈno-genous** [+ -GEN + -OUS] *adjs.*, producing fibrin; **ˌfibrinoˈlysin, fibriˈnolysin** [LYSIN], any enzyme causing fibrinolysis; **fibriˈnolysis** [ad. Fr. *fibrinolyse* (A. Dastre 1893, in *Arch. de Physiol. norm. et path.* 5th Ser. V. 661): see LYSIS], the enzymic conversion of fibrin to soluble products; hence **ˌfibrinoˈlytic** *a.*; **ˌfibrino-ˈplastic** *a.*, concerned in the formation of fibrin; **ˌfibrino-ˈplastin** = GLOBULIN; **ˌfibrino-ˈpurulent** *a.*, containing a mixture of fibrin and pus.

1835–6 TODD *Cycl. Anat.* I. 49/1 *Fibrino-albuminous matter. **1872** HUXLEY *Phys.* iii. 69 *Fibrinogen..is exceedingly like globulin. **1876** *Wagner's Gen. Pathol.* 155 Fibrinogens are not only those coagulating spontaneously, but almost all serous fluids. **1927** Fibrinogen [see FIBRIN 1 a]. **1968** PASSMORE & ROBSON *Compan. Med. Stud.* I. xxvi. 16 Recent work.. has shown that the conversion of fibrinogen to fibrin is not as simple as previously represented. Thrombin is now believed to split fibrinogen into one major component, fibrin monomer, and several minor polypeptide components. **1876** *Wagner's Gen. Pathol.* 155 The humors of the eye..have no *fibrinogenetic property. *Ibid.*, A *fibrinogenic substance peculiar to the intercellular fluids. *Ibid.* 228 Its quantity stands..in almost direct ratio with its contained *fibrinogenous substance. **1915** FLEISHNER & LOEB in *Jrnl. Biol. Chem.* XXI. 497 The above observations make it appear probable that there exist in various species of animals certain tissue substances which have the power to dissolve blood coagulum when it is in direct contact with the tissues. These substances may be called *fibrinolysins. **1958** *Observer* 14 Dec. 4/3 Fibrinolysin is believed to fulfil an important role in removing small clots that form in the blood-stream. **1962** *New Scientist* 16 Aug. 344/3 Fibrinolysin, or plasmin, which is available commercially. **1907** *Jrnl. Physiol.* XXXV. p. xiii, If the carefully washed fibrin is placed into chloroform instead of chloroform-water..*fibrinolysis occurs all the same. **1949** H. W. FLOREY et al. *Antibiotics* I. ix. 383 Neter..reported that actinomycin inhibited fibrinolysis. **1911** *Chem. Abstr.* V. 3842 If fresh fibrin is first heated to 90°, then treated with H_2O_2, the catalase and the *fibrinolytic action is lessened. **1961** *Lancet* 16 Sept. 645/2 The introduction of purified proteolytic and fibrinolytic enzymes made possible a more direct attack on the clot. **1876** *Wagner's Gen. Pathol.* 155 A *fibrinoplastic substance belonging to the contents of cells. **1872** HUXLEY *Phys.* iii. 70 The interaction of two substances ..globulin or *fibrino-plastin, and fibrinogen. **1876** *Wagner's Gen. Pathol.* 259 Abundant admixture of these constitutes the *fibrino-purulent exudation.

fibrinoid (ˈfaɪbrɪnɔɪd). *Path.* [a. G. *fibrinoid* (E. Neumann 1880, in *Arch. f. mikrosk. Anat.* XVIII. 137), f. FIBRIN + -OID.] Any of one or more poorly characterized substances staining like fibrin, found normally in the placenta as well as in various diseased tissues. Also *attrib.*, as ***fibrinoid degeneration, necrosis***.

1910 *Practitioner* Jan. 43 The muscle so invaded stains feebly, and the presence of these cells in them has brought about a fibrinoid or necrotic change. **1958** *Amer. Jrnl. Med. Sci.* CCXXXVI. 373 Most authorities now agree that the term fibrinoid should be reserved for an intensely acidophilic (eosinophilic), homogeneous, dense and refractile substance with staining characteristics similar to those of fibrin. In the long interval since Neumann's publication much investigation..has failed to resolve the conflicting opinions regarding the origin and nature of fibrinoid. **1964** S. DUKE-ELDER *Parsons' Diseases of Eye* (ed. 14) xvii. 226 A proliferative infiltration by chronic inflammatory cells surrounding a central area of fibrinoid necrosis. **1967** C. W. M. ADAMS *Vasc. Histochem.* vii. 265 More severe stenosis..results in rapidly developing hypertension and 'fibrinoid' degeneration. **1970** PASSMORE & ROBSON *Compan. Med. Stud.* II. xxx. 3/2 The term fibrinoid belongs to an age of pathology before the cryostat, the integrating micro-densitometer and the technique of immunofluorescence... In spite of this, the term fibrinoid will probably continue to be used to describe a characteristic appearance under light microscopy in a variety of diseases.

fibrinous (ˈfaɪbrɪnəs), *a.* [f. FIBRIN + -OUS.]

a. Full of or composed of fibrin. b. Of, pertaining to, or of the nature of fibrin.

1830 R. KNOX *Béclard's Anat.* 305 The muscular flesh is less red, and more gelatinous and fibrinous. **1834** J. FORBES *Laennec's Dis. Chest* 563 The fibrinous concretions were softer. **1872** F. G. THOMAS *Dis. Women* 512 About the very existence of the fibrinous polypus there is some doubt.

Hence **fibriˈnosity**, the quality of being fibrinous.

1876 *Wagner's Gen. Pathol.* 228 Schmidt has examined.. 93 transudates with respect to their fibrinosity.

Fibro, fibro (ˈfaɪbrəʊ). **1.** The proprietary name of a viscose rayon staple.

1926 *Trade Marks Jrnl.* 11 Aug. 1880 *Fibro*,..filaments.. supplied in untwisted form for all spinning purposes. Courtaulds, Limited. **1935** *Economist* 23 Nov. 1002/2 The chemist has perfected yet another synthetic textile. The new fibre, technically known as staple fibre and popularised as 'fibro', bids fair, with rayon, to oust the older materials from a wide range of uses. **1941** *Daily Sketch* 22 Apr., The blue fibro dress. **1968** *Woollen Carding* (W.I.R.A.) xv. 143/2 For the Fibro/mungo tests two blends were made of 50 per cent. by weight mungo and 50 per cent. Fibro.

2. = *fibro-cement*: also, a house constructed chiefly with fibro-cement; also as *adj. Austral.*

1953 K. TENNANT *Joyful Condemned* viii. 63 Front balconies glassed in or filled with stray bits of fibro. **1957** *Times* 11 May 7/7 The cheap fibro shacks are giving way to clean-lined pastel-painted homes, most of them pleasantly designed, a few the inevitable excrescences of too much money and too little taste. **1963** A. LUBBOCK *Austral. Roundabout* 66 The new fibro-walled, tin-roofed townships. **1969** *Sydney Morning Herald* 24 May 39/6 (Advt.), Sans Souci old type fibro with iron roof.

fibro- (ˈfaɪbrəʊ), used as a comb. form of FIBRE, employed chiefly in *Phys.* terms, to indicate a fibrous condition. **ˌfibro-adeˈnoma**, an adenoma containing much fibrous tissue; hence **ˌfibro-adeˈnomatous** *a.*; **ˌfibro-adiˈpose** *a.*, consisting of fibrous and adipose tissue. **ˌfibro-aˈreolar** *a.*, consisting of fibrous and areolar or connective tissue. **ˈfibro-ˌblast** [+ -BLAST], one of the cells in which fibrous tissue is immediately formed. **ˌfibroˈblastic** *a.*, of, involving, or relating to fibroblasts. **ˌfibro-bronˈchitis** (see quot.). **ˌfibro-calˈcareous** *a.*, consisting of fibrous tissue and containing calcareous bodies. **ˌfibro-ˈcartilage**, a firm elastic material partaking of the structure and character of fibrous tissue and cartilage; hence **ˌfibro-cartiˈlaginous** *a.*, of the nature of fibro-cartilage. **ˌfibro-ˈcellular** *a.*, composed of fibrous and cellular tissue. **fibro-ceˈment** = *asbestos cement.* **ˌfibro-chonˈdritis**, 'inflammation of a fibro-cartilage' (*Syd. Soc. Lex.* 1884). **ˌfibro-ˈcystic** *a.*, consisting of fibrous tissue and cysts. **ˌfibro-cyˈstoma**, a tumour containing fibrous tissue and cysts. **ˈfibrocyte** [-CYTE], an inactive fibroblast. **ˌfibroeˈlastic** *a.*, consisting of fibrous and elastic tissue. **ˌfibroelaˈstosis**, name given to a congenital heart disease (***congenital*** or ***endocardial fibroelastosis***) characterized by proliferation of fibroelastic tissue in the endocardium. **ˌfibro-ˈfatty** *a.*, 'relating to fibrous tissue and to fat' (*Syd. Soc. Lex.* 1884). **ˌfibro-ˈferrite** (*Min.*), ferric sulphate occurring in fibrous silky tufts and masses of a yellow colour. **ˌfibro-inˈtestinal** *a.*, in '***fibro-intestinal layer***, the innermost of the two layers into which the mesoderm of some Invertebrata divides' (*Syd. Soc. Lex.* 1884). **ˌfibro-ligaˈmentous** *a.*, consisting of fibrous tissue and ligaments. **ˌfibro-liˈpoma**, a lipoma containing much fibrous tissue; hence **ˌfibro-liˈpomatous** *a.*; **ˌfibro-ˈmembrane** (*Bot.*) = *fibro-membranous tissue.* **ˌfibro-ˈmembranous** *a.*, (*a*) 'possessing the nature of fibrous and of mucous membranes' (Ogilv. citing *Dunglison*); (*b*) *Bot.*, consisting of fibrous and membranous tissue. **ˌfibro-ˈmucous** *a.*, consisting of fibrous and mucous tissue. **ˌfibro-ˈmuscular** *a.*, 'pertaining to or consisting of fibrous and muscular tissue' (*Syd. Soc. Lex.* 1884). **ˌfibro-myˈoma**, 'a myoma in which the tumour contains a large proportion of fibrous connective tissue' (*Syd. Soc. Lex.* 1884); whence **ˌfibro-myˈomatous** *a.* **ˌfibro-neuˈroma**, 'the form of neuroma which consists chiefly of fibrous connective tissue' (*Syd. Soc. Lex.* 1884). **ˌfibro-ˈnucleated** *a.*, composed of fibrous tissue mixed with elongated nuclei. **fibroˈplasia** [Gr. πλάσις formation], the proliferation of fibrous tissue, as in the healing of wounds. **ˌfibro-ˈplastic** *a.*, fibre-forming; said *esp.* of a tissue organized from the lymph exuded on wounds. **ˌfibro-sarˈcoma**, a tumour intermediate in character between a fibroma and a sarcoma. **ˌfibro-ˈserous** *a.*, possessing the nature of both fibrous and serous membranes. **ˌfibro-ˈvascular** *a. Bot.* (see quot. 1845).

1892 *Brit. Med. Jrnl.* 23 Apr. 862/2 A large *fibro-adenoma removed from the left breast of a girl. **1961** G. M. BONSER et al. *Human & Experimental Breast Cancer* x. 212 Fibroadenomata are circumscribed, benign tumours. **1894** W. R. WILLIAMS *Dis. Breast* xviii. 472 The *fibro-adenomatous nature of the disease. **1931** CHEATLE & CUTLER *Tumours of Breast* xi. 471 Whole sections of these tumours, however, reveal its epithelial contents and establish the true fibroadenomatous nature of the growth. **1835–6** TODD *Cycl. Anat.* I. 148/2 The dense *fibro-adipose cushion..found in the sole of the foot. **1859** J. TOMES *Dental Surg.* (1873) 43 The superimposed *fibro-areolar tissue. **1876** *Wagner's Gen. Pathol.* 373 Cells in this metamorphosis are called *fibroblasts. **1884** D. MACALISTER tr. *Ziegler's Textbk. Path. Anat.* II. 363/1 (*index*) *Fibroblastic cells in organisation. **1960** W. W. WASHBURN in W. W. Nowinski *Fund. Aspects Norm. & Malig. Growth* viii. 693 The period of active fibroblastic proliferation is followed by one of relatively slow cell division during which collagen is formed. **1875** R. FOWLER *Med. Voc.* (ed. 2), **Fibro-bronchitis*, bronchitis accompanied with the formation and expectoration of solid fibrinous, or tubular membranous, casts of the bronchial tubes. **1878** T. BRYANT *Pract. Surg.* I. 111 With calcareous matter '*fibro-calcareous'. **1835–6** TODD *Cycl. Anat.* I. 250/1 *Fibro-cartilages are useful..as elastic cushions placed between the bones. *Ibid.* 249/2 The triangular cartilage of the wrist joint ..does not appear to me to be *fibro-cartilaginous in its structure. **1839** A. GRAY *Lett.* (1893) 137, I..saw some strange things..*fibrocellular tissue, the most beautiful thing you can imagine. **1878** T. BRYANT *Pract. Surg.* (1879) II. 239 Fibro-cellular tumours..cause much local distress. **1927** *Census Commonw. Austral. 1921* II. (Stat. rep.) 297 The highest average number of inmates for South Australia was shared by dwellings of stone and of *fibro-cement. **1938** *Ann. Reg. 1937* 175 Production of Italian minerals and pyrites, and the replacing of iron by fibro-cement. **1947** *Archit. Rev.* CI. 84/2 The mobile panels, which only occur on the west façade, are of fibro-cement and are painted. **1854** JONES & SIEV. *Pathol. Anat.* iv. 159 Cyst-like cavities, filled with clear fluid are..found in fibrous tumours, constituting thus a *fibro-cystic variety. **1872** PEASLEE *Ovar. Tumours* 26 *Fibro-cystoma. **1911** STEDMAN *Med. Dict.* 312/2 *Fibrocyte. **1927** *Biol. Abstr.* I. 944/1 Results were..especially pronounced upon the fibrocytes and migrating cells in subcutaneous tissue. **1967** K. HASHIMOTO in A. S. Zelickson *Ultrastruct. Norm. & Abnorm. Skin* xi. 229 In the normal skin, fibroblasts are few in number and the majority reside in a quiescent form, *i.e.*, the fibrocyte. The fibrocyte has scanty cytoplasm, inconspicuous ergastoplasm, flattened Golgi complex, and a relatively large nucleus. **1891** FOSTER *Med. Dict.* III. 1584/1 *Fibroelastic. **1941** *Arch. Path.* XXXI. 169 A simple noninflammatory hyperplasia of fibroelastic tissue. **1965** R. P. MOREHEAD *Human Path.* xxiii. 642/2 A thin layer of fibroelastic tissue covered by endothelium. **1943** WEINBERG & HIMELFARB in *Bull. Johns Hopkins Hosp.* LXXII. 299 An analysis of the literature..failed to reveal any unrefutable evidence for.. fetal endocarditis... The purpose of this presentation is..to report the occurrence of two cases of endocardial *fibroelastosis (a much better term in view of the lack of inflammatory stigmata). **1956** *Amer. Heart Jrnl.* LII. 138 Fibroelastosis (fetal endocarditis, endocardial fibrosis, congenital idiopathic hypertrophy of the heart, and congenital fibroelastosis) is a recognized pathologic entity in infants. **1957** *Brit. Heart Jrnl.* XIX. 186 (*heading*) Fibro-elastosis of the heart in adolescence. **1966** WRIGHT & SYMMERS *Systemic Path.* I. i. 46/1 Nothing is yet known of the aetiology or pathogenesis of fibroelastosis of the endocardium. **1844** DANA *Min.* 226 The *Fibro-ferrite of Prideaux. **1884** *Ibid.* 656 *Fibro-ferrite*, delicately fibrous. **1847** YOUATT *Horse* ix. 218 An interposed *fibro-ligamentous substance. **1882** *Syd. Soc. Lex.* II, *Fibro-lipoma. **1889** *Brit. Med. Jrnl.* 11 May 1062/1 Fibro-lipoma of Labia Majora. *Ibid.*, A fibro-lipomatous growth. **1965** R. P. MOREHEAD *Human Path.* xxv. 759/2 As is the case with mesodermal growths in general, they appear in the literature under a wide variety of names: lipoma, fibroma, fibrolipoma, leiomyoma, rhabdomyxoma, etc. **1882** *The Garden* 28 Jan. 69/1 The corm tunic consists of soft *fibro-membrane. *Ibid.*, The tunic consists of soft, *fibro-membranous tissue. **1856** TODD & BOWMAN *Phys. Anat.* II. 3 The entire lining of the bone has been sometimes called a *fibro-mucous membrane. **1878** T. BRYANT *Pract. Surg.* I. 117 *Fibro-nucleated and recurrent tumours. **1929** *Jrnl. Amer. Med. Assoc.* XCII. 44 The phase of *fibroplasia is equally important, for it is during this time that the strength of the wound is developed up to a maximal point. **1933** *Arch. Surg.* XXVII. 846 (*title*) Effect of complete and partial starvation on the rate of fibroplasia in the healing wound. **1969** S. M. LEVENSON in Dunphy & Van Winkle *Repair & Regen.* xxi. 323 Preparations of cartilage powder instilled locally may accelerate fibroplasia. **1857** BULLOCK *Cazeaux' Midwif.* 66 In the oviduct nothing but cellular tissue and *fibro-plastic elements are to be met with. **1878** T. BRYANT *Pract. Surg.* I. 137 The spindle-celled kinds..are most common in *fibro-sarcoma. **1841–71** T. R. JONES *Anim. Kingd.* (ed. 4) 842 The heart, contained in a *fibro-serous envelope. **1845** LINDLEY *Sch. Bot.* x. (1854) 159 Vascular tissue..usually occurs mixed with fibrous tissue, and hence the mixture of the two is called **fibro-vascular*. **1882** VINES *Sachs' Bot.* 420, I was unable to satisfy myself as to the true form of the fibro-vascular system.

fibroid (ˈfaɪbrɔɪd), *a.* and *sb.* [f. FIBRE + -OID.]

A. *adj.* Resembling fibre or fibrous tissue; composed of, or characterized by, fibre or fibrous tissue; ***fibroid change, degeneration***, a morbid change into fibre or fibrous tissue.

1852 PAGET *Surg. Pathol.* ii. 155, I have proposed the name of Recurrent Fibroid tumour. **1854** JONES & SIEV. *Pathol. Anat.* ii. 30 Masses of fibrine..become fibroid tissues. **1874** *Ibid.* iv. 124 Fibroid degeneration is somewhat allied to induration. **1874** FAGGE in *Trans. Path. Soc. London* XXV. 64 A series of cases of fibroid disease of the heart. *Ibid.* 67 Towards the apex of the left ventricle..there was advanced fibroid growth. **1875** B. W. RICHARDSON *Dis. Mod. Life* 30 The simple growths include what are known as ..fibroid tumour. **1918** *Act 8 & 9 Geo. V* c. 14 (*title*) The disease known as fibroid phthisis or silicosis of the lungs. **1967** *Cancer* XX. 134 (*heading*) Neurogenic nature of so-called inflammatory fibroid polyps of the stomach.

B. *sb. Pathol.* A fibroid tumour.

1872 PEASLEE *Ovar. Tumours* 20 Scanzoni considered it an ovarian fibroid. **1876** *Wagner's Gen. Pathol.* 385 Tumor.. So-called fibroma or fibroid.

fibroin (ˈfaɪbrəʊɪn). [f. FIBRO- + -IN.] A chemical substance which is the principal constituent of silk, cobwebs, and the horny skeleton of sponges.

1861 HULME tr. *Moquin-Tandon* II. III. ii. 90 Sponge is composed of an animal matter which has been compared to albumen and to mucous (Fibroine, Mulder). **1878** KINGZETT *Anim. Chem.* 367 In a study of fibroin from silk, Schutzenberger concludes that it differs from ordinary albumin. **1887** J. PATON in *Encycl. Brit.* (ed. 9) XXII. 61/1 Silk fibre consists essentially of a centre or core of fibroin.. Fibroin..has a composition represented by the formula $C_{15}H_{23}N_5O_6$.

Fibrolane (ˈfaɪbrəʊleɪn). The proprietary name of any of a series of wool-like synthetic fibres made from protein.

1946 *Trade Marks Jrnl.* 7 Aug. 416/1 *Fibrolane.* Raw fibrous textile materials. Courtaulds Limited..London. **1954** R. W. MONCRIEFF *Artificial Fibres* (ed. 2) xv. 204 The original Fibrolane, known as Fibrolane A, was very similar to Lanital. A newer product, Fibrolane BX,..is the 'Fibrolane' that is mostly used today. **1957** *Economist* 12

Oct. 158/2 But there is no sign that Courtaulds intends to.. cease production of its milk-based protein fibre, 'Fibrolane'.

fibrolite ('faɪbrəlaɪt). [f. FIBRO- + Gr. λίθος stone; see also -ITE.] A fibrous mineral consisting chiefly of aluminium silicate.

1802 BOURNON in *Phil. Trans.* XCII. 289 Fibrolite.. always.. either of a white colour, or of a dirty gray. **1803** *Nicholson's Jrnl.* IV. 14 Fibrolite accompanying the matrix of corundum. **1884** DANA *Min.* 375 Fibrolite was much used for stone implements.. in the 'Stone age'.

Hence **fibro'litic** *a.*, containing fibrolite.

1879 DANA *Man. Geol.* (ed. 3) 72.

fibroma (faɪ'brəʊmə). *Path.* Pl. **fibromata** (faɪ'brəʊmətə). [mod.L., f. L. *fibra* FIBRE + *-oma*; cf. CARCINOMA, CYSTOMA.] A fibrous tumour.

1847-9 TODD *Cycl. Anat.* IV. 130/2 The nature of fibroma leads it simply to enlarge, without change in, or around, itself. **1876** *Wagner's Gen. Pathol.* 385 Fibromata are for the most part sharply circumscribed.

fibrome ('faɪbrəʊm). [a. Fr. *fibrome.*] = prec.

1872 COHEN *Dis. Throat* 206 The structure.. was altogether similar to that of these fibromes.

fibrose, *a.* ? *Obs.* [ad. mod.L. *fibrōsus*: see FIBRE and -OSE.] = FIBROUS.

1697 J. PETIVER in *Phil. Trans.* XIX. 681 The Roots fibrose and whitish. **1752** *Ibid.* XLVII. 511 Their external appearance will show them fibrose. **1775** in ASH.

fibrose ('faɪbrəʊz), *v. Path.* [f. FIBROSE *a.*] *intr.* To form fibrous tissue. Hence **'fibrosed** *ppl. a.*; **fi'brosing** *vbl. sb.* and *ppl. a.*

1879 *St. George's Hosp. Rep.* IX. 133 Lungs (some fibrosing or caseous). *Ibid.* 156 Indolent fibrosing tubercle at the apices of the lungs. **1897** *Brit. Med. Jrnl.* 11 Dec. 1728/1 The lower lobe of each lung was completely fibrosed. **1909** *Practitioner* Feb. 210 On examination of the fibroid, it is found shrunken and fibrosed throughout. **1956** G. LAPAGE *Vet. Parasitol.* x. 275 The bile ducts become fibrosed and thickened.

fibrosis (faɪ'brəʊsɪs). *Path.* [mod.L., f. L. *fibra* FIBRE: see -OSIS.] The development in an organ of excessive fibrous tissue; fibroid degeneration.

1873 *Brit. Med. Jrnl.* 4 Jan. 4 Arterio-capillary fibrosis. **1886** *Buck's Handbk. Med. Sci.* II. 174/2 Cirrhosis. Synonyms.—Sclerosis,.. Chronic Fibrosis. **1893** *Brit. Med. Jrnl.* 2 Dec. 1214/2 Ordinary fibrosis of the kidney. **1906** *Practitioner* Dec. 730 The fibrosis steadily invades the lung parenchyma. **1920** R. STOCKMAN *Rheumatism & Arthritis* ii. 43 These local fibroses are due to small colonies of microbes invading the tissues. **1968** *Cancer* XXII. 1254 Pathologic examination revealed myocardial fibrosis.

Hence **fi'brotic** *a.*, of, pertaining to, or characterized by fibrosis.

1893 *Brit. Med. Jrnl.* 2 Dec. 1214/2 The difficult problems presented by fibrotic kidneys. **1910** *Practitioner* June 781 Between 45 and 50 the liability to fibrotic metritis, endometritis, and mucous polypi diminishes. **1956** *Nature* 3 Mar. 437/1 In a few specimens the lung tissue.. was cloudy in appearance, possibly fibrotic.

fibrositis (faɪbrəʊ'saɪtɪs). *Path.* [f. FIBROS(E *a.* + -ITIS.] Any rheumatic disorder of the white fibrous tissue that is of unknown or uncertain cause and is characterized chiefly by pain; inflammation of white fibrous tissue. Hence **fibro'sitic** *a.*, of, pertaining to, or suffering from fibrositis.

1904 W. R. GOWERS in *Brit. Med. Jrnl.* 16 Jan. 118/2, I think we need a designation for inflammation of the fibrous tissue which has not such results [*sc.* the production of induration or suppuration]... We may conveniently follow the analogy of 'cellulitis' and term it 'fibrositis'. **1910** *Lancet* 12 Mar. 713/2 Muscular rheumatism.—This affection is always a fibrositis. *Ibid.*, Muscular fibrositis of the shoulder. **1915** LLEWELLYN & JONES *Fibrositis* i. 14 Herein.. lies the most cogent argument that can be adduced in favour of displacement of the term 'chronic rheumatism' by that of 'fibrositis'. **1926** THOMSON & GORDON *Chronic Rheumatic Dis.* iii. 17 The fibrositic change is associated with a certain amount of myxœdema. **1963** *Lancet* 5 Jan. 56/2 Much of the pain in rheumatoid arthritis.. arises.. from anatomically well-defined areas of secondary 'fibrositis' which I have called the 'critical zones'. **1969** W. S. C. COPEMAN *Textbk. Rheumatic Dis.* (ed. 4) xviii. 507 'Weather sensitivity' in the fibrositic patient.

fibroso- (faɪ'brəʊsəʊ), comb. f. of FIBROSE *a.* or next, as in **fi,broso-cal'careous** adj. = *fibro-calcareous*; **fi,broso-carti'laginous** adj. = *fibro-cartilaginous*.

1856-8 W. CLARK *Van der Hoeven's Zool.* I. 83 Gorgonia, the crust polypiferous, fibroso-calcareous, persistent. *Ibid.* II. 69 *Chimæroïdei*, cranium fibroso-cartilaginous.

fibrous ('faɪbrəs), *a.* [ad. mod.L. *fibrōsus*: see FIBRE and -OUS. Cf. FIBROSE and Fr. *fibreux.*]

1. Full of fibres; formed of fibres:

a. in animals. ***fibrous tissue***: the ordinary connective tissue in the body. ***fibrous tumour*** = FIBROID.

1657 S. PURCHAS *Pol. Flying-Ins.* iii. 7 Their [Bees'] back and breast is a kind of reddish fibrous flesh. **1661** LOVELL *Hist. Anim. & Min.* Introd., Their lungs are single, fibrous.. and fungous. **1800** tr. *Lagrange's Chem.* II. 350 Blood.. separates into two portions, the coagulum or fibrous part, and the serum. **1872** HUXLEY *Phys.* ii. 23 Outside the muscular coat is a sheath of fibrous or connective tissue. **1885** CREIGHTON in *Encycl. Brit.* (ed. 9) XVIII. 369/1 The fibrous tumors may become cystic in their interior.

b. in plants.

1626 BACON *Sylva* §616 There are of Roots, Bulbous Roots, Fibrous Roots, and Hursute Roots. **1677** PLOT *Oxfordsh.* 144 Which large Violet from a fibrous root sendeth forth many leaves. **1713** C'TESS WINCHELSEA *Misc. Poems* 232 Branches.. Of fibrous cordage and impending shrouds. **1846** J. BAXTER *Libr. Pract. Agric.* (ed. 4) I. 279 From its fibrous bark we procure the comfort of linen. **1870** HOOKER *Stud. Flora* 300 *Cyclamen hederæfolium*.. tuber fibrous all over.

c. in minerals and metals.

1794 SULLIVAN *View Nat.* I. 452 Fibrous asbestos, alumen plumosum, is mild magnesia, combined with silex, calcareous earth, and a small proportion of argill, and iron. **1805-16** R. JAMESON *Char. Min.* 232 In the fibrous fracture we have to attend to the thickness.. and the position of the fibres. **1813** BAKEWELL *Introd. Geol.* (1815) 217 Thin strata of beautiful white fibrous gypsum occur in marle. **1858** GREENER *Gunnery* 88 The metal has been changed from the molecular to the fibrous.

d. of protein: having an elongated molecular structure showing little folding.

1931 *Nature* 2 May 663/2 X-ray photographs of fibrous proteins. **1954** J. C. KENDREW in Neurath & Bailey *Proteins* IIB. xxiii. 846 Structure protein is often macroscopically fibrous; hence the term 'fibrous protein' is more or less synonymous with structure protein... It has, in fact, become conventional to divide the whole range of proteins into two main classes: the fibrous and the globular. **1968** A. C. T. NORTH in W. G. Crewther *Symposium on Fibrous Proteins* 13 In comparing the relationships between primary sequence and secondary structure found in fibrous and globular proteins, account must be taken of the repetitive nature of fibrous protein sequences.

2. Resembling fibre or fibres; fibre-like.

1707 *Curios. in Husb. & Gard.* 81 There are fibrous Tubes in Trees, for the Sap to mount. **1813** SHELLEY *Q. Mab* I. 94 Yon fibrous cloud.. Were scarce so thin, so slight.

3. *Comb.*, as ***fibrous-rooted*** adj.

1796 C. MARSHALL *Garden.* xx. (1813) 399 Divide fibrous rooted perennial flowers. **1845** LINDLEY *Sch. Bot.* viii. (1858) 134 Generally *bulbous*, sometimes *fibrous*-rooted.

Hence **'fibrously** *adv.*, in a fibrous manner; like fibres; and **'fibrousness**, the state or quality of being fibrous.

1727 BAILEY vol. II, *Fibrousness*, fulness of fibres. **1827** *Westm. Rev.* IX. 174 Fibrousness is its essential character. **1833** J. HOLLAND *Manuf. Metal* II. 342 The fibrousness produced by this operation is again removed. **1854** JONES & SIEV. *Pathol. Anat.* ii. 33 They never show any organized arrangement beyond a low grade of fibrousness. **1881** J. S. in *Art Jrnl.* 102/1 The two faded leaves drawn so very fibrously. **1891** *Harper's Mag.* Jan. 210/1 Low-hanging firs .. all fibrously a-glitter.

fibry ('faɪb(ə)rɪ), *a.* [f. FIBRE + -Y¹.]

a. Resembling a fibre. **b.** Abounding in fibres.

1802 W. FORSYTH *Cult. Fruit Trees* xiv. (1824) 264 Cut off all the small fibry roots with a knife. **1881** *Gard. Chron.* No. 417. 814 Hundreds.. of fibry roots. **1882** *The Garden* 14 Jan. 31/1 Insert them.. in small pots filled with fibry turf.

fibster ('fɪbstə(r)). [f. FIB *v.*¹ + -STER.] One who fibs; a fibber, petty liar.

1848 THACKERAY *Van. Fair* xlviii, You silly little fibster. **1861** H. KINGSLEY *Ravenshoe* I. xx. You wicked old fibster!

fibula ('fɪbjʊlə). Pl. **fibulæ, -as.** [a. L. *fībula*, f. *fīgĕre* to fix, or the synonymous *fīvĕre* (Festus).]

‖**1.** *Antiq.* A clasp, buckle, or brooch.

1673 RAY *Journ. Low C.* 346 Rings, Fibulæ and abundance of other implements. **1736** POPE *Let. to Cromwell* 30 Dec. 1710, His robe might be subnected with a Fibula. **1831** WORDSW. *Highland Broach*, The Fibula, whose shape .. Still in the Highland Broach is seen. **1851** D. WILSON *Preh. Ann.* (1863) I. vii. 226 A small fibula of bone. **1869** T. NICHOLS *Handy Bk. Brit. Mus.* 349 There is also a large collection of fibulas or garment-fastenings.

2. *Anat.* The long or splint bone on the outer side of the leg (app. from its resemblance to the tongue of a clasp, of which the tibia forms the other part).

1706 in PHILLIPS (ed. Kersey). **1741** MONRO *Anat.* (ed. 3) 287 The sharpest Angle of the Fibula is anterior. **1831** R. KNOX *Cloquet's Anat.* 377 It arises.. from the fore part of the inner surface of the fibula. **1872** MIVART *Elem. Anat.* 183 The femur does not articulate with the fibula.

fibular ('fɪbjʊlə(r)), *a.* [f. FIBULA + -AR. Cf. F. *fibulaire.*] †**a.** Resembling the fibula: see FIBULA 2 (*obs.*⁻¹). **b.** Of or pertaining to the fibula.

1729 SCHEUCHZER in *Phil. Trans.* XXXVI. 98 The Bark.. is not so easily roll'd up into a fibular Form. **1831** R. KNOX *Cloquet's Anat.* 731 Anterior Fibular Artery. It.. perforates the inferior extremity of the interosseous ligament. **1854** OWEN *Skel. & Teeth* (1855) 64 A fibular ridge projects slightly from the.. tibia.

fibulate ('fɪbjʊleɪt), *v.* [f. L. *fibulāt-*, ppl. stem of *fībulāre* to clasp, f. *fībula*: see FIBULA.]

†**a.** *intr.* (*nonce-use*) To perform the action of buttoning and unbuttoning; to fiddle with one's buttons (*obs.*⁻¹). †**b.** *trans.* (see quot. 1656-81). **c.** To put a button on (a foil). Hence **'fibulated** *ppl. a.* **fibu'lation** (see quot.).

1640 BROME *Antipodes* II. ii, Your fingers fibulating on your breast. **1656-81** BLOUNT *Glossogr.*, *Fibulate*, to joyn, or fasten together. **1658** PHILLIPS, *Fibulation*, a buttoning, or joyning together. **1832-4** DE QUINCEY *Cæsars* Wks. 1862 IX. 138 Perhaps buttoned, fibulated as in the case of our own foils.

†**fibulous** ('fɪbjʊləs), *a.* In 7 fibulus. [f. FIBULA + -OUS.] Resembling a fibula.

1662 J. BARGRAVE *Pope Alex. VII* (1867) 129 A toung.. with a small fibulus button at the end of it.

-fic, *suffix*, repr. L. *-ficus* '-making, -doing' (f. weakened root of *facĕre* to make, do), forming adjs. (1) from sbs., with the sense 'making, causing, producing', as in *honōrificus*, *pācificus*, or 'performing', as *sacrificus*; (2) from adjs., with the sense 'performing actions of a certain kind', as *magnificus*, also (in late and med.L.) with the sense 'bringing into a specified state', as *beātificus*; (3) from vbs., with the sense 'causing to', as *horrificus*, *terrificus*; (4) from advbs., only in *beneficus*, *maleficus*, adjs. of agency to the phrases *bene*, *male facere* to do good, do ill (to). Except in the two last-mentioned words, and in *venēficus* (contr. for **venēnificus*), the suffix *-ficus* is always preceded by *-i-*, which is either the stem-vowel or a substitute for it, or a connecting-vowel appended to a consonant-stem. Most of the L. adjs. in *-(i)ficus* appear in Fr., the termination being adapted as *-(i)fique*; also in It., Sp., Pg., the form being *-fico*. In Eng. the suffix prob. first occurred in adoptions from Fr., like *magnific*, and was often spelt *-(i)fique* down to the 17th c. In mediæval and mod.L. new formations with *-(i)ficus* were very common, and many of them have passed, in adapted forms, into the Rom. langs. and Eng., as *prolific*, *scientific*. In scientific nomenclature new words are still sometimes formed by the addition of the representative of *-(i)ficus* to L. stems; such words, if accepted at all, are usually of international currency, and it is often uncertain in which lang. they were first used; Eng. examples are *acidific*, *chylific*, *felicific*, *morbific*.

Several L. adjs. in *-ficus* form their comparatives and superlatives, and their nouns of quality, from a stem in *-ficent-*. In Eng. (but not in Romanic) the adapted forms of these words end in *-ficent*, as *beneficent*, *magnificent*, *maleficent*, *munificent*.

ficary ('fɪkərɪ). *rare.* [ad. mod.L. *ficāria* in *Ranunculus Ficaria* the lesser Celandine.]

1848 MARY HOWITT in Tyas *Field Flowers* I. 26 Our garden fence.. With ficaries like a golden rain Shower'd on the earth below.

-fication (fɪ'keɪʃən), *suffix*, repr. L. *-ficātiōn-em*, the regular formative of nouns of action (see -ATION) from vbs. in *-ficāre*: see -FY. Many words of this formation (chiefly post-classical) were adopted in Fr. with their related vbs., the sbs. in learned form with the suffix *-fication*, and the vbs. in semi-popular form with the suffix *-fier*; on the analogy of these many new formations with these suffixes arose in Fr. From the 14th c. F. vbs. in *-fier* with their corresponding agent-nouns in *-fication* have been freely introduced into Eng., as *purify*, *purification*, *sanctify*, *sanctification*; and hence the suffix *-fication* has become the recognized means of forming nouns of action corresponding to vbs. in *-fy*, except such as represent L. vbs. in *-facĕre* (see -FACTION). In general, however, such nouns of action are (unless as mere nonce-wds.) formed only on assumable mod.L. types; but *beautification* has been in use since 17th c., and words like *Frenchification*, *transmogrification*, *uglification* may occasionally be met with. In scientific language the suffix forms many sbs. (some of which have no corresponding vb.); examples are *acetification*, *acidification*, *chylification*, *dentification*, *ossification*, etc.

1799 SOUTHEY *Lett.* (1856) I. 85 Excuse the damned city-country-fication of that word [cottage].

†**ficche**, *v. Obs.* Forms: 4-5 fitch(en, (ficchyn, fichch, fichene, fycche), ficche, fich, (5 fychch), 4-6 fych(e. [a. OF. *fichier* (mod.F. *ficher*) = Pr. *ficar*, Sp. *hincar*, *fincar*, *ficar*, Pg. *fincar*, *ficar*, It. *ficcare*: referred by Diez to a popular L. **figicare*, extension of L. *fīgĕre* to FIX.]

1. *trans.* To fix, fasten, make firm, establish; both in a material and an immaterial sense.

c **1340** *Gaw. & Gr. Knt.* 658 Alle þese fyue syþez.. were.. fyched upon fyue poyntes. *c* **1374** CHAUCER *Boeth.* II. iv. 45 Haue mynde certeynly to ficchyn þi house of a myrie site in a lowe stoone. **1382** WYCLIF *Josh.* iv. 3 In the place of tentis, where ȝe this nyȝt fitchen tentis. **1412-13** HOCCLEVE *Counsel to Hen. V*, 9 God dreede and ficche in him your trust. **1430** LYDG. *Chron. Troy* v. xxxvi, To fyche fynally the date. *c* **1477** CAXTON *Jason* 94 Whan she hadde put al these thinges in a balance and fiched in her engyn she began to recomforte medea. [**1530** PALSGR. 549/1, I Fyche (Lydgat), I stedye or make ferme or stedfaste, *Je fiche*. This terme is nat yet [*i.e.* no longer] admytted.]

b. To stud, furnish *with* something infixed.

impulsive band which proposed to fiddle down the walls of our Social Jericho.

2. *techn.* (See quot.)

1883 GILL in *Encycl. Brit.* (ed. 9) XVI. 244 s.v. *Micrometer*, Each movable web must pass the other without coming in contact with it or the fixed wire and without rubbing on any part of the brass-work. Should either fault occur (technically called 'fiddling') it is fatal to accurate measurement.

3. a. To make aimless or frivolous movements; *esp.* to play, toy *about*, *at*, *on*, *over*, *with* (a thing, *rarely*, a person); to act idly or frivolously. Also ***to fiddle about.***

1530 PALSGR. 549/1 Loke you fydell nat with your handes whan your maister speketh to you. **1604** T. WRIGHT *Passions* IV. ii. §3. 133 Some men you haue alwaies fidling about their garments. **1663** PEPYS *Diary* 13 July, The ladies..talking, and fiddling with their hats and feathers. **1705** W. KING *Art of Love* xii. 13 Her fingers or her tongue would fiddle. **1738** SWIFT *Polite Convers.* ii, He took a pipe in his hand, and fiddled with it till he broke it. **1741** BETTERTON *Eng. Stage* v. 64 Some are perpetually fiddling about their Cloaths. **1761** MRS. SHERIDAN *Sidney Bidulph* (1767) IV. 134, I had pretended to be fiddling at it all the time we were at tea. **1855** BROWNING *Fra Lippo Lippi* 13 You'll take Your hand away that's fiddling on my throat. **1883** H. SMART *Hard Lines* I. iii, They've had him fiddling about so long in the school, he's most likely forgot how to gallop. **1884** *Sat. Rev.* 12 July 40/1 A Ministry fiddling with Franchise Bills.

b. *slang.* (See quot.)

1851 MAYHEW *Lond. Labour* I. 199/1 A lad that had been lucky fiddling (holding horses or picking up money anyhow).

c. trans. ***to fiddle away***: to fritter away.

1667 H. MORE *Div. Dial.* II. xiv. (1713) 132 [They] fiddle away their time as idlely as those that pill Straws. **1861** BERESF. HOPE *Eng. Cathedr. 19th C.* vi. 221 The commonplace way of treating it is that of simply fiddling it away.

4. *trans.* and *intr.* To cheat, swindle; to 'wangle', intrigue; (see also quot. 1850). Also with *into*, *out of*. Now only *slang*.

1604 DEKKER *Honest Wh.* Wks. 1873 II. 170 There was one more that fiddled my fine Pedlers. **1703** DE FOE *Villainy of Stockjobbers* Misc. 268 There People can..Fiddle them out of their Money. **1738** CHESTERF. *Common Sense* 14 Oct., Somebody else would have been fiddled into it again. **1850** *Lloyd's Weekly* 3 Feb. (Farmer), I understand fiddling—that means, buying a thing for a mere trifle and selling it for double or for more. **1851** MAYHEW *Lond. Labour* I. 424 The way the globe man does is to go among the old women and fiddle (humbug) them. **1861** *Ibid.* III. 130 We are generally fiddled most tremendous. *a* **1889** *St. Louis Chron.* in Barrère & Leland *Dict. Slang* (1889) I. 360/1 Bob is the man who fiddled himself into Congress. **1938** F. D. SHARPE *Sharpe of Flying Squad* xv. 169 They fiddled into this job. **1955** *Times* 12 Aug. 5/4 William Alfred Powell, in evidence, said he approached Heard about getting a letter 'fiddled out' for him. **1958** S. SPENDER *Fool & Princess* 172 His own power for 'fiddling' through... His capacity for making deals.

5. *slang.* To take liberties with (a woman).

1632 CHAPMAN & SHIRLEY *Ball* II. iii, Fiddling ladies, you molecatcher!

'fiddle-bow. The stringed bow with which a fiddle is played; = FIDDLESTICK.

1827 W. HERSEE in *Gentl. Mag.* Dec. 484 Thine elbow instinctively moving to the fiddle-bow even after sleep had settled upon thy weary eyelids. **1831** BREWSTER *Nat. Magic* viii. (1833) 180 Drawing a rosined fiddle-bow across it. **1871** B. TAYLOR *Faust* (1875) I. ii. 40 The fiddle bow was playing.

'fiddle-case.

1. The case in which a fiddle is kept. Also *attrib.*, *fiddle-case boots*: boots as big as a fiddle-case.

1647 WARD *Simp. Cobler* 27 To spend their lives in making fidle-cases for futulous womens phansies. **1762** GOLDSM. *Cit. W.* xli, Heads..as empty as a fiddle-case. **1837** LOCKHART *Scott* (1839) VIII. 71 Half a dozen tall footmen each bearing a fiddle case. **1852** R. S. SURTEES *Sponge's Sp. Tour* lxvi. 536 Tweed trousers thrust into fiddle-case boots.

2. *pl.* (See quot.).

1878–86 BRITTEN & HOLLAND *Plant-n.*, Fiddle-cases, *Rhinanthus crista-galli.*

†**'fiddlecome,** *a. Obs.* [short for next, used *attrib.*] Nonsensical, silly, trumpery.

1697 VANBRUGH *Relapse* IV. i. 103 A fiddlecome tale of a draggle-tailed girl. **1777** SHERIDAN *Trip Scarb.* IV. i, Do you think such a fine proper gentleman..cares for a fiddle-come tale of a child?

†**fiddle-come-faddle.** *Obs. rare.* Altered form of FIDDLE-FADDLE, with *come* for CUM.

1663 COWLEY *Cutter of Coleman St.* III. viii, They have their Simpathies and Fiddle-come-faddles in their Brain.

fiddlededee (ˌfɪd(ə)ldɪˈdiː), *int.* and *sb.* [f. FIDDLE *sb.* or *v.*, used in a contemptuous sense with a nonsensical appendage.]

A. *int.* Nonsense!

a **1784** JOHNSON in *Boswell's Life* (1848) Appdx. 837/1 All he [Johnson] said was, 'Fiddle-de-dee, my dear'. **1825** J. NEAL *Bro. Jonathan* I. 182 Fiddle-de-dee then; I'll venter it! **1865** TROLLOPE *Belton Est.* xxix. 352 'He is a man very estimable'..'Fiddle-de-dee. He is an ape,—a monkey.'

B. *sb.* Nonsense, absurdity.

1843 *Ainsworth's Mag.* IV. 176 A large bundle of the latest fiddlededees of ladies' rattletraps hot from London. *c* **1848** PLANCHÉ & DANCE *Blue Beard* i. 6 Don't believe him, it's all fiddlededee.

fiddle-faddle (ˈfɪd(ə)lˈfæd(ə)l), *sb.*, *a.* and *int.* [This and the vb. are reduplications of FIDDLE or FADDLE; cf. Ger. *fickfack*, and contemptuous formations like *flim-flam*, *skimble-skamble*, etc.]

A. *sb.*

1. Trifling talk or action; in *pl.* trivial matters, trifling occupations or objects of attention.

1577 tr. *Bullinger's Decades* 103 This more then neding fiddle faddle smacks somwhat of ambition. **1592** G. HARVEY *Pierce's Super.* Wks. 1884 II. 98 Away with these paultringe fidle-fadles. **1684** tr. *Agrippa's Van. Arts* xxx. 86 The Fiddle-faddles and Trifles of Mathematicians. *a* **1734** NORTH *Exam.* II. v. §141 (1740) 403 Come leave your Fiddlefaddles of Presumptions. *c* **1760** in Macaulay *Ess. Pitt* (1854) 308/2 No more they make a fiddle-faddle About a Hessian horse or saddle. **1827** SCOTT *Jrnl.* 8 July, The fiddle-faddle of arranging all the things was troublesome. **1849** DARWIN *Life & Lett.* (1887) I. 377 Describing species of birds and shells, &c., is all fiddle-faddle. **1861** T. L. PEACOCK *Gryll Gr.* 103 Where you just look on fiddlefaddles while your dinner is behind a screen. **1887** JESSOPP *Arcady* iv. 134 Collecting cards..and all the petty fiddlefaddle that is growing so stale.

2. An idler, trifler; a gossip, chatterbox.

1602 BRETON *Merry Wonders*, Maid Marian in a Morrice-daunce, would put her down for a Fiddle-faddle. **1756** MRS. DELANY *Let. to Mrs. Dewes*, Mrs. Montagu, Mrs. Gosling, and two or three fiddle faddles. **1824** *Westm. Rev.* II. 337 Your true fiddle-faddle Somebody, who would be in high repute among his fellows. **1888** *Berksh. Gloss.* s.v., A 'viddle vaddle or viddle vaddler'.

B. *adj.* Trifling, petty, fussy: said of persons as well as of things.

1617 COLLINS *Def. Bp. Ely* 298 A great deale more of such fiddle-faddle stuffe. **1727** DE FOE *Protest. Monast.* 16 In any other fiddle faddle part of Life. **1712** ARBUTHNOT *John Bull* in Arb. *Garner* (1883) VI. 603 They [liverymen] said, 'She was a troublesome fiddle faddle old woman!' **1834** BECKFORD *Italy* II. 164 So fiddle-faddle and so coquettish. **1855** THACKERAY *Newcomes* II. 69 The fiddle-faddle etiquette of the Court.

C. *int.* Nonsense! Bosh!

1671 SHADWELL *Humorists* v, Fiddle faddle on your Travelling and University. **1705** VANBRUGH *Confed.* II. i, Fiddle, faddle; han't I wit enough already? **1779** MAD. D'ARBLAY *Diary* 11 Jan., *Dr. Johnson*: Pho! fiddle-faddle; do you suppose your book is so much talked of and not yourself? **1876** F. E. TROLLOPE *Charming Fellow* III. xv. 191 Oh, fiddle-faddle, my lord!

fiddle-faddle (ˈfɪd(ə)lfæd(ə)l), *v.* [See the sb.] *intr.* To be busy about petty trifles; to fuss, 'mess about'.

1633 FORD *Broken H.* I. iii, Ye may as easily Outrun a cloud driven by the northern blast As fiddle faddle so. **1776** MRS. DELANY *Lett.* Ser. II. II. 202 Had you been bred up only to fiddle faddle, you would have fiddle faddled all your life. **1870** MISS BROUGHTON *Red as Rose* I. 226 She has..fiddle-faddled about the garden, picking off half-a-dozen dead roses.

Hence **fiddle-faddling** *vbl. sb.* and *ppl. a.* Also **fiddle-faddler**.

1834 T. MEDWIN *Angler Wales* I. Pref. ix, But lest I should chance to be considered here one of the tribe of that fiddle-fadling, dull old prosing pedant. **1846** WORCESTER (citing *Qu. Rev.*), *Fiddle-faddler*, a foolish trifler. **1850** CLOUGH *Poems and Pr. Rem.* (1869) I. 168 Whatsoever your hand findeth to do, do it without fiddle-faddling. **1861** MISS BRADDON *Lady Lisle* (1885) 36, I don't want him to be a fiddle-faddling girl. **1882** *Society* 14 Oct. 11/2 The mistaken notion..that detail is a substitute for spirit and fiddle-faddling for acting.

'fiddle-head. [f. FIDDLE *sb.* + HEAD.]

1. *Naut.* The ornamental carving at the bows of a vessel, the termination of which is a scroll turning aft or inward like the head of a violin.

1799 *Naval Chron.* I. App. State of Navy, *Neptune*, The fiddle-head..had..a bad effect. **1833** MARRYAT *P. Simple* xli, I hope Captain O'Brien will take off her fiddle-head, and get one carved.

2. A local name for a young fern frond.

1882 J. HARDY in *Proc. Berw. Nat. Club* IX. 563 Young fern fronds—'fiddle-heads', as they are named—are greedily devoured as substitutes for green vegetables.

3. A head as empty as a fiddle.

1887 W. F. ANSTEY in *Macm. Mag.* Feb. 262/2 He hasn't two ideas in his great fiddle-head.

'fiddle-ˌheaded, *a.* [f. prec. + -ED².]

a. *Naut.* Having a fiddle-head. **b.** Of a fork, spoon: Having the handle made after the pattern of a fiddle. **c.** Empty-headed. **d.** (see quot. 1883).

1840 HOOD *Kilmansegg, First Step* iii, In short a kind Of fork—that is fiddle-headed. **1851** H. MELVILLE *Whale* viii. 43 A projecting piece of scroll work fashioned after a ship's fiddle-headed beak. **1854** WHYTE MELVILLE *Gen. Bounce* v. (1855) 104 'You've broke it, you fiddle-headed brute!' **1883** G. STABLES *Our Friend the Dog* vii. 60 *Fiddle-headed*, a long, gaunt, wolfish head, like what one sees in some Mastiffs.

'fiddlement. *nonce-wd.* [f. FIDDLE *v.* + -MENT.] The action of fiddling, an instance of this.

1859 SALA *Tw. round Clock* (1861) 157 An egregious fiddler..used to attract large crowds in the street beneath listening to his complicated fiddlements.

fiddler (ˈfɪd(ə)lə(r)). [OE. *fiðelere*, f. **fiðelian* to fiddle, f. **fiðele* FIDDLE *sb.* Cf. ON. *fiðlari.*] One who fiddles.

1. a. One who plays on the fiddle; *esp.* one who does so for hire. ***fiddler's fare, money, pay, wages***: see quots. 1597, 1608, *a* 1700, 1785.

a **1100** *Ags. Voc.* in Wr.-Wülcker 311 Fidicen, fiðelere. *c* **1330** *Arth. & Merl.* 6568 Ther were trumpes and fithelers. **1463** *Mann. & Househ. Exp.* 230 Govyn to a fedelere, the sayd day at nyte, iiij.d. **1532** MORE *Confut. Barnes* VIII. Wks. 735/1 He..fareth as he wer from a frere waxen a fideler. **1597** *1st Pt. Return fr. Parnass.* I. i. 380 He..gave me fidler's wages, and dismiste mee. **1608** MARKHAM *Dumb Knight* III, Let the world know you haue had more than fidlers fare, for you haue meat, money, and cloth. **1644** MILTON *Areop.* (Arb.) 50 The gammuth of every municipal fidler. *a* **1700** B. E. *Dict. Cant. Crew*, *Fidlers-pay*, Thanks and Wine. **1721** BOLINGBROKE in *Swift's Lett.* (1766) II. 20 As fiddlers flourish carelessly, before they play a fine air. **1785** GROSE *Dict. Vulg. Tongue*, *Fidler's money*, all sixpences. **1807–8** W. IRVING *Salmag.* (1824) 350 The fiddler puts the whole assembly in motion. **1886** HALL CAINE *Son of Hagar* II. xvi, The fiddler's function was at an end for the present.

b. ***Fiddler's Green*** (*Naut.*): 'a sailor's elysium, in which wine, women, and song figure prominently' (Farmer).

1825 *Sporting Mag.* XVI. 404 My grannan..used to tell me that animals, when they departed this life, were destined to be fixed in *Fidler's Green*. **1836** W. H. MAXWELL *Capt. Blake* I. xv. *note*, It is..believed that tailors and musicians after death are cantoned in a place called 'Fiddler's Green'. **1837** MARRYAT *Dog-fiend* ix, We shape a course for Fiddler's Green. **1883** J. D. J. KELLY in *Harper's Mag.* Aug. 441/2 The pilotless narrows which lead to Fiddler's Green, where all good sailors go.

2. †**a.** A trifler. *Obs.*

1591 R. CECIL in *Unton's Corr.* (Roxb.) 197 This discorse growes by many fidlers in your cause. **1735** DYCHE & PARDON *Dict.*, *Fidler*..a trifling, foolish, or impertinent Person.

b. *slang.* A swindler, cheat; one who 'wangles'.

1857 'DUCANGE ANGLICUS' *Vulgar Tongue* 8 *Fiddler*, a sharper, or cheat. Thieves. **1932** 'JOCK' *Dartmoor fr. Within* v. 107 B——..was..what is termed in prison 'a clever fiddler'. **1958** *Times Lit. Suppl.* 15 Aug. p. iv/1 He is a 'spiv' or a 'fiddler',..for he has offended against the principles of 'fairness' which is..the virtue nearest to the Englishman's heart. **1962** D. WARNER *Death of Bogey* I. ii. 10 Spivs and pimps, fiddlers and tweedlers.

c. A meddlesome or interfering person.

1952 A. GRIMBLE *Pattern of Islands* vii. 143 Interfering with the customs of simple peoples..can end by leaving them bereft of their national will to live. The fiddler is a killer on a grand scale.

3. *slang.* A sixpence.

1846 *Swell's Night Guide* 119/1 *Fiddler*, a sixpence. **1848** *Sinks of London laid Open* 106 *Fiddler*, a sixpence. **1885** *Household Words* 20 June 155/2 A more easily explained name [for a sixpence] is a Fiddler..probably from the old custom of each couple at a dance paying the fiddler sixpence.

4. a. See quots. 1750 and 1887. **b.** A local name for the Sandpiper (*Tringoides hypoleucus*).

1750 G. HUGHES *Barbadoes* 82 Fiddlers. This fly..much resembles a cockroach. **1885** SWAINSON *Prov. Names Brit. Birds* 196 Fiddler (Hebrides). **1887** *Kent Gloss.*, *Fiddler*, the angel or shark-ray.

c. A small crab of the genus *Gelasimus*. Also ***fiddler-crab***.

1714 J. LAWSON *Carolina* 162, Fidlars are a sort of small Crabs, that lie in Holes in the Marshes. **1867** W. B. LORD *Crab, Shrimp, & Lobster Lore* 29 A 'Fidler-Crab' (as it is sometimes called from the rapidity with which it works its elbows). **1883** S. L. CLEMENS ['Mark Twain'] *Life on Mississippi* xlviii. 429 The drainage-ditches were everywhere alive with little crabs—'fiddlers'.

5. *attrib.* and *Comb.*, as ***fiddler lad***; ***fiddler-like*** adj. and adv.; **fiddler beetle**, an Australian beetle, *Eupœcila australasiæ*, belonging to the family Scarabæidæ.

1824 SCOTT *Redgauntlet* Let. xii, 'Deil's in the fiddler lad' was muttered from more quarters than one. **1628** VENNER *Baths of Bathe* (1650) 359 It is Fidler-like. **1660** HOWELL *Parly of Beasts* 128 He was dismissed Fidler-like, with meat, drink, and money. [**1907** W. W. FROGGATT *Austral. Insects* 161 The Fiddler, *Eupoecila australasiae*,..is black and reddish brown, marked upon the thorax and elytra with green stripes.] **1917** *Austral. Naturalist* Apr. 184 At Tuggerah Lakes in September, 1916, a cluster of cocoons of the Fiddler beetle were found at the base of a hollow stump of a Eucalyptus. **1926** R. J. TILLYARD *Insects Austral. & N.Z.* xx. 231 The Fiddler Beetle, *Eupoecila australasiae* Don..is common in Eastern Australia in November. **1945** K. C. MCKEOWN *Austral. Insects* 145 One of the commonest species is *Eupoecila australasiae* Don., the Fiddler Beetle; it is black with bright green hieroglyphics on the elytra.

†**'fiddlery.** *Obs.* In 6 fidlery. [f. prec. + -Y³.] The art or craft of a fiddler.

1588 FRAUNCE *Lawiers Log.* I. vi. 36 As though Humfrey Crowther were a whole integrall thing made and consisting of these two partes, goodnesse and fidlery.

fiddlestick (ˈfɪd(ə)lstɪk), *sb.* [f. FIDDLE *sb.* + STICK *sb.*]

1. The bow strung with horsehair with which the fiddle is played. ***the devil rides on a fiddlestick***: = here's a fine commotion.

14.. *Nom. MS. Reg.* 17 in Wr.-Wülcker 693 *Hic arculus*, fydylstyk. **1596** SHAKS. *1 Hen. IV*, II. iv. 535 The Deuill rides vpon a Fiddle-sticke. **1653** WALTON *Angler* 106, I lent you indeed my Fiddle, but not my Fiddlestick. **1773** JOHNSON in *Boswell* 15 Apr., Give him a fiddle and a fiddlestick, and he can do nothing. **1842** ABDY *Water Cure* (1843) 210, I might as well inquire whether the fiddle or the fiddlestick makes the tune.

2. *humorously.* Something insignificant or absurd, a mere nothing. Often substituted for another word in derisively repeating a remark. Also, ***fiddlestick's end***. ***not to care a fiddlestick***: to care not at all.

1621 FLETCHER *Pilgrim* III. iv, Shot with a fiddlestick: who's here to shoot ye? **1701** FARQUHAR *Sir H. Wildair* IV.

ii, Golden pleasures! golden fiddlesticks! **1796** GROSE *Dict. Vulg. Tongue* (ed. 3), *Fiddlestick's End*, Nothing. **1807–8** W. IRVING *Salmag.* (1824) 140 We do not care a fiddle-stick.. for either public opinion or private ill-will. **1838** DICKENS *Nich. Nick.* viii, 'We purify the boys' bloods now and then.' 'Purify fiddlesticks' ends,' said his lady. **1855** THACKERAY *Newcomes* x, She..proposed to die of a broken heart..A broken fiddlestick! **1877** BLACK *Green Past.* xxvii. (1878) 214 'Beware the awful fiddlesticks!' she flippantly answered.

3. Hence as *int.* An exclamation equivalent to Nonsense! fiddle-de-dee! Often in *pl.* Also, ***fiddlestick's end!***

1600 NASHE *Summer's Last Will* Wks. (Grosart) VI. 130 A fiddlesticke! ne're tell me I am full of words. **1842** THACKERAY *Miss Tickletoby's Lect.* vii, Do you suppose men so easily change their natures? Fiddlestick! **1854** H. AINSWORTH *Flitch of Bacon* ii. 17 'And she refused you.' 'Fortunately she did, my dear.' 'Fiddlestick's end! I dare say you preferred her.' **1857** HUGHES *Tom Brown* ix. (1871) 186 Fiddlesticks! it's nothing but the skin broken. **1883** STEVENSON *Treasure Isl.* I. ii. (1886) 16 'Wounded? A fiddle-stick's end!' said the doctor. **1887** JESSOPP *Arcady* vii. 219 Once a labourer always a labourer? Fiddlesticks!

'fiddle-string. [f. as prec. + STRING.] One of the strings on a fiddle, which by their vibration produce the sound. Also *fig.*

1728 YOUNG *Love Fame* iii. (1757) 108 Fix'd is the fate of whores, and fiddle-strings! **1733** ARBUTHNOT *Air* iii. §20 A Fiddle-string, moisten'd with Water will sink a Note in a little time. **1835** MRS. CARLYLE *Lett.* I. 43, I do but..fret myself to fiddlestrings. **1884** E. HERON-ALLEN *Violin-making* II. xii. 210 The manufacture of fiddle strings.

fiddley ('fɪd(ə)lɪ). *Naut.* The iron framework round the deck opening that leads to the stoke-hole of a steamer; usually covered by a grating of iron bars; the space below this.

1881 *Standard* 17 Nov. 2/3 The coverings of the fiddleys or openings to the stoke hole. **1885** RUNCIMAN *Skippers & Sh.* I A few men were crouching in the fiddley. **1893** *Westm. Gaz.* I Feb. 4/2 They have had to sleep amidst the 'fiddlies' around the engine boilers.

fiddley-did ('fɪd(ə)lɪdɪd). *Austral. slang.* Also **fiddl(e)y**. [Rhyming slang for QUID *sb.*²] One pound; a pound note.

1941 BAKER *Dict. Austral. Slang* 28 Fiddley. **1957** 'N. CULOTTA' *They're Weird Mob* (1958) iii. 42 Here's a couple and a 'alf fiddley dids. **1966** *Sunday Truth* (Brisbane) 23 Dec. 22/2 And for a sovereign, a quid, a pound, a jimmy-o-goblin or a fiddly. **1967** K. GILES *Death in Diamonds* vii. 132, I said I'd give him four Irish fiddlies and take the chance... I gave him the four quid, sir.

fiddling ('fɪdlɪŋ), *vbl. sb.* [f. FIDDLE *v.* + -ING¹.] The action of the vb. FIDDLE in various senses.

1. Playing the fiddle.

c **1460** *Emare* 390 Bothe harpe and fydyllyng. *a* **1680** BUTLER *Rem.* (1759) I. 7 Th' Arcadians..Whom nothing in the World could bring To civil Life, but fiddling. **1702** ADDISON *Dial. Medals* iii. Wks. 1721 I. 530 We see Nero's fidling and Commodus's skill in fencing on several of their Medals. **1879** BESANT & RICE *Trafalg. Bay* ii. (1891) 22 There could be no fiddling that evening.

2. Fussy trifling; petty adjustment or alteration.

1622 MASSINGER *Virg. Mart.* IV. i, Hell on your fiddling! **1705** W. KING *Art of Love* xii. 68 Some times your hair you upwards furl..All must through twenty fiddlings pass. **1762** *Songs Costume* (Percy Soc.) 240 'Tis so metamorphos'd by your fiddling and fangling, That I scarce know my own. **1878** in *N. Amer. Rev.* CXXVI. 249, I am sick of this fiddling about.

3. Cheating, swindling.

1884 J. GREENWOOD *Little Ragamuffins* xxxii. 300 So sure as a boy of mine takes to fiddling, I'd manoeuvre him into quod before he sleeps that night. **1959** *New Statesman* 11 July 39/1 The Ministry people would not agree because they thought it would lead to [taxi] drivers taking strangers all round the place and doing all sorts of fiddling.

fiddling ('fɪdlɪŋ), *ppl. a.* [f. as prec. + -ING².]

1. That plays the fiddle.

1580 SIDNEY *Arcadia* II. (1590) 217, I curse the fidling finders out of music. **1780** COWPER *Progr. Err.* 111 A cassocked huntsman and a fiddling priest. *a* **1839** PRAED *Poems* (1864) I. 290 He lighted by chance on a fiddling fellow.

2. a. Of persons: Busy about trifles; addicted to futile and petty activity. **b.** Of things: Petty, trifling, unimportant; contemptible, futile.

a. 1660 S. FISHER *Rusticks Alarm* Wks. (1679) 374 The Fruit of their fidling Minds. **1673** WYCHERLEY *Gentleman Dancing-Master* II. ii, You grow so fiddling and so trouble-some there is no enduring you. **1748** RICHARDSON *Clarissa* (1811) II. i. 5 A sort of fiddling, busy, yet..unbusy man.

b. 1652 SIR E. NICHOLAS in *N. Papers* (Camden) 301 Putting himself into every fidling business. *a* **1672** WOOD *Life* (1848) 70 For feare of making their meetings to be vaine and fidling. **1705** W. KING *Art of Love* 62 The most fidling work of knitting. *a* **1745** SWIFT *Direc. to Servants* ii, *Wks.* (1778) II. 358 Good cooks cannot abide what they..call fiddling work, where abundance of time is spent, and little done. **1886** J. R. REES *Pleas. of a Bk. Worm* v. 169 The quantity of fiddling, complaining criticism with which many of our..critical journals abound.

fiddly ('fɪdlɪ), *a. colloq.* Also **fiddley**. [f. FIDDLE *v.* + -Y¹.] Requiring time or dexterity; pernickety.

1926 *Blackw. Mag.* Sept. 403/1 A fiddly sort of way of translating into action the Political's broad exhortation. **1960** *Times* 29 July 4/6 'Fiddly things' should be done by automatic machines. **1964** *Which?* Apr. 43/2 The Commer's [roof]..needed rather a push to get it started and had fiddley catches. **1970** *Amateur Photographer* 11 Mar. 28/3 Working in total darkness to line up those fiddly bits of film.

fide (faɪd), *v. rare*⁻¹. [f. L. *fīd-ĕre* to CONFIDE.] *trans.* To confide or entrust *to*.

1863 LD. LYTTON *Ring Amasis* iv. 66 The..request that her infant daughter might be fided to the care of her friend.

'fideal, *a. rare*⁻¹. [f. L. *fide-* (*fidēs*) + -AL¹.] Pertaining to or based upon faith.

1854 *Notes Biogr. W. Law* p. xxv, His far-seeing fideal realizations.

†**'fideding,** *a. Obs. Sc. rare*⁻¹. [ad. L. *fidē dignus* worthy of credit.] Trustworthy. In quot. *ellipt.* a trustworthy person.

1535 STEWART *Cron. Scot.* III. 432 Schawin him be ane richt fideding, Ane man of gude.

†**fi'deicide.** *Obs.*⁻⁰ [f. L. *fidei*, gen. of *fidēs* faith + -CIDE I.] 'A faith-destroyer; a breaker of word or TRUST' (Blount *Glossogr.* 1656–81).

1676–1717 in COLES.

fidei-commissum (ˌfaɪdiːaɪkɒ'mɪsəm). *Rom. Law.* [a. L. *fidei-commissum*, neut. pa. pple. of *fidei-committĕre*, f. *fidei*, dat. of *fidēs* faith + *committĕre* to entrust, COMMIT.] A bequest which a person made by begging his heir or legatee to transfer something to a third person.

1727–41 in CHAMBERS *Cycl.* **1767** BLACKSTONE *Comm.* II. II. xx. 327 The fidei-commissum..was the disposal of an inheritance to one, in confidence that he should convey it or dispose of the profits at the will of another.

So **ˌfidei-co'mmissary** [ad. L. *fidei commissārius*: see -ARY], of, belonging to, or of the nature of a fidei-commissum. **fidei-co'mmissarily** *adv.* [+ -LY²], in a fidei-commissary or precatory manner; through a fidei-commissum. **ˌfidei-co'mmission**, the action involved in a fidei-commissum; an instance of this. **ˌfidei-co'mmissioner** [+ -ER¹], one who receives a fidei-commissum. **ˌfidei-co'mmissor**, 'he that commits a thing to be disposed of by another' (Blount *Glossogr.* 1656–81).

1751 CHAMBERS *Cycl.* s.v. *Fidei-Commissum*, A prætor was erected, whose business was restrained to the single matter of fidei-commissions. *Ibid.*, The fidei-commissioner refused to accept the trust. **1880** MUIRHEAD *Ulpian* xxv. §3 A fideicommissary gift may be left even by a mere nod. **1880** —— *Gaius* II. §247 Fideicommissary inheritances. *Ibid.* §260 Competent for a testator to bequeath single things by fideicommissary gift. *Ibid.* §289 He cannot be appointed fideicommissarily. **1880** —— *Ulpian* ii. §8 He to whom freedom is given fideicommissarily is a freedman not of the testator's but of the manumitter's.

fideism ('faɪdiːɪz(ə)m). Also **F-**. [f. L. *fides* faith + -ISM.] Any doctrine according to which all (or some) knowledge depends upon faith or revelation, and reason or the intellect is to be disregarded, as **a.** = TRADITIONALISM; **b.** a Roman Catholic theory developed from Kantian idealism; **c.** in Protestant usage, also derived from Kant, with reference to justification by faith. Hence **'fideist, fide'istic** *a.*

1885 [see TRADITIONALISM]. **1895** *Dublin Rev.* Apr. 313 As to Fideism, see Dr. Hettinger's interesting classification of its four stages, as corresponding to the four stages of Rationalism, in his 'Fundamental Theologie', 1879, vol. ii. pp. 348–9. **1903** *Hibbert Jrnl.* I. 556 'Fideism' denotes the material principle—the nature and condition of salvation through Christ. **1908** *Programme of Modernism* 142 Such scepticism destroys the certitude of the fact of revelation and ends in blind fideism. **1909** *Cath. Encycl.* VI. 68/2 Fideism owes its origin to distrust in human reason, and the logical sequence of such an attitude is scepticism. *Ibid.*, For some fideists, human reason cannot of itself reach certitude in regard to any truth whatever. *Ibid.*, It is also a fideistic attitude which is the occasion of agnosticism..and other modern forms of anti-intellectualism. **1912** F. VON HÜGEL *Eternal Life* II. xii. 344 Rome is finely free from all Fideism or Pietism. **1957** *Oxf. Dict. Chr. Ch.* 503/1 Scholastic theologians regularly charged the Modernists with 'Fideism'. **1966** *Cath. Dict. Theol.* II. 296/1 Fideistic tendencies also appeared during the Middle Ages. *Ibid.*, Fideists like the Abbé Louis Bautain... The doctrine of the last-named is the fullest..expression of fideism and indeed has come to be almost identified with fideism. **1967** *Philos.* XLII. 191 (*title*) Wittgensteinian Fideism.

'fideist. *nonce-wd.* [f. L. *fide-* (*fides*) + -IST.] (See quot.)

1881 *Dublin Rev.* Ser. III. V. 250 Writers who have exaggerated the influence of faith..he [Ollé-Laprune] would call..fideists.

fidejussion (faɪdiː'dʒʌʃən). [ad. L. *fidejussiōn-em*, n. of action f. *fide-jubēre*: see next.] A giving or being surety or bail; suretyship.

1657 FARINGDON *30 Serm.* i. 15 If he will be a surety, such is the nature of fidejussion and suretiship, he must.

Hence **fide'jussionary** *a.*

1880 MUIRHEAD *Gaius* IV. §137 [He] gave his fidejussionary undertaking for Lucius Titius for something indefinite.

fidejussor (faɪdiː'dʒʌsə(r), -ɔː(r)). *Civil Law.* [a. L. *fidejussor*, agent-n. f. *fide-jubēre*, f. *fidē*, abl. of *fides* faith + *jubēre* to order.] One who authorizes the bail of or goes bail for another; a surety.

1539 *Sc. Acts Jas. V* (1814) II. 354 Certane vtheris his collegis caucioneris & fide Jussoris. **1647** JER. TAYLOR *Lib. Proph.* xviii. 239 If he would have appointed Godfathers.. to be fidejussors for them [Children]. **1768** BLACKSTONE *Comm.* III. 108 They..take recognizances..of certain fidejussors in the nature of bail. **1880** MUIRHEAD *Gaius* III. §115.

fidejussory (faɪdiː'dʒʌsərɪ), *a.* [ad. L. *fidejussōri-us*, f. *fidejussor*: see prec.] Of or pertaining to surety or bail.

1754 ERSKINE *Princ. Sc. Law* (1809) 325 Relief against the debtor is implied in fidejussory obligations. **1774** BP. HALLIFAX *Anal. Rom. Law* (1795) 18 Any one that offered the Fidejussory Caution.

fidel(e, obs. form of FIDDLE.

†**fi'dele,** *a. Obs.* Also 6 **fydell**, 7 **fidell**. [a. F. *fidèle*, ad. L. *fidēl-is*, f. *fidēs* faith.] Faithful, sincere, true.

1539 HEN. VIII *To Sir T. Wyatt* 10 Mar. (R.), They were true and fidele unto us. **1545** RAYNOLD *Byrth Mankynde* Riv, He is one of the moost fydell & faithfullest Apothecaries in London. **1671** *True Nonconf.* 133 Our Lord ..hath in his fidell discharge..fully defined the former. **1677** GALE *Crt. Gentiles* III. Pref., An humble fidele mind.

†**fi'delious,** *a. Obs.* [f. L. *fidēli-s* + -OUS.] Faithful.

1650 S. SHEPPARD *Candido* 14, I..have found thee cordially fidelious. **1655** *Marrow of Complements* 114 Your fidelious servitour. **1656** S. HOLLAND *Zara* (1719) 16 The Champion and his fidelious. Land-loper Soto.

Fidelism (fɪ'dɛlɪz(ə)m). [ad. Sp. *Fidelismo* (also used), f. the name of *Fidel* Castro Ruz (b. 1927), Cuban politician + -ISM.] The methods and policies of Fidel Castro's political administration in Cuba; = CASTROISM. Hence **Fi'delist** *a.*, of or pertaining to Fidel Castro or to Fidelism; ‖ **Fidelista** (fide'lista), an adherent of Fidel Castro; also *attrib.*

1959 *Washington Post* 24 Nov. A 14/1 Fidelismo has become revolution for revolution's sake. **1960** *Business Week* 3 Dec. 87 'Fidelism', or 'Fidelismo', as the Latin Americans call it..is the Castro-style revolution that's followed by a left-wing, Communist-influenced, perhaps Communist-controlled, government. *Ibid.*, The Fidelistas and Communists. **1961** *Ann. Reg.* *1960* 211 This was fertile ground for 'Fidelismo'. **1961** *Economist* 25 Nov. 723/2 An attempted return to dictatorship in the Dominican Republic, and the chance of a fidelist uprising that might have followed it. **1962** *Listener* 1 Feb. 206/1 *Fidelista* cells began to be formed in the cities, in the universities, in the sugar mills. **1968** *Guardian* 1 Oct. 8/4 That generation is now trying out various kinds of Trotskyism, Maoism, and Fidelism. **1970** 'J. MORRIS' *Candywine Devel.* xviii. 212 It may be..the local Fidelistas. **1971** *N.Y. Rev. Bks.* 28 Jan. 6/4 'El Che' was not Castro's brain, but he was the Fidelista conscience.

fidelity (fɪ'dɛlɪtɪ), *sb.* Forms: 5–6 **fydelite, -itie, -itye, -yte, -ytie,** 6–7 **fidelitie,** (6 **fidelite**), 6– **fidelity.** [a. F. *fidélité*, ad. L. *fidēlitāt-em*, f. *fidēlis* faithful, f. *fidēs* faith.]

1. The quality of being faithful; faithfulness, loyalty, unswerving allegiance to a person, party, bond, etc. Const. *to, towards.*

1508 BARCLAY *Shyp of Folys* (1874) II. 92 Amonge these wasters is no fydelyte. **1520** *Caxton's Chron. Eng.* III. 25/1 They kepte fydelyte to the Romayns. **1553** Q. JANE in Strype *Eccl. Mem.* III. App. ii. 4 Our special trust is in your ..fidelities in this matter. **1659** HAMMOND *On Ps.* 520 Gods mercies..and fidelities to his people. **1683** BURNET tr. *More's Utopia* (1684) 163 They serve those that hire them.. with..great Fidelity. **1791** BENTHAM *Panopt.* Wks. 1843 IV. 225 Fidelity to engagements is a virtue. **1839** THIRLWALL *Greece* VI. 279 The conduct of Arsames raised Alexander's suspicions of his fidelity. **1856** KANE *Arct. Expl.* II. viii. 90 A strict, stanch fidelity to the expedition.

†**b.** *to make fidelity*: to take an oath of fealty.

1494 FABYAN *Chron.* VII. ccxxxviii. 277 That..Kynges of Scotlonde, shuld make theyr homage and fydelyte vnto the Kynges of Englonde. **1609** SKENE *Reg. Maj.* (1774) 79 Ane other fidelitie..salbe..made be the woman, and her heires, in the samine forme and words as homage should be made. *Ibid.* Table 80 He quha maries ane widow, sould make fidelity to the heire of hir first husband.

c. Conjugal faithfulness.

1694 *Acct. Sweden* 70 Some of them are accounted more eminent for Chastity before Marriage, than Fidelity after. **1825** J. NEAL *Bro. Jonathan* III. 227 If we are not barren, our fidelity is proved.

†**d.** Word of honour, oath, pledge; also ***to give, break one's fidelity. by my fidelity***: upon my word. *Obs.*

1531 in W. H. Turner *Select. Rec. Oxford* 105 The benche dyd examen the foresayd [persons] uppon theyre fydelities. **1574** WHITGIFT *Def. Aunsw.* iii. Wks. 1851 I. 306 None is admitted to any degree..but the same is first presented..to the university, by some one..who giveth his fidelity for them. **1581** MARBECK *Bk. of Notes* 165 Pharao..was punished for breaking his fidelitie. **1598** SHAKS. *Merry W.* IV. ii. 160 By my fidelity this is not well.

e. *Ecol.* The degree of association of a species with a plant community.

1932 FULLER & CONARD tr. *Braun-Blanquet's Plant Sociol.* iv. 52 The more or less rigid ties by which the species are bound to certain communities—their fidelity. **1955** *Jrnl. Ecol.* XLIII. 232 Species which are of high fidelity regionally become less faithful in other regions and other different climatic conditions. **1967** M. E. HALE *Biol. Lichens*

iv. 61 A large group of lichens..have high fidelity for limestone and other basic substrates.

2. Strict conformity to truth or fact.

†**a.** Of persons: Honesty, truthfulness, trustworthiness, veracity (*obs.*). **b.** Of a description, translation, etc.: Correspondence with the original; exactness.

1534 MORE *On the Passion* Wks. 1344/2 Ought we to doubte of his fidelitie and testimony? **1597** HOOKER *Eccl. Pol.* v. §19. 29 The principall thing required in a witnesse is fidelitie. **1662** STILLINGFL. *Orig. Sacr.* II. vi. §1 How then can the fidelity of a Prophet be discovered by the event? **1709** STRYPE *Ann. Ref.* I. xxi. 252 He trusting to their Fidelities, set them down as he received them. **1735** POPE *Lett.* 22 Jan. 1709 Be very free of your Remarks..in regard ..to the Fidelity of the Translation. **1847** EMERSON *Repr. Men, Shaks.* Wks. (Bohn) I. 359 The only critics who have expressed our convictions with any adequate fidelity. **1872** DARWIN *Emotions* Introd. 26 By this means [photography on wood] almost complete fidelity is ensured.

c. The degree to which a sound or picture reproduced or transmitted by any device resembles the original; esp. in HIGH FIDELITY. Cf. HI-FI, LO-FI.

1878 G. B. PRESCOTT *Speaking Telephone* i. 12 The apparatus..reproduces the original vibrations with perfect fidelity. **1896** MARCONI *Brit. Pat. 12,039* 6 The space cannot ..be excessively shortened without injuring the fidelity of the transmission. **1918** H. SEYMOUR *Reprod. Sound* 269, I introduced baked carbon sheet for the purpose, with remarkable results as to strength and fidelity of tone. **1923** *Sci. Amer.* July 67/2 For..radio programs..you will..have an extremely sensitive sound converter..which is of an entirely different order of fidelity from that..of [other] microphonic devices. **1931** *Electronics* Oct. 137/1 We find that the same word—Fidelity—can be used both in connection with the excellence of sound reproduction and picture reproduction. **1935** *Discovery* Sept. 278/1 Fidelity of both picture and sound reproduction is good. **1958** *Economist* 26 July 270 The German industry also put its first complete fidelity recorder on to its domestic market in that year [*sc.* 1948].

3. fidelity insurance, insurance taken out by an employer to indemnify him against losses incurred through the dishonesty or non-performance of an employee. So ***fidelity bond, guarantee***, such a bond or contract.

1880 *Encycl. Brit.* XIII. 161/2 *Fidelity Guarantee.* The guarantee of employers against the fraud or insolvency of their servants. **1930** *Economist* 26 Apr. 942/1 Its activities are confined to the transaction of fidelity guarantee insurance. **1970** *Daily Tel.* 28 Sept. 3 The insurance companies..will investigate the staff, checking with previous employers and so on. If their character is good they are given what is known as a fidelity bond.

fidepromissor (ˌfaɪdiːprəʊˈmɪsɔː(r)). *Rom. Law.* [a. L. *fidepromissor*, agent-n. f. *fide-promittĕre*, f. *fides* faith + *promittĕre* to promise.] One who promises or pledges himself as security for another; a bail, surety.

1875 POSTE *Gaius* III. Comm. (ed. 2) 403 The sponsor and fidepromissor have vanished from the legislation of Justinian. **1880** MUIRHEAD *Gaius* Digest 604 Fidepromissors could become accessory only to verbal obligations.

fidfad (ˈfɪdfæd), *sb.* and *a.* [Short for FIDDLE-FADDLE.]

A. *sb.* **a.** One who gives fussy attention to trifles. **b.** A petty matter of detail, a crotchet.

1754 *World* No. 95 The youngest..is, in everything she does, an absolute fidfad. **1875** MRS. LYNN LINTON *Patricia Kemball* II. 31 The fidfads, called improvements, which were not wanted. **1881** B. W. RICHARDSON in *Gd. Words* XXII. 52 He built himself a house, and fitted it with every fidfad that could be suggested.

B. *adj.* Frivolous, fussy, petty.

1830 R. HILL in E. Sidney *Life* (1834) 351 With the tinkling cymbal fid-fad musicians may try to tickle the fancy of such half-witted admirers. **1844** *Blackw. Mag.* LV. 199 From exuberant 4to, down to the fid-fad concentration of 12mo.

fidge (fɪdʒ), *sb. dial.* or *colloq.* [f. next vb.]

1. The action or habit of fidgeting; the state of being fidgety: in phr. *to be in a fidge*; also, a commotion, stir, fuss.

1731 SWIFT *Tim & Fables* Wks. 1778 IX. 158 The twist, the squeeze, the rump, the fidge and all. **1790** J. MACAULAY *Poems* 129 No ane gi'es e'er a fidge or fyke, Or yet a moan. **1832** W. STEPHENSON *Gateshead Local Poems* 56 He's in a fidge To get to Beamish forge. **1887** RUSKIN *Præterita* II. 189 'There'll be such a fidge about you, when you're gone.'

2. A restless person.

1884 in *Cheshire Gloss.*

fidge (fɪdʒ), *v. Obs.* exc. *dial.* See also FIG *v.*[3] [Of obscure origin; the sense closely resembles that of FIKE, but etymological connexion is hardly possible, unless the form has undergone onomatopœic modification. Cf. Ger. *ficken* to move about briskly.]

1. *intr.* To move about restlessly or uneasily; also, ***to fidge about, abroad, to and fro.*** Of a limb: To twitch.

1575 J. STILL *Gamm. Gurton* I. iv. in Hazl. *Dodsley* III. 184 Where ha' you been fidging abroad, since you your nee'le lost? **1577** BRETON *Wks. Young Wit* (T.), Some [dame] would fidge, as though she had the itch. **1667** DRYDEN *Maiden Queen* III. i, What is it, that makes you fidge up and down so? **1700** CONGREVE *Way of World* v. 77 The good Judge..fidges off and on his Cushion. **1728** SWIFT *Mullinix & Timothy*, You wriggle, fidge, and make a rout. **1786** BURNS *Ordination* i, Kilmarnock wabsters fidge and claw. **1883** STEVENSON *Treasure Isl.* I. iii. (1886) 20 'Look..how my fingers fidges.'

b. To be eager and restless. ***to fidge fu' fain***: (*Sc.*) to express pleasurable eagerness by restless movements.

1785 BURNS *To W. Simpson* vi, Auld Coila, now, may fidge fu' fain, She's gotten Poets o' her ain. **1790** —— *Tam O'Shanter* 185 Even Satan glowr'd and fidg'd fu' fain. **1803** R. ANDERSON *Cumberld. Ball.* 57 The barn and the byre.. Will just seem like cronies yen's fidgin to see.

2. *trans.* To twitch, shrug. *rare.*

1786 BURNS *Prayer to Sc. Representatives* vi, Ne'er claw your lug, an' fidge your back, And hum an' haw.

Hence **ˈfidging** *vbl. sb.*

1604 T. M. *Black Bk.* Middleton's Wks. V. 525 The fidging of gallants to Norfolk and up and down countries. *a* **1734** NORTH *Exam.* II. v. §124 (1740) 392 It was by their perpetual fidging about from Place to Place.

fidget (ˈfɪdʒɪt), *sb.* [f. FIDGE *v.*, perh. in imitation of *rickets*.]

1. A condition of vague physical uneasiness, seeking relief in irregular bodily movements. App. first used in ***the fidget(s*** (now always pl.) as if the name of a malady or pathological symptom (sometimes in definite pathological sense: see quot. 1876). Hence *transf.* a condition or mood of impatient uneasiness or restlessness.

1674 N. FAIRFAX *Bulk & Selv.* 134 'Tis a..thing that has got the fidget. **1750** GRAY *Long Story* xxxiv, Jesu Maria! Madam Bridget..(Cried the Square-hoods in woeful fidget). **1753** *World* No. 7. 39 Fits of the fidgets. **1778** MAD. D'ARBLAY *Diary* Aug., I was really in the fidgets from thinking what my reception might be. **1781** COWPER *Conversation* 208 Weavers of long tales Give me the fidgets. **1800** MRS. HERVEY *Mourtray Fam.* I. 45 Their arrival, owing to the fidget and hurry of Mrs. Mourtray, was somewhat premature. **1809** B. H. MALKIN tr. *Le Sage's Gil Blas* (1866) VII. vii. 245 Her tongue was cruelly on the fidget to be let loose. **1837** HOWITT *Rur. Life* VI. viii. (1862) 484 The landlady and her daughter are on the fidgets. **1839** E. FITZGERALD *Lett.* I. 51, I have got the fidgets in my right arm. **1864** J. H. NEWMAN *Apol.* (1865) 41 Palmer..still.. felt..some fidget and nervousness. **1876** BARTHOLOW *Mat. Med.* (1879) 403 Wakefulness from..unrest of the peripheral nerves (fidgets), and similar causes, will generally be relieved by the bromides. **1893** DUNGLISON *Dict. Med.* (ed. 21), *Fidgets.*

2. [From the vb.] One who fidgets or worries unnecessarily, or who causes the fidgets in others.

1816 M. E. BICKNELL *Let.* 19 Mar. in *Constable's Corr.* (1964) II. 182 You know what a sad *fidget* I am. **1837** F. COOPER *Recoll. Europe* I. 208 He..betrayed himself immediately to be a fidget. **1881** LADY HERBERT *Edith* 159 Lord St. Aubyn is a terrible fidget. **1882** *Three in Norway* ii. 10 Dispense with that creaking-booted fidget, the waiter.

3. [From the vb.] The action or habit of fidgeting, bustling about or worrying; also the rustling of a dress, etc.

1860-1 FLO. NIGHTINGALE *Nursing* 36 The fidget of silk and of crinoline. **1890** *Spectator* 15 Nov., The policy of legislative fidget carried to the most mischievous excess.

fidget (ˈfɪdʒɪt), *v.* Pples. **fidgeted, -eting** (often incorrectly with double *t*). [f. prec. sb.]

1. *intr.* To make movements indicative of impatience, restlessness, or uneasiness; to move restlessly to and fro. Also, ***to fidget about.***

1754 [see FIDGETING *ppl. a.*]. **1809** W. IRVING *Knickerb.* IV. iv. (1849) 217 The governor snapping his fingers and fidgeting with delight. **1827** LYTTON *Pelham* iii. 18 Davison fidgeted about in his chair. **1849** DICKENS *Barn. Rudge* i, Joe ..had been fidgeting in his chair with divers uneasy gestures. **1858** R. S. SURTEES *Ask Mamma* xxxiii. 138 The Major..has been fidgetting about pairing parties off. **1867** J. HATTON *Tallants of B.* xviii, The chairman fidgetted uneasily in his seat.

b. To be uneasy; to worry.

1884 *Manch. Exam.* 25 Nov. 5/1 They can but fidget and fume. **1884** MRS. EWING *Mary's Meadow* (1886) 58 Mother fidgetted because I looked ill.

2. *trans.* To cause (a person) to fidget; to make uncomfortable, trouble or worry; *refl.* to take trouble. ***to fidget into***: to force into a specified condition by fidgeting; hyperbolically, ***to fidget to death.***

1785 [see FIDGETING *ppl. a.*]. **1815** JANE AUSTEN *Emma* II. ix. 197 She says I fidget her to death. **1836** T. HOOK *G. Gurney* I. 85 The fever into which I had fidgetted myself. **1845** FORD *Handbk. Spain* I. 55 Spaniards never fidget themselves to get quickly to places where nobody is expecting them. **1847** ALB. SMITH *Chr. Tadpole* xxv. (1879) 229 The heat fidgetted them all by day.

3. To move *about* restlessly and uneasily. *rare.*

1819 *Metropolis* I. 86 Fan-flirting, and fidgetting the body about.

Hence **ˈfidgeted** *ppl. a.*, **ˈfidgeting** *vbl. sb.*

1765 C. SMART *Fable* iv. in *Poems* (1791) II. 11 Susan..all the rites of rage perform'd, As scolding..fidgetting, and fretting. **1775** MAD. D'ARBLAY *Early Diary* (1889) II. 17 'How can you say so, Sir?' cried Bell..colouring, and much fidgetted. **1845** FORD *Handbk. Spain* I. 66 Nothing is gained by fidgeting and over-doing.

†**fidgeˈtation.** *Obs.*[−1] [f. FIDGET *v.* + -ATION.] The action of fidgeting; a fidgety movement.

1742 LADY M. W. MONTAGUE *Lett.* II. 248 Your Grace asks me if I have left off footing, and tumbling down stairs; as to the first, my fidgetations are much spoiled.

fidgetiness (ˈfɪdʒɪtɪnɪs). [f. FIDGETY + -NESS.] The state or quality of being fidgety; nervous restlessness, uneasiness.

1772 FRANKLIN *Wks.* (1887) IV. 529 This fidgetiness (to use a vulgar expression for want of a better) is occasioned wholly by an uneasiness in the skin. **1860-1** FLO. NIGHTINGALE *Nursing* 55 A nurse will be careful to fidgetiness about airing the clean sheets. **1861** HUGHES *Tom Brown at Oxf.* xxviii. (1889) 269 That's some of uncle's fidgetiness.

fidgeting (ˈfɪdʒɪtɪŋ), *ppl. a.* [f. FIDGET *v.* + -ING[2].] In senses of the vb.

1672 WYCHERLY *Love in a Wood* II. i, He is a fidgetting, censorious, gossiping, quibbling wretch. **1754** RICHARDSON *Grandison* (1781) VI. li. 319 My fidgetting Lord thrust in.. his sharp face. **1785** MAD. D'ARBLAY *Diary* 25 Nov., This was rather fidgetting intelligence. **1839-40** W. IRVING *Wolfert's R.* (1855) 5 He had warred for quiet through the fidgeting reign of William. **1865** *Pall Mall G.* 11 Apr. 1 Some fidgeting little matter of exchange.

Hence **ˈfidgetingly** *adv.*, in a fidgeting manner.

1882 'BASIL' *Love the Debt* II. xxviii. 270 A small parcel which Mabel had seen her take up..furtively and fidgetingly half a dozen times. **1892** *Temple Bar Mag.* Dec. 570 Pamela is..fidgettingly handling the little objects.

fidgety (ˈfɪdʒɪtɪ), *a.* [f. FIDGET + -Y[1].]

1. Inclined or disposed to fidget; uneasy, restless.

1730-6 in BAILEY (folio). **1788** MAD. D'ARBLAY *Diary* IV. IV. 187 He declared if I was fidgety he should have no comfort. **1827** SCOTT *Jrnl.* 10 Aug., This is a morning of fidgety, nervous confusion. **1880** MISS BRADDON *Just as I am* xviii, He held the somewhat fidgety horse.

2. Producing fidgetiness, disquieting. *rare*[−1].

1885 *Truth* 11 June 927/1 Dining-rooms..fidgety with glitter.

Hence **ˈfidgetily** *adv.*, in a fidgety manner.

1880 MISS BROUGHTON *Sec. Th.* II. iii, Gillian fidgetily watches her.

fidging (ˈfɪdʒɪŋ), *ppl. a. Sc.* [f. FIDGE *v.* + -ING[2].] That 'fidges', restless, fidgety.

1637 ABP. WILLIAMS *Holy Table* 60 As..manly as he is fidging. **1721** KELLY *Sc. Prov.* 8 A fidging Mare should be well girded. **1821** *Blackw. Mag.* VIII. 619 The fidging Prentices, their elbows claw. **1862** HISLOP in *Scot. Prov.* 5.

b. In phr. ***fidging fain***, eager to restlessness or discomfort. Const. *to* with *inf.*

?*a* **1700** *Maggie Lauder* in *Songs of Scot.* (1851) II. 111 Maggie..I'm fidgin' fain to see thee. **1785** BURNS *Ep. to J. Lapraik* v. **1826** J. WILSON *Noct. Ambr.* Wks. I. 322 The people in the pit, a fidgin fain to see her. **1892** in *Northumb. Gloss.*

‖**ˈfidibus.** [Ger.; of uncertain etymology; for conjectures see Grimm.] A paper match for lighting pipes. Also *attrib.*

1829 LONGF. in *Life* (1891) I. 172, I was just lighting my pipe..the 'fidibus' fell from my hand. **1889** *Pall Mall G.* 24 June 6/1 Sleeping in mosquito curtains and with 'fidibus' pastilles.

†**fiˈdicinal,** *a. Obs.*[−1] [f. L. *fidicin-, fidicen* lute-player + -AL[1].] Of or pertaining to a player on stringed instruments.

1776 SIR J. HAWKINS *Hist. Music* I. III. i. 255 Pulsatile instruments..in contradistinction to those of the fidicinal or stringed kind.

ˌfidimˈplicitary, *a. nonce-wd.* [f. Eccl. L. *fid-es implicita* implicit faith + -ARY.] That puts 'implicit faith' in another's dictum.

1652 URQUHART *Jewel* Wks. (1834) 198 Fidimplicitary gown-men..satisfied with their predecessors' contrivances. **1817** *Blackw. Mag.* I. 470 Fidimplicitary coxcombs.

†**ˈfidious,** *a. Obs.*[−1] Short for PERFIDIOUS.

1640 SHIRLEY *Arcadia* II. i, Oh! fidious rascal! I thought there was some roguery.

†**ˈfidiped,** *a. Obs.*[−1] [badly f. L. *fid-* stem of *findĕre* to split + *ped-, pes.*] = FISSIPED.

1661 LOVELL *Hist. Anim. & Min.* Introd. 4 Sea gull, white, cinerous, piscatorie, black, sterna, fidiped.

FIDO, Fido (ˈfaɪdəʊ). [f. the initials of the words *Fog Investigation Dispersal Operation.*] A system of dispersing fog over aerodromes by heat from petrol-burners.

1945 *Newsweek* 11 June 53/2 Fido stands for 'Fog Investigation Dispersal Operation'. It was suggested in 1942 by Prime Minister Churchill to Geoffrey Lloyd. **1946** D. BANKS *Flame over Britain* vii. 157 We saw the glow of Fido in the night sky. Making a circuit at 1,500 feet above the flames the thick rime on his wind-screen cleared and the runway then became clearly visible through the fog. **1959** *Times* 21 Feb. 7/7 [Passengers] would probably find their first FIDO-aided landing an eerie experience. **1971** *Daily Tel.* 6 Jan. 2/3 With the FIDO (Fog Intensive Dispersal Operation) system used during the war, petrol is burned in troughs on either side of the runway to raise air temperature.

†**fiˈduce.** *Obs.* [ad. L. *fidūcia.*] Confidence.

1582 N. T. (Rhem.) *1 Tim.* vi. 20 *note*, Their [the Protestants'] sole faith, their fiduce, their apprehension of Christs iustice. **1615** BYFIELD *Exp. Coloss.* i. 4 (1869) 35/1 Faith..stands in three things:—desires; fiduce, or confidence; persuasion.

fiducial (faɪˈdjuːʃ(ɪ)əl, fɪˈdjuːʃəl), *a.* [ad. L. *fīdūciāl-is*, f. *fīdūcia* trust, confidence: see -AL[1].]

1. *Theol.* Of or pertaining to, or of the nature of, trust or reliance.

1624 F. WHITE *Repl. Fisher* 164 Such a..Faith, as is both an intellectuall and fiduciall assent to diuine Promises. **1656** H. MORE *Enthus. Tri.* 43 Every thing has..a fiduciall Knowledge of God in it. *a* **1703** BURKITT *On N.T.* John xv. 5 Abide in me..by a real and fiducial adherence. *a* **1711** KEN *Divine Love* Wks. (1838) 312 Teach us to live..with a fiducial dependence on thy fatherly goodness. **1870** SPURGEON *Treas. Dav.* Ps. xxxi. 3 II. 63 The words..appear to..fasten upon the Lord with a fiducial grip.

2. *humorous nonce-use.* Willing to trust.

1847 L. HUNT *Men, Women, & B.* I. ix. 169 Taverns..not hospitable—not fiducial—don't trust.

†**3.** Trusted, trusty. *Obs.*

1647 H. MORE *Song of Soul* II. I. IV. iii, Prop fiduciall Of all those lives and beings cleeped Naturall. **1730–6** in BAILEY (folio).

4. In *Surveying*, *Astronomy*, etc. Of a line, point, etc.: Assumed as a fixed basis of comparison.

1571 DIGGES *Pantom.* (1591) 30 Note the degrees cut by the line fiduciall. **1644** NYE *Gunnery* (1670) 44 The Line Fiduciall, because from this line proceeds the beginning of the degrees in the Circle. **1828** HUTTON *Course Math.* II. 55 These sights and one edge of the index are in the same plane, and that is called the fiducial edge of the index. **1873** MAXWELL in *Life* xiv. (1882) 435 We need some fiducial point or standard of reference.

5. = FIDUCIARY.

1832 in WEBSTER quoting Spelman.

Hence **fiˈducially** *adv.*, in a fiducial manner.

1647 T. HILL *Best & Worst of Paul* (1648) 22 God hath given thee a sweet perswasion of soul to rest fiducially. **1654** WARREN *Unbelievers* 204 Fiducially trusting upon Christ. *a* **1716** SOUTH *Serm.* Wks. 1737 VI. 472 It is the Spirit of God alone, that..enables the soul fiducially to..rest upon that object. **1727** BAILEY vol. II, *Fiducially*, honestly, trustily. **1847** in CRAIG.

†**fiduciˈality.** *Obs.*$^{-0}$ [f. prec. + -ITY.]

a. Trustiness. **b.** A firm reliance; religious confidence.

1727–36 in BAILEY. **1775** in ASH.

fiduciary (faɪˈdjuːʃ(ɪ)ərɪ), *a.* and *sb.* [ad. L. *fīdūciāri-us*, f. *fīdūcia*: see FIDUCIAL and -ARY. Cf. F. *fiduciaire.*

In Rom. Law *fiducia* denoted the transfer of a right to a person subject to the obligation to transfer it again at some future time or on some condition being fulfilled.]

A. *adj.*

1. a. Of a person: In trust of a person or thing; holding something in trust. *Obs.* exc. in *Rom. Law.*

1647 *Bury Wills* (Camden) 197, I doe acknowledge my selfe to be but a fiduciarie possessor of them vnder God. **1652** NEEDHAM tr. *Selden's Mare Cl.* 254 Guthrunus King of the Danes, was..setled in Northumberland as a Fiduciarie Client..to Alfred. **1788** LD. BULKELEY in Dk. Buckhm. *Crt. & Cabinets Geo. III* (1853) I. 445 The Prince..in his quality of Fiduciary Regent. **1880** MUIRHEAD *Ulpian* xi. §5 He who has manumitted a free person..becomes that person's tutor ..and is called a fiduciary tutor.

b. Of or pertaining to a trustee; pertaining to or of the nature of a trusteeship.

fiduciary coemption (Rom. Law): the formal purchase of a married woman, the purchaser being bound by a 'fiducia' to remancipate her to some one of her choice.

1795 WYTHE *Decis. Virginia* 17 The Receivers possession is fiduciary. **1846** MCCULLOCH *Acc. Brit. Empire* (1854) II. 159 The fiduciary system of the Roman Law, adopted by the clerical chancellors. **1863** H. COX *Instit.* II. viii. 495 *note*, It is not every fiduciary possession of property which constitutes a trust. **1875** POSTE *Gaius* I. §166 Fiduciary guardianship arises when a free person..is manumitted by the alienee. **1879** CASTLE *Law of Rating* 71 The persons in actual valuable occupation of property are rateable, though they occupy in a merely fiduciary character. **1880** MUIRHEAD *Gaius* I. §115 *a*, Fiduciary coemption was also had recourse to of old to enable a woman to make a will.

2. a. Of a thing: In trust of a person; held or given in trust.

a **1641** SPELMAN *Admiral-Jurisd.* (1723) 224 The High Admiral himself cannot grant it for longer than his own time, being but a Trust and fiduciary Power. **1660** G. FLEMING *Stemma Sacrum* 41 Scotland was once acknowledged a fiduciary Kingdom to the Crown of England. **1768** BLACKSTONE *Comm.* III. 51 Uses of land.. were considered as fiduciary deposits and binding in conscience by the clergy. **1827** HALLAM *Const. Hist.* (1876) I. vi. 344 Such fiduciary estates were well known to the Roman jurists. **1884** W. S. LILLY in *Contemp. Rev.* Feb. 264 Christianity..regarded authority as limited and fiduciary.

b. Of or pertaining to something held in trust.

1767 BLACKSTONE *Comm.* II. 333 The incidents, that formerly attended it [the land] in its fiduciary state.

†**3.** Of the nature of, proceeding from, or implying trust or reliance. *Obs.*

1640 GAUDEN *Love of Truth* (1641) 32 Fiduciary assurance and the like. **1640** HOWELL *Dodona's Gr.* 19 Elaiana which can relye no where upon meere love and fiduciary obedience. **1648** *Eikon Bas.* 80 That fiduciary and fervent application of their spirits wherein consists the very life and soul of Prayer. **1655** GURNALL *Chr. in Arm.* II. 242 The Christian, when he..hath greatest victory over it [sin], even then must he renounce all fiduciary glorying in this. *a* **1680** CHARNOCK *Attrib. God* (1834) II. 245 It was this..edged the fiduciary importunity of the souls under the altar.

4. Of a paper currency: Depending for its value on the confidence of the public or on securities.

1878 H. H. GIBBS *Corres. in B. Price's Pol. Econ.* 562 It is wholly impossible that a convertible Circulation of fiduciary (or security) notes should ever fall to that point [15 millions]. **1880** *Manch. Guard.* 25 Oct., The system of a fiduciary paper money began in Russia during the Crimean war. **1891** *Pall Mall G.* 3 Dec. 7/1 The fiduciary issue would then stand at 25½ millions. **1892** *Daily News* 13 Sept. 2/3 The fiduciary currency of the United States. **1930** M. CLARK *Home Trade* v. xxx. 240 The £260,000,000 of note issue is known as the fiduciary issue. **1965** SELDON & PENNANCE *Everyman's Dict. Econ.* 172 In the early 1960's the fiduciary issue stood at over £2,200 million.

5. Of or pertaining to a person that is trusted; confidential. *rare.*

1882 F. ANSTEY *Vice Versâ* xii. 216 Every right-minded boy ought to feel himself in such a fiduciary position towards his master.

B. *sb.*

1. One who holds anything in trust; a trustee.

1631 T. POWELL *Tom All Trades* 11 You know they are faithfull fiduciaries in the election. **1821** SCOTT *Kenilw.* xii, Persuade the good Sir Hugh to make me his..fiduciary in this matter.

†**2.** One who identifies justifying faith with assurance of one's own salvation. *Obs.*

1654 HAMMOND *Fundam.* xiii. 120 The second obstructive ..is that of the Fiduciarie..having resolved Faith to be the only instrument of his justification. **1684** T. HOCKIN *God's Decr.* 359 Some bold Fiduciaries..confidently pretend that their names are certainly written in the Book of Life.

†**3.** Something that secures confidence; credentials. *Obs.*

1593 ABP. BANCROFT *Daung. Posit.* III. xiii. 106 Let euerie of them deliuer the instructions from their Churches.. together with the Fiduciary or Letters of credence.

Hence **fiˈduciarily** *adv.* †(*a*) trustfully, confidingly (*obs.*); (*b*) under the conditions of a trust.

1653 W. SCLATER *Fun. Sermon* (1654) 31 He really and fiduciarily intended it. **1863** H. COX *Instit.* II. viii. 497 Equity..has annexed to the fiduciary possession of property a multitude of rules in favour of the persons fiduciarily interested.

†**fiˈduciate**, *v.* *Obs. rare*$^{-0}$. [ad. L. *fīdūciāt-* ppl. stem of *fīdūciāre*, f. *fīdūcia* trust.] *trans.*

1656–81 BLOUNT *Glossogr.*, *Fiduciate*, to commit to trust, or make condition of trust.

‖**fidus Achates** (ˈfaɪdəs æˈkeɪtiːz). [L., = faithful Achates (Virgil *Aen.* VI. 158, etc.).] A devoted follower, henchman.

1603 C. HEYDON *Def. Judic. Astrol.* xx. 411 Yet I haue tied my selfe to be *fidus Achates* to him. **1771** SMOLLETT *Humph. Cl.* I. 125 Dr. Lewis, who is the *fidus Achates* of my uncle. **1839** DICKENS *Let.* 13 May (1965) I. 550 Mr. Macrone and his fidus Achates Mr. Hansard. **1934** *Times Lit. Suppl.* 24 May 377/4 In Portsmouth they arrest the *fidus Achates*.

fie (faɪ), *int.* Forms: 3 fi, 3–8 fy, (4 fyȝ), 5–9 fye, 6–7 phy, 5– fie. [ME. *fi*, *fy*, app. a. OF. *fi*, *fy* (mod.F. *fi*):—L. *fi*, an imitation of the sound instinctively made on perceiving a disagreeable smell. Cf. ON. *fý* (Da. *fy*, also *fy skam dig*, fie shame to you! Sw. *fy*), of similar origin.

The ON. may possibly be a joint source of the Eng. word, but the early instances either occur in translations from Fr. or imitate the Fr. construction *fi de*.]

1. An exclamation expressing, in early use, disgust or indignant reproach. No longer current in dignified language; said to children to excite shame for some unbecoming action, and hence often used to express the humorous pretence of feeling 'shocked'. Sometimes more fully *fie, for shame!* Const. †*of* (= on), *on, upon.*

1297 R. GLOUC. (1724) 390 'Fy a debles', quaþ þe kyng. *c* **1330** *King of Tars* 612 Fy on ow everichon! *c* **1380** *Sir Ferumb.* 1578 'Fy', quaþ Moradas, 'wat ert þow; þat telest of me so lyte?' *c* **1386** CHAUCER *Man of Law's Prol.* 80 Of all swiche cursed stories I say fy. —— *Nun's Pr. T.* 71 Ye ben a very sleper, fy for shame. *c* **1430** *Pilgr. Lyf Manhode* III. xlvi, Chastitee..whan she seeth me seith fy. *c* **1440** *York Myst.* xxxii. 103 Fye on hym, dastard! **1509** HAWES *Past. Pleas.* XI. xxxv, Fy upon slouth, the nourysher of vyce. *a* **1553** UDALL *Royster D.* III. iv. (Arb.) 52 What weepe? Fye for shame! And blubber? **1583** BABINGTON *Commandm.* ix. (1637) 91 Fie of that affection, that damneth our soules! **1592** SHAKS. *Ven. & Ad.* 611 Fie, fie, he saies, you crush me, let me go. **1606** *Sir. G. Goosecappe* III. ii. in Bullen *O. Pl.* III. 53 Fie for shame; I never heard of such an antedame. **1677** GALE *Crt. Gentiles* IV. 113 Phy! how depraved is mans nature altogether! **1749** FIELDING *Tom Jones* VIII. ix, Fy upon it, Mr. Partridge..are you afraid of facing a little cold? **1764** FOOTE *Mayor of G.* II. i, Fye Mr. Bruin, how can you be such a bear to your wife. **1832** LYTTON *Eugene A.* I. ii, Fie, neighbour, fie, what's the good of profaneness. **1861** T. A. TROLLOPE *La Beata* II. xiv. 111 'Fie!' said Beppina in a state of great delight.

2. quasi-*sb.* †**a.** qualified by an adj.: as *double, much fie* (*obs.*). **b.** as *obj.* in *to cry* (†*bid*, †*spit*) *fie upon.*

c **1550** R. WEAVER *Lusty Juventus* in Hazl. *Dodsley* II. 87 Now much fie upon you! how bawdy you are! *c* **1555** HARPSFIELD *Divorce Hen. VIII* (1878) 173 Fie and double fie upon the impudency of this..shameless divine. **1599** BRETON *Author's Dreame*, Follie, he badde Fie upon Wisdome. **1662** J. SPARROW tr. *Behme's Rem. Wks.*, *Def. agst. Rickter* 13 The Libeller spits Fy, and filth, against the Repentance. **1848** THACKERAY *Van. Fair* xvii, 'My relations won't cry fie upon me', Becky said.

3. as *sb.*

1576 GASCOIGNE *Philomene* in Wks. 1870 II. 245 These phyes, and many moe, Pore Philomene may meane. *a* **1643** W. CARTWRIGHT *Ordinary* IV. v. in Hazl. *Dodsl.* XII. 298 What angry pishes, and what fies..The list'ning taper heard there sworn. **1820** SCOTT *Monast.* I. ii. 105 The child reddened..while the mother, with many a fye and nay pshaw [etc.].

†**fie**, *v.*[1] *Obs.* In 4 fye, 5 phy. [ad. Fr. *fier*, Pr. and Sp. *fiar*, It. *fidare*:—popular L. **fīdāre*, f. L. *fīdus* faithful.] *trans.* To trust; also *refl.* = Fr. *se fier.* Const. *in.*

1340 *Ayenb.* 136 He him fyeth more in oþres uirtue þanne ine his. *c* **1485** *Digby Myst.* (1882) III. 1068, I his lover and cavse wyll phy.

†**fie**, *v.*[2] *Obs.* [f. FIE *int.*] *intr.* To say Fie!

c **1394** *P. Pl. Crede* 616 [He] fyeþ on her falshedes þat þei bifore deden.

fieble, obs. form of FEEBLE.

fiedlerite (ˈfiːdləraɪt). *Min.* [ad. G. *fiedlerit* (G. vom Rath 1887, in *Sitzungsber. d. niederrhein. Ges. f. Natur- und Heilkunde zu Bonn* 157), f. the name of K. G. *Fiedler* (1791–1853), German traveller: see -ITE[1].] A hydroxychloride of lead found at Lávrion, Greece, and produced by the action of sea-water on lead-slags.

1892 DANA *Syst. Min.* (ed. 6) iv. 172 *Fiedlerite*...Luster adamantine. Colorless. Transparent... Named after the Saxon Commissioner of Mines, Fiedler, director of the Grecian exploration. **1899** *Jrnl. Chem. Soc.* LXXVI. II. 433 The new mineral, paralaurionite, may at a cursory glance be easily mistaken for laurionite or fiedlerite. **1934** *Mineral. Mag.* XXIII. 583 The crystals of fiedlerite are poor and the angles for any given form show considerable variation.

fief (fiːf), *sb.* Forms: 7 feif, 7–9 feof(f, 7– fief. [First in 17th c.; a. F. *fief*: see FEE *sb.*[2]]

1. = FEE *sb.*[2] 1. ***male fief, fief masculine***: one that could be held by males only.

1611 COTGR., *Fief*, A Fief; a (Knights) fee; a Mannor, or inheritance held by homage. *a* **1613** OVERBURY *Observ. France* Wks. (1856) 238 They pawned all their Feifs to the church. **1671** F. PHILLIPS *Reg. Necess.* 419 An Estate in Tayl or Fief Masculine. **1756** NUGENT *Gr. Tour* II. 27 'Tis he only that can give away the great fiefs of the empire. **1820** SCOTT *Monast.* iii, A male fief. **1838** ARNOLD *Hist. Rome* (1846) I. xiv. 267 Proprietors who received their land as an hereditary fief. **1868** MILMAN *St. Paul's* 43 The cession of the kingdom as a fief of the Holy See.

transf. and *fig.*

1686 DRYDEN *Ode to Mrs. Killigrew* 98 To the next Realm she stretcht her Sway..And the whole Fief, in right of Poetry, she claim'd. **18..** W. SAWYER *New Year Numbers* xii, Not of thy strength nor cunning didst thou come, Into the fief and heritage of life. **1873** SYMONDS *Grk. Poets* i. 27 The cities of Greece became the fiefs of foreign despots.

b. *in fief* = *in fee*: see FEE *sb.*[2] 1 b.

1728 MORGAN *Algiers* II. v. 313 The knights hold the said Islands in Feof from the king of Sicily. **1821** BYRON *Mar. Fal.* v. i, In fief perpetual to myself and heirs. **1871** B. TAYLOR *Faust* (1875) II. Pref. 10 Faust receives the sea-shore in feoff for ever.

2. *Comb.*, as ***fief-holder***, one who holds a fief from a superior.

1864 KIRK *Chas. Bold* II. IV. iii. 419 The fief holders of France..were still more assiduous in the cultivation of martial exercises. **1882–3** SCHAFF *Encycl. Relig. Knowl.* I. 484 The power of the feudal lords or fief-holders increased.

†**fief**, *v.* *Obs.* [f. prec. sb. Cf. FEOFF *v.*] *trans.* To grant as a fief. Also *to fief out.*

1792 A. YOUNG *Trav. France* 327 The seigneurs, who possess the same rights, sell and fief them at a still cheaper rate. *Ibid.* 394 Seigneurs, who will not sell, but only fief out these wastes.

ˈfiefdom. [f. as prec. + -DOM.] = FIEF *sb.* 1.

1814 MRS. J. WEST *Alicia de Lacy* I. 130 To forfeit one of our fiefdoms, is not enough.

†**ˈfieffal**, *a.* *Obs. rare.* [f. as prec. + -AL[1].] Of or pertaining to a fief.

1738 *Hist. Crt. Excheq.* i. 3 The Fieffal is the feudal Jurisdiction, by the Reason of the Fieffs, that is, where the feudal Lord had power to do Right to his Tenants upon any Complaints.

fie-fie (faɪfaɪ), *a.* Also fi-fi. [f. FIE by doubling.] Jocularly used for: Improper, of improper character.

1812 G. COLMAN *Br. Grins, Two Parsons* vii, What would [if we were sinless] become of all the fie-fie ladies? **1837** T. HOOK *Jack Brag* xiv, There is such a long fie-fie story about that. **1860** TROLLOPE *Framley P.* vi, One or two fie-fie little anecdotes about a married lady. **1873** *St. Paul's Mag.* Jan. 9 She was rather fifi.

Hence **fie-fie** *sb.*, a woman of tarnished reputation. **fie-fie** *v.* (*a*) *intr.* To say Fie! (*b*) *trans.* To say Fie! to.

1820 LADY GRANVILLE *Let.* 25 Aug. (1894) I. 164 A mixture of..Dowager Lansdowne, fye-fyes, and venerable peers. **1836** *Libr. Fiction* I. 371 In 'fie, fieing' the excesses of divers gentlemen. **1892** *Punch* 13 Aug. 72/2 Purists may fie-fie, or sneer.

†**fiel**, *a.* *Obs.* [perh. a survival of ME. FELE *a.*[2]] Comfortable.

1792 BURNS *Bessy & Spinnin Wheel* 4 Frae tap to tae that cleeds me bien And haps me fiel and warm at e'en! **1808** A. SCOTT *Poems* (ed. 2) 193 Her blankets air'd a' feil an' dry.

field (fiːld), *sb.* Forms: 1–2 feld, 3–6 feild(e, feld(e, 3 fæld, *south.* vælde, vald(e, (5 falde, feald), 3–4 *south.* veld(e, 3–5 felt(e, fild(e, (5 fyld(e), 4–6 feeld(e, 6–7 fielde, 6– field. [Com.

WGer.; OE. *feld* str. masc. corresponds to OFris. and OS. *feld* masc. (MDu. *velt*, Du. *veld* neut.), OHG. *feld* (MHG. *velt*, mod.Ger. *feld*) neut.:—OTeut. **felþu-z* masc., **felþu* neut. Not found outside WGer., the Sw. *fält*, Da. *felt* being from Ger.; but the Finnish *pelto* field is believed to have been adopted from prehistoric Teut. or pre-Teut.

Prob. related by ablaut and Verner's law to OE. *folde* earth (see FOLD *sb.*³); it is uncertain whether the Teut. **felþu-*, **foldôn-* are formed with *t* suffix from a pre-Teut. root *pel-*, represented in OSl. *polʲe* plain, field, or belong to the Aryan root *pelth* or *pelt*, whence Skr. *pṛthivī* earth, Gr. πλατύς broad.]

I. Ground; a piece of ground.

†**1. a.** Open land as opposed to woodland; a stretch of open land; a plain. *Obs.*

c **1050** *Byrhtferth's Handboc* in *Anglia* VIII. 299 On þære stowe se æðela feld us ȝearcode swete huniȝ. *a* **1123** *O.E. Chron.* an. 1112 Swiðe wistfull on wudan and on feldan. *c* **1200** ORMIN 14568 Wude, & feld, & dale, & dun. **1297** R. GLOUC. (1724) 565 To wodes & to feldes [hii] hulde hom day & nizt. *a* **1300** *Cursor M.* 3608 (Cott.) Bath in feild and in forest. *c* **1386** CHAUCER *Knt.'s T.* 664 That feld hath eyen, and the woode hath eeres. ?*a* **1400** *Arthur* 472 Þe feltes fulle of men yscleyn. **1538** STARKEY *England* I. ii. 52 Wyld Feldys and wodys. **1593** MARLOWE in *Pass. Pilgr.* xix, Hilles and vallies, dales and fields. **1697** DRYDEN *Virg. Georg.* IV. 759 They..strew'd his mangled Limbs about the Field.

b. with reference to that which grows upon the surface. *Obs.*

a **1000** *Boeth. Metr.* vi, Weaxað hraðe feldes blostman. *c* **1200** ORMIN 9225 Itt wass huniȝ off þe feld. *a* **1300** *E.E. Psalter* cii[i]. 15 Als blome of felde sal he [man] welyen awa. *a* **1300** *Cursor M.* 6080 (Cott.) Letus wild, þe quilk þat groues on þe feild. **1382** WYCLIF *Luke* xii. 28 The hey which to day is in the feeld. *c* **1449** PECOCK *Repr.* I. vi. 28 The feld is the fundament of the flouris. **1611** BIBLE *Gen.* ii. 5 Euery plant of the field.

†**2. a.** The country as opposed to a town or village. *Obs.* exc. *arch.* or *dial.*

c **1400** *Rom. Rose* 6237 Fulle many a seynt in feeld & toune. *c* **1400** *Gamelyn* 672 He moste nedes walke in felde þat may not walke in towne. **1526** TINDALE *Mark* xv. 21 They compelled..Simon of Cerene (which cam out of the felde)..to bear hys crosse. **1590** SHAKS. *Mids. N.* II. i. 238 In the Towne, and Field You doe me mischiefe. **1862** BORROW *Wild Wales* III. 160, I don't think your honour is a Durham man either of town or field.

b. That part of the open country which is hunted over (perh. originally *transf.* from sense 8). Cf. *hunting field*.

1732 LAW *Serious C.* xii. (ed. 2) 190 The next attempt after happiness carry'd him into the field..nothing was so happy as hunting. **1801** STRUTT *Sports & Past.* I. i. 6 King John was particularly attached to the sports of the field. **1864** *Field* 2 July 9/3 His [the huntsman's] character in the field..has given the highest satisfaction.

†**3.** The territory belonging to a city. Cf. L. *ager*.

a **1533** LD. BERNERS *Gold. Bk. M. Aurel.* (1539) 140b, In the felde of Elinos, vnder a marble, is the pouders of Sysifo Seteno. **1572** J. JONES *Bathes of Bath* II. 11b, The hot wellse, in the fielde of Padua.

4. a. Land or a piece of land appropriated to pasture or tillage, usually parted off by hedges, fences, boundary stones, etc. Often with defining word prefixed, as ***clover-, corn-, hay-, turnip-, wheat-field***.

c **1025** *Interl. v. Rule St. Benet* (1888) 73 Geswinc felda gif hi nabbað munecas. *c* **1220** *Bestiary* 401 [Þe fox] goð o felde to a furg. **1297** R. GLOUC. (Rolls) 7798 Feldes were vol of corne echon. **1382** WYCLIF *Ruth* ii. 2 Y shall goo in to the feeld and gedre eeris. *c* **1449** PECOCK *Repr.* 275 Feeldis..in which..thei hem silf tilien. **1578** LYTE *Dodoens* IV. lvi. 516 That with the pale..flowers growteth in drie medowes, and in the feeldes also. **1657** AUSTEN *Fruit Trees* I. 56 The Flanders Cherries bear well in Orchards and Feilds. **1765** A. DICKSON *Treat. Agric.* (ed. 2) 94 There is scarcely a field, in which we will not observe weeds of the two first kinds. **1840** DICKENS *Barn. Rudge* iv, Fields..through which the New River took its winding course.

b. pl. ***the fields***, used in collective sense. Formerly sometimes = 2 (cf. F. *les champs*) or 2b.

a **1533** LD. BERNERS *Huon* lxxxvii. 276 He was in the feldes a hawkynge. **1561** NORTON & SACKV. *Gorboduc* V. ii, Children..play in the streetes and fieldes. **1611** BEAUM. & FL. *King & No King* II. ii, How fine the fields be, what sweet living 'tis in the Country! **1856** RUSKIN *Mod. Paint.* III. IV. xiv. §51 The fields!..All spring and summer is in them.

c. ***common, open field***: see those words.

d. A piece of ground put to a particular use, as ***bleach, camping, print-field***: see BLEACH, etc.

e. = AIRFIELD.

1912 *Sci. Amer.* 24 Aug. 156/1 The field was so narrow that the aviators were compelled to start always toward the north regardless of the direction of the wind. **1930** *Techn. News Bull., Bureau of Standards* (U.S.) June 61/1 The angle ..of the high-frequency landing beam has been adjusted so that an airplane may be guided along the proper gliding path to the field. **1958** 'N. SHUTE' *Rainbow & Rose* i. 8 It's not a licensed field.

5. An extent or tract of ground covered with or containing some special natural formation or production. Chiefly with defining word, as ***coal, diamond, gold, oil fields***: see those words.

1859 CORNWALLIS *New World* I. 55 Bowls filled with the precious metal, and..labelled with the name of the field from which it was taken. **1875** WOOD & LAPHAM *Waiting for Mail* 39 You've tried the best Victorian fields.

6. a. The ground on which a battle is fought; a battle-field. More explicitly ***field of battle, conflict, †fight; field of honour***.

a **1300** *Cursor M.* 6432 (Cott.) Wit israel was left þe feild. *a* **1400–50** *Alexander* 450 Þan foundis Philip to þe fyȝt & þe fild entres. *c* **1460** FORTESCUE *Abs. & Lim. Mon.* ix, The Erlis of Lecestir and Glocestre..toke hym and his sonne prisoners in the ffelde. **1592** R. D. *Hypnerotomachia* 22 Instruments of war..for the field. **1604** SHAKS. *Oth.* I. iii. 85 They haue vs'd Their deerest action, in the Tented Field. **1697** DRYDEN *Virg. Georg.* II. 378 As Legions in the Field their Front display. **1718** *Lond. Gaz.* No. 4739/3 The Quarter-Masters of the Army are gone to mark a Field of Battel. **1774** GOLDSM. *Nat. Hist.* (1776) III. 102 The victor is obliged to fight several of those battles before it remains undisputed master of the field. **1824** W. IRVING *T. Trav.* I. 52 My forefathers have been dragoons, and died on the field of honour. **1848** MACAULAY *Hist. Eng.* I. 658 These three chiefs..fled together from the field of Sedgemoor. **1851** E. S. CREASY *15 Decisive Battles* (1864) 22 The Greeks could not stand before the Persians in a field of battle. **1863** KINGLAKE *Crimea* (1876) I. xi. 182 The English Ambassador remained upon the field of the conflict.

b. *fig.*

1340 *Ayenb.* 131 A ueld of uiyȝt huerinne him behoueþ eure to..wyȝte mid dyeulen. **1526** *Pilgr. Perf.* (W. de W. 1531) 72b, Well exercysed in the feelde of vertues and holy workes. **1615** CROOKE *Body of Man* 56 Before we leaue the field, it shall not be amisse to disparkle all the forces of our aduersaries. **1724** SWIFT *Drapier's Lett.* Wks. 1761 III. 75 He is so far master of the field, that no London printer dare publish any paper written in favour of Ireland. **1775** SHERIDAN *Duenna* I. iv, If I could hamper him with this girl, I should have the field to myself. **1848** H. ROGERS *Ess.* I. vi. 322 To drive the sophists from the field. **1886** B. L. FARJEON *Three Times T.* 1, I bade her good-day, and left Captain Bellwood in possession of the field.

c. Phrases: ***to keep, maintain the field***: to continue the fight, *lit.* and *fig.* Also (chiefly *fig.*) ***to conquer the field***: to gain one's point. ***to hold the field***: to hold its ground; not to be superseded or displaced. ***to leave*** (***another***) ***the field***: to give up the argument or contest. ***to leave the field open***: to abstain from interference.

a **1450** *Knt. de la Tour* (1868) 21 Ye wylle speke riotesly.. therfor y wille leve you the felde. **1673** DRYDEN *Marr. à la Mode* II. i, This tongue..may keep the field against a whole army of lawyers. *c* **1686** *Roxb. Ball.* (1886) VI. 125 He conquer'd the field: Then they both were united. **1724** SWIFT *Drapier's Lett.* iii, His Majesty, pursuant to the law, hath left the field open between Wood and the Kingdom of Ireland. **1855** PRESCOTT *Philip II*, I. ii, Four knights were prepared to maintain the field against all comers. **1870** TENNYSON *Pelleas & Ettarre* 161 All day long Sir Pelleas kept the field With honour. **1887** A. BIRRELL *Obiter Dicta* Ser. II. 66 The last edition will..long hold the field.

7. In wider sense: The country which is to be, or has become, the scene of a campaign; the scene of military operations. ***in the field***: engaged in military operations. ***to keep the field***: to remain in the 'field'; to keep the campaign open. ***to take the field***: to commence military operations; to open the campaign.

a **1612** SIR R. CECIL *Let.* in Naunton *Fragm. Reg.* (Arb.) 61 They will..learn the strength of the Rebels, before they dare take the field. **1651** HOBBES *Leviath.* II. xxix. 174 The forces of the Commonwealth keeping the field no longer. **1676** TEMPLE *Let. to Pr. of Orange* Wks. 1731 II. 410, I did not believe Your Highness would do any thing in those kind of Affairs till Your Return from the Field. **1724** DE FOE *Mem. Cavalier* (1830) 10 All the military part of the court was in the field. **1769** *Junius Lett.* ii. 13 A sincere.. attachment to his King and Country..first impelled him to the field. **1835** I. TAYLOR *Spir. Despot.* iii. 85 Their [the Greek people's] eye was directed..to the senate or the field. **1852** THACKERAY *Esmond* III. i, Esmond..took the field.. under Webb's orders. **1863** H. COX *Instit.* III. viii. 713 An army in the field abroad.

transf. and *fig.* **1614** SAUL *Chesse-play* xi. (*heading*), All the men being in the field. **1831** BREWSTER *Newton* (1855) II. xiv. 3 The greatest mathematicians of the age took the field.

8. a. A battle; now *rare* exc. in such phrases as ***a hard-fought, hard-won field. a single field***: a single combat. Also ***to fight, † give, lose, † make, win (a, the) field***. Hence, †Victory, *esp.* in ***to get, have the field***.

?*a* **1400** *Arthur* 480 The falde was hys & Arthourez. *c* **1435** *Torr. Portugal* 213–5 Of the fynd the maystry to haue, Of hym to wyn the fyld..Of hyme he wane the fyld þat day. **1473** WARKW. *Chron.* 6 The Walschmenne loste the felde. **1484** CAXTON *Fables of Æsop* III. iv, The egle..gat the feld and vaynquysshed..the bestes. **1487** WRIOTHESLEY *Chron.* (1875) I. 2 A feild that they made againste the Kinge. **1502** ARNOLDE *Chron.* (1811) p. xxxiv, A felde..bytwene the Kynge and yᵉ Duke of Yorke. **1535** COVERDALE *1 Macc.* x. 50 A mightie sore felde..continuynge till the Sonne wente downe. **1536** BELLENDEN *Cron. Scot.* (1821) II. 43 Ennimes ..of sic strenth and multitud that he micht not weil geif thaim feild. **1556** *Chron. Gr. Friars* (Camden) 25 The commons..made a felde agaynst the kynge and lost it. **1586** WARNER *Alb. Eng.* IV. xx. (1589) 89 The Danes..got the feeld. **1596** SHAKS. *Merch. V.* II. i. 26 This Symitare..won three fields of Sultan Solyman. **1605** VERSTEGAN *Dec. Intell.* v. (1628) 128 Battailes or Foughten Fields. **1667** MILTON *P.L.* I. 105 What though the field be lost? **1816** BYRON *Ch. Har.* III. xlix, In their..single fields, What deeds of prowess unrecorded died! **1843** PRESCOTT *Mexico* (1850) I. 293 Many a bloody field was to be fought.

transf. **1862** J. PYCROFT *Cricket Tutor* 77 Every old player will..recall many a hard-fought field.

†**b.** Order of battle, disposition of men in the field. Phrases, ***to pitch, set a field***, to choose one's battle-ground, to dispose one's men for fighting; ***to gather a field***, to collect an armed force.

1502 ARNOLDE *Chron.* p. xxxiv, Yᵉ Duke of Yorke set his felde at Brent Heth. *c* **1540** *Order in Battayle* A vij, Let him study to breake hys [foe's] felde. **1548** HALL *Chron. K. Hen. VI*, An. 4. 96b, That my saied lorde of Winchester, intended to gather any feld or assemble people, in troublyng of the kynges lande, and against the kinges peace. *a* **1562** G. CAVENDISH *Wolsey* (1893) 274 Who pitched a feld royall ayenst theme. **1600** HOLLAND *Livy* VI. xv. 226 Either part beholding their captaine, as it were in a pight field. **1678** WANLEY *Wond. Lit. World* v. ii. §32. 470/1 Nicephorus.. was slain in a pitch'd Field against the Bulgarians.

†**c.** ***officer of the field*** = FIELD-OFFICER. ***general of the field***: the general commanding in a battle or campaign. *Obs.*

1590 NASHE *Pasquil's Apol.* I. D iij, Equal in respect of theyr fight in..battailes, as the Generall of the fielde and the common Souldiours are. **1647** CLARENDON *Hist. Reb.* VII. (1703) II. 269 There were..above twenty Officers of the Field..slain upon the place.

9. a. With mixture of sense 4: An enclosed piece of ground in which some outdoor games are played, as ***cricket, football field***: see CRICKET, etc.; also *ellipt.* with sb. to be supplied from the context.

c **1742** J. LOVE *Cricket* (1770) III. 18 To such impetuous Might compell'd to yield The Bail, and mangled Stumps bestrew the Field. *a* **1788** CANNING in 'Bat' *Crick. Man.* (1850) 36 The poet will be equally circumstanced in the field. **1849** *Laws of Cricket* ibid. 57 No substitute in the field shall be allowed to bowl. **1882** *Daily Tel.* 12 June, Neither Spofforth nor Boyle were in the field.

b. *Baseball.* The ground in which the fielders stand, divided into INFIELD and OUTFIELD *sb.*

1875 *Encycl. Brit.* III. 406/2 The theory of the game [Base ball] is that one side takes the field, and the other goes in. **1891** N. CRANE *Baseball* vi. 45 The pitcher is the only player whose position on the field is prescribed by the rules.

10. *collect.* Those who take part in any outdoor contest or sport.

a. *Sporting.* Also, in restricted sense: All the competitors in a race except the favourite. ***to bet, back, lay against the field***: to back one (often one's own) dog, horse, etc. against all other competitors.

1742 RICHARDSON *Pamela* III. xxxiii. 315 An hundred Guineas to one against the Field. **1771** P. PARSONS *Newmarket* II. 149 Camillus against the field, for a hundred guineas. **1872** LEVER *Ld. Kilgobbin* lxx, Bet on the field— never back the favourite. **1885** *Truth* 28 May 853/2 The Great Northern Handicap..brought out a better field than usual. **1888** *Daily News* 29 June, Pillarist was backed against the field.

transf. and *fig.* **1860** GEN. P. THOMPSON *Audi Alt.* III. cxxxiii. 101 To speak up for 'Victor Emmanuel against the field'. **1884** *Sat. Rev.* 2 Feb. 139 An historical prize will bring together a much larger 'field'.

b. *Hunting.* Those who take part in the sport. ***to lead the field***: to be first in the chase.

1806–7 J. BERESFORD *Miseries Hum. Life* (1826) III. iv, In hunting..while you are leading the field. **1830** GREVILLE *Mem. Geo. IV* (1874) II. xiii. 77 The field which had been out with the King's hounds. **1841** J. T. HEWLETT *Parish Clerk* II. 15 The hounds and huntsman, with the field at their heels. **1890** *Sat. Rev.* 1 Feb. 135/1 Fields of hunting and riding men are very large.

c. *Cricket.* The 'side' who are 'out' in the 'field': see 9; also the players on both sides.

1744 *Norwich Mercury* 15 Sept., And spread the field at distance wait, To break the striker's force. **1850** 'BAT' *Cricket Man.* 51 The disposition of the field depends entirely upon circumstances. **1857** HUGHES *Tom Brown* II. viii, The ball..sticks..in the fingers of his left hand, to the utter astonishment of himself and the whole field. **1859** *All Year Round* No. 13. 305 Our field worked like tigers. **1862** *Sporting Life* 14 June, On the reappearance of the 'field', H. H. Stephenson took the wicket. **1882** *Daily Tel.* 24 June, The first over was sent down..by Palmer..his field being arranged thus.

d. ***to play the field***: to avoid an exclusive commitment (to any one person, etc.); to devote oneself to many causes, persons, etc. *U.S. colloq.*

1936 L. LEFKO *Public Relations* ii. 18 He hasn't any steady. He plays the field—blonde, brunette, or what have you. **1948** G. VIDAL *City & Pillar* (1949) II. ix. 199 Well, I've come to the conclusion that the only real pleasure is in playing the field. **1966** *New Republic* 3 Mar. 19 Japan Plays the Field. Peace and Trade with Everyone.

11. *Cricket* and *Baseball.* One who stands on the field; one of the side that is 'out'; a fieldsman; also in names descriptive of his position in the field, *e.g.* in Cricket, † ***long field to the hip*** (see quot.). ***long field*** (†***straight***) ***off, on*** (see quots.; now usually *long off, on*). ***in the long field***: at the position of long field off or on. In Baseball: ***in-, out-, right-, centre-, left-field***.

1825 'B. BLACKMANTLE' *Eng. Spy* I. 1. 32 He was accounted..an active *field*. **1830** MISS MITFORD *Village* Ser. IV. (1863) 174 That exceedingly bad field..caught him out. **1833** J. NYREN *Yng. Cricketer's Tutor* (1893) 47 *Long field, straight on*, should stand at some distance out from the bowler's wicket, to save two runs. *Ibid.*, *Long field to the hip.* The fieldsman must stand out to save two runs opposite to the popping-crease. *Ibid.*, *Long field, straight off*, should be an active man..His station is on the off-side between the bowler and the middle wicket. **1850** 'BAT' *Cricket Man.* 48 Long Field Off, On. **1859** *All Year Round* No. 13. 305 Southey..a good bowler and 'field'. **1889** *Pauline* VIII. 24 The out-going batsman..ought to have been caught in the long field. *Ibid.*, A good long field.

II. An extended surface.

12. A large stretch; an expanse:

a. of sea, sky, etc.

1608 SHAKS. *Per.* I. i. 37 Without covering, save yon field of stars. **1697** DRYDEN *Virg. Georg.* IV. 103 The nimble Horsemen scour the Fields of Air. **1732** POPE *Ess. Man* I. 41 Yonder argent fields above. **1813** SHELLEY *Q. Mab* IV. 20 The orb of day..o'er ocean's waveless field Sinks sweetly smiling. **1860** RUSKIN *Mod. Paint.* V. VII. iv. 140 *note*, Detached bars, darker or lighter than the field [of cloud] above.

b. of ice or snow.

1813 BAKEWELL *Introd. Geol.* (1815) 55 Vast masses of rock..are sometimes enveloped in fields of ice. **1818** SIR J. LESLIE in *Edin. Rev.* XXX. 16 *North West Passage*, A very wide expanse of it [salt-water ice] they call a field. **1887** RUSKIN *Præterita* II. 178 The snows round..are the least trodden of all the Mont Blanc fields.

c. of immaterial things; cf. 15.

1577 GOOGE *Heresbach's Husb.* (1586) I. 7 What divinitie there is in it, and what a feeld of the acknowledged benefits of God, you have heard. **1590** GREENE *Never too late* (1600) 60 Loue had..wrapt him in a field of woes. **1712** BLACKMORE *Creation* VI. (1818) 203 Who can this Field of Miracles survey. **1847** L. HUNT *Men Women & B.* II. xi. 265 He discloses to us the whole field of his ignorance. **1867** A. BARRY *Sir C. Barry* vi. 190 The whole field of English history.

13. The surface on which something is portrayed.

a. *Her.* The surface of an escutcheon or shield on which the 'charge' is displayed. Also the surface of one of the divisions in the shield.

c **1400** *Destr. Troy* 6290 Hys feld was of fyn gold, freche to behold, With þre lyons launchond. *c* **1435** *Torr. Portugal* 1120 Sir Torrent ordenyth hym a sheld, It was ryche in every ffeld. **1572** BOSSEWELL *Armorie* II. 56 The field is parted per fesse embattyled. **1610** GUILLIM *Heraldry* II. ii. (1660) 52 The Field is the whole Surface..of the Shield over-spread with some Metall, Colour, or Furre, and comprehendeth in it the Charge. **1705** HEARNE *Collect.* 12 Dec., The Arms..are A field Jupiter. **1802** REES *Cycl.* s.v. *Bar*, When the field is divided into four..or more equal parts, it is then blazoned, barry. **1859** TENNYSON *Elaine* 661 Sir Lancelot's azure lions..Ramp in the field.

fig. **1593** SHAKS. *Lucr.* 72 This silent warre of Lillies and of Roses..in her faire faces field. **1607** HIERON *Wks.* I. 414 A field of sincerity, charged with deedes of piety.

b. The groundwork of a picture, etc.

1634 J. BATE *Myst. Nat. & Art* IV. 162 How to make white letters in a blacke Feild. Take [etc.]. **1695** DRYDEN tr. *Du Fresnoy's Art of Painting* xlv. 51 Let the Field, or Ground of the Picture, be clean. **1849** RUSKIN *Sev. Lamps* vi. §14. 175 Shadow is frequently employed as a dark field on which the forms are drawn.

c. *Numism.* (See quot. 1876.)

1876 HUMPHREYS *Coin-Coll. Man.* vii. 82 The field..is the plain part of the coin not occupied by the principal figure or type. **1879** H. PHILLIPS *Notes Coins* 6 The setting sun is illumining with his rays the whole field of the medal.

d. Of a flag: The ground of each division.

1867 SMYTH *Sailor's Word-bk.* 301 The flags of the British navy were severally on a red, white, or blue field.

†**14.** ***green field***: the green cloth of a counting house. *Obs.* (Can this be the sense in quot. 1599?)

1470 *Liber Niger* in *Househ. Ord.* (1790) 51 And suche dayes as the Kings chappell removeth, every of these children then present receveth iiiid. at the grene feald [*MSS. in Brit. Mus.* read *seald, fald*] of the countyng-house for horse hyre dayly, as longe as they be journeying. [**1599** SHAKS. *Hen. V*, I. iii. 17 His Nose was as sharpe as a Pen, and [? *read* on] a Table of greene fields.]

III. Area of operation or observation.

15. a. An area or sphere of action, operation, or investigation; a (wider or narrower) range of opportunities, or of objects, for labour, study, or contemplation; a department or subject of activity or speculation.

1340 *Ayenb.* 240 Huanne oure lhord wolde by uonded of þe dyeule: he yede in-to desert. uor þe desert of religion: is ueld of uondinge. **1580** SIDNEY *Arcadia* I. (1622) 19 A very good Orator might have a fair field to use eloquence in, if [etc.]. **1626** BACON *Sylva* §228 As for the increase of Vertue generally..it is a large Field, and to be handled by it self. **1674** OWEN *Holy Spirit* (1693) 82 A large and plain Field doth here open it self unto us. **1711** ADDISON *Spect.* No. 160 ¶4 This..Failure..opens a large Field of Raillery. **1750** BEAWES *Lex Mercat.* (1752) 2 The wide field for trade that now lies before us. **1807** T. THOMSON *Chem.* (ed. 3) II. 143 A very interesting field of investigation. *a* **1862** BUCKLE *Civiliz.* (1873) III. v. 350 The philosopher and the practical man..each is in his own field, supreme.

b. (without *a* or *the*.) Scope, opportunity, extent of material for action or operation. ? *Obs.*

1664 DRYDEN *Rival-Ladies* III. i, Thou hast not field enough in thy young breast, To entertain such storms to struggle in. **1681** TEMPLE *Mem.* III. Wks. 1731 I. 343, I thought I had Field enough left for doing them good Offices to the Duke. **1719** SWIFT *To Yng. Clergyman*, The matter..will afford field enough for a divine to enlarge on.

c. Used *attrib.* to denote an investigation, study, etc., carried out in the natural environment of a given material, language, animal, etc., and not in the laboratory, study, or office; also, to denote a person taking part in such an activity, as ***field archæologist, naturalist***, etc. Also in phr. ***in the field***.

1789 MONTAGU *Let.* in G. White *Selborne* (1877) II. 236 You are a field-naturalist. **1898** W. JAMES *Coll. Ess. & Rev.* (1920) 426 In the '50's and '60's Captain Mayne Reid..was forever extolling the hunters and field-observers of living animals' habits, and keeping up a fire of invective against the 'closet-naturalists', as he called them, the collectors and classifiers, and handlers of skeletons and skins. **1904** Field naturalist [see AVICULTURIST]. **1906** *Nature* 1 Mar. 411/1 A handbook in a paper wrapper is hardly fit for use in the field. **1915** J. P. WILLIAMS-FREEMAN *Introd. Field Archæol.* p. viii, A general introduction to Field Archaeology. *Ibid.* p. xix, Hampshire is..a happy hunting-ground for the Field Archaeologist. **1930** E. E. HUNT *Audit of Amer.* 8 We have as yet no method for summing up individual incomes into a family income, exc. that of direct field studies. **1932** H. C. BREARLEY *Homicide in U.S.* 10 There is need of a thorough field survey to determine how accurate are the homicide reports now being made to state and federal bureaus of vital statistics. **1933** *Brit. Birds* XXVI. 363 The elementary co-operative services..a national field centre which can collaborate with other national field centres overseas,—still remain to be provided. **1935** *Discovery* Nov. 346/2 Dr. Margaret Mead, by her studies of certain aspects of primitive societies in New Guinea and Samoa, has already established a reputation as a field anthropologist. **1936** *Brit. Birds* XXIX. 264 (*heading*) Interpretation of field-observations. **1936** *Discovery* Dec. 382/2 It was only a matter of organisation to set up a field laboratory. **1937** R. H. LOWIE *Hist. Ethnol. Theory* ix. 151 They lead to still another extension of traditional field research. *Ibid.* xiii. 231 In contrast to Radcliffe-Brown, Malinowski is first of all a field investigator. *Ibid.*, His field technique conforms to Boas' standards. **1937** J. ORR tr. *Iordan's Introd. Romance Ling.* 5 The Romance tongues are still spoken to-day..and can thus be observed and studied directly, 'in the field', to use a term borrowed from the natural sciences. **1946** *Lancet* 15 June 910/2 The Council for the Promotion of Field Studies have..established..their first residential centre. **1949** M. FORTES *Social Structure* p. vi, Much as the theory owes to Durkheim, its emphasis on synchronic study and its rejection of conjectural history are the results of field experience. **1951** *Archit. Rev.* CIX. 51/2 An extensive 'field-survey' of the monuments and a prodigious accumulation of new or hitherto scattered documentary material. **1956** O. L. ZANGWILL in A. Pryce-Jones *New Outl. Mod. Knowl.* 170 Ethology is concerned with field-observations of behaviour and their systematic interpretation. **1957** *N. & Q.* CCII. 233/1 Shrimpton [is] an extraordinary prodigy, perhaps our first field archaeologist. **1959** *Listener* 5 Mar. 402/2 A university must employ a variety of means far wider than those of the lecture room. Seminars, practical work, field trips, a library with access to original material..are all essential to this. **1960** S. KAUFFMAN *If it be Love* ii. 24 It'd be a help if I had some of the field reports. **1961** *Amer. Speech* XXXVI. 201 Not having ready access to the field records, this reviewer must perforce rely for comparisons on his own published investigations. **1962** H. E. BEECHENO *Introd. Bus. Stud.* ix. 80 It is at this point that 'field research' must be undertaken. **1968** *Times* 14 Oct. 15/1 The fossils were seen by an undergraduate from Rutgers University, New Jersey, during a field trip to study techniques in palaeontology. **1969** *Ibid.* 13 Jan. 11/2 When this virus is put into sheep experimentally it produces a disease identical with that from which it can be recovered in the field. **1970** E. LEACH *Lévi-Strauss* i. 8 By Malinowski standards 'Lévi-Strauss' field research is of only moderate quality.

d. *Math.* An algebraic system with two operations that satisfy certain axioms analogous to those for the multiplication and addition of real numbers; technically, a commutative ring that contains a unit element for multiplication and an inverse for each non-zero element.

1893 E. H. MOORE in *Bull. N.Y. Math. Soc.* III. 75 Suppose that we have a system of symbols or marks,..in number *s*, and suppose that these *s* marks may be combined by the four fundamental operations of algebra..and that when the marks are so combined the results of these operations are in every case uniquely determined and belong to the system of marks. Such a system of *s* marks we call a field of order *s*. **1905** *Trans. Amer. Math. Soc.* VI. 183 Closely connected with the theory of groups is the theory of fields, suggested by Galois, and due, in concrete form, to Dedekind in 1871. The word *field* is the English equivalent for Dedekind's term *Körper*. **1941** BIRKHOFF & MACLANE *Surv. Mod. Algebra* ii. 40 A field F is an integral domain which contains for each element $a \neq 0$ an 'inverse' element a^{-1} satisfying the equation $a^{-1}a = 1$. **1958** K. S. MILLER *Elem. Mod. Abstr. Algebra* ii. 65 A field is an integral domain... In general, an integral domain is not a field. **1963** E. WEISS *Algebraic Number Theory* v. 185 By a global field we mean a field which is either (1) an algebraic number field, or (2) an algebraic function field in one variable over a finite constant field. **1968** E. D. MACDONALD *Theory of Groups* xi. 222 Familiar examples of fields are the real numbers, the rational numbers, and the residue classes modulo a prime.

e. *Logic.* The class comprising the domain and the range or converse domain of a relation.

1903 [see DOMAIN *sb.* 4 f]. **1952** F. B. FITCH *Symbolic Logic* vi. 179 The field of a relation has the same members as the field of the converse of that relation.

f. *Computers.* A set of one or more characters in a record, or a group of columns on a punched card, which together represent a single item of information; an item of information that can be so represented.

1946 P. S. DWYER in *Proc. Research Forum* (I.B.M.) 21/1 By an 'elimination' field I mean a field which eliminates or causes the accounting machine to throw out every variate in any specified accumulation field for which the corresponding variate is missing in the elimination field. **1953** *Proc. Inst. Radio Engin.* Oct. 1337/1 The card columns are grouped in Fields. For example, a very simple invoicing problem would have a Field for Quantity, another for Unit Price,..and maybe a Field for discounts which apply. **1959** *Jrnl. Assoc. Computing Machinery* VI. 7 Figure 3 illustrates a file of payroll data as it would be recorded on magnetic tape. Each record in this file is partitioned into fields. **1966** ABRAMS & CORVINE *Basic Data Processing* ii. 14 A field is one or more characters of data that are meaningful as a unit. The number of children in a family is a field; so is a person's name.

16. a. The space or range within which objects are visible through an optical instrument in any one position.

1747 GOULD *Eng. Ants* 32 Kill her, and..place her Body on the Field of a Microscope. **1765** MATY in *Phil. Trans.* LV. 305 It filled the field of the telescope. **1812–6** J. SMITH *Panorama Sc. & Art* I. 474 The visible field is..twenty degrees in diameter. **1871** TYNDALL *Fragm. Sc.* (1879) II. xiii. 307 Organisms..shooting rapidly across the microscopic field. **1884** F. J. BRITTEN *Watch & Clockm.* 102 A very superior achromatic glass..giving a..flat field.

b. ***field of observation, view*** or ***vision***: the space to which observation, etc. is limited. So ***field of consciousness, perception***.

1812–6 J. SMITH *Panorama Sc. & Art* II. 718 The whole field of view through the foot-wide arch. **1817** CHALMERS *Astron. Disc.* ii. (1852) 53 That circle by which the field of observation is enclosed. **1855** BAIN *Senses & Int.* II. ii. §3 The eye can take in a wide field at once. **1859** REEVE *Brittany* 236 They are not seen in the picture, being much to the left of our field of view. **1862** MERIVALE *Rom. Emp.* (1865) VI. lii. 300 The field of vision is overclouded. **1865** S. HODGSON *Time & Space* vi. 295 It has been shown that the whole field of consciousness is occupied by perception and spontaneous redintegration. **1905** W. JAMES *Ess. Radic. Empir.* (1912) vi. 170 The world experienced (otherwise called the 'field of consciousness') comes at all times with our body as its centre, centre of vision, centre of action, centre of interest. **1933** H. READ *Art Now* ii. 78 Take any field of vision—a land-scape, the scene before you now, if you lift your eyes. **1942** R. HILLARY *Last Enemy* iii. 72, I noticed how small was my field of vision [from an aeroplane]. **1957** H. READ *Tenth Muse* xiii. 109 As the mind perceives, it automatically selects and organizes the field of perception.

fig. **1877** E. R. CONDER *Bas. Faith* ii. 83 No scintillation of its existence twinkles within the field of our knowledge.

c. Photogr. ***depth of field***: the distance between the nearest and the farthest objects that give an image judged to be in focus.

1911 B. E. JONES *Cassell's Cycl. Photogr.* 167 'Depth of field' is sometimes used as synonymous with 'depth of focus' and 'depth of definition', the third expression more correctly indicating what is meant. **1920** C. W. PIPER *J. E. Fearn's Mod. Photogr.* (ed. 6) xiv. 102 The distance between the nearest and farthest objects in focus with any particular stop is called the depth of field for that stop. **1939** HENNEY & DUDLEY *Handbk. Photogr.* iv. 90 A useful accessory included on most miniature cameras and on many larger cameras is a depth-of-field, or depth-of-focus, table. **1951** G. H. SEWELL *Amat. Film-Making* (ed. 2) iii. 28 Objects in front of and behind the main object will throw images of sufficient sharpness, and the magnitude of the distance between these front and back objects is known as 'depth of field'. **1965** *Movie* Spring 34/1, I used a telefoto lens a great deal so as not to have any depth of field.

d. *Television.* A set of equally spaced scanning lines extending over the whole picture area and produced by a single passage of the spot.

1943 D. G. FINK *Telev. Stand. & Pract.* iv. 81 There is some question whether the scanning period should be taken as the field period or the frame period in the case of interlaced scanning. *Ibid.* 76 What is the lowest field frequency that will result in naturalness, smoothness, and nonjumpiness..in the picture? **1950** *Sci. Amer.* Dec. 14/2 The CBS [colour television] system..requires six fields to present a single complete picture (i.e., two interlaced fields in each of the three primary colors). **1967** WHARTON & HOWORTH *Princ. Telev. Reception* iii. 38 Two types of field, 'odd' and 'even', are generated and interlaced to form a complete picture. *Ibid.*, Each complete scan is called a field, and two successive scans which provide the complete picture information are called a picture.

17. a. *Physics.* The area or space under the influence of, or within the range of, some agent; a state or situation in which a force is exerted on any objects of a particular kind (e.g. electric charges) that are present; the action of such a force; the value (or direction) at any point of the force on an object defined as having unit magnitude, or the set of the vectors that represent this force at each point in a region. So ***electric, gravitational, magnetic***, etc., ***field***; also ***field of force***. Phr. ***to be in, out of the field***: see quot. 1884.

The word is freq. used as if it denoted an identifiable causal entity.

1845 FARADAY *Diary* 10 Nov. (1933) IV. 331 Wrought with bodies between the great poles, i.e. in the magnetic field, as to their motions under the influence of magnetic force. **1850** *Ibid.* 23 July (1934) V. 325 When the opposed bodies are on opposite sides of the axis (Magnetic), then the figured forms would give fields of force in which the lines of magnetic power would vary. **1850** W. THOMSON in *Phil. Mag.* 3rd Ser. XXXVII. 251 The 'field of force' [of a magnet] occupied by the mercury and watch-glass. **1863** TYNDALL *Heat* ii. §35 (1870) 37 The exact equivalent of the power employed to move the medal in the excited magnetic field. **1865** J. C. MAXWELL in *Phil. Trans. R. Soc.* CLV. 460 The theory I propose may..be called a theory of the Electro-magnetic Field, because it has to do with the space in the neighbourhood of the electric or magnetic bodies. *Ibid.* 493 The intrinsic energy of the field of gravitation. **1881** —— *Electr. & Magn.* I. 45 The electric field is the portion of space in the neighbourhood of electrified bodies, considered with reference to electric phenomena. **1884** WATSON & BURBURY *Math. Th. Electr. & Magn.* I. 48 In physics a body which is within the range of the action of another body is said to be *in the field* of that other body, and when it is so distant from that other body as to be sensibly out of the range of its action it is said to be *out of the field.* **1897** J. J. THOMSON in *Phil. Mag.* 5th Ser. XLIV. 311 If these corpuscles are..projected from the cathode by the electric field, they would behave exactly like cathode rays. **1903** RUTHERFORD *Ibid.* 6th Ser. V. 179 The magnetic field was applied perpendicular to the plane of the paper and parallel to the plane of the slits. *Ibid.* 184 The rate of

discharge..with the electric field off and on. 1928 A. S. Eddington *Nature Physical World* vii. 153 It is usually considered that when we use these [*sc.* magnets, electroscopes, etc.] we are exploring not space, but a field in space. 1928 Newman & Searle *Gen. Prop. Matter* iii. 75 According to Newton's Law the nature of the attracting masses is unimportant, and it is the magnitude of the mass ..which determines the gravitational field. 1946 *Ann. Reg.* *1945* 355 The stability of ordinary atomic nuclei could be explained only by the existence of a meson field analogous to the electro-magnetic field. 1952 Fitzgerald & Kingsley *Electr. Machinery* i. 6 Voltages are induced..by mechanically rotating a magnetic field past the windings. 1956 E. H. Hutten *Lang. Mod. Physics* iii. 93 Energy is thus contained in the volume of space in which a field exists. 1959 B. I. & B. Bleaney *Electr. & Magn.* i. 4 From Eq. (1.2) we find that $E = q_1/(4\pi\epsilon_0 r^3)r$ is the electric field due to the charge q_1. 1962 J. Dougall tr. *Born's Atomic Physics* (ed. 7) iii. 59 According to Maxwell's electromagnetic theory, light.. consists of a periodically variable, electromagnetic alternating field. 1962 Corson & Lorrain *Introd. Electromagn. Fields* i. 1 The force between two electric charges will be considered as being due to an interaction between one of the charges and the field of the other. 1962 V. H. Booth *Physical Sci.* xxi. 300/1 The strength of the gravitational field is extremely weak compared to electric and magnetic fields.

fig. 1943 H. Read *Educ. through Art* vi. 181 They [*sc.* Jungian archetypes] are centres of influence, or fields of force within the unconscious. 1959 *Times Lit. Suppl.* 23 Jan. 45/3 The present Byronic field of force.

b. That part of an electric generator or motor in which the magnetic flux is produced; a field magnet. (An *absol.* use of *field* used *attrib.* in the preceding sense.)

1893 G. Kapp *Dynamos* x. 226 We can..alter the design altogether so as to obtain enough cooling surface without increasing the weight of the field. 1952 Fitzgerald & Kingsley *Electr. Machinery* i. 11 (*caption*) Part of Boulder Dam hydroelectric station showing wound revolving field (suspended from two cranes) of 82,500-kva..water-wheel generator.

c. *Embryol.* A region of an embryo capable of developing into a particular organ; a supposed system of influences regarded as collectively causing the differentiation of tissue.

1927 G. R. de Beer in *Biol. Rev.* Mar. 189 The only hypothesis which appears tenable is that of a Gradient System or 'field'..for the place of determination of the rudiments of other organs. 1934 Huxley & de Beer *Elem. Exper. Embryol.* viii. 276 The term *field* implies a region throughout which some agency is at work in a co-ordinated way, resulting in the establishment of an equilibrium within the area of the field. 1957 *Encycl. Brit.* VIII. 976/2 Each area or morphogenetic field..is a gradient field in the sense that the capacity for differentiation is highest in the centre and diminishes gradually toward the periphery. 1969 *Jrnl. Theoret. Biol.* XXV. i. 41 It has been a great surprise and of considerable importance to find that most embryonic fields seem to involve distances of less than 100 cells, and often less than 50.

d. *Psychol.* An environment or situation regarded as a system of psychological forces with which an individual interacts.

1934 *Philos. Sci.* I. 328 Since the genesis of ego and superego out of id depend on experience, one might suppose that the activity of these parts of the ego was determined by the structure of the psycho-biological field. 1935 Adams & Zener tr. *Lewin's Dynamic Theory Personality* iii. 79 To understand or predict the psychological behavior..one has to determine for every kind of psychological event..the momentary whole situation, that is, the momentary structure and the state of the person..and of the psychobiological environment... Every fact that exists psychobiologically must have a position in this field. 1950 *Mind* LIX. 569 A stimulus in an environmental field acts upon an organism in such a way as to evoke a 'directional' response, which leads to adaptation to the field—certain 'directional' responses being attitudes, sentiments, and so on. 1952 W. J. H. Sprott *Social Psychol.* i. ii. 30 The central concept in his [*sc.* Kurt Lewin's] scheme is the 'field'. The 'field' can be analysed into 'subjective' and 'objective' elements. 1964 Gould & Kolb *Dict. Soc. Sci.* 270/1 The field concept as specifically used by gestalt psychologists refers to organized conscious behaviour accompanied by a physiological energy pattern and forming part of a larger physiological system.

IV. *attrib.* and *Comb.*

18. General relations: **a.** simple attrib. (sense 1), as ***field-dew***, ***-flower***; (sense 2), as ***field-character***, ***-craft***, ***-dweller***, ***-honour***, ***-mark*** (of a bird), ***-mate***, ***-pastime***, ***-properties*** (of a greyhound), ***-smell***, ***-tent***, (senses 2 and 4) ***field-trial***; (sense 4), as ***field capacity***, ***-crop***, ***-drain***, ***-gate***, ***-hedge***, ***-husbandry***, ***-measure***, ***-name***, ***-noise***, ***-path***, ***-rent***, ***-road***, ***-seed***, ***-stones***; (sense 7), as ***field ambulance***, ***-battalion***, ***-cap***, ***-craft***, ***-duties***, ***-equipment***, ***-evolutions***, ***-exercise***, ***-insignia***, ***kitchen***, ***-movements***, ***post card***, ***punishment***, ***-service*** (also attrib.), ***-telephone***; ***-troops***, ***-watch***; (sense 17), as ***field coil***, ***law***, ***physics***, ***winding***. **b.** objective (sense 4), as ***field-purging*** ppl. adj. **c.** locative (sense 4), as ***field-faring*** ppl. adj. **d.** limitative, as (sense 17) ***field-free*** adj.

1916 F. M. Ford *Let.* 23 Aug. (1965) 69, I have had..a week in *Field Ambulance. 1875 G. P. Colley in *Encycl. Brit.* II. 596/1 An infantry regiment [in the Prussian army] has three *field battalions. 1888 Sir M. Mackenzie *Frederick the Noble* viii. 140 He wore the simple blue cloak of the Prussian Cavalry, with fur cape and *field cap. 1938 Weaver & Clements *Plant Ecol.* (ed. 2) viii. 201 The total amount of water that is held against the downward pull of capillarity and the force of gravity and does not drain through the soil is termed the water-retaining capacity or *field capacity. 1937 *Brit. Birds* XXXI. 84 *Field characters, habitat, song and 'habits' generally. 1953 Bannerman *Birds Brit. Isles* II. 212 Both sexes have the excellent field-character of a long tail. 1892 Crocker & Wheeler *Pract. Managem. Dynamos & Motors* i. 4 Field Magnet.—This consists of one or more iron cores on which are wound the *field coils. 1887 *Pall Mall G.* 26 Sept. 5/2 No one..expects to fill his bag save by *field-craft. 1933 B. H. L. Hart *Future of Infantry* App. ii. 80 The following exercises are of use in developing the individual's field-craft. 1967 *Observer* 14 May 2/5 American troops are poor at fieldcraft. 1860 Gosse *Rom. Nat. Hist.* (1866) 105 The injuries done..in our *field-crops. 1889 *Daily News* 16 Dec. 7/1 Indian agricultural field crop seeds. 1590 Shaks. *Mids. N.* v. i. 422 With this *field dew consecrate. 1933 B. W. Adkin *Land Drainage in Brit.* xx. 348 Open drains are never cut as deep as the ordinary *field drains. 1945 'G. Orwell' *Animal Farm* v. 36 He talked learnedly about field-drains.. and basic slag. 1844 *Regul. & Ord. Army* 127 Subordinate Officers understand their *Field Duties. 1575 in *Russia at close 16th C.* (Hakluyt Soc.) Introd. 9 The..Tartars are barbarowse and *fyilde dwellers. 1808 Wellington in Gurw. *Desp.* IV. 29 A *field equipment with a proportion of horses. 1875 G. P. Colley in *Encycl. Brit.* II. 579/2 The war establishment of a field equipment troop is 6 officers and 233 men. 1853 Stocqueler *Milit. Encycl.*, A regiment is.. instructed in the *field exercise and evolutions. 1892 *Pall Mall G.* 8 Dec. 2/1 A sketch of *fieldfaring women. 1653 Walton *Angler* 214 *Field-flowers..perfum'd the air. 1852 Lytton *Falkland* 59, I see him..gathering the field-flowers. 1955 O. Klein in W. Pauli *Niels Bohr* 116 The *field-free Dirac equation. 1962 *Science Survey* IV. 64 In contrast with the microwave maser, no magnetic field is required because energy levels existing in the field-free atom are used. 1970 G. K. Woodgate *Elem. Atomic Struct.* iv. 70 The beam travels a further distance *l′* in a field-free region to a detector. 1891 S. C. Scrivener *Our Fields & Cities* 33, I was..glad to see the horse turning towards a *field-gate. 1823 in Cobbett *Rur. Rides* (1885) I. 399 A *field-hedge and bank. 1737 M. Green *Spleen* (1738) 5 *Field-honours.. Atchiev'd by leaping hedge and ditch. 1760 J. Eliot (*title*), Essays upon *Field-Husbandry in New England. 1823 J. Badcock *Dom. Amusem.* 34 This stick, or baton..became the *field insignia of a general. 1915 'I. Hay' *First Hundred Thousand* xiv. 191 We might..let the grooms and drivers go with..*field kitchens. 1942 *Penguin New Writing* XIV. 9 The oppressor's soldiers have offered soup from their field-kitchens to those among the inhabitants who are utterly destitute. 1928 A. S. Eddington *Nature Physical World* xi. 236 The *field laws—conservation of energy, mass, momentum and of electric change..are not controlling laws. They are truisms. 1954 Bannerman *Birds Brit. Isles* III. 20 The white wing-bar..was an excellent *field-mark and could be distinguished..at a range of thirty to forty yards. 1786 Burns *Brigs of Ayr* 36 The feather'd *field-mates, bound by Nature's tie. 1857 *Phil. Trans. R. Soc.* CXLVII. 627 The Ordnance Survey Office have used, as standards of reference for *field-measures, two 10-feet iron bars. 1798 Wellington in Gurw. *Desp.* I. 12 Wellesley.. practising them in combined *field movements. 1924 E. Ekwall in Mawer & Stenton *Introd. Surv. Eng. Place-Names* i. iv. 89 A full investigation of *field-names..will probably often tell of a strong Scandinavian influence. 1960 P. H. Reaney *Orig. Eng. Place-Names* x. 207 If we are to be accurate in our use of terms, 'field-names' should be used only of the enclosed areas of arable and pasture land which are never found on the Ordnance Survey maps. *Ibid.* 210 Although not strictly accurate, the term 'field-name' is also used of the innumerable minor place-names found in documents of all periods. 1904 W. Stevens *Let.* 6 Aug. (1967) 78 And it sounds, perfectly, like a *field-noise at harvest. 18.. Wordsw. *Sonnets* (1838) 151 To chase mankind, with men in armies packed For his *field-pastime. 1772 De Foe *Col. Jack* (1840) 66 It was agreed to spread from the *field-path to the road way. 1847 Mary Howitt *Ballads* 294 Through old field-paths we'll wander. 1928 A. S. Eddington *Nature Physical World* xi. 236 The material, gravitational and electromagnetic fields are all included... The quantities enumerated above..obey the great law of *field-physics. 1932 *Discovery* Oct. 338/1 The whole conception of what is called field physics springs from Maxwell and Faraday. 1916 T. E. Lawrence *Let.* 14 Dec. (1954) 332 This is not a letter: only a substitute for a *field post card. 1917 W. Owen *Let.* 1 Jan. (1967) 421 If on my Field Post Card I cross out 'I am being sent down to the base' with a double line..then I shall actually be at the Front. 1883 *Chamb. Jrnl.* 305 The..*field properties of a greyhound. 1907 *Act 7 Edw. VII* c. 2 §10 Amendments of Army Act... The words '*field punishment' shall be substituted for the words 'summary punishment' wherever those words occur in provisoes (9) and (10). 1601 Weever *Mirr. Mart.* E vj b, *Feeld-purging Februarius. 1580 Hollyband *Treas. Fr. Tong, Champart*, *fielde rent. 1864 H. Spencer *Illustr. Univ. Progr.* 418 While along the *field-roads..the movement is the slowest. 1888 *Daily News* 11 Sept. 2/5 A fair amount of business is now being transacted in *field seeds. 1656 J. Harrington *Oceana* 57 The Youth for *field-service..armed and under continual Discipline. 1834 J. S. Macaulay *Treat. Field Fortif.* xi. 225 [Tools required] 1 Field-service level. 1 Six-feet rod [etc.]. 1869 E. A. Parkes *Pract. Hygiene* (ed. 3) 118 On field service..the same duties are enjoined. 1915 F. H. Lawrence in *Home Lett. of T. E. Lawrence* (1954) 660, I am sending a field service post card at the same time as this letter. 1940 *N. & Q.* 28 Sept. 217/2 Field Service Cap. 1818 Shelley *Rosalind* 1110 *Field smells known in infancy. 1799 J. Robertson *Agric. Perth*, *Field stones..were gathered off the land, where it seemed to be fit for tillage. 1892 *Jrnl. Archæol. Inst.* No. 194. 155 Small field-stones concreted with sticky gravel. 1908 E. J. Stevens (*title*) *Field telephones for army use. 1939 Auden & Isherwood *Journey to War* ix. 222 Soldiers installed a field-telephone. 1755 Smollett *Quix.* (1803) IV. 174 Among these trees we have pitched some *field-tents. 1849 Johnston *Exp. Agric.* 60 Such *field-trials as appear to me likely to throw light upon it. 1895 *Westm. Gaz.* 12 Dec. 7/2 That great field-trial authority [on dogs]. 1970 *Encycl. Brit.* IX. 250/1 Field trials are competitions among individual sporting dogs, or gun dogs, as they are called in Great Britain, of the same general type under conditions that approximate or simulate those found in the hunting field. 1875 G. P. Colley in *Encycl. Brit.* II. 595/2 *Field troops [in the Prussian army] in peace time form the standing army. 1871 *Daily News* 13 Jan., The last intermittent French *fieldwatch is definitely ascertained to have quitted Bondy. 1883 Seebohm *Eng. Village Comm.* i. (1884) 4 A common *fieldway gives access to the strips. 1893 D. C. Jackson *Electro-Magn.* v. 123 To know the number of leakage lines is therefore a matter of moment..in calculating the *field windings.

19. Prefixed to the names of many animals, birds, and insects, often in the sense of 'wild', to indicate a species found in the open country as opposed to *house* or *town*, as ***field-ass***, ***-bee***, ***-cricket***, ***-mouse***, ***-rat***, ***-slug***, ***-spider***; **field-duck**, the little bustard (*Otis tetrax*) found chiefly in France; **field-finch** (see quot.); **field-lark** (*Alauda arvensis*); *U.S.* = meadow *lark* (*b*); **field-martin** (*Tyrannus carolinensis*); **field-plover** (*U.S.*), a name for two species of plover, and for a sandpiper (*Bartramia longicauda*); **field-sparrow** (*U.S.*) (*Spizella pusilla* or *S. agrestis*); **field-titling**, †**-tortoise** (*jocular*), **-vole** (see quots.).

1382 Wyclif *Jer.* ii. 24 A *feld asse vsid in wildernesse. 1835 *Chambers's Edin. Jrnl.* 7 Mar. 45/1 Seven species of the genus *apis*; the most remarkable of which are the small *field-bee, [etc.]. 1918 D. H. Lawrence *New Poems* 10 As a field-bee, black and amber, breaks from the winter-cell. 1600 E. Blount *Hosp. Inc. Fooles* A iv, Those *field-Crickets..play the parrats so notably. 1868 Wood *Homes without H.* viii. 161 The black-bodied Field Cricket (*Acheta campestris*). 1892 W. H. Hudson *La Plata* 185 The *field-finch, *Sycalis luteola*. 1678 Ray *Willughby's Ornith.* ii. 207 Mr. Jessop suspects that there is yet another different sort of this bird, which may be called the lesser *field-lark. 1768 Pennant *Brit. Zool.* II. 238 The Lesser Field Lark. *a* 1883 G. W. Bagby *Old Virginia Gentleman* (1910) 126 We hear his gun go off, and he comes back presently bringing a field-lark in his hand. 1580 Baret *Alv.* M 531 A *field mouse with a long snoute. 1861 Mrs. Norton *Lady La G.* iii. 69 The small field-mouse, with wide transparent ears, Comes softly forth. 1562 Turner *Herbal* ii. 60 b, The roote of Myrrhis dronken in wyne helpeth the bytynges of *feldespyders. 1647 H. More *Song of Soul* iv. vi, Unlesse that wiser men make't the field-spiders loom. 1864 J. C. Atkinson *Provincial names of Birds*, *Field Titling, sb., Prov. name for the Tree Pipit, *Anthus arboreus*. 1708 Motteux *Rabelais* iv. lxiii, A *Field-Tortoise, *alias*, eclip'd a Mole. 1868 Wood *Homes without H.* xxxi. 598 The Short-tailed Field Mouse otherwise termed Campagnol or *Field Vole (*Arvicola arvensis*).

20. a. In many names of plants growing in the fields, as ***field-bindweed***, ***-forget-me-not***, ***-mushroom***, ***-rhubarb***, etc.; **field-ash** (*Pyrus aucuparia*); **field-basil**: see basil[1] 2; **field-bromegrass** (*Bromus arvensis*); **field-cypress**: see cypress[1] 2 b; **field-kale** (*Sinapis arvensis*); **field-madder**, †(*a*) rosemary, (*b*) a common modern book-name for *Sherardia arvensis*; **field-nigella** or **nigel-weed** (*Lychnis Githago*); **field-southernwood** (*Artemisia campestris*); **field-weed** (*Anthemis Cotula*, also *Erigeron philadelphicum*) (*Syd. Soc. Lex.* 1884); †**field-wood**, ? gentian (? = OE. *feldwyrt*).

1578 Lyte *Dodoens* vi. lxx. 748 *Feelde Ashe. 1866 *Treas. Bot.* 118 *Field balm, *Calamintha Nepeta*. 1825 Loudon *Encycl. Agric.* §4962. 798 The *field-beet, commonly called the mangold-würzel. 1861 Miss Pratt *Flower. Pl.* IV. 17 *Field Bindweed..this plant is one of the most troublesome weeds. 1846 J. Baxter *Libr. Pract. Agric.* (ed. 4) I. 369 The ..*field-brome grass..is found in some of the best pastures. *Ibid.* I. 151 The..large red *Field Carrot, was the only variety employed for agricultural purposes in England. 1578 Lyte *Dodoens* i. xviii. 28 Called..in English..Ground Pyne ..and *field Cypres. 1867 Sowerby *Eng. Bot.* VII. 105 *Field Forget-me-not. 1861 Miss Pratt *Flower. Pl.* IV. 6 *Field Gentian..contains in every part of it some of the tonic bitter principle common to the tribe. *c* 1000 *Durham Gloss.* in *Sax. Leechd.* III. 305/1 *Rosmarinum*, sun deav & bothen & *feld medere. 1861 Miss Pratt *Flower. Pl.* III. 144 Field Madder, Corolla funnel-shaped. 1832 *Veg. Subst. Food* 331 The *Field Mushroom..is the only species.. cultivated in this country. 1578 Lyte *Dodoens* ii. xi. 160 Cockle or *fielde Nigelweede, hath straight..stemmes. 1591 Percivall *Sp. Dict.*, *Leche de gallina*, white *field onion. 1868 Hereman *Paxton's Bot. Dict.*, *Field Rhubarb. 1838 Clarke in *Proc. Berw. Nat. Club* I. 163 The bank was ..enamelled with..the barren Strawberry and the *Field-Rush. 1861 Miss Pratt *Flower. Pl.* IV. 48 *Field Scorpion-grass..the whole plant is rough with spreading bristles. 1597 Gerarde *Herbal* ii. ix. §3. 190 Common Mustarde, or *fielde Senuie. 1776 Withering *Brit. Plants* (1796) III. 709 *Field Southernwood. 1861 Miss Pratt *Flower. Pl.* III. 262 Field Southernwood..is a very rare plant..The involucre is of a purplish-brown colour. 1826 Miss Mitford *Village* Ser. ii. (1863) 411 The *field-star of Bethlehem,—a sort of large hyacinth of the hue of the misletoe. 1393 Gower *Conf.* II. 262 The *feldwode and verveine, Of herbes ben nought better tweine. 1861 Miss Pratt *Flower. Pl.* III. 159 *Field Woodruff..the flowers are bright blue. *Ibid.* V. 300 *Field Wood Rush..a common plant..has a straight unbranched stem.

b. In designations of crops covering a large area, as ***field-hay***; **field-pea**, *Pisum sativum* var. *arvense*.

1895 C. J. Cornish *Wild Eng.* 242 'Field-hay', as the produce of the rye-grass, sainfoin, clover, and trefoil is called, is a new feature in the country. 1709 J. Lawson *New Voy. Carolina* 77 All the sorts of English Pease..thrive..in Carolina. Particularly..the common Field-Pease. 1858 Field pea [see pea[1] 2 b]. 1892 W. Fream *Elem. Agric.* (ed. 2) 240 The field-pea, of which there are several sorts, distinguished by bearing a blue blossom, should be sown as early as possible in the spring. 1949 G. H. Ahlgren *Forage Crops* xiii. 131 The field pea was brought to America by the early colonists, being reported first in Virginia in 1636.

21. Special comb.: **field-abbot** (see quot.); **field-allowance**, an allowance to an officer, and sometimes to a private, on active service, to meet the increased expenses attendant thereupon; **field-artillery**, light ordnance fitted for travel and for active operations in a campaign; † **field-bar**, the border or limit of the field in a telescope (see 16); **field-battery**, a battery of field-guns; † **field-battle**, a sham-fight; † **field-beast**, an animal used for draught or for ploughing, in *pl.* cattle; † **field-bishop**, transl. Fr. *évêque des champs*, one who is hanged in chains; **field block, blocking** *Surg.*, a technique in which an anæsthetic solution is injected so as to create a zone of anæsthesia around the operative field and block the passage of nerve impulses; **field boot**, a knee-high military boot, usu. laced from the foot to mid-calf; † **field-breadth, -brode**, a short distance; **field-cannon** = *field piece*; **field-carriage**, the carriage for a field-gun, its ammunition, etc.; **field-club**, an association for the study of Natural History by outdoor observation; **field-colours** (*Mil.*), small flags for marking out the ground for the squadrons and battalions; also the colours used by an army when in the field (cf. *camp colours*); **field-cornet**, 'the magistrate of a township in the Cape colony' (Simmonds, 1858); whence **field-cornetcy**, the territory under the jurisdiction of a field-cornet; **field-culverin**, a culverin for use in the field of battle (cf. *field-piece*); † **field-deputy**, a representative attached to an army in the field; **field-derrick** (see quot.); † **field-devil**, used by Coverdale, after Ger. *feldteufel* (Luther), as transl. of Heb. *səʻirim* (A.V. 'satyrs'); **field-dressing**, appliances for dressing a wound in the field; **field-driver** (see quots.); **field-effect transistor**, a semiconductor device in which the majority carriers flow along a channel whose effective resistance is controlled by a transverse electric field produced by a reverse bias applied to a gate region surrounding the channel, the gate and the channel being of opposite conductivity types; **field emission**, the emission of electrons from the surface of a conductor under the influence of a strong electrostatic field as a result of the tunnel effect; hence **field emission microscope**, a device which utilizes this effect to produce an enlarged image of the emitting surface on a fluorescent screen; **field equation** [FIELD *sb.* 17], one of a series of equations established by Maxwell (1865) and Einstein (1950) which describe conditions existing within electromagnetic and gravitational fields respectively; **field events**, certain athletic events (see quots.), as distinguished from events on the running-track; † **field-fight**, a fight in the open, a pitched battle; **field-fleck**, ? *nonce-wd.*, a 'spot' of land; **field-folk**, agricultural workers; † **field-foot**, ? the right foot (of a hawk); **field-fort** (see quot.); **field-fortification**, the constructing of field-works; also *concr.* a fieldwork; **field-geologist**, a geologist who studies by observation in the field; **field goal** esp. *N. Amer.* and *Austral.*, (*a*) in Football, a goal scored from the field of play; (*b*) in Basketball, a goal scored while the ball is in play; (*c*) in other games; **field-grey** [tr. G. *feldgrau*], the regulation colour of the uniform of a German infantryman; **field-gun** = *field-piece*; whence **field-gunner**; **field-hand**, (*a*) a slave who works on a plantation; (*b*) a farm-labourer; **field-hospital**, (*a*) a moving hospital; an ambulance; (*b*) a temporary hospital erected near a field of battle; **field-ice**, ice that floats in large tracts; **field ion microscope**, a device which works on the same principles as the field emission microscope but which uses ions produced at the surface of the emitter or in the gas near by in place of electrons; † **field-keeper**, a scarer of birds from cornfields; **field-kirk** (*Antiq.*; repr. O.E. *feldcirice*) a chapel or oratory in the fields; **field labourer** = *field-hand* (*b*); **field-lens** = FIELD-GLASS 3; **field-lore**, knowledge gained from the fields; **field-magnet** (see quot.); † **field-man**, one who lives or works in the fields, (*a*) a field labourer, a peasant, also *attrib.*; (*b*) a lover of field sports; † **field-mark**, a badge or mark for identification in the field; **field-master** (*Hunting*), master of the hounds; **field-monument** *Archæol.* (see quot. 1954); **field-net** *v.*, *trans.* to catch (ground game) with nets in the fields; **field-notes**, notes made in the field, *e.g.* by a surveyor, naturalist, etc.; **field-park**, 'the spare carriages, reserved supplies of ammunition, tools, etc. for the service of an army in the field' (Wilhelm *Mil. Dict.*); **field pattern**, the way in which the sensitivity or emitted power of a detector or emitter of waves (e.g. a microphone or an aerial) varies with direction; **field-piece**, a light cannon for use on a field of battle; † **field-place**, a level place, a plain; cf. FIELDY *a.*; **field-plot**, (*a*) a plan of a field or piece of land drawn to a scale; (*b*) a plot of land; † **field-pondage** (see quot.); **field-practice**, 'military practice in the open field' (Ogilv.); **field-ranger** (see quot.); whence, **field-ranging** *vbl. sb.*, *attrib.* (see quot.); **field-reeve** (see quots.); **field-regulator, -rheostat** (see quots.); **field-roller**, a roller drawn over a ploughed field to crush the clods and level the ground; † **field-room, -roomth**, open or unobstructed space; also *fig.*; † **field-sconce**, a detached earthwork; † **field-separation**, *collect.* in *Sc. Hist.* separatists who attend field-conventicles; **field-sequential system** *Television*, a system of colour television in which each of the successive fields composing the picture is of a single primary colour; **field-show** = *field-trial*; **field-sketching**, 'the art or act of sketching in plan rapidly, while in the field, the natural features of a country' (Cass.); **field spaniel**, a spaniel trained to retrieve; a variety of spaniel closely allied to but larger than the cocker; **field-sports**, outdoor sports, *esp.* hunting; † **field-staff** (see quots.); **field strength**, the intensity of an electric, magnetic, or other field; **field system** (see quot. 1915); cf. OPEN FIELD; † **field-teacher**, an instructor in military exercises; **field-telegraph**, one used in military operations; **field-test** *v. trans.*, to test in the field (sense 15 c); **field tile**, a tile used in the construction of a field-drain; **field train** (see quots.); **field-trial**, a trial in the open field, *esp.* of hunting-dogs; † **field-ware**, produce of the fields; the crops; **field-whore**, a 'very common whore' (Halliwell); **field-wife**, (*a*) *nonce-wd.* (see quot. and Gen. xxxiv. 1, 2); (*b*) = next; **field-woman**, a woman who works in the fields; cf. *field-man*; † **field-word**, a battle-cry, a watch-word. Also, FIELD-CONVENTICLE, FIELD-DAY, FIELD-MARSHAL, etc.

1833 *Penny Cycl.* I. 13/1 *Field-Abbots..were secular persons, upon whom the sovereign had bestowed certain abbeys, for which they were obliged to render military service. **1853** STOCQUELER *Milit. Encycl.*, Certain extra allowances are granted to them [officers], according to their several ranks, and these are denominated *field allowances. **1644** EVELYN *Mem.* (1857) I. 123 Two pieces of *field-artillery upon carriages. **1879** *Cassell's Techn. Educ.* III. 308 The broad distinction between the field-artillery and the garrison-artillery. **1771** MASKELYNE in *Phil. Trans.* LXI. 538 Let ENWS..represent the *field-bar of the telescope. **1825** J. NEAL *Bro. Jonathan* III. 42 A loose broken irregular line of ditch and parapet-*field batteries. **1834** J. S. MACAULAY *Treat. Field Fortif.* vi. 113 A field battery consists of a parapet pierced with embrasures, with epaulments on the flanks, and traverses..to cover the guns from enfilade fire. *Ibid.*, The artillery accompanying an army in the field are divided into batteries, also called field-batteries. **1875** tr. *Comte de Paris' Hist. Civ. War Amer.* I. 450 Several field-batteries erected in the vicinity of the arsenal. **1697** LUTTRELL *Brief Rel.* (1857) IV. 255 On Wensday next will be..a *feild battle. **1382** WYCLIF *Num.* xxxii. 26 Oure..*feeldbeestis, and howsbeestis we shulen leeue. **1660** R. COKE *Power & Subj.* 185 A freeman who hath Field-beasts valued at thirty pence, shall pay a Peter-peny. **1708** MOTTEUX *Rabelais, Pantag. Prognost.* v, One of those Worthy Persons will go nigh to be made a *Field-Bishop, and, mounted on a Horse that was foal'd of an Acorn, give the Passengers a Blessing with his Legs. **1932** C. L. HEWER *Rec. Adv. Anæsthesia* x. 102 *Infiltration analgesia*, or *field block, where the nerve endings are blocked at or near the site of operation. **1937** *Ibid.* (ed. 2) xii. 134 *Field blocking consists in creating walls of analgesia encircling the operative field. **1963** D. E. HALE *Anesthesiol.* (ed. 2) xiv. 431/1 Some procedures may be done under either local or field block, and in practice, they are often combined. **1905** E. J. C. SWAYSLAND *Boot & Shoe Design & Manuf.* vii. 120 The *field boot..may be fitted by several methods; they have usually a short strap down the front, reaching to the top edge of the tongue, and a back strip covering the back seam. **1926** T. E. LAWRENCE *Seven Pillars* VIII. xciii. 493 Dawnay ..was our best card, with his proved military reputation, exquisite field-boots, and air of well-dressed science. **1938** AUDEN & ISHERWOOD *On Frontier* 41 'If you're foolish enough,' they declare, 'to resist, You shall feel the full weight of fieldboot and fist.' **1969** R. T. WILCOX *Dict. Costume* 37 (*caption*) Leather field boot—English—1940's. **1535** COVERDALE *2 Kings* v. 19 He was gone from him a *felde bredth in the londe. —— *Gen.* xxxv. 16 Whan he was yet a *felde brode from Ephrath. **1865** CARLYLE *Fredk. Gt.* V. XIX. v. 505 With only *field-cannon. **1871** (*title*), Transactions of the Newbury District *Field Club. **1875** G. C. DAVIES (*title*), Rambles and Adventures of our School Field-Club. **1721** BAILEY, **Field colours.* **1812** A. PLUMTRE *Lichtenstein's Trav.* I. 67 *Field-cornet..a magistrate who decides in the first instance little disputes that arise among the colonists. **1863** W. C. BALDWIN *Afr. Hunting* 231, I was asked by a field-cornet what I had in my wagon. **1890** *Pall Mall G.* 20 Jan. 2/1 Her [the Dutch housewife's] brandy liqueur is the praise of the county—or rather the '*field-cornetcy.' **1684** J. PETER *Siege Vienna* 109 Long *Field-Culverin. **1706** *Lond. Gaz.* No. 4280 Messieurs Van Collen and Cuper, two of their High Mightinesses *Field-Deputies. **1874** KNIGHT *Dict. Mech.* I. 838/2 **Field-derrick*, one used for stacking hay in the field. **1535** COVERDALE *2 Chron.* xi. 15 He founded prestes to yᵉ hye places, & to *feldedeuels. **1884** *Syd. Soc. Lex.*, **Field-dressing.* **1826** CUSHING *Newburyport* 119 *Field Drivers, Moses Somerby, Charles Toppan. **1835** *Municip. Corp. 1st Rep.* App. IV. 2109 The Field Drivers [of Bedford] perform the duties of a hayward. **1860** BARTLETT *Americanisms, Field-driver*, a civil officer, whose duty it is to take up and impound swine, cattle, sheep, horses, etc. going at large in the public highways [etc.]. **1888** BRYCE *Amer. Commw.* II. II. xlviii. 229 Hog reeves (now usually called field drivers). **1953** DACEY & ROSS in *Proc. Inst. Radio Engin.* XLI. 970 (*heading*) Unipolar '*field-effect' transistor. *Ibid.*, The 'field-effect' transistor was first proposed by W. Shockley. **1955** —— in *Bell Syst. Techn. Jrnl.* XXXIV. 1150 In essence, a field-effect transistor can be regarded as a structure containing a semi-conducting current path, the conductivity of which is modulated by the application of a transverse electric field. **1970** J. EARL *Tuners & Amplifiers* ii. 33 Trend is towards field effect transistors in the f.m. front-end. **1928** *Proc. R. Soc.* A. CXIX. 173 As the higher temperatures, at which ordinary thermionic emission begins, are approached, the strong *field emission does become sensitive to temperature and finally blends into the thermionic. **1951** *Bell Syst. Techn. Jrnl.* Oct. 910 (*heading*) Description of field emission microscope tube. **1965** *New Scientist* 17 June 781/1 Field-emission diodes could prove very useful at microwave frequencies if they were placed in a superconducting cavity. **1965** PHILLIPS & WILLIAMS *Inorg. Chem.* I. x. 374 In recent years the use of the Field Emission microscope and the Field Ion microscope has shown that diffusion at the surface of metals is considerable at temperatures as low as 0·2T_m. **1922** E. P. ADAMS tr. *Einstein's Meaning Relativity* 52 Repeated application of the *field equations. **1923** J. RICE *Relativity* iv. 95 So strong, however, was the impulse towards making the field equations as alike as possible for all observers..that these values for the moving observer were not regarded with any great favour. **1924** H. L. BROSE tr. *M. Born's Einstein's Theory Relativity* v. 154 Maxwell's 'field equations', as they are called, constitute a true theory of contiguous action or action by contact, for..they give a finite velocity of propagation for electro-magnetic forces. **1955** W. PAULI *Niels Bohr* 34 We assume..for the sake of simplicity the *local* character of the field equation, which means that all field quantities are spinors or tensors of finite rank. **1959** *Listener* 27 Aug. 320/3 The steady-state cosmological theory ..modifies Einstein's field equations. **1899** *Windsor Mag.* IX. 243/1 Irishmen..have established a monopoly in what are described as *field events of late years. **1912** E. H. RYLE *Athletics* 19 'Field events' (*i.e.*, long-, high- and pole-jumping, weight-putting, hammer- and discus-throwing, and hurdling). **1950** *Oxf. Jun. Encycl.* IX. 35/1 *Field Events*. .. This department of athletic sports includes the Long and High Jumps, the Hop, Step, and Jump, Pole Vaulting, Putting the Weight, and Throwing the Discus, the Javelin, and the Hammer. **1955** R. BANNISTER *First Four Minutes* v. 60 To raise the standard of British athletic achievement, particularly in field events. **1600** HOLLAND *Livy* 129 Rather a competent guard for defence of the campe, then a sufficient power to maintain a *field-fight. **1653** H. MORE *Antid. Ath.* III. xii. (1712) 124 Field-fights and sea-fights seen in the Air. **1892** MISS J. BARLOW *Irish Idylls* iii. 32 A meagre *field-fleck and a ramshackle shanty on the hill's wan grey slope. **1886** W. MORRIS tr. *Æneids* VII. 204 Calling to aid the hardy hearts of *field-folk there-about. **1891** HARDY *Tess* II. xxxii. 149 The fatalistic convictions common to field-folk and those who associate more extensively with natural phenomena than with their fellow-creatures. **1681** *Lond. Gaz.* No. 1610/4 Lost..a Tarsell Gentle with..the hind Pounce of the *Field-Foot lost. **1775** ASH, **Field-fort*, a fort towards the field; a fort thrown up in a field. **1851** J. S. MACAULAY *Field Fortification* 6 Those..only wanted for periods not exceeding one or two campaigns..are termed **Field Fortifications.* **1902** *Chicago Record-Herald* 28 Sept. 2/3 A try for a *field goal was made, but..the kick was easily blocked. **1906** *Off. Bk. Rules Govt. Game of Basketball 1906–1907* 13 Flint..has tallied the most field goals. **1947** *Redbook* Oct. 56/3 No man with a bum leg could kick a field goal from the 37-yard line with the wind against him. **1961** J. S. SALAK *Dict. Amer. Sports* 158 *Field goal* (basketball), a basket scored from the floor; has a value of two points. *Field goal* (bowling), on a two split, to send the ball between the pins hitting neither of them. *Field goal* (football), placekicking or dropkicking ball between uprights and over opponent's cross-bar from scrimmage without touching ground or teammate. Three points. **1969** *Eugene* (Oreg.) *Register-Guard* 3 Dec. 1D/6 Shooting: Field goals, 45·3%. **1969** *Sun-Herald* (Sydney) 13 July 36/2 Williams was set up for a field goal on the fourth tackle but his kick was wide and the ball went dead. **1970** *Globe & Mail* (Toronto) 28 Sept. 18/2 Ivan MacMillan converted both Oldham touchdowns and added a 12-yard single on a wide field goal attempt. **1970** *Washington Post* 30 Sept. D4/3 Shugars..has directed the team to just three touchdowns and a field goal. **1915** *Sphere* 17 Apr. 59/2 The men in *field grey tramped past him towards the Aisne. **1929** W. F. MORRIS (*title*) Bretherton, khaki or field-grey? **1828** J. M. SPEARMAN *Brit. Gunner* 179 The detachments for the service of heavy ordnance are told off and numbered in precisely the same manner as for *field-guns. **1907** *Westm. Gaz.* 16 May 7/2 The men of the 'Victory'..give field-gun displays. **1826** *Deb. Congress U.S.* 25 June (1832) 3758/2 The price of labor, *fields [*sic*] hands, from eighty to one hundred and twenty dollars per annum and found. **1835** J. H. INGRAHAM *South-West* II. 254 The third and lowest class consists of those slaves who are termed 'field-hands'. **1845** F. DOUGLASS *Life* (1846) 58, I was now for the first time in my life a field hand. **1856** OLMSTED *Slave States* 46 Able-bodied field-hands were hired out..at the rate of one hundred dollars a year. **1879** FROUDE *Cæsar* ix. 91 These slaves were not ignorant field hands. **1701** *Lond. Gaz.* No. 3713/3 Their *Field-Hospital is arrived here. **1869** E. A. PARKES *Pract. Hygiene* (ed. 3) 635 Movable field hospitals.. to be made of tents. **1796** MORSE *Amer. Geog.* II. 13 The *field-ice is of two or three fathoms thickness. **1875** BEDFORD *Sailor's Pocket-bk.* iv. (ed. 2) 118 The limits of field-ice in March extend from Newfoundland to the Southward as far as 42° N. latitude. **1952** *Sci. Abstr.* A. Mar. 216/1 (*heading*) The *field ion microscope. **1967** *New Scientist* 20 July 134/1 The importance of the field-ion microscope lies in its ability to depict the positions and

arrangement of the individual atoms of a solid surface. **1620** MARKHAM *Farew. Husb.* (1625) 95 If your *Field-keeper.. doe vse to shoot off a Musket, or Harquebush, the report thereof will appeare more terrible to these enemies of corne. **1772** T. SIMPSON *Vermin Killer* 19 Field-keepers are necessary just before the corn is ripe. *a* **1035** *Laws Cnut, Eccl.* IX. iii. (Thorpe), *Feld-cirice, pær leᵹer-stow ne siᵹ, mid þrittiᵹum scillingum. **1857** MRS. GASKELL *C. Bronte* (1860) 4 It is probable that there existed on this ground a field-kirk.. in the earliest times. **1853** MRS. STOWE *Key to Uncle Tom's C.* 17/1 We ask.. whether this does not show that this poor *field-labourer had.. a true mother's heart? **1860** J. S. C. ABBOTT *South & North* 279 A little handful of slaveholders may be exempted from paying wages to.. their field-laborers. **1837** GORING & PRITCHARD *Microgr.* 207 The said slider-holder, with its *field-lens. **1883** *Phil. Mag.* XVI. 144 The intensity of a powerful magnetic field, such as that in the space in which the armature-coils of a dynamo move between the poles of the *field-magnets. **1891** S. P. THOMPSON *Dynamo-El. Mach.* (ed. 4) 2 Every dynamo.. consists of two essential parts, a *field-magnet*, usually a massive stationary structure of iron surrounded by coils of insulated copper wire, and an *armature*.. The function of the field-magnet is to provide a *magnetic field* of great extent and intensity. *c* **1440** *Secrees* 154 Wylde letus pat *feldmen clepyn skarioles. **14..** *Voc.* in Wr.-Wülcker 692 *Hec rustica*, a feldman wyfe. *c* **1475** *Babees Bk.* (1868) 7 Kutte nouhte youre mete eke as it were Felde men. *c* **1575** *Balfour's Practicks* (1754) 536 Feild-men quha has mair nor four ky. **1811** SIR P. WARWICK in Hone *Every-day Bk.* II. 146 He was.. a laborious hunter, or field-man. **1689–90** *Proc. agst. French* in *Select. Harl. Misc.* (1793) 478 A detachment.. landed.. the *field-mark being matches about their left arms. **1680** *Lond. Gaz.* No. 1525/4 A brown bay Gelding.. a Field mark of Tar on the Hip. **1893** *Daily Tel.* 14 Nov. 5/5 Lord Robert Manners.. was acting as *field-master. **1937** *Proc. Prehist. Soc.* III. 266 The care of *field-monuments in the Free State is entrusted to the Office of Public Works. **1954** S. PIGGOTT *Neolithic Cultures* ii. 17 The field monuments of the culture fall into three classes,.. earthwork enclosures.. flint mines.. long barrows. **1890** J. WATSON *Confess. Poacher* v. 62 In *field-netting rabbits, lurchers are equally quick. **1786** WASHINGTON *Diaries* (1925) III. 84 His assistant who had his *field notes.. had not returned. **1806** *Deb. 9th Congr. U.S.* 2nd Sess. 1002 He was retained as a necessary assistant to the principal surveyor in copying field notes. **1841** C. CIST *Cincinnati* 152 From these field-notes, the plats, or maps.. are prepared. **1849** *President's Message Congress* II. 572 United States geological survey of public lands in Michigan—Field notes. **1958** BANNERMAN *Birds Brit. Isles* VII. 210 There have been no recent field-notes published on this species. **1961** *Amer. Speech* XXXVI. 201 Numerous allophonic variations, the accurate transmission of which from informant to fieldworker to field notes.. produces certain problems in communication. **1875** G. P. COLLEY in *Encycl. Brit.* II. 579/2 All tools and implements for a company of engineers, and a '*field-park'. **1936** *Jrnl. R. Aeronaut. Soc.* XL. 191 The radiated field pattern should therefore remain constant from day to day. There was no evidence whatsoever that atmospheric conditions had any effect on the *field patterns. **1962** A. NISBETT *Technique Sound Studio* 265 *Polar characteristic, polar diagram* (Am.: field pattern), the response of a microphone, loudspeaker, etc., showing sensitivity (or volume of sound) in relation to direction. **1590** J. SMYTHE *Concern. Weapons* 35 And the next day he entered the towne and brought in foure and twentie *field peeces. **1863** KINGLAKE *Crimea* (1876) I. xiv. 276 A couple of field-pieces stood pointed towards the barricade. **1382** WYCLIF *Luke* vi. 17 Jhesu.. stood in a *feeld place. **1659** *Burton's Diary* (1828) IV. 470 All original maps, *field-plots, and field books. **1884** *Mag. Art* Mar. 215/2 The velvety green of spring-watered field-plots. **1612** STURTEVANT *Metallica* (1854) 96 *Field-pondage, is a kind of Pipeage, which.. conueigheth.. water into seuerall pastures.. and fields, and.. leaueth a pond of water for cattle and beasts to drink in. **1885** *Pall Mall G.* 17 June 6/1 '*Field Rangers' is a term applied to 'speculative builders' of the lowest class. **1892** *Labour Commission* Gloss., **Field-ranging Houses*, hastily and badly built structures erected on the outskirts of all large towns and cities by 'jerry-builders'. **1617** *Nottingham Rec.* IV. 354 Ouerseers of the feild or *Field Reeues. **1881** *2nd Suppl. Cumbrld. Gloss.*, *Field Reeve*, a person having charge of a stinted pasture belonging to different owners. **1919** W. H. MARCHANT *Wireless Telegr.* (ed. 2) 297 *Field Regulator. A variable resistance forming part of the field circuit of a motor or a dynamo. **1924** *Harmsworth's Wireless Encycl.* 918/2 A field regulator is a device for varying the strength of the field magnets in a dynamo or electric motor. *Ibid.* 919/1 From the wireless point of view, the chief use of field regulators is to provide a convenient means for regulating the charging rate of a dynamo used to recharge accumulators. **1910** *Hawkins' Electr. Dict.*, **Field Rheostat*, an adjustable resistance used to vary the strength of the magnetic field of a shunt wound dynamo or motor. **1943** *Gloss. Terms Electr. Engin. (B.S.I.)* 55 *Field rheostat* (*field regulator*), a rheostat arranged for varying, at will, the current in the field winding of a machine. **1607** ROWLANDS *Famous Hist.* 48 We will not make our prison in this place, As long as there is *field-room to be got. **1612** DRAYTON *Poly-olb.* xii. 204 Falling backe where they Might field-roomth find at large, their ensignes to display. **1672** DRYDEN *Conq. Granada* IV. i, Which Hearts, for want of Field-room, cannot bear. **1673** —— *Marr. a-la-mode* II. i, It is tolerable when a man has field-room to run from it. **1950** *Sci. Amer.* Dec. 14/2 The '*field-sequential' system developed by the engineers of the Columbia Broadcasting System is perhaps the simplest of the three. **1957** *Encycl. Brit.* XXI. 912N/2 Presenting the colours in such rapid succession to the eye that persistence of vision merges them into a single sense impression. The last method is employed in the field-sequential system. **1688** CAPT. J. S. *Fortification* 123 *Field-Skonces, and others Forts with Ramparts. **1680** G. HICKES *Spirit of Popery* Pref. 1 Scottish-Nonconformists, especially those of the *Field-Separation. **1851** J. S. MACAULAY *Field Fortif.* 245 It is presumed that the beginner in *field-sketching has already learned to copy plans. **1867** 'STONEHENGE' *Dogs Brit. Isl.* 36 *Field Spaniels... The heavy, large-eared, well-feathered, short-legged 'field-spaniels', have been known for years as 'springers'. **1897** *Encycl. Sport* I. 319/2 There are four varieties of field spaniels,.. the Clumber, the Sussex, the Black, and the any-other-colour. **1960** *Times* 2 Jan. 9/3 Two varieties now much in a minority are the Sussex and field spaniels. **1674** *Essex Papers* (Camden) I. 210 *Field sports, of wᶜʰ I have ever bin a Lover. **1814** SCOTT *Wav.* iv, Field-sports.. the chief pleasure of his own youthful days. **1721** BAILEY, **Field staff*, a Staff carried by Gunners, in which they skrew lighted Matches. **1847** CRAIG, *Field-staff*, a weapon carried by gunners, about the length of a halberd, with a spear at the end, having on each side ears screwed on, like the cock of a matchlock, where lighted matches are contained when the gunners are on command. **1896** D. C. & J. P. JACKSON *Alternating Currents* xiv. 574 If the *field strength of a motor is so adjusted that the values of the impressed and counter pressures are equal.. then when the motor is switched on.. it will fall back in phase with respect to the impressed pressure, sufficiently to permit the proper load current to pass through the armature. **1946** *Nature* 7 Sept. 332/2 If the field-strength inside the dielectric exceeds a critical value, the insulation breaks down. **1962** F. I. ORDWAY et al. *Basic Astronautics* iv. 164 Sunspot field strengths up to several thousand gauss have been observed. **1915** H. L. GRAY *Eng. Field Syst.* 3 The term '*field system' signifies the manner in which the inhabitants of a township subdivided and tilled their arable, meadow, and pasture land. **1935** *Proc. Prehist. Soc.* I. 10 The archaeological investigation of ancient field-systems. **1962** H. R. LOYN *Anglo-Saxon England* i. 18 The agrarian inheritance in the shape of methods and field-systems was far from negligible from Roman villa to Saxon village. **1623** BINGHAM *Compar. Rom. & Mod. Warres* X ij b, Where are our *Field-teachers? Where is our daily meditation of Armes? **1874** KNIGHT *Dict. Mech.* I. 839/1 The *field-telegraph of the German army consists of [etc.]. **1875** G. P. COLLEY in *Encycl. Brit.* II. 597/2 The field telegraph detachments.. are trained in peace time to everything connected with telegraphy. **1950** in *Amer. Speech* (1956) XXXI. 210 The results were *field tested in the Yukon. **1961** *Times* 15 Aug. 13/5 At present N.C.R. are field-testing their prototype scanner at a chain store. **1970** *Computers & Humanities* IV. 323 To field-test and perfect the DOVACK Model for effectiveness, adaptability, and economic feasibility. **1958** J. S. SCOTT *Dict. Civil Engin.* 138 *Field tile. **1965** G. J. WILLIAMS *Econ. Geol. N.Z.* xx. 364/2 Similar deposits [of clay].. are used for making bricks, field-tiles and refractories at Kamo. **1816** C. JAMES *Milit. Dict.* s.v. *Train*, **Field-train*, a body of men consisting chiefly of commissaries and conductors of stores, which belong to the Royal Artillery. **1864** BURTON *Scot Abr.* I. iv. 156 A field-train of unusual strength for those times. **1562** J. HEYWOOD *Prov. & Epigr.* (1867) 75 *Feelde ware might sinke or swym. **1750** ELLIS *Mod. Husbandm.* II. ii. 136 The farmer's corn, and other of his field ware. *c* **1475** *Pict. Voc.* in Wr.-Wülcker 794 *Hec rustica*, a *fyld-wyfe. **1591** H. SMITH *Prep. Marriage* 35 Not a street-wife, like Thamar, nor a field-wife, like Dinah; but a house-wife. **1891** T. HARDY *Tess* I. 171 A field-man is a personality afield; a *field-woman is a portion of the field. **1645** in Rushw. *Hist. Coll.* (1701) IV. I. 42 The *Field-word for the King was *Queen Mary*: For the Parliament *God our Strength*. *a* **1693** URQUHART *Rabelais* III. x. 83 *Apollo* was the Field-word in the.. Day of that Fight.

field (fiːld), *v.* [f. prec. sb.]

1. *intr.* To go into the field (see FIELD *sb.* 2); of a pigeon: To obtain its food from the field.

1868 DARWIN *Anim. & Pl.* II. 32 Highly improved breeds of the pigeon will not 'field' or search for their own food.

2. *trans.* **a.** To leave (corn) in the field to harden. **b.** *transf.* To expose (malt-wash or gyle in casks) to the action of the air and sun to promote oxidation.

1844 *Jrnl. R. Agric. Soc.* V. I. 267 [The oats] after being well fielded, were thrashed immediately.

†**3. a.** *intr.* To 'take the field' (see FIELD *sb.* 7); to fight. **b.** *trans.* To fight with. *Obs.*

1529 LYNDESAY *Compl.* 355 And feildit vther, in land and burgh. **1535** STEWART *Cron. Scot.* II. 598 How King Malcolme and the Danis feildit agane. **1536** BELLENDEN *Cron. Scot.* (1821) I. 135 It was defendit.. to feild the Romanis with plane battall. **1590** SPENSER *F.Q.* II. vi. 29 Who, soone prepard to field, his sword forth drew.

4. *intr.* To bet on the field (see FIELD *sb.* 10 a) against the favourite.

1886 *Daily News* 4 June 3/3 A marked disposition to 'field' on the Grand Prize of Paris. **1890** *Ibid.* 19 June 6/1 The professionals fielded staunchly.

5. a. *intr.* To act as fielder in base-ball, cricket, etc. **b.** *trans.* To stop and return (the ball).

1823 *Lady's Mag.* July 390/2 How well we fielded! **1824** MISS MITFORD *Village* Ser. I. (1863) 41 Batting, bowling, and fielding, as if for life. **1833** J. NYREN *Young Cricketer's Tutor* 48 The fieldsman.. should not wait and let the ball come to him, but dash in to meet it, fielding it with his right hand. **1880** S. LAKEMAN *What I saw in Kaffir-Land* 57 They fielded for the cannon-shot.. as though they were cricket-balls. **1883** *Daily Tel.* 21 Aug., The ball being sharply fielded at cover-point. *Mod.* Well fielded, Sir!

c. *to field out*: to be or remain in the field as a fieldsman or as the fielding side.

1888 R. H. LYTTELTON in Steel & Lyttelton *Cricket* vi. 280 An eleven that is really A1 in fielding very rarely has to field out for 300 runs. **1921** P. F. WARNER *My Cricketing Life* xii. 225 He hated fielding, and had no wish to field out the whole summer! **1944** BLUNDEN *Cricket Country* 11 Someone was bowling, someone batting, the rest fielding out.

d. *fig.* To deal with (a succession of items), 'catch', 'pick up'.

1902 *Daily Chron.* 2 Sept. 3/1, I would get an agile and hard-skinned man to field the novels as they come. **1908** *Ibid.* 20 Apr. 4/6 From Good Friday to the following Tuesday, if you stay in London, you have to field splashes of paint and skirt ladders. **1909** *Ibid.* 18 Nov. 4/6 The Correctors of the Press are demanding the proper consideration of men who field the mistakes of careless writers. **1969** *Morning Star* 11 Oct. 5/7 A man who has just emerged from two years in solitary confinement cannot be expected to field rapid fire questions from the Press.

6. *trans. Games.* To select (a team or an individual) to play; to put into the field.

1922 *Daily Mail* 1 Dec. 11 The F.A. played four professionals in the defence, but fielded an amateur forward line. *Ibid.* 6 Dec. 12 North Midlands hope to field a powerful fifteen in to-day's match v. Warwickshire. **1925** *Times* 12 June 7/1 It would have been rather futile to field the remnants of the M.C.C.'s Australian team when its leading batsmen.. were not available. **1927** *Morn. Post* 24 Oct. 13/3 The Oxford side fielded against the United Services was a more workmanlike lot. **1948** *Evening Standard* 28 Apr., The Australians are fielding their strongest team. **1955** *Times* 3 Aug. 3/7 Even more significantly, the British side fielded an unfit hooker. **1962** *Listener* 11 Oct. 586/1 The Swedes fielded a new pair in the first half [of a bridge championship].

fieldage (ˈfiːldɪdʒ). *rare.* [f. as prec. + -AGE.] (See quot.)

1880 *Jersey Weekly Press* 23 Oct. 21/6 The fieldage or twelfth sheaf.. upon a portion of land situate on the said fief.

ˈfield-bed.

1. A portable or folding bed chiefly for use in the field; a camp or trestle bedstead.

1580 HOLLYBAND *Treas. Fr. Tong.*, *Lict de camp*, a fielde bed. *c* **1590** GREENE *Fr. Bacon* v. 10 A fair field-bed with a canopy. **1709** STRYPE *Ann. Ref.* I. lv. 604 The Spanyard.. made his brags, that he had turned the English ensigns into Spanish field-beds. **1728** DE FOE *Capt. Carleton* (1841) 33 He ordered his field-bed to be put up near the powder.

2. A bed in the open field or upon the ground.

1592 SHAKS. *Rom. & Jul.* II. i. 40 Ile to my truckle bed, This Field bed is to cold for me to sleepe. **1645** G. DANIEL *Poems* Wks. 1878 II. 42 The night is fled, and Daye's best Chorister Kickes his feild-Bed with Scorne. **1754** A. MURPHY *Gray's-Inn Jrnl.* No. 100 He was making his Brags that he had been in a Field-bed with a young Lady, whose Brother was present.

attrib. **1599** MASSINGER, etc. *Old Law* IV. ii, A 'strumpet' and a 'whore'.. And such fine field-bed words.

ˈfield-book.

1. A book for use in the field.

a. The book in which a land-surveyor notes down the measurements as taken in the field.

1616 A. RATHBORNE *Surveyor* 136 The order of making of a necessary and fitting Field-booke. **1685** PETTY *Will* p. vii, Maps and field-books, the copies of the Downe-survey. **1777** *Barmby Inclos. Act* 9 A proper field book of the said town-ship. **1807** HUTTON *Course Math.* II. 64 Enter the measures in a field-book.

b. A botanist's or naturalist's book for preserving collected specimens while in the field.

1848 W. GARDINER *Flora of Forfarshire* 56 To preserve good specimens, the collector would require to be provided with a field-book. **1849** BALFOUR *Man. Bot.* §1229 (1855) 659.

2. (See quot.)

1853 LYTTON *My Novel* III. xxix, My great-grandfather kept a Field-Book, in which were entered.. the names of all the farmers, and the quantity of land they held.

ˌfield-conˈventicle. An open-air religious meeting. See CONVENTICLE 4 c.

1678 MARVELL *Corr.* ccclxi. Wks. 1872–5 II. 631 They [the Scots] still continue their.. field conventicles. *a* **1715** [see CONVENTICLE *sb.* 4 c]. *a* **1806** C. J. FOX *Hist.* 129 The punishment of death.. had formerly attached upon the preachers at field conventicles only.

transf. **1711** SHAFTESB. *Charac.* (1737) I. 21 If we had.. grave officers and judges, erected to restrain poetical licence.. we shou'd have field-conventicles of lovers and poets.

Hence **ˌfield-conˈventicle** *v.*, *intr.*, to frequent or hold field-conventicles. **ˌfield-conˈventicler**, one who attends or frequents field-conventicles.

1680 G. HICKES *Spirit of Popery* Pref. 3 They [the Scotch] began to Field-Conventicle. *Ibid.* 67 *Jus populi vindicatum*, and *Naphthali* are the Pocket-books of the Field-Conventiclers. **1687** *Lond. Gaz.* No. 2221/1 Those Enemies of Christianity as well as Government and Humane Society, The Field-Conventiclers.

ˈfield-ˌday.

1. a. *Mil.* A day on which troops are drawn up for exercise in field evolutions; a military review.

1747 *Scheme Equip. Men of War* 32 These periodical Intervals of eating and drinking.. are to the Citizens as it were Field Days, for improving.. their Valour. **1832** *Regul. Instr. Cavalry* III. 62 Almost every movement at a Field Day should be followed by an Advance in Line. **1869** E. A. PARKES *Pract. Hygiene* (ed. 3) 624 Our present field-days represent the very acme and culminating point of war.

b. *transf.* and *fig.* A day occupied with brilliant or exciting events; a time of great opportunity or success.

1827 CREEVEY *Let.* 26 Mar. (1934) II. xiii. 236 Saturday was a considerable field day in Arlington Street,.. and a very merry jolly dinner and evening we had. **1848** THACKERAY *Bk. Snobs* xx, The mean pomp and ostentation which distinguish our banquets on grand field-days. **1855** BAGEHOT *Coll. Works* (1965) I. 313 A 'field-day' controversy is a fine thing. **1857** HUGHES *Tom Brown* II. viii, This terrible field-day passed over without any severe visitations in the shape of punishments. **1864** KNIGHT *Passages Work. Life* I. i. 209 Thursday.. is to be a great field-day in the Commons. **1925** E. F. NORTON *Fight for Everest: 1924* II. 45 The two experts, who had for days been working every afternoon, and often late into the night, put in a regular field-day. **1953** A. HUXLEY *Let.* 8 Dec. (1969) 689 Industrial agriculture is having a field day in the million acres of barren plain now irrigated. **1969** *New Yorker* 12 Apr. 98/2 The human-factors men have been having a field day with it.

2. A day spent in the field.

a. *Hunting.* A day on which the hunt meets.

1823 BYRON *Juan* XIII. cviii, Sometimes a dance (though rarely on field days, For then the gentlemen were rather tired).

b. 'A day when explorations, scientific investigations, etc., as of a society, are carried on in the field' (*Cent. Dict.*).

*a***1878** G. G. SCOTT *Recoll.* (1879) viii. 354 We had a delightful field-day in the abbey.

fielded ('fi:ldɪd), *ppl. a.* [f. FIELD *v.* + -ED[1].]

1. Engaged in a field of battle; fighting in the open field, as opposed to 'protected by a fort'.

1607 SHAKS. *Cor.* I. iv. 12 We with smoaking swords may march from hence To helpe our fielded Friends. **1808** J. BARLOW *Columb.* v. 760 Untrench'd..they dare oppose Their fielded cohorts to the forted foes.

2. *Cricket.* Of a ball: Stopped and returned from the field. Also *transf.*

1884 ANSTEY *Giant's Robe* xxxviii, 'I can hold on till the night itself, Bertie, my boy!' with a cleverly fielded yawn. *Mod.* That was a well fielded ball!

3. *Furniture.* Of a panel (see quot. 1940).

1900 in *Eng. Dial. Dict.* **1940** *Chambers's Techn. Dict.* 331/1 *Fielded panel*, a panel which is moulded, sunk, or raised, or is divided into smaller panels. **1952** J. GLOAG *Short Dict. Furnit.* 254 *Fielded panel*, a cabinet-making term that describes a panel with the central space raised so that it projects slightly beyond the surface of its frame. **1961** *Times* 13 Feb. 14/5 The 14 doors have fielded up leather covered panels with enrichments in gilt.

†**'fielden**, *a.* and *sb. Obs.* Also **fieldon(e.** [f. FIELD *sb.* + -EN[4].] **A.** *adj.*

1. Level and open.

1604 EDMONDS *Observ. Cæsar's Comm.* 110 Footemen are not onely of importance in fielden countries, but are necesrarie also in mountenous or woodie places. **1669** WORLIDGE *Syst. Agric.* (1681) 15 Wheat in the Fielden Country is subject to Mildews.

2. Consisting of fields.

1623 FAVINE *Theat. Hon.* III. ii. 336 The whole Uniuersitie being then a fielden and woodie Wildernesse.

3. Of, pertaining to, or characteristic of the field (see FIELD *sb.* 2); rural, rustic.

1620 tr. *Boccaccio's Decameron* 161 Of a fielden clownish lout he would needs now become a judge of beauty. **1620** BRINSLEY *Virgil* 58/2 Now will I meditate a fielden Muse (viz. a pastorall song) with my slender reed. **1623** FAVINE *Theat. Hon.* VII. xiii. 271 With Fagot-sticks they erected a poore Fielden Lodging.

B. *absol.* or *sb.* Field land.

1621–51 BURTON *Anat. Mel.* II. ii. III. 261 Our Townes are generally bigger in the woodland than the fieldone. **1649** BLITHE *Eng. Improv. Impr.* (1653) 15 Those that use to fetch their seed out of Chilterne into other parts or Countries of the Fieldon. **1712** J. MORTON *Nat. Hist. Northampt.* 7 Tillage-land, or Fielden.

fielder ('fi:ldə(r)). [f. FIELD *sb.* and *v.* + -ER[1].]

†**1.** One who works in the field (see FIELD *sb.* 4). *Obs.*

1393 LANGL. *P. Pl.* C. XVIII. 103 Folke boþe sowers [*v.r.* felders] and shupmen.

2. *Sporting.* One who backs the field against the favourite.

1844 *Spirit of Times* 6 Apr. 67 The reliance of the 'fielders' was undoubtedly Norma. **1853** WHYTE MELVILLE *Digby Grand* I. vi, I accommodate a vociferous fielder with six to four in hundreds. **1867** 'OUIDA' *Under Two Flags* I. iii. 46 Taking long odds with the fielders. **1969** *Australian* 24 May 35/3 It appears that the fielders consider the Bernborough Handicap will be dominated by this trio.

3. *Cricket* and *Baseball.* = FIELDSMAN.

1832 P. EGAN *Bk. Sports* 346/1 A bowler and fielder of very great use. **1912** A. A. LILLEY *Twenty-four Years Cricket* iv. 45 A magnificent fielder in the slips.

fieldfare ('fi:ldfɛə(r)). Forms: 1 feldeware, 4–7 feld(e)fare, (4 feldyfare, feldifer, 5–7 fel(e)fare, 6 feldifair, 7 felfar, feldefer, veldefare, 8 feldifire, 9 fell-fare, *dial.* felverd), 7– fieldfare. [ME. *feldefare* (4 syll. in Chaucer):—? OE. **feldefare* (miswritten *feldewar*, only once occurring). Of obscure formation; app. it means 'field-goer', f. *feld* FIELD + *far-* (see FARE *v.*); but the presence of the middle syllable is not accounted for, and this, with the divergent spelling in the OE. gloss, suggests possibility of corruption from popular etymology.

Not related to OE. *feala-, feolufor*, of unknown origin, in glosses rendering *onocrotalus* (pelican), *porphyrio* (some water-bird), and *torax* (of unknown meaning). This must have been the name of some *large* bird.]

A species of Thrush (*Turdus pilaris*), well known as a regular and common autumnal visitor throughout the British Islands.

*a***1100** *Voc.* in Wr.-Wülcker 287 *Scorellus*, clodhamer and feldeware. *c***1325** *Gloss.* in *Rel. Ant.* II. 78 The feldefare, *la greue.* *c***1350** *Will. Palerne* 183 Fesauns & feldfares. *c***1381** CHAUCER *Parl. Foules* 364 The frosty feldefare. *c***1450** HOLLAND *Howlat* 228 The Feldifer in the forest. **1562** TURNER *Herbal* II. 25 a, At the tyme of yeare the feldefares fede only of Iuniper berries the people Eate the feldefares undrawen. **1634** T. JOHNSON *Parey's Chirurg.* XXV. xxii. (1678) 621 It feeds on pepper, as the..Felfars with us do upon Ivy-berries. *a***1670** HACKET *Abp. Williams* I. (1692) 82 Such long wing'd hawks were not to be cast of to fly after field-fares. **1694** *Acct. Sweden* 7 Small Birds..of the bigness of Veldefares. **1785** COWPER *Needless Alarm* 20 Berries.. With which the field-fare, wintry guest, is fed. **1810** SCOTT *Lady of L.* III. v, The fieldfare framed her lowly nest. **1852** M. ARNOLD *Poems, Tristram & Iseult*, Hollies..With scarlet berries gemm'd, the fell-fare's food.

attrib. **1681** CHETHAM *Angler's Vade-m.* xxxv. §3 (1689) 227 The Feather of a Felfare quill.

b. *Proverb.* (See FAREWELL *int.* 2 b.)

*c***1374**, *c***1400** [see FAREWELL]. **1560** ROLLAND *Crt. Venus* IV. 718 Gude nicht now feldifair, Fair on fond fuill.

fieldful ('fi:ldfʊl). [f. FIELD *sb.* + -FUL.] As much as will grow in a field.

1889 *Cornh. Mag.* July 51 A single frost will turn a whole fieldful black.

'field-glass. [f. FIELD *sb.* + GLASS.]

1. A binocular telescope for use in the field. Now usu. in *pl.*

1836 WELLINGTON *Let.* 8 Oct. in Stanhope *Conversations*, I send you one of my field-glasses. **1880** OUIDA *Moths* I. 20 A prolonged gaze through a friend's field-glass. **1888** *Century Mag.* XXXVI. 211/1 A minute examination, with the field-glasses, of all the neighboring mountain. **1911** M. CORELLI *Life Everlasting* vii. 142 Mr. Harland was.. searching for his field-glasses. **1932** *Discovery* Oct. 330/2 The meter reading is recorded by observations carried out with powerful field glasses. **1963** A. SMITH *Throw out Two Hands* xv. 155 Through field-glasses one looks for shapes, and shapes are therefore recognized.

2. 'A small achromatic telescope, usually from 20 to 24 inches long, and having from three to six joints' (Ogilv.).

3. That one of the two lenses forming the eyepiece of an astronomical telescope or compound microscope, which is the nearer to the object glass.

1831 BREWSTER *Optics* xli. 340 A larger lens than any of the other two, called the field-glass. **1867** J. HOGG *Microsc.* I. ii. 40 An amplifying lens by which the field of view is enlarged ..is..called a field-glass.

fielding, *sb. dial.* [f. FIELD *sb.* + ? -ING[1]; but cf. FIELDEN.] (See quot.)

1847 *Jrnl. R. Agric. Soc.* VIII. II. 265 The north-west sandy districts or fieldings.

fielding ('fi:ldɪŋ), *vbl. sb.* [f. FIELD *v.* + -ING[1].]

1. The action of the vb. FIELD.

a. The action or process of exposing corn, malt, etc. to the action of the air. Also *attrib.*

1848 *Jrnl. R. Agric. Soc.* IX. II. 501 The wheat is harvested much greener..Six or seven days is as much fielding as is usually given. **1875** URE *Dict. Arts* III. 1076 When fielding is resorted to [in making vinegar], it must be commenced in the spring months..The fielding method requires a much larger extent of space..than the stoving process.

†**b.** The action of taking the field or fighting.

1526 in Pitcairn *Crim. Trials* I. 237* Ffor.. Insurrectioune and Feilding aganis Johne Duke of Albany.

c. *Cricket* and *Baseball.* The action of stopping or recovering and returning the ball.

1823 *Lady's Mag.* July 391/1 John Strong did very well; his length told in fielding. **1859** *All Year Round* No. 13. 306 Their fielding was first-rate. **1862** J. PYCROFT *Cricket Tutor* 81 Long-stopping requires clean fielding. **1884** H. C. BUNNER in *Harper's Mag.* Jan. 299/1 Somebody will do a little neat fielding [in baseball]. **1955** *Times* 9 May 15/1 The South Africans have been hailed as a great fielding combination.

d. The action of a fielder (sense 2).

1873 HOTTEN *Slang Dict.* 161 s.v. *Field*, Laying against favourites is called fielding, and bookmakers are often known as fielders. **1895** *Daily News* 20 May 3/6 There was a lot of fielding against yesterday's winner.

2. *Comb.*, †**fielding-piece** = *field-piece*; **fielding-plane**, 'a plane used in sinking the margin round a panel' (Jam.).

1582–8 *Hist. James VI* (1804) 132 They..came..in sicht of thair enemie, with twa feilding peeces of guns. **1646** in Rushw. *Hist. Coll.* III. I. 400 The Army followed up after the Fielding Pieces.

Fieldingesque (ˌfi:ldɪŋ'ɛsk), *a.* [f. the name of the novelist Henry *Fielding* (1707–54) + -ESQUE.] Of or pertaining to Fielding, his writings, or his style.

1931 A. HUXLEY *Music at Night* 1. 12 A few Fieldingesque irrelevancies would destroy it [*sc.* 'Othello']. **1933** *Times Lit. Suppl.* 5 Oct. 657/2 The Fieldingesque adventures related by Cibber's own daughter. **1934** *Ibid.* 17 May 356/2 Novels in the Fieldingesque tradition.

†**'fieldish**, *a. Obs.* [f. FIELD *sb.* + -ISH.]

a. Inhabiting the fields. **b.** Level and open.

*a***1541** WYATT '*My Mothers maides*' 2 They sing a song made of the feldishe mouse. **1587** M. GROVE *Pelops & Hipp.* (1878) 31 If there be any wyght that mindes to trye By course of charets on the fieldish playne.

fieldite ('fi:ldaɪt). *Min.* [f. *Field*, name of the geologist who first examined it + -ITE.] A variety of tetrahedrite.

1868 DANA *Min.* 104 Kenngott has named it *Fieldite.*

'field-ˌland. †**a.** A level plain. OE. only. *Obs.* †**b.** Level and unenclosed land. *Obs.*

*c***1000** ÆLFRIC *Deut.* i. 7 Faraþ to Amorrea dune & to oþrum feld landum. **1669** WORLIDGE *Syst. Agric.* (1681) 35 Champain or Field-land. **1707** MORTIMER *Husb.* 234 Field Lands are not exempted from Milldews. **1710** *Lond. Gaz.* No. 4674/7, 65 Acres of..Pasture inclosed, and 80 Acres of Field Land.

c. Land suitable for cultivation. *U.S.*

1851 A. O. HALL *Manhattaner* 129, I have seen a million dollars worth of property..plantations; field lands; sugar-houses.

fieldless ('fi:ldlɪs), *a.* [f. FIELD *sb.* 4 + -LESS.] Without fields.

1890 O. CRAWFURD *Round Calendar in Portugal* 2 A great stretch of hedgeless, fieldless land. **1964** *Economist* 14 Mar. 1016/1 The new concrete, fieldless farms.

'field-'marshal. [After G. *feld-marschall.*] The title of a military officer of high rank.

1. In continental armies (= Ger. *feldmarschall*, F. *maréchal de camp*). In 16th c. and early 17th c., an officer subordinate only to the 'captain-general' or 'general', and charged with the control of the encampment and sustenance of the army. As in the case of other designations of military rank, the application greatly changed in the 17th and following centuries. 'In German-speaking countries and in others (e.g. Russia) which have adopted the term, it is the highest military title, superior to that of general' (N.E.D., 1895).

[**1579** DIGGES *Stratioticos* 126 As shall be ordayned by the Marshals of the fielde. *a***1587** GARRARD *Art War* (1591) 234 The high Marshall of the fielde, or maister of the Campe.] **1614** SELDEN *Titles Hon.* 325 The Tribuni Militum (as it were, Field Marshalls). **1701** *Lond. Gaz.* No. 3692/2 Count Muttoni..is entred into the Emperor's Service, who has made him Lieutenant Field-Marshal-General. **1706** *Ibid.* No. 4201/2 Field-Marshal-General Herbeville continued there. **1710** WHITWORTH *Acc. Russia* (1758) 66 He was made Prince of the Empire in 1706..and Felt Marshal in 1709. **1848** W. H. KELLY tr. *L. Blanc's Hist. Ten Y.* I. 475 The Russian army..had passed under the command of Field-marshal Paskewitch.

2. In the British army, a general officer of the highest rank.

The title was first conferred in 1736 (see quot.); since then the army has always had a few field-marshals, either members of the royal family or generals who have rendered distinguished services. The Army List for 1894 gives the names of six officers of this rank.

1736 *Gent. Mag.* VI. 56 D. of Argyle, and E. of Orkney, Field-Marshals of Great Britain. **1844** *Regul. & Ord. Army* 29 A Field-Marshal is to be saluted with the Standards and Colours of all the Forces, except the Horse and Foot Guards.

Hence **ˌfield-'marshalship.**

1855 in OGILVIE *Suppl.* **1864** in WORCESTER (citing *Q. Rev.*).

'field-ˌmeeting. [f. FIELD *sb.* + MEETING.]

†**1.** A hostile meeting in the open air; a duel.

1603 H. CROSSE *Vertues Commw.* (1878) 14 Whose hot bloud..cannot be cooled without reuenge and field-meetings.

2. A religious meeting in the open air. *Hist.*

1649 G. DANIEL *Trinarch., Hen. V* lvii, The first S[ts]..Had such feild-meetings. **1818** SCOTT *Hrt. Midl.* xv, He..had been present at a field-meeting at Crochmade. **1882** J. TAYLOR *Sc. Covenanters* 72 The bishops sought..to deter the people from frequenting the field-meetings.

Hence **field-'meeter**, one who attends or frequents field-meetings (sense 2).

1680 HICKERINGILL *Meroz* 29 No Thanks..to the Conventiclers and Field-meeters, they show'd their good Will.

'field-night. A night marked by some important gathering, discussion, etc. Cf. FIELD-DAY.

1861 *Falkirk Herald* 2 Mar., Yesterday night was a field night..the beauty of Falkirk was in the Corn Exchange. **1880** TREVELYAN *Early Hist. Fox* v. 196 The debate was remembered as the greatest field night..for a generation.

field officer. 'An officer above the rank of captain, and under that of general' (Stocqueler).

1656 J. HARRINGTON *Oceana* 127 A..field-officer shall be elected..by the Scruteny of the Council of War. **1724** *Lond. Gaz.* No. 6310/2 All the Field Officers having the Honour of being admitted to his Table. **1804** WELLINGTON in Gurw. *Desp.* III. 549 A field officer shall not hold an office upon the staff. **1860** TYNDALL *Glac.* 138 One peak stood like a field-officer with his cap raised above his head.

Hence **field-'officerism.**

1837 CARLYLE *Fr. Rev.* (1857) II. III. v. vi. 310 Spanish Field-officerism struck mute at such cat-o'-mountain spirit.

fieldon, var. FIELDEN *sb. Obs.*

ˌfield-'preacher. [f. FIELD *sb.* + PREACHER.] One who preaches in the open air.

1688 in Ellis *Orig. Lett.* Ser. II. IV. 148 Balfour..is a Scotch field-preacher. **1755** *Connoisseur* No. 86 The spirited harangues of our..field-preachers. **1839** STONEHOUSE *Axholme* 209 He [Wesley] commenced field preacher; and itinerancy followed as a natural consequence.

ˌfield-'preaching. [f. FIELD *sb.* + PREACHING.] The practice of preaching in the open air; an instance of this.

1739 WESLEY *Wks.* (1872) I. 185 Our Lord's Sermon on the Mount (one pretty remarkable precedent of field-preaching). **1814** SCOTT *Wav.* xxxv, Have you..left a great part of your command at a field-preaching? **1882** J. TAYLOR *Sc. Covenanters* 72 At first, these field-preachings were peaceable.

fieldsman ('fi:ldzmən). [f. FIELD *sb.* + MAN.]

a. *Cricket.* One of the side which is in the field; a fielder. **b.** (See quot. 1823.)

1767 R. COTTON *Cricket Song* ix. in F. S. Ashley-Cooper *Hambledon Cricket Chron.* (1924) 184 Ye Fieldsmen look sharp. **1823** 'ION BEE' *Slang* 206 *Fieldsmen* (turf) — those who make it a rule to give odds against the favorite, or any particular horse; they are considered very knowing. **1824** MISS MITFORD *Village* Ser. I. (1863) 176 An uncertain hitter, but a good fieldsman. **1850** 'BAT' *Crick. Man.* 40 The positions of the Fieldsmen are arranged according to efficiency. **1881** *Daily News* 9 July 2 A possible catch to a more plucky fieldsman.

c. A person responsible for the management of various agricultural matters (see quots.).

1750 *Court Baron Rules & Orders* 12 Mar. in *Purefoy Lett.* (1931) II. 435 For every Cow put or turned into the Common or Cow pasture shall be paid yearly to the Fieldsmen..6ᵈ. **1914** W. H. HUTTON *Highways & Byways in Shakespeare's Country* viii. 144 Weston-sub-Edge... Though the lord of the manor seems for all practical purposes to have died out there at the Reformation, the old open field system of husbandry continued. What was practically a corporation of fieldsmen (who have been truly described as the aristocracy of the village and 'did not represent more than one-sixth of the population') managed the agricultural arrangements of the land... The 'fieldsmen' were gradually dying out before the climax of 1852, when the..enclosures were carried out. **1950** H. J. MASSINGHAM *Curious Traveller* xi. 237 The Fields-men, appointed annually by the village, determined the crops of the year, fixed and paid wages, imposed fines for trespass and strayed livestock, [etc.].

fieldspar, obs. form of FELDSPAR.

'fieldstone. [f. FIELD *sb.* + STONE *sb.*] Stone as found in the field, used esp. for building.

1896 *Folk-Lore* Mar. 47 Cybele, the Magna Mater, whose image in the shape of a rough field-stone had been given by the Phrygian priests. **1959** *Times* 19 June (Queen in Canada Suppl.) p. iv/4 Grey Quebec fieldstone. **1968** *Globe & Mail* (Toronto) 13 Jan. 28/4 The handsome panelled and fieldstone walls. **1970** H. BRAUN *Parish Churches* vii. 94 Some parts of England..have as their field-stone flint, lying in great nodules.

field theory. Any theory about fields (see FIELD *sb.* 15 and 17) or in which the idea of a field is the dominant concept. So ˌ**field-theo'retical** *a.*; **'field-theorist**.

1901 L. E. DICKSON (*title*) Linear groups with an exposition of the Galois field theory. **1922** JEFFERY & PERRETT tr. *Einstein's Sidelights Relativity* 23 We ought not ..to reject the possibility that the facts comprised in the quantum theory may set bounds to the field theory. **1929** EINSTEIN in *Nature* 2 Feb. 175/1 The purpose of my work is ..to reduce to one formula the explanation of the field of gravity and of the field of electromagnetism. For this reason I call it a contribution to 'a unified field theory'. **1934** J. F. BROWN in *Philos. Sci.* I. 325 The central idea of a 'field' theory is that the behavior of an object within the field is determined by the field structure or spatial-temporal configuration of the energy within the field. *Ibid.*, By 'class' theory I mean essentially what Lewin has called Aristotelian theory, and by 'field' theory what Lewin has called Galilean theory. *Ibid.* 334 Aristotle was trying to answer the question: 'Why do bodies move?' Galileo, the first thinker in the field-theoretical tradition, attempted the more modest question: 'How do bodies move?' **1961** M. B. HESSE *Forces & Fields* x. 274 Field-theorists who, since Maxwell, have interpreted matter as itself a manifestation of a physically prior field. **1961** POWELL & CRASEMANN *Quantum Mech.* iv. 87 Quantum field theory is the basic discipline in terms of which modern ideas in fundamental-particle physics are expressed. **1964** R. H. ROBINS *Gen. Ling.* ii. 70 The theory ..of the linguistic field, or the field theory of meaning, is concerned to show that the lexical content of a language..is not a mere conglomeration or aggregation of independent items. **1967** L. RÉDEI *Algebra* I. ii. 36 The most important chapters of algebra are group theory, ring theory and the theory of skew fields (in particular field theory).

fieldward, -wards ('fiːldwəd, -z), *adv.* [f. FIELD *sb.* + -WARD(S.] Towards the fields, in the direction of the fields.

1805 WORDSWORTH *Prelude* (1926) 228 The Dame, That field-ward takes her walk in decency. **1820** KEATS *Isabella* xxxix, Glossy bees at noon do fieldward pass. **1862** CALVERLEY *Verses & Tr.* 82 Fieldward winds the lowing herd. **1866** CARLYLE *Remin.* (1881) I. 277 My commonest walk was fieldwards.

'field-'work. [f. FIELD *sb.* + WORK.]

1. Work done in the field or in the fields; *spec.* in *Surveying*.

1767 R. GIBSON *Treat. Surveying* (ed. 2) 173 If the End of the last Station falls exactly in the Point you begin at, the Field-Work and Protraction are truly taken. **1777** ROBERTSON *Hist. Amer.* (1783) III. 277 In Peru..negroes.. are employed in field-work. **1844** MARG. FULLER *Wom. 19th C.* (1862) 35 Those who think it impossible for negresses to endure field-work. **1851** J. S. MACAULAY *Field Fortif.* 245 The beginner in field-sketching..should commence his field-work in a road. **1856** KANE *Arct. Expl.* I. x. 109 Mr. Kennedy..used October and November for Arctic field-work. **1891** N. CRANE *Baseball* vi. 43 There is no department of the game so full of life..as field work. **1901** *Daily Colonist* (Victoria, B.C.) 16 Oct. 5/3 Mr. Carry, who conducted the survey from the summit westward, returned from the Mainland on Monday night, having completed the field work. **1956** P. KISSAM *Surveying Instrum. & Methods* (ed. 2) xi. 192 The procedure (the location survey) is planned to require a minimum of field work.

2. *Mil.* A temporary work or fortification thrown up by troops operating in the field.

1819 REES *Cycl.*, *Field-works* are..for the most part, formed by the excavation of the soil. **1851** J. S. MACAULAY *Field Fortif.* 169 The manner of attacking field-works is very different from that employed in the attack of fortresses.

3. A comprehensive name to describe the practical side of research in archæology, linguistics, the social sciences, etc., carried out in the areas concerned, as distinguished from theoretical or laboratory investigation. Cf. FIELD *sb.* 15 c.

1922 B. MALINOWSKI *Argonauts West. Pacific* 4 This exactly describes my first initiation into field work on the south coast of New Guinea. **1930** *Economist* 24 May 1159/2 He not only played his part in shaping the organisation, but he also did what might be termed important field work for it. **1933** LEAVIS & THOMPSON *Culture & Environment* 18 As 'field-work', pupils might..note the effects of advertising on themselves and their friends. **1936** J. C. BROWN (*title*) Field work with public welfare agencies. **1937** *Oxoniensia* II. 75 The field-work and excavation undertaken in 1935 and 1936 have proved beyond a doubt that this north Oxfordshire Dyke, so far from being a continuous circumvallation, was made up of numerous unconnected sectors. **1940** *Mind* XLIX. 64 He does not sit all day in his arm-chair, he spends at least part of his time in observational field-work. **1959** *Listener* 14 May 868/2 Rehabilitation, Boarding Out, Adoption, Supervision, and other Field work associated with deprived children. **1962** *Amer. Speech* XXXVII. 164 The Banks were not included in the *Linguistic Atlas* field work. **1971** *Observer* 1 Aug. 26/8 In the 1930s Jacques Soustelle did some very fine anthropological and archaeological field-work in Mexico.

'field-worker. [f. FIELD *sb.* + WORKER.] One who performs field-work (senses 1 and 3).

1832 *Chambers's Edin. Jrnl.* I. 115/3 Being then left by him without any provision, she sunk into the condition of a field-worker. **1915** J. WEBSTER *Dear Enemy* (1916) 26 We need a field worker to travel about the country and pick up all the hereditary statistics she can about our chicks. **1922** B. MALINOWSKI *Argonauts West. Pacific* 9 The field worker relies entirely upon inspiration from theory. **1935** *Amer. Speech* X. 4/1 The personal character of the informant..is of great importance. Unless he is hospitable, the fieldworker has little chance of putting the case before him. Unless he is honest, his answers to the fieldworker's questions lose most of their value. **1950** *Oxoniensia* XV. 13 The thin but widespread scatter of Romano-British potsherds which can be picked up from the surface and lynchets of Celtic fields is a phenomenon which the field-worker soon learns to accept as a matter of course in Celtic field areas. **1961** *Evening Standard* 2 Aug. 12/3 (Advt.), Market research part-time field workers..for retailer research.

†**'fieldy,** *a. Obs.* [f. FIELD *sb.* + -Y¹.]

1. Level, open; exposed.

c **1380** WYCLIF *Serm.* Sel. Wks. I. 214 [Crist] stood in a fieldi place. *c* **1449** PECOCK *Repr.* 280 In the feeldi placis of Moab. **1576** FLEMING tr. *Caius' Dogs* in Arb. *Garner* III. 238 In fieldy lands rather than in bushy and woody places. **1598** FLORIO, *Piaggioso*..fieldie.

2. That grows in or inhabits the fields.

1382 WYCLIF *Wisd.* xix. 18 Feeldi wilde thingus in to watri ben turned. **1598** FLORIO, *Camporeccio*, fieldie, that growes in the fields.

3. Forming a field or fields. Cf. FIELD *sb.* 12 a.

1598 SYLVESTER *Du Bartas* II. i. IV. *Handie-Crafts* 451 In fieldy clouds he vanisheth it away.

fiend (fiːnd). Forms: 1–2 féond, *north.* fiond (*pl.* fiend, fýnd, féond, fond, *north.* fiond, fiondas; *dat. sing.* fiend, fýnd, féonde), 3–4 feond (*pl.* feond, fiend, feondes), (3 feont, fond, *south.* veond), 2–7 fend(e, (3 fent), 3–6 find(e, 3–7 feind(e, (4 *south.* vyend), 4–6 feynd, fynd(e, (5 fynt), 4–7 feend(e, (4 fende, 7 feigne), 8 *Sc.* fient, fint, 4– fiend. [Com. Teut.: OE. *féond* = OFris. *fîand*, OS. *fîond*, *fîund* (MDu. *vîant*, Du. *vijand*), OHG. *fîant* (MHG. *vîent*, *vînt*, mod.G. *feind*), ON. *fjánde* (Sw. *fiende*, Da. *fjende*), Goth. *fijands*; originally the pr. pple. of OTeut. **fijêjan* (OE. *féoȝean*, OHG. *fiên*, ON. *fjá*, Goth. *fijan*) to hate. The formation is parallel with that of FRIEND.]

†**1.** An enemy; foe. *Obs.*

Beowulf 2289 Stone þa æfter stane, steareheort onfand feondes fotlast. *c* **975** *Rushw. Gosp.* Matt. v. 43 Hate þine fiond [*c* **1000** and *c* **1160** feond]. *c* **1050** *Byrhtferth's Handboc* in *Anglia* VIII. 323 Gefliȝeorne & godes fynd. *a* **1175** *Cott. Hom.* 231 Bi tweone frend and fend. *a* **1225** *Ancr. R.* 98 Ueond þet þunched freond is swike ouer alle swike. *c* **1320** R. BRUNNE *Medit.* 1124 And þe fende bonde to make to þe. **1340** *Ayenb.* 19 He ys wel renay þet þet land þet he halt of his lhorde deþ into þe hond of his uyende.

2. a. *spec.* The arch-enemy of mankind; the devil. More fully: ***fiend of hell, foul fiend, old fiend.*** †***fiend's limb*** = limb of Satan (see LIMB).

a **1000** *Hymns* viii. 25 (Gr.) Ðu fiond ȝeflæmdest. *c* **1000** *Sax. Leechd.* II. 294 Hit eac deah wiþ feondes costungum yflum. *c* **1175** *Lamb. Hom.* 67 Ure fond nefre ne linnen [cease] for to fonden us mid sunnen. *a* **1225** *St. Marher.* 1 Ouercomen ant akasten..þe feont. *a* **1300** *Cursor M.* 1056 (Cott.) Caim was þe findes fode. *c* **1340** *Cursor M.* 14880 (Trin.) Leuer had þei se þe fend of helle þen him amonges hem to dwelle. *c* **1380** WYCLIF *Sel. Wks.* III. 357 It falliþ ofte..þat a tyraunt and a fendis lyme is put bifore a lyme of Crist. **1393** LANGL. *P. Pl.* C. XXI. 18 Fecche þat þe feond cleymeþ. *c* **1460** *Play Sacram.* 953, I shalle yow blysse to saue yow alle from the fendis blame. **1515** *Scot. Field* 598 in *Chetham Misc.* (1856) II, What it is to be false, and the finde serve! **1526** TINDALE *Luke* viii. 29 And was caryed of the fende into wildernes. **1605** SHAKS. *Lear* III. vi. 9 Beware the foule Fiend. **1667** MILTON *P.L.* x. 233 The Gates.. belching outrageous flame..since the Fiend pass'd through. **1708** *Brit. Apollo* No. 99. 3/2 Drugs of more Force..Than e'er was conceiv'd, by the subtil Old Fiend. **1848** MRS. JAMESON *Sacr. & Leg. Art* (1850) 64 The fiend is the worst part of the picture.

b. In forms of asseveration or execration: † ***the fiend on thee! the foul fiend!*** Also Sc. ***fient a*** (***crum***, etc.), ***fient ane, haet*** = 'Devil, never a one, crumb, whit', etc.

a **1568** A. SCOTT *Poems* (1820) 51 Feind a crum of the scho fawis. **1637** B. JONSON *Sad Sheph.* II. ii, O, the feind, and thee! Gar, take them hence. *a* **1774** FERGUSSON *Rising of Session* Poems (1845) 29 The fient ane there but pays his score. **1787** BURNS *Twa Dogs* 16 The fient a pride, nae pride had he. *Ibid.* 180 Fient haet o' them 's ill-hearted fellows. **1818** SCOTT *Br. Lamm.* vi, What the foul fiend can detain the Master so long?

3. An evil spirit generally; a demon, devil, or diabolical being; more fully ***fiend of hell.***

a **1000** *Guthlac* 392 (Gr.) No þær þa feondas ȝefeon þorfton. *c* **1175** *Lamb. Hom.* 33 Ah a þer is waning and graming..and feonda bitinga. *c* **1250** *Gen. & Ex.* 2961 It was on fendes wise wroȝt. *c* **1386** CHAUCER *Sompn. Prol.* 10 Ffreres and feendes been but lyte a-sonder. *c* **1440** *Generydes* 2520 But suerly they be fendez. **1509** HAWES *Conv. Swearers* 24 To redeme you from the fendes of hell. **1605** CAMDEN *Rem.* 7 They yellen as fends do in hell. **1694** F. BRAGGE *Disc. Parables* iv. 152 Revenge..makes a man a fiend incarnate. **1738** WESLEY *Psalms* lvii. 4 Inflam'd with Rage like Fiends in Hell. **1798** COLERIDGE *Anc. Mar.* VI, A frightful fiend Doth close behind him tread. **1840** MACAULAY *Ranke* Ess. (1854) 545/1 In the language of Goethe's scoffing fiend.

4. *transf.* **a.** A person of superhuman wickedness. (Now only with reference to cruelty or malignity.)

c **1220** *Bestiary* 450 For wo so..ðenkeð iuel on his mod fox he is and fend iwis. *c* **1300** *Havelok* 2229 He with his hend Ne drop him nouth, that sor fend. **1393** LANGL. *P. Pl.* C. XXIII. 58 Freres folweden þat feonde [Antichrist]. *c* **1475** *Rauf Coilȝear* 892 Fy on that foull Feind [*sc.* Mahoun]. **1590** SPENSER *F.Q.* II. vi. 50 That cursed man, that cruel feend of hell. **1799** CAMPBELL *Pleas. Hope* I. 327 Where human fiends on midnight errands walk. **1875** W. S. HAYWARD *Love agst. World* 45 He is at times a perfect fiend.

b. †A grisly monster (e.g. a dragon) (*obs.*). Also applied to baleful or destructive influences or agencies personified.

c **1400** *Destr. Troy* 597 It is playnly your purpos..With suche fyndes to fight. **1590** SPENSER *F.Q.* I. i. 22 Whose corage when the feend [the monster Errour] perceivd to shrinke. **1784** COWPER *Task* II. 185 He calls for famine, and the meagre fiend Blows mildew from between his shrivel'd lips.

c. Applied with jocular hyperbole to a person or agency causing mischief or annoyance. Often with qualifying word or phrase.

1621 BURTON *Anat. Mel.* III. ii. II. iv. (1845) 545 If you do but stir abroad, these fiends [*sc.* women; transl. *umbræ* in Petronius] are ready to meet you at every turn. **1807–8** W. IRVING *Salmag.* (1824) 305 It is that fiend Politics, Asem —that baneful fiend, which bewildereth every brain. **1870** LOWELL *Study Wind, Swinburne's Trag.* (1871) 162 This sorcery which the fiend of technical imitation weaves about his victims. *a* **1896** *Mod.* The autograph-fiend; the cyclist-fiend; the interviewer-fiend; the newsboy-fiend; the organ-fiend. **1889** FARMER *Americanisms* s.v., The free lunch fiend ..is one who makes a meal off what is really provided as a snack. He pays for a drink, but shamefacedly manages in this way to get something more than his money's worth. **1896**, etc. Dope fiend [see DOPE *sb.* 5]. **1904** *Philadelphia Even. Tel.* 25 July 6 The camera fiend is after him, hot foot. **1909** WEBSTER 812/1 *Fiend*...An opium fiend...he is a fiend in mathematics; a botany fiend. **1925**, etc. Drug-fiend [see DRUG *sb.*¹ 1 b]. **1927**, etc. Fresh-air fiend [see FRESH *a.* 6]. **1929** R. GRAVES *Goodbye to All That* xxviii. 377 He had been upset that morning by a letter from an autograph-fiend. **1956** M. SWAN *Paradise Garden* I. i. 7 A neighbour a small-boat fiend. **1962** N. MARSH *Hand in Glove* v. 196 I'm a bit of a camera-fiend myself.

d. A kind of firework.

1634 J. BATE *Myst. Nat. & Art* II. 75 How to make fiends, or fearefull apparitions.

5. *attrib.* and *Comb.*: **a.** simple attrib., as ***fiend-breed, -face.*** **b.** objective, as ***fiend-compelling, -fraying*** adjs. **c.** instrumental, as ***fiend-begotten, -drawn, -tenanted, -tied*** adjs. **d.** originative, as ***fiend-born*** adj. **e.** parasynthetic, as ***fiend-hearted*** adj.

1810 SCOTT *Lady of L.* IV. v, Aught that..Yon *fiend-begotten monk can tell. **1802** SCOTT *Thomas the Rhymer* III. 18 in *Minstr. Scot. Border* II. 289 Brangwain was there.. And *fiend-born Merlin's gramarye. **1586** WARNER *Alb. Eng.* II. xiii. (1597) 62 Brute..suppressed so the state Of all the *Fiend-breed Albinests. **1856** R. A. VAUGHAN *Mystics* (1860) II. 108 Solomon achieved his *fiend-compelling wonders by its aid. **1821** SHELLEY *Prometh. Unb.* I. 126 As one checks a *fiend-drawn charioteer. **1879** BROWNING *Ned Bratts* 56 Horrified, hideous, frank *fiend-faces! **1664** H. MORE *Myst. Iniq.* xviii. 69 The *Fiend-fraying Holy-water. **1847** CRAIG, **Fiendhearted*, having a very wicked or depraved heart. **1892** *Daily News* 21 Sept. 5/5 Who was grasping his *fiend-tenanted fiddle so firmly by the throat. **1754** ARMSTRONG *Forced Marriage* iv. 1 Misc. (1770) II. 80 My quick revenge Shall burst this *fiend-tied most unnatural knot.

†**'fienden,** *a. Obs. rare.* [f. prec. + -EN⁴.] = FIENDISH.

c **1315** SHOREHAM 85 I-schelde ous..Fram alle fendene jewyse. **13..** *E.E. Allit. P.* B. 224 Fylter fenden folk forty dayez lencþe.

†**'fiendful,** *a. Obs. rare*⁻¹. [f. as prec. + -FUL.] Proceeding from fiendish agency.

c **1590** MARLOWE *Faust.* Final Chorus, Faustus is gone, regard his hellish fall Whose fiendful fortune may exhort the wise. **1832** in WEBSTER.

Hence **'fiendfully** *adv.*

1847 in CRAIG.

'fiendhead. [-HEAD] = FIENDSHIP b.
1830 *Westm. Rev.* XII. 356 He will find a more flattering treatment of his fiend-head.

fiendish ('fiːndɪʃ), *a.* (and *adv.*) [f. as prec. + -ISH.] Resembling, or characteristic of, a fiend; superhumanly cruel and malignant. Also as *adv.*, excessively, horribly.
1529 MORE *Comf. agst. Trib.* II. Wks. 1187/1 This woman was so fendish. **1798** COLERIDGE *Anc. Mar.* VII. 6 It hath a fiendish look. **1801** SOUTHEY *Thalaba* VIII. x, Through the vampire corpse He thrust his lance..And..Its fiendish tenant fled. **1823** PRAED *Troubadour* II. 563 And Satan will grin with a fiendish glee. **1861** W. JAMES *Let.* Sept. (1920) I. 38, I have noticed fleeting shades of expression on her face ..*unhuman*, ghoul-like, fiendish-cunning! **1871** FREEMAN *Hist. Ess.* Ser. I. 74 The fiendish brutalities practised by him. **1891** S. HALE *Lett.* (1919) 258 As all the Continent is fiendish cold, we did wisely.
transf. **1836** KINGSLEY *Lett.* I. 35 The wavy lightning glared over the sea with fiendish light.
Hence **'fiendishly** *adv.* (also in trivial use); **'fiendishness.**
1613 BP. HALL *Holy Panegyricke* 39 Those Dames which vnder a cloke of modestie..hide nothing but pride, and fiendishnesse. **1801** SOUTHEY *Thalaba* II. xvii, A smile That kindled to more fiendishness Her hideous features. **1879** BLACK *Macleod of D.* viii, A calm and dignified silence is the best answer to the fiendishness of thirteen. **1879** E. NESBIT *Let.* in D. L. Moore *E. Nesbit* (1933) iii. 47 Remember I am *fiendishly* busy sometimes. **1951** *Mind* LX. 428 A correlation of observations, fiendishly difficult in practice.

fiendism ('fiːndɪz(ə)m). *rare*$^{-1}$. [f. as FIENDISH *a.* + -ISM.] Fiendish spirit or manner.
1852 LD. COCKBURN *Circuit Journeys* (1888) 380 The wretch maintained his domestic fiendism to the last.

†**'fiendkin.** *Obs. rare.* [f. as prec. + -KIN, dim. suffix.] A little fiend or evil spirit.
1377 LANGL. *P. Pl.* B. XVIII. 371 Fendes and fendekynes bifor me shulle stande.

'fiendlike, *a.* [f. as prec. + -LIKE.]
a. Resembling a fiend. **b.** Characteristic of a fiend.
1605 SHAKS. *Macb.* V. viii. 69 His Fiend-like Queene; Who ..by selfe and violent hands, Tooke off her life. **1716** ROWE *Ode New Year* 19 Ev'ry Fiend and Fiend-like Form. **1774** WARTON *Hist. Eng. Poetry* I. 160 The last circumstance recalls a fiend-like appearance drawn by Shakspeare. **1804** J. GRAHAME *Sabbath* 591 Their little ones, Tremble beneath the white man's fiend-like frown! **1854** J. S. C. ABBOTT *Napoleon* (1855) I. viii. 150 With fiendlike ferocity they hurled themselves upon each other.

fiendly ('fiːndlɪ), *a.* [OE. *féondlic*, f. *féond*, FIEND + *-lic*, -LY¹.]
†**1.** Hostile, unfriendly. *Obs.*
After the OE. period perh. always with mixture of sense 2.
c **1050** *Voc.* in Wr.-Wülcker 168 *Hosticus, uet hostilis,* feondlic. *c* **1175** *Lamb. Hom.* 107 [W]e maȝen þurh godes fulste þa fondliche sunnan mid icompe ouercuman. *c* **1205** LAY. 8660 He fusde heom to mid feondliche strengðe. *c* **1386** CHAUCER *Can. Yeom. Prol. & T.* 750 He semed frendly.. But he was fendly, both in werk and thought. **1470–85** MALORY *Arthur* XVI. xvi, He ranne vpon his broder as a fendly man. *a* **1529** SKELTON *Image Hypocr.* 346 To feyne yourselves frindley And be nothinge but fyndly.
2. Resembling or befitting a fiend; fiendlike, devilish, diabolical.
c **1386** CHAUCER *Can. Yeom. Prol. & T.* 605 This feendly wrecche..Out of his bosom took a bechen cole. *c* **1422** HOCCLEVE *Jereslaus' Wife* 784 It manly is to synne, But feendly is longe lye ther-ynne. **1470–85** MALORY *Arthur* XI. i, An horryble & a fyendly dragon. *c* **1510** BARCLAY *Mirr. Gd. Manners* (1570) G v, This is their chiefe study and findly pollicy. **1562** PHAER *Æneid.* VIII. Y j b, Cacus fendly sprite. **1801** SOUTHEY *Thalaba* IX. xxvii, 'Curse thee!' cried the fiendly woman. **1818** SHELLEY *Rev. Islam* VIII. xxi, Yes it is Hate, that shapeless fiendly thing. **1831** WILSON in *Blackw. Mag.* XXX. 554 You talk as if you suspected the Peers of having profited by the Fiendly Advice.
Hence **'fiendliness,** the state of being fiendly.
1860 *Lit. Churchm.* VI. 264/1 The ferocious fiendliness to which the whole..population had been brought.

†**'fiendly,** *adv.* Forms: 1 féondlice, 3 -liche. [OE. *féondlíce*, f. *féond*, FIEND + *-líce*, -LY².] In a fiendly manner. **a.** Like an enemy, angrily. **b.** Like a fiend, terribly.
a **1000** *Juliana* 118 (Gr.) Hyre þa þurh yrre ageaf andsware fæder feondlice. *c* **1205** LAY. 85 Vt of þan fehte þe was feondliche stor, Eneas the duc mid ermde at-wond.

†**fiend-rese.** *Obs.* [OE. *féondrǽs*, f. *féond*, FIEND + *rǽs*, RESE.] Fierce or hostile onset.
a **1000** *Cædmon's Gen.* 900 (Gr.) Ic fracoðlice feondræs ȝefremede. *c* **1205** LAY. 23960 Frolle him to fusden mid his feond ræse.

†**'fiend-scathe.** [OE. *féondscaða*, *-sceaða*, f. *féond*, FIEND + *scaða*, *sceaða* enemy.] A monster.
Beowulf 554 Me to grunde teah fah feondscaða. *c* **1205** LAY. 26039 Aris feond-scaðe to þine sæie-siðe.

fiendship ('fiːndʃɪp). [OE. *féondscipe*, f. *féond*, FIEND + *-scipe*, -SHIP.] †**a.** Enmity (*obs.*). **b.** [A new formation.] The personality of a fiend.
c **900** tr. *Bæda's Hist.* III. xiv. (1890) 208 He..Rædwaldes feondscipe fleah. *c* **1205** LAY. 22966 ȝif on uolke feond-scipe arereð an æur æi time bitweone twon monnen. **1874** M. & F. COLLINS *Frances* I. 104 If we may believe his Fiendship.

†**'fiend-slaught.** *Obs.* In 3 feond-slæht. [ME. *feond-slæht*, f. *feond*, FIEND + *slæht* = OE. *sleaht* slaughter.] Slaughter of foes.
c **1205** LAY. 16456 Fare we heom to-ȝænes & makien feond slæhtes.

†**'fiend-thews,** *sb. pl. Obs.* [ME. *feon-ðewæs*, f. *feon(d*, FIEND + *ðeawes*, pl. of *ðeaw*, OE. *ðéaw* manner.] Evil-conduct.
c **1205** LAY. 579 Monie þar feollen þurh heora feon-ðewæs.

fier, var. of FEER *sb.*¹ 2, FEIR, FERE *a. Obs.*

fierasfer (faɪə'ræsfə(r)). [mod.L. (L. Oken 1817, in *Isis* CXLVIII. 1182/1), f. Pr. *fieras-fèr*, *fielat-fèr*, f. *fieras*, f. OPr. *filat* thread, net (f. L. *filum* FILE *sb.*²) + *fèr* fierce, wild (f. L. *ferus* FEROUS *a.*).] A small parasitic fish of the family Carapidæ, which includes a genus once called *Fierasfer*, found in the Mediterranean and in British waters; also called *pearlfish*.
1843 *Proc. Zool. Soc.* XI. 92 The occurrence in Madeira of a single individual, imposes the necessity of proposing, in lieu of the barbarous vernacular appellation *Fierasfer*, a name founded on an obvious character. **1876** tr. *P. J. van Beneden's Animal Parasites* ii. 5 We see Fierasfers,.. accompanied by Palæmons and Pinnotheres in the same animal. **1936** J. T. JENKINS *Fishes Brit. Isles* (ed. 2) 168 There are two representatives [of *Ophidiidæ*] which wander occasionally into British waters. These are the Bearded Ophidium..and the Fierasfer (*Fierasfer dentatus*). **1969** A. WHEELER *Fishes Brit. Isles & N.W. Europe* 455/1 The pearlfishes or fierasfers are well known for their habit of living within the body of a holothurian (sea cucumber) host.

†**fierce,** *sb. Her. Obs.* (See quot.)
1634 PEACHAM *Gentl. Exerc.* III. 144 This [the Pale] in ancient time was called a *fierce*, and you should then have blazed it thus, hee beares a fierce Sables, between two fierces, or.

fierce (fɪəs), *a.* Forms: 3–6 fers(e, (4 firs), 4–6 fiers(e, fyers(e, 6 fearce, -se, (5 feres, -ys, fuerse, furse, 5–6 feers(e, 6 fayrse, ferse), 3– fierce. See also FEER *a.* [a. OF. *fers*, *fiers* in same senses, nom. form of *fer*, *fier* (mod.F. *fier* proud) = Prov. *fer*, It. and Sp. *fiero*:—L. *ferus* wild (of an animal), untamed, fierce.]
1. Of formidably violent and intractable temper, like a wild beast; vehement and merciless in anger or hostility.
Less emphatic, and less associated with the notion of wanton cruelty, than FEROCIOUS, which was never used, like this word, in a good sense (see 2).
a. of persons, their dispositions or attributes.
a **1300** *Cursor M.* 2197 Nembrot..was fers, prud, and fell. *c* **1374** CHAUCER *Anel. & Arc.* 1 Yow fiers god of armes Mars the rede. **1485** CAXTON *Chas. Gt.* 26 Hys syght and regarde fyers & malycyous. **1570** B. GOOGE *Pop. Kingd.* 10 With countenaunce ferce and grim. **1607** SHAKS. *Cor.* I. iv. 57 A Souldier..not fierce and terrible Onely in strokes. **1667** MILTON *P.L.* II. 44 Moloc..the fiercest Spirit That fought in Heav'n; now fiercer by despair. **1712–4** POPE *Rape Lock* IV. 7 Tyrants fierce that unrepenting die. **1794** MRS. RADCLIFFE *Myst. Udolpho* xxviii, Montoni turned upon him with a fierce and haughty look. **1812** J. WILSON *Isle of Palms* II. 578 Fierce savage men Glare on them. **1852** MISS YONGE *Cameos* I. xxxii. 277 Hugh Lupus, the fierce old Earl of Chester, was likewise a Lord Marcher.
absol. **1820** KEATS *Hyperion* II. 251 Thus wording timidly among the fierce.
b. of animals.
1377 LANGL. *P. Pl.* B. XV. 300 God sent hem fode bi foules and by no fierse bestes. *a* **1400–50** *Alexander* 3922 A beste.. Fere fersere þan an olifaunt. **1583** GOLDING *Calvin on Deut.* xlvii. 281 Swine..bee not so fearce as to fall to rending downe of the tree. **1611** BIBLE *Job* x. 16 Thou huntest me as a fierce Lion. **1697** DRYDEN *Virg. Georg.* IV. 741 Fierce Tigers couch'd around. **1781** COWPER *Retirement* 254 Poetry disarms The fiercest animals with magic charms. **1874** C. GEIKIE *Life in Woods* v. 84 It is amazing how fierce some of the small snakes are.
absol. *c* **1400** *Destr. Troy* 888 So þe fuerse by-flamede all with fyre hote.
c. Of things: forceful; acting strongly or violently.
1912 *Motor Manual* 166 Complaints are occasionally made of what is called a 'fierce' clutch. In other words, the clutch will not slide or slip in, but permits the engine to take hold suddenly, and almost takes the starting control from the driver's hands. **1961** *Listener* 7 Dec. 1007/1 If your oven is inclined to be 'fierce', you may find it best to tie a band of folded brown paper round the outside of the tin. **1971** 'D. HALLIDAY' *Dolly & Doctor Bird* viii. 113 The brake was fiercer than I expected, but the thing was stable enough.
†**2.** High-spirited, brave, valiant. *Obs.*
1297 R. GLOUC. (Rolls) 3910 Al so þe dosse pers Of france were þer echon þat so noble were & fers. **13..** *E.E. Allit. P.* B. 101 Be þay fers, be þay feble for-lotez none. **1475** *Bk. Noblesse* 2 Next after came the feers manly Danysh nacion. **1485** CAXTON *Chas. Gt.* 74 Oliuer was so fyers of fayt. *a* **1533** LD. BERNERS *Huon* lv. 185 Our man is fyers and of gret hardynes. —— *Gold. Bk. M. Aurel.* (1546) F viij, A lusty horse fyerse and flingyng.
†**3.** Proud, haughty. *Obs.* Cf. F. *fier.*
c **1290** *S. Eng. Leg.* I. 272/34 With grete nobleye; swyþe fierce and proute. *c* **1430** *Pilgr. Lyf Manhode* I. xlix. (1869) 30 But of yow j haue no neede; haue your herte neuere þe more feers. *c* **1430** *A B C of Aristotle* in *Babees Bk.* (1868) 11 [Not] to fers, ne to famuler, but freendli of cheere. **1593** SHAKS. *2 Hen. VI*, IV. ix. 45 He is fierce and cannot brooke hard Language.
4. Of natural forces, e.g. fire, wind, etc.; also of passion, disease, conflict, persecution, etc.: Angry, violent, vehemently raging.
a **1300** *Cursor M.* 23239 (Gött.) þa dintes er ful fers and fell. *c* **1340** *Ibid.* 1854 (Trin.) Aboute fyue moneþes hit stode Wiþouten falling þat fers flode. *c* **1350** *Will. Palerne* 436 Saue a fers feintise folwes me oft. *c* **1400** *Destr. Troy* 569 Flamys of fyre han so furse hete. *c* **1450** *St. Cuthbert* (Surtees) 4579 Persecucioun fers and fell. **1490** CAXTON *Eneydos* lxii. 162 The bataylle was fyerse. **1508** FISHER *Wks.* (1876) 279 The assautes of deth was fyers and sharpe. **1508** in *Arnolde's Chron.* (1811) p. xliii, The Duke of Burgon.. was dryuen in to Englond with a ferse streynable wynde. **1611** BIBLE *Jer.* xxv. 37 The fierce anger of the Lord. **1697** DRYDEN *Virg. Past.* II. 14 The..Locusts..fry'd with Heat, and I with fierce Desire. **1708** POPE *Ode St. Cecilia* 118 Music the fiercest grief can charm. **1799** G. SMITH *Laboratory* I. 9 If the rocket burst as soon as it is lighted the charge is too fierce. **1848** MACAULAY *Hist. Eng.* I. 173 A mind heated by a fierce conflict. **1863** BRYANT *Poems, Little People of Snow* 289 Cruel we, Who suffered her to wander forth alone In this fierce cold! **1874** DEUTSCH *Rem.* 419 Two centuries and a half of fierce discussion.
5. a. Ardent, eager; full of violent desire; furiously zealous or active. †Const. *for*, *to*, *upon*, and *to* with *inf.*
1377 LANGL. *P. Pl.* B. v. 67 To affaiten hire flesshe þat fierce was to synne. *c* **1450** *St. Cuthbert* (Surtees) 7260 For to gyue she was full fers. **1513** DOUGLAS *Æneis* x. vii. 102 He on cace was fleand fers as flynt. **1601** B. JONSON *Poetaster* (1602) v. iii, And, Lupus, for your fierce Credulity, One fit him with a paire of larger Eares. **1647** CLARENDON *Hist. Reb.* IV. (1702) I. 239 One of the Fiercest men of the Party. **1654** SIR E. NICHOLAS in *N. Papers* (Camden) II. 149 He is.. fierce for the Duke of Gloucesters returne. **1702** *Eng. Theophrast.* 314 It is not good to be over fierce upon anything. *a* **1744** POPE *Odyssey* VIII, Vengeful slaughter, fierce for human blood. **1871** BROWNING *Balaust.* 1821 The feast was fierce But brief. **1874** MORLEY *Compromise* (1886) 115 The..fiercest hunt after the grosser prizes.
b. *dial.* Brisk, lively, vigorous.
1877 *N.W. Linc. Gloss.*, 'If thoo's so fierce ower thee work i' th' mornin' thoo'll be dauled oot afore neet.' **1881** *Leicestersh. Gloss.*, 'Ah'm glad to see ye luke so feece todee.' **1886** *S.W. Linc. Gloss.*, 'Oh, they were fierce; they were as merry as crickets.'
†**6.** Of a number: Great, immense. *Obs.*
c **1400** *Destr. Troy* 1617 Fuerse was þe nowmber Of lordes of þe lond. *Ibid.* 2271 So fele fightyng folke be a fuerse nowmber.
7. quasi-*adv.* = Fiercely.
a **1300** *Cursor M.* 1765 (Cott.) þe rain it fell sua fers and fast. **1591** SHAKS. *1 Hen. VI*, I. i. 14 Mid-day Sunne, fierce bent against their faces. **1771** GOLDSM. *Hist. Eng.* IV. 164 The war..continued to rage as fierce as ever. **1855** MACAULAY *Hist. Eng.* IV. 102 The war, which was now all but extinguished, might blaze forth fiercer than ever.
8. *attrib.* and *Comb.*: **a.** parasynthetic, as ***fierce-eyed***, ***-faced***, ***-fanged***, ***-minded***, ***-natured***. **b.** adverbial, as ***fierce-descending***, ***-flaming***, ***-looking***, ***-menacing***, ***-rushing***, ***-trotted***.
1735 THOMSON *Liberty* v. 45 By..No *fierce-descending wolf..Disturb'd. **1873** SYMONDS *Grk. Poets* vii. 227 They will slay me, those..*Fierce-eyed..dread goddesses. **1876** GEO. ELIOT *Dan. Der.* IV. liv. 110 A fierce-eyed temptation. **1892** *Pall Mall G.* 21 Jan. 3/1 These..*fierce-faced beasts, with their noiseless footfall. **1851** H. MELVILLE *Whale* xlii. 209 The *fierce-fanged tiger in his heraldic coat. **1740** C. PITT *Æneid* XII. 1337 His Eyes, *fierce-flaming, o'er the Trophy roll. *a* **1859** MACAULAY *Hist. Eng.* V. 23 Accosted by *fierce-looking captains. **1735** SOMERVILLE *Chase* III. 302 Another pard.. Grins.. *fierce-menacing. **1785** CRUTTWELL *Bible, 3 Macc.* vi. 18 Forgetfulness seized his *fierce-minded confidence. **1625–8** *Camden's Hist. Eliz.* II. (1688) 246 This Parsons was..a violent *fierce-natured man. **1725** POPE *Odyss.* XXIII. 75 A Boar *fierce-rushing in the sylvan war.
Hence †**'fiercehead.** [+ -HEAD] = Fierceness.
c **1440** *Promp. Parv.* 156/2 Fercehede, *ferocitas, severitas.*

†**fierce,** *v. Obs.* [f. prec. adj.] *trans.* To make fierce; to inflame.
1565 GOLDING *Ovid's Met.* III. (1593) 63 And for to fierce hir ire, Another thing..there commeth in the nicke.

†**'fierceful,** *a. Obs. rare*$^{-1}$. [f. as prec. + -FUL.] Full of fierceness; ferocious, savage.
1607 TOPSELL *Four-f. Beasts* (1673) 412 If it had as much strength, as..courage, it would be as fierceful as any Bear.

fierceish ('fɪəsɪʃ), *a. rare*$^{-1}$. [f. as prec. + -ISH.] Somewhat fierce; inclined to fierceness.
1840 *Fraser's Mag.* XXI. 82 He strode with..head erect, and rather fierceish glance.

fiercely ('fɪəslɪ), *adv.* [f. as prec. + -LY².] In a fierce manner; furiously, impetuously, violently; †sternly, haughtily.
a **1300** *Cursor M.* 16795 (Gött.) Sua fersli þe erd quock, þe grauis it vndid. **13..** *E.E. Allit. P.* C. 337 Thenne oure fader to þe fysch ferslych biddez. *c* **1350** *Will. Palerne* 1766 Fersely on here foure fet as fel for swiche bestes. **1471** RIPLEY *Comp. Alch.* III. in Ashm. (1652) 142 Fersely brennyng as Fyre of Hell. *a* **1533** LD. BERNERS *Huon* lxxxi, The gayler answered fyersly with grete pryde. **1611** BIBLE *Esther* xv. 7 He looked very fiercely upon her. **1631** GOUGE *God's Arrows* III. §6. 195 The more fiercely Christians are assaulted, the more closely they will cling together. **1715–20** POPE *Iliad* XXI. 703 Fiercely rushing on the daring foe. **1719** YOUNG *Busiris* III. i, Sending his soul out to me, in a look So fiercely kind, I trembled, and retired. **1801** SOUTHEY *Thalaba* VIII. xxix, Up she raised her bright blue eyes, And fiercely she smiled on him. **1829** ALFORD in *Life* (1873) 42 Read mathematics very fiercely being afraid of the paper tomorrow. **1834** PRINGLE *Afr. Sk.* vi. 202 The noon-day sun flamed fiercely down upon us. **1855** MACAULAY *Hist.*

Eng. III. 496 The Parliament was wrangling even more fiercely.
Comb. **1809** WORDSW. *Feelings of the Tyrolese* iii, The gales Of fiercely-breathing war.

fiercen (ˈfɪəs(ə)n), *v. rare.* [f. FIERCE *a.* + -EN⁵.] **a.** *trans.* To make fierce. ***to fiercen up***: to brush up, enliven. *dial.* **b.** *intr.* To become or grow fierce. Hence **ˈfiercening** *ppl. a.*
1831 J. WILSON *Unimore* ii. 150 The Naiad in the fiercening foam her prow Buries. **1881** MYERS *Wordsworth* 73 A metal which can grow for ever brighter in the fiercening flame. *Mod. Staffordsh.*, 'I think it has fiercened her up a bit.'

fierceness (ˈfɪəsnɪs). [f. as prec. + -NESS.] The quality or condition of being fierce.
1. a. Formidable violence; intractable savageness of temper; vehement and merciless fury.
1382 WYCLIF *1 Macc.* iv. 8 Dreede ȝe not inwardli the feersnesse of hem. **1398** TREVISA *Barth. De P.R.* v. xviii. (1495) 123 Yf [the] chynne [of beestes] be broke all theyr cruelnes and fyersnes faylle. **1462** *Pol. Poems* (Rolls) II. 268 God smote the said Henry for his gret fersnesse. **1526** TINDALE *Eph.* iv. 31 Bitternes, fearsnes [θυμός], and wrath. **1553** EDEN *Treat. Newe Ind.* (Arb.) 15 The females are of greater fiercenesse then the males. **1695** LD. PRESTON *Boeth.* II. 74 *note*, The Fierceness of the People being not wholly subdued. **1712** SWIFT *Proposal Corr. Eng. Tongue* 27 The same Defect of Heat which gives a Fierceness to our Natures, may contribute to that Roughness of our Language. **1865** KINGSLEY *Herew.* xxi, The priest looked at him with something of honest fierceness in his eyes. **1875** JOWETT *Plato* (ed. 2) III. 288 He is like a wild beast, all violence and fierceness.
†**b.** Sternness, severity. *Obs.*
1382 WYCLIF *Rom.* xi. 22 Therfore se..the feersnesse of God; sothli feersnesse into hem that felden doun. *c* **1400** *Apol. Loll.* 17 þe fersnes be noþer to mikil ne to litil. **1643** MILTON *Divorce* Introd., To..pacify the fiercenes of this gentle Ordinance.
†**c.** Bravery, high-spirit, mettle. *Obs.*
c **1400** *Destr. Troy* 4825 The fame of our fuersnes fares abrode. *c* **1489** CAXTON *Blanchardyn* iii. 18 The fyersnes of the sayd courser. **1692** E. WALKER *Epictetus' Mor.* xxxi, Who..admires the..manly Fierceness that adorns his Face.
d. Eagerness. †Const. *to* with *inf.*
1533 BELLENDEN *Livy* I. (1822) 73 That uthir limmare.. for fersnes to fle, left the ax stikkand in the kingis hede.
2. Of natural agents, disease; also of passions, conflict, etc.: Intense vehemence, furious activity.
1435 MISYN *Fire of Love* I. xxvii. 58 Grete ferisnes of turmentis. **1541** R. COPLAND *Galyen's Terapeutyke* 2 C ij, Lay vpon the sayd vlceres a playster..vntyll that the yre and fyersnesse be abated. **1665** MANLEY *Grotius' Low C. Warres* 355 It proved very dangerous by the fierceness of the Frost and cold. **1718** ROWE tr. *Lucan* VII. 1040 They..curse the cruel Gods, in fierceness of Despair. **1885** *Manch. Exam.* 29 June 5/2 The present fierceness of trade competition throughout the world. **1891** E. PEACOCK *N. Brendon* I. 271 The fierceness of the storm was over.

†**ˈfiercety.** *Obs.* Forms: 4–6 fe-, fi-, fyerste(e. [f. as prec. + -TY.] = FIERCENESS.
1382 WYCLIF *Judith* iii. 11 And ȝit ner the latere these thingus doende thei myȝten not swagen the feerste of his brest. *c* **1450** *Mirour Saluacioun* 4233 The fierstee of this streit dome is noted be virgines ten. **1494** FABYAN *Chron.* VII. 394 The northyn wynde blewe with suche fyerste. *c* **1500** *Melusine* 119 He considered..the fyerste of hys vysage.

†**ˈfierdhalf.** *Obs.* [f. *fierd*, FOURTH + HALF.] A fourth part, a quarter.
1674 N. FAIRFAX *Bulk & Selv.* 21 Such a kind of somewhatkin, as truckles beneath the very tinyness of an half nothing, and is forsooth a fierdhalf nothing.

ˈfierding. *pseudo-arch.* [a. Sw. *fjerding*:—ON. *fjórðungr*: see FARTHING.
Introduced from a Swedish writer by Blackstone in his disquisitions on Teutonic legal antiquities, and by some later writers mistaken for a term of early Eng. law.]
An alleged name for a quarter of a hundred or of a shire. Also *attrib.* in ***fierding-court.***
1768 BLACKSTONE *Comm.* III. 34 The antient Gothic courts in their lowest instance, or fierding-courts. **1872** E. W. ROBERTSON *Hist. Ess.* 120 *note*, The district between the Hundred and the greater Shire—the Fierding or Quarter. **1889** *Century Dict.*, *Fierding-court*, one of an early class of English courts, so called because [etc.].

‖**fieri** (ˈfaɪəraɪ). [L. *fierī*, inf. to be made, come into being. Cf. *in esse*, *in posse*.] Used in med.L. phrase ***in fieri***: in process of being made or coming into being. †Formerly sometimes treated as an Eng. phrase, as ***in the fieri***, ***in our very fieri.***
1640 BP. HALL *Episc.* I. ii. 8 The Roman Church, then in the fieri of reforming. **1677** PLOT *Oxfordsh.* 117 Many of these formed stones seem now to be in fieri. **1681** *Relig. Clerici* 5 There is a certain magical influence of nature..that tempers us all diversly in our very fieri. **1726** A. HORNECK in *Glanvill's Sadducismus* 363 The things then being in fieri, when it [the book] was printed. **1832** AUSTIN *Jurispr.* II. (1885) 910 The contract is still *in fieri* as between obligor and obligee.

‖**fieri-facias** (ˈfaɪəraɪˈfeɪʃɪæs). *Law.* [L. *fierī-facias* cause to be made, f. *fierī* (see prec.) + *facias* cause, 2nd pers. sing. pres. subj. of *facĕre* to do, make.] 'A writ wherein the sheriff is commanded that he cause to be made out of the goods and chattels of the defendant, the sum for which judgement was given' (Blackstone); the common process for executing a judgement. Often quoted as ***Fi. fa*** (ˈfaɪˈfeɪ).
1463 *Paston Lett.* II. No. 474. 135 A *fieri facias* is come out of the Exchequir for Hue Fen. **1544** tr. *Nat. Brev.* 177 He shal haue execucyon against them by the statute of acton Burnel by a fieri facias. **1685** KEBLE *King's Bench Rep.* I. 947 Recovery of Debt on Fi. fa. direced to the Sheriff into London. **1728** CARTHEW *King's Bench Rep.* (1741) 419 There were two distinct Writs of Fi. fa. brought to the Sheriff. **1818** CRUISE *Digest* (ed. 2) II. 174 Nor were lands originally liable to a private person's debts, nor any execution but by *fieri* or *levari facias.* **1829** MAULE & SELWYN *King's Bench Rep.* VI. 110 The plaintiff claimed as a purchaser of a term, seized and sold by the sheriff under a writ of fi. fa.
†**b.** *punningly.* (Cf. FIERY *a.* 4 b.) *Obs.*
1594 NASHE *Unfort. Trav.* Wks. V. 44 Purseuants with red noses..a purseuant..with the verie reflexe of his firie facias. **1608** *Pennyless Parl.* in *Harl. Misc.* (Malh.) III. 74 They that drink too much Spanish sack shall..be served with a fiery-facias. **1611** [see FACIES 1]. **1667** DRYDEN *Wild Gallant* II. ii, I use to tell him of his Title, Fiery facias.

fierily (ˈfaɪərɪlɪ), *adv.* [f. FIERY *a.* + -LY².] In a fiery manner.
1. With the appearance or colour of fire.
1824 tr. *Hoffmann's Devil's Elixir* I. 75 The rising sun, which now ascended fieryly. **1859** J. C. MANGAN *Poems* 69 The sun ere he fierily sinks. **1885** G. MEREDITH *Diana* III. xv. 304 Her musings on him..fierily brushed her cheeks.
2. With ardour; ardently, eagerly, passionately.
1600 ABP. ABBOT *Exp. Jonah* 37 The Prophet so firily is set, and so hotely enflamed to run from his dutie. **1825** *Blackw. Mag.* XVIII. 448 Long, and eagerly, and fierily I gazed. **1880** G. MEREDITH *Trag. Com.* viii. (1892) 112 He lived with the pulses of the minutes, much as she did, only more fierily.

fieriness (ˈfaɪərɪnɪs). [f. as prec. + -NESS.] The quality or condition of being fiery.
†**1.** The attribute of containing the element fire; igneous nature. *Obs.*
1680 H. MOORE *Apocal. Apoc.* 74 As if a burning Mountain had been cast into the Sea, the earthiness and fieriness thereof being so contrary..to Water.
2. The condition of being hot as fire, or of glowing like fire.
1611 COTGR., *Ignition*..firinesse; the being red-hot. **1698** J. FRYER *E. India & Persia* 104 Water is sprinkled, to mitigate the Fieriness of the Sun.
†**b.** Inflammation; ***fieriness of the face*** = ERYSIPELAS. *Obs.*
1616 SURFL. & MARKH. *Country Farme* 206 It quencheth the firinesse of the face. **1658** A. FOX *Wurtz' Surg.* II. xxiii. 139 All the fieriness and burning is gone [from a wound].
c. Of a liquid or viand: see FIERY 4 c.
1698 J. FRYER *E. India & Persia* 157 Their Relishing Bits have not the Fieriness of ours. **1837** WHITTOCK *Bk. Trades* (1842) 393 Flavour, mellowness and a due strength without fieriness, comprised all that need be desired to produce a British Brandy.
3. Ardour of temper; tendency to 'fire up'.
1625–8 *Camden's Hist. Eliz.* IV. (1688) 568 The Fieriness and Heat of his Youth. **1704** ADDISON *Italy* (1733) 37 Natural Fieriness of Temper. **1842** DICKENS *Lett.* (ed. 2) I. 76 Katey (from a lurking propensity to fiery-ness) [is named] Lucifer Box.

†**ˈfierize,** *v. Obs.*⁻¹ [f. *fier*, FIRE *sb.* + -IZE.] *intr.* To become fire, assume the properties of fire.
1591 SYLVESTER *Du Bartas* I. ii. (1641) 11/2 But Aire turne Water, Earth may Fierize.

fierk, obs. f. of FIRK.

Fiersday, Sc. form of THURSDAY.

fiers(e), obs. forms of FIERCE.

‖**fierté** (fjɛrte). [F. *fierté*, f. *fier*: see FEER *a.*] Haughtiness, pride; high spirit.
1673 DRYDEN *Marr. à la Mode* II. i, I assume something of fierté into my countenance. **1784** HAN. MORE in W. Roberts *Mem.* (1835) I. 353 This preposterous pride Mrs. Palmer seemed to think a noble fierté. **1841** LADY BLESSINGTON *Idler in France* I. 171 A certain fierté..of aspect.

fiery (ˈfaɪərɪ), *a.* Forms: 3 furie, -y, fuyre, -i, -y, 4–6 fyre, -ie, -y, 4–7 firie, -y(e, (5 fery), 6–7 fierie, (6 fyeri), 6–9 fir(e)y, 6– fiery. [f. FIRE *sb.* + -Y¹. Cf. OFris. *fiurech*, Du. *vurig*, Da. *fyrig*, MHG. *viurec*, *viuric* (Ger. *feurig*).]
1. a. Consisting of or containing fire; flaming with fire. ***fiery-drake, -dragon*** = FIRE-DRAKE.
c **1275** *Passion* 660 in *O.E. Misc.* 56 þe holy gost heom com vp-on in fury tunge. *c* **1290** *S. Eng. Leg.* I. 39/175 A fiery Drake þar-opon: a-ȝein heom cominde huy seiȝe. **1393** GOWER *Conf.* II. 183 For to wissen hem by night A firy piller hem alight. **1526** *Pilgr. Perf.* (W. de W. 1531) 3 b, The holy goost appered on yᵉ apostles in fyry tonges. **1611** BIBLE *Dan.* iii. 23 These three men..fell downe bound into the midst of the burning fierie furnace. *a* **1800** COWPER *Heroism* 85 Where no volcano pours his fiery flood. *a* **1822** SHELLEY *Satire upon Sat.* 34 And rains on him like flakes of fiery snow. **1832** DE LA BECHE *Geol. Man.* (ed. 2) 113 One vast flood of burning matter..rolling to and fro its 'fiery surge'. *fig.* **1866** B. TAYLOR *Palm & Pine*, Passion's fiery flood.
b. Fire-bearing; *esp.* of an arrow, dart, etc. *lit.* and *fig.*
c **1300** *St. Brandan* 332 Tho ther com in a furi arewe at a fenestre. *c* **1386** CHAUCER *Knt.'s T.* 706 Loue hath his firy dart so brenningly Ystiked thurgh my..hert. *c* **1500** *Lancelot* 1227 Loues fyre dart..smat one to the hart. **1697** DRYDEN *Virg. Georg.* I. 447 He deals his fiery Bolts about. **1796** H. HUNTER tr. *St. Pierre's Stud. Nat.* (1799) I. 86 The Father of Day, with his fiery shafts. *a* **1822** SHELLEY *To Italy* 3 As the earthquake's fiery flight.
c. In biblical allusions: Attended with or performed by a display of fire.
1847 EMERSON *Poems, Problem* Wks. (Bohn) I. 401 Ever the fiery Pentecost Girds with one flame the countless host. **1850** HARE *Mission Comf.* 9 The firy baptism of the day of Pentecost. **1879** FARRAR *St. Paul* (1883) 233 The awful fiery Law [see *Deut.* xxxiii. 2]..delivered by God Himself.
2. Depending on or performed by the agency of fire; in ***fiery trial*** with reference to the testing of metals; also, †of a metal, tested by fire. †***fiery weapons*** = FIRE-ARMS. ***fiery wound***: a wound inflicted by fire-arms.
1398 TREVISA *Barth. De P.R.* VIII. xxv. (1535) 127/1 He [Mars] dysposethe and makethe able to fyrye werkes and craftes. **1555** PHILPOT in Strype *Eccl. Mem.* III. App. xlviii. 156, I cownsel ye therfor to the fyeri Gold of the Deity of owre Christ. **1598** BARRET *Theor. Warres* I. i. 2 The wars are much altered since the fierie weapons first came vp. *Ibid.* 3 Well wishing in my hart..that this infernall fierie engine had never bin found out. **1611** BIBLE *1 Pet.* iv. 12 Thinke it not strange concerning the fiery triall which is to trie you. **1704** POPE *Windsor For.* 113 The whirring pheasant feels the fiery wound. **1876** FREEMAN *Norm. Conq.* V. xxiv. 395 The fiery trial which England went through.
3. a. Having the appearance of fire; brightly glowing or flaming, of a blazing red.
14.. *MS. Herald's Office* in *R. Glouc.* (1724) 484 *note*, In whiche enetid appered in the West ii. sterres of fuyry colour. **1480** CAXTON *Chron. Eng.* ccxxxii. 252 Many sterres..fyl doun to the erth leuyng behynde hem fery bemes. **1561** *Burn. Paules Ch.* A ij, On Wednesday..was seene a marueilous great fyrie lightning. **1590** SPENSER *F.Q.* I. lxxv. 7 Flyeth firie light. **1601** ? MARSTON *Pasquil & Kath.* I. 208 Your nose is firie enough. **1607** TOPSELL *Four-f. Beasts* (1658) 6 The head, and back parts to the tail, are of a fiery colour. **1727** DE FOE *Syst. Magic* I. iv. (1840) 102 These fiery appearances are nothing but certain collections of matter exhaled by the influence of the sun from the earth. **1791** MRS. RADCLIFFE *Rom. Forest* xi, The sun threw a fiery gleam athwart the woods. **1878** MORLEY *Crit. Misc.*, *Carlyle* 163 Veiled by purple or fiery clouds of anger.
b. *absol.* or quasi-*sb. rare.*
1847 L. HUNT *Men, Women, & B.* I. xiv. 239 Hair amounting to a positive fiery.
c. Of eyes (with mixture of sense 5): Flashing, glowing, ardent.
1568 R. GRAFTON *Chron.* (1812) II. 192 The king..having black eyes, which when he waxed angry, would seeme to be fyrie. **1601** SHAKS. *Jul. C.* I. ii. 186 Cicero Lookes with such Ferret and such fiery eyes. **1819** SHELLEY *Cyclops* 463 So will I, in the Cyclops fiery eye. **1841** W. SPALDING *Italy & It. Isl.* I. 32 The dark fiery eye and marked features of the Neapolitan fisherman.
4. a. Hot as fire; blazing, burning, red hot. †***fiery-triplicity***: see quot. 1730.
c **1290** *S. Eng. Leg.* I. 105/146 Nomen huy pich and brumston..And ope hire nakede tendre bodi al-fuyri it casten. **1297** R. GLOUC. (Rolls) 6866 þat, heo wolde þoru fury yre. **1535** STEWART *Cron. Scot.* II. 461 Ony spark out of ane fyrie brand. **1597** HOOKER *Eccl. Pol.* v. §54. 115 The sword which is made fierie doth not only cut..but also burne. **1697** DRYDEN *Virg. Georg.* I. 157 The fiery Suns too fiercely Play. **1726** tr. *Gregory's Astron.* I. Pref. 5 That the Sun and Stars were fiery or red-hot Stones. **1730–6** BAILEY (folio), Fiery triplicity, are those signs of the zodiack which surpass the rest in fiery qualities, as Leo, Aries, and Sagittarius. **1744** BERKELEY *Siris* §186 The throne of God appeared like a fiery flame. **1836** MACGILLIVRAY tr. *Humboldt's Trav.* xx. 291 The sky became clearer..and the atmosphere more fiery. *fig. a* **1340** HAMPOLE *Psalter* cxviii. 140 þe worde þat is fyry thorgh þe haly gast. **1593** SHAKS. *3 Hen. VI*, I. iv. 87 Hath thy fierie heart so parcht thy entrayles?
b. Of a tumour, etc.: Burning, inflamed. ***fiery face***: one affected by erysipelas.
1600 SURFLET *Countrie Farme* II. xliv. 291 Of these two ointments, the first is better for..skurfs, and firy faces. **1758** J. S. *Le Dran's Observ. Surg. Dict.* (1771) B bb, *Antrax*, a red fiery Tumour. **1784** COWPER *Task* II. 183 Bids a plague Kindle a fiery boil upon the skin.
c. Acting like fire; productive of a burning sensation or inflammation.
1535 COVERDALE *Isa.* xiv. 29 The frute shalbe a fyrie worme. **1577** NORTHBROOKE *Dicing* (1843) 5 This is that fyrie serpent, that as many as looke vpon him should liue. **1611** BIBLE *Num.* xxi. 6 Fierie serpents. **1821** SHELLEY *Hellas* 553 Like a fiery plague breaks out anew. **1855** BAIN *Senses & Int.* II. ii. §15 The fiery taste of alcoholic liquors.
d. *Cricket.* Causing the ball to fly up after pitching. (Cf. FIRE *sb.* A. 15.)
1877 C. BOX *Eng. Game Cricket* xxvi. 450 *Fiery*, one of the ungenerous appellations a ground receives when it is hard, and probably not so verdant as a lawn or smooth as a billiard table. **1882** *Austral. in Eng.* 181 The wicket was fiery and the outfielding rough. **1893** *Baily's Mag.* Oct. 255/1 Fiery wickets are not at all desirable, since they introduce an element of danger into the game which is customarily absent. **1909** *Westm. Gaz.* 7 Aug. 11/2 Mr. Carr is indispensable to an England eleven on any wicket—fast, slow, crumbly, fiery.
5. Of persons, their actions and attributes:
a. Ardent, eager, fierce, spirited.
c **1385** CHAUCER *L.G.W.* 2292 *Philomene*, He caste his fery herte up-on hyre. **1393** GOWER *Conf.* III. 237 Sardanapallus..Was..Fall into thilke firy rage Of love. **1529** MORE *Comf. agst. Trib.* III. Wks. 1219/1 Yᵉ firye affeccion that we beare to our owne filthy fleshe. **1594** SHAKS. *Rich. III*, IV. iii. 54 Then fierie expedition be my wing. **1650** HUBERT *Pill Formality* 24 Very fiery and zealous for the maintenance of

Episcopacy. **1681** DRYDEN *Abs. & Achit.* 156 A fiery Soul, which working out its way, Fretted the Pigmy-Body to decay. **1848** MACAULAY *Hist. Eng.* II. 459 Adventures irresistibly attractive to his fiery nature. **1867** FREEMAN *Norm. Conq.* (1876) I. v. 290 Such fiery zeal implies the firmest belief.

b. Fiercely irritable; easily moved to violent anger.

1590 SHAKS. *Com. Err.* IV. iv. 53 Alas how fiery, and how sharpe he lookes. **1640** in *Hamilton Papers* (Camden) App. 259 His speeches did so fascinate the old fiery little man. **1710** *Tatler* No. 231 ¶2 A terrible Apprehension of his fiery Spirit. **1752** YOUNG *Brothers* I. i, Rome calls me fiery: Let her find me so! **1806** SURR *Winter in Lond.* (ed. 3) II. 273 The signor and this fiery Montagu exchanged some fierce looks. **1852** MISS YONGE *Cameos* II. xv. 163 Charles, in his fiery petulance, declared that he would go.

c. Of a horse: Mettlesome, spirited.

1593 SHAKS. *Rich. II*, V. ii. 8 The Duke..Mounted vpon a hot and fierie Steed. **1697** DRYDEN *Virg. Georg.* III. 130 The fiery Courser..Pricks up his Ears. **1827** LYTTON *Pelham* x, My horse was..the most fiery..in Paris.

6. Of a vapour, *esp.* gas in a mine: Liable to take fire, highly inflammable. Hence of a mine, etc.: Containing inflammable gas, liable to explosions from firedamp.

1751 BP. R. POCOCKE *Trav. Eng.* (1888) I. 206 They are much troubled with what they call fiery air..When it is very bad, they let down a candle by a rope, to set fire to the fiery damp, as they call it. *Ibid.* 207 Nothing but the vapours or fiery damp that come out of the spring. **1851** GREENWELL *Coal-trade Terms Northumb. & Durh.* 27 A furnace of the width of 10 feet..will..be sufficient for any mine, however fiery. **1868** *Daily News* 30 Nov., The seam of coal was known to be..a fiery one. **1887** *Ibid.* 30 May 5/3 Both pits are situated in what the miners..call a 'fiery' district.

7. *attrib.* and *Comb.* **a.** adverbial, as ***fiery-bright, -fierce, -flaming, -hot, -kindled, -liquid, -rash, -red, -seeming, -shining, -short, -sparkling, -twinkling.*** **b.** parasynthetic, as ***fiery-faced, -footed, -helmed, -hoofed, -mouthed, -pointed, -spangled, -spirited, -sworded, -tressed, -visaged, -wheeled, -winged.*** Also, **fiery-new**, †(*a*) = BRAND-NEW *obs.* (cf. *fire-new*); (*b*) of wine, not yet mellowed; **fiery-puissant**, transl. of L. *ignipotens*, working powerfully with fire.

1531 ELYOT *Gov.* II. vi, The eien *firye bright. **1594** SPENSER *Amoretti* xvi, Legions of loves..Darting their deadly arrowes, fyry bright. **1588** FRAUNCE *Lawiers Log.* Ded., A raging and *fireyfaced Aristotelean. **1819** SHELLEY *Cyclops* 486 The Cyclops' eye so *fiery fierce. **1598** SYLVESTER *Du Bartas* II. ii. *Columnes* 469 David..Holds a fierce Lyon's *fiery flaming Crest. **1590** SPENSER *F.Q.* I. xii. 2 Scarcely had Phœbus..harnessed his *fyrie-footed team. **1592** SHAKS. *Rom. & Jul.* III. ii. 1 Gallop apace, you fiery-footed steeds. **1748** THOMSON *Cast. Indol.* II. xxxii, A fiery-footed boy, Benempt Dispatch. **1715–20** POPE *Iliad* xx. 52 In aid of Troy..came, Mars *fiery-helm'd. **1612** DRAYTON *Poly-olb.* i. 3 Where Titan still vnyokes his *fiery-hoofed Teame. **1398** TREVISA *Barth. De P.R.* XI. xiii. (1495) 398 Whan *firy hote yren is quenchyd in water. **14..** HOCCLEVE *Compl. Virgin* 221 Now thow art frosty cold now *fyry hoot. **1850** TENNYSON *In Mem.* cxiv, Some wild Pallas..fiery-hot to burst Al barriers. **1595** SHAKS. *John* II. i. 358 Backe to the stained field You equall Potents, *fierie kindled spirits. **1655** H. VAUGHAN *Silex Scint.* I. *Midnight* (1858) 54 Thy heav'ns ..Are a *firie-liquid light. **1596** SPENSER *F.Q.* V. viii. 40 The *firie-mouthed steedes. **1644** *Feast of Feasts* 2 Take a taste of their new, *fiery-new Divinity. **1842** TENNYSON *Will Water.* 98 The vintage, yet unkept, Had relish, fiery-new. **1593** SHAKS. *Lucr.* 372 The fair and *fiery-pointed sun. **1573** TWYNE *Æneid* x. Eej, Take that shield which..The *fyrypuissant god unvict gaue thee. **1631** WEEVER *Anc. Fun. Mon.* 212 Which *fierie-rash temper of his. **1593** SHAKS. *Rich. II*, II. iii. 58 Here come the Lords..*fierie red with haste. **1846** G. E. DAY tr. *Simon's Anim. Chem.* II. 228 The urine was usually of a fiery-red colour. **1628** F. FLETCHER *Drake's Voy.* (Hakl. Soc.) 149 An infinite swarme of *fierie-seeming wormes flying in the aire. **1594** ? GREENE *Selimus* Wks. XIV. 288 Mars..Mounted vpon his *firie-shining waine. **1847** TENNYSON *Princ.* v. 297 *Fiery-short was Cyril's counter-scoff. **1586** MARLOWE *1st Pt. Tamburl.* v. ii, Even from the *fiery-spangled bed of heaven. **1596** FITZ-GEFFREY *Sir F. Drake* (1881) 63 The *fierie-sparkling precious Chrysolite. **1652** J. WRIGHT tr. *Camus' Nature's Paradox* 266 The *fiery-spirited Beast..carried Liante towards the besieger's Trenches. **1821** BYRON *Cain* I. i, Guarded by *fiery-sworded cherubim. **1745–6** COLLINS *Ode to Liberty* 97 The *fiery-tressed Dane..o'erturn'd the fane. *a* **1649** DRUMM. OF HAWTH. *Poems* Wks. (1711) 15 'Mong ..*fiery twinkling gleams Of warm vermilion swords. **1813** SHELLEY *Q. Mab* VII. 87 The *fiery-visaged firmament expressed Abhorrence. **1632** MILTON *Penseroso* 51 The *fiery-wheeled throne. **1757** DYER *Fleece* IV. 211 *Fiery-winged winds..rous'd by sudden storms.

c. In the names of birds and animals: **fiery-brandtail**, the redstart (*Ruticilla phœnicurus*); **fiery-flare, -flaw** = *fire-flaire*, the sting-ray; **fiery-tangs**, *dial.* (see quot.); **fiery-topaz**, a species of humming bird.

1813 J. HEADRICK *Agric. Surv. Forfars.* App. 55 Both these species [crab and lobster] are called in Angusshire ..*Firy-tangs*. **1867** SMYTH *Sailor's Word-bk.*, *Fiery-flaw* or *fire-flaire*, a northern designation of the sting-ray (*Raia pastinaca*). **1868** WOOD *Homes without H.* xxix. 554 The oddly shaped nest..is made by the Fiery Topaz (*Topaza pyra*). **1879** MISS JACKSON *Shropsh. Word-bk.*, *Fiery-bran'tail*, the Redstart.

ˌfiery ˈcross.

1. = FIRE-CROSS

1615 SIR D. CAMPBELL *Let.* in Pitcairn *Crim. Trials Scot.* III. 23 Sir James the traitour hes latlie directit out ane fyrie croce from the head of Lockerrane to the Tarbart. **1810** SCOTT *Lady of L.* III. xviii, He vanish'd, and o'er moor and moss Sped forward with the Fiery Cross.

2. A burning cross used by the Ku Klux Klan to intimidate people. *U.S.*

1926 *New Masses* July 7/2 Three hundred klansmen are burning a fiery cross on a hillside. **1936** M. MITCHELL *Gone with Wind* lviii. 982 We convinced the hot-heads that watching, waiting and working would get us further than nightshirts and fiery crosses. **1948** *Chicago Tribune* 2 July 1/7 A 10 foot fiery cross was set ablaze in his front yard last night.

fiesta (fiːˈɛstə). [Sp., feast.] In Spain or Spanish America, a religious festival; also, any festivity or holiday. Also *transf.*

1844 J. GREGG *Commerce Prairies* I. 208 These *carretas* ..[are] the 'pleasure-carriages' of the rancheros, whose families are conveyed in them to the towns..or to *fiestas*. **1845** R. FORD *Hand-bk. Trav. Spain* I. III. 332/2 The *Fiestas* are of the highest order. **1910** 'O. HENRY' *Whirligigs* v. 71 There are bathing and fiestas and bull-fights and scandal. **1923** *Blackw. Mag.* Nov. 697/1 The failure of the great June *fiestas* owing to continued rains. **1934** J. B. PRIESTLEY *Eng. Journey* x. 341 An agricultural fiesta. **1966** *Illustr. London News* 26 Feb. 2 Seek out the island of sun, gaiety, carnivals, fiestas, a casino.

Fi.fa, abbrev. of FIERI-FACIAS.

FIFA (ˈfiːfə). Also **F.I.F.A., Fifa.** [Acronym f. the initial letters of *F*édération *I*nternationale de *F*ootball *A*ssociation, established (1904) in Paris, and now based in Zurich.] The name of the administrative body controlling international association football.

1946 *Times* 16 July 2/5 England, Ireland and Wales have already rejoined the F.I.F.A. **1948** *Times* 29 July 2/5 The Congress of F.I.F.A...failed to reach a decision on the definition of amateurism in football. **1953** *Universal Guide for Referees* (Féd. Int. de Football Assoc.) 3 It is remarkable that in each of the seventy-three countries affiliated to F.I.F.A. football is played according to exactly the same laws. **1963** C. D. FAWCETT *Cycl. Initials & Abbrev.* 59/1 *FIFA, Fédération Internat. des Football Assocns*, controlling internat. football competitions. **1972** G. GREEN *Great Moments in Sport: Soccer* ii. 31 England faced a selected F.I.F.A. XI drawn from the stars of Europe. **1973** [see *return leg* s.v. RETURN *sb.* 19]. **1982** *Daily Tel.* 23 Dec. 16/1 UEFA have joined FIFA in their condemnation of the referee clampdown.

fife (faɪf), *sb.* Forms: α. 6 fiphe, fyfe, 6– fife. β. 6–7 phi-, phyfe, -phe. [First appears in 15th c.: it is uncertain whether it is directly a. HGer. *pfeife* (see PIPE *sb.*), or a corruption of F. *fifre* fife, fifer (15th c. in Littré), a. OHG. *pfîfâri* (mod.G. *pfeifer*) piper, fifer, f. *pfîfan* to PIPE.]

1. *Mus.* **a.** A small shrill-toned instrument of the flute kind, used chiefly to accompany the drum in military music.

1555 WATREMAN *Fardle Facions* II. xi. 248 Thei [Turkes] vse a dromme and a fiphe, to assemble their Bandes. **1577** FENTON *Gold. Epist.* 319 Out of little and smal phyfes, come a voice cleare and shrill. **1710** PHILIPS *Pastorals* v. 52 In thee The rudeness of my rural fife I see. **1846** GROTE *Greece* I. viii. (1862) II. 212 Their step was regulated by the fife.

b. (See quot.)

1876 STAINER & BARRETT *Dict. Mus. Terms*, *Fife*, an organ stop. A piccolo, generally of two feet in length.

c. ***fife and drum***: taken as typical instruments of martial music; often *attrib.* in lit. sense, and fig. = martial, militant.

1674 PLAYFORD *Skill Mus.* Pref. 5 When he hears the sound of the Trumpet, the Fife and Drum. **1900** *Westm. Gaz.* 14 Feb. 3/2 The 'Captains Courageous' of the House were by no means unanimous in his favour. The Under-Secretary for War had not many fife-and-drum supporters in their ranks. **1923** B. WHITLOCK *J. Hardin & Son* I. v. 69 In the line there was a fife and drum corps. **1958** *Times* 29 Dec. 9/4 As a curate at St. Giles-in-the-Fields he started a fife-and-drum band for boys.

2. The sound of this instrument; in quots. *transf.*

1627 P. FLETCHER *Locusts* II. iv, And blasts with whistling fifes new rage inspire. **1810** SCOTT *Lady of L.* I. xxxi, The lark's shrill fife may come..from the fallow.

3. One who plays the fife; a fifer.

1548 *Privy Council Acts* (1890) II. 166 For one monthes wages..for iiij drummes and two fyfes, every at xl^s. **1598** BARRET *Theor. Warres* II. i. 18 Instructing the Drummes and Phifes their seuerall soundes. **1625** MARKHAM *Souldiers Accid.* 15 The Phiphes (if there be more then one) the eldest shall march with the eldest Drumme. **1649** *Ann. Barber-Surgeons Lond.* (1890) 406 Paid to the Drumme & Phiffe —12s. *Mod.* They sent the drums and fifes to drown his voice.

4. *attrib.*, as ***fife-bird***. Also, **fife-major** (*Mil.*), a non-commissioned officer who superintends the fifers of a regiment.

1854 WHITTIER *Lit. Rec. & Misc.* 241 I heard a mellow gush of music from the brown-breasted fife-bird. **1802** JAMES *Milit. Dict.*, *Fife-major.*

fife (faɪf), *v.* [f. prec. sb.] **a.** *intr.* To play on a fife. **b.** *trans.* To play (a tune) upon or as upon the fife.

1598 FLORIO *Worlde of Wordes* 462/2 *Zuffolare*, to whistle, to pipe, to fife, to blow hard. **1837** LONGF. *Drift-Wood* Prose Wks. 1886 I. 322 All blowing and drumming and fifing away like mad. **1887** STEVENSON *Underwoods* 17 Winds that in darkness fifed a tune.

Hence **ˈfifing** *vbl. sb.*, the action of the vb.

c **1817** BYRON *To T. Moore* ii, Fifing and drumming..Oh Thomas Moore! **1851** RUSKIN *Stones Ven.* I. xxi. §xx, The fluting and fifeing expire, the drumming remains.

fifer¹ (ˈfaɪfə(r)). [f. as prec. + -ER¹.] One who plays the fife.

1540 in *Vicary's Anat.* (1888) App. xii. 242 Item, for Iohn Pretre, fyfer, wagis..xxs. viijd. **1585** JAS. I *Ess. Poesie* (Arb.) 17 Syne Phifers, Drummes, and Trumpets cleir do craue The pelmell chok with larum loude alwhair. **1659** TORRIANO, *Fifaro*, a piper, a fifer, a fluter. **1809** PINKNEY *Trav. France* 247 This is some fifer who has obtained this leave. **1840** *Act 3–4 Vict.* c. 96 §53 Drummer, trumpeter, fifer. **1868** MORRIS *Earthly Par.* II. (1870) 147 The fifer [must] stop His dancing notes the pensive drone that chid.

Fifer² (ˈfaɪfə(r)). [f. *Fife* + -ER¹.] A native or inhabitant of Fife, a county of Scotland.

1887 P. MCNEILL *Blawearie* ix. 73 He'll be awfu' cunning, for a' the Fifers are burstin' fu' o' that commodity. **1897** *Daily News* 23 Nov. 3/6 He knew that the outside and envious critic was in the habit of telling Fifers that they worked the idea of a kingdom of Fife for a good deal more than it was worth. **1901** *Daily Chron.* 14 Oct. 5/2 The London 'Fifers' do not forget in exile the engaging qualities of their native county. **1908** *Westm. Gaz.* 12 May 7/2 We Scots outside 'the Kingdom' know it takes 'a long spoon to sup wi' a Fifer'. **1927** *Glasgow Herald* 14 May 9 The average Fifer..has more of Gaelic blood in him than the average Lewisman. **1967** I. FINLAY *Lowlands* i. 20 The man of Lothian is far different from the man of Galloway, the Fifer from the Borderer.

fife-rail (faɪfˈreɪl). *Naut.* [Said by sailors to be so called because the fifer sat on this rail while the anchor was being got in.] †**a.** 'Rails forming the upper fence of the bulwarks on each side of the quarter-deck and poop in men-of-war' (Adm. Smyth, 1867) (*obs.*). **b.** The rail round the main-mast, encircling both it and the pumps and furnished with belaying pins for the running rigging.

1721–1800 BAILEY, *Fife Rails.* **1804** A. DUNCAN *Mariner's Chron.* Pref. 19 Drift-rails, fife-rails, sheer-rails, waist-rails, etc. **1881** W. C. RUSSELL *Ocean Free-Lance* II. iv. 168 [It] whitened the rigging and the fife-rails.

fiff (fɪf), *v. nonce-wd.* [Echoic.] To play on the Pandean pipes. (In quot. quasi-*trans.*)

1886 *Tinsley's Mag.* July 65 The man with..the Pandean pipes..trying to fiff himself into a Consumption.

Fifie, fifie (ˈfaɪfɪ). *Sc.* [f. *Fife* in Scotland + -IE.] 'A type of herring fishing boat with vertical stem and stern-posts, common in the second half of the 19th and early 20th cents. on the E. coast, prob. so called from having been first built and used on the Fife coast' (*Scot. Nat. Dict.*).

1905 *Banffshire Jrnl.* 28 Mar., A place for biggin heerin' boats Zulus, Fifies—best afloat. **1914** *Chambers's Jrnl.* Apr. 264/1 The craft at this time were of the 'scaff' or 'fifie' build. **1927** *Glasgow Herald* 3 May 7 Scaffie boats gave way to Zulu and Fifie types. **1934** *Geogr. Jrnl.* LXXXIV. 438 The Scottish craft, the fifies and zulus. **1950** P. F. ANSON *Scots Fisherfolk* viii. 104 The most common type of Scottish fishing vessel until about the introduction of steam was the '*Fifie*'.

Fifish (ˈfaɪfɪʃ), *a. Sc.* [said to be f. *Fife* the name of a Scotch county + -ISH; applied originally as a term of opprobrium to people from that county.] Somewhat deranged.

1822 SCOTT *Pirate* ix, Very, very Fifish, as the east-country fisher-folks say. **1824** —— *Redgauntlet* vii, 'Just Fifish, wowf—a wee bit by the East-Nook or sae.'

fifo (ˈfaɪfəʊ), *sb.* (*a.*) orig. *U.S.* Also **FIFO.** [Acronym f. the initial letters of *first in, first out.*] **a.** *Econ.* (Designating or pertaining to) a method of accounting in which the goods first acquired by a company are valued as though they are the first to be sold; = *first in, first out* (*a*) s.v. FIRST *adv.* 1 g.

1945 *Inland Printer* Jan. 40/1 There are numerous ways to figure inventory: first-in, first-out, last-in, first-out, popularly called the 'fifo' and 'lifo' methods. **1965** *Economist* 31 July 470/2 Most companies in this country use the first-in-first-out (FIFO) system [of stocktaking]. **1975** *Times Lit. Suppl.* 26 Sept. 1083/5 In times of high inflation companies using FIFO for stocks and historical accounts for depreciation can at one and the same time show 'obscene' (but fictional) profits and be heading straight for liquidation. **1980** *Oil Majors in 1979* (Shell Internat. Petroleum Co.) 2 Shell's and BP's relatively large increase in net working capital reflects the application of FIFO-accounting by the two companies.

b. *Computing.* = *first in, first out* (*b*) s.v. FIRST *adv.* 1 g. Also, a device in which this procedure is employed. Freq. *attrib.*

1966 [see FIRST *adv.* 1 g]. **1968** D. E. KNUTH *Art of Computer Programming* ii. 236 Queues are sometimes called ..first-in-first-out ('FIFO') lists. **1968** *Israel Jrnl. Technol.* VI. 378/2 The queueing discipline in all queues is FIFO, and at time O there are K items awaiting service. **1969** P. B. JORDAIN *Condensed Computer Encycl.* 406 It is possible to organize lists with neither LIFO nor FIFO. **1984** J. HILTON *Choosing & using your Home Computer* III. 68 FIFO buffers ..are an extremely common feature of most types of computer software. **1984** H. M. DEITEL *Introd. Operating Systems* (rev. ed.) ix. 219 This..causes pages to be loaded into storage and replaced under FIFO. **1984** *AGARD Conf. Proc.* No. 361. xxix. 4 Each synchronous program stores in a FIFO (in RAM) its own data. **1985** *Electronics* 2 Sept. 51/2

We will burst several words into the FIFO, encrypt, and then burst those words into communication memory on the board.

fift, obs. form of FIFTH.

fifteen (fɪfˈtiːn, ˈfɪftiːn), *a.* and *sb.* Forms: 1 fif-, fýfténe, -týne, 3–6 fif-, fyften(e, 3 *south.* vyftene, (3 fythtene), 3, 5 fiveten(e, 7–8 -een, 5–7 fyvetene, 6–7 fifteene, 9 *Sc.* feifteen, 6– fifteen. [OE. *fífténe*, *-týne* corresponds to OFris. *fîftîne*, OS. *fîftein* (LG. *föftein*, Du. *vijftien*), OHG. *fimf-zehen*, *finfzehan* (MHG. *vünf-*, *fünfzehen*, mod.G. *fünfzehn*), ON. *fimtán* (Sw. *femton*, Da. *femten*), Goth. *fimftaihun*; f. OTeut. **fimfi* FIVE + **tehun* TEN: see -TEEN.]

The cardinal number composed of ten and five, represented by the symbols 15 or xv.

A. as *adj.*

1. In concord with sb. expressed.

Beowulf 1582 (Gr.) He..sloh..fyftyne men. *a* **1000** *Guthlac* 908 (Gr.) He on westenne wiceard ȝeceas fiftynu ȝear. *c* **1160** *Hatton Gosp.* John xi. 18 Ofer fyftena furlenga. *c* **1250** *Gen. & Ex.* 415 For fiftene ȝer hadde adam; ðan caim of eue cam. **1297** R. GLOUC. (1724) 416 A..comete..hym ssewede vyftene nyȝt ywys. *a* **1300** *Cursor M.* 27737 (Cott.) Þir ar þe springes o wreth fythtene. **1340** HAMPOLE *Pr. Consc.* 4564 Aftir þair dede..Anticrist sal regne, yhit fiften days. *a* **1400** *Prymer* (1891) 59 Heere bygynneth the fyftene psalmes. **1548** FORREST *Pleas. Poesye* 472 The beste ffyuetene shealinges not surmowntinge. **1602** WARNER *Alb. Eng.* XI. lxii. 272 Saint Nicholas Bay..fifteene hundred Miles from Mosco is away. **1647** FULLER *Good Th. in Worse T.* (1841) 92 An agitation..to bring down jubilees to fifteen, twelve, or ten years. **1766** PENNANT *Zool.* (1768) II. 235 Taken in clap-nets of fiveteen yards length. **1819** SHELLEY *Peter Bell* vii. 23 For fifteen months. **1883** STEVENSON *Treas. Isl.* I. i, Fifteen men on the dead man's chest.

2. With ellipsis of sb., which may usually be supplied from context. *the Fifteen*: the Court of Session (formerly) consisting of fifteen Judges. Also, the first Jacobite rising (in the year 1715).

c **1050** *Byrhtferth's Handboc* in *Anglia* VIII. 303 Gif þær synt fiftene to lafe todælað þa eall swa þa oðre. *a* **1300** *Cursor M.* 8863 (Cott.) Þis temple..of heght it had fiften [eln]. **1660** SIR B. RUDDIER *Poems* 83 Give me a Virgin of Fifteen. **1712–4** POPE *Rape Lock* IV. 58 Hail, wayward Queen! Who rule the sex to fifty from fifteen. **1769** *Dublin Mercury* 16–19 Sept. 2/2 A Black Gelding..about fifteen high. *a* **1797** H. WALPOLE *Mem. Geo. II*, I. 266 A man engaged in the former rebellion or as the Scotch call it in the Fifteen. **1814** SCOTT *Wav.* lxiv, 'Ye were just as ill aff in the feifteen.' **1815** —— *Guy M.* xxxviii, 'A man's aye the better thought o' in our country for having been afore the feifteen.' **1842** ORDERSON *Creol.* viii. 75 From adolescent fifteen..to mature twenty-five.

†**3.** = FIFTEENTH *a.* *Obs.*

1375 BARBOUR *Bruce* II. 17 On the fyften day. *c* **1430** *Freemasonry* 251 The fyftene artycul maketh an ende, For to the mayster he ys a frende. **1525** LD. BERNERS *Froiss.* II. cxxv. [cxxi.] 356 To be at Hamton the fyftene day of May. **1598** GRENEWEY *Tacitus' Ann.* VI. vi. (1622) 130 The fifteene Kalends of Nouember. **1623** *Bill of Compl.* in *N. Shaks. Soc. Trans.* (1885) 498 In the fifteene yeare of his Maties raigne.

B. as *sb.*

1. *Eng. Hist.* = FIFTEENTH *sb.* 1. *Obs.*

1494 FABYAN *Chron.* VII. 480 In this yere also the Kynge helde his parlyament..in the which was graunted vnto hym thre fyftenys. **1540** *Nottingham Rec.* III. 379 To Master Meyre in money to make owte the Fyften v.*li.* **1593** SHAKS. *2 Hen. VI*, IV. vii. 23. **1643** PRYNNE *Sov. Power Parl.* I. (ed. 2) 23 Both the Houses gave halfe a tenth and halfe a fifteene, to be disposed of as the Lords thought fit, for the defence of the Realme.

2. A set of fifteen persons or things: **a.** A set of fifteen players forming a 'side' at Rugby football.

1878 *Cliftonian* Apr. 232 No O.C. has ever complained of difficulty in accommodating himself to the fifteen game. *Ibid.* 233 There will..be some competition to get into the fifteen. **1880** *Times* 12 Nov. 4/4 The two Universities..always place strong fifteens in the field. **1890** *Daily News* 4 Dec. 2/5 The visitors brought a powerful fifteen, and secured the victory after a splendid game.

†**b.** (see quot.) *Obs.*

1688 R. HOLME *Armoury* III. 231/2 A pair of Beads called Fifteens, containing fifteen Pater Nosters and 150 Aves.

c. *Cribbage.* An exact sum of fifteen pips counted on two or more cards, a court card reckoning as 10.

1674 COTTON *Compl. Gamester* ix. 108 That makes you six Games, because there is two fifteens and a pair. **1830** *Hoyle made familiar* 58 They neither form a pair, a fifteen, a sequence nor a flush.

3. a. A game at cards: see quot.

1884 *Daily News* 13 Feb. 5/6 During a game of fifteen, a species of poker, several cards were marked.

C. *Comb.*, as *fifteen-spined* adj.; **fifteen-pounder**, a gun throwing a shot that weighs fifteen pounds; **fifteen-shilling** *a.*, worth fifteen shillings.

1684 J. PETER *Siege Vienna* 109 *Fifteen pounders. **1855** MACAULAY *Hist. Eng.* IV. 698 The ministers..resolved to issue..*fifteenshilling bills, for the payment of the troops. **1832** JOHNSTON in *Proc. Berw. Nat. Club* I. 7 The *fifteen-spined stickleback.

fifteener (fɪfˈtiːnə(r)). [f. prec. + -ER¹.] A book printed in the fifteenth century.

1830 *Blackw. Mag.* XXVII. 306 An ardent devotee of Fifteeners. **1876** CUTTER *Rules Dict. Catal.* 68 Such..books are fifteeners or the rarest Americana.

fifteenth (fɪfˈtiːnθ, ˈfɪftiːnθ), *a.* and *sb.* Forms: 1 fifteiðe, -éoða, -é(o)ȝða, 3 fiftéoða, *south.* viftethe, vyfteoþe, 3–4 fiftend(e, 4 *south.* vyfteoþe, 6 *Kent* vifftend, 4–7 fiftenth(e, (4 fiftenþe), 5–6 fyfte(n)th(e, (6 -teenth), 6–7 fivete(e)nth, 6– fifteenth. [OE. *fíftéoða* (fem. and neut. *-e*), f. *fífténe* FIFTEEN on the analogy of *téoða* TENTH. From the 14th c. the forms descending from the OE. become rare, being superseded by a new formation on FIFTEEN + -TH¹, which still remains. A third form of the ordinal, *fiftend(e*, appears in the Ormulum, Hampole and the Cursor Mundi, and appears to be due to Scandinavian influence; cf. ON. *fimtánde* (Sw. *femtonde*, Da. *femtende*). The other Teut. langs. agree with the ON. in having the ordinal suffix as *-d-* instead of *-þ-*; OFris. *fîftînde*, OS. **fifteindo* (Du. *vijftiende*), OHG. *funfzêndo* (MHG. *vünfzehende*, mod.Ger. *fünfzehnte*), Goth. *fimfta-taihunda* (= fifth + tenth).] The ordinal numeral belonging to the cardinal fifteen.

A. *adj.*

1. In concord with *sb.* expressed.

c **900** *Bæda's Hist.* IV. xxvii. [xxvi.] (1891) 358 Þy fifteȝðan ȝeare. *c* **1000** *Sax. Leechd.* III. 190 Mone se fifteoða. *c* **1200** ORMIN 9170 Onn hiss fiftende winnterr. **1297** R. GLOUC. (1724) 522 The viftethe peni of hor god. **1382** WYCLIF *Num.* xxviii. 17 In the fiftenthe day. *a* **1440** *Sir Degrev.* 1869 One the fyftethe day. **1535** COVERDALE *2 Kings* xiv. 23 In the fyftenth yeare of Amasias. **1749** FIELDING *Tom Jones* XV. xii, And here we put an end to the fifteenth book. **1851** RUSKIN *Stones Ven.* (1874) I. i. 30 Dull inventions of the fifteenth century.

2. With ellipsis of sb.

1641 MILTON *Ch. Govt.* I. vi. 25 A councell, from which by any thing that can be learnt from the fifteenth of the Acts, no faithful Christian was debarr'd. **1753** N. TORRIANO *Gangr. Sore Throat* 125 She having had a very bad Night from the Fourteenth to the Fifteenth.

3. *fifteenth part*: one of fifteen equal parts into which a quantity may be divided.

1626 BACON *Sylva* §798 A Fifteenth Part of Siluer. **1662** GRAUNT *Bills of Mortality* vii. 42 London..bear[s] the fifteenth part of the charge of the whole Nation in all Publick Taxes.

B. *sb.*

1. A fifteenth part; *esp.* in *Eng. Hist.* A tax of one-fifteenth formerly imposed on personal property.

c **1380** WYCLIF *Eng. Wks.* (1880) 66 Men supposen alle þes passen þre fiftenþes. **1496–7** *Act. Hen. VII*, c. 12 (*title*) An Acte for Fyftenthes and Tenthes. **1518** *MS. Acc. St. John's Hosp., Canterb.*, Payd for ij wrytys for alowans off þe vifftend. **1647** N. BACON *Disc. Govt. Eng.* I. lxiv. (1739) 133 He took a fifteenth which was granted to his Father. **1765** BLACKSTONE *Comm.* I. I. viii. 298 Tenths and fifteenths were temporary aids..granted to the king by parliament. **1879** CASTLE *Law of Rating* 21 The collectors of the tenths and fifteenths granted to the King in the City of London.

2. *Mus.* **a.** (see quot. 1876.) **b.** (see quot. 1880.)

a. **1597** MORLEY *Introd. Mus.* 71 An eight, a twelfth, a fifteenth..and so forth..be perfect cordes. **1609** DOULAND *Ornith. Microl.* 79 Others are tripled, to wit, a fifteenth, which is equall to the sound of an Vnison, and an Eight. **1876** STAINER & BARRETT *Dict. Mus. Terms*, *Fifteenth*, the interval of a double octave.

b. **1613** *Organ Specif. Worcester Cathedral*, In the choir organ..1 smal principal or fifteenth of mettal. **1776** SIR J. HAWKINS *Hist. Music* IV. I. x. 149 Of the stops of an organ, the most usual are the Diapasons..Tenth, Twelfth, Fifteenth [etc.]. **1880** GROVE *Dict. Mus.*, *Fifteenth* is a stop or set of pipes in an organ sounding 2 octaves or 15 notes above the Open diapason.

Hence **fifˈteenthly** *adv.*, in the fifteenth place.

a **1642** SIR W. MONSON *Naval Tracts* III. (1704) 322/1 Fifteenthly, they ought to take Account. **1691–8** NORRIS *Pract. Disc.* (1711) III. 170 When he shall yet further consider Fifteenthly.

fifth (fɪfθ), *a.* and *sb.* Forms: 1 fifta, (fem. & neut. fifte), 2–7 fift(e, (3 fiȝft, 4 fyfft), 3–4 *south.* vifte, 3–6 fyfte, -the, (3 fivet, 5 fyvet), 4–5 fyve(þe, -th(e, (4–5 fifþe, -the), 5–7 fith(e, 6– fifth. [OE. *fífta* = OFris. *fifta*, OS. *fîfto* (Du. *vijfde*), OHG. *fimfto*, *finfto* (MHG. *vunfte*, *vünfte*, mod.Ger. *fünfte*), ON. *fimte* (Sw. and Da. *femte*), Goth. **fimfta*:—OTeut. **fimfton-*, f. pre-Teut. **penqto-* (Gr. πεμπτός, Lat. *quin(c)tus*), f. **penqe* FIVE. The normal form *fift* still survives in dialects; the standard form, which first appears in the 14th c., is due to the analogy of *fourth*.] The ordinal numeral belonging to the cardinal five.

A. *adj.* **1. a.** In concord with *sb.* expressed.

c **1000** ÆLFRIC *Lev.* xix. 25 Ær þam fiftan ȝeare. *c* **1000** *Sax. Leechd.* II. 298 Fifte mæȝen is. *c* **1175** *Lamb. Hom.* 103 Þeo fifte sunne is Tristicia. *a* **1225** *Ancr. R.* 198 Þe vifte hweolp hette Inobedience. *a* **1300** *Cursor M.* 9232 (Cott.) To recken forth þat leuedi kin, þe fift eild wil we be-gin. **1340** *Ayenb.* 12 Þe vifte article zuo is þet [etc.]. *c* **1380** WYCLIF *Sel. Wks.* III. 444 Þe fyfft heresie. *c* **1400** *Destr. Troy* 7553 *heading*, Of the Fyuet Batell in the Felde. **1486** *Bk. St. Albans* E j b, The fithe yere a grete stagge. **1526** *Pilgr. Perf.* (W. de W. 1531) 307 b, By the vertue of the fyfth worde that thou spake for great mystery. **1632** SANDERSON *Serm.* 447 The fift position. **1700** DRYDEN *Pal. & Arc.* III. 168 With smiling aspect you serenely move In your fifth orb, and rule the realm of love. **1781** COWPER *Hope* 414 Just made fifth chaplain of his patron lord. **1857** HUGHES *Tom Brown* I. viii, The fifth form would fag us, and I and some more struck and we beat 'em. **1884** *Syd. Soc. Lex.*, *Fifth ventricle* [of the brain], the cavity which lies between the two layers of the septum lucidum.

b. *to smite, †stab in, under the fifth rib*: to strike to the heart. *lit.* and *fig.*

The Revised Version (agreeing with the older Eng. versions) has 'in the belly'; the translators of 1611 regarded *ḥōmesh* as the same word as *ḥōmesh* fifth part; the two are from different roots, as the other Semitic langs. show.

1611 BIBLE *2 Sam.* ii. 23 Wherefore Abner with the hinder ende of the speare smote him vnder the fift ribbe. **1641** W. HOOKE *New Eng. Teares* 11 Death..stabs them in the fift rib. **1822** SHELLEY *Chas. I*, I. 104 Smiting each Bishop under the fifth rib.

c. *the fifth wheel of a coach, waggon*, etc.: proverbially used for something superfluous. See also *fifth wheel* (*b*) in C. below.

1631 DEKKER *Match me in London* I. 14 Thou tyest but wings to a swift gray Hounds heele, And add'st to a running Charriot a fift wheele. **1891** *Law Times* XCI. 205/2 The functions of the grand juror are too often those of the fifth wheel in the coach. **1902** H. JAMES *Wings of Dove* xvii. 255 'Respect', in their game, seemed somehow..a fifth wheel to the coach. **1960** J. BAYLEY *Characters of Love* iv. 242 Her distress is partly finding herself the fifth wheel of the coach.

2. With ellipsis of sb.

O.E. Chron. an. 827 Fifta was Eadwine Norþan hymbra cyning. *c* **1175** *Lamb. Hom.* 39 Fifte is þet þu scalt forȝeuen þon monne þe wið þe agultet. *a* **1300** *Cursor M.* 23235 (Gött.) Of helle pines..þe fiȝft es vndemes of dint, þat þa wreches þar sal hint. **1584** R. SCOT *Discov. Witchr.* I. viii. 13 Statutes made in the fift of Elizabeth. **1678** B. R. *Let. Pop. Friends* 8 That cursed, unfortunate Fifth of November. **1725** POPE *Odyss.* IX. 395 The lots were cast on four; Myself the fifth. **1818** SHELLEY *Rev. Islam* X. ix. 5 Each fifth shall give The expiaton for his brethren here.

3. *fifth part*: one of five equal parts into which a quantity may be divided.

1480 CAXTON *Chron. Eng.* ccxxv. 230 The kyng axed the fifthe part of all the meoble goodes of englond. **1565–73** COOPER *Thesaurus*, *Cochlearium*..two fift partes. *a* **1687** PETTY *Pol. Arith.* (1690) 73 The same Lands will produce a fifth part more of Food.

4. quasi-*adv.* In the fifth place, FIFTHLY.

1526 *Pilgr. Perf.* (W. de W. 1531) 292 Fyfth, they be mortifyed from the inordynate affeccyon of parentes.

5. *Fifth Estate*, any institution considered as comparable to the four estates (ESTATE *sb.* 7).

1966 *New Statesman* 15 Apr. 526/2 The achievements of the trade union movement,..the pride the government takes in an historic, responsible and independent Fifth Estate.

B. *sb.* **1.** = *fifth part*. See A. 3. Also, a fifth part of moveable goods granted to the king.

1557 RECORDE *Whetst.* B ij b, *Sesquiquinta*, 6 to 5: 12 to 10 ..(1⅕) a fifte more. **1578** T. N. tr. *Conq. W. India* 6 The kings fiftes and revenues. **1674** JEAKE *Arith.* (1696) 209 To set down 3 Fourths and 4 Fifths. **1724** SWIFT *Drapier's Lett.* v. (1725) 147 When the Publick shall have lost..Four Fifths of its Annual Income for ever. **1777** ROBERTSON *Hist. Amer.* (1783) III. 370 The spoil..after setting apart the king's fifth, was divided among 480 persons.

2. *Mus.* **a.** A note five diatonic degrees above or below a given note; the interval of three tones and a semitone, embracing five diatonic degrees of the scale.

1597 MORLEY *Introd. Mus.* 70 A third, a Fift, a Sixt. **1652** *News fr. Lowe-Countr.* 8 He..Knows Thirds, Fifths, Eights, Rests, Moods, and Time. **1737** OZELL *Rabelais* V. 80 *La Quinte*..a Fifth, or the Proportion of Five in Musick. **1825** DANNELEY *Encycl. Music*, *Fifth*, a note in music, of which there are three species, viz. the perfect fifth, called also dominant, the diminished and augmented. **1864** MRS. GATTY *Parables fr. Nature* Ser. IV. 131 All the fifths were either too flat or too sharp.

b. The concord of two tones separated by this interval.

1656 tr. *Hobbes' Elem. Philos.* IV. xxix. 372 The Organ [of hearing] will..make that Concord which is called a Fifth. **1674** [see CONCORD *sb.* 5].

3. *pl.* Articles of the fifth degree in quality; fifth-rate material.

1881 *Daily News* 7 Sept. 3/4 Butter..thirds, 106*s.*; fourths, 99*s.*; fifths, 78*s.* **1893** *Westm. Gaz.* 5 June 6/3 Formerly only as low a quality as good fifths were imported.

4. A fifth part of a gallon of liquor; a bottle containing such a part. *U.S. colloq.*

1938 D. BAKER *Young Man with Horn* (1939) i. 69 Davis pulled the glass stopper out of the square bottle..—Shorty's fifths never came sealed; they never came fifths for that matter. **1967** E. MCGIRR *Here lies my Wife* ii. 63 Bring a fifth —if you drink—and I'll provide ice.

C. *Comb.* **a.** **fifth-chain** (see quot.); **fifth (cranial) nerve** *Anat.*, either of the trigeminal nerves (see TRIFACIAL, TRIGEMINAL *adjs.*), together called the ***fifth pair of nerves***; **fifth-essence** = QUINTESSENCE; **fifth-penny**, = fifth part; **fifth-wheel**, (*a*) (see quot.); (*b*) chiefly *U.S.*, something superfluous (*ellipt.* for sense A. 1 c above); also as *adj.*

1874 KNIGHT *Dict. Mech.* I. 839/2 **Fifth-chain*, the chain by which the single lead horse in a team of five is hitched to the end of the tongue. **1585** JAS. I *Ess. Poesie* (Arb.) 35 Poure out, my frends, there your *fift-essence fyne. **1685** S. COLLINS *Syst. Anat.* II. 1047 The *Fifth pair of Nerves, called by the Antients the Third, are seated below the other pair of Nerves. **1836–9** *Todd's Cycl. Anat.* II. 270 The fifth nerve is attached to the surface of the brain on either side of the pons Varolii, at a distance of three-fourths of an inch from its middle line. **1875** *Encycl. Brit.* I. 881/2 The Trifacial or fifth is the largest cranial nerve. **1931** *Daily Tel.*

19 Jan. 11/3 The Archbishop is suffering from severe fifth nerve neuralgia. **1968** W. H. HOLLINSHEAD *Anat. for Surgeons* (ed. 2) I. 70 The trigeminal, or fifth cranial, nerve is..the largest of all cranial nerves except the optic. **1732** SWIFT *Prop. Pay Nat. Debt*, Wks. (1841) II. 123 The lands of the primacy..are let so low that they hardly pay a *fifth penny of the real value. **1809** BAWDWEN *Domesday Bk.* 416 Torksey and Hardwick paid the fifth-penny of the tax of the city of Lincoln. **1874** KNIGHT *Dict. Mech.* I. 839/2 **Fifth wheel*, a wheel or segment above the fore-axle of a carriage and beneath the bed..the fifth wheel forms an extended support to prevent the careening of the carriage bed. **1881** Fifth wheel [see *wheel-plate* (WHEEL *sb.* 19)]. **1962** *Engineering* 30 Mar. 418/2 The turntable on a tractor is known as the fifthwheel. **1916** O. H. PROUTY (*title*) The fifth wheel: a novel. *Ibid.* xx. 187 (*heading*) The fifth wheel gains wings. **1944** H. S. TRUMAN in M. Truman *Harry S. Truman* (1973) ix. 184 Maybe your dad can make a job out of the fifth wheel office. **1976** *National Observer* (U.S.) 24 Apr. 2/5 The vaunted and proud FSO 'generalist' has become a fifth wheel in many posts.

b. When prefixed to certain sbs., as *form*, *rate*, etc. *fifth* forms a combination, which is used attributively, passing occas. into an *adj.*, and through the absolute use into a *sb.*

1666 *Lond. Gaz.* No. 38/4 A Fifth Rate Fregat, called the Sweepstakes. **1672** LACY *Dumb Lady*, Prol., My less than fifth rate wit. **1689** *Lond. Gaz.* No. 2451/4 Admiral Herbert had with him..10 fourth Rates, 1 fifth Rate, and 2 Tenders. **1747** J. LIND *Lett. Navy* i. (1757) 22 Captains of a fifth rate. **1857** HUGHES *Tom Brown* I. ix, For most of the sixth spent their evenings in the fifth-form room.

c. In Quaker use; *fifth day* (i.e. of the week), Thursday; similarly *fifth month*, May.

1698 S. SEWALL *Let.-Bk.* in *Mass. Hist. Soc. Coll.* (1886) I. 203 Am going to keep Court at Springfield, next Fifth day. **1799** E. FRY in S. Corder *Life* (1853) 63 Fifth Month, 1st. **1821** *Ibid.* 318 My beloved daughter, Rachel, was married last Fifth-day, the 23rd, at Runcton. **1868** G. G. CHANNING *Early Recoll. Newport, R.I.* 231, I went frequently to hear him at the fifth-day meetings.

Hence **'fifthly** *adv.*, in the fifth place.

1526 *Pilgr. Perf.* (W. de. W. 1531) 8 b, Fyfthly, they must despyse ye deuyll with all his pompes. **1681** H. MORE *Exp. Dan.* App. iii. 297 Fifthly, If it be demanded why, etc. **1681–6** J. SCOTT *Chr. Life* (1747) III. 252 Fifthly and lastly, That Christ also was that Jehovah and divine Lord and King ..is evident. **1800** YOUNG in *Phil. Trans.* XCI. 82 Fifthly by immerging the eye in water.

Fifth Avenue. *U.S.* The name of a fashionable street in central New York City, used *fig.* to denote fashion, elegance, or high society. Freq. *attrib.*

[**1857** *San Francisco Call* 15 Mar. 1/2 The class of the '*Fifth Avenuedity!*'.] **1858** *Spirit of Times* 27 Feb. 409/3 The Fifth Avenue does not drive out or walk out on Sunday. They do not consider it to be in good taste. **1869** J. H. BROWNE *Great Metropolis* 520 A charming Fifth avenue belle is soon to be led to the altar by a prominent member of the stock board. **1907** F. H. BURNETT in *Century Mag.* Mar. 673/2 She had understood and cared, American as she was! She had felt it all, even with the hideous background of Fifth Avenue behind her. **1946** *Coronet* Oct. 129/1 Thousands of New Yorkers..satisfy Fifth Avenue tastes on a five-and-ten budget. **1972** D. LEES *Zodiac* 8 His cream sports trousers had a Fifth Avenue look.

fifth column. [tr. Sp. *quinta columna*; cf. COLUMN *sb.* 10.] Orig. the column of supporters which General Mola declared himself to have in Madrid, when he was besieging it in the Spanish Civil War, in addition to the four columns of his army outside the city (see 1936 quots.); hence, allusively, a body of one's supporters in an attacked or occupied foreign country, or the enemy's supporters in one's own country. Also *attrib.* and *transf.* Hence **fifth-columnist**, freq. loosely, a traitor, a spy. Also ***fifth columnism***.

[**1936** *N.Y. Times* 16 Oct. 2/2 Police last night began a house-to-house search for Rebels in Madrid... Orders for these raids..apparently were instigated by a recent broadcast over the Rebel radio station by General Emilio Mola. He stated he was counting on four columns of troops outside Madrid and another column of persons hiding within the city who would join the invaders as soon as they entered the capital.] *Ibid.* 17 Oct. 9/4 Prudence counsels the government to forestall as far as possible the activities of this 'fifth column'. **1938** E. HEMINGWAY (*title*) The Fifth Column. **1939** *War Illustr.* 21 Oct. p. ii/3 This looks to me like the Nazis' 'fifth column' in Belgium ready for the invasion. **1940** W. S. CHURCHILL *Into Battle* (1941) 222 Parliament has given us the powers to put down Fifth Column activities with a strong hand. **1940** *Economist* 20 Apr. 723/1 Now that the news is beginning to reach the outside world of the..extent and..efficiency of the Nazi plot by which the key positions in Norway's cities and harbours were sacrificed to the invader..the other neutrals are attempting..to cope with the problem of their own 'Fifth Columns'. **1940** G. B. SHAW *Platform & Pulpit* (1962) 291 If you call Stalin a bloodstained monster you must be shot as the most dangerous of Fifth Columnists. **1941** E. SNOW *Battle for Asia* 354 Factions..sabotaged the Eighth Route and New Fourth Armies in ways which elsewhere would be called Fifth Columnism. **1941** A. HUXLEY *Grey Eminence* vii. 146 His enemies..accused him of using his missionaries as French agents and anti-Hapsburg fifth-columnists. **1942** *Mind* LI. 166 Hence Prof. Collingwood arrives at the startling conclusion that psychologists are a group of fifth column conspirators, whose real aim is to destroy western civilisation from within. **1958** *New Statesman* 26 Apr. 538/3 After denouncing the Free World's readiness to let Communist fifth columns flourish undisturbed in its midst, he rails [etc.]. **1958** *Times Lit. Suppl.* 15 Aug. p. xxviii/4 Sensational elements began to infiltrate like fifth-columnists into the work of serious novelists. **1967** W. SOYINKA *Kongi's Harvest* 66 I've put him through the standard tests. He's no fifth columnist. **1971** *Daily Tel.* 6 Apr. 1 Most of them had confessed to entering East Pakistan as fifth columnists.

†**fifth monarch.** *Obs.* Christ as the head of the 'fifth monarchy'; see next.

1658 COWLEY *Cutter Coleman St.* Epil. *Wks.* 1710 II. 893 So great and gay a one [Congregation] I ne'er did meet At the Fifth Monarch's Court in Coleman-street. **1660** *Biblioth. Fanat.* in *Harl. Misc.* (1746) VIII. 70/2 He had resolved to keep it till the Coming of the fifth Monarch.

Fifth monarchy. The last of the five great empires referred to in the prophecy of Daniel (Dan. ii. 44), in the 17th c. identified with the millennial reign of Christ predicted in the apocalypse. Also *attrib.*, *esp.* in **Fifth-monarchy man**, one of those in 17th c. who believed that the second coming of Christ was immediately at hand, and that it was the duty of Christians to be prepared to assist in establishing his reign by force, and in the meantime to repudiate all allegiance to any other government.

1657 EVELYN *Diary* 10 Aug., Desperate zealots, call'd the Fifth-Monarchy-Men. **1677** DK. LAUDERDALE in *L. Papers* (1885) III. lvii. 89 How soone they [the disaffected in W. Scotland] may take armes no man can tell; for..they are perfitely fifth monarchye men. **1702** SEWALL *Diary* 31 Jan. (1879) II. 52 William Parsons of 88 years, is buried. Was in the fifth-monarchy fray in London: but slipt away in the Crowd. **1731** E. CALAMY *Life* (1830) I. i. 76 He [Calamy's schoolmaster] was a sort of Fifth Monarchy man.

Hence **Fifth-mo'narchical**, *a.*, of or pertaining to the Fifth-monarchy; **Fifth-'monarchism** *nonce-wd.*, the principles of the *Fifth-monarchy men*; **Fifth-'monarchist** = *Fifth-monarchy man.*

1679 OATES *Narr. Popish. Plot* Ded. A ij b, An Anti-christian pretence of a Fifth Monarchical Soveraignty over all the Kings and Princes of Christendom. **1705** E. WARD *Hud. Rediv.* II. ix., Fifth-Monarchical Fanaticks. **1736** *Plea Sacram. Test* 110 Venner, and the other Fifth-Monarchists in England. **1832–4** DE QUINCEY *Cæsars* Wks. 1862 IX. 9 The fanatics of 1650 who proclaimed Jesus for their king.. were usually styled Fifth-Monarchists. **1870** LOWELL *Among my Bks.* Ser. I. (1873) 235 The turbid zeal of Fifth-Monarchism.

fiftieth ('fɪftɪɪθ), *a.* (*sb.*) Forms: 1–2 fiftigoða, -geða, fifteogoða, -gaðe, 2–3 fiftuða, -ðe, 3 fiftugeðe, 4–6 fif-, fyftith(e, -tyth(e, 6– fiftieth. [OE. *fíftigoða*:—earlier **fíftigunþa*, corresponding to ON. *fimmtugánde* (Sw., Norw. *femtiande*, Da. *femtiende*), f. FIFTY on the analogy of TENTH.

In the other Teut. langs. the ordinal suffix is different: OFris. *fiftichsta* (Du. *vijftigste*), OHG. *fimfzugôsto* (MHG. *vünfzegeste*, mod.Ger. *fünfzigste*.]

The ordinal numeral belonging to the cardinal fifty. *fiftieth part*: one of fifty equal parts into which a quantity may be divided.

c **1000** ÆLFRIC *Gram.* (Z.) 283 *Quinquagesimus* se fifteo-goða. *c* **1175** *Lamb. Hom.* 87 þe fiftuða dei fram þan estertid. *c* **1200** *Trin. Coll. Hom.* 117 þe fiftugeðe dai after estrene dai. **1382** WYCLIF *Num.* viii. 25 Whanne the fyftithe ȝeer of age thei han fulfillid. **1530** PALSGR. 372 *Cinquantiesme*..fyftyth. **1579** FULKE *Heskins' Parl.* 495 The fiftieth Chapter sheweth the understanding of the same text by Effrem. **1611** BIBLE *Lev.* xxv. 11 A Iubile shall that fiftieth yeere be vnto you. **1721** NEWTON *Opticks* III. xxi. (ed. 3) 325 The fiftieth part of an Inch. **1868** LOCKYER *Heavens* (ed. 3) 310 The fiftieth part of a second of arc. **1800** YOUNG in *Phil. Trans.* XCI. 48 Their difference was exactly one-fifth of an inch. To this we must add a fiftieth.

fifty ('fɪftɪ), *a.* and *sb.* Forms: 1 fiftiȝ, 2–4 fifti, 3 *Orm.* fifftiȝ, *south.* vifti, 3–5 fi-, fyfte, 3–6 fyfty, 4–6 fiftie, -tye, (6 fyvetie), 7 fivety, 4, 7– fifty. [OE. *fiftiȝ*= OFris. *fiftich*, *fiftech*, OS. *fiftich* (Du *vijftig*), OHG. *fimfzug* (MHG. *fümfzec*, *fünfzec*, mod.Ger. *fünfzig*), ON. *fimm tigir* (Sw. *femtio*, Norw. and obs. Da. *femti*), Goth. *fimf tigjus*, OTeut. **fimfi* FIVE + **tigiwiz*, pl. of **teguz* decade: see -TY.]

A. *adj.* The cardinal number equal to five tens, represented by 50 or l. Also with omission of sb., and in comb. with numbers below ten (ordinal and cardinal), as *fifty-one*, *fifty-first*, etc.

Beowulf 2733 (Gr.) Fiftiȝ wintra. *c* **1000** ÆLFRIC *Deut.* xxii. 29 Fiftiȝ yntsena seolfres. *a* **1175** *Cott. Hom.* 225 Fifti fedme wid. *c* **1205** LAY. 1285 Fifti scipen fulle. **1297** R. GLOUC. (1724) 518 Arst he adde ileye an erthe vnssrined vifti ȝer. *c* **1325** *Metr. Hom.* 18 A man haht him fifty penis. *c* **1380** WYCLIF *Wks.* (1880) 192 Fourty or fyfty in a queer. *c* **1400** *Destr. Troy* 4064 In hor company come clene shippes fyfté. **1483** *Cath. Angl.* 132/2 Fifte sithe, *quinquagesies*. *a* **1561** G. CAVENDISH *Metr. Vis.* in *Life Wolsey* (1825) II. 31 This fyvetie or threscore yere. **1588** SHAKS. *L.L.L.* IV. iii. 242 A withered Hermite, fiue score winters worne, Might shake off fiftye looking in her eye. **1611** BIBLE *Gen.* ix. 28 And Noah liued after the flood, three hundred and fifty yeeres. **1683** *Pennsylv. Archives* I. 57 To secure the Paeyment of fivety pounds of like money. **1777** ROBERTSON *Hist. Amer.* (1783) II. 377 Near the fifty-third degree of latitude. **1847** TENNYSON *Princ.* v. 305 Some fifty on a side. **1878** MORLEY *Carlyle* Crit. Misc. Ser. I. 199 The disruption of the French monarchy fifty years afterwards.

b. Used indefinitely as a large number.

1818 BYRON *Juan* I. cviii, When people say, 'I've told you fifty times', They mean to scold. **1870** KINGSLEY in *Gd. Words* 204/1 A merchant..who had fifty things to tell us of his own special business.

†**c.** = FIFTIETH. *Obs.*

1539 TONSTALL *Serm. Palm Sund.* (1823) 58 Expoundynge the gospel of John in the fyfty treaty. **1558** KENNEDY *Compend. Treatise* in *Wodr. Soc. Misc.* (1844) 123 The Apostolis ressavit the gift of the Haly Gaist the fyftiday, callit in our language Wytsounday. **1578** TIMME *Caluine on Gen.* 156 As we may read in the fiftie Psalme.

B. *sb.*

1. A set of fifty persons or things.

c **1000** *Ags. Gosp.* Mark vi. 40 Hi þa sæton hundredon & fiftiȝon. **1382** WYCLIF *Luke* ix. 14 Make hem to sitte to mete by feestis, fyftyes. **1611** BIBLE *2 Kings* i. 13 Hee sent againe a captaine of the third fiftie, with his fiftie. —— *1 Macc.* iii. 55 Iudas ordained..captains..ouer fifties, and ouer tennes. **1844** LINGARD *Anglo-Sax. Ch.* (1858) II. ix. 64 Every deacon read..two fifties [fifty psalms]. **1894** *Times* 23 Feb. 8/4 The price rose by fifties to £3,450.

2. a. The age of fifty years. **b.** *the fifties*: the years between fifty and sixty in a particular century or in one's life.

c **1714** POPE *Imit. Hor.*, *Epist.* I. vii. 73 Near fifty and without a Wife. **1855** TENNYSON *Maud* I. vi. 31 Ah, what shall I be at fifty Should Nature keep me alive? **1880** MISS BROUGHTON *Sec. Th.* II. III. iv. 157, I know that I am somewhere in the fifties, and that I was born on a Monday. **1889** R. B. ANDERSON tr. *Rydberg's Teut. Mythol.* 9 A series of works published in the fifties and sixties.

†**3.** A fifty-gun ship. *Obs.*

1778 BURKE *Corr.* (1844) II. 249 Two ships of the line, two fifties, and about four lesser frigates. **1799** *Naval Chron.* I. 292 Ships of the line 188, Fifties 27.

C. *Comb.*, as in *fifty-fold* adj. and adv.; *fifty-gun-ship*; **fifty-pence piece**, a cupro-nickel heptagonal coin worth fifty (new) pence, introduced in the U.K. in 1969 during the conversion to decimal currency; also **fifty-penny piece**; **fifty-per-cent** *a.*, usurious; **fifty-weight**, half a hundredweight.

c **1000** ÆLFRIC *Gram.* (Z.) 285 *Quinquagenarius*, *fiftiȝfeald. **1606** SHAKS. *Ant. & Cl.* I. ii. 70 Till the worst of all follow him laughing to his graue, fifty-fold a Cuckold. **1872** PROCTOR *Ess. Astron.* xi. 156 Exceeding fiftyfold the volume of the Sun. **1806** A. DUNCAN *Nelson* 58 Ten sail of the line, and a *fifty-gun-ship. **1832** MARRYAT *N. Forster* xiii, A fifty-gun ship, frigate, and two corvettes, made their appearance. **1969** *Economist* 18 Oct. 87/2 From this week the new *50p piece will gradually start replacing the old brown 10s notes. **1970** O. NORTON *Dead on Prediction* ii. 34 The fifty-penny pieces still didn't look worth ten shillings to me. **1979** *Washington Post* 10 July A17/6 The British 50-pence piece has seven sides and is unambiguous. **1986** R. RENDELL *Live Flesh* ii. 24 The room heater could be made to function by the insertion of twenty-pence pieces and the water heater fifty-pence pieces. **1825** KNAPP & BALDW. *Newgate Cal.* III. 496/1 No trades-man of a *fifty per cent. conscience. **1667** PRIMATT *City & C. Build.* 105 Nine hundred and *fifty weight of Lead taken up in Ledges and Gutters. **1840** W. S. MAYO *Kaloolah* 140 Packing on my back about fifty weight of iron bolts.

fifty-fifty, *adv.* and *a. colloq.* (orig. *U.S.*). [f. FIFTY *sb.* 1.] **A.** *adv.* On a basis of fifty per cent. (or one half) each; half-and-half, equally. **B.** *adj.* Equal, shared equally; half-and-half.

1913 WODEHOUSE *Little Nugget* vi. 121 Say, Sam, don't be a hawg. Let's go fifty-fifty in dis deal. *Ibid.* xii. 209 Would a fifty-fifty offer tempt you? *Ibid.* xiv. 248 'Fifteen per cent. is our offer,' he said. 'And to think it was once fifty-fifty!' **1916** H. L. WILSON *Somewhere in Red Gap* vi. 263 And she glared at Cousin Egbert with rage and distrust splitting fifty-fifty in her fevered eyes. **1922** E. O'NEILL *Anna Christie* I. 19 Good girl?.. Well, yuh treated me square yuhself. So it's fifty-fifty. **1924** *Daily Mail* 28 Nov. 10/5 [He] did not take a fifty-fifty chance that the bedroom door he would enter by was the right one. It was pointed out to him the day before. **1937** *Times* 13 Apr. p. xxix/4 In many craft the power of the engine is such that one could hardly say into which division she fits; there is, as a fact, a type of motor-sailer which is spoken of as the 'fifty-fifty'. **1949** H. WADMAN *Life Sentence* 47 It will take much of the sting out of the opposition if the ownership is fifty-fifty.

fiftyless ('fɪftɪlɪs), *a.* [f. FIFTY *a.* and *sb.* + -LESS.] Without fifty; in quot. = not fifty years old.

1767 G. CANNING *Poems* 87 Let not your fiftyless lover despair.

fig (fɪg), *sb.*[1] Forms: 3–5 fige, 4–6 fyg(g(e, (4 fijg), 5–8 figg(e, 6–9 *Sc.* and 9 *dial.* feg, 9 *dial.* vig, 5– fig. [a. OF. *fige*, *figue*, ad. Prov. *figa*, *figua* = Sp. *higa* (obs. rare), It. *fica* (rare):—popular Lat. **fica* fig, f. L. *ficus* (*u*-stem) fig-tree, fig. The L. *ficus* was taken into OE. as *fic* (see FIKE *sb.*[1]) and was represented directly in OF. by *fi* (= It. *fico*, Sp. *higo*, Pg. *figo*), and **fica* by *fie*.]

1. a. The fruit of the fig-tree or *Ficus*, esp. the fruit of the *Ficus carica*. †*figs of Pharaoh*: the fruit of the Sycamore Fig (*Ficus Sycomorus*).

a **1225** *Ancr. R.* 150 Swete frut, þet me clepeð figes. *c* **1325** *Coer de L.* 1549 Fyggys, raysyns, in frayel. **1393** LANGL. *P. Pl.* C. III. 29 Ne on croked kene þorne kynde fygys wexe. *c* **1400** MAUNDEV. (1839) v. 50 Fyge trees þat beren no leves but fyges vpon the smale braunches, & men clepen hem Figes of Pharoon. *c* **1430** *Two Cookery-bks.* 15 An sethe fygys in Wyne & grynde hem. **1591** SYLVESTER *Du Bartas* I. iii. 573 The milky Fig, the Damson black and white. **1671** SALMON *Syn. Med.* III. lxxxii. 713 Apply a Cataplasm of Figgs and Raisons stoned. **1730–46** THOMSON *Autumn* 679 Beneath his ample leaf the luscious fig. **1801** SOUTHEY *Thalaba* II. xxxiii, Before their guest They laid..the

FIG 891 FIG-DOTE

luscious fig. **1870** MORRIS *Earthly Par.* I. II. 552 In the orchard hangs aloft The purple fig.

b. = FIG-TREE. Any tree of the genus *Ficus*, esp. *Ficus carica. Indian fig*: the Banyan (*F. indica*), or the Pipal (*F. religiosa*).

1382 WYCLIF *Num.* xx. 5 The whiche ne fige getith, ne vynes, ne powmgarnettis. *c* **1400** *Rom. Rose* 1364 Fyges, & many a date tree There wexen. *c* **1440** *Promp. Parv.* 159 Fygge or fyge tre, *ficus.* **1664** EVELYN *Kal. Hort.* (1729) 222 Figs and Mulberries will be propagated by their Suckers. **1763** CHURCHILL *Gotham* I, The Fig, which..gave our first Parents Cloaths. **1860** DELAMER *Kitch. Gard.* 150 The Fig —*Ficus carica.*

c. In the East and West Indies popularly applied (like the corresponding words in Fr., Sp., and Pg.), to the Banana, also to the Cochineal Cactus.

1582 N. LITCHFIELD tr. *Castaneda's Discov. E. Ind.* ix. 22 Fruites: that is to saye, Pomegranets, Figges of the Indias, Orenges. **1700** S. L. tr. C. Fryke's *Two Voy. into E.I.* 31 Pisang Figgs, which are a long kind of Figg. **1712** tr. *Pomet's Hist. Drugs* I. 17 The Indian Fig..call'd Jamacan..is the same Plant that..bears the Cochineal. **1794** [see COCHINEAL 2]. **1871** KINGSLEY *At Last* ii. 49 At St. Thomas's we had been introduced to bananas (figs, as they are miscalled in the West Indies). **1961** F. G. CASSIDY *Jamaica Talk* xvi. 351 Bananas named for their..flavour and other qualities.. apple or honey (the smallest), fig (very small), plum (small). **1970** *Country Life* 17–24 Dec. 1221/3 In the West Indies a fig is a small banana.

†**2.** A poisoned fig used as a secret way of destroying an obnoxious person. Often *fig of Spain, Spanish, Italian fig. Obs.*

c **1589** *Theses Martinianæ* 21 Have you given him an Italian figge? **1616** R. C. *Times' Whistle* iii. 1151 This boy.. long he shall not soe, if figs of Spain..their force retaine. **16..** NORTH *Theret's Lives* (1657) 45 Tamberlaine..did cause a Fig to be given him, and after his death married his widow. **1670** G. H. *Hist. Cardinals* III. I. 233 Some report he was poyson'd with an Italian Fig. **1691** BETHEL *Provid. God* 33 He..durst not have disobeyed for fear of a Dose, or a Fig.

3. As the name of a disease, from the resemblance in shape. †**a.** In human beings: The disease *Ficus*, or the piles. Also *pl. Obs.*

14.. *Nom.* in Wr.-Wülcker 707 *Hic figus*, the fyge. **1483** *Cath. Angl.* 130/1 þe Figes, *quidam morbus, ficus. c* **1550** LLOYD *Treas. Health* (1585) M ij, It is good if the fygge blede.

b. *Farriery.* An excrescence on the frog of a horse's foot, somewhat resembling a fig.

1607 TOPSELL *Four-f. Beasts* 414 Of the Figge. A Horse having receiued any hurt..in the sole of his foot..there will grow in that place a certain superfluous piece of flesh, like a Figge. **1616** SURFL. & MARKH. *Country Farme* 142 You must pare the hoofe..betwixt the sole of the foot and the figge. **1753** CHAMBERS *Cycl. Supp.*, *Fig* in the manege, is a sort of wart on the frush and sometimes all over the body of a horse. **1823** in CRABB *Technol. Dict.*

4. a. As a type of anything small, valueless, or contemptible; also, † *a dried fig; a fig's end.* In phrases: † ***never a fig*** = not at all; (*to* †*bid, care, give*) ***a fig, or fig's end for***; ***to mind, value*** (***a person or thing***), ***be worth a fig or fig's end.***

c **1400** *Destr. Troy* 12206 He fortherit neuer a fyge with his fight yet. *c* **1450** *Crt. of Love* xcviii, A Figge for all her chastite! **1571** HANMER *Chron. Irel.* (1633) 115 If hee threaten as an enemie, a figge for his Monarchie. *a* **1572** KNOX *Hist. Ref.* Wks. 1846 I. 173 A feg for the fead, and a buttoun for the braggyne of all the heretikis..in Scotland. **1600** ROWLANDS *Let. Humours Blood* i. 7 All Beere in Europe is not worth a figge. **1632** SHERWOOD s.v. *Figge*, Not to care a figge for one, *faire la figue à.* **1634** WITHALS *Dict.* 557 *Fumi umbra non emerim*, I will not give a fig's end for it. **1710** *Brit. Apollo* III. 3/1 No Man Does care a Fig for such a Woman. **1728** VANBR. & CIB. *Prov. Husb.* II. i. 49 Pshah! a Fig for his Mony! **1840** THACKERAY *Catherine* vii, We have it from nature, and so a fig for Miss Edgeworth. **1852** —— *Esmond* III. ii, Nor..is the young fellow worth a fig that would. **1855** ROBINSON *Whitby Gloss.*, A feg's end for it. **1887** *Poor Nellie* (1888) 185 Charlie does not care a fig about it.

†**b.** Used contemptuously; so *fig's end* used as a substitute for some other word. Also as an exclamation. Cf. *fiddlestick*(*s! fiddlestick's end! Obs.*

1604 SHAKS. *Oth.* I. iii. 322 Vertue? A figge, 'tis in our selues that we are thus, or thus. *Ibid.* II. i. 256 *Rodo.* She's full of most bless'd condition *Iago.* Bless'd figges-end. **1752** FOOTE *Taste* II. Wks. 1799 I. 23 This is Mynheer Baron de——. *Lady.* Mynheer Figs-end.

5. *dial.* A raisin.

1787 GROSE *Prov. Gloss.*, *Figs*, raisins, W. **1880** in *W. Cornw. Gloss.* **1882** *Hampsh. Gloss.*

6. *slang.*

1798 EDGEWORTH *Pract. Educ.* I. 315 Coiners give.. names to..the various kinds of false money which they circulate; such as *flats*, or *figs*, or *figthings*.

7. *Soap-making.* (See quots.)

1885 CARPENTER *Manuf. Soap* i. 12 The appearances known as 'grain' or 'strike' in a hard soap and 'fig' in a soft soap, are due to the crystalline character of soap. *Ibid.* vi. 161 To produce a grained soft-soap (or 'fig').

8. *fig* (*of tobacco*): a small piece. Cf. FID.

1837–40 HALIBURTON *Clockm.* (1862) 187 How are you off for tobacco? said Mr. Slick. Grand, said he, got half a fig left yet. **1893** MRS. C. PRAED *Outlaw & Lawmaker* I. 103 Running round to the store for a fig of tobacco.

9. *attrib.* and *Comb.* **a.** simple attrib., as ***fig-box, drum, -juice, -plaster, -skin, -tart, -wasp, -wood, -yard; fig-like*** adj. **b.** objective, as ***fig-gatherer, -lover, -seller.***

1868 *Less. Mid. Age* 126 The one man of the company set his foot upon the old *fig-box. **1864** THOREAU *Cape Cod* x. (1894) 324, I saw a great many barrels and *fig-drums. **1552** HULOET, *Figge gatherer, *ficetor.* **1853** HICKIE tr. *Aristoph.* (1872) II. 637 Pound together garlic with *fig-juice. **1845** LINDLEY *Sch. Bot.* iv. (1858) 28 b, The roots have long *fig-like fibres. **1552** HULOET, *Figge louer, *ficetor.* **1884** BROWNING *Ferishtah* (1885) 56 Try a *fig-plaster: may it ease thy pangs! **1483** *Cath. Angl.* 129/2 A *Fige celler, *ficarius.* **1855** BROWNING *Fra Lippo* 85, I starved..On *fig-skins. **1552** HULOET, *Figge tartes, *collybia.* **1883** G. ALLEN in *Knowl.* 3 Aug. 66/1 The *fig-wasps lay their eggs in the fruit of the caprifico. **1875** POLLEN *Anc. & Mod. Furn.* 33 *Figwood, willow, plane, elm, ash [etc.]. **1570** LEVINS *Manip.* 210/29 The *Fygyeard, *ficetum.* **1874** FARRAR *Christ* 55 Winding thro' the rich figyards and olive groves.

10. Special comb., as **fig-apple**, a kind of apple (see quot.); **fig-banana**, a small variety of the banana common in the West Indies (*Cent. Dict.*); **fig-bean**, a name for several species of *Lupinus*; **fig-bird**, (*a*) = BECCAFICO; (*b*) see quot. 1854; **fig-blue**, soluble blue; **fig-cake** (see quot. 1858); **fig-dust**, finely ground oatmeal, used as food for caged birds (*Cent. Dict.*); **fig-eater**, (*a*) one who eats figs; (*b*) = BECCAFICO; **fig-fauns** = L. *fauni ficarii* (see Forcellini s.v. *ficarius*); **fig-finch** = BECCAFICO; **fig-flower**, a fig of the first crop; **fig-frail**, a frail or basket of figs (see FRAIL *sb.*); **fig-gnat**, a gnat, *Culex ficarius*, injurious to the fig; **fig-marigold**, a name given to several species of the genus *Mesembrianthemum*; **fig-pecker** = BECCAFICO; **fig-peepul**, the Indian Fig (see above, sense 1 b); **fig-shell**, a shell somewhat resembling a fig; **fig-sue** *dial.*, a posset of bread, figs, and ale; **fig-Sunday** *dial.*, Palm Sunday; **fig-water**, a decoction of figs. Also FIG-LEAF, -TREE, -WORT.

1707 MORTIMER *Husb.* 542 The *Fig-apple is also newly propagated, the Tree yielding no Blossoms..nor hath the Fruit in it any Core. **1657** W. COLES *Adam in Eden* ccxii. 333 They are usually called Lupines..yet some call them *Fig-beanes after the Dutch name. **1878–86** BRITTEN & HOLLAND *Plant-n.*, *Fig-Bean.* **1576** NEWTON *Lemnie's Complex.* (1633) 105 *Figge-birds. **1854** J. W. WARTER *Last of Old Squires* xiii. 138 The chiff-chaffs; one of which Sussex people call the fig-bird. **1786** *N.Y. Directory* 26 Coller, Christopher, *fig-blue manufacturer. **1861** MRS. BEETON *Bk. Househ. Managem.* 1010 The linen..should again be rinsed..in abundance of cold water slightly tinged with fig-blue. **1837** WHEELWRIGHT tr. *Aristophanes* II. 29 She once supplied us with *fig-cakes and figs. **1858** SIMMONDS *Dict. Trade*, *Fig-cake*, a preparation of figs and almonds worked up into a hard paste, and pressed into round cakes like small cheeses. **1552** HULOET, *Figge eater, *ficarius.* **1678** RAY *Willughby's Ornith.* 216 The Beccafigo or Fig-eater. **1750** BIBLE (Douay) *Jer.* I. 39 Therefore shall dragons dwell there with the *fig-fauns. **1655** MOUFET & BENNET *Health's Improv.* xviii. 162 The *Fig-finch, the Thrush and the Oisters. **1719** LONDON & WISE *Compl. Gard.* v. 94 Figs bear twice a year, viz. first in July and August, and are usually call'd *Fig-Flowers. **1607** MIDDLETON *Five Gallants* IV. v, Upon paths made of *fig-frails. **1658** ROWLAND *Moufet's Theat. Ins.* 954 *Culex ficarius*, i.e. *Fig Gnat. **1731** MEDLEY *Kolben's Cape G. Hope* II. 255 African *Fig-Marygold with a long triangular leaf and a flesh coloured flower. **1881** E. HOLUB *Seven Yrs. in S. Africa* I. i. 16 Fig-marigolds of various kinds are especially prominent. **1647** R. STAPYLTON *Juvenal* 267 The ficedula or *figpecker, called by the Italian 'beccafico', because it feeds most on figtrees. **1864** A. V. KIRWAN *Host & Guest* i. 2 Several species of dates, fig-peckers, roebuck, and wild boar. **1859** LANG *Wand. India* 303 The tamarind, the *fig-peepul, the pomegranate, and others of the plains. **1752** SIR J. HILL *Hist. Anim.* 151 The *Fig-shell, with the depressed clavicle. **1888** *Riverside Nat. Hist.* I. 352 The species of *Ficula* are known from their shape as fig or pear shells. **1851** *Cumbrld. Gloss.*, **Fig-Sue*, bread and figs boiled in ale. **1850** *N. & Q.* 1st Ser. II. 68/2 *Fig Sunday. **1747** MRS. DELANY *Autobiog.* (1861) II. 480 *Fig-water has cured him.

†**fig** (fig), *sb.*² *Obs.* [ad. F. *figue* (in phrase *faire la figue* to make the gesture described), ad. It. *fica*; cf. Sp. *higa* in *dar la higa* to 'give the fig'.

By some identified with FIG *sb.*¹ (for a story purporting to account for the use, see Littré s.v.). According to others, It. *fica* had an indecent sense: see Tommaseo's Dict.]

A contemptuous gesture which consisted in thrusting the thumb between two of the closed fingers or into the mouth. Also, *fig of Spain*, and ***to give*** (***a person***) ***the fig.***

1579 ULP. FULWELL *Art of Flattery* ii. C iv/1 For a token I thee sende A dotinge Figge of Spayne. **1599** SHAKS. *Hen. V*, III. vi. 62 The Figge of Spaine. **1600** *Shepherd's Slumber* 90 in *England's Helicon* Z iv, With scowling browes their follies check and so giue them the Fig. **1891** C. E. NORTON *Dante's Hell* xxv. 133 The thief raised his hands with both the figs, crying, 'Take that God!'

fig (fig), *sb.*³ [f. FIG *v.*⁴ 2.

It has been asserted that in fashion prints 'Full fig.' (abbreviation for *figure*) and 'Demi-fig.' were formerly used for front and back or side views of the figure; but we have failed to find confirmation of the statement.]

1. Dress, equipment, only in phr. ***in full fig.***

1841 T. HOOK *Fathers & Sons* xxi, In full fig for the ceremony. **1839** DE QUINCEY *Casuistry Rom. Meals* Wks. III. 269 All belted and plumed, and in full military fig. **1866** MOTLEY *Corr.* 14 Aug. II. 247 We all turned out in full fig the other day.

2. Condition, form.

1883 SHERER *At Home in India* 203 Lord Alaric was in great fig. *Mod.*, The horse was in good fig for the race.

†**fig**, *v.*¹ *Obs. rare.* [f. FIG *sb.*¹] *trans.* only in † *to fig away* (a person): to get rid of by means of a poisoned fig. *Obs.* Cf. FIG *sb.*¹ 2.

1609 BP. W. BARLOW *Answ. Nameless Cath.* 23 Cardinals Allen and Tollet; yea Pope Sixtus quintus himselfe, all figg'd away in a trice. *Ibid.* 109 What an excellent veine both Popes haue in Figging each other away.

†**fig**, *v.*² *Obs.* [f. FIG *sb.*²] *trans.* To insult (a person) by giving him the fig: see FIG *sb.*²

1597 SHAKS. 2 *Hen. IV*, v. iii. 123 When Pistoll lyes, do this, and figge me, like The bragging Spaniard.

†**fig**, *v.*³ *Obs.* Also 7 **figge**. [var. of FIKE *v.*¹; cf. also FIDGE *v.*] *intr.* To move briskly and restlessly; to jog to and fro. Also, *to fig about.*

1595 *Enq. Tripe-wife* (1881) 148, I trotted from my trotter stall, And figd about from neates feete neatly drest. **1598** SYLVESTER *Du Bartas* II. i. *Handie-Crafts* 505 Like as a hound that..upon the sent doth ply, Figs to and fro, and fals in cheerfull cry. **1644** QUARLES *Barnabas & B.* (1651) 73 They that..run to sermons, figge to lectures, pray thrice a day [etc.]. *a* **1734** NORTH *Exam.* I. iii. § 125 (1740) 204 Multitudes of factious People incessantly figed about.

Hence '**figging** *vbl. sb.*, and *ppl. a.*

1577 B. GOOGE *Heresbach's Husb.* (1586) 6 Not medling with figging, chopping, & changing, nor seeking their living by handycrafts. **1601** DEACON & WALKER *Answ. to Darel* 190 Your violent fiskings and figgings about those your idle vagaries. *a* **1627** MIDDLETON *Chaste Maid* III. ii, Their short figging little shittle-cock heeles! *a* **1659** OSBORN *Observ. Turks* Wks. (1673) 334 Their daily figging up and down the streets..unattended. *a* **1693** URQUHART *Rabelais* II. xxxii, Their..figging Itch, wrigling Mordicancy. *a* **1734** NORTH *Lives* I. 99 His figging about at the first entrance.

fig (fig), *v.*⁴ [var. of FEAGUE.]

1. *trans.* = FEAGUE *v.* 2 b. ***to fig out*** (***a horse***): to trot out in lively condition. Also ***to fig up***, to make lively or spirited.

1810 *Sporting Mag.* XXXVI. 182 He said the horse..was figged with ginger. **1819** MOORE *Tom Crib's Mem.* 24 In vain did they try to fig up the old lad. **1825** C. M. WESTMACOTT *Eng. Spy* I. 177 Fig out two lively ones [horses].

2. ***to fig out***: to dress, 'get up'. Also ***to fig up***: to furbish up, make 'smart'.

1825 M. WILMOT *Let.* 26 Sept. (1935) 223, I figg'd up the petticoat into a broad sash for Wᵐ's waist. **1837** MARRYAT *Dog-fiend* xx, Landsmen are figged out as fine as Lord Harry. **1841** THACKERAY *Sec. Fun. Nap.* i, Cowards fig themselves out..as 'salvage men'. **1872** *Punch* 9 Nov. 196/1 It [a house] wants a little figging up. **1883** W. C. RUSSELL in *Longm. Mag.* III. 123 The waiter's costume, as he styled the dress I had figged myself out in.

†**3.** ? To stuff. *Obs. rare*⁻¹.

Johnson explains this: 'To put something useless into a person's head. Low Cant.'

1692 R. L'ESTRANGE *Fables* cccciii. 378 Away to the Sow she goes, and Figs her in the Crown with another Story.

†**fig**, *v.*⁵ *slang. Obs.* [Of doubtful origin; perh. (like FEAGUE, FIG *v.*⁴, FAKE) repr. Ger. *fegen*: see FAKE *v.* The spelling *fegge* (see FIG-BOY) seems to support this.] *intr.* To pick pockets. Hence '**figger** (see quot.). '**figging** *vbl. sb.* only in **figging-law** (see quot. 1785).

c **1550** *Dice-Play* B v a, Hyghe law robbery; Figginge law, picke purse crafte. **1611** DEKKER *Roaring Girle* Wks. 1873 III. 220 All his traine study the figging law. **1785** GROSE *Dict. Vulg. Tong.*, *Figger*, a little boy put in a window to hand out goods to the diver. *Ibid.*, *Figging law*, the art of picking pockets.

†**figarde.** *Obs. rare*⁻¹. [corruptly ad. L. *pygarg-us.*] = PYGARG.

1388 WYCLIF *Deut.* xiv. 5 A figarde.

Figaro ('figərəʊ). *slang.* [The name of the hero in *Le Barbier de Séville* and *Le Mariage de Figaro* by Beaumarchais (1732–99), and later in operas by various composers.] A barber.

[**1831** *Figaro in London* 10 Dec. 1/1 As the wood engraving, which distinguishes this page, will appear at the head of every separate publication of the Figaro,..we beg most distinctly to state that..the sketch of the lively *barber* is *not* intended for Sir Edward Sugden.] **1864** HOTTEN *Slang Dict.* 133 *Figaro*, a barber. **1886** *Globe* 18 Mar. 3/2 (Farmer), There is wailing and weeping among a certain section of the army, the Figaros, which has been despoiled at one fell swoop [*viz.* by an order of the French War Minister permitting soldiers to wear their beards]. **1922** *Contemp. Rev.* Mar. 334 [He] one day asked his Figaro who he thought was the richest man in the town.

figary, var. form of FEGARY, vagary.

figate, ? obs. form of FAGGOT.

1645 N. DRAKE *Siege Pontefr.* (Surtees) 69 They made figates, of which they made a barricado. This eevning the enemy was seene to bring..figates.

†'**fig-boy.** *Obs. slang.* [f. stem of FIG *v.*⁵ + BOY.] A pickpocket.

c **1550** *Dice-Play* D v b, Where by fyne fingered Fegge boye..picked shalbe his purse. **1602** W. WATSON *Quodlibets Relig. & State* 61 Practicall science inuented by fig-boyes, and men of the Bernard high lawe.

†'**fig-dote.** *Obs.* Also 5 **-dode**, 7 **-date**. [Conjectured to be ad. Pg. *figo doudo*, wild (lit. 'mad') fig, = Fr. *figue folle*. Cf. Du. *vijghe dote, dodesche vijgh* (Kilian) in same sense. In the S.W. counties *dough-fig* is used for a dried fig,

the word *fig* alone meaning a raisin.] An inferior kind of fig.

1481–90 *Howard Househ. Bks.* (Roxb.) 351 Item, for a topet of fygge dodes ij.*s.* **1552** Huloet, Figge dote, *busicon.* **1655** Moufet & Bennet *Health's Improv.* xxii. 204 Let Dioscorides commend his..yellow figs..and Pratensis his Mariscas or Fig-dates.

†**figee.** *Obs.* Forms: 4–5 fygey(e, 5 figee, figge. [Perh. originally a. OF. *figé* a dish of curds, subst. use of pa. pple of *figer* to curdle; in later use associated with FIG *sb.*[1]] A dish in old cookery: **a.** of fish (see quot. 1381); **b.** of figs, etc.

1381 in S. Pegge *Forme of Cury* (1780) 114 For to make Fygey. Nym Lucys or tenchis and hak hem in morsells [etc.]. **14..** *Noble Bk. Cookry* (Napier 1882) 119 A figge. To mak a figge tak figges and boile them in wyne, then [etc.]. *c* **1450** *Two Cookery-bks.* 94 Ffygey. Take figges and caste hem in a potte And [etc.].

†ˈ**figent,** *a. Obs.* Also 6 figgent, 7 figient, FITCHANT [? f. FIDGE *v.* + -ENT.] Fidgety, restless.

1598 E. Gilpin *Skial.* (1878) 51 He..Is an odd figgent iack called Iealousie. **1605** Chapman, etc. *Eastw. Hoe* III. ii. D iv b, *Quick.* What kind of figent memory haue you? *Pet.* Nay then, what kind of figent wit hast thou? **1613** Beaum. & Fl. *Coxcomb* IV. iii, He was somewhat figent with me. *a* **1616** —— *Fr. Lawyer* III. i, I have known such a wrangling advocate. Such a little figent thing. *a* **1627** Middleton *Chaste Maid* III. iii, I never could stand long in one place yet; I learnt it of my father, ever figient.

†ˈ**figer.** *Obs.* [a. OF. *figier* (mod.F. *figuier*), f. *figue* FIG *sb.*[1]] A fig-tree. Also *figer-tree.*

a **1300** *Cursor M.* 804 (Cott.) Þai cled þam þan in þat mister Wit leues brad bath o figer. *c* **1300** *K. Alis.* 5784 Appel trowes and fygeres. *c* **1320** *Sir Tristr.* 3082 Ful ner þe gat þai abade Vnder a figer tre. *a* **1400** *Pistill of Susan* 86 On Firres and fygers þei fongen heore seetes. **1401** *Pol. Poems* (Rolls) II. 112 The curse that Crist ȝaf to Phariseis, figured in the figre tree.

†ˈ**figetive,** *a. Her. Obs.* Also 5 figityve, 7 figitive. [ad. heraldic Lat. *figitiv-us* irregularly f. L. *figĕre* to fix: see -TIVE.] = FITCHED.

1486 *Bk. St. Albans, Her.* C vj b, Thys cros is founde other while pycche or figityue in armys. **1610** Guillim *Heraldry* II. vii. (1611) 69 Crosses that haue the whole fourth part figitive. **1828–40** Berry *Encycl. Herald.* I, Figetive, fitched.

figged (figd), *ppl. a.* [f. FIG *sb.*[1] + -ED[2].] = FIGGY 2 and 3.

1720 *Humourist* 157 Then they..eat figged pudding. **1839** Ure *Dict. Arts, etc.* s.v. *Soap*, Interspersed with the figged granulations of stearate of potash.

ˈ**figgery,** *sb. rare.* [f. FIG *sb.*[3] or *v.*[4] + -ERY.] Dressy ornament.

1841 Thackeray *Sec. Fun. Nap.* i, Coquettes..cover their persons with figgery, fantastically arranged.

ˈ**figgery-four,** vulgar U.S. pronunc. of *figure-(of-) four* (trap): see FIGURE *sb.* 19 c.

figging (ˈfɪgɪŋ), *sb.* [f. FIG *sb.*[1] + -ING[1].] The granulation produced in soft soap by the addition of tallow in the manufacture.

1839 Ure *Dict. Arts, etc.* s.v. *Soap.*

†ˈ**figgins.** *Obs.* [A variant form of FEGS.]

1653 Urquhart *Rabelais* I. v, By my figgins, godmother, I cannot as yet enter in the humour of being merry. *a* **1693** *Ibid.* III. lii, By my Figgins, I believe it.

†ˈ**figgle,** *v. Obs. rare*[−1]. [Cf. FIG *v.*[3] and DAGGLE, DRAGGLE, etc.] *intr.* To fidget about.

a **1652** Brome *Love-sick Court* V. ii, Our fleecy sheep, Who shake their heads, figgle, and writh their tayls.

†**figgum.** *Obs.* ? Juggler's tricks.

1616 B. Jonson *Devil an Ass* V. viii, *Tay.* See, he spits fire. *Pov.* O no, he plaies at Figgum, The Diuell is the Author of wicked Figgum.

figgy (ˈfɪgɪ), *a.* [f. FIG *sb.*[1] + -Y[1].]

1. Resembling figs, sweet as figs; in quot. *fig.*

1548 Hooper *Declar. 10 Commandm.* iv. 39 A gentle, swete, and fyggie god that..will not see thabhomination.

2. Made with figs, i.e. raisins; see FIG *sb.*[1] 5.

1846 *Spec. Cornish Dial.* 53 A thoomping figgy pudden. **1867** Smyth *Sailor's Word-bk., Figgie-dowdie,* a west-country pudding, made with raisins, and much in vogue at sea among the Cornish and Devon men.

3. In *Soap-making*: Containing white granulations, like the seeds of figs, of stearate of potash.

1862 O'Neill *Dyeing & Calico Print.* 185/1 The quality of soft soap is thought to depend in some measure upon the existence of white particles diffused through the mass, producing the appearance called 'figgy'.

fight (faɪt), *sb.* Forms: *α.* 1 feoht(e, 2–3 fiht(e, 3 fæht(e, fahte, feht(e, *south.* veht, feiht, (feoht, fith, fiþt, fyȝte), 3–5 fiȝt(e, *south.* 3 vihte, 4 vi(y)ȝt, (4 feȝt, ficht, fyhte, *south.* vyhte, fyth), 4–5 fyght, (5 feght, feyghte, fighte), 5–6, 9 *Sc.* fecht, 8 *Sc.* (faught), 9 *dial.* feight, 3, 5– fight. *β.* 1 ȝefeoht, 2–3 ifiht. [f. next vb.; OE. had three words, *feohte* wk. fem., *feoht* and *ȝefeoht* str. neut. Cf. OFris. *fiuchte* wk. fem., OS. and OHG. *fehta* str. fem. (MHG. *vehte* fem.); also Du. *gevecht,* OHG. *gifeht* (MHG. *geveht,* mod.Ger. *gefecht*) str. neut.]

1. a. The action of fighting. Now only *arch.* in phrase (*valiant,* etc.) *in fight.* †*in fight*: engaged in battle.

Beowulf 959 (Gr.) We þæt ellenweorc..feohtan fremedon. *c* **1000** *Ags. Ps.* cxliii[i]. 1 God..tæceþ handa mine to feohte. *c* **1175** *Lamb. Hom.* 151 Beoð stronge on fihte. *c* **1205** Lay. 23208 To-gædre heo fusden and veht heo bigunnen. **13..** *E.E. Allit. P.* B. 275 He watz famed for fre þat feȝt loued best. **1340** *Ayenb.* 219 Moyses ouercom amalec..naȝt be uiȝt: ac be his holy biddinges. *c* **1420** *Anturs of Arth.* xxii, For Fraunse haue ȝe frely with ȝaure fiȝte wonne. **1513** Douglas *Æneis* x. vi. 76 Thar syre that..companȝeon was in fecht To Hercules. **1548** Hall *Chron.* (1809) 296 The Erle of Warwick after long fight, wisely did perceiue his men to be ouerpressed. **1592** Shaks. *Ven. & Ad.* 114 The god of fight. **1666** Evelyn *Mem.* (1857) II. 5 The Duke of Albemarle was still in fight. **1680** Morden *Geog. Rect.* (1685) 88 No River..affordeth more..sufficiency for Fight. **1859** Tennyson *Enid* 223 So that I be not fall'n in fight.

b. In obvious phrases: †*to fang,* †*take* (*the*) *fight, to give fight, to make* (*a*) *fight.*

a **1300** *Cursor M.* 5515 (Cott.) If þai tak agains vs fight. *c* **1450** *Golagros & Gaw.* 762 Of thair strife sa strang, The feght so fellely thai fang. **1831** *Examiner* 89/1 Suppose they..should make fight upon the occasion. **1833** Marryat *P. Simple* x, They..had resolved to 'give fight'. **1847** —— *Childr. N. Forest* xx, We will make a fight for it. **1884** *Times* 5 Mar. 5/2 Apparently..he made a great fight.

†**c.** Method of fighting. *Obs.*

1603 Knolles *Hist. Turks* (1638) 89 After the maner of the fight of that time. **1613** Hayward *William I* 77 Afterward the English, being trained to that fight [i.e. the practice of archery] did thereby chiefly maintaine themselues with honourable aduantage against all nations.

2. A combat, battle.

a. A hostile encounter or engagement between opposing forces; = BATTLE 1. Now *arch.* or *rhetorical.*

c **893** K. Ælfred *Oros.* I. ix. §1 Þæt..ȝefeoht betuh Cretense & Atheniense þam folcum. *c* **1205** Lay. 18693 Alle þa seouen nihte ilaste þat selliche feoht. *c* **1310** in *Pol. Songs* (Camden) 190 Sire Jakes ascapede..Out of the fyhte..in wel muchele drede. **1596** Shaks. *1 Hen. IV,* II. iii. 58 Thou hast talk'd..Of..all the current of a headdy fight. **1600** Holland *Livy* IX. 327 The conflicts and fights at sea, in the first Punick warre. *a* **1671** Ld. Fairfax *Mem.* (1699) 68 This was the issue of Hornsby Fight. **1789** Cowper *Ann. Mem.* 1789, 23 Siege after siege, fight after fight. **1821** Shelley *Hellas* 474 The sea-convulsing fight. **1852** Tennyson *Ode Death Dk. Wellington* 96 He that gain'd a hundred fights.

b. A combat between two or more persons or animals. Not now usually applied (exc. rhetorically) to a formal duel, but suggesting primarily either the notion of a brawl or unpremeditated encounter, or that of a pugilistic combat.

c **1300** *Havelok* 2668 So was bi-twenen hem a fiht Fro þe morwen ner to þe niht. *a* **1400** *Octouian* 1093 The Sarsyns cryde..To hare God Mahone To help her geaunt in that fyght. **1606** Shaks. *Tr. & Cr.* IV. v. 90 As you and Lord Æneas Consent vpon the order of their fight. **1678** Butler *Hud.* III. i. 84 The ancient Errant Knights Won all their Ladies' Hearts in Fights. **1712–4** Pope *Rape Lock* v. 77 Nor fear'd the Chief th' unequal fight to try, Who sought no more than on his foe to die. **1818** Shelley *Rev. Islam* I. viii. 4 An Eagle and a Serpent wreathed in fight. **1826** J. Wilson *Noct. Ambr.* Wks. 1855 I. 174 You hear..faint far-aff echoes o' fechts wi' watchmen. **1840** Blaine *Encycl. Rur. Sports* §4077 (1852) 1229 New rules of the ring..adopted after a fatal fight between [etc.].

c. With various qualifying attributes. *running fight*: a fight kept up while one party flees and the other pursues. *sham fight*: a mimic battle (intended to exercise or test the troops engaged, or simply for display). †*single fight*: a duel. *stand-up fight*: one in which the combatants 'stand up' manfully to each other.

1596 Shaks. *1 Hen. IV,* v. i. 100, I..will..Try fortune with him, in a Single Fight. **1697** Dryden *Æneid* VIII. 751 Herilus in single Fight I slew. **1727** in Bailey vol. II. s.v. *Fights,* Running Fights [at Sea]. **1876** Green *Short Hist.* vii. §4. 411 The running fight between the two fleets lasted throughout the week. **1884** *Pall Mall G.* 9 July 1/1 We can all understand a stand-up fight on a clear issue. **1890** *Spectator* 20 Sept. 362/2 The sham fight near Grosswardein in Hungary.

d. *fight-off,* a contest to decide a tie in a fencing match.

1930 *Morning Post* 14 July 15 In the fight-off, Armstrong worried at his enemy's arm with an incessant attack. **1961** *Times* 9 June 5/3 He then only tied for top place, and in the fight-off Howard..won 5–0.

e. *fight-back,* a retaliation, rally, or recovery (see also quot. 1961). *colloq.*

1953 *Quick* 9 Mar. 16 Butter producers mapped a 'fight back' against substitutes which have made inroads into the butter market. **1960** J. Fingleton *Four Chukkas to Australia* v. 153 The great fight-back..the Englishmen made. **1961** *New Scientist* 17 Aug. 397/1 'Fight-back',..referring to the way in which the cheese pushes back against your thumb when the pressure is released.

3. *fig.* Strife, conflict, struggle for victory; = BATTLE 7.

c **1000** *Bi Manna Mode* 66 (Gr.) Wearð seo feohte to grim. *a* **1225** *Ancr. R.* 162 Ure Louerd sulf stont þer bi þe uihte. *a* **1300** *Cursor M.* 20114 (Gött.) Loued scho nouþer fith na striue. **1340** *Ayenb.* 131 A ueld of uiyȝt huerinne him behoueþ eure to libbe. **1526–34** Tindale *1 Tim.* vi. 12 Fyght the good fyght of fayth. **1667** Milton *P.L.* VI. 30 Well hast thou fought The better fight. **1794** Burns *Contented wi' little* 6 Man is a sodger, and life is a faught. **1818** Shelley *Rev. Islam* v. ii. 7 What secret fight Evil and good..Waged thro' that silent throng.

4. Power, strength or inclination for fighting; pugnacity. Also in *to show fight.*

1812 *Sporting Mag.* XXXIX. 138 Which ultimately took the fight out of him. **1863** H. Kingsley *A. Elliot* I. xv. 188 Until—something or another happens to make little Eleanor show fight. **1886** McCarthy & Praed *Right Hon.* I. vii. 120 Their country had fight enough in her yet. **1892** G. Hake *Mem. 80 Years* lxiv. 272 Marcus Aurelius Antoninus, a man of fight.

†**5. a.** A kind of screen used during a naval engagement to conceal and protect the crew of the vessel. Usually in *pl. Obs.* See also CLOSE-FIGHT.

1598 Shaks. *Merry W.* II. ii. 142 Clap on more sailes, pursue: vp with your fights Giue fire. **1631** Heywood *Fair Maid of West* IV. Wks. 1874 II. 316 Then now up with your fights. **1673** Dryden *Amboyna* III. iii. *Song,* Up with your Fights and your Nettings prepare. **1678** Phillips, *Fightts* in Navigation, are the Waste- [*printed* Mast-] clothes which hang round about the Ship, to hinder men from being seen in fight, or any place wherein men may cover themselves and yet use their Arms. **1721–1800** in Bailey.

†**b.** *foremost fight* (nonce-use): a breastwork on a rampart; = *forefight,* L. *propugnaculum.*

c **1611** Chapman *Iliad* XII. 271 They fiercely set vpon..The Parrapets..ras't euerie formost fight..The Greeks yet stood, and stil repaird the forefights of their wall.

†**6.** A division of an army in battle array. Cf. BATTLE *sb.* 8. *Obs.*

1622 Drayton *Poly. olb.* xxii. 221 The King into three fights his forces doth divide.

7. *Comb.,* as in †*fight-field,* -*time.* Also †**fight-rac't** (? = -*racked*) *a.,* overthrown in battle; †**fight-wite,** a fine for taking part in a disturbance.

1611 Sylvester *Du Bartas* II. iv. IV. *Decay* 931 Till one winding Cave Become the *Fight-Field of two Armies brave. *c* **1611** Chapman *Iliad* IV. 490 His fall was like a *fight-rac't towre. *c* **1400** *Destr. Troy* 6267 Þat our fos with no faulshed in þe *fyght tyme, Sese not our Cité. *c* **900** *Laws Edw. & Guth.* xiii, Þæt *fyht-wite. *c* **1250** *Gloss. Law Terms* in *Rel. Ant.* I. 33 Ficthwite, *quite de medlée de lamerci.*

fight (faɪt), *v. Pa. t.* and *pa. pple.* fought (fɔːt). Forms: *Infin.* 1 feohtan, fehtan *north.* fehta, 3 fehten, *south.* vehten, (3 feahten, fahten, fuhten), 3–5 feȝt(e, (4 fett), 3–6 feghte, 4–8 *Sc.* fecht; 2–3 feihten, (4 feyȝtte), 5–6 feyght(yn, (5 fayȝte, 6 *Sc.* feicht), 6, 9 *dial.* feight; 2–3 fihten, *Orm.* fihhtenn, 3–5 fiȝte(n, fite(n, 4 *south.* viȝte, (4 fiȝhte, fyþt), 4–5 fighte(n, 4–6 fyghte, 9 *dial.* foight, fught, 3– fight. *Pa. t.* 1 feaht, fæht, *pl.* fuhton, (2 feight, 3 faht, fæht, feaht, feht, feoht, feuht, fuht), 3–5 faȝt(e, -ght(e, 3 *south.* vagt, (3 fachte, fagt, faþt), 3–5 foȝte, (5 foghte, fughte), (3 fougte, 4 fouhte, 6 fouȝte, foughted, fowght, 9 fout), 3–5 fauȝte, -ghte, (4 fauht, -th, fawght, 5 faughth, fawte, 6 faucht), (5 fet, 8–9 *dial.* or *vulgar* fit), 6– fought. *Pa. pple.* 1 fohten, 3–6 foghten, (3 fughten), 4 fouȝten, (fooȝte, fouȝte), 5–9 *arch.* foughten, (4 -yn, 6 fochin, 6 fowth, 6– fought), 7–9 *dial.* or *vulgar* fit, fitten. [A Com. WGer. strong vb.: OE. *feohtan* = OFris. *fiuchta,* OS. **fehtan* (not recorded, but cf. the sb. *fehta*; Du. *vechten*), OHG. *fehtan* (MHG. *vehten,* mod.Ger. *fechten*):—OTeut. type **fehtan* (*faht, fuhtum, fohtono-*).

The conjugation of this vb. is peculiar, because in all the other vbs. that have the *u-* and *o-* grades these are caused by the presence of a liquid or nasal; possibly the forms have been influenced by the analogy of *flehtan* to plait. Outside Teutonic the formal equivalent is L. *pectĕre* to comb, though the difference in sense causes some difficulty; see Brugmann *Grundriss* II. §680.]

1. a. *intr.* To contend in battle or single combat.

c **900** *Pol. Laws Alfred* vii, Be ðon ðe mon on cynges healle feohte. *a* **1000** *Riddles* vii. 5 (Gr.) Mec min frea feohtan hateð. *c* **1205** Lay. 3939 Heo bi-gunnen to fuhten. *c* **1250** *Gen. & Ex.* 3227 He ne moȝen fiȝten a-ȝen, for [he] wiðvten wopen ben. *a* **1300** *Cursor M.* 5666 (Cott.) Feghtand fand he Iuus tua. **1352** Minot *Poems* v. 78 Sir Edward, oure gude king..Faght wele on þat flude. *c* **1430** Lydg. *Bochas* VIII. xxix. (1554) 194 b, Howe King Arthur..Fet with his knightes, and liueth in Fayrie. *c* **1489** Caxton *Sonnes of Aymon* xii. 291 Yf we fyghte strongly, he is deed wythout remedy. **15..** *Sir A. Barton* in *Surtees Misc.* (1890) 73 Feight till ye heare my whisstill blowe. **1596** Shaks. *1 Hen. IV,* v. iv. 151 We rose both at an instant and fought a long houre by Shrewsburie clocke. **1603** Florio *Montaigne* I. iii. (1632) 7 Captaine Bayart..having stoutly foughten so long as he could stand. **1700** Congreve *Way of World* III. x, I thought once they wou'd have fit. **1719** De Foe *Crusoe* (1840) II. xii. 263, I..resolved to die fighting to the last gasp. **1869** Blackmore *Lorna D.* ii, Not that I was afraid of fighting..I had..foughten all that time.

b. Const. *against,* †*on* or †*upon, with* (a person); hence, *to fight together.*

O.E. Chron. an. 514 Stuf & Wihtgar fuhtun wiþ Brettas. *c* **1000** *Ags. Gosp.* Luke xiv. 31 Oððe ȝyf hwylc cyningc wyle faran & feohtan aȝen oðerne cyning. *c* **1175** *Lamb. Hom.* 129 Þe King constantinus ouer com al þet folc þe feiht to ȝeines him. *c* **1200** Ormin 1842 He sholde fihhtenn Onnȝæn an drake. *a* **1300** *Cursor M.* 6405 (Cott.) A lauerding hight amalec, þat on þam faght, and þai on him. *c* **1340** *Ibid.* 7462 (Trin.) Ouþer sende he to me hider A mon þat we may fiȝte to gider. *a* **1400** *Burgh Laws* xii. (*Sc. Stat.* I), He may nocht fecht apon þe burges. **1473** Warkw. *Chron.* 6 Ther thei

faughthe strongly togedere. **1535** COVERDALE *1 Macc.* xii. 13 The kynges aboute vs haue foughten agaynst vs. **1611** BIBLE *1 Sam.* xvii. 10 Giue me a man, that we may fight together. **1678** LADY CHAWORTH in *Hist. MSS. Comm.* 12th Rep. App. v. 48 Some of [the King of France'] ships have fought with some Dutch ones. **1715** DE FOE *Fam. Instruct.* (1841) I. iv. 86 It may be your mother may fight with you. **1804** R. ANDERSON *Cumbrld. Ball.* 83 What..a lickin Tou gat when tou fit wi' Tom Wheyte.

c. Const. *for* = on behalf of (a person, etc.); on account of (a thing); hence in indirect passive.

a **1300** *Cursor M.* 15735 (Cott.) Al redi for to fight, On him he su'd ha foghten fore. *c* **1320** *Sir Tristr.* 1034 He fauȝt for ingland. *c* **1440** *Gesta Rom.* xlix. 220 (Harl. MS.), I wolle Fite for hir. **1571** GOLDING *Calvin on Ps.* lv. 19 Angels, whome wee know to feyght in battellray for us. **1672–3** MARVELL *Reh. Transp.* Wks. II. 212, I think the cause was too good to have been fought for. **1782** WOLCOT in J. J. Rogers *Opie* (1878) 22 He..is ready to fight up to his knees in blood for her Majesty. **1847** MRS. A. KERR *Hist. Servia* xx. 364 The principle of emancipating the Christian population, for which the Servians fought.

d. *Proverb.*

? *a* **1300** *Salomon & Sat.* (1848) 272 Wel fyþt þat wel flyþ quoþ Hendyng. *c* **1440** *Gesta Rom.* lvii. 420 (Add. MS.) It is an olde sawe, He feghtith wele that fleith faste.

e. To bring or get (oneself) *into*, *out of*, *to* (a certain condition, etc.) by fighting.

1640 *Lawfulness Expedit. Eng.* 3 We must doe as a man that fighteth himselfe out of prison. **1643** S. MARSHALL *Let.* 26 So many unworthy Gentlemen..fight themselves and posterity into slavery. **1873** *Sat. Rev.* 10 May 630/2 His sentence is to fight himself to death with trained gladiators in the amphitheatre.

f. Phrases. ***to fight with one's own shadow***: to struggle vainly; to talk at random. Cf. Gr. σκιαμαχεῖν. For ***to fight at sharp, to fight (for) one's own hand(s), to fight one's heart out, to fight the tiger, to fight tooth and nail***: see HAND, HEART, SHARP, TIGER, TOOTH. For ***that cock won't fight***: see COCK *sb.*[1] 2 c.

1579 FULKE *Heskins' Parl.* 377 In which argument he fighteth with his owne shadowe.

2. *transf.* and *fig.* **a.** To contend, strive for victory, struggle, engage in conflict. Const. as in 1. Of an animal: to struggle for freedom or mastery. Also *trans.*, to strive with (a horse, etc.) for mastery. *U.S.*

a **1000** *Sal. & Sat.* 499 (Gr.) þonne feohteð se feond. *c* **1175** *Lamb. Hom.* 151 Fihteð wið þe alde neddre. *c* **1200** *Trin. Coll. Hom.* 137 þe flesliche lustes þe fihteð togenes þe soule. *a* **1340** HAMPOLE *Psalter* xviii. 5 His body in þe whilke he faght wiþ þe fend. **1393** LANGL. *P. Pl.* C. XXII. 65 To fighten and fenden ous fro fallyng in-to synne. **1483** CAXTON *G. de la Tour* D iij, Alwey fyghtynge ageynst the fire of lecherye. **1582** BENTLEY *Mon. Matrones* ii. 17 Against whome for my sake thou foughtedst so sore on the crosse. **1611** BIBLE *1 Cor.* ix. 26 So fight I, not as one that beateth the ayre. **1645** E. CALAMY *Indictm. agst. Eng.* 9 Men that fight against a Reformation. **1733** POPE *Ess. Man* III. 305 For Modes of Faith let graceless zealots fight. **1850** 'H. HIEOVER' *Pract. Horsemanship* 179 If you find he at all fights against you..stand now on no ceremony with him. **1855** TENNYSON *Maud* III. vi. 57 It is better to fight for the good than to rail at the ill. **1875** J. C. WILCOCKS *Sea Fisherman* 163 These larger fish fight well, sometimes requiring five or six minutes to kill them. **1908** C. E. MULFORD *Orphan* i. 13 He mounted and fought the animal for a few minutes, just as he always had to fight it. **1920** J. M. HUNTER *Trail Drivers of Texas* 231, I 'fought' cattle for nine years almost night and day.

b. ***to fight up against***: to struggle against (something of overwhelming power).

1768 STERNE *Sent. Journ.* (1778) II. 54 (*Sword*) The Marquis..had fought up against his condition with great firmness. **1817** COLERIDGE *Biog. Lit.* (1847) II. 142 I soon felt that human nature itself fought up against this wilful resignation of intellect. **1838** LYTTON *Alice* VII. v, Lumley fought up against his own sensations.

c. To clash or jar *with*. *rare.*

a **1624** SWINBURNE *Sponsals* (1686) 8 This distinction fighteth with the former definition of Spousals. **1645** RUTHERFORD *Tryal & Tri. Faith* (1845) 81 It cannot be meant of Christ personally, for so it should fight with the scope of Paul. **1876** MISS YONGE *Womankind* xv. 116 One of those tints that 'fight' with the fewest colours.

†**d.** To operate as an argument, 'militate.'

1587 GOLDING *De Mornay* xiv. 213 All the reasons which thou alledgest against the immortalitie of the soule, doe feight directly to the proofe of it.

3. a. quasi-*trans.* with cognate object. Also † ***to fight it.***

a **1300** *Cursor M.* 17090 (Cott.) Hu he again ur wyþerwin, ur bateil tok to fight. **1523** LD. BERNERS *Froiss.* I. xxxi. 45 There was a sore batayle, and well foughten hande to hande. **1526–34** TINDALE *1 Tim.* vi. 12 Fyght the good fyght of fayth. **1593** SHAKS. *2 Hen. VI*, I. iii. 220, I shall neuer be able to fight a blow. **1606** G. W[OODCOCKE] tr. *Ivstin* 68 a, Their was a field fought betweene the fugetiue senators and himselfe. **1697** DRYDEN *Virg. Georg.* ii. 766 His wanton Kids..Fight harmless Battels in his homely Yard. **1769** GOLDSMITH *Roman History* (1786) II. 498 The senate dispatched their ambassadors to Alaric, desiring him..to give them leave to fight it with him in the open field. **1776** HURST in *Trial of Nundocomar* 64/1 The battle of Buzar was fought the 23d of October. **1819** SHELLEY *Peter Bell* VI. ix. 5 I've half a mind to fight a duel. **1847** MARRYAT *Childr. N. Forest* xxvii, A severe action was fought in the streets.

b. To maintain (a cause, quarrel) by fighting. Often *transf.*, ***to fight an action*** (at law), ***a case***, etc.

1600 SHAKS. *A.Y.L.* v. iv. 49, I haue had foure quarrels and like to haue fought one. **1713** ADDISON *Cato* I. i, He fights the cause Of honor, virute, liberty, and Rome. **1784** BAGE *Barham D.* I. 239 We fought this business four whole days. **1868** YATES *Rock Ahead* III. v, Gilbert Lloyd saw that there was no use fighting the question any longer. **1893** *Law Times* XCIV. 559 1 If I had had my way, I would have fought every one of these actions.

c. To win or make (one's way) by fighting.

1859 TENNYSON *Enid* 870, I will not fight my way with gilded arms. All shall be iron. **1861** HUGHES *Tom Brown at Oxf.* iv. (1889) 36 No one knew whether a boy..would have to fight his own way in the world.

4. a. *trans.* To combat; to engage or oppose in battle; to war against.

1697 DRYDEN *Æneid* VII. 655 To fight the Phrygian and Ausonian hosts. **1794** SOUTHEY *Botany-Bay Ecl.* ii, 'Tis a fine thing to fight the French for fame! **1859** TENNYSON *Enid* 221 Then will I fight him and will break his pride.

b. *transf.* and *fig.* ***to fight fire***: cf. FIRE *sb.* B. 2.

1784 COWPER *Task* III. 560 The shifts Which he that fights a season so severe Devises. [**1824** W. OWEN *Diary* (1906) 83 Then they fight it [*sc.* a fire]..endeavouring to overcome it by striking it with clap-boards.] **1835** J. ABBOTT *New Eng. & Institutions* 21 For days and nights together, all the physical force of the village has been arrayed in 'fighting the fire'. **1850** TENNYSON *In Mem.* cxiv. 10 She cannot fight the fear of death. **1852** M. ARNOLD *Tristr. & Iseult* xiv, Some ship that fights the gale. **1860** *Leisure Hour* 1 Nov. 690/2 Fight fire, fight water, fight Farmer Jackson, wagoner and mate. **1865** *Chambers's Jrnl.* 29 July 470/1 They took away from the local firemen their apparatus, and proceeded in their own way to 'fight fire'. **1944** J. S. HUXLEY *On Living in Rev.* ii. 22 There are today thousands who, though they may sometimes grumble, at heart have enjoyed fighting fires or acting as wardens.

c. To beat, flog. Chiefly *absol. Obs.* exc. *dial.*

1573 TUSSER *Husb.* lxxvii. (1878) 169 A wand in thy hand, though ye fight not at all, makes youth to their businesse better to fall. **1875** *Sussex Gloss.*, 'I wants more learning and less fighting.' **1877** *N.W. Linc. Gloss.*, 'I sha'n't let our Bob go to school no more, master feights bairns.'

5. To contend in single combat for (a prize).

1826 SCOTT *Woodst.* xiv, I..have fought prizes. **1835** BROWNING *Paracelsus* IV. 119 While we fight the prize, Troop you in safety to the snug back-seats.

6. To cause to fight; to set on to fight.

c **1680** HICKERINGILL *Wks.* (1716) II. 528 The Prince of Poets..never fights his Champion Achilles, till he has first buckled on him his Armour of Proof. **1828** SCOTT *F.M. Perth* xvi, The nobles and gentry had fought cocks. **1865** DICKENS *Mut. Fr.* I. iv, Rubbish was shot, dogs were fought.

7. To command, manage, or manœuvre (troops, a ship, gun, etc.) in battle.

1779 BURGOYNE *Let. to Constituents* (ed. 3) 15 My intention of fighting my own regiment as colonel. **1812** J. B. SKERRETT in *Examiner* 28 Sept. 615/1 Gallantly fighting his gun. **1843** *Blackw. Mag.* LIV. 216 He fights his vessel well. **1862** GEN. LEE in *Century Mag.* May (1887) 150/1 General A. P. Hill..fights his troops well.

8. With adverbs. ***to fight back***: to resist. ***to fight down***: to overcome. ***to fight off***: (*a*) *trans.* to deliver oneself with effort from; to repel, *lit.* and *fig.*; (*b*) *intr.* to try to back out of anything. † ***to fight over***: to fight one after another. ***to fight out***: to settle (a dispute) by fighting, to fight to the end; often ***to fight it out.***

1548 W. PATTEN in Arber's *Garner* III. 109 If they had meant to fight it out. **1588** SHAKS. *Tit. A.* v. iii. 102 That true hand that fought Romes quarrell out. **1610** SHAKS. *Temp.* III. iii. 103 But one feend at a time Ile fight their Legions ore. *a* **1732** T. BOSTON *Crook in Lot* (1805) 99 It is better to yield to providence, than to fight it out. **1787** BURKE *Corr.* (1844) III. 49 You perceive the manner in which Anderson fights off. **1800** DUNDAS in Owen *Wellesley's Desp.* 556, I must therefore fight it down. **1810** BENTHAM *Packing* (1821) 51 After fighting off till judgment. **1831** *Examiner* 193/2 Stand to, and fight it out without fear. **1833** T. HOOK *Widow & Marquess* (1842) 242 Fight off the wedding, if you please: be ill—make any excuse. **1886** *Law Times' Rep.* LV. 283/1 The issues which are not fought out. **1890** *John Bull* 5 Apr. 229/2 These people were fighting back the diseases manfully.

9. ***to fight shy***: perh. orig. to lose confidence in battle; recorded only in the sense: To keep aloof, avoid intercourse with a person, evade an undertaking, etc. Const. *of*. Similarly in 15th c. ***to fight sore at heart.***

c **1489** CAXTON *Sonnes of Aymon* iv. 125 He knewe well he sayd trouth and beganne to fyghte sore atte his herte. **1778** MAD. D'ARBLAY *Diary* Nov., I fight very shy with Mr. Seward, and..he takes the hint. **1786** MACKENZIE *Lounger* No. 98 ¶2, I fought a little shy, as the saying is. **1821** W. IRVING *Life & Lett.* (1864) II. 44, I have..had to fight shy of invitations that would exhaust time and spirits. **1867** FROUDE *Short Stud.* (ed. 2) 138 The better sort of people fight shy of him.

fightable (ˈfaɪtəb(ə)l), *a.* [f. prec. + -ABLE.] Ready for fight, in fighting trim.

1823 C. WESTMACOTT *Points of Misery* 32 Drover very abusive, coachee very fightable. **1837** *New Monthly Mag.* L. 422 If the chap's fightable, I'm his man. **1864** *Daily Tel.* 11 Nov., The Sanspareil..came out of action a fightable ship.

fighter (ˈfaɪtə(r)). [? OE. *feohtere* (Lye) = OHG. *fehtâri* (MHG. *vehtære*, mod.Ger. *fechter*): see FIGHT *v.* and -ER[1].]

1. a. One who fights; *occas.* a fighting man, a warrior.

c **1300** *K. Alis.* 5703 Alle his gode fightteres. **1375** BARBOUR *Bruce* XI. 102 He had of fechtaris with hym thar Ane hundreth thousand men and ma. **1483** CAXTON *Gold. Leg.* 66/1 This geaunt hath ben a fightar fro his chyldehod. **1685** BAXTER *Paraphr. N.T.* Matt. x. 16 Sheep and Doves are no good fighters against Wolves and Hawks. **1763** CHURCHILL *Ghost* I. 173 Whether repletion is not bad, And fighters with full stomachs mad. **1823** BYRON *Juan* XIV. xx, I've seen them [writers] balance even the scale with fighters. **1883** STEVENSON *Treasure Isl.* I. ii. (1886) 11 He did not look much like a fighter.

fig. *a* **1300** *Cursor M.* 18081 (Cott.) A faint fighter me thinc er þou. *c* **1430** *Life St. Kath.* (Gibbs MS.) 64 My lord ihesu criste whyche is þe hope and croune of alle his fyghters. **1656** S. WINTER *Serm.* 181 Lest you seem to..be found fighters against the Lord of hosts. **1861** TRENCH *Epistles 7 Churches* 86 These daring fighters against God.

†**b.** One employed to fight; a champion, bully.

1611 BEAUM. & FL. *Maid's Trag.* IV. i, Y'are grown a glorious Whore, where be your Fighters? *c* **1683** *Roxb. Ball.* V. 215 Keep Frank still for your writer, And Poulteney for your fighter.

†**2.** A pugnacious person; a brawler. *Obs.*

c **1400** *Destr. Troy* 1751 The fortune of feghters may be fell chaunse. **1413** LYDG. *Pilgr. Sowle* IV. xxxv. (1483) 83 Robbours..fyghters and debatours. **1552** *Act 5–6 Edw. VI*, c. 4 §3 Fray-makers and Fighters. **1557** N. T. (Genev.) *1 Tim.* iii. 3 No fighter, nor couetous.

3. *Aeronaut.* A high-speed military aircraft designed for aerial combat.

1917 [see BOMBER 2]. **1936** *Economist* 8 Feb. 294/2 There will still be..two squadrons of bombing machines..to one squadron of fighters. **1960** C. H. GIBBS-SMITH *Aeroplane* I. xvi. 139 (*caption*) The turbojet Gloster Javelin fighter. **1971** H. F. KING *World's Fighters* xi. 116 Several different armament combinations are possible on the Lightning fighter.

4. *attrib.* and *Comb.*, as ***fighter aerodrome, cover, duty, escort, machine, patrol, pilot, plane, screen, squadron, strip, umbrella.*** Also **fighter-bomber**, an aircraft that combines the functions of a fighter and a bomber; **Fighter Command**, the headquarters controlling the operation of a fleet of fighters.

1941 *Hutchinson's Pict. Hist. War* 19 Mar.–13 May 43 He sent large forces to deal with fighter aerodromes in the south and south-east of England. **1936** *Air Stories* Dec. 544/1 The R.A.F.'s latest fighter-bomber is as fast as any fighter yet in service anywhere in the world. **1959** *Observer* 14 June 16/2 American fighter-bombers equipped with nuclear weapons. **1941** *Aeronautics* Dec. 39/1 'Fighter Command' did not pass into Everyman's vocabulary until well after the beginning of the war. **1942** *Jane's All World's Aircraft 1941* 13a/1 Fighter Command's contribution to the bombing offensive opened on November 1, 1941, when the new Hawker 'Hurricane II' fighter-bomber..went into action. **1941** D. GARNETT *War in Air* 107 The number of Fighters with the Air Component of the B.E.F. was increased..and Fighter cover was given on the Western flank. **1934** *Times* 28 July 9/5 It is a tribute to the success of the Territorial experiment..that these squadrons should have been chosen for fighter duty. **1939** *War Weekly* 24 Nov. 139/4 In the hours of darkness fighter-planes will rarely, if ever, attack bombers, and, therefore, raids carried out entirely in darkness have no need of fighter escort. **1919** N. FLOWER *Hist. Great War* XIII. 121/2 The German aviation service was in extreme need of fighter machines..and aerial machine-gunners. **1917** *Flying* 3 Oct. 161/2 A fighter patrol met a large formation of Albatross scouts. **1936** *Air Stories* Dec. 573/2 The likelihood of securing a hit is in the proportion of 9 to 1 in favour of the fighter pilot. **1939** *Flight* 19 Oct. 309 Fighter pilots in crews' quarters on an aerodrome. **1971** *Sunday Times* 1 Aug. 3/6 The fighter pilot..parachuted to safety. **1935** *Economist* 17 Aug. 320/1 Unless the raiding enemy can be located he is immune..from the defending fighter planes. **1941** *Battle of Britain, Aug.–Oct. 1940* 13 The covering fighter screen flew at very great heights. **1932** *19th Cent.* Feb. 202 The enemy forces which are locked up by attack are fighter squadrons. **1944** *Birmingham* (Ala.) *News* 25 Apr. 1/1 Australian Royal Air Force engineers worked at night under floodlights..to repair the bomber and fighter strips. **1942** *Flight* 27 Aug. 218/2 Everything..depended on the British fighter umbrella.

fighteress (ˈfaɪtərɪs). *rare.* [f. prec. + -ESS.] A female fighter or soldier, an Amazon.

1864 R. F. BURTON *Dahome* II. 69 *foot-n.*, The king..keeps the fighteresses for himself.

fighting (ˈfaɪtɪŋ), *vbl. sb.* [f. FIGHT *v.* + -ING[1].]

1. The action of the vb. FIGHT in various senses; an instance of the same.

a **1225** *Ancr. R.* 228 þe ueorðe uroure is, sikernesse of Godes helpe iðe vihtunge aȝein. **1340** *Ayenb.* 239 He hedde arered and ymad manye werren and manye viȝtinges. **1484** CAXTON *Fables of Æsop*, etc. (1889) II. 310 The fyghtynge of the wymmen. **1535** COVERDALE *1 Esdras* iv. 6 The other y^t medle not with warres and fightinge. **1724** DE FOE *Mem. Cavalier* (1840) 58, I have had fighting enough..upon these points of honour. **1828–40** TYTLER *Hist. Scot.* (1864) I. 172 It was impossible to come to close fighting. **1871** FREEMAN *Norm. Conq.* (1876) IV. xviii. 231 While they were..receiving the rewards of their fightings.

†**2.** An alleged designation for a company of beggars. *Obs.*

1486 *Bk. St. Albans* F vj b, A Fightyng of beggers.

3. *attrib.* and *Comb.* **a.** simple attrib., as ***fighting-day, -face, -gear, -ground, -line, -order, -ship, -song, -strength, -trim, weight.***

1778 *Biog. Brit.* (ed. 2) I. 240 *note*, He was a coward who had his *fighting days. **1879** BROWNING *Halbert & Hob* 58 With an outburst blackening still the old bad *fighting-face. **1816** SCOTT *Pibroch of Donuil Dhu*, Come with your *fighting gear, Broadswords and targes. **1845** JAMES *A. Neil* vii, We might contrive to get into better *fighting ground. **1883** *Daily News* 21 Sept. 5/4 Detachments..all in full *fighting order. **1863** P. BARRY *Dockyard Econ.* 185 No *fighting ship is worth anything now-a-days without coal and speed. **1872** BLACK *Adv. Phaeton* xxviii. 379 Now this is a *fighting song. **1580** SIDNEY *Ps.* xviii. 11 My *fighting strength, by thy strength, strengthned was. **1886** J. K. LAUGHTON in *Dict. Nat. Biog.* VI. 387/1 The urgent necessity of keeping the ship at all times in perfect *fighting trim. **1884** *Boy's Own Paper* 2 Feb. 275/1 Twelve stone two was his *fighting weight. **1938** L. A. G. STRONG *Shake Hands* iv. 43 Willard's height was six feet five, and his fighting weight in the neighbourhood of seventeen stone.

b. Special comb.: **fighting chair** *U.S.*, a fixed chair on a launch, for use when catching large fish; **fighting chance**, an opportunity of succeeding by great effort; **fighting-cock**, see COCK *sb.*[1] 2 b.; **fighting drunk, -tight** *adjs.*, *colloq.*, drunk to a state of quarrelsomeness; **fighting-field** = BATTLE-FIELD; **fighting-fit** *a.*, fit to fight; fit enough to take part in a fight; hence *fighting-fitness*; **fighting fund**, a sum of money raised to finance a cause or campaign; **fighting-lanterns**, lanterns used during night actions; **fighting mad** *a. colloq.* (orig. *U.S.*), furiously angry (cf. MAD *a.* 5); **fighting-sails** (see quot. 1867); †**fighting-school**, a gymnasium; †**fighting-stead** *Sc.*, battle-field; **fighting-stopper** *Naut.* (see quot.); **fighting-top** *Naut.*, a circular platform placed at an elevation on the mast of a warship, on which guns and armed men can be stationed; †**fighting-wise**, battle array.

1950 GABRIELSON & LA MONTE *Fisherman's Encycl.*, Note the fishing chair—or '*fighting chair' as they are sometimes called. **1967** L. JAMES *Chameleon File* (1968) ix. 110 He walked over to a revolving chair bolted to the deck... 'This is the throne from which we catch the marlin... It is called a "fighting chair".' **1889** *Kansas Times & Star* 20 Feb., With a somewhat divided party, but having a *fighting chance of success. **1894** *Outing* (U.S.) XXIV. 295/1 The captain decided to..land the sailor so as to give him a fighting chance for his life in the hospital. **1894** *Congress. Rec.* 1 Feb. 1786/1 He can not be beaten out of hand. He will have a fighting chance. **1971** 'H. CALVIN' *Poison Chasers* xiii. 170 To concoct some fiendish scheme that might like give youse a fightin' chance. **1908** *Daily Chron.* 17 Nov. 4/7 Those who are acting like hooligans or who are '*fighting' drunk. **1909** *Westm. Gaz.* 1 Oct. 3/3 Jim's Sarah she come 'ome fighting drunk the other night. **1676** DRYDEN *Aurengz.* II. i. 935 In *Fighting Fields, where our Acquaintance grew. **1891** KIPLING *Life's Handicap* 313 He did not feel *fighting-fit that morning. **1963** *Lancet* 19 Jan. 174/1 Weatherbeaten 'fighting fit' soldiers. **1894** H. DRUMMOND *Ascent of Man* 267 Fitness in the stormy days of the world's animal youth was necessarily *fighting-fitness. **1940** *Economist* 9 Mar. 411/2 The additional proposal that each industry should raise a '*fighting fund' to assist its exporters. **1940** N. MARSH *Death at Bar* ii. 31 Another ten bob for the fighting fund. **1867** SMYTH *Sailor's Word-bk.*, **Fighting-lanterns*. **1896** W. JAMES *Let.* 5 Feb. (1920) II. 32 If any other country's ruler had expressed himself with equal moral ponderosity would n't the population have gone twice as *fighting-mad as ours? **1952** A. GRIMBLE *Pattern of Islands* 86 Otherwise..the spell..could not succeed in sending Biribe fighting-mad. **1627** CAPT. SMITH *Seaman's Gram.* xii. 58 If you see your chase strip himselfe into *fighting sailes. **1867** SMYTH *Sailor's Word-bk.*, *Fighting-sails*, those to which a ship is reduced when going into action; formerly implying the courses and topsails only. **1535** COVERDALE *2 Macc.* iv. 12 He durst make a *fightinge scole vnder ye castell. **1375** BARBOUR *Bruce* xv. 378 [He] wes ded richt in that ilk *fechting-sted. **1881** *Hamersly's Naval Encycl.*, **Fighting-stopper*, an arrangement of two dead-eyes, connected by rope laniards, and furnished each with a tail of rope. When a shroud is parted in action, the tails embrace the severed parts, and then they are hauled together by the laniard. *a* **1889** *Chicago Tribune* (Barrère & Leland), A quarter of a dollar would buy enough sour mash to make an ordinary man *fighting tight. **1896** *Naval Annual* I. 32 The foremast has two *fighting-tops... The mainmast has only one fighting-top. **1915** *Nature* XCVI. 182/1 On board our battleships a range-finder of this kind is placed in one of the fighting-tops on the masts. **1958** O. WARNER *Portrait Ld. Nelson* xii. 352 Fired from above, from a fighting top in the *Redoutable*, it [*sc.* a cannon-ball] had penetrated deep into Nelson's chest. *c* **1340** *Gaw. & Gr. Knt.* 267 Had I founded in fere, in *feȝtyng wyse, I haue a hauberghe at home and a helme boþe.

fighting ('faɪtɪŋ), *ppl. a.* [f. as prec. + -ING[2].]

1. That fights, able and ready to fight, bearing arms, militant, warlike.

a. of persons, their attributes, etc.

a **1340** HAMPOLE *Psalter* xiv. 1 Tabernakill propirly is þe mansyon of feghtand men. *c* **1400** *Apol. Loll.* 3 Þis fiȝting kirke. ? *a* **1400** *Arthur* 318 Þowsandez ten Of hardy & welle fyghtyng Men. *c* **1500** *Melusine* 128, xx^ti thousand fyghtyng men. **1602** SHAKS. *Ham.* III. iv. 113 O step betweene her, and her fighting Soule. **1663** GERBIER *Counsel* 59 No more ..then Souldiers fight without a fighting Captain. **1855** MACAULAY *Hist. Eng.* III. 233 The fighting men of the garrison.

fig. **1592** SHAKS. *Ven. & Ad.* 345 To note the fighting conflict of her hew, How white and red, ech other did destroy.

b. of natural or mechanical agents.

13.. *E.E. Allit. P.* B. 404 On folde no flesch styryed þat þe flod nade al freten with feȝtande waȝez. **1641** WILKINS *Math. Magick* II. iv. (1648) 173 These fighting images. **1667** MILTON *P.L.* II. 1015 The shock Of fighting Elements.

c. Of words or speeches. Also *transf. colloq.* (orig. *U.S.*).

1876 'MARK TWAIN' *Tom Sawyer* i. 9 You're a fighting liar, and darn't take it up. **1917** R. W. LARDNER *Gullible's Travels* 209 You know they's lots o' words that's called fightin' words. Some o' them starts a brawl, no matter who they're spoke to. **1930** *Economist* 23 Aug. 374/2 The trade.. has a direct interest in the possible findings of the Royal Commission on Licensing, and 'fighting' speeches..should possibly be interpreted with due reference to this fact. **1959** *Listener* 12 Feb. 302/3 Tom Fallon..came out with fighting if rather catchpenny words.

d. Fighting French, a name given to the Free French armed forces during the German occupation of France in the 1939–45 war.

1943 *New Statesman* 20 Nov. 327/1 Between them, the people of the Lebanon and the Fighting French have made an ugly problem for each other and for us. **1957** *Encycl. Brit.* XXIII. 791O/1 Outside France, Gen. Charles de Gaulle had started his 'Free French' (later 'Fighting French') movement as early as June 18, 1940.

2. *Comb.*: **fighting crab** (see quot. 1868); **fighting fish**, a Siamese fish (*Betta pugnax*); **fighting sandpiper**, the ruff (*Machetes pugnax*).

1868 WOOD *Homes without H.* iv. 90 The Fighting Crab (*Gelasimus bellator*).

Hence '**fightingly** *adv.*, pugnaciously.

1632 BROME *Northern Lasse* I. iii, She frown'd..and look'd fightingly. **1841** J. T. HEWLETT *Parish Clerk* I. 60 Why should they be so fightingly inclined?

'**fightist.** *slang* or *jocular.* = FIGHTER.

1877 *Daily News* 8 Oct., Turkey had just acquired reputation enough as a 'fightist' to daunt half a dozen second-rate powers.

†**fight-lac.** *Obs.* [OE. *feoht-lác*: see FIGHT *sb.* and -LOCK.] Fighting, battle.

c **1000** *Laws Ethelred* IX. iv, Si hit þurh feoht-lac si hit þurh reaf-lac. *a* **1250** *Owl & Night.* 1697 Ȝet ich ow alle wolde rede..þat [ȝe] ower fiht-lac leteth beo.

†'**fightless,** *a. Obs.* [f. FIGHT *sb.* + -LESS.] Without fight or fighting.

1595 G. MARKHAM *Trag. Sir R. Grinvile* (Arb.) 69 Yet should we fightlesse let our shyps force flie. *a* **1618** SYLVESTER *Panaretus* 782 Fight-lesse to fight, and without force to force.

'**fighty,** *a.* [f. as prec. + -Y[1].] Pugnacious; †warlike.

c **1250** *Gen. & Ex.* 546 Of hem woren ðe ȝetenes boren, Miȝti men, and fiȝti. **1888** W. B. CHURCHWARD *'Blackbirding' in South Pacific* vi. 108 They annoy me, and then I get bad and fighty. **1941** J. CARY *House of Children* xxxviii. 168 He's so fighty all at once—he sounds absolutely ferocious.

'**fig-leaf.** [f. FIG *sb.*[1] + LEAF.]

1. a. The leaf of a fig-tree; chiefly in reference to Gen. iii. 7.

1535 COVERDALE *Gen.* iii. 7 They..sowed fygge leaues together. **1675** WYCHERLEY *Country Wife* II. (1688) 19, I wou'd as soon look upon a Picture of Adam and Eve, without fig leaves, as any of you. **1854** LOWELL *Jrnl. in Italy* Prose Wks. 1890 I. 116 The evening is so hot that Adam would have been glad to leave off his fig-leaves.

b. *transf. slang.* (See quot.)

1891 FARMER *Slang, Fig-leaf*, an apron. In fencing, the padded shield worn over the lower abdomen and right thigh.

2. *fig.* A device for concealing something shameful or indecorous; a flimsy disguise. Orig. only in *Pl.*

1553 LATIMER *Fruitf. Serm.* (1584) 296 b, It is all but figge-leaues what man can do. **1621** BACON *Submission to Ho. Lords* in Rushw. *Hist. Coll.* (1659) I. 29 Without Fig-leaves I do ingeniously confess and acknowledge, that [etc.]. **1755** LADY M. W. MONTAGU *Lett.* (1893) II. 291 Fig-leaves are as necessary for our minds as our bodies. **1843** LOWELL *Glance bef. Curtain*, For men in earnest have no time to waste In patching fig-leaves for the naked truth. **1850** KINGSLEY *Alt. Locke* xx, They tore off..even the fig-leaves of decent reticence. *c* **1856** EMERSON *Jrnl.* in *Sel. Writ.* (1965) 168 Whipple said of the author of 'Leaves of Grass' that he had every leaf but the figleaf. **1897** *Daily News* 20 Oct. 5/6 Court and country in Spain would rejoice if they succeeded in getting rid of Cuba in a decent..manner. They seek the fig-leaf. **1960** C. W. MILLS *Castro's Cuba* iii. 69 If they had some kind of puppet regime there, they could 'recognize' it and arm it. That would be their fig leaf.

3. *attrib.*, as *fig-leaf covering, defence.*

1648 JENKYN *Blind Guide* iii. 37 The novice hath..driven you to..a meere Figg-leafe defence. **1698** SIDNEY *Disc. Govt.* ii. §21 (1704) 139 These are imperfect Figleave coverings of Nakedness. **1850** WHITTIER *Old Portraits* 2 The tearing off of the fig-leaf covering of its sin.

Hence '**figleaf** *v. trans.*, to cover with a fig-leaf, or fig-leaves. '**fig-leaved** *ppl. a.*, (*a*) made of fig-leaves; (*b*) (see quot. 1820).

1880 S. L. CLEMENS ['Mark Twain'] *Tramp Abroad* I. (1881) 515 Yet these ridiculous creatures have been thoughtfully and conscientiously figleaved by this fastidious generation. **1710** *Brit. Apollo* III. 2/1 Adam made himself a pair of Fig-leav'd Breeches. **1748** RICHARDSON *Clarissa* Wks. 1883 VII. 309 A husband is a charming cloak, a fig-leaved apron for a wife. **1820** GREEN *Univ. Herb.* I. 289 *Chenopodium Serotinum*, fig-leaved Goosefoot.

'**figless,** *a.* [f. FIG *sb.*[1] + -LESS.] Without figs.

1623 T. ADAMS *Barren Tree* Wks. (1629) 968 The Figlesse Fig-tree, the gracelesse Christian, is good for nothing.

†'**figling.** *Obs.* A little fig.

1612 tr. *Benvenuto's Passenger* I. ii. 175, I finde in my selfe daily a great desire to these figges, or fat figlins.

figmalirie, var. of WHIGMALEERY *Sc.*

figment ('fɪgmənt). [ad. L. *figment-um*, f. *fig-* short stem of *fingĕre* to feign, fashion.]

†**1.** Something moulded or fashioned, *e.g.* an image, a figure, a model. *Obs.*

1592 R. D. *Hypnerotomachia* 34 b, The excellencie, dilicatnes and perfection of this figment and woorkmanshippe can-not be suffi[ci]entlie expressed. **1607** TOPSELL *Four-f. Beasts* (1658) 97 Some are of opinion, that this Achaian Hart was but an invention or figment made in bread. **1664** H. MORE *Myst. Iniq.* viii. 24 This Statue is become the..eternal God of Heaven and Earth..though it be really a mere figment.

2. A product of fictitious invention.

a. An invented statement, story, doctrine, etc. †In early use also: A fraudulent device.

1432–50 tr. *Higden* (Rolls) I. 177 [The Greeks] reteyne to them the figmentes of Sinonis, the fallace of Vlixes. **1577** HANMER *Anc. Eccl. Hist.*, The fond figments of hereticall persons. **1598** B. JONSON *Ev. Man in Hum.* IV. iv, *Deliro.* I heard he was to meet your worship here. *Punt.* You heard no figment, sir; I do expect him. *a* **1639** W. WHATELY *Prototypes* II. xxiv. (1640) 9 It is a sin to lie, even for Gods cause, and to defend even his justice with false tales and figments. **1774** J. BRYANT *Mythol.* I. 340 From this abuse of terms the silly figment took its rise. **1862** THACKERAY *Round. Papers, On half a loaf* 235 Have we..invented a monstrous figment about going to shoot pheasants with Mac in the morning? **1874** STUBBS *Const. Hist.* II. xvii. 516 Royal prerogative was not..a figment of theorists.

b. Something which exists only as an arbitrarily framed notion of the mind. Phr. *a figment of (the* or *one's) imagination.*

1624 GATAKER *Transubst.* 33 We have..great reason to reject it, as a figment of mans braine. **1665** GLANVILL *Scepsis Sci.* 71 Therefore [space] has a kind of being that is no arbitrary figment. **1744** BERKELEY *Siris* §335 Beauty, virtue, and such like are not figments of the mind. **1847** C. BRONTË *J. Eyre* II. xxv. 277 The long dishevelled hair, the swelled black face, the exaggerated stature, were figments of imagination. **1875** JOWETT *Plato* (ed. 2) II. 201 We must not conceive that this logical figment had ever a real existence. **1877** E. CAIRD *Philos. Kant* II. xii. 484 A self-conscious being..existing alone in an unconscious world, is a figment of abstraction. **1955** *Bull. Atomic Sci.* Mar. 79/1 This condition is almost certainly a figment of the imagination. **1971** *Nature* 2 Apr. 299/3 Another attempt..to read into prehistoric monuments..patterns and explanations which are simply figments of the observer's imagination.

figmental (fɪg'mɛntəl), *a.* [f. prec. + -AL[1].] Of the nature of a figment; fictitious, imaginary, not real.

1655 H. MORE *Antid.* (1662) 170 These figmental impressions. **1669** W. SIMPSON *Hydrol. Chym.* 74 From this original by figmental additions came the Ganiahen. **1727** in BAILEY, vol. II.

figmentary ('fɪgməntərɪ), *a. rare.* [f. as prec. + -ARY.] = prec.

1887 T. GIFT *Victims* I. x. 276 The same girl who had been wont to start from shadows the most figmentary.

†**figmen'titious,** *a. Obs.*[−1] [f. as prec. + -ITIOUS.] Addicted to the framing of figments.

1660 FISHER *Rusticks Alarm* Wks. (1679) 323 Whence came this Whiffle and Whimzy within the circumference of thy Figmentitious Fancy?

figmentor. *Obs.*[−1] [f. FIGMENT + -OR.] One who makes up figments, or fictitious tales.

1638 T. HERBERT *Trav.* 307 Frier Oderic of Friuli..a contemporary and fellow Traveller and Figmentor with our Sir John [Mandeville].

†**fignade.** *Obs. rare.* ? = FIGEE.

c **1420** *Liber Cocorum* (1862) 43 For stondand fygnade Fyrst play þy water with hony and salt, Grynde blanchyd almondes [etc.]. *Ibid.* 54 For the secunde course..Take ryse and fletande fignade.

†'**figo.** *Obs.* [a. OSp. and Pg. *figo* = FICO.] = FICO in various senses.

1599 SHAKS. *Hen. V*, IV. i. 60 The Figo for thee then. **1600** HAKLUYT *Voy.* III. 740 A fruite which they [natives of the Moluccas] call Figo. *Ibid.* 741 Lemmons, cucumbers, cocos, figu, sagu. **1640** GLAPTHORNE *Ladies Privilege* v, You do not mean to make a gul of me, a figo for a thousand.

†**figonale.** *Obs.* ? Some kind of basket.

c **1450** HOLLAND *Howlat* 833 Syne for ane figonale of frut thai straif in the steid.

'**fig-tree.** [f. FIG *sb.*[1] + TREE.] A tree of the genus *Ficus*, esp. the *Ficus carica*.

a **1340** HAMPOLE *Psalter* civ. 31 He smate þaire vynȝerdis & þaire fige trese. *c* **1430** LYDG. *Chorle & Byrde* (Roxb.) 1 He myght not forsaken his fattenesse Ne the fyge tree his amerous swetenesse. **1667** MILTON *P.L.* IX. 1101 The Fig-tree—not that kind for Fruit renowned, But such as, at this day..In Malabar or Decan spreads her Armes. **1762** WALPOLE *Vertue's Anecd. Paint.* (1765) I. ii. 28 The milk that flows from the leaf of a young fig-tree. **1862** KENDALL *Poems* 119 How lone we sit beneath this old Fig-tree.

attrib. **1552** HULOET, Figge tree staffe or stalcke. *Ibid.*, Figge tree droue, or groue. **1889** *Pall Mall G.* 26 Dec. 3/2 The seventh and ninth columns from the fig-tree corner [of the Ducal Palace].

†'**figulate,** *a. Obs.*[−0] [ad. L. *figulāt-us*, pa. pple. of *figulāre* to fashion as a potter does, f. *figulus* potter, f. *fig-*: see FIGMENT.] (See quot.)

1730–6 in BAILEY (folio), *Figulate*, made of earth or potter's clay.

†'**figulated,** *a. Obs.*[−0] [f. L. *figulāt-us* (see prec.) + -ED[1].] = prec.

1670 in BLOUNT *Glossogr.* (ed. 3). **1721–1800** in BAILEY.

figuline ('fɪgjʊlɪn, -aɪn), *a.* and *sb.* [ad. L. *figulīnus*, f. *figulus* potter.]

A. *adj.* **a.** Such as is produced by the potter; made of earthenware. **b.** Of earth: Suitable for the potter, fictile.

1657 TOMLINSON *Renou's Disp.* 146 Turpentine may not onely be well reserved in an iron or glass vessel, but in a figuline also. **1686** PLOT *Staffordsh.* 124 The Smectic and figuline Earths. **1697** EVELYN *Numism.* viii. 280 Improving ..Figuline Ware by Palissy's White Glaze. **1790** PENNANT *London* (1813) 171 Wedgewood..making it the repository of his figuline ware.

B. *sb.*

1. An earthen vessel; in *pl.* pottery.

1878 LONGF. *Kéramos* 106 This Potter..whose figulines and rustic wares scarce find him bread.

2. Potter's clay.

1859 R. F. BURTON *Centr. Afr.* in *Jrnl. Geog. Soc.* XXIX. 383 The figuline, a greyish-brown clay, is procured from river-beds.

‖**figura** (fɪ'gjʊərə). [mod.L., ad. L. *figūra* FIGURE *sb.*] **1.** *Theol.* = TYPE *sb.*¹ Cf. FIGURE *sb.* 12.

1959 MANHEIM & GARVIN tr. *Auerbach's Sc. fr. Drama Europ. Lit.* 34 Moses is no less historical and real because he is an *umbra* or *figura* of Christ.

2. *Literary.* A person who represents some higher or supervening reality.

1959 MANHEIM & GARVIN tr. *Auerbach's Sc. fr. Drama Europ. Lit.* 71 Virgil in the *Divine Comedy* is the historical Virgil himself, but then again he is not; for the historical Virgil is only a *figura* of the fulfilled truth that the poem reveals. **1968** *Eng. Studies* XLIX. 404 The poet..wants us to connect the Troy legend with the theme of his poem and to see in Aeneas a *figura* of his own hero.

b. An act or deed that is representative or symbolic.

1959 MANHEIM & GARVIN tr. *Auerbach's Sc. fr. Drama Europ. Lit.* 66 Cato's voluntary choice of death rather than political servitude is here introduced as a *figura* for the eternal freedom of the children of God. **1964** *Eng. Studies* XLV. 111 His [*sc.* Orsino's] sudden dismissal of the music ..is a *figura* that sets the pattern of his behaviour.

figurability (ˌfɪgjʊərə'bɪlɪtɪ). [f. next; see *-bility*, -ITY.] The quality of being figurable.

1730–6 BAILEY (folio) Pref., *Figurability* of Body or Matter, is that universal Disposition thereof, whereby it is under a Necessity, of appearing or putting on some Sort of Figure. **1794** G. ADAMS *Nat. & Exp. Philos.* IV. App. 492 What are..properties of matter? 1. Extension or magnitude, and consequently figurability. **1848** in CRAIG.

figurable ('fɪgjʊərəb(ə)l), *a.* [f. FIGURE *v.* + -ABLE.]

1. Capable of receiving a definite figure or form.

1605 Z. JONES tr. *De Loyer's Specters* 45 Much lesse can they take a body of the Ayre for that is not figurable. **1644** DIGBY *Nat. Bodies* xvi. (1645) 177 Wax remaineth figurable, whether it be melted or congealed. **1755** JOHNSON s.v. Thus lead is *figurable*, but not water. In mod. Dicts.

2. Capable of being represented figuratively.

1880 G. MEREDITH *Trag. Com.* xvi. (1892) 228 He waited, figureable by nothing so much as a wild horse in captivity.

figural ('fɪgjʊərəl), *a.* Also 6 figurall(e. [a. OF. *figural*, ad. late L. **figūrālis* (implied in *figūrālitās*), f. *figūra* FIGURE *sb.*]

1. = FIGURATIVE 1, 4. Cf. FIGURA.

c **1450** HENRYSON *Mor. Fab.* 22 Ouerhailled with types figurall. *c* **1555** HARPSFIELD *Divorce Hen. VIII* (1878) 142 Scripture is to be expounded..by the allegoricall or figurall ..and by the tropologicall sense. **1621** W. SCLATER *Tythes* (1623) 82 Their caeremonies..were shadowy and figurall. **1953** W. R. TRASK tr. *Auerbach's Mimesis* 195 A figural schema permits both its poles—the figure and its fulfillment —to obtain the characteristics of concrete historical reality, in contradistinction to what obtains with symbolic or allegorical personifications. *Ibid.* 196 Far more prevalent in the Christian life of the High Middle Ages is the figural realism which can be observed in full bloom in sermons, the plastic arts, and mystery plays. **1955** R. JAKOBSON in Saporta & Bastian *Psycholinguistics* (1961) 424/2 The two varieties of figural speech—metaphor..and metonymy. **1959** *Encounter* Nov. 78/2 A 'figural' interpretation, as if every particular event signified precisely 'something other'. .. Modern 'realism' lacks this 'figural' quality. **1968** E. SALTER in *Proc. Brit. Acad.* LIV. 85 The essential messages of *Piers Plowman* are conveyed at their greatest intensity by figural or typological means, as are those of the Bible.

†**2.** *Arith.* Of numbers: Representing some geometrical figure, such as a square, cube, etc.; consisting of factors. Cf. FIGURATE *a.* 3 a. *Obs.*

figural arithmetic: in quot., the arithmetic of 'figural' numbers.

1551 RECORDE *Pathw. Knowl.* I. A ij b, Defin., Formes [*sc.* produced by arrangements of points in rows]..whiche I omitte..considering that their knowledg appertaineth more to Arithmetike figurall, than to Geometrie. **1557** —— *Whetst.* A ij b, Many nombers are referred to some figure.. So if I saie that .16. is a square nomber, bicause it is made of .4. multiplied by .4. then is .16. here to be called a figuralle nomber. **1674** JEAKE *Arith.* (1696) 173. **1704** in HARRIS *Lex. Techn.*

quasi-*sb.* **1696** *Lond. Gaz.* No. 3183/4 Treatise of Arithmetick in all its Parts, viz. Integers, Fractions.. Figurals, etc.

3. †**a.** Pertaining to figure or shape (*obs.*). **b.** Of or pertaining to figures. *rare.*

1650 SIR T. BROWNE *Pseud. Ep.* (ed. 2) VI. xiv. 287 Yet equall incongruities have been commonly committed by Geographers and Historians, in the figurall resemblances of severall regions on earth. **1813** W. TAYLOR *Eng. Synonyms* (1856) 175 Keeping is a bad word, though a painter's term for figural perspective. **1884** SCHLIEMANN in *North Amer. Rev.* CXXXIX. 526 We also see in the wall-paintings figural representations.

c. (In present technical use.)

1952 D. T. RICE *Eng. Art 871–1100* 83 Sculptures of a monumental figural character are quite different from those of a decorative or ornamental nature. **1958** *Times Lit. Suppl.* 3 Jan. 4/4 Similar not to the Book of Lindisfarne or the Book of Durrow, but to the figural sculpture on the Ruthwell Cross. **1970** M. SWANTON *Dream of Rood* 12 The broad principal faces of the shaft are carved with figural subjects surrounded by identifying Latin inscriptions.

4. *Mus.* = FIGURATE *a.* 4.

a **1897** [In mod. Dicts.]. **1938** *Oxf. Compan. Mus.* 316/2 Often the word 'florid' is a good translation of 'Figural'. **1959** *Listener* 17 Dec. 1093/2 As well as this simple liturgical form (*Choral*-passion, implying unaccompanied monody), composers cultivated the *Figural*-passion.

†'**figurally**, *adv. Obs.* [f. prec. + -LY².]

1. By way of a figure, figuratively.

c **1380** WYCLIF *Serm.* Sel. Wks. II. 6 [Joon] is Hely figurali. *c* **1450** *Mirour Saluacioun* 77 This fortakened a virginis ymage with hir childe figurelly. **1541** COVERDALE *Old Faith* vi, He came and performed all things in deed that they had figurally in their sacrifices. **1550** HUTCHINSON *Image of God* iii. (1842) 23 Who doth not see that these things are to be taken figurally of God?

2. See FIGURAL 2. ***to multiply figurally***: to multiply into itself, so as to raise to a higher power.

1674 JEAKE *Arith.* (1696) 206 When a Fraction is given to be multiplyed Figurally, multiply the Numerator by himself ..and the Denominator likewise.

†'**figurance.** *Obs.*—⁰. [f. FIGURE *v.* + -ANCE.] The action of figuring or expressing some form or shape.

1730–6 in BAILEY (folio). **1775** in ASH.

‖**figurant** (figyrɑ̃) *masc.*, **figurante** (figyrɑ̃t) *fem.* [Fr. *figurant, figurante*, pr. pple. of *figurer* to FIGURE.

The pl. masc. was formerly sometimes written *figurans.* It is often impossible to determine whether *figurante* is intended for the F. or the It. word: see next.]

1. A ballet-dancer.

1790 COMBE *Devil upon Two Sticks* (1817) I. 126 The lascivious agility of his figurantes. **1807** T. HORNE tr. *Goede's Trav.* II. 264 The theatre at Paris..its statists and figurants. **1837** MAJOR RICHARDSON *Brit. Legion* ii. (ed. 2) 42 A sort of ballet the figurans and figurantes in which were inmates of a mad-house. **1859** SMILES *Self-Help* iii. (1860) 52 The poor figurante must devote years of incessant toil to her profitless task.

2. A supernumerary character on the stage who takes no prominent part, and has little or nothing to say.

1775 H. WALPOLE *Lett.* (1857) VI. 195 Plays, in which comedians, singers, dancers, figurantes, might all walk at a coronation. **1816** J. SCOTT *Vis. Paris* (ed. 5) 342 The women can be little more than the figurantes, receiving a mock reverence merely to carry on the drama. **1886** *Athenæum* 2 Jan. 15/1 [In the play] Shakspeare is a mere *figurant.*

transf. **1893** *Nation* 21 Sept. 211/2 They were but figurants in the great drama.

‖**figurante** (figu'rante). Pl. -ti, *occas.* -tes. [It. *figurante*, pr. pple. of *figurare* to FIGURE.] = prec. 1.

1782 MISS BURNEY *Cecilia* (1809) I. viii. 81 The figuranti will divert you beyond measure. **1821** BYRON *Juan* IV. lxxxv, As for the figuranti, they are like The rest of all that tribe. **1826** HEBER *Journ. India* (1828) II. xxviii. 283 The bundles of red cloth which swaddle the figuranté of Hindostan.

transf. **1830** SCOTT *Demonol.* i. 20 The green figurantés.. came capering and frisking..with great glee. **1870** O. W. HOLMES *Old Vol. of Life* (1891) 269 The spangles of conversational gymnasts and *figurantes.*

figurate ('fɪgjʊəreɪt). *ppl. a.* and *sb.* [ad. L. *figūrāt-us*, pa. pple. of *figūrāre* to form, fashion, f. *figūra* FIGURE.]

A. *ppl. a.*

†**1.** Framed according to, or exemplifying, 'figures' of grammar or rhetoric. *Obs.*

1530 PALSGR. 394 *Auoyr course*..for *auoyr courouse*, and many suche be figurate by syncopa. **1669** MILTON *Accedence Grammar* Wks. 1738 I. 607 Of figurate Construction, what is useful, is digested into several Rules. **1674** PETTY *Disc. Dupl. Proportion* Ded. A v, Figurate and measured periods.

†**b.** = FIGURATIVE 4. *Obs.*

1548 UDALL, etc. *Erasm. Par. Luke* xviii. 34 In these woordes..there laie priuely hidden some figurate & mistical manier of speaking. *a* **1677** BARROW *Serm.* Wks. 1716 II. 363 Some do scarce admit those figurate senses. **1728** in Earbery tr. *Burnet's St. Dead* II. 47 The Diction of holy Scripture is figurate.

†**c.** As *pa. pple.*: Figured, prefigured. *Obs.*

1563 WINȜET *Four Scoir Thre Quest.* Wks. 1888 I. 85 The sacramentis of the Euangell exhibitis in deid and veritie thai graces figurat only and hoipit for in the Auld Testament.

d. Expressed by figures as opposed to letters.

1830 *Westm. Rev.* XIII. 229 That system [of numerical signs] is neither literal, like the Grecian..nor altogether figurate, like the Arabic.

2. a. Having definite form or shape.

Now only in medical use, as *figurate fæces* (opposed to *diffluent*).

1626 BACON *Sylva* §602 Plants are all Figurate and Determinate, which Inanimate Bodies are not. **1678** CUDWORTH *Intell. Syst.* 801 Tertullian..drives the business so far, as to make the Soul itself..Figurate. **1755** JOHNSON, *Figurate*, resembling anything of a determinate form, as figurate stones retaining the forms of shells in which they were formed by the deluge.

b. Formed into figures or patterns.

1867 J. HOGG *Microsc.* I. ii. 133 The symmetrical and figurate depositions of siliceous crystals.

3. *Math.* †**a.** = FIGURAL 2. *Obs.*

1614 T. BEDWELL *Nat. Geom. Numbers* i. 1 A rationall figurate number is a number that is made by the multiplication of numbers betweene them-selues. **1636** *Recorde's Gr. Artes* 559 A Figurate Number is a number made by the multiplication of one number or more by another. **1674** JEAKE *Arith.* (1696) 179 Figurate Fractions are deferred to the Fourth Chapter.

b. ***figurate numbers***: numbers, or series of numbers, formed from any arithmetical progression in which the first term is a unit, and the difference a whole number, by taking the first term, and the sums of the first two, first three, first four, etc., terms as the successive terms of a new series, from which another may be formed in the same manner, and so on. So ***figurate arithmetic***, the science of such numbers.

Thus from the arithmetical series 1, 2, 3, 4, etc., a second series 1, 3, 6, 10, etc. ('triangular' numbers) is formed as above described; and from this again a third series, 1, 4, 10, 20 ('pyramidal' numbers).

1706 W. JONES *Syn. Palmar. Matheseos* 163 The Sums of Numbers in a Continued Arithmetic Proportion from Unity are call'd Figurate..Numbers. **1785** HUTTON *Math. Tables* 7 The several orders of figurate numbers, which he [Vieta] calls triangular, pyramidal, etc. **1816** tr. *Lacroix's Diff. & Int. Calculus* 528 Ex. 2 The sum of the *x* first terms of any progression of figurate numbers being required.

1666 COLLINS in Rigaud *Corr. Sci. Men* (1841) I. 122 As to Figurate Arithmetic, it is largely handled in Maurolycus.

4. *Music.* = FLORID. Cf. FIGURED 7 a.

1708 J. HARRIS *Lex. Techn.* s.v. *Descant, Figurate* or *Florid Descant*, is that wherein Discords are concerned, as well (though not so much) as concords. **1795** MASON *Ch. Mus.* 28 *Figurate*..we now employ to distinguish florid from more simple Melody. **1833** *New Monthly Mag.* XXXVIII. 199 Haydn's masses are more figurate than those of his predecessors.

B. *sb.*

†**1.** Something possessing form or shape. *rare.*

1610 W. FOLKINGHAM *Art of Survey* II. ix. 62 The Content Solid is of Timber, Stone, and other Bodies or Figurates.

2. A figurate number: †**a.** a number consisting of factors; *esp.* an integral power of any number. ***equilater figurate***: a square number. Cf. A. 3 a. *Obs.*

1614 T. BEDWELL *Nat. Geom. Numbers* i. 4 The figurate 4 is made by one multiplication of one number by it selfe. *Ibid.*, An equilater figurate is made of equall numbers, or of one number multiplied by it selfe.

b. (See A. 3 b.)

1796 HUTTON *Math. Dict.* I. 469 Malcolm's Arithmetic, p. 396, where the subject of Figurates is treated in a very.. perspicuous manner.

†'**figurate**, *v. Obs.* [f. L. *figūrāt-* ppl. stem of *figūrāre* to FIGURE.]

1. *trans.* To give figure or shape to; to shape.

1615 CROOKE *Body of Man* 265 The harder and more solide parts are figurated together, but not together perfected. For of the bones some are sooner perfected, some later. *Ibid.* 307 Sixe dayes it is in Milke..Twelue figurate the flesh. **1623** in COCKERAM.

2. To present in figure, outline, or visible shape.

1704 HEARNE *Duct. Hist.* (1714) I. 38 So do Chronological Tables figurate to us the Series and Concatenation of Times.

3. a. To represent by a figure or emblem; to typify. **b.** To speak of in a figure, or figuratively. **c.** To treat as figurative. **d.** To liken or compare *to.*

a. **1533** COVERDALE *Lord's Supper* 451 They did in their gesture and rite figurate a certain image of a sacrifice. **1602** MARSTON *Ant. & Mel.* v. Wks. 1856 I. 62 The glowe worme figurates my valour. **1609** BIBLE (Douay) *Gen.* xiv. Comm., Melchisedec..knew how to figurate his eternal priesthood. **1654** JER. TAYLOR *Real Pres.* 274 The Fathers..call the figure, by the name of the thing figurated.

b. **1643** R. O. *Man's Mort.* v. 22 It is well figurated in Scripture by sleepe.

c. *a* **1806** S. HORSLEY *Serm.* (1811) 408 Those..who have improved upon St. Austin's hint of figurating this passage.

d. *c* **1450** HENRYSON *Mor. Fab.* 22 This feinȝit Foxe may well bee figurate To flatterers.

4. To furnish with figures of speech.

1652 URQUHART *Jewel* Wks. (1834) 292 There is neither definition, distribution..or any scheme figurating a speech.

5. *Math.*: cf. FIGURATE *a.* 3 a and FIGURAL 2.

1674 JEAKE *Arith.* (1696) 289 To Figurate any Cossick is Cossically to multiply the same..by it self.

Hence '**figurated** *ppl. a.*; in quots. = FIGURATE.

1642 F. POTTER *Interpr. of No. 666*, 195 The number 30 is a figurated number, because three times ten, or five times six, make this number. **1660** INGELO *Bentiv. & Ur.* II. (1682) 202 After the dissolution of Figurated matter. **1848** CRAIG, *Figurated*, having a determinate form.

†'**figurately**, *adv. Obs.* [See -LY².]

1. = FIGURATIVELY 1 and 2.

1533 FRITH *Disput. Purgat.* II. G iij/1 He dare not vnderstonde this thynge as figuratelye spoken. *a* **1677** BARROW *Serm.* (L.), Doing it then mediately and figurately by his prophets.

2. According to a grammatical figure.

1530 PALSGR. 402 They use *voult* fyguratly by Syncopa for *voulut.*

3. (*to multiply*) ***figurately*** = FIGURALLY 2.

1674 JEAKE *Arith.* (1696) 249 Let then 100 be multiplyed Figurately to the 10th Power.

figuration (fɪgjʊə'reɪʃən). Also 5 figuracion. [a. F. *figuration*, ad. L. *figūrātiōn-em*, n. of action f. *figūrāre* to fashion, FIGURE.]

1. a. The action or process of forming into figure; determination to a certain form.

1561 T. NORTON *Calvin's Inst.* II. xiv. (1634) 230 Finally the figuration of Christ, hath with them the place of

begetting. **1656** H. MORE *Enthus. Tri.* 4 The inward figuration of our brain or spirits into this or that representation. **1677** GREW *Anat. Fruits* vi. §2 The Vessels serve for the Figuration of the Fruit. **1856** R. A. VAUGHAN *Mystics* (1860) II. 230 A mysticism like that of Tauler strives to escape all image and 'figuration'.

b. quasi-*concr.* The resulting form or shape; contour, outline.

1432-50 tr. *Higden* (Rolls) I. 199 The chiefe cite..is callede Brundusium..in that hit holdethe in the figuracion of hit the similitude of the hede of an herte. **1563-87** FOXE *A. & M.* (1596) 77/1 Constantine caused a Crosse after the same figuration to be made of gold and precious stones. **1658** SIR T. BROWNE *Gard. Cyrus* iii. 53 Quincuncial forms..are also observable in animall figurations. **1697** T. SMITH in *Lett. Lit. Men* (Camden) 249 The different shapes and figurations of letters in several ages of the world. **1728** PEMBERTON *Newton's Philos.* 8 The figuration and the motion of bodies strike our senses more immediately than most of their other properties. **1842** DE QUINCEY in *Blackw. Mag.* LI. 13 Their very figurations now appeared to reflect and repeat each other. **1890** J. H. STIRLING *Gifford Lect.* iv. 71 Finite things were the figurations, the lineamentations of extension.

2. a. The action of representing figuratively; an allegorical or figurative representation.

1561 DAUS tr. *Bullinger on Apoc.* Pref. (1573) 12 It [this Apocalips] sheweth vs also sondry descriptions and figurations of matters most weightie. **1579** FULKE *Heskins' Parl.* 266 The sacrament is not a bare figuration of the flesh of Christ. **1664** H. MORE *Myst. Iniq.* 213 In Prophetick Figurations one individual Beast signifies a Multitude of men. **1737** WATERLAND *Eucharist* (1739) 28 The..dark Intimations of the legal Types or Figurations. **1840** LYTTON *Pilgr. Rhine* xxvi, The..faun has been made the figuration of the most implacable of fiends. **1871** MACDUFF *Mem. Patmos* xix. 256 The island-home..may have possibly added power and reality to the figuration.

b. The figurative style of painting. Cf. FIGURATIVE *a.* 2 b.

1962 *Listener* 19 July 93/2 Some painters who persisted with figuration during the nineteen-fifties when it was least in favour.

3. The action of framing figures or shapes: **a.** in dreams; in quot. quasi-*concr.* **b.** Ornamentation by means of figures or designs. *rare.*

1652 GAULE *Magastrom.* 176 There is neither vertue nor efficacy in such fabrications, or figurations, from God, Angels, nature. **1730-6** BAILEY (folio), *Figuration*, a chimerical vision. **1866** J. G. MURPHY *Comm. Ex.* xxvi. 36-7 The figuration is wrought not by the loom, but by the needle.

†**4.** *Math.* **a.** The making of arithmetical figures. **b.** The multiplying of a number into itself (see FIGURATE *v.* 5); involution. *Obs.*

c **1430** *Art of Nombrynge* (E.E.T.S.) 2 Ffigure is clepede for protraccione of figuracione. **1674** JEAKE *Arith.* (1696) 373 Figuration of the Sinister part of the Divisor.

5. *Music.* Employment of figurate or florid counterpoint; alteration of a theme or counterpoint by the introduction of passing-notes, rapid figures, etc.

1597 MORLEY *Introd. Mus.* 90 *Phi.* What is Figuration? *Ma.* When you sing one note of the plain-song long, and another short, etc. *a* **1646** J. GREGORY *Nicene Creed* Wks. (1649) 53 The Singing of the Nicene creed..with all the Ornaments and figurations of Harmonie. **1883** PARRY in Grove *Dict. Mus.* III. 759 The process is rather that of free figuration of two or three parts, giving in general a contrapuntal effect to the whole. **1889** *Ibid.* IV. 761 The mixed style, in which the figuration introduced consists chiefly of suspended concords [etc.].

6. A member of the Figures form (see FIGURE *sb.* 22 b).

1904 *Ushaw Mag.* XIV. 200 Whilst the Grammarians scored 16 the High Figurations scored 7.

figurative ('fɪgjʊərətɪv), *a.* Also 4-5 **figuratif**, 4-6 **fygurative, -tyf, -tyve**. [a. Fr. *figuratif, -ive*, ad. late L. *figūrātīvus*, f. *figūrāre* to FIGURE.]

1. Representing by a figure or emblem; emblematical, typical.

1398 TREVISA *Barth. De P.R.* VI. xxvii. (1495) 217 Dremes ben somtyme wrappyd in fyguratyf mystyk. **1504** tr. *De Imitatione* IV. xi, This royall souper, in the which thou hast nat purposed to be eten the fyguratyue lambe. **1597** HOOKER *Eccl. Pol.* V. xv. (1611) 208 This they will say was figuratiue, and serued but for a time. **1650** BULWER *Anthropomet.* 174 The Nails were made..for a figurative token. **1853** MARSDEN *Early Purit.* 22 They were a part of the divinely appointed constitution of the Jewish church, and had passed away with the rest of its figurative and mystic ceremonial.

2. a. Pertaining to, or of the nature of, pictorial or plastic representation.

1607 TOPSELL *Four-f. Beasts* (1658) 156 Serpents..in whose heads are many pretious stones, with such naturall seals or figurative impressions as if they were framed by the hand of man. **1843** PRESCOTT *Mexico* (1850) I. 77 This is the *representative* or *figurative* writing, which forms the lowest stage of hieroglyphics. **1889** J. HIRST in *Archæol. Inst. Jrnl.* No. 181. 34 Transmission of both geometric as well as animal and figurative decorated forms from East to West.

b. Of a style of the visual arts; esp. applied to painting in which the forms are recognizably derived from objective sources without necessarily being clearly representational; ***figurative painter***: one who paints in this style.

1960 *Guardian* 2 Feb. 7/4 'Figurative' is a comparatively new word in the critical vocabulary of contemporary art. It implies a kind of painting that is not abstract and..not necessarily representational. **1962** *Listener* 19 July 93/1 There is a new interest in figurative painting today. *Ibid.* 94/1 The work of three figurative painters who have recently shown in London: Francis Bacon, Sidney Nolan, and Arthur Boyd. *Ibid.* 94/2 In their use of chance in the act of painting figurative painters today undoubtedly owe much to abstract expressionism.

†**3.** Pertaining to the use of graphic symbols. ***figurative arithmetic***: algebra. Also, Of the nature of a symbolic diagram. *Obs.*

1690 LEYBOURN *Cursus Math.* 335 Division is done in Figurative Arithmetick..by applying some Line of Separation between the Dividend and the Divisor. **1800** tr. *Lagrange's Chem.* I. 13 Let us still exhibit a figurative table.

4. a. Of speech: Based on, or involving the use of, figures or metaphors; metaphorical, not literal.

14.. *Prose Legends* in *Anglia* VIII. 134 Legeauns & figuratif spekynges. *a* **1568** COVERDALE *Hope Faithf.* xxvii, By a figurative and borrowed speech he declareth the horror ..of the damned. **1589** PUTTENHAM *Eng. Poesie* I. iv. (Arb.) 24 The vtterance in prose..is also not so voluble..nor in fine allowed that figuratiue conueyance..as meeter is. **1607** TOPSELL *Serpents* (1653) 653 A witty check, or a figurative flout. **1711** J. GREENWOOD *Eng. Gram.* 217 Customary or Figurative Syntax is that which is used in the Forms of Speech..wherein Words are put together according to a Metaphorical or borrowed Sense. **1785** REID *Int. Powers* 15 There is a figurative sense in which things are said to be in the mind. **1845** H. J. ROSE in *Encycl. Metrop.* II. 891/1 Will it be contended that this was not figurative language? **1859** *Ecce Homo* iii. (ed. 8) 26 The mistake of confounding a figurative expression with a literal one.

b. Metaphorically so called.

14.. *Prose Legends* in *Anglia* VIII. 118 The figuratif body of Chryste þat is holy chirche. **1577** HANMER *Anc. Eccl. Hist.* (1619) 5 Also Princes, whom the prophets..have..made figurative Christs. **1832** LEWIS *Use & Ab. Pol. Terms* v. 44 Confound real with figurative Sovereignty. **1842** S. LOVER *Handy Andy* ii, He saw a real instead of a figurative blister.

5. Abounding in or addicted to figures of speech.

1589 PUTTENHAM *Eng. Poesie* III. vii. (Arb.) 166 Which thing made the graue iudges Areopagites..to forbid all manner of figuratiue speaches..to be vsed before them in their consistorie of Iustice. **1693** DRYDEN *Juvenal* Pref., Sublime subjects ought to be adorned with the sublimest and with the most figurative expressions. **1740** J. CLARKE *Educ. Youth* (ed. 3) 88 Tho' they are..easy Authors, yet they are more Figurative than Cæsar. **1783** H. BLAIR *Lect.* I. xiv. 274 They will pour forth a torrent of Figurative Language. **1789** BELSHAM *Ess.* I. ii. 25 Shakespeare..is the most figurative writer..in our language. **1878** BROWNING *Poets Croisic* 113 La Roque..broke bounds Of figurative passion.

†**6.** *Mus.* = FIGURATE *a.* 4. *Obs.*

1744 *Suppl. Harris's Lex. Techn.* s.v. *Counterpoint*, Counterpoint is divided into simple and figurative.. Figurative Counterpoint is of two Kinds, in one, Discords are introduced occasionally, as passing Notes..in the other, the Discord bears a chief Part of the Harmony.

figuratively ('fɪgjʊərətɪvlɪ), *adv.* [f. prec. + -LY[2].] In a figurative manner.

1. In or by means of a figure or emblem.

1393 LANGL. *P. Pl.* C. XVII. 294 And þow fynde hym bote figuratifliche a ferly me þynkeþ. *c* **1430** *Speculum* (1888) 33 In Gedeones flece was this shewed figuratively. **1508** FISHER *7 Penit. Ps.* ooiij, There be thre partes of penaunce whiche this holy prophete sheweth derkely and fyguratyuely by the symylitude of thre dyuers byrdes. **1646** SIR T. BROWNE *Pseud. Ep.* III. vii. 121 The sense is still the same; for therein are figuratively intended Vzziah and Ezechias. **1780** G. HORNE *Disc.* (1794) III. xvii. 379 Figuratively and sacramentally presented in the temple on earth.

2. By or as a figure of speech; metaphorically.

1533 FRITH *Disput. Purgat.* (1829) 151 He dare not understand this thing as figuratively spoken. **1651** HOBBES *Leviath.* III. xxxv. 220 Figuratively, those men also are called Holy. **1749** FIELDING *Tom Jones* VII. ii, To express myself less figuratively, he determined to go to sea. **1867** MISS BROUGHTON *Not wisely* II. 282 It is very, very difficult figuratively to get inside another person.

'figurativeness. [f. as prec. + -NESS.] The quality of being figurative.

a **1729** S. CLARKE *Serm.* II. cxxii. 45 From the figurativeness..of these expressions. **1816** J. GILCHRIST *Philos. Etym.* 227 Dispense with the figurativeness of Bacon's style! **1837** HALLAM *Hist. Lit.* III. iv. §8 The precepts..of Revelation, notwithstanding their brevity and figurativeness. **1881** *Athenæum* No. 2811. 328/2 The figurativeness of another kind of which..Rossetti's sonnets are so full.

†**'figurature.** *Obs. rare*[−1]. [as if ad. L. **figūrātūra*, f. *figūrāre* to FIGURE: see -URE.] Form, make, shape.

1642 BP. T. MORTON *Presentm. Schismatic* 2 One may see the face of another, and yet not discern the linaments and figurature.

figure ('fɪgə(r), -jʊə(r)), *sb.* Forms: 3-4 **vig(o)ur**, (3 **wygur**), 4-5 **fig(o)ur**, (5 **fegure**), 4-6 **fygure**, 3- **figure**. [a. Fr. *figure* (= Pr., Sp., It. *figura*), ad. L. *figūra*, f. **fig-* short stem of *fingĕre*: see FEIGN.

The L. word was the ordinary rendering of Gr. σχῆμα (see SCHEME) in its many technical uses; several of the senses below are traceable, wholly or in part, to Greek philosophy.]

I. Form, shape.

1. a. The form of anything as determined by the outline; external form; shape generally; *spec.* ***figure of the earth***: see GEOID and quot. 1931.

1393 GOWER *Conf.* III. 52 But yet it [a statue] was as in figure Most lich to mannes creature. **1477** EARL RIVERS (Caxton) *Dictes* 141 A man that is in a derke kaue may not se his propre figure. **1535** COVERDALE *Ezek.* x. 22 The figure of their faces was, euen as I had sene them. **1626** BACON *Sylva* §221 The Figure of a Bell partaketh of the Pyramis. **1697** DAMPIER *Voy.* (1729) I. 537 Their Faces are of a flat oval Figure. **1698** KEILL *Exam. Th. Earth* (1734) 289 The Theorist..had deduced its [the Earth's] true Figure from its true causes. **1705** [see OBLATE *a.*]. **1756** NUGENT *Gr. Tour* I. 164 The figure of the city is an oblong square. **1830** KATER & LARDN. *Mech.* i. 5 Bodies having very different volumes may have the same figure. **1878** HUXLEY *Physiogr.* xix. 318 In addition to this change of size..the figure of the ship suffers a change. **1931** *Bull. Nat. Res. Counc.* LXXVIII. vii. 113 Figure of the Earth.—The defining elements of the mathematical surface which approximates the geoidal surface. The figure of the earth has been proved to be approximately an oblate spheroid.

b. In generalized sense, as an attribute of body.

1471 RIPLEY *Comp. Alch.* III. in Ashm. (1652) 141 Both fygure and ponderosyte. **1690** LOCKE *Hum. Und.* II. xxxi. §2 Solidity and Extension, and the Termination of it, Figure. **1744** HARRIS *Three Treat.* (1841) 29 Such things..as are peculiarly characterized by figure and colour. **1831** BREWSTER *Optics* xvii. §90. 147 Crystals whose..simplest form had only one axis of figure. **1875** JOWETT *Plato* (ed. 2) I. 275 Figure is the only thing that always follows colour.

†**c.** Appearance, aspect; also, attitude, posture.

1513 DOUGLAS *Æneis* V. xiii. 13 The seis figur wes abhominable. **1658** SIR T. BROWNE *Hydriot.* iv. 58 Some Christians..decline the figure of rest, and make choice of an erect posture. **1684** CHARNOCK *Attrib. God* (1834) II. 577 To have devout figures of the face, and uncomely postures of the soul.

d. *transf.* The 'shape', state (of a matter). *rare.*

1858 CARLYLE *Fredk. Gt.* (1865) I. III. iii. 150 As to Friedrich's Pomeranian quarrel, this is the figure of it.

2. *Geom.* A definite form constituted by a given line or continuous series of lines so arranged as to enclose a superficial space, or by a given surface or series of surfaces enclosing a space of three dimensions; any of the classes or species of such forms, as the triangle, circle, cube, sphere, etc.

1340 *Ayenb.* 234 Ine þe rounde figure: þe ende went ayen to his ginninge. **1551** RECORDE *Pathw. Knowl.* I. Defin., Figures..be made of pricks, lines or platte formes. **1570** BILLINGSLEY *Euclid* I. xv. 3 Of all figures a circle is the most perfect. **1603** HOLLAND *Plutarch's Mor.* 814 A Figure is the superficies, circumscription, and accomplished lineament of a bodie. **1714** STEELE *Englishman* No. 46 That beautiful Figure in Architecture called a Pyramid. **1809-10** COLERIDGE *Friend* (1865) 97 A circle is..a figure constituted by the circumvolution of a straight line with its one end fixed. **1823** H. J. BROOKE *Introd. Crystallogr.* 137 The new figures would be octahedrons. **1840** LARDNER *Geom.* 134 A figure may be constructed similar to a given figure.

†**3.** The proper or distinctive shape or appearance (of a person or thing). *Obs.*

a **1300** *Cursor M.* 22148 (Cott.) O thinges sere þair naturs [anticrist sal do] turnd to be in sere figurs. **1340** HAMPOLE *Pr. Consc.* 2320 A devel in hys fygur right. *c* **1386** CHAUCER *Monk's T.* 232 Than..God..him [Nebuchadnezzar] restored to his regne and his figure. *c* **1400** MAUNDEV. (Roxb.) iv. 13 Scho bad hem þat he schuld..hafe na drede of hir, what figure so euer he sawe hir. *a* **1400-50** *Alexander* 360 þe figour of a freke he sall take eftire. **1475** *Bk. Noblesse* (1860) 21 Wonderfulle entreprises..that Hercules did, whiche is writen in figure of a poesy. **1599** SHAKS. *Much Ado* I. i. 15 Doing in the figure of a Lambe, the feats of a Lion. **1611** BIBLE *Isa.* xliv. 13 The carpenter..maketh it after the figure of a man.

4. a. Of a living being: Bodily shape, occas. including appearance and bearing. Now chiefly of persons.

13.. *E.E. Allit. P.* A. 746 Quo formed þe þy fayre fygure? **1483** CAXTON *Gold. Leg.* 283 b/1 A monk of a ryght honourable fygure and parure. **1484** —— *Fables of Æsop* IV. iv, To the [the pecok] they [the goddes] haue gyuen fayr fygure. *a* **1533** LD. BERNERS *Huon* xlii. 140 Yf I shold dyscryue his foule fygure at length. **1637** NABBES *Microcosm.* II. C ij, When other creatures..Look downwards on't, [thou] hast an erected figure. **1740** CHESTERF. *Lett.* I. lxii. 174 [Poets] represent as persons, the passions, and many other things that have no figures nor persons belonging to them. **1774** GOLDSM. *Nat. Hist.* (1776) II. 106 There is little known exactly with regard to the proportion of the human figure. *Ibid.* IV. 24 Few readers.. are not as well acquainted with the figure of a Squirrel. **1863** FR. A. KEMBLE *Resid. in Georgia* 42 The figures of some of the women are handsome. **1869** BOUTELL *Arms & Arm.* vii. 109 This hauberk was adjusted to the figure by a belt. **1888** BURGON *Lives 12 Gd. Men* I. ii. 140 His dignified aspect and commanding figure.

b. The bodily frame, considered with regard to its appearance.

1715-20 POPE *Iliad* IX. 71 Wise Nestor then his reverend figure rear'd. **1728** —— *Dunc.* II. 62 So lab'ring on, with shoulders, hands, and head, Wide as a windmill all his figure spread.

5. a. An embodied (human) form; a person considered with regard to visible form or appearance.

c **1250** *Gen. & Ex.* 1006 In ðe dale of mambre, saȝ abraham figures ðre. *c* **1420** *Anturs of Arth.* xi, Ho was a figure of flesche, fayrest of alle. *c* **1450** LONELICH *Grail* xliii. 303 The fegure þat there-owt gan gon. **1602** SHAKS. *Ham.* I. i. 109 This portentous figure Comes armed through our watch. **1673** DRYDEN *Marr. à la Mode* III. i, What a figure of a man is there! **1730** A. GORDON *Maffei's Amphith.* 50 Two Figures..in the Action of going into the Amphitheatre. **1754** RICHARDSON *Grandison* IV. xxi. 153 She is a very fine figure of a woman. **1768** STERNE *Sent. Journ.* (1782) II. 81 A tall figure, of a philosophic, serious, adust look. **1877** RITA *Vivienne* I. iv, He saw a figure leaning against the embrasure of one of the windows.

b. *colloq.* A person of grotesque or untidy appearance. ***figure of fun***: a ludicrous personage, an oddity.

1774 MAD. D'ARBLAY *Early Diary* (1889) I. 322, I.. obtained leave to come down, though..quite a figure. **1811** MISS L. M. HAWKINS *C'tess. & Gertr.* (K.O.), Figure of fun. **1813** LADY BURGHERSH in *Lett.* (1893) 61 Words can't

describe the figures the women dress here of a morning. 1840 Mrs. F. Trollope *Widow Married* vii, what..can have induced you to make such a figure of yourself? 1861 Hughes *Tom Brown at Oxf.* xviii. (1889) 173 The figure of fun was a middle-aged man of small stature. 1886 Burton *Arab. Nts.* I. 82 Each of them is a figure o' fun after his own fashion.

6. *transf.* A person as an object of mental contemplation; a personage. ***father-figure***: see FATHER *sb.* 12.

1734 Watts *Reliq. Juv.* (1789) 216 She had rather bear an inconvenience herself, than give an uneasiness even to the meaner figures of mankind. 1847 Emerson *Repr. Men, Goethe* Wks. (Bohn) I. 389 And he flung into literature, in his Mephistopheles, the first organic figure that has been added for some ages. 1874 Green *Short Hist.* vi. §6. 335 This utter absence of all passion..makes the figure of [Thomas] Cromwell the most terrible in our history. 1888 Bryce *Amer. Commw.* II. liii. 327 The disappearance of this brilliant figure [Hamilton].

7. Conspicuous appearance. In phrase ***to make*** (familiarly ***to cut***) ***a figure***:

a. in neutral sense, with qualifying adj.: To present a (good, bad, splendid, ridiculous, etc.) appearance; to produce an impression of specified character on the beholder.

1699 Bentley *Phal.* 361 Any Metaphor at all makes but a very bad Figure. 1710 Steele *Tatler* No. 57 ¶1 To understand among what Sort of Men we make the best Figure. 1727 A. Hamilton *New Acc. E. Ind.* I. xii. 134 The City makes a good figure from the Sea. 1766 Goldsm. *Vic. W.* x, When Moses has trimmed them a little, they will cut a very tolerable figure. 1791 'G. Gambado' *Ann. Horsem.* V. (1809) 87 London Riders,..who cut..so smart a figure in a country town. 1882 Serjt. Ballantine *Exper.* I. 456 Witnesses of this kind cut but an awkward figure in the hands of a skilful counsel. 1883 S. C. Hall *Retrospect* I. 240 He made but a poor figure in the House.

b. To appear in a ridiculous aspect.

1726 *Adv. Capt. R. Boyle* 212 It was as much as I could do to keep my Countenance at the Figure he made. 1854 Felton *Fam. Lett.* xlvi. (1865) 343 There is nothing more comical than the figure an English scholar cuts when he first comes to Athens.

c. To occupy a conspicuous or distinguished position; to play a prominent or important part; to attract admiration or respect. Cf. F. *faire figure*.

1691 J. Wilson *Belphegor* v. i. Dram. Wks. (1874) 368 And what figure do you make in this house? 1697 Dryden *Æneid* II. 116 While his arms..rul'd the Counsels of the Court, I made some figure there. 1711 Addison *Spect.* No. 92 ¶8 Gentlemen that make a Figure at Will's. 1736 Butler *Anal.* I. iii, Revolutions, which make a figure even in the history of the world. 1749 Chesterf. *Lett.* II. 233, I am very willing that you should make, but very unwilling that you should cut, a figure..; the cutting a figure being the very lowest vulgarism in the English language. 1762–71 H. Walpole *Vertue's Anecd. Paint.* (1786) I. 223 The first painter who seems to have made any figure in this reign. 1809 Syd. Smith *Wks.* (1859) I. 171/2 Boys, who make a considerable figure at school..often make no figure in the world. 1824 W. Irving *T. Trav.* I. 187 If they did not make much figure in talking, they did in eating. 1864 Burton *Scot Abr.* I. iv. 206 Kirkaldy of Grange..cut some figure in politics.

8. a. Importance, distinction, 'mark'. Now only with reference to persons, in phrases (somewhat *arch.*) ***man, woman of figure***, a person of rank and station.

1692 Dryden *St. Evremont's Ess.* 192 Persons of the greatest Figure make every thing valued according to their Fancy. 1703 Maundrell *Journ. Jerus.* (1732) 44 Another River, of no inconsiderable figure. 1711 Addison *Spect.* No. 122 ¶7 The speech..was..designed..to give him a Figure in my Eye. 1769 *De Foe's Tour Gt. Brit.* II. 63 Wallingford..a Place of great Figure. c1800 K. White *Rem.* (1837) 379, I met him..in company with persons of apparent figure. 1851 Carlyle *Sterling* II. i. (1872) 89 Mr. Sterling, a private gentleman of some figure.

b. Style of living, ostentation, display. *arch.*

1602 *Ld. Cromwell* III. iii. 2 Our County now exceeds the figure Of common entertainments. 1720 De Foe *Capt. Singleton* xx. (1840) 342 He obliged her not to increase her figure, but live private. 1807 *Fielding's Tom Jones* I. Life 11 Fond of figure and magnificence, he incumbered himself with a large retinue. 1851 Carlyle *Sterling* I. ix. (1872) 55 Lieutenant-General Barton of the Life-guards..lived in a certain figure here in town.

II. Represented form; image, likeness.

9. a. The image, likeness, or representation *of* something material or immaterial.

a1340 Hampole *Psalter* xxii. 4 Ill men..beris þe figure of ded. c1400 Maundev. (Roxb.) vii. 25 Euermare in þe middes of þam es funden þe figure of þe crosse. 1481 Caxton *Myrr.* I. iii. 9 He fourmed hym [man] to his figure and semblaunce. 1531 Elyot *Gov.* I. xxvi, There is nat a more playne figure of idlenesse, than playinge at dise. 1608 Shaks. *Per.* v. iii. 92 In Helicanus may you well descry A figure of truth, of faith, of loyalty. 1658 Sir T. Browne *Hydriot.* iii. 40 The mystical Figures of Peacocks, Doves and Cocks. 1791 Burke *App. Whigs* Wks. VI. 30 He is their standard figure of perfection. 1878 B. Taylor *Deukalion* Argt. 10 She is no figure of the Faith of her day.

†**b.** An imaginary form, a phantasm. *Obs.*

c1384 Chaucer *H. Fame* I. 48 Or if the soule..warnith al and some..Be avisions or be figures. 1598 Shaks. *Merry W.* IV. ii. 231 To scrape the figures out of your husbands braines.

10. *esp.* An artificial representation of the human form.

a. In sculpture: A statue, an image, an effigy.

† ***to work by the figure*** (quot 1598): perh. to operate on a wax effigy of a person, for the purpose of enchantment (Schmidt); some have referred it to sense 14.

a1300 *Cursor M.* 2290 (Cott.) Lik til his fader þat was ded A wygur was mad. a1300 *E.E. Psalter* xcvi[i] 7 Alle schende be..þat mirthen in þar vigours [*in simulacris*] als. c1400 *Destr. Troy* 4349 The Figur of his fader was falsly honouryt. 1483 Caxton *Cato* A iij b, To adoure the ymages and other fygures humayn. 1535 Lyndesay *Satyre* 4087 *Stage Direct.*, Heir sal Dissait be drawin up, or ellis his figure. 1598 Shaks. *Merry W.* IV. ii. 185 A witch..She workes by Charmes, by Spels, by th' Figure. 1611 Bible *1 Kings* vi. 29 Carued figures of Cherubims. 1697 Dryden *Virg. Georg.* II. 646 The breathing Figures of Corinthian Brass. 1717 Lady M. W. Montagu *Lett.* II. xlvi. 35 All the figures have their heads on. 1807–8 Scott *Wav.* App. ii, I tried..to frighten her..by introducing a figure through a trap-door. 1851 Hussey *Papal Power* iii. 158 The use of figures in Churches.

b. In painting, drawing, etc.: A representation of human form (as opposed to landscape, still life, etc.). Now restricted to representation of the whole or greater part of the body.

c1400 Maundev. (Roxb.) xi. 43 A boist of grene iasper with foure figures and viii. names of oure Lord þerin. c1440 *Promp. Parv.* 159/2 Fygure, or lykenesse. 1676 *North's Plutarch* Add. Lives 75 His Cabinet, furnished with many Pourtraitures and Figures of those who had been Travellers. 1695 Dryden tr. *Du Fresnoy's Art of Painting* Pref. 37 In the principal Figures of a Picture..consists the principal beauty of his [the Painter's] Work. 1705 Addison *Italy* 13 Tapestry, in which are wrought the Figures of..great Persons. 1821 Craig *Lect. Drawing* viii. 428 If your subject be of figures. 1832 G. Downes *Lett. Cont. Countries* I. 14 On the front are the figures of his wife and child.

c. *Her.* (Cf. F. *figure* the face.)

1727–41 Chambers *Cycl.*, *Figure*, in heraldry, a bearing in a shield, representing or resembling a human face; as a sun, a wind, an angel, etc.

†**11. a.** Represented character; part enacted; hence, position, capacity. *Obs.*

1610 Shaks. *Temp.* III. iii. 83 Brauely the figure of this Harpie, hast thou Perform'd. 1673 Dryden *Marr. à la Mode* v. i, Since he is King, methinks he has assumed another Figure. 1675 Temple *Let. to Sir J. Williamson* Wks. 1731 II. 314 His Majesty would upon no Occasion quit the Figure of Mediator. 1711 Steele *Spect.* No. 262 ¶6 Those who appear in the higher Figures of Life. 1721 De Foe *Mem. Cavalier* (1840) 113 Your majesty..shall be served by me in any figure you please.

b. One acting a part. *Obs. rare.*

1494 Fabyan *Chron.* VII. ccxxviii. 258 She was there as a fygure, a woman werynge that habyte without professyon of ordre.

c. A person dressed in character. *Obs.*

1767 J. Penn *Sleepy Serm.* v, Horse-jockeys, Italian figures, rope-dancers, and ballad-singers.

12. An emblem, type. † ***in figure***: in emblematical representation. † ***to be in figure***: to be typical. † ***in figure to***: emblematic *of*.

a1340 Hampole *Psalter* cxlvi. 8 He hilys halywrit wiþ figurs forto stire men to seke. c1366 Chaucer *A.B.C.* 169 Ysaak was figure of his [Christ's] deth certeyn. c1450 *St. Cuthbert* (Surtees) 697 þe ship þat beres vs in þe se, Of haly kyrke þe figure be. 1497 Bp. Alcock *Mons Perfect.* A ij, This mount is in figure and sygnefyeth relygyon. 1532 More *Confut. Tindale* Wks. 385/1 Al thing vnto them came in figures. 1607–12 Bacon *Ess. Counsel* (Arb.) 312 The auncient tymes doe sett fourth in Figure..the incorporacion ..of Councell with Kinges. 1637 Nabbes *Microcosm.* I. C, Oh gentle power..Figure of peace. 1647 Saltmarsh *Sparkles Glory* (1847) 149 A rest or peace in figure to that glory and fulness to be revealed in us. 1651 C. Cartwright *Cert. Relig.* I. 122 The Rock..was a Type and a Figure of Christ. 1730–6 in Bailey (folio). 1855 Macaulay *Hist. Eng.* IV. 453 It has long been usual to represent the imagination under the figure of a wing.

III. Delineated or devised form; a design or pattern.

13. A delineation illustrating the text of a book; a diagram, an illustration. When used as a reference usually abbreviated to *fig.*

The L. *figura* = Gr. σχῆμα as applied to mathematical diagrams; but the mod. use is influenced by sense 9.

c1391 Chaucer *Astrol.* I. §3 For the more declaracioun, lo here the figure. 1545 Raynold *Byrth Mankynde* (1564) B ij, Not onely in wordes, but also in liuely and expresse fygures. 1551 Recorde *Pathw. Knowl.* II. Pref., The charges in cuttyng of the figures. a1660 W. Oughtred (*title*), Mathematicall Recreations, or a Collection of sundry Problemes..illustrated with divers Brasse Figures. 1703 Moxon *Mech. Exerc.* 173 As you see in the Figure at *b*. 1849 *Sk. Nat. Hist., Mammalia* IV. 113 Two figures of skulls (Fig. 71 and 72). 1851 P. L. Simmonds (*title*), Ure's Cotton Manufacture..in two volumes with one hundred and fifty original figures. 1885 Leudesdorf *Cremona's Proj. Geom.* 81 Let in the first figure a transversal *m* be drawn to cut *a, b, c, d* in *A, B, C, D* respectively.

14. *Astrol.* A diagram of the aspects of the astrological houses; a horoscope. ***a figure of heaven*** or ***the heavens***: a scheme or table showing the disposition of the heavens at a given time. ***to cast, erect, set a figure***: see the vbs.

1393 Gower *Conf.* III. 79 He..Through his carectes and figures The maistry and the power hadde. 1610 B. Jonson *Alch.* IV. iv, By erection of her figure, I gest it. 1651 tr. *Bacon's Life & Death* 1 The Figures of Heaven, under which they were born. 1678 Butler *Hud.* III. i. 455 He set a Figure to discover If you were fled to Rye or Dover. 1716 Addison *Drummer* II. i, They are casting a figure. 1831 Brewster *Newton* (1855) I. ii. 21 He bought a book on Judicial Astrology..and in..perusing it he came to a figure of the Heavens.

15. a. An arrangement of lines or other markings forming an ornamental device; one of the devices combined into a decorative pattern; also applied to similar markings produced by natural agency. Also *collect.* † ***in figure***: so as to form a pattern.

1597 Shaks. *Lover's Compl.* 17 Oft did she heave her napkin to her eyne..Laundering the silken figures in the brine. 1625 Bacon *Ess. Friendship* (Arb.) 175 It was well said..That speech was like Cloth of Arras, opened, and put abroad; Whereby the Imagery doth appeare in Figure; whereas in Thoughts, they lie but as in Packs. 1637 Milton *Lycidas* 105 His bonnet sedge, Inwrought with figures dim. 1665 G. Havers *Sir T. Roe's Voy. E. Ind.* 447 This Seal..the Great Mogul, either in a large, or lesser figure causeth to be put into all Firmanes. 1833 Ht. Martineau *Loom & Lugger* II. vi. 118 A beautiful figure that velvet has, to be sure. 1855 Tennyson *Brook* 103 Sketching with her slender pointed foot Some figure..On garden gravel. 1860 Tyndall *Glac.* II. i. 232 The luminous figure reflected from such a surface is exceedingly beautiful.

transf. 1667 Milton *P.L.* VII. 426 Part more wise In common, rang'd in figure, wedge thir way. 1718 Lady M. W. Montagu *Let.* 10 Apr. (1861) I. 358 He..begins a sort of solemn dance. They all stand about him in a regular figure.

b. *spec.* in wood (see quots.).

1875 *Trans. N.Z. Inst.* VII. 185 The..point of insertion of the main lateral branches [of the kauri tree]..is cross-grained, the straight 'grain' of the lower part of the tree being twisted round the 'knots' into a great variety of..lines, and showing what cabinet-makers call 'figure'. 1904 P. Macquoid *Hist. Eng. Furnit.* ii. 35 What is called 'figure' in oak was obtained by cutting the wood... This so-called figure in wood has the appearance of hard diagonal splashes. 1953 H. L. Edlin *Forester's Handbk.* ii. 29 The beautiful *figure* found in certain woods is simply a representation of the intricate structure of the timber. It varies according to the way in which the log is cut up.

16. *Dancing.* One of the evolutions or movements of a dance or dancer; also, a set of evolutions; one of the divisions into which a set dance is divided.

1636 Massinger *Gt. Dk. Florence* IV. i, Keep your figure fair, And follow but the sample I shall set you. 1806–7 J. Beresford *Miseries Hum. Life* (1826) III. xvii, Blundering in the figure all the way down a country dance. 1825 *Anal. Lond. Ball-room* 62 The figure and tune being selected, the M.C. should be informed of it. 1874 Mrs. H. Wood *Mast. Greylands* I. 84 Such was the commencement of the figure.

17. *Skating.* 'A movement, or series of movements, beginning and ending at the centre' (*Badm. Libr., Skating* 145). (In quot. 1854 with joc. allusion to sense 7.).

1854 J. R. Planché *Camp at Olympic* i. 18 Like a bold wench, resolved at any price To cut a figure, though it's but on ice. 1869 Vandervell & Witham *Syst. Figure-skating* ix. 164 To commence a figure the skaters stand opposite each other, as on the sides of a square.

IV. A written character. Cf. 15.

†**18.** *gen.* Applied, e.g., to a letter of the alphabet, the symbol of a musical note, a mathematical symbol, etc. *Obs.*

1597 Morley *Introd. Mus.* Annot., Figures in time shorter than minimes cannot be tied or enter in ligature. 1607 Shaks. *Timon* v. i. 157 Shall..write in thee the figures of their loue Euer to read them thine. *Ibid.* v. iii. 7 The Charracter Ile take with wax, Our Captaine hath in euery Figure skill. 1609 J. Douland *Ornithop. Microl.* 39 A Breefe is a Figure, which hath a body foure-square, and wants a tayle ▬. 1660 Barrow *Euclid* II. i. Schol., Seeing by reason of the figure—, that A is not [etc.].

19. a. A numerical symbol. Originally, and still chiefly, applied to the ten symbols of the so-called Arabic notation. ***two*** (or ***double***), ***three, four***, etc. ***figures***; a number amounting to ten or more, a hundred or more, a thousand or more, etc.; a sum of money indicated by such a number. ***man of figures***: one versed in arithmetic or statistics.

In Cricket, (*a*) phr. ***to get into*** or ***reach double*** or ***three figures*** = to make ten or a hundred runs; (*b*) a bowler's average.

a1225 *Ancr. R.* 214 þe ȝiscare..makeð þerinne figures of augrim. c1305 *Edmund Conf.* 223 in *E.E.P.* (1862) 77 Arsmetrike radde in cours..& his figours drouȝ aldai. c1369 Chaucer *Dethe Blaunche* 447 And recken with his figures ten. c1425 *Craft Nombrynge* 1 In þis craft ben vsid teen figurys. 1542 Recorde *Gr. Artes* (1575) 42 There are but ten Figures, that are vsed in Arithmetike. 1600 T. Hill *Arith.* 5 b, The Cipher (for so the figure o is peculiarly named, although it be generally called and accompted as a figure). 1674 Playford *Skill Mus.* I. xi. 36 The Figures usually placed over Notes in the Thorough-Bass of Songs. 1746–7 Hervey *Medit.* (1818) 72 Arithmeticians have figures, to compute all the progressions of time. 1817 Tierney in *Parl. Deb.* 1357 The noble lord..could not disprove figures. 1884 *Punch* 5 Apr. 161/1 Mr. B., A.R.A., sends a 'single figure', —for which he asks three figures. 1884 *Lillywhite's Cricket Ann.* 64 Lancashire could not reach three figures either time. 1955 *Times* 9 May 15/1 His figures..were rather battered about by Perks, who hit him far and wide against the spin.

b. ***figure of eight***: see EIGHT 3. Also *attrib.*, as in ***figure of eight bandage, shield, suture***; ***figure of eight moth***: (see quot.).

1604 Marston *Malcontent* IV. ii, [The brawl] Why, 'tis but singles on the left, two on the right..a figure of eight. 1815 Kirby & Sp. *Entomol.* I. 196 The figure-of-eight-moth (*Bombyx cæruleocephala*, F.). 1871 Holmes *Syst. Surg.* (ed. 2) V. 508 The figure of eight bandage is formed of a single continuous roller. 1939 J. D. S. Pendlebury *Archaeol. Crete* v. 271 The great figure-of-eight shield (φώτε πύργος) protected the warrior from the neck to the feet. 1958 L. Cottrell *Anvil of Civilisation* viii. 114 Such symbols as the Double-Axe, the Figure-of-Eight Shield, and the Trident, which figure prominently in Minoan buildings of the Middle Minoan period.

c. ***figure* (*of*) *four***: a trap for catching animals, the trigger of which is set in the shape of the figure 4. Also ***figure four trap***.

1743 J. ISHAM *Observ. Hudson's Bay* (1949) 162 One more trap their is a figure of 4 trap, which is 2 Logs Squar'd for the sides, and a Log for the top of one foot wide, which is call'd a figure of 4 trap. **1785** T. B. HAZARD *Diary* 14 Feb. (1930) 76/2, I made and Sott atrap with a figger 4 for quails. **1834** J. J. AUDUBON *Ornith. Biogr.* II. 60 Many of these birds are frequently offered for sale.., they being easily caught in 'figure-of-four traps'. **1838** J. C. NEAL *Charcoal Sks.* I. 38 The most beautiful notions are all lost for want of a trap; an intellectual Figgery Four. **1862** *Trans. Ill. Agric. Soc.* (1865) V. 734 Boys..capture them by means of a 'figure four' trap. **1872** O. W. HOLMES *Poet. Breakf.-t.* i. (1885) 10 Rabbits are entrapped in 'figgery fours'. **1889** FARMER *Americanisms*, *Figure Four*, a hunter's trap for large game. Also called a *dead-fall*. **1919** H. L. WILSON *Ma Pettengill* viii. 243 Lew Wee..made a figure-four trap, and put something for bait on the pointed stick and set the trap.

20. a. Hence, An amount, number, sum of money expressed in figures.

1842 *Punch* II. 118/2 He may put a better dessert upon his table at a lighter figure than now. **1848** THACKERAY *Bk. Snobs* x, Accommodating a youngster..with a glandered charger at an uncommonly stiff figure. **1869** TYNDALL *Notes Lect. Light* §127 The index of refraction..reached..so high a figure as 2.4.

b. ***to do things on the big figure***, ***to go*** (or ***come***) ***the big figure***: see BIG *a.* B. 2; ***to go the whole figure*** U.S., to go the whole way; to act in a thoroughgoing fashion.

1834 *Sun* (N.Y.) 25 Mar. 2/3 (*heading*) Going the whole figure. **1839** *Havana* (N.Y.) *Republ.* 21 Aug. 369 (Th. s.v. *hull*), I was determined to go the hull figure, and see all. **1840** J. P. KENNEDY *Quodlibet* (1872) xii. 180, I can tell you that he goes the whole figure against rotation in this individual.. case. **1855** T. C. HALIBURTON *Nat. & Hum. Nat.* II. xii. 142 Sally was death on lace, and old Aunt Thankful goes the whole figure for furs. **1864** J. T. TROWBRIDGE *Cudjo's Cave* iii. 37 The time may come when we will have to..go the whole figure with the free north, or drift with the cotton states. *a* **1916** H. JAMES *Ivory Tower* (1917) 309 The.. momentous season or scene,..in which she goes the whole figure.

c. ***figure of merit***: a general term for a numerical expression taken as representing the performance or efficiency of a device or material (see also quot. 1865). Cf. *factor of merit* (FACTOR *sb.* 8 b).

1865 BRANDE & COX *Dict. Sci., Lit., & Art* I. 889/1 *Figure of merit*, in rifle-shooting at a target, the number denoting the individual success of any rifle. **1881** H. R. KEMPE *Handbk. Electr. Testing* (ed. 2) iii. 37 The degree of sensitiveness of any galvanometer, or its 'figure of merit', is determined by the amount of current which will produce one division or degree of deflection. **1911** *Encycl. Brit.* XXVII. 173/2 The hysteresis loss should not exceed 3·0 watts per kilogram of iron measured at a frequency of 50∼ and a flux-density of 10,000 lines per square centimetre. This is now called the 'figure of merit' of the iron. **1930** *Engineering* 7 Mar. 303/2 If figures of merit could be assigned for the various attributes of an engine..a collective efficiency or merit curve might be constructed. **1952** DRYSDALE & JOLLEY *Electr. Measuring Instrum.* (ed. 2) I. ii. 66 When an instrument has been designed, the designer wishes to have some criterion by which he can judge whether his design will be satisfactory in service. Some 'figure of merit' or means of judgment therefore appears to be necessary. **1958** CONDON & ODISHAW *Handbk. Physics.* iv. 109/1 Frequently the inverse of the loss tangent, the quality factor *Q* of the dielectric,..serves as the figure of merit, especially in waveguide problems.

V. In various uses, representing the technical applications of Gr. σχῆμα.

21. *Rhet.* **a.** Any of the various 'forms' of expression, deviating from the normal arrangement or use of words, which are adopted in order to give beauty, variety, or force to a composition; e.g. Aposiopesis, Hyperbole, Metaphor, etc. Also, ***figure of speech***.

c **1386** CHAUCER *Clerk's Prol.* 16 Your termes, your coloures, and your figures, Kepe hem in store, til [etc.]. **1589** PUTTENHAM *Eng. Poesie* III. vii. (Arb.) 166 Figures be the instruments of ornament in euery language. **1596** HARINGTON *Metam. Ajax* (1814) 11 And minding to speak it shorter, by the figure of abbreviation. **1609** BIBLE (Douay) *Ps.* cxiii. Comm., By the figure Apostrophe he speaketh to the sea, river, and hilles. *c* **1633** HOBBES *Rhet.* (1840) 519 A figure is garnishing of speech in words, or in a sentence. **1665** BOYLE *Occas. Refl.* Pref. (1848) 22 That noble Figure of Rhetorick call'd Hyperbole. **1766** CHESTERF. *Lett.* 188 The Egotism is the usuall and favourite figure of most people's Rhetorick. **1824** L. MURRAY *Eng. Gram.* (ed. 5) I. 486 Figures of Speech imply some departure from simplicity of expression. **1878** BOSW. SMITH *Carthage* 161 The proverb 'as many slaves, so many enemies' was, in their case, no figure of rhetoric but the stern and simple truth.

b. In a more restricted sense (with mixture of senses 9 and 12): A metaphor or metaphorical mode of expression; an image, similitude.

1435 MISYN *Fire of Love* 3 þe flaume, whilk vndyr fygure I cald fyer. **1526** *Pilgr. Perf.* (W. de W. 1531) 1 Declareth it by the similitude and fygure of the passage of the chyldren of Israel from Egypte. **1611** BIBLE *1 Cor.* iv. 6 These things ..I haue in a figure transferred to my selfe. **1727** POPE, etc. *Art of Sinking* 77 That..destroyer of fine figures, which is known by the name of common sense. **1782** PRIESTLEY *Corrupt. Chr.* I. II. 156 [These] expressions have much the air of figure and allusion. **1855** BRIMLEY *Ess.* 44 Simile and figure may be regarded as a natural short hand. **1875** JOWETT *Plato* (ed. 2) III. 96 The old Pythagorean ethical symbols still exist as figures of speech among ourselves.

22. a. *Grammar.* Any of the permitted deviations from the normal forms of words (e.g. Aphæresis, Syncope, Elision), or from the ordinary rules of construction (e.g. Ellipsis). †Formerly also *figure of speech.*

1669 MILTON *Accedence Gram.* Wks. 1851 VI. 467 Words are sometimes encreast or diminisht by a Letter or Syllable ..which are call'd Figures of Speech. **1721-1800** in BAILEY.

b. *pl.* The name of the first form in certain Jesuit schools and colleges, divided into High (or †Great) and Low (or †Little) Figures: corresponding to the Rudiments or Accidence of other places.

1629 WADSWORTH *Pilgr.* iii. 12, I was promoted to the first forme called the Figures. **1713** in B. Ward *Hist. St. Edmund's Coll.* (1893) iv. 58 What we call the Accidence they call Figures, which they divide into two years, one for the lower, the second for the higher. **1716** M. DAVIES *Athen. Brit.* III. 2 Their Humanity-Schools..are sub-divided, and call'd Little Figures..then great Figures or Rudiments. **1786** T. HAYDOCK *Let.* 12 Jan. in J. Gillow *Haydock Papers* (1888) 83 He was in low-figures before. **1893** B. WARD *Hist. St. Edmund's Coll.* iv. 58 The two classes of 'Figures' were changed very shortly after this [1713] into three classes of 'Rudiments'... At Ushaw the older title of 'Figures' is now in use. **1913** *Ushaw Mag.* Dec. 170 The Rev. William Lamb, who for a year had taught High Figures as a professor. **1951** *Ibid.* Mar. 60 Low Figures *Historical Society* is now in its ninth year.

23. *Logic.* (See quot. 1837–8.)

1551 WILSON *Logike* (1567) 286 Examples of the firste figure and the modes thereof. **1589** *Pappe w. Hatchet* B b, 'Tis neither in moode nor figure. **1628** T. SPENCER *Logick* 258 Aristotle delivers the forme of Syllogismes..and divides them into three figures. **1663** EVELYN *Mem.* (1857) III. 141 A Reverend Father..has put Mr. Cressy's rhapsody into moode and figure. **1708** SWIFT *Sacramental Test*, As to that argument..I wonder by what figure those gentlemen speak. **1837-8** SIR W. HAMILTON *Logic* xx. (1866) I. 400 The forms determined by the different position of the middle term..in the premises of a syllogism, are called figures,—a name given to them by Aristotle.

24. *Mus.* 'Any short succession of notes, either as melody or a group of chords, which produces a single, complete, and distinct impression' (Grove).

1884 R. PRENTICE *Musician* III. 29 The first Invention is founded entirely on the opening eight-note figure.

VI. *attrib.* and *Comb.*

25. a. simple attrib. (sense 10), as ***figure-action***, ***-art***, ***-artist***, ***-composition***, ***-incident***, ***-painting***, ***-picture***, ***-piece***, ***-sculpture***, ***-study***, ***-subject***. **b.** objective (sense 4), as ***figure-training***; (sense 10), as ***figure-painter***; (senses 10, 15) as ***figure-carver***, ***carving***, ***-stamper***, ***-weaving***.

1860 RUSKIN *Mod. Paint.* V. IX. i. 198 Heroic [landscape] ..is frequently without architecture; never without *figure-action, or emotion..Contemplative [landscape]..requires ..*figure incident. **1903** *Burlington Mag.* Sept.–Oct. 3/1 Poetry and the *figure arts seldom keep pace in their evolution. **1857** 'C. BEDE' *Verdant Green* III. ii. 12 Young-lady *figure-artists, who usually limit their efforts to chalk-heads and crayon smudges. **1935** *Burlington Mag.* Nov. 211/1 In the sphere of *figure-composition and light-treatment. **1868** G. STEPHENS *Runic Mon.* II. 511 The *figure-stampers and *figure carvers of the Early and still more of the Later Iron Age. **1849** SOUTHEY *Comm.-pl. Bk.* Ser. II. 345 To cut up a fowl in the air..This sort of *figure-carving implies abominable cookery. **1770** J. WEDGWOOD *Let.* 12 May (1965) 92 The fine *figure Painters are another order of beings. **1947** WYNDHAM LEWIS *Let.* Apr. 405 Down a third [road]..the figure of a figure-painter. **1873** HAMERTON *Intell. Life* VII. 239 The wife is with you always ..the world, to you, is a *figure-picture in which there is one figure, the rest is merely background. **1816** JANE AUSTEN *Emma* I. vi. 86 Has not Mrs. Weston some inimitable *figure-pieces in her drawing-room? **1864** A. MCKAY *Hist. Kilmarnock* (ed. 4) 250 He excelled..in..landscapes, and figure-pieces. **1874** MICKLETHWAITE *Mod. Par. Churches* 111 Whether or not *figure-sculpture ought to be employed in ecclesiastical architecture. **1884** RUSKIN in *Pall Mall G.* 10 Dec. 11/1 The vast irruption of sensual *figure-study. **1877** W. JONES *Finger-ring* 374 An ivory patch-box, with *figure-subject carved in relief. **1871** (*title*), *Figure Training. **1831** G. PORTER *Silk Manuf.* 234 *Figure-weaving is the art of producing various patterns in the cloth.

26. Special comb.: **figure-maker**, (*a*) one who casts or moulds figures; (*b*) a maker of wooden anatomical models for artists; **figure-servant**, *nonce-wd.*, a commercial clerk; **figure-six** *a.* (see quot. 1851); **figure-skater**, one who practises figure-skating; **figure-skating**, the art or practice of skating in figures (see FIGURE *sb.* 17); **figure-stone** (*Min.*) = AGALMATOLITE. Also FIGURE-CASTER, FIGURE-DANCE, FIGURE-FLINGER, etc.

1769 J. WEDGWOOD *Let.* 25 June (1965) 76 If we get these painters, and the *figure makers, we shall do pretty well in those branches. **1850** J. H. NEWMAN *Diffic. Anglic.* 205 Operatives, journeymen, *figure-servants and labourers. **1851** MAYHEW *Lond. Labour* I. 36/2 The hair, they [coster-lads] say ought to be..done in *figure-six curls. **1892** T. M. WITHAM *Figure-skating* in *Skating* (Badm. Libr.) iii. 45 Dry cracks..are very dangerous to the *figure-skater. **1852** H. SPENCER *Gracefulness* Ess. 1891 II. 384 Early attempts..in *figure-skating, are..fatiguing. **1892** T. M. WITHAM *Figure-skating* in *Skating* (Badm. Libr.) iii. 57 A figure-skating club..the members of which are mostly English. **1805** R. JAMESON *Char. Min.* II. 604 It is brought from China, and has received the name *Figure-stone. **1852** L. OLIPHANT *Journey to Katamandu* 174 Amongst other minerals are corundum, figure-stone, and talc.

figure (ˈfɪgə(r), -jʊə(r)), *v.* [f. prec. sb.; cf. OF. (and mod.Fr.) *figurer* (= Pr. and Sp. *figurar*, It. *figurare*, ad. L. *figūrāre*, f. *figūra* FIGURE *sb.*), which is probably the source of some of the senses.]

†1. a. *trans.* To give figure to; to form, shape; to bring into shape. *Obs.*

? *a* **1400** *Morte Arth.* 2151 The faireste fygured folde that fygurede was ever. **1555** EDEN *Decades* 261 The damme..by lyttle and lyttle figurethe the informe byrthe. **1645** EVELYN *Mem.* (1819) I. 186 Piedestals exquisitely cast and figur'd. *c* **1790** IMISON *Sch. Art* II. 155 The bed of hones should be ..very little larger than the metal intended to be figured upon it.

b. With complement: To shape into; also to shape *into* (a specified form). *Obs.*

c **1430** *Pilgr. Lyf Manhode* I. lxxii. (1869) 42 Flesh and blood it is in sooth, but bred it and wyn it is figured. **1626** BACON *Sylva* §352 Some [shining wood] was found to be Firm and hard; so as it might be figured into a Cross.

2. a. To represent in a diagram or picture.

c **1380** WYCLIF *Sel. Wks.* III. 456 Þo holy Trinity in no manere schulde be fygurid..in þat fourme by whiche comynly hit is peyntid. *c* **1391** CHAUCER *Astrol.* I. §9 Next this folwyth the cercle of the dayes that ben figured in maner of degrees. *c* **1430** *Pilgr. Lyf Manhode* IV. ii. (1869) 175 Ordeyned j haue that peynted it [the beste] be heere and figured. *c* **1500** *Melusine* 364 Ryche pictures where as were fygured many a noble hystory. **1591** SPENSER *Muiop.* 277 Arachne figur'd how love did abuse Europa like a bull. **1776** WITHERING *Brit. Plants* (1796) IV. 111 *Fucus fastigiatus* of Wulfen, figured in Jacq. coll. iii. 14. 2, is perhaps the plant of Linnæus. **1814** WORDSW. *White Doe of Ryl.* II. 20 The sacred Cross; and figured there The five dear wounds our Lord did bear. **1851** CARPENTER *Man. Phys.* (ed. 2) 531 The Perch, whose Encephalon is here figured. **1882** MINCHIN *Unipl. Kinemat.* 17 Some such curve as that figured.

b. To trace, mark (a design, letter, etc.).

1526 TINDALE *2 Cor.* iii. 7 The ministracion of deeth thorowe the letters figured in stones. **1801** SOUTHEY *Thalaba* v. xii, Whose windows lay in light, And of their former shape..Rude outline on the earth Figured.

3. To picture in the mind; to imagine. Const. with simple *compl.* and object clause.

(Sometimes *to figure to oneself*: cf. F. *se figurer*.)

1603 SHAKS. *Meas. for M.* I. ii. 53 Thou art alwayes figuring diseases in me; but..I am sound. **1637** NABBES *Microcosm.* 111, I am transform'd into a happiness Cannot be figured. **1718** LADY M. W. MONTAGU *Lett.* (1861) I. 367 He..had..already figured his bride to himself with all the deformities in nature. **1760** H. WALPOLE *Corr.* (ed. 3) III. cccxlvii. 332 You cannot figure a duller season. **1831** CARLYLE *Sart. Res.* i. 2 In all speculations they have tacitly figured Man as a Clothed Animal. **1851** —— *Sterling* I. iv. (1872) 27, I figure him a brilliant..creature. **1868** AIRY *Pop. Astron.* iii. 123 There is no difficulty at all in figuring to ourselves..that [etc.]. **1886** MRS. LYNN LINTON *Paston Carew* xlii, All the pains and griefs his imagination had ever figured.

4. To portray or represent by speech or action.

1475 *Bk. Noblesse* 21 Aventurous dedis that Hercules, as it is figured..in..the .v. booke of Boecius, toke uppon him. **1594** SHAKS. *Rich. III*, I. ii. 194 *Anne.* I would I knew thy heart. *Glo.* 'Tis figur'd in my tongue. **1634** FORD *P. Warbeck* I. i, Thy heart Is figur'd on thy tongue. *a* **1668** ? DAVENANT in Dryden *Prose Wks.* 1800 I. II. 214 An heroic poem should be..like a glass of nature, figuring a more practicable virtue to us than was done by the ancients. **1894** R. H. SHERARD in *Westm. G.* 13 June 2/1 The *aficionados* do all in their power to figure a Spanish audience..but these simulated enthusiasms have but a hollow ring.

†5. 'To prefigure, foreshow' (J.). *Obs.*

1593 SHAKS. *3 Hen. VI*, II. i. 32 Three glorious Sunnes, each one a perfect Sunne..In this, the Heauen figures some euent.

6. To be an image, symbol, or type of; to represent typically.

1401 *Pol. Poems* (Rolls) II. 63 Two perfit lyves, that actif and contemplatif comounli ben callid, ffulli figurid by Marie and Martha. **1447** BOKENHAM *Seyntys* (Roxb.) 10 These sexe vertuhs be fyguryd mystyly In the sexe wengys..Of the cherubyns. **1450-1530** *Myrr. our Ladye* 250 The body of her blyssed sonne..was fygured by the sayde arke. **1604** DEKKER *King's Entert.* Wks. 1873 I. 280 A Personage, figuring, The Counsell of the City. **1653** H. COGAN tr. *Pinto's Trav.* xxxii. 129 This boy leaned on his elbow upon the Chaems chair and figured mercy. **1697** DRYDEN *Virg. Georg.* II. 593 Soft Peace they [olives] figure, and sweet Plenty bring.

†7. To display the form of; to exhibit a resemblance to. *Obs.*

1567 MAPLET *Gr. Forest* 34 Birdes tongue is an Herbe.. It figureth the tong of a Birde, whereof it hath his name. In his top it figureth a taile to looke to. **1779** FORREST *Voy. N. Guinea* 54 A high island..which remarkably figures a cock's comb.

†8. To represent as resembling; to liken (a person or thing) *to* (another). *Obs.*

1393 GOWER *Conf.* III. 118 Taurus..figured is Unto a bulle. **1520** *Caxton's Chron. Eng.* III. 24 b/1 This man was cursed every ynche, and therfore he was fygured to Ante-cryst. **1523** LD. BERNERS *Froiss.* I. cccxcix. 691 Sermons made..figurynge them to the people of Israell, whome kynge Pharaon kepte long in seruytude.

9. †a. To predicate in a metaphorical sense (*obs.*). **b.** To express by a metaphor or image.

c **1386** CHAUCER *Pars. T.* ⁋922 (Ellesmere) Mariage is figured betwixe Crist and holy chirche. **1836** EMERSON *Nat., Prospects* Wks. (Bohn) II. 171 The difference..is happily figured by the schoolmen, in saying that the knowledge of man is an evening knowledge..but that of God is a morning knowledge. **1857** BUCKLE *Civiliz.* I. vii. 225 That image of desolation under which the noble old man figured his immeasurable grief.

†**10.** To frame (a discourse) according to rhetorical figures; to adorn with figures of speech. *Obs.*

1652 URQUHART *Jewel* Wks. (1834) 292 Ironical.. cromatick, or any other way of figuring a speech by opposition, being formules of oratory. **1727** BAILEY vol. II. s.v. *Figures* (*Theatrical*), Orators..figure their Discourses.

11. To adorn or mark with figures; to embellish or ornament with a design or pattern.

1480 *Wardr. Acc. Edw. IV* (1830) 116 Blue velvet figured with tawny. **1595** SHAKS. *John* v. ii. 53 Had I seene the vaultie top of heauen Figur'd quite ore with burning Meteors. **1609** BIBLE (Douay) *Isa.* xl. 19 Hath the goldsmith figured it with gold? **1725** POPE *Odyss.* IV. 808 A goblet of capacious mold, Figur'd with art to dignify the gold. **1883** *Truth* 31 May 769/2 Crimson satin, figured with velvet flowers.

12. a. *trans.* to mark with (numerical) figures; to express or indicate by figures. Also, †*to figure* (a sum of money) *on* (a person): (*slang*) to total up against.

1683 DRYDEN & LEE *Duke of Guise* v. 11 So what was figured twelve, to thy dull sight Appeared full twenty-one. **1773** *Gentl. Mag.* XLIII. 654 His antagonist..figured on him (as his phrase is) at the game of two-handed whist, about £200. **1781** COWPER *Let. to J. Hill* 3 Oct., Your draft is worded for twenty pounds, and figured for twenty-one.

b. *intr.* To use figures in arithmetic. Also *trans.*: *to figure up* (also with *down*): to reckon up with figures; to reckon, calculate, understand, ascertain. Also with obj. clause, and *absol.*, esp. in colloq. phr. *it* (or *that*) *figures*, it is reasonable, likely, or understandable; it makes sense (orig. and chiefly *U.S.*). *to figure out*: see 15 c.

1854 H. MILLER *Sch. & Schm.* iii. (1858) 52 He wrote and figured well. **1865** *Congress. Globe* 9 Feb. 671/3, I have not figured the number of square miles that there will be. **1884** *Bread Winners* 245 I'll figure it all up and take my pay. **1891** *Fur, Fin & Feather* Mar. 170 By this time Sagebrush and I had got the whole thing figured down pretty fine in our own minds. **1901** *Chambers's Jrnl.* Sept. 633/1 Only this morning I was figuring that the work should bring us enough to put all straight and sow next year again. **1913** *N.Y. Even. Post* 8 Sept. 1/6 Yale men figure that the bones have lain where found from 5,000 to 20,000 years. **1935** R. STOUT *League of Frightened Men* xiii. 155, I couldn't figure the runt at all. **1947** [see GET *v.* 74 c]. **1952** B. WOLFE *Limbo* (1953) IV. 213 That figures, all right... It's kind of a startling idea, but it figures. **1967** *Boston Sunday Herald* 30 Apr. III. 10/4 Everyone has to figure her own way. **1969** C. WATSON *Flaxborough Crab* iii. 33 'She's not complained to us.' 'That figures.' **1970** *Globe & Mail* (Toronto) 26 Sept. 40/4 As Champlain's party cut a wide swath through these parts, it figures that a calling card was left behind in the naming of a lake.

(*b*) *to figure on* or *upon* (fig.): to think over, consider; to count on, anticipate, expect. *U.S.*

1837 *Congress. Globe* App. 247/1, I..cannot understand the Secretary's report. I figured upon its data until I threw down my slate in despair. **1877** BARTLETT *Dict. Amer.* (ed. 4) s.v., 'Figure on that' means to consider it; to think it over. Western. **1904** G. STRATTON-PORTER *Freckles* 241 In figuring on their not coming that day he failed to reckon with the enthusiasm of the Bird Woman. **1905** *Smart Set* Oct. 17/1 But I'm figurin' on gettin' hold of some more land. **1906** *N.Y. Even. Post* 13 Oct. 5 He is not figuring on any extensive defection on their part. **1907** *Smart Set* Feb. 96, I hadn't figured on that. **1909** *N.Y. Even. Post* 7 Jan. (Th.), We always figure on supplying more lenses in July and August than in all the rest of the year. **1911** *Chambers's Jrnl.* Jan. 57/1 My brother and I have never figured on building large passenger-carrying machines. **1934** J. W. HUTCHISON *North to Rime-Ringed Sun* x. 104 Ira had 'figured' (as they say in Alaska) on landing to trade at a native house.

c. trans. *Mus.* To write figures over or under (the bass) in order to indicate the intended harmony. Cf. FIGURED *ppl. a.* 7.

1674 PLAYFORD *Skill Mus.* III. 5 You find here only mentioned and figured a third, fifth, and eighth. **1881** G. A. MACFARREN *Counterpoint* v. 20 It is recommended to figure the bass throughout these exercises.

13. intr. *Dancing.* To perform a figure or set of evolutions (see FIGURE *sb.* 16). Also, *to figure away, down, out* (see 15 d).

1744 *Coll. Country Dances* 2 Foot it again and half figure. **1780** COWPER *Progr. Err.* 366 We..Teach him to fence and figure twice a week. **1820** W. IRVING *Sketch Bk., Christmas Eve* (1865) 251 The squire himself figured down several couple with a partner. **1828** LONGF. in *Life* (1891) I. 139 One passing regret that he cannot..figure away in the dance with the best of them.

14. *intr.* **a.** To make an appearance, to appear; often with *as*: To appear in the character of, stand for; also, to look like. †*to figure for*: (*a*) to pose as a claimant for, pretend to; (*b*) to stand for, represent. *to figure in*: to come upon the scene. Cf. FIGURE *sb.* 6.

1602 WARNER *Alb. Eng.* x. lvii. (1612) 253 The Duke of Guize, who earst had figur'd for the Crowne. **1634** D'AVENANT *Temple of Love* Dram. Wks. 1872 I. 287 On the other side an Asiatique in the habit of an Indian borderer.. figured for the Asian monarchy. **1762** GOLDSM. *Nash* 50 When he first figured at Bath, there were few laws against this destructive amusement. **1812** H. & J. SMITH *Rej. Addr.* xvii. (1873) 162 Like great Jove, the leader figuring in, Attunes to order the chaotic din. **1815** W. H. IRELAND *Scribbleomania* 106 *note*, This gentleman..formerly figured as shopman at an oil warehouse. **1826** DISRAELI *Viv. Grey* II. xiii, On the door of one of the shabbiest houses in Jermyn Street the name of Mr. Stapylton Toad for a long time figured. **1837** —— *Venetia* I. viii, The intervening woods figured as the forests of Thessaly. **1871** MORLEY *Voltaire* (1886) 11 One of those robust and incisive constitutions, to which doubt figures as a sickness. **1893** *Law Times* XCIV. 454/1 Propositions of this kind will not figure upon the Statute-book yet awhile.

b. To make a distinguished appearance; to be conspicuous or notable. Also, *to figure away, off*: to 'show off'. Cf. FIGURE *sb.* 7.

1736 BOLINGBROKE *Patriot.* (1749) iii. 233 Persons who figured afterwards in the rebellion. **1762** CHURCHILL *Ghost* IV, Whilst my Lord figur'd at a race. **1771** MAD. D'ARBLAY *Early Diary* 8 May (1889) I. 112 Dr. King..came in and figured away to his own satisfaction before Mr. Garrick. **1803** T. JEFFERSON *Writ.* (1830) III. 501 We shall get entangled in European politics, and figuring more, be much less happy. **1812** FOSTER *Let.* 7 Feb., in *Life & Corr.* (1846) I. lxxxv. 426 Without obtaining, against the monopolists of the bar, even the opportunity of fairly figuring off in this jabber. **1814** CHALMERS *Evid. Chr. Revel.* v. 147 Such a testimony would have figured away in all our elementary treatises. **1879** *Cassell's Techn. Educ.* IV. 236/1 Yorkshire then begins to figure as a cloth-making county.

15. figure out.

†**a.** *trans.* To display or exhibit in visionary forms or shapes. Also, To exhibit obscurely, shadow forth. *Obs.*

1602 DANIEL *Hymen's Tri.* III. ii, No Time..for me to.. leave for Sleep to figure out the rest. **1721** R. KEITH tr. *T. à Kempis' Solil. Soul* xiii. 207 If.. thou dost figure out by such a Document..somewhat..both just and reasonable.

†**b.** To portray, represent.

1657 W. RAND tr. *Gassendi's Life Peiresc* I. 59 He never.. refused to suffer himself to be painted or figured out in a Statue. **1702** ADDISON *Dial. Medals* Wks. 1721 I. 490 The Emperor..holds a Globe in his hand, to figure out the Earth.

c. To work out (a sum) by means of figures; more widely, to estimate or calculate; hence, to work out, make out. Chiefly *U.S.*

1833 C. A. DAVIS *Lett. J. Downing* (1834) 41 As I said before, I'm stump'd about that Bank of U.S.; and I want you to help me figure it out. **1873** C. H. SMITH *Bill Arp's Peace Papers* 32 Matthy Mattiks nor his daddy couldn't figger out how long it will take you to get through accordin to your feebul progress. **1884** *Punch* 15 Mar. 125/1 Whitewash..on which you could..figure out a sum. **1888** 'R. BOLDREWOOD' *Robbery under Arms* xlvii, We took a couple of days figuring it out at the Hollow. Starlight had a map, and we plotted it out, and marked all the stages which could be safely made. **1902** G. H. LORIMER *Lett. Merchant* i. 5 You can't have to be very bright to figure out which one started the demand. **1903** *N.Y. Sun* 1 Nov. 5 The telegraph lines began to have trouble, and for a while the experts couldn't figure out what was the matter. **1905** *Smart Set* Oct. 17/2 'I'll figure it out after a while,' he said. 'It ain't exactly worryin' me sick yet.' **1910** W. M. RAINE *B. O'Connor* 12 Now, this is how I figured it out. **1919** H. JENKINS *John Dene of Toronto* x. 156, I don't seem to be able to figure things out here as I did at T'ronto. **1966** 'J. HACKSTON' *Father clears Out* 87, I figured it out that he was staring at the top of the old gumtree opposite.

d. *intr.* To step out and perform a figure in dancing.

1753 FOOTE *Eng. in Paris* I. Wks. 1799 I. 36 When 'twas her turn to figure out, souse she flapp'd on her back.

'figure-,caster.

†**1.** One who practises the casting of figures (see CAST *v.* 39 and FIGURE *sb.* 14); 'a pretender to astrology' (J.). *Obs.*

1584 R. SCOT *Discov. Witchcr.* XI. xxi. 169 The vaine and trifling tricks of figure-casters. **1642** MILTON *Apol. Smect.* (1851) 306, I, by this figure-caster must be imagin'd in.. distresse.

2. One who casts up figures (see FIGURE *sb.* 19).

1831 SCOTT *Ct. Robt.* vii, Movable troops for which this figure-caster [the Logothete] makes no allowance. **1880** SWINBURNE *Stud. Shaks.* i. (ed. 2) 10 A whole tribe of finger-counters and figure-casters.

'figure-,casting, *vbl. sb.* The action or practice of casting a figure (see CAST *v.* 39).

1600 ABP. ABBOT *Exp. Jonah* 287 Figure casting..to judge of nativities..is a lying vanity. **1625** HART *Anat. Ur.* II. xi. 123 Figure-casting, with a world of other forbidden trash. **1868** MILMAN *St. Paul's* 299 Foolish fears..from the ..opposition of planets, and from figure-casting.

figured ('figəd, -jʊəd), *ppl. a.* [f. FIGURE *v.* and *sb.* + -ED¹ and ².]

1. In various senses of the vb.: Shaped into a figure or figures; represented by figures, etc.

1552 HULOET, Figured like an Image, *imaginatus.* **1599** SHAKS. *Pass. Pilgr.* 52 He refus'd to take her figur'd proffer. **1697** DRYDEN *Æneid* v. 704 This Goblet, rough with figur'd Gold. **1710** POPE *Windsor For.* 335 The figur'd Streams in Waves of Silver roll'd.

2. Having a particular figure or shape. In comb. with advbs., as *fair, foul, ill figured.*

?*a* **1400** *Morte Arth.* 2151 The faireste fygured folde that fygurede was ever. *c* **1430** *Pilgr. Lyf. Manhode* IV. ii. (1869) 175 Thilke beste was..so foule figured that [etc.]. *a* **1533** LD. BERNERS *Huon* clv. 593 Thoughe they were ones fayre now they be fowle and yll fygured. **1821** T. DWIGHT *Travels* II. 141 Its summits are finely figured, and richly diversified.

†**3.** Having definite shape; also, formed into figures or patterns. Cf. FIGURATE A. 2. *Obs.*

1626 BACON *Sylva* §588 Trees and Herbs, in the growing forth of their Boughs and Branches are not figured and keep no order. **1786** R. WILLAN in *Med. Commun.* II. 118 He had a figured natural stool, and..two or three loose motions. **1789** G. WHITE *Selborne* (1853) II. xli. 272 Geese and cranes ..move in figured flights.

4. Adorned or ornamented with patterns or designs. *figured card* = COURT CARD.

c **1489** CAXTON *Blanchardyn* ii. 15 Riche tapysserye of the destruction of Troye, Well and alonge fygured. **1593** SHAKS. *Rich. II.* III. iii. 150 Ile giue..My figur'd Goblets, for a Dish of Wood. **1596** HARINGTON *Metam. Ajax* 36 Fugerd sattin and velvet. **1611** COTGR., *Velours a fond de satin*..Figured Satin. **1777** SHERIDAN *Sch. Scand.* II. i, A pretty figured linen gown. **1821** SHELLEY *Prometh. Unb.* IV. i, The figured curtain of sleep. **1882** *Mrs. Raven's Tempt.* II. 87 She wore ..a figured shawl.

5. Adorned with rhetorical figures; figurative.

1500–20 DUNBAR *Poems* lxvi. 10 Figurit speiche, with faceis tua. *c* **1698** LOCKE *Cond. Underst.* §32 (1762) 127 Figured and metaphorical expressions do well to illustrate more abstruse and unfamiliar ideas. **1727** POPE, etc. *Art of Sinking* 108 Style is divided by the rhetoricians into the proper and the figured. **1861** M. ARNOLD *Pop. Educ. France* 170 The figured language of which he is a master.

6. Of a dance: Consisting of figures.

1711 SHAFTESB. *Charac.* III. 91 Enthusiasm, which is.. wrought upon by Chalices, Candles, Robes, and figur'd Dances. **1879** GEO. ELIOT *Coll. Breakf. P.* 95 Nor any missing of their figured dance.

7. *Mus.* **a.** = FLORID. **b.** *figured bass* = thorough bass: see BASS *sb.*⁵

1801 T. BUSBY *Dict. Mus.* s.v. *Figured.* A bass, accompanied with numerical characters, denoting the harmony formed by the upper or superior parts of the composition, and directing the chords to be played by the organ, harpsichord, or piano-forte, is called a *figured* bass. **1879** GROVE *Dict. Mus.* s.v., Figured Counterpoint is where several notes of various lengths, with syncopations and other ornamental devices, are set against the single notes of the Canto fermo; and Figured melody, or *Canto figurato*, was the breaking up of the long notes of the church melodies into larger or more rapid figures or passages. **1948** G. B. SHAW *How to become Mus. Critic* (1960) 325 Seventy years ago I filled up the figured basses in Stainer's textbook of harmony quite correctly.

8. *Her.* (See quot. and cf. FIGURE *sb.* 10 c.)

1830 in ROBSON *Brit. Her.* III. Gloss. **1889** ELVIN *Dict. Her.* s.v., Charges on which human faces are depicted, are blazoned Figured, as the Sun, Crescents, etc.

Hence **'figuredly** *adv.*

1636 ABP. WILLIAMS *Holy Table* i. 11 Not so figuredly and distinctly in the later.

'figure-dance. A dance, or exhibition of dancing, consisting of several distinct figures or divisions (see quot. 1801).

1801 STRUTT *Sports & Past.* III. v. 175 The grand figure-dances..are..pantomimical representations of historical and poetical subjects, expressed by fantastic gestures. *fig.* **1816** COLERIDGE *Lay Serm.* 327 The giddy figure-dance of political changes.

'figure-,dancer.

1. A performer in a figure-dance.

1753 A. MURPHY *Gray's-Inn Jrnl.* No. 25 They all had the Honour of Kissing a Figure Dancer. **1779** SHERIDAN *Critic* I. i, French spies..disguised like fiddlers and figure dancers. **1819** *Metropolis* II. 202 The figure-dancers, flower-girls, characters [etc.].

2. *slang.* (See quot.)

1796 GROSE *Dict. Vulg. Tongue, Figure Dancer*, one who alters figures on bank notes, converting tens to hundreds.

'figure-,flinger. A contemptuous synonym of FIGURE-CASTER 1.

1587 FLEMING *Contn. Holinshed* III. 1271 Simon Penbrooke..a figureflinger, and vehementlie suspected to be a coniurer. **1652–62** HEYLIN *Cosmogr.* III. (1674) 113/1 Every Astrologaster or Figure-flinger was called a chaldean. **1712** HEARNE *Collect.* (Oxf. Hist. Soc.) III. 407 Mr. Gadbury the Figure Flinger mentions the Custom in one of his Almanacks.

So **'figure-,flinging** *vbl. sb.* = FIGURE-CASTING.

a **1625** BOYS *Wks.* (1629) 734 Not by starre-gazing, or figure-flinging, or conjuring, or any curious act. **1652** GAULE *Magastrom.* 60 A fantasticall figure-flinging. **1723** HEARNE in *Rem.* 1 July (ed. 2) II. 165 Being much addicted to astrology, he gave over his trade and set up the trade of figure flinging and publishing of almanacks.

'figure-'head.

1. A piece of ornamental carving, usually a bust or full-length figure, placed over the cut-water of a ship.

1765 *Ann. Reg.* 185 His Majesty's ship..will soon have a new figure-head. **1833** MARRYAT *P. Simple* (1863) 113 If her figure-head..be finished off by the same builder, she's perfect. **1887** BESANT *The World went* xxvii. 207 The beautiful carved group..once served for a figure-head.

b. humorously for: Face (of a person).

1840 MARRYAT *Poor Jack* v, [It] had..knocked his figure-head all to smash. **1884** PAE *Eustace* 91 If you don't want your figure-head spoiled.

2. Said depreciatingly of one who holds the position of head of a body of persons, a community, society, etc., but possesses neither authority nor influence. Also *attrib.*

1883 *Congregationalist* Dec. 1019 Mere diocesan figure-heads with no opinions at all. **1885** *Harper's Mag.* Mar. 610/2 A mere figure-head president. **1891** *Spectator* 12 Dec. 832 A mere figure-head to the Government.

3. *Arch.* A grotesque head, animal, etc. carved in stone on the corbel of a building; a corbel-head.

1874 *Archæol. Assoc. Jrnl.* Dec. 416 The row of figure-heads is continued inside that portion of the church.

Hence **figure-'headless** *a.*, without a figure-head. **figure-'headship**, the position of figure-head.

1878 BESANT & RICE *Celia's Arb.* I. xv. 219 The figure-headless ironclads of the present degenerate days. **1884** *Pall Mall G.* 14 May 3/1 The figure-headship of the Opposition.

figureless ('fɪgəlɪs, -jʊəlɪs), *a.* [f. FIGURE *sb.* + -LESS.] Without figure or a figure.

1. Without shape, shapeless.

1606 SYLVESTER *Du Bartas* II. iv. I. (1641) 198/2 If heer.. I write.. These Figures figure-less. **1892** W. S. LILLY *Gt. Enigma* 287 They are figureless and formless.

2. Not bearing a figure.

1849 ROCK *Ch. of Fathers* II. vi. 262 The plain, figureless, wooden cross, borne in procession during Passion-tide.

3. *Mus.* Devoid of figure (see FIGURE *sb.* 24).

1887 E. GURNEY *Tertium Quid* II. 30 Figureless counter-pointless see-sawings.

figurement ('fɪgəmənt, -jʊəmənt). *rare.* [f. FIGURE *v.* + -MENT.] **a.** Presentation of figures to the mind. **b.** Introduction as a figure or ornament.

1850 BLACKIE *Æschylus* II. 237 But yesternight, with figurement most clear, I dreamt. **1879** G. MEREDITH *Egoist* I. xiv. 255 An embellishment.. such truly as should one day gain for them an inweaving and figurement—in the place of bees, ermine tufts [etc.].. upon the august great robes.

'figurer. [f. as prec. + -ER¹.] One who figures. †**a.** One who serves as a figure or type *of*. †**b.** One who makes use of a figure or type. †**c.** One who figures or counterfeits; an imitator. †**d.** = FIGURE-DANCER. **e.** = *figure-skater*.

1548 GEST *Pr. Masse* 104 Aaron.. was a fygurer of Christ. **1565** JEWEL *Repl. Harding* (1611) 331 And whatsoeuer they were that vsed this word, Figura, in this matter of the Sacrament, D. Steuen Gardiner scornfully calleth them Figuratores, Figurers. **1665** HERBERT *Trav.* (1677) 383 Parrat.. painful figurer of humane voice. **1782** T. VAUGHAN *Fashionable Follies* I. 204 The prettiest figurer at the opera. **1882** N. & A. GOODMAN *Fen skating* 10 The contempt felt by figurers for fen skaters.

figuresome ('fɪgəsəm, -jʊəsəm), *a.* [f. as prec. + -SOME.] Bent upon making a (prominent) figure.

1884 BLACKMORE *Tommy Upm.* I. xv. 234 A figuresome member of the Opposition.. had given notice of a question.

figurette (,fɪgjʊə'rɛt). *rare*⁻¹. [f. FIGURE *sb.* + -ETTE] = FIGURINE.

1850 LEITCH tr. *Müller's Anc. Art* §307. 349 The silver inlaid work on bronze figurettes in the museum at Naples.

†**figu'retto.** *Obs. rare*⁻¹. [? error for It. *figurato* figured (stuff).] (See quot. 1678.)

1662 *Stat. Ireland* (1765) II. 473 Figurettoes with silk or copper. **1678** PHILLIPS, *Figuretto*, a kind of stuff so called from the flowres or other figures which are wrought upon it. **1721** in BAILEY. **1775** in ASH.

figurial (fɪ'gjʊərɪəl), *a.* 'Represented by figure or delineation' (Craig 1847).

Whence in mod. Dicts.

figurine (fɪgjʊə'riːn). [a. F. *figurine*, ad. It. *figurina*, dim. of *figura*: see FIGURE and -INE.] A small carved or sculptured figure.

1854 tr. *Lamartine's Celebr. Char.* II. 333 Copper frames ornamented with wooden figurines representing personages from history. **1883** *Pall Mall G.* 15 Mar. 2/2 A Roman girl .. selling figurines at the doors of a temple.

figuring ('fɪgərɪŋ, -jʊərɪŋ), *vbl. sb.* [f. FIGURE *v.* + -ING¹.]

1. The action of the vb. FIGURE. Also with *out*.

1534 MORE *On the Passion* Wks. 1335/1 Hys blessed bodye and bloude in the sacrament, thoughe they seme dead, for the more ful representacyon and fygurynge of the same bodye and bloude remaynynge deade on the crosse. **1648** W. MOUNTAGUE *Devout Ess.* xiii. §6. 168 Chaines which vain Lovers forge for the figuring out the powerfulnesse of beauty. **1859** GEO. ELIOT *A. Bede* 5 'There's the sperrit o' God in all things.. i' the figuring and the mechanics.' **1881** KRAUS in *Metal World* No. 24. 371 The apprentice should acquire a knowledge of.. practical figuring.

attrib. **1752** N. DUKES (*title*), A concise and easy Method of learning the Figuring part of Country Dances.

†**2. a.** ? Configuration, form (or perhaps emblematic significance). **b.** An impressed shape. *Obs.*

c **1385** CHAUCER *L.G.W.* 298 This flour.. bereth our alder pris in figurynge. **1665** GLANVILL *Sceps. Sci.* xxii. 221 Let us consider.. the divers figurings of the brain.

3. = *figure-skating*.

1869 VANDERVELL & WITHAM *Figure-skating* i. 24 From these two figures [3 and 8].. we get the terms 'figure-skating', or 'figuring'.

†**'figurist.** *Obs.* [f. as prec. + -IST.] One who maintains the figurative nature of something (e.g. of the presence of Christ in the Eucharist).

1585–7 T. ROGERS 39 *Art.* (1607) 289 The Symbolists, Figurists, and Significatists.. are of opinion that the faithful at the Lord's supper do receive nothing but naked and bare signs. **1625** BP. MOUNTAGU *Appeale to Cæsar* 297 The Figurists, Significatists, Symbolists, taught you this Doctrine. **1737** WATERLAND *Eucharist* (ed. 2) 453 Dr. Cudworth's notion is in no way favourable to the Figurists, or Memorialists.

†**Figuristian.** *Obs.* (Meaning not clear).

1716 M. DAVIES *Athen. Brit.* II. To Rdr. 45 The infimous Class of Mechanick Figuristians.

†**'figurize,** *v. Obs.*⁻¹ [f. FIGURE *sb.* + -IZE.] *intr.* To indulge in figures of speech.

1649 H. LAWRENCE *Some Consid.* ii Will the way to helpe our selves be to fall a Figurizing and Allægorizing?

'figury, *a.*¹ *Obs.* [a. OF. *figuré* figured.] = FIGURED (of satin, velvet, tinsel, etc.).

1467 *Nottingham Rec.* II. 262 Duas manicas de saten figur'. **1473** in *Ld. Treas. Accts. Scot.* I. 73 A govne.. of blac satyne figory. **1480** *Wardr. Acc. Edw. IV* (1830) 116 Velvet russet figury. **1502** *Priv. Purse Exp. Eliz. of York* (1830) 69 A gowne of sattyn fygure. *a* **1577** GASCOIGNE *Wks.* (1587) 302 Cloth of gold or tinsel figurie.

figury ('fɪgərɪ, -jʊərɪ). *a.*² [f. FIGURE *sb.* + -Y¹.] Having plenty of 'figure' or pattern.

1893 *Times* 12 June 13/5 Small plain logs are difficult to sell, but large and figury logs are scarce and wanted.

'fig-wort. [See FIG *sb.*¹ 3 a.] The name of certain plants reputed to cure the 'fig'. **a.** The pilewort (*Ranunculus Ficaria*). **b.** The genus *Scrophularia*, esp. *S. aquatica* and *S. nodosa*.

a. 1548 TURNER *Names of Herbs* (E.D.S.) 42 The second kynde called in latine *Chelidonium minus* is called in englishe Fygwurt. **1578** LYTE *Dodoens* I. xx. 31 The lesser [celandyne] is called.. in English Pyleworte or Figworte.

b. 1597 GERARDE *Herbal* II. ccxxxiv. 579 There is another Figwoort called *Scrophularia Indica*. **1668** WILKINS *Real Char.* II. iv. §5. 105 Figwort, an Herb [*Scrophularia*]. **1758** MRS. DELANY *Life & Corr.* III. 507 Matfellon and figwort flourish here remarkably. **1865** GOSSE *Land & Sea* (1874) 7 The figwort with its brown bead-like blossoms.

Fijian (fiː'dʒiːən), *sb.* and *a.* Also 9 **Feegeean, Feejeean, Fejean.** [f. *Fiji*, native name of the principal island of the Fiji archipelago + -AN.]

A. *sb.* **1.** A native or inhabitant of the Fiji archipelago. **2.** The language of the Fijian people. **B.** *adj.* Of or pertaining to the Fiji archipelago, the Fijians, or their language.

1809 J. DAVIES *Jrnl. Missionaries* 16 Nov. in Im Thurn & Wharton *Jrnl. W. Lockerby* (1922) 135 What we have seen as yet of the Fejeans gives us no favourable opinion of them. **1838** J. WILLIAMS *Miss. Enterpr. S. Sea Isl.* p. xviii, Cruel Rite of the Fijians. **1846** in *Wesleyan-Meth. Mag.* (1847) Apr. 221/1 Thus is laid the foundation of another Feejeean war. **1856** J. LUBBOCK *Pre-Hist. Times* xi. 356 The fortified towns of the Feegeeans had an earthen rampart. **1860** MRS. SMYTHE *10 Months in Fiji Isl.* (1864) 112 He wrote a letter to him, which Mr. Waterhouse read aloud, in Fijian. **1861** *Ibid.* 206 A narrow patch of ground supplies the wants of a Fijian household. **1875** W. S. JEVONS *Money* 25 Among our interesting fellow-subjects, the Fijians, whale's teeth served in the place of cowries. **1879** *Encycl. Brit.* IX. 157/1 The Fijian character was till lately proverbial for every savage abomination. **1885** R. H. CODRINGTON *Melanes. Lang.* 4 It is desirable to use the term Polynesia strictly to indicate the region of the East Pacific to the West of which Melanesia begins with the Fijian group. **1885** *Encycl. Brit.* XIX. 423/2 In Fijian the word *luve* means either a son or a daughter. **1921** W. DEANE *Fijian Soc.* 208 It is at feast-time that the Fijian earns for himself the reputation of being a good eater. **1933** BLOOMFIELD *Lang.* iv. 71 The second, Melanesian, branch of Malayo-Polynesian includes many languages of smaller island groups, such as the languages of the Solomon Islands and Fijian. **1951** R. FIRTH *Elem. Social Organiz.* iii. 102 A Fijian woman had twins, and the mother's milk was not sufficient to feed them both. **1957** P. WORSLEY *Trumpet shall Sound* 13 Today Indians bid fair to outnumber the native Fijians. **1965** J. KNOX-MAWER *Gift of Islands* ii. 15 Eroni repeated the question in Fijian. *Ibid.* v. 43 For the Fijians the grand climax of their stay came with an excursion to Windsor Castle. *Ibid.*, The European had established himself as a permanent and familiar feature of Fijian life.

†**fike,** *sb.*¹ *Obs.* Forms: 1 fic, 3, 5 fike(s, 5 fyke. [OE. *fíc*, ad. L. *fic-us.*] **a.** A fig; also *attrib.*, as *fike-tree*. **b.** A fig-tree.

c **975** *Rushw. Gosp.* Matt. xxi. 19 And forwisnade sonæ se fic. —— *John* i. 48 Miððy ðu were under ðæm fictree ic ȝisæh. *a* **1300** *Cursor M.* 804 (Gött.) þai clad þaim.. wid leuis of a fike tre. **14..** *Nom.* in Wr.-Wülcker 713 *Hec ficus*, a fyke or a fikes.

fike (faɪk), *sb.*² *Sc.* Also 7–9 **fyke.** [f. FIKE *v.*¹]

†**1.** Something that causes one to fidget; *esp.* the itch. Also, *the fikes* = the fidgets. *Obs.*

In first quot. possibly a different word; ? the piles. Cf. FICUS.

a **1605** MONTGOMERIE *Flyting* 313 The frencie, the fluxes, the fyke and the felt. **1736** RAMSAY *Sc. Prov.* (1750) xliii. 87 Ye have gotten the fikes in your arse or a waft clew. *a* **1758** RAMSAY *Address of Thanks* xxii, A Briton.. as his fancy takes the fykes, May preach or print his notions. **17..** LADY DALRYMPLE in *Lives of Lindsays* (1849) II. 322 Your mother's cold was another of my fykes.

b. A restless movement.

1790 MACAULAY *To Cheerfulness* Poems 129 No ane gies e'er a fidge or fyke Or yet a moan.

2. Anxiety about what is trifling, fuss, trouble.

1719 HAMILTON *2nd Epist. to Ramsay* i, O sic a fike and sic a fistle I had about it! **1790** BURNS *Tam o'Shanter* 193 As bees bizz out wi' angry fyke. **1808** E. HAMILTON *Cottagers of Glenburnie* 169, I dinna fash wi' sae mony fykes. **1827** SCOTT *Surg. Dau.* ii, Have I been taking a' this fyke about a Jew.

3. Dalliance, flirtation.

1808–80 JAMIESON, 'He held a great fike wi' her.' **1810** J. COCK *Simple Strains* 144 (Jam.) They had a fyk thegither.

fike (faɪk), *v.*¹ Chiefly *Sc.* and *north. dial.* Forms: 4, 5, 7–9 **fyke**, (6 **fyk**), 3, 7– **fike.** [? a. ON. *fíkja* (rare in Icel.) = MSw. *fikja* to move briskly, be restless or eager. Cf. ON. *fíkenn* eager. See FIG *v.*³, FITCH *v.*, FIDGE *v.*]

1. *intr.* To move restlessly, bustle, fidget: *fig.* to be fussy or restless, vex oneself. Also, to flinch, shrink. *to fike and fling*: to caper about; also *fig.*

c **1220** *Bestiary* 656 Fikeð and fondeð al his miȝt ne mai he it forðen no wiȝt. *c* **1325** *Coer de L.* 4749 The Sarazynes fledde, away gunne fyke. *c* **1340** *Gaw. & Gr. Knt.* 2274 Nawþer fyked I, ne flaȝe, freke, quen þou myntest. *c* **1440** *Promp. Parv.* 160/1 Fykin a-bowte. **1595** BUREL *Pilgr.* in Watson *Collect.* II. 26 The Bee.. From hole to hole did fyke. **1697** W. CLELAND *Poems* 105 We forsooth must fyke and fling, And make our Pulpits sound and ring With bulkie words, against the Test. **1786** BURNS *On a Sc. Bard* 21 Wha can do nought but fyke an' fumble. **1801** MACNEILL *Poems* (1844) 88 Nae langer grane nor fyke, nor daidle, But brandish ye the lang-shanked ladle. **1818** SCOTT *Hrt. Midl.* x, To fyke and fling at piper's wind and fiddler's squealing. **1825** BROCKETT *N.-C. Words, Fike*, to fidget, to be restless. **1883** MRS. OLIPHANT *Wizard's Son* vii, Old Blairallan comes fyking.

b. To dally, flirt.

1804 TARRAS *Poems* 58 No to fike wi' yon wild hizzie Janet's dochter i' the glen.

2. *trans.* To vex, trouble. *to fike one's noddle*: to trouble one's head. Also, to shrug (the shoulders).

1572 in *Satir. Poems Reform.* xxxi. 124 Blind Jamie tauld me ells That quyetly yai news did fyk yame. **1808–80** JAMIESON, 'This will fike him.' **1809** *Christmas Ba'ing* in J. Skinnner *Misc. Poetry* 123 Some baith thair shou'ders up did fyke. **1837** R. NICOLL *Poems* (1843) 263 It snoozes on thro' rain and snaw, Nor fykes its noddle.

†**fike,** *v.*² *Obs.* [? repr. OE. **fícian* (? *fíc*-); cf. OE. *befícian* (? *befícian*) to deceive, *ȝefic* deceit; prob. cognate with FAKEN.] *intr.* To flatter, fawn, act or speak deceitfully.

a **1225** *St. Marher.* (1862) 13 Thu fikest quoth ha ful thing. *a* **1225** *Ancr. R.* 206 þe scorpiun.. fikeð mid te heaued & stingeð mid te teile. *c* **1250** *Meid. Maregrete* xiii, Meidan Maregrete nulle we nout mitte fike. *c* **1325** *Advice to Women* in Wright *Spec. Lyr. Poetry* 46 Wymmon, war the with the swyke, That feir ant freoly ys to fyke.

Hence **'fiking** *ppl. a.*, fawning.

a **1225** *Ancr. R.* 256 Leouere me beoð hire wunden þen uikiinde cosses.

fike, var. FYKE.

fikel(e, obs. form of FICKLE.

†**'fikenung.** *Obs. rare*⁻¹. [f. **fiken(en)* vb., extension of FIKE *v.*²] Deceit.

c **1175** *Lamb. Hom.* 103 Idelȝelp.. þenne mon.. mid fikenunge fearð and deð for ȝelpe mare þenne for godes luue.

fikery ('faɪkərɪ). *Sc.* [f. FIKE *v.* + -ERY.] Fidgetiness, fussiness: fuss.

1823 GALT *Entail* I. 306, 'I canna understand.. what for a' this fykerie's about a lump o' yird.' **1823** *Petticoat Tales* I. 330 'I couldna be fashed wi' sic fikery.' **1850** CARLYLE in Froude *Life in London* xviii. (1884) II. 51 His fussiness and fikery has brought angry growlings.

fikie, fiky ('faɪkɪ), *a. Sc.* [f. FIKE *sb.* + -Y.¹] Fidgety, restless. Also, That costs much trouble, minutely elaborate.

1768 ROSS *Helenore* I. 28 Your fiky dress. **1823** GALT *Ringan Gilhaize* I. xiv. 154 My Lord there is hyte and fykie. **1825** BROCKETT *N.-C. Words, Fikey.* **1830** GALT *Lawrie T.* II. v. (1849) 55 Sooth to say, I was disturbed and fykie.

fikiness ('faɪkɪnɪs). *Chiefly Sc.* Also **feikieness, fykiness.** [f. FIKIE *a.* + -NESS.] Restlessness, agitation; the action of taking much trouble.

1889 BARRIE *Window in Thrums* xiv, Her feikieness ended in his surrender. **1892** N. DICKSON *Auld Sc. Min.* 128 I'm sure ye ken as weel as me that love's just an unco fykiness o' the mind.

†**filace.** *Law. Obs.* Also 5 **filas**, 6 **fylas**, 8 **filaze.** [a. AF. *filaz*, ad. med.L. *filacium*, either f. L. *filum* thread, FILE *sb.*², or perh. shortened from late L. *chartophylacium* (ad. late Gr. χαρτοφυλάκιον) place for keeping papers.] = FILE *sb.*² 3 b.

[**1292** BRITTON II. xvii. §12 Et si le bref soit perdu ou remué maliciousement de filaz, adounc cesse le poer la Justice.] **1434** *Proc. & Ordin. Priv. Council Eng.* (1835) IV. 269 A cedule annexed to þe articles þat remayne in þe filas in þoffice of þᵉ prive seal. *a* **1483** *Liber Niger* in *Househ. Ord.* (1790) 33 Other lettres and remembraunces be kept upon a filace. **1509–10** *Act 1 Hen. VIII*, c. 8 Yf the clerke of the petie bagge.. wyll not receyve the same office.. and putt yt on the fylas to remayne of recorde. **1537** in *State Pap.* (1834) II. 501 The fylaceis and recordes of the Chauncery.

Hence †**filace** *v. trans.*, to place on a file, to file.

1537 in *State Papers* (1834) II. 499 Before a bille of compleinte be exibytid and filaceid with the Master of the Rolles clerke.

†**fi'laceous,** *a. Obs.* [f. L. *filum* thread + -ACEOUS.] Consisting of thread-like parts.

1626 BACON *Sylva* §614 It is the Stalk that maketh the Filaceous matter. **1694** WESTMACOTT *Script. Herb.* (1695) 194 Of the filacious matter of the Bark.. Cables.. are made.

filacer, filazer ('fɪləsə(r), -zə(r)). Forms: α. 6 **felyssour, filliser**, 7–8 **filizer, filizar**, 9 **fyliser**, 7– **filacer, -azer.** β. 7–8 **philaser, -azer, -iser, -izer.** [f. FILACE + -ER².] A former officer of the superior courts at Westminster, who filed original writs, etc. and issued processes thereon.

Also a corresponding officer of the Irish superior courts.

[**1432** *Act 10 Hen. VI*, c. 4 Que null Filicer, Exigenter, ne autre officer desore enavaunt fera tiel entree en ascun seute.] **1512** *Act 4 Hen. VIII*, c. 4 §1 The Felyssour or exigenter in whose offyce suche sute is taken. **1562** *Act 5 Eliz.* c. 1 §5 All Attornies, Protonotaries and Philizers. **1613** SIR H. FINCH *Law* (1636) 23 The profits of the office of a Filizer, &c. cannot be put in execution. **1667** WOOD *Life* (Oxf. Hist. Soc.) II. 105 John Hickmote of Windsore in Berks, esq. a philiser. **1708** J. CHAMBERLAYNE *St. Gt. Brit.* II. III. (1743) 266 A List of the Philazers of the Court of Common Pleas, with the counties belonging to each respective Philazer. **1818** HALLAM *Mid. Ages* (1872) III. 88 A petition..to..forbid filazers..from practising. **1827** BINGHAM *Reports* IV. 63 A præcipe into Cambridgeshire had been filed with the filacer of the County of Cambridge. **1837** *Act 7 Will. IV. & 1 Vict.* c. 30, Sched. A, Offices abolished by this Act..On the Plea Side of the Court of Queen's Bench: The Office of ..Filacer..In the Court of Common Pleas: The Office of.. Filacers for the several Counties, Cities, and Towns in England and Wales. **1883** *General Advertiser* 2 June, William Woodlock, Esq...Solicitor, formerly Filazer of the Court of Equity.

†**filacery.** *Obs.* In 7 filizarie. [f. prec. + -Y[3].] The office of a filacer.

1625 SIR H. FINCH *Law* (1636) 358 In an assize of an office as of a filizarie.

filagree: see FILIGREE.

filament (ˈfɪləmənt). [ad. mod.L. *fīlāment-um*, f. late L. *fīlāre* to spin, f. *fīlum* thread. Cf. F. *filament*.]

1. a. A tenuous thread-like body, resembling a fibre of tow; a minute fibre. Often in scientific use, as applied to animal or vegetable structure.

1594 T. B. *La Primaud. Fr. Acad.* II. 31 The..filaments.. are litle long threeds, slender & white, solide & strong. **1664** POWER *Exp. Philos.* I. 66 Those long filaments of which the substance of Brain..consists. **1671** GREW *Anat. Plants* I. vi. §9 (1682) 43 Every one having a Seed appendent to it, whose Coats it entreth by a double Filament. **1774** J. BRYANT *Mythol.* I. 364 The rivers conveyed down their streams fine filaments of brass. **1791** HAMILTON *Berthollet's Dyeing* I. I. II. i. 123 Differences in wool consist in the length and fineness of its filaments. **1841** H. MILLER *O.R. Sandst.* i. 12 The stone..was of..filamentary texture, the filaments radiating in straight lines from the centre to the circumference. **1854** J. SCOFFERN in *Orr's Circ. Sc.* Chem. 6 The suspending filament should be..unspun silk. **1855** BAIN *Senses & Int.* I. ii. §14 The part where the filaments of the nerve are distributed. **1876** ROCK *Text. Fabr.* i. 1 The filaments drawn out of the leaves of plants.

fig. = 'Scrap', 'shred'.

1870 LOWELL *Among my Bks.* Ser. I. (1873) 356 Is there the least filament of truth in it? **1875** EMERSON *Lett. & Soc. Aims, Quot. & Orig.* Wks. (Bohn) III. 214 From the slenderest filament of fact a good fable is constructed.

b. *spec.* The infusible conductor (orig. some form of carbon; now commonly tungsten), placed in the glass bulb of an incandescent electric lamp and raised to incandescence by the passage of the current; a similar conductor in a thermionic valve that serves as a heater or as a directly heated cathode.

1881 S. P. THOMPSON *Elem. Less. Electr.* §374 In these lamps the carbon filament is mounted upon conducting wires..which pass into a glass bulb, into which they are sealed, the bulbs being afterwards exhausted of air. **1885** *Proc. R. Soc.* XXXVIII. 219 If a galvanometer G be connected between *a*, the positive electrode, and *e*, a derived current will be observed to pass..through the rarefied space *ec* when the main current is increased to a certain strength, and the filament reaches a certain degree of incandescence. **1904** FLEMING *Brit. Pat. 24,850* I An appliance which.. constitutes..an electrical valve. I construct it as follows:—In a glass bulb, I seal two or more carbon filaments... These filaments each have their own separate terminals. **1930** *Engineering* 28 Nov. 671/3 The filaments of all the five valves are connected in parallel. **1950** P. PARKER *Electronics* xviii. 900 Hum may be introduced into the output of a valve by the magnetic and electric fields of its filament or heater. **1965** M. MANDL *Fund. Electronics* (ed. 2) xi. 200 The heater filament is placed sufficiently close to the cathode so that the heater will raise the temperature of the cathode to the point where it will emit electrons.

c. *Zool.* The shaft of a down feather.

1869 [see BARBULE 2]. **1959** VAN TYNE & BERGER *Fund. Ornith.* iii. 71 It is probable that in their evolutionary history birds began with a covering of scales and a few feather filaments (cryptoptiles) scattered between them.

d. *Textiles.* A thread of man-made fibre.

1927 T. WOODHOUSE *Artificial Silk* 34 The introduction of small pumps near the filament-forming tubes. **1955** *Times* 10 May 18/3 More inquiry continues to come forward for filament rayon and staple yarns. **1957** R. W. MONCRIEFF *Man-Made Fibres* xxii. 342 The fibre is spun from the molten polymer..through a spinneret with circular holes; the individual filaments solidify almost immediately.

2. a. *transf.*, e.g. in *filament of air, light*, etc.; also in *Hydromechanics* (see quot. 1850).

1646 SIR T. BROWNE *Pseud. Ep.* II. iv. 80 Effluvium passing out in a smaller thred and more enlengthened filament..stirreth not the bodies interposed. **1712** BLACKMORE *Creation* II. (1718) 51 The ever-rolling Orb's impulsive Ray On the next Threads and Filaments does bear. **1810** VINCE *Elem. Astron.* xxi. 229 Part of that exceedingly fine filament of light was intercepted. **1822–56** DE QUINCEY *Confess.* (1862) 73 Slender as a filament of air. **1828** J. M. SPEARMAN *Brit. Gunner* (ed. 2) 200 The lateral pressure of a filament of fluid is equal to its vertical pressure. *c* **1850** *Rudim. Navig.* (Weale) 154 A Filament is an imaginary portion of a stream, of very small breadth, consisting of a row of corpuscles, or of an indefinite number of particles, following each other in the same direction. **1860** TYNDALL *Glac.* I. xxi. 146 The fog was drawn away in long filaments by the wind. **1879** G. PRESCOTT *Sp. Telephone* 128 The action of the helix..upon filings, consists in grouping them under the forms of filaments parallel to the axis.

b. *Astr.* A narrow thread-like streamer from the sun's chromosphere or in its corona.

a **1869** J. NASMYTH in E. Dunkin *Midnight Sky* (1869) 224 The filaments in question are seen..at the edges of the luminous surface. **1871** *English Mechanic* 24 Nov. 243/1 The chromosphere is surmounted by filaments like brilliant hairs. **1902** *Encycl. Brit.* XXVII. 630/2 The drawings in the volume quoted show its polar rays, wings, interlacing filaments, and rifts as they are now known to be, as well as the forms and details of the prominences. **1955** *Sci. Amer.* Feb. 44/3 Certain hydrogen clouds in the sun's atmosphere known as 'filaments'. **1968** P. MOORE *Sun* ix. 81 The prominences..can..be examined when full on the disk, when the Sun is observed or photographed in hydrogen light, but they then look rather like dark snakes, and are called filaments.

3. *Bot.* That part of the stamen which supports the anther; also (see quot. 1884).

1756 P. BROWNE *Jamaica* 123 Vegetables that have three distinct Filaments or male generative parts in every flower. **1759** B. STILLINGFLEET *Misc. Tracts Nat. Hist.* Introd. (1762) 30 Six long thready substances called the filaments each terminated by an oblong body..called the anthera. **1776** WITHERING *Brit. Plants* (1796) I. 22, 10 Stamens in each, and the Filaments not united. **1858** CARPENTER *Veg. Phys.* §9 The filaments of the Berberry stamen. **1884** *Syd. Soc. Lex.*, *Sexual Filament*, the one-celled stalk of the oogonium of some Algæ when it also bears an antheridium.

4. *nonce-uses.* **a.** A thread-like band. **b.** (with etymological reference) A spun thread.

1715 tr. *Pancirollus' Rerum Mem.* I. IV. ii. 157 The Pagan Priests had a Cap upon their Heads, which..they bound.. with a woollen Filament. **1791** COWPER *Odyss.* VIII. 345 Hung them numerous from the roof diffused Like spider's filaments.

5. *attrib.* and *Comb.*, as ***filament bulb***, ***-cathode***, ***current***; **filament battery**, a battery that provides the current for the filament of a valve; **filament lamp**, an electric light bulb in which the light is produced by an incandescent filament.

1919 *Radio Rev.* Oct. 47 The filament battery is used to supply the anode circuit voltage, as well as for lighting the filament. **1949** A. V. EASTMAN *Fund. Vacuum Tubes* (ed. 3) iii. 45 A 45-volt battery is used to supply the plate voltage, its negative terminal being connected to the negative terminal of the filament battery. **1904** FLEMING *Brit. Pat. 24,850* 2 The above described multiple carbon filament bulb ..may be used as a receiving instrument in wireless telegraphy. **1966** R. G. KLOEFFLER *Electron Tubes* i. 6 Directly heated filament-cathodes require comparatively little heating power and are used in tubes designed for use with dry batteries. **1885** *Proc. R. Soc.* XXXVIII. 227 Returned to 90 volts and repeated the experiments. Filament current readings the same as before. **1921** W. H. ECCLES *Contin. Wave Wireless Telegr.* I. 266 The filament current and the length of the filament which could be used directly on a 10-volt battery at a temperature of 2,300°K. **1885** *Proc. R. Soc.* XXXVIII. 220 The lamp..was a short (75 mm.) filament lamp, with a platinum plate. **1908** *Chem. Abstr.* II. 1929 The hourly expense of the metallic filament lamp is 60% less than that of the carbon. **1952** H. HEWITT *Mod. Lighting Techn.* 33 This rapid development in electric lamps has derived from the employment of several different principles, the incandescence of the filament lamp being followed by the luminescence of the discharge tube.

filaˈmentar [f. prec. + -AR[1].] = next.

18.. *Jrnl. Microsc. Sc.* XXVIII. 425 (Cent. Dict.) Even such slips of mesentery..often exhibit a filamentar (craspedal) thickening.

filamentary (fɪləˈmɛntərɪ), *a.* [f. as prec. + -ARY.] Of, pertaining to, or of the nature of a filament or filaments.

1841 [see FILAMENT 1]. **1858** T. R. JONES *Aquarian Nat.* 277 Its head..is provided with numerous filamentary tentacula. **1860** TYNDALL *Glac.* II. xxx. 407 They should change the expressions which refer..the structure to the sliding of 'filaments' past each other..Such filamentary sliding may take place in a truly viscous body. **1867** F. FRANCIS *Angling* vi. (1880) 197 A series of small filamentary appendages, serving as fins. **1875** BLAKE *Zool.* 322 In the higher organized Entozoa a filamentary nervous system has been recognised.

filamented (ˈfɪləməntɪd), *a.* [f. as prec. + -ED[2].] Provided with filaments.

1889 BUCK *Handbk. Med. Sc.* IV. 626 The cells were larger and were not filamented.

filamentiferous (ˌfɪləmənˈtɪfərəs), *a.* [f. as prec. + -(I)FEROUS.] 'Bearing a filament or filaments; filiferous' (*Cent. Dict.*).

ˈfilamentless, *a.* Without a filament.

1934 *Amer. Year Bk. 1933* 697/2 The demonstration of 'filamentless' tubes, not commercially available as yet. **1935** *Economist* 29 June 1509/2 That way of street lighting was due to the filamentless lamp which they called 'Osira'.

filamento-, comb. form of FILAMENT. In ***filamento-cribrate***, having sieve-like openings fringed with filaments.

1846 DANA *Zooph.* (1848) 513 Parietes filamento-cribrate.

filamentoid (fɪləˈmɛntɔɪd), *a.* [f. FILAMENT + -OID.] Having the appearance of a filament; like a filament.

1884 in *Syd. Soc. Lex.*

filamentose (ˌfɪləmənˈtəʊs), *a.* [f. as prec. + -OSE.] = FILAMENTOUS.

1848 in CRAIG. **1854** WOODWARD *Mollusca* II. 194 Gills filamentose..along the sides of the back. **1874** COOKE *Fungi* 15 The anatomical filamentose elements of lichens.

filamentous (fɪləˈmɛntəs), *a.* [f. as prec. + -OUS.]

1. a. Composed of or containing filaments or thread-like parts. **b.** Resembling a filament or thread; thread-like.

1671 GREW *Anat. Plants* I. ii. §8 (1682) 12 The filamentous Extremities of some Roots. **1727** BRADLEY *Fam. Dict.* s.v. *Alum*, Stone alum; it is nothing but a filamentous Talk soft to the touch. **1789** A. CRAWFORD in *Med. Commun.* II. 355 A saturated solution of the..salt..shoots into long filamentous chrystals. **1827** FARADAY *Chem. Manip.* iv. 101 A small platina wire or other piece of filamentous matter. **1831** R. KNOX *Cloquet's Anat.* 609 A layer of dense and close filamentous cellular tissue unites the muscular to the mucous membrane. **1860** GOSSE *Rom. Nat. Hist.* 165 Ranging among the filamentous leaves of the Myriophyllum. **1871** DARWIN *Desc. Man* II. xiii. 74 The backs of the feathers..are filamentous or plumose.

2. Of a plant: Bearing filaments or thread-like parts.

1835 LINDLEY *Introd. Bot.* (1848) II. 125 Some of the filamentous tribes. **1872** OLIVER *Elem. Bot.* II. 295 Many of these filamentous species [of Algæ]..multiply themselves by the contents of the cells which form their filaments.

3. Of or pertaining to a filament or filaments.

1860 TYNDALL *Glac.* II. xxxiii. 421 The seams..were developed..where..filamentous sliding was entirely out of the question.

filaˈmentule. *rare*[−1]. [f. as prec. + -ULE.] A small filament: *spec.* (see quot).

1837 MACGILLIVRAY *Hist. Brit. Birds* I. Introd. 78 These filamentules have the same relation to the filament, their shaft, that the barbules of the feathers have to their barb.

filamo(r)t: see FILEMOT.

filander[1] (fɪˈlændə(r)). Chiefly *pl.* Forms: 5 fylaundris, 7 felanders, fillanders, -enders, fylanders, 6– filander(s. [a. OF. *filandre*:—popular L. **filandula*, dim. f. (*lāna*) *fīlanda* wool to be spun.

The word is used in mod.F. for a gossamer thread, also for various fibres in animal and vegetable organisms.]

In *plural*, Thread-like intestinal worms causing a disease in hawks; the disease so caused.

1486 *Bk. St. Albans* B vij b, A medecyne for wormys in an hawke wiche sekenesse is called the Fylaundris. **1575** TURBERV. *Faulconrie* 252 These filanders..are smal as threedes. **1615** LATHAM *Falconry* 7 These occasions of extraordinary and vntimely heate, may..ingender the fillanders. *a* **1682** SIR T. BROWNE *Hawks* Misc. (1684) 115 This..may probably destroy that obstinate Disease of the Filander or back-worm. **1891** HARTING *Gloss.* in *Bibl. Accipitraria* 222 Filanders, intestinal worms.

†**fiˈlander**[2]. *Obs. rare.* [ad. late L. *phellandrion*, Gr. φελλάνδριον.] The plant Stavesacre (*Delphinium Staphisagria*).

1575 TURBERV. *Faulconrie* 286 To scowre by medicine. Take..graines of filander otherwise called Stauesaker.

filander[3] (fɪˈlændə(r)). A name given to a species of *Macropus* (*M. Brunii*). Also, ***filander kangaroo***.

1737 tr. *C. De Bruyn's Trav. Mosc. & Persia* II. 101 When I was at our general's country seat [in Java] I saw a certain animal called Filander. **1841** WATERHOUSE *Marsupialia* 225 Filander Kangaroo, *Macropus Brunii*.

filander, *v.*: see PHILANDER.

filar (ˈfaɪlə(r)), *a.* [f. L. *fīl-um* thread + -AR.] Of or pertaining to a thread; *esp.* in ***filar micrometer***, ***microscope***, one having threads or wires across its field of view.

1874 KNIGHT *Dict. Mech.*, *Filar-micrometer*. **1879** NEWCOMB & HOLDEN *Astron.* 90 By the filar micrometer we can determine the distance apart in seconds of arc of any two stars A and B. **1884** KNIGHT *Dict. Mech.* IV, *Filar suspension* (Electricity), said of a magnetic needle, which is suspended by a filament of silk.

filaria (fɪˈlɛərɪə, fɪˈlɑːrɪə). Pl. filariæ (occas. filarias). [mod.L. (O. F. Müller 1787, in *Naturforscher* XXII. 64), f. L. *fīlum* thread.] A parasitic nematode worm belonging to the genus *Filaria* or to genera closely related to it. Also *attrib.*

1834 H. MCMURTRIE tr. *Cuvier's Animal Kingdom* 473 The Filariæ in their external appearance are very similar to the Gordii. **1883** P. MANSON *Filaria Sanguinis Hominis* 51 Filarial periodicity is an adaptation of the habits of the filaria to those of the mosquito. **1897** *Daily News* 8 Feb. 6/2 From its decaying body the filaria larvæ escape into the water. **1922** *Nature* 23 Mar. 379/1 The filarias and their allies, which live in the connective tissues. **1924** C. MACKENZIE *Old Men of Sea* vii. 101 If he could have injected *filariæ* into Biscoe and induced elephantiasis he would have done so. **1934** T. W. M. CAMERON *Internal Parasites of Domestic Animals* I. 11 Filaria larvae, found in the blood of man at night, were actually abstracted from this closed circuit by a blood-sucking insect. **1956** —— *Parasites & Parasitism* 260 Mosquitoes carrying filariae are widespread.

filarial (fɪˈlɛərɪəl), *a.* [f. mod.L. *fīlāri-a*, f. *fīl-um* thread + -AL[1].] Of or pertaining to the genus

Filaria of parasitic worms. ***filarial periodicity*** (see quot.).

1881 *Athenæum* 5 Feb. 203/3 A paper by Dr. Manson, 'On the Periodicity of Filarial Migration to and from the Circulation,' was communicated by Dr. Cobbold. **1883** B. W. RICHARDSON *Prev. Med.* vii. 788 In the filarial disease the filarial embryos are found in the blood of the person affected by them. **1884** *Syd. Soc. Lex.*, *F. periodicity*, Cobbold's term for the phenomena of the periodical daily appearance, in the blood, of the embryos of the *Filaria sanguinis hominis* during the night or the hours of sleep, and their absence during the daytime or the hours of waking.

filarian (fɪˈlɛərɪən), *a.* [f. as prec. + -AN.] = prec.

In some mod. Dicts.

filariasis (fɪlɛərɪ-, fɪlɑːrɪˈeɪsɪs). *Path.* Also filariˈosis. [f. FILARI(A + -ASIS.] Any disease resulting from infection with filariæ.

1879 *Veterinarian* LII. 401 (*heading*) Facts in Filariasis. **1888** *Brit. Med. Jrnl.* 29 Sept. 728/2 The term 'filariosis', he [*sc.* Dr. Lancereaux] applies to the entire group of pathological conditions resulting from infection of the organism by the *filaria sanguinis hominis*. **1900** G. H. F. NUTTALL in C. Watson *Encycl. Med.* III. 464 Though the term 'filariasis' has been usually applied in medical works only to diseases due to *Filaria Bancrofti*, it appears advisable so to extend the term that it may include all diseases, both of man and animals, which are due to the presence and action of filariae. **1949** H. W. FLOREY et al. *Antibiotics* II. xxxi. 1062 Filariasis in man has been treated with penicillin without effect. **1957** L. F. R. WILLIAMS *State of Israel* 131 Some 20 per cent of the Cochin population suffered from filariasis. **1966** WRIGHT & SYMMERS *Systemic Path.* II. xxxiv. 1189 *Wuchereria bancroftii*, one of the causative organisms of filariosis, behaves in two respects like the malarial parasite.

fiˈlariate, *v.* [f. as FILARIAL *a.* + -ATE³.] *trans.* To infect with filariæ. Hence **fiˈlariated** *ppl. a.*

1884 MANSON in *Trans. Linn. Soc.* Ser. II. Zool. II. 368 We may settle the relationship of the mosquito to the Filaria ..By filariating a man..by means of Filariæ metamorphosed in passing through the mosquito. *Ibid.* 369 The blood of a filariated man.

filariform (fɪˈlærɪfɔːm), *a.* [f. as prec. + -FORM.] Of the form of *Filaria*.

filariid (fɪˈlɛərɪɪd, fɪˈlɑːrɪɪd), *a.* [f. FILARI(A + -ID³.] Of or pertaining to a family of parasitic nematode worms, the Filariidæ.

1929 H. A. BAYLIS *Man. Helminthol.* II. 205 The name *Filaria*, however, continues to be largely used, in a loose sense, for Filariid worms. **1946** *Nature* 20 July 98/2 *Litomosoides carinii* is a filariid parasite of the cotton rat, *Sigmodon hispidus*. **1956** T. W. M. CAMERON *Parasites & Parasitism* 138 Some of the filariid worms live in similar habitats.

filarioid (fɪˈlɛərɪɔɪd, fɪˈlɑːrɪɔɪd), *a.* [f. FILARI(A + -OID.] Of or pertaining to a superfamily of parasitic nematode worms, the Filarioidea.

1930 E. C. FAUST *Human Helminthol.* xxviii. 438 Filarioid species are classified under two families. **1956** G. LAPAGE *Vet. Parasitol.* viii. 216 The usual habitat of filarioid roundworms is the body cavity, the lymphatic system or the connective tissue of their hosts.

filarious (fɪˈlɛərɪəs), *a.* [f. as FILARIFORM *a.* + -OUS.] Infected with *Filariæ*.

1883 MANSON *Filaria Sang. Hom.* 48 Hooihoah, a highly filarious district. **1884** —— in *Trans. Linn. Soc.* Ser. II. Zool. II. 370 My..filarious patients.

filasse (filas). [Fr., = TOW *sb.*¹ Cf. FILLIS.] Vegetable fibre prepared for manufacture.

1858 in SIMMONDS *Dict. Trade*. **1895** *Daily News* 3 Dec. 2/3 Ramie, whose fibre produces a substance called filasse, similar to flax.

filate (ˈfaɪlət), *a.* *Entom.* [f. L. *fīl-um* thread + -ATE².] (See quots.)

1826 KIRBY & SP. *Entomol.* IV. 294 Margin..*Filate*.. when the edge is separated by a channel, often producing a very slender threadlike margin. *Ibid.* IV. 324 *Filate*..when inversatile antennæ have neither a terminal nor a lateral bristle.

filaterie, obs. form of PHYLACTERY.

filatory (ˈfɪlətərɪ). [ad. med.L. *fīlātōri-um*, f. *fīlāre* to spin, f. L. *fīlum* thread.] A machine for forming or spinning threads.

?**18..** TOOKE (Webster 1832), This manufactory has three filatories, each of 640 reels.

filature (ˈfɪlətjʊə(r)). [a. F. *filature* (as if ad. L. **fīlātūra*; cf. It. *filatura*), f. late L. *fīlāre* to spin, f. *fīlum* thread.]

1. The action of forming or spinning into threads; the reeling of silk from cocoons.

1783 BURKE *Rep. Affairs India* Wks. 1842 II. 27 Buying up the cocoons for the Italian filature. **1860** URE *Dict. Arts* II. 277 *Floss-silk* is the name given to the portions of ravelled silk broken off in the filature of the cocoons.

b. *attrib.* in ***filature-silk*** = floss-silk.

1804 COLEBROOKE *Husb. Bengal* (1806) 153 The prime-cost of fileture-silk [*sic*].

2. An establishment for reeling silk.

1759 *Chron.* in *Ann. Reg.* 165/1 The public filature at Savannah. **1772** FRANKLIN *Lett.* Wks. 1887 IV. 477 *note*, Fifty-four pounds [of silk] had been reeled at the filature of private persons. **1851** L. D. B. GORDON in *Art Jrnl. Illust. Catal.* 11**/1 The process of Reeling the Silk from the Cocoons is carried on..in establishments called filatures. **1880** MISS BIRD *Japan* I. 270 In the rear of the filature is a large fireproof building.

filaw, obs. form of FELLAH.

filaze, filazer: see FILACE, FILACER.

filbert (ˈfɪlbət). Forms: α. 4 philliberd, 6–7 philbert, (7 -ibert), (8 philberd, -bud). β. 5 fel-, 5–6 fyl-, 6–9 filberd(e, (7 -burd, fillberd), 6–9 *dial.* filbeard(e, (6 fyl-), 6 filberte, (fylbert), 6–7 filbird(e, (6 fylbyrd). 4– filbert. [prob. short for *filbert* (i.e. *Philibert*)-*nut*, dial. Fr. *noix de filbert* (Moisy *Dict. Patois Normand*) from being ripe near St. Philibert's day, Aug. 22 (O.S.). Cf. Ger. *Lamberts-nuss*.]

1. a. The fruit or nut of the cultivated hazel (*Corylus avellana*).

[**1292** BRITTON II. xxiv. §1 Et as foiles, et as flours (*v.r.* e a philbers).] *a* **1400** *Pistill of Susan* 92 þe fyge and þe filbert were fode med so fayre. *c* **1440** *Promp. Parv.* 160 Fylberde, notte, *fillum*. **1533** ELYOT *Cast. Helthe* (1539) 21 b, Fylberdes and hasyll nuttes..are more stronge in substance than wall nuttes. **1620** VENNER *Via Recta* vii. 127 Filberds are wholsomer then the common Hasell-Nuts. **1712** E. COOKE *Voy. S. Sea* 70 Something bigger, and more oval than a Filbeard. **1774** GOLDSM. *Nat. Hist.* (1776) IV. 29 The acorn, the philberd, the chesnut, and the wilding. **1846** J. BAXTER *Libr. Pract. Agric.* (ed. 4) I. 264, I grew two hundred weight of filberts..upon fifty-seven trees.

b. *slang*. The head (cf. NUT *sb.*¹ 7).

1886 H. BAUMANN *Londinismen* 54/1 *Cracked in the filbert*, ..dotty. **1936** J. CURTIS *Gilt Kid* xx. 198 Get that into your old filbert.

2. The tree bearing the nut; = *filbert-tree*.

1393 GOWER *Conf.* II. 30 And after Phillis philliberd This tre was cleped in the yerd. *c* **1450** LYDG. *Compl. Loveres Life* 68 The filbert eke, that lowe doth encline Her bowes grene. ?*c* **1475** *Sqr. lowe Degre* 37 The fylbyrdes hangyng to the ground. **1523** FITZHERB. *Husb.* §140 Fylberdes and walnuttes may be set on the nuttes in a gardeyn. **1616** SURFL. & MARKH. *Country Farme* 341 Filberts..doe grow of smal shoots. **1796** C. MARSHALL *Garden.* vi. (1813) 80 Filberds are raised from nuts or suckers. **1858** GLENNY *Gard. Everyday Bk.* 21 Filberts must be planted by the same rules.

3. *attrib.* and *Comb.* **a.** simple attrib:, as ***filbert-grove, -hedge, -nut, -tree, -walk***. **b.** similative, as ***filbert nails; filbert-formed, -shaped*** adjs. Also, †**filbert-mouse**, the common dormouse (*Muscardinus avellanarius*), so called from its fondness for filberts.

'Filbert nails' are often referred to as a beauty, but sometimes regarded as a symptom of consumptive tendencies.

a **1845** BARHAM *Ingol. Leg.*, *Lady Rohesia*, A pretty little hand with..*filbert-formed nails. **1552** HULOET, *Filberde groue, *coryletum*. **1742** FIELDING *J. Andrews* III. iv, A short Walk, shaded on each side by a *Filbert Hedge. *a* **1821** KEATS *Poems*, '*I stood tiptoe*' 35 A filbert hedge with wild briar overtwined. **1607** TOPSELL *Four-f. Beasts* 545 Of the Nut-mouse, Hasell-mouse, or *Filburd-mouse. **1861** TROLLOPE *Framley P.* I. i. 9 Clear white hands, *filbert nails. **1552** HULOET, *Filberd nutte, *abellina*. **14..** *Nom.* in Wr.-Wülcker 715 *Hec morus*, a *fylberdtre. **1551** TURNER *Herbal* I. (1568) Miij a, The gardyne nutt tree [is] called the fylberde tree. **1751** *Phil. Trans.* XLVII. 176 The fruit of the nut and filberd-tree will be most numerous. **1879** MISS JACKSON *Shropsh. Word-bk*, 'I never sid the filbyard-trees covered ooth lamb-tails [catkins] as they bin this ear' [1879].

filch (fɪlʃ, fɪltʃ), *sb.* [Belongs to next vb. It is uncertain whether the sb. in sense 1 was the source of the vb., or derived from it; in the other senses it is f. the vb.]

†**1.** A staff with a hook at one end, used to steal articles from hedges, open windows, etc. *Obs.*

1622 FLETCHER *Beggar's Bush* II. i, Thus we throw up our Nab-cheats..And then our filches. **1632–48** DEKKER *Eng. Villanies* M iij/2 [He] carries a short staffe..which is called a Filch. *a* **1700** B. E. *Dict. Cant. Crew*, *A good Filch*, a Staff, of Ash or Hazel, with a Hole through, and a Spike at the bottom, to pluck Cloathes from a Hedge or anything out of a Casement. **1725** in *New Cant. Dict.*

2. That which is filched or stolen; also, 'a good taking'.

a **1627** MIDDLETON *More Dissemblers besides Women* IV. ii, Save ev'ry hour a filch or two, Be it money, cloth or pullen. **1798** WOLCOTT (P. Pindar) *Tales of Hoy* Wks. 1812 IV. 424 He put a fine parcel of money into the pockets of the proprietors: quite a Filch.

†**3.** One who filches or steals: a filcher. *Obs.*

1775 in ASH. **1810** POOLE *Hamlet Travestie* II. iii, A very Filch, that more deserves to hang, Than any one.

4. The action of filching or stealing

1877 *Five Years' Penal Servit.* iii. 246 She were an out and outer in going into shops on the filch.

filch (fɪlʃ, fɪltʃ), *v.* Also 6 filche, filtch, fylche. [Of unknown origin; see prec. sb.

Originally slang, and, like many other slang words, first recorded in 16th c. The following passage is often quoted as an earlier instance, but the various reading *fliched* ('flinched', 'given way') seems preferable, and in any case the present vb. yields no good sense:—

?*c* **1300** *Song* in Langtoft *Chron.* (Rolls) II. 264 In toune herd I telle, Thair baghel and thair belle Ben filched and fledde.]

1. *trans.* To steal, *esp.* things of small value; to pilfer. Occas. in weaker sense: To take away surreptitiously.

1561 AWDELAY *Frat. Vacab.* 3 Or els filtch Poultry, carying them to the Alehouse. **1596** H. CLAPHAM *Briefe Bible* I. 65 Let such as haue filtched Church-liuings, marke this. **1602** *2nd Pt. Return fr. Parnass.* I. ii. (Arb.) 9 Those eggs which haue ben filcht from the nest of Crowes and Kestrells. *a* **1677** BARROW *Serm.* Wks. 1716 II. 155 From him they filcht that proud..uncivil humour. **1714** GAY *Trivia* III. 58 The wily Fox..Who lately filch'd the Turkey's callow Care. **1785** PALEY *Mor. Philos.* (1818) I. 94 If he filched a book out of a Library. **1810** T. JEFFERSON *Writ.* (1830) IV. 138 A mere contrivance to filch wealth and power to themselves. **1856** MRS. BROWNING *Aur. Leigh* VI. 671 I did not filch,—I found the child. **1873** SYMONDS *Grk. Poets* vii. 212 He would filch me hence.

absol. **1567** HARMAN *Caveat* 32 They be..skilfull in.. filching. **1688** LD. DELAMER *Wks.* (1694) 26 For when Servants are pincht, they will be filching. **1866** GEO. ELIOT *F. Holt* 56 If I don't lie and filch somebody else will.

b. with *away, off*.

1577 *Test. 12 Patriarchs* (1604) 52 Ye shall purloin the Lord's offering, and filch away pieces of it. **1678** BUTLER *Hud.* III. i. 1176 What made thee..filch the Ladie's Heart away? **1829** LYTTON *Disowned* 4 The rascals would not filch off the corner of your garment. **1843** PRESCOTT *Mexico* V. ii. (1864) 283 He..succeeded in filching away much of the territory of his royal kinsman.

†**c.** To introduce stealthily *into*. *Obs. rare*⁻¹.

1589 NASHE *Almond for Parrat* 3 Thou shouldst filche thyselfe..into our gouernement.

2. To rob (*of* something). *rare*.

1567 HARMAN *Caveat* 29 If they meete with a woman.. such they filche and spoyle. **1837** HOWITT *Rur. Life* III. iii 243 No man is in danger of..being filched of his purse.

†**3.** To beat, strike. *Obs.*

1567 HARMAN *Caveat* 84 *To fylche*, to beate, to stryke. **1610** ROWLANDS *Martin Mark-all* (1874) 38 *Filch*, to beate.

Hence **filched** *ppl. a.*

1567 DRANT *Horace Epist.* xiii. E iv, Drunken Pyrrhe beares her wool her flycesie filched gaine. *a* **1625** FLETCHER *Chances* I. ix, I foster up your filch'd Iniquities! **1809** SCOTT *Poacher* 74 The filched lead the church's roof affords. **1856** BOKER *Poems*, *Anne Boleyn* I. i, This same haughty moon That floods our prospect with her filched beams.

filcher (ˈfɪlʃə(r), ˈfɪltʃə(r)). [f. prec. + -ER¹.] One who filches; a petty thief, pilferer.

1573 TUSSER *Husb.* (1878) 25 Purloiners and filchers, that loueth to lurke. **1621** MOLLE *Camerar. Liv. Libr.* I. xii. 39 Begins to fall upon these filchers. **1702** W. J. *Bruyn's Voy. Levant* xxxviii. 152 The Arabians are the greatest Filchers in the World. **1860** J. P. KENNEDY *Swallow B.* xxxviii. 376 A filcher of caps and napkins from a washerwoman's basket.

Hence **ˈfilchery**, the art or practice of a filcher.

1607 R. C[AREW] tr. *Estienne's World of Wonders* xv. 82 Feates of filchery and cunning coueyance.

ˈfilching, *vbl. sb.* [f. as prec. + -ING¹.]

1. The action of the verb FILCH.

1567 DRANT *Horace Epist.* E viij b, Thy facte not lesse in this thy filchinge meanes. **1597** J. PAYNE *Royal Exch.* 35 Avoyde filchinge and robbinge.

2. *concr.* That which is filched or stolen.

1834 LYTTON *Pompeii* IV. ii, By what reserved filchings from marketing..hast thou been enabled to make them serve thee? **1872** GEO. ELIOT *Middlem.* xlvi, To pay some call where she distributed her small filchings.

3. *attrib.* and *Comb.*, as ***filching-sack, -trade***.

a **1592** GREENE *James IV* (1861) 192 The filching trade when time serves. **1836–48** B. D. WALSH *Aristoph.*, *Knights* I. iii, I'll flay you for a filching-sack.

ˈfilching, *ppl. a.* [f. as prec. + -ING².] That filches; pilfering.

1570 B. GOOGE *Pop. Kingd.* IV. 54 To looke that no disorder be, nor any filching hande. **1592** WYRLEY *Armorie* 151 Ah filching death, thou felonous bloodie thiefe. **1659** *Gentl. Calling* (1660) 110 This filtching Devil, that thus steals from men their precious hours. *a* **1700** B. E. *Dict. Cant. Crew*, *Filching-cove*, a Man-thief.

†**ˈfilchingly**, *adv.* *Obs.* [f. prec. + -LY².] In a filching manner; stealthily, surreptitiously.

1583 GOLDING *Calvin on Deut.* clviii. 978 They will not go filchingly to cut downe a patche of medowe. **1598** FLORIO, *Arúba*, by stealth, filchingly. *a* **1693** URQUHART *Rabelais* III. xviii. 149 Cull'd by fervent Lovers filchingly.

†**ˈfilchman**. *Obs.* [f. FILCH *v.* (? or *sb.*) + *-man* as in many other slang words; cf. *darkmans*, *fakeman*, etc.] = FILCH *sb.* 1.

1561 AWDELAY *Frat. Vacab.* 4 An Upright Man is one that goeth wyth the trunchion of a staffe, which staffe they cal a Filtchman. **1673** R. HEAD *Canting Acad.* 60 A short Truncheon..which he calls his Filch-man.

fild(e, obs. form of FIELD.

†**fildor**. *Obs.* In 4 fildore, fyldor. [a. Fr. *fil d'or* thread of gold.] Gold thread. Also *attrib.*

a **1310** in Wright *Lyric P.* ix. 33 A fyldor [*printed* fyld or] fax to folde. **13..** *E.E. Allit. P.* A. 106 As fyldor fyn her b[o]nkes brent. *c* **1340** *Gaw. & Gr. Knt.* 189 Folden in wyth fildore aboute þe fayre grene.

file (faɪl), *sb.*¹ Forms: 1 fil, féol, 3 *south.* vile, (5 vyle), 4–7 fyle, 4– file. [OE. *féol* (Anglian *fíl*) = MDu., MLG. *vîle* (Du. *vijl*, LG. *file*), OHG. *fîla, fîgila, fîhala* (MHG. *vîle, vîgel*, mod.Ger. *feile*); ON. with anomalous initial consonant *þél* (mod.Icel. *þjöl*, MSw. *fäl*, MDa. *fel*; the mod.Sw. and Da. *fil* are prob. adoptions from LG. or HG.).

The OTeut. **fihlâ* is commonly referred to the Aryan *pink*, nasalized form of the root *peik*, to which the primary sense 'to scratch, mark' is assigned; cf. OSl. *pĭsati* to write, L. *pingĕre* to point. The OSl. (also Russian, Bohemian, etc.) *pila* file, saw, Lith. *pela, pėlyczià* file, have a remarkable

similarity of sound to the Teut. word, but etymological affinity cannot be affirmed.]

1. a. A metal (usually steel) instrument, having one or more of its surfaces covered with numerous small raised cutting edges or teeth, for abrading, reducing, or smoothing surfaces. ***to bite, gnaw a file***: *fig.* to make an attempt that can result only in vexatious failure (in allusion to the fable); similarly ***to lick a file*** (see quot. 1647).

a **800** *Corpus Gloss.* (Sweet) 1234 *Lima*, fiil. *c* **1000** *Riddles* lxx. 4 (Gr.) Ic..eom..laf fyres and feole. **1382** WYCLIF *Isa.* xliv. 12 The yren smyth with the file wroȝte. **1432** *E.E. Wills* (1882) 91 A vyle, and a forser with loke and kye. **1484** CAXTON *Fables of Æsop* III. xii, She [the serpent] fond a fyle whiche she beganne to gnawe with her teethe. **1549** *Compl. Scot.* iii. 28 Ane file is ane instrument to file doune yrn. **1647** H. MORE *Song of Soul* I. II. cxii, Like the mistaken Cat that lick'd the file. **1649** J. H. *Motion to Parl. Adv. Learn.* 26 As soone as they have done licking of this file. **1697** EVELYN *Numism.* vi. 214 The File..which they use for the smoothing of the edges. **1786** BEATTIE *Minstr.* II. xiv, So gnaw'd the viper the corroding file. **1824** TREDGOLD *Ess. Cast Iron* 90 These bars yielded freely to the file. **1880** W. CORY *Mod. Eng. Hist.* I. 105 He bit at the file of English obstinacy, and broke his teeth.

b. *fig. esp.* with reference to the polish imparted by a file. (Cf. the use of L. *lima.*)

a **1225** *Ancr. R.* 284 He is þi uile þet misseið þe oðer misdeð þe. **1621** B. JONSON *Gipsies Metamorph.* Wks. (Rtldg.) 628/1 From a tongue without a file Heaps of phrases and no style. *a* **1639** WOTTON in *Reliq. Wotton.* (1685) 341 If it shall pass the file of your Judgment. **1749** AKENSIDE *Odes* II. i, The nice touches of the critic's file.

†**2.** = *file-shell. Obs.*⁻¹

1705 J. PETIVER in *Phil. Trans.* XXV. 1955 The fine blush Jamaica File.

3. *slang.* An artful, cunning, or shrewd person. Also, a man, 'fellow', 'cove'.

[Cf. Fr. slang *lime sourde*, lit. 'a silent file', in similar sense.]

1812 J. H. VAUX *Flash Dict.*, *File*, a person who has had a long course of experience in the arts of fraud..is termed *an old file upon the town*;..a man who is extremely cunning..is a *deep file.* **1819** *Metropolis* I. 61 You're an old file. I know you well; you're as deep as Garrick. **1838** DICKENS *O. Twist* (1850) 233 The Dodger..desired the jailer to communicate 'the names of them two files as was on the bench'. **1848** THACKERAY *Van. Fair* lv, All the old files of the Ring were in it. **1857** HUGHES *Tom Brown* I. iv. (1871) 84 Old Blow-hard was a dry old file. **1877** *Holderness Gloss.*, 'A deep awd file.'

4. *attrib.* and *Comb.*: **a.** simple attributive, as ***file-chisel, -cut, -dust, -handle, -smith, -stroke, -trade.*** **b.** objective, as ***file-cleaner, -cutter, -grinder, -maker; file-cutting, -finishing, -grinding, -nibbling, -tempering*** vbl. sbs.

1874 KNIGHT *Dict. Mech.*, *File-chisel. *Ibid.*, *File-cleaner. **1888** HASLUCK *Mech. Workshop Handybk.* 86 This method of crossing the *file-cuts..is recommended. **1677–83** MOXON *Mech. Exerc.* 58 *File-cutters also use it to make their Chissels. **1890** *Pall Mall G.* 2 Sept. 4/2 The knife-grinders and file-cutters in Sheffield. **1819** REES *Cycl.* s.v. *File*, The most likely machine for *file-cutting. **1601** HOLLAND *Pliny* II. 519 The *file dust which commeth of lead. **1876** VOYLE *Milit. Dict.* (ed. 3) s.v. *File*, Little shavings or shreds..called file dust. **1883** *Daily News* 25 June 2/8 The *file-grinders still stand out. **1874** KNIGHT *Dict. Mech.*, **File-grinding Machine*, a machine for surfacing forged or rolled file-blanks to bring them to form previous to cutting. **1888** *Lockwood's Dict. Terms Mech. Eng.*, **File-Handle.* **1842** *Bk. Trades* 230 Some *File-makers are in the habit of using the coal of burnt leather. **1869** *Times* 1 Jan. 4 Mighty little will be done by such *file-nibbling or tinkering over law of entail. **1865** *Pall Mall G.* 19 Oct. 4 A meeting of the *File-smiths' Union. **1677** MOXON *Mech. Exerc.* 15 The Smooth file is to take out those cuts, or *file-stroaks, that the fine file made. **1888** HASLUCK *Mech. Workshop Handybk.* 84 Without stopping the file-strokes. **1874** KNIGHT *Dict. Mech.*, **File-tempering.* **1887** *Daily News* 20 June 2/6 In the *file trade there is apparently a slight change.

5. Special comb., as **file-blank**, a piece of soft steel, shaped and ground ready for cutting, to form a file; also *attrib.*; **file-card**, a card used for cleaning files; **file-carrier** (see quot): † **file-fast** *adv.*, ? securely; **file-shell**, a species of *Pholas*, so called from the roughness of its shell; **file snake**, a non-poisonous colubrid snake of the genus *Mehelya*, found in South Africa; **file-stripper** (see quot.). Also FILE-FISH.

1874 KNIGHT *Dict. Mech.*, **File-blank.* **1892** SIMMONDS *Dict. Trade* Suppl., *File-blank Forger*, a workman who prepares the crude material for the file-cutter. **1884** KNIGHT *Dict. Mech.* IV, **File Card.* **1888** HASLUCK *Mech. Workshop Handybk.* 86 These file cards are used in the same way as the scratch brushes. **1874** KNIGHT *Dict. Mech.*, **File-carrier*, a tool-holder like the stock of a frame-saw. *a* **1225** *Ancr. R.* 244 Þe ueond..wearð ibunden *uileueste mid te holie monnes beoden. **1752** SIR J. HILL *Hist. Anim.* 177 The West Indian *File-shell. [**1908** *Ann. Transvaal Museum* I. 23 *Simocephalus capensis* (Smith). Three-cornered Snake. Vijlslang.] **1912** F. W. FITZSIMONS *Snakes S. Afr.* iv. 96 Three-cornered or File Snakes..although found in most parts of South Africa, seem to be rather rare everywhere. **1931** *Discovery* Mar. 74/2 A file snake captured a frog. **1962** R. M. ISEMONGER *Snakes Afr.* 98 The file snake is generally feared by Africans, who associate its entry to their house with the death of a relative or friend. **1874** KNIGHT *Dict. Mech.*, **File-stripper*, a machine in which a worn-out file after being softened by heat, and slow cooling, is smoothed to prepare it for being re-cut.

file (fail), *sb.*² Also 6–7 fyle. [Properly two different words, ultimately of identical etymology: (1) a. Fr. *fil* = Pr. *fil*, It. *filo*, Sp. *hilo*:—L. *fīlum* thread; (2) a. Fr. *file* = Pr., and It. *fila*, Sp. *hila*:—Com. Romanic **fila*, fem. sing.; according to some scholars a vbl. sb. f. *filare*, to spin, draw out threads, f. L. *fīlum*.]

I. Senses chiefly repr. F. *fil.*

†**1.** A thread. **a.** *fig.* The thread of life. **b.** *transf.* Of the nerves: A nerve-cord. *Obs.*

1606 N. BAXTER *Sidney's Ourania* N ij b, The fatall Sisters would not cut her file. **1607** TOPSELL *Four-f. Beasts* (1658) 223 A dubble file or threed to the top of the tail.

†**2.** The thread, course, or tenor (of a story, argument, etc.). *Obs.*

1560–1 *Schort Somme 1st Bk. Discipl. Ch. Scot.* §14 Following the file and dependance of the text. **1596** SPENSER *F.Q.* VII. vi. 37 Ill fitting for this file To sing of hills and woods 'mongst wars and knights. **1612** SHELTON *Quix.* III. x. I. 209 You must promise me that you will not interrupt the File of my doleful Narration. *a* **1639** WOTTON in *Reliq. Wooton.* (1685) 223 Let me resume the File of my Relation. **1647** N. BACON *Disc. Govt.* I. xlv. (1739) 73 If the file of his purposes be rightly considered.

3. a. A string or wire, on which papers and documents are strung for preservation and reference. In recent use extended to various other appliances for holding papers so that they can be easily referred to.

1525 in *Vicary's Anat.* (1888) App. viii. 214 Thapothecaries shall kepe the billis that they serue, vpon a fyle. **1649** *Lanc. Tracts* (Chetham Soc.) 233 Their examinations remaining still upon fyle in Manchester. **1666** PEPYS *Diary* 9 Dec., Burning all the unnecessary letters which I have had upon my file for four or five years backward. **1732** *Acc. Workhouses* 175 Keep the tradesmen's notes upon a file. **1768** FOOTE *Devil on 2 Sticks* II. Wks. 1799 II. 259 There are some of their names, I am sure, that I never desire to see on my file. **1866** W. COLLINS *Armadale* II. IV. iii. 277 Some place in the City where all the papers are kept, as he calls it, in file. **1882** BLACK *Shandon Bells* vi. A printed slip which the latter pulled off a file.

fig. **1581** J. BELL *Haddon's Answ. Osor.* 275 We hang uppe this accusation also upon the file of your other slaunderous lyes. **1659** J. ARROWSMITH *Chain Princ.* 200 This commination standeth upon the file in holy Scripture.

b. *esp.* one in a court of law to hold proceedings or documents in a cause, etc.; the list of documents, etc., in a cause.

In the Court of Chancery the pleadings themselves were filed; in the Common Law Courts the pleadings and judgements were *enrolled*, and only affidavits and collateral documents were filed.

1607 in COWEL *Interpr.* **1631** *Star Chamb. Cases* (Camden) 42 The sentence of the court was..that the bill should be taken off the fyle, that [etc.]. **1718** PRIOR *Solomon* II. 722 Causes unjudg'd disgrace the loaded file. **1818** CRUISE *Digest* (ed. 2) V. 285 They will not, however, order the fine to be taken off the file. **1833** MYLNE & KEEN *Reports* II. 247 This was the only bill upon the file relative to the testator's estate. **1885** *Law Times' Rep.* LII. 681/2 A motion was made to take the affidavits off the file.

†**c.** A catalogue, list, roll. *Obs.*

1566 PARTRIDGE *Hist. Plasidas* D iij, Thus ended they their mortall race, their file was at an ende. **1597** SHAKS. *2 Hen. IV*, I. iii. 10 Our present Musters grow vpon the File To fiue and twenty thousand men of choice. **1620** DEKKER *Dreame* 10 With Pens of Steele, Eternall Files to keepe Of euery Nation, since the Earth began. **1697** DRYDEN *Disc. Epic Poetry* Prose Wks. 1800 III. 441 The file of heroick poets is very short. **1702** C. MATHER *Magn. Chr.* III. III. (1852) I. 544 It would not be improper under this file to lodge the singular and surprising successes of his prayers. **1795** BURKE *Regic. Peace* iv. Wks. IX. 335 Catalogued files of murders.

4. a. A collection of papers placed on a file, or merely arranged in order of date or subject for ready reference.

a **1626** BACON *Adv. Villiers* Wks. 1740 III. 566 After you have ranked them into several files, according to the subject matter. **1699** GARTH *Dispens.* 32 Then from the Compter he takes down the File And with Prescriptions lights the solemn Pile. **1806** *Naval Chron.* XV. 113 Files of newspapers. **1806** WILBERFORCE in G. Rose *Diaries* (1860) II. 212 Having just this moment got a file of letters. **1847** LD. HOUGHTON in *Life* (1891) I. ix. 401 You can get at..the newsroom a file of the *Times.* **1851** D. JERROLD *St. Giles* xii. 121 A man who has a file of receipts to show for everything. **1860** MRS. GASKELL *C. Brontë* 301 She sent to Leeds for a file of the 'Mercuries' of 1812, '13 and '14.

b. *Computers.* A collection of related records stored for use by a computer and able to be processed by it. Also *attrib.* and *Comb.*

1954 *Jrnl. Assoc. Comput. Mach.* I. 8/2 A 'master' tape..contains the file of unit records as at the last date of processing. **1967** COX & GROSE *Organiz. Bibl. Rec. by Computer* 19 A file sequence may contain only one file, and this is generally the case when updating procedures are being carried out. **1969** *Computers & Humanities* III. 132 This search (once through the file), whether for a single interrogation or for several, is called a file-pass.

5. *Her.* = LABEL (but sometimes distinguished: cf. quot. 1727). [So in Fr.]

1562 LEIGH *Armorie* (1597) 107 He beareth Argent a fyle with iij Lambeaux Azure, for a difference. Some will call them a Labell of three pointes. *c* **1640** J. SMYTH *Lives Berkeleys* (1883) I. 120 The Cheveron..distinguished by a file with five labels to shew that he was a fifth brother. **1710** HEARNE *Collect.* 5 May, A Shield with a Cross Saltire and a File of 3 Points. **1727** BRADLEY *Fam. Dict.* s.v. *File*, Some distinguish File and Label, calling the File the upper horizontal Line, and the Label the Point that issues from it. **1889** ELVIN *Dict. Herald.*, *File* or Label.

6. A disease, ? from its producing an appearance of lines or threads: †**a.** in trees—Fr. *fil* (*obs.*); **b.** in cattle. *dial.*

1600 SURFLET *Countrie Farme* III. xlvii. 520 The file is a disease in trees that fretteth their barkes. **1688** in R. HOLME *Armoury* II. 86/1. **1892** *Northumberland Gloss.* s.v. *File*, 'File in the foot' is a disease peculiar to cattle and sheep.

II. Senses repr. Fr. *file.*

7. *Mil.* **a.** The number of men constituting the depth from front to rear of a formation in line, etc. ***in file***: one behind the other. For ***Indian, single file*** see those adjs. ***rank and file***: see RANK.

The front of a file is one man (the *file-leader*), the depth may be any number; but in the modern English formation of infantry it is only two, consisting of the front and the rear rank men.

1598 BARRET *Theor. Warres* III. i. 37 By file, I vnderstand all the line..of all the souldiers standing consequently one after another, from front to the traine. **1625** MARKHAM *Souldier's Accid.* 6 A File..ought neuer to be aboue ten persons deepe. **1633** T. STAFFORD *Pac. Hib.* ii. (1821) 524 It was impossible for men to march but in file. **1667** MILTON *P.L.* VI. 339 His Chariot..stood retir'd From off the files of warr. **1734** tr. *Rollin's Anc. Hist.* V. 9 Each squadron had..8 in depth, for that was the usual depth of the files. **1790** BURNS *Sheriffmuir* 15 Great Argyle led on his files. **1796–7** *Instr. & Reg. Cavalry* (1813) 34 The others..will first cover in file with precision. **1810** WELLINGTON in Gruw. *Desp.* VI. 208 The 16th are very strong; when I saw them the other day they were 59 file a squadron. **1816** BYRON *Siege Cor.* xxiii, Even as they fell, in files they lay. **1838** PRESCOTT *Ferd. & Is.* (1846) I. x. 406 Riding along their broken files. **1864** SKEAT *Uhland's Poems* 243 The brave Fernando, Searching through the files of war.

transf. and *fig.* *a* **1613** OVERBURY *A Wife* (1638) 109 Hunger and cold ranke in the same file with him. **1649** BP. HALL *Cases Consc.* (1650) 15 That we be not in the first file of enhancers. **1650** R. STAPYLTON *Strada's Low C. Warres* II. 44 He was by the Emperour valued in the first file of Nobility. *c* **1665** MRS. HUTCHINSON *Mem. Col. Hutchinson* (1846) 31 In all his actions it [valour] ever marched in the same file with wisdom. **1700** BLACKMORE *Song of Moses*, The foaming files o'ertook them in the chase. **1713** YOUNG *Last Day* II. 142 The radiant files of angels. **1842** TENNYSON *Locksley Hall* 178, I the heir of all the ages, in the foremost files of time.

b. Phrases: † ***to accept the files***, to open one's own ranks for a charging enemy to enter. ***to double the files***: to put two files in one and so make the ranks smaller; also *fig.* ***to close their files***, see CLOSE *v.* 10 b. ***to take the right-hand file***, to take precedence.

1616 BINGHAM *Ælian's Tactics* xxix. 137 *notes*, Double your files to the right or left hand. **1629** MASSINGER *Picture* III. v, There are Many..who may take..the right-hand file of you. **1642** FULLER *Holy & Prof. St.* I. i. 3 In her husbands absence she is wife and deputy-husband, which makes her double the files of her diligence. **1706** PHILLIPS (ed. Kersey) s.v. *File*, To Double the Files. **1868** KINGLAKE *Crimea* IV. v. 163 It used to be said of the foreigners that they 'accepted the files'.

c. A small body of men, formerly varying in number from two to twelve or more, but now usually two. Also, when 'marching in files' (see *file-marching* in 11), the two soldiers walking abreast.

1616 BINGHAM *Ælian's Tactics* xxix. 136 *notes*, When 16 men (that is a file) are so extended, that they possesse as much length as 32 should doe (that is, as 2 files). **1624** CAPT. SMITH *Virginia* VI. 239 They met with a file of Saluages that let fly their Arrowes. **1647** SPRIGGE *Anglia Rediv.* II. iv. (1854) 105 Twelve files of men with firearms and pikes. **1702** STEELE *Funeral* v. 70 A file of Men, Bumpkin, is six Men. **1769** *Junius Lett.* xxxi. 142 The general was escorted by a file of musqueteers. **1832** *Regul. Instr. Cavalry* III. 45 *A File*, two Soldiers placed one behind the other when formed in ranks, but abreast when marching in file. **1836** MARRYAT *Midsh. Easy* viii, I shall send a sergeant and a file of marines to fetch you. **1844** *Regul. & Ord. Army* 262 A Non-commissioned Officer, with a file of men.

d. An individual soldier.

1903 *Med. Record* 7 Feb. 227 (Cent. Dict. Suppl.), The poor file who has to carry it, as well as his gun and various other accoutrements. **1916** 'BOYD CABLE' *Action Front* 105 'Dusty Miller', the next file on his left,..spoke to him.

8. A row of persons, animals, or things placed one behind the other. ***the common file*** = 'the common herd' (*obs.* or *arch.*) ***in file***: one after another, in succession.

1603 SHAKS. *Meas. for M.* III. ii. 144 The greater file of the subiect held the Duke to be wise. **1607** —— *Cor.* I. vi. 43 The common file..did budge From Rascals worse then they. **1656** tr. *Hobbes' Elem. Philos.* 364 This Hoarse Sound..seemeth to be nothing but the dividing of the air into innumerable and very small Files. **1712–4** POPE *Rape Lock* I. 137 Here files of pins extend their shining rows. *a* **1734** NORTH *Lives* III. 134 He furnished..one state-apartment of divers rooms in file. **1740** SOMERVILLE *Hobbinol* III. 230 Before him march in Files The rural Minstralsy. **1794** WORDSW. *Guilt & Sorrow* iv, Long files of corn-stacks. **1826** DISRAELI *Viv. Grey* III. viii, I push my way into court through files of attorneys. *Ibid.* VI. i, A double file of wine-glasses and goblets. **1834** H. MILLER *Scenes & Leg.* xviii. (1857) 264 An endless file of bare gloomy cliffs. **1838** PRESCOTT *Ferd. & Is.* (1846) I. xi. 432 Whose military prowess had raised him from the common file. **1845** DARWIN *Voy. Nat.* ii. (1879) 35 When the ants came to the road they changed their course, and in narrow files reascended the wall. **1856** KANE *Arct. Expl.* I. xvi. 192 The men were standing in silent file on each side of it. **1867** LADY HERBERT *Cradle L.* iv. 121 A file of camels.

9. *Chess.* One of the eight lines of squares extending across the board from player to player. ***an open file***: one on which no piece or pawn of either colour is standing. ***to seize the***

open file: to place a rook or the queen on the first square.

1614 SAUL *Chesse-play* i. 3 Imagine that the blacke King for his first draught playeth his owne Pawne into the third house in his owne file. **1680** COTTON *Compl. Gamester* iv. (ed. 2) 39 The Rook goes backward and forward in any file. **1860** PARDON *Handbk. Chess* 15 The horizontal rows of squares are termed *ranks* and the vertical squares *files*.

10. The run or track of a hare; also, *to run her file* (see quot. 1838).

1815 *Sporting Mag.* XLV. 109 It is strictly necessary to look into the hares' files for wires. **1838** HOLLOWAY *Provincialisms*, When sportsmen say the hare runs her File, that is runs round the same track continually to foil or deceive the dogs.

11. *attrib.* and *Comb.*, as *file-closer, -leader* (†*-lead*), *-mark*; (sense 4) *file card, copy, cover, signal*. Also **file-fire, -firing**, firing by files, now called independent firing (opposed to volley-firing); **file-marching**, marching in files, by turning from a formation in line to the right or left, so that the line becomes a series of files facing to the right or left flank; †**file-wort**, Gerarde's rendering of botanical L. *filāgo*, the name of a genus of plants.

1966 *English Studies* XLVII. 200 It is as though a scholar ..were to decide to re-arrange a mountainous stack of *file-cards. **1836** J. HILDRETH *Dragoon Campaigns Rocky Mts.* I. vi. 48 Next in order of inspection came the adjutant, and, commencing at the right of the line, 'told off' the battalion by equal troops, the subalterns taking their stations in the rank of *file-closers. **1888** *Harper's Mag.* Apr. 788/1 The.. officers hidden as file-closers behind their companies. **1899** *Daily News* 23 Jan. 4/7 Prudent swains might find a *file copy extremely useful in general emergencies. **1909** *Daily Chron.* 2 Sept. 4/7 The file copy of 'The Daily Chronicle' of the same date. **1968** V. C. C. BADDELEY *My Foe Outstretch'd* ii. 27, I don't know why Miss Cragg couldn't give you a tape. .. I suppose..she's only got a file copy. **1925** J. G. BRUCE in E. F. Norton *Fight for Everest, 1924* VI. 349 A few *file covers are useful to keep the correspondence on various subjects separate. **1857** *New Boy at Styles's* in *Househ. Words* 9 May 436 The usual *file-fire of glances was exchanged. **1837** CARLYLE *Fr. Rev.* III. VI. iii. 324 His Jurymen are charged to make feu de file, *file-firing till the ground be clear. **1847** *Infantry Man.* (1854) 40 Independent or file firing may commence. **1775** ASH, **File-lead*..the foremost man in the file. **1616** BINGHAM *Ælian's Tactics* v. 42 Hee that leadeth the file, who is also called the *file-leader. **1796–7** *Instr. & Reg. Cavalry* (1813) 18 The file leaders preserve such distances as they ought from which ever hand they are to dress to. **1809** W. IRVING *Knickerb.* (1861) 135 Most people require a..file-leader. **1847** *Infantry Man.* (1854) 49 *File marching may be adopted. **1961** *Lebende Sprachen* VI. 69/2 Office furniture, machines and supplies. *File signal. **1597** GERARDE *Herbal* App, *Filewort is *Filago minor*.

†**file**, *sb.*^{3} *Obs.* [a. OF. *file* (Fr. *fille*) girl:—L. *filia* daughter.] A girl, woman; also in a bad sense, a concubine, a whore.

1303 R. BRUNNE *Handl. Synne* 4540 To rage wyþ ylka fyle [*gl.* maydgerle]. **1393** LANGL. *P. Pl.* C. VII. 135 Dame purnele a prestes file, prioresse worth hue neuere.

†**file**, *sb.*^{4} *Obs.* [a. ON. *fýla* foulness, fig. foul person, f. *fúll* FOUL *a.*] A worthless person (male or female); a rascal.

a **1300** *Cursor M.* 715 (Cott.) Sorful bicom þat fals file. *c* **1300** *Havelok* 2499 Men mithe thethen a mile Here him rore, that fule file. *c* **1330** R. BRUNNE *Chron.* (1810) 95 þat did Roberd trauaile for nouht, he was a file. *c* **1450** *Douce MS.* 559 (Bodleian) Quest. 240 My brotheres wyfe may be a fyle.

†**file** (faɪl), *sb.*^{5} *slang. Obs.* Also 7 foyl, 8 foile. [First appears in the longer form *foyl-cloy* (later *file-cloy*); possibly this is not a comb. of *file* sb., but the original from which the latter is shortened; but the etymology is unknown. Cf. *to file a cly* (FILE *v.*^{4}).] A pick-pocket. Also, *file-cloy, -lifter*.

1673 R. HEAD *Canting Acad.* 191 The sixth is a Foyl-cloy. **1676** *Warning for Housekprs.* Title-p., Budg and Snudg, File-lifter, Tongue-padder, the private Theif. **1695** KENNETT *Par. Antiq.* Gloss. s.v. *Putta*, A file, or pick-pocket whore. **1708** MOTTEUX *Rabelais* (1737) V. 218 Pickpockets, Divers, Buttocking-Foiles. **1721** BAILEY, Bulk and File, is when one jostles you while another picks your pocket. **1725** *New Cant. Dict., File-Cloy*, a Pickpocket, Thief or Rogue. **1743** FIELDING *Jon. Wild* IV. xiii, A Pick-pocket, or, in truer Language, a File.

†**file**, *sb.*^{6} *Obs.* Apparently = *Fylde*, proper name of a district in Lancashire.

1775 SIR E. BARRY *Observ. Wines* 416 The..files of Lancashire.

file (faɪl), *sb.*^{7} *U.S. local.* [app. a. Du. *feil*, given in Bomhoff's Dict. as variant or synonym of *dweil* floor-cloth, corresp. to ON. *þvegill* towel:—OTeut. **þvagilo-z* f. **þwahan* (OE. *þwéan*) to wash.] A cloth used for wiping a floor or a table after scrubbing, a house-flannel.

1851 ELIZ. WARNER *Wide W. World* II. xxii. (1852) 368 'A file!' said Ellen..'O I remember now..I didn't know what you meant. Margery calls it a dish-cloth, or a floor-cloth, or something else'. **1860** in BARTLETT *Dict. Amer.* **1889** in FARMER *Americanisms*.

file (faɪl), *v.*^{1} Forms: 3 *south.* vile, 4–7 fyle, (5 fylin), 6 fill, 5– file. [f. FILE *sb.*^{1}; cf. OHG. *fîlôn* (MHG. *vîlen*, mod.G. *feilen*), Du. *vijlen*.]

1. *trans.* To rub smooth, reduce the surface of, with a file. *to file* (*one's*) *teeth*: (*fig.*) to render harmless. *to file in* (or †*a*) *two*: to cut in two by filing.

In the contextual use 'to sharpen' (weapons) sometimes associated with AFFILE.

a **1225** *Ancr. R.* 284 And nis þet iren acursed þet iwruðeð þe swarture & þe ruhure so hit is ofture & more iviled? *c* **1340** *Gaw. & Gr. Knt.* 2225 A denez ax..Fyled in a fylor. *c* **1420** *Chron. Vilod.* 354 And a file to file þis nayle a two. **1542–3** *Act 34–5 Hen. VIII*, c. 6 Pinnes..shal..haue..the point well and rounde, filled, canted and sharped. **1553** EDEN *Treat. Newe Ind.* (Arb.) 16 He fyleth and whetteth his horne on a stone. **1599** *Broughton's Lett.* i. 6 It is..time enough to file your teeth, or muzzle you. **1696** LUTTRELL *Brief Rel.* (1857) IV. 65 Some persons are committed for fyling the edges of new shillings. **1787** HOLCROFT tr. *Life Baron Trenck* (1886) II. 33, I filed the iron which passed through it on the outside. **1876** VOYLE *Milit. Dict.* (ed. 3) s.v. *File*, Leaving the surface that has been filed more or less smooth.

absol. **1680** COTTON *Compl. Gamester* i. (ed. 2) 10 Others have made them [false dice] by filing and rounding. **1888** HASLUCK *Mech. Workshop Handybk.* 85 Take an old file and file away steadily.

b. *fig.* To remove the roughness of; to smooth, polish, elaborate to perfection. Also, to wear *down*; to bring *into* (a certain condition) as if by filing.

c **1400** *Rom. Rose* 3812 His tunge was fyled sharpe & square. **1551** RECORDE *Pathw. Knowl.* title-p., All fresshe fine wittes by me are filed. **1568** T. HOWELL *Arb. Amitie* (1879) 101 Nor he that files his smoothed speeche. *c* **1600** SHAKS. *Sonn.* lxxxv, Precious phrase by all Muses fil'd. **1700** DRYDEN *Fables* Pref. Wks. (Globe) 494 Dante had begun to file their language, at least in verse. **1757** WESLEY *Wks.* (1872) IX. 192 The Treatise..which he has had leisure for many years to revise, file, correct, and strengthen against all objections. **1820** SCOTT *Ivanhoe* ii, And file your tongue to a little more courtesy. **1837** DICKENS *Pickw.* xlii, His bones [were] sharp and thin..the iron teeth of confinement and privation had been slowly filing them down for twenty years. **1889** *Temple Bar Mag.* Nov. 406 Lads who would be filed into business shape.

2. To remove (roughnesses, part of a surface, etc.) by filing. Now only with *away, off*. Also *fig.*

a **1225** *Ancr. R.* 184 He is þi uile & uileð awei al þi rust. **1597** HOOKER *Eccl. Pol.* v. xxvii. (1611) 241 They that would file away most from the largenesse of that offer. *a* **1618** RALEIGH *Advice of Son* (1651) 7 Death hath already filed from you the better part of your natural forces. **1625** FLETCHER *Noble Gent.* I. i, That..Files off all rudeness and uncivil 'haviour. **1670** CLARENDON *Ess.* Tracts (1727) 216 He will never file away the stain. **1707** NORRIS *Treat. Humility* iii. 154 It [Humility]..files off the roughnesses of our passions. **1833** J. HOLLAND *Manuf. Metal* II. 291 They adjusted the balance by filing away some of the thickness of the longest part of the beam. **1850** H. ROGERS *Ess.* II. iv. 204 What was required was to file away asperities [in language]. **1859** TENNYSON *Vivien* 621 So grated down and filed away with thought.

file (faɪl), *v.*^{2} Forms: 2–3 fulen, 3 filen(n, 3–6 fele, 4–8 fyle, (6 fyll, 7 feel), 3– file. [OE. **fýlan*, in combs. *a-, be-, ȝefýlan*) = MDu. *vuilen*, OHG. *fûlen*:—OTeut. **fûljan*, f. **fûlo-* FOUL *a.*

In early southern ME. the spelling *fule-n* represents both this vb. (the *u* being sounded (y)) and the originally intransitive vb. FOUL:—OE. *fúlian*.]

1. *trans.* To render (materially) foul, filthy or dirty; to pollute, dirty; to destroy the cleanness or purity of; = DEFILE *v.*^{1} 2. *Obs.* exc. *dial.*

13.. *E.E. Allit. P.* B. 136 No festiual frok but fyled with werkkez. **1340** HAMPOLE *Pr. Consc.* 2348 A thyng es fouler þat may file þan þe thyng þat it fyles. *c* **1475** *Rauf Coilȝear* 446 Oft fylit my feit in mony foull fen. **1494** FABYAN *Chron.* VI. cxcvii. 202 He felyd the holy lyker with the fruyte of his wombe. **1523** FITZHERB. *Husb.* §41 If any shepe..be fyled with dounge about the tayle. **1611** G. WILKINS *Miseries Inforced Marr.* v. in *Old Plays* (1825) V. 86 As not to file my hands in villain's blood. **1721** KELLY *Sc. Prov.* 384 You need not file the House for want of Legs to carry you to the Midding. **1753** *Stewart's Trial* App. 84 A piece which is laid by foul, will..file one's finger. **1792** BURNS *Willie's Wife* iv, Her face wad fyle the Logan Water. **1825** SOUTHEY *Tale Paraguay* III. 44 No art of barbarous ornament had..'filed her face. **1888** ELWORTHY *W. Somerset Word-bk., File*, to defile.

fig. **1607** TOURNEUR *Rev. Trag.* II. Wks. 1878 II. 644 A word that I abhorre to file my lips with. **1606** BRYSKETT *Civ. Life* 78 He will not vouchsafe himselfe to file his hands vpon so base..a person.

b. *Proverbs.*

a **1250** *Owl & Night.* 100 Dahet habbe that ilke beste, That fuleth his owe nest. **1568** *Jacob & Esau* II. iii. in Hazl. *Dodsley* II. 216 Claw a churl by the tail and he will file your hand. **1823** GALT *Entail* II. xx. 190 It's a foul bird that files its ain nest.

†**c.** *intr.* for *refl.* To become soiled. *Obs.*

1565 CALFHILL *Answ. Treat. Cross* (1846) 132 His garments never filed; nor his shoes..waxed old.

†**d.** *absol.* Also *intr.*, to void excrement. *Obs.*

1560 BECON *New Catech.* Wks. (1844) 62 If doves, or any other fowls or beasts file upon their [i.e. the images] heads, they perceive it not. **1611** G. WILKINS *Miseries Inforced Marr.* III. in *Old Plays* (1825) V. 40 Oaths are..like smoak from a chimney that files all the way it goes.

†**2.** *trans.* To taint with disease, infect. Obs.

1456 *Sc. Acts James II* (1814) §6 And not lat þame pas away fra þe place..to fyle þe cuntre about thame.

3. To render morally foul or polluted; to destroy the ideal purity of; to corrupt, taint, sully; = DEFILE *v.*^{1} 3. *Obs.* exc. *arch.*

[*c* **1175** *Cott. Hom.* 205 Ich habbe..mid flesches fulðe ifuled me.] *c* **1200** ORMIN 1959 þatt nan ne shollde filedd ben Wiþþ hæpenndom þurrh macche. *c* **1290** *S. Eng. Leg.* I. 287/314 Alle þo..þat his ordre fuylden ouȝt with..worldes feo. *a* **1340** HAMPOLE *Psalter* Prol., To confourme men þat are filyd in adam til crist in newnes of lyf. **1434** MISYN *Mending of Life* 129 No man filys hym-self with wardly bisynes after þat he truly has ioyd in lufe euerlastyng. **1513** DOUGLAS *Æneis* IV. Prol. 104 Is that trew luif, guid faith and fame to fyle? **1605** SHAKS. *Macb.* III. i. 65 For Banquo's Issue haue I fil'd my Minde. **1816** BYRON *Ch. Har.* III. cxiii, Had I not filed my mind, which thus itself subdued. **1860** TROLLOPE *Framley P.* xxxiii. 539 Why had he thus filed his mind?

†**4.** To violate the chastity of, to deflower; to debauch. *Obs.* = DEFILE *v.*^{1} 4.

? *a* **1400** *Morte Arth.* 978 He has forsede hir and fylede. *c* **1460** *Towneley Myst.* (Surtees) 75 For me was she never fylyd. **15..** *Peebles to Play* xviii, 'Ye fyl'd me; fy, for shame!' quoth she.

†**5.** To sully the honour of, dishonour. *Obs.* = DEFILE *v.*^{1} 6.

c **1250** *Gen. & Ex.* 3498 Tac ðu noȝt in idel min name[n] Ne swer it les to fele in gamen. *c* **1400** *Destr. Troy* 8120 Euery lede will þe lacke and þi lose file. *c* **1440** *Gesta Rom.* xvii. 62 (Harl. MS.) He made the new lawe, & fylid not þat othir. *c* **1470** HARDING *Chron.* CCXVIII. v, They the trewce had broken and did fyle. *c* **1500** *Doctr. Gd. Servaunts* 10 A good name that none dooth fyle. **1502** *Ord. Crysten Men* (W. de W. 1506) IV. xxi. 251 If he hath broken and fyled the preuyleges of the chyrche. **1594** JAS. VI in Tytler *Hist. Scot.* (1864) IV. 217 That so wise and provident a prince [Elizabeth]..should be so fyled and contemned by a great number of her own subjects. *a* **1668** D'AVENANT *Siege* III. (1673) 75 The bold warrier, that hath deserv'd Fame..once feel'd [*mod. ed.* fil'd] his victories Are quite forgot.

†**6.** To charge with a crime, accuse. *Obs.*

c **1460** *Towneley Myst.* (Surtees) 273 To thare prynces thay can hym fyle. *c* **1560** *Durham Depositions* (Surtees) 64 Mr. Ratlyf was in great greif that Doon shuld fyll his man Dixon for certain shepe. **1721** KELLY *Sc. Prov.* 376 You are busy to clear your self when no Body files you. **1759** FOUNTAINHALL *Decisions* I. 14 They..were ready to file, by their delation, sundry gentlewomen.

†**b.** To find guilty, condemn. *Obs.*

c **1330** R. BRUNNE *Chron.* (1810) 173 þe courte opon him sat, þe quest filed him & schent. **1525** in Pitcairn *Crim. Trials Scot.* I. *131 Quhil þai had..fylit þame of þe said slauchtir. **1609** SKENE *Reg. Maj.* IV. i. §5 Gif anie man is fyled or condemned of that crime. **1673–50** ROW *Hist. Kirk* (1842) 387 He was noted as if he had fylled him.

Hence †**filed** *ppl. a.*

1483 *Cath. Angl.* 130/2 Filed, *deturpatus*. **1590** SPENSER *F.Q.* III. i. 62 She lightly lept out of her filed bedd, And to her weapon ran. **1593** Q. ELIZ. *Boeth.* (E.E.T.S.) 95 His fyled conscience.

file (faɪl), *v.*^{3} Also 5–7 fyle, (fill, fyll). [f. FILE *sb.*^{2}]

1. a. *trans.* †To string upon a thread (*obs.*); to place (documents) on a file; to place (papers) in consecutive order for preservation and reference. Also, † *to file together, up* (obs.).

1601 HOLLAND *Pliny* II. 613 Their maner is to bore holes through them, and then to file them vp into chains and collars. **1625** B. JONSON *Staple of N.* I. i, They..sort and file And read the news and issue them. **1653** H. COGAN tr. *Pinto's Trav.* xxxvi. 142 At her arm-pits hung a many of little idols..filed together. **1682** GREW *Anat. Plants* Pref. 3 A Letter..now filed amongst others in the Custody of the Royal Society. **1770** FRANKLIN *Wks.* (1887) IV. 364 No care is taken to file the newspapers. **1865** DICKENS *Mut. Fr.* III. ii, Miss Abbey filed her receipts.

transf. and *fig.* **1581** J. BELL *Haddon's Answ. Osor.* 292 Let not this accusation of Osorius be filed uppe amongst the other hys false reproches and lyes. **1596** SPENSER *F.Q.* IV. ii. 32 Dan Chaucer..On fames eternall beadroll worthie to be fyled. **1632** MASSINGER *Maid of Hon.* IV. iii, I am no churchman: Such a one must file it on record. **1647** FANSHAWE *Pastor Fido* 187 Thou dost file One Lye upon another well. **1753** SHORT in *Phil. Trans.* XLVIII. 14 F. Frisi..files it up, as the sixth of the errors, which he says have been discovered in the Principia. **1778** *Arminian Mag.* I. 201 Lest I should be filed upon that chain.

b. *spec.* To place (a document) in a due manner among the records of a court or public office; esp. *to file a bill* (*in Chancery*), *an information*. Also, † *to file up* (*obs.*).

1511–2 *Act 3 Hen. VIII*, c. 23 §3 The same accomptes.. to be taken and filed up in the Pipe. *Ibid.* §5 The Kinges said lettres missives annexed and fyled to the same Accomptes. **1529** MORE *Dyaloge* III. Wks. 213/1 He..therwith brought in those letters and filed them amonge the recordes of the court. **1677** *Lond. Gaz.* No. 1211/4 If they do not forthwith File and Enter all such their Proceedings. **1769** BLACKSTONE *Comm.* IV. 305 When an information is filed. **1776** *Trial of Nundocomar* 80/1 An office copy of the executors' accounts ..filed the first of October, 1774. **1818** CRUISE *Digest* (ed. 2) II. 20 Leaving two daughters, who..afterwards filed a bill in Chancery against the trustees. **1835** T. P. GRANGER *Tomlins' Law-Dict.* (ed. 4) I. s.v. *Bankrupt* 11, *By what Acts ..a Trader may become a Bankrupt*... If any..trader shall file..a declaration..that he is insolvent..the..secretary of bankrupts..shall sign a memorandum that such declaration hath been filed. **1853** MARSDEN *Early Purit.* 387 The king.. cancelled the judgments filed against him. **1886** WILLIAMS in *Encycl. Brit.* (ed. 9) XX. 342/1 The difference between filing and registration is that the documents filed are filed without alteration, while only an epitome is usually registered. **1957** *Encycl. Brit.* III. 66/2 An act of bankruptcy is committed..if he [*sc.* the debtor] files in court a declaration of inability to pay his debts. **1966** *Times* 12 Aug. 14/4 About 80 of the world's larger foreign companies whose shares are traded in the United States have filed public financial information about their operations.

fig. **1619** MIDDLETON *Inner-Temple Masques* C i b, Thy faire desires in Vertue's Court are fil'de. **1742** YOUNG *Nt. Th.* vii. 502 Let conscience file the sentence in her court.

c. *N. Amer.* To file a claim *on* or *upon*, assert a title to, apply for (a piece of land or a mining claim); also *absol.*

1871 *Scribner's Monthly* II. 254 The half-breed who had 'filed on' the claim alongside Lindley's. **1879** [see FILE *v.*³ 4 c]. **1893** *Congress. Rec.* 11 Feb. 1470/1 Many persons filed upon these lands. **1910** W. A. FRASER *Red Meekins* (1921) 194 First thing in the mornin' we'll hike to the outside an' file the claim. **1911** J. F. WILSON *Land Claimers* 2 The relinquishment has been made in Portland where you filed. **1932** T. G. SPRINGER *Sagebrush Buckaroo* (1933) xxii. 252 You thought to stake out all the locations, file on them with dummies, and.. get the cream! **1948** *Sat. Even. Post* 4 Dec. 70/2 He.. had assays made and was on the way to file his claim, but I got him drunk and filed myself. **1968** R. M. PATTERSON *Finlay's River* 29 F. H. Davis was the first man alert enough to stake the fraction and get in first to the mining recorder's office to file.

d. Of a newspaper reporter: to transmit (a story, information, etc.) to his newspaper.

1954 D. DODGE *Lights of Skaro* ii. 57 A reporter could file one, and only one, story the Party didn't like before they cancelled his visa. **1964** *New Statesman* 13 Mar. 387/2 They agreed not to file their stories for that morning's British papers.

†**2.** To arrange in consecutive order. *Obs.*

c **1450** *Bk. Curtasye* 435 in *Babees Bk.* 313 Gromes palettes shyn fyle and make litere. *c* **1470** HARDING *Chron.* VII. i, In balade thus it shall be made and fyled. **1607** FLETCHER *Woman-hater* I. ii, I would have my several courses and my dishes well filed. **1676** GREW *Anat. Flowers* i. §4 (1682) 164 Not being filed one just over another but alternately.

†**3.** To arrange (men, soldiers) in a file, or files.

1598 BARRET *Theor. Warres* III. i. 44 The other halfe is to be brought vnto the traine of the pikes, and there filed in like maner. **1623** BINGHAM *Xenophon* 87 They stood a hundred deepe.. filing themselues one opposite to the other. **1642** FULLER *Holy & Prof. St.* III. xviii. 200 The King of Sweden never filed his men above six deep in one company. **1643** SIR T. BROWNE *Relig. Med.* II. §1 One man is ranked with another, another filed before him, according to the quality of his desert.

4. a. *intr.* To march or move in file. Also with *away*, etc. *to file off*, 'to wheel off by files from moving in a spacious front, and march in length' (Stocqueler *Mil. Encycl.*).

1616 BINGHAM *Ælian's Tactics* xix. 109 *notes*, The first [kind of Rhombe] both filed and ranked, this neither fileth, nor ranketh. **1703** *Lond. Gaz.* No. 3914/5 Some of their Battalions filed up several steep and narrow Passages. **1704** *Ibid.* No. 4054/1 At night they filed and stood to the Northward. **1708** *Ibid.* No. 4475/3 The Enemy filed off.. towards the Thickets. **1749** FIELDING *Tom Jones* IX. iii, This fair creature entering the field of battle, immediately filed to that wing where [etc.]. **1796–7** *Instr. & Reg. Cavalry* (1813) 89 The whole divisions then file from their reverse flanks. **1808** SCOTT *Marm.* I. xxxi, Till, filing from the gate, he past That noble train. **1813** WELLINGTON in Gurw. *Desp.* XI. 101 *note*, The French troops shall file out tomorrow morning. **1858** HAWTHORNE *Fr. & It. Jrnls.* (1872) I. 70 A party of Americans filed into his studio. **1876** F. E. TROLLOPE *Charming Fellow* I. iv. 48 The players file off in the wake of the host. **1883** E. E. HALE in *Harper's Mag.* Dec. 145/2 They filed away for the south.

†**b.** To march in line, keep pace *with*; in quot. *fig. Obs.*

1613 SHAKS. *Hen. VIII*, III. ii. 171 My endeauors Haue euer come too short of my Desires Yet filld [*mod. edd.* filed] with my Abilities. **1619** FLETCHER *M. Thomas* I. ii, Too light .. To fyle with her affections.

c. U.S. *to file upon*: to march upon, occupy (vacant land).

1879 H. KING in *Scribner's Mag.* Nov. 132/1 Intervals not yet 'filed upon' or 'opened up'.

5. *trans.* To cause or order (soldiers) to file *off*.

1831 *Examiner* 338/1 When the soldiers had returned.. they were filed off in four divisions to receive billets for the night.

Hence **'filing** *ppl. a.*

1616 BINGHAM *Ælian's Tactics* xix. 110 *notes*, The filing Rhombe began at the front point & reare-point & proceeded to the flanks.

†**file,** *v.*⁴ *slang. Obs.* [Cf. FILE *sb.*⁵] To pick pockets. Also, *to file a cly*.

a **1700** B. E. *Dict. Cant. Crew* s.v. *Tout, Do you Bulk and I'll File*, if you'll jostle him, I will Pick his Pocket. *Ibid.* s.v. *Cly, Filed a Cly*, Pickt a Pocket.

Hence **'filer**, a pick-pocket. **'filing** *vbl. sb.*, the action of the vb. FILE, in comb. *filing-lay*, pocket-picking.

1674 COTTON *Compl. Gamester* i. (1680) 5 Filers, Budgies, Droppers.. &c... may all pass under the general.. appellation of Rooks. **1719** D'URFEY *Pills* III. 100 A filer my Sister, a Filcher my Brother. **1743** FIELDING *J. Wild* IV. ii, I am committed for the Filing-Lay.

file, obs. var. of VILE, FOIL *sb.*

filed (faɪld), *ppl. a.* [f. FILE *v.*¹ + -ED¹.] In senses of the vb.: chiefly *fig.* of speech, etc.: Polished, smooth, neatly finished off or elaborated; fine (now *rare*). Also with defining word prefixed as *fair-filed*, *true-filed* adjs.

c **1530** LD. BERNERS *Arth. Lyt. Bryt.* (1814) 477 Thy tong is fayre fyled. **1548–77** VICARY *Anat.* Pref. Verse, That fyled phrase. **1570** B. GOOGE *Pop. Kingd.* II. 22 b, Their eloquence, and filed tongue. **1599** A. M. tr. *Gabelhouer's Bk. Physicke* 379/2 Take filed Iron. **1603** KNOLLES *Hist. Turks* (1621) 328 Wee goe not about with filed speech and rich rewards to circumvent thee. **1623** B. JONSON *Pref. Verses* in *1st Fo. Shaks.*, In his well torned, and true-filed lines. **1823** SCOTT *Quentin D.* xxx, Thou hast a better filed tongue than either Crèvecœur or I. **1888** HASLUCK *Mech. Workshop Handybk.* 87 With regard to finishing filed work. **1892** *Nation* 4 Aug. 88/3 Mr. Aldrich's filed lines.. show his even power.

file-fish. [f. FILE *sb.*¹ + FISH *sb.*] †**a.** = *file-shell* (FILE *sb.*¹ 5). *Obs.* **b.** A fish of the genus *Balistes*, having its skin granulated like a file.

1774 GOLDSM. *Nat. Hist.* VII. iv. 61 The latter [kind] are called Pholades or File Fish. **1815** *Trans. Lit. & Philos. Soc. N.Y.* I. 467 Tut-mouthed file-fish. *Balistes broccus.* **1839–47** TODD *Cycl. Anat.* III. 977/2 The incisors of the File-fish. **1962** K. F. LAGLER et al. *Ichthyology* vi. 192 Both the dorsal and the anal fins are moderately long-based in the triggerfishes and filefishes (Balistidae). **1969** A. WHEELER *Fishes Brit. Isles & N.-W. Europe* 565 Trigger-fish (File-fish).

filemot ('fɪlɪmɒt), *a.* and *sb.* Forms: α. 7–8 feuill(e)mort, (7 fueillemort), f(i)eulamo(r)t, fi(l)-amo(r)t, -imot, (8 foliomort), 8–9 fillemot, 8–filemot. β. 7 philia-, phylia-, phyllamort, 7–8 philemort, 7–9 philamot, (8 -mort), -omot, 9 phil(l)imot. [A corruption of FEUILLEMORTE.]

A. *adj.* = FEUILLEMORTE *a.*

1647 R. STAPYLTON *Juvenal* 98 Her fieulamort old gownes he begs. **1688** R. HOLME *Armoury* II. 247/1 The Wings of a Feuill-mort colour. **1698** J. PETIVER in *Phil. Trans.* XX. 334 They are of a Tawny or Phyllamort Colour. **1702** *Lond. Gaz.* No. 3835/4 A Feulamort Persian Silk. **1712** ADDISON *Spect.* No. 265 ¶5 One of them was blue, another yellow, and another Philomot. **1794** MARTYN *Rousseau's Bot.* xvii. 239 The leaves fade first to purple, and then to feuillemort colour. **1840** BROWNING *Sordello* II. 313 Let Vidal change.. His murrey-coloured robe for philamot, And crop his hair. **1880** L. WALLACE *Ben-Hur* 177 Each compartment crowded with labelled folios all filemot with age and use.

b. Comb. ***filemot-coloured*** adj.

1681 CHETHAM *Angler's Vade-m.* xxxiv. §8 (1689) 188 Philomot coloured Mohairs. **1847** JAMES *J. Marston Hall* xxvii, A fillemot-coloured cloak lined with light blue.

B. *sb.* The name of a colour, viz. that of a dead or faded leaf; (may have a plural).

1655 W. ROKEBY in *Surtees Misc.* (1858) 16, I would have it trimmed with a.. philamot or some pretty colour. **1657** R. LIGON *Barbadoes* (1673) 3 Instead of the fresh and lively greens.. these [islands] were apparrel'd with Russets, or at best Phyliamorts. **1659** LOVELACE *Poems* (1864) 169 Lucasta ..'stills new life in fields of fueillemort. **1703** M. MARTIN *Descr. W. Isl.* (1716) 135 It's of a dark colour, and only dyes a Philamot. **1721** CIBBER *Double Gallant* I, A mottly crowd of Blacks, Tawny, Olives, Feulamots, and pale Blues. *a* **1745** SWIFT *Direct. Servants, Footman*, The colours you ought to wish for are blue, or filemot, turned up with red. **1841** *Brand's Pop. Antiq.* II. 173 The Egyptians [use] yellow, or fillemot. **1844** JAMES *Agincourt* I. 37 His tight-fitting hose were of a light philimot, or brownish yellow.

filer¹ ('faɪlə(r)). [f. FILE *v.*¹ + -ER¹.] One who files or works with a file; *spec.* †one who files down gold and silver coin.

1598 FLORIO, *Limaro*, a filer or maker of files. **1660** HOWELL *Lexicon*, A Filer, *limeur*. **1692** LUTTRELL *Brief Rel.* (1857) II. 554 Severall clippers, coinners, and filers taken up in the Mint on Sunday last, and sent to Newgate. **1882** *Birm. Weekly Post* 24 June 5/5 Gun-action Filers wanted. **1884** *Birm. Daily Post* 23 Feb. 3/5 Spur Filer and Finisher wanted.

filer² ('faɪlə(r)). [f. FILE *v*³ + -ER¹.] **a.** One who places something upon a file. **b.** An apparatus for filing or holding papers.

1880 *Libr. Univ. Knowl.* (N.Y.) XI. 377 Notice is given to the filer of the *caveat*. **1874** KNIGHT *Dict. Mech.*, *Filer*, an office device for holding bills and loose papers.

filer³: see FILE *v.*⁴

filet ('fɪlɪt). Also fillet. [a. F. *filet* thread.]

1. A kind of net or lace having a square mesh. Also *attrib.*, as *filet lace*, *net*, *veiling*.

1881 C. C. HARRISON *Woman's Handiwork* I. 82 Drawn-work, with darned filet and cut-work. **1904** GOODCHILD & TWENEY *Technol. & Sci. Dict.* 221/1 *Fillet ground*, a net with absolutely square holes, similar to canvas, but more defined and 'lacey' in appearance. **1907** *Westm. Gaz.* 9 Mar. 13/2 The lace might be of cream silk filet. **1907** *Daily Chron.* 25 June 8/3 The new filet designs. **1907** *Westm. Gaz.* 24 Aug. 13/1 A nice tea-gown.. with filet laces. **1908** *Ibid.* 8 Aug. 13/2 The square spotted filet veiling. *Ibid.* 28 Dec. 5/1 A brown filet net trimmed with small rosettes of velvet. **1931** *Evening Standard* 29 Jan. 5/3 Fadeless artificial silk filet net. **1953** M. POWYS *Lace & Lace-Making* iv. 33 Lacis or filet, 16th century. A rare pointed pattern made for collars or to border a cover. The groundwork is the knotted filet mesh made like a fish net and with the same implements.

2. (‖file) *Cookery.* = FILLET *sb.* 6 a, c. Also in phr. *filet de bœuf*.

1841 THACKERAY *Misc. Ess.* (1885) 385 The beefsteak cut from the filet, as is usual in France. **1861** MRS. BEETON *Bk. Househ. Managem.* 918 Entrees, Filet de Bœuf and Spanish Sauce. **1864** G. MEREDITH *Let.* 24 Feb. (1970) I. 245 Smooth flow the Sauces!—may the filets tender be! **1951** E. DAVID *French Country Cooking* 114 Your beef.. should be a fine piece of *filet*. **1962** *Harper's Bazaar* Aug. 69/1 Tournedos steaks cut from the tail end of a *filet de boeuf*.

b. ***filet mignon***: a slice cut from the small end of the tenderloin of beef.

1906 'O. HENRY' *Four Million* (1916) 67 'We'll have oysters to-night.' 'And filet mignon with champignons.' **1960** L. COOPER *Accomplices* III. iv. 176 A delightful meal —caviare, an iced consommé, a filet mignon. **1961** J. HELLER *Catch-22* (1962) xxii. 233 Yossarian and Orr.. went.. to eat shrimp cocktails and filet mignon in a very fine restaurant.

filet(e), obs. form of FILLET.

‖**fili** ('fɪlɪ). Also fileadh, filid(h. [Ir. *filí*, *fileadha*, *filidh*, pl. forms of *file* poet.] The name given in Irish to an ancient order of poets.

1876 *Encycl. Brit.* V. 303/1 The Fili truly represents the Οὐάτεις, or vates, who formed one of the orders of Druids, mentioned by Strabo. **1880** *Ibid.* XIII. 250/2 The *filid*, whom we shall conventionally call bards.. were part of the transformed Druidic order... An ollam fili, the highest grade of the order, was entitled to a large retinue of pupils. **1898** J. HERON *Celtic Ch.* 30 Entrance into the ranks of the Ollamhs and the Fileadh (or poets). **1933** *Times Lit. Suppl.* 26 Jan. 53/1 The *filid*, the poet-seers who have descendants in the land. **1957** *Ibid.* 25 Oct. 636/2 The bards were reciters, employed by the *fili*, or professional poets.

filial ('fɪlɪəl), *a.* Also 6 feliall, fyliall, 6–7 filiall. [ad. late L. *filiāl-is*, f. *fili-us* son. Cf. F. *filial.*]

1. Of or pertaining to a son or daughter.

a. Of sentiments, duty, etc.: Due from a child to a parent. *filial fear*: see FEAR *sb.*¹ 3 d.

1393 LANGL. *P.Pl.* C. IX. 216 Ys no final [*v.r.* filial] loue with þis folke. **1532** MORE *Confut. Tindale* Wks. 700/1 Christen people receiue the spirit of feliall loue. **1667** MILTON *P.L.* XII. 306 Disciplin'd.. from servil fear To filial. **1759** ROBERTSON *Hist. Scot.* I. VII. 494 James had hitherto treated his mother with filial respect. **1834** HT. MARTINEAU *Demerara* xii, Now her filial cares were ended. **1857** H. REED *Lect. Eng. Poets* II. xi. 67 The filial piety of her children for poor auld Scotland.

†**b.** That is the due of a son or daughter. *Obs.*

1558 *Wills & Inv. N.C.* (Surtees) II. 175, I giue to my said Sonne Rob'rt in full contentacion & payment of his fyliall porcion.. of all my goodes. **1635** QUARLES *Embl.* II. xv. (1718) 121 At length corrected by the filial rod Of his offended, but his gracious God. **1795** WYTHE *Decis. Virginia* 6 The sum of the plaintiff Mary's filial portion.

c. Of a relation, designation, etc.: Characteristic of a son or daughter.

1659 PEARSON *Creed* (1839) 150 The primitive Christians did.. include this filial title of our Saviour together with his names into the compass of one word.

transf. **1874** STUBBS *Const. Hist.* (1875) I. iii. 52 The foundation of new villages.. standing in a filial relation to the original settlement.

2. a. 'Bearing the character or relation of a son or daughter' (J.) Now only *transf.* and *fig.* of a thing: That is the offspring of something else. ***filial generation*** Biol., the offspring of a cross, the ***first filial*** (or F_1) ***generation*** being the immediate offspring of the organisms selected for crossing, the ***second filial*** (or F_2) ***generation*** being produced usually by self-fertilisation or intercrossing of F_1 individuals, and so on.

1667 MILTON *P.L.* VI. 722 Thus the filial Godhead answering spake. *a* **1711** KEN *Psyche* Wks. 1721 IV. 185 Paternal God gave filial God to die. **1718** PRIOR *Celia to Damon* 102 Where the old Myrtle her good Influence sheds; Sprigs of like Leaf erect their Filial Heads. **1762** tr. *Busching's Syst. Geog.* IV. 213 A collegiate-church, to which .. belong four other filial churches. **1889** *Times* 13 Aug. 3/1 The size of the parent seed was reproduced in the filial seed. **1902** [see F. III. 1 i]. **1909** W. BATESON *Mendel's Princ. Heredity* i. 8 Mendel took a pair of varieties of which one was tall.. and the other was dwarf... These two were then crossed together... In our modern terminology such a cross-bred, the first filial generation, is called F_1. **1938** E. B. FORD *Study of Heredity* ii. 30 If we cross a black bird with a white, all the offspring are grey... These are the 'first filial' generation of our cross. *Ibid.*, If we mate the grey F_1 birds with one another, we obtain a 'second filial generation' (F_2). **1969** *Dict. Gardening Suppl.* (R. Hort. Soc.) 454/2 The plants obtained in this first Hybrid Filial (F_1) generation are all tall like one of the parents.

†**b.** Entertaining the sentiments of a son or daughter. *Obs. rare.*

1754 RICHARDSON *Grandison* V. ii. 20 Your ever affectionate and filial friend.

†**c.** *absol.* (quasi sb.) An off-shoot. *Obs.*

1538 LELAND *Itin.* (1711) VII. 48 The Body of the Cathedral Chyrch [in Carlisle] is of an older Building then the Quyer. And yt ys as a Filial deriveid from S. Oswalds fast by Pontfreyt. **1762** tr. *Busching's Syst. Geog.* IV. 214 This church is a filial of the parish of St. Veit.

filiality (fɪlɪ'ælɪtɪ). [f. prec. + -ITY. Cf. Fr. *filialité.*] **a.** The relation of a son or daughter to a parent. **b.** The quality of being filial.

1615 T. ADAMS *Two Sonnes* 70 There are that chalenge a filialitie—as the Jewes—'we have one Father even God'. **1633** —— *Exp. 2 Peter* i. 4. 75 Infinite good things we partake, if we be sonnes; but all lies in the assurance of this filialitie. **1775** in ASH. **1829** JAS. MILL *Hum. Mind* (1869) II. xiv. 53 Paternity connotes filiality. **18..** R. THOMAS in *Chr. World Pulpit* No. 432. 87 Irreligion is as unnatural as want of filiality in a child.

filially ('fɪlɪəlɪ), *adv.* [f. as prec. + -LY².] In a filial manner; with filial feeling or affection.

1613 BP. HALL *Holy Panegyrick* 25 There is no seruant of God, but feares filially. **1702** C. MATHER *Magn. Chr.* III. II. xxx. (1852) 520 His prayers were observable for the.. filially familiar strains of them. **1843** GLADSTONE *Glean.* V. i. 37 Dutiful affection filially accorded to their own [Church].

filialness ('fɪlɪəlnɪs). [f. as prec. + -NESS.] The quality of being filial; filial affection or conduct.

1727 in BAILEY vol. II. **1775** in ASH. **1874** BP. MAGEE in *Hansard* CCXIX. 27 There is something very one-sided in this cry for fatherliness from the Bishops when they meet with no filialness.

filiate ('fɪlɪeɪt), *v.* [f. med.L. *filiāt-* ppl. stem of *filiāre* to have a child, f. *fili-us* son: see -ATE³.]

trans. = AFFILIATE *v.* **to filiate itself**: (*fig.*) to declare its author.

1791 HAMPSON *Mem. J. Wesley* II. 191 The language, in several passages, filiates itself. **1824** *Examiner* 11/2 A young girl..brought..before a Magistrate, in order to filiate her expected offspring. *a* **1843** SOUTHEY *Doctor* ccxxxi. (1848) 624/1 Many parts..bearing so strong a likeness that no one can hesitate at filiating them upon the *ipsissimus* Luther.

Hence **ˈfiliated** *ppl. a.*

1810 T. JEFFERSON *Writ.* (1830) IV. 139 On these the filiated societies model their opinions. **1839** BAILEY *Festus* xix. (1848) 217 The great paternal..fire..wherein All filiated nature ceaseth work.

filiation (fɪlɪˈeɪʃən). Also 6 filiacion. [a. F. *filiation*, ad. med.L. *filiātiōn-em*, n. of action f. *filiāre*, recorded in sense 'to give birth to', f. L. *fili-us* son.]

1. *Theol.* The process of becoming, or the condition of being, a son.

Many Dicts. have a sense 'adoption as a son', illustrated by the first of our quots. from Donne. The sense is etymologically justifiable, and may probably exist; but quot. 1628 seems to show that it was not intended by Donne.

a **1529** SKELTON *Prayers, To the Father* 18 The only Sonne of God by filiacion. **1628** DONNE *Serm.* vi. (1640) 56 God hath forgot all these paternities, all these filiations..all these inviscerations of Israel into his owne bosome. *Ibid.* 57 God shall forget his former Paternities and our former Filiations. **1720** WATERLAND *Eight Serm.* 155 Those Expressions of Image, or Form of God, relate to Christ's Sonship or Filiation. **1893** FAIRBAIRN *Christ in Mod. Theol.* 491 Continuous incarnation is progressive filiation.

2. The designating (of a person) as a son; ascription of sonship.

1659 PEARSON *Creed* (1741) 105 After our Saviour's nomination immediately followeth his filiation.

3. The fact of being the child of a specified parent. Also, a person's parentage; 'whose son one is'.

1611 SPEED *Hist. Gt. Brit.* IX. xix. §4 Yee be borne within this Land..and all the three Estates of the Land haue..knowledge of your birth and filiation aforesaid. **1799** MALONE in *Boswell's Johnson* an. 1744, Mr. Cust's reasoning, with respect to the filiation of Richard Savage. **1855** H. SPENCER *Princ. Psychol.* (1872) II. VIII. v. 569 Where the monogamous relation makes filiation clear.

4. The fact of being descended or derived, or of originating *from*; descent, transmission *from*.

1799 KIRWAN *Geol. Ess.* 323 The resemblance..by no means evinces the filiation of the latter from the former. **1850** MERIVALE *Rom. Emp.* (1865) I. Pref. 13 The..institutions of modern Europe are derived by more direct filiation from those of Rome. **1874** MAHAFFY *Soc. Life Greece* vii. 199 The filiation of Aristophanes' comedies from these choruses.

5. The relation of one thing to another from which it may be said to be descended or derived; position in a genealogical classification.

1794 KIRWAN *Min.* I. p. xv, The intricate filiation and connection of these productions. **1859** DARWIN *Orig. Spec.* xiv. (1873) 371 And would give the filiation and origin of each tongue. **1864** H. SPENCER *Illustr. Univ. Progr.* 131 This he asserts to be the true filiation of the sciences.

6. Formation of branches or offshoots; chiefly *concr.*, a branch or offshoot of a society or language.

1777 W. DALRYMPLE *Trav. Sp. & Port.* 110 The order of Alcantara was instituted a filiation of Calatrava. **1814** BERINGTON *Lit. Hist. Mid. Ages* v. (1846) 231 The northern dialects..were filiations from one Common Stock. **1832** *Blackw. Mag.* XXXI. 65 The democratical party, with their numerous filiations, in the towns. **1890** J. T. FOWLER *Cistercian Statutes* 5 That great system of filiation and visitation which went so far to make up what has been called the 'Cistercian idea'.

7. = AFFILIATION 3. *lit.* and *fig.*

1561 in *Child-Marriages* (E.E.T.S.) 86 Margaret Wilkinson came to the Vicar of Budworth with a filiacion. **1839** LD. BROUGHAM *Statesm. Geo. III* (ed. 2) 60 A mandamus to the Justices to make an order of filiation upon a foreign ambassador's secretary.

fig. **1791** BOSWELL *Johnson* an. 1761, The filiation of a literary performance is difficult of proof. **1887** SAINTSBURY *Hist. Elizab. Lit.* xxii. (1890) 448 The direct filiation of euphuism on Spanish originals is no doubt erroneous.

filibeg (ˈfɪlɪbɛg). *Sc.* Also 8 philebeg, 8–9 philabeg, -ibeg, fillibeg, feilbeg, 9 philiberg, phillibeg. [ad. Gael. *feileadh-beag* the kilt of modern shape, f. *feileadh* a fold, plait + *beag* little, as distinguished from *feileadh-mor* the large kilt of primitive form.] A kilt.

1746 *Act 19–21 Geo. II*, c. 39 §17 The..philebeg, or little kilt. **1771** PENNANT *Tour Scotl.* I. (1790) 211 The feil beg, i.e. little plaid, also called kelt..is a modern substitute for the lower part of the plaid. **1773** JOHNSON *Lett. to Mrs. Thrale* 24 Sept., Old Malcolm in his filibeg. **1794** BURNS *Jolly Beggars, John Highlandman*, His philabeg and tartan plaid. **1828** LANDOR *Imag. Conv.* III. 203 Persian robes and Scotch phillibegs.

filibuster (ˈfɪlɪbʌstə(r)). *sb.* Forms: 6 flibutor, 8–9 flibustier, 9 filibustier, fillibuster, filibuster. [The ultimate source is certainly the Du. *vrijbuiter* in Kilian *vrij-bueter* (see FREEBOOTER). It is not clear whether the 16th c. Eng. form *flibutor*, of which we have only one example, was taken from Du. directly or through some foreign lang. Late in the 18th c. the F. form *flibustier* was adopted into Eng., and continued to be used, with occasional variations of spelling, until after the middle of the nineteenth century. About 1850–54, the form *filibuster*, ad. Sp. *filibustero*, began to be employed as the designation of certain adventurers who at that time were active in the W. Indies and Central America; and this has now superseded the earlier *flibustier* even with reference to the history of the 17th c.

The mutual relation of the forms is involved in obscurity. It is possible that the corruption of *fri-* into *fli-* may be due to the influence of the word FLYBOAT (Du. *vlieboot*, whence F. *flibot*, Sp. *flibote*); but against this it may be urged that in our first quot. the word seems to be applied to marauders on land. In Fr. the form *fribustier* (which may be a corruption of Eng. *freebooter*) occurs in Du Tertre *Hist. des Ant-Isles* (1667) III. 151; but *flibustier* is app. first recorded in A. O. Oexmelin (Esquemeling) *Hist. des Avanturiers* (1686); this writer says that it comes from the Eng. *flibuster* 'corsair'; in the earlier ed. of the work in Dutch (1678) the word does not occur. It is possible on the one hand that the corrupt form of the Du. word may be of Eng. origin, and may have been taken into F. from its use in the Eng. colonies in the W. Indies; or, on the other hand, that the F. form arose in the European wars of the 16th c., and is the immediate source of Garrard's *flibutor*. In any case the insertion of the *s* probably originated in Fr. as a mere sign of vowel-length, though from the *Dictionnaire de Trévoux* we learn that the *s* was already pronounced in 1704. In the *Dict. étymologique* of Ménage (who died in 1692), s.v. *flibot*, the form *flibutier* occurs, with the explanation (doubtless erroneous) 'celui qui gouverne un *flibot*'. The Sp. *filibustero* is presumably ad. F. *flibustier*.]

†**1.** *gen.* = FREEBOOTER. *Obs. rare*$^{-1}$.

a **1587** GARRARD *Arte Warre* (1591) 236 Such..as bring wares to the campe, he [the High Marshall of the Field] must take order that they be courteously..vsed..procuring them a conuoy..to the intent they may..remaine..satisfied, without suspect of being robbed..of theeues and flibutors. *Ibid.* 154 Clearing..the hye wayes..from fleebooters.

2. *spec.* **a.** One of a class of piratical adventurers who pillaged the Spanish colonies in the West Indies during the 17th c.

1792 BURKE *Heads for Consid.* Wks. VII. 93 The Flibustiers..about a century back..brought..calamities upon the Spanish colonies. **1822–56** DE QUINCEY *Confess.* (1862) 6 This..man is a buccaneer, a pirate, a flibustier.

b. A member of any of those bands of adventurers who between 1850 and 1860 organized expeditions from the United States, in violation of international law, for the purpose of revolutionizing certain states in Central America and the Spanish West Indies.

1854 LOWELL *Camb. 30 Y. Ago* Prose Wks. 1890 I. 85 He who was ordained to-day might..accept a colonelcy of filibusters to-morrow. **1855** THOREAU *Let.* in *Atlantic Mo.* (1893) LXXII. 744/1 The gold-diggers and the Mormons, the slaves and the slaveholders and the flibustiers. **1856** WHITTIER *Panorama, Haschish* ix, A raving Cuban filibuster!

attrib. **1857** GEN. P. THOMPSON *Audi Alt.* I. ii. 6 To avoid a collision with the filibuster power [i.e. the U.S.A.].

c. In wider sense: One who resembles a 'filibuster' (sense a or b) in his actions; now *esp.* one who engages in unauthorized and irregular warfare against foreign states.

1860 W. G. CLARK *Vac. Tour* 31 The contrast which these filibusters [Garibaldians] presented to the royal troops was exceedingly striking. **1863** DRAPER *Intell. Devel. Europe* iv. (1865) 95 The Greek colonists were filibusters; they seized by force the women wherever they settled. **1896** E. DOWSON *Let.* 5 July (1967) 372 Yet they have always their Austin, & his praise of *filibustiers*.

d. *nonce-use.* A vessel employed in filibustering; a pirate craft.

1860 MOTLEY *Netherl.* (1868) II. xviii. 455 The coast of..Dunkirk swarmed with their..craft, from the flyboter or filibuster of the rivers to the larger armed vessels.

3. *U.S.* One who practises obstruction in a legislative assembly: see FILIBUSTER *v.* 2.

1889 *Boston* (Mass.) *Jrnl.* 14 Jan. 2/2 A humiliating 'treaty' with a single determined filibuster.

4. An act of obstruction in a legislative assembly. Chiefly *U.S.*

1890 *Congress. Rec.* 11 Feb. 1217/2 A filibuster was indulged in which lasted..for nine continuous calendar days. **1915** *Morn. Post* 13 Feb. 8/3 It has been decided..to suspend the filibuster in order to attend to important appropriations. **1917** *Daily Chron.* 5 Mar. 1/7 The bill..was talked to death. Its last hours were spent in a filibuster against Senator Lafollette. **1923** E. F. WYATT *Invis. Gods* III. iii. 121 There was a three hours' filibuster against the civil service clause. **1965** *Daily Tel.* 5 Apr. 23/3 Need we tolerate the use of 'filibuster' as meaning 'obstruction' instead of 'obstructionist'?

filibuster (ˈfɪlɪˌbʌstə(r)), *v.* [f. prec. sb.]

1. a. *intr.* To act as a filibuster.

1853 LONGF. in *Life* (1891) II. 247 Youths..rather inclined to filibustering in Cuba. **1862** S. LUCAS *Secularia* 135 He prayed with fervour as he went fillibustering.

b. quasi-*trans.* Also *trans.* To subject to the methods of a filibuster.

1862 B. TAYLOR *Home & Abr.* Ser. II. ii. 67 When the inmates [of a prison] have enjoyed a satisfactory period of rest and seclusion, they join in companies, and filibuster their way out. **1887** L. OLIPHANT *Episodes* 122, I was..endeavouring to filibuster a constituency. **1955** C. E. CARRINGTON *Rudyard Kipling* ix. 228 Dr. Jameson's attempt to filibuster the Transvaal Republic into the British Empire was defeated.

2. *U.S.* To obstruct progress in a legislative assembly; to practise obstruction.

1853 *Congress. Globe* 4 Jan. 194/1, I saw my friend..filibustering, as I thought, against the United States. **1882** SIR M. H. BEACH in *Standard* 24 Mar. 3/2 The objectionable practices of 'filibustering' and 'stone-walling'. **1885** *Boston* (Mass.) *Jrnl.* 20 Feb. 2/3 Ex-Confederates Filibuster to Prevent a Vote on the Bill.

Hence **filiˈbustering** *vbl. sb.*, also *attrib.* and *ppl. a.*; also **filiˈbusterer**, one who filibusters.

1856 *Tait's Mag.* XXIII. 433 They are willing to find a safety valve for a portion of their filibusterers and loafers. **1856** *Gentl. Mag.* New Ser. I. 111/1 The President has recognised Walker, the filibustering chief of Nicaragua. **1857** GEN. P. THOMPSON *Audi Alt.* I. xxiv. 89 America has long been engaged in two courses of avowed and notable injustice, 'filibustering' and slave-dealing. *Ibid.*, Nobody would look..for economy..to a filibustering nation. **1859** JEPHSON *Brittany* ii. 14 Palmy days of..filibustering prosperity. **1885** *Times* (weekly ed.) 23 Jan. 1/2 A filibustering expedition to Cuba is being prepared. **1888** BRYCE *Amer. Commw.* I. I. x. 137 Systematic obstruction, or, as it is called in America, 'filibustering'. **1893** *Columbus* (Ohio) *Dispatch* 5 Dec., He found that the men..were high-minded, law-abiding citizens instead of filibusterers.

filibusterism (fɪlɪˈbʌstərɪz(ə)m). [f. FILIBUSTER *sb.* + -ISM.] The practice of filibustering; inclination to, or tendency to support, filibustering.

1862 J. SPENCE *Amer.* 74 Filibusterism is another branch of the same tree [as Repudiation]. **1880** *American* XII. 361 Filibusterism had excited the troubles.

filibusterous (fɪlɪˈbʌstərəs). [f. as prec. + -OUS.] Resembling the conduct of a filibuster.

1883 *St. James's Gaz.* 19 Apr. 3 It would be hard to say why that was a design less filibusterous than the occupation of New Guinea. **1890** *Sat. Rev.* 19 July 64/2 In a manner gallant but slightly filibusterous—the word deserves coining—he broke down the resistance of the Mexicans.

filical (ˈfɪlɪkəl). *a.* [f. L. *filic-*, *filix* fern + -AL[1].] Of or pertaining to ferns.

1835 LINDLEY *Introd. Bot.* (1848) II. 93 The Filical alliance, consisting of vascular Acrogens.

filicauline (fɪlɪˈkɔːlaɪn), *a.* [f. L. *fili-*, *filum* thread *caul-em* stalk + -INE.] Having a threadlike stem.

1884 in *Syd. Soc. Lex.*

filicetum: see FILIX.

filicic (fɪˈlɪsɪk), *a. Chem.* Also filixic. [ad. G. *filixsäure* filicic acid (E. Luck 1851, in *Jahrb. f. prakt. Pharm.* XXII. 130), f. L. *filic-*, *filix* fern + -IC.] ***filicic acid***, a mixture of phloroglucinol derivatives obtained from the rhizome of various ferns (chiefly the common male fern, *Dryopteris filix-mas*), and one of the anthelmintic agents in the drug Male Fern (*filix mas*) (the name was orig. given to the crude extract of the fern, now called *filicin*). Similarly **ˈfilicin** [a. G. *filicin* (E. Poulsson 1891, in *Arch. f. exper. Path. & Pharm.* XXIX. 9)], (*a*) the crude extract of anthelmintic principles obtained from male fern; (*b*) the therapeutically inactive lactone of filicic acid; also loosely applied to the acid itself.

1865 BRANDE & COX *Dict. Sci., Lit. & Art* (ed. 4) I. 890/1 *Filicic acid*, an acid obtained from fern root. **1874** FLÜCKIGER & HANBURY *Pharmacographia* 669 The medicinal ethereal extract, of which the rhizome yields about 8 per cent., deposits a colourless, granular, crystalline substance, noticed by Peschier as early as 1826, and subsequently designated by Luck, Filicic Acid. **1892** *Jrnl. Chem. Soc.* LXII. I. 380 The poisonous properties of fern extract are due to an amorphous substance which is the true filicic acid. The acid is readily converted into its lactone, by simply boiling its ethereal solution. The lactone is named filicin. **1941** *Thorpe's Dict. Appl. Chem.* (ed. 4) V. 181/2 Filicin (filicic acid)..consists of three..ketone nuclei. **1958** *Progress in Org. Chem.* IV. 120 The ultra-violet absorption spectrum of filixic acid indicates a structure in which the three phenolic nuclei are separated by a methylene group. **1959** *Chem. Abstr.* LIII. 14324 Filicin prepd. with $Ba(OH)_2$ showed lower toxicity for warm-blooded animals and higher toxicity for cold-blooded animals. **1963** *Brit. Pharm. Codex* 449 Filicin is the name given to the ether-soluble product obtained in the assay of the drug [*sc.* Male Fern] and the extract. **1963** *Acta Chem. Scand.* XVII. 191 Naturally occurring filixic acid, the characteristic phloroglucinol derivative from *Dryopteris filix mas*, has been shown to be a mixture of six homologues, which differ from each other in regard to the acyl side chains of the filicinic acid nuclei. **1968** J. H. BURN *Lect. Notes Pharmacol.* (ed. 9) 123 Castor oil..aids the absorption of the filicic acid in the extract of male fern.

filicide[1] (ˈfɪlɪsaɪd). [f. L. *fili-us*, *filia* son, daughter + -CIDE: see -CIDE 1.] One who kills a son or daughter; a slayer of his own child.

1823 *Douglas* III. xx. 267 Fearful of being discovered by the intended filicide. **1848** LOWELL *Fable for Critics* Poet. Wks. (Moxon) 365, I told how it [the aloe]..discharging its pistil..shot The botanical filicide dead on the spot.

filicide[2] (ˈfɪlɪsaɪd). [f. as prec.: see -CIDE 2.] The action of killing a son or daughter.

1665 J. WEBB *Stone-Heng* (1725) 217 Homicide, Filicide, Fratricide. **1839** F. BARHAM *Adamus Exul.* 47 Let not the race Of mortal men..Utterly perish, thro' our filicide. **1879** A. E. SPROUL in *Boston Herald* 3 May, Additional details of the Pocasset filicide are given below.

Hence **fili'cidal** *a.* concerned with the slaughter of sons and daughters.
1852 J. B. OWEN in *Ld. Ingestre's Meliora* I. 133 His ruin realized the filicidal fable of Saturn.

filiciform (fɪ'lɪsɪfɔːm), *a.* [f. L. *filic-*, *filix* fern + -(I)FORM.] Having the form of a fern; fern-shaped.
1846 in SMART *Suppl.*, and in mod. Dicts.

filicoid ('fɪlɪkɔɪd), *a.* and *sb.* [f. as prec. + -OID.]
A. *adj.* Resembling a fern.
1847 in CRAIG. **1876** PAGE *Adv. Text-bk. Geol.* xiv. 268 The same gigantic coniferous and filicoid plants are found.
B. *sb.* A plant having the appearance of a fern.
1847 in CRAIG.

filicology (fɪlɪ'kɒlədʒɪ). [f. L. *filic-*, *filix* fern + Gr. -λογια discoursing: see -(O)LOGY.] The science or study of ferns.
1884 in *Syd. Soc. Lex.*

filiety (fɪ'laɪɪtɪ). *rare.* [ad. late L. *fīlietāt-em* sonship, f. *fīlius* son.] = FILIATION 2.
1851 MILL *Logic* (ed. 3) I. I. ii. §7. 45 The concretes, father and son, have, or might have, the abstracts, paternity, and filiety, or filiation.

filife: see FIVE-LEAF.

filiferous (faɪ'lɪfərəs), *a.* [f. L. *fīl-um* thread + -(I)FEROUS.] Bearing or provided with thread-like parts.
1841–71 T. R. JONES *Anim. Kingd.* (ed. 4) 61 The presence of a prehensile apparatus of filiferous capsules. **1846** DANA *Zooph.* (1848) 513 Cells..filiferous within.

filiform ('faɪlɪfɔːm), *a.* [f. as prec. + -(I)FORM, cf. F. *filiforme.*] Having the form of a thread; thread-like.
1757 PULTNEY in *Phil. Trans.* I. 66 The style is filiform. **1811** PINKERTON *Petral.* II. 310 The amorphous lava..sprinkled with filiform crystals of felspar. **1887** RUSKIN *Præterita* II. 152 This [inlet] was crossed..by the delicatest of filiform suspension bridges.
Hence **'filiformed** *ppl. a.* in same sense.
1851 DARWIN *Cirripedia* I. 9, I distinctly saw a long filiformed organ, bearing excessively fine hairs in lines.

filigrane ('fɪlɪgreɪn), *sb.* Forms: α. 7–9 filigrain(e, fillagreen, (7 filagram, fil'gran, filegreen, filograin, 8 filagrain, -green), 8 filigreen, filligrane, -grean, -green, 8– filigrane. β. 7 philigrin, 7–8 philagrain, -green, -grin. [a. Fr. *filigrane* (in 17th c. often *-gramme*), ad. It. *filigrana*, f. L. *fīlum* thread and *grānum* grain.]
1. = FILIGREE *sb.* 1.
1668 LADY CHAWORTH in *12th Rep. Hist. MSS. Comm.* App. v. 10 A cabinet of cristall and philigrin. *a* **1680** BUTLER *Rem.* (1759) I. 183 As if it had been wrought in Filograin. **1682** *Lond. Gaz.* No. 1721/1 Coco-nut Cups set in Fillagreen. **1713** *Phil. Trans.* XXVIII. 226 Their Embroiderers work in Filigreen very curiously. **1794** W. COMBE *Boydell's Thames* I. 90 Taste has run into the contrary extreme of frippery and filigrane. **1850** LONGF. *Blind Girl of Castèl-Cuillè* iii. 68 The crown of filigrane suspended from the low-arched portal.
b. *transf.* *esp.* of architectural ornament.
1727 BRADLEY *Fam. Dict.* s.v. *Caramel*, The Sugar thickens and..a kind of curious Filigreen or Net-work, will be form'd. **1762–71** H. WALPOLE *Vertue's Anecd. Paint.* (1786) I. 194 For airy towers of almost filigraine we have none to be compared with those of Rheims. **1775** —— *Let. to Sir H. Mann* 22 Apr., Adam, our most admired, is all gingerbread, filigraine, and fan-painting.
2. *attrib.* = FILIGREE 2. Also **filigrane-work** = FILIGREE-WORK.
1680 ASHMOLE *Diary* 358 A gold chain..composed..of philagreen links in great knobs. **1687** E. BROWNE *Trav.* (ed. 2) 147 A curious Filegrane Handkerchief, and two fair Filegrane Plates. *a* **1689** A. BEHN *Novels* (1722) II. 194 This case shall be..like those delicate ones of Filligrin Work, which do not hinder the sight. **1690** *Songs Costume* (Percy Soc.) 194 In filgran casset. **1696** tr. *Du Mont's Voy. Levant* x. 122 A golden Sun of Filagram-Work. **1710** STEELE *Tatler* No. 245 ¶2 A small Cabinet..in which were..several Filagrain Curiosities. **1715** tr. *Mad. D'Anois' Wks.* 416 All in large Flaskets of Filagreen Gold. **1742** MRS. DELANY *Autobiog.* (1861) II. 169 A fine present in a large filligrane silver box. **1753** HOGARTH *Anal. Beauty* viii. 96 The great number of its filligreen ornaments. **1786** tr. *Beckford's Vathek* (1823) 67 Drawing from a fillagreen urn, a parchment. **1847** ANSTED *Anc. World* viii. 144 Their edges appear like golden filigrane-work.

†**'filigrane**, *v.* *Obs.* = FILIGREE *v.* Hence †**'filigraned** *ppl. a.*
1690 EVELYN *Fop's Dict.*, *Fil-grain'd*, Dressing-boxes..or whatever else is made of silver wire-work.

filigree, filagree ('fɪlɪgriː, -əgriː), *sb.* Forms: α. 7–9 fillagree, 8–9 filligree, 7– filagree, 9 filigree. β. 8 phillagree, phil(l)igree, -grew. [Abbreviated from *filigreen*: see FILIGRANE.]
1. a. 'Jewel work of a delicate kind made with threads and beads, usually of gold and silver' (*Encycl. Brit.*).
1693 EVELYN *Diary* 13 July, A cabinet of silver fillagree. **1721** *Lond. Gaz.* No. 6014/3 Fine chac'd Philigrew and Houshold-Plate. **1789** MRS. PIOZZI *Journ. France* I. 118 Ear-rings of silver fillagree finely worked. **1821** BYRON *Juan* III. lxiii, Gold cups of filigree. **1821** SCOTT *Kenilw.* vi, A beautiful Venetian mirror, in a frame of silver filigree.
transf. **1873** BROWNING *Red Cott. Nt.-cap* 69 Palace-panes Pinholed athwart their windowed filagree By twinklings sobered from the sun outside.
b. The art of making this work.
1800 *Spirit Pub. Jrnls.* (1801) IV. 366 Having her daughters taught French and filagree.
2. *attrib.* (= made of, or worked in, filigree); **filigree glass** (see quot.); **filigree paper, paper work**: see quot. 1960. Also FILIGREE-WORK.
1747 H. WALPOLE *Let. to Conway* 8 June, It is set in enamelled meadows, with phillagree hedges. **1779** FORREST *Voy. N. Guinea* 299 Goldsmiths, who make filligree buttons. **1796** M. EDGEWORTH *Parent's Assist.* (ed. 2) II. II. 7 The shop where the filigree paper was to be bought. **1797** MRS. RADCLIFFE *Italian* xi, Enclosed within a filigree screen of gold, lay the image of the saint. **1803** *Gent. Mag.* in *Spirit Pub. Jrnls.* (1804) VII. 44 Fillagree tea-caddies. **1843** LYTTON *Last Bar.* II. ii, A collar or necklace of uncut jewels set in filagree gold. **1872** YEATES *Techn. Hist. Comm.* 264 Filigree glass..consisted of spirally-twisted white and coloured enamel glasses, cased in transparent glass. **1886** SHELDON tr. *Flaubert's Salammbô* 4 Gold filigree baskets containing flowers. **1960** H. HAYWARD *Antique Coll.* 117/2 *Filigree paper work.* Throughout the 18th cent. filigree was a popular amateur ornament for small cabinets... This was achieved solely with tiny rolls of paper.

filigree ('fɪlɪgriː), *v.* [f. prec. sb.] *trans.* To ornament with filigree work, to work in filigree. Hence **'filigreed** *ppl. a.*
1831 TRELAWNY *Adv. Younger Son* lvi, A little filagreed basket of fruit. **1847** *Tait's Mag.* XIV. 383 Vestiges of pre-Adamite existence found filagreed into fossils, or intaglioed on stones. **1872** 'MARK TWAIN' *Innoc. Abr.* xiv. 95 A domed and filagreed white temple..burst upon us.

'filigree-,work. [f. FILIGREE *sb.* + WORK.]
1. Work in filigree.
1773 *Gentl. Mag.* XLIII. 433 A thick board cut through like filligree-work. **1848** LYTTON *Harold* I. i, An uncut jewel, set in Byzantine filagree work.
fig. **1818** HAZLITT *Eng. Poets* iv. 96 The Rape of the Lock..the most exquisite specimen of filigree work ever invented.
2. *transf.* Stone-work resembling filigree.
1790 PENNANT *London* (1813) 94 Quatre-foils of philligree-work. **1857** H. MILLER *Test. Rocks* i. 38 Columns of an elder Alhambra, roughened with..exquisite filagree work.

'filiism. *nonce-wd.* [f. L. *fīli-us* + -ISM; after NEPOTISM.] Undue partiality for one's own son.
1823 in *Examiner* 681/2 The *filiism* and *secretaryism* of the Earl of Eldon here are as great evils as nepotism ever was in Rome.

filing ('faɪlɪŋ), *vbl. sb.*[1] [f. FILE *v.*[1] + -ING[1].]
1. The action of FILE *v.*[1] *lit.* and *fig.*
1398 TREVISA *Barth. De P.R.* XVI. xlv. (1495) 568 The powdre that fallyth fro the yren wyth fylynge. **1557** RECORDE *Whetst.* Bij b, The filyng, sharpenyng, and quickenyng of the witte. **1683** MOXON *Mech. Exerc.* 53 An Instrument of great use for flat Filing. **1694–5** PEPYS *Let.* 10 Jan. in *Academy* (1890) 9 Aug. 111/1 Our Friend's Learning..wants a little fileing.
attrib. **1774** FOOTE *Cozeners* I. Wks. 1799 II. 147 The clipping and filing affair compels him to keep a little private.
2. *concr.* usually *pl.* One of the particles rubbed off by the action of the file.
1398 TREVISA *Barth. De P.R.* XVI. iv. (Tollem. MS.), The vilynge of golde take in mete. **1591** PERCIVALL *Sp. Dict.*, *Limaduras*, the filings. **1646** SIR T. BROWNE *Pseud. Ep.* III. xxii. 165 For medicall uses, wee take downe the filings of Iron or steele. **1661** LOVELL *Hist. Anim. & Min.* 79 The filings of the foremost hoofes given with water help the frettings in Horses. **1772** PRIESTLEY in *Franklin's Wks.* (1887) IV. 489 A mixture of iron filings and brimstone. **1812** SIR H. DAVY *Chem. Philos.* 259 Filings of copper are usually employed. **1855** MILMAN *Lat. Chr.* (1864) II. III. vii. 154 The minutest filings from the chains of St. Peter.
3. *Comb.*, as **filing-block**, a block of wood grooved to hold small rods or bars while being filed; **filing-machine** (see quot.); **filing-pin**, a piece of hard wood used in silver manufacture to file against.
1874 KNIGHT *Dict. Mech.* I. 843/1 **Filing-block*..**Filing-machine*, 1. A machine used in the mint to reduce the weight of coin planchets, when above the standard..2. A machine in which a file is mounted as a jig-saw; or to reciprocate in a manner similar to that of a file in the hands of a workman.

'filing, *vbl. sb.*[2] [f. FILE *v.*[2]] The action of the vb. FILE; †*concr.* excrement.
1340 HAMPOLE *Pr. Consc.* 2345 Now er þai made foule and ugly Thurgh fylyng of þair syn anly. *c* **1460** *Urbanitatis* 52 in *Babees Bk.* (1868) 14 Kepe þy hondys fayre & welle Fro fylynge of the towelle. **16..** *Childe Waters* in Evans *O.B.* (1784) II. xxxv. 213 And take her up in thine armes twaine, For filing of her feete. *a* **1622** R. HAWKINS in *Hawkins's Voy.* (1878) 196 Nor in any of their nestes, was to be found..the filing of any fowle.

filing ('faɪlɪŋ), *vbl. sb.*[3] [f. FILE *v.*[3] + -ING[1].] The action of FILE *v.*[3]; an instance of this. **a.** The action of putting a document on a file. **b.** *Mil.* The action of forming a file or files.
a. 1712 ARBUTHNOT *John Bull* I. xi, Fees..for enrollings, exemplifications..filings of words. **1888** *Law Times* LXXXV. 132/2 The filing by a debtor of his own petition.
b. 1796 *Instr. & Reg. Cavalry* (1813) 8 Filings, formings, and in general the movements of manœuvre. **1832** *Regul. Instr. Cavalry* II. 9 Filing is an operation of the squadron.
c. *attrib.*, as ***filing cabinet, clerk, system.***
1907 G. B. SHAW *J. Bull's Other Island* I. 3 (*stage direction*) A filing cabinet, with a cupboard on it. **1911** H. S. HARRISON *Queed* xxv. 329 West went to a filing cabinet in the corner of the room. **1930** *Daily Express* 6 Nov. 3/2 There are scores of new type-writers..and filing cabinets, telephone instruments and..telephone boxes for the use of the ninety delegates and their staffs. **1964** *English Studies* XLV (Suppl.). 26, I have selected a number of details that might..have remained in my filing cabinet. **1922** S. LEWIS *Babbitt* ii. 16 Verona had for six months been filing-clerk at the Gruensberg Leather Company offices. **1956** A. H. COMPTON *Atomic Quest* 338 From filing clerks to administrators. **1926** *Daily Colonist* (Victoria, B.C.) 10 Jan. 6/3 A central filing system is being contemplated. **1936** *Discovery* Nov. 346/2 A New Filing System. **1958** Filing system [see *brain-child* s.v. BRAIN *sb.* 6].

†**'filiole**[1]. *Obs.* Forms: α. 4 fylyole, 5 felyole. β. 6 fyall, -ell, phioll. [a. OF. *filloele*, *-elle*, *fillole*, also *fiole*, *-lle*, *fyole*, app. a column, turret.] ? A column, turret, or pinnacle.
13.. *E.E. Allit. P.* B. 1462 Þe coperounes of þe canacles..Wer fetysely formed out in fylyoles longe. ?*c* **1475** *Sqr. lowe Degre* 835 Your curtaines of camaca, all in folde, Your felyoles all of Golde. **1501** DOUGLAS *Pal. Hon.* III. xvii, Pinnakillis, Fyellis, Turnpekkis..Gilt birneist torris. **1513** —— *Æneis* XII. Prol. 71 Euery fyall, fane, and stage.

†**'filiole**[2]. *Obs.*[−1] In 6 filliole. [a. OF. (and mod. dial. Fr.) *filliole* (Fr. *filleule*):—L. *filiola*, dim. of *filia* daughter.] A god-daughter.
15.. *Wyse Chylde & Emp. Adrian* (W. de W., repr. 1860) 14 It were synne to take his cosynne vnto wyfe..or his filliole, or ony of his lygnage.

filionymic (,fɪlɪəʊ'nɪmɪk). *rare.* [f. L. *fīli-us* son; after PATRONYMIC.] A name derived from that of a son.
1870 LUBBOCK *Orig. Civiliz.* ix. 316 The Rejangs among whom the filionymic is not so common.

filio-pietistic (,fɪlɪəʊpaɪɪ'tɪstɪk), *a.* [f. L. *filius* son + PIETISTIC.] Marked by excess of filial piety. (*contemptuous.*)
1893 C. F. ADAMS *Massachusetts* 49 The historians of the Massachusetts filio-pietistic school. **1897** *Q. Rev.* Apr. 532 The 'filio-pietistic' school [of American historians]. **1902** *Daily Chron.* 19 June 4/1 The 'filio-pietistic' spirit of the New England writers in American history. **1962** *Times Lit. Suppl.* 6 July 485/3 The age of Jared Sparks with his highly selective filiopietistic approach to biography and history.

‖**filioque** (fɪlɪ'əʊkwiː). [L.] The word (= 'and from the Son') inserted in the Western version of the Nicene creed to assert the doctrine of the procession of the Holy Ghost from the Son as well as from the Father, which is not admitted by the Eastern Church. Also *attrib.*, as ***filioque clause, question.***
1876 C. M. DAVIES *Unorth. Lond.* 90 With reference to the 'Filioque' clause, 'One branch of the Church Catholic affirms on this point, whilst the other declares to affirm'. *Ibid.* 239 The 'Filioque' question.

filip, obs. form of FILLIP.

‖**filipendula** (fɪlɪ'pɛndjuːlə). *Obs.* exc. as botanical Latin. Also 6 **philypendula**. [mod.L. fem. of *fīlipendulus* hanging by a thread, f. *fīlum* thread + *pendulus* hanging, f. *pendēre* to hang. Cf. Fr. *filipendule.*] The drop-wort (*Spiræa Filipendula*).
?**1540** tr. *Vigo's Lyttel Practyce* Aiij/2 Rotes of Philypendula. **1548** TURNER *Names of Herbs*, Oenanthe is called boeth of the Herbarics and of al our countrey men Filipendula. **1655** MOUFET & BENNET *Health's Improv.* (1746) 364 What Shepherd is ignorant that his Flock feedeth upon Filipendula, Daisies [etc.]? **1706** in PHILLIPS (ed. Kersey).

filipendulous (fɪlɪ'pɛndjʊləs), *a.* [f. mod.L. *fīlipendul-us* (see prec.) + -OUS.] Hanging or having the appearance of hanging by a thread.
1864 in WEBSTER. **1889** in WAGSTAFFE *Mayne's Med. Dict.*

Filipinize ('fɪlɪpɪnaɪz), *v.* Also -ise. [f. FILIPINO + -IZE.] *trans.* To convert to operation by Filipinos. Hence **Filipini'zation.**
1923 *Glasgow Herald* 28 Apr. 8 The administrative services have been almost completely Filipinised. **1924** *Life & Work* Feb. 30/1 A Dual Government for eight years marked by a sweeping Filipinisation of the services. *Ibid.* 31/1 A Reserve Fund of 41 million dollars was handed over by the Americans to the Filipinised Government.

Filipino (fɪlɪ'piːnəʊ), *sb.* and *a.* Also **Filipina** (-'iːnə) fem. [Sp., f. (*las Islas*) *Filipinas* the Philippine islands.] **A.** *sb.* A native or inhabitant of the Philippine islands, especially one of Spanish or mixed blood. **B.** *adj.* Of or pertaining to Filipinos or the Philippine islands.
1898 *Daily News* 16 Dec. 4/6 Though there may be no guarantee of American citizenship for the Filipinos, the islands will become a part of the Union. **1899** R. R. LALA *Philippine Islands* 86 (*caption*) A high-born Filipina. **1900** H. W. LAWTON in Forbes *Philippine Islands* (1945) iii. 61 If I am shot by a Filipino bullet, it might as well come from one of my own men. **1902** *Encycl. Brit.* XXXI. 668/2 Filipinos had for generations been ordained in the priesthood. *Ibid.*, Ever ready to join issue against any Filipino movement. **1909** 'O. HENRY' *Roads of Destiny* xxi. 352 A Southerner is as good as a Filipino any day. **1918** E. S. FARROW *Dict. Mil. Terms*, *Filipino ration*, the ration for use of Filipino scouts, consisting of 70 per cent of fresh beef or canned meat, 20 per cent of bacon, and 10 per cent of fish. **1936** G. A. MALCOLM *Commonwealth of Philippines* ii. 36 The fair Filipina of today dresses smartly, whether in dainty native costume or the

latest Paris mode. **1944** J. S. Huxley *On Living in Revol.* i. 13 The United States..in its encouragement of the Filipino's development towards independence. *Ibid.* v. 66 Certain Filipino tribes. **1959** *Chambers's Encycl.* X. 657/2 Filipinos, ethnically related to Malays..but christianized by long association with Spaniards, form 93% of the inhabitants.

filix ('faılıks, 'fılıks). *Bot.* Usu. in pl. **filices**. [a. L. *filix* fern.] The group of plants in the division Pteridophyta that includes the ferns. Hence **fili'cetum** [-etum], a collection of living ferns.

1731 P. Miller *Gardeners Dict.*, *Filix*: Fern. There are great Varieties of this Plant in the different Parts of the World. **1789** G. White *Selborne* I. v. 11 These..scenes..delight the naturalist..with their curious *filices* with which they abound. **1832** J. Lindley *Introd. Bot.* iii. 195 Filices, or ferns, are plants consisting of a number of leaves, or fronds, as they are called, attached to a stem. **1856** *Athenæum* 19 Jan. 73/1 Every garden its Filicetum for the cultivation of those species which will bear exposure in our climate. **1869** S. Hibberd *Fern Garden* i. 1 The ferns or *filices* are the most noble of all. **1891** G. Massee *Evol. Plant Life* vii. 213 Filices (*Ferns*)..includes some of the largest of Cryptogams living at the present day. **1965** Bell & Coombe tr. *Strasburger's Textbk. Bot.* III. 572 Some of the Filices have distinct long shoots.

filixic, var. filicic *a.*

filix mas ('faılıks mæs, 'fılıks mæs). [f. the Latin name of the male fern, *Dryopteris filix-mas*.] An anthelmintic drug prepared from the rhizome of *Dryopteris filix-mas*, the male fern.

1789 W. Cullen *Treat. Materia Medica* II. 41 Filex [*sic*] mas..has long been celebrated as an anthelmintic. **1880** Bentley & Trimen *Medicinal Plants* IV. 300 Filix Mas; the dried rhizome with the bases of the foot-stalks and portions of the root fibres. **1907** J. H. Parsons *Dis. Eye* xvii. 384 Tobacco, alcohol, quinine, filix mas, carbon disulphide, and other poisons sometimes produce defective vision. **1940** J. H. Gaddum *Pharmacol.* xx. 320 The tapeworms in his [*sc.* man's] intestine are removed by Filix mas, pelleterine, and cusso.

filizar, -er, obs. ff. of filacer, -zer.

fill (fıl), *sb.*[1] For forms see the vb. Also 4 folle, *south.* volle. [OE. *fyllo*, *fyllu* fem. = OHG. *fulli* fem. (MHG. *vülle*, Ger. *fülle* fem.), ON. *fyllr* (*fylli*) fem. (Da. *fylde* masc. and fem., Sw. *fylle* neut), Goth. (*ufar*) *fullei*:—OTeut. **fullîn-*, n. of state f. **fullo-* full *a.* But in Eng. the word has, from similarity of sound, always been associated with the vb. fill. Senses 2–4 strictly belong to a distinct word, f. the vb.]

I. 1. a. A full supply of drink or food; enough to satisfy want or desire. Since OE. only in ***to drink, eat, have, take,*** etc. ***one's fill***. Const. *of*; also in apposition to *obj.*

Beowulf 562 (Gr.) Næs hie ðære fylle ȝefean hæfdon. *c* **893** K. Ælfred *Oros.* II. iv. §8 Drinc nu ðine fylle. *c* **1175** *Lamb. Hom.* 53 To eten hire fulle. *c* **1220** *Bestiary* 485 Fret hire fille. *a* **1300** *Cursor M.* 3536 (Cott.) Lang es siþen I ete my fill. **14..** *Sir Beues* (MS. M.) 2473 Of that water he dranke his fyl. **1508** Fisher *Wks.* (1876) 234 He coude not haue his fyll of pesen and oke cornes. **1549–62** Sternhold & H. *Ps.* civ. 259 Beastes of the mountaynes thereof drinke their fils. **1611** Bible *Deut.* xxiii. 24 Thou mayest eate grapes thy fill. **1697** Dryden *Virg. Past.* x. 114 Away, my goats, away: for you have browz'd your fill. **1810** Scott *Lady of L.* I. i, The stag at eve had drunk his fill. **1817** Shelley *Revolt of Islam* VII. xix, She sucked her fill even at this breast.

transf. and *fig.* *c* **1200** *Trin. Coll. Hom.* 51 Hie hadden þe fulle of wurldes richeise. *c* **1340** *Cursor M.* 23547 (Trin.) Vche mon shal haue þe folle of al þat he aftir wilne wolle. **1551** Crowley *Pleas. & Pain* 615 Of blysse or of payne they shall haue theyr fyll. **1611** Bible *Prov.* vii. 18 Let vs take our fill of loue vntill the morning. **1653** Holcroft *Procopius* I. 6 Having had their fill of mourning. **1775** Johnson *Lett. to Mrs. Thrale* (1788) I. cxx. 259 The hay..to-day has its fill of sunshine. **1821** Shelley *Adonais* vii, He takes his fill Of deep and liquid rest. **1861** Hughes *Tom Brown at Oxf.* Introd. (1889) 1 He was having his fill of hunting.

b. Hence used with intransitive vbs. as an adverbial phrase: 'to (his) heart's content'.

c **1300** *Havelok* 954 Þe children..with him leykeden here fille. *c* **1340** *Cursor M.* 10475 (Trin.) Þere she myȝte sorwe hir fille. *c* **1400** *Melayne* 213 They had foughten thaire fill. **1548** Udall, etc. *Erasm. Par. John* xix. 113 That ye may looke your fyl upon hym. **1642** H. More *Song of Soul* I. III. xliii, They danc'd their fills. **1770** Gray in *Corr. N. Nicholls* (1843) 107 Talk your fill to me and spare not. **1808** Scott *Marm* VI. xv, Let my boy-bishop fret his fill. **1866** Mrs. Gaskell *Wives & Dau.* xi. (1867) 119 She burst into a passion of tears, and cried her fill.

2. a. A quantity sufficient to fill a receptacle or empty space; a filling, charge. *lit.* and *fig.*

1555 *Ludlow Churchw. Acc.* (Camden) 62 Paid for a fylle of tymber..x.d. **1849** Grote *Greece* II. lxxiv. (1862) VI. 473 It imparted to her a second fill of strength. **1881** Stevenson *Virgin. Puerisq.* 102 If there is a fill of tobacco among the crew..pass it round. **1884** Eissler *Mod. High Explosives* 265 The earth and clay for the fill were obtained from Fruitvale.

b. An embankment to fill up a gully or hollow.

1850 *Congress. Globe* Apr., App. 531/1 It was like..making deep cuts and large fills with a view to construct a railroad. **1873** J. H. Beadle *Undevel. West* xxiv. 507 There is not..a difficult 'cut' or 'fill' for over two hundred miles. **1884** *Lisbon* (Dakota) *Star* 18 July, The fill will be 150 feet long. **1887** M. Roberts *Western Avernus* 71 They made a 'fill' or embankment eighty feet high.

c. In Poker: the act of filling one's hand. Cf. fill *v.* 1 c.

1866 *Wilkes' Spirit of Times* 10 Mar. 28/3 In a game of draw-poker on the draw or fill, a party..discovers that he has only four cards. **1887** S. Cumberland *Queen's Highway* 276 If I drew for a 'fill' I 'filled', it is true, only to find that some one at the table had drawn a 'full hand' of a higher denomination.

d. Auxiliary or secondary material inserted to ensure continuity in music, literature, etc.

1934 S. R. Nelson *All about Jazz* ii. 46 The pianist used to fill up, with 'breaks'... In fact, the excellence of the player was determined by the nature of these 'fills'. **1962** C. Watson *Hopjoy was Here* xvi. 176 He knew..what would tickle a sub-editor's fancy and help meet the insatiable demand for short 'fills'.

e. *Archæol.* The body of material found in a pit, ditch, etc., in excavation, of a later period than the digging of the feature itself.

1952 *Antiquity* XXVI. 118 The levels beneath it and associated with it are pre-pottery, while two deep later fills against its face are still pre-pottery. **1955** *Times* 24 Aug. 9/6 In the fills behind each of the walls were found rich deposits of pottery and votive offerings.

3. The action of filling (*esp.* a cup or glass). *lit.* and *fig.* *rare.*

a **1732** T. Boston in Spurgeon *Treas. Dav.* Ps. lxxxi. p. 10 A fill proposed and offered to empty sinners. *a* **1810** Tannahill *Poems* (1846) 68 I'll treat you wi' a Highland gill, Though it should be my hindmaist fill.

4. †Of a river: The point at which its stream is filled, the head-waters; in quot. opposed to *fall*. Hence *transf.* in proverbial use, ***neither fill nor fall***: neither head nor tail, not a trace (*dial.*).

1622 Drayton *Poly-olb.* xix. (1748) 333 A stream, that from the fill to fall, Wants nothing that a flood should be adorn'd withal. **1887** *Kent Gloss.* s.v., 'My old dog went off last Monday, and I can't hear neither fill-nor-fall of him.'

II. With adverbs forming combs. expressing the action of the corresponding verbal combinations (fill *v.* V).

5. fill-in. a. Something put in as a substitute or to fill a vacancy.

1918 in C. W. Cunnington *Eng. Women's Clothing* (1952) iv. 141 Fill-in or vest or waistcoat is an absolute necessity. **1928** *Sunday Express* 15 Apr. 11/5, I can hardly say my interest was aroused in the 'new art', except as a fill-in for the stage. **1936** N. Coward *To-night at 8.30* I. 101 This date's only a fill-in for us. **1944** R. Lehmann *Ballad & Source* 141 'Well no, not really,' I murmured, realising that she had forgotten she was talking to me, but feeling that some non-committal fill-in was required. **1958** *Listener* 6 Nov. 722/2 At twelve there was a fill-in term at a rather arty school. **1968** [see Bircher].

b. A briefing.

1946 *Sat. Rev. Lit.* 20 July 24/3 George Holmes..had given the President a fill-in on Stimson's literary background. **1953** Pohl & Kornbluth *Space Merchants* (1955) ii. 18, I gave him a fill-in on what Schocken Associates was up to.

c. = sense 2 d. Also *attrib.*

1952 B. Ulanov *Hist. Jazz in Amer.* (1958) iv. 29 You may get two-bar phrases with two-bar fill-ins. **1955** L. Feather *Encycl. Jazz* ii. 55 The French horns join with the xylophone to provide a 'fill-in' phrase before the three themes resume in Bar 5. **1965** *Crescendo* Oct. 10/1 Hasaan's piano runs at times are extremely dazzling... Roach's explosive fill-ins seem to spark him along to experiment further.

d. *Photogr.* (See quot. 1955.)

1955 M. Reifer *Dict. New Words* 81/2 *Fill-in*, a supplementary light to illuminate shadows. **1957** T. L. J. Bentley *Man. Miniat. Camera* (ed. 5) v. 78 A smaller bulb having one half this guide number will be about right for the fill-in flash. **1958** *Amat. Photographer* 31 Dec. 897/2 The strength of the main light in relation to the strength of the fill-in light is also worthy of much consideration.

6. fill-out = fill *sb.*[1] 1 a.

1838 Dickens *O. Twist* II. xxv. 87 Produce the sustainance, and let's have a quiet fill-out for the first time these three days!

† **fill** (fıl), *sb.*[2] *Obs.* exc. *dial.* Also 6 phil, 7 fil. [var. of thill.]

1. *pl.* The thills or shafts of a cart. *sing.* The pair of shafts, 'the space between the shafts' (J.).

1606 Shaks. *Tr. & Cr.* III. ii. 48 And you draw backward weele put you i'th fils. **1632** Rowley *Woman never V.* iii, I will Give you the fore Horse place, and I wilbe in the Fill's. **1707** Mortimer *Husb.* 164 This Mule being put in the Fill of a Cart..ran away. **1755** in Johnson. **1845** D. Webster *Priv. Corr.* (1856) II. 202 He could not follow them any more than a dray-horse can jump out of the fills. **1904** F. Crissey *Tattlings Retired Politician* 247 Father's old clay-bank mare..[had never] laid down in his stall, in the fills, or in double harness.

2. *Comb.*, as **fill-horse** = shaft-horse.

1596 Shaks. *Merch. V.* II. ii. 100 Thou hast got more haire on thy chin, then Dobbin my philhorse has on his taile. **1648** Herrick *Hesper.* (1844) II. 38 Some cross the fill-horse. **1695** Kennett *Par. Antiq.* Gloss. s.v. *Pullanus*, The horse which goes in the rods is commo[n]ly called the fillar, and the fill-horse. *a* **1825** in Forby *Voc. E. Anglia.*

fill (fıl), *v.* Pa. t. and pa. pple. filled (fıld). Forms: 1 fyllan, 2 fellen, 3–5 full(e(n, fille(n, (3 felen, 4 *south*, velle), 4–6 fyll(e, 3– fill. [ME. *fullen*(*ü*):—OE. *fyllan* = OFris. *fullia*, *fella*, OS. *fullian* (Du. *vullen*), OHG. *fullen* (MHG. *vüllen*, Ger. *füllen*), ON. *fylla* (Sw. *fylla*, Da. *fylde*), Goth. *fulljan*:—OTeut. **fulljan*, f. **fullo-* full *a.*]

I. To make full.

1. To supply with as much as can be held or contained; to put or pour something into (a receptacle) till no more can be received. Also, *to fill full.* Const. †*mid*, †*of* (= OE. *genitive*), *with*.

a. in material sense.

c **1000** *Ags. Ps.* lxxx[i]. 10 Ontyn þinne muð and ic hine teala fylle! *c* **1160** *Hatton Gosp.* Luke xv. 16 Ða ȝe-wilnede he his wambe fellen of þam bean-coddan þe þa swin æten. *c* **1205** Lay. 20507 Me feolden heom [scipene] mid folke. *c* **1250** *Gen. & Ex.* 1225 A fetles wið water fild. *c* **1320** *Cast. Love* 731 A welle þat..fulleþ þe diches a-boute þe wal. **1393** Gower *Conf.* II. 204 That o kist Of fine golde..anone he filde full. *c* **1440** Capgrave *Life St. Kath.* v. 1962 Of laumpes hangynge..fillt with þat oyle. **1599** Marston *Sco. Villanie* II. vii. 205 That they their paunch may fill with Irus blood. **1645** Rutherford *Tryal & Tri. Faith* (1845) 11 Jesus Christ..was full of grace a vessel filled to the lip. **1697** Dryden *Virg. Georg.* III. 283 Who fill'd the Pail with Beestings of the Cow. **1875** Jowett *Plato* (ed. 2) I. 249 At the tale of pity my eyes are filled with tears. **1886** D. C. Murray *Cynic Fortune* vi, The broken..gentleman..filling his pockets with fairy bank-notes.

b. in immaterial sense.

a **1000** *Andreas* 523 (Gr.) He..wuldres fylde beorhtne boldwelan. *c* **1200** *Trin. Coll. Hom.* 117 Þe holi gost com uppen þe apostles and filde ful þat hus þere hie inne seten. *a* **1300** *Cursor M.* 852 (Cott.) God..fild þis werld al wit his grace. **13..** *Poems fr. Vernon MS.* 71 Ffullyng hem of þi fatnesse Of inward saunctite. *c* **1430** *Hymns Virg.* (1867) 27 Of grace my þouȝt þou fille. **1471** Ripley *Comp. Alch.* v. in Ashm. (1652) 158 Theyr howsys wyth stench they fyll. **1561** Norton & Sackv. *Gorboduc* I. i. (1571) A iv/1 His enuious hart..Filled with disdaine. **1667** Milton *P.L.* I. 495 Ely's Sons, who fill'd With lust and violence the house of God. **1697** Dryden *Virg. Georg.* III. 522 Linnets fill the Woods with tuneful Sound. **1710** Addison *Tatler* No. 220 ¶1 Having received many Letters filled with Compliments. **1744** Bp. Warburton *Wks.* (1811) XI. 244 *note*, The public therefore cannot be as impatient for their conviction as this decipherer is for filling his subscription. **1812** Southey *Life* (1850) III. 338 Surely such a subscription might soon be filled. **1848** Macaulay *Hist. Eng.* II. 29 Three more years filled with injuries.

c. Phrases: † ***to fill the hands of*** (a Hebraism): to invest with an office. ***to fill one's pipe***: to attain to easy circumstances or wealth (*slang*).

1535 Coverdale *Judg.* xvii. 5 Micha..fylled yᵉ handes of one of his sonnes. **1821** P. Egan *Tom & Jerry* vi. 84 Such persons..have lived just long enough, according to a vulgar phrase, to fill their pipe, and leave others to enjoy it.

d. ***to fill a ship's bottom*** (see quot. 1867). ***to fill the ice*** (see quot. 1892).

1867 Smyth *Sailor's Word-bk.*, *Filling a ship's bottom*, implies covering the bottom of a ship with broad-headed nails, so as to give her a sheathing of iron. **1892** J. Kerr *Gloss. Curling Terms, Curling* 380 *Fill the ice*, place stones on the way to the tee.

e. *Sc.* In hand-loom weaving, *absol.* = to fill the 'pirns' or bobbins with yarn, thus making them ready to be placed in the shuttle.

1889 J. M. Barrie *Window in Thrums* xii. 108 Nanny went to the loom in his place, filling as well as weaving.

f. In Poker: to complete (a 'full house', flush, straight, etc.) by drawing the necessary cards; also, to improve (one's hand) by drawing complementary cards; *intr.* or *absol.*, to make a flush, etc.; also, (of the flush, etc.) to become complete.

1865 'Mark Twain' *Sk. New & Old* (1875) 74 His last acts was to go his pile on 'kings-*and*' (calklatin' to fill, but which he didn't fill,) when there was a 'flush' out agin him. **1882** *Poker* 31 Scott drew to 'fill a straight and a flush both'. **1885** H. Jones in *Encycl. Brit.* (ed. 9) XIX. 283/1 The dealer then asks each in rotation who have chipped whether they will fill their hands (i.e. whether they will exchange any cards for an equivalent number from the top of the pack) or play the hand dealt. **1887** [see fill *sb.*[1] 2 c]. **1889** R. Guerndale *Poker Bk.* 25 To fill your hand, to improve it by the draw. **1895** 'Templar' *Poker Manual* 43 Sometimes the ante-man or the straddler will come in, if there has been no raise, on three to a straight or flush, drawing two cards. Such hands rarely fill. **1901** D. Curtis *Sci. Draw Poker* 56 If the three cards held be the Queen, Jack and nine it is evident that either the ten and eight, or the King and ten, would fill. *Ibid.* 78 Theoretically, the Flush should be filled oftener than the Straight. *Ibid.* 79 If B then fills he is getting 11 to 1. **1913** 'A. B. Lougher' *Poker* 13 The next process is that of drawing to fill the hands. **1928** *Amer. Mercury* Oct. 136/2 I'd made maybe a straight flush, [h]a[ve] filled somehow anyway, and cleaned him. **1957** *Encycl. Brit.* XVIII. 129/1 The odds are..39 to 8 against 'filling a bob-tail straight'.

†**2.** To impregnate. Cf. full *a.* *Obs.*

1607 Topsell *Four-f. Beasts* (1658) 48 They desire the Cow at eight months old, but they are not able to fill her till they be two years old. **1645** Milton *L'Allegro* 23.

3. a. *intr.* To become full, either in a material or immaterial sense. Of the bosom: = *fill out* (16 b).

1607 Shaks. *Timon* IV. iii. 244 The one is filling still, neuer compleat. **1685** Cotton tr. *Montaigne* I. 211 A soul stretches and dilates itself proportionably as it fills. **1713** *Guardian* No. 171 In a few weeks, when the town fills. **1751** R. Paltock *P. Wilkins* (1884) I. ix. 93 Upon launching my boat I perceived she was very leaky, so I let her fill. **1803** J. Davis *Trav. Amer.* 57 A bosom just beginning to fill. **1850** Tennyson *In Mem.* xix, Twice a day the Severn fills.

†**b.** Of a list, etc.: To be filled up. *Obs.*

1710 *Lond. Gaz.* No. 4661/3 The Lottery for two Millions of Florins fills with great Success.

c. *intr.* Of the eyes: to fill with tears.

1871 *Two Little Bruces* ix, 'I'm..tired..,' said Clemmie, with filling eyes. **1905** *Westm. Gaz.* 14 Jan. 2/3 The blue-grey eyes filled as the girl got quietly into bed.

4. *Naut.* **a.** *trans.* Of the wind: To cause (the sails) to swell; to distend.

1610 Shaks. *Temp.* Epil. 12 Gentle breath of yours my Sailes Must fill. **1735** *Phil. Trans.* XLI. 536 The Sailor

concerns himself no farther with the Wind, than as it fills his Sails. **1887** BOWEN *Virg. Æneid* III. 268 South winds filling the sails.

b. *intr.* Of a sail: To become full of wind.

1835 MARRYAT *Pirate* i, The jib filled as the frigate rounded to.

c. trans. *to fill the sails*: 'to brace the yards so that the wind strikes the after side of the sails, and advances the ship in her course' (Smyth).

1794 *Rigging & Seamanship* II. 312 Fill the sails. **1847** SIR J. C. ROSS *Voy. S. Seas* II. 168 By backing and filling the sails we endeavoured to avoid collision. **1875** BEDFORD *Sailor's Pocket-bk.* x. (ed. 2) 354 Fill the head sails.

d. *absol.*; also *to fill away*.

1681 *Lond. Gaz.* No. 1628/1 In the mean time, the Admiral who had been beaten off, filled and laid them Aboard the second time. **1832** MARRYAT *N. Forster* xli, The commodore made the signal to fill. **1840** R. H. DANA *Bef. Mast* xxxv. 133 Each vessel filled away, and kept on her course. **1860** G. BALMANNO in *Merc. Marine Mag.* VII. 369 Thinking there must be room ahead I filled again.

5. To stock or store abundantly.

c **1000** *Cædmon's Gen.* 196 (Gr.) Tudre fyllað eorðan ælgrene. **1388** WYCLIF *Gen.* i. 22 Wexe ȝe, and be ȝe multiplied, and fille ȝe the watris of the see. **1667** MILTON *P.L.* VII. 397 Be fruitful, multiply, and in the Seas And Lakes and running Streams the waters fill. **1782** COWPER *Progr. Err.* 480 The wriggling fry soon fill the creeks around. **1855** MACAULAY *Hist. Eng.* III. 203 This parliament was filled with Dermots and Geohegans [etc.]. **1856** EMERSON *Eng. Traits, Ability* Wks. (Bohn) II. 42 The rivers..are artificially filled with the eggs of salmon.

6. To charge or make up with some foreign material; hence, to adulterate.

1887–1890 [see FILLED *ppl. a.* 1 b.].

II. To occupy completely.

7. a. To occupy the whole capacity or extent of; also, to spread over or throughout, pervade.

a **1300** *Leg. Rood* (1871) 28 þe suotnesse þat þer-of com velde al þat lond. *a* **1400–50** *Alexander* 3065 His folke fellis all þe flode a forelange o brede. **1608–11** BP. HALL *Medit. & Vows* I. §34 The heart of man is..so infinite in desire, that the round globe of the world cannot fill the three corners of it. **1646** P. BULKELEY *Gospel Covt.* I. 130 Water which fills the sea. **1690** LOCKE *Hum. Und.* II. iv. §2 The Idea [which] belongs to Body, whereby we conceive it to fill space. **1768** JOHNSON *Let. to F. A. Barnard* 28 May, The maps..fill two Atlantic folios. **1848** MACAULAY *Hist. Eng.* I. 397 The fame of her great writers filled Europe. **1860** TYNDALL *Glac.* I. ii. 17 Glaciers which once filled the valley. **1884** tr. *Lotze's Logic* 444 The discussion which fills the XIIth book of Aristotle's Metaphysics. **1892** *Daily News* 17 Oct. 2/7 Wherever there is sufficient business between the two [towns] to 'fill' a wire.

b. In immaterial sense: To be all that is contained in.

1890 J. MARTINEAU *Seat Authority Relig.* Pref. 6 The mere resort to testimony for information beyond our province does not fill the meaning of 'authority'.

c. slang. *to fill the bill*: (*a*) *Theatrical*: see quot. 1891. (*b*) *U.S.* 'To do all that is desired, expected, or required; to suit the requirements of the case' (*Cent. Dict.*). See also BILL *sb.*[3] 8 d.

1882 *Chicago Tribune*, 'Affable Imbecile' would about fill the bill for you. **1891** FARMER *Slang Dict.*, *Fill the bill*, to excel in conspicuousness: as a star actor whose name is 'billed' to the exclusion of the rest of the company.

8. To hold or occupy (a position); to discharge the duties of (an office, place, post, etc.). In *to fill a chair, place, seat*, etc. with mixture of sense 7. So †*to fill the time*: to do what is wanted at the time.

c **1400** *Apol. Loll.* 1 þe pope..filliþ not in dede, ne in word, þe office of Petir in ȝerþ. **1601** SHAKS. *All's Well* I. ii. 69, I fill a place, I know't. *Ibid.* III. vii. 33 In fine, deliuers me to fill the time, Her selfe most chastly absent. **1697** DRYDEN *Virg. Georg.* IV. 294 Thus make they Kings to fill the Regal Seat. **1711** STEELE *Spect.* No. 2 ¶1 He fills the Chair at a Quarter-Session. **1769** GOLDSM. *Rom. Hist.* (1786) II. 105 His assiduity in filling the duties of each [employment]. **1821** BYRON *Juan* IV. xv, They were not made in the real world to fill A busy character in the dull scene. **1848** MACAULAY *Hist. Eng.* II. 608 Perth..filling the great place of Chancellor. **1871** FREEMAN *Norm. Conq.* (1876) IV. xviii. 216 Stamford, like Lincoln..fills a prominent place in the wars of Edward. **1876** GLADSTONE *Homeric Synchr.* 49 Who fills the Chair of Chemistry at Athens. **1885** *Law Times* LXXIX. 170/2 The post which is now filled by Mr. Ilbert.

9. a. To occupy or furnish the means of occupying (what is vacant). †*to fill the room of*: to take the place of.

1562 TURNER *Herbal* II. 67 a, The asshes may fill the rome of spodium. **1875** JOWETT *Plato* (ed. 2) III. 235 Amusements which fill a vacant hour.

b. To put a person or thing into (a vacant place).

1593 SHAKS. *3 Hen. VI*, III. i. 16 No Harry..'tis no Land of thine, Thy place is fill'd. **1868** FREEMAN *Norm. Conq.* (1876) II. App. 588 The people at large claimed a voice in filling the episcopal chair.

III. To satisfy; to fulfil, complete.

10. a. To produce a sense of fullness in; to satiate, satisfy, glut; in both material and immaterial sense. Chiefly of a personal agent; occas. of a thing. Const. *with*.

a **1300** *Cursor M.* 6842 (Cott.) þe pour men hunger for to fill. *Ibid.* 17227 (Cott.) Mi flexsli lust to fill. **1340** *Ayenb.* 77 Hi onderstondeþ þet al þe worlde ne is naȝt a guod snode: uor mannes herte to uelle. *c* **1440** *Promp. Parv.* 160/1 Fyll wythe mete, *sacio*. **1485** CAXTON *Paris & V.* 31 Coude not be contente ne fylled to beholde hyr fayre loue. **1559** *Mirr. Mag., Dk. Suffolk* xvii, How fast she fylde me both with prayes and prayse. **1607** SHAKS. *Timon* I. i. 271 To see meate fill Knaues, and Wine heat fooles. **1607** TOPSELL *Four-f. Beasts* (1658) 360 A Lion..when he is satisfied and filled he layeth aside that savage quality. **1661** PEPYS *Diary* 23 July, I sat before Mrs. Palmer..and filled my eyes with her. **1715** CHEYNE *Philos Princ. Relig.* II. ii. 70 Nothing..but the absolute and increated Infinite, can adequatly fill and super-abundantly satisfy it [the desire]. **1821** KEATS *Isabel* ii, Her full shape would all his seeing fill.

†**b.** *intr.* To become satisfied or satiated. *Obs.*

c **1330** R. BRUNNE *Chron. Wace* (Rolls) 2392 Sone afterward þey fillede of Leyre. **1592** SHAKS. *Ven. & Ad.* 548 Glutton-like she feeds, yet never filleth.

†**11.** To make satisfaction for, atone for (a fault).

a **1300** *Cursor M.* 24700 (Gött.) Suilk fautis mai men fill.

12. †**a.** To carry out in or to its fullness, execute, perform (a command, duty, promise, etc.); to fulfil (a prophecy, etc.). Also *to fill forth*. *Obs.*

c **1000** *Azarias* 42 (Gr.) Fyl nu þa frumspræce. *c* **1200** ORMIN 917 He ne namm nan gom To fillenn all hiss wikenn. *a* **1225** *Ancr. R.* 386 Luue fulleð þe lawe. *c* **1250** *Gen. & Ex.* 1463 Ðat he sulde fillen ðat quede ðat he abraham quilum dede. *a* **1300** *Cursor M.* 14531 (Cott.) He com for..þe prophecies to fill. *c* **1340** *Gaw. & Gr. Knt.* 1405 To fylle þe same forwardez þat þay by-fore maden. *c* **1380** WYCLIF *Serm.* Sel. Wks. I. 324 Goddis wille is fillid asideli. *c* **1400** *Destr. Troy* 602 But this forward to fille, first ye me sweire. *c* **1500** *Lancelot* 3353 Thai..All redy war to fillyng his command. **1578** *Scot. Poems 16th C.* II. 131 To fulfill his Fathers will, Till fill furth that he said. **1836** *Congress. Globe* Jan., App. 50/2 From age to age, they [*sc.* the Negroes] have filled this saying ['Cursed be Canaan'].

†**b.** To make perfect, accomplish, complete, finish (a work, period of time, 'one's days'). Also with *inf.* as *obj.* *Obs.*

c **1175** *Lamb. Hom.* 39 Þet seofeðe is cherite, heo fulleð alle þa oðre þing and endeð. *c* **1300** *Havelok* 354 Deth him tok þan he best wolde Liuen, but hyse dayes were fulde. *c* **1330** R. BRUNNE *Chron.* (1810) 34 Auht ȝere was he kyng, his daies alle filled. **1382** WYCLIF *Ex.* xxxvi. 8 Alle the wise men in herte maden to fille the werk of the tabernacle. **1388** —— *Jer.* li. 63 Whanne thou hast fillid to rede this book. *c* **1400** *Destr. Troy* 1109 To fillyn our fare & our fos harme. **1611** BIBLE *Isa.* lxv. 20 An olde man, that hath not filled his dayes.

c. *Comm.* To execute (a trade order). Also (*U.S.*), to make up (a prescription).

1860 *Richmond Enquirer* 2 Nov. 1/7 The Executive of the State is making the most strenuous efforts to fill the orders for arms that come to him from all parts of the State. **1866** LOWELL *Lett.* (1894) I. 369, I sat down and did what I could to answer ('fill', I think, is the proper word) your order. **1891** *Pall Mall G.* 15 Oct. 7/2 In order to fill this one order by a single firm. **1891** H. TUCKLEY *Under the Queen* 25 The individual who fills their prescriptions. **1926** D. L. COLVIN *Prohibition in U.S.* 171 During the campaign he filled one hundred and twenty-five speaking engagements. *a* **1940** F. SCOTT FITZGERALD *Last Tycoon* (1947) v. 104 If you were in a drug store..having a prescription filled. **1968** *Globe & Mail* (Toronto) 17 Feb. 12 (Advt.), Phone orders filled for city and suburban delivery only.

IV. With the introduced contents as *obj.*

†**13.** To put (wine, etc.) into a vessel with the view of filling it; hence, To pour out. Also, *to fill about, out* (see 16 c). *Obs.* exc. *arch.* (Cf. Ger. *füllen*.)

c **1450** *Erle Tolous* 314 Fylle the wyne, wyghtly he badd. **1530** PALSGR. 549/2, I fyll drinke..*Je verse a boyre*. **1615** MARKHAM *Eng. Housew.* II. i. (1668) 12 Having filled it [Milk] into a clean vessel. **1637** T. MORTON *New Eng. Canaan* III. xiv. 134 Fill sweet nectar freely about. **1705** W. BOSMAN *Guinea* 230 Brandy in the Morning and Palm-Wine in the Afternoon are very briskly filled about. **1710** STEELE *Tatler* No. 141 ¶4, I..desire the young lady may fill tea one week longer. [**1840** FONBLANQUE *Life & Lab.* (1874) 318 Let there be well-paid publicans to fill gills of whiskey.]

absol. *c* **1510** *Robin Hood* 1, 'Fyll of the best wyne' sayd Robyn. **1594** MARLOWE & NASHE *Dido* I. i, I fill'd into your cups. **1611** BIBLE *Rev.* xviii. 6 In the cup which she hath filled fill to her double. **1820** SCOTT *Ivanhoe* xxi, He hath no pleasure save to fill, to swill, and to call for more.

14. a. To fill a receptacle with (any material); to put or take a load of (corn, water, etc.) on board a ship. *to fill powder* (see quot. 1867).

1297 R. GLOUC. (1724) 13 He lette sende hys messageres in to al Grece..And lette fulle corn, and oyl, & wyn, by iche syde. **1496** [See FILLER 1.] **1557** W. TOWRSON in Hakluyt *Voy.* (1589) 114 Here we filled water, and after set saile. **1697** DAMPIER *Voy.* I. xv. 404 Having fill'd our Water, cut our Wood, and got our Ship in a sailing posture. **1725** DE FOE *New Voy.* (1840) 35 Having the long-boat and the shallop, with about six-and-thirty men with them, away they went to fill water. **1797** NELSON in Nicolas *Disp.* II. 224 Eighteen rounds of powder filled. **1867** SMYTH *Sailor's Word-bk.*, *Filling powder*, taking gunpowder from the casks to fill cartridges.

b. *Dentistry.* = STOP *v.* 4 d.

1848 *Lit. Amer.* 29 July 64/2 Teeth filled with gold (if preferred), extracted and cleaned. **1859** J. TOMES *Syst. Dental Surg.* 334 In the treatment of caries, filling must ever be regarded as the great remedy. *Ibid.*, There is perhaps no other operation..which is attended with the same unqualified success as that of filling teeth. **1945** L. BAKER *Party Line* 92 Dick not only filled and pulled teeth, but he went modern and practiced orthodontia. **1963** C. R. COWELL et al. *Inlays, Crowns & Bridges* iii. 17 Any caries remaining is excavated and these localized excavations are filled with cement.

c. To put or throw *into* (a receptacle) by way of filling it.

1884 *Encycl. Brit.* XVII. 742 Measured quantities..of [oil-seed] meal are filled into woollen bags. **1906** *Springfield Weekly Republ.* 12 Jan. 13 The New Englander curses gold mining. Billions of good, hard New England cash have been filled into those little black holes.

V. Idiomatically combined with adverbs. (For non-specialized combinations, see the simple senses and the advbs.)

15. fill in.

a. *trans.* To complete (an outline). **b.** To put in, *esp.* by speech or in writing, what will occupy a vacancy or vacant place. **c.** *Naut.* (see quot.).

1840 CLOUGH *Amours de Voy.* III. 178 A chamber filled-in with harmonious, exquisite pictures. **1867** SMYTH *Sailor's Word-bk.*, *Filling-in*, the replacing a ship's vacant planks opened for ventilation, when preparing her, from ordinary, for sea. **1878** BOSW. SMITH *Carthage* 269 The outline is commanding..and there is no detail with which our materials enable us to fill it in at all, which is not in perfect harmony with the whole. **1883** *Sat. Rev.* 8 Sept. 302 The aposiopesis is seldom filled in. **1893** SIR J. W. CHITTY in *Law Times' Rep.* LXVIII. 430/1 He had left the date blank for the plaintiff to fill in. **1962** *Rep. Comm. Broadc.* 224 in *Parl. Papers 1961–2* (Cmnd. 1753) IX. 259 The material to fill-in the programmes when local items were not being broadcast would..be obtained by switching in to one or other of the three national sound services. *Ibid.* 231 The form of organisation envisaged by the BBC—that is, of local stations providing their own programmes, and filling in with centrally provided material.

d. *to fill in (the) time*: to occupy oneself during a period of inaction. Also *transf.*

1905 W. BODIE *Bodie Bk.* 135 It is simply to fill in the time while I am deciding how to act. **1939** *War Illustr.* 201 Nurses usefully filling in time while they are off duty. **1966** *Listener* 15 Dec. 898/2 The film sags, filling in time tediously.

e. *to fill* (someone) *in on*: to make (a person) conversant with. Also *intr.* and without *on*. orig. and chiefly *U.S.*

1945 E. NEWHOUSE *Many are Called* (1952) 192 Can you fill me in on them? **1951** *Time* 19 Mar. 46/3 He felt chipper enough to spend an hour..with General MacArthur 'filling in' on U.S. affairs. **1951** L. HOBSON *Celebrity* (1953) vi. 78 He had called Roy Tribble and asked to be filled in on Jim Hathaway. **1955** *Bull. Atomic Sci.* Sept. 248/3 It would be incorrect and unfair to say that the AEC has altogether failed to 'fill in' reporters who have called upon its information division for guidance. **1960** 'R. EAST' *Kingston Black* xix. 178, I filled in for Kitty. **1962** H. BURNETT *Nothing Sacred* (*caption*), You've been candid about my faults, so I'd be glad to fill you in about your own!

f. (See quot. 1948.) *slang.*

1948 W. GRANVILLE in Partridge *Dict. Forces' Slang* 69 *Fill in, to*, to give someone a good hiding... (Lower-deck.) **1959** *Times* 3 Mar. 3/4 A naval rating accused of murdering..an antique dealer..was alleged to have..said: 'I filled in a chap and took his money.'

16. fill out.

a. *trans.* To enlarge or extend to the desired limit. Cf. 4.

a **1700** DRYDEN (J.), Whom pomp and greatness sits so loose about, That he wants majesty to fill them out. **1707** NORRIS *Treat. Humility* vi. 278 They may not..so fill out the sails of our reputation in this world.

b. *intr.* To become distended, or rounded in outline.

1851 CARPENTER *Man. Phys.* (ed. 2) 360 As each set of muscles is relaxed, the veins..fill out again. **1888** *Illustr. Sport. & Dram. News* 21 Jan. 511/1 Merry Hampton [horse] is thickening and filling out. **1937** V. WOOLF *Years* 334 How nice to see you—you've filled out.

c. *trans.* To pour out (wine, etc.). Cf. 13.

1602 MARSTON *Ant. & Mel.* II. Wks. 1856 I. 28 Fill out Greeke wines. **1749** FIELDING *Tom Jones* VIII. v, Filling out a glass of wine. **1864** G. DYCE *Bella Donna* II. 145 The tea was filled out and getting cold.

d. = *fill up* (see 17 g), *fill in* (see 15 b).

1880 [see FILLED *ppl. a.* 2]. **1903** W. E. CURTIS *True Abraham Lincoln* 59 Mr. Lanman forwarded to him a blank to be filled out with facts and dates. **1941** *Amer. Speech* XVI. 310/1 The borrower fills out a call card. **1963** H. GARNER in R. Weaver *Canad. Short Stories* (1968) 2nd Ser. 44, I filled out a 'first off' tag and attached it to the inspected part. **1967** *Boston Sunday Globe* 23 Apr. (*Parade*) 27/4 (Advt.), So fill out the coupon and send it to us. We'll send you all the details about Canada '67.

17. fill up.

'*Up* is often used without much addition to the force of the verb' (J.).

a. *trans.* To fill to repletion. **b.** To complete the process of filling; to fill the vacant parts or places in (anything); to supply the deficiencies in.

1605 SHAKS. *Macb.* IV. iii. 62 Your Wiues, your Daughters..could not fill up The Cesterne of my Lust. **1712** STEELE *Spect.* No. 432 ¶11 When you want a Trifle to fill up a Paper. **1780** A. MCDOUGALL in Sparks *Corr. Amer. Rev.* (1853) III. 136 They have passed very decisive laws for filling up their regiments for the war. **1803** SCOTT *Bonnie Dundee*, Come fill up my cup, come fill up my can. **1824–9** LANDOR *Imag. Conv.* (1846) II. 209 He has left us a design to fill up. **1891** S. C. SCRIVENER *Our Fields & Cities* 72 These people could fill up their time at agriculture.

c. To supply (a deficiency, a vacancy); to provide an occupant for (a vacant post).

1596 SHAKS. *1 Hen. IV*, IV. ii. 35 Such haue I to fill vp the roomes of them that haue bought out their seruices. **1611** BIBLE *Col.* i. 24 Who..fill vp that which is behind of the afflictions of Christ in my flesh. **1694** F. BRAGGE *Disc. Parables* v. 181 A numerous progeny to..fill up the vacancies left by the fall of the rebel angels. **1891** *Law Times* XC. 419/2 He has had to fill up two High Court judgeships.

†**d.** To come up to the measure of; to equal.

1588 SHAKS. *L.L.L.* v. ii. 193 How many inches doth fill vp one mile?

†**e.** To complete the measure of. *Obs.*

1611 BIBLE *1 Thess.* ii. 16 Forbidding us to speak to the Gentiles, that they might be saved, to fill up their sins alway.

1642 CHAUNCY in Bradford *Plymouth Plantation* (1856) 396 God sometimes hids a sinner until his wickednes is filled up.

†**f.** To fulfil, satisfy. *Obs.*

1596 SHAKS. *Merch. V.* IV. i. 160 Comes..to fill vp your Graces request in my sted.

g. To write what is requisite in the blank space or spaces of a cheque, form, etc. Cf. 15 b.

1802 LD. ELDON in *Vesey's Reports* VII. 78 A blank, left for the name of the person..was not filled up. **1885** *Act 48 Vict.* c. 15 Sched. II. Forms, Part ii. Form (A), You are hereby required to fill up accurately the under-written form. **1885** *Manch. Exam.* 3 June 4/7 One of them [cheques] he filled up for £1,000.

h. To stop up; to do away with (a hole) by filling.

1596 SHAKS. *1 Hen. IV*, III. ii. 116 To fill the mouth of deepe Defiance vp. **1611** —— *Wint. T.* v. iii. 101 Ile fill your Graue vp. **1818** CRUISE *Digest* (ed. 2) III. 96 A commoner cannot fill up rabbit burrows made by the lord. *Mod.* There was a pond here, but it has been filled up.

i. *intr.* 'To grow full' (J.) Of (the bed of) a sea: To silt up.

1695 WOODWARD *Nat. Hist. Earth* I. (1702) 49 Neither the Palus Mœotis..nor any other Seas, fill up, or by degrees grow shallower.

VI. 18. *Comb.* The vb.-stem is prefixed to various sbs., forming sbs. with the sense 'he who or that which fills something', as **fill-basket**, a name applied by gardeners to certain large or prolific kinds of peas, potatoes, etc.; **fill-belly**, a glutton; **fill-(the)-dike, -ditch** *a.*, epithets of the month February; †**fill-knag**, ? a drunkard; **fill-paunch** (see quot.); **fill-pot**, ? a tippler; **fill-sack, fill-space** (see quots.); †**fill-square** (*Geom.*), one of the complements of a square.

1881 *Oxfordsh. Gloss.* Suppl., **Fill basket*, a large kind of pea. **1553** BECON *Reliques of Rome* (1563) 49* They are *fylbellyes and Epicures. **1611** COTGR., Wee call it [February], *Fill-dike. **1879** JEFFERIES *Wild Life in S.C.* 314 In February—*'fill-ditch', as the old folk call it. *a* **1605** POLWART *Flyting w. Montgomerie* 790 Buttrie bag, *fill knag! **1659** TORRIANO, *Tira-pancia*, a stretch-gut, a gulch-bellie, a *fill-panch. **1609** *Ev. Woman in Hum.* I. i. in Bullen *O. Pl.* IV. 315 *Host.* There, my fine *fil-pots; give the word as you passe. *a* **1635** NAUNTON *Fragm. Reg.* (Arb.) 55 The people then called him, *Fill-sack, by reason of his great wealth. **1827** LAMB *Lett.* (1888) II. 194 The artist (who had clapt in Miss merely as a *fill-space). **1551** RECORDE *Pathw. Knowl.* I. xvi, When there are more then one [square] made about one bias line, the *filsquares of euery of them muste needes be equall.

fill(e, obs. pa. t. of FALL *v.*

'fillable, *a.* [f. prec. + -ABLE.] Capable of being filled.

1483 *Cath. Angl.* 130/2 Fyllabylle, *saciabilis*. **1870** *Graphic* 14 May 563/2 When the white hands of April are fillable With blossoms.

†**'fillady, filliday.** *Obs.* Some bird in Newfoundland.

1622 N. H. *Let.* 18 Aug. in Whitbourne *Newfoundland*, The Fowles and Birds of the Land are Partriges, Curlues, Fillidayes..and such like. **1623** *Ibid.* 7 Filladies, Nightingales, and such like small birds. **1674** J. JOSSELYN *Two Voy. to N.-E.* 100 Filladies are small singing Birds.

fillamo(r)t, -ander, obs. ff. FILEMOT, FILANDER¹.

†**'fillatrice.** *rare*⁻¹. [a. F. *filatrice*, woman who spins; also (17th c.) a stuff with a woof of floss-silk, f. *filer* to spin.] *attrib.* in ***fillatrice-stuff***, a sort of stuff ? made of floss silk.

1714 *Fr. Bk. of Rates* 41 Fillatrice-Stuff, as mercery, per 100 Weight.

†**fille**¹. *Obs.* [OE. *fille*, app. shortened from *cerfille*, CHERVIL.] ? = CHERVIL.

In Wr.-Wülcker 323 (*c* 1050) it glosses *serpillum*, which properly means thyme. Halliwell's Dict. has '*Fill*, the plant Restharrow', but gives no authority.

c **1000** *Sax. Leechd.* 34 Fille and finule. *a* **1310** in Wright *Lyric P.* xiii, The fenyl ant the fille.

†**fille**². *Obs.* [a. F. *feuille*.]

1. A leaf.

c **1450** *Med. Rec.* in *Thornton Rom.* p. xxxvi, Take vervayne or vetoyne, or filles of wormod, and make lee therof.

2. As the type of something worthless. [Perh. another word.]

1297 R. GLOUC. (1724) 297 Al nas worþ afylle. *c* **1305** *Pilate* 87 in *E.E.P.* (1862) 113 Pilatus..ne ȝaf noȝt worþ afille.

filled (fɪld), *ppl. a.* [f. as prec. + -ED¹.]

1. a. In various senses of the vb. *U.S.* (quot. 1843): stuffed.

1580 BARET *Alv.* F 494 Filled, satisfied, *saturatus*. **1769** FALCONER *Dict. Marine* (1789) Y y iij, The filled cartridges. **1772** *Ann. Reg.* 9/1 A Chinese..offered me a filled tobacco pipe. **1843** 'R. CARLTON' *New Purchase* viii. 51 Why should we trespass on patience with the account of..steaks, filled chickens, plum puddings, and the curious dish of what-nots? **1882** *Pall Mall G.* 12 July 8/2 Barges laden with filled shell are arriving. **1892** LOCKWOOD *Mech. Engin. Dict.*, *Filled Rail*, a point rail, or a stock rail, which has one or both sides filled up flush.

b. Made up by the addition of foreign materials; adulterated. Of cotton fabrics: Faced or sized with certain preparations serving to give the appearance of greater substance.

1887 *Pall Mall G.* 25 June 12/1 A word in defence of the much abused 'filled' cottons. **1888** *Nature* 26 July 294/1 The methods of production of 'filled' (*i.e.* adulterated and watered) soaps. **1890** *Daily News* 25 Apr. 5/3 A mysterious product analogous to margarine, known to the trade as 'filled cheese'. **1934** WEBSTER, Filled milk. **1959** *Observer* 8 Feb. 4/6 'Filled milk'—that is, milk in which the natural animal fats are replaced by special vegetable fats.

2. With adverbs: see FILL *v.* 15–17.

1849 *Florist* 264 The variety caused by numerous petals and a filled-up outline. **1865** *Cornhill Mag.* Feb. 179, I will ..take them before and after my filled-up hours. **1866** HOWELLS *Venet. Life* xvi. 248 A filled-up canal. **1880** *Daily News* 26 Aug. 2/3 The booking clerk gives him a filled-out memorandum. **1899** *T. Eaton & Co. Catal.* Spring & Summer 218 Fine English China tea sets..with filled-in colors. **1905** *Westm. Gaz.* 15 July 12/2 That..filled-in look [of a bodice]. **1951** AUDEN *Nones* (1952) 42 Halting at each of the now filled-in shafts. **1968** H. HARMAR *Chihuahua Guide* 237 *Filled-up face*, one in which the cheek muscles are well developed, such as in the Staffordshire.

‖**fille de chambre** (fij də ʃɑ̃br). [Fr.] A chambermaid; a lady's personal maid.

1675 H. WOOLLEY *Gentlew. Comp.* 79 Their *Filles de Chambre*..attending their beauties. **1768** STERNE *Sent. Journ.* I. 141 Madame de L***..rang up her *fille de chambre* to ask about it. **1809** [see AGACERIE]. *a* **1846** B. R HAYDON *Autobiogr.* (1927) III. xiii. 231 The *fille de chambre*, Rose Armande, was a very interesting girl.

‖**fille de joie** (fij də ʒwa). [Fr.] A prostitute.

1705 [see ENTRE NOUS]. **1755** C. CHARKE *Life* 135 At this Time, my Lord kept in the House with him a *Fille de Joye*. **1867** 'OUIDA' *Under Two Flags* II. ii. 31 The grisette charms of little tobacconists, milliners,..bonbon-sellers and filles de joie. **1901** A. E. TAYLOR *Probl. Conduct* iv. 212 The mere purposelessness and joylessness of the routine life led by the professional 'fille de joie'. **1964** C. MACKENZIE *My Life & Times* III. iii. 92 That production in which the four *filles de joie* were played by Jean MacKinlay, [etc.]. **1970** *Daily Tel.* 8 Oct. 16/2 A string of odious street pick-ups when she embarks finally and inevitably on the career of a fille de joie.

fillemot, -ender, obs. ff. FILEMOT, FILANDER.

filler¹ ('fɪlə(r)). [f. FILL *v.* + -ER¹.]

1. a. One who or that which fills: in various senses of the verb, *spec.* in *Mining*.

1496 *Nottingham Rec.* III. 291 To þe fillers þat filled grauell at Trent side. **1541** R. COPLAND *Guydon's Quest. Chirurg.*, The fyller and nouryssher of the other. **1641** BEST *Farm. Bks.* (Surtees) 59 Hee that forketh the waine is to stande on the stacke [? waine] and forke to the stacke and fillers. **1755** YOUNG *Centaur* Wks. 1762 IV. 197 Centre of all good! Filler of immensity! **1816** BYRON *Let. to Moore* 5 Jan., The fifteen hundred fillers of hot rooms, called the fashionable world. **1883** GRESLEY *Gloss. Coal-m.*, *Filler*, one who fills at a working place or in a stall. **1886** *Pall Mall G.* 5 Oct. 14/1 The peaches come in large pans, and each 'filler' selects with a fork only the perfect halves. **1921** *Dict. Occup. Terms* (1927) §042 *Filler*.., shovels coal into trams or tubs or upon conveyor at coal face. **1928** *Observer* 12 Feb. 21/4 The full effect of the reduction will be felt only by the hewers, fillers, and a few others. **1955** *Times* 3 May 10/1 The unofficial miners' strike in the Doncaster area arises out of dissatisfaction with the pay of fillers (the men who load coal on the conveyor belts).

b. *Sc.* A funnel.

1782 SIR J. SINCLAIR *Observ. Scot. Dial.* 118 *A filler*, a funnel. **1847** in CRAIG.

c. A filling machine or apparatus. Also *attrib.*, as ***filler cap***, the cap closing the pipe leading to the petrol tank of a motor vehicle; ***filler hose***, the hose of a petrol pump at a garage.

1895 *Army & Navy Co-op. Soc. Price List* 15 Sept. 252/2 Boiler Fillers, galvanized, 2 gall. *Ibid.* 309 Oil Fillers, 1 pint. **1901** *Daily Chron.* 10 Sept. 9/1 Mineral Waters.—Experienced respectable young man, accustomed Riley's filler. **1927** Filler-cap [see AIR-LOCK b]. **1962** *Which? Car Suppl.* Oct. 139/2 Petrol filler hoses had damaged the paint finish..and the paintwork was discoloured next to the filler cap.

2. Something used to fill a cavity, stop a gap, complete a load or charge, make bulk, etc.

1591 GREENE *Disc. Coosnage* (1592) 22 Laying in the mouth of the sack certaine choise coles, which they call fillers, to make the sack shew faire. **1697** DRYDEN *Æneid* Ded. (1709) 297 It [an epithet] is a mere filler, to stop a vacancy in the Hexameter. **1867** SMYTH *Sailor's Word-bk.*, *Filler*, a filling piece on a made mast. **1874** *Congress. Rec.* 10 Jan. 558/1 They will not give beyond so much for a certain class of fillers and a certain class of wrapper. **1884** *Pall Mall G.* 17 May 4 A cigar consists of three parts, the wrapper, the bunch, and the filler. **1885** *Harper's Mag.* Mar. 608/2 It consists of..marble blocks inclosing a 'filler' of cemented granite stones. **1895** *Street Railway Jrnl.* Apr. 252 'Filler' wire strand, consisting of 19 wires of the same size with the small wires inserted so as to make the outer wires of the strand tangent to the circumscribed circle. **1904** GOODCHILD & TWENEY *Technol. & Sci. Dict.* 221/1 *Filling up*, the process of bringing a surface to a level before painting or between the application of the coats... A good filler for a plastered surface is made by mixing fine plaster of Paris, whiting, and warm size... A paste filler..is used to fill the grain of the wood. **1904** *Electr. Rev.* 11 Sept. 450 (Cent. Dict. Suppl.), The floor framing consists of six sills, the four centre ones being six-inch 'I' beams with wood fillers extending the entire length of car. **1913** *Writer's Mag.* Dec. 247/1 Fillers of a few hundred words in this field..are desirable in this department. **1916** J. W. TOUMEY *Seeding & Planting* 70 The original cost of the seeding or planting can be materially reduced by the use of so-called fillers, i.e. inexpensive species which serve to occupy a portion of the area, but which are removed in the early thinnings. **1930** *Engineering* 25 Apr. 545/3 The effects of trass as a pozzuolanic material and as a merely inert filler. **1935** *Economist* 7 Dec. 1142/2 Plastics..may be divided into three main groups: Phenolic and fillers, [etc.]. **1941** E. CULBERTSON *Contract Bridge Complete* (ed. 3) iii. 48 Minor intermediate values, or 'fillers'. These fillers consist of isolated jacks, tens and even nines. **1942** H. A. MADDOX *Dict. Stationery* (ed. 2) 40 *Filler*, (also known as stuffer), a small inset which is used nowadays as a popular advertising device to enclose in letters or with other literature. A cheap and effective medium of publicity with a saving of postal cost. **1946** *N. & Q.* CXCI. 238/2 While he was editor.. there appeared a series of brief papers (obviously fillers) called 'Omniana'. **1951** R.. MAYER *Artist's Handbk.* ii. 89 The inert fillers or extenders are..white or nearly white pigments which have low refractive indices and, therefore, when ground in oil in the manner of the usual artist's colour, have little or no opacity or tinctorial effect. **1954** *Paper Terminol.* (*Spalding & Hodge*) 36 *Loading*, mineral material added to paper pulp..imparting solidity and a good printing surface to the paper... Also called Filler. **1958** *Listener* 18 Dec. 1055/2 Primer, filler, undercoat, and finish. **1959** F. W. HOUSEHOLDER in Saporta & Bastian *Psycholinguistics* (1961) 25/1 The 'filler' part [of a tagmeme] is either another formula..or a list. **1961** *John o' London's* 13 Apr. 417/3 The American is given the job as a filler while he waits for the post of judge to fall vacant. **1964** M. A. K. HALLIDAY et al. *Linguistic Sci.* 193 Exclamations and 'fillers' such as *oh, ah, quoi!*

3. With adverbs, as ***filler-in, filler-up***.

1726 LEONI *Alberti's Archit.* I. 44 b, Those parts which.. lie between these principal parts, are very properly call'd fillers up. **1735** POPE *Let. to Cromwell* 17 Dec. 1710, A Mixture..of forc'd and inextricable Conceits, and of needless fillers-up. **1776** 'COURTNEY MELMOTH' *Pupil Pleas.* I. 217 Detraction is a necessary filler-up of the vacuum. **1877** *N.W. Linc. Gloss.*, *Fillers in*, small stones in the inside of a rubble-wall.

4. *Comb.*: **filler-box**, a receptacle for prepared clay in a brick machine.

1884 C. T. DAVIS *Bricks & Tiles* v. 177 It is impossible to fill the charge-boxes, or as they are also termed, the 'filler-boxes', with any degree of regularity in dry-clay machines.

filler² ('fɪlə(r)). Also 7 **fillar**, 9 **viller**. [f. FILL *sb.*² + -ER¹.] A thill- or shaft-horse. Also *attrib.* as **filler-horse**.

1695 KENNETT *Par. Antiq.* Gloss. s.v. *Pullanus*, The horse which goes in the rods is commo[n]ly called the fillar. **1852** C. W. H[OSKINS] *Talpa* 3 Just as the filler-horse was congratulating himself that it was all plain sailing now. **1888** *Berksh. Gloss.*, *Viller*.

‖**filler**³ ('filleːr). Also **fillér**. [Hungarian *fillér*.] A Hungarian coin, the hundredth part of a forint.

1904 *Statesman's Year-Bk.* 416 Nickel:—The twenty-heller (20-fillér) piece. **1927** *Observer* 9 Oct. 11/3 Buyers of the fifty-filler 'Trianon' brooch. **1928** *Ibid.* 15 Apr. 12 Nádosy earned four *filler* a day. **1947** *Statesman's Year-Bk.* 1001 A decree of 26 July, 1946, issued by the Hungarian Government..instituted a new monetary unit, the 'forint', subdivided into 100 'fillér'.

filleroy, obs. form of PHILLYREA.

fillet ('fɪlɪt), *sb.*¹ Forms: 4 **filete, philett**, 4–5 **felet(t**, 5 **filett**, 5–6 **fi-, fylette**, *south.* **vylette**, 6 **fyllet(t**, (6 **fylet, fillott**, 7 **filot**, 7–8 **fillit(t)**, 6–7 **phillet**, 4–7 **fillet**, 6– **fillet**. [a. Fr. *filet* = Pr. *filet*, Sp. *filete*, It. *filetto*, a Com. Romanic diminutive of L. *filum* thread.]

1. A head-band. **a.** A ribbon, string, or narrow band of any material used for binding the hair, or worn round the head to keep the headdress in position, or simply for ornament.

Also *fig.*, esp. with reference to the *vitta* with which in classical antiquity the heads of sacrificial victims were adorned, or to the 'snood' formerly worn as a badge of maidenhood.

a **1327** *Pol. Songs* (Camden) 154 Habbe he a fauce filet, he halt hire hed heȝe. *a* **1400–50** *Alexander* 4338 Oure paramours vs to plese ne pride þaim bewenes, Nouthire ffurrers, filetts, ne frengs. *c* **1467** *Paston Lett.* No. 568 II. 298 She wuld fayne have a new felet. **1530** PALSGR. 200/1 Fyllet for a maydens heed, *fronteau*. **1553** EDEN *Treat. Newe Ind.* (Arb.) 18 All..of the kinges bande, haue a silken fyllet of scarlet colour tied about their heades. **1626** T. H[AWKINS] *Caussin's Holy Crt.* 93 Euen those, which haue yet the fillet of shamefastnesse vpon theyr browes, suffer themselues..to runne, after the torrent of Examples. **1697** DRYDEN *Virg. Georg.* II. 675 Ye sacred Muses..Whose Priest I am, whose holy Fillets wear. **1704** POPE *Windsor For.* 178 A belt her waist, a fillet binds her hair. **1795** BURKE *Let. to Elliot* Wks. 1842 II. 241 These priests..begin by crowning me with their flowers and their fillets. **1839** MRS. HEMANS *Poems, Lady of Castle*, Those long fair tresses..Bursting their fillet. **1879** BEERBOHM *Patagonia* vi. 91 Their hair is kept from falling over their faces by a fillet tied round the head.

attrib. **1847** EMERSON *Poems, Mithridates* Wks. I. 140 Ivy for my fillet band; Blinding dog-wood in my hand.

†**b.** (See quot.) ? *nonce use* (transl. Gr. διάδημα).

1688 R. HOLME *Armoury* III. 3/1 Of a Crown, the Diadem, or Royal Fillet, is that part which compasseth the head.

c. In the harness of a horse (see quot.).

1607 MARKHAM *Caval.* II. ii. 12 Cauezan, or any other binding fillet ouer the nose of the horse.

2. a. A strip of any material suitable for binding; a band or bandage; †the edging or list of cloth.

1601 HOLLAND *Pliny* I. 259 The brims & borders of the sea, called for the resemblance of fillets or lists in a cloth, Tæniæ. **1633** P. FLETCHER *Purple Isl.* x. xxxvii. 144 Her daintie breasts, like to an Aprill rose From greene silk fillets yet not all unbound. **1734** tr. *Rollin's Anc. Hist.* (1827) I. II. i. 226 The body was swathed in lawn fillets. **1769** MRS. RAFFALD *Eng. Housekpr.* (1778) 301 When it is almost cold bind it up with a fresh fillet. **1834** LYTTON *Pompeii* I. ii, She

will bind the door-posts of her husband with golden fillets. **1865** LIVINGSTONE *Zambesi* v. 114 Fillets of the inner bark of a tree wound spirally round each curl.

transf. **1796** H. HUNTER tr. *St.-Pierre's Stud. Nat.* (1799) I. 7 Yellow *antheræ* of flowers, suspended by fillets of white.

b. A surgical bandage.

1802 PALEY *Nat. Theol.* viii. (1805) 122 The fillet is almost always strapped across [a fracture] for the sake of giving firmness and strength to the bandage. **1807–26** S. COOPER *First Lines Surg.* (ed. 5) 409 A band, or fillet, which goes round the head.

c. *Obstetr.* (see quot. 1884.)

1753 N. TORRIANO *Midwifry* 35 In this Case a Fillet is necessary. **1884** *Syd. Soc. Lex., Fillet*..a loop or noose used from very ancient times for the extraction of the head of the child.

3. A thin narrow strip of any material. In many mechanical applications, e.g. in *Coining*, the ribbon of metal out of which the blanks or planchets are punched; in the *Carding-engine*, a strip of card-clothing; 'a perforated curb to confine the curds in making cheese' (Knight); etc.

1663 GERBIER *Counsel* 15 A fillet of Lead. **1724** SWIFT *Prometheus*, The Mixture [i.e. the metal for Wood's halfpence]..In Fillets roll'd, or cut in Pieces, Appear'd like one continu'd Spec'es. **1779** BAILEY *Adv. Arts* II. 14 An iron Fillet [of a plough] six inches and a quarter long; its extreme breadth is two inches and a half, and three sixteenths of an inch thick. **1859** *All Year Round* 2 July 239/1 Fillets, or ribands of gold [for coining]. **1893** *Daily News* 9 June 5/4 Some of them [coins] perhaps have been cut from the..cracked parts of the fillets.

†**4.** In etymol. sense (after Fr. *filet*): A thread or string: **a.** *fig. pl.* The 'threads' of life. **b.** In plants: A fibre of the root; a rib or vein of a leaf; the pistil or stamen of a flower. **c.** The 'string' of the tongue. *Obs.*

1590 GREENE *Orl. Fur.* (1599) 19 Seek not..To..slice the slender fillets of my life. **1601** HOLLAND *Pliny* I. 557 All other corne.. haue many small fillets or strings appendant to the roots. **1660** HEXHAM, *Ribbekens die door de bladers loopen*, Fillets or Sprouts which run through the leaves of Trees or Hearbes. *a* **1693** URQUHART *Rabelais* III. xxxiv. 287 To have the Fillet of her Tongue untied. **1730–6** BAILEY (folio), *Filet* is used to signify those threads that are usually found in the middle of flowers, as the Lily, Tulip, etc. **1735** DYCHE & PARDON, *Fillet*..in Anatomy, 'tis the Extremity of the Ligament under the Tongue, called the *Frenum*.

5. A band of fibre, whether muscle or nerve; a flap of flesh: †**a.** A muscle. *Obs.*

1533 ELYOT *Cast. Helthe* (1541) 85 b, Excessive multitude of humors..do extende the muscules or fyllettes. **1543** TRAHERON *Vigo's Chirurg.* I. i. 1 b, A muscle is a membre compounde of synnowes, ligamentes, and fleshie fyllettes, or as it were, threads fylled wᵗ fleshe.

b. (See quots.)

1840 G. ELLIS *Anat.* 27 A band of fibres is continued from its nucleus to the fibres of the lateral part of the medulla on which it lies; this band is the *fillet* of Riel. **1884** *Syd. Soc. Lex., Fillet*, a tract of obliquely-curved white nerve-fibres seen on the surface of the pons Varolii, and occupying a triangular area at the side of the tegmentum.

†**c.** A lobe of the liver. Cf. FIBRE 1 a. *Obs.*

1607 TOPSELL *Four-f. Beasts* (1658) 402 The..fillets of the liver of a mouse. *a* **1656** USSHER *Ann.* vi. (1658) 279 The liver of it had no filets. **1692** R. L'ESTRANGE *Josephus' Antiq.* III. ix. (1733) 70 The Fillets of the Liver.

d. pl. ***the fillets***: the loins (of an animal, *rarely* of a man).

? *a* **1400** *Morte Arth.* 1158 His [Arthur's] flawnke and his feletez, and his faire sydez. **1483** *Cath. Angl.* 130 A Felett of þe bakke, *pala.* **1523** FITZHERB. *Husb.* §76 The .ix. propertyes of an hare..the .ix. to haue two good fyllettes. **1611** MARKHAM *Country Content.* (1649) 6 His [the hound's] fillets would be thick and great. **1615** CROOKE *Body of Man* ii. 65 The Loynes..the fleshy parts on either side are called in Greeke ψόα, *Pulpa à palpando*, in imitation whereof wee call it the Fillet, as it were Feele it. **1737** BRACKEN *Farriery Impr.* (1757) II. 27 The Reins of a Horse, or what we commonly stile the Fillets. **1790** BURNS *Let. to Nicol* 9 Feb., She had been quite strained in the fillets beyond cure. **1892** *Northumberl. Gloss., Fillets*, the hollow between a horse's ribs and haunch bones.

†**e.** (See quot.; app. a misunderstanding.)

1638 R. HOLME *Armoury* II. 154/1 The Fillets, are the fore-parts of the shoulders next the Breast. Whence **1721** in BAILEY.

6. *Cookery.* **a.** A fleshy portion of meat near the loins or ribs of an animal, easily detachable; the 'undercut' of a sirloin or rump of beef; a similar fleshy part in the body of a fowl. **b.** One of the thick slices into which a fish is easily divided; also, a thick slice of meat, tongue, etc.

The fillet of beef is sometimes cooked like the fillet of veal (sense c): see quot. 1747. In the above senses sometimes with Fr. spelling : see FILET.

c **1420** *Liber Cocorum* (1862) 31 Take filetes of porke and half hom rost. *c* **1430** *Two Cookery-bks.* 49 Take lardes of Venysoun..or of a Bere, & kerue hem þinne as Fyletes of Porke. **1658** T. MAYERNE *Archimag. Anglo-Gall.* xiii. 7 The Phillets..of Beef. **1725** BRADLEY *Fam. Dict.* s.v. *Pike*, A Pike Filets fry'd. **1741** *Compl. Fam. Piece* I. ii. 174 Cut a Fillet of Veal into 3 or 4 Fillets. **1747** MRS. GLASSE *Art of Cookery* 21 A Fillet of Beef..is the Inside of the Surloin: You must carefully cut it all out from the Bone..roll it up tight; tye it with a Packthread. **1824** BYRON *Juan* xv. lxvi, Young partridge fillets. **1846** SOYER *Gastron. Regen.* 166 A small fillet of tongue. *Ibid.* 266 Take out the fillet from beneath a rump of beef. *Ibid.* 329 Carefully skin and bone the breast [of a turkey] without separating the fillets. *Ibid.* 360 Pass a knife down the back bone [of a hare]..keeping it close to the ribs till you have extracted the fillet. **1853** KANE *Grinnell Exp.* xvii. (1854) 130 The filet of a large Ivory one [sea-gull] is a morceau between a spring chicken and our own unsurpassed canvas back.

c. A 'joint' consisting of the middle part of a leg of veal, boned, rolled and tied with a string or 'fillet'; a piece of beef, fish, etc. prepared in a similar manner.

1700 DRYDEN *Fables* 213 The rest They cut in Legs and Fillets for the Feast. **1732** FIELDING *Miser* III. iii, A fillet of veal roasted. **1747** MRS. GLASSE *Art of Cookery* 93 To Roast a Fillet or Collar of Sturgeon. Take a Piece of fresh Sturgeon..take out the Bones, and cut in Lengths..then begin to roll it up as close as possible..and bind it round with a narrow Fillet. **1769** MRS. RAFFALD *Eng. Housekpr.* (1778) 100 Take a fillet of a cow calf, stuff it well. **1835** MARRYAT *Jac. Faithf.* III. i, We dine at half-past three—fillet of veal and bacon—don't be too late for dinner.

attrib. **1841** J. T. HEWLETT *Parish Clerk* I. 125 Firmly united by a fillet-of-veal skewer.

7. Any object having the appearance of a fillet or band.

1611 SPEED *Theat. Gt. Brit.* I. xvi. 31/1 From a split cloue ..a white blewish Flowre shortly springeth from whence Fillets of Saffron are gathered before the Sunne, and dried. **1696** AUBREY *Misc.* (1721) 35 The two Filots, which cross the greater Circle..were of a pale colour. **1817** COLERIDGE *Biog. Lit.* 247 Above the moon was a huge volume of deep black cloud, while a very thin fillet crossed the middle of the orb. **1862** TYNDALL *Mountaineer*, vi. 43 We once halted beside a fillet of clear spring water to have a draught. **1863** —— *Heat* v. §192 (1870) 153 Every fillet of mercury freezes the water with which it comes into contact.

8. *Arch.* **a.** A narrow flat band used for the separation of one moulding from another; a fascia. **b.** A small band between the flutes of a column.

[**1379** *Mem. Ripon* (Surtees) III. 101 Item fac. filetes et alia necessaria pro clo—— totam sept. 3s.] **1473** *Churchw. Acc. St. Mich. Cornhill*, For sconcheons and a felet for the same pewes. **1563** SHUTE *Archit.* D j b, At the toppe of the pillor lieth Astragalus and his fillet being half so high as the Astragalus. **1639** *Contract* in *Proc. Soc. Antiq.* 8 June (1893) 374 The fillitts of the Moulds..fairly guilt. **1789** P. SMYTH tr. *Aldrich's Archit.* (1818) 108 Reason would place the small fillet of the architrave upon the greater. **1815** ELPHINSTONE *Acc. Caubul* (1842) I. 107 A fillet, formed by stones projecting a very little from the wall. **1879** SIR G. G. SCOTT *Lect. Archit.* I. 248 The heaviness of large roll mouldings was often relieved by fillets.

9. *Her.* **a.** A horizontal division of a shield, one-fourth of the depth of a CHIEF. †**b.** A band running round near the edge of a shield, one-third or one-fourth of the breadth of a BORDURE or an ORLE (*obs.*). †**c.** A band usually drawn from the sinister chief across the shield; usually called ***fillet of bastardy*** (*obs.*).

1572 BOSSEWELL *Armorie* 11 b, A Fillet..conteyneth the fower parte of the cheefe. **1634** PEACHAM *Gentleman's Exerc.* III. 151 A Fillet the fourth of an Orle. **1751** CHAMBERS *Cycl., Fillet* is also used for an ordinary, drawn like the bar, from the sinister point of the cheif across the shield; in manner of a scarf: though it is sometimes also seen in the situation of a bend, fesse, cross, etc. **1756–7** tr. *Keysler's Trav.* (1760) I. 185 Two coats of Arms; one, three wheels and a sword; in the other two fillets and six balls. **1766** PORNY *Heraldry* (1787) 53 The Chief is an Ordinary..Its Diminutive is a fillet, the content of which is not to exceed one fourth of the Chief. **1882** CUSSANS *Heraldry* iv. 57, I cannot recall to my memory any instance of a Fillet being employed in English Armory.

10. *Ent.* and *Ornith.* **a.** A coloured band or stripe. **b.** In a spider: The space between the eyes and the base of the mandibles or cheliceræ.

1668 WILKINS *Real Char.* 153 Grey plover..which hath a black fillet about the eyes. **1841** E. NEWMAN *Hist. Brit. Ins.* ii. 175 A fillet is a longitudinal stripe, and a band or fascia is a transverse one.

11. In various technical uses:

a. A raised rim or ridge on any surface, *esp.* 'a ring on the muzzle and cascabel of a gun' (Adm. Smyth); also, the thread of a screw.

1703 MAUNDRELL *Journ. Jerus.* (1732) 90 These Stones are let into each other with a fillet fram'd round about the cavity. **1874** BOUTELL *Arms & Arm.* v. 78 The [sockets] of these javelin heads are..finished with a circular raised fillet. **1881** RAYMOND *Mining Gloss., Fillet*, the rounded corner of a groove in a roll.

b. *Carpentry.* A narrow strip of wood fastened upon any surface to serve as a support, etc. or to strengthen an angle formed by two surfaces.

1779 *Projects* in *Ann. Reg.* 101/1 These fillets will..form, as it were, a sort of small ledge on each side of all the joists. **1856** S. C. BREES *Terms, Fillets* are also used as stops to room and closet doors. **1881** *Every Man his own Mechanic* §1281 Nail or screw a fillet 1 in. square down the centre of the three rafters.

c. *Bookbinding.* A plain line impressed upon the cover of a book. Also, a rolling tool used for impressing the line.

1641 *Camilton's Disc.* in *Harl. Misc.* (Malh.) V. 111 Curiously bound up in leather or parchment, with fillets of silver or gold. **1880** *Print. Trades Jrnl.* XXXI. 13 The black outer level is surrounded in turn by a gilt fillet or line. **1890** ZAEHNSDORF *Bookbinding* xxiii. (ed. 2) 118 Tools and Materials required for Finishing—Rolls, fillets, pallets.

d. *Printing.* 'A rule with broad or broad and narrow lines, principally used as a border' (Knight).

e. *Gilding* and *Painting.* (See quots.)

1730–6 BAILEY (folio), *Fillets*, a little rule or riglet of leaf-gold, drawn over certain mouldings, or on the edge of frames, pannels, &c. **1794** W. FELTON *Carriages* II. Gloss., *Fillet*, a narrow painted border, not exceeding one inch broad.

f. *Aeronaut.* (See quot. 1950.)

1935 *Jrnl. R. Aeronaut. Soc.* XXXIX. 143 Graphical curves of lift, drag and moment as a function of incidence show comparisons of a low wing and a dropped wing without fillet, with three unsuccessful fillets and with a so-called optimum fillet. **1950** *Gloss. Aeronaut. Terms (B.S.I.)* I. 14 *Fillet*, a fairing at the junction of two surfaces to improve the air-flow. **1966** D. STINTON *Anat. Aeroplane* xi. 206 The remaining shape of an aeroplane is largely non-structural, in that it consists of fairings, cowlings and fillets.

12. *attrib.* and *Comb.*, as **fillet gutter**, 'a sloping gutter, with a learboard and fillet thereon, to divert the water' (Gwilt); **fillet-plane**, a moulding-plane for dressing a fillet or square bead (Knight, 1874); **fillet steak**, a steak cut from the fillet (sense 6 a); **fillet-swift** (see quot.); **fillet weld** (see quot. 1965).

1877 E. S. DALLAS *Kettner's Bk. Table* 63 Perhaps the most prized of all..the fillet-steak. **1963** N. MARSH *Dead Water* (1964) 27 We never order fillet steak. **1861** SWINHOE *N. China Camp.* 16 The anxious screech of the fillet swift (*Cypselus vittatus*). **1929** *Engineering* 22 Nov. 688/3 The plate is welded..with the final $\frac{3}{8}$-in. fillet weld. **1965** *Welding Terms & Symbols (B.S.I.)* I. 51 *Fillet weld*, a fusion weld, other than a butt, edge or fusion spot weld, which is approximately triangular in transverse cross-section.

†**'fillet**, *sb.*^{2} *Obs. rare*$^{-1}$. (See quot.)

1587 HARRISON *England* II. xv. (1877) I. 272 Which bill [of dishes] some doo call a memoriall, other a billet, but some a fillet, bicause such are commonlie hanged on the file.

fillet ('fɪlɪt), *v.* [f. FILLET *sb.*^{1}] Pples. **filleted**, **filleting**.

1. *trans.* To bind with or as with a fillet.

a. To bind or tie up (the hair) with or as with a fillet (see FILLET *sb.* 1); also with *up*.

1604, 1638 [see *ppl. a.*^{1}]. **1692** R. L'ESTRANGE *Josephus' Antiq.* v. x. (1733) 127 That Experiment..of filleting and twisting up his Locks. **1821** *Blackw. Mag.* X. 513 For whom do you comb, brush, and fillet your tresses? **1852** MOIR *Poems, Remembered Beauty*, Her golden tresses..Were filleted up with roses.

b. †To bind or tie up, to confine or swathe with a bandage (*obs.*). Also *Surg.* To bandage (a limb).

1633 FORD *Broken H.* v. ii, Quick fillet both his arms. **1758** J. S. *Le Dran's Observ. Surg.* (1771) 288 Stop the Blood, by ..filletting the Arm. **1764** HADLEY in *Phil. Trans.* LIV 8 The feet were filleted..being first bound separately, and then wrapped together.

c. *gen.* To encircle or gird with an ornamental band: also with *about*.

1611 BIBLE *Ex.* xxxviii. 28 He made hookes for the pillars, and ouerlaide their chapiters, and filleted them. **1784** COWPER *Task* v. 402 A stump..filletted about with hoops of brass. **1860** *All Year Round* No. 46. 459 Amber mouthpieces filleted with 'sparklers', as the English cracksman..calls diamonds.

transf. **1603** KNOLLES *Hist. Turks* (1638) 342 The great round roofe..being all enameled and fillited, with the pictures of Saintes.

2. *Cookery.* To divide (a fish) into fillets. Also, to cut the fillets out of (a fowl, etc.).

1846 SOYER *Gastron. Regen.* 103 Fillet a brill by passing a good knife from the head to the tail of the fish close to the middle bone [etc.]..Proceed in like manner until you have got off all the meat from the bones. *Ibid.* 332 Fillet a poularde by splitting the skin up the breast, and passing your knife down the bone, keeping close to the ribs until you have scooped them [i.e. the fillets] out.

3. *Building* and *Carpentry.* To close or cover the interstices between boards, slates, etc. with fillets. Cf. FILLET *sb.* 11 b.

1843 HILL in *Jrnl. R. Agric. Soc.* IV. II. 358 In filleting, the under edge of each floor-board is cut away, and a fillet, one inch wide, and three-fourths of an inch thick, is introduced.

4. To mark or ornament with fillets; now chiefly in *Bookbinding*.

1621 QUARLES *Argalus & P.* (1678) 88 Armors of Steel, fair filletted with Gold. **1642** FULLER *Holy & Prof. St.* III. xxiv. 227 The second edition of the Temple by Zorobabel, as it was new forrelled and filleted with gold by Herod, was a statelier volume then that first of Solomon. **1665** T. HERBERT *Trav.* (1677) 250 His *Argyraspides* who had their Armour damasked and filletted with Silver. **1747** FRANKLIN *Let.* 1 Sept. Wks. 1887 II. 91 A book whose covering is filleted with gold.

Hence **'filleter**, one who fillets: senses 2, 4.

1884 *Birm. Daily Post* 23 Feb. 3/4 Japanners—Wanted, a good Cash-box Filleter. **1961** *Guardian* 18 Jan. 9/4 Filleters will tell you that the bobbers..who unload the trawlers have the best job.

filleted ('fɪlɪtɪd), *ppl. a.*^{1} [f. as prec. + -ED^{1}.]

1. Bound with or as with a fillet or fillets. Also, ***filleted about***. Of a victim: Having the head bound with a fillet.

1604 DEKKER *King's Entert.* Wks. 1873 I. 318 Her haire —filletted about with snakes. **1638** T. HERBERT *Trav.* 338 They weare their heare very long, and filleted. **1755** T. AMORY *Mem.* 1769 II. 221 We..had a sight of the filleted subject [a mummy]. **1768** FOOTE *Devil* I. Wks. 1799 II. 255 The purple pinions, and filletted forehead. **1879** BROWNING *Pheidippides* 47 The filleted victim.

2. *Cookery.* Cut into fillets.

1871 *Daily News* 29 May, Dinner, which consisted of filleted soles, boiled chicken, and cold beef.

3. Marked or decorated with a fillet: see FILLET *sb.* senses 8, 10, 11 c.

1611 COTGR., *Vetade*, the filletted Cockle. **1812–6** J. SMITH *Panorama Sc. & Art* I. 149 These kinds of piers have

their shafts sometimes filleted. **1880** *Print. Trades Jrnl.* xxx. 20 The binding will be artistic..filletted in gold, and lettered.

†'**filleted**, *ppl. a.*² *Obs.* [f. as prec. + -ED².] Having fillets (see FILLET *sb.* 5 d); only in comb., as ***broad-, full-, narrow-filleted.***

1617 MARKHAM *Caval.* VI. 3 Your running Horse.. somwhat long filletted between the huckle bones, and the short ribbes. **1657** R. LIGON *Barbadoes* (1673) 81 The men ..are..well filletted. **1737** BRACKEN *Farriery Impr.* (1757) II. 27 The strait or narrow filletted Horse. *Ibid.* 124 The muscular flesh full upon the Loins or Fillets, which is what we call Broad-filletted.

filleting ('fɪlɪtɪŋ), *vbl. sb.* [f. as prec. + -ING¹.]

1. The action of the vb. FILLET in various senses.

1598 *Vestry Bks.* (Surtees) 274 To the mason for the filleting of the church, ijs. iiijd. **1823** P. NICHOLSON *Pract. Build.* 400 Filleting..consists in covering the meeting-joints with fillets of slates. **1962** J. TUNSTALL *Fishermen* iii. 62 Hand filleting is not a simple job.

attrib. **1643** *Vestry Bks.* (Surtees) 192 Six dayes and a halfe worke in fillitting and playstering worke.

2. *concr.* **a.** A woven material for binding; tape; a piece of the same; a band or bandage.

1639 DE GRAY *Compl. Horsem.* 79 Take a peece of Filliting and bind it above the Pastern-joynt. **1658** A. FOX *Wurtz' Surg.* II. xxviii. 197, I tied..on the roulers two fillettins. **1764** HADLEY in *Phil. Trans.* LIV. 6 The filleting.. went round the upper part of the body. **1778** *Eng. Gazetteer* (ed. 2) s.v. *Manchester*, Tapes, filleting, and linen cloth. **1882** CAULFEILD & SAWARD *Dict. Needlewk.*, *Filletings*, an unbleached and very heavy description of Holland Tape.

b. A head-band; = FILLET I.

1648 HERRICK *Hesper.* (1844) II. 218 Put on thy holy fillitings.

c. Fillets or ornamental lines, e.g. of gilding on the covers of a book.

1747 FRANKLIN *Let.* 1 Sept. Wks. 1887 II. 91 The whole filleting round the cover [of the book].

3. *Aeronaut.* = FILLET *sb.*¹ 11 f.

1935 *Jrnl. R. Aeronaut. Soc.* XXXIX. 835 Eleven photographs show..four types of glider with filleting between wings and body.

‖**fillette** (fijɛt). [Fr.] A young girl.

1847 C. BRONTË *J. Eyre* I. xv. 288 Unluckily the Varens.. had given me this fillette Adèle. **1888** MRS. H. WARD *R. Elsmere* I. I. iii. 77 A *fillette*, unformed, inexperienced. **1928** C. A. NICHOLSON *Hell & Duchess* I. v. 94 As for your *fillette*, she is quite charming.

filli-, see also FILI-.

filling ('fɪlɪŋ), *vbl. sb.* [f. FILL *v.* + -ING¹.]

1. The action of the vb. in various senses. Also with advbs., as ***filling in, out, up***: cf. FILL *v.* V. Only gerundial.

c **1440** *Promp. Parv.* 160/2 Fyllynge, *implecio.* **1486** *Nottingham Rec.* III. 253 Fullyng vp of þe dyke. **1580** HOLLYBAND *Treas. Fr. Tong*, *Remplissement*, a filling. *a* **1610** HEALEY *Cebes* (1636) 147 They..imagine the filling of that [the belly] the full fruite of all their expected good. **1712** J. JAMES tr. *Le Blond's Gardening* 209 This Wall being made all round, you begin the Filling in of the Bottom. **1726** LEONI *Alberti's Archit.* I. 38 b, One thing is proper..for the outward Face of the Wall, another for the cramming and filling up the middle Parts. **1793** SMEATON *Edystone L.* §114 The interior filling of the walls was with rough Rubble. **1816** CHALMERS *Let.* in *Life* (1851) II. 31 Such a filling up of the time as will keep you away from the evil communications. **1870** LOWELL *Study Wind.* (1886) 190 He ..does his filling-in rather shabbily. **1884** *Birm. Daily Post* 23 Feb. 3/4 Wanted, several Boys, used to Filling-in and Finishing. **1888** *Lockwood's Mech. Engin. Dict.*, *Box Filling*, the filling up of a moulding box with its body of sand enclosing a pattern. **1958** *Spectator* 4 July 13/2 As 'ribbon development' is now a dirty phrase, the new horror is called 'filling in'. **1959** *Gloss. Packaging Terms (B.S.I.)* 35 *Filling-in*, a process for applying paint or other materials to a recessed design to obtain a contrasting colour effect. **1967** *Gloss. Paper/Ink Terms for Letterpress Printing (B.S.I.)* 5 *Filling in*, the spreading of the printed image, to the point where the small white spaces are obliterated.

2. *concr.* Also *pl.* **a.** That which fills or is used to fill a cavity or vacant space, to stop a tooth or a hole, to make up a bank or road, the interior of a wall, etc.; also in *Dentistry*, a quantity of this in one tooth. Also, †a full supply or 'fill' (of food, etc.).

a **1400-50** *Alexander* 4265 Þat is þe filling of fode þat ilk flesch askis. *c* **1430** *Pilgr. Lyf Manhode* IV. xix. (1869) 185 We hadden many goode vesselles in whiche we hadden put fillinge [*emplage*] of the grete tresores of Paradys. **1596-7** S. FINCHE in *Hist. Croydon* App. (1783) 153 Great flinte and chalke for the buildinge, and small for fillinge. **1611** BIBLE *Ex.* xxviii. 17 Thou shalt set in it settings [*marg.* fill in it fillings] of stones. **1640** SANDERSON *Serm.* II. 174 Binding them [the stones] with fillings and cement. **1641** BEST *Farm. Bks.* (Surtees) 59 The foreman to lye the courses [of hay]; another to lye the fillinge and to fill after him. **1776** G. SEMPLE *Building in Water* 119 The Bank of any common filling. **1830** J. HODGSON in J. Raine *Mem.* (1858) II. 174 A few feet of the fillings of its foundation walls. **1848** *Lit. Amer.* 29 July 64/2 Indestructible filling for the teeth. **1851** RUSKIN *Stones Ven.* I. xviii. §1 The fillings of the aperture are unimportant. **1878** L. P. MEREDITH *Teeth* 74 The enamel at the margin of the filling is fractured. **1892** *Daily News* 17 Nov. 3/3 The excavated material will form good 'filling'. **1943** WYNDHAM LEWIS *Let.* 5 Dec. (1963) 371 My wife was greatly impressed by the number of your 'fillings'.

b. Something of inferior quality put in to occupy space.

1640 FULLER *Joseph's Coat* vii. (1867) 176 [Heraldic coats] of a later edition..are so full of filling that they are empty of honour. **1733** SWIFT *On Poetry*, The prefaces of Dryden.. meerly writ at first for filling To raise the volume's price a shilling. **1737** BENTLEY *Remarks Disc. Free-thinking* III. 6 §54 Why that spiteful Character given to all Crowds? meer Fillings of his own, without warrant from his Original. **1860** WORNUM *Anal. Ornament* 19 All such superficial decoration is..mere filling. **1887** *Pall Mall G.* 25 June 12/1 The practice of putting into higher class goods..even the smallest quantity of filling.

3. a. Similarly in various technical uses (see quots.); *spec.* in cigar-making and mining.

1812 *Niles' Weekly Reg.* II. 9/1 Much of it [*sc.* wool]..may be wrought into..worsted chain or warp for woolen weft or fillings. **1839** J. R. LOWELL *Let.* Sept. (1894) I. 52 The filling of cigars now belies the wrapper. **1858** SIMMONDS *Dict. Trade*, *Fillings*, prepared wort, added in small quantities to casks of ale to cleanse it. **1864** *Congress. Globe* 3 June 2706/3 Cigars are made of Connecticut grown wrappers and the best qualities filled with Cuba filling. **1874** KNIGHT *Dict. Mech.* I. 844/1 *Filling*, an embankment of stone, gravel, earth, etc, to make a raised bed for a road, railroad track, or canal. An artificial, elevated way. *Ibid.* I. 844/2 *Filling (Weaving)*, the weft-thread which fills up the warp. **1883** R. HALDANE *Workshop Receipts* Ser. II. 439 For this coat, which is called filling, use one half ground lead and any good mineral. **1883** GRESLEY *Gloss. Coal-m.* 106 *Filling*, the places where trams are loaded in the workings. **1898** *Westm. Gaz.* 15 Dec. 2/1 'Fillins! What may they be?' 'Why, they're the inside of noo cigars, of course.' **1901** *Chambers's Jrnl.* May 302/2 Each leaf will give on an average two 'wrappers' or outside covers for cigars and when used for such the remainder of the leaf is used for 'filling'. **1940** *Chambers's Techn. Dict.* 332/1 *Filling*, the loading of tubs or trucks with coal, ore, or waste.

b. *Naut.* (See quots.)

1794 *Rigging & Seamanship* I. 24 *Fillings* are pieces fayed to the side of the mast, edges of the front-fish, and cheeks. **1857** P. COLQUHOUN *Comp. Oarsman's Guide* 30 The oar or scull is 'filled' with harder wood between the shank and loom, called the upper and under fillings. *c* **1860** H. STUART *Seaman's Catech.* 67 What is termed the 'filling'?..the intervals between the frame timbers are filled up solid..so that if the outside planks be injured a watertight surface would remain.

4. *attrib.* and *Comb.*, as ***filling-earth, -machine, -room, -stones.*** Also **filling-nail** (see quot. 1850 and quot. 1867 s.v. FILL *v.* 1 d); **filling-station** orig. *U.S.*, a depot for the supply of petrol, oil, etc. to motorists; a petrol station; **filling-thread**, one of the threads for the woof or tram; **filling-timber** (see quot.); **filling-transom** (see quot.).

1634 T. JOHNSON *Parey's Chirurg.* 1165 Their fellowes.. put them, yet alive, in the mines, which served them for so much *filling earth. **1884** *Health Exhib. Catal.* 110/2 Meat Cutting and Sausage-Making Machines..*Filling Machines. **1772-84** COOK *Voy.* (1790) VI. 1945 Some expert swimmers were one day detected under the ships, drawing out the *filling nails from the sheathing. *c* **1850** *Rudim. Navig.* (Weale) 134 *Filling nails* are generally of cast iron, and driven very thick in the bottom planks instead of copper sheathing. **1799** CAPT. WATKINS in *Naval Chron.* I. 206 It was impossible to fill cartridges as fast as they wanted them, though the *filling rooms were crouded. **1921** *Outing* (U.S.) May 66/2 He should not attempt the trip without a small reserve can of gasoline..enough to carry him to a *filling station in case of leakage. **1931** EARL OF MAYO et al. *Regional Planning Rep. on Oxfordshire* v. 73 No Filling Station..shall be permitted by the occupier thereof to be visible unless [etc.]. **1935** *Amer. Speech* X. 5/2 The garage mechanic.., or the filling-station attendant, usually knows the town as well as anybody. **1951** J. B. PRIESTLEY *Festival at Farbridge* ii. 272 Roadhouses..and filling stations were brave in new paint. **1585** HIGGINS tr. *Junius' Nomenclator* 202 The *filling-stones, rubbish conveyed betweene the two outsides of a wall. **1639** FULLER *Holy War* I. xiii. (1647) 20 Hungary might bring filling-stones to this building. **1642** —— *Holy & Prof. St.* II. xviii. 116 Their walls though high, must needs be hollow, wanting filling-stones. **1886** *Pop. Sc. Monthly* XXVIII. 483 To make one yard of cloth, a shuttle carrying the *filling-thread is thrown across the web perhaps 1,500 times. *c* **1850** *Rudim. Navig.* (Weale) 118 **Filling-timbers*, the intermediate timbers between the frames that are got up into their places singly after the frames are ribanded and shored. **1867** SMYTH *Sailor's Word-bk.*, **Filling-transom*, is just above the deck transoms, securing the ends of the gun-deck plank and lower-transoms.

filling ('fɪlɪŋ), *ppl. a.* [f. as prec. + -ING².] That fills or is adapted to fill.

1626 BACON *Sylva* §300 Things that are Sweet and Fat, are more Filling. **1674** P. HENRY *Diaries & Lett.* (1882) 267 The world to come, not this, is the filling world. **1691-8** NORRIS *Pract. Disc.* IV. 179 Can a Man Sin with this great and filling Thought before him? **1837** DICKENS *Pickw.* xliv, 'Crumpets is not wholesome'..'But they're so cheap..and so wery fillin' at the price.' **1872** *Daily News* 5 Nov., The most convenient, not to say filling, luncheon.

Hence '**fillingly** *adv.*, in a filling manner.

1611 COTGR., *Fillingly*, compleatly, perfectly.

fillip ('fɪlɪp), *sb.* Forms: α. 6 fillippe, -op(pe, fyl(l)ippe, -yp(pe, -op, 6–9 filip, (6 -op), (8 fillup), 6– fillip. β. 6–7 phillip, (6 phil(l)ippe, phylyp, 7 philip, -lop). [app. onomatopœic; cf. FLIP, FLIRT, used in similar sense. The sb. and vb. appear nearly contemporaneously in 16th c.; it is uncertain which is the source of the other.]

1. A movement made by bending the last joint of a finger against the thumb and suddenly releasing it (so as to propel some small object, or merely as a gesture); a smart stroke or tap given by this means.

1530 PALSGR. 220/1 Fyllippe with ones fyngar, *chicquenode.* **1589** *Pasquil's Ret.* 20 Their Bookes be Glasse, giue them but a filip, they run to powder. **1594** PLAT *Jewell-ho.* III. 44 Gestures..or actions, as..a crosse made on the forehead for a C, a phillip for D. **1619** RICH *Irish Hubbub* (1623) 24 Hee..gives the cup a phillip to make it cry Twango. **1721-1800** BAILEY, *Fillip*, a throw of a Piece of Money with one's Finger or Nail. **1791** BOSWELL *Johnson* 10 Apr. an. 1772, The Prince..by a fillip, made some of it [wine] fly in Oglethorpe's face. **1862** MERIVALE *Rom. Emp.* (1865) IV. xxxvi. 234 He could..draw blood from a slave's head with a fillip.

b. Something of small importance; a trifle. Also, a short space of time, a moment.

1621 MOLLE *Camerar. Liv. Libr.* v. xvii. 386 The rest is not worth a fillip with the finger. **1633** D. R[OGERS] *Treat. Sacraments* I. 171 If the Lord then crosse thee so, not in some petty filip of a finger, but in a tedious sort. **1821** BYRON *Sardan.* I. ii, Eat, drink, and love; the rest's not worth a fillip. **1880** GRIFFIS *Jap. Fairy World* xvii. (1887) 150 The tortoise ..in a fillip of the finger was down in the gardens of Riu Gu.

2. In a wider sense: A smart blow (with the fist, etc.). Now *rare.*

1543 BECON *Invect. agst. Swearing* 28 a, Suche a fylyppe, as shal fylyppe them downe into the botome of hell fyre. **1575** J. STILL *Gamm. Gurton* v. ii. in Hazl. *Dodsley* III. 238 There was a knave not far, Who caught one good filip on the brow with a door-bar. **1618** FLETCHER *Chances* III. iv, One, if foule play Should fall upon us..Will not flie back for phillips. **1772** tr. *Galland's Arab. Nts.* IV. 151 One give poor Bakbarah a filip on the nose with all her strength.

fig. **1788** T. JEFFERSON *Writ.* (1859) II. 250 The Marquis de la Fayette, with several others, have lately received a fillip for having assembled to sign a memorial to the King.

3. Something that serves to rouse, excite, or animate; a stimulus.

a **1700** B. E. *Dict. Cant. Crew*, *Give Nature a Fillip*, to Debauch a little now and then with Women, or Wine. **1740** CHEYNE *Regimen* 80, I willingly allow, that fermented.. Liquors, are excellent Remedies, temporary Filips, Whips or Spurs. **1817** COLERIDGE *Biog. Lit.* 238 This *bon mot* gave a fillip to my spirits. **1837** WHITTOCK *Bk. Trades* (1842) 273 A remission of two-thirds the duty on flint-glass..has given the trade a fillip. **1847** J. WILSON *Chr. North* (1857) I. 144 Without the filip of a little scandal.

fillip ('fɪlɪp), *v.* [See the sb.]

1. *trans.* To put into motion by a fillip; to toss (a coin) with a fillip. Also with *away, down, forth, off.*

1543 [see FILLIP *sb.* 2.] **1584** R. SCOT *Discov. Witchcr.* XIII. xxx. 338 When he hath filipped the monie..he must saie; What is it? **1622** DONNE *Serm.* xvi. 157 Not be able to nip or fillip away one of his own wormes. *a* **1680** CHARNOCK *Attrib. God* (1834) II. 70 That can..fillip nature with his finger into that nothing whence he drew it. **1783** MAD. D'ARBLAY *Diary* 9 Dec., I was forced to begin filliping off the crumbs ..from my muff. **1831** A. FONBLANQUE *Eng. under 7 Administ.* (1837) II. 155 Had our aforesaid merchant filliped a nut sharply against his bullying giant. **1871** TYLOR *Prim. Cult.* I. 61 The use of an elastic switch to fillip small missiles with.

transf. and *fig.* **1535** JOYE *Apol. Tindale* (Arb.) 17 These playn testimonyes..wolde take no place with Tindal for.. he..agenst me fylipt them forth betwene his fynger and his thombe. **1624** BP. MOUNTAGU *Gagg* iii. 42, I like not that the ancient Fathers should so be philipped off, and sent away. **1689** *Answ. Lords' & Commoners' Sp.* 21 Those Tests [etc.] ..which..were so easily filliped down by his Vigorous Successor.

b. To stimulate, urge. Also with *forward.*

1551 T. WILSON *Logike* C viij a, They will..with good indeuoure, filip nature forward. **1819** SHELLEY *Cyclops* 145 Pour: that the draught may fillip my remembrance.

2. To strike with a fillip; to tap smartly with the nail-joint of the finger. Also with *out.*

1580 BARET *Alv.* F 505 To fillip one, *talitrum impingere, incutere, infringere alicui.* **1586** J. HOOKER *Girald. Irel.* in *Holinshed* II. 86/1 There is not a meane subject that dare extend his hand to fillip a peere of the realme. **1626** BACON *Sylva* §725 If you fillip a Lute-string, it sheweth double, or Treble. **1681** *Depos. Cast. York* (Surtees) 249 My Lorde.. did arise from his seate and phillipped him over the nose. **1786** tr. *Beckford's Vathek* (1834) 49 Others poised themselves over a fire, and without mercy filliped their noses. **1851** D. JERROLD *St. Giles* xxviii. 288 Like earthen vessels; that properly filliped.. should perforce reveal a.. fracture. **1862** H. W. FULLER *Dis. Lungs* 35 A good example of it may be obtained by filiping the inflated cheeks.

transf. and *fig.* **1607** SHAKS. *Cor.* v. iii. 59 Then let the Pibbles on the hungry beach Fillop the starres. **1667** DENHAM *Direct. Paint.* II. ii. 66 How the hard Pellets fell away as dead, By our inchanted Timber filliped. **1857** READE *Course of True Love* ii. (1868) 42 Patrick..could not bear to be filliped. **1876** T. HARDY *Hand of Ethelberta* I. 148 To escape the risk of having his eyes filliped out by the twigs that impeded his progress.

3. *gen.* To strike smartly.

1577 HOLINSHED *Chron.* (1808) IV. 220 There was one [stone] that lent him a blow on the shoulder, an other of them philipped him on the fingers. **1597** SHAKS. *2 Hen. IV*, I. ii. 255 If I do, fillop me with a three-man-Beetle.

4. *intr.* To make a fillip with the fingers. Also, ***to fillip with (one's) fingers***, and ***to fillip it.***

1577 B. GOOGE *Heresbach's Husb.* (1586) II. 110 b, If you do but fillip with your finger upon the other end. **1599** PORTER *Angry Wom. Abingd.* in Hazl. *Dodsley* VII. 300 When he scarce can trim His gouty fingers, thus he'll phillip it. **1626** BACON *Sylva* §183 If you..fillip upon the Brim, or outside. **1670** LASSELS *Voy. Italy* II. 407 Of such a rare timber, that one filipping upon one end of them, you heare it easily at the other end. **1842** TENNYSON *Godiva* 25 He laugh'd..Then fillip'd at the diamond in her ear. **1871** B. TAYLOR *Faust* (1875) II. I. iii. 40 Just see me fillip with my fingers.

b. quasi-*trans.* To give a fillip with (the fingers).

1712 HEARNE *Collect.* III. 371 Then filip your Finger and Thomb.

Hence ˈ**filliped** *ppl. a.*, ˈ**filliping** *vbl. sb.*

1611 COTGR., *Chiquenaudé*, fillipped. 1622 MASSINGER *Virg. Mart.* v. i, Tush, all these tortures are but fillipings, Fleabitings. *a* 1693 URQUHART *Rabelais* III. xx. 169 Interlarded with a double row of bobs and finger filipings. 1856 DOBELL *Eng. in Time of War, Shower in War Time,* The drip Did whip the filliped pool.

fillipeen, var. of PHILIPPINE, a game of forfeits.

fillis (ˈfɪlɪs). Also **phillis**. [Var. FILASSE.] A kind of loosely-twisted string, made of hemp (***hemp fillis***) or the jute (***jute fillis***), used by horticulturists as a tying material.

1900 *Oxford rope-dealer's price-list,* Fillis, Hemp, and Jute. 1954 A. G. L. HELLYER *Encycl. Garden Work* 91/1 Fillis. Soft string used for tying. 1954 E. R. JANES *Vegetable Garden* 242 Soft fillis string is the best material for securing tomatoes to their stakes. 1961 *Catal. E. J. Woodman & Sons, Pinner* 62/2 *Fillis,* plain, soft, balls, 1 lb. 4/3. 1969 E. B. LE GRICE *Rose Growing* vi. 79 Sisal or fillis should be weather-proofed.

filliser, obs. form of FILACER.

fillister (ˈfɪlɪstə(r)). [Of unknown origin.]

a. A rabbeting plane used in making window-sashes, etc. **b.** (See quot. 1874.)

1819 *Rees' Cycl.* XXVII. s.v. *Plane,* There is also a third sort [of rebating planes], called *fillisters,* used for sinking, or cutting away the edge of the piece of wood to form the rebate. 1874 KNIGHT *Dict. Mech.* I. 844/2 *Fillister,* the rabbet on the outer edge of a sash-bar, to hold the glass and the putty.

† ˈ**fillock**. *Obs.* Forms: 5, 6 fillok, (6 fyllok), 6, 8 fillock. [Of obscure formation; the original sense is perh. 'filly' (cf. Welsh *ffilawg* filly, wanton girl, in Salesbury 1547 *filoc,* which may be an early adoption from Eng.). The word may be f. FILL-Y + -OCK, or represent (with Northern pronunciation) an OE. **fylece* wk. fem., corresponding to OHG. *fulihha*:—OTeut. **fulikôn-*, f. **ful-*, *fol-*: see FOAL.]

A wanton young girl. Also *attrib.*

? *c* 1450 *Hoccleve's Let. Cupide* 262 [MS. Arch. Seld. B 24] Swyche fillokes [*other texts* filthes] as weren vertulesse. 1500–20 DUNBAR *Poems* xiv. 74 So mony fillok with fuck sailis Within this land was nevir hard nor sene. 15.. *Hye way to Spyttel Hous* 142 in Hazl. *E.P.P.* IV. 29 Mychers, hedge-creepers, fylloks, and lushes. 1569 E. HAKE *Newes Powles Churchyarde* (1579) G j b, Yong fillock Jylles, and bawdie Jacks.

fillop, fillott, obs. forms of FILLIP, FILLET.

fillowite (ˈfɪləʊaɪt). *Min.* [Named by Brush and Dana 1879 after *A.N. Fillow*: see -ITE.] A phosphate of manganese, iron, calcium and sodium, found in transparent yellow or brown crystals.

1879 *Amer. Jrnl. Sc.* Ser. III. XVII. 363 Fillowite occurs in granular crystalline masses.

fill-up, *sb.* [f. verbal phr. *to fill up*: see FILL *v.* For the stress see BREAK-DOWN.] That which serves to fill up a hollow or stop a gap.

1853 E. TWISLETON *Let.* 6 Feb. (1928) iv. 69 The three first [men] are cousins..and the latter is a fill-up [at a dinner-table]. 1872 *Daily News* 2 Sept., They are falling by spadefuls into the cart, and have now to do service..as a fill-up for some pestilential ditch. 1883 *Pall Mall G.* 12 Sept. 4/2 The incident of the 'Sempiternal Club'..looks..a little like a 'fill-up'. 1899 *Sketch* 1 Nov. 48/1 For years the flower would figure in the 'fill-up par.'. 1908 *Chambers's Jrnl.* Oct. 767/1 Compressing them [*sc.* exhibits in a museum] within the allotted space in accordance with what may be..described as a 'fill-up' policy. 1941 *B.B.C. Gloss. Broadc. Terms* 12 *Fill-up,* stop-gap material broadcast in an interval between the end of one programme and the beginning of the next. 1948 *Scrutiny* XV. 336 The French pianist Monique Haas has made a record of Bach's Italian Concerto with Rameau's *Les Cyclopes* as fill-up. 1960 *John o' London's* 7 Apr. 414/4 As the fill-up is a rather laboured..performance of Wolf's delicious Italian *Serenade,* I cannot recommend this record. 1970 J. FLEMING *Young Man, I think you're Dying* xi. 141 He had breakfast and a fill-up with petrol and oil in a motorway restaurant.

filly (ˈfɪlɪ), *sb.* Forms: α. 4 (in *Comb.*), 6 fely, (6 felee, felly), 5–8 fillie, (6 file, fille, fyllye, 8 filley), 6– filly. β. 7 philly. [? a. ON. *fylja* wk. fem.:—**fuljôn-*, f. *ful-*, *fol-*: see FOAL.]

1. A young mare, a female foal.

? *a* 1400 *Chester Pl.* (Shaks. Soc.) I. 51 Atter and foxe, fillie, mare alsoe. 1525 *Test. Ebor.* (Surtees) 206 To Thomas Miller, hir sone, a file with a white foite. *a* 1641 SUCKLING *Answ. to Let.* Wks. (1696) 99/2 An unback'd Filly may by chance give thee a fall. 1709 *Lond. Gaz.* No. 4591/4 Stoln or stray'd..a black Fillie, two years old. 1848 KINGSLEY *Saint's Trag.* III. iii. 93 What's good for the filly, is good for the mare, say I.

b. *to slip her filly*: *transf.* of a woman, to miscarry.

1665 PEPYS *Diary* 31 Mar., My Lady Castlemaine is sick again—people think, slipping her filly.

2. *transf.* Applied to a young lively girl.

1616 BEAUM. & FL. *Scornful Lady* III. i, A skittish filly will be your fortune, Welford. 1668 SEDLEY *Mulb. Gard.* I. i, I believe nobody will be very fond of a Hide-Park Filly for a Wife. 1711 ADDISON *Spect.* No. 211 ¶9, I am joined in Wedlock for my Sins to one of those Fillies who are described in the old Poet. 1849 MISS MULOCK *Ogilvies* I. (1875) 390 Katharine's a young filly that will neither be led nor driven. 1881 BESANT & RICE *Chapl. of Fleet* I. 41 You are but a filly yet.

3. *attrib.* and *Comb.*, as ***filly-foal***; † **filly-stag**, a filly foal.

1523 FITZHERB. *Husb.* §68 It is a horse foole, bycause a horse gate it, though it be a *felly fole. 1884 *W. Sussex Gaz.* 25 Sept. Advt., Brown draught brood mare, with filly foal. 1378 *Will of J. Delmarshe* in *Test. Karl.* (1893) 125 Item, Johanni, filio Thomæ Sympson, unum *felystag.

Hence † ˈ**filly** *v.*, to give birth to a filly. ˈ**fillying**, *vbl. sb.*

1598 FLORIO, *Partorire*..to calue..to fillie. *Parto*..a caluing,..a fill[y]ing, etc.

filly, obs. form of (FELLOE), FELLY.

filly-folly (ˈfɪlɪˌfɒlɪ). [One of the onomatopœic reduplications expressing the notion of something trivial; cf. FAL-LAL.] A foolish or ridiculous notion; a foolish hobby.

1565 JEWEL *Def. Apol.* (1611) 511 Ye doe but trifle with your Filly Follies. 1765 STERNE *Tr. Shandy* VIII. xxxi, 'Tis the sporting little filly-folly which carries you out for the present hour,—a maggot, a butterfly..a fiddle-stick.

film (fɪlm), *sb.* Forms: 1 fil-, fylmen, 5 vilm, 5–6 fylme, (6 philome), 6–7 filme, 7– film. [OE. *filmen* str. neut., membrane, caul, prepuce, cognate with OFris. *filmene* skin: the WGer. **filmin(n)i* is an extension (with suffix repr. OTeut. *-jo-*) of **felmen-*, *-on-* (OE. *ǽʒ-felma* skin of an egg), f. the same root as FELL *sb.*[1]]

† **1. a.** A membrane, animal or vegetable. *Obs.*

c 1000 *Sax. Leechd.* II. 204 Her sint tacn aheardodre lifre, ʒe on þam læppan, & healocum & filmenum. *c* 1400 *Lanfranc's Cirurg.* (MS. A) 241 Rethina þat is þe þinne skyn ..þat is clepid þe vilm of þe ize. *c* 1440 *Promp. Parv.* 160/2 Fylme, of a notte, or oþer lyke, *folliculus.* 1530 PALSGR. 220/1 Fylme that covereth the brayne, *taye.* 1562 TURNER *Herbal* II. 31 b, Rounde cornes diuided one from an other by filmes yᵗ rynne betwene. 1610 BARROUGH *Meth. Physick* I. ix. (1639) 13 The filmes and tunicles of the stomack. 1693 EVELYN *De la Quint. Compl. Gard.* 47 In a Wallnut..one part goes to make a Green, Tough, and Bitter Bark, another part the Shell lin'd with Films. 1743 *Lond. & Country Brew.* III. (ed. 2) 193 Twelve Eggs, their Shells being only bruised, but the Films not broken. 1764 HARMER *Observ.* I. vii. 313 The papyrus, a sort of bulrush..whose stalk was covered with several films, or inner skins, on which they wrote.

b. Applied to the tongue. *Obs. rare*⁻¹.

1644 BP. HALL *Serm.* 9 June Rem. Wks. (1660) 101 This loose and busie filme, which we carry in our mouths.

2. a. An extremely thin pellicle or lamina of any material.

1653 QUARLES *Embl.* II. x. (1718) 102 The painted film but of a stronger bubble. 1747 GOULD *Eng. Ants* 54 These wings are composed of exceeding fine and thin Films. *a* 1799 BLACK *Lect. Chem.* (1803) II. 677 An ingot..appears fine, even when cut through with a chizel, because this carries a film along with it from the surface, which covers the rest. 1831 BREWSTER *Optics* xvi. 138 Even silver and gold, when beaten into thin films, are transparent. 1853 HERSCHEL *Pop. Lect. Sc.* vi. §29 (1873) 245 As if the two media were separated by an exceedingly thin film of air. 1860 EMERSON *Cond. Life, Fate* Wks. (Bohn) II. 318 A tube made of a film of glass. 1860 TYNDALL *Glac.* I. vi. 44 The small bubbles of air ruptured the film of water.

b. Often applied to the emanations from the surface of bodies ('Simulacra..Quae quasi *membranæ* summo de corpore rerum Direptæ volitant', Lucr. IV. 35), which in the philosophy of Epicurus were supposed to be the objects of perception.

1682 CREECH tr. *Lucretius* IV. 38 Images of Things Which like thin films from bodies rise in streams. 1692 BENTLEY *Folly of Ath.* (ed. 4) 8 Those fleeting superficial films of bodies. 1785 REID *Int. Powers* II. xx, The films of Epicurus ..are the productions of human fancy.

3. a. *esp.* A thin pellicle forming a coating or overlying layer.

1577 GOOGE *Heresbach's Husb.* (1586) IV. 184 The Hony.. is covered with a thinne rine, or filme. 1665 *Phil. Trans.* I. 34 A slimy film floated on the top of the water. 1704 F. FULLER *Med. Gymn.* (1711) 18 Cover'd with an oily Film of several Colours. 1726–46 THOMSON *Winter* 724 An icy gale ..o'er the pool Breathes a blue film. 1784 COWPER *Task* IV. 292 The sooty films that play upon the bars. 1806 *Med. Jrnl.* XV. 148 A semi-transparent white film, which proved to be new cuticle. 1812 SIR H. DAVY *Chem. Philos.* 294 A reddish film which burns like phosphorus is deposited. 1851 RUSKIN *Stones Ven.* (1874) I. xx. 218 The pearly film of the Nautilus shell. 1863 LYELL *Antiq. Man* 34 The film of matter which is thrown down annually upon the plain during the season of inundation.

b. *Photography.* A thin pellicle or coating of collodion, gelatin, etc. spread on photographic paper or plates, or used by itself instead of a plate. Now *esp.* a thin, flexible, transparent material consisting essentially of a plastic base or support (formerly of celluloid, now commonly of cellulose acetate) coated on one side with one or more layers of emulsion and sold as a rolled strip and as separate sheets; also, a single roll of this material, allowing a small number of exposures for use in still photography or a large number for use in cinematography.

1845 THORNTHWAITE *Guide Photogr.* 52 The film of isinglass..peels off and will be found to bear a minute copy of the original. 1883 *Hardwick's Photogr. Chem.* (ed. 9) 175 If..the sensitive film of Iodide be allowed to lie loosely upon the surface of the Collodion, the picture will be very feeble. 1890 WOODBURY *Encycl. Photogr., Film Negative Process,* or film photography, is a term applied to processes in which flexible films are used instead of glass plates. 1895 *Montgomery Ward Catal.* 217/1, 1 Roll Film, for 25 exposures. 1897 *Sears, Roebuck Catal.* 473/2 The Hand Camera is the simplest form of photographic camera... Some are constructed for the use of films only, others for both films and dry plates... A roll of film weighs but a few ounces. 1897 [see CINEMATOGRAPH *sb.* b]. 1902 *Encycl. Brit.* XXXI. 687/2 Instead of glass plates, flexible films of celluloid and other materials are available in single sheets like plates, or in rolls enclosed in opaque paper. 1903 A. WATKINS *Photogr.* (ed. 2) 50 The great convenience of daylight changing with rollable films. 1910 *Punch* 15 June 433/1 Messrs. Pathé, who have conceived the idea of showing the news of the week on films at the cinematograph theatres. 1918 *Photo-Miniature* Mar. (Gloss.) s.v., Roll film, flat or cut film. 1928 *Daily Express* 12 Apr. 8/6 A length of film, comprising a number of small photographs, is placed in the transmitter. 1946 W. CLARK *Photogr. by Infrared* ii. 12 Plates and film for general infrared photography require no greater care in storage than do panchromatic materials. 1950 J. HUNT *Introd. Med. Photogr.* x. 188 Filmstrips either of X-ray or photographic films can be made in a similar manner. 1954 C. WALLACE *Enjoy your Photogr.* viii. 101 Loading by touch is quite simple... The photograper should try it with an old film. 1961 K. REISZ *Technique Film Editing* (ed. 9) i. 58 Editing of visually telling strips of film. 1966 LACOUR & LATHROP *Photo Technol.* vii. 77/1 Photography as we know it today, would not have achieved its present popularity, were it not for the introduction of roll film. 1969 M. J. LANGFORD *Adv. Photogr.* xv. 317 The top, blue sensitive layer of a multilayer colour film is also sensitive to near ultra-violet radiation.

c. A cinematographic representation of a story, drama, episode, event, etc.; a cinema performance; *pl.* the cinema, the 'pictures', the movies. (See also 7 c.)

1905 *Westm. Gaz.* 21 Jan. 3/2 A firm who took cinematograph films of his operations... The films once obtained have been sold and even exhibited at country fairs. 1911 *Times* 22 Sept. 6/2 The great majority of heroic and patriotic films shown here make United States sailors and roughriders the heroes. 1912 [see CINEMA c]. 1913 *Punch* 14 May 388/2 When half-a-dozen persons in the same film write letters they all do it in the same hand-writing. 1923 F. A. TALBOT *Moving Pictures* 72 The films emanating from the European studios. 1927 *Times* 23 Dec. 11/4 The American film *The King of Kings.* 1954 I. MURDOCH *Under Net* ii. 33 Anna never tried to get into films.

d. Film-making considered as an art-form.

1920 *Q. Rev.* July 185 The Film as Caricaturist opens up a new and slightly more encouraging vista—though it is hard to resist the impression that many of the more serious creations of the studio are really intended for caricatures even now. 1929 [see *art-form* s.v. ART *sb.* 18]. 1962 *Listener* 12 Apr. 645/2 Is film any more fundamentally mechanical than, say, architecture?

4. A morbid growth upon the eye. Also said of the growing dimness in the eyes of a dying person; sometimes ***film of death***.

1601 HOLLAND *Pliny* II. 367 The webs, filmes, and cataracts which trouble the eyesight. 1712 POPE *Messiah* 39 He from thick films shall purge the visual ray. 1762 STERNE *Tr. Shandy* VI. x, The film forsook his eyes for a moment. 1822 HAZLITT *Table-t.* I. vii. 147 An odd fancy, like a film before the eye. 1877 L. MORRIS *Epic Hades* II. 104 O'er his glaring eyes the films of death Crept.

fig. 1626 T. H[AWKINS] *Caussin's Holy Crt.* 60 The euill spirit, instantly spreadeth a filme ouer theyr eyes. *a* 1711 KEN *Psyche* Poet. Wks. 1721 IV. 253 From sensual Films when free'd, she saw strange sights. 1846 GROTE *Greece* I. xvi. (1862) I. 370 They looked at the past with a film of faith over their eyes.

5. *transf.* A slight veil or covering of haze, mist, or the like. *lit.* and *fig.*

1833 L. RITCHIE *Wand. by Loire* 31 The interminable vineyards of the Loire, already covered with the film of early twilight. 1837 SYD. SMITH *Let. to Singleton* Wks. 1859 II. 265/1 A slight film thrown over convenient injustice. 1847 H. MILLER *First Impr.* xiv. (1857) 244 An incipient frost, in the form of a thin film of blue vapour. 1883 *Times* 10 Aug. 2/3 The brown..walls show through a film of peach and almond blossoms.

6. A fine thread or filament, as of gossamer, silk, etc. *lit.* and *fig.*

1592 SHAKS. *Rom. & Jul.* I. iv. 63 Her Whip of Crickets bone, the Lash of Philome. 1781 COWPER *Anti-Thelyphthora* 73 When..floating films envelope every thorn. *a* 1822 SHELLEY *Unf. Drama* 230 Floating on the line Which, like a film in purest space, divided The heaven beneath the water from the heaven Above the clouds. 1845 DARWIN *Voy. Nat.* viii. (1879) 161 They were..in undulations like films of silk blown by the wind. 1849 RUSKIN *Sev. Lamps* iv. §10. 102 A riband..spoils all that is near its wretched film of an existence. 1859 I. TAYLOR *Logic in Theol.* 203 We must not trust ourselves to any such films of correspondence.

7. a. *Comb.*, as ***film-like***, ***-winged*** adjs.; also † **film-broke**, ruptured; † **film-bursting**, hernia; **film-colour** *Psychol.*, an expanse of colour that has a filmy appearance, neither being transparent nor seen as being on the surface of an object or at a definite distance (opp. *surface-colour*); **film-cooling** (see quot.); **film-fern**, a fern with filmy fronds, *esp.* one of the genus *Hymenophyllum*; **film-free** *a.*, free from film, not obscured, clear.

c 1400 *Lanfranc's Cirurg.* 281 Men þat weren *filme broke. 1578 LYTE *Dodoens* I. lvi. 83 The leaues pound and layde too healeth *filme [*printed* filine] burstings [Fr. *hergnes*]. 1922 *Psychol. Bull.* XIX. 574 'Uncertainty'..may quite well be a property of visual phenomena, as Katz..maintained for the

'distance' of his so-called '*film'-colors (*Flächenfarben*). **1951** R. H. THOULESS *Gen. & Soc. Psychol.* (ed. 3) xii. 190 Katz would call the colour..seen in the spectroscope a film colour. **1962** M. D. VERNON *Psychol. of Perception* v. 83 It will appear as 'film' colour and not as surface colour. The colour cannot be definitely localized as belonging to the surfaces of objects, but seems to be soft and hazy and to lie over them like a film. **1964** *Amer. Philos. Q.* I. 7/1 The term 'film-color' will do as an example. To get the reader to understand this technical term of visual phenomenology, we instruct him to look at some fairly distant object through a paper tube. **1950** *Sci. News* XV. 82 *Film cooling [in a space rocket]... Small holes are drilled through the wall of the combustion chamber so that fuel can leak through from the jacket... It boils and forms a protective film of comparatively cool vapour between these gases and the metal wall. **1865** GOSSE *Land & Sea* (1874) 352 Out of the crevices many species of *Film-ferns..project their tufts of pellucid fronds. **1880** BROWNING *Dram. Idylls, Pan & Luna* 19 From each web of mist Utterly *film-free—entered on her race The naked Moon. **1865** TYLOR *Early Hist. Man.* i. 9 Dreams..are *film-like images which fly off from the surfaces of real objects. **1875** LANIER *Poems, Symphony* 139 All shynesses of *film-winged things.

b. In sense 3 b, as ***film-base, camera, -carrier, -holder, magazine, -maker, -punch, roll, side, speed, -wind, -winding***; **film badge, ring**, a device containing photographic film which registers the amount of the wearer's exposure to radiation; **film cement** (see quots.); **film pack**, an assemblage of cut films fitted in a case or holder; **film recording** (see quot. 1941); **film stock**, unexposed film; **film strip**, a length of film bearing a sequence of still frames, used esp. as a teaching aid.

1945 H. D. SMYTH *Gen. Acct. Devel. Atomic Energy Mil. Purposes* viii. 90 The Health Division later introduced 'film badges', small pieces of film worn in the identification badge. **1955** *Gloss. Terms Radiol.* (*B.S.I.*) 67 *Film badge*, a photographic film used as a radiation monitor. It is often partially shielded to differentiate between types and quantities of ionizing radiation. *Film ring*, a film badge worn as a ring to measure the dose of radiation, usually beta radiation, received by the fingers. **1968** *Brit. Med. Bull.* XXIV. 260/2 Counting of breaks and dicentrics is a surer index of damage than film-badge monitoring. **1923** F. A. TALBOT *Moving Pictures* 62 It was necessary to discover..a new film-base. Cellulose could not be avoided as the basic constituent. **1897** *Sears, Roebuck Catal.* 473/2 The film cameras are most convenient for the traveller. **1920** *Edin. Rev.* July 73 Charlie Chaplin must practise his own funniments before the film camera. **1890** *Anthony's Photogr. Bull.* III. 312 We have to use 'film carriers' which up to date have been complicated, unsafe. **1897** C. M. HEPWORTH *Animated Photogr.* xi. 87 The 'solution' or 'film cement' with which the joints of film are effected is either a solution of celluloid and, possibly, one or two other substances, in a solvent such as acetone or amyl, acetate, or else the latter chemical used alone. **1959** W. S. SHARPS *Dict. Cinematogr.* 95/1 *Film cement*, a solution that will partially dissolve film base and so enable two pieces of film to be joined together in a splice. **1918** Film-holder [see *film pack*, below]. **1967** E. CHAMBERS *Photolitho-Offset* viii. 106 Vacuum filmholders permit the use of contact screens. **1931** B. BROWN *Talking Pictures* x. 247 The film magazines..were found to accentuate vibration and noise from the camera mechanism. **1859** *National Mag.* VI. 332/1 Solution rapidly takes place, and the photographic film-maker is constituted. **1903** *Brit. Jrnl. Photogr.* 19 June 490/2 The Film Pack consists of a light tight sheath made of black press board, with an opening in one side corresponding in size to the exposure, into which are folded thirteen strips of black, chemically pure paper..; each of twelve of these..has fastened to the inner side of a sheet of film. **1918** *Photo-Miniature* Mar. (Gloss.) 20 *Film pack*, a cardboard or metal holder containing, usually, 12 cut films so placed in it that, by pulling in succession projecting paper tabs, the films are brought into position... The device is..a magazine film-holder. **1961** A. L. M. SOWERBY *Dict. Photogr.* (ed. 19) 308 Film packs are no longer made in Great Britain, but imported packs are from time to time available. **1923** F. A. TALBOT *Moving Pictures* 88 The film-punch for indicating exposure changes upon the edge of the film in a camera. **1931** B. BROWN *Talking Pictures* x. 216 Thus film recording ..'starts right', and..has no real limitation whatsoever, since it is easy to increase film speed, and thus raise the maximum frequency. **1941** *B.B.C. Gloss. Broadc. Terms* 12 Film Recording: (1) Process of registering sound by electro-mechanical means for reproduction by photo-electric means, the recording medium being transparent ribbon coated with an opaque substance. (2) (Also Film.) Ribbon on which sound has been so recorded. (3) (By extension.) Programme material so recorded. **1890** *Anthony's Photogr. Bull.* III. 22 When a film roll is used, one is tempted to make a great many utterly useless pictures. **1889** *Ibid.* II. 361 The film side of the plate. **1915** B. E. JONES *Cinematograph Bk.* iv. 32 Round the inner movable dial [of the exposure meter] are scales relating to film speed and stop. **1911** C. N. BENNETT et al. *Handbk. Kinematography* I. App. 108 Long strips of photographically-coated celluloid, known as 'film stock'. **1920** *Stage Year Bk.* 51 Film stock in particular became scarce, for there was no plant for manufacturing this in Britain at the time. **1930** P. ROTHA *Film till Now* 341 On the film strip, a frame is three-quarters of an inch high by one inch wide. **1962** *Engineering* 16 Nov. 649 Three new filmstrips, intended for training student electronic engineers. **1962** *Unesco Bull. Libr.* XVI. 10 The 35 mm. filmstrip, which carries a sequence of pictures to be projected. The size of the frames on the strip is usually 18 × 24 mm. Filmstrips are mainly used for teaching purposes. **1958** M. L. HALL *Newnes Compl. Amat. Photogr.* 55 All 35 mm. cameras have film-wind mechanisms. *Ibid* 61 In one camera all the necessary actions—film wind, exposure counter, shutter tensioning..are combined. **1936** *Discovery* Aug. 238/2 Automatic Film-Winding.

c. In sense 3 c, as ***film actress, clip, company, composer, crew, critic, cue, -editing, editor, fan, festival, hero, magazine, -maker, -making*** ppl. adj. and vbl. sb., ***music, producer, production, rights, script, set, society, -struck*** adj., ***studio, super, trade, unit***; **film-goer**, a frequenter of the cinema; hence **film-going** *ppl. a.*; **film star**, a star actor or actress for the cinema.

1921 *Punch* 12 Jan. 21/1 Two leading film actresses have made runaway marriages. **1958** Film clip [see CLIP *sb.*[2] 2 c]. **1962** *Sunday Times* 26 Aug. 25/5 The sort of film clips which only political popagandists would dream of using. **1918** H. CROY *How Motion Pictures are Made* ii. 35 Charles Pathé, of Paris,..later came to head the world's premier film company. **1948** *Penguin Music Mag.* Feb. 67 Vaughan Williams is, as a film composer, best at moments such as these. **1976** *Facts on File* 14 Aug. 592/2 Sudan barred the entry into the country of a British Broadcasting Co. film crew. **1982** T. BARR *Acting for Camera* iv. xxvi. 188 The film crew, whether it be for a TV episode or a feature film, is large. **1931** *Punch* 8 Apr. 384/1 The film-critic of *The Daily Telegraph*. **1918** H. CROY *How Motion Pictures are Made* vi. 134 The director..gives him what might be called his film cues. **1922** *Moving Picture Stories* 23 June 25/1 Film editors and splicers are working as they haven't done in many months. **1953** T. DICKINSON in K. Reisz *Technique Film Editing* 7 The pivotal contribution of the film editor has never been analysed objectively. Film editing has only been dealt with in the personal theories of Eisenstein, Pudovkin and others. **1918** R. WAGNER *Film Folk* i. 12 But that was before the film fans became oversophisticated. **1951** N. MITFORD *Blessing* II. i. 162 She discouraged Hughie from following her to Venice, saying vaguely that she would be taken up with the film festival. **1919** *Fortn. Rev.* CVI. 455 Some owners of cinema theatres are doing their best to attract a better intellectual class of film-goer. **1927** *Sunday Express* 26 June 4 Every film-goer likes to feel that he is up-to-date in cinema affairs. **1929** *Evening News* 18 Nov. 12/4 They should realise that the film-going public have brains. **1925** W. DEEPING *Sorrell & Son* xv. §1, He hated crowds, he —the crowd's film-hero. **1939** C. DAY LEWIS *Child of Misfortune* III. ii. 271 Alice, looking up from her film magazine. **1919** *Fortn. Rev.* CVI. 456 Many film-makers.. have set their faces against this appeal. **1960** *Guardian* 27 Oct. 8/2 Certain products of Hollywood—about which French film-makers were traditionally contemptuous. **1938** *Observer* 26 June 12/6 A first-class film-making nation. **1944** J. S. HUXLEY *Living in Rev.* iii. 37 Wartime film-making, especially perhaps in Canada, is making the movie a comprehensive and faithful mirror for the wartime life and purpose of peoples. **1927** *Melody Maker* Sept. 938/2 The art of cue film-music compilers in the fitting of films with appropriate music. **1914** R. GRAU *Theatre of Science* iv. 85 He will prove a greater asset to the film producer a year from now. **1920** *Q. Rev.* July 182 The only kind of ending the film-producers can think of for this or any other type of drama. **1927** P. D. HUGON *Morrow's Word Finder* 205 Terms used in film production. **1935** H. G. WELLS *Things to Come* 13 The incorporation of original music in film production is still..an unsolved problem. **1913** *Writer's Mag.* Dec. 263/1 Contracts with..today's most famous authors for the film rights to their..stories. **1933** A. BRUNEL *Filmcraft* 194 Selling the film rights at an immensely exaggerated figure. **1970** L. MEYNELL *Curious Crime of Miss Julia Blossom* xv. 180 Serial rights. American rights, and I saw a para in last night's *Standard* saying somebody was after the film rights too. **1948** DYLAN THOMAS *Let.* 17 Nov. (1966) 323 My fee for my next unspecified filmscript. **1952** ELIOT & HOELLERING *Film of Murder in Cathedral* 7 That is in itself a justification for publishing this film script. **1933** C. WINCHESTER *World Film Encycl.* 475/2 The first film sets were called 'flats'. **1931** *Week-end Review* 14 Feb. 212/2 The Film Society. **1968** *Guardian* 27 Dec. 4/8 Film societies.. have increased in membership. **1914** R. GRAU *Theatre of Science* iii. 50 The greatest film stars in the world. **1923** *Chambers's Jrnl.* Mar. 180/1 A number of very beautiful women have earned untold riches as 'film-stars'. **1963** *Times Lit. Suppl.* 26 Apr. 313/5 The film-star treatment of the Royal Family. **1923** *Weekly Disp.* 28 Jan. 1 She had become absolutely 'film-struck'. **1913** *Writer's Bulletin* July 11 The great photoplays of the future will be those that are created within the confines of the film studio. **1935** *Discovery* Oct. 309/1 In film studios the necessity for absolute silence demands an air-tight enclosure. **1924** GALSWORTHY *White Monkey* II. ii, The lurid professions—film super, or mannequin. **1914** *Even. News* 8 Oct. 2/1 It is 'up to' the American film trade to see that the evidence of the camera gets a fair reception. **1951** 'M. INNES' *Operation Pax* III. vii. 113 Film units..descend upon the place.

Hence **'filmcraft**, the technique of making films; **'filmdom** [-DOM], the realm of cinematographic production, producers, and stars, the cinema world; **'filmland**, (*a*) = *filmdom*; (*b*) Hollywood, or a specific locality associated with the film industry.

1928 *Observer* 15 Apr. 5/4 Filmcraft is little understood. **1963** *Guardian* 9 Feb. 5/5 Its sixty minutes contain no remarkable feat of filmcraft. **1914** *Writer's Bulletin* Feb. 35/1 Even in filmdom..there are a dozen who hold the art of the silent drama in reverence. **1927** *Sunday Express* 12 June 18/3 One of filmdom's finest mansions is Pickfair. **1930** *Daily Express* 9 Sept. 8/3 A strange trail of thought in filmdom. **1914** R. GRAU *Theatre of Science* p. vii, There are not a few celebrities in film-land averse from publicity. **1928** *Punch* 21 Nov. 578/3 How Filmland Regards a Royal Commission. 'English Royal Group...'—*Los Angeles Paper*.

film (fɪlm), *v.* [f. prec. sb.]

1. *trans.* To cover with or as with a film. Also, *to film over*, †*up*.

1602 SHAKS. *Ham.* III. iv. 147 It will but skin and filme the Vlcerous place. *a* **1656** BP. HALL *Rem. Wks.* (1660) 251 Grosse infidelity that hath filmed up thine eyes. **1700** C. DAVENANT *Disc. Grants* Introd. 7 They do but film over a sore which breaks out afterwards with greater rancour. **1794** COLERIDGE *Relig. Musings* Wks. (1829) I. 90 And curse your spells, that film the eye of Faith. **1876** FARRAR *Marlb. Serm.* xxix. 290 Would you linger by the stagnant pool because its surface is filmed with the iridescence of decay?

2. *intr.* for *refl.* To become covered with a film (as the eyes); to grow dim or obscure as though covered with a film; hence (*poet. rare*) of distant objects, to become hazy, fade away. Also, *to film over*.

1844 MRS. BROWNING *Dead Pan*, Straight her eyeballs filmed with horror. **1850** NEALE *Med. Hymns* (1867) 53 Eyes are filming o'er in death. **1877** LANIER *Poems, Florida Ghost* 5 Past far-off palms that filmed to nought.

3. *trans.* To photograph for use in a cinema or cinematographic device; to exhibit as a cinematographic production; to put on 'the films' or 'the screen'.

Quot. 1899 refers to a 'mutoscope'.

1899 *Westm. Gaz.* 21 Sept. 4/1 Professors of medicine are 'filming' their patients' muscles. **1912** F. A. TALBOT *Moving Pictures* xv. 174 He succeeded in persuading Sir Herbert Beerbohm Tree to let him film the Shakespearean production of Henry VIII. **1915** A. S. NEILL *Dominie's Log* viii, I have seen *Hamlet* filmed. **1915** W. IRWIN *Men, Women & War* 15 We filmed a Belgian troop of cavalry going into action. **1920** *Q. Rev.* July 183 Hallo, here's a big success, let's film it! **1920** *Glasgow Herald* 11 Sept. 7 Churchmen are invited to write thrilling Biblical scenarios to be filmed for exhibition at afternoon services. **1934** W. SAROYAN *Daring Young Man* (1935) 26, I am not expecting Paramount Pictures to film this work. **1971** *Daily Tel.* 20 Oct. 12/8 Cameras were allowed for the first time to film their lordships inside their red-carpeted sanctum.

4. *intr.* To be (well or ill) suited for film-acting or for reproduction on film.

1920 *Punch* 31 Mar. 246/3 This incident should 'film' well. **1927** E. HEMINGWAY *Fiesta* I. vi. 60 He's leaving me. He's decided I don't film well. **1928** *Observer* 26 Feb. 20/2 [He] 'films' very well indeed. **1934** W. SAROYAN *Daring Young Man* (1935) 204, I always knew I had the sort of face that would film well and look good on the screen.

Hence **'filming** *ppl. a.* and *vbl. sb.*

1889 *Anthony's Photogr. Bull.* II. 292, I drew a plan of the filming instrument. **1912** F. A. TALBOT *Moving Pictures* xi. 120 The procession drew within the field of the camera and the filming commenced. **1918** H. CROY *How Motion Pictures are Made* 110 The filming of this is put last to give the carpenters time to complete it. **1933** *Discovery* Dec. 359/2 The hunting, filming and capture of wild beasts.

filmable ('fɪlməb(ə)l), *a.* [f. FILM *v.* 3 + -ABLE.] Capable of being filmed or adapted to the cinema; well suited to reproduction on film.

1920 V. STEER *Secrets Cinema* ii. 27 Even if one posseses ..filmable features, the beginner will discover that the work is..exceedingly precarious. **1921** *Glasgow Herald* 25 Mar. 7 Full of 'filmable' incident. **1926** *Spectator* 17 July 88/2 A reason, incidentally, why Dickens is not really filmable. **1961** *Guardian* 14 Sept. 10/5 Gestures which are extremely filmable.

filmart, -mert, obs. and dial. ff. FOUMART.

filmed, *ppl. a.* [f. FILM *v.* and *sb.* + -ED.]

a. Covered with a film. **b.** Having films.

1637 NABBES *Microcosm.* IV. E iij, Colours do not take My filmed eyes. **1649** G. DANIEL *Trinarch., Hen. V* cxci, Soe the Autumnall Gossamere..knitts the Sun, (within his narrow film'd Cordage) to all his wealth. **1878** B. TAYLOR *Deukalion* IV. iii, Wash thine filmed eyes And look around thee.

filmic ('fɪlmɪk), *a.* [f. FILM *sb.* 3 c + -IC.] Of or pertaining to cinematography; suggestive of the cinema; filmable. Hence **'filmically** *adv.*

1929 I. MONTAGU tr. *Pudovkin's On Film Technique* ii. 19 The problem was the expression, filmically, of his joy. **1930** *Time & Tide* 23 Aug. 1080 They do seem to have an eye for the filmic possibilities of subjects. **1930** *Times Lit. Suppl.* 18 Sept. 728/2 Debating the merits of various types of 'filmic' art. **1936** *Archit. Rev.* LXXIX. 137 But while reading this book one frequently feels that Mr. Rotha has more interest in his social message than in his filmic means. **1948** 'E. CRISPIN' *Buried for Pleasure* iii. 22 His blonde visitant's filmic radiance. **1953** *New Statesman* 14 Nov. 599/1 The most gorgeous of them [*sc.* Shakespeare films], and after fearful struggles, the most filmic..was *Henry V*. **1958** *Times Lit. Suppl.* 15 Aug. p. xxviii/2 Arthur Calder-Marshall (whose early novel *About Levy* was a perfect example of filmic-construction). **1962** *Listener* 23 Aug. 273/2 Most people felt that filmically this was an untidy work.

filmiform ('fɪlmɪfɔːm), *a.* [f. FILM *sb.* + -(I)FORM.] In the form of a film, film-like.

1831 [POTE] *Assassins of the Paradise* 43 The loaded air.. Floats filmiform.

filmlet ('fɪlmlɪt). [f. FILM *sb.* 3 c + -LET.] A short film for cinema or television.

1931 *Punch* 18 May, In very advanced cases the 'trailer'.. is a specially made filmlet. **1958** *Bookseller* 8 Nov. 1905 (*caption*) Scene from the Book Tokens 'filmlet' which will be televised during the coming weeks. **1959** *Times Lit. Suppl.* 13 Nov. 662/3 One is reminded of those filmlets and television commercials which so often win prizes.

‖ **film noir** (film nwar). [Fr., lit. 'black film'.] A cinematographic film of a gloomy or fatalistic character.

1958 *Spectator* 25 July 134/2 It [*sc.* a play] tries to be a parody of a *film noir*. **1960** *Times* 9 May 16/4 A school-boy adventure story which turns suddenly and surprisingly into a bleak film noir.

'filmograph. [f. FILM *sb.* + -(O)GRAPH.] A name given by Pumphrey to a camera adapted for the use of films (1890 Woodbury *Encycl. Photogr.*).

filmography (fɪl'mɒgrəfɪ). [f. FILM *sb.* 3 c, after BIBLIOGRAPHY.] **a.** A list of the films of a particular director, producer, actor, etc., or of those dealing with any particular theme. **b.** The systematic description of, and information about, films.

1962 *Movie* Sept. 30/3 We hope to include also a complete filmography of Preminger, with details of the availability of the films. **1963** *Amer. N. & Q.* II. 10/1 *Film Composers in America*..will contain biographies, filmographies, discographies, and bibliographies. **1968** P. GRAHAM *Dict. Cinema* 5 The filmographies that follow each director, actor, scriptwriter, etc., listed in the dictionary are complete.

filmot, var. of FILEMOT.

'filmset, *v.* *Printing.* [f. FILM *sb.* + SET *v.* 72.] *trans.* To compose (matter) by projecting images on to photographic film in a photocomposing machine. So **'filmset** *ppl. a.*, **'filmsetting** *ppl. a.* and *vbl. sb.*

1954 *Printing Rev.* XVIII. LXV. 41/2 The Keybar frames ..can be used without alteration for film-setting on a 'Monophoto'. **1956** *Print in Britain* IV. 234/1 Protype provides the..printer with the opportunity of installing a simple film-setting system. **1958** *Times Lit. Suppl.* 18 Apr. 209/3 In 1954 an Italian novel was filmset in Europe, on the Westover Rotofoto. In the United States, two (not one) books were filmset on the Intertype Fotosetter before the end of 1951. **1959** *Penrose Ann.* p. xviii, It is to be hoped that examples of filmset books..will be seen in the National Book League's exhibitions of book design. **1963** D. BLAND in O. Simon *Introd. Typogr.* (ed. 2) p. v, The increasing use of slug-setting and film-setting for bookwork. **1963** *Printing & Mind of Man* 113 This [*sc.* the Rotophoto], the first British filmsetting machine to be placed on the market, was the invention of..George Westover, and was first shown in 1948. **1966** *Print* (Wynkyn de Worde Soc.) ii. 18 Type is still largely the basis of non-pictorial printing, whether the job be done from the type itself..or from a filmset or 'cold-type' basis.

filmy ('fɪlmɪ), *a.* [f. FILM *sb.* + -Y[1].]

†**1.** Of membranous structure. *Obs.*

1661 LOVELL *Hist. Anim. & Min.* Introd. 37 The ventricle ..is filmy, and therefore cold, hard, dry, and glutinous. **1665** EVELYN *Diary* 9 Feb., Its lower beak..being filmy, stretches to a prodigious wideness when it devours a great fish.

2. Forming a thin pellicle or coating.

1628 WOTTON *Let.* 14 Dec. in *Reliq. Wotton.* (1685) 441 A little Excrescence..upon the uttermost ball of his Eyes, a filmy matter, like the rudiment of a Pin and Web. **1735** N. TORRIANO *Gangr. Sore Throat* 94 As these filmy Membranes came away, the Weasand or Throat became freer. **1772** PRIESTLEY in *Phil. Trans.* LXII. 219 The water ..had deposited a filmy kind of matter. **1853** KANE *Grinnell Exp.* xxxvii (1856) 344 The area of filmy ice. **1885** R. BUCHANAN *Annan Water* iii, Encrusting its black sides with a species of filmy salt.

3. Resembling a film, of extremely delicate texture, gauze-like; consisting of slender filaments, as of gossamer.

1604 DRAYTON *Owle* 764 The Spiders..in his traine their filmie netting cast. **1664** POWER *Exp. Philos.* I. 30 Another pair of filmy Tiffany long wings. **1740** SOMERVILLE *Hobbinol* II. 190 The luxurious Wasp His filmy Pennons struggling flaps in vain. **1813** SCOTT *Trierm.* III. xi, It seem'd a veil of filmy lawn. *a* **1839** PRAED *Poems* (1864) II. 21 The filmy shroud Of many a mild transparent cloud. **1871** R. ELLIS *Catullus* lxix. 3 Some robe most filmy.

fig. **1794** COLERIDGE *Lines on Friend who died of Fever*, Vanity her filmy net-work spread. **1820** HAZLITT *Lect. Dram. Lit.* 75 A veil of words and filmy abstractions. **1856** R. A. VAUGHAN *Mystics* (1860) II. IX. i. 120 The filmiest evanescence of the feeling has to be..anatomized.

b. ***filmy-fern, filmy-leaf***, names of a genus of ferns, *Hymenophyllum*. (Cf. *film-fern*, FILM *sb.* 7.)

1829 LOUDON *Encycl. Plants* 886 Hymenophyllum, Filmy-Leaf. **1861** MISS PRATT *Flower. Pl.* VI. 154 Order Filices..(Filmy Fern). **1882** *The Garden* 5 Aug. 111/3 The Filmy Fern House in the Pine-apple Nursery.

4. Covered with or as with a film; beclouded, dim, hazy.

1825 J. NEAL *Bro. Jonathan* III. 345 With eyes no longer white or filmy. **1833** HT. MARTINEAU *Briery Creek* i. 3 The filmy orb of the moon. **1864** LOWELL *Fireside Trav.* 132 Gradually the filmy trees defined themselves.

5. *Comb.*

1821 SHELLEY *To Night* iv, Thy sweet child Sleep, the filmy-eyed.

Hence **'filmily** *adv.*; **'filminess.**

1727 BAILEY vol. II, *Filminess.* **1831** *Fraser's Mag.* III. 483 The haze and filminess dropped from our 'optic nerve'. **1870** H. MACMILLAN *Bible Teach.* xiii. 262 The milk-white filminess of the onyx. **1890** *Harper's Mag.* Oct. 803/2 Something that filmily wavers before their senses.

Filofax ('faɪləʊfæks). [Repr. colloq. pronunc. of *file of facts*: see FILE *sb.*[2] and FACT.] A proprietary name for a portable filing system for personal or office use, consisting of a loose-leaf notebook with separate sections for appointments, notes, addresses, etc., usu. in a wallet with spaces for pens, credit cards, and other personal items.

Long established, but not widely known until the 1980s.

1931 *Trade Marks Jrnl.* 6 May 647/1 *Filofax*..Loose leaf binders. **1983** *Financial Times* 16 Apr. 13/5 Filofax..has been going for years... Entirely British, based in Essex, it was started sometime in the 1920s... Basically it is a looseleaf system of keeping almost all the personal documentation you need up to date and in order, all in one small portable package... A standard pack would probably consist of a diary, address book and spare notepaper. **1985** *Trade Marks Jrnl.* 9 Oct. 2588/2 *Filofax*..Stationery, printed matter; printed forms; diaries; covers..index cards; card index cabinets (not being furniture). **1985** *Company* Dec. 9/1 Paul Smith was first to spot and stock the now ubiquitous Filofax, which the media crowd took so completely to their hearts and pockets. **1986** *Private Eye* 2 May 14 *Out* goes the Militant Tendency—or rather it doesn't. *In* come a lot of new-style ad-men in suits with computers and Filofaxes. **1987** *Independent* 23 Mar. 1/4 The company itself started in 1921..[at] Sandhurst... Filofaxes were standard issue. In military circles they were known as vade-mecums—an article carried on the person.

‖**filon** (filɔ̃). *Mining.* [a. F. *filon* vein, lode, f. *fil* thread (see FILE *sb.*[2]).] A mineral or metallic vein, a lode.

1845 GIBSON in *Cambrian Jrnl.* (1863) 149 The collaterals cross the main filon in angles of incidence.

filoplumaceous (ˌfaɪləpluːˈmeɪʃəs), *a.* *Ornith.* [f. mod.L. *filoplūma* (see next) + -ACEOUS.] Of the nature of a filoplume.

1890 COUES *Field & Gen. Ornith.* II. §3. 128 Types of Feathery Structure..3. The hairy, bristly, or filoplumaceous.

filoplume ('faɪləpluːm). *Ornith.* [ad. mod.L. *fīloplūma*, badly f. L. *fīlum* thread + *plūma* feather. (The correct L. form would be **fīliplūma*.)] (See quot. 1890.)

1884 *Syd. Soc. Lex.*, *Filoplume.* **1890** COUES *Field & Gen. Ornith.* II. §3. 128 Different kinds of Feathers. 4. *Filoplumes, filoplumæ*, or thread-feathers, have an extremely slender, almost invisible stem..and usually no vane, unless a terminal tuft of barbs may be held for such..These are the nearest approach to hairs that birds have.

filose (faɪ'ləʊs). *Bot.* and *Zool.* [as if ad. L. **fīlōs-us*, f. *fīlum* thread.] Having a thread-like termination.

1823 CRABB *Technol. Dict.*, *Filose*, ending in a thread-like process; an epithet applied to insects and plants. **1884** *Syd. Soc. Lex.*, *Filose*, in Botany.

†**filo'sella.** *Obs.* exc. *Hist.* Forms: 7 file-, filozella, 8 filosella. Also 7 philizella, philosella. [Corruptly ad. It. *filosello*, according to Mussafia a perversion (after *filo* thread) of **folisello*:—popular L. **follicellus* cocoon (whence OF. *foucel*), dim. of L. *follis* bag.] A kind of stuff; = FILOSELLE b.

1611 COTGR., *Filoselle*..the stuff Filozella. **1619** PURCHAS *Microcosmus* xxvii. 269 The new deuised names of Stuffes and Colours..Veletato, Philizello, Paragon. **1640** in Entick *London* II. 169 Silk say calimancoes and phillosellas, broad, the dozen yards os. 4*d*. **1678–96** PHILLIPS, *Filozella*, a kind of Stuff.

filoselle ('fɪləsɛl). Forms: 7 fil(l)-, fyllozel, 7–9 filosel(l, (7 filiosell), 9 filoselle. Also 7 philiselle. [a. F. *filoselle*, fem., OF. *filloisel* masc., ad. It. *filosello*: see prec.] **a.** 'Ferret or floss silk; grogram-yarn' (Simmonds).

1612 *Sc. Bk. Customs* in *Halyburton's Ledger* (1867) 326 Filosell or ferrett silk the pound viiili. **1662** *Stat. Ireland* (1765) II. 464 Fyllozell or Paris silk. **1876** M. M. GRANT *Sun-Maid* iv, It was a wonderful piece of work of woven gold and silver and filosel.

attrib. **1892** *Pall Mall G.* 27 Oct. 1/2 It is a wide ribbon, which has the appearance of plaited filoselle silk.

†**b.** A kind of stuff (? a mixture of silk and wool).

a **1605** in Beck *Draper's Dict.* 16 *note*, The paragon, peropus, and philiselles may be affirmed to be double chambletts. *Ibid.*, To make this a philiselle, a peropus, a paragon, or a buffyn is but to alter the breadth.

†**filo'setta.** *Obs.* Also fillizetta. [App. altered from It. *filosello* by substitution of the It. suffix *-etta* for *-ello*. But cf. Sp. *filoseda* mixture of silk and wool.] ? = prec.

1598 FLORIO, *Filisello*, a kinde of course silke which we call, filosetta or flouret silke. **1623** J. TAYLOR (Water P.) *Praise Hempseed* 4 Shag, Fillizetta, Damaske and Mockado.

filosofe, -phie, obs. forms of PHILOSOPH, -Y.

filot, obs. form of FILLET.

†**'filour**, *Obs.* Forms: 4–5 fylor, -oure, -owre, 5 fillour. [Shortened ad. OF. *affiloir*:—med.L. *affīlātōrium*, f. *affīlāre*: see AFFILE *v.*] A tool for sharpening steel, a hone or whetstone.

c **1340** *Gaw & Gr. Knt.* 2225 With a borelych bytte.. Fyled in a fylor, fowre fote large. *c* **1440** *Promp. Parv.* 160/2 Fylowre, of barbowrs crafte *acutecula, filarium*. **1483** *Cath. Angl.* 130/2 A Filoure, *affilatorium*.

Hence †**'filour**, *v.* *Obs.*[−0] *trans.* To whet, sharpen.

1483 in *Cath. Angl.* 130/2.

filour, var. of FELOURE *Obs.* foliage.

a **1400–50** *Alexander* 3690 Gilden platis, Flamband all in filour & fewlis en-blanchid.

[**filour**, explained in some Dicts. as 'a curtain-rod,' is from *Bk. of Curtasye* 447, where *fylour* is prob. a bad reading for *sylour*, CELURE.]

filozofe, -fie, obs. forms of PHILOSOPH, -Y.

‖**fils** (fiːs). [Fr., son.] The son, junior: appended to a name to distinguish between a father and son of the same name.

1886 *Athenæum* 30 Oct. 565/1 Athanase Coquerel *fils* does not seem to have had any great distinction..of style. **1889** E. DOWSON *Let.* 24 Mar. (1967) 54 Dumas fils easily first. **1936** OGDEN & RICHARDS *Meaning of Meaning* (ed. 4) v. 89 Mill *fils* in his editorial notes on this passage holds [etc.]. **1965** *House & Garden* Mar. 42 Russell *père* had been in banking. .. Russell *fils*..thought this a bit-too-cramping project.

†**'filsen**, *v.* *Obs.* Forms: 3 filstnen, 4 fulsun, fylsen, 5 felsen, -yn, filsom, fylsy(n. [ME. *fils(t)ne-n*, f. FILST *sb.*; cf. -EN[5].] *trans.* To minister to, aid, support; to further, promote.

c **1200** ORMIN 6170 Himm birrþ þe fillstnenn wiþþ þin fe. *c* **1220** *Bestiary* 44 His fader him filstnede swo ðat he ros fro dede. *c* **1325** *E.E. Allit. P.* B. 1644 Þe souerayn of heuen Fylsened euer þy fader. *c* **1400** *Destr. Troy* 4871 Yche freike is þere frynd to filsom þere spede. *a* **1400–50** *Alexander* 4669 ȝe..fage ay þe flesche & felsen it wele.

†**'filsne**, *v.* *Obs. rare*[−1]. [f. ON. *fylgsni* (sb pl.) hiding-place (cf. Goth. *fulhsni* sing. in same sense), f. OTeut. **fulg-* ablaut-var. of **felh-* to hide: see FEAL *v.*] *intr.* To lurk.

? *a* **1400** *Morte Arth.* 881 Sire, see ȝe ȝone farlande, with ȝone two fyrez, þar filsnez þat fende.

†**filst**, *sb.* *Obs.* Forms: 1 fullǽst, fullést, fylst, 2–3 fulst. [OE. *fullǽst, fullést, fylst* = OFris. *folliste, folste, fulliste*, OS. *fullêsti*, OHG. *folleist, follist*; connected with next verb.] Assistance, support, furtherance.

a **1000** *Boeth. Metr.* xxiii. 14 Mid Godes fylste. *a* **1000** *Cædmon's Exod.* 554 (Gr.) Is..mægenwisa trum, fullesta mæst. *c* **1175** *Lamb. Hom.* 113 He ne mei habben nane mihte ..butan godes fulste. *c* **1205** LAY. 1747 Þa Corine of wode com..Brutun to fulste. *c* **1230** *Hali Meid.* 17 Hire forme fulst is sihðe.

†**filst**, *v.* *Obs.* Forms: 1 fullǽstan, fullésten, fylstan, 2 felsten, 3 fulsten, *south.* vulsten, filsten. [OE. *fullǽstan, fulléstan, fylstan* = OS. *fullêstian*, OHG. *folleisten*.

The word is a compound of the OTeut. vb. **laistjan* to follow, attend upon; with regard to the prefixed element see FOLLOW *v.*]

trans. To aid, help.

c **893** K. ÆLFRED *Oros.* III. xi. §10 Pirrus him..fylste. *c* **1000** *Ags. Gosp.* Luke v. 7 Hiȝ bicnodon hyra ȝeferan..þæt hi comun ant him fylston [*c* **1160** *Hatton* felsten]. *c* **1200** *Trin. Coll. Hom.* 29 Þese two þe ben leihter and lust uulsted þe þridde þat is þe flesliche lust. *a* **1275** *O.E. Misc.* 135 Þe bet sal he þe felsten to don al þine wille.

b. *refl.* To give one's aid *to*.

c **1200** *Trin. Coll. Hom.* 193 He deleð him fro gode and fulsteð him to ðe deuel.

filtch obs. f. of FILCH.

filter ('fɪltə(r)), *sb.* Forms: 5–9 filtre, (6 fylter, -ture), 6– filter. Also 7 philter. [ME. *filtre*, a. OF. *filtre*, ad. med.L. *filtrum*: see FELT]

†**1.** = FELT *sb.* Also a piece of felt. *Obs.*

c **1400** MAUNDEV. (Roxb.) xxvi. 125 Þan es he sette apon a blak filtre, with þe whilk þai lift him vppe and settez him in his trone. *Ibid.* xxxiv. 152 Þai dwell all in tentez made of blakk filtre.

2. a. A piece of felt, woollen cloth, paper, or other substance, through which liquids are passed to free them from matter held in suspension.

Now only with reference to chemical manipulation, where the filter is usually of unsized paper.

1563 T. GALE *Antidot.* II. 76 b, Distill them by a fylture or thorowe a lyttle bagge, or by a peece of clothe. **1683** PETTUS *Fleta Min.* I. (1686) 214 Dissolve the Vitriol and purify it through a Filtre. **1769** LANE in *Phil. Trans.* LIX. 220 The clear liquor being decanted, the remainder was passed through a filter. **1812** SIR H. DAVY *Chem. Philos.* 285 The whole is then to be poured upon a filtre of cloth. **1846** J. BAXTER *Libr. Pract. Agric.* (ed. 4) I. 53 Collected on a filter, washed and dried.

b. 'A twist of thread' (or a strip of cloth) 'of which one end is dipped in the liquor to be defecated, and the other hangs below the bottom of the vessel, so that the liquor drips from it' (J.). *Obs.* exc. in ***capillary filter***.

1559 MORWYNG *Euonym.* 75 Distillacion by a filter, or a list of wollen cloth. **1660** BOYLE *New Exp. Phys. Mech.* xxxv. 263 We resolved, instead of a List of Cotton, or the like Filtre, to make use of a Siphon of Glass. **1727–41** in CHAMBERS *Cycl.* **1874** KNIGHT *Dict. Mech.* I. 455/2 *Capillary-filter*, a simple mode of freeing water of its larger impurities by means of a cord of loose fiber.

c. In wider sense: Any contrivance for freeing liquids from suspended impurities; *esp.* an apparatus consisting of a vessel in which the liquid is made to pass through a stratum of sand, charcoal, or some porous substance.

1791 J. PEACOCK *Patent* No. 1844 The filters will be cleansed by drawing out the head or body of water or fluid. **1834** S. BAGSHAW *Patent* No. 6708 An improved filter for water or other liquids. **1872** BAKER *Nile Tribut.* xx. 339 Nevertheless the natives had scraped small holes in the sand, as filters. **1879** A. B. MACDOWALL in *Encycl. Brit.* (ed. 9) IX. 167/2 The filter was occasionally cleaned with an exhausting and condensing pump.

d. *transf.* and *fig.*

1605 TIMME *Quersit.* I. v. 20 The common salt..passing thro' the philter of the earth. **1802** PALEY *Nat. Theol.* xii.

(1803) 241 This natural filter [the bills of a duck]. **1840** ALISON *Hist. Europe* (1850) VIII. l. §39. 159 The whole information..was strained through the imperial filters. **1873** TRISTRAM *Moab* xii. 228 A heavy conversation of ponderous compliments passed through the dragoman filter.

3. a. A contrivance for arresting dust, smoke, disease-germs, etc. in the air which is breathed.

1874 KNIGHT *Dict. Mech.* s.vv. *Filter, Air-filter.*

b. *Photogr.* A screen to cut out rays which interfere with correct colour-rendering; = *colour-filter* (see COLOUR *sb.*[1] 18).

1900, 1902 [see COLOUR *sb.*[1] 18]. **1912** E. J. WALL *Dict. Photogr.* (ed. 9) 335 Most makers of orthochromatic..plates also supply filters specially adapted for use with their plates. **1948** [see COLOUR *sb.*[1] 18]. **1958** M. L. HALL *Newnes' Compl. Amat. Photogr.* viii. 97 Light filters are transparent, coloured discs which are attached to the camera lens for the purpose of modifying the colour quality of the light transmitted but which do not otherwise affect the image formed by the lens.

c. In a cigarette: a pad of absorbent material fitted at the unlit end to purify the smoke. Also, a cigarette so fitted.

1908 *Lancet* 21 Mar. 907/2 A pad of cotton wool is inserted into the paper casing of these cigarettes, which effectually prevents dust and shreds of tobacco entering the mouth, besides which a large proportion of the objectionable oils formed during smoking is arrested in the wool filter. **1958** *Amer. Speech* XXXIII. 147 A new cellulose fiber for.. cigarette filters. **1963** N. FREELING *Gun before Butter* II. 96 Yes, I do smoke but only filters.

d. *Radiol.* and *Nuclear Sci.* A sheet or block of material inserted in the path of a beam of X-radiation or elementary particles in order to reduce the intensity of radiation of certain wavelengths or energies.

1917 ARTHUR & MUIR *Man. Pract. X-Ray Work* (ed. 2) x. 313 For skin treatment it is well to use a weak filter—such as thick paper—which will absorb the softest rays which.. might otherwise produce dangerous over-effects. **1957** *Encycl. Brit.* XVIII. 898/1 In some of the work for which X-rays are used, the quality or penetrating ability of the radiation is expressed..in terms of its absorbability in filters of standard composition and thickness. **1969** G. E. BACON *Neutron Physics* x. 127 We can..use a sufficiently thick block of graphite as a filter which..removes all neutrons with a wavelength greater than 0·67 nm.

e. *Electronics.* A passive circuit that attenuates all signals except those within one or more frequency bands.

1920 *Radio Rev.* July 505 By a combination of the two types of filter only currents between the two frequency limits are transmitted. **1922**, etc. [see BAND *sb.*[2] 14]. **1938** F. E. TERMAN *Fund. Radio* x. 267 The pulsating voltage delivered by the rectifier output can be smoothed into a steady direct-current voltage..by being passed through an electrical network called a filter, which ordinarily consists of series inductances and shunt condensers. **1955** G. M. GLASFORD *Fund. Telev. Engin.* xvii. 581 There must be employed in the video section a 4·5-Mc rejection filter to remove the audio carrier and its sidebands from the video signal. **1959** *Engineering* 30 Jan. 153/3 A conventional voltage doubler serves as the high voltage rectifier, with sufficient capacitance employed in the filter to reduce the r.m.s. ripple to 0.5 per cent.

4. A material for filtering. *rare.*

1823 J. BADCOCK *Dom. Amusem.* 26 The burning it over and over again..produces a better filtre than at first. **1870** TYNDALL in *Nature* 27 Jan. 341 This [cotton-wool] was the filter used by Schrœder in his experiments on spontaneous generation.

5. *attrib.* and *Comb.*, as ***filter-shop***; also **filter aid**, any substance added to a liquid or to a filtering medium in order to improve filtration by preventing the formation of an impervious filter cake; **filter-arrow**, a device forming part of a traffic signal (cf. FILTER *v.* 3 b); **filter-bed**, a pond or tank with a false bottom covered with sand or gravel, serving as a large filter; also *fig.*; **filter cake**, the insoluble residue deposited on a filter; so ***filter-caked*** adj.; **filter circuit** *Electronics* = 3 e above; **filter condenser** *Electronics*, a capacitor forming one of the chief elements in a filter circuit; **filter factor**: see FACTOR *sb.* 7 c; **filter-faucet** (see quot.); **filter-feeder**, an animal that obtains its nourishment by means of filter-feeding; **filter-feeding** *vbl. sb.*, the filtering and ingestion of nutrient matter suspended in water; also as *adj.*; **filter-paper**, porous paper to be used for filtering; **filter-passer**, a filter-passing 'organism', esp. a virus; **filter-passing** *a.*, not retained by a filter, esp. by one that does retain bacteria; **filter-press**, (*a*) a filter in which the liquid is forced through by pressure; (*b*) a machine for extracting oil from fish; **filter reactor** *Electronics*, a reactor forming one of the chief elements in a filter circuit; **filter shot** *Photogr.*, a photograph taken through a colour-filter; **filter tip** = 3 c above; hence **filter-tipped** *a.*, **filter-tipping** *vbl. sb.*

1946 DICKEY & BRYDEN *Theory & Pract. Filtration* iii. 47 A precoat and/or a *filter aid are often necessary, to prevent the deposited particles from being carried..into the interstices of the filter medium, or filter cake. **1951** KIRK & OTHMER *Encycl. Chem. Technol.* VI. 510 Materials such as kieselguhr or diatomite, asbestos fibres,..and sawdust flour are examples of materials used as filter aids. **1963** *Times* 24 May p. xiv/1 (Advt.), Filteraids and chemicals to purify most pipe-borne liquids. **1965** PRIESTLEY & WISDOM *Good Driving* xi. 77 A *filter-arrow allowing left-turning vehicles to proceed. **1874** KNIGHT *Dict. Mech.* I. 846/2 **Filter-bed*, a settling pond whose bottom is a filter. **1885** *Weekly Notes* 7 Feb. 24/2 The water..was filtered through filter-beds on their premises. **1892** *Pall Mall G.* 25 May 2/1 All that is known here of the Transvaal..comes through the political filter-beds of Cape Town. **1912** *Mining & Engin. World* 20 Apr. 863/3 In forming a *filter cake with any material there is a certain point where the rate of filtration begins to drop off very rapidly due to the resistance offered by the cake. **1967** *Filtration & Separation* IV. 471 Most filter cakes show some degree of compressibility. **1956** K. IMHOFF et al. *Disposal of Sewage* xii. 202 The *filter-caked sludge may be dried finally by heat and sold as fertilizer. **1920** *Radio Rev.* July 505 A number of special *filter circuits designed with the object of allowing certain frequencies to pass and cutting out others. **1962** A. NISBETT *Technique Sound Studio* iv. 82 Correction of a whole range of faults, such as noise, distortion, and unsatisfactory frequency response, is often attempted by means of filter circuits. **1922** A. F. COLLINS *Book of Wireless Telegraph & Telephone* III. iv. 197 Connect the filter reactor and the *filter condensers to the mid-taps of the filament secondaries. **1951** S. DEUTSCH *Theory & Design Telev. Receivers* xii. 406 The size of the various filter condensers is determined by consideration of tolerable ripple. **1921** *Filter factor [see FACTOR *sb.* 7 c]. **1958** M. L. HALL *Newnes' Compl. Amat. Photogr.* vii. 98 Filters reduce the light transmitted to form the image and require a compensating exposure increase; with certain very pale filters..this filter factor is..small enough to be ignored... The increase is specified as a multiplying factor. **1874** KNIGHT *Dict. Mech.* I. 846/2 **Filter-faucet*, one having a chamber containing sand, sponge, or other material to arrest impurities. **1928** *Trans. R. Soc. Edin.* LV. I. 235 Besides being a *filter feeder, Hemimysis also feeds from large solid masses of food. **1959** A. HARDY *Fish & Fisheries* v. 109 The most elaborately developed suspension-feeders are the bivalve (lamellibranch) molluscs. They are filter-feeders. Their gills have been enormously enlarged..as sieving devices to collect the fine particles of food from the water which is propelled through them by cilia. **1931** *Trans. R. Soc. Edin.* LVI. III. 537 A study of the feeding mechanisms and physiology of digestion in Polychaetes has..been begun, choosing a *filter-feeding form as a starting point. **1963** R. P. DALES *Annelids* 11 With loss of motility we find more selective methods of feeding, this evolution culminating in the filter-feeding fan or feather-duster worms. **1849** D. CAMPBELL *Inorg. Chem.* 18 A few grains of recently-heated spongy platinum, in a small piece of *filter paper. **1892** *Photogr. Ann.* II. 109 Dried on pure filter paper. **1913** J. MCFADYEAN in *XVIIth Internat. Congress Med.* IV. I. 50 The term '*filter passers' has been adopted.. as the preferable name for the micro-organisms which.. were..called the ultra-visible or invisible viruses. **1919** *Nature* 6 Nov. 210/2 The infective agents of the common exanthemata..are at some period of their life-history so small as to be included amongst the 'filter-passers'. **1946** *Nature* 21 Sept. 398/1 Bacteria, filter-passers, viruses, protozoan and metazoan parasites or fungi. **1915** *Lancet* 4 Dec. 1241/2 Attempts were made to demonstrate the presence of non-pathogenic *filter-passing viruses. **1930** *Morning Post* 24 Nov. 3 'Ultra-microscopic' or 'filter passing' virus. **1947** AUDEN *Age of Anxiety* (1948) v. 107 No filter-passing Virus invade. **1957** G. E. HUTCHINSON *Treat. Limnol.* I. vi. 385 They give the percentage effect of suspended or retained and dissolved or filter-passing material on the absorption. **1889** *Pall Mall G.* 2 May 7/1 The sludge is next forced into a *filter press. **1922** A. F. COLLINS *Book of Wireless Telegraph & Telephone* III. iv. 194 The purpose of a *filter reactor is to smooth out the pulsating direct current after it is produced by the rectifier tube. **1842** DICKENS *Amer. Notes* II. iv. 112, I have seen water like it at the *Filter shops. **1951** J. B. PRIESTLEY *Festival at Farbridge* I. iii. 126 We got some lovely *filter and scrim shots. **1932** *Daily Mail* 12 Oct. 8/4 (Advt.), The *Filter Tip that holds throat irritants in check. **1953** *Wall St. Jrnl.* 1 Oct. 1/4 The work on a filter-tip cigaret began early in 1951. The company was seeking a non-mineral material to filter the smoke and finally decided upon a highly purified alpha cellulose tip. **1957** *New Yorker* 23 Nov. 100/2 When I ran out of American filter-tips, I chose the nearest equivalent I could find—a Bulgarian make. **1957** *Times* 28 Dec. 4/2 A substantial increase in the sales of filter-tip cigarettes was a common feature of tobacco sales in Britain and the United States in 1957. **1954** *Newsweek* 16 Aug. 72/3 The American Tobacco Co...brought out a *filter-tipped version of Herbert Tareyton, its king-size and cork-tipped brand. **1954** *Wall St. Jrnl.* 18 Nov. 10/2 American Machine Foundry Co. has developed a new method of applying filter tips to cigarets which it claims 'renders obsolete all other *filter tipping devices currently used in the tobacco industry'.

filter ('fɪltə(r)), *v.* Forms: 7 fylter, 7–9 filtre, 6– filter. Also 6 philter. [ad. mod.L. *filtrāre*, f. *filtrum* FILTER *sb.* Cf. F. *filtrer.*]

1. a. *trans.* To pass (a liquid) through a filter, or some porous medium, for the purpose of removing solid particles or impurities. Also with *off.* Also *absol.*

1576 G. BAKER *Jewell of Health* I. i. 2 The dropping caused by a Lyste, or piece of Woollen cloth..which maner of dooing the Chymistes name Fyltring. **1594** PLAT *Jewell-ho., Chim. Concl.* 23 Some use to filter this Lee divers times. **1605** TIMME *Quersit.* I. ix. 36 They dissolue many times, they fylter, and coagulate. **1671** GREW *Anat. Plants* I. i. §31 The Sap..not being filtred through so fine a Cotton. **1747** WESLEY *Prim. Physic* (1762) 86 Filtre the Tincture thro' Paper. **1784** COWPER *Task* II. 507 Sages strove In vain to filter off a crystal draught Pure from the lees. **1812–6** J. SMITH *Panorama Sc. & Art* II. 355 Putrid and stinking water may be rendered sweet by filtering it through charcoal-powder. **1838** T. THOMSON *Chem. Org. Bodies* 200 We then filter, washing the blue-coloured sulphate of lime remaining on the filter till it becomes red. **1853** SOYER *Pantroph.* 27 The liquid was several times filtered.

b. *transf.* and *fig.*

1830 GEN. P. THOMPSON *Exerc.* (1842) I. 291 The Chamber of Deputies, though filtered through every process which policy could invent. **1856** EMERSON *Eng. Traits, First Visit* Wks. (Bohn) II. 5 The passage would no doubt strike you more in the quotation than in the original, for I have filtered it. **1885** *Manch. Exam.* 10 Jan. 5/3 At present his instructions to counsel are filtered through a solicitor. **1892** *Pall Mall G.* 4 May 1/3 Each of these images is 'filtered' through a colour screen.

c. Said of the filtering material.

1854 WOODWARD *Mollusca* (1856) 37 The sea-weed filters the salt-water. **1882** WATTS *Dict. Chem.* II. 648 Paper which filters slowly may be improved in quality by this treatment.

d. *Electronics.* To pass (an electrical signal, etc.) through a filter (FILTER *sb.* 3 e) as a means of removing or attenuating components of undesired frequencies or undue prominence. Also with *out*: to select or remove (a component of a signal) by means of a filter.

1921 B. LEGGETT *Wireless Telegr.* xiii. 399 Zenneck has proposed..to filter out and utilise this harmonic by means of a tuned circuit. **1937** W. G. DOW *Fund. Engin. Electronics* xxi. 487 The greater the number of anodes, the smaller is the ripple to be filtered out. **1959** ZIMMERMANN & MASON *Electronic Circuit Theory* iv. 130 The effects of a poorly filtered power supply on an audio system can be heard directly in the form of an objectionable hum.

2. To cause (a liquid) to pass drop by drop, or slowly, through a porous medium (now only in *passive*); also, †to give forth through the pores, exude. *rare.*

1583 STANYHURST *Æneis* III. (Arb.) 71 The tre..of swart blud filtred abundance. **1644** DIGBY *Two Treat.* I. xx. 183 That streame [of atoms]..clymbing and filtring it selfe along the stones streame. **1860** MAURY *Phys. Geog. Sea* x. §466 Rivers..some of which are filtered through soils.. which yield one kind of salts.

3. a. *intr.* To pass as through a filter; to percolate; also with *away*, *down*.

Cf. F. *filtrer*, used *refl.* and *intr.* in this sense.

1798 W. BLAIR *Soldier's Friend* 100 The water..will filter through the sand. **1864** MARSH *Man & Nature* 438 A stratum of snow..causes almost all the water that composes it to filter down into the earth. **1882** VINES *Sachs' Bot.* 687 Water will filter through the cell-walls into the cavities of the wood.

transf. and *fig.* **1821** CLARE *Vill. Minstr.* I. 207 The sunbeams, filtering small, Freckling through the branches fall. **1868** YATES *Rock Ahead* II. iii, A perpetual stream of.. people..would filter..through her..drawing-rooms. **1944** *Times* 29 Apr. 3/3 Here the enemy succeeded in temporarily filtering through our lines. **1958** HAYWARD & HARARI tr. *Pasternak's Dr. Zhivago* II. viii. 231 Although the station area was cordoned off..passengers for the local trains had managed, in some unaccountable way, to 'filter through' (as we would say now). **1969** *Listener* 27 Feb. 281/2 Meanwhile foreign literature (Ibsen and Chekhov notably) and painting (the Post-Impressionist Exhibition) were slowly filtering in. **1971** *Daily Tel.* 16 June 11/5 Hints..of an upsurge in Government spending on new by-passes..have filtered out with unusually effective timing.

b. *spec.* Of road vehicles: to join another line of traffic at a road junction, usu. by deviating from the main stream which is held up by traffic lights.

1928 *Traffic Signals to be used by Police & Drivers of Vehicles* (*H.M.S.O.*) ii. 10 At road junctions, when one stream of traffic has been halted, constables should, so far as may be safe or practicable, permit drivers who wish to do so to turn to the left and so filter into the cross stream of moving traffic. **1937** V. WOOLF *Years* 334 He filtered slowly round the corner. **1971** *A.A. Continental Handbk.* 396 Some crossroads have traffic lights with a flashing yellow arrow which allows drivers to filter off in the direction of the arrow.

4. a. To obtain by filtering. Also *transf. rare.*

1794 PEARSON in *Phil. Trans.* LXXXIV. 387 The liquid filtered from these solutions had a sweetish and bitterish taste. **1845** DARWIN *Voy. Nat.* i. (1879) 5 Fine dust, which appeared to have been filtered from the wind by the gauze of the vane at the mast-head.

b. *to filter out* (trans.): to separate or prevent the passage of by, or as by, filtering.

1908 [see SCRATCH *sb.* 6 b]. **1917** G. W. C. KAYE *X Rays* (ed. 2) ix. 116 By filtering out the soft rays from the primary beam by the use of a suitable screen, the polarisation can be doubled. **1921, 1937** [see 1 d above]. **1927** DAVIS & KAYE *Acoustics of Buildings* i. 7 In suitable circumstances it is possible to filter out undesired harmonics. **1936** *Discovery* July 224/1 These [stops] change the tone-colour..the original note produced being deliberately made very rich in overtones, which in turn are filtered out as required. **1951** KIRK & OTHMER *Encycl. Chem. Technol.* VI. 516 The sand acts as the filter medium and filters out suspended solids. **1961** G. MILLERSON *Technique Telev. Prod.* iii. 43 Sound reproduction begins to lose crispness as higher audio notes are filtered out. **1965** N. CHOMSKY *Aspects of Theory of Syntax* 224 An extraneous factor..filters out certain latent intepretations provided by the deep structures. **1967** M. FRAYN *Towards End of Morning* viii. 151 He seemed unaware of the noise Damian was making. Bob's head ached ..at the effort of filtering the adult conversation out from it. **1971** *Daily Tel.* 4 Mar. 3/3 Continued flights..could reduce the ozone layer that filters out cancer-producing ultra-violet rays.

Hence **'filtered, 'filtering** *ppl. adjs.* Also **'filterer**, that which filters or serves as a filter.

1727 BAILEY vol. II, *Filtered*, strained through a Paper, Cloth, etc. **1794** SCHMEISSER in *Phil. Trans.* LXXXIV. 421 The remaining filtered liquor was saturated with purified pot-ash. **1809** J. F. ARCHBOLD *Patent* No. 3225 It [sea water] is passed through a filterer. **1821** CLARE *Vill. Minstr.* II. 162, I love to watch thy [an hour-glass's] filtering burthen pass. **1830** TENNYSON *Ode to Memory* iv, The filtered tribute of the rough woodland. **1853** SOYER *Pantroph.* 412 Eight barrels of filtered water. **1859** CORNWALLIS *New World* I. 38 The stretcher might have been directly under this water filterer.

filter, var. form of FELTER *v.*, PHILTRE.

filterability (ˌfɪltərəˈbɪlɪtɪ). Also **filtrability**. [f. next: see -ITY.] The quality or state of being filterable.

1910 *Jrnl. Exper. Med.* XII. 242 The filterability of the virus. **1928** T. M. RIVERS *Filterable Viruses* i. 10 Others, however, do not seem to be so small and concerning the filterability of these there is much discussion. **1952** *Genetics* XXXVII. 724 The infective transmission of F^+ at once calls to mind the latent bacterial viruses... However, the filtrability of bacteriophage at once differentiates it from the F^+ agent.

filterable (ˈfɪltərəb(ə)l), *a.* Also **filtrable**. [f. FILTER *v.* + -ABLE.] Able to pass through the pores of a filter, esp. one that retains bacteria; ***filterable virus*** (see VIRUS).

1908 M. H. HAYES tr. *Friedberger & Fröhner's Vet. Path.* (ed. 6) II. 425 The causative agents in fowl-pox belong to the group of so-called filtrable agents of infection. **1912** *Jrnl. Med. Res.* XXVII. 1 The diseases caused by filterable viruses include many of the most important of man and animals. *Ibid.* 3 There is also another protozoan which has a filterable stage. **1922** *Glasgow Herald* 21 Feb. 10 A number of animal diseases besides foot-and-mouth disease are caused by filterable viruses. **1928** *Daily Tel.* 10 July 9/4 Dr. Gye's theory of the causation of cancer by a filtrable virus. **1928** T. M. RIVERS *Filterable Viruses* i. 3 To designate the active agents discussed in the book the term 'filterable viruses' was chosen from a long list of unsatisfactory names. For many reasons the term 'viruses' is preferable to 'filterable viruses'. **1952** G. H. BOURNE *Cytol. & Cell Physiol.* (ed. 2) ix. 402 A filterable tumour, on crushing to a pulp and mixing with saline, yields by Berkefeld-filtration a cell-free filtrate. **1955** *Sci. Amer.* Mar. 65/1 They [*sc.* viruses] were first distinguished from bacteria by the fact that they were filtrable, whereas the pores of the ordinary porcelain filter blocked the passage of bacteria. **1965** T. M. BELL *Introd. Gen. Virol.* i. 2 Today The Viruses are exclusively the 'filterable viruses' and are considered apart from The Microbes.

filtering (ˈfɪltərɪŋ), *vbl. sb.* [f. FILTER *v.* + -ING¹.]

1. The action of the verb FILTER.

1830 M. DONOVAN *Dom. Econ.* I. 191 The filtering of this rain through the ground. **1845** J. WILKINSON *Patent* No. 10,984 The whole process of filtering is effected by pressure. *fig.* **1876** GEO. ELIOT *Dan. Der.* III. xlii. 235 There's been a good filtering of our blood into high families.

2. *attrib.* and *Comb.*, as ***filtering-apparatus, -bag, -box, -funnel, -material, -medium, -paper, -stand, -vessel***; also **filtering-basin** (see quot. 1874); **filtering-cup**, a cup of porous wood used to illustrate the pressure of the atmosphere; **filtering-press** = *filter-press*; **filtering-stone**, any porous stone through which water is filtered; **filtering-tank** = *filtering-basin* (Knight).

1845 J. WILKINSON *Patent* No. 10,984 Which [a cistern] must be considerably above the level of the *filtering apparatus. **1874** KNIGHT *Dict. Mech.* I. 846/2 **Filtering-basin*, the chamber in which the water from the reservoir of waterworks is received and filtered previous to entering the mains. **1792** G. COWEN *Patent* No. 1920 A quantity of sand, or any other *filtering material. **1791** J. PEACOCK *Patent* No. 1844 The ascent of the fluid through the *filtering medium. **1757** LEWIS in *Phil. Trans.* L. 163 The colourless sorts of *filtering-paper are preferable for this use to the coloured. **1876** HARLEY *Mat. Med.* 311 Filtering Paper is an almost pure form of cellulin. **1874** KNIGHT *Dict. Mech.* I. 846/2 **Filtering-press*, a press in which the passage of a liquid through a body of filtering material is expedited by pressure applied thereto; a pressure-filter. **1827** FARADAY *Chem. Manip.* i. 17 The *filtering stands are of this kind. **1812** J. SMYTH *Pract. Customs* (1821) 234 *Filtering Stones,—Duty —for every £100 value. **1811** J. ASHLEY *Patent* No. 3472 An improved *filtering vessel for purifying.. water.

filth (fɪlθ), *sb.* Forms: 1 **fýlþ**, 2–4 **felðe**, 4 *south.* **veolthe**, 5 **felthe**, 3–4 **fulðe**, 3–6 **fylth(e**, (3 **fuylþe**, 6 **faylt, fylt**), 3–5 **filthe**, 3– **filth**. [OE. *fýlð* str. fem. = OS. *fûlitha* (Du. *vuilte*), OHG. *fûlida*:—OTeut. **fûliþâ*, n. of quality f. **fûlo-* FOUL *a.*]

†**1.** The quality or state of being foul; a filthy state or condition; filthiness; in *pl.* foul treatment, indignities. *Obs.*

c **1300** *K. Alis.* 6370 Veolthe loveth al heore lynage. **1481** CAXTON *Godfrey* 304 What fylthes the turkes made them to suffre. **1579** LYLY *Euphues* (Arb.) 38 The Lacedemonians were wont to shewe their children dronken men.. that by seing their filth, they might shunne the lyke fault.

2. *concr.* Foul matter.

†**a.** Putrid matter, corruption, rottenness; in later use, purulent matter, pus. *Obs.*

c **1000** *Ags. Gosp.* Matt. xxiii. 27 Ant hiȝ synt innan fulle deadra bana, and ealre fylðe [**1160** *Hatton* felðe]. *a* **1050** *Liber Scintill.* viii. (1889) 38 þænne fylð [*putredo*] seo þe innan wealð byþ utaworpen to hæle sar byð ȝeopenud. *c* **1430** *Life St. Kath.* (1884) 49 þe temporal kyng.. whiche ys now proude in hys power and to-morwe schal be fylthe and wormes. **1526** *Pilgr. Perf.* (W. de W. 1531) 240 b, He scraped yᵉ stynkyng fylth & corrupcyon of her deed body. **1561** HOLLYBUSH *Hom. Apoth.* 11 To draw the fylt out of the head. **1696** PECHY tr. *Sydenham's Wks.* III. ii. 116 The Inflammation which the Small-Pox has impressed upon the Blood.. no less indicates Blood-letting than the filth [L. *colluvies*] which has been gathered together does Purging.

b. Uncleanly matter, dirt. Now only in stronger sense, expressing violent disgust: Loathsome dirt. Rarely in *pl.* filth of various kinds, filthy matters.

c **1290** *S. Eng. Leg.* I. 191/52 þare feol out of eiþer eiȝe Fuylþe ase þei it were slym. *a* **1300** *Cursor M.* 22397 (Cott.) All þe filthes of his maugh sal brist vte. *c* **1340** *Ibid.* 468 (Trin.) In þat court þat is so clene No fulþe may dwelle ne be sene. *c* **1430** LYDG. in Turner *Dom. Archit.* III. 39 Voydynge fylthes lowe into the grounde. *c* **1440** *Promp. Parv.* 161/1 Fylthe of mannys nose, snotte, *polipus*. **1555** *Nottingham Rec.* IV. 109 He.. swffares mwke and fylthe to be powered yn yᵉ hy strett. **1626** BACON *Sylva* §397 Waters .. found in Rising Grounds of great Cities.. must needs take in a great deale of Filth. **1721** STRYPE *Eccl. Mem.* III. xxii. 180 The Chamber.. on one side of which was the Sink and Filth of all the House. **1836** EMERSON *Nat., Prospects* Wks. (Bohn) II. 173 The sordor and filths of nature, the sun shall dry up. **1873** OUIDA *Pascarel* I. 30 A palace with superb staircases reeking in filth.

c. Vermin (†formerly *pl.*). In mod. use (? *dial.*) restricted to insect parasites.

c **1400** MAUNDEV. (1839) v. 61 In that Abbeye ne entrethe not no Flye ne Todes ne Ewtes.. For there were wont to ben many suche manere of Filthes. *Mod.* (Yorks.) A dirty brute, with his head swarming with filth. The currant bushes are covered with filth.

3. *fig.* **a.** Moral defilement, vileness; corruption, pollution; obscenity.

a **1023** WULFSTAN *Hom.* (Napier) xxxiii. 161 *note*, To maneȝe.. ane cwenan ȝemænum ceape bicȝað.. and wið þa ane fylþe adreoȝaþ an æfter anum. *a* **1225** *Ancr. R.* 84 þe bacbitare.. openeð so þet fulðe þ hit stinkeð wide. *a* **1300** *Vox & Wolf* 165 in Hazl. *E.P.P.* I. 63 And liuie in fulthe and in sunne. *c* **1380** WYCLIF *Wks.* (1880) 299 þei ben blaunchid wiþ-oute as sepulcris, and wiþ-inne ful of fylþe. *a* **1450** *Knt. de la Tour* (1868) 77 The prince.. suffered suche felthe to be done. **1638** *Penit. Conf.* viii. (1657) 209 The filth of sin is purged by the Laver of tears. *a* **1704** T. BROWN *Sat. agst. Woman* Wks. 1730 I. 56 Wallowing in all the filth of boundless luxury. **1813** SHELLEY *Q. Mab* v. 159 Every slave now dragging through the filth Of some corrupted city his sad life. **1860** HOOK *Lives Abps.* I. v. 226 Forbidding.. all the filth of the wicked.

†**b.** *pl.* Moral impurities, corrupt or impure actions, transgressions. *Obs.*

c **1200** *Vices & Virtues* (1888) 131 Holi maiden of þanke, and clane of alle felðes. *a* **1225** *St. Marher.* (1862) 3 Biwite thou mi bodi the is al bitahte from fleshliche fulthen. *c* **1340** *Cursor M.* 10105 (Trin.) To make me falle in fulþes fele. *c* **1440** *York Myst.* xx. 180 All filthes of flesshely synne. **1583** *Satir. Poems Reform.* xlv. Pref. 60 Compared to swyne returning to the myre, In thair awin filthes to get thair fames defyled.

c. Foul or obscene language; vile or loathsome imputations.

1730 SWIFT *Traulus* I. 25 Among the rout He wildly flings his filth about. **1879** FROUDE *Cæsar* xv. 237 Instead of scolding and flinging impotent filth.

4. a. Said of a person: A vile creature; a scoundrel; a slut, drab, whore. *Obs.* exc. *dial.*

c **1350** *Will. Palerne* 2542 Lest þat foule felþe schuld have hem founde þere. **1402** HOCCLEVE *Letter of Cupid* 262 These ladyes.. were noon of thoo.. but swyche filthes as weren vertulesse. **1565** HARDING in Jewel *Def. Apol.* (1611) 27 Ioan of Kent, that filth.. was she a sister of yours? **1607** SHAKS. *Timon* IV. i. 6. **1608** —— *Lear* (Qo. 1) IV. ii. 39 Filths sauor but themselues. **1612** R. SHELDON *Serm. St. Martin's* 65 Their filthes lie by their sides to satisfie their abhominable pleasures. **1790** MRS. WHEELER *Westmld. Dial.* (1821) 13 Nea yan can bide wie him, an arrant filth! **1869** *Lonsdale Gloss., Filth*, a disreputable woman, a scoundrel. **1871** R. ELLIS *Catullus* xlii. 13 O ugly filth, detested Trull.

b. *collect.* The police. *Criminals' slang.*

1967 *Times* 23 Nov. 8/3 'It's the filth,' cried one of the robbers. **1970** G. F. NEWMAN *Sir, you Bastard* 271 Hurting the filth wasn't easy, not when they were DI's. **1979** J. WAINWRIGHT *Duty Elsewhere* xxxix. 102 He's a big wheel in the filth, Mr Nolan. Y' know.. assistant chief constable and all that. **1982** *Observer* 15 Aug. 22/5 A 'face', or well-known and celebrated criminal, has done a trade with the 'filth', or police, to get off a serious crime.

5. *attrib.* and *Comb.*, as ***filth-disease, -ferment***; ***filth-created, -fed, -sodden*** adjs.

1852 DR. GUY in Ld. Ingestre *Meliora* I. 96 *Filth-created fever and disease. **1885** *Science* VI. 101/1 Typhoid-fever and other preventable *filth-diseases. **1891** *Daily News* 5 Oct. 5/5 How.. is the *filth-fed oyster to be distinguished? **1891** C. CREIGHTON *Hist. Epidemics* 589 Spots of soil.. so situated in cups of the hills as to retain and multiply the *filth-ferment. **1871** NAPHEYS *Prev. & Cure Dis.* I. viii. 264 A *filth-sodden porous earth.

Hence **ˈfilthless** *a.* [-LESS], without filth; undefiled. **ˈfilthous** *a.* [-OUS] = FILTHY.

14.. *Balade in Commend. our Lady* 51 (Chaucer's Wks. 1561) Fountain al filthlesse, as birell current clere. **1546** BALE *Eng. Votaries* II. (1550) 9 b, And so sent hym forth abrode.. to maynteyne all kyndes of ydolatry and fleshly fylthouse lyvynge.

filth, *v.* Now *poet.* [f. prec. sb.] *trans.* To make foul, defile.

c **1450** LONELICH *Grail* xliii. 21 Alle blak becomen they.. and i-fylthed. **1598** E. GILPIN *Skial.* (1878) 31 Filthing chaste eares with theyr pens Gonorrhey. **1955** W. DE LA MARE *Beginning* 211 You merely filthed and made vile the most sacred misfortune.

†**ˈfilthery**. *Obs. rare*⁻¹. [f. as prec. + -ERY.] = FILTHINESS.

a **1656** USSHER *Ann.* (1658) 370 Wallowing in all filthery of gluttony and luxury.

†**ˈfilthhead, -hood**. *Obs.* Forms: α. 3 **fulþhede**, 4–5 **filth-, filt-, fylthede, -heed**, (5 **filthet**). β. 6 **filthood**. [f. FILTH *sb.* + -HEAD, -HOOD.] Filthiness, uncleanness. *lit.* and *fig.* Also *concr.* filth. ***to do one's filthhood***: to void excrement.

1297 R. GLOUC. (1724) 290 þe chyld.. dude hys kunde fulþ-hede. **1382** WYCLIF *Lev.* xviii. 7 The filth-heed [Vulg. *turpitudinem*] of thi fader, and the filth-heed of thi moder thow shalt not discover. Ibid. *Rom.* i. 27 Mawlis in to mawlis worchinge filthhede. *c* **1440** tr. *Girald. Hist. Irel.* (E.E.T.S.) 31 The fylthede of the lond folk yn whych thay ladde har lyf. **1583** STANYHURST *Æneis* II. (Arb.) 52 With dust al powdred, with filthood dustye bedagled.

filthify (ˈfɪlθɪfaɪ), *v.* [f. FILTHY *a.* + -FY.] *trans.* To make filthy; *lit.* and *fig.*

1790 J. WILLIAMS *Shrove Tuesday* (1794) 13 Filthified they flounder to Remorse. **1821** BENTHAM *Wks.* (1843) X. 524 He was.. covering my clean napkin with his 'flag of abomination' filthified. **1828** WHEWELL in Todhunter *Account of Writings*, etc. (1876) II. 94 Mathematics with which Mr. Thompson has filthified his subject.

filthily (ˈfɪlθɪlɪ), *adv.* [f. FILTHY *a.* + -LY².] In a filthy manner.

1552 HULOET, Filthilye, *fœde*. **1596** DALRYMPLE tr. *Leslie's Hist. Scot.* II. (1887) 144 In the ix ȝeir of his regne, quhilke sa filthilie he had ruled. **1633** PRYNNE *Histrio-Mastix* I. VI. iii. 366 For the liberty of doing filthily and obscenely, is next to the liberty of speaking filthily and obscenely. **1709** STEELE *Tatler* No. 31 ¶1 The ancient Romans would scold, and call Names filthily. **1812** BYRON *Ch. Har.* I. xvii, For hut and palace show like filthily.

filthiness (ˈfɪlθɪnɪs). [f. as prec. + -NESS.] The condition of being filthy.

1. In physical sense: Foulness, uncleanliness.

? *a* **1500** *Wycket* (1828) 15 The puttynge awaye of fylthenes of the fleshe. **1558** BP. WATSON *Sev. Sacram.* xiii. 78 The prieste washeth his handes, that no outward filthynes should seclude hym from the communion. **1611** BIBLE *2 Macc.* ix. 9 The filthinesse of his smell was noysome to all his army.

†**b.** *concr.* Filth; *spec.* matter, pus. *Obs.*

1531 TINDALE *Exp. 1 John* (1537) 8 Yᵉ water once in the yeare casteth al fylthynesse unto the sydes of it. **1580** BARET *Alv.* F 511 The matter, or filthinesse that commeth out of a bile. **1611** BIBLE *Isa.* xxviii. 8 All tables are full of vomite and filthinesse. **1649** DRYDEN *Upon Death of Ld. Hastings* 54 Was there no milder way but the Small Pox, The very Filth'ness of Pandora's Box?

2. Moral corruption or pollution; obscenity; vileness, wickedness.

1526 *Pilgr. Perf.* (W. de W. 1531) 185 b, Than the deformite & fylthynes of synne is taken away. **1684** *Contempl. State of Man* II. x. (1699) 246 This deformity and filthiness of sin. **1741** RICHARDSON *Pamela* I. 138 A Woman that seems to delight in Filthiness. **1834** LYTTON *Pompeii* I. vi, Men reeking with all the filthiness of vice.

†**ˈfilthish**, *a.* *Obs.*⁻⁰ [f. FILTH *sb.* + -ISH.] Filthy.

1530 PALSGR. 312/2 Fylthysshe as ones eyes be that haue whyte slyme in them, *chassieux*. *Ibid.*, Fylthysshe as mysse women of yll lyuyng, *putairie*.

filthy (ˈfɪlθɪ), *a.* [f. FILTH *sb.* + -Y¹.]

1. a. Full of filth; besmeared or defiled with filth; dirty, foul, nasty, unclean. †***the filthy parts***: the private parts.

In early use often hardly more emphatic than the mod. *dirty*; it is now a violent expression of disgust, seldom employed in polite colloquial speech. Cf. the similar development in FILTH *sb.* 2 b; also in FOUL *a.*

1382 WYCLIF *Zech.* iii. 3 Jhesus was clothid with filthi clothis. **1398** TREVISA *Barth. De P.R.* XVIII. xcv. (1495) 842 A serpent.. louyth fylthi places. **1553** EDEN *Treat. Newe Ind.* (Arb.) 17 The inhabitantes.. haue almost no apparel, couering onely theyr fylthy partes. **1581** MULCASTER *Positions* xxxv. (1887) 132 To go home thorough stinking streates, and filthy lanes. **1682** OTWAY *Epil. 21 Apr.*, From the filthy dunghill-faction bred, New-form'd rebellion durst rear up its head. **1712** STEELE *Spect.* No. 509 ¶3 The benches around are so filthy, that no one can sit down. **1832** TENNYSON *Pal. of Art* 201 In filthy sloughs they roll. **1865** KINGSLEY *Herew.* xiv, He was filthy and ragged.

†**b.** Of air or clouds: Murky, thick. *Obs.*

1599 SHAKS. *Hen. V*, III. iii. 31 The coole and temperate Wind of Grace O're-blowes the filthy and contagious Clouds. **1605** —— *Macb.* I. i. 12 Houer through the fogge and filthie ayre.

c. Of weather: extremely unpleasant.

1875 L. TROUBRIDGE *Life amongst Troubridges* (1966) xi. 127 It was a most filthy day, pouring hard. **1895** 'G. MORTIMER' *Tales fr. Western Moors* 290 You'm only half a notion o' weather till you'm atop of Darteymoor when 'tis filthy. **1955** *Times* 3 May 5/2 In filthy weather.

2. Fond of filth, delighting in filth.

1526 *Pilgr. Perf.* (W. de W. 1531) 18 The fylthy and stynkynge lust of the body. **1635** SWAN *Spec. M.* Pref. (1643) 1 Like a filthie flie she seeks all over the body for a soare. **1778** BP. LOUTH *Transl. Isaiah* Notes (ed. 12) 156 The filthy animals that frequent such places.

3. Morally foul or polluted; obscene.

1535 COVERDALE *Zeph.* iii. 1 Wo to the abhominable, fylthie and cruel cite. **1596** SHAKS. *1 Hen. IV*, II. ii. 49 Ballads.. sung to filthy tunes. **1611** BIBLE *Col.* iii. 8 You also put off all these, anger.. filthy communication out of your mouth. **1682** BUNYAN *Holy War* 264 Being filthy, arch, and slie they quickly corrupted the families. **1712** ADDISON *Spect.* No. 271 ¶4 The Matron.. commended the Discretion of the Writer, for having thrown his filthy Thoughts into Greek. **1871** ALABASTER *Wheel of Law* 213 From this heaven the filthy one.. descends to the earth to tempt and excite to evil. *a* **1897** *Mod.* He could not stand their filthy talk.

4. †**a.** Disgraceful, contemptible, low, mean, scurvy, disgusting. *Obs.*

c **1400** *Destr. Troy* 10362 Neuer so filthy a fare hade fallyn in his hond. **1545** BRINKLOW *Compl.* xxiv. (1874) 65 Antychryst had fownd out that fylthy auricular confessyon. **1577–87** HOLINSHED *Scot. Chron.* (1805) II. 419 This murther.. was one of the most filthiest acts that ever was done. **1596** SHAKS. *1 Hen. IV*, III. iii. 79 Doulas, filthy Doulas. **1610** BP. CARLETON *Jurisd.* 166 Taking other

errours from other filthie heretiques. **1648** MILTON *Tenure Kings* 42 The filthy love of gaine. **1728** VANBR. & CIB. *Prov. Husb.* v. ii. 97 What's his filthy Name? **1828** SCOTT *F.M. Perth* xvi, Thou filthy weaver of rotten worsted.

b. ***filthy lucre***: dishonourable gain = Gr. αἰσχρὸν κέρδος (Tit. i. 11). Sometimes jocularly used for: Money; also *absol.* 'The filthy'.

1526–34 TINDALE *Titus* i. 11 Teachinge thinges which they ought not, because of filthy lucre. **1680** HICKERINGILL *Meroz* 30. **1709** ADDISON *Tatler* No. 116 ¶7, I did not make that Judgment for the Sake of filthy Lucre. **1855** TROLLOPE *Warden* xi. 175 No man lived less addicted to filthy lucre than the warden. **1877** BLACKMORE *Cripps* (1887) 225, I can catch my own without any appeal to 'the Filthy'. **1928** A. HUXLEY *Let.* 19 July (1969) 301 A considerable sale.. and a corresponding quantity of filthy lucre. **1931** WODEHOUSE *If I were You* ii. 27 Just trying to make a bit of the filthy.

5. quasi-*sb.* A filthy person.

1681 OTWAY *Soldiers Fort.* I. i, Damn'd Whores, hout ye filthies.

6. quasi-*adv.* = FILTHILY.

1616 *Rich Cabinet* 93 b, Modesty shutteth a young mans lippes.. so that he will not talke filthy. **1650** BULWER *Anthropomet.* xi. 180 Which makes them shew filthy fine. **1843** *Knickerbocker* XXI. 122 His trousers [were] 'filthy dirty' and pulled up above the tops of his boots. **1940** M. BANNING *Enough to live On* ix. 168 He's filthy rich and didn't earn a cent of it. **1954** J. B. PRIESTLEY *Magicians* ii. 28, I organise these parties for her—she's filthy rich. **1970** *Globe & Mail* (Toronto) 28 Sept. 1/3 He told me he was filthy rich.

7. *Comb.*

1823 in Cobbett *Rur. Rides* (1885) I. 318 Filthy-looking people. **1824** J. SYMMONS tr. *Agamem. Æsch.* 70 Where filthy-handed Mammon dwells. **1946** R. LEHMANN *Gipsy's Baby* 125 Filthy tempered woman.

filthy ('fɪlθɪ), *v.* [f. the adj.] *trans.* To make filthy.

1917 J. MASEFIELD *Old Front Line* v. 67 All this mess of heaps and hillocks is strung and filthied over with broken bodies and ruined gear. **1952** C. DAY LEWIS tr. *Virgil's Aeneid* III. 60 They tear the banquet to pieces, filthying all with their bestial Touch. **1967** 'LA MERI' *Sp. Dancing* (ed. 2) xi. 137 Cigarette butts and spilled liquids filthied the floor.

filtrability, filtrable, varr. FILTERABILITY, FILTERABLE *a.*

filtrate ('fɪltreɪt), *sb.* [ad. mod.L. *filtrātum*, f. *filtrāre*: cf. FILTER *v.* and -ATE[1].] **a.** The liquor which has been passed through a filter.

1845–6 G. E. DAY tr. *Simon's Anim. Chem.* II. 125 The lead contained in solution in the filtrate was separated. **1875** DARWIN *Insectiv. Pl.* vi. 89 The filtrate contained as much of the fibrin as had been digested.

b. *attrib.*, as **filtrate factor**, any soluble unidentified substance in a filtrate, esp. such a substance affecting the growth of an organism.

1937 EDGAR & MACRAE in *Biochem. Jrnl.* XXXI. 893 The second constituent was present in the filtrate after fuller's earth treatment of the yeast extract; this we have called the yeast fuller's earth filtrate factor. **1965** *Mycologia* LVII. 273 For *M[orchella] crassipes* the beneficial effect is accounted for mainly.. by the minerals supplied by the natural product, especially Mn and Ca. These two elements make up the 'filtrate factor' previously reported for this fungus.

filtrate ('fɪltreɪt), *v.* Also 7 **filterate**. [ad. mod.L. *filtrāt-* ppl. stem of *filtrāre* to FILTER.]

1. *trans.* = FILTER *v.* 1.

1612 WOODALL *Surg. Mate* Wks. (1653) 245 Calcine them, and after inbibe and filtrate them, etc. **1764** HARMER *Observ.* XXVII. iv. 192 They filtrate it [the wine of Schiras] through a cloth, and then it is very clear. **1852** TH. ROSS *Humboldt's Trav.* II. xxiv. 439 Leaves of the plantain.. used to filtrate the liquids. *c* **1865** LD. BROUGHAM in *Circ. Sc.* I. Introd. Disc. 23 The process of vegetation filtrates or distils the liquid, so as to produce from the worst, the purest water. *fig.* **1776** JOHNSON in Boswell *Life* II. 408 He never clarified his notions, by filtrating them through other minds. **1885** H. N. OXENHAM *Short Studies* 331 A Christianity filtrated of all its sectarian dogmas.

2. To cause to percolate; = FILTER *v.* 2.

1661 BOYLE *Spring of Air* II. Index, A vessel by which Air may be filtrated thorough water. **1794** SULLIVAN *View Nat.* I. 68 The waters, filtrated through these bodies.

3. *intr.* = FILTER *v.* 3.

1725 BRADLEY *Fam. Dict.* s.v. *Milk*, A white Liquor which filtrates thro' the Glands of Women's Breasts. **1780** SCHOTTE in *Phil. Trans.* LXX. 480 Digging a pit into the sand.. into which the water filtrates from all sides. **1834** PRINGLE *Afr. Sk.* v. 210 Through which the stream.. filtrates silently and unperceived.

fig. **1876** *Tinsley's Mag.* XVIII. 43 The corruptions of the higher stratum of society had been slowly filtrating to the lower.

Hence **'filtrated** *ppl. a.*, **'filtrating** *vbl. sb.* in quots. *attrib.*

1665 HOOKE *Microgr.* 128 The filterated Oyl. **1730** STUART in *Phil. Trans.* XXXVI. 356 A small Quantity of filtrated Bile. **1772** MONRO *ibid.* LXII. 30 The water being taken up by the spungy filtrating paper. **1811** J. ASHLEY *Patent* No. 3472 The water.. ascends through the filtrating medium. **1836** MACGILLIVRAY tr. *Humboldt's Trav.* xxiv. 350 The filtrated water losing itself in the crevices.

filtration (fɪl'treɪʃən). Also 7 **filteration**. [a. Fr. *filtration*, f. *filtrer* to FILTER.]

1. The action or process of filtering.

1605 TIMME *Quersit.* II. iii. 115 Chymical workings, as distillations.. filtrations. **1758** *Elaboratory laid open* Introd. 60 Filtration is generally practised, by means either of flannel cloth, or paper. **1822** IMISON *Sc. & Art* II. 7 Filtration is a finer species of sifting. **1862** STANLEY *Jew. Ch.* (1877) I. v. 100 Vessels of stone, used.. for the filtration of the delicious water from the sediment of the river-bed. **1943** *Gloss. Terms Electr. Engin.* (*B.S.I.*) 142 *Filtration*, of X-rays, the absorption of the longer wavelengths to a greater extent than the shorter wavelengths by placing an absorbing medium in the path of the beam. **1970** D. F. SHAW *Introd. Electronics* (ed. 2) x. 220 If a current of more than one milliamp is to be delivered by the rectifier, *L—C* filtration must be used.

fig. **1843** PRESCOTT *Mexico* I. vi. (1864) 55 It is not easy to render his version into.. English rhyme, without the perfume of the original escaping in this double filtration.

2. A gradual movement like that of water passing through a filter; percolation.

1664 POWER *Exp. Philos.* I. 70 For Motion the Spirits move impetuously down the Nervous filaments.. but for Sensation they onely creep by a filtration down their Coats. **1707** *Curios. in Husb. & Gard.* 69 If we pursue this Sap in its incomprehensible Filtration through the Pores of Plants. **1794** G. ADAMS *Nat. & Exp. Philos.* II. xxi. 414 [The pervasiveness of light and heat] has been overlooked as an accidental filtration.

3. *transf.* (Cf. FILTER *v.* 3 b.)

1932 *Evening Standard* 21 Jan. 4/4 'Filtration' at a crossing takes place whenever the lights give the 'All Clear' at a crossing; many vehicles in the stream which is let loose turn left or right despite the fact that in the road into which they are turning the traffic lights show red.

†**'filtrature.** *Obs.*[−1]. [f. FILTRATE *v.* + -URE.] = FILTRATION 2.

1670 W. SIMPSON *Hydrol. Ess.* 145 The sabulous matter.. by its various filtratures and percolations.

‖**filtre** (filtr). [Fr.] A filtering appliance, fitted over a pot or cup, for making coffee by the passage of boiling water through ground coffee. Also, the coffee so prepared (see CAFÉ 3).

1940 'M. INNES' *Secret Vanguard* xx. 217 Orchard was.. measuring coffee into a *filtre*. **1959** *Guardian* 9 Nov. 3/2, I have sat in a French café watching a 'filtre' deliver the coffee drop by drop into my cup. **1966** P. V. PRICE *France* 35 Cona coffee will cost slightly more than a *filtre*.

filtz, var. form of FITZ.

fimashing: see FUMISHING.

fimble ('fɪmb(ə)l), *sb.*[1] Also 5–6 **femble**, 6 **fembull, femle, ffemble, (fyrble)**. [a. Du. *femel*, LG. *fimel*, a. F. (*chanvre*) *femelle*, lit. 'female hemp', this name being popularly applied to what modern botanists call the male plant.]

1. The male plant of hemp, producing a weaker and shorter fibre than the CARL HEMP or female plant. Formerly also the fibre of this as prepared for use. Also more fully, ***fimble hemp***.

1484 *Churchw. Acc. Wigtoft, Boston* (Nichols 1797) 78 Paide for femble, and for makyng thar of in bell-ropes, 1*s.* 5*d.* **1577** *Wills & Inv. N.C.* (Surtees) I. 415 Tenn dosen femle hempe vij*l*. **1577** B. GOOGE *Heresbach's Husb.* I. 39 b, The Female or fyrble Hempe. **1669** WORLIDGE *Syst. Agric.* (1681) 277 Gather the Fimble, or earliest Hemp and Flax. **1707** MORTIMER *Husb.* 118 The light Summer-hemp, that bears no Seed, is called Fimble hemp. **1731–59** MILLER *Gard. Dict.* (ed. 7) s.v. *Cannabis*, The Fimble Hemp.. is the male Plants. **1877** *N.-W. Linc. Gloss.*, The fimble, or female hemp, was applied to.. domestic purposes. **1877** [see CARL HEMP 1].

2. *attrib.*

a **1519** *Invent.* in *Gentl. Mag.* Apr. (1864) 501 Ij payr of ffembull Shetts, ij[s] viij[d]. **1548–9** *Will of A Peyrson* (Somerset Ho.), A payre of shettes a lynnyne & a Femble. **1622–3** *Invent.* in Best *Farm. Bks.* (Surtees) 162 *note*, Three [pound] of femble harne, 4*s.*

†**'fimble**, *sb.*[2] *Obs.* [? var. of THIMBLE.] App. a ring for fastening a gate.

1597 *Althorp MS.* in Simpkinson *Washingtons* App. p. xxxviii, For a hoke and fimble for Great Norrells gate.

†**'fimble**, *v. Obs.* exc. *dial.* [app. an onomatopœic variant of FAMBLE or FUMBLE, altered to express a more delicate movement.] **a.** *intr.* To move the fingers lightly and frequently over anything. **b.** *trans.* To touch lightly and frequently with the ends of the fingers. See also quot. *a* 1825.

1577 DEE *Relat. Spir.* I. (1659) 6 She is much fimbling about the Stone on her breast. **1647** H. MORE *Song of Soul* I. II. lxxxiii, When he the black silk rope soft fimbling felt. *a* **1825** FORBY *Voc. E. Anglia*, *Fimble*, to pass through without cutting. Ex. 'My scythe fimble the grass.'

‖**fimbria** ('fɪmbrɪə). [L. *fimbria* thread, fibre, fringe.] A fringe: *spec.* **a.** *Anat.* the fringed end of the Fallopian tube; **b.** *Bot.* (see quot. 1847).

1752 SIR J. HILL *Hist. Anim.* 304 There runs all round the sides of the fish a kind of fimbria. **1754–64** SMELLIE *Midwif.* I. ii. §2. 97 The cavity of each [of the Fallopian tubes] ends in an open mouth.. from the brim of which is expanded the Fimbria. **1847** CRAIG, *Fimbria*, in Botany, the dentated or fringe-like ring of the operculum of mosses, by the elastic power of which the operculum is displaced. **1872** F. G. THOMAS *Dis. Women* 625 The Fallopian tube of each side is connected with the ovary by one fimbria.

fimbrial ('fɪmbrɪəl), *a.* [f. prec. + -AL[1].] Of or pertaining to a fimbria.

In some mod. Dicts.

fimbriate ('fɪmbrɪeɪt), *a.* [ad. L. *fimbriāt-us* fringed: see -ATE[2].] **a.** *Her.* = FIMBRIATED.

b. *Bot.* and *Zool.* Fringed; bordered with hairs or filiform processes.

1829 LOUDON *Encycl. Plants* 33 *Eleusine*.. Scales truncate, fimbriate. **1846** DANA *Zooph.* (1848) 666 Tentacles long fimbriate. **1870** HOOKER *Stud. Flora* 50 *Dianthus plumarius*.. petals fimbriate. **1870** ROLLESTON *Anim. Life* 59 The fimbriate.. portion of the mantle.

fimbriate ('fɪmbrɪeɪt), *v.* [f. L. *fimbria* fringe + -ATE[3]. Cf. L. *fimbriātus* fringed.] *trans.* To finish or decorate with a border of any kind.

1486 [see FIMBRIATED]. **1639** FULLER *Holy War* v. xxiv. 271 Besides the divers tricking or dressing [heraldick crosses]; as piercing, voiding, fimbriating.

fimbriated ('fɪmbrɪeɪtɪd), *ppl. a.* [f. prec. + -ED[1].] **a.** *Her.* Of a bearing: Bordered with a narrow band or edge. **b.** *gen.* Having a fringe; fringed. Chiefly in scientific applications, as *Anat.*, *Bot.*, *Zool.*

a. **1486** *Bk. St. Albans, Her.* D j a, Thys cros fimbriatit or borderit. **1586** FERNE *Blaz. Gentrie* 174 He beareth B on a crosse Gewles fimbriated or bordured Argent. **1610** GUILLIM *Heraldry* II. vii. (1611) 73 In the crosse fimbriated the edges thereof doe occupie the least portion therof. **1864** BOUTELL *Heraldry Hist. & Pop.* xxi. §1 (ed. 3) 356 A pall of the last, fimbriated and fringed gold.

b. **1698** J. PETIVER in *Phil. Trans.* XX. 405 A Calyx whose Divisions are fimbriated. **1752** SIR J. HILL *Hist. Anim.* 153 The small, flatted, and, as it were, fimbriated Porcellana. **1797** M. BAILLIE *Morb. Anat.* (1807) 401 The fimbriated extremity of the Fallopian tubes. **1862** DARWIN *Fertil. Orchids* vi. 283 The labellum is covered with longitudinal and fimbriated ridges. **1877** HUXLEY *Anat. Inv. Anim.* iii. 154 Tentacles, which may be slender and conical, or short, broad and fimbriated.

fimbriation (fɪmbrɪ'eɪʃən). [f. as prec. + -ATION.] The condition or fact of being fimbriated; in quots. *concr.* a fringe or border.

1864 BOUTELL *Heraldry Hist. & Pop.* xxxii. (ed. 3) 475 A red fimbriation to represent the red field of the National Flag itself. **1881** *N.Y. Nation* XXXII. 376 The error consists in the width of the white border or fimbriation of the St. George's cross.

fimbriato- (fɪmbrɪ'eɪtəʊ), used as combining form of FIMBRIATE *a.*

1866 *Treas. Bot.*, *Fimbriato-laciniate*, having the edge cut up into divisions which are fimbriated.

fimbricate ('fɪmbrɪkeɪt), *a.* [Erroneous var. of FIMBRIATE *a.*, perh. due to association with *imbricate*.] = FIMBRIATE *a.*

1846 WORCESTER (citing *P. Cyc.*), *Fimbricate* (*Bot.*), fringed; jagged. **1884** *Syd. Soc. Lex.*, *Fimbricate*.

Hence **'fimbricated** *a.*

1879 *Cassell's Techn. Educ.* IV. 154/1 The ciliary organs or fimbricated margin of its [the oyster's beard.

‖**fimbrilla** (fɪm'brɪlə). *Bot.* and *Phys.* [mod.L. dim. of FIMBRIA: see -IL.] A minute fringe.

1884 [see next].

fimbrilliferous (fɪmbrɪ'lɪfərəs), *a. Bot.* [f. prec. + -(I)FEROUS.] Bearing small fringes.

1866 *Treas. Bot.*, *Fimbrilliferous*, bearing many little fringes, as the receptacle of some composites. **1884** *Syd. Soc. Lex.*, *Fimbrilliferous*, having small fringes or a fimbrilla.

fimbrillose (ˌfɪmbrɪ'ləʊs), *a.* [f. as prec. + -OSE.] Bearing a fimbrilla.

1884 in *Syd. Soc. Lex.*

†**'fimbrious,** *a. Obs.* [f. L. *fimbri-a* + -OUS.] = FIMBRIATE *a.*

1657 TOMLINSON *Renou's Disp.* 295 With broad, mucronated, fimbrious, crisped leaves. **1662** J. CHANDLER *Van Helmont's Oriat.* 246 The tongue is cloathed with a fimbrious or seamy coat.

†**fime.** *Obs.* [ad. L. *fimus* dung.] Dung.

1460–70 *Bk. Quintessence* 11 Renewe þe fyme oonys in þe wike. **1599** A. M. tr. *Gabelhouer's Bk. Physicke* 319/1 Take nue Horse fime. **1607** TOPSELL *Four-f. Beasts* (1658) 203 The fime or dung of such Females as live in the Mountains. **1647** H. MORE *Poems* 73 Inward parts.. Lie close upwrapt in that dull sluggish fime.

fimetarious (fɪmiː'tɛərɪəs), *a.* [f. L. *fimēt-um* dunghill + -ARIOUS.] Growing on or amidst dung.

1866 in *Treas. Bot.* **1884** in *Syd. Soc. Lex.*

fimetic (fɪ'mɛtɪk), *a. nonce-wd.* [f. as prec. + -IC.] Pertaining to or concerned with dung.

1880 RUSKIN in *19th Cent.* VII. 944 The necessary obscurities of fimetic Providence.

fimicolous (fɪ'mɪkələs), *a.* [f. L. *fim-us* dung + *col-ĕre* to inhabit + -OUS.] Inhabiting dung.

1874 COOKE *Fungi* (1875) 245 Only seven or eight.. do not occur on dung, whilst fifty-six are fimicolous.

fin (fɪn), *sb.*[1] Forms: 1 **finn**, 3–7 **finne**, (7 **finn**), 4–5 **fyn(ne**, (*south.* **vyn(ne**), 7– **fin**. Also 7 **phin**. [OE. *finn* str. masc., cognate with the synonymous MDu. *vinne* (mod.Du. *vin*) fem., MLG. *finne* fem.; the mod.Ger. *finne* is prob. adopted from LG. The L. *pinna* fin is prob. the same word.]

1. a. An organ attached to various parts of the body in fishes and cetaceans, which serves for propelling and steering in the water. With prefixed adj., as *anal*, *caudal*, *dorsal*, *pectoral*,

ventral, etc., indicating the part to which the organ is attached. Applied also to similar organs in other animals, as the flipper of a seal, the modified wing of a penguin, etc.

c **1000** ÆLFRIC *Lev.* xi. 9 Ne ete ȝe fisc buton þa þe habbaþ finnas & scilla. *a* **1225** *St. Marher.* 9 þe fisches þat i þe flodes fleoteð wið finnes. *c* **1300** *K. Alis.* 6591 They liveth, so theo heryng..Feet and hond buth heore vynnes. *c* **1400** *Rom. Rose* 7008 Swimme..Bet than a fish doth with his finne. *c* **1450** *Two Cookery-bks.* 104 Take a Sturgeon, and kut of the vyn fro the tayle to þe hede, on þe bakke. **1599** HAKLUYT *Voy.* II. I. 107 The..fish had on euery side a wing, and toward the taile two other lesser as it were finnes. **1671** MILTON *P.R.* II. 345 All fish..of shell or fin. **1699** HACKE *Coll. Voy.* II. 62 Penguins..have..only two Fins or Flaps, wherewith they are helped to swim. **1802** PALEY *Nat. Theol.* xii. (1803) 253 If you cut off the pectoral fins, i.e. the pair which lies close behind the gills, the head falls prone to the bottom. **1883** W. H. FLOWER in *Encycl. Brit.* XV. 395/1 *Balænoptera* [has] a small falcate dorsal fin.

b. (*fish*) *of every fin*: = of every species. Cf. FEATHER.

1725 POPE *Odyss.* XIX. 134 Fish of every fin thy seas afford.

c. A finned animal; a fish.

1549 LATIMER *6th Serm. bef. Edw. VI* (Arb.) 178 Wee..haue not caught one fynne. **1881** *Leicestersh. Gloss.*, Theer 'asn't a fin i' the stank. **1893** *Daily News* 15 Dec. 5/3 It is to be hoped that Mr. Watson will add him to his list of fins.

†**d.** Phrase, *to put out one's fins*: *fig.* ? to bestir oneself eagerly.

1461 MARG. PASTON in *Lett.* No. 369 I. 544 And now he and alle his olde felaweship put owt their fynnes, and arn ryght flygge and mery.

2. Something resembling a fish's fin.

a. *jocularly.* The arm and hand (of a man), or simply the hand.

1785 GROSE *Dict. Vulg. Tongue*, *Fin*, an arm. **1801** NELSON in A. Duncan *Life* (1806) 140, 'I am Lord Nelson; see, here's my fin'..shewing the stump of his right arm. **1855** SMEDLEY *H. Coverdale* ii. 12 Lend us a fin, old man, for I feels precious staggery-like. *Mod.* (*slang*), Tip us your fin (= shake hands).

†**b.** The lid (of the eye). *Obs.*

1604 MARSTON *Malcontent* I. iii, Here's a knight..shall..ride at the ring Till the fin of his eyes look as blue as the welkin. **1623** WEBSTER *Duchess of Malfy* II. i, The fins of her eye-lids look most teeming blue.

c. The baleen of a whale (? *obs.*). Hence, a blade or thin strip of whalebone.

1634 T. JOHNSON *Parey's Chirurg.* XXV. xxi. 1013 The finnes that stand forth of their [whales'] mouths, which are commonly called Whale-bones, being dryed and polished, serve to make buskes for women. **1706** *Lond. Gaz.* No. 4238/4 Cut-Whalebone..in Fins. **1858** SIMMONDS *Dict. Trade*, *Fin*, a blade of whalebone.

d. *pl.* Rubber flippers for the feet, to assist underwater swimming.

1960 *News Chron.* 9 July 6/7 You'd need a pair of fins (£1), a mask (£1) and a breathing tube. **1967** J. SEVERSON *Great Surfing* Gloss., *Fins*, rubber flippers used as aids in swimming or body surfing; called swim fins.

3. A projecting part.

†**a.** A lobe of the liver or lungs. *Obs. rare.*

1615 CROOKE *Body of Man* 131 In bruite beasts it [the Liuer] is diuided into foure, fiue, or six Lobes or Finnes. *Ibid.* 385 Each Lung is diuided into two Lobes or Finnes.

b. A sharp lateral projection on the share or the coulter of a plough.

1653 BLITHE *Eng. Improv. Impr.* 197 Be carefull in keeping your..Share phin as sharp as may be. **1677** [see CHEP]. **1717** *Dict. Rust.* s.v. *Plough*, Some set on the right side of the Coulter a small Wing or Fin, which cuts in two the bottom of the Roots. **1759** tr. *Duhamel's Husb.* I. viii. (1762) 44 A hollow plow-share..has a fin both ways; which fins must also begin at the point. **1807** VANCOUVER *Agric. Devon* (1813) 115 When the land is designed to be ploughed clean..a long pointed share, with a small fin or wing, is used.

c. *Mech.* (see quots.).

1874 KNIGHT *Dict. Mech.* I. 846/2 *Fin*, a slip inserted longitudinally into a shaft or arbor, and left projecting so as to form a guide for an object which may slip thereon, but not rotate. *Ibid.* I. 847/1 *Fin*, a tongue on the edge of a board. **1876** AITKEN *Guns* (*Brit. Manuf. Industr.*) 21 Presses fitted up with cutting-out tools, punch out, trim, and relieve the stampings from the superfluous metal, or 'fins' left after stamping.

d. In aircraft and rockets, esp. as a stabilizer (see quots.).

1835 *Nautical Mag.* IV. 612 An internal balloon is fitted for the purpose of ascending and descending at will, and the whole is intended to be propelled by fins, paddles, or wings. **1852** *Illustr. London News* XX. 468/1 By means of the handles at the outer sides, the apparatus contained in the case can be turned round at pleasure, and the position of the fins altered, thus enabling the operator to steer the balloon. **1910** C. C. TURNER *Aerial Navig.* iv. 54 Leppig's Balloon, 1812. It was to be driven by a fin propeller, worked by hand. **1911** *Chambers's Jrnl.* I. 57/2 An aeroplane..supported largely by the pressure against its body, its wings reduced to mere fins, serving to guide its motion. **1920** *Discovery* Mar. 78/1 An elliptically-shaped gas-bag provided with a conical-shaped tail filled with air, to which a rudder and stabilising fins are attached. **1935** [see ANTI-ICER]. **1935** *Jrnl. Brit. Interplanetary Soc.* Oct. 13 Fin—wing-like device for stabilizing flight. **1950** *Gloss. Aeronaut. Terms* (*B.S.I.*) I. 49 *Fin. a.* A fixed surface outside the envelope or outer cover of a lighter-than-air aircraft providing aerodynamic stability. *b.* Those parts of the stabilizers of a kite balloon providing stability in pitch.

e. A fin-like appendage to a ship's bottom; a fin-keel; also, a centreboard.

1885 *Marine Engineer* 1 Apr. 8/1 But it is possible to fit fins, flappers, or shutters.., to the run of a ship so as to be flush with the plates. **1893** *Outing* (U.S.) XXII. 147/1 The fin is of Tobin bronze, one-quarter inch thick, six feet long on upper edge. **1897** *Ibid.* XXX. 468/1 Their hulls..are enormously strong, so as to restrain the heavy weight of the fin. **1949** *Jane's Fighting Ships 1949–50* 36 Fin stabilisers will be fitted to prevent rolling.

f. On a motor vehicle. Hence *fin-tailed* adj.

1959 *Listener* 4 June 982/1 Even family cars are now made impressive with the fins which were once the distinguishing mark of sharks. **1960** *Guardian* 11 Oct. 8/4 The reluctant mums..are induced to step gingerly out of the fintailed cars. **1968** P. M. POSTAL *Aspects Phonol. Theory* xiii. 283 There is no more reason for languages to change than there is for automobiles to add fins one year and remove them the next.

4. *dial.* The herb restharrow. Also *fin-weed*.

1649 BLITHE *Eng. Improv. Impr.* xviii. (1653) 120 They bear plenty of..Phins, Moss, and Shargrase. **1790** W. MARSHALL *Midl. Count.* Gloss., *Fin*, *anonis arvensis*, rest-harrow. **1821** CLARE *Vill. Mistr.* I. 204 Where the blushing fin weed's flower Closes up at evening hour.

5. *attrib.* and *Comb.*: **a.** simple attributive, as *fin-apparatus*, *-membrane*; **b.** objective, as *fin-cutting* vbl. sb.; **c.** parasynthetic and similative, as *fin-shaped*, *-tailed*, *-winged*; *fin-like* adjs.

1847–9 TODD *Cycl. Anat.* IV. 173/2 The connexion which exists between the *fin-apparatus and the body of Clio. **1886** *Pall Mall G.* 16 Aug. 5/2 Discovering that the pike gorged our perch ravenously with and without their fins..we gave up the *fin-cutting. **1666** DRYDEN *Ann. Mirab.* 157 Ere..*fin-like oars did spread from either side. **1889** T. H. EMERSON *Eng. Idylls* 43 He stood in his boat rubbing his fin-like hands. **1874** WOOD *Nat. Hist.* 569 The *fin-membranes are brown. **1835–6** TODD *Cycl. Anat.* I. 651/2 *Fin-shaped caudal processes. **1892** LD. LYTTON *King Poppy* Prol. 319 Tritons stall Their *fin-tail'd steeds in azure caverns. **1820** SHELLEY *Vision of Sea* 150 A blue shark..The *fin-wingèd tomb of the victor.

6. Special comb.: **fin-back** = FINNER; also *attrib.*, as *finback calf*, *whale*; also *fin-backed whale*; **fin-fish** = FINNER; **fin-foot**, (*a*) a swimming-foot; a pleiopod; (*b*) a name for birds of the genera *Heliornis* or *Podica*; **fin-footed** *a.*, *Ornith.* (*a*) web-footed; (*b*) having the toes furnished with flaps or lobes, lobate-footed; (*c*) 'in Mollusca, pteropod' (*Cent. Dict.*); **fin-keel**, a keel shaped like a dorsal fin inverted; **fin-leg**, the leg of an aquatic insect, used as a fin; **fin-ray**, one of the hard spiny or soft jointed processes which support the skin of the fins; †**finscale**, another name for the RUDD[1]; **fin-spine**, a spine or spiny ray of a fish's fin; **fin-spined** *a.*, having spiny fins, acanthopterygious; **fin-toed** *a.* = *fin-footed* (*b*); **fin-weed** (see sense 4); **fin-whale** = FINNER.

1725 DUDLEY in *Phil. Trans.* XXXIII. 258 The *Finback Whale is distinguished from the right Whale, by having a great Fin on his Back. **1851** H. MELVILLE *Whale* xxxi. 151 The Fin-back is not gregarious. **1843** *Zoologist* I. 33 *Fin-backed whale (*Balænoptera boops*). **1694** NARBOROUGH in *Acc. Sev. Late Voy.* II. 3 A *Fin-fish swam by our Ship. **1787** HUNTER in *Phil. Trans.* LXXVII. 375 When they [whales] are of a certain size, they are brought to us as Porpoises; when larger, they are called Grampus, or Fin-fish. **1843** *Zoologist* I. 34 It [a whale] is well known among fishermen..by the names of finner, fin-back, fin-fish. **1849** tr. *Cuvier's Anim. Kingd.* 423 Which appendages..are used in swimming, or are *fin-feet. **1886** *Encycl. Brit.* XX. 223/2 The..group formed by the..Heliornis, and the..Podica..to which the name 'Finfoots' has been applied. **1646** SIR T. BROWNE *Pseud. Ep.* v. i. 234 It [the Pelecan] is..*fin-footed like Swannes. **1804** BEWICK *Brit. Birds* (1847) II. 153 Linnæus..describes it as a genus distinct from..waders in general, on account of its being fin-footed. **1893** *Westm. Gaz.* 21 Feb. 11/2 Boats..exhibiting all the most recent devices in bulb and *fin keels. **1843** *Zoologist* I. 57 The *fin-legs could not be well made out. **1863** *Spring Lapl.* 162 The same, both in shape, colour, number of scales, and *finrays. **1677** PLOT *Oxfordsh.* 184 A Fish of the squammous kind, which they call a *Finscale, somwhat like a Roach. **1771** FORSTER in *Phil. Trans.* LXI. 318 *note*, The fish..is supposed to be the same with the rud or finscale. **1876** PAGE *Adv. Text-bk. Geol.* xiii. 228 Detached *fin-spines known to the palæontologist as ichthyodorulites. **1674** RAY *Collect. Eng. Words* 91 Such whose toes are divided, which I may call *Fin-toed. **1847** HILL in Gosse *Birds of Jamaica* 439 A bird with fin-toed feet. **1885** S. TROMHOLT *Aurora Borealis* II. 283 The family of whales which have been named *'fin' whales, from a fin on the back.

fin (fɪn), *sb.*[2] *slang.* = FINNIP (see also quot. 1925). Also *U.S.*, a five-dollar note; the sum of five dollars.

1868 *Temple Bar* XXIV. 538 'What are "fins"?' 'Five-pound notes, or flash notes.' **1925** *Flynn's* 24 Jan. 119/1 *Fin*, ..five dollars; a five-year term. **1949** *Penguin New Writing* XXXVI. 97 We slipped them a fin apiece. **1953** W. R. BURNETT *Vanity Row* xv. 101 Costs a fin just to check your hat.

fin (fɪn), *v.* [f. FIN *sb.*[1]]

1. *trans.* **a.** To cut off the fins from (a fish). **b.** To cut up (a chub).

1513 *Bk. Keruynge* in *Babees Bk.* (1868) 265 Fynne that cheuen. **1799** *Sporting Mag.* XIV. 10 Fin a chub, cut him up. **1853** *Fraser's Mag.* XLVIII. 694 When he puts the slice into a fish, he truncheons eel, fins chub, [etc.].

2. *nonce-use.* To keep supplied with fish. Cf. FIN *sb.*[1] 1 c.

1808 J. BARLOW *Columb.* VIII. 484 Swarms..Repeople still the shoals and fin the fruitful tide.

3. *U.S.* Of a fish: To wound with its fins. Also *intr.* of a whale, *to fin* (*out*): to lash the water with its fins when dying.

1889 *Columbus* (*Ohio*) *Dispatch* 15 Feb., He had never been bitten by a dog, but..had been finned by fish.

4. *intr.* To swim, as a fish; hence used of underwater swimmers. Also *trans.*, *to fin it*, *to fin a* (or *one's*) *passage*, *way*.

1807 J. BARLOW *Columb.* VIII. 285 Renascent swarms by nature's care supplied, Repeople still the shoals and fin the fruitful tide. *a* **1861** T. WINTHROP *Canoe & Saddle* (1862) 134 In midsummer salmon fin it along the reaches of Whulge. **1894** *Outing* (U.S.) XXIV. 140/1 For this [stump] the rascal [trout] steers, as fast as he can fin his way. **1928** T. HARDY *Coll. Poems* 591 Fishes might seem to fin a passage. **1933** W. DE LA MARE *Lord Fish* 36 He grew hungrier and hungrier as he finned softly on. **1964** B. GASTON *Drifting Death* ii. 24, I jack-knifed down to beyond twenty and finned hard for the yacht. **1964** *Guardian* 20 May 7/6 You fin slowly down, 15 to 20 feet now.

5. *trans.* To provide with fins (sense 3). Usu. as *vbl. sb.*

Hence **'finning** *vbl. sb.*

1883 *Fisheries Exhib. Catal.* 197 Finning and flitching knives. **1933** *Meccano Mag.* Mar. 193/1 The finning of the head has also received special attention. **1962** *Times* 8 May 16/5 Pininfarina's finning is sufficient to assist stability and guide the driver when parking.

fin, obs. f. FINE.

finable, fineable ('faɪnəb(ə)l), *a.*[1] [f. FINE *v.* + -ABLE.] Liable or subject to a fine.

1. Of a person, also of an offence: Liable to be punished by a fine.

1485 *Act 1 Hen. VII.* c. 7 The said Offences of Huntings ..[shall] be..but Trespass finable. **1592** in *Vicary's Anat.* (1888) App. xv. 276 All suche aliantes and straungers being founde withe a faulte..shall be fyneable. **1647** N. BACON *Disc. Govt. Eng.* I. lxix. (1739) 180 Before this Law, this crime was but finable. **1761** HUME *Hist. Eng.* I. App. i. 100 If any of them..give him assistance they are finable to the king. **1860** WYNTER *Curios. Civiliz.* 503 The Legislature should make it a fineable offence to work a dry stone without a fan.

2. Of a tenure: Subject to the payment of a fine on renewal. Of a tenant: Liable to pay such a fine. Also of a writ: On which a fine or fee has to be paid.

c **1600** NORDEN *Spec. Brit.*, *Cornw.* (1728) 25 Their tenure is ad voluntatem Domini, and at euery taking finable at the Lordes pleasure and heriotable. **1611** COTGR., *Questable*, finable, taxable, as some tenants are at the pleasure of their Lords. **1641** *Termes de la Ley* 84 b, Some Copyhold is fineable..that which is fineable, the Lord rateth at what fine he pleaseth. **1646** *Grant* in Ld. Campbell *Chancellors* (1857) III. lxvii. 308 A grant was made..of all such part of fineable writs..as former Lord Keepers have had.

Hence **'finableness.**

1727 BAILEY vol. II, *Finableness*, liableness to be fined, or to pay a Fine or Amercement.

finable ('faɪnəb(ə)l), *a.*[2] [f. FINE *v.*[2] + -ABLE.] Capable of being clarified, refined, or purified.

In mod. Dicts.

†**'finably**, *adv. Obs.* [f. OF. *finable* final + -LY[2]. Cf. OF. *finablement.*] = FINALLY.

1483 CAXTON *Gold. Leg.* 361/1 In such wise..finably she myghte come to heuen. **1541** R. COPLAND *Galyen's Terapeutyke* D iv, Fynably of the Elebore what it is.

finagle (fɪ'neɪg(ə)l), *v. colloq.* (orig. *U.S.*). Also fin(n)agel, finaygle, phe-. [ad. Eng. dial. *fainaigue* to cheat. See *E.D.D.* and cf. RENEGUE *v.*] *intr.* To use dishonest or devious methods to bring something about; to fiddle. Also *trans.*, to 'wangle', to scheme, to get (something) by trickery. So **fi'nagling** *vbl. sb.*

1926 in H. Wentworth *Amer. Dial. Dict.* (1944) 216/1 Finagle, U.S. political cant. **1926** ANDERSON & STALLINGS *What Price Glory* 111, I'm a weary man, and I don't want any finnagelling from you. **1933** P. CAIN *Fast One* (1936) vii. 250 Turn her over to me in the open and without any finaygling. **1936** *Writer's Digest* Oct. 4 Discounting any possible editorial finageling..the solid fact remains that opposing politically minded people do cancel subscriptions. **1941** *Time* 9 June 19/3 Months of diplomatic finagling necessary to interview key men. **1941** *Word Study* Nov. 1/2 *Variety*..insists on describing Bergen's high art [*sc.* ventriloquism] as 'tonsilar phenagling'. **1954** J. B. PRIESTLEY *Magicians* vi. 120 All the time trying it on, fiddling and finagling, selling anybody out for fourpence. **1955** W. W. DENLINGER *Compl. Boston* 173 Any attempt to fudge or finagle or to get ahead of the other fellow will be recognized by the judge for what it is. **1955** *Publ. Amer. Dialect Soc.* XXIV. 164 Big business is trying..to phenagle us all out of a dollar. **1959** *Spectator* 11 Sept. 320/1 The Western members [of the Security Council] managed to finagle their resolution..out of reach of the Soviet Union's veto. **1966** *Punch* 28 Dec. 954/2, I soon finagled my way past the innumerable porters.

final ('faɪnəl), *a.* and *sb.* Also (4 fenal), 4–6 fynal(l, 4–7 finall(e. [a. F. *final*, ad. L. *fīnāl-is* of or pertaining to an end, f. *fīnis* end.]

A. *adj.*

1. a. Coming at the end (of a word, a series).

1530 PALSGR. Introd. 28 Every feminyn plurell endeth in S, added to the E fynall of his singular. **1821** SHELLEY *Hellas* note, The final Chorus is indistinct and obscure. **1838** DE MORGAN *Ess. Probab.* 202 A colon placed after the final letter. **1865** GEIKIE *Scen. & Geol. Scot.* xiii. 340 In this final chapter let me present the reader with a brief summary. **1881** *Football Annual* 91 In the final tie they were beaten by the Walsall Swifts.

†**b.** *Her.* in *quadrate final*, according to Ferne a field bearing a 'token of arms' other than a representation of a living creature. *Obs.*

[1486 see FINIAL *a.*] 1586 FERNE *Blaz. Gentrie* 206 The armes called Quadrates were nine in number, and they were either finall, or Royall.

c. Law. ***final process*** (see quot.). ***final proof***: (U.S.) the process observed in paying for pre-empted land after six months' occupancy.

1768 BLACKSTONE *Comm.* III. xix. 279 Mesne process is.. sometimes put in contradistinction to final process, or process of execution. 1884 *Milnor* (Dakota) *Teller* 5 Sept., He.. makes final proofs and attends to all business of that kind.

d. ***final drive*** (see quot. 1968).

1907 R. B. WHITMAN *Motor-car Princ.* ix. 138 From the change-speed mechanism the power is passed to the driving wheels by the final drive. 1912 J. ARMSTRONG *Motor* ix. 173 The final drive.. is achieved mostly through the medium of bevel-gear, that.. is very nearly as wear-resisting as a pair of constantly mated spur-wheels. 1968 *Practical Motorist* Nov. 333/1 *Final drive*, the last part of the transmission, consisting of the crown wheel and pinion, differential gears and axle drive shafts.

2. a. Marking the last stage of a process; leaving nothing to be looked for or expected; ultimate.

*c*1365 CHAUCER *L.G.W.* 2101 *Ariadne*, This is the fynal ende of al this thyng. *c*1440 *Govt. Lordschipes* (E.E.T.S.) 48 He made many morales epistels to Aristotel of greet delyt to haue his secree fynal. 1504 ATKYNSON tr. *De Imitatione* III. lxiv, Dyrecte it by thy grace contynually in this lyfe vnto the fynall countrey of euerlastyng peace. *a*1535 MORE *Wks.* 578/1 By his word electes, he meneth the finall and eternall electes. 1649 MILTON *Eikon* Pref., A Person.. who hath.. payd his finall debt both to Nature and his Faults. 1736 BUTLER *Anal.* I. ii. 38 Delay of punishment is no sort nor degree of presumption of final impunity. 1805 FOSTER *Ess.* I. iii. 37 The final basis of all character. 1871 MORLEY *Voltaire* (1886) 9 Philosophic candour and intelligence are supposed to have hit their final climax.

b. ***final demand***, (*a*) an account for goods or services rendered that is the creditor's final attempt to recover the money owed before proceeding to legal action or withdrawing the service; (*b*) *Econ.*, (a measure of) demand for current output as measured by sales to final buyers, and excluding additions to stock or inventories; also *attrib.*

1969 *U.S. Federal Reporter* CCCCXI. 876/1 One form is called 'Final Demand for the Payment of Debt' and warns the debtor that 'This Demand is made to give you a last opportunity to pay.' 1975 *Business Week* 10 Feb. 20 The recession has already begun to put some real pressures on the price side because of the shrinkage of final demand. 1982 *Financial Times* 2 Jan. 4/8 Relative to final demand, inventories of most metals are low throughout the supply chain. 1982 *Financial Times* 30 Mar. I. 18/5 Make sure the factor informs the client when it is sending final demands and solicitors' letters to customers.

3. a. Putting an end to something (rarely const. *of*, *to*); putting an end to strife or uncertainty; not to be undone, altered, or revoked; conclusive.

Formerly often in phr. ***final peace*** or ***concord*** = med.L. *finalis pax*, *concordia*.

*c*1330 R. BRUNNE *Chron.* (1810) 338 þe parties wold mak a finalle pes. *c*1386 CHAUCER *Frankl. T.* 259 Taak this for fynal answere as of me. *c*1489 CAXTON *Blanchardyn* x. 40 His resolucion fynall was. 1559 *Mirr. Mag.*, *Dk. Suffolk* xi, But syth we could no fynall peace induce. 1590 SPENSER *F.Q.* I. ix. 51 At last, resolv'd to work his finall smart, He lifted up his hand. 1625 BACON *Ess.*, *Greatn. Kingd.* (Arb.) 489 Examples, where Sea-Fights have beene Finall to the warre. 1660 R. COKE *Power & Subj.* 95 Treason does ever produce fatal and final destruction to the offender. 1771 *Junius Lett.* xlix. 255 You would long since have received your final dismission and reward. 1797 G. WASHINGTON in Sir J. Sinclair *Corr.* (1831) II. 26 Nothing final in Congress has been decided respecting the institution of a National Board of Agriculture. 1827 HOOD *Mids. Fairies* xxxiv, Time shall be final of all things. 1860 TYNDALL *Glac.* I. xii. 89 We made a series of final measurements.

b. ***final solution*** [tr. G. *endlösung*]: name given to the German policy, from 1941, of exterminating Jewish people in Europe; the process of massacring these victims.

1947 *Trial German Major War Criminals* (H.M.S.O.) XI. p. ix, Final solution of the Jewish question. 1949 D. MACARDLE *Children of Europe* vi. 110 As the 'final solution', camps fitted with gas-chambers, electrocution plants and huge crematoria were erected in Poland. 1953 G. REITLINGER (*title*) The final solution. 1961 *Observer* 17 Dec. 10/3 The formal adoption of the Final Solution, ordaining the extermination of European Jewry,.. on July 31, 1941.

4. Having regard to end or purpose: chiefly in ***final cause*** (see CAUSE *sb.* 4 b); ***final clause*** (Gram.), a clause expressing purpose or intention.

*c*1400 *Test. Love* II. (1560) 281 b/2 Aristotle supposeth that the actes of every thing been in a manner his finall cause. 1583 *Exec. for Treason* (1675) 42 The very causes final of these Rebellions.. have been to depose her Majesty from her Crown. 1606 *Sir G. Goosecappe* III. ii. in Bullen *O. Pl.* III. 53 Wer't not for women, who of all mens pompes Are the true final causes. 1878 MORLEY *Condorcet* Crit. Misc. 76 All predispositions are destined to develope themselves according to their final purpose. [See also CAUSE *sb.* 4 b.]

B. *sb.*

1. the adj. used *absol.* †**a.** ***for final*** = finally, conclusively. ***in final*** = in conclusion (*obs.*). **b.** That which comes last; completion, end, finish. Now *rare*.

*c*1374 CHAUCER *Troylus* IV. 145 Thembassadours ben answered for fynal. 1393 GOWER *Conf.* III. 383 And now to speke as in finall Touchend that I undertoke. 1582 N. LICHEFIELD tr. *Castanheda's Conq. E. Ind.* 20 b, Those two Pilots had.. trauailed to bring to finall and execution their diuellish intent. 1617 COLLINS *Def. Bp. Ely* II. x. 427 The heele is the finall, the bottome of Gods workemanship. 1854 SYD. DOBELL *Balder* xxv. 186 Finish each stern power To such an exquisite final that it ends A plumèd feeling.

2. In various applications due to elliptical uses of the adj.: e.g. **a.** The final letter of a word. †**b.** *Music.* (see quot. 1885). **c.** *Athletics.* The deciding game, heat, or trial. **d.** The last of a series of examinations; also *pl.* (Oxford *colloq.*).

1609 DOULAND *Ornith. Microl.* 15 Euery Song ending in the Finals, is regular and not transposed. *Ibid.* 41 Euery crooked Finall, whether it ascend or descend, is a Breefe. 1627 ABP. USSHER *Lett.* (1686) 383 Without any difference of Initials and Finals. 1880 A. GIBSON (*title*), Aids to the Final [Law examination]. 1880 *Amateur Athletic Assoc. Laws for Meetings* 21 The best three competitors of the first trial shall be allowed three more tries each for the final. 1885 W. S. ROCKSTRO in *Encycl. Brit.* XIX. 169/1 The intervals of each 'mode' [of plain chant] are derived from a fundamental sound, called its 'final.' (*Note.* Analogous to the tonic or key-note of the modern scale.) 1894 GRANT ALLEN in *Westm. Gaz.* 20 June 2/1 Taking a pass degree in Finals. *a*1897 *Mod.* The initials and finals of these words form a double acrostic. 1933 BLOOMFIELD *Lang.* viii. 132 In a form like *test* or *text* we call the [-t] a main final. 1963 [see ENVIRONMENT 2 c].

e. The last edition of an issue of a daily newspaper.

1931 *Sat. Rev.* 4 July 17/1 The difference between the English play called 'Inquest' and the American play called 'Late Night Final' is a fundamental one. 1938 F. THAYER *Newspaper Managem.* 82 The *Daily News* published nine regular editions as follows... Final.. 3:25 P.M.

finale (‖fi'nale, fɪ'nɑːleɪ). [It. *finale* adj. (used subst.):—L. *fīnālem*: see prec.]

1. *Music.* **a.** 'The last movement of a symphony, sonata, concerto, or other instrumental composition.' **b.** 'The piece of music with which any of the acts of an opera are brought to a close' (Grove).

[1724 *Explic. Foreign Words in Music* 31 *Fin*, *Finis*, or *Finale*, is the End or last Note of a Piece of Musick.] 1783 MAD. D'ARBLAY *Diary* 1 Jan., The conclusion [of the opera] is a long historical finale. 1784 *New Spect.* No. 21. 3/2 Several of them [the new airs] were encored, as was the finale. 1800 MRS. HERVEY *Mourtray Fam.* II. 147 He has treated me with the overture of the piece.. we shall have a grand *finale* at home. 1837 DICKENS *Pickw.* ii, The finale concluded, the dancers promenaded the room. 1866 ENGEL *Nat. Mus.* i. 10 Weber.. has introduced in the Finale of the first act, an Arabian melody. 1875 OUSELEY *Mus. Form* x. 51 A fugue on the original theme will often make a good finale to a set of variations.

fig. 1810 BENTHAM *Packing* (1821) 57 This, the finale of his praises, sounded in his ears.. by his sergeant trumpeter [etc.].

2. The last scene or closing part of a drama or any other public entertainment.

1814 BYRON *Let.* 14 Feb. in Moore *Life*, It doubtless gratifies me much that our *finale* has pleased, and that the curtain drops gracefully. 1851 LONGF. in *Life* (1891) II. 209 Scherb has promised to read his lecture on Faust by way of finale.

3. The conclusion, end; the final catastrophe. Also *transf.*

1785 MRS. A. M. BENNETT *Juv. Indiscr.* (1786) II. 114 Her finale of the matter was, that [etc.]. 1816 *Gentl. Mag.* LXXXVI. I. 60 In the real battle.. we are most pleased with the *finale*. 1821 SYD. SMITH *Wks.* (1859) I. 340/1 It seems to us no bad *finale* of the pious labours of those who [etc.]. 1874 L. TROUBRIDGE *Life amongst Troubridges* (1966) ix. 92 All the 'homeites' rush downstairs and the grand finale takes place. 1878 BOSW. SMITH *Carthage* 166 The natives remembered the crucifixion of 3000 of their countrymen, the finale of their.. attempt at revolt.

fi'nale, *v.* *intr.* *nonce-wd.* [f. prec.] To conclude, wind up.

1797 MRS. A. M. BENNETT *Beggar Girl* (1813) I. 199 Mrs. Brown.. generally finaled with, 'God knew, hundreds soon went'.

finalism ('faɪnəlɪz(ə)m). [f. FINAL *a.* and *sb.* + -ISM.] **1.** The belief that the end or limit has been reached.

1883 J. PARKER *Tyne Ch.* 18 The infallibility of this finalism was most obnoxious to a mind so strong-minded.

2. The doctrine that natural processes (e.g. evolutionary changes) are directed towards some end or goal.

1909 W. R. SORLEY *Interpr. Evol.* 24 'The organization of nature', says Kant, 'has in it nothing analogous to any causality we know'. It is not mechanism; nor, again, is it finalism. 1917 A. S. PRINGLE-PATTISON *Idea of God* xix. 370 He develops his own account of 'creative' evolution in contrast with the two rival theories of mechanism and finalism. 1952 G. SARTON *Hist. Sci.* I. xx. 515 The purpose of a being is revealed by the study of its genesis and evolution. We are falling back upon the theory of finalism (or teleology). 1966 *Philos.* XLI. 129 It only leaves the quite obvious streak of finalism in Hegel harder to understand.

finalist. [f. FINAL *a.* and *sb.* + -IST.]

1. One who believes that the end or limit has been reached.

1883 J. PARKER *Apost. Life* II. 265 They were not finalists; they felt that something more might be added to it.

2. Any of the competitors that are left in for the final contest; also, a candidate in the last of a series of examinations (see FINAL *sb.* 2 c and d).

1898 *Bury Times* 2 Nov. 2/3 Two of the finalists,.. just before the race started, publicly appealed to the Baths Committee to withdraw the objectionable clause. 1902 *Westm. Gaz.* 1 July 4/3 The finalists in the Gentlemen's Doubles Championships. 1906 *Daily Chron.* 25 May 1/7 The finalists in the Amateur Golf Championship. 1930 *Daily Express* 6 Sept. 2/3 Those aspidistras which seem possible finalists. 1959 *Times* 4 Feb. 2/3 Law Graduate or C.I.S. Finalist.. preferred. 1970 *Globe & Mail* (Toronto) 28 Sept. 29/3 (Advt.), Blue chip Toronto based mining firm requires an accounting graduate or finalist.

finalistic (faɪnə'lɪstɪk), *a.* [f. FINALIST + -IC.] Of or pertaining to finalism (sense 2).

1927 *Mod. Philology* Nov. 225 But the fact that we are not omniscient.. is no warrant for a finalistic hypothesis. 1958 *New Scientist* 16 Oct. 1076/3 The 'mechanistic' and the 'finalistic' descriptions of biological phenomena.

finality (faɪ'nælɪtɪ). [ad. Fr. *finalité*, ad. late L. *fīnālitātem*, f. *fīnālis*: see FINAL and -ITY.]

†**1.** An end in view; a guiding object. *Obs.*⁻¹

1541 R. COPLAND *Galyen's Terapeutyke* 2 D iv b, Thou shalt prepose two fynalytees of curacyon.

2. The relation of being an end or final cause; the principle of final cause viewed as operative in the universe.

1859 DARWIN in *Life & Lett.* (1887) II. 247 On the contrary he [Naudin] brings in his principle of finality. 1877 E. CAIRD *Philos. Kant* II. xii. 486 A relation between the parts of a living being, which can only be expressed by the category of finality.

3. The quality, condition, or fact of being final; the condition of being at the limit; also the belief that something is final. (First used in this sense with regard to the Reform Bill of 1832.)

1833 CROKER in *Croker Papers* (1884) II. 200 Althorp's explanation as to the finality.. of the Bill. 1842 GROVE *Corr. Phys. Forces* (1874) 160 Instead of approaching finality, the more we discover the more infinite appears the range of the undiscovered. 1846 S. B. WILLIAMS *Princ. Railw. Managem.* 26 Let us not devise our future works and arrangements with the idea of 'finality' to cramp our exertions. 1873 C. M. DAVIES *Unorth. Lond.* 167 They claim finality for the revelation of Emmanuel Swedenborg. 1878 BAYNE *Purit. Rev.* I. 21 Calvin.. fell into the error of finality.

b. *concr.* Something that is final, a final action, state, or utterance.

1833 JEFFREY in Ld. Cockburn *Life* I. 352 I have just taken my last peep into that.. heart-stirring House of Commons .. There is something sad in these finalities. 1859 HAWTHORNE *Fr. & It. Jrnls.* II. 293 I cannot bear to say that word as a finality. 1860 O. W. HOLMES *Elsie V.* 225 Each propagandist ready with his bundle of finalities.

4. *attrib.*

1839 *Tait's Mag.* VI. 630 John Russell.. To Reform he has been detrimental.. He is our own Finality John. 1844 DISRAELI *Coningsby* VI. iii, Odious distinctions were not drawn between Finality men and progressive Reformers. 1856 EMERSON *Eng. Traits, Lit.* Wks. (Bohn) II. 115 The perceptive class and the practical finality class are ever in counterpoise.

Hence **fi'nalityship**, *nonce wd.* (cf. quot. 1839 in 4).

1839 *Tait's Mag.* VI. 631 The vehement patriotic desire, entertained by his Finalityship [Lord J. Russell], to keep out the Radicals and the Tories.

finalize ('faɪnəlaɪz), *v.* [f. FINAL *a.* + -IZE.] *trans.* To complete, bring to an end, put in final form; to approve the final form of. Also occas. *intr.*, to bring something to completion, to conclude. Hence **ˌfinali'zation**, the action or process of finalizing; an instance of finalizing.

1922 *Private Let. Standard Publishing Co., Melbourne* (G. & C. Merriam Co. files) 4 May, Our Mr. S. Jaboor writing from New Zealand advises that he was in communication with you again in March last, with a view to our acting as your representatives in Australasia, and says that you are still finalizing matters with Mr. Forbes. 1926 J. DOONE *Timely Tips for New Australians* 7 The established usage of the word 'finalise' (to complete) is.. illustrative of the Australian variations of the English language... To 'finalise a deal' is an expression in daily use throughout the island-continent. 1927 *U.S. Naval Inst. Proc.* May 606 Communication tests are being continued, and negotiations are proceeding in relation to finalised traffic arrangements. 1930 *John o' London's* 25 Jan. 656/1 The plaintiff.. complained that her lover had promised to marry her but failed to 'finalize' matters. 1931 *Times* 26 Mar. 14 (Austral. correspondent) It is expected that these motions will be carried, thus finalizing the split between the New South Wales and the Federal organizations. 1936 F. CLUNE *Roaming round Darling* x. 90 Banjo.. finalizes: And on misty moonlight evenings, while the dingoes howl around, [etc.]. 1936 P. MONCRIEFF *N.Z. Birds* (ed. 2) p. xii, Finalization of our New Zealand species has by no means been reached. 1937 I. L. IDRIESS *Forty Fathoms Deep* (1941) 51 If we don't finalize tonight, those two coons will get suspicious and sell to someone else. 1945 *Devel. & Welfare in West Indies 1943–1944* (Colonial No. 189. 1945), The plans for British Guiana and British Honduras have not yet been finalized, but those of the former colony are well advanced. 1952 *N.Y. Times* 17 Feb. 29 Other efforts which will lead to the finalization of a sound doctrine set forth in service manuals. 1953 N. BIRKETT *Magic of Words* 8 When I hear of.. things being adumbrated, or visualized, or finalized.. I think of that other aim of this [English] Association, 'To uphold the standards of English writing or speech.' 1955 *Times* 15 July 15/2 Our claims for refund of taxation.. were finalized with the Inland Revenue, resulting in a net repayment of £76,347. 1960 *New Left Review* Nov.–Dec. 12/2, I personally would not agree to any finalisation of those matters with two powers... Only this assembly should finalise them. 1966 *New Statesman* 18 Feb. 215/3 If Russia does finalise her break with China soon, [etc.]. 1971 *Financial Mail* (Johannesburg) 26 Feb. 719/1 Subject to

finalisation of certain conditions they had agreed to acquire the trading assets.

finally (ˈfaɪnəlɪ), *adv.* Also 4 **fynaly**, 5–6 **-ally**, 5 **fynallich**. [f. FINAL *a.* + -LY[2].]

1. In the end, lastly, at last, ultimately.

c **1374** CHAUCER *Troylus* III. 1006 For þer-with mene I fynaly þe peyne..Fully to slen. *c* **1400** *Beryn* 1521 Fynallich, to the end of hir accordement. **1447** BOKENHAM *Seyntys* (Roxb.) 2 What was the entent Of the auctour fynally. *a* **1533** LD. BERNERS *Huon* lix. 206 Fynally the forse of the paynyms was so gret that at length they coude not abyde it. *a* **1610** HEALEY *Cebes* (1636) 134 And finally, confirmeth the body in perfect soundnesse. **1729** BUTLER *Serm.* Wks. 1874 II. 36 Evil prevailing finally over good. **1825** J. NEAL *Bro. Jonathan* I. 8 Finally, after having beaten him at everything else, he beat him at his own..game. **1860** TYNDALL *Glac.* I. ix. 64 We finally swerved to the right.

b. Indicating the last point or conclusion of a discourse, treatise, etc.

1526 *Pilgr. Perf.* (W. de W. 1531) 2 Fynally, I beseche all..to pray for me wretche. **1611** BIBLE 2 Cor. xiii. 11 Finally, brethren, farewell. **1743** J. MORRIS *Serm.* vii. 206 Finally, let us all fear God.

quasi-*sb.* **1874** ALDRICH *Prud. Palfrey* x. (1885) 164 The poor old parson's interminable ninthlies and finallies.

2. So as to make a complete end; in a manner not to be reversed or altered; once for all, decisively, conclusively.

c **1400** *Destr. Troy* 10802 Lest his folke in the feld were fynally distroyet. **1512** *Act 4 Hen. VIII* c. 18 §14 All manner of Officers..[shall] be utterlye acquyted & fynallye discharged for ever. **1650** FULLER *Pisgah* III. ix. 430 Devils he cast out of men so finally, that they entred no more into them. *a* **1716** SOUTH *Serm.* (1737) II. 229 Many men are finally lost. **1801** FOSTER in *Life & Corr.* (1846) I. 130 Finally settle the great account. **1884** *Manch. Exam.* 28 May 5/4 The arrangement..would..deal finally and effectually with a national question.

finance (fɪ-, faɪˈnæns, ˈfaɪ-), *sb.*[1] Forms: 5 fenaunce, 5–6 fin-, fynaunce, (5 fynance), 5– finance. [a. OF. *finance*, n. of action f. *finer* to end, to settle a dispute or a debt, pay ransom, to bargain for, to furnish, procure, f. *fin*: see FINE *sb.* The senses now current are adopted from mod.Fr.

Johnson 1755 and some mod. Dicts. mark the stress on the first syllable, though all editions of Bailey (1721–90) have the stress on the second syllable; 'now usual' (N.E.D., 1897).]

†**1.** Ending, an end. *Obs. rare.*

a **1400** *Cov. Myst.* (1841) 223 God, that alle thynge dede make of nowth..puttyst each creature to his fenaunce. **1616** in BULLOKAR.

†**2. a.** Settlement with a creditor; payment of a debt; compensation or composition paid or exacted. *Obs.*

c **1400** *Beryn* 2534 To make for yeur wrongis to ȝew riȝte hiȝe fenaunce. **14..** *Lament, Mary Magd.* (*Chaucer's Wks.* 1561), There is no more, but dethe is my fynaunce. *c* **1470** HENRY *Wallace* VIII. 926 Thar finance maid, delyuerit gold full sone.

b. *esp.* A payment for release from captivity or punishment; a ransom. Phrase, ***to put to*** (***one's***) ***finance*** = Fr. *mettre à finance*. *Obs.*

1439 *Rolls Parl.* V. 22/1 Where as the seid Countesse.. hath made a Lone of a MCCli. to the seid Erle of Somerset, for the payment of his fenaunce. **1475** *Bk. Noblesse* 14 The said King Johan was put to finaunce and raunsom of thre millions of scutis of gold. **1523** LD. BERNERS *Froiss.* I. cccxi. 193 Yᵉ other knyghtes..were put to their fynaunce. **1568** GRAFTON *Chron.* II. 120 The sayde Foulkes after he had lyen a certaine of tyme in prison, was for his finance delivered. **1597** *Guistard & Sismond* B ij, I for your finaunce give that ye love best.

†**3.** Supply (of goods); stock of money; treasure, substance. ***to make finance*** [= OF. *faire finance*]: to furnish supplies. *Obs.*

1475 *Bk. Noblesse* 9 Thoroughe lak of provision of men of armes, tresour, and finaunce of suffisaunt nombre of goodes. **1489** *Act Dom. Conc.* 129 That nain of thaim..supple the said James in making of fynance or vtherwais. **1502** *Ord. Crysten Men* (W. de W. 1506) IV. xxi. 225 Yf the procurer or tuter of ony faderlesse chyldren gyueth theyr fynaunce unto usurye. **1692–1732** in COLES.

†**4.** Borrowing of money at interest. *Obs.*

1552 CHAMBERLAIN *Let.* 8 Jan. in Strype *Eccl. Mem.* II. xiii. 349 The Emperor..sought..to have what he could by finance and other means. **1721** STRYPTE *Ibid.* II. xiii. 350 There was no money to be had at finance in Antwerp under 16 in the hundred for one year.

†**5.** A tax; taxation; the revenues of a sovereign or state (in *pl.* passing into 6). *Obs.*

1489 CAXTON *Faytes of A.* III. xiv. 200 A prynce..ought before hande to..see where and how hys fynaunce shal be made and taken. **1548** HALL *Chron.* (1809) 161 In like robes folowed the Lordes..of the finaunce. *c* **1598** LAMBARDE *Office of Alienations* in Bacon's Wks. 1778 II. 401 All the finances or revenues of the imperial crown..be either extraordinary or ordinary. **1670** COTTON *Espernon* II. VII. 306 Bulion..Sur-Intendant of the Finances.

6. *pl.* The pecuniary resources, **a.** *primarily*, of a sovereign or state; **b.** *transf.* of a company or an individual.

a. 1781 GIBBON *Decl. & F.* II. 33 To their wisdom was committed the supreme administration of justice and of the finances. **1845** MCCULLOCH *Taxation* III. ii. (1852) 444 The management of the finances of a great nation.

b. 1739 CIBBER *Apol.* (1756) I. 169 The finances of the other house held it not above one season more. **1766** COWPER *Wks.* (1837) XV. 13 My finances will never be able to satisfy these craving necessities. **1783** FOX *Sp. E. India Bill* 1 Dec. in *Sp.* (1815) II. 247 The finances of the East India company. **1842** BARHAM *Ingol. Leg., Sir Rupert* 16 These, and a few less defensible fancies Brought the Knight to the end of his slender finances.

¶**c.** Expenditure. ? *nonce-use.*

1730 GAY *Let. to Swift* 6 Dec. (1766) II. 118 The duchess is a more severe check upon my finances than ever you were.

7. The management of money, *esp.* public money; the science which concerns itself with the levying and application of revenue in a state, corporation, etc. †***man of finance*** = FINANCIER.

1770 *Junius Lett.* xxxix. 201 His first enterprise in finance. **1814** WELLINGTON in Gurw. *Desp.* XII. 119 The law on finance yesterday passed the House of Peers. **1816** BENTHAM *Law Taxes* Wks. 1843 II. 581 It is too much to expect of a man of finance, that [etc.]. **1845** MCCULLOCH *Taxation* III. i. (1852) 417 No scheme of finance can be bottomed on sound principles which disguises these necessary consequences of war.

8. *attrib.* and *Comb.*, as ***finance-chamber***, ***committee***, ***-minister*** (sense 7); †***finance-making*** vbl. sb. (sense 2 b); **finance bill**, a legislative bill containing financial provisions; **finance company**, **house**, a company that is primarily concerned with the financing of hire-purchase transactions.

1901 L. H. COURTNEY *Working Const. U.K.* 24 What used to be called the Customs and Inland Revenue Bill, received in 1894 the name of the *Finance Bill. **1959** *Chambers's Encycl.* X. 451/1 Even finance bills are often declared not to be money bills. **1971** *Money Which?* Mar. 4/1 The tax changes the Chancellor proposes in his speech are set out in detail in the Finance Bill—published about a fortnight later. **1845** S. AUSTIN *Ranke's Hist. Ref.* III. 251 The emperor had ..been required to restore to the empire its *finance chambers (Kammern). **1807** *Morn. Chron.* in *Spir. Publ. Jrnls.* (1808) XI. 112 That *Finance Committee. **1926** *Economist* 9 Oct. 576/2 This credit is passed on by the sellers of the goods either to banks with which they have established relations or to one of the many '*finance' companies which have been established solely to cater for this sort of business. **1968** *Listener* 6 June 725/2 Large companies..in turn are often owned by finance companies much larger than themselves. **1929** *Economist* 27 July 181/2 He declared that the hostility at one time evoked by the idea of hire-purchase or installment selling was passing..and that the long-term credit bank or *finance house had an essential contribution to make to the national welfare. **1958** *Spectator* 22 Aug. 262/3 A Birmingham hire-purchase finance house. *a* **1467** GREGORY *Chron.* 152 Withowte anny of *fynaunce makynge or ramsom. **1790** BURKE *Fr. Rev.* Wks. 1808 V. 405 The plain obvious duty of a common *finance minister. **1845** MCCULLOCH *Taxation* III. iii. (1852) 468 Our finance ministers can claim no credit for peculiar.. ability in this respect.

†**finance**, *sb.*[2] *Sc. Obs.* Also 6 **fynance**. [? a. AF. **finance*, f. *finer* to refine, f. *fin* FINE *a.*] Fineness (of precious metals).

1473 *Sc. Acts Jas. III* (1814) II. 105/1 Þe new pennyis.. haue þe course..vnto þe tyme þat þe fynance of þame be knawne. **1478** *Ibid.* (1814) II. 118/2 His hienes..sall..mak a sett & Reuyle [rule] of his moneye baith gold & siluer of þe wecht & finance þat It sall halde. **1555** *Sc. Act. Mary* (1814) II. 499/1 That na goldsmyth mak..siluer vnder the iust fynance of elleuin penny fyne vnder the pane of deid.

finance (fɪ-, faɪˈnæns), *v.* [f. FINANCE *sb.*[1]]

†**1. a.** *trans.* To put to ransom. **b.** *intr.* To pay ransom. *Obs.*

1478 *Plumpton Corr.* p. lxii, Some of them labored and treated by them to make them fynance, as they had bene the Kings enemies. **1494** FABYAN *Chron.* VII. 562 [They] caryed away with theym many of the cytezeyns, beynge ryche, and fynauncyd theym at great summes of money.

2. *trans.* To furnish with finances or money; to find capital for.

1866 *Times* 2 Feb. 7/5 To finance a business..a new verb ..is to supply it with capital to make a daring speculation. **1883** F. P. HENRY in *Law Times* 28 July 247/2 It was alleged that Manning..had financed or backed Hannam, a cattle dealer, lending him money to trade with.

3. *intr.* To conduct or engage in financial operations, to manage monetary affairs; to provide oneself with capital.

1827 [see next]. **1885** *Daily News* 12 Feb. 5/7 He financed, in the most successful manner, with paper money.

Hence **fiˈnancing** *vbl. sb.*; also *attrib.*

1827 HONE *Every-day Bk.* II. 12 They [our ancestors] had no counting-houses, no ledgers, no commerce, no.. financing. **1866** *Morn. Star* 17 Mar., The old board allowed this man to do what was sometimes called financing. **1881** CARLYLE in Froude *Life in Lond.* II. xxiv. 481 Those millions you have heaped together with your financing work.

financeer, var. of FINANCIER *v.*

†**fiˈnancer**. *Obs.* [f. FINANCE *sb.* + -ER[1].] = FINANCIER 1.

a. 1630 *R. Johnson's Kingd. & Commw.* 166 His Financers and Officers used for the collection. **1656** BLOUNT *Glossogr*, *Financer*, an Exchequer-man, Receiver, Under-Treasurer or Teller in the Exchequer. **1666** *Lond. Gaz.* No. 37/2 The Financers and Partisans were here [Paris] for some time in a little ease. **1769** GOLDSM. *Hist. Rome* I. 421 The financers or farmers of the public revenue.

financial (fɪˈnænʃəl), *a.* [f. as prec. + -(I)AL.]

1. Of, pertaining, or relating to finance or money matters. ***financial year***: the annual period for which accounts are made up.

1769 BURKE *State of Nation* Wks. 1808 II. 112, I shall make no objections whatsoever, logical or financial, to this reasoning. **1812** G. CHALMERS *Dom. Econ. Gt. Brit.* 102 A financial operation was performed..which gradually relieved the embarrassments of the State. **1861** LINCOLN in Raymond *Life* 168 The financial year ending on the 30th of June 1861. **1882** MISS BRADDON *Mt. Royal* I. i. 16 She had hardly ever given a thought to her financial position.

2. Of a member in a society: That pays (his subscription), 'paying' as opposed to 'honorary'. Also, that is not in arrear with his payments.

1892 *Daily News* 29 Feb. 5/5 The Miners' Federation.. contains in round numbers 180,000 paying or 'financial' members, as they are called, among the 'bottom workers'.

3. In possession of money. *Austral.* and *N.Z. slang.*

1926 J. DOONE *Timely Tips for New Australians* 11 In Australia, to describe a man as being 'financial' is to describe him as being possessed of means. **1936** M. E. C. SCOTT *Barbara & N.Z. Backblocks* 96 Paddy, who had been harvesting for neighbours, was magnificently financial. **1940** W. S. GILKISON *Peaks, Packs & Mountain Tracks* 104 In my 'varsity days I dragged my old 'omnibus' over many a trail where, had I been more financial, I would surely have saved myself much trouble and toil by employing motor car or pack-horse. **1961** P. WHITE *Riders in Chariot* xi. 410 'Shall I tell you, Alf,' he called, 'how us girls got to be financial?'

Hence **fiˈnancially** *adv.*, in relation to financial matters, from a financial point of view.

1795 BURKE *Thoughts on Scarcity* Wks. 1808 VII. 414, I consider..the stopping of the distillery, œconomically, financially, commercially..as a measure rather well meant than well considered. **1864** BP. OF LINCOLN *Charge* 5 Financially, the diminution of grants received..has not been..great. **1882** *Macm. Mag.* XLVI. 439 Progress in this respect must be attempted only when financially safe.

financialist (fɪˈnænʃəlɪst). [f. FINANCIAL + -IST.] = FINANCIER 2.

1864 *Daily Tel.* 27 Apr., The astute financialist who created this great agency [the Crédit Mobilier]. **1884** *Truth* 4 Sept. 374/2 Certain great cosmopolitan financialists who hold large amounts of Unified Bonds.

financian (fɪˈnænʃɪən). *rare*[−0]. [f. FINANCE *sb.* + -(I)AN.] = FINANCIER.

1846 WORCESTER (citing *Month. Rev.*).

†**fiˈnancical**, *a. Obs. rare.* [f. as prec. + -IC + -AL[1].] = FINANCIAL.

1800 *Ann. Reg.* 230 The financical difficulties of France.. formed the proximate cause. [And elsewhere in same vol.]

financier (fɪˈnænsɪə(r)). [a. F. *financier*, f. *finance*: see FINANCE *sb.*[1]]

†**1.** *Fr. Hist.* An administrator, collector, or farmer of taxes before the Revolution. *Obs.*

1678 in PHILLIPS App. **1741** HUME *Ess.* xv. 185 The only Gainers by it [the oppressive fiscal system in France] are the *Financiers*, a Race of Men..hated by..the whole Kingdom. **1755** JOHNSON *Dict.*, *Financier* [in italics as a foreign word], one who collects and farms the public revenue.

2. One who is concerned with finance; one who is skilled in levying and managing public money.

1618 BACON *Let. to Jas. I*, 2 Jan. Wks. (Spedding) XIII. 453, I..whom only love and duty to your majesty..hath made a financier. **1681** COLVIL *Whigs Supplic.* (1751) 136 So we may prove Financiers thieves. **1770** LD. MALMESBURY *Diaries & Corr.* (1844) I. 52 His [Charles III of Spain] own subjects are starving, and his financiers are at their wits' ends. **1790** BURKE *Fr. Rev.* 330 The objects of a financier are ..to secure an ample revenue; to impose it with judgment.. to employ it œconomically [etc.]. **1824** BYRON *Juan* XVI. xcviii, Most orators, but very few financiers. **1874** GREEN *Short Hist.* ix. §10. 710 Walpole..was the first English Minister who was a great financier.

3. A capitalist concerned in financial operations.

1867 *Pall Mall G.* 26 July 7 A financial combination of London financiers and financial houses. **1880** DISRAELI *Endym.* xxxviii, Forty years ago the great financiers had not that..position in society which they possess at present.

Hence **fiˈnanciery**, the practice or occupation of a financier.

1881 *Blackw. Mag.* CXXIX. 176 Speculative customers who had an instinctive *flaire* for accommodating financiery, began to find him out.

financier (ˌfɪnænˈsɪə(r)). *v.* Also **financeer**. [f. prec. sb.; first in vbl. sb. and ppl. adj. *financiering*, after *engineering*, etc.] **a.** *intr.* To play the part of a financier; to conduct financial operations. Chiefly in contemptuous use; now often (*esp.* in *U.S.*), to swindle, cheat. Also quasi-trans. ***to financier away***, ***out of***. **b.** *trans.* = FINANCE *v.* 2. Hence **finanˈciering** *vbl. sb.* and *ppl. a.*

1800 *Morn. Chron.* in *Spirit Pub. Jrnls.* (1801) IV. 163 Your financiering genius. **1822** *Examiner* 290/1 The unspeakable financiering of the 'heaven-born'. **1843** *Blackw. Mag.* LIV. 245 The financiering economist of 'cheese parings and candle ends'. **1864** CARLYLE *Fredk. Gt.* IV. XVI. vii. 339 Expenditures and financierings. **1865** *Ibid.* VI. XX. vi. 147 Endless sore business he doubtless has, of recruiting, financiering, watching and providing. **1864** SALA in *Daily Tel.* 27 Sept., At least one-fifth of the five millions of dollars..has been 'financiered' away to private uses. **1865** —— *Diary in Amer.* I. 129 He tried hard..to financeer us out of an additional forty cents. **1884** *N.Y. Herald* 27 Oct. 4/3 Railroad construction and financiering. **1892** *Harper's Mag.* Feb. 429/2 This region..does its financiering in Chicago. **1894** *Daily News* 3 Oct. 6/5 Intent upon persuading her husband to financeer the Onofalga Company.

financist (fɪˈnænsɪst). [f. FINANCE *sb.*[1] + -IST.] = FINANCIER *sb.* 2 and 3.

1881 *Daily News* 18 Nov. 5/4 Financists hastened a little what must have happened soon or late. **1887** *Ibid.* 30 May 5/4 The financists..wanted to keep their concession. **1888** *Univ. Rev.* Oct. 218 Mexico was looked upon as an El Dorado by the financists of the St. Simonian school.

†**financy.** *Obs. rare.* [f. F. *finance*: see FINANCE *sb.*[1] and -ANCY.] = FINANCE *sb.*[1] 3, 6.

1656 in BLOUNT *Glossogr.* [citing BACON]. **1727** ARBUTHNOT *Anct. Coins, Diss. Navig.* 227 When he was straitned in his Financies at the Siege of Byzantium.

finary, obs. f. FINERY[2] a puddling furnace.

‖**finca** (ˈfiːŋkə, ˈfɪ-). [Sp., f. *fincar*: see FICCHE *v.*] In Spain and Spanish America: landed property, (country) estate; a ranch.

1909 in *Cent. Dict.* Suppl. **1922** *Glasgow Herald* 18 Apr. 3 Ministerial 'conclaves' at Andalucian fincas. **1934** A. HUXLEY *Beyond Mexique Bay* 147 A few years ago..the coffee *fincas* were in full production. **1955** *Sci. News Let.* 8 Jan. 26/2 From these mountain coffee 'fincas' come 15,000 to 20,000 tons of coffee a year. **1963** W. MCGIVERN *Choice of Assassins* (1964) iii. 31 The few wealthy men of the village had come down from their *fincas*..for the Sunday bullfights in Málaga.

finch (fɪnʃ). Forms: 1 finc, 5–6 fynche, 4– finch. [OE. *finc* str. masc. = MDu. *vinke* (Du. *vink*), OHG. *fincho* wk. masc. (MHG. *vinke*, Ger. *fink*); not recorded in ON. (Sw. *fink*, Da. *finke*).

The OTeut. **finki-z*, *finkjon-*, would correspond to a pre-Teut. **ping-*, which Fick finds in Gr. πίγγα young bird (Hesych.), and in various Indo-European words denoting colour: OSl. *pęgŭ* particoloured, Skr. *pinga* brown, reddish, also young animal, *pinjára* gold-coloured, *pingalá* brown, brown animal (cf. Gr. πίγγαλος lizard). Cf. also SPINK, the chaffinch = Gr. σπίγγος and σπίζα (:—**spingja*). Of similar sound and meaning, but not demonstrably connected, are F. *pinson*, Sp. *pinchon*, *pinzon*, Catal. *pinsá*, It. *pincione*:—med.Lat. *pinciōn-em*; also Welsh *pinc*, Eng. dial. *pink*, Breton *pint*, *tint*, the chaffinch; and Russian *penka* willow-wren (and cognates in other mod. Slav. langs.) It seems possible that some at least of these words are of echoic origin; the call-note of the male chaffinch is, in England, often represented as 'spink' or 'pink'.]

1. a. A name given to many small birds of the order *Passeres*, esp. to those of the genus *Fringilla* or family *Fringillidæ*. † *to pull a finch*: to swindle an ignorant or unsuspecting person (cf. *to pluck a pigeon*).

a **700** *Epinal Gloss.* 423 Fringella, finc. *c* **1050** *Ags. Voc.* in Wr.-Wülcker 286 *Fringilla*, finc. *c* **1386** CHAUCER *Prol.* 654 Ful prively a finch eke coude he pull. *c* **1400** *Rom. Rose* 658 In many places were nyghtyngales, Alpes, fynches, and wodewales. *c* **1532** DEWES *Introd. Fr.* in *Palsgr.* 912 The fynche, *le pinchon.* **1590** SHAKS. *Mids. N.* III. i. 133. **1655** MOUFET & BENNET *Health's Improv.* (1746) 188 Finches for the most part live upon Seeds. **1720** GAY *Poems* (1745) II. 176 And pecking finches scoop the golden rind. **1847** LYTTON *Lucretia* 31 The linnet and finch sang still from the neighbouring copses. **1878** BROWNING *Poets Croisic* 71 Brisk as any finch He twittered.

b. With defining words, forming popular names of species of *Fringillidæ* and of other birds of similar appearance, as **fallow finch**, the wheat-ear; **mountain finch**, the brambling; **purple finch** (U.S.), (see quot. 1884); **storm finch**, the stormy petrel; **thistle finch** (= F. *chardonneret*), **yellow finch**, rare names for the goldfinch. Also BULLFINCH, CHAFFINCH, GOLDFINCH, GREENFINCH.

1678 RAY *Willughby's Ornith.* 255 The great pied Mountain-Finch..is of the bigness of a yellow Finch. **1708** MOTTEUX *Rabelais* IV. lix. (1737) 244 Snytes..Thistle-Finches. **1768** PENNANT *Zool.* II. 434 Like the storm-finch, they are dispersed over the whole Atlantic ocean. *a* **1826** LONGF. *Autumn* 23 The purple finch. **1828** STARK *Elem. Nat. Hist.* I. 245 The Mountain Finch. **1884** COUES *N. Amer. Birds* (ed. 2) 346 *Carpodacus purpureus*, Purple Finch (better Crimson Finch). *Ibid.* 347 *C. Cassini*..Cassin's Purple Finch.

c. *S. Afr.* = WEAVER[1] 4. Cf. FINK *sb.*[1]

1801 J. BARROW *Trav. S. Afr.* I. iv. 247 Different species of small birds, chiefly sparrows, finches, and grossbeaks. **1833** S. KAY *Trav. Caffraria* iii. 85 The long-tailed finches ..were here seen flying about. **1944** *Cape Times* 14 Oct. 6/7 Cape canaries, finches (their woven nests are hanging from the trees this month) and bush doves. **1963** MACKWORTH-PRAED & GRANT *Birds S. Third Afr.* II. 673 Southern Africa is very well supplied with Finches, particularly in the south.

2. *attrib.* and *Comb.*, as †*finch-bird*, *-tribe*. Also † **finch-egg**, a contemptuous epithet.

1552 HULOET, Finche byrde, *achantis.* **1606** SHAKS. *Tr. & Cr.* V. i. 41 *Patr.* Out, gall! *Ther.* Finch Egge! **1802** BINGLEY *Anim. Biog.* (1813) II. 168 Of the Finch tribe in general.

finch, obs. form of FINISH *v.*

ˈ**finch-backed,** *a.* ? *Obs.* = next.

1796 W. MARSHALL *Midland Counties* Gloss., Finch-backed, white on the back; as cattle.

finched (fɪnʃt), *ppl. a.* [? f. FINCH + -ED[2]; but the meaning is not accounted for.] (See quots.)

1786 CULLEY *Live Stock* 56 They [Long-horned Cattle].. have (in general) a white streak or lace along their back, which the breeders term finched. **1794** WEDGE *Agric. Surv. Chester* 31 Their [cows'] prevailing colours are red, brindled and pied; with almost universally 'finched', or white backs. **1825** in LOUDON *Encycl. Agric.* §6108. 954 (quoting CULLEY).

finchery (ˈfɪnʃərɪ). [f. FINCH + -ERY.] A place for finches, a decoy.

1887 *Eng. Illust. Mag.* Sept. 779, 4,425 finches were caught in this finchery alone.

†ˈ**finction.** *Obs. rare.* [a. OF. *finction*, *fincion*, ad. vulgar L. **finctiōn-em* (class. L. *fictiōnem*): see FICTION *sb.*] A fiction, invention.

a **1529** SKELTON *Image Ipocr.* II. 283 That frames his finctions Into distinctions.

†ˈ**fincture.** *Obs.* [ad. It. *finctura* (mod. *fintura*), a. vulgar L. **finctūra*, f. *fingĕre* to FEIGN. Cf. OF. *finture.*] = FEINT *sb.* 1 a.

1595 SAVIOLO *Practice* H iv a, If he use any fincture or false thrust, answer him not. **1599** MARSTON *Sco. Villanie* III. xi. 226 Of counter times, finctures, sly passataes.

find (faɪnd), *sb.* [f. next vb.]

1. An act or instance of finding; in hunting language, the finding of a fox, etc.; in wider use, a discovery, e.g. of minerals, treasure, archæological remains, etc. Somewhat *colloq.*

1825 SOUTHEY *Let.* 30 Aug. (1856) III. 498, I only hope 'twill fit the man that finds it. And a good find he had; for it [a hat] was a new one. **1852** W. JERDAN *Autobiog.* I. 157 The public, as fox-hunters say, shall have the benefit of the 'find'. **1868** G. STEPHENS *Runic Mon.* I. 195 We need not despair of fresh finds. **1883** E. PENNELL-ELMHIRST *Cream Leicestersh.* 299 They realised the find of a fox. **1884** *The American* VII. 220 The Paris *Figaro* announces a 'find' of letters by Beaumarchais. **1887** R. MURRAY *Geol. Victoria* 159 The Frying-pan gold-field, where some good finds were made.

2. a. *concr.* That which is found.

1847 in HALLIWELL. **1858** MCCOMBIE *Hist. Victoria* xv. 218 The great 'finds' of gold were..first discovered on the old Golden Point on Forest Creek. **1865** LUBBOCK *Preh. Times* i. (1869) 12 Bronze weapons are entirely absent from the great finds of the Iron Age.

b. A person who is 'discovered' or brought to public notice; a valuable discovery. orig. *U.S.*

1890 *Sporting Life* (Phila.) 8 Jan. 7/1 As to Secretary Rogers' two 'finds', Day and Anderson, little can be said in their favor. **1914** R. GRAU *Theatre of Science* 139 Miss Snow ..must be set down as a Thanhouser 'find'. **1915** GALSWORTHY *Punch & Go*, Miss Hellgrove's a find, I think. **1917** W. OWEN *Let.* 14 Oct. (1967) 499 Graves was mightily impressed, and considers me a kind of *Find*!!

3. *a sure find*; **a.** *Sporting*, a place where a 'find' is sure to be made; **b.** *colloq.* one who or something which is sure to be found.

1838 THACKERAY *Yellowplush Papers* vii, His son was a sure find (as they say) during his illness. **1866** H. W. WHEELWRIGHT *Sporting Sketches* 335 There are certain.. coverts which are sure finds.

4. *Comb.*, as **find-place** = *find-spot*; **find-spot**, the place of finding.

1939 *Burlington Mag.* Oct. p. vi/1 A map showing find-places and centres of manufacture. **1962** *N. & Q.* Dec. 450/2 Drake was unable to learn the exact find-place. **1971** E. OKASHA *Hand-list of Anglo-Saxon Non-Runic Inscr.* 43 Find-place and date, where known, with brief details of the find. **1876** J. FERGUSSON *Indian Archit.* I. vii. 170 *note*, He could only ascertain the 'find spot' of five or six [specimens]. **1938** *Oxoniensia* III. 49 Mortarium. Hard white ware, colour-washed. Find-spot unrecorded. Early second century. **1960** K. M. KENYON *Archæol. in Holy Land* i. 33 The Samaria ostraca..provide limits for the reigns of the king to which they refer, but their find-spot was not accurately recorded with reference to the structural phases of the town.

find (faɪnd), *v.* *Pa. t.* and *pple.* found (faʊnd). Forms: α. 1. find-an, 2–4 find-en, 3–7 finde, fynd(e(n, 2–4 *south.* vinde, vynde, (2 fundan, 3 findin, feind, 5 fende, fyne, 9 *dial.* fine, *Sc.* and *north.* 3–9 fin, 4–5 fon(d), 3– find. *β.* 1 ȝefindan, 2–3 ifinden, *south.* ivinden, 4 ifind, yfynde. *Pa. t. sing.* α. 1 fand, also wk. form funde, 4 *south.* vand, 3–4 faand, 1–5 fond, (3–5 fonde, 3 *south.* vond, 4–5 foond, 3–5 fande, funde, 5 faunde, 6 fund), 3–6 founde, 5– found, (4 fon, funn, 5 fune, 5–8 *Sc.* fand, 9 *dial.* fan), *β.* 2–3 ȝe-, ifund(e, *south.* ivunde, 3 ifond, -nt. *south.* ivond, 5 yfonde, 3–5 i-, yfound(e. *pl.* 1 fundon, (2 fyndon), 2–4 -en, 3–7 founden, (4 found-, fundyn, 6 *Sc.* fundin), 4–5 fonden, 3–5 founde, 5– found, *Sc.* 4– fand, (9 *dial.* fant). *β.* 2–3 ifunden. *Pa. pple.* α. 1–5 funden, (3 fundun), 4–6 founde, (4 fownde, 4–5 founden, fond(en, -in, -yn), 5– found; (also 4 fonte, 5 fon, 8 *dial.* fawnd, *Sc.* 4–6 fundin, -yn, 6 -ing, 4–9 fun, 9 fan, fund). *β.* 1 ȝefunden, 3 ifonden, ifunde(n, 4 yfounde(n, *south.* yvonde. [A Com. Teut. str. vb.: OE. *findan* (pa. t. *fand*, *fǫnd*, pl. *fundon*, pa. pple. *funden*) = OFris. *finda*, OS. *findan*, *fīthan* (MDu., Du. *vinden*), OHG. *findan* (MHG. *vinden*, mod.G. *finden*), ON. *finna* (Sw. *finna*, Da. *finde*), Goth. *finþan*, f. Teut. root **finþ-*:—pre-Teut. **pent-* whence OIrish *étaim* I find.

Some regard this *pent-* as a nasalized form (with an *n* originally belonging to the present stem only) of the root *pet-* of L. *petĕre* to seek, aim at. Others would identify it with the widely represented Indo-European root *pent-* (:*pont-*, *pnt-*) to go, journey, whence OTeut. **fanþjon* (OHG. *fendo*, OE. *fēða*) footsoldier, pedestrian; on this supposition the development of sense is similar to that of L. *invenire* to come upon, to find.

The OTeut. conjugation, *finþan*, *fanþ-*, *fundum*, *fundono-* (Goth. *funþum*, *funþans* are due to the analogy of the forms with *þ*), should by phonetic law have yielded OE. **fīðan*, **fōð*, *fundon*, *funden*; as this would have been an apparently unique ablaut-series the vb. was naturally affected by the analogy of vbs. like *bindan*, *grindan*, *windan*. For the short forms *fin*, *fan*, *fun* (chiefly *Sc.*) and for the survival of *fand* as pa. t. cf. remarks on BIND.]

I. To come upon by chance or in the course of events.

1. a. *trans.* To come across, fall in with, meet with, light upon. Primarily of persons, and implying perception of the object encountered; hence of things viewed as agents.

Beowulf 2136 (Gr.) Ic..grundhyrde fond. *a* **1000** *Boeth. Metr.* xiii. 38 Seo leo..Nimð eall ðæt hio fint. *c* **1175** *Lamb. Hom.* 83 Þe sunne scineð þurh þe glesne ehþurl..and ho nimeð al swuch hou alse ho þer on vint. *Ibid.* 107 He mei findan fele þe beoð bet iþoȝen and istoȝen þene he. *c* **1205** LAY. 12303 Heo..iuunden þene king þær he wes an slæting. *a* **1300** *Cursor M.* 1183 (Cott.) Quen adam abel bodi fand For soru on fote moght he noght stand. *c* **1394** *P. Pl. Crede* 631 Whoso for-gabbed a frere y-founden at þe stues. *c* **1400** MAUNDEV. (Roxb.) viii. 29 In þat ryuer er oft tymes funden many precious stanes. *c* **1489** CAXTON *Sonnes of Aymon* xxiv. 526 Men shold fynde in the worlde but fewe suche knyghtes as he is one. **1513** DOUGLAS *Æneis* VIII. ii. *heading*, The sow with grisis..Eneas fand. **1660** BOYLE *New Exp. Phys. Mech.* xxxv. (1682) 138 Which impels the water it findes in its way. **1705** ADDISON *Italy* Pref., Many new Subjects that a Traveller may find to employ himself upon. **1883** *Century Mag.* XXVI. 911/2 They might find traces of European sojourn on the island.

absol. **1340** *Ayenb.* 38 Yef þe vinst and naȝt ne yelst: þou hit stelst. **1611** BIBLE *John* xxi. 6 Cast the net on the right side of the ship, and yee shall find.

b. with †*obj.* and *inf.*; or with *obj.* and *compl.*

a **1000** *Juliana* 364 (Gr.) Ic hine finde ferð staðelian. *c* **1275** *Pass. Our Lord* 325 in *O.E. Misc.* 46 Þesne mon we funde vorbeoden vre lawe. *c* **1340** *Cursor M.* 6827 (Trin.) Þin enemyes beest þou fyndes o stray. *c* **1385** CHAUCER *L.G.W.* 1798 *Lucretia*, Ryghte as a wolfe that fynt a lamb allone. *c* **1450** *Merlin* 4 He was founden dede. **1552** LYNDESAY *Monarche* 5517 Geue thare sall ony man, or wyue, That day be funding upon lyue. **1670** LADY M. BERTIE in *12th Rep. Hist. MSS. Comm.* App. v. 21, I..could not find her at hom. **1826** J. WILSON *Noct. Ambr.* Wks. 1855 I. 179 He has..been fun' lying in the middle of the road.

c. To meet with in records. †Also *absol.*

c **1175** *Lamb. Hom.* 47 We uindeð in halie boc þet ieremie þe prophete stod..in þe uenne up to his muðe. *a* **1300** *Cursor M.* 356 (Cott.) Þis elementz þat al thinges bindes Four er þai, als clerkes findes. **1340** HAMPOLE *Pr. Consc.* 7176 Als in som boke wryten es fonden. *c* **1400** *Destr. Troy* 13494 Fro the towne of Thessaile..Eght furlong, I fynd. **1678** ABP. SANCROFT in D'Oyly *Life* (1821) II. 406 There we find the holy man in a great strait of affliction. **1712** ADDISON *Spect.* No. 415 ¶3 We find Semiramis leading her three Millions to the Field. **1861** M. PATTISON *Ess.* (1889) I. 34 In 1276, we find the Emperor and the King of England in constant communication.

d. To come upon, begin acquaintance with or operation upon (any object), when it is in a specified condition; often contrasted with *leave*.

c **1460** *Towneley Myst.* (Surtees) 59 In the state thou it fand Thou shal it turne. *a* **1568** ASCHAM *Scholem.* (Arb.) 133 He found that Colledge spending scarse two hundred markes by [the] yeare: he left it spending a thousand markes and more. *a* **1656** BP. HALL *Rem. Wks.* (1660) 179 Affliction never leaves us as it findes us. **1784** COWPER *Task* III. 386 The morning finds the self-sequester'd man Fresh for his task. **1827** *Examiner* 481/1 They can only administer the law as they find the law. **1884** GLADSTONE in *Standard* 29 Feb. 2/6 That is the state of things we found established.

2. a. To discover the whereabouts of (something hidden or not previously observed); sometimes with implied notion of picking up or carrying off. Cf. 9.

c **1250** *Gen. & Ex.* 1878 Salamon findin is sal, And his temple sriðen wið-al. *a* **1572** KNOX *Hist. Ref.* Wks. 1846 I. 360 The multitude had fundin, bureid in the Kirk, a great number of idollis. **1656** COWLEY *Misc.*, *Gold* 11 A curse on him who found the Oare! *Mod.* I found a shilling on the floor.

b. *euphem.* To steal. *slang.*

1865 T. ARCHER *Pauper, Thief & Convict* ii. 22 Too little moral restraint to go back to their miserable lodging with an empty stomach if they can '*find*' anything that will procure them a meal. **1884** J. GREENWOOD *Little Ragamuffins* xvi. 139 Pinchin', findin', gleanin', some coves calls it. **1936** *Punch* 2 Dec. 640/1 Certain portions have been 'found' in the literal Army sense of the word, which is a polite way of describing petty theft. **1945** G. MILLAR *Maquis* viii. 155 He left in a rush and flurry on a brand-new woman's bicycle that he had 'found' in Besançon.

3. a. To meet with, come to have, obtain, receive, get (chiefly, something desirable or needful). *to find favour, grace, mercy*: see the sbs. *to find one's account in* (something): to receive advantage from (a course of action), to experience to be profitable (= Fr. *trouver son compte*).

a **1000** *Cædmon's Gen.* 1456 (Gr.) Heo..no..reste fand. *c* **1230** *Hali Meid.* 7 Swuch swetnesse þu schalt ifinden in his luue. *c* **1374** CHAUCER *Anel. & Arc.* 106 Hir fredome fonde Arcyte. *c* **1475** *Rauf Coilȝear* 294 The worthie harberie that I haue fundin heir. **1581** J. BELL *Haddon's Answ. Osor.* 380 b, What heresy [was ever] so absurde, that found not creditte..somewhere? **1596** DALRYMPLE tr. *Leslie's Hist. Scot.* II. (1887) 169 Finding occasioune to win honour.. blythlie he apprehendes it. **1611** BIBLE *Transl. Pref.* 1 But yet [it] findeth but cold intertainment in the world. **1737** BRACKEN *Farriery Impr.* (1757) II. 231, I have always found my Account in such Method. **1767** BLACKSTONE *Comm.* II. 369 Upon a petition preferred to the lord in his court baron the party grieved shall find remedy. **1781** COWPER *Charity*

557 No works shall find acceptance in that day. **1813** MACAULAY *Epitaph on Martyn*, The Christian hero finds a Pagan tomb. **1853** F. W. NEWMAN *Odes of Horace* Pref. 5, I ..despair of finding readers among those who seek solely for amusement. **1861** M. PATTISON *Ess.* (1889) I. 47 Such commodities..found little market.

absol. **1611** BIBLE *Job* xxxiv. 11 He [shall]..cause euery man to finde according to his wayes.

†**b.** with *inf.* as *obj. Obs. rare.*

1375 *Cantic. de Creatione* 851 in *Anglia* I, þat y may fynden glad to be in al my lyf tyme ones.

4. To gain or recover the use of (one's limbs, powers, etc.). ***to find one's feet***: lit. of a child: To be able to stand; *fig.* to become conscious of or develop one's powers. Cf. FEEL *v.* 6 d.

a **1535** MORE *Wks.* 1254 The bitch had founde the foote agayn: and on she came. **1593** SHAKS. *2 Hen. VI*, II. i. 147 We must haue you finde your Legges. Sirrha Beadle, whippe him till he leape ouer that same Stoole. **1642** FULLER *Holy & Prof. St.* v. xix. 438 They thought it high time for the Cow to find her horns. **1667** MILTON *P.L.* VIII. 97 His [the Sun's] beams, unactive else, thir vigor find. **1673** *Ess. Educ. Gentlewom.* 26 Children..when they find their own feet, will not abide the tedium of a School. **1827** KEBLE *Chr. Y.* 23 Trin. xi, The groveling worm Shall find his wings. **1868** HOLME LEE *B. Godfrey* ii. 8 Olive was just beginning to find her feet.

5. a. To discover or perceive on inspection or consideration; to perceive or recognize the presence of. Sometimes approximating to the sense of Fr. *trouver*: To consider (a quality, circumstance) to be present. ***to find fault***: see FAULT *sb.* 6.

1382 WYCLIF *Luke* xxiii. 4, I fynde no thing of cause in this man. *c* **1400** MAUNDEV. (Roxb.) vii. 25 Euermare in þe middes of þam es funden þe figure of þe crosse. **1486** *Bk. St. Albans* E j b, Ther in fyndyn wee suche dyuersite. **1553** WILSON *Rhet.* (1580) Prol. A iv b, Malitious folke, that love to finde faults in other mennes matters. **1735** BERKELEY *Def. Free-thinking in Math.* §30, I find no sense or reason in what you say. **1848** MACAULAY *Hist. Eng.* I. 354 Nor did the world find anything ludicrous in the pomp which..surrounded him.

b. with complement or infinitive.

c **1200** *Trin. Coll. Hom.* 87 And cumeð þerto [the huse] and fint hit emti. **13..** *E.E. Allit. P.* A. 870 On alle her forhedez wryten I fande, þe lombez nome. *c* **1380** *Sir Ferumb.* 522 Or we departye henne; al hool þou schalt me vynde. **1597** MONTGOMERIE *Cherrie & Slae* 1256 For he esteemt his faes defate, Quhen anes he fand them fald. **1724** RAMSAY *Tea-t. Misc.* (1733) I. 34 When we fand our purses toom. **1879** GEO. ELIOT *Coll. Breakf. P.* 292, I..find no scheme Content them both.

c. *refl.* To perceive oneself to be in a specified place or position, or condition of body or mind. Also in weaker sense: To come to be (in the course of events). ***how do you find yourself?*** how are you? Cf. Fr. ***se trouver***, Ger. ***sich befinden***.

c **1386** CHAUCER *Pard. Prol.* 385 Who so fyndeth hym out of swich fame. **1447** BOKENHAM *Seyntys* (Roxb.) 26 Than fynt he hymself..More strong to performyn his journe. *c* **1489** CAXTON *Blanchardyn* ii 14 Blanchardyn fonde hym self in aduyses wyth his mayster, walkynge wythin the paleys. **1600** FAIRFAX *Tasso* XV. lii. 277 On the mountaines top themselues they fand. **1633** BP. HALL *Hard Texts* 212 Do not ye find yourselves perplexed herein? **1692** R. L'ESTRANGE *Fables* xcv. 89 Pray, Sir, How d'ye Find your self? **1791** MRS. RADCLIFFE *Rom. Forest* xii, Tell me how you find yourself. **1816** J. SCOTT *Vis. Paris* 43 He was quite sure of finding himself comfortable. **1823** F. CLISSOLD *Ascent Mt. Blanc* 21 We found ourselves opposed by a parapet of congealed snow. **1873** BLACK *Pr. Thule* xii. 183 Lavender found himself..entering a drawing-room.

6. a. To discover, come to the knowledge of (a fact or state of things) by experience or trial. Const. with simple obj. (*obs. rare*), obj. and inf. or complement, or clause as obj. Also, in a more subjective sense (cf. Fr. *trouver*): To feel to be (agreeable, disagreeable, etc.), to consider or regard as (ridiculous, excellent, etc.).

a **1300** *Cursor M.* 25180 (Cott.) Bot þat es man-hed mast o mede, be funden treu in ilk nede. *c* **1400** *Rom. Rose* 2707 They thee fande Curteis and wys. **1435** MISYN *Fire of Love* 20 He has fun þam worþi to haue hym-self. *a* **1533** LD. BERNERS *Huon* lxx. 240 Ye shall fynde the mater other wyse then Gerarde his brother hath sayd. **1570** BUCHANAN *Chamæleon* Wks. (1892) 49 He fand to be trew in deid all yat he suspectit afoir. **1607** TOPSELL *Serpents* (1608) 596 Cadmus, not finding their return, went likewise to the same fountain. **1611** BIBLE *Dan.* v. 27 Thou are weighed in the balances, and art found wanting. **1626** BACON *Sylva* §22 We finde that Violets..yeeld a pleasing Sent. **1711** STEELE *Spect.* No. 6 ⁋2 He finds Rest more agreeable than Motion. **1768** STERNE *Sent. Journ.* (1778) II. 83 (*Character*) How do you find the French? **1831** KEBLE *Serm.* v. (1848) 120 When his severe trials came..he was found wanting in some qualities. **1886** *Manch. Exam.* 27 Feb. 5/2 Deer forests have been found to pay better than sheep grazing.

b. Often in phrases, ***to find (it) †fit, impossible, necessary,*** etc. ***to (do so and so)***.

1629 *S'hertogenbosh* 5 They found fit to build there the fourth chiefe Towne. **1776** *Trial of Nundocomar* 16/2 Whatever contingent expenses you may find it necessary to disburse in Calcutta. **1879** B. TAYLOR *Stud. Germ. Lit.* 11 Hildebrand finds it impossible to decline the defiance.

7. In certain senses of FEEL: †**a.** To suffer, undergo (punishment, pain) (*obs.*). **b.** To suffer from, feel unpleasantly (cold, etc.); now *colloq.* or *dial.*; also, *to find of.* **c.** To perceive (a smell, taste) (*Sc.*). Cf. also 16.

a **1300** *Cursor M.* 6295 (Gött.) Oft þai fand his wrake. *c* **1400** MAUNDEV (1839) iii. 17 At the Cop of the Hille..Men may fynde no Wynde. **1633** BP. HALL *Hard Texts* 369 Before she findes the throwes of her travell. **1723** *Present State Russia* II. 24 We did not find the Cold..very sensibly. **1771** GOLDSM. *Hist. Eng.* II. 298 Henry found little uneasiness at Perkin's irruption. **1826** J. WILSON *Noct. Ambr.* Wks. 1855 I. 274 Do you fin' the smell o' burnin, sir. **1884** JEFFERIES *Red Deer* xiii. 154 Even those who are hardened to it find of the cold.

†**8.** = *find out* (20 c). *Obs.*

c **1200** *Trin. Coll. Hom.* 5 Forleteð ȝure synne þat ȝe ne be ifunden on sunne. **13..** *E.E. Allit. P.* B. 547 War þe now.. In þe fylþe of þe flesch þat þou be founden neuer. *a* **1400** *Octouian* 229 Sche was founde with the dede. **1530** PALSGR. 550/1 Howe canste thou denye it, wast thou nat founde with the maner? **1611** HEYWOOD *Golden Age* I. Wks. 1874 III. 19 This imposture neuer shall be found. **1692** LOCKE *Educ.* §124 The first time he is found in a Lye, it should rather be wondered at as a monstrous Thinge in him. **1741–3** WESLEY *Extract of Jrnl.* (1749) 83 O, I find you, I find you! I know where you are. Is not your name Wesley? *a* **1774** FERGUSSON *Election* Poems (1845) 42 Had some laird his lady fand In sic unseemly courses.

II. To discover or attain by search or effort.

9. a. To discover or obtain by searching.

c **950** *Lindisf. Gosp.* Matt. xxvi. 60 All ðiu somnung ȝesohton leas witnessa wið ðonehælend..& ne fundon. *c* **1000** *Ags. Ps.* lxxvi. 16 [lxxvii. 19] (Gr.) Ne bið þær eðe þin spor on to findanne. *a* **1200** *Moral Ode* 243 in *Trin. Coll. Hom.* 227 Hie secheð reste þar non nis ac hie hies ne muȝen ifinden. **1375** BARBOUR *Bruce* I. 60 Thar mycht succed na female, Quhill foundyn mycht be ony male. *c* **1386** CHAUCER *Sqr.'s T.* 462 Herbes shal I ryght ynowe yfynde To hele with your hurtes. *c* **1420** *Pallad. on Husb.* I. 10 To write..For husbondry how water shal be fonde. **1553** WILSON *Rhet.* (1580) 98 Is his Lease long inough..Then..I will finde a hole in it I warrant thee. **1656** COWLEY *Friendsh. in Absence* ix, A Bird..Finding at last no passage out, It sits and sings. **1785** BURNS *To W. Sampson* xv, The Muse, nae Poet ever fand her, Till by himsel he learn'd to wander. **1848** MACAULAY *Hist. Eng.* I. 534 The exiles..tried to find another leader. **1870** C. F. GORDON CUMMING in *Gd. Words* 133/2 The slope [is] so rapid that you can scarcely find footing.

absol. *c* **1250** *Gen. & Ex.* 3190 He..hauen soȝt, And funden, and hauen up-broȝt ðe bones. **1340** *Ayenb.* 24 Clier wyt wel uor to understonde, and sotil wyt wel uor to vynde. **1382** WYCLIF *Matt.* vii. 7 Seke ȝe, and ȝe shulen fynde.

b. To discover (game) in hunting. Also *absol.*

c **1420** *Avow. Arth.* xxxi, The bore brittunt thay funde Was colurt of the kingus hunde. **1486** *Bk. St. Albans* E v b, When she shall with houndes be foundyn and soght. **1565–73** COOPER *Thesaurus*, Good hounds..open not but where they finde. **1848** MRS. JAMESON *Sacr. & Leg. Art* (1850) 196 The dogs..found. **1883** SHERAR *At Home & in India* 207 Lady Montego..heard the view hallo..They had found.

c. To come again into view of, to recover (something lost).

a **1225** *Ancr. R.* 48 Louerd..min heorte is icumen aȝein eft: ich hire habbe ifunden. *a* **1300** *Cursor M.* 4108 (Cott.) He went him forth and forþer soght Til he þam faand he finid noght. **13..** *E.E. Allit. P.* A. 327 Now haf I fonte þat I for-lete. **1382** WYCLIF *Luke* xv. 5 Whanne he hath founden it, he ioyinge puttith on his shuldris. *c* **1440** *Generydes* 53 He wyste not them [his knyghtes] to fynde. **1596** SHAKS. *Merch. V.* I. i. 143 By adueturing both [shafts] I oft found both. **1667** MILTON *P.L.* VIII. 479 She disappeerd..I wak'd To find her, or for ever to deplore Her loss. **1791** 'G. GAMBADO' *Ann. Horsem.* ix. (1809) 106, I..soon found the hounds again.

d. *fig.* in phrase. ***to know where to find him, you***, etc. So, ***†where may we find you?***

1581 J. BELL *Haddon's Answ. Osor.* 153 Set downe your mynde whereunto you will stand, that we may know once where we may finde you. **1602** W. WATSON *Decacordon* 147 Whereby father Parsons and his adherents did so square their actions, as neuer..any man liuing can tell where to find them. *a* **1626** SCLATER *On Rom.* iv. (1650) 25 *Versipelles!* Where may we finde you? **1856** J. H. NEWMAN *Callista* 61 He did not understand his nephew, or (to use a common phrase) know where to find him.

e. *refl.* To discover and attain one's special place, power, or vocation.

1647 H. MORE *Poems* 294 [The soul] infinitely has fun Herself, her deep'st desire unspeakably hath wonne. **1889** *Spectator* 14 Dec. 839 Browning may be said almost to have found himself in the delight he had in reading other persons' souls. **1893** *Academy* 11 Mar. 222/1 It was as assistant to Bain that Minto found himself.

f. Of a letter, etc.: to reach (a person); of an address: to be adequate to enable correspondence to reach (a person). Also ***†to find out*** (obs.).

1605 T. MATTHEW *Let.* 29 May in Mathew & Calthrop *Life Sir T.M.* (1907) iii. 45, I hope you will acquaint me with your mind, by letter, wch wth direction at Signore Thomaso Yonge,..will find me out. **1922** W. B. YEATS *Let.* 7 July (1954) v. 687, 82 Merrion Square will always find us.

10. a. To succeed in obtaining (something needed or desired); to procure (money, bail, sureties, etc.). Cf. 18.

1552 HULOET, Finde suerties, *vadio.* **1609** SKENE *Reg. Maj.* 110 Gif sic borgh may not be founden, he sall pas to the knawledge of ane assise. **1640–1** *Kirkcudbr. War-Comm. Min. Bk.* (1855) 81 They find suretie to uthers, as accords of the law. **1821** *Examiner* 350/1 You shall find security for your good behaviour. **1868** *Act 31–2 Vict.* c. 54 §5 It shall not be necessary..to find Security for Expenses.

b. To get or obtain (opportunity, time, etc.) by arrangement or management.

a **1225** *Ancr. R.* 330 Him nis no þing leouere þen þet he muwe ivinden ancheisun uorto ȝiuene. **1535** COVERDALE *Haggai* i. 4 Ye youre selues can fynde tyme to dwell in syled houses. **1656** COWLEY *Imit. Martial's Epigr.* 21 If we for Happiness could leisure finde. **1711** STEELE *Spect.* No. 76 ⁋3 He would find an Opportunity to take some favourable Notice of him. **1760** H. WALPOLE *Corr.* (ed. 3) III. ccclviii. 376, I just found a moment to write you a line. **1868** J. H. BLUNT *Ref. Ch. Eng.* I. 466 The volume had not been long in print before the king found time to read it.

c. To summon up (courage, resolution, etc. to do something). ***to find in one's heart***: to be inclined or desirous; to prevail upon oneself (to do something); in present use chiefly, to be hard-hearted enough. ***†to find one's countenance***: to assume a certain demeanour.

c **1374** CHAUCER *Troilus* III. 979 He..took a light, and fond his contenaunce As for to loke upon an old romaunce. *c* **1440** *Gesta Rom.* lxx. 324 (Harl. MS.) He slepte..so savourly, þat þe preste ne non othir myȝt fynde in hire herte to wake him. **1551** ROBINSON tr. *More's Utop.* (Arb.) 26 They can not fynde in their hertes to loue the author therof. **1611** BIBLE *2 Sam.* vii. 27 Therfore hath thy seruant found in his heart to pray this prayer vnto thee. **1711** STEELE *Spect.* No. 27 ⁋1 They..cannot find in their Hearts to relinquish it. **1861** GEO. ELIOT *Silas M.* xiv. 255 Not as I could find i' my heart to let him stay i' the coal-hole more nor a minute. *a* **1897** *Mod.* At last he has found courage to speak.

11. Of things: **a.** To obtain as if by effort. So ***to find expression, ingress, outlet, place***, etc. Also occasionally, to have in a specified place.

1810 SCOTT *Lady of L.* III. ix, The billow..That far to seaward finds his source. **1813** H. & J. SMITH *Horace in London* 90 Clouds..Which quickly find vent in a deluge of tears. **1819** SHELLEY *Cenci* V. iv. 99 The only ill which can find place Upon the giddy, sharp and narrow hour Tottering beneath us. **1860** W. F. COLLIER *Gt. Events Hist.* v. (1871) 173 The devotion of the people found vent chiefly in pilgrimages. **1875** JOWETT *Plato* (ed. 2) III. 696 An opening sufficient to enable the largest vessels to find ingress.

b. To reach, arrive at as a destination.

a **1340** HAMPOLE *Psalter* xx. 8 þi righthand fynd [L. *inveniat*] all þat has þe hated. **1646** SIR T. BROWNE *Pseud. Ep.* II. iii. 72 The iron being..guided toward the stone, untill it find the newtrall point wherein its gravity just equalls the magneticall quality. **1801** SOUTHEY *Thalaba* VII. xx, Yet may a dagger find him.

c. To come home to, take hold of, reach the understanding or conscience of.

a **1834** COLERIDGE *Conf. Inquiring Spirit* i. (1840) 10 Whatever *finds* me, bears witness for itself that it has proceeded from a Holy Spirit. **1865** M. ARNOLD *Ess. Crit.* i. (1875) 37 As long as his new casting so fails more fully to commend itself, more fully (to use Coleridge's happy phrase about the Bible) to *find* us. **1891** DRUMMOND in *Pall Mall G.* 17 Oct. 7/2 The books of which I have been speaking found me and taught me.

12. a. To ascertain or attain by mental effort; to discover by study or attention.

a **1000** *Cynewulf's Christ* 183 (Gollancz) Hu mæȝ ic.. andsware æniȝe findan Wraþum to-wiþere. *c* **1175** *Lamb. Hom.* 103 Eaðe mei þe mon fundan hu he hine seolf amerre. *a* **1250** *Owl & Night.* 705 þe niȝtingale..hadde andsuere gode ifunde. *c* **1320** *Seuyn Sag.* (W.) 2371 Ac thai ne couthe nowt i-find, Whi th' emperour was blinde. **1481** CAXTON *Godfrey* cxxxvii. 204 The duc..bad hym saye that he hath founden. **1538** STARKEY *England* I. ii. 68 We may perauenture fynd some mean to restore our cuntrey. *a* **1631** DONNE *Poems* (1650) 3 Teach me to..finde What winde Serves to advance an honest minde. **1678** PHILLIPS, *To Find the Ships Trim*, a term in navigation to find how she will sail best. **1697** DRYDEN *Virg. Georg.* III. 701 This Remedy the Scythian Shepherds found. **1812–6** J. SMITH *Panorama Sc. & Art* I. 481 We must rest contented with viewing the true figure of an object, without expecting to find its natural colour.

b. ***to find religion*** (and similar phrases): to experience religious conversion.

1877 *Independent* 4 Jan. 11/3 He said that at least 200 boys had found Jesus in the Tabernacle. **1932** H. J. LASKI *Let.* 21 Aug. in *Holmes-Laski Lett.* (1953) II. 1402 He..asked me in a loud voice..if I had found Christ. I said that I was.. exempt from religious experience. **1957** J. S. HUXLEY *Relig. without Revelation* i. 22 If..we have in any true sense of the phrase, 'found religion', it means that we shall have so organised our minds that, for flashes at least, we attain to a sense of interpenetration with the reality around us.

13. To ascertain by calculation; to get at or obtain (the solution of a problem).

c **1391** CHAUCER *Astrol.* Prol. 1 Conclusiouns that han ben fownde. *c* **1500** *Lancelot* 497 We have fundyne so. **1714** WHISTON *Euclid* (ed. 3) III. i, To find [BILLINGSLEY **1570** *has* To finde out] the Center of a given Circle. **1840** LARDNER *Geom.* 141 We find the point *B* on the second parallel from *OY* at a certain distance above the fifth parallel from *OX*.

14. ***to find one's way***: ***primarily***, to make out one's way by observation or inquiry; to contrive to reach one's destination. Hence in weaker sense, said of persons and things: To go or be brought to a place in spite of difficulties, or not quite as a matter of course.

[*a* **1225** *Ancr. R* 66 þe ueond..ivond wei touward hire of hire uorlorenesse. *c* **1250** *Gen. & Ex.* 3246, xii. weiȝes ðer-in..ðat euerilc kinde of israel Mai ðor his weiȝe finden wel. **1393** GOWER *Conf.* I. 265 If thou wolt finde a siker weie To love, put envie awaye. **1667** MILTON *P.L.* IV. 889 Who would not, finding way, break loose from Hell?] **1746–7** HERVEY *Medit.* (1818) 71 That fatal javelin..finds its way to the hearts of all the sons of Adam. **1803** J. BRISTED *Pedestrian Tour* II. 655 Her cousins..had been bankrupted ..and had found their way up to London. **1827** *Examiner* 792/2 English corn is finding its way into Holland. **1835** THIRLWALL *Greece* I. 11 A weak and sluggish river, which.. scarcely finds its way to the sea. **1847** MARRYAT *Childr. N. Forest* iv, Could you find your way home? **1875** JOWETT *Plato* (ed. 2) I. 340 Notions which have found their way into the drama.

†**15.** To contrive, devise, invent; to discover (a scientific fact, etc.). Also with *forth, up*. *Obs.*

O.E. Chron. an. 918 Se cyng hæfde funden, ðæt [etc.]. *a* **1240** *Ureisun* in *Cott. Hom.* 199 þet þu bringe þene Munuch to þire glednesse þet funde ðesne song bi ðe. *a* **1300**

Cursor M. 1469 (Cott.) Enoch..was þe first þat letters fand. *c* **1380** WYCLIF *Wks.* (1880) 279 Tradicions founden vp of synful wrecchis. **1393** GOWER *Conf.* II. 161 The first in thilke londe..whiche the melodie fonde Of reedes. **1430** LYDG. *Chron. Troy* I. iii, Famous Argus..fyrst that art yfonde. *c* **1449** PECOCK *Repr.* 534 For this eende religioun weren founde and foundid. *c* **1450** HENRYSON *Mor. Fab.* 77 At the last hee finds fourth a wyle. **1568** GRAFTON *Chron.* II. 145 Many..have found suggestions..to bring this your realme into subversion. **1655–60** STANLEY *Hist. Philos.* (1701) 106 About this time..Anaximander found the obliquity of the Zodiack.

16. *dial.* To feel (a pulse); also *intr.* to feel, grope.

1826 J. WILSON *Noct. Ambr.* Wks. 1855 I. 164 You wad hae fan' a pulse with Æsculapian solemnity. **1892** *Northumb. Gloss.*, It's that dark, aa'll he' to fin' for the sneck.

17. *Law.* †**a.** *intr.* To determine. (Only in OE.)

a **1000** *Laws Alfred* §18 in Thorpe *Laws* (1840) I. 72 Swa we ær be læwdum men fundon.

b. †To determine and declare (an offence) to have been committed (*obs.*); to determine and declare (*an issue*) to be (so and so).

1495 *Act 11 Hen. VII*, c. 3 Pream., The seid offences..myght not..be punysshed except it were first founde and presented by the verdite of xij men. **1515** WRIOTHESLEY *Chron.* (1875) I. 9 They saide he hanged himselfe, but it was fownde contrarie. **1602** SHAKS. *Ham.* v. i. 5 The Crowner hath sate on her, and finds it Christian buriall. **1647** N. BACON *Disc. Govt. Eng.* I. lxvii. (1739) 168 If it were found for the supposed Offender, he was bailed till the next coming of the Justices. **1675** C. HATTON in *Hatton Corr.* (1878) 121 Yᵉ crowner's inquest have found it only manslaughter. **1817** W. SELWYN *Law Nisi Prius* (ed. 4) II. 1223 Judgment shall be given for defendant, although the issue be found against him.

c. To determine and declare (a person) *guilty* or *innocent*.

c **1400** *Apol. Loll.* 45 Þe Holi Goost, wan He comiþ, schal find þis world of dome. *c* **1475** *Rauf Coilȝear* 290 He will be found in his fault, that wantis forouth weir. **1531–2** *Act 23 Hen. VIII*, c. 1 Anie personne..founde gyltie of any abbettement. **1613** SHAKS. *Hen. VIII*, II. i. 7 Is he found guilty? **1784** COWPER *Task* II. 12 He finds his fellow guilty of a skin Not colour'd like his own. **1821** *Examiner* 544/1 The Jury found the defendants guilty.

d. To agree upon and deliver, 'bring in' (a verdict). Also with obj. sentence introduced by *that*.

1574 tr. *Littleton's Tenures* 100a, The Graund Assise ought by the law to finde that [etc.]. *a* **1657** SIR J. BALFOUR *Ann. Scot.* (1824–5) II. 58 The said courte..fand that the said edicte did no wayes extend towardes the subiectes of the kingdome of Scotland. **1848** MACAULAY *Hist. Eng.* II. 37 The jury..found a verdict of guilty. **1888** *Law Times* LXXXV. 132/2 The jury at the trial found that the managing director..had ratified the contract.

absol. **1622** BACON *Hen. VII*, 210 They would..inforce them to finde as they would direct. **1891** *Law Times* XC. 283/1 The jury..found for the plaintiff.

e. To ascertain the validity of (an indictment, etc.). ***to find a (true) bill***: see BILL *sb.*³ 4.

1512 *Act 4 Hen. VIII*, c. 10 Any office or offices found before Eschetour or Eschetours. **1534** *Act 26 Hen. VIII*, c. 2 An inditement of .xii. men lawfully founden. **1647** CLARENDON *Hist. Reb.* VI. (1703) II. 99 This Indictment and Information was found by the Grand Jury. **1769** BLACKSTONE *Comm.* IV. xxiii. 301 To find a bill, there must at least twelve of the [grand] jury agree. **1845** STEPHEN *Laws Eng.* II. 484 An indictment for treason..must be found within three years after the commission of the act of treason.

III. 18. a. To procure (something) for the use of (somebody): with direct (or direct and indirect) obj.; to supply, provide, furnish. ***all found*** (also, chiefly *U.S.*, simply *found*) (in regard to servants): with all customary articles of food, etc., provided.

c **1200** *Trin. Coll. Hom.* 215 Wi sholdest þu þis finden þe noht ne fost þerof. *a* **1225** *St. Marher.* 20 Hwa so..makeð chapele oðer chirche oðer ifindeð in ham liht oðer lampe. **1297** R. GLOUC. (1724) 297 Þat euere eyȝte hyde lond an man hym ssolde fynde. *a* **1300** *Cursor M.* 13277 (Cott.) Wit þair scipp þai fand þam fode. *c* **1386** CHAUCER *Knt.'s T.* 1555 And euer more..Eterne fyr I wol bifore the fynde. *c* **1430** *Pilgr. Lyf Manhode* II. xix. (1869) 82 He wolde that..here herkeners..founden hem here vitailes. **1543–4** *Act 35 Hen. VIII*, c. 11 §3 Boroughes..not findinge burgesses for the parliament. **1563** *Richmond. Wills* 167 My thre natural sonns..shalbe fownden meate and drynke. **1603** JOHNSON *Kingd. & Commonw.* 152 No more then every horseman [is accounted] a rider, or able to finde himselfe armour. **1647** N. BACON *Disc. Govt. Eng.* I. lxxi. (1739) 192 For every Plough, every man should find two compleat Horses. **1762–71** H. WALPOLE *Vertue's Anecd. Paint.* (1786) III. 253 The subscription was but ten shillings a year: Britton found the instruments. **1814** COL. HAWKER *Diary* (1893) I. 122 The hotels do not find breakfast. **1826** [see *field-hand*]. **1830** S. SMITH *Major Downing* 13, I get 12 dollars a month and found. **1839** DICKENS *Nickleby* xii. 107 An annual salary of five pounds..and 'found' in food and lodging. **1853** B. F. TAYLOR *Jan. & June* (1871) 273 A story..he wouldn't have whispered for twelve dollars a month 'and found'. **1867** FREEMAN *Norm. Conq.* (1876) I. App. 662 The government required each county to find its quota of ships. **1884** *Punch* 8 Mar. 118/2 Wages £18, all found but beer. **1923** 'B. M. BOWER' *Parowan Bonanza* iv. 48, I got him cheap for yuh. Three dollars and found.

b. with immaterial object.

1664 BUTLER *Hud.* II. ii. 386 Honour is like that glassy Bubble That finds Philosophers such trouble. **1771** *Junius Lett.* xlix. 254 The perpetration..of new crimes will find employment for us both. **1858** BUCKLE *Civiliz.* (1873) II. viii. 574 The forms of constitutional government they could bestow, but they could not find the traditions and the habits by which the forms were worked.

19. a. To support, maintain, provide for (a person, *rarely* an institution). ***to find in***: to supply with. †***to find to school***: to maintain at school.

[App. from 18 by conversion of indirect into direct obj.]

1375 BARBOUR *Bruce* I. 322 Nane..Wald do sa mekill for him, that he Mycht sufficiantly fundyn be. **1393** LANGL. *P. Pl.* C. VI. 36 My frendes founden me to scole. *c* **1430** *Hymns Virg.* (1867) 59, I wole þee fynde til þou be oolde. *a* **1529** SKELTON *Replyc.* 147 Exhibicyon Therewith to be founde At the universite. **1599** HAKLUYT *Voy.* II. II. 73 Condemned persons..are found by the king as long as they do liue. **1713** STEELE *Guardian* No. 58 ¶3 The king of Sweden finds me in clean linen. **1795** BURKE *Thoughts Scarcity* Wks. 1842 II. 249 Unless the labourer is well fed, and otherwise found with such necessaries of animal life. **1830** GEN. P. THOMPSON *Exerc.* (1842) I. 212 Decline finding paupers in venison. **1857** R. TOMES *Amer. in Japan* viii. 183 Boatmen's wages are from one-and-a-half to two-and-a-quarter dollars per month, when *found*.

b. So ***to find oneself***: to provide for one's own living or needs. †Also said *transf.* of a war.

c **1386** CHAUCER *Nun's Pr. T.* 9 Sche fond hirself. **1466** *Mann. & Househ. Exp.* 346 Item, to ij. fellers of tymbre, and to fynde them selffes, viij.*d.* **1553** BECON *Reliques of Rome* (1563) 24b, Such poore..as haue not wherof to fynde themselues. **1585** WASHINGTON tr. Nicholay *Voy. Turkie* III. iv. 76b, They have..4 Aspres of pension by the day, but upon that they must fynde themselves. **1624** BACON *War with Spain* (1629) 45 The war in continuance will finde it selfe. **1653** H. COGAN tr. *Pinto's Trav.* xxxiii. 133 A certain pay to find himself withal, and to live upon. **1754** FIELDING *Voy. to Lisbon* Wks. 1882 VII. 99 It was expected the passengers should find themselves in several things. **1847** MARRYAT *Childr. N. Forest* vi, They..found themselves, as fowls can always do when they have a great range of ground to go over.

†**c.** To serve to maintain. *Obs.*

1483 *Festivall* (W. de W. 1515) 59 Of yᵉ wheet was so grete plente yᵗ it founde all yᵉ people..for thre yere. **1523** FITZHERB. *Surv.* 2b, It is to be enquered..what maner of beestes or catell it [the medowe] is most necessary vnto, and howe many it wyll fynde. **1586** T. B. *La Primaud. Fr. Acad.* 429 He gave to every citizen as much wheate as would finde him three moneths.

d. In Harrow School phraseology (see quot. 1905). Also as *sb.* (see quot. 1881).

1881 M. J. RENDALL in C. E. Pascoe *Everyday Life in our Public Schools* 210 In a large House there are usually four Sixth Form 'finds' (a Harrow term signifying a mess of three or four senior boys who take tea and breakfast in a room separate from the hall). **1889** BARRÈRE & LELAND *Dict. Slang* I. 362/2 *To find*, to mess together. **1905** H. A. VACHELL *Hill* x. 218 You will find together. Of course Scaife can find with you, if you wish. *Footnote.* 'Finding' is the privilege, accorded to the Sixth Form, of having breakfast and tea served in their own rooms instead of in Hall. *Ibid.* xi. 244 They no longer shared No. 7..but they still 'found' together.

IV. With adverbs.

20. find out.

a. To discover by attention, scrutiny, study, etc.; to devise, invent; to unriddle, solve.

1552 HULOET, Finde out by studye, *excudo.* **1568** GRAFTON *Chron.* II. 637 Johannes Fauscius..first found out the noble science of Imprintyng. **1611** BIBLE *2 Chron.* ii. 14 A man of Tyre, skilfull to..find out euery deuice which shall be put to him. **1667** MILTON *P.L.* II. 406 Who shall..through the palpable obscure find out His uncouth way. **1712** ADDISON *Spect.* No. 542 ¶1 Since the circulation of the blood has been found out. **1744** HARRIS *Three Treat.* II. (1765) 363 *note*, They found out Laws. **1871** R. H. HUTTON *Ess.* (1877) I. 38 It aims..at finding out how they may be really united.

b. To come upon by searching or inquiry; to discover (what is hidden). Cf. 9.

1551 WILSON *Logike* (1580) 36b, Thei..doe searche narrowlie..and..at lengthe finde out the Mine. **1611** BIBLE *Job* xi. 7 Canst thou by searching finde out God? **1625** BACON *Ess. Truth* (Arb.) 499 The..Labour, which Men take in finding out of Truth. **1634** HERBERT *Trav.* 217 A..proofe that Madoc ap Owen Gwynedd first found out that Continent now call'd America. **1712** STEELE *Spect.* No. 308 ¶5, I was very much surprized..that any one should find out my Lodging. **1749** FIELDING *Tom Jones* VII. vii, As she is a woman of very great note, I shall easily find her out. **1816** SCOTT *Antiq.* xxiv, 'Whenever Misticot's grave was fund out, the estate..should be lost.'

c. To detect in an offence; to detect, discover (a fraud, etc.); to penetrate the disguise of, discover the identity or true character of. Cf. 8.

1711 STEELE *Spect.* No. 51 ¶7 If at the Catastrophe he were found out for a Traitor. **1741** RICHARDSON *Pamela* I. 65 Pray don't reveal yourself till he finds you out. *a* **1853** ROBERTSON *Serm.* Ser. III. viii. 108 When once a man has found himself out he cannot be deceived again. **1883** *Stubbs' Mercantile Circular* 8 Nov. 982/2 The worthlessness of..clayed cottons is now being found out by the consumer.

†**d.** To provide, supply. *Obs.*⁻¹.

a **1715** BURNET *Own Time* (1823) I. 528 It was not possible for them to find out funds for so great an expense.

e. *absol.* or *intr.* To make a discovery; to discover a fact, the truth, etc.; also with prep. *about*.

1862 G. MACDONALD *D. Elginbrod* II. ii, 'I don't like the pigs—I don't know where they are.' 'Well, we must find out.' **1881** C. E. L. RIDDELL *Senior Partner* xxxi, 'Who might that one be?' 'I am thinking ye'll have to find out for yourself.' **1893** M. E. MANN *In Summer Shade* xix, 'He has found out about Mrs. Le Grice's bill,' said Lally to herself. **1894** B. HARRADEN *Varying Moods* 132 Perhaps death brings peace. I shall soon find out about that. **1913** W. M. GALLICHAN *Like Stars that Fall* xi, Supposing your husband found out? There might be a devil of a row. **1927** M. SINCLAIR *Anthony Waring* xviii, Tony determined to find out. Aunt or no aunt, he would go to her.

21. find up. To discover by search.

Said to be 'a Norfolkism' (W. Taylor in Robberds *Mem.* II. 135). 'Still common in Suffolk' (F. Hall).

[Cf. *c* **1380** in 15 and **1430** in FINDER 1 c.] **1799** W. TAYLOR in Robberds *Mem.* I. 260 You have a mind..to find up 'More Reliques of Rowley'. **1817** —— *Monthly Mag.* XLIV. 314 Jerom..found-up a Hebrew original of the first book of Maccabees. **1832** HT. MARTINEAU *Each & All* vii. 96, I am going into the depths of the city to find up a money lender.

findable ('faɪndəb(ə)l), *a.* [f. as prec. + -ABLE.] That may be found: see senses of FIND *v.*

c **1449** PECOCK *Repr.* I. viii. 41 Many mo of hem ben fyndeable and knoweable by mannis resoun. *a* **1661** FULLER *Worthies* I. (1662) 75 I return such persons to have nothing more to be said of them, findable by all my endevours. **1791** WARING in *Phil. Trans.* LXXXI. 152 The series findable as above mentioned. **1843** MRS. CARLYLE *Lett.* I. 232 I felt about for pillows, none were findable. **1887** T. A. TROLLOPE *What I remember* I. vii. 151 There exists—still findable I suppose..a large lithographed portrait of her.

† '**findal.** *Obs.* Forms: 1 fyndele, 3 find-, fundles, 6–7 *pl.* findelles, findal(l)s, fyndalls. [OE. *fyndele* str. masc., f. *fund-* ablaut-stem of *find-an* to FIND; quot. *a* 1225 points to a form **findels*, f. the pres.-stem (cf. Da. *findelse*).]

a. Invention. **b.** That which is found; treasure-trove.

a **1000** *Scintilla* 108 *Ad inventionem*, to fyndele. *a* **1225** *Ancr. R.* 6 Þe vttre riwle..is monnes findles. *Ibid.* 8 Monnes fundles. **1525** in Boys *Sandwich* (1792) 775 Findalls to be ordered by the mayor, bailiffs, and jurats, where they happen [etc.] **1570** *Ibid.*, Wrecks and fyndalls floating, and the half of all wrecks and fyndalls jottsome. *a* **1598** tr. *Charter Edw. I to Cinque Ports* in Hakluyt *Voy.* I. 117 And that they [Barons] shall haue their findelles in the sea and in the land. **1629** in Boys *Sandwich* (1792) 775 Wrecks and findals.

finder ('faɪndə(r)). [f. FIND *v.* + -ER¹.]

1. a. One who or that which finds, in various senses of the vb.; one who comes upon or discovers by chance or search; †one who contrives or invents, an inventor, deviser; †one who discovers (a country, a scientific truth, etc.).

c **1300** *K. Alis.* 4794 Beheldeth me therof no fynder; Her bokes ben my shewer. *c* **1369** CHAUCER *Dethe Blaunche* 1168 Pictagoras..the firste fynder was Of the art. *a* **1420** HOCCLEVE *De Reg. Princ.* (Roxb.) 179 The first fynder of our faire langage..maister Chaucer. *c* **1430** *Life St. Kath.* (1884) 46 Þe fynder of all euels þe fende. **1487** *Act 4 Hen. VII*, c. 2 §1 The Kyng therof to have the on half, and the fynder the other halfe. **1526** *Pilgr. Perf.* (W. de W. 1531) 81b, The fynder of the ryght waye to heuen. **1555** EDEN *Decades* 77 Christophorus Colonus the fyrst fynder of those landes. *Ibid.* 134 The Chaldeans beynge the fyrst fynders of letters. **1660** FULLER *Mixt Contempl.* (1841) 184 The first finders, founders, and forgers of false reports. **1711** MRS. CENTLIVRE *Marplot* v, By Marplot's direction [I found you]; you know he's a very good finder. **1765** BLACKSTONE *Comm.* I. ix. 349 Concerning treasure trove, he is..to enquire who were the finders. **1870** EMERSON *Soc. & Solit.* xii. 269 Time..is the finder, the unweariable explorer.

b. One whose occupation it is to find; spec. *slang*, One who picks up the refuse of the meatmarkets.

¶ In *Termes de la Ley* 1641, and hence in certain Dicts., erroneously said to be an early synonym for SEARCHER (as the designation of a Custom-house official); in 14 Ric. II. cap. 10, and other statutes, the AF. *tronour* (trone-keeper) was misread as *trovour* (finder), whence the mistake.

1752 *Low Life* (1764) 16 The whole Company of Finders..are marching towards all the markets. **1839** MARRYAT *Diary Amer.* Ser. I. II. 129 Finders, who would search all over the country for..every appearance on the surface of a good vein of metal. **1851** MAYHEW *Lond. Labour* I. 255 Leadenhall-market..was infested..with 'finders'. They carry bags round their necks, and pick up bones or offal.

c. In comb. with advbs., as ***finder-out***, †***-up***.

c **1430** LYDG. *Bochas* I. ii (1544) 5b, He [Nimrod]..was fynder up of false religion. **1553** UDALL *Flowers Latin Speaking* (1560) 103/2 The deuiser and fynder out..of all my pleasures. **1611** SHAKS. *Wint. T.* v. ii. 131 Had I beene the finder-out of this Secret. **1612** WOODALL *Surg. Mate* Pref. Wks. (1653) 1 The..first finders out of the Science.

d. Colloq. phr. ***finders keepers***, whoever finds something is entitled to keep it (cf. *findings* (*are*) *keepings*, FINDING *vbl. sb.* 6).

[**1825** J. T. BROCKETT *Gloss. N. Country Words* 89 No halfers—findee keepee, lossee seekee. **1828** D. M. MOIR *Mansie W.* xi. 98 According to the auld Scotch proverb of 'he that finds keeps, And he that loses seeks'.] **1856** C. READE *Never too Late* III. xiii. 127 We have a proverb—'Losers seekers finders keepers'. **1923** G. E. KELLY (*title*) Finders-Keepers. **1961** B. E. WALLACE *Death packs Suitcase* vi. 60 In this game it's going to be finders keepers. **1969** *Daily Express* 17 Mar. 9/3 Where I come from it's finders keepers, losers weepers.

2. *Sporting.* †A dog trained to find and bring game that has been shot; a 'water-spaniel', retriever (*obs.*). Also, one used to discover the track of, or 'put up', game for the sportsman.

1576 FLEMING tr. *Caius' Dogs* in Arb. *Garner* III. 266 The Water Spaniel..is..called a Finder because..he findeth such things as be lost. **1681** HICKERINGILL *Wks.* (1716) I. 214 This Couple or pair usually Hunt together..as..a Grey-Hound and a Finder. **1766** PENNANT *Zool.* (1768) I. 54. **1803** *Ann. Reg.* 800 One or two small dogs called finders, whose scent is very keen, and always sure of hitting off a track. **1824** MISS MITFORD *Village* Ser. I. (1863) 95 Dash..is a capital finder, and will beat a cover with any spaniel in England.

3. A contrivance or instrument for finding.

†**a.** An index. *Obs.*

1588 J. MELLIS *Brief Instr.* C iv b, Vnto which Leager it shalbe necessary to ordein or make a calender, otherwise called a Repertory or a finder.

b. A small telescope attached to the large one for the purpose of finding an object more readily.

1784 HERSCHEL in *Phil. Trans.* LXXV. 41 The finder of my reflector. **1871** tr. *Schellen's Spectr. Anal.* liii. 244 Janssen left the spectroscope to look for a moment through the finder, or small telescope.

c. A microscopic slide divided by crossed lines, so that any point in the field can be identified readily.

1867 J. HOGG *Microsc.* I. iii. 187 A finder, as applied to the microscope, is the means of registering the position of any particular object in a slide.

d. *Photogr.* A supplementary lens attached to a camera, to locate the object in the field of view.

[**1889** P. H. EMERSON *Naturalistic Photogr.* I. i. (1890) 133 The handiest view finder for quick exposure work is to fit a double convex lens..to the front of the camera.] **1892** in L. de Vries *Victorian Advts.* (1968) 76/1 The 'artist', ½-plate camera Containing Euryscope lens working at F/6, large Finder with Hood. **1894** *Brit. Jrnl. Photogr.* XLI. 83 Cameras..in which the finders were..carelessly fixed. **1894**, etc. [see BRILLIANT *a.* 1 b]. **1915** B. E. JONES *Cinematograph Bk.* iii. 15 A finder is provided for focusing purposes, consisting of a long narrow tube..running right across the camera and having a cap..outside. **1951** G. H. SEWELL *Amateur Film-Making* (ed. 2) iii. 33 Generally the finder looks along a line different from the axis of the taking-lens, but parallel to it.

‖**fin de siècle** (fɛ̃ də sjɛkl). [Fr.] A phrase used as an adj. in sense: Pertaining to, or characteristic of, the end of the (nineteenth) century; characteristically advanced, modern, or decadent. Hence **fin-de-siècl(e)ism**, the state or quality of being characteristically *fin de siècle*.

1890 *Daily News* 29 Dec. 2/2 The finance of the year has been special—*fin de siècle.* **1891** *Melbourne Punch* 4 June 377/1 The *fin de siècle* ballet. **1893** [see ARGONAUT 1 b]. **1896** W. CALDWELL *Schopenhauer's Syst.* 523 What is called *Fin-de-Siècle-ism.* **1898** *Westm. Gaz.* 4 July 1/2 These days, which pessimists call *fin-de-siècle* with some sort of idea that the phrase indicates a weariness and weakening of purpose. **1908** *Daily Chron.* 22 Apr. 4/6 He has recreated for us the Versailles of Louis XIV. in that fin-de-siècle epoch when the glories of the Grand Monarque were fading. **1930** *Punch* 30 Apr. 498 This charming old comedy can be trusted to delight us on its own merits. *Fin-de-siècle* trimmings are alien to its spirit. **1948** H. ACTON *Mem. Aesthete* vi. 119, I had started sweeping away *fin-de-siècle* cobwebs with a paper called *The Oxford Broom.* **1965** *Listener* 25 Nov. 863/1 He..ignores the aspects of Proust that do not interest him personally; the realist, the chronicler of *fin de siècle* society, and the student of inversion are hardly mentioned. **1966** *New Statesman* 27 May 786/1 [The description] conveys none of his fin-de-sièclism. **1967** R. CROFT-COOKE *Feasting with Panthers* viii. 166 Even French phrases carried sinister meanings and when people called the literary pseudo-movement of the Nineties *fin-de-siècle* it added an ominous purple hue to the earlier writings of Wilde and of those..who imitated him.

ˈ**find-fault.** *Obs.* exc. *dial.* [f. FIND *v.* + FAULT *sb.*] One who finds fault (see FAULT *sb.* 6); a fault-finder, censorious person.

1577 NORTHBROOKE *Dicing* (1843) 17 Frantike findefaults, dispraysing and condemning euery good endeauour. **1656** TRAPP *Comm. Matt.* vii. 4 Hypocritical find-faults, that can say such things to others, when themselves are most obnoxious. **1863** G. MELLY *Sp. Soirée L'pool Co-op. Assoc.* 17 Feb., We have a good old Lancashire saying, that one mend-fault is better than nine find-faults.

attrib. **1598** FLORIO, *Cacafiori*, a vaine, self-conceited, others-scorning, find-fault foole.

†**find-faulting,** *vbl. sb. Obs. rare*$^{-1}$. [f. phr. *find fault* (treated as if one word) + -ING[1].] The action of finding fault. In quot. *attrib.*

1654 WHITLOCK *Zootomia* 347 She doth not set Businesse back by unquiet branglings, and findefaulting Quarrells.

findhorn: see FINNAN.

†ˈ**findible,** *a. Obs.*$^{-0}$ [ad. L. **findibilis*, f. *findĕre* to split.] That may be split or cleft. Hence ˈ**findibleness**, capability of being split.

1656 BLOUNT *Glossogr.*, Findible. **1721–90** in BAILEY. **1730–36** BAILEY (folio), Findibleness.

finding (ˈfaɪndɪŋ), *vbl. sb.* [f. FIND *v.* + -ING[1].]

1. a. The action of the vb. FIND in its ordinary senses; an instance of the same. Also with *out.*

c **1340** *Cursor M.* 5365 (Trin.) Joseph..I haue founden here. Of his fyndynge þonke I god so. *c* **1449** PECOCK *Repr.* I. xiii. 70 Into whos fynding and grounding doom of mannys resoun may suffice. **1611** BIBLE *Eccl.* xiii. 26 The finding out of parables is a wearisome labour of the minde. **1870** MRS. RIDDELL *Austin Friars* ii, 'You speak as though my misfortunes had been of my own seeking'..'They have been of your own finding'.

b. That which is found or discovered; also, a find, a discovery.

1598 FLORIO *Trouadelli*, findlings, children found, findings. **1644** MILTON *Areop.* 36 When a man hath bin labouring..in the deep mines of knowledge, hath furnisht out his findings. **1805** W. TAYLOR in *Monthly Mag.* XX. 339 The findings at Pompeii, preserved in the Museum of Portici. **1876** TAIT *Rec. Adv. Phys. Sc.* xiii. (ed. 2) 322 To Joule we owe the first precise findings on the subject.

2. The action of inventing or devising; a device, invention. Now only with *out*; formerly also with *up.*

a **1300** *Cursor M.* 27661 (Cott.) O nith cums..finding of il. **1340** HAMPOLE *Pr. Consc.* 1557 Þai styrd God tyll wreth, In þair new fyndynges of vanité. *c* **1380** WYCLIF *Wks.* (1880) 77 Here owene fyndynge vp, þat crist & apostlis spoken not of. *c* **1400** *Destr. Troy* 4296, I will tell here a tale..Of þe fyndyng of false goddes. **1578** TIMME *Caluine on Gen.* 151 The finding out of Harps and such like Musical Instruments. **1642** ROGERS *Naaman* 182 Beseech the Lord not to leaue thee to thine owne findings.

3. The action of providing or supplying.

c **1449** PECOCK *Repr.* 358 He ȝaf a certein of possessioun for fynding of liȝtis. **1580** BARET *Alv.* F 556 A finding..of things that one lacketh.

4. a. The action of maintaining or supporting (a person or an institution). †*at a person's finding(s*: at his own cost or expense. Cf. FIND *v.* 19.

a **1300** *Cursor M.* 3223 A sergaunt..þat had ben ay at his finding, Euer siþen þat he was child ȝeing. **1494** FABYAN *Chron.* v. cxiii. 86 He gaue possessions for the fyndyng of hir. **1535** GARDINER *Let. to Cromwell* in Strype *Eccl. Mem.* I. xxx. 213 The finding of young children to school. **1642** ROGERS *Naaman* 369 We will be at our owne findings. **1709** STRYPE *Ann. Ref.* I. xxvi. 309 An annuity..for the finding of a school in Guilford. **1840** THACKERAY *Catherine* vii, She will be very glad to..pay for the finding of him.

†**b.** Keep, maintenance, provision, support. *Obs.*

1393 LANGL. *P. Pl.* C. VII. 293 [To] haue my fode and my fyndynge of false menne wynnynges. *c* **1449** PECOCK *Repr.* III. v. 305 He myȝte haue askid his lijflode and fynding of hem to whom he prechid. **1470–85** MALORY *Arthur* VII. i, That he hadde al maner of fyndynge as though he were a lordes sone. **1565–73** COOPER *Thesaurus*, *Annona*, finding in meate, drinke or apparell.

c. in *pl.* (*a*) (See quots.) Also *attrib.* in *finding-store* (U.S.).

1846 WORCESTER (citing CHUTE), *Findings pl.*, the tools and materials used by shoemakers. **1858** SIMMONDS *Dict. Trade*, *Findings*, the wax, thread and tools which a journeyman shoemaker has to supply himself with for his work. *Ibid.*, *Finding-stores*, an American name for what are termed in England grindery-warehouses; shops where shoemakers' tools, etc. are vended.

(*b*) (See quot. 1939.) *U.S.*

1896 *Godey's Mag.* Feb. 222/2 The cost of findings for a waist. **1939** M. B. PICKEN *Lang. Fashion* 57/2 *Findings*, threads, tapes, buttons, bindings, hooks and eyes, slide fasteners, Featherbone, belting, braids, and other sewing essentials used in garment making; carried in notion departments. **1971** *Lebende Sprachen* XVI. 11/1 US findings-BE/US sewing things.

5. The result of a judicial examination or inquiry; the verdict of a jury, the decision of a judge or arbitrator.

1859 LANG *Wand. India* 364 The court-martial still adheres to its finding of murder. **1865** *Pall Mall G.* 17 May 11 Fitly says Sir Joseph Arnould, in his eloquent finding. **1884** G. HASTINGS in *Law Times Rep.* 5 Apr. 175/1 The findings of an official referee have always been considered as equivalent to the findings of a jury.

6. Proverbial phr. *findings* (*are*) *keepings.* Also in *sing.* form. Cf. FINDER 1 d.

1863 J. H. SPEKE *Discov. Sources of Nile* v. 121 The scoundrels said, 'Findings are keepings, by the laws of our country; and as we found your cows, so we will keep them.' **1904** *Daily Chron.* 27 Sept. 1/7 Harsh sentences of imprisonment for 'findings-keepings' offences. **1959** I. & P. OPIE *Lore & Lang. Schoolch.* viii. 134 Articles may be acquired..by 'finding-keeping'.

7. *Comb.*, **finding-list** (see quot. 1961).

1889 in *Cent. Dict.* **1930** *Library* XI. iii. 260, I had prepared a skeleton finding-list only. **1961** T. LANDAU *Encycl. Librarianship* (ed. 2) 142/2 *Finding list*, a list of books, often of a special kind or by a particular writer, represented in a library or in the libraries within a given area.

findling, obs. var. of FOUNDLING.

findon, findram: see FINNAN.

findrinny (ˈfɪndrɪnɪ). [ad. Ir. *findruine* (Roy. Irish Acad. *Dict. Irish Lang.*), f. OIr. *findbruine*, f. OIr. *find* (mod.Ir. *fionn*) white + **bruine* of unknown meaning: ultimate origin obscure.] White bronze.

[**1873** E. O'CURRY *Manners & Customs Anc. Ir.* I. p. ccccl xv, In Norse shields the rim was of iron, but in the descriptions of shields to be found in Irish poems and prose tales, the material of the rim is almost always *Findruini.* *Ibid.*, *Findruini* was probably bronze coated with tin or some white alloy. *Ibid.* III. 100 She had presented him at the outset with..a bracelet of *Findruine* or carved white metal (silver bronze) to fit his left wrist.] **1895** W. B. YEATS *Poems* 6 On a horse with bridle of findrinny. *Ibid.* 22 With hoofs of the ruddy findrinny. **1934** J. JOYCE *Let.* 16 Oct. (1957) 348 A 30-year wedding should be called a 'findrinny' one. Findrinny is a kind of white gold mixed with silver.

†ˈ**findy,** *a. Obs.* Also 3 findiȝ, findige, fundie. [ME. *findiȝ*, *fundi*(ü); cf. OE. *ȝefyndiȝ* capable, Da. *fyndig* powerful, solid, f. *fynd* strength, substance.] Firm, solid, weighty. Of a harvest: Plentiful.

c **1200** ORMIN 4149 Crist iss strang & stedefasst & findiȝ & unnfakenn. *c* **1200** *Trin. Coll. Hom.* 119 Þus hie segen þe holi gost on tungene euene, and þerefore weren fundie on speche. *Ibid.* Bidde we nu þe holigost þat he..giue us..findige speche. *a* **1677** *Proverb* in Junius *Etymologicum* (ed. Lye 1743) s.v. *Fyndie*, A May cold and windy maketh the barn full and fyndie.

fine (faɪn), *sb.*[1] Forms: 3 fin, 3–6 fyn(e, 3– fine. [ME. *fin*, a. OF. *fin* = Pr. *fin-s*, *fi-s*, Sp. *fin*, Pg. *fim*, It. *fine*:—L. *finem*, *finis* end.

In med.L. and OF. the word has the senses 'ending of a dispute, settlement, payment by way of composition'; hence the various applications in branch II.]

I. End. (Obs. exc. in phr. *in fine.*)

†**1.** Cessation, end, termination, conclusion, finish. Phr. *to bring to fine, set the fine of.* *Obs.*

c **1200** *Trin. Coll. Hom.* 258 Pine wiðute fin. **1297** R. GLOUC. (Rolls) 8547 Þis stalwarde cristine volc þis worre broȝte to fine. **13..** *E.E. Allit. P.* A. 634 Why schulde he not ..pay hym at þe fyrst fyne? *c* **1460** *Pol. Rel. & L. Poems* 73 When þat pyte..hath sett the fyne of al myn heuynesse. *c* **1500** *Lancelot* 1388 Deth that neuer shal haf fyne. **1560** ROLLAND *Crt. Venus* III. 724 And sa to bring my argument to fine I can not find [etc.]. **1601** SHAKS. *All's Well* IV. iv. 35 Still the fine's the Crowne. **1664** *Flodden F.* i. 2 A lucky fine and end to make. **1839** BAILEY *Festus* xxx. (1848) 348 Open thine arms O death! thou fine of woe.

b. Phrase, *in* (†*the*) *fine*; also rarely †*a*, †*at*, †*of fine*: †(*a*) in the end, at last; (*b*) to conclude or sum up, finally; also, in short.

(*a*) **1297** R. GLOUC. (1724) 91 Þe noble Constantyn, (þat was kyng here of þis lond, & emperour atte fyn). *c* **1450** *Merlin* 286 But in the fyn he mote yeve grounde a litill. *c* **1450** R. MORICE in *Lett. Lit. Men* (Camden) 24 In fyne he was perceyved to affixe one of the papers upon the dore. **1575** J. STILL *Gamm. Gurton* v. ii. in Hazl. *Dodsley* III. 246 My cockis, I thank Christ, safe and well a-fine. **1693** *Mem. Ct. Teckely* I. 41 In fine after a Months obstinate defence.. the Turks took the Fort by assault.

(*b*) **1401** *Pol. Poems* (Rolls) II. 91 I can telle wel a fyn what heresie amounteth. **1550** CROWLEY *Epigr.* 917 Ye must saye as they saye, be it wrounge or ryght. In fine, ye must prayse them. **1649** MILTON *Eikon.* Wks. 1738 I. 408 In fine, he accuses Piety with the want of Loyalty. *a* **1704** T. BROWN *Sat. French King* Wks. 1730 I. 60 In fine, the Government may do its will. **1849** RUSKIN *Seven Lamps* vii. §8. 195 We have, in fine, attained the power of going fast.

†**c.** The latter part (of time), close. *Obs.*

c **1400** *Sowdone Bab.* 306 The daie passed to the fyne. **1599** HAKLUYT *Voy.* II. I. 200 About the fine of September. **1615** G. SANDYS *Trav.* 101 Vntill the fine of December.

†**2.** End of life, decease, death. *to do, take* (one's) *fine*: to die. *Obs.*

c **1250** *Gen. & Ex.* 3852 Alle [ðe] olde deden ðor fin. *a* **1300** *Floriz & Bl.* 441 Hi beden God ȝiue him uuel fin þat so manie flures dude þerin. *a* **1300** *Cursor M.* 3905 (Cott.) He was þe chesun of hir fine. *Ibid.* 21102 (Cott.) Þer tok he fine. *c* **1330** R. BRUNNE *Chron.* (1810) 189 Or I ȝit do my fyn. *c* **1330** *Assump. Virg.* (Add. MS.) 777 He wolde haue ben at hure fyne ȝif he myȝt haue come bi tyme. **1494** FABYAN *Chron.* II. xxxi. 24, I haue here shewed vnto you, the fyne or ende of Brennius. **1548** HALL *Chron.* 151 b, Choked and brought to his fatall fine. **1556** LAUDER *Tractate* 209 Geue ȝe Indure vnto ȝour fyne.

†**3.** The extreme part or limit of anything; a boundary. Also *fig.* extreme case, extremity. *Obs.*

a **1300** *Cursor M.* 23200 (Gött.) Þe pitt of hell pine It es suo depe, widuten fine, þat end ne bes þar neuer apon. *c* **1400** *Rom. Rose* 1558 Of the welle, this is the fyn. **1586** J. HOOKER *Girald. Irel.* in *Holinshed* II. 135/2 Vpon the fines and marches in Ulster. **1596** DALRYMPLE tr. *Leslie's Hist. Scot.* (1885) 114 Our King nevir to that fine, at ony tyme to haue beine brocht, that [etc.]. **1859** I. TAYLOR *Logic in Theol.* 139 The 'settled fine' to which each aspires to rise.

†**4.** End in view, aim, purpose, object; *esp.* in phr. *to what fine.* Hence, the purpose for which a thing exists. *Obs.*

c **1374** CHAUCER *Troylus* II. 745 To what fine is soche loue, I can not seen. *c* **1386** —— *Merch. T.* 862 Sche knew eek the fyn of his entent. **1413** LYDG. *Pilgr. Sowle* IV. xx. (1483) 65 To what ende or fyn Engendred ye me? **1533** BELLENDEN *Livy* I. (1822) 38 To schaw to quhat fine thay war cummin. **1562** WINȜET *Cert. Tract.* iii. Wks. 1888 I. 31 For thair abusing of the samyn to ane vther fine than He [God] institute tham. **1603** DEKKER, etc. *Patient Grissell* (1841) 42 Our fine be now to apparel all these former in some light sarcenet robe of truth.

†**5.** Final issue, consequence, result. *Obs.*

1513 DOUGLAS *Æneis* IV. Prol. 130 ȝit luffis ony to that fyne, quharby Thi self or thaim thow frawart God removis. **1549** *Compl. Scot.* x. 84 Pirrus..past to the oracle of appollo til inquyre of the fyne of the veyris that vas betuix hym and the romanis. **1605** *Lond. Prodigal* III. ii, There's the fine.

II. 6. *Law.* A 'final agreement'; 'an amicable composition or agreement of a suit, either actual or fictitious, by leave of the king or his justices' (Blackstone).

[**1299** *Act 27 Edw. I*, c. 1 Quia Fines in Curia nostra levati finem litibus debent imponere et imponunt, & ideo fines vocantur, maxime cum post duellum & magnam assisam in suo casu ultimum locum & finalem teneant & perpetuum.]

b. *spec.* The compromise of a fictitious or collusive suit for the possession of lands: formerly in use as a mode of conveyance in cases where the ordinary modes were not available or equally efficacious.

The procedure was as follows. The person to whom the land was to be conveyed sued the holder for wrongfully keeping him out of possession; the defendant (hence called the cognizor) acknowledged the right of the plaintiff (or cognizee); the compromise was entered on the records of the court; and the particulars of it were set forth in a document called the *foot of the fine* (see FOOT). This method of conveyance was resorted to by married women (who could not alienate land by any other process), and as a means of barring an entail. The cognizor was said to *acknowledge* or *levy a fine*; sometimes the vb. *to levy* was used intrans. with *fine* as the subject. Also *to sue a fine.*

[**12..** BRACTON *De Legibus Angliæ* v. IV. viii. §3 VI. 70 Item sufficit finis factus in curia domini regis [etc.]. **1292**

BRITTON II. iii. §14 Par acord del purchaceour et del donour covendra lever fin en nostre court.] **1483** *Act 1 Rich. III*, c. 7 §1 Notes and fynes to be levied in the Kinges Court.. shold be openly and solempnly radd. **1509–10** *Act 1 Hen. VIII*, c. 19 Pream., Your said Oratour..levyed severall Fynes of all the foresaid Manours. **1602** SHAKS. *Ham.* v. i. 114 His Statutes, his Recognizances, his Fines, his double Vouchers, his Recoueries. *a* **1626** BACON *Max. & Uses Com. Law* (1636) 51 A Fine is a reall agreement, beginning thus, 'Hæc est finalis concordia, etc.' **1751** LADY LUXBOROUGH *Let. to Shenstone* (1775) 281 A lawyer..to see me execute a fine, in consequence of my parting with my house in London. **1773** E. BONHOTE *Rambles Mr. Frankly* (1797) I. 81 He forbade me his house, sued a fine, and cut me off with a shilling. **1818** CRUISE *Digest* (ed. 2) VI. 138 A fine was levied accordingly.

†**c.** Hence used *gen.* for: A contract, agreement.

c **1330** R. BRUNNE *Chron.* (1810) 106 Sir Henry mad þe fyne, and mad þe mariage. **1362** LANGL. *P. Pl.* A. II. 51 Meede In Mariage was [I-feffed] To beo fastnet with fals þe fyn was arered.

III. A composition paid.

7. a. *Feudal Law.* A fee (as distinguished from the rent) paid by the tenant or vassal to the landlord on some alteration of the tenancy, as on the transfer or alienation of the tenant-right, etc. **b.** *Mod. Law.* A sum of money paid by a tenant on the commencement of his tenancy in order that his rent may be small or nominal.

c **1435** *Torr. Portugal* 1086 Omage thou shalte none nor ffyne. **1523** FITZHERB. *Surv.* Prol., To cause them to pay more rent or a gretter fyne than they haue ben acustomed to do in tyme past. **1625** *Act 1 Chas. I*, c. 2 §1 His Majestie having received divers Fines and sommes of Mony, according to the said Contracts. **1710** PRIDEAUX *Orig. Tithes* ii. 82 Reckoning in their Fines as well as their Rents. **1818** CRUISE *Digest* (ed. 2) I. 351 Where a fine is certain, the tenant is bound to pay it immediately upon his admittance. **1862** LD. BROUGHAM *Brit. Const.* x. 138 The fines paid by his vassals on succession to or alienation of their fees. **1877** *Act 40 & 41 Vict.* c. 18 §4 On every such lease shall be reserved the best rent..that can be reasonably obtained..without taking any fine or other benefit in the nature of a fine.

8. †**a.** In phr. ***to make (a) fine***: to make one's peace, settle a matter, obtain exemption from punishment or release from captivity, *esp.* by means of a money payment. *Obs.* exc. *Hist.*

1297 R. GLOUC. (1724) 511 Some hii lete honge Bi hor membres an hey..Vort hii adde fin imad. *c* **1325** *Coer de L.* 3350 Charges mules..Off brende gold..For our heyres to make fyn. *c* **1325** *Metr. Hom.* 46 To mak the fin For sin. *c* **1330** R. BRUNNE *Chron. Wace* (Rolls) 15966 When Penda hadde to Cadwalyn Obliged hym, & mad his fyn. *c* **1380** WYCLIF *Wks.* (1880) 184 It is lijttere to make a fyn for moche money þan to purge hym. **1422** J. YONGE *Privytye* 204 And there this McMahons, with dyuers othyr enemys, fynes with hym makid, pees forto haue. **1574** in W. H. Turner *Select Rec. Oxford* 351 Richard Lloyde..shall make fyne for his contemptuous..wordes. **1891** *Northumb. Assize Rolls* (Surtees) Pref. 25 The matter..settled by the Swethops making a fine with Dionisia for 20 marks.

†**b.** A sum of money offered or paid for exemption from punishment or by way of compensation for injury. *Obs.*

[**1292** BRITTON I. xii. §7 Sur peyne de raunceun et de fin.] *c* **1340** *Cursor M.* 6753 (Trin.) If þef haue no fyn ny ȝift..he shal be solde. **1628** EARLE *Microcosm., Meere Gull Citizen* (Arb.) 94 A harsh scholemaster, to whom he..payes a fine extraordinary for his mercy.

c. A certain sum of money imposed as the penalty for an offence. † ***to put to (one's) fine***: to fine.

1529 MORE *Supplic. Soulys* Wks. 296/2 The v. C. poundes whych he payed for a fyne by the premunire. **1542–3** *Act 34–5 Hen. VIII*, c. 27 §84 No persone..for murther or felonie shall be put to his fine, but suffer accordinge to the lawes. **1647** CLARENDON *Hist. Reb.* I. (1843) 10/1 He was..condemned in a great fine. **1719** W. WOOD *Surv. Trade* 302 Which cannot fail of bringing many more to the Church, than is possible by Fines and Imprisonments. **1827** HALLAM *Const. Hist.* (1876) III. xvii. 327 Fines to the amount of £85,000..were imposed on the Covenanters. **1861** M. PATTISON *Ess.* (1889) I. 47 A blow..subjected the offender to a fine.

d. *transf.* A penalty of any kind. *arch.* † ***to pass a fine***: *fig.* to pronounce sentence.

1503 HAWES *Examp. Virt.* v. 59 Deth is fyne of euery synne. **1580** LUPTON *Sivqila* 14 To pay the fine of damnation for euer. *a* **1680** BUTLER *Rem.* (1759) I. 141 Two Self-admirers..may pass a Fine Upon all Judgment. **1697** DRYDEN *Eneid* XI. 1222 Too dear a Fine, ah much lamented Maid, For warring with the Trojan hast thou paid. **1705** ADDISON *Italy* 501 Fines..set upon Plays, Games, Balls and Feastings. **1876** BLACKIE *Songs Relig. & Life* 195 We stood for our faith, when our life was the fine.

†**9.** A fee or charge paid for any privilege. Also, probate duty on a will. *Obs.*

[**1422** *E.E. Wills* (1882) 51 & soluerunt pro fine iiijor nobilia.] **1434** EARL OF OXFORD in Ellis *Orig. Lett.* Ser. II. I. 110 That the said Shipp, without any fyn or fee..may have licence..to make the furst viage unto St. James. **1521** *Bury Wills* (Camden) 120 Item to Mr. Miles, for the aquitans at thys cownt makyng in Fornham and for ye fyne of ye testament..v š. viij d. *c* **1744** *Parl. Bill* in Hanway *Trav.* (1762) I. v. lxxi. 323 All persons..should be admitted into the freedom of the said company, upon paying a fine of fifty pounds.

IV. 10. *Comb.*, **fine-rolls** (= *rotuli oblatorum* or *finium*; see quot. 1891); **fine-setting** *vbl. sb.*, fining, mulcting.

1800 *1st Rept. Public Records* 54 The Fine Rolls. **1853** THOMAS *Handbk. Publ. Rec.* 39 The Fine Rolls of King John. **1891** SCARGILL-BIRD *Guide to Public Records* 35 The Rolls upon which were entered the sums of money (or other property..) offered to the king by way of oblation or fine for the passing or renewal of charters or grants, and for the enjoyment of lands, offices, wardships, exemptions..and other marks of royal favour, were called Oblata or Fine Rolls. The first of these appellations fell into disuse after the reign of John, the latter only being thenceforward retained. **1657** *Burton's Diary* (1828) II. 17 This fine-setting is no breach of privilege.

‖**fine** ('fɪnɪ), *sb.*2 *Irish Hist.* [Irish.] An Old Irish family or sept.

1873 SULLIVAN *Introd. O'Curry's Anc. Irish* I. 79 The clan..comprised several Fines. **1875** MAINE *Hist. Inst.* iv. 105 My own..opinion is that the 'Fine'..is neither the Tribe..nor..the modern Family..but the Sept.

fine (faɪn), *a.* Forms: 3–5 fin, fyn, 4–6 fyne, (4 fyin), 4– fine. [a. F. *fin* = Pr. *fin-s*, Sp., Pg., It. *fino* (also It. *fine*):—Com. Rom. *fino* (med.L. *fīnus*), prob. a back-formation from *finire* (pa. pple. *finito*) to FINISH. On the analogy of the many Rom. vbs. in *-ire* derived from adjs. (e.g. *grossire* to make thick, f. *grosso* thick) the vb. *finire* seems to have been felt to presuppose an adj. *fino*. Similar back-formations (from adjs. of ppl. form) are Sp. *cuerdo* intelligent from L. *cordātus*, It. *manso* gentle from L. *mansuētus*. The Rom. word has passed into all the Teut. langs.; cf. OHG., MHG. *fīn* (mod.G. *fein*), MDu., Du. *fijn*, Icel. (15th c.) *finn*, Sw. *fin*, Da. *fiin*.

In Fr. the word now chiefly expresses delicate and subtle perfection, as opposed to all that is gross or clumsy. In Eng. the senses derived from this notion are still current, but the word came to be used as a general expression of admiring approbation, equivalent to the Fr. *beau*, which it renders in many adopted locutions.]

A. *adj.*

I. Finished, consummate in quality.

1. Of superior quality, choice of its kind.

a **1300** *Cursor M.* 2870 (Gött.) Men findis lompis on þe sand Of ter, nan finer in þat land. **1377** LANGL. *P. Pl.* B. II. 9 With pelure þe finest vpon erthe. *c* **1385** CHAUCER *L.G.W.* 673 *Cleopatras*, She..made..a shryne Of alle the rubies and the stones fyne In al Egypte that she coude espye. *c* **1440** *Promp. Parv.* 161/1 Fyne wyne, *falernum*. **1653** WALTON *Angler* 130 Certain fields..make the Sheep that graze upon them..bear finer Wool. **1872** YEATS *Growth Comm.* 31 Elba remarkable to this day for the fine iron it produces.

absol. ? *a* **1400** *Morte Arth.* 3372 Ffonde of þe fyneste,..And reche to the ripeste.

2. Free from foreign or extraneous matter, having no dross or other impurity; clear, pure, refined.

a. Of metals: Free from dross or alloy.

a **1300** *Cursor M.* 16453 (Cott.) Quen þai þe fine gold for-soke. *c* **1384** CHAUCER *H. Fame* III. 258 Of gold As fyne as ducat in venyse. *c* **1450** *Mirour Saluacioun* 1148 This reuerent Throne was made..of finest gold. **1557** N. T. (Genev.) *Rev.* i. 15 And his fete lyke vnto fyne brasse. **1611** BIBLE *Ezra* viii. 27 Two vessels of fine copper, precious as gold. **1757** JOS. HARRIS *Coins* 31 Coins..should contain certain assigned quantities of pure or fine silver. **1867** *Chamb. Jrnl.* XXXVIII. 105 'Fine' gold being purer than 'standard'. **1881** RAYMOND *Mining Gloss.*, *Fine metal*, the iron or plate-metal produced in the refinery.

fig. **1727** SWIFT *Further Acc. E. Curll*, Mixing a greater quantity of the fine metal of other authors with the alloy of this society.

b. Of gold or silver: Containing a given proportion of pure metal, specified respectively in 'carats' (see CARAT) or 'ounces' (*sc.* per lb. troy).

1594 PLAT *Jewell-ho.* III. 85 The golde being 24 Carots high, & the siluer 12 ounces fine. **1666** *Act 18 Chas. II*, c. 5 §1 For every pound troy of gold or silver..that shall be finer upon assay than crown gold or standard silver. **1820** G. G. CAREY *Funds* 95 Gold of twenty two carats fine signifies that twenty two parts of the whole mass is pure gold and two parts of some other metal. **1862** E. W. ROBERTSON *Hist. Ess.* I. i. 3 The purest gold, 24 carats fine.

fig. **1581** [See CARAT 3].

c. Of liquids; Free from turbidity or impurity, clear. Also occas. of air: Pure.

1481 CAXTON *Myrr.* I. i. 6 The good wyn that is aboue abideth alway clere and fyn. **1567** R. EDWARDS *Dam. & Pith.* in Hazl. *Dodsley* IV. 35 Methinks this is a pleasant city..The air subtle and fine. **1596** DALRYMPLE tr. *Leslie's Hist. Scot.* (1885) 27 Ane..spring, of fyne, freshe and fair water. *a* **1637** B. JONSON *Rules Tavern* v, Let our wines without mixture or stum be all fine. **1671** GREW *Anat. Plants* I. ii. (1682) 15 Which transient Sap..thus becomes fine. **1723** SWIFT *Stella at Woodpark*, She view'd the wine To see that ev'ry glass was fine. **1745** R. POCOCKE *Descr. East* II. i. 5 They..brought fine oil of olives. **1819** SHELLEY *Cyclops* 47 Here the air is calm and fine.

†**3.** Pure, sheer, absolute; perfect. In phrases adopted from OF., esp. (*of*, *with*, *by*) ***fine force***, (by) absolute necessity, also (by) main force; ***fine love***, ***fine heart***, etc. *Obs.*

c **1320** *Cast. Love* 1405 Ther was never fadur to his child Of fyne love so meke and myld. *c* **1330** R. BRUNNE *Chron.* (1810) 35 Kymak..com for fyne awe. *c* **1340** *Gaw. & Gr. Knt.* 1139 Me be-houez of fyne. force, Your seruaunt be. *c* **1450** *Merlin* 156 By fyn strengthe. *c* **1475** *Partenay* 3831 Whom I so loued with hert Fyn. **1564** HAWARD *Eutropius* VII. 61 Cesar..of fine force caused the Romaynes to create hym consull. **1670** COTTON *Espernon* I. II. 45 To effect that by fine Force, he could not obtain by the more moderate ways of Addresses, and Treaty. **1706** PHILLIPS (ed. Kersey), *Fine Force* (Fr. Law Term) an absolute unavoidable Necessity or Constraint. **1721–1800** in BAILEY.

4. Of persons: †**a.** Consummate in virtue or excellence. Chiefly as rime-word. *Obs.*

13.. *E.E. Allit. P.* A. 1203 A god, a lorde, a frend ful fyin. *c* **1330** R. BRUNNE *Chron.* (1810) 257 A baron bold & fyn. *c* **1400** *Rowland & O.* 14 Sir Cherlles gud & fyne. *c* **1450** *St. Cuthbert* (Surtees) 1901 Twa halymen and fyne, Saint benet and bischop Marcellyne.

†**b.** Used with reproachful designations: Consummate, 'egregious'. *Obs.* Cf. 12 c.

c **1425** WYNTOUN *Cron.* VI. vi. 18 A schrewe fyne. **1598** SHAKS. *Merry W.* v. i. 19 That same knaue (Ford hir husband) hath the finest mad diuell of iealousie in him..that euer gouern'd Frensie. **1604** — *Oth.* IV. i. 155, I was a fine Foole to take it.

c. In good health, well. (Cf. FIDDLE *sb.* 1 b.)

1791–1897 in *Eng. Dial. Dict.* (chiefly northern and Sc.). **1959** *Listener* 9 July 59/1 The sleepy subjects felt fine during the complex interesting tests. *a* **1968** H. HOOD in R. Weaver *Canad. Short Stories* 2nd Ser. (1968) 220 There's nothing wrong with my heart. I've just had my checkup and I'm fine, just fine.

5. Of persons or actions: Consummately skilful, highly accomplished. Now only as a contextual use of 12: Admirably skilful.

c **1320** *Orfeo* 265 To her harpyng that was fyne. *c* **1400** *Destr. Troy* 7716 A fyn archer. **1535** STEWART *Cron. Scot.* III. 436 To seik him leichis that wer fyne and gude, To heill his woundis. **1601** SHAKS. *Jul. C.* I. i. 10 In respect of a fine Workman, I am but..a Cobler. **1837** DISRAELI *Venetia* I. iii, A fine musician. **1880** L. STEPHEN *Pope* v. 133 Pope was a really fine judge of literature.

II. Delicate, subtle.

6. a. Exquisitely fashioned; delicately beautiful.

13.. *E.E. Allit. P.* A. 170 Her fygure fyn. *c* **1450** *Why I can't be a nun* 113 in *E.E.P.* (1862) 141, I fylle Among the herbes fresche and fyne. **1530** PALSGR. 312/2 Fyne as any worke that is small and subtylly wrought, *soubtil*. **1596** SPENSER *Prothalamion* 27 They..with fine fingers cropt..The tender stalks. **1610** SHAKS. *Temp.* I. ii. 317 Fine apparision: my quaint Ariel Hearke in thine eare. **1819** SHELLEY *Cenci* IV. i. 133 Warp those fine limbs To loathèd lameness. **1867** TENNYSON *Window* 88 Fine little hands, fine little feet.

b. Of immaterial things, e.g. emotion or feeling: Delicate, elevated, refined. Cf. 10.

1606 SHAKS. *Tr. & Cr.* IV. ii. 24 Some ioy too fine..For the capacitie of my ruder powers. **1797** MRS. RADCLIFFE *Italian* xxxiii. (1824) 713 A moment of finer joy. **1842** TENNYSON *Locksley H.* 46 What is fine within thee growing coarse to sympathise with clay.

7. a. Delicate in structure or texture, delicately wrought; consisting of minute particles or slender threads or filaments. Opposed to COARSE.

Often contextually coincident with sense 1.

c **1386** CHAUCER *Prol.* 453 Hire coverchiefs weren ful fine of ground. *a* **1400** *Sir Perc.* 453 He fande a lofe of brede fyne. **1558** *Bury Wills* (Camden) 151, J fyne hone. **1660** *Act 12 Chas. II*, c. 4. Sched. s.v. *Brushes*, Fine, or head brushes. **1721** BERKELEY *Prevent. Ruin Gt. Brit.* Wks. III. 199 More fine linen is wore in Great Britain than in any other country. **1737** BRACKEN *Farriery Impr.* (1756) I. 118 Any Thing that is termed fine Work. **1842** BISCHOFF *Woollen Manuf.* II. 192 The wool is fit for clothing purposes or for making fine flannels. **1884** A. R. PENNINGTON *Wiclif* vi. 187 They were..written on fine vellum.

b. In minute particles, comminuted.

1535 COVERDALE *Lev.* ii. 1 A meat offerynge..of fyne floure. **1589** *Pappe w. Hatchet* D ij b, They haue..got themselues the fine meale. **1602** SHAKS. *Ham* v. i. 116 Full of fine Dirt. **1820** SHELLEY *Witch* xliv. 6 Interwoven with fine feathery snow. **1885** *Manch. Exam.* 4 May 5/3 The air is in fact quite misty with the fine impalpable dust which it contains.

c. Attenuated, of small density, subtle, rare.

1626 BACON *Sylva* §761 When the Eye standeth in the Finer Medium. **1712–4** POPE *Rape Lock* II. 61 Transparent forms, too fine for mortal sight, Their fluid bodies half dissolved in light. **1783** POTT *Chirurg. Wks.* II. 219 The exudation of a fine fluid. **1860** MISS MULOCK *Parables* 30 in *Poems* 273 Air so rare and fine.

d. Very small in bulk or thickness; extremely thin or slender.

c **1400** MAUNDEV. (1839) iii. 17 Upon the Body lay a fyn plate of Gold. **1552** HULOET Fine threde, *arachnion*. **1577** GOOGE *Heresbach's Husb.* (1586) II. 68 Make..a fine hole..in the stocke. **1590** SPENSER *F.Q.* I. iv. 21 Like a crane his neck was long and fyne. *c* **1790** IMISON *Sch. Art* I. 223 The fine membranes between a frog's toes. **1821** SHELLEY *Prometh. Unb.* II. i. 116 Thine eyes..underneath Their long fine lashes.

fig. **1588** SHAKS. *L.L.L.* V. i. 19 He draweth out the thred of his verbositie finer then the staple of his argument. **1845** LD. HOUGHTON in *Life* (1891) I. viii. 360, I think my own finer [lines of judgment] just as distinct. **1884** *Manch. Exam.* 26 May 5/1 Margins of profit are so fine. **1891** FARMER *Slang*, *Cut fine*, to narrow down to a minimum.

e. *Athletics.* Reduced in fat to the proper degree by training.

1815 *Sporting Mag.* XLVI. 44 The gentleman who brought him [Oliver] so fine into the ring in his combat with Painter. **1887** R. L. STEVENSON *Pastoral* in *Longm. Mag.* IX. 598 With a certain strain in the expression, like that of a man trained too fine and harassed with perpetual vigilance.

f. With advb. force in *Cricket*: behind the wicket and near the line of flight of the ball (opp. *square*).

1867 *J. Lillywhite's Cricketers' Compan.* 9 His [*sc.* the fieldsman's] own judgement will tell him..to play fine at one time, and square at another. **1888** STEEL & LYTTELTON *Cricket* iii. 147 It is a golden rule for every bowler..on these wickets to have a short-slip 'finer' than on ordinary occasions. **1891** W. G. GRACE *Cricket* x. 263 Short-leg..must be quick to detect..whether he means to play it fine,

square, or more in the direction of mid-on. **1961** F. C. Avis *Sportsman's Gloss.* 119/2 *Fine leg*, the position of a fieldsman on the leg side but behind the wicket. **1963** A. Ross *Australia 63* vii. 129 Harvey swung across the line of the next ball, and it went straight in and out of Sheppard's hands at short fine leg.

g. In colloq. expressions such as *to cut fine, to run fine*, with advb. force: with a very slight margin (of time, space, etc.).

1871 *Chambers's Jrnl.* 9 Sept. 563/1 For purposes of concealment we sometimes ran it very fine. **1884** *Boy's Own Paper* Xmas no. 40/2 In endeavouring to round a headland the Crystal cut matters too fine, got on to rough ice. **1890**, **1892** [see run *v.* 36 d]. **1896** *Daily News* 24 July 8/6 The making of clothes was, he added, 'cut very fine'. **1899** *Chambers's Jrnl.* 30 Sept. 694/1 If by..chance I was cutting it fine. **1908** *Pearson's Weekly* 5 Mar. 606/2 Running it fine. **1930** W. S. Churchill *My Early Life* vii. 107 This was running things very fine, but it was not until my journey was half completed that I realised that I should be almost certainly late for dinner. **1950** 'W. Cooper' *Scenes Provincial Life* I. v. 72 Robert had ordered himself to come last. Tom argued with Robert about cutting it fine.

h. Of a ship's bow: slender.

1927 G. Bradford *Gloss. Sea Terms* 64/1 *Fine*, knife-like forward, where a vessel enters the water. The more a vessel departs from the shape of a box, the finer her lines.

i. ***fine print***: applied to those detailed clauses of a contract, warranty form, etc., that are printed in small type and specify the limits, qualifications, etc., of the agreement. Also *fig.*

1960 J. Carswell *S. Sea Bubble* i. 19 He produced the 'fine print' which it is peril to leave unread. **1966** *Guardian* 28 Nov. 1/1 A careful reading of the fine print of Mr Smith's latest proposals is likely. **1968** D. Hitchens *Cabin of Fear* i. 13 He was a fanatic about the fine-print..and he didn't get where he was by being careless.

j. ***fine chemicals***: see chemical *a.* 6 b.

8. Of a tool, weapon, etc.: Sharp-pointed, keen-edged; sharp. Also *fig.* (see also point *sb.*[1] B. 1 d).

c **1400** *Destr. Troy* 5824 He..frusshit at Philmene with a fyn launse. **1611** Shaks. *Wint. T.* v. iii. 78 What fine Chizzell Could euer yet cut breath? **1848** Macaulay *Hist. Eng.* I. 342 Those exquisitely fine blades which are required for operations on the human frame. **1871** Morley *Voltaire* (1886) 8 A fine sword, very fatal to those, who [etc.].

fig. *c* **1600** Shaks. *Sonn.* lii. 4 For blunting the fine point of seldom pleasure. **1622** Bacon *Hen. VII* 51 The finer edges or points of wit.

†**9.** Of bodily constitution: Delicate, sensitive, tender. *Obs.*

1607 Topsell *Four-f. Beasts* (1658) 583 Some fine or delicate person which cannot endure so gross a medicine. **1661** Lovell *Hist. Anim. & Min.* Introd., [Meats] fit for fine complexions, idle and tender persons.

10. a. Of distinctions, reasoning, objects of perception, etc.: Subtle, delicate, refined. **b.** Of senses, organs, instruments: Capable of delicate perception or discrimination; sensitive to delicate or subtle impressions.

1567 R. Edwards *Dam. & Pith.* in Hazl. *Dodsley* IV. 17 Now mens ears are finer. **1580** Baret *Alv.* F 544 A subtile and fine distinction, *distinctio tenuis & acuta*. **1606** Shaks. *Tr. & Cr.* I. iii. 338 For here the Trojans taste our dear'st repute With their finest palate. **1693** Dryden *Juvenal* Ded. 41 The..most delicate touches of Satire consist in fine Raillery. **1712** Addison *Spect.* No. 409 ⁋1 Gratian very often recommends the fine Taste, as the utmost Perfection of an accomplished Man. **1784** Cowper *Task* vi. 562 Grac'd with polish'd manners and fine sense. **1801** Southey *Thalaba* iii. xi, The subtile sounds, Too fine for mortal sense. **1855** Bain *Senses & Int.* ii. ii. §8 The part endowed with the finer tactile power feels the other. **1879** Thomson & Tait *Nat. Phil.* I. i. §431 A fine balance should turn with about a 500,000th of the greatest load which can safely be placed in either pan. **1885** *Law Times* LXXIX. 171/2 The distinction between motive and intention is perhaps a little fine.

†**11.** Intellectually subtle, clever, ingenious. In bad sense, Cunning, artful. *Obs.*

1377 Langl. *P. Pl.* B. x. 247 Had neuere freke fyne wytte þe feyth to dispute. *c* **1450** *St. Cuthbert* (Surtees) 7870 In all doyng discrete and fyne. **1559** *Mirr. Mag., Fall R. Tresilian* xii, To crepe into whose fauour we were full fyne and slye. **1579–80** North *Plutarch* (1676) 159 Soon after he understood they were counterfeit Letters, made by Hannibals fine device to have drawn him out. **1607–12** Bacon *Ess. Empire* (Arb.) 298 The wisedome of all theis latter tymes, in Princes' affaires, is rather fine Deliveryes, and shiftinges of daungers and mischeifes..than solid and grounded courses to keepe them aloofe. **1610** Bp. Carleton *Jurisd.* 6 Some of the finer Iesuits..are growen more cunning in the manner of deliuering it. **1701** Rowe *Amb. Step-Moth.* ii. ii. 942 One fine project of the Statesman's Brain. **1766** [Anstey] *Bath Guide* viii. (1807) 57 Men of fine heads, and nice calculations.

III. Senses developed in Eng. (chiefly = Fr. *beau*).

12. a. Used as a general expression of admiration: Excellent; admirable in quality; of rare or striking merit. In phr. ***fine and dandy***: see dandy *a.* 2.

c **1440** *Promp. Parv.* 161/1 Fyne, or ryght goode. **1580** Sidney *Arcadia* (1622) 116 To my conceite the fine cleanenesse of bearing it was exceeding delightfull. **1671** Lady Mary Bertie in *12th Rep. Hist. MSS. Comm.* App. v. 22 Two very fine new plays. **1676** Cotton *Angler* ii. i. 5 As fine Rivers, and as clear from..encumbrance to hinder an Angler, as any you ever saw. **1729** Law *Serious C.* i. (1815) 9 You see them..pleased with fine preachers. **1751** Chatham *Lett. Nephew* ii. 7 They [Homer and Virgil] contain the finest lessons for your age to imbibe. **1756–7** *Keysler's Trav.* (1760) IV. 451 Part of the fine paintings.. have already been brought from Dusseldorp. **1794** Southey *Botany Bay Ecl.* ii 'Tis a fine thing to fight the French for fame! **1829** Lytton *Devereux* i. iii, Candour no longer seemed to me the finest of virtues. **1833** Ht. Martineau *Manch. Strike* i. 9 Shake hands, my fine fellow. **1836** W. Irving *Astoria* II. 314 He accordingly fitted out a fine ship of four hundred and ninety tons. **1863** Kingsley *Water-Bab.* (1878) 5 He thought of the fine times coming when he would be a man.

b. Of thoughts, sayings, etc.: Admirably conceived or expressed.

1676 Hobbes *Iliad* Pref. (1686) 10 Two or three fine sayings are not enough to make a Wit. **1695** Dryden *Parall. Poetry & Paint.* Prose Wks. 1800 III. 348 The word *æs*, or brass, was taken for a trumpet, because the instrument was made of that metal,—which of itself was fine. **1712** Steele *Spect.* No. 288 ⁋1 Saying as many fine Things as their Stock of Wit will allow. **1875** Jowett *Plato* (ed. 2) III. 569 According to his own fine expression, 'the thought of God made God'.

c. Often used *ironically*.

1581 J. Bell *Haddon's Answ. Osor.* 36 How say you fine man? **1613** Shaks. etc. *Hen. VIII*, v. iv. 74 Y' haue made a fine hand, fellowes. **1679** Ld. Chancellor in R. Mansel *Narr. Popish Plot* 40 You are a fine Fellow; first to come to His Majesty..then to the Lord Powis. **1683** in Wood *Life* (O.H.S.) III. 70 That 'to execute penal lawes upon dissenters was'—speaking ironically—'a fine way to unite us'. **1797** Mrs. Radcliffe *Italian* xvi, Fine plots they would lay. **1855** Browning *Fra Lippo* 201 A fine way to paint soul, by painting body So ill. **1861** T. A. Trollope *La Beata* I. iv. 74 It is all very fine, but one must live. **1890** W. A. Wallace *Only a Sister?* 323 Telling your mates of your fine goings-on.

d. Of printing: intended for display as much as for reading; of the condition of a book: see quot. 1948; of an edition of a book: printed on better-quality paper, esp. in ***fine-paper copy***.

1867 [see press-work]. **1874** *Art of Paper-Making* iii. 23 In a fine-paper mill, the increase of manual labour..is more than compensated by the greater purity of the resulting product. **1912** A. W. Pollard (*title*) Fine books. **1948** J. Carter *Taste & Technique in Book-Collecting* xii. 172 In its most absolute sense..the term 'fine', applied to any book of any period, could be said to mean no more (if no less) than that all its leaves were present, clean, whole and amply margined; that it was sound and undisturbed in its binding; and that that binding, whatever its material, was fresh and unblemished and, if of leather, of a sufficient elegance to raise it above the modest category of 'neat'. **1952** E. J. Labarre *Dict. Paper* (ed. 2) 104/1 *Fine paper*,..indicates the printing of a book on better paper than the bulk of the edition. **1957** R. L. Collison *Book Collecting* 197 Formerly very popular, this process [*sc.* marbling] is now mostly confined to account books and ledgers, though since the war it has also been used in fine printing. **1964** F. Bowers *Bibliogr. & Textual Crit.* iii. vi. 84 One perhaps aberrant fine-paper copy. **1970** *Sotheby's Catal. Sale Children's Books* 16 Mar. 29 The Golliwogg Books, a complete set of 13 vol., the last eight first editions, coloured illustrations, original cloth-backed boards, pictorial upper covers, seven covers slightly spotted, otherwise a very fine set.

13. a. Remarkably good-looking, handsome. Said both of persons and things.

In the 18th c. the expression 'a fine woman' (= *une belle femme*) was very often used where we should now rather say 'beautiful' or 'pretty'.

1340–70 *Alex. & Dind.* 591 But hit [a tomb] fair be & fin, folie ȝe holden. **1598** Yong *Diana* 36 A Shepherdesse so fine perdie, So liuely yoong and passing faire. **1726** Franklin *Jrnl.* Wks. 1887 I. 106 From the battlements of this upper castle..you have a fine prospect. **1749** Fielding *Tom Jones* viii. viii, [She] is still a very fine woman. **1791** Mrs. Radcliffe *Rom. Forest* x, She is a fine girl. **1828** Scott *F.M. Perth* xxx, To make yourself acceptable to a fine woman. **1833** Ht. Martineau *Brooke Farm* iv. 43 As fine a set of lads and lasses as could be seen. **1867** Miss Broughton *Cometh up as Flower* xxx. (1878) 334 A monstrous fine woman. **1868** Lockyer *Elem. Astron.* i. (1879) 34 The finest ring-nebula is the 57th in Messier's catalogue.

b. Of the features, etc., in a more elevated sense: 'Beautiful with dignity' (J.).

1801 Southey *Thalaba* ix. ii, Her fine face raised to Heaven. **1849** C. Brontë *Shirley* ii, He seems unconscious that his features are fine. **1878** Hutton *Scott* i. 4 His father was a man of fine presence.

14. a. Of handsome size or growth.

1590 Greene *Never too late* (1600) 3 The finest buds are soonest nipt with frosts. **1703** Maundrell *Journ. Jerus.* 40 Orange Trees..all of so fine a growth..that one cannot imagine anything more perfect in this kind. **1796** C. Marshall *Garden.* xvii. (1813) 279 Some sorts [of fruit trees] grow finest in..a warm soil. **1870** Mrs. H. Wood *G. Canterbury* II. i. 9 A fine child you call him..He is not a fine child, for he is remarkably small; but he is a very pretty one.

b. Colloquially often with derisive notion: Very large; also followed by *large, big*, etc.

1833 Ht. Martineau *Berkeley* i. iii. 53 You had a fine slice of bread and honey just before Miss Berkeley came in.

15. a. Of the weather, a day, etc.: In which the sky is bright, or comparatively free from cloud. Often merely in the sense: Free from rain. Also *Naut.* of the wind (see quot. 1867).

[= F. *beau*; F. has also *un temps fin* bright and cloudless weather, but this seems not to have influenced the Eng. use.]

1704 Cuningham in *Phil. Trans.* XXV. 1688 Fair and pleasant weather, with fine gales at S.E. **1732** Berkeley *Alciphr.* ii. §1 The weather was so fine they had a mind to spend the day abroad. **1836** M. Scott *Cruise Midge* I. ii. 39 A fine breeze, that..was nearly a fair wind up the river. **1867** Tennyson *Window* 153 'Cuck-oo! Cuck-oo!' was ever a May so fine? **1867** Smyth *Sailor's Word-bk.*, *Fine breezes*, said of the wind when the flying-kites may be carried but requiring a sharp look-out. **1872** Wood *Insects at Home* iii. 337 On a fine day, it is very interesting to watch the ants [etc.].

b. *one of these fine days*, etc. (= F. *un de ces beaux jours*): often used playfully or derisively with reference to the occurrence of some unlooked for event. Also ***some fine day***, one day in the future.

1846 G. E. Jewsbury *Sel. Lett. to Mrs. Carlyle* (1892) 189 Some fine day she will let you inside that moral mystery, and will hate you for it afterwards. **1853** Miss Mulock *Agatha's Husb.* I. iii. 65 Miss Bowen set off one fine morning, hoping [etc.]. **1854** Dickens *Hard T.* i. xi. 89 You'll get yourself into a real muddle, one of these fine mornings. **1890** [see money *sb.* 3 a].

16. Of dress: Highly ornate, showy, smart. Hence of persons: Smartly dressed. Chiefly in disparaging use. Prov. ***fine feathers make fine birds***.

1526 *Pilgr. Perf.* (W. de W. 1531) 84 With fayre and fyne clothes. **1596** Shaks. *Tam. Shr.* ii. i. 319, I will be sure my Katherine shall be fine. **1665** Boyle *Occas. Refl.* v. v. (1845) 313 A Colour'd suit, that but last Week, would have been thought a fine one. **1721** Kelly *Sc. Prov.* 109 Fine Feathers make fine Birds. **1730** Swift *Death & Daphne*, Fine as a col'nel of the guards. **1771** Mrs. Harris in *Priv. Lett. Ld. Malmesbury* I. 214 A dress which was pretty and fine. **1798** Jane Austen *Northang. Abb.* (1833) I. ii. 7 She had a harmless delight in being fine.

17. Characterized by or affecting refinement or elegance; polished, dainty, refined, fastidious, etc.

1546 J. Heywood *Prov.* (1562) Ijb, Lyke one of fond fancy so fyne and so neate, That would haue better bread than is made of wheate. *a* **1555** Latimer *Serm. & Rem.* (1845) 109 Those fine damsels thought it scorn to do any such thing unto Mary. **1732** Pope *Ep. Bathurst* 73 Soft Adonis, so perfum'd and fine. **1774** Mrs. Harris in *Priv. Lett. Ld. Malmesbury* I. 279 She is too fine to come to town till the day before the birthday. **1786** Burns *Holy Fair* xv, His English style, an' gesture fine Are a' clean out o' season. **1800** Mrs. Hervey *Mourtray Fam.* I. 55 Since she had been admitted into the society of her fine neighbours. **1814** Wordsw. *Excursion* vi, Yet farther recommended by the charm Of fine demeanor. **1885** Besant *Children of Gibeon* ii. xxxii, He's only a working-man, you see. He hasn't got your fine ways.

18. a. Of speech, writing, etc.: Affectedly ornate or elegant.

1773 Mrs. Chapone *Improv. Mind* (1774) II. 113 Idle gallantry and unmeaning fine speeches. *c* **1800** K. White *Lett.* (1837) 334 Never make use of fine or vulgar words. **1837** J. H. Newman *Par. Serm.* (ed. 3) I. xiii. 202 A price for the indulgence of fine speaking. **1867** Freeman *Norm. Conq.* (1876) I. App. 610 By way of fine writing.

b. Flattering, complimentary.

1848 Macaulay *Hist. Eng.* I. 168 When this haggling was very obstinate and very skilful it was called by some fine name. **1865** Mill in *Morn. Star* 6 July, I hope you don't suppose that I think all the fine things true about me which have been said [etc.]. **1874** Morley *Compromise* (1886) 169 Hardly..more than a fine name for self-indulgence.

B. *sb.* (The adj. used absol.) †**a.** A fine woman. †**b.** Fine quality. **c.** The fine part of anything. **d.** Fine weather.

1607 Tourneur *Rev. Trag.* iii. v, Me thinkes she makes almost as faire a fine. **1638** Ford *Lady's Trial* iii. i, Fairs, fines, and honies, are but flesh and blood. **1669** J. F. *Merchant's Ware-ho.* 15 What it wants in the fine, you have compleated in the strength. *a* **1834** Lamb *Final Mem.* viii. To H. C. Robinson 264 You go about, in rain or fine, at all hours. **1886** G. Allen *Maimie's Sake* xviii, The fine of the day will all be gone by that time.

e. *pl.* Very small particles: used in various technical senses. (See also quot. 1880).

1880 J. Dunbar *Pract. Papermaker* 14 Fines consist of fine white cottons [*sc.* rags]. **1904** *Westm. Gaz.* 28 July 3/2 Breaking up much waste rock into fines. **1908** *Ibid.* 22 Oct. 13/1 All fines [*sc.* fine ores] are discharged into the tank over the head of the funnel with great force. **1930** *Engineering* 4 Apr. 449/2 The fines are entirely withdrawn from the coal. **1950** *Ibid.* 13 Jan. 53/2 It was..found possible to stabilise a powder by mixing it with dry stearic acid or zinc stearate in small amounts... The chief objection to the process was that the flowing properties of the treated powder were poor, the deterioration being more marked than would have been expected from the slight increase in the proportion of 'fines' during the milling. **1951** *Gloss. Terms Plastics (B.S.I.)* 21 *Fines*, a qualitative description of the extremely small particles which may be present in a granular powder. The presence of this very fine material in substantial amount may in some instances be undesirable. **1957** *Brit. Commonw. Forest Terminol.* ii. 73 *Fines*, in pulping, the very short or fragmented fibres. **1965** G. J. Williams *Econ. Geol. N.Z.* xvi. 266/2 Many of the quartz sand deposits contain too much fines (i.e. passing 100 mesh BSS) for glass manufacture. **1969** *Times* 2 May (Suppl.) p. iv/6 All companies with the exception of the Savage River group produce iron ore lump and fines. **1970** *Nature* 24 Jan. 325/2 The word fines is accepted in lunar research as describing all those solid particles with a size less than 1 cm. *Ibid.* 326/1 Several others also reported the gradual loss of adhesion on exposure of fines material to a gaseous atmosphere.

f. See fine champagne.

C. *adv.* = Finely: **a.** In a fine manner, elegantly, etc.; as, to talk fine. **b.** Well, very well; completely, fully; also in †***full fine***; †***well and fine***: to one's satisfaction, thoroughly (*obs.*). *dial.* and *colloq.* **c.** Delicately, mincingly, subtly, with nicety.

a. **1508** Dunbar *Tua Mariit Wemen* 31 Annamalit fine with flouris Off alkin hewis under hewin. **1708** *Lond. Gaz.* No. 4496/4 A strong Bay Horse that..goes fine. **1730** Swift *Paneg. on the Dean*, The neighbours who come here to dine, Admire to hear me speak so fine. **1751** *Female Foundl.* II. 46 Nothing could be imagined finer turned than the Praises which he gave me. **1773** *Hist. Ld. Ainsworth* I. 9 Servants who drest finer than their mistresses. **1812** W. Taylor in

Monthly Rev. LXXIX. 384 All the personages talk fine. 1812 L. Hunt in *Examiner* 14 Dec. 785/2 They spoke finest.

b. c1385 Chaucer *L.G.W.* 1715 *Lucrece*, The husbonde knew the estris wel and fyn. c1400 *Destr. Troy* 7168 Iche freike was fyn hole of þere fell hurttes. c1470 Harding *Chron.* c. v, Rulyng that lande in peace and lawe full fine. c1554 *Interl. Youth* in Hazl. *Dodsley* II. 12 Your brother and you together Fettered fine fast! 1889 Barrie *Window in Thrums* 168, I believe fine ye mean what ye say. 1890 W. A. Wallace *Only a Sister?* 327, I could see all fine from behind the curtains. 1932 T. S. Eliot *Sweeney Agonistes* 18 We like London fine. 1947 Partridge *Usage & Abusage* 118/2 *Fine* as an adverb ('He's doing fine') is dialectal and colloquial.

c. 1588 Shaks. *L.L.L.* v. i. 22 Such rackers of ortagriphie, as to speake dout fine, when he should say doubt. 1611 —— *Cymb.* i. i. 84 Dissembling curtesie! How fine this Tyrant Can tickle where she wounds! 1676 Cotton *Angler* ii. v. 35 To fish fine, and far off is the..principal Rule for Trout Angling. 1704 J. Trapp *Abra-Mulé* iii. i. 1191 Thy Plot was wrought Too fine for my dull Sight.

D. *Comb.*

1. Of the adj. **a.** With pr. pples. forming adjs., as *fine-appearing* (U.S. dial.), *-looking*..

1879 Howell *L. Aroostook* (1883) II. 59 'She is very *fine-appearing,' said Lydia. Staniford smiled at the countrified phrase. 1799 Malthus *Jrnl.* 2 June (1966) 44 We saw a great number of healthy *fine looking children. 1844 J. Cowell *30 Yrs. among Players* (1845) i. x. 25/2 A fine-looking young man and a beautiful girl. 1922 Joyce *Ulysses* 734 Killing any finelooking men there were.

b. In parasynthetic derivatives, as *fine-baited, -boned, -eyed, -feathered, -featured, -fleeced, -furred, -haired, -jointed, -leaved, -mouthed, -nosed, -paced, -skinned, -spirited, -textured, -threaded, -timbered, -toned, -tongued, -tubed, -witted, -woolled*.

1598 Shaks. *Merry W.* ii. i. 99 Lead him on with a *fine baited delay. 1927 Joyce *Pomes Penyeach*, I wrap him warm And touch his trembling *fineboned shoulder. 1959 J. Wain *Travelling Woman* iii. 22 The chin..at the same time fine-boned and intellectual. 1815 Keats *Epistle to G. F. Mathew* 35 The *fine-eyed maid. 1751 R. Paltock *P. Wilkins* (1884) II. ii. 18 A very *fine-feathered creature. 1657 Cokaine *Obstinate Lady* iii. i, *Fine-featur'd Mars. 1835 Ure *Philos. Manuf.* 131 The high prices at which the *fine-fleeced animals were sold. 1630 Drayton *Noahs Floud* 97 The *fine-furd Ermin. 1711 *Lond. Gaz.* No. 4890/4 Very Fat and *fine hair'd. 1849 Parker *Goth. Archit.* i. i. (1874) 16 *Fine-jointed masonry. 1885 T. Baines (*title*) Green-house & stove plants, flowering and *fine-leaved, palms, [etc.]. 1952 A. G. L. Hellyer *Sanders's Encycl. Gardening* (ed. 22) 174 [*Edraianthus*] *tenuifolius*, blue fine-leaved. a1700 B. E. *Dict. Cant. Crew*, *Fine-mouth'd, nice dainty. 1811 *Sporting Mag.* XXXVIII. 111 Should the executioner be too fine-mouthed. 1655 Fuller *Ch. Hist.* vi. ii. §1 The Monks themselves were too *fine-nosed to dabble in Tan-fatts. 1625 B. Jonson *Staple of N.* i. i, A *fine-paced gentleman. 1701 *Lond. Gaz.* No. 3748/4 A black Gelding..*fine Skin'd. 1714 Mandeville *Fab. Bees* (1733) II. 315 Many *fine-spirited creatures. 1890 Child *Ballads* vii. ccxi. 145/2 It is a fine-spirited ballad as it stands. 1901 *Fine-textured [see textured *a.*]. 1958 *Yearbk. Agric. 1957* (U.S. Dept. Agric.) 758/1 *Fine-textured soil*, roughly, clayey soil containing 35 percent or more of clay. 1833 Herschel *Astron.* ii. 84 A *fine-threaded screw. 1634 Massinger *Very Woman* ii. iii, This day the market's kept for slaves; go you, And buy you a *fine-timber'd one to assist me. 1864 A. McKay *Hist. Kilmarnock* (1880) 120 A *fine-toned organ. 1580 Sidney *Arcadia* (1622) 238 My *fine-witted wench Artesia. 1797 *Fine-woolled [see woolled *a.* 2]. 1868 Darwin *Anim. & Pl.* I. iii. 99 Fine-woolled sheep.

2. Of the adv. **a.** With pr. pples., forming adjs., as *fine-dividing, -feeling, -sounding, -tapering*.

1879 Geo. Eliot *Coll. Breakf. P.* 610 Brains and *fine-dividing tongue. 1795 *Jemima* I. 4 This..is your amiable.. your *fine-feeling Miss Jemima. 1845 Ford *Handbk. Spain* i. 35 The names of the animals are always *fine-sounding. 1728–46 Thomson *Spring* 384 The rod *fine-tapering with elastic spring.

b. With pa. pples., forming adjs., as *fine-bred, -dressed, -set, -sifted, -spoken, -tricked, -wrought*.

1667 Dryden *Wild Gallant* iii. ii, A *fine-bred woman. 1710 Palmer *Proverbs* 111 Many a fine-bred gentleman has been ruin'd by a title. 1681 Otway *Soldier's Fort.* ii. i, A dainty *fine-drest coxcomb. 1703 Moxon *Mech. Exerc.* 111 **Fine-set*, the Irons of Planes..are set Fine, when..in working they take off a fine-shaving. 1823 P. Nicholson *Pract. Build.* 223 *Fine-set*. 1824 Miss Mitford *Village* Ser. i. (1863) 197 The *fine-sifted mould of the shrubberies. 1666 Pepys *Diary* 1 Apr., I find him a very *fine-spoken gentleman. 1853 Lynch *Self-Improv.* v. 105 The talk and airs of fine-spoken reputable people. 1600 J. Lane *Tom Tel-troth* 235 These mincing maides and *fine trict truls, ride post To Plutoes pallace. 1691 Norris *Pract. Disc.* 239 As the laborious Spider weaves her *fine-wrought Web. 1725 De Foe *Voy. round World* (1840) 198 Fine-wrought China silks. 1816 Shelley *There is no work* 21 The fine-wrought eye and the wondrous ear.

c. With verbs, forming verbs, as *fine-burnish*.

1833 Holland *Manuf. Metal* II. 40 Women, who carefully *fine-burnish the bows with a polished steel instrument.

3. Special comb.: **fine-arch** (see quot.); **fine-axe** *v. trans.*, to face (stone) to a smooth surface by tapping with a mason's axe; **fine-boring** *vbl. sb.*, the process of giving a fine bore to a gun; **fine-edge** *v.* to put a fine edge upon, sharpen; **fine entrance, entry**, a slender ship's bow; **fine-fingered** *a.*, (*a*) delicate, fastidious; (*b*) light-fingered; **fine-groove** , the groove on a long-playing gramophone record; usu. *attrib.*, as *fine-groove record*; **fine-headed** *a.*, (*a*) given to making fine distinctions; (*b*) clear-headed, clever; †**fine-palated** *a.*, pleasing to the palate; **fine-sight** (see quot.); **fine stuff** (see quots.); **fine-toothed** *a.*, (*a*) of a file or a saw: having fine teeth; (*b*) of persons: delicate or epicurean in matters of taste or palate; **fine world** = beau-monde. Also fine-art, fine gentleman, fine lady, fine-spun, fine-weather, etc.

1874 Knight *Dict. Mech.* I. 847/1 **Fine-arch*, the smaller fritting-furnance of a glass-house. 1886 H. C. Seddon *Builder's Wk.* 82 *Fine axed is a more careful description of single axed work. 1895 *Daily News* 18 June 6/4 All kinds of Scotch granites, polished and fine-axed. 1891 *Pall Mall G.* 30 May 7/2 The process called '*fine-boring'. 1824 *Mechanic's Mag.* No. 46. 280 Easy mode of *fine-edging a Razor. 1869 *Fine entrance [see entrance *sb.* 6]. 1961 F. H. Burgess *Dict. Sailing* 86 **Fine entry, fine entrance*, a lean bow. A quality possessed by any vessel with long tapered bows to offer less resistance. 1549 Coverdale *Erasm. Par. 1 Tim.* 13 To professe Christ, is not an ydle nor a delycate *fine fyngred matter. c1559 in Strype *Ann. Ref.* I. xiv. 189 These finefingered rufflers with their sables about their necks. 1603 Breton *Mad World* (Grosart) 11/1 Taking me for a fine fingreed companion. 1956 (*title*) Reproducing equipment for *fine-groove records. (B.B.C.) 1957 *B.B.C. Handbk.* 52 A further development during 1956 was the introduction of 'fine groove' long-playing disk recording equipment. 1958 *Chambers's Techn. Dict.* 967/1 (s.v. *coarse groove*). Fine groove, or microgroove, used for vinylite long-playing discs. 1579 Tomson *Calvin's Serm. Tim.* 1007/2 Some *fine headed and learned fellowe. 1583 Golding *Calvin on Deut.* li. 307 Some..which are so fine headded that they will make God a lyer. 1603 Florio *Montaigne* ii. xvii. (1632) 366 The finer-headed, and more subtle-brained a man is. 1742 *Lond. & Country Brew.* i. (ed. 4) 37 The desired End of enjoying *fine-palated wholesome Drink. 1859 *Musketry Instruct.* 34 **Fine-sight* is when the line of sight is taken along the bottom of the notch of the back-sight, the fine point of the fore-sight being only seen in the alignment. 1825 J. Nicholson *Operat. Mechanic* 611 *Fine stuff..is merely pure lime, slaked first with a small quantity of water, and afterwards [etc.]. 1858 Simmonds *Dict. Trade*, *Fine-stuff*, the second coat of plaster for the walls of a room, composed of finely sifted lime and sand mixed with hair. 1601 Holland *Pliny* I. 430 As they say that be *fine-toothed, and have a delicate tast. 1842 *Bk. Trades* 231 The fine-toothed files. 1960 *Farmer & Stockbreeder* 8 Mar. (Suppl.) 5/1 Cut very carefully using a fine-toothed saw. 1801 Han. More *Wks.* VIII. 181 Persons who are pleased exclusively to call themselves..the *fine world.

†**fine**, *v.*[1] *Obs.* Forms: 3–6 fine, (3 fin, 4 fyn), fyn(e(n. Often with strong pa. t.: 3–4 fan(e, (3 fayne), 4 fon, 5 fyne. [ad. OF. *finer* = Cat., Sp., Pg. *finar*, It. *finare*, com. Rom. *finare*, f. L. *fin-is* end.]

1. *intr.* Of persons and other agents: To cease, stop, give over, desist. Const. *inf.* with *to*.

1297 R. Glouc. (1724) 140 Heo ne fynede neuer mo ar þo oþer ware at gronde. a1300 *Cursor M.* 3309 (Cott.) Bot ai þe quils he ne fan To be-hald þat leue maidan. c1375 *Sc. Leg. Saints*, *Jacobus* 338 For-þi þe lele mene, ore þa fane, Thinkand na ewil vent to þe hill. 1430 Lydg. *Chron. Troy* i. ii, He wolde not fyne Playnely to worke to his conclusyon.

2. To come to an end, fail, pass away, end. Also, to come to the end of one's life, to die.

a1300 *Cursor M.* 22268 (Cott.) Sua sal cristen kingrik fine. 13.. *E.E. Allit. P.* A. 328 Schal I efte forgo hit er euer I fyne? 14.. Lydg. *Temple of Glas* 372 In short tyme hir turment shulde fyne. c1500 *Lancelot* 2081 This Is hy mycht that neuer more shall fyne. 15.. *Bk. Fair Gentlewom.* in *Laneham's Let.* (1871) Introd. 96 Here Fineth Lady Fortune.

3. *trans.* To bring to an end, complete, conclude, finish.

c1374 Chaucer *Troylus* iv. Proeme 26 Father of Qwyrine! This ferthe book me helpith for to fyne. 1426 *Pol. Poems* (Rolls) II. 134 Alle oure trouble to enden and to fyne. a1512 Fabyan *Chron.* vii. 682 An ende of thys boke..Here is now fyned, whereof the sence precedyth. 1593 Shaks. *Lucr.* 936 Time's office is to fine the hate of foes.

b. To finish off (a part of a building).

1448 *Will of Hen. VI* in Willis & Clark *Cambridge* I. 369 Euery boterace fined with finialx. *Ibid.*, Smale tourettis.. fined with pynacles.

Hence **fined** *ppl. a.*, '**fining** *vbl. sb.*

c1300 *K. Alis.* 8015 God geve alle good fynyng! c1448 *Avyse of Hen. VI* in Willis & Clark *Cambridge* I. 367 Fro the Crest unto the fynyng of the pynnacles. 1571 T. Fortescue *Forest of Hist.* 64 b, Considering what we reade of their fined labours. 1596 Drayton *Legends, Robert* cxv, In fined things such meruails infinite.

fine (faɪn), *v.*[2] Also 3–7 fyne. [f. fine *sb.*[1]]

†**1.** *trans.* To pay as a fine or composition. *Obs.*

1297 R. Glouc. (1724) 463 Me..bounde men & enprisonede, vorte hii fynede raunson. *Ibid.* 528 So þat vor þe manslaȝt..þe clerkes finede wiþ him gret raunson inou. 1599 Shaks. *Hen. V*, iv. vii. 72 Know'st thou not That I have fined these bones of mine for ransom?

†**2.** To impose (a tax) *upon*. *Obs.*

1563–87 Foxe *A. & M.* (1596) 307/1 Shortlie after a tax was fined upon the countrie of Norfolke.

†**3.** *intr.* To pay a penalty, ransom, or composition. Const. *with* (a person). *Obs.*

1297 R. Glouc. (1724) 511, & wo so nolde aȝen hom at hor wille fine, Hii barnde hous & other god. 1526 *Customs of Pale* (Dillon 1892) 85 Unto that theie have ffined with him for theire trespas. 1548 Hall *Chron.* (1809) 9 He made them fine of newe. 1561 Stow *Eng. Chron.* (1565) 155 b, He was deteyned in prison..vntyll he had fyned with the kyng for 8000 poundes. 1563–87 Foxe *A. & M.* (1684) III. 761 Except you fine with me, I will put a Collar about your Neck.

transf. and *fig.* 1580 Sidney *Ps.* lv. 18 He ransom'd me, he for my safetie fin'd In fight. 1634 Shirley *Examples* iv. i, A challenge! Some young gentlemen that have Strong purses and faint souls do use to fine for 't.

b. *esp.* to do this in order to escape the duties of an office. Const. *for*, esp. in *to fine for* (*the office of*) *alderman, sheriff*, etc. Also, †*to fine off*.

1557 *Order of Hospitalls* B vj, Except he be such a one as have borne th' Office of an Alderman, or hath fined for the same. 1663 Pepys *Diary* 1 Dec., Mr. Crow..hath fined for Alderman. 1682 *Enq. Elect. Sheriffs* 41 Charlton..chose rather to Fine than to run the risk of being confirmed by the Commons to hold. 1706 Estcourt *Fair Examp.* v. i, You.. are able to Fine for Sheriff upon occasion. 1751 Johnson *Rambler* No. 116 ¶3 Some have fined for Sheriffs. 1761–2 Hume *Hist. Eng.* (1806) V. lxix. 179 Box apprehensive of the consequences which might attend so dubious an election, fined off.

fig. a1680 Butler *Rem.* (1759) I. 82 So sadly dull And stupid, as to fine for Gull.

†**4.** Of a magistrate: *to fine with* (a person). To accept a money payment as the price of connivance. *Sc.*

1609 Skene *Reg. Maj.* 135 Gif any Lord of Regalitie sells any theif: or fines with him for theift done.

5. †**a.** To pay a fine on the renewel of tenure. (Cf. fine *sb.*[1] 7.) *Obs.* **b.** *trans. to fine down* or *off*: to arrange for a reduction of (rent) upon payment of a fine. So, *to fine down a lease*.

1670 Walton *Lives* i. 50 Our Tenant.. offered to fine at so low a rate as held not proportion with his advantages. 1705 *Lond. Gaz.* No. 4183/3 The Tenant fining down a Part. 1709 *Ibid.* No. 4540/5 Fining off part of the Rent after the rate of ten Years Purchase. 1880 [see fining below].

6. *to fine and recover*: see recover.

1831 Scott *Jrnl.* (1890) II. 401, I believe I have fined and recovered, and so may be thankful.

7. To pay a consideration for a specified privilege, or for appointment to an office.

1548 Udall, etc. *Erasm. Par. John* xviii. 13 Beeyng a benefice sette to sale it [the high-priesthood] was fined for euery yere to the princes. 1776 Adam Smith *W.N.* i. x. (1869) I. 130 Such adulterine guilds..were..obliged to fine annually to the king for permission to exercise their usurped privileges. 1813 Scott *Rokeby* ii. xxx, Nobles and knights ..Must fine for freedom and estate. 1818 Hallam *Mid. Ages* II. viii. ii. 117 In England, women, and even men, simply as tenants in chief, and not as wards, fined to the crown for leave to marry whom they would. 1876 S. Dowell *Taxes in Eng.* I. iv. 33 In the fifth year of King Stephen, the Londoners fined in C marks of silver, that they might have sheriffs of their own choosing.

8. *trans.* To punish by a fine; to mulct. Hence simply, to punish (*obs.*). With the penalty or amount expressed as a second object, or introduced by *in*.

1559 Fabyan *Chron.* (1811) 615 Of the whiche prysoners some were after fyned, and some punysshed by longe imprysonment. 1603 Shaks. *Meas. for M.* iii. i. 115 If it were damnable, he being so wise, Why would he for the momentarie tricke Be perdurablie fin'de? 1662 Stillingfl. *Orig. Sacr.* i. i. §11 He was..fined five talents. 1679 Burnet *Hist. Ref.* I. ii. 166 He was..fined in 400 Pound. 1692 Locke *Consid. Money* 12 To Fine Men one Third of their Estates..seems very hard. 1722 Sewel *Hist. Quakers* (1795) I. iii. 153 They were fined for not taking off their hats. 1794 S. Williams *Vermont* 294 Others have been fined in large sums. 1827 Hallam *Const. Hist.* (1876) III. xiii. 9 It was against law to fine a jury for giving a verdict contrary to the court's direction. 1874 Green *Short Hist.* iv. §5. 198 The King was strong enough to fine and imprison the Earls. *Mod.* The magistrate fined him forty shillings.

Hence **fined** *ppl. a.*, in *fined-down* (sense 5); '**fining** *vbl. sb.*, the action of the verb, an instance of this; also *fining down*, in quot. *attrib.*

1599 Massinger, etc. *Old Law* iv. ii, Your smiles deserve a fining. 1660 Fisher *Rusticks Alarm* Wks. (1679) 125 Fineing, banishing..and such like. 1880 *Daily Tel.* 31 Dec. 3/5 Many of the tenants have paid large sums for fined-down leases. *Ibid.*, The fining-down system, by which reductions of rent were bought out by lump sums.

fine (faɪn), *v.*[3] Also 4–6 fyne(n. [f. fine *a.*] To make or become fine.

1. *trans.* To make fine or pure; to purify from extraneous or impure matter; to clarify, refine. Also *to fine down*. †*to fine chaff*: to drive it off in the process of cleansing the wheat.

1340 *Ayenb.* 106 Ase deþ þet uer [þet] clenzeþ and fineþ þet gold. c1440 Hylton *Scala Perf.* (W. de W. 1494) ii. xxix, Also sone as the wyne is fyned & clered thenne it stondeth styll. 1487 *Act 4 Hen. VII*, c. 2 Preamb., To fine and part all Gold and Silver. 1520 Whitinton *Vulg.* (1527) 15 This rynlet of malvesy is not fyned. 1579 Spenser *Sheph. Cal.* Dec. 125 As the chaffe should in the fan be fynd. 1613 J. Rovenzon *Treat. Metallica* D iij, The Sowe-Iron may be fined at one time. 1686 Plot *Staffordsh.* 338 They have a knack of fineing it [ale] in three days time to that degree, that [etc.]. 1761 Franklin in J. Adams *Wks.* (1850) II. 82 *note*, The porter.. is..fined down with ising-glass. 1797 Downing *Dis. Horned Cattle* 22 That will help to fine and thin the blood. 1823 J. Badcock *Dom. Amusem.* 103 To 'fine down' Spirits. 1843 Ure *Dict. Arts* (ed. 3) 1302 In the month of January the clear wine is racked off, and is fined by a small quantity of isinglass. 1859 Sala *Gas-light & D.* vi. 71 Has it been adulterated, 'fined', doctored. 1906 Mrs. Beeton *Bk. Househ. Managem.* lxix. 1790 There are various methods of fining wine; eggs, isinglass, gelatine and gum Arabic are all used. *Ibid.*, A cask of clarified wine will fine thirteen dozen bottles of port or sherry.

fig. 1340 Hampole *Pr. Consc.* 2634 For in heven may na saul be sene, Unto it be fyned and clensed clene. 1628 Coke *On Litt.* 97 a, The Law of England..hath beene fined and refined by an infinite number of graue and learned men. 1663 Blair *Autobiog.* ii. (1848) 49 The Lord is pleased by

trials to fine the faith of his servants. **1871** BROWNING *Pr. Hohenst.* 1324 Fined and thrice refined I' the crucible of life.

2. *intr.* To grow or become fine or clear; to clarify. *lit.* and *fig.* Also, *to fine down.*

1552 HULOET, Fine, reste, or settle, as wine dothe or other licoure, *sido.* **1664** EVELYN *Pomona* Gen. Advt. (1729) 89 It will work so long, that when it fines, the Cider will be hard. **1719** *Free-thinker* No. 134 ¶6 The perpetual violent Motions..hinder his Mind from fining. **1756** C. LUCAS *Ess. Waters* I. 46 Water..which..appears muddy and foul, will fine..upon standing. **1822** IMISON *Sc. & Art* II. 159 The liquor is now suffered to stand for some time to fine (or become transparent). **1859** HUGHES *Scouring of White Horse* iv. 62 [The ale] hadn't had quite time to fine down.

†**3.** *trans.* To make beautiful, handsome, or elegant. Also, *to fine up*: to furbish up, smarten. *Obs.*

c **1400** *Rom. Rose* 1696 For it so wel was enlumyned With colour reed, as wel fyned, As nature couthe it make faire. **1567** *Trial Treas.* in Hazl. *Dodsley* III. 263 Though the style be barbarous, not fined with eloquence. **1627–77** FELTHAM *Resolves* I. xxviii. 48 He does fine up his homely house. **1655** GURNALL *Chr. in Arm.* xii. (1669) 47 To bestow a great deal of cost in fining up an old Suit. **1664** J. WILSON *Cheats* II. iv, He does not fine up himself, as he was wont.

†**4.** To improve in quality. *Obs.*

1683 PENN in R. Burton *Eng. Emp. Amer.* vii. (1685) 111 Whether it be best to fall to Fining the Fruits of the Country ..or send for foreign Stems or Sets already good. **1712** MORTIMER *Husb.* II. v. 23 It fines the Grass, but makes it short, tho' thick.

5. To make small, thin, or slender.

a. To break into fine or small particles. *Obs.* exc. *techn.*

1548 UDALL, etc. *Erasm. Par. Luke* Pref. 9 b, They fyne and beate to powder..not receiptes of theyr owne, but of Christes. **1725** BRADLEY *Fam. Dict.* s.v. *Ploughing of Land*, If the Land mounts full of Clots..you must fine it by harrowing it when Rain comes. **1880** LOMAS *Alkali Trade* i. 9 The large pieces must first be..fined by the small tods used for road metal.

b. To make keen or subtle.

1839 BAILEY *Festus* xxix. (1848) 337 Senses fined And pointed brilliantwise.

c. *to fine away, down*: to make gradually finer; to thin off, whittle away or down (either a material or an immaterial thing).

1801 STRUTT *Sports & Past.* Introd. §33. 39 The author.. endeavours to fine away the objections of its opponents. **1826** *Granby* II. iii. 34 You fine down her good qualities so dexterously. **1844** MRS. BROWNING *Child Asleep* viii, To fine down this childish beauty To the thing it must be made. **1866** FERRIER *Grk. Philos.* I. v. 34 So imperceptibly are they [the changes] fined away into each other. **1868** HELPS *Realmah* xvi. (1876) 449 Fining down his original statement. **1872** BROWNING *Fifine* iii, The human beauty..Tricot fines down if fat. **1887** FENN *Off to Wilds* xxix, The sharp stake formed by fining down a good-sized tree.

6. *intr.* **a.** To become comminuted. *dial.*

1868 ATKINSON *Cleveland Gloss.*, *Fine*, to become fine and powdery, in consequence of having been slaked.

b. To become attenuated or delicate.

1889 *Eng. Illust. Mag.* Dec. 255 The wind fined into light, delicate curls of shadow upon the sea.

c. *to fine away, down, off*: to become gradually fine, thin, or less coarse; to dwindle away to the vanishing-point..

1858 BUSHNELL *Serm. New Life* 416 The low superstitions, the coarse and sensual habit..have gradually fined away. **1873** C. M. YONGE *Pillars of House* xlvii. 332 Matilda was..better looking at two-and-thirty than at two-and-twenty, for she had somewhat fined down. **1876** R. F. BURTON *Gorilla L.* I. 124 Fining imperceptibly away till lost in the convexity of the waters. **1881** *Daily Tel.* 5 July 2/2 Fining away with delicate keenness at the forefoot. **1884** *St. James's Gaz.* 29 May 6/1 Beauchamp..had fined down very much since the Two Thousand.

7. Of the weather: To clear. (In Australia const. *up*). *rare.*

1888 *Scott. Leader* 12 July 7 [*Sailor says*] The weather fined a bit. **1966** BAKER *Austral. Lang.* (ed. 2) xvi. 350 *Bogaduck weather* for heavy rain and *to fine up*, (of weather) to become fine, are other Australianisms.

8. *trans.* To bring into good condition.

1835 SIR G. STEPHEN *Adv. Search Horse* ii. 27 'He was brought out half an hour before, Sir, with legs like millstones..They trotted him up and down..just to *fine his legs*.'

Hence **fined** *ppl. a.*; **'fining** *ppl. a.*

1483 *Cath. Angl.* 131/1 Fynde, *defecatus, meratus.* **1555** in Strype *Eccl. Mem.* III. App. xliv. 123 Not with pure and most fined gold. **1599** A. M. tr. *Gabelhouer's Bk. Physicke* To Rdr. 1 Euerye fined and perpolite witte. **1613** CHAPMAN *Masque Inns of Court* Wks. III. 113 O blow away, Al vapours from the fined ayre. *a* **1661** FULLER *Worthies* I. (1662) 245 Fined Silver in Wedges. **1839** BAILEY *Festus* (1854) 469 How mind will act with..senses fined..we know not. **1888** *Daily News* 4 Apr. 3/1 A gradually fining river.

fine, dial. form of FIND.

fineable, var. form of FINABLE.

fine art. [*Orig.* in *pl.* as transl. of F. *beaux-arts*; cf. FINE *a.* III.]

1. In *plural*, the arts which are concerned with 'the beautiful', or which appeal to the faculty of taste; in the widest use including poetry, eloquence, music, etc., but often applied in a more restricted sense to the arts of design, as painting, sculpture, and architecture. Hence in *sing.* one of these arts; also *transf.* an art or employment requiring refined and subtle skill comparable to that required in the practice of 'the fine arts'.

1767 [see ART *sb.* 11]. **1821** CRAIG *Lect. Drawing* i. 4 Our advancement in the fine arts. **1839** DE QUINCEY *Wks.* (1864) IV. 1 (*title*) On Murder, considered as one of the Fine Arts. **1856** EMERSON *Eng. Traits, Aristocracy* Wks. (Bohn) II. 85 Often they have been the friends and patrons..of the fine arts. **1884** GLADSTONE *Sp. in Parl.* 28 Apr., At that period the art of obstruction was not so much of a fine art as it is now. **1890** WATSON *Conf. Poacher* v. 58 Poaching is one of the fine arts..and the man who would succeed must be a specialist.

2. *collect. sing.* In generalized sense: The fine arts as constituting a department of practice or study. Also *attrib.* (often hyphened *fine-art*).

1855 GEO. ELIOT *Let.* 16 July (1954) II. 210 Literature is Fine Art, and the man who writes mere literature with insolent slovenliness is..inexcusable. **1856** *Art-Jrnl.* 57/3 Glasgow Fine-Art Association... The paintings..were exhibited in the St. Vincent Street Fine-Art Gallery. **1863** [see *art gallery* s.v. ART *sb.* 18]. **1942** BLUNDEN *Romantic Poetry & Fine Arts* 17 Mrs. Hemans must have kept a sharp look-out for fine-arts literature. **1955** R. BLESH *Shining Trumpets* (ed. 3) i. 6 A hybridized popular music rather than a fine-art form. **1966** *Penrose Ann.* XIX. 164 One has met fine art students..aware of their awe-inspiring heritage.

‖**fine champagne** (fin ʃɑ̃paɲ). [Fr., = eau-de-vie *fine* de la *Champagne* 'fine brandy of the Grande Champagne and Petite Champagne vineyards' (of the department of Charente).] Old liqueur brandy (from the vineyards mentioned above). Also abbreviated *fine* (*de la*) *maison*, old brandy 'of the house'; so *fine*, (French) brandy.

1868 G. A. SALA *Notes & Sk. Paris Exhib.* 167 We shall require sixty bottles of cognac, *fine champagne.* **1875** H. VIZETELLY *Wines of World* 19 The Enrageat,..Folle Blanche, or crazy vine, which prevails so extensively in the Deux-Charentes, and from whose fruit *fine champagne* cognac is distilled. **1923** E. E. CUMMINGS *Let.* 15 Sept. (1969) 103, I prefer fine to calvados. **1927** E. HEMINGWAY *Fiesta* i. 12 We had several *fines* after the coffee. **1928** A. E. W. MASON *Prisoner in Opal* xxiii, So! Some coffee and some *fine de la maison*? **1928** *Observer* 11 Mar. 12/2 The wine waiter has had the habit of insidiously proposing a 'fine maison' to the customer who wants an old brandy. **1951** N. BALCHIN *Way through Wood* xii. 174, I ordered two fines. **1964** E. KELEN *Peace in Their Time* xiii. 350 He was afraid that if he bought somebody a *fine* he would one day die of starvation.

fine-cut, *a.* and *sb.* [FINE *adv.*]

A. *adj.* **a.** Finely cut, delicately chiselled. **b.** Cut so as to be fine; *fig.* cut down to narrow limits.

1837 *Knickerbocker* IX. 268 He ejected a quid from his mouth, that would have shamed in size the largest paper of Lorillard's fine-cut chewing tobacco. **1878** *Congress. Rec.* 5 June 4164/2 Gentlemen of fortune..can very well afford.. to chew their fine-cut tobacco. **1894** *Daily News* 9 Jan. 5/2 These days of fine-cut profit on safe monetary business.

B. *sb.* **a.** A kind of fine-cut tobacco.

1844 *Knickerbocker* XXIII. 288, I thrust a ball of 'Mrs. Miller's fine cut'..between the sub-maxillary bone and its carnal casement. **1864** *Congress. Globe* 3 June 2707/3 On tobacco, cavendish, plug, twist, fine cut, and manufactured of all descriptions. **1909** 'O. HENRY' *Roads of Destiny* xxi. 355 Haven't got a chew of fine-cut on you, have you? **1939–40** *Army & Navy Stores Catal.* 84/3 Smoking mixtures..(coarse and fine cuts).

b. (See quot.)

1959 W. S. SHARPS *Dict. Cinematogr.* 96/1 *Fine cut*, in editing,..the term used for the workprint after the rough cut has been further edited.

fine-draw, *v.* [f. FINE *a.* and *adv.* + DRAW *v.* The stress is equal or variable.]

1. *trans.* To draw or sew together (two edges of a rent, two pieces of tapestry, etc.) so finely that the join is not noticed; to mend (a garment) neatly.

[**1713** (Implied in *fine-drawer*: see below).] **1755** in JOHNSON. **1756** ROLT *Dict. Trade* s.v., It is now prohibited to fine-draw pieces of foreign manufacture upon those made in Great Britain. *a* **1774** GOLDSM. tr. *Scarron's Comic Rom.* (1775) I. 83 Had not a bungling taylor advised him to get his hat fine-drawn. **1833** MARRYAT *P. Simple* (L.), It was in my best pair of kerseymeres, but, thanks to the skilful little seamstress, I got them finedrawn. **1852** JAMES *Pequinillo* III. 196 Did you ever buy a coat without looking through it to see that it wasn't fine-drawn?

2. To draw out to minute fineness, tenuity, or subtlety. *lit.* and *fig.* Somewhat *rare.*

1761 CHURCHILL *Rosciad* Poems 1763 I. 57 Let wits, like spiders, from the tortured brain Fine-draw the critic-web. **1845** MRS. S. C. HALL *Whiteboy* iv. 35 The rude but genuine hospitality was being fine-drawn in every direction.

b. *intr.* (*nonce-use.*) To execute elaborate variations.

1859 G. MEREDITH *R. Feverel* II. iv. 44 To gentlemen and ladies he fine-draws upon the viol, ravishingly.

Hence **fine-drawing** *vbl. sb.*, the action of the vb., also *concr.* (see quot. 1888). Also **fine-drawer**, one who fine-draws.

1713 *Phil. Trans.* XXVIII. 225 If you tare a piece of Muslin into two Pieces, and give it to one of their Fine-Drawers to set it together again. **1735** DYCHE & PARDON *Dict.*, *Fine Drawing*, a..Way of mending Rents in Cloaths, a particular Part of the Taylor's Art, and commonly a distinct Employment. **1871** G. MEREDITH *H. Richmond* lv. (1889) 524 Toss common-sense overboard, there's no end to your fine-drawings. **1883** *Almondbury Gloss.*, *Finedrawer.* **1888** ELWORTHY *W. Somerset Word-bk.*, *Fine-drawing*, the name of one of the sorts of long or combing wool, sorted out of the fleece.

'fine-'drawn, *ppl. a.* [f. FINE *a.* and *adv.* + *drawn*, pa. pple. of DRAW.

When used *attrib.* it may have chief stress on first syll.]

Drawn fine; drawn out to extreme thinness, tenuity or subtlety. *lit.* and *fig.* Also in *Racing* and *Athletics*: Reduced in weight or fat by exercise and 'training'.

1840 BLAINE *Encycl. Rural Sports* IV. vi. §1699. 484 He may go through a very long and severe run, and yet return comparatively but little finer drawn than when he went out. **1869** E. A. PARKES *Pract. Hygiene* (ed. 3) 387 Many men are 'overtrained', i.e., too fine-drawn from absorption of fat. **1876** T. S. EGAN tr. *Heine's Atta Troll, etc.* 249 The fine-drawn aristocrats. **1884** R. MARRYAT in *19th Cent.* May 840 Struggling against that fine-drawn network of circumstance. **1887** H. SMART *Cleverly Won* ii. 14 She was in training, and rather fine drawn to boot. **1887** LOWELL *Democr.* 23 Fine-drawn analyses of the Rights of Man. **1888** ELWORTHY *W. Somerset Word-bk.*, That story is too fine-drawn—*i.e.* grossly exaggerated.

†**fi'neer**, *v.*[1] *Obs.* Also 8 **finnier.** [early form of VENEER.] = VENEER. *lit.* and *fig.* Hence **fi'neered** *ppl. a.*; **fi'neering** *vbl. sb.*

1708 *New View of London* I. 98/2 The Communion Table is neatly Finnierd. **1716** *Prot. Mercury* 18 May 6 Chests of Drawers..of the Newest Fashion and best Fineer'd Work in Walnut-Tree. **1778** R. TICKELL *Wreath of Fashion* 98 See Palmerston fineer his *Bout's Rhimeès.* **1780** *Descr. Tunbridge Wells* 11 The yew especially is of late become very fashionable, and the goods fineered with it are certainly excessively pretty. **1781** HAYLEY *Tri. Temper* II. 144 Our young lord..Fineer'd the mean interior of his mind. **1832** GELL *Pompeiana* II. 74 This sort of fineering with rare marbles.

†**fineer**, *v.*[2] *Obs. rare*[−1]. [app. ad. Du. *finieren*, *fijneren* to collect money or riches (Oudem.), ad. Of. *finer*; cf. FINE *v.*] (See quot.)

1758–65 GOLDSM. *Ess.*, *Biog. Mem.*, The second method of running into debt is called *fineering*; which is getting goods made up in such a fashion as to be unfit for every other purchaser; and if the tradesman refuses to give them upon credit, then threaten to leave them upon his hands. *Ibid.*, The young man..could face, fineer and bring custom to a shop with any man in England.

Fine Gael (ˌfiːnə 'geɪl). *Pol.* [Ir., lit. 'Tribe of Gaels'.] An Irish political organization and party which was formed after the collapse of the United Ireland Party, and entered Dail Eireann in 1937.

The Cumann na nGaedheal Party (formed in 1923) and the United Ireland Party (formed in 1933) were the political predecessors of Fine Gael, and are sometimes referred to as Fine Gael; however, the Party did not officially adopt this name until 1937.

1938 *Encycl. Brit. Bk. of Year 1937* 341/1 The general election..gave 69 seats to Fianna Fáil, 48 to Fine Gael, 13 to Labour, and 8 to Independents. **1940** D. O'SULLIVAN *Irish Free State* xxvii. 474 The title of United Ireland Party had long ago been supplanted in ordinary use, by Fine Gael, which means Tribe of Gaels, though the one cannot..be regarded as the equivalent of the other. New Fine Gael was but old Cumann na nGaedheal writ small. **1956** *Encycl. Brit.* XII. 628/2 De Valera refused to enter into any coalition..,though his Fianna Fail had won 68 seats and Mulcahy's Fine Gael had only 31. **1966** *Ann. Reg. 1965* 280 The chief Opposition party, Fine Gael, presented a comprehensive social programme. **1979** J. J. LEE *Ireland 1945–70* 175 Fianna Fáil and Fine Gael continued to dominate the political landscape. **1983** *Whitaker's Almanack 1984* 569/1 The general election in the Irish Republic resulted: Fianna Fail 75 seats; Fine Gael 70; Labour 16; Workers' Party 2; others 3.

fine 'gentleman. a. A gentleman of polished manners and refined tastes. **b.** A gentleman of fashion, one who is distinguished for elegance and correct style in dress and habits of life; now usually in sarcastic use. Also *attrib.* or as *adj.*

1583 C. HOLLYBAND *Campo di Fior* 207 You fine gentelman, do you leane on the table? **1628** EARLE *Microcosm.* xxxvi, *A Blunt Man*..is a great enemy to the fine Gentleman. **1728** GAY *Beggar's Opera* I. iv. 4 How many fine Gentlemen have we in Newgate every Year? **1732** BERKELEY *Alciphr.* I. §11 Men of pleasure, men of fashion, and fine gentlemen. **1848** MACAULAY *Hist. Eng.* I. 368 The fine gentleman's ornaments, his embroidered coat, his fringed gloves. **1879** FROUDE *Cæsar* ix. 90 Fine gentlemen could once more lounge in their clubs. **1928** *Smart Set* Sept. 49/1 Your fine-gentleman airs sit ridiculously on you.

Hence **fine-'gentlemanish** *a.*, foppish; so **fine-'gentlemanism, fine-'gentlemanship.**

1865 *Spectator* 29 Apr. 471/1 Some highly affected and fine-gentlemanish verbosity which we have not met before. **1866** *Athenæum* 24 Nov. 676/2 The evanescent air of fine gentlemanism. **1874** L. CARR *Judith Gwynne* xvii, That boredom is one of the necessary traits of fine gentlemanism. **1833** *Contemp. Rev.* June 899 The spirit of fine gentlemanship.

fine-grain, *a.* [f. FINE *a.* 7 + GRAIN *sb.*[1]] Having a fine grain (GRAIN *sb.*[1] 12–15); consisting of particles that are very small (GRAIN *sb.*[1] 7); *spec.* in *Photogr.*, containing or composed of particles smaller than normal, so that considerable enlargement of the photograph is possible without any graininess becoming apparent; suitable for producing such photographs.

1927 *Brit. Jrnl. Photogr. Alm. 1928* 758 (*Index*) Fine-grain images, metol developer, Eastman formula. **1928** *Ibid. 1929*

247 *Fine-grain developers*,..the following metol developer is advocated..for giving greater contrast than the fine-grain developers usually quoted. **1934** J. L. BARING tr. *Heering's Rolleiflex-Bk.* 61 Miniature photography has compelled the industry..to produce fine-grain film. **1937** *Discovery* Jan. 22/2 Users of the popular miniature cameras may remember that some years ago their choice lay between a fine-grain emulsion with a slow speed, necessitating a longer exposure, and a coarse-grained one that did not enlarge so well but had a faster speed. **1963** C. R. COWELL et al. *Inlays, Crowns & Bridges* ii. 6 It is important, therefore, to use a fine-grain cement. **1966** *Lancet* 31 Dec. 1429/1 X-rayed separately with an aluminium step-wedge on fine-grain industrial film.

Also **fine-grained** *a.* (also *fig.*).

1538 LELAND *Itin.* (1744) VII. 81 Very fayre and fyne greynyd Okes. **1634** PEACHAM *Gentl. Exerc.* I. iv. 15 They are more blew and finer grained then the other coales. **1799** KIRWAN *Geol. Ess.* 148 All the houses of Malta are built of a fine grained limestone. **1838** J. M. SPEARMAN *Brit. Gunner* (ed. 2) 252 The proof of fine-grained, or small-arm powder, is with a charge of two drachms from a carbine barrel. **1859** F. A. GRIFFITHS *Artil. Man.* (1862) 92 Fine grained, or musket powder. **1894** W. JAMES *Coll. Ess. & Rev.* (1920) 342 In this sense he *is* original, for no one has yet attained to writing up the subject in as fine-grained a way as this. **1906** *Jrnl. Geol.* XIV. 695 Phanerocrystalline rocks have been described as coarse, medium, or fine grained, with little effort to fix absolute values for these terms. **1911** B. E. JONES *Cassell's Cycl. Photogr.* 280 Process dry plates are relatively slow in order to secure a fine-grained emulsion. **1939** A. JOHANNSEN *Descr. Petrogr.* (ed. 2) I. iii. 31 If the grains are less than a cubic millimeter in size, but recognizable as individuals, the rock is said to be fine-grained. **1949** J. E. GARSIDE *Process & Physical Metall.* xvii. 288 Resulting from variation in grain size, it is possible to distinguish between fine- and coarse-grained steels. **1965** *Language* XLI. 202 A single fine-grained quantization of acoustic space.

fine hair, *sb.* [FINE *a.* 7.] (See quot. 1901.)

1897 C. T. DAVIS *Manuf. Leather* (ed. 2) 109 Besides the hair proper, the animal hide is covered with a short down, similar to what is found on the arms and legs of the human body. This down is known to the tanners as fine-hair. **1901** F. T. ADDYMAN tr. *Villon's Leather Industry* 359 *Fine hair*, long, fine but coarser than wool, as the rabbit. **1962** STUBBINGS & FLEISCH in F. O'Flaherty et al. *Chem. & Technol. Leather* III. xxxviii. 245 The shorter the unhairing process, usually the more fine hair is left on the sides.

Hence **fine-hair** *v. trans.*, to remove the fine hair or down from (a skin).

1897 C. T. DAVIS *Manuf. Leather* (ed. 2) 158 The best time for fine-hairing is after the drenching, as the grain of the skins is then cleaner and the fine hairs more easily seen. **1903** H. R. PROCTER *Princ. Leather Manuf.* 180 After bating, the hides are usually 'worked' ('scudded', 'fine-haired') on the beam, to remove dirt and grease.

fine-hand, *a.* [FINE *a.* 7 d.] Written in a fine or delicate hand. Also *fig.*

1845 C. M. KIRKLAND *Western Clearings* 154, I want a fine-hand copy. **1846** *Knickerbocker* XXVII. 279 How many recollections of early school-days,..of coarse and fine-hand pens. **1878** B. F. TAYLOR *Between Gates* 228 From this rock the horse-trail climbs to the right for Nevada Fall and a fine-hand affair, a foot-trail, trends up to the left of Vernal Fall.

fineish ('faɪnɪʃ), *a.* Also 6–9 **finish**, 7 **fynish**. [f. FINE *a.* + -ISH.] †**a.** Affecting refinement, fastidious (*obs.*). **b.** Somewhat fine, in various senses of that word.

1583 STANYHURST *Æneis, etc.* (Arb.) 145 Tyndarus.. Would needs bee finish, with bitter frumperye taunting. *a* **1639** W. WHATELY *Prototypes* II. xxx. (1640) 103 An idle, coy, finish maide is so much the more disdained of wise persons. **1647** WARD *Simp. Cobler* 86, I have here and there taken a few finish stitches. **1650** B. *Discolliminium* 48 My habit is somwhat fynish as other Gentlemen are. **1832** MISS MITFORD *Village* Ser. v. (1863) 344 A fineish girl. **1867** CARLYLE *Remin.* (1881) II. 165 He was the leanest of mankind..face and head fineish..and of a Jew type rather.

fine 'lady. A lady of quality or refinement; a lady of fashion. Often applied sarcastically to a woman who dresses showily, imitates the manners of a class above her own, or is devoted to display and disdains useful work. Also attrib. (hyphened *fine-lady*).

1707 M. LOVETT *Let.* 26 Mar. in M. M. Verney *Verney Lett. 18th Cent.* (1930) I. xii. 200 There was all the Beaux and fine Ladys in town. **1728** GAY *Beggar's Opera* I. iv. 6 She loves to imitate the fine Ladies. **1801** MAR. EDGEWORTH *Belinda* (1832) II. xxi. 82 The poor gardener, who had been cheated by some fine ladies out of his aloe. **1862** MRS. CARLYLE *Lett.* III. 145, I had got a little girl..in place of my fine-lady housemaid. **1893** MISS K. SIMPSON *Jeanie o' Biggersdale* 115 Romany lasses could not expect to lead fine-lady lives.

Hence **fine-'ladically** *adv.*, after the manner of a 'fine lady'; **fine-'ladyish** *a.*, like or proper to a 'fine lady', finical; **fine-'ladyism**, the disposition and behaviour of a 'fine lady', also *concr.* a fad or crotchet of a 'fine lady'; **fine-lady-like** *a.* = *fine-ladyish*; **fine-'ladyship**, the condition of being a fine lady.

1777 MAD. D'ARBLAY *Early Diary* (1889) II. 189 Rather than appear finical and fine-ladyish, I got out. **1784** R. BAGE *Barham Downs* II. 40 Assuming a certain degree of fine-lady-like effrontery. **1811** BYRON *Let. to Hodgson* 13 Oct. Wks. (1846) 549/1, I am growing..fine-ladically *nervous*. **1834** *Tait's Mag.* I. 596/1 The upstart affectation of her fine-ladyism was fulsome. **1848** THACKERAY *Van. Fair* lxiv. 588 She resumed her fine-ladyship, and tried to look and feel as if she was in May Fair once more. **1866** GEO. ELIOT *F. Holt* (1868) 64 'One sort of fine-ladyism is as good as another', said Felix. **1867** H. KINGSLEY *Silcote of Silcotes* xlviii, A little too fine-ladyish.

fineless ('faɪnlɪs), *a. rare.* [f. FINE *sb.*[1] + -LESS.] Boundless, infinite, unlimited.

1604 SHAKS. *Oth.* III. iii. 173 But Riches finelesse is as poore as Winter, To him that euer feares he shall be poore. **1839** BAILEY *Festus* xix. (1848) 214 All fineless as the future. **1878** BROWNING *La Saisiaz* 45 That which dropped the dew its fineless food.

finely ('faɪnlɪ), *adv.* Forms: 4 fin(e)-, fynliche, 5–6 fyn(e)ly(e, 4, 6– **finely**. [f. FINE *a.* + -LY[2].] In a fine manner (see senses of the adj.).

†**1.** In a consummate degree; perfectly, completely. *Obs.*

c **1320** *Cast. Love* 1132 Hou fynliche in herte God loueþ þe. **1340–70** *Alisaunder* 1201 Fende mee finliche well to fonde my strength. **1655** CULPEPPER *Riverius* VII. i. 152 The Tumor vanished, and she was finely cured.

2. With consummate skill, with beautiful workmanship or admirable finish. In mod. use merged in 6.

c **1340** *Cursor M.* 6563 (Fairf.) Hit ys of gold fineli diȝt. **14**.. *Tundale's Vis.* 1656 Of red gold fynly ennamelyd. **1587** TURBERV. *Trag. T.* (1837) 169 And finely finisht up the ship.

3. In a state of fine division; to a fine point or edge; so as to be subtle or delicate in structure; delicately, minutely.

c **1550** LLOYD *Treas. Health* (1585) T viij, Make them into pouder fynelye. **1578** LYTE *Dodoens* I. i. 4 The leaves are much more jagged..finelier cut. **1606** PEACHAM *Drawing* iv. 10 Get you black lead, sharpened finelie. **1718** LADY M. W. MONTAGU *Let. Ctess. Mar.* 4 Jan., Napkins..as finely wrought as the finest handkerchiefs. **1816** L. HUNT *Rimini* III. 16 The other finelier spun. **1847** JOHNSTON in *Proc. Berw. Nat. Club* II. No. v. 222 The skin is very finely striolate. **1863** LYELL *Antiq. Man.* 46 Finely laminated sand.

fig. **1693** DRYDEN *Orig. of Sat.* Prose Wks. 1800 III. 212 Here is the Majesty of the heroick finely mixed with the venom of the other. **1885** *Bookseller* 5 Mar. 240/2 The distinction in these mixed races seems very finely drawn.

4. With respect to action, speech, etc.: With delicacy and nicety; delicately, subtly, nicely.

1548 HALL *Chron.* 18 He would that poinct should be.. more fynely and closely handled. **1608** *Yorksh. Trag.* I. ii, Chide me? Do't finely then. **1710** HEARNE *Collect.* II. 369 In yᵉ City of Rome they spoke more finely..than in Provinces. **1712** ADDISON *Spect.* No. 345 ¶21 The new Passion that was awakened in him [Adam] at the sight of her [Eve] is touch'd very finely. **1851** MRS. BROWNING *Casa Guidi Windows* 2 Who..touched the heart of us So finely that the pity scarcely pained. **1867** F. FRANCIS *Angling* iii. (1880) 79 The angler is compelled to fish as finely as possible. **1883** *Kendal Mercury & Times* 23 Nov. 5/1 An elevating or finely humanising tendency.

†**5.** Cleverly, cunningly, shrewdly. *Obs.*

1542 UDALL *Erasm. Apoph.* II. (1877) 326 The argument of his frendes he did moste finely wrest to the contrarie of their menyng. **1579–80** NORTH *Plutarch* (1676) 154 Whereas he himself by Hannibal was first finely handled and deceived. *a* **1639** WOTTON *Essex & Dk. Buckhm.*, Wee rate this one secret as it was finely carried at 4000*l.* in present money.

6. a. In a manner fitted to call forth admiration; admirably, beautifully, excellently, splendidly.

1690 W. WALKER *Idiomat. Anglo-Lat.* 330 Thou hast plaid thy part finely. **1759** tr. *Duhamel's Husb.* II. i. (1762) 128 The crop came up finely. **1807** G. CHALMERS *Caledonia* I. iv. 135 Lockhart-hall..is finely situated on the right bank of the Clyde. **1850** LYNCH *Theo. Trin.* 81 Greenish tints, finely contrasting with its [the moon's] own soft white.

b. *ironically.*

1579 FULKE *Heskins' Parl.* 222 He scoffeth finely at our spirituall sifting of the sacrament so fine. **1598** SHAKS. *Merry W.* v. iii. 22 Wee'll betray him finely. **1691** SOUTH *Serm. Nat. & Meas. of Conscience* ii, I doubt not but you will find that kingdom..finely governed in a short time. **1778** MAD. D'ARBLAY *Diary* Sept., When we are away, I suppose she pays us off finely. **1883** STEVENSON *Treas. Isl.* I. iv, My heart was beating finely when we two set forth.

c. *dial.* Used predicatively as quasi-*adj.*: Very well in health.

1818 TODD *Johnson* s.v. *Finely* 7 In Cumberland a man in good health being asked how he is, answers 'he is finely'. **1840** SPURDENS *E. Anglian Wds.*, 'How is your wife, John, after her groaning?' 'Finely, sir, thank 'ee.' **1878** in *Cumberld. Gloss.*

7. With respect to dress: Showily, handsomely.

1665 BOYLE *Occas. Refl.* (1845) 354 Many of them as finely and as richly dress'd, as if [etc.].

8. *Comb.* With pples. forming adjs., as ***finely-arched***, ***-bred***, ***-chequered***, ***-cut***, ***-pinnated***, ***-situated***, ***-tempered***, ***-timed***, ***-varied***, ***-veined***, ***-wrought***; ***finely-axed***, fine-axed (FINE *a.* D. 3).

1876 GEO. ELIOT *Dan. Der.* III. xxxv. 35 Each *finely-arched chapel. **1902** *Daily Chron.* 13 Oct. 7/1 The pedestal is of *finely-axed Kemnay granite. **18..** TRISTRAM in *Queen's Printers' Bible-Aids* 54 A swift or *finely-bred camel. **1728–46** THOMSON *Spring* 776 The *finely-checkered duck. **1835** *Court Mag.* VI. 7/1 Her *finely-cut features. **1952** A. G. L. HELLYER *Sanders' Encycl. Gardening* (ed. 22) 5 [*Acer Hersii*] *laciniatum*, finely-cut leaves. **1870** KINGSLEY in *Gd. Words* 239 *Finely-pinnated mimosa leaves. **1875** W. MCILWRAITH *Guide Wigtownshire* 94 The ..*finely-situated..Endcliffe House. **1869** BOUTELL *Arms & Arm.* vii. 120 Their *finely-tempered blades. **1658–9** *Burton's Diary* (1828) III. 558 His was a *finely-timed speech. **1876** GEO. ELIOT *Dan. Der.* IV. li. 23 Her voice..in its *finely-varied tones. **1763** COLLINSON in *Phil. Trans.* LIV. 65 Four *finely-veined transparent wings. **1873** HAMERTON *Intell. Life* III. iii. (1876) 91 The *finely-wrought texture of the verse.

fineness ('faɪnnɪs). [f. FINE *a.* + -NESS.] The quality or state of being fine.

1. a. Choice or superior quality.

c **1400** *Test. Love* II. (1560) 291/1 Margarite..sheweth in it selfe by fineness of colour, whether [etc.]. **1523** FITZHERB. *Surv.* 3 The fynenesse of the grasse. **1612** DRAYTON *Poly-olb.* xii. 515 For finenesse of her turfe surpassing. **1847** TENNYSON *Princ.* II. 133 Some men's [heads] were small; not they the least of men; For often fineness compensated size.

†**b.** *concr.* Articles of good quality. *Obs.*

1579–80 NORTH *Plutarch* (1676) 40 Such other like costly furniture and fineness.

2. Freedom from foreign admixture, purity.

a. in metals: generally in the sense of comparative freedom from alloy; now *spec.* the number of parts per thousand of gold or silver in an alloy.

1487 *Act 4 Hen. VII*, c. 2 Pream., It causeth Money..to be made worse in Fineness than it should be. **1555** EDEN *Decades* 38 Of lyke finenes to that wherof the florenes are coyned. **1638** PENKETHMAN *Artach.* K iv, The finenesse of their Coine, which did farre exceed ours. **1704** *Royal Procl.* 18 June in *Lond. Gaz.* No. 4029/1 The Currency of all Pieces ..shall..stand Regulated, according to their Weight and Fineness. **1843** URE *Dict. Arts* (ed. 3) 74 In estimating or expressing the fineness of gold, the whole mass spoken of is supposed to weigh 24 carats. **1855** MACAULAY *Hist. Eng.* IV. 640 The money of the kingdom should be recoined according to the old standard..of fineness. **1862** G. H. MAKINS *Man. Metallurgy* viii. 144 From numerous examinations of the quality of the fine silver..the author finds that the average fineness is about 998 parts in the thousand. **1957** *Encycl. Brit.* II. 555/2 The gold present is reported as so many parts of gold in 1,000 parts of alloy. This is called 'Fineness', and British gold coinage is said to be '916·6 fine'.

b. Of a liquid: Clearness.

1657 HOWELL *Londinop.* 13 The fineness of the River. **1664** EVELYN *Pomona* Gen. Advt. (1729) 87 Broach the Vessel..and see what Fineness it is of.

3. Fine or striking appearance, handsomeness. Of dress: Showiness, splendour.

1553 EDEN *Treat. Newe Ind.* (Arb.) 14 The chiefe cytie.. is in situacion and fynenes much lyke vnto the cytie of Milayne. **1667** *Decay Chr. Piety* v. 87 The fineness of Cloaths destroys the ease. *a* **1704** T. BROWN *Praise Wealth* Wks. 1730 I. 84 The fineness of his address. **1719** LONDON & WISE *Compl. Gard.* p. xxv, In the beauty and fineness of the Trees. **1749** FIELDING *Tom Jones* XVI. v, He greatly admired the fineness of the dresses. **1841** L. HUNT *Seer* II. (1864) 76 He wrote to the Prince of Orange upon the fineness of his troops.

4. a. Slenderness, tenuity, thinness. Of a point or edge: Keenness, sharpness.

1533 ELYOT *Cast. Helthe* II. (1540) 17/1 By fourme is vnderstand grossenesse, fynenesse, thicknesse, or thynnesse. **1657** J. SMITH *Myst. Rhet.* 69 Litotes, λιτότης.. smalness or finenesse, derived from λιτός (*litos*..small or fine). **1703** MOXON *Mech. Exerc.* 193 A Screw, whose Thread shall be of the same fineness that the Screw and the Shank is of. **1825** J. NICHOLSON *Operat. Mechanic* 352 The wire is..then in the proper state for being reduced to the utmost degree of fineness it is capable of sustaining. **1837** LANDOR *Pentameron* Wks. 1846 II. 312 As little as a silkworm knows about the fineness of her thread.

b. fineness ratio *Naut.* and *Aeronaut.* (see quot. 1915).

1911 *Reports & Mem.* (Adv. Comm. Aeronaut.) No. 43. 58 With a view to deciding upon the best fineness ratio for a non-rigid airship, the same calculation has been made for the case of constant *net* lift. **1915** W. E. DOMMETT *Submarine Vessels* ii. 10 Another matter which has been experimented upon is the value of the ratio between the length divided by the diameter (or width). This ratio is known as the 'fineness ratio'. **1930** *Engineering* 8 Aug. 169/1 A streamline body of 5·45 fineness ratio.

5. The quality of being composed of fine particles, filaments, threads, or material in general: the opposite of *coarseness*.

1634 SIR T. HERBERT *Trav.* 182 Taffataes of transparent finenesse. **1770** CHESTERF. *Misc. Wks.* II. lxix. 538 Irish linen..much about the same fineness and price of the last. **1846** MCCULLOCH *Acc. Brit. Empire* (1854) I. 505 Without injuring the fineness of the fleece. **1860** RUSKIN *Mod. Paint.* V. IX. vii. 268 Fineness of structure in the body..renders it capable of the most delicate sensation. **1879** *Cassell's Techn. Educ.* IX. 158 The degree of fineness to which this grinding is carried varies.

6. a. Of immaterial things, e.g. of thought and speech: Subtly-refined quality, delicacy, subtlety.

1606 SHAKS. *Tr. & Cr.* I. iii. 209 Those that with the finenesse of their soules, By Reason guide his execution. **1607** R. C. *World of Wonders* To the Reader A iv, The finenesse, fitnesse, and featnesse of the phrase. **1654** JER. TAYLOR *Real Pres.* 205 It were a finenesse of Spirit to be able to believe the two parts of a contradiction. **1689–90** TEMPLE *Ess. Learning* Wks. 1731 I. 167 That Language [the French] has much more Fineness and Smoothness at this Time. **1718** PRIOR *Wks.* Pref., The Softness of Her Sex, and the Fineness of Her Genius, conspire to give Her a very distinguishing Character. **1780** MAD. D'ARBLAY *Diary* Apr., He..played with a fineness that resembled the man we looked at at Piozzi's benefit. **1856** MASSON *Ess.* x. 452 Those peculiar finenesses and flights of intellectual activity which are native to verse. **1878** E. JENKINS *Haverholme* 98 The delicate fineness and fragrance of her flattery.

b. A nice or subtle point or matter; a subtlety.

1622 MABBE tr. *Aleman's Guzman d' Alf.* II. ii. 17 Thinking that..there was no need of these finenesses and niceties betweene them. *a* **1716** SOUTH *Serm. Extemp. Prayers* (1737) II. iv. 130 In matters of wit, and finenesses of imagination.

7. Subtlety, astuteness, cunning; a stratagem, artifice. Cf. FINESSE 3, 4. Now *rare*.

1546 *St. Papers Hen. VIII*, XI. 374 He said that the fynenesse of the Frenchemen was suche, that they wold gyve a thowsande to wynne a myllion. **1581** T. HOWELL *Deuises* (1879) 233 Your curious hed may finenesse frame. **1658** CLEVELAND *Rustick Rampant* (1687) 469 By this Fineness they are gained to quit the Gates. **1663** *Flagellum; or O. Cromwell* (1672) 55 For his party had tryed all ways to over-reach the Presbyterean with fineness and Artifice. **1685** H. MORE *Cursory Refl.* A 1 a. Against all the Finenesses of Rome. **1872** TENNYSON *Gareth & Lynette*, And so fill up the gap where force might fail With skill and fineness.

finer[1] ('faɪnə(r)). [f. FINE *v.*[3] + -ER[1].] One who or that which fines or refines, a refiner.

1489 *Act 4 Hen. VII*, c. 2 Pream., Fynours and parters of golde and silver by fire and water. **1577** B. GOOGE *Heresbach's Husb.* (1586) II. 110 The finers rather desier the coles that are made of the pine tree. **1647** HAWARD *Crown Rev.* 23 Chiefe Finer [in the Mint]: Fee, 10*l.* 0*s.* 0*d.* **1815** *Specif. of Hushet's Patent* No. 3944 Finers' iron, or metal of a quality fit for the purposes of the puddling furnace. **1858** BUSHNELL *Serm. New Life* 280 Is it a finer's fire?

finer[2] ('faɪnə(r)). *dial.* [f. FINE *v.*[2] + -ER[1].]

1891 *Labour Commission* Gloss., *Finer*, the one who fines; a name given to the inspector by Lancashire factory hands.

finery[1] ('faɪnərɪ). [f. FINE *a.* + -ERY; perh. on the analogy of BRAVERY.]

1. †a. 'Fine' appearance; beauty or elegance viewed disparagingly (*obs.*). b. Smartness, stylishness, affected or ostentatious elegance or splendour (now *rare*).

1729 LAW *Serious C.* iv. 57 They want..to maintain their families in some such figure and degree of finery as a reasonable Christian life has no occasion for. **1741** WATTS *Improv. Mind* I. xv. §4. 214 Don't chuse your constant Place of Study by the Finery of the Prospects. **1741** MIDDLETON *Let. fr. Rome* Postscr. 244 To gaze at the finery of these paintings. **1792** WOLCOTT (P. Pindar) *More Money* Wks. 1812 II. 496 Never wish to keep a thing for finery. **1847** JAMES *Convict* iii, There was a looking for comfort rather than finery. **1865** MERIVALE *Rom. Emp.* VIII. lxvi. 250 They represent..a certain fantastic finery of manners.

2. *concr.* Gaudy or showy decoration; showy dress. Also in *pl.*

1680 MISS A. MONTAGUE in *Hatton Corr.* (1878) 240, I doe not heare of much finnery, and what I shall have will not deserve that name. **1726** AMHERST *Terræ Fil.* v. 25 Sciences and arts have declin'd in Oxford, in proportion as their fineries have increased. **1751** JOHNSON *Rambler* No. 170 ¶4 My sisters envied my new finery. **1805** N. NICHOLLS *Let.* in *Corr. w. Gray* (1843) 53 When Mr. Walpole added the gallery, with its gilding and glass, he said, 'he had degenerated into finery'. **1849** RUSKIN *Sev. Lamps* i §7. 16, I would not have that useless expense in unnoticed fineries or formalities. **1858** HAWTHORNE *Fr. & It. Jrnls.* I. 192 Children rendered stiff..by the finery which they wear.

†3. *pl.* Instances of fine or delicate workmanship.

1713 DERHAM *Phys. Theol.* VIII. iv. 407 The minute Curiosities and inimitable Fineries, observable in those lesser Animals.

4. *Comb.*: **finery folks**, people stylishly dressed; **finery-ironer, -machinist** (see quots.).

1828 W. DYOTT *Jrnl.* Apr. (1907) II. 22 Dick and I.. became lookers-on at the assembled crowds and the finery folks going to S[t] James's. **1895** *Westm. Gaz.* 16 Apr. 3/2 Of the ironers: four made incomplete weeks; one worked 72,.. and one (the finery ironer) 75¾. **1908** *Daily Chron.* 12 June 9/6 Laundry.—Wanted finery ironers. **1921** *Dict. Occup. Terms* (1927) §918 *Finery machinist*, general term for any person ironing delicate articles by machine in a laundry.

finery[2] ('faɪnərɪ). Also 7-8 **finary**. [a. Fr. *finerie*, f. *finer* to refine, FINE *v.*[2]; see -ERY.]

1. A hearth where cast iron is made malleable, or in which steel is made from pig-iron.

1607 COWELL *Interpr.* s.v. *Blomary*, One of the forges belonging to an iron mill..called a Finary. **1613** J. ROVENZON *Treatise of Metallica* C 4 The furnaces may be made with conuenient places therein for the Finery and Chaffery. **1697** *View Penal Laws* 255 Any Iron-Mill Furnace, Finary or Bloomary for the making of iron or metal. **1831** J. HOLLAND *Manuf. Metal* I. 80 One man and a boy at the finery should make two tons of iron in a week. **1864** PERCY *Iron & Steel* 579 Before the introduction of [puddling] the conversion was always effected in a finery.

2. The action of refining iron. *rare.*

1839 URE *Dict. Arts* 699 The finery..is executed in peculiar furnaces called running-out fires.

3. *Comb.*, as **finery-cinder** (see quot. 1826); **finery-furnace** (see quot. 1874); **finery-hearth** = *finery furnace*.

1788 PRIESTLEY in *Phil. Trans.* LXXVIII. 154 Also when the scale of iron, or *finery cinder, is heated. **1810** HENRY *Elem. Chem.* (1840) II. 21 Iron thus treated [with water when red-hot]..may be crumbled down into a black powder, to which the name of *finery cinder* was given by Dr. Priestley. **1791** BEDDOES in *Phil. Trans.* LXXXI. 173 The reverberatory has been substituted in the place of the *finery furnace. **1874** KNIGHT *Dict. Mech.* I. 847/2 *Finery-furnace*, a species of forge-hearth in which gray cast-iron is smelted by fuel and blast, and from which it is run into iron troughs for sudden congelation. **1693** LISTER in *Phil. Trans.* XVII. 866 Bars..taken up out of the *Finnery Harth, or second Forage, are much better Iron than those which are made in the Bloomary.

‖**fines herbes** (finz ɛrb), *sb. pl.* [Fr., lit. 'fine herbs'.] A mixture of herbs used in cooking. Freq. in adj. phr. with *aux*, as *omelette aux fines herbes*, a savoury omelette flavoured with herbs.

1846 A. SOYER *Gastronomic Regenerator* 474 (*heading*) Omelette aux fines herbes. **1861** MRS. BEETON *Bk. Househ. Managem.* 169 (*heading*) Whiting aux fines herbes. **1908** G. B. SHAW *Let.* 27 Aug. (1956) 137 *What* a lunch! *Sweet* omelette (fines herbes, indeed!) and crab apples. **1936** LUCAS & HUME *Au Petit Cordon Bleu* 129 For a 'fines herbes' add 1 large tablespoon of chopped herbs with a little onion. **1965** *House & Garden* Dec. 84/3 *Fines herbes.* This means a mixture of fresh, chopped parsley, tarragon, chives and chervil.

'fine-,spun, *a.* [f. FINE *adv.* + SPUN *ppl. a.*]

1. Spun or drawn out to extreme tenuity; delicate in texture, flimsy.

1674 N. FAIRFAX *Bulk & Selv.* Ep. Ded., When men had wrought up all the Woman within them that was feeble and glowing, into a fine-spun thread. **1704** F. FULLER *Med. Gymn.* (1718) 20 The Solids are so fine-spun. **1798** SOTHEBY tr. *Wieland's Oberon* (1826) II. 152 Fine-spun as if aërial spiders wove a web to deck, not hide the form of love. **1856** R. A. VAUGHAN *Mystics* (1860) I. 33 The fine-spun, gay-coloured ribbons of allegory.

2. *fig.* Elaborated to flimsiness, excessively subtle or refined.

1647 SIR R. FANSHAW tr. *Guarino's Pastor Fido* II. vi. 13 That Mistresse in the art of making The fine-spun lyes, that sels so deer False words, false hopes and a false leer. **1719** W. WOOD *Surv. Trade* 161, I am an Enemy to the fine-spun Notions, some Men do..advance concerning them. **1842** EMERSON *Nat., Transcendentalist* Wks. (Bohn) II. 280 The materialist..mocks at fine-spun theories.

finesse (fɪ'nɛs), *sb.* Forms: 6 **fynes(se**, 7-8 **fines(s**, 6- **finesse**. [a. F. *finesse* = Pr. and Sp. *fineza*, Cat. *finesa*, It. *finezza*:—Com. Rom. **finitia*, f. *fino* FINE *a.* (Many of the early examples may belong to FINENESS; cf. the spellings *playnes*, *prophaness* for *plainness*, *profaneness*.)]

†1. a. = FINENESS in various senses; purity, degree of purity (of precious metals); clearness (of a liquid); slenderness, delicacy of structure or texture.

1528 PAYNEL *Salerne's Regim.* H b, Wyne made hotte, by reason of the clerenes and fynes, ouer cometh a mans brayne the soner. **1549** LATIMER *1st Serm. bef. Edw. VI* (Arb.) 35 The fynes of the Silver I can not se. **1562** TURNER *Herbal* II. 59 b, Tamarisk hath much finesse in the partes. **1605** BACON *Adv. Learning* I. iv. §5. 20 Copwebs of learning, admirable for the finesse of thread and worke. **1609** SKENE *Reg. Maj.*, *Stat. David II*, 44 That it be equivalent, & conforme to the current money of England in wecht & fines. **1665** *Phil. Trans.* I. 66 Sand and Powders of several finesses. **1700-1** *Act 12-13 Will. III*, c. 4 §3 Silver Vessell Plate..less in finess then according to the Standard of this Kingdom.

†b. Ostentatious elegance or splendour. *Obs.*

1549 OLDE *Erasm. Par. Eph.* Prol. ij, Therefore where vnnecessary fynesse wanteth, accept true meanyng playnesse. **1589** PUTTENHAM *Eng. Poesie* III. xxiii. (Arb.) 273 Too much finesse and curiositie is not commendable in an Embassadour..I haue knowen..such of them, as studied more vpon what apparell they should weare..then they did vpon th' effect of their errant.

2. Delicacy or subtlety of manipulation or discrimation; refinement, refined grace.

Now *rare*, and only as a foreign word.

1564 A. B. tr. *Jewel's Apol.* L v, The old fynesse and eloquence that Cicero and Cesar vsed..in the Latin tonge. **1580** FRAMPTON *Dial. Yron & Steele* 148 b, I doe not speake of the finesse and delicatenesse that there is in sodering of it. **1704** F. FULLER *Med. Gymn.* Pref., The Perfection of an Operation shall depend upon a certain Finesse. **1727-41** CHAMBERS *Cycl.*, *Finesse*..among us, it is chiefly used to denote that peculiar delicacy or subtlety perceived in works of the mind..This man understands all the *Finesses* of his art. The substance and necessary part of a language is learnt at a little expence: It is the *Finesses* and delicacies that cost the most. **1750** CHESTERF. *Lett.* III. ccxxiv. 15 To understand all the force and finesse of those three languages. **1782** COWPER *Table-t.* 652 His musical finesse was such. **1791** MAD. D'ARBLAY *Diary* 2 Aug., Her smile, which was rare, had a finesse very engaging. **1821** HAZLITT *Table-t.* I. iv. 90 *Tact, finesse*, is nothing but the being completely aware of the feeling belonging to certain situations, passions, etc. **1878** *Masque Poets* 31 Where the gold festal goblets stand Carved by Lysippus' rare finesse.

3. Artfulness, cunning, subtle strategy.

1530 in Ellis *Orig. Lett.* Ser. III. I. 298, I knaw ellis the fynes of the man and nayn mayr dowbyll in our realm. **1647** N. BACON *Disc. Govt. Eng.* I. v. (1739) 12 Nor could Austin with his miracles or finesse settle one footstep of his Church-policy amongst them. **1713** STEELE *Guardian* No. 174 ¶4 Nor shall I speak dishonourably of some little artifice and finesse used upon these occasions. **1798** JANE AUSTEN *Northang. Abb.* (1833) I. v. 21 She was not experienced in the finesse of love. **1869** RAWLINSON *Anc. Hist.* 202 He was a master of finesse.

4. a. An artifice, stratagem, trick.

1562 J. SHUTE *Cambine's Turk. Wars* 4 When the Turcke dyd understande this fynesse of Scanderbeg. **1615** DANIEL *Hymen's Tri.* (1717) 111 Full of their Finesses, Serve their own Turns in others Businesses. **1756** *Monitor* No. 27 ¶12 The project..is..as delicate a Finesse in politicks as has been played for many a year. **1790** BEATSON *Nav. & Mil. Mem.* 281 By way of finesse, she saluted the Admiral. **1839** *Times* 6 Apr. in *Spirit Metrop. Conserv. Press* (1840) I. 196 Though cordially sensible to the merits of a bold finesse.

b. In whist: (see quot. 1862). In bridge: (see quot. 1959).

1862 'CAVENDISH' *Whist* (1870) 28 A finesse is an endeavour, by the second or third player, to obtain or keep the command of a suit by heading a trick with an inferior card, though holding a higher one of the suit not in sequence. **1902** *Encycl. Brit.* XXVI. 371/1 (s.v. *Bridge*), Deep finesses should be made when there is no other way of stealing a trick. **1958** *Listener* 18 Dec. 1053/2 West could look for twelve top tricks and the club finesse at worst. **1959** REESE & DORMER *Bridge Player's Dict.* 89 A finesse is an attempt to profit from a favorable lie of the cards. A player tries to win or establish a trick with a card that is not the highest held by his side.

finesse (fɪ'nɛs), *v.* [f. prec. sb.]

1. a. *intr.* To use finesse, artifice, or stratagem.

1778 *Conquerors* 61 The flights finesse. **1803** *Edin. Rev.* II. 103 But our author can hector as well as finesse. **1867** MISS BRADDON *Aur. Floyd* i. 15 She diplomatized and finessed with them as if she had been canvassing the county.

b. *trans.* To conduct by artifice; to bring or modify by finesse or delicate handling *into* (a specified state). Also with *away*.

1814 JANE AUSTEN *Watsons* Concl. (1879) 290 Till such time as Reginald de Courcy could be talked, flattered and finessed into an affection. **1851** RUSKIN *Stones Ven.* I. xiv. §16 A battlement..may be decorated..or finessed away into traceries. **1885** L. WINGFIELD *B. Philpot* II. iii. 75 The Bill had been finessed through the first stage.

2. a. *Whist* and *Bridge. intr.* To attempt to take a trick by finesse; also *trans.* To play (a particular card) for the purpose of finessing.

1746 HOYLE *Whist* (ed. 6) 4 He finesses upon your Partner. *Ibid.* 40 Your Adversary finesses the Knave. **1752** A. MURPHY *Gray's-Inn Jrnl.* No. 7 ¶4, I can now return my Partner's Suit, lead through the Honour, Finesse [etc.]. **1837** DICKENS *Pickw.* xxxv, Mr. Pickwick had not..finessed the heart. **1885** PROCTOR *Whist* vii. 86 You may finesse more deeply in trumps than in plain suits. **1902** *Encycl. Brit.* XXVI. 371/1 (s.v. *Bridge*), It is in general unsound to finesse against a card that must be unguarded. **1960** J. BETJEMAN *Summoned by Bells* i. 5 If you'd finessed my heart And played your diamond.

b. *Croquet. intr.* To play one's ball out of the adversary's way.

1875 J. D. HEATH *Croquet Player* 65 Blue's best game would be to finesse to the corner near him.

Hence **fi'nessed** *ppl. a.*; **fi'nessing** *vbl. sb.* Also **fi'nesser**, a schemer, strategist.

1746 HOYLE *Whist* (ed. 6) 68 *Finessing*, means the endeavouring to gain an Advantage by Art and Skill. **1774** GOLDSM. *Retal.* 106 If they were not his own by finessing and trick. **1835** MISS SEDGWICK *Linwoods* (1873) I. 212 Contriving..like an expert finesser. **1851** RUSKIN *Stones Ven.* I. xxi. §11 Educated imbecility and finessed foolishness. **1861** *Macm. Mag.* Dec. 134 Finessing is scarcely ever admissible in quadrille, the number of cards being too limited.

fine-still, *sb.* [f. FINE *a.* + STILL *sb.*] A vessel used in distilling spirit from treacle.

1731-3 P. SHAW *Chem. Lect.* xii. (1755) 247 Coarse-Stills and Fine-Stills.

Hence **fine-still** *v.*, to distil spirit from treacle or the like; **fine-stiller**, one who fine-stills; **fine-stilling** *vbl. sb.*

1731-3 P. SHAW *Chem. Lect.* xii. (1755) 248 There needs no particular Experiment to shew the business of the Fine-Stiller; this being no more than working..from a Wash made by fermenting Treacle with Yeast. **1847** CRAIG, *Fine-stiller. Fine-stilling*..is employed in distilling spirit from treacle, or other preparations..of sugar.

fine structure. [tr. G. *feinstruktur* (A. Sommerfeld 1916, in *Ann. d. Physik* LI. 2).]

1. *Physics.* a. (The presence of) multiplets of closely spaced lines in atomic spectra that appear as single lines under low resolution; usu. applied to multiplets that result from the splitting of energy levels by the electron spin-orbit coupling, in contrast with *hyper-fine structure*.

1918 *Phil. Mag.* Oct. 345 Here a^2 is the small quantity $(2\pi e^2/hc)^2$, (where e is the electronic charge, h Planck's constant, and c the velocity of light) occurring again as a universal constant in the discussion of the fine structure of lines. **1936** *Discovery* Nov. 363/1 The fine-structure of spectral lines frequently arises through the nuclei of the atoms, to which the spectrum is due, having a spin. **1942** J. D. STRANATHAN *'Particles' of Mod. Physics* vi. 224 The details of fine structure differ from one element to another, both as regards the number of lines in the multiplet and the spacing of these lines. **1962** H. D. BUSH *Atomic & Nuclear Physics* iii. 58 If the fine structure is examined with the aid of very high resolution instruments, each component of the fine structure is resolved into further components with separations of the order of 1 cm^{-1} (*hyperfine structure*).

b. Similar groups of lines or energies in other spectra.

1930 *Proc. R. Soc.* A. 3 Sept. 229 To examine the fine structure of the α-rays, Rosenblum has employed the focussing method so much used in the examination of β-ray spectra. **1942** J. D. STRANATHAN *'Particles' of Mod. Physics* viii. 344 The previously supposed homogeneous α-rays emitted from ThC actually fall into five distinct groups. The rays are said to have a fine structure. **1955** R. D. EVANS *Atomic Nucleus* xiii. 424 Energy levels in the product nucleus determine the 'fine structure', or energy groups, of the reaction products.

2. *gen.* Small-scale variation in structure, texture, appearance, etc.

1933 *Nature* 17 June (*heading*) Fine-structure of the ionosphere. **1935** *Discovery* Apr. 108/1 This [X-ray] technique yields information on the fine-structure of bodies, of a sub-microscopic order, while the radiographic method reveals the gross structure. **1946** *Nature* 12 Oct. 519/1 An account was given of the examination of..a cleavage face of a selenite crystal... Only low magnifications..were used, yet it was observed that the fringes were extremely ragged, indicative of a complex surface 'fine-structure'. **1967** R. MICHARD in J. N. Xanthakis *Solar Physics* v. 116 One can

see that these flocculi are organized in a large cellular network..visible mainly on average-quality pictures where the fine structure is smoothed out. **1968** *Brit. Med. Bull.* XXIV. 236/1 The fine structure of proteins has also been subjected to taxonomic analysis to estimate the relationships between the constituent amino acids. **1971** *Sci. Amer.* July 19/1 Even more striking than the differences among the states was the shifting of populations at the county level—the changes in what might be called the fine structure of the population distribution.

3. *attrib.*, as ***fine-structure constant***.

1923 H. L. Brose tr. *Sommerfeld's Atomic Struct. & Spectral Lines* viii. 497 Our representation of the L-doublet is fully determined and expressed rationally by the fine-structure constant..by the Rydberg frequency..and by the nuclear charge. **1930** Ruark & Urey *Atoms, Molecules & Quanta* v. 134 Introducing the dimensionless fine-structure constant, $\alpha = 2\pi e^2/hc = (7{\cdot}284 \pm 0{\cdot}006) \cdot 10^{-3}$, we get [etc.]. **1935** A. S. Eddington *New Pathways in Sci.* xi. 234 The fine-structure constant..has reference to the structure of spectral lines, but the constant occurs more widely; just as the velocity of light occurs in many problems unconnected with optics. The fine-structure constant is really the ratio of two natural units or atoms of action. **1935** S. Tolansky *Fine Structure in Line Spectra and Nuclear Spin* ii. 5 In general the fine structure components of a line lie very closely together. **1970** *Sci. Amer.* Oct. 63/1 The fine-structure constant is the basic constant of quantum electrodynamics.

fine-tooth, *a.* [FINE *a.* 7 d.] Of a comb: having fine and closely-set teeth. Also in *fig.* phrases. So **fine-tooth-comb** *v. trans.*, to comb (the hair of someone) with such an article; also *fig.* Hence **fine-tooth-combing** *vbl. sb.*

1839 H. Malcom *Trav.* I. ii. 37 Friends who wish to make little presents to the Karen Christians, might send fine-tooth combs. **1849** *Rep. Comm. Patents* (U.S.) (1850) 267 Improvement in making Ivory fine-tooth Combs. **1878** B. F. Taylor *Between Gates* 246 As slender in the distance as a fine-tooth comb. **1889** G. B. Shaw *London Music in 1888–89* (1937) 197 That lady benevolently clothed it [*sc.* a child], fine-tooth-combed it. **1891** *Century Mag.* Feb. 595 I'll go through this town like a fine-tooth comb but what I'll find him. **1935** 'N. Blake' *Question of Proof* xi. 221 We've been over the whole ruddy caboodle with a fine tooth comb. **1949** 'N. R. Nash' *Young & Fair* II. ii. 71 But I'm going to fine-tooth-comb this school. **1957** *Times Lit. Suppl.* 22 Nov. 710/2 The general reader may..skip the fine-tooth combing of evidence. **1966** A. Firth *Tall, Balding, Thirty-five* xvii. 216 We've gone through the remains of the helicopter with a fine-tooth comb, but there wasn't much left.

finetop. *U.S.* [FINE *a.* 7.] The meadow and pasture grass of eastern North America (*Agrostis tenuis*), also known as *herds-grass*, etc.

1856 *Rep. Mass. Board Agric.* I. 26 Redtop, Finetop, Burden's Grass, Dew Grass, Herds Grass of Pennsylvania and Southern States. **1889** G. Vasey *Agric. Grasses* (ed. 2) 46 *Agrostis vulgaris* (Redtop, Finetop, Herds Grass, Bent Grass, etc.).

fine-tune, *v.* orig. *U.S.* Also fine tune. [Back-formation from FINE TUNING *vbl. sb.*]

a. *trans.* To adjust (an instrument, measurement, etc.) very precisely.

1969 *Program & Abstr. URSI Spring Meeting* (U.S. National Comm.) 81 The operation of the all-pass network will be explained..including..how to measure and fine tune such structures. **1975** *New Yorker* 31 Mar. 26/3 Normally, we only change the pressurization in the cabin every thousand feet.., but after he let out that holler we fine-tuned the pressurization all the way. **1979** *Sci. Amer.* Sept. 8/2 In each generating plant there is a pendulum-regulated clock that fine-tunes the speed of the alternators to exactly 60 hertz before they are put on line. **1980** *SLR Camera* July 39/1 The most useful filters to carry with you are all gentle in their effects and are for fine tuning the tonal and colour response of the film. **1982** *Sci. Amer.* Nov. 148/3 Two other effects may be said to 'fine-tune' the drumhead frequencies, because their role is minor compared with the effect of air-mass loading.

b. *fig.* To make delicate adjustments to (the economy, a situation) so as to bring about a desired improvement.

1969 *Washington Post* 16 Apr. A23/3 To say that we can 'fine-tune' the economy so that the addition of another $1 billion or so in surplus makes a difference—we're not that smart. **1971** *Daily Tel.* 20 Jan. 15 We delude ourselves if we believe that we can neatly fine-tune the money supply or interest rates precisely as we would like. **1977** *Nat. Westminster Bank Q. Rev.* Aug. 8 Macro economic management..has tended to exacerbate this problem with clumsy attempts at 'fine tuning' the economy by innumerable changes in monetary and fiscal measures. **1983** *Listener* 15 Sept. 6/3 It's not on if you're seriously trying to fine-tune a superpower confrontation in such a way that you can stop short of something nasty happening. **1984** *Times* 26 Nov. 17/1 (*heading*) Fed fails to fine tune economy.

fine 'tuning, *vbl. sb.* Also fine-tuning. [f. FINE *a.* + TUNING *vbl. sb.*] **a.** Minute adjustment of a radio receiver, instrument, etc., so as to achieve exactly the tuning required; the facility for this. Also *attrib.* **b.** *fig.* The policy or process of making a series of fine adjustments to a situation (*esp.* the economy).

1924 *Wireless World & Radio Rev.* 3 Sept. 659/1 There are many occasions when..it is essential to employ fine tuning adjustments. **1925** *Wireless World* 11 Mar. 170/2 Fine tuning can be obtained in a variometer-tuned set. **1959** K. Henney *Radio Engin. Handbk.* (ed. 5) xix. 45 Tuning by means of push buttons offers freedom from fine tuning. **1968** *Economist* 16 Mar. 79/1 The movement from a sluggish economy to an uninterrupted growth..led many to expect even greater triumphs to come as a result of what is deceptively called the introduction of 'fine tuning'. **1976** *Globe & Mail* (Toronto) 29 Nov. 6/3 God may have fashioned us all in His image but does that mean we shouldn't do a little fine-tuning of our own? **1983** *Nat. Westminster Bank Q. Rev.* Feb. 33 The time has come to abandon the concept of fine tuning involving very detailed management of the national economy by means of fiscal policy measures. **1985** *Sci. Amer.* Apr. 104/2 Parsons..equipped his governor with a fine-tuning mechanism that depended directly on the dynamo voltage.

Also **fine tuner**, a device for fine tuning; *fig.*, a person who advocates fine tuning of the economy, etc.

1967 W. E. Pannett *Dict. Radio & Television* 101 *Fine tuner*, control enabling a signal to be tuned in accurately after the main tuning control has been set. **1976** *Business Week* 19 July 12/2 Will Burns live up to his reputation as a monetary fine-tuner *par excellence* or will he again reach for those brakes? **1984** *Forbes* (N.Y.) 27 Aug. 169 The point about the postwar era that the Keynesian fine-tuners have missed is that..those policies are no longer politically reversible.

† **'finew**, *sb. Obs.* exc. *dial.* Forms: 6 fenowe, 7–8 finnow, finew, 8 vinew, vinnow, 9 *dial.* vinny. [f. FINEW *v.*] Mouldiness, mould.

1556 Withals *Dict.* Nij a/1 Fenow or horenesse in bread, *mucor, -coris.* **1658** Evelyn *Fr. Gard.* (1675) 230 Endamaging the beans by a musty finnow, which bespots them. **1669** Boyle *Contn. New Exp.* II. (1868) 68 The fruits were covered with a kind of mucor or Finew. *a* **1722** Lisle *Observ. Husb.* (1757) Gloss., *Vinnow*, mouldiness.

† **'finew**, *v. Obs.* exc. *dial.* Forms: 6–7 fenow, finnew, vinew, 8 finnow, 9 *dial.* vinny. [OE. *fyneȝian*, f. *fyniȝ* mouldy (see FINNY *a.*^{2}), f. *fyne*: see FEN *sb.*^{2}] **a.** *intr.* To become mouldy or musty. **b.** *trans.* To cause to become mouldy. Also *fig.*

c **1000** *Canons Ælfric* §36 Þæt þæt haliȝe husel sceole fyneȝian. **1581** Pettie *Guazzo's Civ. Conv.* I. (1586) 30 Secretes which he suffered to mould and vinew within it. *a* **1633** Lennard tr. *Charron's Wisd.* I. xxxi. §1 (1670) 88 With time it [sadness] rusteth and fenoweth the soul. *a* **1722** Lisle *Observ. Husb.* (1757) 206 Whereby the undermost corn..finnows [*marg. gloss* molds].

Hence **'finewing** *vbl. sb.*

1552 Huloet, Vinewing, or molinge of breade or wyne for stalenes, *mucor.* **1609** C. Butler *Fem. Mon.* (1634) 174 It [syrup of violets] may be kept a year without finnewing or corruption.

fine-weather, *a.* Fit or suitable only for fine weather.

1829 Marryat *F. Mildmay* iii, A..frigate ran on board of us..and left her fine-weather-jib hanging on our fore-yard.

† **'finewed**, *a. Obs.* exc. *dial.* Forms: α. 6–7 fenoed, fen(n)owed, finnowed, 7 finewed. β. 6–9 vin(n)ewed, (6 ven-, vinued, 7 whinid, vinnowed), 9 vinned, -ied. [f. FINEW *sb.* or *v.* + -ED.] Mouldy.

α. **1574** Hellowes *Gueuara's Fam. Ep.* (1577) 94 Bread long kept groweth finnowed. **1669** Boyle *Contn. New Exp.* II. (1682) 42 The paste was finewed or mouldy.

β. **1552** Huloet, Vynued, *mucidus.* Vynewed wyne. **1606** Shaks. *Tr. & Cr.* II. i. 15 Speake then you whinid'st leauen speake. **1880** *W. Cornw. Gloss.* s.v., Blue-ripe cheese is called vinnied cheese.

b. *fig.*

α. **1571** *Mirr. Mag., Ld. Hastings* xxviii, A Souldiers hands must oft be dyed with goare, Least, starke with rest, they finewd wax and hoare. **1619** Favour *Antiq. Triumphing* xiii. §10. 334 The foisty and fenowed Festival. **1655** E. Terry *Voy. E. Ind.* 117 Who instead of the two Breasts of the Church, the Law and the Gospel, are fed with mouldy and finnowed Traditions.

β. **1602** F. Beaumont in Speght *Chaucer*, That many of his words are become (as it were) vinewed & hoarie with ouerlong lying.

Hence † **'finewedness.**

1580 Baret *Alv.* H 460 Hoarnesse, or vinewednesse.

† **'finewy**, *a. Obs.* Also finnowy, vinnowy. [f. FINEW *sb.* + -Y^{1}.] Mouldy. Hence **'finewiness**.

α. **1722** Lisle *Observ. Husb.* (1757) 54 The moldiness and finnowyness of the grass. *Ibid.* 82 The seed-beans were finnowy. *Ibid.* Gloss., *Finnowy, vinnowy, vinnewed, vinney*, mouldy.

‖ **fingan, finjan** (fɪn'gɑːn, -'dʒɑːn). Also 7 fin-ion, 9 fingian. [Arab. *finjān*, in Egypt *fingān*.] A small porcelain coffee-cup, used in the Levant.

1609 W. Biddulph in T. Lavender *Trav. Englishmen* 66 A Fin-ion or Scudella of Coffa. **1836** Lane *Mod. Egyptians* I. 168 The coffee-cup (which is called *finga'n*) is small..and, being without a handle, is placed within another cup, of silver or brass. **1842** Lady H. Stanhope *Mem.* (1845) I. iii. 81 The pipe, coffee and a finjàn of orange-flower water.

fingent ('fɪndʒənt), *a. rare*$^{-1}$. [ad. L. *fingent-em*, pr. pple. of *fingĕre* to fashion, form.] Given to fashioning or moulding.

1837 Carlyle *Fr. Rev.* (1857) I. I. i. ii. 7 Man is the most fingent, plastic of creatures.

finger ('fɪŋgə(r)), *sb.* Forms: 1 finger, 3 fenger, fingre, finker, 3–5 *south.* ving(e)re, 3–7 finguer, 4–5 fyngir, -yr, fin-, fyngur, fingere, fyngre, 4–6 fynger, 6 fin-, fyngar, 3– finger. [Com. Teutonic. OE. and OFris. *finger*, OS. *fingar* (Du. *vinger*), OHG. *fingar* (MHG. *vinger*, Ger. *finger*), ON. *fingr* (Sw., Da. *finger*), Goth. *figgrs*:—OTeut. **fingro-z*.

The pre-Teut. antecedent is uncertain; of various forms that are phonologically possible the most likely, on the ground of meaning, is **penqrós*, related to **penqe* FIVE.]

I. 1. a. One of the five terminal members of the hand; in a restricted sense, one of the four excluding the thumb. In this latter sense, the fingers are commonly numbered first to fourth, starting from that next the thumb. Also ***fore-finger, index-finger***, the first; ***middle finger*** (†***fool's finger***), the second; ***ring finger*** (***annular***, †***leech-***, †***medical***, †***physic-finger***), the third; ***little finger*** (***ear-finger***), the fourth.

c **950** *Lindisf. Gosp.* Matt. xxiii. 4 Mið fynger..hiora nallas ða [byrðenna hefiȝa] ymbcerræ. *c* **1050** *Byrhtferth's Handboc* in *Anglia* VIII. 326 Þæt þu cume to þæs læstan fingres nægle. *c* **1175** *Lamb. Hom.* 13 Þas .x. bebode þe godalmihti seolf idihte and awrat mid is aȝene fingres. *c* **1290** *S. Eng. Leg.* I. 309/320 Þeos fif fingres þe deuel hath. **1362** Langl. *P. Pl.* A. II. 11 Hir Fyue Fyngres weore frettet with Rynges. *c* **1400** *Lanfranc's Cirurg.* 158 Bitwene þe litil fyngir and þe leche fiyngir. **14..** *Camb. MS.* Ff. v. 48 lf. 82 (Cath. Angl. 131/2) The fifte fynger is the thowmbe. **1526** *Pilgr. Perf.* (W. de W. 1531) 34 b, Caused..a meruaylous swete sauour to respyre and smell aboute his fyngers. **1549** *Bk. Com. Prayer, Matrimony*, To put it vpon the fowerth finger of the womans left hande. **1611** Cotgr., *Le doigt sale*, the middle finger, which we (after the Latines) call the fooles finger. **1621** Molle *Camerar. Liv. Libr.* v. ii. 321 His fourth finger called the Ring-finger or Physicke-finger. **1653** Urquhart *Rabelais* I. viii, Upon the medical finger of the same hand, he had a ring. **1707** Floyer *Physic. Pulse-Watch* 229 They lay their four Fingers along the Artery. **1794** Cowper *Let.* 5 Jan., My pen slips out of my fingers. **1804** *Med. Jrnl.* XII. 24 Contractions..so small as only to admit the passage of the little finger. **1819** Shelley *Cenci* III. i. 83 Those pallid hands whose fingers twine With one another. **1861** Hulme tr. *Moquin-Tandon* I. ii. 4 The fingers are 5 in number in each hand: they are named thumb, index, middle, ring, and little finger.

b. *little finger*: used to signify the smallest member of the body.

1611 Bible *2 Chron.* x. 10 My little [**1382** Wyclif, lest] finger shall be thicker then my father's loynes. **1670** Ray *Eng. Prov.* 175 He hath more in's little finger, then thou in thy whole body. **1736** Ramsay *Scot. Prov.* xiv. 34 He has mair wit in his little finger than ye have in a' your bouk.

2. a. *transf.* and *fig.*

1612 Bacon *Ess., Judicature* (Arb.) 458 An ancient Clearke..is an excellent finger of a Court, and doth many times point the way to the Iudge himselfe. *a* **1661** Fuller *Worthies* (1840) III. 216 The least finger thereof [body of lies] finding credit could prove heavy enough to crush any innocence with posterity. **1827** Pollok *Course T.* VII. 327 Touched by the mortal finger of decay. **1814** Wordsw. *Excurs.* vi. 19 Spires whose solemn finger points to Heaven. **1862** B. Taylor *Poet's Jrnl.* III. 112 The fingers of the rain In light staccatos on the window played. **1891** B. Harte *First Family of Tasajara* II. i. 27 On whose mute brown lips Nature seemed to have laid the finger of silence.

b. Viewed as 'the instrument of work' (J.); *esp.* (after Heb. use) as attributed to God.

c **825** *Vesp. Psalter* viii. 4 Ic ȝesie heofenas werc fingra ðinra. *a* **1340** Hampole *Psalter* viii. 4, I sall see þi heuens werkes of þi fyngirs. **1577** B. Googe *Heresbach's Husb.* (1586) I. 5 b, All things handled with honest and vertuous fyngers prosper the better. **1585** Abp. Sandys *Serm.* (1841) 288 He cast out devils by the finger of God. **1611** Bible *Ex.* viii. 19 The Magicians said vnto Pharaoh; This is the finger of God. **1645** Waller *Epist. Vandike* 18 Foole, that forget'st her stubborne looke This softnesse from thy finger tooke. **1727** De Foe *Syst. Magic* I. iii. (1840) 77 What they did by their sorcery..was not done by the finger of God.

3. Phrases: **a.** † ***to bring up on the finger***: = 'to bring up (young animals) by hand'; see HAND. † ***to have most fingers***: to be in the greatest need. ***to keep*** (or ***to have***) ***one's fingers crossed***: to crook one finger over another to bring good luck; hence *fig.*, to hope for success or good fortune; also ***with fingers crossed*** (and similar phrases). ***to lay*** or ***put a finger upon*** (***a person***): to 'touch', meddle with however slightly. ***to lay*** or ***put one's finger upon***: to indicate with precision. ***to lift, throw,*** or ***turn up the little finger***: to drink heavily. ***to look through the*** or ***one's fingers*** (***at, upon***): to take no heed, pretend not to see; also, to see indistinctly. (***to point the***) ***finger of scorn***: see POINT *v.*^{1} 12 and SCORN *sb.* 1 c. ***to pull*** (or ***take***) ***one's finger out***: (slang) to get a move on, get 'cracking'; freq. in *imp.* ***to put the finger on***: (slang, orig. *U.S.*) to inform against, to denounce to the police; to identify (a victim) to an assassin; also *transf.* ***to put*** (†***set***) ***one's finger in one's eye***: see EYE *sb.* 2 c. ***with one's finger in one's mouth***: (*a*) helplessly inactive; (*b*) with nothing accomplished, 'looking foolish'. † ***to speak at one's fingers of***: to speak off-hand about. ***to stir a finger***: to make the least effort; also (***not***) ***to lift*** (or ***move***) ***a finger***. ***to turn*** or ***twist*** (***a person***) ***round one's*** (***little***) ***finger***: to make subservient to one's will or caprice.

1617 Markham *Caval.* II. 109 Those that neuer suck their dams, but..are..brought vp vpon the finger. **1677** Yarranton *Eng. Improv.* 171 It is we poor Men that have most Fingers. **1924** *Ladies' Home Jrnl.* Jan. 24/1 This is the year to keep your fingers crossed and announce yourself from Missouri. **1938** 'N. Shute' *Ruined City* xii. 246 I've

got my fingers crossed. I keep them that way all the time. **1940** F. SCOTT FITZGERALD *Let.* 24 Aug. (1964) 122, I have my fingers crossed but.. I think my stock out here is better. **1945** *Penguin New Writing* XXIII. 16 We'll.. duck when we hear a mortar, and keep our fingers crossed. **1966** D. SHANNON *With a Vengeance* (1968) x. 141 I'll go see your Papa. With fingers crossed. **1865** R. S. HAWKER *Prose Wks.* (1893) 41 He wished he'd.. never laid a finger on him to save his life. **1889** *Repent. P. Wentworth* III. 236 Any definite complaint on which a physician could have put his finger. **1894** DOYLE *S. Holmes* 120 You lay your finger upon the one point which we [etc.]. **1824** SCOTT *Redgauntlet* II. xiii. 311 Nanty likes the turning up of his little finger unco weel. **1845** J. S. LE FANU *Cock & Anchor* III. 143 Has he been throwing up the little finger, my dear?.. He used to be raythere partial to brandy. **1890** F. M. PEACOCK *Soldier & Maid* i. 9 The best of fellows,.. but liquors a bit..; lifts his little finger. **1549** LATIMER *4th Serm. bef. Edw. VI* (Arb.) 105 If the kynge.. shoulde loke through his fingers, and wynke at it. **1550** COVERDALE *Spir. Perle* xx. 193 As thoughe God must.. loke thorowe the fingers vpon the wicked world. **1579** GOSSON *Sch. Abuse* (Arb.) 24 To shew you that.. which I see in a cloude, loking through my fingers. **1941** BAKER *Dict. Austral. Slang* 28 *Pull out your finger!* Hurry up! **1942** *Observer* 4 Oct. 7/3 We stooged about a bit above our target.. and then we pulled our fingers out, and pranged it. **1944** J. H. FULLARTON *Troop Target* i. 16 For Christ's sake pull your finger out, Bill. **1956** T. SUTHERLAND *Green Kiwi* i. 22 'They're tigers for toil,' he went on. 'The bloke that takes a job with them wants to be able to pull his finger out.' **1961** *Times* 18 Oct. 8/2 (Duke of Edinburgh) I think it is about time we pulled our fingers out. **1962** *Spectator* 2 Nov. 680 If the publicity.. would 'take its finger out' and show railways.. as.. if they were a new idea. **1963** *Listener* 21 Feb. 320/2 We have come to a pretty pass when even royalty tells us to pull our fingers out. **1926** J. BLACK *You can't Win* vii. 84 If I'm grabbed with this junk I'll rot in jail before I put the finger on you. **1929** D. HAMMETT *Red Harvest* xxiv. 236 You think I killed them, don't you, Dick?.. Going to put the finger on me? **1930** in *Amer. Speech* (1951) XXVI. 155/2 *Put a finger on*, mark for killing. **1951** PARTRIDGE *Dict. Slang* Suppl. 1047 *Put the finger on*, to point (a wanted man) out to the police. **1959** *Times Lit. Suppl.* 25 Dec. 753/2 In one episode Brett puts the finger on a 'loaded' script depicting juvenile crime. **1971** *Daily Tel.* 2 July 15/1, I have not heard of anyone who wants to put the finger on me. *a* **1568** COVERDALE *Bk. Death* III. v. (1579) 263 Many.. which.. haue set finger in the eye, knocked vpon there breastes [etc.]. **1649** CROMWELL *Lett.* 14 Nov., To stand with our fingers in our mouths. **1874** in *Spectator* (1891) 28 Mar. 443 He returned to Ireland with his finger in his mouth. **1607** TOPSELL *Four-f. Beasts* Pref., He was an unskilful Divine.. which could not at his fingers speak of these things. **1833** A. FONBLANQUE *England under Seven Administr.* (1837) II. 321 We don't believe that he would have moved a finger to procure the return of the only man for the chair. **1854** H. MILLER *Sch. & Schm.* (1858) 338, I.. would not stir a finger in assertion of.. alleged rights. **1863** GLADSTONE *Let.* 12 Nov. in P. Guedalla *Palmerston Papers* (1928) 269, I believe he has not himself lifted a finger in the matter. **1955** D. GARNETT *Flower of Forest* ii. 14 Could anyone honestly say that we should have allowed Paris to be occupied and France defeated without lifting a finger? **1855** MOTLEY *Dutch Rep.* v. iii. (1866) 698 Margaret.. had already turned that functionary round her finger.

b. with reference to the capacity or condition of the fingers. †*to have a fine finger*: to be apt at 'fingering' bribes. †*to have fingers made of lime-twigs*: to be thievish. *my fingers itch*: I am eager or impatient. †*each finger is a thumb*; *his fingers are all thumbs*: he is extremely clumsy. *with a wet finger*: with the utmost ease.

1542 UDALL *Apophth.* To Rdr., Whereby.. to any good matter in the booke conteined, readie waie and recourse maie with a weate finger easily be found out. **1546** J. HEYWOOD *Prov.* (1562) G iij b, Whan he should get ought, eche fynger is a thumbe. **1549** LATIMER *5th Serm. bef. Edw. VI* (Arb.) 151 Brybes wyl make you peruert iustice. Why you wil say. We touche none. No mary. But my Mystres your wyfe hath a fyne fynger she toucheth it for you. **1573** G. HARVEY *Letter-bk.* (Camden) 10 Ani quæstion which I culd not shew with a wet finger out of sum excellent.. writer. **1596** HARINGTON *Metam. Ajax* (1814) 65 A certain gentleman that had his fingers made of lime-twigs, stole a pice of plate. **1600** HOLLAND *Livy* XXXVIII. xli. (1609) 1009 They had lesse store of pillage and bootie with them to set their.. fingers on itching. **1754** FOOTE *Knights* I. Wks. 1799 I. 69 If Dame Winifred were here she'd make them all out with a wet finger. **1796** NELSON in Nicolas *Disp.* II. 280, I thought it most proper not to take him (although my fingers itched for it). **1861** HUGHES *Tom Brown at Oxf.* vii, It makes one's fingers itch to think of it.

c. with reference to 'taking part in', 'interference' or 'meddling'. *to burn one's fingers*: see BURN *v.* 14, 14b; so *to put one's finger in the fire*, † *in a hole*. *to put* or *dip one's finger(s in*: to meddle in (a matter). *to have a finger in*: to have something to do with; to take some part in (a business); so *to have a finger in the pie*.

1546 J. HEYWOOD *Prov.* (1562) F iv, It were a foly for mee.. to put my finger to far in the fyre, Betweene you. *Ibid.* H ij b, To make me put my fynger in a hole. **1591** LAMBARDE *Archeion* (1635) 83 Whatsoever other Commissioners.. will dip their owne fingers in the Suits. **1600** ABP. ABBOT *Exp. Jonah* 416 The High Priest had a finger both in the Trumpet and the Fast. **1659** B. HARRIS *Parival's Iron Age* 75 Lusatia.. must needs, forsooth, have her Finger in the Pye. **1672** R. WILD *Declar. Lib. Consc.* 10 None.. durst begin, for fear they should burn their Fingers. **1828** SCOTT *F.M. Perth* vii, You will needs put your fingers in the fire. **1861** W. S. PERRY *Hist. Ch. Eng.* I. vi. 258 The King.. had a finger.. in all the disputes in Europe. **1886** MISS TYTLER *Buried Diamonds* xii, Susie.. liked to have a finger in every pie.

d. with reference to grasping or holding. *in one's fingers*: in one's grasp or power. *to let (a thing or person) slip through one's fingers*: to let go one's hold of (*lit.* and *fig.*). †*out of (a persons's) fingers*: out of his clutches. †*to hang long betwixt the fingers*: to be long in hand.

1623 BINGHAM *Xenophon* 139 Let vs be gone out of their fingers. *c* **1645** HOWELL *Lett.* (1655) I. v. 216, I am one of them, who value not a curtesie that hangs long betwixt the fingers.

e. (For phrases referring to the 'fingers' ends', see FINGER-END.) See also FINGER-TIP.

4. †**a.** One of the divisions of the foot in reptiles. **b.** One of the articulations of a bat's wing.

1607 TOPSELL *Serpents* (1653) 738 The fingers of their [Lizards'] feet were very small, being five in number. *Ibid.* (1608) 794 They [Tortoises] have four legs.. every foot having five fingers or divisions. **1626** BACON *Sylva* §360 On each Foot he [the Chameleon] hath five Fingers. **1883** G. ALLEN in *Knowl.* 22 June 368/1 Between these fingers, and from them to the hind legs, stretches the membrane by means of which the bat flies.

c. 'One of the two parts forming a chelate or forceps-joint, expecially the smaller part, which hinges on the other' (*Cent. Dict.*).

5. As a measure. **a.** The breadth of a finger. Also as a definite measure = $\frac{3}{4}$ inch.

c **1400** MAUNDEV. (Roxb.) xxi. 97 Nere a fote lang and v. fyngers on brede. **1561** EDEN *Arte Nauig.* I. xviii. 19 Foure graines of barlye make a fynger: foure fingers a hande: foure handes a foote. **1607** TOPSELL *Four-f. Beasts* 19 Their tayle is about three fingers long. **1719** LONDON & WISE *Compl. Gard.* 167 You must lay a Finger thick of Moss upon those Shelves. *c* **1850** *Arab. Nts.* (Rtldg.) 236 The lady.. had on a rose-coloured girdle at least four fingers in width. **18..** HALL *Mexican Law* 79 (Cent. Dict.) A finger, in Mexican law, is the sixteenth part of a foot.

†**b.** *Astron.* = DIGIT. *Obs.*

1561 EDEN *Arte Nauig.* II. viii. 35 The Astronomers deuide into .xii. equall partes, as well the Diameter of the Sunne as of the Moone. And these partes they call fyngers, punctes or prickes.

c. *slang.* (orig. *U.S.*) A 'nip' of liquor. [So F. *doigt*.]

1856 *Porter's Spirit of Times* 4 Oct. 73/1 We each took a first mate's drink—i.e. three fingers. **1888** *Newport Jrnl.* 25 Feb. (Farmer), 'Which is correct, spoonfuls or spoons-ful?'.. 'In Denver.. we say fingers.' **1940** L. MACNEICE *Plant & Phantom* (1941) 53 Three fingers of Scotch and a cube of ice. **1959** 'J. WELCOME' *Stop at Nothing* xiii. 185, I poured out another four fingers and handed the tumbler to him.

d. In *U.S.*, the length of a finger (about $4\frac{1}{2}$ inches).

6. a. That part of a glove which is made to receive a finger.

1565 COOPER *Thesaurus, Digitalia*, thinges couering the fingars.. fingers of gloues. **1655** MRQ. WORCESTER *Cent. Inv.* §89 White Silk knotted in the fingers of a Pair of white Gloves. **1884** *Chester Gloss., Finger-stall*, a covering.. made by cutting off the finger of an old glove.

b. *dial.* in *pl.* The foxglove.

1888 ELWORTHY *W. Somerset Word-bk., Fingers*, Foxglove.

7. Skill in fingering (a musical instrument); touch.

1741 RICHARDSON *Pamela* (1824) I. cii. 499 Miss L——.. has an admirable finger upon the harpsichord. **1751** R. PALTOCK *P. Wilkins* (1884) I. xxiv. 245 Softness and easiness of finger. **1850** MRS. F. TROLLOPE *Petticoat Govt.* 78 Her brilliant finger on the piano-forte.

II. Something which resembles a finger.

8. a. A finger-like projection; *esp.* such a part either of the fruit, foliage, or root of a plant. *spec.* a banana.

1702 J. PETIVER in *Phil. Trans.* XXIII. 1264 Having its Spikes or Fingers shorter. **1864** BROWNING *Jas. Lee's Wife* III. ii, Our fig tree.. has furled Her five fingers. **1888** *Encycl. Brit.* (ed. 9) XXIX. 662/2 Some of these [varieties of Turmeric] consist.. of the somewhat cylindrical lateral tubers, which are distinguished in trade as 'fingers'. **1894** J. E. HUMPHREY in *Pop. Sci. Monthly* XLIV. 497 A hand may contain from a dozen to twenty fruits or 'fingers'. **1895** *Daily News* 26 Aug. 5/2 This.. is a shorter and stouter plant than the tropical banana, and often bears from 150 to 250 'fingers' in a bunch. **1961** F. G. CASSIDY *Jamaica Talk* v. 99 A single banana or plantain (a 'finger' of the hand) is often called a *seed*.

b. 'A cartilaginous slender appendage sometimes observable in fishes between the pectoral and ventral fins' (Crabb 1823).

c. A long narrow pier, etc. (e.g. a feature of airport architecture).

1951 *Progressive Archit.* Jan. 49 The pair of two-level 'finger' concourses allows passage to plane-loading points almost wholly under cover. **1954** *Civil Engin.* (U.S.) Sept. 56 Work on the terminal building and its fingers. **1958** *Times* 30 May 7/6 Aircraft can taxi to the.. 900 ft. long glazed pier, or 'finger', which stretches out from the terminal to provide completely enclosed passenger access. **1962** *Economist* 15 Dec. 1131/2 Narrow, cluttered 'finger' piers such as those in New York. **1965** *New Statesman* 20 Aug. 261/3 Half-a-dozen well-detailed finger-plan airports. **1970** *Times* 18 Mar. (Liberia Suppl.) p. v/5 An additional 750 ft. 'finger' pier was built at Monrovia to accommodate two further ore-carrying vessels.

9. a. A short and narrow piece of any material. **b.** Short for *finger-biscuit* (see 14b).

1846 FRANCATELLI *Mod. Cook* 397 Fingers, or Naples biscuits. **1865** *Athenæum* No. 1989. 803/2 Elderberry wine and fingers of toast.

10. a. Something which performs the office of a finger: the 'hand' of a clock (now *dial.*); in *Mech.*, any small projecting rod, wire, or piece which is brought into contact with an object in order to initiate, direct, or arrest motion, or to separate or divide materials.

1496 in *Acc. Ld. High Treas. Scot.* I. 292 Item.. for lokkis, fyngeris, and boltis to the bombartis. **1784** COWPER *Task* IV. 118 Fancy, like the finger of a clock, Runs the great circuit. **1855** MRS. MARSH *Heiress of Haughton* II. iv, One cannot discern the finger moving on the dial plate. **1878** A. BARLOW *Weaving* 214 In Webster's loom a temporary race is formed by means of 'fingers', inserted and withdrawn at proper times, and two shuttles may be thrown separately or simultaneously. **1884** F. J. BRITTEN *Watch & Clockm.* (1892) 204 A small gold finger, projecting far enough to reach the edge of the smaller roller.

b. (*a*) A policeman or detective; (*b*) an informer; (*c*) a contemptible or eccentric person; (*d*) a pickpocket; (*e*) one who supplies information or indicates victims to criminals. *slang.*

1899 'J. FLYNT' *Tramping with Tramps* 393 *Finger*, a policeman. **1914** JACKSON & HELLYER *Vocab. Criminal Slang* 33 *Finger*,.. An informer; an investigator for officers. **1916** C. J. DENNIS *Songs Sentimental Bloke* 122 *Finger*, an eccentric or amusing person. **1925** *Flynn's* 24 Jan. 119/1 *Finger*, a pickpocket. **1926** *Ibid.* 16 Jan. 638/2 If th' stunt was pulled right an' th' Finger does call you, you know th' getaway is in th' clear. **1932** *Ibid.* 28 May 36/2 The café owner had taken me for a professional finger, one of the scouts of the underworld. **1933** G. INGRAM '*Stir*' 8 *Finger*, a term of contempt for man or woman. **1938** F. D. SHARPE *Sharpe of Flying Squad* xiv. 156 They [*sc.* pickpockets] work in pairs; one is 'the fingers', the other obstructs and jostles. **1960** K. HOPKINS *Dead against my Principles* xix. 129 He's a finger, works in Fulham mostly. Small profits, quick returns. **1962** *John o' London's* 25 Jan. 82/3 A man who identifies a suspect at an identification parade.. is called a *finger*.

11. *Printing.* **a.** One of the grippers which hold the paper in a printing-machine. **b.** (See quot.)

1869 S. T. DAVENPORT in *Eng. Mech.* 31 Dec. 377/2 Filling in the separate colours [in coloured printing].. by small inking-rubbers, known as thumbs and fingers.

12. In a reaping machine: (see quots.).

1860 *Gard. Chron.* 14 July 658/3 The fingers [of the reaping machine].. having sharp points, flat vertical sides. **1873** *Daily News* 13 Aug., By the addition of what are called 'fingers', the 'reaper' will cut corn, however much it may be laid. **1878** URE *Dict. Arts* IV. 18 The knife.. consists of a serrated blade, at first straight, but afterwards waved, and passing through pointed sheaths now called 'fingers'.

13. With various defining words prefixed, *esp.* in popular names of plants, as *bloody (man's) finger*, *dead man's (men's) finger(s*, *devil's*, *dog-*, *fairy-*, *fox-*, *king's*, *lady's*, *lords' and ladies'*, *purple fingers*: see the different words.

III. *attrib.* and *Comb.*

14. General relations: **a.** simple attrib., as *finger-fillip*, *-game*, *-gesture*, *-joint*, *-ring*, *-sign*, *-work*; **b.** similative, chiefly in the sense of resembling a finger in shape, as *finger-biscuit*, *-muffin*, *prayer-book*, *-shell*; *finger-like*, *-shaped* adjs.; **c.** objective, as *finger-licking*, *-pointing*, *-wagging*; *finger-squeezing* adj.

1846 FRANCATELLI *Mod. Cook* 397 The *finger biscuits must be immediately placed on a baking sheet, and put in the oven. **1884** YATES *Recoll.* II. vi, On the other side of the newspaper came a *finger-fillip. **1871** TYLOR *Prim. Cult.* I. 68 The ancient Egyptians.. used to play at some kind of *finger-game. **1930** R. PAGET *Babel* 49 Hand- and *finger-gestures. **1938** R. G. COLLINGWOOD *Princ. Art* xi. 242 Italians.. have a long tradition of controlled finger-gesture, going back to the ancient game of *micare digitis*. **1838** DICKENS *Nich. Nick.* iv, Cracked his *finger-joints as if he were snapping all the bones in his hands. **1860** G. H. K. *Vac. Tour* 139 There is no patting.. on his part, or cringing and *finger-licking on that of colly. **1776** WITHERING *Brit. Plants* (1796) III. 735 Outer scales of the calyx with *finger-like divisions. **1860** TYNDALL *Glac.* I. ii. 20 The lower glacier, cleft.. into finger-like ridges. **1842** CHARLES WHITEHEAD *Richard Savage* (1845) II. ix. 294 There was my devilish mother in a side-box, gay and giggling, *finger-pointing [etc.]. **1860** EMERSON *Cond. Life, Power* 44 Their instincts are a finger-pointing of Providence. **1889** (*title*), The *Finger Prayer Book. **1535** COVERDALE *Esther* viii. 2 The kynge put of his *fynger rynge.... & gaue it vnto Mardocheus. **1879** MACLEAR *Celts* ii. 13 Costly finger-rings. **1857** WOOD *Com. Obj. Sea-shore* vi. 116 *Alcyonium digitatum*, or the *Finger-shaped Alcyonium. **1953** J. S. HUXLEY *Evol. in Action* iv. 110 She [*sc.* Helen Keller].. realized that this particular combination of *finger-signs '*meant* the wonderful cool something' that she was feeling. **1770** JENNER *Placid Man* II. 92 For one cold, bleak, *finger-squeezing night. **1931** *Times Lit. Suppl.* 6 Aug. 607/3 The inconsequent *finger-wagging information, the all too 'noble' priggishness. **1965** G. MCINNES *Road to Gundagai* vi. 107 We were the object of finger-wagging lectures.

15. Special comb.: as **finger-alphabet**, an alphabet consisting of certain dispositions of the fingers as a means of communication between the deaf and dumb; a deaf and dumb alphabet; **finger-bar**, the bar which carries the fingers of a reaping machine (sense 12); **finger-board**, (*a*) 'the flat or slightly rounded piece of wood attached to the neck of instruments of the violin and guitar class, on to which the strings are pressed when stopped by the fingers' (Stainer & Barrett); (*b*) a key-board, manual; (*c*) *U.S.* = FINGER-POST; (*d*) a gradient indicator; **finger-bowl** = *finger-glass*; **finger-breadth** (also *finger's-breadth*) the width of a finger used as a measure; **finger-brush** (see quot.); **finger-cold**

a. dial., cold enough to benumb the fingers; **finger-coral**, a millepore (*Millepora alcicornis*); **finger-counting**, calculation by means of the fingers; **finger-cymbals** (see quot.); **finger-director**, 'a metallic cylinder tapering towards the extremity, and open in front; used in the rectangular operation of lithotomy' (*Syd. Soc. Lex.* 1884); **finger-fed** *a. Sc.*, 'delicately brought up, pampered' (Jam.); **finger-fern**, the name of a kind of Spleenwort (*Asplenium Ceterach*); **finger-fish**, the star-fish; cf. *five fingers*; **finger-flower**, the fox-glove (*Digitalis purpurea*); **finger food**, food which may be eaten with the fingers; food so served that it can conveniently be eaten without cutlery, esp. as a snack; **finger-glass**, (*a*) a glass vessel to hold water, for rinsing the fingers after dessert; (*b*) *pl.* = HARMONICA 1 a; **finger-grass**, grass of genus *Digitaria* (N.O. *Gramineæ*); *red finger-grass*, *Digitaria sanguinalis*; **finger-grip** (see quot.); **finger-guard**, the quillons of a sword, recurved towards the pommel as a protection to the fingers; **finger-hold**, something by which the fingers can hold; also *transf.* and *fig.*; **finger-hole**, one of a series of holes in a wind-instrument, which are opened and closed by the fingers in playing; **finger-impression**, a term formerly used for *finger-print*; **finger lake** [f. *Finger Lakes*, name of a group of lakes in New York State], any long narrow lake in a glaciated valley; **finger-language**, language expressed upon the fingers by means of the finger-alphabet; **finger-length**, the length of a finger used as a measure; **finger-lickin', -licking (good)** *a.* orig. *U.S.* [f. the proprietary slogan 'It's finger lickin' good'], tasty or appetizing; also *fig.*; **finger-light** *a.*, (of motor-vehicle steering) susceptible to pressure by the fingers alone; †**finger-loping** (see quot.); **finger man** *U.S. slang* = FINGER *sb.* 10 b (*e*); **finger-mark**, the mark left upon a surface where the finger has touched it; also, a term formerly used for *finger-print*; **finger-mark** *v.*, *trans.* to mark with a (dirty) finger (also in quasi-passive sense); hence *finger-marked* ppl. adj.; **finger-mirror**, a dentist's mouth-mirror fitted with a clasp or attachment to the finger; **finger-nut** (cf. *finger-screw*); **finger-orchis** (see quot.); **finger paint**, a jelly-like paint used chiefly by children; **finger-paint** *v. intr.*, to apply paint (to a canvas or other surface) with the finger; also *transf.*; so **finger-painting** *vbl. sb.*; **finger-parted** *a. Bot.*, divided into lobes more or less resembling the fingers of the hand; **finger-passage** *Mus.*, a passage suited to the study and practice of fingering; **finger-piece**, a piece actuated by the finger; **finger-plate**, a plate of metal or porcelain fixed on either side of a door above and below the handle to prevent finger-marks; **finger-play**, (*a*) a game involving an intricate use of the fingers (see also quot. 1945); (*b*) the use of the fingers for caressing or sexual stimulation, *spec.* of the genital parts; †**finger-plum**, a kind of plum; **finger-print** = *finger-mark*, also *fig.*; now with specific reference to the recording by the police of impressions taken from the finger-tips of criminals and suspects; hence **finger-print** *v. trans.*, to take the finger-prints of; **finger-printing** *vbl. sb.*; **finger-puff** (*Hair-dressing*), 'a long and slender puff, often made by rolling the hair over a finger' (*Cent. Dict.*); **finger-reading**, a method of reading, practised by the blind, by passing the fingers over raised letters; **finger-root** = *finger-flower*; **fingers-and-thumbs**, a popular name for *Lotus corniculatus*; **fingers-and-toes** (*a*) = prec.; (*b*) = ANBURY 2 (also *finger-and-toe*); **finger-screw**, one made with wings so that it may be turned by the fingers; a thumb-screw; †**finger-shade**, the action of concealing the mouth with the fingers; **finger-shield** (see quot.); **finger-smith** *slang*, (*a*) a midwife; (*b*) a pickpocket; **finger-snap**, a snap of the fingers; whence **finger-snapping**; **finger-speech** = *finger-language*; **finger-spin**, spin imparted to a ball by the fingers (as in Cricket and Table Tennis in bowling and serving); hence **finger-spinner**; **finger-sponge**, a sponge with finger-shaped lobes or branches; **finger-steel** (see quot.); **finger-stocks** (see quot.); **finger-style** *a.* and *adv.*, using the fingers alone (not a plectrum) in playing certain stringed instruments; **finger-talk** = *finger-language*; so **finger-talking**; **finger-tight** *adv.*, as tightly as possible by hand; **finger-tray**, †**finger-watch** (see quots.); **finger-wave** *Hairdressing*, a wave set in wet hair with the fingers; so **finger-waving** *vbl. sb.*; **finger-work**, (*a*) work executed with the fingers; (*b*) the play of, or manipulation by, the fingers. Also FINGER-END, -POST, -STALL, -STONE.

1751 SMOLLETT *Per. Pic.* (1779) III. lxxxiii. 285 She asked, by the help of the *finger-alphabet. **1865** TYLOR *Early Hist. Man.* ii. 17 To spell out sentences with the finger-alphabet. **1865–6** *Trans. Ill. Agric. Soc.* VI. 52 Patent Cold Rolled Reaper and *Mower Finger Bars. **1893** *Jrnl. R. Agric. Soc.* Dec. 710 The finger-bar was necessarily carried higher. *a* **1672** WOOD *Life* (O.H.S.) I. 257 The *finger-board of the violin. **1804** *Fredericktown* (Md.) *Herald* 11 Feb. 3/1 Holding the finger board in a wrong direction for Carter's Mountain. **1845** in D. Drake *Pioneer Life Kentucky* (1870) x. 235 At their..forks there were no finger boards, and not many living fingers to point out the true way. **1879** STAINER *Music of Bible* 15 In the guitar the finger-board forms a back or strip of wood behind the strings for their whole length. **1883** F. S. WILLIAMS *Our Iron Roads* iv. 95 Gradients..vary considerably as we may see by the finger-boards placed on the lines for the guidance of the engine-driver. **1864** WORCESTER, **Finger-bowl*. **1884** *Harper's Mag.* July 309/1 Guests..unused to finger-bowls. **1594** BLUNDEVIL *Exerc.* III. II. vi. (ed. 7) 382 Foure barley kernels couched close together side by side..are said to make a *finger breadth. **1659** B. HARRIS *Parival's Iron Age* 179 Spain was indeed within her fingers breadth of destruction. **1721–1800** BAILEY, *Fingers-breadth*, a Measure of two Barley Corn's Length, or 4 laid side to side. **1817** COLERIDGE *Biog. Lit.* 205 It does not desire a single finger-breadth more than what is necessary. **1885** CRANE *Bookbinding* x. 87 The *'finger-brush'..is..about the size of a shaving-brush, of stiff hairs cut square at the ends. The brush, being dipped in the colour, is drawn across the fingers, so as to jerk the colour off in spots. **1862** THOREAU *Excursions* (1863) 302 It is *finger-cold. **1887** *Kent Gloss.*, ''Twas downright finger-cold first thing this marning.' **1884** GOW *Grk. Math.* §8 That..more complicated system of *fingercounting. **1888** STAINER & BARRETT *Dict. Mus. Terms* 126 Small cymbals are sometimes attached to the fingers and are hence called *finger-cymbals. **1578** LYTE *Dodoens* III. lxvii. 408 This herbe [Ceterach] is called in English..*Finger ferne. **1621** BURTON *Anat. Mel.* (1624) 300 For the spleene, maiden-haire, fingerfearne. **1796** MORSE *Amer. Geog.* I. 228 Star Fish or *Finger Fish. **1629** PARKINSON *Paradisus* xcvii. 383 Some..doe call them [foxgloves] *Finger-flowers, because they are like vnto the fingers of a gloue, the ends cut off. **1949** A. L. HILL *Compl. Bk. Table Setting* xix. 248 Asparagus used to be considered a *finger food, but today, happily, the tips are cut off with the fork and eaten with it. **1965** *Harper's Bazaar* Feb. 59/2 What a nauseating expression 'Finger Food' is! **1977** P. LEACH *Baby & Child* iii. 145 At this age all but finger-foods will have to be smoothly pureed. **1985** *N.Y. Times* 9 Aug. C20/3 'Finger foods', intriguing little appetizers that can be picked up and eaten with the hands. **1814** JANE AUSTEN *Mansf. Park* III. xv. 296 She was meditating much upon silver forks, napkins, and *finger glasses. **1831** BREWSTER *Optics* vii. 71 Blue glass, like that generally used for finger glasses. **1868** G. M. HOPKINS *Jrnl.* 20 June (1959) 167 Madle. Vogt [played] the finger-glasses (Mattauphône), and certainly that instrument is chromatically more perfect than the violin. **1821** *Mass. Hist. Soc. Coll.* 2nd Ser. IX. 149 Plants, which are indigenous in the town of Middlebury, [Vermont, include] *Finger grass. **1856** *Rep. Mass. Board Agric.* I. 85 The stems of the finger grass are from one to two feet high. **1943** R. PEATTIE *Great Smokies* 168 In the first year after abandonment.. horseweed and finger grass predominate. **1874** KNIGHT *Dict. Mech.* I. 848/1 **Finger-grip*, a tool for recovering rods or tools dropped into a bored shaft. **1883** GRESLEY *Gloss. Coal Mining*, *Finger Grip*, a tool used in boring for gripping the upper ends of the rods. **1909** *Daily Chron.* 21 Aug. 7/4 Wherever it [*sc.* samphire] can get *finger-hold in the rough face of the cliff, it shows in abundance. **1923** A. TRAIN *His Children's Children* xviii. 219 The relief of him who, having plunged part way down the face of a precipice, has caught a finger-hold in a crevice. **1923** H. L. WILSON *Oh, Doctor!* xii. 135 'Yes,' assented Seaver; 'one of these movie actors that can bite nails in two and throw a horse over a fence and climb up the side of a church with only a finger hold.' **1964** M. MORSE *Unattached* v. 158 There seemed nothing I could do about this without endangering the fingerhold I had gained. **1879** STAINER *Music of Bible* 96 Four of its tubes have small lateral *finger-holes. **1903** *Westm. Gaz.* 16 Nov. 5/1 Witness told him that his *finger-impression had been found on a pane of glass on the roof of the building. **1906** *Daily Chron.* 24 Oct. 1/7 Two men who are so much alike that they can be distinguished only by their finger impressions. **1931** C. C. CARTER *Landforms & Life* xix. 122 Ten or more..radial streams and valleys may be counted and named from the map; most of them expand into *finger lakes. **1939** A. K. LOBECK *Geomorphol.* viii. 273 The long finger lakes of central and northern Sweden on the eastern side of the Scandinavian Highland correspond to the fiords of Norway on the western side. **1968** R. W. FAIRBRIDGE *Encycl. Geomorphol.* 435/2 Where the ice sheet passed over an escarpment, it left extra-deep finger lakes. **1842** DICKENS *Amer. Notes* I. iii. 93 She often soliloquizes in the **finger language*. **1874** SAYCE *Compar. Philol.* i. 52 The finger-language of the deaf and dumb. **1857** MRS. CARLYLE *Lett.* II. 329 The baby is about three *finger-lengths long. [**1896** *Dialect Notes* I. 420 *Licking* (adv.), very. 'Licking good', of pie, candy, etc.] **1958** *Amer. Restaurant Mag.* June 64 (in picture) Featuring..Kentucky Fried Chicken..'It's *finger lickin' good.' **1963** *Official Gaz.* (U.S. Patent Office) 20 Aug. TM137/2 Kentucky Fried Chicken, Inc...*'it's finger lickin' good'*. For freshly prepared chicken and gravy packaged and sold in retail trade. First use April 1952. **1970** *Times* 9 Mar. 8/5 A chain of shops selling southern fried chicken to take away finds 'finger-lickin' an effective adjective to describe their products. **1976** *New Musical Express* 12 Feb. 43/1 Eric and his chums consumed the lot and fell over without picking a single finger-lickin' note. **1978** *Forbes* (N.Y.) 23 Jan. 51/2 Massey went on to take over Kentucky Fried Chicken..and..sell out to Heublein at a finger-licking $45 million profit. **1927** *Observer* 15 May 21 But no special skill is needed in directing this car, the steering of which is *finger-light. **1958** *Times* 22 Oct. 5 Finger-light power assisted steering ensures perfect control. **1644** BULWER *Chiron.* 110 The wagging and impertinent extension of the Fingers in speaking..Cresollius condemnes this *Finger-loping gesture as very uncomely. **1930** *Flynn's* 15 Mar. 624/2 Martin was knocked off... It was thought Butch Swang had brought in the *finger men to put Martin on the spot. **1951** I. SHAW *Troubled Air* viii. 127 They're using you. You're their finger man. You're their respectable front. **1968** E. MCGIRR *Lead-Lined Coffin* ii. 80 He was right to concentrate on Fall. There could have been the fingerman watching him. **1840** DICKENS *Barn. Rudge* ii, Dirty *finger-marks upon his face. [**1880** HERSCHEL in *Nature* 25 Nov. 76/2, I have been taking sign-manuals by means of finger-marks for now more than twenty years.] **1889** *Daily News* 10 Dec. 7/9 Brilliant, lasting polish. Will not finger mark. **1891** GALTON in *Proc. R. Soc.* 28 May 540 Methods of indexing Finger-Marks. **1884** KNIGHT *Dict. Mech.* IV. 334/2 **Finger-mirror*. **1598** GERARDE *Herbal* I. ciii. §2. 170 Roiall Satyrion or *finger Orchis, is called of the Latines *Palma Christi*. **1950** WEBSTER Add., *Finger paint (*sb.*). **1966** 'E. V. CUNNINGHAM' *Helen* (1967) xii. 176, I dreamed that I was a little boy using finger paints. **1951** C. HAYES *Ape in House* (1952) xxiv. 210 She learned..to *fingerpaint on the rugs with butter and orange juice. **1971** *Guardian* 9 July 7/5 Teachers learning to finger paint at the York Teachers' Centre. **1950** WEBSTER Add., *Finger painting. **1959** J. VERNEY *Friday's Tunnel* iii. 34 Splodgy finger paintings in paste and powder colour. **1829** LOUDON *Encycl. Plants* 17 Lower leaves [of *Veronica triphyllos*] entire: middle *finger-parted. *Ibid.* 1099/1 *Finger-parted*, divided into lobes having a fanciful resemblance to the five fingers of a human hand. **1883** PARRY in Grove *Dict. Mus.* III. 584 The familiar outlines..of the principal harmonies afford the most favourable opportunities for..*finger-passages. **1881** GREENER *Gun* 201 This gun is loaded by turning the *finger-piece, which lies in the fore-part of the stock, round to the top of the barrel. **1851** *Ord. & Regul. R. Engineers* §19. 91 Brass Sashes are not to be allowed; nor *Finger Plates, except for one or two rooms in a House. **1879** *Cassell's Techn. Educ.* IV. 298/2 Finger plates for doors. **1945** C. V. GOOD *Dict. Educ.* 171/2 **Finger play*, a dramatization of a verse or poem with appropriate finger movements, used as an attention-getting device with young children. **1963** *Times* 3 June 11/6 A book of fingerplays (great for idle moments),..and some books of riddles and puzzles. **1965** P. & E. KRONHAUSEN *Sexual Response in Women* vi. 137 His finger-play on my clitoris helps. **1966** BEREITER & ENGELMANN *Teaching Disadvantaged Children* i. 14 Some time is usually devoted to group games, finger-plays, and the like. **1970** *Sunday Times* 15 Nov. 32/3 Pepys was highly susceptible to any available charmer, but contented himself as a rule with mutual fingerplay. **1577** B. GOOGE *Heresbach's Husb.* II. 96 The *fynger Plomes..being of the length of a mans fynger. **1859** *North Amer. Rev.* LXXXVIII. 492 The chapel of St. Verena, where the *finger-prints of the young maiden still remain in the rock. **1884** J. PARKER in *Chr. World* 15 May 360/4 The word 'dogma'..seems to me to bear the *finger-prints of the pedant or the priest. **1891** GALTON in *19th Cent.* XXX. 304 My..collection of analysed finger-prints. **1891** *19th Cent.* Aug. 304 Finger-prints have been proposed..as a means of identification. **1903** *Daily Chron.* 9 Feb. 8/7 The finger-print system of identification. **1905** *Ibid.* 13 Sept. 7/4 A prisoner..seldom objects to being finger-printed. **1923** *Glasgow Herald* 2 Nov. 6 Demanding that every new-born child be finger-printed when registered. **1937** *Oxoniensia* II. 6 The large vessels..with finger-print decoration on the shoulder. **1955** *Wall St. Jrnl.* 1 Nov. 9/3 These methods of 'finger printing' chemical compounds often are considered better evidence of the existence of large molecules like those of natural rubber than physical evaluations. **1956** V. M. INGRAM in *Nature* 13 Oct. 793/2 It was decided to call the resulting chromatogram the 'finger print' of the protein. **1961** J. SINGH *Ideas Mod. Cosmol.* vii. 96 The measurement ..enables us to compute the curvature. In other words, space curvature leaves its fingerprint on the pattern of galactic distribution in depth over the sky. **1969** *Nature* 23 Aug. 832/2 Fig. 1 shows a 'fingerprint' (peptide chromatogram) of the tryptic peptides of normal myoglobin. **1970** *Daily Tel.* 27 Feb. 4/8 The technique uses the radioactive 'fingerprint' of elements to determine their age and origin or to compare one substance with another. *Ibid.* 4 Mar. 17/8 When I realised it might be used in evidence against me I asked for it to be finger-printed. **1970** *Nature* 21 Mar. 1131/2 Fingerprints of the T_1 ribonuclease digestion products of 16S and 23S RNAs are very different, thus indicating dissimilar primary structures. **1922** *Glasgow Herald* 2 Nov. 6 The big Danish prisons, where *fingerprinting is an important factor. **1958** *Sci. Amer.* Jan. 19/3 The electrophoretic 'fingerprinting' technique..to distinguish the hemoglobin of men, horses and whales. **1882** FRIEND *Devonsh. Plant-n.*, *Fingers and Thumbs, *Lotus corniculatus* L., or *Cypripedium Calceolus* L. **1750** *Fingers-and-toes [see ANBURY 2]. **1812** W. SPENCE (*title*), Observations on the Disease in Turnips, termed in Holderness 'Fingers and Toes'. **1875** W. T. THORNTON in *Encycl Brit.* (ed. 9) I. 367 The roots present a thickened, palmated appearance, giving rise to the popular name for the disease, 'fingers and toes'. **1883** *Daily News* 18 Sept. 2/5 Stunted growth..and finger-and-toe. **1825** J. NICHOLSON *Operat. Mechanic* 320 Unturning the *finger-screw. **1711** PUCKLE *Club* 28 Brethren in iniquity [gamesters] using *Finger-shade, Mouth-spirt, or Shoulder-dash. **1882** CAULFEILD & SAWARD *Dict. Needlework*, **Finger-shield*, a silver appliance made to fit the first finger of the left hand.. It is employed to protect the finger from the needle. **1812** J. H. VAUX *Flash Dict.*, **Finger-smith*, a midwife. **1884** *Gd. Words* June 401/1 A couple of 'finger-smiths'—pickpockets. **1821** *Blackw. Mag.* IX. 71 Coats of finest nap, For which I ne'er receiv'd a *finger-snap. **1884** *Pall Mall G.* 8 Nov. 2/2, I do not value Government Reports..at a finger-snap. **1882** *Society* 14 Oct. 12/1 The cousin's song..with a *finger-snapping accompaniment, goes very well. **1858** J. MARTINEAU *Stud. Chr.* 37 The *finger-speech of ceremony. **1905** *Westm. Gaz.* 1 July 2/3 Bowlers with plenty of *finger-spin are most likely to take wickets on the mat. **1906** *Ibid.* 8 May 2/1 Finger-spin bowlers like Schwarz, Faulkner, and Vogler. **1927** *Observer* 17 Apr. 17/4 [He] only needs more power of finger-spin to be a match-winning bowler. **1938** *Encycl. Brit. Bk. Yr.* 623/1 It is now no longer legal [in Table Tennis] to use the finger-spin in serving. **1958** *Listener* 16 Oct. 604/2 The wrist-spinner..is inevitably less accurate than the *finger-spinner. **1884** KNIGHT *Dict. Mech.* IV. 334/2 **Finger-steel*, a steel instrument like a skewer or awl, used for restoring the edge of the currier's knife while

in use. **1686** PLOT *Staffordsh.* 390 *Finger-Stocks; into which the Lord of misrule, used formerly to put the fingers of all such persons as committed misdemeanours. **1934** S. R. NELSON *All about Jazz* ii. 53 When the banjo was first introduced into the dance band, the players were *finger-style performers. **1955** L. FEATHER *Encycl. Jazz* (1956) vii. 77 Plays unamplified Spanish concert guitar, finger style. **1656–81** BLOUNT *Glossogr., Dactylogie*, *finger-talk, speech made with the fingers. **1843** J. T. HEWLETT *College Life* II. xxix, Having had the difficulties..explained to him in dumb-show and finger-talk. **1855** H. CLARKE *Dict.* s.v. *Finger*, *Finger-talking. **1940** 'N. SHUTE' *Old Captivity* v. 148 Bolts were put on *finger-tight... Finally..the bolts were tightened down and locked. **1961** *Lancet* 19 Aug. 410/2 Retention is ensured by screwing the female end-piece fingertight over the male. **1884** KNIGHT *Dict. Mech.* IV. 334/2 ***Finger-tray**, a small pan, attached by a clasp to the finger, used by dentists for carrying amalgam or plastic filling. *a* **1680** BUTLER *Rem.* (1759) II. 393 He [an Hypocrite] is the Devil's *Finger-Watch, that never goes true, but too fast, or too slow, as he sets him. *a* **1718** PENN *Maxims* Wks. 1726 I. 842 A Finger Watch, to be set forwards or backwards, as he pleases that has it in keeping. **1934** WEBSTER, Finger wave. **1936** J. STEINBECK *In Dubious Battle* 299 Her hair was damp..and little, uneven *finger-waves were pressed into it. **1950** J. B. LOHLE in Foan & Wolters *Art & Craft Hairdressing* (ed. 3) v. 267 If the natural wave is rather weak..the older type of blow dryer may be used to give a finger-wave. **1963** M. MCCARTHY *Group* xii. 286 A finger wave in her majestic coiffure. **1926** *Amer. Hairdresser* May 6 The subject of '*Finger Waving'. **1932** L. GOLDING *Magnolia St.* III. iii. 508 They were masters of the latest methods of permanent marcel, water and finger waving. **1849** ROCK *Ch. of Fathers* III. x. 354 A..rich pall of silk.. the *finger-work of some queen. **1906** *Practitioner* Dec. 826 The great drawback of this treatment is that it..must be minutely carried out, demanding..a great deal of finger-work. **1906** *Westm. Gaz.* 10 Aug. 3/1 There was never before so clear an exposition of balance, of swing, and of finger-work in bowling. **1927** *Observer* 29 May 14/5 [His] first recital showed promise... Mozart does not suit his style: it needs better finger-work and not so much arm and body and pedal. **1967** *Antiquaries Jrnl.* XLVII. 208/1 Simpler finger-work,..companion thus to cord-impression.

finger ('fɪŋgə(r)), *v.* [f. prec. sb. Cf. Ger. *fingern.*]

†**1.** *trans.* To point at with the finger. *Obs.*

c **1450** [see FINGERING *vbl. sb.* 1]. **1483** *Cath. Angl.* 131/2 To Finger, *digitare.*

2. a. To hold or turn about in one's fingers; to put one's fingers upon, touch with the fingers; also, to do this repeatedly or restlessly.

1590 SPENSER *F.Q.* III. ii. 6 To finger the fine needle and nyce thread. **1690** DRYDEN *Don Sebastian* III. ii, You would fain be fingering your rents beforehand. **1762** GOLDSM. *Cit. W.* cii, In China, our women..are never permitted to finger a dice-box. **1853** KINGSLEY *Hypatia* vii. 92 Philammon, fingering curiously the first coins which he ever had handled. **1861** HUGHES *Tom Brown at Oxf.* xiii, The..crew fingered their oars. **1870** *Mod. Hoyle* 46 To finger the squares of the [chess-]board whilst planning your move is strictly legal but a most villanous habit. **1887** R. N. CAREY *Uncle Max* xxx. 244 She was never weary of fingering her silks and satins.

fig. **1883** T. H. GREEN *Proleg. Ethics* §297 To be always fingering one's motives is a sign..of an unwholesome preoccupation with self. **1885** W. B. YEATS in *Dublin Univ. Rev.* Apr., For the dawn the foliage fingereth. **1929** D. H. LAWRENCE *Pansies* 61 My body need not be Fingered by the mind. **1956** *Kenyon Rev.* XVIII. 417 Often they [*sc.* skilful poets] 'finger' the speech flow.

b. To touch or handle (money) with unworthy motives. †Also *absol.*

1581 MULCASTER *Positions* xxxvii. 159 They [the Romains] fell to fingering [context speaks of 'receiuing giftes and rewarde']. **1651** JER. TAYLOR *Serm. for Year* I. xxi. 264 It is a huge dishonour..to be too busie in fingring money in the matters of religion. **1884** TENNYSON *Becket* I. iii. 56 The cardinals have finger'd Henry's gold.

†**c.** To lay hands upon, apprehend (a person). Also to handle roughly, 'claw'. *Obs.*

1624 SIR R. ALDWORTH *Let.* 27 Dec. in *Lismore Papers* (1888) Ser. II. III. 136 The two Releeuers feighin [Fagan] and lyney [Leyne] I knowe and Dout not but to finger on Thursday next. **1670** W. WALKER *Idiomat. Anglo-Lat.* 200 How would I finger him! *Quibus illum lacerarem modis!*

3. *intr.* To make restless or trifling movements with the fingers (const. *at*); also, to play or toy *with*. †*to finger for*: (*fig.*) to grope for, hanker after.

1655 GURNALL *Chr. in Arm.* xi. (1669) 130/1 Thy heart is fingering for more of these than God allows thee. **1816** L. HUNT *Rimini* II. 119 They stood with their old foreheads bare, And the winds fingered with their reverend hair. **1858** KINGSLEY *Poems, Sappho* 22 She flung her on her face..And fingered at the grass. **1869** TENNYSON *Pelleas & Ettarre* 433 Pelleas..Fingering at his sword-handle.

4. a. *trans.* To lay the fingers upon or touch with a view to plunder; to pilfer, filch. Also const. *from*: To take or remove fraudulently *from.*

1530 PALSGR. 550/2 Beware of hym, for al that he can fyngar gothe with hym. **1577–87** HOLINSHED *Chron.* III. 1136/1 So likewise did the Spanish soldiers..that could come to finger anie thing of value. **1593** SHAKS. *3 Hen. VI*, v. i. 44 But whiles he thought to steale the single Ten, The King was slyly finger'd from the Deck. **1655** FULLER *Ch. Hist.* III. ii. §6 His Predecessors..grasp it fast in their fist, in defiance of such Popes as would finger it from them. **1693** *Mem. Ct. Teckely* I. 17 The Troops..took away all they could finger without paying for it.

†**b.** To cheat (a person) *out of* (a thing).

1709 *Brit. Apollo* II. No. 70. 2/2 Three Thornbacks.. artfully finger'd me out of five Guineas.

c. To indicate (a victim) or supply (information) to criminals; to inform on or identify (a criminal) to the police. *U.S. criminals' slang.*

1930 *Flynn's* 13 Dec. 194/1 Frank Lee..had 'fingered' many, many dealers to the Feds. **1936** *Ibid.* 12 Dec. 8/2 Matt Prance has got me fingered... They're going to kill me. **1949** R. CHANDLER *Little Sister* xxxiii. 242 She's on her way back..with..the pocket money she got..for fingering her brother. **1954** H. ROTH *Content Assignment* xxii. 139 She.. couldn't finger them for any crime.

5. a. To play upon (an instrument) with the fingers.

1515 BARCLAY *Egloges* iv. (1570) C iij/2 Yet could he pipe and finger well a drone. **1603** DRAYTON *Odes* I. 61 To seeke, Of Pindar that Great Greeke, To Finger it [the harp or lyre] aright. **1641** EVELYN *Mem.* (1857) I. 27 He had fingered an organ. **1873** C. KEENE *Let.* in G. S. Layard *Life* vii. (1892) 152 A dummy bagpipe chanter..I carried in my pocket, and fingered on every possible occasion.

b. To play (a passage of music) with the fingers used in a given way (where there is a choice of methods of execution).

c. To mark (a piece of music) with figures indicating the fingers with which the notes are to be played.

1816 *Gentl. Mag.* June 539/2 All the lessons are sufficiently fingered. **1891** *Times* 22 Oct. 14/2 The latest issues..of Bach's organ works..are carefully edited and fingered.

6. a. To manipulate with the fingers, 'to perform any work exquisitely with the fingers' (J.); *fig.* to elaborate, bestow minute labour on. Also with *up. rare.*

1816 J. GILCHRIST *Philos. Etym.* 185 If they can finger up, or arrange words into..soft, smooth, pretty, insignificant composition. *Ibid.* 236 Addison's composition..is.. carelessly irregular..but nevertheless much-laboured and fingered.

b. *intr.* for *pass.* To be manipulated with the fingers.

1927 W. W. BISHOP *Pract. Handbk. Mod. Libr. Catal.* (ed. 2) 33 The tests of a card are the cleanness and speed with which it 'fingers' in consultation, and the fastness of its color.

†**7.** ***finger out***: **a.** To read carefully or with effort, passing the finger along the lines. **b.** To point out as with the finger. *Obs.*

1680 JENKINS in Mansel *Narr. Popish Plot* 101 He received all the Tryals that were printed, and had fingerd them out. **1767** W. HANBURY *Charities Ch.-Langton* 134 Amity of dunce with dunce, Fingers out genius all at once.

8. ***finger up*** (nonce-use): *intr.* to run up in finger-like extensions.

1854 HOOKER *Himal. Jrnls.* I. xi. 264 Peninsulas, between which the misty ocean seemed to finger up like the fiords of Norway.

Hence '**fingerable** *a. rare*, that can be fingered. '**fingerative** *a.*, apt to 'finger', thievish. '**fingerer**, one who fingers; *esp.* a pilferer, thief.

1561 AWDELAY *Frat. Vacab.* 8 A Fyngerer, an olde beaten childe, not onely in such deceites but, etc. **1674** JOSSELYN *Voy. New Eng.* 98 The Indians are very fingurative or thievish. **1891** G. DU MAURIER in *Harper's Mag.* Aug. 383/1 Four strings; but not the fingerable strings of Stradivarius. **1893** *Scribner's Mag.* May 614/2 Dencombe was..a fingerer of style.

fingered ('fɪŋgəd), *ppl. a.*[1] [f. FINGER *v.* + -ED[1].] In senses of the vb. In *Music*: Marked with figures showing what finger is to be used for producing each note.

1775 ASH *Fingered*..touched, stolen. **1823** CRABB *Technol. Dict., Fingered*, a term applied to piano-forte exercises.

fingered ('fɪŋgəd), *ppl. a.*[2] [f. FINGER *sb.* + -ED[2].] Having or provided with fingers.

1. a. Of a person; chiefly in parasynthetic derivatives, as ***light-***, ***rosy-***, ***three-fingered.***

a **1529** SKELTON *Elynour Rummyng* 41 How she is gumbed, Fyngered and thumbed, Gently ioynted. **1865** DICKENS *Mut. Fr.* I. ii, The great looking-glass..reflects.. Mrs. Veneering; fair, aquiline-nosed and fingered.

b. Of a glove etc.; also in parasynthetic derivatives, as ***cut-fingered***: see CUT *ppl. a.* 12.

1591 [see CUT *ppl. a.* 12]. **1739** MRS. DELANY *Life & Corr.* (1861) II. 35 Six pair of cut fingered gloves. **1849** SOUTHEY *Comm.-pl. Bk.* Ser. II. 584 The stalks of the leaves furnished stockings, and ladies fingered gloves.

2. *Bot.* **a.** Of a leaf or plant: Digitate. **b.** Of the fruit or root: Shaped like a finger.

1668 WILKINS *Real Char.* II. iv. 98 A fingered leaf, being from one foot-stalk divided into many segments. **1758** *Phil. Trans.* I. 590 *Spongia Americana capitata et digitata*; The fingered sponge of Plumier. **1861** MISS PRATT *Flower. Pl.* VI. 40 Fingered Sedge. **1883** *Evang. Mag.* Nov. 511 The carpels fail to unite, and we get what are called 'fingered citrons'.

finger-'end, finger's 'end. Pl. finger-ends, fingers'-ends. The end or tip of the finger.

c **1400** *Destr. Troy.* 8795 Folowand the fell to þe fyngur endys. *c* **1400** *Lanfranc's Cirurg.* 28 þe skyn of the fyngris endis. **1598** SHAKS. *Merry W.* v. v. 88 With Triall-fire touch me his finger end. **1655** SIR E. NICHOLAS in *N. Papers* (Camden) II. 321, I will never desert whilst I can wagg nose, toes, or finguers end. **1712** tr. *Pomet's Hist. Drugs* I. 135 Fruit, about the size of ones Finger End. **1825** SCOTT *Jrnl.* 20 Nov., His finger-ends can describe..what he cannot bring out clearly..in words.

b. Phrases: † ***to arrive at one's fingers' ends***: to come to gnawing one's fingers' ends; to reach the extremity of poverty. ***at one's finger(s') ends***: ready at hand. ***to have*** (or †***know***), ***at*** (or †***on one's finger(s' ends*** or ***tips***: to have thorough familiarity with (a subject, branch of knowledge, etc.). (***to live***) ***by one's fingers' ends***: by industry or manual labour. †***to suck*** (***anything***) ***out of one's own fingers' ends***: to arrive at by one's own ingenuity. ***to one's finger-ends***: completely, entirely, quite. †***to get upon the finger ends*** (= Fr. *avoir sur les doigts*): *fig.* to incur a sharp reprimand, to 'catch it.'

1546 J. HEYWOOD *Prov.* (1562) E ij, I suck not this out of my owne fingers eends. **1553** LATIMER *Serm.* (1575) III. 181 He forgetteth them not, but hath them at hys finger's-ende (as they say). **1561** HOBY tr. *Castiglione's Courtyer* I. C b, You haue at your fingers endes that belongeth thereto. *a* **1568** COVERDALE *Bk. Death* xl. (1579) 194 He maie be the better aquainted with them, and have them on his fingers endes. **1577** tr. *Bullinger's Decades* (1592) 581, I..knowe at my fingers ends, what kind of men..are in this citie. **1579** GOSSON *Sch. Abuse* (Arb.) 36 If any parte of Musick haue.. aried by fortune at their fingers endes. **1621** BURTON *Anat. Mel.* Democr. to Rdr. (1676) 32/2 Thousands..live singular well by their fingers' ends. **1662** GREENHALGH in Ellis *Orig. Lett.* Ser. II. IV. 14 Their Service-books..they have at their fingers' end. **1693** *Apol. Clergy Scot.* 37, I am afraid I may get upon the Finger-ends, because I did not name my Witnesses. **1711** STEELE *Spect.* No. 156 ¶5 Names which a Man of his Learning has at his Fingers-Ends. **1816** EARL OF DUDLEY *Lett.* (1840) 143, I already have all these authors completely at my fingers' ends. **1862** CARLYLE *Fredk. Gt.* (1865) III. IX. ii. 82 All manner of Military Histories, we perceive, are at his finger-ends. **1883** *Harper's Mag.* Jan. 322/2, I would be Duchess to my finger-ends.

fingerful ('fɪŋgəfʊl). [f. FINGER *sb.* + -FUL.] As much as can be held on one finger or between two fingers at one time; hence, a small quantity (*of* something).

1889 H. JOHNSTON *Chrons. Glenbuckie* ii. 19 Just put a fingerfu' o' poother i' the pan. **1923** U. L. SILBERRAD *Lett. J. Armiter* vi. 138 At first I could get them to do nothing more than suck a finger; and it is quite hopeless to try to get enough milk into them by finger-fulls. **1958** *Listener* 13 Nov. 768/1 They put the final fingerful of colour on to our faces. **1968** H. C. RAE *Few Small Bones* II. v. 114 He peeped out of the side window through a fingerful of curtain.

fingering ('fɪŋgərɪŋ), *sb.* Also 7–8 *Sc.* fingram, 8 *Sc.* fingrim, fingrine, fingrum, -om, 9 fingerin. [The oldest forms *fingram* etc., combined with the difficulty of connecting the sense with that of *finger*, suggest that the word may be an early corruption of F. *fin grain*, lit. 'fine grain' (cf. *grogram* from *gros grain.*)]

1. A kind of wool or yarn used chiefly in knitting stockings; 'worsted spun of combed wool, on the small wheel' (Jam.). Also *attrib.*

1681 COLVIL *Whigs Supplic.* (1751) 107 There fingram stockings spun on rocks lyes. **1808** JAMIESON, *Fingerin.* **1875** *Plain Needlework* 10 Fingering Yarn. **1885** *Bazaar* 30 Mar. 332/1 Stocking..knitted with German fingering wool. **1894** *Westm. Gaz.* 10 May 3/3 Stockings made from the best 'fingerings'.

†**2.** A kind of woollen cloth. *Sc. Obs.*

1707 G. MIEGE *Pres. State Gt. Brit.* II. 24 Large Flocks of Sheep they have in Scotland produce abundance of Wool, from whence come..Fingrines, Serges [etc.]. **1719** *Act 6 Geo. I*, c. 13 An Act for..preventing Frauds..in manufacturing Serges..and Fingrums. **1733** P. LINDSAY *Interest Scot.* 105 At Aberdeen, and Countries adjacent, large Quantities of our own coarse tarred Wooll are manufactured into coarse Serges, called Fingrams.

fingering ('fɪŋgərɪŋ), *vbl. sb.* [f. FINGER *v.* + -ING[1].]

1. The action of the vb. FINGER in various senses.

c **1450** *Bk. Curtasye* 249 in *Babees Bk.* 306 Bekenyng, fynguryng, non þou use. **1553** T. WILSON *Rhet.* (1580) 144 As when one hath..got his livyng with light fingeryng. **1567** DRANT *Horace Epist.* Bj, Measure the lawe of sounde by fingering, or by eare. **1621** SANDERSON *Serm.* I. 214 Uzza had better have ventured the falling, than the fingering of the ark, though it tottered. **1760** *Impostors Detected* I. 251 He shall not have the fingering of her any more than myself. **1818** JAS. MILL *Brit. India* (1840) I. I. iii. 80 The Directors ..had expected the fingering of the money. **1872** O. W. HOLMES *Poet Breakf.-t.* i. (1885) 28 Covers browned..with ..the fingering of..book-misers.

†**b.** Work done with the fingers. Cf. FINGER *v.* 6.

1590 SPENSER *Muiopotmos* 366 Nor anie skil'd in loupes of fingring fine.

2. *Mus.* **a.** The action of using the fingers in playing upon an instrument; the proper method of doing this.

c **1385** CHAUCER *L.G.W.* Prol. 91 As an harpe obeieth to the honde, And maketh it soune after his fingering. **1545** ASCHAM *Toxoph.* (Arb.) 39 Instrumentes..whyche standeth by fine and quicke fingeringe. **1593** *Pass. Morrice* 78 Shee tooke her lute, singing to her fingering this sonnet. **1674** PLAYFORD *Skill Mus.* II. 103 The Rule of true Fingering. **1856** MRS. BROWNING *Aur. Leigh* I, I learnt much music.. fine sleights of hand And unimagined fingering.

b. The indication, by figures set against the notes of a piece of music, of the way in which the fingers are to be used in its performance.

1879 GROVE *Dict. Mus.* I. 527/2 The earliest German fingering..was the same as the present English system.

3. *attrib.*

1603 HOLLAND *Plutarch's Mor.* 1252, I am better acquainted with the fingring Musicke and manuall practise than otherwise. *a* **1680** BUTLER *Rem.* (1759) I. 255 A cheat, That lets his false Dice freely run.. But never lets a true one stir Without some fingering Trick or Slur. **1883** BLACKIE in *Contemp. Rev.* June 814 Not from any fingering induction of external details.

fingering ('fɪŋgərɪŋ), *ppl. a.* [f. FINGER *v.* + -ING².] That fingers (an instrument); also, addicted to 'fingering' or petty manipulation.

1712 *Spectator* No. 338 ⁋2 Those fingering Gentlemen should be informed that they ought to suit their Airs to the Place. **1799** WORDSW. *Poet's Epitaph* v, Philosopher! a fingering slave. **1816** [see FINICALNESS].

fingerish ('fɪŋgərɪʃ) *a. nonce-wd.* [f. FINGER *sb.* + -ISH.] Of or pertaining to the fingers.

1892 M. NORTH *Recoll. Happy Life* I. vii. 259 Fingers were their only tools and.. by the end of the day the saucers must have had a strong fingerish flavour.

fingerless ('fɪŋgəlɪs), *a.* [See -LESS.] Without fingers.

1838 DICKENS *Nich. Nick.* xxxi, After putting on his fingerless gloves with great precision. **1895** *Chambers's Jrnl.* XII. 628/1 They showed their blotched and swollen bodies, fingerless hands, and toeless feet.

fingerlet ('fɪŋgəlɪt). *nonce-wd.* [See -LET.] A small or delicate finger.

1854 W. JOHNSON *Ionica* (1858) 77 Those straying fingerlets that clutched At good and bad.

fingerling ('fɪŋgəlɪŋ). Also 8 **fingerin**. [f. FINGER *sb.* + -LING. Cf. Ger. *fingerling* glove-finger, thimble (MHG. *fingerlinc* ring).]

†**1.** One of the fingers of a glove; a finger-stall.

c **1440** *Promp. Parv.* 161/2 Fyngyrlynge of a glove, *digitabulum.* **1530** PALSGR. 220/1 Fingerlyng of lether, *delot.* **1580** HOLLYBAND *Treas. Fr. Tong, Vn doigtier*, a thimble, a fingerling.

2. A very diminutive being; used to translate Ger. *Däumerling* (Goethe *Faust*).

1835 ANSTER *Faustus* II. II. (1887) 128 Pigmies, emmets, fingerlings, And other active little things. **1867** *Contemp. Rev.* VI. 50 Thumblings and Fingerlings whom the Pygmies have enslaved.

3. A name for the parr (*Salmo salmulus*). Cf. BRANDLING 2.

a **1705** RAY *Synop. Method. Piscium* (1713) 63 Salmulus, *The Samlet* Herefordiensibus, *Branlin & Fingerin* Eboracensibus. **1836** YARRELL *Brit. Fishes* II. 43 The transverse dusky bars from which this fish has obtained the name of Brandling and Fingerling.

attrib. **1888** *Pall Mall G.* 7 Apr. 6/1 A couple of wretched fingerling smolts.

†'**fingerly**, *a. Obs. rare*⁻¹. [f. FINGER *sb.* + -LY¹.] Of or pertaining to the fingers.

1619 SIR J. SEMPILL *Sacrilege Handl.* 81 They poynted him out, as by a fingerly demonstration.

'**finger-'nail.** One of the nails of the fingers. *to one's finger nails*: completely, thoroughly.

a **1240** *Wohunge* in *Cott. Hom.* 281 þat te blod wrang ut at tine finger neiles. **1842** TENNYSON *E. Morris* 22 He seem'd All-perfect, finish'd to the finger nail. **1884** —— *Becket* III. i, He's as like the King as fingernail to fingernail. **1888** *Graphic* Summer No. 21/1, I was a theosophist to my finger-nails.

'**finger-post**, *sb.* A post set up at the parting of roads, with one or more arms, often terminating in the shape of a finger, to indicate the directions of the several roads; a guide-post.

1789 MRS. PIOZZI *Journ. France* II. 291 The words *Route de Belgrade* upon a finger-post. **1857** TOULM. SMITH *Parish* 357 The Highway Surveyors ought to put up finger posts.. where they are likely to help travellers.

transf. and *fig.* **1793** BEDDOES *Math. Evid.* 158 It had pleased him to christen the pronouns, the finger-posts of language. **1857** STANLEY *Mem. Canterb.* i. 31 So many finger-posts, pointing your thoughts, along various roads, to times and countries far away.

b. *slang.* (See quot.)

1785 GROSE *Dict. Vulg. Tongue, Finger post*, a parson, so called, because like the finger post, he points out a way he.. probably will never go, i.e. the way to heaven.

Hence '**finger-posted** *ppl. a.*, having a finger-post; in quot. *fig.* '**finger-postless** *a.*, without a finger-post.

1885 H. O. FORBES *Nat. Wand. E. Archip.* 88 Flowers.. with.. a beautifully painted and finger-posted labellum. **1873** MISS BROUGHTON *Nancy* III. 147 A labyrinth of cross-roads, fingerpostless, guideless.

finger-post, *v.* [f. the sb.] *trans.* To indicate by means of a finger-post. Also *fig.*

1908 *Councils' Jrnl.* 17 The Parish Council of Orrell-with-Ford.. is properly proud of having 'name-plated all the roads, finger-posted all the footpaths,' [etc.]. **1926** T. E. LAWRENCE *Seven Pillars* (1935) 7 The contents seem to me to be adequately finger-posted by this synopsis. **1944** *Ess. & Stud.* XXIX. 52 In the drama the playwright may be 'explicit' in finger-posting parts of plot, situation, or character.

'**finger-stall.** A cover or protection for the finger, usually of leather, e.g. the finger of a glove, used in some handicrafts, in dissection, or when the finger is injured or diseased.

1483 *Cath. Angl.* 131/2 A Fyngyr stalle, *digitale.* **1578** LYTE *Dodoens* II. xxiv. 175 Foxe glove hath.. fayre, long, round, hollow floures fashioned like fingar stalles. **1606** HOLLAND *Sueton.* 74 The fore finger of his right hand hee perceived.. to be so weake, that.. he could hardly set it to any writing, with the helpe of an hoope and finger-stall of horne. **1643** I. STEER tr. *Exp. Chyrurg.* xv. 64 Finger-stalls made of Leather. **1832** BABBAGE *Econ. Manuf.* I. (ed. 3) 14 The child puts on the forefinger of its right hand a small cloth cap or finger-stall. **1879** MISS JACKSON *Shropsh. Word-bk.* 148, I cut my finger, but I clapt a finger-stall on.

'**finger-stone.**

†**1.** A stone sufficiently small to be cast by the hand. Also *attrib. Obs.*

c **1400** MAUNDEV. (Roxb.) xi. 46 A lytil þeine, as it ware a fynger stane cast, es anoþer chapell. **1688** I. CLAYTON in *Phil. Trans.* XVII. 984 They are so nigh the Shoar, that a Man may almost fling a Finger-stone on Board.

2. A cylindrical stone, convexly tapering to a point; a belemnite.

1773 JOHNSON (ed. 4), *Finger-stone*, a fossil resembling an arrow. **1802–3** tr. *Pallas's Trav.* (1812) II. 229 A whimsical mixture of broken belemnites, or finger-stones.

'**finger-tip.** The tip of a finger; used *attrib.* to indicate length (of a garment) or sensitivity (of an object) to pressure, and *spec.* in *Archæol.* designating ornamentation made with the tips of the fingers; hence **finger-tipping** *vbl. sb.* Phr. *to the* (or *one's*) *finger-tips* = through one's whole body, 'from top to toe', throughout; ***at one's finger(s') tips*** = 'at one's finger-ends'.

1842 TENNYSON *Launcelot & Q. Guin.*, As she sway'd The rein with dainty finger-tips. **1870** *Harper's Mag.* Nov. 864/1 The best learning that the world affords, my Bert has at his fingers' tips. **1883** E. PENNELL-ELMHIRST *Cream Leicestersh.* 314 There was a bite at one's fingertips. **1886** KIPLING *Departmental Ditties* 45, I redden to my finger-tips. **1905** *Strand Mag.* June 702/1 He has at his finger-tips every stroke in the game. **1907** *Daily Chron.* 21 Jan. 3/5 Alive with science to the finger tips. **1928** CRAWFORD & KEILLER *Wessex fr. Air* 10 If it was constructed, as he concludes, by the finger-tip people. *Ibid.* 200 The fragment of a typical finger-tip urn. **1929** F. HACKETT *Henry VIII* VIII. 417 He was a magnate to his finger-tips. **1929** V. G. CHILDE *Danube in Prehist.* 364 Biconical or open urns with finger-tip ornament. **1935** *Times* 28 Nov. 19/5 Finger-tip coat and frock. **1937** *Times* 13 Apr. p. xxii/4 A 'finger-tip' adjustment for setting the brake shoes to the correct clearance. **1937** *Oxoniensia* II. 28 Rough grey-brown smoky ware with finger-tipping on the shoulder. **1956** A. H. COMPTON *Atomic Quest* 54 He had at his fingertips the most recent experimental values of the constants. **1959** *Observer* 7 June 31/1 A great bout of finger-tip handling right across the Australian goalmouth. **1960** *News Chron.* 19 Feb. 8/7 The fingertip light switch. **1961** *Antiquaries Jrnl.* XLI. 36 Two shoulder sherds.. with stick impression or impressed finger-tip decoration. **1961** J. MCCABE *Mr. Laurel & Mr. Hardy* (1962) iii. 75 He was an artist to his fingertips once he got going.

fingery ('fɪŋgərɪ), *a.* [f. FINGER *sb.* + -Y¹.] Branching into fingers or finger-like divisions.

1821 MOIR in *Blackw. Mag.* VIII. 527 The broad fern with its fingery leaf. **1840** *Jrnl. R. Agric. Soc.* I. IV. 403 Turnips.. grow fingery and of little value.

fingian: see FINGAN.

fingle-fangle. [reduplication of FANGLE. Cf. FIDDLE-FADDLE.] A trifle; something whimsical or fantastic. Also *attrib.*

a **1652** BROME *Covent Garden* I. 13 This comes of your new fingle-fangle fashion. **1678** BUTLER *Hud.* III. iii. 221 To wrangle, About the slightest fingle fangle. **1710** *Brit. Apollo* III. No. 61. 3/1 A Woman.. I Love; A kind of Female Fingle, Fangle. **1900** *Daily News* 26 Nov. 4/1 A lot of fingle-fangle, like piano-playing. **1963** *Brewer's Dict. Phr. & Fable* 359/2 *Fingle-fangle*.. is not heard nowadays, except as an archaism.

Hence '**fingle-fangled** *ppl. a.*

1651 BIGGS *New Disp.* ⁋11 The upstart fingle-fangl'd Paracelsian.

Fingo ('fɪŋgəʊ). Also **Fengu** ('fɛŋguː). [f. Bantu *amaMfengu* destitute people in search of work, f. *fenguza* to seek service.] A Negro people of South Africa, now resident in the eastern Cape Province, representing a coalescence of various groups of fugitives driven from Natal in the 1820's.

1829 C. ROSE *4 Years S. Afr.* viii. 193, I saw many of the fugitives, who are called *Fingos*, wanderers. **1836** *Grahamstown Jrnl.* 109 (Pettman), The Fingoes residing on the missionary station, displayed.. considerable firmness and courage. **1850** J. W. APPLEYARD *Kafir Lang.* 41 The term *Amafengu* is a conventional national epithet, first applied to the *Fingoes* by the Kafirs, but now in general use amongst themselves. **1883** *Encycl. Brit.* XVI. 517/1 The South African races, Hottentots and Kaffres, Fingoes and Bechuanas, Basutos and Zulus. **1902** *Ibid.* XXX. 3/1 The formerly degraded but now respected and civilized Fingos or Fengus, who give their name to the district of Fingoland. **1955** M. GLUCKMAN *Custom & Conflict in Afr.* iii. 76 A similar attitude was shown by some Fingo elders.

fingram, obs. variant of FINGERING *sb.*

fingrigo ('fɪŋgrɪgəʊ). The name in Jamaica for a prickly climbing shrub, *Pisonia aculeata.*

1707 SLOANE *Jamaica* I. p. liv, They grind the roots of Fingrigo and Limetree between two stones. **1756** P. BROWNE *Jamaica* 252 Fingrigo or Thorny Mimosa. This prickly shrub is frequent in most of our sugar colonies.

†'**fingure.** *Obs.*⁻¹ [irreg. f. L. *fing-ĕre* to frame + -URE.] A fabrication, coinage.

1592 NASHE *P. Penilesse* E iij b, Doctor Watson, retorting verie merilie his owne licentious fingures upon him.

finial ('fɪnɪəl), *a.* and *sb.* Forms: 4–6 **fynial**(l, **-yal**(l, 5–7 **finiall**, 6– **finial**. [A variant of FINAL, app. of Eng. origin, as no similar form has been found in OE. or med.Lat.]

A. *adj.*

†**1.** = FINAL. *Obs.*

? *a* **1400** *Chester Pl.* (Shaks. Soc.) I. 157 Rittes ceremoniall,.. Shall utterlye cease, and take ther ende fyniall. **1426** AUDELAY *Poems* 50 There was faythfolé made a feneal code. **1447** BOKENHAM *Seyntys* (Roxb.) 116 Graunt them to dyen in fynial grace. **1460** *Pol. Rel. & L. Poems* 105 Fynyal blyse. **1486** *Bk. St. Alban's, Her.* B iij a, Ther be ix. quadratis for to consider. v. quadrate finiall and iiij royall.

2. [Suggested by the sb.] Forming the crown or completion; crowning. *rare*⁻¹.

1888 A. S. WILSON *Lyric Hopeless Love* 182 Until.. life erects its finial part, The formulation of the heart.

B. *sb. Arch.* An ornament placed upon the apex of a roof, pediment, or gable, or upon each of the corners of a tower, etc.; a similar ornament serving as a termination to a canopy or the like, or to the end of an open seat in a church.

1448 *Will of Hen. VI* in Willis & Clark *Cambridge* I. 369 Euery boterace fined with finialx. **1572** *Indenture* 4 Jan. in H. Walpole *Vertue's Anecd. Paint.* (1765) I. App., All the seid fynyshing and performyng of the seid towre with fynyalls. **1591** SYLVESTER *Du Bartas* I. i. 223 From this faire Palace then he takes his Front, From that his Finials. **1600** HOLLAND *Livy* XXXV. x. (1609) 894 Gilded shields.. were set up on the finiall or lanterne of Jupiters temple. **1601** —— *Pliny* XXXV. xii. 552 To set up Gargils or Antiques at the top of a Gavill end, as a finiall to the crest tiles. **1811** J. MILNER *Eccl. Archit.* vii. 105 Pinnacles.. surmounted with an elegant flower, called a finial. **1853** TURNER *Dom. Archit.* II. vi. 255 The finish of the northern gable with its beautiful finial. **1870** F. R. WILSON *Ch. Lindisf.* 31 The low open seats are ornamented with finials.

b. *transf.* and *fig.*

1591 SYLVESTER *Du Bartas* I. v. 985 As the Phœnix on my Front doth glister, Thou shalt the Finials of my Frame illustre. **1632** HOLLAND *Cyrup* 206 The absolute perfection and finiall of many noble and excellent Actions. **1876** R. F. BURTON *Gorilla L.* I. 96 Monotheism, the finial of the spiritual edifice. **1880** BLACKMORE *M. Anerley* III. iii. 33 An ivied bush, which served as the finial of the garden-hedge.

Hence '**finialled** *ppl. a.*, having, or decorated with, finials.

1850 T. INKERSLEY *Romanesque Archit. France* 323 An external Pointed arch, surmounted by a triangle crocketed and finialled.

†'**finially**, *adv. Obs.* [f. FINIAL *a.* + -LY².] = FINALLY.

1588 J. READ *Compend. Method* 110 b, Finially all affects that are called Rumatick.

finical ('fɪnɪkəl), *a.* [Connected with FINICK *v.*, FINICKING; as *finical* is the earliest recorded, it may be the source of the other words; in any case ultimate derivation from FINE *a.* seems probable.] Of persons, their actions and attributes: Over-nice or particular, affectedly fastidious, excessively punctilious or precise, in speech, dress, manners, methods of work, etc. Also of things: Over-scrupulously finished; excessively or affectedly fine or delicate in workmanship.

1592 NASHE *P. Penilesse* (ed. 2) 10 b, She is so finicall in her speach. **1607** R. C. *World of Wonders* 50 Women gorgeously apparelled, finicall and fine as fippence. **1650** HOWELL *Ep. Ho-El.* I. I. i, Expressions made up of a bombast of words and finical affected complements. **1660** H. MORE *Myst. Godl.* To Rdr. 11 More trim and elegant fancies, who are so nice and finical that they would not come near a sore. **1709** STEELE *Tatler* No. 82 §6 Your open Sleeves.. made a much better Show than the finnikal Dress I am in. **1727** POPE, etc. *Art of Sinking* 111 The Finical Style.. consists of the most curious, affected, mincing metaphors. **1754** RICHARDSON *Grandison* (1781) II. ii. 11 Lord G. seems a little too finical in his dress. **1820** MISS MITFORD in L'Estrange *Life* II. v. 119 Such a pretty, little, delicate, ladylike, finical gentleman! **1840** THACKERAY *Crit. Rev.* Wks. 1886 XXIII. 167 It might be painted with a good deal less finical trifling with the pencil. **1887** SAINTSBURY *Hist. Elizab. Lit.* v. (1890) 189 The finical scholarship of the present day.

absol. *a* **1845** HOOD *Compass* xxii, Fear quitted the most finical.

Hence †'**finical** *v.*, *nonce-wd. trans.* to dress or 'get (oneself) *up*'. '**finically** *adv.*, in a finical manner, affectedly, fastidiously. '**finicalness**, (*a*) the quality of being finical; (*b*) a finical thing, a refinement. **fini'cality**, (*a*) finical quality; (*b*) something finical.

1594 NASHE *Unfort. Trav.* 15, I was ordained Gods scourge from aboue for their daintie finicalitie. **1659** TORRIANO, *Stringáto*.. finicaly drest up. **1670** COVEL *Diary* (1893) 261 We had no such finicallnesse as knives or forkes, onely.. our hands and teeth. **1682** MRS. BEHN *False Count* I. ii. 20 You think yourself a very fine fellow now, and finical yourself up to be thought so. **1762–71** H. WALPOLE *Vertue's Anecd. Paint.* (1786) V. 206 His works have no more merit than finicalness.. can give them. **1777** ROBERTSON *Hist. Amer.* (1778) I. IV. 372 Finically attentive to dress. **1816** J. GILCHRIST *Philos. Etym.* 217 [He] would arrest the press to alter a comma; yet with all this fingering finicalness, has not left a single well-constructed paragraph in his whole writings! **1819** *Sporting Mag.* V. 60 After sipping with all

the finicallity of spinsterian consequence her sixth cup of the enlivening liquid. **1826** *Blackw. Mag.* XIX. 655 To cut joints..neither in slices too thick, nor in such as are finically thin. **1884** J. PAYN *Lit. Recoll.* 256 He..sometimes exhibited a whimsical finicality.

finicism (ˈfɪnɪsɪz(ə)m). [f. next + -ISM.] Finical affectation.

1844 *N. Brit. Rev.* II. 65 Notwithstanding..of this theatrical finicism, he was always himself again before an audience. **1862** *Temple Bar Mag.* VI. 132 There was no finicism in the Author of Waverley.

finick (ˈfɪnɪk), *sb.* [? Back-formation from FINICAL; in sense 2 more prob. f. next vb.]

1. A finical person.

1706 *Reflex. upon Ridicule* 103 Does he think to be courted for acting the finick and conceited? *Ibid.* 119 She's an affected Finick. **1861** G. MEREDITH *Evan Harrington* iii. 29 The ladies..signalized him as a 'finick'. **1949** S. GIBBONS *Match-maker* xxx. 370 No one would have credited such a finnick as Mrs Hoadley with being a first-class cook.

2. *dial.* 'Mincing, affected manners' (*S. Chesh. Gloss.* 1887).

finick (ˈfɪnɪk), *v.* orig. *dial.* Also **finnick**; in glossaries spelt **finnack, -ock**, etc. [See FINICAL, FINICKING.] *intr.* 'To execute work in a fastidious manner, wasting time over unnecessary details' (*Holderness Gloss.*); 'to mince, affect airs' (*S. Chesh. Gloss.*); to behave in a fastidious or finicky manner. Hence **ˈfinicking** *vbl. sb.*

1857 G. MEREDITH *Farina* 153 The Demon..pointed his feet, and finicked a few steps away. **1869** E. WADHAM *Eng. Versificat.* 147 The verse laughs at such finnicking, and asserts its true division. *a* **1916** E. P. OPPENHEIM *Golden Beast* (1926) I. xxiv, She's all brain and fancies and temperament. That sort of person finicks with the marriage question. **1931** V. WOOLF *Waves* 76, I do not finick about fearing what people think of 'my father a banker at Brisbane' like Louis.

finickiness (ˈfɪnɪkɪnɪs). Also **finn-**. [f. FINICKY *a.* + -NESS.] The quality or condition of being finicky; excessive concern over trifles, over-fastidiousness.

1833 J. NYREN *Young Cricketer's Tutor* (1902) 114 It was thought a piece of finnikinness by those simple and homely yeomen. **1920** *Glasgow Herald* 23 Dec. 4 Sensitive to the point of finnickiness. **1930** *John o' London's* 18 Jan. 618/2, I received a letter..which supplies me with a fine example of this grammatical 'finickiness'.

finicking, finikin (ˈfɪnɪkɪŋ, -ɪn), (*ppl.*) *a.* and *sb.* Also **finnicking, finnikin**, (9 **finican**). [Of somewhat doubtful etymology; most likely f. FINICK *v.* + -ING²; the chief difficulty is that the adj. is recorded from the middle of 17th c., while the vb. is known only from a very recent period.

It has been suggested that *finikin* is the original form, and is of Du. origin; cf. MDu. *fijnkens* adv. accurately, neatly, prettily (Kilian). On this hypothesis the words *finical* and *finick* sb. and vb. must in some way have been evolved from *finikin.* The conjecture however is unsupported by evidence, and *finical* appears 70 years earlier than the earliest known instance of *finikin.*]

A. *adj.* Affecting extreme refinement; dainty, fastidious, mincing; excessively precise in trifles. Also of things: Over-delicately wrought or finished; also, insignificant, paltry, trifling.

1661 A. BROME *Leveller* i. Poems 72 Your Madams and Lords, And such finikin words. *c* **1680** *Roxb. Ball.* (1891) VII. 467 He's a finikin' vapouring Taylor. **1741** E. POSTON *Pratler* (1747) I. 230 Thou finicking Stuff, Put thy Hands in a Muff. **1822** *Blackw. Mag.* II. 444 To apply their finican hands and utensils to the laborious task. **1831** *Fraser's Mag.* II. 745 Quiet and finikin as his [Horace's] satire is. **1837** DICKENS *Pickw.* xix, With all the finicking coxcombry of youth. **1865** G. MEREDITH *R. Fleming* x, Out..came the old, broad, bent figure, with little finicking steps. **1886** T. HARDY *Mayor Casterbridge* xii, Such finnikin details.

†**b.** In eulogistic sense: Dainty, pretty. *Obs.*

c **1749** *Robin Hood & Allen a Dale* xviii. in Child *Ballads* v. cxxxviii. 174/1 A finikin lass, Did shine like glistering gold.

B. *sb.* (in form *finikin, finnikin*).

†**1.** A finicking person. *Obs.*

1744 MRS. E. HEYWOOD *Female Spect.* (1748) I. 82 Every public place so abounded with coxcombs and finikins.

†**2.** A variety of pigeon. *Obs.*

1725 BRADLEY *Fam. Dict.* s.v. *Pigeon,* Many sorts of pigeons, such as Carriers..Finikins. **1765** *Treat. Dom. Pigeons* 136 The Finnikin. These Pigeons are possessed of certain whimsical gestures when salacious. **1867** TEGETMEIER *Pigeons* 175 The Finnikin.

Hence **ˈfinickingly** *adv.*

1880 VERN. LEE *Italy* IV. ii. 153 Finickingly finished like a fan-painting.

finicky (ˈfɪnɪkɪ), *a.* orig. *dial.* and *U.S.* [f. FINICK *v.* + -Y¹.] = FINICKING *a.*

1825 BROCKETT *Gloss. N. Country Words, Finniky,* trifling, scrupulously particular. **1839** POE *Wks.* (1865) II. 388 He was really the most finnicky little personage that had ever been seen in Vondervotteimittiss. **1859** *Trans. Ill. Agric. Soc. 1857–8* III. 473 We desire to be neither coarse or finicky. **1873** E. EGGLESTON *Myst. Metrop.* xxxv. 303 You a'n't so finicky 'bout vittles as you was. **1887** *Critic* (N.Y.) 9 Apr., A great number of the rules..seem equally what New England matrons call 'finicky'. **1892** B. MATTHEWS *Americanisms & Briticisms* 24 Professor Freeman.. frequently finicky in his choice of words. **1895** *Rev. Reviews* Oct. 355/1 The fine or finicky ear of the critic in the study. **1934** *Brit. Jrnl. Psychol.* July 59 A prolix writer, finicky I am told, about literary style.

†**ˈfinifest.** *nonce-wd.* [f. L. *fini-s* end + *festum* FEAST.] (See quot.)

1551 R. ROBINSON tr. *More's Utop.* (Arb.) 153 The whyche woordes may be interpreted primifeste and finifest, or els in our speache, first feaste and last feast.

finific (faɪˈnɪfɪk), *a.* [f. L. *fini-s* + -FIC.] Putting a limit to; limiting; in quot. *absol.* or quasi-*sb.*

1830 COLERIDGE in *Lit. Rem.* (1836) III. 2 The eternally self-affirmant self-affirmed..whose definition is the essential finific in the form of the infinite.

finifugal (faɪˈnɪfjʊgəl), *a.* *nonce-wd.* [f. L. *fini-s* end + *fug-a* flight + -AL¹.] Of or pertaining to shunning the end (of anything).

1883 L. A. TOLLEMACHE in *Jrnl. Educ.* 1 Sept. 307 In modern as well as in ancient times, the finifugal tendency.. is apparent.

ˈ**finify,** *v.* *Obs.* exc. *U.S.* and *dial.* Also 7 **finefy, finifie.** [f. FINE *a.* + -(I)FY.] *trans.* To make fine; to adorn, deck, 'trick up'. *to finify it*: see quot. 1611.

1586 WARNER *Alb. Eng.* II. x, Her rotten trunk and rustie face she finified than. **1611** COTGR. *Pimper,* to sprucifie, or finifie it; curiously to pranke, trimme, or tricke vp himselfe. **1678** MRS. BEHN *Sir P. Fancy* IV. iii, Get you gone, and finefy your knacks. **1708** MOTTEUX *Rabelais* IV. x. (1737) 41 Some..dress'd the Pages in Womens Cloths, and finified them like any Babies. **1847** J. S. ROBB *Streaks of Squatter Life* 73 (Bartlett), If this new judge is the slicked up, finefied sort on a character they pictur' him, I don't want to see him. **1891** *Harper's Mag.* Jan. 222/1 They [*sc.* women] air obleiged ter set out a table all tricked up an' finified off. **1895** RYE *E. Anglian Gloss., Finify,* to be over-nice in doing anything.

Hence **ˈfinified** *ppl. a.*; **ˈfinifying** *vbl. sb.*

1628 WITHER *Brit. Rememb.* II. 2067 Some..parted from Our City walls..so finifi'd, As if their meaning was, to shew their pride In Country Churches. **1655** GURNALL *Chr. in Arm.* viii. (1669) 267/2 Now while thou art in a natural estate (though never so finified) Old Adam is thy father. **1674** DRYDEN *Mall* II. iii, Such licking, patching, and finifying.

Finiglacial (fɪnɪˈgleɪʃ(ɪ)əl), *a.* *Geol.* Also **Fini-glacial, finiglacial.** [f. L. *fini-s* end + GLACIAL *a.*] Epithet of the last of the three divisions or 'sub-epochs' of the Late Glacial epoch in north-western Europe, when the ice-sheet left Finland and retreated across the Gulf of Bothnia to central Sweden.

1910 G. DE GEER in *Geol. Förening. Stockholm Förhandl.* XXXII. 1146 The last part of the late glacial epoch, when the ice receded from the great moraines to eastern Jämtland at the point of the first bipartition of the vanishing ice-remnant, may be called the *finiglacial* age. **1946** L. D. STAMP *Brit. Struct.* xiv. 170 The Fini-Glacial lasted from about 8500 B.C. to 6500 B.C. and was the period of the retreat of the ice from Finland. **1957** J. K. CHARLESWORTH *Quaternary Era* II. xlii. 1158 The Daniglacial may have equalled the Gotiglacial and Finiglacial in length. **1965** F. J. MONKHOUSE *Dict. Geogr.* 122/2 *Finiglacial stage,* the third stage in the retreat of the continental ice-sheet from Scandinavia.

†**finiˈgraphical,** *a.* *humorous.* *nonce-wd.*

1594 NASHE *Unfort. Trav.* Wks. (Grosart) V. 37 In their sincere and finigraphicall cleane shirts and cuffes. **1596** —— *Saffron Walden* Ep. Ded. *heading,* To..the sincere & finigraphicall rarifier of prolixious rough barbarisme [i.e. a barber].

finikin, var. form of FINICKING.

fining (ˈfaɪnɪŋ), *vbl. sb.* [f. FINE *v.*³ + -ING¹.] The action of the vb. FINE.

1. The operation or process of refining (metals); *esp.* that of converting cast iron into wrought iron by heating it in contact with charcoal and so removing the carbon.

1502 *Priv. Purse Exp. Eliz. of York* (1830) 38 Certain personnes..that wrought in fynyng of iron. **1585** ABP. SANDYS *Serm.* (1841) 366 The fining of gold in the furnace. **1864** PERCY *Iron & Steel* 579 It seems somewhat absurd to designate the process of incomplete decarburization as refining, and that of..complete decarburization as only fining. *Ibid.*, I..apply the word fining to the operation of converting cast into malleable iron..in a hearth or open fire urged by a blast of air with charcoal as the fuel.

2. The operation or process of clarifying (a liquid; *esp.* beer, wine, etc.). Also the process by which a liquid becomes fine or clear.

1607 DEKKER *Wh. Babylon* Wks. 1873 II. 215 No Vines could please our taste, But of her fining. **1683** *Lond. Gaz.* No 1862/8 New Experiments, for Fyning and Improving of Syder. **1707** MORTIMER *Husb.* xvi. 339 It [Beech] is good also for Fuel..not to omit the Shavings of it for the fining of Wine. **1846** J. BAXTER *Libr. Pract. Agric.* I. 137 The operation of fining will be unnecessary to such beer. **1864** *Reader* 9 Jan. 53 To investigate the cause of this fining of the blood.

b. *concr.* Anything used for this purpose. Usu. *pl.*

1772 JACKSON in *Phil. Trans.* LXIII. 5 One ounce and a half of good isinglass..was converted into good fining. **1822** IMISON *Sc. & Art* II. 160 A preparation of isinglass and sour beer, called finings, is put into it. **1851** MAYHEW *Lond. Labour* I. 184 The coffee is made of a dark colour by means of what are called 'finings' which consist of burnt sugar. **1885** *Act* 48–9 *Vict.* c. 50 §8 Finings for the purpose of clarification [of beer].

3. *Comb.*: **fining-forge** (see quot.); **fining-pot,** a crucible in which metals are refined; **fining-roller** (see quot.).

1874 KNIGHT *Dict. Mech.* I. 848/2 **Fining-forge*..an open hearth with a blast by which iron is freed of impurities or foreign matters. **1611** BIBLE *Prov.* xvii. 3 The *fining pot is for siluer, and the furnace for gold. **1879** SIR G. G. SCOTT *Lect. Archit.* I. 134 Let us throw them boldly into the fining-pot. **1874** KNIGHT *Dict. Mech.* I. 848/2 **Fining-roller* (*Paper-making*), a cylindrical wire-cloth sieve in the paper-making machine, which allows the finely ground stuff to pass, but restrains the coarse fibers and knots.

finion var. form of FINGAN.

finis (ˈfaɪnɪs). [a. L. *finis* end.]

1. The Latin word for 'end', formerly, and still occasionally, placed at the end of a book.

Almost universally used in the earlier half of 19th century; in recent books 'End' or 'The End' is substituted.

[? *a* **1400** *Chester Pl.* xii. *Temptation,* Finis paginæ duodecimæ.] *c* **1460** *Play Sacram.*, Finis. **1523** FITZHERB. *Husb.*, Finis. **1621** BURTON *Anat. Mel.*, Finis. **1697** EVELYN *Medals* vii. 255 And now I have but a Word to add before I come to *Finis.* **1839** BAILEY *Festus,* Finis.

2. Hence, the conclusion, end, finish; end of life, death.

1682 D['URFEY] *Butler's Ghost* I. 47 To deck the *Finis* of his Face. **1719** —— *Pills* (1872) IV. 328 Under this Stone lies one who writ his Finis. **1865** CARLYLE *Fredk. Gt.* IX. xx. x. 169 Next Year..must be the finis of this long agonistic tragedy. **1871** CARLYLE in *Mrs. Carlyle's Lett.* III. 200 Fast falling into imbecility and finis, poor man. **1874** LONGF. in *Life* (1891) III. 223 Though that may be the proper finis of the book.

3. End in view, ultimate destination. *rare.*

1850 CARLYLE *Latter-d. Pamph.* v. (1872) 162 Which is itself a *finis* or kind of goal.

finish (ˈfɪnɪʃ), *sb.* [f. next vb.]

1. a. The conclusion, last stage, termination; also (*colloq.* or *vulgar*) the 'end' of a man.

1790 A. M. JOHNSON *Monmouth* III. 140 To look upon death..as the finish of your sorrows! **1806** SOUTHEY *Lett.* (1856) I. 361 The fit and worthy finish of such a life. **1814** MAD. D'ARBLAY *Wanderer* V. 318 And here..is the finish of all I have to recount. **1826** *Sporting Mag.* XVII. 321 You would like to hear what was the finish of the noted Will Barrow. **1827** *Ibid.* XXI. 78 The finish of the hunting season I unfortunately lost.

b. *elliptically* in *Sporting*: The end of a hunt, race, etc.; the death of a fox; also in phrase, ***to be in at the finish.*** Also *fig.*

1875 W. S. HAYWARD *Love agst. World* 13 The old squire was determined to be in at the finish. **1879** JEFFERIES *Wild Life in S.C.* 133 Think for a moment of a finish as it is in reality. **1891** H. LE CARON *25 Years in Secret Serv.* (1893) 188 It was..in the speeches from start to finish.

2. a. That which finishes, or serves to give completeness or perfection to anything.

1779 J. WEDGWOOD *Let.* 23 Nov. (1965) 245 We have formed a..school, which I have..some notion of.. continuing instead of sending them [*sc.* children] from home again, unless by way of finish. **1793** *Copper-Plate Mag.* No. 13, The choir received it's embellishments and finish from Henry the Eighth. **1823** GR. KENNEDY *Father Clem.* i. 20 To obtain that finish to his education which it was..thought could only be acquired by travelling [etc.]. **1868** FREEMAN *Norm. Conq.* (1876) II. x. 515 Two smaller towers were designed as the finish of the building. **1890** *Century Mag.* Jan. 362/1 To have an American finish put to her education and manners.

b. *Building.* The last coat of paint or plaster laid upon a surface.

1823 P. NICHOLSON *Pract. Build.* 417 Over this a coat of oil-colour..called the finish, is laid.

3. The condition or quality of being finished or perfected.

c **1805** MAR. EDGEWORTH *Wks.* (Rtldg.) I. 354 There was a want of *finish,* as the workmen call it, in my manufacture. **1857** H. MILLER *Test. Rocks* vi. 229 They could not, compatibly with such nicety of finish, be laid over each other. **1876** HUMPHREY *Coin-Coll. Man.* xxvi. 397 High finish could not be obtained in the mode by which this massive money was produced. **1885** NEWHALL in *Harper's Mag.* Jan. 278/2 They [gloves] are tanned with sumac and gambier..as these produce softer finishes. **1885** *Manch. Exam.* 22 Feb. 5/3 Mr. Reeves sang with perfect finish. **1888** CROSS & BEVAN *Text-bk. Paper-Making* x. 159 The degree of smoothness or 'finish' that can be given to the paper by the calenders, depends..upon the degree of moisture which it contains. **1962** F. T. DAY *Introd. to Paper* 115/1 *Finish.* This is the degree of smoothness applied to a paper. Finishes may vary: rough antique, smooth, mill finish, super calender, highly glazed or gloss finish.

4. *slang.* A house of entertainment, where the night is finished.

1796 GROSE *Dict. Vulg. T.* (ed. 3) *The finish,* a small coffee-house, in Covent-Garden market,..open very early in the morning. **1840** *Fraser's Mag.* Oct. 399/1 The pleasures of the metropolis—the theatres, the Cider-cellars, the Finish. **1859** SALA *Tw. round Clock* (1861) 17 The innumerable finishes and saloons. **1860** THACKERAY *Lovel* (1869) 204 A weakly little man..whose pallid countenance told of Finishes and Casinos.

5. (See quot.)

1875 *Ure's Dict. Arts* I. 58 Methylated spirit can be procured also in small quantities..containing in solution 1 oz. to the gallon of shellac, under the name of 'finish'. **1888** *Dumfries Standard* 22 Feb. 3 The traffic in methylated spirit or 'finish' as it is popularly called.

6. ***finish line,*** a real or imaginary line which marks the end of a race.

1899 *Daily News* 4 Oct. 3/4 Both yachts being then about three miles from the finish line. **1959** M. SHADBOLT *New Zealanders* 86 The leaders in the junior race flashed across

the finish-line. **1968** *Guardian* 28 June 1/5 Williams had been declared the winner, both for crossing the finish line first and on a corrected time basis.

finish ('fɪnɪʃ), *v.* Forms: 4 finch, 4–6 fenys, fen-, fynissh, -ysch, -ysh, -ysshe, -esch, 4 finisch, 6– finish. [ME. *fenys, finisch*, a. OF. *feniss-* (Fr. *finiss-*) lengthened stem of *fenir* (*finir*) = Pr. *fenir*, Cat. *finir*, It. *finire*:—L. *finire*, f. *finis* end.]

1. a. *trans.* To bring to an end; to come to the end of, go through the last period or stage of. Often with gerund (formerly with inf.) as object: To 'make an end of', cease (doing something). †Also, *rarely*, To put an end to, cause to cease.

c **1350** *Will. Palerne* 3934 Then was þat ferli fiȝt finched þat time. ? *a* **1400** *Morte Arth.* 4255 Qwene they had ffenyste þis feghte. **1481** Caxton *Myrr.* I. xx. 60 The sonne the whiche..neuer shal fynysshe to goo with the heuen. *a* **1533** Ld. Berners *Huon* lv. 185 Who so euer dyd fyght agaynst him were lyke myserably to fynysshe his days. **1603** Drayton *Bar. Wars* vi. 87 In Death what can be..That I should fear a Couenant to make With it, which welcom'd, finisheth my Woe? **1697** Dryden *Virg. Georg.* iv. 674 His Griefs with Day begun, Nor were they finish'd with the setting Sun. **1796** H. Hunter tr. *St. Pierre's Stud. Nat.* (1799) III. 567 That calm ambition of gold, in which all the ambitious finish their course. **1847** Marryat *Childr. N. Forest* viii, Edward..had just finished a hearty meal. **1891** E. Peacock *N. Brendon* I. 256 As he finished speaking.

b. ***to finish off***: to provide with an ending (of a certain kind).

1834 H. N. Coleridge *Grk. Poets* (ed. 2) 51 Plutarch finishes off the story in his usual manner.

2. To bring to completion; to make or perform completely; to complete. Also with *off*, †*up*. † ***to finish to*** (do): to succeed completely in (doing).

a **1400–50** *Alexander* 2144 For quen I done haue with Dary & my dede fenyschid. *c* **1489** Caxton *Blanchardyn* xi. 41 Hys enterpryse that ful sore he desyred to fynysshe. *a* **1533** Ld. Berners *Huon* lxii. 217 Whan the sacrement of baptysme was fynyshyd. **1556** *Chron. Gr. Friars* (Camden) 84 In August [1553] was the aulter in Powlles set up agayne, and fenysyd in September. **1593** Shaks. *3 Hen. VI*, ii. v. 28 How many Dayes will finish vp the Yeare. **1594** Carew *Huarte's Exam. Wits* (1616) 269 When Nature hath finished to forme a man in all perfection. **1648** W. Mountague *Devoute Ess.* i. xviii. §3. 336 They expose themselves to the reproach of having begun what they were unable to finish. **1669** Worlidge *Syst. Agric.* (1681) 185 Yet have I not finished to attain the right Method, or way of ordering them. **1761–2** Hume *Hist. Eng.* (1806) III. xlvii. 694 The marriage of the princess Elizabeth with Frederic..was finished some time after the death of that prince. **1816** J. Smith *Panorama Sc. & Art* II. 686 Finish sowing greenhouse plants. **1828** Scott *F. M. Perth* iii, He cuts all his gloves out for the right hand, and never could finish a pair in his life. **1848** C. K. Sharpe *Let.* 7 Feb. (1888) II. 590 That bloody-minded person who finished off the work.

absol. **1611** Bible *1 Chron.* xxvii. 24 Ioab..began to number, but he finished not. **1856** Ruskin *Mod. Paint.* III. iv. ix. §5 God alone can finish.

3. a. To deal with or dispose of the whole or the remainder of (an object); to complete the consumption of (food, one's stock of anything), the reading of (a book, etc.).

1526 Tindale *Matt.* x. 23 Ye shal nott fynysshe all the cites of israhel tyll the sonne of man be come. **1856** Kane *Arct. Expl.* I. xxxi. 434 He and Brooks will doubtless finish the two [potatoes]. **1884** F. M. Crawford *Rom. Singer* I. 72 Would you mind finishing the canto?

b. To complete the destruction of; to dispatch, kill. Also in weaker sense: To complete the discomfiture or defeat of; to reduce to complete exhaustion or helplessness. Now chiefly *colloq.*

1611 Bible *Dan.* v. 26 God hath numbred thy kingdome, and finished it. **1755** *Mem. Capt. P. Drake* I. xvii. 187 Five Germans, who were resolved to finish me. **1816** *Sporting Mag.* XLVIII. 181 Lancaster..was completely finished. **1840** Goodrich *P. Parley's Ann.* 188 They were for finishing him [a wounded man] outright with their bayonets. **1864** Lowell *Fireside Trav.* 308 If he still obstinates himself, he is finished by [etc.]. **1884** E. P. Roe *Nat. Ser. Story* ix, The moist sultriness..finished the ox-heart cherries.

4. a. To perfect finally or in detail; to put the final and completing touches to (a thing). Also with *off, up*.

1551 T. Wilson *Logike* (1580) 39 b, Those [the hands, arms and feet] bee..the partes whiche finishe the whole and make it perfecte. *c* **1555** Harpsfield *Divorce Hen. VIII* (1878) 80 To perfect and finish our answer. **1611** Bible *2 Cor.* viii. 6 Wee desired Titus, that as he had begun, so hee would also finish in you the same grace also. **1683** Soames tr. *Boileau's Art of Poetry* ii. 20 A faultless Sonnet, finish'd thus, would be Worth tedious Volumes of loose Poetry. **1703** Moxon *Mech. Exerc.* 249 They finish the plastering.. by Trowelling and brishing it over with fair Water..and also brish over their new Plastering when they set, or finish it. **1713** Steele *Englishm.* No. 7. 45 To a good natural Discernment Art must therefore be joined to finish a Critick. **1807** W. Taylor in *Ann. Rev.* V. 713 He was compelled by his father to finish up his pottery minutely. **1816** J. Smith *Panorama Sc. & Art* I. 17 The hole may be finished with a file. **1842** [see finger-nail].

absol. **1852** Mrs. Carlyle *Lett.* II. 187 The plasterers were..finishing off, and clearing away their scaffoldings.

b. To complete or perfect the education of (a person).

1734 tr. *Rollin's Anc. Hist.* (1827) IX. v. 169 She sent her most illustrious citizens to be finished and refined in Greece. **1796** Dr. Burney *Metastasio* I. 214 Most of the great singers ..had been formed or finished by him. **1814** Jane Austen *Watsons* vii. (1879) 215 The accomplishments which are now necessary to finish a pretty woman. *a* **1839** Praed *Poems* (1864) II. 158 Where were you finished?

c. To complete or perfect the fatting of (cattle).

1841 *Jrnl. R. Agric. Soc.* II. ii. 226 The cattle..by means of the turnip are 'finished out' and in a proper state for the butcher in the spring. **1851** *Ibid.* XII. ii. 334 Many flock-masters 'finish' their sheep before selling. **1865** *Ibid.* Ser. ii. I. ii. 259 If the lambs are well summered it will answer to finish them off in the house or yards.

†**d.** With complement or *into*: To make *into* by a final operation. *Obs.*

1704 Swift *Battle of Bks.* Wks. 1778 I. 427 Polite conversation has finished thee a pedant. **1812** W. Taylor in *Monthly Mag.* XXXIV. 410 This earth is to be finished up into one vast terrestrial paradise.

5. a. *intr.* To come to an end, reach the end; to cease, leave off. Also with *off, up*. Also, to end *in* (something), to end *by* (doing something).

c **1450** *Merlin* iii. 54 They sey thei shull neuer fenisshe till thei haue auenged the deth of Aungis. *c* **1489** Caxton *Sonnes of Aymon* ix. 248 And beganne to make so grete a sorowe as thoughe all the worlde had fynyssed a fore his eyen. **1503** Hawes *Examp. Virt.* xi. 212 Infernall payne that shall not fynysshe. **1527** R. Thorne *His Booke* in Hakluyt *Voy.* (1589) 253 Which maine land..finisheth in the land which we found. **1563** Shute *Archit.* D j a, Wherwith finisheth the first. **1591** Shaks. *1 Hen. VI*, iii. i. 201 Exeter doth wish His dayes may finish, ere the haplesse time. **1788** Franklin *Autobiog.* Wks. 1840 I. 143 Partnerships often finish in quarrels. **1829** Landor *Wks.* (1868) I. 205/2 If we begin to reinstate old words, we shall finish by admitting new ones. **1863** Kingsley *Water Bab.* 10 Finishing off somewhere between 12 and 4. **1878** *Harper's Mag.* Nov. 892/2 Shall we finish up and have done with it, with a song at the end? **1902** R. Machray *Night Side London* i. 21 Others vanish into the night..finishing up..at some night-club, or in some other den.

b. ***to finish with***: (*a*) To cease to deal with, have done with; (*b*) to complete one's work at or upon.

1782 Miss Burney *Cecilia* (1809) IV. 62 He approved..of her finishing wholly with the old Don. **1823** Southey *Life* (1850) V. 139 To-night I shall finish with Queen Mary's reign. **1939** G. B. Shaw *Good King Charles* ii. 102 How often have you told me that you are finished with all women!

†**c.** To die. *Obs.*

1578 T. N. tr. *Conq. W. India* Pref. 4 Considering that all flesh must finish, I seek for no quiet rest in this transitorie life. **1611** Shaks. *Cymb.* v. v. 36 Who with wet cheekes Were present when she finish'd.

d. Of a competitor in a sporting contest: to come to the end of a course or race (in a certain condition or 'place').

1881 *Sat. Rev.* 25 June 818/1 Kermesse..finished a couple of lengths in front of Kingdom. **1894** G. Moore *Esther Waters* ii, He told me..to bring the colt along and finish up close by where he would be standing. **1929** *Star* 21 Aug. 16/2 Every horse he has backed has finished out of the first three. **1971** *Daily Tel.* 29 Oct. 29/1 Lithiot finished threequarters of a length behind Gold Rod to be third in this big mile race. *Ibid.* 31/5 Randle finished third in the 350 cc Italian Grand Prix at Monza.

†**6.** *trans.* (After L. *finire*.) To assign a limit or boundary to; to limit. *Obs. rare*⁻¹.

1587 Golding *De Mornay* iv. 47 So as he finish or bound himselfe.

finishable ('fɪnɪʃəb(ə)l), *a. rare.* [f. finish *v.* + -able.] Capable of being finished.

1831 Carlyle *Let.* 26 Feb. in Froude *Life* (1882) II. vii. 141, I purpose seriously inclining heart and hand to the finishing of 'Teufelsdröckh'—if indeed it is finishable. **1933** G. Stein *Autobiogr. Alice B. Toklas* ii. 27 Picasso thereupon brought out a smaller picture..very unfinished and not finishable. **1933** *Punch* 8 Nov. 524/1, I cannot pretend that if I had a daughter of finishable age I should care to send her to Geneva to *Madame Domini's*.

finished ('fɪnɪʃt), *ppl. a.* [f. as prec. + -ed¹.]

1. In senses of the vb.: **a.** Brought to a conclusion, ended. **b.** Completed. **c.** That has passed through the last process or stage of manufacture or elaboration.

1583 Stanyhurst *Aeneis* iii. (Arb.) 93 At leingth kept he silence, with finnished historye resting. **1682** Creech *Lucretius* (1683) 62 End their almost finisht race, and die. **1801** Southey *Thalaba* vii. xxx, From the finish'd banquet now The wedding guests are gone. **1833** J. Holland *Manuf. Metal* II. vii. 185 It is not an uncommon thing..to purchase a finished stove, take it to pieces, and use the.. pieces as models. **1857** Mrs. Carlyle *Lett.* II. 338 They most likely will not live to see the finished book. **1875** Jowett *Plato* (ed. 2) V. 7 Rather the materials for a work.. than a finished composition. **1887** *Daily News* 23 Nov. 2/7 Bleached and finished linens are in good request.

2. Consummate, perfect, accomplished.

1709 Steele *Tatler* No. 126 ⁋1 Lydia is a finished Coquet. **1718** J. Chamberlayne *Relig. Philos.* Pref. (1730) 42 If not by finished Atheists, yet at least by unsettled and wavering Minds. **1831** Henslow *Let. Darwin* in *Darwin's Life & Lett.* (1887) I. 167 Not in the supposition of your being a finished naturalist, but as amply qualified for collecting. **1844** Disraeli *Coningsby* iii. ii, The finished gentleman. *c* **1850** *Arab. Nts.* (Rtldg.) 236 He possessed a countenance of the most finishd beauty.

finisher ('fɪnɪʃə(r)). [f. as prec. + -er¹.]

1. One who or that which finishes (in the different senses of the vb.).

1526 Tindale *Heb.* xii. 2 Jesus the auctor and fynnyssher of oure fayth. **1587** Golding *De Mornay* Ep. Ded., God the verie founder, furtherer and finisher of trueth. **1597** Hooker *Eccl. Pol.* v. xlii. 85 The other a finisher of all his troubles. **1667** Milton *P.L.* xii. 375 O Prophet of glad tidings, finisher Of utmost hope! **1786** Sir J. Reynolds *Disc.* xiii. (1876) 69 A portrait by Denner, or any other high finisher. **1827** *Sporting Mag.* XX. 267 By way of a finisher, washing..the flax in the rivers kills hundreds of fish. **1875** Lowell *Spenser* Prose Wks. (1890) IV. 297 *note*, With all his abundance, he was evidently a laborious finisher. **1963** P. Drackett *Motor Rallying* 90 To be classed as a finisher a car must arrive at the final control..within half an hour or such other period of time as may be specified.

2. *spec.* **a.** In various trades: The workman, or machine, that performs the final operation in manufacture.

1691 Southerne *Sir A. Love* iii. i, I am poor Courtant your Taylor's finisher. **1835** Ure *Philos. Manuf.* 169 This finisher carding-engine is furnished with finer teeth than the scribbler. **1869** T. Leicester in *Eng. Mech.* 3 Dec. 282/1 It is then passed on to the finisher or workman. **1875** *Ure's Dict. Arts* I. 425 The 'forwarder' then passes the book on to the 'finisher', whose duty it is to add the required lettering and ornament. **1884** *Standard* 14 Apr. 3/7 A strike..has commenced among the 'lasters and finishers' of the boot trade.

b. ***finisher of the law***: jocularly, the hangman, executioner.

1708 Motteux *Rabelais* v. Prol. (1737) 57 The Finisher of the Law. **1734** *Grub St. Jrnl.* 2 May 1/1, I imagine..that in point of order..the finisher of the law ought to draw up the conclusion. **1833** *Fraser's Mag.* VIII. 30 Thistlewood was suspended by the finisher of the law. **1835** *Tait's Mag.* II. 168 It [the Newspaper Press] is the grand inquistor—the expositor—the flagellator—the finisher!

c. *colloq.* Something that finishes, discomfits, or 'does for' any one; 'a settler'. In *Pugilism*, one who gives a blow that ends a fight; the blow so given.

1771 C. Burney *Pres. State Mus. France & Italy* I. 27 But the last chorus was a *finisher* with a vengeance! it surpassed, in clamour, all the noises I had ever heard in my life. **1817** *Sporting Mag.* L. 54 As a finisher, there is a great analogy between Randall and the late Dutch Sam. **1827** *Ibid.* XX. 60 He gave him..four or five such finishers, as [etc.]. **1832** Marryat *N. Forster* xliv, This *conversazione* was a finisher to Dr. Feasible. **1876** Besant & Rice *Gold. Butterfly* III. 106 When I saw her marriage..I thought it was a finisher.

finishing ('fɪnɪʃɪŋ), *vbl. sb.* [f. as prec. + -ing¹.]

1. The action of the vb. finish. Also with *off*.

a **1535** Fisher *Prayer* E iij/1 The Smyth..vseth the hammer..towardes the finishyng of his worke. **1614** T. Jackson *Comm. Apostles Creede* II. 216 The accomplishment or finishing of his glory. **1672** C. Manners in *12th Rep. Hist. MSS. Comm.* App. v. 24, I haesten on Mr. Cooper all I can to the finishing of my Lady Exesters picture. **1757** Foote *Author* i. Wks. 1799 I. 135 A sketch can never convey him. His peculiarities require infinite labour and high finishing. **1886** *Athenæum* 18 Dec. 832/1 The cuts are..as good as photography, delicate finishing, and choice modern cutting can make them. **1940** *Chambers's Techn. Dict.* 167/2 *Cleaning-up*, the operation of preparing the finished surface of joinery work. Also called *finishing-off*. **1942** W. S. Churchill *Secret Session Speeches* 23 Apr. (1946) 74 The defeat of Hitler left the finishing-off of Japan merely a matter of time and trouble.

2. *concr.* That which completes or gives a finished appearance to any kind of work. In *Building* and *Carpentry*, decoration, ornamental work. In *Bookbinding*, the lettering and ornamental work on the covers.

1663 Gerbier *Counsel* 15 If the Builder..will have the Building to have no other finishing. **1712** Addison *Spect.* No. 285 ⁋3 Give the last Finishing to every Circumstance in so long a Work. **1766** Entick *London* IV. 287 The wainscot and finishing very neat. **1785** J. Phillips *Treat. Inland Navig.* 25 To have a lawn terminated by water..is a finishing, of all others the most desirable. *c* **1850** *Rudim. Navig.* (Weale) 118 *Finishings*, the carved ornaments of the quarter-galleries. **1884** H. P. Spofford in *Harper's Mag.* Jan. 181/1 The house is..of a pale cream-color, with white finishings.

3. *attrib.* and *Comb.*, as ***finishing governess, machine, master, mortar, wood***. Also **finishing-card** (see quot.); **finishing cloth**, calico prepared for 'finishing'; so ***finishing goods, linens***; **finishing-coat**, in *Building*, the last coating of plaster; **finishing-hammer**, the last hammer used by the gold-beater; **finishing-post**, the post or place which marks the finishing point of a race; **finishing-press** (*Bookbinding*), a small press used in the process of 'finishing'; **finishing-rolls**, a second set of rolls in a rolling-mill; **finishing-school**, a school where a pupil's (usually young lady's) education is 'finished'.

1874 Knight *Dict. Mech.* I. 848/2 **Finishing-card*, a machine in which the process of carding is repeated. **1892** *Daily News* 19 Mar. 5/5 Printers' and *finishing cloths slow. **1892** *Ibid.* 6 Aug. 6/4 Printing and *finishing goods slow. **1862** *Times* 2 Jan., A *finishing daily governess wishes to devote three or four hours every afternoon to the instruction of pupils. **1892** *Daily News* 5 Mar. 2/7 Cross Channel demand for..*finishing linens. **1869** *Ibid.* 10 Dec., Double-blast thrashing and *finishing machines. **1799** Han. More *Fem. Educ.* (ed. 4) I. 79 All..have the honour to co-operate with a *finishing master. **1662** Gerbier *Princ.* 19 Bricks to be daubed over with *finishing Morter. **1703** Moxon *Mech. Exerc.* 250 The finishing Morter to represent Stone, should be made of the strongest Lime. **1895** *Daily Tel.* 26 Sept. 3 The referee was sent on ahead to the Bricklayers' Arms, the *finishing-post. **1931** *Times Lit. Suppl.* 29 Jan. 83/3 Unable to make out exactly where the finishing-posts are. **1881** Raymond *Mining Gloss.*, **Finishing-rolls*. **1836–7** Dickens *Sk. Boz* (1850) 204/2 I'll bring in a bill for the abolition of *finishing-schools. **1863** Miss Braddon *Eleanor's Vict.* iii, He sent his daughters to the most expensive finishing-school in Paris. **1887** *West Shore* 427 The white..cedar, a splendid *finishing wood.

finishing, *ppl. a.* [f. as prec. + -ING².] That finishes; *esp.* in (*to put, give, receive*) *the finishing* (†*hand,*) *stroke* or *touch.*

1705 STANHOPE *Paraphr.* II. 296 The finishing, or the First, act of Repentance. **1707** *Reflex. upon Ridicule* 330 A Mind well turn'd, receives the finishing stroke and polishing from Science. **1754** A. MURPHY *Gray's-Inn Jrnl.* No. 71 ⁋4 In each Species of Writing I have given the finishing Hand to some Pieces. **1771** WALPOLE *Anecd. Painting* IV. 145 (*On Gardening*), We tire of all the painter's art when it wants these finishing touches. **1831** KEBLE *Serm.* v. (1848) 106 With the finishing touch..he completes his picture of that intense depravity. **1858** R. S. SURTEES *Ask Mamma* lxxxi. 354 To enable them to put the finishing stroke to their respective arrangements.

† **'finishment.** *Obs.* [f. as prec. + -MENT.] End, finishing, completion; death.

c **1340** *Gaw. & Gr. Knt.* 499 þe forme to be fynisment foldez ful selden. **1448** *Will of Hen. VI* in Willis & Clark *Cambridge* I. 353 After the finisshement of the edifications of oon of the same Colleges. *c* **1450** *Merlin* 23 Merlyn began to telle of the fynyshment of Ioseph. **1559** ABP. PARKER *Corr.* (Parker Soc.) 105 To the finishment and stay of that offendicle. **1648** W. MOUNTAGUE *Devoute Ess.* I. xviii. §3. 336 None must undertake this edifice, but after computation of the pertinences requisite for the finishment. **1872** E. EGGLESTON *End of World* viii. 59 This 'rithmetic preacher can't make a finishment of this sublunary *speer* by addition. **1873** C. G. LELAND *Egypt. Sketch-Bk.* 103, I should say, in finishment of this chapter, that one leaves the dervish performance with mixed emotions.

finitary ('faɪnɪtərɪ), *a. Math.* [f. FINITE *a.* after *unitary*, translating G. *finit* (Hilbert & Bernays *Grundl. d. Math.* (1934) I. 32).] Of methods, proofs, etc: involving only a finite number of steps, a finite number of well-defined objects, and so on; capable of being completed within the concrete domain.

1952 S. C. KLEENE *Introd. Metamath.* iii. 63 Methods, called finitary by the formalists, which employ only intuitively conceivable objects and performable processes. (We translate the German 'finit' as 'finitary', since the English 'finite' is used for the German 'endlich'.) **1963** G. T. KNEEBONE *Math. Logic* vii. 205 We can now reformulate in finitary terms the usual arguments. **1965** A. S. & E. H. LUCHINS *Log. Found. Math.* ix. 145 Hilbert did not offer a precise specification of what procedures were regarded by him as finitary.

finite ('faɪnaɪt), *a.* and *sb.* Also 5–6 **fynyte.** [ad. L. *fīnīt-us*, pa. pple. of *fīnīre* to put an end to, bound, limit, f. *fīnis* end, limit.]

A. *adj.*

† **1.** Fixed, determined, definite. *Obs.*

1493 *Festivall* (W. de W. 1515) 79 There was made a fynyte loveday betwene the kyng & Thomas. **1603** HOLLAND *Plutarch's Mor.* 1191 Giving us assurance of that which is finite and determinate. **1680** H. MORE *Apocal. Apoc.* 334 A finite vast number is here put for an indefinite numerous multitude.

2. a. Having bounds, ends, or limits; bounded, limited; opposed to *infinite.*

1587 GOLDING *De Mornay* iv. 42 For if any of them [perfections] be finite, then he is not infinite. **1651** HOBBES *Leviath.* I. iii. 11 Whatsoever we imagine, is Finite. **1692** BENTLEY *Serm. Folly of Atheism* vi. 21 That supposed Infinite Duration will..be limited at two Extremes..and consequently must needs be Finite. **1854** MOSELEY *Astron.* iii. (ed. 4) 11 The surface of the earth is finite in every direction.

b. Having an existence subject to limitations and conditions.

1633 G. HERBERT *Temple, Artillerie* iv, I am but finite, yet thine infinitely. **1712** ADDISON *Spect.* No. 421 ⁋7 The whole Heaven or Hell of any finite Being. **1809–10** COLERIDGE *Friend* (1865) 67 Of eternity and self-existence what other likeness is possible in a finite being, but immortality and moral self-determination? **1875** JOWETT *Plato* (ed. 2) I. 416 Of the absolute goodness of any finite nature we can form no conception.

3. *Math.* Of a line: Terminated. Of a quantity, number, distance: Limited, neither infinite nor infinitesimal. Of a group: Containing a limited number of substitutions. Of a solution: Resulting in a finite quantity. ***finite difference***: a difference between two quantities that is finite; *spec.*, any of the differences between the successive values of a function when its independent variable takes on the values of an arithmetical progression. ***finite points***: such as are not at an infinite distance apart. ***finite series*** (see quot. *c* 1865). ***finite state***: used *attrib.* in communication theory of any system limited to a finite number of alternative states, or of a type that, even if it contains an infinite number of parts, is producible by a generative device so limited.

1570 BILLINGSLEY *Euclid* I. Post. ii. 6 To produce a right line finite, straight forth continually. **1660** BARROW *Euclid* I. i, Upon a finite right line..to describe an equilateral triangle. **1807** Finite difference [see DIFFERENCE *sb.* 2]. **1840** LARDNER *Geom.* 276 The distance V F, remains finite. **1860** G. BOOLE *Calculus of Finite Differences* viii. 137 It is not true that every result of the Calculus of Finite Differences merges when the increments are indefinitely diminished into a result of the Differential Calculus. *c* **1865** *Circ. Sc.* I. 573/1 A series is called a finite series when it has an assignable last term. **1885** LEUDESDORF *Cremona's Proj. Geom.* 139 Two other finite points on the curve. *Ibid.* 265 The finite segment *FF'* is cut or not by the tangents according as the conic is a hyperbola or an ellipse. **1885** WATSON & BURBURY *Math. Th. Electr. & Magn.* I. 38 It may be proved that $\frac{d^kP_i}{d\mu^k}$ is the only finite integral solution in μ of the equation. **1893** A. R. FORSYTH *Th. Functions* 587 These finite discontinuous groups are of importance on the theory of polyhedral functions. **1910** *Encycl. Brit.* XIV. 545/1 The theorem [*sc.* Taylor's theorem] was first given by Brook Taylor in his *Methodus Incrementorum* (1717) as a corollary to a theorem concerning finite differences. **1949** SHANNON & WEAVER *Math. Theory of Communication* 27 The output of a finite state transducer driven by a finite state statistical source is a finite state statistical source. **1957** N. CHOMSKY *Syntactic Structures* iii. 18 Suppose that we have a machine that can be in any one of a finite number of different internal states... Any language that can be produced by a machine of this sort we call a finite state language; and we can call the machine itself a finite state grammar. **1957** L. FOX *Two-point Boundary Probl.* ii. 21 The rigorous theory of finite differences attaches a remainder term to every finite-difference formula and sometimes..the formula diverges and gives no useful result. **1969** *Listener* 10 July 44/1 Finite-state rules are the simplest kind of grammar rule; they can be as simple as 'after "the" produce any noun at all'. **1971** *Mathematical Rev.* Feb. 278/1 The authors treat some elementary aspects of the theory of finite differences.

4. *Gram.* Of a verb: Limited by number and person; not in the infinitive mood.

1795 L. MURRAY *Gram.* Syntax 86 A simple sentence has in it but one subject, and one finite verb. **1798** *Ibid.* (ed. 4) III. 113 *note*, Finite verbs are those to which number and person appertain.

5. *Music.* (See quot.)

1869 OUSELEY *Counterp.* xv. 105 If the canon is concluded by a coda, it is called Finite.

¶ App. misused for *infinite.*

a **1400** *Cov. Myst.* (Shaks. Soc.) 93 That it may plese his fynyte deyte Knowleche in this to sendyn us.

B. quasi-*sb.*

1. a. The adj. used absolutely.

1687 DRYDEN *Hind & P.* I. 105 But how can finite grasp Infinity? **1690** LOCKE *Hum. Und.* II. xv. §12 Finite of any Magnitude, holds not any proportion to infinite. **1825** COLERIDGE *Aids Refl.* (1836) 155 Reasoning from finite to finite, on a basis of truth..will always lead to truth. **1847** EMERSON *Poems, Threnody* Wks. (Bohn) I. 492 My servant Death, with solving rite, Pours finite into infinite.

b. *the finite*: that which is finite.

1845 MAURICE *Mor. & Met. Philos.* in *Encycl. Metrop.* II. 575/1 The finite and the infinite are both alike thoughts of our own. **1875** JOWETT *Plato* (ed. 2) IV. 9 To us, the notion of infinity is subsequent rather than prior to the finite.

2. A finite thing; a finite being: see A. 2.

a **1619** FOTHERBY *Atheom.* II. x. §4 (1622) 309 All termes, and all indeterminations, all finites and all infinites. **1648** BOYLE *Seraph. Love* xxvi. (1700) 154 It being impossible for an Aggregate of Finites to comprehend..one Infinite. **1846** [see FINITED *ppl. a.*].

3. *Gram.* A finite verb or verb-form.

1924 H. E. PALMER *Gram. Spoken Eng.* II. 91 A Finite is that part of a sentence which predicates, exclusive however of complements, objects or modifiers. **1963** F. T. VISSER *Hist. Syntax* I. iv. 497 The verbs *shall, can, may*..called anomalous finites or auxiliary verbs. **1965** *Language* XLI. 208 If we consider the range of 'finites' that can operate at X in the sequence *He X (to) come every day.*

finite ('faɪnaɪt), *v.* [f. prec.; or f. ppl. stem of L. *fīnīre.*] *trans.* To make finite; to subject to limitations.

1628 T. SPENCER *Logick* 47 The matter doth finite, and contract the amplitude of the forme. **1847** BUSHNELL *Chr. Nurt.* II. v. (1861) 318 The Lord to be is there, there to personate and finite himself. **1867** *Eng. Leader* 20 Apr. 224 There are two sides—a divine side and a human side.. the latter being finited, attempered, and dimmed.

Hence **'finited** *ppl. a.*

1846 CLISSOLD tr. *Swedenborg's Principia* I. iii. 81 In relation to things much finited and compounded, this finite is as it were nothing;..nevertheless it is a something and a finited ens. **1868** *Contemp. Rev.* VIII. 617 To find God finited in Nature. **1884** *Gosp. Divine Humanity* iii. 60 Man in his finited state is dust of the ground.

[**finiteless**: a spurious word in the Dictionaries.

Cited by Johnson from Sir T. Browne (*Pseud. Ep.* I. ii, where the real reading is 'fruitlesse').]

finitely ('faɪnaɪtlɪ), *adv.* [f. FINITE + -LY².] In a finite manner or degree.

1654 JER. TAYLOR *Real Presence* xi. 216 Christ moved finitely by dimensions, and change of places. **1677** HALE *Prim. Orig. Man.* I. v. 114 Within such a compass as is finitely distant from this hour. **1736** BUTLER *Anal.* v. 130 Such creatures would be made upright or finitely perfect. **1748** HARTLEY *Observ. Man* II. ii. 185 The Balance will ultimately be in favour of each Individual finitely. **1965** J. J. ROTMAN *Theory of Groups* xii. 257 A group is finitely presented in case it has a presentation with only a finite number of generators and a finite number of relations. **1968** P. A. P. MORAN *Introd. Probability Theory* iv. 197 We have defined ϕ_c as a finitely additive set function on the field of all cylinders in Ω_o.

finiteness ('faɪnaɪtnɪs). [f. as prec. + -NESS.] The quality or condition of being finite; the condition of being limited in space, time, capacity, etc.

1601 DEACON & WALKER *Spirits & Divels* 89 It ariseth.. from the finitenesse, and dimensiuenesse of the angelicall nature. **1708** BERKELEY *Commonpl. Bk.* Wks. 1871 IV. 490 Finiteness of our minds no excuse for the geometers. **1886** PROCTOR *Fam. Sc. Stud.* 5 No theory of the finiteness of space can possibly be more utterly inconceivable than the idea of infinite space itself.

finitesimal (faɪnɪ'tɛsɪməl), *a. Math.* [f. FINITE *a.*, after *millesimal*, etc.] Denoted by the ordinal of a finite number.

1861 H. J. S. SMITH *Th. Numbers* III. in *Rep. Brit. Assoc.* 326 Any term which occupies a finitesimal place in any one arrangement should occupy a finitesimal place in every other arrangement.

¶ ? Erroneously used for *infinitesimal*, in the sense 'exceedingly minute'.

1836 E. HOWARD *R. Reefer* xxxvii, A spasmodic contraction of the finitesimal nerves.

† **fi'nitimate,** *a. Obs.* [f. L. *finitim-us* bordering upon + -ATE².] Bordering, neighbouring, close by. Const. *to.*

1578 BANISTER *Hist. Man* I. 21 We finde the seuenth [vertebra]..finitimate, and next adioyning to the Vertebres of the brest. *Ibid.* II. 9 This middle Cartilage is to the bony ..diuision of the nose aunswerable, and very finitimate.

finitism ('faɪnaɪtɪz(ə)m). [f. FINITE *a.* + -ISM.] **a.** *Philos.* and *Theol.* The belief that the world, or some realm, or God, is finite. **b.** *Math.* The doctrine that only methods involving a finite number of steps should be used in mathematics; the rejection of actual infinities.

1922 W. R. INGE *Outspoken Ess.* II. 19 Finitism and Infinitism are equally demonstrable and equally refutable. **1935** A. AMBROSE in *Mind* XLIV. 186 (*title*) Finitism in mathematics. **1956** G. E. M. ANSCOMBE tr. *Wittgenstein's Remarks Found. Math.* II. 63 Finitism and behaviourism are quite similar trends... Both deny the existence of something, both with a view to escaping from a confusion. **1964** J. A. BENARDETE *Infinity* i. 25 With the return to finitism, the infinite series is no longer viewed as *actually* infinite.

finitist ('faɪnaɪtɪst), *a.* and *sb. Philos.* and *Math.* [f. as prec. + -IST.]

A. *adj.* Characterized by, or relating to, finitism.

1904 W. JAMES *Let.* 12 June (1920) II. 203 My philosophy ..is finitist; but it does not attribute to the question of the Infinite the great methodological importance which you and Renouvier attribute to it. **1914** B. RUSSELL *Our Knowl. External World* vi. 155 There is no longer any reason to struggle after a finitist explanation of the world. **1931** F. P. RAMSEY *Found. Math.* 243 Provable..means provable in any number of steps, and on finitist principles the number must in some way be limited, e.g. to the humanly possible. **1935** *Mind* XLIV. 186 These present to the finitist school of mathematicians difficulties. **1940** *Mind* XLIX. 243 He will use only 'finitist' methods. **1966** *Mathematical Rev.* Jan. 9/2 *F* is complete with respect to some distinguished notion of proof, such as finitist or predicative.

B. *sb.* An exponent or adherent of finitism.

1897 B. RUSSELL in *Mind* VI. 118 When the finitist objects that an infinite collection can never be..really a whole, the infinitist replies that..number itself must be contradictory. **1900** J. ROYCE *World & Indiv.* I. 558 Couturat, in his dialectical discussion between the 'finitist' and the 'infinitist',..gives full room to..these arguments. **1935** *Mind* XLIV. 186 Denials by the finitists which the formalist and logistic schools contest. **1960** S. KÖRNER *Philos. of Math.* v. 111 Finitists such as Aristotle, Gauss, and the older and the newer intuitionists, deny all 'real' content or even 'intelligibility' to such mathematical notions as are not characteristic either of finite aggregates or at most of potentially infinite.

Hence **fini'tistic** *a.*

1937 *Mind* XLVI. 58 Gödel..seemed to have destroyed for ever Hilbert's hope that he would carry out his programme of establishing with finitistic means the non-contradictoriness of mathematics. **1959** E. W. BETH *Found. Math.* iii. 73 Complete induction ranked high among the forms of argument admitted in finitistic meta-mathematics.

† **'finitive,** *a. Obs.* Also 6 **finative, finityve.** [ad. L. *finitiv-us* defining.]

1. a. Definitive, final. **b.** Defining.

1593 RICH *Greenes Newes* F b, Richard had no sooner thus added his finative conclusion, but [etc.]. **1656** BLOUNT *Glossogr.*, *Finitive*, which defines or determines. **1730–6** BAILEY (folio,) *Finitive*, defining.

¶ **2.** Erroneous uses: **a.** Put for L. *finitimus*: Of or belonging to the frontier. **b.** ? = FINICAL.

1549 *Compl. Scot.* xx. 166 The fyrst sort of battellis and veyris that broucht the romans to ruuyne, vas callit battellis finityuis, A finibus. **1640** R. BRATHWAIT ('Phil. Panedonius') *Boulster Lect.* 67 The Tale of that Finitive Girle [app. = affecting fine language].

finitize ('faɪnaɪtaɪz), *v.* [f. FINITE *a.* + -IZE.] *trans.* To make finite. Hence **'finitizing** *vbl. sb.*

1906 S. S. LAURIE *Synthetica* II. 85 The Unconditional has been under a necessity to finitise Itself. **1917** A. S. PRINGLE-PATTISON *Idea of God* xvi. 321 Professor Howison ..seems to use the idea of self-consciousness entirely as a principle of separation and exclusion, which finitizes even what he calls 'the Supreme Instance', the 'absolutely perfect mind, or God'. **1930** *Monument to St. Augustine* 257 In his account of Kant, Hegel reproaches him with a shallow finitizing, whereas Spinoza represents for him an impracticable infinitizing.

† **finitor.** *Obs. Astron.* [a. L. *fīnītor*, agent-n. f. *fīnīre* to bound; a literal transl. of Gr. ὁρίζων HORIZON.] The horizon.

1594 BLUNDEVIL *Exerc.* VI. Introd. (ed. 7) 604 The other Crosse Diameter..signifieth the Horizon, which for distinctions sake is otherwise called the Finitor. **1671** FLAMSTEED in Rigaud *Corr. Sci. Men* (1841) II. 124 Not thinking but that the appearance..would be invisible as celebrated under our finitor. **1688** R. HOLME *Armoury* III. 147/1 In Terms of Art used by Limners..Finitor [is the]

Horizon. **1704** J. HARRIS *Lex. Techn.*, *Finitor*, the same with Horizon.

finitude ('fɪnɪtju:d). [f. FINITE + -TUDE.] The condition or state of being finite; the condition of being subject to limitations; = FINITENESS.

1644 R. HARWOOD *David's Sanct.* 13 The finitude of the King's presence. **1677** GALE *Crt. Gentiles* II. IV. 514 Void of al power and composition, and therefore of al finitude and limitation. **1733** CHEYNE *Eng. Malady* I. viii. §4 (1734) 73 It seems Precision is a Contradiction to Finitude. **1836** SIR G. HEAD *Home Tour* 128 Those catastrophes which..serve to remind man of the finitude of his wisdom. **1842** DE MORGAN *Diff. & Int. Calculus* 66 The values of *x* which satisfy such a condition are separated by intervals of finitude. **1878** NEWCOMB *Pop. Astron.* IV. iii. 505 This idea of the finitude of space.

finity ('fɪnɪtɪ). [ad. OF. *finité*, f. *fini* (pa. pple. of *finir* to bound) FINITE *a.*] = prec. Also semi-*concr.*, an instance of finiteness.

1675 BURTHOGGE *Causa Dei* Ep. Ded. A iij b, The Finity of Sin, that in its own Nature cannot Merit an Infinite Punishment. **1813** BUSBY *Lucretius* I. 1081 The laws of nature Finity oppose. **1855** MISS COBBE *Intuit. Mor.* 17 Creatures..exposed by the finity of their natures to continual temptations. **1899** H. WRIGHT *Depopulation* 57 There seemed no finity to the vista of country the eye followed. **1903** B. HARRADEN *Kath. Frensham* II. x. 199 Infinities which one..could see were finities blending with each other imperceptibly.

finjan: see FINGAN.

fink (fɪŋk), *sb.*[1] *S. Afr.* [ad. Afrikaans *vink* FINCH.] = WEAVER[1] 4. Cf. FINCH I c.

1834 A. SMITH *Diary* 9 Dec. (1939) I. 168 Red vink and Caffer fink common along the streams. **1853** *Edin. New Philos. Jrnl.* LV. 82 The yellow and green *finks* may be seen disporting in multitudes..and entering every now and then into their grass-woven nests. **1896** E. CLAIRMONTE *Africander* 2 A flock of long-tailed mousebirds, called *finks*, would dash past to settle in a *rooihout* tree. **1897** A. PAGE *Afternoon Ride* 62 The Kafir fink swaying on the grass. **1908** HAAGNER & IVY *Sk. S. Afr. Bird-Life* 70 The Red Bishopbird or Kaffir-fink. **1931** [see *bishop-bird*]. **1936** R. CAMPBELL *Mithraic Emblems* 34 The scarlet fink, the chook, the sprew, That seem to call me by my name.

fink (fɪŋk), *sb.*[2] *U.S. slang.* [Origin unknown.] A pejorative term of wide application, esp. **a.** An unpleasant or contemptible person. **b.** An informer; a detective. **c.** A strike-breaker.

1903 ADE *People you Know* 60 Anyone who goes against the Faculty single-handed is a Fink. **1914** JACKSON & HELLYER *Vocab. Criminal Slang* 33 *Fink*,..an unreliable confederate or incompetent sympathizer. **1925** *Amer. Speech* I. 151/2 'Dick' and 'bull' and 'John Law' have become established as names for the police, while 'fink' and 'stool' and 'fly-dick' denote the plain-clothes men. **1926** *Amer. Mercury* Jan. 63/1 Dating from the famous Homestead strike of 1892 is the odious *fink*. [It] according to one version was originally *Pink*, a contraction of Pinkerton, and referred to the army of strikebreakers recruited by the detective agency. **1929** E. BOOTH *Stealing through Life* xi. 259 'That guy..is a rat.'.. 'So's the fink with him.' *a* **1940** F. SCOTT FITZGERALD *Last Tycoon* (1949) vi. 143 A fink? That's a strike-breaker or a company tec. **1940** R. CHANDLER *Farewell, My Lovely* v. 25 Now he's looking for the fink that turned him up eight years ago. **1959** C. WILLIAMS *Man in Motion* viii. 106 Except for being a rat, a fink, a scab, a thug, and a goon, he's one of the sweetest guys you'll ever meet. **1970** *New Yorker* 15 Aug. 66/2 The film, in sudden want of a through-and-through-fink type, forgets that it has established two..hippies as loyal.

fink (fɪŋk), *v.*[1] Colloq. corruption of THINK *v.*[2]

1888 KIPLING *Wee Willie Winkie* (1890) 12, I don't fink I'll ever want to kiss big girls. **1913** B. MOORE in E. Pertwee *Reciter's Second Treasury Verse* 226, I really fink, 'tween me and you, I'd raver be a little girl. **1941** H. G. WELLS *You can't be too Careful* III. ii. 115 That boy is still as pure as the driven snow. (I *don't* fink. I saw his face.) **1962** N. MARSH *Hand in Glove* vi. 202 Makes you fink, don't it?

fink (fɪŋk), *v.*[2] *U.S. slang.* [f. FINK *sb.*[2]] *intr.* To inform *on*.

1925 *Flynn's* 24 Jan. 119/1 *Fink*, to squeal; to inform on. **1953** W. R. BURNETT *Vanity Row* v. 43 Only a rat co-operated with the police; only a rat finked! **1953** R. CHANDLER *Long Good-Bye* ix. 57 Suppose you had to hire a private eye... Would you want one that finked on his friends? **1969** *Rolling Stone* 28 June 4/2 The gang tries to sell their smack to a black hippie pusher who finks on them.

finkle ('fɪŋk(ə)l). *Obs.* exc. *dial.* Forms: 3 fenecel, 4 fenkil, 5 fenkylle, 4–6, 9 fenkel, 5–6 fenkell(e, 6 fyncle, 6, 9 finckle, 6 finkil, 7–9 finkel, finkle. See also FENNEL. [ME. *fenecel*, ad. L. *fæniculum*: see FENNEL. The immediate source may be continental Teut.; cf. Du. *venkel*, OHG. *fenachal*, *finachal*, mod. Ger. *fenchel*.] = FENNEL I.

c **1265** *Voc.* in Wr.-Wülcker 556 *Feniculum*, fenecel. *c* **1440** *Promp. Parv.* 155/2 Fenkylle, *feniculum*. **1567** MAPLET *Gr. Forest* 42 Fenkell is an Herbe of the Gardaine and fielde common to them both. **1659** ROWBOTHAM *Gate Lang. Unl.* xii. §132 These are spices; Pepper..fenil or finkel, thyme. **1883** *Almondbury Gloss.*, *Finkel*, fennel.

attrib. *c* **1350** *Med. MS.* in *Archæol.* XXX. 351 Take yᵉ jus of fenkel rote And droppyn in yᵉ eyne. **1362** LANGL. *P. Pl.* A. v. 156 A Ferþing-worþ of Fenel-seed [*v.r.* fenkil seed].

finks: see FENKS.

Finlander ('fɪnlændə(r)). Now *rare*. [f. *Finland*, name of a country in N.E. Europe + -ER[1].] A native or inhabitant of Finland.

The usual form now is *Finn*.

1727 P. KINCK in *Phil. Trans. R. Soc.* XXXV. 357 A Letter to James Theobald, Esq., giving an Account of the Norwegian Finns, or Finlanders. **1808** in W. Monteith *Narr. Conq. Finland* (1854) 53 The Finlander regiments entering the service of His Imperial Majesty shall not be employed against Sweden..during the present war. **1838** *Penny Cycl.* X. 274/1 The Laplander is of the same extraction as the Finlander, and calls himself a 'Samelada or Same'. **1854** [see FINN]. **1920** *Contemp. Rev.* Dec. 792 Finnish-speaking Finlanders.

Finlay process. *Photogr.* [f. the name of C. L. *Finlay*, a British photographer.] (See quot. 1935.)

[**1911** *Encycl. Brit.* XXI. 519/1 In C. L. Finlay's 'Thames' colour plate (1908) the tricolour screen is formed by rows of circular dots coloured alternately orange-red and green and the intermediate spaces blue.] **1931** F. R. NEWENS *Technique Colour Photogr.* iv. 92 The Finlay process is a duplicating process... One of the fundamental necessities for success in the Finlay process, is the closest possible contact between the squares of the taking screen and the emulsion of the negative plate. **1935** *Discovery* July 188/2 All photographers are familiar with..the Finlay screen plate process... The ruled colour screen is on a separate plate which is exposed in contact with the photographic plate; from the negative so exposed a transparency print in black and white is made, and this is finally viewed bound in register with a ruled colour screen plate similar to that which was used when the negative was exposed. **1940** A. L. M. SOWERBY *Wall's Dict. Photogr.* (ed. 15) 142 Shorter exposures are required by the Finlay and Dufaycolor processes than with the earlier screen-plates.

finless ('fɪnlɪs), *a.* [f. FIN *sb.*[1] + -LESS.] Without a fin or fins.

1596 SHAKS. *1 Hen. IV*, III. i. 151 A finne-lesse Fish. **1775** in ASH. **1863** C. A. JOHNS *Home Walks* 159 A thin cylindrical fish..with a blunt head and finless tail.

finlet ('fɪnlɪt). [dim. of FIN.] A small fin.

1874 J. G. WOOD *Nat. Hist.* 579 Delicate filamentary finlets..decorate the tail in some species.

Finn, Fin (fɪn). [OE. *Finnas* pl., corresponding to ON. *Finnr*, Sw., Da., Ger. *Finne*.

In the first and second centuries the name is recorded as L. *Fenni* (Tac.) Gr. *φίννοι* (Ptol.). Presumably of Teut. origin; some have conjectured that it is related by ablaut to FEN *sb.*]

The name used by the Teut. nations for an individual of a people in North-Eastern Europe and Scandinavia, calling themselves *Suomi* or *Suomelaisset*, and speaking a language of the Ural-Altaic class. Often applied more widely to include other peoples closely allied ethnically and linguistically to the Finns proper or Suomi.

c **893** K. ÆLFRED *Oros.* I. i. (Sweet) 17 þa Finnas..& þa Beormas spræcon neah an ʒeþeode. **1599** tr. *K. Ælfred's Oros.* in Hakluyt *Voy.* I. He iudged, that the Fynnes and Biarmes speake but one language. **1854** LATHAM in *Smith's Dict. Cl. Geog.* I. 894 Finn is not the name by which either the Finlanders or the Laplanders know themselves. It is the term by which they are known to the Northmen.

finn: see FINNIP.

finnac(k: see FINNOC.

finnan ('fɪnən). Also findhorn, findram, fintrum, findon, finnon. [A place-name used *attrib.* app. orig. the name of the river *Findhorn*, or of a place so called on its banks; but confused with *Findon*, the name of a village in Kincardineshire.] A haddock cured with the smoke of green wood, turf, or peat earth. More fully *finnan-haddock* (*-haddie*), *-spelding*.

a **1774** FERGUSSON *Leith Races* Poems (1845) 33 The Buchan bodies..Their bunch o' findrams cry. **1811** W. THOM *Hist. Aberdeen* II. 170 Findon haddocks are.. esteemed a great delicacy. **1816** SCOTT *Antiq.* xxvi, The elder girl..was preparing a pile of Findhorn haddocks (that is, haddocks smoked with green wood). **1861** RAMSAY *Remin.* v. (ed. 18) 121 'Findon,' or 'Finnan haddies,' are split, smoked, and partially dried haddocks. **1873** J. G. BERTRAM *Harvest of Sea* 205 Genuine Finnans, smoked in the original way by means of peat-reek. **1893** *Times* 13 Dec. 3/6 Central Fish Market..Aberdeen finnons sold well.

finned (fɪnd). [f. FIN *sb.*[1] + -ED[2].] Having a fin or fins (see senses of FIN *sb.*[1]). Also in parasynthetic derivatives, as *prickly-*, *red-finned*.

1340–70 *Alex. & Dind.* 298 Of þe finnede fihcs our fode to lacche. **1611** COTGR., *Perche de mer*, a wholesome, rough-find..rocke-fish. **1707** MORTIMER *Husb.* 61 They..plough up the Turf with a broad finned Plough. **1774** GOLDSM. *Nat. Hist.* (1776) VI. 303 The fish that have bony prickly fins, are called Prickly Finned Fish. **1785** GROSE *Dict. Vulgar Tongue* s.v. *Fin*, A one finned fellow, a man who has lost an arm. **1864** BOUTELL *Heraldry Hist. & Pop.* xxi. §11. (ed. 3) 369 Dolphins..finned and ducally crowned or. **1868** MORRIS *Earthly Par.* I. 313 Seeing The red-finned fishes o'er the gravel play. **1938** *Archit. Rev.* LXXXIII. 32 'Finned' pipes have been carried under the clerestorey behind a splayed capping on top of the upper stacks as a precaution against down draught. **1958** *Times Rev. Industry* Feb. 68/2 The liquified ammonia..enters another system of finned tubes. **1970** *Cryogenics* X. 239 (*heading*) A new form of finned-tube heat exchanger.

finner ('fɪnə(r)). [f. FIN *sb.*[1] + -ER[1].]

1. A name given to whales of the genus *Balænoptera*, esp. the Rorqual, from the fact of their having a dorsal fin. Also *finner-whale*.

1793 *Statist. Acc. Scotl.* V. 190 These [whales] commonly measure from 60 to 90 feet in length and are denominated finners. **1822** SCOTT *Pirate* ii, The Berserkars used to..snap them [swords and spears] all up into pieces, as a finner would go through a herring net. **1855** E. FORBES *Lit. Papers* v. 152 The mighty finners (*Balænoptera*), whose prodigious fleetness makes them too dangerous to encounter. **1865** *Athenæum* No. 1987. 732/3 Skeleton of a finner whale. **1880** *Daily News* 8 Dec. 6/7 The great northern Rorqual Razorback, or 'Finner'.

2. = FINNOC.

1803 J. MACKENZIE *Prize Ess. Highl. Soc.* II. 377 Finners or finnocs, which usually abound in every salmon river, have fins of a yellow colour.

‖**finnesko, fin(n)sko** ('fɪnskəʊ). [ad. Norw. *finnsko*, f. *Finn* FINN + *sko* shoe.] A boot made of birch-tanned reindeer skin with the hair left on the outside.

1890 tr. *Nansen's 1st Crossing Greenland* I. 47 The two Lapps had two pair of 'finnesko' each. **1911** R. F. SCOTT *Diary* 20 Jan. in *Last Exped.* (1913) iv. 132 We have..served out two pairs of finnesko (fur boots) to each traveller. **1928** *Daily Tel.* 27 Nov. 10/6 Leather boots to replace the finsko which the men were wearing.

finney ('fɪnɪ). Local name of finnan haddock. Also **finnie haddie**.

1851 MAYHEW *Lond. Labour* I. 77/1 Smoked or dried haddocks (often called 'finnie haddies'). **1906** *Daily Chron.* 10 May 1/4 Finneys, kippers, bloaters, 2s. 6d. per box... Fish Docks, Grimsby. **1966** 'L. LANE' *ABZ of Scouse* 36 Got a face like a stale finny-addy.

Finnic ('fɪnɪk), *a.* Also 7 Finnonick. [f. FINN + -IC. The form *Finnonick* is ad. mod.L. *Finnonicus*, f. *Finno* FINN; cf. *Lapponic*.]

a. Pertaining to the Finns, Finnish. **b.** Now usually, Pertaining to the group of peoples ethnically allied to the Finns, or to that division of the Ural-Altaic languages to which Finnish belongs.

1668 WILKINS *Real Char.* I. i. §iii. 4 The Finnic [language] used in Finland and Lapland. **1674** tr. *Scheffer's Lapland* 76 The Finnonick Language. **1878** *N. Amer. Rev.* CXXVI. 368 The Lesghian and other tongues of the Caucasus, by some pretended to be of Finnic origin.

Hence '**Finnicize** *v. nonce-wd.*, to give a Finnish form to.

1827 *Westm. Rev.* VII. 320 The foreign names..have been gradually finnicized, and *Biblia* is now written Piplia.

finnicking, finnikin: see FINICKING.

finnier, var. of FINEER *v.*, *Obs.*

†**finnimbrun.** *Obs. rare*[−1]. [Of arbitrary formation: cf. *conimbrum*, var. of CONUNDRUM.] A trifle, a gimcrack.

1653 WALTON *Angler* (1676) 263 He saw Ribbins and Looking-glasses..and Hobbyhorses..and all the other finnimbruns that make a compleat Country Fair.

'**finnip.** *slang.* Also finn, finny, fin(n)if(f), finnup, finuf. [Said to be a Yiddish pronunc. of Ger. *fünf* five.] A five-pound note. Also *U.S.*, five dollars.

1839 W. A. MILES *Poverty, Mendicity & Crime* 112 If he finds any 'finnips' (5*l.* notes)..he gives them to Nelson to fence. **1846** R. L. SNOWDEN *Magistr. Assist.* 346, I..got six Finnips and a Cooter for the Yacks. **1859** HOTTEN *Slang Dict.* 39 *Finuf*, a five-pound note. **1859** G. W. MATSELL *Vocabulum* 32 *Finniff*, five dollars. **1865** MAYHEW *Lond. Labour* III. 396 The notes were all finnies (£5 notes), and a good imitation. **1879** *Macm. Mag.* Oct. 505/1 Fifty quid in double finns. **1889** BARRÈRE & LELAND *Dict. Slang* I. 343/1 *Finnup ready*, a five-pound note. **1931** D. RUNYON *Guys & Dolls* (1932) vii. 141 He asks me if I happen to have a finnif on me, but of course I am not giving finnifs to guys like Feet Samuels, and finally he offers to compromise with me for a deuce, so I can see things must be very bad with Feet for him to come down from five dollars to two. **1966** R. STOUT *Death of Doxy* (1967) v. 47, I..got out my wallet and extracted a finif.

Finnish ('fɪnɪʃ), *a.* [f. FINN + -ISH; cf. ON. *Finnskr*, Sw., Da. *Finske*, Ger. *Finnisch*.]

a. Pertaining to the Finns; rarely in wider sense = FINNIC b. **b.** *absol.* quasi-*sb.*, the Finnish language. **c.** In adjectives of the type *Finnish-Ugrian* = Finnish and ——. Also *Finnish Spitz*, a small, stocky breed of dog, with a coarse, reddish-brown coat. Also *Finnish-speaking* adj.

1789–96 MORSE *Am. Un. Geog.* XI. 84 The Ostiaks, who are likewise a Finnish race. *a* **1845** HOOD *Sir J. Bowring* 24 Although you should begin in Dutch, and end (like me) in FINNISH. **1856** *Gazetteer of the World* III. 359 The Finnish peasantry. **1911** FRAZER *Golden Bough* (ed. 3) II. ix. 10 The tribes of the Finnish-Ugrian stock. **1920** [see FINLANDER]. **1930** E. C. ASH *Pract. Dog Bk.* ii. 22 The Finnish Spitz... They have been known on the Continent for many years, but have only recently been introduced into this country. **1933** BLOOMFIELD *Lang.* iv. 68 We find, to the east of the Indo-European languages.., the great Finno-Ugrian family... The first [branch] is the Finnish-Lapponic. **1945** C. L. B. HUBBARD *Observer's Bk. Dogs* 68 The Finnish Spitz ..was introduced into England in 1927. **1947** WYNDHAM LEWIS *Let.* 15 Nov. (1963) 419 With your Finnish-Irish ancestry and American birth. **1965** B. VESEY-FITZGERALD

Dog Owner's Encycl. 88 The Finnish Spitz characteristics are eagerness to hunt, courage and fidelity.

Finno- ('fɪnəʊ), used as comb. form of FINN or FINNIC to designate race combinations and language groups of Finns or Finnish with other elements.

1864 *Smithsonian Inst. Ann. Rep. 1863* 110 The Scythian family..is divided into five principal branches: 1. The Ugrian, or Finno-Hungarian, [etc.]. **1877** *Illustr. London News* 23 May 2/2 If the surrounding Finno-Swedish atmosphere has had any influence on him, it has been to develop his inborn Russian patriotism. **1879** *Encycl. Brit.* IX. 219/1 The term Finns..being, with its adjective Finnic or Finno-Ugric or Ugro-Finnic, the collective name of the westernmost branch of the great Uralo-Altaic family. **1880** A. H. SAYCE *Introd. Sci. Lang.* II. vi. 9 The roots of the Finno-Ugrian dialects exhibit the same vowel-harmony. **1885** *Encycl. Brit.* XVIII. 779/2 The nearer relation of the Samoyed is with the Finno-Hungarian. **1888** *Ibid.* XXIV. 1/1 The Ural-Altaic, Finno-Tatar, or 'Turanian' languages. **1895** A. H. KEANE *Ethnol.* 200 We have in Europe..mixed Finno-Slavs, Slavo-Teutons, Kelto-Teutons, but no Finno-Slav, Slavo-Teutonic or Kelto-Teutonic tongues. **1933** [see FINNISH *a.*]. **1955** *Proc. Prehist. Soc.* XXI. 91 The kinship system belongs to the Finno-Ugric system, characterized by bilateral descent and division into age groups. **1961** L. F. BROSNAHAN *Sounds of Language* v. 92 The zone of slight affrication..Greek, Romance, Germanic, and Finno-Ugrian.

finnoc ('fɪnək). Also 8 finnac(k, -eck, -ock, 8–9 phin(n)ock. [a. Gael. *fionnag*, f. *fionn* white.] 'A white trout, a variety of the *Salmo fario*' (Jam.).

1771 PENNANT *Tour Scotl.* (1794) 230 Phinocs are taken here in great numbers. **1792** *Statist. Acc. Scotl.* III. 360 A trout called a finneck..appears in..July and August. **1834** JARDINE in *Proc. Berw. Nat. Club* I. No. 2. 51 This fish I consider to be the Salmo albus of Fleming..the Phinnock of the north and west of Scotland. *c* **1850** *Nat. Encycl.* I. 38 The river abounds with trout, finnock, eels.

finny ('fɪnɪ), *a.*[1] [f. FIN *sb.*[1] + -Y[1].]

1. Provided with or having fins; finned.

1590 SPENSER *F.Q.* III. viii. 29 Proteus..Along the fomy waves driving his finny drove. **1695** BLACKMORE *Pr. Arth.* IV. 52 The Finny or the Feather'd Kind. **1850** BLACKIE *Æschylus* I. 142 With finny monsters teems the sea.

b. *nonce-use.* Of a person: With arms like fins.

1883 F. M. CRAWFORD *Dr. Claudius* vii, Miss Skeat..looked tall and finny.

2. Of the nature of a fin; like a fin.

1648 HERRICK *Hesper.* (1869) 338 Never againe shall I with finnie-ore Put from or draw unto the faithfull shore. **1668** WILKINS *Real Char.* 133 Finny substances, standing out from each side like wings.

3. a. Of or pertaining to fish. **b.** Teeming with fish. Cf. FIN *sb.*[1] 1 c.

1764 GOLDSM. *Trav.* 187 He..With patient angle, trolls the finny deep. **1831** *Blackw. Mag.* XXX. 965 Instinctive all with finny life. **1867** J. B. ROSE tr. *Virgil's Æneid* 99 The headlong osprey..skims the finny flood.

† **'finny, 'vinny,** *a.*[2] *Obs.* exc. *dial.* [OE. *fyniȝ*, f. *fyne* mould. Cf. FENNY.] Mouldy.

a **1722** Vinney [see FINEWY]. **1861** RAMSAY *Remin.* Ser. II. p. xxix, 'I can't eat un [a loaf], zur: it be soa vinny.' I discovered that he meant 'mouldy'. **1863** BARNES *Dorset Dial.* 97 Blue vinny, or vinnied, cheese.

finny: see FINNIP.

fino ('fiːnəʊ). [Sp. *fino* FINE *a.*] A type of dry sherry; a glass of such sherry.

1846 R. FORD *Gatherings from Spain* xiv. 155 Those [sherries] only which exhibit great delicacy, body, and flavour are called *finos* or fine. **1888** *Encycl. Brit.* XXIV. 607/1 The Amontillado class may be..subdivided into Fino and Oloroso. **1959** W. JAMES *Word-Bk. Wine* 78 The finos which the Spaniards..drink are considerably drier than those which they export. **1961** [see AMONTILLADO]. **1962** *Times* 7 May 13/4 Old fino sherry. **1964** G. SIMS *Terrible Door* xxvii. 144, I had two double finos in Martinez.

‖**finochio** (fɪ'nɒkɪəʊ). Also 8 fenochia, -io, -occhio, finocha, finochi, 8–9 fin(n)ochia. [It. *finocchio*:—popular L. *fēnoclum*: see FENNEL.] The sweet fennel (*Fœniculum dulce*); also called the dwarf or French fennel.

1723 R. DIGBY *Let. to Pope* 14 Aug. How spring the Brocoli and the Fenochio. **1767** J. ABERCROMBIE *Ev. Man own Gardener* (1803) 658/1 *Finochio*, or French fennel; for soups, sallads, etc. **1796** C. MARSHALL *Garden.* xvi. (1813) 267 Finochio is a sort of dwarf fennel. **1847** CRAIG, *Finnochia*, a variety of fennel.

Finsen ('fɪnsən). The name of Niels R. *Finsen* (1860–1904), Danish physician, used *attrib.* and in the possessive to designate the method introduced by him of treating skin diseases by ultra-violet light, and also the apparatus he devised for the purpose.

1899 *Brit. Med. Jrnl.* 30 Sept. 825/1 (*heading*) Remarks on Finsen's phototherapy. **1902** *Westm. Gaz.* 12 Mar. 9/3 A Finsen lamp for the new treatment of lupus. **1902** *Brit. Med. Jrnl.* 31 May 1324/2 A small ulcerating surface, which resisted treatment by Finsen's light. **1903** *Ibid.* 3 Jan. 24/1 The Finsen treatment in lupus vulgaris. **1907** *Practitioner* Nov. 721 The Finsen-light treatment of lupus. **1911** *Albutt's Syst. Med.* IX. 480 Intra-nasal lupus can be rarely reached with Finsen's apparatus. **1934** DORE & FRANKLIN *Dis. Skin* xxiv. 343 For small growths ultra-violet light applied with either the Finsen or Kromayer compression lamp is sometimes successful. **1961** *Brit. Med. Dict.* 561/1 *Finsen apparatus*, or *lamp*, a source of ultra-violet-light radiation designed for the local treatment of lupus. It consists of a carbon-arc lamp of high amperage. *Ibid.*, *Finsen treatment*, the treatment of lupus vulgaris by local ultraviolet irradiation with the Finsen lamp; this is now seldom employed.

† **'finter-'fanter.** *Obs.* [A jingling reduplication of unmeaning sounds. Cf. FIDDLE-FADDLE.] The name of a herb.

? *a* **1400** [see FETTERFOE].

‖**fi'occo.** *Obs.* Also 7 *erron.* fiocchio. [It. *fiocco* (pl. *fiocchi*): see FLOCK *sb.*[2]] A tassel.

1694 S. JOHNSON *Notes Past. Let. Bp. Burnet* I. 2 Fiocchio's or Cardinals Horse-top-knots. **1714** *Hist. Mitre & Purse* 30 A Cardinals Horse with his Fiocco upon him.

† **'fiole.** *Obs.* Also 4–5 fyole, viol(e, fiolle, 6 fyoyle. [a. OF. *fiole, phiole* = Pr. *fiola*, med.L. *fiola* (class. L. *phiala*, Gr. φιάλη): see PHIAL, VIAL.] A bowl, cup, or phial.

13.. *E.E. Allit. P.* B. 1476 Fyoles fretted with flores & fleez of golde. *a* **1375** *Joseph Arim.* 290 Sencers..and a viole of sence. **1382** WYCLIF *Num.* vii. 13 A siluern fiole [**1388** viol], hauynge seuenti sicles aftir the peyse of the seyntuarye. *c* **1400** MAUNDEV. (Roxb.) xi. 43, xii fiolles of gold. **14..** *Voc.* in Wr.-Wülcker 583 *Fiola*, a ffyole or a cruet. **1490** CAXTON *Eneydos* xiii. 47 The fyole fulle of the holi libacion. **1541** R COPLAND *Guydon's Quest. Chirurg.*, A glasse full, or the mountenaunce of a fyoyle.

fion. A piece cut from a fish and used for bait.

1875 WILCOCKS *Sea-Fisherm.* 137 This [mackerel] bait is termed a last, lask, float, or fion.

fiond, obs. form of FIEND.

fiord, fjord (fjɔəd). Also 8 fuir, 9 fyord. [a. Norw. *fiord* :—ON. *fjǫrðr* :—prehistoric **ferþu-z*.] A long, narrow arm of the sea, running up between high banks or cliffs, as on the coast of Norway.

1674 tr. *Scheffer's Lapland* 147 Till it comes to Titus-fiord. **1742** MIDDLETON in *Phil. Trans.* XLII. 167 These Shores have many Inlets or Fuirs. **1818** E. HENDERSON *Iceland* I. p. vi, The Faxe Fiord abounds with lava. **1853** KANE *Grinnell Exp.* xlviii. (1856) 447 Those great indentations known as the Fiords. **1865** LUBBOCK *Preh. Times* 81 In the sheltered and shallow fjords of Denmark, the sea is generally calm.

b. *attrib.*, as ***fiord-mouth***: ***fiord-like*** adj.

1885 *Pall Mall G.* 7 May 4/2 Coal Harbour is situated on the same fiordlike Burrard Inlet. **1887** *Ibid.* 23 Aug. 6/1 Islands..lying in the fjord-mouths.

fiorin ('faɪərɪn). [App. a corruption of Ir. *fiorthán* long coarse grass.] A species of grass (*Agrostis stolonifera* or *alba*). Also ***fiorin-grass***.

1809 W. RICHARDSON in *Farmer's Mag.* X. 503 The variety of Irish grass called Fiorin. **1812** *Examiner* 7 Sept. 563/2 The wheat has been fairly eaten out by the couch and *fiorin* grass. **1856** W. ALLINGHAM in *Athenæum* 26 July 931 The clover and the fiorin deep. **1866** *Evening Star* 24 Mar., The fiorin grass, which some farmers anathematise as a weed.

fiorite (fɪ'ɔəraɪt). *Min.* [Named by Thomson 1796 from *Santa Fior-a*, its locality; see -ITE.] An incrustation formed from the decomposition of the siliceous minerals of volcanic rocks about fumaroles, or from the siliceous waters of hot springs.

1808 T. ALLAN *Min. Nomen.* 52 Müller's glass, or Lava glass..Fiorite. **1830** LYELL *Princ. Geol.* I. 214 A siliceous incrustation, first noticed by Dr. Thompson under the name of fiorite. **1884** DANA *Min.* 199 The original fiorite..occurs in tufa.

‖**fioritura** (fjori'tura). Pl. fioriture. [It. *fioritura*, f. *fiorire* to flower.] A florid ornament or embellishment in music. Usually *pl.*

1841 LADY BLESSINGTON *Idler in France* I. 220 The only defect I can discover in her singing is an excess of *fiorituri*. *a* **1859** DE QUINCEY *Conversation* Wks. XIV. 155 These *impromptu* torrents of music create rapturous *fioriture*.

transf. **1873** SYMONDS *Grk. Poets* x. 323 The modern poet [endeavours]..to embroider their materials with the dazzling *fioriture* of his invention.

fip (fɪp). *U.S.* [short for *fipenny bit*.] (See quot. 1860 and next.)

1822 *Philad. Freeman's Jrnl.* 5 Sept. (Th.), A dispute now commenced between two persons respecting some cents and a 'fip'..: one asserting that there were two 'fips', and the other that there was but one. **1833** in *Indiana Mag. Hist.* (1919) XV. 244 He would not let us pass through the fense without a 'fip', that is 4½ cents. **1837–47** [see LEVY *sb.*[2]]. **1860** BARTLETT *Dict. Amer.*, Fippenny Bit, or contracted, *Fip*, fivepence. In Pennsylvania, and several of the Southern States, the vulgar name for the Spanish half-real. **1876** T. HILL *True Order Studies* (1878) 49 The..fips and eleven-penny bits of fifty years ago.

Hence **'fipsworth**, as much as may be bought or sold for a 'fip'.

1844 MAURY *Let. to A. Maury* 23 June, in Corbin *Life* (1888) 48 If nonsense will sell at all, I am sure you have here three fipsworth of it.

fipenny ('fɪpənɪ). *slang.* Also fi'penny, fippen(n)y. [Corruption of FIVE-PENNY.] (See quots.) **fipenny bit** *U.S.* = FIP. (*Disused.*)

1802 *Port Folio* (Phila.) 27 Feb. 6/2 We shall gather *fipenny-bits* from every parsley bed. **1812** J. H. VAUX *Flash Dict.*, *Fi'penny*, a clasp-knife. **1856** MRS. STOWE *Dred* I. 235 What do we want to send our girls there, to get fipenny-bit ideas? **1889** BARRÈRE & LELAND *Slang*, *Fipenny* (thieves), a clasp knife. The term is in common use in Australia, where it was introduced by the convicts.

'fippence. *Colloq.* [Corruption of *five pence*.] = Five pence.

1607 R. C. *World of Wonders* 50 Women gorgeously apparelled, finicall and fine as fippence. **1721** J. KELLY *Scot. Prov.* 18 As fine as Fippence, you'll give a Groat raking. **1823** *Blackw. Mag.* XIII. 457 On leaving the lush-crib, we can figure them giving fippence to the drawer.

fipple ('fɪp(ə)l), *sb.* Also *Sc.* **faiple**. [Cf. Icel. *flipi* lip of a horse.]

1. The plug at the mouth of a wind-instrument, by which its volume was contracted. Also *attrib.*, as **fipple flute** (see quot. 1956).

1626 BACON *Sylva* §161 Let there be a Recorder made with two Fipples, at each end one. **1911** *Encycl. Brit.* XXII. 966/2 (*heading*) Recorder, Fipple Flute or English Flute. *Ibid.*, This channel is so constructed within the mouthpiece that the stream of air impinges with force against the sharp edge of a lip or fipple. **1956** *Oxf. Compan. Music* (ed. 9) 865/1 Flutes of the end-blown variety are..known as fipple flutes.

2. *north. dial.* 'The underlip in men and animals, when it hangs down large and loose' (Jam.). ***to hang a (the, one's) fipple***: to look disappointed, discontented, or sulky; also, to weep.

1805 A. SCOTT *Poems* 23 (Jam.) Condemned to hang a faiple. **1825** BROCKETT *N. Country Gloss.*, 'See how he hangs his fipple.' **1892** *Northumb. Gloss.* s.v. 'What a fipple!'—what a face you're making.

3. *dial.* (See quot.)

1892 *Northumb. Gloss.*, After stooks of corn remain standing for a time, the bottoms of the sheaves become naturally longer on the outside than the inside, which is called their 'fipple'.

† **'fipple,** *v. Sc. Obs.* Also 6 fepple. [Cf. Sw. *flipa* to weep with distortion of the mouth.] *intr.* ? To whimper, whine; ? to slaver, dribble.

14.. *Peebles to Play* xxv, He fippilit like ane faderles fole. **1508** DUNBAR *Tua Mariit Wemen* 114 He feppillis like a farcy aver, that flyrit on a gillot.

fir (fɜː(r)). Forms: 3–8 firr, 4 fer, *south.* ve(e)r, 4–5 fyr(re, *south.* vyrre, 4–7 firre, (6 fire, 7 fyre), 7 fur, 4– fir. [ME. *firr, firre*, perh. repr. OE. **fyre* or ON. *fyri-* (in combs. *fyriskógr* fir-wood, etc.; cf. Da. *fyr*):—OTeut. **furhjôn-* f. **furhâ, forhâ*, whence OE. *furh(wudu)*, OHG. *forha* (MHG. *vorhe*, Ger. *föhre*), ON., Norw., Sw. *fura*. For the formation cf. BEECH, OE. *béce*:—**bôkjôn* f. *bôkâ* (Ger. *buche*).

A form differing in ablaut-grade is OHG. *vereh-eih* (rare early mod.Ger. *ferch*), Lombard *fereha*, all denoting a kind of oak (L. *æsculus*). The L. *quercus* oak is doubtless cognate.]

1. The name given to a number of coniferous trees, of different genera. **Scotch fir** (*Pinus sylvestris*), a native of Arctic Europe and Asia; perhaps indigenous in a few spots of northern Britain; called also *Scotch Pine.* **silver fir** (*Abies pectinata*), a native of the mountainous parts of middle and southern Europe; so called from its whiteness under the leaves. ***silver fir of Canada*** (*Abies balsamea*), a small tree which furnishes 'Canada balsam.' **spruce fir** (*Picea excelsa*), a native of northern and mountainous central Europe; called also *Norway Spruce.*

(The first quot. is doubtful: the word may be FAR.)

a **1300** *Cursor M.* 11501 (Gött.) [Rekels]..es a gum þat cummes of firr. *c* **1381** CHAUCER *Parl. Foules* 179 The sayling firr. **1398** TREVISA *Barth. De P.R.* XVII. iv. (Tollem. MS), Veer [**1535** Fer] is a tre þat streccheþ in lengþe upwarde. *a* **1490** BOTONER *Itin.* (1778) 175 Arbores et mastys de vyrre cum anchoris jacent. **1530** PALSGR. 220/2 Fyrre a tree, *sappin*. **1590** SPENSER *F.Q.* I. i. 9 The firre that weepeth still. **1624** CAPT. SMITH *Virginia* I. 19 The rocky clifts..overgrown with Firre. **1713** C'TESS WINCHELSEA *Misc. Poems* 188 The silver Firr dotes on the stately Pine. **1777** HUNTER in *Phil. Trans.* LXVIII. 47 Spruce fir, Scotch fir, Silver fir, Weymouth fir. **1794** MARTYN *Rousseau's Bot.* xxviii. 446 Silver Fir is so named from the whiteness of the leaves underneath. **1846** J. BAXTER *Libr. Pract. Agric.* I. 267 'As a nurse'..'no other tree equals the Scotch fir.' **1877** BRYANT *Odyss.* v. 290 Firs that reach the clouds.

2. a. The wood of any of these trees. ***fir-in-bond***, 'a name given to lintels, bond-timbers, wall-plates, and indeed all timbers built in walls' (1846 Buchanan *Technol. Dict.*).

1398 TREVISA *Barth. De P.R.* XVII. cxxi. (1495) 684 The ver rotyth anone vnder erthe. **1611** BIBLE *1 Kings* vi. 15 Hee ..couered the floore of the house with plankes of firre. **1677** YARRANTON *Engl. Improv.* 69 Many Cities are built of Fir. **1823** P. NICHOLSON *Pract. Build.* 261 The fir which is mostly used in carpentry is distinguished by the name of Memel Fir.

b. *Sc.* = *candle-fir*: see CANDLE *sb.* 7.

1813 W. BEATTIE *Entertain. & Instruct. Tales* I. 31 Pate..but-a-house dare hardly look, But had, and snuff the fir.

3. *attrib.* and *Comb.* **a.** simple attrib.: (sense 1), as ***fir-bark***, ***-clump***, ***-cone*** (hence *fir-coning*, nonce-wd.), ***-green***, ***-plantation***, ***-seed***, ***-top***, ***-wood***; (sense 2), as ***fir-lathing***, ***-plank***, ***-pole***, ***-timber***; **b.** instrumental or parasynthetic, as ***fir-bordered***, ***-built***, ***-scented***, ***-topped*** adjs.

1840 MRS. NORTON *Dream* 2 The changeful beams still play'd On the *fir-bark. **1891** *Daily News* 7 Sept. 2/1 Along the *fir-bordered road. **1867** SMYTH *Sailor's Word-bk.*, **Fir-built*, constructed of fir. **1842** FABER *Styrian Lake* 356 Groupes of birch..Rise up..Among the *fir-clumps dark. **1818** KEATS *Endym.* I. 256 Oak-apples, and *fir-cones brown. **1819** MISS MITFORD in *Life* (1870) II. 56, I like it [reading]..better than *fir-coning—better than violeting. **1884** *Girl's Own Paper* 29 Nov. 136/1 The newest greens are called cresson and '*fir-green'. **1884** *Health Exhib. Catal.* 84/1 Webbing made of reed and used in substitution of *fir-lathing. **1855** H. CLARKE *Dict.* s.v. *Fir*, *Fir-plank. **1824** MISS MITFORD *Village* Ser. I. (1863) 61 The dark verdure of the *fir-plantations. **1703** MOXON *Mech. Exerc.* 177 The Pole is commonly made of a *Fir-pole. **1823** P. NICHOLSON *Pract. Build.* 223 Fir-poles, small trunks of fir-trees. **1880** OUIDA *Moths* II. 384 He was thinking of green, cool, dusky, *fir-scented Ischl. **1664** EVELYN *Kal. Hort.* (1729) 196 *Fir-seeds. **1858** *Skyring's Builders' Prices* 62 Memel and all other *fir timbers. **1855** KINGSLEY *Heroes* II. 212 Upon the *fir-tops hung the bones of murdered men. **1886** *Pall Mall G.* 28 Aug. 3/2 The *fir-topped hill that shuts out the view of the lake. *c* **1540** LELAND *Itin.* VII. (1744) 22 Ther be founde in Morisch and Mossy Grounde..*Fyr-woodde Rootes. **1611** BIBLE *2 Sam.* vi. 5 Instruments made of Firre-wood. **1877** BLACK *Green Past.* ii. (1878) 12 That distant line of firwood on the horizon.

4. Special comb.: as **fir-apple, -ball**, the fruit of the fir-tree; a fir-cone; **fir balsam**, the silver fir of Canada, *Abies balsamea*; † **fir-beech**, the lime or linden tree (L. *tilia*); **fir-bob** = *fir-apple*; **fir-brush** (see quot.); **fir-candle** = FIR 2 b; **fir-cedar** (see quot.); **fir club-moss** = *fir-moss*; **fir-deal**, a deal or plank of fir; also, fir-wood cut in planks; **fir-marigold** (see quot.); **fir-moss** (see quot.); **fir-needle** (see quot.); **fir-pine** = 1; **fir-rape**, a parasitic plant on roots of fir and beech (*Hypopithys multiflora*); **fir-spell** *dial.* = FIR 2 b (in quot. referring to fir-roots so used). Also FIR-TREE.

1712 J. JAMES tr. *Le Blond's Gardening* 147 The Fir-Tree ..bears a scaly Fruit of a piramidal Figure, call'd the *Fir-Apple. **1878** BRITTEN & HOLLAND *Plant-n.* 184 Fir Apple ..*Fir Balls..Fir-bob. **1810** MICHAUX *Arbres* I. 18 Sylvir fir,..*Fir balsam,..[ou] Balsam of Gilead tree. **1899** S. O. JEWETT *Queen's Twin* 16 Fir balsams comin' up over the hill all green an' hearty. **1854** *Househ. Words.* IX. 327/2 The fire was always in that state when somebody had..to unload his pockets of fir-bobs, which..threw beautiful dancing lights. **1577** B. GOOGE *Heresbach's Husb.* II. (1586) 101 b, The Fyrre, the Oke, the Chestnutte, the *Fyrrebeeche. **1879** MISS JACKSON *Shropsh. Word-bk.*, **Fir-brushes*, the needle-foliage of fir trees. **1601** HOLLAND *Pliny* II. 179 The great Cedar, called by the Greeks Cedrelate, as one would say, the *Fir-Cedre, yeeldeth a certain pitch or parrosin named Cedria. **1855** MISS PRATT *Ferns* 138 Order Lycopodiaceæ, *L. Selago* (*Fir Club-moss, Upright Fir-moss). **1450, 1558, 1604, 1618** *Fir-deal [see DEAL *sb.*[3] 1, 1 b]. **1834** PRINGLE *Afr. Sk.* ix. 308 The *fir-marigold [mesembryanthemum] was expanding its radiated crowns over thousands of acres. **1879** PRIOR *Plant-n.* 80 **Fir-moss*, a mossy looking plant like a little fir-tree, *Lycopodium Selago*. **1883** *Hampsh. Gloss.*, **Fir-needles*, the leaves of the Scotch Fir. **1843** MARRYAT *M. Violet* xxxv. 290 The *fir-pines..told us that we had reached the highest point of the hills. **1861** MISS PRATT *Flower. Pl.* III. 384 Order Monotropeæ..(Yellow Bird's-nest)..called also *Fir-rape. **1884** *Evangelical Mag.* Feb. 60 The Fir-Rape..grows at the foot of beech and fir trees. **1697** *Phil. Trans.* XIX. 382 Examine the *Fir-spells, as they call them, who are brought up the River Ouse by the Turff-men and sold at York.

fir, var. form of FUR.

Firbankian (fɜːˈbæŋkɪən), *a.* [f. the name of Ronald *Firbank* (1886–1926), English author.] Of, pertaining to, or characteristic of Ronald Firbank or his works and opinions.

1931 C. BEATON *Diary* Feb. (1961) 226 Firbankian intrigues. **1958** *Times Lit. Suppl.* 19 Dec. 733/4 A delightfully absurd, almost Firbankian day-dream. **1963** *Listener* 10 Jan. 92/1 The Firbankian name of Mirabeau Buonaparte Lamar.

Firbolg (fɪəˈbɒlg, in Irish firˈbɔləg). [Ir., ulterior etym. obscure: perh. f. OIr. *fir* pl. of *fear* man + *bolg* gen. pl. of *bolg* bag, belly, thus 'men of the bags (or bellies)'; or possibly (Pokorny) cogn. w. Gaulish *Belgae*:— IE. **bhelgh-*/**bhol-gh-*.] A name given in Irish legend to an early colonizing people of Ireland. Also *transf.* Hence **Firˈbolgian** *a.*, of or pertaining to this people.

1797 *Encycl. Brit.* IX. 313/1 The Firbolgs were..expelled or totally subdued..by the Tuath de Dannans. **1863** *Chambers's Encycl.* V. 626/1 According to ancient native legends, I[reland] was in remote times peopled by tribes styled Firbolgs and Danauns, eventually subdued by Milesians or Gaels. **1916** JOYCE *Portrait of Artist* v. 210 The rude Firbolg mind of his listener had drawn his mind towards it and flung it back again. **1936** M. FRANKLIN *All that Swagger* i. 8 Families of the reverberating cognomens and Firbolgian descent. **1938** L. MACNEICE *I crossed Minch* II. xvi. 240 Flora..answered..that Firbolgs were prehistoric and anyway ought to be called Ciuthachs. **1968** *Times* 15 Oct. 13/5 Production of fairyland lustre began in November 1915: gnomes, pixies,..fey creations, including the 'firbolgs', a peculiarly unappealing class of little men with big eyes. **1971** *It* 2–16 June 24/1 The..Formorians, Fir-Bolgs and de-Danaans are all remembered as being of semi-human stock.

† **ˈfirdon**, *v. Sc. Obs.* Also firdoun, frid(d)oun. [ad. F. *fredonn-er*.] *intr.* To warble, to quaver in singing. Hence **ˈfirdoning** *vbl. sb.*

1599 A. HUME *Hymnes, Day Estivall* 18 Their firdoning the bony birds In banks they do begin. **16..** MONTGOMERIE *Cherrie & Slae* vii. (in *Ever Green* 1724) Compleitly mair sweitly Scho fridound flat and schairp.

fire (faɪə(r)), *sb.* Forms: 1 fýr, 2–4 fur(e, 3–5 fuyr(e, 4 fuir(e, 5 feure, 2–5 fer(e, 3 *south.* ver(e, (5 feer), 2–7 fier(e, (3 feir), 4–6 fyr(e, (5 fyyr, 5–7 fyer(e, (5 feyer, 6 fyar, fieare), 2–5 fir, 3– fire. [Com. WGer.: OE. *fýr* str. neut. = OFris. *fiur*, *fior*, OS. *fiur* (Du. *vuur*, Flem. *vier*), OHG. *fiur*, *fûir* (MHG. *viur*, *fiwer*, Ger. *feuer*); the Icel. *fúr-r* str. masc., *fýre* str. neut., fire, and Sw., Da. *fyr*, lighthouse, beacon, may be of German or Eng. origin. The OTeut. **fûir-* (cons. stem) corresponds to Gr. *πῦ-ιρ*, *πῦρ*, Umbrian *pir*, Arm. *hūr*, of same meaning; cf. Skr. *pū*, *pāvaka* fire.]

In poetry sometimes as two syllables (ˈfaɪə(r)).

A. As simple *sb.*

1. a. The natural agency or active principle operative in combustion; popularly conceived as a substance visible in the form of flame or of ruddy glow or incandescence.

c **825** *Vesp. Psalter* xvii. 9 [xviii. 8] Astag rec in eorre his & fyr from onsiene his born. *a* **1000** *Cædmon's Exod.* 93 (Gr.) Him beforan foran fyr and wolcen. *c* **1175** *Lamb. Hom.* 89 On þisse deie com þe halie gast on fures heowe to godes hirede. *c* **1200** ORMIN 17414 He swallt þurrh firess wunde. *c* **1250** *Gen. & Ex.* 1140 Đo meidenes herden quilum seien, Đat fier sulde al ðis werld forsweðen. **1297** R. GLOUC. (1724) 151, Y formed as a dragon, as red as þe fuyr. **1340** *Ayenb.* 265 Þer me geo uram chele in to greate hete of uere. *c* **1380** WYCLIF *Sel. Wks.* III. 102 Þanne maist þou wiþ tendre gete fuyre of þat stone. **1447** BOKENHAM *Seyntys* (Roxb.) 21 The feer wych owt dede renne From his [the dragon's] mouth. **1526** *Pilgr. Perf.* (W. de W. 1531) 3 Whiche from yᵉ gyrdell downwarde was all lyke fyre. **1607** HIERON *Wks.* I. 364 Fier is knowne to be fier by the heat, though for the time it haue no flame. **1622** MABBE tr. *Aleman's Guzman d'Alf.* I. 49 With a face as red as fire. **1781** GIBBON *Decl. & F.* III. lxxi. 802 Fire is the most powerful agent of life and death. **1837** J. H. NEWMAN *Par. Serm.* (1839) I. i. 9 Fire does not inflame iron, but it inflames straw.

b. as one of the four 'elements'.

a **1300** *Fragm. Pop. Sc.* (Wright) 121 Next the mone the fur is hext. **1576** BAKER *Jewell of Health* 170 a, Mans blood ..out of which draw, according to Art, the fowre Elements ..The water of it auayleth in all sicknesses..The Ayre also distylled of it much auayleth vnto [etc.]..But the fyre purchased of it is more precious..This fyre is named the Elixir vitæ. **1700** DRYDEN *Fables, Pythag. Philos.* 517 The force of fire ascended first..Then air succeeds.

c. with reference to hell or purgatory; sometimes in *pl.* Also in Alchemy, † *Fire of Hell* = ALKAHEST.

c **975** *Rushw. Gosp.* Mark ix. 44 Ðer..þ fyr ne bið ȝidrysnad. *c* **1000** *Ags. Gosp.* Matt. v. 22 Se ðe segð, þu stunta, se byð scyldiȝ helle fyres. *a* **1175** *Cott. Hom.* 221 Þat ece fer. *a* **1300** *Cursor M.* 29165 (Cott.) þe fier of purgatori. **1577** FULKE *Confut. Purg.* 102 But what doctrine is tryed.. by the fire of purgatory? **1657** G. STARKEY *Helmont's Vind.* 241 The sweet oyl..by cohobation with the fire of Hell (that is, the Alchahest) becomes volatile. **1667** MILTON *P.L.* I. 48 In Adamantine Chains and penal Fire. **1829** A. FONBLANQUE *Eng. under 7 Administ.* (1837) I. 273 [A child-witness] 'knows that people who swear falsely in a Court of Justice go to brimstone and fire'.

fig. **1847** TENNYSON *Princ.* v. 444 The fires of Hell Mix with his hearth.

d. Volcanic heat, flame, or glowing lava; †a volcanic eruption.

c **1582** SKORY in *Nature* XXVII. 316 The fyers doe ofte breake forth from out the hole in the topp of this hill. **1632** LITHGOW *Trav.* IX. 391 This last and least fire [of Etna] runne downe in a combustible flood. **1734** POPE *Ess. Man* IV. 124 Shall burning Ætna..Forget to thunder and recall her fires? **1811** W. J. HOOKER *Iceland* (1813) II. 106 Hecla, from the frequency of its fires..has been..the most celebrated. **1845** DARWIN *Voy. Nat.* i. 1 The volcanic fires of a past age ..have..rendered the soil unfit for vegetation.

† **e.** *farriery.* = Cautery. Cf. *to give the fire* in 1 f. *Obs.*

1635 MARKHAM *Faithf. Farrier* (1638) 103 The Actuall fire stoppeth corruption of members, and stancheth blood.. The Potentiall fires are Medecins Corosive, Putrefactive, or Caustick. **1737** BRACKEN *Farriery Impr.* (1740) II. 199 As Horses must submit to Fire. *Ibid.* 218 Is not this Oil, in a great measure, what we call potential Fire?

f. Phrases. † *to give fire* (*to*): (*a*) to apply a match *to*, set light *to*; to kindle, *lit.* and *fig.*; also *absol.*; (*b*) in *Farriery* (also, *to give the fire*), to cauterize; in quots. *absol.* *to set* (†*a*) *fire to* (†*of*, †*in*, †*on*, †*upon*): to apply fire to, kindle, ignite. *to strike* (or †*smite*) *fire*: see the verbs.

c **1430** LYDG. *Minor P., Agst. Idlen.* xx, Peryodes..From flyntes smote fuyre, darying in the roote. **1568** GRAFTON *Chron.* II. 107 b, Thei set fire in their lodgynges, and departed in good ordre of battail. **1580** BARET *Alv.* F 450 To strike fire with a flint, *excutere silicis scintillam.* **1580** BLUNDEVIL *Horsemanship* IV. clxxxv. (*heading*), Of Cauterization, or giuing the fire. **1590** SIR J. SMYTH *Disc. Weapons* 21 The Harquebuziers giving fire with their matches..to the touchpowder. **1604** E. GRIMSTONE *Hist. Siege Ostend* 45 A firie Bullet..set fire of a barrell of Poulder. **1607** A. BREWER *Lingua* IV. i, He..gives fire to the touch-hole. **1623** BINGHAM *Xenophon* 50 All arose and..set fire on the Carts, and Tents. **1633** BP. HALL *Hard Texts* 549 Who shall invade their country and set a fire on their chief city. **1635** MARKHAM *Faithf. Farrier* (1638) 103 There are two waies to give fire. **1669** STURMY *Mariner's Mag.* v. 85 These Fuses are very certain to give Fire. *a* **1674** CLARENDON *Hist. Reb.* XIII. (1704) III. 354 The Lady.. having given fire her self to the Cannon. **1700** TYRRELL *Hist. Eng.* II. 786 They set Fire on the Suburbs. **1725** *Lond. Gaz.* No. 6447/4 One of the said Persons did strike Fire. **1737** BRACKEN *Farriery Impr.* (1757) II. 217 The absurdity of giving the Fire for the Cure of Bog-spavins. **1761** GRAY *Let. to Brown* 24 Sept. Fire was given to all the lustres at once by trains of prepared flax.

g. In exclamatory phrases (cf. 1 c).

[**1601, 1604**: see BRIMSTONE 1 b.] **1825** J. NEAL *Bro. Jonathan* II. 91 Fire an' brimstone! lay hold o' the trumpet, I say. **1840** DICKENS *Barn. Rudge* I, Fire and fury, master! ..What have we done, that you should talk to us like this!

h. Proverbs. † *do not put fire to flax or tow.* † *there is no fire without smoke*: i.e. everything has some disadvantages. *there is no smoke without fire* (see quot. 1670).

a **1450** *Knt. de la Tour* 25 It wille make her do and thenke the worse, as it were to putte fere in flexe. **1539** TAVERNER *Erasm. Prov.* (1552) 57 Put not fyer to fyer..This prouerbe is touched in Englyshe where it is sayde, that we ought not to put fyre to towe. **1546** J. HEYWOOD *Prov.* (1562) Hj, There is no fyre without some smoke. **1670** RAY *Prov.* 143 No smoke without some fire, *i.e.* There is no strong rumour without some ground for it. **1888** F. HUME *Mad. Midas* II. xii, 'There is no smoke without fire', replied Rolleston, eagerly.

2. a. State of ignition or combustion. In phrases: *on fire* (also †*of a fire*, †*in* (*a*) *fire*): ignited, burning; *fig.* inflamed with passion, anger, zeal, etc. *to set* (or †*put*) *on fire* (also † *in* (*a*) *fire*, † *on a fire*): to ignite, set burning; also *fig.* to inflame, excite intensely. *to set the Thames on fire*: to make a brilliant reputation. See also AFIRE.

Not found in OE., nor is there anything analogous in German; F. has *en feu*. The phrases in lit. sense chiefly refer to destructive burning: cf. 5.

c **1400** *Apol. Loll.* 3 For þoo þre chimneis ich low of þe fendis blowing is sett in fire. *a* **1400–50** *Alexander* 2470 Fest I all on [*v.r.* in] a fire þe foly is ȝoure awen. *c* **1485** *Digby Myst.* (1882) III. 742 Goo in-to þis howsse, & loke ye set yt on a feyer. *c* **1489** CAXTON *Sonnes of Aymon* i. 17, I shall sett all his londes in fyre. *c* **1500** *Melusine* 228 He..sware his goddes that he shuld putte al on fyre. **1548** HALL *Chron.* 107 b, The fortresse..thei toke and set it on fire. **1553** T. WILSON *Rhet.* (1580) 136 No mans nature is so apt, straight to be heated, except the Oratour hymself be on fire. **1559** *Mirr. Mag., Jack Cade* xvii. 6 Set much part on fire. **1641** SHUTE *Sarah & Hagar* (1649) 148 Certainly, if God's mercy be in a fire, our thankfulness must not be in a frost. *a* **1680** CHARNOCK *Wks.* (1864) I. 195 Water poured on lime sets it on fire by an antiperistasis. **1697** DAMPIER *Voy.* I. xv. 414 The Sea seemed all of a Fire about us. **1724** DE FOE *Mem. Cavalier* (1840) 142 They were all on fire to fall on. **1818** SHELLEY *Rev. Islam* VI. iv, For to the North I saw the town on fire. **1857** TROLLOPE *Three Clerks* vii, When Sir Gregory ..declared that Mr. Fidus Neverbend would never set the Thames on fire, he meant to express his opinion that that gentleman was a fool. **1871** FREEMAN *Norm. Conq.* (1876) IV. xvii. 80 Enough was carried beyond the sea to set on fire the minds of all.

b. *to catch, take fire*, († *set on fire*): to become ignited (see CATCH *v.* 44, TAKE *v.*). Also (*colloq.* or *vulgar*), *to catch on fire.*

1644 DIGBY *Two Treat.* I. 183 The Indian canes..if they be first very dry, will of themselves set on fire. **1886** CONWAY *Living or Dead* x, Now, don't catch on fire like that, Philip.

3. a. Fuel in a state of combustion; a mass of burning material, e.g. on a hearth or altar, in a burning furnace, etc. † *to keep one's fire*: to stay at home. *coals of fire*: see COAL 1 b. Also *ellipt.* for *gas fire*, *electric fire*, etc.

a **1000** *Cædmon's Gen.* 322 (Gr.) Laȝon þa oðre fynd on þam fyr. *c* **1205** LAY. 1196 He halde þa milc in þat fur. *c* **1290** *S. Eng. Leg.* I. 12/373 Ouer a gret fuyr and strong. *c* **1350** *Will. Palerne* 907 Sum-time it hentis me wiþ hete as hot as ani fure, but quicliche so kene a cold comes þer-after. *c* **1430** *Two Cookery-bks.* 42 Do hem on a potte ouer þe fyre. *c* **1460** *Play Sacram.* 682 To make an ovyn as redd hott as euer yt can be made wᵗ fere. *c* **1500** *Melusine* xxxvi. 264 To long he had kept his fyre. **1533** GAU *Richt Vay* (1883) 31 As the gold is prouine in the fyr. ? *c* **1558** CAVENDISH *Wolsey* (1825) I. 204 Go down again, and make a great fire in your lodge, against I come to dry them. **1634** PRYNNE *Documents agst. Prynne* (Camden) 24 He condempnes the booke to the fyer. **1697** DRYDEN *Æneid* II. 398 The Wreaths and Relicks of th' Immortal Fire. **1717** BERKELEY *Tour in Italy* Wks. 1871 IV. 564 Cold weather; forced to have a fire. **1735** POPE *Donne Sat.* II. 112 No kitchens emulate the vestal fire. **1823** SCOTT *F.M. Perth* ii, A good fire, with the assistance of a blazing lamp, spread light and cheerfulness through the apartment. **1854** H. MILLER *Sch. & Schm.* v. (1857) 95 The second apartment..had..its fire full in the middle of the floor, without back or sides. **1895** *Army & Navy Co-op. Soc. Price List* 334 Ball Fire without Fender and Trivet, 15/9. **1926–7** *Ibid.* 344/2 A small 1-unit fire... One bar (1,000 watts). **1939–40** *Ibid.* 271 All fires are wired complete. *Ibid.*, Well designed 2 kw. fire with hammered copper reflector. **1968** 'J. LE CARRÉ' *Small Town in Germany* v. 70 'Very gadget-minded, Mr Harting is... He had a *tea* machine.' ..'What else?' 'A fire. The new fan type with the two bars over.'

b. *transf.* and *fig.*; also in phr. *near the fire.* Phr. *fire in the* (or *one's*) *belly*: ambition, driving force, initiative.

1560 DAUS tr. *Sleidane's Comm.* 408 The other Princes and states, especially suche as are nere the fire. **1596** HARINGTON *Metam. Ajax* (1814) 116 You may make a great fire of your gains and be never the warmer. **1611** BIBLE *Jas.* iii. 6 The tongue is a fire, a world of iniquitie. **1633** P. FLETCHER *Purple Isl.* v. iii, So shall my flagging Muse to heav'n aspire..And warm her pineons at that heav'nly fire. **1639** LAUD in Rushw. *Hist. Coll.* (1721) III. II. 899 Let him

make a happy use of coming so near the Fire, and yet escape. **1665** HOOKE *Microgr.* 210 The excellent contrivance of Nature, in placing in Animals..a fire..nourished..by the materials conveyd into the stomach. **1709** POPE *Ess. Crit.* 195 Some spark of your celestial fire. **1951** N. ANNAN *L. Stephen* ix. 275 There is no fire in the belly, no sense of urgency. **1960** *20th Cent.* Nov. 390 If they rebel..then they are crackbrained, want a pretext for a rave, or have fire in their belly. **1970** *Guardian* 10 Aug. 9/8 Her success is due, she says, 'to the fact that I have fire in my belly'.

†**c.** *fire of joy*: a bonfire; = FEU DE JOIE 1.

a **1674** CLARENDON *Relig. & Policy* (1711) I. vi. 314 Preparations..by the magistrates for making fires of joy.

d. The same serving as a beacon. [Cf. Da. *fyr* lighthouse.]

1711 *Lond. Gaz.* No. 4893/3 The Fire [in a lighthouse] will be lighted..from the First Day of September.

e. Proverbs. ***a burnt child dreads the fire***: see BURNT 3 b. † ***a soft fire makes sweet malt***: said as a recommendation of gentleness or deliberation. ***the fat is in the fire***: see FAT *sb.*² 3 c.

?*a* **1300** *Salomon & Sat.* (1848) 276 Brend child fur dredeþ, quoth Hendyng. **1340** *Ayenb.* 116 þe yberned uer dret. *c* **1530** R. HILLES *Common-Pl. Bk.* (1858) 140 A softe ffyre makyth swete malte. **1550** COVERDALE *Spir. Perle* xiii. (1588) 141 A Burnt hande dreadeth the fire. **1663** BUTLER *Hud.* I. iii. 1251 Soft fire, They say, does make sweet Malt, Good Squire.

†**f.** *transf.* in enumerations: A household. *Obs.*

1630 *R. Johnson's Kingd. & Commw.* 214 Parishes; in some of which..a thousand housholders or fires doe inhabit. **1653** H. COGAN tr. *Pinto's Trav.* xviii. 63 A town of fifteen hundred fires.

g. ***to play with fire***: to trifle with dangerous matters, esp. at the risk of moral disaster or emotional distress.

1887 J. GRANT (*title*) Playing with fire. **1887** KIPLING *Plain Tales fr. Hills* (1888) 139 There is no sort of use in playing with fire, even for fun. **1907** *Daily Chron.* 9 Oct. 4/6, I should like to sound a note of warning, for, as one who plays with fire, he can only expect to get burnt. **1925** A. S. M. HUTCHINSON *One Increasing Purpose* III. xvi, Looking back upon herself in those fire-playing days. **1928** GALSWORTHY *Swan Song* v. 33 If—on second thoughts, she wanted to play with fire. **1957** L. P. HARTLEY *Hireling* xix. 149 She led me on, she played with fire, but she wouldn't have me.

†**4. a.** The means of lighting a fire or setting something alight; a live coal. **b.** Firing, fuel.

a **1300** *Cursor M.* 3163 (Gött.) Suord ne fir forgat he noght, And yong ysaac a fagett broght. **1540** *Act 33 Hen. VIII*, c. 6 With quarelles gunpouder, fyre, and touche. **1611** BIBLE *Gen.* xxii. 7 Behold the fire and wood; but where is the lambe for a burnt offring?

b. 1547 *Nottingham Rec.* IV. 91 In exspenses for fyar and candelle. **1635** W. BRERETON *Trav.* (1844) 96 There is a mighty want of fire in these moors. **1793** SMEATON *Edystone L.* §274 Little extra expence..except a little more Lead, and a little more Fire.

5. a. Destructive burning, *esp.* of any large extent or mass of combustible material, e.g. a building, forest, etc.; a conflagration. Also in phr. ***fire and sword***, († ***iron and fire***); also *attrib.* ***at fire's-length*** (rare): at a safe distance in the event of fire. For (*to set*) *on fire*, etc. see 2.

a **1175** *Cott. Hom.* 239 Wic drednesse wurð þer þan þat fer to for him abernð þat middernad. *c* **1205** LAY. 2159 He fuhten wið his leoden mid fure & mid here. *c* **1325** *Know Thyself* 30 in *E.E.P.* (1862) 131 Hit fareþ as fuir of heth. **1393** LANGL. *P. Pl.* C. IV. 96 Fur on here houses. **1504** WRIOTHESLEY *Chron.* (1875) I. 5 A great fier at the ende of London Bridge. **1568** GRAFTON *Chron.* II. 314 Spoylyng the Countrie with yron and fyre as he went. **1577** B. GOOGE *Heresbach's Husb.* I. (1586) 9 b, These offices (for feare of fyre) you see, are all severed from the house. **1600** HOLLAND *Livy* VII. 269 In euerie place nothing but fire and sword. **1667** WATERHOUSE (*title*), A short narrative of the late dreadful fire in London. **1724** T. RICHERS *Hist. R. Geneal. Spain* 53 They..put all to Fire and Sword. **1738** JOHNSON *London* 14 Now a rabble rages, now a fire. **1780** in *Lett. 1st Earl Malmesbury* (1870) I. 465 This night we are quiet, and I hear no attempts at fire have been made. **1781** COWPER *Conv.* 756 Till the last fire burn all between the poles. **1820** SHELLEY *Ode to Naples* 148 The fields they tread look black and hoary With fire. **1830** *Westm. Rev.* XIII. 313 'The dissolution of social order,' which our fire-and-sword logicians so long and confidently preached. **1855** TROLLOPE *Warden* xix, That would be saving something out of the fire. **1862** H. MARRYAT *Year in Sweden* II. 428 Wooden houses, wisely placed at fire's-length from each other.

fig. **1548** HALL *Chron.* 99 b, The greate fire of this discencion, betwene these twoo noble personages, was..utterly quenched out. **1654** tr. *Scudery's Curia Pol.* 3 To see this fire extinguished, before the flame grew higher.

b. Sc. Law. ***letters of fire and sword***: before the Union, an order authorizing the sheriff to dispossess an obstinate tenant or proceed against a delinquent by any means in his power.

1681 VISCT. STAIR *Instit. Law Scot.* IV. xxxviii. §27 (1693) 662 Letters of Fire and Sword are given out against them. *a* **1768** ERSKINE *Instit.* IV. iii. §17 (1773) 691 If a party was so obstinate as to..continue his possession in despite of the law, the Scots privy council..granted letters of fire and sword, authorising the sheriff to..dispossess him by all the methods of force. **1861** W. BELL *Dict. Law Scot.* s.v.

c. An exclamation used as a call for aid at a conflagration.

1682 N. O. *Boileau's Lutrin* IV. 201 One cryes, Fire! Fire! Fire! the Church doth burn. **1819** T. MOORE *Tom Crib's Mem.* 21 As a man would cry 'fire!'

d. ***to go through fire***: to submit to the severest ordeal or proof; ***to go through fire and water***: to encounter or face the greatest dangers or hardest chances.

c **825** *Vesp. Psalter* lxv[i]. 12 We leordun ðorh fyr & weter. **1534** HERVET tr. *Xenophon's Householde* 61 b They wolde gladly folowe theym through fyre and water, and throughe all maner of daunger. **1590** SHAKS. *Mids. N.* II. ii. 103 And run through fire I will for thy sweet sake. **1598** —— *Merry W.* III. iv. 107 A woman would run through fire & water for such a kinde heart. **1660** JER. TAYLOR *Worthy Communicant* ii. §1. 119 We also are to examine..how we have passed through the fire? **1781** COWPER *Expost.* 521 [They] Would hunt a Saracen through fire and blood. *a* **1796** BURNS *Ronalds of Bennals* 19 The Laird o' Blackbyre wad gang through the fire If that wad entice her awa, man.

e. ***a brand from*** (or ***out of***) ***the fire***, see BRAND *sb.* 3 b; ***to save out of the fire***, to preserve as a remnant from a disaster or catastrophe; ***to pull*** or ***snatch out of the fire*** [after Jude 23], to rescue from disaster or ruin.

1855 TROLLOPE *Warden* xix, To be sure Puddingdale is only four hundred, but that would be saving something out of the fire. **1893** H. HUTCHINSON *Golfing* 85 It is wonderful what matches these strong souls now and again pull out of the fire. **1924** G. LAMBTON *Men & Horses* 120 Well, I pulled that race out of the fire. **1927** *Daily Tel.* 11 Oct. 5/6 The winner pulling the match out of the fire after being down 2 sets to 1. **1928** *Observer* 10 June 27/4 The best snatcher of a match out of the fire that we ever had. **1932** C. MORGAN *Fountain* I. i. 9 A man who..pulls a business out of the fire isn't an incompetent.

f. ***to pull the chestnuts out of the fire***: used (with reference to the fable of the monkey using the cat's paw to extract roasting chestnuts from the fire) of the employment of another to undertake the dangerous part of an enterprise. (See *N. & Q.* 6th Ser., 1883, VII. 286, VIII. 34.)

[**1586** G. WHITNEY *Emblems* 58 The ape, did reache for Chestnuttes in the fire,..he with a whelpe did close, And thruste his foote, into the Embers quick, And made him, pull the Chestnuttes out perforce.] **1657** [see CAT'S PAW 2]. [**1754** RICHARDSON *Grandison* III. 358 He makes her fight his battles for him; and become herself the cat's paw to help him to the ready-roasted chestnuts.] **1886** [see UNIONIST A. I. c]. **1930** J. C. SNAITH *Unforeseen* II. xxi, He was the guy who pulled the financial chestnuts out of the fire. **1957** *Economist* 28 Sept., The Germans cannot be expected to pull our chestnuts out of the fire.

g. ***where's the fire?***: jocular phrase said to a person who is in a hurry.

1924 P. CRESWICK *Beaten Path* xxxvi. 195 A husky voice enquired of me: 'Where's the fire?' **1963** J. F. STRAKER *Final Witness* xvi. 174 'Where's the fire, dear boy?' he drawled. 'Do we really have to run for it?' **1971** 'H. CALVIN' *Poison Chasers* ix. 124 'Where's the fire?' he snarled.

6. Torture or death by burning. Also, ***fire and faggot***: see FAGGOT 2. Hence † (***to persuade***) ***by fire***: by extreme inducements.

1646 SIR T. BROWNE *Pseud. Ep.* I. iii. 9 And are not sometime perswaded by fire beyond their literalities. **1718** PRIOR *Charity* 8 Did Shadrach's Zeal my glowing Breast inspire, To weary Tortures, and rejoice in Fire.

7. Lightning; a flash of lightning; a thunderbolt. More fully, † ***levenes fire, fire of heaven***. † ***electrical fire***: the electric fluid, electricity.

1154 *O.E. Chron.* an. 1122 Com se fir on ufenweard þone stepel. *c* **1250** *Gen. & Ex.* 3046 Ðhunder, and hail, and leuenes fir. *c* **1300** *Cursor M.* 19613 (Cott.) þe fire of heuen þar has him stunt. **1393** LANGL. *P. Pl.* C. IV. 102 þenne falleth þer fur on false menne houses. **1747** FRANKLIN *Lett.* Wks. 1840 V. 186 He imagined that the electrical fire came down the wire from the ceiling to the gun-barrel. **1748** *Ibid.* 215 Vapors, which have both common and electrical fire in them. **1820** SHELLEY *Ode W. Wind* ii. 14 From whose solid atmosphere Black rain, and fire, and hail will burst.

8. a. An inflammable composition for producing a conflagration or for use in fireworks; a firework. More fully ***artificial fire*** = Fr. *feu d'artifice*. *Obs.* exc. in ***false fire***: see FALSE *a.* 14 b.

1602 DEKKER *Satiro-Mastix* E iij, We must have false fiers. **1653** H. COGAN tr. *Pinto's Trav.* xx. 71 Nine hundred pots of artificial fire. **1662** J. DAVIES tr. *Mandelslo's Trav.* 51 The Artificial Fires, which are made use of to frighten these Creatures. **1700** J. JACKSON in Pepys *Diary* VI. 232 The rockets, and other smaller fires, were in abundance. **1777** G. FORSTER *Voy. Round World* II. 92 We let off some false fires at the mast-head.

b. ***Greek fire***: a combustible composition for setting fire to an enemy's ships, works, etc.; so called from being first used by the Greeks of Constantinople. Also ***wild fire***: see WILDFIRE.

a **1225** *Ancr. R.* 402 þis Grickische fur is the luue of ure Lourde. *c* **1477** CAXTON *Jason* 101 b, Sparkklyng and brennyng as fyre grekyssh. **1855** HEWITT *Anc. Armour* I. 90 The receipt for the composition of the Greek Fire may be found in the Treatise of Marcus Grecus.

9. *Coal Mining* = FIREDAMP.

1883 in GRESLEY *Gloss. Coal. Mining.*

10. a. Luminosity or glowing appearance resembling that of fire.

1591 SHAKS. *1 Hen. VI*, I. i. 12 His sparkling Eyes, repleat with wrathfull fire. **1605** —— *Macb.* I. iv. 51 Starres, hide your fires, Let not Light see my black and deepe desires! **1735** POPE *Prol. Sat.* 5 Fire in each eye, and papers in each hand. **1821** SHELLEY *Prometh. Unb.* I. 762 Their soft smiles light the air like a star's fire. **1865** J. C. WILCOCKS *Sea Fisherm.* (1875) 271 Should the 'brime' or 'fire' show itself, the fish will not be likely to strike the nets. **1873** BLACK *Pr. Thule* x. 164 A great fire of sunset spread over the west.

b. ***fires of heaven, heavenly fires***: (*poet.*) the stars. ***fires of St. Elmo***: see CORPOSANT. † ***fatuous, foolish fire*** (obs.) = IGNIS FATUUS.

1563 W. FULKE *Meteors* (1640) 11 b, *Ignis fatuus*, foolish fire. **1607** SHAKS. *Cor.* I. iv. 39 Or by the fires of heauen, Ile leaue the Foe. **1667** MILTON *P.L.* XII. 256 Before him burn Seaven Lamps as in a Zodiac representing The Heav'nly fires. **1774** GOLDSM. *Nat. Hist.* (1862) I. xxi. 134 Floating bodies of fire..the fires of St. Helmo, or the mariner's light. **1847** TENNYSON *Princess* IV. 255 Like the mystic fire on a mast-head.

11. Heating quality (in liquors, etc.); *concr.* in jocular use, 'something to warm one', ardent spirit. Also (see quot. 1819).

1737 FIELDING *Hist. Reg.* II. Wks. 1882 X. 223 We'll go take a little fire for 'tis confounded cold upon the stage. **1819** REES *Cycl.* s.v. *Fire*, Also the heat of fermenting substances ..has often been called their fire. **1851** THACKERAY *Eng. Hum.* ii, [He] was of a cold nature, and needed perhaps the fire of wine to warm his blood. **1883** STEVENSON *Silverado Sq.* 37 One corner of land after another is tried with one kind of grape after another..Those lodes and pockets of earth.. that yield inimitable fragrance and soft fire..still lie undiscovered.

12. Burning heat produced by disease; fever, inflammation. Also disease viewed as a consuming agency. ***St. Anthony's fire***: a name for one or more inflammatory or gangrenous diseases of the skin, variously identified with erysipelas, ergotism, etc.; also † ***wild fire***, WILDFIRE. † ***St. Francis' fire*** (Spencer): ? = St. Anthony's fire.

c **1386** CHAUCER *Parson's T.* ¶427 By the fyr of seint antony or by cancre. *c* **1400** *Lanfranc's Cirurg.* 223 Panaricium is an enpostym..aboute þe nail and is swiþe hoot and..ful of fier. **1527** etc. [see ANTHONY (St.)]. **1580** BARET *Alv.* F 447 S. Antonies fire, *ignis sacer.* **1580** BLUNDEVIL *Horsemanship* IV. clxv. 69 You must get it [the pellet] out with an instrument..Then to kill the fire. Take [etc.]. **1590** SPENSER *F.Q.* I. iv. 35 The shaking palsey, and Saint Fraunces fire. **1686** LADY RUSSELL *Lett.* I. xxxvi. 94 Ill of St. Anthony's fire. **1697** DRYDEN *Virg. Georg.* III. 727 When the thirsty Fire had drunk Their vital Blood. **1737** BRACKEN *Farriery Impr.* (1756) I. 301 The Inflammation, which they term Fire. **1843** SIR T. WATSON *Lect. Physic* II. lxxxix. 767 Erysipelas..called..St. Anthony's fire. **1866** G. MACDONALD *Ann. Q. Neighb.* xxvi. (1878) 460 The unseen fire of disease.

13. In certain figurative applications of sense 1.

a. A burning passion or feeling, *esp.* of love or rage.

a **1340** HAMPOLE *Psalter* Prol., þai..kyndils þaire willis wiþ þe fyre of luf. **1435** MISYN *Fire of Love* 1 Hampole hys boke has named *Incendium Amoris*, þat is to say 'þe fyer of lufe'. **1598** SHAKS. *Merry W.* II. i. 68 The wicked fire of lust. **1694** F. BRAGGE *Disc. Parables* xii. 408 Rage, and fury, and impatience..are frequently attended with the epithet of fire. **1780** COWPER *Table T.* 606 The victim of his own lascivious fires. **1818** SHELLEY *Rev. Islam* x. xl, With an inward fire possesst, They raged like homeless beasts. **1859** TENNYSON *Enid* 955 He fain had..loosed in words of sudden fire the wrath..that burnt him all within.

b. Ardour of temperament; ardent courage or zeal; fervour, enthusiasm, spirit.

1601 SHAKS. *Jul. C.* I. ii. 177, I am glad that my weake words Haue strucke but thus much shew of fire from Brutus. **1709** STEELE *Tatler* No. 61 ¶ 1 Among many Phrases which have crept into Conversation..[is] that of a Fellow of a great deal of Fire. **1814** *Sporting Mag.* XLIV. 92 Both were full of fire and courage. **1865** KINGSLEY *Herew.* xx, Hereward was haranguing them in words of fire.

c. Liveliness and warmth of imagination, brightness of fancy; power of genius, vivacity; poetic inspiration.

1656 COWLEY *Pindar. Odes, To Mr. Hobs* vi, Nor can the Snow which now cold age does shed Upon thy reverend Head, Quench or allay the noble Fires within. **1680-90** TEMPLE *Ess. Poetry* Wks. 1731 I. 237 The Poetical Fire was more raging in one, but clearer in the other. **1737** POPE *Hor. Ep.* II. i. 274 Corneille's noble fire. **1847** *Illust. Lond. News* 10 July 27/1 As an actress, she has fire and intelligence. **1869** J. MARTINEAU *Ess.* II. 228 For the poet there is a season of inward fire. **1877** R. W. DALE *Lect. Preach.* i. 26 They have neither the fire of a human genius nor the fire of a Divine zeal.

14. a. The action of firing guns, etc.; discharge of fire-arms; also in phrases, † ***to give, make*** (***a***) ***fire***. ***to open fire***: to begin firing. ***between two fires***: lit. and fig. ***under fire***: within the range of an enemy's guns; also *fig.*, criticized. † ***weapon of fire*** = FIRE-ARM.

[The similar use of F. *feu* shows that this is not (as is often said) a separate word F. FIRE *v.*, but a transferred use of the sb. as it occurs in the phrase *to give fire* (see 1 f) = F. *faire feu*.]

1590 J. SMYTHE *Concern. Weapons* 27 Liking the aforesaid weapons of fire, because [etc.]. **1600** *Sir John Oldcastle* v. ix, Unconstant fate, That hast reserved him from the bullet's fire. **1657** R. LIGON *Barbadoes* (1673) 8 Some of the Soldiers of the Castle gave fire upon them. **1706** *Lond. Gaz.* No. 4243/1 We made..great fire all Night with our Cannon. **1709** STEELE *Tatler* No. 80 ¶9 The Charge began with the Fire of Bombs and Grenades. **1815** SCOTT *Paul's Lett.* (1839) 112 One fire..struck down seven men of the square. **1816** *Sporting Mag.* XLVIII. 237 A learned Barrister was practising a fire at a mark. **1847** MARRYAT *Childr. N. Forest* iv, You shall have the first fire. **1855** MACAULAY *Hist. Eng.* IV. 280 Most of Mackay's men had never before been under fire. **1859** F. A. GRIFFITHS *Artil. Man.* (1862) 248 *A direct fire* from a battery is when the line of fire is perpendicular to the parapet. **1885** *Times* 20 Feb. 5/6 He was about to find himself placed between two fires—viz. the Mahdi and the reinforced garrison of Metammeh.

fig. **1792** BURKE *Corr.* (1844) IV. 17 If they have received the fire of the grand juries with a good countenance. **1848** THACKERAY *Gt. Hoggarty Diam.* ix, Miss Belinda opening the fire, by saying she understood Mrs. Hoggarty had been

calumniating her. **1886** 'MARK TWAIN' *Lett. to Publishers* 19 Mar. (1967) 196 It isn't good policy for anybody connected with our publishing firm to be under a fire of newspaper criticism this year. **1965** *New Statesman* 19 Mar. 430/3 Their chief..has recently been under fire because it appeared he had joined the Nazi Party in his student days. **1968** *Time* 17 May 66 University ties with IDA have also come under fire at Columbia.

b. *false fire*: see FALSE *a.* 14 b. ***reverse, running fire***: see the adjs. Also transf. ***Kentish fire***, a mode of applauding by 'volleys' of handclapping, etc.: see KENTISH.

c. ***to hang, miss fire***: see the vbs.

15. *Cricket.* Tendency (of a ball) to fly up erratically or (of the ground) to cause the ball to fly up.

1888 A. G. STEEL in Steel & Lyttelton *Cricket* iii. 161 A good long run..gets way and 'fire' on to the ball. **1897** K. S. RANJITSINHJI *Jubilee Bk. Cricket* 70 Coming from a high elevation, a ball..has more fire or 'devil' in it. *Ibid.* 80 There is something to be done with the ball when..the wicket has fire in it.

B. Fire- in *Comb.*

I. General relations.

1. attributive. **a.** *gen.* (sense 1), as ***fire-chariot, -colour, -crag, -flame, -flash, -flood, -folk, -glance, hazard, -heat, †-leme, -mist, -ordeal, -season, -stream***; (sense 3), as ***fire-beacon, -blaze, -coal, -glow, -link, season, -shine, -signal***; (sense 14), as ***fire-shock***.

1804 *Edin. Rev.* III. 430 The Amonian *firebeacons. **1605** VERSTEGAN *Dec. Intell.* iii. (1628) 80 A torch, or as they terme it a *fire-blase. **1849** SOUTHEY *Comm.-pl. Bk.* II. 391 Elijah dropping his cloak as the *fire-chariot carries him away. **1640** *Witt's Recreations, Epit., On a Candle*, And with it a *fire-coale. *a* **1672** P. S[TERRY] *Wks.* (1710) II. 283 The Fire-Coals, which our Saviour taught his Disciples to cast on their Enemies. **1802** BEDDOES *Hygëia* v. 17 *P.* How hot! *N.* She has been like a fire-coal these two hours. **1811** PINKERTON *Petral.* II. 96 One pretty large, of the scarce *fire-colour with the purple tinge. **1821** SHELLEY *Prometh. Unb.* IV. 333 My cloven *fire-crags. **1817** COLERIDGE *Sibyl. Leaves* (1828) II. 304 The shadows..By the still dancing *fire-flames made. **1586** FETHERSTONE (*title*), Brutish Thunderbolt, or rather Feeble- *Fier-Flash of Pope Sixtus the Fift, against Henrie..of Navarre. **1632** LITHGOW *Trav.* I. 35 Earthquakes, thunder, and fire-flashes. **1842** BARHAM *Ingol. Leg., Smuggler's Leap*, The fire-flash shines from Reculver cliff. **1821** JOANNA BAILLIE *Metr. Leg., Wallace* xxvi, To see the *fire-flood in their rear. **1877** G. M. HOPKINS *Poems* (1918) 26 O look at all the *fire-folk sitting in the air! *a* **1835** MRS. HEMANS *Poems, League of Alps* iv, Where the sun's red *fire-glance earliest fell. **1907** *Westm. Gaz.* 18 Dec. 2/3 What's amiss with the *fire-glow, what is awry with the light? **1926** *Daily Colonist* (Victoria, B.C.) 8 July 4/1 Logging methods such as will tend to reduce the *fire hazard that now prevails. **1935** *Discovery* Nov. 316/2 The film used will be of the safety type, which presents somewhat less fire hazard than ordinary newsprint. **1823** J. BADCOCK *Dom. Amusem.* 65 *Fire-heat at 212° of Fahrenheit produced detonation. *a* **1000** *Satan* 128 (Gr.) *Fyrleoma stod ȝeond þæt atole scræf. **1494** FABYAN *Chron.* VII. ccxxiv. 250 Many..vncouthe syghtes were this yere seen in Englonde, as hostis of men fyghtyng in the skye, & fyre lemys. **1579–80** NORTH *Plutarch* (1676) 884 Tying Torches of *Fire-links unto their horns. **1875** G. H. LEWES *Problems* II. 393 We begin an inquiry which may lead back to the primeval *fire-mist. **1878** W. JAMES *Coll. Ess. & Rev.* (1920) 47 Back of him [*sc.* the polyp] lay the not-yet-polyp, and, back of all, the universal mother, fire-mist. **1711** SHAFTESB. *Charac.* (1737) III. 41 That new kind of *fire-ordeal. **1892** *Work* IV. 58/1 The mantleshelf in the '*fire season' is the dustiest place in the room. **1901** *Wide World Mag.* VIII. 194/2 The long grass was as inflammable as tinder; but this not being the 'fire' season we anticipated no danger. **1871** ROSSETTI *Poems, My sister's sleep* v, By vents the *fireshine drove And reddened. **1824** J. SYMMONS tr. *Æschylus' Agam.* 31 *note*, This description of the *fire-signals is very finely imagined. **1811** W. J. HOOKER *Iceland* (1813) II. 142 The *fire-stream over-ran the southern district.

b. Of or pertaining to the worship of fire, as ***fire-deity, -god, -spirit, -temple***. Also FIRE-WORSHIP, -WORSHIPPER.

1871 TYLOR *Prim. Cult.* II. xvi. 252 A distinct *fire-deity. *Ibid.* 253 The *Fire-spirit. **1815** MOORE *Lalla R.* (1817) 260 By the *Fire-God's shrine. **1741** D. WRAY in *Athen. Lett.* (1792) II. 470 He will..lay the foundation of a *fire-temple.

c. In the names of various receptacles for burning fuel, as ***fire-bag, -basket, -cage, -chauffer***.

1843 PORTLOCK *Geol.* 682 On the outside [of the kiln]..a niche is formed to receive the fuel, and is called a *fire-bag. **1855** H. CLARKE *Dict.*, **Fire-basket*, portable grate. **1874** KNIGHT *Dict. Mech.* I. 862/2 **Fire-cage*, a skeleton box or basket of iron for holding lighted fuel. **1558** *Inv. R. Hyndmer* in *Wills & Inv.* (Surtees) 162, Ij *fyer chavffers.

d. Pertaining to the fire of a hearth or furnace, as ***fire-bellows, -block, -blower, -brush, -cheek, †-cricket, -door, -grate, -nook, -rake, -set, †-stock, -stove***.

c **1475** *Pict. Voc.* in Wr.-Wülcker 779 *Hoc reposilium*, a *fyirbelowys. **1836** F. MAHONEY *Rel. Father Prout* ii. (1859) 247, I..made the kindling *fireblocks shine. **1884** *Health Exhib. Catal.* 65/1 Patent *Fire Blower, for..regulating the draught in ordinary grates. *a* **1745** SWIFT *Direct. Servants, Footman*, Clean away the Ashes from betwixt the Bars with the *Fire-Brush. **1884** *Health Exhib. Catal.* 82/1 *Fire Cheeks and Hearths of Marble Mosaic. **1530** PALSGR. 220/2 *Fyre crycket, *cricquet*. **1838** *Civil Engin. & Archit. Jrnl.* Sept. 326/2 It produced more steam than was required, and with the *fire-door kept open. **1859** RANKINE *Steam Engine* §304 The fire-door, which closes the mouth-piece or doorway. **1664** EVELYN *Kal. Hort* (1729) 229 Let..the *Fire-grate stand about three Feet higher than the Floor. **1840** MARRYAT *Poor Jack* xlix, I..went to the fire-grate. **1845** R. W. HAMILTON *Pop. Educ.* ii. (ed. 2) 21 Their huts are seen and their *fire-nooks exposed. **1660** HEXHAM, *Een kam-stock*, a *Fire-rake which Brewers and Bakers use. **1855** H. CLARKE *Dict.*, **Fire-set*, fire-irons. *c* **1440** *Promp. Parv.* 161/2 *Fyyr stok. **1756** TOLDERVY *Hist. Two Orph.* III. 205 He came with..his head into the *fire stove.

e. In the names of implements or instruments bearing, containing, or sending forth fire, as ***fire-arrow, -cane, -gun, -shaft, -spear, -weapon***.

1720 DE FOE *Capt. Singleton* xvii. (1840) 291 They would ..shoot *fire-arrows at you. **1809** *Naval Chron.* XXII. 374 We should indulge them..with a few shot and shell, not forgetting Congreve's fire arrows. **1887** *Graphic* 17 Dec. 662/1 He..had produced a '*fire-cane', which warmed its owner's hand, and supplied him with lighting for his cigar. **1680** H. MORE *Apocal. Apoc.* 88 They let off their *Fireguns and Pistols. **1628** (*title*), A new invention of Shooting *Fire-Shafts in Long-Bowes. **1549** *Compl. Scot.* vi. 42 Mak reddy ȝour..*fyir speyris, hail schot, lancis, pikkis. **1616** BINGHAM *Tactics Ælian* ii. 25 *note*, The *fire-weapons haue theire advantages. **1860** HEWITT *Anc. Armour* Supp. 489 The analogous fire-weapons.

f. In the names of various kinds of fireworks, as ***fire-cracker, †-lance, †-sword, †-target***.

1858 SIMMONDS *Dict. Trade*, **Fire-cracker*. **1958** *Punch* 22 Jan. 150/3 Nine weeks ago firecrackers were thrown into the gangway and among neighbouring seats. **1634** J. BATE *Myst. Nat. & Art* II. 89 The description and making of three sorts of *Fire-lances. *Ibid.* II. 88 How to make a *fire sword. *Ibid.* II. 94 How to make a *Fire-target.

g. Pertaining to a conflagration (sense 5), (*a*) *gen.* as ***fire-bell, -drum, -gown, -ladder, -loss, -shell, -telegraph, -watch, -year***; (*b*) used in kindling a conflagration, as ***fire-bavin, -fagot, -mixture***; (*c*) concerned with the extinction of a conflagration, as ***fire-apparatus, -barrow, -boat, -bucket, -call, -chief, -float, -main, -marshal*** (U.S.), ***-pipe, -pump***.

1901 *Daily Colonist* (Victoria, B.C.) 6 Oct. 2/1 Loss about $225,000, with 25 per cent. insurance. There was no *fire apparatus. **1890** *Daily News* 9 Jan. 2/5 *Fire barrows and hose were quickly on the spot. **1832** WEBSTER, **Firebavin*, a bundle of brush-wood, used in fireships. *a* **1626** MIDDLETON *Changeling* v, Buckets! ladders!.. The *fire-bell rings. **1867** DICKENS *Lett.* 22 Dec. (1880) II. 320, I have heard the fire bells dolefully clanging all over the city. **1876** *N.Y. Nautical Gaz.* in *Pract. Mag.* VI. 73 An iron *fire-boat. **1585** HIGINS *Junius' Nomenclator* 279 *Incendiarij siphones*..*Fire buckets. **1844** DICKENS *Mart. Chuz.* xxvii, Rows of fire-buckets for dashing out a conflagration in its first spark. **1897** *Daily News* 30 Nov. 5/1 Our *fire-call system in London. **1906** *Westm. Gaz.* 26 Apr. 7/1 Within a very few minutes of the fire-call being rung. **1889** *Kansas Times & Star* 21 Sept., Our gallant *fire chief was elected first vice-president. **1814** SCOTT *Wav.* xxxiv, A kind of rub-a-dub-dub like that with which the *fire-drum alarms the slumbering artizans. **1828–40** TYTLER *Hist. Scot.* (1864) I. 137 Piles of *fire-fagots, mixed with bundles of pitch and flax..were in readiness. **1887** *Daily News* 18 June 3/5 Five *fire-floats were quickly sent from ships in the harbour. **1874** MRS. WHITNEY *We Girls* xii. 249 Mrs. Hobart has a '*fire-gown'..she made it for a fire, or for illness, or any night-alarm. **1832** *Examiner* 700/1 It was 20 minutes.. before the *fire-ladders were brought. **1891** *Daily News* 30 Nov. 5/4 A professional *fire-loss assessor. **1855** H. CLARKE *Dict.*, **Fire-main*, water-pipe for occasions of conflagration. **1894** STEAD *If Christ came to Chicago* 295 *Fire-Marshal Swenie has remained in command of the firemen for many years. **1855** HEWITT *Anc. Armour* I. 90 These early *fire-mixtures. *c* **1865** LD. BROUGHAM in *Circ. Sc.* I. Introd. 6 Water..forced out of a pump, or from a *fire-pipe. **1892** *Pall Mall G.* 9 Feb. 2/1 The *fire-pump..has a throwing power of sixty feet above the highest pinnacle of the hotel. *a* **1818** M. G. LEWIS *Jrnl. W. Ind.* (1834) 70 A *fire-shell is blown, and all the negroes..hasten to give their assistance. **1694** *Acc. Sweden* 27 There is also a *Fire-Watch by Night. **1673** F. KIRKMAN *Unlucky Citizen* A iij b, The next year 1666 being the *Fire year.

2. objective (sense 1), as ***fire-bringer, -spewer, -striker, -user; fire-bearing, -belching, -breathing, -darting, -foaming, -resisting, -spitting, -using*** adjs.; (sense 3), as ***fire-holder, -keeper, -kindler, -trimmer; fire-making*** vbl. sb.; ***fire-kindling*** vbl. sb. and adj.; (sense 5), as ***fire-annihilator, -extinguisher, -extinguishing, -fighter, -fighting, -quencher, -quenching; fire-resistant*** adj.; ***fire-retardant*** adj. and sb.

1849 *Mech. Mag.* LI. 424 The so-called *Fire Annihilator of Mr. Phillips. **1853** GROTE *Greece* II. lxxxiv. XI. 153 They set fire to the city..with *fire-bearing arrows. **1591** SYLVESTER *Du Bartas* I. iv. 22 Their *Fire-breathing Horses. **1837** CARLYLE *Fr. Rev.* I. VI. i. 267 On a sudden.. rises Sansculottism, many-headed, fire-breathing. **1594** MARLOWE & NASHE *Dido* I. i, Exhal'd with thy *fire-darting beames. **1769** GOLDSM. *Hist. Rome* (1786) I. 199 The fire-darting eyes of the Romans. **1849** *Mech. Mag.* LI. 381 The patentee next describes a portable *fire-extinguisher. **1928** GALSWORTHY *Swan Song* III. xiii. 319 He..seized a fire extinguisher... He knew vaguely that you dashed the knob on the floor and sprayed the flames. **1876** *N.Y. Nautical Gaz.* in *Pract. Mag.* VI. 73 This boat and her *fire-extinguishing apparatus deserve detailed description. **1903** *Westm. Gaz.* 16 June 4/3 The 'invention' and arrangement of the display..is the work of a practical *fire-fighter of great experience..who has been for a long time the chief officer of the Hampton Fire Brigade. **1904** *Forum* Oct. 274 The most modern equipment should be at the command of the fire fighters. **1945** S. SPENDER *Citizens in War* 26 The work of fire-fighters depended greatly on the prompt reporting of fires. **1970** *Globe & Mail* (Toronto) 25 Sept. B7/2 (Advt.), A well equipped Fire Department with a present strength of over 80 Fire Fighters. **1897** L. J. GAGE in *Open Court* XI. 213 The *fire-fighting force is divided into 109 companies. **1897** *Westm. Gaz.* 22 Nov. 9/1 Chemical engines, water-towers, and other time-saving and fire-fighting apparatus. **1903** *Daily Chron.* 5 May 7/1 The present week is an interesting one in the history of fire-fighting. **1959** *Times Rev. Industry* Sept. 50/1 The standard of fire-fighting equipment has improved. **1971** *Guardian* 7 July 1/8 Fire fighting equipment..must be available. **1565** GOLDING *Ovid's Met.* II. (1593) 31 His *fier-foming steedes..They take from manger trimly dight. **1872** H. W. TAUNT *Map Thames* 49/1 A frying-pan, pot, and kettle, all to fit a *fireholder. **1881** GREENER *Gun* (ed. 2) 45 These fire-holders were usually attached to the girdle. **1873** L. WALLACE *Fair God* v. iv. 278 When my sword is at the throats of the *fire-keepers [of an Aztec temple]. **1643** [ANGIER] *Lanc. Vall. Achor* 21 To darken and smother the *fire-kindlers. **1849** E. C. OTTÉ tr. *Humboldt's Cosmos* II. 508 *note*, The 'fire-kindler', Prometheus. *Ibid.*, The *fire-kindling Titan on the Caucasus. **1884** Q. VICTORIA *More Leaves* 107 Brown begged I would drink to the '*fire-kindling'. *c* **1386** CHAUCER *Can. Yeom. Prol. & T.* 369 Som sayd it was long on the *fuyr-makyng. **1865** TYLOR *Early Hist. Man.* ix. 228 The art of fire-making. **1690** NORRIS *Beatitudes* (1692) 178 The business of a *Fire-quencher, who..may..rescue the pile of building from the devouring Flames. **1718** J. CHAMBERLAYNE *Relig. Philos.* (1730) II. xvii. §25 The Pumps in a *Fire-quenching Engine. **1902** *Science* 12 Sept. 424 The treatment of wood with a view of making it *fire-resistant is not a matter of recent years. **1946** *Nature* 19 Oct. 462/2 The treatment of the boards to render them fire-resistant. **1612** STURTEVANT *Metallica* (1854) 116 Maintained with such *fier-resisting meanes that it cannot possibly melte or burne down. **1850** CHUBB *Locks & Keys* 24 Safes which were sold as fire-resisting. **1915** *Proc. Nat. Fire Protection Assoc., 19th Ann. Meeting* 108 There is nothing new in the idea of treating wood to make it *fire retardant. **1952** *Dict. Fire Technol.* (Inst. Fire Engin.) (Advt.), 'Faspos' fire retardants for fireproofing wood. **1961** *Engineering* 6 Oct. 447/2 The properties of bentonite as a fire retardant. **1962** *Punch* 17 Oct. 560/3 A wise pilot dips his overalls in fire-retardant liquid. **1483** *Cath. Angl.* 132/1 A *Fire spewer, *igniuomus*. **1631** T. FULLER *David's Heinous Sin* xxxix, *Fire-spitting cannons. **1483** *Cath. Angl.* 132/1 A *Fire stryker, *fugillator*. **1891** *Daily News* 26 Sept. 2/5 Prisoner and Jensen joined the ship..as *fire-trimmers. **1865** TYLOR *Early Hist. Man.* ix. 235 Any known race of *fire-users. **1862** D. WILSON *Preh. Man* v. (1865) 82 Man is peculiarly *fire-using.

3. a. instrumental, locative, and originative, as ***fire-baptism; fire-armed, -baptized, -bellied, -born, -burning, -burnt, -clad, †-coached, -cracked, -crowned, -footed, -gilt, †-given, -hardened, -hoofed, -lighted, -lipped, -lit, -marked, -mouthed, pitted, -robed, -scarred, -scathed, -scorched, -seamed, -shot, -swept, -tinged, -warmed, -wheeled, -winged, -wrought*** adjs.

1598 SYLVESTER *Du Bartas* II. i. I. *Eden* 249 A *fire-arm'd Dragon. **1682** DRYDEN & LEE *Dk. of Guise* III. i, I'll meet him now, though fire-armed cherubins Should cross my way. **1831** CARLYLE *Sart. Res.* II. vii, My Spiritual New-birth, or Baphometic *Fire-baptism. *Ibid.* II. viii, The *fire-baptized soul..here feels its own Freedom. **1892** *Daily News* 5 May 5/4 The little '*fire-bellied toad', of.. poisonous properties. **1846** R. CHAMBERS *Vestiges Creat.* vi. (ed. 5) 95 The numerous upbursts and intrusions of *fire-born rock. *c* **1275** *Death* 216 in *O.E. Misc.* (1872) 180 Swo he me wule for-swolehen þe *fur-berninde drake. *c* **1290** *S. Eng. Leg.* I. 290/86 *Fur-barnd he was þoru Iuggemont. **1573** TWYNE *Æneid* XI. Kk iij, Poales of length firebrent at end. **1615** SYLVESTER *Hymne Almes* 55 The *Fire-Coacht Prophet. **1836–48** B. D. WALSH *Aristoph., Acharnians* IV. ii, It rings With a harsh jar, like *fire-cracked things. **1870** TENNYSON *Window* 151 The *fire-crown'd king of the wrens. **1565** GOLDING *Ovid's Met.* II. (1593) 39 My *firefooted horse. **1613** CHAPMAN *Rev. Bussy D'Ambois* Plays 1873 II. 148 Hee draue as if a fierce and *fire-giuen Canon Had spit his iron vomit out amongst them. **1627** MAY *Lucan* III. 536 (1635) E iij b, Stakes, and *fire harden'd oaks. **1621** G. SANDYS *Ovid's Met.* II. 393 Those *fire-hooft steeds. **1850** LYNCH *Theo. Trin.* v. 80 A..*fire-lighted room. **1839** BAILEY *Festus* iv. (1848) 33 Mountain, and wood, and wild, and *fire-lipped hill. **1849** MISS MULOCK *Ogilvies* (1875) 109 The pleasant *fire-lit room. **1705** *Lond. Gaz.* No. 4114/4 A brown Mare..*fire-marked I.I. in the near Buttock. **1590** SPENSER *F.Q.* I. ix, 52 That *fire-mouth'd Dragon. **1759** MOUNTAINE in *Phil. Trans.* LI. 290 The sheets..[were] scorched and *fire-pitted in like manner. **1611** SHAKS. *Wint. T.* IV. iv. 29 The *Fire-roab'd-God Golden Apollo. **1853** KINGSLEY *Hypatia* xiii. 147 A doleful *fire-scarred tower. **1848** MRS. JAMESON *Sacr. & Leg. Art* (1850) 64 Swarthy red, as if *fire-scathed. *a* **1892** WHITTIER *Poet. Works* (1898) 309/1 The *fire-scorched stones. **1815** MILMAN *Fazio* (1821) 79 Thy..*fire-seamed visage. **1927** *Observer* 18 Dec. 19/3 Mr. Richard Goolden's *fire-shot devil. **1898** G. B. SHAW *Man of Destiny* in *Plays Pleasant & Unpleasant* II. 155 Napoleon Bonaparte.. rushed the *fireswept bridge. **1930** BLUNDEN *Poems* 40 The naked fire-swept windows. **1907** *Daily Chron.* 19 Sept. 4/4 The dark pines..dripped *fire-tinged dews. **1856** KANE *Arct. Expl.* I. xv. 173 Our only *fire-warmed apartment. **1822** MILMAN *Martyr of Antioch* 121 His *fire-wheel'd throne. **1591** SYLVESTER *Du Bartas* I. ii. 656 Then like a Squib it falls, Or *fire-wing'd shaft. **1826** MILMAN *A. Boleyn* (1827) 41 The fire-wing'd ministers of Heaven's just wrath. *a* **1892** WHITTIER *Poet. Works* (1898) 324/2 Its *fire-wrought language. **1905** *Daily Chron.* 9 Dec. 8/1 Mr. Jones's fire-wrought temperament.

b. In names of occupations, processes, etc., carried on by the aid of fire, as ***†fire-trade; fire-fishing, -gilding, -offering, -polishing, -silvering*** vbl. sbs. Also forming verbs, as ***fire-hollow***.

1831 J. HOLLAND *Manuf. Metal* I. 295 Persons employed in *fire-gilding. **1864** TENNYSON *En. Ard.* 570 Enoch's comrade..*Fire-hollowing this in Indian fashion, fell Sun-stricken. *c* **1870** J. G. MURPHY *Comm. Lev.* i. 9 A *fire-offering; a firing, or offering made by fire. **1849** PELLATT *Curios. Glass Making* 31 By rewarming, technically called *fire polishing, the glass preserves its refractive brilliancy.

1621 BURTON *Anat. Mel.* Democr. to Rdr. (1657) 63 *Fire-trades, as Smiths, Forge-men [etc.].

4. parasynthetic and similative, as ***fire-angry***, ***-bright***, ***-burning***, ***-flowing***, ***-hearted***, ***-like***, ***-opalescent***, ***-souled***, ***-spirited***, ***-swift***, ***-tongued*** adjs.

c **1489** CAXTON *Sonnes of Aymon* xxii. 476, I am well sure that Charlemagne shall wexe *fyre angry for it. **1916** A. HUXLEY *Burning Wheel* 15 My *fire-bright window-pane. **1562** COOPER *Answ. Priv. Masse* (Parker Soc.) 66 But your scalding hot and *fireburning charity may be more justly charged with the continuance thereof. **1820** SHELLEY *Vis. Sea* 19 Like whirlpools of *fire-flowing iron. **1902** *Westm. Gaz.* 24 Feb. 2/3 Each minute *Fire-hearted followed. **1931** V. WOOLF *Waves* 319 The watery fire-hearted jewel. **1567** MAPLET *Gr. Forest* 56 The Peare tree..is called Pyrus, for that it is in his fashion and kinde of growth, Piramidall or *firelike. **1875** TENNYSON *Q. Mary* I. v, I'll have it burnish'd firelike. **1882** MYERS *Renewal of Youth, etc.* 94 *Fire-opalescent wilderness! **1876** SWINBURNE *Erechth.* (ed. 2) 47 Wrath of a *fire-souled king. **1839** BAILEY *Festus* xvii. (1848) 159 Things hidden, seen alone by eyes *Fire-spirited. **1876** SWINBURNE *Erechth.* (ed. 2) 16 *Fire-swift wheels That whirl the four-yoked chariot. *a* **1892** WHITTIER *Poet. Works* (1898) 486/2 The *fire-tongued miracle.

II. Special comb.

5. a. fire-action, the action of firing, *esp.* skirmishing in line; **fire-adjuster** (see quot.); **fire-alarm**, (*a*) an automatic arrangement by which notice of fire is given, also *attrib.*; (*b*) *N. Amer.* a warning of fire; **fire-altar**, 'an altar upon which burnt sacrifices were offered, as distinguished from one used for incense only' (*Cent. Dict.* Suppl. 1909); † **fire-amel**, enamel produced by fire; **fire-ant** (see quots.); **fire assay** *U.S.*, an assay in which intense heat is applied to a material; **fire-back**, (*a*) the back wall of a furnace or fire-place; (*b*) a pheasant of the genus *Euplocamus* (*E. ignitus*); hence ***fire-backed*** adj. (*Cent. Dict.*); **fire-balloon**, a balloon whose buoyancy is derived from the heat of a flaming combustible suspended at its mouth; **fire-bank** (see quot.); **fire-bar**, one of the iron bars of a grate or of a boiler furnace; **fire-barrel**, a cylinder filled with combustibles, used in fire-ships; **fire-bay** *Mil.*, a trench with a concealed parapet from which firing takes place; **fire-beater** (for *-beeter*: see BEET *v.* II) *dial*, a stoker; **fire-bill** (see quot.); **fire-blast**, a disease of certain plants, giving them a scorched appearance; **fire-blight**, (*a*) a disease of hops; (*b*) (chiefly *U.S.*), a bacterial disease affecting (esp. pear and apple) trees, producing a scorched appearance of the leaves; **fire-blitz**, an air attack with incendiary bombs; so ***fire-blitzed*** ppl. a.; **fire-board**, (*a*) a board used to close up a fireplace in summer, a chimney board; (*b*) (see quot. 1883); **fire-boat** = FIRE-SHIP 1; **fire-bolt**, a thunderbolt; hence ***fire-bolted*** adj., struck with lightning; **fire-bomb**, an incendiary bomb; hence as *v. trans.*, to attack or destroy with these bombs; also **fire-bombing** *vbl. sb.*; † **fire-bome** (? *bome* = BOMB *sb.* 1), a beacon; **fire-boom** *Naut.* (see quot. 1867); **fire-boss** (*N. Amer.*) *Mining* (see quot.; cf. FIREMAN 5); **fire-bottle**, an early application of phosphorus for the purpose of fire-lighting; **fire-break** orig. *N. Amer.*, an obstacle to the spread of (grass or forest) fires, as cleared or ploughed land; also *fig.*; **fire-brick**, a brick capable of withstanding intense heat without fusion, also *attrib.*; **fire-bridge** (see quot. 1874); † **fire-brief**, a circular letter asking assistance for sufferers by fire; **fire-brigade**, an organized body of firemen; also *fig.*; † **fire-broil**, the heat of a conflagration; **fire-bug** (*U.S.*), an incendiary; † **fire-cane** (see quot. 1644); **fire-cask**, a cask of water, provided as a resource against fire on board ship; **fire certificate**, a certificate issued by a local authority, confirming that the current statutory fire precautions have been complied with at the premises inspected; **fire-chamber** (see quot.); † **fire-chemise** (see quot.); **fire-churn** = *fire-drill*; **fire-clay**, a clay capable of resisting great heat, used for fire-bricks, etc.; **fire-club**, † (*a*) a kind of firework; (*b*) *U.S.* a club of firemen (?); **fire-cock**, a cock or spout to give water to extinguish a fire; † **fire-coffer**, a kind of fireship; **fire-company**, (*a*) a fire-brigade; (*b*) a fire insurance company; **fire-control**, the regulation or control of the fire of guns (esp. in batteries); also, the station from which a commanding or gunnery officer may exercise such control; **fire-crack**, a crack formed by heat, *spec.* in metal when it is being reheated or annealed; hence **fire-cracking** *vbl. sb.*; **fire-crome** = FIRE-HOOK a; **fire-crook** = FIRE-HOOK; **fire-cure** *v. trans.*, to cure (tobacco or leather) over a fire; hence ***fire-cured*** ppl. a., ***fire-curing*** vbl. sb.; **fire-curtain**, (*a*) a fire-proof curtain in a theatre, etc.; (*b*) *Mil.* = CURTAIN *sb.*[1] 3 b; **fire-department**, (*a*) the department in an insurance office which deals with insurances against fire; (*b*) *U.S.* a body of firemen; **fire-discipline** *Mil.*, the training of men to fire exactly as directed by the commander, so that the work of a unit is co-ordinated; **fire-dog** = ANDIRON; † **fire-dragon** = FIRE-DRAKE; **fire-drill**, (*a*) the name given by Tylor to a primitive contrivance, consisting of an obtuse-pointed stick which is twirled between the hands with the point in a hole in a flat piece of soft wood till fire is produced; hence ***fire-drilling*** vbl. sb.; (*b*) the rehearsal of action to be taken in the event of fire; **fire dropper**, a man who removes the fire from the fire-box of a locomotive at the end of a journey; **fire-edge**, *lit.* the edge of a weapon hardened in the fire; hence *fig.* (now only *dial.*) fire, spirit, 'freshness'; **fire-escape**, an apparatus for facilitating the escape of persons from a building on fire; **fire-fan**, (*a*) a small hand fire-screen (*obs.*); (*b*) (see quot. 1874); **fire-fiend**, (*a*) fire personified as an evil spirit of destruction; (*b*) a fire-god; (*c*) an incendiary (*colloq.*); **fire-fight** *Mil.*, the struggle to establish fire superiority over the enemy; † **fire-fit** *a.*, fit for burning; **fire-flag**, (*a*) a meteoric flame; (*b*) a flag of distress, when a ship is on fire; **fire-flair**, the sting-ray, *Trygon Pastinaca* or *Raia Pastinaca*; † **fire-flyer**, a kind of firework; **fire-free** *a.*, safe from fire, fire-proof; **fire-grappling**, a grappling iron with which to capture fireships; **fire-guard**, (*a*) a wire frame or semicircular railing put in front of a fireplace, to keep children or others from accidental injury; also a grating placed before the bars of a fire to prevent the coals from falling out; (*b*) *N. Amer.* a member of a fire-brigade or fire-watching group; (*c*) *N. Amer.* = *fire-break*; **fire-guard** *v. trans.*, to surround (land) with a *fire-guard* (*c*); **fire hall** *N. Amer.*, a fire station; **fire-hat** *U.S.*, a hat for a fireman; **fire-hole**, (*a*) a furnace; (*b*) (see quot. 1835); † **fire-hoop**, a hoop made of brushwood steeped in tar, etc., set on fire and thrown into an enemy's ship; **fire-hose**, a hose-pipe for conveying water to a fire; **fire-insurance**, insurance against losses by fire; also *attrib.*; **fire-isle**, a volcanic island; **fire-junk**, a kind of fireship; **fire-king**, (*a*) fire personified as a monarch; (*b*) a champion fire-eater; **fire-lamp**, *Mining*, a basket of burning coals used (*a*) to give light to banksmen where gas is not used, (*b*) to create a draught; **fire-lighter**, (*a*) one who kindles a fire; (*b*) material for lighting fires; **fire-line** = *fire-break*; **fire-lute**, a composition or lute capable of resisting great heat; **fire-maker**, one who lights or makes fire or a fire; **fire-marble**, *Min.* = LUMACHELLA; **fire-mark**, the mark left by a branding-iron; **fire-measure** = PYROMETER; **fire-money**, a payment for firing at school; † **fire-night**, a night round the fire-side; **fire-opal**, a variety of opal showing flame-coloured internal reflections; **fire-piece**, (*a*) = FIRE-ARM; (*b*) a picture having as its subject a fire; **fire-pile**, a pile of wood on which a person is burnt to death, or a corpse is cremated; **fire-piston**, a device for making fire (see quot. 1951); **fire-plough** (see quots.); **fire-plug**, a contrivance for connecting a hose, or the supply-pipe of a fire-engine, with a water-main in case of fire; **fire-policy**, the official certificate received from an insurance office, guaranteeing the payment of a certain sum in the case of loss of property by fire; **fire-porr**, **fire-prong** *dial.*, a poker; **fire position** *Mil.*, a position from which fire is opened by an attacking force during an advance; **fire-power** *Mil.*, the total effectiveness of the fire of guns, missiles, etc., of a military force; **fire-raft**, a raft for setting an enemy's shipping on fire; **fire-raid**, an air-raid with incendiary bombs; **fire-ranger** *N. Amer.*, an official who keeps watch against the occurrence of forest fires; **fire-risk**, (*a*) the risk of loss by fire; (*b*) the obligation of a fire-insurance company to make good loss by fire; (*c*) property insured against fire; **fire-roll** (*Naut.*), a peculiar beat of the drum on an alarm of fire; **fire-room**, (*a*) a room containing a fire-place; (*b*) a furnace-room of a building or stokehold of a ship; † **fire-salt** *a.*, pungently salt; **fire-setting**, the softening or cracking of the working-face of a lode, to facilitate excavation, by exposing it to a wood fire built close against it (Raymond *Mining Gloss.*); † **fire-snort** *a.*, sending forth fire through the nose; **fire-spout**, a jet of volcanic fire (cf. *waterspout*); **fire-sprit** (*dial.*) = FIRE-BRAND; † **fire-spy**, one who is on the look out for a fire; **fire station**, the headquarters of a fire brigade, housing fire engines, etc; **fire-steel** (see quot.): **fire-step** = *firing-step*; **fire-stick**, (*a*) a burning brand; (*b*) = *fire-drill*; (*c*) an implement used for stirring up a fire; **fire-stink**, *Mining* (see quot. 1881); **fire-stop**, a device designed to stop the spread of fire; *spec.* incombustible material placed in the open parts of a structure; **fire-storm**, (*a*) *poet.*, a storm of fire; (*b*) *spec.* a high wind or storm following a conflagration caused by incendiary or nuclear bombs; **fire-swab** (*Naut.*), the wet bunch of rope-yarn used to cool a gun in action and swab up any grains of powder; **fire-swallower**, one who entertains by swallowing or pretending to swallow fire; **fire-swart** *a.*, † (*a*) blackening with fire; (*b*) blackened by fire; **fire-syringe**, a piston and cylinder employed to produce combustion by means of the heat resulting from the compression of air; **fire-teazer**, a stoker; **fire-tile**, a tile capable of resisting great heat; **fire-tower**, (*a*) a tower with a beacon on its top, serving the purpose of a light-house; (*b*) a watch-tower to guard against fires in towns; **fire-trace** = *fire-break*; **fire-trap**, a place with insufficient means of egress in case of fire; **fire-tree**, (*a*) a kind of firework; (*b*) = *flame-tree*; (*c*) in New Zealand the *Metrosideros tomentosa* (*Cent. Dict.*); **fire-trench** *Mil.*, a deep and narrow trench from which firing takes place; † **fire-trunk**, (*a*) a kind of projectile or 'fire-work'; (*b*) *Naut.* (see quots.); **fire-tube**, a pipe-flue; **fire-vessel**, (*a*) a receptacle for fire, a fire-pan; (*b*) = FIRE-SHIP; **fire-walk**, the ceremony of walking barefoot over hot stones, performed as a religious rite by the Fijians and others, and formerly as an ordeal in European countries; so **fire-walker**, **-walking**; **fire-wall** orig. *U.S.*, a fireproof wall to prevent the spreading of fire; **fire-ward**, = *fire-warden* (*a*); **fire-warden**, (*a*) *U.S.* the chief officer of a fire-brigade; (*b*) *N. Amer.*, an official concerned with the prevention or extinction of fires; **fire-watcher**, (*a*) one who tends a fire; (*b*) one who is engaged in fire-watching; **fire-watching** *vbl. sb.*, keeping on the alert, esp. at night, to watch for and report the occurrence or spread of fires, esp. those caused by aerial bombardment; hence **fire-watch** *v. intr.*, † **fire-waterwork**, the name given by the Marquess of Worcester to a rude steam-engine which he invented; **fire-well** (see quot.); † **fire-wheel**, a kind of fire-work, a catherine-wheel; **fire-wind** = *fire-storm* (*b*); **fire-woman**, a woman member of a fire brigade; **fire-worm**, (*a*) = FIRE-FLY; (*b*) a glow-worm; **fire-wreath** = *fire-hoop*; **fire-zone**, an area swept by gunfire.

1875 CLERY *Min. Tact.* ix. 100 *Fire-action was the actual means of victory. **1882** SALA *Amer. Revis.* (1885) 229 *note*, A '*Fire Adjuster' is a gentleman..who is continually ..'adjusting' claims for losses by fire. **1849** *Mech. Mag.* LI. 425 A difficulty which has proved fatal to all our *fire alarms. **1874** KNIGHT *Dict. Mech.* I. 849/2 *Fire-alarm Telegraph.* **1876** *Wide Awake* (Boston, Mass.) Apr. 262/1 The three churchbells that give the fire alarm. **1921** *Daily Colonist* (Victoria, B.C.) 7 Apr. 9/4 Fire Chief Parkin reported the department had answered four fire alarms during the month of March. **1926** 'M. LEINSTER' *Dew on Leaf* 30 *Fire-altar wreathed in clouds of incense. **1935** *Burlington Mag.* Jan. 30/1 The fire-altar on the coinage of the later Kushan princelings. **1423** JAS. I *Kingis Q.* xlviii, Hir nek, quhite as the *fyre amaille. **1796** STEDMAN *Surinam* II. xx. 91 Small emmets, called here *fire-ants, from their painful biting. **1863** BATES *Nat. Amazon* ix. (1864) 241 Fire-ants (*formiga de fogo*) under the floors. **1869** C. L. BRACE *New West* 167 Mills..guarantee 75 per cent. returns on the *fire assay. **1847** *Rep. Comm. Patents 1846* (U.S.) 249 The *fire-backs of fireplaces have been made separate. **1862** WOOD *Illustr. Nat. Hist.*, Birds 613 The very handsome Fireback is an Asiatic bird, inhabiting Sumatra. **1874** KNIGHT *Dict. Mech.* I. 862/1 *Fire-back.* **1822** IMISON *Sc. & Art* I. 170 *Fire-balloons, or those raised by heated air. **1847** TENNYSON *Princ.* Prol. 74 A fire-balloon Rose gem-like. **1888** J. PAYN *Myst. Mirbridge* ix, A fire-balloon which he had sent up on a Guy Fawkes' Day. **1883** GRESLEY *Gloss. Coal Mining*, **Fire-bank*, a spoil-bank which takes fire spontaneously. **1703** MOXON *Mech. Exerc.* 13 A course sort of Iron..fit for *Fire-bars. **1844** *Proc. Inst. Civ. Eng.* III. 312 The fuel is spread over a large surface of fire-bar [in a furnace]. **1881** F. CAMPIN *Mech. Engineering* xii. 168 At *a* are fire-bars forming the grate. **1704** *Lond. Gaz.* No. 4082/3 Throwing down *Fire-Barrels. **1917** *Chambers's Jrnl.* Mar. 174/1 They look for the *firebays, which are, of course, on the German side. **1940** J. BROPHY *Home Guard* 64 In a fire-trench, to be manned with rifles and machine-guns, the sections facing the expected advance of the enemy are known as fire-bays. **1883** *Manch. Guardian* 17 Oct. 5/2 A determined attempt was made by a *firebeater..to murder his wife. **1867** SMYTH *Sailor's Word-bk.*, **Fire-bill*, the distribution of the officers and crew in the case of the alarm of fire. **1727** DESAGULIERS in *Phil. Trans.* XXXIV. 269 *Fire-Blasts..may be occasion'd by Solar Rays reflected from, or condens'd by Clouds. **1824** FORSYTH *Fruit Trees* xxvii. 373 This is what

is called a fire-blast. **1750** Ellis *Mod. Husbandm.* IV. i. vi. 74 They [hops] are subject to the..*Fire-blight, and the Mould or Dwindle. **1817** W. Coxe *View Cult. Fruit Trees* 175 The fire blight frequently destroys [pear] trees. **1869** *Trans. Ill. Agric. Soc.* VII. 503 There are several distinct diseases, all grouped together under the general name of 'Fire Blight'. **1958** *New Scientist* 20 Nov. 1301/1 The recent outbreak of Fire Blight in this country is alarming... It is caused by a bacterium, *Erwinia amylovora*, that usually attacks the fruit trees in the spring. **1941** A. O. Pollard *Bombers over Reich* vi. 64 This total of fire-bombs seemed to be the mark, in Nazi eyes, of a super '*fire-blitz'. **1940** *Daily Express* 31 Dec., The *fireblitzed area. *a* **1828** D. Wordsworth *Tour Continent* in *Jrnls.* (1941) II. 316 She replied 'Oh Madame! you will soon be warm here!' taking down a *fire-board. **1855** H. Clarke *Dict.*, *Fire-board*, chimney-board. **1883** Gresley *Gloss. Coal Mining*, *Fire-board*, a piece of board with the word *fire* painted upon it.. to caution men and lads not to take a naked light beyond it. **1885** A. T. Slosson in *Harper's Mag.* Apr. 804/1 There was a..fire-place, but it was closed by a fire-board. **1826** Mrs. Shelley *Last man* II. ii. 51 *Fire-boats were launched from the various ports. **1583** Stanyhurst *Æneis, etc.* (Arb.) 137 A clapping *fyerbolt (such as oft, with rownce robel hobble, Ioue toe the ground clattreth). **1832** Bryant *Hurricane* 37 As the fire-bolts leap to the world below. **1839** Bailey *Festus* (1848) 16/2 The root of oak *firebolted. **1895** G. Griffith *Outlaws of Air* xxiii. 207 The conflagration that his *fire-bombs had started. **1940** *Flight* 24 Oct. 339/2 Many fire-bombs were dropped, as well as high explosives. **1970** *Guardian* 14 May 2/4 More than twenty buildings have been fire-bombed. **1966** *Economist* 30 July 442/3 The disorders were mostly confined to the hit-and-run *fire-bombing.. and to isolated shooting incidents. **1969** K. Vonnegut *Slaughterhouse-Five* v. 87 The greatest massacre in European history..was the fire-bombing of Dresden. *c* **1440** *Promp. Parv.* 29 Beekne or *fyre-bome, *far* (*pharus* P.). **1769** Falconer *Dict. Marine* (1789), In which sense it [*boute dehors*] is usually called *fire-boom. **1867** Smyth *Sailor's Word-bk.*, *Fire-booms*, long spars swung out from a ship's side to prevent the approach of fire-ships..or vessels accidentally on fire. **1883** Gresley *Gloss. Coal Mining*, **Fire-bosses* (U.S.A.), underground officials who examine the mine for gas, and inspect every safety-lamp taken into the colliery. **1898** 'R. Connor' *Black Rock* 87 Mr. Shaw, fire-boss of the mines. **1955** J. S. Gowland *Smoke over Sikanaska* x. 180 There's a Greek who used to be a fire boss in the mine. **1823** J. Badcock *Dom. Amusem.* 122 A most useful application of phosphorus..is the art of making the *fire bottle, that affords immediate light. **1841** *Newfoundland Ho. Assembly Jrnl.* App. 178 The lane opposite Messrs. Codner & Jennings's *firebreak. **1885** *Boston* (Mass.) *Jrnl.* 26 Sept. 4/1 Fears are entertained for the safety of the town, and teams are out plowing fire-breaks around it. **1930** Billis & Kenyon *Pastures New* viii. 120 Large areas of grass were often saved by burning fire-breaks ..round extensive sections of good grass land. **1934** *Bulletin* (Sydney) 17 Oct. 20/3 Doesn't 'T. T.' know that a firebreak is always burnt against the wind? **1935** *Discovery* Mar. 64/1 Fire-breaks are..left open in the new plantations. **1959** *Economist* 31 Jan. 391/1 Independence behind a firebreak of Belgian..paternalism. **1965** H. A. Kissinger *Probl. Nat. Strategy* vi. 120 His [*sc.* A. C. Enthoven's] basic argument is that the most reliable 'fire break' is between conventional and nuclear weapons and that once that threshold is crossed, rapid escalation is probable. **1793** *Trans. Soc. Encourag. Arts* IV. 123 Let the whole of the cylinder..be lined with *fire bricks. **1865** *Daily Tel.* 21 Oct. 5/1 The fire-brick footway. **1854** Ronalds & Richardson *Chem. Technol.* I. 263 Admitting a current of air behind, or through the *fire-bridge. **1874** Knight *Dict. Mech.* I. 862/2 *Fire-bridge*, a plate or wall at the back of the furnace to..prevent the fuel being carried over. *a* **1643** W. Cartwright *On the Great Frost* 51 We laugh at *fire-Briefs now, although they be Commended to us by his Majesty. **1838** *Penny Cycl.* X. 279 Within a few years the firemen belonging to the different insurance companies in London have been formed into a body—the *Fire Brigade. **1959** *Daily Tel.* 10 Apr. 19/2 S.E.A.T.O. will probably get the 'fire brigade' that Asian members have so long been calling for. **1583** Stanyhurst *Æneis* iii. (Arb.) 75 Then my holye domesticall housgods, In last nights *fyrebroyls, that from Troy skorched I saulued. **1872** O. W. Holmes *Poet Breakf.-t.* i. (1885) 7 Political *firebugs we call 'em. **1883** *Pall Mall G.* 6 Sept. 12/1 It is believed there exists an organized band of 'firebugs'. **1931** *Times Lit. Suppl.* 24 Sept. 719/2 An even more elusive foe of the fire office than petrol is 'the cold-blooded fire-bug' who trades in arson. **1962** *Punch* 14 Mar. 439/1 Robert Morley as a dedicated firebug is notable. **1644** Digby *2 Treat.* i. xvii. 147 Indian canes (..called *firecanes), being rubbed with some other sticke of the same nature,.. will of themselues sett on fire. **1670** Lassels *Voy. Italy* I. Pref., They bring home nothing but firecanes, parots, and Monkies. **1804** A. Duncan *Mariner's Chron.* III. 101 The only article we now wanted was water. I recollected the *fire-cask in the mizen-chains. [**1891** *Factory & Workshop Act* 54 & 55 Vict. c. 75 §7(1) Every factory of which the construction is commenced after the first day of January [1892], and in which more than forty persons are employed, shall be furnished with a certificate from the sanitary authority of the district..that the factory is provided.. above the ground floor with such means of escape in case of fire for the persons employed therein as can reasonably be required.] **1963** *Offices, Shops & Railway Premises Act* c. 41 §29(1) A certificate (hereinafter in this Act referred to as a '*fire certificate') issued..by the appropriate authority.. that the premises are provided with such means of escape in case of fire for the persons employed to work therein..as may reasonably be required. **1985** *Financial Times* 10 Apr. iv. 20 The need for a fire certificate and meeting planning requirements impose another set of demands. **1847** *Rep. Comm. Patents 1846* (U.S.) 211, I also claim the air passage below the *fire chamber. **1859** Rankine *Steam Engine* §303 In the External Furnace Boiler, the furnace or fire-chamber is wholly outside of..the water vessel or boiler. **1874** Knight *Dict. Mech.* I. 863/1 *Fire-chamber* (*Puddling*), the chamber at the end of the puddling-furnace. **1727–41** Chambers *Cycl.* s.v. *Chemise*, **Fire-Chemise* is a piece of linen cloth, steeped in a composition of..combustible matters; used at sea, to set fire to the enemy's vessel. **1865** Tylor *Early Hist. Man.* ix. 253 Churning fiercely at the *fire-churn. **1819** Rees *Cycl.* s.v., A very excellent *fire-clay. **1869** E. A. Parkes *Pract. Hygiene* (ed. 3) 309 The radiating power of the small barrack grate is aided..by a fireclay back. **1634** J. Bate *Myst. Nat. & Art* ii. 92 The description and making of two sorts of *Fire-clubs. **1826** Cushing *Newburyport* Pref., The fire-clubs and engine societies [of the town]. **1856** Emerson *Eng. Traits, Cockayne* Wks. (Bohn) II. 67 To carry the boisterous dulness of a fire-club into a polite circle. **1707** *Act 6 Anne* c. 58 §1 To the Intent such Plugs or *Fire Cocks may always upon Occasion of any Fire be opened. **1844** *Proc. Inst. Civ. Eng.* III. 318 In enclosed premises..firecocks are much to be preferred [to plugs]. **1804** *Naval Chron.* XII. 331 Four *Fire-coffers filled with combustibles. **1744** *Penna. Gaz.* 14 Dec. 4/2 The Union *Fire-Company of Philadelphia. **1792** *Fayetteville* (N.C.) *Gaz.* 16 Oct., Proposals from the Maryland Insurance Fire-company. **1832** Webster, *Fire-company*, a company of men for managing an engine to extinguish fire. **1835** *Southern Lit. Messenger* I. 259 The remaining expenses are on account of the public markets, fire companies, salaries of officers, [etc.]. **1880** *Harper's Mag.* July 208/2 Several of the members belonged to the volunteer fire-companies, then in the height of their glory. **1915** *Cincinnati Ann. Rep. 1914* 343 Temporary quarters have been provided for Fire Company No. 54. **1886** J. H. A. Macdonald *Common Sense on Parade* 118 What is wanted is the conviction in the mind of every instructor..that his men should never leave a parade without having gained something in fire discipline,—that is, that *fire control drill be one of the main points in view as a necessary part of the work to be performed on every occasion when men are being drilled, [etc.]. **1907** *Westm. Gaz.* 3 May 7/1 Stand on the deck amidships, look up at the vast tripod which supports the fire-control. *a* **1928** in C. F. S. Gamble *N. Sea Air Station* (1928) xv. 241, I had a very pleasant minute or so wondering which I was going to hit—the wireless masts or the monitor's fire-control top. **1935** *Jrnl. R. Aeronaut. Soc.* XXXIX. 875 Thirty diagrams illustrate problems of fire control arising out of attacks by fighter formations on light bombing formations. **1862** *Catal. Internat. Exhib.* II. x. 12 Cliff's patent enamelled clay retort is..adapted for the use of gas works, by its..freedom from *fire-cracks. **1898** *Engineering Mag.* XVI. 147/2 The Influence of Bismuth on Brass, and its Relation to Fire-Cracks. **1959** *Jrnl. Iron & Steel Inst.* CXCIII. 388/3 It is shown that thermal stresses were responsible for the appearance of fire-cracks. **1923** Glazebrook *Dict. Appl. Physics* V. 424/2 This '*fire-cracking' can be entirely prevented by a previous heat treatment at a much lower temperature. **1960** D. J. O. Brandt *Manuf. Iron & Steel* (ed. 2) iv. xxix. 221 *Fire-cracking*, that is, the development of a series of little crazy cracks on the surface caused by alternate heating and cooling. **1846** *Fire-croom [see crome, cromb *sb.*]. **1899** *Athenæum* 2 Sept. 329/2 The head of a great fire-hook or fire-crome was noted. *a* **1668** Davenant *Seige Rhodes* (1673) 20 The *Fire-crooks are too short! **1899** *Atlantic Monthly* LXXXIII. 758/2 The pliant sandals of *fire-cured skin. **1900** *Rep. U.S. Dept. Agric.* lxv. 34 Tobaccos that have been fire-cured, as the plug tobaccos. **1962** *Times* 12 Oct. (Standard Bank Suppl.) p. vii/3 Dark fire-cured tobacco. **1848** *Rep. Comm. Patents 1847* (U.S.) 170 *Fire-curing is not necessary. **1912** P. McKeon *Fire Prevention* 153 The proscenium arch has a *fire curtain. **1932** G. B. Shaw *Emperor & Little Girl* in *Wks.* VI. 15 These curtains..were really shells, showers of bombshells... They were called fire curtains. **1940** *War Illustr.* 19 Jan. 620/1 Two great steel fire-curtains..can be dropped in a few seconds to subdivide each of the hangars where the machines are housed thus localizing any fire outbreak. **1855** H. Clarke *Dict.*, **Fire department*, body of firemen. **1886** *Fire discipline [see *fire-control*]. **1897** *Cavalry Tactics* xvii. 121 Fire discipline must be strictly enforced, both to ensure accurate shooting at the indicated object and to control the ammunition expenditure. **1923** Kipling *Irish Guards in Great War* I. 11 Our fire-discipline, as we fell back, gave them the impression that the forest was filled with machine-guns. **1792** *Massachusetts Spy* 1 Mar. 3/1 [He] caught a *fire-dog, which he threw with such force that he knocked down one of the ruffians. **1840** Dickens *Barn. Rudge* x, The fire-dogs in the common room. **1556** *Chron. Gr. Friars* (Camden) 3 In the ayre was sene *fyere draggons and sprettes flyenge. **1865** Tylor *Early Hist. Man.* ix. 228 The use of the *fire-drill. **1911** *Daily Colonist* (Victoria, B.C.) 13 Apr. 20/1 Chief Davis submitted a report on the time occupied by the children in fire drill in clearing the school houses. **1913** J. Vaizey *College Girl* xviii. 264 [It's] the fire drill! They've had an alarm, and she's told to shut off draughts. **1959** C. V. Good *Dict. Educ.* 230/1 *Fire drill*, practice in the systematic, safe evacuation of the children and teachers..upon the sounding of the fire alarm. **1865** Tylor *Early Hist. Man.* ix. 237 It comes much nearer than '*fire-drilling' to the yet simpler process of striking fire with two pieces of split bamboo. **1898** *L'pool Weekly Courier* 9 Apr. 2/7 He was a *fire dropper—drawing the fires from locomotives. **1614** Markham *Cheap Husb.* i. ii. (1668) 29 [To put a horse to these lessons] after his *fireedge is taken away, will but bring him to a loathing of his instruction. *a* **1684** Leighton *Comm. 1 Pet.* (ed. Valpy) 388 Blunt that fire-edge upon your own hard..hearts. **1878** *Cumberld. Gloss.*, 'He gallop't his laal nag till t' fire edge was off.' **1788** *Specif. Dufour's Patent* No. 1652. 1 A Machine called a *Fire escape. **1832** *Examiner* 678/1 They..rush to the fire-escapes. *a* **1700** B. E. *Dict. Cant. Crew*, **Fire-fanns*, little Hand-Skreens for the Fire. **1706** Collier *Refl. Ridic.* 43 They praise..the Fire-Fan that is offer'd them. **1874** Knight *Dict. Mech.* I. 867/2 *Fire-fan*, a small blast apparatus adapted to a portable forge. **1815** Moore *Lalla R.* (1817) 251 'Tis he..The fellest of the *Fire-fiends' brood. **1899** *Westm. Gaz.* 23 Nov. 2/1 The excitement of a *fire-fight at short ranges. **1968** *Listener* 26 Dec. 871/2 One savage, roaring, banging, howling 'fire-fight'. **1595** Chapman *Ovid's Banq. Sence* C j b, That lye like *fire-fit blocks. **1798** Coleridge *Anc. Mar.* v. vi, A hundred *fire-flags sheen. **1879** *Ann. Reg.* 22 The red ensign reversed (fire-flag) was run up. *a* **1705** Ray *Syn. Method. Piscium* (1713) 24 *Pastinaca marina*..the *Fire-Flaire. **1861** J. Couch *Brit. Fishes* (1862) I. 74 The Torpedo and Fire flair have soft and sweet flesh. **1799** G. Smith *Laboratory* I. 30 Charges for *fire-flyers and wheels. **1650** Fuller *Pisgah* ii. v. 122 So *firefree they could not be burned. **1853** Sir H. Douglas *Milit. Bridges* (ed. 3) 111 Light boats were constantly kept in readiness, with *fire-grapplings, to meet and anchor anything that might be drifted down the stream. **1833** *Niles' Reg.* XLIV. 259/2 There were twenty-three engine and hose companies,..and four divisions of *fire guards. **1852** Burn *Nav. & Mil. Tech. Fr. Dict.* ii. 96 *Fire-guard.* **1874** J. C. McCoy *Hist. Sk.* 217 An impassable barrier would be created between the unburned grass within the encircled tract, and that upon the outside of the 'fire-guard'. *Ibid.*, A large adjacent tract of land..will be 'fire-guarded', in order to secure a winter range from the ravages of prairie fires. **1912** Fire-guard [see back-fire *v.* 1]. **1926** *Daily Colonist* (Victoria, B.C.) 15 July 7/1 It was stated that the fire on the southwest side of the river was practically under control, while a fire guard had been placed between the fire zone and the city watershed. **1963** R. D. Symons *Many Trails* 40 The smoky air..choked us as we feverishly plowed fire-guards. **1881** A. Begg *Gt. Canad. North West* 103 A handsome *fire hall centrally located. **1966** *Kingston* (Ont.) *Whig-Standard* 26 Jan. 6/3 Council decided to increase the insurance on the fire hall. **1851** C. Cist *Cincinnati* 213 George E. Minister..makes..*fire hats. **1823** P. Nicholson *Pract. Build.* 362 The *fire-hole, or furnace. **1835** Sir J. C. Ross *Narr. 2nd Voy.* Explan. Terms p. xvi, *Fire-hole*, a hole in the ice, kept open in order to obtain water to extinguish fire. **1876** Davis *Polaris Exp.* ix. 217 The crew..had been employed in..keeping the fire-hole open. **1585** Higins *Junius' Nomenclator* 279 *Malleoli* ..*fire hoopes. **1867** Smyth *Sailor's Word-bk.*, *Fire-hoops*. **1883** *Century Mag.* XXVII. 33 The stream might have played, like a *fire-hose, on the Toll House roof. **1822** *Lond. Directory* 6 Norwich Union *fire-insurance Society. **1858** Ld. St. Leonards *Handy Bk. Prop. Law* vii. 45 A word of advice about your Fire Insurance. **1818** Shelley *Rev. Islam* vii. viii. 8 From the *fire-isles came he. **1884** *Chr. World* 28 Aug. 641/3 The burning gunboats and *fire-junks. **1829** Carlyle *Misc.* (1857) II. 101 The Birmingham *Fire-king has visited the fabulous East. **1861** *Leisure H.* 17 Oct. 661 Thus aided [by the wind], the fire-king marched victoriously from east to west. **1876** *Chamb. Jrnl.* 11 Nov. 733 The fire-king devoured flaming brimstone by way of dessert. **1883** Gresley *Gloss. Coal Mining*, **Fire-lamp*. **1779** *Hist. Europe* in *Ann. Reg.* (1780) 127/1 Will..the Clerks, or even the *fire-lighter come to prove it? **1853** Geo. Eliot *Let.* 5 Nov. (1954) II. 123 Will you..send me the address of the London agent for the Firelighters? **1897** *Daily News* 4 June 8/2 Firelighters, specially prepared,..to light all the bonfires throughout the country. **1957** *Times* 9 Sept. 11/5 New-fangled, oil-soaked, 'fire-lighters' and suchlike meretricious aids are nothing but barefaced cheating. **1902** A. C. Laut *Story Trapper* (1912) 147 The game..must be moving away from the *fire line. **1905** *Terms Forestry & Logging* 10 *Fire line*, a strip kept clear of inflammable material as a protection against the spread of forest fire. **1927** W. H. Todd *Tiger, Tiger!* 108, I walked down a jungle ride, or fire line. **1953** *Brit. Commonw. Forest Terminol.* I. 53 *Fire line*, (*a*) the portion of a control line or fire trace from which inflammable materials have been removed... (*b*) A clear felled permanent firebreak..[Ind]. (*c*) A line round an active fire..to..control it [Can]. **1758** *Elaboratory laid open* Introd. 51 The *fire-lute. **1710** Palmer *Proverbs* 61 Even from the *fire-makers and necessary-women, to the groom of the stole. **1865** Tylor *Early Hist. Man.* ix. 228 The wide-spread legends of first fire-makers. **1816** W. Phillips *Min.* (1818) 97 It has obtained the name of *Fire marble. *a* **1661** Holyday *Juvenal* 253 What learns his Son, who does ..*Fire-marks, and Country-jails with joy admire? **1690** *Lond. Gaz.* No. 2571/4 Lost..a brown Gelding..a Flower-de-luce Fire mark on the near Hip. **1833** N. Arnott *Physics* II. 115 The apparatus has been called Wedgewood's Pyrometer, or *fire-measure. **1721** in Picton *L'pool Munic. Rec.* (1886) II. 74 All gratuities..such as entrance money, cockpenny, *fire money, and quarteridge. **1653** *Noctes Hibernæ* i. 3 Some have learned more of their Teacher..on a *fire-night, than sitting at the desk all day. **1816** R. Jameson *Char. Min.* I. 238 Third Sub-species, *Fire Opal. **1738** [G. Smith] *Curious Relat.* II. 358 Twenty-seven Foresters, with *Fire-Pieces in their Arms. **1775** J. Wright *Let.* in *Athenæum* 10 July (1886) 56/3 A report that I paint fire-pieces admirably. **1664** H. More *Myst. Iniq.* xv. 167 Multitudes..martyred..either at one common *fire-pyle, or else in barns and dwelling-houses. **1863** *Blackw. Mag.* Sept. 292 Hercules..who has ascended from the fire-pile to the Nectar Hall of Olympus. **1920** *Brit. Mus. Return* 64 A *fire-piston of buffalo horn from the Kachin, Upper Burma. **1951** *N. & Q. Anthropol.* (ed. 6) iii. 240 The *fire-piston* depends for its working on the development of heat by the sudden compression of air in a confined space. **1893** *Funk's Stand. Dict.*, *Fire-plow. **1934** E. Eyre *European Civilisation* I. i. 39 The methods of fire-making in use are: the fire-plough (the rubbing up and down of a piece of hard wood in a groove of soft timber), which may well be the oldest device of its kind. **1955** *Antiquity* XXIX. 132 In the fire-plough a pointed stick is rubbed vigorously along a groove or depression in a piece of wood laid flat on the ground. **1713** *Lond. Gaz.* No. 5116/11 Scarcity of Water, occasion'd by the want of *Fire-Plugs in the Street. **1840** Dickens *Old C. Shop* xx, The pony looked with great attention into a fire-plug which was near him. **1855** Ogilvie *Suppl.*, **Fire-policy*. **1558** *Inv. R. Hyndmer* in *Wills & Inv.* (Surtees) 162 A *fyer porre, a payre of tonges [etc.]. **1855** *Whitby Gloss.*, *Fire-porr*. **1905** *Westm. Gaz.* 15 May 4/1 Cavalry could do next to nothing, and artillery could seldom find really effective *fire-positions. *Ibid.* 13 June 3/1 The most favourable spot for your individual fire-position. **1913** R. Meinertzhagen *Army Diary* 6 Oct. (1960) 55 What I should have liked to see is more automatic *fire-power in the hands of both the battalion commander and the company commander. **1928** *Daily Tel.* 11 Sept. 12/4 The greatest possible strength of fire-power—from guns and machine guns—should be concentrated rapidly on one part of the front only. **1955** *Bull. Atomic Sci.* Mar. 94/1 The authors readily admit that the tactical A-bomb has grave limitations, yet they feel that it grants us superior firepower to counter the conventional strength of the Soviets. **1967** *New Scientist* 17 Aug. 328/1 A lieutenant colonel of the Viet-cong.. confessed himself unimpressed by the white men's mobility in jungle conditions, but he had no doubts about the effectiveness of their firepower. **1568** *Inventory W. Strickland* in *Richmond Wills & Inv.* (Surtees) 222 A *fyer pronge. **1776** T. Jefferson *Lett.* Writ. 1893 II. 83 One of the two *fire-rafts..grappled the Phoenix ten minutes. **1844** H. H. Wilson *Brit. India* III. 52 To..destroy any armed boats or fire-rafts they might meet with. **1945** *Daily Tel.* 20 July, Over 600 of the giant bombers visited four cities, including Hitachi, with *fire raids. **1960** Koestler *Lotus & Robot* ii. vi. 177 The two conventional fire-raids on Tokyo, earlier in the same year, had claimed another 100,000 victims. **1909** A. D. Cameron *New North* 82 The *Fire-

Ranger of the district..has his barley and rice spread out on sheeting. **1920** *Outing* June 137/2 If you discover a fire, put it out if possible. If you cannot, get word to the nearest U.S. Fire Ranger or State Fire Warden. **1928** *Daily Express* 29 Aug. 2/5 The British Columbia fire ranger, whose lookout station is on Mount Cartier, 9,000 feet above sea level. **1865** *Atlantic Monthly* XV. 86 Joint-stock companies for the underwriting of *fire-risks. **1867** C. J. Bunyon *Law of Fire Insurance* iii. 40 Gasworks are esteemed a fire risk of special hazard. **1907** *Install. News* Mar. 7/1 The Gunpowder Manufactory at Minden, where Simplex Screwed Conduits have been used because of the fire risk. **1966** *Lancet* 24 Dec. 1405/2 Little is known of the fire-risks to man in oxygen-rich environments. **1830** Marryat *King's Own* lii, He desired the '*fire-roll' to be beat by the drummer. **1632** *Inventory* 9 Apr. in M. W. Barley *Eng. Farmhouse & Cottage* (1961) App. 278 Itim in the Chamber over the *fire roume a trundle bedstedle. **1805** Forsyth *Beauties Scotl.* (1806) III. 123 One wing of a new castle..in which there are between fifty and sixty fire-rooms. **1836** *Southern Lit. Messenger* II. 734 Passing the fire-room, where they were just firing up, I stopped. **1880** *Harper's Mag.* Oct. 793 Yet even on the *Seawanhaka* it appears that the fireroom..was unprotected. **1903** A. H. Lewis *Boss* i. 8 As for a bed, if it should be summer time, what should be finer than the docks? Or if winter, than the fire-rooms of the tugs? **1650** Fuller *Pisgah* II. xii. 246 Partly because the water hereof was salt with a witness, *fire-salt, as I may say. **1611** Sylvester *Du Bartas* II. iv. III. *Schisme* 629 The *fire-snort Palfreys. **1794** Sullivan *View Nat.* II. 184 Three *fire-spouts broke out. **1811** W. J. Hooker *Iceland* (1813) II. 128 Several fire-spouts were distinctly seen. **1848** C. Brontë *J. Eyre* (1857) 267, I have seen what a *fire-sprit you can be when you are indignant. **1676** C. Hatton in *Hatton Corr.* (1878) 141 One of my Ld Craven's *fire-spyes. **1877** *Fireman* June 2/1 (*heading*) The new metropolitan central *fire station. **1979** N. Wallington *Fireman!* 15 A world that normally lies hidden behind the closed doors of a fire station until suddenly they crash open and one or two bright-red appliances emerge. **1585** Higins *Junius' Nomenclator* 244 *Igniarium*..a *fire-steele wherewith to strike fire out of a flint. **1916** *War Illustrated* 23 Dec. 449/1 Bill got upon the *fire-step, placed his rifle against the wall, [etc.]. **1954** W. Faulkner *Fable* (1955) 54 Two British privates were resting on the firestep of a frontline trench. *c* **1300** *Havelok* 966 Was it nouth worth a *fir sticke. **1587** Golding *De Mornay* xi. 158 The babe, who thinkes his Nurce does him wrong..when sometimes shee plucks a firestick from him. **1794-6** E. Darwin *Zoon.* (1801) I. 30 If a fire-stick be whirled round in the dark. **1833** Sturt *Exped. S. Australia* I. iii. 105 Several carried fire-sticks. **1865** Tylor *Early Hist. Man.* ix. 238 For many years, flint and steel could not drive it [the fire-drill] out of use among the natives, who went on carrying every man his fire-sticks. **1896** J. C. Harris *Sister Jane* 100 Sister Jane, armed with a fire-stick (a heavy piece of metal weighing four or five pounds)..was..making an effort to get to the door. **1900** *Ann. Rep. Smithsonian Inst.* (Nat. Mus.) 180 In the same plate are included a pair of wooden fire sticks or tongs [of the Tulare Indians]. **1881** Raymond *Mining Gloss.*, **Fire-stink*, the stench from decomposing iron pyrites, caused by the formation of sulphuretted hydrogen. **1897** F. C. Moore *How to build Home* 7 The ceiling should be plastered on metallic lathing. This will be an effectual *fire-stop in case of fire starting in the cellar. **1926** C. E. Mulford *Cassidy's Protégé* iv. 41 The farms he had dreamed of were now no more than memories, their boundary furrows and fire-stops rank with triumphant bunchgrass. **1581** Marbeck *Bk. of Notes* 478 Helias..was taken vp into Heauen in a *fire storme. **1905** *Westm. Gaz.* 13 May 6/2 Glowing embers as it were of the fire-storm [*i.e.*, a grass fire]. **1945** in *Amer. Speech* (1951) XXVI. 236/2 These storms soon combined in an immense 'fire storm' (high winds blowing inwards toward the center of a large conflagration) similar to those caused by ordinary mass incendiary raids. **1959** *Times* 26 June 11/2 Nearly half of these could be expected to die instantly, killed by blast or incinerated in the fire-storms caused by the explosions. **1855** Ogilvie *Suppl.*, **Fire-swab.* **1924** A. Huxley *Little Mexican* 57 Fat women, *fire-swallowers, elastic men. **1932** 'R. Crompton' *William—the Pirate* vi. 134 'My hubby's just gone to have a drink with the fire swallower,' continued Mrs. Tom Thumb. *a* **1000** *Crist* 984 (Gr.) Færeð æfter foldan *fyrswearta leȝ. *a* **1849** W. Taylor in Southey *Comm.-pl. Bk.* IV. 93 Thy shatter'd fire-swart hall. **1863** Tyndall *Heat* i. 13 The *fire syringe. **1827** *Westm. Rev.* VII. 279 The..*fire-teazer who holds the soul of the steam-boat..in his hands. **1843** Mill *Logic* I. i. iv. §1. 105 The fire-teazer of a modern steam-engine. **1854** Ronalds & Richardson *Chem. Technol.* (ed. 2) I. 348 The under-surface of the cylinder being protected by *fire tiles from the direct and too powerful action of the fire. **1827** G. Higgins *Celtic Druids* Pref. 46 They have of late obtained the names in general of *fire towers. **1891** W. Schlich *Man. Forestry* II. iii. 192 Protection is afforded by removing all inflammable matter, or clearing *fire-traces around the area. **1953** *Brit. Commonw. Forest Terminol.* I. 55 *Fire trace*, a cleared (often burnt) line used as a base from which to counterfire; also frequently as a syn[onym] for *firebreak*. **1887** *Spectator* 28 May 722/2 The building appears to have been a regular *fire-trap. **1801** Strutt *Sports & Past.* IV. iii. 332 Exhibitions..consisting chiefly in *fire-trees, jerbs, and rockets. **1909** *Strand Mag.* Apr. 365/2 He dived down into the *fire-trenches. **1916** 'Boyd Cable' *Action Front* 103 The deep ditch with a narrow platform along its front that was the forward fire trench. **1928** Blunden *Undertones of War* xviii. 193 Men..asleep in narrow chilly firetrenches. **1639** J. C[ruso] *Art of Warre* 154 To make a *fire-trunk. Take a piece of light wood..bore it through..with a hole of an inch in diameter;..place at the one end an half pike..To charge the trunk, put a charge of beaten powder in the bottome [etc.]. **1687** J. Richards *Jrnl. Siege Buda* 26 Stones, Granadoes, Arrows, Bullets, and Fire-Trunks. **1769** Falconer *Dict. Marine* (1789), *Sausisson*, the trough.. which communicates the flame from the train to the fire-trunks or powder-barrels in a fire-ship. **1830** *Falconer's Dict. Marine*, *Fire-trunks* are wooden funnels fixed in fire-ships under the shrouds, to convey the flames to the masts, rigging, and sails. **1855** H. Clarke *Dict.*, **Fire-tube.* **1382** Wyclif *Ex.* xxvii. 3 Toonges, and hokes, and *fyer vessels. **1827** *Examiner* 723/2 The *Dartmouth* sending a boat to one of the fire-vessels. **1898** *Westm. Gaz.* 26 July 3/2 The Fijian *fire-walk. **1900** *Proc. Soc. Psychical Res.* Feb. 11 Colonel Haggard saw the fire-walk done in Tokio, on April 9th, 1899. **1895** *Folk-Lore* Sept. 246 A photograph of the *fire-walkers. **1898** *Westm. Gaz.* 28 June 4/3 The fire-walkers then approached..and..walked leisurely across and around the oven. **1938** *Times Lit. Suppl.* 1 Jan. 5/4 He is inclined to attribute the immunity of the fire-walkers to the power of faith. **1899** *Daily News* 25 Jan. 4/6 There was a *fire-walking ceremony at Benares the other day. **1904** *Athenæum* 13 Feb. 216/1 An interesting lecture on 'The Fijians and their Fire-Walking'. **1963** *Times* 2 Mar. 10/6 A Chinese fire-walking ceremony. **1851** C. Cist *Cincinnati* 230 Three smoke-houses..are separated by twelve inch walls.. with *fire-walls on the roof. **1947** *Aircraft Engin.* Jan. 15/1 The firewall is a stout bulkhead. **1763** J. Adams *Diary* Feb. Wks. 1850 II. 144 Collectors, wardens, *fire-wards, and representatives, are regularly chosen. **1832** Webster, *Fire-ward, Firewarden.* **1724** *New-Eng. Courant* 10-17 Aug. 2/2 Leave first obtain'd from the *Firewardens. **1817** *Upper Canada Gaz.* (York, Ont.) 12 June 95/5 The said Fire Warden shall..carry about with him on occasion of Fires, a staff or some other visible distinguishing badge of office. **1875** *Chicago Tribune* 2 July 3/4 The seven Fire Wardens were..abolished. **1968** R. M. Patterson *Finlay's River* 41 Truly this butte was..well sited for the fire warden's lookout. **1941** R. Greenwood *Mr. Bunting at War* xix. 269 I've got to *fire-watch. **1910** W. de la Mare *Three Mulla-Mulgars* xvi. 217 *The fire-watcher raised his sad countenance. **1941** *Ann. Reg. 1940* 95 All factories employing not less than thirty persons must have fire watchers. **1944** *Times* 31 Jan. 2/3 In the cities and towns the Home Guard give a good deal of help in the Civil Defence services, as fire-watchers now. **1941** *Manch. Guardian Weekly* 10 Jan. 18 Everyone now realises the great importance of *fire-watching and fire prevention. **1952** O. R. Gurney *Hittites* vii. 150 There were even regulations about fire-watching and nightly patrols. **1663** Mrq. Worcester *Cent. Inv.* Index, A *Fire Water-work 68. **1879** Geikie in *Encycl. Brit.* (ed. 9) X. 250/1 Emanations of carburetted hydrogen, which, when they take fire, are known as *Fire-wells. **1634** J. Bate *Myst. Nat. & Art* II. 77 How to make Gironells or *fire wheeles. **1799** G. Smith *Laboratory* I. 27 The fire wheels that are used on land, turn upon an iron pin or bolt, drawn or screwed into a post. **1945** in *Amer. Speech* (1951) XXVI. 236/2 The wind velocity in the city had been less than 5 miles per hour before the bombing, but the *fire-wind attained a velocity of 30-40 miles per hour. **1899** *Westm. Gaz.* 15 Apr. 8/1 A brigade of *fire-women should be attached to the staff of such sisterhoods. **1964** *Guardian* 29 May 2/4 The Fire Brigades' Union executive today promised to examine firewomen's conditions of service. **1567** Maplet *Gr. Forest* 111 Another which is called the *fier Worme, & semeth as it were to be a kinde of Spider. **1821** Byron *Cain* II. i, I have seen the fire-flies and fire-worms. **1639** J. C[ruso] *Art of Warre* 93 Fire-balls, granadoes, *fire-wreathes, and fire-trunks. **1862** H. Marryat *Year in Sweden* II. 346 *note*, Fire-arrows shot from the bows, as well as fire-wreaths cast into the vessels of the enemy. **1916** *Brit. Dominions Year Bk. 1917* 248 The pilot..can only secure these valuable pictures by making a dash into the *fire-zone. **1923** Kipling *Irish Guards in Great War* I. 125 All four companies worked their way..out of the fire-zone.

b. In various plant-names, as **fire-bush** (see quot.); **fire-grass** *dial.*, parsley piert (*Alchemilla arvensis*), so called because used as a remedy for erysipelas (J. Smith, *Dom. Bot.* 1871); **fire-leaves**, (*a*) *Plantago media*; (*b*) *Scabiosa succisa*; **fire-pink** (see quot.); **fire-weed**, applied to various plants (see quots.) that spring up on burnt land.

1882 *Garden* 13 May 322/2 The *Fire Bush (*Embothrium coccineum*)..which thrives so well in..Devonshire. **1860** *Gard. Chron.* 11 Aug. 738 **Fire-leaves.* In Gloucestershire the name is given to the leaves of Plantains; and we have heard it in Herefordshire used for the *Scabiosa succisa* (Devil's bit). **1882** *Garden* 6 May 307/2 The *Fire Pink (*Silene virginica*).—The flowers of this Catchfly are unsurpassed as regards brilliancy by those of any other plant. **1792** J. Belknap *Hist. New-Hampsh.* III. 133 No other culture being necessary..but the cutting of the *fire-weed. **1829** Loudon *Encycl. Plants* 706 *Senecio hieracifolius* ..in North America, as *S. vulgaris* in Europe..is known by the name of the Fire-weed. **1857** Thoreau *Maine W.* (1894) 350 There were great fields of fire weed (*Epilobium angustifolium*) on all sides. **1861** Miss Pratt *Flower. Pl.* II. 104 In Virginia, the Thorn-Apple is called Fireweed. **1866** *Treas. Bot.*, *Fireweed*, an American name for *Erechthites hieracifolia*. **1892** R. Kipling in *Times* (weekly ed.) 24 Nov. 13/3 The fire-weed glows in the centre of the driveways.

c. In provincial or local names of birds and insects, as **fire-beetle** = cucuy; **fire-brat**, a bristle-tail (*Thermobia domestica*), found in hot parts of buildings; **fire-bug**, (*a*) *U.S.*, the fire-fly; (*b*) an insect of the family Pyrrhocoridæ; **fire-crest**, a warbler (*Regulus ignicapillus*), closely resembling the gold-crest; also ***fire-crested wren***; **fire-finch**, a name given to several African weaver birds from the red plumage of the male in the breeding season; **fire-flirt**, the redstart (*Ruticilla phœnicurus*); **fire-hang-bird**, the Baltimore oriole (see fire-bird); **fire-tail**, (*a*) the redstart; (*b*) a small finch-like bird of Tasmania; also, ***fire-tailed finch***; (*c*) (see quot. 1868); **fire-worm** *U.S.*, the larva of any of several moths belonging to the superfamily Tortricoidea.

1842 T. W. Harris *Insects Injur. Veget.* 49 *Elater* (*Pyrophorus*) *noctilucus*, the night-shining Elater, is the celebrated *cucuio* or *fire-beetle of the West Indies. **1855** K. Büchele *Land Nord-Amerika* 32 Den Feuerkäfer (*fire beetle*), 1 Zoll lang, in Louisiana und Texas. **1895** *Cambr. Nat. Hist.* V. 186 The bakers call these Insects [sc. *Thermobia furnorum*] *fire-brats, apparently considering them to be fond of heat. **1955** *Sci. News Let.* 22 Jan. 62/3 The firebrat..preferring to live in the vicinity of a fireplace, furnace or other hot spot. **1789** J. Morse *Amer. Geogr.* 62 Fire Fly or *Bug. **1877** J. M. Bailey *Folks in Danbury* 40 (Th.), [The lamp] don't give more light than a fire-bug. **1921** E. Step *Brit. Insect Life* 169 A striking representative of this family is a Bug that is known in France as the Beadle and the Soldier (*Pyrrhocoris apterus*), and mentioned sometimes as Fire-bug. **1959** Southwood & Leston *Land & Water Bugs* iv. 72 The firebug occurs throughout much of Europe and is..found in gregarious masses on various mallows and limes. **1843** J. D. Hoy in W. Yarrell *Hist. Brit. Birds* I. 324 By the early part of November you will rarely find the *Fire Crest. **1885** Swainson *Prov. Names Birds* 229 Fire crest. **1889** *Cent. Dict.*, *Fire-finch. **1905** G. E. Shelley *Birds Afr.* IV. i. 260 These Fire-finches are represented in the British Museum by a full plumaged male. **1966** C. Sweeney *Scurrying Bush* x. 140 Little birds, such as cordon-bleus and firefinches, used to come to the crocodiles' pool to drink. **1885** Swainson *Prov. Names Birds* 13 Redstart..*Fire flirt. **1855** Lowell *Let. to Stillman* 21 May, The linnets, catbirds, *fire hang-birds, and robins. **1802** G. Montagu *Ornith. Dict.* (1833) 412 *Fire-tail..the Redstart. **1865** Gould *Hdbk. Birds Australia* I. 406 *Zonæginthus bellus*, Fire-tailed Finch..Fire-tail. **1867** *Cornh. Mag.* XV. 593 'There's a firetail', said the boy. **1868** Wood *Homes without H.* xxv. 481 Those splendid insects which are popularly called Ruby-tailed Flies or Fire-tails and scientifically are termed *Chrysididæ*. **1869** A. S. Packard *Guide Study Insects* 339 These larvæ, called the Cranberry-vine worms, hatch about the first of June... Before reaching their full size they, if very numerous, almost wholly destroy the leaves and tender shoots, giving the whole bog a dark dry appearance as though a fire had been over it. This is why they are in some places known as '*fire-worms'. **1954** Borror & DeLong *Introd. Study Insects* xxvi. 531 The cranberry black-headed fire-worm, *Rhopobota naevana* Hübner, is a serious pest of cranberry plantings in the Eastern states.

fire (faɪə(r)), *v.*[1] Forms: 1 fýrian, 3 furen(ü), 4-7 fyre, (4 fijre, 5 firin), 6-7 fier, 4- fire. [f. fire *sb.*; OE. had *fýrian* (once, in sense 1); cf. OHG. *fiurên* to be on fire, *fiuren* to set on fire (MHG. *viuren*, mod.G. *feuern*).]

†**1.** *trans.* To supply with firing. (Only OE.)

c **970** *Canons of Edgar, Penitents* §14 Fede þearfan and scryde and husiȝe and fyriȝe, baðiȝe and beddiȝe.

2. a. *trans.* To set on fire, so as to damage or destroy; sometimes, to consume or destroy by fire.

a **1400-50** *Alexander* 2217 A full thousand he fangid to fire þe foure ȝatis. *c* **1440** *Promp. Parv.* 162/1 Fyrin, or sette on a fyre, or brinnyn. *c* **1490** *Adam Bel* 117 in Ritson *Anc. Pop. P.* 9 They fyred the house in many a place. **1592** Lyly *Midas* I. i, Least desiring things above my reach, I be fiered with Phaeton. **1699** Bentley *Phal.* 77 Cylon fired the Pythagorean College. **1840** Thirlwall *Greece* VII. lvi. 180 He fired his camp. **1848** Kingsley *Saint's Trag.* III. ii. When all your stacks were fired, she lent you gold.

b. To light, kindle, ignite (anything intended for the purpose; now only a beacon, or something explosive).

1393 Gower *Conf.* I. 81 Sinon..Withinne Troie..a tokne hath fired. *c* **1489** Caxton *Sonnes of Aymon* xvii. 399 He toke a torche and fyred it. **1571** Digges *Pantom.* Pref. A iij b, He hath..sundrie times by the Sunne beames fired Powder. **1665** *Sir T. Roe's Voy. E. Ind.* 428 They fire an innumerable company of lamps. **1795** *Phil. Trans.* LXXXV. 461 Twenty..white lights, which were fired at Beachy Head. **1860** Tyndall *Glac.* II. iii. 242 Gunpowder could easily be fired by the heat of the sun's rays converged.

†**c.** *to fire about*: to surround with fires. *Obs.*

c **1440** *Bone Flor.* 709 The Grekys had fyred hym abowte, That he myght on no syde owte.

†**d.** Used in the imperative as an imprecation.

1752 Foote *Taste* II. Wks. 1799 I. 23 Fire me, my Lord, there may be more in this than we can guess. **1760** —— *Minor* I. ibid. I. 241 Fire him, a snub-nos'd son of a bitch.

3. *fig.* **a.** To set (a person) on fire; to inspire *with* passion or strong feeling or desire; to inflame, heat, animate. Also, to kindle or inflame (a passion, etc.).

a **1225** *St. Marher.* 18 Wið þe halwunde fur of þe hali gast moncunne froure fure min heorte. *c* **1385** Chaucer *L.G.W.* 1013 *Dido*, That al the world her beute hadde y-fyred. *a* **1420** Hoccleve *De Reg. Princ.* 3835 They kyndlen ire, and firen lecherie. **1602** Marston *Antonio's Rev.* II. iii, What danke marrish spirit, But would be fyred with impatience? **1697** Dryden *Virg. Past.* VIII. 99 Verse fires the frozen Veins. **1728** Young *Odes to King* Wks. 1757 I. 176 What hero's praise Can fire my lays, Like His? **1749** Fielding *Tom Jones* xv. iv, Perceiving she had fired the young Lord's pride. **1775** Johnson *Tax. no Tyr.* 22 The nations of Europe were fired with boundless expectation. **1813** Scott *Rokeby* I. xii, Fired was each eye, and flushed each brow. *a* **1862** Buckle *Misc. Wks.* (1872) I. 13 Venice, that land so calculated to fire the imagination of a poet. **1881** Mallock *Romance Nineteenth Cent.* II. 62 These imaginations fired him with a new longing for her.

†**b.** = feague *v.* 2 b.

1737 Bracken *Farriery Impr.* (ed. 2) II. 61 You may chance to get a View of the Horses without the Dealer's having first put them upon their Mettle, or fired them, as it is called; for the last of these they will do, if possible, unless the Horse happens to set his Tail naturally.

4. a. *intr.* To catch fire, to be kindled or ignited; †also, to be consumed by fire. Of a coal mine: (see quot. 1892). ***to fire up***: (of a volcano) to burst into flame.

a **1618** Raleigh *Apol.* 29 For I will fire with the Gallioones if it come to extreamity. **1681** *Lond. Gaz.* No. 1628/2 In this Fight, the Frigat fired twice. **1731** S. Hales *Stat. Ess.* I. 270 As in the case where houses are first beginning to fire. **1774** Goldsm. *Nat. Hist.* (1862) I. viii. 39 Gunpowder will readily fire with a spark. **1869** Phillips *Vesuv.* iii. 59 On the 20th of April rain came with the Sirocco, and the mountain, as usual, fired up. **1892**

Northumberld. Gloss. s.v. A pit is said to have fired when an explosion of gas has taken place.

b. *transf.* Of flax: To become covered with black spots as if burnt.

1814 W. S. Mason *Surv. Ireland* I. xiii. ix. 265 They find from experience that the latter [American flax-seed] fired much more than the former [Dutch flax-seed].

c. Said of a cylinder of an internal-combustion engine when the fuel inside it is ignited.

1894 W. J. Lineham *Textbk. Mech. Engin.* x. 699 The first practical gas engine..was double-acting, charging with air and gas during a half stroke, firing during the remaining half. **1902** J. E. Hutton in A. C. Harmsworth et al. *Motors* viii. 139 Two cylinders out of the four fire in each revolution. **1959** *'Motor' Manual* (ed. 36) iii. 61 As soon as the engine fires, the left-hand disc valve is drawn to the right. *Ibid.* ii. 38 When No. 1 is firing or on its power stroke, No. 2 is taking in its fresh charge.

5. *fig.* To become inflamed, heated, or excited. *to fire up*: to show sudden heat or anger.

1568 T. Howell *Arb. Amitie* (1879) 38, I rage and rewe, I fire and freese. **1604** Marston *Malcontent* v. ii, Women are flax, and will fire in a moment. **1749** Fielding *Tom Jones* v. x, The parson..fired at this information. **1798** Jane Austen *Northang. Abb.* (1833) I. vi. 25 If I were to hear any one speak slightingly of you, I should fire up in a moment. **1824** W. Irving *T. Trav.* I. 261 She fired up at the arrogance of the squire. **1832** *Examiner* 388/1 His heart swells, and his imagination fires. **1840** Dickens *Barn. Rudge* xli, I should have fired and fumed!

6. *transf.* **a.** *trans.* To redden or cause to glow as if on fire; to suffuse with a fiery hue.

1593 Shaks. *Rich. II*, iii. ii. 42 When..He [the sun] fires the prowd tops of the Easterne Pines. **1633** P. Fletcher *Purple Isl.* ii. 10 The flaming bloud, Which fir'd her scarlet cheek with rosie dies. **1784** Cowper *Task* v. 2 The sun.. Ascending, fires th' horizon. **1878** B. Taylor *Deukalion* ii. ii. 59 As a strong sunset fires the unwilling East.

b. *intr.* To glow as if on fire; to grow as red as fire.

1865 J. C. Wilcocks *Sea Fisherm.* (1875) 118 When the water fires, or, as the fishermen term it, 'brimes'. **1886** A. Lang *Lett. to Dead Authors* xvii. 177 Watching..the dawn as it fired.

7. a. *trans.* To affect (the body) with a burning sensation. ? *Obs.* **b.** *intr.* To become heated or inflamed. ? *U.S.*

1673 Ray *Journ. Low C.* 459 Olives..are of a horrid.. taste, firing the throat and palate. **1889** *Century Dict.* s.v., His feet fire easily in walking. (Colloq.)

8. a. *trans.* To drive (any one) away from a place by fire; with *out*, *out of*, *from*, or equivalent const. Also *fig.* *Obs.* or *rare*.

1530 Palsgr. 551/1 Come out, or I shall fyre the out. **1590** Marlowe *Edw. II*, iii. ii, March to fire them from their starting-holes. **1605** Shaks. *Lear* v. iii. 23 He..shall bring a Brand from Heauen, And fire vs hence, like Foxes. **1615** Byfield *Expos. Col.* iii. 5 Lust will not usually out of the soul ..till it be fired out with confession. **1677** W. Hubbard *Narrative* 128 The rest of the Enemy being first fired out of their strong hold, were taken. **1728** Swift *Let. Dubl. Wkly. Jrnl.* 21 Sept., The law is like the wooden houses of our ancestors..where you..are very often fired out of all you have.

†**b.** To force (a way) by fire. *Obs.*

1671 Crowne *Juliana* ii. Dram. Wks. 1873 I. 53 Ha! the gates fastened!..Fetch me a torch, I'll fire my way to 'um.

9. *trans.* To subject to the action of fire; to prepare by heat; e.g. to bake (pottery, bricks, etc.); to dry or cure (tea or tobacco) by artificial heat.

1662 R. Mathew *Unl. Alch.* lxxxix. 159 The gentlier thou dost fire, the better wil thy Work be. **1782** Wedgwood in *Phil. Trans.* LXXII. 307 The kiln in which our glazed ware is fired furnishes three measures. **1805** J. Nicol *Poems* I. 28 (Jam.) The dough is then rolled thin, and cut into small scones, which, when fired, are handed round the company. **1825** *Beverley Lighting Act* ii. 18 Hoop, fire, cleanse, wash or scald any cask. **1875** *Sat. Rev.* XL. 553/1 For green tea the leaf is 'fired' within two hours of picking. **1883** *U.S. 10th Census Report Agric.* Tobacco 92 If a damp spell occurs after the barn is filled with tobacco it is sometimes fired with wood to save it. **1888** *Pall Mall G.* 19 Nov. 2/1 The work is fired, again painted with enamels, again fired, and so on.

10. *Farriery.* To burn; cauterize.

1607 Topsell *Four-f. Beasts* (1658) 299 Then to give him the fire, which Absyrtus doth not allow, saving the Spleen lyeth so, as it cannot easily be fired, to do him any good. **1677** *Lond. Gaz.* No. 1201/4 A..Hunting Gelding..fired for the Spaven..on the near leg behind. **1737** Bracken *Farriery Impr.* (1756) I. 320, I see no Harm in Firing or Cauterizing young Colts. **1869** E. Farmer *Scrap Bk.* (ed. 6) 27 They'll be most of them 'blistered' or 'fired', and turned out!

11. a. To supply (a furnace, etc.) with fuel; to attend to the fire of (an engine).

1760 Goldsm. *Cit. W.* xciii. ¶3 [He] might as well send his manuscript to fire the baker's oven. **1862** Smiles *Engineers* III. 25 George firing the engine at the wage of a shilling a day. **1890** *Daily News* 26 Dec. 5/7 The Edinburgh Works have as much coal as will fire the retorts for at least eight or ten days. **1894** *Chamb. Jrnl.* 30 June 414/1 The boilers were fired by oil.

b. *absol.* Also with *up*: To make up a fire; to light up the fire of a furnace; hence *colloq.* to light one's pipe; *fig.*, to stimulate or fill with enthusiasm (*U.S. colloq.*). Also *trans.*

1836 *Southern Lit. Messenger* II. 734 Passing the fire-room, where they were just firing up, I stopped. **1857** E. Stone *Life Howland* xii. 267 The time required to 'fire up', and set the engine again in motion, delayed the arrival. **1867** *Trans. Ill. Agric. Soc.* VI. 320 It can be attached..in less time than is required to fire up a steam fire engine. **1879** Baring-Gould *Germany* II. 368 In the depth of winter..it is quite enough to fire up twice in the twenty-four hours. **1881** M. Reynolds *Engine-Driving Life* 17 He allows the fireman to find out how to fire, when to fire, and where to fire. **1890** *Century Mag.* 127/2 When we had fired up he grew more and more in cordial mood. **1893** *Catholic News* 21 Oct. 6/5, I had been firing on the line for five years back. **1903** *N.Y. Even. Post* 13 Oct. 1 Then the two statesmen fired up their cigars. **1976** *National Observer* (U.S.) 16 Oct. 10/3 He fired up his investigators, offered deals to suspects who would turn state's evidence, and played off the knowledge of one suspect against the other. **1978** *Detroit Free Post* 5 Mar. C4/1 When you're fired up and want to play, Vandy's style won't let you play.

c. *to fire off* (a kiln): to cause it to cease burning.

1884 C. T. Davis *Bricks, etc.* 283 When the first kiln has been fired-off.

12. a. To apply fire to (a charge of gunpowder) in order to cause its explosion; to discharge or let off (a gun, firework, etc.), explode (a mine, etc.). Also, *to fire off*.

to fire a salute, to fire a certain number of guns as a salute; *to fire a broadside*, to fire all the guns on one side of a ship. Also *fig.*

1530 Palsgr. 550/1 Fyer this pece..*affustez ceste piece.* **1602** Shaks. *Ham.* v. ii. 281 Let all the Battlements their Ordinance fire. **1699** W. Hacke *Coll. Voy.* iv. 37 They load them with loose Powder..and they fire them with Stoneshot. **1705** Berkeley *Cave Dunmore* Wks. 1871 IV. 506, I desired one of our company to fire off his gun. **1799** G. Smith *Laboratory* I. 17 These sorts of rockets are fired on a board or stand. **1840** R. H. Dana *Bef. Mast* xxvii. 91 At sundown, another salute of the same number of guns was fired. **1847** Marryat *Childr. N. Forest* xv, Edward fired his gun into the body of the man. **1883** J. Gilmour *Among Mongols* xxvi. 315 A grey-headed old man comes out and fires off crackers. **1886** Mrs. Lynn Linton *Paston Carew* xl, Only when Mary fired a broadside into her character..did Mrs. Richard give tongue in her behalf.

b. *causal.* To cause to discharge a fire-arm.

1847 *Infantry Man.* (1854) 42 The instructor will fire each recruit *singly*.

13. a. *intr.* or *absol.* To discharge a gun or other fire-arm; to shoot. Const. *at*, *upon*, *into*, etc.

Fire! as a word of command, is now apprehended as the vb. in the imperative; originally it was prob. the sb. (= Fr. *feu*).

c **1645** T. Tully *Siege of Carlisle* (1840) 47 Stradling.. threatened to fire upon them. **1719** De Foe *Crusoe* (1840) II. iv. 93 He fired, and hit two. **1721** —— *Col. Jack* (1840) 227 We had orders not to fire upon the burghers. **1794** Southey *Botany Bay Ecl.* ii, I fired, they fell. **1848** Macaulay *Hist. Eng.* II. 250 Devonshire..had been fired at from Colepepper's windows. **1855** Haliburton *Nat. & Hum. Nat.* I. viii. 231 He has fired into the wrong flock this time. **1885** *Law Times* 9 May 29/2 The plaintiff..fired at him, but did not hit him.

b. *transf.* (*Bell-ringing.*) To ring all the bells in a peal at once.

1788–1880 [cf. firing 6 b].

c. fig. *to fire away*: to start off and proceed (in a speech or action) with energy and rapidity; to 'go ahead'. *colloq.*

1775 Mad. D'Arblay *Early Diary* 4 Mar., Mr. Burney fired away in a voluntary. **1840** Marryat *Poor Jack* xvii, Now then, Billy, fire away. **1841** E. FitzGerald *Lett.* (1889) I. 67 Then Edgeworth fires away about the Odes of Pindar. **1880** Payn *Confid. Agents* III. 156 You tell it to me, and I will tell it to him. Fire away.

14. a. *intr.* Of a gun, etc.: To go off.

1668 *Lond. Gaz.* No. 260/4 The Gun fired, killing two men. **1799** *Naval Chron.* I. 440 A quantity of six-inch live shells fired. **1816** *Sporting Mag.* XLVII. 194 The keepers.. heard a gun fire.

b. *fig.* To go *off* in an explosion of passion.

1848 Thackeray *Van. Fair* lxiv, Madame de Belladonna ..fired off in one of her furies.

15. a. *trans.* To eject or propel (a missile) from a gun or other fire-arm. *to fire away*: to consume (ammunition) by firing.

1588 Shaks. *L.L.L.* iii. i. 63 Is that Lead slow which is fir'd from a Gunne? **1864** Macdougall *Modern War* vii. 176 He paralysed one half of his army by shutting it in behind the ravine, where it did not fire a shot. *Ibid.* xiii. 428 There is a tendency in the soldiers..to fire away their ammunition in a reckless and aimless manner. **1885** *Times* 23 Jan. 9/2 A man who had never commanded a regiment or fired a shot in anger.

b. *transf.* To propel or discharge (a missile) as from a gun. Also *absol.* (cf. 13.)

1708 Ockley *Saracens* (1848) 143 The Persian archers firing on them all the while. **1849** *Pitman's Ghost* in *Bards of the Tyne* 409 (Northumb. Gloss.) They fired styens at him. **1878** A. Hamilton *Nerv. Dis.* x. 270 A boy having fired a brick at her. **1885** *Times* 4 Feb. 4/4 If you want something to eat, fire a stone through a window.

c. *fig.*; also, *to fire off*.

1850 J. W. Croker in *Croker Papers* (1884) III. xxvii. 214 He had a most effective style of firing off his joke. **1859** Reade *Love me Little* I. i. 29 Her ardent aunt..fired many glowing phrases in at the [carriage] window. **1861** Hughes *Tom Brown at Oxf.* ii, He..would not notice the looks of recognition which Tom kept firing at him. **1873** *Argosy* XVI. 443 'Miss Timmens is not worth her salt', fired Tod. **1888** Bryce *Amer. Commw.* III. cxi. 600 The great set speeches being fired off..with a view to their circulation in the country.

d. *Photogr.* To release (the shutter). Also *intr.* in *to fire away* or *off*, to take a photograph.

1892 *Photogr. Ann.* II. 51 What is the object of firing off at a street view..with the shutter set at $\frac{1}{70}$ second when $\frac{1}{25}$ would be fast enough? *Ibid.* 349 The shutter release.. appears to lift the mirror and fire the shutter much more efficiently. **1900** *Daily News* 21 June 5/1, I..fired away at some Tommies trying to catch a pig. **1958** M. L. Hall *Newnes Complete Amat. Photogr.* iv. 60 There is no doubt that the 35mm. user, with 36 frames on his roll, is much more apt to fire away indiscriminately.

16. *U.S. slang.* To turn (any one) out of a place; to eject or expel forcibly; to dismiss or discharge peremptorily; to reject (a picture sent in for exhibition). Frequently with *out*.

It has been suggested that this sense is derived from 8, but this seems unlikely.

1885 *Milner* (Dakota) *Free Press* 25 Apr. 5/2 If..the practice is persisted in, then they [pupils] should be fired out. **1887** *Lisbon* (Dakota) *Star* 11 Feb. 4 Postmaster Breed says the next time such a thing occurs he will fire the offender bodily. **1889** *Pall Mall G.* 29 Apr. 2/1 A Commissioner who should be discovered to have reported a subordinate unjustly would be fired from his high post. **1892** *Nation* (N.Y.) 15 Dec. 447/2 Artists of genuine ability have found their canvases fired.

fire, *v.*[2] Obs. variant of veer.

1536 Bellenden *Cron. Scot.* iv. xiv, Thay fyrit thair takillis, and sank down in yᵉ middis of yᵉ see.

'fireable, *a.* [f. fire *v.* + -able.] Capable of being fired or set on fire.

1662 J. Chandler *Van Helmont's Oriat.* 137 If Iron be not throughout its whole Body fireable, but a Coal altogether fireable. **1898** *Westm. Gaz.* 26 May 4/2 The *Don Juan de Austria* had only two fireable guns. **1900** *Times* (weekly ed.) 3 Aug. Suppl. p. iii/4 American coal, in consequence of being very firable, is not screened out.

'fire-arm. Usually *pl.* [f. fire *sb.* + arm *sb.*[2]] A weapon from which missiles are propelled by the combustion of gunpowder or other explosive. (The sing. is late and rare in use.)

1646 Evelyn *Diary, Brescia*, Here I purchas'd..my fine carabine..this citty being famous for these fire-armes. **1647** Clarendon *Hist. Reb.* ii. (1702) I. 92 Nor had they Ammunition to supply their few Fire-Arms. **1719** De Foe *Crusoe* (1840) I. xvii. 331 I left them my fire-arms; viz. five muskets. **1840** Thackeray *Paris Sk.-bk.* (1872) 197 He heard the report of a fire-arm. **1879** *Cassell's Techn. Educ.* III. 267 Battles are more and more fought out with fire-arms.

Hence **'fire-armed** *ppl. a.*, provided with fire-arms.

1869 Petherick *Trav.* I. 139 The negroes..having only clubs and lances, they were soon overpowered by the fire-armed Arabs.

'fire-ball. [f. fire *sb.* + ball *sb.*[1]]

1. a. A ball of fire or flame; applied *esp.* to certain large luminous meteors, and to lightning in a globular form.

1555 Eden *Decades* 217 The fyer baule or starre commonly cauled saynt Helen. **1611** Speed *Hist. Gt. Brit* 616/2 There was such a Tempest & thunder with great firebals of lightning. **1835** Browning *Paracelsus* i. *'I go to prove'*, Unless God send His hail Or blinding fireballs. **1862** Tyndall *Mountaineer.* i. 8 Sometimes the lightning seems to burst, like a fireball. **1883** H. A. Newton in *Encycl. Brit.* XVI. 108/1 Another class of luminous meteors known as shooting or falling stars, fire balls [etc.]. **1888** P. G. Tait *ibid.* XXIII. 330/1 The most mysterious phenomenon is what goes by the name of 'globe-lightning' or 'fire-ball'.

b. *spec.* The ball of flame resulting from the explosion of a nuclear device.

1955 *Bull. Atomic Sci.* Feb. 45/2 The exploding super-bomb produces a 3 to 4 mile diameter fireball. **1957** *Times* 18 May 6/4 The base of the fireball was well above the surface of the sea.

2. a. *Mil.* A ball filled with combustible or explosive materials, used as a projectile, either to damage the enemy by explosion or to set fire to their works.

1595 Barnfield *Cassandra* xli, Vulcan darted Against their Tower his burning fier-bals. **1609** Holland *Amm. Marcell.* xxiv. iv. 249 Tumbling downe huge stones, with firebrands, and fireballs [*malleolis*]. **1684** *Scanderbeg Rediv.* v. 120 They shot above 2000 Cannon Bullets into the Town, and 500 Fireballs. **1753** Chambers *Cycl. Supp.*, *Fire balls* are bags of canvas filled with gunpowder, sulphur, saltpetre, pitch, &c. **1841** Elphinstone *Hist. Ind.* I. 505 A fire-ball struck the rája's elephant.

b. *fig.*

1675 Traherne *Chr. Ethics* xxv. 390 Virulent speeches are a fire-ball tossed to and fro, of them that love death. **1718** Hickes *J. Kettlewell* ii. xxix. 131 At this Time there were Fire-Balls of Dissention flung..all over the Kingdom.

c. *Her.* (See quot.)

1830 Robson *Brit. Her.* III. Gloss. s.v. *Ball, Fire Ball*, or *Ball fired proper*, is always represented with the fire issuing from the top. When otherwise, it should be so expressed in the blazon; as, *a ball fired* in four places.

3. a. A ball of coal-dust and clay or other material, used for kindling fires. **b.** A ball of fire-brick, put into a fire to save fuel.

'fire-bird. Also 6 fieres-bird.

1. †**a.** A bird which stays by or hovers round the fire (quot. 1593). **b.** (See quot. 1865.)

1593 *Tell-troth's New Y. Gift* 12 This weather-beaten fieres-bird. **1865** Tylor *Early Hist. Man.* ix. 252 The story of the fire-bird..a bird which pecked at it [a tree] and made fire come forth.

2. a. *U.S.* A popular name of the Baltimore oriole, *Icterus galbula*. **b.** A kind of bee-eater.

1824 W. Irving *T. Trav.* (1849) 436 The fire-bird streamed by them with his deep-red plumage. **1856** Bryant *Poems, Indian Story* viii, The hollow woods..Ring shrill with the fire-bird's lay. **1892** *Pall Mall G.* 12 Nov. 3/1 You may watch the red fire-bird (a kind of bee-eater) as it sweeps ..round the bush-grown moat of the fortress.

ˈfire-blende. *Min.* [translation of Ger. *feuerblende* (Breithaupt in 1832), f. *feuer* FIRE + *blende*: see BLENDE.] = PYROSTILPNITE.

1850 DANA *Min.* 543. **1875** *Ure's Dict. Arts* (ed. 7) II. 393.

ˈfire-boot, †-bote. *Law. Obs.* exc. *Hist.* [f. FIRE *sb.* + BOOT *sb.*^{1} Cf. OE. *fýr-béta* one who 'beets' or mends a fire.] The repair or mending of a fire; wood used for this purpose, fuel (granted by the landlord to the tenant); the right of a tenant to take fire-wood from off the landlord's estate.

1484 *Lease of Manor of Scotter* (N.W. Linc. Gloss.), 12 carect subbosci pro le heybote et octo focal pro fyrbot. **1557** TUSSER *100 Points Husb.* lxv, A blocke at the harthe.. Shall helpe to saue fier bote. **1559** *Will of E. Boraston* (Somerset Ho.), My saide wyf shall..have certayne underwoodes appoynted to her by my executours towardes her fyreboote. **1657** SIR H. GRIMSTONE in *Croke's Reports* I. 477 Those trees were long since..fit only for fire-boot. **1726** AYLIFFE *Parergon* 506 If a Man cuts Trees for..Cartboot, Ploughboot, and Fireboot. **1824** HITCHINS & DREW *Cornwall* II. 214 Gathering for fire-boot and house-boot.. branches of oak trees. **1888** *Athenæum* 12 May 596/3 The privilege of firebote in the lord's wood, that is gathering sticks for fuel.

fire-box. [BOX *sb.*^{2}]

†**1.** A box with materials for procuring fire, a tinder-box. *Obs.*

1555 EDEN *Decades* 291 Euery man caryeth with hym..a fyre boxe. **1806-7** J. BERESFORD *Miseries Hum. Life* (1826) Post. Groans No. 43 Comforts of a fire-box. **1840** DICKENS *Old C. Shop* xlvii, He carried in his pocket, too, a fire-box.

†**2.** A kind of firework. *Obs.*

1634 J. BATE *Myst. Nat. & Art* II. 75 How to make fire Boxes..In these boxes you may put golden rayne, starres, serpents petrars [etc.].

3. The chamber of a steam-boiler in which the fuel is burnt.

1830 STEPHENSON & LOCKE *Locomotive & Fixed Engines* 65 Those [wheels] on which the 'fire-box' rests. **1887** J. A. EWING in *Encycl. Brit.* XXII. 516/1 The boiler..is fitted with a cast-iron internal fire-box.

ˈfire-brand. [f. FIRE *sb.* + BRAND *sb.*]

1. A piece of wood kindled at the fire.

c **1205** LAY. 25608 Sloȝen [floȝen ?] of heore hæȝene swulc fur-burondes. *c* **1300** *K. Alis.* 6848 Theo kyng sygh a lem, so a fuyrbrond. *c* **1400** MAUNDEV. (Roxb.) xiii. 57 A wikked man..kest a brynnand fyrebrand at oure Lord. **1591** SPENSER *Virg. Gnat* 343 Tisiphone..doth shake..Her flaming fire brond. **1684** BUNYAN *Pilgr.* II. (1862) 296 As the Proverb is, he could have bit a Fire-brand, had it stood in his way. **1786** tr. *Beckford's Vathek* (1868) 6 Eyes which glowed like firebrands. **1828** BERRY *Encycl. Her.* I, *Fire-brand inflamed ppr.*, fire brands, borne in coat-armour, are generally represented raguly. **1887** BOWEN *Virg. Æneid* I. 525 We..Pray thee the firebrand fell from the Trojan vessels to keep.

†**b.** *transf.* One who is doomed or deserves to burn in hell; usually ***firebrand of hell.*** Obs.

1340 HAMPOLE *Pr. Consc.* 7421 Or he us made for noght els to dwelle In erth, bot to be fyre brandes in helle. **1551** CROWLEY *Pleas. & Pain* 270 Eternall fyre is redy for eche hell fyrebrande. **1560** BECON *New Catech.* Wks. 1844 II. 204, I was by nature..a very firebrand of hell.

2. *fig.* One who, or a thing which, kindles strife or mischief, inflames the passions, etc.

1382 WYCLIF *Isa.* vii. 4 Thin herte be not ferd of the two tailes of these smokende fyr brondis. **1581** SAVILE *Tactius' Hist.* II. lxxxvi. (1591) 104 This man..became a principall fire-brande of the warre. **1583** *Exec. for Treason* (1675) 16 Dr. Sanders the Popes firebrand in Ireland. **1647** CLARENDON *Hist. Reb.* IV. (1702) I. 293 And so this firebrand of Priviledge inflamed the City at that time. **1690** NORRIS *Beatitudes* (1692) 67 Meer Firebrands in Society, that kindle and lay waste where-ever they come. **1791** BURKE *Corr.* (1844) III. 278 These fierce republicans, even the very firebrands of the Jacobins. **1860** MOTLEY *Netherl.* I. iv. 132 Not peace, but a firebrand..had the King held forth to his subjects.

†**3.** = BRAND-MARK. *Obs.*

1675 *Lond. Gaz.* No. 1049/4 A speckled Mare..marked with a Fire-brand on the near shoulder. **1704** *Ibid.* No. 4037/8 A..Cart Gelding..a Firebrand on the near Shoulder.

4. A local name for the redstart.

1890 in *Gloucest. Gloss.*

5. *attrib.* ***firebrand-new*** (dial.) = BRAND-NEW.

c **1420** *Pallad. on Husb.* IV. 328 Umbidelve The rootes, and dryve ynne a firbronde pynne. **1606** SHAKS. *Tr. & Cr.* II. ii. 110 Our fire-brand Brother Paris burns vs all. **1882** *W. Worc. Gloss., Fire-brand-new*..quite new.

Hence **ˈfire-branded** *ppl. a.*, (*a*) = BRAND-MARKED (*obs.*); (*b*) furnished with fire-brands. **ˈfire-brandism** (*nonce-wd.*), the disposition or behaviour of a (social) fire-brand.

1673 *Lond. Gaz.* No. 764/4 The Gelding is brown..the Letter R firebranded on the farther buttock. **1818** KEATS *Endym.* III. 7 Who..will see unpack'd Fire-branded foxes to sear up and singe Our gold and ripe-ear'd hopes. **1887** *Sat. Rev.* 5 Nov. 643 Firebrandism of this kind is..an act either of unpardonable folly or..wickedness.

†**ˈfire-ˌcrancel.** *Obs.* [Cf. Ger. *feuerkranz* in same sense; also *kränzel*, dim. of *kranz* wreath.] = *fire-hoop, -wreath*: see FIRE *sb.* B. 5.

1755 MAGENS *Insurances* II. 444 Cannons, Muskets.. Granadoes, Fire-Crancels, pitched Hoops.

ˈfire-cross. [See CROSS 13.] A signal used anciently in Scotland, and more recently in the Highlands, to summon the men to a rendezvous on the sudden outbreak of war.

It was called in Gaelic *cros-táraidh* or *crann-táraidh* = cross or beam of gathering, and consisted of a cross or piece of wood burnt at one end and dipped in blood at the other —symbolical of fire and sword—which was handed from clansman to clansman, each man immediately on receiving it running with it to his nearest neighbour, so as to spread the alarm over a district in a short time. (Poetical references to it are often mere guesses founded on the name.)

1547 in *Reg. Privy Seal* XXI. 45 (Jam.) The fire Croce being borne throw the hale Realme. **1548** W. PATTEN *Exped. Scotl.* Pref. sig. a viii, Caused yᵉ fier crosse..to be caried: whearof the solempnitee is never vsed, but in an vrgent nede. **1641** MILTON *Reform.* II. (1851) 51 To..proclaime a fire-crosse to a..perpetuall civill warre. **1826** LINGARD *Hist. Eng.* (ed. 4) VII. 16 Arran had dispatched the fire-cross from clan to clan.

fired (faɪəd), *ppl. a.* [f. FIRE *v.* + -ED^1.]

1. Set on fire or alight, kindled.

c **1420** *Pallad. on Husb.* I. 929 The fyred nuttes smolder. **1556** J. HEYWOOD *Spider & F.* lvii. 130 Euerie peece..Hath a spider gonner; with redy fired mach. **1665** MANLEY *Grotius' Low-C. Warres* 957 The Holland ships also attempted to succour their fired Vessels. **1719** D'URFEY *Pills* I. 197 To quench a fir'd House. **1884** *Pall Mall G.* 30 Dec. 2/1 The gases from the fired gunpowder.

†**2.** As transl. of L. *ignitus*: **a.** Tried in the fire.

1382 WYCLIF *Rev.* iii. 18, I counseile thee, for to bye of me gold fyrid.

†**b.** Full of fire, fiery. (*lit.* and *fig.*) *Obs.*

a **1300** *E.E. Psalter* cxviii. [cxix.] 140 Fired þi speche es swithe wele. *a* **1340** HAMPOLE *ibid.*, Ffyrid gretly þi worde ..þat is, þi worde þat is fyry thorgh þe halygast. **1388** WYCLIF *Num.* xxi. 6 The Lord sente firid serpentis in to the puple.

3. Of flax: (see quots. and FIRE *v.*^{1} 4 b).

1789 *Trans. Soc. Encourag. Arts* I. 204 Except fired or mildewed flax, both of which..being improper for linen cloth. **1814** MASON *Surv. Ireland* I. XIII. ix. 264 The leaves ..are, by the wet, laid flat upon the stem, the flax instantly appears fired (which is a number of black specks appearing upon the stem).

4. *Her.* Of a fire-ball: Represented with fire issuing from the surface. See FIRE-BALL 2 c.

5. ***fired off***: said of a kiln when the fire has ceased to burn, but before the heat is exhausted.

1884 C. T. DAVIS *Bricks, etc.* 284 If it is desired to admit hot air to the upper part of any kiln, this may be done by opening the dampers..at the top of a fired-off kiln.

6. Of the case of a cartridge: used, having had the cartridge discharged.

1892 W. W. GREENER *Breech-loader* 65 Such processes as cocking the locks and taking out the fired cases. **1902** *Encycl. Brit.* XXX. 402/2 The extractor holds a cartridge and a fired case ready to be pushed into the empty breech and ejector-tube respectively... The lock is withdrawn taking with it the fresh cartridge from the belt and the now fired case.

ˈfire-damp. [See DAMP *sb.*] A miner's term for carburetted hydrogen or marsh-gas, which is given off by coal and is explosive when mixed in certain proportions with atmospheric air.

1677 *Phil. Trans.* XII. 895 The Fire-damp did by little and little begin..to appear in crevisses and slits of the Cole. **1710** *Brit. Apollo* III. No. 3. 2/2 What Miners relate concerning Fire-damps. **1774** PENNANT *Tour Scotl. in* 1772, 49 The..colliers dare not venture with a candle in spots where fire-damps are supposed to lurk. **1879** *Cassell's Techn. Educ.* I. 143 Two different gases, known by the miners as fire-damp and choke-damp.

attrib. **1867** W. W. SMYTH *Coal & Coal-mining* 200 The ingenious 'fire-damp indicator' of Mr. Ansell. **1874** KNIGHT *Dict. Mech.* I. 863/1 *Fire-damp-alarm*, one which indicates the presence of dangerous quantities of gas or fire-damp in coal workings.

ˈfire-drake. [OE. *fýr-draca*, f. *fýr*, FIRE *sb.* + *draca* dragon.]

1. A 'fiery dragon': a mythical creature belonging to Germanic superstition.

Beowulf 5371 þa wæs..frecne fyr-draca, fæhða ȝemyndiȝ. **1393** GOWER *Conf.* III. 95 Sometime the fire-drake it semeth. **1522** SKELTON *Why not to Court* 978 That he wolde than make The devyls to quake Lyke a fyerdrake. **1683** CROWNE *City Politiques* II. i, Were not your writings like so many Fire-drakes?..no person [would] come near 'em. **1865** KINGSLEY *Herew.* xiii, He expected the enchanter to enter on a fire drake. **1883** *Longm. Mag.* Sept. 517 Woodcuts, representing..fire-drakes, and other fearful wild-fowl.

†**2. a.** A fiery meteor. **b.** A will-o'-the-wisp.

1563 W. FULKE *Meteors* (1640) 10 Flying Dragons, or as Englishmen call them, fire Drakes, be caused in this maner. **1607** G. WILKINS *Miseries Enforced Marr.* in Hazl. *Dodsley* IX. 572 Who should be lamps to comfort out our way, And not like firedrakes to lead men astray. **1631** CHAPMAN *Cæsar & Pompey* Wks. 1873 III. 159 So have I seen a firedrake glide at midnight Before a dying man to point his grave. **1851** SIR F. PALGRAVE *Norm. & Eng.* I. 127 He deals in signs, portents, fire-drakes..armies fighting in clouds.

†**3.** A kind of firework. *Obs.*

1607 MIDDLETON *Five Gallants* III. ii. 82 But, like fire-drakes, Mounted a little, gave a crack, and fell. **1634** J. BATE *Myst. Nat. & Art* 80 How to make fire Drakes. **1706** in PHILLIPS (ed. Kersey).

†**4.** *transf.* **a.** An alchemist's assistant. **b.** A man with a fiery nose. **c.** One who is fond of fighting; = FIRE-EATER 2. **d.** A fire-man. **e.** = FIRESHIP 2.

1610 B. JONSON *Alch.* II. i, That's his fire-drake, His lungs, his Zephyrus, he that puffes his coales. **1613** SHAKS. *Hen. VIII*, V. iv. 45 Twenty of the Dog-dayes now reigne in 's Nose..that Fire-drake did I hit three times on the head. *c* **1626** *Dick of Devon.* I. ii. in Bullen *O. Pl.* II. 14 Our shipps Carrying such firedrakes in them that [etc.]. *a* **1670** HACKET *Abp. Williams* II. (1692) 146 It is not strange that such fire-drakes as he writes of could not forbear to threaten the nation. **1631** DEKKER *Match mee* I. Wks. 1873 IV. 140 Another Fire-drake! More Salamanders! *a* **1700** B. E. *Dict. Cant. Crew, Fire-drakes*, Men with a Phenix for their Badge, in Livery, and Pay from the Insurance-Office, to extinguish Fires. **1710** *Brit. Apollo* II. Q. No. 3. 7/1 A Fire-drake of Spain [might]..put you in the same Plight.

ˈfire-ˌeater.

1. A juggler who eats or pretends to eat fire.

1672 EVELYN *Diary* 8 Oct., Richardson the famous Fire-eater..before us devour'd brimston on glowing coales, chewing and swallowing them. **1762** GOLDSM. *Cit. W.* lxxxv, Stage-players, fire-eaters..and wire-walkers..ought not entirely to be despised. **1827** G. HIGGINS *Celtic Druids* 221 Like the celebrated fire-eater in London.

2. One fond of fighting, a duellist; one who seeks occasion to quarrel or fight.

1804 *Morning Herald* in *Spirit Pub. Jrnls.* (1805) VIII. 249 The Sieur W-d-m, fire-eater in ordinary to the troop. **1827** BARRINGTON *Personal Sk.* II. 8 About the year 1777, the 'Fire-eaters' were in great repute. **1840** THACKERAY *Paris Sk.-bk.* (1869) 25 He killed a celebrated French fire-eater. **1864** *Spectator* No. 187. 627 Sober-minded men..not fire-eaters wishing to fight for pure fighting's sake.

b. (*U.S.*) Before the Civil War: A violent Southern partisan.

1863 HAWTHORNE *Our Old Home* (1883) I. 55 The newcomer proved to be..as he pleasantly acknowledged, a Southern Fire-Eater. **1879** TOURGEE *Fool's Err.* vii. 30 An original Secesh, a regular fire-eater.

3. *Trade slang.* A quick worker.

1841 SAVAGE *Dict. Printing, Fire-eater*, Compositors who are expeditious workmen are styled Fire Eaters. **1889** BARRÈRE & LELAND *Dict. Slang, Fire-eater*, (Tailors), one who does a great amount of work in a very short time.

So **ˈfire-ˌeating** *vbl. sb.* and *ppl. a.*

1819 *Metropolis* II. 207, I would as soon sit down in company with my butcher as with these fire-eating fellows. **1848** THACKERAY *Van. Fair* xvii, A fire-eating and jealous warrior. **1863** HAWTHORNE *Our Old Home* (1883) I. 55 My fire-eating friend has had ample opportunities to banquet on his favorite diet. **1882** W. HASLAM *Yet not I* (1883) 8 He did not like that fire-eating kind of preaching. **1890** *Spectator* 4 Jan., The absence of fire-eating among the leading statesmen of Europe.

ˈfire-engine. [f. FIRE *sb.* + ENGINE.]

1. A machine for throwing water to extinguish fires.

c **1680** *Sir S. Morland's Pumps* Broadside, Brit. Mus. 816 m. 10. 90 For a Fire Engin with one Pair of Handles.. Twenty three pound. **1725** DESAGULIERS *Exper. Philos.* (1744) II. 505–519 *heading*, Mr. Newsham's Fire-Engine. **1755** FRANKLIN *Let.* Wks. 1887 II. 405 A stream [of water] from a fire-engine will force through the strongest panes of a window. **1806** O. GREGORY *Mech.* (1807) II. 175 Fire engine [is] the name now commonly given to a machine by which water is thrown upon fires to extinguish them. **1836** DICKENS *Sk. Boz, Our Parish* i, The services of that particularly useful machine, a parish fire-engine, are required.

2. A steam-engine. *Obs.* exc. *local.*

1722 BARNES in Brand *Hist. Newcastle* (1789) II. 685 *note*, The charge of water was calculated as if to be drawn by horses, whereas it may be done much cheaper by help of a fire engine. **1750** FRANKLIN *Wks.* (1887) II. 164 They waited for a fire-engine from England to drain their pits. **1806** O. GREGORY *Mech.* (1807) II. 353 This [i.e. the steam engine] has often been called the Fire-engine, because of the fire used in boiling the liquid. **1867** W. W. SMYTH *Coal & Coal-mining* 6 Newcomen appears..to have first tried his 'fire-engine' on the large scale at a colliery near Wolverhampton. **1880** *W. Cornw. Gloss., Fire-engine*, a steam-engine.

†**3.** A heating apparatus. *Obs. rare.*

1708 J. CHAMBERLAYNE *St. Gt. Brit.* I. I. iii. (1743) 9 One fire-engine conveys warm air to every individual Part of the Machine [Lombe's machine for thrown silk].

ˈfire-eyed, *a.* Having eyes glowing as with fire.

1596 SHAKS. *1 Hen. IV*, IV. i. 114 To the fire-ey'd Maid of smoakie Warre..will wee offer them. **1601** *Downfall Earl of Huntington* IV. i. in Hazl. *Dodsley* VIII. 178 Anon comes forth the fire-eyed dreadful beast. **1602** MARSTON *Antonio's Rev.* V. v, Grim fier-eyed rage Possess us wholly. **1823** MOORE *Fables* 137 Like certain fire-eyed minstrel maids. **1831** CARLYLE *Sart. Res.* (1858) 64 Only at rare intervals did the young soul burst forth into fire-eyed rage.

ˈfire-fang, *sb.* [f. next vb.] The state of being fire-fanged or overheated.

1813 W. LESLIE *Surv. Nairn* 454. **1855** *Jrnl. R. Agric. Soc.* XVI. II. 328 Suppose the oxygen had been supplied to the decaying mass..would there have been any firefang?

ˈfire-fang, *v. Obs.* exc. *dial.* [f. FIRE *sb.* + FANG *v.*^{1}] *trans.* To lay hold of with fire; to singe, scorch; in quot. *absol.* Also jocosely of the burning of heretics. *Obs.* in gen. sense.

1562 SCOTT *N.Y. Gift to Quene* x. in *Bannatyne Poems* (1770) 245 And quha eit flesch on Fridayis was fyre-fangit. **1618** M. BARET *Horsemanship* I. 37 A hasty fire does not only firefange..but also taketh away the true rellish. **1896** *Vermont Agric. Rep.* XV. 72 There is danger if ensilage contains more than 25 per cent of dry matter that it will fire-fang in the silo.

Hence **ˈfire-fanged** *ppl. a.*, † (*a*) *gen.* caught by the fire, singed, scorched (*obs.*); (*b*) *spec.* of barley, oatmeal, etc., of manure and straw; also of cheese: Having a scorched or singed appearance, smell, or taste, as if overheated. **ˈfire-fanging** *vbl. sb.*, the action of the vb.

1513 Douglas *Æneis* XII. v. 202 This Chorineus.. Ruschit on his fa, thus fyrefangit and onsaucht. **1615** Markham *Eng. Housew.* II. vii. (1668) 166 Too..hasty a fire scorcheth and burneth it [i.e. the Malt], which is called among Maltsters Fire-fang'd. **1725** Bradley *Fam. Dict.* s.v. *Malt*, With a moderate Fire, for fear of Fire-fanging. **1790** Grose *Prov. Gloss.* (ed. 2), *Fire-fanged*, fire-bitten. Spoken of oatmeal &c. that is overdried. North. **1808** Jamieson *s.v.*, Cheese is said to be *firefangit*, when it is swelled and cracked, and has received a peculiar taste, in consequence of being exposed to much heat before it has been dried. **1869** *Lonsdale Gloss., Fire-fanged*, of oats or barley too hastily dried in the kiln.

'fire-flaught. Orig. *Sc.* [f. fire *sb.* + flaught. Cf. fireslaught.]

1. Lightning; a flash of lightning; a storm of thunder and lightning.

c **1375** ? Barbour *Troy-bk.* I. 468 Ande fyre-flauthtis our þe feldes flee Ine syk fladdanis & flambys briht. *c* **1425** Wyntoun *Cron.* VI. v. 33 A gret fyre flawcht..Ðan hapnyd in Rome. **1552** Lyndesay *Monarche* 5556 Than sall ye sone of god discend: As fyreflaucht haistely glansyng. **1645** Rutherford *Tryal & Tri. Faith* (1845) 149 Reasons work not in a moment, as fire flaughts in the air. **1816** Scott *Old Mort.* xxxviii, He passed by me like a fire-flaught. **1876** Miss Yonge *Three Brides* (ed. 3) I. xi. 167 She passes like—like a fire-flaught, whatever that is—just bows.

b. The northern lights; *aurora borealis.*

1787 Grose *Prov. Gloss., Fire-flaught*..the northern lights.

2. *transf.* **a.** A sudden burst or rush.

1637 Rutherford *Lett.* (1862) I. civ. 265 A fire-flaught of challenges will come in at mid-summer and question me. **1880** Swinburne. *Study Shaks.* 173 Even Goneril has her one splendid hour, her fireflaught of hellish glory.

b. A fiery glance.

1802 Jamieson *Water Kelpie* viii. in Scott *Minstr. Scott. Bord.* (1869) 538 From ilka ee the fire-flauchts flee And flash alangis the flude. **1826** J. Wilson *Noct. Ambr.* Wks. 1855 I. 136 Every coorser flingin' fire-flaughts frae his een.

'fire-fly. [f. fire *sb.*]

1. A lampyrid or elaterid insect which has the property of emitting phosphorescent light.

1658 Rowland *Moufet's Theat. Ins.* 1019 Of the Fire-fly. **1756** P. Browne *Jamaica* 432 The larger Fire Fly. **1814** Cary *Dante's Inf.* xxvi. 31 Fire-flies innumerous spangling o'er the vale. **1880** Ouida *Moths* II. 262 Where the fire-flies flash amongst the lemon blossoms and the myrtle.

2. a. *attrib.* and *Comb.*

1806 Moore *Lake Dismal Swamp* ii, Her fire-fly lamp I soon shall see. **1858** Bushnell *Serm. New Life* 189 A mere fire-fly spark in comparison. **1876** Ouida *Winter City*, vii. 183 Such as echo through the firefly-lighted corn.

b. *fig.*

[**1897** *Sears, Roebuck Catal.* 162/2 The 'Fire-Fly' Single Wheel Hoe.] **1948** A. Toynbee *Civilization on Trial* i. 9 Those pages teeming with firefly flashes of historical insight. **1965** *Sunday Mail Mag.* (Brisbane) 15 Aug. 5/2 The nearest firefly flash of expression came into the generalissimo's face.

'fire-fork. *Obs.* exc. *dial.* [f. as prec.] A fork-shaped instrument used for stirring up the fire, putting on fuel, etc.

c **1440** *Promp. Parv.* 161/2 Fyyr forke, *ticionarium.* **1483–4** *Act 1 Rich. III*, c. 12, Fireforkes. **1547** *Lanc. Willis* I. 108 Ij yrnes for the oven mouthe and a fire-fork. **1627** Drayton *Agincourt* 179 The women eager as their husbands were With Spits and Fireforkes. **1727** De Foe *Hist. App.* ix. (1735) 169 A fourth came out, not with a Sword, but a Fire-Fork. **1875** in *Sussex Gloss.* **1887** in *Kent Gloss.*

fig. **1685** Crowne *Sir C. Nice* III. Wks. 1874 III. 301 *Bell.* Who brought this picture? *Hot.* The common fire-fork of rebellion.

'fire-hearth. [f. as prec.]

1. The pavement of brick or stone on which a fire is made; the hearth in front of a fireplace.

c **1440** *Promp. Parv.* 161/2 Fyyr herthe, *focarium.* **1615** Crooke *Body of Man* 45 The Testicles are..the Feu-place or Fire-hearth, where the Lares or houshold-Gods of the body, do solace and disport themselues. **1703** T. N. *City & C. Purchaser* 43 Bricks are frequently used in Paving of.. Sinks, and Fire-hearths. **1769** R. Price *Observ. Revers. Payments* (1792) II. 276 *note*, There was a tax of two shillings on every fire-hearth.

2. A kind of cooking range or stove for ships.

1676 *Lond. Gaz.* No. 1127/4 The..Invention of Iron Fire-Hearths for Ships. *c* **1850** *Rudim. Navig.* (Weale) 118 *Fire-hearth*, the fire-place and conveniences in the galley for cooking the provisions for the people.

'fire-hook. [f. as prec.] **a.** A large hook used in pulling down burning buildings. **b.** (See quot. 1874).

1467 in *Eng. Gilds* (1870) 385 That ther be v. fuyre hokes. **1585** Higins *Junius' Nomenclator* 279 *Hama*..a fire hooke. **1620** *Nottingham Rec.* (1889) IV. 371 We present the townes fyer hookes to be decayd for want of steales [handles]. **1788** Franklin *Autob.* Wks. 1887 I. 205 Fines..apply'd to the purchase of fire-engines, ladders, fire-hooks. **1812** H. & J. Smith *Rej. Addr., Tale Drury Lane* 89 The engines thunder'd through the street, Fire-hook, pipe, bucket, all complete. **1874** Knight *Dict. Mech.* I. 867/2 *Fire-hook* (Steam-engineering), a kind of hook for raking and stirring the furnace fire.

† **'fire-'hot,** *a.* [f. as prec.] **a.** Of material things: Hot as fire; red-hot. **b.** *fig.* Inflamed with zeal, passion, or lust. *Obs.*

a **1000** *Elene* 937 (Gr.) Fyrhat lufu. **1398** Trevisa *Barth. de P.R.* x. iv. (Tollem. MS.), As it farep in fyre hoot yren and in brennynge cole. **1483** Caxton *Gold. Leg.* (1892) 979 Whan it was fyre hote. **1589** R. Harvey *P. Perc.* 17, I dare saie..(with that firehot Preacher) that [etc.]. **1595** J. Weever in *Shaks. C. Praise* 16 Faire fire-hot Venus. **1605** T. Hutton *Reas. Refusal* 37 In the daies of firehot persecution. **1678** R. R[ussell] *Geber* III. II. III. v. 224 That the Plates may be kept fire-hot.

'fire-house. [f. as prec. Cf. ON. *eldhús.*] **a.** A house with a fireplace in it, as distinguished from the out-buildings. *Obs.* exc. *dial.* Sometimes, †the particular room in which the family fire was.

c **1000** Ælfric *Gloss.* in Wr.-Wülcker 184/26 *Caminatum*, fyrhus. **1530** *Test. Ebor.* (Surtees) V. 292 Every fyer howse wt in the parishing of Acclome. **1632** in S. O. Addy *Hall of Waltheof* (1893) 182 *note*, The Hall or Fierhouse of the now mansion house of the said John Parker. **1635** Pagitt *Christianogr.* (1646) I. 237 Ive (or Ine)..granted to the pope, that every Fire-house within his Kingdome should yearly pay him a peny. **1680** in *N. & Q.* 3rd Ser. (1866) IX. 452/1 All that ancient Messuage or Firehouse wherein one C.M. now dwelleth. **1878** *Cumberld. Gloss., Fire-house*, the dwelling—in contradistinction to the outbuildings.

b. *U.S.* (Now usu. as one word.) = ***fire station*** s.v. fire *sb.* 5.

1901 *Rep. Fire Dept. N.Y. 1900* 6 A number of sites for new fire-houses..have been acquired. **1902** *Scribner's Mag.* Oct. 452/1 Our American fire-houses compare favorably with those in Europe. **1945** *Sat. Rev.* 7 July 21/1 Sometimes it's as elevated as the conversation in back of the firehouse in Salem, Ohio. **1961** [see bong]. **1979** R. Jaffe *Class Reunion* (1980) II. xi. 296 'What's it like in the firehouse?'..'Like an army barracks.' **1984** *New Yorker* 18 June 76/2 Firemen in Washington, D.C., were growing it [*sc.* corn]..in vacant lots next to their firehouses.

'fire-hunting, *vbl. sb.* *U.S.* [fire *sb.* B. 3 b.]

a. The firing of timber to drive out game. **b.** Hunting by night in which lights are used to attract or reveal the game. Hence (in sense b) **'fire-hunt** *sb.*, **'fire-hunt** *v. trans.* and *intr.*, **'fire-hunter**.

1705 R. Beverley *Hist. Virginia* II. 39 They [*sc.* Indians] had a better Way of killing the..greater Game, by a method which we call Fire-Hunting: that is,..they wou'd Fire the Woods. **1788** M. Dewees *Jrnl.* (MS.) 17v Had Several Gentlemen to dine..expecting a fire hunt of some deer. **1814** *Sporting Mag.* XLIV. 62 The method of approaching ..the red deer..by means of fire-hunting them. **1833** *Amer. Turf Reg.* Feb. 305 Here we took our first drive; but..a '*fire hunter*' had anticipated us the previous night. **1852** Haliburton *Traits Amer. Humor* III. 171 The fire-hunt was Sam's hobby. **1875** E. King *Southern States N. Amer.* 417 The sportsman..may 'fire-hunt' the deer in the forests. **1885** T. Roosevelt *Hunting Trips* v. 158 Fire-hunting is never tried in the cattle country. **1891** *Outing* Dec. 236/1 No sooner had he eaten his supper each day than he began to importune the younger men of the party to join him in a 'fire hunt'... Beverly carried the gun, his chief the torch, consisting of 'lightwood' knots blazing in the bowl of a long-handled frying pan. **1948** E. N. Dick *Dixie Frontier* 35 Fire hunting..was most effective on a dark night.

'fire-iron. [Cf. MHG. *viurisern.*]

† **1.** An iron (or a steel) for striking a light. *Obs.*

c **1300** *St. Brandan* 639 He browȝte a fur-ire and a ston Forto smyte fur therwith. *c* **1440** *Promp. Parv.* 161/2 Fyyre yryn, to smyte wythe fyre, *fugillus.* *c* **1500** *Melusine* 23 Raymondin..hadd kyndled the fyre with hys fyre-yron. **1530** Palsgr. 220/2 Fyre yron to stryke fyre with, *fusil.*

2. *pl.* Implements for tending a domestic fire, usually shovel, tongs and poker.

1812 *Specif. G. Babb's Patent* No. 3526, A new Method of producing..fire irons. **1848** C. Bronte *J. Eyre* xxi, The grate and fire-irons were burnished bright. **1886** J. K. Jerome *Idle Thoughts* (1889) 36 Hammering, shouting and rattling the fire-irons.

† **fire-isle.** *Obs. rare*$^{-1}$. [f. fire *sb.* + OE. *ysla, ysela* hot ashes.] In *pl.* Ashes, embers.

c **1250** *Gen. & Ex.* 1130 Oc quane here apples ripe ben, fier-isles man mai ðor-inne sen.

fireless ('faɪəlɪs), *a.* [f. fire *sb.* + -less.] Devoid of fire, without a fire.

† **1.** Unlit, not flaming. *Obs.*

1649 Stanley *Europa* etc. 29 With hizzing firelesse Torches.

2. a. Having no fire, without a fire.

1661 Brome *Epist. to Mr. J. B.* 6 My fireless chymnies catch the cold. **1775** Mad. D'Arblay *Early Diary* (1889) II. 117 This cold season, when there is no writing in a fireless room. **1789** Wordsw. *Evening Walk*, When..fireless are the valleys far and wide. **1852** Hawthorne *Blithedale Rom.* I. v. 81, I went shivering to my fireless chamber.

b. Of a tribe: Having no knowledge of or means of procuring fire.

1865 Tylor *Early Hist. Man.* ix. 228 The mention of a fireless race. *ibid.* 229 A fireless people.

c. ***fireless cooker***, an insulated chamber brought to a heat suitable for cooking and capable of maintaining sufficient heat to cook with; also, = *hay-box* (hay *sb.*[1]).

1908 E. A. Huntington (*title*) The fireless cooker. **1945** R. Molloy *Pride's Way* 291, I believe Mrs. Wilson approves of a fireless cooker. **1965** G. McInnes *Road to Gundagai* v. 83 The other gadget was the Fireless Cooker.. a wooden box filled with straw.

3. *fig.* Without energy, life, or animation.

The alleged example from **1598** Sylvester *Du Bartas* II. i. I. (1641) 86/1 is an error for sireless *a.*, q.v.

1656 Trapp *Comm. Matt.* iii. 11 The Latines call a dull dronish man, a fireless man.

'fire-light. **a.** The light given by a fire or fires. † **b.** Lightning (*obs.*). **c.** (quot. 1845) = aurora 5.

Beowulf 3037 He..Fyr-leoht ȝeseah. *c* **1340** *Cursor M.* 22680 (Trin.) As þondir doþ wiþ fire liȝt. **1769** *De Foe's Tour Gt. Brit.* III. 210 It takes its Name from Flam, a British Word for a Fire-light. **1800** Herschel in *Phil. Trans.* XC. 480 Their disposition to transmit candle-light or fire-light. **1845** Hirst *Com. Mammoth* 21 Flashed, like the fire-lights of the North, When Winter rules the frozen earth. **1860** Tyndall *Glac.* I. v. 41 The ruddy fire-light gleaming over the walls.

† **'fireling.** *Obs.*$^{-1}$ [see -ling.] A little fire.

15.. *Image Ipocr.* 108 in Skelton *Wks.* (ed. Dyce) II. 415 For many a hyerlinge With a wilde fyerlinge..Shall pryck owt as a post.

'firelock. [See lock *sb.*]

1. A gun-lock in which sparks were produced (either by friction or percussion) to ignite the priming.

The name was at first given to the wheel-lock; in the 17th cent. it became transferred to the flint-lock.

1547 *Inventory* in Meyrick *Antient Armour* III. 15 One chamber pece blacke..with a fier locke. **1625** G. M[arkham] *Souldiers Accid.* 53 Pistolls, Petronells, or Dragons..all these are with fire-lockes, and those fire-lockes (for the most part) Snap-hances. **1639** R. Ward *Animadv. Warre* I. 293 The Firelocke is surest to give fire, and not so apt to be out of kilter; besides they will indure Spand 24 houres together without hurting them. **1655** Mrq. Worcester. *Cent. Inv.* No. 44 A perfect Pistol..with Prime, Powder and Fire-lock. **1677** Ld. Orrery *Art of War* 31 In the Fire-lock the motion is so sudden, that what makes the Cock fall on the Hammer, strikes the Fire, and opens the Pan at once.

2. A musket furnished with such a lock.

1590 Sir J. Smyth *Disc. Weapons* 47 Whereby they [the stones] should faile to strike iust vpon the wheeles being fire-lockes, or vpon the hammers or steeles, if they be Snap-hances. **1625** G. M[arkham] *Souldiers Accid.* 41 They [cuirassiers] shall haue a case of long Pistolls, firelockes (if it may be) but Snaphaunces, where they are wanting. **1630** R. *Johnson's Kingd. & Commw.* 382 Part..carried Fire-lockes of two foot, and the residue Pikes. **1662** J. Davies tr. Mandelslo *Trav. E. Ind.* 51 They have no fire Armes with wheeles, nor yet Fire-locks. **1703** Luttrell *Brief Rel.* (1857) V. 305 An agent..is arrived here, to buy 30,000 fire-locks. **1811** Gen. Doyle in Napier *Penins. War* (Rtldg.) II. App. 427 Six months have passed without a fire-lock being made! **1869** E. A. Parkes *Pract. Hygiene* (ed. 3) 324 The English army have extemporised tents..by suspending blankets over their firelocks.

3. A soldier armed with such a weapon.

1645 R. Symonds *Diary Civ. War* (Camden) 181/2 Colonel John Russell, with..the Prince's fferelockes, assaulted. **1704** *Collect. Voy.* (Church.) III. 728/2 Where they posted 12 Firelocks. **1801** Wellington in Gurw. *Desp.* I. 285 The other corps..will amount to about 2000 firelocks. **1844** H. H. Wilson *Brit. India* II. 342 The detachment.. scarcely mustered nine hundred and fifty firelocks.

4. *attrib.*, as ***firelock musket, firelock piece.***

a **1577** Gascoigne *Compl. Gr. Knt.* Weedes (1587) 183 My chaunce was late to haue a peereles firelock peece. **1631** *Schedule of Prices* in Meyrick *Ant. Arm.* III. 101 For a pair of firelock pistols. *a* **1672** Wood *Life* (1848) 24 Capt. Bunce returned safe..with..six fire-lock musquets.

† **'firely,** *a.* and *adv.* *Obs.* [f. fire *sb.* + -ly.]

A. *adj.* Ardent, furious.

B. *adv.* Ardently, with fierce eagerness.

1340 *Ayenb.* 55 Þe þridde boȝ of þise zenne is to uerliche yerne to þe mete. **1435** Misyn *Fire of Love* II. iv. 75 Þe qwhilk fyrely & opynly is byrnyd with fyre of lufe.

Hence † **'firelihead**, ardour, eagerness.

1340 *Ayenb.* 55 Þe more þet is þe ilke uerlichhede [*ardeur*] þe more is þe zenne.

fireman ('faɪəmən).

† **1.** One who uses fire-arms; a gunner. *Obs.*

1626 *Rawleigh's Ghost* 4 The best experienced soldiers or firemen. *a* **1648** Ld. Herbert *Life* (1770) 51 Notwithstanding all that our Firemen speak against it [archery]. **1724** De Foe *Mem. Cavalier* (1840) 181 The cannoneers and firemen were killed. **1727** A. Hamilton *New Acc. E. Ind.* I. xxii. 263 The fire Men place themselves at convenient Distances along the skirts of an Hill.

2. One who attends to a furnace or the fire of a steam-engine.

1657 R. Ligon *Barbadoes* (1673) 53 One or two of these were Firemen that made the fires in the furnaces. **1784** Wedgwood in *Phil. Trans.* LXXIV. 367 The fire about the oven was..kept as even and steady as possible, by an experienced fireman, under my own inspection. **1849** F. B. Head *Stokers & Pokers* vii. 62 It [*sc.* a locomotive] proceeds to the fire-pit, over which it stops. The fireman here opens the door of his furnace. **1885** *Manch. Exam.* 19 Feb. 4/7 The fireman jumped off..but the driver..and a brakesman.. were killed.

† **3.** *fig.* A 'fellow of fire'; see fire *sb.* 13 b.

1709 Steele *Tatler* No. 61 ¶ 1, I had last Night the Fate to drink a Bottle with Two of these Fire-men.

4. One who is employed to extinguish fires.

1714 Gay *Trivia* III. 362 The Fire-man sweats beneath his crooked Arms. **1766** Entick *London* IV. 262 This office keeps in its service 30 fire-men. **1855** O. W. Holmes *Poems* 140, I asked the firemen why they made Such noise about the town.

5. *Mining.* One whose duty it is to examine the workings of a mine to see that no fire-damp is present, to attend to the blasting, etc.

1866 J. Hogg in *Intellect. Observer* IX. 2 As there was no great quantity [of inflammable air] detected, the 'fireman' thought it sufficient precaution to put up a 'danger-signal'. **1885** *Law Times* LXXIX. 119/2 The fireman should not

allow any shot to be fired without seeing the charge put in, and without first carefully examining the place.

6. *Comb.*, as ***fireman-waterman***.

1836 DICKENS *Sk. Boz, Tales* vii, 'Did you want to be put on board a steamer, sir?' inquired an old fireman-waterman.

Hence **'firemanship** (*nonce-wd.*), the craft or function of a fireman.

1874 *Daily News* 17 Mar. 5 The amateur firemanship of a nobleman. **1881** M. REYNOLDS *Engine-driving Life* 66 Now is the time for the display of good enginemanship,—ah! and good firemanship.

'fire-master.

†**1.** An officer of artillery who superintended the manufacture of explosives or fireworks. *Obs.*

1622 F. MARKHAM *Dec. Warre* III. ii. 87 The Fier-master being he that hath the art how to make and compound all manner of Fire-workes. **1688** CAPT. J. S. *Fortif.* 132 By this, a Fire-Master may lay his Granado.. at any place. **1692** *Capt. Smith's Seaman's Gram.* II. xiv. 110 Discovered by Mr. Valentine Pyne, late Fire-Master of England. **1708** CHAMBERLAYNE *St. Gt. Brit.* II. III. (1743) 108 Mr. Watson, Firemaster to the Grenadiers. **1824** BYRON *To Hancock* 7 Feb., A firemaster (who is to burn a whole fleet).

b. (See quot.)

1876 VOYLE *Mil. Dict.* s.v., The designation of fire-master is still known in the ordnance branch of the service; he is an officer of the royal artillery, and is entrusted with the inspection of ordnance stores at foreign stations.

2. A local title given to the chief officer of a fire-brigade.

1865 *Ann. Reg.* 5 The fire-master [in Edinburgh] and others had reason to be grateful for their deliverance.

†**'firen,** *a. Obs.* Forms: 1 fyren, 2-3 furen, (3 fern, 3-5 firen, fyren (-in, -un). [OE. *fýren*, OHG. *fiurîn* (MHG. *viuren*):—OTeut. **fûirîno-*, f. **fûir*, OE. *fýr*, FIRE *sb.*] Consisting of or containing fire; flaming with fire.

971 *Blickl. Hom.* 43 þonne bið he ȝeteald to þære fyrenan ea. ? *c* **1000** *Martyrologium* 4 (1894) Ond Romanen ȝesawon fyren cleowen ȝefeallan of heofonum. *c* **1175** *Lamb. Hom.* 89 Wes iseȝen biforan heore elche swilc hit were furene tungen. *c* **1205** LAY. 18863 Of his eȝene scullen fleon furene gleden. *a* **1300** *Cursor M.* 22680 (Cott.) All þe stanes.. aboue þe erth and beneþen.. sal smitt togedir wit sli maght, als thoner dos wit firen slaght. **1382** WYCLIF *2 Kings* ii. 11 Loo! the fijren chaare and the fijren hors deuyden euer either. *c* **1400** *Apoll. Loll.* 98 Taking þe scheld of þe feiþ, in þe wilk we may sleckun all the firun dartis of the enemy. *c* **1440** *Jacob's Well* (E.E.T.S.) 157 þat prynce of deuelys.. ȝaf hym drynken of a fyren cuppe brynnyng drynk wyth brymston.

'fire-new, *a. arch.* [Cf. Ger. *feuerneu*; also BRAND-NEW.] † Fresh from the fire or furnace (*obs.*); hence, perfectly new, brand-new.

1594 SHAKS. *Rich. III*, I. iii. 256 Your fire-new stampe of Honor is scarce currant. **1599** H. BUTTES *Dyet's drie Dinner* N v b, Curdes.. fire-newe: for these be most digestible. **1615** SYLVESTER *Hymn Alms* 195 Fire-new Fashion in a Sleeve. **1713** ADDISON *Guardian* No. 113 ⁋2 Another suit fire-new, with silver buttons to it. **1800** COLERIDGE *Piccolom.* IV. vii, Duke Friedland is as others A fire-new noble. **1842** BROWNING *Solil. Sp. Cloister* iii, A fire-new spoon.

fire-office. An office for issuing policies for insurance against fire; a fire-insurance company.

1684 H. S. (*title*) An answer to a letter.. giving an account of the two insurance-offices. The Fire-Office and Friendly Society. **1716** *Lond. Gaz.* No. 5488/8 Hand-in-Hand Fire-Office. **1727** SWIFT *What passed in Lond.*, All the fire-offices were required to have a particular eye upon the bank of England. **1842** SYD. SMITH *Lett.* Wks. 1859 II. 324/1 Leave me to escape in the best way I can, as the fire-offices very kindly permit me to do. **1861** DICKENS *Gt. Expect.* xxxi, Insured in some extraordinary Fire Office.

'fire-pan. [OE. *fýrpanne*, f. *fýr*, FIRE + *panne*, PAN.]

1. A pan or receptacle for holding or carrying fire, e.g. a brazier, a chafing dish, a portable grate.

c **1000** ÆLFRIC *Gloss.* in Wr.-Wülcker 124 *Arula, uel batilla* fyrpanne. **1382** WYCLIF *Ex.* xxxviii. 3 Fleshhokes, hokes, and fier pannes. **1432** *E.E. Wills* (1882) 91 A vergyous barell, and a fyerpanne. **1567** *Inv. Sir G. Conyers* in *Wills & Inv. N.C.* (Surtees) 267 A poer, a fier pann and a pair of tonngs xx^{d}. *a* **1639** SPOTTISWOOD *Hist. Ch. Scot.* VI. xiii. (1655) 306 That.. the watch-tower called Repentance, be repaired, a great bell and firepan put into it. *a* **1661** HOLYDAY *Juvenal* 58/1 The Romans.. had fire-pans, or chafing dishes, placed in their baskets. **1767-9** S. PATERSON *Another Traveller!* II. 141 He next takes the pipe in one hand and the fire-pan in the other. **1833** J. HOLLAND *Manuf. Metal* II. 158 The portable brazier, or fire-pan, which might be used in any apartment requiring to be warmed.

†**2.** A pan for heating anything over a fire. *Obs.*

1607 TOPSELL *Four-f. Beasts* (1658) 285 Hold it in a fire-pan over the fire untill it be baked so hard as it may be made in powder. **1638** RAWLEY tr. *Bacon's Life & Death* (1650) 44 To poure them upon a Fire-pan somewhat heated.

†**3.** The pan which held the priming of a flintlock gun. *Obs.*

1613 T. JACKSON *Comm. Apost. Creede* I. 192 This was but as a little flash in the fire-panne.

†**4.** A kind of firework. *Obs.*

c **1793** in *Spirit Pub. Jrnls.* (1799) I. 91 They ran about.. letting off fire-pans of all sizes; firing crackers [etc.].

5. *Mining.* 'A kind of fire-lamp' (Gresley *Gloss. Coal Mining* 1883).

†**'fire-pike** *Obs.*

1. An instrument for stirring or making up a fire.

1413 LYDG. *Pilg. Sowle* III. vii. (1483) 55 With fyre pykes they cast them in the forneis. **1532** *Inv.* in Noake *Worcester Monast.* (1866) 157 Two awndyerns, a fyer pycke. **1563-87** FOXE *A. & M.* (1596) 65/1 When this triumphant martyr had beene pressed downe with firepikes.

2. A fire-bearing pike or lance used in sea-fights. Also used as a signal of distress.

1630 J. TAYLOR (Water P.) *Wks.* (Spenser Soc.) 528 The Frigots.. threw fire pots in at the Ports and stucke fire pikes in her sides. **1635** LD. LINDSEY in Sir W. Monson *Naval Tracts* III. (1704) 335/1 If your Ship should happen to run aground.. in the night, You shall burn a Fire-Pike. **1644** PRYNNE & WALKER *Fiennes' Trial* App. 10 They made their often attempts with Scaling Ladders, Fire-pickes, Granadoes.

'fire-place. A place for a fire, *esp.* the partially enclosed space at the base of the chimney appropriated to the fire; a hearth.

1702 T. SAVERY *Miner's Friend* 34 An Engine of a three Inch-bore.. requires a Fire-place of not above twenty Inches deep. **1710** SWIFT *Lett.* (1767) III. 39, I have no fire-place in my bed-chamber. **1825** J. NEAL *Bro. Jonathan* II. 28 They sat round the great fire-place. **1844** *Mem. Babylonian P'cess* II. 117 A temporary fire-place constructed with loose stone.

'fire-pot. †**a.** An earthen pot containing combustibles or explosives used as a missile. *Obs.* exc. *Hist.* **b.** The receptacle for the fire in a furnace or heating-stove. **c.** A crucible (Knight *Mech. Dict.* 1874).

1627 CAPT. SMITH *Seaman's Gram.* xii. 57 You must be carefull to cleare the decks with.. fire-pots. **1669** STURMY *Mariner's Mag.* v. 86 Fire-Pots.. may be made of Potters-Clay, with Ears baked, and to it hang lighted Matches. **1753** CHAMBERS *Cycl. Supp.*, *Fire-pots.*

b. 1871 NICHOLS *Fireside Science* 229 Around the ash-chamber and fire-pot [of furnace]. **1874** KNIGHT *Mech. Dict.*, *Base-burning Stove*, one having a magazine to hold a supply of fuel, which falls out at the bottom as that in the fire-pot becomes consumed.

'fire-pote. *dial.* [f. FIRE *sb.* + POTE *v. dial.* to push] A poker, an iron bar for stirring the fire.

1651 *Depos. Cast. York.* (Surtees) 51 Mending the fire with the fire-poite. **1855** ROBINSON *Whitby Gloss.*, *Fire-poat*, the poker. **1865** WAUGH *Goblin's Grave* 15 Iv aw'd had a red-whot fire-pote or two.

'fire-proof, *a.* [f. FIRE *sb.* + PROOF *a.*] Proof against fire; incombustible. *spec.* of paper.

a **1638** MEDE *Paraphr. 2 Pet.* iii. App. Wks. (1672) III. 618 That such as had departed out of this life not fully purged.. should not be found fire-proof at that day. **1642** FULLER *Holy & Prof. St.* II. iv. 159 The one of brick fire-proof. **1823** J. BADCOCK *Dom. Amusem.* 184 To render Wood Fire-proof.. or.. incombustible. **18..** MOORE *Case of Libel* x, A grim old dandy, seen about With a fire-proof wig. **1922** *Pulp & Paper Mag. Canada* 15 June 494/3 Paper and board may be rendered partially fireproof by treatment with magnesium-sulphate solution. **1962** F. T. DAY *Introd. to Paper* 115/1 *Fireproof papers...* Most are made of asbestos or are suitably treated with standard solutions and recipes.

fig. **1830** CARLYLE *Misc.* (1857) II. 152 Perennial, fire-proof Joys, named Employments.

Hence **'fire-proof** *v. trans.*, to render proof against fire. **fire-proofing** *vbl. sb.*, (*a*) the action or process of rendering fire-proof or incombustible; (*b*) material for use in making anything fire-proof; (*c*) *attrib.*

1867 A. BARRY *Sir C. Barry* vi. 167 The 'fire-proofing' ordered by Government. **1883** *Pall Mall G.* 13 Dec. 3/2 He carefully examined my fire-proofing work on the dome [of St. Paul's Cathedral]. **1884** *Health Exhib. Catal.* 831 Models showing application of 'Silicate Cotton' for fire-proofing. **1887** *Pall Mall G.* 29 Oct. 5/1 With the aid of electric light and all the fire-proofing appliances of to-day.

firer ('faɪərə(r)). [f. as prec. + -ER¹.] One who or something which fires, in senses of the vb.

1. One who sets anything on fire; also, one who superintends the 'firing' of glass.

1882 *Pall Mall G.* 29 June 2/1 On the hills the 'firers' are at work, burning off the scrub. **1890** *Ibid.* 9 Feb. 6/1 One is the chemist, another the decorator, a third the 'firer'.

fig. **1823** ROSCOE *Sismondi's Lit. Eur.* (1846) I. xiv. 401 Silvia, the forest's honor, the soul's firer.

b. An incendiary. *Obs.* exc. const. *of.*

1602 CAREW *Cornwall* II. 156/2 Others.. burned.. Mouse-hole, the rest marched as a gard for defence of these firers. **1716** *Glossogr. Angl. Nova*, *Boutefeu*, a wilful Firer of Houses. **1841** J. T. HEWLETT *Parish Clerk* II. 136 A bully, and a firer of ricks.

2. One who discharges a fire-arm. Also applied to the fire-arm itself, usu. in *comb.*, as ***single-firer***, a gun that can be fired only once without reloading.

1868 *Daily News* 6 Oct., One can never be sure that the firer has exercised sufficient caution in regard to the exclusion of bullets. **1885** *Manch. Exam.* 19 Oct. 5/5 The rifles can then be discharged.. at the option of the firer. **1887** *Sci. Amer.* (N.Y.) 21 May 320/2 Theoretically it [magazine gun] has a great advantage over the single firer.

b. A contrivance for firing a gun. Only in *comb.*, as ***quick-firer***.

1887 *Daily News* 10 Mar. 2/5 The rifle and its quick-firer should be ordinarily used in this way.

'fire-'raising, *vbl. sb.* Orig. a technical term in Sc. law. [f. FIRE *sb.* + RAISING *vbl. sb.*, f. RAISE.] The action or crime of kindling an incendiary fire; arson, incendiarism.

1685 in *Lond. Gaz.* No. 2032/3 We hereby fully Pardon and Indemnifie them for ever, of all Slaughter, Blood, Mutilation, Fire-raising, burning of Ships. **1754** ERSKINE *Princ. Sc. Law* (1809) 31 Rape, murder, and wilful fire-raising. **1820** SCOTT *Monast.* ix, Doest thou menace the holy Church's patrimony with waste and fire-raising? **1855** MACAULAY *Hist. Eng.* III. xvii. 113 Outrages, robberies, fireraisings, assassinations.

So **fire-raiser**, an incendiary.

1891 *Daily News* 1 Dec. 5/3 The exemplary sentences passed.. at the Central Criminal Court on two fire-raisers.

fire-red, *a.* and *sb.* [f. as prec. + RED *a.* Cf. MHG. *viurrot.*]

A. *adj.* Red like fire. Also, reddened by fire.

1382 WYCLIF *Lev.* xiv. 49 He shal take.. fier reed silk. *c* **1386** CHAUCER *Prol.* 624 A Sompnour.. That hadde a fire-red cherubinnes face. **1601** HOLLAND *Pliny* I. 154 People borne with eies like owles, whereof the sight is fire red. **1626** SANDYS tr. *Ovid's Met.* XIV. 779 Iron, boyld In fire-red furnaces. **1896** 'MARK TWAIN' in *Harper's Mag.* Aug. 356 Cotton-velvet westcot, fire-red and yaller squares. **1931** V. WOOLF *Waves* 98 The fire-red windows.

B. *sb.* A commercial name for a brilliant red monoazo pigment characterized by strong resistance to oil and light.

1955 H. A. LUBS *Chem. Synthetic Dyes & Pigments* xi. 633 Aktien Gesellschaft für Anilinfabrikation (AGFA) disclosed that replacement of *p*-nitroaniline by 2-chloro-4-nitroaniline.. gave the product (12), Fire Red. **1967** KARCH & BUBER *Offset Processes* vii. 269 *Para reds*, and *Fire reds* are quite 'dirty' in color, are semi-transparent and used mostly in poster and label inks.

'fire-screen.

1. A movable screen, whether hanging, standing, or for use with the hand, to intercept the heat of the fire.

1758 JOHNSON *Idler* No. 13 ⁋8 We have twice as many fire-screens as chimneys. **1824** SCOTT *St. Ronan's* xxii, A couple of her ladyship's drawings, made up into fire-screens. **1833** N. ARNOTT *Physics* II. 44 In our drawing-rooms it is common to have plate-glass fire-screens, which, while they allow the light to pass, defend the face from the heat.

2. A wire frame placed in front of a fire to keep back sparks, falling cinders, etc.; a fire-guard.

1874 KNIGHT *Dict. Mech.* I. 871/1 *Fire-screen.*

3. *Naut.* (see quot.)

1815 *Falconer's Marine Dict.* (ed. Burney) 436 s.v. *Screen*, Fire-screens are pieces of fearnought.. hooked round the magazine passages, and also round the hatchways, where it is necessary to pass the powder. **1867** in SMYTH *Sailor's Word-bk.*

'fire-ship.

1. A vessel freighted with combustibles and explosives, and sent adrift among ships, etc. to destroy them.

1588 PARKE tr. *Mendoza's Hist. China* 170 Captayne of the fire shippes of Chincheo. **1628** MEADE in Ellis *Orig. Lett.* Ser. I. III. 270, I cannot hear of above some two or three of our fireships lost. **1709** STEELE *Tatler* No. 21 ⁋16 Sir Edward Whitaker, with five Men of War, four Transports and two Fireships, was arrived at that Port. *a* **1859** MACAULAY *Hist. Eng.* V. 20 Montague bitterly described him as a fireship, dangerous at best, but on the whole most dangerous as a consort.

2. *slang.* One suffering from venereal disease; a prostitute.

1672 WYCHERLEY *Love in Wood* II, Are you not a Fire-ship, a Punk, Madam? **1673** R. HEAD *Canting Acad.* 18 Thy Sweep-stakes still shall bare the Bell, No Fire-ship yet aboard it fell. **1738** SWIFT *Polite Conv.* ii Wks. 1883 IX. 447 No; damn your fire-ships, I have a wife of my own. **1748** SMOLLETT *Rod. Rand.* I. xxiii, 'A fire-ship!.. more like a poor galley in distress that has been boarded by such a fire-ship as you.'

'fire-shovel. [OE. *fýr-scofl*, f. *fýr*, FIRE + *scofl*, SHOVEL.] A shovel for placing coals on a fire or for removing coal or ashes.

c **1000** ÆLFRIC *Gloss.* in Wr.-Wülcker 358 *Batilla*, fyrscofl. **1543** in Rogers *Agric. & Prices* III. 572/1 Fireshovel 1/8. **1567** *Inv. E. Hutton* in *Wills & Inv.* (Surtees) 250 A paire of tonges, a porr & a fyer shule. **1612** *Sc. Bk. Customs* in *Halyburton's Ledger* (1867) 304 Fire shooles the dozen. **1719** DE FOE *Crusoe* I. (1883) 227, I took a Fire Shovel and Tongs. **1838** DICKENS *O. Twist* ix, The Jew, tapping the fire-shovel on the hearth.

fireside (faɪə'saɪd, *attrib.* 'faɪəsaɪd). [f. FIRE *sb.* + SIDE.]

1. The side of a fire-place; *originally*, the place occupied by the two seats right and left of the fire under the chimney; hence, the space about the fire: the hearth.

1563 O. FOXE in *Child Marr.* 58 This contract was made toward evening nere the fireside. *a* **1639** T. CAREW *Poems, Spring* 20 Love no more is made By the fire side. **1705** HICKERINGILL *Priest-cr.* II. i. 12 The news.. coming to the Pope, as he was saying his Beads by the Fire-side. **1798** MALTHUS *Popul.* (1817) III. 74 The warm house, and the comfortable fireside, would lose half of their interest. **1859** W. COLLINS *Q. of Hearts* (1875) 3 My brothers had made my place ready for me by their fireside.

2. *transf.*

a. As a symbol of home and home-life.

1848 MACAULAY *Hist. Eng.* I. 149 They would fight manfully for their shops and firesides. **1894** *Daily News* 6 June 6/4 The English are regarded as the nation most appreciatory of the home, the fireside.

†**b.** *collect.* Those who sit round one's fire or hearth; one's household. *Obs.*

1720 *Lett. from Lond. Jrnl.* 13 He has a numerous Fireside of squabbling Brats. **1722** POPE *Lett.* (1735) I. 276 Enjoy your own Fire-side..that is, all those of your Family who make it pleasing to sit and spend whole Wintry Months together. **1785** MAD. D'ARBLAY *Lett.* 3 Jan., A very happy new year to you and your fireside. **1839** F. REYNOLDS *Let.* 13 May in A. Bunn *Stage* (1840) III. vi. 218 For so many years he formed a part of my fireside.

3. *attrib.* (quasi-*adj.*) Also applied *spec.* (orig. in the U.S.) to informal broadcast talks to the nation.

1740 MRS DELANY *Life & Corr.* (1861) II. 137, I own such a downright fire-side epistle from her disappointed me. **1807** CRABBE *Par. Reg.* III. 621 The fire-side chair, still set, but vacant still. **1840** DICKENS *Barn. Rudge* i, The fire-side group. **1871** LOWELL *My Study W., A. Lincoln,* The simple confidence, the fireside plainness, with which Mr. Lincoln always addresses himself to the reason of the American people. **1885** H. JAMES *Little Tour in France* (1900) vii. 70 The sixty years that preceded the [French] Revolution were the golden age of fireside talk. **1926** R. MACAULAY *Crewe Train* II. x. 196 Her fireside chats about the characters and intimate histories of her friends and relations were famed in London. **1935** *Amer. Mercury* July 325/2 Now and again.. one may find a half-hearted Hoosier who turns from the lamp to listen to a 'Fireside Chat'. **1939** *Ann. Reg. 1938* 301 In a 'fireside' radio talk he [*sc.* the President] announced that the Administration would initiate a 4 million dollars 'spending and lending' programme. **1963** AUDEN *Dyer's Hand* 344 The fireside-chat I'm-a-plain-fellow manner is still irritating. **1966** *Observer* 7 Aug. 28/4 Fireside chats from Number 10 Downing Street.

Hence (*nonce-wds.*) **fire'sider**, one who sits by the fireside. **fire'sideship**, the personality of one who sits by the fireside.

1817 HAZLITT *Round Table* in *Q. Rev.* XVII. 157 Fire-sider [cited by the reviewer as coined by Hazlitt.] *a* **1859** L. HUNT *Fancy Concert*, What concert 'twould please his Firesideship to have.

†**'fire-slaught.** *Sc. Obs.* [f. FIRE *sb.* + ME. *slaht.* OE. *sleaht* stroke, blow: see SLAUGHT.] A flash of fire or lightning: lightning.

a **1300** *Cursor M.* 1769 (Cott.) Fire slaght fell wit thoner and rain. *c* **1375** *Sc. Leg. Saints, Laurentius* 16 Alsa it has vertu..Fore to resyst agane fyre-slacht. **1549** *Compl. Scot.* vi. 60 The fyir slaucht vil consume the vyne. **1872** TENNANT *Papistry storm'd* 24 As thunder on the fire-slacht's back.

'fire-stone. [OE. *fýrstán* (= Ger. *feuerstein*), f. *fýr*, FIRE + *stán*, STONE.]

†**1.** A stone capable of being used in striking fire: **a.** A popular name for iron pyrites. **b.** A flint, *esp.* the flint of a fire-lock. *Obs.*

c **1000** ÆLFRIC *Gloss.* in Wr.-Wülcker 148 *Pirites, uel focaris lapis*, fyrstan. *c* **1440** *Promp. Parv.* 161/2 Fyyr-stone, for to smyte wythe fyre, *focaris.* **1579** LILY *Euphues* (Arb.) 121 Ye fire-stone in Liguria, though it be quenched with milke, yet againe it is kindled with water. **1671** J. WEBSTER *Metallogr.* 114 Marchasites or Fire Stones. **1728** J. WOODWARD *Catal. Fossils* (1729) I. 176 In Yorkshire, where these [Pyritæ] are called Fire-Stones. **1865** TYLOR *Early Hist. Man.* ix. 246 Iron pyrites..shared with flint, the name of Fire-stone.

b. **1530** PALSGR. 220/2 Fyre stone, *pierre a fev.* **1586** WITHALS *Dict.* H vij/2 A fire-stone to strike fire with, *silex.* **1700** ASTRY tr. *Saavedra-Faxardo* I. 283 The Prince's Heart should resemble the Fire-stone or Flint. **1833** J. HOLLAND *Manuf. Metal* II. v. 87 Afterwards a firestone was screwed into the cock..This 'firestone' was not at first of a vitreous nature..but a compact pyrites or marcasite.

2. a. A stone that resists the action of fire; one used for lining furnaces, ovens, etc. **b.** A local name for certain calcareous sandstones found in the carboniferous and cretaceous strata. **c.** A local name for granite, tufa, etc.

a. *c* **1475** *Pict. Voc.* in Wr.-Wülcker 805 *Hic abbestus* a fyirstone. **1651** R. CHILD in *Hartlib's Legacy* (1655) 75 Sandy stones commonly called fire-stones, because they will endure strong fires. **1674** I. STURDIE in *Phil. Trans.* XVII. 696 A Wall of the best Fire-stone to keep off the force of the Fire from the Walls of the Furnace. **1702** SAVERY *Miner's Friend* 26 The Furnace being made of..Fire-stone. **1862** G. P. SCROPE *Volcanos* 384 Employed, under the name of Bakofenstein, as a fire-stone for the lining of ovens.

b. **1707** MORTIMER *Husb.* vi. 95 Any soft Stone as Fire-stone, Limestone, etc., if broke small, and laid on cold Lands, must be of advantage. **1833** LYELL *Princ. Geol.* III. 286 An inferior deposit called, provincially, 'Firestone,' and by English geologists the 'Upper green-sand.' **1839** MURCHISON *Silur. Syst.* I. xxxiv. 452 A subordinate band of reddish sandstone, the *firestone* of the country people. **1892** SIMMONDS *Dict. Trade* Suppl., *Firestone*, a local name in Surrey for the soft calcareous sandstone..sold..under the name of hearthstone.

c. **1776** G. SEMPLE *Building in Water* 56 The Carriage-way ..was to be paved with Fire-stone. **1860** *Ecclesiologist* XXI. 143 The walling generally is built of a volcanic stone called [in the West Indies] firestone.

3. A hearth-stone.

1613 ROVENZON *Treat. Metal.* D iij, The furnace may bee pulled downe, & a new fire-stone or hearth put in. **1842** S. C. HALL *Ireland* II. 6 The stones..have been removed by the peasantry to make 'Fire-stones.'

'fire-tongs. *pl.* [OE. *fýrtang*, f. *fýr*, FIRE + *tang*, TONG.] Tongs used for handling ignited combustibles.

a **1100** *Gerefa* in *Anglia* (1886) IX. 263 Fyrtange, wæipundern; and fela towtola. **1463** *Rolls Parl.* V. 507/1 Eny of theese Wares..That is to sey, eny..Fyretonges. **1671** J. WEBSTER *Metallogr.* xvii. 250 Of which [Brass] is made fire-tongs. **1853** J. D. DALE tr. *Baldeschi's Ceremonial* 199 Two thuribles, with the boats and fire-tongs.

'fire-water.

1. 'A name given to alkahest' (Chambers *Cycl. Supp.* 1753).

2. Any strong liquor or ardent spirits.

Originally used by (or attributed to) the North American Indians: chiefly current with reference to the pernicious effects of alcoholic liquors on barbarous races, or in vituperative or jocular use.

1826 J. F. COOPER *Mohicans* xi, His [Magua's] Canada fathers..taught him to drink the fire-water, and he became a rascal. **1849** WHITTIER *Marg. Smith's Jrnl.* Prose Wks. 1889 I. 32 Never taste of the strong fire-water, but drink only of the springs. **1861** HUGHES *Tom Brown at Oxf.* x, His father..had a horror..of the fire-water which is generally sold to the undergraduate.

'fire-wood, 'firewood. Wood for burning; fuel. Also *attrib.*

1496 *Nottingham Rec.* III. 290 For brekyng of fire wodde in the owte wodes. **1553** EDEN *Treat. Newe Ind.* (Arb.) 19 This tree serueth them for firewood. **1602** FULBECKE *2nd Pt. Parall.* 52 And the termor hath house-wood..and fire-woode belonging to his tearme of common right. **1719** DE FOE *Crusoe* (1840) I ix. 143 I..placed my fire-wood all round it. **1815** ELPHINSTONE *Acc. Caubul* (1842) II. 175 During the day, they issue forth in swarms to search for forage and fire-wood. **1889** *Evening News* 3 Dec. 4/5 Firewood Cutters.

'fire-work, 'firework.

†**1.** Work done by, in, or with fire.

1601 HOLLAND *Pliny* II. 467 But for that the..smoke.. may stifle and choke them..they are forced to giue ouer such fire-work. **1607** BRETON *Murmurer* D iiij, His heart the Anuile wheron the deuill frames his fireworke. **1609** ROWLANDS *Crew Kind Gossips* 15 Ile vndertake, The credit of this fire-worke [tobacco-smoking] quite to shake. **1686** PLOT *Staffordsh.* ix. §10. 336 To the fire-works succeed the Arts relating to water.

†**2.** An apparatus for working with fire, a furnace; also, a place where the material for fire is obtained. *Obs.*

1607 DEKKER *Knt's. Conjur.* (1842) 21 The map of a country that lyes lower..than the cole-pits of Newe castle, is farre more darke..then the colliers of those fire-workes are. **1613** ROVENZON *Treat. Metal.* C iv, The furnaces or fire-workes may be made rounde. **1674** PETTY *Disc. Dupl. Proportion* 36, I know that in Fire-works great Fires are more profitable than small; as in Brewers Coppers.

3. †A combustible or explosive composition for use in war (*obs.*); a projectile or other machine charged with such composition.

1560 WHITEHORNE *Ord. Souldiours* title-p., And moreover how to make Saltpetre, Gunpowder, and divers sorts of Fireworks or Wild Fire. **1636** FEATLY *Clavis Myst.* xiv. 189 Granadoes and other fire-works..do more harm to them that cast them than to the enemie. **1676** *Lond. Gaz.* No. 1119/3 The Enemy set fire to a Firework they had prepared in the Court of Guard of the said Bastion. *c* **1710** in *Torrington Mem.* (1889) 140 Some boats mann'd, arm'd, and with fireworks..to burn a French privateer. **1777** BURKE *Corr.* (1844) II. 142 The construction of all fireworks is understood at the ordnance-office. **1851** J. S. MACAULAY *Field Fortif.* 181 In the attack of fortified houses, the fire of the loop-holes may be stopped by the introduction of small rockets, or any other artificial firework, that will create.. smoke.

fig. **1633** G. HERBERT *Temple, Starre* iii, First with thy fire-work burn to dust Folly. **1679** *Establ. Test.* 3 These Men of Tempestuous Principles are continually making their Fireworks in our very Intrals.

4. Any contrivance for the use of fire to produce a pleasing or scenic effect. †**a.** A 'set piece'; an arrangement of pyrotechnic contrivances to form a pictorial or ornamental design. Also *piece of firework.*

1575 GASCOIGNE *Pr. Pleas. Kenilw.*, At which time there wer fire-works shewed upon the water; the which were both strange and wel executed. **1590** WEBBE *Trav.* (Arb.) 29, I my selfe was there constrained to make a cunning peece of fire work framed in form like to ye Arke of Noy. **1644** EVELYN *Mem.* (1857) I. 137 The night ended with fire-works..The first appeared to be a mighty rock. **1675** *Lond. Gaz.* No. 1027/4 A rare Fire-work was erected on the little Isle.. representing the Alliance of the Confederates. **1795** in *Ld. Auckland's Corr.* (1862) III. 314 The shrubs of the island were rooted out to make a place for a fire-work.

b. A single piece of pyrotechnic apparatus, e.g. a rocket, squib, etc.

1611 MIDDLETON & DEKKER *Roaring Girl* V. 1, A justice.. used that rogue like a firework, to run upon a line betwixt him and me. **1684** *Contempl. State of Man* II. ix. (1699) 232 A Wheel of Squibs and Fire-Works. **1731** SWIFT *Answ. to Simile*, Like fire-works she can burn in water. **1849** F. B. HEAD *Stokers & Pokers* x. (1851) 93 Sparks created by the sudden ignition of a sackful of fire-works.

c. *pl.* (formerly also *sing.*) A pyrotechnic display. Also *transf.*, *spec.* in *Services' colloq.* (see quots.).

1588 SHAKS. *L.L.L.* v. i. 119 The King would haue mee present the princesse..with some delightfull ostentation.. or fire-worke. **1625** K. LONG tr. *Barclay's Argenis* III. xxiv. 228 In expectation of fire-workes, which hee had promised not farr from the shore. **1761** FOOTE *Lyar* I. Wks. 1799 I. 287 After supper a ball; and to conclude the night, a firework. **1848** MACAULAY *Hist. Eng.* I. 476 The banquet [was followed] by brilliant fireworks, and the fireworks by much bad poetry. **1851** D. JERROLD *St. Giles* xx. 206 The omission of the bonfires and the fireworks did pain me.

transf. **1872** HUXLEY *Phys.* ix. 222 The remarkable display of subjective fireworks which follows a heavy blow upon the eyes. **1925** FRASER & GIBBONS *Soldier & Sailor Words* 94 *Fireworks*, the familiar name for the display of search-lights, star-shells, rockets, etc., over the front-line and No Man's Land, on the occasion of night bombardments. **1943** HUNT & PRINGLE *Service Slang* 32 *Fireworks.* Bomber crews give this name to intensive anti-aircraft fire. It is also used for flare dropping.

d. *fig.*

1670 EACHARD *Cont. Clergy* 31 He has neither squibs nor fireworks..the curs'd carrier lost his best book of phrases. **1682** DRYDEN *Abs. & Achit.* II. 450 In fireworks give him leave to vent his spite; Those are the only serpents he can write. **1883** F. M. CRAWFORD *Dr. Claudius* ix, Barker turned on the fireworks of his conversation for the amusement of Claudius. **1889** BARRÈRE & LELAND *Slang Dict.*, *Fireworks (tailors)*, a great disturbance, a state of intense excitement.

5. *attrib.* and *Comb.*, as ***firework-factory***, ***-maker***.

1885 *Pall Mall G.* 4 Nov. 4/1 Norwood, where Mr. Brock has his thirty acres of *firework factories. **1892** *Ibid.* 1 Nov. 5/2 We are busy manufacturing the smaller *fire-work goods all the year round. **1803** tr. *Lebrun's Monsieur Botte* II. 230 The *fire-work maker loaded ten porters with grenades. **1885** *Pall Mall G.*, 4 Nov. 4/1 None more healthy than the firework maker.

Hence **'fire,workless** *a.*, devoid of fireworks. **'fire,worky** *a.*, like a firework, abrupt, jerky.

1856 DICKENS *Lett.* (1880) I. 437 Whom I found with some fireworkless little boys in a desolate condition. **1887** *Graphic* 15 Jan. 66/2 The Major departed in his usual fireworky way. **1889** in *Pall Mall G.* 13 May 6/2 He disported himself..in his kaleidoscopic and fireworky fantasia.

'fire-,worker. [f. FIRE *sb.* + WORKER, after FIREWORK.]

†**1.** One who has to do with fireworks or explosives in war; *spec.* an artillery officer, under the fire-master. *Obs.*

1626 PURCHAS *Pilgrimage* (ed. 4) 527 They tooke some of these Fire-workers, & one of which being examined, confessed after M. Prings Relation thus. **1686** *Lond. Gaz.* No. 2124/2 They will be 8000 fighting Men, besides.. Gunners and Fire-workers. **1703** *Ibid.* No. 3913/2 A Lieutenant, with 5 Fireworkers, killed. **1800** DUNDAS in Owen *Wellesley's Desp.* 564 Each company to have an additional Lieut.-Fireworker.

2. One who makes fireworks; a pyrotechnist.

1772 in J. T. Smith *Bk. Rainy Day* (1861) 52 Torre the fireworker divided the receipts at the door with the proprietor. **1835** BURNES *Trav. Bokhara* (ed. 2) I. 176 All the fire-workers of Lahore seemed to be exerting their talents in pyrotechny.

So †**fire-working** *vbl. sb.*, the management of fireworks or explosives (*obs.*); **fire-working** *ppl. a.*, working with fire.

1758 WHITWORTH *Acc. Russia* 60 He..understands navagation, shipbuilding, fortification, and fire-working. **1850** W. MAGINN *Homeric Ball.* 169 A vessel wrought By the fire-working god.

'fire-,worship. [f. as prec. + WORSHIP *sb.*] The worship or adoration of fire.

1774 J. BRYANT *Mythol.* I. 210 Here was the source of fire-worship. **1871** TYLOR *Prim. Cult.* II. 254 The fire-worship of Assyria, Chaldea, Phœnicia.

So **'fire-,worshipper**, one who worships fire, a follower of Zoroaster.

1806 T. MAURICE *Fall Mogul* Introd. 19 Persees, who, though in these pages denominated fire-worshippers, are [etc.]. **1879** SIR G. G. SCOTT *Lect. Archit.* I. 13 The Fire-worshippers of ancient Persia.

firing ('faɪərɪŋ), *vbl. sb.* [f. FIRE *v.* + -ING¹.]

1. a. The action of setting on fire or alight.

1548 HALL *Chron.* 18 b. Perceyving by the firyng of the beacons that the people began to assemble. **1677** YARRANTON *Engl. Improv.* 16 The ruine of some thousand Families since the firing of London. **1817** COBBETT *Wks.* XXXII. 150 Those meetings led..to the firing and pulling down of houses.

b. The action of catching fire or becoming ignited. *Obs.* or *rare.*

1588 G. FLETCHER in *Hakluyt's Voy.* (1598) I. 480 The greatest inconuenience of their wodden building is the aptnesse for firing, which happeneth very oft. **1641** BEST *Farm. Bks.* (Surtees) 61 Then doe wee drawe up a leape aboute the middle of each roomstead..whearby the dainger of firing is prevented. **1677** HALE *Prim. Orig. Man.* I. iii. 95 By the eruption of..Sulphureous Vapours, and the firing thereof, these protuberances of Mountains and Hills may be made. **1750** ELLIS *Mod. Husb.*, III. i. 87 *Firing*, the spontaneous combustion of hay when stacked damp.

c. The ignition of the fuel in a cylinder of an internal-combustion engine.

1888 *Lockwood's Dict. Mech. Terms* 140 *Firing*, the ignition of a charge in a gas engine. **1902** J. E. HUTTON in A. C. Harmsworth et al. *Motors* viii. 153 When the moment of firing arrives the striker..is caused to drop smartly. **1934** A. D. MERRIMAN *Romance of Engineering* vii. 108 Methods for ..compressing the charge before firing were greatly improved upon when Degrand in 1858 suggested compression in the cylinder by the motor piston. **1966** JACKSON & MORTON *Reed's Gen. Engin. Knowledge for Marine Engineers* ii. 41 The time interval between fuel injection and firing, called ignition delay, must not be too long.

2. The action of subjecting to the operation of fire; preparation, baking, or curing by heat.

1782 WEDGWOOD in *Phil. Trans.* LXXII. 307 Their use is confined to a particular structure of furnaces, and mode of firing. **1839** STONEHOUSE *Axholme* 228 This window has had four firings at a very high temperature. **1885** *Harper's Mag.* Apr. 679 1 The glazing and firing of pottery has been a fine art. **1888** *Times* (weekly ed.) 23 Nov. 9/4 The process called 'firing' [of tea]..is a kind of roasting.

3. *Farriery.* Cauterizing. (See FIRE *v.* 10.)

1644 PRYNNE & WALKER *Fiennes' Trial* 65 Who should not use cauteries or firing till the utmost extremity. **1866** ROGERS *Agric. & Prices* I. xv. 282 In 1385..firing was used

to cure horses of spavin. **1891** *Daily News* 21 Apr. 5/4 Firing, for curb especially, need not be a severe operation.

4. Applied to a disease in tobacco and in flax: see quots. and cf. FIRE *v.* 4 b.

1688 J. CLAYTON in *Phil. Trans.* XVII. 947 What they call Firing is this: When..there has been a very wet and cold Season, and very hot Weather suddenly ensues, the Leaves [of tobacco] turn brown, and dry to dust. **1812** DUBOURDIEU *Agric. Surv. Antrim* 197 Flax is subject to a disease called firing, which often attacks it when near ripe. **1888** PATON & DITTMAR in *Encycl. Brit.* XXIII. 424/2 Tobacco plants.. have been subject to..a disease called 'firing,' caused by the long continuance of very wet or very dry weather.

5. The action of supplying with fire; the feeding and tending of a fire or furnace.

1892 *Labour Commission* Gloss., *Firing*, attending to the fires and keeping them up to the required heat for carbonising coal.

6. a. The discharging a fire-arm, a mine, etc.

1603 KNOLLES *Hist. Turks* (1638) 69 All things being now in readinesse for the firing of the mine. **1684** *Scanderbeg Rediv.* vi. 143 The fierce Firings of the said Battalions. **1790** BEATSON *Nav. & Mil. Mem.* I. 157 Night coming on, the firing on both sides ceased. **1885** *Manch. Exam.* 3 Oct. 4/7 The train drew up..amid..the firing of guns.

b. *transf.* in *Bell-ringing*. The ringing of all the bells in a peal at once.

1788 W. JONES, etc. *Clavis Campanalogia* 4 Those *clamberings* and *firings* (as it is called) that destroy all music. **1880** in GROVE *Dict. Mus.*

7. a. *concr.* Material for a fire, fuel.

a **1555** RIDLEY in *Contemp. Rev.* (1878) XXXI. 771 To give him both meat, drink, clothing, and firing. **1591** GREENE *Disc. Coosnage* (1592) 23 Fewel or fiering, being a thing necessary. **1667** PEPYS *Diary* 24 Aug., The bells rung; but no bonfires..any where,—partly from the dearness of firing. **1796** MORSE *Amer. Geog.* II. 212 Want of firing is the greatest inconveniency that both islands labour under. **1833** HT. MARTINEAU *Brooke Farm* ii. 18 Their mother explained that the boys cut firing on the common.

†**b.** A quantity of burning fuel. *Obs. rare.*

c **1485** *Digby Myst.* (1882) II. 433 Here shall entere a-nother devyll..with a fyeryng.

8. *attrib.* and *Comb.*, as (sense 1) ***firing-chamber***; (sense 3) ***firing-iron***; (sense 5) ***firing-door, -hole, -machine, -tool***, etc.; (sense 6) ***firing line, -pin***, etc.; **firing-bay** = *fire-bay*; **firing-glass**, a table-glass with an unusually thick base; **firing order**, the order in which the cylinders in a motor engine operate; **firing-party** (see quot. 1867); **firing-place**, a fire-place (*obs.*); also, the place from which a gun is fired; **firing point**, (*a*) the temperature at which an inflammable oil is liable to spontaneous combustion; (*b*) in target shooting: the position from which the firing is done; **firing squad**, (*a*) = *firing party*; (*b*) a squad of soldiers detailed to shoot a condemned man; **firing-step** *Mil.*, a board or ledge in a trench, upon which soldiers stand when firing.

1923 KIPLING *Irish Guards in Great War* I. 222 The wreck of a *firing-bay. **1892** *Lockwood's Dict. Mech. Engin.*, **Firing Chamber* or *Lighting Chamber*, the small cavity or chamber through which the charge of a gas engine is ignited. **1892** *Pall Mall G.* 13 Dec. 6/2 A small but well-preserved hypocaust, with its *firing-door. **1905** P. BATE *Eng. Table Glass* 72 '*Firing' glasses..having a thick and massive base with which to knock on the table when applause was to be given. **1923** *Weekly Disp.* 30 Sept. 7/4 Short Jacobite firing-glasses. **1892** *Lockwood's Dict. Mech. Engin.*, **Firing Hole*, the door in the side of a reverberatory furnace through which the fuel is introduced to the grate area. **1753** CHAMBERS *Cycl. Supp.*, s.v., When the farrier has made his *firing-iron red hot in his forge, he applies the thinnest part to the horses skin. **1881** LD. HARTINGTON in *Daily Tel.* 6 May 2, General Stewart was obliged to put every reserve man into the *firing line. **1910** A. WILLIAMS *Engin. Wonders of World* III. 33/1 The *firing order of the cylinders of a seven-cylinder engine is 1, 3, 5, 7, 2, 4, 6, 1, [etc.]. **1959** '*Motor*' *Manual* (ed. 36) ii. 38 The firing order usually is 1, 5, 3, 6, 2, 4. **1859** F. A. GRIFFITHS *Artil. Man.* (1862) 48 The *firing party move to the grave. **1867** SMYTH *Sailor's Word-bk.*, *Firing-party*, a detachment of soldiers, marines, or small-arm men selected to fire over the grave of an individual buried with military honours. **1890** J. G. SMITH in *Upland Shooting* 138 Carry an extra *firing-pin, as you may break one. **1715** LEON *Palladio's Archit.* (1742) II. 99 Hearths and *Firing-places. **1879** BROWNING *M. Relph* 78 The turf marked out for the party's firing-place. **1878** *Ure's Dict. Arts* IV. 570 Mineral oil, one or two degrees above the standard *firing-point, may, if stored in a populous locality, cause sad disaster. **1900** *Times* 12 July, The wind has not blown straight from the firing point to the targets. **1958** J. A. BARLOW *Elem. Rifle Shooting* (ed. 5) iii. 38 The register keeper at the firing-point then shouts out the firer's name and the value of his shot. **1904** CONRAD *Nostromo* II. i. 114 The irregular report of the *firing squad would be heard. **1917** A. G. EMPEY *Over Top* 291 *Firing squad.* Twelve men picked to shoot a soldier who has been sentenced to death by courts-martial. **1959** T. S. ELIOT *Elder Statesman* I. 27 The ones who don't get out in time Find themselves in gaol..Or before a firing squad. **1916** 'BOYD CABLE' *Action Front* 254 He..leaped on the *firing step, and hurled himself over after him.

†**'firish**, *a.* *Obs.*—⁰. [f. FIRE *sb.* + -ISH.] Savouring of fire. Hence †**'firishness**.

1568 TURNER *Herbal* III. 65 There is a firishnes in it.

†**firk, ferk**, *sb. Obs.* [f. next vb.]

1. A smart sudden blow or stroke, as with a whip; a flick, flip; a cut or thrust (with a sword).

a **1634** RANDOLPH *Muses Looking-glasse* I. iv, My Apish imitation..Does as good service..As your proud whip, with all his ferkes, and jerkes. *a* **1679** EARL ORRERY *Guzman* (1693) 40 Both of them had a Fierk at each of my Haunches.

2. A trick, dodge, subterfuge. Also, a freak, prank, caprice.

1611 BARREY *Ram-Alley* III. in Hazl. *Dodsley* X. 329 Leave this firk of law. **1636** DAVENANT *Witts* in Dodsley *Old Plays* (1780) VIII. 498 This was such a firk of piety I ne'er heard of. **1682** H. MORE *Annot. Glanvill's Lux O.* 211 A pretty juvenile Ferk of Wit.

3. ? A dance; ? a partner for a dance.

1632 SHIRLEY *Hyde Park* II. ii, Come, choose your firk, for dance you shall.

firk, ferk (fɜːk), *v.* Forms: α. 1 færcian, fercian, 4 ferkien, 4–6 ferke, (5 fark), 7– ferk. β. 6–7 firke, (7 firck), 9 *dial.* virk, 6– firk. [OE. *fercian, færcian*, prob. f. *fær* (see FARE *sb.*[1]).

In OE. known only in one example in the sense 'to bring, conduct'; but the vb. *fercian* to support, feed, may perh. be the same word, as this sense may have developed from that of supplying with provisions for a journey (cf. FARE *sb*[1] 8.)]

†**1.** *trans.* To bring, carry, conduct; to help *forward* on one's way. *Obs.*

O.E. Chron. an 1009 þet folc..færcodon [v.r. fercodon] ða scipo eft to Lundene. *c* **1350** *Will. Palerne* 3630 þei.. bisiliche fondede fast to ferke him forþward. **1393** GOWER *Conf.* III. 295 This lord..The which upon the see she [Fortune] ferketh. *c* **1400** *Destr. Troy* 614 The flese for to fecche, and ferke it away. *Ibid.* 3840 So bolnet was his body, þat þu then hade ynoghe The fete of þat freke to ferke hym aboute. *Ibid.* 6032 All necessaries..[þai] ffechit fro the flete, & ferkit to bonke.

2. †**a.** To urge, press hard; to drive, drive away. *Obs.*

1340–70 *Alisaunder* 66 By force of hur fight ðei firked hym ðennes. *Ibid.* 85 [þei] Felled þe falsse folke, ferked hem hard. **1606** CHAPMAN *Gentleman Usher* I. i, The red fac'd Sunne hath firkt the flundering shades. **1640** BROME *Antipodes* III. ii, This shall serve To firke your adversary from court to court. **1674** N. FAIRFAX *Bulk & Selv.* 74 There is somewhat in it, that firks us more at such a nick of time to wake.

b. With advbs.: To drive, force, or move sharply and suddenly *off, out, up*; †to cut *off* (some one's head). Also *dial.* to drive or 'ferret' *out* (vermin), to clear *out* (a burrow, etc.). ***to firk up*** (*fig.*): to stir up, rouse. † ***to firk to death, (out) of life***: to put to death.

c **1400** *Destr. Troy* 145 He caste in his thoghte The freike vpon faire wise ferke out of lyue. *Ibid* 5260 With a fouchon felle to ferke of his hede. *Ibid.* 12191 þe fell kyng of Frigie I ferkid of lyue. *Ibid.* 12362 With hor fos to be felly ferkit to dethe. **1610** B. JONSON *Alch.* II. i, He..puffes his coales, Till he firke nature vp, in her owne center. **1640** BROME *Antipodes* II. ii, As Tumblers doe; when betwixt every feat They gather wind, by firking up their breeches. **1644** DIGBY *Two Treatises* (1645) I. 377 He [the badger] will pisse upon his taile, and by firking that up and downe, will endeavour ..to make their eyes smart. **1817–8** COBBETT *Resid. U.S.* (1822) 249 These vermin our friend *firks out* (as the Hampshire people call it). **1823** *New Monthly Mag.* VIII. 496 If I do not ferk you out of all likelihood of ringing the beauty, why mandamus me! **1878** P. ROBINSON *Indian Garden* 106 Not all the marigolds of Cathay will firk up Christmas spirits. **1891** *Sheffield Gloss.* Suppl., *Ferk*, to clear out..'Come, lass, let's ferk all them nooks out!'

†**c.** To contrive to get or 'raise' (a living); to get (money) *from* a person. Also, to cheat, rob (any one). ***to firk up***: to hatch or vamp up (a business). *Obs.*

1604 DEKKER *Honest Wh.* in Dodsley *Old Plays* (1780) III. 344 As from poor clients lawyers firk money. *a* **1616** BEAUM. & FL. *Little Fr. Lawyer* III. ii, A fine lawyer, sir, And would have firk'd you up a business, And out of this court into that. **1622** FLETCHER *Beggars' Bush* III. i, Were ever fools so ferk'd? **1624** —— *Rule a Wife* III. iv, These five years she has firkt a pretty Living. **1709** *Brit. Apollo* II. No. 65. 3/2 She Firkt a Living upon Earth.

†**3.** *refl.* and *intr.* To urge oneself forward; to move quickly, hasten. † ***to firk (oneself) up***: to start up, set oneself in motion. ***to firk out with (a sword)***: to draw hastily. *Obs.*

13.. *E.E. Allit. P.* B. 897 Fast þe freke ferkez vp ful ferd at his hert. *c* **1340** *Gaw. & Gr. Knt.* 173 þe fole þat he ferkkes on. *Ibid.* 2013 þat oþer ferkez hym vp & fechez hym his wedez. **1340–70** *Alex. & Dind.* 300 Ne fourre-fotede best [we] ferke to kill. *c* **1400** *Melayne* 484 He ferkes owte with a fawchon And hittis the Sawdane one the crownn. *c* **1400** *Destr. Troy* 6585 The freke þen in fuerse hast ferkid on horse. *a* **1400–50** *Alexander* 766 He..Farkis to see Philip & fangis his leue. *Ibid.* 926 Philip..Ferkis furth with a fewe folk. **1599** NASHE *Lenten Stuffe* Wks. (Grosart) V. 244 The bonnie Northren cobbles..with their Indian canaos.. firking as flight swift thorow the glassy fieldes of Thetis, as if it were the land of yce.

†**b.** *intr.* To move about briskly; to dance, jig; to flaunt or frisk about: to be lively, frisky, or 'jiggish'. Also ***to firk it***. *Obs.*

1596 NASHE *Have with you* Ep. Ded., Wks. (Grosart) III. 17 Neuer surcease flaunting and firking it in fustian. **1606** *Sir G. Goosecappe* II. i. in Bullen *O. Pl.* III. 32 Your dauncers legges bow for-sooth, and Caper, and jerke and Firke. *a* **1625** FLETCHER *Woman's Prize* II. vi, They have got a stick of Fiddles and they firke it In wondrous waies. *c* **1630** B. JONSON *Expost. Inigo Jones*, How would he firk, like Adam Overdo, Up and about. **1672** VILLIERS (Dk. Buckhm.) *Rehearsal* (Arb.) 115 We'l frisk in our shell, We'l firk in our shell. *a* **1679** EARL ORRERY *Guzman* IV. (end), Well since I am restrain'd a while from doing, I'll ferk it with thinking.

4. *trans.* To beat, whip, lash, trounce, drub. *Obs.* exc. *arch.*

1567 EDWARDS *Damon & Pithias* in Hazl. *Dodsley* IV. 164 O, I had firk'd him trimly, thou villain, if thou hadst given me my sword. **1599** SHAKS. *Hen. V*, IV. iv. 29 M. Fer: Ile fer him, and firke him, and ferret him. *a* **1625** FLETCHER *Women Pleas'd* III. iv, I have paid her, I have so ferk'd her face. **1638** FORD *Lady's Trial* II. ii, He has firk'd And mumbled the rogue Turks. **1708** *Brit. Apollo* No. 9. 3/1 Who..Bound up a tingling Rod, and firk'd his Tail. **1722** SEWEL *Hist. Quakers* IV. 128 At this the Judge said, 'Take him away, Prevaricator! I'll ferk him'. **1736** AINSWORTH *Lat. Dict.* I, To firk, *flagello*. **1863** SALA *Capt. Dangerous* I. iv. 97, I would sooner see a poor rogue soundly firked at the post.

†**b.** To play (a fiddle). *Obs.*

1668 DAVENANT *Man's the Master* III. ii, Firk your fiddles!

Hence **'firking** *vbl. sb.* and *ppl. a.* Also **'firker**, one who firks. **'firkery** (see quot. 1611).

1594 NASHE *Unfort. Trav.* Wks. (Grosart) V. 70 Why should I goe gadding..after firking flantado Amphibologies? **1602** MARSTON *Ant. & Mel.* III. Wks. 1856 I. 34 He would proove a rare firking Satyrist. **1611** COTGR., *Bichecoterie*..firkerie, an odde pranke, or ierke, in whoorisme. **1611** BARREY *Ram-Alley* IV. i. Fiv, She shall haue bayle..And a firking writte Of false imprisonment. *a* **1625** FLETCHER *Mad Lover* V. iv, No firking out at fingers ends. **1632** ROWLEY *Woman never Vext* IV. i. 51 These briske factors are notable firkers. **1636** DAVENANT *Witts* (1673) 197 Sir, these are the firkers of the City Fiddles. **1654** GAYTON *Pleas. Notes* III. i. 68 Your soberest Jades are firkers in Corners. **1664** BUTLER *Hud.* II. II. 448 Give thy outward-fellow a ferking. *a* **1704** T. BROWN *Sat. French King* Wks. 1730 I. 59 That I had the firking of thy bumb with holly. **1719** D'URFEY *Pills* (1872) IV. 263 In Paul's Churchyard.. dwells a noble Firker. Take heed..Lest you taste of his Lash.

†**'firkett.** *Obs.* = next.

1523 *Nottinghm. Rec.* No. 1396, 6 Unum cadum, Anglice a firkett, nigri sopi.

firkin ('fɜːkɪn), *sb.* Forms: 5 ferdekyn, ferken, 6 fi-, fyrken, fyrkin, *Sc.* ferrekyn, (7 firking, 8 ferkin), 9 *Sc.* firikin, 6– firkin. [In 15th c. *ferdekyn*, app. a. MDu. **vierdekijn*, dim. of *vierde* fourth, fourth part: see -KIN.]

1. A small cask for liquids, fish, butter, etc., originally containing a quarter of a 'barrel' or half a 'kilderkin'.

1423 *Act 2 Hen. VI*, c. 14 Ferdekyns de Harank. **1502** ARNOLDE *Chron.* (1811) 85 To enacte that euery..barell, kilderkyn and firken of ale and bere kepe ther full mesur. **15..** *Aberdeen Reg.* (Jam.), Ane ferrekyn of saip. **1653** WALTON *Angler* 223 Put them..into some tub or firkin. **1745** *De Foe's Eng. Tradesman* (1841) I. xxvi. 258 Butter, in firkins. **1817** W. SELWYN *Law Nisi Prius* II. 1177 He carried the firkins as far as Bowes. **1879** J. BURROUGHS *Locusts & W. Honey* 10 As the dairy-maid packs butter into a firkin. **1886** *Pall Mall G.* 20 Aug. 4/1 The farm labourer carries his day's allowance to the field in a sort of miniature cask, known to him as a 'firkin', which may hold from a quart to a gallon.

b. humorously applied to a person.

1630 J. TAYLOR (Water P.) *Wks.* III. 78/2 Most of them are transformed to Barrels, Firkings, and Kinderkins, alwayes fraight with Hamburge beere. *a* **1700** B. E. *Dict. Cant. Crew*, *Firkin of foul Stuff*, a..Coarse Corpulent Woman. **1830** GALT *Lawrie Todd* II. VI. viii. 315 Rather than see our school defiled with yon firikin of foul stuff.

2. Used as a measure of capacity: Half a kilderkin. (The 'barrel', 'kilderkin', and 'firkin' varied in capacity according to the commodity.)

1465 *Mann. & Househ. Exp.* 299 Paid for a fferken ale, x.d. **1525** TINDALE *John* ii. 6 Pottes of stone..contaynynge two or thre fyrkyns a pece. **1542** RECORDE *Gr. Artes* (1575) 204 Of Ale the Fyrken conteineth 8 gallons. **1600** T. HYLL *Arith.* I. xiii. 66 b, 8 gallons in measure make 1 firkin of ale, sope, herring; 9 gallons..1 firkin of beere; 10½ gallons, 1 firkin of salmon or Eeles. **1668** DENHAM *Second West. Wonder* 4 in Poems 107 Another..was done with a Firkin of powder. **1713** WARDER *True Amazons* 32 Honey, that will make us a Ferkin of good Mead. **1727** BRADLEY *Fam. Dict.* s.v., Two Firkins make a Kilderkin. **1828** SCOTT *F.M. Perth* xvi, 'They made me drink a firkin of Malvoisie.'

3. *attrib.* and *Comb.*, as **firkin-man, -trade** (see quot. 1706); **ale-firkin**: see ALE.

1670 J. SMITH *England's Improv. Reviv'd* 164, 4 wooden Vessels of Firkin size. **1706** PHILLIPS (ed. Kersey), *Firkin-man*, one that trades with a Brewer for small Beer, to furnish his own Customers. **1743** *Lond. & Country Brew.* II. (ed. 2) 158 The honest Brewer or Firkin-man. *Ibid.*, This Monster in Iniquity sold his Firkin-Trade.

Hence (*nonce-wds.*) **'firkin** *v.*, *trans.* to store *up* in firkins. **firki'neer** [see -EER[1]], one who sells by the firkin.

1563–87 FOXE *A. & M.* (1684) III. 732, I cannot firken up my butter..and let the poor want. **1842** *Blackw. Mag.* LII. 468 The orders—the princely prices, came from kingdoms that were magnificent—not from costermongering republics ..not from illiberal guilds of salt-butter firkineers.

firlot ('fɜːlɒt). *Sc.* Forms: 5 ferlot, 6 feirt-, fert-, ferthelett, fertleitt, furlet, fyrlot, 7–8 furlot, 8 farlet, 6– firlot. [First in L. *ferthelota*, app. repr. ON. *fiórþe hlotr* fourth part: see LOT.

The OE. *hlot* does not appear to have been used in the sense of '(fractional) part'.]

1. A measure of capacity for corn, etc., the fourth part of a boll.

[**1264** *Comput. Vicecom. de Forfar* (Jam.), In servicio regis iij celd. ij boll. et j ferthelota.] **1426** *Sc. Acts Jas. I* (1597) §70 They ordaned..foure firlotts to conteine a boll. **1484** *Act Audit.* 36/2, iii ferlotis of mele. *c* **1540** in W. H. Maxwell *Sports & Adv. Scotl.* xxviii. (1855) 229 Oats, 47 chalders 1 boll 2 firlots. **1708** J. CHAMBERLAYNE *St. Gt. Brit.* II. III. ii. 510 The Firlot of Linlithgow..contains Thirty-one Pints Sterling Jugg, for the Measuring of Wheat, Rye, Meal, etc. **1824** *Mech. Mag.* No. 46. 279 You can determine the weight of a firlot of grain in the short space of half a minute. **1876** GRANT *Burgh. Sch. Scotl.* II. 458 *note*, Another [gives] a firlot, and another two firlots of meal.

b. A certain measure used for other commodities; also, a great quantity.

1549 *Inv. of Brine* (Somerset Ho.), xij ferthelettes of grece butter. 1585 *Inv. of Postilthwaite* (Somerset Ho.), Itm v. feirtletts couerlete ȝarne. *a*1832 *Fire of Frendraught* iii. in Child *Ballads* VII. cxcvi (1890) 46/1 Ye's hae a firlot o the gude red gowd. 1883 J. PURVES in *Contemp. Rev.* Sept. 353 Poachers.. who in a night secure a 'firlot' of partridges.

2. A vessel used to measure a firlot of corn, etc.

1573 TYRIE *Refut. Answ. Knox* 40 b, Na man doth licht ane lanterne, putting it vnder ane firlot. 1577–95 *Descr. Isles Scotl.* in Skene *Celtic Scotl.* III. App. 437 To take sa mony firlotts as micht stand side by side. 1670 RAY *Prov.* 287 Mony words fills not the furlot. 1815 SCOTT *Guy M.* ii, The old castle, where the family lived, in their decadence, as a mouse lives under a firlot.

firm (fɜːm), *sb.*[1] Also 6 firme. [ad. It., Sp. and Pg. *firma*, a Com. Rom. n. of action f. L. *firmāre* to confirm, in late L. to ratify by one's signature, f. *firm-us* FIRM *a.* Cf. FARM *sb.*[2], which is another form of the same word. The word first occurs in translations from Sp. writers; in sense 2 it was prob. taken, like other commercial words, from Italian.]

†**1.** Signature, sign-manual. *Obs.*

1574 HELLOWES *Gueuara's Fam. Ep.* 62 The firme of my hand I cannot denie. *Ibid.* 257 This letter.. is.. without date or firme. 1588 PARKE tr. *Mendoza's Hist. China* 81 He .. doth firme the petition with his own firme with red inke. [1613 PURCHAS *Pilgrimage* (1864) 50 The Articles.. were confirmed by the King's Firma.] 1688 *Lond. Gaz.* No. 2354/2 He.. puts the Grand Signior's Firm or Name to all Imperial Commands. 1707 FREIND *Peterborow's Cond. Sp.* 143 We order these Presents to be passed with our Royal Firm. 1755 tr. *Italian certificate* in Magens *Insurances* I. 304 The frequent knowledge we have of his Firm and Signature.

2. a. The 'style' or name under which the business of a commercial house is transacted. **b.** A partnership of two or more persons for carrying on a business; a commercial house.

1744 in Hanway *Trav.* (1762) I. v. lxvi. 301 We are come to the unanimous resolution of fixing one house, under the firm of Messieurs Hanway and Mierop. 1785 MRS. BENNETT *Juvenile Indiscret.* (1786) II. 135 He could not oppose the wishes of the respectable partners without altering the firm of the house. 1802 MAR. EDGEWORTH *Moral T.* (1816) I. xix. 163 All we want to know, is the number of your note, and the firm of the house. 1817 W. SELWYN *Law Nisi Prius* II. 1065 An action brought by the other parties in the firm, for goods sold and delivered. 1861 W. BELL *Dict. Law Scot.* 387/1 A proper or personal firm is a firm designated by the names of one or more of the partners.. A descriptive firm has reference to some such circumstance as the place where the company is established, or the transactions in which it is engaged. 1864 MRS. RIDDELL *George Geith* I. ii. 9 Trading under the firm of 'Grant & Co.' 1870 DICKENS *E. Drood* viii, My small patrimony was left a part of the capital of the Firm I am with. 1882 SERJT. BALLANTINE *Exper.* viii. 81 A respectable firm of solicitors.

c. *transf.* Applied (chiefly in sarcastic use) to a number of persons regarded as associated for the promotion of their common interest. Also used *gen.* of a group of persons working together.

*a*1797 BURKE (T.), The bill was carried by a very small majority, consisting of partners in the firm. 1819 *Metropolis* II. 209 He won a little money in Bennet Street, (where, to be sure, it seldom happens that any one, not of the firm, does win). 1862 MERIVALE *Rom. Emp.* (1865) VII. lx. 291 The plebeian emperor, the head of the Flavian firm. 1909 *Westm. Gaz.* 16 Aug. 7/3 The general surgical and medical work is in charge of a medical and surgical 'firm', each consisting of two visiting and one house physician or surgeon. 1933 J. HILTON *Lost Horizon* x. 218 Moderation, y'know—the motto of the firm. 1952 E. F. DAVIES *Illyrian Venture* ii. 35 Our organisation [*sc.* SOE], which was known as 'The Firm', had equipped a hut with every item of kit we were likely to want. 1964 G. L. COHEN *What's Wrong with Hospitals?* vi. 125 Each consultant heads a firm usually comprising registrar and houseman, who get their own beds allocated *en bloc*. 1964 G. LYALL *Most Dangerous Game* xxv. 218 He's one of the Firm... He's not going to talk. 1969 *Daily Tel.* 8 Feb. 13/6 The Kray 'firm' were like income-tax inspectors in assessing what 'pension' or protection money a club should pay them. 1971 R. BUSBY *Deadlock* x. 159 Put in for a transfer to the Met, we could use a good man in my firm.

d. *long firm.* (See quot. 1882.)

1869 *Orchestra* 2 Jan. 235/1 The doings of 'the Long Firm', a body of phantom capitalists who issue large orders to supply an infinite variety of goods. 1882 OGILVIE s.v. *Firm, Long Firm*, a term given to that class of swindlers who obtain goods by pretending to be in business in a certain place, and ordering goods to be sent to them, generally from persons at a distance, without any intention of payment. 1888 RIDER HAGGARD *Mr. Meeson's Will* xv, John would give James briefs, and James's reflected glory would shine back on John. In short, they were anxious to establish a legal long firm of the most approved pattern.

firm, *sb.*[2] *Hist.* [ad. med.L. *firma*: see FARM *sb.*[2]] Occasionally used instead of FARM *sb*[2] in translations of med.L. documents.

1859 A. JEFFREY *Roxburghsh.* III. iv. 111 He granted to Sir Robert Erskine £100 out of his firms in Aberdeen. 1875 W. MCILWRAITH *Guide Wigtownshire* 54 James III granted to his Queen the whole Lordship of Galloway, with the customs and firms of the burghs of Kirkcudbright and Wigtown, as well as the Castle of Thrieve.

firm (fɜːm), *a.* and *adv.* Forms: 4–6 ferm(e, 6 fyrme, 6–7 firme, 6– firm. [ME. *ferme*, a. OF. (and Fr.) *ferme*:—L. *firmus*.]

A. *adj.*

1. Having a close consistence, of solid or compact structure or texture; not readily yielding to pressure or impact.

1611 BIBLE *Job* xli. 24 His heart is as firme as a stone. 1614 RALEIGH *Hist. World* III. §5 To dry up the abundant slime and mudde of the Earth, and make the Land more firme. 1667 MILTON *P.L.* I. 350 Down they light On the firm brimstone. 1726 SHELVOCKE *Voy. round World* 28 To case it all over with firm thick plank. 1727 SWIFT *Gulliver* III. ii. 187 Upon the firm earth. 1812–16 J. SMITH *Panorama Sc. & Art* I. 5 Cast steel takes a fine firm edge. 1823 F. CLISSOLD *Ascent Mt. Blanc* 20 The surface of the snow was of so firm a consistence that [etc.]. 1854 BADHAM *Halieut.* 170 The flesh is rather too firm when fresh.

2. Securely or steadily fixed, not easily moved or shaken, stable.

1597 SHAKS. *2 Hen. IV*, IV. v. 204 Yet, though thou stand'st more sure, than I could do, Thou art not firme enough. 1598 —— *Merry W.* III. ii. 49 It is as possitiue, as the earth is firme. 1694 NARBOROUGH in *Acc. Sev. Late Voy.* 46 They lie in Veins in the Earth, and in the firm Rocks. 1784 COWPER *Task* V. 156 So stood the brittle prodigy, though smooth And slipp'ry the materials, yet frost-bound Firm as a rock. 1791 MRS. RADCLIFFE *Rom. Forest* ii, The glass was yet firm in the windows. *Mod.* Try whether the post is firm in the ground.

3. That does not shake, quiver, or waver; steady in motion or action; having control of the muscular forces of the body, not relaxed or nerveless.

1593 SHAKS. *2 Hen. VI*, III. i. 190 King Henry throwes away his Crutch, Before his Legges be firme to beare his Body. 1614 BP. HALL *Recoll. Treat.* 102 This firme and beautifull light [the Sun]. 1656 COWLEY *Davideis* III. 504 The Lion's royal whelp.. leaves the rugged Bear for firmer claws. 1667 MILTON *P.L.* VI. 534 Him soon they met Under spred Ensignes moving nigh, in slow But firm Battalion. 1697 DRYDEN *Virg. Georg.* III. 121 Upright he walks on Pasterns firm and straight. 1809 ROLAND *Fencing* 22 Extend the longe.. provided you feel yourself firm and steady in that position. 1834 MEDWIN *Angler in Wales* I. 273, I never heard but one woman who had so firm a touch [on the piano]. 1840 *P. Parley's Ann.* I. 176 A wise man's feet are always firm in the stirrup. 1870 BRYANT *Iliad* I. IV. 120 O aged man, would that thy knees were firm As is thy purpose.

4. Healthy, robust; sound, undecayed. (Cf. *infirm.*) ? *Obs.*

1577 B. GOOGE *Heresbach's Husb.* III. (1586) 124 b, If the Horse have an ache [*si febrit*], give it him with water, if he be ferme [*si non febrit*] with good strong Wine. 1715–20 POPE *Iliad* XVII. 348 Lamented youth! in life's firm bloom he fell. 1776 G. SEMPLE *Building in Water* 84 Those which were painted were all quite rotten, but those that were not painted continued firm. 1798 MALTHUS *Popul.* (1817) I. 428 In the firmest stages of life.

5. a. Of non-material things: Fixed, settled, established. Of a decree, law, or sentence: Immutable.

*c*1374 CHAUCER *Boeth.* III. vi. 78 I ne trowe nat þat þe pris and grace of þe poeple.. ne is ferm perdurably. *c*1400 MAUNDEV. (Roxb.) xvi. 74 Þou.. sall hafe were withouten ferme pees all way. 1538 STARKEY *England* I. i. 16 The law of nature ys.. in al cuntreys fyrme and stabul. 1568 GRAFTON *Chron.* II. 173 We.. promise to observe and holde his deede firme and stable. 1600 SHAKS. *A.Y.L.* I. iii. 85 Firme and irreuocable is my doombe. 1625 BURGES *Pers. Tithes* 64 If the Law bee.. firme for Personal Tithes. 1660 MILTON *Free Commw.* 430 The happiness of a Nation must needs be firmest and certainest in a full and free Council of thir own electing. 1837 WHEWELL *Hist. Induct. Sc.* (1857) I. 229 This apotelesmatic or judicial astrology obtained firm possession of men's minds.

†**b.** Assured, secure (as a possession, etc.). Also of a person: Assured *of* a thing. *Obs.*

1375 BARBOUR *Bruce* IX. 755 The King.. Send hym to be in ferm keping. 1483 CAXTON *Gold. Leg.* 285 b/1 They mette and were ferme of the lignage promysed. 1594 *First Pt. Contention* (1843) 39 You shall have your firme rewarde. 1671 CHARENTE *Let. Customs* 64 He who was Governour at the time.. did not.. deliver it up to the King of Portugal, but kept it firm to the King of Spain. 1737 WHISTON *Josephus' Antiq.* VII. ix. §6 The kingdom would be firm to him when David was dead.

†**c.** Well-ascertained, certain, sure. Of an argument: Well-founded, valid. *Obs.*

1377 LANGL. *P. Pl.* B. XII. 283 Þorough fuire is fullyng and þat is ferme bileue. 1581 J. BELL *Haddon's Answ. Osor.* 494 Alleadgyng no firme, or honest proofe of yᵉ crimes. 1596 SHAKS. *Merch. V.* IV. i. 53 There is no firme reason to be rendred Why [etc.]. 1616 SURFL. & MARKH. *Country Farme* 27 If the drops of Water comming from the roofes of Houses doe fall one a good while after another, he shall hold it for firme, that cold is neere at hand. 1693 SOUTH *Serm.* II. 187 If the sole use of Words.. were to inform the Person, whom we speak to, the Consequence would be firm and good.

6. a. Of a person, his attributes, etc.: Immovable or not easily moved; constant, steadfast; unflinching, unshaken, unwavering; resolute, determined.

1377 LANGL. *P. Pl.* B. XV. 341 Wherfore folke is þe feblere and nouȝt ferme of bileue. *c*1400 *Rom. Rose* 5229 If he be so ferme & stable, That fortune chaunge hym not. 1490 CAXTON *Eneydos* xii. 43 Make thy selfe ferme wyth hope. 1552 ABP. HAMILTON *Catech.* (1884) 4 Thairto gyf ferme credens. 1598 SHAKS. *Merry W.* IV. v. 28 Her Mother, (euen strong against that match And firme for Doctor Caius). 1637 *Decree Star Chamb.* §24 in Milton *Areop.* (Arb.) 20 The Court doth hereby declare their firme resolution. 1659 B. HARRIS *Parival's Iron Age* 245 The people of Liedge are very firm Roman Catholicks. 1751 T. SHARP in *Lett. Lit. Men* (Camden) 375 A firm and lasting friendship. 1838 LYTTON *Alice* I. ix, Lady Vargrave, though touched, was firm. 1848 MACAULAY *Hist. Eng.* I. 225 Those classes which had been the firm allies of the monarchy. 1852 H. ROGERS *Ecl. Faith* (1853) 181 [They] were firm believers in the theory of insight. 1873 HELPS *Anim. & Mast.* (1875) 4 It is my firm belief that [etc.].

b. Steadfast in attachment *to* (a person, cause, or the like).

1705 WALSH *Hor. Odes* III. iii. 2 The man that's resolute and just, Firm to his principles and trust. *a*1715 BURNET *Own Time* I. 393 While the Parliament was so firm to the King. 1726–46 THOMSON *Winter* 482 Phocion the Good.. To virtue still inexorably firm.

c. Indicating steadfastness or resolution.

1802 MAR. EDGEWORTH *Moral T.* (1816) I. 211 'I am the count', replied he, in a firm tone. 1844 *Mem. Babylonian P'cess* II. 253 The firm voice of the captain giving his orders. 1878 B. TAYLOR *Deukalion* II. iv. 81 Pity shines From those firm eyes.

7. *Comm.* **a.** Of prices: Maintaining their level; with no downward tendency. Of commodities: Not depressed in market value. Also *transf.* applied to the market, a season of trade, etc. **b.** *a firm offer*: one which the person making it is resolved not to increase.

1846 *Times* 19 Nov. 6/2 The trade is very firm, and the prices of Friday are fully maintained. *Ibid.* 30 Nov. 3/3 The wool trade is flat, and few sales can be effected, although prices are firm. 1883 *Daily News* 7 Nov. 4/7 American prices were firm. 1887 *Ibid.* 7 June 2/6 English wheats in the country markets are somewhat irregular, though most generally firm. 1887 *Times* 25 Aug. 9/1 The Money Market has been a little less firm to-day. 1891 *Daily News* 23 Nov. 2/7 There is no probability of the market becoming weaker. Indeed, a continued firm winter and a good spring is looked forward to.

†**8. firm land, firm-land**: dry land, solid earth; the mainland (as opposed to an island), a 'continent'. *Obs.* as a recognized phrase. [= med.L. *terra firma*. F. *terre ferme*.]

1553 EDEN *Treat. Newe Ind.* (Arb.) 8 They see the continente or fyrme lande, extended euen to the North Pole. 1594 BLUNDEVIL *Exerc.* V. (ed. 7) 574 The South firme Land is called of some Magellanica. 1612 BREREWOOD *Lang. & Relig.* x. 93 Thus it is.. in the firm land of Asia: but in the islands about Asia [etc.]. 1667 MILTON *P.L.* II. 589 A frozen continent.. which on firm land Thaws not. 1682 WHELER *Journ. Greece* I. 22 It is joyned.. to the Firm-land by a Woodden one [bridge]. 1872 BROWNING *Fifine* lxxxii. 5 No more to do But tread the firmland, tempt the uncertain sea no more.

†**9.** *ellipt.* quasi-*sb.* = prec. *Obs.*

1598 HAKLUYT *Voy.* I. 438 No such Islands may bee found in the Scithian sea toward the firme of Asia. 1612 DRAYTON *Poly-olb.* ii. 407 Betwixt the fore-land and the firme, Shee [Wight] hath that narrow Sea, which we the Solent tearme. 1615 G. SANDYS *Trav.* I. 19 Ashore on the firme of Asia.

B. *adv.* and quasi-*adv.*

1377 LANGL. *P. Pl.* B. XIX. 116 That she furste and formest ferme shulde bilieue. 1667 MILTON *P.L.* XII. 127 He .. firm believes. 1703 MOXON *Mech. Exerc.* 137 The shorter all the Bearings of Timbers are, the firmer they Bear. 1768–74 TUCKER *Lt. Nat.* (1852) II. 304 Charity.. is built firmest upon faith and prudence. 1801 SOUTHEY *Thalaba* XI. iv, Her rosy feet press firmer, as she leaps Upon the wing.

b. Chiefly in phr. *to stand firm* (lit. and fig.), and *to hold firm* (*to*).

*a*1340 HAMPOLE *Psalter* xviii. 10 Þat þai be halden ferme. 1570 BILLINGSLEY *Euclid* I. Def. iv. 2 A right lyne is that which standeth firme betwene his extremes. 1611 BIBLE *Josh.* iv. 3 The place where the Priests feet stood firme. 1611 SHAKS. *Cymb.* II. i. 67 Heel'd make the Heauens hold firme The walls of thy deere Honour. 1626 BACON *Sylva* §900 Wee that hold firme to the Works of God. 1724 DE FOE *Mem. Cavalier* (1840) 277 He, an old tried soldier, stood firm. 1856 EMERSON *Eng. Traits, Manners* Wks. (Bohn) II. 45, I find the Englishman to be him of all men who stands firmest in his shoes. 1857 SPURGEON *Serm. New Park St.* II. 132 Those who hold truth pretty firm and will not let it go.

C. *Comb.*

1. Of the adj.: **a.** with sb., as †*firm-wood* (used as adj.). Also **firm-land** (see A. 8).

1745 tr. *Columella's Husb.* III. xvii, Authors who denied that the upper firm-wood branch is fit for bearing fruit.

b. In parasynthetic adjs., as *firm-based*, *-bodied*, *-faced*, *-featured*, *-framed*, *-lipped*, *-minded*, *-natured*, *-nerved*, *-paced*, †*-proposed*, *-sinewed*, *-souled*, *-textured*; also **firm-footed**, *spec.* in Cricket = *fast-footed* (a); **firm-hoofed**, having hoofs not cloven.

1820 KEATS *Hyperion* II. 138 My *firm-based footstool. 1915 D. H. LAWRENCE *Rainbow* 315 She was *firm-bodied as Diana. 1918 E. POUND *Pavannes & Divisions* 39 One of those *firm-faced inspecting women. 1916 JOYCE *Portrait of Artist* v. 273 Cranly's *firm featured suffering face. 1907 *Westm. Gaz.* 20 Aug. 3/2 A hitter of the *firm-footed school. 1928 *Daily Tel.* 15 May 19/1 He attempts, firm-footed, to drive the ball which is pitched a couple of feet wide of the off-stump. 1961 *Times* 22 May 3/3 He lost Teague, bowled firm-footed. 1877 BLACK *Green Past.* iii. (1878) 20 He was a bony *firm-framed young man. 1646 SIR T. BROWNE *Pseud. Ep.* VI. vi. 297 Solipes, or *firme hoofed creatures, as Horses, Asses, Mules, &c. 1870 BRYANT *Iliad* v. 286 Thy firm-hoofed [Gr. μώνυχας] coursers. 1921 W. DE LA MARE *Crossings* 27 *Firm-lipped, round-browed, keen-eyed. 1913 J. MASEFIELD *Daffodil Fields* 60 He should not have a woman sick with ghosts, But one *firm-minded to be his. 1858 BAGEHOT *Coll. Works* (1965) I. 319 They [*sc.* Whigs] are emphatically pure-natured and *firm-natured. 1821 JOANNA BAILLIE *Met. Leg., Wallace* xxxvii, The *firm-nerved youth's exerted force. 1799 CAMPBELL *Pleas. Hope* I, *Firm-paced and slow, a horrid front they form. 1599 SHAKS. *Hen. V*, V. ii. 462 The King hath graunted euery Article.. According to their *firm proposed natures. 1884

BLACK *Jud. Shaks.* viii, His *firm-sinewed figure. **1918** W. B. YEATS *Per Amica Silentia Lunae* xvi. 79 Some *firm-souled man. **1854** HAWTHORNE *Eng. Note-bks.* (1883) I. 553, I..found her sensible..and *firm-textured, rather than soft and sentimental.

2. Of the adv. with pa. pples., forming adjs., as ***firm-braced, -compacted, -planted, -rooted*** (hence ***firm-rootedness***), ***-set, -written.***

1847 EMERSON *Poems* (1857) 47 *Firm-braced I sought my ancient woods. **1779** POTTER *Æschylus* I. 142 (*Supplicants*) Their *firm-compacted ships. **1870** BRYANT *Iliad* I. XII. 382 Oaks..*Firm-planted. **1808** MRS. E. H. ILIFF *Poems* (1818) 97 *Firm-rooted in the yellow sands. **1860** PUSEY *Min. Proph.* 587 The allusion..is to its *firm-rootedness. **1605** SHAKS. *Macb.* II. i. 56 Thou sure and *firme-set Earth Heare not my steps. **1863** I. WILLIAMS *Baptistery* II. xxiii. (1874) 85 O firm-set, ever-during scene! **1649** G. DANIEL *Trinarch., Hen. V* ccxv, *Firme-written destinie Reverts the Breath of Kings.

firm (fɜːm), *v.* Now *rare* exc. in technical use. Forms: 4 **ferme**, 5–7 **firme**, 6 **fyrme**. [Partly ad. (either through F. *fermer* or directly) L. *firmāre*, f. *firmus* FIRM *a.*; partly a new formation on the adj.]

1. a. *trans.* To make firm or fast; to set or fix firmly or securely; also, to hold (a thing) fast.

c **1374** CHAUCER *Boeth.* I. v. 14 (Camb. MS.) Fastne and ferme thise erthes stable with thilke bonde by whiche thow gouerneste the heuene. *a* **1400–50** *Alexander* 1369 And þat [tower] he fiches & firmes sa fast to þe wall. **1609** BIBLE (Douay) *Gen.* vii. 16 *Annot.*, The dore..was to be firmed without..for better induring the forcible waters. **1615** CHAPMAN *Odyss.* XIII. 246 He..to a stone Turn'd all her sylvan substance; all below Firm'd her with roots, and left her. **1669** BOYLE *Contn. New Exp.* II. (1682) 46 The Reciever seemed to admit the external air..therefore I firmed the cover with Turpentine. **1670** WALTON *Lives* I. 77 The stones..were again by the masons art so levelled and firm'd, as they had been formerly. **1808** J. BARLOW *Columb.* VII. 735 They firm the base Of Freedom's temple, while her arms they grace. **1855** SINGLETON *Virgil* II. 70 With its griping fang The anchor firmed the ships. **1885** *Birm. Weekly Post* 7 Feb. 1/7 Keep spring flowers well firmed in the ground. **1890** HOSIE *West China* 166 Men..removing with their toes the weeds from the roots of the young shoots, and firming the latter in the ground.

†**b.** To fasten or fix (the eye) upon (something). *Obs.*

1590 SPENSER *F.Q.* II. vii. 1 As pilot..Upon his card and compas firmes his eye.

†**c.** To steady, support. *Obs. rare.*

1646 SIR T. BROWNE *Pseud. Ep.* v. xvi. 258 The staffe of his [Christ's] direction, whereon if he firmeth himselfe, he may be able to overcome the billows of resistance.

2. To make firm in consistence; to compact, solidify.

1580 NORTH *Plutarch* (1676) 85 The force of the water..did firm and harden it, and made it grow so to Land. **1605** B. JONSON *Volpone* II. i, The powder..clear'd her wrinkles, firm'd her gums, fill'd her skin, colour'd her hair. **1610** W. FOLKINGHAM *Art of Survey* I. x. 24 Boggie and spungie grounds are..setled, fastened and firmed by frequent overflowing them with Fords. **1757** DYER *Fleece* III. 137 Ever and anon, to firm the work, Against the web is driv'n the noisy frame. **1842** *Jrnl. R. Agric. Soc.* III. I. 125 By every means firm the land after wheat-sowing. **1882** *Garden* 18 Mar. 185/3 Plant carefully, well firming the soil about their roots with the hand. **1890** HOSIE *West China* 19 Drums for firming the paper as it comes from the pulp-troughs.

†**3.** *trans.* To strengthen, make robust. *Obs.*

1592 GREENE *Palmer's Verses* viii. Wks. (Rtldg.) 303/2 When in the Virgin's lap earth's comfort sleeps..Both corn and plants are firmed.

†**4.** To establish, settle, confirm (a person, etc.); to strengthen (in resolution), encourage. *Obs.*

1303 R. BRUNNE *Handl. Synne* 9889 God ȝyue vs grace..Yn þe beleue to ferme vs ryȝt. **1639** G. DANIEL *Ecclus.* xxii. 52 The heart Which firmed is by what the Wise impart, Fear cannot daunt. **1650** W. BROUGH *Sacr. Princ.* (1659) 545 Solid knowledge will..Firm the Mind in Truth. **1682** N. O. *Boileau's Lutrin* III. 171 Thy Valour firm'd the wavering Troops that day.

†**5. a.** To make (an agreement, etc.) firm; to establish firmly, settle, strengthen. *Obs.*

c **1425** WYNTOUN *Cron.* VIII. i. 40 Twa Erlys..Come chargyd in Scotland..To tret, and ferme a Marriage. **1577–87** HOLINSHED *Chron.* III. 1184/1 It was further concluded also, that a peace should be firmed..betwixt the realmes of England and Scotland. **1594** LODGE *Wounds Civil War* III. in Hazl. *Dodsley* VII. 135 And we will firm our honours by our bloods. **1659** H. L'ESTRANGE *Alliance Div. Off.* 486 These testimonies firm the comparison betwixt such persons and Adam. **1673** DRYDEN *Amboyna* II. i, Hold back your Hand, from firming of your Faith. **1729** SAVAGE *Wanderer* I. 294 He won the Belgic Land..And firms the Conquest with his fenceful Mound. **1808** J. BARLOW *Columb.* II. 294 Ten wide provinces..Bless the same king, and daily firm the sway.

†**b.** To make (a possession, title, etc.) sure; to assure, secure; also, to attach (a person) securely. Const. *to, unto. Obs.*

1530 R. WHYTFORD *Werke for Househ.* E, The blessynge of the parentes dothe fyrme and make stable the possessyons and the kynred of the chylder. **1624** T. SCOTT *Belg. Souldier* 18 That [he] be especially carefull to firme and contract unto himselfe..the King of Poland. **1664** J. WILSON *A. Comnenius* v. iii, Since your joint unanimous concent Has firm'd that title. **1669** J. OWEN in T. Gale *Jansenisme* Pref., That ground shall be firmed to them speedily by new Briefs.

†**c.** *gen.* To ratify formally; to confirm. *Obs.*

1599 NASHE *Lenten Stuffe* 15 When hee [William I] firmed and rubrickt Kentishmen's gauill-kind of the sonne to inherite at fifteene. **1659** H. L'ESTRANGE *Alliance Div. Off.* 435 Solemn leagues..solemnly firmed by oaths. **1685** DRYDEN *Albion & Albanius* I. 8 Jove has firm'd it with an Awfull Nod. **1703** POPE *Thebais* 591 Be present still, oh Goddess!..Proceed, and firm those omens thou hast made.

†**6. a.** To make (a document) valid by authoritative seal, indorsement, signature, stamp, or the like; to subscribe, sign. Also, ***to firm with the hand.***

1510 *Will of J. Deram* (Somerset Ho.), Fyrmed..wᵗ my hand. **1574** HELLOWES *Gueuara's Fam. Ep.* 62 To firme it with the hand, is meere follie. *Ibid.* 64 If..Catiline and other his fellowes had not firmed the letter of their coniuration. *Ibid.* 231, I caused your bill to be firmed by the Queene. **1588** *Ord. Sp. Fleet* in *Harl. Misc.* (1744) I. 111 These my instructions are..firmed by my hand. **1613** HAYWARD *Norm. Kings, Will. I*, 98 Charters and deeds..were firmed by the parties speciall seale. **1641** *Termes de la Ley* 156b, Writings..were wont to be firmed in England with Crosses of gold. **1690** DRYDEN *Don Sebastian* v. 120 Your Father's hand, Firm'd with his Signet.

†**b.** To affix, 'sign' (one's name) to a document or writing. *Obs.*

1529 *Will of A. Chew* (Somerset Ho.), In witness whereof we..haue fyrmed our names. **1582** N. LICHEFIELD tr. *Castanheda's Conq. E. Ind.* 153 He..firmed therevnto his name.

absol. **1529** *Will of A. Chew* (Somerset Ho.), Because here is noo space to fyrme on this side we haue fyrmed on the other side. **1620** SHELTON *Quix.* IV. ii. 10 Another shall firm for me.

7. a. *intr.* To become firm.

1882 in OGILVIE. **1883** [see *ppl. adj.* below]. **1887** *S. Chesh. Gloss., Firm*, to grow firm. A cheese-making term.

b. *Comm.* Of prices that vary with a market, as share prices, rates of exchange, etc.: to become firm (FIRM *a.* 7a); to rise (slightly), esp. after being weak. Usu. with *up*. Also *fig.* Hence **'firming-up** *vbl. sb.*

1896 [see UP *adv.*[1] 18b]. **1899** *Daily News* 30 Oct. 2/6 A gradual firming-up of prices. **1907** *Daily Chron.* 9 Dec. 1/7 One or two Argentine Rails firmed up. **1929** *Daily Express* 7 Nov. 2/7 Then all firmed up on trade and Cuban buying. **1938** *Times* 13 Apr. 20/3 Shortly before the close of business they firmed up considerably. **1952** *Sat. Rev.* 20 Sept. 9/3 The firming up of prices resulting from the impact effect of the deficit. *a* **1969** R. WILLIAMS in D. Knight *100 Yrs. Sci. Fiction* (1969) 305 The whole picture was beginning to firm up in my mind now. **1971** *Daily Tel.* 18 June 23/1 Eurodollar rates firmed up yesterday. **1971** *Timber Trades Jrnl.* 21 Aug. 34/1 The Scandinavian market, which has been fairly weak over recent months, is now showing faint signs of firming. **1986** *Washington Post* 17 Apr. E2/6 As the economy gathers more noticeable strength through the second half, these investment plans may firm up soon.

8. *trans.* With *up*: to make firm (an agreement, etc.); to settle, establish, confirm. *colloq.*

1970 *Guardian* 22 June 20/7, I..firmed it up with the 'Statesman'. **1974** *Economist* 31 Aug. 48/1 The EEC is now preparing..to firm up its economic ties with..Greece and Portugal. **1979** S. WILSON *Greenish Man* 11 We'll firm up the deal later. **1983** *Listener* 10 Feb. 27/1 Like all comic draughtsmen he discovered running-gag characters who firmed up his style.

Hence **firmed** *ppl. a.* (*spec.* in *Falconry*: see quot. 1706). **'firming** *ppl. a.* (*a*) *trans.* That confirms or ratifies. (*b*) *intr.* That is becoming firm: see FIRM *a.* 7.

1574 HELLOWES *Gueuara's Fam. Ep.* 36 It [a letter] had not come firmed or with superscription. **1625** BP. MOUNTAGU *App. Cæsar.* Ep. Ded., I did it with a firmed purpose to leave all private opinions. **1649** G. DANIEL *Trinarch., Hen. IV*, ccclxv, Belgia, only (in a firmed state Wrought out by others) has been fortunate. **1706** PHILLIPS (ed. Kersey), *Firmed* or full Firmed (in Falconry), well fledged or well cover'd with Feathers. **1816** L. HUNT *Rimini* iv. 96 A noble word! exclaimed the Prince, and smote Preparingly on earth his firming foot. **1839** BAILEY *Festus* (1854) 332 A vital wind invisible, Yet firmed and bounded in a beauteous form. **1883** *Scotsman* 9 May 10/1 Sold at firming prices.

†**'firmable**, *a. Obs.* [f. FIRM *v.* + -ABLE.] ? Worthy to be ratified.

1584 R. W. *Three Ladies of London* in Hazl. *Dodsley* VI. 282 You will make an ill matter seem good and firmable.

firmament ('fɜːməmənt). Forms: 4–6 **fer-, fyrmament(e**, 3– **firmament**. [ad. L. *firmāmentum* f. *firmā-re* to strengthen, f. *firmus* firm. Cf. OF. *firmament*.

In class. Lat. the word means 'something which strengthens or supports' (cf. 3). In the Vulgate it was adopted, in imitation of the στερέωμα of the LXX (properly 'firm or solid structure', f. στερεόειν to make firm or solid, f. στερεός firm, solid), as the rendering of Hb. *rāqīaᶜ*, applied to the vault of the sky. The Heb. word prob. means 'expanse', from the root *rāqaᶜ* which in the Bible has the senses 'to tread', 'to beat out (metals)', 'to spread out'; but in Syriac the vb. means 'to condense, make firm or solid', whence the Gr. and Lat. renderings of the sb.]

1. a. The arch or vault of heaven overhead, in which the clouds and the stars appear; the sky or heavens. In mod. use only *poet.* or *rhetorical.*

[*c* **1050** *Byrhtferth's Handboc* in *Anglia* (1885) VIII. 309 On þam oðrum dæge he ȝeworhte firmamentum þæt ys þeos heofon.] *c* **1250** *Gen. & Ex.* 95 Ðo god bad ben ðe firmament. *c* **1290** *S. Eng. Leg.* I. 226/248 þat huy ne yseiȝen no-þing bote þe se ant þe firmament. *c* **1386** CHAUCER *Merch. T.* 975 Bright was the day, and bliew the firmament. **1555** EDEN *Decades* 35 That lyttle sleepe that they had was..abrode vnder the firmamente. **1667** MILTON *P.L.* IV. 604 Now glow'd the Firmament With living Saphirs. **1693** LUTTRELL *Brief Rel.* (1857) III. 192 This morning a rainbow seen in the firmament. **1846** tr. *Schlegel's Phil. Hist.* 80 The northern firmament possesses by far the largest and most brilliant constellations. **1877** BRYANT *Poems, Receive thy Sight* ii, The pleasant rays That lit the glorious firmament.

b. Heaven, as the place where God dwells. *Obs.* exc. in Biblical and liturgical phrases.

13.. *E.E. Allit. P.* B. 221 Thikke þowsandez..Fellen fro the fyrmament, fendez ful blake. **1388** WYCLIF *Ps.* cl. 1 Herie ȝe þe lord in hise seyntis! herie ȝe him in þe firmament of his vertu! **1535** COVERDALE *Song 3 Childr.* 33 Blessed be thou in yᵉ firmament of heauen. **1611** BIBLE *Ps.* cl. 1 Praise him in the firmament of his power.

c. *transf.* and *fig.*

1526 *Pilgr. Perf.* (W. de W. 1531) 104 Pite, whiche may wele be called the firmament of perfeccyon, for it is the stablysshment of all holy conuersacyon, whereby man..discerneth waters from waters. **1643** MILTON *Divorce* II. xxii. (1851) 127 That it may be suffer'd to stand in the place where God set it amidst the firmament of his holy Laws. **1667** —— *P.L.* II. 175 What if..this Firmament Of Hell should spout her Cataracts of Fire? **1871** E. F. BURR *Ad Fidem* vi. 97 A whole firmament of twinkling philosophers and philosophies.

†**2. a.** In old Astronomy: The sphere containing the fixed stars; the eighth heaven of the Ptolemaic system.

c **1400** MAUNDEV. (Roxb.) xi. 43 þe xii. signez of þe firmament. **1450–1530** *Myrr. our Ladye* 93 A nother heuen ys called the fyrmamente, where are the sterres. **1551** RECORDE *Cast. Knowl.* (1556) 7 Aboue these seuen planetes, is there an other heauen or skie, which commonly is named the Firmament, and hath in it an infinite numbre of starres. **1635** N. CARPENTER *Geog. Del.* I. iv. 79 The distance of the Firmament, wherein are placed the fixt Starres is not measurable by mans industrie. **1665** BOYLE *Occas. Refl.* (1845) 15 Those Stars that shine in the Firmament or highest visible Heaven.

†**b.** Hence, applied sometimes to the other celestial spheres. ***first firmament***: the ***Primum mobile***.

c **1386** CHAUCER *Man of Law's T.* 197 O firste moving cruel firmament, With thy diurnal swegh that croudest ay. **1393** GOWER *Conf.* III. 2 He can..yiven every Jugement, Which longeth to the firmament..Both of the sterre and of the mone. **1551** RECORDE *Cast. Knowl.* (1556) 11 This motion is..called of auncient writers the motion of the First firmament.

c. *transf.* in *Alchemy*. (Cf. HEAVEN.)

1610 B. JONSON *Alchemist* II. iii, Your sunne, your moone, your firmament, your adrop.

†**3. a.** In the literal etymological sense: Anything which strengthens or supports; a substratum, a firm support or foundation. *lit.* and *fig.*

1554 KNOX *Godly Let.* B viij, Here is the firmamente of my fyrst cause. *a* **1555** PHILPOT *Exam. & Writ.* (Parker Soc.) 382 Paul calleth the church the firmament and pillar of truth. **1578** BANISTER *Hist. Man* I. 17 [That] this same bone ..might be vnto Larinx as a firmament, and foundation. **1615** CROOKE *Body of Man* 388 It was not safe that his thinne coat should runne along without some Firmament. *a* **1626** BACON *Interpr. Nature* i. Wks. 1857 III. 218, I thought it good..to make a strong..bank..to guide the course of the waters; by setting down this position or firmament, namely, That all knowledge is to be limited by religion. **1649** JER. TAYLOR *Gt. Exemp.* II. ix. 121 This duty to parents is the very firmament and bond of commonwealths. **1701** S. SEWALL *Diary* 30 June (1879) II. 38 The absence of him who was the Firmament and Ornament of the Province.

b. The process of strengthening or making firm.

1650 BULWER *Anthropomet.* 144 The tongue hath a ligament or bridle for two causes: First for the firmament of its Basis.

†**4.** (See quot.)

1690 EVELYN *Mund. Muliebris* 7 Pins tipt with Diamond Point, and head, By which the Curls are fastened, In radiant Firmament set out. —— *Fop-Dict.* 18 *Firmament*, Diamonds, or other precious Stones heading the Pins which they stick in the Tour, and Hair, like Stars.

5. *Comb.*

1593 NASHE *Christ's Tears* Wks. (Grosart) IV. 70 Theyr Firmament-propping foundation, shal be adequated with the Valley of Iehosaphat. **1883** 'MARK TWAIN' *Life on Mississippi* 244 A firmament-obliterating irruption of profanity.

Hence **'firmament,wards** *adv.*, towards the firmament; heavenwards.

1886 BURTON *Arab. Nts.* I. 188 Then she flew firmamentwards to circle it.

firmamental (fɜːmə'mɛntəl), *a.* [f. prec. + -AL[1].]

1. Of or pertaining to the firmament.

1600 *Dr. Dodypoll* I. i. in Bullen *O. Pl.* III. 100 Looke on the heavens colour'd with golden starres, The firmamentall ground of it all blew. **1621** BURTON *Anat. Mel.* III. iv. I. v, If there be infinite planetary and firmamental worlds. **1657** COKAINE *Obstinate Lady* II. i, He was an intricate prognosticator of firmamental eclipses. **1869** TYNDALL in *Fortn. Rev.* 1 Feb. 240 To obtain the most perfect polarisation of the firmamental light. **1874** T. HARDY *Madding Crowd* II. vii. 81 In the vast firmamental hollows overhead.

†**b.** *Alchemy.* ***firmamental water***: liquid as pure as the firmament; app. rectified *Aqua Vitæ*.

1559 MORWYNG *Evonym.* 97 These..make disceitful image and likeliness of youth: the firmamentall water dothe it in dede. [**1666** DRYDEN *Ann. Mirab.* 281 An hollow crystal pyramid he takes, In firmamental waters dipt above.]

2. Of the nature of a supporting framework or permanent substratum: cf. FIRMAMENT 3.

1696 BROOKHOUSE *Temple Open.* 40 The Flesh is the Incremental or Changeable Part, and the Spirit the Firmamental or Immoveable Part. **1825** COLERIDGE *Lit. Rem.* (1836) II. 357 *note*, The firmamental law that sustains and disposes the apparent world.

†firma'mentary, *a. Obs. rare.* [f. as prec. + -ARY.] = prec.

1633 T. ADAMS *Exp. 2 Peter* ii. 7 Some by that firmamentary division of the waters, have dreamt of a watery heaven above the stars. **1690** BOYLE *Chr. Virtuoso* I. 69 And much more must they do so..who believe..there were..Firmamentary comets.

firman ('fɜːmən, ‖fɛr'mɑːn). Forms: α. (7 firma, 8 firhman), 8–9 fermaun, firmaun, 7– firman, 20 farman. β. 7 phirman, 7–9 phirmaund. [a. Pers. *fermān*, OPers. **framāna* (so in Pehlvi) = Skr. *pramāṇa* command.] An edict or order issued by an Oriental sovereign, *esp.* the Sultan of Turkey; a grant, licence, passport, permit.

1616 SIR T. ROE in Purchas *Pilgrims* (1624) I. IV. xvi. 541 Then I moued him for his fauour for an English Factory to be resident in the Towne, which hee willingly granted, and gaue present order to the Buxy to draw a Firma..for their residence. **1634** SIR T. HERBERT *Trav.* 50 But upon sight of his Phirman (or Letter of command) hee agreed willingly. **1704** *Collect. Voy.* (Church.) III. 571/2 Your Majesty's Firman, or Letters Patent. **1710** PITT *Let.* in *Edin. Rev.* (1893) 151, I had..a phirmaund under his great seal. **1816** *Gentl. Mag.* LXXXVI. I. 325 A translation of the fermaun itself has since been forwarded by Dr. Hunt. **1863** KINGLAKE *Crimea* (1877) I. xvii. 369 Having caused the Porte to issue firmans. **1932** *Times Lit. Suppl.* 10 Nov. 842/2 This volume contains photographic reproductions of seventeen farmans granted to the head of the Vallabha sect of Vaishnavas. **1962** *Economist* 13 Jan. 115/1 No such *farman* or decree has actually been issued by HM the Shah personally.

transf. **1835** HOOD *Poetry, Prose, & Worse* iv, He bows to the metrical firman, As dulcet as song of the South. **1840** BARHAM *Ingol. Leg.*, *St. Odille* iii, A German..Paid his court to her father, conceiving his firman Would soon make her bend.

†'firmance. *Sc. Obs.* Also 6 fermans, firmans, 7 fermance. [ad. OF. *fermance* (1) an enclosure, (2) a guarantee, f. *fermer* to shut, confirm, secure:—L. *firmāre*: see FIRM *v.*]

1. The state or condition of being confined; confinement, imprisonment; chiefly in phrase: (*to keep, put*) *in firmance*. Also *concr.* An enclosure.

1513 DOUGLAS *Æneis* XII. Prol. 176 Within fermans and parkis cloys of palys. *c* **1565** LINDESAY (Pitscottie) *Chron. Scot.* (1728) 63 Himself to be put in sicker Firmance. **1613** BP. FORBES *On Revel.* xx. 221 The surenesse is cleered in the person apprehender, and manner of fermance. **1679** in G. Hickes *Spirit of Popery* 64 We..do Command..all Sheriffs ..to Search for..the Persons afternamed..and put them in sure Ward and Firmance. **1721** WODROW *Hist. Ch. Scot.* (1829) II. II. xiii. 485 Three men in firmance for robbery. **1752** J. LOUTHIAN *Form of Process* (ed. 2) 137 The Rebels.. put them in sure Ward, Firmance and Captivity.

2. Assurance, confidence; also, a source of confidence. ***to make firmance to***: to give a pledge of faithfulness to.

1536 BELLENDEN *Cron. Scot.* Proheme Cosmogr. vi, So lang I swomit in hir seis deip That sad auising with hir thochtfull lance Couth find na port to ankir hir firmance. *Ibid.* II. i. 10 b, For the fame of ane nobyll prince is ane grete firmance to his realme. *Ibid.* II. xvi. 21 b, Als sone as Gillus was maid kyng..to stabil the realme to him with sickir firmance, he tuk þe aithis of his pepil.

b. Firmly established condition, stability.

1533 BELLENDEN *Livy* (1822) 107 The Romanis..ar brocht to sic firmance, that they may..sustene the plesand frute of libertie.

firmary, var. of FERMERY, *Obs.*, infirmary.

†fir'mation. *Obs.* [ad. L. **firmātiōn-em*, n. of action f. *firmāre* to make firm, f. *firmus* FIRM.]

1. The action of making firm or fixing steadily.

1646 SIR T. BROWNE *Pseud. Ep.* IV. i. 179 If we define sitting to be a firmation of the body upon the Ischias.

2. Ratification, confirmation.

1684 T. HOCKIN *God's Decrees* 153 The incarnation, passion, and resurrection of our blessed Saviour..being the firmation and seal of all.

firme, *a. Her.* (See quot. 1889.)

1688 R. HOLME *Armoury* I. v. §31 A Cross Patee Entyre (or Fixed or Firme). **1889** ELVIN *Dict. Her.* 61 *Firme*, a term used for a cross pattée, when it extends to each side of the shield: the same as a cross pattée throughout, or entire.

firme, var. of FORME *Obs.*, first.

firment, obs. form of FERMENT.

firmer ('fɜːmə(r)). [ad. F. *fermoir* chisel for making mortices, altered form (as if f. *fermer* in obs. sense to fasten, secure) of *formoir*, which was earlier anglicized as FORMER.] Used only in comb., **firmer-chisel, -gouge, -tool** (see quots.).

[**1688, 1727–51, 1764**: see FORMER.] **1823** P. NICHOLSON *Pract. Builder* 239 The firmer chisel is a thin broad chisel, with the sides parallel to a certain length, and then tapering, so as to become much narrower towards the shoulder. It is used by being driven by the blows of a mallet on the handle. **1876** GWILT *Encycl. Archit.* Gloss. 1243 *Firmer Tool*, a chisel used by joiners with a mallet, by which the sides of mortises are formed. **1888** *Lockwood's Dict. Mech. Engin.*, *Firmer Tools*, the ordinary short chisels and gouges of wood workers, so termed in order to distinguish them from paring tools.

firmest, obs. form of FOREMOST.

†'firmify, *v. Obs. rare.* [f. FIRM *a.* + -(I)FY.] *trans.* To make firm. *intr.* To become firm.

1578 BANISTER *Hist. Man* I. 5 You shall not dread, to finde the examples of Syssarcosis very playne, in the fleshy firmifieng of the teeth in their Celles. *Ibid.* 17 Os Hyoides.. is so firmified in the middest, as to neither part it easely slippeth.

†firming chisel = *firmer-chisel*.

1799 *Trans. Soc. Encourag. Arts* XVII. 337 Work off the remaining wood with a large firming chissel.

firmish ('fɜːmɪʃ), *a.* [f. FIRM *a.* + -ISH.] Somewhat firm.

1839 *Fraser's Mag.* XX. 718 Let's see..if the cits stand firmish. **1924** J. MASEFIELD *Sard Harker* III. 124 The hop took him to firmish tussock.

†'firmitude. *Obs.* [ad. L. *firmitūdō*, f. *firm-us* FIRM *a.*] The quality or state of being firm, in the various senses of the adj.; firmness, solidity, stability, strength; stability of purpose, resolution.

1541 R. COPLAND *Galyen's Terapeutyke* 2 Ej, They do vse these names, Dyspathies, Metasyncrises, Imbecyllitees, fyrmytudes [Lat. *firmitudines*], and sondry other such names. **1579** TWYNE *Phisicke agst. Fort.* II. cxiv. 308 a, Vnlesse the minde..had put on the same firmitude and constancie agaynst it [the payne]. **1603** HOLLAND *Plutarch's Mor.* 1340 The stability and stedy firmitude of those broad flat faces which it [the cube] hath. **1668** H. MORE *Div. Dial.* I. §4 (1713) 10 So great a firmitude is there in Life against all the subtle attaques of shifting Reason. **1701** W. NICHOLS *Consol. to Parents* 112 What great Firmitude of Mind they have to oppose against such a cutting misfortune.

†'firmity[1]. *Obs.* Also 5–6 fermete, -itie, 6–7 firmitie, -yte. [a. OF. *fermeté*, f. *ferme* FIRM *a.*; refashioned after FIRM and -ITY.]

1. Firmness, solidity, stability. Also, moral firmness, firm allegiance, constancy.

a **1450** *Knt. de la Tour* (1868) 83 [It] were to long to compte the tenthe party of her fermete, for they ouercome the deuelle and hys temptaciones. **1480** *Bury Wills* (1850) 59 For the more fermete and stedfastenes therof, and that yt perpetually shulde indure. **1563** W. FULKE *Meteors* (1640) 25 b, There was no firmity or strength in it [the ayre] to beare them [birds] up. **1589** PUTTENHAM *Eng. Poesie* II. (Arb.) 113 The square..for his owne stay and firmitie requireth none other base then himselfe. **1638** CHILLINGWORTH *Rel. Prot.* I. vi. §7. 329 The strength and firmity of my assent. *a* **1656** USSHER *Ann.* VI. (1658) 337 Pyrrhus, doubting the firmity of the Macedons unto him, yielded thereto. *c* **1729** EARL OF AILESBURY *Mem.* (1890) 51 His firmity and presence of mind.

2. A means of strengthening; an assurance.

1523 *St. Papers Hen. VIII*, IV. 94 If mariage myght be goten on this side and that side, it woll be..good for bothe the realmes, and a firmyte of kindnes.

†'firmity[2]. *Obs.*—[1] Aphetic f. INFIRMITY.

1426 AUDELAY *Poems* 31 To socour ham, in here fyrmeté.

†firmless ('fɜːmlɪs), *a. Obs.* [f. FIRM *a.* + -LESS.] Unsteady, shifting.

1598 SYLVESTER *Du Bartas* II. II. iv. *Columnes* 667 In Egypt it [Astronomy] erects A famous School, yet firm-lesse in affects. **1605** *Ibid.* II. III. iii. *Lawe* 926 We float On firm-lesse sands of this vaste Desart. *a* **1744** POPE (Webster), Does passion still the firmless mind control?

firmly ('fɜːmlɪ), *adv.* [f. as prec. + -LY[2].] In a firm manner.

1. With little possibility of movement; so as not easily to be shaken or dislodged; fixedly, securely, strongly; steadily, immovably.

c **1374** CHAUCER *Troylus* III. 1439 (1488), I wist..That your humble seruant..Were in your harte yset so fermely As ye in mine. *a* **1533** LD. BERNERS *Huon* lv. 187 Euery man praysed gretely Huon that he helde hym selfe so fermely. **1591** SPENSER *Muiopotmos* 58 His breast-plate..Before his noble hart he firmely bound. *c* **1630** JACKSON *Creed* IV. xi, Charity..firmlier rooted..in their hearts. **1704** NEWTON *Opticks* (1721) III. i. 365 How such very hard Particles..can stick together..so firmly. **1776** GIBBON *Decl. & F.* I. 334 The dangerous frontier of Rhætia he so firmly secured, that [etc.]. **1860** TYNDALL *Glac.* I. xviii. 127 To fix at each step my staff firmly in the consolidated snow. **1880** GEIKIE *Phys. Geog.* ii. 7 The atmospheric envelope clasps the planet firmly.

2. Without wavering, hesitation, or doubt; constantly, resolutely, steadfastly.

c **1425** WYNTOUN *Cron.* VIII. xv. 29 Þe lele Scottis men.. To-gyddyr stood sa fermly. **1552** ASCHAM in *Lett. Lit. Men* (Camden) 12, I am thus firmelie persuaded. **1647** CLARENDON *Hist. Reb.* I. (1843) 14/2 He was..firmly resolved never to trust him. **1751** JOHNSON *Rambler* No. 177. ¶9 A copy..which he firmly believed to be of the first edition. **1781** GIBBON *Decl. & F.* III. 119 The Goth, on whose fidelity he firmly relied. **1848** MACAULAY *Hist. Eng.* I. 110 The nation was firmly attached to hereditary monarchy. **1871** MORLEY *Voltaire* (1886) 11 It was time to trust firmly to the free understanding of men for guidance. **1887** *Daily News* 7 June 2/6 Foreign wheats firmly held.

3. *Comb.*, as ***firmly-braided, -closed, -rooted***.

1877 BLACK *Green Past.* xxi, The sunlight touched the *firmly-braided masses of hair. **1888** F. HUME *Mad. Midas* I. iii, With *firmly-closed lips. **1768–74** TUCKER *Lt. Nat.* (1852) II. 249 The *firmly-rooted Christian may say.

firmness ('fɜːmnɪs). [f. as prec. + -NESS.] The state or quality of being firm.

1. Solidity, cohesion, resistance to pressure.

1653 HOLCROFT *Procopius* II. 53 Which encreasing by degrees, crumbled and brake the firmeness of the stones. **1661** BOYLE *Spring of Air* III. xxxi. (1682) 82 In the short history we have published of Fluidity and Firmness. **1799** KIRWAN *Geol. Ess.* 108 Firmness is that coherence which resists percussion, and its opposite is brittleness, or fragility. **1851** CARPENTER *Man. Phys.* (ed. 2) 155 The requisite firmness and solidity are given to the animal fabric.

2. The quality of being to a large extent unmoved or immovable; fixedness, stability.

1597 SHAKS. *2 Hen. IV*, III. i. 48 Make the Continent (Wearie of solide firmenesse) melt it selfe Into the Sea. *a* **1627** HAYWARD *Edw. VI* (1630) 13 Both the easinesse and firmnes [of the union] might be coniectured. **1703** MAUNDRELL *Journ. Jerus.* 89 The whole work seems to be endued with such absolute firmness, as if it had been design'd for Eternity. **1802** PALEY *Nat. Theol.* viii. §3 (1819) 86 By firmness I mean not only strength but stability.

3. The state or quality of being firm in mind; resolution, steadiness, steadfastness.

Hence, in *Phrenology*, the 'bump' or 'organ' supposed to indicate the possession of this quality.

1561 tr. *Calvin's Foure Serm.* ii. D ij b, That constauncye and firmnes of minde. *a* **1684** EARL ROSCOMMON *Wks.* (1753) 42 Nor can th' Ægyptian Patriarch blame my muse, Which for his firmness does his heat excuse. **1741** MIDDLETON *Cicero* I. VI. 518 Cæsar is said to have born the news of her death with an uncommon firmness. **1874** GREEN *Short Hist.* iv. §1. 162 Terrible..as were the sufferings of the English army, Edward's firmness remained unbroken.

†b. Steadfastness of attachment *to* a person or cause; faithfulness, fidelity. *Obs.*

a **1627** SIR J. BEAUMONT *To the Prince* 14 Your noble firmenesse to your friend. **1653** SIR E. NICHOLAS in *N. Papers* (Camden) II. 11 His Majesty's affection to religion and his firmness to his word. **1667** MILTON *P.L.* IX. 279 But that thou shouldst my firmness therfore doubt To God or thee..I expected not to hear.

4. *Comm.* Steadiness in price, or of prices.

1880 *Globe* 5 Mar. 5/4 The feature in Foreign Government Securities is the firmness of Peruvian Bonds. **1883** *Manch. Exam.* 14 Dec. 4/1 There being little inclination to take short bills, owing to a belief that the present firmness will not last. **1890** *Daily News* 16 Sept. 3/4 The outlays on behalf of this pair did not affect the firmness of Signorina and Nunthorpe, who maintained their Saturday rates.

firmor, firmorie, var. of FERMERER[2], -Y.

a **1618** RALEIGH in Gutch *Coll. Cur.* I. 83 A mere tenant at will, or firmor of the profits.

firmware ('fɜːmwɛə(r)). *Computing.* [f. FIRM *a.*, after SOFTWARE.] A permanent form of software built into certain kinds of computer.

1968 *World Bk. Year Bk.* 274/2 Efforts were also made to transfer some of the functions of software..to small high-speed memories which could operate as 'assistants' to computer processing circuitry... This function..was given the new label 'firmware'. **1971** *New Scientist* 7 Jan. 27/1 A modular construction..to which is added the right hardware and firmware for the particular job, allows the user to buy a computer that has exactly the capacity he needs. **1977** C. J. SIPPL *Microcomputer Handbk.* vii. 294 Massive libraries of programs developed on cards, blocks, strips, boards..are available... They are called 'firmware' because they are software made 'firm' by being electronically fixed or burned into ROM chips. **1980** *Sci. Amer.* July 90/3 (Advt.), The system's firmware relieves the user from having to write application routines to utilize the graphic capability. **1985** *Listener* 9 May 35/1 It must have on-board computer power and programming software incorporated at the time of manufacture as 'firmware'.

‖firn (fɪrn). [Ger. *firn*, *firne*, lit. 'last year's' (snow), subst. use of *firne* adj. 'of last year': see FERN *a.*] A name given to snow above the glaciers which is partly consolidated by alternate thawing and freezing, but has not yet become glacier-ice. Also *attrib.* and *Comb.*

1853 KANE *Grinnell Exp.* viii. (1856) 61 The 'firn', or consolidated snow of the Alpine glaciers. **1855** J. D. FORBES *Tour Mt. Blanc* 33 Magnificent is the prospect which these firns sometimes present. **1878** HUXLEY *Physiogr.* 155 The imperfectly consolidated substance, partly snow and partly ice, is known in Switzerland as *Névé* or *Firn*. **1934** *Geogr. Jrnl.* LXXXIV. 283 The firn-field, as we know it in the Alps. **1937** *Discovery* Feb. 35/2 The 'firn stoss' or 'ice-quake'. **1958** *Jrnl. Glaciology* III. 265 The firn line..is rather lower than the equilibrium line of the smallest glaciers.

Hence **firnifi'cation**, the conversion of snow into firn.

1923 AHLMANN & TVETEN in *Geogr. Annaler* V. 55 We imagine the process in the firnification of the snow, and its further glaciation to consist mainly in a sublimation, caused by the various vapour pressures on different forms and different sizes of crystals. **1937** *Nature* 30 Jan. 187/1 *Firnification*, or the changes of the snowflake after lying on the ground.

†'firous, *a. Obs. rare.* In 6 fierous, fyrous. [f. FIRE + -OUS.] = FIERY 4.

1503 HAWES *Examp. Virt.* xii. 237 In to the sygne of the fierous lyon. *Ibid.* xiv. 296 He dyd vs lyght with his pure bemys Quenchynge of mars the fyrous lemys.

firre, obs. form of FIR.

†'firren, *a. Obs.* In 4 firrene, 6 *Sc.* firrin, firron. [f. FIR + -EN.] Made of fir.

c **1300** *Havelok* 2078 A fayr firrene wowe. **1513** DOUGLAS *Æneis* II. vi. 17 The firryne closouris opnys, but noyise or dyn, And Greikis, hid the hors coist within, Patent war maide. **1578** *Inventories* (1815) 255 Ane thik firrin plank.

firret(te, obs. form of FERRET.

firring: see FURRING.

firry (ˈfɜːrɪ), *a.* [f. FIR + -Y¹.] **a.** Abounding in firs. **b.** Of or pertaining to the fir.

1833 LAMB *Elia, Blakesmoor*, Thy firry wilderness. **1843** TENNYSON *Miller's Dau.* 6 Oft I heard the tender dove In firry woodlands making moan. **1842** HOOD *Elm Tree* III. xvi, With many a fallen acorn-cup, And mast, a firry cone.

firs, obs. form of FIERCE *a.*

first, *sb. Obs.* exc. *dial.* in comb. Forms: 1 first, fyrst, 3 firste, *south.* virste. [OE. *fyrst* str. fem. = OHG. *first* (MHG. *virst*, Ger. *first*):—**fersti-z*; cf. the ablaut-var. Du., LG. *vorst*:—**fursti-z*, of same meaning, which corresponds phonetically to Skr. *pṛshṭí* fem. rib; in sense it is nearer to the (prob. cognate) Skr. *pṛshṭá* back.]

The inward roof or ceiling of a chamber; also, a ridge-pole; = *first-piece*.

c **1000** ÆLFRIC *Gloss.* in Wr.-Wülcker 126 *Laquear*, fyrst. *c* **1275** *Death* 155 in *O.E. Misc.* (1872) 179 Þe rof and þe virste schal ligge on þine chynne. **1378** *Durham Halm. Rolls* (Surtees) 149 In manu Johannis fil. Gilberti x spars et j first, et in gardino præd. Thomæ sunt v ribs et firsts.

b. *Comb.*, ***first-piece*** (*Chesh. Gloss.*), ***-pole***, (*Shropsh. Wordbk.*), the ridge piece of roof-timbers.

first (fɜːst), *a.* (*sb.*) and *adv.* Forms: 1 fyrst, fyrest, first, 2–6 fyrst, 3 *Orm.* firrst, *south.* vorst, 4 forst, 3–4 ferst, (3 feirst, ferest, -ist, *south.* verst), 3–5 firste, (3 fireste, -ist, *south.* virst), furst(e, 3–7 frist, (4 freste), 4–5 fryst, (6 fruist), 3– first. [OE. *fyrst, fyrest*, OFris. *ferost, -est, -st*, OS. **furist*, used absol. as *furisto* wk. masc., prince (MDu. *vorste*, mod.Du. *vorst* prince), OHG. *furist* foremost, first, highest, absol. *furisto* prince (MHG. *vürste*, mod.G. *fürst* sb., prince), ON. *fyrstr* (Sw. *första*, Da. *förste*; the sbs. Sw. *furste*, Da. *fyrste*, prince, are adapted from Ger.):—Com. Teut. **furisto-*, a superlative formation on the stem **fur-, for-* (see FORE *adv.*, FOR *prep.*). The corresponding comparative occurs in OHG. *furiro*, ON. *fyrre*, earlier. From the same stem, with different superlative suffix, is formed OE. *forma* first, whence the double superlative form *fyrmest*: see FORMER, FOREMOST.

The OTeut. *fur-, for-*, represents OAryan *pr-*, whence in most of the Aryan langs. words meaning 'first' are derived, chiefly with superlative suffixes. Cf. Skr. *prathama*, OSl. *prĭvŭ*, Gr. πρῶτος, πρώιστος, L. *prīmus*.]

A. *adj.* That is before all others; earliest in time or serial order, foremost in position, rank, or importance. Hence often serving the function of a numeral adjective, the ordinal of ONE, in which use it may be written 1st.

In Eng., as in most other langs., the number *one* has no regularly formed ordinal, and in OE. the want was supplied by the use of various superlative adjs. meaning 'foremost' or 'earliest', viz. *fyrst, forma, fyrmest* (also *formest*, Northumbrian *forðmest*) and *ærest*. In middle English the other words became obsolete, or lost their ordinal sense, so that *first* became the sole representative of the ordinal of *one*. This is now its most prominent use, and colours all the applications of the etymological sense; but the word can still be applied (like L. *primus*, F. *premier*, etc.) in contexts where a true ordinal would be inadmissible, as in 'the first days of the year', 'one of the first men in the country', etc.

I. As simple adjective.

1. a. In regard to time: Prior to all others in occurence, existence, etc.; happening, existing, or presenting itself before the others; earliest.

a **1000** *Cædmon's Exod.* 399 (Gr.) Fyrst ferhðbana. *c* **1220** *Bestiary* 675 Ðus fel adam..vre firste fader. **1345** in Heath *Grocers' Comp.* (1829) 45 The freste Wardynes that euer were, of owre fraternyte. *c* **1440** *Promp. Parv.* 162/1 Fyrste be-getynge, *primogenitura*. **1483** *Cath. Angl.* 132/1 Þe Firste martyr, *prothomartir*. **1500–20** DUNBAR *Poems* lxxxi. 5 Sen oure first father formed was of clay. *a* **1626** BACON *Max. & Uses Com. Law* (1636) 23 This maner of gaining lands was in the first dayes, and is not now of use in England. **1662** STILLINGFL. *Orig. Sacr.* I. iv. §7 Cadmus Milesius, supposed to be the first writer of History. **1698** VANBRUGH *Prov. Wife* I. i, He is the first aggressor, not I. **1848** MACAULAY *Hist. Eng.* II. 16 Another planted the first vines in the neighbourhood of the Cape of Good Hope. **1868** LOCKYER *Elem. Astron.* v. (1879) 193 The first clock in England was made about 1288.

b. With the application defined by a relative clause, for which in mod.Eng. *to* with *infinitive* is often substituted.

c **1200** ORMIN 797 He wass þe firrste mann þat brohhte word onn eorþe. *a* **1300** *Cursor M.* 1469 (Cott.) Enoch..was þe first þat letters fand. *c* **1400** *Destr. Troy* 4330 The furst þat was founden of þes fals goddes. **1568** TILNEY *Disc. Mariage* A vij, I will not be the first, that shall disobey. **1798** COLERIDGE *Anc. Mar.* II, We were the first that ever burst Into that silent sea. **1857** BUCKLE *Civiliz.* I. xii. 658 [Voltaire] was the first who popularized in France the philosophy of Newton. *Mod.* You were the first person to explain the matter. He is always the first to find fault. This part of the system was one of the first to be developed, and one of the first to disappear.

c. Said of anything which occurs or presents itself next after a given point of time expressed or implied in the sentence.

1607 MARSTON *What you Will* v, The first thing her bounty shall fetch is, my blush-colour satin suit from pawn. **1719** DE FOE *Crusoe* (1840) II. ii. 42 The first business was to get canoes. **1732** BERKELEY *Alciphr.* III. §6 Make an experiment on the first man you meet. **1834** L. RITCHIE *Wand. by Seine* (1835) 138 The first thing to be done was to secure lodgings. **1848** MACAULAY *Hist. Eng.* II. 138 One of his first acts, after he became King, was to recall Ormond from Ireland. **1871** M. COLLINS *Mrq. & Merch.* I. viii. 240, I shall get back to London by the first train.

d. With emphatic force, where it is implied that the first event or occurrence is the only one to be regarded or waited for.

1399 LANGL. *Rich. Redeles* III. 56 Þey ffolwith þe vois at þe ffrist note. **1506** *Pylgrym. Sir R. Guylforde* (Camden) 16 To euery pylgryme at the firste fote that he setteth on londe there is graunted plenary remyssion. **1607** SHAKS. *Cor.* I. viii. 5 Let the first Budger dye the others Slaue. **1675** MARVELL *Corr.* Wks. 1872–5 II. 433 ['*Mock speech*' *of Charles II*], I have made Crew, Bishop of Durham, and, at the first word of my Lady Portsmouth, Prideaux, Bishop of Chichester. **1699** HACKE *Coll. Voy.* II. 39 Some Men of War lay ready to put out after us upon the first News of our being near. *a* **1822** SHELLEY *Unfin. Drama* 153 Like a child's legend on the tideless sand, Which the first foam erases half and half Leaves legible.

e. In phr.: ***at*** (†***the***) ***first sight*** (***or view***), ***at*** (***the***) ***first blush***. (Also, †***at first dash, push***.)

a **1300** *Cursor M.* 8029 (Cott.) He kneu þam at þe first sight. **1579** LYLY *Euphues* (Arb.) 52 Euphues at the first sight was so kindled with desire, that [etc.]. **1583** GOLDING *Calvin on Deut.* ix. 51 True it is that we perceiue it not at the first push. *a* **1593** MARLOWE *Hero & Leander* I. 176 Who ever lov'd, that lov'd not at first sight? **1611** MIDDLETON *Roaring Girl* IV. i, *Sir A.* You can play any lesson [music]? *Moll.* At first sight, sir. **1665** SIR T. HERBERT *Trav.* (1677) 139 At first view I thought they had some resemblance with those four monsters. **1670** COTTON *Espernon* II. v. 202 So brisk an Article as this at first dash, and before the King would proceed to any further Treaty..would startle the Spanish Gravity. **1702** C. MATHER *Magn. Chr.* I. ii. (1833) I. 54 They saw no Indians..but such as at the first sight always ran away. **1702** *Eng. Theophrast.* 575 A fool may so far imitate the mien..of a wise man, as at first blush to put a man at a stand what to make of him. **1875** JOWETT *Plato* (ed. 2) I. 426 There is more of system in the Phaedo than appears at first sight.

f. (***the***) ***first thing***: advb. phrase = as the first thing that is done.

[**1596** SHAKS. *1 Hen. IV*, III. iii. 205 Rob me the Exchequer the first thing thou do'st. **1720** *Humorous Lett.* in *Lond. Jrnl.* (1721) 50 My fancy..carried me, the first thing it did..to Rome.] **1836** DICKENS *Sk. Boz* 2 Go to this woman the first thing in the morning. **1885** ANSTEY *Tinted Venus* 74 I'll buy a cloak for her the first thing to-morrow morning. **1893** *Pall Mall Mag.* II. 79, I was to..hand it over to him the moment we pulled up..so that he might give it to the little one first thing.

g. *ellipt.* for 'the first of the season'.

1599 H. BUTTES *Dyets drie Dinner* G iij b, The first buds, or yong braunches shooting from the roote. **1860** GOSSE *Rom. Nat. Hist.* 8 The first cuckoo, the first swallow, sent a thrill through our hearts which is not repeated.

h. After the name of a day of the week: Next, following, *north. dial.*

1781 D. RITCHIE in *Southey's Life of A. Bell* (1844) I. 252, I..must prepare a new sermon for Sabbath first. **1868** ATKINSON *Cleveland Gloss.*, '*Sat'rda' first*' for Saturday next. **1890** *Glasgow Herald* 24 Mar. 1/1 Tickets for the special service in the Cathedral, on Thursday first.

2. a. Preceding all others in a series, succession, order, set or enumeration.

O.E. Chron. an. 963 On þe fyrste sunnon dæʒ of Aduent. *a* **1300** *Cursor M.* 7219 (Cott.) Sampson, þi first wijf lerd þe witte. **1380** *Lay Folks Catech.* (Lamb. MS.) 171 The furst part [of the Hail Mary] contenys þe wordys of Gabriel. *c* **1400** *Lanfranc's Cirurg.* 11 We seie is hoot in þe firste degree þat is I-heet of kyndely heete. **1484** CAXTON *Fables of Æsop* II. Proem, A fable whiche is the fyrst and formost of this second book. **1599** H. BUTTES *Dyets drie Dinner* L v, He maketh Quaile the first dish of the first course. **1670** LADY M. BERTIE in *12th Rep. Hist. MSS. Comm.* App. v. 22 The second part..is then the first time acted. **1773** GOLDSM. *Stoops to Conq.* II, The first blow is half the battle. **1827** JARMAN *Powell's Devises* II. 291 The testator had a first marriage in contemplation. **1834** L. RITCHIE *Wand. by Seine* 124 The first thing that fixes our eye is the noble river covered with boats. **1850** TENNYSON *In Mem.* lxxxv. 108 First love, first friendship, equal powers, That marry with the virgin heart. **1874** CHADWICK *Base Ball Man.* 28 When a player is on the first base and one on the third. *Mod.* Take the first turning on the right.

b. in dates, with ellipsis of *day*. Also in sporting language. ***the First***, spec. the first of September (when partridge-shooting begins). (See also quot. 1944.)

1593 SHAKS. *2 Hen. VI*, II. iv. 71, I summon your Grace, to his Maiesties Parliament, Holden at Bury, the first of this next Moneth. **1673** *S' too Him Bayes* 20 Do'st thou take this to be the first of April? **1818** JAS. MILL *Brit. India* II. v. v. 525 He encamped on the 1st of June within three miles of the place. **1922** H. TITUS *Timber* xxii. 201 Humphrey was going down state the first of the week to hunt an investor. **1926** *Publishers' Weekly* 16 Jan. 147 When the first of the year had passed. **1944** H. W. HORWILL *Dict. Mod. Amer. Usage* (ed. 2) 132/2 In Eng. one may speak of *the first* of the month, meaning the first day of it. In Am. one may speak also of *the first* of the year, or of the week; not, however, meaning the first day of this period but the first part of it.

c. ***in the first place***: an adverbial phrase = first, firstly: see PLACE.

1665 SIR T. HERBERT *Trav.* (1677) 393, I shall therefore in the first place see what [etc.].

d. ***the first*** = even, or so much as, the first; even one, a single (*U.S.*). ***the first thing***: the elements or rudiments, esp. in phr. ***not to know the first thing about***.

1849 *Let.* in *N.Y. Tribune* 23 May 2/2 On my knees, which I couldn't move the first inch. **1857** W. A. GILBERT *Sp.* in *Ho. Reps.* 27 Feb. (Bartlett), I am not aware of having committed the first act which would bring upon me the displeasure of the house. **1935** *Punch* 24 July 97/3 But I couldn't start up the car. I don't know the first thing about car-engines. **1938** 'E. CAMBRIDGE' *Spring always Comes* II. xii. 267, I don't know the first thing about painting.

e. With a cardinal numeral. In this combination three varieties of word-order have been used. (*a*) The earliest recorded form is ***the two*** (***three***, etc.) ***first*** (= Fr. *les deux premiers*, Ger. *die zwei ersten*). This still survives, though it is now rarely used where numbers above 3 or 4 are concerned. †(*b*) In 15–16th c. ***two*** (***three***, etc.) ***the first*** occasionally occurs. (*c*) In 16th c. the growing tendency to regard *first* as an ordinal led to the introduction of the form ***the first two*** (***three***, etc.), corresponding to 'the second two (or three, etc.)'. This is now the universal form in the case of high numbers; but for numbers up to 3 or 4 many writers use it only when the number specified is viewed as a collective unity contrasted with the second or some succeeding 2, 3, or 4 in the series.

(*a*) **1340** *Ayenb.* 11 Þe þri verste. **1526** *Pilgr. Perf.* (W. de W. 1531) 1 Of the whiche thre bokes, the two first be but as prefaces. **1650** R. STAPYLTON *Strada's Low C. Warres* I. 13 The two first dayes the King..had the Victory. **1779–81** JOHNSON *L.P., Pope* Wks. IV. 136 Each of the six first lines of the *Iliad* might lose two syllables. **1781** GIBBON *Decl. & F.* III. 197 During the five first ages of the city.

(*b*) **1447** SHILLINGFORD *Lett.* (Camden) 28 As ye have..alleged by two the furst divers articulis. **1531** ELYOT *Gov.* I. xi, Two the fyrste bokes of the warke of Aristotell. **1540–1** —— *Image Gov.* 79 In eight the first yeeres of his empire.

(*c*) **1593** FALE *Dialling* 35 Omitting likewise yᵉ first three, &c. **1661** BRAMHALL *Just Vind.* i. 2 For the first six hundred years and upwards. **1704** HEARNE *Duct Hist.* (1714) I. 134 He wrote the Life of Alexander in x Books, whereof the first two are lost. **1860** ELLICOTT *Life Our Lord* viii. (1865) 373 The first two Evangelists.

3. a. Foremost or most advanced in position (said of things either at rest or in motion). In OE. as an independent sense, = 'front'; subsequently as a special use of sense 2, *first* opposed to *second*, *third*, etc.

a **1000** *Laws Ethelbert* §51 Æt ðam feower toþum fyrestum. **1647** R. STAPYLTON *Juvenal* 218 The first-file of orators. **1704** MARLBOROUGH in *Lond. Gaz.* No. 4045/2 With..the Foot of the First Line, I passed the Lech. **1801** JAMES *Milit. Dict.* s.v. *Line*, In order that the first line..may ..not endanger the disposition of the second line, by precipitately crowding upon it. *Mod.* He was sitting in the first row of seats. The first horse in the race.

b. In adverbial phrases (where *foremost* may be substituted), ***head first, feet first***, etc., i.e. with the head, feet, etc., foremost.

1877 SPURGEON *Serm.* XXIII. 46 We used to dip our toes in the waves instead of taking a plunge head first.

4. a. Foremost, preceding all others, in dignity, rank, importance, or excellence. Also in phr. ***of the first order*** [F. *du premier ordre*]; (***to put*** or ***do***) ***first things first***: (to give) first place to the most important things.

1382 WYCLIF *Mark* ix. 34 If any man wole be the firste among ȝou. **1548** PATTEN *Exped. Scot.* in Arb. *Garner* III. 118 It was counted for the first part of medicine to have it [i.e. the finger] cut quite away. **1670** G. H. *Hist. Cardinals* I II. 37 The Apostles were all first, and all last, without any difference of priority. **1720** OZELL *Vertot's Rom. Rep.* II. XIV. 346 Courage, a General's first Quality. **1770** LANGHORNE *Plutarch* (1879) II. 639/1 Eumenes..raised himself to the first military employments. **1794** [see ORDER *sb.* 4]. **1798** *Anti-Jacobin* xxxi. 182 The song of Rogero..is admitted on all hands to be in the very first taste. **1821** W. TAYLOR in *Monthly Rev.* XCV. 538 Fruit and vegetables, articles of the first necessity at Naples. **1837** HT. MARTINEAU *Soc. Amer.* III. 30, I was told a great deal about 'the first people in Boston'. **1848** MACAULAY *Hist. Eng.* I. 370 There were coffee houses where the first medical men might be consulted. **1894** G. JACKSON (*title*) First things first; addresses to young men. **1895** *Bookman* Oct. 33/1 A diplomatist of the first order. **1920** W. RILEY *Yorkshire Suburb* 136 The dear lady was..incapable..of putting first things first. **1922** 'SAPPER' *Black Gang* xiv. 217 The whole thing is a boss shot of the first order. **1931** *News Chron.* 28 Apr. 3/3 'First things first' must be the guiding principle. **1961** L. VAN DER POST *Heart of Hunter* xviii. 245 The lion's sense of first-things-first decides the issue: it will go to the water before it eats. **1971** *Scope* (S. Afr.) 19 Mar. 124/4 Let's do first things first.

b. In official titles, etc., indicating that the person designated has precedence over colleagues, as ***first minister*** (more commonly 'prime minister'); ***First Lord of the Admiralty, of the Treasury***; also *ellipt.*; ***first lieutenant***, etc.

1753 HANWAY *Trav.* (1762) II. II. i. 70 The first minister ..is a kind of representative on behalf of the regal prerogative. **1782** *Ann. Reg.* 255 Royal Oak—Mr. Gwatkin, first lieutenant, killed. **1814** JANE AUSTEN *Mansf. Park* II. vii. 155, I would rather find him private secretary to the first Lord than any thing else. **1843** CARLYLE *Past & Pr.* II. xvii. 174 Of whom as First Lord of the Treasury..we could be so glad and proud. **1858** SIMMONDS *Dict. Trade*, First mate, the chief officer of a merchant vessel; the next in rank to the captain. **1866** H. COPPEE *Grant & his Campaigns* 25 His first-lieutenancy dated from Sep. 16, 1847. **1884** *Manch. Exam.* 19 Feb. 5/2 The plaintiff..was engaged as first tenor at the Comedy Theatre. **1963** *Times* 26 Apr. 19/4 There is no truth in the allegation that the presence of another spy inside the Admiralty was known to the First Lord and his Service chiefs for 18 months before Vassall's arrest.

II. *absol.* (quasi-*sb.*)

5. In certain absolute uses.

a. *the first*: the thing or person first mentioned. (Where only two are mentioned, *the former* is now commonly preferred.)

1579 Lyly *Euphues* (1607) B iv, I am neither so suspitious to mistrust your good wil, nor so sottish to mislike your good counsaile, as I am therefore to thanke you for the first, so it stands me vpon to thinke better of the latter. **1774** Pennant *Tour in Scotl. in 1772*, 238 They yield bear and potatoes, much of the first is used in distillation.

b. *spec.* in *Her. the first* = that tincture which is first mentioned in a blazon.

1562 Leigh *Armorie* (1597) 28 b, I sayde, voyded of the first, because Argent was the first that was named. **1705** Hearne *Collect.* 8 Dec., Sable, A Cross argent, charg'd with another of the first. **1828–40** Berry *Encycl. Her.* II, *Filshed* quarterly or. and az.; on the second and third quarters, an eagle, displayed, of the first.

c. *the first* = the first part, the beginning (*obs.* or *dial.* in ordinary phrases). Esp. in phrases *the first of the ebb, flood,* or *tide*.

a **1586** Sidney *Arcadia* II. xxvii. (1590) 220 b, But now perceiuing the flood of their furie began to ebbe, he thought it policie to take the first of the tide. **1670** Narborough in *Acc. Sev. Late Voy.* (1711) 44 At the first of the Flood we caught five hundred Fishes. **1761** *Brit. Mag.* II. 446 The six prames..dropt down upon the first of the ebb. **1784** *Unfort. Sensibility* II. 67 It was boiling from the first of the morning, till they wanted their dinners. **1798** *Invasion* II. 14, I had.. from the first of his entrance, kept retreating to the other side of the room. **1840** Marryat *Poor Jack* xxii, We shall be able to stem the *first* of the flood.

d. *Printing.* (See quots.)

1683 Moxon *Mech. Exerc.* II. 319 The one they distinguish by the name of First, the other his Second, these call one another Companions: The First is he that has wrought longest at that Press. **1888** Jacobi *Printers' Vocab.*, *First*, the senior or leading partner of the two men who work at a hand-press.

e. *first and last*: all, 'one and all'.

1589 R. Harvey *Pl. Perc.* 2 First and last, helpe, quench all.

6. In adverbial phrases with a preposition:

a. *from the first*: from the beginning, at the outset, to start with. *from first to last*: from beginning to end, throughout.

1611 Bible *Luke* i. 3 Hauing had perfect vnderstanding of things from the very first. **1737** Bracken *Farriery Impr.* (1757) II. 18 Their Practice, from the first, is ill grounded. **1849** Grote *Greece* II. lxxii. (1862) VI. 347 The mainstay of the Thirty from first to last. **1885** *Manch. Even. News* 16 July 3/1 The disaffected section..made a dead set against him from the first. **1893** *Strand Mag.* VI. 473/1 Mr. Gladstone was..in his place from first to last.

b. *at first* (also, *at the first*, now *rare*): †(*a*) first, for the first time; †(*b*) in the first place; †(*c*) at once, immediately; (*d*) at the beginning, at the first stage.

(*a*) *a* **1300** *Cursor M.* 12605 (Gött.) Wid þe grete maistris þus he badd Till mari had hir iornai made, þan at þe frist on him toght scho. *c* **1340** *Ibid.* 1558 (Fairf.) And now at first wakkenes woghe. **1682** Creech *Lucretius* II. 576 In Phrygia Corn at first took birth.

(*b*) **1340** *Ayenb.* 46 Of þise ȝenne uondeþ þe dyeuel in vif maneres..Auerst ine fole ziȝþe efterward ine fole wordes [etc.]. *c* **1380** Wyclif *Sel. Wks.* III. 359 We graunten at þe firste, þat [etc.].

(*c*) **1362** Langl. *P. Pl.* A. vii. 159 And hoped aftur hunger þo, þat herde him atte furste. *a* **1626** Bp. Andrewes 7 *Serm.* iv. (1627) 65 He bids them..but whistle for an Angell, and they will come at first. **1643** Prynne *Sov. Power Parl.* III. 132 How little coherence there is in this Argument, the silliest childe may at first discern.

(*d*) **1577** B. Googe *Heresbach's Husb.* iv. (1586) 185 Their broode lieth very small at the first. **1599** H. Buttes *Dyets drie Dinner* B iv, This fruite was at first white. **1611** Bible *John* xii. 16 These things vnderstood not his disciples at the first. **1671** Milton *Samson* 883 Why then Didst thou at first receive me for thy husband? **1712** Steele *Spect.* No. 455 ¶3, I am no more delighted with it than I was at the very first. **1776** *Trial of Nundocomar* 23/1 He was at first very ill, then got better. **1845** M. Pattison *Ess.* (1889) I. 25 The assurance he had at first displayed was now succeeded by an air of embarrassment. **1874** Boutell *Arms & Arm.* xi. 216 At the first they made petards with it.

†**c.** *with the first*: among the first (persons or things); hence, chiefly, especially (cf. L. *cum primis*).

1611 Abp. Ussher *Lett.* (1686) 15 Of which we will not fail to certifie you with the first. **1621** T. Bedford *Sinne unto Death* 34 This is *apprimè necessarium*, necessary with the first. **1660** F. Brooke *Le Blanc's Trav.* 270 The servant.. coming in with the first.

7. Elliptical uses passing into quasi-*sb.* (admitting of plural).

a. Anything that is first (*nonce-uses*).

1587 Golding *De Mornay* vi. 71 There are two Firsts: the one is Gods worde, and the other is God. **1892** *Daily News* 1 Dec. 2/3 The 1st June and December are the two quietest 'firsts' in the year.

b. Comm. *first of exchange*: the first of a set of bills of exchange of even tenor and date.

[The ellipsis of *bill* is common to all the European langs.; but the phrase is often written in full, both in Eng. and in the other langs.]

1809 R. Langford *Introd. Trade* 27 Three months after date, pay this my first of Exchange (second and third not paid) to the order of Mr. R. Rich. **1866** Crump *Banking* v. 137 In case of delay of the arrival of a first of exchange.

c. A place in the first class in an examination-list; the first place in an athletic contest. Also, a man who has taken a place in the first class.

1850 Clough *Dipsychus* IX. 110 Philip returned to his books..Got a first, 'tis said. **1861** Hughes *Tom Brown at Oxf.* iv. (1889) 32 He'll be a safe first, though I don't believe he reads more than you or I. **1885** M. Pattison *Mem.* 26 The men who got firsts would have done so equally at any college. **1885** *Cyclist* 19 Aug. 1089/1 He..won four firsts and a second last week.

d. *Mus.* (See quot. 1823).

a **1774** Goldsm. *Exper. Philos.* (1776) II. 159 The performers on glasses..who play firsts, seconds, and sometimes a base altogether. **1823** Crabb *Technol. Dict.*, *First* (*Mus.*), the upper part of a duett, trio [etc.].

e. *Base-ball*: = first base.

f. *pl.* Used to denote the best quality of certain articles of commerce, e.g. butter.

1825 J. Nicholson *Operat. Mechanic* 535 The finest marls, called firsts, are selected for the arches of doorways, &c. **1832** Porter *Porcelain & Glass* (Lardner) 186 Crown glass is sold, according to its quality, under four different denominations—firsts, seconds, thirds, and fourths. **1887** *Times* 27 Aug., Butter:—Firsts, 119*s.*; seconds, 113*s.*

g. A first edition; a first-class railway carriage or compartment; the first known or discovered example or specimen of a thing; a first instance or occurrence.

1922 M. Sadleir *Excurs. Vict. Bibliogr.* 6, I have contrived..to keep myself fairly supplied with 'reading firsts'. **1924** *G. McLeish's Catal.* 13 Essential to the collection of 'modern firsts'. **1925** B. Travers *Mischief* iv, The train arrived and Eleanor..was easily spotted, being alone in the firsts. **1931** Buck & Anthony *Bring 'em back Alive* 215 There is no bigger thrill in the game than bringing back rare 'firsts' [i.e. an animal that has not been seen alive before in the country to which it is brought]. **1955** *Times* 20 June 8/7 Another important French 'first' was the arrival of the Caravelle, the country's first jet airliner. **1960** *Analog Science Fact/Fiction* Dec. 83 Echo I, the sateloon that went up last August, was a true First in space flight. **1960** J. Betjeman *Summoned by Bells* vi. 58 Perhaps one day I'll find a 'first' of Keats. **1963** J. F. Straker *Final Witness* iv. 48 'I'm sorry about that, Paul.' That made another first: they had not used Christian names before. **1970** *Guardian* 27 Feb. 8/5 Those were days of high adventure: every programme was a first..breaking new ground. **1971** L. Black *Death has Green Fingers* ix. 100 I'm in a first, next carriage along the train.

h. The first or lowest gear on a motor vehicle or bicycle.

1909 J. S. V. Bickford *Faults & how to find Them* §1173 If, however, the change from first to second (not through the gate we are assuming) has to be done quickly, [etc.]. **1935** G. Heyer *Death in Stocks* iv. 40 Antonia slammed the gear-lever into first and started with a jerk. **1968** P. Dickinson *Weathermonger* vi. 66 He wrenched the gear into first and banged through, misjudging it slightly.

B. *adv.* [OE. *fyrst*, the accus. neut. of the adj. Cf. ON. *fyrst*, OHG. *furist*.]

1. a. Before any other or anything else, in time, serial order, rank, etc; before anything else is done or takes place. Also in strengthened phr. *first of all, first and foremost*.

O.E. Chron. an. 963 Se biscop com þa fyrst to Eliȝ. *c* **1200** Ormin 6876 Forrþi comenn þeȝȝ himm firrst To sekenn i þatt ende. **1297** R. Glouc. (1724) 383 To chyrche & to pouere men he ȝef vorst, as he ssolde. *c* **1340** *Cursor M.* 22879 (Trin.) Bi his wille doþ þat kyng out of þe harde tre to spryng forst þe leef & þenne þe flour and siþen fruyt. **1375** Barbour *Bruce* I. 542 Julius Cesar..Off Rome wes fryst maid Emperour. **1377** Langl. *P. Pl.* B. xix. 116 þat she furste & formest ferme shulde bilieue. *c* **1450** *St. Cuthbert* (Surtees) 732 þai straue wha first to lande myght wynne. **1553** T. Wilson *Rhet.* (1580) 5 [He] must fasten his mynde firste of all, upon these five especiall pointes. **1635** R. N. tr. *Camden's Hist. Eliz.* II. xii. 110 She wished them, first and formost to get the Queene's assent. **1667** Milton *P.L.* I. 377 Who first, who last Rous'd from the slumber, on that fiery Couch. **1718** Prior *Alma* III. 397 Who first offend will first complain. **1776** *Trial of Nundocomar* 68/1 Having received that money, I will pay you first, and after that will pay others. **1814** Wordsw. *Excursion* I. Poems (1888) 422/1 Oh, Sir! the good die first. **1841** Keble *Serm.* xi. (1848) 275 The two who first saw our Lord. **1874** Stubbs *Const. Hist.* I. xii. 492 Consent of the historians..makes him, first and foremost, a legislator. **1884** W. C. Smith *Kildrostan* 88 Your wet ropes..give blisters first And then a horny hand.

b. proverb. *first come, first served*. Also as *attrib. phr.*

1545 Brinklow *Compl.* xvii. E iij, First come first serued, so one or ij shal be all payed, & yᵉ rest shal haue nothing. **1632** Massinger *Maid of Hon.* I. ii, And you know, First come first serv'd. **1860** *Macm. Mag.* June 113 The sailors.. rushed away to the boat. First come, first in. **1887** *Times* (weekly ed.) 24 June 7/4 It was..a case of first come, first served. **1960** R. B. Gregg *Power of Nonviolence* (ed. 2) i. 38 Passengers were seated on a first-come, first-served basis. **1964** *Sun* (Brisbane) 23 July 9/1 The Administration Bill would substitute the quota system with one based on a first-come, first-served basis.

c. In a statement, discourse, or argument, where points or topics are enumerated: In the first place, as the first thing to be mentioned or considered, firstly.

c **1380** Wyclif *Sel. Wks.* III. 441 þai say furst, þat [etc.]. *c* **1386** Chaucer *Melib.* ¶275 Ffirst and forward ye han erred in thassemblynge of youre conseillours. **1393** Langl. *P. Pl.* C. vii. 15 For ich formest and ferst..Haue ybe vnboxome. **1583** Babington *Commandm.* v. (1637) 41 First & formest.. let them [etc.]. **1644** H. Parker *Jus Pop.* 39, I make answer First..Secondly..Thirdly. **1711** Addison *Spect.* No. 89 ¶4 First of all I would have them seriously think on the Shortness of their Time. **1847** [see firstly 1].

†**d.** At first, originally. *Obs.*

c **1100** tr. *Bull of Pope Agatho* in *Cod. Dipl.* V. 30 Ic Saxulf, ðe wæs first abbot and nu eam biscop. *a* **1300** *Cursor M.* 5373 (Gött.) First was he here as vr thrall, Nou vnder me es he mast of all. **1598** Grenewey *Tacitus' Ann.* II. xviii. (1622) 58 Plancina growing more insolent then first. *a* **1721** Prior (J.), Heav'n, sure, has kept this spot of earth uncurst, To shew how all things were created first.

e. *first and last*: taking one thing with another, at one time and another, reckoned altogether, in all. *first or last*: at one time or another, sooner or later.

1678 Lady Chaworth in *12th Rep. Hist. MSS. Comm.* App. v. 45 Lord Shrewsbery is like to marry Mr. Chiffens his daughter who will be first and last made worth 40,000*l.* to him. **1699** Dampier *Voy.* II. II. 2 The Bay of Campeachy, where I lived first and last about 3 Years. *a* **1700** Dryden (J.), All are fools and lovers first or last. **1719** De Foe *Crusoe* (1840) I. iv. 65, I brought away all the sails first and last.

f. *first off*: at the first blush, in the first place, to begin with. *U.S. colloq.*

1880 'Mark Twain' *Tramp Abroad* xx. 193 First-off, I thought it would certainly give me the botts. **1897** W. D. Howells *Landlord at Lion's Head* 445 First off, you know, I thought I'd sell to the other feller. **1910** W. M. Raine *B. O'Connor* 39 Fox's right. First off Neil, then the fellow I took to be the Wolf. **1915** *Nation* (N.Y.) 10 June 646/1 Men of science..no longer admit first off what simple good sense shows to us.

g. *first in, first out*: (*a*) = fifo *sb.* (*a.*) a.

1934 *Jrnl. Accountancy* Nov. 344. Shall cost be on the basis of 'first in, first out'? **1936** N. L. Burton *Introd. Cost Accounting* vii. 109 When the first-in, first-out method is used, goods received are entered at actual cost—invoice price plus freight, etc.... Subsequent issues are priced at the cost of the second shipment received. **1945, 1965** [see fifo *a.* (*sb.*) a]. **1978** J. Kellock *Elements of Accounting* iii. 66 *First in, first out*, the calculation used in this method is based on the principle that the oldest unit costs are the first units sold.

(*b*) *Computing.* (Pertaining to, using, or designating) a procedure in which the item removed from a buffer, queue, etc., is always the one that has been in it the longest.

1966 *IBM Systems Jrnl.* V. 84 Another Class-1 algorithm, called fifo (first in, first out), has been investigated. fifo always replaces the block having spent the longest time in memory. **1969** P. B. Jordain *Condensed Computer Encycl.* 406 The next item to be retrieved will be the item that was inserted earliest in the list, resulting in a first-in, first-out structure. **1973** P. B. Hansen *Operating Syst. Princ.* v. 188 The simplest replacement algorithm is first-in, first-out, which is used in the B5500 system. **1977** E. E. Klingman *Microprocessor Systems Design* iv. 91 (*heading*) First-in-first-out buffers. **1984** H. M. Deitel *Introd. Operating Systems* (rev. ed.) ix. 218 In the first-in-first-out page replacement, we time-stamp each page as it enters primary storage. When a page needs to be replaced, we choose the one that has been in storage longest. *Ibid.*, First-in-first-out is likely to replace heavily used pages because the reason a page has been in primary storage for a long time may well be that it is in constant use.

2. a. Before some other specified or implied thing, time, event, etc.

a **1300** *Cursor M.* 1625 (Gött.) Bot first a tre, ar i bigine, I sal here sett of noe kinne. **1567** *Satir. Poems Reform.* vii. 189 Conarus was inclosit First being dewlie for his fault deposit. **1597** J. Payne *Royal Exch.* 38 Although it be long fyrst..yet..they come. **1611** Bible *2 Sam.* xiii. 13 Thou shalt not see my face, except thou first bring Michal Sauls daughter. **1618** Bolton *Florus* (1636) 251 They wasted the puissance of Sertorius in battell, though it was long first. **1662** J. Davies tr. *Olearius' Voy. Ambass.* 7 Ask'd..when those of Holstein would be receiv'd; he told him..it would be three weeks first. **1748** Richardson *Clarissa* (1811) VIII. 15 Mr. Pocock undertakes to deliver this; but fears it will be Saturday night first. **1766** Goldsm. *Vic. W.* xxviii, I wounded one who first assaulted me. **1855** Dickens *Dorrit* v, She had this bit of work to begin first..that bit of work to finish first. **1884** A. R. Pennington *Wiclif* ix. 297 It is impossible for the priest to remit the sins of any unless they are first remitted by Christ.

b. In preference to something else; rather, sooner (than do something specified or implied, or allow it to be done).

1580 A. Melville in *Life* (1819) I. ii. 87 They shall have all the blood of my body first. *a* **1625** Fletcher *Hum. Lieutenant* II. iv, My noble childe, thou shalt not fall in virtue, I and my power will sink first. **1797** Frere & Canning in *Anti-Jacobin* ii. 11, I give thee sixpence? I will see thee d—d first! **1819** Shelley *Cenci* v. iii. 99 O weak, wicked tongue..would that thou hadst been Cut out and thrown to dogs first! **1869** Browning *Ring & Bk.* IV. x. 311 Die? He'll bribe a gaoler or break prison first!

3. For the first time, then and not earlier (with reference to a specified time, place, etc.).

c **1300** *St. Brandan* 246 After than that seint Brendan furst this yle i-seȝ. *c* **1350** *Will. Palerne* 648 þus was ferst here sad sorwe sesed þat time. *c* **1400** Maundev. (1839) xi. 126 From þenne, Pylgrymes mowen fyrste se vn to Jerusalem. *a* **1461** *Pol. Poems* (Rolls) II. 249 Whan seyntes felle fryst from hevene. *c* **1600** Shaks. *Sonn.* civ. 2 For as you were when first your eye I eyde, Such seemes your beautie still. **1732** Berkeley *Alciphr.* I. §1, I knew him first at the Temple. **1776** *Trial of Nundocomar* 25/1 When was it that you first heard mention of the bond? **1850** Tennyson *In Mem.* xl, A maiden in the day When first she wears her orange-flower!

4. ellipt. for *first class* (in travelling by railway, etc.).

1889 J. K. Jerome *Three Men in Boat* iv. 50 They would ..pay the difference and go first. **1919** D. Ashford *Young Visiters* ii. 23 They traveled 2nd class in the train and Ethel was longing to go first but thought perhaps least said soonest mended. **1922** M. Arlen *Piracy* II. xix. 288 Travelling 'first' with a 'third' ticket. **1967** 'J. Munro' *Money that Money can't Buy* vi. 75 They..went aboard their Trident..Loomis had insisted on travelling first.

C. *Comb.*

1. Chiefly of *adv.* with ppl. adjs., as *first-begot*, *-begotten* (whence *first-begottenship*), *-built*, *-conceived*, *-created*, *-done*, *-endeavouring*,

-famed, *-formed*, *-found*, *-framed*, *-gendered*, *-gotten*, *-grown*, *-intended*, *-invented*, † *-kinned* (= FIRST-BORN), *-made*, *-mentioned*, *-moving*, *-named*, etc. Also with ordinary adj., as *first-ripe*. Also with vbl. nouns, as *first-beginner*, *-beginning*, *-comer*, *-mover*, *-running*. The combs. **first-movable**, **-moved**, **-mover**, **-moving** have all been used as equivalents for the *primum mobile* of the old astronomy.

1587 GOLDING *De Mornay* vi. 71 Hee calleth him the *Firstbeginner. **1860** MUNRO *Lucretius* (1864) I. 55, I.. will open up the *first-beginnings of things. **1671** MILTON *P.R.* I. 89 His *first-begot we know. **1382** WYCLIF *Zech.* xii. 10 In deth of the *first bygoten. *c* **1440** *Promp. Parv.* 162/1 Fyrste begoton, *primogenitus*. **1583** GOLDING *Calvin on Deut.* cxcv. 1212 Hee was not of the common sort, but had as it were a *first-begottenship. **1887** BOWEN *Virg. Æneid* III. 17, I.. Found my *first-built walls in an evil hour on the shore. **1868** LOWELL *Shaks.* Pr. Wks. 1890 III. 45 The privilege which only *first-comers enjoy. **1880** *Libr. Univ. Knowl.* X. 368 The foundling named by the first-comer. **1593** SHAKS. *2 Hen. VI*, III. ii. 44 The *first-conceiued sound. **1552** HULOET, *First created, *protoplastes*. **1671** MILTON *Samson* 83 O first-created beam. **1552** HULOET, *First done or spedde, *præuersus*. **1627** MILTON *Vacat. Exerc.* 2 Hail Native Language, that by sinews weak Didst move my *first-endeavouring tongue to speak. **1859** TENNYSON *Guinevere* 321 The two *first-famed for courtesy. **1497** BP. ALCOCK *Mons Perfect.* B iij, Our *fyrst fourmed faders. **1874** DARWIN in *Life & Lett.* (1887) III. 194, I have found first-formed theories erroneous. **1594** BLUNDEVIL *Exerc.* II. (ed. 7) 109 So shall you have the *first found number. **1633** EARL MANCH. *Al Mondo* (1636) 12 Our *first-framed father Adam. **1388** WYCLIF *Ps.* civ. [cv.] 36 He killide ech the *firste gendrid thing in the lond of hem. **1382** *Ibid.*, He smot alle the *firste goten in the lond of hem. **1785** J. PHILLIPS *Treat. Inland Navig.* 47, 900*l.* less than the *first-intended expence. **1827** G. HIGGINS *Celtic Druids* 35 The *first invented letters. *a* **1300** *E.E. Psalter* civ. [cv.] 36 He smate al *first-kinned in land of þa. **1630** DRAYTON *Noah's Flood* 203 The earthly Heauen, where he had plac't That *first-made Man. **1877** J. D. CHAMBERS *Divine Worship* 390 The *first-mentioned formularies are the more ancient. **1594** BLUNDEVIL *Exerc.* III. I. iii. (ed. 7) 281 The tenth [sphere] is called the *first movable. **1667** MILTON *P.L.* III. 483 That Crystalline Sphear whose ballance weighs The Trepidation talkt, and that *first mov'd. *Ibid.* VII. 500 As the great *first-Movers hand First wheeld thir course. **1771** SMOLLETT *Humph. Cl.* (1815) 118 The opposition cursed him, as the indefatigable drudge of a first-mover. **1796** HUTTON *Math. Dict.*, *First Mover* in the old Astronomy, is the *Primum Mobile*. *c* **1625** MILTON *On Death fair Inf.* 39 Whether above that high *first-moving sphere Or in the Elysian fields. **1838** DICKENS *O. Twist* xviii, The *first-named young gentleman. **1599** H. BUTTES *Dyets drie Dinner* C ij, In Latine Præcocia, or Præmatura. Id est. Soone ripe, or *first ripe. **1611** BIBLE *Num.* xiii. 20 Now the time was the time of the first ripe grapes. **1764** FOOTE *Patron* II. Wks. 1799 I. 341 When.. the sprightly *first-runnings of life are rack'd off, you offer the vapid dregs to your deity.

2. a. In syntactical combs. of a permanent nature or with a special meaning: for many of these, as ***first cause***, ***cousin***, ***intention***, ***magnitude***, ***person***, ***principle***, ***water***, see the respective sbs. Many of them are used *attrib.* and as adjs., and are then regularly written with the hyphen: see esp. ***first chop*** (CHOP *sb.*^{5} 4), FIRST-CLASS, FIRST-RATE. Also, **first aid** (*to the wounded*), assistance given on the spot in the case of street-accidents and the like, before proper medical treatment is procured; also *fig.*; **first-aider**, one who is skilled in first aid; **first ascent**, the ascent of a particular mountain for the first time; **first base** (see BASE *sb.*^{1} 15 d); **first birth**, a first-born child; also *fig.*; hence †***first-birth-right***; **first blood**, in Pugilism, the first drawing of blood; also *fig.*; **first coat**, the first layer of plaster or paint; hence **first-coated** *a.*; **first cost**, prime cost; also *attrib.*; **first cross**, the crossing of two pure breeds; the offspring of such a cross; **first-day cover**, an envelope bearing, or designed to bear, stamps postmarked on the day when they were first issued (see COVER *sb.*^{1} 2 d); **first derivative** *Calculus*, the derivative of a function obtained by differentiating it once; **first-ever** *a.* (see EVER *adv.* 7 f); **first feature**, the main feature in a cinema programme; **first-fleeter** *Austral. slang* (see quots); **first-foot** (*north.*), the person who first enters a house after the beginning of the new year; hence *first-footing*; **first-footer**, one who goes first-footing; **first form**, (*a*) the lowest form in a school; (*b*) in *Printing* (see quots.); **first futtocks** (*Naut.*; see quot.); **first gear**, the lowest gear (cf. GEAR *sb.* 7 b); **first lady**, the most important lady; in the U.S., spec. the wife of the President; in full *the first lady in the land*; **first light** orig. *Mil.*, the time when light first appears in the morning (see also quot. 1952); **first line**, those fighting forces that are most advanced or of the highest quality; **first love**, (*a*) the first time one falls in love; the emotion felt at such a time; (*b*) one's favourite occupation, pastime, possession, etc.; **first man** (*Mining*; see quot.); **first motion** (*Mech.*; see quot.); **first night**, the night on which a play, or a particular representation of a play, is first produced on the stage; also *attrib.*; hence **first-nighter** (one who assists at a 'first night'), **first-nighting**; **first novel**, the first novel written by a particular author; **first offender** (see OFFENDER *note*); † **first penny** (see PENNY); **first pointed** *a. Arch.*, = Early English (see EARLY *a.* 4 b); **first polar** *Math.*, (of a point $(a_0, a_1, \ldots a_n)$ with respect to a curve described by the homogeneous function $f(x_0, x_1, \ldots x_n) = 0$) the curve represented by the equation $\Sigma_i a_i \partial f/\partial x_i = 0$; **first position**, (*a*) the lowest possible position of the hand on the fingerboard of a stringed instrument; (*b*) *Dancing* (see quot. 1884); **first refusal**, an agreement with a prospective customer that goods, etc., will not be on sale to others until he has refused them (cf. REFUSAL 3); also *transf.* and *fig.*; **first run** *U.S.*, the first showing or première of a film; **first school** *Educ.*, a primary school for children aged between five and eight years; **first sergeant** *U.S.*, the highest ranking non-commissioned officer in a company or equivalent unit; **first sight**, (*a*) see sense 1 above; (*b*) that which is seen for the first time (*nonce-use*); also *attrib.*; whence **first-sighted** *ppl. a.* (*nonce-wd.*); **first-spear**, in pig-sticking, the first thrust which draws blood; also, the man who makes it; **first story** = FIRST FLOOR; **first-strike**, a first aggressive attack with nuclear weapons; freq. *attrib.*; **first-time buyer**, a buyer of property who has not previously owned a home, and therefore has no house to sell; **first timer**, one who does or is something for the first time; also, something done for the first time or at the first attempt; **First World War**, now the more usual term for the *Great War* (b); **first youth**, early youth; esp. in phr. ***in*** or ***past one's first youth***. Also FIRST DAY, etc;

1882 PRINCESS CHRISTIAN tr. Esmarch's (*title*) *First aid to the injured. **1892** *Medical Annual* 602 Dressing (First Aid). **1926** W. DEEPING *Sorrell & Son* i. §2 The porter applied first aid to their piece of luggage. **1944** *Living off Land* v. 101 The *First Aider should keep cool. **1956** J. A. C. BROWN *Soc. Psychol. Industry* 142 The knowledgeable first-aider. **1935** D. PILLEY *Climbing Days* xvi. 321 Recent chronicles of the French Alpine Club are filled annually with notes of his *First Ascents and other exploits. **1398** TREVISA *Barth. De P.R.* IX. xxxi. (1495) 366 The vertue of the angell that slewe the *fyrste byrthes were wythstonde therby. **1827** HARE *Guesses* Ser. I. (1847) 55 Those twin firstbirths of Poetry. **1650** J. TRAPP *Clavis to the Bible* I. 299 Then came forth Perez.. who took the *first-birth-right and kingdom by force. **1809** *First blood [see KNOCK-DOWN B. *sb.* 2]. **1899** R. KIPLING in *McClure's Mag.* May 11/2 First blood to me. You flushed, Ansell. You wriggled. **1964** C. WILLOCK *Enormous Zoo* iii. 52 Before first blood was drawn it was decided to see what could be done to the ruined grazing of certain areas by simply keeping the hippo out. **1823** P. NICHOLSON *Pract. Build.* 390 **First Coat* of two-coat work, in plastering, is denominated *laying* when on lath, and *rendering* when on brick. **1870** *Eng. Mech.* 11 Feb. 385/1 The laths are 'primed' or *first-coated. **1772** FRANKLIN *Lett.* Wks. 1887 IV. 547 Which, at the *first cost here, can scarce be reckoned at less than half a guinea a head per annum. **1778** T. JEFFERSON *Lett.* Wks. 1893 II. 156 The master had once sold the whole cargo.. for 5*s.* 3*p.* the livre, first cost. **1840** *L'pool. Jrnl.* 4 July 1/4 Quantity of soiled account books.. at first cost prices. **1862** W. YOUATT *Sheep* vii. 260 The *first cross evidently detracted much from the beauty of the English sheep. **1910** T. ALLEN *Profitable Pig Breeding* ii. 13 A first cross of pure-bred stock, judiciously selected, is hard to beat. **1937** C. FORMAN *Pig Breeding* iii. 27 Other first crosses might be made with equal success. **1947** J. STEVENSON-HAMILTON *Wild Life S. Afr.* xxi. 165 The two best dogs.. I ever possessed.. were a first-cross between a pointer and a bull-terrier, and a first-cross between Great Dane and Irish terrier. **1962** W. E. BOWDEN *Beef Breeding* ii. 64 Milk yields from the first cross would be less than one would expect. **1938** *First-day cover [see COVER *sb.*^{1} 2 d]. **1951** J. L. GRUMBRIDGE *Introd. Stamps* ix. 103 This quite intelligible demand for first-day covers as items of philatelic interest. **1971** D. POTTER *Brit. Eliz. Stamps* vi. 66 To accompany the new stamps, a very simple first-day cover envelope was prepared by the Post Office. **1834** *Rep. Brit. Assoc. 1833* 338 If $f(x) = 0$, or $X = 0$ be the equation, $f'(x)$, $f''(x)$, or X', X'' its *first and second derivatives. **1852** T. G. HALL *Differential & Integral Calculus* (ed. 5) iii. 31 This process is called successive differentiation, and du/dx, dp/dx, dq/dx, &c. are called the first, second, third, &c. differential coefficients, or the first, second, third, &c. derivatives of u. **1881** First derivative [see DERIVATIVE B. 3]. **1953** P. FRANKLIN *Differential & Integral Calculus* iii. 50 If this function is differentiable, its derivative.. will be a new function of x. Suppose that this new function is differentiable. Then the derivative of the *first* derivative is called the *second* derivative of the original function. **1936** *World Film News* May 28/2 To sell a film as a *first-feature, a producer must have a personality.. well enough known to induce the public to go to the.. theatres. **1958** *Observer* 9 Mar. 4/6 This film—a first feature on its first release round a big circuit— was badly presented. **1830** D. MCLEOD in *Hist. Rec. Australia* (1922) 1st Ser. XV. 371 One of the *first Fleeters died a few Years ago. **1848** H. W. HAYGARTH *Recoll. Bush Life Austral.* viii. 93 A man who, by his own account, is of so long standing in the neighbourhood as to have been what is called in the colony a 'first fleeter'. **1850** DICKENS in *Househ. Words* I. 418/2 He was a 'first fleeter', that is, came over with Governor Phillips in the first fleet. **1805** NICOL *Poems* I. 33 (Jam.) Ere new years' morn begin to peep At doors, the lasses sentrie keep, To let the *first-fit in. **1883** J. PARKER *Tyne Ch.* 4 How glad.. the dear soul was when she had a good 'first-foot' on New Year's morning. **1897** *Daily News* 23 Sept. 2/6 Scottish '*first-footers' in the fifteenth century awoke the night echoes with a mild and 'soughing' Tra-la-la. **1926** *Glasgow Herald* 30 Dec. 6 The red herring which your Dundee 'first-footer' carries with him as a lucky emblem. **1864** A. McKAY *Hist. Kilmarnock* (ed. 4) 112 Another custom.. was that of *first-footing on the morning of New-year's day. **1883** BLACK in *Harper's Mag.* Dec. 63 At midnight 'first-footing' begins, and it is considered very lucky if your first visitor should be a dark-haired man. **1683** MOXON *Mech. Exerc.* II. 376 **First Form*, the Form the White Paper is Printed on, which generally by Rule ought to have the First Page of the Sheet in it. **1888** JACOBI *Printers' Vocab.*, *First Forme*, the inner or outer [forme] of a sheet —whichever is printed off first. **1867** SMYTH *Sailor's Wordbk.*, **First Futtocks*, timbers in the frame of a ship which come down between the floor-timbers almost to the keel on each side. **1909** R. W. A. BREWER *Motor Car* xii. 120 On changing down to the *first gear the power of the engine due to its increased rate of revolution rises to 20 B.H.P. **1965** *Motoring Which?* Oct. 136/2 The effect of changing to low ratio is to make all gears lower, so that, for example, in the Land-Rover you then have three gears lower than the ordinary first gear. **1853** LYTTON *My Novel* I. IV. ix. 306 She was so beautiful.. and not proud she! though she looked like the *first lady in the land. **1861** W. H. RUSSELL *Diary* 3 Nov. (1863) II. 393 Some charming little pieces of gossip about 'the first Lady in the Land'. **1948** *Chicago Tribune* 26 June I. 1/4 Mrs. Thomas E. Dewey disclosed today what kind of first lady she will be. **1950** 'E. CRISPIN' *Freq. Hearses* i. 27 Madge is one of the First Ladies of British Films. **1965** *Sunday Times* 7. Nov. Suppl. 13/1 [Mrs. Kennedy] disapproved of the term 'First Lady', which had come into semi-official usage in the previous administration. **1970** *Washington Post* 30 Sept. B2/1 The First Lady of the United States was questioned by Italian women reporters today. **1946** *Amer. Speech* XXI. 209 Orders [in the Eighth Army] for an early start never mentioned dawn but instead used **first light*... There might be some squabble about just what time constituted dawn. There couldn't be any at all about *first light*, at least not in the desert. **1952** *Brewer's Dict. Phr. & Fable* 364/1 *First light*, roughly, dawn. Used in World War II to signify the earliest time at which infantry can see to make their way forward. **1969** *Daily Colonist* (Victoria, B.C.) 6 July 1/6 A search-light equipped helicopter was to press the search overnight, with the full armada out in force again at first light today. **1914** H. M. BUIST *Aircraft in German War* 78 They are accounting for such large numbers of the enemy's *first line of airmen. **1741** RICHARDSON *Pamela* III. xiv. 63 It was a *first Love on both Sides; and so he could not appear to her as a practised Deceiver. **1825** H. WILSON *Mem.* II. 91 First love is all powerful in the head and heart of such an ardent character as Worcester's. **1954** E. MCLEOD tr. *Colette's Vagabond* II. viii. 129 You couldn't mistake it; it was love indeed, *first love*. That was what it was and never again will be. **1971** *Radio Times* 27 May 5/1 Despite a recent ITV series his first love remains radio. **1971** *Daily Tel.* 21 June 19/2 However, she is put off by the apparently poor prospects of a career in biology, her first love. **1883** GRESLEY *Gloss. Coal Mining*, **First man*, the head butty or coal getter in a stall, who.. is responsible for the safety of the men working under him and for the proper working of the coal. **1888** *Lockwood's Dict. Mech. Engin.*, **First-motion*, a term of general application, as first motion shafts, first motion belts, first motion wheel, &c., meaning the one which first receives, and then communicates, power to its successors. **1711** *First Night [see NIGHT *sb.* 4 b]. **1894** *Westm. Gaz.* 3 Apr. 2/3 A 'first-night' notice. **1882** *First-nighter [see NIGHTER]. **1886** *Boisgobey's Steel Necklace* v. 79 All the first-nighters had turned out in force. **1887** *Daily News* 3 May 6/1 The social philosophy of *first nighting. **1876** *Gentl. Mag.* Oct. 412 *Daniel Deronda*.. is as much a *first novel, from a fresh hand and mind, as if no scene of clerical life had ever been penned. **1906** *Daily Chron.* 18 Oct. 3/3 One of the best first-novels of recent years. **1942** E. WAUGH *Put out More Flags* iii. 213 'It won't do,' he always said whenever Mr Bentley produced a new author, 'no one ever reads first novels.' **1849** *Chambers's Edin. Jrnl.* 3 Nov. 283/2 In the assize-yard there was a considerable number of what are called *first-offenders. **1935** *Economist* 18 June 1353/1 Not at Borstal only, but in at least one of the prisons for first offenders, the humanising influence is at work. **1674** MARVELL *Corr.* Wks. 1872–5 II. 424 E of Pembroke marryed to Madame Qerronal's [*sic*] sister. The King gives 1000 *first peny. **1875** *Encycl. Brit.* II. 427/1 The *First Pointed, Lancet, or Early English style to which the transitional work thus led up. **1886** F. G. LEE *Edw. VI.* i. 58 A first-pointed chapel and charnel-house. **1877** *Encycl. Brit.* VI. 720/2 If the given curve has a node, the *first polar passes through this node,.. and.. if the curve has a cusp, the first polar passes through the cusp, touching the curve there. **1949** SEMPLE & ROTH *Introd. Algebraic Geom.* i. 11 The first polar of an arbitrary point Q with respect to a primal V_{r-1}^{n} is a primal of order $n-1$, which meets V_{r-1}^{n} in the locus of points of contact of tangent lines from Q. **1880** H. E. KREHBIEL tr. *Courvoisier's Technics of Violin Playing* (1881) iii. 14 (*caption*) Correct position of the thumb and fingers in the *first position. **1884** D. ANDERSON *Compl. Ball-Room Guide* 10 *First position*, heels together, and toes turned out at a right angle. **1957** G. B. L. WILSON *Dict. Ballet* 124 In the First Position the legs are together and the heels touching but not overlapping, with the feet fully turned out in a straight line. **1966** tr. *Flesch's Violin Fingering* I. 9 The basic position of the hand at the lower end of the fingerboard, with the first finger naturally poised to produce a second above the open string, constitutes the 'first position'. **1871** G. H. LEWES *Let.* 5 Apr. (1955) V. 139 We want £100 for the early sheets—the poem to appear in America in June—and of course we give you the *first refusal. **1887** First refusal [see REFUSAL 3]. **1966** *Listener* 9 June 833/1 Sometimes I am asked why we have a month's first refusal agreement with ABC. Could we not sell more in an open field? **1970** M. KELLY *Spinifex* i. 12, I made damn sure this department got the first refusal of your services. **1912** *First run [see sense C 2 b]. **1921** *Moving Picture World* 29 Oct. 1067/3 Vitagraph's manager.. wrote contracts for first runs in twenty-eight towns. **1939** L. JACOBS *Rise of Amer. Film* iv. 53 A 'first run', for instance, cost the exhibitor twenty times as much as a 'twentieth run'. **1976** D. SPOTO *Art of Alfred Hitchcock* xxix. 291 The first time I saw Alfred Hitchcock's *Vertigo* was in 1958, its first run. **1967** *Primary Educ. in Wales* (Dept. Educ. & Sci. Central Advisory Council Educ., Wales) iv. 23 We recommend the following long-term plan

for primary education: Nursery stage (part-time, voluntary) ..3 to median 5:6..Infants stage (*First school) Median 5:6..to median 8:6..Junior stage (Middle school) Median 8:6 to median 12:6. **1973** *New Society* 10 May 294/1 The eight to twelve year old middle school was first seriously discussed in the early 1960s, when it was rumoured that the Plowden committee might eventually consider a system of first schools for the five to eight year olds. **1986** *Guardian* 17 Feb. 6/2 The village would consent to the school becoming a first school, rather than a primary. **1874** J. K. Polk in *Amer. Speech* (1957) XXXII. 209 *First Sergeant W. Peat, of this company, who acted with extraordinary daring, lost one of his legs. **1969** I. Kemp *Brit. G.I. in Vietnam* vi. 117 First Sergeant Bryant, the senior N.C.O. in 'A' Force. **1773** Goldsm. *Stoops to Conq.* III, Then your *first sight deceived you; for I think him one of the most brazen first sights that ever astonished my senses. **1859** Farrar *J. Home* 27 Without any first-sight vows of eternal friendship. **1748** Richardson *Clarissa* (1811) I. 305 To compliment our own sagacity, in our *first-sighted impressions. **1898** *Encycl. Sport* II. 92 The object of the run is to kill the pig, and not entirely for getting the honour of '*first spear'. *Ibid.*, First spear... Transferred frequently to the man who makes it. **1920** *Blackw. Mag.* Jan. 112/2 Much of the supreme joy in pig-sticking lies in the successful struggle for first-spear and in outgeneraling and outriding one's friends. *Ibid.*, A first-spear which merely pricks the pig in the buttock, is a matter for shame. **1662** J. Davies tr. *Mandelslo's Trav.* 137 The River which often overflowes drowns them sometimes to the *first story. **1834** L. Ritchie *Wand. by Seine* (1835) 181 [The prisons] were sometimes placed in the first story of the donjon. **1860** Bartlett *Dict. Amer.* s.v. *Story*, In the United States the floor next the ground is the first story. [Cf. first-floor 2.] **1962** *Listener* 5 Apr. 605/2 A Russian *first strike. **1973** *Times* 9 Oct. 4/4 The Building Societies Association was taken unawares by the Government's specific proposals to help *first-time buyers. **1986** *What Mortgage* June 8/2 Two out of every five applicants for new mortgages were first time buyers. **1961** Webster *First timer, s.v. *timer*. **1976** *Evening Post* (Nottingham) 15 Dec. 15/4 (Advt.), Cheery bright house, ideal for first timers. **1977** *Hongkong Standard* 12 Apr. 11/2 He centred to Leung Kam-fat who, from just 12 yards out, did well with his first-timer. **1986** *Sunday Tel.* (Colour Suppl.) 2 Feb. 29/4 She's got a good eye for pictures... I thought they were excellent—not only for a first-timer, but it shows that you can get really good pictures with an ordinary compact. **1931** S. Jameson *Richer Dust* xix. 552 The salvage of what a dear dead and let us piously hope well-damned colonel preferred to call the *First World War. **1947** *Partisan Rev.* XIV. 237 The mystique of the working class has faded somewhat since the First World War. **1958** *Listener* 19 June 1020/2 The outbreak of the first world war in the present century. **1390** *Ferste youthe [see youth 3]. **1789** H. More *Let.* (1925) 126 She is past her first youth..and subject to caution. **1878** H. James *Europeans* I. i. 7 She was not pretty... Neither was she in her first youth.

b. In attrib. uses of syntactical collocations; see also first class, first-class B, First-day, etc.; generation 4 b.

1741 Richardson *Pamela* IV. lxiii. 419 Has extraordinary Notions of a First-sight Love. **1840** [see *first cost* s.v. first C. 2]. **1859** [see *first sight* s.v. first C. 2]. **1861** E. Cowell *Diary* (1934) 244 The small audience was one of the usual 'first night' 'critical' ones. **1892** W. W. Greener *Breech-loader* 174 Loaded with first quality powder. **1894** [see *first night* s.v. first C. 2]. **1897** *Daily News* 1 June 3/2 To establish themselves once more in their former first line positions. **1904** Conrad *Nostromo* III. xiii. 476 A knot of night prowlers..hung about the door of the first-aid hospital. **1904** *Westm. Gaz.* 28 May 2/3 First-category Cossacks of the Chitinsk, Argunsk, and Veckhni Udinsk regiments. **1905** *Ibid.* 14 Mar. 12/1 Any privileges which go with a first-cabin ticket. *Ibid.* 9 June 10/1 A first edition copy of 'Richard III'. *Ibid.* 13 Nov. 12/1 The only first-magnitude star in the track of the moon. **1906** *Daily Chron.* 21 July 1/7 The third best first-wicket stand on record. **1909** *Ibid.* 23 July 6/7 Suitable employment, treatment &c., for first-stage patients. *Ibid.* 9 Aug. 6/4 At least nineteen first-order stations for agricultural investigations. **1912** J. F. Hodges *Opening & operating Motion Picture Theatre* 13 A film being exhibited for the first time is called 'first run' film. **1912** L. J. Vance *Destroying Angel* xvi, A light-house—probably a first-order light—with its characteristic flash, not duplicated anywhere along this section of the Atlantic coast. **1926** *Daily Colonist* (Victoria, B.C.) 18 July 9/5 First Aid Kits. For the camp or your car. In metal box, up from 75¢. **1930** *Flight* 24 Jan. p. ii, First-line machines, ready for war, over 1,000; reserves, about 800; total, 1,800. **1933** *Mind* XLII. 312 It is certain that P_n will have an eternal first-order Secondary Part. **1934** F. Scott Fitzgerald *Let.* 10 May (1964) 307 It did not have as large a proportion of first-flight stories. **1936** *World Film News* May 28/2 And so we reach the figure of £30,000 as the normal minimum cost of a first-feature film. **1936** *Mind* XLV. 171 The difference between a first-order proposition and a second-order proposition (or proposition of second intention)..is that the former says something about the realm of facts, while the latter says something about 'propositions'. **1940** 'G. Orwell' *Inside Whale* 56 The two first-person novels are also good stories. **1950** *N.Y. Times* 20 Apr. 1/2 Dr. Sander, accused by the state of first degree murder. **1957** L. Fox *Two-point Boundry Probl.* v. 106 First-order equations are generally amenable only to step-by-step methods. **1960** *New Left Rev.* July–Aug. 2/1 First-strike nuclear weapons. **1961** C. C. T. Baker *Dict. Math.* 131 *First-order equation*, a differential equation containing only the first differential coefficient *dy/dx*. **1969** *Daily Tel.* 17 Nov. 14 The most sinister aspect of Russia's nuclear expansion is her concentration on a variety of giant 'first-strike' weapons, designed to knock out American launchers and control centres. **1970** *Nature* 12 Dec. 1031/2 The reaction follows first-order kinetics. **1971** B. de Ferranti *Living with Computer* 87 *First generation computer*, an early machine built in the 1950s or early 1960s using valves. **1971** *It* 9–23 Sept. 21/2 The First New York Erotic Film Festival..will be held in first-run Manhattan cinemas.

first (fɜːst), *v.* [f. first *a.*]

†**1.** *nonce uses.* **a.** *intr.* As rendering of Gr. πρωτεύειν: To have the first place, be first. **b.** *trans.* With allusion to the vb. *to second* (see context): To advance (a person) to the first place.

1625 Gill *Sacr. Philos.* iv. 49 That Hee may bee Ἐν πᾶσι πρωτεύων firsting, or having the first place or preheminence in all things. **1656** S. H. *Gold. Law* 11 These also will befool you..to gain you to second the King, that so ye may second, and so first them.

†**2.** *trans.* To propose (a resolution), 'move' (as opposed to 'seconding'). *Obs.*

1656 *Burton's Diary* (1828) I. 66 The question in the morning, which was firsted and seconded. **1658** *Ibid.* III. 193 The question which is firsted and seconded.

3. *dial.* To 'set out' with the hoe.

1860 *Jrnl. R. Agric. Soc.* XXI. II. 386 The swedes..were not 'firsted' until August 6th.

first: see frist *sb.* and *v.* *Obs.*

'first-born, *a.* [f. first *adv.* + born *a.*]

1. That is born first, eldest.

1382 Wyclif *Luke* ii. 7 Sche childide her firste born sone. **1413** *Pilgr. Sowle* (Caxton 1483) III. viii. 55 Cayn the fyrst borne child. **1611** Bible *Deut.* xxi. 15 If the first borne sonne be hers that was hated. **1847** Mrs. A. Kerr *Hist. Servia* 250 He often called him 'Son'; saying, 'Alexa, his first-born son, was not dearer to him'.

transf. **1784** Cowper *Task* IV. 701 The firstborn efforts of my youthful Muse. **1807** Crabbe *Newspaper* 449 Read your first-born work a thousand times.

b. *nonce-use.* That is the right of the first-born.

1770 Goldsm. *Des. Vill.* 256 Spontaneous joys..The soul adopts, and owns their first-born sway.

2. *absol.* (quasi-*sb.*)

a **1340** Hampole *Psalter* cxxxiv. 8 He smote þe first borne of egipt fro man til best. **1587** Golding *De Mornay* vi. 71 The Firstborne of God. **1667** Milton *P.L.* I. 489 Jehovah ..equal'd with one stroke Both her first born and all her bleating Gods. **1712** Steele *Spect.* No. 263 ¶1 Camillus and his first-born dwell together. **1837** Lytton *E. Maltrav.* III. iv, Teresa was trying to teach her first-born to read.

transf. **1830** Tennyson *Ode Mem.* 92 The love thou bearest The first-born of thy genius.

b. *rarely* as sb. with plural ending.

1866 J. H. Newman *Gerontius* ii. 21 All praise to Him.. By whom proud first-borns from their thrones are cast.

first chop, first-chop: see chop *sb.*⁵.

'first 'class, first-class.

A. (as two words).

a. The first of a series of classes in which things or persons are grouped. Usually implying priority in importance; *esp.* in fixed or technical applications, e.g. the highest grade of accommodation for travellers by railway or steamboat, the highest division in an examination-list.

1789 A. Young *Jrnl.* 17 Aug. in *Travels* (1792) I. 165 In the first class of French families..they undoubtedly are. **1807** [see class *sb.* 4]. **1846** *Commercial Mag.* Oct. 135 There is a first-class for those who are willing to pay for the superior comfort.

b. *ellipt.* A place in the first class of an examination list (cf. class *sb.* 4.); one who has obtained such a place; first-class accommodation or fare.

1838 *British Mag.* VI. 100 There was no double First-Class [Referring to Oxford]. **1851** H. W. Dulcken tr. *Pfeiffer's Visit Holy Land* i. 23 The first-class to Constantinople costs 120 florins. **1859** Farrar *J. Home* 186 My getting a first class in the May examination. **1885** *Oxford Univ. Cal.* 40 Candidates must have obtained..a First Class in Litt. Gr. et Lat. at the First Public Examination. **1930** E. Pound *XXX Cantos* xviii. 82 And Mr. Oige was very choleric in a first-class From Nice to Paris.

B. *attrib.* or *adj.* (written with the hyphen).

(In attributive use sometimes with stress on the first syll.; in predicative use the stress is equal or on the last.)

1. a. Of or belonging to the first class in a recognized series of grades: as, a first-class (railway) carriage, a first-class man (in an examination: also written ***first-classman***).

1837-8 [see second-class *a.* 1]. **1846** *Commercial Mag.* Oct. 133 His Lordship..refused to travel in the first-class carriages, and went as a second-class passenger. **1852** *Ann. Reg.* 207 A 'composite' carriage, the centre being a first-class compartment. **1860** *All Year Round* No. 74. 560 An Oxford first-class man. **1869** Dunkin *Midn. Sky* 14 The first-class star Capella. **1871** Smiles *Charac.* ii. (1876) 33 A first-classman at Oxford. **1887** *Spectator* 25 June 860/1 A Balliol Scholar, a first-classman.

b. In *U.S.* sometimes used of the lowest or least important grade: as, a first-class clerk (= one who receives the lowest salary).

2. a. *gen.* Of the highest grade in importance, value, or excellence; of the first or best quality.

1858 R. S. Surtees *Ask Mamma* xlv. 199 First-class servants who had fallen into second-class circumstances. **1872** Raymond *Statist. Mines & Mining* 147 The first-class ores were shipped to Reno and San Francisco. **1878** *Rep. Postmaster-Gen.* (U.S.) 33 The efficiency and security of the registry system of first-class mail matter suggested the propriety of extending its provisions to valuable matter of the third class. **1879** McCarthy *Own Times* II. xxviii. 351 Only one first class reputation of a military order had come out of the war. **1885** *Leeds Mercury* 24 June 4/4 Unless some foreign question of first-class importance should arise. **1887** *Postal Laws U.S.* 138 A 'drop letter'..is first-class matter and should be returned to the writer, if unclaimed. **1924** H. A. Blackman *Business Mail* 15 In this connection it is well to remember that first-class postage is never an odd number of cents. **1968** *Times* 19 Mar. 2/1 A two-tier system providing a first class letter service for 4d.

b. *colloq.* Extremely good, 'first-rate'.

1879 Spurgeon *Serm.* XXV. 90 When he was on the road to Damascus to hunt the saints, he was on first-class terms with himself.

3. quasi-*adv.* **a.** By first-class conveyance, etc. **b.** *colloq.* Excellently, very well indeed (cf. *first-rate*).

1847 *Illustr. London News* 22 May 328 (*caption*) Epsom races—1847. The railway—first class. **1895** *Month* Feb. 197 She looks first-class and healthy. *a* **1897** *Mod.* To travel first-class. How are you getting on? Oh, first-class. **1971** A. Price *Alamut Ambush* x. 124 He borrowed a fivepenny stamp off me..because he wanted it [*sc.* a letter] to go first class.

First-day. The name given (chiefly by members of the Society of Friends) to Sunday, as being the first day of the week.

a **1690** G. Fox *Jrnl.* (1694) I. 168 Upon the first-day after, I was moved to go to Aldenham steeple-house. *a* **1713** Ellwood *Autobiog.* (1765) 101 One First day in four there was a more general Meeting. **1843** Whittier *First Day in Lowell* Prose Wks. 1889 I. 369 One must be here of a pleasant First day at the close of what is called the 'afternoon service'.

attrib. **1773** *Hist. Brit. Dom. N. Amer.* II. iv. 278 First-day Baptists, whose weekly holiday is the Sunday. **1872** Whittier *Penn. Pilgrim* 385 Fair First-Day mornings.

†**'firsten,** *a.* *Sc. Obs.* Also **firstin.** [Lengthened form of first *a.*, ultimately due to the analogy of eightin.] = first *a.*

1594 *Battell of Balrinness* in *Scot. Poems 16th C.* II. 351 The firstin man in counsall spak Good Errol it was he. *Ibid.* II. 353 The firsten shot was to neir..The nixtin shot thair foes hurt.

†**'firster,** *a.* *Obs.* [f. first + -er. Cf. G. *erstere*.] Earlier, former.

1608 *Certif.* in Peel *Spen Valley* (1893) 125 Followynge the same brooke untyl yt come to the firster boundarye where yt begun. **1633** *Puritanisme the Mother* Ep. Ded., In those firster times of Protestancy, the name of Puritan was scarce heard of.

first-floor.

1. The floor or story of a building next above the ground floor.

1865 Dickens *Mut. Fr.* I. iv, This is the gentleman who has taken your first-floor.

2. The floor or story which is built on or just above the ground; a ground floor. Now only *U.S.*

1663 Gerbier *Counsel* 101 The first Floore of a building should not lye level with the ground. **1860** Worcester, *First-floor*, the basement of a building [U.S.].

3. *colloq.* The person who occupies the first floor.

1861 Mrs. Carlyle *Lett.* III. 83 A piano hired in by 'the first floor' yesterday.

4. *attrib.*, as ***first-floor-room, -window***.

1840 Dickens *Old C. Shop* viii, An oval board over the front first-floor window. **1877** Black *Green Past.* iii. (1878) 19 In the first-floor room of a small house in Piccadilly.

'first-fruit. Chiefly *pl.* [Orig. as two words; used as transl. of L. *primitiæ*.]

1. The fruits first gathered in a season; the earliest products of the soil; *esp.* with reference to the custom of making offerings of these to God or the gods.

1382 Wyclif *Num.* xviii. 12 What euer thing thei shulen offre of first fruytis to the Lord. **1483** *Cath. Angl.* 132/1 Firste Frute, *primicie*. **1535** Coverdale *Lev.* ii. 14 Yf thou wilt offre a meatofferynge of the first frutes vnto yᵉ Lorde. **1667** Milton *P.L.* XI. 435 Thither anon A sweatie Reaper from his Tillage brought First Fruits. **1725** Pope *Odyss.* XIV. 497 The first-fruits to the gods he gave. **1870** Bryant *Iliad* I. IX. 292 The first-fruits of his fertile field.

2. *transf.* and *fig.* The earliest products, results, or issues of anything; the first products of a man's work or endeavour.

1597 Hooker *Eccl. Pol.* v. lvi. (1611) 309 The first fruites of Christs Spirit. **1653** Walton *Angler* 56 It is a good beginning of your art to offer your first-fruits to the poor. **1677** Waller *Loss Dk. Camb.*, As a First-fruit, Heaven claim'd that Lovely Boy; The next shall live, and be the nation's joy. **1718** Prior *Poems* Postscript to Pref., The blooming Hopes..[of] my then very Young Patron have been confirmed by most Noble First-Fruits. **1866** J. H. Newman *Gerontius* iii. 25 That calm and joy uprising in thy soul Is first-fruit to thee of thy recompense. **1868** Freeman *Norm. Conq.* II. vii. 72 One of the first-fruits of the great national reaction.

3. *Eccl.* and *Feudal Law.* A payment, usually representing the amount of the first year's income, formerly paid by each new holder of a feudal or ecclesiastical benefice, or any office of profit, to some superior.

The first-fruits of the English bishoprics and other benefices were paid before the Reformation to the Pope, afterwards to the Crown: see annates.

c **1380** Wyclif *Wks.* (1880) 66 It is symonye to..ȝeue hym [the Pope]..þe frystefruytes for ȝifte of a chirche. *c* **1394** *P. Pl. Crede* 729 þey [freres] freten vp þe fu[r]ste-froyt. **1545** Brinklow *Compl.* 2 b, Of first frutes, both of benefices and of lordes landes. **1587** Harrison *England* II. i. (1877) I. 24 Our first fruits, which is one whole yeares commoditie of our living. **1622** Bacon *Hen. VII*, 16 The King did vse to rayse them [Bishops] by steps; that hee might not loose the profit of the First-fruits. **1710** Swift *Let. to Harley* 7 Dec. Wks. 1841 II. 455 The first-fruits paid by all incumbents upon their promotion amount to £450 per annum. **1767**

BLACKSTONE *Comm.* II. 67 The king used to take..the first fruits, that is to say, one year's profits of the land.

4. *attrib.*, as ***first-fruit offering***; **first-fruits-book**, a record of first-fruits.

1655 FULLER *Ch. Hist.* I. x. vii. §2 That there were in England foure thousand five hundred Benefices with Cure, not above ten, and most of them under eight pounds in the first fruits-book. **1695** CONGREVE *Love for L.* Prol. 25 We.. bring this day The first fruit offering of a virgin play.

Hence **first-fruit** *v. trans.*, to offer or pay as first-fruits; **first-fruitable** *a.* (*nonce-wds.*).

1621 BP. MOUNTAGU *Diatribæ* 465 It was giuen them in charge, to first-fruit their Tenths..of whatsoeuer the ground brought forth. *Ibid.* 302 Euery herbe was Titheable ..and if so, then shew reason why not first-fruitable also.

first hand.

A. adv. phr. *at first hand* (also *at first-hand*): From the first source or origin, without intermediate agency or the intervention of a medium; direct from the maker, producer, or original vendor. Also with *at* omitted.

1732 FIELDING *Miser* I. vii, All bought at the first hand too. **1811** *Sporting Mag.* XXXVII. 76 Gave ninety guineas for that, which he might have purchased at first hand for five-and-forty. **1840** CARLYLE *Heroes* (1858) 219 Such a man is what we call an original man; he comes to us at first-hand. **1852** DICKENS *Bleak Ho.* xxiv, Asking Phil Squod..what it [the rifle] might be worth, first-hand. **1865** M. ARNOLD *Ess. Crit.* viii. (1875) 337 Matters we cannot well know at first-hand.

B. *adj.* (*first-hand*). Of or belonging to the first source, original; coming direct from the first source and not through an intermediate channel or agency; obtained direct from the producer or original vendor.

1748 RICHARDSON *Clarissa* (1811) I. 338 Second-hand messengers, and first-hand insults. **1861** M. PATTISON *Ess.* (1889) I. 31 Dr. Pauli's study of first-hand sources gives.. a correctness to his language, which [etc.]. **1871** R. H. HUTTON *Ess.* (1877) I. 83 What knowledge you have of such beings is not direct, not first-hand at all. **1890** *Spectator* 31 May 765/1 The author has had access to some first-hand information.

first-handedness (fɜːstˈhændɪdnɪs). Also **firsthandness**. [f. FIRST HAND + -ED + -NESS.] The quality or condition of being first-hand or of an original character.

1905 *Daily Chron.* 3 May 8/5 It may breed distrust as to the first-handedness of some brilliant toilettes whose origin we could never account for. **1926** M. BARING *Daphne Adeane* x, That first-handedness; that habit..of taking nothing for granted. **1950** *Scrutiny* XVII. I. 39 For what looks like carelessness..is actually precision and vivid firsthandness.

†ˈ**first-head, -hood.** *Obs.* [f. FIRST *a.* + -HEAD, -HOOD.] The position of one who is first; primacy.

1382 WYCLIF *Ecclus.* xxiv. 10 [6] In alle folc of kinde the firsthede I hadde. **1619** W. WHATELY *God's Husb.* I. (1622) 66 Diotrephes..desired to be reputed the onely man (which is the louing of first-hood, as the Apostle calls it). *a* **1679** T. GOODWIN *Exp. Eph.* vi. Wks. 1681 I. 83 In Election Christ held the Primacy, the First-hood.

†ˈ**firsting.** *Obs. rare*⁻¹. [? f. FIRST *a.* + -ING³ as in *sweeting*, etc.; or misprint for *firstling*.] = FIRSTLING.

1607 TOPSELL *Four-f. Beasts* 233 Their firstinges, or those which are first of all engendered.

firstling (ˈfɜːstlɪŋ). [f. FIRST *a.* + -LING.] The first of its kind to be produced, come into being, or appear; the first product or result of anything. Usually in collect. pl., like *first-fruits*.

In its earliest recorded use, perh. after G. *erstling*.

1535 COVERDALE *Prov.* iii. 9 Honoure the Lorde..with yᵉ firstlinges of all thine encrease. **1574** tr. *Marlorat's Apocalips* 9 Christ is therefore called the..firstlings of them that ryse againe. **1605** SHAKS. *Macb.* IV. i. 147 The very firstlings of my heart shall be The firstlings of my hand. **1684** BUNYAN *Pilgr.* II. Introd., Perhaps..they will imbrace Thee, as they did my firstling. **1830** J. G. STRUTT *Sylva Brit.* 110 Lord Chancellor Bacon..procured the firstlings of the species [the Plane] from Sicily. **1861** SALA *Dutch Pict.* viii. 120 She had sacrificed her youth, the firstlings of her beauty.

b. *esp.* The first offspring of an animal, the first-born of the season.

1593 DRAYTON *Eclogues* III. 130 Beta shall have the firstling of the Fold. **1697** DRYDEN *Virg. Past.* I. 9 The tender Firstlings of my Woolly breed. **1725** POPE *Odyss.* IV. 841 The firstlings of the flock are doom'd to dye. **1839** MRS. HEMANS *Poems, Forest Sanctuary*, No fair young firstling. **1879** BUTCHER & LANG *Odyss.* 141 Each kind was penned by itself, the firstlings apart.

c. *attrib.*

1611 BIBLE *Deut.* xv. 19 All the firstling males that come of thy heard. **1814** CARY *Dante's Paradise* xxiv. 142 From this germ, this firstling spark, The lively flame dilates. **1863** *Macm. Mag.* Mar. 349 On our soil her foot is set With the firstling violet. **1870** BRYANT *Iliad* I. IV. 109 A hecatomb Of firstling lambs.

firstlin(g)s, *adv. Sc.* [see -LINGS] = FIRST *adv.* I.

1827 TENNANT *Papistry Stormed* 23 Firstlins ae cork, than the tither, Hetly they chasit ane anither.

firstly (ˈfɜːstlɪ), *adv.* [f. as prec. + -LY².]

1. In the first place, before anything else, first. Used only in enumerating heads, topics, etc. in discourse; and many writers prefer *first*, even though closely followed by *secondly*, *thirdly*, etc.

The word is not in Johnson's Dict. Smart (1846) s.v. *First* has the note: 'Some late authors use *Firstly* for the sake of its more accordant sound with secondly, thirdly, etc.'

c **1532** DEWES *Introd. Fr.* in *Palsgr.* 928 Fyrstly, *premierment.* **1562** J. HEYWOOD *Prov. & Epigr.* (1867) 216 Walke thou fyrstly, walke thou lastly: Walke in the walke that standeth fastly. **1668** WILKINS *Real Char.* 393 The Adverb, Firstly, secondly, thirdly. **1723** LADY M. W. MONTAGU *Lett.* (1893) I. 466 A most delightful [ballad].. which has been laid firstly to Pope, and secondly to me. **1726** *Ibid.* I. 495 Firstly, she was pleased to attack me in very Billingsgate at a masquerade. **1816** SCOTT *Old Mort.* iv, The consequence thereof..will be, firstly, that I will tweak thy proboscis or nose. **1847** DE QUINCEY *Sp. Mil. Nun* §5 First (for I detest your ridiculous and most pedantic neologism of *firstly*). **1857** GLADSTONE *Oxf. Ess.* I These objects are twofold: firstly, to promote [etc.].

†**2.** In the beginning, originally. *Obs.*⁻¹

1591 SYLVESTER *Du Bartas* I. v. (1621) 108 To save-vs And salue the wounds th' old Serpent firstly gave-vs.

3. quasi-*sb.* The word *firstly* used in making subdivisions of a subject.

1698 FARQUHAR *Love & Bottle* IV. ii, They hate to hear a fellow in church preach methodical nonsense, with a firstly, secondly, and thirdly. **1759** GOLDSM. *Polite Learning, Lit. Decay*, The most diminutive son of fame..has his *we* and his *us*, his *firstlies* and his *secondlies.* **1846** LOWELL *Lett.* (1894) I. 113 In the next place (turn back a page or two and you will find that I have laid down a 'firstly').

†ˈ**firstmost,** *a. Obs.*⁻¹ [f. as prec. + -MOST.] First, foremost.

c **1400** *Lanfranc's Cirurg.* 9 Þe science of elementis, whiche þat ben firstmoost force of natural þingis.

first name. A person's first or Christian name. Also as *attrib. phr.* Hence as *v. trans.*, to address (a person) by the first name; ***first-naming*** vbl. sb.

c **1250** [see NAME *sb.* I]. **1598** FLORIO *Worlde of Wordes* 291/2 Prenome, the first name, the name given at the font. **1839** C. F. BRIGGS *Adv. H. Franco* I. 74 'My first name is Harry,' I said. **1914** 'E. BRAMAH' *Max Carrados* 66 This, Parkinson,..is a photograph of a Mr. ——. What first name, by the way? **1935** *Punch* 7 Aug. 142/2 He called her by her first name for the first time. **1940** S. LEWIS *Bethel Merriday* xxv. 267 Zed and..Bill Mattocks..were already first-naming each other as though they had been intimates for years. **1952** P. BONNER *SPQR* (1953) viii. 71 We are not even on a first-name basis. **1959** A. HARRINGTON *Life Crystal Palace* (1960) vii. 109 The company's democratic social organization..permits him to first-name..those several ranks higher. **1968** MRS. L. B. JOHNSON *White House Diary* 23 May (1970) 677 Nearly everybody was on a first-name basis.

ˈ**firstness** (ˈfɜːstnɪs), [f. as FIRSTMOST *a.* + -NESS.] The quality or state of being first.

c **1380** WYCLIF *Sel. Wks.* (1869) I. 172 Oo firstnesse of love shulde we have to us silf, and to oure fadir and oure modir. **1626** W. SCLATER *Expos. 2 Thess.* (1629) 106 This firstnes, or precedence of Apostasie, to the day of Christ. **1659** HAMMOND *Dispatcher Disp.* Pref. Wks. 1660 II. 163 When I give..a firstness of Precedency and Presidency to the Pope. **1675** BROOKS *Gold. Key* Wks. 1867 V. 183 Oh! the firstness, the freeness..the matchlessness of Christ's love to fallen man in becoming man! **1895** MRS. W. K. CLIFFORD *Flash of Summer* vii, Daffodils..—the bell-like single ones: and their tender firstness appealed to her. **1924** *Glasgow Herald* 4 Sept. 4 A first novel,..with a freshness and spontaneity not always synonymous with 'first-ness' in novel-writing. **1927** *Blackw. Mag.* June 828/2 An odd kind of distinction should halo the person who is the very first to see something or to do something which hitherto humanity has not seen or done. .. The value of these 'firstnesses' is by no means equal.

first rate, first-rate, *phr.*, *a.* (*adv.*), and *sb.*

A. As *phrase* and *adj.*

1. *first rate*: the highest of the 'rates' (see RATE *sb.*) by which vessels of war are distinguished according to size and equipment. In phrase *of (the) first rate*, also from an early date used *transf.* (now *rare*; superseded by the attributive use 2).

1666 *Lond. Gaz.* No. 65/2 Twelve new Ships, all of the first Rate. **1697** VANBRUGH *Relapse* I. iii, Now has he ruined his estate to buy a title, that he may be a fool of the first rate. **1749** FIELDING *Tom Jones* III. iii, His natural parts were not of the first rate. **1810** *Sporting Mag.* XXXVI. 230 He having struggled hard with Crib and other boxers of first-rate. **1816** SCOTT *Old Mort.* ii, Ere Folly..cut down her vessels of the first-rate.

2. *attrib.* (passing into *adj.*) *first-rate*: of the first rate (said of vessels); hence *gen.* Of the highest class or degree of excellence.

1671 EVELYN *Mem.* (1857) II. 66 A few of his Majesty's first-rate frigates. *a* **1681** J. LACY *Sir H. Buffoon* II. iv, There are your first, second, third, fourth, and fifth-rate wits too. **1714** MANDEVILLE *Fab. Bees* (1733) II. 149 A first-rate man of war. **1732** BERKELEY *Alciphr.* I. §11, I never saw a first-rate picture in my life. **1853** BRIGHT *Sp. India* 3 June, The question is one..of first-rate importance. **1888** DUFF *Pol. Surv.* 5 As long as France remained a first-rate power.

3. Hence used as an emphatic expression of praise or approval: Extremely good, excellent.

1812 KNOX & JEBB *Corr.* II. 90 Worthington was a first-rate christian; but I think he was not a first-rate divine. **1879** F. W. ROBINSON *Coward Conscience* II. ix, 'Miss Hilderbrandt is first-rate, and no mistake.'

4. quasi-*adv.* (*colloq.*) Excellently, very well. Also, in excellent health, quite well.

1844 W. T. THOMPSON *Major Jones' Courtship* 168 (Bartlett) Mary liked all the speakers first rate. **1857** BORTHWICK *Three Yrs. California* xii. 211 As if you really wanted to know the state of their health, they [Indians] invariably answer 'fuss-rate'. **1880** HOWELLS *Undisc. Country* iv. 79, I want to go away to-morrow feeling first-rate. **1884** PAE *Eustace* 15 'Dod, sir, my claes fit ye first-rate.'

B. *sb.*

1. *Naut.* A war vessel of the first rate; used *esp.* of the old three-deckers carrying 74 to 120 guns.

1708 MOTTEUX *Rabelais* IV. lxii. (1737) 254 The biggest First Rate. **1790** BEATSON *Nav. & Mil. Mem.* I. 72 She was larger than any of our first rates. **1825** BENTHAM *Ration. Rew.* 76 The command of a first-rate is accepted by those only who cannot obtain a frigate. **1878** BROWNING *Poets Croisic* 154 Forced to put about the first-rate.

2. *transf.* A person or thing of the highest class or rank.

a **1683** OLDHAM *Art Poetry*, Poets have been held a sacred name, And plac'd with first Rates in the Lists of Fame. **1706** FARQUHAR *Recruiting Officer* III. ii, She [a woman] is called the Melinda, a first-rate, I can assure you. **1781** COWPER *Let. to Newton* 22 July, Our great wheelbarrow, which may be called a first rate in its kind, conveyed all our stores. **1828** D'ISRAELI *Chas. I*, II. xi. 274 In the House, these leaders of party were both firstrates.

Hence **first-rately** *adv.*; **first-rateness**, the state of being first-rate, first-rate quality; **first-rater**, one who or something which is first-rate.

1806 *Sporting Mag.* XXVII. 243 Who may be deservedly titled first raters in their profession. **1837** DICKENS *Pickw.* xli, 'He must be a first-rater,' said Sam. **1843** *Blackw. Mag.* LIV. 713 Of all instruments the violin, first-rately played, is the most..heavenly. **1882** *Pall Mall G.* 19 June 5/1 The note of first-rateness, of permanence, is hardly here.

†ˈ**firstship.** *Obs.* [f. FIRST *a.* + -SHIP.] The position of being first.

1632 LYNDE *Via Tuta* 39 Peter had a Primacy of order, that is, a First-ship among the Apostles. *a* **1661** FULLER *Worthies, Suffolk* (1662) III. 67 Two Firstships met in this Man [Necton], for he Handselled the House-Convent.. Secondly, He was the first Carmelite, who [etc.].

firth¹ (fɜːθ). Chiefly *northern. Obs.* or *arch.* Forms: 4 **firþe**, **fyrþe**, 4-6 **fyrth**, 6- **firth.** [Metathesis of FRITH *sb.*²] A synonym of FRITH *sb.*² in some of its senses: A deer-forest, hunting-ground; a piece of ground covered with brushwood with a few trees; a coppice, small wood. In poetry frequent in alliterative phrases, ***firth and fell***, ***firth and field***, ***firth and fold***: see FRITH *sb.*²

c **1375** *Sc. Leg. Saints, Blasius* 77 Þane send he ma knychtis..To hwnt in [to] þat sammyne fyrth. ? *a* **1400** *Morte Arth.* 1708 We have foundene in ȝone firthe..ffifty thosandez of folke of ferse mene of armez. *c* **1425** WYNTOUN *Cron.* I. xiii. 52 Ane Lande..Of Fyrth, and Felde. *c* **1475** *Rauf Coilȝear* 682 Fyne foullis in Fyrth. **1513** DOUGLAS *Æneis* VII. Prol. 162 Quhen frostis days ourfret bayth fyrth and fauld. **1535** STEWART *Cron. Scot.* II. 593 The fox that rynnis in the firth. **1581** SAVILE *Agric.* (1622) 192 The firths and the thickets he proued the first in his owne person. **1794** BURNS *A Vision* (1st version) 17 Looking over firth and fauld, Her horn the pale-fac'd Cynthia rear'd.

firth² (fɜːθ). Also 5 **fyrth.** See also FRITH *sb.*³ [app. a. ON. *fiǫrðr*: see FIORD.

Firth or *frith* was originally a Sc. word, introduced into English literary use *c* 1600.]

An arm of the sea; an estuary of a river.

c **1425** WYNTOUN *Cron.* VI. xx. 108 Þai..of fors, as wynd þame movyd, Come in þe Fyrth. **1513** DOUGLAS *Æneis* III. vi. 123 The ile of Cecill devidit hes allhaile, Ane narrow fyrth flowis..Betuix thai costis. **1535** STEWART *Cron. Scot.* (1858) I. 9 So hapnit tham..to wend Out throw ane firth endlang ane cragie cost. **1601** HOLLAND *Pliny* I. 43 In many firths and armes of the sea. **1637** RUTHERFORD *Lett.* (1862) I. lxxxiv. 215 Glad may our souls be that are safe over the firth. **1774** NICHOLLS *Corr. w. Gray* (1843) 175 The Castle, from whose summit the Firth of Forth is seen for many miles. **1839** W. CHAMBERS *Tour Holland* 31/1 A neck of sea.. possessing all the appearance of a navigable firth. **1865** GEIKIE *Scen. & Geol. Scot.* 125 The sea runs inland in long narrow firths.

Firthian (ˈfɜːθɪən), *a.* and *sb.* [f. the name of J. R. *Firth* (see below) + -IAN.] **A.** *adj.* Of, pertaining to, or characteristic of the British linguist John Rupert Firth (1890–1960) or his theories (see quots.). **B.** *sb.* One who subscribes to Firth's theories. Cf. *Neo-Firthian* adj. and sb. s.v. NEO- I a.

1961 *Jrnl. Canad. Linguistic Assoc.* VI. 169 In a Firthian analysis, congruence of statement is clearly necessary. **1964** R. H. ROBINS *Gen. Linguistics* p. xix, One aspect of transformational grammar constitutes an interesting link with Firthian theory. **1967** *Word* XXIII. 434 Most of the first generation of British linguists were directly influenced by Firth, and the second generation at least by Firth's own students. Hence the identification of the name 'Firthian Linguistics' with the London school of linguistics, or, in some cases, with British linguistics as a whole. **1972** HARTMANN & STORK *Dict. Lang. & Linguistics* 30/2 J. R. Firth..also developed prosodic phonology and a 'contextual' theory of meaning (*Firthian linguistics*). **1981** *Internat. Jrnl. Sociol. Lang.* 72 The Firthian approach to language seeks the appropriateness of the behavior of participants in a language-event, and the whole background of their coming together which determines their use of language in a certain way in a particular context. *Ibid.* 79 The main concentration of the Firthians has traditionally been at the School of Oriental and African Studies of London University.

ˈ**fir-tree.** [f. FIR + TREE.] = FIR I.

1382 WYCLIF *Isa.* xiv. 8 Fyrre trees also gladeden vp on thee. **1430–50** tr. *Higden* (Rolls) I. 335 There be bryddes

whiche thei calle bernacles..whom nature producethe ageyne nature from firre trees. **1577** B. GOOGE *Heresbach's Husb.* II. (1586) 101 b, In the mountaines delighteth the Fyrre tree. **1664** EVELYN *Kal. Hort.* (1729) 196 A little after the Equinox, prune Pine and Fir-trees. **1712** tr. *Pomet's Hist. Drugs* I. 148 They grow in Clusters upon a Kind of Turpentine or Fir-Tree. **1855** LONGF. *Hiaw.* VII. 63 Give me of your balm, O Fir-Tree!

firy, obs. form of FIERY.

firze, obs. form of FURZE.

fisc, fisk (fɪsk). Also 7 fisque. [a. Fr. *fisc*, or independently ad. L. *fiscus* rush-basket, purse, treasury. The current spelling in Sc. Law is *fisk*, in other uses *fisc*.]

1. *Antiq.* The public treasury of Rome; under the Empire, the imperial treasury or privy purse of the Emperor.

1598 GRENEWEY *Tacitus' Ann.* II. xi. (1603) 49 Cæsar.. bestowed the goods of Aemilia Musa, a rich woman, fallen to the fisque; vpon Aemilius Lepidus. **1601** HOLLAND *Pliny* II. 463 The Fisque or city chamber by that means was soone acquit of all debts. **1679** BURNET *Hist. Ref.* I. 274 The endowments of the heathenish temples were..adjudged to the fisc, or the Emperor's exchequer. **1865** MERIVALE *Rom. Emp.* VIII. lxiii. 55 The endowment of the professors.. seems to have been made from the fisc.

b. Any royal or state treasury; an exchequer. Now *rare* (*Hist.* or with allusion to 'confiscation'). Also *attrib.* in *fisc-lands* (*Hist.*) = *fiscal lands*.

1599 *Broughton's Lett.* iii. 11 As if your inuentions were al Treasure trouue, fiske royal. **1606** SYLVESTER *Du Bartas* II. iv. ii. *Magnificence* 609 Peru..By yeerly Fleets into his Fisk doth flow. **1697** EVELYN *Numism.* vii. 233 The Fisque and publick Treasure. **1788** PRIESTLEY *Lect. Hist.* v. xlviii. 360 A fine must therefore be paid to the fisc. **1801** A. RANKEN *Hist. France* I. 251 Public or fisc lands, which formed the revenue of the government. **1854** MILMAN *Lat. Chr.* I. III. ii. 287 King Chlotaire demanded for the fisc the third part of the revenue of the churches. **1868** MILL in *Star* 13 Mar., How can that be confiscation by which the fisc is not to receive anything.

c. *jocosely.* A man's purse or 'exchequer'.

1820 LAMB *Elia* Ser. I. *Two Races of Men*, The streams were perennial which fed his fisc.

2. *Scots Law.* The public treasury or 'Crown', to which estates lapse by escheat: in the phrase 'as to the fisc' (translating *quoad fiscum*), i.e. so far as the Crown rights of escheat are concerned. †Hence incorrectly used for: The right of the Crown to the estate of a rebel.

[**1641** *Sc. Acts Chas. I* (1870) V. 415 § 107 Provyding allwayes that..the bandis or contractes heirby ordeened to perteene to þe neerest of kine..shall not fall wnder þe compas of escheat nor ȝit any pairt therof perteene to þe relict jure relictæ Bot shall remaine in þe owne nature quoad fiscum et relictam as they wer befor þe making of this acte]. **1680** in *Fountainhall's Hist. Notices* (1848) I. 269 The King ..was sending..a letter converting the sentence to banishment, and confiscating his ship and all his goods, but preferring his creditors theirin to his fisk. **1754** ERSKINE *Princ. Sc. Law* II. ii. §11 Personal bonds are now moveable in respect of succession, but heritable as to the fisk, and husband and wife. **1773** —— *Instit. Law Scot.* II. ii. §10 *heading*, By the word *fisk* in this statute [see quot. 1641] is meant the crown's right to the moveable estate of persons denounced rebels.

3. = FISCAL *sb.* †**a.** *Sc. Law* (obs.) **b.** Used by Browning after It. *fisco*.

1732 J. LOUTHIAN *Form of Process* iii. 19 Every Sheriff or Fisk of Court, to whom the Execution of the Warrand is committed, orders a Party..for the Prisoner's safe transportation..and gives Receipt to the Fisk of the County he receives him from. **1868** BROWNING *Ring & Bk.* IX. 14 The Court Requires the allocution of the Fisc.

fiscal (ˈfɪskəl), *a.* and *sb.* Also 6 fyscall, 6–7 fiscall, (7 phiscall). [a. Fr. *fiscal*, Sp. *fiscal*, It. *fiscale*, ad. late L. *fiscālis*, f. *fiscus* FISC.]

A. *adj.*

1. a. Of or pertaining to the fisc or treasury of a state or prince; pertaining to the public revenue.

1563 FOXE *Martyrs* 333 (1632) I. 475/2 Which excludeth all right both fiscall and Ecclesiasticall. *a* **1618** RALEIGH *Cab. Council* xix. (1658) 50 It behoveth the Prince to have a vigilant eye on..such fiscal Ministers. **1652** HOWELL *Revol. Naples* II. 49 That he should send a Trumpet for the Fiscal Proctor. **1765** BLACKSTONE *Comm.* I. 281 We proceed now to examine the king's fiscal prerogatives, or such as regard his revenue. **1838** PRESCOTT *Ferd. & Is.* (1846) II. xvi. 113 Alonso de Quintanilla..a fiscal officer of the crown. **1863** FAWCETT *Pol. Econ.* IV. iii. (1876) 549 The last remnant of Protection has been banished from our fiscal system.

b. *fiscal lands* (transl. of L. *terræ fiscales*): in Frankish history, lands belonging to the king.

In some mod. Dicts.

c. *fiscal agent*, 'a bank or trust company acting as the financial representative of a corporation or service organization' (Webster 1961); also *fig.*

1841 in X. D. MacLeod *Biogr. F. Wood* (1856) 75 For forty years this Government has tried a national bank as its fiscal agent. **1856** *Househ. Words* 1 Mar. 153/1 There are.. several buffets in Paris where you can be supplied with the cool and cunning drink known..as a Fiscal Agent. **1877** BARTLETT *Dict. Amer.* (ed. 4) 357 The various compounds or mixtures of spirituous liquors and wines served in the United States... Fiscal Agent. **1931** *Times Trade & Engin. Suppl.* 5 Sept. 534/2 Inquiries concerning the heavy fall in the securities of this group have led to the publication of a statement by the British fiscal agents.

2. Of or pertaining to financial matters in general. ***fiscal year***: a financial year: see FINANCIAL *a.* 1. (Chiefly *U.S.*)

1865 H. PHILLIPS *Amer. Paper Curr.* II. 44 The estimates for the fiscal year were only calculated to the tenth of June. **1872** RAYMOND *Statist. Mines & Mining* 99 The above figures represent the condition of the company at the close of the fiscal year ending June 30. **1880** E. KIRKE *Garfield* 42 The work of the past fiscal year.

B. *sb.*

†**1.** = FISC 1 b.

1590 LAMBARDE *Compos. for Alienations* in *Bacon's Wks.* (1740) III. 549 War..as it is entertained by diet, so can it not be long maintained by the ordinary fiscal and receipt.

2. As the title of an official, in various connexions.

†**a.** A minister or official of the treasury; a treasurer. *Obs.*

1652 HOWELL *Revol. Naples* II. 50 The Captain propos'd to the Fiscal, That..a Tax should be impos'd upon all the Nobles. **1665** SIR T. HERBERT *Trav.* 60 To those onely his Fiscal or Treasurer yearly giving out above forty millions of Crowns. **1676** W. HUBBARD *Happiness of People* 26 Inferiour Officers, such as are Fiscalls and Treasurers.

b. In Italy, Spain, Spanish colonies, etc., the title given to legal officials of various ranks, having the function of public prosecutors; under the Holy Roman Empire, the highest law officer of the crown.

1539 T. PERY in Ellis *Orig. Lett.* Ser. II. II. 147 Myne acwzacyon presentyde by the fyscall. **1622** R. HAWKINS *Voy. S. Sea* (1847) 103 That suite, which in Spaine is prosecuted by the kings atturney, or fiscall. **1757** *Hist. Europe* in *Ann. Reg.* (1758) 15/1 The King of Prussia was condemned for contumacy and the Fiscal had orders to notify to him that he was put under the ban of the Empire. **1779** H. SWINBURNE *Trav. Spain* xlii. 379 Don Pedro Rodriguez Campomanès, fiscal of the council of Castille. **1845** S. AUSTIN *Ranke's Hist. Ref.* I. 199 The emperor caused the plenipotentiaries of the city to be cited before the fiscal of the empire. **1868** BROWNING *Ring & Bk.* IX. 133 Exactly so have I..Your Fiscal, made me cognizant of facts.

c. In Holland and Dutch colonies: A magistrate whose duty it is to take cognizance of offences against the revenue.

1653 SIR E. NICHOLAS in *N. Papers* (Camden) II. 18 The children's late insurrection in this town for having their trumpet taken from them by the Fiscal. **1700** S. L. tr. *Fryke's Voy. E. Ind.* 114, I never saw him more; without doubt he run away for fear the Fiscael should call him to an account for the death of my Companion. **1772–84** COOK *Voy.* (1790) IV. 1241 They waited on the governor, the lieutenant-governor or the fiscal. **1796** W. TAYLOR in *Monthly Rev.* XXI. 514 Peter Paulus, a man of forty years of age, originally Fiscal of the Admiralty. **1842** ORDERSON *Creol.* viii. 83 The Fiscal..consigned him to the penal gang.

d. *Sc.* Short for PROCURATOR FISCAL.

1681 in *Lond. Gaz.* No. 1649/2 All Sheriffs..Officers of the Mint, Commissars and..their Clerks and Fiscals. **1818** SCOTT *Hrt. Midl.* xviii, 'Is it only you?'..answered the fiscal. **1885** C. GIBBON *Hard Knot* I. xvii. 237 The eyes of the Sheriff and the Fiscal were turned to Sarah.

3. The name given in Cape Colony to a shrike (*Lanius collaris*). Also, ***fiscal-bird***.

1801 J. BARROW *Trav. S. Afr.* I. i. 29 Turtle doves, a thrush called the Sprew, and the fiscal bird, the *Lanius Collaris*, frequent the gardens near the town. **1822** LATHAM *Hist. Birds* II. 23 The Canary-Biter, or Fiscal-bird..the tail feathers in the cinereous species are twice as broad as in the Fiscal. **1884** SHARPE *Layard's Birds S. Africa* 374 Fiskal Shrike.

fiscalism (ˈfɪskəlɪz(ə)m). [f. FISCAL + -ISM.] Fiscal principles or policy, esp. in relation to the questions of free trade and protection.

1892 A. C. MORANT tr. *Schäffle's Imposs. Soc. Democr.* 193 The old-fashioned fiscalism. **1902** *Daily Chron.* 15 July 8/7 Two out of every three members spoken to declared that they will fight regardless of fiscalism for the House of Representatives having effective control of the purse. **1906** *Ibid.* 27 Mar. 6/7 Seeing that they are Free Traders, and most of us are Protectionists, their talking fiscalism would not be very helpful.

fiscality (fɪˈskælɪtɪ). [f. as FISCAL *a.* and *sb.* + -ITY. Cf. Fr. *fiscalité*.] Exclusive regard to fiscal considerations. Also, fiscal policy; *pl.* fiscal matters.

1825 BENTHAM *Ration. Rew.* 301 We shall have ceased to consider colonies with the greedy eyes of fiscality. **1831** PEACOCK *Crotchet Castle* ix, The other classes of society, combined by gunpowder, steam, and fiscality. **1887** J. C. MORISON *Serv. of Man* 35 A grinding fiscality which, at last, exterminated wealth. **1904** W. D. GAINSFORD *What is Fiscal Question?* 7 Such is Cobden Club Fiscality. **1904** *Westm. Gaz.* 13 Jan. 9/1 The rascalities of the Education Act would be set aside by the fiscalities of the food-tax. **1904** *Fabian News* XIV. 4/1 Fiscalities occupy much space. **1905** *Daily Chron.* 14 Dec. 4/6 One eye on Fiscalities and the other on Mr. John Burns's costume.

fiscalize (ˈfɪskəlaɪz), *v. rare*$^{-0}$. [f. FISCAL *a.* + -IZE.] *trans.* To deal with fiscally; to cause to yield revenue. Hence **fiscaliˈzation**.

1886 H. C. DENT *Year in Brazil* 315 Which, under careful fiscalization, would give an annual sum of over one million milreis to the Treasury.

fiscally (ˈfɪskəlɪ), *adv.* [f. as prec. + -LY².] In a fiscal manner; from a fiscal point of view.

1845 MIALL in *Nonconf.* V. 197 Society, fiscally considered, is an insurance association. **1864** *Daily Tel.* 7 Oct., Raisins, molasses, and hewn timber also figure for lessened totals, but fiscally they are comparatively unimportant.

†**ˈfiscelle.** *Obs.* Also 5 fyschelle. [a. F. *fiscelle*, ad. L. *fiscella*, dim. of *fiscus* basket.] A little basket.

The quot. from the *Promptorium* apparently shows misapprehension of the meaning of the word. Way's ed. reads 'fyschelle of fyschew or festu', and explains this as meaning 'basket of osier'; but this is obviously incorrect.

[*c* **1440** *Promp. Parv.* (1499), Fysshell, fysshewe or festu, *festuca*.] **1483** CAXTON *Gold. Leg.* 55/1 She saw the lytyl crybbe or fiscelle. **1491** —— *Vitas Patr.* (W. de W. 1495) I. xxxvii. 43 b/1 He made fyscellis wouen wyth Rede and Ionkes.

fischerite (ˈfɪʃəraɪt). *Min.* [Named in 1844 after *G. Fischer*: see -ITE.] A hydrous phosphate of aluminium, found in green veins in sandstone.

1846 *Amer. Jrnl. Sc.* Ser. II. II. 415 Fischerite is a phosphate of alumina.

Fischer-Tropsch (ˈfɪʃə trɒpʃ). The names of F. J. E. *Fischer* (1877–1948), German chemist, and H. *Tropsch* (1889–1935), German chemist born in Czechoslovakia, used *attrib.* to denote a process introduced by them for the production of hydrocarbons by the catalytic hydrogenation of carbon monoxide.

1933 *Brit. Chem. Abstr.* B. 49/2 The saturated hydrocarbons of a benzine prepared by the Fischer-Tropsch process have been shown to consist of about 33% of hydrocarbons containing *tert.*-bound C atoms and 67% of hydrocarbons unattacked by $SbCl_5$ [etc.]. **1951** KIRK & OTHMER *Encycl. Chem. Technol.* VI. 965 The first commercial Fischer-Tropsch plant at Oberhausen-Holten. **1964** N. G. CLARK *Mod. Org. Chem.* v. 83 The preparation of straight-chain paraffins and olefins by the Fischer-Tropsch process, originating in Germany in 1925.

‖**fiscus** (ˈfɪskəs). [L.: see FISC.] = FISC 1, 1 b.

1650 JER. TAYLOR *Fun. Serm.* 31 So have I seen a river.. paying to the *Fiscus*, the great Exchequer of the Sea..a tribute large and full. **1861** PEARSON *Early & Mid. Ages Eng.* 195 Four years were sufficient [bar] against the imperial fiscus.

fise. Also foise, fice. [Cf. Sw. *fis*, Da. *fiis*.]

†**1.** = FIST *sb.*² 1.

14.. *Nominale* in Wr.-Wülcker 679 *Hec lirida*, a fyse. **1823** EGAN *Grose's Dict. Vulgar Tongue*, *Fice* or *Foyse*, a small windy escape backwards.

†**2.** attrib. *fise-ball* = *fist-ball*.

a **1300** *Cursor M.* 2879 (Cott.) Þar-bi groues sum apell tre, Wit appuls selcut fair to se, Quen þai ar in hand, als a fise bal, To poudir wit a stink þai fal.

fisetin (fɪˈsiːtɪn, ˈfɪsɪtɪn). *Chem.* [ad. G. *fisettin*, f. *fisett(holz)* young fustic + -IN¹.] A yellow crystalline compound, $C_{15}H_{10}O_6$, formerly obtained from young fustic (*Rhus cotinus*) and various other trees for use as a dye.

1865 *Chem. News* 17 Mar. 126/1 M. Chevreul, who has been almost alone in his chemical researches on fustic, found in it—1. A yellow colouring matter, presenting itself when pure in the form of small crystalline needles, and which he called fissetine [*rendering* fisettin], or fisetic acid; 2. A red substance. **1959** N. CAMPBELL in E. H. Rodd *Chem. Carbon Compounds* IVB. viii. 907 A number of naturally occurring hydroxyflavones such as quercetin, luteolin, fisetin, etc. were used as yellow dyestuffs for many centuries.

fisgig(g, var. of FIZGIG.

fish (fɪʃ), *sb.*¹ Forms: 1–2 fisc, 3 *Orm.* fissk, 3–4 fis(s(e, fix, (4 fizs), *south.* viss, vyss, 3–5 fich, 5–6 fych(e, 3–5 fissh(e, (3 fishsh, fischsch), 4–6 fysch(e, -ssh(e, (6 fiszsh), 5–6 fysh(e, 4–6 fishe, 3– fish. [Com. Teut.; OE. *fisc* str. masc. = OFris. *fisk*, OS. *fisc* (Du. *visch*), OHG. *fisc* (MHG. *visch*, Ger. *fisch*), ON. *fiskr* (Sw. and Da. *fisk*), Goth. *fisks*:—OTeut. **fisko-z*:—pre-Teut. **pisko-s*, cogn. with L. *piscis* and OIr. *iasc* (:—**peiskos*).]

I. 1. a. In popular language, any animal living exclusively in the water; primarily denoting vertebrate animals provided with fins and destitute of limbs; but extended to include various cetaceans, crustaceans, molluscs, etc. In modern scientific language (to which popular usage now tends to approximate) restricted to a class of vertebrate animals, provided with gills throughout life, and cold-blooded; the limbs, if present, are modified into fins, and supplemented by unpaired median fins.

Except in the compound *shell-fish*, the word is no longer commonly applied in educated use to invertebrate animals.

c **825** *Vesp. Psalter* viii. 9 Fuglas heofenes & fiscas saes. *c* **1175** *Lamb. Hom.* 129 Alle þe fiscas þe swummen in þere se. *c* **1200** *Trin. Coll. Hom.* 177 Fishshes and fugeles. *c* **1250** *Gen. & Ex.* 160 God made..ilc fuel and euerilc fis. *c* **1290** *S. Eng. Leg.* I. 10/302 A fair ȝwater with grete fischsches. *c* **1386** CHAUCER *Prol.* 180 A Monk, whan he is recchelees, Is likned til a fissh þat is waterlees. **1485** CAXTON *Chas. Gt.* 205 Fysshes alle blacke. **1535** COVERDALE *1 Kings* iv. 33 He talked..of foules, of wormes, of fiszshes. **1653** WALTON *Angler* 179 He [the Pearch] is one of the fishes of prey. **1695** WOODWARD *Nat. Hist. Earth* III. i. (1723) 153 Whales..and other great Fishes. **1719** W. WOOD *Surv. Trade* 334 Shells of Fishes, known by the Name of Cowries. **1726** GAY *Fables* I. iv. 37 The Fishes..skim beneath the main. **1774** GOLDSM. *Nat. Hist.* IV. 3 The whale, the limpet, the tortoise and the

oyster.. as men have been willing to give them all the name of fishes, it is wisest for us to conform. **1842** H. MILLER *O.R. Sandst.* iii. (ed. 2) 68 Fishes seem to have been the master existences of five succeeding formations, ere the age of reptiles began.

b. *collect. sing.* used for *pl.*

a **1300** *Cursor M.* 9395 (Cott.), Foghul and fiche, grett thing and small. *c* **1400** MAUNDEV. (Roxb.) xiii. 57 Criste.. filled þaire nettes full of fisch. **1486** *Bk. St. Albans* F vij a, A scoll of ffysh. **1556** *Chron. Gr. Friars* (1852) 48 Herrynge and other fyche that was tane on the see. **1563** *Myrr. Mag., Somerset* xxiii, For the fyshe casting forth his net. **1611** BIBLE *Num.* xi. 22 Shal all the fish of the sea bee gathered together for them? **1667** MILTON *P.L.* VII. 401 Fish.. with thir Finns and shining Scales Glide under the green Wave. **1715-20** POPE *Iliad* XXI. 136 Let the Fish surround Thy bloated Corse. **1780** COWPER *Let. to Mrs. Newton* 2 June, When I write to you, you answer me in fish. I return you many thanks for the mackerel and lobster. **1802-3** tr. *Pallas' Trav.* (1812) II. 132 Such port is frequented by fish of passage. **1808** FORSYTH *Beauties Scotl.* v. 384 Herrings.. mackerel, cod-fish, whitings, hadocks, and some others, may with propriety be called fish of passage.

c. phr. ***a nice*** or ***pretty kettle of fish*** (colloq.): an awkward state of things, a 'muddle'. ***to be*** or ***feel like a fish out of water***: to be or feel out of one's element. ***drunk*** (***dull, mute***) ***as a fish***: very drunk (etc). ***to drink like a fish***: to drink excessively. ***to feed the fishes***: (*a*) to meet one's death by drowning; (*b*) to be sea-sick. ***all is fish that comes to*** or †***in*** (***his***) ***net***: i.e. nothing comes amiss to him, he turns everything to account.

1523 LD. BERNERS *Froiss.* I. ccccxvi. 727 Suche as came after toke all.. for all was fysshe that came to net. **1613** PURCHAS *Pilgrimage* VI. xii. 636 The Arabians out of the desarts are as Fishes out of the Water. *c* **1620** Z. BOYD *Zion's Flowers* (1855) 48 All's fish that comes in net. **1654** GATAKER *Disc. Apol.* 7 He is as mute as a fish. **1700** CONGREVE *Way of World* IV. ix, Thou art both as drunk and as mute as a fish. **1744** GRAY *Let.* 26 Apr. in *Wks.* (1807) II. 35 Mr. Trollope and I are in a course of Tar-water;.. I drink like a Fish. **1769** FALCONER *Dict. Marine* (1789) Ggg ij, To cruise as a pirate; to make all fish that comes to the net. **1821** J. G. LOCKHART *Let.* 13 July, He.. drinks like a fish. **1840** MARRYAT *Poor Jack* xi, You're as mute as a fish. **1837** HOOD *Drinking Song* xi, He's the.. drinker that verily 'drinks like a fish!' **1865** J. G. BERTRAM *Harvest of Sea* (1873) 228 Being a commission agent, it is all fish that comes to my net. **1870** H. MEADE *Ride N. Zealand* 313 His first act was to appease the fishes.. by feeding them most liberally. **1879** [see DRINK *v.*¹ 11 a]. **1886** BARING GOULD *Court Royal* vi, The lawyer.. was as a fish out of water here. **1889** BRIDGES *Feast of Bacchus* IV, And there you stand, As dull as a fish! **1937** A. J. CRONIN *Citadel* I. ii. 19, I better anticipate the gay tidings—I drink like a fish.

d. In other proverbial expressions.

1546 J. HEYWOOD *Prov.* (1562) D ij b, Fishe is caste awaie that is cast in drie pooles. *a* **1625** FLETCHER *Mons. Thomas* I. iii, No swearing; He'll catch no fish else. **1630** J. TAYLOR (Water P.) Wks. I. 117/2 The Prouerbe sayes, If you sweare you shall catch no fish. **1710** *Brit. Apollo* III. No. 29 3/2 'Tis good Fish, if it were but Caught. **1857** TROLLOPE *Three Clerks* xvi, There were still as good fish in the sea as had ever yet been caught out of it.

†**e.** in the quasi-oath ***God's fish!*** (more commonly ODDS-FISH).

c **1728** EARL AILESBURY *Mem.* 649 Gods fish! when two rogues fall out, their master then is like to know the truth.

f. Applied to the turtle.

1898 *Westm. Gaz.* 9 Nov. 3/1 The sea round about the West Indies is the happiest hunting-ground for green turtle. The fish (the dealers describe them as fish) are usually taken in the manner described. **1908** *Daily Chron.* 6 Nov. 7/3 The 'fish', as they are called in the trade, are probably as tenacious of life as any animal.

g. *U.S. slang.* A dollar.

1920 *Collier's* 5 June 44/4, I.. shoved my way Through the howlin' mob on the en route to the box office To collect our four hundred fish. **1934** WODEHOUSE *Thank you, Jeeves* xii. 168 She was heiress to a sum amounting to more than fifty million fish. **1949** N. ALGREN *Man with Golden Arm* 11 Used to get fifteen fish for an exhibition of six-no-count.

h. *Naut. slang.* (In full ***tin fish.***) A torpedo; also, a submarine.

1925 FRASER & GIBBONS *Soldier & Sailor Words* 282 *A tin fish*, a torpedo. **1928** *Papers Mich. Acad. Sci. & Arts* X. 293 *Fish*, torpedo;.. submarine. **1943** *Penguin New Writing* XVI. 19 The air seemed full of falling bombs, and tinfish like carelessly dropped cigarettes splashed among the crowded ships. **1946** R. HARLING *Steep Atlantick Stream* ii. 29 They do say the old QM's had a tin-fish under her tail. **1967** B. KNOX *Blacklight* i. 16 The Navy didn't like losing a torpedo... Each 'fish' represented some £3,000 in cash.

2. In combination with various qualifying words, as *lantern-, lump-, monk-, pipe-, rock-, toad-, whistle-, wolf-*: see those words. **blubber-fish**, fish yielding blubber, as the whale, porpoise, etc. **royal-fish**, also ***fish-royal*** (see quots.). Also ANGEL-, FLAT-, FLYING-, GOLD-, JELLY-, SHELL-, SUN-, SWORD-FISH.

1756 R. ROLT *Dict. Trade & Comm., Royal fish*, are dolphins and sturgeons; as also in France, are salmon and trout; so called, because they belong to the King, when cast upon the sea-shore.. *Blubber-fish* are whales, porpoises, tunnies, sea-calves, and other fat fish. **1776** *Customs Manor of Epworth* in Stonehouse *Axholme* (1839) 145 When any *fish royal be taken in the river of Trent, within this Manor.. it belongs to the Lord of the Manor. **1867** SMYTH *Sailor's Word-bk., Royal Fish*, whale and sturgeon.

3. a. Applied *fig.* to a person (also *collect.* to persons) whom it is desirable to 'catch' or 'hook'.

1722 DE FOE *Col. Jack* (1840) 116 The subtle devil.. found us proper fish for her hook. **1753** FOOTE *Eng. in Paris* II. Wks. 1799 I. 42 The fish [a rich young booby] is hook'd. **1885** *Boy's Own Paper* 5 Sept. 771/1 People would think he was an easy fish to catch.

b. Used (with prefixed adj.) unceremoniously for 'person'.

1750 COVENTRY *Pompey Litt.* II. ix. (1785) 67/2 They.. smoaked him for a queer fish, as the phrase is. **1771** FRANKLIN *Autobiog.* Wks. 1887 I. 137 He was an odd fish. **1820** LAMB *Elia, South-Sea-House*, Humourists, for they were of all descriptions.. Odd fishes. **1831** *Examiner* 395/2 The lady, who was a 'loose fish,' became acquainted with him. **1857** HUGHES *Tom Brown* I. (1882) 19/2 The queerest, coolest fish in Rugby. **1871** J. H. BANKA *State Prison Life* iv. 60 'Fresh fish' is the name applied to all newcomers. **1920** F. SCOTT FITZGERALD *This Side of Paradise* I. i. 36 I'm tired of being nice to every poor fish in school. **1930** A. CHRISTIE *Murder at Vicarage* x. 79 Well—of all the poor fish! If I'd committed a murder, I wouldn't go straight off and give myself up. **1958** *Listener* 9 Oct. 568/1 The old man is revealed as having been a very cold fish.

4. a. The flesh of fish, *esp.* as used for food; opposed to *flesh*, i.e. the flesh of land-animals, and *fowl*, that of birds.

a **1300** *Cursor M.* 13502 (Gött.) þis bred and fisse was delt abute. **1393** LANGL. *P. Pl.* C. VII. 159 Hij eteþ more fisch þan flesh. **1398** TREVISA *Barth. De P.R.* XIII. xxvi. (1495) 461 Female fysshes ben more longe than male fysshes and haue more harde fysshe. *c* **1400** *Lanfranc's Cirurg.* 60 Salt fisch. *c* **1460** LYDG. & BURGH *Secrees* 1653 In etyng of ffyssh make no contynuaunces. **1568** GRAFTON *Chron.* II. 232 Ships.. furnished with Bisket.. freshe Water, salt Fishe. **1650** SIR T. BROWNE *Pseud. Ep.* (ed. 2) III. xxv. 143 We mortifie ourselves with the diet of fish. **1756** R. ROLT *Dict. Trade & Comm., Green Fish* is that which is just salted, and yet moist. **1768** TRAVIS in Pennant *Zool.* (1777) IV. 12 The fish of a Lobster's claw is more tender, delicate, and easy of digestion than that of the tail. **1813** SIR H. DAVY *Agric. Chem.* (1814) 288 Fish forms a powerful manure.

b. Meat having the qualities of fish.

1607 TOPSELL *Four-f. Beasts* (1658) 444 The taile of a Beaver is fish, but the taile of an Otter is flesh.

c. phr. ***neither fish nor flesh*** (***nor good red herring***), also ***neither fish, flesh, nor fowl***: i.e. neither one thing nor another; without the particular qualities (or merits) of either. ***to have other fish to fry***: to have other business to attend to. ***to make fish of one and flesh*** (or ***fowl***) ***of another***: to make an invidious distinction; to show partiality. ***to cry stinking fish***: see CRY *v.* 5 b.

1528 *Rede me & be nott wrothe* I iij b, Wone that is nether flesshe nor fisshe. **1546** J. HEYWOOD *Prov.* (1562) C ij b, She is nother fyshe nor fleshe, nor good red hearyng. **1596** SHAKS. *1 Hen. IV*, III. iii. 144. **1600** HOLLAND *Livy* XXIV. xlv. (1609) 540 He had the party himselfe in jelousie and suspition, as one neither fish nor flesh, a man of no credit. **1660** EVELYN *Mem.* (1857) III. 132, I fear he hath other fish to fry. **1682** DRYDEN *Duke of Guise* Epilogue 40 Damned neuters, in their middle way of steering, Are neither fish nor flesh nor good red-herring. **1721** J. KELLY *Sc. Prov.* 220, I will not make Fish of one, and Flesh of another. **1885** *Manch. Exam.* 21 May 5/2 This is making fish of one and fowl of another with a vengeance. **1889** MRS. OLIPHANT *Poor Gent.* xliv, 'I've got other things in hand.. I've got other fish to fry'.

5. *Astron.* **a.** *the Fish* or *Fishes* (L. *Pisces*), a zodiacal constellation, situated between Aquarius and Aries. **b.** *the Southern* (†*South*) *Fish* (L. *Piscis australis*, anciently *Piscis notius major*), a southern constellation, bounded on the north by Capricorn and Aquarius.

c **1386** CHAUCER *Sqr.'s T.* 265 Now dauncen lusty Venus children dere, For in the fyssh her lady sat ful hye. **1551** RECORDE *Cast. Knowl.* (1556) 267 Laste of the 12 signes commeth the Fyshes. *Ibid.* 271 The Southe fyshe, containynge 12 starres.

II. *attrib.* and *Comb.*

6. General relations: **a.** simple attrib. (sense 1), as ***fish-bone, -bowl, -egg, -guts, -haunt, -shell, -skin, -spawn***; (sense 4), as ***fish-dinner, -meal, tea.***

1530 PALSGR. 220/2 *Fysshebonne, *areste*. *a* **1653** GOUGE *Comm. Heb.* xiii. 1 Fish-bones.. in the dark make a bright lustre. **1772-84** COOK *Voy.* (1790) I. 228 The points of these lances are sometimes made of fish-bone. **1906** S. W. BUSHELL *Chinese Art* II. viii. 32 A large garden *fish-bowl.. is decorated in the usual style with enamel colours. **1964** *Listener* 23 Apr. 682/1 The Chinese made their fishbowls out of porcelain. **1661** LOVELL *Hist. Anim. & Min.* Introd., Before the eating of a *fish-dinner, the body is not to be heated with exercise. *a* **1680** EVELYN *Diary* *c* Feb. an. 1646 (1955) II. 474 The famous Anna Rencha, whom we invited to a Fishdinner, after 4 daies in Lent. **1865** J. G. BERTRAM *Harvest Sea* (1873) 66 The collection and distribution of *fish-eggs. **1768** TRAVIS in Pennant *Zool.* (1777) IV. 12 The bait is commonly *fish-guts tied to the bottom and middle of the net. **1833** J. RENNIE *Alph. Angling* 50 The angler.. must find these *fish-haunts. **1597** SHAKS. *2 Hen. IV*, IV. iii. 99 Making many *Fish-meales, they fall into a kind of Male Greene-sicknesse. **1601** HOLLAND *Pliny* II. 307 The said hairs burnt in some earthen pan or *fish-shell. **1774** GOLDSM. *Nat. Hist.* (1776) VII. 366 They are impregnated in the manner of *fish-spawn. **1930** *Daily Express* 16 Aug. 8/7 If there is any Guards officer who is forced to indulge in *fish teas, [etc.].

b. connected with the catching or selling of fish, as ***fish-bag, -bait, -bar, -basket, -boat, -boy, -craft, -creel, -frail, -line, -market, -net,*** †***-officer, -salesman,*** †***-shambles,*** †***-ship, -shop, -spear, -stall, -street, -trap, -van, -wagon, -woman.***

1815 *Sporting Mag.* XLVI. 11 If my *fish-bag should fall in the way of such a man. **1870** 'F. FERN' *Ginger-Snaps* 275 Won't the laundress rub the skin off her knuckles when she tries to get the *fish-bait off your ruffled skirt. **1887** *Mod. London* 195/1 A *fish bar where those tempting little fish luncheons popularly denominated 'snacks' may be had at all hours. **1838** DICKENS *O. Twist* xxi, Women with *fish-baskets on their heads. **1663** SPALDING *Troub. Chas. I* (1829) 82 Eighteen gentlemen.. passing the water of Findhorn in a *fish-boat, were pitifully drowned. **1919** J. MASEFIELD *Reynard* 117 Like a fish-boat beached. **1853** READE *Chr. Johnstone* xiii. 217 The *fish-boys struck up a dismal chant of victory. **1480** CAXTON *Descr. Brit.* 12 Seuarn is swyft of streme, *fishecraft is therin. **1866** *Game Laws Conn.* in *Fur, Fin & Feather* (1872) 34 Shall forfeit the value of the seine and fish-craft used for said purpose. **1953** DYLAN THOMAS *Under Milk Wood* (1954) 33 In you reeled, my boy, as drunk as a deacon with.. a *fish-frail full of stout. **1639** in *Archives Maryland* IV. 79, 2. *fish lines. **1864** J. T. TROWBRIDGE *Cudjo's Cave* xliii. 451 Arms and head hung down, causing him to resemble.. a frog hooked on for bait at the end of a fish-line. **1913** J. LONDON *Valley of Moon* III. i, Hall had sent out fish-lines and a swimming suit. **1552** HULOET, *Fishe market and fishe streate. **1863** MISS BRADDON *Eleanor's Vict.* i, The slimy and slippery fish market. *a* **1000** *Boeth. Metr.* xix. 21 Hwy ȝe nu ne settan on sume dune *fisc net eowru. *c* **1200** *Trin. Coll. Hom.* 175 Werpinde ut here fishnet in þe se. **1955** E. POUND *Classic Anthol.* I. 20 Goose to get in a fish-net set! **1472** *Presentmts. of Juries* in *Surtees Misc.* (1890) 23 þt þy sell noy feche wt owt yt be abyld be *fyche offesers. **1868** PEARD *Water-Farm.* xv. 154 An eminent *fish-salesman. **1601** HOLLAND *Pliny* I. 243 The Maquerels.. furnish the *fish shambles. **1676** *Lond. Gaz.* No. 1144/1 Several English *Fish Ships are arrived. **1827** HONE *Every-day Bk.* II. 58 Pedestrians.. turn in to sup at the *fish-shops. **1611** BIBLE *Job* xli. 7 Canst thou fill.. his head with *fish-speares? **1837** R. M. BIRD *Nick of Woods* II. xi. 144 Upon this pillar.. were laid or suspended sundry Indian utensils of the kitchen and the field,.. wooden bowls.. fish spears [etc.]. **1908** E. J. BANFIELD *Confessions of Beachcomber* I. iv. 150 To enjoy it to perfection, extricate the creature from his lurking place far down in the blue crevice of the coral, with a fish-spear. **1818** *Sporting Mag.* II. 100 Well pleas'd with the bargain, she left the *fish-stall. **1837** W. IRVING *Capt. Bonneville* III. 44 Trout and other fish, which they catch.. in '*fish traps'. **1858** SIMMONDS *Dict. Trade*, **Fish-van*, a light spring-cart for transporting fish; a railway truck set apart for fish. **1865** TYLOR *Early Hist. Man.* i. 11 The *fish waggon comes by. **1698** J. CRULL *Muscovy* 141 You may hear them.. Abuse one another like *Fish-Women. **1855** MACAULAY *Hist. Eng.* IV. 170 In those private letters.. the Princess expressed the sentiments of a fury in the style of a fish-woman.

c. in the names of dishes, etc., composed of fish, as ***fish-ball,*** †***-broo, -broth, -cake, -chowder,*** †***-pickle, -pie, -pudding, -soup, -stock.***

1854 B. P. SHILLABER *Mrs. Partington* 100 The breakfast was waiting for him, the *fishballs were getting cold. **1872** E. A. HART *Runaway* iii. 67 The viands that it might be possible to carry out to Olga. Soup?.. Fish-balls? **1883** *Fisheries Exhib. Catal.* 316 Fish Balls, with Brown Sauce. **14..** *Nominale* in Wr.-Wülcker 740 *Garus*, a *fysc-browe. **1660** HOWELL *Lex. Tetrag.*, *Fish-broth, or fish-pickle, *murette de poisson*. **1854** *Harper's Mag.* May 802/1 The favorite comestible was the *piroga*, a very unctuous kind of *fish-cake. **1883** *Fisheries Exhib. Catal.* 316 Fishcakes in Curry. **1838** E. C. WINES *Trip to Boston* 79 We had 'clam chowder' and '*fish chowder'. **1897** KIPLING *Capt. Cour.* 84 Harvey stuffed himself to the brim on fish-chowder and fried pies. **1725** BRADLEY *Fam. Dict.*, **Fish Pie*, a Dish usually serv'd upon Days of Abstinence. **1883** *Fisheries Exhib. Catal.* 316 *Fish Pudding, in tins. **1723** J. NOTT *Cook's & Confect. Dict.* No. 136 B, Strain it through a Sieve.. and use it to simmer *Fish-soops. **1886** *Sat. Rev.* 6 Mar. 328/1 Fish soup is made out of the 'trimmings' of fish. **1787** J. FARLEY *Lond. Art of Cookery* (ed. 4) 166 Take what quantity may be wanted of *fish-stock. **1883** A. THOMAS *Mod. Housewife* 51 The receipt for a fish-stock which is as strengthening and succulent as can well be desired.

d. objective, as ***fish-breeder, -cadger, -catcher, -curer, -frier, -hawker, -seller; fish-breeding, -packing***, vbl. sbs.; ***fish-eating, -producing, -selling***, ppl. adjs.

1860 *Rep. U.S. Comm. Patents: Agric. 1859* 232 Practical hints to *fish breeders. **1883** E. R. LANKESTER *Adv. Science* (1890) 214 So far as it affects the procedure of fish-catchers, fish-breeders, or fish-culturists. **1860** *Rep. U.S. Comm. Patents: Agric. 1859* 232 The best methods of securing success in artificial *fish breeding. **1889** BARRIE *Window in Thrums* 189 Hendry had been to the *fish-cadger in the square. **1530** PALSGR. 220/2 *Fysse catcher, *peschevr*. **1847-8** H. MILLER *First Impr.* x. (1857) 166, I have seen a *fish-curer's vat throwing down its salt when surcharged with the mineral. **1835-6** TODD *Cycl. Anat.* I. 323/1 The *fish-eating Osprey. **1892** *Encycl. Cookery* I. 660/1 Larger fish require a vessel called a *fish-fryer, which is fitted with a perforated or wire strainer. **1893** *Daily News* 14 Apr. 6/6 The wife of a fish-frier. **1866** *Cornh. Mag.* May 616 *Fish-hawkers wrangle and organ-grinders count their ill-gotten coppers. **1890** *Westm. Gaz.* 30 Sept. 3/1 The *fish-producing lakes and rivers. *c* **1440** *Promp. Parv.* 163/1 *Fysch sellare, *piscarius*. **1768-74** TUCKER *Lt. Nat.* (1852) I. 475 *Fish-selling rhetoricians.

e. similative, as †***fish-drunk, -eyed, -faced, -haunted, -like, -shaped***, adjs.

1591 PERCIVALL *Sp. Dict., Embarbascar*, to make *fishe drunke. **1937** L. C. DOUGLAS *Forgive our Trespasses* x. 199 Its *fish-eyed challenge that dared any man to speed its heart. *a* **1940** W. J. TURNER *Sea Music* in P. M. Jones *Mod. Verse* (1940) 138 Thro' the fish-eyed meadows Flows the herd-pasturing ocean. **1963** WODEHOUSE *Stiff Upper Lip, Jeeves* xviii. 143 He's no worse than that *fishfaced blighter. **1887** MORRIS tr. *Homer's Odyssey* x. 458, I myself, I know, How on the sea *fish-haunted ye bore a weight of woe. **1952** C. DAY LEWIS tr. *Virgil's Aeneid* XI. 248 The fish-haunted river Padusa. **1610** SHAKS. *Temp.* II. ii 27 A very ancient and *fish-like smell. **1835-6** TODD *Cycl. Anat.* I. 93/2 The elongated fish-like form of those amphibia. **1840** DICKENS *Barn. Rudge* (1849) 3/2 Dull fish-like eyes. **1878** H. H. GIBBS *Ombre* 8 The counters should be long or *fish-shaped.

f. instrumental and originative, as ***fish-derived, -fed, -feeding***, adjs.

1883 *Fisheries Exhib. Catal.* p. xxxvi, *Fish-derived products. **1614** SYLVESTER *Bethulian's Rescue* v. 297 *Fish-fed Carmanians. **1835–6** TODD *Cycl. Anat.* I. 280/1 The *fish-feeding *Grallæ.*

g. appositive, as ***fish-god, -goddess.***

1856 STANLEY *Sinai & Pal.* v. (1856) 256 Dagon the *Fish-god. *Ibid.*, Derceto, the *Fish-goddess.

7. Special comb.: **fish and chips**, a dish consisting of fried fish and fried chipped potatoes; also *ellipt.* for a shop at which this dish may be bought ready-cooked; also *attrib.*, esp. in form ***fish-and-chip***; **fish-backed** *a.*, shaped like a fish's back, swelling upwards; † **fish-basil** (see quot.); **fish-basket**, (*a*) a basket used for carrying fish (see 6 b); (*b*) *U.S.*, a creel for catching fish; **fish-bed**, a deposit containing the fossil remains of fishes; **fish-bellied** *a.*, shaped like a fish's belly, 'curved underneath, the depth of curve increasing towards the centre' (Lockwood); **fish belly**, (*a*) see quot. 1878; (*b*) *attrib.*, = *fish-bellied*, adj.; (*c*) used *attrib.* of a degree of whiteness; **fish-berry**, a name for *Cocculus indicus*, the fruit of *Anamirta cocculus*, used for stupefying fish; **fish-blooded** *a.*, cold-blooded; **fishbone-stitch** (see quot. 1957); **fish-bone-thistle** = *fish-thistles*; **fish-bone-tree**, 'the *Panax crassifolium*, a small araliaceous tree of New Zealand' (*Cent. Dict.*); **fish-brine**, a fish-sauce; **fish-broth** (see 6 c), *humorously*, salt-water; **fish-car**, a box in which fish are carried alive in the water; **fish-carle** *Sc.*, a fisherman (Jam.); **fish-carrier**, (*a*) a vessel used to transport the 'catch' from the fishing-boats to the shore; (*b*) a contrivance for keeping fish alive whilst transporting them from place to place; **fish-carver**, a carving knife for fish; *pl.* a carving knife and fork for fish; † **fish-climber**, ? = *fish-berry*; **fish-coop**, (*a*) = *fish-pot*; (*b*) 'a box about three feet square used in fishing through ice' (*Cent. Dict.*); **fish-crow** (*U.S.*), a crow (*Corvus ossifragus*) that feeds mainly on fish; **fish-culture**, the artificial breeding of fish, pisciculture; hence **fish-cultural** *a.*, of, pertaining to, or concerned in fish-culture, piscicultural; **fish-culturist**, one engaged in fish-culture, a fish-breeder, a pisciculturist; **fish dive** (see quot. 1952); **fish-eagle**, an eagle that preys upon fish; † **fish-ear** (see quot.); **fish-eater**, (*a*) one who lives chiefly upon fish; (*b*) chiefly *pl.* a knife and fork to eat fish with; **fish-eye**, (*a*) (also *fish's eye*) a variety of moonstone; a diamond or imitation diamond; (*b*) (see quot. 1958); (*c*) used *attrib.* or as *adj.* of a wide-angle lens with a curved front resembling a fish's eye; also *ellipt.*; **fish-eye-stone** *Min.*, obs. synonym of APOPHYLLITE; **fish-face**, a term of abuse; **fish-fag**, a female hawker of fish, a fishwife; **fish-farm**, a place where fish-culture is carried on; hence **fish-farmer**, **fish-farming**; † **fish-fast**, the observance of fish-days (see FISH-DAY); **fish-finder**, a device for locating fish; **fish finger**, a small finger-shaped or rectangular section of fish coated in batter or breadcrumbs; **fish-flake** (*U.S.*), a frame upon which fish is laid to dry; **fish-flour**, (*a*) = *fish-meal*; (*b*) 'a dry inodorous fertilizer made from fishes, used for manure' (*Cent. Dict.*); **fish-fly** *U.S.*, any of various small insects belonging to the order Megaloptera and family Corydalidæ, especially those included in the genus *Chauliodes*; **fish food**, (*a*) = FISH *sb.*^{1} 4; (*b*) the food eaten by fishes; **fish-fry**, (*a*) *U.S.*, a picnic where fish is fried and eaten; (*b*) = FRY *sb.*^{1} 3; **fish-gaff**, a pole with an iron hook at the end by means of which heavy fish are secured when caught with a line; **fish geranium** *U.S.*, a garden variety of geranium, *Pelargonium hortorum*; **fish-globe**, a spherical glass vessel in which fish are kept; **fish-glue**, glue obtained from the bladders and sounds of fish, isinglass; **fish-gorge**, a primitive implement for catching fish, consisting of something (e.g. a stone) fastened by a string for the fish to swallow; **fish guano** = *fish-manure*; **fish-hack**, a name of the *Gobius niger* (Adm. Smyth); **fish-hatchery**, a place for the rearing of fish by artificial means; so **fish-hatching** *vbl. sb.*; **fish-hawk**, the osprey, or bald-buzzard (*Pandion haliaëtus*); **fish-horn**, a tin horn used on fishing-boats or by sellers of fish; **fish-house**, †(*a*) a place where fish are kept; (*b*) a place where fish is sold; **fish insect** = SILVER-FISH 2; **fish-kettle**, a long oval vessel for boiling fish; **fish-knife**, a broad knife, usually of silver, for cutting and serving fish at table; also, a knife for eating fish with; **fish-ladder**, a series of steps to enable fish to ascend a fall or dam by a succession of leaps; **fish-leaves**, the pondweed *Potamogeton natans*, the flat leaves of which were formerly supposed to give shelter to fish; † **fish-leep**, a fish-basket; **fish-liquor**, the liquid in which a fish has been boiled; **fish-liver-oil**, a term applied to the oil obtained from other fish than the cod (*Syd. Soc. Lex.* 1884); **fish-lock** = *fish-weir*; **fish-louse**, a general name for crustaceans parasitic on fishes; **fish-man**, †(*a*) one who makes a meal of fish; (*b*) a fish hawker; (*c*) a fisherman; (*d*) a student of ichthyology; **fish-manure**, a manure or fertilizer composed of fish; † **fish-mariner**, the sail-fish; **fish-maw**, the sound or air-bladder of a fish; **fish-meal**, dried fish ground to a meal; **fish-meter** (see quot.); † **fish-mint**, water-mint; **fish-moth** = SILVER-FISH 2; **fish-net**, used *attrib.* of an open-meshed fabric or garment; **fish-oil**, oil obtained from fishes and marine animals, *spec.* cod-liver oil and whale oil; **fish-owl**, an eared fishing owl, of the genus *Ketupa*, with rough feet; **fish paper**, (*a*) paper on which cooked fish is laid; (*b*) (see quot. 1924); **fish-pass** = *fish-way*; **fish paste** = PASTE *sb.* 1 d; **fish-pearl**, an artificial pearl (see quot.); **fish-plate**, the perforated draining plate of a fish-kettle; **fish-poison**, a name given to various plants which have an intoxicating effect upon fish, causing them to float helplessly on the surface of the water; **fish pole** *U.S.*, a pole used as a fishing-rod; **fish-pomace**, the refuse of fish after the oil has been expressed, used as a fertilizer; **fish-pot**, a wicker basket for catching fish, *esp.* eels, also crabs, lobsters, etc.; **fish-potter**, one who uses or has charge of fish-pots; † **fish-range**, a place for catching and drying fish; **fish-room** (see quots.); **fish-sauce**, sauce made to be eaten with fish; **fish sausage**, a sausage made with fish; **fish-scrap**, fish refuse, used as a fertilizer; **fish-slice**, a fish-carving knife; also, an implement used by cooks for turning fish in the pan; **fish-slide**, 'a fish-trap for shallow rivers and low waterfalls: used in the southern United States' (*Cent. Dict.*); **fish-sound**, the swimming bladder of a fish; † **fish-stew** = FISH-POND: see STEW; **fish stick**, (*a*) (see quot. 1875); (*b*) *N. Amer.* = *fish finger*; † **fish-stone**, ? a stone table for the sale of fish; **fish-story**, an incredible tale or 'yarn'; † **fish-stove** = *fish-stew*; **fish-strainer**, (*a*) 'a metal cullender with handles for taking fish from a boiler; (*b*) an earthenware slab with holes, placed at the bottom of a dish to drain the water from cooked fish' (Simmonds); **fish supper**, a supper meal with fish as the main course; *spec.* (esp. *Sc.*), a meal of fish and chips bought from a take-away restaurant; **fish tank**, a tank to hold live (esp. ornamental) fish, an aquarium; **fish-thistles**, the *Chamæpeuce casabonæ* (*Syd. Soc. Lex.* 1884); **fish-tiger**, a bird that preys upon fish; **fish-tongue**, 'an instrument sometimes used for the removal of the wisdom-teeth: so named from its shape' (*Syd. Soc. Lex.* 1884); **fish-torpedo**, a torpedo resembling a fish in shape and with an automatic swimming action; **fish-trowel**, a fish-carver in the shape of a trowel; **fish-warden** (*U.S.*), 'an officer who has jurisdiction over the fisheries of any particular locality' (*Cent. Dict.*); **fish-way**, an arrangement for enabling fish to ascend a fall or dam; **fish-weir**, †(*a*) a draught of fishes; (*b*) = FISH-GARTH; **fish-wood**, (*a*) (see quot.); (*b*) 'the strawberry bush, *Euonymus americanus*' (*Cent. Dict.*); **fish-worker**, 'a fishculturist' (*Cent. Dict.*); **fish-working**, 'fish-culture' (*Cent. Dict.*); **fish-works**, (*a*) 'the appliances and contrivances used in fish-culture; (*b*) a place where the products of the fisheries are utilized; a fish-factory' (*Cent. Dict.*); **fish-worm** *U.S.* = EARTHWORM 1; cf. WORM 8 b; † **fish-yard** = FISH-GARTH. Also FISH-DAY, -GIG, -HOOK, -MONGER, -POND, -POOL, -SKIN, -TAIL, -WHOLE, -WIFE.

1876 in *Listener* (1965) 3 June 826/3 *Fish and chip shops were a considerable source of nuisance. **1913** ROWNTREE & KENDALL *How Labourer Lives* iii. 169 Fish and chips.. 3[d.]. **1928** D. SAYERS *Unpleasantness at Bellona Club* x. 122 We'll go and see 'George Barnwell' at the Elephant and have a fish-and-chips supper afterwards. **1940** *Economist* 26 Oct. 517/2 The fish and chips sellers have been blessed by the Ministry of Food. **1948** J. BETJEMAN *Coll. Poems* (1958) 219 Ask at the fish and chips in the Market Square. **1961** E. A. POWDRILL *Vocab. Land Planning* iii. 44 A study of social rank will normally involve an examination of population,.. poverty shops (fish and chips, secondhand dealers, pawnbrokers, etc.). **1970** *Which?* Mar. 68/2 If it is classified as a dwelling house, you can't use it as a fish and chip shop without first getting planning permission. **1825** J. NICHOLSON *Operat. Mechanic* 644 *Fish-backed rail. **1597** GERARDE *Herbal* II. ccxiii. 549 L'Obelius..calleth it [another wilde Basill] *Corcoros*, which we have Englished *Fish Basill. **1814** H. M. BRACKENRIDGE *Views Louisiana* 179 They unite, and thus form a semicircle like a *fish basket. **1844** S. S. HALDEMAN in Schele de Vere *Americanisms* (1872) 351 Various species are abundantly caught..in fish-baskets, made of lath-work, with diverging walls of stone. **1867** *Game Laws Penn.* in *Fur, Fin & Feather* (1872) 100 It shall not be lawful to take, catch, or kill..any fish, by means of any fish-basket. **1955** E. POUND *Classic Anthol.* I. 16 So come not near my dam and weir, Let my fish-basket be. **1869** *Rep. Comm. Agric. 1868* (U.S.) 75 Bones of marine animals are so abundant as to have induced Professor L. Agassiz, twenty years ago, to call it the '*fish bed' of the Charleston Basin. **1834** *Edin. Rev.* LX. 118 *Fish-bellied instead of parallel rails. **1862** SMILES *Engineers* III. 282 The line was..laid with fish-bellied rails. **1878** W. DICKINSON *Cumbld. Gloss.* 33/1 **Fish belly*, the *Cnicus heterophyllus* plant. The underside of the leaf is white, and turns up in the wind. **1884** 'MARK TWAIN' *Huck. Finn* 31 A tree-toad white, a fish-belly white. **1888** GREENWELL *Gloss. Coal-trade terms* (ed. 3) 38 Malleable iron rails of the fish-belly pattern. **1927** A. CONAN DOYLE *Case Bk. S. Holmes* 63 Fish-belly whiteness. **1898** *Westm. Gaz.* 14 Jan. 3/1 Not that the historian is *fish-blooded and without predisposition. **1923** *Daily Mail* 27 Feb. 8 The Ministerial policy of fish-blooded neutrality. **1932** D. C. MINTER *Mod. Needlecraft* 182/2 Note *fish-bone stitch on frayed edges. **1957** M. B. PICKEN *Fashion Dict.* 131/1 *Fishbone-stitch*, series of diagonal single-purl stitches zigzagged across an unmarked line. **1882** *Garden* 1 Apr. 220/1 *Chamæpeuce* (*Fish-bone Thistle). *c* **1000** ÆLFRIC *Gloss.* in Wr.-Wülcker 128 *Liquamen, uel garum*, *fiscbryne. **1820** W. TOOKE tr. *Lucian* I. 553 From inadvertence pour the fish-brine into their lentil-soup. **1599** NASHE *Lenten Stuffe* 44 The churlish frampold waues gaue him his belly-full of *fish-broath. **1883** *Fisheries Exhib. Catal.* 199 Model of *fish-car towed by the smack for keeping the catch alive. **1804** TARRAS *Elegy on Sautie* 11 Poems 143 Ye *fish-carles never lift an oar, In codlin greed. **1886** *Pall Mall G.* 29 June 4/1, I went out to the fleets on board a steam *fish-carrier. **1888** *Ibid.* 27 Dec. 2/2 Among Mr. Burgess's other notions, however, one took the form of a fish carrier. The carrier he has invented is made of zinc. **1855** E. ACTON *Mod. Cookery* (rev. ed.) p. xxxvii, (*caption*) *Fish Carvers. **1697** DAMPIER *Voy.* (1729) III. I. 447 *Fish-Climer has a welted Stalk..its Beans are red, with a black Kernel: these being bruised and cast into Rivers intoxicate the Fish. **1803** S. PEGGE *Anecd. Eng. Lang.* 277 A *fish-coop..for taking fish in the Humber, made of twigs, such as are called eel pots in the south. **1812** A. WILSON *Amer. Ornith.* V. 27 *Fish-crow: *Corvus ossifragus*. **1870** *Amer. Naturalist* III. 287 The Fish-crows..are running over the wet sands. **1883** *Century Mag.* Sept. 682/2 The fish-crow fishes only when it has destroyed all the eggs and young birds it can find. **1865** J. G. BERTRAM *Harvest of Sea* (1873) 61 The art of *fish-culture is almost as old as civilization itself. **1872** (*title*), Transactions of the American *Fish Cultural Association. **1874** *Amer. Cycl.* III. 219 This method has been extensively adopted by American *fish culturists. **1943** K. AMBROSE *Ballet-Lover's Pocket Bk.* iii. 40 A lift from the climax of the Aurora *pas de deux*; known to dancers as the '*fish dive'. **1952** KERSLEY & SINCLAIR *Dict. Ballet Terms* 78 *Poisson*, a position of the body in which the dancer arches her back, lifts her head, and bends back her legs with the feet crossed. This pose may be sustained while jumping..or in double work when the girl is supported in this position and the term *pas poisson* or *fish dive* is used. **1959** *Times* 26 Jan. 6/5 Her dancing betrayed signs of unsteadiness only in the exacting 'fish-dives' in the final *pas-de-deux*. **1678** RAY *Willughby's Ornith.* II. 59 A Fisher-man of Strasburgh..sets forth the Bald Buzzard under the title of *Fish-Eagle. **1890** H. M. STANLEY in *Pall Mall G.* 28 June 2/2 Fish eagles. **1748** *Phil. Trans.* XLV. 233 The other [order of Fishes] is furnish'd with Organs analogous to Lungs, which we call *Fish-Ears, or Gills. **1741** CHAMBERS *Cycl.*, *Ichthyophagi*, *Fish-eaters. **1849** SOUTHEY *Comm-pl. Bk.* Ser. 11, Babylonian Fish-eaters. **1883** *Fisheries Exhib. Catal.* 78 Fish Eaters, Fish Carvers. **1882** E. W. STREETER *Prec. Stones* (ed. 3) 96 The '*Fish's Eye' becomes red by transmitted light, undergoing the same changes as a bead of Schmetze paste. **1914** JACKSON & HELLYER *Vocab. Criminal Slang* 33 *Fish eye*,..a diamond. **1916** F. B. WADE *Diamonds* vi. 139 The stone that is too thin will have a ring of brilliancy around a black and empty centre producing the so-called 'fish eye' effect. **1942** *Metal Progress* XLII. 201 (*heading*) Fish-eyes in steel welds caused by hydrogen. *Ibid.* 203/2 'Coarsely crystalline fracture' surrounded by normal fibrous metal in tensile and impact specimens showing 'flakes', 'snowflakes', 'fish-eyes', and such variously named seats of hydrogen embrittlement.. can be immediately recognized by that outstanding characteristic whereby the affected zones stand out brilliantly against the darker fibrous background. **1958** A. D. MERRIMAN *Dict. Metallurgy* 94/11 *Fish eyes*, a term used in reference to micro-fissures occurring in steel. **1961** R. SCHREYER et al. *Dict. Photogr.* 192/2 Fish-eye lens. **1969** *Amat. Photogr.* 28 May 73/1 The range of lenses is immense. The widest angle is given by fish-eye types which reduce the image scale at the edges more than in the centre. **1971** *Pop. Photogr.* Aug. 60 (Advt.), A fisheye conversion lens. *Ibid.* 90/1 The fisheye could be used to obtain an even broader coverage. **1805** R. JAMESON *Char. Min.* II. 601 Ichthyophthalmite or *Fish-eye-stone. *a* **1625** FLETCHER *Hum. Lieutenant* I. i, Whether would you, *fish face? **1914** C. MACKENZIE *Sinister St.* II. III. ix. 687 O, shut up, fish-face. **1786** WOLCOTT (P. Pindar) *Bozzy & Piozzi* 21 With vulgar *fish-fags to be forc'd to chat. **1860** *Times* 8 Mar. 8/4 We rail away at one another..with the impotence of fish-fags. **1865** J. G. BERTRAM *Harvest of Sea* (1873) 238 *Fish-farms for the cultivation of the oyster alone. **1876** *All Year Round* 29 Apr. 162/1 Broad-leaved aquatic plants are a real blessing to the *fish farmer. **1869** *Rep. Comm. Agric. 1868* (U.S.) 330 Area for *fish-farming. **1969** *Guardian* 20 Nov. 7/3 Flat fish..spawn only once a year, a productivity level unacceptable to those interested in fish farming. **1554** T. SAMPSON in Strype *Eccl. Mem.* III. App. xviii. 49 *Fish-fasts, vows, pilgrimages. **1961** *New Scientist* 9 Nov. 362/1 In ordinary trawling the *fish-finder apparatus has its transducer set in the hull of the ship. **1962** *Ibid.* 2 Aug. 251/1 An ingenious use of a small magnetic memory drum is made in a new type of fish-finder for trawlers. **1962** *Listener* 22 Mar. 510/1 Cornflakes and frozen *fish-fingers, oven-ready chickens, and wrapped, sliced bread. **1970** *Which?* Apr. 105/1 Fish fingers are white fish fillets, coated with crumbs.

Ibid. 106/1 All the fish fingers are a valuable source of protein. Three fish fingers will give an 8-year-old child a fifth of his or her daily protein requirement. **1837–40** Haliburton *Clockm.* (1862) 195 A sort o' *fish flakes. **1865** Thoreau *Cape Cod* x. 197 The houses here were surrounded by fish-flakes, close up to the sills. **1880** G. B. Goode *Menhaden* 141 (Cent. Dict.) Biscuits made from *fish-flour..were in good condition after having been kept for ten years in an unsealed jar. **1956** *Nature* 17 Mar. 512/2 Much attention is being given [in S. Africa] to the production of fish flour in a form suitable for enriching bread. **1963** *Spectator* 15 Feb. 191 Fish flour, which has been developed in the US, would seem to be everything that a cheap, protein-rich food should be. **1968** M. Pyke *Food & Society* ii. 19 An argument about fish 'flour'. This is a product composed of fat-extracted, dried and powdered fish. **1969** N. W. Pirie *Food Resources* v. 140 Initially the product was called 'fish flour'; now however, because of protests from flour millers, it is called 'fish protein concentrate' or FPC. **1866** *Prairie Farmer* 16 June 412/1 (*heading*) Large *Fish Fly. **1902** L. O. Howard *Insect Bk.* 211 The so-called comb-horned fish-fly..is the commonest form throughout the United States. **1955** *Sci. News Let.* 14 May 313/2 The fishfly, which begins its slow, nocturnal flights about this time of the year, is among the earliest insects with complete metamorphosis, fossil records show. **1883** A. Shea *Newfoundland Fisheries* 12 Their excellence would give them a high place in the *fish-food market. **1909** *Westm. Gaz.* 14 Aug. 2/2 Fish-food from the sea. **1926–7** *Army & Navy Stores Catal.* 1149/3 Zoological department... Fish Food—per pkt.— 1½. **1936** *Discovery* Feb. 43/1 On northern streams the Stone Fly and Alder Fly are more numerous, among aquatic insects forming fish food, than the May Fly. **1967** V. Canning *Python Project* ix. 175 Bags of hound meal, fish and bird food were stacked on the floor. **1824** 'A. Singleton' *Lett.* 66 *Fish-fries are held about once in a fortnight. **1936** M. Mitchell *Gone with Wind* ii. 25 For two years he had squired her about the County, to balls, fish fries, picnics and court days. **1951** W. de la Mare *Winged Chariot* 10 Tiniest fish-fry in a rock-bound pool. **1887** *Pall Mall G.* 28 June 6/2 His two sisters..were cut and stabbed with a *fish-gaff. **1865** *Trans. Ill. Agric. Soc.* V. 581, I remarked..on viewing some *fish geraniums..how much their scent was like that emitted from the scales of a fresh fish. **1901** L. H. Bailey *Cycl. Amer. Hort.* III. 1261/2 Fish or Bedding Geraniums. **1946** M. Free *All about House Plants* xvii. 163 House Geraniums (*P[elargonium] hortorum*), also known as Bedding, Horseshoe, Fish and Zonal Geraniums. **1601** Holland *Pliny* II. 438 This *fish-glew [Ichthyocolla] is thought to be best, that is brought out of Pontus. **1676** Worlidge *Cyder* (1691) 151 Isinglass, or Fish-glew. **1861** Hulme tr. *Moquin-Tandon* II. III. 181 Isinglass or Fish-glue is the prepared air-bladder or swimming-bladder of the sturgeon. **1883** B. Phillips in *Century Mag.* Apr. 900/1 Starting with the crude *fish-gorge, I can show, step by step, the complete sequence of the fish-hook. **1856** *Rep. Maine Board Agric.* 81 The manufacture of '*fish guano', as recently attempted. **1884** C. W. Smiley in *U.S. Commiss. of Fish & Fisheries, Report for 1881* 665 Six farmers used about five sacks each of fish guano. **1885** *Fish hatchery [see hatchery]. **1862** *London Society* Aug. 134 All that can be at present done by the press is to show the ease with which a *fish-hatching apparatus can be established. **1869** *Rep. Comm. Agric. 1868* (U.S.) 319 The Chinese..have practised fish-hatching successfully for centuries. **1883** G. B. Goode *Fish. Indust. U.S.* 59 This being needed for fish-hatching purposes, another larger steamer..has just been built. *a* **1813** A. Wilson *Osprey* Poet. Wks. (1846) 280 God bless the *fish-hawk and the fisher! **1848** Thoreau *Maine W.* (1894) 35 Fish-hawks were sailing overhead. **1856** F. S. Cozzens *Sparrowgr. Papers* iii. 38 Mrs. Sparrowgrass asked me who that was 'blowing a *fish-horn'. **1860** J. G. Holland *Miss Gilbert's Career* xix. 351 The instrument leaping out into various angular flourishes, as if a fish-horn had got above its business and were ambitious of the reputation of a key-bugle. **1913** W. W. Thompson *Sea Fisheries Cape Col.* iv. 82 The tuneless reverberations of the archaic fish-horn. **1947** L. G. Green *Tavern of Seas* (1952) i. 7 The fish horn is music only in the ears of those who love Cape Town. *c* **1000** *Ælfric's Gloss.* Supp. in Wr.-Wülcker 184 *Piscinale*, *fischus. **1483** *Cath. Angl.* 132/2 A Fische house, *piscarium*. **1701** *Lond. Gaz.* No. 3748/4 A sand..stretcheth from the South end of the Town to the most Southern Fish-houses. **1877** S. O. Jewett *Deephaven* 224 Going to market was apt to use up a whole morning, especially if we went to the fish-houses. **1905** *Daily Chron.* 21 July 2/7 A common *fish insect, which had been injuring photographs and photographic material. **1948** 'P. Woodruff' *Whatever Dies* 170 There were old copies of the..*Field*, half eaten away by fish-insects. **1681** Grew *Musæum* I. §1. 2 A long Cauldron like a *Fish-kettle. **1823** J. Badcock *Dom. Amusem.* 16 Over the pan, or fish kettle, put a gridiron. **1403** *Nottingham Rec.* II. 20, j. *fyschknyff, ij d. **1825** T. Cosnett *Footman's Directory* 129 Have two soup-ladles and fish-knives. **1826** *The Ass* 1 Apr. 2 You there with the pinking eyes and the fish-knife nose. **1865** *Mich. Gen. Statutes* (1882) I. 574 Sufficient and permanent shutes or *fish ladders to admit of the free and uninterrupted passage of fish over such dam or dams. **1885** Bompas *Life F. Buckland* ix. 189 Many fish-ladders had proved useless. **1886** Britten & Holland *Dict. Eng. Plant-Names* 184 Fish leaves. *c* **1440** *Promp. Parv.* 163/1 *Fysch leep, *nassa*. **1832** Miss Mitford *Village* Ser. v. (1863) 365 He's actually discussing the whole concern! fish, *fish-liquor, bread, and butter, and parsley. **1661** *N. Riding Rec.* VI. 43 The milner of Brignall presented for that he do usually keep in the back beck a *fish-lock. **1540** Sir R. Sadler *State Papers* I. 48, I eat eggs and white meats, because I am an evil *fishman. *a* **1584** *Hist. Tom Thumb* in Hazl. *E.P.P.* II. 220 Tom..is caught by a Fishman. **1794–6** E. Darwin *Zoon.* (1801) IV. 145 A fishman asleep on his panniers. **1805** *Sporting Mag.* XXV. 72 My fish-man of whom I constantly purchase. **1856** L. Agassiz in Bence Jones *Life Faraday* (1870) II. 378 The enthusiastic fish-man whom you met at Dr. Mantell's. **1788** Washington *Diaries* (1925) III. 330 The effect of the *fish Manure w[hi]ch was put into the Corn hills in May last was visible with the Wheat. **1868** *Rep. Mass. Board Agric.* I. 105 Fish manures, the product of the oil-fisheries on our coast.. sell at about forty-five dollars per ton. **1591** Sylvester *Du Bartas* I. v. 381 Thou *Fish-Mariner [*side note* The Sayle-Fish], Thou Boat-Crab. **1840** Malcom *Trav.* 30/1 I tried sharks' fins, birds' nests, *fish-maws. **1858** Simmonds *Dict. Trade*, Fish-maws..are sent to China and used as glue, &c. **1854** Badham *Halieut.* 23 They ate it [fish] raw, dried, or ground down in whalebone mortars into *fish-meal bread. **1967** *Times* 12 Apr. 28/4 Previously fishmeal was used mainly as a fertilizer, but now it is employed as an indispensable ingredient of animal feed. **1880** *Daily News* 8 Nov. 2/5 The officers (*fishmeters as they are called) appointed by the Court of the Fishmongers' Company seized..18 tons 7 cwt. of fish as unfit for human food. **1578** Lyte *Dodoens* II. lxxiv. 245 The seconde wilde kynde..is called..in English *Fisshe Mynte, Brooke Mynte. **1859** R. J. Mann *Natal* viii. 171 It is one of nature's beneficent compensations that the *fish-moth is devoid of wings. **1942** E. O. Essig *College Ent.* v. 70 The silver fish moth, *Lepisma saccharina* Linnaeus, is now almost cosmopolitan in distribution, being known in North America, Europe, China, Japan, and the Hawaiian Islands. **1881** C. C. Harrison *Woman's Handiwork* I. 57 *Fish-net fringe..can be made of *écru* cord..in ordinary fish-net stitch, in large meshes. **1897** *Sears, Roebuck Catal.* 238/2 Hot Weather Specialities... Men's Fish Net Undershirts..with short sleeves. **1933** D. L. Sayers *Murder must Advertise* x. 182 My dear! and got up regardless..fish-net stockings and all. **1861** Hulme tr. *Moquin-Tandon* II. III. 188 Whale oil, known under the name of *Fish oil, is obtained from the Common Greenland Whale. **1887** *Pall Mall G.* 22 Nov. 2/2 The duty-free admission into the States of..fish-oils. **1867** A. L. Adams *Naturalist in India* 114 We were startled one night by the unpleasant laugh of the *fish-owl (*Ketupa ceylonensis*). **1868** M. Jewry *Warne's Model Cookery* 98/2 Slide it [*sc.* the turbot] gently on to a hot dish, on which a folded damask napkin or ornamental *fish paper has been placed. **1924** C. J. West *Class. & Def. Paper* 38 Fish paper, a term applied to a chemically treated board; used..as insulation in building dynamos and motors. **1928** *Daily Mail* 9 Aug. 3/5 Always serve fried fish as hot as possible, dish it on a fish paper, [etc.]. **1873** *Act 36–7 Vict.* c. 71 §17 No person shall ..wilfully scare or hinder salmon from passing through any *fish pass. **1885** Bompas *Life F. Buckland* ix. 189 Varying weirs required different forms of fish-pass. **1920** *Peace Handbks.* (Foreign Office) LXII. 55 Sturgeon..are made into *fish-pastes for local consumption. **1939** T. S. Eliot *Old Possum's Pract. Cats* 31 A spoon and a bit of fishpaste. **1960** A. E. Bender *Dict. Nutrition* 50/1 *Fish paste* legally must contain not less than 70% fish. **1853** Ure *Dict. Arts* II. 361 In Saxony, a cheap but inferior quality [of pearls] is manufactured..They are known by the name of German *fish pearls. **1747** H. Glasse *Art of Cookery* 88 When the Water boils, lay the Turbot on a *Fish-plate. **1802** J. Drayton *View South-Carolina* 67 *Fish poison, horse chesnut, or buck's eye. (*Æsculus Pavia.*) **1846** Lindley *Veget. Kingd.* 384 Serjania triternata is also employed as a fish poison. **1866** Lindley & Moore *Treas. Bot.*, Fish-poison, *Lepidium Piscidium*. Jamaica, *Piscidia Erythrina*. **1884** W. Miller *Dict. Eng. Names Plants* 46/2 Fish-poison-plant. **1834** *Visit to Texas* ix. 88 We touched [a flame] to a few of the tall canes, at this season as dry as *fish poles. **1841** J. F. Cooper *Deerslayer* xiv. 99 Deerslayer..played with the end of a fish-pole in the water. **1957** R. Ruark *Old Man & Boy* 261 'Just the cast net and some fish poles, Lottie,' the old man said sweet as pie. *a* **1555** Philpot *Exam. & Writ.* (Parker Soc.) 336, That *fish-pot or net in the which both good and naughty fishes be contained. **1681** R. Knox *Hist. Ceylon* 28 They place Fish-pots between the Rocks. **1847** Gosse *Birds Jamaica* 430 It was brought to him alive, having been knocked off a fish-pot-buoy. **1820** Southey *Lett.* (1856) III. 183 The *fish-potters being unanimously of opinion that this is not the season. **1699** Dampier *Voy.* II. II. 12 A little to the East of this River is a *Fish-Range.. Here are Poles to hang their Nets on, and Barbecues to dry their Fish. **1815** *Falconer's Dict. Marine*, **Fish-room*, that place between the after-hold and the spirit-room. *c* **1850** *Rudim. Navig.* (Weale) 118 *Fish-room*, a place parted off in the after-hold..It was formerly used for stowing the salt-fish to be consumed on board. **1728** E. Smith *Compl. Housewife* 70 English katchop..is good to put into *Fish Sauce. **1818** Byron *Beppo* vii, I would recommend The curious in fish sauce..to bid their cook..buy..Ketchup. **1937** *N.Y. Times* 16 Mar. 15/2 In Frankfort, the hot dog's home town,..*fish sausage had been introduced on the market. **1965** *Punch* 12 May 682/1 Technology Minister Frank Cousins gave the Commons an interim report on current progress towards the development of the fish sausage. **1969** N. W. Pirie *Food Resources* vii. 163 Also in Japan, 150,000 tons of fish sausage are eaten annually though it was almost unknown a few years ago. **1881** *N.Y. Times* in G. B. Goode *Amer. Fishes* (1888) 112 These smacks are engaged..for the oil-rendering and *fish-scrap works on Barren Island. **1748** H. Glasse *Art of Cookery* (ed. 2) v. 118 Have your *Fish-Slice ready. **1850** Dickens *Dav. Copp.* lxi. 602 We pick out the spoons and forks, fish-slices..and sugar-tongs. **1886** *Punch* 20 Nov. 252/2 The unavoidable absence of the fish-slice. **1879** *Encycl. Brit.* X. 133/1 Gelatin-yielding substances..comprising..bladders and *fish sounds. **1552** Huloet, *Fishe..stewe, *icthyotrophia*. **1885** *Chamb. Jrnl.* 75 A proposal to revive the fish stews or ponds which in bygone times were so plentiful in this country. **1875** J. C. Wilcocks *Sea Fisherm.* 57 A *fish-stick consists generally of a young holly bush deprived of its bark, and the branches left about a foot in length at bottom, diminishing to six inches at the top, the fish being thrust on through a hole in the back. **1953** *Time* 12 Oct. 103 Birds Eye brought out fish sticks (fresh fish coated with a special batter, breaded, fried, packed and then frozen). **1955** *Kingston* (Ont.) *Whig-Standard* 6 Apr. 25/2 The newly developed frozen fish fillets known as fish sticks. **1822** in Picton *L'Pool Munic. Rec.* (1886) II. 379 The erection of such a number of *Fish Stones in Derby Square..as they may think proper for the accommodation of the neighbourhood. **1819** *St. Louis Enquirer* 8 Dec. (Th.), A *fish story!.. In consequence of the shoals of white-fish which occupied and choaked the channel between Bois Blanc Island and Amherstburgh, the steamboat could not pass. **1823** *Missouri Intelligencer* 28 Jan. (Th.), That's 'a fish story', but mine's a true one. **1867** *Harper's Mag.* July 183/1 A friend who does not tell fish stories, says he has seen them [*sc.* herring] in such schools that he could not row his boat through them. **1887** C. F. Holder *Living Lights* 97 Exaggerations are often termed 'fish-stories', for the reason perhaps that improbable tales are related concerning the denizens of the sea. **1615** Sandys *Journey* IV. 255 The *fish-stoues by him hewne out of the rocke, and built. **1829** P. Egan *Boxiana* 2nd Ser. II. 179 Short and sweet to the Sheenies—better than a prime *fish supper to their palates; their blunt had been laid out right. **1974** *News & Press* (Darlington, S. Carolina) 25 Apr. 1/1 The Darlington Handicapped Chapter's fried fish supper will be held Friday night. **1985** *Times* 5 Nov. 15/4 [Sc. correspondent] Nor did he treat himself to a fish supper at my expense. **1957** *Encycl. Brit.* II. 159/2 Most of these [temperate-water] fishes..are not good candidates for domestic *fish tanks. **1984** *N.Y. Times* 27 Aug. B3/5 A Manhattan man and his wife were moving their daughter's 10-gallon fish tank..when it suddenly slipped from their hands and smashed. **1879** E. Arnold *Lt. Asia* I. (1886) 20 The pied *fish-tiger hung above the pool. **1878** *N. Amer. Rev.* CXXVII. 236 The Shah..sent a *fish-torpedo against the Huascar. **1855** H. Clarke *Dict.*, **Fish-trowel*. **1826** Cushing *Newburyport* 118 **Fishwardens*. Messrs. Offin Boardman, [etc.] **1845** *Mass. Acts. & Resolves 1843–45* 434 Whenever a *fishway shall be constructed..all former laws relating to fishways at said dam shall be repealed. **1870** *Law Rep.* V. 671 No mill is prejudiced by the making of a fishway in the dam. *c* **1000** *Ags. Gosp.* Luke v 4 Lætað eowre nett on þone *fisc-wer. *a* **1100** *Gerefa* in *Anglia* (1886) IX. 261 Fiscwer and mylne macian. **1387** Trevisa *Higden* (Rolls) I. 423 Tweye grete fische werys. **1883** *Harper's Mag.* Aug. 376/1 Fish-weirs along the rocks. **1861** Miss Pratt *Flower. Pl.* II. 73 The celebrated *fish-wood (*Piscidia erythrina*) used for the purpose of intoxicating fish. **1854** Thoreau *Walden* 223, I catch shiners with *fishworms. **1933** *Amer. Speech* VIII. IV. 15/2 The term *fishworm* has a wide distribution throughout New England. **1971** *Daily Hampshire Gaz.* (Northampton, Mass.) 27 Aug. 1 Billy Middleton..was planning on going fishing when he had the chance to dangle a long fat fishworm in front of Sandra Dobbs. **1685** in Picton *L'pool Munic. Rec.* (1883) I. 287 Allowing Mr. Maior..all the fish taken in yᵉ *fish yards in one tide. **1789** *Ibid.* II. 241 To destroy the Fish Yards now set upon the..river Mersey.

fish (fɪʃ), *sb.*² [Of doubtful etymology.

The comb. *fish-paunch*, synonymous with sense 1, suggests that the word was a transferred use of fish *sb.*¹; the appropriateness of the name on this supposition is not obvious, but the same may be said of many nautical terms of undisputed etymology. On the other hand, it is possible that the word is a. F. *fiche* (see next); it is not known that the F. word was ever used in sense 1, but its etymological sense is 'a means of fixing.']

1. *Naut.* 'A long piece of hard wood, convex on one side and concave on the other' (Adm. Smyth), used to strengthen a mast or yard; a fish-piece.

1666 *Lond. Gaz.* No. 59/3 We put hard hands on Jury Masts and Fishes. **1692** in *Capt. Smith's Seaman's Gram.* I. xvi. 79 Lash the Fish on to the Mast. **1748** *Anson's Voy.* III. vii. 367 His fore-mast was broken asunder..and was only kept together by the fishes which had been formerly clapt upon it. **1749** Chalmers *Phil. Trans.* XLVI. 367 The Spikes, that nail the Fish of the Mainmast. **1854** G. B. Richardson *Univ. Code* v. 2143 Can you let me have a fish for my mast? *c* **1860** H. Stuart *Seaman's Catech.* 73 One fore and one aft fish dowelled and bolted to spindle and side trees.

transf. **1833** M. Scott *Tom Cringle* xvi. (1859) 410 A black paw with fishes or splints whipped round it by a band of spunyarn.

2. A flat plate of iron, wood, etc. laid upon a beam, rail, etc., or across a joint, to protect or strengthen it; in railway construction = *fish-plate*.

1847 *Specif. Adams & Richardson's Patent* No. 11 715. 2 To connect the two iron rails together we use wood or iron fishes. **1875** R. F. Martin tr. *Havrez' Winding Mach.* 4 Rods..tied together by oak fishes of the same scantling as the rods. **1875–6** *Proc. Inst. Civ. Engin.* XLVI. 202 The original road had been laid with fishes 16 inches long.

3. *attrib.* and *Comb.*, as **fish-bar, -beam, -bolt, -hoop,** (see quots.); **fish-joint**, a joint or splice made with fish-plates (also ***fish-plate joint***); hence **fish-joint** *v.*, **-jointed, -jointing; fish-front, -paunch,** = sense 1; **fish-piece** = 1, 2 above; **fish-plate**, one of two plates bolted together through the ends of two rails on either side of their meeting-point to cover and strengthen the joint; hence **fish-plating**.

1872 W. S. Huntington *Road-Master's Assistant* (ed. 2) 27 Expansion..is supposed to have been provided for at the rolling-mill, by elongating the bolt-hole both in the rail and *fish-bar. **1874** Knight *Dict. Mech.* I. 872/1 *Fish-bar*, the splice bar which breaks the joint of two meeting objects, as of railroad rails or scarfed timber. **1892** *Northumb. Gloss.* s.v., A '*fish beam' is a composite beam, where an iron plate is sandwiched between two wood beams. **1875** J. W. Barry *Railw. Appliances* (1890) 61 The nuts of the *fish-bolts are apt to shake loose with the jar of passing trains. **1888** *Lockwood's Dict. Mech. Engin.*, *Fish-bolt*, a bolt employed for fastening fish plates and rails together. **1815** *Falconer's Dict. Marine* (ed. Burney), **Fish-front*, or Paunch is a long piece of oak or fir timber, convex on one side, and concave on the other, used to strengthen the lower masts or yards, when they are sprung. **1794** *Rigging & Seamanship* I. 24 At the lower end of the fish is driven on a hoop, called a *fish-hoop, which is beat close to the sides of the mast. **1849** J. Samuel in *Proc. Inst. Civ. Engin.* VIII. 265 A number of these *fish joints had been laid down. **1868** *Daily News* 5 Nov., The almost universal adoption of the new 'fish-joint rail'. **1892** *Northumb. Gloss.* 286 A 'fish joint' is a joint made by bolting or riveting a plate on each side near the ends. **1855** Dempsey *Pract. Railw. Engineer* (ed. 4) 265 A portion only of the lines of this kingdom being as yet *fish-jointed.. It is obvious that with the same rail a fish-jointed road is much stronger. *Ibid.* 267 Mr. Ashcroft has accomplished the *fish-jointing of 150 miles of line without accident. **1867** Smyth *Sailor's Word-bk.*, **Fish-piece*. **1869** Sir E. J. Reed *Ship-build.* vi. 102 The fish pieces or covering plates. **1855** Dempsey *Pract. Railw. Engineer* 268 The chairs are cast so that one side forms a *fish-plate. **1889** G. Findlay *Eng. Railway* 42 In 1847 Mr. Bridges Adams introduced the suspended joint with fish plates. **1889** *Life of Vignoles* xiii. 183 Vignoles always claimed to have been one of the earliest to introduce the fish-plate joint. **1881** Young *Every Man his*

own Mechanic §437 An exemplification of this fish-joint or *fish-plating is to be seen on any railway.

fish (fɪʃ), *sb.*³ [ad. F. *fiche* (of same meaning; also peg), f. *ficher* to fix; see FICCHE *v.*]

A small flat piece of bone or ivory used instead of money or for keeping account in games of chance; sometimes made in the form of a fish.

Popularly confused with FISH *sb.*; hence the collective *sing.* is used for *pl.*

1728 VANBR. & CIB. *Prov. Husb.* I. i, I am now going to a party at Quadrille..to piddle with a little of it [money], at poor two guineas a fish. **1751** ELIZA HEYWOOD *Betsy Thoughtless* I. 230 She was just going to call for the cards and fishes. **1766** ANSTEY *Bath Guide* viii. 90 Industrious Creatures! that make it a Rule To secure half the Fish, while they manage the Pool. **1816** *Sporting Mag.* XLVII. 297 A notorious gamester..at a game of loo, accumulated a large quantity of fish. **1825** HONE *Everyday Bk.* I. 91 Mother-o'-pearl fish and counters. **1878** H. H. GIBBS *Ombre* 9 A penny a fish will be found sufficiently high play.

fish (fɪʃ), *sb.*⁴ [f. FISH *v.*; the senses are unconnected.]

1. An act of fishing. *colloq.*

1880 *Scribner's Mag.* XX. 542/2, I will go find Tim..and have a fish.

2. a. The purchase used in 'fishing' or raising the flukes of an anchor to the gunwale. **b.** (See quot. 1892.)

1825 H. B. GASCOIGNE *Nav. Fame* 51 The tricing Fish the careful Gunners hook, No time is lost, it firmly grasps the Fluke. **1892** *Northumb. Gloss.*, *Fish*, a tool used for bringing up a bore rod or pump valve.

3. *attrib.* and *Comb.* The sb. in sense 2, or the vb.-stem, occurs in various technical terms (chiefly *Naut.*): **fish-back**, a rope attached to the hook of the fish-block, and used to assist in 'fishing' the anchor; **fish-block**, the block of a fish-tackle; **fish-davit**, a davit for fishing the anchor; **fish-fall**, the tackle depending from the fish-davit; **fish-head**, **-martingale**, **-pendant** (see quots.); †**fish-rope** = *fish-fall*; **fish-tackle**, that used for fishing the anchor; **fish wire**, a stiff wire, usu. looped at the end, used for pulling or 'fishing' wires through conduits, etc.; also **fish tape**. Also FISH-HOOK 2.

1862 NARES *Seamanship* 74 **Fish-back*, from the fore-castle, and secured to the back of the fish hook. **1627** CAPT. SMITH *Seaman's Gram.* ii. 10 The Dauid is a short peece of timber, at the end whereof..they hang a blocke in a strap called the *Fish-block, by which they hale up the flook of the Anchor to the Ships bow. **1840** R. H. DANA *Bef. Mast* xxxi. 120 The..*fish-davit [was] rigged out. **1882** NARES *Seamanship* (ed. 6) 93 Iron..fish davits are now fitted to nearly all ships. **1862** *Ibid.* 74 It [the fish martingale] keeps the davit from topping up as the *fish fall is hauled taut. **1842** *Proc. Inst. Civ. Eng.* II. 171 The *'fish-head' for drawing a 'drowned clack.' **1883** GRESLEY *Gloss. Coal Mining* 109 *Fish-head*, an apparatus for withdrawing the clacks of pumps through the column. **1862** NARES *Seamanship* 74 **Fish martingale*, a large jigger, the double block secured to one of the bolts in the davit head, the single block hooked down to a bolt in the ship's side. **1750** T. R. BLANCKLEY *Naval Expositor*, **Fish Pendant* hangs at the end of the Davit. **1867** SMYTH *Sailor's Word-bk.* 234 The upper end [of the fish-davit] being properly secured by a tackle from the mast-head; to which end is hung a large block, and through it a strong rope is rove, called the fish-pendant. **1630** J. TAYLOR (Water-P.) *Wks.* I. 81/1 Cables, hawsers, *Fish and Cattrope..Halliers, Ropeyarns..were all of rare stuffes of great price. **1841** R. H. DANA *Seaman's Man.* 105 **Fish-tackle.* **1907** W. S. IBBETSON *Electr. Wiring* x. 186 If the *fish wires are not put through the whole of the tubing, it is certainly better to put them at the difficult parts round bends, etc. **1958** *Van Nostrand's Sci. Encycl.* (ed. 3) 1820/2 A fish tape or wire, a tempered steel wire of rectangular cross-section, is pushed through the conduit until its end appears at the farther end. A draw line is then attached to it and..the line is drawn through the conduit.

fish (fɪʃ), *v.*¹ Pa. t. and pa. pple. **fished** (fɪʃt). Forms: 1 fiscian, 3 fissen, *Orm.* fisskenn, 4–5 fysshe(n, fis(s)he(n, 4–6 fisch(e, fishe, (4 fihche, fyschyn), 6 fyshe, 6– fish. [OE. *fiscian* = OFris. *fiskia*, OS. *fiskôn* (Du. *visschen*), OHG. *fiskôn* (MHG. *vischen*, mod.Ger. *fischen*), ON. *fiska* (usually *fiskja* of differing conjugation; Sw. *fiska*, Da. *fiske*), Goth. *fiskôn*:—OTeut. **fiskôjan*, f. **fisko-z* FISH *sb.*¹]

I. *intr.*

1. a. To catch or try to catch fish; to use nets or other apparatus for taking fish. Const. †*after*, *for*.

c **888** K. ÆLFRED *Boeth.* xxxii. §3 Ðonne ȝe fiscian willaþ. *c* **1200** ORMIN 13297 To fisskenn affterr fisskess. *a* **1300** *K. Horn* 1136 Ihc am a fissere, Wel feor icome bi este For fissen at þi feste. *c* **1305** *St. Andrew* 3 in *E.E. Poems* (1862) 98 As hi fischede aday Bi þe see oure louerd com. *c* **1386** CHAUCER *Reeve's T.* 7 Pipen he coude, and fisshe, and nettes bete. *c* **1440** *Promp. Parv.* 163/1 Fyschyn, *piscor.* **1546** J. HEYWOOD *Prov.* (1562) D j b, He hath well fysht and caught a frog. **1674** tr. *Scheffer's Lapland* 107 Their way of fishing alters with the season. **1727** SWIFT *Gulliver* III. i. 181, I beheld some people fishing with long angling rods. **1848** *Life Normandy* (1863) I. 283 They fish for them very much in the same manner.

b. *fig.* (with reference to Mark i. 17).

1413 *Pilgr. Sowle* (Caxton 1483) v. xiv. 80 These tonges were taken them as for theyr pryncipal Instrument for to fysshen with. **1552** LATIMER *Serm.* vii. (1562) 125 b, Their special callyng is to fishe, to preache the worde of God.

c. *to fish in troubled waters*: *fig.* to take advantage of disturbance or trouble to gain one's end.

1568 GRAFTON *Chron.* II. 102 Their perswasions which alwayes desyre your unquietnesse, whereby they may the better fishe in the water when it is troubled. **1625** BP. MOUNTAGU *App. Cæsar.* v. 43 They..fare full and fatt by Fishing in troubled waters. **1722** SEWEL *Hist. Quakers* (1795) I. IV. 276 You delight to fish in troubled waters. **1797** *Spirit Pub. Jrnls.* (1799) Though drunk as fish our rulers be, The thing sure little matters; Only it forces you and me To fish in troubled waters.

2. To search by dredging, diving, or other means *for* something that is in or under water, *e.g.* sunken treasure, pearls, coral, etc.

1655 F. W. in *W. Fulke's Meteors* 166 Gold..found in Waters and Rivers is fished for, and is in form of little Grains. **1690** LUTTRELL *Brief Rel.* (1857) II. 129 The..grant for fishing for silver at a wreck in the West Indies. **1697** DAMPIER *Voy.* I. vi. 134 A very rich Ship..lies to this day; none having attempted to fish for her.

3. a. To use artifice to obtain a thing, elicit an opinion, etc. Const. *after*, *for*. Phr. *to fish for a compliment*; also *absol.*

1563–87 FOXE *A. & M.* (1684) III. 239 They both did come but to fish for some things which might make a shew that my L. Chancellor had justly kept him in prison. **1583** STANYHURST *Æneis* IV. (Arb.) 108 Crosse thee seas: fish for a Kingdoom. **1638** *Penit. Conf.* vii. (1657) 190 To fish..after secrets. **1752** FIELDING *Amelia* VIII. x, The Half Guinea, for which he had been fishing. **1803** *Lett. Miss Riversdale* I. 264, I feared he would think I was fishing for a compliment. **1806–7** J. BERESFORD *Miseries Hum. Life* (1826) III. xxiii, At the game of commerce losing your life in fishing for aces. **1814** JANE AUSTEN *Mansf. Park* II. xi. 252, I am not fishing; don't compliment me. **1848** THACKERAY *Van. Fair* iv, The first woman who fishes for him, hooks him. **1886** MALLOCK *Old Order Changes* II. 217, I should have fished for you to ask me. **1961** W. BUCHAN *Helen All Alone* 183 'Don't fish!' Helen said childishly.. 'But please—what is "fish"?'..'Fish for compliments—make people say nice things about you.'

b. *to fish for oneself*: to get all one can; to seek one's own profit exclusively; to rely on one's own efforts.

1647 N. BACON *Disc. Govt. Eng.* I. iii. (1739) 8 This raised the price of the Clergy, and taught them the way to fish for themselves. **1653** BAXTER *Chr. Concord* 117 Such men fish most for themselves. **1867** LADY HERBERT *Cradle L.* ii. 48 He leaves you to fish for yourself among his miscellaneous stores. **1892** *Northumb. Gloss.*, 'Aa'll gan an fish for mesel.'

c. *Harvard College Slang* (see quot. 1851): *absol.* to curry favour, strive to ingratiate oneself with another.

1774 T. HUTCHINSON *Diary* 10 Oct. I. 261 He courts me a good deal, and fishes. I fish in return; and I think neither of us meets with much luck. **1851** B. H. HALL *College Words and Cust.*, *Fish.* At Harvard College, to seek or gain the good-will of an instructor by flattery,..or officious civilities; to curry favor..Students speak of fishing for parts, appointments, ranks, marks, &c.

II. *trans.*

4. a. To catch or try to catch (fish); to take as fish are taken; to collect (corals, pearls) from the bottom of the sea.

1585 T. WASHINGTON tr. *Nicholay's Voy.* IV. vii. 118 b, The Misidan Sea..whereas are fished great quantitie of Pearles. **1611** BIBLE *Jer.* xvi. 16, I will send for many fishers ..and they shal fish them. **1667** HY. OLDENBURG in *Phil. Trans.* II. 432 Red Coral..is fished from the beginning of April till the end of July. **1828** SCOTT *F.M. Perth*, Thou hast fished salmon a thousand times. **1865** J. G. BERTRAM *Harvest of Sea* (1873) 233 There is a period every year during which the oyster is not fished.

transf. and *fig.* *c* **1374** CHAUCER *Troylus* v. 777 To fisshen hire, he layde out hook and lyne. *c* **1400** *Rom. Rose* 7494 To fisshen sinful men we go.

b. To use as a bait in fishing.

1922 *Times Lit. Suppl.* 27 Apr. 273/3 Fishing the floating fly with a very fine cast. **1927** *Observer* 24 July 26/3 Mackerel skin, on a single hook, cast and fished like a fly.

5. *transf.* **a.** To draw or pull *out of* water, mud, etc.; to discover and bring *out of* a heap of lumber, a deep place, or the like. Also with *out*, *up*.

1632 J. LEE *Short Survey* 21 The inhabitants fish out of the bottomes of their lakes a certaine rude matter. **1653** D. OSBORNE *Let.* 22 Jan. (1903) 36 Where have you fished him out, for I think he is..little known in the world. **1707** *Lond. Gaz.* No. 4304/1, 29 Brass Guns, lately fished up. **1727** A. HAMILTON *New Acc. E. Ind.* II. I. 224 We..fished up some small Fir-trees, which we had converted into Masts. **1778** FOOTE *Trip Calais* I. Wks. 1799 II. 343 My wife fished out a large piece of blue apron upon the top of her fork. **1822** BYRON *Werner* II. i. 29 He..help'd to fish the baron from the Oder. **1834** MEDWIN *Angler in Wales* I. 219 He was fished by his disciples out of the mud. **1880** LOMAS *Alkali Trade* 200 The crystals..are drawn out..or 'fished', and allowed to drain. **1889** J. K. JEROME *Three Men in Boat* 64 We had to ..fish them out of the bag. **1953** H. MILLER *Plexus* (1963) vi. 212, I fished out the money..and handed it to Sadie's brother.

fig. **1652** J. WRIGHT tr. *Camus' Nature's Paradox* 10 Sometimes he fished wealth at Court, sometimes in his Government. **1886** *Edin. Rev.* CLXIII. 177 [A service] either fished up from some ancient 'use', or invented afresh, like some of the fancy litanies we have heard of. **1889** *Spectator* 23 Nov. 712/2 Out of the vast reservoir of facts.. something might be fished up..of interest.

b. Naut. *to fish the anchor*: to draw up the flukes to the gunwale.

1769 FALCONER *Dict. Marine* (1789), *To fish the Anchor*, to draw up the flukes upon the ship's side after it is catted. **1890** W. C. RUSSELL *Ocean Trag.* I. iii. 57 They..were fishing the anchor forwards.

absol. **1893** R. KIPLING *Many Invent.* 364 (*Envoy*), Stop, seize and fish, and easy on the davit-guy.

c. *Coal-mining.* (See quot.)

1888 GREENWELL *Gloss. Coal-trade Terms* (ed. 3) 38 *Fish*, to catch up a drowned clack by means of a fish-head.

d. To pull (a wire) through a conduit or between floors or walls by means of a stiff looped wire or other device pushed in from the nearer end.

1896 R. ROBB *Electr. Wiring* v. 118 Wires are said to be 'fished' when they are started in at one end of a concealed space and then, so that they may be pulled through, are felt for, or 'fished' for, from the other end, with a hooked wire or other contrivance. *Ibid.*, Wire in a flexible conduit may be fished just as the wire alone would be fished. **1914** H. PENDER *Amer. Handbk. Electr. Engineers* 1957 Flexible conduit possesses the advantage over rigid conduit in that it ..may be fished between partitions or floors. **1930** MOYER & WOSTREL *Indust. Electr. & Wiring* vi. 151 In small houses ..the boards can be taken up through the doorways, and the wires fished to the ceiling outlets and switches.

6. a. To try to catch fish in (a pool, stream, etc.). (Cf. similar use of *shoot*, etc.) *to fish out*: to exhaust the fish from.

c **1440** LYDG. *Secrees* 579 Lyk hym that..fyssheth a bareyn pool. **1539** *Act 31 Hen. VIII*, c. 2 §1 Vnreasonable persones..haue..fished the said pondes..as well by night as by daie. **1676** COTTON *Angler* vi. 47 Do but Fish this stream like an Artist. **1772** *Poetry* in *Ann. Reg.* 224 She fish'd the brook. **1838** JAMES *Robber* ii, You are quite welcome to fish the stream. **1866** *Daily Tel.* 5 Jan. 5/1 Rye Bay..is more fished perhaps than any piece of sea bottom in the world. **1892** *Daily News* 12 Apr. 2/1 Whether the Thames is over-fished, or, as the very gloomy prophets say, fished out.

b. *transf.* To search through (a receptacle, region, etc.) *for* (something material or immaterial).

1727 SWIFT & POPE *Pref. to Miscel.*, Some have fished the very jakes for papers left there by men of wit. **1728** POPE *Dunc.* II. 80 Oft, as he fish'd her nether realms for wit, The goddess favour'd him. **1865** MASSON *Rec. Brit. Philos.* iv. 260 Nowhere else are the various sciences so fished for generalizations.

7. Chiefly with *out*: To get by artifice or patient effort; to ascertain, elicit (a fact or opinion). Const. *from*, *out of*. Cf. L. *expiscari*.

c **1374** CHAUCER *Troylus* III. 1113 (1162) He that nedis most a cause out fisch. **1531** *Instr* in Elyot *Gov.* (1883) Life 72 To fish out..what opinion the Emperor is of us. **1541** *St. Papers Hen. VIII.* I. 663 We maye fyshe out of them, whither they were procured or sent hither by any maner of meanes. **1590** GREENWOOD *Collect. Sclaund. Art.* B b, They ..haue..commaunded certaine theire priests..to fish farther cause of accusation. **1663** PEPYS *Diary* 7 Sept., I could not fish from him..what was the matter. **1709** STRYPE *Ann. Ref.* I. xxiii. 271 Hoping by this means to have fished out money either of the king or him. **1713** ADDISON *Guardian* No. 71 ¶4 An admirable knack of fishing out the secrets of his customers. **1770** in Doran *Mann & Manners* (1876) II. ix. 211 To desire a Lady to fish out of me whether I actually intended to go or not. **1866** MRS. H. WOOD *St. Martin's Eve* xxxii. (1874) 412 She was trying to fish out.. what real business he..had at Hatherton.

III. 8. [A new formation on the sb.] *trans.* To dress (land) with fish-refuse as a fertilizer. *U.S.*

1651 R. CHILD in *Hartlib's Leg.* (1655) 36 In the North parts of New-England, where the fisher men live, they usually fish their Ground with Cods-heads. **1894** E. EGGLESTON in *Cent. Mag.* Apr. 851/2 In New England the peculiar mode of fertilizing learned from the Indians introduced a new verb; the first comers 'fished' their corn ground.

9. *intr.* Of water: to provide (good or bad) sport for anglers.

1898 *Daily News* 4 Oct. 9/3 The Arun continues to fish badly. **1904** *Daily Chron.* 13 Jan. 5/2 It is a loch that fishes best in the early part of the year. **1910** *Westm. Gaz.* 26 Feb. 16/4 The Avon was fishing well for roach.

fish (fɪʃ), *v.*² [f. FISH *sb.*²]

1. *trans.* To fasten a piece of wood, technically called a fish, upon (a beam, mast, yard, etc.) so as to strengthen it; to mend (a broken spar, etc.) with a fish or fishes. Also *to fish together.*

1626 CAPT. SMITH *Accid. Yng. Seamen* 3 Ready for.. fishing or splicing the Masts or Yards. *Ibid.* 13 A Jurymast ..is made with yards, rouftrees, or what they can..fished together. **1748** *Anson's Voy.* III. i. 295 We were obliged to fish our fore-mast. **1823** P. NICHOLSON *Pract. Build.* 120 Sometimes the pieces that are applied on the sides are made of wood; in this case, it is called fishing the beam. **1840** R. H. DANA *Bef. Mast* xxv. 83 All hands were now employed.. fishing the spritsail yard. **1875** R. F. MARTIN tr. *Havrez' Winding Mach.* 5 Fishing the rods with the wooden fishes.

b. To fasten (a piece of wood) *on.*

1711 S. SEWALL *Diary* 10 Sept. (1879) II. 322 Our Axel-tree..broke quite off..Fish'd on a piece in the morning.

2. To join (the rails) with a fish-joint.

1850 C. H. GREGORY in *Proc. Inst. Civ. Engin.* IX. 405 'Fishing' the joints of the rails with two pieces of cast or wrought iron secured by bolts or rivets. **1866** W. H. BARLOW *ibid.* XXV. 409 It would not do..to fish old rails.

fishable (ˈfɪʃəb(ə)l), *a.* [f. FISH *v.*¹ + -ABLE.]

a. That may be, or admits of being, fished in. **b.** Of the weather: Suitable for fishing. *rare.*

1611 COTGR., *Pescheable*, fishable, which may be fished in. **1819** *Blackw. Mag.* V. 591 The water..was fishable. **1867** F. FRANCIS *Angling* ix. (1880) 315 A..river, fishable from the shore. **1892** *Illust. Sporting News* 14 May 328/3 Warm, genial, and withal eminently fishable weather.

'fish-day. [f. FISH *sb.*^{1} + DAY.] A day on which fish is eaten, usually in obedience to an ecclesiastical ordinance; a fast-day.

a 1327 *Pol. Songs* (Camden) 151 On fyhshe day launprey ant lax. *c* 1440 *Anc. Cookery* in *Househ. Ord.* (1790) 429 Take almondes and..tempur hom, on fyssheday wyth wyn, and on flesheday with broth of flesh. 1564 *Act 5 Eliz.* c. 5 It shall not be lawfull..to eate any flesh vpon any dayes now vsually obserued as fish dayes, or vpon any Wednesday now newly limited to be obserued as fish day. 1641 'SMECTYMNUUS' *Vind. Answ.* §2. 12 In the Calendar Fish dayes are now called Fasting days. 1699 T. BROWN in R. L'Estrange *Colloq. Erasm.* (1711) 358 If it happened to be a fish-day, we had sometimes three whitings.

fished (fɪʃt), *ppl. a.*^{1} [f. FISH *v.*^{1} + -ED^{1}.] Only in ***fished-up*** fig. brought up.

1849 DARWIN in *Life & Lett.* (1887) I. 366, I feel sure that the newly fished-up names would not be adopted.

fished (fɪʃt), *ppl. a.*^{2} [f. FISH *v.*^{2} + -ED^{1}.] Strengthened, or fastened together, with a fish or fishes. ***fished-beam*** (see quot. 1846).

1846 BUCHANAN *Techn. Dict.*, *Fished-beam*, a beam bellying on the underside. 1875–6 PRICE WILLIAMS in *Proc. Inst. Civ. Engin.* XLVI. 160 The relative strength of the fished ends of the rail as compared with that of the solid part. 1882 NARES *Seamanship* (ed. 6) 235 Fished yards are heaviest on the damaged side. 1888 *Lockwood's Dict. Mech. Engin.* 141 *Fish joint*, or *Fished joint*.

fished (fɪʃt), *ppl. a.*^{3} [f. FISH *sb.*^{1} + -ED^{2}.] Supplied with fish.

1630 *R. Johnson's Kingd. & Commonw.* 365 Savoy. Many and large lakes it hath, and those very well fisht. 1846 MCCULLOCH *Acc. Brit. Empire* (1854) I. 641 Not one had a full cargo, only one or two being half fished. 1882 F. DAY *Fishes of Gt. Brit.* II. 215 The trawl-net boats..were very poorly fished.

fisher^{1} ('fɪʃə(r)). Forms: 1 fiscere, 2 fixere, 3 fiscære, 3–4 fissar(e, -er, *south.* vyssare, vissere, 3–5 fisch-, fyschar(e, -er(e, (5 fecher, fychere), 4–6 fissh-, fyssher(e, (5 fysshyer, 6 fiszher), 4– fisher. [OE. *fiscere*, OFris. *fisker*, OS. *fiskari* (Du. *visscher*) = OHG. *fiscâri* (MHG. *vischer*, Ger. *fischer*), ON. *fiskari* (Sw. *fiskare*, Da. *fisker*):—OTeut. **fiskărjo-*, f. **fisko-z* FISH *sb.*^{1} Like other OTeut. sbs. with this suffix it has become an agent-noun related to the vb.: see -ER^{1}.]

1. a. One who is employed in catching fish. Now *arch.*; superseded in ordinary use by FISHERMAN.

c 893 K. ÆLFRED *Oros.* i. i. 17 [Ðær] huntan ȝewicodon, oþþe fisceras, oþþe fuȝel[er]as. *c* 1175 *Lamb. Hom.* 97 Petrus wes fixere. 1297 R. GLOUC. (1724) 265 Hys vyssares come to hym, & so gret won of fyss hym broȝte. 1382 WYCLIF *Isa.* xix. 8 And mowrne shul the fissheres. 1553 EDEN *Treat. Newe Ind.* (Arb.) 22 The inhabitantes are great fyshers on the sea. 1704 POPE *Windsor For.* 137 The patient fisher takes his silent stand, Intent, his angle trembling in his hand. 1758 *Descr. Thames* 227 Fishers distinguish their Herrings into six different sorts. 1851 KINGSLEY *Song*, Three fishers went sailing away to the West.

b. *transf.* and *fig.* (esp. after Matt. iv. 19).

c 1000 *Ags. Gosp.* Matt. iv. 19 Cumeð æfter me, & ic do þæt ȝyt beoð manna fisceras. *a* 1300 *Cursor M.* 13325 (Cott.) Fra þis dai forth i sal þe ken for to be fissar god o men. 1663 COWLEY *Ess.* etc. (1669) 133 They found them Hunters and Fishers of wild creatures, they have made them Hunters and Fishers of their Brethren. 1664 H. MORE *Apol.* iii. §3 Who profess myself a Fisher for Philosophers, desirous to draw them to..the Christian Faith.

2. a. An animal that catches fish for food.

1562 BULLEYN *Bk. Simples* (1579) 78 Herones, Bitternes, [etc.]. These fowles be Fishers. 1576 FLEMING tr. *Caius' Dogs* in Arb. *Garner* III. 245 The Dog called the Fisher.. seeketh for fish by smelling among rock and stone. 1823 BYRON *Island* IV. ii, The feather'd fishers of the solitude.

b. *spec.* The pekan or Pennant's marten (*Mustela pennanti*) of North America (also ***fisher marten, fisher weasel***). Also, the fur of this animal.

1796 MORSE *Amer. Geog.* I. 200 The fisher has a general resemblance to the martin, but is considerably larger. 1879 M. M. BACKUS in *Encycl. Brit.* IX. 838/1 *Fisher*, size, 15 by 30 inches..glossy dark and durable. 1882 BECK *Draper's Dict.*, *Fisher* (fur), these skins are larger than sables, and the fur is longer and fuller. 1883 W. H. FLOWER in *Encycl. Brit.* XV. 577/2 *Mustela pennanti*..the Pekan or Pennant's Marten, also called Fisher Marten.

†3. A fishmonger. *Obs.*

a 1400 in *Eng. Gilds* (1870) 353 No ffysshyere ne no pulter ne shal bygge ffysche ne pultrye [etc.]. 1582 in W. H. Turner *Select. Rec. Oxford* 420 Any fisher that occupieth any standinge or shoppe.

†4. An implement used by tanners (see quot.).

1688 R. HOLME *Armoury* III. 350/2 The Fisher..is an Iron with Nett-work, made from side to side of it with strong Iron Wyers, with this the Bark is taken out of the Water. 1726 *Dict. Rust.* (ed. 3) s.v.

5. A fishing-boat; a vessel employed in fishing.

1864 THOREAU *Cape Cod* ix. (1894) 211 We saw countless sails of mackerel fishers abroad on the deep.

6. *attrib.* and *Comb.*: **a.** simple attrib., as ***fisher-bark, -house, -keel, -net, †-pan, -ship, -stall, -town.*** **b.** appositive (= that is a fisher, belonging to the class of fishers), as ***fisher boy, -carl, -child, -folk, -girl, -people, -swain, -train, -wife, -woman.*** Also ***fisher's coat.***

1862 H. MARRYAT *Year in Sweden* II. 341 The passage of small *fisher barks down to Carlskrona. 1621 LADY M. WROTH *Urania* 308 From a Run-away and poore *Fisher-boy he made me a King. 1867 SMYTH *Sailor's Word-bk.*, *Fisher-boys*, the apprentices in fishing vessels. 1870 MORRIS *Earthly Par.* III. IV. 212 A few rough *fisher-carles there were. *Ibid.* 227 The *fisher children hand in hand. 1854 H. MILLER *Sch. & Schm.* xxii. (1857) 481 Some of our Cromarty *fisher-folk. 1888 *Daily News* 18 Dec. 3/6 Here fisherboys and *fishergirls..crowd the stage. 1525 LD. BERNERS *Froiss.* II. xlvii. 162 Without the towne there were certayne *fissher houses. 1870 MORRIS *Earthly Par.* III. IV. 227 And *fisher-keel on fisher-keel The furrowed sand again did feel. 1601 HOLLAND *Pliny* II. XIX. i. 4 Thread, passing good for to be twisted and knit into *fisher-nets. 1890 *Daily News* 15 Feb. 6/4 A black fisher-net dress trimmed..with well-imitated mimosa. 1535 COVERDALE *Amos* iv. 2 Youre posterite caried awaye in *fyssher pannes. 1885 *Truth* 28 May 848/2 *Fisherpeople hauling their boat through the surf. 1611 BIBLE *John* xxi. 7 He girt his *fishers coate vnto him. 1614 *Eng. Way to Wealth* in *Harl. Misc.* (Malh.) III. 235 Busses, bonadventures, or *fisher-ships. 1572 *Nottingham Rec.* IV. 145 A *fyssher stalle that Thomas Reve stans in. 1627 P. FLETCHER *Apollyonists* III. xxi, Those *fisher-swaynes..by full Jordan's wave. 1538 LELAND *Itin.* (1744) VII. 55 A lytle prety *Fyssher Town cawled Wyrkinton. 1647 CLARENDON *Hist. Reb.* VII. (1703) II. 306 In Dorset-shire..little fisher Towns, Poole and Lyme. 1725 POPE *Odyss.* XXII. 425 When by hollow shores the *fisher-train Sweep with their arching nets the hoary main. 1868 M. E. BRADDON *Dead-Sea Fruit* xxxix, The rough fishermen and brawny *fisherwives. 1887 RUSKIN *Præterita* II. vi. 200 A fisher-wife doll from Calais. 1895 *Month* Sept. 52 All the fisher-wives we dressed alike in short petticoats of blue stuff. 1816 SCOTT *Antiq.* xxvi. *note*, The *fisherwomen..put in their claim. 1863 BATES *Nat. Amazon* ix. (1864) 258 The two dusky fisherwomen marched down to their canoe.

7. Special combs.: **fisher-fish** (see quot.); **† fisher's berry** = *fish-berry*; **† fisher's folly**, an angler's house in the country; **fisher's-knot**, a slip knot, the ends of which lie horizontally, and will not become untied (Davies); **fisher's ring or seal** = *fisherman's ring.* Also FISHER-BOAT, FISHERMAN.

1867 SMYTH *Sailor's Word-bk.*, **Fisher-fish*, a species of Remora, said to be trained by the Chinese to catch turtle. 1787 BEST *Angling* (ed. 2) 67 *Coculus indicus*..called also *baccæ piscatoriæ*, *fisher's berries. 1638 BRATHWAIT *Surv. Hist.* 183 As one who had taken a surfeit of the City, h'as built himself a new *Fishers folly in the Countrey. 1611 MARKHAM *Countr Content.* I. x. (1668) 53 A *Fishers knot, which is your ordinary fast knots, foulded four times about, both under and above. 1741 *Compl. Fam. Piece* II. ii. 331 You may tie your Links together with the Fishers or Weavers Knot. 1689 *Lond. Gaz.* No. 2486/1 He afterwards broke the *Fishers Ring, and caused the Lead of the Bulls to be likewise broke.

Fisher^{2} ('fɪʃə(r)). *colloq.* [f. the name of Sir Warren *Fisher*, Permanent Secretary to the Treasury 1919–39.] Temporary name for a currency note (esp. of £1). Cf. BRADBURY.

1922 *Daily Mail* 18 Dec. 7 A 'Bradbury' or a 'Fisher' are terms that have practically passed into the language. 1923 *Motor Cycling* 14 Nov. 35/2 The Bench mulcted him of a couple of Fishers and warned him as to his future behaviour.

'fisher-boat. A boat used by fishermen.

c 1440 *Promp. Parv.* 162/2 Fyscharys boote, *phaselus.* 1541 *Act 33 Hen. VIII*, c. 2 The great diminucion of the Kinges nauie, fisherbotes and mariners. 1662 J. DAVIES tr. *Olearius' Voy. Ambass.* 395 To send the Baggage by Sea, in six great Fisherboats. 1741–3 WESLEY *Extract of Jrnl.* (1749) 110 It seem'd strange to me, to attempt going in a fisher-boat, fifteen leagues upon the main ocean. 1874 FARRAR *Christ* 136 The rough fisher-boats of Bethsaida.

fig. 1663 COWLEY *Pindar. Odes, To Mr. Hobs* iv, The Baltique..and the Caspian..Seem narrow Creeks to thee, and only fit For the poor wretched Fisher-boats of Wit.

'fisheress. *rare.* [See -ESS.] A female fisher.

1611 COTGR., *Pescheresse*, a fisheresse, a woman fisher. 1685 EVELYN *Mrs. Godolphin* 210, I would sometymes call her the fisheress of her sex.

fisherman ('fɪʃəmən). [f. FISHER^{1} + MAN.]

1. One whose occupation is to catch fish.

1526 TINDALE *Luke* v. 2 The fisshermen..were wasshynge their nettes. 1605 SHAKS. *Lear* IV. vi. 17 The Fishermen that walk'd vpon the beach Appeare like Mice. 1780 HARRIS *Philol. Enq.* Wks. (1841) 429 Massinello who in a few days, from a poor fisherman rose to sovereign authority. 1855 MILMAN *Lat. Chr.* (1864) II. IV. v. 293 St. Gall was a skilful fisherman and supplied the brethren with fresh fish from the lake.

transf. 1878 *Fraser's Mag.* XVIII. 628 The natives are splendid fishermen of money.

2. An animal that catches fish. (Cf. also *fisherman-diver* in 4.)

1634 T. JOHNSON *Parey's Chirurg.* (1649) 51 Of the Fish called the Fisherman. This fish is called the Fisherman, because he hunts and takes other Fishes. 1963 B. VESEY-FITZGERALD *Cat Owner's Encycl.* 63 Some [cats] are expert fishermen.

3. A fishing-boat; a vessel employed in the business of taking fish.

1604 E. GRIMSTONE *Hist. Siege Ostend* 185 There entred six Fisher-men into the Towne whereof one was sunke. 1700 S. L. tr. *Fryke's Voy. E. Ind.* 356 The 15th we met with an English Fisherman that was coming from Ysland; he was loaden with Salt-fish. 1927 G. BRADFORD *Gloss. Sea Terms* 64/2 *Fisherman*, a fishing vessel, particularly applied to a schooner.

4. *attrib.* and *Comb.*, as ***fisherman apostle, pilot***; also, **fisherman-diver**, the merganser; **fisherman's bend**, a kind of knot; **fisherman's daughter**, rhyming slang for water; **fisherman's knit**, a type of thick ribbed knitting; **fisherman's knot** (see quots.); **fisherman's nightingale**, a name for the sedge-warbler; **fisherman's ring** (see quots.); **fisherman's walk** (see quot.).

1653 WALTON *Angler* i. 28 His four *Fishermen Apostles. 1885 G. ALLEN *Babylon* vi, We call him a *fisherman-diver. 1886 *Pall Mall G.* 8 Sept. 8/2 The suggestion that a *fisherman pilot should be placed on board each of the four cruisers. *c* 1860 H. STUART *Seaman's Catech.* 2 A *fisherman's bend. 1867 SMYTH *Sailor's Word-bk.*, *Fisherman's Bend*, a knot, for simplicity called the king of all knots. 1880 D. W. BARRETT *Life & Work among Navvies* II. ii. 41 If he wants water, he makes a demand for 'the *fisherman's daughter'. 1960 *News Chron.* 19 July 6/4 Classic shaped sweaters in heavy *fisherman's knit silk. 1961 S. PRICE *Just for Record* v. 35 I'd..slide into my jeans and fisherman's knit sweater. 1876 G. E. VOYLE *Mil. Dict.* 139/2 **Fisherman's knot*, a knot used in pontooning to fasten the cables to the rings of the anchors. 1961 F. H. BURGESS *Dict. Sailing* 88 *Fisherman's knot*, used to bend two small lines together. It is made by forming an overhand knot in the end of each line, in such a way that each contains the other line; both knots are then pulled close to each other, forming one knot. 1884 *Public Opinion* 5 Sept. 299/1 My old angler friends call this bird [the sedge warbler] the *fisherman's nightingale. 1727–41 CHAMBERS *Cycl.* s.v. *Seal*, The pope has two kinds of seals: the first used in apostolical briefs, and private letters, &c. called the *fisherman's ring.—This is a very large ring, wherein is represented St. Peter, drawing his net full of fishes. 1877 W. JONES *Finger-ring* 198 The 'Fisherman's Ring' is the Pope's ring of investiture. 1867 SMYTH *Sailor's Word-bk.*, **Fisherman's Walk*, an extremely confined space, 'three steps and overboard', is often said of what river yachtsmen term their quarter-decks.

fishery ('fɪʃərɪ). [f. FISH *v.*^{1} + -ERY, or f. FISHER^{1} + -Y^{3}.]

1. The business, occupation, or industry of catching fish, or of taking other products of the sea or rivers from the water.

In this and the following senses often preceded by some defining word, as *bank-*, *bay-*, *coast-*, *cod-*, *pearl-*, *river-*, *salmon-*, *sea-*, *whale-fishery.*

1677 YARRANTON *Eng. Improv.* 142 We have not one fourth part of Moneys sufficient to drive the Trade of England, and set up the neglected Fishery. 1769 *Lloyd's Evening Post* 22 Sept. 295/2 The British fishery at Iceland has this year turned out but poorly. 1890 *Pall Mall G.* 2 June 2/1 The French fishery upon the coast of Newfoundland, once very large, has fallen away to a mere nothing.

2. A place or district where fish are caught; fishing-ground.

1699 DAMPIER *Voy.* II. II. 124 It is a great Fishery, chiefly for Snooks, which they catch in the Lake. 1792 G. WASHINGTON *Lett.* Writ. 1891 XII. 245 The landing by Bishop's house, which used to be, and no doubt still is, good fishery. 1823 BYRON *Juan* IX. xxxi, Where God takes sea and land, Fishery and farm, both into his own hand.

3. A fishing establishment; *collect.* those who are engaged in fishing in a particular place.

1710 *Lond. Gaz.* No. 4713/3 Some English Gallies had destroyed the French Fishery there. 1788 T. JEFFERSON *Writ.* (1859) II. 539 This produced an outcry of the Dunkirk fishery. 1885 E. R. SCIDMORE *Alaska* iv. 35 The Kasa-an fishery has distanced its rivals.

4. *Law.* The right of fishing in certain waters. ***free fishery***, an exclusive right of fishing in public water, derived from royal grant; ***several fishery***, an exclusive right to fish derived from ownership of the soil; ***common of fishery***, the right of fishing in another man's water; ***common fishery***, the right of all to fish in public waters.

1748 LADY M. W. MONTAGU *Lett.* (1893) II. 167 The fishery of this part of the river belongs to me. 1767 BLACKSTONE *Comm.* II. 39 A free fishery, or exclusive right of fishing in a public river, is also a royal franchise..He that has a several fishery must also be the owner of the soil. 1817 W. SELWYN *Law Nisi Prius* II. 772 A plea, which prescribed for a several fishery in an arm of the sea. 1832 MISS MITFORD *Village* Ser. v. (1863) 462 Colonel Talbot..possesses a right of fishery for some mile or two up the river.

5. *collect.* Fish of different kinds (*nonce-use*).

1828 MISS MITFORD *Village* Ser. III. (1863) 491 Martha Glen having been long his constant customer, dealing with him in all sorts of fishery and fruitery.

6. *attrib.* and *Comb.*, as ***fishery house, industry, law***, etc.; ***fisheries act, exhibition***; **fishery-salt** (see quot. 1884).

1528 in *Archæologia* LIII. 380 The fyssherye house at Guisnes. 1864 *Glasgow Daily Herald* 24 Sept., I have been stationed here as fishery officer. 1865 ESQUIROS *Cornwall* 132 The fishery women pointed out to me the surface of the bay striped with red. 1868 PEARD *Water-farm.* xiii. 128 There were no fishery laws in France. 1883 E. R. LANKESTER *Adv. Science* (1890) 215 More accurate knowledge of fishery-animals shall be provided. 1883 *Fisheries Exhib. Catal.* 74 Fishery Salt. 1884 *Chesh. Gloss.*, *Fishery Salt*, coarse salt made specially for curing fish. 1894 *Daily News* 19 Jan. 5/3 As an outcome of the County Fisheries Exhibition held last year at Truro, the Technical Instruction Committee of the Cornwall County Council.. resolved to establish a fisheries school.

fishet ('fɪʃɪt). *nonce-wd.* [see -ET^{1}.] A little fish.

1823 LAMB *Lett.* (1888) II. 84, I wash my hands in fishets that come through the pump thick as motelings.

fishew, *Obs.*, var. of FICHU.

1755 MRS. DELANY *Let. to Mrs. Dewes* 364, I brought a little cold from Longleat, and lost my good fishew.

fishful ('fɪʃfʊl), *a.* [f. FISH *sb.*[1] + -FUL.] Abounding in fish.

1550 PHAER *Æneid* IV. (1558) Kj, Most lyke a byrd that.. his haunting kepes Among the fyshfull rocks. **1605** CAMDEN *Remains* (1638) 1 Fishfull and navigable rivers. **1652–62** HEYLIN *Cosmogr.* II. (1682) 147 Not far from a Fishful Lake. **1860** *All Year Round* 5 May 79/2 Rising from the fishful Thames. **1889** HISSEY *Tour in Phaeton* 227 The fishful-looking river Bure.

fishgarth ('fɪʃgɑːθ). [f. as prec. + GARTH.] A garth or inclosure on a river or the seashore for preserving fishes or taking them easily.

1454 *Let.* in Burton & Raine *Hemingbrough* 393 Oon fysshgarth.. is at yis tyme void of take. **1532** *Act 23 Hen. VIII*, c. 18 Certaine engines for taking of fish in the said riuer.. commonly called fishgarthes. **1634** FORD *P. Warbeck* IV. i, The earl shall deliver from his ransom The town of Berwick to him, with the fishgarths. **1771** in Picton *L'pool. Munic. Rec.* (1886) II. 240 The several fish garths erected within this Port. **1894** R. S. FERGUSON *Hist. Westmorland* 199 There was a perpetual quarrel about a fishgarth in the Esk.

'fish-gig. [var. of FIZGIG, the first element being modified after FISH, from its use in catching fish.] (See quot. 1788.) = FIZGIG 4.

a **1642** SIR W. MONSON *Naval Tracts* VI. (1704) 532/2 These Fishes are taken with.. Fishgigs. **1788** FALCONBRIDGE *Afr. Slave Tr.* 41 The fish-gig.. an instrument used for striking fish.. consists of several strong barbed points fixed on a pole, about six feet long, loaded at the end with lead. **1802** BARRINGTON *Hist. N. South Wales* i. 16 The men fish with a fish-gig. **1866** *Atlantic Monthly* Mar. 278/2 They were prevented from ascending by what appears to have been an ordinary fish gig.

'fishhood. *rare.* [f. FISH *sb.*[1] + -HOOD.] The state or condition of a fish.

1866 F. BUCKLAND *Cur. Nat. Hist.* Ser. 3 I. 125 Thousands.. of your babies have I reared up to fishhood. **1887** *Story of a Kiss* I. vi. 95 A shark in the bloom of early fishhood.

'fish-hook. [f. FISH *sb.*[1] and *v.* + HOOK.]

1. A barbed hook used for catching fish.

1387 TREVISA *Higden* (Rolls) IV. 295 [A] goldene fisch-hook. **1482** *York Myst.* Introd. 40 Those that makes pynnes.. or maketh ffisshe-hukes. **1555** EDEN *Decades* 201 Crooked like a fysshehooke. **1611** BIBLE *Amos.* iv. 2. *a* **1732** T. BOSTON *Crook in Lot* (1805) 12 Aptness to catch hold and entangle, like.. fish-hooks. **1872** YEATS *Techn. Hist. Comm.* 342 The manufacture of English fish-hooks is computed at one-sixth that of needles.

2. *Naut.* An iron hook forming part of the tackle used to raise the anchor to the gunwale of a ship.

1627 CAPT. SMITH *Seaman's Gram.* vii. 30 Hitch the fish-hooke to the Anchors flooke. **1805** A. DUNCAN *Mariner's Chron.* III. 206 In fishing the anchor, the fish-hook gave way. *c* **1860** H. STUART *Seaman's Catech.* 56 The fish tackle consists of two double blocks, and one single block; the lower one is fitted with a fishhook.

3. *attrib.* and *Comb.*, as ***fish-hook maker***; **fish-hook cactus** *U.S.*, any of several cacti with hooked spines; **fish-hook wire**, a wire consisting of twisted strands, with a piece of wire resembling a fish-hook inserted at intervals; also ***fish-hooked wire***.

1696 *Lond. Gaz.* No. 3206/4 Tim. Kirby, the Son of Charles Kirby, Fish-hook Maker. **1846** *30th Congress 1 Sess. H.R. Ex. Doc.* No. 41, 612 The fish-hook cactus is found here [*sc.* in California]. **1892** *Star* 20 Sept. 4/3 All knowledge of the use of this fishhook wire was disclaimed by the defendants.. This fishhooked wire is manufactured, and.. finds a market. **1947** *Southern Sierran* (Los Angeles) May 4/2 Rare and very beautiful, the Mohave Fishhook or Pineapple Cactus, *Echinocactus Polyancistrus*, with clustered iridescent magenta-pink blossoms.

fishify ('fɪʃɪfaɪ), *v.* [f. FISH *sb.*[1] -(I)FY.] *trans.* To turn (flesh) into fish.

1592 SHAKS. *Rom. & Jul.* II. iv. 40 O flesh, flesh, how art thou fishified. **1768** *Poetry* in *Ann. Reg.* 241 Ev'ry dish Seem'd transmuted.. There was fishified flesh, and fleshified fish. **1865** *Examiner* 11 Mar. 151/3 We have, in an English version.. the good flesh of Moliere's shrewd simple prose fishified by Mr. Kenney into.. verse.

fishily ('fɪʃɪlɪ), *adv.* [f. FISHY + -LY[2].] In a fishy manner.

1851 *Fraser's Mag.* XLIV. 439 Naples.. is as fishily inclined as ever. **1879** F. W. ROBINSON *Coward Consc.* III. i, Marcus shook hands fishily all round.

fish-in ('fɪʃɪn). [See -IN *suff.*[3]] A form of protest by American Indians against the loss of fishing rights, characterized by fishing in prohibited waters.

1964 *Post-Herald* (Birmingham, Ala.) 3 Mar. 2/3 They took part in an Indian protest 'fish-in' on the Puyallup River. **1966** *New Statesman* 15 Apr. 530/1 In resisting the injunction, the Indians have staged pathetic 'fish-ins'. **1968** *Daily Tel.* 4 June 22/3 Dick Gregory, the Negro comedian and Civil Rights leader.. was sentenced for taking part in a 'fish-in' along the Nisqually river to support local Indians protesting against a State ban on net fishing.

fishiness ('fɪʃɪnɪs). [f. as FISHILY *adv.* + -NESS.]

1. The quality or fact of being fishy.

1766 PENNANT *Zool.* (1812) II. 17 Its [the bittern's] flesh has.. nothing of the fishiness of that of the heron. **1834** BECKFORD *Italy* I. 31 I am not greatly surprised at the fishyness of their site. **1853** KANE *Grinnell Exp.* xxvi. (1856) 214 The fishiness.. is no longer disagreeable.

2. *fig.* 'Shadiness', questionableness. *colloq.*

1919 WODEHOUSE *Damsel in Distress* xiv. 163 The extreme fishiness of Albert's sudden production of a cousin from America.

fishing ('fɪʃɪŋ), *vbl. sb.*[1] [f. FISH *v.* + -ING[1].]

1. The action of the vb. FISH.

a. The action, art, or practice of catching fish.

c **1300** *Cursor M.* 13278 (Cott.) Petre and andreu.. wit þair fissing war þai fedd. **1464** *Nottingham Rec.* II. 374 For a lyne boght for the same fisshyng. **1570** *Act 13 Eliz.* c. 11 §3 Such Cods and Lings as they shall happen to take.. by their own fishing. **1632** LITHGOW *Trav.* III. 105 The best fishing that the whole Ocean yeeldeth, is upon the coasts of Orkney and Zetland. **1762** H. WALPOLE *Vertue's Anecd. Paint* II. i. 19 Representations in miniature of the.. huntings, fishings, and productions of the country. **1814** SCOTT *Wav.* iv, Of all diversions.. fishing is the worst qualified to amuse a man who is at once indolent and impatient.

b. *proverbs.*

1546 J. HEYWOOD *Prov.* (1562) Div, It is.. yll fyshyng before the net. **1614** BP. HALL *Recoll. Treat.* 695 There is no fishing so good as in troubled waters. *a* **1665** J. GOODWIN *Filled w. the Spirit* xiii. (1670) 362 Those Proverbial Sayings; There is no fishing like to a fishing in the sea, no service like the Service of a King. **1671** F. PHILLIPS *Reg. Necess.* 432 It grew into a Proverb amongst us not yet forgotten, No fishing to the Sea, no Service to the King.

c. *transf.* and *fig.* Also with advbs., as *about*, *out*, *up* (see senses of the vb.).

1548 UDALL, etc. *Erasm. Par. Matt.* iv. 19 The newe fyshyng, whiche serued.. wyth the nette of the Gospell to catche men. **1641** HINDE *J. Bruen* vii. 27 Witnesse hereof, in parents such fishing for heires. **1720** *Lond. Gaz.* No. 5909/2 Forbidding.. either the fishing up, or receiving any of the.. Effects that might be driven on the Coast. **1741** RICHARDSON *Pamela* (1824) I. 79 Why.. is all this fishing about for something when there is nothing? **1889** *Century Dict.*, *Fishing out*, the removal of fish from a fish-pond, the 'drawing' of a pond.

2. *to go* (also ME. *wade*) *a-fishing*: **a.** *lit.* (OE. had *on fiscoð gán*).

1297 R. GLOUC. (Rolls) 2198 For ȝe beþ men bet iteiȝt to ssofle & to spade To cartstaf & to ploustaf & a wissinge [*v. rr.* a fischyng, in fuschinge, to fysschynge] to wade.

b. *transf.* (*nonce-use*) To rob on the highways.

1608 *Pennyless Parl.* in *Harl. Misc.* (Malh.) III. 78 Soldiers, that have no means to thrive by plain dealing.. go a-fishing on Salisbury Plain.

3. The privilege or right of catching fish in certain waters; ***common*** and ***several fishing*** = *common* and *several fishery*: see FISHERY 4.

1495 *Act 2 Hen. VII.* c. 62 §1 The Mede called the Kingis Mede and half the fysshing of the Watir called Temise. **1523** FITZHERB. *Surv.* 9 Also of mylnes seuerall fysshinges and commen fysshinges what they be worthe. **1607** NORDEN *Surv. Dial.* 110 Hath the Lord of the Mannor any peculiar fishing within any river. **1788** *Filey Inclos. Act* 24 Wrecks, fishings, and all other royalties.

4. A place or facilities for catching fish; fishing-ground, fishery.

1596 SPENSER *State Irel.* (1633) 95 A good towne, having.. a plentifull fishing. **1641** in J. Knox *View Brit. Emp.* (1785) II. 397 The Imployment of the Fishermen.. till they come to their Fishings outwards bound. **1795** J. RICHARDSON in J. Robertson *Agric. Perth* 377 Upon the Tumble.. there are scattered fishings belonging to different proprietors. **1815** SCOTT *Guy M.* vii, Ellangowan's hen-roosts were plundered.. and his fishings poached.

5. *attrib.* and *Comb.*: **a.** simple attrib. (sense 1) as ***fishing-bark, -basket, -boat, -box, -craft, expedition, -gear, -ground, -hook, -house, -hutch, -light, -limit, -line, -net, -party, -pen, -port, rights, -season, -ship, -smack, -spear, -tackle, -town, -trade, trip, -village, -weir, -worm.***

1841 W. SPALDING *Italy & It. Isl.* III. 349 The list.. included *fishing-barks and small coasters. **1838** JAMES *Robber* i, The *fishing-basket under the arm. **1732** BERKELEY *Alciphr.* v. §1 Several *fishing-boats and lighters, gliding up and down. **1836** MARRYAT *Midsh. Easy* xiii, They had received information from the men of a fishing-boat. **1870** *Law Rep.* Comm. Pleas V. 659 A *fishing-box.. so arranged that a fish going into it cannot get out. **1699** DAMPIER *Voy.* II. II. 31 If they are not provided with Hooks, Lines or Harpoons or any other *Fishing-Craft. **1875** W. MCILWRAITH *Guide Wigtownshire* 91 Stranraer was the rendezvous of the.. fishing craft. **1961** E. S. GARDNER *Case Bigamous Spouse* (1967) xv. 203, I am not going to permit counsel to go on a *fishing expedition. **1966** A. SACHS *Jail Diary* iii. 38 They.. seemed to be on a fishing expedition. **1839** *Knickerbocker* XIII. 406 To throw by my *fishing gear, and sit upon rocks. **1863** LYELL *Antiq. Man* 19 The Swiss archæologist has found abundant evidence of fishing-gear. **1641** in J. Knox *View Brit. Emp.* (1785) II. 397 They are to.. make them [nets].. in a readinesse against they come to the *fishing grounds. **1725** DE FOE *Voy. round World* (1840) 350 They had neither *fishing-hook or nets. **1799** G. SMITH *Laboratory* I. 237 Your small fishing hooks. **1676** COTTON *Angler* i. 9, I have lately built a little *Fishing House upon it [the river], dedicated to Anglers. **1778** *Eng. Gazetteer* (ed. 2) s.v. *Selsey*, This peninsula has several fishing-houses towards the shore. **1868** *Law Rep.* Queen's B. III. 289 The water.. is used to supply the mill.. and also a *fishing-hutch or trap. **1832** T. W. MAGRATH *Let.* Jan. in T. Radcliff *Lett. f. Upper Canada* (1833) xiii. 215 At night the shore was brilliant with the *fishing lights in the canoes. **1845** C. M. KIRKLAND *Western Clearings* 120 Nobody broke his windows or pulled the shingles off his roof to make fishing-lights or quail-traps. **1963** *Times* 14 Jan. 6/7 The Anglo-Danish *fishing-limit compromise. **1466** *Mann. & Househ. Exp.* 212 My mastyr paid hym for v. *fyshenge lynes. **1865** LUBBOCK *Preh. Times* 375 Their fishing-lines were made of the bark of the Erowa. **1530** in Weaver *Wells Wills* (1890) 145 A vowlyng nett and a *ffyshing nett. **1699** DAMPIER *Voy.* II. II. 105 He would soon destroy their Canvas and Fishing-Nets. **1864** TENNYSON *En. Ard.* 17 Enoch Arden.. play'd Among.. swarthy fishing-nets.. and boats up-drawn. **1765** *Jrnl. French Traveller* 20 June in *Amer. Hist. Rev.* (1922) XXVII. 72 We went to a *fishing party out in the Bay. **1838** C. GILMAN *Recoll. Southern Matron* xxvi. 176 Fishing parties, and the chase soon occupied his leisure moments. **1849** F. PARKMAN *Calif. & Oregon Trail* 35 She sat down and entertained us.. with anecdotes of fishing-parties. **1791** W. JESSOP *Rep. Thames & Isis* 20 The Sills of the old Lock and *Fishing Pen may be raised 18 Inches. **1897** KIPLING *Capt. Cour.* 253 Some sort of poem about a *fishing-port called Brixham. **1930** *Daily Express* 8 Sept. 9/5 He reached Porthleven, a fishing port in Mount's Bay, at ten o'clock on Tuesday morning. **1936** *Discovery* May 139/2 The rivers and the *fishing rights belong to the riparian owners. **1699** DAMPIER *Voy.* II. II. 12 Where the Indian Fishers.. lye in the *Fishing-Seasons. **1785** J. KNOX *View Brit. Emp.* I. 319 Several *fishing-ships from Kinsale take abundance of ling every year. *Ibid.* I. 302 *Fishing-smacks from Harwich. **1876** J. SAUNDERS *Lion in Path* vii, The tiny fleet of fishing-smacks were all hauled up together on the shingle. **1840** C. F. HOFFMAN *Greyslaer* I. xi. 122 The torches.. enable them.. to approach sufficiently near to destroy him with their *fishing spears. **1703** *Lond. Gaz.* No. 3935/4 A Vellum Pocket-Book, with some *Fishing-Tackle in it. **1813** *Examiner* 15 Feb. 102/1 B. George.. fishing-tackle-maker. **1699** in J. Picton *L'pool Munic. Rec.* (1883) I. 325 It was formerly a small *fishing-town. **1662** J. SMITH *England's Improv. Reviv'd* (1670) 258 The *Fishing-Trade, being in our own Seas, and on our own ground. **1909** 'O. HENRY' *Roads of Destiny* 36 Mr. Robert mentioned his intended *fishing-trip. **1943** J. S. HUXLEY *TVA* vii. 51 About a million and a half individual fishing trips.. were made on the new TVA lakes. **1699** DAMPIER *Voy.* II. II. 124 At this Opening is a small *Fishing Village. **1870** *Law Rep.* Comm. Pleas V. 659 A *fishing-weir.. of solid masonry. **1884** 'MARK TWAIN' *Huck. Finn* xxxvii. 376 Curled him up like a fishing-worm.

b. Special comb., as **fishing admiral**: see ADMIRAL *sb.* 4; **fishing-breeze**, one favourable for fishing; **fishing-crib** (see quot.); **fishing-flake** = *fish-flake*; **fishing-float** (see quots.); **fishing-pole**, a pole used as a fishing-rod; **fishing-room** (see quot.); **fishing tool** (see quot. 1963); **fishing-tube** (see quot.); **fishing-wand** (*Sc.*) = FISHING-ROD.

1888 E. J. MATHER *Nor'ard of Dogger* 279 There has been a 'smart *fishing-breeze' during the night, resulting in a heavy catch. **1886** C. ADAMS in *Longm. Mag.* VII. 652 Owing to the increase of fixed engines, called *fishing-cribs. **1861** L. L. NOBLE *After Icebergs* 20 We are glad to jump ashore at Mrs. Bridget Kennedy's *fishing-flake. **1727–41** CHAMBERS *Cycl.*, **Fishing-floats*, are little appendages to the line, serving to keep the hook and bait suspended at the proper depth. **1893** *Standard Dict.*, *Fishing-float*, [U.S.], a scow used in seine-fishing, from which an apron is let down to the bed of the river for the more convenient handling of the seine. **1791** T. B. HAZARD *Diary* 12 Sept. (1930) 127/1, I broke my *Fishing Pole Cought 4 Pickrel 3 Eeels and 6 Trout. **1873** T. B. ALDRICH *Marj. Daw* 75 He rigged himself up a fishing-pole. **1931** J. BUCHAN *Blanket of Dark* 52 He was.. able to spend long days.. on the meres with his fishing pole. **1946** H. S. PEARSON *Countryman's Cookbook* 78 Our hooks and lines were ready, and we had made several fishing poles from slender saplings during the winter. *a* **1728** in J. Reeves *Hist. Newfoundland* (1793) II. 76 In such case should the ships *fishing rooms of that harbour be taken up before he arrives. **1732** E. FALKINGHAM *Let.* 4 Oct. in *Calendar State Pap. Amer. & W. Indies* (1939) 223 And by that means stake out the very best of the antient fishing room and by that pretence claim a right. **1879** E. W. H. HOLDSWORTH in *Encycl. Brit.* IX. 266 'Fishing rooms' or portions of the shore set apart for the curing and storing of fish. **1886** *Century Mag.* July 330/1 The '*fishing tools'.. come into important service when the drilling apparatus or the rope breaks in the well. **1963** *Gloss. Mining Terms* (*B.S.I.*) III. 10 *Fishing tools* or *tackle*, tools used to recover objects lost or stuck down a borehole. **1874** KNIGHT *Dict. Mech.* I. 873/2 **Fishing-tube* (Microscopy), an open-ended glass tube for selecting a microscopic object in a fluid. **1889** BARRIE *Window in Thrums* 96, I was in the garden putting some rings on a *fishing-wand.

'fishing, *vbl. sb.*[2] [f. FISH *v.*[2] + -ING[1].] The action of strengthening or supporting with a fish; see FISH *sb.*[2] ***fishing-key***, a kind of fish-plate.

1798 NELSON in Nicolas *Disp.* (1845) III. 132 The.. two masts, by good fishing will hold fast. **1837** MARRYAT *Dog-fiend* xii, I wish I had the fishing of your back that is so bent. **1852** *Specif. Bruff's Patent* No. 14096. 2 Into this metal clip, which I term a fishing key, the ends of each rail at its junction with the preceding or succeeding rail are received.

fishing ('fɪʃɪŋ), *ppl. a.* [f. as prec. + -ING[2].] That fishes.

1. Of an animal: That catches fish. (The names of such animals are sometimes hyphened.)

fishing frog, a fish: = ANGLER[1] 2; ***fishing eagle, hawk, owl*** = *fish-eagle, -hawk, -owl* (FISH *sb.*[1] 7).

1688 CLAYTON in *Phil. Trans.* XVII. 989 The Fishing Hauk is an absolute Species of a Kings-fisher. **1766** PENNANT *Zool.* (1769) III. 94 The fishing frog grows to a large size. **1785** T. JEFFERSON *Notes Virginia* (1787) 72 *Accipiter piscatorius*.. Fishing hawk. **1795** S. HEARNE *Journey from Prince of Wale's Fort* 398 Eagles of several sorts are found in the country bordering on Hudson's Bay during the Summer; but none, except the common brown Fishing Eagle, ever frequent the Northern parts. **1835** R. M. BIRD *Hawks of Hawk-hollow* I. vi. 85 They are no true fishing-hawks, after all. *Ibid.* vii. 94 The Solitude.. [was] broken by.. the plaintive scream of the fishing eagles. **1883** *Fisheries Exhib. Catal.* (ed. 4) 153 The Fishing cat.. is very common in Lower Bengal about Calcutta. **1934** *Jrnl. R. Aeronaut. Soc.* XXXVIII. 837 This is the fishing owl of tropical Asia, which goes by the Latin name of Ketupa Flovipes. **1953** G. DURRELL *Overloaded Ark* xiii. 220 The Fishing-Eagles,

their black-and-white livery standing out..and their canary-yellow beaks and feet bright in the sun.

2. Of an accusation, inquiry, etc.: Preferred or put forward in order to elicit information which cannot be gained directly.

1831 PEACOCK *Crotchet Castle* xv, He again threw out two or three fishing questions. **1844** LD. BROUGHAM *A. Lunel* I. ii. 37 So she framed what our lawyers call her fishing question. **1863** H. G. WILSON *Sp. bef. Privy Council* 3 Merely colourable and fishing Articles of accusation.

Hence **'fishingly** *adv.*

1837 LOCKHART *Scott* (1839) VIII. 23 One of the College librarians yesterday told Sir W., fishingly, 'I have been so busy that I have not yet read *your* Redgauntlet'. **1893** *Field* 27 May 771/1 The onlooker who is not fishingly inclined.

'fishing-rod. [f. FISHING *vbl. sb.*]

1. A long slender tapering rod to which a line is attached for angling. Formerly called also ANGLE-ROD.

1552 HULOET, Fishing rodde, *calamus*. **1591** PERCIVALL *Sp. Dict.*, *Veleta*, the toppe of a fishing rodde, *tragula*. **1706** FARQUHAR *Recruiting Officer* IV. ii, You have some-thing like a fishing-rod there. **1861** W. F. COLLIER *Hist. Eng. Lit.* 175 Izaak Walton, who wielded pen and fishing-rod with equal love and skill, was born at Stafford in 1593.

2. *attrib.* and *Comb.*

1892 *Vermont Agric. Rep.* XII. 135 At Thetford a large fishing rod manufactory has been quite successful. **1896** *Daily News* 17 June 7/5 The car is to be driven by electricity conveyed by overhead wires, the current being caught by a fishing-rod projection from the car. **1904** *Westm. Gaz.* 1 July 4/1 There is no novelty..in the fishing-rod [golf] clubs. **1953** J. S. HUXLEY *Evol. in Action* iv. 101 Fitting two sticks together by a fishing-rod joint.

fishless ('fɪʃlɪs), *a.* [f. FISH *sb.*[1] + -LESS.] Without fish; devoid of fish.

1591 FLORIO *2nd Fruites* 109 Where you shall have the aire birdles, the sea fishles. **1655** FULLER *Ch. Hist.* VI. 339 The rapid seas shall sooner fishless slide. **1879** WALFORD *Londoniana* II. 38 Fishless ponds and ragged turf.

fishlet ('fɪʃlɪt). *rare.* [f. as prec. + -LET.] A very small fish.

1886 *Contemp. Rev.* June 856 We might have filled a boat in an hour with..queer fishlets. **1890** *Q. Rev.* July 221 The fishlets are fed from time to time with yolk of egg.

fishling ('fɪʃlɪŋ). *rare.* [f. as prec. + -LING, dim. suffix.] A small or young fish.

a **1861** T. WINTHROP *Life in Open Air* (1863) 33 Only petty fishlings, weighing ounces. **1884** *Manch. Exam.* 30 Aug. 5/2 The curious fishling which wants to find out what is behind the door. **1893** *Field* 4 Feb. 152/2 The unhappy fishling.

†**'fishly,** *adv. Obs.* [f. as prec. + -LY[2].] Like fish, fishily.

1699 COWLEY *Voy.* in *Cook's Voy.* (1790) III. 846 Which fowles..tasted somewhat fishly.

fishmonger ('fɪʃmʌŋgə(r)). [f. as prec. + MONGER.] One who deals in fish.

1464 *Mann. & Househ. Exp.* 243 The ferst day off Marche at the Fyshemongerys howse. **1594** PLAT *Jewell-ho.* I. 9 This maketh the Fishmongers Wiues so wanton. **1725** BAILEY *Erasm. Colloq.* 309 It was at a time when 'tis the Fishmonger's Fair. **1865** DICKENS *Mut. Fr.* I. xvii, The fishmonger pulls off his hat with an air of reverence.

Hence **'fishmongering** *vbl. sb.*, in quot. *attrib.*

1862 H. MARRYAT *Year in Sweden* I. 160 Abraham Cabeliau, known in the fishmongering world, from a cod which still bears his name.

fishpond ('fɪʃpɒnd). [f. as prec. + POND.]

1. a. A pond in which fish are kept.

c **1440** *Promp. Parv.* 163/1 Fisshe ponde, *vivarium*. **1653** WALTON *Angler* ii. 42 An herb Benione, which being hung in a linen cloth near a Fish Pond..makes him [an otter] avoid the place. **1777** W. DALRYMPLE *Trav. Sp. & Port.* liv, There is a terrass on the south side, with a fish-pond. **1855** MACAULAY *Hist. Eng.* IV. 723 A small country seat, surrounded by pleasant gardens and fishponds.

fig. **1669** WOODHEAD *St. Teresa* I. xix. 117 To make so filthy a Fish-pond, as I was, so pure.

b. Applied jocularly to the sea (cf. *herring-pond*).

1604 DEKKER *Honest Wh.* I. Wks. 1873 II. 9 I had not saild a league in that great fishpond but I cast up my very gall. **1661** OGILBY *His Majesty's Entert.* 18 The great Fish-pond Shall be thine. **1866** G. MACDONALD *Ann. Q. Neighb.* i. 3 Our queer German brothers over the Northern fish-pond.

2. A depression in a card-table to contain 'fish' (see FISH *sb.*[3]) or counters.

1785 COWPER *Let. to Newton* 19 Mar., When covered with a table-cloth, the fish-ponds are not easily discerned.

3. A game in which participants try to catch toy fish; also, a receptacle at a fair, etc., from which small parcels can be extracted by means of a fishing-rod.

1892-3 *T. Eaton & Co. Catal.* Fall & Winter 67/2 Games .. Fish ponds. **1904** E. NESBIT *Phoenix & Carpet* iv. 81 Anthea and Jane went off..to fish in the fishpond, and dive into the bran-pie. **1921** *Daily Colonist* (Victoria, B.C.) 29 Mar. 6/3 Plain and fancy articles will be on sale, also home cooking and a fish pond. **1939-40** *Army & Navy Stores Catal.* 825/3 Magnetic fishponds..with pond, fishing rods and everything complete.

'fish-pool. [f. FISH *sb.*[1]] A pool of water to contain fish; a fishpond.

c **950** *Lindisf. Gosp.* John v. 7 In þæt fiscpol [L. *in piscinam*]. *c* **1000** *Suppl. Ælfric's Voc.* in Wr.-Wülcker 178 *Uiuarium*, fiscpol; *Euripus uel piscina*, fiscpol. *c* **1425** *Seven Sag.* (P.) 883 To a fische-pole he come. **1529** *Supplic. to King* 48 Fyshe pooles well stored with dyuerse kyndes of fyshes. **1616** SURFL. & MARKH. *Country Farme* 77 The.. Fish-poole, which we haue appointed to be in the midst of our Court. **1718** PRIOR *Solomon* II. 638 To the large Fish-pools, or the glassy Floods.

b. (See quot.)

1718 STEELE & GILLMORE (*title*) An Account of the Fish-Pool: consisting of a Description of the Vessel so call'd, lately invented and built for the Importation of Fish alive.

'fish-scale. [f. FISH *sb.*[1]]

1. One of the scales of a fish's skin. Chiefly *attrib.* (in quot. 1834 referring to ichthyosis: cf. *fish-skin disease* below); **fish-scale tile,** a tile shaped like a fish scale.

a **1661** HOLYDAY *Juvenal* 61 Was this a price for fish-scales? **1834** GOOD *Study Med.* (ed. 4) IV. 465 One case is recorded, in which the face was the only part exempted from the fish-scale covering. **1873** LADY C. SCHREIBER *Jrnl.* (1911) I. 186 Found a pretty German Enamel étui—pink fish-scale ground. **1881** YOUNG *Every Man his own Mechanic* § 1260 Fish-scale tile slabs, £12 10s. per 100. *Ibid.* § 1261 The fish-scale slabs..are notched or rebated on the lower edge. **1882** CAULFEILD & SAWARD *Dict. Needle-work* 207 *Fish Scale Embroidery*.. The principal parts of the design..are covered over with brightly tinted Fish scales sewn to the foundation with coloured silks. **1930** E. POUND *XXX Cantos* iv. 16 Like a fish-scale roof. **1940** *Archit. Rev.* LXXXVII. 12 Fish-scale slates are shown used in the upper part of a shop in the High Street and in a detail of their setting-out. **1961** S. SITWELL *Golden Wall & Mirador* vi. 124 The pair of towers have their columns pitted with a fish-scale.

2. *Metallurgy.* (See quot. 1958.)

1932 *Jrnl. Iron & Steel Inst.* CXXV. 587 Fish-scale in high-speed steel is the result of abnormal grain growth in the austenite due to critical strains. **1958** A. D. MERRIMAN *Dict. Metallurgy* 94/1 *Fish scale*, a defect sometimes encountered in vitreous enamel coatings. It..is often associated with flaking of minute areas of enamel.

fish-skin ('fɪʃskɪn). [f. FISH *sb.*[1]]

1. The skin of a fish.

1651 J. HALL *Grounds of Monarchy* II. 31 Hanging fish skins about the wals of the Chamber. **1759** COLEBROOKE in *Phil. Trans.* LI. 43 A piece of old wainscoat..was smoothed with a fish-skin. **1859** LOWELL *Biglow Papers* Gloss., Fish-skin, used in New England to clarify coffee. **1909** *Westm. Gaz.* 15 May 15/1 The last thing in leather is pearl-tinted fish-skin.

2. *attrib.* and *Comb.*: **fish-skin disease** (also shortened *fish-skin*), ichthyosis; **fish-skin grain,** grain (in leather) resembling the skin of a fish.

1703 *Lond. Gaz.* No. 3896/4 He..had about him a Fish skin Plaister-Box with Silver Instruments. **1814** T. BATEMAN *Cutan. Dis.* (ed. 3) 49 The *Ichthyosis*, or fish-skin disease. **1834** GOOD *Study Med.* (ed. 4) IV. 463 *Lepidosis Ichthyiasis*. Fish-skin. **1879** *Eng. Mech.* 11 Feb. 534/2 Steel rollers, for making the 'fish skin' grain.

'fish-tail, *sb.* [f. FISH *sb.*[1]] **a.** The tail of a fish. Chiefly *attrib.* of things resembling a fish's tail in shape or action, e.g. a spreading flame from a kind of gas-burner, hence called ***fish-tail burner, -jet*** (also shortened *fish-tail*); **fish-tail wind** (see quot. 1875).

1840 *Mech. Mag.* XXXII. 343/2 The best small light is.. the fish-tail jet. **1852** J. BOURNE *Screw Propeller* 56 Fowles's Fish-tail Propeller. **1864** SALA in *Daily Tel.* Oct., I turned on a fishtail burner. *c* **1865** LETHEBY in *Circ. Sc.* I. 128/2 In the case of cannel coal, the holes are small; and for common London gas they are rather large. The former are known by the name of Lancashire or Scotch fish-tails. **1872** O. W. HOLMES *Poet Breakf.-t.* x. (1885) 247 We have no more reverence for the sun than we have for a fish-tail gas burner. **1875** *Times* 16 July 5/5 A nasty shifting breeze blowing down the ranges all day, now on this side, now on that,—a 'fishtail' wind. **1882** *Daily News* 15 Sept. 6/1 The day was bright with a strong fish-tail wind. **1892** *Daily News* 29 Mar. 6/6, I spliced it to the bedstead, in what they call a fishtail knot. **1931** [see FISH-TAIL *v.*]. **1939** M. B. PICKEN *Lang. Fashion* 57/3 *Fish-tail*, shaped like tail of fish; having cut-out V in end.—*f*[*ish-tail*] *drapery*, train, as on a formal gown, shaped like fish-tail. **1963** *Gloss. Mining Terms* (*B.S.I.*) III. 8 *Drag bit* (fishtail bit, pilot bit), a rotary bit which has two or more cutting blades or wings with hard-faced cutting edges. (Various types are the two-wing, three-wing, fishtail and pilot bits.)

b. Hence as predicative *adj. rare.*

1891 *Daily News* 28 Mar. 5/6 The wind was very fish-tail and tricky.

'fish-tail, *v.* [f. the sb.] *intr.* To cause the tail of an aircraft or the back of a motor-car to swing from side to side (in aircraft in order to reduce the landing speed; also said of the aircraft or car itself). Hence **'fish-tailing** *vbl. sb.*

1927 *N.Y. World* 23 July 2/6 She looped,..fish-tailed and then swooped some. **1931** *Vanity Fair* Nov. 78/2 *Fishtailing*, which is swishing the machine from side to side to reduce the forward speed, explains a *fishtail landing* as zig-zagging after touching ground, in order to slow down when coming into a small field. **1942** J. ALDRIDGE *Signed with their Honour* 14 He put his flaps down and fish-tailed in. **1957** *Life* 29 Apr. 132/1 Causing his rear wheels to spin or the rear end to 'fish-tail', that is, swing back and forth. **1967** L. FORRESTER *Girl called Fathom* xi. 129 She..sat there, stiffly swaying as the car fish-tailed, straightened out. **1971** *Daily Colonist* (Victoria, B.C.) 28 Jan. 31/6 One of the cars appeared to be fishtailing.

†**'fish-whole,** *a. Obs.* [f. FISH *sb.*[1]] As sound as a fish; thoroughly sound or healthy.

a **1225** *Juliana* 59 Heo ase fischhal as þah ha nefde no-wher hurtes ifelet. *c* **1400** MAUNDEV. (Roxb.) xii. 52 He was clensed of lepre and made fisch hale. *c* **1430** *Chev. Assigne* 353 Þ Fyve cheynes I haue & þey ben fysh hole. **1599** H. BUTTES *Dyets drie Dinner* M, As sound as a Trout. And another phrase, Fish-whole, I think is most ment of the Trout.

fishwife ('fɪʃwaɪf). [f. as prec. + WIFE.] A woman who sells fish.

1523 J. ROPER *Will* in *Archæol. Cant.* (1859) II. 154, I bequethe to the making of an horse way, for the fisshe wyves. **1662** J. DAVIES tr. *Olearius' Voy. Amb.* 80 They..abuse one another like Fish-wives. **1739** J. MILLER *Jests* cxv, She bid the Fish-Wife about half what she asked. **1867** J. MACGREGOR *Voy. Rob Roy* (1868) 72, I took the tow-line thrown down from the quay by some sturdy fishwives.

fishy ('fɪʃɪ), *a.* [f. as prec. + -Y[1].]

1. Abounding in fish. Now *poet.* or *humorous.*

1552 HULOET, Fishye, or full of fishe..*piscosus, pisculentus*. **1632** J. LEE *Short Surv.* 20 Hath many fishie rivers and lakes. **1725** POPE *Odyss.* IV. 499 Bait the barb'd steel, and from the fishy flood Appease th' afflictive fierce desire of food. **1833** *Blackw. Mag.* XXXIII. 853 On the banks of that fishy loch we stood. **1870** BRYANT *Iliad* I. IX. 265 As when two winds upturn the fishy deep.

2. a. Resembling a fish or something belonging to a fish; fish-like.

1611 BIBLE *1 Sam.* v. 4 Only the stump [*marg.* fishy part] of Dagon was left. **1646** SIR T. BROWNE *Pseud. Ep.* v. xix. 260 The Mermaids..with womans head above, and fishy extremity below. **1703** MAUNDRELL *Journ. Jerus.* (1721) Add. 2 Two Syrens, which twining their fishy Tails together, made a Seat. **1863** N. MACLEOD *Remin. Highland Par.* in *Gd. Words* 505 Lachlan had become so accustomed to this kind of fishy existence. **1868** HELPS *Realmah* iii. 47 I know nothing of these fishy, half-under-water people.

Comb. **1825** J. NEAL *Bro. Jonathan* II. xxvi, Getting over the ground upon a pair of droll, fat, fishy looking legs.

b. Of the eye: Dull, vacant of expression. Also in comb. ***fishy-eyed*** adj.

1836 T. HOOK *G. Gurney* III. 23 The door was opened by a tall, fishy-eyed maid. **1847** ALB. SMITH *Chr. Tadpole* xv. (1879) 136 The same vacant faces, looking with the same fishy stare into the lecturer's countenance. **1862** SALA *Seven Sons* I. vi. 128 A pallid young man with a fishy eye. **1877** A. B. EDWARDS *Up Nile* xi. 291 The Sheykh of the Cataract —a flat-faced, fishy-eyed old Nubian.

3. Of odour, taste, etc.: Characteristic of or proceeding from fish.

1616 CHAPMAN *Musæus* 383 It is enough for thee To suffer for my love the fishy savours. **1667** MILTON *P.L.* IV. 168 Better pleas'd Then Asmodeus with the fishie fume. **1791** COWPER *Odyss.* IV. 546 Which the fishy scent subdued. **1837** M. DONOVAN *Dom Econ.* II. 211 An example of a pure fishy taste without the slightest degree of rankness.

4. Having the savour, smell, or taint of fish.

1547 BOORDE *Brev. Health* § 292 Clawe nat the skyn with fyshye fyngers. **1667** H. STUBBE in *Phil. Trans.* II. 501 A Bird..called a Pellican, but a kind of Cormorant, that is of taste Fishy. **1791** MAD. D'ARBLAY *Diary* 8 Aug., The part by the sea..was so..fishy that I rejoiced when we left it. **1837** HAWTHORNE *Twice-told T.* (1851) II. vi. 90 The very air was fishy.

5. Consisting of fish; produced from fish.

1699 DAMPIER *Voy.* II. I. ii. 28 Soy is made partly with a Fishy composition. **1725** POPE *Odyss.* IV. 64 Watery fowl, that seek their fishy food. **1879** CHR. ROSSETTI *Seek & F.* 279 In connexion with the fishy family. **1884** *Illust. Lond. News* 13 Dec. 571/3 The guests..washed down their fishy repast with Latour Blanche.

6. *colloq.* or *slang.* **a.** (? With the notion 'slippery as a fish', or perh. with allusion to meat with a 'fishy' taste.) Of dubious quality, unreliable, questionable, 'shady'. **b.** Having 'fishy' eyes (see 2 b); hence, languid or 'seedy', *esp.* as the result of a debauch.

1840 J. P. KENNEDY *Quodlibet* 75 Jesse being..a little amphibious in his politics, or, in Mr. Fog's expressive language, *rather fishy*. **1844** DISRAELI *Coningsby* I. ix, I thought it was all up..The most fishy thing I ever saw. **1865** J. C. WILCOCKS *Sea Fisherm.* (1875) 117 There he lay.. certainly doosed fishy about the eyes. **1880** J. PAYN *Confid. Agent* III. 151 Langton's French is very fishy. **1882** BLACK *Shandon Bells* xi, I always heard he was fishy about money matters. **1882** *American* V. 83 Altogether, the story is too fishy.

fisic, fisician, obs. ff. PHYSIC, PHYSICIAN.

fisk: see FISC.

†**fisk,** *v. Obs.* Also 4-6 fysk(e, 6-8 fiske. [Possibly a frequentative (formed with *k* suffix as in *walk*, *talk*, *lurk*) of OE. *fýsan* to hurry, or of *fésian*, *fýsian* FEEZE *v.* Cf. the synonymous Sw. *fjäska*, a frequentative of *fjäsa* to bustle, make a fuss.] *intr.* To move briskly, scamper about, frisk, whisk; also with *about*, *abroad*, *in and out*, *to and fro*.

Quot. 1906 is a deliberate archaism.

c **1340** *Gaw. & Gr. Knt.* 1704 & he fyskez hem by-fore, þay founden hym sone. **1393** LANGL. *P. Pl. C.* x. 153 What frek of þys folde fiskeþ þus a-boute? *c* **1440** *Promp. Parv.* 162/2 Fiskin a-bowte yn ydilnesse, *vagor*. **1549** LATIMER *4th Serm. bef. Edw. VI* (Arb.) 104 Than he is busi..then he fyskes a brode. **1575** J. STILL *Gamm. Gurton* I. ii. in Dodsl. *O. Pl.* II. 10 Tome Tannkard's Cow..fysking with her taile. *c* **1620** Z. BOYD *Zion's Flowers* (1855) 114 Why feare yee so, thus fisking in and out? *a* **1700** B. E. *Dict. Cant. Crew*, *Gadding-Gossips*, way-going Women, Fidging and Fisking everywhere. **1721-1800** in BAILEY. **1906** KIPLING *Puck of Pook's Hill* 120 Take *me* from Pevensey to fisk and flyte through fern and forest.

quasi-*trans.* **1556** J. HEYWOOD *Spider & F.* lvii. 242 If he scaped this, at all times to be ware, With faint fond flies, to fiske agayne a warfare.

Hence 'fisking *vbl. sb.* and *ppl. a.* Also 'fisker, one who frisks or scampers about.

c**1440** *Promp. Parv.* 162/2 Fyscare a-bowte ydylly, *discursor, discursatrix, vagulus vel vagator.* **1523** FITZHERB. *Husb.* §45 If a shepe haue mathes, ye shall perceyue it by her bytynge, or fyskynge. **1592** G. HARVEY *Pierce's Super.* 175 Not such an other mutterer..or a fisking will. **1601** DEACON & WALKER *Answ. to Darel* 190 Being growne very wearie with your violent fiskings. **1611** COTGR. s.v. *Trotiere*, A fisking huswife, a raunging damsell. c**1620** Z. BOYD *Zion's Flowers* (1855) 91 Thoughts..Come buzzing so within my ..breast, With fisking traine. **1675** *Rules of Civility* v in *Antiquary* (1880) II. 58/2 Madam..fisking and pratling are but ill ways to please.

fisnamy, fisonomie, obs. ff. PHYSIOGNOMY.

†**fiss-buttocked,** *a.* ? *Obs.*

1552 HULOET, Fissebuttocked sowe, *tarda mulier, trossa.*

fissenless, var. of FOISONLESS.

fissi-, less correctly fisso-, used as combining form of L. *fissus*, pa. pple. of *findĕre* to split, employed in *Biol., Phys., Zool.*, in terms formed chiefly on the analogy of late L. *fissipēs* (see FISSIPED) to indicate the condition of being cleft. ˌ**fissi'costate** *a.* [L. *costa* rib: see COSTATE], having the nervures or ribs divided (*Syd. Soc. Lex.*). ˌ**fissi'dactyl, -yle** *a.* [Gr. δάκτυλ-ος finger], having the digits divided. ˌ**fissige'mmation,** a mode of reproduction intermediate between fission and gemmation. ˌ**fissi'lingual** *a.* [L. *lingua* tongue + -AL¹], having the tongue cleft; said of a suborder of saurian reptiles, hence called *Fissilinguia.* ˌ**fissi'palmate** *a.* [see PALMATE], partially web-footed; semipalmate. Hence ˌ**fissipal'mation,** partial palmation, or incomplete webbing of the toes. ˌ**fissipartu'rition,** the action of giving birth to young by fission (in quot. *transf.*). ˌ**fissi'rostral** *a.* [L. *rostr-um* + -AL¹], having a deeply cleft beak; belonging to the order of birds thence called *Fissirostres.* ˌ**fissi'rostrate** *a.* [as prec. + -ATE²] = prec.

1835-6 TODD *Cycl. Anat.* I. 268/1 Families of the Fissirostral tribe. **1856-8** W. CLARK *Van der Hoeven's Zool.* II. 377 Natatores.—Feet..palmate or fisso-palmate. **1881** O. FISHER in *Nature* XXV. 243 The act of fissiparturition by which the moon was born must have been sudden.

fissibility (fɪsɪ'bɪlɪtɪ). [badly f. L. *fiss-* ppl. stem of *findĕre* to split, cleave + *-(i)bility* -ITY.] The quality of being easily cleft.

1798 PENNANT *Hindoostan* I. 144 They [bamboo canes] are often made use of for frames of houses, for which their ready fissibility, and their lightness, peculiarly adapt them. **1908** W. SCHLICH *Man. Forestry* (ed. 2) V. 86 The property of wood owing to which it may be split..is termed fissibility, and depends chiefly on the direction in which the force acts.

fissile ('fɪsɪl, now usu. 'fɪsaɪl), *a.* Also 7 fissel, 8 fissil. [ad. L. *fissil-is*, f. *findĕre* to cleave: see -ILE. Cf. Fr. *fissile.*]

1. Capable of being divided or split; cleavable; inclined or tending to split.

1661 LOVELL *Hist. Anim. & Min.* Introd., Some are Fissil, as the spectacle stone; others not, as mettals. **1756** C. LUCAS *Ess. Waters* II. 128 It springs slowly through a soft, fissil rock. **1830** LYELL *Princ. Geol.* (1875) II. III. xlviii. 572 Layers of drift peat, sand or fissile clay. **1857** H. MILLER *Test. Rocks* xi. 427 They communicate often a fissile character to the stone in which they occur. **1887** BOWEN *Virg. Æneid* VI. 180 Ash-hewn timbers and fissile oaks with the wedges are rent.

2. *spec.* in *Nuclear Physics.* Capable of undergoing nuclear fission; sometimes used specifically of materials capable of fission upon absorption of a slow (as opposed to a fast) neutron.

1945 *Nature* 29 Dec. 768/1 The first bomb had not been dropped but..large production plants were rapidly accumulating the fissile material which it was planned to use. **1950** [see FISSIONABLE *a.*]. **1950** J. COCKCROFT in Crammer & Peierls *Atomic Energy* iv. 75 Fast reactors require considerable quantities of scarce fissile material such as U 235. **1953** *Economist* 14 Nov. 508/1 These ['breeder' reactor] plants, which create fissile fuel out of normally non-fissile materials at a faster rate than they are used up, are in the early stage of development. **1957** *Observer* 7 July 11/8 The 'gaseous diffusion' process used during the war to separate fissile uranium-235 for atomic bombs from natural uranium was based on this work [of Professor S. Chapman]. **1958** *Listener* 19 June 1005/1 There are fissile materials (such as plutonium, and uranium-235) which can undergo nuclear chain-reactions. **1965** [see FISSION *v.* 2].

Hence '**fissileness** = next.

1727 BAILEY vol. II, *Fissileness*, aptness to be cleaved.

fissility (fɪ'sɪlɪtɪ). [f. FISSILE + -ITY.] The quality of being fissile or cleavable.

1670-81 in BLOUNT *Glossogr.* **1689** G. HARVEY *Curing Dis. by Expect.* xxii. 178 The knowledge of..the fissility of a stone. **1837** J. MACCULLOCH *Attributes God* III. xlv. 202 Had the fissility of slate not been known it would scarcely have been credited. **1882** GEIKIE *Text-bk. Geol.* II. II. §6. 121 This superinduced fissility or 'cleavage' has resulted from an internal rearrangement of the particles. **1955** J. A. WHEELER in W. Pauli *Niels Bohr* 175 The slow neutron fissility of 28 nuclei.

fission ('fɪʃən), *sb.* [ad. L. *fissiōn-em*, n. of action f. *findĕre* to split.]

1. The action of splitting or dividing into pieces.

1865 *Pop. Sc. Rev.* Jan. 177 Fission or the separation of cuttings is used to perpetuate the same variety.

2. *spec.* in *Biol.* The division of a cell or organism into new cells or organisms, as a mode of reproduction.

1841-71 T. R. JONES *Anim. Kingd.* 49 In some elongated species the fission is effected in a longitudinal direction. **1846** PATTERSON *Zool.* 38 A Medusa may actually be generated..by fertile ova, by gemmation, and by spontaneous fission.

transf. **1883** ABBOTT *Alphabet*, Vau had the singular fate of generating four other letters by a sort of spontaneous fission. **1950** R. A. KNOX *Enthusiasm* 68 Yet the schism went on; and, as is the way of schisms, propagated itself by fission.

3. *spec.* in *Astr.* The breaking up of one star into two others, as postulated in one theory of the origin of binary stars.

1919 J. H. JEANS *Probl. Cosmogony & Stellar Dynamics* xi. 246 (*heading*) The evolution of binary and multiple stars: the process of fission. **1924** H. DINGLE *Mod. Astrophysics* xv. 236 A binary star may originate in the division, or fission, of a single star which, by its contraction, acquires such a high rotational velocity as to become unstable. **1957** A. W. TITHERLEY *Orig. Solar Syst.* ii. 9 As Algol and most other eclipsing binaries have very short periods..it cannot be doubted that before fission the dense central core had previously become elongated. **1964** R. H. BAKER *Astron.* (ed. 8) xiv. 421 The fission theory..was favored in former times, and some recent efforts have been made to revive it in amended form.

4. *spec.* in *Nuclear Physics.* The splitting, either spontaneously or under the impact of another particle, of a heavy nucleus into two (very rarely three or more) approximately equal parts, with resulting release of large amounts of energy.

1939 MEITNER & FRISCH in *Nature* 11 Feb. 239/2 By bombarding thorium with neutrons, activities are obtained which have been ascribed to radium and actinium isotopes. Some of these periods are approximately equal to periods of barium and lanthanum isotopes resulting from the bombardment of uranium. We should..like to suggest that these periods are due to a 'fission' of thorium. *Ibid.* 240/1 'Fission' of the nucleus. **1942** J. D. STRANATHAN *'Particles' of Mod. Physics* xi. 443 Neutron bombardment of uranium causes the uranium nucleus to split into two parts not far different in mass. This approximately equal splitting is called fission. **1947** J. HAYWARD *Prose Lit. since 1939* 17 It remains to be seen whether man's discovery and immediate abuse of the cataclysmic energy released by atomic fission will fortify or weaken his transcendental aspirations and nournal gropings. **1957** *Encycl. Brit.* II. 648/2 The fission of one pound of uranium yields about 10,000,000 kw. hr... To produce this same amount of energy would require the combustion of 3,000,000 lb. of coal. **1965** J. S. STRETTAN *Ionizing Radiations* vii. 123 If the neutrons produced by one fission are slowed down sufficiently before they meet the next U^{235} atom, fission will continue and the chain reaction will be established. **1967** ROY & NIGAM *Nuclear Physics* v. 162 Most heavy nuclides undergo spontaneous fission in competition with the emission of an *a*-particle.

5. *attrib.* and *Comb.*, as (sense 4) ***fission bomb, chain reaction, fragment, -fusion-fission, neutron, process, product, reactor, spectrum, yield.***

1941 in H. D. Smyth *Gen. Acct. Devel. Atomic Energy Mil. Purposes* (1945) iv. 42 A fission bomb of superlatively destructive power will result from bringing quickly together a sufficient mass of element U-235. **1957** *Encycl. Brit.* II. 651/1 In a fission bomb the uranium or plutonium explode simultaneously if a sufficient amount of material is assembled. **1950** F. GAYNOR *Encycl. Atomic Energy* 37 The fission chain reaction occurring in the atomic bomb, in which a neutron is captured by a uranium nucleus. **1950** *Amer. Speech* XXV. 26 The process of fission has..created such phrases as..fission spectrum, fission yield, fission fragments. **1965** *Gloss. Atomic Terms* (*H.M.S.O.*) 25 *Fission fragments*, freshly produced fission products before they have been slowed down by nearby matter. **1955** *Sci. Amer.* Aug. 46/3 Speculation about the 'fission-fusion-fission' bomb..was indirectly confirmed last month by Atomic Energy Commissioner Willard F. Libby. This weapon is said to consist of a fission bomb which triggers a thermonuclear reaction which in turn causes ordinary uranium (238) to fission. In a speech at the University of Chicago, Libby mentioned 'a nuclear explosion releasing 10 megatons of fission energy'. **1966** *Observer* 15 May 2/5 'Fission-fusion-fission' means a three-stage bomb with a uranium or fission trigger, a hydrogen or fusion intermediate stage..and an outer case of 'natural' uranium 238. **1956** A. H. COMPTON *Atomic Quest* 26 A means of slowing down the fission neutrons. **1939** MEITNER & FRISCH in *Nature* 11 Feb. 239/2 It seems..possible that the uranium nucleus has only small stability of form, and may, after neutron capture, divide itself into two nuclei of roughly equal size... The whole 'fission' process can..be described in an essentially classical way. **1939** *Nature* 13 May Suppl. 794 (*heading*) Decay curves of uranium and thorium fission products. **1955** *Sci. News Let.* 5 Mar. 147/1 Fission products are atoms of chemical elements newly formed, during the explosion, out of the fragments of uranium and plutonium atoms. **1948** *Physics Abstr.* 488 Nuclear fission reactors. **1955** *Newsweek* 1 Aug. 11/2 A new type reactor seems to be under development in which fusion—the H-bomb principle—supplements the energy provided by the usual fission reactor. **1960** *Gloss. Atomic Terms* (*H.M.S.O.*) 25 *Fission spectrum*, the wide range of elements and isotopes formed in fission is called the fission spectrum. Up to 35 elements may be formed [etc.]. *Ibid.*, *Fission yield*, the fraction of fissions giving rise to one particular group of fission products all having the same mass number.

fission ('fɪʃən), *v.* [f. the sb.]

1. *intr.* To undergo fission; to split or divide into a small number of parts comparable in size.

1929 J. H. JEANS *Universe around Us* 226 The development of the hypothetical chaos has now been traced through five generations of astronomical bodies, chaos—nebulae—stars—binary systems—sub-systems, to which a sixth generation must be added if the stars of the sub-system happen to fission further. **1971** *Sci. Amer.* June 87/1 The bubble is pinched at the waist and finally fissions into two bubbles.

2. *trans.* and *intr.* In *Nuclear Physics*: to split or break up into fission products; to cause (a nucleus) to undergo fission.

1947 *Sci. News Let.* 20 Sept. 181 (*heading*) Lighter elements fissioned. **1949** *Nucleonics* May 6/1 The isotope uranium-235..is the only naturally occurring substance that can be fissioned with most of the neutrons available within a pile. **1950** A. C. CLARKE *Interplanetary Flight* 84 This is necessary to maintain the chain reaction in normal uranium, which is fissioned only by slow-moving ('thermal') neutrons. **1955** *Wall St. Jrnl.* 24 Feb. 5/2 Uranium atoms would fission in the graphite core of the proposed reactor. **1965** G. R. KEEPIN *Physics Nucl. Kinetics* i. 3 We shall adopt the convention recommended by the American Nuclear Society. Thus 'fissile' will herein refer to those heavy nuclides which can be fissioned by thermal neutrons. **1967** W. E. MEYERHOF *Elem. Nucl. Physics* v. 219 Another process can start when U^{237} can be created with sufficient excitation energy to fission.

Hence '**fissioning** *vbl. sb.* and *ppl. a.*

1955 *Sci. News Let.* 23 July 51/3 Fissioning of uranium 235 atoms in solution provides the gamma rays and neutrons for medical treatment and other research. **1965** G. R. KEEPIN *Physics Nucl. Kinetics* ii. 13 We find that the mass of a fissioning U^{236} nucleus is greater than the total mass of its ..fission products.

fissionable ('fɪʃənəb(ə)l), *a.* [f. FISSION *v.* + -ABLE.] Capable of undergoing nuclear fission. Also *fig.* Hence ˌ**fissiona'bility.**

1945 H. D. SMYTH *Gen. Acct. Devel. Atomic Energy Mil. Purposes* i. 17 Plutonium 239 is the nucleus rightly guessed to be fissionable by thermal neutrons. **1946** *Physical Rev.* 2nd Ser. LXX. 108 Determining the thermal fissionability of several nuclear species. **1948** *Times* 9 Mar. 3/3 The new fissionable element is uranium of the atomic weight of 233. **1950** *Amer. Speech* XXV. 24 Reactors may be named according to fuel (uranium reactor)..addition of fissionable fuel (enriched reactor)..and so on. *Ibid.* 26 *Fissile* and *fissionable*..are sometimes distinguished, with fissile assigned to material that will undergo fission upon absorption of a neutron and *fissionable* reserved for material that fissions spontaneously. **1953** *Ann. Rev. Nuclear Sci.* II. 399 For convenience, this first section on the fissionability of nuclides has been divided into two parts: the first part deals with heavy elements from thorium on up, while the second part deals with medium elements from bismuth on down. **1958** *Spectator* 15 Aug. 211/1 Mr. John Wardle and the Yorkshire Cricket Club continued to throw fissionable material at one another, heedless of the fall-out. **1959** *Times* 22 Jan. 11/2 Parties with an ideology are always more 'fissionable' than those without one. **1968** F. KERTESZ *Lang. Nuclear Sci.* (Oak Ridge Nat. Lab. TM 2367) 18 Fissionable materials were shipped in containers held in a birdcage.

fissiparous (fɪ'sɪpərəs). [f. mod.L. type *fissiparus* (f. FISSI- + L. *parĕre* to bring forth; incorrectly on analogy of *viviparus*) + -OUS.]

a. Of organisms: Producing new individuals by fission. **b.** Of or pertaining to the process of reproduction by fission. Hence **fi'ssiparously** *adv.*

1835-6 TODD *Cycl. Anat.* I. 145/2 The first of these modes of reproduction is entitled fissiparous. **1872** NICHOLSON *Palæont.* 94 The polypes produced fissiparously resemble one another in organization. **1887** W. HOOPER in *Encycl. Brit.* XXII. 464 Organisms which are fissiparous, and when cut in two form two fresh independent organisms.

transf. **1874** MORLEY *Compromise* (1886) 70 All error is what physiologists term fissiparous. **1890** *Times* 21 Nov. 9/2 Scotch Home Rule and, perhaps, half-a-dozen other fissiparous developments of 'national life'.

So ˌ**fissipa'ration,** the process of fissiparous reproduction. **fi'ssiparism** = prec. ˌ**fissi'parity,** the attribute of being fissiparous. **fi'ssiparousness** = *fissiparity* (in examples *fig.*).

1864 *Athenæum* No. 1920. 216/1 Fissiparation and gemmation. **1868** E. P. WRIGHT *Ocean World* iv. 77 This is what Naturalists term generation by division—fissiparism or fission. **1872** DANA *Corals* i. 57 This dividing one's self in two, for the sake of an increase of population, is the process called spontaneous fission or fissiparity. **1891** *Monist* I. 627 The change from fissiparity to sexuality. **1931** A. L. ROWSE *Politics & Younger Generation* x. 295 In England and France the [Communist] party has been reduced to a negligible quantity by its own fissiparousness. **1961** *Times* 14 Jan. 7/6 India, haunted as it is by the fear of 'fissiparousness'.

fissiped, fissipede ('fɪsɪpɛd, -piːd), *a.* and *sb.* [ad. late L. *fissiped-em*, f. *fiss-us*, pa. pple. of *findĕre* to split + *ped-em, pēs* foot.]

A. *adj.* Having the toes separated.

1656 BLOUNT *Glossogr*, *Fissiped*, cloven-footed. **1847** CRAIG, *Fissiped.* **1882** W. A. FORBES in *Nature* No. 639. 287 The three great groups of fissiped Carnivora.

B. *sb.* An animal having its toes divided.

In the two first quots. the word may be Latin.

1646 SIR T. BROWNE *Pseud. Ep.* v. i. 234 It is discribed like fissipedes, or birdes which have their feet or clawes divided. **1688** R. HOLME *Armoury* II. 309 2 Fissipedes, or having open Toes..[are] Aquatick Birds living much in Water. **1847** CRAIG, *Fissiped.* **1854** *Encycl. Brit.* VII. 542 The second subdivision, denominated Fissipedes, are destitute of pincers.

Hence **fi'ssipedal** *a.*, **fi'ssipedate** *a.* = FISSIPED *a.*

1883 W. H. FOWLER in *Encycl. Brit.* XV. 434/1 The Fissipedal Carnivora were divided by Cuvier into two groups. **1884** *Syd. Soc. Lex.*, *Fissipedate.*

fissive ('fɪsɪv), *a.* [f. L. type **fissīvus*, f. *findĕre* (pa. pple. *fissus*) to split.] Pertaining to, or of the nature of, fission.

1875 HUXLEY & MARTIN *Elem. Biol.* v. 29 The whole plant is built up by the fissive multiplication of the simple cell in which it takes its origin.

fissle, fistle ('fɪs(ə)l), *sb. Sc.* [f. next vb.] 'Bustle, fuss' (Jam.).

1719 HAMILTON *Ep. to Ramsay* 24 July, O sic a fike and sic a fistle I had about it. **1768** ROSS *Helenore* I. 35 The oddest fike an' fisle that e'er was seen.

fissle, fistle ('fɪs(ə)l), *v. Sc.* and *dial.* Also fisle, fissil. [echoic: cf. FIZZLE.]

1. *intr.* To make a slight continued noise; to rustle; to move with such a noise.

1721 RAMSAY *Wks.* I. Gloss. *Fistle* to stir. **1789** DAVIDSON *Seasons, Winter* 232 Or icicle drop frae the bended twig, Wi' fissling din, amang the leafless bri'rs. **1816** SCOTT *Antiq.* ix, 'He heard the curtains o' his bed fissil'. **1823** GALT *R. Gilhaize* III. 65 The wind again began to fisle, and the signs of a tempest were seen. **1851** GREENWELL *Coal-trade Terms, Northumb. & Durh.* 26 *Fissle, Fistle*, to make a crepitant noise or faint crackling. **1856** T. AIRD *Poet. Wks.* 132 The little mouse.. Creeps from her hole and fissles through the grass. **1859** *All Year Round* No. 34. 179 The dead leaves were fistling in troops down the lanes.

2. To move about restlessly or uneasily; to fidget.

1785 BURNS *Ep. to J. Lapraik* xxii, Twa lines frae you wad gar me fissle. **1855** ROBINSON *Whitby Gloss.*, *Fizzling*, fidgeting as a person in a state of bodily uneasiness. **1863** ROBSON *Bards of Tyne* 319 Whole patriot bands.. Do fyke and fistle sair about her.

fissle, dial. form of THISTLE.

fissural ('fɪʃʊərəl), *a.* [f. FISSURE *sb.* + -AL[1].] Of or pertaining to a fissure, also, inclined to form or having fissures.

1881 WILDER & GAGE *Anat. Techn.* 501 (Cent. Dict.), To confine the discussion of the fissural pattern to a brief statement of what appear to be the constant and inconstant fissural characters. **1884** *Syd. Soc. Lex.*, *Fissural angeioma*, angeioma of the natural fissures of the body.

fissuration (fɪʃʊ'reɪʃən). [a. F. *fissuration*, n. of action f. *fissurer*: see FISSURE *v.* and -ATION.]

1. The action of fissuring or splitting asunder; the state of being fissured or cleft.

1864 *Intell. Observ.* No. 33. 193 A slight fissuration of the caudal end. **1887** *Amer. Jrnl. Psych.* I. 342 Whether fissuration be due to mechanical causes or [etc.].

2. *Biol.* = FISSION *sb.*

1867 J. HOGG *Microsc.* II. ii. 403 The multiplication of the species is effected in some by spontaneous division or fissuration. **1884** *Syd. Soc. Lex.*, *Fissuration.*

fissure ('fɪsjʊə(r), 'fɪʃə(r)), *sb.* [a. F. *fissure*, ad. L. *fissūra*, f. *findĕre* (pa. pple. *fissus*) to cleave.]

1. a. A cleft or opening (usually rather long and narrow) made by splitting, cleaving, or separation of parts; 'a narrow chasm where a breach has been made' (J.).

1606 R. CAWDREY *Table Alph.*, *Fissure*, rift, cleft, or pertition. **1677** PLOT *Oxfordsh.* 235 Of but few gallons of water forced through a narrow Fissure, he could raise a mist in his Garden. **1695** WOODWARD *Nat. Hist. Earth* (1723) 6 Those Strata were divided by parallel Fissures. **1730–46** THOMSON *Autumn* 811, I see.. The gaping fissures to receive the rains. **1814** CARY *Dante, Inf.* XIV. 107 Each part, except the gold, is rent throughout; And from the fissure tears distil. **1856** STANLEY *Sinai & Pal.* ii. (1858) 112 The vast fissure of the Jordan valley.

b. *fig.* (of non-material cleavage).

1876 DOUSE *Grimm's L.* §61. 150 A dialectic fissure, as it were, was originated. **1890** *Spectator* 5 July, They.. were.. divided by too deep a social fissure from the Indians whom they were expected to convert.

2. *spec.* **a.** *Path.* A narrow solution of continuity produced by injury or by ulceration; also, an incomplete fracture of a bone, without separation of parts. (*Syd. Soc. Lex.*)

c **1400** *Lanfranc's Cirurg.* 270 Whanne þe bowels fallip adoun þoruȝ a fissure .i. a brekynge. **1601** HOLLAND *Pliny* XXI. xx, [It cureth] the Fissures in the seat. **1676** WISEMAN *Surg.* v. ix. 379 By a Fall or Blow the Scull may be fissured or fractured.. this Fracture or Fissure may be under the Contusion, or [etc.]. **1706** PHILLIPS (ed. Kersey), *Fissure*.. In Surgery a kind of Fracture, or breaking of a Bone, that happens in the length of it. **1767** GOOCH *Treat. Wounds* I. 249 The best Authors.. divide the injuries, of which the skull is susceptible, into five kinds, as a *fissure*, a *fracture*, [etc.] . **1876** DUHRING *Dis. Skin* 49 Fissures are linear wounds having their seat in the epidermis or corium.

b. *Anat.*, *Bot.* etc. A natural cleft or opening in an organ or part; e.g. one of the *sulci* or depressions which separate the convolutions of the brain.

1656–74 BLOUNT *Glossogr.*, *Fissure*, a cleft, a division, a parted leaf. **1713** DERHAM *Phys.-Theol.* IV. ii. 101 In other Animals the Fissure of the Pupil is erect. **1797** M. BAILLIE *Morb. Anat.* (1807) 184 The mouth of the earth worm consists of a small longitudinal fissure. **1871** DARWIN *Desc. Man* I. i. 10 Bischoff.. admits that every chief fissure and fold in the brain of man has its analogy in that of the orang. **1884** *Syd. Soc. Lex.*, *Fissure*.. in Botany, the line of cleavage of seed vessels and anthers, and the clefts of a divided leaf.

c. *Her.* A diminutive of the bend sinister, being one fourth of its width. †Also, a riband, or eighth part of a bend (*obs.*).

1486 *Bk. St. Albans, Her.* E vij b, Thys fyssure is calde a staffe, and in french it is cald a baston. **1562** LEIGH *Armorie* 110 b, A ribande.. conteineth in bredeth, the eight parte of yᵉ bende.. This ys also called a Fissure. **1610** GUILLIM *Heraldry* II. v. (1611) 53 It is commonly called a Fissure.. in that it cuts or rents the coat armour in twaine. **1828–40** BERRY *Encycl. Herald.* I, *Fissure* is the fourth part of the bend sinister and by some called a *staff*.

3. The action of cleaving or splitting asunder; the state of being cleft; cleavage.

1633 T. ADAMS *Exp. 2nd Peter* i. 11 226 The apertion of heaven.. in these places signifies.. a visible fissure of heaven. **1853** KANE *Grinnell Exp.* xxviii. (1856) 232 On striking the surface with a walking-pole.. lines of fissure radiated from the point of impact.

4. *attrib.* and *Comb.*, as ***fissure theory***; **fissure claim, -eruption, -needle, vein** (see quots.).

1871 TYNDALL *Fragm. Sc.* (1879) I. ix. 281, I had heard the Via Mala cited as a conspicuous illustration of the fissure theory. **1874** KNIGHT *Dict. Mech.*, *Fissure-needle*, a spiral needle for catching together the gaping lips of wounds. **1881** RAYMOND *Mining Gloss*, *Fissure-vein*, a fissure in the earth's crust filled with mineral. **1882** A. GEIKIE *Text-Bk. Geol.* III. 198 In many parts of the earth.. there have been periods.. when the crust was rent into innumerable fissures over areas thousands of square miles in extent, and when the molten rock.. welled out from the vents, and flooded enormous tracts of country... Of these 'fissure-eruptions',.. no examples have occurred within the times of human history, unless some of the lava-floods of Iceland can be so regarded. **1886** *York Herald* 4 Aug. 1/4 As usual in such fissure veins ..as the workings increase in depth the lode will considerably increase both in thickness and richness. **1894** *Westm. Gaz.* 4 May 6/1 The reef.. is reported.. to be a true fissure claim.

fissure ('fɪʃjʊə(r)), *v.* [f. prec. sb.]

1. *trans.* To make a fissure or fissures in; to cleave, split.

1656 RIDGLEY *Pract. Physic* 173 When the inward place is Fissured, the outward remaining unhurt. **1676** [see FISSURE *sb.* 2]. **1841** LEVER *C. O'Malley* xlvii, The French cannon had fissured the building from top to bottom. **1863** LYELL *Antiq. Man* xi. (ed. 3) 202 By that convulsion the region around Natchez was.. much fissured. **1869** PHILLIPS *Vesuv.* viii. 237 The strata would be fissured and displaced.

2. *intr.* To break into, or open in, fissures; to become cleft or split.

Hence **'fissuring** *vbl. sb.* and *ppl. a.*

1830 LYELL *Princ. Geol.* I. 419 The rending and fissuring of the ground. **1859** TODD *Cycl. Anat.* V. 49/2 The process of fissuring or segmentation. **1862** G. P. SCROPE *Volcanos* 47 The fissuring effect upon solid rocks.

fissured ('fɪʃjʊəd), *ppl. a.* [f. FISSURE *sb.* or *v.* + -ED.] Having a fissure or fissures; broken up by fissures.

1788 T. TAYLOR *Comment. of Proclus* I. p. cxii, Quadrupeds having solid or many fissured hoofs. **1816** SHELLEY *Alastor* 579 Ivy clasped The fissured stones with its entwining arms. **1845** DARWIN *Voy. Nat.* xvi. (1873) 352 Fluids that escape from the fissured ground. **1872** OLIVER *Elem. Bot.* I. iii. 21 Which lobes, after the expansion of the flower, become fissured near their margins.

fissureless ('fɪʃjʊəlɪs), *a.* [f. FISSURE *sb.* + -LESS.] Without a fissure or fissures.

1875 BENNETT & DYER tr. *Sachs' Bot.* III. iii. 650 The fissureless pieces of ice.

fissuriform (fɪ'ʃjʊərɪfɔːm), *a.* [f. FISSURE *sb.* + -(I)FORM.] Resembling a fissure in form.

1861 HULME tr. *Moquin-Tandon* II. VII. xii. 388 The two lateral pits.. are fissuriform.

fissury ('fɪʃjʊərɪ), *a. nonce-wd.* [f. as prec. + -Y[1].] Having, or full of, fissures.

1825 *Blackw. Mag.* XVII. 339 Should the rock.. happen to be loose or fissury.

fist (fɪst), *sb.*[1] Forms: 1 fýst, (fæst), 2–6 fest(e, (3 *south.* veste), 3–5 fust(e, (3 *south.* vuste), 4–5 feest, 4–6 fyst(e, 4, 6–7 fiste, 5– fist. [OE. *fýst* str. fem. corresponds to OFris. *fêst*, MLG. *fûst* (Du. *vuist*), OHG. *fûst* (MHG. *vûst*, mod.Ger. *faust*):—WGer. **fûsti*.

By some scholars this is referred to an OTeut. form **fûhsti-z*, **funhsti-z*:—pre-Teut. **pnqstis* (whence OSl. *pęstĭ* of same meaning), f. ablaut-variant of **penqe* FIVE.]

1. The hand clenched or closed tightly, with the fingers doubled into the palm:

a. *gen.*, *esp.* for the purpose of striking.

a **900** *Lorica Gloss.* 49 in *O.E. Texts* (1885) 173 *Pugnas*, fyste. *c* **1000** ÆLFRIC *Exod.* xxi. 18 Gif men cidaþ & hira oþer hys nextan mid.. fyste sticþ. *c* **1050** *Monastic Sign-language* in *Techmer's Internat. Zeitschr. f. allg. Sprgsch.* II. 124 Rær up þine fæste. *c* **1160** *Hatton Gosp.* Mark xiv. 65 Sume.. mid festen hine beaten. *c* **1205** LAY. 22785, & seodden þa uustes uusden to sweoren. *a* **1225** *Ancr. R.* 106 He þolede.. þet te Giws dutten.. his deorewurde muð mid hore dreori fustes. *c* **1400** *Lanfranc's Cirurg.* 105 þe fyngris of his hand ben folden into his fist. **1490** CAXTON *Eneydos* xxvii. 107 Smytynge her brestes wyth her handes and fustes. **1526** *Pilgr. Perf.* (W. de W.) 253 b, They layde on hym with theyr fystes and other wepens. **1588** *Marprel Epist.* (Arb.) 4 You will shortly.. haue twenty fistes about your eares. **1626** J. PORY in Ellis *Orig. Lett.* I. 331 III. 239 The Queen.. brake the glasse windowes with her fiste. **1650** BULWER *Anthropomet.* 175 He only fights with a closed fist. **1740** SOMERVILLE *Hobbinol* II. 294 His Iron Fist descending crush'd his Skull. **1840** DICKENS *Old C. Shop* v, Testifying ..a vehement desire to shake her matronly fist at her son-in-law. **1865** KINGSLEY *Herew.* II. ii. 36 Which we inherited by right of fist.

b. for clasping or holding something within. Hence also, grasp, grip, clutches. Now chiefly *jocular*.

Cf. F. *poing*, still the ordinary word in this sense. In Eng. *hand* is now commonly used.

1297 R. GLOUC. (1724) 345 Boþe hys honden he nom Vol of þe poudre & of þe erþe.. And closedes to gader & hys fustes boþe adrou. *c* **1320** R. BRUNNE *Medit.* 212 He þat þou seest yn þe prestes fest. *a* **1400** *Prymer* (1891) 18 He.. hooldith the world in his feest. *c* **1400** *Destr. Troy* 10995 Philmen the fre kyng, þat he in fyst hade. **1483** CAXTON *G. de la Tour* E vij, She with her fyst tooke hym fast by the mantell. *c* **1500** *Melusine* xxxviii. 302 The geaunt, that held his syþe in his fyst. **1568** GRAFTON *Chron.* II. 2 He that a little before perswaded himselfe to have helde all England in his fist, now [etc.]. **1590** SPENSER *F.Q.* II. vii. 34 More light then Culver in the Faulcons fist. **1676** HOBBES *Iliad* (1677) 244 Lycon.. broke his sword: one part staid in his fist; The other flew. **1727–38** GAY *Fables* II. ix. 10, I know, that in a modern fist, Bribes in full energy subsist. **1807–8** SYD. SMITH *Plymley's Lett.* Wks. 1859 II. 139/2 No eel in the well-sanded fist of a cook-maid.. ever twisted.. as [etc.]. **1833** MRS. BROWNING *Prometh. Bound* Poems (1850) I. 182 To shatter in Poseidon's fist The trident-spear. **1864** SIR F. PALGRAVE *Norm. & Eng.* III. 19 The leash in his fist.

c. In various phrases: ***to grease the fist*** or (one) ***in the fist***: to bribe, pay well; so, † ***to mollify the fist***. ***to make a*** (***good, poor***, etc.) ***fist***: colloq. (orig. *U.S.* and *dial.*) to make a (good, etc.) attempt ***at*** or ***of*** something. Also, ***hand over fist, hand to fist***: see HAND.

1598 BP. HALL *Sat.* IV. v. 2 That some fat bribe might grease him in the fist. **1698** FRYER *Acc. E. India & P.* 98 Till a right understanding be created.. which commonly follows when the Fist is mollified. **1700** S. L. tr. *Fryke's Voy. E. Ind.* 111, I had now and then greased the Chief Surgeons Fist. **1833** A. GREENE *Dod. Duckworth* ii. 8 You hadn't ought to tax any thing.. seeing you've made such a fist of it. **1838** C. GILMAN *Recoll. Southern Matron* v. 46 He reckoned he should make a better fist at farming than edicating. **1841** W. G. SIMMS *Kinsmen* II. 24 (Th.), You made a poor fist of this business. **1869** A. C. GIBSON *Folk-sp. Cumb.* 177 Thoo *hes* mead a fist on't. **1876** HARDY *Ethelberta* xlvi, 'Tis a poor fist I can make at hearing anything. **1880** HOWELLS *Undisc. Country* v. 87 Mrs. Burton is really making a very pretty fist at a salon. **1920** GALSWORTHY *In Chancery* iii, He made a poor fist of sleeping. **1950** E. A. MCCOURT *Home is Stranger* (1951) ii. 31 He doesn't make much of a fist at farming. **1965** *Listener* 2 Dec. 934/2 You could make a much better fist of it than the experts.

d. in *Falconry*, with reference to carrying hawks.

1482 *Monk of Evesham* xxxiii. (Arb.) 75 Sothely he bare there on hys fyste a lytyll byrdde lyke a sparhauke. **1486** *Bk. St. Albans* D j b, When ye haue yowre hawke on yowre fyst. **1562** J. HEYWOOD *Prov. & Epigr.* (1867) 214 They [falcones] wyll check oft, but neuer come to the fist. **1828** J. S. SEBRIGHT *Observ. Hawking* 47 The goshawk is termed a hawk of the fist, because it is from thence, and not from the air, that he flies at his game. **1865** KINGSLEY *Herew.* xv, He will have his hawks to sit on his fist.

e. Used occasionally for: †(*a*) A blow with the fist (*obs.*); (*b*) the art of using the fists, boxing.

1767 H. BROOKE *Fool of Qual.* I. iii. 74 Harry gave him such a sudden fist in the temple as drove him staggering backward. *Ibid.* I. vi. 206 [He] gave him such a sudden fist in the mouth. *a* **1839** PRAED *Poems* (1864) II. 13 Skilful in fencing and in fist.

2. a. The hand, not necessarily clenched or closed. *Obs.* exc. in jocular use.

a **1300** *Fragm. Pop. Sc.* (Wright) 322 Thelbowes to the schare, the fustes to the chynne. *c* **1314** *Guy Warw.* (A.) 4059 Mani he smot of fot & fest. **1393** LANGL. *P. Pl.* C. xx. 124 The fader is þenne as þe fust with fynger and with paume. *a* **1400–50** *Alexander* 4674 With ilka fingire on ȝoure fist. **1583** STANYHURST *Aeneis* I. (Arb.) 28 This fist shal sacrifice great flocks on thy sacred altars. **1586** J. HOOKER *Girald. Irel.* in *Holinshed* II. 24/2 She.. did wring hir fists, and cried out with a lowd voice. **1628** FORD *Lover's Mel.* II. i, Humbly on my knees I kiss your gracious hand. I have a fist for thee too, stripling. **1650** BULWER *Anthropomet.* II. 113 The people of Numidia eat out of their Fist. **1708** MOTTEUX *Rabelais* IV. v. (1737) 20 Panurge and his Antagonist shak'd Fists. **1719** D'URFEY *Pills* (1872) III. 105 Each Lad took his Lass by the Fist. *Mod. colloq.* Give us your fist, old fellow: *i.e.* shake hands.

b. *Print. slang.* An index mark ☛.

1888 in JACOBI *Printer's Vocab.* s.v.

3. The 'hand' that one writes; handwriting. Now only *jocular*.

[**1524** R. DOLPHINE *Let.* 19 Apr. in M.A.E. Wood *Lett. R. Ladies* (1846) II. 23 The letter is subscribed and signed 'By the rude fist of your servant.. Richard Dolphine'.] *a* **1553** UDALL *Royster D.* III. v. Loke you on your owne fist, and I will looke on this. **1567** TURBERV. *Ovid's Ep.*, *Ulysses to Penelope* U j b, I knewe thy freendly fist at first. *c* **1690** in *Bagford Ballads* (1877) 757 Several Yards of Fist Were wanting to compleat the List. **1864** *Derby Day* i. 8 Your friend writes a tolerable fist.

4. *attrib.* and *Comb.*, as ***fist-like*** adj.; ***fistwise*** adv.; **fist-ball** (see quot.); **fist-fight**, a duel with fists; so ***fist-fighter, -fighting***; **fist-free** *a.*, unharmed by blows; **fist-law** (= Ger. *faustrecht*), the right of the strongest; **fist-mate**, an opponent in a boxing-match; † **fist-meat**, in phr. ***to eat fist-meat***, to receive a blow in the mouth from a fist; **fist-note**, in *Printing*, matter of particular importance signalled by a symbol in the shape of a hand with the index finger

extended; **fist-work**, fighting with the fists. Also CLOSE-FIST.

1585 HIGINS tr. *Nomenclator* 296 *Follis*..a *fist ball or a wind ball beaten with the fists to and fro in play. **1603** HOLLAND *Plutarch's Mor.* v. iv. 773 At hurl-bats and *fist-fight. **1873** J. H. BEADLE *Undevel. West* iv. 88 Dances, drunks and fist-fights met with a sudden interruption. **1961** A. MILLER *Misfits* xi. 128 A blasted look is on Gay's face, as though he had been beaten in a fistfight in a cause he only half-believed. **1950** J. DEMPSEY *Championship Fighting* xvi. 89 They [*sc.* shovels] are particularly valuable for the *fist-fighter. *Ibid.* i. 9 Exploding body-weight is the most important weapon in *fist-fighting or in boxing. **1615** TOMKIS *Albumazar* v. ix, Neuer a sute I wore today, but hath been soundly basted. Onely this faithfull Countrey-case 'scap't *fist-free. **1831** *Examiner* 436/1 It was probably acquired..by *fist-law (the *jus gladii*, or *Faustrecht*, of the old Civilians). **1856** R. A. VAUGHAN *Mystics* (1860) I. 35 A rough age of fist-law. **1647** R. STAPYLTON *Juvenal* 214 Hie [His?] *fist-like dowcets. **1834** LANDOR *Wks.* (1846) II. 239/2 A third [fights] because the next parish is an eyesore to him, and his *fist-mate is from it. **1563** *Jack Juggler* (Grosart 1873) 47 Gentlemen are you disposed to eat any *fist-mete? **1934** WEBSTER, *Fist-note. **1967** *Dict. Canadianisms* xix/2 Within many entries are short notes (identified by this symbol ☛ and called 'fist-notes'). **1393** LANGL. *P. Pl.* C. xx. 150 As my hand and my fyngres, Vnfolde oþer yfolde, a *fust-wise oþer elles, Al is hit bote on hand. *a* **1603** T. CARTWRIGHT *Confut. Rhem. N.T.* (1618) 514 The same hand which being first stretched forth palm-wise, is after gathered fist-wise. **1819** T. MOORE *Tom Crib's Mem.* (ed. 3) 6 A Ring and fair *fist-work at Aix-la-Chapelle.

fist (faɪst), *sb.*² Forms: 5 **fyyst**, 5–7, 9 **fiste**, 6–7 **fiest, fyest, fyst(e**, 9 *Sc.* **feist**, 7, 9 **fist**. Also FOIST. [First appears in 15th c., though OE. has the vbl. sb. *fisting* (see under FIST *v.*²). The various WGer. langs. have synonymous words representing the three ablaut-types *faist-*, *fist-*, *fist-*: MDu. *veest*, mod.Du. *vijst*, MLG. *vîst*, mod.HG. *fist*. Cf. ON. *físa* (Da. *fise*) to break wind, and see FISE *sb.*

A view widely held is that OTeut. **fisti-* is f. **fest:*—OAryan **pezd-* whence L. *pēdere*, Gr. βδέω (from *bzd-*), Lith. *bezdyti*, and that the root *fis* was evolved from this; but the hypothesis does not clearly account for the facts.]

† **1.** A breaking wind, a foul smell, stink. *Obs.*

1440 *Promp. Parv.* 163/1 Fyyst, stynk, *lirida.* **1511** *Demaundes joyous* in Kemble *Salomon* (1848) 288 It is fartes and fyestes. *a* **1529** SKELTON *Elynour Rummyng* 343 Jone sayne she had eaten a fyest; By Christ, sayde she, thou lyest, I haue as swete a breth As thou. **1605** JONSON, etc. *Eastward Hoe* IV, F iv b, Marry, fyste o' your kindnesse. I thought as much. **1611** COTGR., *Secrette*..a fiste. **1664** COTTON *Scarron.* 44 With that he whistled out most mainly. You might have heard his Fist..From one side of the skie to th' t' other.

† **2.** The fungus usually known as puff-ball (*Lycoperdon bovista*). Also called BULLFIST, PUCKFIST (see those words) and ***wolves' fist***. *Obs.*

1597 GERARDE *Herbal* III. clxii. 1386 Puffe Fistes are commonly called in Latine *Lupi crepitus* or Woolfes Fistes. **1611** COTGR., *Vesse de loup*, the dustie or smoakie Toad-stole called..Bull fyste, Puffyst, wolues fyste.

3. *U.S. dial.* A small dog. Cf. *fisting-hound*.

1860 BARTLETT *Dict. Amer.*, *Fiste* (*i* as in *mice*).

4. Comb., **fist-ball** = FUZZ-BALL, PUFF-BALL.

1635 HERRICK *K. Obron's Feast* Poems (1869) 471 A little fust-ball [**1648** *Hesper.* 137 Fuz-ball] pudding standes By. **1640** PARKINSON *Theat. Bot.* XIV. lxiv. 1324 The Fusse balls or rather Foist or Fist balls.

fist (fɪst). *v.*¹ [f. FIST *sb.*¹]

† **1.** *intr.* To fight with the fists. *Obs.*

? *a* **1300** *Salomon & Sat.* (1848) 272 þou most fist and fle ylome wiþ eye ant wiþ herte. **1705** [see FISTING *vbl. sb.*].

2. a. *trans.* To strike with the fist, beat, punch.

1597 SHAKS. *2 Hen. IV*, II. i. 23 If I but fist him once. **1681** DRYDEN *Sp. Friar* v. ii, I saw him spurning and fisting her most unmercifully. **1876** TENNYSON *Harold* I. i, The boy would fist me hard.

b. spec. in *Football.* Also *absol.*

1909 *Daily Chron.* 1 Feb. 8/5 The latter unobserved by the referee fisted the ball into the net..and a goal was allowed. **1937** *Times* 15 Feb. 6 Bigot first hooked the ball in when Hankey had fisted out a troublesome free-kick by Payen. **1970** *Times* 30 Sept. 15/4 Ferencvaros continued to press —Clemence fisted clear.

3. To grasp or seize with the fist; to handle. Now *esp. Naut.* † *to fist about*, to hand round.

1607 SHAKS. *Cor.* IV. v. 131 We haue beene downe together in my sleepe..fisting each others Throat. **1685** COTTON tr. *Montaigne* I. 621 Neither is it [the Bible] a book for every one to fist. **1701** FARQUHAR *Sir H. Wildair* II. i, I warrant they [salvers] were fisted about among his dirty levee of disbanded officers. **1840** R. H. DANA *Bef. Mast* 124 We had to fist the sail with bare hands. **1867** SMYTH *Sailor's Word-bk.*, *Fist*, to handle a rope or sail promptly. **1870** MEADE *Ride N. Zealand* 356 To see me take off my coat and fist an oar.

† **4.** *to fist* (a person) *with*: to place in his hand, to make to accept. *Obs. rare.*

1599 *Life Sir T. More* in Wordsw. *Eccl. Biog.* II. 85 For all theire importunate pressinge of him they could by no means fist him with one penny thereof.

Hence **'fisting** *vbl. sb.*, the action of the vb.

1608 SHAKS. *Per.* IV. vi. 177 To the choleric fisting of every rogue Thy ear is liable. **1705** E. WARD *Hud. Rediv.* I. I. 88 Each Zealot's Purity consisting In bitter Words, and sometimes fisting.

† **fist**, *v.*² *Obs.* Forms: 5 **fyistyn**, 6 **fyest**, (**fiesten, fysthe**), 6–7 **fyst(e**. [? OE. **fīstan* (? implied in *fīsting* vbl. sb.), f. **fīst* sb. (see prec.); cf. Du. *vijsten*, *veesten*, MHG. *visten.*]

intr. To break wind.

c **1440** *Promp. Parv.* 163/1 Fyistyn, *cacco, lirido.* **1530** PALSGR. 549/1 Beware nowe thou fysthe nat. **1570** LEVINS *Manip.* 92/25 To Fyest, *pedere.* **1605** MARSTON *Dutch Courtezan* IV. v. G ij, I must fiddle him till he fyst. **1611** COTGR., *Vessir*, to fyste, to let a fyste.

Hence **'fisting** *vbl. sb.* Also **'fister**, one who fists.

c **1000** ÆLFRIC *Gloss.* in Wr.-Wülcker 162/43 *Fesiculatio*, fisting. *c* **1440** *Promp. Parv.* 163/1 Fyystynge, *liridacio.* **1527** ANDREW *Brunswyke's Distyll. Waters* F ij, As with fystynge and shytyng. **1580** HOLLYBAND *Treas. Fr. Tong*, *Cest vn gros, vn grand vesseur*, a great farter or fyster. **1611** COTGR., *Venneur*, a fizzler or fyster.

fisted ('fɪstɪd), *ppl. a.* [f. FIST *sb.*¹ + -ED².] Having or possessed of fists, fighting with the fists.

1806 *Sporting Mag.* XXVII. 243 The fisted knights being well matched.

b. In combination with some defining prefix, as ***close-***, ***clumsy-***, ***hard-fisted***: see those words.

'fister. [f. as prec. + -ER¹.] A blow with the fist.

1825 COLERIDGE *Lit. Rem.* IV. 281 A partizan enjoying every hard thump and smashing fister he gives the adversary.

fistful ('fɪstfʊl), *sb.* [f. as prec. + -FUL.] As much as a fist will hold, a handful.

1611 COTGR., *Poignée*, a handfull, fistfull. **1862** TROLLOPE *Orley F.* I. xxii, Felix..brought forth a fistful of fruit. **1872** BESANT & RICE *Ready-Money M.* xviii, Sometimes with a fistful of money, sometimes without a dollar.

fistiana (fɪstɪ'ænə, -'eɪnə). *humorous.* [f. as prec. + -(I)ANA: cf. *boxiana.*] Matters relating to the fists and boxing.

1840 (*title*) Fistiana or the Oracle of the Ring. **1857** KINGSLEY *Two Y. Ago* II. 129 When you are driven against the ropes, 'hit out', is the old rule of Fistiana and common sense. **1881** R. BUCHANAN in *Illust. Lond. News* 3 Oct. 355/1 In matters of fistiana, science, combined with pluck, is everything.

† **'fistic**, *sb. Obs.* Forms: 6 **fistike**, (**festike, fystike**), 6–7 **fistick**, 7, 9 **fistic**. [ad. (through med.L. *fisticum*) Arab. *fistuq*, *fustuq*, *-aq*, a. Pers. *pistah*, whence ultimately PISTACHIO.] = PISTACHIO. Also, ***fistic nut***, ***tree***.

1548 TURNER *Names of Herbes* 63 Pistacia are called of the poticaries Fistica, they may be called in english Fistikes or Festike nuttes. *c* **1550** LLOYD *Treas. Health* (1585) C ij, Oyle of Fystikes healeth the hemicrane. **1562** TURNER *Herbal* II. 91 b, The figure of yᵉ fistic tre is almost rounde. **1578** LYTE *Dodoens* VI. lviii. 734 The tree which bringeth fourth Fistick Nuts. **1640** PARKINSON *Theat. Bot.* XVI. xx. 1416 The Fisticke Nut groweth to be a tree of a reasonable large sise. **1655** MOUFET & BENNET *Health's Improv.* (1746) 300 Fisticks..are Nuts growing in the Knob of the Syrian or Egyptian Turpentine-tree. **1708** MOTTEUX *Rabelais* IV. lx. (1737) 247 Pistachoes, or Fistick-Nuts.

fistic ('fɪstɪk), *a.* Not in dignified use. [f. FIST *sb.*¹ + -IC] Pertaining to or concerned with the fists or their use in boxing; pugilistic.

1806 *Sporting Mag.* XXVIII. 146 Having a little knowledge of the fistic science. **1812** S. JONES in D. E. Baker *Biog. Dram.* III. 451 The fistic hero in this afterpiece was several times interrupted by hisses. **1865** DICKENS *Mut. Fr.* II. xii, This was another common procedure of the ladies, when heated by verbal or fistic altercation.

fistical ('fɪstɪkəl). [f. as prec. + -AL¹.] = prec.

1767 A. CAMPBELL *Lexiph.* 33 Having instantaneous recurrence to fistical ratiocination. **1823** *Blackw. Mag.* XIV. 65 The man I sing, who..in a fistical combat, beat..the butcher of Bristol.

fisticuff ('fɪstɪkʌf), *sb.* Also **fisty-**. [f. FIST *sb.*¹ + CUFF *sb.*²; the form may be imitated from *handiwork.*]

1. In *pl.* Blows or fighting with the fists.

1605 ARMIN *Foole upon F.* (1880) 23 The foole..falls at fisty cuffes with him. **1613** T. GODWIN *Rom. Antiq.* (1658) 92 In this kinde of fight succeeded fisticuffes. *a* **1625** BEAUM. & FL. *Little French Lawyer* IV. iv, To revenge my wrongs at fisty-cuffs. *a* **1745** SWIFT (J.), My invention and judgment are perpetually at fisticuffs, till they have quite disabled each other. **1812** *Sporting Mag.* XXXIX. 34 Fighting men and lovers of fisty-cuffs. **1858** R. A. VAUGHAN *Ess. & Rev.* I. 23 The blows..are not mere fisticuffs. **1877** SYMONDS *Renaiss. Italy* v. 243 It now and then happened that the literary gladiators came to actual fisticuffs.

2. *attrib.* (quasi-*adj.*)

1749 FIELDING *Tom Jones* IV. viii, It is lucky for the women, that the seat of fistycuff war is not the same with them as among men. **1810** *Naval Chron.* XXIV. 369 The fistycuffs art. **1848** J. GRANT *Adv. Aide-de-C.* xxxiii, Many a fisticuff battle and bicker.

fisticuff ('fɪstɪkʌf), *v.* [f. prec. sb.] **a.** *trans.* To strike or cuff with the fists. Also *fig.* **b.** *intr.* To fight or spar with the fists.

1650–3 HALES *Dissert. de Pace* in *Phenix* (1708) II. 351 This Writing will be so fisty-cuff'd by many. **1833** *New Monthly Mag.* XXXVII. 488 A brace of judges fisticuffing on the bench. **1885** M. PATTISON *Mem.* 52 He would..have fisticuffed me round the room for my pains.

Hence **'fisticuffing** *vbl. sb.* Also **'fisticuffer**, a pugilist; **'fisti,cuffery**, fighting.

1823 *Blackw. Mag.* XIV. 527 On the moral propriety of conjugal fistycuffery I had prepared some copious remarks. **1854** HAWTHORNE *Eng. Note-bks.* (1883) II. 173 The miscellaneous assaults and batteries, kickings, fisticuffings ..which the inferior officers continually perpetrate. **1878** JEFFERIES *Gamekeeper at H.* 196 The keeper himself is not altogether averse to a little fisticuffing. **1888** *Century Mag.* Feb. 562/1 Every..fisticuffer..had heard of Bob's strength.

fistify ('fɪstɪfaɪ), *v. humorous nonce-wd.* [f. FIST *v.* + -(I)FY.] *intr.* To fight with the fists.

1860 THACKERAY *Round. Papers, Late Gt. Victories* (1876) 38 There has been fistifying enough.

† **'fisting**, *ppl. a. Obs.* [f. FIST *v.*²] That fists: applied as a contemptuous epithet. ***fisting cur***, ***dog***, ***hound***: a small pet dog (cf. *foisting hound*).

1529 MORE *Comf. agst. Trib.* III. Wks. 1262/2 A lyttle fysting curre. **1535** LYNDESAY *Satyre* 2141 Quhat kynd of woman is thy wyfe?..Ane fistand flag, a flagartie fuffe. **1546** BALE *Eng. Votaries* I. (1550) 49 Where as your fisting Nonnes were of Antichrist and the deuill. **1576** FLEMING tr. *Caius' Dogs* in Arb. *Garner* III. 267 This cur [the Spaniel gentle] which some frumpingly term Fisting Hounds serve in a manner to no good use. **1611** COTGR., *Vessaille*, a fysting; or a crue of fysting slouens or sluts. **1630** J. TAYLOR (Water P.) *Wks.* II. 227/1 No Daintie Ladies fisting-hound. **1688** R. HOLME *Armoury* II. 186/2 The Puppy, or Fisting-Dog, [is] such as Ladies delight in.

† **'fistinut.** *Obs.* Also 7 **fistenut**. [corrupted form of *fistic nut*: see FISTIC *sb.*]

1676–1732 COLES, *Fiste-nuts.* **1775** ASH, *Fistinut.*

fistle, var. of FISSLE and dial. f. THISTLE.

fistle: see FISTULA.

† **'fistmeal.** *Obs.* [f. FIST *sb.*¹; cf. OE. *fótmǽl* measure of a foot.] The breadth of the fist.

1621 BOLTON *Stat. Irel.* 37 (an. 3 Edw. iv) Every English man..shall have an English Bow of his own length and one fistmele at the least betwixt the neckes.

† **'fistock.** *Obs. rare*⁻¹. [dim. of FIST *sb.*¹: see -OCK.] A fist.

1565 GOLDING *Ovid's Met.* IX. (1593) 227 Scarce able for to stay His fistocke from his servants face.

† **'fistucate**, *v. Obs.*⁻⁰ [f. L. *fistūcāt-* ppl. stem of *fistūcāre* to use a *fistūca* or rammer: see -ATE³.] (See quot.)

1623 COCKERAM II. E ⁋v, To Ramme downe stones, *fistucate.*

‖ **fistula** ('fɪstjʊlə), *sb.* Forms: α. 5–6 **fystel**, (6 **fistle, fystle, -yl**), 6–7 **fistule**, (6 **fystule**). β. 6 **fystela, fistulay, -ey, fistelow, -olo(e, phistilo**, 6–7 **fistulo(e**, 7 **fistila**, 6– **fistula**. [a. L. *fistula* pipe, flute (also in pathological sense = 1), of which the popular representative in OF. was *festre*, FESTER *sb.*

In Eng. the word appears first in adapted forms, perh. taken from OF. *fistle*, *fistule.*]

1. a. *Pathol.* A long, narrow, suppurating canal of morbid origin in some part of the body; a long, sinuous pipe-like ulcer with a narrow orifice.

α. **1481** CAXTON *Reynard* (Arb.) 82 Colyk, stranguyllyon, stone, fystel or kanker or ony other sekenes. **1527** ANDREW *Brunswyke's Distyll. Waters* C iv, It is good for to wasshe the fystules with the same water twyse in a daye. **1547** BOORDE *Brev. Health* §236 A fystle. **1599** A. M. *Gabelhouer's Physick* 318/2 This cureth all wounds, and all fistles.

β. [**1398** TREVISA *Barth. de P.R.* VII. lix. (1495) 274 *Fistula*, the fester is a postume that..rootyth wythin.] **1563** T. GALE *Antidot.* II. 25 This vnguent..doeth also profyte muche in Fistulays. *c* **1570** SIR H. GILBERT *Q. Eliz. Acad.* (1869) 5 Towching all kindes of Vlcers, Sores, Phistiloes, wowndes, &c. **1579** LANGHAM *Gard. Health* (1633) 12 It is good for all wounds, fistilaes, and sores of the mouth. **1671** SALMON *Syn. Med.* III. xxii. 423 It cools Feavers and cures Ulcers, Fistulas, Cancers. **1732** ARBUTHNOT *Rules of Diet* 360 It happens sometimes to end in a Fistula. **1879** GREEN *Read. Eng. Hist.* xviii. 89 Henry, notwithstanding his fistula and his fever, was able to sit on horseback.

fig. **1581** J. BELL *Haddon's Answ. Osor.* 389 b, Fosteryng continually this fretting Fistula within the Bowels of the Christian commonweale. **1622** W. WHATELY *God's Husb.* II. 48 An heart diseased with that grievous fistula of hypocrisie. **1644** BULWER *Chiron.* 5 The mouth is but a running sore and hollow fistula of the minde.

b. in animals, birds, etc.

1607 MARKHAM *Caval.* VII. xxvi. 45 *heading*, Of the Poll euill or Fistula in the Necke. **1614** —— *Cheap Husb.* VIII. xvi. (1668) 133 The Fistula in hawks is a cankerous, hollow Ulcer in any part of a hawks body. **1678** *Lond. Gaz.* No. 1311/4 A sorrel Gelding..having formerly had a Fistula. **1861** G. F. BERKELEY *Sportsm. W. Prairies* x. 162 Sylph [a mare]..having been blistered too severely on the withers where a fistula had evidently been apprehended.

c. Also applied to certain passages in the body made surgically.

1892 KEEN & WHITE *Text-bk. Surg.* II. III. vi. 691 An intentional gastric fistula may require surgical treatment for its closure if the object for which the fistula was made has been accomplished, as when it has been undertaken with a view of dilating a cicatricial stricture of the cardiac orifice. **1963** W. V. McDERMOTT in R. Warren *Surgery* xxvi. 825/1 In 1877 Nikolai Eck conducted a series of experiments on dogs in which he diverted the portal blood into the inferior vena cava... This type of shunt has commonly been referred to as the Eck fistula.

2. *Bot.* = *cassia fistula*: see CASSIA 4.

1812 J. SMYTH *Pract. of Customs* (1821) 62 This is the purgative fruit or pods of the Cassia Fistula, black or purging Fistula.

3. A natural or normal pipe or spout in cetaceous animals, insects, etc. (see quots.).

1646 SIR T. BROWNE *Pseud. Ep.* III. xix. 154 Like cetaceous animals and Whales, the Lamprey hath a fistula spout or pipe at the back part of the head. **1658** *Ibid.* III. xxvi. 215 The Fistula or spout [of the Whale]. **1661** LOVELL *Hist. Anim. & Min.* Introd., The Mollusca..have a fistule above the head. **1848** MAUNDER *Treas. Nat. Hist.* Gloss. App., *Fistula*, the intermediate subquadrangular pipe, in insects, formed by the union of the two branches of the *antlia* which conveys the nectar to the pharynx.

4. *Eccl.* A tube through which in early times communicants received the consecrated wine; now used by the Pope only.

1670 LASSELS *Voy. Italy* II. 53 The fistula, or pipe of gold wherwith the Pope receiues the consecrated blood of our Sauiour in the Chalice. **1848** *Ecclesiologist* VIII. 99 He held the chalice with his right hand, and the fistula in the chalice with his left, while the brethren in order imbibed.

‖**5.** *Mus.* A reed instrument or pipe of the ancient Romans.

1717 LADY M. W. MONTAGU *Lett.* (1893) I. 301 A rural instrument, perfectly answering the description of the ancient fistula, being composed of unequal reeds. **1722** J. RICHARDSON *Statues Italy, etc.* 185 One sits upon a Rock playing on a Fistula. **1727** POPE *Mem. M. Scriblerus* I. v. Wks. 1741 II. 19, I will have it [the Whistle] exactly to correspond with the ancient Fistula.

† **'fistula,** *v. Obs.* In 6 fystle. [f. prec. sb.] *intr.* To form or become a fistula.

1547 BOORDE *Brev. Health* vi. 9 If this impediment do encrease, and a remedy by tyme not had, it wyll fester and fystle. **1646** J. WHITAKER *Uzziah* 39 Till at last it fistula or gangrene.

† **'fistula'd,** *ppl. a. Obs.* Also 6 **fystyled, fystuled,** 7 **fistuled.** [f. FISTULA, *fistule* + -ED².] Formed into, or accompanied by, a fistula.

1547 BOORDE *Brev. Health* Pref. 4 Woundes that be festered and fystyled. *Ibid.* §377 Some be playne woundes, & some fystuled, & some be festered. **1656** EARL MONM. *Advt. fr. Parnass.* 147 Wounds that are fistuled, and incurable cancars. *Ibid.* 155 Fistula'd. **1662** R. MATHEW *Unl. Alch.* §16. 10 Sundry stinking Fistula'd Ulcers running in it.

fistular ('fɪstjʊlə(r)), *a.* [ad. L. *fistulār-is*, f. *fistula*: see FISTULA *sb.* and -AR¹.]

1. *Bot.* Hollow and cylindrical like a pipe or reed, tube-like. Also, consisting of tube-like parts.

1704 J. HARRIS *Lex. Techn.* s.v. *Flower*, Compounded Flowers, are either, Discous..Planifolious..Fistular, which is compounded of many long, hollow, little Flowers like Pipes. *a* **1722** LISLE *Husb.* (1757) 150 The fibres and fistular parts of a plant. **1845** LINDLEY *Sch. Bot.* viii. (1858) 150 Leaves fistular. **1870** HOOKER *Stud. Flora* 149 Umbelliferæ. Herbs. Stems usually fistular, solid at the nodes.

2. *Path.* Pertaining to, or of the nature of, a fistula.

1706 PHILLIPS (ed. Kersey), *Fistular, Fistulary*, or *Fistulous*, belonging to a Fistula. **18..** tr. *Bichat's Physiol.* (L.), Such, too, is the character of the mucous membrane in fistular canals.

† **'fistulary,** *a. Obs.* [See -ARY².] = prec.

1616 CHAPMAN *Homer's Hymns, Hermes* Wks. (1625) 83 Apollo..Gaue him the farr-heard fistularie Reede. **1656** BLOUNT *Glossogr.*, *Fistulary*, belonging to that disease [Fistula] or to a pipe.

† **'fistulate,** *v. Obs.* [f. L. *fistulāt-* ppl. stem of *fistulāre*, f. *fistula*: see FISTULA *sb.* and -ATE³.]

1. *intr.* (in *Path.*) To form or grow to a fistula.

1607 TOPSELL *Four-f. Beasts* (1658) 322 That the upper part of the wound heal not faster then the bottom, for fear of Fistulating. **1663–76** BULLOKAR, *Fistulate*, to turn or grow to a Fistula.

2. *trans.* To make tubular.

1751 *Student* II. 378 It [*chalal*] signifies..to perforate or fistulate. *Ibid.* 379 Their tubes, pipes or ducts, fistulated, or hollowed, to circulate the blood and juices.

Hence **'fistulated** *ppl. a.*; **'fistulating** *vbl. sb.* and *ppl. a.* Also **fistu'lation**, the formation of a fistula.

1612 WOODALL *Surg. Mate* Wks. (1653) 79 Cure old and fistulated sores. **1617** MARKHAM *Caval.* VII. 64 There many times followeth cankerous sores and fistulating. **1638** A. READ *Chirurg.* xxix. 213 Wounds tending to fistulation. **1656** EARL MONM. *Advt. fr. Parnass.* 312 Cankers and fistulated wounds must be cured by fire. **1659** BP. GAUDEN *Slight Healings* (1660) 2 The old sores and fistulating ulcers of this Church and State.

fistule: anglicized form of FISTULA, q.v.

fistulidan (fɪ'stjuːlɪdən). *Zool.* [f. mod.L. *fistulid-es* (see FISTULA and -ID) + -AN.] (See quot. 1842.)

1835 KIRBY *Hab. & Inst. Anim.* I. vi. 214 The third and last section of the Echinoderms..are the Fistulidans. **1842** BRANDE *Dict. Sc. Lit. & Art*, *Fistulidans*..a tribe of Echinodermatous animals, comprehending those which have an elongated cylindrical tube-like body.

fistuliform ('fɪstjʊlɪfɔːm), *a.* [f. FISTULA + -(I)FORM.] Of the form of a reed or tube.

1823 W. PHILLIPS *Introd. Min.* (ed. 3) Introd. 88 Minerals occurring in round hollow columns are termed fistuliform.. Stalactites and iron pyrites occur fistuliform.

fistulose (fɪstjuː'ləʊs). *a.* [ad. L. *fistulōs-us*, f. *fistula*: see -OSE.] = next.

c **1420** *Pallad. on Husb.* I. 375 For bylding better is the harder myne The fistulose and softer lete it goone To cover with. **1846** WORCESTER (citing HOOKER), *Fistulose*, formed like a fistula; fistular. **1881** *Nature* XXIII. 426 A mass of fistulose coral.

fistulous ('fɪstjʊləs), *a.* [ad. L. *fistulōs-us*: see prec. and -OUS.]

1. *Path.* Of or pertaining to a fistula; of the nature of a fistula; attacked by a fistula.

1611 COTGR., *Injection*..a squirting, or conueying of a liquid medicine..into a hollow and fistulous vlcer. **1721** S. SEWALL *Diary* 13 Mar. (1882) III. 284 His fistulous thigh. **1797** BAILLIE *Morb. Anat.* (1807) 337 A fistulous orifice is gradually formed. **1869** E. A. PARKES *Pract. Hygiene* (ed. 3) 98 Fistulous sores are apt to be produced.

2. a. Resembling a pipe or tube in form, tubular. **b.** Having or containing a tube or tubes; honey-combed with small tubes. **c.** Of a flower: Having many long hollow florets.

1578 BANISTER *Hist. Man* IV. 48b, The flesh of it [the tongue] is rare, Fistulous, & soft. **1601** HOLLAND *Pliny* I. XI. i. 310 Hanging togither only by a little pipe and fistulous conveiance. **1603** —— *Plutarch's Mor.* 1009 As for the flesh of the Polype, it is to see to, fistulous, and spongeous, like unto hony-combs. **1671** GREW *Anat. Plants* I. v. (1682) 39 The Fistulous Pouches of Wake-Robin, or of Dragon. **1688** J. CLAYTON in *Phil. Trans.* XVIII. 128 Vipers..have I believe their Poisonous Teeth Fistulous. **1712** tr. *Pomet's Hist. Drugs* I. 185 The Flowers..having their lower Part fistulous. **1830** LINDLEY *Nat. Syst. Bot.* 159 Stems fistulous rooting. **1858** *Times* 4 Nov. 7/3 The careworn soil..pierced with fistulous passages of miles of hard piping.

fisty ('fɪstɪ), *a.* [f. FIST *sb.*¹ + -Y¹.] Of or pertaining to fists, or their use in boxing.

1681 COLVIL *Whig's Supplic.* (1751) 34 A fisty strife Between a preacher and his wife. **1821** BYRON *Juan* XI. lv, Like to the champion in the fisty ring. **1840** THACKERAY *Paris Sk. Bk.* (1867) 409 He engages in a fisty combat with a notorious boxer.

fit, fytte (fɪt), *sb.*¹ *Obs.* exc. *arch.* Forms: 1 fitt, 4–5 fyt(t, 4–6 fitt(e, 5–6, 9 fytte, 5–8 fit. [OE. *fitt* str. fem. = OS. **fittia*, preserved in latinized form in the preface to the *Hêliand*: 'Juxta morem vero illius poematis, omne opus per *vitteas* distinxit, quas nos lectiones vel sententias possumus appellare'.

Some regard the word as identical with OHG. *fiza* list of cloth, mod.Ger. *fitze* skein of yarn, also explained in the 17th c. as 'the thread with which weavers mark off a day's work'; the sense 'division or canto of a poem' might well be a transferred use of this. The Ger. word corresponds to ON. *fit* str. fem., hem, also 'web' of a bird's foot:—OTeut. **fitjâ*, of unknown origin: see remarks under next sb.]

1. A part or section of a poem or song; a canto.

c **888** K. ÆLFRED *Boeth.* xxxi. §1 (Gr.) Se wisdom þa þas fitte asungen hæfde. **1362** LANGL. *P. Pl.* A. I. 139 Cumse[þ] þer a Fitte. *c* **1386** CHAUCER *Sir Thopas* 177 Lo, lordes, heer is a fyt; If ye wil eny more of it, To telle it wol I fonde. *a* **1400–50** *Alexander* 5626 Now fynes here a fitt & folows a nothire. *c* **1450** *Bk. Curtasye* 349 in *Babees Bk.* 309 Of curtasie here endis þe secunde fyt. **1589** PUTTENHAM *Eng. Poesie* I. xxvi. (Arb.) 65 This Epithalamie was deuided by breaches into three partes to serue for three seuerall fits or times to be song. **1771** JOHNSON *Let. to Langton* 20 Mar. in *Boswell*, Dr. Percy has written a long ballad in many fits. **1812** BYRON *Ch. Har.* I. xciii, Here is one fytte of Harold's pilgrimage. **1864** SKEAT *Uhland's Poems* 213 The first 'fytte' here is ended.

2. A strain of music, stave. Also, *to dance a fit.*

a **1500** *Iak & his step dame* in Herrig's *Archiv* XC. 78, I shall yow shewe of my gle: Ye shall haue a fytte. ? *a* **1548** *King Estmere* 243 in *Percy Reliq.* (1765) I. 68 To playe my wiffe and me a fitt. *c* **1550** R. WEVER *Lusty Iuventus* in Hazl. *Dodsley* II. 48, I would fain go dance a fit. **1578** *Gude & G. Ball.* (1868) 182 Sa sall thay pype ane mirrie fit. **1673** *True Worship God* 65 An afternoon Sermon..many times.. serves only like a fit of Musick, to Lull them asleep after their Dinner. **1681** W. ROBERTSON *Phraseol. Gen.* (1693) 611 Come now, strike up and give us a fit.

fit (fɪt), *sb.*² Forms: 1 fitt, 4–7 fitt(e, 5–6 fytt(e, 4, 6– fit. [OE. *fitt*, str., of uncertain gender; recorded only once; the sense 'conflict' seems probable from the context.

The OTeut. type **fitjo-, -jâ* is not found in any other lang. with any of the senses explained below. It is possible, however, that the word may be cognate or even identical with prec., and that the primitive sense may have been 'juncture', 'meeting'; cf. the vbs. Icel. *fitja* to knit, early mod.Du. *vitten* 'to accomodate, to fitt, to serve' (Hexham); on this supposition FIT *sb.*³, *a.*, and *v.* would also be cognate.]

† **1.** Conflict, struggle. Only in OE. *rare*⁻¹.

a **1000** *Cædmon's Gen.* 2072 (Gr.) [Abraham] sloh and fylde feond on fitte.

† **2. a.** A position of hardship, danger, or intense excitement; a painful, terrible, or exciting experience. *Obs.*

In quot. 1550 there is an apparent re-development of the OE. sense.

c **1325** *Song Yesterday* 93 in *E.E.P.* (1862) 135 þat ferful fit may no mon fle. *c* **1386** CHAUCER *Reeve's T.* 264 We han had an yvel fit today. *Ibid.* 310 So mery a fit ne had she nat ful yore. —— *Wife's Prol.* 42 This noble king.. The firste night had many a mery fitte With eche of hem. *c* **1400** *Rom. Rose* 5197, I mene not that [love], which..bringith thee in many a fitte, And ravysshith fro thee al thi witte. *a* **1440** *Sir Eglam.* 254 An hardere fytt never ye had. ? *a* **1500** *Chester Pl.* (E.E.T.S.) 205 And now that fitt may I not flee. *Ibid.* 390 Four wyndes they be..Which shall blow..before Christ.. ther is none so fell their fitt may flee. **1550** BALE *Eng. Votaries* II. H vij b, The first fit of Anselme with kynge William Rufus. **1601** HOLLAND *Pliny* I. 8 In this fearefull fit also of an eclipse.

† **b.** In 16th c. occas.: A mortal crisis; a bodily state (whether painful or not) that betokens death.

1579 LYLY *Euphues* (Arb.) 181 The patient..is yᵉ neerest death when he thinketh himself past his disease, and the lesse griefe he feeleth yᵉ greater fits he endureth. **1590** SPENSER *F.Q.* II. vii. 66, The life did flit away out of her nest, And all his senses were with deadly fit oppress. **1591** —— *Ruines Time* 598 Feeling the fit that him forewarnd to die.

3. a. A paroxysm, or one of the recurrent attacks, of a periodic or constitutional ailment. In later use also with wider sense: A sudden and somewhat severe but transitory attack (of illness, or of some specified ailment).

a **1547** SURREY *Faithf. Louer declareth, Songs & S.* (1585) 15 b, As sick men in their shaking fits procure them selues to sweat. **1601** SHAKS. *Jul. C.* I. ii. 120 He had a Feauer..And when the Fit was on him, I did marke How he did shake. **1667** D. ALLSOPP in *12th Rep. Hist. MSS. Comm.* App. v. 8 Taken with a fit of the collicke. **1691** BLAIR in W. S. Perry *Hist. Coll. Amer. Col. Ch.* (1860) I. 6 The Bishop of London ..was..taken..with a fit of the stone. **1725** N. ROBINSON *Th. Physick* 146 The Fits of Intermittent Fevers. **1771** SMOLLETT *Humph. Cl.* (1815) 3, I expect to be laid up with another fit of the gout. **1806–7** J. BERESFORD *Miseries Hum. Life* (1826) IV. xvi, A violent fit of coughing. **1855** BAIN *Senses & Int.* II. ii. §3 (1864) 123 A cut or a scald is different from a fit of rheumatism or gout.

fig. **1567** DRANT *Horace's Art Poet.* C j b, Sawes there be to cure thy greedie care: To master thyne assaltynge fyttes.

† **b.** *spec.* A paroxysm of lunacy (formerly viewed as a periodic disease). *Obs.*

1588 SHAKS. *Tit. A.* IV. i. 17 Vnlesse some fit or frenzie do possesse her. **1590** —— *Com. Err.* IV. iii. 91 Belike his wife acquainted with his fits On purpose shut the doores against his way. **1697** DRYDEN *Æneid* III. 565 In her frantick Fitts. **1722** WOLLASTON *Relig. Nat.* ix. 201 Cruel tyrants..who (at least in their fits) divert themselves with the pangs and convulsions of their fellow-creatures.

c. A sudden seizure of any malady attended with loss of consciousness and power of motion, or with convulsions, as fainting, hysteria, apoplexy, paralysis, or epilepsy. In 18th c. often used *spec.* without defining word = 'fainting-fit' or 'fit of the mother' (i.e. of hysteria: see MOTHER); in recent use it suggests primarily the notion of an epileptic or convulsive fit.

1621 BURTON *Anat. Mel.* III. iii. III. 689 A iealous woman that by this meanes had many fits of the Mother. **1650** BULWER *Anthropomet.* 141 Who..fell straightway into a Convulsion and Epileptical fits. **1681** OTWAY *Soldier's Fort.* I. i, One Kiss of him were enough to cure Fits of the Mother. **1702** STEELE *Funeral* I. (1734) 20 Fits are a mighty help in the Government of a good-natured Man. **1762** GOLDSM. *Cit. W.* xxi. §15 Observe the art of the poet..When the queen can say no more, she falls into a fit..take my word for it, that fits are the true aposiopesis of modern tragedy. **1789** W. BUCHAN *Dom. Med.* (1790) 629 Convulsion fits often constitute the last scene of acute or chronic disorders. **1833** HT. MARTINEAU *Loom & Lugger* I. v. 76 When the fainting fit came on in which she died. *Mod.* 'Has she fainted?' 'No, I fear it is a fit.'

d. Hence *colloq.* in various hyperbolical phrases, as *to scream oneself into fits, to throw (a person) into fits.* Also, *to beat (a person, a thing) into fits*: to defeat or excel thoroughly, 'beat hollow'; *to give (a person) fits*: to inflict humiliating defeat on; in *U.S.* to rate or scold vigorously.

1839 HOOD *Tale Trumpet* xxix, It beats all others into fits. **1848** THACKERAY *Bk. Snobs* xx, Till the little wretch screams herself into fits. **1859** FARRAR *Jul. Home* i, He beat you to fits in the Latin verse. **1860** L. HARCOURT *Diaries G. Rose* II. 104 Such a proposal..would have thrown him into fits. **1861** DICKENS *Gt. Expect.* I. iv, If you could only give him his head, he would read the clergy-man to fits. **1861** J. BLACKWOOD *Let.* 23 Dec. in Geo. Eliot *Lett.* (1954) III. 474 Your account of Caliban's exploit..has put me into fits. Archie is in an extasy with it. **1872** E. EGGLESTON *Hoosier Schoolm.* xii. 66, I rather guess as how the old man..will give particular fits to our folks to-day. **1877** S. O. JEWETT *Deephaven* iii. 53 She used to take a notion to set in the dark. ..I should have forty fits, if I undertook it. **1885** RUNCIMAN *Skippers & Sh., Old Pirate* 87 We goes out and tackles a East Indiaman..and he gives us fits. **1906** J. LONDON *Let.* 20 Oct. (1966) 213 Bailey Millard is throwing fits all around the shop..because of the way you worded your announcement. **1924** C. BEATON *Diary* 12 Apr. (1961) II. 44, I had fits at the back of the car because Papa kept shouting.

4. In various uses originally *transf.* from 3.

a. A sudden and transitory state of activity or inaction, or of any specified kind of activity, feeling, inclination, or aptitude.

1586 WARNER *Alb. Eng.* I. ii. 20 His seruants fear his solemn fittes. **1591** SYLVESTER *Du Bartas* I. iii. 186 The Sea hath fits, alternate course she keeps From Deep to Shore and from the Shore to Deeps. **1634** MILTON *Comus* 546 Wrapt in a pleasing fit of melancholy. **1667** FLAVEL *Saint Indeed* (1754) 143 We have our hot and cold fits by turns. **1697** BP. PATRICK *Comm. Ex.* xx. 8 Stedfastly resolve not in a Fit but constantly. **1744** BERKELEY *Siris* §213 Certain persons have fits of seeing in the dark. *a* **1764** LLOYD *A Tale* Poet. Wks. 1774 I. 73 Who..to Tottenham Court In furious fits of zeal resort. **1807–8** W. IRVING *Salmag.* xvii. (1860) 391 This outrageous merriment..threw the whole family into a violent fit of wondering. **1852** MISS YONGE *Cameos* I. ii. 11 He had many fits of devotion. **1882** PICTON *Cromwell* ii. 25 The boy had fits of application alternating with fits of idleness.

b. *spec.* in *Optics.* (see quot. 1704).

1704 NEWTON *Optics* II. III. (1721) 256 The returns of the disposition of any Ray to be reflected I will call its Fits of easy Reflexion, and those of its disposition to be transmitted its Fits of easy Transmission, and the space it passes between every return and the next return, the Interval of its Fits. 1803 *Edin. Rev.* I. 455 The law of the fits..might be fancifully resolved into a still more general law. 1831 BREWSTER *Optics* xv. §83. 126 In virtue of which they possess at different points of their path fits or dispositions to be reflected or transmitted by transparent bodies.

c. Often in phr. ***by fits (and starts)***: by irregular impulses or periods of action, at varying intervals, fitfully, spasmodically. Also more rarely, †***at***, †***upon, fits, by fits and girds*** (obs. exc. *dial.*), †***spasms***, or †***turns***; †***by halves and fits***.

1583 GOLDING *Calvin on Deut.* vii. 39 He doth not thinges by fittes as Creatures doe but he continueth alwayes in one will. 1615 G. SANDYS *Trav.* 72 A lazy people, that worke but by fits. *a*1617 HIERON *Wks.* II. 489 Vpon fits you shall haue them talke like angels, and yet..are deuils indeede. 1620 SANDERSON *Serm. ad Pop.* i. (1681) 145 If thou hast these things only by fits and starts. 1635 SWAN *Spec. M.* (1670) 363 The swallow..sleepeth but by 'halves and fits' (as we say) which is no sound kind of rest. 1650 FULLER *Pisgah* I. ii. 5 That froward people worshiped him by fits and girds. 1664 POWER *Exp. Philos.* I. 25 Without any saliency or leaping, without any fits or starts in its Progression. 1678 CUDWORTH *Intell. Syst.* I. iv. §17. 303 To suppose that Orpheus had by Fits and turns been of different humours. 1782 MAD. D'ARBLAY *Let.* 19 Mar., Let me murmur as I will by fits, I would not, if I could, change your destination. 1785 T. JEFFERSON *Corr.* Wks. 1859 I. 426 No particular State, acting by fits and starts, can harass the trade of France, Holland, &c. 1791 BURKE *Th. French Affairs* Wks. VII. 49 The non-payment..is only by fits and spasms. 1805 SOUTHEY *Madoc in W.* x, As the flashes of the central fire At fits arose. 1850 TENNYSON *In Mem.* xxiii, Breaking into song by fits. 1862 MRS. H. WOOD *Mrs. Hallib.* I. xiv, Jane was..more hopeful by fits and starts than continuously so. 1884 *Chesh. Gloss.* s.v., 'The clock strikes by fits and gurds.'

d. †The time during which a 'fit' lasts, a 'spell', short period (*obs.*). Also, a spell of weather of a specified kind (*obs.* exc. *dial.*).

1583 FULKE *Defence* iii. 205 After you have railed a fit. 1615 DYKE *Myst. Self-Deceiving* 116 Which is not settled and rooted, but onely for a fitte. *a*1625 FLETCHER *Hum. Lieutenant* IV. iv, I will not leave ye for a fit. *a*1628 PRESTON *New Covt.* (1634) 213 He may for a fit, put out his hand to wickedness. 1685 TEMPLE *Ess. Garden.* Wks. 1731 I. 188 Attended by some Fit of Hot and Dry Weather. 1685 DRYDEN *Horace, Ode* III. xxix. iv, Sometimes 'tis grateful to the Rich, to try A short vicissitude, and fit of Poverty. 1721 SWIFT *Corr.* Wks. 1841 II. 556 A fit of good weather would tempt me a week longer. 1868 ATKINSON *Cleveland Gloss.* s.v., 'A strange dry fit we've had for seear.'

e. A capricious impulse, humour, mood.

*a*1680 BUTLER *Rem.* (1759) I. 174 Invention..Disdains t' obey the proudest Wit, Unless it chance to b' in the Fit. 1786 BURNS *To J. S.* iv, Just now I've taen the fit o' rhyme. 1787 MAD. D'ARBLAY *Diary* 6 Mar., I assured him I was seized with a silent fit. 1869 MRS. STOWE *Oldtown Folks* iv. 30 When the fit was on him, he would shoe a horse better than any man in the county.

f. A violent access or outburst of laughter, tears, rage, etc.

1654 WHITLOCK *Zootomia* 47 The Doctresse would have a shaking fit of Laughter at you presently. 1676 HOBBES *Iliad* (1677) 377 Achilles, when his fit of tears was laid..came from his throne. 1678 WANLEY *Wond. Lit. World* v. ii. §12. 469/2 In one of his drunken fits he was buried alive. 1778 MAD. D'ARBLAY *Diary* 26 Aug., [She] took me into a back room, and burst into a hearty fit of laughter. 1816 SHELLEY *Alastor* 171 Her breath Tumultuously accorded with those fits Of intermitted song. 1874 CARPENTER *Ment. Phys.* I. vii. (1879) 325 A prolonged fit of grumbling. 1886 J. K. JEROME *Idle Thoughts* 64 He would go off into fits of merriment over every word you uttered.

5. *Comb.*, as †**fit-meal** *adv.*, by fits and starts (cf. PIECE-MEAL); **fit-weed** (see quot.).

1593 NASHE *Christ's T.* 34 a, Rather..then day-diuersifying Agues..should fit-meale feede on them. 1756 P. BROWNE *Jamaica* 185 The stinking Eryngo or Fittweed.. All parts of this plant are reckoned very powerful anti-histerics.

†**fit**, *sb.*³ *Obs. rare*⁻¹. In 3 fitte (2 syll.). [ME. *fitte*, perh.:—OE. **fitta*, of obscure origin; possibly f. OE. *fitt*, FIT *sb.*²

It might be supposed to be a subst. use of FIT *a.*, but that word has not been found before the 15th c., and is perhaps a derivative of this.]

An adversary of equal power; one's 'match'.

*a*1250 *Owl & Night.* 782 Thou deth mid strengthe and mid witte That other thing nis non his fitte.

fit (fit), *sb.*⁴ [f. FIT *v.*¹]

1. The process of fitting or rendering fit. †**a.** In the phrase ***out of fit***, app. meaning 'fitted out, settled in life' (*obs. rare*⁻¹). **b.** A preparation or fitting *for* something (U.S.). Cf. *outfit*.

*a*1688 BUNYAN *Heav. Footman* (1698) 42 Till my children are out of Fit. 1883 *New Eng. Jrnl. Educ.* XVII. 133 [This Academy] has for many years given an excellent fit for college.

2. a. A fitting or adaptation of one thing to another, *esp.* the adjustment of dress to the body; the style or manner in which something is made to fit. ***to a fit***: to a nicety.

1823 W. T. MONCRIEFF *Tom & Jerry* I. iv, A tight fit, not much hunting room. 1868 E. YATES *Rock Ahead* II. iii, He noticed all these details down to the fit of her gloves. 1884 W. C. SMITH *Kildrostan* 69 A man May be ashamed too of his rustic fit. 1890 C. M. WOODWARD *Manual Train.* xv. 247 How to saw to a fit on the right or left of a line.

b. *concr.* A garment that fits.

1831 *Examiner* 11/2 It's rather a tight fit. 1849 THACKERAY *Pendennis* xvii, It [the gown] was an excellent fit.

3. *Soap-making.* The condition of the liquid soap in the operation of 'fitting'; see FIT *v.* 10.

1885 W. L. CARPENTER *Manuf. Soap* vi. 173 Practice and observation alone enable the operator to obtain 'a good fit'. *Ibid.*, A fine fit gives a very large nigre.

4. ***a fit-out***: a furnishing with all that is requisite, *esp.* in dress; an equipment.

1830 G. COLMAN *Random Rec.* II. vii. 214 A complete Fit-Out, on my return to London, at my father's cost. 1836 MARRYAT *Midsh. Easy* xx, They condescended to have a regular fit-out—and it so happened that the fit-out was not far from a regular fit. 1844 DICKENS *Mart. Chuz.* xxiii, Who says we ain't got a first-rate fit-out?

5. *Comb.*, as **fit-rod** (see quot.).

1867 SMYTH *Sailor's Word-bk.*, *Fit-rod*, a small iron rod with a hook at the end..to ascertain the length of the bolts or treenails required to be driven in.

fit (fit), *a.* Forms: 5 fyt, 6 fitte, 6–7 fytt(e, 6– fit. [First recorded *c* 1440; possibly f. FIT *sb.*³, though as that word is known only from a solitary instance the derivation is very doubtful. The adj. is recorded a century earlier than the modern verb, and appears to be its source; the view that it is a pa. pple. of the vb. *fitte* to marshal troops (see FIT *v.*¹ 1) is tenable only on the assumption that the vb. had an unrecorded wider sense. To some extent the adj. appears to have been influenced in meaning by FEAT *a.*]

1. a. Well adapted or suited to the conditions or circumstances of the case, answering the purpose, proper or appropriate. Const. *for* (also, rarely, with ellipsis of *for*) or *to* with *inf.*

*c*1440 *Promp. Parv.* 163/1 Fyt, or mete, *congruus*. 1550 BALE *Image Both Ch.* xxi. Hh v b, Nothinge faire apered this stones..whan they were hewen, squared and made fitte foundacion. 1594 WILLOBIE in *Shaks. C. Praise* 10 No tyme or fit occasion leave. 1597 SHAKS. *2 Hen. IV*, I. ii. 17 Thou art fitter to be worne in my cap, then to wait at my heeles. 1599 H. BUTTES *Dyets drie Dinner* M v, Tench..is fittest meate for labouring men. 1613 SHAKS. *Hen. VIII*, II. ii. 117 Prethee call Gardiner to me, my new Secretary. I find him a fit fellow. *a*1616 BEAUM. & FL. *Bonduca* III. i, Steel us both with angers, and warlike executions fit thy viewing. 1634 T. JOHNSON *Parey's Chirurg.* XXVI. xxxvi. (1678) 654 The time fittest for the use of Apophlegmatisms is the morning. 1639 FULLER *Holy War* v. xxix. (1647) 281 A Spaniard.. proposed the French Tongue as most fit. 1663 BUTLER *Hud.* I. i. 865 This is no fit Place Nor time, to argue out the Case. 1710 PRIDEAUX *Orig. Tithes* ii. 53 What is the fittest portion of our Substance to be set apart. 1852 MISS YONGE *Cameos* I. ii. 14 Until he could find a fit opportunity of quitting Normandy. 1862 H. SPENCER *First Princ.* I. v. §32 (1875) 119 Forms of religion..must be fit for those who live under them. 1875 JOWETT *Plato* (ed. 2) III. 251 Those stories are not fit to be repeated.

b. *absol.*; esp. in ***survival of the fittest***.

1843 CARLYLE *Past & Pr.* II. viii. 111 There is in every Nation and Community a fittest, a wisest, bravest, best. 1867 H. SPENCER *Biol.* §193 II. 53 By the continual survival of the fittest, such structures must become established.

2. a. Befitting the person or the circumstances, agreeable to decorum, becoming, convenient, proper, right. Const. as above. Now only in predicative use, as ***it is fit that***, etc., or *to* with *inf.*

*c*1440 *York Myst.* i. 65 Fetys and fayre and fygured full fytt. 1554–9 *Songs & Ball. Ph. & Mary* (1860) 4 In hyme voyd was nothyng that was nydfull and fytt. 1601 SHAKS. *All's Well* III. vi. 14 It were fit you knew him, least..he might at some great and trustie businesse..fayle you. 1607 —— *Cor.* III. ii. 83 Say to them Thou..Hast not the soft way, which thou do'st confesse Were fit for thee to vse. 1625 BACON *Ess., Innovations* (Arb.) 526 What is setled by Custome, though it be not good, yet at least it is fit. 1649 BP. HALL *Cases Consc.* (1650) 203 There are Theologicall verities fit for us to know and beleeve. *a*1715 BURNET *Own Time* (1766) I. 102 While he was balancing in his mind what was fit for him to do. 1787 BENTHAM *Def. Usury* x. 94 It is one thing, to find reasons why it is fit a law should have been made: it is another to [etc.].

absol. 1681 DRYDEN *Abs. & Achit.* 765 If the Croud be Judge of fit and just, And Kings are onely Officers in trust, Then [etc.]. 1810 D. STEWART *Philos. Ess.* II. I. i. 215 The idle generalities we meet with..about the ideas of the good, the fit, and the becoming.

b. In phrases, ***to see, think fit***.

1611 BIBLE *2 Macc.* iv. 19 Which..the bearers therof thought fit not to bestow vpon the sacrifice. *a*1687 PETTY *Pol. Arith.* (1690) 95 All these things may be done, if it be so thought fit by the Sovereign Power. 1711 STEELE *Spect.* No. 43 ⁋3 Where and in what manner we see fit. 1761 HUME *Hist. Eng.* III. lxi. 322 Cromwell thought fit to indulge a new fancy. 1815 MRS. SHERWOOD *Susan Gray* 73 If God sees fit ..that I should marry, in his due time he will provide me with a worthy husband. 1875 JOWETT *Plato* (ed. 2) I. 477 The Athenians have thought fit to condemn me.

†**c.** Needing, requiring, or calling for (action of some kind). Const. *to* with *passive inf.* *Obs.*

1621 ELSING *Debates Ho. Lords* (Camden) 54 Fytt to be so done, but the matter of Yelverton..cannot be paste over. 1661–2 MARVELL *Corr.* xxxiii. Wks. 1872–5 II. 77 Wherein you shall find it [the Petition] fit to be alterd, be pleased to returne it corrected to us. 1756 BURKE *Subl. & B.* Wks. 1842 I. 53 Good sense and experience..find out what is fit to be done in every work of art.

†**3.** Of a manufactured article: Of the right measure or size; made to fit, accurate in fit, well or close-fitting. *Obs.*

1530 PALSGR. 312/2 Fytte as a garment or other thynge. 1588 SHAKS. *L.L.L.* IV. i. 50 One a these Maides girdles for your waste should be fit. 1596 HARINGTON *Metam. Ajax* (1814) 8 To which you must have a hollow key with a worm fit to that screw. 1641 FRENCH *Distill.* i. (1651) 6 The stopple ..ground very smooth and fit to the mouth of the Vessell. 1646 CRASHAW *Poems* 118 Her garments, that upon her sit.. close and fit. 1703 MOXON *Mech. Exerc.* 169 A square hole made fit to it in the hithermost Cheek.

4. Possessing the necessary qualifications, properly qualified, competent, deserving. Const. as above; also †*of*. For phr. ***fit to hold a candle to***: see CANDLE 5 c.

1573 G. HARVEY *Letter-bk.* (Camden) 44 Having now at the lenght so fit a barer as I have. 1591 SHAKS. *Two Gent.* I. ii. 45 'Tis an office of great worth, And you an officer fit for the place. *a*1592 H. SMITH *Wks.* (1866–7) I. 476 They thought themselves fitter to govern than he. 1607–12 BACON *Ess., Youth & Age* (Arb.) 258 Yonge Men are fitter to invent, then to iudge; fitter for execution, then for Councell. 1621 LADY M. WROTH *Urania* 421 None..how much soeuer condemn'd, but may liue to be fit of commiseration and respect. 1670 TEMPLE *Let. to Earl Northumberland* Wks. 1731 II. 220 Nothing makes Men fit to command, like having learn'd to obey. 1722 DE FOE *Relig. Courtsh.* I. i. (1840) 22, I think my father is the fittest to give him his answer. 1771 FRANKLIN *Autobiog.* Wks. 1840 I. 89 This is a business I am not fit for. 1855 BROWNING *Fra Lippo* 107 Let's see what the urchin's fit for. 1868 BAIN *Ment. & Mor. Sc.* (1875) 624 Every man..being fitter to take care of himself than of another person.

5. a. In a suitable condition for doing or undergoing something; prepared, ready. Const. *for*, or *to* with *inf.*; otherwise *Obs.* exc. *dial.*

[*c*1534 tr. *Pol. Verg. Eng. Hist.* (Camden 1846) I. 102 Brittaine seemed..feete for the invasion of hostilitie.] 1568 GRAFTON *Chron.* II. 113 The sayde Lewes was in all pointes fit for their handes. 1596 SHAKS. *Merch. V.* v. i. 85 The man that hath no musicke in himselfe..Is fit for treasons. 1603 —— *Meas. for M.* III. i. 266 The Maid will I..make fit for his attempt. 1604 —— *Oth.* III. iv. 166 If I doe finde him fit, Ile moue your suite. 1678 BUNYAN *Pilgr.* I. (1847) 4 If I be not fit to go to Prison, I am not fit..to go to Judgement. 1681 W. ROBERTSON *Phraseol. Gen.* (1693) 610 Is the money fit? 1703 MOXON *Mech. Exerc.* 212 Having prepared the Work fit for the Lathe. 1784 COWPER *Let.* 10 Feb., When I am..more fit for mental occupation than at any other time. 1796 MRS. GLASSE *Cookery* xix. 300 They will be fit to eat in two or three days. 1823 CRABB *Technol. Dict.*, *Fit for service* (Mil.), an epithet for healthy men capable of undergoing the fatigues of service. *a*1825 FORBY *Voc. E. Anglia*, 'Come, stir, make yourself fit.' 1846 J. BAXTER *Libr. Pract. Agric.* (ed. 4) II. 345 Which makes the land perfectly clean and fit for the wheat crop.

b. Inclined, disposed. Now chiefly *colloq.* and *dial.* in stronger sense: Angry or troubled enough *to* (do something desperate or violent); exhausted enough, 'ready' *to* (sink to the ground, etc.). Also, ***fit to be tied*** (slang), extremely angry, hopping mad.

1580 BARET *Alv.* F 603 Fitte..inclined, disposed, *accomodatus*. 1585 ABP. SANDYS *Serm.* (1841) 308 When men are heavy laden with grief and sorrow, then are they fittest to call for and to receive refreshing. 1728 DE FOE *Syst. Magic* (1840) 251, I am fit to hang myself because I can't find it out. 1787 BURNS *To W. Creech* 50 And Calvin's folk are fit to fell him. 1821 CLARE *Vill. Minstr.* II. 24 To look at things around he's fit to freeze. 1848 J. H. NEWMAN *Loss & Gain* II He..keeps you standing till you are fit to sink. 1856 *Knickerbocker* Oct. 433 Then she laughs fit to kill. 1866 'OLD STAGER' *Stage Reminisc.* vii. 92 The smoke and fumes ..came up through the chinks of the stage, fit to choke a dozen Macbeths. 1878 *Cumberld. Gloss.*, 'They war fit to feyt about her.' 1894 SOMERVILLE & 'ROSS' *Real Charlotte* II. xxviii. 177 The old devil was fit to be tied. 1916 E. F. BENSON *David Blaize* v. 101 Cruikshank's awfully pi: fit to burst. 1922 JOYCE *Ulysses* 754, I was fit to be tied. 1938 R. FINLAYSON *Brown Man's Burden* 30 The roundabout with its hurdy-gurdy shrieking fit to raise the dead. 1953 'E. FERRARS' *Murder in Time* xxi. 189 Mad at you. Fit to be tied. 1956 C. SIMAK *Strangers in Universe* (1958) 193 It threw the place into a tizzy... The boss is fit to be tied. When he gets hold of you...

quasi-*adv.* 1808 in *Spirit Pub. Jrnls.* (1809) XII. 301 It made us laugh fit to kill ourselves.

c. of things: Likely, 'enough' (to). *colloq.*

1776 BENTHAM *Wks.* I. 276 We hear now and then of a sort of Government fit to break one's teeth, called an Ochlocracy.

6. In *Racing* or *Athletics*: In good 'form' or condition; hence *colloq.* in good health, perfectly well. ***fit as a fiddle***: see FIDDLE *sb.* 1 b.

1869 BRADWOOD *The O.V.H.* (1870) 28 Vale House was not as 'fit' inside as modern conveniences might have made it. 1876 OUIDA *Winter City* vi. 124 To hear the crowd on a race-day call out..'My eye, ain't she fit!' just as if I were one of the mares. 1885 *Manch. Exam.* 17 Jan. 5/5 General Stewart with his men and camels, all apparently well and fit. 1891 DIXON *Dict. Idiom. Phr.* s.v. *Fit*, 'How are you?'—'Very fit, thank you; never felt better.'

7. quasi-*adv.* = FITLY.

*c*1440 [See sense 2 above.] 1581 J. BELL *Haddon's Answ. Osor.* 200 This would have accorded farre fitter with your exposition. 1591 SHAKS. *Two Gent.* IV. iv. 167, I was trim'd in Madam Iulias gowne Which serued me as fit..As if the garment had bin made for me. 1613 W. BROWNE *Brit. Past.* II. i. Wks. 1772 II. 33 Limos..fed well.. Which serv'd Marina fit. 1630 M. GODWYN tr. *Bp. Hereford's Ann. Engl.* 153 The mention of Poole falls fit with our time. 1657 W. RAND tr. *Gassendi's Life Peiresc* II. 75 One cup would go fit into the other.

8. *Comb.*, as †***fit-forked*** adj.

1598 SYLVESTER *Du Bartas* II. i. IV. *Handy-crafts* 214 Their fit-forkéd stems.

fit (fit), *v.*¹ Forms: 5 fitte, 7 fitt, fyt(t, 6– fit. [Sense 1, found only in the *Morte Arthur c* 1400,

is of uncertain etymology, but may possibly be f. FIT *sb.*³ Apart from this use, the word first appears late in 16th c. when it was presumably a new formation on FIT *a.* The coincidence of form and meaning with the 16–17th c. Du. and Flemish *vitten* to suit, agree, adapt, is remarkable, but most probably the two words have developed their identical sense independently by different processes, though they may be from the same ultimate root.

In mod. editions of 15th c. works, the words *sit, besit* (= to be becoming), *sitting* (= becoming) are often misprinted *fit, befit, fitting*; the latter do not appear to be older than the Elizabethan period, but when once introduced they rapidly superseded the older synonyms; probably owing to their obvious connexion with FIT *a.*, they were felt to express the meaning more forcibly.]

†**I. 1.** *trans.* To array, marshal (soldiers). *Obs.* Only in the Morte Arthur.

? *a* **1400** *Morte Arth.* 1755 Thus he fittez his folke. *Ibid.* 1989 The kynge..ffittes his fote-mene, alles hym faire thynkes. *Ibid.* 2455 Þe frekke men of Fraunce folowede thare aftyre, ffaire fittyde one frownte.

II. To be fit, becoming, or suitable (to).

†**2. a.** *intr.* To be fit, seemly, proper, or suitable. Chiefly *impers.* or quasi-*impers. Obs.* or *arch.*

(The first examples given under the trans. sense 3 may belong here, as the obj.-pronoun is probably *dative.* Cf. similar use of *sit.*)

1574 H. G. tr. *Cataneo's Most briefe Tables* A iij a, Howe to determine vppon a sodayne fitteth well to eueryе one that hath anye doinges. **1592** SHAKS. *Rom. & Jul.* I. v. 77 It fits when such a Villaine is a guest. **1594** SPENSER *Amoretti* liv. 5 Sometimes I joy when glad occasion fits. **1594** *First Pt. Contention* (1843) 8 Whose Church-like humours fits not for a Crown. **1594** CAREW *Huarte's Exam. Wits* (1616) 130 This fitteth not to be remembered to the Preachers of our time. *c* **1620** Z. BOYD *Zion's Flowers* (1855) 5 Amittais Sonne fites for what I intend. **1632** MILTON *Penseroso* 78 If the air will not permit, Some still removed place will fit. **1671** —— *Samson* 1318 To appear as fits before th' illustrious lords. **1663** GERBIER *Counsel* 99 None will deny but that Greatnesse and Conveniency being conjoynt fits best. **1725** POPE *Odyss.* III. 83 The genial banquet o'er, It fits to ask ye, what your native shore, And whence your race?

†**b.** To agree or harmonize *with. Obs.*

1588 SHAKS. *Tit. A.* III. i. 266 Why dost thou laugh? it fits not with this houre. **1605** —— *Lear* III. ii. 76 He..Must make content with his Fortunes fit. **1594** CAREW *Huarte's Exam. Wits* (1616) 119 A name, which might fit well with a furious Giant.

3. *trans.* Chiefly *impers.* or quasi-*impers.* To be suited or suitable to, be proper for; to be in harmony with, become, befit.

a **1586** SIDNEY *Arcadia* II. x. 142 b, How euill fits it me to haue such a sonne. **1590** MARLOWE *Edw. II.* III. ii, Things of more weight Than fits a prince so young as I to bear. **1593** SHAKS. *Lucr.* 1613 Few words..shall fit the trespasse best. **1671** MILTON *Samson* 1236 This insolence other kind of answer fits. **1703** ROWE *Ulyss.* III. i. 1240 This Boldness does not fit a Stranger. **1725** POPE *Odyss.* III. 57 Thee first it fits, oh stranger! to prepare The due libation. **1806** H. SIDDONS *Maid, Wife, & Widow* II. 239 What the contents of Middleton's letter were it fitted me not to inquire. **1852** TENNYSON *Death Dk. Wellington* iii, Lead out the pageant: sad and slow, As fits an universal woe. **1866** GEO. ELIOT *F. Holt* I. i. 49 Her person..would have fitted an empress in her own right.

†**4.** To be well adapted or suitable for; to answer or satisfy the requirements of; to answer, suit. Also, † *to fit it*, † *to fit one's turn*: to serve one's turn. *Obs.*

1571 HANMER *Chron. Irel.* (1633) 179 Little Iohn came to Ireland..and found in the woods enough to fit his humours. **1598** SHAKS. *Merry W.* II. i. 166 Trust me, I thought on her; shee'll fit it. **1603** SIR G. FENTON in *Lismore Papers* Ser. II. (1887) I. 74 A coursse which may ease you, and yet will fytt my turne. **1677** HORNECK *Gt. Law Consid.* iv. (1704) 126 A temptation which will fit one, will not fit another. **1703** MOXON *Mech. Exerc.* 197 Of these Rowlers they have several ..that upon all occasions they may chuse one to fit their purpose. **1749** FIELDING *Tom Jones* VIII. iv, There is a piece of cold buttock and carrot, which will fit you.

5. a. To be of the right measure or proper shape and size for; to be correctly shaped or adjusted to. Said *esp.* of dress; also *fig.* Often *absol. the cap fits*: see CAP *sb.*¹ 9. *to fit to a T*: see T.

1581 PETTIE tr. *Guazzo's Civ. Conv.* II. (1586) 51 b, To finde a fashion for a saddle to fit anie Horse. **1603** SHAKS. *Meas. for M.* IV. ii. 46 Euerie true mans apparrell fits your Theefe. *a* **1691** BOYLE *Firmness* Wks. 1744 I. 278 As much of the stone, as was contiguous to the marchasite..fitted the marchasite so close as if [etc.]. **1795** BURNS *Song, Last May, a braw wooer*, And how her new shoon fit her auld schachl't feet. **1828** SCOTT *F.M. Perth* xxxiv, [The] armour..is light, and will fit thee well. **1842** TENNYSON *Walk to the M.* 57 Those manners next That fit us like a nature second-hand. **1846** GREENER *Sc. Gunnery* 207 A leaden ball to fit the bore. **1849** C. BRONTË *Shirley* I. iii. 49 You cannot always cut out men to fit their profession. **1863** W. C. BALDWIN *African Hunting* vi. 152 The only utensil..big enough to cook him in was a soap-boiler, which he just fitted. **1885** J. DE GRIEZ in *Law Times* LXXX. 138/2 A suit of clothes, which the latter..refused to accept, on the ground that the clothes did not fit him. *Mod.* Your description fits him to a T.

absol. **1782** COWPER *Gilpin* xlvii, My head is twice as big as yours, They therefore needs must fit. **1889** BRIDGES *Feast of Bacchus* III. 47 *Pam*, I like the hat. *Ph.* Is it comfortable? *Pam.* It fits like fun.

b. *intr.* To be of such size and shape as to fill exactly a given space, or conform properly to the contour of its receptacle or counterpart; to be adjusted or adjustable to a certain position. Often with *in* (adv. and prep.), *into, in with.*

1694 *Acc. Sev. Late Voy.* II. (1711) 142 On the upper Lip is a cavity or hole which the lower [*printed* upper] Lip fits exactly into. **1703** MOXON *Mech. Exerc.* 283 Then your Wainscot will fit exactly between any two lines of the Arch. **1867** FREEMAN *Norm. Conq.* (1876) I. App. 644 A statement which curiously fits in with our story. **1891** *Speaker* 11 July 37/1 The..complicated mechanism invented in the library would not fit into modern life. *Mod.* This peg fits into this hole.

III. *trans.* To make fit.

6. a. To make fit or suitable; to adapt to the object in view; to make ready, prepare; †*rarely* with *up*. Const. *for, to* with *sb.* or *inf.*: otherwise *dial.* only.

1600 HAKLUYT *Voy.* III. 200 A notable strong ship..in all thinges fitted for a man of warre. **1611** BIBLE *Rom.* ix. 22 The vessels of wrath fitted to destruction. **1628** DIGBY *Voy. Medit.* (1868) 5 In like manner wee fitted our seleues for fight. **1634** EARL CORK *Diary* in *Lismore Papers* Ser. I. (1886) IV. 43, I rodd with my daughter..to fyt the howse against her removall thither. **1670** NARBOROUGH *Jrnl.* in *Acc. Sev. Late Voy.* (1711) 28, I judged this a very fit Harbour to fit the Ship in. **1674** tr. *Scheffer's Lapland* 66 Skins, either plain or fitted up for use. **1677** YARRANTON *Eng. Improv.* 53 There is much in preparing and fitting of the Flax. **1703** MOXON *Mech. Exerc.* 74 You must know how to grind, and whet them, for they are not so fitted when they are bought. **1715–20** POPE *Iliad* II. 186 They urge the Train, To fit the Ships. **1737** BRACKEN *Farriery Impr.* (1756) I. 33 This..fits the Glands to perform their Office. **1784** COWPER *Task* I. 374 Winds from all quarters..fit the limpid element for use. **1877** MRS. OLIPHANT *Makers Flor.* i. 1 The action of time may fit Rome..for becoming the capital of Italy. **1880** *W. Cornw. Gloss.* s.v., 'When shall I fit the dennar?'

b. To render (a person) competent or qualified. Const. as above.

1597 HOOKER *Eccl. Pol.* v. i. §1 [If] that which fitteth them bee their vertues. **1647** TRAPP *Comment. on Epist.* 681 Such as fits a man for some particular calling. **1671** MILTON *P.R.* I. 73 Who..Pretends to..fit them so Purified to receive him pure. **1720** OZELL *Vertot's Rom. Rep.* II. IX. 48 To fit himself to shine in it more conspicuously. **1820** W. IRVING *Sketch Bk.* I. 174 Accomplishments, fitting him to shine both in active and elegant life. **1888** BRYCE *Amer. Commw.* III. lxxx. 54 It..does not completely fit him to weigh the real merits of statesmen.

absol. (U.S. only.)

1878 *Scribner's Mag.* XV. 426/2 There are schools that fit for Harvard. There are those that fit for Yale.

7. To fashion, modify, or arrange so as to conform or correspond to something else. Const. *to*, formerly also †*into*, †*for*.

1580 LYLY *Euphues* (Arb.) 473 For as thou framest thy manners, so wil thy wife fit hers. **1590** SHAKS. *Mids. N.* I. i. 118 To fit your fancies to your Fathers will. **1615** R. BRUCH tr. *Gerhard's Soule's Watch* title-p., Heavenly Meditations ..fitted to all the Dayes in the Weeke. *c* **1645** HOWELL *Lett.* IV. xiv. 19, I return here enclos'd the Sonnet..rendered into Spanish, and fitted for the same Ayr it had in English. **1665** BOYLE *Occas. Refl.* (1845) 36 Scarce any thought will puzzle him to fit words to it. **1718** (*title*) A Book of Psalms in Blank Verse fitted into the tunes commonly used. **1850** TENNYSON *In Mem.* lxxv. 6 Expert In fitting aptest words to things. **1855** H. REED *Lect. Eng. Lit.* i. (1878) 36 How exquisitely the individual man and the external world are fitted to each other. **1877** HUXLEY *Amer. Addr.* i. 29, I have no reason to suppose that she [Nature] is bound to fit herself to our notions.

8. a. To fix, apply, adjust, or insert (something) so that it fills exactly the required place, or conforms to the contour of its receptacle or counterpart. Const. *in, into, on, to, upon*; also with *in* adv. Also *fig.* Freq. *refl.* of persons, and const. *to, into.*

1611 BIBLE *1 Kings* vi. 35 Gold, fitted vpon the carued worke. **1628** DIGBY *Voy. Medit.* (1868) 86 The Jonas (to whom wee continually fitted saile). **1667** MILTON *P.L.* VI. 543 Let each..Fit well his Helme. **1670** NARBOROUGH *Jrnl.* in *Acc. Sev. Late Voy.* (1711) 30 The rest of the seamen fitted Rigging. **1703** MOXON *Mech. Exerc.* 136 Having.. fitted in the Bressummers, Girders, Joysts, etc. **1719** DE FOE *Crusoe* I. 242 He had a Bow and Arrow, and was fitting it to shoot at me. **1796** H. HUNTER tr. *St.-Pierre's Stud. Nat.* (1799) I. 31 The tyrant..who fitted the unhappy traveller to his bed of iron. **1867** SMYTH *Sailor's Word-bk.*, *Fit rigging*, to cut or fit the standing and running rigging to the masts, etc. **1879** *Cassell's Techn. Educ.* IV. 78/1 The practice of fitting them [water-tight bulkheads] has since become common. **1883** *Knowledge* 13 July 30/1 A dressmaker would fit the belt best. **1885** *Law Times* LXXIX. 366/2 Hoods will also be fitted over the tops of the doors.

fig. **1875** JOWETT *Plato* (ed. 2) V. 14 The accuracy with which the question and answer are fitted into one another. **1919** M. K. BRADBY *Psycho-Analysis* 52 His consequent difficulty in fitting himself in to life. *Ibid.* 247 He cannot fit himself in happily to his surroundings.

b. *to fit on*: to try on (a garment, etc.) with the view of ascertaining whether it fits the person. (Also *colloq.* with the person as *obj.*) *to fit the cap on*: to take some allusion as applying to oneself.

1842 WHITTOCK, etc. *Bk. Trades* 431 When the suits are commanded to be fitted on. **1842** TENNYSON *St. S. Stylites* 206 The crown! the crown! So now 'tis fitted on and grows to me. **1856** READE *Never too Late* xxiv, The truth is when a searching sermon is preached, each sinner takes it to himself..I am glad the prisoners fitted the cap on.

c. *to be fitted*: *absol.*, to have a garment, etc., fitted on one.

1926 N. COWARD *Queen in Parlour* I. i. 18, I shall have to go and be fitted. **1958** B. NICHOLS *Sweet & Twenties* 128 Far too busy to come and be fitted in person.

†**9. a.** To appoint, determine, or settle as may be fitting. *Obs.*

16.. BEAUM. & FL. *Laws Candy* I. i, My prisoner..I surrender: Fit you his ransom. —— *Mad Lover* III. i, If by my meanes Your busines may be fitted. **1621–31** LAUD *Sev. Serm.* (1847) 10 This time is in God to fit.

†**b.** *Sc.* To adjust or balance (an account); also, to examine, test, or audit (accounts). *Obs.*

1653 *Burgh Rec. Glasgow* (Rec. Soc.) II. 269 To meit with Mr. George Young and to fitt and cleir ane compt with him.

10. *Soap-making.* To bring (a mass of fluid soap) into such a condition that it will separate into two strata, the upper purer than the lower.

1866 TOMLINSON *Cycl. Useful Arts* II. 539 The soap is *fitted*, *i.e.* the contents of the copper are fused in a weak lye or in water. **1885** W. L. CARPENTER *Manuf. Soap* vi. 173 The English practice is to fit rather 'fine.' **1887** *Encycl. Brit.* XXII. 204/1 It is impossible to 'fit' or in any way purify soft soap.

IV. 11. a. To supply, furnish, or provide *with* what is fit, suitable, convenient, or necessary. ? *Obs.* when obj. is a person.

1591 SHAKS. *Two Gent.* II. vii. 42 Fit me with such weedes As may beseeme some well reputed Page. **1595** —— *John* III. iii. 26, I had a thing to say, But I will fit it with some better tune. **1627–77** FELTHAM *Resolves* I. xxv. 44 Those [senses] which carry the most pleasing tasts, fit us with the largest reluctations. **1653** WALTON *Angler* 71, I wil fit him to morrow with a Trout for his breakfast. **1660** BOYLE *New Exp. Phys.-Mech.* Proem 7 The last nam'd Person fitted me with a Pump. **1703** MOXON *Mech. Exerc.* 32 Having fitted yourself with a Hole in your Screw-plate. **1737** BRACKEN *Farriery Impr.* (1757) II. 61 They will pretend..that they can fit you to a Title with such a Horse. **1892** *Law Times Rep.* LXVII. 251/1 A steamship of 1074 tons net, fitted with steam steering gear.

b. †refl. *to fit oneself*: to suit oneself, get suited. Also pass. *to be fitted*: to be suited. *dial.*

1667 PEPYS *Diary* 29 Jan., He..promised she should stay till she had fitted herself. **1786** BURNS *To G. Hamilton* 14 If sae be ye may be Not fitted otherwhere. **1877** *N.W. Linc. Gloss.*, I'm just fitted where I am. **1882** *Lanc. Gloss.*, *Fitted*, suited, served.

c. *to fit out*: to supply with what is necessary; to equip, rig out. *Obs.* exc. *Naut.* or *transf.* from that use.

1670 R. COKE *Disc. Trade* 63 A Dutch Ship..may be built and fitted out to Sea for half the terms an English Ship can. **1722** DE FOE *Plague* (1754) 9 All loaded with Baggage and fitted out for travelling. **1741** RICHARDSON *Pamela* I. 21 My poor honest Dress, with which you fitted me out. **1776** *Trial of Nundocomar* 70/2, I saw Maha Rajah..order the house to be fitted out for him. **1824** LANDOR *Imag. Conv.* Wks. 1846 I. 106/2 If they had, they would fit out a cutter. **1840** THIRLWALL *Greece* VII. 183 The Athenians, in addition to the galleys which they had before, fitted out others. **1893** STEVENSON *Catriona* 2 At a merchant's in the Luckenbooths I had myself fitted out.

d. *to fit up*: to supply with necessary fittings, furniture, or stores.

1670 R. COKE *Disc. Trade* II. 56 The Dutch..do fit up more Ships for Navigation, and cheaper than the English. **1728** POPE *Let. to Swift* 20 June, He has fitted up his farm. **1821** SHELLEY *Epipsych.* 515, I have fitted up some chambers there. **1823** J. CONSTABLE *Let.* 29 Aug. (1964) II. 285 Any beautifull Gothick building magnificently fitted up with crimson & gold. **1859** JEPHSON *Brittany* xv. 243 The kitchen was fitted up with large boilers and ovens.

trans. **1869** J. MARTINEAU *Ess.* II. 156 Their neighbouring skies are fitted up with moons.

12. To visit (a person) with a fit penalty; to punish. *Obs.* exc. *Australian.* Also *dial.* with *out*.

a **1625** FLETCHER *Hum. Lieutenant* IV i, If I do not fit ye let me frie for't. **1685–8** *Roxb. Ball.* VII. 470 His Lass then presently devis'd to fit him for his whoring. **1782** MISS BURNEY *Cecilia* (1809) II. 229 With a look that implied—I'll fit you for this! **1889** BOLDREWOOD *Robbery under Arms* (1890) 3 A sergeant of police was shot in our last scrimmage, and they must fit some one over that. *Mod.* (Derbyshire) I'll fit you out for this.

† **fit**, *v.*² *Obs. rare*⁻¹ [f. FIT *sb.*²] *trans.* To force by fits or paroxysms *out of* (the usual place).

c **1600** SHAKS. *Sonn.* cxix, How haue mine eies out of their Spheares bene fitted In the distraction of this madding feuer?

fit (fɪt), *v.*³ [Sc. pronunciation of FOOT.] In the game of *Curling* (see quots.).

1831 *Blackw. Mag.* Dec. 985 Fit fair and rink straight. **1892** J. KERR *Hist. Curling* 361 The crampit or the hack is immoveable, and no advantage must be taken by changing to a place from which the shot could be more easily taken. This is fit fair. *Ibid.*, He must first fit the tee, i.e. he must so place himself that his eye travels along the central line toward the farther tee, while his right foot rests in the hack or on the heel of the crampit.

fit, Sc. and dial. var. of FOOT; also var. (dial. or vulgar) of *fought*: see FIGHT *v.*

fitch (fɪtʃ), *sb.*¹ *Obs.* exc. *dial.* Forms: 4–5 ficche, fetch, 5–6 fiche, 6 feche, fytch, fitche, 5– fitch. [var. of VETCH.]

1. = VETCH; the plant *Vicia sativa*, or its seed. Also *attrib.*, as *fitch-grass*.

1382 WYCLIF *Isa.* xxviii. 25 Barly, and myle, and ficche [**1388** fetchis] in her coestes. *c* **1420** *Pallad. on Husb.* I. 550 Fitches flynge afore hem [briddes] ofte. **1559** BP. AYLMER *Harborowe* H j, Satan..soweth tares and fytches of heresies and sectes continually. **1611** BIBLE *Isa.* xxviii. 25 Doth he not cast abroad the fitches? **1725** BRADLEY *Fam. Dict.* s.v. *Sand*, It was sowed with Oats and Fitches. **1789** *Trans. Soc. Encourag. Arts* (ed. 2) II. 57 Rib-grass, fitch-grass..and rye-grass. **1876** in *Whitby Gloss.*, *Fitches.*

†**b.** With reference to the size of a vetch-seed.
1590 BARROUGH *Meth. Phisick.* I. xxxvii. 61 Put in a peece of a spunge as much as the fiche. **1634** PEACHAM *Gentl. Exerc.* I. xxii. 69 A little eare-waxe to the quantitie of a fitch.

†**2.** *transf.* Something resembling the seed of a vetch. *Obs.*
1625 HART *Anat. Ur.* II. viii. 102 Red Vetches or Fitches in the residence..are recorded..to signifie..great inflammation of the Liuer.

fitch (fɪtʃ), *sb.*^{2} Also 6 **fyȝche, feche, fyche, fiche.** [a. (perh. through an unrecorded OF. form) MDu. *visse, fisse*, whence OF. *fissel* FITCHEW.]
1. = FITCHEW.
1550 J. COKE *Eng. & Fr. Heralds* §213 (1877) 118 We have marterns..otters, fitches, squerelles, etc. **1607** TOPSELL *Four-f. Beasts* (1658) 172 They say 'they stink like an Iltis,' that is, a fitch, or poul-cat. **1661** LOVELL *Hist. Anim. & Min.* 49 Fitch..The part of use taken from them is the skinne. **1706** PHILLIPS (ed. Kersey), *Fitch*, a Polecat.
2. The fur or hair of a polecat.
1502 *Will of Sowerby* (Somerset Ho.) [Furred with] fyȝches. **1663–73** BULLOKAR, Fitch, the furr of the Polecat. **1879** M. M. BACKUS in *Encycl. Brit.* IX. 838/1 *Fitch* Size about that of the American mink. **1884** J. C. STAPLES in *Girl's Own Paper* 8 Mar. 354/3 Some [brushes] are made of sable, fitch, and other hairs.
3. A brush made of the hair of a fitchew or polecat; also, a small brush made of hog's hair.
1873 SPON *Workshop Rec.* Ser. I. 106 The smallest hog-hair brushes are called fitches.
4. *attrib.*, as ***fitch-brush, -hair.***
1840 THACKERAY *Paris Sk. Bk., French Sch. Paint.* (end), Can you describe it? No, not if pens were fitch-brushes.

fitch (fɪtʃ), *sb.*^{3} Also fetch. [Origin unknown.] In basket-making, a kind of plait in which two canes or osiers are twisted together in the same direction so as to enclose a crossing weft at each half-turn. Also = *fitch-rod*, one of the canes so used. Hence **fitch** *v.*^{2}
1907 *Jrnl. Society Arts* 11 Jan. 190/2 The strokes chiefly used are termed: a slew when two or more rods are woven in together.., a fitch when two are woven alternately one under the other. *Ibid.*, Some fitched basket chairs..are nearly 3,000 years old. **1910** *Encycl. Brit.* III. 482/2 The 'fitch'..employed for skeleton work such as cages and waste-paper baskets. **1912** *Rep. Cambr. Anthropol. Exped. Torres Straits* IV. 64. **1953** A. G. KNOCK *Willow Basket-Work* 21 When a round of fitching is completed, the remainder of the two rods may be worked out as a pair. *Ibid.*, The size of the fitch rods is generally a little smaller than that of the stakes.

fitch, *v.*^{1} *Sc.* and *north. dial.* [app. an intermediate form between FIKE and FIDGE.]
1. *intr.* 'To move by slow succussations from one place to another' (Jam.). Cf. FIDGE *v.*
1637 GILLESPIE *Eng. Pop. Cerem.* IV. viii. 35 They are so nettled therewith, that they fitch hither and thither. **1790** A. WILSON *Poems* 63 A speakin' Pack's owre learnt for me, Or ane that steers an' fitches.
2. *trans.* 'To move any thing a little way from its former place' (Jam.).
1892 *Northumb. Gloss., Fitch* that flake—remove that hurdle.
b. 'To lift and lay down again, to touch a thing frequently' (Jam.); = FIDGE *v.*
[**1692** J. CURATE *Sc. Presbyt. Eloquence* iii. 99 This John [Simple] was ordinarily called Fitch-cape and Claw-poll, because in the time of Preaching, or Praying he used to claw his Head, and rub his Callet.]

†**'fitchant,** *a. Obs.* [var. of FIGENT: cf. FITCH *v.*] Nimble, restless.
c **1600** BEAUMONT *Grammar Lecture* Sloane MS. 1709 f. 17 To visit often the pagan puppett playes, and to behold their fitchant anticks.

fitché, -ée (ˈfɪtʃeɪ), *a. Her.* Also anglicized FITCHY. [ad. Fr. *fiché, fichée*, pa. pple. of *ficher* to fix.] Fixed: applied to a cross, the lower extremity of which is sharpened to a point.
1572 BOSSEWELL *Armorie* II. 64 b, S. beareth Sable twoo Delphines d'Argent, addorsez hariant, betwene sixe Crosses Botony Fitche. *a* **1661** FULLER *Worthies* (1662) 141 A Cross Patee fitchee betwixt the Attire. **1864** BOUTELL *Heraldry Hist. & Pop.* vi. 29 When the shaft of any Cross is pointed at the base, it is said to be Fitchée.

fitched (fɪtʃt), *a. Her.* Also 7 **fitchet.** [f. prec. + -ED^1.] = prec.
1562 LEIGH *Armorie* 57 a, The field Azure a crosse formye fitched Or. **1611** COTGR., *Croix fichée*, a crosse Fitchet. **1688** R. HOLME *Armoury* III. 145/1 Pencils of all sorts..as Duck Quill pointed and Fitched. **1705** HEARNE *Collect.* 21 Dec., A Fesse..between three Crosses fitched Gules. **1889** in ELVIN *Dict. Her.*, s.v. *Fitché.*

fitcher (ˈfɪtʃə(r)), *v. Mining. intr.* (See quot.)
1865 GARLAND *W. Cornw. Words* in *Jrnl. Roy. Inst. Cornw.* Apr. 48 *Fitchered*, to be baulked, stopped short. The word is mostly used in mining, where some difficulty occurs in the boring of a hole for blasting.

fitchet (ˈfɪtʃɪt). Also 6 **fechet,** 7–8 **fichat.** [dim. of FITCH *sb.*^{2}]
1. = FITCHEW 1, 2.
1535 in Weaver *Wells Wills* (1890) 29 My blew furryd gowne of fechets. **1653** WALTON *Angler* I. i. 14 The Fichat..and the like creatures. **1772** T. SIMPSON *Vermin-Killer* 23 The Polecat, Fitchat, Fitchew, Formet. **1885** [see FITCHEW 1].
†**2.** Incorrectly: The weasel. *Obs.* exc. *dial.*
1693 RAY *Synops. Animal.* 195. **1713** RICHARDSON in *Phil. Trans.* XXVIII. 170 He [Ray] says that *Mustela vulgaris* is called here a Foumart or Fitchet. **1881** *Leicester Gloss., Fitchet*..sometimes incorrectly applied to a weasel.

fitchew (ˈfɪtʃuː). Forms: 5 **fechu, fychew,** (*plural* **fecheus, fychews, -eux**), 6 **fechowe, ficheuxe, fitchewe,** 7 **fitcholl, fitchaw,** 8 **fi(t)cher, fitchole,** 4– **fitchew.** [a. OF. *fissel* (pl. *fissiaulx*), later *fissau* (Cotgr.), a diminutive formation on the word which appears in Du. of 16–17th c. as *fisse, visse, vitsche* (see Kilian and Hexham).]
1. A foumart, polecat.
1418 *E.E. Wills* (1882) 34 My furre of Fycheux. **1486** *Bk. St. Albans* B vij b, That no fulmertis nor fecheus..com nott in to hir. **1577** HARRISON *England* III. iv. (1878) II. 25, I might here intreat..of..the weasell..fitchew, and such like. **1688** in A. L. Humphreys *Hist. Wellington* (1889) 125 Pd. for killing of a fitcholl and a hedgehogg 8*d.* **1752** SIR J. HILL *Hist. Anim.* 547 They all call it..Mustela; we the Weasel, the Foumart, or the Fitcher. **1787** GROSE *Provinc. Gloss., Fitchole*, a polecat, fitchet or ficher. **1788** WOLCOTT (P. Pindar) *Peter's Pension* Wks. 1812 II. 18 Your fowls have suffer'd by the fitchews. **1885** *Encycl. Brit.* XIX. 332/1 To this [its fetid smell] it is indebted for its..English names *fitchet, fitchew.*
b. Used as a term of contempt.
1604 SHAKS. *Oth.* IV. i. 150 'Tis such another Fitchew.
2. The fur of the polecat.
c **1394** *P. Pl. Crede* 295 A cote haþ he furred Wiþ foyns or wiþ fitchewes oþer fyn beuer. **1493** *Will of Squyer* (Somerset Ho.) Penulatam cum fychew pollys. **1502** *Will of Grene* (Somerset Ho.) (Gown furred with) Ficheuxe. **1534** in Weaver *Wells Wills* (1890) 98 My gowne furryd with ffechowe. **1721** BAILEY, Fitchow, a Pole-cat..also the skin of it.

†**'fitchew,** *v. Obs.*$^{-1}$
a **1650** MAY *Satir. Puppy* (1657) 85 Yet this is she..whom Pride did become as a full Oath doth a desperate Gallant: that fichew'd with a degenerate posture of the Chinne.

†**'fitchock.** *Obs.* Also **fich-, fytchock, fitchuk.** [f. FITCH *sb.*^{2} + dim. suffix -OCK.] = FITCHEW; also as a term of contempt.
a **1615** BEAUM. & FL. *Bonduca* I. ii, And make ye fight like fichocks. —— *Scornful Lady* V. i, Farewell, fytchock! **1804** DUNCUMB *Herefordsh.* I. 213 A fitchock, a pole-cat. **1847** HALLIWELL, *Fitchet*, a polecat, also called..fitchuk.

†**'fitchy,** *a.*^{1} *Obs.* [f. FITCH *sb.*^{1} + -Y^1.] Resembling a fitch or vetch.
1610 HEALEY *St. Aug. Citie of God* 612 There is..*lenticula* of *lens*, a little fitchie kind of pease.

fitchy (ˈfɪtʃɪ), *a.*^{2} *Her.* [Anglicized form of FITCHÉ.] = FITCHÉ. Also *transf.*
1650 FULLER *Pisgah* IV. iv. 68 Silver sockets..made fitchy, or picked, to be put into the earth. **1763** *Brit. Mag.* IV. 638 Three cross croslets, fitchy. **1864** BOUTELL *Heraldry Hist. & Pop.* xv. (ed. 3) 215 Crusily fitchy or.

†**'fitelfoot.** *Obs. rare*$^{-1}$. [? Cf. FITTLE *a.*] An alleged designation for the hare.
a **1325** *Names of Hare* in *Rel. Ant.* I. 133 The sittere, the gras-hoppere, The fitelfot, the foldsittere.

fitful (ˈfɪtfʊl), *a.* [f. FIT *sb.*^{2} + -FUL. A word used once by Shakspere, and popularized by writers of the beginning of the 19th century.]
1. Of a disease: Characterized by fits or paroxysms. *Obs.* exc. in Shakspere's phrase.
1605 SHAKS. *Macb.* III. ii. 23 Lifes fitfull Feuer. **1744** ARMSTRONG *Preserv. Health* I. 131 Quartana..this fitful pest With feverish blasts subdues the sickening land.
2. Characterized by irregular fits of activity or strength; coming and going by fits and starts; full of irregular changes; spasmodic, shifting, changing, capricious.
1810 SCOTT *Lady of L.* I. Prol., And down the fitful breeze thy numbers flung. **1816** BYRON *Siege Cor.* xxi, So seen by the dying lamp's fitful light. **1832** HT. MARTINEAU *Each & All* ii. 18 His impulses were generous, but fitful. **1841** MIALL *Nonconf.* I. 1 The fitful and convulsive energy they have at times displayed. **1874** MOTLEY *Barneveld* I. i. 5 The first fitful years of peace.

fitfully (ˈfɪtfʊlɪ), *adv.* [f. prec. + -LY^2.] In a fitful manner; by fits and starts.
1792 WORDSW. *Descr. Sketches* Poems (1888) 17/2 Fitfully, and in flashes, through his soul, Like sun-lit tempests, troubled transports roll. **1834** MRS. SOMERVILLE *Connect. Phys. Sc.* xxxvii. (1849) 424 Here we have a star fitfully variable. **1889** RUSKIN *Præterita* III. 181 The fireflies..shone fitfully in the still undarkened air.

fitfulness (ˈfɪtfʊlnɪs). [f. as prec. + -NESS.] Fitful condition or quality.
1825 LYTTON *Falkland* 12 Fitfulness of temper. **1859** SMILES *Self-Help* x. (1860) 264 A habit of fitfulness and ineffective working.

fithel(e, -ul, obs. forms of FIDDLE.

'fitly, *a. rare.* [f. FIT *a.* + -LY^1.] = FIT *a.*
1573 TUSSER *Husb.* (1878) 183 Giue childe that is fitly. **1840** BROWNING *Sordello* VI. 441 'Twere fitliest maintain the Guelfs in rule.

fitly (ˈfɪtlɪ), *adv.* [f. FIT *a.* + -LY^2.]
1. In a way that is fit; properly, aptly, becomingly, suitably, appropriately.
c **1550** in Strype *Cranmer* (1694) App. No. 49. 138 Their heads [standith] most fyttely on London bridge. **15..** TURBERVILE *Compl. lost Dove, Epitaphes* etc. (1567) 130 b, Eche part so fitly pight as none mought chaunge his place. **1607** SHAKS. *Cor.* IV. ii. 34 Cats that can iudge as fitly of his worth, As I can of those Mysteries. **1667** MILTON *P.L.* VIII. 394 So fitly them in pairs thou hast combin'd. **1732** BERKELEY *Alciphr.* I. §2 The mind of man may be fitly compared to a piece of land. *a* **1822** SHELLEY *Cyclops* 193 Well, is the dinner fitly cooked and laid? **1870** SWINBURNE *Ess. & Stud.* (1875) 277 Seen fitlier by starlight than by sunlight.
†**b.** At the fitting time or season. *Obs.*
1605 SHAKS. *Lear* I. ii. 184 From whence I will fitly bring you to heare my Lord speake. **1611** BIBLE *Prov.* xxv. 11 A word fitly spoken is like apples of gold in pictures of siluer. **1623–6** COCKERAM II, *Fitly*, opportunely.
2. *Comb.*, as ***fitly-contrived, fitly-fair.***
1598 SYLVESTER *Du Bartas* II. ii. IV. *Columnes* 375 Our Learned Elders..Heav'n's shining Signes imagin'd fitly-fair. **1677** GILPIN *Demonol.* (1867) 182 A fitly-contrived subject.

fitment (ˈfɪtmənt). [f. FIT *v.* + -MENT.]
†**1.** A making fit, preparation. *Obs.*
1611 SHAKS. *Cymb.* V. v. 409 'Twas a fitment for The purpose I then follow'd.
†**2.** That which is fitting or proper; duty. *Obs.*
1608 SHAKS. *Per.* IV. vi. 6 When she should doe for clyents her fitment..shee [etc.].
3. A piece of furniture. Usually in *pl.* Fittings.
1851 *Ord. & Regul. R. Engineers* §4. 19 The expense of repairs of Fences, Fixtures, Fitments, &c. **1862** MRS. FRESHFIELD *Grisons & Bern.* xvii. 282 In keeping with the other fitments of the room. **1888** *Illustr. Lond. News* 29 Dec., Every variety of Fitment and Furniture. **1891** *Times* 22 Oct. 16/5 The library has an enamelled wood fitment.

fitness (ˈfɪtnɪs). [f. FIT *a.* + -NESS.]
1. a. The quality or state of being fit or suitable; the quality of being fitted, qualified, or competent. *spec.* the quality or state of being physically fit. Often *attrib.* and *Comb.*
1580 BARET *Alv.* F 604 Ablenesse, fitnesse, handsomnesse, *habilitas.* **1597** HOOKER *Eccl. Pol.* V. vi. (1611) 193 Competent to shew their conueniencie and fitnesse. **1601** SHAKS. *All's Well* II. ii. 31 Haue you, I say, an answere of such fitnesse for all questions? **1748** HARTLEY *Observ. Man* II. ii. 158 The Harmonies, and mutual Fitnesses, of visible things. **1783** BURKE *Affairs India* Wks. 1842 II. 11 His fitness for the supreme council. **1845–6** TRENCH *Huls. Lect.* Ser. I. iii. 49 Every other man has..fitnesses for one task rather than another. **1875** JOWETT *Plato* (ed. 2) IV. 132 Their fitness as instruments of thought to express facts. *a* **1935** T. E. LAWRENCE *Mint* (1950) II. xxii. 158 So I dodge the last weeks of depot training and the orgy of fitness-tests with which it closes. **1939** *Ann. Reg. 1938* 100 The 'fitness' campaign which had recently been launched.
b. The state of being morally fit; worthiness.
1647 W. LYFORD *Transl. Sinner* (1648) 3 Not because of our works, or fitnesse, or betternesse of disposition in us. **1745** WESLEY *Answ. Ch.* 36 No Fitness is required at the Time of communicating. **1858** J. MARTINEAU *Stud. Chr.* 332 To insist..on a mere moral fitness.
2. a. The quality or condition of being fit and proper, conformity with what is demanded by the circumstances; propriety.
1597 HOOKER *Eccl. Pol.* V. §7. 13 In things the fitnes whereof is not of it self apparent. **1613** SHAKS. *Hen. VIII* II. iv. 231 The Queene being absent, 'tis a needfull fitnesse That we adiourne this Court till further day. **1784** COWPER *Task* V. 672 Make him hear Of rectitude and fitness. **1820** BYRON *Let.* Wks. 1846, 153/1 Their system has its rules, and its fitnesses, and its decorums.
b. *the (eternal) fitness of things*: a phrase extensively used in the 18th c. with reference to the ethical theory of Clarke, in which the quality of moral rightness is defined as consisting in a 'fitness' to the relations inherent in the nature of things. Hence popularly used (at first with playful allusion) for: What is fitting or appropriate.
Clarke's own usual phrase is 'the eternal *reason* of things'; but the words *fit* and *fitness* are constantly used by him as synonyms of 'reasonable' and 'reason'.
1705 CLARKE *Nat. & Rev. Relig.* (1706) 52 They [the Hobbists] have no way to show how Compacts themselves come to be obligatory, but by inconsistently owning an eternal Fitness in the thing itself. **1730** M. TINDAL *Christianity old as Creation* 357 His [God's] Commands are to be measured by the antecedent Fitness of Things. **1749** FIELDING *Tom Jones* IV. iv, The rule of right, and the eternal fitness of things. **1749** LADY LUXBOROUGH *Let. to Shenstone* 29 Nov. (1775) 148 My writing a Postcript after so long a letter is not according to the *fitness of things... Note.* Be it known, these words thus applied are fashionable. **1885** *Manch. Exam.* 15 Sept. 4/7 Mr. Slagg..showed a characteristic sense of the fitness of things by confining his attention [etc.].
†**3.** The quality of fitting exactly (cf. FIT *a.* 3); correspondence of size and shape. *Obs.*
1658 A. FOX *Wurtz' Surg.* II. xxv. 150 Have a good Knife also about you, in case you have need to cut the splinters to a fitness. **1719** DE FOE *Crusoe* (1840) I. xi. 188 If there was any similitude or fitness, that I might be assured it was my own foot. **1793** SMEATON *Edystone L.* §235 Where there was the least want of fitness..either the stone or the rock was cut, till each stone would come into its exact relative position.
†**4.** Readiness, inclination. (Cf. FIT *a.* 5, 5 b.)
1604 SHAKS. *Ham.* V. ii. 209 (Qo 2) I am constant to my purposes, they followe the Kings pleasure: if his fitnes speakes, mine is ready.

fitsides (ˈfɪtsaɪdz), *adv. Sc.* ? *Obs.* [f. *fit*, Sc. form of FOOT + SIDE.] Only in phr. *to be fitside(s*

with (a person): to be on the same footing *with*, to be 'upsides' or quits *with*.

1609 *Burgh Rec. Glasg.* (Rec. Soc.) I. 304 And thou wart out of thy office, I sould be fit syde with the. **1752** A. B. STEWART in *Scots Mag.* July (1753) 338/2 He would be fit-sides with Glenure, where-ever he met him.

fitt (fɪt). *v. local.* [Of uncertain origin: identity with FIT *v.* 1 is possible.] To vend and load (coals); to load (a vessel) with coals for transport.

1600–1 *Order of Hostmen's Comp.* in Brand *Newcastle* II. 272 *note*, None shall fitt any keell..without the consent of the owner thereof. **1625** *Ibid.* 28 Apr., To fitt and load coles abord of the keeles. **1825** in Brockett *N.C. Words.*

Hence **'fitting** *vbl. sb.*; in quot. *attrib.*

1843 T. WILSON *Pitman's Pay, etc.* 108 The Faithers o' the fittin' trade The Quayside a'ways pacin'.

fittable ('fɪtəb(ə)l), *a. rare*⁻⁰. [f. FIT *v.* + -ABLE.] That may be fitted.

1611 COTGR., *Accommodable*, fittable, aptable, appliable. **1660** HOWELL *Lexicon*, Fittable, *accommodable.*

fittage ('fɪtɪdʒ). *local.* [f. FITT *v.* + -AGE.] The commission allowed a fitter or coal shipper.

1708 J. C. *Compl. Collier* (1845) 49 Their pretence is to have and get no more than two Shillings and six Pence per Chaldron..for Fittidge. **1892** in *Northumb. Gloss.*

attrib. **1797** *Monthly Mag.* III. 73 Mr. A. Baker, staith-man and fittage agent to the Beamish South-Moor Colliery.

fitted ('fɪtɪd), *ppl. a.* [f. FIT *v.* + -ED¹.]

a. In various senses of the vb.; also *fitted-up*. **b.** Often used predicatively with the ppl. sense somewhat obscured: Adapted, 'calculated', likely. Const. *to* with *inf.*

1736 BUTLER *Anal.* I. Wks. 1874 I. 101 Circumstances peculiarly fitted to be, to them, a state of discipline. **1777** WATSON *Philip II* (1793) I. II. 26 How much soever Philip's power and character were fitted to excite jealousy. **1810** *Sporting Mag.* XXXVI. 156 Elegantly fitted-up pleasure boats. **1860** *Ure's Dict. Arts* (ed. 5) III. 713 A white, uni-coloured or fitted soap would be the result. **1867** SMYTH *Sailor's Word-bk.*, *Fitted Furniture*..articles of spare supply, sent from the dockyard. **1888** *Times* 26 June 12/5 Advt., Fitted plate chests.

c. *fitted carpet*, a carpet cut to fit exactly the floor of a room; **fitted sheet**, a bed-sheet with box ends which fit closely round the mattress.

1898 D. C. PEEL *New Home* iii. 24 In no room would I allow a fitted carpet. **1950** *Vogue* Aug. 98/2 Intellectuals can't afford a fitted carpet. **1963** *Good Housek. Home Encycl.* (ed. 5) 30 *Fitted Tailored Sheets*, those with boxed ends simplify bed-making and are a boon to the restless sleeper. **1969** *Which?* Nov. 372/1 You can get nylon fitted sheets for less than this. **1970** EDWARDES & SMEDLEY *Good Housek. Running Home* 72 Are you going to have a fitted carpet—or not?

Hence **'fittedness**, the state of being fitted.

1611 H. D *Disc. Liturgies* (1661) 77 The singing then used, and its fittedness to the duty of Christians in praising God. **1645** T. COLEMAN *Hopes Deferred* 3 There is no fittednesse to receive. **1894** DRUMMOND *Ascent of Man* 267 Fitness to survive is simply fittedness.

†**'fitten**, *sb. Obs.* Forms: 5 fyton, 6 fytten, fitton(e, 6–7 fitten. [Of unknown origin.

The suggestion that it is a corruption of *fiction* is inadmissible. The form coincides curiously with the corruption of L. *python* found in various Teut. langs.: ON. *fitón*, MDu. *fytoen* necromancy, sorcery.]

An untruth, a lie, an invention.

c **1440** *Promp. Parv.* 163/1 Fyton, or lesynge, *mendacium.* **1530** PALSGR. 220/2 Fytten, *mensonge, menterie.* *a* **1577** GASCOIGNE *Fruites of Warre* 24 Wks. (1587) 118 Let not dame flattery in your bosome creepe, To tel a fittone in your Landlords eares. **1599** B. JONSON *Cynthia's Rev.* I. iv, He doth feed you with fittons, figments and leasins. **1654** GATAKER *Disc. Apol.* 69 Others of them may wel be deemed Fittons of his own framing, as [etc.]. **1825** J. BRITTON *Beauties Wiltsh.* III. 373 *Fitten*, a feint, a pretence.

'fitten, *a. Obs.* exc. in *U.S. dial.* [as if a pa. pple. (strong formation) f. FIT *v.*]. Suitable, fit.

1642 H. MORE *Song of Soul* IV. xxx, Sensation The soul some fitten hint doth promptly lend To find out plantall life. **1873** 'MARK TWAIN' & WARNER *Gilded Age* 32 It was fitten to make a body's heart break. **1876** 'MARK TWAIN' *Tom Sawyer* 120, I reckon I ain't dressed fitten for a pirate. **1932** W. FAULKNER *Light in August* vi. 98 He would see fitten to reveal it. **1938** M. K. RAWLINGS *Yearling* ii. 19 The scrub's a fitten place for the game to raise, and all the wild things.

†**'fitten**, *v. Obs.* Also 6 fiton. [f. FITTEN sb.] *intr.* To utter falsehoods, fib, tell lies.

1577–87 HOLINSHED *Chron.* II. 15/2 Least the apostle should haue beene thought to haue fitoned. *c* **1580** LODGE *Answ. to Gosson* Wks. 1879 III. 30 Yf Boetyus fitten not. **1624** H. MASON *Art of Lying* v. 104 How can I tell that they doe not fitten and deuise all that vpon their fingers ende?

fitter ('fɪtə(r)), *sb.*¹ [f. FIT *v*¹. + -ER¹.]

1. One who or that which fits (see the vb.). Also with adverbs, as *fitter-out, up.*

1660 HEXHAM, *Een geriever*, a Fitter, an Applier, or an Accommodatour. **1707** MORTIMER *Husb.* ix. 146 Sowing.. with French Furze seed, they reckon a great Improver of their Land, and a fitter of it for corn. **1859** SALA *Tw. round Clock* (1861) 224 Nothing more can be done for a palace than the fitters-up of a modern club have done for it.

2. a. *spec.* in various trades (see quots.). Also in *Comb.*, as *gas-fitter, hot-water-fitter*, etc.

1851 C. CIST *Cincinnati* (Advt.), Brass and iron founders; fitters of wrought iron welded pipe, for steam, gas, etc. **1888** *Lockwood's Dict. Mech. Engin.*, *Fitter* or Engine Fitter—a working engineer whose duties consist in the fitting together of machine or engine parts. **1892** *Labour Commission* Gloss., *Fitters*, term applied to those persons..who paste together the portions cut out to form the boot-upper, to prepare them for sewing. **1905** *Terms Forestry & Logging* 37 *Fitter*, 1. one who notches the tree for felling and after it is felled marks the log lengths into which it is to be cut; 2. one who cuts limbs from felled trees and rings and slits the bark preparatory to peeling tanbark. **1948** L. LEVY *Music for Movies* iii. 22 Films being given a preview to the conductor (or as he was sometimes ingloriously known, the 'fitter'), with the object of making some attempt at fitting the music to the mood of the film.

b. One who is engaged to supervise the cutting out and making of garments, or the alteration of ready-made garments to suit customers' requirements.

1858 SIMMONDS *Dict. Trade*, *Fitter*..a weigher at the mint; a tailor, one who tries on and adjusts articles of dress. **1885** *Law Times* LXXX. 8 1 A cutter and fitter of wearing apparel. **1896** *Daily News* 10 Dec. 7/2 She will find that the fitter who receives her presides..at the table where her orders are being carried out. **1906** *Daily Chron.* 17 July 5/2 She sent the defendants notice that unless they sent a fitter up to make the dress right on the Monday it would be of no use to her. **1921** *Dict. Occup. Terms* (1927) §405 *Fitter, dressmaker's fitter*, in charge of workrooms in large establishment..; fits garments requiring alterations and takes customers' measurements for length of skirt, etc. **1931** *Times Lit. Suppl.* 16 Apr. 805/2 The women in the workrooms, the fitters, the mannequins.

fitter ('fɪtə(r)), *sb.*² *local.* [f. FITT *v.* + -ER¹.] One who vends and loads coals; a coal-broker.

1678 in Brand *Newcastle* (1789) II. 669 The customers, collectors, fitters, and other..officers..in the said port. **1739** *Enquiry Reasons Advance Price Coals* 31 The Host-men or Fitters at Newcastle are an incorporated Company. **1843** T. WILSON *Pitman's Pay, etc.* 108 The 'Runnin' Fitters' stannin' still. *Ibid.* 117 Mourn, a' the fitters o' the Quay!

†**'fitter**, *v. Obs. rare.* [Perh. cognate with MHG. *vetze*, mod.G. *fetzen* rag, scrap, and ON. *fit* hem (see FIT *sb*¹); the vb. (perh. first used in pa. pple.: see next) is formed with frequentative suffix -ER⁵ common in vbs. expressive of the action of breaking into small pieces.] *intr.* To break into small fragments.

c **1380**, *c* **1450** [? implied in next]. **1600** ABP. ABBOT *Exp. Jonah* 319 When Sampson was disposed he brake the cordes and ropes wherewith he was tyed; they fittered and dissolved even as the flaxe which is burnt with the fire.

†**'fittered**, *ppl. a. Obs.* [f. prec. + -ED¹.] Ragged, wearing rags; also of clothes, slashed, cut into tags or streamers.

c **1380** WYCLIF *Wks.* (1880) 60 Many raggid & fittrid squyeris. *c* **1450** MYRC 1146 Hast þou ben prowde..Of fytered clothes as foles done?

'fitters, *sb. pl. Obs.* exc. *dial.* See also FLITTERS. [f. FITTER *v.*] Fragments, pieces, atoms. In various obvious phrases, as *to tear to fitters, to break in(to fitters*, etc. *to be in fitters*: *fig.* to be broken up into small parties.

1532 MORE *Confut. Tindale* Wks. 374/2 Whiche the deuil hath by yᵉ blast of his mouth..frushed al to fitters. **1614** RALEIGH *Hist. World* II. 292 Which Image..was with Fire from Heaven broken into fitters. **1639** FULLER *Holy War* IV. xxxii. 225 They were in fitters about prosecuting their titles to this city. **1715** tr. *Pancirollus' Rerum Mem.* II. i. 273 That Sarsaparilla is to be chosen which is..hard to be broken but when it falls into Fitters. **1869** *Lonsdale Gloss.*, *Fitters*, very small pieces, fragments. **1886** in *S.W. Linc. Gloss.*

fitting ('fɪtɪŋ), *vbl. sb.* [f. FIT *v.* + -ING¹.]

1. a. The action of the vb. FIT in various senses. Also gerundially with omission of *in*. Also with *advs.*

1607 HIERON *Wks.* I. 301 There should be also..a fitting of this generall truth touching Christ to his owne particular. **1719** *Freethinker* No. 154, I am fitting out for one of the most compleat Beaus in Christendom. **1746–7** HERVEY *Medit.* (1818) 73 They saw the fatal arrow fitting to the strings. **1829** MARRYAT *F. Mildmay* xxiii, The ship was fitting. **1862** DANA *Man. Geol.* 583 In the final fitting up of the earth with life there was still a reference to him [Man]. **1886** RUSKIN *Præterita* I. vi. 179 The perfect fitting of windows.

b. The action or an act of fitting on a garment in tailoring and dressmaking.

1900 *Daily Express* 22 June 5/3 Messrs. —— gave her eight fittings. **1930** *London Mercury* Feb. 320 They had had to cancel two fittings and three dress shows. **1942** D. POWELL *Time to be Born* (1943) xi. 274 It was an exciting adventure to lie about a 'fitting'..and then make her dignified dash.

2. *concr.* Anything used in fitting. Usually in *pl.*: Fixtures, apparatus, furniture. Also *fitting-up.*

a **1817** JANE AUSTEN *Persuasion* (1818) III. xi. 233 The varieties in the fitting-up of the rooms. **1823** J. BADCOCK *Dom. Amusem.* 77 Bladders filled with a quantity of this gas ..and the neck, or fitting-up of its end, made capable of being closed or opened. **1860** HAWTHORNE *Marb. Faun* xxxi. (1883) 321 These fittings-up of polished marble. **1864** BP. OF LINCOLN *Charge* 7, 42 grants for fittings and books. **1868** FREEMAN *Norm. Conq.* (1876) II. viii. 207 All the roofs, floors, and fittings were burned.

3. *Mech. Engin.* (see quot. 1888).

1878 W. ALLAN *Rose & Thistle* 131 What though your labour is merely stone-breaking, Turning or fitting, or wielding the spade. **1888** *Lockwood's Dict. Mech. Engin.*, *Fitting*, that section of mechanical engineering devoted to the bringing together and adjusting of the different portions of engines, machines, &c.

4. *Soap-making.* See FIT *v.* 10.

1860 *Ure's Dict. Arts* (ed. 5) III. 713. **1885** W. L. CARPENTER *Manuf. Soap* vi. 172 The finishing operation for yellow soaps is termed 'fitting' in England.

5. *attrib.*, as *fitting-out basin, fitting(-out)-shop, fitting-room.*

1909 *Daily Chron.* 23 Feb. 1/9 The vessel was..towed to one of the fitting-out basins. **1961** F. H. BURGESS *Dict. Sailing* 88 New vessels..launched and 'taken in hand' for completion, usually in a 'fitting-out' basin. **1840** MARRYAT *Poor Jack* xii, I went to a fitting-out shop. **1888** *Lockwood's Dict. Mech. Engin.*, *Fitting-Shop*, the shop in which the operations of fitting are carried on. **1909** in A. Adburgham *Shops & Shopping* (1964) xxi. 249 The Costume Department (to which luxurious fitting-rooms are attached). **1962** L. S. SASIENI *Optical Dispensing* ix. 205 Such faults can be corrected in the fitting-room. **1969** R. JAFFE *Fame Game* xiv. 196 He went into a fitting room.

fitting ('fɪtɪŋ), *ppl. a.* [f. as prec. + -ING².]

That fits: **a.** Becoming, appropriate, proper, suitable. **b.** That conforms to the contour or size of something; now only with prefixed advbs. (often hyphened), as *close(-ly)-, well-, ill-fitting.*

Many examples in editions of 15th c. works are spurious, the reading of the MSS. being *sitting*, which was formerly used in the same sense. It is doubtful whether the reading of our first quot. is not similarly incorrect, as FIT *v.*¹ has not otherwise been found so early.

1535 STEWART *Cron. Scot.* III. 486 Thre men war clad in fitand [coit-] armour. **1595** SHAKS. *John* v. vi. 19 News fitting to the night, Blacke, fearefull, comfortlesse. **1617** E. OWENS in *Lismore Papers* (1887) Ser. II. II. 113 Thus much I thought fytinge to acqueynt your Lordshipp. **1705** STANHOPE *Paraphr.* II. 355 Use all fitting means of putting it to Shame. **1825** SOUTHEY *Paraguay* III. 44 Which seem'd to be for beasts a fitting lair. **1845** M. PATTISON *Ess.* (1889) I. 20 Counsel..such as is fitting a bishop should give. **1866** GEO. ELIOT *F. Holt* (1868) 10 Her tight-fitting black dress was much worn. **1881** RITA *My Lady Coquette* xvii, It's the fittingest name.

Hence **'fittingly** *adv.*, in a fitting manner; **'fittingness**, the state of being fitting.

1641 JOS. SHUTE *Sarah & Hagar* (1649) 106 Let us carry our selves fittingly. **1653** JER. TAYLOR *Gt. Exemp.* I. vi. II. §28 (1667) 182 He..need not question the fittingness of Godfathers promising in behalf of the Children for whom they answer. **1863** BATES *Nat. Amazon* II. 95 The fire-ant, which might be fittingly termed the scourge of this fine river. **1866** ARGYLL *Reign Law* vii. (ed. 4) 377 Whose labours were to match with a curious fittingness into his.

fitting, Sc. form of FOOTING.

fittish, obs. form of FETISH *sb.*

1744 W. SMITH *Voy. Guinea* 196 They are kept in Fittish-houses or Churches built for that Purpose in a Grove.

†**fittle**, *a. Obs. rare*⁻¹. See quot.

1552 HULOET, Fittle or runninge witted, *futilis.*

fitty ('fɪtɪ), *a.*¹ *Obs.* exc. *dial.* [? f. FIT *a.* or *v.* + -Y¹; but cf. FEATOUS, FEATISH, and FEATY of which it may be a corruption.] Fitting, becoming, proper, suitable; hence, nice, trim, neat.

1589 PUTTENHAM *Eng. Poesie* III. ix. (Arb.) 169 Others strained themselues to giue the Greeke wordes Latin names, and yet nothing so apt and fitty. **1746** *Exmoor Scolding* 73 Thy buzzom Chucks are pretty vittee. *Ibid.* 569 Tha stewarliest and vittiest Wanch that comath on tha Stones o' Moulton. *a* **1800** *Ballad* in *Edin. Mag.* Oct. (1818) 328 The fittie fairies liftit her. **1880** *W. Cornw. Gloss.*, 'Your dress isn't looking fitty.'

Hence **'fittily** *adv.*; **'fittiness**; **'fittyways, -wise** *adv.*, properly.

1746 *Exmoor Scolding* 209 Tha hast..no Vittiness in enny keendest Theng. **1810** *Devon & Cornw. Voc.* in *Monthly Mag.* XXIX. 435 That coat is fittily made. **1880** *W. Cornw. Gloss.*, 'Do behave fitty-ways.' **1893** COUCH *Delectable Duchy* 50 We'm going to do the thing fittywise.

'fitty, *a.*² [f. FIT *sb.*². + -Y¹.] Subject to fits.

1811 E. NARES *Thinks I* II. 161 They..turned out so sickly and fitty that there was no rearing them anyhow.

fittyland ('fɪtɪlænd). *Sc.* [f. *fit*, Sc. form of FOOT *v.* + LAND.] 'The near horse of the hinder pair in the plough, which "foots" the unploughed "land" while its neighbour walks in the furrow' (Reid *Burns Concord.* 1889).

1787 BURNS *Auld Farmer's Mare* xi, Thou was a noble fittie-lan'.

fit-up ('fɪtʌp). *Theatr. slang.* [f. verbal phr. *to fit up* (see FIT *v.*¹ 11 d).] A stage or other theatrical accessory that can be fitted up for the occasion. Hence (in full *fit-up company*), a travelling theatrical company which carries makeshift scenery and properties that can be fitted up for the occasion.

1864 P. PATERSON *Glimpses Real Life* xxxiv. 333 The theatre was what is called 'a fit-up', erected in the large room at..a small hotel of the town. **1883** *Referee* 22 July 7/3 The 'fit-up towns'..are the towns which do not boast a theatre, [etc.]. **1885** J. K. JEROME *On Stage* v, He had been a member of a fit-up company that travelled with a complete Shaksperian *répertoire* and four set scenes. *Ibid.* xvii, However, I never did join a booth... The nearest I approached to anything of the kind was this fit-up. **1901** *Westm. Gaz.* 4 Nov. 10/1 His early, struggling, happy days with his father when they took the road with a little fit-up show. 'Fit-up, indeed!' he used to say with a laugh; 'why, our whole fit-up went into a couple of brown-paper parcels!' **1934** S. R. NELSON *All about Jazz* vi. 135 He spent a long time playing in fit-up shows, with a speaking part thrown in gratis. **1957** J. OSBORNE *Entertainer* x. 75, I was..on the

Irish fit-ups. **1970** *Daily Tel.* 14 Feb. 12 Today there are some 40 off-Broadway houses. You might add another 40 off-off-Broadway clubs and fit-ups.

‖**Fitz** (fɪts). Forms: 3–4 **fiz**, (3 **fyz**), (5 **fice**, **fytz**), 4– **fitz**. [AF. spelling of OF. *fiz* (pronounced fits):—earlier *filz*:—Lat. *fīlius* son.

The form is due to the phonetic law in OF. that a palatalized *l* caused a succeeding *s* to become *ts* (written *z*).]

The Anglo-French word for 'son'; chiefly *Hist.* in patronymic designations, in which it was followed by the name of a parent in the uninflected genitive. Some of these survive as surnames, e.g. *Fitzherbert*, *Fitzwilliam*, etc.; in later times new surnames of the kind have been given to the illegitimate children of royal princes. †Also in 12–15th c. used occas. in adopted AF. phrases, ***beau fitz*** = 'fair son'; ***fiz a putain*** = 'whoreson'.

1297 R. GLOUC. (1724) 432 Syre Roberd le Fyz Haim my fader name was. *a* **1300** *Signa ante Judicium* 179 in *E.E.P.* (1862) 12 Merci ihsu fiz mari. *a* **1300** *Cursor M.* 11879 (Gött.) 'Fiz a putaines', he said, 'quat er ȝe?' **1393** LANGL. *P. Pl.* C. x. 311 'Beau fitz', quaþ þe fader, 'we shulleþ for defaute'. *c* **1435** *Torr. Portugal* 2098 Antony fice Greffown. *c* **1450** *Merlin* 299 Leff the lady, traitour fitz aputain! *c* **1470** HARDING *Chron.* CCXLI. iii, Henry le Fytz Empryce. **1655** FULLER *Ch. Hist.* IX. Ded. 49 You shall be even in the language of the Apostle himself, Fitz-Dieu, A Son Of God. **1814** MRS. WEST *Alicia de Lacy* II. 92 The contentions of Henry Fitz-empress with Eleanora of Guienne.

b. *nonce use.* One whose surname begins with Fitz; i.e. an Irishman of Anglo-Norman extraction.

1848 MACAULAY *Hist. Eng.* vi. (1858) II. 130 The Fitzes sometimes permitted themselves to speak with scorn of the O's and Macs.

FitzGerald (fɪts'dʒɛrəld). [The name of George Francis *FitzGerald* (1851–1901), Irish physicist.] ***FitzGerald contraction*** or ***effect***, the contraction or foreshortening of a moving body in a direction parallel to its direction of motion, small except at speeds comparable to that of light, that was postulated independently by G. F. FitzGerald and H. A. Lorentz in 1892. (The effect is freq. named after Lorentz or after the two men jointly.)

1905 *Phil. Mag.* IX. 680 (*heading*) Report of an Experiment to detect the FitzGerald-Lorentz Effect. **1920** A. S. EDDINGTON *Space, Time & Gravit.* i. 22 Let the reader suppose that he is travelling through the aether at 161,000 miles a second vertically upwards... For this speed the FitzGerald contraction is just ½, so that every object contracts to half its original length when turned into the vertical position. **1967** J. L. ANDERSON *Princ. Relativity Physics* vi. 133 Several attempts were made to explain the negative results of the Michelson-Morley experiment. One of these was the Fitzgerald-Lorentz contraction hypothesis, which postulated that material bodies were contracted as they moved through absolute space.

Fitzrovia (fɪts'rəʊvɪə). [f. *Fitzrovius*, Latinized form of the name *Fitzroy* + -IA.] A Bohemian area of London around Fitzroy Square, west of Tottenham Court Road (see quots.).

1958 [see DOWN AND OUT adj. phr.]. **1971** J. MANTON *Sister Dora* xix. 328 The Medical and Surgical Home, 15 Fitzroy Square... Here among the Italians and artists of Fitzrovia the two friends had opened one of London's first private nursing homes. **1971** *Guardian* 3 Feb. 8/1 That pub-crawling area of London that Tambi called Fitzrovia, from Fitzroy Square and, more important, the Fitzroy Tavern.

‖**fiumara** (fju'mara). [It.] A flooded river, a mountain torrent: also the dry bed left by it.

1820 T. S. HUGHES *Trav. Sicily* II. x. 244 The road was no more than a fiumara, over which at this time a torrent from the melted snow was flowing. **1833** NEWMAN *Lett.* (1891) I. 396 We passed various fiumaras .. dry, of course. **1859** R. F. BURTON *Centr. Afr.* in *Jrnl. Geog. Soc.* XXIX. 104 The burns .. descending from the upper heights form fiumaras of considerable extent.

five (faɪv), *a.* and *sb.* Forms: 1–2 **fíf**, 3–5 **fif**, (3 **fifve**, 4 **fijf**, **fyf**, 5 **feyffe**, **fiffe**), 3–4 *south.* **vif**, 2–3 *south.* **vyve**, 3–6 **fyve**, 7 *Sc.* **fywe**, 3– **five**. [Com. Teut. and Aryan: OE. *fíf*, inflected *fífe* (ME. *five*, *vyve*), *fífa*, *fífum* (ME. *fiven*, *viven*) = OFris. and OS. *fîf* (Du. *vijf*), OHG. *fimf*, *finf*, *funf* (MHG. *vünf*, mod.Ger. *fünf*), ON. *fimm* (Sw. and Da. *fem*), Goth. *fimf*:—OTeut. **fimf*(*i*:—pre-Teut. **pempe*, modified by assimilation of consonants from OAryan **penqe*, whence Skr. *pañca*, Lith. *penkì*, Gr. πέντε, πέμπε, Lat. *quīnque*, OIrish *cóic*, Gaulish *pempe*, OWelsh *pimp* (mod. Welsh *pump*).]

The cardinal number next after four, represented by the symbols 5 or V.

A. as *adj.*

1. a. In concord with a sb. expressed.

the Five points, (*a*) the principal points of controversy between the Calvinists and Arminians, relating to predestination, satisfaction, regeneration, grace, and final perseverance; (*b*) the reforms demanded by the 'People's Charter' of 1838 (see CHARTER *sb.* 1 d). The ***Five Ports***: the CINQUE PORTS. ***the five senses, wits***: see the sbs.

c **1000** *Ags. Gosp.* Matt. xvi. 9 Ne ȝe ȝeþenceað þæra fif hlafa and fif þusend manna. *c* **1050** *Byrhtferth's Handboc* in *Anglia* (1885) VIII. 298 Nim þas an hund tida & þas fif & wyrc fif daȝas. *c* **1250** *Gen. & Ex.* 746 Fif burges wer ðor-inne bi tale, ðer-fore it hiȝte pentapolis. **1297** R. GLOUC. (Rolls) 7888 Ac þe vif pors of engelond. **1340** *Ayenb.* 179 Vif þinges specialliche destorbeþ zoþe ssriffþe. **1422** J. YONGE *Priv. Priv.* in *Secreta Secret.* (E.E.T.S.) 180 If þou fynde noght ffyue vpberers þat be lykynge to þe. **1631** WEEVER *Anc. Fun. Mon.* 268 Lord Warden of the fiue ports. **1845** DISRAELI *Sybil* (1863) 182 The national petition .. praying the House to take into consideration the five points in which the working classes deemed their best interests involved; to wit, universal suffrage, vote by ballot, annual parliaments, salaried members, and the abolition of the property qualification.

b. Phrases. ***to know how many (blue) beans make five*** (see BEAN *sb.* 6 d); †***to come in with (one's) five eggs*** (see EGG *sb.* 4).

2. a. With ellipsis of sb., which may usually be supplied from context. †***a*** or ***o five***, in five (parts): see A *prep.*[1] 6.

c **1000** *Ags. Gosp.* Matt. xxv. 2 Hyra fif wæron dysiȝe, and fif gleawe. *c* **1205** LAY. 25891 þæs bures dure he warp adun: þat heo to-barst a uiuen. *a* **1225** *Juliana* 71 Alle italde bitale seoue siðe tene & forðre ȝet fiue. *a* **1200** *Moral Ode* 28 in *Lamb. Hom.* 289 Betere his on almesse before þanne ben after vyue. *c* **1330** *King of Tars* in *Eng. Stud.* XI. 33 Him þouȝt his hert is brast o fiue. **1591** in Nichols *Progr. Q. Eliz.* III. 117 In this square they .. played, five to five, with the hand-ball. **1611** BIBLE *Isa.* xxx. 17 At the rebuke of fiue, shall ye flee. **1823** BYRON *Juan* X. xxxiii, Thermometers sunk down to ten, Or five, or one, or zero.

b. *esp.* of the hour of the day, as ***five o'clock***, etc.

1552 HULOET, Ffiue of the clocke, *hora quinta.* **1603** SHAKS. *Meas. for M.* IV. ii. 127 Let me haue Claudios head sent me by fiue. **1737** POPE *Hor. Epist.* II. i. 162 A sober Englishman would knock His servants up, and rise by five o'clock. **1842** TENNYSON *W. Waterproof* i, How goes the time? 'Tis five o'clock.

3. Coupled with a higher cardinal or ordinal numeral following, so as to form a compound (cardinal or ordinal) numeral.

a **1000** *Cædmon's Gen.* 1131 (Gr.) Wintra hafde fif and hund-teontiȝ. *a* **1225** *Leg. Kath.* 2530, I Nouembris moneð þe fif & twentuðe dai. **1297** R. GLOUC. (1724) 3 Fyue and þritti schiren heo maden in Engelonde. **1535** COVERDALE *Josh.* xiv. 10 This daie am I fyue and foure score yeare olde. **1579** FULKE *Heskins' Parl.* 382 The fiue and twentieth Chapter proceedeth vpon the same text. **1610** SHAKS. *Temp.* III. ii. 16, I swam ere I could recouer the shore, fiue and thirtie Leagues off and on. **1786** BURNS *Cry to Scotch Represent.* xxiv, Now, ye chosen Five-and-Forty, May still your mither's heart support ye.

4. = FIFTH 1 and 2.

c **1550** R. WEVER *Lusty Juventus* in Hazl. *Dodsley* II. 94 Read the Five to the Galatians. **1660** BLOOME *Archit.* B, The five part of one such part.

B. as *sb.*

1. The abstract number five.

1398 TREVISA *Barth. De P.R.* XIX. cxviii. (1495) 922 One done to foure makyth the seconde odde nombre, that is the nombre of fiue and hyghte Quinarius. **1876** MASON *Eng. Gram.* (ed. 21) §62 *note*, We say 'twice five is ten'.

2. A set of five things. **a.** *Cards* and *Dominos.* A card or domino marked with five pips.

1674 COTTON *Gamester* vi. 80 The Deuces, Treys, Fours, and Fives. **1870** HARDY & WARE *Mod Hoyle* 81 Suppose your hand consists of a four, five, and six of spades. *Ibid.* 95 The next player then plays 5/5 to the single five.

b. *Cricket.* A hit for which five runs are scored.

1859 *All Year Round* No. 13. 306 The loose balls we hit for fours and fives.

3. *pl.* †**a.** = *five cards*; see C 2.

1674 COTTON *Gamester* 150 All-fours is play'd in Kent, and Fives in Ireland.

b. The five fingers; also, ***bunch of fives***: the fist, the hand; ***to use (one's) fives***: to fight with (one's) fists. ***a fives*** (slang): a street fight (Farmer).

1825 C. M. WESTMACOTT *Eng. Spy* I. 290 With their bunch of fives. **1837** DICKENS *Pickw.* ii, Smart chap that cabman—handled his fives well. **1863** READE *Hard Cash* xxxiv, Now look at that bunch of fives.

c. (See FIVES[2].)

4. †**a.** *pl.* Five-penny nails. **b.** *pl.* Gloves, shoes, etc., of the fifth size. **c.** Short for *five-pound note.* **d.** *pl.* Short for *five-per-cents.* **e.** Short for *five minutes*, a five-minute break, in phr. ***to take five***: see TAKE *v.* 52 c.

a. 1629 *MS. Acc. St. John's Hosp. Canterb.*, For one hundred of fiues and one hundred of sixes, xj*d*.

b. 16.. *Description of Love* (1629) *I loued a Lasse*, Her wast exceeding small, The fiues did fit her shooe. *Mod.* What size gloves does she take? Fives.

c. 1837 DICKENS *Pickw.* ii, Want change for a five. **1860** F. W. ROBINSON *Grandmother's Money* II. IV. iii. 290 I'll bet ten to one in fives upon it.

d. 1848 THACKERAY *Van. Fair* xx, Look .. what the French fives were when I bought for the account.

C. *Comb.*

1. a. Combined with sbs., forming adjs., as ***five-act***, ***-bar***, ***-card***, ***-day***, ***-guinea***, ***-minute***, ***-pound***, ***-power***, ***-storey***, ***-wheel***, ***-year-old***.

1773 J. HOADLY *Let.* in *Corr. Garrick* (1831) I. 506, I have not yet had a sight of Dr. G—'s *five-act farce. **1882** L. TENNYSON in *Daily News* 10 Oct. (1892) 2/2 The contrast of action that can be provided in a busy five-act tragedy full of incident. **1709** STEELE *Tatler* No. 37 ¶2 [She] moves as if she were on her Nag, and going to take a *Five-Bar Gate. **1823** BYRON *Juan* VIII. lv, So was his blood stirr'd .. As is the hunter's at the five-bar gate. **1870** HARDY & WARE *Mod. Hoyle* 81 No hand in *five-card cribbage can be made to count so many. **1850** MRS. BROWNING *Poems* I. 256 God's *five-day work he would accept. **1706** *Lond. Gaz.* No. 4208/3 A Purse, with 3 *Five-Guinea Pieces. **1884** F. J. BRITTEN *Watch & Clockm.* 224 *Five minute repeaters give after the hour the number of five minutes past it. **1691** *Lond. Gaz.* No. 2626/4, 100*l.* in Old Gold and *Five Pound Pieces. **1806** T. S. SURR *Winter in Lond.* III. 255, I have inclosed you a five pound bank note. **1887** *Roy. Proclam.* in *Standard* 18 May 3/2 Every Five pound Piece should have .. our effigy. **1945** W. S. CHURCHILL *Victory* (1946) 151 A *five-Power conference bringing in Russia and China. **1679** *Exec. Bury* 6 Four *Five-shilling pieces they will afford for Fifteen shillings good Money. **1870** RAMSAY *Remin.* vi. (ed. 18) 202 He dropped .. a five-shilling-piece. **1769** *St. James' Chron.* 10–11 Aug. 3/4 *Five-year-olds 9 st. **1892** *Daily News* 26 Feb. 5/7 Taylor saw Robinson pick up a five-year-old girl.

b. In parasynthetic adjs. with suffix -ED[2], as ***five-barred***, ***-beaded***, ***-cornered***, ***-foiled***, ***-lobed***, ***-pointed***, ***-rayed***, ***-toed***, ***-toothed***.

1733 SWIFT *On Poetry* 15 A founder'd horse will oft debate Before he tries a *five-barr'd gate. **1820** CLARE *Rural Life* (ed. 3) 177 The five-barr'd gate with ease they leap. **1864** TENNYSON *Aylmer's Field* 186 The tender pink *five-beaded baby-soles. **1483** *Cath. Angl.* 132/2 *Fyve cornerd, *pentagonum.* **1658** SIR T. BROWNE *Gard. Cyrus* iii, The circular branches of the Oak .. five-cornered in the tender annual sprouts. **1860** RUSKIN *Mod. Paint.* V. VI. vii. §13 The *five-foiled star. **1823** CRABB *Techn. Dict.*, *Five-lobed, *quinquelobatus.* **1777** PENNANT *Zool.* IV. 54 Asterias [Beaded] .. smooth above the aperture: below *five-pointed. **1802** BINGLEY *Anim. Biog.* (1813) III. 435 The .. *five-rayed star-fish. **1854** OWEN in *Circ. Sc.* (*c* 1865) II. 82/1 The *five-toed or pentadactyle structure. **1877–84** F. E. HULME *Wild Fl.* p. vii, Calyx tubulate, *five-toothed.

c. In parasynthetic sbs. with suffix -ER[1] (chiefly *colloq.*), denoting individuals of a certain rank or size, as ***five-boater***, ***-master***, ***-rater***.

1887 *Pall Mall G.* 25 July 2/1 The iron-sheathed five-masters the *Agincourt* and the *Minotaur.* **1889** *Century Dict.*, *Five-boater*, a whaling-vessel carrying five boats; a large whaler. **1892** *Daily News* 24 May 2/6 The new Gosport five-rater.

d. Comb. in advbl. sense (= in five parts) with pa. pples., imitating scientific L. words with *quinque-* or *quinqui-*.

1823 CRABB *Techn. Dict.*, Five-cleft, *quinquefidus.* *Ibid.* Five-parted, *quinquepartitus.*

2. Special comb., as **five-acre**, a piece of land consisting of five acres; **five-and-ten (cent store)** *N. Amer.*, a store where all the articles were orig. priced at either five or ten cents; also *colloq.*, ***five-and-dime store***; † **five-cards** (see quot.); **five-corner(s** (*Austral.*), the fruit of *Styphelia triflora*, or the plant itself; **five-day week**, a working week of five days; † **five-double** *a.*, (*a*) five-fold; (*b*) consisting of five twice over; also *adv.*; **five-eighth** *Rugby Union* and *Rugby League Football* (*N.Z.* and *Austral.*), one of two players stationed between the scrum-half and the centre three-quarter; **five-figure** *a.*, (*a*) evaluated to or containing tabular entries of five significant figures or five decimal places; (*b*) worth ten thousand pounds or more; † **five-foot** = FIVE-FINGER 2; **five hundred** orig. *U.S.*, a variety of euchre in which five hundred points constitute a game (Webster Addenda 1918); **five-lined** *a.*, consisting of or marked with five lines, *esp.* of a parliamentary 'whip' with five underlinings to denote urgency; **five-maled** *a.*, *nonce-wd.* having five male organs or stamens, pentandrous; **Five-mile Act**, an act passed in 1665 forbidding Non-conformist teachers who refused to take the non-resistance oath, to come within five miles of any town, etc.; **Five Nations** [NATION *sb.*[1] 5 d], five confederated tribes of North American Indians collectively known as the IROQUOIS; later joined by the Tuscaroras to become the Six Nations (SIX *a.* 1 d); **five-nine**, a type of shell used by the German forces in the 1914–18 war; a gun that fires such a shell; **five percenter** *U.S.*, an agent who, in return for a percentage fee, assists businessmen to obtain Government contracts, etc.; **five-per-cents.**, stock or shares paying five per cent. interest on their nominal value; † **five-piece**, a five-pound piece; **five-score**, rarely used for 'a hundred' (Shaks.); **five-shooter**, a five-chambered revolver; so **five-shot** *a.*, having five cartridge chambers; **five-spot** *U.S. slang*, (*a*) a five-dollar note; (*b*) a playing-card having five pips; **five-star** *adj.*, (*a*) applied to a hotel classified as first-class and designated by five asterisks; also *transf.* and *fig.*; (*b*) *U.S.*, applied to a general or admiral whose badge of rank includes five stars; **five stones** = *chucks* s.v. CHUCK *sb.*[3] 5; **five-stroke** (*Billiards*), a stroke by which five points are scored; **five-to-two** *Rhyming slang*, a Jew; **five-yearly** *a.*, celebrated every five years, quinquennial; **five-year plan**, a scheme for the economic development of the U.S.S.R. over a period of five years, inaugurated in 1928; later of other countries and repeated in the U.S.S.R. Also, **five-o'clock** (see A. 2 b), used *attrib.* in **five o'clock shadow** (see quot. 1937), **five-o'clock tea** (colloq. shortened ***a five o'clock***).

1863 Tennyson *Grandfather* xx, Harry is in the *five-acre. 1880 in *Sat. Even. Post* (1940) 10 Feb. 23/3 Woolworth Bros. *5 & 10 Cent Store. 1907 'O. Henry' *Trimmed Lamp* 115 Did you ever notice me..peering in the window of the five-and-ten? 1922 L. Mumford in H. Stearns *Civilization in U.S.* 9 In the five and ten cent store it is possible for the circumscribed factory operative to obtain the illusion of unmoderated expenditure. 1924 *Antiques* May 229/2 Of course, we are all familiar with the ordinary pink, white and baby blue celluloid thimble of the present-day five-and-ten-cent store! 1934 J. T. Farrell *Young Manhood* in *Studs Lonigan* (1936) i. 160 A small American flag which he'd copped from the nearby five-and-dime store. 1945 S. Lewis *Cass Timberlane* (1946) xxv. 166 The lone goldfish in a bowl which she sheepishly brought home from the Five and Ten. 1674 Cotton *Gamester* 123 *Five Cards is an Irish game.. There are but two can play at it, and there are dealt five cards apiece. 1826 J. Atkinson *Agric. & Grazing N.S.W.* 19 The native cherry, *five corners, jibbong, and others, are merely tasteless berries. 1888 Boldrewood *Robbery under Arms* xxxiii, You won't turn a five-corner into a quince..dig and water as you like. 1926 *Sat. Rev.* 2 Oct. 367/2 Mr. Ford has inaugurated a *five-day working week... The five-day week cannot be isolated from the whole Ford policy. 1930 *N.Y. Times* 5 Dec. 3/2 The universal adoption of the five-day week by American industry would have the..effect of returning to employment all..now out of work. 1935 *Discovery* Aug. 221/1 The five-day week has already arrived, the four-day week will come and there will be increasing leisure to be employed. 1552 Huloet, *Ffyue double, *quincuplex*. 1591 Sylvester *Du Bartas* i. ii. 1103 O fair, five-double Round. 1594 *2nd Report Dr. Faustus* xxviii in Thoms *Prose Rom.* (1828) III. 103 Every archer being five double furnished. 1905 *Westm. Gaz.* 5 Oct. 10/2 Their three three-quarters and two '*five-eighths' gave them..a three-quarter line of five men. 1906 Gallaher & Stead *Complete Rugby Footballer* 76 During very many matches of the British tour, one of the present writers (Stead) played five-eighth to Roberts. 1927 *Daily Tel.* 27 Sept. 14/1, I place no value at all on the fact that they indulged in five-eighths, and multiplied the number of potential attackers immediately in rear of the scrummage. 1958 *Times* 22 Oct. 14/3 He has played for Australia against New Zealand in the stead of no less a five-eighth than A. Summons. 1969 *Australian* 24 May 36/4 The class of Balmain five-eighth, Dave Bolton, should be the deciding factor in the backs. 1969 *Sydney Morning Herald* 24 May 28/2 The move of captain Terry Rigney from full-back to five-eighth several weeks ago was one of the trumpets that heralded Gordon's renewed vigour. 1842 *Penny Cycl.* XXIII. 499/1 Lalande, 'Tables de Logarithmes'... *Five-figure tables throughout, and no mistake has ever been found in them. *Ibid.* 499/2 'Tables for Nautical Men.' Contains five-figure logarithms, neatly printed. 1861 Knight *Eng. Cycl., Arts & Sci.* VII. 1006 The necessity of dispensing with printed differences is alone almost fatal to the attempt at giving five-figure logarithms on one sheet. *Ibid.* 1007 The first British five-figure table.. which gives Gauss's table. 1929 Hall & Rideal (*title*) Cambridge Five-Figure Tables. 1948 C. Attwood *Pract. Five-Figure Math. Tables* p. iv, Mean proportional parts have been provided for five-figure values of cubes or areas of circles. 1971 E. Lemarchand *Death on Doomsday* vi. 85 They've got some pictures... One or two in the five-figure class at present values. 1706 Phillips (ed. Kersey), *Five-foot [*printed* foor] or Star-fish. 1659 Torriano, *Stellione*, the star-fish, or *five-foot-fish. 1920 S. Lewis *Main Street* 195 What do you say we go down to Jack Elder's and have a game of *five hundred? 1936 'R. Hyde' *Passport to Hell* 118 'Five hundred' and louse-catching were the major sports of Gallipoli. 1959 *Sunday Times* 22 Feb. 16/4 *Five Hundred*..never had much success in this country. 1787 Sir J. Hawkins *Johnson* 418 Roubiliac called for paper, and scored thereon a few *five-lined staves. 1884 *L'pool Mercury* 18 Feb. 5/6 The following five-lined whip..has been issued to members. *a*1794 Sir W. Jones *Tales* (1807) 171 This *five-mal'd single-femal'd flow'r. 1672 Marvell *Reh. Transp.* i. Wks. (Grosart) III. 224, I thought he deserved to be within the '*five-mile Act', and not to come within that distance of any corporation. 1689 *Apol. Failures Walker's Accus.* 24 Five-mile-Acts. 1684 L. A. Lahontan *Let.* 18 June in *New Voy. N. Amer.* (1703) I. 58 [It was a] pipe of the *five nations. 1688 *Pennsylv. Arch.* (1852) 1st Ser. I. 104 The five Nations or Cantons of Indians. 1713 *Col. Rec. N. Carolina* II. 24 To fly to the Indians and hire them to be mediators of a peace..would be derogatory to Her Majesty's honor, and might encourage the five nations to set Indians against Her Majesty's subjects. 1789 *Deb. Congr. U.S.* 25 May (1834) 41 *Resolved.* That the Superintendent of Indian Affairs..inform the Five Nations, the Hurons, and other Indian nations,..that Congress..received their said representation. 1852 J. Reynolds *Pioneer Hist. Illinois* 35 The bitter hostility of the Iroquois or Five Nations to the French. 1884 *Encycl. Brit.* XVII. 454/1 (New York) Forming permanent settlements about the headwaters of the streams which gave them passage to the heart of the country, they organized the political league or confederacy known as the Five Nations. 1959 *Chambers's Encycl.* VII. 754/1 *Iroquois* was the name of a great confederation of North American tribes, formed about 1570... At first called the 'Five Nations' (Cayuga, Mohawk, Oneida, Onondaga and Seneca), they became the 'Six Nations' of the 'Long House' when the Tuscarora joined them in 1715. *a*1918 W. Owen *Poems* (1963) 55 Deaf even to the hoots Of tired, outstripped *Five-Nines that dropped behind. 1930 Blunden *Summer's Fancy* 49 The five-nines drop like hail. 1960 J. Betjeman *Summoned by Bells* iii. 27 When Poperinghe and Zillebeke and Mons Boomed with five-nines. 1869 L. M. Alcott *Little Women* II. x. 143 Mrs. Kirk asked me if I wouldn't go down to the *five-o'clock dinner. 1872 Ld. Shaftesbury in Hodder *Life* (1886) III. 307 Five o'clock tea, that pernicious, unprincipled and stomach-ruining habit. 1882 *Worc. Exhib. Catal.* iii. 4 Five o'clock tea sets in fine porcelain. 1886 *Punch* 16 Jan. 36/2 Ladies invite their friends to 'a five-o'clock'. 1960 O. Manning *Great Fortune* ii. x. 115 The café..was crowded for the 'five-o'clock', which here [*sc.* in Bucharest] meant coffee or chocolate, and cakes. 1937 *Time* 11 Oct. 33/1 (Advt.), '*5 o'clock Shadow'—that unsightly beard growth which appears prematurely at about 5 P.M., looks bad. 1969 *New Yorker* 6 Sept. 115/1 Mr. Nixon, however, was given a deep five-o'clock shadow by the Rumanian artist. 1949 *Life* 24 Oct. 97/2 Be unswervingly loyal to all his party friends, even if they turn into *five-percenters. 1667 Pepys *Diary* 21 Sept., This day also came out first the new *five-pieces in gold, coined by the Guiny Company. 1848 *Gem of Prairie* (Chicago) 30 Sept. 6/2 These desperadoes are..well armed with the formidable '*five-shooter'. *c*1900 R. L. Hale *Log of Forty-Niner* 92, I had seen in his belt a bowie, and a five shooter. 1897 *Westm. Gaz.* 30 Nov. 4/3 The Mouzin *five-shot magazine rifle of 3 in. 1903 R. L. McCardell *Conversat. Chorus Girl* 42 Della's had a bunch of Broadway blooms that must have cost him a *five spot. 1913 C. E. Mulford *Coming of Cassidy* vii. 118 As the Queen slid off a five-spot showed. 1936 J. Dos Passos *Big Money* 78 They went into a hotel..to have a little supper and that just about cleaned his last fivespot. 1913 *Autocar Handbk.* (ed. 5) xxiii. 297 The Association has classified on a '*five star' basis a very large number of British hotels. 1949 *Manch. Guardian Weekly* 20 Oct. 15/3 Fleet Admiral William Halsey, the only five-star officer who will be called. 1951 I. Shaw *Troubled Air* xxii. 380 It doesn't make any difference..whether a five-star general or an ambassador to England sat next to you. 1953 P. Frankau *Winged Horse* iv. iii. 261 We always celebrate the moment..with a five-star quarrel. 1959 *Times* 10 June 12/6 An island where a five-star hotel caters for people who like deep-sea fishing. 1970 *New Scientist* 2 Apr. 5/2 Oysters, salmon and other five-star seafood. 1900 in *Eng. Dial. Dict.* II. 373/2 They are lakin' [= playing] at *fahv steeans. 1916 *Banffshire Jrnl.* 25 Apr. 3/3 Recollections. School Life in 1857... Early arrival was common..and the time left available was spent in the resting game of 'Five Stanes'. 1948 H. M. Gunn *Silver Bough* xix. 144 'What's five-stones?' 'Och, just a lassie's game!' 1985 *Sunday Tel.* (Colour Suppl.) 1 Sept. 12/2 He could shoot a marble farther than I could, but I always won the game of five stones (for which, surely, greater skill is needed). 1848 Thackeray *Van. Fair* xxii, 'How well he made that *five stroke, eh?' 1914 *Five-to-two [see *big-mouthed* s.v. big *a.* B.2]. 1932 P. P. *Rhyming Slang* 21 *Five to two*, Jew. 1941 G. Kersh *They die with their Boots Clean* i. 40 A Five is a Five-to-Two, or Jew. 1948 E. Waugh *Loved One* 7 They respect us. Your five-to-two is a judge of quality. 1618 Bolton *Florus* ii. vii. (1636) 114 This proclamation was made..at the Quinquennal, or *five-yeerely playes. 1929 *Times* 9 July 15/3 Soviet Industries. Failure of *Five-Year Plan. *Ibid.*, A special conference to consider how far Soviet organizations have succeeded during the past eight months in carrying out the five-year economic plan. 1932 *Ann. Reg. 1931* ii. 220 The Cabinet [of Romania]..drew up a 'five-year plan' for agriculture. 1938 *Time* 10 Jan. 20/1 The second Five-Year Plan ended last week, and the Soviet Union entered 1938 by starting on a third. 1969 N. W. Pirie *Food Resources* i. 36 The Indian Government is sometimes condemned because the fourth Five Year Plan..envisages only a 1 per cent increase.

†**five**, *v. Obs.* [f. prec.] **a.** In the game of Five-cards: *to five it* (see quot.). **b.** *trans.* (*nonce-use.*) To count by fives.

1674 Cotton *Gamester* xiii. 123 Before you play, ask whether he will five it, if he speaks affirmatively turn up the next Card of the Pack under that first turn'd up, and that must be trumps; if not play it out. 1769 R. Wood *Ess. Homer, Lang. & Learning*, When therefore I say that he *fived* them I take the liberty of coining a word.. corresponding precisely with the old Greek term [πεμπάσσεται].

'five-ˌfinger. [OE. *fīffingre* wk. fem. (sense 1), f. *fīf* five + finger.]

1. A name for various plants. **a.** The cinquefoil (*Potentilla reptans* and other species). **b.** The oxlip (*Primula elatior*). **c.** *Lotus corniculatus.*

*c*1000 *Sax. Leechd.* III. 123 Ac ceowe hwytes cuduwys sæd & fiffingran ælce dæȝ ær he etan. *a*1825 Forby *Voc. E. Anglia* 114 Five-fingers, oxlips, *primula elatior.* 1845 S. Judd *Margaret* iii. (1851) II. 295 The leaves of the five-finger draw together to shelter the flower when it rains. 1866 *Treas. Bot.*, Five-fingers, *potentilla reptans* and *canadensis.*

d. Any of several New Zealand trees with five-lobed leaves.

1926 *Trans. N.Z. Inst.* LVI. 701 *Nothopanax arboreum*, five-finger. 1960 B. Crump *Good Keen Man* 32 There wasn't a live five-finger or mangeo left in the valley.

2. A popular name for a species of star-fish.

1678 Phillips, *Five-finger*, a Fish resembling a Spur-rowel, which gets into Oysters, when they open and sucks them out. 1850 Hawthorne *Scarlet L.* xv. (1883) 213 She ..made prize of several five-fingers.

†**3.** *Card-playing.* The five of trumps. Also *five-fingers. Obs.*

1611 Chapman *May-Day* v. ii. Wks. 1873 II. 400, I..lost it [the set] hauing the varlet and the fiue finger to make two tricks. 1674 Cotton *Gamester* xiii. 123 The five fingers (*alias*, five of trumps) is the best Card in the pack.

4. *Comb.* **five-finger discount** *U.S. slang*, the activity or proceeds of stealing or of shop-lifting; **five-finger exercise**, a piece of music written for the purpose of affording practice in the movement of the fingers in pianoforte playing; also *transf.* and *fig.*, something very easy; **five-finger-grass** = 1 a; **five-finger-tied** *a.* (*nonce-wd.*), ? tied with all the fingers of the hand.

1966 J. M. Brewer in A. Dundes *Mother Wit* (1973) 241/2 *Five-finger discount (stealing) pays off. 1976 Lieberman & Rhodes *Compl. CB Handbk.* v. 119 The perfect 'gift' for the 'midnight shopper' looking for a 'five-finger discount'. 1983 Neaman & Silver *Dict. Euphemisms* 184 If it fell off the back of a lorry.., Americans might describe it in CB English as a five finger discount (stolen merchandise). 1903 *Daily Chron.* 20 July 3/3 Teaching small pupils the *five-finger exercises. 1936 T. S. Eliot *Coll. Poems 1909–35* 145 (*title* of series of short poems) Five-Finger Exercises. 1959 W. Golding *Free Fall* xii. 234 Leave happiness to the others, Sammy. It's a five-finger exercise. 1963 B. W. Aldiss *Airs of Earth* 64 Early news bulletins had spoken of rioting and arrests here and there, but these were mere five-finger exercises for what was to come. 1640 Parkinson *Theat. Bot.* 398 In English Cinkefoile..and *five finger grasse, or five leafed grasse. 1879 Prior *Plant-n.*, Five-finger-grass or Five-leaf, a plant so called from its five leaflets, *potentilla reptans.* 1606 Shaks. *Tr. & Cr.* v. ii. 157 And with another knot *five finger-tied, The fractions of her faith..are bound to Diomed.

Hence **five-fingering** *vbl. sb.* (see quot.).

1889 A. T. Pask *Eyes Thames* 58 They go out 'five-fingering', *i.e.* catching star-fish for manure.

'five-ˌfingered, *a.* [f. five + finger + -ed².] Having five divisions more or less resembling the fingers of the hand. *five-fingered grass* = five-finger 1 a. *five-fingered root* (see quot. 1746).

1562 Turner *Herbal* ii. 110 b, Cinkfoly or fyuefyngred grasse. 1578 Lyte *Dodoens* i. lvi. 83 Cinquefoyle is called.. in English..of some..Fiuefingred-grasse. 1746 Howell in *Phil. Trans.* XLIV. 228, I found it to be the *Oenanthe aquatica cicutæ facie* of Lobel which..is called by the inhabitants [of Pembrokeshire] five-finger'd Root. 1896 *Westm. Gaz.* 8 Feb. 2/1 *Uraster rubens*, the Five-fingered one. 1910 W. B. Yeats *Green Helmet* 21 An old five-fingered trick to tumble you out of the place.

fivefold ('faɪvfəʊld), *a.* and *adv.* Forms: 1–3 fiffeald, (fifeald), 2–3 fiffald, -fold, 6 fivefolde, -fould, 7– fivefold. [OE. *fīffeald*, f. *fīf* five + *-feald* -fold.] **A.** *adj.*

1. Consisting of five together, comprising five things or kinds.

*c*1000 Ælfric *Gram.* (Z.) 284 *Quinarius*, fiffeald. *c*1175 *Lamb. Hom.* 75 Heore fif-falde mihte hom wes al binumen. *c*1200 Ormin 7836 Himm birrþ off all hiss sinne beon þurrh fiffald þine clensedd. 1601 Shaks. *Twel. N.* i. v. 312 Thy tongue, thy face, thy limbes, actions, and spirit, Do giue thee fiue-fold blazon. 1624 Quarles *Job* (1717) 183 He hath torn me with the five-fold knot Of his sharp scourge. 1860 Pusey *Min. Proph.* 398 He pronounces a five-fold woe on the five great sins of the Chaldæans.

2. Five times as great or numerous; quintuple.

1557 Recorde *Whetst.* Bij, Quintupla. 5 to 1: 10 to 2.. Fiuefolde. 1612–15 Bp. Hall *Contempl. O.T.* iii. v, All the brethren are intertained bountifully, but Benjamin hath a fiue-fold portion. 1830 Bentham in *Westm. Rev.* XIII. 431 As the quantity of business-time is five-fold, so is the quantity of delay-time five-fold.

B. *adv.* In five-fold proportion.

1571 Digges *Pantom.* iv. xxv. Hh, The diameter of this body is fiuefolde in power greater than the side of his inscribed Cube. 1885 *Manch. Exam.* 20 July 6/1 London itself has increased fivefold since the century began.

Hence **'fivefold** *v. rare. trans.* To quintuple.

1858 Bushnell *Serm. New Life* 165 The capacity of religion may be five-folded.

'five-leaf. Forms: 1 fifléafe, 3 fiflef, 4 fivelef, 5 filife, 6 fyvelefe, 7 fiveleafe. [OE. *fīfléafe* wk. fem., f. *fīf* five + *léaf* leaf.] The plant cinquefoil (*Potentilla reptans*).

*c*1000 *Sax. Leechd.* II. 72 Þa wyrt þe hatte fifleafe. *c*1265 *Gloss. Names Plants* in *Rel. Ant.* I. 36/2 *Quinquefolium*.. fiflef. *c*1425 *Voc.* in Wr.-Wülcker 645 *Pentifolium*, filife. 1562 Turner *Herbal* ii. 110 b, Quinquefolium is named in.. English..herbe fyuelefe. 1579 Langham *Gard. Health*, Fiueleafe. The root boyled in water..helpeth the raging ach of the teeth. 1884 *Syd. Soc. Lex.*, *Five-leaf*, the *potentilla reptans*, from its five leaflets.

'five-leaved, *a.* [f. five + leaf + -ed².] Having five leaves.

1658 Sir T. Browne *Gard. Cyrus* iii. 155 The five-leaved flowers of Henbane. 1698 J. Petiver in *Phil. Trans.* XX. 316 Five leaved Mock-Mustard. 1704 *Lond. Gaz.* No. 4068/4 Two five Leav'd Lacker'd Screens.

b. *five-leaved grass* = five-leaf.

1526 *Grete Herbal* cccxlvii, Peenthafilon is an herbe called fyue leued. 1578 Lyte *Dodoens* i. lvi. 83 Cinque-foyle is called..of some Fyueleaued Grasse. 1614 Markham *Cheap Husb.* i. (1668) Table Words, Quinque-folio..is that Herb which is called Five-leaved Grass. 1884 *Syd. Soc. Lex.*, *Five-leaved grass*, or *Potentilla reptans.*

fiveling ('faɪvlɪŋ). [f. as prec. + -ling, dim. suffix.] 'A twin crystal consisting of five individuals' (*Cent. Dict.*).

fivepence ('faɪvpəns). Also *colloq.* fippence. [f. five + pence.] **a.** A sum of money, equal in value to five pennies. Phrase. *as fine as fivepence*: see fine *a.* 16. See also fippence. **b.** *U.S.* The value of 5 cents or 2½*d.* (*Cent. Dict.*).

1564 Bullein *Dial. agst. Fever* (E.E.T.S.) 62 Out of the countree..as fine as fippence! 1662 I. T. *Grim Collier Croydon* ii. in *Gratiæ Theatrales* sig. G12ᵛ, As a man would say, finer than Five pence, or..more proud than a Peacock. 1672 Wycherley *Love in Wood* v. 80 His Mistress is as fine as fippence, in her embroidered Satens. 1793 W. B. Stevens *Jrnl.* 21 Feb. (1965) 69 *Unde derivatur* as fine as Fivepence *vulgo dict* Fippence? 1805 E. Cavanagh *Let.* 4 Oct. in M. & C. Wilmot *Russ. Jrnls.* (1934) II. 187 All sorts of Music playing *as fine as five Pence*!

fivepenny ('faɪvpənɪ), *a.* [f. five *a.* + penny.] Valued at or amounting to fivepence. *a fivepenny rate, tax*: one at fivepence in the pound.

1799 in *Deb. 7th Congr. U.S.* 2 Sess. 1410, I was like-wise informed that this was done, and a fivepenny-bit each paid freely for a copy. 18.. [see tenpence]. 1968 *Guardian* 24 Apr. 3/3 The woman at the till took the new fivepenny piece.

1971 A. Ross *Huddersfield Job* 51 A fistful of fivepenny pieces.

fiver ('faɪvə(r)). *colloq.* [f. FIVE + -ER¹.]

1. A five-pound note. In U.S. a five-dollar note.

1843 *Spirit of Times* 7 Jan. 536/2 If any man heard more than a double X bet, he was in a livelier crowd than we met with. But in *'fivers'* something was done. 1853 WHYTE MELVILLE *Digby Grand* i, Spooner.. loses a five-pound note, or, as he calls it, a fiver. 1894 DOYLE *S. Holmes* 62 I'll lay you a fiver.. that.. you will never.. hear from him again. 1931 M. DE LA ROCHE *Finch's Fortune* xxiv. 315 Renny won a fiver off me.

2. Anything that counts as five (as a hit for five at cricket).

3. *Thieves' slang.* A fifth (term of imprisonment).

1872 *Daily News* 27 Apr. 3/4 They announced that they were in for a 'fiver' or a 'sixer', according to the number of their visits to a particular gaol.

†**fives**¹. *Obs.* = AVIVES.

1596 SHAKS. *Tam. Shr.* III. ii. 54 His horse.. past cure of the Fiues. 1639 T. DE GRAY *Compl. Horsem.* 79 This terme Avives we have also gotten from the French.. *secundum vulgus*, it is called the Fives or Vives.

fives² (faɪvz). [pl. of FIVE *sb.*, used as *sing.*

The reason for the name is obscure. The conjecture that the game may originally have been played by five persons on each side appears to be unsupported by evidence; the 16th. c. game of BORD-AND-CORD (see quot. s.v.) is stated to have been on one occasion played 'five against five'; but the two games had apparently nothing in common except that they were games of ball played with the hands. The slang use of *fives* for the hand (see FIVE B 3 b) has not been found until long after the appearance of the name of the game; otherwise it would afford a plausible explanation: cf. Fr. *jeu de paume*, which originally denoted hand-tennis, though afterwards transferred to the later tennis played with rackets. The statement common in Dicts., that the name was given 'because three fives, or fifteen, are counted to the game', is unsatisfactory: the number of 'points' in the Eton game is 15, but they are not divided into groups of five, and in other varieties there are 11, 20, or 25 points.]

1. A game in which a ball is struck by the hand against the front wall of a three-sided court. A variety of the game, in which a wooden bat is used, is called ***bat-fives***.

1636 *Div. Trag. lately acted* 8 He had a purpose.. to goe on the Lords day.. to play at a sport, called fiues. 1726 AMHERST *Terræ Fil.* xxxiv. (1741) 179 The old ball-court, where I have had many a game at fives. 1801 STRUTT *Sports & Past.* II. iii. 88 Hand-tennis.. is now called fives. 1862 H. KINGSLEY *Ravenshoe* xxxv, The little man was playing at fives against the bare wall.

2. *attrib.* and *Comb.*, as ***fives-ball, -bat, -player***; **fives-court**, a prepared court where the game of fives is played; also *collect.* for the persons who frequent a fives-court.

1825 in Hone *Every Day Bk.* I. 863 I made the first *fives-ball. 1857 HUGHES *Tom Brown* I. ix. (1871) 184 A favourite old *fives-bat. 1822 HAZLITT *Table-t.* I. ix. 205 Cavanagh was the admiration of all the *fives-courts. 1819 *Sporting Mag.* III. 210 Cavanagh, the famous hand *fives-player.

fivesome ('faɪvsəm), *a.* (quasi-*sb.*) and *sb. Sc.* Also 4 **fiff-sum.** [f. FIVE + -SOME.]

A. *adj.* (quasi-*sb.*) Five in all, five together.

1375 BARBOUR *Bruce* VI. 149 Fiff-sum in the furd he slew. ?16.. *Ballad, Kinmont Willie* 11 They guarded him fivesome on each side.

B. *sb. Golf.* A round in which five players take part.

1928 *Collier's* 10 Nov. 6/2 The idea was not to play a fivesome on a crowded course.

†'**five-square**, *a.* and *sb. Obs.* [f. FIVE after the logically correct *four-square*; cf. *three-square*.]

A. *adj.* Having five (equal) sides; equilaterally pentagonal.

1552 HULOET, Ffiue square, *quinquangulus.* 1560 BIBLE (Genev.) *1 Kings* vi. 31 The vpper poste & side postes were fiue square. 1657 W. COLES *Adam in Eden* lxiii, The seed-vessel, when it is ripe is formed five square.

B. *sb.* A (regular) pentagon.

1587 GOLDING *De Mornay* xv. 241 A fiuesquare conteineth both a Fowersquare, and a Triangle.

Hence '**five-squared** *ppl. a.* = FIVE-SQUARE A.

1535 COVERDALE *1 Kings* vi. 31 He made two dores.. with fyue squared postes. 1562 TURNER *Herbal* II. 7 The twygges [of Broome] are roughe and fiuesquared.

,**five-'twenty.** *U.S.* Used *attrib.* in ***five-twenty bonds*** (or shortly ***five-twenties***), certain bonds issued by the U.S. government in 1862, 1864, and 1865; so called from being redeemable at any time after *five* years from date of issue and payable in full at the end of *twenty* years.

1886 in WEBSTER *Suppl.*

fivety, obs. form of FIFTY.

fix (fɪks), *sb.* See also FIXES. [f. the vb.; the senses have no mutual connexion.]

1. (orig. *U.S.*) A position from which it is difficult to escape, a 'tight place'; a difficulty, dilemma, predicament. Also, condition, state; (working) order (*U.S.*).

1816 HORRY & WEEMS *Life Gen. F. Marion* (ed. 4) xiv. 124 They are in a mighty good fix. 1818 E. P. FORDHAM *Pers. Narr. Trav.* (1906) 167 The fire went out and it got quite dark. I was in a bad *fix*, as they say in the back-woods. 1834 D. CROCKETT *Narr. Life* vi. 50, I believe.. we should all have been genteelly licked that time, for we were in a devil of a fix. 1834 W. A. CARRUTHERS *Kentuckian in N.Y.* I. 29, I couldn't get my hands in no sort of a comfortable fix. 1836 *Pleasant Peregrinations* 50 (Th.), Tables and settees are put into a sleeping fix in the twinkling of a bedpost. 1839 MARRYAT *Diary Amer.* Ser. I. II. 166 The Americans are never at a loss when they are in a *fix*. 1839 *Spirit of Times* 27 Apr. 90/3 The filly is a keener, but looked out of fix. 1839 C. BRONTË *Let.* 14 Aug. in W. Gérin *C. Brontë* (1967) x. 153 It so happens that I can get no conveyance.. so I am in a fix. 1842 BARHAM *Ingol. Leg.*, *St. Medard*, A Stranger there, Who seem'd to have got himself into a fix. 1852 C. H. WILEY *Life in South* 126 I'll be delighted to be in your company in any fix (*i.e.* costume). 1854 E. FORBES *Let.* in Wilson and Geikie *Life* xiv. 532 The Scottish authorities have run me into a fix. 1868 H. WOODRUFF *Trotting Horse* xi. 113 In getting a whole stable of horses into fix to trot races, there will seldom be two whose treatment during their preparation ought to be the same. 1873 BLACK *Pr. Thule* vii. 101 And is this the fix you wish me to help you out of? 1895 *Outing* (U.S.) XXVI. 356/1 George's rod is splintered, and the Kid's reel out of fix. 1931 *Kansas City Times* 7 Dec. 16 What a fix this old world might have been in if our boys had not made it safe for democracy.

2. The material used for lining a puddling-furnace; fettling.

1871 *Trans. Amer. Inst. Mining Eng.* I. 327 In puddling 30 per cent. less 'fix' was required. 1881 RAYMOND *Mining Gloss.* 35 Fettle or line with a fix or fettling, consisting of ore scrap and cinder.

3. a. A reliable indication of the position of a ship, aircraft, etc., obtained by determining the bearings, visually or by radio, of objects whose position is known (as fixed points on land, or celestial objects); the position so obtained; also, the action of obtaining a 'fix'.

1902 *Encycl. Brit.* XXXIII. 97/2 The 'station-pointer' is the instrument used in plotting fixes. 1919 H. SHAW *Textbk. Aeronaut.* xviii. 208 An 'absolute' fix is one in which all the observations are taken together, while if a considerable interval of time is allowed to elapse between the taking of the observations, a 'running' fix is obtained, which is not so reliable. 1925 F. C. BOWEN *King's Navy* 182 On a well-lighted coast night navigation can be easier than by day since there will always be lights from which to take compass bearings and so to get a 'fix'. 1935 *Travel* Sept. 8/1 Throughout the flight position reports will be made every thirty minutes, based on these 'fixes', radio bearings and dead reckoning. 1942 J. A. HAMMERTON *ABC of RAF* (ed. 2) 110/1 When the landmark is recognized, then the airman is said to have obtained a 'visual fix'; the word 'fix' merely means the position of the aircraft. *Ibid.* 110/2 If the weather is bad and clouds hide the ground the navigator cannot obtain a visual fix, but there are other kinds of fix. He may obtain a 'radio fix' by getting in touch with two wireless stations. *Ibid.*, With clear sky above, the navigator may use the stars and get an 'astro' fix. 1950 A. P. HERBERT *Independent Member* xxxi. 196 If two or three reported the same splash from different angles.. there might even be an accurate 'fix'. 1958 *Observer* 12 Oct. 1/1 The Jodrell Bank radio telescope has been following the American moon rocket out into space. After tracking ended.. 65 'fixes' of the rocket's position had been made. 1963 *Times* 14 Jan. 13/7 There was only one fix on the trawler's chart for that day and no time was given for the fix. 1971 *Daily Tel.* 17 June 17/4 Using radio-direction finding equipment he obtained a 'fix' from the signals and traced the transmitter to Westmoreland Road, Bromley.

b. An estimate; an agreed or established point (of time, size, price, or the like); *spec.* on the London bullion market, a twice-daily ritual at which the price of gold is determined by the main bullion dealers.

1965 *Chem. & Engin. News* 10 May 88/1 Neither of the major companies that make rare earth polishes.. will say how much they make, so it is difficult to get an accurate fix on the size of this market. 1971 *Sci. Amer.* Oct. 67/3 It is noteworthy that the earliest astronomical fix is at 4000 years ago, that all older dates have errors. 1974 *Times* 9 Nov. 1/5 From a morning fix of $177½ an ounce the price climbed to $183 at the afternoon fix. 1982 *Times* 24 Aug. 11/2 Heavy buying was reported by dealers who said that the afternoon fix was particularly busy. 1985 *Daily Tel.* 22 Oct. 18/6 Gold price. 1st fix $326.50. 2nd fix $326.15.

4. *slang* (orig. *U.S.*). A dose of a narcotic drug. Also **fix-up**. Cf. FIX *v.* 16 c.

[1867 W. H. DIXON *New Amer.* I. 191 Claret-cobbler.. eye-opener, fix-ups, or any other Yankee deception in the shape of liquor.] 1934 *Flynn's* 21 Apr. 113/2 A package of narcotics is called a deck or a bindle; a shot is a geezer,.. or fix-up. 1936 *Amer. Speech* XI. 121/1 *Fix-up*, a ration of dope, especially one which has just been taken. 1938 *Ibid.* XIII. 184/1 *Fix*, var. of *fix-up*. A ration of narcotics, especially one to be injected. 1949 N. ALGREN *Man with Golden Arm* (1959) I. 57 'Don't vomit, student,' he taunted Frankie to remind him of the first fix he'd had. 1958 *Oxf. Mail* 29 July 6/7 A weird scene where the dope peddlers gather to beat up Johnny, who gets more into debt with each 'fix'. 1966 *Evening News* 17 Nov. 10/5 Hardly a week goes by without a report of drug-taking and 'fix' parties among teenagers.

5. A bribe; bribery; an illicit arrangement (e.g. amongst politicians, or between policemen and criminals). *U.S. slang.*

1929 *Flynn's* 20 Apr. 793/2, I can put the fix on for you so you can run your stuff over the line and straight into Chicago. 1930 E. D. SULLIVAN *Chicago Surrenders* (1931) ii. 48 It's impossible to scare tough hombres who can get $55 a barrel for beer that costs them $7. There's plenty leeway for the 'fix'. 1950 H. E. GOLDIN *Dict. Amer. Underworld Lingo* 70/2 *Fix.* 1. An agreement, secured through bribery, chicanery, intimidation, whereby a criminal indictment is quashed, or the severity of a sentence or of a charge lessened. .. 2. Any arrangement by which laws, rules, or regulations are circumvented... 'his mob got a license (police permission) to hustle (steal) on the cannon (picking pockets) here. The fix is in solid.' 1953 W. P. MCGIVERN *Big Heat* x. 124 He had come up through the ranks of a society that was founded on the fix.

†**fix**, *a.* (and *adv.*). *Obs.* [ad. L. *fix-us*, pa. pple. of *fīgĕre* to fix, fasten; the immediate source may have been OF. *fix* (13th c. in Hatzf.). Cf. mod. F. *fixe* (16th c. in Littré), Sp. *fijo* (earlier *fixo*), Pg. *fixo*, It. *fisso*.]

A. *adj.* = FIXED in various senses: a. As applied to the stars. b. Firmly placed or settled; not easily moved; not liable to fluctuation or change. c. Of a substance: Not volatile.

c1374 CHAUCER *Troylus* I. 298 His fixe and depe impression. c1391 —— *Astrol.* II. §3 *heading*, The sterres fixe. c1430 LYDG. *Min. Poems* 235 With eye fyx looke on his visage. c1449 PECOCK *Repr.* 393 Curatis.. schulden haue a stable fix endewing of lyflode. c1532 DEWES *Introd. Fr.* in Palsgr. 1054 All the starres fixe. 1660 tr. *Paracelsus' Archidoxes* I. x. 142 Take then the fix Element that remained after the separation of the Three Imperfect Elements. 1673 *Phil. Trans.* VIII. 5188 Those Salts being rendered so fix, that by a gentle fire they are not so much as at all moved.

B. *adv.* Fixedly, steadily.

1601 T. WRIGHT *Passions* (1621) 305 Why cannot many abide that you looke fixe in their eies.

fix (fɪks), *v.* Pa. t. and pa. pple. **fixed** (fɪkst). [Ultimately f. L. *fīx-us* (see FIX *a.*), pa. pple. of *fīgĕre* to fix, fasten. The proximate origin is uncertain; it may have been an Eng. formation on FIX *a.*, or ad. med.L. *fixāre* or F. *fixer* (if the latter existed in 15th c.; Hatzf. quotes Montaigne c 1590 for the earliest known use). Cf. Sp. *fijar* (earlier *fixar*), Pg. *fixar*, It. *fissare*.

The earliest recorded use is 'to fix (one's eyes) upon an object'; this is the oldest and still the most prominent application of the corresponding verb in Italian, and it appears in Du Cange's only example of med.L. *fixare*. The use in alchemy is nearly as old in Eng.; it is found in the Romanic langs. and in the med.Lat. writers on alchemy (e.g. R. Lulli *Ep. ad Robertum*). While in Romanic the verb has only the senses derived from L. *fixus*, it was in Eng. taken as the representative of L. *fīgĕre*, superseding the earlier FICCHE, and (in some applications) FAST and FASTEN *vbs.*]

I. To make firm or stable.

1. a. *trans.* To fasten, make firm or stable in position; to place, attach, or insert and secure against displacement. Const. *in*, *on*, *to*. etc.

to fix bayonets (Mil.): to attach them to the mouth of the musket or rifle.

14.. *Songs & Carols 15th C.* (Percy Soc.) vi. 6, I thouȝt in mynd I schuld ay fynd The wehle of fortunat fyxyd fast. 1489 *Barbour's Bruce* (Edin. MS.) x. 402 Thair ledderis.. maid ane clap, quhen the cruchet Wes fixit [*older text* festnyt] fast in the kyrnell. 1548 HALL *Chron.* 160 His head to be fixed on a poole. 1634 SIR T. HERBERT *Trav.* 213 The Bats.. hang.. (by clawes fixed to their wings.) 1659 B. HARRIS *Parival's Iron Age* 39 The Forts.. could not.. hinder them from fixing their cluches in the flat country. 1665 HOOKE *Microgr.* Pref. F ij, Fixing both the Glass and Object to the Pedestal. 1694 *Acc. Sev. Late Voy.* II. (1711) 5 We fixed our Ship with Ice-hooks to a large Ice-field. 1772 FRANKLIN *Exper.* Wks. 1887 IV. 509 In Philadelphia I had such a rod fixed to the top of my chimney. 1842 TENNYSON *Gardener's Dau.* 126 Holding the bush, to fix it back, she stood. 1860 TYNDALL *Glac.* I. xxvii. 210 The last stake being fixed, the faces of the men were turned homeward. 1892 *Law Times Rep.* LXV. 582/1 The posts of the gantry stand on planks, and are fixed thereto by iron dogs and dowels.

†b. ***to fix the foot*** or ***footing***: to obtain or take a sure foothold. *lit.* and *fig. Obs.* (Cf. FASTEN *v.* 1, and Lat. *figere gradum.*)

1583 STANYHURST *Aeneis* III. (Arb.) 89 He stutted, apaled; And fixt his footing. 1607 SHAKS. *Cor.* I. viii. 4 Fix thy foot. 1641 J. JACKSON *True Evang. T.* II. 98 The more weary [the Oxe] is, the more strong doth he fixe his footings. 1654 tr. *Martini's Conq. China* 52 The Tartars could never fix a foot in China. 1681 DRYDEN *Sp. Friar* I. i, I'll plant my colours down In the mid-breach, and by them fix my foot.

†c. To affix (a seal), attach (a codicil) *to*. *Obs.*

1568 GRAFTON *Chron.* II. 173 All the Nobilitie of Scotland .. entered into bond.. whereunto were fixed their severall seales. *Ibid.* 434 To be fixed as a Scedule to his last will and testament. 1776 *Trial of Nundocomar* 24/2, I have seen him .. wet two.. papers, and fix his seal to them.

d. In immaterial sense: To attach firmly; to implant securely (principles, etc.).

a1533 LD. BERNERS *Gold. Bk. M. Aurel.* xxxviii. (1539) 70 As sone as the goddes haue gyuen theim a doughter, forthwith they ought to fyxe in theyr hartes a newe remembraunce. 1672 J. LACY *Dumb Lady* To Rdr., You are fixed to the freehold never to be parted. 1712 BUDGELL *Spect.* No. 319 ¶4, I resolved.. to fix his Face in my Memory. 1789 W. BUCHAN *Dom. Med.* (1790) 25 Early application.. often fixes in the mind an aversion to books. 1855 BAIN *Senses & Int.* III. i. §5 While the mind is elsewhere, there is no progress in fixing them [lessons].

e. To 'fasten' (an imputation, responsibility, etc.) *on* a person.

1665 SIR T. HERBERT *Trav.* (1677) Ded. A iij b, The worst Reproach, Malice.. can fix upon your Name. 1694 *Acc. Sweden* 90 The Odium.. was easily fix'd upon the Ministers. 1744 BERKELEY *Siris* § 353 It will not seem just to fix the imputation of Atheism upon those philosophers. 1809 SCOTT *Fam. Lett.* 10 Sept. (1894) I. 148 Ellis fixes on me an article about Miss Edgeworth's Tales.

f. *intr.* for *refl.* To become firmly attached or implanted; to adhere *to*. *lit.* and *fig.* ? *Obs.*

1682 D'URFEY *Butler's Ghost* 159 For, salve the matter how you will, I fix to my Narration still. 1715 DESAGULIERS *Fires Impr.* 43 They pass over them, without fixing to them. 1748 RICHARDSON *Clarissa* (1811) VII. 299 Prejudices in

disfavour of a person at his first appearance, fix deeper.. than prejudices in favour.

2. a. To secure from change, vacillation or wandering; to give stability or constancy to (the mind, thoughts, affections, purposes).

1604 SHAKS. *Oth.* v. i. 5 Thinke on that..fixe most firme thy Resolution. **1605** BACON *Adv. Learn.* II. xi. §3 Images are said by the Roman church to fix the cogitations..of them that pray before them. **1642** FULLER *Holy & Prof. S.* III. xxi. 212 A constant impression of Gods omnipresence is an excellent way to fix mens souls. **1793** *Object. to War Examined & Refuted* 37 What other system is likely to fix your fluctuating opinions? **1851** DIXON *W. Penn* xvii. (1872) 143 At length his mind began to fix itself. **1875** McLAREN *Serm.* Ser. II. vii. 120 Thy tremulous and vagrant soul shall be braced and fixed.

b. To make (a person) constant in attachment. Const. *to*, *in*. ? *Obs.*

1710 PRIDEAUX *Orig. Tithes* Reasons for Bill 7 They are seldom well fixed to Virtue and sober Behaviour. **1738** JOHNSON *London* 145 How..Can surly virtue hope to fix a friend? **1747** in *Col. Rec. Pennsylv.* V. 153 To improve this favourable opportunity for fixing these Indians in the English Interest. **1749** FIELDING *Tom Jones* XVIII. xii, Can the man who is in possession of these be inconstant? Impossible!..they would fix a Dorimant. **1796** JANE AUSTEN *Pride & Prej.* vi, If a woman conceals her affection..from the object of it, she may lose the opportunity of fixing him.

c. To settle immovably the purpose or conviction of (a person). Const. *to* with inf.; also *on*, *for*, *against*. Now only in *passive*.

1671 MILTON *Samson* 1481, I am fixed not to part hence without him. **1697** DRYDEN *Virg. Georg.* IV. 126 They challenge, and encounter Breast to Breast; So fix'd on Fame. **1700** —— *Fables, Ceyx & Alcyone* 48 If fate has fix'd thee obstinate to sail. **1701** W. WOTTON *Hist. Rome* iii. 50 Marcus was fixt upon taking him. **1766** FRANKLIN *Let.* Wks. 1887 III. 456 The ministry are fixed for us. **1856** DARWIN in *Life & Lett.* (1887) II. 68, I am fixed against any periodical.

†d. With *complement*: To render unchangeably (so and so). *Obs.*

1726 W. R. CHETWOOD *Adv. Boyle & Castelman* 59 This Interview had fix'd my Heart intirely hers. **1744** S. FIELDING *David Simple* (ed. 2) I. 44 The Girl was commanded..to receive him in such a manner, as to fix him hers. **1777** *Hist. Eliza Warwick* I. 238 That important one [*sc.* day] which fixed me wretched for ever.

e. *Genetics.* To establish (a character, or the gene responsible for it) as a permanent property of subsequent generations.

1900 *Jrnl. R. Hort. Soc.* XXIV. 142 Seeds were again selected from the plants producing smooth seed and planted the third year, and so on through five generations, when the character was fully fixed, and all the plants came true, producing only the smooth black seed. **1902** BATESON & SAUNDERS *Rep. Evol. Committee R. Soc.* I. 131 It has long been known to breeders that certain forms cannot be fixed by selection indefinitely continued. **1905** *Jrnl. R. Hort. Soc.* XXIX. 418 Whenever it is desired in a cross-bred strain to fix a *dominant* character selection must always be made of *single* families containing no recessive members. **1957** *Ann. Math. Statistics* XXVIII. 891 The gene A will ultimately be fixed in the population or completely lost from it. **1969** *Times* 17 Feb. 6/7 The breed was created after 17 years of 'fixing' a type from a beef Shorthorn-Highland cross. **1970** R. GORER *Devel. Garden Flowers* i. 34 The recessive genes are always the easiest to fix, once they have been brought out.

3. a. To direct steadily and unwaveringly, fasten, set (one's eyes, attention, affections, etc.) *on*, *upon*, †*to* (an object). Also *refl.*

*c*1430 LYDG. *Min. Poems* 35 Hyr eyen she fixethe on him. **1509** HAWES *Past. Pleas.* xxx. xix, Specially I gyve to you a charge To fyxe your love, for to be true and stable Upon your lady. **1593** SHAKS. *2 Hen. VI* I. ii. 5 Why are thine eyes fixt to the sullen earth? **1665** SIR T. HERBERT *Trav.* (1677) 44 Could but these Idolaters fix their mind upon Heaven. **1709** BERKELEY *Th. Vision* §83 The more we fix our sight on any one object. **1792** G. WASHINGTON *Lett.* Writ. 1891 XII. 197 The enemy's attention would be less fixed to it. **1802** MAR. EDGEWORTH *Moral T.* (1816) I. viii. 60 The hand, upon which every eye was fixed. **1838** DICKENS *O. Twist* xliv, A mind unable..to detach itself from old.. associations, though enabled to fix itself steadily on one object. **1866** J. MARTINEAU *Ess.* I. 173 We fix attention on a single fundamental problem. **1904** L. T. MEADE *Love Triumphant* IV. vii, Her eyes fixed themselves on Leonora's face.

b. *absol.* To concentrate one's attention or mind *on*. Also *intr.* for *refl.* (said of the eyes, attention, etc.).

1663 GERBIER *Counsel* E vija, You..could not suffer your Eyes to fix on slight objects. **1690** LOCKE *Hum. Und.* III. vi. §28 In most other bodies, not propagated by Seed, 'tis the Colour we most fix on, and are most led by. **1760** JOHNSON *Idler* No. 97 ⁋7 He will find nothing [in these books] on which attention can fix.

c. Of an object of vision or thought: To 'rivet', attract and hold fast (the eye, the attention, etc.).

1752 *Hist. Jack Connor* I. 231 The Major gave a loud Hem, and having fix'd Sangfroid's Eyes, call'd out, [etc.] **1781** J. MOORE *View Soc. It.* (1790) I. xl. 437 Your admiration is fixed by the animated equestrian statue. **1792** C. SMITH *Desmond* I. 53 There is not in the world another [subject] that really fixes my attention an instant. **1823** BYRON *Island* IV. vii, A shrine would fix The eye upon its seeming crucifix. **1888** BRYCE *Amer. Commw.* II. xlvi. 206 That which chiefly fixes his attention is the influence of a State Victory on an approaching national contest.

d. To make (the eyes, features, etc.) motionless or rigid (as in death). Also *intr.* for *refl.*

1821 SHELLEY *Prometh. Unb.* I. 600 Fix those tortured orbs in peace and death. **1842** *Punch* II. 20 Ere death her charms should fix. **1877** W. G. WILLS *Love that Kills* xxi. Her heart stops, and her eyes fix.

e. To make (a person) motionless with astonishment or other feeling, to hold spellbound.

1664 J. WILSON *A. Comnenius* I. i, She fixt me, Ducas. **1795** *Fate of Sedley* II. 76 Paulinus was fixed in astonishment. **1802** *Helen of Glenross* IV. 18 At the first view of her I was fixed in admiration.

4. a. *trans.* To deprive of volatility or fluidity.

Orig. in *Alchemy*, to fasten a volatile spirit or essence by combination with a tangible solid or fluid; also, to render (mercury) solid by combination with some other substance.

1460-70 *Bk Quintessence* 15 Also it is needeful þat he vse ofte good wiyn at his mete and at þe soper, in þe which be fixid þe 5 essence of gold as I tauȝte ȝou to. **1471** RIPLEY *Comp. Alch.* Ep. in Ashm. (1652) 115 Dyssolve, Dystill, Sublyme..and Fyxe, With Aquavite. **1698** FRYER *Acc. E. Ind. & P.* 53 The Earth..penetrating the rarified Cuticle, fixes the Humours by intercepting their free concourse. **1700** ASTRY tr. *Saavedra-Faxardo* I. 42 He will have a fancy to fix Mercury. **1702** C. MATHER *Magn. Chr.* II. vii. (1852) 145 The animal spirits are..fixed with acid, bilious, venemous ferments in the blood. **1727** FIELDING *Love in Sev. Masques* v. x, Women, like quicksilver, are never fixed till they are dead. **1805** CHENEVIX in *Phil. Trans.* XCV. 111 Mercury can be fixed..by platina. **1885** HERVEY tr. *Behrens' Microsc. in Bot.* iii. §4. 178 The cell wall..becomes rigid, and the protoplasm with slight contraction is 'fixed'.

b. *intr.* for *refl.* To lose volatility or fluidity; to become firm, rigid, or solidified; to congeal, set.

1626 BACON *Sylva* §847 The Quicke-Siluer will fix, and runne no more. **1715-20** POPE *Iliad* v. 1114 When the fig's press'd juice, infused in cream, To curds coagulates the liquid stream, Sudden the fluids fix. **1777** ROBERTSON *Hist. Amer.* (1778) I. IV. 328 The blood fixes and congeals in a moment.

c. *trans.* Of a plant or micro-organism: to assimilate (the nitrogen or carbon dioxide of the atmosphere) by causing it to become combined in a non-gaseous metabolizable form. Hence, to cause (an element, esp. nitrogen) to form a compound, whether gaseous or not, as the first step in some biological or industrial process.

1850 *Jrnl. Hort. Soc. Lond.* V. 59 For a given quantity of water evaporated the amount..of the *nitrogenous* proximates fixed is..about *twice* as great in the Leguminosæ as in the Graminaceæ. **1862** *Phil. Trans. R. Soc.* CLI. 448 The Nitrogen might enter directly into the organism of the plant, provided its green parts were adapted to fix it. **1887** *Chem. News* 4 Mar. 104/2 According to the author's [*sc.* Berthelot's] experiments arable soil continually fixes free atmospheric nitrogen. **1906** *Jrnl. Soc. Chem. Industry* 30 June 568/2 The electro-chemical processes which have been proposed for fixing atmospheric nitrogen are..very numerous. **1928** F. A. ERNST *Fixation of Atmospheric Nitrogen* i. 9 Calcium carbide at red heat will absorb free nitrogen as a sponge will water, thus fixing the nitrogen in the form of calcium cyanamide. **1930** BUCHANAN & FULMER *Physiol. & Biochem. Bacteria* III. xvii. 174 The nitrogen fixed by microörganisms is used at once in the synthesis of the cell proteins. **1931** H. G. WELLS et al. *Science of Life* VI. iv. 558 The green plant is good at fixing carbon, the bacterium at fixing nitrogen. **1940** *Jrnl. Biol. Chem.* CXXXV. 790 *Escherichia coli* and *Propionibacterium pentosaceum* fix CO_2 with formation of succinic acid. **1946** *Nature* 28 Sept. 447/2 Application of phosphate fertilizers together with any substances which..stimulate the soil microflora will tend to increase the total amount of phosphorus fixed. **1947** J. R. PORTER *Bacterial Chem. & Physiol.* ix. 831 The most important bacteria capable of fixing atmospheric nitrogen belong to the genera *Rhizobium* (symbiotic root-nodule bacteria) and *Azotobacter* (nonsymbiotic bacteria). **1971** *Sci. Amer.* Sept. 62/3 Photosynthesis fixes carbon in the leaf and stores solar energy in the form of carbohydrate.

d. To preserve and harden biological material, esp. before microscopic examination.

1878 *Jrnl. R. Microsc. Soc.* I. 189 The property which osmic acid has of fixing the histological elements instantaneously in their actual form. **1969** BROWN & BERTKE *Textbk. Cytol.* iii. 16/1 Formaldehyde..is probably the most widely used chemical for fixing tissues.

e. *Immunol.* To bring about the fixation of (complement).

In early use occas. const. *to* and used as if belonging to sense 1.

1902 *Jrnl. Hygiene* II. 257 The plague bacillus in the presence of the anti-plague immune body of the horse fixed complement of the normal guinea-pig and caused its disappearance from the mixture. **1903** *Lancet* 15 Aug. 447/2 In Tube B the complement becomes fixed to the treated corpuscles before sufficient immune-body can pass to the untreated corpuscles; as a matter of fact, immune-body does pass over, but by the time this has occurred all the complement has been fixed. **1964** M. HYNES *Med. Bacteriol.* (ed. 8) vii. 85 As little as 0·00001 ml. of human serum..will fix complement in the presence of 0·1 ml. of human antiserum. **1970** PASSMORE & ROBSON *Compan. Med. Stud.* II. xxii. 12/1 Both IgG and IgM molecules have the capacity to fix complement.

5. a. *trans.* To make (a colour, a drawing, photographic image, etc.) fast or permanent.

1665 HOOKE *Microgr.* 79 Colours..capable of being..fixt with several kinds of *Saline menstruums*. **1750** FRANKLIN *Let.* Wks. 1887 II. 170 This color, given by the flash from two jars only, will wipe off, but four jars fix it. **1845** *Athenæum* 22 Feb. 203 The first who succeeded in fixing the images taken by the camera. **1859** GULLICK & TIMBS *Paint.* 316 There is no satisfactory method of 'fixing' pastel paintings. **1875** tr. *Vogel's Chem. Light* i. 6 No means were then known to make the pictures durable..or as we now say, to fix them.

†b. To set down in writing (F. *fixer par écrit*).

1630 CAPT. SMITH *Trav.* Ded. Wks. (1884) 808 Sir Robert Cotton..requested me to fix the whole course of my passages in a booke. **1656** *North's Plutarch, Add. Lives* 76 The Laws..(on Paper fixt)..pass the Seas.

c. To give permanent form to (evanescent images).

*a*1834 LAMB *Acting of Munden* O for the power of the pencil to have fixed them when I awoke!

6. a. To force into or overtake in a position from which escape is difficult; to 'corner', 'nail'. *lit.* and *fig.*

1736 LEDIARD *Life Marlborough* 406 It was his opinion.. that they should fix the Rebels at Preston. **1741** RICHARDSON *Pamela* (1742) III. 371 As I entered one Room he went into another..At last I fixed him speaking to Rachel.

b. To hold (a person) engaged or occupied, so as to prevent his leaving the spot.

1668 ETHEREDGE *She Would if She Could* I. ii, When Mr. Courtal has fixed 'em with a beer-glass or two, he intends to steal away. **1764** FOOTE *Patron* I. Wks. 1799 I. 334 Fix the old fellow so that she may not be miss'd.

c. ***to fix (a person) with one's eyes***: to direct upon him a steady gaze from which he cannot escape.

Cf. F. *fixer avec l'œil*, condemned by Littré as incorrect.

1792 MAD. D'ARBLAY *Diary* 27 June, Mrs. Wells..fixed her eyes on Mrs. Crewe..Mrs. Crewe fixed her in return.. with a firm, composed..look. **1879** F. W. ROBINSON *Coward Consc.* III. xix, Ursula..'fixed' Mrs. Coombes with a steady, searching stare. **1894** MRS. H. WARD *Marcella* I. 142 Marcella fixed him with her bright frank eyes.

d. Of the eyes: To arrest (an object of vision) with the gaze, i.e. to have a steady vision of it.

1791 MAD. D'ARBLAY *Diary* 4 Jun. (1842) V. 211 His eyes ..could not fix any object steadily.

†7. To transfix. [After L. *figere*.] *Obs. rare*$^{-1}$.

1638 G. SANDYS *Job* xx. in *Divine P.* 27 While from the raging sword he vainely flyes, A Bow of Steele shall fixe his trembling thighes.

II. To place definitely.

8. a. To place in a definite and more or less permanent position; to set, station. ***to fix up***: to set up.

1568 GRAFTON *Chron.* II. 18 The Citizens..fixed on his grave stone this Epitaph. **1633** MARMION *Fine Companion* III. ii, Were I a goddess..I would..fix you up A monument for your hypocrisy. **1634** SIR T. HERBERT *Trav.* 8 The Pole-star..is..fixt in the tip of the little Beares taile. **1653** WALTON *Angler* i. 7 Hee shall finde it fix'd before the Dialogues of Lucian. **1674** *Dryden's Mall* Ded. Wks. 1884 VIII. 508 The Glory I take in seeing your Name fixt in the Frontispiece. **1766** GOLDSM. *Vic. W.* xvi, It [a picture] was so very large that we had no place in the house to fix it. **1768** STERNE *Sent. Journ.* (1778) II. 199 The beds..were fixed up ..near the fire. **1796** T. TWINING *Trav. Amer.* (1894) 3 The dining-table was fixed in the middle of the room.

b. To place, install (a person, oneself) in a position, with preparations for a stay; in early military use, †to set (oneself) in a posture of defence. ***to fix (a person) up*** (colloq.): to 'put (him) up', provide with quarters.

1697 DAMPIER *Voy.* I. 5 We..fixt ourselves against our Enemies, if we should be attack'd. **1825** SCOTT *Fam. Lett.* (1894) II. 349 After he has had his umbrella and portmanteau accommodated, and himself comfortably fixed [in a coach]. **1867** TROLLOPE *Chron. Barset* I. xxxvi. 316 She fixed herself at her desk to write her letter. **1889** MRS. C. PRAED *Rom. of Station* 161 He'd..fix up Mr. Sabine comfortably for the night.

c. To establish (a person) in a place of residence, a position or office; to take up (one's quarters, abode); to locate, settle (an industry, etc.) in a certain place. In *passive*, to be (comfortably or otherwise) 'placed' or circumstanced.

1638 SIR H. WOTTON in *Four C. Eng. Lett.* 54 In any part where I shall understand you fixed. **1659** B. HARRIS *Parival's Iron Age* (ed. 2) I. xv. 27 John Calvin..fixed his Chayre at Geneva. **1665** SIR T. HERBERT *Trav.* (1677) 353 Noah..fixed his Quarters somewhere in Mergiana. **1677** YARRANTON *Eng. Improv.* 134 Here this Trade of making Mum may be first fixt with very great advantage. **1694** DRYDEN *Love Triumphant* Ep. Ded., Our decay'd Gentry..look about them for some illustrious Family, and there endeavour to fix their young Darling. **1702** C. MATHER *Magn. Chr.* IV. (1853) II. 10 Conforming to the ceremonies of the church of England, he was fixed at Biddiford. **175.** *Hist. Young Lady of Distinction* II. 214 He is fixing himself, as if he was to live here for ever. **1759** ROBERTSON *Hist. Scot.* I. II. 145 They determined to fix their residence at Edinburgh. **1803** SOUTHEY in Robberds *Mem. W. Taylor* I. 475 We are fixed here for some time. **1844** *Jrnl. R. Agric. Soc.* V. I. 282, I am happy to see them all comfortably fixed. **1861** M. PATTISON *Ess.* (1889) I. 39 The Hanse..fixed their factories in Lisbon, Bergen, and Novogorod.

9. *intr.* for *refl.* To settle, take up a position; *esp.* to settle permanently, take up one's abode.

1638 SIR T. HERBERT *Trav.* 102 Bidding farewell to the world..[he] fixes at Zirmol. **1710** STEELE *Tatler* No. 263 ⁋4 The Dinner has crept..from Twelve o'clock to Three, and where it will fix no Body knows. **1737** WHISTON *Josephus' Antiq.* XVIII. vi. §5 Those [Governors] are not to fix there, but to stay a short time. **1760** GOLDSM. *Cit. W.* xxv. ⁋7 Wherever luxury once fixes, no art can either lessen or remove it. **1796** JANE AUSTEN *Pride & Prej.* (1885) I. vi. 21, I had once some thoughts of fixing in town. **1801** SOUTHEY *Thalaba* VI. xiii, The solitary Bee..Seeking in vain one flower, whereon to fix. **1862** T. L. PEACOCK *Wks.* (1875) III. 300 Well, let us fix here.

10. a. To take up one's position mentally. ? *Obs.*

1623 MASSINGER *Dk. Milan* II. i, Take heed That you fix here, and feed no hope beyond it. **1646** H. LAWRENCE *Comm. Angels* 170 Your hope fixeth upon seeing him in heaven. **1655** *Nicholas Papers* (Camden) II. 332 *Mais Dieu sur tout*; and there I fix and pray. **1757** CHESTERF. *Lett.* IV.

cccxxi. 94, I am lost in astonishment and conjectures, and do not know where to fix.

b. *to fix on* or *upon*: to settle one's choice *on* or *upon*; to decide upon, choose, select.

1653 H. COGAN tr. *Pinto's Trav*, lxxvi. 311, I was nominated unto him as the fittest he could fix upon. **1712** POPE *Vertumnus* 82 Of all these lovers.. Fix on Vertumnus and reject the rest. **1823** H. J. BROOKE *Introd. Crystallogr.* 229 Our choice would probably fix on that which was most predominant. **1855** COSTELLO *Stor. Screen* 74 The night which Laloubière fixed upon for the carrying out of his plot.

c. To decide, determine *to* (do something); also const. *for* with gerund, or with subord. sentence.

1788 *Trifler* 206 He fix'd to come with some eclat to Town. **1794** MISS GUNNING *Packet* IV. 35 They fixed for going to the parsonage early the next morning. **1813** SOUTHEY *Nelson* I. 132 It was immediately fixed that the brigadier should go. **1834** KEBLE in *Card. Newman's Lett.* (1891) II. 23, I have fixed to go to London next week. **1866** *Times* 29 Dec. 10/3 The lady had entirely fixed to lead a life of celibacy.

11. a. To appoint or assign the precise position of; to refer (something) to a definite place, time, etc.; †to appoint or attribute exclusively *to* (some particular person, thing, etc.).

1662 STILLINGFL. *Orig. Sacr.* I. v. §1 [The ancients had various estimates of the length of the year;] what certainty can we possibly have which of them to fix their accounts to? **1692** LOCKE *Educ.* §15 When Custom has fixed his Eating to certain stated Periods, his Stomach will expect Victuals at the usual Hour. **1737** JOHNSON in *Boswell* (1791) I. 52 Here will I fix the limits of transgression. **1776** T. JEFFERSON *Let.* Writ. 1893 II. 88 The commissions.. do not fix the officers to any particular battalion. **1790** PALEY *Horæ Paul.* ii. 11 We have these circumstances each.. fixed to a particular time. **1874** NEWMAN *Tracts Theol. & Eccl.* 340 The full moon is not fixed to any certain day in either month. **1875** JOWETT *Plato* (ed. 2) IV. 271 Wherever we fix a limit, space is springing up beyond.

b. To allocate, determine the incidence of (a responsibility, liability, etc.). Also, *to fix* (a person) ***with costs, liability***, etc.: to impose upon him the obligation of meeting or paying them.

1833 LD. BROUGHAM in Mylne & Keen *Rep.* II. 248 No degree of mistake.. would entitle the Court to fix a next friend with costs. **1850** *Florist* June 159 Take care to fix your judges with the full responsibility of their decisions. **1884** SIR J. BACON in *Law Times' Rep.* LII. 568/2 The liability with which the plaintiffs seek to fix them. **1888** BRYCE *Amer. Commw.* III. lxxxvi. 151 The American plan of dividing powers.. makes it hard to fix responsibility.

12. To settle definitely; to appoint or assign with precision; to specify or determine. Const. *at*, *for*, *to*.

1660 R. COKE *Power & Subj.* 134 After some reasonable time fixt. **1694** MOLESWORTH *Acc. Denmark* 223 The prices of all these Drugs are fixed. *a* **1715** BURNET *Own Time* II. 303 What definition or standard should be made for fixing the sense of so general a term. **1719** *Free-Thinker* No. 120 ¶6 The ordinary Meetings of the Senate.. were fixed to the Day of the Calends. **1739** CHESTERF. *Wks.* (1892) V. 500 Chronology.. fixes the dates of facts. **1769** GOLDSM. *Rom. Hist.* (1786) I. 319 He afterwards fixed the price of corn to a moderate standard. **1772** FRANKLIN *Wks.* (1887) IV. 431 The opening of the session.. is fixed for next Tuesday. **1821** SOUTHEY *Life* (1849) I. 42 This recollection.. fixes the date to 1778, when I was four years old. **1825** SCOTT *Fam. Lett.* 13 May (1894) II. 265 Mr. Chantrey.. has been down here fixing the place for the King's statue. **1869** E. A. PARKES *Pract. Hygiene* (ed. 3) 5 The War Office authorities have fixed the daily supply.. at 8 gallons. **1876** GLADSTONE *Homeric Synchr.* 9 An endeavour to fix the place of Homer in History.

absol. **1748** in Sir J. Picton *L'pool. Munic. Rec.* (1886) II. 167 To paint an Altar Piece in such scripture-historical manner as the said Committee shall fix.

13. To settle or determine the form of, give a permanent form to (language or literature).

1712 SWIFT *Proposal* 31 That some Method should be thought on for ascertaining and fixing our Language for ever. **1752** HUME *Ess. & Treat.* (1777) I. 223 Eminent and refined geniuses.. fix the tongue by their writings. **1837** HALLAM *Hist. Lit.* I. iii. §57. 241 The use of printing fixed the text of a whole edition. **1874** MAURICE *Friendship Bks.* iii. 75 It [Wycliffe's Translation of the Bible] has fixed the language.

14. a. To adjust, make ready for use (arms, instruments, etc.); to arrange in proper order. †*to fix a shell*: to fit it with a fuse. Also with *up*.

1663 PEPYS *Diary* 12 July, I found.. the arms well fixed, charged, and primed. **1666** EARL ORRERY *State Papers* (1743) I. 241 We have in every garrison one gunsmith.. who buys arms for us, and fixes them up privately. **1697** DAMPIER *Voy.* I. iii. 45 We went back.. to fix our Rigging, which was shattered in the Fight. **1701** FARQUHAR *Sir H. Wildair* II. i, Are all things set in order? the toilet fixed, the bottles and combs put in form? **1769** FALCONER *Dict. Marine* (1776) D d, No shells, fixed during the service, are to be kitted. **1779** FORREST *Voy. N. Guinea* 287, I thought it a good opportunity to fix my german flute. **1797** WASHINGTON *Let.* Writ. 1892 XIII. 417 To have the press fixed for copying.

b. In wider sense (chiefly U.S. *colloq.*): To arrange, get ready, put in order; to put to rights, make tidy, 'rig up'; *spec.* to prepare (food or drink). Also with *off*, *over*, and *up* and const. *for* (doing something). *to fix out*, 'to set out, display, adorn, supply, fit out' (*Cent.*); ***to fix the table*** (see quot. 1842²); ***to fix one's face***, etc.: to put on or rearrange one's make-up, etc.

1725 S. WILLARD in H. S. Nourse *Early Rec. Lancaster, Mass.* (1884) 237, I fixed the men out with stores. [**1769** BICKERSTAFF *Dr. Last* II. vii, We'd fix things directly; I'll settle whatever you please upon her.] **1783** JAS. SMITH *Tour* 1 Dec. in *Ohio State Archaeol. & Hist. Q.* (1907) XVI. 360 After having fixed up our luggage and taken breakfast we started from Capt. Owsley's. **1804** W. CLARK in Lewis & Clark *Orig. Jrnls.* (1905) VII. 301 Captain Lewis.. has been detained at St. Louis to fix off the Osage chiefs. **1832** MACAULAY *Life & Lett.* (1883) I. 272 As soon as I was fixed in my best and had breakfasted. **1839** MARRYAT *Diary Amer.* Ser. I. II. 228 'Shall I fix your coat or your breakfast first?' **1839** F. TROLLOPE *Dom. Manners* (1949) 414 You must fix me a drink. **1842** DICKENS *Amer. Notes* (1850) 101/2 You are advised to have recourse to Doctor so and so, who will 'fix you' in no time. **1842** —— *Amer. Notes* II. ii. 46 You call upon a gentleman in a country town, and his help informs you that he is 'fixing himself' just now, but will be down directly: by which you are to understand that he is dressing. *Ibid.*, You inquire.. whether breakfast will be ready soon, and he tells you.. they were 'fixing the tables': in other words, laying the cloth. **1853** J. G. BALDWIN *Flush Times Alabama* 99 Tom had unfortunately fixed him for visiting his mother on crutches. **1856** *Knickerbocker* June XLVII. 617 Only point me out your traps, and I'll send them up to the hotel, and fix you off all as square as a box. **1860** O. W. HOLMES *Elsie V.* (1887) 77 Come here, girls, and fix yourselves in the glass. **1873** C. M. YONGE *Pillars of House* IV. xlv. 278 He examined the last roll of proof.. and said.. 'I can fix off a sheet for you.' **1882** MRS. A. EDWARDS *Ballroom Repent.* I. 4 None of the physicians in Europe can fix her up. **1883** 'MARK TWAIN' *Life on Mississippi* 286 The feud.. could have been fixed up, easy enough. **1884** MISS WILKINS in *Harper's Mag.* July 304/2 I'll hev to fix me up some thoroughwort tea. **1889** 'MARK TWAIN' *Connecticut Yankee* 21 We fixed up an agreement. **1891** B. HARTE *First Family of Tasajara* ii, Mother'll fix you suthin' hot. **1893** W. TIREBUCK *Sweetheart Gwen* II. iii. 223 It's the weekly meeting and I fix the table. **1908** R. W. CHAMBERS *Firing Line* xxi. 367 Use a sponge and cold water and fix your hair and put on your shoes. **1917** C. MATHEWSON *Second Base Sloan* 279 Tell him to show that to the man at the ticket office and he will fix him out. **1928** A. WAUGH *Last Chukka* 87 Why don't we go into the club now, and fix it up? **1933** A. CHRISTIE *Ld. Edgware Dies* ii. 23 Come in here and talk to me while I fix my face. **1936** WODEHOUSE *Laughing Gas* ii. 23 They come to take me out to some party, and they find me in my kitchen in a gingham wrapper, fixing a Welsh rarebit. **1941** J. P. MARQUAND *H. M. Pulham, Esq.* xxiv. 385 When we did have a guest, Gladys had to move.. into the old nursery, which we never had got around to fixing over. **1947** AUDEN *Age of Anxiety* (1948) v. 103 Cutting sandwiches and fixing drinks. **1953** N. GORDIMER *Lying Days* II. vii. 69 In my room.. I fixed my hair this way and that. **1962** K. ORVIS *Damned & Destroyed* xiii. 88, I should go and fix my face. **1969** A. GLYN *Dragon Variation* iii. 74 She.. went to the bathroom, bathed her face and fixed it.

c. Orig. and chiefly *U.S.* ***to fix*** (a person): to deal with, settle or 'do for' (a person); to kill (a person). ***to fix it***: to arrange matters. ***any way you can fix it***: whatever you do, contrive as you may. ***to fix (another's) flint***: to settle or 'do for' him.

1836 *Col. Crockett's Exploits* 125 The people in Texas would have nothing to do with that affair, nohow they could fix it. **1840** HALIBURTON *Clockm.* Ser. III. xii, Their manners are rude.. They want their flints fixed for 'em. **1842** DICKENS *Amer. Notes* II. ii. 46 You beg a porter to collect your luggage, and he entreats you not to be uneasy, for he'll 'fix it presently'. **1843** HALIBURTON *Sam Slick in Eng.* I. ii, A wet day is considerable tiresome.. any way you can fix it. **1859** O. W. HOLMES *Prof. Breakf.-t.* i. (1891) 15 If you can't fix it so as to be born here [Boston], you can come and live here. **1860** HOTTEN *Slang Dict.* (ed. 2) 140 To fix one's flint for him, *i.e.*, to settle his hash. **1874** 'MARK TWAIN' *Let.* (1917) I. 216 I'll close the door against them all—which will 'fix' all of the lot. **1875** *Chicago Tribune* 25 Sept. 7/1 McDonald.. said, 'I'll fix you, Fiddler Neary.' He drew a weapon. **1876** C. C. ROBINSON *Gloss. Mid-Yorksh.* 42/1 To 'fix' the flint of any person, is to serve him out. **1942** WODEHOUSE *Money in Bank* (1946) xii. 106 'Don't you worry. I'll fix him.'.. 'How do you mean, fix?' 'Just fix.' 'You wouldn't croak him?' Mrs Molloy laughed merrily at the whimsical thought. **1957** *Times Lit. Suppl.* 8 Nov. 670/3 He tries to 'fix' her by another [lawsuit], but she wins that too. Unhappily, Seymour 'fixes' it so that her besotted husband gets custody of the younger child.

d. orig. *U.S.* 'To make favourable to one's purposes' (Bartlett), to 'square', usu. by illegal means, esp. bribery.

1790 in *Jrnl. Wm. Maclay* (1927) 248 It is expected of us that we should fix the Governor of Pennsylvania. **1872** G. P. BURNHAM *Mem. U.S. Secret Service* 72 When Biebusch saw *this* man in Court, whom he fancied he had 'fixed' for certain, the criminal wilted. **1881** *Standard* 7 Sept. 5/2 It is true that they talk of 'fixing' a horse, but they also use 'nobbling' in the same sense. **1886** *Boston* (Mass.) *Jrnl.* 15 July, An organized attempt is being made to fix the jury. *Ibid.* 24 Aug. 4/3 Fixing Legislatures. **1908** *Atlantic Monthly* Aug. 230/2 A jockey or a pugilist is 'fixed'. **1941** L. A. G. STRONG *Bay* ix. 229 She had ignored the difficulty of fixing Muriel. **1959** *Daily Tel.* 10 Dec. 20/3 He was told that a [driving] test could be 'fixed' for £10. **1960** *Guardian* 18 Oct. 8/2 The mere suspicion that matches were being 'fixed' would be disastrous for the game.

e. To mend, repair. orig. *U.S.*

a **1762** S. NILES *Wars* in *Mass. Hist. Soc. Coll.* (1861) II. 401 A number of hands came to fix our whale-boats. **1870** 'MARK TWAIN' *Sk. New & Old* (1875) 20 [I] finally took the watch to another watchmaker... He fixed it, and gave it a fresh start. **1947** 'N. SHUTE' *Chequer Board* iii. 59 They fixed the vicar's Austin Seven. **1949** F. SARGESON *I saw in my Dream* 37 Arnold was fixing his motor bike.

f. To castrate, sterilize (an animal).

1930 D. H. LAWRENCE *Nettles* 21 Is he a gentleman or a lady?—Neither, my dear! I had him fixed. It saves him from so many undesirable associations. **1962** *Coast to Coast 1961–62* 13 Many years ago he had chosen Silvanus from a litter of kittens, and Brett had 'fixed' it, as he had 'fixed' so many male animals on the farm. **1970** *Washington Post* 30 Sept. B7 'If you fix a stallion,' said Dawnita, 'something happens. He just doesn't have as much action.'

15. (See quot.)

1881 RAYMOND *Mining Gloss.*, *Fix*, to *fettle* or line with a *fix* or *fettling*.. the hearth of a puddling furnace.

16. *intr.* **a.** To intend; to arrange, get ready, make preparations, *for* or *to do* something. Also with *out* and *up*. *U.S.*

1716 B. CHURCH *Hist. Philip's War* (1865) I. 140 He fixes for another Expedition. **1779** D. LIVERMORE in *Coll. New Hampsh. Hist. Soc.* (1850) VI. 335 Troops are busy in clearing and fixing for laying the foundations of the huts. **1829/30–1943** in WENTWORTH *Amer. Dial. Dict.* **1854–5** in N. E. Eliason *Tarheel Talk* (1956) iv. 136 Aunt Lizy is just fixing to go to church. **1871** MRS. STOWE *Old Town Fireside T.* 55 He was a fixin' out for the voyage. **1875** 'MARK TWAIN' *Speeches* (1923) 55 You fix up for the drought. **1907** *Springfield* (Mass.) *Weekly Republ.* 22 Aug. 6 What a pretty night! The moon is fixing to shine! **1914** G. ATHERTON *Perch of Devil* I. 32, I meet.. schoolgirls.. so painted up they look as if they was fixin'.. to be bad. **1935** J. B. PRIESTLEY *Wonder Hero* iv. §3. 121, I may be able to fix up for you both to go out to supper afterwards. **1970** H. E. ROBERTS *Third Ear* 6/2 *Fixin' to*, about to do something; to be ready or to intend to.

b. (Usually with *up*.) To put oneself in proper trim; to dress up; to spruce up.

1783 JAS. SMITH *Tour* 7 Dec. in *Ohio State Archaeol. & Hist. Q.* (1907) XVI. 361 We fixed up and started from our encampment as soon as it was well light. **1834** D. CROCKETT *Narr. Life* vii. 51, I fixed up, and joined old Major Russell again. **1845** S. JUDD *Margaret* III. 393 Pa and Ma.. were for fixing up a little. *a* **1852** F. M. WHITCHER *Widow Bedott Papers* (1883) xxvi. 116 She looked as if she'd fixed in a wonderful hurry. **1873** J. H. BEADLE *Undevel. West* x. 177 When we can build larger houses it will be time to fix up. **1929** W. FAULKNER *Sartoris* III. iii. 202 You better go to the bathroom and fix up. **1964** MRS. L. B. JOHNSON *White House Diary* 26 Feb. (1970) 75 They were readying a press conference... I fixed up a bit and went down with Lynda.

c. *intr.* and *trans.* To inject (oneself) with narcotics. (Cf. FIX *sb.* 4.) *slang* (orig. *U.S.*).

1938 *Amer. Speech* XIII. 184/1 *To fix*, to take narcotics. **1962** K. ORVIS *Damned & Destroyed* ix. 59 No wonder you're setting there so smug and relaxed. You fixed this morning. You're floating! **1963** A. TROCCHI *Cain's Book* 78 The one vital coil in him is the bitter knowledge that he can choose to fix again. **1967** M. M. GLATT et al. *Drug Scene* vii. 87 At first I 'fixed' only once a week, then more often, and after about six months I was addicted. **1969** *Guardian* 8 July 18/1 The Association for the Prevention of Addiction's centre.. shelters addicts and allows them to 'fix' themselves from 10.30 a.m. to 10.30 p.m.

fixable ('fɪksəb(ə)l), *a.* Also 5 **fixabull**, **-ibill**, 8–9 **fixible**. [f. FIX *v.* + -ABLE.] Capable of being fixed: in various senses of the vb.

In quot. 1486 = FITCHÉ (*Her.*)

1486 *Bk. St. Albans, Her.* C ij b, Hit is calde a cros patee fixible. **1648** W. MOUNTAGUE *Devout Ess.* I. ix. §2 Since they cannot then stay what is transitory, let them attend to arrest that which is fixable. **1785** *Phil. Trans.* LXXV. 370 The stock K is to slide in a rebated.. groove AD, and be fixable to any part thereof by the screw O. **1796** *Hist.* in *Ann. Reg.* 49 The highest extent.. was fixable by the magistrate. **1817** COLERIDGE *Biog. Lit.* 76 The chemical student is taught not to be startled at disquisitions on.. latent and fixible light. **1837** CARLYLE *Fr. Rev.* (1857) I. I. I. ii. 7 For ours is a most fictile world.. A world not fixable.

b. Capable of being made non-volatile. †*fixable air*: carbonic acid gas.

1766 LEE in *Phil. Trans.* LVI. 100 The quick-lime, attracting fixable air, was reduced. **1794** SULLIVAN *View Nat.* I. 267 The air in animals is mostly inflammable, but that in vegetables fixible. **1887** *Sat. Rev.* 8 Jan. 65 Substances.. which have a.. fixable odour.

†'**fixal**, *a.* (and *sb.*) *Her. Obs.* Also 5 **fixiale**. [f. L. *fix-us* FIX *a.* + -AL¹.] (See quots.)

1486 *Bk. St. Albans, Her.* B j b, Fixall in armys is calde the thirde degre by the right lyne from the right heyre by line male. *Ibid.* B ij, The bastarde of the fixiales. **1586** FERNE *Blaz. Gentrie* I. 255 The fourth coat-armor perfect.. is called Fixall [p. 250 *arma fixa*]. This did alwaies belong to that personne, which was the next of the third degree, to the right heyre male.

fixate ('fɪkseɪt), *v.* [f. L. *fix-us* (see FIX *a.*) + -ATE³.]

1. *trans.* To fix; to render stable.

1885 *Mind* X. 560 The percipient.. often judges on general grounds without laboriously fixating the sensation. **1887** *Science* 16 Dec. 293 To fixate and hold one sensation is an art that must be learned.

2. *intr.* To become fixed.

1888 *Amer. Jrnl. Psychol.* I. 506 Some subjects fixate first and then the eyes close, or are closed by the operator.

3. a. *trans.* To direct the eyes upon, concentrate the gaze directly on.

1889 *Amer. Jrnl. Psychol.* II. 639 Carefully fixate the point marked, keeping the eye entirely from wandering. **1924** R. M. OGDEN tr. *Koffka's Growth of Mind* iii. §5. 71 In fixation, the eye is turned until the fixated object falls upon the place of clearest vision. **1931** *Brit. Jrnl. Psychol.* July 9 Let a subject fixate a point between two discs of different shades of grey. **1951** G. HUMPHREY *Thinking* ix. 268 Instructions were: to fixate no special point, but if fixation is necessary to direct attention towards the middle of the dividing line, [etc.]. **1971** *Sci. Amer.* June 36/3 The subject must move his eyes and look around the picture, fixating each part he wants to see clearly.

b. *Psychol.* Orig., in Freudian theory, to cause (a component of the libido) to be arrested at an immature stage leading a person to abnormal attachments to people or things, etc.; hence, to cause (a person) to react automatically to stimuli in terms which relate to a previous strong

emotional experience; to establish (a response) in this way. Usu. *pass.* or as **fixated** *ppl. a.*, established or responding in this way; also *loosely*, obsessed with. Cf. FIXATION 3 b.

1926 W. McDougall *Outl. Abnormal Psychol.* 133 According to this theory [*sc.* the theory of the Œdipus complex] the *libido*..of every infant normally becomes fixated upon the parent of the opposite sex. **1945** 'G. Orwell' *Crit. Ess.* (1951) 185 It is clear that for many years he remained 'fixated' on his old school. **1951** N. E. Miller in S. S. Stevens *Handbk. Exper. Psychol.* 443 When animals that have learned a specific habit..are given a few electric shocks at the choice point, it 'fixates' their behaviour. **1952** W. J. H. Sprott *Social Psychol.* ix. 180 Furthermore.. frustration may give rise to a response..which gets 'fixated' and is repeated in the frustrating situation over and over again, irrespective of its uselessness. **1955** *Bull. Atomic Sci.* Jan. 14/1 As a nation, we became fixated to the transitory moment of our victory. **1957** C. M. Anderson *Beyond Freud* i. 13 The person who is 'fixated at the anal level' has traits supposedly characteristic of the child from one to three years. **1958** *Times Lit. Suppl.* 21 Mar. 159/3 The build-up is good: a rich, crippled husband, fixated on his only son; a nymphomaniac wife, [etc.]. **1962** C. E. Buxton in Hilgard *Introd. Psychol.* (ed. 3) xvii. 480/1 An individual may in some sense have remained immature by being fixated or caught at one stage of development.

fixation (fɪkˈseɪʃən). Also 5 fixacioun. [ad. med.L. *fixātiōn-em* (used in *Alchemy*), n. of action f. *fixāre* to FIX.]

1. a. The action of fixing, in various senses (see FIX *v.*).

1652–6 Heylin *Cosmogr.* i. (1682) 89 The fixation of the Popes in the Metropolis. **1671** F. Phillips *Reg. Necess.* 67 After the fixation of the Common Pleas or Actions of the people to a certain place in the Kings Palace at Westminster. **1671** *Phil. Trans.* VI. 2132 Some observations, touching Colours, in order to the Increase of Dyes, and the Fixation of Colours. **1776** Adam Smith *W.N.* ii. iv. (1869) I. 360 If this legal rate should be fixed below the lowest market-rate, the effects of this fixation must be [etc.] **1810** Bentham *Packing* (1821) 90 The fixation of the punishment not lying within the province of the jury. **1832** Austin *Jurispr.* (1879) II. lvi. 924 Procure the fixation of the stamp to the evidentiary instrument. **1864** Bowen *Logic* iv. 84 Language ..has an important influence in the regulation and fixation of Thought. **1874** Carpenter *Ment. Phys.* i. i. §20. (1879) 21 The 'training'..mainly consists in the fixation of the Attention on the audible result. **1886** Blackie *What does Hist. Teach?* 24 The fixation of the order of succession to the throne. **1953** *Brit. Commonw. Forest Terminol.* i. 56 *Fixation*, the process of stabilizing soil, particularly shifting sand, against erosion. **1968** *Gloss. Terms Timber Preservation* (*B.S.I.*) 21 *Fixation*, the act or state of fixing a preservative in the timber so that it will not leach. **1971** *Novum Testamentum* Jan. 56 The fixation in writing of a cycle of oral tradition. **1971** *Nature* 2 Apr. 289/1 Species formation through genetic divergence and its fixation by reproductive isolating mechanisms is a slow process.

b. The fact or condition of being fixed.

a **1631** Donne in *Select.* (1840) 219 Three enemies to that fixation and entireness of the heart. **1660** Fuller *Mixt Contempl.* xlix. (1841) 211 Which giveth the fixation to a colour and setteth it in the cloth. **1683** Dr. Fitzwilliam *Let.* in *Lady Russell's Lett.* (1773) 9 When your thoughts have been saddened..by a long fixation on the doleful object. **1831** Carlyle *Misc.* (1857) II. 301 Yet it had attained no fixation or consistency. **1894** *Westm. Gaz.* 17 Jan. 7/2 The first of a course of lectures on locomotion and fixation in plants and animals.

c. A fixed habitation or location (*obs.*); a fixed proportion or standard.

1614 Raleigh *Hist. World* i. 8 For to Light created in the first day, God gave no proper place or fixation. *a* **1661** Fuller *Worthies Suffolk* iii. (1662) 68 He..was buried at York, far..from Ipswich his first fixation. **1774** Franklin *Ess.* Wks. 1840 II. 412 No everlasting, invariable fixation for coining can be made. **1836** *Blackw. Mag.* XXXIX. 63 The Prussian tariff pretends to proceed upon an *ad valorem* fixation.

2. a. *esp.* in scientific uses: The action of depriving of volatility or fluidity: see FIX *v.* 4. †In *Alchemy*: The process of reducing a volatile spirit or essence to a permanent bodily form; the conversion (of mercury) into a solid by amalgamation or combination. In mod. use: The process of rendering solid a liquid or semi-liquid substance; coagulation; also, the process of causing (a gas) to combine with a solid.

1393 Gower *Conf.* II. 86 Do that there be fixation With tempred hetes of the fire. **1477** Norton *Ord. Alch.* in Ashm. (1652) 58 Without him Generation shall be none; Neyther of our Tinctures fixation. **1576** Baker *Jewell of Health* 166 b, This besides serveth to fixation in Alchemye matters. **1594** Plat *Jewell-ho.* iii. 38 For the better fixation of the Mercurie. **1610** B. Jonson *Alch.* ii. i, Two Of our inferior works are at fixation. **1646** Sir T. Browne *Pseud. Ep.* ii. i. 50 The determination of quick-silver is properly fixation. **1665** Glanvill *Scepsis Sci.* vii, Salt dissolved, upon fixation returns to its affected cubes. **1759** B. Martin *Nat. Hist. Eng.* I. *Somerset* 85 A Fixation of cold phlegmatic Humours. **1805** R. Chenevix in *Phil. Trans.* XCV. 104 The fixation of mercury by platina is by many regarded as visionary. **1813** J. Thomson *Lect. Inflam.* 645 The stiffness of a frost-bitten part..may be owing..to the fixation by cold, of the oil contained in the cellular membrane. **1813** Sir H. Davy *Agric. Chem.* ii. (1814) 57 The fixation of oxygene by the combustible body in a solid form. **1872** Oliver *Elem. Bot.* i. ii. 18 This fixation of the carbon and liberation of the oxygen of carbonic acid has been termed vegetable respiration.

†b. The quality or condition of being non-volatile or able to resist the action of fire. *Obs.*

1626 Bacon *Sylva* §328 Gold hath these Natures: Greatnesse of Weight; Closenesse of Parts; Fixation; [etc.]. *a* **1691** Boyle *Wks.* IV. 307 Adding fixation to a body, that was before either volatile, or less fixed. **1721** W. Gibson *Farrier's Dispens.* ii. Introd. 74 Fixation..where the Surfaces of the Particles of Bodies are so small..that they cannot be raised by the Force of Fire.

†c. *concr.* A product of fixation. *Obs.*

1669 W. Simpson *Hydrol. Chym.* 114 *Mercurius Precipitatus Diaphoreticus*, which is a fixation or Precipitate.

d. The process of fixing nitrogen or another substance as part of a biological or industrial process; see FIX *v.* 4 c. Cf. *nitrogen fixation*.

1850 *Jrnl. Hort. Soc. Lond.* V. 57 The suspicion that the water evaporated had a more definite quantitative relationship to the fixation of the *non*-nitrogenous than to that of the nitrogenous constituents of the plants. **1862** *Phil. Trans. R. Soc.* CLI. 468 The question whether or not the assimilation of free Nitrogen by plants may account for all, or a part, of the otherwise unexplained fixation, is seen to be left in a dilemma almost inexplicable. **1888** *Ann. Bot.* I. 351 Experiments to determine the fixation of atmospheric nitrogen by vegetable substances. **1914** J. Knox *Fixation of Atmospheric Nitrogen* ii. 73 A great advantage of the NH_3 synthesis for the fixation of nitrogen is that the amount of energy required for the process is small. **1927** S. A. Waksman *Princ. Soil Microbiol.* xxii. 558 Fixation of nitrogen in the soil is carried on largely by bacteria. **1930** Buchanan & Fulmer *Physiol. & Biochem. Bacteria* III. xvii. 178 In aerobic nitrogen and oxygen fixation there is a competition between nitrogen and oxygen to act as hydrogen acceptors. **1941** *Jrnl. Biol. Chem.* CXXXIX. 375 The fermentation of glucose by propionic acid bacteria was accompanied by fixation of $C^{13}O_2$ in the succinate. **1966** *New Statesman* 2 Dec. 824/3 A celebrated chemical process, on which all food supplies ultimately depend, is the 'fixation' of nitrogen from the air to fertilise the soil or the sea.

e. The process of fixing biological specimens (cf. FIX *v.* 4 d).

1891 *Jrnl. R. Microsc. Soc.* 287 Sublimate fixation produced excellent results. **1929** C. E. McClung *Handbk. Microsc. Technique* i. 8 Living protoplasm is a gelatinous or semi-fluid material, and after fixation it becomes a solid. **1969** Brown & Bertke *Textbk. Cytology* iii. 15/2 The most important single step in the preparation of tissues is fixation.

f. *Immunol.* = *complement-fixation.*

1905 *Centralblatt f. Bakteriol.* (*Originale*) XXXIX. 603 (*heading*) The fixation of alexines by specific serum precipitates. **1970** Passmore & Robson *Compan. Med. Studies* II. xxii. 12 The activation or fixation of complement ..depends upon changes in configuration of immuno-globulin molecules when they are brought into close apposition during reaction with antigen.

3. a. The concentration of the gaze upon some object for a given time with the intention of holding the retinal image upon the area of direct vision. Cf. FIXATE *v.* 3.

1889 H. H. Ellis tr. *Moll's Hypnotism* (1890) i. 2 Indian yogis and fakirs..throw themselves into the hypnotic state by means of fixation of the gaze. **1896** G. F. Stout *Anal. Psychol.* I. 214 For the most part, however, the fixation of images is not accompanied by overt movement or by any very appreciable muscular strain. **1924** [see FIXATE *v.* 3]. **1941** *Nature* 13 Sept. 321/1 Reading ordinary type an average adult reader traverses a line of print 3½ in. long in about six stages or fixations. **1951** [see FIXATE *v.* 3]. **1971** *Sci. Amer.* June 35/1 During normal viewing of stationary objects the eyes alternate between fixations, when they are aimed at a fixed point in the visual field, and rapid movements.

b. *Psychol.* In Freudian theory, the arresting of the development of a libidinal component at a pregenital stage, so that psychosexual emotions are 'fixed' at that point. Also *loosely*, an obsession, an *idée fixe*. Cf. FIXATE *v.* 3 b.

1910 A. A. Brill tr. *Freud's Three Contribs. to Sexual Theory* i. 11 A phase of very intense but short-lived fixation on the woman (usually on the mother). *Ibid.* 27 We find feelings of inversion in the unconscious psychic life, fixation of libido on persons of the same sex. **1925** A. & J. Strachey tr. *Freud's Coll. Papers* III. iv. 447 In my *Drei Abhandlungen zur Sexualtheorie* I have expressed the opinion that each stage in the development of psycho-sexuality affords a possibility for the occurrence of a 'fixation' and thus for the laying down of a disposition to illness in later life. *Ibid.* 453 Fixation can be described in this way. One instinct or instinctual component fails to accompany the rest along the anticipated normal path of development. **1946** O. Fenichel *Psychoanal. Theory of Neurosis* i. v. 65 They represent, rather, pathological cases with special oral-sadistic fixations. **1947** A. Huxley *Let.* 9 Mar. (1969) 567 Marlow is one of those classical cases, so dear to psychoanalysts, with a fixation on his mother, about which he feels subconsciously guilty, so that he can't associate sex with respectability. **1957** F. Alexander *Psychoanal. & Psychotherapy* v. 103 According to this view there is a reciprocal relationship between fixation and regression. **1963** *Daily Tel.* 15 May 25/8 A young man with a fixation about boats. **1970** *Ibid.* 21 Feb. 8/3 Victorian taste had a fixation with the Gothic.

c. *Med.* The immobilization and holding in place of a limb or joint or the parts of a fractured bone; the holding in place of a displaced or floating organ by means of sutures.

1897 W. J. Walsham *Surg.* (ed. 6) 829/1 (Index), Fixation of kidney. **1906** Walsham & Spencer *Surg.* (ed. 9) iii. 254 Fixation of a fracture by open operation. **1908** Rose & Carless *Man. Surg.* (ed. 7) xix. 476 The fixation of the fracture in a good position is provided for by the application of suitable splints. **1926** *Jrnl. Bone & Joint Surg.* VIII. 496 (*caption*) Vanadium (author's design) steel plate with transfixion of bone, giving maximum fixation and security. **1948** F. W. Holdsworth in *Brit. Surg. Pract.* IV. 192 Internal fixation is, therefore, advisable by plating the fracture of the radius with a 4-screwed vitallium plate. **1951** Dorland *Med. Dict.* (ed. 22) 566 *Internal fixation*, the fastening together and fixation of the ends of a fractured bone by means of wires, plates, screws or nails applied directly to the fractured bone. **1957** R. Nissen in Mulholland *Current Surg. Managem.* 57 (*title*) Repair of esophageal hiatal hernia by fixation to the abdominal wall. **1966** J. S. Batchelor in R. Furlong *Fractures & Dislocations* 215, 85 fractures treated by early fixation within six days of injury gave a non-union of 23 per cent. **1968** S. Taylor et al. *Short Textbk. Surg.* (ed. 2) xxv. 379 In the past, fixation of the kidney (nephropexy) was performed for such symptoms as aching in the loins. *Ibid.* xxx. 449 Pathological Fracture... Treatment includes immobilization by internal fixation of the fracture if that is feasible.

4. *attrib.* and *Comb.* **fixation-point**, the point at which an eye is directed, so that its image falls on the most sensitive part of the retina; also, the most sensitive part of the retina.

1890 Billings *Med. Dict.*, *Fixation-point*.., the point of sight—*i.e.* the point of which the retinal image is on the centre of clearest vision; the crossing-point in outer space of the lines of regard. **1909** E. B. Titchener *Text-bk. Psychol.* i. 81 The object first becomes visible as a patch of black;.. finally, as it approaches the fixation-point, it appears in its true colour. **1932** W. S. Duke-Elder *Text-bk. Ophthalmol.* I. xiii. 580 A position in which the eyes are both directed upon the same fixation point situated straight ahead and infinitely far away. **1950** *Sci. News* XV. 24 Seven different fixation points were discovered, for the following spectral regions. **1971** *Nature* 11 June 395/1 The subject fixated a central point in the pre-exposure field and after a 'ready' signal the stimulus was presented briefly to the left or right of the fixation point.

fixative (ˈfɪksətɪv), *a.* and *sb.* [f. FIX *v.* + -ATIVE. Cf. Fr. *fixatif*.]

A. *adj.* Tending to fix.

1644 Nye *Gunnery* ii. (1647) 29 Opium is of a congealing and fixative nature. *a* **1832** Bentham *Wks.* (1843) VIII. 30 But for these fixed and fixative signs, nothing that ever bore the name of art or science could ever have come into existence. **1870** *Eng. Mech.* 25 Feb. 576/1 One of the..uses of this fixative process is supposed to be the preserving of the ..colour of..drawings from decay.

B. *sb.* **1.** That which serves to set or fix; *spec.* a preparation used to fix colours, or charcoal or crayon drawings.

1870 *Eng. Mech.* 11 Mar. 638/3 There are some papers which absorb the fixative with difficulty. **1930** R. Campbell *Adamastor* 64 Speed, motion, flight!.. Fixative of blurred effects. **1959** *Times* 3 Aug. 9/6 Moustache fixatives.

2. Any substance or preparation used to fix biological specimens. Cf. FIX *v.* 4 d.

1891 *Jrnl. R. Microsc. Soc.* 287 As a fixative, the author has the highest opinion of the value of osmic acid. **1929** C. E. McClung *Handbk. Microsc. Technique* i. 8 Some fixatives preserve nuclear conditions especially well, others those of the cytoplasm. **1969** Brown & Bertke *Textbk. Cytol.* iii. 16/1 Acetic acid is a rapid penetrant but a poor fixative.

3. A liquid that serves to reduce the rate of evaporation of more volatile components in a mixture of odoriferous liquids, esp. a perfume.

1923 E. J. Parry tr. *Durvelle's Prep. Perfumes & Cosmetics* iv. 123 Fixatives..are bodies which serve to render more permanent odours of a fugitive nature, such as those of most flowers... Amongst the classic fixatives are ambergris, civet and musk. **1949** R. W. Moncrieff *Chem. Perfumery Materials* xiii. 203 The fixative need not itself be strongly odorous, for benzyl benzoate is an excellent fixative and yet has only a faint scent. **1971** *Nature* 16 Apr. 433/2 Deer musk is a direct preputial gland secretion and a fixative for secondary odours.

fixator (fɪkˈseɪtə(r)). [agent-n. f. FIX *v.* after Latin analogies. Cf. Fr. *fixateur*.] That which fixes; a fastener, fixer.

1874 Roosa *Dis. Ear* 217 Rüdinger considers this thin muscle to be a fixator of the medium cartilaginous plate. **1884** in *Syd. Soc. Lex.*

†fixatory, *a. Obs.* In 7 fixatorie. [f. FIX *v.* after Lat. analogies: see -ORY.] Serving to fix; having the property of fixing.

1605 Timme *Quersit.* ii. iii. 112 Salt peter..being now put into a fixatorie fire, you shal see that it conteineth within it all maner of colours.

fixature (ˈfɪksətjə(r)). [f. as prec. after the analogy of CURVATURE, etc.] A gummy preparation for fixing the hair.

1860 Thackeray *Lovel the Widower* ii, A barber, with his tongs and stick of fixature for the mustachios. **1883** E. Lynn Linton *Ione* I. xi. 263 No brushing could make it smooth; no fixature keep it straight.

fixed (fɪkst), *ppl. a.* [f. FIX *v.* + -ED[1].]

1. a. Placed or attached firmly; fastened securely; made firm or stable in position.

1577 B. Googe *Heresbach's Husb.* iv. (1586) 179 b, The fixed or standing Hives, bee discommodious. **1593** Shaks. *2 Hen. VI*, iii. ii. 313 Bitter searching termes..Deliuer'd strongly through my fixed teeth. **1647** Cowley *Mistress, Inconstancy*, The most fixt Being still does move and fly. **1694** *Acc. Sev. Late Voy.* ii. (1711) 51 Where the firm or fixed Ice lies. **1805** T. Lindley *Voy. Brasil* (1808) 273 By means of two fixed pieces of wood. *c* **1850** *Rudim. Navig.* (Weale) 118 *Fixed blocks*, those blocks that come through the sides and are bolted, as the sheet, tack, and brace blocks. **1882** Minchin *Unipl. Kinemat.* 71 When a body, *M*, rolls on a fixed surface, *AB*.

b. *Her.* Of a cross: Having its limbs attached to the edges of the escutcheon: = FIRME.

1688 R. Holme *Acad. Armory* i. v. §31 A Cross Patee Entyre (or Fixed or Firme)..This term (Fixed, or Entyre) must be added, to shew that..they are joyned to the sides of the Escochion. **1828–40** Berry *Encycl. Her.* I s.v., Crosses which are usually borne in the centre of the escocheon without extending to the sides, when attached thereto are termed fixed, as a cross pattée fixed.

2. In immaterial sense: Firmly attached or implanted; securely established; secured against alteration or dislodgement. In early use often (now rarely) of persons: Firmly resolved; constant, steadfast; bent, set, or intent upon anything. ***fixed idea***: an idea firmly rooted in the brain, with a tendency to become unduly dominant [F. *idée fixe*]. ***fixed fact***: a well-established fact (*U.S.*).

1580 BARET *Alv.* F 632 Mindes certeinly fixed, to trie the matter by dint of sword. **1625-8** tr. *Camden's Hist. Eliz.* III. (1688) 385 A Lady fixed and constant in her Religion. **1627-77** FELTHAM *Resolves* I. xlv. 71 How fixt he was to Jonathan! **1655** SIR E. NICHOLAS in *N. Papers* (Camden) II. 348 This man is.. a fast fixt Catholike. **1706** HEARNE *Collect.* 7 Mar., A Man of no fixt Resolution. **1712-4** POPE *Rape Lock* v. 5 Not half so fix'd the Trojan could remain, While Anna begg'd. **1821** SHELLEY *Prometh. Unb.* I. 262, I defy thee with a calm fixed mind. **1829** H. C. ROBINSON *Diary* 13 Aug. (1967) 102 [Goethe] repeated.. one of his fixed ideas that it is by the most laborious collection of facts that even a poetical view of nature is to be corrected. **1831** CARLYLE *Sart. Res.* III iv. (1858) 139 A deadly fear of Population possesses the Hofrath; something like a fixed-idea. **1847** *Boston Post* June (Bartlett), That he did dispose of a large quantity of oil, and afterwards desert from the vessel are fixed facts. **1849** MACAULAY *Hist. Eng.* II. 165 For all persecution he felt a fixed aversion. **1860** MOTLEY *Netherl.* (1868) I. i. 4 Philip.. seemed to become.. more fixed in his determination. **1868** FREEMAN *Norm. Conq.* (1876) II. vii. 153 The fixed purpose of raising forces. **1875** JOWETT *Plato* (ed. 2) V. 28 The lawgiver.. was a fixed idea in the mind of the Greek.

3. a. Of a person's eyes, thoughts, etc.: Steadily or intently directed towards or 'fastened' upon an object.

1552 HULOET, Fixed, *intentus*. **1616** CHAPMAN *Musæus* 358 A tower so high, As soon would lose on it the fixedst eye. **1643** DENHAM *Cooper's H.* 112 But my fixt thoughts my wandring eye betrays. **1725** POPE *Odyss.* XIII. 35 All, but Ulysses, heard with fix'd delight. **1791** MRS. RADCLIFFE *Rom. Forest* viii, He regarded her with a fixed attention. **1850** HARE *Mission Comf.* 124 Disease and death are glaring with fixt eyes upon them.

quasi-*adv.* **1649** G. DANIEL *Trinarch., Rich. II*, clxviii, Kites.. cannot looke the Sun fixt in the face.

b. Of a person, his countenance, etc.: Made rigid or immobile (as by strong emotion or resolution, or in death).

1608 D. T[WIL] *Ess. Pol. & Mor.* 67 That Vertue is but weake.. that cannot with a fixed countenance out-stare the threatening eye of Danger. **1801** SOUTHEY *Thalaba* I. iv, Looking up to her fix'd countenance. **1824** LAMB *Elia* Ser. II, *Blakesmoor in H—shire*, As fixed and motionless as the marble effigies that kneel.. around thee. **1833** HT. MARTINEAU *Manch. Strike* x. 109 The papers in his hand shook; but his countenance was fixed and his attitude firm. **1888** W. BLACK *Lochaber* III. viii, Her eyes.. were fixed and staring.

4. a. Deprived of volatility. †***fixed air***: a name given by Black in 1754 to *carbonic dioxide* (*carbonic acid*); see AIR *sb.* 2.

1766 CAVENDISH in *Phil. Trans.* LVI. 141 By fixed air, I mean that particular species of factitious air, which is separated from alkaline substances by solution in acids or by calcination. **1807** T. THOMSON *Chem.* (ed. 3) II. 187 To this species of air he gave the name of fixed air, because it existed in these bodies in a fixed state.

b. Not easily volatilized; not losing weight under the influence of fire. ***fixed alkali***: see ALKALI 3, 6. †***fixed nitre*** = *potassium carbonate*.

1641 FRENCH *Distill.* v. (1651) 171 Little fixed salt can be extracted from them, onely volatile. **1669** BOYLE *Contn. New Exp.* II. (1682) 135, I put *Aqua Fortis* with fixed Nitre into a Receiver. **1685** —— *Salubr. Air* 111 The fixedest of Metals, Gold itself. **1688** J. CLAYTON in *Phil. Trans.* XVII. 944 The fixeder Saline Particles of the Marine Salt. **1727-51** CHAMBERS *Cycl.* s.v., Of all metals, gold and silver alone are fixed; i.e. on remaining a long time exposed to the most intense flame, they alone lose nothing of their weight. **1744** BERKELEY *Siris* §8 Fixed salts are much the same in all bodies. **1757** A. COOPER *Distiller* I. i. (1760) 6 Only a fixed husky matter remains. **1830** FARADAY *Exp. Res.* xxxiv. 207 Mercury is volatile at temperatures above 30° but fixed at temperatures below 20°.

c. Of acids and oils: That cannot be distilled or evaporated without decomposition.

1800 tr. *Lagrange's Chem.* II. xlix. 215 Fixed oils. **1805** W. SAUNDERS *Min. Waters* 324 The iron is held in union with a fixed acid. **1812** J. SMYTH *Pract. of Customs* (1821) 160 Oils.. are divided by Chemists into two kinds; fixed or fat oils, and volatile or essential oils. **1859** GULLICK & TIMBS *Paint.* 206 The Fixed Oils.. are so called because they do not almost entirely evaporate in drying.

5. Of a colour, photographic image, etc.: Fast, lasting, permanent. Said also of the photographic plate.

1791 HAMILTON *Berthollet's Dyeing* I. Introd. 10 Mordants [serve] to render the colour more fixed. **1875** JOWETT *Plato* (ed. 2) III. 51 Colours which are dyed in this way become fixed. **1888** ABNEY *Instr. Photog.* xxii. 190 The plate is known to be fixed by looking at the back of it, which should appear black. *Ibid.* xxxv. 278 When the prints are fixed they will appear colourless in the whites.

6. a. Definitely and permanently placed; stationary or unchanging in relative position. ***fixed point***: (*a*) a place where a policeman is permanently stationed; freq. *attrib.*; cf. *point-constable, -policeman* (POINT *sb.*[1] D. 14) and POINT-DUTY; (*b*) *Physics*, a temperature of some well-defined and reproducible physical process, such as a change of phase of a pure substance, used in defining a scale of temperature; (*c*) *Math.*, a point that is unchanged by a given transformation or by each of a given set of transformations; (*d*) *Broadcasting* (see quot. 1941); (*e*) *Computers*, designating a method of representing numbers by a single sequence of digits with a fixed or constant position for the radix point; usu. *attrib.*

1559 W. CUNNINGHAM *Cosmogr. Glasse* 19 And is this Horizont a fixed Circle or not? It is fixed, and without motion. **1665** SIR T. HERBERT *Trav.* (1677) 221 Houses and fixed Inhabitants. **1667** MILTON *P.L.* III. 669 In which of all these Orbes hath Man His fixed seat, or fixed seat hath none. **1704** J. HARRIS *Lex. Techn., Fixed Line of Defence*, in Fortification is drawn along the Face of the Bastion, and terminates in the Courtine. **1848** J. CURWEN *Gram. Vocal Music* (1866) p. xxiv, Unlike the 'fixed Do' of the old notation, the 'movable Do'.. is no difficulty whatever. **1858** *Merc. Marine Mag.* V. 30 A Fixed Red Light will be shown at the head of the.. Breakwater.

1896 *Daily News* 15 Feb. 3/1 'Fixed point' constables. **1900** *Daily Chron.* 15 Aug. 5/1 City Police on fixed-point duty. **1904** *Ibid.* 16 Sept. 4/5 Fixed-point constables, whose imperious arms will later indicate the right of way.

1778 *Phil. Trans. R. Soc.* LXVII. 844 In the following pages we have thrown together the practical rules, which we would recommend to be observed in adjusting the fixed points of thermometers. **1849** R. V. DIXON *Treat. Heat* I. 10 Sir Isaac Newton first pointed out the advantage to be obtained by this method of graduating temperature scales, and at the same time proposed as the fixed points in the graduation the temperatures of melting ice and boiling water. **1966** *Units & Standards of Measurement: Temperature* (H.M.S.O.) (ed. 2) 3 The International Practical Scale of Temperature is based on six reproducible temperatures (defining fixed points) to which numerical values are assigned and on formulae establishing the relation between the temperature and the indications of instruments calibrated by means of the values assigned to the six defining fixed points.

1893 A. R. FORSYTH *Theory Functions Complex Variable* xix. 514 If we assume that w and z are two points in the same plane, then there will in general be two different points which are unaltered by the transformation; they are called the *fixed* (or *double*) points of the transformation. **1963** G. F. SIMMONS *Introd. Topol.* 337 A topological space X is called a fixed point space if every continuous mapping f of X into itself has a fixed point. **1968** E. T. COPSON *Metric Spaces* viii. 111 The problem of solving an algebraic equation $f(z) = 0$ can be expressed as a fixed point problem. The relation $w = z + f(z)$ maps the complex plane into itself; and the fixed points are the zeros of $f(z)$.

1941 *B.B.C. Gloss. Broadc. Terms* 13 *Fixed point*, time set apart over a continuous period for the broad-cast, at regular intervals, of programmes of a similar type over a particular network, or for successive contributions to a regular series. **1969** *Radio Times* 18/25 Dec. 94/2 There are not many fixed-points in transmission times, but obviously they have to be strictly adhered to.

1948 *Math. Tables & Other Aids to Computation* III. 318 The position of the radix point in the fixed-point representation is a matter of some importance since it determines what combinations of operand values are permissible for multiplication and division. **1955** *Jrnl. Assoc. Comput. Mach.* Jan. 57 Both floating binary point and fixed point operation are included. **1964** F. L. WESTWATER *Electronic Computers* ix. 143 Soon, 'libraries' of standard subroutines were available for each particular computer and ..sets of subroutines to be performed in 'floating-point' rather than the fixed-point mode arithmetic. **1970** *Math. Rev.* XXXIX. 215/1 This paper examines the distribution of the binary digits of a number representation that is supplied to a conversion routine in decimal form (all in fixed point).

b. ***fixed star***: a star which appears always to occupy the same position in the heavens (and so distinguished from a *planet*).

Cf. FIX *a.*, earlier used in the same sense.

.. *Almanack for Year* 1386 (1812) 8 Al planetys and sternes fyxt. *c* **1430** LYDG. *Min. Poems* 153 *Stelle eratice*, nat fixed. **1561** EDEN *Arte Nauig.* Pref., The Sunne & Moone & the other Planetes & fixte Starres. **1697** DRYDEN *Virg. Georg.* I. 209 Sailers.. found a Name For ev'ry fix'd and ev'ry wandring Star. **1812** WOODHOUSE *Astron.* viii. 51 The transits of fixed stars are used for regulating clocks.

absol. **1667** MILTON *P.L.* III. 481 They pass the Planets seven, and pass the fixt.

c. ***fixed capital***: see CAPITAL *sb.* 3 c; ***fixed property***: that which consists in immovables, as land and houses; ***fixed asset***: an asset which cannot be promptly converted into cash (cf. LIQUID *a.* 6); freq. *pl.*; ***fixed odds***: used *attrib.* of a bet on association football results that is paid off at predetermined odds, as opp. to a bet on a football pool; ***fixed trust***, an investment trust or unit trust in which the investment of funds is restricted to a fixed list of securities.

1845 MᶜCULLOCH *Taxation* I. ii. (1852) 74 Land and other fixed property. **1848** MILL *Pol. Econ.* I. vi. §1 Capital which exists in any of these durable shapes.. is called Fixed Capital. **1863** FAWCETT *Pol. Econ.* I. iv. (1876) 41 Fixed capital may continuously repeat the assistance which it lends to industry. **1898** L. R. DICKSEE *Auditing* (ed. 3) vii. 275 (*heading*) Fixed assets. *Ibid.* 276 It would have seemed more natural to have placed Plant before Stock-in-trade, as being, properly speaking, a 'fixed asset'. **1907** *Act 7 Edw. VII* c. 50 §21 Every company.. shall include.. a summary of.. its assets, giving such particulars as will disclose.. how the values of the fixed assets have been arrived at. **1930** *Economist* 8 Nov. 865/1 The 'fixed trust'.. holds a fixed number of common stocks and participation in the trust takes the form of certificates authenticated by a trust company and specifying a fractional interest in a block or unit of the fixed common stocks held by the trust company. These fixed investment trusts first came into public notice about 1924. **1935** *Ibid.* 6 Apr. 795/2 The stream of new investment which has come under fixed trust control has been directed predominantly into the shares of well-established.. companies. **1950** *Sporting Investor* Feb. 20 (Advt.), The superb methods for the smaller pools and fixed-odds coupons provide the steady solid income for the small or large investor. **1951** R. W. JONES *Thomson's Dict. Banking* (ed. 10) 280/2 *Fixed assets*, assets (such as land, buildings, plant, machinery), which are not turned into cash, but are used indirectly for the purpose of providing the income of a business. **1959** *Times* 14 Jan. 13/6 Early Unit Trusts had a fixed unit of investment, as their name, Fixed Trusts, implied. It was of the essence of those trusts that unit certificates were issued only against successive deposits of a fixed portfolio of securities, the unit of investment. **1964** *Daily Tel.* 15 Apr. 1/6 (*heading*) Fixed odds tax shocks book-makers. *Ibid.*, The turn-over on fixed odds football betting was well over £60 million last year.

d. ***fixed-head***: (*a*) of a car body, having a fixed roof (opp. *drop-head* (b)); (*b*) of a car engine, having a fixed cylinder-head; ***fixed light*** (*Naut.* and *Aeronaut.*): see quot. 1960.

1889 L. DELBOS *Naut. Terms* 31 Fixed light. **1948** R. DE KERCHOVE *Int. Maritime Dict.* (1958) 264 *Fixed light*, a coastal light in which the illuminating apparatus gives a continuous light of uniform intensity. **1960** *Guide Civil Land Aerodrome Lighting* (*B.S.I.*) 9 *Fixed light*, a light having constant luminous intensity when observed from a fixed direction. **1962** *Times* 14 Mar. 15/4 A full width rear bench seat in the fixed-head coupé. **1963** BIRD & HUTTON-STOTT *Veteran Motor Car* 96 Delahaye.. never made fixed-head engines and never, apparently, had trouble with their detachable heads. **1971** *Daily Tel.* 20 Oct. 6 The new 350 SLC fixed head coupé—a stretched version of the sports car with.. room for five.

7. Definitely appointed or assigned; not fluctuating or varying; definite, permanent.

a **1698** SIR W. TEMPLE *Misc.* III. i, One loves fixed Laws, and the other arbitrary Power. **1741** MIDDLETON *Cicero* (1742) II. VII. 201 He [Cicero] laid it down as the fixt rule of his administration. **1838** THIRLWALL *Greece* III. 191 A fixt and uniform rent. **1861** M. PATTISON *Ess.* (1889) I. 47 Every Hanse town was in its turn represented, according to a fixed cycle. **1882** R. BITHELL *Counting-House Dict.* s.v. *Trust* 309 It is recommended that one half-yearly coupon should be *fixed* [bearing a fixed rate of interest] and the second variable. **1884** tr. *Lotze's Logic* 434 The conceptions of good and bad, just and unjust, are fixed and unchanging. **1935** *Planning* III. LII. 7 The Board is financed by the issue of fixed-interest stock which carries no voting rights. **1971** *Daily Tel.* 19 Oct. 19 The demand for fixed interest stocks is still running strongly.

8. Prepared, put in order. †Of a shell: Fitted with a fuse. '***fixed ammunition***: a charge of powder and shot inclosed together in a wrapper or case ready for loading' (Knight).

1638 *Penit. Conf.* vii. (1657) 145 The Trent Fathers.. plant their fixt Canon, to discharge Anathema's. **1769** FALCONER *Dict. Marine* (1789) Cc iv b, The fixed shell is placed upon the wad.

9. Corrupted, bribed, 'squared'; tampered with; of a sporting contest, having the result dishonestly prearranged. (Cf. FIX *v.* 14 d.) *slang* (orig. *U.S.*).

a **1889** *San Francisco News Letter* (Farmer), His friends on the grand jury.. acted precisely as fixed jurors had been known to act. **1901** *Denver Republican* 26 Aug. 3/4 'Fixed' roulette wheels, 'squeeze' faro boxes, loaded dice and marked cards. **1931** L. STEFFENS *Autobiogr.* I. v. 37 Being in with the stables, I soon began to hear about 'fixed races'. **1960** *Guardian* 18 Oct. 8/2 (*heading*) 'Fixed' football.

10. In predicative use: situated materially or financially. *colloq.* (orig. *U.S.*).

1844 [see FIX *v.* 8 c]. **1873** J. H. BEADLE *Undevel. West* 791 From these figures I think they should be better fixed than they are. **1875** *Chicago Tribune* 25 Aug. 8/1 He was very well 'fixed' both in money and in whisky. **1904** H. R. MARTIN *Tillie* 47 I'm well fixed. I got money plenty. **1906** *Springfield* (Mass.) *Weekly Republ.* 25 Jan. 1 The new Connecticut senators are much better fixed financially than their predecessors. **1963** M. LAURENCE in R. Weaver *Canad. Short Stories* 2nd Ser. (1968) 134 Sabina had once had a wealthy lover—well, not wealthy, perhaps, but certainly nicely fixed. **1970** *Guardian* 31 Dec. 11/4 Ali will come out of this fight very well fixed.

11. Special comb.: **fixed bayonet**, a bayonet fixed to the mouth of a musket or rifle; also *attrib.*; **fixed focus** *Photogr.*, a focus on a camera that is fixed by the design and cannot be adjusted by the user; also *attrib.*; **fixed income**, an unvarying income derived from fixed-interest investments, a pension, etc., as distinct from a salary or wage; **fixed link**, a (projected) permanent means of transit between Great Britain and France, esp. by road or rail; a bridge, tunnel, etc., built to accommodate this; cf. CHUNNEL; **fixed-pitch airscrew, propeller** *Aeronaut.*, a propeller with blades whose pitch cannot be varied; **fixed price**, (*a*) the price charged for a set meal at a restaurant (cf. Fr. *prix fixe*); also *attrib.*; (*b*) used *attrib.* of a 'bazaar' type shop at which all articles are sold at or below a stated price; (*c*) a net price not subject to discount; **fixed seat**, a rowing-seat without a slide; **fixed-wing aircraft, plane**, an aeroplane of the conventional type as opposed to a rotating-wing aircraft such as a helicopter.

1802 C. JAMES *Mil. Dict.* s.v. Manual §vi, The first motion of the charge is the position which the soldier will.. take, in order to advance on an enemy, whom it is intended to attack with *fixed bayonets. **1815** J. SIMPSON *Visit Flanders* 173 Eight battalions of the guard debouched with fixed

bayonets. **1858** *Leisure Hour* 660/1 We essay to enter the waiting-room but are stopped by a..soldier, armed with musket and fixed bayonet. **1908** *Daily Chron.* 3 Oct. 4/6 The Royal Marines..enjoy the same fixed bayonet rights in the City. **1909** *Ibid.* 1 Oct. 4/6 Other fixed-bayonet corps in the City are the Honourable Artillery Company,..the 'Buffs', or East Kent Regiment, and the 'Royal Fusiliers' (City of London Regiment). **1892** *Photogr. Ann.* II. 320 Those who object to *fixed focus cameras. **1904** *Westm. Gaz.* 27 Aug. 14/2 It will be found that with the majority of lenses the best fixed focus is at about a distance of 20 ft. **1951** G. H. SEWELL *Amateur Film-Making* (ed. 2) iii. 27 The simplest and most inexpensive cameras are equipped with what is known as 'fixed-focus' lenses. **1970** *Which?* July 217/2 Most of the lenses were fixed focus, that is to say you could not vary the distance setting. **1858** TROLLOPE *Three Clerks* III. xii. 213 You will not object to state whether or no you possess any *fixed income? **1929** A. HUXLEY *Do what you Will* 110 So much middle-class pride on such small fixed incomes. **1933** B. ELLINGER *This Money Business* xi. 107 All people who are in receipt of fixed incomes (whether it be from investments in Government securities or in debentures, or landlords in receipt of long-term fixed rents, or old age pensioners) benefit from the fall in prices. **1967** *Listener* 16 Mar. 359/2, I am a fixed income pensioner. **1974** *Economist* 30 Nov. 90/2 As so much of the traffic will be road vehicles and their passengers, it is worth asking whether a rail tunnel is the best form of a *fixed link with France, rather than a road bridge or bridge/tunnel. **1985** *Financial Times Survey* 16 Dec. p. ii./7 The debate was dominated by the doubts of the Kent MPs about the impact of any Channel fixed link on the economies of the coastal towns, especially the ferry ports, as well as environmental considerations. **1931** *R.A.F. Quart.* July 397 Various types of *fixed pitch airscrew were tried. **1934** *Flight* 8 Feb. 124/2 As a fixed-pitch airscrew does not possess satisfactory characteristics for both take off and speed in high-speed aircraft, a variable-pitch airscrew is usually fitted to the latest Northrop models. **1968** MILLER & SAWERS *Techn. Devel. Mod. Aviation* iii. 68 The performance suffered from the use of fixed-pitch propellers, so the Hamilton-Standard variable pitch propeller..was quickly adopted. **1907** *Baedeker's Paris & Environs* (ed. 16) 17 Among the *Brasseries* and *Tavernes*..some are elegant establishments à la carte, while others (charges indicated) have *fixed prices. **1909** *Bradshaw's Railway Guide* Apr. 1097 All 'fixed price' meals served in Restaurant. **1933** D. C. E. PEEL *Life's Enchanted Cup* xvi. 211 A special dining-room for those who wished for lunch at a fixed price of 3.50 francs. **1935** *Economist* 6 Apr. 798/2 Though the principle of the 'chain chemists' has allowed Boots to build up an excellent business..it does not seem to offer the opportunity for rapidly expanding profits which, say, Woolworth and Marks and Spencer have discovered in the fixed-price store. **1960** *Farmer & Stockbreeder* 22 Mar. 104 With the lowest price in its class, low running costs, and low fixed-price maintenance and parts costs the Fordson Dexta is a great cost saver. **1965** J. L. HANSON *Dict. Econ.* 180/1 For most consumers' goods the custom of the fixed or specified price has replaced the older custom of haggling over price. **1970** N. FREELING *Kitchen Bk.* iii. 27 There was nothing so vulgar as a fixed-price menu in this hotel. Everything was à la carte. **1889** W. B. WOODGATE *Rowing* 103 The mechanical power gained by a sliding seat is so great that even if he who uses it sets at defiance all recognised principles of *fixed-seat rowing, he can still command more pace than if he adhered to fixed-seat work. *Ibid.*, Oarsmen of the fixed-seat school. **1907** *Daily Chron.* 27 July 9/3 It would be a good thing if all junior races could be rowed on fixed seats. Many novices who promised well have lost all style and cultivated wrong methods by having rowed races on sliding seats before knowing how to work on a fixed seat. **1950** *Chambers's Encycl.* XII. 15/2 The boats first used were in-rigged with fixed seats and clinker-built. **1949** *Aero Digest* Sept. 120 Picking up fuel supplies dropped by parachutes from *fixed-wing aircraft. **1955** *Oxf. Jun. Encycl.* VIII. 4/1 For fixed-wing aircraft..the varying requirements of speed, altitude, and range affect the choice of engine. **1958** *Times* 1 Mar. 7/3 It [*sc.* a helicopter] may be slower than the fixed wing aircraft. **1966** *Times* 19 July 11/1 So far..B.E.A. has bought fixed-wing types [of American aircraft].

fixedly ('fɪksɪdlɪ), *adv.* [f. prec. + -LY².] In a fixed manner; firmly, securely, steadfastly; attentively, earnestly; intently, steadily.

1598 SYLVESTER *Du Bartas* II. i. IV. *Handy-crafts* 643 On Gods face his eyes he fixtly bears. **1654** EARL ORRERY *Parthen.* (1676) 217 He..would only look fix'dly upon her. **1661** MARVELL *Corr.* xxix. Wks. 1872–5 II. 72 His Majesty is most fixedly honorable. **1690** LOCKE *Hum. Und.* III. vi. §22 If we pretend that the distinction of Species..is fixedly establish'd. **1702** C. MATHER *Magn. Chr.* (1853) II. 167 It was his manner..to meditate..fixedly upon some truth. **1849** MACAULAY *Hist. Eng.* II. 230 The old man looked fixedly at the King. **1865** TROLLOPE *Belton Est.* xxviii. 335 It was almost impossible for him to make up his mind fixedly to any purpose.

fixedness ('fɪksɪdnɪs). [f. as prec. + -NESS.]

1. The quality or condition of being fixed in various senses. **a.** Of material things: Immobility, steadiness of position, stillness, permanence.

1641 BP. HALL *Serm.* in *Rem. Wks.* (1660) 66 The Earth was made for fixednesse and stability. **1647** H. MORE *Song of Soul* III. I. xxxiii, What eye could bear in contemplation So long a fix'dnesse? *a* **1711** KEN *Hymnotheo* Poet. Wks. 1721 III. 170 The..Fix'dness of a Star. **1812–16** J. SMITH *Panorama Sc. & Art* II. 448 The beauty and fixedness of the colours. **1845** MAURICE *Mor. Phil.* in *Encycl. Metrop.* 590/1 The Eleatic 'fixedness', which was the formal opposite of the Heracleitan 'flux'. **1859** O. W. HOLMES *Prof. Breakf.-t.* xii. 274 The fixedness of the smileless mouth.

b. Of immaterial things: Definiteness, invariability. Of persons and their attributes: Firmness, resoluteness, steadfastness (*in*); steadfast adherence *to* (a cause); intentness, attentiveness.

1612–15 BP. HALL *Contempl. O.T.* XX. x, The fixednesse of his terme, is no lesse mercie than the protraction. **1680** R. MANSEL *Narr. Popish Plot* 12 A person whose fixedness to the true Interest of his Majesty..they well knew. **1784** J. BROWN *Hist. Brit. Churches* I. 110 That notwithstanding her fixedness in her own religion, she would compel none to it. **1823** *Examiner* 709/2 The fixedness of her despair. **1837** CARLYLE *Fr. Rev.* I. VII. v, All hearts set, with a moody fixedness, on one object. **1863** G. ELIOT *Romola* I. xv, He was looking at her with mild fixedness while he spoke. **1875** JOWETT *Plato* (ed. 2) V. 122 The great defect of both his [Plato's] constitutions is the fixedness which he seeks to impress upon them.

†**2.** The quality of resisting the action of heat, or of being non-volatile. *Obs.*

1665 HOOKE *Microgr.* 28 The Proprieties of Gold (such as are the Malleableness..Fixtness in the fire). **1764** HEBERDEN in *Phil. Trans.* LV. 58 The natron..resembles the vegetable alkali in taste and fixedness. **1812–16** J. SMITH *Panorama Sc. & Art* II. 365 The fixedness of platina admirably fits it for crucibles.

fixen(e, obs. forms of VIXEN.

fixer ('fɪksə(r)). [f. FIX *v.* + -ER¹.]

1. One who fixes. Now, esp. one who arranges or adjusts matters (often illicitly).

1885 *Instr. to Census Clerks* 69 [Workmen employed in the] Dye-House: Fixer, Dunger, Washer. *Ibid.* 95[Workmen in the Zinc Trade] Fixer. **1889** *Amer. Mission.* Dec. 363 Where the 'boss' and the fixer of elections are unknown. **1892** *Daily Chron.* 28 Apr. 8/1 Blind Fixers wanted. **1900** 'FLYNT' & WALTON *Powers that Prey* III. i. 64 Do you know what fixers are travelin'? **1909** W. IRWIN *Confess. Con Man* ii. 52 At the head of the outfit stood the 'fixer', whose job it was to bribe or stall city officials so that the gamblers could proceed with reasonable security. **1914** JACKSON & HELLYER *Vocab. Criminal Slang* 33 *Fixer*,..one who acts as go-between for thieves and bribe takers. Example: 'If you get a rumble, send for Jones, the mouthpiece; he's a sure-shot fixer and can square anything short of murder.' **1926** J. BLACK *You can't Win* xii. 155 Lawyers haggling at the desk about releases for prisoners, 'fixers', hawk-eyed and rapacious, lurked about. **1930** *Observer* 14 Sept. 15 The Americans have a word for the professional collaborator: they call him a 'fixer'; and his business is to remove the technical defects from a play. **1931** *Economist* 15 Aug. 302/2 A corps of lawyers and lobbyists who enjoyed a high reputation at Ottawa and Quebec as political 'fixers'. **1952** *Country Life* 12 Dec. 1959/2 The most successful dog..has the commanding eye, enabling him to hypnotise the sheep, which earns him the name of fixer. **1959** *Listener* 25 Mar. 561/1 The second [group in Parliament] are the onlookers, the fixers, and the rank and file. **1971** *Guardian* 21 Jan. 3/3 Victor Louis who was the principal contact man and fixer.

2. Something used for fixing (a volatile substance, a drawing, a colour or dye.) Also in *Photogr.*

1849 JOHNSTON *Exper. Agric.* 129 Experiments with gypsum as a fixer of ammonia. **1882** HAMERTON *Graphic Arts* 123 The fixer [for charcoal drawing]..is simply a very weak solution of gum-lac in spirits of wine. **1885** *Westmld. Gaz.* 13 June 8/6 The albumen..is used as the fixer of bright aniline dyes in calicoes. **1922** C. BEATON *Diary* 28 Dec. (1961) 29, I..went to Kodak's and bought a portrait attachment, some gas-light paper, developers and fixers. **1935** KINGSBURY & JOHANNSEN *Histol. Technique* 1 A fixer may be defined as a fluid (or gas) in which the living, or at least very fresh, tissue is placed in order to preserve the structure of its elements as nearly as possible as in life. **1941** J. D. CORRINGTON *Working with Microscope* 161 Zenker's fluid, one of the most efficient and widely used of all fixers in animal histology. **1968** *Gloss. Terms Offset Lithogr. Printing (B.S.I.)* 15 *Fixer*, a solution which changes undeveloped light-sensitive material into a water-soluble form for subsequent removal from the photographic layer by washing.

†**'fixes**, *sb. pl. Obs.* [? f. FIX *v.*; or a corruption of **fæxes*, Eng. pl. of FÆX: cf. FÆCES.] (See quot.)

The discrepancy of the explanations in the two quots. is prob. due to some error.

1594 PLAT *Jewell-ho.* III. 79 Aquafortis, whose faeces (fixes the Goldsmiths vnproperly tearme them) haue beene first stricken down with some fine siluer. **1819** REES *Cycl.* XIV, *Fixes* is a name given by the workmen in gold and silver to a solution in [? read *of*] silver, from its use in carrying down and fixing the heterogeneous acids mingled with aqua-fortis.

fix-fax¹ ('fɪksfæks). Also 9 *dial.* fic-fac, fig-fag. [See the variant PAX-WAX.]

The thick tendon in the neck of cattle or sheep.

[*c* **1280** W. DE BIBLESWORTH in *Promp. Parv.* 388 *Et si ad le wenne* (fex .wex) *au col derere.*] *c* **1460** J. RUSSELL *Bk. Nurture* 444 In þe nek þe fyxfax þat þow do away. [*c* **1500** *Fr.-Eng. Glossary* (Harl. MS. 219, f. 150) in *Promp. Parv.* 388 *Le vendon*, the fax wax.] **1691** RAY *Creation* (1714) 157 Which aponeurosis is taken notice of by the vulgar by the name of Fixfax—or Packwax. **1737** BRACKEN *Farriery Impr.* (1756) I. 317 The Fix-fax of the Neck. **1869** *Lonsdale Gloss.*, *Fixfax*. **1878** *Cumbrld. Gloss.*, *Fic-fac, fig-fag*.

†**'fix-fax.**² *Sc. Obs. rare*⁻¹. [Onomatopœic; the reduplication expresses hurried and repeated movements; cf. FIDFAD, Ger. *fickfack*, etc.] 'Hurry, the middle of any business' (Jam.).

1768 ROSS *Helenore* II. 326 When the're just i' the fix fax o' their din.

fixial(e: see FIXAL *Her.*

fixidity (fɪk'sɪdɪtɪ). Now *rare.* [badly f. FIX *a.* or FIXED *ppl. a.*, after *fluidity*.] = FIXITY.

R. cites an example from Boyle's *Works* (1772) III. 78, where the orig. reading is *fixity*: see FIXITY 1 quot. 1666.

1762 tr. *Busching's Syst. Geol.* I. 45 Copper retains its fixidity the longest in the fire next to Iron. **1778** W. PRYCE *Min. Cornub.* I. iii. 51 Quicksilver..has every property of Metal except fixidity. **1872** W. F. BUTLER *Great Lone Land* xiii. (1875) 198 Assuming greater fixidity of purpose.

†**'fixily**, *a. Her. Obs.* App. = FITCHÉ.

1486 *Bk. St. Albans, Her.* B iij b, Of theym [croslettis] ther be iiij dyuerse..Cros fixyly, Cros paty [etc.].

fixing ('fɪksɪŋ), *vbl. sb.* [f. as prec. + -ING¹.]

1. a. The action of the verb FIX in various senses. Also with advbs., as ***fixing out, up***; and gerundially with omission of *in*.

1605 BACON *Adv. Learn* II. xxii. §14 The fixing of the good [hours of the mind] hath been practised by two means: vows ..and observances or exercises. **1666** EARL ORRERY *State Papers* (1743) I. 251, I find multitudes of arms are fixing amongst the Irish gunsmiths. **1769** FALCONER *Dict. Marine* (1789) D d, The filling and fixing of the shells. **1792** in Picton *L'pool. Munic. Rec.* (1886) II. 267 To superintend the fixing up of the said figure. **1817** KEATS *Lett.* Wks. 1889 III. 53 Another reason of my fixing is, that I am more in reach of the places around me. **1883** MRS. ROLLINS *New Eng. Bygones* 157 For the daughters..table-linen and bedding were to be stored away for their fixing out. **1910** *Jrnl. R. Hort. Soc.* XXXVI. 28 This enables the breeder to dispense entirely with the old and laborious method of so-called 'fixing' by continuous selection. **1929** C. E. McCLUNG *Handbk. Miscroscop. Techn.* i. 7 Fixing is the process of preserving, by means of coagulation, the normal structural characters of organs, tissues and cells. **1939** *Times* 10 July 13/1 Gold to the amount of £183,000 was dealt in at the fixing. **1965** J. L. HANSON *Dict. Econ.* 202/1 *Gold fixing*, determining the price of gold on the London Gold Market. *Ibid.* 264/1 The traditional 'gold-fixing' is carried out [at the premises of N. M. Rothschild in London] by representatives of four firms of bullion dealers. **1967** *Times* 18 Mar. 16/5 At the fixing in London the gold price was lowered 1d. to 251s. 5½d.

b. *Photogr.* The process of rendering (a negative, etc.) permanent; *concr.* that which fixes.

1853 *Family Her.* 3 Dec. 510/2 In the next operation, the fixing, it will become much lighter. *c* **1865** J. WYLDE in *Circ. Sc.* I. 146/1 Hyposulphite of soda is largely prepared for photographic 'fixing'. **1879** *Cassell's Techn. Educ.* III. 65 For the fixing of the image we should recommend the use of a dipping bath.

c. A method or means of fixing. *rare.*

1660 JER. TAYLOR *Duct. Dubit.* II. ii. I. 360 [The Jewish feasts] were..only..fixings of their thoughts, apt to wander to the Gentile Customes. **1793** SMEATON *Edystone L.* 121 To cut the rock..so as to get a firm fixing for our work.

2. *concr.* **a.** In *pl.* (orig. *U.S.*) Apparatus, equipment; trimming of a dress; the adjuncts to any dish, garnishing. Also (*Australian slang*), strong liquor (Barrère and Leland 1889). Also *transf.*

1820–1 R. FLOWER *Let.* in R. G. Thwaites *Early Western Trav.* (1904) X. 126 'There wife,' said he, 'did you ever see such fixings?' He felt the paper, looked in a mirror.., and gazed with amazement. **1827** J. F. COOPER *Prairie* I. ii. 30 'Your fixen seem none of the best for such a calling.' **1839** MARRYAT *Diary Amer.* Ser. I. II. 228 White wheat and chicken fixings. **1840** *Kentucky Rifle* (Danville, Ky.) 31 Oct. 110/2 Let every man that can play a fiddle or blow a horn, bring his fixins along and make music. **1842** DICKENS *Amer. Notes* (1850) 101/1 Said my opposite neighbour, handing me a dish of potatoes..'will you try some of these fixings?' **1847** J. S. ROBB *Streaks of Squatter Life* 31 Throw yourself wide on the literary fixins and poetry, for the galls. **1851** MAYNE REID *Scalp Hunt.* ii, Delicious frog 'fixings'. **1855** BROWNING *Men & Wom.*, *Bp. Blougram's Apol.* 212 Neat ship-shape fixings and contrivances. **1861** LOWELL *Biglow P.* Poems 1890 II. 230 We don't make no charge for the ride an' all the other fixins. **1864** BAGEHOT *Coll. Works* (1965) II. 333 There is a setting of surroundings—as the Americans would say, of *fixings*—without which the reality is not itself. **1882** B. HARTE *Flip* ii, He's..lost his rod and fixins. **1957** *N.Z. Timber Jrnl.* Mar. 52/1 *Fixings*, certain items like plugs, pallets, nogs and backings used to fix joinery. **1963** WODEHOUSE *Stiff Upper Lip, Jeeves* v. 40 She was undeniably an eyeful, being slim, svelte and bountifully equipped with golden hair and all the fixings.

b. = FIX *sb.* 2.

1874 in KNIGHT *Dict. Mech.* I. 874/2.

3. *attrib.* and *Comb.*, as ***fixing agent, fluid, process, solution*** (Photogr.); **fixing-bath**, (*a*) *Photogr.*, the bath in which a developed negative or positive is plunged in order to fix it; (*b*) *Tanning* (see quot.).

1855 T. F. HARDWICH *Man. Photogr. Chem.* v. 52 The Iodide and Bromide of Potassium have both been employed as *fixing agents. **1878** W. ABNEY *Treat. Photogr.* iv. 28 In determining the fixing agent to employ in silver printing. **1919** *Brit. Jrnl. Photogr. Alm.* 248 The fixing agent is hypo. **1936** C. J. WALLIS *Pract. Biol.* 6 Immerse the object in several times its own volume of the fixing agent. **1944** B. J. ORBAN *Oral Histol. & Embryol.* xvi. 326 The length of time necessary for a fixing agent to act upon a tissue varies. **1968** C. E. ENGEL *Photogr. for Scientist* v. 254 The fixing agent must not affect the silver of the developed image. **1868** M. C. LEA *Photogr.* 35 The negative *fixing-bath consists of a strong solution of hyposulphite of soda. **1885** C. T. DAVIS *Manuf. Leather* xxxix. 601 [The tanner] prepares a new liquor termed the 'fixing-bath', consisting of water sufficient to cover the skins [etc.]. **1927** H. E. JORDAN *Text-bk. Histol.* (ed. 4) xx. 727 An excellent *fixing fluid for general embryologic work. *c* **1865** J. WYLDE in *Circ. Sc.* I. 141/2 The *fixing process is intended to dissolve away that portion of the silver salt which has not been acted on by the light. **1872** W. F. STANLEY *Photogr.* 21 The quantity of *fixing solution required will be in proportion to the number of prints to be fixed.

'fixing, *ppl. a.* [+ -ING².] That fixes.
(Often difficult to distinguish from the vbl. sb. used *attrib.*: see prec. 3.)
1641 FRENCH *Distill.* i. (1651) 10 By the adding of some fixing thing to it [any volatile body]. **1873** HAMERTON *Intell. Life* x. x. 387 The gradual fixing power of habit.

†'fixion. *Obs.* [ad. med.L. *fixiōn-em*, n. of action f. L. *figĕre* to FIX. Cf. OF. *fixion*.] = FIXATION 3.
1555 EDEN *Decades* 340 This is a token of purenesse and fixion. **1605** TIMME *Quersit.* I. xiv. 67 A propertie belonging to the most fixed salts, and a token of their assured and most constant fixion. *a* **1631** DONNE *Serm.* (1640) lxiv. 648 There must be a Fixion, a settling thereof, so that it shall not evaporate into nothing.

fixion(e, obs. forms of FICTION *sb.*
1599 THYNNE *Animadv.* 32. **1615** G. SANDYS *Trav.* 152.

fixity ('fɪksɪtɪ). [ad. assumed L. **fixitātem*, f. *fixus*: see FIX *a.* and -ITY. Cf. Fr. *fixité*.] The quality or condition of being fixed.

1. Originally *spec.* in *Physics*: The property of enduring heat without volatilization or loss of weight.
1666 BOYLE *Orig. Formes* 282 So much do the Fixity [*Wks.* **1772** III. 78 fixidity] and Volatility of Bodies depend upon Texture. **1757** WALKER in *Phil. Trans.* L. 129 This cremor was found to have a great degree of fixity. **1811** PINKERTON *Petral.* II. 220 Tartarin, notwithstanding its fixity, is.. found in soot. **1826** FARADAY *Exp. Res.* xxxii. 205 Retaining them in a state of perfect fixity.

2. a. *gen.* The condition of not being liable to displacement or change; stability or permanence in situation, condition, or form.
1791 HAMILTON *Berthollet's Dyeing* I. I. I. ii. 40 The oxyd of tin.. increases the brightness and fixity of several [colours]. **1807** W. TAYLOR in *Ann. Rev.* V. 575 The translation of the Bible.. gave fixity to the tongue of the new religion. **1858** FROUDE *Hist. Eng.* III. xvii. 525 The unbending fixity of a law of nature. **1877** C. O'NEILL in *Encycl. Brit.* VII. 579/1 The aniline purples.. are only fitted for use where great fixity is not demanded. **1885** CHITTY in *Law Times Rep.* LII. 690/1 Irresolution and want of fixity of purpose.

b. *fixity of tenure*: the condition of having a fixed, permanent tenure.
1844 MISS M. HENNELL *Social Syst.* 82 The expediency of giving fixity of tenure to the tillers of the soil in Ireland.

c. *concr.* Something fixed.
1817 COLERIDGE *Biog. Lit.* I. 296 Fancy, on the contrary, has no other counters to play with, but fixities and definites.

d. Fixedness (of look).
1895 *Cornhill Mag.* Nov. 519 Dark, restless eyes, that could.. fasten upon one with a disagreeable fixity.

fixive ('fɪksɪv), *a. rare*⁻¹. [Lat. type **fixīvus* f. *figĕre* to FIX.] Adapted to fix, tending to fix. (Cf. FIXATIVE 1).
a **1834** COLERIDGE *Biog. Lit.* (1847) I. 322 App., When it acts as a Solid.. it exerts the same fixive power.

†'fixly, *adv. Obs.* [f. FIX *a.* + -LY².] = FIXEDLY.
1591 SYLVESTER *Du Bartas* I. v. 583, I know thy constant sight Can fixly gaze against Heav'ns greatest Light. **1604** T. WRIGHT *Passions* IV. ii. §4. 132 To stare fixly vpon one.. commeth from blockishnesse, as in Rustickes.

†fixnet. *Obs. rare*⁻¹. ? A swaggerer (other edd. published in the author's lifetime read *Thraso*).
1583 STUBBES *Anat. Abus.* C iij, [Silks, velvets, etc.] may be worne.. of the nobylity.. but not of every proud fixnet indifferentlie.

fixture ('fɪkstjʊə(r)). [Altered form of FIXURE, after the analogy of *mixture*.]

1. a. The action of fixing; the process of fixing or settling, or of becoming fixed or settled. ? *Obs.*
1598 SHAKS. *Merry W.* III. iii. 67 The firme fixture [*so F. 1 and Q. of* 1630; *the later Ff. have* fixure] of thy foote, would giue an excellent motion to thy gate. **1791** SMEATON *Edystone L.* §277 Employed in fixing and completing the fixture of the iron-work. **1797** WASHINGTON *Let.* Writ. 1892 XIII. 430 We must.. yield to the time she requires to prepare for her fixture here. **1817** G. S. FABER *Eight Dissert.* (1845) II. 202 The ultimate fixture of the sacred floating island appears in the greek legend of Delos.

b. The condition of being fixed; fixedness, fixity.
1809–10 COLERIDGE *Friend* (1818) III. 235 It was the Roman instinct to appropriate by conquest and to give fixture by legislation. **1850** L. HUNT *Autobiog.* II. xv. 167 They [Wordsworth's eyes] were like fires half burning, half smouldering, with a sort of acrid fixture of regard.

c. *concr.* A means of fixing or setting fast.
1791 SMEATON *Edystone L.* §223 Two Lewis holes upon the upper surface of each stone, those served as temporary fixtures for the work of the succeeding course.

2. a. Anything fixed or securely fastened in position; anything made firm, stable, or immobile.
1812 COLERIDGE in Southey *Omniana* II. 17 Features, which are looks become fixtures. **1831** DE QUINCEY *Dr. S. Parr* iii. Wks. 1862 V. 139 Even the most absolute fixtures (to use that term) in an English structure, must often be unsettled.. in a thoroughly Latin composition. **1841–44** EMERSON *Ess., Circles* Wks. (Bohn) I. 125 There are no fixtures in nature. The universe is fluid and volatile. **1858** GLENNY *Gard. Every-day Bk.* 125/1 The side cloths are in some Tulip-houses fixtures. **1878** SPURGEON *Treas. Dav.* Ps. civ. 5 The earth.. remains as stable as if it were a fixture.

b. *U.S.* in *pl.* Appendages, apparatus, 'fixings'.
1767 in *Archives State New Jersey* XX. 547 Tables, chests of drawers, fixtures, &c. **1849** N. KINGSLEY *Diary* (1914) 66 Saw a man that had died, and the fixtures and mode of preparation for burial. **1854** BARTLETT *Mex. Boundary* I. ii. 12 The blacksmiths.. were employed in making many small fixtures to the wagons. **1874** COUES *Field Ornith.* I. vi. 41 When travelling your fixtures must ordinarily be limited to a collecting-chest.

3. *Law.* In *plural*, 'Things of an accessory character annexed to houses or lands, which become, immediately on annexation, part of the realty itself' (Wharton *Law Lex.*).
1758 GRAY *Let. to Wharton* 21 Feb., I am much puzzled about the bishop and his fixtures. **1770** *Junius Lett.* xxxvi. 179 Tenants, who have had warning to quit.. destroy the fixtures. **1861** KENT *Comm.* (1873) II. xxxv. 345 The right to what are ordinarily called fixtures or articles of a personal nature affixed to the freehold. **1882** E. ROBERTSON in *Encycl. Brit.* XIV. 274/2 In respect of fixtures.. the tenant may sometimes remove them.
transf. **1786–89** BENTHAM *Wks.* (1843) II. 542 *Glebæ ascriptitii*, fixtures to the soil on which they are born.

4. A person or thing permanently confined to or established in a particular place or position.
1788 MAD. D'ARBLAY *Diary* 6 Nov., Miss Goldsworthy was a fixture at her side. **1812** BYRON *Ch. Har.* II. App. Dj, All the Franks who are fixtures, and most of the English.. etc. of passage, came over.. to their opinion. **1818** HAZLITT *Eng. Poets* v. (1870) 128 His sentiments have very much the air of fixtures. **1821** TICKNOR *Life, Lett. & Jrnl.* (1838) II. ix. 162 Mrs. Grant.. from age and its infirmities.. is a fixture. **1889** LOWELL *Lett.* (1894) II. 376 We have.. an American circus that seems a fixture.

5. *Athletic* and *Sporting*, rarely *Commercial*. An appointment or date for a meet, race, etc.; hence, the meet, race, etc. itself. Also attrib. *fixture-card, -list*. Also *transf.* and *fig.*
1825 *Sporting Mag.* XV. 346 Appointments have been substantiated into fixtures. **1826** —— XVIII. 111 Owthorpe —not the fixture of that name in Nottinghamshire. **1862** 'SCRUTATOR' (Horlock) *Country Gentleman* 146 Our next fixture is made already for Frampton Wood. **1869** *Times* 26 Feb. 10/2 Fixtures of the principal.. yachting clubs. **1882** *Daily News* 4 Mar., Bristol Wool Fair and the opening of the Colonial sales in London. These important 'fixtures' had been looked forward to. **1886** *Cycl. Tour. Club Gaz.* May 173/1 A neat fixture card from the Dublin.. Club. **1890** E. DOWSON *Let.* 11 Feb. (1967) 136, I hope to have it complete for your criticism when you come here on Thursday. For you will come—must come... Let me have a card to-morrow to acquaint me if it is a fixture. **1905** *Strand Mag.* Sept. 298/1 We always take it last on our fixture-list. **1914** C. MACKENZIE *Sinister St.* II. III. vii. 638 A gilt mirror.. stuck round with the fixture cards of the university and the college. **1923** [see BET *sb.* 1]. **1946** M. C. SELF *Horseman's Encycl.* 453 The 'fixture card' is sent to all members of a hunt and tells them what coverts are to be drawn on what days. **1955** *Times* 5 Aug. 4/5 Although their fixture list includes as many as 13 schools, they have not been beaten by another school since July, 1953. **1964** C. WILLOCK *Enormous Zoo* ix. 161 The annual fixture in which one tribe comes over to steal its neighbours' cows, the return match being played for the attackers' women.

fix-up ('fɪksʌp). *U.S.* [f. verbal phrase *to fix up*: see FIX *v.* 8 and 14 b.] Something 'fixed up'; a contrivance or 'get-up'. See also FIX *sb.* 4.
1832 *Polit. Examiner* (Shelbyville, Ky.) 8 Dec. 4/1 She says Mr. Bunker sit down, well I thought I would whilst she was getting her fixups off. **1855** *Knickerbocker* XLVI. 84 The old gentleman looked at me very disdainfully, and then in his most staid accents drawled out: 'Well, if this isn't one of the curiousest fix-ups ever I did see!' **1861** *N.Y. Tribune* 27 Nov. (Chipman's Bartlett), The 'Albany Argus', still hoping for some sort of a compromise or fix-up with the rebels, says [etc.]. **1867** W. H. DIXON *New Amer.* I. 191 Claret-cobbler, .. eye-opener, fix-ups, or any other Yankee deception in the shape of liquor. **1873** J. MILLER *Life Modocs* (1876) x. 149 The lady who has the least amount of natural hair has invariably the largest amount of artificial fix-ups on her head.

fixure ('fɪksjʊə(r)). *Obs.* or *arch.* See FIXTURE. [ad. late L. *fixūra*, f. *figĕre* to FIX].
Fixed condition, position, or attitude; fixedness, stability.
1603 DRAYTON *Bar. Wars.* I. xxxiii, This dreadfull Commet.. Whose glorious fixure in so faire a sky Strikes the beholder with a chilly feare. **1606** SHAKS. *Tr. & Cr.* I. iii. 101 Rend.. The vnity.. of States Quite from their fixure [*Ff.* 3 *and* 4 fixture]. **1611** —— *Wint. T.* v. iii. 67 The fixure of her Eye ha's motion in't. **1648** W. MONTAGUE *Devout Ess.* I. vi. §3. 62 The unfaithfulnesse of all materiall goods, in point of duration and fixure. **1680** *Hon. Cavalier* 7 Those Wandring Stars who have no Fixure from Heaven. **1753** *Gray's-Inn Jrnl.* (1756) II. No. 53 The Fixure of her Eyes, and Feebleness of her whole Person. **1817** COLERIDGE *Lay Sermon* in *Ch. & St.* (1839) 404 The very habit and fixures .. that had been impressed on their frames by the former.. winters.

fizenless, fizzenless, obs. ff. FOISONLESS.

fizgig, fisgig ('fɪzgɪg). Forms: 6 fisegig, fysgygge, 6–7 fisgigg, 7 fisguigge, 9 fizzgig, 6– fisgig, 7– fizgig. [A compound of GIG, which had the senses: 1. frivolous person (Chaucer); 2. whipping-top (Shaks.); the first element is obscure, but may perh. be identical with FISE. The Swiss-Ger. *fisigugg*, foolish busybody, can hardly be connected. Sense 3 seems to have been suggested by that of FIZZ without regard to the second element. Sense 4 was app. taken from Sp. *fisga* harpoon.]

1. A light, frivolous woman, fond of running or 'gadding' about; = GIG. Also *attrib.* or as *adj.* = flighty.
a **1529** SKELTON *Elinour Rumming* 538 Than sterte forth a fysgygge, And she broughte a bore pygge. **1596** GOSSON *Pleasant Quippes for Gentlewomen* 13 When you looke for praises sound, Then are you for light fisgiggs crownde. **1611** *Cotgr.*, *Trotiere*, a raumpe, fisgig. **1656** S. HOLLAND *Zara* (1719) 140 A Fis-gig, a flurt, a fickle.. foolish Female. **1872** BROWNING *Fifine* xxxiii. 46 In short, prefers to me.. this fizgig called Fifine! **1877** *N.W. Linc. Gloss.*, *Fizgig*, an ugly woman; a woman dressed in a strange or unbecoming manner. **1928** GALSWORTHY *Swan Song* III. xii. 308 Like all these 'fizz-gig' young moderns, she was just fluttering without basic purpose or direction.

2. (See quots.)
1656–81 BLOUNT *Glossogr.*, *Fizgig* [1681 *Fisgig*] is a kind of Top, which boyes play with. **1883** *Hampsh. Gloss.*, *Fizgig*, a whirligig; a round piece of iron or brass, serrated at the rim; through two holes near the centre, a piece of whipcord is passed. When set in motion by the twisting of the string, either in the air or in water, it makes a whizzing, hissing, or fizzing noise.

3. A kind of firework; a squib.
1644 NYE *Gunnery* II. (1647) 91 How to make Fisgigs, which some call by the name of Serpents. **1668** J. WHITE *Rich Cab.* (ed. 4) 87 The serpents or fisgigs are made about the bignesse of ones little finger, by rowling a paper upon a small rowler.. and choaking the paper coffin an inch from the end, then fill it three inches with powder dust. **1886** DOWDEN *Shelley* I. vii. 306 Fiery fizgigs in the hands of a pair of gleeful boys.

4. A kind of harpoon.
Perverted into FISHGIG. The GIG which appears in this sense from 18th c. is perh. a shortened form.
1565 J. SPARKE in Hakluyt *Voy.* III. 520 Those bonitos.. being galled by a fisgig did follow our shippe.. 500 leagues. **1668** D. SMITH *Voy. Constantinople* in *Misc. Cur.* (1708) III. 31 A Fisgig, a kind of barbed Iron, at the End of a Pole tyed fast to a Rope. **1798** *Acc. Bks.* in *Ann. Reg.* 460 Spears, fizgigs, or other articles. **1947** *Yr. Bk. Arts N.Z.* III. 166 Steal their canoes, Smash their fishing fiz-gigs.

5. In various senses suggested by the grotesque sound of the word or by association with FIZZ: **a.** A piece of tawdry finery, a gimcrack. **b.** A silly notion, an absurd crotchet. **c.** *to make fizgigs*: app. some drawing-room pastime (perh. in sense 2).
1822 SOUTHEY in *Q. Rev.* XXVIII. 26 Modes of devotion, with their outward and visible signs.. the banderoles, and humgigs, and fizzgigs of superstition. **1824** *Blackw. Mag.* XVI. 287 You soon take a fine fizgig into your head. **1825** T. LISTER *Granby* viii. (1826) 104 The Miss Cliftons.. were always *au courant du jour*.. were the first who made fizgigs, or acted charades.

6. An informer. *Austral. slang.*
1902 *Daily Chron.* 21 Aug. 5/2 Each detective [in Melbourne] had a criminal in his employ, who was known as a 'fizz-gig'. **1953** BAKER *Australia Speaks* v. 124 A stool pigeon or informer, otherwise known as a fizgig, fizzer, shelf and topoff.

Hence **†'fizgig** *v. intr.*, to run or gad about.
1594 NASHE *Vnfort. Trav.* 32 Why should I goe gadding and fisgigging after firking flantado amphibologies?

fizz, fiz (fɪz), *sb. colloq.* Also 8 phiz. [f. next vb. Cf. the earlier FISE.]

1. A hissing sound.
1812 J. & H. SMITH *Rejected Addr.* 69 The water when he was baptized gave a fizz. **1842** S. LOVER *Handy Andy* i, Every fizz it [the soda-water] made. **1855** O. W. HOLMES *Poems* 177 No rubbing will kindle your Lucifer match If the fiz does not follow the primitive scratch. **1870** THORNBURY *Tour Eng.* II. xxx. 268 A palpable devil.. flew off in a fizz of fire.

2. a. A disturbance, fuss.
a **1734** NORTH *Exam.* I. ii. §83 (1740) 74 What a Phiz of a Scandal is here upon the King. **1804** TARRAS *Poems* 107 'Douce wife', quoth I, 'what means the fizz?'

b. Animal spirits or 'go'.
1856 MRS. STOWE *Dred.* I. xvii. 235 Just enough fizz in her to keep one from flatting out. **1884** *Pall Mall G.* 2 Apr. 5 Mr Little has fizz and go enough to make excellent capital out of a broomstick.

3. a. *concr.* Something that fizzes; an effervescing drink, *esp.* champagne. Also any alcoholic or non-alcoholic effervescing drink.
1864 *Punch* XLVII. 100 We.. ordered some fizz. **1879** E. K. BATES *Egyptian Bonds* II. ix. 226 Let's have a bottle of fiz, old fellow. **1889** *Cent. Dict.*, *Fizz, fiz*,.. a light frothy liquid; specifically, in the United States, soda-water or other effervescent water. **1891** Gin fiz [see GIN *sb.*² 2]. **1906** MRS. BEETON *Househ. Managem.* xlviii. 1512 *Silver fizz*,.. 1 wineglass of gin, the juice of ½ a lemon, the white of 1 egg, 1 teaspoonful of icing sugar, a pinch of carbonate of soda, pounded ice. **1942** V. M. COTTRELL *Lost Cave of Pukerangi* ix. 81 A bottle of 'fizz' each. **1955** G. FREEMAN *Liberty Man* I. i. 17 I'll 'ave a coke... No I won't, I'll 'ave a raspberry fizz. **1958** A. L. SIMON *Dict. Wines* 76/2 *Fizzes*, American 'long' drinks made up of various kinds of spirits and some sugar or syrup.. served in tall glasses which are then filled with a syphon.

b. fizzbang = WHIZZ-BANG *sb.* 1.
1916 'BOYD CABLE' *Action Front* 67 He has a confused memory.. of drumming rifle fire.. and, then, immediately after, the rush and crash of a couple of German 'Fizz-Bang' shells. *Ibid.* 186 This cellar roof is too thin to stop an ordinary Fizzbang.

fizz, fiz (fɪz), *v.* [Echoic; cf. FIZZLE *v.*]
a. *intr.* To make a hissing or sputtering sound.

1685 CROWNE *Sir Courtly Nice* III, I kiss'd all the wenches as I came along, and made their moyst lips fiz again. **1687** COTTON *Burlesque upon B.* (ed. 2) 136 Thou oft hast made thy fiery Dart Fizz in the hollow of his heart. **1786** BURNS *Scotch Drink* 57 O rare! to see thee fizz an' freath I' th' lugget caup. **1827** PRAED *Red Fisherm.* 213 And the water fizzed as it tumbled in! **1839** MARRYAT *Diary Amer.* Ser. I. I. 286 Some black fellow..brings out the leather hose..and fizzes away with it till the stream has forced the dust into the gutter. **1861** HUGHES *Tom Brown at Oxf.* v. (1889) 38 His host put the kettle on the fire..and then, as it spluttered and fizzed, filled up the two tumblers.

b. To move with a fizzing sound.

1864 *Reader* 3 Dec. 707/2 The bluebottle..fizzes fussily into some poor man's cottage. **1880** SIR S. LAKEMAN *What I saw in Kaffir-Land* 48 Up and down the lines he used to fizz with his fat podgy legs.

c. *trans.* (*causal.*)

1665 COTTON *Scarron.* Æn. IV. 80 There will I stand with flaming taper, To Fizze thy tail instead of paper.

d. Also with *out*. Cf. FIZZLE *v.* 3.

1847 *Punch* 4 Sept. 87/2 Jenny Lind..has created a *fureur*, but it has fizzed out. **1941** BAKER *Dict. Austral. Slang* 29 *Fizz out on*, to let down, fail in a promise.

Hence **ˈfizzing** *vbl. sb.*

1842 C. WHITEHEAD *R. Savage* (1845) II. iv. 217 Such a roaring, and fizzing, and chuckling. **1877** WRAXALL *Hugo's Misérables* IV. xxv. 15 The children heard the phizzing of a match.

fizzen, var. of FOISON.

fizzer (ˈfɪzə(r)). [f. FIZZ *v.* or *sb.* + -ER[1].]

1. a. *slang.* Anything excellent or first-rate.

1866 *Lond. Misc.* 19 May 235/2 If the mare was such a fizzer why did you sell her? **1889** BOLDREWOOD *Robbery under Arms* (1890) 318 That was a regular fizzer of a spree.

b. *Cricket.* A very fast ball; also, one that deviates with unexpected speed after pitching. *colloq.*

1904 *Daily Chron.* 9 May 7/3 It will be good fun watching Tom keeping his fingers out of the way of a springing 'fizzer' of Lockwood. **1929** A. CONAN DOYLE *Maracot Deep* 251 Challen sent down another over of fizzers. **1956** R. ALSTON *Test Commentary* 44 Lock's first ball..was an absolute 'fizzer' which broke sharply.

2. = FIZZ *sb.* 3; *attrib.*, as ***fizzer-man***, ***-brigade***.

1894 *Westm. Gaz.* 11 Sept. 3/2 I may explain that the 'fizzer-man' is a species of camp-follower who..takes every opportunity of disposing of his wares, consisting generally of sherbet-and-water. In hot weather Tommy Atkins patronises the fizzer brigade very largely.

3. Usu. in phr. ***on a*** (or ***the***) ***fizzer***. A charge-sheet. *Services' slang.*

a **1935** T. E. LAWRENCE *Mint* (1950) I. xi. 39, I got back after..twelve, and they shoved me on the fizzer! **1940** *Daily Mail* 7 Sept. 3/8 Here are some current military phrases, interpreted...'On a fizzer'—On a charge. **1966** *New Society* 9 June 25/1 Feeling I was on a fizzer (army talk for a disciplinary charge).

4. a. A firecracker that fails to go off. *U.S. colloq.* and *dial.*

1914 *Dialect Notes* IV. 106 *Fizzer*, a firecracker that explodes with a hiss. **1978** D. BALL *Great Austral. Snake Exchange* 107 When we brought them home..to break the wickless ones in half for 'fizzers', we never felt disappointment in these small gleanings after the profusion of the night before.

b. A disappointing failure; a fiasco or 'wash-out'. *Austral. slang.*

1957 R. S. PORTEOUS *Brigalow* xiii. 101 Good old Carson, I thought. You may be a bit of a fizzer, but you'll do me. **1967** PARTRIDGE *Dict. Slang* Suppl. 1120/2 *Fizzer*, a failure, esp. *it's a fizzer*, 'The traditional c[atch] p[hrase] when a mechanical device..fails to work'..: Australian: since ca. 1920. **1969** W. DICK *Naked Prodigal* xix. 236 We all went to a New Year's Eve party in Goodway, but it was a fizzer. It never even got off the ground. **1974** *Courier-Mail* (Brisbane) 21 Nov. 2/2 Even the Country Party leader..called it [*sc.* a mass protest by farmers] a badly-organised fizzer. **1986** *Sunday Sun* (Brisbane) 25 May 84/5 (*heading*) A Team debut fizzer by George. **1986** *Facts on File* 4 July 487/3 John Howard..ridiculed the prime minister's address as the biggest fizzer since Halley's Comet.

fizzing (ˈfɪzɪŋ), *ppl. a.* [f. FIZZ *v.* + -ING[2].]

1. That fizzes.

1841 S. C. HALL *Ireland* I. 71 Endeavouring to divert the attention from the fizzing train. **1860** SALA *Lady Chesterf.* v. 76 He always associated that fizzing..wine with Jacobinism. **1877** M. M. GRANT *Sun-maid* viii, A shining salver bore a small fizzing urn.

2. *slang.* First-rate, excellent; chiefly quasi-*adv.*

1885 *Daily Tel.* 1 Aug. 2/2 'She'll do fizzing', remarked Mr. Menders, 'to stick up at the end of the barrer.'

fizzle (ˈfɪz(ə)l), *sb.* [f. next vb.]

1. a. The action of breaking wind quietly.

1598 FLORIO, *Sloffa*, a fizzle, a fiste, a close farte. *a* **1700** B. E. *Dict. Cant. Crew*, *Fizzle*, a little or low-sounding Fart. **1739** R. BULL tr. *Dedekindus' Grobianus* 208 Now let a Fizzle steal in Silence forth. **1836–48** B. D. WALSH *Aristoph. Knights* II. iv, And then in court they poisoned one another with their fizzles.

b. The action of hissing or sputtering.

1842 BARHAM *Ingold. Leg.*, *Auto-da-Fé*, Whose beards..Are smoking, and curling, and all in a fizzle. **1852** MRS. STOWE *Uncle Tom's C.* xiii. 118 The chicken and ham had a cheerful and joyous fizzle in the pan.

2. A failure or fiasco; *U.S. college slang*, a failure in recitation or examination. Also with *out*.

1846 *Yale Banger* 10 Nov. in Hall *Coll. Words & Cust.* (1851) 130 To get just one third of the meaning right constitutes a *perfect fizzle*. **1861** O. W. NORTON *Army Lett.* (1903) 23 The Erie Regiment is one grand fizzle out. **1884** *L'pool Daily Post* 13 Sept. 5/7 The affair will be a simple fizzle. **1958** *Spectator* 8 Aug. 185/2 A Suez-type fizzle-out.

fizzle (ˈfɪz(ə)l), *v.* Also 6 fysel(l, 7 fisle. [f. FISE: see -LE. Cf. also FIZZ and FISSLE.]

†**1. a.** *intr.* To break wind without noise. *Obs.*

c **1532** DEWES *Introd. Fr.* in *Palsgr.* 957 *Uencr* to fysel. **1601** HOLLAND *Pliny* II. 286 As for Onopordon, they say if Asses eat thereof, they will fall a fizling and farting. **1711** E. WARD *Quix.* I. 415 He gap'd and fizzl'd twice or thrice. **1739** R. BULL tr. *Dedekindus' Grobianus* 268 To fart and fizzle in the Time of Need.

b. quasi-*trans.* (with cognate obj.)

1721 D'URFEY *Two Queens Brentford* Epil., I fizzle such small puffs of Wind.

2. *intr.* To make a hissing sound; to hiss or sputter (as a wet combustible, or a fire-work).

1859 *All Year Round* No. 36, 222 The black oil fizzles. **1881** *Daily News* 7 Nov. 5/1 Unambitious rockets which fizzle doggedly downwards.

3. *fig.* **a.** *intr.* (chiefly *U.S. colloq.*) To fail, make a fiasco, come to a lame conclusion; in *U.S. college slang*, to fail in a recitation or examination. Also, ***to fizzle away***, ***out***. **b.** *trans.* *U.S. college slang.* To cause (a person) to fail in examination, or the like.

1847 *Yale Banger* 22 Oct. in Hall *Coll. Words & Cust.* (1851) 130 My dignity is outraged at beholding those who fizzle and flunk in my presence tower above me. *a* **1848** *Cincinnati Gaz.* (Bartlett), The factious and revolutionary action of the fifteen has..disgraced the actors, and fizzled out! **1850** *Yale Lit. Mag.* XIII. 321 *Ibid.* 131 Fizzle him tenderly, Bore him with care. **1854** *Olympia* (Wash.) *Pioneer* 15 Apr. (Th.), The Stellacoom gold excitement has entirely fizzled out. **1866** *Richmond Enquirer* (De Vere), The enterprise fizzled out in the most contemptible manner. **1878** *Cumbld. Gloss.*, *Fizzle*, to work busily but ineffectively. **1884** *Melbourne Punch* 4 Sept. 98/2 Another of Mr. Mirams' pet fads has fizzled ignominiously out. **1893** *Sat. Rev.* 11 Nov. 538/2 A general recognition by the Chicagoans that their show had to some extent fizzled. **1910** R. BROOKE *Coll. Poems* (1928) Mem. p. li, I've several times started to write to you a notable..letter, but my life has been too jerky to admit of much connected thought lately, so the letter always fizzled away.

Hence **ˈfizzling** *vbl. sb.* and *ppl. a.*

1616 B. JONSON *Devil an Ass* v. iii, It is the easiest thing, Sir, to be done As plain as fizzling. **1638** BROME *Antipodes* III. iv, Fah on your passages, Your windy workings, and your fislings at The barre. **1758** GRAY *Lett.* Wks. 1884 II. 368 That old fizzling Duke is coming here again. **1815** tr. *Paris Chit-Chat* (1816) II. 22 The fizzling of the bacon she was frying. **1893** A. WALTERS *Lotos Eater* vii. 157 The more complicated set pieces..lay in a fizzling, sputtering, snorting heap.

fizzle, var. of FISSLE.

†**ˈfizzler.** *Obs.* [f. prec. + -ER[1].] One who fizzles or breaks wind without noise.

1582 *MS. Cott. App.* xlvii. (Fenton's Voyage) f. 36 A fyzeler. **1611** COTGR., *Venneur*, a fizzler, or fyster.

fizzy (ˈfɪzɪ) *a.* and *sb.* [f. FIZZ *v.* + -Y[1]]. Given to fizz. Also *fig.*

1855 *Sat. Rev.* 17 Nov. 45/2 It is a very good article, this rollicking, noisy, fizzy letter. **1955** *Times* 20 Aug. 7/6 With their N.A.A.F.I.'s and their bus stops, their parlour games and their fizzy lemonades, the soldiers strike a staid and respectable note. **1963** WODEHOUSE *Stiff Upper Lip, Jeeves* xviii. 143 A very different Bassett from the fizzy rejoicer who had exited so short a while before.

Also *sb.*, a fizzy drink, e.g. champagne.

1896 KIPLING *Seven Seas* 209 The Captain stood a limberful of fizzy—Somethin' Brutt. **1970** 'M. UNDERWOOD' *Shem's Demise* v. 35 Can I have something to drink, Mum?.. Is there any fizzy?

‖**fjeld** (fjɛld). [a. Norw. *field*:—ON. *fiall*: see FELL *sb.*] An elevated rocky plateau, almost devoid of vegetation.

1860 GOSSE *Rom. Nat. Hist.* 51 The wildest and most barren of those snowy fjelds. **1882** *Three in Norway* vii. 53 We rambled on across the fjeld.

fjord, var. of FIORD.

fl. = L. *floruit* he flourished (FLOURISH *v.* 4).

1879 LEWIS & SHORT *Latin Dict.* p. xi/1, F. Vegetius Renatus, writer on the art of war, fl. A.D. 386. **1905** F. H. COLLINS *Author & Printer* 124/1 *fl.*, *floruit* (flourished). **1959** *Webster's Biogr. Dict.* 808/1 Kay.., John. fl. 1733–1764. English inventor of flying..shuttle.

fla, var. of FLO, *Obs.*, an arrow.

fla, obs. form of FLAW *sb.*[1], FLAY, FLEA.

flab (flæb), *sb.* Also **flap**. [f. onomatopœic stem *flab*, expressing the notion of something thick and broad; cf. *flap*, *dab*, *slab*.]

1. *dial.* (See quot. 1825).

? **18..** *Receipts in Cookery* 45 (Jam. Suppl. 1825) To make Catchup. Gather your large flabs, cut off the root ends, and take off the rough skins; knock them to pieces; and put them in an earthen jar [etc.] *a* **1825** FORBY *Voc. E. Anglia*, *Flaps* pl. large broad mushrooms.

2. *slang.* Fat, flabbiness; *spec.* at Christ's Hospital, butter. (See also quot. 1959.)

1923 *Glasgow Herald* 15 Nov. 8 Other terms in every day use [at Christ's Hospital] are 'flab', butter [etc.]. **1958** *Globe Mag.* 27 Sept. 17/5 He ballooned to 175 pounds of flab and was a poor advertisement for his product. **1959** I. & P. OPIE *Lore & Lang. Schoolch.* ix. 168 The unfortunate fat boy..is known as..flab. **1966** K. GILES *Big Greed* 136 She looks pretty good..no flab round the thighs yet.

†**flab**, *v.* *Obs.* [Onomatopœic; cf. FLAP *v.*] *trans.* To flap (the wings).

1765 GIRTON *Compl. Pigeon-fancier* 107 The smiter..has a particular manner of falling and flabbing its wings.

†**ˈflabberdeˌgasky**, *v.* *Obs. nonce-wd.* [var. of FLABBERGAST *v.*]

1822 *New Monthly Mag.* IV. 37 I lay like a log, Quite flabber-de-gasky'd, as sick as a dog!

ˈflabbergast, *sb.* ? *Sc. rare.* [f. next; for the sense cf. '*flabrigast* to gasconade. Perthshire' (Jam.).] Bombast.

1831 *Fraser's Mag.* IV. 161 The 'Asiatic style of oratory' with..its meretricious flabbergast,—its diluvial verbiage.

flabbergast (ˈflæbəgɑːst, -æ-), *v.* *colloq.* Also 8 **flaba-**, 9 **flaber-**. [First mentioned in 1772 as a new piece of fashionable slang; possibly of dialectal origin; Moor 1823 records it as a Suffolk word, and Jamieson, *Suppl.* 1825, has *flabrigast* to gasconade, *flabrigastit* worn out with exertion, as used in Perthshire. The formation is unknown; it is plausibly conjectured that the word is an arbitrary invention suggested by FLABBY or FLAP and AGHAST.]

trans. To put (a person) in such confusion that he does not for the moment know what to do or say; to astonish utterly, to confound.

1772 *Ann. Reg.* II. 191 *On New Words*, Now we are *flabbergasted* and *bored* from morning to night. **1801** MAR. EDGEWORTH *Angelina* iv. (1832) 77 They quite flabbergasted me. **1840** DISRAELI 15 July in *Corr. w. Sister* (1886) 158 My facts flabbergasted him. **1878** MOZLEY *Ess. Hist. & Theol.* I. 89 It perfectly flabbergasted the Commons.

Hence **ˌflabbergaˈstation**, the action of flabbergasting; the state of being flabbergasted.

1856 *Punch* 13 Dec. XXXI. 240/1 We scarcely remember to have ever seen any respectable party in a greater state of flabbergastation.

flabbiness (ˈflæbɪnɪs). [f. next + -NESS.] The state or condition of being flabby, flaccidity.

1727 BAILEY vol. II, *Flabbiness*, limberness with Moisture, Staleness, &c. **1774** GOLDSM. *Nat. Hist.* (1776) II. 197 The fat, and the flabbiness of that, seems to give an appearance of softness. **1834** *Brit. Husb.* I. 140 A certain want of spirit and flabbiness of flesh. **1856** G. MEREDITH *Shav. Shagpat* 370 The lion came trundling along in utter flabbiness, raising not his head.

b. In immaterial things: Want of vigour, feebleness, laxness, slackness.

1883 *Solicitor's Jrnl.* 24 Nov. 63/1 The practice of the courts..has..tended to establish a general vagueness and flabbiness. **1889** H. F. WOOD *Englishman of Rue Cain* i, Weakness of character, or flabbiness of intellect.

flabby (ˈflæbɪ), *a.* [An onomatopœic modification of the earlier FLAPPY; the voiced ending in *flab-* as compared with *flap-* gives to the syllable a feebler effect suited to the meaning. Cf. Du. *flabberen* (of a breeze) to flutter; Sw. dial. *fläbb* the hanging underlip of an animal. With sense 2 cf. *slabby*.]

1. Hanging loose by its own weight, yielding to the touch and easily moved or shaken, flaccid, limp, soft; said chiefly of or with respect to flesh.

[**1598**, see FLAPPY.] **1697** DRYDEN *Virg. Georg.* III. 780 His flabby Flanks decrease. **1740** E. BAYNARD *Health* (ed. 6) 10 Loose and flabby, wrinkled skin. **1752** H. WALPOLE *Corr.* (1837) I. 163 The town is empty, nothing in it but flabby mackerel. **1766** SMOLLETT *Trav.* 165 Ducks..very fat and flabby. **1813** J. THOMSON *Lect. Inflam.* 545 Her tongue had become yellow, swollen, and flabby. **1858** HOLLAND *Titcomb's Lett.* vi. 58 Their muscles are flabby. **1865** DICKENS *Mut. Fr.* III. iii, This flabby lump of mortality.

2. Of language, character, etc.: Weak, wanting 'back-bone'; nerveless, feeble.

1791 BOSWELL *Life Johnson* (1831) IV. 356 *note*, Garrick, after listening to him for a while..turned slily to a friend, and whispered him, 'What say you to this?—eh? Flabby, I think.' **1855** *Sat. Rev.* 10 Nov. 35/2 Flabby hebdomadal drivel. **1861** *Ibid.* 14 Dec. 596 The flabby talk of people who are expressly told to keep their minds clear of all knowledge of the principles which it involves. **1864** CARLYLE *Fredk. Gt.* IV. XII. viii. 181 An indolent flabby kind of creature. **1880** *Standard* 22 Dec., Flabby logic like this.

3. Damp, clammy.

c **1780** M. MONSEY *Let. to Mrs. Montague* in J. C. Jeaffreson *Bk. about Doctors* II. 87 How do you stand this flabby weather? **1849** DICKENS *Dav. Copp.* (C.D. ed.) 157 There was a flabby perspiration on the walls.

4. *Comb.* **a.** In parasynthetic adjs., as ***flabby-breasted***, ***-jowled***, ***-mouthed***.

1965 H. GOLD *Man who was not with It* xxix. 266 A gutty, chicken-necked, *flabby-breasted manager. **1932** W. FAULKNER *Light in August* xiii. 290 *Flabbyjowled and darkcaverneyed. **1905** *Daily Chron.* 1 June 5/7 Those bleareyed, *flabby-mouthed swillers.

b. With pr. pple. forming adj., as ***flabby-looking***.

1895 J. ASHBY-STERRY *Tale of Thames* 43/2 A flabby-looking, unhealthy person. **1947** W. DE LA MARE *Coll. Stories for Children* 201 Rather flabby-looking mackerel.

Hence **ˈflabbily** *adv.*, in a flabby manner.

1846 WORCESTER *Flabbily*, in a flabby manner. **1856** G. MEREDITH *Shav. Shagpat* 325 His tawny skin hung flabbily and his jaw drooped.

† **ˈflabel,** *sb. Obs.* Also 6 **flable.** [ad. L. *flābell-um* fan, dim. of **flābrum*, pl. *flābra* gusts of wind, f. *flāre* to blow.] **a.** A fan. **b.** *Entom.*, in grasshoppers (see quot. 1658).

1552 HULOET, Flable and fanne *idem.* **1570** LEVINS *Manip.* 56 A Flabel, *flabellum.* **1628** VENNER *Tobacco* (1650) 402 The lungs which are the flabel of the heart. **1658** ROWLAND *Moufet's Theat. Ins.* 992 They [Grashoppers] sing not with their mouth.. but by the reverberation of a little membrane under the flabells; (so they call those two coverings behinde the hinder thighs cleaving to the belly). **1656–81** BLOUNT *Glossogr.*, *Flabel*, a Fan.

† **flabel,** *v. Obs. rare*⁻¹. [f. prec. sb. Cf. OF. *flabeller*, ad. late L. *flābellāre.*] *trans.* To fan.

1653 URQUHART *Rabelais* I. xxxix. 176 It is continually flabbell'd [= Fr. *éventé*], blown upon, and aired by the north winds.

flabellate (fləˈbɛlət), *a. Bot.* and *Zool.* [f. L. *flābell-um* (see FLABEL) + -ATE².] Like a fan in form, fan-shaped.

1819 G. SAMOUELLE *Entomol. Compend.* 197 *Rhipiphorus*.. *antennæ* pectinated or flabellate. **1853** G. JOHNSTON *Nat. Hist. E. Bord.* I. 214 The branchlets.. of the Elms [are] alternate zigzag, and flabellate. **1856** W. CLARK *Van der Hoeven's Zool.* I. 235 Branchiæ two flabellate.

flabellation (flæbəˈleɪʃən). *Surg.* [a. F. *flabellation*, n. of action f. L. *flābellāre* to fan, f. *flābellum* fan.] The action of fanning.

1658–78 PHILLIPS, *Flabellation* a fanning with a Flable or fan. **1884** *Syd. Soc. Lex.*, *Flabellation* the act of fanning, employed to keep injured parts and the dressings covering them cool.

flaˈbelli-. combining form of L. *flābellum* fan, used to indicate a fan-like form or arrangement, as in ***flabellifoliate, flabellinerved*** adjs.

1880 GRAY *Struct. Bot.* iii. §4. 92 Flabellinerved, where straight nerves and ribs radiate from the apex of the petiole, as in Fan-palms. **1884** *Syd. Soc. Lex.*, *Flabellifoliate* having leaves which fold like a fan, as those of *Oxalis acetosella.*

flabelliform (fləˈbɛlɪfɔːm), *a. Bot.* and *Zool.* [f. L. *flābell-um* fan + -(I)FORM.] Having the form of a fan, fan-like.

1777 MILLER in *Phil. Trans.* LXVIII. 179 A palm with flabelliform leaves. **1828** STARK *Elem. Nat. Hist.* II. 295 Antennæ flabelliform or pectinated. **1861** HULME tr. *Moquin-Tandon* II. VII. 408 They have an anterior flabelliform filament. **1880** C. & F. DARWIN *Movem. Pl.* 206 The branches are flat, or flabelliform.

‖ **flabellum** (fləˈbɛləm). Pl. **flabella** (erroneously **-i**). [L. *flābellum* fan: see FLABEL *sb.*]

1. A fan; applied *esp.* to a fan carried in religious ceremonies.

1875 MASKELL *Ivories* 91 The bishop's pastoral staff, again, has not dropped out of use like.. the flabellum. **1889** C. D. BELL *Winter on Nile* xvi. 154 Officers wave round the shrine flabella and fans.

2. *Science.* A fan-shaped part of anything.

1867 J. HOGG *Microsc.* II. i. 270 The frond consists of olive-coloured irregularly-divided flabelli.

† **ˈflaber,** *a. Obs. rare*⁻¹. [Cf. FLAB *sb.*] ? = FLABERKIN.

1687 MRS. BEHN *Lucky Chance* II. i, There's no other way of quenching the fire in her flaber chops.

† **ˈflaberˌgudgion, ˌflaberˈgullion.** *Obs.* [The assonance of these forms with CLAPPERDUDGEON, SLUBBERDEGULLION (also *slabber-*), and the similarity of sense, suggest that they may either be variants of one word, or at least belong to the same group of experiments in the invention of grotesque words.] (See quots.)

1611 COTGR., *Baligaut*, an unweldie lubber.. mishapen lowt, ill fauoured flabergullion. *Ibid.*, *Trainquenailles*, scoundrells, ragamuffins, base rascalls, flabergudgions. **1677** MIEGE *Eng.-Fr. Dict.*, Flabergullion or (rather) Slaberdegullion, *un sot, un impertinent.*

† **ˈflaberkin,** *a. Obs. rare*⁻¹. [? f. FLABER (recorded later, but perh. in dial. use) + -KIN.] Puffed out, puffy.

1592 NASHE *P. Penilesse* (ed. 2) 2 a, Nature hath left him a flaberkin face, like one of the foure winds.

† **ˈflabile,** *a. Obs. rare.* [ad. L. *flābil-is*, f. *flāre* to blow.] Of musical instruments: Played upon by blowing; wind-. Also *transf.*

1727 BAILEY vol. II, *Flabile*, easily blown. **1728** R. NORTH *Mem. Musick* (1846) 24 These [instruments] were either flabile or nervous; the former were either trumpets (*tuba*), tibia, or fistula, and the other divers sorts of harps. *Ibid.* 78 As for.. mercenary musick, it was cheifly flabile.

flabotomye, obs. form of PHLEBOTOMY.

† **flacˈcescency.** *Obs. rare*⁻¹. [f. L. *flaccēscent-em*, pr. pple. of *flaccēscĕre* to wither, f. *flaccēre* to be flabby, f. *flaccus* flabby: see -ENCY.] The quality of becoming flaccid.

1664 POWER *Exp. Philos.* II. 117 The reason of its flaccescency, upon admission of external Ayr, is, because [etc.]. **1721–1800** in BAILEY.

flaccid (ˈflæksɪd), *a.* Also 7 **flaccide,** (8 **flacid**). [a. F. *flaccide* (Cotgr.), ad. L. *flaccidus*, f. *flaccus* flabby.]

1. Wanting in stiffness, hanging or lying loose or in wrinkles; limber, limp; flabby. Chiefly of flesh and similar structures: rarely of a person.

1620 VENNER *Via Recta* v. 87 The one it maketh flaccide, and the other subiect to putrefaction. **1660** BOYLE *New Exp. Phys. Mech.* iv. 46 The sides of the Bladder grew flaccid. **1704** F. FULLER *Med. Gymn.* (1711) 32 Yet are the Muscles not Flaccid, but Tense and Firm. **1751** JOHNSON *Rambler* No. 117 ¶8 The flaccid sides of a football. **1848** THACKERAY *Bk. Snobs* Wks. IX. 385 His double chin over his flaccid whitey-brown shirt collar. **1848** —— *Van. Fair* lxi, The flaccid children within. **1879** FROUDE *Cæsar* xv. 234 His hair moist, his eyes heavy, his cheeks flaccid.

b. Of vegetable organs and tissues: Bending without elasticity, also, relaxed from want of moisture; drooping.

1626 BACON *Sylva* §493 The part, against which the Sun beateth, waxeth more faint and flaccide in the Stalk, and thereby less able to support the Flower. **1776** WITHERING *Brit. Plants* (1796) II. 233 Stem flaccid, rough with strong hairs. **1875** DARWIN *Insectiv. Pl.* ix. 226 The leaf being flaccid and apparently dead. **1882** VINES *Sachs' Bot.* 675 The current of water also ceases as soon as the tissues which have become somewhat flaccid are again turgescent.

2. Of immaterial things: Wanting vigour and nervous energy, limp, feeble.

1647 H. MORE *Song of Soul* II. i. II. xli, What's dull or flaccid, nought illustrative. **1855** TENNYSON *Maud* I. i. 20 A scheme that had left us flaccid and drain'd. **1875** FARRAR *Silence & V.* viii. 140 It is because his resolutions have been feeble, and his purposes flaccid.

Hence **ˈflaccidly** *adv.*, in a flaccid manner; **ˈflaccidness,** the state of being flaccid, flaccidity.

1727 BAILEY vol. II, *Flaccidness.* **1847** CRAIG, *Flaccidly.* **1876** tr. *Wagner's Gen. Pathol.* 238 The flaccidness of the tissues. **1883** MISS BROUGHTON *Belinda* I. I. xii. 218 Belinda has thrown herself flaccidly into a chair.

flaccidity (flækˈsɪdɪtɪ). [f. FLACCID *a.* + -ITY. Cf. F. *flaccidité.*]

1. The quality or condition of being flaccid; want of stiffness or tension, limpness, looseness.

1676 WISEMAN *Surgery* VI. ii. 444 There is neither Fluxion nor Pain, but Flaccidity joyned with an Insensibility. **1725** CHEYNE *Ess. Health* vii. 173 The Viscidity of the Juices and the Flaccidity of the Fibres, would.. be removed. **1800** YOUNG in *Phil. Trans.* XCI. 62 The flaccidity of the eye after death. **1882** VINES *Sachs' Bot.* 689 So long as no actually perceptible amount of flaccidity, *i.e.* of withering.. takes place.

b. Of immaterial things: Want of firmness and vigour; limpness, flabbiness.

1778 BP. LOWTH *Isaiah, Dissert.* liii, The Prophet would express the drowsiness and flaccidity.. of his countrymen. **1806–7** J. BERESFORD *Miseries Hum. Life* II. xvi, The flaccidity of mind with which you [etc.]. **1875** LIGHTFOOT *Comm. Col.* (ed. 2) 124 A vagueness, a flaccidity, of conception betrays itself in their language.

2. Used to render It. *flaccidezza*, Fr. *flacherie*: A disease of silkworms.

18.. RILEY *Silk-Culture* 36 (Cent. Dict.) The worms are attacked by flaccidity.

flacco(u)n, obs. Sc. form of FLAGON.

flache, obs. form of FLASH.

‖ **flacherie** (flaʃri). [F. *flacherie* (Littré Supp.) a disease of silkworms.] = FLACCIDITY 2.

1885 LADY CLAUD HAMILTON tr. *Life Pasteur* 152 A characteristic specimen of the disease called morts-flats or flacherie. **1888** E. A. BUTLER *Silkworms* v. 71 It is possible for flacherie to become hereditary.

flachet, var. of FLATCHET, *Obs.*

Flacian (ˈfleɪʃɪən), *a.* and *sb. Eccl. Hist.* Also 6 **Flaccian.** [f. *Flaci-us* + -AN.]

A. *adj.* Of or pertaining to Flacius Illyricus, a Protestant divine of the 16th c., who opposed the adiaphorist views advocated by Melanchthon. **B.** *sb.* A follower of Flacius Illyricus; an anti-Adiaphorist. Hence **ˈFlacianism,** the doctrine or principles of Flacius Illyricus and his followers; **ˈFlacianist** = FLACIAN *sb.*

1565 T. STAPLETON *Fortr. Faith* 146 Thus write the Flaccians and zelous Lutherans. **1619** BRENT tr. *Sarpi's Counc. Trent* VI. (1629) 527 Whole Parishes of Lutherans, Zuinglians, Flacians, Anabaptists. **1847** F. PRANDI tr. *Cantu's Ref. Europe* I. 98 Hence arose the heresy of the Flacians or substantialists. **1872** SHIPLEY, etc. *Gloss. Eccl. Terms* s.v. *Adiaphoristic Controversy*, His [Melanchthon's] supporters were called Philippists; his opponents, Flacianists. **1882–3** SCHAFF *Encycl. Relig. Knowl.* III. 1827 Pure Lutheranism, free from all Flacian extravagances.

flack (flæk), *sb.*¹ *dial.* [echoic; cf. F. *flac* in same sense.] A blow, slap, or stroke.

1823 MOOR *Suffolk Words, Flack*, a blow. *a* **1825** FORBY *Voc. E. Anglia, Flack*, a blow, particularly with something loose and pliant.

flack (flæk), *sb.*² *slang* (chiefly *U.S.*). [Origin unkn.] A press agent; a publicity man.

1946 'S. STERLING' *Where there's Smoke* xiii. 99 That publicity flack is here. **1961** A. BERKMAN *Singers' Gloss. Show Business* 23 *Flack*, a member of the Publicity Department (usually of a motion picture studio); press agent. **1966** L. CHARBONNEAU *Way Out* xiv. 102 And all of a sudden my flack friend believes in his own fairy tales. **1968** C. DRUMMOND *Death & Leaping Ladies* v. 120 They were booked to do ten matches in Mexico City; Bull, their flack, had lined up the opposition.

flack (flæk), *v. Obs.* exc. *dial.* [ME. *flacken*, of onomatopœic formation = MDu. *vlacken* (Kilian), Icel. *flaka* to flap, hang loose.]

1. *intr.* To flap, flutter; to flap the wings; to throb, palpitate.

1393 GOWER *Conf.* III. 315 Her herte.. [began] to flacke and bete. **1567** MAPLET *Gr. Forest* 71 The Crow.. flieth and flacketh about his eies and face. **1788** W. MARSHALL *Yorksh.* Gloss., *Flack*, to flicker as a bird; to throb as a wound. **1876** *Mid. Yorksh. Gloss.*, *Flack*, to pulsate heavily.

2. To hang loosely. *dial.*

a **1825** FORBY in *Voc. E. Anglia.* **1847** in HALLIWELL.

3. *trans.* To move or shake intermittently; to flap, flick; also, to flap or flick *with* (something). (Connoting a clumsier instrument and a 'flatter' blow than *flick.*)

1751 R. PALTOCK *P. Wilkins* (1884) I. xii. 137, I observed it.. frequently flacking its short tail. **1819** *Metropolis* I. 58 He now flacked his boot with a silk handkerchief. **1859** SALA *Gas-light & D.* xxxiii. 385 Flacking his horsewhip. **1870** *Daily Tel.* 20 Aug. 3 Flacking his cloak in the eyes of a huge bull.

4. *Agric.* To beat with a flail; also to rake (hay).

1744–50 W. ELLIS *Mod. Husbandm.* VI. iii. 71 They.. flack the Heap of Corn not only once as it lies, but they turn it, and thrash it again and again. **1891** *Rutland Gloss.*, *Flack in*, to rake hay in a long row.

Hence **ˈflacking** *vbl. sb.*, the action of the vb.

1844 *Zoologist* II. 500 The flight was quite distinct from the 'flacking along the water' of which Mr. Parsons speaks.

flacker (ˈflækə(r)), *v. Obs.* exc. *dial.* [ME. *flakeren* (possibly repr. OE. **flacorian*; cf. *flacor* adj., flying, fluttering, and *flicorian* FLICKER *v.*), corresponding to MDu. *flackeren*, ON. *flǫkra* to flutter (Da. *flagre*), MHG. *vlackern* (mod.G. *flackern*) to flicker; a frequentative f. the onomatopœic stem *flak-*: see FLACK *v.*

The OHG. *flagorôn*, Flemish *vlaggheren* (Kilian) to flutter, may be compared as parallel onomatopœic formations.]

1. *intr.* To flap, flutter, throb; *esp.* of birds, to flap the wings, to fly flutteringly. In mod. dial. also *trans.* To flap (the wings) (*Whitby Gloss.*).

13.. *E.E. Allit. P.* B. 1410 Foles in foler flakerande bitwene. **1535** COVERDALE *Isa.* vi. 2 From aboue flakred the Seraphins. **1631** R. H. *Arraignm. Whole Creature* xviii. 321 As two Birds, that are flackering, and flying at the two ends of a threed. **1785** [HUTTON] *Bran New Wark* 75 (E.D.S.) How strangely the mind of man flackers and flounces? **1877** *Holderness Gloss.* s.v., 'Ther was a lot o' bods altegither, and didn't they flacker, mun, when Ah let gun off amang em?'

† **2.** = FLATTER *v. Obs. rare*⁻¹. (Perh. a corrupt reading; cf. however the similar sense of FLICKER *v.*).

a **1225** *Ancr. R.* 222 Men.. þet flakered [*v.r.* faltreð, flattereð] hire of freolac.

Hence **ˈflackering** *vbl. sb.* and *ppl. a.*

c **1440** *Gesta Rom.* xxvi. 100 (Harl. MS) Þe Faucon seynge this, makethe a flakeryng with his wynges. **1565** GOLDING *Ovid's Met* VIII. (1593) 192 Within the compasse of this pond great store of osiers grew.. and flackring flags. **1855** ROBINSON *Whitby Gloss.*, A flackering at the heart.

flacket (ˈflækɪt), *sb.*¹ *Obs.* exc. *dial.* Forms: 4–5 **flacked,** 4–6 **flak(k)et(t(e, flag(g)et(te,** (5 **flagot**), 5–7 **flackett,** (4 **flackette**), 6 *Sc.* **flacat,** 6– **flacket.** [a. ONF. **flaquet*, *flasquet* (= Central OF. *flaschet, flachet*), dim. of *flasque* (*flache, flasche*): see FLASK *sb.* and -ET¹.]

A flask, bottle, or vessel; now applied in dial. use to a barrel-shaped vessel for holding liquor.

c **1320** *Sir Beues* 1298 Bred & flesc out of his male And of his flaketes win & ale. *c* **1350** *Will. Palerne* 1893 Þe flagetes he let falle. **1387** TREVISA *Higden* (Rolls) III. 171 A flakett ful of manis blood. **1465** *Mann. & Househ. Exp.* 490 My master payd fore a flaket of sylver, xx. s. **1539** BIBLE (Great) *1 Sam.* xvi. 20 Isai toke an asse laden with breed, and a flacket of wyne. **1673** *Depos. Cast. York* (Surtees) 196 She gott a flackett of ale. **1753** MAITLAND *Hist. Edin.* I. iii. 37 Two Flackets of eight pounds weight. **1936** W. JAMES *Gangways & Corridors* v. 51 A verse my grandfather used to repeat to me.. When I was a boy No bigger than a flacket Half a yard of flannel Would make me a jacket.

† **ˈflacket,** *sb.*² *Obs. rare.* [? f. next vb.] A bunch (of hair). Cf. FLAGGAT.

1599 HAKLUYT *Voy.* II. I. 113 Sixe goodly yong ladies.. had vpon their heads caps of Goldsmiths worke, hauing great flackets of haire, hanging out on each side.

flacket (ˈflækɪt), *v. dial.* and *U.S.* [freq. of FLACK *v.*: cf. ON. *flǫkta* of same meaning.] *intr.* To flap *about.*

1823 MOOR *Suffolk Words* s.v., Womens ribbons or loose geer are said to 'Flacket about'. It is more expressive than *flap*.. A dressy loose woman would have the former word figuratively applied to her 'She'll go flacketen about'. **1863** A. D. WHITNEY *Faith Gartney* v. 45 You go flacketting out, bareheaded, into the streets, after a topping jade like that. **1885** J. SPILLING *Daisy Dimple* ix. 72, I see her go past flackerting with him last night.

flackoun, flacon, obs. forms of FLAGON.

‖ **flacon** (flakɔ̃). [F. *flacon*; the word was adopted in wider sense in ME.; see FLAGON.] A

small stoppered bottle; *esp.* a scent-bottle or smelling-bottle.

1824 Scott *Redgauntlet* Let. xii, The exercise of the fan, the *flacon* and the other duties of the *Cavaliere Serviente.* **1841** Lady Blessington *Idler in France* I. 251 A flacon of rock crystal. **1872** Longf. in *Life* (1891) III. 208 An oblong ebony tray, with two glass *flacons* for the ink.

‖**fladbrod, -bröd** (ˈflatbrøː, ˈflɑːbrøː). [Da. (Norw.) *fladbröd*, mod.Norw. *flatbröd*, lit. flat bread.] A type of thin unleavened bread eaten in Norway.

1799 Malthus *Jrnl.* 12 June (1966) 60 The Norwegians who are used to the flad brod made of oatmeal always find the rye bread disagree with them. **1881** P. B. Du Chaillu *Land Midnight Sun* I. 394 *Fladbröd* is made from an unfermented dough of barley and oat-meal, often mixed with pea-flour. **1903** B. Harraden *Kath. Frensham* II. v. 144 To-morrow Mette makes Fladbröd. **1963** 'G. Carr' *Lewker in Norway* iv. 82 Two packets of the thin but nourishing Norwegian biscuit-bread called *fladbrod.*

flae, Sc. form of FLEA.

flael(le, obs. form of FLAIL.

flaff (flæf), *sb.* Chiefly *Sc.* [cf. next vb.] A flutter or flapping of the wings; also, a puff, gust.

1827 Wilson *Noct. Ambr.* (1855) I. 277 The snow was.. giving them sair flaffs and dads on their faces. **1827** W. Tennant *Papistry Storm'd* 25 He..gave his wings a flaff. **1833** M. Scott *Tom Cringle* xviii. 509 Merely helping themselves over the top by a small flaff of their wings. **1834** —— *Cruise Midge* (1836) I. ii. 50 When with a flaff and a rustling brush through the topmost leaves he [the owl] came down. **1894** Crockett *Raiders* 301 A flaf o' wind.

flaff (flæf), *v. Sc.* [onomatopœic; cf. FLAP.]

1. *intr.* To flap, make a flapping; to flutter. Of the lungs or heart: To pant or throb.

1513 Douglas *Æneis* XII. xiii. 175 This vengeabill wraik.. Evyn in the face..of Turnus Can fle and flaf. **1786** Burns *Addr. of Beelzebub* 47 Flaffan wi' duds..Frightin' awa your deucks an' geese [etc.]. **1815** G. Beattie *John o' Arnha'* in *Life* (1863) 252 The watchfu' mate flaff'd i' the gale Wi' eerie screech. **1880** *Antrim & Down Gloss., Flaff*, to flutter or flap.

2. *trans.* To flap (the wings).

1827 W. Tennant *Papistry Storm'd* 5 Thou..flaff'd thy wings, and in a crack Flew frae th' unsicker stance!

Hence ˈ**flaffing** *vbl. sb.* and *ppl. a.*

1513 Douglas *Æneis* X. vii. 63 All the blayd, vp to the hylt and hand, Amyd hys flaffand longis [*in tumido pulmone*] hyd hes he. **1584** Hudson *Du Bartas' Judith* 708 A thousand flaffing flags. **1833** Moir *Mansie Wauch* xii. 79 A severe shaking of the knees and a flaffing of the heart.

flaffer (ˈflæfə(r)), *v. north. dial.* [f. FLAFF *v.* + -ER[5].] *intr.* To move with a rustling motion; to flutter. Also with *out.*

17.. *Colin Clout* in Aitken *Scott. Song* 189 Mony a birdie ..Flaffered briskly roun about. **1863** Robson *Bards of Tyne* 342 Oft fra its nest..It flaffer'd out at neets, man.

flafte, obs. var. of FLAUGHT *sb*[1].

flag (flæg), *sb.*[1] Also 4–7 **flagg(e,** (5 **flegge**). [Of obscure origin; cf. Du. *flag*, occurring in Bible 1637, *Job* viii. 11 *margin* (the Eng. Bible has the same word in this passage), also mod.Da. *flæg* (in *Dansk Ordb.* 1802, but not found in MDa., which has *flæ, flæde* in the same sense).]

1. a. One of various endogenous plants, with a bladed or ensiform leaf, mostly growing in moist places. Now regarded as properly denoting a member of the genus *Iris* (esp. *I. pseudacorus*) but sometimes (as in early use) applied to any reed or rush.

1387 Trevisa *Higden* (Rolls) IV. 157 þere herdes fond hym among mory flagges and sprayes, and sente hym to Silla. *c* **1440** *Promp. Parv.* 165 Flegge, *infra in* S. *idem quod* Sedge. *a* **1533** Ld. Berners *Gold. Bk. M. Aurel.* (1546) Q, The drye flaxe will brenne in the fyre, and the grene flagge smoke in the flame. **1563** B. Googe *Eglogs* viii. (Arb.) 64 He that once preserued in Flags, the sely suckyng Chylde. **1624** Capt. Smith *Virginia* II. 26 The chiefe root they haue for food..groweth like a flagge in Marishes. **1763** Churchill *Duellist* I, On Lethe's Stream, like flags, to rot. **1842** *Guide to Trade, Cooper* 74 A flag or rush should be put round the groove. **1873** G. C. Davies *Mount. & Mere* ii. 6 Gazing with a feeling akin to awe at..the tall rushes and flags.

b. With words indicating the species, as **garden flag** (*Iris germanica*); **sweet smelling flag,** spicewort (*Acorus Calamus*); **water flag, yellow flag** (*Iris pseudacorus*). Also CORN-FLAG.

c **1550** Lloyd *Treas. Health* (1585) E iv b, The ioyce of yeolowe flagge put into thine eare is of the same operation. **1578** Lyte *Dodoens* II. xxxv. 193 That kinde [of Iris] whose flower is purple and blewe is called..of some..garden flagges. **1580** Baret *Alv.* F 639 The water Flagge, or the yellowe wild Iris. **1640** Parkinson *Theat. Bot.* I. xlviii. 139 The sweet smelling Flagge. **1831** J. Davies *Manual Mat. Med.* 373 The American Blue Flag, *Iris versicolor.*

c. In *pl.* or *collect. sing.* A kind of coarse grass.

1577 Holinshed *Chron.* I. 185 The hay of our low meadows is..also more rooty, foggy and full of flags. **1639** Horn & Rob. *Gate Lang. Unl.* xxxii, Arable ground being.. cleared from the roots of the flag. **1847** Halliwell, *Flag*.. also applied to the small pieces of coarse grass common in some meadows. **1878–86** Britten & Holland *Plant-n., Flag* (3)..Probably *Aira cæspitosa* L.

¶ **d.** Used for ALGA. *Obs.*

1778 Milne *Bot. Dict., Algæ*, Flags. **1807** J. E. Smith *Phys. Bot.* 402 *Algæ*, Flags, whose herb is likewise a frond.

2. The blade or long slender leaf of a plant, e.g. of *Iris* and of cereals.

1578 Lyte *Dodoens* II. xxxv. 193 The narrow leaved Ireos, his flagges be long and narrowe. **1599** T. M[oufet] *Silkwormes* 34 Sweetest Iris beareth shortest flagges. **1750** W. Ellis *Mod. Husbandm.* II. i. 38 This Oat has not only a strong large Stalk and Ear to nourish, but also a broad Flag besides. **1850** Bromfield in *Phytologist* III. 1006 The green leaves [of *Typha latifolia*]..are used..for mats, chair-bottoms and basket-work, under the name of flags. **1880** Jefferies *Gt. Estate* 8 The wheat was then showing a beautiful flag.

†**3.** ? = *flag-basket. Obs.*

1640 in Entick *London* (1766) II. 182 For every twenty sugar flags. **1812** J. Smyth *Pract. of Customs* (1821) 23 Annotto, Package tared, and 6 per Cent. allowed for Flags.

4. *attrib.* and *Comb.* as ***flag-bed, -flower, -grass*** (U.S.), ***-pond, -root; flag-bottomed, -fenced,*** †***-shaggy*** adjs. Also **flag-basket** *dial.*, a basket made of reeds, chiefly used by workmen for carrying their tools; **flag-broom** (see FLAG *sb.*[2] 5); **flag-leaf,** an iris; **flag-lily,** the common yellow flag, *Iris pseudacorus*, and other irises; **flag-reed** (see quot.); **flag-worm,** a worm found in the roots of flags and used by anglers.

1747 H. Purefoy *Let.* 9 Dec. (1931) II. 280 Pray bring a *flag Basket or Wallet to take them [*sc.* books] away with you. **1859** Geo. Eliot *A. Bede* 262 Emptying his tools out of the flag-basket. **1656** Trapp *Comm. Eph.* vi. 4 Like Moses in the *flag-bed. **1840** R. H. Dana *Bef. Mast* xxviii. 96 Furniture, including a dozen *flag-bottomed chairs. **1878** Smiles *Robt. Dick* vii. 79 Beyond them the *flag-fenced fields in the distance. **1753** Chambers *Cycl.* Supp., **Flag-flower*. See *Iris*. **1801** Southey *Thalaba* XI. xxxiv, The flag-flower blossom'd on its side. **1848** W. H. Emory *Notes Milit. Reconn.* 92 It [*sc.* the island] was overgrown with willow, cane, Gila grass, *flag grass, &c. **1827** Clare *Sheph. Cal.* 53 Mint and *flagleaf, swording high Their blooms to the unthinking eye. **1884** 'C. E. Craddock' *In Tenn. Mts.* I. 18 Among their roots *flag-lilies..and devil-in-the-bush mingled in a floral mosaic. **1922** A. S. Macmillan *Pop. Names Flowers Somerset* 107 Flag Lily. Yellow Iris, *Iris Pseudacorus*. **1652** *Rec. Providence, R.I.* (1893) II. 64 John Field shall have the *Flagge-pond. **1680** *Portsmouth* (R.I.) *Rec.* 204 The flag pond where the fence now stands. **1837** T. C. Haliburton *Clockmaker* 1st Ser. ix. 66 He chases [the horses]..over ditches, creeks, wire holes, and flag ponds. **1833** Sturt *S. Australia* II. vii. 181 The reeds are the broad *flag-reed (*arundo phragmatis*). **1707** J. Mortimer *Husb.* (1708) 287 At D is a spade..the Edges of which are as sharp as a knife, which makes it easie to cut *Flag-roots. **1881** S. P. McLean *Cape Cod Folks* v. 107 Grandma fed him with bits of unsweetened flag-root. **1605** Sylvester *Du Bartas* II. iii. IV. *Captains* 123 Th' agéd Floud..pensive leaning his *flag-shaggie head Upon a Tuft. **1653** Walton *Angler* 178 He will also in the three hot months..bite at a *Flag-worm, or at a green Gentle. **1787** Best *Angling* (ed. 2) 19 Flag-worms, or Dock-worms. Found among flags.

flag (flæg), *sb.*[2] Also 5, 7 **flagg(e.** [Cf. Icel. *flag* neut. the spot where a turf has been cut out, ON. *flaga* wk. fem. slab of stone (cogn. with FLAY *v.*); these appear in Eng. as FLAW *sb.*[1], but some dialects have app. retained *-ag-* in adoption of ON. words. Cf. also FLAKE *sb.*[2], FLAUGHT[1].].

1. a. A piece cut out of or pared off the sward; a turf, sod. Also *collect.* Now *dial.* (*E. Anglian*).

c **1440** *Promp. Parv.* 16 Flagge of þe erthe..*terricidium.* **1633** P. Fletcher *Purple Isl.* VIII. lvi. 120 Upon his shield an heap of fennie mire In flagges and turfs..Did smoth'ring lie, not burn. **1691** Ray *S. & E.C. Words* (E.D.S.), *Flags*, the surface of the earth, which they pare off to burn; the upper turf. *Norf.* **1847** *Jrnl. R. Agric. Soc.* VIII. II. 306 The flags are burnt in small heaps. *Ibid.* Ser. II. III. II. 659 Covered with grass flag, cut 3 inches thick.

b. The slice of earth turned over by the plough-share; also, the ground thus made ready for sowing. *dial.* (*E. Anglian*) only.

1787 Marshall *E. Norf. Words* (E.D.S.), *Flag*, the furrow turned. **1795** *Annals Agric.* XXIII. 27 To dibble beans, one row on each flag. **1800** *Trans. Soc. Encourag. Arts* XVIII. 109 The plough..turned over a flag of nine inches. **1823** Moor *Suffolk Words, Flag*..the portion of clover land turned at once by the plough. *a* **1825** Forby *Voc. E. Anglia, Flag* 2, The surface of a clover lay of the second year, turned up by the plough. The wheat for the next year's crop is dibbled into the *flag.* **1845** *Jrnl. R. Agric. Soc.* V. II. 340 Nothing rose to cover the ground after the first mowing, so as to make a flag for the wheat.

2. a. A flat slab of any fine-grained rock which may be split into flagstones; a flagstone.

1604 *Vestry Bks.* (Surtees) 282 A cesse of iij*d.* the pound shalbe levied for the winninge of flaggs. **1658** in Picton *L'pool Munic. Rec.* (1883) I. 188 That a new flagge be laid over the watercourse. **1774** Pennant *Tour Scotl. in 1772*, 297 A stone chest formed of six flags. **1799** J. Robertson *Agric. Perth* 34 The brown flags..were at one period used.. in covering houses. **1839** E. D. Clarke *Trav.* 33/1 The new promenade..is paved with large flags. **1871** Tyndall *Fragm. Sc.* (1879) I. xii. 308 With a hammer and chisel I can cleave them into flags.

b. *pl.* A flagged foot-pavement.

1802 Mar. Edgeworth *Moral T.* (1816) I. xiii. 106 Dancing dogs, that he was exhibiting upon the flags. **1850** Clough *Dipsychus* II. iv. 3 Shall I..like the walking shoe-black roam the flags To see whose boots are dirtiest?

3. *Salt-mining.* 'A very hard kind of marl found near the first bed of rock salt' (*Chester Gloss.* 1884).

1883 Gresley *Gloss. Coal Mining.* **1892** *Cornhill Mag.* Sept. 263 A shaft is sunk till the 'flag' or 'bean metal' has been pierced.

4. *Glass-making.* (See quot.)

1883 Chance in Powell *Principles Glass-making* 111 These grate-rooms are sunk several feet below the level of the bed of the furnace, and are separated from each other by a portion of the bed, which is called the flag.

5. *attrib.* and *Comb.*, as ***flag-way; flag-like, -paved*** adjs. Also ? **flag-broom** (see quots.; perh. belongs to FLAG *sb.*[1]); **flag-harrow,** a harrow for thoroughly breaking up the flag (sense 1 b); **flag-sandstone,** sandstone that may be split into flags (sense 2). And FLAG-STONE.

1697 Dampier *Voy.* I. 150 The Leaves that make the brush part of the *Flag-brooms which are brought into England..are..a small kind of Palmeto. **1755** Johnson, *Flag-broom*, a broom for sweeping flags or pavements.. commonly made of birch-twigs, or of the leaves of the dwarf palm. **1845** *Jrnl. R. Agric. Soc.* V. II. 333 The land..may be broken down by a *flag-harrow, called by some a crab-harrow. **1849** Murchison *Siluria* vii. 125 These *flaglike strata. **1895** *Daily News* 21 Nov. 6/2 The street is *flag-paved. **1926** W. J. Locke *Old Bridge* II. vii, A narrow flag-paved street. **1843** Portlock *Geol.* 505 The micaceous *flag sandstones of the old red are highly calcareous. **1800** in *Spirit Public Jrnls.* (1801) IV. 263 The *flag-way is pleasant to saunter and idle. **1875** Le Fanu *Will. Die* xix. 116 He walked slowly up and down the silent flagway.

flag (flæg), *sb.*[3] [perh. subst. use of FLAG *a.*, though that is not recorded so early. Cf. FAG *sb.*[2] 1.]

1. a. *pl.* The quill-feathers of a bird's wing; in quot. 1486 the cubital or secondary feathers of a hawk's wing. Also *attrib.* **b.** (See quot.)

a. 1486 *Bk. St. Albans* B j, The federis at the wynges next the body be calde the flagg or the fagg federis. **1575** Turberv. *Faulconrie* 274 Otherwhile it chaunceth, through the hurte of a Hawkes wing, that one or twoo of hir Flagges ..are broosed. **1615** Tomkis *Albumazar* II. iv, If I mue these Flagges of Yeomanry. **1635** Quarles *Embl.* III. i. (1818) 138 Like as the haggard, cloister'd in her mew..to renew Her broken flags. **1678** Ray *Willughby's Ornith.* 84 The flag-feathers of the Wing [of the Kestrel] are in number twenty four. **1741** Chambers *Cycl.* s.v. *Feather*, The vanes or webs in the flag part of the wing. **1858** W. Clark *Van der Hoeven's Zool.* II. 379 Wings acute, with flag-feathers often short.

b. 1890 Coues *Ornith.* II. iii. 182 Crural feathers are.. sometimes long and flowing, as in the 'flags' of most hawks.

2. *pl.* (See quot.)

1892 Simmonds *Dict. Trade* Suppl., *Flags*, a technical name for a variety of quills.

flag (flæg), *sb.*[4] Also 5–7 **flagge.** [A word found in all mod.Teut. langs., but app. first recorded in Eng.; cf. Da. *flag* (1569 in Kalkar), Sw. *flagg, flagga* (not in Söderwall *MSw. Dict.*), Du. *vlag* (*vlagghe* in Kilian 1599), Ger. *flagge* (17th c.; also *flacke*).

Whether the word originated in Eng., Du., or Scandinavian, it may plausibly be supposed to be an onomatopœic formation, expressing the notion of something flapping in the wind; cf. FLACK *v.*, FLAG *v.*[1], MDu. *vlaggheren* to flutter. If the word be of Eng. origin, there are other possibilities: it might be a transferred use of FLAG *sb.*[1]; or, if the primary sense were 'square of cloth' or the like, it might be the same word as appears in OE. *flacg* 'cataplasma' (Wr.-Wülck. 386) and *flage*, recorded in 1139 as an Eng. name for a baby's garment (Du Cange s.v.).]

1. a. A piece of cloth or stuff (usually bunting), varying in size, colour, and device, but most frequently oblong or square, attached by one edge to a staff or to a halyard, used as a standard, ensign or signal, and also for decoration or display.

For ***black, red, white, yellow flag***, see the adjs. ***bloody flag*** (Shaks. *K. Hen. V*, I. ii. 101): cf. quot. 1724.

[**1481–90** *Howard Househ. Bks.* (Roxb.) 42, ij. stremers, standartes, and ij. fagges.] **1530** Palsgr. 220/2 Flag or baner of a felde, *guidon.* **1595** Shaks. *John* II. i. 207 These flagges of France..Haue hither march'd to your endamagement. **1612** W. Parkes *Curtaine-Dr.* (Grosart) 47 Each Play-house aduanceth his flagge in the aire. **1676** Dryden *Aurengz.* V. i, In either's Flag, the golden Serpents bear, Erected Crests alike. **1702** *Royal Proclam.* in *Lond. Gaz.* No. 3872/1 Any other Flags, Jacks, Pendants or Ensigns. **1724** R. Falconer *Voy.* (1769) 118 They consented to hoist the bloody Flag, and neither to give or take Quarter. **1783** W. Thomson *Watson's Philip III*, VI. 442 The flag of rebellion is displayed throughout all Bohemia. **1834** M. Scott *Tom Cringle* 304 Don't cease firing, although his flag be down—it was none of his doing. **1840** Dickens *Old C. Shop* xix, Flags streamed from windows and house-tops.

transf. and *fig.*

1592 Shaks. *Rom. & Jul.* V. iii. 96 Beauties ensigne yet Is Crymson in thy lips..And Deaths pale flag is not aduanced there. **1604** —— *Oth.* I. i. 157, I must show out a Flag and signe of Loue. **1663** Sir G. Mackenzie *Religious Stoic* xx. (1685) 160 Who would not..bow the flag of his private opinion to the commands of the Church. **1737** Bracken *Farriery Impr.* (1756) I. 351, I have often..been sorry to see a Flag of Horse-Soles hung out upon every silly Smith's Door. **1825** Hone *Every-day Bk.* I. 1254 A white apron may be the 'flag' of the 'Licensed Victualler's profession', but it is not the barber's 'flag'. **1881** Miss Braddon *Asph.* II. 318 She..'blushed celestial red'..her lover..hung out a rosy flag on his own side.

b. ***flag*** (***of truce***): a white flag, carried by a messenger or hoisted on a vessel, to express a wish for parley with the enemy. Hence, the person or the ship dispatched with a flag of truce.

1582 N. Lichefield tr. *Castanheda's Conq. E. Ind.* xlii. 98 Then the enimies helde up a flagge. [*Margin*] This flag was a sign and request of peace. **1627** Capt. Smith *Seaman's Gram.* xiii. 62 They hang out a flag of truce. **1775** R.

MONTGOMERY in Sparks *Corr. Amer. Rev.* (1853) I. 495 Firing upon a flag of truce. **1779** T. JEFFERSON *Let.* Writ. 1893 II. 259 A flag sails hence to-morrow..to negotiate the exchange of some prisoners. **1810** WELLINGTON in Gurw. *Desp.* VI. 107 He should fire upon all flags in future. **1842** CAMPBELL *Napoleon & Brit. Sailor* 62 He gave the tar a piece of gold, And, with a flag of truce, commanded He should be shipp'd to England Old.

c. In various nautical phrases, as ***to give*** (***deny, refuse,*** etc.) ***the honour of the flag***: to make (or refuse) an acknowledgement of supremacy by striking the flag to another; ***to lower*** or ***strike one's flag***: to take it down, *esp.* in token of respect, submission, or surrender; ***the flag of defiance is out!*** (naut. slang) (see quot. 1700); ***to keep the flag flying***: to refuse to haul down one's flag and surrender; to carry on the fight; chiefly *fig.*; ***to show the flag***: (of one of H.M. ships) to make an official visit to a foreign port or elsewhere, showing the White Ensign; also *transf.* and *fig.*; hence ***flag-showing*** vbl. sb. and ppl. a.

1644 MANWAYRING *Sea-mans Dict.* s.v. *Flaggs*, At sea to lower or strike ones Flagg in fight is a token of yeelding, but otherwise of great obedience and respect. **1673** LD. SHAFTESBURY *Parl. Sp.* in *Collect. Poems* 235 They came to that height of insolence, as to deny the Honour and right of the Flag. *a* **1700** B. E. *Dict. Cant. Crew* s.v. *Flagg*.. *The Flag of Defiance is out*, (among the Tars) the Fellow's Face is very Red, and he is Drunk. **1779** F. HERVEY *Naval Hist.* II. 146 Firing upon a Dutch man of war who refused him the honour of the flag. **1802** WINDHAM *Sp. Definit. Treaty* 13 May, Sp. (1812) III. 428 The notion that peace would hush up all our dangers had induced us to give up to Holland the honour of the flag. **1881** PALGRAVE *Visions Eng.* 275 Above the war-thunder came shouting, as foe struck his flag after foe. **1914** J. W. STALKER (*song title*) Keep the old flag flying. **1918** A. HURD *Brit. Fleet Gt. War* iv. 48 It was only..by releasing 11,000 or 12,000 trained officers and men from non-fighting ships—vessels that 'showed the flag', to quote the phrase of the moment—that it became possible..to obtain crews for what was to become the Grand Fleet. **1919** BEERBOHM *Seven Men* 20 Neither he nor his work received the slightest encouragement; but he persisted in behaving as a personage: always he kept his dingy little flag flying. **1931** *Times Lit. Suppl.* 1 Oct. 740/3 Professor Warfield kept the flag flying in the theological seminary of Princeton. **1937** PARTRIDGE *Dict. Slang* 281/1 *Show the flag*, to put in an appearance, just to show that one is there. **1957** D. MACINTYRE *Jutland* iii. 36 There had been flag-showing cruises. **1959** *Listener* 14 May 826/2 'Showing the flag' means a British ship going to a foreign port. **1963** *Times* 7 Feb. 18/6 This was a genuine effort on the bank's part to show the flag at a time when they thought it should be shown. A series of six British products would be advertised. **1965** A. NICOL *Truly Married Woman* 29 They had formed a literary club to keep the flag of culture flying.

d. A metal plate bearing the words 'For Hire' affixed to the meter of a taxi.

The flag is raised when the vehicle is disengaged, and when engaged is lowered to start the meter and register the fare due for the distance travelled.

1909 *Daily Chron.* 26 June 6/2 Taxi-cab 'flag up' case... A taxicab driver..was found guilty of defrauding his employers..by driving a cab of the company with the flag up, thus putting into his own pocket money that should have gone to the company. **1910** *Punch* 14 Dec. 421/1 Or in the pouring rain..a taxi will go by with the flag up. **1924** C. MACKENZIE *Old Men of Sea* i. 3, I would walk by the kerb and peer with futile optimism at the drooping flags of the many taxis. **1969** 'J. MORRIS' *Fever Grass* i. 5 The driver.. did not lean across to lift the little red metal flag of the meter mounted on the dashboard by the left front window.

e. *Sporting.* A flag used chiefly to indicate the start or finish of a race; also, a device on a chess-clock which falls when the time-limit is reached. So ***to drop the flag***, to give the signal for the start or finish; also, ***the flag falls***.

1856 'STONEHENGE' *Man. Brit. Sport* viii. 203 The Duties of the Flag-Steward are to..see that the flagman hoists the right flag... The Field-Stewards..should have one or two flagmen with blue flags. **1890** 'R. BOLDREWOOD' *Col. Reformer* xx, He will be there, or thereabouts, when the flag falls, I'll lay. **1890** in A. E. T. Watson *Turf* (1898) 232 Every horse shall be considered as having started which is under the Starter's orders when the advance flag has been raised. **1895** MANSON *Sporting Dict.* s.v. *Distance Judges*, When the first horse reaches the winning post, one of the judges there drops a flag. **1898** in A. E. T. Watson *Turf* iv. 113 It had been supposed by many that no horse of this age could win with so heavy a burden; but there was never any doubt as to the result after the flag had fallen. **1925** E. F. NORTON *Fight for Everest, 1924* 200 It would be a great help to the leader of a future expedition in making up his mind when to 'drop the flag'. **1930** *Brit. Chess Mag.* I. 48 In a time-scramble.. the Hungarian's flag actually fell. **1951** 'ASSIAC' *Adv. in Chess* III. ii. 93 Reshevsky..would remain quite unperturbable by the nerve-racking need to make half a dozen moves or more with the 'flag' on his clock about to drop in a matter of seconds. **1969** A. GLYN *Dragon Variation* ii. 49 Carl's clock flag had now fallen, but it didn't matter any more. The game was over.

f. ***flag of convenience***: a foreign flag under which a ship is registered in order to avoid certain duties, charges, etc.

1956 *Times* 20 Aug. 7/2 'We Greeks didn't invent the so-called flag of convenience,' he said, somewhat indignantly. **1957** *Britannica Bk. of Yr.* 416/2 The phenomenal growth of merchant fleets registered under the flags of such non-maritime countries as Liberia and Panama began [in 1956] to cause alarm... The ownership of such vessels, under what came to be known as 'flags of convenience', was vested mainly in U.S. and Greek companies and citizens of other nationalities. Owners of ships registered in such countries were able to avoid the high rates of taxation applicable in most of the traditional maritime countries, or, in the case of U.S. companies, the handicaps of U.S. shipping legislation. **1971** B. CALLISON *Plague of Sailors* iii. 94 'Owners?' I queried. 'Greek firm—it's a flag of convenience set-up—called Manentis Shipping.'

g. A statement of the name, ownership, etc., of a publication, or of its name alone, as printed on the editorial page or the front page.

1956 E. C. ARNOLD *Functional Newspaper Design* vi. 108 Some papers have dropped the article *The* from their flag. **1967** *Boston Globe* 18 May 27/5 The New York Times recently made a sensational change in its 'flag' across the top of Page One.

h. *Computers.* A symbol or symbols used to indicate some property of the data in a record.

1959 *Jrnl. Assoc. Comput. Mach.* VI. 147 It is necessary to define the information with flag words inserted directly in the physical records. *Ibid.* 148 There are a number of end flags which indicate the end of a string of information. **1967** Cox & GROSE *Organiz. Bibl. Rec. by Computer* 151 The fields and their 'flags' are specified..to ensure consistency in input.

2. *Naut.* **a.** A flag carried by a flagship to indicate that an admiral is in command, an admiral's emblem of rank afloat. Hence, of the admiral, ***to hoist*** or ***strike one's flag***: to enter upon, or relinquish command.

1695 *Lond. Gaz.* No. 3088/4 A Squadron of Dutch Ships, whereof 3 carried Flags. **1697** *Ibid.* No. 3329/4 Sir George Rooke hoisted his Flag on Board the Defyance. **1707** *Ibid.* No. 4390/3 This Morning he struck his Flag on board the Nassau. **1769–89** FALCONER *Dict. Marine* s.v. *Admiral*, Admirals that have carried no flag. **1796** NELSON in Nicolas *Disp.* II. 187 The Admiral thinks I shall be ordered to hoist my Flag here. **1809** SIR A. HAMMOND in G. Rose *Diaries* (1860) II. 359, I never meant to charge him with having deprived me of my flag. **1867** SMYTH *Sailor's Word-bk.*, *Flag*..Also, a certain banner by which an admiral is distinguished at sea from the inferior ships of his squadron.

b. A ship carrying an admiral's flag, a flagship.

1652 *Perfect Account* No. 101. 2065 The Garland..was engaged by two Dutch Flags. **1710** *Lond. Gaz.* No. 4755/2 That they did not do it is attributed to the Loss of their two Flags. **1829** MARRYAT *F. Mildmay* vii. (Rtldg.) 67, I.. quitted the flag with a light heart.

c. Applied to the admiral himself. Also, ***flag!*** the answer returned to a sentry's challenge by an admiral's boat.

1665 PEPYS *Diary* (1879) III. 274 Not giving to all the Commanders, as well as the Flaggs. **1719** SIR E. BYNG in *Torrington Mem.* (1889) p. xi, My whole pay as a flag of the fleet. **1747** J. LIND *Lett. Navy* (1757) I. 23 If more than two flags, then the commander in chief is to have one half of the eight. **1867** SMYTH *Sailor's Word-bk.*, *Flag*.

d. *pl.* A flag-lieutenant. *Naut. slang.*

1929 F. C. BOWEN *Sea Slang* 49 *Flags*, a Flag Lieutenant. **1936** *S.P.E. Tract* XLVII. 257 His Admiral and perhaps others will continue to call him 'the Flag Lieutenant' (familiarly 'Flags').

3. *slang.* An apron.

1851 MAYHEW *Lond. Labour* (1861) I. 218 *Flag*, an apron. **1882** *Echo* 29 Aug. 1/5 Ere long we may expect to hear that a Congress of Servant-girls has been discussing the use of the 'flag'.

4. *Sporting.* The tail of a setter or Newfoundland dog. Also of a deer; occas. of a horse. Cf. quots. under FLAG *a*.

1859 'STONEHENGE' (J. H. Walsh) *Dog* I. iv. 97 The stern, or flag [of the setter]..is furnished with a fan-like brush of long hair. **1883** G. STABLES *Our Friend the Dog* vii. 60 *Flag*, the tail, applied to Setters and Newfoundlands. **1891** R. KIPLING *Plain Tales* 148 A switch-tailed demirep of a mare called Arab because she has a kink in her flag.

5. ? = FAG *sb.*[2] 2.

1874 KNIGHT *Dict. Mech.* I. 875/2 *Flag*, the uneven end of an uncut tuft of hair in a brush. **1893** *Standard Dict.*, *Flag*, the split end of a bristle.

6. *Printing.* A mark made by the corrector of a proof, showing an omission by the compositor of some words which are written by the corrector in the margin; an 'out'.

7. *attrib.* and *Comb.*, as ***flag-bearer, -case, -planter, -planting, -pole***; ***flag-bedecked, -bedizened, -decked, -hung*** adjs.; ***flag-wise*** adv. Also **flag-boat**, a mark-boat in sailing or rowing matches; **flag-captain**, the captain of a flagship; **flag-day**, (*a*) *U.S.*, the anniversary of the adoption by Congress of the Stars and Stripes as the American national flag on June 14th, 1777; (*b*) a day on which money is raised for a cause by the sale of small paper flags or other tokens which are worn as evidence that the wearer has contributed; **flag discrimination** *Comm.*, the application of differential duties or charges according to a ship's nationality; **flag-dues** (see quot.); **flag-fall**, the falling or dropping of a flag to indicate the start of a race (see 1 e); †**flag-fallen** *a.*, unemployed; said of actors in allusion to the lowering of the play-house flag as a sign of closing; **flag-flying**, (*a*) the flying of flags; (*b*) *colloq.*, over-bidding at Bridge; so ***flag-flier***; (*c*) *slang* (see quot. 1889); **flag-furling** *a.* (*fig.*), disposed to cease fighting, pacific; **flag-lieutenant**, an officer acting as an aide-de-camp to an admiral; **flag line** *U.S.*, a transport line flying the flag of a specified country; **flag-list**, the roll of flag-officers or admirals; **flag-pay**, the pay of a flag-officer or admiral; **flagpole sitter**, one who sits on top of a flag-pole, for exhibition, etc.; **flag-raising** *vbl. sb.* (*U.S.*), a ceremonious hoisting of a party flag; **flag-rank**, the rank of admiral; **flag-share**, an admiral's share (one-eighth) of prize-money; **flag-signal** *v.*, to signal by means of flags; so **flag-signaller**; **flag-station** (*Railways*), a place where trains stop only when signalled to do so; **flag-wagger** *slang*, (*a*) a flag-signaller; (*b*) = *flag-waver*; **flag-wagging**, (*a*) *Milit. slang*, signalling with flags held in the hand; also *attrib.*; (*b*) = *flag-waving*; also *attrib.*; **flag-waver**, one who tries to arouse popular enthusiasm; so **flag-waving** *vbl. sb.* Also FLAG-OFFICER, FLAGSHIP, FLAGSTAFF.

1835 LYTTON *Rienzi* II iii, The different servitors and *flag-bearers ranged themselves on the steps without. **1904** *Daily Chron.* 12 Aug. 5/7 The *flag-bedecked town. **1906** *Ibid.* 9 May 7/4 The flag-bedecked fleet. **1937** KOESTLER *Spanish Testament* i. 29 Bending over a flag-bedecked map with Colonel Questa and a German airman. **1887** *Times* (weekly ed.) 24 June 4/4 The houses..were largely *flag-bedizened. **1815** *Sporting Mag.* XLVI. 187 The Caroline passed first round the *flag-boat. **1829** MARRYAT *F. Mildmay* vii. (Rtldg.) 66, I..saw the *flag-captain. **1870** COLOMB & BOLTON *Flashing Signals* 39 The *flag-case is made of strong patent leather. **1894** *Chicago Tribune* 17 June 1/7 American *Flag Day has come to stay. **1905** *N.Y. Even. Post* 10 June 9 Flags shall fly from the City Hall on June 14 in observance of Flag Day. **1914** *Scotsman* 5 Oct. 10/3 The Flag Day effort organised to help the Belgian Relief Fund. **1919** G. B. SHAW *Heartbreak House* p. xvii, The passionate penny collecting of the Flag Days was brought under some sort of regulation. **1899** *Daily News* 18 July 6/3 In *flag-decked cages. **1926** M. LEINSTER *Dew on Leaf* 41 Flag-decked floating temple. **1928** *Britain's Industr. Future* (*Liberal Ind. Inquiry*) I. v. §2. 50 They pointed out the disadvantages of indirect methods of Protection, such as subsidies, *flag discrimination, [etc.]. **1959** *Listener* 28 May 920/1 Other governments assist their National Flag lines by ship-building subventions, operating subsidies, and flag discrimination. **1892** SIMMONDS *Dict. Trade* Suppl., **Flag Dues*, a charge on ships, in some harbours, for hoisting flags. **1899** *Westm. Gaz.* 16 May 5/3 At Newmarket,..in two consecutive races, the favourite was practically out of the race at *flagfall. **1922** E. WALLACE *Flying Fifty-Five* xxvi. 153 But Besse o' the Barn was not favourite at flag-fall. **1609** ROWLEY *Search for Money* B iij/1 Foure or fiue *flag-falne Plaiers. **1927** *Observer* 29 May 25 The more sober and sane *flag-fliers who calculate risks. **1889** BARRÈRE & LELAND *Dict. Slang*, **Flag flying* (tailors) is used in reference to a bill posted up when hands are required. **1904** *Westm. Gaz.* 10 Aug. 2/3 There was some diversity in the flag-flying on the various official and semi-official buildings. **1917** E. BERGHOLT *Royal Auction Bridge* 101 'Flag-flying'. In the early days of Auction, it was considered a very heroic thing, when you saw that the opponents would make game on their call, to rush in with an overbid that you were sure would fail, in order to keep the game alive. **1918** *Ibid.* (ed. 2) 152 As this is an instructive example of 'flag-flying' it is as well to compare the two results in figures. **1928** *Daily Express* 21 May 3/7 Jack, with a pitying smile for Sam's heroic flag-flying, doubled—and Sam made a grand slam. **1947** S. HARRIS *Fund. Princ. Contract Bridge* I. iii. 31 The business double..can obviously be used with great effect against reckless flag-flying. **1802** in *Spirit Public Jrnls.* (1803) VI. 174 A fresh assortment of *flag-furling orations, expected by the pacific packet. **1897** E. L. VOYNICH *Gadfly* III. viii, The sunlit blaze of carpeted street and *flag-hung walls. **1905** *Daily Chron.* 25 Dec. 3/5 The Rev. Michael Adler preached a sermon from the flag-hung pulpit. **1798** NELSON in Nicolas *Disp.* III. 2 Your note..about the *Flag Lieutenant. **1944** B. HERSHEY *Skyways of Tomorrow* v. 83 To this observer it becomes clear that unlimited competition for routes by various United States *flag lines would tend very strongly toward weakening the ability of any United States aviation company to compete. **1873** COLOMB *Let.* 11 June in *Fifteen Yrs. Naval Retirement* (1886) 13 A large nominally active *Flag List. **1719** SIR E. BYNG in *Torrington Mem.* (1889) p. ix, My *flag pay. **1901** *Westm. Gaz.* 28 Oct. 2/2 The Frenchman..is an indefatigable *flag-planter. **1899** *Daily News* 12 July 4/4 Foreign politics in these regions, not content with pinpricks and *flag-plantings. **1901** *Westm. Gaz.* 10 Oct. 3/1 This plan of flag-planting is distinctly ingenious. We shall have to speak of planting out flags (instead of pegging out claims) for posterity. **1884** *Pall Mall G.* 9 Sept. 3/2 That is a contretemps to which annexation by *flagpoles is occasionally exposed. **1931** *Kansas City Star* 18 Sept., A man who would do that would do most anything, even to being a *flagpole sitter. **1939** A. KEITH *Land below Wind* x. 171 The flagpole sitter rests on the top of his flagpole. **1864** SALA in *Daily Tel.* 18 Nov., *Flag-raising consists in stretching a big banner..across a street, and this banner contains a colossal transcription of the particular 'ticket' which the flag-raisers support. **1894** *Westm. Gaz.* 7 Sept. 8/2 His profession of the Protestant faith having prevented his attaining *flag rank. **1867** SMYTH *Sailor's Word-bk.*, **Flag-share*. **1888** KIPLING *Soldiers Three* (1889) 15 As if he were *flag-signallin' to t' world at large. **1910** H. G. WELLS *Mr. Polly* vi. 130 His mind passed to Mrs. Larkins and the bonnet that was to gain such a hold upon him; it seemed to be flag-signalling as she advanced. **1930** *Daily Express* 6 Sept. 5/5 To make the robot swing his arms and go through the *flag-signaller's alphabet. **1852** *Hist. etc. County Oxford* 681 Here [Gosford] is a *flag station on the Oxford and Bletchley branch of the London and North-Western Railway. **1919** *Athenæum* 11 July 582/2 *Flag-wagger. **1966** *Guardian* 30 Sept. 6/8 An imperialist, a flagwagger. **1971** *Daily Tel.* 18 June 14/6 No mere flag wagger, Mr Marten adopted the cool advocacy of a barrister presenting a well-studied brief. **1887** *Pall Mall G.* 24 Mar. 11/1 So..slow a process as that of '*flag wagging'. **1898** *Westm. Gaz.* 21 Sept. 2/2 Flag-taking (like 'flag-wagging') is more exhilarating than remunerative. **1908** *Ibid.* 20 Nov. 2/2 Flag-wagging rhetoric. **1915** G. ADAM *Behind Scenes at Front* 130 The old name of Army Signals still exists, but flag-wagging is to Signals what Euclid is to mathematics. **1916** 'BOYD CABLE' *Action Front* 152 Wally and me was both in the flag-wagging class. **1928** *Daily Express* 6 June 13 To

live among them without flag-wagging or publicity. **1956** BANNERMAN *Birds Brit. Isles* V. 121 The approaching birds scattered..and no amount of frantic flag-wagging by the flankers would turn them. **1958** *Times* 1 Feb. 3/3 That is not a threat, is not flag-wagging, and it is not bluff. **1894** *Westm. Gaz.* 28 June 2/3 The Pretoria *flag-wavers. **1892** *Pall Mall G.* 12 Nov. 2/2 *Flag-waving is all very well, but it is a miserable proceeding when influenced by such sordid motives. **1849** D. ROCK *Ch. of Fathers* II. I. vii. 490 Figures ..fastened *flag-wise upon staves. **1906** *Westm. Gaz.* 8 June 2/1 One leaf left, flagwise, on its battered stem.

†**flag**, *sb.*[5] *Sc. Obs.* [Cf. ON. *flagð* similarly used.] An opprobrious term applied to a woman.

1500-20 DUNBAR *Poems* xiv. 71 Sic fartingaillis on flaggis als fatt as quhailis. **1535** LYNDESAY *Satyre* 2137 Ane fistand flag. **1866** EDMONDSTOUN *Shetland & Orkn. Gloss.*, *Flaag*, a large clumsy woman.

†**flag**, *sb.*[6] *Sc. Obs.* [var. of FLAW; cf. Sw. *flaga*, *wind flaga*, Du. *vlaag*, earlier *vlaeghe*, *vlage*.] A blast or gust (of wind); a squall. ***flag of fire***: a flash of lightning.

1513 DOUGLAS *Æneis* I. iii. 61 With fluidis ourset the Troianis, and at vndir By flaggis and rayne did fra the hevin descend. *Ibid.* VII. Prol. 49 Dym skyis oft furth warpit feirfull levyne, Flaggis of fyir and mony felloun flawe. **1535** STEWART *Cron. Scot.* (1858) I. 9 In mony flag that furius wes and fell.

flag (flæg), *sb.*[7] [Cf. MLG. *vleger*, 'coin worth somewhat more than a Bremer groat' (Schiller & Lübben).] A groat, fourpence.

1567 HARMAN *Caveat* 85 A flagge, a wyn, and a make (a grot, a penny, and a halfe penny). *a* **1700** B. E. *Dict. Cant. Crew*, *Flagg*, a Groat. **1851** MAYHEW *Lond. Labour* (1861) I. 251 A tremendous black doll bought for a flag of a retired rag-merchant.

†**flag**, *a. Obs.* [Perh. a. OF. *flac* (:—L. *flaccus*) of same meaning. For the change of *c* into *g* cf. *flagon*, *flaget*, repr. earlier *flacon*, *flaket*. See next vb.]

Hanging down, drooping, pendulous; *esp.* of hair, and a horse's or dog's tail. Also in comb., as ***flag-eared***, ***-thighed***, ***-winged***.

1591 PERCIVALL *Sp. Dict.*, *Encapotado de orejas*, flag eared, *flaccidus*. **1613** HEYWOOD *Brazen Age* II. ii, The fierce Thessalian hounds With their flagge eares. **1637** A. WARWICK *Spare Min.* 112 He [the heron] strave to get above her [the hawk] labouring..to make her flagge-winged, and so escape. **1668** *Lond. Gaz.* No. 273/4 About 17 years of Age, bright flag hair. **1683** BP. OF FERNS in *Wicked Contriv. S. Blackhead* in *Select. Harl. Misc.* (1793) 521 His hair.. hangs flag without any curls. **1683** *Lond. Gaz.* No. 1866/8 A Sorrel Gelding..with a bald Face..and a long flag Tail. **1765** *Treat. Dom. Pigeons* 91 The feathers on their thighs hang loose, whereby they are said to be flag-thigh'd.

flag (flæg), *v.*[1] Also 6-7 **flagge**. [? f. FLAG *a.*; cf. OF. *flaquir* to become flaccid. But prob. there is a mixture with an onomatopœic formation, expressing the same notion as *flap*, *flack*, but implying less energetic movement.]

1. *intr.* To hang down; to flap about loosely.

1545 [see FLAGGING *ppl. a.*]. **1609** BIBLE (Douay) *Exod.* xxxix. 19 Which a lace of hyacinth ioyned, lest they should flagge loosely. **1650** BULWER *Anthropomet.* 178 Least the heavy Breasts should flag down too low. **1655** *Theophania* 2 He discovered a tall Ship with her sayls flaging about her masts. **1801** SOUTHEY *Thalaba* III. xviii, When the out-strain'd tent flags loosely. **1818** SHELLEY *Rev. Islam* III. xvii. 3 Its sails were flagging in the breathless noon.

†**b.** To sink *down* heavily. *Obs.*

1617 ABP. ABBOTT *Descr. World*, *Peru* V iv, Which bedds are deuised of Cotten wooll, and hung vp betweene two trees ..in the which flagging downe in the middle, men and their wiues and their children doe lie together.

†**c.** *trans.* To allow to droop: to hang down, drop (the head, ears, tail, etc.). *Obs.* Cf. 5

1637 HEYWOOD *Dial.*, *Anna & Phillis* Wks. 1874 VI. 310 No one but droopes her wings, and flags her tayle. **1644** QUARLES *Sheph. Oracl.* vii, Whereby I was compelled To flag my sailes. **1725** BRADLEY *Fam. Dict.* s.v. *Celery*, It warps and flags its Head too much. **1757** W. THOMPSON *R.N. Advoc.* 20 Dogs..have flaged their Tails..and would not even smell to it.

2. *intr.* To become limp or flaccid. Now only of plants: To droop, fade.

1611 COTGR., *Flestrir*..to fade, wither; flag, droope. **1644** DIGBY *Nat. Bodies* (1645) I. xii. §4. 127 When the string [of a bow] beginneth to flag. **1667** BEALE in *Phil. Trans.* II. 424 The Cherry-Blossoms then flagging, but not much altering their Colour. **1668** CULPEPPER & COLE *Barthol. Anat.* II. iii. 92 The Lungs flag and become small again. **1767** *Nat. Hist.* in *Ann. Reg.* 106/1 Having made an aperture in the bladder, it flagged immediately of itself. **1846** *Jrnl. R. Agric. Soc.* VII. II. 523 The white crops flag, and the turnip-leaves turn yellow. **1860** DELAMER *Kitch. Gard.* 79 They may be cut out with balls of matted fibres, and being then well watered, will scarcely flag at all.

†**3.** *intr.* Of wings: To move feebly or ineffectually in attempting to fly. Of a bird: To move its wings feebly (in early use also *trans.* with *wings* as obj.); to fly unsteadily or near the ground. *Obs.*

1590 SPENSER *F.Q.* To Earl Essex, My Muse, whose fethers..Doe yet but flagg and slowly learne to fly. **1596** —— *Hymn Heav. Beauty* 30 The..faulcon..flags awhile her fluttering wings beneath. **1603** B. JONSON *Sejanus* V. iii, Croking Ravens Flag'd up and downe. **1624** GATAKER *Transubst.* 220 Like eagles wee must soare aloft up to heaven, and not flagge downward. **1635** COWLEY *Davideis* III. 330 The Wings of Time flagg'd dully after it.

fig. **1644** BULWER *Chiron.* 5 Speech divided from the Hand ..flags and creeps upon the ground. *a* **1683** OLDHAM *Art of Poetry* (1686) 3 Others..flag low, and humbly sweep the dust. *a* **1764** LLOYD *Ode to Genius* Poet. Wks. 1774 II. 174 Whose nerveless strains flag on in languid tone.

b. ? To fly level, without soaring; or perh. (after FLAG *sb.*[4]) to fly with long sweep of wing.

1846 KINGSLEY *Saint's Trag.* V. iii, One bird Flags fearful onward. **1849** —— *Misc.* (1859) II. 308 Long strings of sea-fowl are flagging on steadily at railroad pace.

4. To become feeble or unsteady in flight. Hence in wider sense (in early use perh. consciously *transf.*): To be unable to maintain one's speed; to lag, or fall into a halting pace, through fatigue; to become languid, lose vigour or energy.

1639 FULLER *Holy War* IV. xi. (1640) 188 No wonder then if the wings of that armie did quickly flag, having so heavy a weight of curses hanging upon them. **1665** BOYLE *Occas. Refl.* II. v. (1845) 113 Too commonly our Resolutions flagg with our Joys. **1691** NORRIS *Pract. Disc.* 312 We shall be.. far from flagging in our Duty. **1692** LOCKE *Educ.* §15 (1699) 23 His Stomach..flagging into a downright want of Appetite. **1745** *De Foe's Eng. Tradesman* vi. (1841) I. 44 His credit by degrees flags and goes off. **1780** MAD. D'ARBLAY *Lett.* July, She does not suffer one's attention to rest, much less to flag, for hours together. **1810** SCOTT *Lady of L.* I. vi, 'Twere long to tell what steeds gave o'er. Who flagged upon Bochastle's heath. **1821** SHELLEY *Boat on Serchio* 94 The boat..flags with intermitting course, And hangs upon the wave. **1853** SOYER *Pantroph.* 394 The major-domo perceived that appetite began to flag. **1856** KANE *Arct. Expl.* I. xii. 127 The dogs began to flag; but we had to press them. **1874** L. STEPHEN *Hours in Lib.* (1892) I. ii. 63 His zeal in setting forth an example never flags for an instant.

b. Of an author, or his works, a diversion, game, conversation, etc.: To fall off in vigour or interest, to grow dull or languid.

1678 CUDWORTH *Intell. Syst.* 253 Yet doth he sometimes ..seem to flag a little, and speak more Languidly and Sceptically about it. *a* **1745** SWIFT (J.), The pleasures of the town begin to flag and grow languid. **1767** GRAY *Let.* Poems (1775) 325 The diction is..not loaded with epithets and figures, nor flagging into prose. **1773** MRS. CHAPONE *Improv. Mind* (1774) II. 99 Suffering the conversation to flag, for want of..a subject. **1838** DICKENS *Nich. Nick.* vi, When this topic flagged, he turned to the grey-headed gentleman, and asked if he could sing. **1861** HUGHES *Tom Brown at Oxf.* xlvii, By degrees the cricket flagged, and most of the men went off. **1881** BESANT & RICE *Chapl. Fleet* I. x. (1883) 83 Come, gentlemen, we let the glasses flag.

†**c.** ***to flag in money***: to be slow to pay it.

1608 *Yorksh. Trag.* B j a, Shall it be said in all societies, That I broke custome, that I flagd in monie?

†**5.** *trans.* **a.** *lit.* Of a bird, etc.: To cease to ply vigorously, relax the efforts of (its wings) from fatigue. Of conditions, circumstances, etc.: To render (the wings) incapable of soaring; to clog, impede. **b.** Hence To allow or cause to become languid; to be tardy in prosecuting (a purpose); to deprive of vigour, animation, or energy; to depress, enfeeble. *Obs.*

a. 1622 F. MARKHAM *Bk. War* V. ix. 197 The minde..if still it be ouerlaid with its owne toile, must..either flag her wings or stoope to a faulse prey. **1687** DRYDEN *Hind & P.* III. 509 Nor need they fear the dampness of the sky Should flag their wings, and hinder them to fly. **1709** PRIOR *Ode* iii, The Thousand Loves, that arm thy potent Eye, Must..flag their Wings, and die. **1715** MRS. BARKER *Exilius* I. 93 Our Roman Eagles..began to flag their wings.

b. 1602 MARSTON *Antonio's Rev.* III. iii, O, for thy sisters sake, I flagge revenge. **1656** S. HOLLAND *Zara* (1719) 140 A kind of fulsome Recreation, that flags our Crests. **1670** EACHARD *Cont. Clergy* 22 There is nothing that flags the Spirits..as intense Studies. **1720** WELTON *Suffer. Son of God* II. xxi. 571 How forcible this Wretched Spirit of contradiction is..to Quell and Flag the inclinations of doing Good. **1757** W. THOMPSON *R.N. Advoc.* 9 The bloody Brine ..flags by its softer and raw Juices, the Strength of the Pickle.

c. ***to flag rein***: to slacken speed. *rare.*

1848 LYTTON *Harold* II. ii, Took ship from Cherbourg and have not flagged rein, till I could say [etc.].

flag (flæg), *v.*[2] [f. FLAG *sb.*[1]]

†**1.** *trans.* To plant *about* with flags or reeds.

1685 EVELYN *Diary* 22 Oct., The waters are flagged about with *Calamus aromaticus*.

2. To tighten (the seams of a barrel) by means of flags or rushes.

1757 W. THOMPSON *R.N. Advoc.* 15 A Cask..which was not well flag'd. **1842** *Guide to Trade*, *Cooper* 50 Inside joints ..must be flagged. **1846** SIR T. D. LAUDER in *Encycl. Brit.* (ed. 8) IX. 639/1 After which it [the barrel] should be flagged, headed, blown, and tightened.

3. To cut off the flag or blade of (wheat).

1846 *Jrnl. R. Agric. Soc.* VII. II. 538, I had to flag my wheat three times..and then it was partially laid.

Hence **'flagging** *vbl. sb.* Also *attrib.*

1842 *Guide to Trade*, *Cooper* 73 Pulling off from the head, with the flagging iron, the stave or staves that [etc.]. **1846** *Jrnl. R. Agric. Soc.* VII. II. 299 So rank will be the corn-crop there, that in spite of two or three flaggings, it is almost sure to go down and spoil.

flag (flæg), *v.*[3] Also 7 **flagge**. [f. FLAG *sb.*[2]] *trans.* To pave with or as with flagstones. Also of a stone or stones: To form the floor or paving of. ***to flag over***: to cover with a pavement.

1615 G. SANDYS *Trav.* 130 The stones so great, that eight floores it..eight flagge the ends, and sixteene the sides. *Ibid.* 177 The wals are flagged with large tables of white marble. **1682** WHELER *Journ. Greece* II. 187 It is flagged also within with white Marble, and paved in like manner. **1709** STEELE *Tatler* No. 179 ¶8 What Ground remains..is flagged with large Quarries of white Marble. **1810** *Ann. Reg.* 755 The streets in Paris are not flagged on the sides, as in London. **1855** MRS. GATTY *Parab. Nat.* Ser. I. (1869) 125 The hearthstone that flagged the grand old chimney arch of ancient times. **1884** G. H. BOUGHTON in *Harper's Mag.* Oct. 714/1 They..flagged the dead over with their own grave-stones.

flag (flæg), *v.*[4] [f. FLAG *sb.*[4]]

1. a. *trans.* To place a flag over or upon; to decorate or adorn with flags. ***to flag out*** (a racecourse): to mark out by flags.

1875 'STONEHENGE' *Brit. Sports* II. II. i. §6. 511 In a steeplechase, where the ground is not flagged out. **1889** *Times* 1 Oct. 3/3 In honour of the day all the official buildings here were flagged.

b. To mark with a small flag or tag so that relevant items may be readily found. Also *transf.*

1934 H. NICOLSON *Curzon: Last Phase* 74 Instead of being placed in a jacket of its own, each paper as it arrived was affixed to the top of its own file, and these files were encased in a large folder. Any previous paper mentioned in the minutes had to be 'flagged'. It was this flagging process which caused such pain and irritation. The flags consisted of tabs of thick scarlet paper marked 'A' 'B' 'C' 'D' and so on through the letters of the alphabet. These tabs had to be affixed to any back page in the file to which reference was made in the current minute. **1966** *New Statesman* 28 Jan. 113/3 This phrase..purports to embody *Brown and Jones*, 2 B & C 1827, which I have flagged for your Lordship. **1967** *Amer. Speech* XLII. 70 The arrangement follows the method and apparatus of Thompson's revised *Motif-Index*, with the 'new' variants of motifs flagged by an asterisk.

c. In *Computers*: see FLAG *sb.*[4] 1 h.

1959 *Jrnl. Assoc. Comput. Mach.* VI. 128 Symbolic coding —in which only those instructions and data which are referred to by other instructions need be flagged. **1966** C. J. SIPPL *Computer Dict. & Handbk.* (1967) 129/2 *Flag operand*, the third operand of a symbolic instruction, designating which digits of the object-level instruction will be flagged (IBM 1620).

2. a. To inform or warn by flag-signals. *spec.* To stop (a train) by signalling with a flag. Hence, to stop (a vehicle, person, etc.) by waving or signalling. Also *absol.* So ***to flag down***, ***in***. **b.** To communicate (information) by flag-signals. **c.** To inform by flag-signals *that*. **d.** To decoy (game, *esp.* deer) by waving some object like a flag to excite the animal's attention or curiosity.

1856 *N.Y. Herald* 12 Jan. 1/3, I flagged the Albany express train..with my white flag. **1871** *Scribner's Monthly* II. 433 Old Tom, who flagged at the Cherry street crossing. **1884** G. O. SHIELDS in *Harper's Mag.* Aug. 367/2, I will give you a point or two on flagging antelope. **1885** T. ROOSEVELT *Hunting Trips* vi. 181 One method of hunting them [antelopes] is to..flag them up to the hunters by waving a red handkerchief..to and fro in the air. **1886** *Leeds Mercury* Nov., At Mineke some men working in a limekiln flagged the train on account of an obstruction on the track. **1887** *Pall Mall G.* 24 Mar. 11/1 A map of the battle of Hasheen..was flagged across Wimbledon Common. **1893** CAPT. KING *Foes in Ambush* 51, I flagged old Feeny half an hour ago that they hadn't come through here. **1899** A. H. QUINN *Pennsylvania Stories* 168 At Broad Street the outfit was flagged by a Sergeant. **1915** WODEHOUSE *Something Fresh* iii. 63 George, that nice, fat carver is wheeling his truck this way. Flag him, and make him give me some more of that mutton. **1932** W. FAULKNER *Light in August* xii. 270 And I flagged that car with my right hand. **1932** *Kansas City Times* 18 Feb. 22 Fellows who flag a newspaper man down in order to.. pay a subscription. **1940** R. STOUT *Over my Dead Body* xi. 149 A taxi appeared and I flagged it. **1943** N. COWARD *Middle East Diary* 23 Sept. (1944) 100 The car broke down.. however we flagged a passing lorry..and whirled off. **1945** E. BOWEN *Demon Lover* 93 Eric, do you think you could flag the *maître d'hôtel*? **1954** L. KLEMANTASKI tr. *Fraichard's Le Mans Story* viii. 80 Faroux flags in Chinetti's 2 litre Ferrari. **1957** S. MOSS *In Track of Speed* vi. 86 His pit attendants.. flagged him in after the race had been in progress for some time. **1966** *Listener* 6 Jan. 23/1, I was driving along Holland Park Avenue..when I was flagged down by three women. **1970** 'H. CARMICHAEL' *Remote Control* ii. 22 Mrs. Melville managed at last to flag a passing taxi.

flagan, obs. form of FLAGGON.

†**'flagartie**, *a. Obs. Sc.* [Cf. FLACKET *v.*] Flouncing; boisterous.

1535 LYNDESAY *Satyre* 2137 Ane fistand flag, a flagartie fuffe.

fla'gary, var. of FEGARY = VAGARY.

1828 *Blackw. Mag.* XXIII. 46 None of your bantering and flagaries; for have him you must.

†**'flagel.**[1] *Obs.* Also 4 **flegel**. [a. OF. *flageol*, *flagel*, *flajol*, a. Pr. *flajol*, *flaujol*; of unknown origin: the vulgar Lat. type would be *flaviolus*. Diez's suggestion of derivation from Rom. *flauto* flute is untenable on phonological grounds.]

= FLAGEOLET.

c **1325** *Coer de L.* 6681 They herde no pype, ne flagel. *a* **1330** *Fragm. Alexander* in *Rouland & V.* (1836) p. xx, The waite gan a flegel blawe.

flagel.[2] Used with etymological allusion for FLAIL, q.v.

1647 FULLER *Good Th. in Worse T.*, *Occas. Med.* x. 218, I finde two sad Etymologies of Tribulation. One from (*Tribulus*) a three forked Thorn..The other, from *Tribulus*, the Head of a Flail, or Flagell.

flagellant (flə'dʒɛlənt, 'flædʒələnt), *sb.* and *a.* [ad. L. *flagellant-em*, pr. pple. of *flagellāre* to whip, f. *flagellum*: see FLAGELLE *sb.*]

A. *sb.*

1. One who scourges himself by way of religious discipline or penance; *esp.* one of a sect of fanatics (L. *flagellantes*) that arose in the 13th c. Usually *pl.*

1563-87 FOXE *A. & M.* (1596) 139/2 Flagellants going bare-foot in long white linen shirts, with an open place in the backe. **1664** H. MORE *Myst. Iniq.* 323 In their Ninevites or Flagellants. **1782** PRIESTLEY *Corrupt. Chr.* II. IX. 213 There arose..a sect..called the Flagellants, or whippers. **1857** MISS WINKWORTH *Tauler's Life & Serm.* 126 Then appeared the ghastly processions of the Flagellants.

2. In wider sense (chiefly *transf.* from 1): One who flagellates (himself or others).

1785 BURKE *Sp. Nabob Arcot's Debts* 9 These modern flagellants are sure..to whip their own enormities on the vicarious back of every small offender. **1855** PLANCHÉ tr. *C'tess D'Aulnoy's Fairy Tales, Gracieuse & Percinet* (1858) 8 The flagellants so fatigued themselves, that they could no longer lift their arms. **1879** GEO. ELIOT *Theo. Such* ii. 29 That modern sect of Flagellants who make a ritual of lashing—not themselves but—all their neighbours.

fig. **1849** BP. OF EXETER in *Croker Papers* (1884) III. xxvi. 194 This coincidence of opinion avowed by his [Macaulay's] intending panegyrist with that of his actual flagellant.

Comb. **1876** GRANT *Burgh. Sch. Scotl.* II. v. 199 The unhappy teacher had sometimes to perform the duties of a flagellant-general.

B. *adj.*

Given to flagellation, flagellating.

1880 SWINBURNE *Study Shaks.* i. 27 The broad free sketches of the flagellant head-master of Eton.

fig. **1891** G. MEREDITH *One of our Conq.* II. x. 253 So flagellant of herself was she.

Hence **fla'gellantism.**

1855 MILMAN *Lat. Chr.* (1864) IX. XIV. i. 8 Wretched peasantry..maddened to Flagellantism. **1856** KINGSLEY *Misc., Froude's Hist. Eng.* II. 74 The philosopher..may look on wars as in the same category with flagellantisms.

flagellar (flə'dʒɛlə(r)), *a.* [f. L. *flagell-um* + -AR[1].] *Entom.* 'Pertaining to the flagellum of an antenna' (*Cent. Dict.*).

flagellate ('flædʒəleɪt), *pa. pple. rare.* [ad. L. *flagellāt-us*, pa. pple. of *flagellā-re* to whip.] Flagellated, scourged.

1876 J. ELLIS *Cæsar in Egypt* 145 Christ..was one time bound, With scorn assail'd, and flagellate with thongs.

flagellate ('flædʒələt), *a.* and *sb.* [f. FLAGELL-UM + -ATE[2].]

A. *adj.*

1. *Biol.* a. Furnished with vibratile flagella. b. = FLAGELLIFORM.

1867 *Mem. Boston Soc. Nat. Hist.* I. 306 The whole question..hinges upon the determination as to the animal or vegetable nature of the Monad-like, or so-called flagellate infusoria. **1877** HUXLEY *Anat. Inv. Anim.* ii. 79 Those flagellate Infusoria which are termed 'monads'. **1878** BELL *Gegenbaur's Comp. Anat.* 21 The cell runs out into a fine process, and forms a flagellate cell.

2. *Bot.* Having runners or runner-like branches.

1882 VINES *Sachs' Bot.* 379 The male branch may..become an ordinary flagellate branch.

B. *sb.* A microscopic protozoan organism of the class Mastigophora (or Flagellata), characterized by the possession at some stage of its life of one or more flagella that are used for locomotion.

1879 *Q. Jrnl. Microsc. Sci.* XIX. 100 Sometimes the movements of the flagellum are energetic, and the organism then begins to move like a Flagellate, by help of its flagellum. **1897** H. M. BERNARD in A. H. Miles *Concise Knowl. Nat. Hist.* 718 It is impossible to draw any hard and fast line between the lowest plant and animal cells, and..such simple Flagellates may be regarded as belonging to a border land. **1924** H. J. VAN CLEAVE *Invertebr. Zool.* ii. 28 Relatively constant body form with usually one or two chromatophores characterize these small flagellates. **1949** C. A. HOARE *Handbk. Med. Protozool.* v. 111 In addition to the flagellates of the alimentary and genital tracts,..human beings may be infected with flagellates living in the blood and cells of the reticulo-endothelial system. **1963** H. SANDON *Ess. Protozool.* ii. 25 If we could trace the ancestry of all multicellular plants and animals back beyond the time of the earliest creatures capable of leaving fossil remains, most people agree that we should come to organisms which, if they lived today, would be included among the flagellates.

flagellate ('flædʒəleɪt), *v.* [f. L. *flagellāt-* ppl. stem of *flagellā-re*, f. *flagellum*: see FLAGELLE *sb.*] *trans.* To scourge, whip.

1623 in COCKERAM. **1721-82** in BAILEY. **1771** SMOLLETT *H. Clinker* II. 173 To be insulted, flagellated, and even executed as a malefactor. **1837** LANDOR *Pentameron* Wks. 1846 II. 313/2 [That] the angels were created only to flagellate and burn us. **1858** R. S. SURTEES *Ask Mamma* iii. 9 The outside passengers..proceeded to flagellate themselves into circulation.

fig. **1804-8** FOSTER in *Life & Corr.* (1846) I. lxi. 341, I flagellated myself in great anger. **1830** *Westm. Rev.* XII. 274 The Quarterly could for once..flagellate an opponent without having recourse to its old art of wilful misrepresentation. **1856** EMERSON *Eng. Traits*, Wks. (Bohn) II. 39 Their drowsy minds need to be flagellated by war.

Hence **'flagellated** *ppl. a.*

1836 E. HOWARD *R. Reefer* xiii, The flagellated boys contrived to hush up their sobs. **1884** *Pall Mall G.* 29 July 3/2 The flagellated flesh visibly shuddered.

flagellated ('flædʒəleɪtɪd), *a. Zool.* and *Biol.* [f. FLAGELLATE *a.* + -ED[1].] Provided with flagella.

1874 *Monthly Microsc. Jrnl.* XI. 70 Free-swimming and flagellated monads. **1887** W. J. SOLLAS in *Encycl. Brit.* XXII. 418/2 The flagellated chambers of all other sponges. *Ibid.*, Collared flagellated cells or *choanocytes.*

flagellation (ˌflædʒə'leɪʃən). Also 5 **flagellacyon,** 6 **-cion.** [ad. L. *flagellātiōn-em*, n. of action f. *flagellāre* to FLAGELLATE.]

1. a. The action of scourging; a flogging, whipping.

1526 *Pilgr. Perf.* (W. de W. 1531) 13 Suffrynge..intollerable turmentes, flagellacyons, and moost cruell and bytter deth. **1664** H. MORE *Myst. Iniq.* 466 Excoriating their bodies in processionary Flagellations. **1765** STERNE *Tr. Shandy* VIII. xxxi, Speaking of his abstinence, his watchings, flagellations. **1838** DICKENS *Nich. Nick.* xiii, A fearful instrument of flagellation, supple, wax-ended. **1875** H. C. WOOD *Therap.* (1879) 161 Mild flagellations..may be used to keep up the external capillary circulation.

fig. **1490** CAXTON *Eneydos* xx. 73 In all the places of thy flagellacyons, peynes and tormentes. **1502** *Ord. Cryst. Men* (W. de W. 1506) IV. v. 175 By sykenesses, losses of goodes, warres, and other flagellacyons.

b. *spec.* The scourging of Christ; a picture representing this.

1426 AUDELAY *Poems* 55 Vij blodes Crist he bled..The thred in his flagellacion. **1630** DONNE *Deaths Duell* (1632) 33 In his flagellation and thornes. **1703** MAUNDRELL *Journ. Jerus.* (1732) 72 The first place they visited was that of the Pillar of Flagellation. **1741** CHAMBERS *Cycl.* s.v. *Flagellation*, We say..a Flagellation to denote a picture, or print, representing the torment inflicted on the Saviour.

2. *Biol.* a. The arrangement of flagella on an organism.

1893 J. TUCKEY tr. *Hatschek's Amphioxus* 164 The flagellation of the body.

b. = EXFLAGELLATION.

1898 *Jrnl. Exper. Med.* III. 94 The process of flagellation presented by the elongate organism is remarkable. **1926** C. M. WENYON *Protozool.* II. II. 881 In the typical coccidia the male gametocyte produces male gametes after a relatively slow process of nuclear multiplication, while in the hæmosporidia the male gametes are formed by a violent process known as flagellation or exflagellation, which occurs in the stomach of the invertebrate.

flagellative ('flædʒəleɪtɪv), *a. rare.* [f. as prec. + -IVE.] = FLAGELLATORY.

1836 E. HOWARD *R. Reefer* ix, He attended to no department of the school but the flagellative. **1903** *Daily Chron.* 19 Feb. 3/5 All the officers actively concerned in inflicting the late illegal flagellative punishments..should be promptly dealt with.

flagellator ('flædʒəleɪtə(r)). [agent-n. f. L. *flagellāre* to FLAGELLATE.] One who scourges or flogs. (In quot. 1691 = FLAGELLANT A 1.)

1691 G. D'EMILIANE *Frauds Rom. Monks* 358 In the midst of these Flagellators was carried a Representation of the Scourging of our Saviour. **1824** *Examiner* 103/2 He was the flagellator of the boy Lynch. **1876** GRANT *Burgh Sch. Scotl.* II. v. 198 The flagellator having been summoned before the Council, declares that the fault was not his.

fig. **1830** G. CROLY *George IV*, vi. 76 The rise of this grand flagellator [the newspaper press].

flagellatory ('flædʒələˌtərɪ). [f. L. type **flagellātōrius*: see prec. and -ORY.] Pertaining to flagellation or flogging.

1838 *Fraser's Mag.* XVIII. 399 We quote one flagellatory paragraph. **1844** TUPPER *Twins* ii. 16 Often had he screened his bad twin brother from the flagellatory consequences of sheer idleness. **1890** *Sat. Rev.* 30 Aug. 266/1 The unwilling specimen of so much flagellatory skill.

†**flagelle,** *sb. Obs.* [ad. L. *flagellum* dim. of *flagrum* scourge.] A scourge.

c **1430** LYDG. *Bochas* I. (1544) 15 a, Their olde offences to punishe..As a flagell. *c* **1430** —— *Min. Poems* (Percy Soc.) 146 Thu must of righte yeve hym is penaunce, With this flagelle of equite and resoun.

†**flagelle,** *v. Obs.* [ad. L. *flagellāre*, f. *flagellum*: see prec.] *trans.* To scourge.

1550 BALE *Eng. Votaries* II Riij/1 A man wold thinke..that Sathan wer sent..to flagelle the church.

†**flage'lliferan.** *Obs.* [f. med.L. *flagellifer* (f. *flagellum* scourge + *-fer* bearing) + -AN.] = FLAGELLANT *sb.* 1.

1607 T. ROGERS 39 *Art.* 167 The Baptisme of water is now ceased: and the Baptisme of voluntary blood by whipping is come in place thereof, without which none can be saued, as the Flagelliferans [*printed* -erians, *corrected in later Edd.*] published.

flagelliferous (flædʒə'lɪfərəs), *a. Zool.*, etc. [f. L. *flagell-um* + -(I)FEROUS.] Bearing a flagellum or flagella; flagellate.

1868 tr. *Figuier's Ocean World* 99 Flagelliferous Infusoria.

flagelliform (flə'dʒɛlɪfɔːm). *a. Zool.* and *Bot.* [f. FLAGELLUM + -(I)FORM.] Having the form of a FLAGELLUM.

1826 KIRBY & SP. *Entomol.* (1828) IV. xlii. 155 First, flagelliform ovaries consisting of conical tubes. **1875** BLAKE *Zool.* 200 The tail is flagelliform, very long. **1882** VINES *Sachs' Bot.* 356 Flagelliform branches.

flagellin (flə'dʒɛlɪn). *Biochem.* [f. FLAGELL(UM + -IN[1].] A fibrous protein isolated from bacterial flagella.

1955 W. T. ASTBURY et al. in *Symp. Soc. Exper. Biol.* IX. 292 We propose, therefore, to call this new member of the k-m-e-f group 'flagellin'. **1969** S. T. LYLES *Biol. Microorganisms* viii. 191 Flagella are uniform throughout their length and are composed of fibrous protein called flagellin.

flagellist ('flædʒəlɪst). *rare.* [f. L. *flagell-um* + -IST.] One who scourges himself.

1833 I. TAYLOR *Fanat.* v. 113 The Christian flagellist might..draw as much blood from his back in a year. **1926** H. NICOLSON *Let.* 21 July (1966) 31 They were followed by half-naked flagellists.

flagellomania (ˌflædʒələʊ'meɪnɪə). [f. FLAGELL(UM + -O + -MANIA.] Enthusiasm for flogging. Hence ˌ**flagello'maniac** *sb.* and *a.*, (one who is) enthusiastically in favour of flogging.

1895 G. B. SHAW in *Daily Chron.* 24 Feb. 8/5 Flagellomania has been victorious by seven votes to five on the Industrial Schools Committee. **1899** —— in *Humanity* May 136/2 The male flagellomaniac—who is sometimes, unfortunately, a judge—craves intensely for the flogging of women. **1908** *Humanitarian* Sept. 66/2 We are constantly assured by the flagellomaniac section of the Press that crime is 'stamped out' by the 'cat'. **1917** G. B. SHAW in *New Republic* 6 Jan., Any newspaper can get up a flagellomaniac garotting scare. **1952** R. HUGHES *Swinburne's Lesbia Brandon* 553 It is not mere flagellation in the void,..as is usually the case with flagellomaniacs.

‖**flagellum** (flə'dʒɛləm). Pl. **flagella.** [L. *flagellum* whip, scourge.]

1. In humorously pedantic use: A whip, scourge.

1807 'BEN BLOCK' (*title*) Flagellum flagellated. **1830** LYTTON *P. Clifford* iii, Boxing-gloves, books, fly-flanking flagellum. **1842** BARHAM *Ingol. Leg., Ingol. Penance*, The Knight..Received the first taste of the Father's flagellum.

2. a. *Bot.* A runner or creeping shoot.

[**1398** TREVISA *Barth. De P.R.* XVII. cxviii. (1495) 682 The hyghest braunches of a vyne hyghte Flagella.] **1887** BENTLEY *Bot.* (ed. 5) 117 The Runner or Flagellum..is an elongated, slender, prostrate branch, sent off from the base of the stem, and giving off at its extremity leaves, and roots, and thus producing a new plant.

b. *Zool.* and *Biol.* A lash-like appendage.

1852 DANA *Crust.* I. 227 Outer antennæ as long as the front, flagellum 10-jointed. **1878** BELL *Gegenbaur's Comp. Anat.* 79 The flagella..are modifications of the cilia. **1885** *Athenæum* 12 Dec. 773/3 A cholera bacillus showing a flagellum at either end.

flageolet[1] (flædʒə'lɛt, 'flædʒəlɪt). Forms: 7 **flajolet, flageollet, -eret, flagolet,** 7-9 **flagelet, -llet,** (8 **flagelate),** 7- **flageolet.** [a. Fr. *flageolet*, dim. of OF. *flajol*: see FLAGEL *sb.*[1]]

1. A small wind instrument, having a mouthpiece at one end, six principal holes, and sometimes keys.

1659 LEAK *Water-wks.* 27 A Cyclope plaies upon a Flajolet. **1711** ADDISON *Spect.* No. 5 ⁋3 The Musick proceeded from a Consort of Flagelets. **1788** COWPER *Death Bullfinch* 12 Well-taught he all the sounds express'd Of flagelet or flute. **1840** DICKENS *Old C. Shop* xix, Vagabond groups..add their uproar to the shrill flageolet.

transf. **1662** TATHAM *Aqua Tri.* 11 To shew they [the winds] were Joves Flagerets.

†2. A player on the flageolet. *Obs.*

1676 ETHEREDGE *Man of Mode* III. iii., That's one of the walking Flajolets.

3. A stop in an organ having a tone similar to that of the flageolet.

1852 SEIDEL *Organ* 97 Flageolet..imitates the tone of the instrument bearing the same name.

4. *attrib.*, as *flageolet-master, -tone* (see quot.).

1667 PEPYS *Diary* 1 Mar., I find the flageolet-master come, and teaching my wife. **1888** STAINER & BARRETT *Dict. Mus. Terms, Flageolet tones*, the natural harmonics of stringed instruments, so called from their pure flute-like quality of tone.

‖**flageolet**[2] (flædʒəʊ'lɛt, flaʒɔlɛ). [Fr. *flageolet*, corruption of *fageolet*, dim. of *fageol*:—L. *faseolus*. Cf. FASELS.] A species of kidney-bean.

1877 E. S. DALLAS *Kettner's Bk. Table* 243 Haricot beans.—These are the seeds: first, the flageolets, which are green and are to be had fresh from July to October, or dried always. **1885** *Pall Mall. G.* 9 Sept. 4/2 Flageolets, the *pièce de résistance*, are the next cause of amusement. **1951** E. DAVID *French Country Cooking* 235 Pour the whole contents of a tin of *flageolets* into a pan.

flaget, var. of FLACKET, *Obs.*, a bottle, cask.

flaggan: see FLAGON[2].

†**flaggat.** *Obs. rare.* [? var. of FLACKET *sb.*[2]; but cf. FAGGOT.] A bundle, faggot.

1375 BARBOUR *Bruce* XVII. 615 Gret flaggatis tharof thai maid.

flagged (flægd), *ppl. a.*[1] [f. FLAG *sb.*[2] + -ED[2].] Paved with flags or slabs of marble, stone, etc.

1634-5 BRERETON *Trav.* (1844) 86 The daintiest flagged channels. **1777** W. DALRYMPLE *Trav. Sp. & Port.* iii, Our apartment..had a flagged floor. **1852** R. S. SURTEES *Sponge's Sp. Tour* lxii. 350 They paced backwards and forwards under the flagged verandah.

flagged (flægd), *ppl. a.*^{2} [f. FLAG *sb.*^{4} + -ED^2.] Having a flag, decorated with a flag.

1791 COWPER *Yardley Oak* 96 The deck Of some flagged admiral. **1874** PAPWORTH *Coats of Arms* 364 A turret arg. flagged gu.

flagger^1 (ˈflægə(r)). *Anglo-Irish.* [Cf. FLAG *sb.*^{1}; also FLIGGER and OF. *flechiere, flequiere, flagiere* water plants, flags collectively.] = FLAG *sb.*^{1}

1842 S. LOVER *Handy Andy* xv, Its banks sedgy, thickly grown with flaggers and bulrushes. **1843** LEVER *J. Hinton* xx, The sedgy banks, whose tall flaggers bow their heads beneath the ripple that eddies from the bow.

ˈflagger^2. [f. FLAG *v.*^{3} and *sb.*^{2} + -ER^1.]

1. One who flags or lays down flagstones.

1868 WHITMAN *Poems, To Working Men* 6 Flagging of side-walks by flaggers.

2. *slang.* A street-walker.

1865 *Daily Paper*, Police Report (Farmer), She wasn't a low sort at all—she wasn't a flagger as we call it.

flagger^3 (ˈflægə(r)). [f. FLAG *sb.*^{4} + -ER^1.] A man who carries a flag before a traction-engine to warn drivers of vehicles, etc.

1892 *Scott. Leader* 9 Jan. 4 The 'flagger', who turned up some time after in hot pursuit of the fugitive [engine].

flagget, var. of FLACKET *Obs.*, bottle.

flagging (ˈflægɪŋ), *vbl. sb.*^{1} [f. FLAG *v.*^{1} + -ING^1.] The action of the vb. FLAG^1.

1611 COTGR., *Alachissement*..a flagging, or falling downe, through feeblenesse. **1668** CULPEPPER & COLE *Barthol. Anat.* II. vi. 102 The swelling of the Heart and the Flagging thereof. **1855** H. SPENCER *Princ. Psychol.* (1870) I. II. v. 236 That flagging of the circulation which accompanies the decline of life. **1865** M. ARNOLD *Ess. Crit.* i. 36 He was inclined to regret, as a spiritual flagging, the lull which he saw.

ˈflagging, *vbl. sb.*^{2} [f. FLAG *v.*^{3} + -ING^1.]

1. The action of paving with flagstones.

1656 H. WEBB in D. King *Vale Royall* II. 209 The Flagging of the long West Ile..was this year begun by Dean Mitter. **1824** in Picton *L'pool Munic. Rec.* (1886) II. 341 The paving and flagging of streets. **1893** *Birkenhead News* 9 Dec. 1/2 Tenders for the Flagging, Channelling, and Sewering of various Passages in the Borough.

2. *concr.* The material used in paving; hence, the pavement. (The two first quots. are doubtful.)

1622 *Vestry Bks.* (Surtees) 178 For making upp a wall and flagging about the bells floore for five dayes att x d. per diem, iiij s. ij d. **1660** *Ibid.* 197 For setting upp the fount and flagging about itt, 8 s. 6 d. **1825** *Beverley Lighting Act* ii. 27 The flagging and other materials thereof to be taken up. **1851** LONGF. *Gold. Leg.* II. i. 50 He..heard angelic feet Fall on the golden flagging of the street. **1861** HOLLAND *Less. Life* iii. 39 Stretched at her length upon the flagging.

3. *attrib.*, as ***flagging stone***.

1830 N. S. WHEATON *Jrnl.* 366 A vault covered with a coarse flagging stone. **1868** LOSSING *Hudson* 172 Almost inexhaustible quarries of flagging stone.

†**ˈflagging,** *vbl. sb.*^{3} *Obs.* [? f. FLAG *sb.*^{4} + -ING^1.] ? A long flowing hat-band.

1695 *Lond. Gaz.* No. 3045/4 His Coat whitish, with black Triming, a black Hat and Flaging.

flagging (ˈflægɪŋ), *ppl. a.* [f. FLAG *v.*^{1} + -ING^2.] That flags; hanging down, drooping; failing, languid.

1545 RAYNOLD *Byrth Mankynde* (1564) C j, That her brestes..be neyther to great, soft, hangyng, and flaggyng. *c* **1620** Z. BOYD *Zion's Flowers* (1855) 10 Against the yard The flagging mainsaile flapt. **1636** B. JONSON *Discov.* Wks. (Rtldg.) 759/1 The language is thin, flagging, poor, starved. **1715–20** POPE *Iliad* XXIII. 1039 The wounded bird..With flagging wings alighted on the mast. **1838** WORDSW. *Sonnets* x, Dull, flagging notes that with each other jar. **1874** L. STEPHEN *Hours in Lib.* (1892) I. v. 189 He..had recourse to ..stimulants to rouse a flagging imagination.

Hence **ˈflaggingly** *adv.*

a **1693** URQUHART *Rabelais* III. v. 54, I would come off but very faintly and flaggingly.

†**ˈflaggish,** *a. Obs.* [f. FLAG *a.* + -ISH.] Somewhat 'flag' or lank; = FLAGGY *a.*^{2} 1.

1669 *Lond. Gaz.* No. 402/4 Of a brown flaggish Hair. **1685** *Ibid.* No. 2058/4 A tall slender man, flaggish lank Hair.

flaggon, var. of FLAGON.

flaggy (ˈflægɪ), *a.*^{1} [f. FLAG *sb.*^{1} + -Y^1.]

1. Abounding in flags or reeds.

1382 WYCLIF *Exod.* ii. 3 He..putte the litil faunt with ynne, and sette out hym in the flaggi place of the brinke of the flode. **1552** *Nottingham Rec.* IV. 104 For the flaggy peyse of grounde lyeng..in Estcrofte. **1610** G. FLETCHER *Christ's Vict.* xlix, Old Chamus flaggy banks. **1641** BEST *Farm. Bks.* (Surtees) 40 There is a little flaggie piece towardes the west ende. **1821** CLARE *Vill. Minstr.* I. 125 The rings went whirling round, Till they touch'd the flaggy bank. **1884** *Public Opinion* 5 Sept. 299/2 Its favourite flaggy haunts.

2. Consisting or made of flags or reeds.

1621 G. SANDYS *Ovid's Met.* IX. (1626) 176 The rupture of his browes He shades with flaggie wreathes, and sallow boughes. **1698** J. FRYER *E. India & Persia* 17 Their Flaggy Mansions: Flags..upheld with some few Sticks, supplying both Sides and Covering to their Cottages. *a* **1711** KEN *Edmund* Poet. Wks. 1721 II. 200 Cam will ere long his flaggy Tresses rear. **1831** W. HOWITT *Bk. Seasons* iv. 94 The large flaggy nests of the water-hen.

3. Resembling a flag or reed, flag-like.

1577 B. GOOGE *Heresbach's Husb.* (1586) III. 120 Rather soft sweete grasse, then hie and flaggy. **1597** GERARDE *Herbal* I. xxxiv. 45 The common Flower-de-luce hath long and large flaggie leaues, like the blade of a sworde. **1652** CULPEPER *Eng. Physic.* 95 (*Flower-de-luce*) The flaggy kindes thereof have the most physical uses. *c* **1730** BURT *Lett. N. Scotl.* (1760) II. xxvi. 310 A kind of short flaggy grass.

4. Of corn, straw, etc.: Having a large flag (see FLAG *sb.*^{1} 2).

1842 *Jrnl. R. Agric. Soc.* III. II. 300 Straw bright and reedy, not flaggy. **1850** *Ibid.* XI. II. 691 My corn being too strong and flaggy.

flaggy (ˈflægɪ), *a.*^{2} *Obs.* exc. *dial.* [f. FLAG *v.*^{1} + -Y^1. Cf. FLAG *a.*, FLAGGISH.]

1. Hanging down limply or lankly, drooping, pendulous.

1576 NEWTON *Lemnie's Complex.* (1633) 151 The cheekes seeme flaggy and hanging downe. **1590** SPENSER *F.Q.* I. xi. 10 His flaggy winges when forth he did display, Were like two sayles. *c* **1620** T. ROBINSON *M. Magd.* I. 238 Curlinge ye flaggy lockes of the Neptunia plaine. **1681** *Lond. Gaz.* No. 1614/4 A Tall Man with Brown flaggy Hair. **1697** DRYDEN *Virg. Georg.* IV. 40 Basking in the Sun thy Bees may lye, And resting there, their flaggy Pinions dry. **1725** DE FOE *Voy. Round World* (1840) 135 Her breasts were plump and round, not flaggy and hanging down. **1814** H. BUSK *Fugit. Pieces* 229 The flaggy sail Chides the dull absence of the quickening gale. **1821** CRAIG *Lect. Drawing* i. 52 A large head with..wide-spread, flaggy wings..to represent a Jupiter Pluvius.

2. Soft and flabby, having no firmness, flaccid.

a **1565** SIR T. CHALONER in *Q. Eliz. Boethius* (E.E.T.S.) 147 My skynne do sagg in wrinkles slacke, my flaggy lymbes do tremble. **1626** BACON *Sylva* §453 It will beare a great flaggy Apple. **1634** T. HORNE *Janua Ling.* (ed. 8) 9 Lillies.. Wither and grow flaggy. **1668** CULPEPPER & COLE *Barthol. Anat.* II. iii. 91 It [the Heart] becomes soft and flaggy, and gives no pulsation. **1705** BOSMAN *Guinea* 238 The flesh is so flaggy and the Bacon so sorry. **1888** ELWORTHY *W. Somerset Wordbk.*, *Flaggy*, flabby, limp.

Hence **ˈflagginess**, the state of being flaggy.

1654 Z. COKE *Logic* Ded. (1657) A iij b, Through the flagginesse of her Pinion. **1684** tr. *Bonet's Merc. Compit.* XIV. 480 When there is a weakness of the Stomach, especially a flagginess. **1736** BAILEY *Househ. Dict.* 60 The lungs, by their flagginess fastening themselves to the sides. **1755** JOHNSON *Flagginess*, laxity, limberness, want of tension.

flaggy (ˈflægɪ), *a.*^{3} [f. FLAG *sb.*^{2} + -Y^1.] Cleaving readily into flags, capable of being split up, laminate.

1847 ANSTED *Anc. World* iii. 23 A grayish-coloured sandy stone, often slaty or flaggy. **1877** A. H. GREEN *Phys. Geol.* ii. §7. 85 A rock which is regularly and not very thickly bedded, so that it can be split up into slabs for paving, is called Flaggy, or a Flagstone.

flagitate (ˈflædʒɪteɪt). *v.* [f. L. *flāgitāt-* ppl. stem of *flāgitāre* to demand earnestly, f. root *flăg*: see FLAGRANT.] *trans.* To entreat (a person) earnestly; to importune (*rare*).

1623 COCKERAM, *Flagitate*, earnestly to importune. **1656** BLOUNT *Glossogr.*, *Flagitate*, to ask instantly, to desire earnestly. **1862** CARLYLE *Fredk. Gt.* III. XIV. iii. 639 Carteret himself shall go and flagitate the Dutch. **1865** *Ibid.* V. xviii. i. 7 Schmettau earnestly flagitating the Hanoverian Officialities.

flagitation (flædʒɪˈteɪʃən). Also 5 **flagitacyon.** [ad. L. *flāgitātiōn-em*, n. of action f. *flāgitāre*: see prec.] The action of asking or demanding with earnestness or passion.

1658 PHILLIPS, *Flagitation*, an earnest begging. **1727** in BAILEY vol. II.

¶ A mistake for FLAGELLATION 1.

1490 CAXTON *Eneydos* xxvii. 96 The tourment and flagitacyon wherof the see was bette in righte grete violence.

†**flaˈgition.** *Obs.* [badly f. L. *flāgitium*: see FLAGITIOUS.] Flagitious conduct; flagitiousness.

1598 J. KEEPER *Courtiers Acad.* 244 [Riches] being the infamous offspring of couetousnesse, and guilty euen of the same flagition. **1600** E. BLOUNT *Hosp. Incur. Fooles* 158 A woman..stuffed..with all kinde of flagition and villanie.

†**flaˌgitiˈosity.** *Obs.*$^{-0}$ [f. L. *flāgitiōs-us* (see next) + -ITY.] Flagitiousness.

1727 BAILEY vol. II, *Flagitiosity*. **1775** in ASH.

flagitious (fləˈdʒɪʃəs), *a.* Also 4–6 flagicious(e. [ad. OF. *flagicieux, flagitieux*, or L. *flāgitiōsus*, f. *flāgitium* shameful crime. also importunity; related to *flāgitāre*: see FLAGITATE *v.*]

1. Of persons: Guilty of or addicted to atrocious crimes; deeply criminal, extremely wicked.

1382 WYCLIF *2 Macc.* vii. 34 Thou cursid..of alle men most flagiciouse. **1581** CAMPION in *Confer.* I. (1584) C ij, That flagitious Apostata. *a* **1617** BAYNE *On Coloss.* (1634) 98 Is it fit the Wife should be kept under the government of a flagitious servant? **1715–20** POPE *Iliad* XIII. 788 Crimes shall ..whelm in ruins yon flagitious town. **1879** GLADSTONE *Glean.* III. i. 16 The most flagitious of mortals.

absol. **1796** BP. WATSON *Apol. Bible* 3 You will have annihilated in the minds of the flagitious all their fears of future punishment.

¶ **b.** Loosely used for: Infamous.

1741 RICHARDSON *Pamela* (1742) IV. 364 The common Executioner, who is the lowest and most flagitious Officer of the Commonwealth.

2. Of actions, character, principles, etc.: Extremely wicked or criminal: heinous, villainous.

1550 VERON *Godly Saiyngs* (1846) 142 Flagitiouse doinges and factes. **1651** *Raleigh's Ghost* Pref., Men, of so flagitious lives, that [etc.]. **1701** ROWE *Amb. Step-Moth.* II. i, This Age, Of most flagitious Note. **1726** DE FOE *Hist. Devil* I. iv. (1840) 51 Having committed a flagitious crime. **1781** GIBBON *Decl. & F.* II. xxxii. 247 His faith is pure, though his manners are flagitious. **1823** LINGARD *Hist. Eng.* VI. 232 His principles..were of the most flagitious description. **1875** BRYCE *Holy Rom. Emp.* ix. (ed. 5) 134 The flagitious life of the pontiff.

flagitiously (fləˈdʒɪʃəslɪ), *adv.* [f. prec. + -LY^2.] In a flagitious manner; atrociously, villainously.

1612–15 BP. HALL *Contempl. O.T.* (1622) VI. XVI. iv. 79 If Amasa were now..justly..payd for the arerages of his late rebellion..it was flagitiously cruell. **1679** J. GOODMAN *Penit. Pardoned* III. vi. (1713) 391 Such men as have lived flagitiously and wickedly. **1845** LD. CAMPBELL *Chancellors* (1857) V. cxvii. 346 Some of the scenes..are most flagitiously indecent. **1849** MACAULAY *Hist. Eng.* I. 562 A sentence so flagitiously unjust.

flagitiousness (fləˈdʒɪʃəsnɪs). [f. as prec. + -NESS.] The quality of being flagitious.

1692 BENTLEY *Boyle Lect.* i. 3 The corruption and Flagitiousness of Life which naturally attend it. **1750** *Student* I. 176 A and others would intentionally avoid all acts of flagitiousness and villany. **1855** MILMAN *Lat. Chr.* (1864) IV. VII. ii. 72 The flagitiousness of his life as Pope.

flagless (ˈflæglɪs), *a.* [f. FLAG *sb.*^{2} and ^{4} + -LESS.] Destitute of a flag or flags.

1. Not paved with flagstones.

1840 R. BREMNER *Excursion Denmark*, etc. II. 350 The rough-paved flagless thoroughfare.

2. Not bearing a flag or ensign; unadorned by flags or banners.

1866 *Morning Star* 10 July, Within an hour or so, Milan, now so dejected and flagless, will rejoice and be adorned again. **1880** BARING-GOULD *Mehalah* 141 He pointed sadly to his flagless staff, and shook his head.

ˈflaglet. [f. FLAG *sb.*^{4} + -LET.] A small flag.

1872 *Daily News* 25 Mar., The light blue flaglet on the forepeak of the Cambridge boat.

flag-man. [f. FLAG *sb.*^{4} + MAN.]

†1. An admiral, a flag-officer. *Obs.*

1666 PEPYS *Diary* (1879) III. 428 To Mr. Lilly's the painter's; and there saw the heads..of the Flaggmen in the late great fight. **1713** [DARRELL] *Gentleman Instructed* III. (ed. 5) 409 He was a kind of Flagman, a Vice-Admiral, in all those Expeditions of Good-fellowship.

2. One who has charge of or carries a flag; one who signals with a flag.

1832 *Lincoln Herald* 13 Jan. 1 The crowd all rushed into the yard, with Beck, the flagman. **1875** 'STONEHENGE' *Brit. Sports* II. I. xiv. § 1. 487 The Starter is..allowed an assistant, besides a flagman. **1890** *Pall Mall G.* 14 Jan. 6/1 The flagman..obeyed the order.

flag-officer. *Naut.* [f. FLAG *sb.*^{4} + OFFICER.] An officer who carries a flag. **a.** An admiral, vice-admiral, or rear-admiral. **b.** In U.S. navy 1857–1862 the official title of an officer in actual command of a squadron (*Cent. Dict.*).

1665 EVELYN *Diary* 30 June, I went on board the Charles, to which..came all the flag-officers to his Majesty. **1796** MORSE *Amer. Geog.* II. 341 He formerly appointed the flag officers. **1806** A. DUNCAN *Nelson* 119 The rank of a flag-officer. **1859** in *Gen. Navy Reg. U.S.A.* (1888) 931 The commission of senior flag officer of the United States Navy. **1870** COLOMB *Let.* Apr. in *Fifteen Years Naval Retirement* 5 Fifty Flag Officers is too few.

flagon^1 (ˈflægən). Forms: 5 **flagan, flakon,** 6 **flaccon(e, flaccoun,** (*Sc.* **flackoun**), 6 **flagone,** 5–9 **flaggon,** 6– **flagon.** [ME. *flakon*, ad. OF. *flacon*:—earlier *flascon*:—med.L. *flascōn-em*: see FLASK *sb.*]

1. A large bottle for holding wine or other liquors; in early use sometimes *spec.* a metal bottle with a screw top, such as was carried by pilgrims (cf. FLACON, and quots. 1578, 1647, 1653). *arch.*

1470–85 MALORY *Arthur* VII. xiv. 234 And there shalt thou bere with the of my wyn in two flagans of siluer they ar of two galons. **1494** FABYAN *Chron.* VII. 540, .ii. flaggonys of golde. **1527** ANDREW *Brunswyke's Distyll. Waters* B ij b, Take a flatte flaccon or botell of glas. **1578** LYTE *Dodoens* V. xxxii. 592 Gourdes..be oftentimes used (espe-cially of the Pilgrimes) in steede of flagons or bottelles. **1603** DRAYTON *Odes* v. 25 Bring forth your Flaggons (fill'd with sparkling Wine). **1647** R. STAPYLTON *Juvenal* 226 With thy netted knapsack, bisket, wine, And bursten-bellied flaggons. **1653** URQUHART *Rabelais* I. v. 26 What difference is there between a bottle and a flaggon? great difference, for the bottle is stopped..with a stoppel, but the flaggon with a vice. *a* **1794** SIR W. JONES *Hymn to Indra* Wks. 1799 VI. 340 While from their diamond flagons The feasting Gods exhaustless nectar sip. **1847** JAMES *J. Marston Hall* ix, Having..divided the last drop in the flagon equally between himself and me.

b. Recently applied by wine-merchants to a glass bottle of flattened globular shape with a neck, holding nearly twice the quantity of an ordinary wine-bottle.

2. A large vessel containing a supply of drink for use at table; now *esp.* one with a handle and spout, and usually a lid.

1512 *Act 4 Hen. VIII*, c. 7 §7 Basons, Flaggons, Bottles.. or any other such Wares of Tin or Pewter. **1663** BUTLER *Hud.* I. II. 115 Did they coyn.. Bouls, and Flaggons, Int' Officers of Horse and Dragoons. **1828** SCOTT *F.M. Perth* ii, He set the flagon on the table, and sat down. **1883** *Manch. Exam.* 30 Oct. 8/4 They were supplied with beer in the usual stately German flagons with pewter covers.

b. *spec.* A vessel of this description, used to hold the wine at the Eucharist.

1485 *Churchw. Acc. St. Mary's Hill, Lond.* (Nichols 1797) 114 A leeske of laton with a flakon. **1662** *Bk. Com. Prayer* Communion, And here to lay his hand on every vessel (be it Chalice or Flagon). **1686** *Lond. Gaz.* No. 2164/4 Stole.. out of the Parish Church of Ashborne.. a Silver gilt Flagon. **1872** O. SHIPLEY *Gloss. Eccl. Terms, Flagon*, the vessel 1. on the credence for the wine at mass; 2. on the altar, if the chalice be too small.

3. As much as a flagon will hold; also, a flagon and its contents; hence, as a measure of capacity (see quot. 1858).

1602 SHAKS. *Ham.* v. i. 197 A pour'd a Flaggon of Renish on my head once. **1703** *Lond. Gaz.* No. 3906/2 They sent his Grace 36 Flagons of Wine. **1750** JOHNSON *Rambler* No. 49 ⁋10 He had.. drank many a flaggon. **1830** JAMES *Darnley* xxxviii, Sending over many a flaggon of wine and hypocras. **1858** SIMMONDS *Dict. Trade, Flagon*.. a measure of two quarts.

4. *attrib.* as **flagon-bracelet, -chain**, ? a chain-bracelet to which a smelling-bottle (F. *flacon*) could be attached.

1564–78 BULLEYN *Dial. agst. Pest.* (1886) 11 Here is also a Flagone chaine of the hundred angelles that you did giue me in your laste greate Feuer. **1598** *Lanc. Wills* II. 97 One flagon cheane viij[li].. twoe flagon cheane braselette iiij[li]. **1606** MARSTON *Parasitaster* IV. i, I was a simple countrie Ladie, wore golde buttons, trunck-sleeues, and flaggon bracelets.

flagon[2] ('flægən). *Anglo-Irish.* Also **flaggan.** [Corrupted form of FLAGGER[1].] = FLAG *sb.*[1]

1878–86 BRITTEN & HOLLAND *Plant-n.*, Flaggan, *Iris Pseudacorus* L.—Ireland (Belfast). **1882** *Hardwicke's Science Gossip* Feb. 43 Local names of plants. Co. Fermanagh.—Iris, 'Flagons'.

†**'flagonal**, *a.* *Obs. rare*[−1]. In 7 **flaggonal.** [f. FLAGON[1] + -AL[1].] Of or pertaining to a flagon.

1653 URQUHART *Rabelais* I. v. 26 This is called a cup of dissimulation, or flaggonal hypocrisie.

†**'flagonet.** *Obs.* [f. as prec. + -ET[1].] A small flagon; a flagon-shaped vessel.

1599 BP. HALL *Sat.* VI. i. 84 With a big-bellied gallon flagonet. **1648** HERRICK *Hesper., Invitation*, In a burnisht flagonet stood by Beere small as comfort, dead as charity.

flagonless ('flægənlɪs) *a.* [f. as prec. + -LESS.] Wanting or not having a flagon.

a **1849** J. C. MANGAN *Poems* (1859) 459 Wifeless, friendless, flaggonless, alone.

†**'flagrable**, *a.* *Obs.*[−1] [f. L. *flagrā-re* to blaze (see FLAGRANT) + -BLE.] Tending to blaze; capable of being set on fire.

1669 W. SIMPSON *Hydrol. Chym.* 251 *Sal Alkali* made out of spirit of Wine which before was Flagrable.

flagrance ('fleɪgrəns). *rare.* [ad. (either directly or through OF. *flagrance*) L. *flagrantia*, n. of quality f. *flagrant-em* FLAGRANT.]

1. *lit.* Blazing or glowing condition.

1847 *Blackw. Mag.* LXI. 735 We had been brought now to the very flagrance of the dog-star. **1892** BARING-GOULD *Roar of Sea* III. liii. 235 Some vent had been found, and the attic was in full flagrance.

2. Of an offence: The quality or state of being flagrant; glaring shamefulness.

1612–15 BP. HALL *Contempl. N.T.* IV. xv, They bring to him a woman taken in the flagrance of her adultery. **1863** MRS. C. CLARKE *Shaks. Char.* xiii. 321 The shuffling sophistry.. is the very flagrance and crassitude of baseness.

flagrancy ('fleɪgrənsɪ). [ad. L. *flagrantia*: see prec. and -ANCY.]

1. *lit.* The quality of being flagrant; glowing or blazing condition. *Obs.* or *arch.*

1626 BACON *Sylva* §722 Lust causeth a Flagrancie in the Eyes. **1822** T. TAYLOR *Apuleius* 300 So many various stars are beheld supernally in ether, i.e. in the most clear flagrancy of fire.

b. *fig.*

1599 SANDYS *Europæ Spec.* (1632) 240 To draw the modest beauty of a Virgin out of the flagrancy of Harlots. **1650** TRAPP *Clavis To Bible* III. 56 So they dyed in the flagrancy of their lust.

2. Of an offence, crime, evil, etc.: Heinousness, enormity, outrageousness.

1714 STEELE *Apol.* Pref., Polit. Writ. (1715) 215 The Flagrancy and dangerous Consequence of what was doing. **1760** DERRICK *Lett.* (1767) I. 64 A punishment.. which was greatly inadequate to the flagrancy of his crime. *a* **1797** H. WALPOLE *Mem. Geo. III* (1845) II. x. 221 Ministers.. were borne down by the flagrancy of the provocation. **1810** BENTHAM *Elem. Art of Packing* (1821) 245 To do what can be done.. towards holding up to view the flagrancy of the disease.

flagrant ('fleɪgrənt), *a.* [ad. L. *flagrant-em*, pr. pple. of *flagrāre* to burn, f. root *flăg-*, Aryan *bhleg-* to blaze.]

1. *lit.* Blazing, burning, flaming, glowing. *arch.*

1513 BRADSHAW *St. Werburge* II. 334 Torches were caried on eche syde flagrant. **1626** G. SANDYS *Ovid's Met.* VIII. 161 His mother snatcht it.. Out of the fire; and quencht the flagrant brand. **1692** R. L'ESTRANGE *Josephus' Antiq.* IV. iv. (1733) 82 It [a Fire] was clear and flagrant. **1814** SOUTHEY *Roderick* v. 10 Round the crackling hearth, Where heath and cistus gave their flagrant flame. **1856** T. AIRD *Poet. Wks.* 352 Forthwith burst The flagrant lightnings.

†**b.** Of a fluid: Fiery, hot. Hence, *in flagrant blood*, opp. to *in cold blood*. *Obs.*

1614 RALEIGH *Hist. World* III. 73 The Lacedæmonians.. would in cold bloud perform what the Athenians did usually in flagrant. **1676** BEAL in *Phil. Trans.* XI. 588 More sober allayers of thirst, than their Flagrant kill devil.

c. *fig.*

1627–77 FELTHAM *Resolves* II. xlvi. 249 They, who to others seemed flagrant in their tongues, had Ice congealed in their frozen hearts. **1634** HERBERT *Trav.* 108 Quenching his flagrant thirst at the streame. **1822–56** DE QUINCEY *Confess.* (1862) 132 Flagrant health, health boiling over in fiery rapture.

2. a. Of war: Raging; actually in progress. **b.** *in flagrant delict* (= L. *flagrante delicto*): in the very act. *rare.*

1818 HALLAM *Mid. Ages* (1872) III. 157 Except in moments of flagrant civil war. **18..** PALFREY (Webster 1864), A war with the most powerful of the native tribes was flagrant. **1872** E. W. ROBERTSON *Hist. Ess.* 137 When an offender was taken in flagrant delict.

†**3.** Of feelings, passions, etc. (*rarely* of persons): Ardent, burning, intensely eager or earnest. *Obs.*

1515 BARCLAY *Egloges* iv. (1570) C v/4 By flagrant ardour inflamed. **1597** HOOKER *Eccl. Pol.* v. xxxix. (1611) 262 A thing which stirreth up flagrant desires and affections. **1675** MARVELL *Corr.* ccxlix. (1872–5) II. 467 Strangways, a flagrant churchman, made privy counsellor. **1708** OZELL tr. *Boileau's Lutrin* iv. 62 Give Energy to my Enervate Tongue, While the fir'd Chanter's flagrant Rage is sung. **1784** COWPER *Task* III. 794 He burns with most intense and flagrant zeal To serve his country.

4. In occasional uses referring to the visible aspect of flame. †**a.** Resplendent, glorious. *Obs.*

? *a* **1500** *York Myst., Innholders* 39 O flagrant fader! graunte yt myght so be.

†**b.** Burning red from a flogging. *Obs.*

1718 PRIOR *Henry & Emma* 452 The Beadle's Lash still flagrant on their Back. **1728** POPE *Dunc.* II. 128 T[utchin] flagrant from the lash. **1812** SOUTHEY *Lett.* (1856) II. 264 Half.. went over red-hot from the conventicle; the other half, flagrant from Bridewell. *c* **1838** DE QUINCEY *Shakspeare* Wks. 1863 XII. 57 A young man yet flagrant from the lash of the executioner or the beadle.

c. Flaring, gaudy.

1858 CARLYLE *Fredk. Gt.* (1865) II. VI. iii. 164 A highgoing.. Dowager (who dresses, if I recollect, in flagrant colours).

5. Of an offence, crime, etc.; also of an offender: Glaring, notorious, scandalous, 'flaming into notice' (J.).

1706 DE FOE *Jure Div.* Pref. 25 The constant Enormities committed by such flagrant Wretches. **1712** STEELE *Spect.* No. 430 ⁋3 The Fault I speak of was so very flagrant. **1746** SMOLLETT *Reproof* 96 You are a flagrant misanthrope. **1771** FLETCHER *Checks* Wks. 1795 II. 260 Many individuals.. were cut off on account of their flagrant wickedness. **1824** DIBDIN *Libr. Comp.* 746 Ney—an indifferent General, and a flagrant traitor. **1838** THIRLWALL *Greece* II. xi. 22 They had been guilty of a flagrant violation of religion. **1893** F. HALL in *Nation* (N.Y.) LVII. 142/2 Nor.. are his errors less numerous or less flagrant than those of Mr. B.

†**6.** = FRAGRANT. *Obs.*

[The L. vbs. *flagrare* and *fragrare* were often confused in MSS.; cf. F. *flairer* to smell, which in form represents the former. The last quot., however, is burlesque.]

1450 *Pol. Poems* II. 232 The monethe of May.. Flagrant in her floures. *c* **1530** LD. BERNERS *Arth. Lyt. Bryt.* (1814) 376 In the flagraunt odour therof, bothe the body & the herte is reioysed. **1611** BEAUM. & FL. *Knt. Burning Pestle* IV. v, For now the flagrant flowers do spring.

Hence **'flagrantness.**

1727 in BAILEY vol. II.

flagrantly ('fleɪgrəntlɪ), *adv.* [f. prec. + -LY[2].] In a flagrant manner or degree; glaringly, notoriously, scandalously.

1756 J. WARTON *Ess. Pope* ii. (1772) 61 An epigram of four lines; [is] a species of wit flagrantly unsuitable to the dignity.. of the epic muse. **1818** COBBETT *Pol. Reg.* XXXIII. 701 You will see how flagrantly the honour.. and glory, of our country.. are all sacrificed to the selfish views of the Boroughmongers. **1874** MOTLEY *Barneveld* II. xx. 332 A privilege which had been flagrantly interfered with.

†**'flagrate**, *v.* *Obs.* [f. L. *flagrāt-* ppl. stem of *flagrāre* to burn.]

1. *intr.* To burst into flame; to DEFLAGRATE.

1756 C. LUCAS *Ess. Waters* II. 101 It does not flagrate or fulgurate, as nitre does.

2. *trans.* To injure by fire; to burn.

Hence **'flagrating** *ppl. a.*

1705 GREENHILL *Art Embalming* iii. 336 Typhon's destructive and flagrating Power.. was made more temperate.

†**fla'gration.** *Obs.* [as if ad. L. **flagrātiōn-em*, agent-n. f. *flagrāre* to blaze.] The action of bursting into flame or blazing up; burning; a conflagration.

1669 W. SIMPSON *Hydrol. Chym.* 142 Unless the Hydropick moisture.. be exhausted by flagration. **1694** WESTMACOTT *Script. Herb.* (1695) 214 If it [Spirit] take Fire.. and Consume even to the Flagration and Explosion of the Gun-powder. **1727** in BAILEY vol. II. **1847** in CRAIG.

fig. **1679** G. R. tr. *Boyatuau's Theat. World* II. 186 For it fortuned so after the Universal Flagration of Italy.

'flag-root. *U.S.* [f. FLAG *sb.*[1]] The root of the sweet flag (*Acorus Calamus*); the plant itself.

1851 THOREAU *Autumn* (1894) 77 Flagroot, a plant which looks like a cock's tail or a peacock's feather in form.

‖**flagrum** ('fleɪgrəm). *Zool.* [Lat. *flagrum* whip.] A part of the jaw-feet of some crustaceans.

1855 *Eng. Cycl., Nat. Hist.* III. 86/2 They [Hippides] have neither flagrum (fouet) nor palp.

'flagship, *sb.* (*a.*) Also **flag-ship.** [f. FLAG *sb.*[4] + SHIP *sb.*]

1. A ship bearing an admiral's flag.

1672 *Lond. Gaz.* No. 684/4 We.. believe there are several other sunk, and amongst the rest a Flagship. **1740** JOHNSON *Life Blake* Wks. IV. 369 With the loss of one flagship, and six other men of war. **1887** *Spectator* 30 July 1019/1 The 'Inflexible', the flagship for the Admiral.

2. a. *transf.* and *fig.* A leader; something that is or is held to be the best of its kind; *spec.* the major product, model, etc., in a company's range.

1933 M. ARLEN *Man's Mortality* xiii. 261 Knut Helgar sat drinking lager in the control-room of his flagship, I. A. *Valkyr* [*sc.* an aircraft]. **1955** *Wall St. Jrnl.* 13 Jan. 3/1 'Flagship' of the network is.. what Allied calls 'the greatest regional shopping center the nation has ever seen'. **1968** *Listener* 23 May 669/1 The *Mirror* in the past has always been the Fleet Street flagship of the Socialist party. **1976** *Milestones* Winter 31/1 BMW's largest six-cylinder range... Engine sizes range from the 2500 up to the 3.3-litre unit fitted to this, their flagship. **1985** *Listener* 14 Feb. 3/3 The flagship of the devolution strategy, the resiting of one of London's four publicly funded symphony orchestras in Nottingham, seems stuck in the Thames mud.

b. *attrib.* or as *adj.* Representing the leading product, etc., in a range; specially promoted.

1977 *Listener* 20 Oct. 502/1 Flagship programmes on BBC TV were offered as remedies. **1978** *Daily Tel.* 4 Oct. 14/5 Opel's new flagship model, the three-litre Monza coupé. **1981** *Times* 7 Dec. 13/8 THF's flagship hotel, Grosvenor House. **1985** *Truck & Driver* June 18/4 They now found themselves short of flagship trucks to sell.

'flag-staff, 'flagstaff. Pl. (-staves), -staffs. [f. FLAG *sb.*[4] + STAFF.] A pole or staff on which a flag is hung.

a **1613** OVERBURY *Characters, Saylor* Wks. (1856) 76 He.. cannot sit unlesse he beare a flag-staffe. **1698** FRYER *Acc. E. Ind. & P.* 82 Flying the several Colours.. on Flag-Staffs erected for that purpose. **1706** PHILLIPS (ed. Kersey), *Flag-staves.* **1790** BEATSON *Nav. & Mil. Mem.* II. 166 Hoist a red flag on the flag-staff. **1848** DICKENS *Dombey* ix, It began with the erection of flag-staffs.

'flag-stone, 'flagstone. [f. FLAG *sb.*[2] + STONE.]

1. a. A flag or flat stone suitable for paving, etc.; hence often in *pl.* = pavement. **b.** Sandstone capable of being split up into flags.

a. 1730 A. GORDON *Maffei's Amphith.* 359 A Pavement of large Flag-Stones. **1791** BOSWELL *Johnson* (1848) 807/2 Over his [Johnson's] grave was placed a large blue flag-stone with this inscription. **1840** MRS. F. TROLLOPE *Widow Married* xii, Enjoying the sea-breeze on the broad flag-stones of the Marine Parade.

b. 1812–16 J. SMITH *Panorama Sc. & Art* I. 220 If.. a block of flag-stone were converted into a pillar. **1868** LOSSING *Hudson* 184 Extensive quarries of flagstone.

attrib. **1842** H. MILLER *O.R. Sandst.* x. (ed. 2) 229 The flagstone quarries of Caithness and Carmylie.

2. flagstone artist = *pavement-artist* (see PAVEMENT *sb.* 4).

1861 MAYHEW *Lond. Labour* Extra vol. (1862) 436/2 They arrested these flag-stone artists with others. **1891** KIPLING *Light that Failed* iv. 54 They believed I was a self-taught flagstone artist.

Hence **'flagstoned**, paved with flag-stones.

1885 S. O. JEWETT *Marsh Isl.* xi, From whence one could look across the flagstoned court.

flaich, var. of FLEECH *v.* to flatter.

flaid, obs. pa. t. and pple. of FLAY, FLEY, *vbs.*

flaik, obs. Sc. or dial. form of FLAKE.

flail (fleɪl), *sb.* and *a.* Forms: 1 **fliȝel**, 3 *Orm.* **fleȝȝl**, 4–5 **fleil(e, -yl(e**, 4–6 **flaill**, 5 **flayel, flaylle, flaelle**, 5–7 **flayl(e**, 6 **flale, flael**, 6–8 **flaile**, 7 **fleale, fleyle**, (8 **flay**), 4– **flail.** [The late OE. *fliȝel* is possibly a corruption of **flegil*, corresponding to MDu., Du., LG. *vlegel*, OHG. *flegel* (MHG. *vlegel*, mod.Ger. *flegel*):—WGer. **flagil*, prob. ad. L. *flagellum* lit. 'scourge,' but already in the Vulgate used for 'flail'. Some scholars have thought that the WGer. word may be f. OTeut. root **flah-*, *flag-*:—pre-Teut. **plak-* (cf. Lith. *plàkti* to strike, Gr. πληγνύναι); but this appears improbable. Cf. the synonymous Rom. forms, OF. *flaiel*, *flael*, *fleel* (mod.F. *fléau*), Pr. *flagel*, *flachel*, Sp. *flagelo*, Pg. *flagello*, It. *fragello*:—L. *flagellum*. The 15th c. spelling *flayel*, and perh. some earlier forms, are influenced by the OF. word.]

A. *sb.* **1. a.** An instrument for threshing corn by hand, consisting of a wooden staff or handle, at the end of which a stouter and shorter pole or club, called a swingle or swipple, is so hung as to swing freely.

a **1100** *Gerefa* in *Anglia* (1886) IX. 264 To odene fliȝel and andlamena fela. *c* **1200** ORMIN 1500 þa þresshesst tu þin corn wiþþ fleȝȝl. **1362** LANGL. *P. Pl.* A. VII. 174 Faytors.. flapten on with fleiles from morwe til euen. **1481** CAXTON *Reynard* (Arb.) 15 Alle ranne theder..some with a rake, some with a brome..some with a flayel. **1526** *Pilgr. Perf.* (W. de W. 1531) 134 b, The flayle tryeth ye corne from the chaffe. **1635** COWLEY *Davideis* IV. 170 Nor did great Gideon his old Flail disdain, After won Fields. **1727** SWIFT *Gulliver* III. ii. 183 A blown bladder fastened like a flail at the end of a short stick. **1868** ROGERS *Pol. Econ.* x. (1876) 24 Thirty years ago all corn, or nearly all corn, was threshed by the flail.

Proverb. **1674**, **1730** [see FENCE *sb.* 3].

b. *fig.* Also in phrase ***to be threshed with your own flail***: to be treated as you have treated others.

c **1489** CAXTON *Blanchardyn* xxxii. 121 Beten wyth the flayel of fortune. **1589** *Pappe w. Hatchet* (1844) 23 Faith Martin, you shall bee thresht with your owne flaile. **1682** DRYDEN *Mac Fl.* 82 A scourge of Wit, and flayle of Sense. **1781** COWPER *Expost.* 302 Flails of oratory thresh the floor. **1831** CARLYLE in Froude *Life* (1882) II. 208 A tall, loose.. vehement-looking flail of a man.

2. A military weapon resembling a threshing-flail in construction, but usually of iron or strengthened with iron, and often having the striking part armed with spikes. Cf. MORNING-STAR.

Also ***Protestant flail*** (Eng. Hist.): a weapon consisting of a short staff, loaded with lead, attached to the wrist by a strap; it is said to have been carried during the excitement of the 'Popish Plot' (1678–81) by persons who professed to be in fear of murderous assaults by 'Papists'.

c **1475** *Partenay* 2999 Flaelles thre of yre. *c* **1500** *Melusine* xxxviii. 303 The geaunt toke hys flayel of yron, & gaf geffray a grete buffet. **1596** SPENSER *F.Q.* v. ix. 19 He with his yron flaile Gan drive at him, with..might and maine. **1633** P. FLETCHER *Purple Isl.* XI 24 She..Drove farre their flying troops, & thresht with iron flail. ?*c* **1682** *Ballad* in *Roxb. Ball.* IV. 35 Listen a while, and I'll tell you a tale Of a new Device of a Protestant Flayl. *a* **1734** NORTH *Exam.* (1740) 572 A certain Pocket Weapon..called a Protestant Flail. **1887** *Dict. Nat. Biog.* XI. 332 [S. College] made himself notorious..by inventing a weapon..which he called 'the protestant flail'.

† **3.** [After F. *fléau.*] Something that swings on a pivot. **a.** A swing-bar for a gate. **b.** A beam like that of a balance (by which two buckets can be lowered alternately into a draw-well). **c.** A lever with the free extremity weighted, forming part of a cider-press. *Obs.*

c **1450** *Merlin* 206 Merlin caught the flayle of the yate and plukked it to hym and yede oute as lightly as it hadde not haue ben lokked. *c* **1450** HENRYSON *Mor. Fab.* x. 177 Lawrence gird downe [the well]..The other bade aboue and held the flaill. **1691** WORLIDGE *Cyder* (ed. 3) 113 The Flail-Press..with heavy Weights or Stones at the end of the Flail.

† **4.** As transl. of L. *flagellum*: A scourge. *Obs.*

1432–50 tr. *Higden* (Rolls) I. 139 Takenge a flayle in theire honde.

5. *attrib.* and *Comb.*, as ***flail-man***; ***flail-finned***, ***-like*** adjs. Also, **flail-cap** (= Du. *vlegelkap*, Ger. *flegelkappe*), the cap (CAP *sb.*^{1} 12) or CAPLIN of a flail; **flail-capping** *dial.* = prec.; **flail(-type) harvester**, a type of harvesting-machine for forage-grass (see quot.); **flail-joint** *Med.*, a joint showing grossly excessive mobility; † **flail-press** (see 3 c); † **flail-staff**, the part of the flail held in the hands; **flail-stone**, an elongated stone with a hole at one end, for use as a flail-swingle; † **flail-swinger**, a thresher; **flail-swingle**, the swinging or freely-moving part of the flail; **flail tank**, a type of tank used for clearing a mine-field.

c **1440** *Promp. Parv.* 165/1 *Fleyl cappe, *cappa*. **1878** *Cumbld. Gloss.*, **Flail cappin'*, the leather attached to the upper end of the flail soople. **1630** DONNE *Progress Soul* xxxvi. Poems (1669) 302 The *Flail-finn'd Thresher and steel-beak'd Sword-fish. **1959** *Farmer & Stockbreeder* 12 May 70 (*heading*) With a *flail harvester. *Ibid.* 70/1 The true flail-type harvester has a horizontal rotor to which is attached a number of free-swinging flails or cutters. [These flails] cut the grass by high speed impact. **1876** *Trans. Clin. Soc.* IX. 173 A *flail joint, *i.e.* union by a fibrous bond, more or less long, between the bones of thigh and leg. **1967** A. R. SHANDS et al. *Handbk. Orthopaedic Surg.* x. 190 Useful procedures in the surgical treatment of polio-myelitis and other types of flaccid paralysis..restore stability to flail joints. **1880** BROWNING *Dram. Idylls* Ser. II. 224 A human sheaf it thrashed *Flail-like. **1855** J. HEWITT *Anc. Armour* I. 327 The *flail-man in our engraving is engaged in the assault of a castle. **1864** LD. PALMERSTON in *Daily Tel.* 16 Dec., When the first threshing machines were introduced there was a revolt..among the flail-men. *c* **1440** *Promp. Parv.* 165/2 *Fleyl staffe, or honde staffe, *manutentum*. **1851** D. WILSON *Preh. Ann.* (1863) I. 190 Like the ruder *flail-stone, the morning-star, when efficiently wielded, must have proved a deadly weapon. *c* **1515** *Cocke Lorell's B.* (Percy Soc.) 4 Adam auerus *flayle swenger. *c* **1440** *Promp. Parv.* 165/2 *Fleyle swyngyl, *virga*. **1944** *Hutchinson's Pict. Hist. War* 12 Apr.–12 Sept. 423 (*caption*) The enemy has sown mines and the *flail tank in the distance is clearing them away.

B. *adj.* [f. the sb. used *attrib.* as in *flail-joint* (see above).] Of a part of the body, esp. a joint: exhibiting grossly excessive mobility as a result of the loss or absence of normal muscular control.

1876 [see *flail-joint* above]. **1919** R. C. ELMSLIE *After Treatment Wounds & Injuries* vi. 61 A flail but mobile hip joint can be supported by..a Thomas Caliper splint. *Ibid.* xiv. 206 A flail condition of the hip joint results from removal of the head of the femur. **1959** A. G. APLEY *System of Orthopaedics & Fractures* viii. 78 Where the muscles controlling a joint are all equally weakened..the joint becomes flail. **1961** G. PERKINS *Orthopaedics* xx. 300 A Charcot's elbow is also flail, but it is unlike the flail elbow caused by surgical excision. **1968** A. B. FERGUSON *Orthopaedic Surg.* (ed. 3) vii. 605 The foot, if completely flail, must be supported on both sides, as well as anteriorly and posteriorly, by a double upright brace. **1968** S. TAYLOR et al. *Short Textbk. Surg.* (ed. 2) xvi. 202 When a number of ribs are doubly fractured and a segment of the chest wall cannot be used in respiration it is usually referred to as a flail chest.

flail (fleɪl), *v.* Also 5 **flayle**, 7 **fleyle**. [f. prec. sb. In early examples of sense 1 perh. ad. OF. *flaeler*:—L. *flagellāre* to FLAGELLATE.]

1. *trans.* To scourge, whip; to beat or thrash. Also ***to flail along***, to drive by beating.

14.. *Songs & Carols* (Percy Soc.) lx. 72 They hym naylyd and yl flaylyd, Alas, that innocent! **1839** K. H. DIGBY *Mores Catholici* IX. xi. 373 He flails me, and makes all my body burn with his fire. **1873** HOLLAND *A. Bonnic.* v. 85 That's the way my mother always flailed me. **1888** BOLDREWOOD *Robbery under Arms* (1890) 7 We soon got sharp enough to flail him [a pony] along with a quince stick.

2. To strike with or as with a flail.

1583 STANYHURST *Æneis*, etc. (Arb.) 138 For Mars they [the Cyclopes] be sternfulye flayling Hudge spoaks and chariots. **1622** H. SYDENHAM *Serm. Sol. Occ.* II. 97 If we can fleyle down the transgressions of the time. **1878** STEVENSON *Inland Voy.* 165 The misery..made me flail the water with my paddle like a madman. **1878** *Cumbld. Gloss.*, *Flail*, to hit; to beat with a down stroke. **1883** *Blackw. Mag.* Nov., With giant stroke she flails about, And heaps a score of dead.

3. To thresh (corn) with a flail.

1821 SIR J. D. PAUL *Rouge et Noir* 24 Clod..Pens verses on the sheaves he should be flailing.

fig. **1857** WHITTIER *What of the Day* 30 See..through its cloud of dust, the threshing-floor, Flailed by the thunder, heaped with chaffless grain!

4. *intr.* To move in the manner of a flail. Also *fig.*

1874 J. S. BLACKIE in A. M. Stoddart *J. S. Blackie* (1895) II. xvii. 99 Carlyle..is flailing about him in the same one-sided magnificently unreasonable way that you know. **1951** M. MCLUHAN *Mech. Bride* 122/2 She comes flailing along, head back, toes pointed.

† **ˈflaily**, *a.* *Obs.* *rare*$^{-1}$. In 7 **flaly**. [f. FLAIL *sb.* + -Y^1.] Acting like a flail.

1632 VICARS *Aeneid* v. 123 At once all furrows plow..with flaly-oares and slicing foredecks fierce.

flain, obs. pa. pple. of FLAY.

flair (flɛə(r)), *sb.*^{1} [a. OF. and F. *flair*, f. *flairier*, *flairer* to smell:—popular L. *flāgrāre*, altered form of *frāgrāre*: see FRAGRANT.]

† **1.** An odour, a smell. *Obs.*

1340 HAMPOLE *Pr. Consc.* 9017 Alle swete savours..War noght bot als stynk to regard of þat flayre. ?*a* **1400** *Morte Arth.* 772 Syche a vennymous flayre flowe fro his lyppez.

2. [mod.Fr.] Power of 'scent', sagacious perceptiveness, instinctive discernment. Also in weakened senses: (*a*) special aptitude or ability; (*b*) liking, taste, enthusiasm. (Both senses freq. const. *for*.)

1881 MRS. LYNN LINTON *My Love* I. 291 Gip, with the keen 'flair' of her kind, saw how things stood. **1885** MISS BRADDON *Wyllard's Weird* II. ii. 47, I see you have the true flair. **1925** S. LEWIS *Martin Arrowsmith* ix. 106 You have a real flair for investigative science. **1926** FOWLER *Mod. Eng. Usage* 182/1 Mrs. —— has homely accomplishments; a f[lair] for cooking goes with her f[lair] for writing. **1932** *McCall's Mag.* July 96 Her flair for adventure and conquest was rising at the thought of great, strange cities. **1942** *Burlington Mag.* June 134/1 One explanation offered by the psychologist is that this special insight or 'flair' is only found in the repressed or frustrated artist. **1955** *Times* 17 June 3/5 The 'flair' for producing unexpected lobs. **1959** T. S. ELIOT *Elder Statesman* III. 98 Michael's head is well screwed on. He's got brains, he's got flair.

flair (flɛə(r)), *sb.*^{2} Also **flare.** [Cf. OF. *flair* (14th c.) some kind of flat fish.] The ray or skate.

1668 WILKINS *Real Char.* II. v. §3. 133 Flare, Thornback. *a* **1672** WILLUGHBY *Ichthyogr.* (1686) Tab. C.N. 5 The Skate or Flair. **1710** SIBBALD *Hist. Fife* ii. 50 *Raia lævis*, the Skate or Flair. **1740** R. BROOKES *Art of Angling* II. v. 105 The Scate or Flare..is a gristly Fish, with a flat smooth, and very broad Body. **1862** COUCH *Brit. Fishes* I. 87.

flair, var. form of FLARE.

flair (flɛə(r)), *v.* [f. FLAIR^1.] *trans.* To scent. Also *absol.* and *fig.*

1921 *Glasgow Herald* 22 Jan. 4 With a strange and peculiar zest we flair survivals of phrase and intonation lurking in the speech..of very aged persons. **1923** J. MASEFIELD *Poems* 560 The sharp nose flaired them heed-fully. *Ibid.* 563 His ears were cocked and his keen nose flaired. *Ibid.* 565 The fox drew in and flaired with his muzzle. *Ibid.* 569 He flaired the air, then he padded out.

† **ˈflairing**, *ppl. a.* *Obs.* In 3 **fleirand.** [pr. pple. of **flair* vb., a. OF. *flairier*: see FLAIR^1 *sb.*] Smelling; odorous, scented.

a **1300** *Cursor M.* 3695 (Cott.) Quen he had feld his fleirand cloth.

flaitchment: see FLEECHMENT.

† **flaite**, *v.*^{1} *Obs.* *rare*$^{-1}$. [? for **flate*, FLAT *v.*^{4}] *intr.* ? To flatter.

c **1430** *Hymns Virg.* (1867) 74 Quod ouerhope, 'þan y flatir, & sumtyme flaite þou schalt lyue, and þi silf it haue'.

flaite (fleɪt), *v.*^{2} *Obs.* exc. *dial.* Also 6 **flaight**, 7 **flayte.** [var. of FLIGHT *v.*] *trans.* To frighten, scare, terrify. Hence **ˈflaited** *ppl. a.*

1565 GOLDING *Ovid's Met.* II. (1593) 39 His steades that yet for feare doth run Like flaighted fiends. **1642** ROGERS *Naaman* 138 Till the Lord by his terrors flaite her. **1674** RAY *S. & E.C. Words* (1691) 98 *Flaite.* **1721** in BAILEY.

flaith (flɑː). *Irish Hist.* [Irish.] The chief of an ancient family or *fine*.

1861 E. O'CURRRY *Lect. MS. Materials Anc. Ir. Hist.* ix. 202 The hereditary proprietors, the *Flaiths* (pronounced 'flahs'), or landlords. **1876** *Encycl. Brit.* V. 799/2 An *aire* whose family held the same land for three generations was called a *flaith*. *Ibid.* 800/1 The rank of a *flaith* depended upon the number of his *ceiles*. **1898** J. HERON *Celtic Ch.* 15 The 'nobles' or 'flaiths' possessed not only cattle but deis.

flak (flæk). Also **flack.** [G., f. the intials of the elements of **fl***iegerabwehr***k***anone* 'pilot-defence-gun'.]

a. An anti-aircraft gun; also (the usual sense in Eng.), anti-aircraft fire. Also *attrib.* So **flak-happy** *a.*, mentally affected by flak (cf. *bomb-happy* adj., -HAPPY); **flak jacket**, a protective jacket of heavy fabric containing metal strips or plates; **flak ship**, a German anti-aircraft vessel.

1938 *Jane's Fighting Ships* 218/2 [On a German vessel] *A.A. guns.* 4·1 inch, 3·5 inch on H.A. mounts ('Flak'). **1940** *Times Weekly* 23 Apr. 2 Heavy and accurate anti-aircraft fire from the flak ships. **1940** *Times* 16 Sept. 2/3 The word 'Flak' is probably used in every Bomber Command pilot's report after a raid on Germany. **1940** *Flight* 19 Sept. 224/1 One of the British bombers which raided Berlin..had been damaged when diving through heavy *Flak* fire. **1941** D. GARNETT *War in Air* x. 99 Every motorised column of troops..had its own 'Flak' detachment of anti-aircraft guns. **1941** *Times* 30 Sept. 4/7 Blenheim and Beaufort aircraft of Coastal Command flew through intense flak. **1943** in *Amer. Speech* (1944) XIX. 60 *Flak Happy.* **1943** *Hutchinson's Pict. Hist. War* 12 May–3 Aug. 50 One of Hitler's hush-hush flak-towers designed for high elevation defence against raiding aircraft. **1944** *Amer. Speech* XIX. 10 *Flak-happy*..was used to designate the mental confusion of an airman exposed to severe *flak*. **1956** W. A. HEFLIN *U.S.A.F. Dict.* 207/1 Flak curtain... Flak jacket. *Ibid.* 207/2 Flak suit... Flak vest. **1957** J. BRAINE *Room at Top* xxviii. 230 The bomb-aimer got a faceful of flak. **1961** J. HELLER *Catch-22* (1962) xiv. 141 He left his flak suit and parachute there. **1968** *Observer* 4 Feb. 1/1 No man ventures out without a gun and a flak jacket. **1970** *Guardian* 10 July 11/1 Experienced reporters here [*sc.* in Belfast]..have been sending to London for flak jackets. **1971** *Daily Tel.* 5 Aug. 8/7 The burst of orgasms coming as incessantly as a barrage of flak leave one a little sex-shocked.

b. *fig.* (A barrage of) abuse, adverse criticism.

1968 *N.Y. Times* 20 May 46 In spite of the current flak between Mayor Lindsay and..the..administrator of Boston and New Haven.., the potential for the city is unlimited. **1969** A. LURIE *Real People* 163 Well, all right. So why all the flak? **1972** *New Yorker* 16 Jan. 41 (*caption*) Getting much flak from Women's Lib? **1975** *High Times* Dec. 111/2 You may find yorself gathering flack from more vigilant foes of the herb. **1976** T. STOPPARD *Dirty Linen* 25 Isn't that going to cause rather a lot of flak in the..P.L.P.? **1981** *Times* 19 Oct. 17/8 When someone left the office lights on during a power crisis, they..got a good deal of flack in the morning. **1985** A. BLOND *Book Book* ix. 143 Trade pressure groups like the Book Marketing Council have received flak from such pundits as Bernard Levin.

flake (fleɪk), *sb.*^{1} Forms: 4–6 **flek(e**, 5–6 **fleyke**, 6 **fleake**, *Sc.* **flaik**, 7–8 **fleak**, (7 **fleack**), 5– **flake.** *dial.* 9 **fleigh, fleak, flaik.** [? a. ON. *flake*, *fleke* wk. masc., hurdle, wicker shield (Da. *flage* hurdle), corresponding to MDu. *vlāke* fem. (mod.Du. *vlaak* hurdle on which wool is beaten), MLG. and mod.LG. *flake* sort of fishing net. The senses of the word seem to point to some root meaning to plait; a connexion with OTeut. **flehtan* (= L. *plectĕre*, f. root **plek-*; cf. Gr. πλέκειν) to plait, is suggested by the Ger. synonym *flechte* (cf. Ger. *käseflechte* = *cheese-flake* in 2 below), but involves phonological difficulties. The L. *plăga* net, is prob. cognate.]

1. a. A wattled hurdle. Now *dial.* ; in some places applied in wider sense to a hurdle of any kind.

c **1330** R. BRUNNE *Chron.* (1810) 321 A brigge he suld do wrihte, Botes & barges ilkon, with flekes mak þam tighte. **1415** *Churchw. Acc. Somerset* (1890) 68 For fityng off flakes and hurdylls..vj*d.* *c* **1470** HARDING *Chron.* CLXXVII. 1 When they were ouer ye quake of mosse & mire, They drewe the flekes ay after as they went. **1511** *Nottingham Rec.* III. 330, ij. fleykes to be set bytwen ye masons and the wynde. **1513** DOUGLAS *Æneis* XI. ii. 14 Sum of Eneas feris bessely Flakis to plet thame pressis by and by. **1743** *Lond. & Country Brew.* IV. (ed. 2) 322 If the Wind blows there are set Fleaks to shelter the Heap. **1863** GREAVES in *N. & Q.* Ser. 3 III. 96 This [oblong mound] is surrounded by iron fleaks or hurdles.

b. The same used as a temporary gate.

c **1514** *Exam. C. More* in *Chetham Misc.* II. 16 Never ȝate ..but a letull fleke that was for the most parte teyed fast. **1669** WORLIDGE *Syst. Agric.* (1681) 325 A Fleack, a Gate set up in a Gap. **1847** HALLIWELL, *Flake*..a temporary gate or door.

2. a. A frame or rack for storing provisions, in mod. use *esp.* oat-cakes. Cf. *bread-flake*.

c **1420** *Pallad. on Husb.* XII. 248 Plommes summen drie, And hem on fleykes kepe. **1519** HORMAN *Vulg.* 156 b, Ley this meate in trayes and flekis. **1578** *Richmond Wills* (Surtees) 281, iiij chesis and a flake, iiijs . . A chese flake, iiij^{d}. **1641** BEST *Farm. Bks.* (Surtees) 171 One peare of fleakes. **1800** *Trans. Soc. Encourag. Arts* XVIII. 335 Netted frames, resembling the flakes used in Yorkshire for drying oat-cakes. **1865** B. BRIERLEY *Irkdale* I. 91 A 'flake' or 'fleigh', well thatched with cresp-looking and nicely browned oatcakes.

b. A stage or frame used for drying produce, *esp.* fish; a fish-flake. ***upland flake***: a flake for drying codfish, built permanently upon the shore.

1623 WHITBOURNE *Newfoundland* 57 Flakes whereon men yeerely dry their fish. **1649** BLITHE *Eng. Improv. Impr.* xxxv. (1653) 230 When it [Woad] is ground it is to be . . laid upon the fleakes to dry. **1792** J. BELKNAP *Hist. New-Hampsh.* III. 215 The fish is . . spread on hurdles, composed of brush, and raised on stakes, about three or four feet from the ground; these are called flakes. **1876** BANCROFT *Hist. U.S.* II. xxxvi. 393 Wherever safe inlets invited fishermen to spread their flakes.

3. *Naut.* (See quot.)

1867 SMYTH *Sailor's Word-bk, Flake*, a small shifting stage, hung over a ship's side to caulk or repair a breach.

†**4.** A flap on a saddle to keep the rider's knee from touching the horse. [Perh. a distinct word. Cf. FLET *sb.*^{2}] *Obs.*

1568 TURBERV. in Hakl. *Voy.* I. 388 Of birch their saddles be, Much fashioned like the Scottish seates, broad flakes to keepe the knee From sweating of the horse.

5. *Mining.* A framework of boards, used as a shelter against rain and wind.

1653 MANLOVE *Lead-mines* 8 Fleaks, Knockings, Coestid. **1747** HOOSON *Miner's Dict.* I j b, *Fleaks* [are] those very useful things that the Miner uses to make for Shilter, when he has as yet no Côe to hold off the Wind and Rain from his Shaft. **1824** in MANDER *Derbysh. Miners' Gloss.*

6. *attrib.* and *Comb.*, as ***flake-hurdle***; also **flake-room, flake-yard**, 'an inclosure in which flakes for drying salt are built, and in which fish are dried' (*Cent. Dict.*);

1890 *Gloucestersh. Gloss.*, **Flake or Vlake hurdle*, a wattled hurdle. **1894** MORRIS *Wood beyond World* xvii. 132 A tall fence of flake-hurdles. **1856** J. REYNOLDS *Peter Gott* (Bartlett), The owners of vessels have a *flake-yard in the vicinity of the landing-places, to which the fish are carried on being landed.

flake (fleɪk), *sb.*^{2} Forms: 6–8 **fleak(e**, 9 *dial.* **fleak**, *Sc.* **flaike**, 4– **flake**. [Of difficult etymology: possibly several distinct words have coalesced, though ultimate derivation from the Aryan root *plăg-* (cf. Gr. πλήγνύναι to beat), parallel and synonymous with *plăk-* (cf. Lith. *plakù* I beat) may plausibly account for all the senses, and also for the fact that most of these resemble senses belonging to FLAW or FLAUGHT, or to related words in other Teut. langs. (f. Aryan root *plak-*). Sense 1 has not been found earlier than Chaucer, though Junius cites an OE. '*flacea* 7 *flæðra*, flaws or flakes of snow'; it appears to be cognate with ON. *flóke* flock of wool, lock of hair, and perh. with OHG. *floccho* of same meaning (if this be genuinely a Teut. word, repr. a pre-Teut. **plǝgnén-*, and not an adoption of L. *floccus*); the OE. *flacor*, fluttering, has also been compared. The Da. *flage, sneflage*, usually cited as equivalent to E. *flake*, perh. corresponds rather to FLAW (Da. *g* representing ON. *g* as well as ON. *k*); the *Dansk Ordbog* 1800 explains it as a *large* mass of falling snow, as opposed to *flok* which means a 'flake' in the Eng. sense. The senses expressing the notion of 'something peeled or split off' may be compared with FLAY *v.* (OTeut. **flah-*:—OAryan **plak-*). There is possibly a third primary sense, 'something flat'; cf. OHG. *flah* adj. (mod.Ger. *flach*), Du. *vlak* flat, Sw. *flaka* plate, Norw. *flak* ice-floe. But the mutual relation of the Eng. senses is very uncertain.]

1. a. One of the small flocculent pieces in which snow falls.

c **1384** CHAUCER *H. Fame* III. 102 As flakes fallen in great snowes. **1589** *Pappe w. Hatchet* 2 For your flakes of snowe weele pay you with stones of hayle. **1597–8** BP. HALL *Sat.* I. vii, White as . . flakes new blowne. *a* **1649** DRUMM. HAWTH. *Poems* Wks. (1711) 5 Temples spread with flakes of virgin snow. **1784** COWPER *Task* IV. 326 The downy flakes Descending . . Assimilate all objects. **1820** SHELLEY *Sensitive Plant* III. 26 The rose-leaves, like flakes of crimson snow, Paved the turf.

b. A light fleecy tuft; a small piece of some light loosely-cohering substance, as down or fluff; a flock; a fleecy streak (of cloud).

1653 H. MORE *Antid. Ath.* II. vii. (1712) 61 All the Businesses of Men do very much depend upon these little long Fleaks or Threads of Hemp and Flax. **1665** HOOKE *Microgr.* 202 Looking most like to a flake of Worsted prepar'd to be spun. **1712** tr. *Pomet's Hist. Drugs* I. 153 In the Flake [orig. *flocon*] there are seven Seeds as large as Lupins. **1741** STACK in *Phil. Trans.* XLI. 600 Some small Fleaks of Clouds. **1833** HT. MARTINEAU *Manch. Strike* i. 14 You had rather see her covered with white cotton flakes than with yellow ribands. **1855** KINGSLEY *Heroes* I. (1868) 5 Rocks and breakers and flying flakes of foam. **1877** BLACK *Green Past.* xxxv. (1878) 278 There was not a flake of cloud in the sky.

c. ? Gossamer thread. *rare*$^{-1}$.

1817 KIRBY & SP. *Entomol.* II. xxiii 336 They pull in their long thread . . so as to form it into a ball . . of flake.

2. A portion of ignited matter thrown off by a burning or incandescent body; a detached portion of flame; †a flash (of lightning).

13.. *E.E. Allit. P.* B. 954 Flakes of soufre. **1590** SPENSER *F.Q.* III. ii. 5 The rosy red Flasht through her face, as it had beene a flake Of lightning through bright heven fulmined. **1601** WEEVER *Mirr. Mart.* E viij b, Which all at once doe vomit Sulphure flakes. **1602** MARSTON *Antonio's Rev.* I. iii, All the upper vault Thick lac't with flakes of fire. **1660** HOWELL *Lexicon*, Flakes that flee from hammered red hot iron. **1697** DRYDEN *Virg. Georg.* IV. 254 Huge Flakes of Flames expire. **1876** GEO. ELIOT *Dan. Der.* I. 303 Like falling flakes of fire. **1877** BRYANT *Poems, Voice of Autumn* i, Forest leaves . . fall, like flakes of light.

3. A minute exfoliated piece of something, a scale, flattish fragment; †a splinter (of wood). In the first quot. app. *fig.*, a 'bit', small portion.

c **1500** *Maid Emlyn* 109 in Hazl. *E.P.P.* IV. 86 A frere dyd she gyue Of her loue a flake. **1533** MORE *Apol.* i. Wks. 845/2 Sifted to ye vttermost flake of branne. **1599** T. M[OUFET] *Silkwormes* 69 Some graines of muske and Ambres flake. *a* **1648** DIGBY *Closet Open.* in *Leisure H.* (1884) 377/1 Three or four flakes of Mace. **1676** GREW *Anat. Plants* (1682) 263 Flakes or Grains of Bay-Salt. **1705** ADDISON *Italy* 370 Little Flakes of Scurfe. *c* **1720** W. GIBSON *Farrier's Guide* II. lxxxix. (1738) 252 A Prick of a Nail, a Stub, or a Fleak. **1799** G. SMITH *Laboratory* I. 21 Fine iron flakes.

4. a. A thin broad piece peeled or split off from the surface of something. In recent use also *spec.* a chip of hard stone used in prehistoric times as a cutting instrument; cf. FLINT-FLAKE.

1591 G. FLETCHER *Russe Commw.* (Hakluyt Soc.) 14 They . . teare it [a rock] into thin flakes . . and so use it for glasse-lanthorns. **1601** HOLLAND *Pliny* II. 467 The flint or rock . . will cleaue in length, and come away by the sides in broad flakes. **1607** TOPSELL *Serpents* (1658) 675 A thin fleak of a horn, which being laid over black, seemeth black. **1703** MOXON *Mech. Exerc.* 218 The Beam and Tooth . . cut and tore away great Flakes of the Mettal. **1845** DARWIN *Voy. Nat.* xvi. (1852) 369 The shells . . scaling off in flakes. **1865** LUBBOCK *Preh. Times* i. (1878) 13 We have a list comprising . . 310 long flakes and about 2000 small ones. **1875** LYELL *Princ. Geol.* II. III. xlvii. 367 Flint Flakes having a fine cutting edge . . are met with.

b. A piece of skin or flesh peeled or torn off; †a torn strip (of a garment).

1611 SYLVESTER *Du Bartas* II. iv. III. *Schisme* 236 Her mantle (tattered all in flakes). **1802** *Med. Jrnl.* VIII. 30 The skin, instead of becoming branny, separated in large flakes. **1877** BRYANT *Odyss.* v. 520 Flakes of skin . . Were left upon the rock. **1894** *Daily News* 26 June 8/2 The flesh hung in flakes . . on his arm.

c. *pl.* Short for *cornflakes* (CORN *sb.*^{1} 11).

1951 *Good Housek. Home Encycl.* 371/2 Crisp flakes with cold milk and sugar.

5. a. A stratum, lamina, or layer. (In quot. 1616 applied to the shell of an oyster.)

1577 B. GOOGE *Heresbach's Husb.* (1586) I. 21 b, The Plowe . . breakes it not small yenough, but turneth up great flakes. **1613** PURCHAS *Pilgrimage* VI. v. §2 (1626) 649 A Sedgie Reed . . called Papyrus, which easily diuides it selfe into thinne flakes. **1616** BROWNE *Brit. Past.* II. iii. 56 And claps it twixt the two pearle hiding flakes Of the broad yawning Oyster. **1828** STARK *Elem. Nat. Hist.* II. 485 Flakes or thin laminæ. **1843** PORTLOCK *Geol.* 543 A dark green, talcose, clayey matter, disposed in irregular flakes. **1882** *Garden* 14 Jan. 27/3 Thymes and Veronicas grow over stones in great flakes when let alone.

b. *pl.* (See quot.)

1883 GRESLEY *Gloss. Coal Mining, Flaikes*, shaly or fissile sandstone.

6. A (loose) sheet of ice; a floe.

1555 EDEN *Decades* 305 The flakes or pieces of Ise doo flote aboue the water. **1685** LUTTRELL *Brief Rel.* (1857) I. 297 Vast flakes of ice of severall miles. **1796** MORSE *Amer. Geog.* I. 139 To coast . . in small vessels, between the great flakes of ice and the shore. **1820** W. SCORESBY *Arct. Reg.* I. 243 Immense flakes of ice . . resembling fields in the extent of their surface.

7. *pl.* The portions into which the flesh, *esp.* of certain fish, naturally falls.

1611 BIBLE *Job* xli. 23 The flakes of his flesh are ioyned together. **1622** DRAYTON *Poly-olb.* xxvi. (1748) 371[The salmon] whose grain doth rise in flakes with fatness interlarded. **1698** TYSON *Opossum* in *Phil. Trans.* XX. 139 Laminæ [of fat] . . easily separable from one another, in broad Fleaks. **1892** H. HUTCHINSON *Fairway Isl.* 19 The salmon . . was insipid . . though Mr. Trewin . . showed the curd between its flakes.

8. A bundle of parallel threads or fibres; a lock or band of hair not twisted or plaited. *arch.*

1592 LYLY *Midas* III. ii, Your mustachoes . . hanging downe to your mouth like goates flakes. **1697** DAMPIER *Voy.* I. 37 Maho . . Whose Bark is made up of strings or threads . . You may draw it off either in flakes or small threads. **1713** STEELE *Guardian* No. 86 ¶5 The flakes of hair which naturally suggest the idea of lightning. **1792** DIBDIN *Female Crusoe* in *Naval Chron.* XXIV. 464, I dressed some . . cotton into . . thin flakes. **1839** MARRYAT *Phantom Ship* viii, His hair . . fell in long flakes upon his shoulders. **1870** SWINBURNE *Ess. & Stud.* (1875) 363 The heavy straying flakes of unfilleted hair.

transf. **1658** ROWLAND *Moufet's Theat. Ins.* 908 That Honey is best for substance, which . . if you lift it up . . falls to the earth still homogeneous, unsevered, no way parted asunder, but remaines in one continued flake or line.

9. A kind of carnation with striped petals.

1727 BRADLEY *Fam. Dict.* s.v. *Carnation*, The Flakes are of two Colours only, and those always strip'd. **1822** LOUDON *Encycl. Gardening* III. II. 977 The varieties of this flower [carnation] are now arranged in three classes: flakes, bizarres, and picotées.

10. a. [from the vb.] A small fracture or 'chip'.

1866–7 G. STEPHENS *Runic Mon.* I. 205 A mere accidental flake, and not touching the letter itself.

b. [Back-formation f. FLAKY *a.* 4.] One who is 'flaky' or liable to act in an eccentric or crazy manner, a 'screwball'; also, a foolish, slow-witted, or unreliable person. *slang* (chiefly *U.S.*).

1968 *Time* 9 Feb. 71/1 He has a well-deserved reputation as something of a flake. During an exhibition ski jump in Switzerland, Jean-Claude shocked spectators by dropping his trousers in mid-air. **1968–70** *Current Slang* (Univ. S. Dakota) III–IV. 47 *Flake*, a dumbbell; one who is not very bright. — College students, both sexes, New Hampshire. **1973** *Globe & Mail* (Toronto) 13 July 36/1 Richard Quincy Thornton is always considered by squares, as the finest flake outside of a box of breakfast cereal. **1974** R. B. PARKER *Godwulf MS* vii. 58 'There's a lot of flakes in that department. There's a lot of flakes in most departments, if you really want to know.' . . 'Okay, but who is the flakiest?' **1980** *Christian Science Monitor* 10 Apr. 22/2 The media, normally in love with articulateness for the sake of articulateness, stopped quoting Brown, dismissing him as a 'flake' — a rap that stuck despite all the banker's suits and ties and one of the shortest haircuts in the race. **1982** W. SAFIRE in *N.Y. Times Mag.* 24 Oct. 16 Out in California, Gov. Jerry Brown—often called a *flake*—was campaigning against San Diego Mayor Pete Wilson for United States Senator . . . Larry Liebert . . quoted an anonymous Brown aide as asking: 'Why trade a flake for a wimp.' **1983** *Easyriders* Feb. 77/3 Gotta git rid of that flake Bobby Joe. He's just too gutless for the big time.

11. a. *attrib.* in the trade names for varieties of certain products, as ***flake-manna, -tapioca, -tobacco***, from their flaky appearance.

1886 *Daily News* 24 Dec. 2/6 Tapioca . . Singapore flake sold at rather firmer prices. **1889** *Syd. Soc. Lex.* s.v. *Manna, Flake Manna*, a term employed in English commerce to denote the larger fragments and better qualities of manna. **1894** *Westm. Gaz.* 14 Feb. 2/1 Flake tobaccos . . are growing . . in popularity.

b. *Comb.*, as ***flake-heaped*** ppl. a.; also **flake-feather**, a plumule of extreme fineness and silky texture, found in falconine birds; hence ***flake-feathered*** adj. (in quot. *transf.*); **flake-stand**, the cooling-tub of a still-worm; **flake-white**, a pigment made from the purest white-lead in the form of flakes or scales.

1837 W. MACGILLIVRAY *Brit. Birds* I. Introd. 79 If it be necessary to give these feathers a name, they may be called *flake-feathers. **1848** D. GREENWELL *Poems* 35 The *flake-feathered trees show like giant plumes. **1880** BROWNING *Dram. Idylls* Ser. II. *Pan. & Luna* 38 *Flake-heaped how or whence, The structure of that succourable cloud, What matter? **1830** DONOVAN *Dom. Econ.* I. 255 The mash-tun and *flakestand might both be worth twelve shillings. **1660** *Albert Durer Revived* 18 White Lead, or *Flake White. **1752** LADY LUXBOROUGH *Let. to Shenstone* 6 Nov., My great parlour . . is painted with flake-white. **1883** J. PAYN *Thicker than Water* xxix. (1884) 229 Her whole face with a pallor on it like flake white or dead white.

c. *attrib.* and *Comb.* uses in *Archæol.* (see sense 4 above) as ***flake-knife***, etc.; **flake culture**, a prehistoric culture using flake implements.

1865 TYLOR *Early Hist. Man.* viii. 195 The flake-knives are very rude. **1924** M. C. BURKITT *Our Forerunners* 81 If small flakes have been taken off round a flint core which is then split in half, the result is a flat under-surface . . on the other side of which are flake scars. **1926, 1935** [see CORE *sb.*^{1} 5]. **1927** PEAKE & FLEURE *Hunters & Artists* iv. 42 Flake implements, or those formed by working up the edges of the flakes struck from a core, only came into gradual use in Acheulian times, and even then were not common. **1928** D. A. E. GARROD in *Proc. Prehist. Soc. E. Anglia* V. III. 266 From what I have called the 'blade-culture'-group we turn to the great cycle of 'flake-industries'. **1935, 1943** [see BLADE *sb.* 6 b]. **1937** [see BIFACE]. **1937** GARROD & BATE *Stone Age Mt. Carmel* I. i. iii. 32 Flake-scrapers . . are flakes with scraper retouch round some part of the edge. The majority are rough and shapeless. **1947** J. & C. HAWKES *Prehist. Brit.* (ed. 2) i. 10 White flake cultures are predominantly Eastern, extending right across Asia, the core cultures have an African bias. **1957** CHILDE *Dawn Europ. Civilization* (ed. 6) i. 11 Flake-axes . . mounted as adze-blades in perforated antler sleeves. **1957** L. MACNEICE *Visitations* 29 Flake-tool; core-tool. **1959** *Antiquity* XXXIII. 17 A flake-blade industry of Neolithic type.

†**flake**, *sb.*^{3} *Obs.* [Cf. Du. *vlak* blot, speck; also FLECK *sb.*] A blemish, flaw, fleck.

13.. *E.E. Allit. P.* A. 946 Hys flok is with-outen flake. **1555** EDEN *Decades* 233 They espie in theim euery smaule spot or flake.

†**flake**, *sb.*^{4} *Obs. rare*$^{-1}$. [? a. F. *flaque* or Du. *vlacke* (Kilian).] A shallow pool, salt-marsh.

1598 tr. *Linschoten's Disc. Voy.* I. iii. 5/2 Vpon the coast of Brasillia . . lieth great flakes or shallowes, which the Portingales call Abrashos.

†**flake**, *sb.*^{5} *Obs.* Also **fleake**. [Cf. OHG. *flec* blow, stroke, also Du. *vlaag* gust of wind, FLAW.] **a.** ? A heavy blow. **b.** A gust of wind.

1559 *Mirr. Mag., Salisbury* xxxix, A pellet came, and drove a myghty fleake, Agaynst my face. **1626** CAPT. SMITH *Accid. Yng. Seamen* 17 A flake of wind.

flake (fleɪk), *sb.*^{6} [Cf. FAKE *sb.*^{1}, and Ger. *flechte* of same meaning.] = FAKE *sb.*^{1}

1626 CAPT. SMITH *Accidence* 27 Coyle your cable in small flakes [*printed* slakes]. **1891** H. L. WEBB in *Electr. in Daily Life, Making a Cable* 178 The cable is arranged in flat coils . . each coil is technically known as a 'flake'.

flake (fleɪk), *sb.*^{7} [Perh. f. FLAKE *sb.*^{2}] A name under which dogfish is marketed for food.

1906 *Daily Chron.* 1 Mar. 5/5 A meeting of the Sea Fisheries Committee..had approved of the change of the name from dogfish to flake, and after the dinner the company unanimously affirmed that flake was a most excellent..form of food. **1932** *Times Lit. Suppl.* 7 Apr. 242/4 There is also long-line fishing for dog-fish (renamed 'flake' for marketing). **1959** *Chambers's Encycl.* XII. 458/2 Spotted Dog-fish and Spiny Dog-fish..are sold as 'flake'or 'rock salmon'.

†**flake**, *a. Obs.* Also flact. [app. a var. of ME. WLAK:—OE. *wlæc*.] Tepid.

c **1400** *Lanfranc's Cirurg.* 255 Fille his eere ful of flact watir. *c* **1430** *Two Cookery-bks.* 21 Wasshe hem [Rys] clene in flake Water.

flake (fleɪk), *v.*^{1} Also 9 fleak. [f. FLAKE *sb.*^{2}]

1. *intr.* †**a.** Of snow: To fall in flakes. *Obs.* **b.** *transf.* To fall like flakes of snow.

1430 LYDG. *Chron. Troy* IV. xxxiv. (1513) X vj, Snowe that flaketh fro Iupyters toure. **1598** FLORIO, *Affioccare*, to flake as snowe doth. **1852** MOIR *Winter Wild* iii. Poet. Wks. II. 219 Butterflies..Down flaking in an endless stream. **1890** W. C. RUSSELL *Ocean Trag.* III. xxvi. 19 Red stars trembled in the silver lamps..flaking, as it seemed, upon the eye out of the mirrors.

2. *trans.* **a.** To cover with or as with flakes (of snow, etc.); to fleck. **b.** *nonce-use.* To form (snow) into flakes.

1602 MARSTON *Ant. & Mel.* III. Wks. 1856 I. 30 The shuddering morne that flakes, With silver tinctur, the east vierge of heaven. **1725** POPE *Odyss.* IV. 773 No winds inclement..flake the fleecy snow. **1845** HIRST *Poems* 70 The arching azure overhead Was flaked with gems. **1858** LONGF. *M. Standish* i. 14 His russet beard was already Flaked with patches of snow, as hedges sometimes in November.

3. a. †To break into small pieces (*obs.*). **b.** To break flakes or chips from; to chip. Also, *spec.* in *Archaeol.* (see quot. 1879). **c.** To break or rub *away* or *off* in flakes; to take *off* in flakes or layers.

1627–77 FELTHAM *Resolves* II. xlv. 247 Negligence..flakes away more of its [the Soul's] steel and hardness, than all the hackings of a violent hand can perform. **1632** HEYWOOD *Iron Age* II. I. Wks. 1874 III. 362 Fall on the murderer, And flake him smaller then the Lybean sand. **1665** HOOKE *Microgr.* 110 Large pieces of the Shell..sticking on to them, which were easily to be broken or flaked off by degrees. **1667** WATERHOUSE *Fire Lond.* 69 Chapels, Churches, Monuments: all which it..flaked and enervated. **1855** BROWNING *Men & Wom., Old Pictures at Florence* xxiv, Their ghosts..Watching each fresco flaked and rasped. **1864** *Realm* 2 Mar. 8 The Cyclopean blocks [of newspapers] are flaked off in reams and quires. **1865** TYLOR *Early Hist. Man.* viii. 198 Most stone knives of the kind seem to have been used, as they were flaked off. **1879** *Nature* 18 Sept. 483/2 Arrow-heads could in this way be flaked even into the most delicate..shapes. **1887** W. RYE *Norfolk Broads* p. iv, Watermen..are believed to flake off their dirt..by rubbing themselves against the sharp angles of square flint church towers. **1954** S. PIGGOTT *Neolithic Cultures* x. 288 The axes were flaked or chipped on the spot in large quantities. **1955** *Sci. Amer.* May 110/2 Large pebbles were flaked to give a cutting edge. Flaking is a kind of chipping or peeling, analogous to the whittling of wood.

4. *intr.* for *refl.* To come *away* or *off* in flakes; to scale or chip off.

1759 COLEBROOKE in *Phil. Trans.* LI. 45 It flaked off from the board. **1859** W. S. COLEMAN *Woodlands* (1866) 109 Covered with reddish bark that flakes off readily on being touched. **1877** A. B. EDWARDS *Up Nile* ii. 29 Its stuccoed cupola was flaking off piecemeal. **1879** [see FLAKY 2]. **1885** *Law Times* 14 Feb. 285/1 The enamel surface had..flaked away in several places.

5. *trans.* To mark with flakes or streaks.

1615 HEYWOOD *Foure Prentises* Wks. 1874 II. 240 Wee'll flake our white steeds in your Christian blood. **1857** H. MILLER *Test. Rocks* iv. 182 Jupiter..is known..by the dark, shifting bands..fleaking his surface in the line of his trade winds.

6. (*Anglo-Irish.*) To beat, flog. In quot. *absol.*

1841 S. C. HALL *Ireland* II. 316 *note*, My back was sore with the flaking..Flake away, my jewil.

7. *intr. dial.* (See quots.) [Perh. belongs to next vb.]

c **1746** J. COLLIER (Tim Bobbin) *View Lanc. Dial.* Gloss., *To Fleak*, to bask in the sun. **1876** *Whitby Gloss.*, 'Fleeak'd i'bed', laid naked. *Ibid.*, 'Fleeaking in bad weather', going out too thinly clad. **1879** MISS JACKSON *Shropsh. Word-bk.*, 'I seed a ruck o' lads an' dogs flakin' o' that sunny bonk.' **1884** *Chesh. Gloss.*, One who is lazy in the morning and will not get up is described as 'lying flaking i' bed'.

flake, *v.*^{2} [var. of FLACK, FLAG.]

†**1.** = FLAG *v.* in various *intr.* senses. To become languid or flabby. Of a garment: To fall in folds. *Obs.*

1480 *Robt. Devyll* 13, I will contynewe and never wyll flake Thoughe I therfore my lyfe lose shoulde. **1545** RAYNOLD *Byrth Mankynde* II. vii. (1634) 137 If the right brest flake and flagge. **1592** WYRLEY *Armorie* 100 Downe to the ground doth sweeping vestment flake.

2. *to flake* (*out*): to faint, fall asleep (from exhaustion, drunkenness, etc.). So *flaked* (*out*) ppl. adj., exhausted; unconscious, asleep. *colloq.*

1942 L. KENNEDY *Sub-Lieutenant* vi. 39 During the week's [P.T.] course, two of them broke their ankles; the others usually flaked out from exhaustion before the end of the afternoon. **1943** 'H. GREEN' *Caught* 21 There is a man flaked out at your feet. **1953** F. ROBB *Sea Hunters* xiii. 200 'Olley, where's old Drum?' 'Flaked out.' **1958** H. JOHNSTON *Phantom Limb* viii. 71 'Can we go to bed soon?' she asked. 'I'm absolutely flaked out.' **1960** B. CRUMP *Good Keen Man* 139, I flaked out more thoroughly than a man who is blind drunk. **1961** S. PRICE *Just for Record* vii. 60 When it was over I was flaked. **1971** *Guardian Weekly* 17 July 14/3 The nuns are still there, looking a bit flaked out now but bearing up.

flaked (fleɪkd), *ppl. a.* [f. FLAKE *sb.*^{2} or *v.*^{1} + -ED^1 or ^{2}.] **a.** Arranged in or formed into flakes or layers. **b.** Marked with flakes or streaks.

1577 HARRISON *England* III. viii. (1878) II. 31 It is not cloued as the lillie, nor flaked as the scallion. **1703** T. N. *City & C. Purchaser* 107 Chimney-pieces of Egyptian, or black Fleak'd-marble. **1849** *Florist* 261 A bizarre Carnation..is considered to belong to a higher class than the simpler flaked kinds. **1859** R. F. BURTON *Centr. Afr.* in *Jrnl. Geog. Soc.* XXIX. 112 A sea of purest azure, flaked by fleecy opal-tinted vapours. **1860** RUSKIN *Mod. Paint.* V. VI. ix. 80 The spire of the cypress, and flaked breadth of the cedar. **1888** *Wine, Spirit & Beer* 8 Mar. Advt., Flaked rice malts.

'flakelet. [f. FLAKE *sb.*^{2} + -LET.] A small flake.

1887 T. G. BONNEY in *Jrnl. Geol. Soc.* XLIV. 17 Flakelets of fragmental mica or earthy matter.

flaker ('fleɪkə(r)). [f. FLAKE *v.*^{1} + -ER^1.]

1. One who flakes; *spec.* one who strikes off flakes of flint to be used as gun-flints.

1879 *Encycl. Brit.* IX. 326/1 An expert flaker will make 7000 to 10,000 flakes in a day of twelve hours.

2. An implement for flaking flint.

1891 D. WILSON *Right Hand* 51 A..wooden flaker sufficed for the Aztecs in shaping the easily-worked obsidian. **1891** *Ardrossan Her.* 30 Oct. 2 Flint implements and weapons, including..flakers, &c.

flaking ('fleɪkɪŋ). *ppl. a.* [f. FLAKE *v.*^{1} + -ING^2.] That flakes, in various senses of the vb.

1836 LYTTON *Athens* (1837) II. 561 The wild steeds..from their fiery breath..Scatter the flaking foam. **1870** HOOKER *Stud. Flora* 115 *Potentilla fruticosa*..bark flaking.

flaking ('fleɪkɪŋ), *vbl. sb.* [f. FLAKE *v.*^{1} + -ING^1.] The action of the vb.; the condition of being flaked or flecked; *spec.* an adventitious appearance of light flecks on animals. Also *attrib.*

1829 G. GRIFFIN *Collegians* xxxix. 184 I'm only sorry I didn't give him a thing more..an' that was a good flaking. **1841** S. C. HALL *Ireland* II. 316 *note*, My back was sore with the flaking..Flake away, my jewil. **1879** *Nature* 18 Sept. 483/2 He [Mr. F. H. Cushing] accidentally discovered that small fragments could be broken off from a piece of flint with much greater..precision, by pressure with a pointed rod of bone or horn, than by blows with a hammer-stone..To this process Mr. Cushing gives the name of flaking, to distinguish it from chipping produced by percussion. **1902** W. BATESON et al. *Rep. Evol. Comm. Roy. Soc.* I. 47 Flower-colour of First Cross-bred Generation... In connection with the question of colour one point of interest may be briefly mentioned here, viz., the occurrence of 'flaking'... Such flaking was recorded in thirty-one out of thirty-nine combinations in the first year. **1904** GOODCHILD & TWENEY *Technol. & Sci. Dict.* 224/1 *Flaking*, a defect in distemper in which the paint flakes off, owing to imperfect adhesion with the surface to which it is applied. **1920** *Chambers's Jrnl.* 591/2 The automatic carrier once more picks them up, to transfer them to the flaking-machine. **1921** *Ibid.* 173/2 The entire flint armoury of Philip Bentley, along with his fire-drills and flaking-tools. **1954** S. PIGGOTT *Neolithic Cultures* x. 293 A small flaking-site at Stake Pass near the Langdale Pikes in Westmorland.

flakon, obs. form of FLAGON.

flaky ('fleɪkɪ), *a.* Also 6 flakie, 8 fleaky, 8–9 flakey. [f. FLAKE *sb.*^{2} + -Y^1.]

1. a. Consisting of flakes, or of what resembles flakes; said *esp.* of snow.

1580 SIDNEY *Ps.* CXXXV. iii, In flaky mists, the reaking vapors rise. **1594** SHAKS. *Rich. III*, v. iii. 86 Flakie darkenesse breakes within the East. **1665** HOOKE *Microgr.* 110 A white coat, or flaky substance on the top, just like the outsides of such Shells. **1714** GAY *Trivia* II. 199 She bids the Snow descend in flaky Sheets. **1802** *Med. Jrnl.* VIII. 435 A flakey sort of milk. **1819** CRABBE *T. of Hall* x. Wks. 1834 V. 23 Snow-white bloom falls flaky from the Thorn. **1823** E. SMITH *Let.* in Bray *Tamar & Tavy* (1838) I. 209 A mass of flaky..white fog. **1839** MARRYAT *Phantom Ship* xi, The sky was covered with flaky clouds. **1856** KANE *Arct. Expl.* I. xxi. 270 A snow, moist and flaky.

b. Of a flame: cf. FLAKE *sb.*^{2} 2.

1776 W. COMBE *Diaboliad* 7 With flaky flames the distant region glow'd.

2. a. Separating easily into flakes; flake-like. *flaky-spar*, a local name for CALCITE.

1672 BOYLE *Ess. Gems* 22 Diamonds themselves have a grain or a flaky Contexture, not unlike the fissility, as the schools call it, in wood. *c* **1720** W. GIBSON *Farrier's Dispens.* II. II. (1734) 93 The genuine true Salt is transparent and fleaky. **1748** tr. *Vegetius' Distempers Horses* 107 Scissile or flaky Alum. **1758** *Descr. Thames* 171 A flat, luscious and flaky Fish like the Salmon. **1784** J. TWAMLEY *Dairying* 98 It is warmth that..causes Cheese to cut Flakey. **1837** M. DONOVAN *Dom. Econ.* II. 5 The flesh [of the cod] when boiled becomes firm and flaky. **1841–71** T. R. JONES *Anim. Kingd.* (ed. 4) 728 The flaky lateral muscles of the caudal region disappear. **1872** BLACK *Adv. Phaeton* xii. 162 The flaky red surface of the old tower. **1879** MISS JACKSON *Shropsh. Word-bk.*, *Flaky-spar*..the local name given to this spar is very likely due to the manner in which its beautiful rhomboidal prisms sever or flake.

b. *spec.* Of pastry: consisting when baked of thin delicate flakes or layers.

1837 HAWTHORNE *Twice-told T.* (1851) I. viii. 179 Pies, with such white and flaky paste. **1857** DICKENS *Dorrit* II. xxxiv. 619 A pie as far from flaky as the present. **1865** *Harper's Mag.* Apr. 610/1 Crisp 'short-cakes' or 'flaky' pie-crust. **1904** *Daily Chron.* 14 Sept. 8/4 A pie that has not made up its mind whether it is to be short or flaky is not worth eating. **1943** A. SIMON *Conc. Encycl. Gastron.* IV. 92/1 Indian flaky pastry. **1969** *Harper's Bazaar* Oct. 12/2 Quails wrapped in ham and cooked in flaky pastry.

3. Full of locks or tufts of hair.

1803 *Pic Nic* No. 7 (1806) II. 32 His [an ass's] flaky ears prick'd up withal. **1877** BLACK *Green Past.* xxxviii. (1878) 304 His beard in twisted and flaky tangles.

4. *slang* (orig. *U.S.*). **a.** [Cf. *to flake* (*out*) s.v. FLAKE *v.*^{2}] Of a person: liable to act in an odd or eccentric manner (as though exhausted or under the influence of drink or drugs); crazy, 'screwball'; feeble-minded, stupid.

1964 *N.Y. Times* 26 Apr. v. 2/7 The term 'flake' needs explanation. It's an insider's word, used throughout baseball, usually as an adjective; someone is considered 'flaky'. It does not mean anything so crude as 'crazy', but it's well beyond 'screwball' and far off to the side of 'eccentric'. **1974** A. LURIE *War between Tates* vi. 128 'I figure I would have flipped out pretty soon.' She makes the gesture of someone exhausted or insane, flipping a pancake, in demonstration. 'I was really flaky.' **1976** M. MACHLIN *Pipeline* xl. 434 She'd become so flakey and so hostile to the world around her that Larry had found it hard to communicate with her. **1979** *Sunday Sun* (Brisbane) 1 July 49/2 What changed my mind was that Players is the first film to show tennis stars in a realistic way. Not as flaky guys or playboys. **1983** 'J. LE CARRÉ' *Little Drummer Girl* I. iv. 78 We hear she's currently allied with a very flakey anarchist guy, some kind of crazy. **1986** *New Yorker* 20 Jan. 19/2 People can choose their own words to describe Qaddafi's mental state—President Reagan called him 'flaky', and later denied that he considered Qaddafi mentally unbalanced.

b. Of an object, idea, etc.: characteristically eccentric or crazy; outrageous, unusual; also, unreliable or erratic.

1972 *Newsweek* 10 Jan. 25/1 'The majority of citizen-filed bills are pretty flaky,' observes State Senate president Kevin Harrington. **1977** C. MCFADDEN *Serial* (1978) xvi. 39/2 Angela and her flaky 'extended family concept'. **1978** *Consumer Reports* Mar. 174/2 'We know the EPA numbers [on gas mileage] are flaky,' says a Ford Motor Co. public-relations man. **1986** *Guardian* 16 Jan. 13/8 British Telecom's Multi-User dungeon adventure..is playable, but still too flakey for BT to charge people for playing it.

Hence **'flakily** *adv.*, in a flaky manner; **'flakiness**, the quality or condition of being flaky.

1831 J. WILSON in *Blackw. Mag.* XXIX. 306 A better day for a [snowball] Bicker never rose flakily from the yellow East. **1748** *Phil. Trans.* XLV. 364 Brine-Salt hath evermore two main Defects, Flakyness and Softness. **1853** DICKENS in *Househ. Words* (Christmas No.) 1/1 Look at the pie-crust alone. There's no flakiness in it. It's solid—like damp lead.

flale, obs. form of FLAIL.

flam (flæm), *sb.*^{1} and *a.* Also 7 flamm(e. [See FLAM *v.*]

A. *sb.*

†**1.** A fanciful notion, caprice, whim. *Obs.*

a **1625** FLETCHER *Hum. Lieutenant* IV. i, Presently With some new flam or other..She takes her chamber. **1672** EACHARD *Hobbes' State Nat.* Lett. 20 It may be convenient for you to call this..a flam, a whisker, a caprice.

†**2.** A fanciful composition; a conceit. *Obs.*

a **1637** B. JONSON *Underwoods, Execr. Vulcan* 36 Anagrams, Or Eteosticks, or your finer flams Of eggs and halberts. **1725** SWIFT *Let. to Pope* Wks. 1761 VIII. xii. 46 Philips writes little flams (as Lord Leicester called those sort of verses) on Miss Carteret. **1755** GRAY *Let. to Wharton* 9 Mar., Must they too come out in the shape of little six-penny flams, dropping one after another, till Mr. Dodsley thinks fit to collect them..into a pretty volume?

3. A sham story, fabrication, falsehood; a piece of deception, a trick.

1632 SHERWOOD, A flam, or a flimflam tale, *riotte.* **1637** POCKLINGTON *Altare Chr.* 22 The Lincolneshire minister can devise no flamme (as he speaks) to shift off these..cleare places in Origen. **1655** FULLER *Ch. Hist.* I. ii. §9. 12 His Flamens and Arch-Flamens, seeme..Flamms and Arch-Flamms, even notorious Falshoods. **1760** FOOTE *Minor* II. Wks. 1799 I. 257 Had the flam been fact, your behaviour was natural enough. **1826** J. WILSON *Noct. Ambr.* Wks. 1855 I. 5 And all that comes after a flim and a flam. **1888** D. C. MURRAY *Danger. Catspaw* 164 The letter's a flam.

b. Humbug, deception; flattery, 'blarney'.

1692 SOUTH *Conscience* Serm. 1737 II. xii. 443 All pretences to the contrary are nothing but cant and cheat, flam and delusion. **1825** BROCKETT *N. Country Wds.*, *Flam*, flattery bordering on a lie. **1851** MAYHEW *Lond. Labour* I. 367 'There are very few who take money; indeed they profess to take none at all. But that is all flam', said my informant. **1878** *Cumbld. Gloss.*, *Flam*, flattery—equivalent to blarney.

†**B.** *adj.* [Developed from an attrib. use of the sb.; cf. FANCY *adj.* C.] That is intended to deceive; counterfeit, fictitious, sham. *Obs.*

1678–9 C. HATTON 18 Mar. in *Hatton Corr.* (1878) I. 184 His Lo^{pp}e had been impos'd on by a flamm report. **1692** *Contriv. S. Blackhead* in *Select. Harl. Misc.* (1793) 516 She addeth a flam story, that she had got his hand by corrupting one of the letter-carriers. **1692** R. L'ESTRANGE *Josephus' Antiq.* XVI. vi, He could not so conveniently impose upon his Father with flam Stories against his Brothers.

Hence †**flam-flirt** *int.* (cf. FLIM-FLAM-FLIRT), nonsense.

1590 R. W. *3 Lords & Ladies* B iij b, Fly, flam flurt: why? Can a flie doo hurt?

flam (flæm), *sb.*^{2} [Prob. echoic.] (See quot. 1819.)

1796 GROSE *Dict. Vulg. Tongue*, *Flam*, a single stroke on a drum. **1819** REES *Cycl.* XII. s.v. *Drum*, The Flam is a beat made by the two sticks striking almost at the same instant on

the head, but so as to be heard separately. **1848–9** in SOUTHEY *Comm.-pl. Bk.* IV. 434 In beating the drum there is the roll, the swell, the flam and the ruffle. **1876** in VOYLE *Milit. Dict.* (ed. 3). **1931** G. JACOB *Orchestral Technique* vii. 71 Very characteristic of the side-drum are the strokes known as 'the flam' and the 'drag'.

flam (flæm), *sb.*³ [Of uncertain origin; possibly identical with FLAMBE flag, iris; 'the flams' may have been used for the place where these plants grow, and the meaning of the sing. may have been wrongly deduced.] (See quots.)

1725 HEARNE *R. Brunne's Chron.* Gloss. s.v. *Flom*, It is withall remarkable, that low, watry, rushy places are frequently call'd Flams by persons..in and about Oxford. **1791** *Rep. Navig. Thames & Isis* Estimate 3 The Flam or Close to be cut through, and Gangways to the Bridge for the Towing-Horses. **1872** H. W. TAUNT *Map of Thames* p. x, The reedy flams which line its left bank.

†**flam**, *sb.*⁴ *Obs.*⁻¹ ? Short for FLAMBEAU.

1755 AMORY *Memoirs* 449 We had but one flam left. An accident might likewise extinguish it, and then what could we do?

flam (flæm), *sb.*⁵ Variant of FLAN *sb.*¹.

1711 R. SIBBALD *Descr. Ork. & Zetl.* ix. 36 *Ronis-voe*.. could Harbour many Ships, were it free from the Flams of Wind, which come from the Mountain. **1820** *St. Kathleen* III. 110 It blows squally, as the flams o' reek flappin' doun the lum may tell ye. **1903** *Northern Ensign* 28 July 2/1 'Er's a flam o' win' doon 'e shimley.

flam (flæm), *v.* [Belongs to FLAM *sb.*¹; if sense 1 below be not a different word, the vb. is the earlier. Cf. FLIM-FLAM and FLAMFEW, of either of which *flam* may be a shortened form.]

†**1.** *trans.* ? To counterfeit, 'mock'. *Obs.*

c **1500** *Ratis Raving* etc. 3687 Flam not the flouris at wyll faid, To mend hir mak at god has maid.

2. To deceive by a sham story or trick, or by flattery; also, *to flam off, up. Obs.* exc. *dial.* or *U.S.*

1637 HEYWOOD *Dial.* ii. Wks. 1874 VI. 112 You do not well to jeere and flam Me. *a* **1658** FORD, etc. *Witch Edmonton* II. ii, Was this your cunning?—and then flam me off With an old witch. **1660** BOND *Scut. Reg.* 188 Damnable Usurpers.. flaming the people in the mouth with a tale. **1692** SOUTH *Serm.* (1697) 465 A God, who is not to be flamm'd off with Lyes. **1760** C. JOHNSTON *Chrysal* (1822) II. 296 No such tricks for me. I am not to be flammed so neither. **1837–40** HALIBURTON *Clockm.* (1862) 153 Few would accept it.. without some sponsible man to indorse it, that warn't given to flammin. **1876** *Whitby Gloss.*, *Flam up*, to cajole. **1884** *Chesh. Gloss.*, *Flam*, to humbug, or deceive. 'He's only flammin.'

flam, var. of FLAMM, FLAN.

†'**flaman, flammant.** [a. F. *flamant*: see FLAMINGO.] A flamingo.

1706 PHILLIPS (ed. Kersey), *Flamet* or *Flammant*, a large and fine Fowl, as big as a wild Goose, having the Legs and Neck very long. **1708** MOTTEUX *Rabelais* IV. xli. (1737) 166 A Phenicoptere (which in Languedoc they call Flaman). **1737** OZELL *Rabelais* II. i. II. 14 You would have said they had been Cranes, or Flamans (*note* a flame-coloured Bird with long red legs). **1730–6** in BAILEY (folio).

flamant, flammant ('flæmənt). [a. OF. *flam(m)ant*, f. *flam(m)er* to FLAME.] Flaming. *Obs.* exc. *Her.*

1607 TOPSELL *Four-f. Beasts* 485 This constellation is stiled..as heate-bearing..hot, flammant. —— *Serpents* (1658) 751 The second is reddish, like fire flamant. **1610** GUILLIM *Heraldry* III. iv. 95 He beareth seuen Fire brands Flammant and Scintillant, Proper. **1889** ELVIN *Dict. Her.*, *Flamant, Flammant*..Flaming or Burning.

†**fla'mation.** *Obs.*⁻¹ [f. FLAME *v.* + -ATION.] Hence **fla'matious** *a.* [-OUS]. (See quot.)

1688 R. HOLME *Armoury* II. 387/2 A Flamation, or Flamatious feeling; as the pain of burning and scalding.

flamb (flæm), *v. Sc.* Also 5–6 **flawme**, 6 **flame**, 6, 8 **flamm**. [a. F. *flambe-r* to singe; originally a var. of *flam(m)er* to FLAME.] *trans.* To baste ('with flaming lard', Jam.).

c **1440** *Anc. Cookery* in *Househ. Ord.* (1790) 450 Take fygges..and frie hom, and flawme hom with honey. ? *a* **1550** *Freiris of Berwik* 137 in *Dunbar's Poems* (1893) 289 Scho.. bad the madin..To flawme, and turne, and rost thame tenderly. *c* **1568** LAUDER *Godlie Tractate* 460 Euerie fatt Souch fedis and flammis ane vther. **1818** SCOTT *Br. Lamm.* xiii, The iron ladle, with which she had just been *flambing* (*Anglicè*, basting) the roast of mutton.

Proverb. **1721** KELLY *Sc. Prov.* 93 Every Man flamms [*note* basteth] the fat Sow's Arse. They will be sure to get most Gifts that least want them.

flamb(e, obs. forms of FLAME.

†**flambant** ('flæmbənt), *a. Obs.* exc. *Her.* [a. F. *flambant*, pr. pple. of *flamber* to flame.] **a.** *Her.* Flaming, on fire. **b.** (See quot. 1597.)

1597 GERARD *Herbal* I. lxxxvii. (1633) 144 There is another to be seen with a floure mixed with streakes of red and yellow, resembling a flame of fire, whereupon we have called it flambant. *a* **1661** FULLER *Worthies* IV. (1662) 46 An Urn with an Heart flambant [*printed* flamboul] supported by two Angels. **1889** ELVIN *Dict. Her.*, *Flambant*, Flaming or burning.

†**flambe.** [a. OF. *flambe* (var. of *flamme* FLAME *sb.*), still used in Fr. as the name of the plant.] **a.** A torch. **b.** The yellow flag (*Iris pseudacorus*); in quot. *attrib.*

c **1430** LYDG. *Bochas* II. xxvii. (1554) 63 b, No flambes nor brondes clere shining To bren his body wᵗ fiers funeral. **1486** *Bk. St. Albans* C v, Take smale flambe rotis.

‖**flambé** (flɑ̃be), *a.* [Fr., pa. pple. of *flamber* to singe, pass through flame.]

1. Of a certain type of Chinese porcelain: iridescent from the effects of a special process of firing, or from the irregular application of glaze; of a (usu. reddish or bluish) glaze so applied. Also as *sb.*, a piece of porcelain decorated in this way.

1886 S. W. BUSHELL *Chinese Porcelain* 4 Prince Kung one day admired a glazed Buddha from the ruins of the Summer Palace, taking it for old flambée porcelain. **1888** *Harper's Mag.* Oct. 658 The comparison of these *flambé* vases with onyx or precious stones is to the advantage of the brilliant porcelain. **1904** *Daily Chron.* 31 May 3/1 A dozen specimens of 'flambé', which exhibit the splashed reds, browns, and purples, due to a special process of firing. **1904** E. DILLON *Porcelain* 42 In the case of the *flambé* or 'transmutation' glazes, the strange caprices of colour have their origin, in part at least, in the contrast of the red sub-oxide and the green silicate of copper. **1959** G. SAVAGE *Antique Coll. Handbk.* 80 The reign of Ch'ien Lung saw the manufacture of *flambé* glazes in great variety.

2. *Cookery.* Applied to a dish covered with spirit and served alight.

[**1906** MRS. BEETON *Househ. Managem.* lxii. 1659 *Flamber* (Fr.). To singe poultry or game. To cover a pudding or omelet with spirit and set it alight.] **1914** N. NEWNHAM-DAVIS *Gourmet's Guide to London* lvi. 363, I enjoyed the *sole Monico*,..a woodcock *flambé* and a salad. **1935** M. MORPHY *Recipes of all Nations* 87 Crêpes Suzettes..are usually served *flambées*—hot Curaçoa being poured over them and set alight just before serving. **1958** *Times* 16 June 11/5 Americans..have made more use of spectacular flambé dishes in their homes.

flambeau ('flæmbəʊ). Forms: 7 **flambo, -oy**, 8 **-oe**, 7– **flambeau**; *pl.* 7 **flamboys**, 7–8 **-o(e)s**, 7– **flambeaus, -eaux.** [a. F. *flambeau* (= med.L. *flambellum*), f. *flambe* FLAME *sb.*]

1. a. A torch; *esp.* one made of several thick wicks dipped in wax; a lighted torch.

1632 *St. Trials, Ct. Coningsmark, etc.* 11, I had a flambeau in my hand. **1638** SIR T. HERBERT *Trav.* (ed. 2) 133 Others fired their flambeauxes [*sic*]. **1697** *C'tess D'Aunoy's Trav.* (1706) 148 After the Collation was ended, Flamboys were brought in. **1749** FIELDING *Tom Jones* VII. xiv, Eyes as big ..as two large flambeaux. **1816** SCOTT *Antiq.* xxv, An open grave, with four tall flambeaux..placed at the corners. **1840** DICKENS *Barn. Rudge* xvi, Many a private chair..preceded by running-footmen bearing flambeaux.

b. A fire-signal or beacon.

1688 WOOD *Life* (1894) III. 533 A great flambo on Combs his house..was seen as far as Newnham.

2. *transf.* and *fig.* (Cf. *torch, firebrand.*)

1670 EACHARD *Cont. Clergy.* (1705) 132 Receiving some benediction from the flambo's of your Eyes. *a* **1670** HACKET *Abp. Williams* I. ccxxvi. (1693) 220 Our Laws of Correction against such dangerous Flambeaux. **1685** *Gracian's Courtier's Orac.* 54 The sayings of Alexander are the Flamboes of his deeds. **1936** R. CAMPBELL *Mithraic Emblems* 25 Silent and vertical and dim The lunar flambeau of a prayer. **1939** A. E. HOUSMAN *Coll. Poems* 107 The chestnut casts his flambeaux.

3. A large decorated candlestick.

(In mod. Dicts.)

4. *South. U.S.* 'One of the set of kettles used in the open-kettle process of sugar-making, so called because the flames of the furnace strike it with most force' (*Cent. Dict.*). [So in Fr.]

5. *attrib.* and *Comb.*, as ***flambeau-bearer, -light.***

1806 A. DUNCAN *Nelson's Funeral* 25 The men worked by candle and flambeau light. **1859** DICKENS *T. Two Cities* II. ix, Monsieur the Marquis, with his flambeau-bearer going on before, went up the staircase to a door in a corridor.

Hence '**flambeaued** *ppl. a.*, furnished with or lighted by flambeaux.

1852 *Meanderings of Mem.* I. 166 Flambeaued folly of the long procession.

flamberg, flamberge ('flæmbɜːg, flɑ̃bɛrʒ). [a. OF. *flamberge*, proper name of the sword of the Paladin Roland and of that of Renaud of Montauban; hence, generally, a sword; the form *Floberge* occurs earlier, and is prob. more correct; of unknown (presumably Teut.) etymology.] A kind of fencing-sword or rapier.

1885 E. CASTLE *Schools & Masters of Fence* (1892) 271 The sword..is a transition rapier of the Flamberg type. *Ibid.* 333 The special character of this so-called Flamberg is the comparative simplicity of the hilt.

†'**flamble**, *v. Obs. rare*⁻¹ [f. OF. *flamble*:—L. *flammula*, dim. of *flamma* flame.] *intr.* To be in flames; to flame.

1557 *K. Arthur* (Copland) v. iv, Lyke as yᵉ land and water had flambled [*Caxton has* flammed] all on fyre.

flamboyance (flæm'bɔɪəns). [f. as next: see -ANCE.] The quality of being flamboyant.

1891 *Athenæum* 17 Jan. 86/1 Flamboyance..may be a better augury of right richness when chastening comes than conventional moderation. **1909** *Daily Chron.* 2 July 4/7 Its architectural flamboyance. **1940** W. S. MAUGHAM *Books & You* i. 26 The flamboyance of Elizabethan English.

flamboyancy (flæm'bɔɪənsɪ). [f. next: see -ANCY.] = prec.

In mod. Dicts.

flamboyant (flæm'bɔɪənt), *a.* and *sb.* Also 9 **flambeauant.** [a. F. *flamboyant*, pr. pple. of *flamboyer*, OF. *flambeiier*, f. *flambe* FLAME *sb.*

The OF. word may however descend from the pop. L. **flammidiāre* (whence It. *fiammeggiare*) or the recorded late L. *flammigāre* (Gellius).]

A. *adj.*

1. *Arch.* Characterized by waved lines of contrary flexure in flame-like forms (Gwilt): of the style prevalent in France in the 15th and the first half of the 16th c. Also *absol.* (quasi-*sb.*).

1832 RICKMAN in *Archæologia* XXV. 182 They are of all dates, from Early French to the latest Flamboyant. **1836** H. G. KNIGHT *Archit. Tour Normandy* 215 A change..which has recently acquired the fanciful appellation of Flamboyant. **1848** RICKMAN *Archit.* 153 A tendency to the Flamboyant style of tracery is frequently observable. **1861** BERESF. HOPE *Eng. Cathedr. 19th C.* 31 The exuberant Flamboyant of the continent. **1883** *Gd. Words* 503 Etchingham church, with its..curious flamboyant window.

b. In loose and transferred use: Florid, floridly decorated.

1879 DOWDEN *Southey* i. 9 That flamboyant penmanship admired by our ancestors. **1883** L. WINGFIELD *A. Rowe* I. v. 94 Sir Francis Burdett indulged in flamboyant perorations. **1887** SAINTSBURY *Hist. Elizab. Lit.* ii. 42 Although he [Sidney] seldom or never reaches the beauties of the flamboyant period of prose.

2. Of wavy form, suggesting the outline of a flame. Said chiefly of a sword.

1876 GEO. ELIOT *Dan. Der.* 362 With massive face, flamboyant hair. **1878** BROWNING *La Saisiaz* 80 He there with the brand flamboyant. **1879** *Cassell's Techn. Educ.* III. 152 A Siamese grotesque head..[with] flambeauant ears. **1885** E. CASTLE *Schools & Masters of Fence* (1892) 334 By some writers it [the name Flamberg] is restricted to the flamboyant Spadone or Zweyhänder.

3. Flamingly or gorgeously coloured.

1851 LONGF. *Gold. Leg.* III. xli, See, too, the Rose, above the western portal Flamboyant with a thousand gorgeous colours. **1867** D. G. MITCHELL *Rural Studies* 3 Whose daughters, in flamboyant ribbons, were among the belles of the parish. **1888** *Punch 13 Oct.* 170/3 Oh, the flamboyant flare of those fiendish designs, With their sanguine paint-splashes.

B. *sb.* A name for certain plants with flame-coloured flowers.

1879 MRS. BISHOP *Sk. Malay Pen.* i. in *Leisure H.* (1883) 20/2 That wonderful flowering tree variously known as the 'flamboyant' and 'the flame of the forest' (*Poinciana regia*). **1885** LADY BRASSEY *The Trades* 141 The richly-coloured orange and yellow flowers of the flamboyante (*Poinciana*).

Hence **flam'boyantly**, *adv.*

1894 *Speaker* 26 May 586/2 Upon this canvas they are radiantly and flamboyantly alive.

flamboyantism (flæm'bɔɪəntɪz(ə)m). [f. as prec. + -ISM.] Flamboyant style.

1846 *Ecclesiologist* VI. 72 The west window in..its Flamboyantism, much resembles the eastern.

flamboyantize (flæm'bɔɪəntaɪz). *v.* [f. FLAMBOYANT *a.* and *sb.* + -IZE.] **a.** *intr.* To become flamboyant. **b.** *trans.* To render flamboyant.

1846 *Ecclesiologist* VI. 70 Just when Middle-Pointed in France, was beginning to Flamboyantize. **1857** *Ibid.* XVIII. 229 Two great marigolds; one Flamboyantised.

flam'buginous, *a. rare*⁻¹. [A burlesque formation on FLAM.] Of the nature of a 'flam'.

1813 *Sporting Mag.* XLII. 19 The..flambuginous sea-monster, known by the name of the Non-Descript.

flamdoodle (flæm'duːd(ə)l). *U.S.* [An arbitrary formation.] = FLAPDOODLE *sb.* 2.

1888 *N.Y. Sun* (Farmer), We..planted [= buried] Uncle George in ship-shape and proper manner. We wasn't goin' to have any highfalutin' flamdoodle business over him. **1921** H. CRANE *Let.* 28 Jan. (1965) 52 M. Ray will allow the Dada theories and other flamdoodle of this section run him off the track.

flame (fleɪm), *sb.* Forms: 4 **flaume**, 4–5 **flamme**, (5 **flome**), 4–6 **flawme**, **flaumbe**, 5–7 **flambe**, (7 **flam**), 4– **flame**. [a. OF. *flambe, flamme*:—L. *flamma*, of disputed etymology; according to some scholars for **flāgma*, f. root **flăg-* in *flagrāre* to blaze; according to others for **flāma*, f. *flā-re* to blow.]

1. Vapour heated to the point of combustion; ignited gas. Also, †*flame of fire.*

a. without plural.

c **1384** CHAUCER *H. Fame* II. 261 Flaumbe ys but lyghted smoke. **1398** TREVISA *Barth. De P.R.* x. iv. (1495) 376 Flamme is fyre in ayry matere. *c* **1400** MAUNDEV. (Roxb.) viii. 29 Oute of þe whilk commes flawme of fire. **1563** FULKE *Meteors* (1640) 23 Where earthquakes have beene, great abundance of smoke, flame, and ashes, is cast out. **1678** HOBBES *Decam.* vi. 60 Flame is nothing but a multitude of Sparks. **1704** NEWTON *Opticks* III. xi. 134 Is not flame a vapour, fume, or exhalation heated red hot, that is, so hot as to shine? **1831** BREWSTER *Newton* (1855) II. xxv. 368 Flame consists of particles of carbon brought to a white heat,—an opinion of Sir Humphry Davy's.

b. with plural: A portion of ignited vapour, often spire-like or tongue-like. †*to put to flames*: to set on fire.

a **1340** HAMPOLE *Psalter* xxviii. [xxix.] 7 þe voice of lord sherand þe flaume of fire. **1377** LANGL. *P. Pl.* B. XVII. 239 þe weyke and fyre wil make a warme flaumbe. *c* **1400** *Destr. Troy* 12009 Flammes of fyre fuerse to behold. *c* **1450** LONELICH *Grail* xlviii. 174 Fir and flambes they casten echedel vppon Moys there that he sat. *a* **1533** LD. BERNERS *Huon* lxiv. 221 His vysage became lyke a flame of fyer. **1697** DRYDEN *Virg. Georg.* IV. 554 Thrice to the vaulted Roof the Flames aspire. **1722** SEWEL *Hist. Quakers* (1795) I. IV. 272 The flames ascended above my head. **1800** tr. *Lagrange's Chem.* II. 245 The acid burns with a blue flame. **1874** MORLEY *Compromise* (1886) 17 The sky of Paris was red with the incendiary flames of the Commune.

c. *fig.* (see also 6.)

1548 HALL *Chron. Hen. VI*, 154 The inhabitauntes.. perceyuing, that the great flamme of the Englishe force was extinct and consumid. **1601** SHAKS. *All's Well* I. ii. 59 Let me not liue..After my flame lackes oyle. **1623** FAVINE *Theat. Hon.* II. i. 61 Saint Hierome, the..cleare flame of the Church. **1887** BOWEN *Virg. Æneid* I. 263 War's great flame he shall kindle in Italy.

d. *pl.* (with *the*) = fire. Chiefly with reference to death or destruction by burning. Phrase, *to commit to the flames*.

1483 CAXTON *Gold. Leg.* 249/2 The blessid chyldren wente thorugh the flambes. **1656** COWLEY *Poems, Misc.* 10 Pity him Jove, and his bold Theft allow, The flames he once stole from thee grant him now. **1713** STEELE *Englishman* No. 55. 354 He was put into the flames with the General Acclamation of the Multitude. **1782** PRIESTLEY *Corrupt. Chr.* II. IX. 191 Ziska..condemned the rest to the flames. **1817** SHELLEY *Revolt of Islam* XII. xxv. 1 When the consuming flames had wrapt ye round.

e. with reference to hell or purgatory.

1382 WYCLIF *Luke* xvi. 24 Send Lazarus that he..kele my tunge; for I am turmentid in this flawme. *c* **1575** W. FULKE *Confut. Doctr. Purgatory* (1577) 182 To quench the flambes of purgatory. **1637–50** ROW *Hist. Kirk* (1842) 304 By hellish flams thy soule..devoured bee. **1832** TENNYSON *Sisters* 7 She died: she went to burning flame.

†**f.** *vital flame* (see quot.). *Obs.* in scientific use.

1706 PHILLIPS (ed. Kersey), *Vital Flame*, a kind of subtil gentle kindled Heat which some suppose to be in the Heart of Living-Creatures.

2. The condition of visible combustion. In phrases, *on flame*, † *on* or *of a flame*, *in a flame*, *in flames*: blazing, on fire; *transf.* of a wound, etc., inflamed; *fig.* inflamed with anger, passion, or zeal. Also *to put* or *set on* or *in* (†*a*) *flame*, *to burst into flame*(*s*, etc. See also AFLAME.

1490 CAXTON *Eneydos* ii. 14 The cyte was cruelly sette a fyre, and on a flamm. **1638** SIR T. HERBERT *Trav.* (ed. 2) 297 Redolent gums..incendiated or put to flames, wherein the dead body is laid. **1652** J. WADSWORTH tr. *Sandoval's Civ. Wars Spain* 351 The timber of the Church taking fire therewith, all was immediately of a flame. **1658** A. FOX *Wurtz' Surg.* III. i. 220 If a wound be in a flame when drest. **1656** COWLEY *Poems, Mistress* 15 [My heart] 'tis all on flame. **1676** HOBBES *Iliad* (1677) 182 Set the Argives hollow ships on flame. **1685** CROWNE *Sir C. Nice* v. 49 What a flame had your negligence put me into. **1697** DAMPIER *Voy.* I. 116 They found their Boat all in flames. **1721** DE FOE *Mem. Cavalier* (1840) 47 The town..was all on a flame. **1764** GOLDSM. *Trav.* 219 Unknown those powers that raise the soul to flame. **1790** BEATSON *Nav. & Mil. Mem.* I. 74 Setting the nation in a flame against the Minister. **1790** WILLOCKS *Voy.* 11 Immediately his face was all over in a flame. **1818** SHELLEY *Rev. Islam* III. xvi. 8 Below the smoke of roofs involved in flame. **1847** TENNYSON *Princ.* VI. 348 The day..Now set a wrathful Dian's moon on flame. **1879** M. PATTISON *Milton* 53 Once, at twenty, he [Milton] was all on flame by the casual meeting..with a damsel.

3. *transf.* **a.** A bright beam or ray of light (*esp.* from a heavenly body).

c **1374** CHAUCER *Boeth.* II. Metr. iii. 39 þe flamus of þe sonne þat ouer comeþ þe sterre lyȝt. **1572** BOSSEWELL *Armorie* II. 132 These starres..cast from them flambes in maner of heares. **1611** BIBLE *Wisd.* xvii. 5 Neither could the bright flames of the starres endure to lighten that horrible night. **1710** POPE *Windsor For.* 390 Where clearer flames glow round the frozen Pole. **1842** LONGF. *Sp. Stud.* III. v, When the moon began to show her silver flame. **1877** BRYANT *Poems, Little People of Snow* 184 The northern lights, such as thou seest In the midwinter nights, cold, wandering flames.

b. Applied humorously to 'red' hair. Also to one who has such hair. Cf. CARROT *sb.* 3.

1823 'J. BEE' *Slang, Flames*, red haired people receive this appellation..'vho should I fling my precious ogles upon but Flames—she as lived at the Blue Posts?' **1959** I. & P. OPIE *Lore & Lang. Schoolch.* ix. 170 Red heads attract a barrage of nicknames:..fire head, flame, flarey, [etc.].

4. *fig.* Bright or glowing light; brilliance, brilliant colouring.

1781 COWPER *Friendship* ii, That jewel of the purest flame. **1873** OUIDA *Pascarel* II. 162 The flame of roses burns on every handsbreadth of untilled ground.

5. Something resembling a flame of fire: †**a.** A flame-shaped ornament. **b.** A streak or patch of colour or the like.

1602 SEGAR *Hon. Mil. & Civ.* II. xvii. 88 Mantelets of greene cloth of siluer..bordered about with flambes of golde. **1680** *Lond. Gaz.* No. 1562/4 A Bright Bay Gelding.. a white Flame from the Forehead almost to the Nostrils. **1820** SHELLEY *Witch* vi. 3 The sly serpent, in the golden flame Of his own volumes intervolved. **1888** MISS BRADDON *Fatal Three* I. vi, The yellow stonecrop made a flame of colour on the top.

c. The colour of flame, flame-red.

1711 tr. *H. van Oosten's Dutch Gardener* (ed. 2) III. xiv. 151 The Fire..in this Plant [*sc.* tulip], leaves only its own Colour, which is Flame or Gold. **1921** *Queen* 13 Aug. 198 The buds are of extraordinarily deep colour with a suggestion of flame. **1923** *Daily Mail* 16 July 16 In Peach, Brown, Mastic, Royal, Flame, Gold. **1971** *Rose Ann.* 192 Mojave. 1954. Deep orange and reddish flame. *Ibid.* 197 Shepherd's Delight. 1958. Flame, orange and yellow.

6. In certain figurative applications of sense 1.

a. A burning feeling or passion, *esp.* of love: *to fan the flame*: to heighten its intensity by artificial or artful means.

a **1340** HAMPOLE *Psalter* cxxxvii. 1 Alle kyndul þou in þe flawme of þi luf. *c* **1386** CHAUCER *Pars. T.* ¶279 Thanne feeleth he anoon a flambe of delit. *a* **1450–1530** *Myrr. our Ladye* 212 Thre flaumbes of charyte. **1601** SHAKS. *All's Well* I. iii. 217 So true a flame of liking. **1667** MILTON *P.L.* v. 807 Abdiel..Stood up, and in a flame of zeale severe The current of his fury thus oppos'd. **1702** POPE *Sapho* 20 Ah youth ungrateful to a flame like mine! **1708** ROWE *Royal Convert* Prol., The same Flame, by different Ways express'd, Glows in the Heroe's and the Poet's Breast. **1783** J. O'KEEFFE *Birth-day* 17 The lovely town-bred dame, Dear cause of many a flame. **1800** MRS. HERVEY *Mourtray Fam.* IV. 212, I..neglected no opportunity of fanning the flame. **1814** CARY *Dante, Paradise* III. 69 She seemed With love's first flame to glow. **1885** MABEL COLLINS *Prettiest Woman* ix, This flame of ardent ambition kept her alive.

b. quasi-*concr.* The object of one's love. Formerly *poet.*; now only *jocular*.

1647 COWLEY *Mistress, Eccho* ii, Thy flame, whilst living, ..Was of less beauty. **1709** PRIOR *Ode*, Euphelia serves to grace my Measure; But Cloe is my real Flame. *a* **1760** J. BROWNE *Poems, Let. to Corinna* (1768) 109 My earliest flame, to whom I owe All that a Captain needs to know. **1807** W. IRVING *Salmag.* (1824) 263 This little damsel..was my uncle John's third flame. **1840** THACKERAY *Paris Sk.-bk.* (1872) 237 Her heart remains faithful to her old flame, the doctor.

†**c.** Brightness of fancy, power of genius, vigour of thought. *Obs.*

1642 DENHAM *Cooper's H.* 88 As thine his fate, if mine had beene his [Homer's] Flame. **1672** VILLIERS (Dk. Buckhm.) *Rehearsal* 1, Persons of Quality..that understand what Flame and Power in writing is. **1702** ROWE *Tamerl.* Prol., Like him (tho' much unequal to his Flame) Our Author makes a pious Prince his Theme.

†**7.** A name of a variety of carnation. (See quot.)

1727 BRADLEY *Fam. Dict.* s.v. *Carnation*, The Flames have a red Ground always strip'd with Black or very dark Colours.

8. A name given to certain British moths.

1819 G. SAMOUELLE *Entomol. Compend.* 399 *Noctua putris*, the Flame. *Ibid.* 422 *Geometra rubiadata*, the Flame. **1862** MORRIS *Brit. Moths* II. 15 *Anticlea rubidaria*, the Flame.

9. *attrib.* and *Comb.* **a.** simple attrib., as ***flame-banner***, ***-heat***, ***-lamp***, ***-light***, ***-signal***, ***-tongue***.

1880 TENNYSON *Columbus*, The great *flame-banner borne by Teneriffe. **1812–6** J. SMITH *Panorama Sc. & Art* I. 11 In changing the form of iron, the white *flame heat is used. **1888** *Daily News* 10 May 3/1 Miners' electric lamps.. so convenient..that it would really seem to be nothing short of criminal folly to run the slightest risk with *flame lamps. **1611** SPEED *Hist. Gt. Brit.* VI. ix. 75 The search of Tyrants by the *flame-light of Persecutions. **1921** W. DE LA MARE *Crossings* 47 A fire-place, its brass and steel merrily twinkling in the flame-light. **1923** D. H. LAWRENCE *Birds, Beasts & Flowers* 170 Three great elephants..in the torch-light, Slowly sailing in gorgeous apparel through the flame-light. *a* **1835** MRS. HEMANS *League of Alps* xxvi. Poems (1875) 237 *Flame-signals through the midnight sprung. **1876** GEO. ELIOT *Dan. Der.* VIII. lxiv, Where the flowers are no better than a crop of *flame-tongues burning the soles of our feet.

b. objective, as ***flame-breathing***, ***-darting***, ***-snorting***, ***-throwing***, also ***flame-devoted***.

1621 G. SANDYS *Ovid's Met.* VII. (1626) 235 *Flame-breathing buls you tam'd. **1611** SYLVESTER *Du Bartas* II. iv. III. *Schisme* 403 The Welkin's studded with new Blazing-Stars, *Flame-darting Lances. **1767** W. L. LEWIS *Statius' Thebaid* VI. 76 They crown with Cypress..the *Flame-devoted Bier. **1614** SYLVESTER *Du Bartas, Bethulia's Rescue* III. 1 *Flame-snorting Phlegon's ruddy breath began Reducing Day. **1952** C. DAY LEWIS tr. *Virgil's Aeneid* VI. 125 The *flame-throwing Chimaera.

c. instrumental and originative, as ***flame-bred***, ***-burnt***, ***-feathered***, ***-flushed***, ***-irradiated***, ***-robed***, ***-sparkling***, ***-tipped***, ***-uplifted***, ***-winged***.

1606 SYLVESTER *Du Bartas* II. iv. II. *Magnificence* 361 If I live, I live her *Flame-bred-Flie. **1841** *Civil Engin. & Arch. Jrnl.* IV. 340/2 When the bricks were intended to be ..*flame-burnt,..no addition was made to the clay. **1917** D. H. LAWRENCE *Look!* 101 We near the flame-burnt porches. **1591** SYLVESTER *Du Bartas* I. iv. 272 With his *flame feath'red arrow. **1923** D. H. LAWRENCE *Birds, Beasts & Flowers* 66 *Flame-flushed, enraged, splendid salvia. **1937** W. DE LA MARE *This Year, Next Year*, Its drowsy eye Fixed on the flame-flushed company. **1649** G DANIEL *Trinarch., Hen. V*, xciii, High-wrought drosse Shines from his [the Sun's] *flame-irradiated Earth. **1752** H. M[OORE] *To Memory of Dr. Doddridge* vii, [He] midst the *flame-rob'd Bands a Seraph glows. **1625** K. LONG tr. *Barclay's Argenis* v. xx. 402 Thy chaste *flame-sparkling eyes. **1836** KEBLE in *Lyra Apost.* (1849) 215 Some *flame-tipt arrow of the Almighty falls. **1842** SIR A. DE VERE *Song of Faith* 52 The legion hands Of *flame-uplifted Demons. **1621** G. SANDYS *Ovid's Met.* XIV. (1626) 890 Ioue..with *flame-winged thunder earth affrights. *a* **1881** ROSSETTI *House of Life* ix, One flame-winged brought a white-winged harp-player.

d. parasynthetic and similative, as ***flame-eyed***, ***-faced***, ***-haired***, ***-like***, ***-shaped*** adjs.; ***flame-like***, ***-wise*** advs.; limitative, as ***flame-proof***.

1609 B. JONSON *Masque of Queens* Wks. (Rtldg.) 568/2 *Flame-ey'd Rage. **1871** PALGRAVE *Lyr. Poems* 50 That *flame-faced patriot band. *c* **1605** ROWLEY *Birth Merl.* IV. v. 343 Above yon *flame-haired beam that upwards shoots, Appears a dragon's head. **1567** MAPLET *Gr. Forest* 5b, The Chrusoprase is..in the night time..*flamelike, in the day time yelow. **1621** G. SANDYS *Ovid's Met.* XV. (1626) 718 Rouling about his eyes that flame-like blaz'd. **1886** *Illustr. Lond. News* 2 Jan., The materials had been made *flame-proof. **1876** D. WILSON *Preh. Man* vii. (ed. 3) 193 One *flame-shaped arrow-head. **1865** SWINBURNE *Atalanta* 37 My heart Takes fire and trembles *flame-wise.

10. a. Special comb.: **flame-bearer**, a book-name for the genus *Selasphorus* of humming-birds, characterized by the great brilliancy of the gorgets of the males; **flame-bed** (*Steam-engine*) (see quot.); **flame-box**, 'sometimes applied to that portion of the shell of a steam boiler which contains the smoke or flame tubes' (Lockwood 1892); **flame-bridge**, 'a wall rising from the floor of a furnace to cause the flame to impinge upon the bottom of the boiler' (Knight 1874); **flame-cap**, a pale cap-like appearance which the upper part of the flame of a safety-lamp or fire-damp indicator assumes, and which indicates the presence of gas; **flame carpet**, the moth *Coremia propugnaria*; **flame-cell**, a small cavity in the excretory canal of a flat-worm (see quot.); **flame-chamber** (see quot.); **flame-engine**, 'an early name for the gas-engine, in which the piston is moved by the expansion due to the sudden combustion of a body of gas in the cylinder' (Knight 1874); **flame float**, a buoyant pyrotechnic device used for illumination or as a signal, etc.; **flame-flue**, 'the combustion flue of a horizontal boiler, so named to distinguish it from the smoke or return flues which are built in brick-work' (Lockwood 1892); **flame-furnace**, a furnace in which the ore or metal is exposed to the action of flame, but is not in contact with the fuel; †**flame-god**, ? the sun; **flame gun**, a flame-throwing gun, used to destroy weeds, etc.; **flame-kiln** (cf. *flame-furnace*); **flame machine** = *flame-thrower* (a); **flame manometer** (see MANOMETER); **flame-plates**, the top or crown plates of a boiler flue or fire-box (Lockwood 1888); **flame-plating** *Engineering* (see quots.); so (as a back-formation) **flame-plate** *v.*; **flame projector** = *flame-thrower* (*a*); **flame-proof** *v. trans.*, to render flame-proof (Webster 1934); so **flame-proofing** *vbl. sb.* and *ppl. a.*; ***flame-proofed*** ppl. adj.; **flame-red** *a.* and *sb.*, (of) a vivid orange-red shade; **flame-resistant**, **-retardant** *adjs.*, not readily inflammable; so ***flame-resistance***; **flame-shoulder**, the moth *Noctua plecta*; **flame spectrum**, a spectrum of the light produced when a substance is vaporized in an otherwise non-luminous flame; **flame-thrower** [cf. G. *flammenwerfer*], (*a*) a weapon consisting essentially of a reservoir from which a long spray of flame can be ejected against the enemy; (*b*) = *flame gun*; **flame-trap** (see quot. 1949[1]); **flame-ware**, a type of cooking equipment, often of glass, that can withstand the heat of an open flame.

1882 OGILVIE s.v., The little *flame-bearer (*Selasphorus scintilla*) inhabits the inner side of the extinct volcano Chiriqui, in Veragua. **1859** RANKINE *Steam Engine* §304 The flame chamber..has often a floor of fire-brick, called the *flame bed. **1893** *Dublin Rev.* July 653 The wick of the lamp has to be pulled down until the flame becomes pale and non-luminous. In this condition it is small and of low temperature, and therefore ill-suited to produce *flame caps. **1862** MORRIS *Brit. Moths* II. 18 *Coremia propugnaria*, *Flame Carpet. **1888** *Encycl. Brit.* XXIII. 537/1 The spaces between the round connective-tissue cells of the body are star-shaped in form, and into these the finest excretory tubules..open by funnels, into each of which projects a vibratile cilium, thus constituting the so-called '*flame-cells'. **1859** RANKINE *Steam Engine* §304 The *flame-chamber, being the space immediately behind the bridge in which the combustion of the inflammable gases that pass over the bridge is or ought to be completed. **1862** *Atlantic Monthly* July 70/2 Ericsson..soon discovered that his *flame-engine, when worked by the combustion of mineral coals, was [etc.] **1942** T. RATTIGAN *Flare Path* II. ii. 135 It got in the way of a *flame float I was throwing out. **1943** 'T. DUDLEY-GORDON' *Coastal Command* xvii. 167 They hurriedly signalled her [*sc.* the ship] to the spot, dropping flame floats all round the U-boat. **1946** *Jrnl. R. Aeronaut. Soc.* L. 49/2 At night, flame floats were dropped to observe wind. **1888** *Lockwood's Dict. Mech. Engin.*, *Flame-furnace, a reverberatory furnace. **1599** MARSTON *Sco. Villanie* I. ii. 175, I thinke the blind doth see, the *flame God rise From Sisters couch, each morning to the skies. **1931** *Times Lit. Suppl.* 1 Oct. 743/3 *Flame guns which had at first been.. used against them [*sc.* locusts]. **1948** *Times* 20 Mar. 6/7 Even a flame-gun has been devised for their [weeds'] destruction. **1952** E. R. JANES *Flower Garden* 51 Seedlings..looking as if they had been scorched by a flame gun. **1807** VANCOUVER *Agric. Devon* (1813) 28 This limestone..is burnt in what are called *flame-kilns. **1917** *Times* 19 Feb. 7/2 The Germans have used *flame machines for the first time in the Balkans. **1954** *Steel* 5 Apr. 130/3 Productive life of steel core rods has been increased..by having them *flame-plated. **1959** *Engineering* 9 Jan. 59/1 A leading American cable company has saved over $1,500 per year..by having its aluminium alloy pulleys flame-plated to increase their wear resistance. **1954** *Steel* 5 Apr. 130/3 *Flame-plating is a method of

applying tungsten carbide to metal parts... Low temperature deposition is a major advantage of this new process. **1956** *Jrnl. Iron & Steel Inst.* CLXXXIV. 100/1 Flame-plating is a process whereby layers of tungsten carbide/cobalt.. may be applied, by powder deposition, to a wide variety of base metals. **1959** *Engineering* 9 Jan. 59/1 The flame-plating process is a surfacing operation in which particles of tungsten carbide are blasted on to the surface of the workpiece. **1915** *War Illustr.* 4 Sept. 70 German 'Flammenwerfer' (*flame-projector) in action. **1955** *Sci. News Let.* 27 Aug. 143/3 Chemicals.. used.. for *flame-proofing cotton. **1962** *Listener* 25 Jan. 198/2 Most electric blankets are now made of *flame-proofed fabric. **1929** *Chem. Abstr.* 4353 *(heading)* Waterproofing and *flameproofing composition for use on textile fabrics. **1938** *Encycl. Brit. Bk. of Yr.* 332/1 A new flame-proofing material for textile fabrics and paper was announced. **1963** A. J. HALL *Textile Sci.* V. 257 The flameproofing of textile materials has in recent years aroused considerable attention. **1382** WYCLIF *Lev.* xiv. 4 *Flawm reed silk. **1906** L. CLAREMONT *Gem-Cutter's Craft* 77 The beautiful 'flame red' variety which displays the extraordinary effect of a burning coal. **1956** G. DURRELL *My Family* ii. 28 Roses dropped petals that seemed as big and smooth as saucers, flame-red.., glossy and unwrinkled. **1959** *B.S.I. News* May 6/1 The durability of *flame-resistance of such treated fabrics can be seriously affected by washing. **1947** *Amer. Dyestuff Reporter* XXXVI. 135/2 A *flame-resistant or flame-retardant fabric is one which 'exhibits appreciable resistance to afterflaming'. **1959** *Listener* 16 Apr. 695/2 A textile that is claimed to be flame resistant. **1961** *B.S.I. News* Nov. 9/2 The law makes it an offence to sell fabrics and garments as flame-proof or flame-resistant unless they comply with these standards. **1947** *Flame-retardant [see *flame-resistant*]. **1966** *Listener* 15 Dec. 893/2 Thanks to the flame-retardant finish, which public health authorities insist on, the paper dress will char but not flare up when a lighted match is held to it. **1862** MORRIS *Brit. Moths* II. 141 *Noctua plecta*, *Flame-shoulder. **1862** *Chem. News* 26 Apr. 234/1 The broad band in the *flame-spectrum of calcium named Ca β, is replaced in the spectrum of the intense calcium-spark by five green lines. **1907** *Proc. R. Soc.* A. LXXIX. 243 The spectra of the glow from metallic vapours have been photographed repeatedly in the oxy-hydrogen flame spectra of all the alkali metal salts. **1962** R. E. DODD *Chem. Spectroscopy* i. 12 Flame spectra are.. either line spectra of neutral atoms or bands of very closely spaced lines arising from molecules. **1917** P. GIBBS *Battles of Somme* 178 There were eight of these *flame-throwers brought against the Sussex lads. **1944** *Living off Land* vii. 154 To start a backfire rapidly under difficult conditions, flame-throwers are used. **1945** *Reader's Digest* Oct. 84/1 Flame throwers kill the weeds. **1956** A. H. COMPTON *Atomic Quest* 303 Those burned by flame throwers. **1932** *Jrnl. R. Aeronaut. Soc.* XXXVI. 854 It seemed.. that *flame traps were one of the things they could leave off for the moment in their struggle against the weight of engines. **1949** *Gloss. Aeronaut. Terms (B.S.I.)* II. 11 *Flame trap [Induction flame damper]*, a device fitted in the induction system to prevent the passage of flame in the event of a 'backfire' or 'blow-back'. **1949** *Hansard Commons* 15 Mar. 1932 Can he tell the House whether the problem of flame traps for jet aircraft at night has been overcome? **1938** *Trade Marks Jrnl.* 23 Nov. 1420 *Flameware. Made in JP Pyrex Brand JP England. Registration of this Trade Mark shall give no right to the exclusive use, either separately or in combination, of the letters 'J.P.' and the word 'Flame-ware'. **1941** C. J. PHILLIPS *Glass* xii. 281 Pyrex-brand Flameware is made from a special glass of relatively low expansion which has been treated to give it added mechanical strength and resistance to thermal shock. **1967** *House & Garden* Jan. 8/3 A complete range of oven- and flameware in multicolour.. design. *Ibid.* Mar. 79/1 There is a steady demand for good oven-ware and flameware.

b. in some names of plants with vivid scarlet or crimson flowers: **flame-flower**, a species of *Kniphofia* (*Tritoma*); **flame lily** (see quot.); **flame-tree**, (*a*) the *Sterculia acerifolia* of New South Wales; (*b*) the *Nuytsia floribunda* of Western Australia, also called *fire-tree*; (*c*) the *Butea frondosa* or palash tree.

1882 *Garden* 14 Jan. 19/2 We came across several colonies of Pampas Grass.. associated with *Flame flowers (Tritoma). **1841** MRS. LOUDON *Ladies' Flower-Gard.* 129 *Pyrolirion*, the *Flame Lily. **1866** *Treas. Bot.*, *Flame tree, *Brachychiton acerifolium*. **1883** *Cassell's Fam. Mag.* Oct. 685/1 The palash is a fair-sized tree, and its flowers are very bright scarlet, from which it is frequently spoken of as the 'flame-tree'. **1885** MRS. C. PRAED *Australian Life* 96 There are flame-trees, showing in spring vivid patches of crimson.

flame (fleɪm), *v.* Forms: 4–5 **flambe, flaumbe, flaume, flawme, flamme**, 4– **flame**. See also FLAMB. [ME. *flambe, flamme*, a. OF. *flambe-r, flam(m)er*, f. *flambe, flamme* FLAME *sb.*]

1. a. *intr.* To burn with a flame or with flames; to emit flames; to blaze. Also with *away, forth, out, up*.

1377 LANGL. *P. Pl.* B. XVII. 205 A fyre flaumende forth oute of boþe. *?a***1400** *Morte Arth.* 1975 Owre kyng gerte felschene his fyrez, flawmande fulle heghe. **1481** CAXTON *Myrr.* II. iii. 67 Fyre brennyng.. goth flammyng vnto the clowdes. **1548** HALL *Chron.* 195 b, Other causes.. made yͤ fyre to flame. **1601** SHAKS. *Jul. C.* I. iii. 16 His left Hand which did flame.. Like twentie Torches. **1632** LITHGOW *Trav.* x. 479 Fire lying hid under ashes, and touch'd will flame. **1654** H. L'ESTRANGE *Chas. I* (1655) 165 The Admiral of Portugal began to flame being fired with two Holland fire ships. **1667** MILTON *P.L.* I. 62 A Dungeon horrible, on all sides round As one great Furnace flam'd. **1725** DE FOE *Voy. round World* (1840) 242 A volcano.. flamed out that night. **1774** GOLDSM. *Nat. Hist.* (1862) I. viii. 39 Spirits of wine will flame with a candle, but not with a spark. *c***1839** LANDOR *Imag. Conv., Southey & Porson* II, There is a paleness in intense fires; they do not flame out or sparkle. **1853** KANE *Grinnell Exp.* xxxix. 356 Lard lamps flaming away vigorously.

b. *fig.*

1377 LANGL. *P. Pl.* B. XVII. 225 Þanne flaumbeth he [þe holygoste] as fyre on fader & on filius. **1614** BP. HALL *Recoll. Treat.* 976 Cruelty hath but smoaked before, now it flames up. **1752** YOUNG *Brothers* I. i, Sparks of war, Which might one day flame up to strong revenge. **1770** LANGHORNE *Plutarch* (1879) II. 591/1 The Servile war.. wanted but little fuel to make it flame out again. **1793** *Object. to War Examined & Refuted* 27 The Republic.. flames out in many parts with Civil War. **1890** *Century Mag.* Jan. 362/1 Alien blood flamed in her veins.

†**c.** *transf.* To emit a smell (also, of a smell, to issue) with violence like that of flame.

1377 LANGL. *P. Pl.* B. xii. 255 Whan his caroigne shal come in caue to be buryed, I leue it flaumbe ful foule þe folde al aboute. **14..** *MS. Laud* 656 fol. 4 b, A flauour flambeþ þerfro, þey felleden hit alle.

d. *to flame out*: spec. of a jet engine, to cease operation through extinction of the flame in the combustion chamber. So ***flame-out*** sb.

1950 *Nat. Geogr. Mag.* Sept. 307/2 If that boy.. had blasted his throttle forward fast, he would have got what we call a 'flameout'. **1951** *Britannica Bk. of Yr.* 686/1 *Flame-out*, of a jet plane, to exhaust its supply of fuel. **1957** *Wall St. Jrnl.* 15 July 7/4 Curtiss-Wright Corp. announced it has successfully conducted tests with fuels which ignite on contact with air and which can re-light jet engines which have 'flamed-out' at high altitude. **1957** *Aeroplane* 1 Feb. 149/1 When the aircraft was about 90 minutes out of Salisbury, all four engines began 'bumping' and four flame-outs occurred in the space of five minutes. **1960** *Guardian* 30 June 10/4 The nature of the fuel gave the engine a strong tendency to 'flame out'. **1965** *New Scientist* 27 May 577/2 Some of the combustion troubles associated with flame velocities which cause flame-outs in jet engines, especially at great heights.

2. *fig.* **a.** Of the passions, etc.: To burn like flames. ***to flame out***: to burst out violently.

*a***1591** R. GREENHAM *Wks.* (1599) 22 Though he keep thy sinne from flaming out. *a***1625** BEAUM. & FL. *Lover's Progress* I. i. (Rtldg.) 637/2 Lascivious fires, should such flame in you. **1707** NORRIS *Treat. Humility* vi. 240 Here and there where their malice flames out. **1849** MACAULAY *Hist. Eng.* II. 244 The rage of James flamed high.

b. Of persons: To burn (with envy, fury, indignation, etc.); to look angrily or passionately *upon*. ***to flame out, up***: to break out into open anger or indignation; to 'fire up'.

1548 UDALL, etc. *Erasm. Par. Matt.* xxii. 106 Whiche wholy flame with enuy and hatred. **1681** CROWNE *Hen. VI*, IV. 49, I flame with fury to be at it. *a***1701** SEDLEY *Happy Pair* (1766) 16 With heat of loue he flam'd upon his mate. **1754** RICHARDSON *Grandison* V. xiv: 112 If the alliance.. take effect.. how will she flame out! **1849** MACAULAY *Hist. Eng.* I. 195 He flamed with indignation. **1858** CARLYLE *Fredk. Gt.* (1865) I. III. vi. 180 An *Osianderism*.. much flamed-upon by the more orthodox *ism*. **1858** *Ibid.* (1865) II. V. viii. 132 Queen Sophie.. did once.. lose her royal patience and flame out.

3. *transf.* To glow like flame or as with flames; to shine brightly, gleam ruddily. Also with *away, forth, up*, etc.

13.. *E.E. Allit. P.* A. 768 Maskellez bryd þat bryȝt con flambe. **1530** PALSGR. 551/1, I have sene the yerthe flame a nyght season lyke any fyre. **1535** STEWART *Cron. Scot.* II. 320 The face of Phebus flamand fair. **1621** BEAUM. & FL. *Thierry & Theodoret* III. ii. (Rtldg.) 417/2 There's anger yet Flames in your eyes. **1698** CROWNE *Caligula* I. Dram. Wks. 1874 IV. 360 Cæsar [led] A flying camp of ranting concubines, Who flam'd, and gave a lustre to the day. *c***1710** C. FIENNES *Diary* (1888) 257 Diamonds wᶜʰ flamed at yᵉ Least motion. **1740** DYER *Ruins Rome* 21 The rising sun Flames on the ruins. **1777** MAD. D'ARBLAY *Diary* Oct., This .. room was.. flaming with velvet. **1807** W. IRVING *Salmag.* (1824) 133 Fling.. a red shawl over the figure of a fashionable belle, and let her flame away with it in Broadway. **1826** SYD. SMITH *Wks.* (1859) II. 74 The mud is flaming with the scarlet curlew. **1882** EDNA LYALL *Donovan* xv, She felt the colour flame up in her cheeks. **1883** STEVENSON *Silverado Sq.* 15 The dentist.. flamed forth in his second dress as a captain of banditti.

4. a. *intr.* To move as or like flame.

1633 P. FLETCHER *Purple Isl.* XI. iv, Those holy Fishers once amongs Thou flamedst bright with sparkling parted tongues. **1732** POPE *Ess. Man* II. 65 Meteor-like, flame lawless thro' the void. **1892** TENNYSON *Death of Œnone* 38 (*Akbar's Dream*) Once again thou flamest heavenward.

b. *trans.* To send forth or convey by flaming.

14.. LYDG. *Balade of our Ladie* ix, Flambe down þe doleful light of thyn influence. **1610** SHAKS. *Temp.* I. ii. 200 In euery Cabyn, I flam'd amazement: sometime I'ld diuide, And burne in many places. **1892** T. A. COOK *Old Touraine* I. 91 An old system of signalling by beacon fires.. which flamed messages along the valley.

5. To burn, set on fire, consume with flames. Also *fig.*

1583 STANYHURST *Æneis* III. (Arb.) 79 Sundry hostes are flamed on altars. **1590** SPENSER *F.Q.* III. ix. 18 Malbecco seeing them resolvd.. To flame the gates. **1612** N. FIELD *Woman's a Weather-cock* I. i, The Masculine Element of Fire Shall flame his Pyramids downe to the Earth. **1737** WHISTON *Josephus' Antiq.* Diss. III. xiii, Some were nailed to crosses, and others flamed to death. **1942** T. S. ELIOT *Little Gidding* i. 7 The brief sun flames the ice, on pond and ditches.

†**6.** To cause to glow with enthusiasm. zeal, etc.; to kindle, inflame, excite, animate. *Obs.*

*c***1380** WYCLIF *Sel. Wks.* III. 36 Þe swete odour þerof schulde flawme mennys hertis. **1596** SPENSER *F.Q.* V. i. 14 Flam'd with zeal of vengeance inwardly, He ask'd [etc.]. **1627–77** FELTHAM *Resolves* I. xiv. 22 That sacred vigour which had wont.. To flame the Poets noble brest. **1640** SHIRLEY *Coronation* II. D j b, Their courage is so nobly flamed.

7. To subject to the action of flame. Cf. *Sc.* FLAMB.

1875 *Ure's Dict. Arts* III. 88 After flaming, the pieces are successively laid on an inclined table exposed to the fire. **1885** DOLLEY *Bacteria Investigation* I. 69 The pipette is first thoroughly sterilized by flaming every portion of it.

flame, obs. form of FLEAM.

'flame-,colour. The colour of flame; a bright reddish yellow or orange.

1608 B. JONSON *Masque of Beauty*, Splendor in a robe of flame colour. **1712** ADDISON *Spect.* No. 265 ¶7 Melesinda wraps her Head in Flame Colour. **1858** J. MARTINEAU *Stud. Chr.* 143 The preternatural flame-colour mingled in the crucibles of hell.

b. *attrib.* or *adj.* = next.

1763 DEL PINO *Sp. Dict.*, *Caballo de color morado*, a flame colour horse.

'flame-coloured, *a.* Of the colour of flame.

1596 SHAKS. *1 Hen. IV*, I. ii. 11 A faire hot Wench in Flame-coloured Taffata. **1647** STAPYLTON *Juvenal* 22 He.. Weares a fring'd petticote & flame-colour'd veyle. **1704** SWIFT *T. Tub* ii, Flame-coloured Satin. **1876** GEO. ELIOT *Dan. Der.* IV. liii. 96 Her dusky, flame-coloured garment. *fig.* **1784** R. BAGE *Barham Downs* I. 113 Damnation! swore my Lord, and a few other flame-coloured ejaculations.

flamed (fleɪmd), *ppl. a.* [f. FLAME *v.* and *sb.* + -ED[1], [2].]

1. Aflame, burning.

1413 *Pilgr. Sowle* III. viii. (Caxton 1483) 55 A furnoys.. alle flammed with fyre. **1583** STANYHURST *Æneis* II. (Arb.) 54 The.. Greeks thee flamd citty with ruthlesse victorye ransack. **1634** HABINGTON *Castara* (Arb.) 61 A flamed dart shot from her eye.

2. Furnished with flames.

1851 E. J. MILLINGTON tr. *Didron's Chr. Archæol.* I. 452 Wheels which are both winged and flamed.. to express the extreme of velocity.

3. Of a tulip: Bearing flame-like marks.

1665–76 RAY *Flora* 94 The flowers are.. yellow.. and some striped, feathered, or flamed. **1846** J. BAXTER *Libr. Pract. Agric.* (ed. 4) I. 302 A Tulip, is called flamed, when a broad irregular stripe runs up the middle of the petals, with short abrupt projecting points, branching out on each side.

†**'flameful**, *a.* *Obs. rare*$^{-1}$. [f. FLAME *sb.* + -FUL.] Full of flame. In quot. *fig.*

1598 SYLVESTER *Du Bartas* II. i. I. *Eden* 401 When pale Phlegm, or saffron-colour'd Choler.. print upon our Understanding's Tables; That, Water-wracks; this other, flamefull Fables.

flameless ('fleɪmlɪs), *a.* [f. FLAME *sb.* + -LESS.] Devoid of flame; burning without flame.

1606 SYLVESTER *Du Bartas* II. iv. I. *Trophies* 55 A fire so great Could not live flameless long. **1638** G. SANDYS *Par. Div. Poems, Lament. Jer.* ii. 7 Jehova.. forsakes His flamelesse Altar. **1837** CARLYLE *Fr. Rev.* (1857) I. I. VII. x. 219 It burns.. flameless, as charred coals do. **1884** SWINBURNE in *19th Cent.* May 775 The flameless fire of imaginative thought.

'flamelet. [f. as prec. + -LET.] A small flame.

1849 LONGF. *By the Fireside, K. Witlaf's Drinking-Horn* viii. 3 The flamelets flapped and flickered. **1871** B. TAYLOR *Faust* (1875) II. IV. ii. 251 Upon our phalanx' shining lances A nimble host of flamelets dances.

flamen ('fleɪmɛn). Forms: 4–5 **flamyn(e** (*erron.* **flaume**), 4–7 **flamin(e**, 7 **flammin(g**, 7– **flamen.** [a. L. *flāmen*, of doubtful etymology; some modern scholars believe it to stand for **flădmen*, f. *flăd-*:—W Aryan **bhlād-* as in Goth. *blôt-an*, OE. *blót-an* to sacrifice; others regard it as standing for *flăgmen*, f. root *flăg-* to burn (from burning sacrifices).]

1. *Rom. Antiq.* A priest devoted to the service of a particular deity. †***flamin diall*** = L. *flamen dialis*, the flamen of Jupiter.

1533 BELLENDEN *Livy* I. (1822) 34 Yit he institute the sacrifice that pertenit to the flamin diall. **1607** SHAKS. *Cor.* II. i. 229 Seld-showne Flamins Doe presse among the popular Throngs. **1644** MILTON *Areop.* (Arb.) 37 The Romans.. knew of learning little but what their Augurs and Flamins taught them. **1733** POPE *Ess. Man* III. 266 Then first the Flamen tasted living food. **1880** MUIRHEAD *Gaius* I. §112 No person is elected to the office of one of the greater flamens, i.e. a flamen of Jupiter, Mars, or Quirinus.. unless born of farreate parents.

2. *transf.* Applied to other priests, etc.

*c***1400** MAUNDEV. (1839) xii. 141 The Archiflamyn or the Flamyn, as oure Erchebisshopp or Bisshopp.. seythe thus. **1650** BULWER *Anthropomet.* 210 Egyptian Priests and other Flamines of the Natural Law used Circumcision. **1660** HICKERINGILL *Jamaica* (1661) 79 The Muses and their Flamens they cashiere. **1789** BURNS *Let. to Mrs. Dunlop* 13 Dec., Ye venerable sages, and holy flamens, is there probability in your conjectures? **1808** J. BARLOW *Columb.* IV. 316 Let the poor guardless natives never feel The flamen's fraud.

3. The L. *flamen* and *archiflamen* (see ARCH-FLAMEN) were used by Geoffrey of Monmouth to denote the two grades of alleged sacerdotal functionaries in heathen Britain, whose place was taken on the conversion of the island by bishops and archbishops. Hence pseudo-*Hist.* in Eng. writers.

*c***1330** R. BRUNNE *Chron. Wace* (Rolls) 5756 Eyght & twenty flamins men tolde. **1387** TREVISA *Higden* (Rolls) II. 111, 28 bisshoppis icleped flamynes. **1480** CAXTON *Descr. Brit.* 25 To these archbisshops sees were subgette xxviij bisshops and were called flamines. **1612** DRAYTON *Poly-olb.* viii. 112 With Fanes vnto her Gods, and Flamins

euerywhere. **1652** COLLINGES *Caveat for Prof.* (1653) 132 It holds as much for Bishops and Archbishops (instead of Flammins and Archflammins).

4. *attrib.*, as ***flamen-priest***.

a **1533** LD. BERNERS *Gold. Bk. M. Aurel.* II. v. (1535) 114 b, Their gownes long lyke flamine prestes.

Hence ˈ**flamenship**, the office of a flamen.

1600 HOLLAND *Livy* XXVI. xxiii. (1609) 601 C. Claudius, the Arch-flamine of Jupiter, lost his Flamineship. **1610** HEALEY *St. Aug. Citie of God* (1620) 71 Flamines, inheritors of the ancient Flamine-ship.

flamenco (fləˈmɛŋkəʊ). [Sp., = FLAMINGO.] A Spanish gipsy style of singing or dancing; a song or dance in this style.

1896 *Daily News* 8 June 4/2 A few steps from the flamenco, or wild Spanish dance. **1923** *Blackw. Mag.* July 28/1 Gramophone records of flamenco-singing. *Ibid.* Oct. 503/2 Spanish flamenco music. **1925** *Ibid.* Jan. 80/2 The nasal eastern flamenco which gives to Spanish singing its most marked character. **1950** *Ballet Ann.* IV. 32 There is no clear distinction in people's minds between *flamenco* dancing and the classical or 'school' dancing of Spain. **1952** B. ULANOV *Hist. Jazz in Amer.* ii. 11 The intensity.. resembles..flamenco dances in Spain. **1959** F. NEWTON *Jazz Scene* i. 14 There is a great difference between the first flamenco songs of the 1860s and the flamenco of today.

flamenco, -go, obs. forms of FLAMINGO.

flamer (ˈfleɪmə(r)). [f. FLAME *v.* + -ER¹.]

1. One who or that which flames.

1591 SYLVESTER *Du Bartas* I. ii. 996 And then no more you would the Aire allow For Element, then th' hot bright Flamer now. **1612** STURTEVANT *Metallica* (1854) 110 The Scottish coal is the best flamer. **1887** *Pall Mall G.* 9 Dec. 5/2 Armed only with an electric battery, or was it only a flamer? with which he signalled to the magic lantern.

2. *slang.* A person or thing glaringly conspicuous.

1809 *Spirit Pub. Jrnls.* (1810) XIII. 163 Dick Daredevil.. sported a brace of *flamers* (wenches) on his coach-box. **1840** H. COCKTON *Val. Vox* ii. 5 A criticism on the evening's performance which certainly was..'a regular flamer.'

flamery, obs. form of FLUMMERY.

ˈ**flameship.** *nonce-wd.* [f. FLAME *sb.* + -SHIP.] The personality or dignity of (the god of) flame.

a **1637** B. JONSON *Underwoods, Execration Vulcan*, Pox on your Flameship, Vulcan.

†**flamet.** *Obs.* [a. F. *flamet* (also in Pr.).] = FLAMINGO.

1706 [see FLAMAN.]

flamfew (ˈflæmfjuː). Also 6 **flamefew**, 9 *Sc.* **flamfoo.** [Corruption of F. *fanfelue*:—med.L. *famfalūca* bubble, lie, app. ad. Gr. πομφόλυξ bubble. Cf. mod.F. *fanfreluche*.] A gewgaw, trifle, fantastic thing.

Also *Sc.* 'Any gaudy trapping in female dress,' 'a gaudily dressed female' (Jam.).

1580 BARET *Alv.* F 614 A Flamefew, or the mooneshine in the water. **1583** STANYHURST *Æneis*, etc. (Arb.) 138 Voyd ye fro theese flamfews..set a part the begun wurck. **1890** *Temple Bar Mag.* Nov. 430 Fancy..had bodied forth a curious flamfew.

†ˈ**flaminal**, *a. Obs.* [ad. L. *flāminālis*, f. *flāmen* FLAMEN.] Of or pertaining to a flamen.

a **1693** URQUHART *Rabelais* III. xlviii. 385 The Flaminal Mists, and mysterious Flamens.

flamineous (fleɪˈmɪnɪəs), *a.* Also **flaminious.** [f. L. *flāmin-*, FLAMEN + -EOUS, -IOUS. Cf. L. *flāminius*.] Of or pertaining to a flamen.

1846 WORCESTER *Flamineous* (citing MORE). **1864** WORCESTER *Flaminious.* [? Error for *flammeous*, in H. More.]

flaming (ˈfleɪmɪŋ), *vbl. sb.* [f. FLAME *v.* + -ING¹.] The action of the verb FLAME. Also *concr.*, something which flames or resembles a flame.

c **1400** *Destr. Troy* 970 The flammyng of þe flese was ferly to see. **1546** BALE *Eng. Votaries* I. 39/1 A..starre, whiche semed with flamynges of fyre to fall into the sea. **1703** tr. *H. van Oosten's Dutch Gardener* III. ii. 153 Concerning the Striping or Flaming, it must be low, beginning from the bottom of the Flower. **1854** RUSKIN *Lect. Archit.* Add. 128 Wherever colour is introduced, ornamentation..may consist in mere spots, or bands, or flamings.

flaming (ˈfleɪmɪŋ), *ppl. a.* Also 4 **flammande, flawmbeand,** 5 **flawmand.** [f. as prec. + -ING².]

1. a. That flames; in flames or on fire, as a combustible; *esp.* in ***flaming sword***.

c **1400** MAUNDEV. (Roxb.) xxxiii. 150 þe flawmand swerde þat Godd ordaynd þare before þe entree. **1509** HAWES *Past. Pleas.* XLIII. ix, Thus in flamynge tonges all aboute I flye. **1611** BIBLE *Gen.* iii. 24 A flaming sword. **1781** GIBBON *Decl. & F.* III. 137 The spoil, and cattle, of the flaming villages. **1821** SHELLEY *Prometh. Unb.* I. 88 Nor yon volcano's flaming fountains.

fig. **1422** tr. *Secreta Secret., Priv. Priv.* (E.E.T.S.) 191 A flawmyng vertu dwellys yn þe hert. **1509** HAWES *Joyf. Medit.* 17 O flambynge honour of euery hardy herte. **1748** RICHARDSON *Clarissa* (1811) VIII. ii. 16 O these flaming spirits! **1874** MORLEY *Compromise* (1886) 264 The flaming hopes of its friends.

†**b.** ***flaming chapel*** = F. *chapelle ardente*: a chapel or chamber thickly set with lighted tapers.

1802 *Paris as it was* II. lxvii. 318 A flaming chapel was constructed at the entrance of the house.

c. ***flaming onions***, an anti-aircraft projectile consisting of about ten balls of fire shot upwards in succession, so called from its resemblance to a string of onions (see also quot. 1943). *Services' slang.*

1918 V. DRAKE *Above Battle* vi. 118 These 'flaming onions' were huge rockets of balls of phosphorus which burst at the top of their climb and spread out into a great umbrella shaped curtain of flame, and sank slowly down, the idea being that any machine in its path would be instantly set fire to by the burning phosphorus. **1925** FRASER & GIBBONS *Soldier & Sailor Words, Flaming onions*, a colloquial name for a German anti-aircraft projectile. **1928** C. F. S. GAMBLE *N. Sea Air Station* xxii. 384 One of the flying-boats..came into a heavy barrage of 'flaming onions'. **1943** HUNT & PRINGLE *Service Slang* 32 *Flaming onions*, tracer fire from the ground.

2. a. Burning hot, inflamed, fiery. Used euphemistically for a profane epithet. Also as *adv.*

1697 DRYDEN *Virg. Georg.* III. 841 Red Blisters..And flaming Carbuncles. **1786** BURNS *'Once fondly lov'd'*, Who, distant, burns in flaming torrid climes. **1871** R. ELLIS *Catullus* lxiv. 354 As some labourer..Under a flaming sun. **1895** 'G. MORTIMER' *Like Stars that Fall* xv, Yes, by God, I'll get flaming drunk. **1922** D. H. LAWRENCE *England, my England* 230 I've never been patient to no flaming doctor, and hope I never shall be. **1936** *Punch* 10 June 646/1 Some flaming person has gone and stolen my flaming bicycle-pump, flame it all! **1944** *Coast to Coast 1943* 188 It was lovely work Patsy, but, stone the flamin' crows! you can't do that at your age. **1946** *Coast to Coast 1945* 163 Brand new line, and you're too flaming lazy to get the lot! **1960** *Analog Science Fact/Fiction* Oct. 174/1 Miss Fulton says..'Not bad, but Chandler has done better...' Too flaming right he has. **1966** 'J. HACKSTON' *Father clears Out* 61 To hell with the flaming place. **1969** *Private Eye* 9 May 14 He's saved my life if he only flamin' knew it.

b. quasi-*adv.*, as ***flaming-hot***. *lit.* and *fig.*

1638 SIR T. HERBERT *Trav.* (ed. 2) 32 The wind less'ned, and weather grew flaming hot. **1681** BAXTER *Apol. Nonconf. Min.* 111 Flaming-hot Disputer.

3. *transf.* a. Emitting rays of light, flashing, glowing, brilliant. †***flaming fly*** = FIREFLY.

13.. *E.E. Allit. P.* B. 1468 Alle þe fruyt in þo formes of flaumbeande gemmes. ? *a* **1400** *Morte Arth.* 198 Ffesauntez enflureschit in flammande silver. *c* **1400** *Destr. Troy* 3986 Hir ene flamyng fresshe, as any fyne stones. **1686** PLOT *Staffordsh.* 116 Our English Glow-wormes, as well as the American, or flaming-flyes, have a luminous juice in their tailes. **1744** BERKELEY *Siris* §187 The glory of the Lord, which was wont to appear in a flaming light. **1826** DISRAELI *Viv. Grey* III. vii, The large yellow eye grew more flaming and fiery.

b. in regard to colour: Resembling flame, very bright or vivid.

c **1450** *Crt. of Love* 793 Her mouth is short..Flaming somedele, not over red. **1638** SIR T. HERBERT *Trav.* (ed. 2) 297 The Bannana's..from a dark-greene, mellow into a flaming yellow. **1718** PRIOR *Solomon* I. xxxvi, At Noon in flaming Yellow bright. **1863** MISS BRADDON *Eleanor's Vict.* II. i. 3 The flaming poppies among the ripening corn. **1865** CARLYLE *Fredk. Gt.* VI. XVI. xii. 282 Voltaire has used his flamingest colours on this occasion.

†**c.** Of a person: Gaudy, 'loud', flaring.

1781 R. KING *London Spy* 95 A serjeant of the guards entered..with a flaming wench.

4. *fig.* a. Highly coloured, highflown; startling, extravagant.

1606 SHAKS. *Tr. & Cr.* I. ii. 115 He hauing colour enough, and the other higher, is too flaming a praise for a good complexion. **1720** DE FOE *Capt. Singleton* xi. (1840) 191, I had heard some flaming stories of Captain Avery, and the fine things he had done in the Indies. **1796** JANE AUSTEN *Pride & Prej.* x. (1813) 224 The good lady..did give him a most flaming character. **1850** PRESCOTT *Peru* II. 6 The flaming pictures..given by the natives of the riches of the land. **1868** HELPS *Realmah* II. xvii. 287 There comes out a flaming attack against some poor man.

b. ***flaming youth*** [Shakes. *Ham.* III. iv. 84]: a collective term for young persons, alluding to their characteristically vigorous and unrestrained behaviour or ways. Chiefly *U.S.*

1923 'W. FABIAN' (*title*) Flaming youth. **1937** *Time* 6 Sept. 40/2 The traditional belief that flaming youth is guilty of most drunken driving accidents was last week scouted by the results of a six-month survey. **1960** J. MITFORD *Hons & Rebels* viii. 58 The Bright Young People had faded from the London scene..as their transatlantic counterparts, the Flaming Youth, had no doubt disappeared from the American scene with the passing of the 'twenties. **1962** *Amer. Speech* XXXVII. 27 The hectic era of Prohibition, bootleggers, flappers, and flaming youth. *Ibid.* 31 The age of flaming youth.

5. Flagrant, glaring, monstrous. ? *Obs.*

1706 COLLIER *Reply to Dr. Filmer* (1730) 412 The most flaming Instances of Vice. **1737** WATERLAND *Eucharist* 583 A flaming Absurdity.

6. Like waving flame in appearance; flamboyant.

1375 BARBOUR *Bruce* XI. 192 Vith baneris richt freschly flawmand. **1686** *Lond. Gaz.* No. 2176/4 A Silver Hilted Sword, with the Blade waved or flaming. **1874** BOUTELL *Arms & Arm.* ix. 177 The blade of this sword not uncommonly affected a wavy or flaming (*flamboyante*) outline.

Hence ˈ**flamingly** *adv.*

1627–77 FELTHAM *Resolves* I. xx. 37 How quaint and flamingly amorous [is Solomon] in the Canticles. **1681** BAXTER *Acc. Sherlocke* v. 203 Why would he meddle (and so flamingly meddle) with what he understands not? **1834** H. AINSWORTH *Rookwood* I. iv. (1878) 31 A flamingly gilt dial. **1888** *Harper's Mag.* Nov. 838/1 You are flamingly patriotic.

‖**Flamingant** (flamɪŋgɑ̃), *sb.* and *a.* [Fr., = Flemish-speaking, f. **flameng*, fem. *flamenge*, ad. Du. *Vlaming* FLEMING¹.] **a.** *sb.* An advocate of the recognition of Flemish as an official language of Belgium, or of the exclusive use of Flemish in certain parts of Belgium. **b.** *attrib.* or as *adj.* Of or pertaining to such advocates or their policies. Hence ˈ**Flamingantism**, the policy of furthering the use of Flemish.

1920 *Contemp. Rev.* Jan. 86 While the chauvinists were badly beaten, the Parliamentary power of both Socialism and Flamingantism was increased tremendously. **1921** *Ibid.* Nov. 700 The aim of the Flamingant programme has been to obtain equal rights, both in theory and practice for the Flemish language. **1922** *Ibid.* Feb. 244 They [*sc.* the Walloons] consider the Flamingants to be unpatriotic and 'pro-German'. *Ibid.* Dec. 786 The result is that the Flamingant officials are rapidly promoted. **1964** P. GEYL *Hist. Low Countries* ix. 199 The Flamingants (as the conscious and active Flemings were called) indulged freely in romanticism. *Ibid.* 200 In Antwerp..the town hall was brought under Flamingant sway. *Ibid.* 201 Militant Flamingantism had been able to come to power in some municipalities.

flamingo (fləˈmɪŋgəʊ). Forms: 6 (**fleming**), **flemengo,** 7–8 **flemingo, flamenco,** 7– **flamingo.** See also FLEMING, FLAMAN. [a. Pg. *flamengo*, Sp. *flamenco*, Pr. *flamenc*, according to Hatzf.-Darm. f. Rom. *flama* FLAME *sb.* + suffix *-enc* (a. Teut. *-ing*) often appended in Pr. and occas. in OF. to sbs. of L. origin. The F. name, *flamant*, is believed to be an alteration of the Pr. form; cf. OF. *ferrant* iron-gray, from *ferrenc*. So called from the colour.]

1. a. A bird of the genus *Phœnicopterus*, with bright scarlet plumage, extremely long and slender legs and neck, and a heavy bent bill.

1565 J. SPARKE in Hakluyt *Voy.* III. 520 The fowle of the fresh riuers..whereof the Flemengo is one, hauing all redde feathers. **1634** SIR T. HERBERT *Trav.* 212 Sundry other Birds, as..Passe-flemingoes. **1697** DAMPIER *Voy.* (1729) I. 70, I saw a few Flamingo's, which is a sort of large Fowl. **1867** JEAN INGELOW *Songs on Voices Birds, Sandmartins*, Where rosy-winged flamingos fish all day.

b. The deep pink colour of the flamingo.

1897 *Westm. Gaz.* 5 June 7/1 The poor little flamingo-caped lassies. **1923** *Daily Mail* 29 Jan. 1/4 In shades of Powder Blue,..Cyclamen,..Flamingo, Pink. *Ibid.* 12 June 15 Favourite Colour of the Season is Flamingo. **1927** V. WOOLF *To Lighthouse* I. 41 Lovely evenings, with all their flamingo clouds and blue and silver.

2. *attrib.* and *Comb.*, as ***flamingo-legged*** adj.; **flamingo flower** or **plant**, a name for *Anthurium scherzerianum*.

1862 THORNBURY *Turner* I. 14 A flamingo-legged footman. **1882** *Garden* 1 Apr. 212/2 The Flamingo flower. *Ibid.* 9 Sept. 226/1 The Flamingo plant.

†**flaˈminical**, *a. Obs.* [f. L. *flāmin-*, *flāmen* FLAMEN + -IC + -AL¹.] Of or pertaining to a flamen.

1641 MILTON *Ch. Govt.* Wks. 1738 I. 63 Superstitious Copes and flaminical Vestures.

flamm, flam, ? incorrect form of FLAWN. (But cf. FLAMMICK.)

1819 SCOTT *Bride Lammerm.* x, A tart—a flam—and some nonsense sweet things. **1820** —— *Monast.* xvi, The wafers, flamms, and pastrymeat.

flammaˈbility. Also 7 **flamability.** [f. next; see *-bility*, -ITY.] = INFLAMMABILITY. Revived in modern use to avoid the possible ambiguity of *inflammability*, in which the prefix *in-* might be taken for a negative (IN- *pref.*³).

1646 SIR T. BROWNE *Pseud. Ep.* VI. xii. 335 The oily fat and unctuous parts wherein consist the principles of flammability. **1669** W. SIMPSON *Hydrol. Chym.* 246 The same Essential properties of Flamability. **1942** *Jrnl. R. Aeronaut. Soc.* XLVI. 471 That intense combustion in Diesel engines probably occurs only in regions in which local concentration of fuel at least equals a certain minimum value analogous to the lower limit of flammability. **1959** *Scotsman* 1 May 7/6 Scientists at the Government's research establishment at Boreham Wood are carrying out flammability tests on some of the materials used in Glasgow tramcars. **1961** *Times* 1 Mar. 21/7 The flammability of clothing fabrics has caused much concern. **1963** *B.S.I. News* July 10/1 *Inflammability* is unquestionably capable of being misunderstood... The fire research interests on the.. committee were particularly anxious that we should standardize on *flammability* in order to prevent such misunderstanding.

flammable (ˈflæməb(ə)l), *a.* [f. L. *flammāre* to set on fire: see -ABLE.] = INFLAMMABLE. Revived in modern use: cf.prec.

1813 BUSBY tr. *Lucretius* I. 731 That igneous seeds, no longer linked To matter flammable, become extinct. **1867** *Morning Star* 12 Apr., Their houses are built of much less flammable materials than ours. **1959** *Gloss. Packaging Terms* (*B.S.I.*) 10 In order to avoid any possible ambiguity, it is the Institution's policy to encourage the use of the terms 'flammable' and 'non-flammable' rather than 'inflammable' and 'non-inflammable'. **1970** *Which?* May 136/2 The plastic linings provided for the kitchen areas..will do little to stop your tent catching fire, because they also are highly flammable.

† **fla'mmation.** *Obs.* In 7 flamation. [n. of action f. L. *flammāre*: see prec.] Exposure to fire.

1646 Sir T. Browne *Pseud. Ep.* II. v. 90 White or Cristaline arsenick..sublimed with salt, will not endure flamation.

‖ **flammenwerfer** (flamən'vɛrfər). [G., f. *flamme* FLAME *sb.* + *werfer* thrower, mortar, f. *werfen* to throw.] = *flame-thrower* (a).

1915 *War Illustr.* 4 Sept. 70 German 'Flammenwerfer' (flame-projector) in action. **1917** P. Gibbs *Battles of Somme* 178 It was against the Sussex men that the Germans used their 'flammenwerfer' or flame-jets. **1957** G. Barker *Coll. Poems 1930–55* 130 The flammenwerfer and the fish And also I acknowledge him creator.

flammeous ('flæmɪəs), *a.* Now *rare.* [f. L. *flamme-us* (f. *flamma* flame) + -OUS.]

1. Of the nature of flame.

1664 H. More *Myst. Iniq.* 45 An inanimate and unintelligent mass of flammeous matter. **1686** Goad *Celest. Bodies* II. vii. 245 Comets are Flammeous, or Lucid Expirations..produced by the Planets. **1775** in Ash.

2. Resembling flame or its attributes; flamelike; hence, shining, resplendent.

1646 Sir T. Browne *Pseud. Ep.* III. xxv. 177 This flammeous light [of the Glow-worme]. **1672** *Phil. Trans.* VII. 4071 The flammeous Life of the Bloud. **1728** Earbery tr. *Burnet's St. Dead* II. 34 The Glory of the Person of Christ is..described..as lucid and flammeous.

3. Flame-coloured.

1656–81 Blount *Glossogr.*, *Flammeous*, somewhat coloured like a flame of fire. **1867** A. L. Adams *Wand. Nat. India* 113 The flammeous flycatcher (*Pericrocotus flammeus*) ..red is the prevailing hue of the former [males].

flammery, obs. var of FLUMMERY.

† **'flammick.** *Obs. rare*$^{-1}$. [a. F. *flamiche.*] A confection made with butter, eggs, and cheese.

1600 Surflet *Countrie Farme* v. xxii. 720.

† **'flammid,** *a. Obs. rare*$^{-1}$. [ad. L. *flammid-us*, f. *flamma* flame.] Flame-coloured; red.

1610 W. Folkingham *Art of Survey* I. iii. 5 The flammid Carbuncle, purple Amethyst.

fla'mmiferous, *a. rare*$^{-0}$. [f. L. *flammifer* bearing flame (f. *flamm-a* FLAME + *-fer* bearing) + -OUS.] Bearing or producing flame.

1656–81 in Blount. **1721–1800** in Bailey. In mod. Dicts.

fla'mmigerous, *a. rare.* Also 6 flamigerous. [f. L. *flammiger* bearing flame (f. *flamma* + *-ger* bearing) + -OUS.] Bearing flame; in quots. *fig.*

1592 R. D. *Hypnerotomachia* 44 One of these flamigerous Nymphes. **1596** R. L[inche] *Diella* v, With that inrag'd (flamigerous as he is). **1775** in Ash.

fla'mmivomous, *a. rare.* [f. L. *flammivomus* (f. *flamm-a* flame + *-vomus* vomiting) + -OUS.] Vomiting out flame.

1663–76 Bullokar, *Flammivomous*, vomiting or belching flames of fire. **1745** W. Thompson *Sickness* II. 284 Hark, how the anvils thunder round the dens Flammivomous!

flammulated ('flæmju:leɪtɪd), *a.* [f. mod.L. *flammulatus*, f. L. *flammula*, dim. of *flamma* FLAME.] Of a reddish colour, ruddy. So **flammulation** (flæmju:'leɪʃən), a small flame-like marking.

1860 *Ibis* II. 41 The nearest ally of the present species [sc. *Malacoptila veræ pacis*] is Lafresnaye's *Malacoptila panamensis*, from which it may be distinguished by the absence of any flammulations below. **1872** E. Coues *N. Amer. Birds* 203 Flammulated owl. Above grayish-brown, obscurely streaked with black.

† **'flampoint.** *Obs.* Forms: 4 flaumpeyn, 5 flampoynte, flampayn, -peyn, -poyne, 6 flampett. [? a. F. **flan pointé.*] A pie or tart ornamented with pointed pieces of pastry.

c **1390** in Pegge *Forme of Cury* (1780) 54 To make Flaumpeyns. **14..** in *Househ. Ord.* (1790) 443 Flampoyntes. **1494** Fabyan *Chron.* VII. 587 Flampeyn flourisshed with a Scochounr oyall. **1525** in Pegge *Forme of Cury* (1780) 173 Item, a Flampett.

flamy ('fleɪmɪ), *a.* Forms: 5–7 flammy, 6 flambye, 7 flamie, 6– flamy. [f. FLAME *sb.* + -Y[1].]

1. Of or pertaining to flame or flames; consisting of flames; beset with flames.

1494 Fabyan *Chron.* VI. clxiii. 156 The hydde fyre in processe breketh oute and shewith great lyghte and flammy blase. **1558** Bp. Watson *Sev. Sacram.* xvi. 100 The fyerye floude..dothe ouerflowe with his flambye waues. **1621** G. Sandys *Ovid's Met.* II. (1626) 225 He..foure times assaild To sack the flamie Pile. **1752** H. M[oore] *To Memory of Dr. Doddridge* vi, The flamy Car, fire-breathing Coursers drew. **1814** Cary *Dante, Paradise* xxv. 133 The flamy circle at that voice so rested.

2. Resembling flame; flame-like.

1626 Bacon *Sylva* §30 Vital spirits..are a substance compounded of an airy and flamy matter. **1638** Sir T. Herbert *Trav.* (ed. 2) 47 A flammy rednesse will orespread the heavens. *a* **1661** Holyday *Juvenal* (1673) 22 The.. flamy vail he wears. **1715–20** Pope *Iliad* XIV. 400 And flamy crocus made the mountain glow. **1801** Southey *Thalaba* IX. vii, Her flamy hairs curl up. **1875** H. R. Proctor in *Encycl. Brit.* III. 94/2 Should the aurora be flamy, and shoot out rays.

fig. a **1586** Sidney *Arcadia* II. xvii. 176 b, My thoughts.. With flamie breathes doo issue oft in sound. **1845** Carlyle *Cromwell* (1871) IV. 3 A very flamy, fuliginous set of doctrines.

† **3.** Performed by the agency of flame. *Obs.*

c **1611** Chapman *Iliad* VII. 69 His body I'll resign To be disposed by his friends in flamy funerals. **1635** Swan *Spec. M.* vi. §2 (1643) 202 [Water] can..keep our mansions from ..a flamie conversion into ashes.

4. *Comb.*, as ***flamy-glittering.***

1581 Sidney *Astr. & Stella* lxxvi, Her flamy-glittering lights increase with time and place.

flan (flæn), *sb.*[1] *Sc.* Also 8–9 flann, 9 flam *sb.*[5] [cf. Icel. *flan* sudden rush, *flana* to rush.] **a.** A sudden gust or puff of wind. **b.** A puff of smoke driven down the chimney by a gust of wind.

c **1475** *Rauf Coilȝear* 2 Thair fell ane ferlyfull flan within thay fellis wide. **1701** J. Brand *Descr. Orkney, etc.* 81 Tho' the wind be not so strong, there will come Flanns and Blasts off the Land. **1742** J. Mill *Diary* (1889) 13 The boat was laid under water by a sudden flan. **1866** Edmondstoun *Shetland & Orkn. Gloss.*, *Flan, Flann*, a gust of wind. S.

flan (flæn), *sb.*[2] *Coining.* [a. F. *flan* (OF. *flan, flaon*: see FLAWN) orig. a round cake, but *transf.* to this sense from the similarity in shape.] A disc of metal before stamping; a blank.

1868 G. Stephens *Runic Mon.* II. 511 That round stampt flan or lamina which thus is mounted. **1880** B. Head *Guide Coins B.M.* 2 The form of the ingot (*flan*) of most of the early coins was bean-shaped or oval.

flan (flæn), *sb.*[3] *dial.* Also **flam.** [f. FLAN *a.*] **a.** A shallow. **b.** A broad-brimmed hat (= *flan-hat*: see the adj.).

a. 1790 Grose *Prov. Gloss.* (ed. 2), *Flan*, a shallow. *North.* **1867** Smyth *Sailor's Word-bk.*, *Flam*, a shallow.
b. 1877 *Holderness Gloss.* s.v., 'Sun's si parlus hot Ah'll put mi flam on'.

flan (flæn), *sb.*[4] *dial.* Also **flam.** A net used in ferreting rabbits. Also *attrib.*, as ***flam-net.***

1801 W. B. Daniel *Rural Sports* I. 352 After the holes are ..covered with Purse-Nets called Flans, the Ferret should be put in. **1876** *Surrey Gloss.*, *Flam* or *Flam-net*, a small net used in ferreting rabbits.

flan (flæn), *sb.*[5] [Fr.: see FLAWN.] An open tart containing fruit or other filling.

1846 A. Soyer *Gastronomic Regenerator* 502 A Flan of Puff Paste... Have a plain round or oval flan mould. **1858** Thackeray *Virginians* ix, The sweets and *flans*, Madam Esmond prepared herself. **1906** Mrs. Beeton *Househ. Managem.* 897 A 6-inch diameter flan or paste-ring. *Ibid.* 899 There are two ways of making a flan without the aid of a ring. **1951** *Good Housek. Home Encycl.* 344/1 Line the flan ring..with the pastry.

flan (flæn), *a. dial.* Also 9 **flam.** [Of unknown etymology. There is a remarkable coincidence of sense with F. *flanier* slightly concave (said of a grindstone), according to Hatzf.-Darm. f. *flan* tart, FLAWN; but it is difficult to assume a parallel derivation for the Eng. dialect word.] Broad, flat, and shallow; also, 'shallow with sloping sides' (*Lonsdale Gloss.*).

1781 Hutton *Tour to Caves* Gloss., *Flan*, shallow. **1787** Grose *Provinc. Gloss.*, *Flan*, broad. **1825–79** Jamieson, *Flan*, 'flat, not very hollow'. **1876** *Mid. Yorksh. Gloss.*, *Flan-hat* is a summer-hat with a flapping brim, worn by the farmer's wives. **1878** *Cumbld. Gloss.* s.v., They gave us fry't eggs and collops in a flan dish.

flan (flæn), *v. dial.* [Connected with FLAN *a.* Cf. FLANCH, FLANGE *vbs.*] *intr.* **a.** Of a vessel, etc.: To expand towards the top, to widen upwards. Also, *to flan out.* **b.** Of a window-jamb: To splay or bevel internally. Cf. FLANNING.

1788 W. Marshall *E. Yorksh.* Gloss., *Flan*, to spread wide as the sides of a bowl or scuttle. **1876** *Mid-Yorksh. Gloss.* s.v., 'How she does flan with that gown of hers!'..A flower vase 'flans out' at the top.

flan, obs. form of FLANE, FLAY.

'flancard. *Obs.* exc. *Hist.* Also 6 ? flaunkart, flankett, 8 flankart, 9 (*Hist.*) flanchard. [a. OF. *flancard*, f. *flanc* FLANK *sb.*[1]]

1. a. A piece of armour for the thigh. **b.** In horse-armour, one of the side-pieces covering the flanks.

c **1489** Caxton *Sonnes of Aymon* vi. 142 His swerde..cut thrugh..an hundred mayles of his flancardes. **1513** Douglas *Æneis* VII. xi. 76 Burnist flaukartis [? *read* flan- *or* flaun-] and leg harnes. **1548** Hall *Chron.* 12 a, Some had.. the guissettes, the flancardes droped & gutted with red. **1555** Eden *Decades* 188 A barbed horse with his barbes and flankettes. **1870** Black tr. *Demmin's Weapons War* 350 The side pieces or flanchards..which joined the front plate or breast-piece to the thigh-pieces and croupière.

2. = FLANKER *sb.*[1]

1767 T. Hutchinson *Hist. Mass.* II. ii. 163 And firing briskly from the flankarts, saved the house.

flanch (flɑ:nʃ, -æ-), *sb.*[1] *Her.* Also **flaunch, flanque.** [? a. OF. *flanche* fem., = *flanc* masc., FLANK.]

A sub-ordinary formed on each side of the shield by a line arched or convex towards the centre, always borne double or in pairs.

We have not been able to find direct evidence that *flanche* was used in Fr. in the heraldic sense; but the form *flanque*, and the adjs. *flanché, flanqué*, are in Geliot (ed. Palliot 1664).

1562 Leigh *Armorie* (1597) 70 b, He beareth Ermin, ij Flaunches, Vert. This is one degree vnder the aforesaide Flasques. **1688** R. Holme *Armoury* I. iv. 39 He beareth Gules, two Flanches Argent. **1727** Bradley *Fam. Dict.* s.v., *Flanches* are always born by Pairs; the Flanch bends more than the Flask. **1828–40** Berry *Encycl. Herald.* I, *Flanch, Flanque*, or *Flasque*. Leigh would make flanch and flasque two distinct subordinate ordinaries, but Gibbon very judiciously accounts them both as one.

Hence **flanched** *ppl. a.*, having flanches.

1688 R. Holme *Armoury* I. ix. 93 He beareth Vert, a Pile, and two demy ones Imbowed or Flanched. **1889** Elvin *Dict. Her.* s.v., A shield of Fitz-Alan, flanched ar.

flanch (flɑ:nʃ, -æ-), *sb.*[2] Also **flaunch.** [This and its variant FLANGE are prob. f. FLANCH, FLANGE *vbs.* The usual explanation is that the sb. is ad. OF. *flanche* fem. = *flanc* masc., FLANK; but the sense is hardly suitable.]

1. = FLANGE 2.

1726 Desaguliers in *Phil. Trans.* XXXIV. 81 With a Shoulder or Flaunch screw'd within the Circle O O by 4 other Screws. **1784** Darwin *ibid.* LXXV. 3 Another leaden ring or flanch was soldered round the leaden pipe. **1862** Smiles *Engineers* III. 8 With flanches cast upon the tire of the waggon-wheels to keep them on the track.

2. *Comb.* as **flanch-chuck, -mill** (see quots.).

1833 J. Holland *Manuf. Metal* II. x. 249 Coffee is ground by what is called a flanch mill, having the body composed of rolled iron, and being screwed against a post in the kitchen. **1842** Francis *Dict. Arts*, etc., *Flanch Chuck*, a ..chuck, formed like a flanch; but instead of holes being bored in it..furnished with several points, upon which the article to be turned is fixed.

Hence **flanched** *ppl. a.*, having a flanch.

1793 Smeaton *Edystone L.* 196 The flanched border.. which surrounds the face of the pillars. **1851** Greenwell *Coal-trade Terms Northumb. & Durham* 7 Tubs having flanched wheels.

flanch (flɑ:nʃ, -æ-), *v.* Also **flaunch,** FLANGE *v.* [Of obscure origin; there would seem to be some connexion with the synonymous FLAN *v.*; but the relation between the two words is not explained by any known process of derivation. Assuming the primary sense to be 'to extend laterally', *flanch* might conceivably be derived from F. *flanc* FLANK; but no vb. **flancher* of similar sense has been discovered in Fr. of any period.

An OF. *flanchir, flangir, flainchir* occurs as a synonym (perh. a variant) of *flechir* to bend (cf. FLINCH). Can the Eng. vb. be an adoption of this in a specialized sense?]

intr. To spread, widen out; to slope outwards towards the top. Also with *out, off.* ***to flanch up***: to slope inwards towards the top; applied especially to the outsides of chimney-shafts.

1776 Withering *Brit. Plants* (1796) IV. 357 Dark grey and smooth within; the border flanching out. **1802** *Trans. Soc. Enc. Arts* XX. 288 The sides, from the floor-heads to the top of the gunwale, flaunch off on each side. **1833** Loudon *Encycl. Archit.* §234 Each flue to have a Roman cement chimney shaft..flanched up (sloped in a way to throw off wet).

Hence **'flanching** *ppl. a.*

1802 Capt. Reed in *Naval Chron.* VII. 490 The curvature of the keel and the flaunching sides..render it almost impossible to be upset.

flanching, *vbl. sb.* Also **flaunching.** [See FLANCH *v.*] **a.** The action or state of spreading outwards. **b.** The sloping fillet of cement or mortar in which the base of a chimney-pot is bedded. Also called ***flanched work.***

1802 *Gentl. Mag.* Apr. 325/1 The boat is about 30 feet long..built in a flaunching manner. **1803** *Naval Chron.* IX. 283 The flaunching, or spreading form of the boat..gives her a considerable bearing. **1833** Loudon *Encycl. Archit.* §234 Sections of the flanchings. **1904** Goodchild & Tweney *Technol. & Sci. Dict.* 226/2 *Flaunching* or *flaunc[h]ed work*, the cement fillet round the bed of a chimney pot.

flanconade ('flæŋkəˌneɪd). *Fencing.* Also 7 flancanade, -konade, 9 flanconnade. [a. F. *flanconade*, f. *flanc*: see FLANK.] A thrust in the flank or side.

1664 J. Wilson *Cheats* IV. i. Dram. Wks. (1874) 68 Observe—how true it bends! Ah! for a pass in flanconade! **1698** Farquhar *Love & a Bottle* II. ii, Sa! sa! defend flankonade, madam. **1779** Sheridan *Critic* II. ii, Hah! thrust in tierce parried..then flankonade..and a palpable hit. **1889** Pollock etc. *Fencing* ii. (Badm. Libr.) 53 This is the famous thrust known as flanconnade or *liement d'octave.*

attrib. **1809** Roland *Fencing* iv. 74 This flanconade thrust cannot be well made use of, unless [etc.].

† **'flandan.** *Obs.* [Of unknown origin; some of the quots. suggest that it was supposed to be originally a term of fortification.] A part of a lady's head-dress (see quots.).

1690 Evelyn *Mundus Muliebris* 6 Monté la haut, and Palisade, Sorti, Flandan..Burgoigne, Jardiné, Cornett. —— *Fop-Dict.* 18 *Flandan*, a kind of Pinner joyning with the Bonnet. *a* **1693** Urquhart *Rabelais* III. xlvi. 375 Great Ladies..with their Flandan, Top-knots and Sultana's. **1694** N. H. *Ladies Dict.* 10 s.v. *Apparel*, A Flandan is a kind of Pinner join'd with a Cornet. *Ibid.* 425 s.v. *Top-knots*, Will it not be convenient to attack your Flandan first, says the Maid? More Anger yet? still Military Terms?

†'Flanderkin. *Obs.* (See also FLOUNDERKIN and FLANDRICAN *a.*) [f. next + -KIN.]

1. An inhabitant of Flanders, a Fleming. Also *attrib.* (quasi-*adj.*) = Flemish. *Obs.*

1694 S. JOHNSON *Notes Past. Lett. Bp. Burnet* I. 32 Till we are in the Condition of the Flanderkin Towns, he need not urge us with their Practice and Example. **1698** LUTTRELL *Brief Rel.* (1857) IV. 432 The Flanderkins have laid a duty of 3 guilders upon every £100 of Irish wool that is imported there. **1810** JANE PORTER *Scot. Chiefs* III. xv. 342 The Flanderkins.. suddenly giving way with cries of terror. **1821** HOGG *Jacobite Relics* Ser. II. ii. 8 But Flanderkins they have nae skill To lead a Scottish force, man.

2. *slang.* (See quots.)

a **1700** B. E. *Dict. Cant. Crew, Flanderkin*, a very large Fat Man or Horse. **1811** *Sporting Mag.* XXXVIII. 63 Florikins are amongst the *nondescripta*.. in ornithology.. You read of them.. under the name, I believe, of Flanderkins.

Flanders ('flɑːndəz, -æ-). [ad. Du. *Vlaanderen* pl.; the name of an ancient countship now divided between Belgium, France, and Holland.]

†1. Short for: **a.** *Flanders-lace*; **b.** *Flanders-horse*.

1690 EVELYN *Mundus Muliebris* 3 Four Cushion-Cloths are scarce enough, Of Point, and Flanders. **1718** CIBBER *Nonjuror* II. ii, Does he keep his Chariot and Berlin, with six flouncing Flanders?

2. *attrib.* as **a.** *Flanders chest, field, flax, lace* (whence *-laced*), *make, mare, mud, shape, wagon*. **b. Flanders baby**, a small doll manufactured in the Low Countries to display fashionable dress, or for use in a puppet show; **Flanders brick** = *Bath-brick*; **†Flanders colour**, ? tawny orange; **Flanders counter**: see COUNTER *sb.*³ 3; **Flanders doll** = *Flanders baby*; **†Flanders-fortunes, -pieces** (see quots.); **Flanders poppy**, a poppy of Flanders, the emblem of the Allied soldiers who fell in the war of 1914–18; also, one of the artificial poppies worn in Britain on Remembrance Sunday, in November; **†Flanders tile** (*a*) = *Flanders brick*; (*b*) = *Dutch tile*.

1823 J. GALT *Entail* I. xix. 156 Yon *Flanders baby is no for a poor man's wife. **1899** A. M. EARLE *Child Life in Colonial Days* xviii. 365 'Flanders babies' had a cherished old age. **1969** E. H. PINTO *Treen* 206 Leslie Daiken considered that Dutch dolls, known in 17th- and 18th-century England as 'Flanders babies', and in America as 'peg dolls', really originated in the Thuringian Forest in Germany. *a* **1700** EVELYN Diary an. 1670 22 July (1955) III. 555 Here my Lord & his Partner had built two or 3 roomes with *flanders white brick, very hard. **1858** SIMMONDS *Dict. Trade, Flanders-brick.* **1875** *Ure's Dict. Arts* II. 401 *Flanders Bricks*, commonly called Bath bricks. [**1433** *Nottngham Rec.* II. 140 Unam cistam Flaundr'.] **1460** *Inv.* in *Ripon Ch. Acts* 365 De j *flandyrs kist, 3*s.* **1652** *Inv. T. Teanby of Barton-on-Humber* (*N.W. Linc. Gloss.*), One fflaunders chist. **1721** STRYPE *Eccl. Mem.* II. xii. 338 His standard an unicorn silver ermine.. and his pensils *Flanders colour. **1557** *Wills & Inv. N.C.* (Surtees 1835) 158 In the Halle ij *flanders counters wᵗʰ ther carpetts xxˢ. **1801** *Monthly Mirror* Aug. 139 Her stage appearance.. might be mistaken for a *Flander's doll, moved by wires. **1915** J. MCCRAE in *Punch* 8 Dec. 468/3 In *Flanders fields the poppies blow Between the crosses, row on row. **1842** MCCULLOCH *Dict. Commerce* s.v. *Flax*, *Flanders or Dutch flax is.. of the finest quality. *a* **1700** B. E. *Dict. Cant. Crew*, **Flanders-fortunes*, of small Substance. **1664** *Newsman* 26 May in Mrs. Palliser *Lace* vii. 102 A black lute-string gown with a black *Flanders lace. **1690** EVELYN *Mundus Muliebris* 3 With a broad Flanders Lace below. **1686** *Lond. Gaz.* No. 2170/4 An open *Flanders.lac'd Neck-cloth. **1799** MALTHUS *Jrnl.* 29 May (1966) 36 The country girls have a little of the *Flanders make in their persons. **1613–16** W. BROWNE *Brit. Past.* I. v. 505 A stubborne Nagge of Galloway.. or a *Flaunders Mare. **1816** SCOTT *Old Mort.* ii, A wheel-carriage.. dragged by eight long-tailed Flanders mares. **1918** KIPLING in *Metropolitan* Dec. 46/2 One man lurched in—helmet, *Flanders mud, accoutrements and all. **1933** A. G. MACDONELL *England, their England* i. 13 An eleven-inch or eight-inch howitzer, both fortunately rare in Flanders mud. *a* **1700** B. E. *Dict. Cant. Crew*, **Flanders-pieces*, Pictures that look fair at a distance, but coarser near at Hand. **1921** *Times* 21 Oct. 13/6 Australia, Canada, France, and the United States, as well as Newfoundland, have adopted the *Flanders poppy as the national remembrance flower. *Ibid.*, All will be able to buy a Flanders poppy. *Ibid.* 29 Oct. 11/5 The King.. has expressed his desire to include Flanders poppies in his wreath to be placed on the Cenotaph on that day. **1971** *Guardian* 21 May 2/8 Mr. Heath.. laid a wreath on the tomb of the unknown soldier beneath the Arc de Triomphe.. a simple circle of Flanders poppies. **1664** DRYDEN *Rival Ladies* III. i, He lov'd that *Flanders shape, that lump of Earth And Phlegm together. **1544** *Liber Magnus C.C.C. Oxon.* (MS.), Impensa sacelli It' pro oleo et *flawnderstele ad mundanda candelabra sacelli, iiij d. **1577** B. GOOGE *Heresbach's Husb.* IV. (1586) 161 b, To beate in powder Bricke, or Flaunders Tyle. **1600–1** *Trinity Coll. Acc.* in Willis & Clark *Cambridge* (1886) II. 483 Flaunders tyles to paue the chimney in the.. great chamber. **1876** VOYLE *Milit. Dict.* (ed. 3), **Flanders Wagon*, a wagon suited to the transport of all light stores.

Flandrian ('flɑːndrɪən, -æ-), *a.* and *sb.* [f. FLANDERS + -IAN.] **A.** *adj.* **a.** Of or pertaining to Flanders or its inhabitants. *rare.* **b.** *Geol.* Of, pertaining to, or designating the period since the retreat of the ice sheet and the rise in sea-level at the end of the last glaciation in northwestern Europe. **B.** *sb.* **a.** An inhabitant of Flanders. *rare.* **b.** *Geol.* The Flandrian period.

1637 J. SHIRLEY *Lady of Pleasure* II. D2. 62 *Celestina.* But some one noble bloud or lusty kindred, Claps in, with his gilt coach, and Flandrian trotters, And hurries her away to be a Countesse. **1670** in J. W. Draper *Cent. Broadside Elegies* (1928) No. 52, Proud France! no more thy Flandrian Conquests borst [*sic*]. **1886** J. H. BLUNT *Dict. Sects* 163/2 *Flandrians*, Flemings. **1934** R. A. DALY *Changing World of Ice Age* v. 169 Table XXII.. includes the Flandrian stage, named by him [*sc.* Dubois] to represent the time and processes involved by the melting of the last great Pleistocene ice-caps. **1937** WOOLDRIDGE & MORGAN *Physical Basis Geogr.* xxiii. 421 The evidence of emergence during the last glaciation, followed by the great submergence, which has been called by Dubois the 'Flandrian transgression'. **1952** *Proc. Prehist. Soc.* XVIII. 109 It would be particularly useful to associate the three stages of the Flandrian transgression with mesolithic or neolithic industries. **1958** F. E. ZEUNER *Dating Past* (ed. 4) 100 Interglacial beach deposits.. to the east of Calais, round the corner where the Flandrian plains begin. **1968** R. G. WEST *Pleistocene Geol. & Biol.* xii. 281 Many raised bogs show the development of *Sphagnum* peats during the middle Flandrian, above earlier lake sediments. **1971** *Nature* 1 Jan. 43/2 The survival of the Teesdale rarities through the Flandrian period.

†'Flandrican, *a. Obs.* Also Flandrikan. [f. FLANDERS + -IC + -AN; but prob. an etymologizing alteration of FLANDERKIN.] = FLEMISH.

1800 J. MILNER *Lett. Prebendary* (1813) 165 John Hooper.. married a Flandrican woman. **1824** MCCULLOCH *Highl. & W. Isles Scotl.* I. 57 It is in vain.. to affect to despise it as Tudesque or Flandrikan (in style of architecture).

†'Flandrish, *a. Obs.* exc. *arch.* Forms: 4–5 **flaunderich, -drissh(e, -dryssh,** 9 **flaundrish.** [f. as prec. + -ISH.] = FLEMISH.

c **1386** CHAUCER *Prol.* 272 Vp on his heed a fflaundryssh beuere hat. **1632** LITHGOW *Trav.* x. 480 The Gentlemans seruant, a Flandrish Fleming. **1809** W. IRVING *Knickerb.* (1861) 234 In rich apparel of the antique flaundrish cut.

†flane. *Obs.* Forms: 1–4 **flan,** 3–4 **flon,** 4–5 **flone,** 5–9 *Sc.* **flane,** 5–6 **flain(e,** (6 **flayn).** [OE. *flán* masc. and fem. = ON. *fleinn* masc., cognate with OE. *flá*: see FLO. The word survived longest in Sc.; otherwise the normal form would have been *flone*.] An arrow.

Beowulf 2438 (Gr.) Syððan hyne Hæðcyn of hornbogan his freawine flane ȝeswencte. *a* **1000** *Byrhtnoth* 71 (Gr.) þurh flanes flyht. *a* **1225** *Juliana* 7 þe flan þe of luue fleoð. *c* **1340** *Gaw. & Gr. Knt.* 1161 At vche [þat] wende vndir wande wapped a flone. *c* **1450** HENRYSON *Mor. Fab.* iv. 152 His bow he bent, ane flane with fedderis gray He haillit to the heid. **1567** *Satir. Poems Reform.* iii. 32 Ane flaine lat fle with bow in tyme of neid. **1724** *Poems on Royal Company of Archers* 34 Burnished swords and whizzing flanes.

flanel, obs. form of FLANNEL.

‖flânerie (flɑnri). [F. *flânerie*, f. *flâner* to lounge, saunter idly.] The disposition or practice of an idler or lounger.

1873 HAMERTON *Intell. Life* x. vii. (1876) 371 Intellectual flânerie. **1875** H. JAMES *Transatl. Sketches* 126 The aimless flânerie which leaves you free to follow capriciously every hint of entertainment.

‖flâneur (flɑnœr). [F. *flâneur*, f. *flâner*: see prec.] A lounger or saunterer, an idle 'man about town'. Also *transf.* Hence **flane, flâne, flané, flâné** *v. intr.*, to saunter, to laze.

1854 *Harper's Mag.* Aug. 411/2 Did you ever fail to waste at least two hours of every sunshiny day, in the long-ago time when you played the *flaneur*, in the metropolitan city, with looking at shop-windows? **1872** E. BRADDON *Life in India* vi. 236 He will affect a knowledge of London life that only comes to the regular flâneur after years of active experience. **1876** OUIDA *Winter City* vi. 149 An existence which makes the life of the Paris flâneurs look very poor indeed. **1876** L. TROUBRIDGE *Life amongst Troubridges* (1966) xi. 143 Shopped the whole morning—*flanéed* down Regent Street. **1894** G. DU MAURIER *Trilby* III. VIII. 155 They are going to laze and flane about the boulevards. **1896** G. B. SHAW *Our Theatres in Nineties* (1932) II. 217 The boundary which separates the clever *flâneur* from the dramatist. **1897** G. DU MAURIER *Martian* IV. 175 To his great surprise he saw Bonzig leisurely flâning about. **1938** H. G. WELLS *Apropos of Dolores* i. 13 In Paris, in London I have been a happy flâneur; I have flâné-d in New York and Washington and most of the great cities of Europe. **1954** I. MURDOCH *Under Net* xv. 203 The fishermen were fishing, and the *flâneurs* were flaning. **1969** *Computers & Humanities* IV. 29 The electronic age may yet see every man a *flaneur*.

flang (flæŋ). A two-pointed pick used by miners.

1858 in SIMMONDS *Dict. Trade.* **1874** in KNIGHT *Dict. Mech.*

flang, obs. and dial. pa. t. of FLING *v.*

flange (flændʒ), *sb.* [See FLANCH *sb.*²]

1. A widening or branching out; the part that widens out: **†a.** in a pan; **b.** in a metallic vein.

1688 R. HOLME *Armoury* III. vii. 320/2 The top that goes out wider than the bottom, is called the Flang of the Pan. **1747** HOOSON *Miner's Dict.* I j b, *Flange* [is] a Place where a Vein takes a run out of Course into one, and sometimes both Sides, insomuch that the Ore lies more scattered. **1881** RAYMOND *Mining Gloss.*, *Flange*, applied to a vein widening.

2. A projecting flat rim, collar, or rib, used to strengthen an object, to guide it, to keep it in place, to facilitate its attachment to another object, or for other purposes.

1735 DYCHE & PARDON *Dict.*, *Flange*, those Side Pieces that are cast on to Iron Pipes or Barrels to screw 'em fast, or to hang 'em by. **1833** J. HOLLAND *Manuf. Metal.* II. 247 At each end of this cylinder there is a deep flange or margin. **1838** SIMMS *Public Wks. Gt. Brit.* 70 The flange or rib on the tire shall not project more than one inch. **1879** *Cassell's Techn. Educ.* IV. 207/1 The whole are firmly secured by two metal flanges.. which are tightly screwed up.

3. Hence **a.** Any rim or projecting surface. **b.** A flattened-out disc. Also, ***blank-flange***.

1876 VOYLE *Milit. Dict.* (ed. 3) s.v., The rim of metal round the mouth of gun caps used with percussion muskets is called a flange. **1877** *Holderness Gloss.*, *Flange*, the brim of a hat. **1884** KNIGHT *Dict. Mech.* IV, *Flange*, a plate for covering.. the end of a pipe or cylinder.

c. *transf.* Of natural objects: a rim or fan which stands out from the main part of the object. Also *fig.*

1880 'MARK TWAIN' *Tramp Abroad* 393 Stepping on an outlying flange of her foot. **1897** M. KINGSLEY *Trav. W. Afr.* 607 The brown water.. striking a ridge of higher rock.. flew up in a lovely flange some twelve feet or so high. **1930** AUDEN *Poems* 25 Nowise withdrawn by doubting flinch Nor joined to any by belief's firm flange.

4. *attrib.* and *Comb.*, as ***flange-coupling, -joint; flange-maker; flange-hilted*** adj.; **flange-bushing** (see quot.); **flange-pipe** (*U.S.*), pipe in sections with flanges for fixing together; **flange-pulley**, a flanged pulley; **flange-rail**, (*a*) a rail with a flanged base; (*b*) *U.S.* (see quot. 1864); **flange-wheel**, a flanged wheel.

1884 KNIGHT *Dict. Mech.* IV, **Flange Bushing*, a flange carrying a shell which acts as a bushing to a hole. *Ibid.*, **Flange Coupling*, a device for connecting pipes at any angle from 0° to 90°. **1930** V. G. CHILDE *Bronze Age* iii. 86 Early versions of the *flange-hilted leaf-shaped sword.. are very common in Northern and Central Europe. **1864** WEBSTER, **Flange-joint*, a joint in pipes etc. made by two flanges bolted together. **1884** KNIGHT *Dict. Mech.* IV, **Flange Pipe*, **Flange Pulley.* **1864** WEBSTER, **Flange-rail*, a rail having on one side a flange to keep wheels, etc., from running off. **1888** *Lockwood's Dict. Mech. Engin.*, *Flange Rail*, a flat-bottomed or flat rail, as distinguished from a double-headed rail.

flange (flændʒ), *v.* [See FLANCH *v.*; in senses 2 and 3 f. prec. sb.]

1. *intr.* To widen out. Also, with *out*.

1820 WILBRAHAM *Chesh. Gloss.*, *Flange*, or flange out, to spread, diverge, to increase in width or breadth. **1878** STEVENSON *Inland Voy.* 167 The east-end of a church.. as it flanges out in three wide terraces.

2. To take the form of a flange. (In recent Dicts.).

3. *trans.* To supply with a flange, attach a flange to, form a flange upon.

1873 R. WILSON *Steam Boilers* 92 By flanging either the barrel or end plate.

flanged (flændʒd), *ppl. a.* [f. prec. sb. or vb.] Made or fitted with a flange.

1797 J. CURR *Coal Viewer & Engine Builder* 51 The angle of the flanged end of the communicating pipes. **1852** T. WRIGHT *Celt, Roman, & Saxon* (1861) 166 Flanged tiles were not unfrequently used for this purpose.

flangeless ('flændʒlɪs), *a.* [f. FLANGE *sb.* + -LESS.] Having no flange.

1903 W. M. CAMP *Notes Track Constr.* v. 247 With all but four of the drivers flangeless. **1927** T. WOODHOUSE *Artificial Silk* 116 This machine is intended to beam warps on flangeless beams.

flanger ('flændʒə(r)). [f. FLANGE *v.* + -ER¹.]

1. (See quot.)

1893 *Labour Commission* Gloss., *Flangers*, also called 'boiler-smiths', are men, in the shipbuilding industry, who bend the plate edges where angles cannot be made to fit.

2. *U.S.* A vertical iron or steel bar for scraping snow and ice from the inside of rail-heads to make room for the wheel-flanges (*Standard Dict.*).

flanging ('flændʒɪŋ), *vbl. sb.* [f. FLANGE *v.* + -ING¹.] The action of the vb. FLANGE.

1861 W. FAIRBAIRN *Iron* 150 It will bear punching and flanging like a sheet of copper. **1869** SIR E. J. REED *Shipbuild.* vi. 105 To facilitate the flanging.

b. *attrib.* and *Comb.*, as ***flanging-hammer, -machine, -press***.

1874 KNIGHT *Dict. Mech.* I. 876/1 *Flanging-machine.* **1884** *Ibid.* IV, *Flanging Hammer*, a machine for turning flanges on sheet-metal for boilers, tanks [etc.]. *Ibid.*, *Flanging Press.*

flanging ('flændʒɪŋ). *ppl. a.* [f. as prec. + -ING².] That flanges or has a flange.

1880 H. C. ST. JOHN *Wild Coasts Nipon* 152 The house-fly's proboscis.. has a broad or flanging end.

flank (flæŋk), *sb.*¹ Forms: 1 **flanc,** 4–7 **flanke,** (4 **flaunke, flawnkke),** 6–7 **flanck(e,** 5– **flank.** [a. F. *flanc*, = Pr. *flanc*, It. *fianco* (Sp., Pg. *flanco*, only in transferred senses, appears to be from French):—pop. Lat. **flancum*.

The ulterior etymology is disputed. The most probable hypothesis appears to be that it is adopted from the Teut. word which appears in OHG. *hlancha, lanka*, MDu. *lanke*, early ME. LONKE; instances of Romanic *fl-* from Teut. *hl-* are believed to occur in some proper names, as F. *Floovent*, med.L. *Flodoardus.* Diez regarded the word as a nasalized form of the L. *flaccus* flaccid, comparing, for the

development of sense, Ger. *weiche* flank from *weich* soft; but no adj. **flancus* is known in L. or Rom.]

I. As denoting a part of the body.

1. a. The fleshy or muscular part of the side of an animal or a man between the ribs and the hip.

a **1100** *Prudentius Glosses* cited by Napier in *Academy* XLV. 457 *Ilia*, flances. *c* **1330** *Arth. & Merl.* 9247 Schuldir and side and flaunke also. *c* **1400** *Lanfranc's Cirurg.* 269 þou muste ordeyne..fastnyngis tofore & bihinde & in hise flankis. **1541** R. COPLAND *Guydon's Quest. Chirurg.* IV. iv. P ij b, The .x. place is in the flankes for the rupture. **1583** HOLLYBAND *Campo di Fior* 187 The poore jawde..Which hath no fleshe on his flancs. **1639** MASSINGER *Unnat. Combat* I. i, Charge her home in the flank. **1691** RAY *Creation* II. (1704) 387 The Hedgehog hath his Back-sides and Flanks set with strong and sharp prickles. **1782** COWPER *Gilpin* 127 Which made his horse's flanks to smoke. **1866** ROGERS *Agric. & Prices* I. xxi. 532 They [marking-irons] may have been employed to brand the flanks of colts and cattle.

b. A part of the same sold as *thick* or *thin flank*.

1747 MRS. GLASSE *Art of Cookery* xxi. 160 A Bullock... The Hind Quarter..the Thin and Thick-flank. **1796** —— *Cookery* xviii. 289 Take a piece of thin flank of beef and bone it.

c. in *Arachnida* and *Crustacea*: The *pleura* or side of the tergum and thorax.

1835-6 TODD *Cycl. Anat.* I. 202 The flancs (*pleuræ*).. have mutually approximated and become united..If the carapace is raised in a crab, the flancs or pleuræ are seen beneath.

†**2.** The belly; the womb. *Obs.*

1398 TREVISA *Barth. De P.R.* XVIII. i. (1495) 738 An olyphaunt hath tetys vnder the breste: and the maare in the flanke bitwene the thyes behynde. **1481** CAXTON *Myrr.* II. vi. 76 They bere them ii yere in their flankes.

3. In the *Leather* trade: That part of the hide or skin which covered the flank of the animal.

1874 KNIGHT *Dict. Mech.*, *Flank* 3. The thin portion of a skin of leather. **1885** C. T. DAVIS *Manuf. Leather* I. i. 38 The parts of hides are called butts, backs, flanks, etc.

4. *pl.* (See quots.) [Cf. F. *mal de flancs*.]

1706 PHILLIPS (ed. Kersey), *Flanks* (among Farriers) a Wrench, Crick, Stroke or other Grief in the Back of a Horse; also a kind of Pleurisy, proceeding from his being over-run with too much Blood. **1810** JAMES *Milit. Dict.* (ed. 3), *Flanks* in farriery, a wrench or any other grief in the back of a horse.

II. Transferred uses (with gen. sense 'side'.)

5. *gen.* The side or lateral part of anything, e.g. of a building, a mountain, etc.

1624 WOTTON *Archit.* (1672) 17 When the Face of the Building is narrow, and the Flank deep. *Ibid.* 29 They [i.e. Pilasters] are commonly narrower in Flank, then in Front. **1859** TENNYSON *Vivien* 674 So long, that mountains have arisen since With cities on their flanks. **1892** WOODWARD & BURNETT *Heraldry* II. 687 *Flanks* (F. *flancs*) the sides of the escucheon.

6. *Mil.* The extreme left or right side of an army or body of men in military formation; a wing. † *a flank* (see also AFLANK), *in flank*: at the side. *to turn the flank* (of an enemy): see TURN.

1548 PATTEN *Exped. Scotl.* I ij b, The Master of the ordinaunce..did gall them with hailshot..and certeyn other gunners with there peces, a flanke, from our Rerewarde. **1568** GRAFTON *Chron.* II. 1309 Whilest he and his horsemen gave the charge on the flanke of their battaille. **1600** in *Lismore Papers* Ser. II. (1887) I. 33 He drew vpp that squadron..to chardge them in fflancke. **1667** MILTON *P.L.* VI. 570 He scarce Had ended, when to Right and Left the Front Divided, and to either Flank retird. **1726** LEONI *Alberti's Archit.* I. 69 Whoever offers to approach between these towers, is exposed to be taken in flank and slain. **1810** JAMES *Milit. Dict.* (ed. 3), *Flank en potence* is any part of the right or left wing formed at a right angle with the line. **1810** WELLINGTON in Gurw. *Desp.* VI. 316 The enemy having it thus in their power to throw their whole force upon both flanks of this army. **1844** H. WILSON *Brit. India* II. 271 They..were taken in flank by a troop of cavalry.

7. *Fortification.* Any part of a work so disposed as to defend another by a flanking fire; *esp.* the part of a bastion reaching from the curtain to the face and defending the opposite face.

1590 MARLOWE *2nd Pt. Tamburl.* III. ii, It must have.. store of ordnance, that from every flank May scour the outward curtains of the fort. **1672** LACEY tr. *Tacquett's Milit. Archit.* iii. 4 The flanques of the Bulwork and Courtine. **1704** *Lond. Gaz.* No. 4082/3 The Ditch is doubly Palisadoed, with very good Flanks within. **1704** J. HARRIS *Lex. Techn.*, *Flank of the Courtine* or Second Flank, is that part of the Courtine, between the Flank, and the Point where the Fichant Line of Defence ends. **1810** JAMES *Milit. Dict.* (ed. 3) s.v. *Fortification*, *Flanks of the Bastion* are the parts between the faces and the curtain. **1868** KINGLAKE *Crimea* (1877) III. v. 364 At the flanks of the bastions.

8. In other technical uses: **a.** *Arch.* (See quot. 1874). **b.** *Mech.* (See quot. 1842).

1842 FRANCIS *Dict. Arts*, etc., *Flank*, the straight part of the tooth of a wheel which receives the impulse. **1874** KNIGHT *Dict. Mech.* I. 876/1 *Flank* (Architecture) the haunch of an arch; the shoulder between the crown and the springing.

III. 9. *attrib.* and *Comb.*, as ***flank-piece***; (senses 6, 7) as ***flank attack***, ***company***, ***defence***, ***file***, ***fire***, ***guard***, ***march***, ***movement***, ***officer***; ***flank-wise*** adv. Also, **flank angle** *Mech.* (see quot. 1954); **flank-bone**, the ilium or haunch-bone; **flank forward** *Rugby Football* (orig. *S. Afr.*), a wing forward; so ***flank***, used *absol.*, **flank-wall**, a side wall.

1951 *Engineering* 21 Sept. 369/3 A screw thread has.. seven elements of shape and size: major diameter, minor diameter, effective diameter, pitch, *flank angles, [etc.]. **1876** VOYLE *Milit. Dict.* (ed. 3), **Flank-attack*..one of the modes of attack whereby the side or flank of an army..is attacked. **1954** *Defs. for Use in Mech. Engin.* (*B.S.I.*) 17 *Flank angles*, the angles between the individual flanks and the perpendicular to the axis of the thread measured in an axial plane section. **1668** CULPEPPER & COLE *Barthol. Anat.* IV. xvi. 351 Os Innominatum..which some term..the *Flank-bone. **1809** WELLINGTON in Gurw. *Desp.* IV. 324 The *flank companies of the 29th, 43rd and 52nd Regiments. **1851** J. S. MACAULAY *Field Fortif.* 150 If the church is not built on a plan favourable to *flank defence. **1810** JAMES *Milit. Dict.* (ed. 3), **Flank-files* are the two first men on the right and the two last men on the left, telling downwards from the right. **1810** WELLINGTON in Gurw. *Desp.* VI. 331 Be prepared, particularly with your *flank fire every morning. [**1937** *Rand Daily Mail* 10 Apr. 18/2 Of the flank or back rankers Strachan cannot be left out.] *Ibid.* 25 June 22/1 Van der Berg will probably be one of the flank forwards. **1956** V. JENKINS *Lions Rampant* i. 19 Scotland's Greenwood, at flank-forward, saw to it that his country's honour was not besmirched. **1960** E. S. & W. J. HIGHAM *High Speed Rugby* p. xx, We have adopted the name 'flank' instead of the more common 'wing forward' as being less likely to cause confusion between wing forward and wing three-quarter. *Ibid.* xii. 154 The Flanks (wing forwards): These are the open play specialists. **1901** 'LINESMAN' *Words by Eye-witness* (1902) 305 Here they are spotted by the self-constituted British *flank-guard. **1918** E. S. FARROW *Dict. Mil. Terms* 234 *Flank guard*, a detachment detailed to cover the flank of a column marching past, or across the front of an enemy. **1930** *Nation* 6 Dec. 327/2 To Hutchinson..the *Shelleyans* are indebted for the fullest one-volume edition, and the *Elians* for the best cheap substitute for, or flankguard to, Mr. Lucas's *Works of Charles and Mary Lamb*. **1866** E. B. HAMLEY *Operat. War* vi. 404 Thus Bulow's march to the field of Waterloo was a *flank march. **1796** *Instr. & Reg. Cavalry* (1813) 39 In the *flank movements of ranks by three's or by two's. **1601** COTGR., *Soubspoictrine*, the *flanke-peece, or bottome of the brisket of an Oxe, &c. **1703** MOXON *Mech. Exerc.* 265 If the House had stood by it self, then we might have had light to the Stairs from the *Flank Wall. **1819** REES *Cycl.*, *Flank-walls*, in Engineery, are the same with wing or return-walls of a lock or bridge. **1603** FLORIO *Montaigne* (1634) 148 He pursued them, and charged them *flank-wise. **1863** KINGLAKE *Crimea* II. 279 Battalions of infantry which.. Mentschikoff had been moving flankwise.

flank (flæŋk), *sb.*² *Obs.* exc. *dial.* Forms: 4 **flaunke**, 6 **flanke**, 9 *dial.* **vlank**. [Cf. FLAKE *sb.*², of which this may be a nasalized form; Sw. has (*snö*) *flanka* a snowflake.] = FLAKE *sb.*² 2.

13.. *E.E. Allit. P.* B. 954 Felle flaunkes of fyr & flakes of soufre. **1586** J. HOOKER *Girald. Irel.* in *Holinshed* II. 148/1 His companie..carried vpon the ends of their poles flankes of fier. **1888** ELWORTHY *W. Somerset Word-bk.*, The vlanks was blowin all over the place.

flank (flæŋk), *v.* Also 6-7 **flanck(e**, **flanke**, (7 **flanque**). [f. FLANK *sb.*¹ Cf. Fr. *flanquer*.]

†**1.** *intr.* To shoot on the flank or sideways; to deliver a raking fire. *Obs.*

1548 W. PATTEN *Exped. Scotl.* N vij, Loopholes as well for shooting directly foorthward as for flankyng at hand.

2. *trans.* To guard, protect, strengthen, or defend on the flank.

1596 SPENSER *F.Q.* IV. xi. 36 A brasen wall, Which mote the feebled Britons strongly flancke Against the Picts. **1598** BARRET *Theor. Warres* III. ii. 70 Some do vse to flanke the two sides of the battell with sleeues of shot. **1608** GRIMSTONE *Hist. France* (1611) 464 The Brittons horse that flanked the armie, growes amazed, and leaues the foote naked. **1638** SIR T. HERBERT *Trav.* (ed. 2) 34 A Castle.. flanckt with Ordnance. **1662** J. DAVIES tr. *Mandelslo's Trav.* 215 The Walls are very broad, and flank'd with Towers. **1666** DRYDEN *Ann. Mirab.* xxvi, Our perfum'd prey.. flank'd with rocks, did close in covert lay. **1704** *Hymn Vict.* lx, This Wing the Woods may flank, the Castle that. **1783** WATSON *Philip III* (1839) 95 A strong intrenchment, flanked with bastions. *a* **1837** H. T. COLEBROOKE in *Life* (1873) 409 The parts of the wall do not well flank each other. **1878** BOSW. SMITH *Carthage* 385 It was flanked throughout its length by towers at equal distances of two hundred feet. *fig.* **1680** J. SCOTT *Serm.* Wks. 1718 II. 24 We cannot.. Flank and Rear our Discourses with Military Allusions. **1757** *Monitor* No. 100 ¶8 Ambitious men flank and fortify one crime with another. **1884** *Chr. World* 25 Dec. 995/1 Flanking himself with an apt quotation from the Psalms. *absol.* **1644** PRYNNE & WALKER *Fiennes' Trial*, App. 11. Fortified with a gallant Parrapet well flanking. **1672** LACEY tr. *Tacquett's Milit. Archit.* iii. 4 Each part of the Fortification must flanque and be flanqued.

3. To menace or attack the flank of; to take in flank. Of artillery: To fire sideways upon, to rake.

1599 HAKLUYT *Voy.* II. I. 123 Flancking and scouring all the ditch with their harquebussie. **1600** HOLLAND *Livy* xxv. 564 Beaten back affront, beset behind, flanked on the sides ..and environned round. **1736** LEDIARD *Life Marlborough* III. 40 The Enemy had, from hence, very much flank'd the Right of the Approaches. **1782** P. H. BRUCE *Mem.* I. 29 One of our own guns..unhappily missing that object, the ball flanked our own trenches. **1820** SCOTT *Monast.* i, An advanced angle..with shot-holes for flanking the door-way. *absol.* **1654** tr. *Scudery's Curia Pol.* 70 To leave no enemy in the rear to march after, and so to flank or offend.

†**b.** To place (artillery, a battery) on the flank, for either attack or defence. *Obs. rare.*

1653 H. COGAN tr. *Pinto's Trav.* v. 12 They had moored up the Galley, and by it raised up a platform, whereupon they had flanked 25 Pieces of Ordnance.

4. To take up or be posted in a position at the flank of; to be placed or situated on either side of. Also pass., ***to be flanked by*** or ***with***: to have situated or stationed on the flanks or sides.

1651 DAVENANT *Gondibert* III. II. xvi, Prostrate Meads, With Forrests flank'd, where shade to darkness grew. *a* **1748** C. PITT *Ep. to Mr. Spence* 34 Where stately colonades are flank'd with trees. **1779** J. MOORE *View Soc. Fr.* (1789) I. xxiv. 188 A well made road..flanked on each side by very high hills. **1838** DICKENS *Nich. Nick.* xv, These viands being flanked by a bottle of spirits & a pot of porter. **1860** TYNDALL *Glac.* I. iii. 23 High mountains flanked us on either side. **1871** L. STEPHEN *Playgr. Eur.* iv. §3. 231 A mountain, flanked by real precipices.

†**b.** *intr.* To occupy a flank position, border *on* or *upon*. *Obs.*

1604 GRIMSTONE *Hist. Siege Ostend* 192 Ten others [embrasures]..flanke vppon the approches. *a* **1680** BUTLER *Milford-haven* Rem. (1759) I. 417 That Side which flanks on the Sea and Haven needs no Art to fortify it. **1828** WEBSTER, *Flank*, v. i. to be posted on the side.

5. *trans.* To march past or go round the flank of; in quot. *transf.*

1893 *Westm. Gaz.* 22 Dec. 2/3 Did they flank the snow and go round to the right, or did they bring the whole avalanche down on top of them?

b. *U.S. slang.* To dodge, etc. (see quot.)

1872 DE VERE *Americanisms* v. 286 The term *to flank*, which, from the strategy of the generals, descended in the mouth of privates to very lowly..meanings. When the men wished to escape the attention of pickets and guards by slipping past them, they said they *flanked* them; drill and detail and every irksome duty was *flanked*, when it could be avoided by some cunning trick. Soon..the poor farmer was *flanked* out of his pig and his poultry.

6. In various nonce-uses. **a.** To strike on the flank or side. **b.** Of a ship: To present the flank or broadside to (a gale). **c.** ***to flank down***: to bring *down* upon the flanks or hips.

1601 HOLLAND *Pliny* I. 501 As the said wind may flanke it on the side. **1704** SWIFT *Batt. Bks.* (end), Flanking down his Arms close to his Ribs, hoping to save his Body. **1762** FALCONER *Shipwr.* II. 298 For this assault should either quarter feel, Again to flank the tempest she might reel.

flank (flæŋk), *v.*² [Onomatopœic; cf. *flick*, *spank*.] *trans.* To whip with a light, sudden stroke, to flick; also, to crack (a whip).

1830 LYTTON *P. Clifford* iii, He then, taking up the driving whip, flanked a fly from the opposite wall. **1833** *Anglo-sapphic Ode* in Whibley *Cap and Gown* 136 Kicks up a row, gets drunk or flanks a tandem-Whip out of window. **1861** MRS. PENNY *Romance Dull Life* vii. 52 He still eased his feelings by flanking everything in the room with a very dusty pocket-handkerchief.

†'**flankard.** *Obs. Hunting.* [a. OF. (*noeud*) *flancar(d*, f. *flanc* FLANK. Cf. FLANCARD.] See quot. 1576; also ? *transf.* a wound in the side.

1567 HARMAN *Caveat* (Shaks. Soc.) 29 Some preuye wounde festred with a fylthy firy flankard. **1576** TURBERV. *Venerie* 128 Two [knottes or nuttes] whiche are in the flankes of the Deare and are called flankardes. **1616** in BULLOKAR.

flanked (flæŋkt), *ppl. a.*¹ [f. FLANK *v.* + -ED¹.] In senses of the vb.

1706 PHILLIPS (ed. Kersey), *Flanked Angle*, the Angle made by the two Faces of the Bastion. *Ibid.*, *Flank'd* or *Double Tenaille*. See *Tenaille*. **1828** J. M. SPEARMAN *Brit. Gunner* (ed. 2) 44 The barbette batteries must be established in the flanked angles of the bastions.

flanked (flæŋkt), *ppl. a.*² [f. FLANK *sb.*¹ + -ED².] Having a flank or flanks: only with defining word, as ***full-flanked***.

1634 HEYWOOD *Witches Lanc.* IV. Wks. 1874 IV. 223 He's broad buttock'd and full flanck'd.

flanker ('flæŋkə(r)), *sb.*¹ Also 6 **flancker**, 7 **flankier**. [f. FLANK *v.*¹ + -ER¹.]

1. A fortification projecting so as to flank or defend another part, or to command the flank of an assailing enemy.

1550-1 EDWARD VI. *Lit. Rem.* (Roxb.) II. 307 Also for flankers at the kepe of Guisnes willed to be made. **1647** SPRIGGE *Anglia Rediv.* (1854) 181 The west-gate, wherein were four pieces of ordnance, and two in the flanker. **1698** FRYER *E. India & Persia* 59 The Castle is seated towards the bottom of the Bay, commanding it every way from the Points and Flankiers. **1753** J. BOWDOIN *Let. to Franklin* 12 Nov. in *Franklin's Wks.* (1887) II. 317 *note*, At each corner a flanker, in which is a couple of canon. **1813** SCOTT *Trierm.* III. xv, Embattled high and proudly towered, Shaded by ponderous flankers.

†**2.** A cannon posted so as to flank a position.

1575 CHURCHYARD *Chippes* (1817) 107 The flankers then in murdring holes that lay Went of and slew, God knowes stout men enew. **1577-87** HOLINSHED *Chron.* III. 1191/2 Capteine Vaughan..entered the ditches, and viewed the flankers; whereupon the French shot off the same flankers.

3. One posted or stationed on either flank. **a.** *Mil.* One of a detachment of skirmishers thrown out on the flanks of an army when marching, to guard the line of march. Usually *pl.* [= F. *flanqueur*.]

1586 J. HOOKER *Girald. Irel.* in *Holinshed* II. 159 Setting out his flankers in seuerall places. **1635** BARRIFFE *Mil. Discip.* lxi. (1643) 16 The Pikes being the Flanquers. **1796** STEDMAN *Surinam* II. xx. 96 With a few flankers or rifle-men outside the whole. **1863** *Cornh. Mag.* Jan. 52 Their services as scouts and flankers proved invaluable.

b. in non-military uses.

1827 LADY MORGAN *O'Briens & O'Flahertys* I. 219 Lady Honoria was still excluded..by a blockade of carriages, and her old flanker the Castleknock. **1893** *Standard Dict.*, *Flanker* 2. In grouse-driving, one of the men walking on the flanks of the line of drivers, to keep the birds in the desired line of flight.

c. A trick, a swindle. *slang* (orig. *Mil.*).

1923 MANCHON *Le Slang* 124 Flanker...3. une échappatoire; he's done us a flanker, il nous a trompés, nous

a attrapés, ou (rare) nous a échappé. **1937** PARTRIDGE *Dict. Slang* 282/1 Do a flanker..; work a flanker. **1962** *Observer* 27 May 3/8 An Army spokesman said: '..he has certainly pulled a flanker on the Army'. **1962** B. KNOX *Little Drops of Blood* ii. 47 This bloke wasn't content wi' just fiddling the h.p. He'd been workin' another flanker.

d. = *flank forward* (FLANK *sb.*^{1} 9). Also in American and Canadian football (see quot. 1961^2).

1953 H. MULLER *Tot Siens to Test Rugby* 180 My first-choice flanker would be Des O'Brien. **1961** *Auckland Weekly News* 5 July 53/1 As a wingforward and later a flanker he will always be remembered. **1961** J. S. SALAK *Dict. Amer. Sports* 165 *Flanker* (football), an offensive end or back who lines up five or more yards wide of his own end. **1962** *Times* 12 June 3/5 Pask for J. Douglas as the blindside flanker in the pack. **1968** [see END *sb.* 3 g]. **1970** *Toronto Daily Star* 24 Sept. 18/7 Waivers were asked on flanker Tom Bland and nobody picked him up.

4. Anything which flanks or adjoins laterally: *esp.* **a.** a side-wall of a courtyard; a wing of a building; †**b.** a side-piece of timber; **c.** a side-piece of armour (see quot. 1659), = FLANCARD; †**d.** a footpath by the side of a highway, a side-walk; **e.** one of the side horses in a three-horse vehicle.

1600 SURFLET *Countrie Farme* II. liv. 377 *To make them [citron-trees] a hood and flankers of Bay trees. **1611** COTGR., *Flanchere*, A flanker, side peece, or flanking peece of timber, in building. **1631** EARL CORK *Diary* in *Lismore Papers* Ser. I. (1886) III. 102 He bwylding..an english howse..with 2 fflankers. **1659** TORRIANO, *Fiancari*, flankers, or sidepieces for an armed man or barbed horse. **1682** WOOD *Life* (1894) III. 25 The highway..pitched..the middle part with peebles, and the two collateralls or flankers with hard white stone. **1823** SCOTT *Let to D. Terry* 29 Oct. in *Lockhart*, The front of the house is now enclosed by a court-yard wall with flankers of 100 feet. **1879** O'DONOVAN in *Daily News* 16 Apr. 3/1 While the central animal is..running along a deep narrow cutting, the flankers are on the top of high banks on either side; or *vice versa*.

'flanker, *sb.*^{2} [f. FLANKER *v.*^{2}] (See quots.)

1840 GOSSE *Canadian Nat.* 11 They..throw out lighted fragments, 'flankers', as they are called. **1847** HALLIWELL, *Flanker*, a spark of fire. *West.*

flanker ('flæŋkə(r)), *v.*^{1} *Obs.* exc. *arch.* [f. FLANKER *sb.*^{1}; cf. however Du. *flankeeren*, ad. F. *flanquer* to FLANK.]

1. *trans.* To support or protect on the flanks; to defend or command from a flanker; to strengthen with flankers.

1598 BARRET *Theor. Warres* IV. i. 96 At euery angle of the battell..a good squadron of Muskets..to flanker it euery way. **1624** CAPT. SMITH *Virginia* V. 191 He began his first peece of fortification, vpon a Rocke which flankers the Kings Castle. **1633** T. STAFFORD *Pac. Hib.* II. xxi. 233 The ground ..was flankered from the Earles quarter by the Cannon. **1665** SIR T. HERBERT *Trav.* (1677) 40 The City is compassed with a thick Stone Wall, flanker'd and moated about. **1721–1800** in BAILEY, To *Flanker*, to fortify the Walls of a City with Bulwarks or Countermures.

fig. **1612** tr. *Benvenuto's Passenger* II. i. §27. 433 The Philosopher also flanckers this intention of ours. **1621** EARL CORK in *Lismore Papers* Ser. II. (1888) III. 18 This purchase will..secure and flanker yt [property] in tyme of trouble.

2. *intr.* To make an attack on the flank.

1603 KNOLLES *Hist. Turks* (1621) 619 One of these great mounts he cast up directly against the face of the towne, and the other at a corner of the same, to flanker alongst the wall. **1664** EVELYN *Sylva* (1679) 20 Where those sharp winds do rather flanker than blow fully opposite upon our plantations.

Hence **'flankered** *ppl. a.*

1860 WHITTIER *Truce of Pis.* 18 The grim, flankered block-house, bound With bristling palisades.

†**'flanker**, *v.*^{2} *Obs.* [f. FLANK *sb.*^{2} + -ER^5; cf. *flacker, flicker.*] *intr.* To sparkle. Hence **'flankering** *ppl. a.*

1567 TURBERV. *Epitaphes*, etc. 127 The fits of love And flanckring sparkes of Cupids fire. **1577** T. KENDALL *Flowers of Epigr.* 49 By flanckeryng flame of firie love, to cinders men are worne.

'flanking, *vbl. sb.* and *ppl. a.* [f. FLANK *v.* + -ING^1 and ^{2}.] In senses of the vb. *flanking party* (see quots. 1802, 1918).

1704 *Lond. Gaz.* No. 4082/3 There is a Flanking Line which runs from the Round Tower. **1802** C. JAMES *Mil. Dict.*, *Flanking-party*, a select body of men on foot or on horseback, whose object is to harrass and perplex the enemy, to get upon his wings, or by any manœuvre to hang upon the flank of an opposing force. **1813** SCOTT *Rokeby* V. iii, The flanking guns dismounted lie. **1841** LEVER *C. O'Malley* xc, Who poured in a flanking fire. **1864** BURTON *Scot Abr.* I. v. 294 When he has built his first flanking works, he wants to protect these works in the same way. **1870** *Daily News* 20 Oct., This distant flanking of their line of communication made the defences that they raised all the easier to examine. **1886** WILLIS & CLARK *Cambridge* II. 508 The flanking turrets. **1888** KIPLING *Departm. Ditties* (1890) 79 Sent out a flanking-party. **1918** E. S. FARROW *Dict. Mil. Terms* 234 *Flanking party*, any body of men detached from the main army to act upon the flanks of an enemy.

flanky ('flæŋkı), *a. Tanning.* [f. FLANK *sb.*^{1} + -Y^1.] Of a skin: loose and coarse.

1903 L. A. FLEMMING *Pract. Tanning* 116 Some classes of skins are naturally more flanky than others.

flanky: see FLUNKEY.

flann: see FLAN *sb.*^{1}

flannel ('flænəl), *sb.* Forms: 6–8, 9 (*dial.*) flan(n)en, 6–7 flan(n)ing, flan(n)ell, (7 flannion), 7, 9 (*dial.*) flannin, 8 *Sc.* flainen, 6– flannel. [Of uncertain etymology. App. first recorded in Eng., whence the continental forms were prob. adopted: F. *flanelle* (late 17th c.), It. *frannella, frenella, fiannella*, Sp. *flanela, franela*, Pg. *farinella* (? influenced by *farinha* flour), Ger. *flanell* (1715), Du. *flanel, flenel*. As flannel was already in 16th c. a well-known production of Wales, a Welsh origin for the word seems antecedently likely. Some scholars have conjectured that the form *flannen* is the original, and is a corruption of Welsh *gwlanen* 'a flannel' (O. Pughe), f. *gwlân* wool (= Ir. *olann*:—OCeltic **ulanā*:—older **wlanā*). This is plausible, but involves some difficulties: the Welsh word is not originally a name for the material, but (as is indicated by its formation with the individualizing suffix *-en*) means literally an article or piece of material made of wool; and the assumed change of *flannen* into *flannel* is perh. less explicable than would be the contrary change, which might be ascribed to the analogy of *linen, woollen*. Another suggestion is that the word is an AF. diminutive of OF. *flaine* blanket or coverlet.]

1. a. An open woollen stuff, of various degrees of fineness, usually without a nap.

1503 *Privy Purse Exp. Eliz. of York* (1830) 94 For iiij yerdes of fflanell..iiijs. *a* **1586** SIDNEY *Arcadia* II. ii. §1 99 She found Dorus, apparelled in flanen. **1597** T. J. *Serm. Paules C.* 54 Thou shalt haue course flaning to be thy best attyre. **1652** *Sessions Rec. Wenlock* 9 Aug. in Jackson & Burne *Shropsh. Folk-lore* xxxii. (1883) 480 John Eavens badger of flanen. **1677–8** MARVELL *Corr.* cccxxii. Wks. 1872–5 II. 581 Greater penaltyes upon those that do not bury in flannell. **1704** F. FULLER *Med. Gymn.* (1711) 212 Flannel is scarce necessary or convenient on this side old Age. **1790** BURNS *Tam o' Shanter* 153 Had..their sarks, instead o' creeshie flannen, Been snaw-white seventeen hunder linnen! **1849** CLARIDGE *Cold Water-cure* 69 Mr. Priessnitz expects all his patients to leave off wearing flannel ..next to the body. **1882** BECK *Draper's Dict.* s.v. *Flannel*, Such [Flannels] as have the pile raised on one side..are termed Raised Flannels; when both sides are so covered they are Double-raised Flannels.

b. *pl.* Different kinds of flannel; flannel goods in general.

1581 *Act 23 Eliz.* c. 9 §1 Logwood..wherewith divers Dyers..dye..Caps, Flannels. **1643** PRYNNE *Open. Gt. Seale* 21 All Worsteds and Flannins within these Townes and their Suburbs. **1875** *Ure's Dict. Arts* II. 401 In Ireland a few varieties of low flannels and coatings, called Galways, are manufactured from Irish grown wool.

†**c.** With reference to the obligation of burying in woollen (18 & 19 Chas. II, c. 4): A shroud. *Obs.*

a **1683** OLDHAM *Sat.* in *Poems & Transl.* (1684) 174 He could not save Enough to purchase Flannel, and a Grave. **1683** TRYON *Way to Health* 320/1 If they escape the Wooden Tenement and Flannel.

d. Ludicrously used to designate a Welshman.

1598 SHAKS. *Merry W.* V. v. 172 I am not able to answer the Welsh flannel.

e. A piece of flannel (or other fabric) for washing the face or hands, etc., or washing the floor, etc.

1819 KEATS *Let.* 20 Sept. (1958) II. 201 The door steps always fresh from the flannel. **1906** MRS. BEETON *Househ. Managem.* 1911 If there is much cheesy-looking substance on the body [of a newly born child] it may be removed with a little sweet oil, and then well soaped with a soft flannel. **1914** D. H. LAWRENCE *Widowing of Mrs. Holroyd* III. 87 She takes a flannel and soap and towel. **1926** I. M. PEACOCKE *His Kid Brother* 10 He gasped and spluttered, as the inexorable soapy 'flannel' passed over his rosy face. **1945** MENCKEN *Amer. Lang. Suppl.* (1948) II. 486 Several English correspondents say that the English for *wash-rag* is really *flannel*, but others deny it. **1962** M. DUFFY *That's how it Was* xxiii. 194 'I've soaped the flannel.' I took it from her and.. washed the pitiful back.

f. *slang.* Nonsense, 'hot air'; flattery, unnecessary ostentation; (see also quot. 1943). (Cf. *flannel-mouth* (*c*) s.v. sense 6 and FLANNEL *v.* d.)

1927 *Daily Express* 11 Oct. 3/4 One day his sister died sudden. Up he comes to ask for fourteen days' leave..'to mourn over the body..according to the Jewish faith'... The padre wired to a rabbi..and..it was all flannel..just flannel from beginning to end. **1943** HUNT & PRINGLE *Service Slang* 32 *Flannel*, honeyed words or small gifts made to N.C.O.s with intent to ask favours. **1945** *Penguin New Writing* XXIII. 49 The ship's company know what is coming. Jimmy the One is going to give us a pep talk. Tons of flannel. **1958** *Sunday Times* 9 Feb. 4/3 The only book I've read about flying that isn't flannel. **1970** *Daily Tel.* 17 Apr. 4 (Advt.), This coupon will bring you our 'all facts—no flannel' brochure telling you all about us.

2. *pl.* **a.** Underclothing made of flannel; also, pieces of flannel used for bandages, etc.

1722 DE FOE *Col. Jack* (1840) 296 Having..my flannels taken off my legs. **1771** SMOLLETT *Humph. Cl.* I. 17 Apr., She forgot to pack up my flannels. **1841** EMERSON *Nat., Conservative* Wks. (Bohn) II. 274 A universe in slippers and flannels.

b. Garments of flannel, for boating, cricket etc.; *spec.* flannel trousers. ***to get*** or ***receive one's flannels*** (see quot. 1889).

1888 J. PAYN *Myst. Mirbridge* ix, He had worn cricketing flannels. **1889** *Boy's Own Paper* 24 Aug. 746/1 Careless schoolboys..lightly dressed in flannels. **1889** BARRÈRE & LELAND *Slang, Flannels* (Harrow), to get one's flannels is to obtain promotion to the school cricket, or football eleven. **1911** L. J. VANCE *Cynthia* 145 The Brazilian had changed to a costume of white flannels, white shirt of silk, and white leather shoes. **1935** *Discovery* May 148/1 Two pairs of flannels were insufficient to prevent their [*sc.* mosquitoes'] drawing blood. **1958** I. MURDOCH *The Bell* i. 19 He wore dark grey flannels and a white open-necked shirt.

c. *sing.* A person who has got his flannels as a member of the Harrow cricket or football team.

1901 *Harrovian* 30 Mar. 35/1 In addition to the good batsmen we have among our old flannels, it seems likely that the Eleven will be stronger in batting than in bowling. **1923** *Daily Mail* 13 July 11 Unfortunately for Harrow, they have not the same eleven available. In fact, only two old 'flannels' are left.

3. (See quot.)

1884 KNIGHT *Dict. Mech.* IV. 346/1 *Flannel*, the first stage in the manufacture of plain cloth.

4. *transf.* **a.** ***natural flannel*** (see quot. 1856). **b.** In popular names of certain woolly-leaved plants: ***Poor Man's Flannel*** = ADAM'S FLANNEL; ***Our Lord's*** or ***Our Saviour's Flannel***: *Ecticum vulgare* (Britten & H.). **c.** *slang* (see quot. 1823).

1823 'J. BEE' *Slang, Flannel* (warm), grog, punch, or gin-twist, with a dash of beer in. **1856** GRIFFITH & HENFREY *Microgr. Dict.* 265 *Flannel, Natural*, a harsh fibrous texture, sometimes found covering meadows, rocks, etc., after an inundation. It consists of the interwoven filaments of Confervæ, with adherent or entangled Diatomaceæ, Infusoria, crystals of carbonate of lime, etc.

5. *attrib.* or *adj.* **a.** Made of flannel.

1585 HIGINS *Junius' Nomenclator* 164 A flanell peticoate. **1611** FLORIO, *Bambagina*, bumbasine. Also a flanell wast-cote. **1618** BRATHWAIT *Rem. after Death, Descr. Death* v, He weares No mantle, flanning trowses. *a* **1700** ? DRYDEN *Suum cuique* In flannen robes the coughing ghost does walk. **1758** *Newport* (R.I.) *Mercury* 26 Dec. 3/1 An old brown Jacket, a Flannel Jacket and Flannel Shirts. **1784** JOHNSON *Let. to Mrs. Thrale* 9 Feb., I have just be-spoke a flannel dress. **1857** HUGHES *Tom Brown* II. viii, In white flannel shirt and trousers. **1905** *Grand. Mag.* I. 116 The Duke's flannel suit. **1908** [see ASCOT]. **1915** T. S. ELIOT *Prufrock* (1917) 15, I shall wear white flannel trousers, and walk upon the beach. **1946** J. IRVING *Royal Navalese* 76 'Have you got flannel ears?' is a rather brutal way of saying 'Can't you pay attention?'

b. In *nonce-uses*: Resembling flannel.

1764 WALPOLE *Lett.* (1820) III. 9, I have little fevers every night, which bid me repair to a more flannel climate. **1795** WOLCOTT (P. Pindar) *Pindariana* Wks. 1812 IV. 186 A pair of flannel cheeks composed her face.

6. *attrib.* and *comb.* as ***dance, flannel-maker, trade, -weaver, -weaving***; also ***flannel-clad, -slacked, -suited*** adjs.; †**flannel-act** (cf. 1 c); **flannel-cake**, a kind of thin griddle-cake; **flannel-flower, -plant**, (*a*) the mullein; (*b*) an Australian plant, *Actinotus helianthi*, the involucre of which resembles a snipped piece of white flannel; hence **flannel-leaf**; **flannelgraph**, a sheet of flannel to which (paper or cloth) cut-outs will adhere, used as a teaching aid; **flannel-mouth**, (*a*) a large species of cat-fish common in North American rivers, esp. the Mississippi and the Great Lakes; (*b*) any of various grunts of the genus *Hæmulon* or *Bathystoma* found off the south Atlantic coast of North America and having the inside of the mouth red, esp. the tomtate (*B. aurolineatum*); (*c*) *U.S. fig.*, used contemptuously of a person; in later quots. *spec.* a braggart or empty talker, a flatterer (cf. 1 f and FLANNEL *v.* d); so ***flannel-mouthed*** adj.; **flannel rash** (see quot.); **flannel-weed**, some water-plant.

1678 T. JONES *Of Heart & Soveraign* 403 (By a Canonical *Flannel Act) [it] must be buried out of the way, as useless. **1792** *Munchhausen's Trav.* xxix. 131 Ten thousand thousand Naples biscuits, crackers, buns, and *flannel-cakes. **1847** 'H. FRANCO' *Trippings Tom Pepper* I. 112 A very delicate species of food, which I tasted then for the first time, called flannel cakes. **1909** 'O. HENRY' *Options* (1916) 212 We..then parted, after Château Margaux, Irish stew, flannel-cakes, [etc.] . **1885** WARREN & CLEVERLY *Wand. Beetle* 59 The Beetle and her *flannel-clad crew. **1898** *19th Cent.* Dec. 993 Its [*sc.* Oxford's] sun-burnt, flannel-clad youth. **1948** J. BETJEMAN *Coll. Poems* (1958) 153 Alfred Brown Remembers courting days in Gospel Oak And takes her to the *Flannel Dance. **1895** J. H. MAIDEN *Flowering Plants N.S.W.* I. 9 We only know one truly local name for this plant, and that is the '*Flannel Flower'. **1911** A. E. MACK *Bush Days* 29 The summer flowers—the Christmas bells, Christmas bush, and flannel flowers. **1944** *Guatemala News* Oct.–Nov. 28 An interest aroused among the Sunday School teachers in the use of *flannelgraph materials. **1955** E. BLISHEN *Roaring Boys* III. 119 The flannelgraph..was a large sheet of flannel that, after some difficulty with drawing-pins, he managed to attach to the blackboard. **1968** *Listener* 27 June 844/2 Glimpses of the evangelism of the street corner, of 'flannelgraph' classes for children. **1821** CLARE *Vill. Minstr.* I. 114 Antique mullein's *flannel-leaves. **1702** *Lond. Gaz.* No. 3776/4 John Judd..*Flannel-maker. **1882** JORDAN & GILBERT in *Bull. U.S. Nat. Mus.* XVI. 108 *I. lacustris* (Walbaum)..Cat-fish of the Lakes; Great Fork-tailed Cat; Mississippi Cat; Florida Cat; *Flannel-mouth Cat... Abundant in all large bodies of water. One of the largest of the cat-fishes, reaching a weight of 100 pounds. [*Ibid.* 882 On page 108, instead of *Ictalurus lacustris*, read:..*I. nigricans* (Le S.).] **1884** G. B. GOODE *Nat. Hist. Aquatic Anim.* I §133. 398 Several species of small

fish, belonging to the genus *Diabasis*..are distinguished by the brilliant red color of the inside of the mouth and throat, from which they have sometimes been called Red Mouths, or Flannel Mouths. **1912** T. Dreiser *Financier* 8 You do, and I'll kick your head off, you flannel mouth. **1929** A. Ellis *Life* 202 George starts to complain that it was run by a bunch of 'flannel mouths'. **1933** *Amer. Speech* VIII. iv. 51/1 [In Nebraska] a *flannel mouth* was one who talked much with little sense or who was a braggart. **1966** *Publ. Amer. Dial. Soc.* 1964 XLII. 39 *Chaw-mouth*..refers to the Irishman's talkativeness and parallels the more common *flannel-mouth*. **1884** G. B. Goode *Nat. Hist. Aquatic Anim.* I §133. 398 The Red-mouth Grunt, *Diabasis aurolineatus*, is probably the '*Flannel-mouthed Porgy', familiar to Florida fishermen. **1893** *Funk's Stand. Dict.* I. 690/3 *Flannel-mouthed.* 1. Having a large mouth. 2. (Slang.) Talking thickly or with a brogue; also loud-mouthed. **1934** Webster *Flannel-mouthed*, orig., talking thickly with or as with a brogue; now, smooth-spoken; oily-tongued;—often contemptuous. **1848** W. A. Bromfield in *Phytologist* III. 598 *Verbascum thapsus*..from the texture of the leaves known here [Hampshire] sometimes as the '*flannel-plant'. **1888** W. A. Jamieson *Dis. Skin* iii. (1891) 41 The '*flannel rash' which Hutchinson and others have noticed on the chest..is another instance of an eruption due to clothing. **1948** J. Betjeman *Coll. Poems* (1958) 180 Her sturdy legs were *flannel-slack'd. **1917** S. McKenna *Sonia* vii. §3. 297 A group of barristers, *flannel-suited for the Long Vacation. **1879** *Encycl. Brit.* IX. 292/1 Blankets, a special branch of the *flannel trade. *Ibid.* Nearly the whole population..finds occupation in *flannel weaving. **1893** *Pall Mall G.* 10 July 10/3 The rains..have put a little more water into the river, and there is not so much *flannel weed to contend with.

flannel ('flænəl), *v.* [f. prec. sb.] ***trans.*** **a.** To wrap in flannel. **b.** To rub with flannel.

1836–9 Dickens *Sk. Boz, Our Parish* vi, The children were yellow-soaped and flannelled. *Ibid., Tales* i, The second-floor front was scrubbed, and washed, and flannelled.

c. *intr.* To put on flannels.

1919 W. T. Grenfell *Labrador Doctor* (1920) ii. 19 Each boy..had to 'flannel' and run round the Aylesbury Arms.

d. *slang.* To flatter, curry favour; so **flannelling** *vbl. sb.* (Cf. flannel *sb.* 1 f.)

1941 *New Statesman* 30 Aug. 218/3 (*list of war slang*) *Flannel*—To flatter. **1945** Partridge *Dict. R.A.F. Slang* 26 *To flannel; flannelling*: (to use) flattering or wheedling words. **1957** J. Braine *Room at Top* v. 46, I managed to flannel him into the belief that I approved of his particular brand of efficiency.

Hence **'flannelled** *ppl. a.*

1778 H. More *Let.* (1834) I. i. iv. 136 The doctor..consented on condition that I should be well furred and flannelled. **1784** J. Belknap *Belknap Papers* (1877) I. 383 She knows what it is to tend a flannelled pair of legs and hands. *a* **1845** Hood *To Grimaldi* i, Joseph! they say thou'st left the stage, To..taste the flannell'd ease of age. **1898** *19th Cent.* XLIV. 994 The single..trotting figures of flannelled men. **1902** Kipling *Five Nations* (1903) 135 Then ye contented your souls With the flannelled fools at the wicket or the muddied oafs at the goals. **1967** T. C. Worsley (*title*) Flannelled fool.

flannelette (flænə'lɛt). Also **flannellette.** [f. flannel + -ette.] **a.** (See quot. 1882.) **b.** A cotton fabric, made in imitation of flannel.

1882 Caulfeild & Saward *Dict. Needlework, Flannellette*, a description of a very soft Flannel, measuring 28 inches in width. **1887** *Daily News* 12 Jan. 3/1 Huge stacks of a poverty-stricken article called flannelette. **1893** *Lady* 17 Aug. 172/2 Flannelette is not flannel.

flannelly ('flænəlɪ), *a.* [f. flannel + -ly[1].] Characteristic or of the nature of flannel; flannel-like. Also *fig.* (In quot. 1842 quasi-*adv.*)

c **1839** Landor *2nd. Convers. Southey & Landor* Wks. 1846 II. 174/1 The dreary hydropathy and flannelly voices of the swathed and sinewless. **1842** Bischoff *Woollen Manuf.* (1862) II. 148 It [the wool] works more flannelly. **1889** H. A. Dodds *Rep. Paris Exhib.* 5 The sooty 'flannelly' appearance of the manipulation in some of the exhibits.

flanning ('flænɪŋ), *vbl. sb.* [f. flan *v.* + -ing[1].] (See quots.)

1849–50 Weale *Dict. Terms, Flanning*, the internal splay of a window-jamb. **1852** Raine *North Durham* referred to in *Dict. Arch.* (Arch. Publ. Soc. 1862). **1874** Knight *Dict. Mech.* I. 876/2 *Flanning* (Building), the internal flare of a window jamb. The *embrasure.* Or of a fireplace *Coving.*

flanque, flanqued *Her.*: see flanch *sb.*[1]

flant, obs. form of flaunt.

†**flan'tado.** *Obs.* [? f. flaunt *v.* with pseudo-Sp. ending.] ? Flaunting. Also *attrib.*

1583 Stanyhurst *Æneis* i. (Arb.) 18 Thee Troian nauye ..the sea salte foaming wyth braue flantadoe dyd harrow. **1594** [see firking].

†**flantitanting,** *ppl. a. nonce-wd.* [A reduplicated formation on *flanting* = flaunting. Cf. flaunt-tant.] Flaunting.

1596 Nashe *Saffron Walden* 71 In that flourishing flantitanting goutie omega fist.

flap (flæp), *sb.* Forms: 4–7 flappe (6 flepe), 7–8 flapp, 5– flap. [f. next vb.; cf. Du. *flap* blow, fly-flapper, lid of a can.]

I. The action of the vb. flap.

†**1. a.** A blow, slap, stroke. Also *fig. Obs.*

c **1330** *Arth. & Merl.* 8084 With fauchouns, axes and battes, Ich gaue other sori flappes. **1377** Langl. *P. Pl.* B. xiii. 67 This freke..Preched of penaunces..And flappes of scourges. *c* **1460** *Towneley Myst.* (Surtees) 206, I shalle lene you a flap, My strengthe for to kythe. **1535** Stewart *Cron. Scot.* I. 382 Thair freikis fell with mony fercie flap.

b. A blow given with something broad and loose (cf. 2). Also *fig.* † ***a flap with a fox tail***: *fig.* ? a contemptuous dismissal; a trivial rebuke (cf. flap *v.* 2 d).

1553 T. Wilson *Rhet.* (1580) 38 So that he [the lawyer] gaineth alwaies..whereas the other get a warme Sonne often tymes, and a flappe with a Foxe taile, for all that euer thei haue spente. **1598** Florio, *Faggiolata*, a flim-flam tale..a flap with a foxetaile. **1653** A. Wilson *Inconst. Lady* iii. i, Liquorish flies do sometimes meet with flaps. **1717** *Will of S. Jackson*, If the Beadle make any demand..send him away with a Flapp of a Fox taile. **1726** Swift *Gulliver* iii. ii. 17 This Flapper is..employed..to give him a soft Flap on his Eyes. **1727** Gay *Lady & Wasp* 8 The slightest flap a fly can chase. *a* **1734** North *Exam.* i. ii. §84 (1740) 75, I found another Flap for the House of Peers.

2. a. 'The motion of something broad and loose' (J.), as a wing or a fly-flapper; the noise produced by its motion, or by contact with some other object. Cf. flap *v.* 5.

1774 Goldsm. *Nat. Hist.* (1776) V. 9 The flap of a swan's wing would break a man's leg. **1816** Byron *Siege Cor.* xxii, The flap of the banners, that flit as they're borne. **1823** Scott *Peveril* ix, The flap of their wings must have been gracious in the ear of the famished prophet. **1859** Kingsley *Misc.* (1860) I. 152, I can hear the flap and snort of the dogs' nostrils. **1860** Tyndall *Glac.* ii. i. 226 A gnat can execute many thousand flaps of its little wings in a second.

b. A consonant sound produced by a flapping motion of the tongue.

[**1867** A. M. Bell *Visible Speech* 57 The subsequent removal of the centre obstruction is attended with a slightly percussive *flap*, which is the essential characteristic of the class of 'Divided' Consonants.] **1887** *Encycl. Brit.* XXII. 383/1 Glides to and from Flaps.—Flaps are consonants where there is a slack organ which flaps with the breath as it passes. **1888** H. Sweet *Hist. Eng. Sounds* 12 The most distinct glide-consonants are the flaps, of which the Norwegian 'thick' *l* is an example. **1950** D. Jones *Phoneme* p. xiii, Single flap tongue-tip r. **1968** P. M. Postal *Aspects Phonol. Theory* ii. 24 Both are pronounced with the same voiced flap [D] as medial consonant.

c. *colloq. fig.* A state of worry, agitation, fuss, or excitement. Esp. in phrases, ***to be in, get in(to), a flap.*** Also *spec.*, an alert (military sense). (Cf. flap *v.* 10 b; unflappable *a.*)

1916 *In Northern Mists* xliv. 188 Sometimes our departures are more than usually sudden and unexpected. The whole proceeding then becomes what is known amongst us as 'a Flap'. **1925** Fraser & Gibbons *Soldier & Sailor Words* 95 *A flap*: the familiar Navy term for the sudden 'liveliness' on board ship on the arrival of an emergency order involving general activity at extreme high pressure... Also, an airman's term for an air-raid. **1936** *Punch* 2 Sept. 265/1 At the moment there is a flap because the price of bread is going up. **1939** *Ibid.* 30 Aug. 231 Now don't go and get into a flap or anything, Mother, but Joan's broken her arm. **1940** 'Gun Buster' *Return via Dunkirk* i. x. 78 Then happened one of our monthly 'flaps' (invasion scares). **1942** W. Simpson *One of our Pilots is Safe* ii. 39 From then on until the 10th May, when the blitz started in Holland and Belgium, we were subjected to a series of 'flaps'. *Ibid.* 40 Get your flight up right away, there's a flap on. **1945** E. Waugh *Brideshead Revisited* 14 'D'you think it's the real thing?' 'No.' 'Just a flap?' 'Yes.' **1949** H. Pakington *Young Wm. Washbourne* xx. 186 There was a sense of something afoot. 'What's the flap?' asked William of the man whose watch he was relieving. 'Only our battle-cruisers engaging the enemy,' replied the other. **1956** W. Slim *Defeat into Victory* xi. 236 Everything was working smoothly, there was no flap. **1960** *Cambr. Rev.* 7 May 510/2 It is quite untrue to say that emotionally vulnerable patients who 'get into a flap' over exams will subsequently panic when a real situation threatens them in later life.

II. Concrete uses.

†**3.** Something broad to strike with; *esp.* a fly-flapper. *Obs.*

c **1440** *Promp. Parv.* 163 Flappe, instrumente to smyte wythe flyys. *c* **1515** *Cocke Lorell's B.* (Percy Soc.) 2 In his hande he bare a flap for flyes. **1558** Phaer *Æneid* v. Argt. L iv b, Ye game called Cœstus (which is fighting with bagges or flappes of leather hanging by stringes, wherin is either lead or sand). **1624** Heywood *Captives* i. i. in Bullen *O. Pl.* IV, The butchers wyves..stood with theire flapps in theire hands like fanns. **1726** Swift *Gulliver* iii. ii. 19 A young Man with a Flap came up to my side, and flapt me gently on the Right Ear.

4. a. 'Anything that hangs broad and loose, fastened only by one side' (J.).

1522 Skelton *Why not to Court* 1166 With a flap afore his eye. **1606** Shaks. *Tr. & Cr.* v. i. 36 Thou greene Sarcenet flap for a sore eye. **1668** Wilkins *Real Char.* 131 The lesser ..having small roundish flapps on either side of the body. **1704** *Lond. Gaz.* No. 4058/6 A Negro Boy..the Flap of one of his Ears being cut off. **1849** Parkman *Oregon Tr.* (1872) 192, I put aside the leather flap that covered the low opening. **1891** Kipling *Light that Failed* x, [He] gave him a letter with a black M on the envelope flap.

b. A pendant portion of a garment, hat, or cap. Hence applied to the garment or hat itself (*slang*).

1530 Palsgr. 220/2 Flappe of a gowne, *cappe.* **1590** Greene *Mourn. Garm.* (1616) 11 His coat was greene.. Turned ouer with a flappe. **1632** Sherwood, The flap, or back point of a friers cowle, *cabuër.* **1699** Dampier *Voy.* II. iii. 64 We spread abroad the Flaps of our Coats. **1707** Hearne *Collect.* 14 Sept., An armfull of ym he took home, covering them with one flap of his Gown. **1713** Swift *Frenzy J. Dennis*, The flap of his breeches dangled between his legs. **1792** Mad. D'Arblay *Let. to Mrs. Phillips* Nov., An old-fashioned suit of clothes, with long flaps to a waistcoat [etc.]. **1875** *Plain Needlework* 18 The old-fashioned shift with flaps. **1892** C. T. Dent *Mountaineering* iv. 104 Tying the flaps of his hat over his ears.

c. Of a saddle; also *transf.*

1849 Murchison *Siluria* v. 95 A geological saddle, having one thin and partly metamorphosed flap only on the east side. **1886** *Encycl. Brit.* XXI. 142/1 The saddle..consists of the tree..the seat, the skirts, and the flaps.

d. The tail of a crustacean.

1774 Goldsm. *Nat. Hist.* VI. 373 The spawn..sticks to the barbs under the flap, or more properly the tail [of the crab]. **1842** H. Miller *O.R. Sandst.* viii. (ed. 2) 173 The terminal flap of this gigantic crustacean was..continuous.

e. (See quot.)

1669 Hacke *Orig. Voy.* (1699) III. 62 Penguins..have neither Feathers nor Wings, but only two Fins or Flaps, wherewith they are helped to swim.

5. a. Something broad and flat, hanging or working (vertically) on or as on a hinge.

1565–73 Cooper *Thesaurus* s.v. *Biforis, Bifore fenestræ*.. with two flappes. **1754** A. Murphy *Gray's Inn Jrnl.* No. 103 ¶9 One Table, the Flap broken. **1825** J. Nicholson *Operat. Mechanic* 140 He makes each sail..to consist of six or eight flaps or vanes..moving upon hinges. **1840** Dickens *Barn. Rudge* iv, It [the cellar] had a great black wooden flap or shutter. **1859** *Musketry Instr.* 71 The first and second class men..should be trained to fire at 300 and 400 yards with the flap of back-sight down. **1867** Trollope *Chron. Barset* I. iv. 27 There was a table..one flap of it was gone altogether.

b. A valve. ***tide flap***: a valve used to shut off the tide-water from a sewer.

1824 R. Stuart *Hist. Steam Engine* 151, *c,c,c*, are the valves or flaps. **1869** *Lonsdale Gloss., Flap*, the leather or valve of a pump. **1884** *Health Exhib. Catal.* 55/2 A Collection of Sanitary Iron work, such as..tide flaps, &c. **1892** *Pall Mall G.* 7 Sept. 1/3 We descend to the other side of the 'flap'—the men's term for a 'penstock'.

c. *Anat.* †(*a*) The epiglottis. *Obs.* (*b*) In fishes: The operculum or gill-cover; a similar cover for the nostril.

c **1550** H. Lloyd *Treas. Health* H iv, Agaynst al grefes in the flap beinge in the mouth whyche couereth the wind pipe. **1681** W. Robertson *Phraseol. Gen.* (1693) 1224 The cover or flap of the throat, *epiglossis.* **1802** Bingley *Anim. Biog.* (1813) I. 37 They fill their mouth with water, then throw it backwards with so much force as to lift open the great flap, and force it out behind. **1881** Günther in *Encycl. Brit.* XII. 637 Nostrils of *Raia lemprieri*, with nasal flaps reverted.

d. One of the floats of a paddle-wheel.

1840 Thackeray *Catherine* vi, The Ensign's arms were working up and down..like the flaps of a paddle wheel.

e. *Aeronaut.* (Also ***wing-flap***) = aileron. (The word has been applied to various kinds of hinged or sliding sections at the leading or trailing edge of the wing or tail of an aircraft, the primary function of which is to modify the lift.)

1906 *Sci. Amer.* 18 Aug. 116/3 One part of the wing..is formed of a series of longitudinal flaps, fixed at the edges to a wire gauze network, so that the flap is made to close when the wing is brought down, but keeps open when the wing is raised. **1909** *Flight* 27 Nov. 755/2 Small triangular planes are fitted above the extremities of the wings... The rudder is put over for steering to the right and simultaneously the flap above the extremity of the right-hand wing-tip is raised. **1911** *Reports & Mem.* (*Adv. Comm. Aeronaut.*) Nov. 100 It would be useful to know..whether the wing flaps should be additional to the width of the wing,..or whether the extra efficiency of warping indicates the abandonment of flaps altogether. **1921** *Aeronaut. Jrnl.* June 274 Flap Experiments with Slotted Aerofoil. An increase in the lift coefficient can be obtained by the use of a plane with flaps and altering the angle of incidence of these flaps. **1930** *Engineering* 14 Feb. 189/2 The vertical top and bottom flaps, which form the rudders, and the horizontal port and starboard flaps, which form the elevators, have each a span of about 44 ft. **1941** A. O. Pollard *Bombers over Reich* xi. 154 With flaps out of action. **1971** *Air Enthusiast* June 22/1 Possibilities of modifying the wing leading edge profile or using a leading-edge flap were eventually discarded.

6. a. Something broad and loose, irrespectively of connexion with anything else; *esp.* an overlying layer; a broad piece of any material.

1603 Florio *Montaigne* (1634) 187 We are all framed of flaps and patches and of so shapelesse and diverse a contexture, that [etc.]. *a* **1634** Randolph *Hey for Honesty* v. Wks. (1875) 474 A rump or a flap of mutton were a fee For Jove's own breakfast. **1764** Foote *Mayor of G.* i. Wks. 1799 I. 173 The damn'd fat flaps of shoulders of mutton. **1843** Thackeray *Contrib. to 'Punch'* Wks. 1886 XXIV. 145 The flap of a shoulder of mutton..I ate cold. **1848** —— *Bk. Snobs* i, We..had flaps of bread for plates. **1866** *Daily Tel.* 18 Jan. 5/2 Large flaps of swine's flesh..make their appearance at breakfast. **1884** Bower & Scott *De Bary's Phaner.* 114 The great flaps of cork on the cortex of Boswellia papyrifera. **1889** Barrère & Leland *Slang, Flap* (thieves), sheet lead for roofs.

b. A large, broad mushroom. Also flab 1.

1743 Pickering in *Phil. Trans.* XLII. 598 The thin Filament is that to which the Edges of the Head of the Mushroom adhere, while it is, what is commonly called, a Button, and from which it separates by expanding to a Flap. **1769** Mrs. Raffald *Eng. Housekpr.* (1778) 361 Scrape large flaps..and boil them in their own liquor. **1854** *Eng. Cycl.* I. 90/1 The common mushroom..in this state..is called a flap.

†**c.** *collect.* Scraps. *Obs.*—0.

1730–6 Bailey (folio), *Flap*, moist meat for hogs.

d. A loose covering for the lower part of the abdomen. *U.S.*

[**1701** C. Wolley *Jrnl. N.Y.* (1860) 29 A piece of Cloth about a yard and a half long, put between their groins, tied with a Snake's Skin about their middle, and hanging down with a flap before.] **1813** *Niles' Weekly Reg.* V. 270/1 The fort was attacked by 725 Indians..; they were entirely naked, except a flap. **1846** J. J. Hooper *Adv. Simon Suggs* 113 Generally there are two or three hundred [Indians].. engaged in the sport at once; all naked except the 'flap'. **1919** C. G. Raht *Romance Davis Mts.* 54 The clothing.. consisted usually of leggings..the breech clout, or 'flap'.

7. *Surg.* **a.** A portion of skin or flesh, separated from the underlying part, but remaining attached at the base.

1807–26 S. COOPER *First Lines Surg.* (ed. 5) 377 Placing the flap of the cornea in regular contact with the part with which it was naturally joined. **1856** KANE *Arct. Expl.* II. xii. 127 A flap let down from his forehead. **1878** T. BRYANT *Pract. Surg.* I. 536 The flaps were reflected and a large gland enucleated.

b. A piece of flesh or skin grafted upon an injured or defective part.

1813 J. THOMSON *Lect. Inflam.* 225 The mode of repairing noses by a flap or portion of flesh taken from the arm. **1894** *Westm. Gaz.* 31 Aug. 3/1 The grafting upon the injured.. part of flaps of skin taken.. from a neighbouring surface.

8. *pl.* in *Farriery.* A disease in the mouth of horses.

1587 L. MASCAL *Govt. Cattel* II. (1600) 163 Giges or flappes, is pimples or teates in the inside of his [a horse's] mouth. **1610** MARKHAM *Masterp.* I. xii. 32 Swelling in the mouth, a signe either of canker, flaps, or lampasse. **17..** *Farrier's Dict.* (J.), When a horse has the flaps, you may perceive his lips swelled on both sides of his mouth. **1847** YOUATT *Horse* viii. 206 The sublingual glands.. sometimes enlarge.. and are called *gigs*, and *bladders*, and *flaps in the mouth*.

9. *dial.* or *slang.* A woman or girl of light or loose character.

1631 MABBE *Celestina* IX. 110 Fall to your flap, my Masters, kisse and clip. *Ibid.* 112 Come hither, you foule flappes. **1892** *Northumbld. Gloss.* s.v., A young giddy girl is called a flap, or a woman who does not settle down to her domestic duties.

III. *attrib.* and *Comb.*

10. General relations, as ***flap-basket, -board, -door, -down, ear(s), -seat, -shutter, -top, -trap, -valve, -window*** (sense 5); ***flap-eared*** adjs.

1862 *Sat. Rev.* XIV. 186/2 He goes out to all Lancashire with his little *flap-basket, and doles out.. his two ounces of tea. **1833** LOUDON *Encycl. Archit.* §2031 A *flap-board. **1899** W. C. MORROW *Bohem. Paris* 269 The bleeding trunk of the victim lying upon the flap-board. **1844** *Zoologist* II. 748 The *flap-door of a glass hive is opened. **1881** RAYMOND *Mining Gloss., Flap-door*, a man-hole door. **1937** *Archit. Rev.* LXXXII. 57/1 The drinks-cupboard is in mahogany, and has a rubber-faced *flap-down serving-board. **1922** JOYCE *Ulysses* 170 Look at his mouth. Could whistle in his own ear. *Flap ears to match. **1959** I. & P. OPIE *Lore & Lang. Schoolch.* x. 183 Nosey people are known as: Flap-ears, Keyhole Kates, Nosey-Parkers [etc.]. **1596** SHAKS. *Tam. Shr.* IV. i. 160 A horson beetle-headed *flap-ear'd knaue. **1891** *Daily News* 4 Feb. 3/4 Mr. Samuel asked why *flap-seats were permitted at Drury-lane Theatre. **1867** SUTTON & DAWSON *Dict. Photogr.* 156 Some use *flap-shutters in front of the lens. **1927** R. A. FREEMAN *Certain Dr. Thorndyke* xv. 225 A large, old-fashioned *flap-top desk. **1858** *Skyring's Builders' Prices* Advt., *Flap Traps.. always kept in Stock. **1867** W. W. SMYTH *Coal & Coal-mining* 211 The chambers are fitted.. with *flap valves. **1874** KNIGHT *Dict. Mech.* I. 876/2 *Flap-valve*, a valve which opens and shuts upon one hinged side. A clack-valve. **1825** *Beverley Lighting Act* ii. 19 Leave open.. the door, hatchway or *flap-window.

11. Special comb.: **flap-apple** = FLAP-JACK 1 b; **flap-dock** (also *flap-dick, flap-a-dock*), local names for the foxglove; **flap-fracture** = *compound fracture*; **flap-hat**, one having flaps or a flapping brim; **flap-holder** (see quot.); **flap-leg**, the leg that supports a flap of a table; **flap-mouth**, a mouth with broad, hanging lips (whence ***flap-mouthed*** adj.); **flap-operation** *Med.* (see quot. 1884); **flap-sight**, in a rifle, one that turns up or down on a hinge; **flap table**, one with a hinged flap, a leaf table; **flap-wing** *dial.*, the swift.

1750 W. ELLIS *Country Housewife* 25 Turnover, or *Flap-Apple, or Meat Pasties. **1846** *E. Anglia Gloss.* Suppl., **Flapdock*, foxglove. **1658** A. FOX *Wurtz' Surg.* II. xxvi. 165, I call this a *Flap-fracture, when the Wound of the broken leg goeth onely through the flesh and skin, and cometh forth with the one end. **1866** BROWNING in Mrs. Orr *Life* (1891) 275 Great black *flap hats. **1884** KNIGHT *Dict. Mech.* IV. 346/1 **Flap Holder* (Surgical), a delicate prehensile instrument for holding flaps of sutures in confined situations. **1882** SALA *Amer. Revis.* (1885) 98 A *flap-leg was let down; and.. a table was improvised. **1631** P. FLETCHER *Sicelides* III. iv, F ij b, So, haue you done? Fie *flapmouth. Triton, thou beslauerest me. **1592** SHAKS. *Ven. & Ad.* 920 Another *flapmouthd mourner.. wolls out his voyce. **1602** *2nd Pt. Return fr. Parnass.* IV. ii. (Arb.) 51 Begin thou Furor, and open like a phlaphmouthd hound. **1785** T. JONES in *Med. Commun.* IX. 326 (*title*) Case of a *Flap Operation, united by first Intention. **1884** *Syd. Soc. Lex.* s.v. *Flap operation*, a method of amputation in which a.. portion of the skin is reflected from the subjacent soft parts before these and the bones are divided. **1887** RIDER HAGGARD *Allan Quatermain* (1888) 66 One of the repeaters.. fitted with ordinary *flap sights. **1833** LOUDON *Encycl. Archit.* §613 An ironing-board, or *flap table. **1924** KIPLING *Debits & Credits* (1926) 183 His pitch-pine-lined caravan, with.. its flap-table. **1834** H. O'BRIEN *Round Towers Irel.* 38 This, it may be said, is applying a steam engine to crush a *flapwing.

flap (flæp), *v.* Also 4–6 flapp(e. [prob. of onomatopœic origin; cf. *clap, slap, flack*, etc. Equivalent words in form and sense are Du. *flappen* to strike, clap, Ger. *flappen* to clap, applaud.]

†**1. a.** *trans.* To strike with a sudden blow. Also with *down, in sunder.* In later use chiefly implying a stroke with a blunt weapon. *Obs.* exc. *dial.*

?*a* **1400** *Morte Arth.* 2782 Alle þe flesche of þe flanke he flappes in sondyre. *c* **1477** CAXTON *Jason* 67 b, A grete whirling or tourbillion cam sodaynly and flapped him on the visage. **1526** SKELTON *Magnyf.* 1525, I shall flappe hym as a fole to fall at my fete. **1843** T. WILSON *Pitman's Pay* II. lxxvii, Flap her doun at yence wi' pouther.

†**b.** *intr.* or *absol. Obs.*

1362 LANGL. *P. Pl.* A. VII. 174 And flapten on with fleiles from morwe til euen. **1398** TREVISA *Barth. De P.R.* XII. ix. (1495) 419 A storke.. smytyth other flappyth with his bylle. *c* **1400** *Destr. Troy* 7674 Tedius.. flappit at hym felly with a fyne swerde. *c* **1460** *Towneley Myst.* (Surtees) 206 Now falle I the fyrst to flap on hys hyde.

†**c.** ***to flap in the mouth (with a lie)***: to tell a barefaced falsehood to. Also, ***to flap the lie in one's teeth.*** *Obs.*

1579 LYLY *Euphues* (Arb.) 68, I will flappe Ferardo in the mouth with some conceipt. **1611** COTGR., *Emboucher d'vn mensonge*.. to.. flap in the mouth, with an (apparant) lie. *c* **1645** HOWELL *Lett.* (1650) III. xxiii. 37 They will flap the lie in Truths teeth. **1654** FULLER *Comm. Ruth* (1868) 162 So many children flap their parents in the mouth with a lie.

2. a. To strike with something flexible and broad (*e.g.* a fly-flapper); to drive *away* or *off*; to put *out* (a light) as with a blow so given.

c **1400** *Destr. Troy* 11795 Ten tymes be-tyde.. þat hit fest was on fyre, & flappit out onone Vnto smorther & smoke. *c* **1440** *Promp. Parv.* 164 Flappyn wythe a flappe, *flabello.* **1553** T. WILSON *Rhet.* (1580) 201 When many flies stode feedyng vpon his rawe fleshe.. he was contented.. to haue them flapte awaie. **1603** HOLLAND *Plutarch's Mor.* 966 With the rest of his taile he flapped and beat her legges. **1677** *Compl. Servant-Maid* 68 Take a clean linen cloth and gently flap it [the lace] over oftentimes. **1726** SWIFT *Gulliver* III. ii. 16 With these Bladders they now and then flapped the Mouths and Ears of those who stood near them. **1735** POPE *Prol. Sat.* 309 Yet let me flap this bug with gilded wings. **1842** TENNYSON *St. Simeon Stylites* 172 They flapp'd my light out as I read. **1843** LE FEVRE *Life Trav. Phys.* I. I. i. 7, I was assured that two men would run before me to flap away the flies.

b. Of a bird: To strike with the flat of the wing; also to drive *off* (etc.) by flapping.

1585 J. B. tr. *Viret's Sch. Beastes* D j, When the female tarieth over long in the feeldes, they [Pygeons] flappe them with their winges. **1601** HOLLAND *Pliny* I. 271 Flapping the water with their wings. **1694** R. L'ESTRANGE *Fables* ccclxxviii, The Eagle Flapt off the former [the Beetle], and Devoured the other [the Hare]. **1813** BUSBY *Lucretius* IV. 847 The cock.. flaps away the darkness with his wings. **1819** WIFFEN *Aonian Hours* (1820) 76 Night's shrieking bird Flaps the friezed window with her wing. **1827** TENNANT *Papistry Storm'd* 62 They [doves] forc'd and flappit to the yird That spulyier and fae.

c. *fig.* To call the attention of, as if with a flap; to prompt, remind. Cf. quot. 1726 in 2 and FLAPPER 1.

1790 MAD. D'ARBLAY *Diary* 20 May, 'He wants nothing.. but a flapper'. 'Yes, and he takes flapping inimitably'. **1888** *Contemp. Rev.* LIII. 13 They.. despatched an agent to London to 'flap' the Colonial Office.

d. *intr.* To make a flap or stroke. Also with *down.* † ***to flap at (something) with a fox's tail***: said *fig.* of a lenient or pretended reproof.

1581 LAMBARDE *Eiren.* IV. xvi. (1588) 582 This is but.. to strike or flap at a fault with a Foxe taile, and none other. *c* **1839** LANDOR *Imag. Conv.* Wks. (1846) II. 108, I flap down with the border of my glove, and brush away.. these gossamer pretensions.

†**3. a.** *trans.* To clap (the hands). **b.** *intr.* To clap, applaud. Also quasi-*trans.* To clap (applause); to signify by clapping. *Obs.*

1382 WYCLIF *Prov.* xvii. 18 A fool man shal for ioȝe flappe with hondis. —— *Jer.* v. 31 Prestus flappeden for ioȝe their hondes. **1583** STANYHURST *Aeneis* I. (Arb.) 42 Thee Moors hands clapping, the Troians, *plaudite*, flapped.

4. a. *trans.* To toss with a smart movement; to throw *down* suddenly; to fold *together* roughly. Also, to toss (a pancake). *Obs.* exc. *dial.*

c **1320** *Seuyn Sag.* (W.) 766 The greihond.. hente the adder in strong ger, And flapped here al aboute his er. **1644** R. CULMER *Cathedrall Newes Canterbury* 5 The maid.. went to bed, leaving the Ruffe flapt together as her mistris had stampt it. **1847** HALLIWELL, *Flap* a froize, to turn it in the pan without touching it. **1877** *N.W. Linc. Gloss.*, 'He flapped th' newspaper doon upo' th' floor.'

b. *intr.* To fall or throw oneself *down* suddenly; to flop. *colloq.*

1660 FISHER *Rusticks Alarm* Wks. (1679) 448 He.. flaps suddainly down into a piece of Cow-dung. **1753** FOOTE *Eng. in Paris* I. Wks. 1799 I. 36 Souse she flapp'd on her back. **1834** S. R. MAITLAND *Voluntary Syst.* (1837) 89 They.. flap down on their knees before the Bishop. **1865** CARLYLE *Fredk. Gt.* VIII. XVIII. xiii. 50 Soldiers flap-down to drink it from the puddles.

5. a. *intr.* Of anything attached at one extremity or loosely fastened: To swing or sway about loosely; to flutter or oscillate as when moved by the wind. Often with the additional notion of making a noise by striking against something, or by the reciprocal concussion of the parts.

1529 SKELTON *Elynour Rummyng* 136 Naked pappes, That flyppes and flappes. *c* **1620** Z. BOYD *Zion's Flowers* (1855) 9 I'le let the Main Saile flap against the yard. **1635** QUARLES *Embl.* III. xi, My Canvace torn, it flaps from side to side. **1644** DIGBY *Nat. Bodies* (1645) 370 This Diaphragma.. flappeth upon all occasions, as a drum head would do, if it were slack and moyst. **1796** SOUTHEY *Ball. & Metr. T., Rudiger* Poems VI. 21 The long streamer fluttering fast, Flapp'd to the heavy gale. **1805** WORDSW. *Waggoner* Concl. 50 When windows flap. **1815** J. W. CROKER in *Croker Papers* (1884) July, We are now lying at sea with our sails flapping. **1840** DICKENS *Barn. Rudge* lv, The cheery deep-red curtains flapped and fluttered idly in the wind. **1876** E. JENKINS *Blot Queen's Head* 7 Proud of their sign-board wherever it flapped and shone. **1877** *Holderness Gloss., Flap*, to close or shut with violence. 'Shut deear or it'll flap teea, ther's sike a wind.'

b. *trans.* (*causal*) To cause to flap; to move (any surface) percussively. Also, to shut (a door) *to* sharply.

1565–73 COOPER *Thesaurus* s.v. *Plango*, Windes flap togither wide garments in the aire. **1727** SWIFT *Further Acc. E. Curll*, His books.. flapping their covers at him. **1801** SOUTHEY *Thalaba* III. ix, I hear the wind, that flaps The curtain of the tent. **1801** *Lusignan* II. 164, I.. flapped my door to, and locked it.

6. a. *intr.* Of a hat: To have the flap or flaps swaying up and down or drooping.

1679 *Trials of White, & Other Jesuits* 82 He had an old black Hat on that flapp'd. **1712–3** *Guardian* No. 11 ¶9 He was so ill that his hat began to flap.

b. *trans.* To pull down the flaps of (a hat).

1751 SMOLLETT *Per. Pic.* (1779) III. lxxviii. 41 They had flapped their hats over their eyes. **1758** JOHNSON *Idler* No. 49 ¶3 It began to rain.. he flapped his hat. **1840** DICKENS *Barn. Rudge* i, Wearing a hat flapped over his face.

7. a. *trans.* To move up and down, beat (the wings).

1567 GOLDING *Ovid's Metam.* VI. 116 But that she clad in feathers white hir lazie wings must flap. **1703** DAMPIER *Voy.* III. 115 They flew flapping their Wings like Lap-wings. **1740** SOMERVILLE *Hobbinol* II. 190 The luxurious Wasp.. in the viscous Nectar plung'd, His filmy Pennons struggling flaps in vain. **1874** WOOD *Nat. Hist.* 287 The Swift does not flap its wings so often as the Swallow.

b. *absol.* and *intr.* To beat the wings; to make movements like the beating of wings. Also of wings: To move up and down, beat.

1697 DRYDEN *Æneid* Ded. d iv, The Dira.. flapping on the shield of Turnus. *a* **1704** R. L'ESTRANGE (J.), 'Tis common for a duck to run flapping and fluttering away. **1821** CLARE *Vill. Minstr.* I. 87 They [leaves] flap and whistle down. **1823** BYRON *Island* IV. xiii, While o'er them flapp'd the sea-birds' dewy wing. **1842** HOOD *Turtles* vii, Five splendid Turtles.. Were flapping all alive. **1865** TYLOR *Early Hist. Man.* ii. 21 Flap with the arms. **1874** T. HARDY *Madding Crowd* II. vii. 81 A light flapped over the scene, as if reflected from phosphorescent wings.

c. *fig.* colloq. phr. ***to have one's ears flapping*** and var., to listen attentively.

1925 WODEHOUSE *Carry on, Jeeves* i. 26 It was the work of a moment with me to.. dive into a bush.. and stand there with my ears flapping. **1937** M. ALLINGHAM *Dancers in Mourning* ix. 124 The next thing Konrad heard—and he must have sat there with his ears flappin'—was Sutane sayin', 'I don't want you.' **1955** M. GILBERT *Sky High* vi. 80 We never.. ask any questions but.. we manage to keep our ears flapping. **1959** G. MITCHELL *Man who grew Tomatoes* x. 137 I'm sure he followed us. Didn't you notice him flapping his ears when you were talking to the receptionist? **1967** 'M. ERSKINE' *Case with 3 Husbands* ii. 33 You get on and explain them... Harris, I can see, has his ears positively flapping.

8. *intr.* (with advb. extension). **a.** Of a bird: To make way by flapping the wings. **b.** Of a ship: To make way with the sails flapping. (Cf. 5.)

1775 CLAYTON in *Phil. Trans.* LXVI. 104 They.. only swim and flap along on the water at an extraordinary rate. **1853** KANE *Grinnell Exp.* ix. (1856) 63 We pursued our way, flapping lazily alongside of the 'pack'. **1870** KINGSLEY in *Gd. Words* 1 June 38/1 A slate-blue heron.. flapped fifty yards up the creek.

9. †**a.** trans. ***to flap open***: to throw open like a flap: see FLAP *sb.* 5. **b.** *intr.* To move like a flap.

1669 W. SIMPSON *Hydrol. Chym.* 97 Gas.. getting passage.. flaps open the Œsophagus. **1834–5** TODD *Cycl. Anat.* I. 658/1 The valves flap together and close that opening.

10. a. *slang.* (See quots.)

1885 *Daily Tel.* 18 Aug. 3/1 £70.. obtained by flapping a jay. **1889** BARRÈRE & LELAND *Slang, Flap the dimmock*, to pay. *Ibid., Flap*, to rob, to swindle; 'to flap a jay', to swindle a greenhorn.

b. *intr. colloq.* To speak (anxiously) *about*; to be upset; to become agitated; to fuss; to panic. (Cf. FLAP *sb.* 2 c.) Also (*trans.*) ***to flap one's mouth.***

[**1870** G. MEREDITH *Let.* 27 Jan. (1970) I. 415 Out flaps the big girl with a whinny, Fire! Fire!] **1910** H. G. WELLS *Mr. Polly* vii. 166 You go flapping your silly mouth about me, and I'll give you a poke in the eye. **1912** KIPLING *Diversity of Creatures* (1917) 40 'We're a nice lot to flap about governing the Planet,' De Forest laughed. **1927** J. ELDER *Thomasina Toddy* ix, 'Anne's a jolly nice person,' she said to Stella. 'Not bad. Nothing to flap about,' said Stella. *Ibid.* xxii, 'It's beastly, being so little,' she said crossly. Anne.. said 'But it *doesn't* matter, Tom. You mustn't let it. It's silly to flap about things which can't be remedied.' **1943** HUNT & PRINGLE *Service Slang* 32 A person who can't 'cope' or who is very nervous is told to stop 'flapping'. **1952** J. CANNAN *Body in Beck* viii. 171 My mamma flaps about my climbing, he said, and I said.. it's no more dangerous than crossing the Corn. **1959** J. VERNEY *Friday's Tunnel* iii. 39 Mummy.. burst into tears. I put my arm round her waist. 'Please don't flap.'

†**11.** The verb stem used adverbially: With a flap or clap. *Obs.*$^{-1}$ Cf. FLOP.

1716 CIBBER *Love makes Man* I. i, About eight a Clock.. flap! They all sous'd upon their Knees.

flapdoodle (flæp'duːd(ə)l), *sb. colloq.* [An arbitrary formation; cf. FADOODLE.]

1. (See quot. 1833.)

1833 MARRYAT *P. Simple* (1863) 210 'The gentleman has eaten no small quantity of flapdoodle in his lifetime.' 'What's that, O'Brien?' replied I... 'Why, Peter,' rejoined he, 'it's the stuff they feed fools on.' **1863** KINGSLEY *Water-bab.* vi. (1878) 266 Where flapdoodle grows wild.

2. a. Nonsense; 'bosh'; humbug. Also as *interj.* **b.** A trifling thing, a gewgaw.

1878 BESANT & RICE *Celia's Arb.* II. iii. 43 A bit of lace now, or any other fal-lal and flap-doodle. *Ibid.*, III. vii. 101 'Fudge and flapdoodle!' **1884** MARK TWAIN *Huck. Finn* xxv, A speech, all full of tears and flapdoodle.
attrib. **1891** B. HARTE *First Family Tasajara* II. vii, Reading flapdoodle stories and sich.

Hence **flap-'doodle** *v. intr.*, to talk nonsense; to maunder. **flap-'doodler** [-ER[1]] (see quot.).

1889 BARRÈRE & LELAND *Slang*, *Flapdoodlers* (journalistic), charlatan namby-pamby political speakers. **1893** *Westm. Gaz.* 11 July 2/1 He flapdoodled round the subject in the usual Archiepiscopal way.

† **flap-dragon** ('flæpˌdrægən), *sb. Obs.* [f. FLAP *v.* + DRAGON.
The original sense may have been identical with a dialectal sense of *snapdragon*, viz. a figure of a dragon's head with snapping jaws, carried about by the mummers at Christmas; but of this there is no trace in our quots.]

1. a. 'A play in which they catch raisins out of burning brandy and, extinguishing them by closing the mouth, eat them' (J.); = SNAPDRAGON. **b.** A dish of the material used in the game.

1599 B. JONSON *Cynthia's Rev.* v. iii, From stabbing of armes, Flap-dragons..and all such swaggering Humors. **1604** DEKKER *Honest Wh.* xiii. Wks. 1873 II. 83 Give me that flap-dragon. Ile not give thee a spoonefull. **1622** FLETCHER *Beggar's Bush* v. ii, I'le go afore and have the bon-fire made, My fire-works, and flap-dragons, and good back-rack.

c. A raisin or other thing thus caught and eaten.

1588 SHAKS. *L.L.L.* v. i. 45 Thou art easier swallowed then a flapdragon. **1599** MASSINGER, etc. *Old Law* III. ii, I'd had..my two butter-teeth Thrust down my throat instead of a flap-dragon. **1791–1823** D'ISRAELI *Cur. Lit.* (1866) 287 Such were flap-dragons, which were small combustible bodies fired at one end and floated in a glass of liquor, which an experienced toper swallowed unharmed, while still blazing.

d. As a type of something valueless.

1700 CONGREVE *Way of World* III. xv, A flap-dragon for your service, Sir!

2. A contemptuous name for a German or Dutchman. Also *attrib.*

1622 FLETCHER *Beggar's Bush* IV. i, You shall not sink for ne'er a sous'd flap-dragon, For ne'er a pickled pilcher of 'em all, sir. **1630** J. TAYLOR (Water P.) *Wks.* II. 264/2 As bumsie as a fox'd flapdragon German. **1644** *Nest Perfidious Vipers, etc.* in *Harl. Misc.* (Malh.) V. 437 The Commons of England will remember thee, thou flap-dragon, thou butter-box.

3. *slang.* (See quots.)

a **1700** B. E. *Dict. Cant. Crew*, *Flap-dragon*, a Clap or Pox. **1785** in GROSE *Dict. Vulg. Tongue.*

Hence **'flapdragon** *v.* (*nonce-wd.*) *trans.*, to swallow as one would a flap-dragon.

1611 SHAKS. *Wint. T.* III. iii. 100 To see how the Sea flap-dragon'd it [the Ship].

flapjack ('flæpdʒæk). [f. FLAP *v.* (sense 4 a) + JACK.]

1. a. A flat cake, a pan-cake. **b.** An apple turnover or flat tart, an 'apple-jack'.

c **1600** DAY *Begg. Bednall Gr.* v. (1881) 114 My Mother.. could have taught thee how to a made butters and flap-jacks. **1620** TAYLOR (Water-P.) *Jack-a-Lent* Bij, A Flap-iack, which in our translation is call'd a Pancake. **1641** BROME *Joviall Crew* II. Wks. 1873 III. 376 Flapiacks, and Pan-puddings. **1825** J. NEAL *Bro. Jonathan* I. 272 Like a flap-jack in a fryin' pan. **1842** HAWTHORNE *Amer. Note-bks.* (1883) 303 We had a splendid breakfast of flapjacks, or slapjacks, and whortleberries. **1871** M. A. BARKER *Christmas Cake in Four Quarters* 294 We told Munro we'd have his flap-jacks for second course. **1945** A. P. HARPER *Camping & Bushcraft in N.Z.* i. 21 To make a flap-jack, mix some flour and baking powder into a thick paste.
Comb. **1872** C. KING *Mountain. Sierra Nev.* vii. 135 Longhurst came upon the boards as a flapjack-frier.

c. A biscuit usu. containing rolled oats, syrup, etc. (Not known to some correspondents in S. England.)

1935 M. STRUAN *Pop. Home Cookery* 234 *Date Flap-jacks.* .. Cream the butter and sugar and when they are soft work in the rolled oats. Press half the mixture in a well-buttered tin, and spread with the dates. **1942** *Radiation Cookery Bk.* (ed. 24) 149 Flap Jacks. Ingredients. 6 oz. butter or margarine. 8 oz. rolled oats. 6 oz. Demerara sugar. Pinch of salt. **1950** *Good Housek. Tea-Time Fare* 34 Syrup Flapjack. .. Melt the margarine, sugar and syrup together, add the rolled oats..and bake it in a moderately hot oven. When the flapjack is golden-brown, remove it from oven. **1962** *Guardian* 17 Nov. 12/6 A proper recipe for genuine oats-and-treacle flapjacks.

2. a. A kind of hydraulic machine (see quot. 1842). **b.** *dial.* The lapwing.

1842 TAYLOR in *Proc. Inst. Civ. Eng.* II. 102 For low falls [of water] there were many machines..for instance..the old 'flap-jack', with a reservoir of water at one end of a beam and a pump at the other. **1847** HALLIWELL, *Flap-jack*, the lapwing. *Suffolk.*

3. A vanity case for face-powder.

1934 *Punch* 16 May 553/3 A flapjack with a powder-puff Might well be indiscreet [as a present]. **1941** S. GIBBONS *Rich House* vii. 75 Slowly opening her handbag and taking out her flapjack.

flapless ('flæplɪs), *a.* [f. FLAP *sb.* + -LESS.] Without a flap.

1916 JOYCE *Portrait of Artist* iv. 195 His Norfolk coat with the flapless sidepockets. **1928** *Daily Express* 2 May 8 Your tailor may insist..that pocket flaps break the line of the waist and will cut your lounge jacket with jetted, or flapless, pockets.

flapped (flæpt), *ppl. a.* [f. FLAP *sb.* + -ED[2].]

1. Of the cheek or ear: Formed like a flap; pendulous.

1661 K. W. *Conf. Charac.*, *Informer* (1860) 47 Why his reverend ears would serve very well for two leathern patches, to sow to each side his flapt jaws. **1840** DICKENS *Old C. Shop* xlviii, The dwarf put his hand to his great flapped ear.

2. Of a hat or garment: Having a flap or flaps.

1748 RICHARDSON *Clarissa* (1811) V. viii. 90, I turned up my flapt slouched hat. **1780** J. ADAMS *Diary* 1 Jan. Wks. 1851 III. 246 A little hat covered with oil cloth, flapped before. **1848** MRS. JAMESON *Sacr. & Leg. Art* (1850) 141 The scallop-shell..on his flapped hat. **1860** HAWTHORNE *Fr. & It. Jrnls.* II. 303 Square-skirted coat, flapped waist-coat, and all the queer costume of the period.

flapper ('flæpə(r)), *sb.*[1] [f. FLAP *v.* + -ER[1].] One who or that which flaps, in senses of the vb.

1. One who flaps or strikes another. Hence (after Swift): A person who arouses the attention or jogs the memory; a remembrancer. Also, of a thing: A reminder.

1726 SWIFT *Gulliver* III. ii. 17 [The absent-minded philosophers of Laputa] always keep a *Flapper*..in their Family..And the Business of this Officer is..gently to strike with his Bladder the Mouth of him who is to speak, and the Right Ear of him..to whom the Speaker addresseth himself. **1747** CHESTERF. *Lett.* xcix. (1774) I. 291, I write to you..by way of flapper, to put you in mind of yourself. **1852** *Blackw. Mag.* LXXI. 85 There is some advantage in having a flapper to remind us of our faults.

2. a. Something flat to strike with; a fly-flap.

1570 LEVINS *Manip.* 72/2 A flapper, *flabellum.* **1783** WOLCOTT (P. Pindar) *Ode R. Academicians* ii. Wks. 1812 I. 55 For flies most charming flappers. **1884** *Pall Mall G.* 15 Aug. 4/2 The captain sat..with a flapper specially made for the slaughter of the vermin at his right hand.
fig. **1612** tr. *Benvenuto's Passenger* I. v. 35 An effectuall flapper to driue away the Flies of all worldly vanities.

b. Something broad and flat used for making a noise by striking.

1825 SCOTT *Talism.* xi, They..clanged their flappers in emulation of each other. **1888** ELWORTHY *W. Somerset Word-bk.*, *Flappers*, clappers for frightening birds. The loose parts are generally called the flappers. **1889** *Cent. Dict.*, *Flapper*..5. *pl.*, very long shoes worn by negro minstrels.

3. A young wild duck or partridge.

1747 MRS. GLASSE *Art of Cookery* xxi. 162 Wild Ducks, called Flappers or Moulters. **1773** G. WHITE *Selborne* xxxix. 99, I saw young teals taken alive..along with flappers, or young wild-ducks. **1809** MAR. EDGEWORTH *Tales Fashion. Life*, *Manœuvring* xiv, Lightbody happened to be gone out to shoot flappers. *a* **1825** in FORBY *Voc. E. Anglia.* **1888** *Berksh. Gloss.*, *Vlapper*, a young partridge just able to fly.

4. a. Something hanging flat and loose; *spec.* the striking part of a flail, a swingle.

1854 LOWELL *Jrnl. Italy* Prose Wks. 1890 I. 194 He lifts the heavy leathern flapper over the door. **1862** THORNBURY *Turner* I. 5 Her hair is..surmounted by a cap with large flappers. **1893** BARING-GOULD *Cheap Jack Z.* I. 37 Runham, flourishing his flail over his head, and throwing out the flapper in the direction of Drownlands.

b. A broad fin or flipper; the tail of a crustacean.

1836 MARRYAT *Midsh. Easy* xxiv, With hands as broad as the flappers of a turtle. **1876** MISS BUCKLEY *Short Hist. Nat. Sc.* xl. 421 The hand of a man, and the flapper of a porpoise. **1880** HUXLEY *Crayfish* i. 20 These two plates on each side, with the telson in the middle, constitute the flapper of the crayfish.

c. *slang.* The hand. (Cf. *flipper*).

[**1768–74** TUCKER *Lt. Nat.* (1852) I. 441 He thrust out a couple of broad arms, or rather flappers.] **1833** MARRYAT *P. Simple* (1863) 201 'My dear Mr. Simple, extend your flapper to me'. **1868** *Lessons Mid. Age* 19 'Come, Frank, and extend the flapper of friendship'.

d. (See quot.)

1856 WHYTE MELVILLE *Kate Cov.* xviii, Two well-mounted officials, termed..'flappers' by disrespectful sportsmen; but whose duty, it appears, is to keep the chase in view till it either beats them off for pace, or leaves them 'planted' at some large awkward impediment.

e. *Racing slang.* = FLAPPING *vbl. sb.* 4.

1928 *Weekly Dispatch* 24 June 2 No flapper meetings for me.

5. Something hanging or working by or as by a hinge. In *pl.* = CLAPNET.

1796 J. OWEN *Trav. Europe* I. 265 The stranger came up, claimed the flappers, and told us, they were 'pour attraper les papillons'. **1839–47** TODD *Cycl. Anat.* III. 958/1 The opercular bones, forming flappers which open and shut the openings of the branchiæ. **1883** GRESLEY *Gloss. Coal Mining* 110 The flappers or doors..fall to or close of themselves.

6. *attrib.* and *Comb.* as ***flapper-shooting*** (sense 3); also **flapper-bag** (see quot.); **flapper-dock**, (*a*) = *flap-dock*; (*b*) (see quots.); **flapper-skate** (see quot.).

1871 *N. & Q.* Ser. IV. VIII. 143/1 *Flapper-bags, burdocks, or what is better known in Scotland as docken. **1886** BRITTEN & HOLLAND *Plant-n.* Suppl., *Flapper Dock, the large leaves of the Colt's foot. Probably *Petasites vulgaris.* **1865** *Standard* 43 July 5 Mr. Clutterbuck.. proceeded..up the Brousa for the purpose of *flapper shooting. **1839** YARRELL *Brit. Fishes* II. Suppl. 66 *Raia intermedia*, *Flapper Skate. **1886** GÜNTHER in *Encycl. Brit.* XX. 299/2 The Flapper Skate (*R. macrorhynchus*).

Hence **'flapper** *v. intr.*, to move like a flapper, i.e. with a loose flapping motion.

1835 HOGG in *Fraser's Mag.* XI. 359 The two serpents came flappering on. **1862** J. F. CAMPBELL *Tales W. Highlands* IV. 140 The three great flappering sails. **1869** *Lonsdale Gloss.*, *Flapper*, to quiver, flutter.

flapper ('flæpə(r)), *sb.*[2] *slang.* [Commonly supposed to be a fig. use of sense 3 ('young wild duck or partridge') of FLAPPER *sb.*[1] (cf. the G. equivalent *backfisch* perch, fish for frying); but the earlier use ('immoral young girl') app. connects the word with mod. north. dial. (Northumb. and Durham) *flap* ('an unsteady young woman', Halliwell); see FLAP *sb.* 9.]

† **1.** (See quots.) *Obs.*

1889 BARRÈRE & LELAND *Dict. Slang*, *Flippers, flappers*, very young girls trained to vice. **1893** FARMER *Slang*, *Flapper*..(3) A very young prostitute. **1909** J. R. WARE *Passing Eng.*, *Flapper*, a very immoral young girl in her early 'teens'.

2. A girl in her late teens, orig. one with her hair down in a pigtail; a young woman, esp. with an implication of flightiness or lack of decorum. *slang* or *colloq.*

1888 B. LOWSLEY *Berkshire Gloss.*, *Vlapper*,..applied in joke to a girl of the bread-and-butter age. [**1893** FARMER *Slang*, *Flapper.* 2... A little girl.] **1903** D. F. T. COKE *Sandford of Merton* iii, There's a stunning flapper. **1905** D. SLADEN *Playing Game* I. ix, A red-faced flapper, with a lot of freckles and a pigtail. **1906** *Varsity* 18 Oct. 23/1 Here we were in tight uniforms stepping out to raucous bugles beneath the eyes of many 'flappers'. **1909** *Tatler* 30 June 149 The first appearance of a 'flapper' at a ladies' golf championship was in 1895,..in these two long-haired, long-legged colleens were the two most famous lady golfers the world has yet produced. **1915** *Home Chat* 6 Nov. 237/1 She was the jolliest flapper I had seen, with her long plait of hair down her back. **1927** *Punch* 30 Nov. 591 'Flapper' is the popular press catch-word for an adult woman worker, aged twenty-one to thirty, when it is a question of giving her the vote under the same conditions as men of the same age. **1928** *Ibid.* 30 May 605 Attention was called in the Upper House to the conspicuous absence of the Peer who had violently attacked what he was pleased to call the 'Flappers' Vote' in his Press. **1929** H. A. VACHELL *Virgin* i. 22 She had behaved like a flapper. **1936** F. CLUNE *Roaming round Darling* ix. 76 A modern flapper, wearing slacks and a beret, riding a man's bicycle, passed.

b. *attrib.*, as ***flapper cousin***, etc.; **flapper-bracket, -seat**, a seat at the back of a bicycle to accommodate a young woman; **flapper vote**, a contemptuous expression for the parliamentary vote which was granted to women of 21 years and over by Act of Parliament in 1928; so ***flapper voter***.

1909 *Tatler* 30 June 149/2 The flapper brigade is a force [at golf] which grows every year. **1916** B. RUCK *Girls at his Billet* ii, As long as [I] can persuade her to let me take her out on the flapper-bracket of my motor-bike. **1917** *Church Q. Rev.* July 317 Educated India..is still possibly at the flapper age, a little awkward..but full of the joy of life. **1921** S. THOMPSON *Rough Crossing* ii. §3 The..attention bestowed ..by her 'flapper' cousins on these ordinary, pleasant-faced young men. **1923** U. L. SILBERRAD *Lett. J. Armiter* xiii, She was thrown off the flapper-seat of a motor-cycle. **1928** *Hansard Commons* 29 Mar. 1414 As to all this talk about the flapper vote, I want to know whether the flapper vote is to keep off the register these 2,000,000 women who are merely excluded at the present moment by a technicality. **1928** *John Blunt* 11 Aug. 2/1 Ten thousand new flapper voters. **1933** O. SITWELL *Miracle on Sinai* 353 An old..opponent of—as it had been called—the Flapper Vote. **1957** *Observer* 8 Sept. 7/2 Mrs. Rosenthal, who launched the 'Maiden-form' brassiere thirty-three years ago at the height of the flapper era.., sent me over from New York the original sketch of this most modest, flattened bust-line.

Hence **'flapperdom**, (*a*) = *flapperhood*; (*b*) flappers collectively; **'flapperhood, 'flapperism**, the condition of being a flapper; **'flapperish** *a.*, pertaining to or characteristic of a flapper or flappers.

1907 'I. HAY' *Pip* I. vi. 157 She was in the last stages of what slangy young men call 'flapperdom', and her hair was gathered on the nape of her neck with a big black bow. *Ibid.* II. vii. 216 The flapper going so far as to ask her two admirers for a quotation of odds—in the current coin of flapperdom, chocolates. **1922** M. SADLEIR *Excurs. Vict. Bibliogr.* 5 Brought up on Jane Austen, Scott, and Dickens, I read, during my years of flapperdom, Marryat, Trollope, and Wilkie Collins. **1905** D. SLADEN *Playing Game* II. ix, That was during her childish beauty, before she passed into red-faced flapperhood. **1921** *Times Lit. Suppl.* 16 June 377/2 The first full-grown, full-blown stories which their mothers considered suitable for their years of flapperhood. **1920** W. J. LOCKE *House of Baltazar* xvii, Her inconsequence and flapperish immaturity. **1927** *Manch. Guardian Weekly* 2 Dec. Suppl. p. xiii/1 This array of flapperish literature, which makes our desk look younger than it has done for years. **1961** I. MURDOCH *Severed Head* xxvii. 235 'Oh, I *do* love you!' She embraced me in a flapperish manner, lifting one high-heeled foot impetuously behind her. **1909** *Tatler* 30 June 149/2 Whilst the elder [sister]..wears her hair on high, the younger..has still a year or more of flapperism. **1927** *Sunday Express* 14 Aug. 4 She represents the essence of youth and flapperism.

† **flappet** ('flæpɪt). *Obs.* In 7 flapet, 8 flappit. [f. FLAP *sb.* + -ET[1].] A little flap (FLAP *sb.* 4 b, and 5); also in *pl.* finery, fallals.

1575 LANEHAM *Let.* (1871) 24 Yet durst he..wype hiz face, with the flapet of his fatherz iacket. **1611** BEAUM. & FL. *Knt. Burn. Pestle* I. iii, What brave spirit could be content to sit in his shop with a flapet of Wood, and a blew Apron before him. **1728** VANBR. & CIB. *Prov. Husb.* I. i, They sell ribbons and flappits, and other sort of geer for gentle-women.

flapping (ˈflæpɪŋ), *vbl. sb.* [f. FLAP *v.* + -ING[1].]
†**1.** The action of knocking or beating; also *attrib. Obs.*
1629 GAULE *Pract. Th.* 335 He's made their flapping, flouting, spawling Sport. *a* **1693** URQUHART *Rabelais* III. xl. 331 The banging and flapping of him.
2. The action of moving (wings) up and down.
1398 TREVISA *Barth. De P.R.* XII. xiii. (1495) 422 By contynual flappynge of wynges the gnatte makyth noyse in the ayre. **1824** LAMB *Elia* Ser. II. *Blakesmoor in H——shire*, The hum and flappings of that one solitary wasp. **1843** LEVER *J. Hinton* xxxiv, The heavy flapping of strong wing would point the course of a heron.
3. a. The action of swaying or working to and fro something broad and loose.
1631 J. TAYLOR (Water P.) *Turn. Fort. Wheel* (1848) 13 They hold your blessinge in no more avayle Then is the flapping of a fox his taile! **1841–71** T. R. JONES *Anim. Kingd.* (ed. 4) 603 By vigorous flappings of this extensive organ, the animal [the poulpe] actively impels itself through the water in a backward direction.
b. *Aeronaut.* The angular up-and-down oscillation of the blade of a helicopter about its hinge. Also *attrib.*
1937 *Jrnl. R. Aeronaut. Soc.* XLI. 820 Although the airscrew may be at an angle, I will call the first flapping 'vertical flapping' and the second 'horizontal flapping'. **1940** H. E. BAUGHMAN *Aviation Dict.* 80/1 *Flapping angle*, the difference between the coning angle and the instantaneous angle of the span axis of a blade of a rotary wing system. **1949** *Aircraft Engin.* Feb. 33/1 Don Juan de la Cierva, father of rotating wing aircraft, introduced a very ingenious but simple invention, the flapping blade. **1950** *Gloss. Aeronaut. Terms (B.S.I.)* I. 44 *Flapping angle*, the angle between the tip-path plane and the plane normal to the hub axis. *Ibid.* 45 *Flapping hinge*, a pivot which allows the zenithal angle of the blade to be varied with respect to the rotor head. **1955** LIPTROT & WOODS *Rotorcraft* v. 43 In forward flight the advancing blade moves upwards about the hinge..the retreating side moves downward... It is this motion about the mean coning position, due to this dissymmetry of lift, which is known as 'flapping'.
4. *Racing slang.* A form of racing which is not subject to Jockey Club or National Hunt Committee regulations, or, in greyhound racing, to those of the National Greyhound Racing Club.
1911 *Queen* 8 Apr. 581/1 In racing parlance there are three sorts of racing, 'the flat', 'over the sticks', and 'flapping'. The first is the spring, summer, and autumn sport, the second is the winter sport of steeplechasing, and the third either form of racing which takes place neither under Jockey Club nor National Hunt regulations. **1916** *Daily Express* 9 Sept. 3/5 There was trouble at the 'flapping' meeting at Blaydon..on Saturday. **1928** *Daily Tel.* 14 Feb. 11/5 'Flapping Meetings'..will not be exempted by the bill from the provisions of the Betting Act, 1853. **1947** F. TOMLINSON in *Police Jrnl.* July–Sept. (*title*) The 'Flapping Track' [of a greyhound-racing stadium]. **1955** *Daily Tel.* 27 Apr. 7/3 The Inspr. said: 'By injecting them [*sc.* greyhounds] with this stuff?' and Selby said 'Yes.' Asked if he realised it was illegal, Selby replied: 'Never. I only do it at flapping tracks.' **1969** C. DRUMMOND *Odds on Death* vi. 136 The old 'flapping' meetings.

ˈ**flapping**, *ppl. a.* [+ -ING[2].] That flaps. Applied *spec.* to the upward and downward movement of the wings of birds and, formerly, of flying machines. So ***flapping flight***, etc.
1592 WYRLEY *Armorie* 144 The flapping brace strikes off his setled hood. **1706** *Lond. Gaz.* No. 4236/4 A dark brown Mare..with flapping Ears. **1711** GAY *Trivia* I. 128 Beneath his flapping Hat secures his Hair. *a* **1857** G. CAYLEY *Let.* in C. H. Gibbs-Smith *Cayley's Aeronaut.* (1962) xlii. 135 You must mind, when you couple the flapping wings to the handle that works them, that the connecting rod takes [?] into the butt end of the wing rod at such a distance from the hinge of the wing as to allow the hand of the person working [it] to go through two feet, whilst the tip end of the wing just completes its full range. **1859** GEO. ELIOT *A. Bede* 414 Totty trotted off in her flapping bonnet. **1864** MISS BRADDON *H. Dunbar* I. xvi. 285 She took the great flapping ears of the animal in her two hands. **1899** *Aeronaut. Jrnl.* July 59/1 (*title*) On Flapping Flight of Aeroplanes. *Ibid.*, The older mathematical investigation by Navier of the problem of flapping flight, seems to be quite discredited. **1906** *Sci. Amer.* 18 Aug. 117 (*caption*) The Florencie Orthopter, or Flapping-Wing Machine. **1909** *Flight* 20 Feb. 99/2 The question is..what fundamental qualities of a flapping-flight machine assimilates its wings to those of the bird. **1921** *Ibid.* 15 Sept. 621/2 (*title*) Problem of Flapping Flight. **1954** BANNERMAN *Birds Brit. Isles* III. 133 The feathers are raised, the tail widely spread and raised and lowered at various angles..and the flapping flight indulged in.

†**flappish** (ˈflæpɪʃ), *a. Obs.*[−1] [f. FLAP *v.* + -ISH[1].] Inclined to swing or toss loosely about.
1665 HOWARD *Committee* IV. 119 You are so flappish, you throw um [your keys] up and Down at your tail.

flappy (ˈflæpɪ), *a.* [f. FLAP *v.* + -Y[1].]
†**1.** = FLABBY *a.* 1. *Obs.*
1598 FLORIO, *Impassire*..to grow flappy, withered, or wrimpled [**1611** to grow flappie and wrimpled].
2. *dial.* (See quots.)
1846 BROCKETT *N.C. Words* (ed. 3) *Flappy*, wild, irregular, unsteady. 'An old flappy body'. **1892** *Northumbld. Gloss.*, *Flappy*, uneven, unsteady. 'The carpet's lyin' aall flappy'.
3. That flaps.
1905 CHESTERTON *Club of Queer Trades* iii. 91 He rose.. flapping like a seal... He flapped a plaid shawl over his.. arm..he flapped his eyelids... He was a..clergyman, of a flappy and floppy type. **1908** *Daily Chron.* 9 Oct. 7/1 Sailors, with bare feet and flappy blue trousers. **1924** *Scribner's Mag.* Aug. 200/2 A flappy little bag of gray and silver beads. **1965** M. BRADBURY *Stepping Westward* iv. 205 Old ladies in flappy dresses.

†ˈ**flap-sauce.** *Obs.* [f. FLAP *v.* + SAUCE *sb.*] A glutton.
1540 PALSGR. *Acolastus* III. i. N iv b, Nowe hathe this glutton .i. this flappe sawce (the thyng) that he may plentuously swallowe downe hole.

†**flapse** (flæps). *Obs.* [Cf. Ger. *flaps* of similar meaning.] An impudent fellow.
a **1652** BROME *New Acad.* IV. ii, You are a Flapse to terme my sonne so.

flare (flɛə(r)). *sb.*[1] Also (in sense 4) 9 **flair.** [f. FLARE *v.* Not in Johnson or Todd.]
1. a. The action or quality of flaring, or giving forth a dazzling and unsteady light; dazzling but irregular light, like that of torches; a sudden outburst of flame. Also *fig.* Obtrusive display, ostentation, etc.; *spec.*, a sudden or loud noise, a fanfare.
1814 SCOTT *Ld. of Isles* I. xxviii, Lighted by the torches' flare. **1834** DICKENS *Let.* 3 Sept. (1965) I. 40 An unpremeditated flare at the English Opera House last night with the ladies. **1837** CARLYLE *Fr. Rev.* (1857) I. I. III. viii. 80 Gardes Suisses: marching..in the flare of torchlight. **1848** THACKERAY *Van. Fair* xix, We should all come home after the flare, and the noise, and the gayety. **1888** *Pall Mall G.* 6 Sept. 8/2 Flares of dazzling crimson and purple shot up from the mouth of the crater. **1888** *Sci. Amer.* N.S. LVIII. 21 Too modest for business push and flare. **1916** E. POUND *Lustra* 97 Since he died My wit and worth are cobwebs brushed aside In the full flare of grief. **1928** *Daily Tel.* 17 Jan. 10/7 After the service was over, amid a flare of trumpets, the procession returned through the Cathedral. **1946** MEZZROW & WOLFE *Really Blues* xv. 264 Flares were always in the right places, to help build up the pulse. **1962** A. NISBETT *Technique Sound Studio* 242 s.v. *Bass*, The most efficient way of producing bass is an acoustic exponential horn, preferably with a low rate of flare.
b. *Astr.* A sudden increase in brightness of part of the sun as seen at certain visible and ultra-violet wavelengths. Also *solar flare*.
1937 *News Service Bull., School Ed.* (Carnegie Inst. Washington) 24 Oct. 153/3 Bright flares of hydrogen light were visible on the Sun. *Ibid.*, It is believed that all of these fade-outs occur simultaneously with solar eruptions—absence of solar observations some times accounting for the failure of any astronomer to report observation of a flare. **1956** H. SPENCER JONES in A. Pryce-Jones *New Outl. Mod. Knowl.* 121 A violent disturbance will not infrequently occur, in which a localized region of the Sun becomes intensely bright. Coincident with this eruption or *flare*, as it is termed, there is a sudden and complete fading on short-wave radio transmissions in channels passing over the sunlit face of the Earth. **1963** H. J. & E. v. P. SMITH *Solar Flares* p. xii, Flares occur in the solar atmosphere and are closely associated with sunspots and other aspects of solar activity.
c. *Astr.* Any sudden and short-lived increase in the overall brightness of a star other than the sun. So ***flare star***, a star in which flares occur from time to time.
1949 *Publ. Astron. Soc. Pacific* LXI. 179 The plate with the Selected Area shows the star in the process of one of its flares. **1951** *Ibid.* LXIII. 142 Krüger 60 B..is the only flare star for which the mass is known. **1956** C. PAYNE-GAPOSCHKIN *Introd. Astron.* xi. 264 A solar flare brightens the whole light of the sun only slightly, but on a cool star a flare may more than double the star's total brightness. **1964** *New Scientist* 19 Mar. 760/1 A flare star is a particular type of variable star which produces an almost undetectable burst of radio emission at the same time as it flares up to become visually brighter.
2. *Naut.* **a.** = FLARE-UP 3. Also in military, aeronautical, and general use; also *attrib.* (see quots. 1918 and 1956 and FLARE PATH). **b.** A combustible made to be burnt as a night-signal at sea, and formerly as a railway fog-signal.
1883 W. C. RUSSELL *Sailor's Lang.* 52 *Flare*, a light made by firing a tar-barrel, etc. **1883** *Fisheries Exhib. Catal.* 41 Boat Launching Flare. **1885** *Law Times Rep.* LIII. 60/1 The I.C.U...burnt flares over her quarter. **1887** *Pall Mall G.* 10 Jan., 'Flares' were burned for the purpose of warning the drivers of trains. **1889** W. RYE *Cromer* 10 'Flares' are burned sometimes to warn mariners on bad nights. **1912** *Aeroplane* 5 Dec. 565/1 Were the flares lighted in order that our own airship should know where to alight? **1915** *Times* 14 Apr. 7/6 The enemy fires some flares across to us, and this is a good sign, for it shows they are afraid of an attack from us. **1916** 'BOYD CABLE' *Action Front* 48 Magnesium flares. **1918** E. S. FARROW *Dict. Mil. Terms* 235 *Flare*, an unsteady, dazzling light used as an illumination and in signaling: in aëronautics, a guide for landing. *Flare lights*, lights used in combination with obstacles, either protected or screened, to prevent the enemy removing them. They are screened in rear so that the defenders may remain in shadow. *Flare pistol*, a large pistol, which looks like a sawed-off shot-gun, from which flares are fired. **1925** N. E. ODELL in E. F. Norton *Fight for Everest, 1924* 134 We watched till late that night for some signs of Mallory and Irvine's return, or even an indication by flare of distress. **1941** *Times Weekly* 15 Oct. 6 Flares dropped by British air-craft hung almost stationary in the air, causing a bright glow over the French coast. **1942** *Aeroplane Spotter* 23 Apr. 101 Flare chutes. **1943** T. HORSLEY *Find, Fix & Strike* 81 In conjunction with dive bombing, and collateral with it, their [Albacores'] suitability as flare droppers was equally well marked. **1944** *Conc. Oxf. Dict.* Add., *Flare*,.. container of combustible material, dropped from aircraft to illuminate target area etc. **1956** W. A. HEFLIN *U.S.A.F. Dict.* 208/1 *Flare chute*, a parachute attached to a flare for letting the flare down slowly. **1965** *Observer* 11 July 1/1 American 'flare-ship' aircraft..continually illuminated our positions at night.
3. *Photogr.* (See quot. 1968). Also, a similar appearance in the object-glass of a telescope.
1867 SUTTON & DAWSON *Dict. Photogr.* (ed. 2) 119 *Flare*, stray light falling upon the sensitive plate during its exposure in the camera. When certain forms of double or triple compound lenses are used, and the camera is turned towards a strong light,..a circular spot of flare is sometimes seen in the centre of the ground glass. **1868** LEA *Photogr.* 88 Flare or ghost in the camera is an indistinct image of the diaphragm. **1878** LOCKYER *Stargazing* II. xi. 140 A 'flare' appearing, shows a want of a slight alteration of the setting screw, on the same side of the object-glass as the 'flare' or elongation appears. **1968** *Gloss. Terms Offset Lithogr. Printing (B.S.I.)* 14 *Flare*, non-image light that reaches the light-sensitive material in the camera, usually caused by surface reflections in the optical system, extraneous light and/or reflection from sources other than the original. **1971** *Amateur Photographer* 13 Jan. 54/1 Of his dozen or so entries about 10 were ruined because of considerable flare—caused by internal lens reflections.
4. a. *Ship-build.* Gradual swell or bulging outwards and upwards. Cf. FLARE *v.* 4.
1833 T. RICHARDSON *Merc. Marine Archit.* 1 To give them more flair in the stem-head. **1882** PAYNE-GALLWEY *Fowler in Irel.* 25 The sides are nearly upright with little flare.
b. *transf.* A gradual widening or spreading outwards; also, that part which spreads. Also *attrib.* In *pl.*, flared trousers (orig. *U.S.*).
a **1910** 'O. HENRY' *Trimmed Lamp* (1916) 8 Her skirt is shoddy, but has the correct flare. **1916** STANFORD & FORSYTH *Hist. Music* 186 The shawm-player prefers to place his lips..on the widened rim or 'flare' at the top of the pipe. **1929** *Star* 21 Aug. 2/4 Cut..with the new smart waist line and full flare skirt. **1964** *N.Y. Post* 10 Nov. 72 (Advt.), Belted coats, skimmers, flares, demi-fits, the 'in' silhouettes for dress and casual wear! **1970** *Toronto Daily Star* 24 Sept. 19/1 (Advt.), Flares..cords..denim bells. **1973** *To our Returned Prisoners of War* (U.S. Office of Secretary of Defense) 4 *Flares*, pants which widen as they get to the ankle. Almost like the Navy Bell Bottoms. **1985** S. LOWRY *Young Fogey Handbk.* vi. 52 The rest of the male world sported peach cord flares.
c. = FLARE-OUT 2.
1967 J. FAY *Helicopter* (ed. 2) viii. 120 Whereas at high speed a flare could..produce a momentary climb the only practical result of a flare at low speed would be to change the fuselage attitude. **1967** D. P. DAVIES *Handling Big Jets* vii. 213 Keep the stabiliser in trim so that full elevator effectiveness is available for the flare. **1969** I. KEMP *Brit. G.I. in Vietnam* iii. 53 Gradually the nose came up and our speed dropped until we were barely moving forward and beginning to go into a 'flare'—that is when the helicopter's nose is up and the tail down, just before she starts to hover.
5. *attrib.* and *Comb.*, as ***flare-light***; also **flare-lamp**, a lamp with an unprotected flame; **flare-spot** (= sense 3); **flare-tin**, a tin vessel in which powder or other combustible material is burnt as a signal at sea.
1891 R. KIPLING *City Dreadf. Nt.* 83 We don't know what fire-damp is here. We can use the *flare-lamps. **1894** *Westm. Gaz.* 1 Dec. 6/3 A *flare light was observed from the barque. **1893** ABNEY *Photogr.* xxxi. (ed. 8) 219 *'Flare spot.' **1884** W. C. RUSSELL *Jack's Courtsh.* III. xiii, There was a *flare-tin aboard, and from time to time we burnt this over the rail.

flare (flɛə(r)), *sb.*[2] *dial.* [Of unknown origin; cf. the synonymous FLEED.] The 'leaf' or fat about the kidneys of a pig. Also *attrib.*
1847 HALLIWELL, *Flare*, fat round a pig's kidney. **1851** MAYHEW *Lond. Labour* I. 199 Flare-cakes..are round cakes, made of flour and 'unrendered' (unmelted) lard, and stuck over freely with currants. **1881** *Oxfordsh. Gloss.* Suppl., *Fleeurn*, the leaf of a pig (Holton), *fleeur* (Yarnton.) **1888** *Lond. Tradesm. Advt.* This Lard..is made from the best Pork Flare only.

flare, *sb.*[3]: var. of FLAIR *sb.*[2], the skate.

flare (flɛə(r)), *v.* Also 6 **fleare**; 7 **flaire**, 7–9 **flair.** [Of unknown etymology; the mod.Norw. *flara* 'to blaze, to flaunt in gaudy attire' (Ivar Aasen) has been compared; but sense 5, with which this agrees, is app. a somewhat late development.]
1. *trans.* †**a.** To spread out (hair); to display in an expanded form. Also with *out. Obs.*
c **1550** *Robin Conscience* 289 in Hazl. *E.E.P.* III. 244 To dye and to fleare your haire so abroad..you doo it shamfully use. **1553** BECON *Jewel Joy* J vj b, It is inough for chast and pure maydes to weare..simple apparell..wythout the flaringe out and coleryng of theyr heare.
b. To spread out to view, display; occas. with mixture of sense 5. Hence, To wave to and fro (or *round*). ***to flare a handkerchief*** (slang): to whisk it out of a person's pocket.
a **1774** GOLDSM. *Surv. Exper. Philos.* (1776) II. 182 In seeing a flaming torch, if flared round in a circle, it appears as a ring of fire. **1838** POE *A.G. Pym* Wks. 1864 IV. 116 We ..began instantly to make every signal in our power, by flaring the shirts in the air. **1851** MAYHEW *Lond. Labour* I. 411/1 Just after that I flared it (whisked the handkerchief out). **1862** BURTON *Bk. Hunter* (1863) 292 Those who flare their qualities before the world. **1884** F. J. BRITTEN *Watch & Clockm.* 96 Hardening the drill by flaring it in the air.
†**2.** *intr.* Of hair, etc.: To spread out conspicuously, to stream or wave in the wind. *Obs.*
1579–80 NORTH *Plutarch* (1676) 667 This Lady..shewing her mourning Apparell, and hair of her head flaring about her eyes. **1598** SHAKS. *Merry W.* IV. vi. 42 Ribonds-pendant, flaring 'bout her head. **1602** MARSTON *Antonio's Rev.* III. ii, Let flare my loosed hair. **1676** HOBBES *Iliad* (1677) 336 His plume by Vulcan made of golden hair..ore his shoulders terribly did flare. **1837** COOPER *Recoll. Europe* II. 131 Her cap flared in the wind.
†**3.** To display oneself conspicuously. *Obs.*

1633 T. ADAMS *Exp. 2 Peter* i. 6 The daughters of Moab and Midian..light housewives, dancing, frisking, and flaring. **1709** PRIOR *Hans Carvel* 90 The Truth is this I cannot stay Flaring in Sun-shine all the Day.

4. a. *intr.* Of the sides of a vessel: To swell or bulge out gradually upwards; also, ***to flare over***.

1644 *Sea-man's Dict.* 40 When a ship is a little howled in neere the water, and above that the work doth hang over againe..they say, that the worke doth Flaire over. **1836** W. IRVING *Astoria* (1849) 86 Their gunwales flare outwards. **1883** *Harper's Mag.* July 934/2 It will be best to have the sides of our oblong diving-bell flare a little.

b. *trans.* To cause to spread gradually outwards.

1857 COLQUHOUN *Compl. Oarsman's Guide* 1 A skiff..can be more conveniently flared, which gives buoyancy. **1858** MAURY *Phys. Geog. Sea* ii. §61 These pipes are then flared out so as to present a large cooling surface. **1888** WOODGATE *Boating* 143 The gunwale was..flared out wide at these points.

c. *intr.* To open or spread outwards, as the sides of a bowl, a skirt, the mouth of a horn.

1835 C. F. HOFFMAN *Winter in Far West* II. 246 Finally, it [*sc.* the vault] flares upward, so that the edges of the arch lose themselves in the projecting face of the cliff. **1857**, etc. [see FLARING *ppl. a.* 3]. **1899** *Daily News* 27 Feb. 6/6 The fronts of the short coat flare open to show a gathered lace vest. **1930** *Times* 17 Mar. 15/6 A skirt slightly flared about the hem. **1968** J. IRONSIDE *Fashion Alphabet* 44 A culotte skirt..is any divided skirt, though usually one flared from the hip.

d. *intr.* To make the glide path of an aircraft about to land gradually less steep until it is parallel to the ground; to raise the nose of an aircraft when doing this; also *trans.*, to cause (an aircraft) to descend in this way. Also with *out*.

1935 [implied at *flared ppl. a.* below]. **1944** W. LANGEWIESCHE *Stick & Rudder* xii. 216 Because of this steeper glide, the heavily wing-loaded ship has more upward turning to do in the flare-out. This makes it necessary to flare out even earlier, even higher. **1951** *Jrnl. R. Aeronaut. Soc.* LV. 526/1 The pilot shuts off power, glides down on to the deck, flares out just before contact. **1967** J. FAY *Helicopter* (ed. 2) viii. 120 Flaring, i.e...easing back on the stick and flattening the glide path. *Ibid.* 121 At high speed, the helicopter is flared gradually with the collective-pitch lever held down all the time. **1967** D. P. DAVIES *Handling Big Jets* vii. 213 From the threshold on, simply flare (if necessary), reduce to idle thrust, *push* off drift (if necessary), then land. **1969** I. KEMP *Brit. G.I. in Vietnam* iii. 72 Hayes followed the routine procedure of 'flaring' the helicopter before descent—letting the tail drop and the nose come up to reduce airspeed—and then dropping her vertically with the collective.

5. a. *intr.* Of a candle, lamp, etc.: To burn with a spreading, unsteady flame, as when blown by the wind; to shine as such a flame does; to glow with or as with flame. Also with *about*, *away*, *out*, and quasi-*trans.* with cognate *obj.* ***to flare into***: to pass with a flare into.

1632, 1633, 1661 [see FLARING *ppl. a.*] *a* **1700** B. E. *Dict. Cant. Crew, Flare*, to Shine or glare like a Comet or Beacon. **1727** BAILEY vol. II, *Flaring*, wasting or consuming wastfully; as a Candle. **1794** MRS. RADCLIFFE *Myst. Udolpho* xxvi, The wind made the torch flare. **1801** SOUTHEY *Thalaba* XII. xviii, The unpruned taper flares a longer flame. **1819** SHELLEY *Medusa* 32 The midnight sky Flares. **1859** TENNYSON *Lancelot & Elaine* 1020 Lo! the blood-red light of dawn Flared on her face. **1874** GREEN *Short Hist.* ii. §4. 72 Town and hamlet flaring into ashes. **1879** BEERBOHM *Patagonia* viii. 132 The fire..flared away without emitting any warmth.

transf. and *fig.* **1837** J. H. NEWMAN *Par. Serm.* (1839) I. xi. 165 Before the flame of religion in the heart is purified..it will flare about. **1868** MILMAN *St. Paul's* 305 The Queen's Protestant zeal flared out against these idolatrous images. **1871** R. ELLIS *Catullus* lxviii. 141 Juno's self..Crushes her eager rage, in wedlock-injury flaring. **1876** GREEN *Stray Stud.* 3 A gilded vane flares out above the grey Jacobean gables.

b. *nonce-use* (with *on*). To go emitting flames.

1820 KEATS *Hyperion* I. 217 His flaming robes streamed out..On he flared, From stately nave to nave.

c. *trans.* To light up with a flare. Also (*causative*) To cause (a candle) to burn with a flare. ***to flare out***: to send forth by means of a flaring flame.

1745 MRS. HAYWOOD *Female Spect.* (1748) III. 309 For fear of flaring or putting out his beloved lights. **1853** KANE *Grinnell Exp.* xxviii. (1856) 238 The south-western horizon is flared with red streaks. **1861** DICKENS *Gt. Expect.* liii, He flared the candle at me again, smoking my face and hair. **1874** GREEN *Short Hist.* vii. §6. 409 The English beacons flared out their alarm along the coast.

6. ***to flare up***: **a.** to burst into a sudden and temporary blaze; also *fig.* Hence of persons: **b.** to break out into sudden anger; Also with *out*, quasi-*trans.* with quoted words. (Cf. FLARE-OUT 1.) **c.** to have a 'jollification', make merry boisterously.

a. 1846 THACKERAY *Crit. Rev.* Wks. 1886. XXIII. 99 Is a man..to despond because he can't in his person flare up like the sun? **1867** SMILES *Huguenots Eng.* 428 They [persecutions] flared up again..with increased fury. **1886** SIR F. H. DOYLE *Remin.* 388 The grass suddenly flared up. **b. 1840** MRS. CARLYLE *Lett.* 5 Oct. (1883) I. 119 It is just because I love you..that I flare up when [etc.]. **1870** MRS. RIDDELL *Austin Friars* iv, You flare up like a bull at sight of a red cloak. **1907** *Smart Set* Feb. 95 'Your name is Ougheltree,' he suddenly flared out. **c. 1869** C. KEENE *Let.* in G. S. Layard *Life* vi. (1892) 138 We flared up again last night, and hailed the New Year with the usual ceremonies.

Hence **flared** *ppl. a.*

1928 *Daily Mail* 31 July 1/2 Delightful Lace Tunic with the new Flared Skirt. **1935** *Jrnl. R. Aeronaut. Soc.* XXXIX. 863 Unexpectedly high lift and drag force coefficients were developed in the latter stages of the flared landings.

flareless ('flɛəlɪs), *a.* [f. FLARE *sb.*[1] + -LESS.] **a.** Not producing a flare (FLARE *sb.*[1] 1). **b.** Of a garment: having no flare (FLARE *sb.*[1] 4 b).

1932 *N.Y. Times* 21 Feb. (*headline*) Japan using new smokeless and flareless powder. **1954** W. FAULKNER *Fable* (1955) 32 The simple flareless breeches.

flare-out. [See FLARE-UP and FLARE *v.*]

1. = FLARE-UP 2 b.

1879 MCCARTHY *Donna Quixote* xvii, Paulina had a hard struggle many a time to keep down her temper, and not to have what she would have called a flare-out.

2. *Aeronaut.* A lessening of the steepness of the glide path of an aircraft about to land (see FLARE *v.* 4 d).

1944 [see FLARE *v.* 4d]. **1958** *Times* 17 Oct. 3/4 An automatic landing is completed with the aid of a Standard Telephones radio altimeter which gives an accurate measurement of height above ground and is used for the 'flare-out' (levelling off to land). **1963** *Spectator* 22 Mar. 351 With BLEU the flare-out is beautifully smooth and accurate. The judgement of the touchdown point is exact.

flare path. *Aeronaut.* [FLARE *sb.*[1] 2.] A line of lights on an airfield or elsewhere to guide aircraft in taking off or coming in to land; an illuminated runway.

1919 R. H. REECE *Night Bombing with Bedouins* 56 The answer received, the machine taxies..turns, hurtles down the flare-path and leaves the ground. **1936** *Jrnl. R. Aeronaut. Soc.* XL. 91 On a fine clear night the flare path is visible for about 50 miles. **1942** T. RATTIGAN (*title*) Flare path. **1943** R. HILLARY *Last Enemy* ii. 46 Across about a hundred yards from us lay the flare path, a straight line of dimly glowing light.

flare-up (flɛərʌp). [f. verbal phrase *flare up*: see FLARE *v.* The stress is variable (cf. BREAKDOWN), but most commonly falls on the first syll.]

1. A sudden breaking out into flame.

1859 M. NAPIER *Life Dundee* I. II. 351 The star of Lauderdale..well nigh consumed the patriot Duke [Hamilton] with the fierceness of its flare-up. **1864** *Realm* 13 Apr. 2 The percussion and flare up of lucifer-matches.

2. *fig.* **a.** A brilliant but temporary access (of popularity, etc.). **b.** A vehement outbreak of anger; a violent commotion. **c.** An uproarious merrymaking, a 'spree'.

a. *a* **1866** MRS. CARLYLE *Lett.* III. 327 That flare-up of popularity in Edinburgh. **1850** ROSSETTI *Let.* 3 Sept. (1965) I. 92 *The Guardian*..contains a flare-up review of *The Gurm.* **1960** *Times* 2 Mar. 11/2 A border flare-up not directly concerned with the water issue. **1970** F. MCKENNA *Gloss. Railwaymen's Talk* 35 A flare-up usually took place on a Saturday night when the men enjoyed themselves after a week of tension and hard work. **b. 1837-40** HALIBURTON *Clockm.* (1862) 239 Some of our young citizens..got into a flare-up with a party of boatmen ..a desperate row it was too. **1839** SIR C. NAPIER in Bruce *Life* iv. (1885) 133 The men would have been destroyed or defeated, and a pretty flare-up would have run like wildfire to Carlisle. **1845** W. IRVING *Life & Lett.* (1866) III. 381 The President's Message..has not been of a tone to create any flare-up in England. **1884** *Manch. Exam.* 7 May 5/3 When the Council..shows a determination to have a decisive voice ..there is a flare up. **c. 1844** ALB. SMITH *Adv. Mr. Ledbury* vii. (1886) 21 We ought to have a flare-up in our rooms. **1851** MAYHEW *Lond. Labour* I. 160 Some have been having a flare-up.

3. *Naut.* A night-signal made by burning some highly inflammable material. Also ***flare-up light***.

1858 *Adm. Reg.* in *Merc. Marine Mag.* V. 103 Pilot-vessels ..are to exhibit a Flare-up Light every 15 minutes. **1880** C. B. BERRY *Other Side* 11 At night she [a pilot boat] burns a 'flare up' whenever she sights a ship's light. **1883** *Daily News* 25 June 5/6 Rockets were at once sent up and blue lights and flare-ups burned.

flaring ('flɛərɪŋ), *vbl. sb.* [f. FLARE *v.* + -ING[1].] *concr.* in *pl.* Gaudy or showy trimmings. *rare.*

1881 BLACKMORE *Christowell* xii, Two girls..with their Sunday stripes and flarings on.

flaring ('flɛərɪŋ), *ppl. a.* [f. as prec. + -ING[2].]

†**1.** Of the hair, etc.: Spreading out or waving conspicuously, flaunting. Of a mirror: Giving a bulging or enlarged outline; exaggerating. *Obs.*

1593 NASHE *Christ's Teares*, Wks. (Grosart) IV. 211 Thy flaring frounzed Periwigs. **1618** BOLTON *Florus* (1636) 33 Marching forward..with..flaring head-tyres speckled like skins of serpents. **1635** QUARLES *Embl.* II. vi. (1718) 85 This flaring mirrour represents No right proportion, view, or feature. **1641** MILTON *Ch. Govt.* I. (1851) 23 In a flaring tire [they] bespeckl'd her with all the gaudy allurements of a Whore.

2. Over-conspicuous, glaring, showy, gaudy; †extravagant, irregular. Now used as *transf.* from 4.

1610 G. FLETCHER *Christ's Vict. on Earth* liv, To search for flaring shells. *a* **1659** OSBORN *Characters &c.* (1673) 630 Such a Flaring and intemperate a Course, as that of a Souldier. **1717** PRIOR *Alma* ii. 518 A young flaring painted whore. **1746-7** MRS. DELANY *Let. to Mrs. Dewes* 446 Crimson and yellow flaring hangings of paper. **1769** GRAY *Let.* Poems (1775) 365 No flaring gentleman's house, or garden-walls, break in upon the repose of this..paradise. **1820** HAZLITT *Lect. Dram. Lit.* 346 The language is a mixture of metaphysical jargon and flaring prose. **1891** E. PEACOCK *N. Brendon* II. 313 This flaring Anonyma, as he called her.

3. Of a vessel, etc.: That has its sides curving gradually outwards from the base. Also of a pan or dish (cf. FLARE *v.* 4 c).

1627 CAPT. SMITH *Seaman's Gram* xi. 52 If she were laid out aloft, and not flaring. *c* **1850** *Rudim. Navig.* (Weale) 118 It is said that a ship has a flaring bow when the topside falls outward from a perpendicular. **1857** *Trans. Ill. Agric. Soc.* II. 158, I..allow a little of the milk to pass along into a large flaring pan. *a* **1877** KNIGHT *Dict. Mech.* I. 876/2 *Flaring*... Increasing in diameter upwards as of an upwardly expanding pan. *Ibid.* III. 2633/2 *Trumpet*... The flaring mouth of a railway-car draw-head. **1883** W. C. RUSSELL *Sea Queen* III. iii. 57 A good-looking vessel, having what sailors call a flairing bow, which made her appear as round as an apple forward. **1895** *Montgomery Ward Catal.* 434/2 Flaring Pails—Tin..6 quarts [to]..14 quarts.

4. Burning with a broad irregular flame; shining brightly and fitfully.

1632 MILTON *Penseroso* 132 And when the sun begins to fling His flaring beams. **1633** G. HERBERT *Temple, Ch. Windows* iii, Speech alone Doth vanish like a flaring thing. **1661** DAVENPORT *City Night-Cap* III. i, I have tugg'd with tempests..Out-star'd the flaring lightning. **1764** GOLDSM. *Trav.* 400 Flaring tapers brightning as they waste. **1834** HT. MARTINEAU *Farrers* i. 18 He put out his flaring candle.

fig. **1884** PAE *Eustace* 67 He stared at the speaker for several moments with a flaring countenance.

Hence **'flaringly** *adv.*, in a flaring manner; gaudily. In mod. Dicts.

flary ('flɛərɪ), *a. rare.* [f. FLARE *sb.* + -Y[1].] Gaudy, showy.

1866 CARLYLE *Remin.* (1881) I. 157 They were not so well dressed as their Edinburgh sisters; something flary, glary, colours too flagrant and ill-assorted. **1873** —— in *Mrs. Carlyle's Lett.* I. 263 Flary, staring, and conceited, stolid-looking girls.

flaser ('flɑːzə(r)). *Geol.* [a. G. *flaser*, dial. form of *flader* streak, vein.] Used *attrib.* to denote the presence of lenses of little-altered rock in a streaky parent rock that has been metamorphosed by shearing under pressure; it is found mainly in gabbro, gneiss, and granite; so ***flaser-gabbro***, ***granite***, ***rock***, ***schist***, ***structure***.

1889 C. LAPWORTH *Page's Geol.* (ed. 12) 108 A curious very or banded structure (flaser structure). **1888** J. J. H. TEALL *Brit. Petrogr.* vii. 177 In speaking of the foliated gabbros it is convenient to recognise two principal types which may be designated by the terms *flaser-gabbro* and *gabbro-schist*. *Ibid.* 245 In some of these a flaser structure has been developed by interstitial movement. **1891** G. A. J. COLE *Aids Pract. Geol.* 210 This structure..appears to arise by interaction of the minerals when subjected to earth-pressures ('Flaser-gabbros', etc.). **1930** PEACH & HORNE *Geol. Scotl.* 58 Flaser structure with abundant phacoids of felspar and hornblende. **1951** TURNER & VERHOOGEN *Ign. & Metamorph. Petról.* xxi. 543 There is continuous transition from mylonites to a group of rocks variously referred to as augen schists, mylonite gneisses, flaser rocks, and blastomylonites. **1954** H. WILLIAMS et al. *Petrogr.* XI. 204 The terms flaser gabbro and flaser granite have long been applied by European petrologists to cataclasites in which granulated streaks and laminae swirl around and between streamlined eyes of undestroyed gabbro or granite.

flash (flæʃ), *sb.*[1] Forms: 5 flasche, 5-6 flassh(e, 9 *dial.* flass, 7- flash. [Of onomatopœic origin; cf. the synonyms *flosche* (FLOSH), FLASK *sb.*[2] (which are earlier recorded), PLASH (= MDu. *plasch*), which seem to imitate the sound of 'splashing' in a puddle. The synonymous F. *flache* may have influenced the Eng. word; it is commonly regarded as a subst. use of *flache*, fem. of OF. *flac* adj. soft:—L. *flaccus*.]

1. A pool, a marshy place. *Obs.* exc. *local.*

c **1440** *Promp. Parv.* 403 Plasche, or flasche, where reyne water stondythe..*torrens, lacuna.* **1523** FITZHERB. *Husb.* §70 The..flasshes, and lowe places, and all the holowe bunnes and pypes that growe therin. **1622** DRAYTON *Poly-olb.* xxv. 60 They [birds] from flash to flash, like the full Epicure Waft, as they lou'd to change their Diet euery meale. *c* **1746** J. COLLIER (Tim Bobbin) *Lanc. Dialect* Gloss., *Flash*, a lake. **1826** H. N. COLERIDGE *Six Months W.I.* 280 A long flash, as they call it, or river with a large bay. **1867** SMYTH *Sailor's Word-bk.*, *Flash*..Also, a pool, Also, in the west, a river with a large bay, which is again separated from the outer sea by a reef of rocks. **1870** E. PEACOCK *Ralf Skirl* II. 111 'Hev' ye forgotten..when we was a duckin' on Ferry Flash?'

attrib. **1882** *Lanc. Gloss.*, *Flash-pit*, a pit nearly grown up with reeds and grass.

2. [Cf. F. *flache* place where a paving-stone has sunk.] (See quot.)

1888 GRESLEY *Gloss. Coal Mining*, *Flash* (Cheshire), a subsidence of the surface due to the working of rock salt and pumping of brine.

flash (flæʃ), *sb.*[2] [f. FLASH *v.*[1]]

I. Burst of light or flame (and senses thence derived); cf. FLASH *v.*[1] III.

1. a. A sudden outburst or issuing forth of flame or light; a sudden, quick, transitory blaze. ***flash in the pan*** (see quot. 1810); *fig.* an abortive effort or outburst; cf. FLASH *v.*[1] 5 c.

1566 PAINTER *Pal. Pleas.* I. 108 Astouned like one that had been stroken with a flashe of lightening. **1635** SWAN *Spec. M.* vi. (1643) 300 It fired with a sudden flash. **1697** DRYDEN *Virg. Georg.* IV. 712 Three flashes of blue Light'ning. **1705** BOSMAN *Guinea* 318 Missing his shot by a flash in the Pan. **1725** DE FOE *Voy. round World* (1840) 309 Our men saw

plainly the three flashes of the guns. **1810** JAMES *Milit. Dict.* (ed. 3), *Flash in the pan*, an explosion of gunpowder without any communication beyond the touch-hole. **1833** MARRYAT *P. Simple* lviii, I now discharged grape alone, waiting for the flash of the fire to ascertain their direction. **1858** *Merc. Marine Mag.* V. 60 It is a Fixed White Light, varied by a Red Flash every half minute.

b. *slang. **flash of lightning***: a glass of gin.

1789 GEO. PARKER *Life's Painter* 149. **1801** *Sporting Mag.* XVII. 34 That fashionable liquor called flashes of lightning. **1830** LYTTON *P. Clifford* II. iv. 112 The thunders of eloquence being hushed, flashes of lightning, or, as the vulgar say 'glasses of gin' gleamed about.

c. *transf.* The quick movement of a flag in signalling.

1870 COLOMB & BOLTON *Flashing Signals* 30 To make a short flash, the flag is moved from *a* to *b*.. To make a long flash, the flag is waved from *a* to *c*.

d. A brief telegraphic news dispatch, usually as a preliminary to a fuller report; a brief item of broadcast news. So ***news flash***, orig. *U.S.* (in telegraphic sense).

1857 *Richmond* (Va.) *D. Whig* 31 Aug. 3/1 The first flash came across the ocean by the Submarine Telegraph at noon to-day. **1904** *Post Express* (Rochester, N.Y.) 12 Sept. 3 News Flashes from All Over. **1933** *Evening Standard* 19 Apr. 6/2 The 'C[entral] N[ewsagency]' had the news.. from the tape machines.. in this form. *Flash* 11.28 P.M. *Moscow Trial.* **1934** H. N. ROSE *Thesaurus of Slang* vii. 48/2 Brief News Bulletin.. *a flash.* **1938** *Manch. Guardian Weekly* 21 Oct. Suppl. i/3 There was little hope that.. a.. news flash would break in.. but her voice all at once receded. 'Flash!' a masculine announcer put in. **1940** P. FLEMING *Flying Visit* 118 The Censorship, after passing a news agency 'flash' stating that the *New York Morning Post* had published an amazing dispatch in which its London correspondent alleged [etc.]. **1965** *New Statesman* 5 Nov. 694/1 It often got out 'flashes' quicker which enabled us to.. save valuable time on big stories.

e. *Cinematography.* Exposure of a scene; a scene momentarily shown on the screen.

1913 E. W. SARGENT *Technique of Photoplay* (ed. 2) ii. 14 We know what is in the letter, so just a *flash* about three feet long is used. **1922** A. C. LESCARBOURA *Cinema Handbk.* i. 23 *Flash*, a short scene, usually not more than three to five feet of film. **1944** *Ann. Reg. 1943* 344 Propaganda shorts.. came in a steady flow,.. their length varying from a flash to five minutes.

f. = *flash-lamp* (b).

1913 D. E. ADAMS in F. H. Harris *Dartmouth out o' Doors* 40 A pocket flash was the only light on hand. **1943** R. CHANDLER *Lady in Lake* (1944) xxxiv. 178 'Got a flash?' 'No.' I said: 'There's one in the car pocket on the left side.' Shorty fumbled around and metal clicked and the white beam of a flashlight came on.

g. A flash-light photograph; also, = *flash-gun*, *flash-lamp* (a).

1945 WAKEFIELD & SMITH *Synchronized Flashlight Photogr.* v. 72 The flash is fixed to the camera. **1959** J. CARY *Captive & Free* lxiii. 287 A camera man held up his reflector and took a flash. **1963** L. DEIGHTON *Horse under Water* xvi. 66 He brought it [*sc.* a camera] complete with flash and a green filter. **1971** *Amateur Photographer* 13 Jan. 42 A man came into the shop and said he would like to buy a small electronic flash he had seen in the window.

h. The brief pleasurable sensation received immediately after an injection of certain narcotic drugs. *slang.*

1967 M. M. GLATT et al. *Drug Scene* iii. 39 He no longer got a 'kick' or 'flash' from taking drugs. **1970** *Observer* 3 May 3/3 The pleasure comes apparently from the half-dreamlike state between consciousness and sleep which the addict calls his 'flash' or 'buzz'. **1971** *Oz* XXXVI. 40/1 More & more people started shooting it to get the flash all the real hip suckers were talking about.

2. *transf.* The brief period during which a flash is visible: †**a.** ***for a flash***: for a brief moment; while the fit lasts (*obs.*). **b.** ***in a flash***: immediately, instantaneously.

1625 BACON *Ess. Greatness Kingd.* (Arb.) 485 The Persians, and Macedonians, had it for a flash. **1648** MILTON *Tenure Kings* (1650) 3 Most men are apt enough to civill wars and commotions as a noveltie, and for a flash hot and active. **1801** *Spirit Pub. Jrnls.* (1806) IX. 372 To the helm, my boy, in a flash. **1858** O. W. HOLMES *Aut. Breakf.-t.* vi. 160 A thoroughly popular lecture ought to have nothing in it which five hundred people cannot all take in a flash.

3. A brief outburst or transient display of something regarded as resembling a flash of light.

1602 SHAKS. *Ham.* v. i. 210 Your flashes of Merriment that were wont to set the Table on a Rore. **1652–62** HEYLIN *Cosmogr.* III. (1673) 8/2 A brave flash of vain-glorious hospitality. **1665** BOYLE *Occas. Refl.* v. iv. (1845) 309 An unseasonable disclosure of flashes of Wit. **1819** BYRON *Juan* II. xxxviii, But now there came a flash of hope once more. **1873** BLACK *Pr. Thule* ii. 27 A sort of flash of expectation passed over Lavender's face.

4. a. Superficial brilliancy; ostentation, display; also †brilliant distinction, 'éclat' (*obs.*). †Phr. ***to cut a flash*** (cf. DASH *sb.* 10).

1674 S. VINCENT *Yng. Gallant's Acad.* 97 Whose Entertainments to those of a higher rank are.. not only flash and meer Complement. **1711** ADDISON *Spect.* No. 59. ¶1 Pedants.. are apt to decry the Writings of a polite Author, as Flash and Froth. **1755** *Gentl. Mag.* XXV. 118 Berry gave him a crown.. to make a flash with to the boys. **1780** MAD. D'ARBLAY *Diary* June (1891) I. 271 Miss Weston, whose delicacy gave way to gaiety and flash, whether she would or not. **1782** C. A. BURNEY *Jrnl.* 15 Jan. in Mad. D'Arblay *Early Diary* II. 306, I had not a very entertaining evening, but I would not but have been there, for the *flash* of the thing. **1795** *Fate of Sedley* I. 50 Some men.. cut a flash without any fortune. **1827** R. H. FROUDE *Rem.* (1838) I. 445, I.. shall be drawn.. into foolishness and flash, and everything that is disgusting. **1880** WEBB *Goethe's Faust* Prel. Theat. 8 Mere flash a moment's interest engages.

†**b.** A piece of showy talk; a vain, empty phrase or vulgarism. *Obs.*

1605 B. JONSON, etc. *Eastward Hoe* IV. i, Sir Petronell Flash, I am sory to see such flashes as these proceede from a Gentleman of your Quality. **1649** MILTON *Eikon.* xii. (1851) 433 Hee next falls to flashes, and a multitude of words. **1735** DYCHE & PARDON *Dict., Flash*.. a Boast, Brag, or great Pretence made by a Spend-thrift, Quack, or Pretender to more Art or Knowledge than a Person has.

†**5.** A brilliant or 'showy' person; usually in contemptuous sense, one vain of his accomplishments or appearance, a coxcomb, fop. *Obs.*

1603 B. JONSON *Sejanus* II. i, Such a spirit as yours, Was not created for the idle second To a poor flash, as Drusus. **1652** BENLOWES *Theoph.* XI. lix. 200 Thou, inconsid'rate Flash, spend'st pretious Dayes In Dances, Banquets, Courtisms, Playes. **1677** MIEGE *Eng.-Fr. Dict.*, A Flash, an empty shallow-brained fellow. **1764** *Low Life* 65 The Jemmies,Brights, Flashes.. and Smarts of the Town. **1807–8** W. IRVING *Salmag.* (1824) 78 She is the highest flash of the ton—has much whim and more eccentricity.

†**6.** *slang.* A wig. *Obs.*

*a***1700** B. E. *Dict. Cant. Crew, Flash*, a Periwig. **1760** BAILEY vol. II. (ed. 5) Canting Words, *Flash*, a Peruke, *Rum Flash*, a long, full, high-priz'd Wig. *Queer Flash*, a sorry, weather-beaten Wig.

7. a. An ornament consisting of three short pieces of black velvet ribbon sewn to the collar of a full-dress tunic, and hanging down the back; supposed to be the remains of the bow which fastened the 'queue'. Now worn only by the officers of the 23rd Royal Welsh Fusiliers. (*N. & Q.* 8th Ser. VII. 20 Apr. 1895).

1837 T. HOOK *Jack Brag* III. 115 A.. young man, dressed in the uniform of some volunteer corps of cavalry, wearing flashes.

b. A patch of cloth sewn on a military uniform, usu. on the upper arm or shoulder, with a device to indicate the unit or country, etc., to which the wearer belongs.

1918 (*title*) Flashes of 53rd Division Prior to Aug. 18 (*chart in Imperial War Museum Libr.*). **1927** W. DEEPING *Kitty* xi. 142 A captain wearing the ribbon of the Military Cross, and black and white chess-board flashes. **1943** *Stars & Stripes* 15 June 2/5 Here's how the British and American armies describe different items: *American.* Insignia, shoulder, sleeve. *British.* Divisional sign or flash. **1944** *Times* 6 July 5/7 One cannot fail to notice the interest the Germans display in shoulder-flashes bearing the name Australia worn by the few A.I.F. officers who are here. *Ibid.*, They nearly all ask where the rest of the Australians are when they see my flashes. **1952** C. DAY LEWIS tr. *Virgil's Aeneid* II. 42 Change shields with these dead Greeks, put on their badges and flashes!

8. A preparation of cayenne pepper or capsicum with burnt sugar, used for colouring spirits.

1820 ACCUM *Adult. Food* 10 The substance which they [brandy merchants].. purchase under the delusive name of *flash*, for strengthening and clarifying spirituous liquors.. is in reality a compound of sugar with extract of capsicum.

†**9.** A small piece; ? a dash or sprinkling.

1615 LATHAM *Falconry* II. viii. 95 Put into it.. one flash or two of Saffron.

10. *pl.* The new shoots of a tea-plant.

1880 ELIOT JAMES *Indian Industries* xxviii. 344 The new shoots.. or 'flashes', as they are called, come on four, sometimes five, times between April and October.

II. Sudden movement of liquids, etc. (cf. FLASH *v.* I).

†**11. a.** A sudden movement of a body of water, a splash; a breaker. *Obs.*

1627 CAPT. SMITH *Seaman's Gram.* x. 47 Which make the Sea.. rebound in flashes exceeding high. **1632** SHERWOOD, A flash of water, *gaschis d'eau.* **1713** DERHAM *Phys. Theol.* IV. xv. 245 The Miller.. with his Man.. were so washed with Flashes of Sea water, that they were almost strangled therewith.

b. A sudden rush of water, let down from a weir, to take a boat over the shallows of a river.

1677 PLOT *Oxfordsh.* ix. §46. 234 Were there a convenient number of Locks, or Holds for water.. to let down flashes as occasion should serve. **1689** S. SEWALL *Diary* 29 Mar. (1882) I. 302 Flashes to help them over the Shallow places. **1758** *Descr. Thames* 162 But this is a Charge only in Summer, and paid for Flashes when the Water is low. **1867** SMYTH *Sailor's Word-bk.* s.v., *To make a flash*, is to let boats down through a lock. **1884** KNIGHT *Dict. Mech.* IV. 76/1 The substitution of a continuous navigation upon the upper Seine.. by the aid of movable dams, for the intermittent navigation by flashes.

†**12.** *transf.* A sudden burst of rain, wind, steam, etc.; a fit of activity, a spurt. *Obs.*

1653–4 WHITELOCKE *Jrnl. Swed. Emb.* (1772) II. 362 Yett the wind being by flashes large, they went.. twenty leagues up and downe. **1685** WOOD *Life* (Oxf. Hist. Soc.) III. 156 Waters extreame low, tho' many flashes of raine. Rivers almost dried up. **1706** PHILLIPS (ed. Kersey), *Flash*, a sudden Spurt. **1808** J. B. DABNEY in *Naval Chron.* XXI. 107 Some few.. were scalded by flashes of steam.

13. A contrivance for producing a 'flash' (senses 11, 11 b). (See quots. and FLASH-BOARD.)

1768–74 TUCKER *Lt. Nat.* (1852) I. 32 The miller, when he takes up his flashes, lays them it may be on the bank. **1841** BREES *Gloss. Civ. Engin., Flashes*, a description of sluice, erected for the purpose of raising the water over any shoals while craft are passing. **1861** SMILES *Engineers* I. II. iv. 122 In some cases these drainage waters were conveyed.. over it [the New River] by what were termed flashes. *Note.* The flash.. consisted of a wooden trough about twelve feet wide .. extending across the river.

III. *attrib.* and *Comb.*

14. a. simple attributive, as ***flash-lock***, ***-mark***, ***-water***, ***-weir*** (senses 11, 11 b).

1788 *Act 28 Geo. III.* c. 51 §14 All the old Flash Locks or Weirs thereon. **1791** W. JESSOP *Rep. Navig. Thames & Isis* 9 Water at the flash mark 4ft. 6 on the Sill. **1793** R. MYLNE *Rep. Thames* 29 The Time of Flash-waters coming down.

b. Special comb., as **flash boiler** = FLASHER 6; **flash bomb** (see quot.); **flash-bulb** *Photogr.*, a glass bulb producing the light used for taking flash-light photographs; **flash burn**, a burn caused by sudden intense heat, esp. that generated by a nuclear explosion; **flash-butt welding** *Metallurgy* (see quot. 1958); also ***flash weld(ing)*** (cf. *butt-weld(ed)*); **flash card** (see quot. 1945); **flash colour**, a patch of bright colour on an animal's body which is visible only when the animal is in motion; so ***flash-colouring*** vbl. sb.; **flash cube** *Photogr.*, a small cube with a bulb and reflector in each of four faces, for attaching to a camera to provide up to four flashes in rapid succession; **flash-dry** *v. trans.*, to dry in a very short time; so ***flash-drying*** vbl. sb.; **flash-flood** [cf. sense 11 a, b] *Phys. Geogr.*, a sudden, destructive flood; so ***flash flooding*** vbl. sb.; †**flash-flown** *a.*, ? uttered in idle talk; **flash-flue** (see quot.); **flash freezer**, a machine for performing flash freezing; **flash freezing**, the very rapid freezing of food in order to preserve its flavour and texture by avoiding the formation of ice crystals; so **flash-freeze** *v. trans.*, to subject to this process; also *transf.*; **flash-frozen** *ppl. a.*; **flash generator** = FLASHER 6; **flash-gun** *Photogr.*, a device that can be attached to a camera to hold and operate a flash-bulb; **flash-lamp** (*a*) (*Photogr.*), a lamp used to give a flash-light; (*b*) a portable electric lamp which produces a light by the pressure of a button, etc.; **flash-light**, (*a*) a light so arranged as to give forth sudden flashes, used for signals and in lighthouses; (*b*) *Photogr.* (see quot. 1890); (*c*) chiefly *U.S.* = *flash-lamp* (b); also as *v. trans.*, to photograph by flash-light (also *fig.*); hence ***flash-lighting*** vbl. sb.; **flash-meter**, a device similar to the shutter of a camera which permits momentary exposure of slides for teaching purposes; **flash-pan**, (*a*) the pan in an old flint-lock for holding the priming by which the charge is exploded; (*b*) a small copper pan with a handle, in which powder is flashed as a signal (*Cent. Dict.*); **flash pasteurization**, a method of pasteurization in which the substance is suddenly raised to a higher temperature than in normal pasteurization but for a shorter period; **flash photolysis** *Chem.*, the use of a very short, intense flash of light to bring about chemical decomposition or dissociation; so **flash-photolyse** *v.*, to decompose by this means; ***flash-photolysed*** ppl. adj.; **flash-pipe** (see quot. 1874); **flash-point** (*a*) = *flashing-point*; (*b*) *fig.*, a point of climax, indignation, etc. (cf. *boiling-point*); **flash powder**, powder used in flash-light photography; also extended uses; **flash process** = *flash pasteurization*; **flash-rim** (see quot. 1867); **flash roasting** *Metallurgy* (see quot. 1958); so ***flash-roast*** v. trans.; **flash spectroscopy** *Chem.*, spectroscopic examination of rapid chemical reactions initiated by a very short, intense flash of light; **flash spectrum**, (*a*) a spectrum of the chromosphere which appears at the beginning and end of totality of a solar eclipse; (*b*) a spectrum of the reactants and reaction products obtained in flash spectroscopy; **flash-spotting** *Mil.*, the locating and reporting of hostile battery positions by observation of their gun-flashes; hence ***flash-spotter***; **flash steam generator** = *flash generator*; **flash-test**, a test to determine the flashing-point of kerosene, etc.; **flash tube** *Photogr.*, a tube, filled usually with xenon under reduced pressure, by means of which a flash is produced when an electrical current is suddenly passed through the gas; **flash-wheel** (see quot.). Also FLASH-BOARD.

1902 *Lockwood's Dict. Mech. Engin.* (ed. 3), *Flash Boiler, a rapidly steaming boiler in which the steam is generated in coils of small tubes. **1906** *Daily Chron.* 3 Mar. 3/6 Water is converted into steam in a tubular boiler, called a flash boiler. **1940** *Flight* 26 Dec. b/2 *Flash bombs are dropped to illumine the target. **1935** *News Chron. Amateur Photogr.* II. iii. 200 The flashlight need not be situated directly behind the camera.. particularly if a *flash-bulb is available. **1937** *Pop. Sci.* Aug. 86/1 (*heading*) Using two flash bulbs for portrait photos. *Ibid.*, Any flash-bulb holder, operated by batteries, may be easily adapted. **1939** HENNEY & DUDLEY *Handbk. Photogr.* iv. 93 Synchronized flash guns are devices which enable the photographer to fire off a flash bulb at the

same instant the shutter of his camera is opened. **1954** X. Fielding *Hide & Seek* ix. 113 Half a dozen sheep stood there motionless for a second, as though posing for a flash-bulb photograph. **1946** *Nature* 3 Aug. 152/1 An attack by atomic bombs would, no doubt, cause some casualties by '*flashburn', although even ordinary clothing appears to offer substantial protection against it. **1951** *Ann. Reg. 1950* 420 The three major effects [of atomic warfare] were blast, flash-burn, and radiological. **1933** *Welding Ind.* Aug. 224/2 On *flash butt welding machines, the transformer if inside the housing is exposed to the damage which may be caused by the unavoidable considerable sparking. **1958** A. D. Merriman *Dict. Metallurgy* 95/1 *Flash-butt welding*, a resistance welding process in which an arc is struck and maintained between the joint members until welding heat is attained. The current is then shut off and the weld made by forcing the parts together. **1923** *Cumulative Book Index* Apr. 18 *Flash cards for rapid word drills. **1945** C. V. Good *Dict. Educ.* 173/2 *Flash card*, a small card of heavy cardboard having on it written or printed letters, words, phrases, numerals, or combinations of numerals for computation; used as an aid to learning, the teacher holding each card up for the class to see for a brief interval. **1953** Wittich & Schuller *Audio-Visual Materials* iii. 53 Flash cards.. ultimately create relationships and understandings of the symbols and the objects for which these symbols stand. **1964** *Listener* 12 Nov. 775/2 The raising of children's 'flash-cards': what do you think of this?—two seconds to answer. **1928** T. H. Savory *Biol. Spiders* viii. 160 Coloration may assist concealment.. by the exhibition of the so called *flash-colours. **1935** —— *Spiders* 28 When the spider has been disturbed and is running away, these quickly moving bright joints are conspicuous. But suddenly it stops and draws in its legs: the bright colours are hidden, and the spider becomes almost invisible—a method of protection known as '*flash-colouring'. **1965** *Perspective* VII. 244/2 *Multiple flash bulb*, a so-called *flash cube introduced for a low-priced amateur still camera consists of four tiny blue flash bulbs set in their own reflectors in four faces of a cube. **1967** *Boston Sunday Herald* 30 Apr. vi. 8/5 The Retina S-1 camera, designed to use flashcubes. **1977** J. Hedgecoe *Photographer's Handbk.* 24 The most basic peel-apart film cameras.. offer scale focusing, a flash cube mounting, and usually have automatic exposure control. **1985** *N.Y. Times* 12 May 1. 59/1 The Minox LX.. has a built-in exposure meter and a flashcube attachment. **1946** *Nature* 10 Aug. 194/1 Considerable progress had been made in drying; and spray-drying, *flash-drying and drum-drying have been developed with considerable success. **1950** *Time* 26 June 10 Big heating ovens.. flash-dry the ink almost instantly. **1960** *Times* 20 Sept. (Pure Food Suppl.) p. xx, Because the food is flash-dried in a high vacuum the moisture takes nothing away with it. **1940** *Words* Apr. 55/1 Harry Burns.. died in a '*flash' flood which raced down Wheeling creek. **1963** N. Freeling *Gun before Butter* ii. 79 Flash floods of eleven centimetres of rain in an hour and a half. **1939** *Nature* 17 June 1028/1 A two feet deep band of boulders and sand, deposited in a period of *flash flooding. **1632** Lithgow *Trav.* viii. 339 Let not surmisers thinke, ambition led My second toyles, more *flash-flowne praise to wed. **1888** *Lockwood's Dict. Mech. Engin.*, **Flash Flue*, the flue underneath an egg-end or similar externally fired boiler. **1984** *Tampa* (Florida) *Tribune* 28 Mar. 17c/10 (Advt.), Restaurant equip. for sale;..dbl refrig., *flash freezer, ice cream machine [etc.]. **1942** Woolrich & Bartlett *Quick & Flash Freezing of Foods* 13 This led to the discovery of 'polyphase freezing' or what some prefer to call '*flash freezing'. **1968** *New Scientist* 29 Aug. 436/2 Any temperature between −120°C and −196°C can be produced in the flash-freezing section. The flash-freezing process can be fully controlled within that temperature range. **1984** *N.Y. Times* 9 Apr. c11/2 Flash freezing of fish at temperatures approaching 40 below zero lengthens their shelf life appreciably. **1973** *Publishers Weekly* 26 Feb. 122/3 Kiley is shot during a student riot, but since he happens to be close to a friend's cryogenic lab, he is immediately *flash-frozen. **1976** *National Observer* (U.S.) 12 June 1/1 Their clothes.. look flash-frozen out of the '50s. **1977** *Time* 23 May 54/1 Passengers doze over their drinks, eat flash-frozen steaks. **1903** *Work* 28 Feb. 58/3 The cylinder constituting alternately a gas-engine and a *flash generator. **1913** W. E. Dommett *Motor Car Mech.* 141 Flash generators are really a particular case of water-tube boilers, in which the tubes serve not only for the production of steam but simultaneously act as super-heaters. **1930** *Pop. Sci.* July 46/3 *(caption)* New *flash gun and camera which it clicks, at the instant trigger fires flashlight cartridge. **1939** Flash gun [see *flash-bulb*]. **1959** *Which?* May 25/2 The cameras tested could be used with flashguns—an advantage for anyone wanting to take indoor pictures. **1890** Woodbury *Encycl. Photogr.* 373 The electric lamp, magnesium lamp, and *flash lamp. **1891** H. L. Webb in *Electr. in Daily Life, Making a Cable* 188 Flag-signalling had to be exchanged for flash-lamps. **1908** *Model Engin. & Electrician* 11 June 570/2 Flashlamp batteries. **1914** G. W. Young *From Trenches* xi. 234 Electric flash-lamps. **1928** *Daily Express* 11 Oct. 8 Tom shone his flashlamp on the knife. **1886** *Sci. Amer.* N.S. LIV. 16/2 A *flash-light, that is to say, one which can be made to glow or disappear at pleasure. **1890** Woodbury *Encycl. Photogr.* 289 *Flashlight*, usually made by blowing magnesium powder through a small flame. **1892** Marg. Stokes *Six Months in Apennines* 163, I was compelled to photograph these most interesting bas-reliefs by the flash-light. **1901** *Field & Stream* Jan. 774/2 The Comet Baby Flash Light. **1902** A. Bennett *Grand Babylon Hotel* xiii. 144 Rocco had photographed the corpse by flashlight. **1906** *Westm. Gaz.* 19 Mar. 3/1 To attempt to flashlight him at night is an invitation.. to trample the photographer and his camera into a jumble of mutilated fragments. **1913** Kipling *Diversity of Creatures* (1917) 205 We were studying the interior of a soul, flash-lighted by the dread of 'losing its position'. **1919** F. Hurst *Humoresque* 233 A gold-handled umbrella with a bachelor-girl flash-light attachment. **1940** E. Caldwell *Trouble in July* xii. 179 Several men rushed inside, flashlighting the room. **1958** 'A. Gilbert' *Death against Clock* 65 Carry a flash-light by any chance? **1959** H. Barnes *Oceanogr. & Marine Biol.* 183 Electronic *flash-lighting with a G.E.C. flash-tube is again employed, the camera mechanism being synchronized to the flash. **1957** D. T. Herman et al. in Saporta & Bastian *Psycholinguistics* (1961) 538/2 A Keystone Model 1045 projector equipped with an Ilex *flashmeter was used. **1959** J. W. Brown et al. *A-V Instructional Materials Man.* iv. 157 Keystone overhead projector setup, with tachistoscope (flash meter) and mask in place, ready to project reading slides. **1921** M. Mortenson *Managem. Dairy Plants* xi. 150 It requires approximately 17 per cent more heat for *flash pasteurization than for vat pasteurization. **1927** H. E. Ross *Care & Handling of Milk* viii. 101 Flash pasteurization is often used in pasteurizing milk and cream for manufacturing purposes where high temperatures may be used without injuring the product. **1940** *Economist* 28 Dec. 798/1 Ordinary pasteurisation imparts an objectionable cooked flavour... But there are certain methods such as flash pasteurisation, film evaporation and freezing which are not open to these objections. **1971** G. Herzberg *Spectra & Struct. Simple Free Radicals* 13 Almost the first absorption spectrum of *flash-photolyzed diazomethane showed a new transient feature.. which turned out to be the spectrum of CH_2. **1950** G. Porter in *Proc. R. Soc.* A. CC. 284 A new technique of *flash photolysis and spectroscopy has been developed. **1962** R. E. Dodd *Chem. Spectroscopy* v. 310 An important kinetic technique which relies upon spectrophotometry is flash photolysis. **1971** G. Herzberg *Spectra & Struct. Simple Free Radicals* 8 *(caption)* Apparatus for the study of absorption spectra of free radicals in the vacuum ultraviolet by flash photolysis. **1971** *Nature* 1 Jan. 41/1 The technique was checked by flash photolysing a 3:1 mixture of hydrogen and nitrogen dioxide. **1874** Knight *Dict. Mech.*, **Flash-pipe*, a mode of lighting gas by means of a supplementary pipe pierced with numerous small holes throughout its length. **1878** *Ure's Dict. Arts* Suppl. IV. 570 The legal *flash-point of petroleum. **1955** *Times* 26 Aug. 3/3 What actually happens is that the idealist is horrified by what he learns of police methods, his social conscience is brought to the flash-point of concentration by a love affair. **1958** *Economist* 13 Sept. 817/1 China's tactics seemed to be to build up heat to near flash-point and then suddenly lower the temperature. **1963** *Ann. Reg. 1962* 132 The flashpoint of East-West relations in 1962 was reached on 22 October. **1889** *Brit. Jrnl. Photogr.* 805 The characteristic of *flash powder is that it contains within itself the elements by which the flash is produced. **1952** Granville *Dict. Theatr. Terms* 77 *Flash powder*, a chemical substance through which is passed an electric current producing a flash and a cloud of smoke. Used for explosive effects in war plays. **1966** F. H. Brightman *Oxf. Bk. Flowerless Plants* 56/2 The spores form a very fine, bright-yellow powder called 'lycopodium powder', which was formerly used as a constituent of 'flash powder'. **1910** Ayers & Johnson in *Bull. U.S. Dept. Agric. Bur. Animal Ind.* cxxvi. 14 Experiments were made, using both the '*flash' process, which consists of heating flowing milk for from thirty to forty seconds and then cooling, and the 'holder' process, where the milk is heated in a tank and held for thirty minutes before cooling. **1867** Smyth *Sailor's Word-bk.*, **Flash Rim*, in carronades, a cup-shaped enlargement of the bore at the muzzle. **1926** D. M. Liddell *Handbk. Non-Ferrous Metallurgy* II. 1428/2 *(Index)* *Flash roasting. **1951** *Engineering* 20 July 75/2 Hydrogen sulphide in town's gas can be obtained by flash-roasting iron pyrites. **1958** A. D. Merriman *Dict. Metallurgy* 95/1 *Flash roasting*, a process for removing sulphur from ores by blowing the pulverised concentrates through a combustion chamber. **1952** *Proc. R. Soc.* A. CCX. 440 *Flash spectroscopy makes possible the recording of absorption spectra in a time less than 50 microseconds. **1953** *Ibid.* CCXVI. 165 The explosive oxidation of acetylene, initiated homogeneously by the flash photolysis of a small quantity of nitrogen dioxide, has been investigated by flash spectroscopy. **1899** C. A. Young *Gen. Astron.* 267 The '*flash-spectrum' was successfully photographed at a number of stations. **1900** *Proc. R. Soc.* LXVII. 373 The centre of the flash spectrum arcs was.. midway between the edges of the spectrum in the photographs obtained at mid-eclipse. **1926** H. Macpherson *Mod. Astron.* 32 Confirmatory observations of this 'flash spectrum', as the phenomenon of reversal from dark to bright was called, were secured at subsequent eclipses. **1950** *Proc. R. Soc.* A. CC. 299 Effect of capacity on flash spectra of krypton and hydrogen. **1930** Blunden *De Bello Germanico* 78, I believe our observers or *flash-spotters used it. **1922** *Encycl. Brit.* XXX. 253/1 Any gun which fired at night within direct view of the enemy was liable to be marked down by the '*flash-spotting' section... It was therefore necessary to introduce flashless powder. **1907** *Westm. Gaz.* 19 Nov. 4/2 The *flash steam generator, which is of the Serpollet type. **1945** Wakefield & Smith *Synchronized Flashlight Photogr.* ix. 109 The light-producing unit is a coiled glass tube filled with pure xenon... The *flash-tube. **1946** *Electronic Engin.* 113 *(title)* Electronic flash tubes in high-speed photography of explosions. **1957** T. L. J. Bentley *Man. Miniat. Camera* (ed. 5) v. 74 The practical uses of electronic flash sets are governed by the characteristics of the modern xenon-filled flash tube. **1959** Flash-tube [see *flash-lighting*]. **1959** *Jrnl. Iron & Steel Inst.* CXCII. 401/2 *Flash welds gave the highest and most consistent results. **1933** *Welding Ind.* Feb. 4/1 Butt welding may be divided into (*a*) direct or upset method... (*b*) *flash welding, in which the material is brought together and an arc is drawn between the parts to be welded. This arc plays along the material in a continuous flash and the pieces are moved together during this flashing period and when in the plastic state the current is interrupted and pressure applied. **1943** *Jrnl. R. Aeronaut. Soc.* XLVII. 289 Flash welding is a type of butt weld in which the two parts to be joined are connected to the secondary terminals of a low-voltage high-current transformer, are then brought into close proximity, and the voltage applied. **1874** Knight *Dict. Mech.*, **Flash-wheel*, a water-raising wheel having arms radial or nearly so to its axle, and revolving in a chase or curved water-way by which the water passes from the lower to the higher level as the wheel rotates.

15. Excess metal or plastic that is forced between facing surfaces as the two halves of a two-part die or mould close up, forming a thin projection on the resulting object.

1910 *Encycl. Brit.* X. 665/1 A large amount of metal is squeezed out beyond the concavity of the forging dies... There are two methods adopted for removing this 'fin', or 'flash' as it is termed. **1936** H. W. Rowell *Technol. Plastics* xxi. 158 If the width [of the land] is made greater to reduce pounds pressure per sq. in., the thickness of flash may exceed the desirable ·004 in. **1952** J. Wulff et al. *Metall. for Engin.* xxvii. 521 Excess metal, called flash, is squeezed from the die faces at the parting line and is subsequently trimmed or ground from the part. **1966** Walker & Martin *Injection Moulding of Plastics* iv. 132 Moulds for nylon usually have to be well bedded together to prevent flash.

16. A thin layer (of glass, chromium, etc.). (Cf. flash *v.*[1] 14a, c.)

1909 Webster, *Flash*.., a layer of glass flashed on. **1950** J. Osborne *Dental Mech.* (ed. 3) xxii. 369 One important modification must be made, however, to prevent any flash being present at the all-important fitting edge. **1959** *Times* 11 Nov. 6/3 What matters most with chromium plating is the layer of nickel under the top 'flash' of chromium. **1961** *B.S.I. News* Apr. 9/2 The durability of chromium-plating depends largely on the thickness and quality of the layer of nickel which is applied under the final 'flash' of chromium.

†**flash**, *sb.*[3] *Obs.* [The examples of 16–17th c. prob. echo Henryson; possibly the copy in *Chaucer's Wks.* 1561 may be correct in reading *fasshe*, a. OF. *fais* or *faisse* bundle, sheaf.] A bundle or sheaf (of arrows).

c **1450** Henryson *Test. Cres.* 167 in *Poems & Fables* (1865) 81 Undir his girdill ane flasche of felloun flanis. **1600** Fairfax *Tasso* xi. xxviii. 201 Her ratling quiuer at her shoulders hong, Therein a flash of arrowes feathered weele. **1671** Skinner *Etym. Ling. Angl.* iv., Flash of flames [*read* flaines], expl. a Sheaf of Arrowes. **1678–1706** Phillips, *Flash of Flames* (old word), a Sheaf of Arrows.

flash, *sb.*[4] [Of doubtful origin; possibly an application of flash *sb.*[2] 13.] = flashing *vbl. sb.*[2]

1574–5 *Jesus Coll. Accts.* in Willis & Clark *Cambridge* (1886) III. 611 Item to the Plummer.. for settinge in lead over the chappell.. where the flasshes were taken awaye. **1614–15** *Trinity Coll. Accts.* ibid. II. 488 Laying the leads after the masons, setting on flashes and sodering.

†**flash**, *a.*[1] *Obs.* In 5 flasch, flaisch. See also flake *a.* [The forms, compared with those given under flake *a.*, suggest that the word may be a confusion of OF. *flac*, *flache* 'feeble, insipid' (see next) with the similar-sounding ME. *wlake*, *wlache* tepid.] Lukewarm, tepid. Also ***flash-hot***.

c **1400** *Lanfranc's Cirurg.* 265 Boile hem in a double vessel & distille it in his eere flaisch. *Ibid.* 266 Loke þat alle þingis þat þou leist þerto be flasch hoot.

†**flash**, *a.*[2] *Obs.* Also 6 flashe. [? ad. OF. *flac*, *flache* (mod.F. with unexplained alteration *flasque*) flabby, weak, insipid:—L. *flaccus*: see flaccid. Cf. flashy.]

1. Weak, wanting in tone.

1562 Turner *Herbal* ii. 30a, If the stomack be so flashe and louse that it can hold no meat. *Ibid.* ii. 74a, Oxys is geuen vnto a flashe, louse or weike stomacke.

2. a. Of food: Insipid. **b.** *fig.* Of speech, reasonings, etc.: Trashy, void of meaning.

a. 1601 Bp. Barlow *Defence* 89 The white of an egge, without salt, is flash and unsavery. **1642** J. Eaton *Honey-combe Free Justif.* 84 The mingling and mixing together of wine and water.. maketh flash matter of both.

b. 1612 Brinsley *Lud. Lit.* 166 Matters vnfit for an Epistle, flash and to little purpose; but very childish. **1622** S. Ward *Life Faith in Death* 101 Loath I am to mingle Philosophicall Cordialls with Diuine, as water with wine, least my Consolations should bee flash and dilute. **1640** Fuller *Joseph's Coat* viii. (1867) 189 Flash in his matter, confused in his method, dreaming in his utterance.

flash (flæʃ), *a.*[3] Chiefly *colloq.* [f. flash *sb.*[2]]

1. Gaudy, showy, smart. Of persons: Dashing, ostentatious, swaggering, 'swell'. Also ***Flash Harry***: see Harry *sb.*[2] 2c.

1785 *European Mag.* VIII. 96 One of that numerous tribe of flash fellows, who live nobody knows where. **1836** J. H. Newman *Lett.* (1891) II. 200 If I could write a flash article on the subjunctive mood, I would, merely to show how clever I was. **1838** C. Sumner in *Mem. & Lett.* (1878) II. 23 Bulwer was here a few minutes ago in his flash falsetto dress. **1860** Trollope *Framley P.* ix, This flash Member of Parliament. **1867** Smyth *Sailor's Word-bk.*, *Flash Vessels*, all paint outside and no order within. **1877** Black *Green Past.* xliii. (1878) 348 A bit of flash oratory on the part of a paid pleader. **1882** *Illustr. Sporting News* 4 Feb. 502/2 A flash young rider.. frightens his horse out of his stride before they have well reached the distance.

b. Of an hotel, etc: First-class, fashionable, 'crack', 'swell'.

1840 Thackeray *Paris Sk.-bk.* (1872) 89 He.. frequented all the flash restaurateurs and boarding-houses. **1841** in Col. Hawker *Diary* (1893) II. 210 We then got into Meurice's flash hotel.

2. Counterfeit, not genuine, sham.

1812 *Sporting Mag.* XXXIX. 210 How could'st thou be so silly, Flash screens to ring for home-spun rope. **1821** *Ann. Reg.* 193 Passed for the purpose of suppressing the 'Fleet' or 'flash-notes'. **1837** Hood *Agric. Distress* vii, 'A note', says he ..'thou'st took a flash 'un.' **1863** R. B. Kimball *Was he Successful?* xii. 138 The difference between the real and the flash fashionable.

3. *slang.* Knowing, wide-awake, 'smart', 'fly'.

1812 J. H. Vaux *Flash Dict.*, *Half-flash and half-foolish*.. applied.. to a person, who has a smattering of the cant language, and.. pretends to a knowledge of life which he really does not possess. **1818** *Sporting Mag.* II. 217 Immense sums of money have been lost by the very flashest of the cognoscenti. **1839** H. Ainsworth *J. Sheppard* I. xii. 339 'Awake!—to be sure I am, my flash cove!' replied Sheppard.

4. Belonging to, connected with or resembling, the class of sporting men, *esp.* the patrons of the 'ring'.

1808 *Sporting Mag.* XXX. 126 A sort of flash man upon the town. **1809** *Ibid.* XXXIII. 228 Crib, who was backed by what is termed the flash side. **1823** BYRON *Juan* XI. xvii, Poor Tom was.. Full flash, all fancy. **1838** DICKENS *Nich. Nick.* xix, A gentleman with a flushed face and a flash air. **1862** WHYTE MELVILLE *Inside Bar* iv. (ed. 12) 267 After the departure of the flash butcher. **1880** G. R. SIMS *Three Brass Balls* xi, One of the flash young gentlemen who haunt suburban billiard-rooms.

5. Connected with or pertaining to the class of thieves, tramps, and prostitutes. Chiefly in *Comb.*, as ***flash-case*** (= FLASH-HOUSE), ***-cove***, ***-crib***, ***-ken***. Also FLASH-HOUSE, FLASH-MAN.

a **1700** B. E. *Dict. Cant. Crew, Flash-ken*, a House where Thieves use, and are connived at. **1718** C. HITCHIN *Receivers & Thief-Takers* 8 A Ken or House frequented by the Thieves and Thief-Takers, or, in their own dialect, thoroughly Flash. **1800** *Sporting Mag.* XVI. 26 Mack and I called at a flash ken in St. Giles's. **1819** *Ibid.* V. 122 The flash part of the creation. **1823** EGAN *Grose's Dict. Vulg. Tong., Flash Cove* or *Covess*, the master or mistress of the house. **1832** *Examiner* 684/1 She has been the associate of 'flash thieves'. **1839** H. AINSWORTH *J. Sheppard* I. xi. 322, I know the house.. it's a flash crib. *Ibid.* III. xii. 28 I've been to all the flash cases in town.

b. *esp.* of the language spoken by thieves: Cant, slang. Also quasi-*sb.*

A statement made by Dr. Aikin, *Country round Manchester* (1795) 437, that 'flash' language was so called because spoken by pedlars from a place called Flash near Macclesfield, is often repeated, but is of no authority.

1746 *Narr. Exploits H. Simms* in Borrow *Zincali* (1843) II. 129 They.. began to talk their Flash Language, which I did not then understand. **1756** TOLDERVY *Hist. Two Orph.* II. 79 Copper learnt flash, and to blow the trumpet. **1782** G. PARKER *Hum. Sk.* 34 No more like a Kiddy he'll roll the flash song. **1812** J. H. VAUX *Flash Dict.* (1819) 173 To speak good flash is to be well versed in cant terms. **1840** HOOD *Miss Kilmansegg, Her Misery* xviii, His comrades explain'd in flash. **1847** EMERSON *Repr. Men, Montaigne* Wks. (Bohn) I. 343 He will.. use flash and street ballads. **1858** O. W. HOLMES *Aut. Breakf.-t.* (1891) 257, I used all the flash words myself just when I pleased.

Hence ˈ**flashly** *adv.* (*slang*), in a flash manner; handsomely, elegantly. Also, in flash language.

1812 *Sporting Mag.* XXXIX. 19 A sort of despondency flashly termed fencing. **1857** *Song* in Ducange Anglicus *Vulg. Tongue* 42 Your fogle you must flashly tie.

flash (flæʃ), *v.*[1] Forms: 4–5 **flas(s)(c)he**, 6– **flash**. [app. of onomatopœic origin; with senses 1–2 cf. *plash, dash, splash*; the 13th c. variant FLASK has been referred to an alleged OF. **flasquer*, a supposed older form of Fr. *flaquer*. With sense 4 cf. *flap* and *slash*. The use of the word to express movement of fire or light (branch III), which is now the most prominent application, has not been found (unless in one doubtful example) before the second half of the 16th c. It seems to have originated in a transferred or extended use of sense 1; the coincidence of the initial sounds with those of *flame* may have helped the development of sense; cf. Sw. dial. *flasa*, Eng. dial. *flaze*, to blaze.]

I. Expressing movement of a liquid.

1. *intr.* Of the sea, waves, etc.: To rush along the surface; to rise and dash, *esp.* with the tide. Also with *up*. In later use with mixture of sense 9.

1387 TREVISA *Higden* (Rolls) *Ibid.* II. 369 Þe wawes of þe see Siculus, þat flascheþ and wascheþ vppon a rokke þat hatte Scylla. **1577–87** HOLINSHED *Chron.* I. 181/2 The sea.. also flashed vp vnto his legs and knees. **1613** W. BROWNE *Brit. Past.* II. iii, Yet will a many little surges be Flashing upon the rocke full busily. **1634–5** BRERETON *Trav.* (1844) I. 166 Sometimes the waves flashed into the ship at the loop-holes at stem. **1727–46** THOMSON *Summer* 601 The tortured wave.. Now flashes o'er the scattered fragments. **1833** M. SCOTT *Tom Cringle* (1859) xvii. 473 The roaring surf was flashing up over the clumps of green bushes. **1834** MEDWIN *Angler in Wales* II. 245 The Tivy.. flashed in a sheet of foam through the chasm. **1850** TENNYSON *In Mem.* lxx. 15 The cataract flashing from the bridge, The breaker breaking on the beach.

†**2.** *trans.* To dash or splash (water) *about, abroad, upon* something. *Obs.* exc. with mixture of sense 11.

c **1460** J. RUSSELL *Bk. Nurture* 985 Rynse hym with rose watur warme & feire vppon hym flasche. **1528** PAYNEL *Salerne Regim.* H b, The spume [froth of wine] to be thynne and soone flashed. **1590** SPENSER *F.Q.* II. vi. 42 With his raging armes he rudely flasht The waves about. **1602** CAREW *Cornwall* 266 Somewhat before a tempest if the sea-water bee flashed with a Sticke or Oare the same casteth a bright shining Colour. **1611** COTGR., *Gascher*, to dash, plash, flash (as water in rowing.) **1638** SIR T. HERBERT *Trav.* (ed. 2) 20 The wave flashing upon our decks.. much salt water. **1813** SCOTT *Rokeby* II. vi. 11 Flashing her sparkling waves abroad.

3. *trans.* To send a 'flash' or rush of water down (a river); also *absol.* Also, to send (a boat) down by a flash.

1791 W. JESSOP *Rep. Thames & Isis* 20 Every Inch that can be gained.. will save much time and water in flashing from above. **1840** MRS. BROWNING *Drama Exile* Poems 1889 I. 69 We [earth spirits].. Flash the river, lift the palm-tree, The dilated ocean roll. **1874** KNIGHT *Dict. Mech.*, s.v. *Flashing*, The gunboats were flashed over the falls at Alexandria by means of a wing-dam.

†**II. 4.** *trans.* To slash, strike swiftly; also, to dash, throw violently down. *Obs.*

?*a* **1400** *Morte Arth.* 4238 The ffelonne with the ffyne swerde freschely he strykes, The ffelettes of the fferrere syde he flassches in sondyre. **1548** UDALL, etc. *Erasm. Par. Luke* iv. 35 With muche great roaryng flashyng hym on the grounde.

III. With reference to fire or light.

5. a. *intr.* Of fire or light: To break forth suddenly. Of lightning: To break forth repeatedly, to play. Of a combustible, a gun, etc.: To give out flame, or sparks; to burst *into* flame. Also with *about, off, out, up*, etc.

The first quot. is difficult; possibly it gives a transferred use of sense 1. The passage is our only example of branch III before 16th c.

c **1400** *Destr. Troy* 12498 A thoner and a thicke rayne þrublet in the skewes.. All flasshet in a ffire the firmament ouer. **1548** [see FLASHING *ppl. a.* 1]. **1596** SPENSER *F.Q.* V. v. 8 So did Sir Artegall upon her lay.. That flakes of fire.. Out of her steely armes were flashing seene. **1618** ELTON *Exp. Rom. vii* (1622) 214 They shall feele the flames of Hell flashing vp in their owne soules. **1650** S. CLARKE *Eccl. Hist.* (1654) I. 9 The flame vehemently flashed about; which was terrible to the beholders. **1661** BOYLE *Phys. Ess., Salt Petre* §21. 121 The Nitre will immediately take fire, and flash out into blewish and halituous flames. **1791** MRS. RADCLIFFE *Rom. Forest* viii, The lightning began to flash along the chamber. **1858** CARLYLE *Fredk. Gt.* (1865) I. III. xi. 206 The gun flashed off, with due outburst, and almost with due effect. **1860** TYNDALL *Glac.* I. ii. 12 Lightning flashed about the summits of the Jungfrau. **1887** BOWEN *Virg. Æneid* III. 199 From the clouds fire flashes again and again.

b. Of a hydro-carbon: To give forth vapour at a temperature at which it will ignite.

1890 *Daily News* 22 Oct. 5/5 The low temperature at which both flashed.

c. ***to flash in the pan***: *lit.* said of a gun, when the priming powder is kindled without igniting the charge; *fig.* to fail after a showy effort, to fail to 'go off'.

1687 SETTLE *Refl. Dryden* 20 If Cannons were so well bred in his Metaphor as only to flash in the Pan, I dare lay an even wager that Mr. Dryden durst venture to Sea. **1741** *Compl. Fam. Piece* II. i. 320 It will occasion it oft-times to flash in the Pan a great while before it goeth off. **1792** GOUV. MORRIS in Sparks *Life & Writ.* (1832) I. 377 Their majesties flashed in the pan yesterday. **1830** GALT *Lawrie T.* III. ix. (1849) 114 Flashing in the pan scares ducks. **1852** W. JERDAN *Autobiog.* IV. xiii. 237 Cannon attempted a joke which flashed in the pan.

†**6.** *trans.* ? To scorch with a burst of hot vapour. *Obs. rare*$^{-1}$.

1600 HOLLAND *Livy* XXVIII. xxiii. 685 Others flashed and half senged with the hote steem of the vapour and breath issuing from the light fire.

7. *intr.* To emit or reflect light with sudden or intermittent brilliance; to gleam. Said also of the eyes.

1791 MRS. RADCLIFFE *Rom. Forest* ii, The almost expiring light flashed faintly upon the walls of the passage. **1820** SHELLEY *Let. to M. Gisborne* 281 Like wingèd stars the fire-flies flash and glance. **1834** MEDWIN *Angler in Wales* I. 268 Rapid zigzags, that flashed each like a plate of silver. **1854** TENNYSON *Charge Light Brigade* iv, Flash'd all their sabres bare, Flash'd as they turn'd in air. **1857** HOLLAND *Bay Path* xviii. 207 Her eyes flashed. **1868** FREEMAN *Norm. Conq.* (1876) II. vii. 26 The prince who had never seen steel flash in earnest.

8. a. *trans.* To emit or convey (light, fire, etc.) in a sudden flash or flashes. Also with *forth, out*.

1610 HOLLAND *Camden's Brit.* I. 274 They flashen fire from either hand. **1639** S. DU VERGER tr. *Camus' Admir. Events* 100 Yet ere he thundred by deeds he flasht out lightning by threats. **1697** DRYDEN *Æneid* VIII. 39 The glitt'ring Species.. on the Pavement play, And to the Cieling flash the glaring Day. **1744** GRAY *Let.* Poems (1775) 176 If any spark of Wit's delusive ray Break out, and flash a momentary day. **1842** TENNYSON *Locksley Hall* 186 Rift the hills, and roll the waters, flash the lightnings, weigh the Sun.

transf. and *fig.* **1592** SHAKS. *Ven. & Ad.* 348 But now her cheeke was pale and by and by It flasht forth fire. **1665** SIR T. HERBERT *Trav.* (1677) 179 Who flashes him this thundring retort, For thy ambition. **1854** J. S. C. ABBOTT *Napoleon* (1855) II. xxi. 397 His eyes flashed fire.

b. To send back as a flash from a mirror; to reflect. More fully ***to flash back***.

1716 POPE *Iliad* VIII. 54 Of heaven's undrossy gold the god's array, Refulgent, flash'd intolerable day. **1808** J. BARLOW *Columb.* v. 201 Then waved his gleamy sword that flash'd the day. **1808** SCOTT *Marm.* I. i, Their armour.. Flash'd back again the western blaze.

c. *transf.* To cause to appear like a flash of lightning; to send forth swiftly and suddenly. Also with *out*. Const. *in, into, on* or *upon*.

1589 GREENE *Menaphon* (Arb.) 32 She.. flashed out such a blush from her alabaster cheeks that they lookt like the ruddie gates of the morning. **1638** SIR T. HERBERT *Trav.* (ed. 2) 105 His name would flash terrour into the hearts of his most potent adversaries. **1700** FARQUHAR *Constant Couple* v. iii, Methinks the motto of this sacred pledge should flash confusion in your guilty face. **1794** COLERIDGE *Death Chatterton* vi, Thy native cot she flash'd upon thy view. **1813** SHELLEY *Q. Mab* III. 145 Red the gaze That flashes desolation, strong the arm That scatters multitudes.

d. ***to flash dead***: to strike dead with a flash.

1682 DRYDEN & LEE *Duke of Guise* IV. iii, This one departing glance shall flash thee dead. **1690** DRYDEN *Don Seb.* III. i, Now flash him dead, now crumble him to ashes.

e. ***to flash a glance, a look, one's eyes***.

1886 'M. GRAY' *Silence of Dean Maitland* I. ix, Cyril flashed upon him one of his droll glances, and laughed. **1888** MRS. H. WARD *R. Elsmere* xiii, She flashed a quick, defiant look at him. **1903** R. LANGBRIDGE *Flame & Flood* xvii, The young man.. flashed his insolent eyes.. at her.

f. *trans.* and *intr.* To switch (lights on a motor vehicle) on and off in order to communicate a warning, a direction, etc.; to signal in this way (*trans.* and *intr.*).

1957 J. KEROUAC *On Road* (1958) III. ix. 233 The guy shot by us.. and tooted his horn and flashed the tail lights for challenge. **1962** L. DEIGHTON *Ipcress File* xxviii. 180, I flashed the headlights and got an answering signal from the brake actuated red rear lights of a vehicle parked there. **1963** *Guardian* 23 Jan. 10/3 After having my head-lights adjusted, I started driving with them dipped. Having been 'flashed' by large numbers of drivers I can only assume that they are.. annoyed. **1965** 'W. HAGGARD' *Hard Sell* ix. 100 The Merc suddenly flashed him and he drew in. **1971** *Daily Tel.* (Colour Suppl.) 22 Oct. 23/4 Hold straight until you are quite sure you are in charge, flashing your brake lights if necessary.. so as to warn following traffic. *Ibid.* 26, I suspect he is the same man who flashes me frenziedly when I dare to use my head-lights before ten o'clock on a summer's night.

9. a. *intr.* To come like a flash of light; to burst suddenly into view or perception. Also with *forth, in, out*, etc.

1590 SPENSER *F.Q.* III. ii. 5 Ever and anone the rosy red Flasht through her face. **1683** DRYDEN *Life Plutarch* I. 118 The arguments.. flash immediately on your imagination, but leave no durable effect. **1781** GIBBON *Decl. & F.* II. xxxiv. 281 A martial ardour flashed from the eyes of the warriors. **1852** MRS. STOWE *Uncle Tom's C.* xv, A sudden recollection seemed to flash upon him. **1856** MASSON *Ess.* v. 165 In 1720.. he [Swift] again flashed forth as a political luminary. **1861** THACKERAY *Four Georges* iii. (1876) 75 Garrick flashing in with a story from his theatre. **1866** MRS. GASKELL *Wives & Dau.* xi. (1867) 111 Molly's colour flashed into her face. **1874** F. C. BURNAND *My Time* viii. 68 It flashed across me that almost the last name I had heard.. was this identical one. **1879** *Cassell's Techn. Educ.* III. 186 The picture flashes out almost instantly.

b. To move like a flash, pass with lightning speed. Also with cognate obj. ***to flash its way***. Also with *round*.

1821 SHELLEY *Hellas* 956 When desolation flashes o'er a world destroyed. **1839–40** W. IRVING *Wolfert's R.* (1855) 151 The French intellect.. flashes its way into a subject with the rapidity of lightning. **1853** KINGSLEY *Hypatia* v, The steel-clad apparition suddenly flashed round, and vanished. **1859** KINGSLEY *Misc.* (1860) II. 141 The lurchers flashed like grey snakes after the hare. **1877** BLACK *Green Past.* ii. (1878) 11 The swallows dipped and flashed and circled over the bosom of the lake. **1893** M. E. MANN *In Summer Shade* xvi, 'He must be paid.' 'How?' demanded Mary, flashing round upon him. **1903** R. LANGBRIDGE *Flame & Flood* iii, Susette flashed round upon him with a brilliant smile.

c. ***to flash back***: to jump back, as when a flame in a Bunsen burner retreats down the tube and burns at the air-inlet; to 'light back'.

1902 *Encycl. Brit.* XXVIII. 596/2 A still further addition of air causes the mixture to become so highly explosive that it flashes back into the tube of the burner.

10. a. To break out *into* sudden action; to pass abruptly *into* a specified state. Also with *forth, out*, and quasi-*trans.* with quoted words.

1605 SHAKS. *Lear* I. iii. 4 Euery howre He flashes into one grosse crime, or other. **1711** H. FELTON *Diss. Classics* (1713) 8 They flash out sometimes into an irregular Greatness of Thought. **1859** TENNYSON *Idylls, Enid* 273 Whereat Geraint flash'd into sudden spleen. **1862** G. P. SCROPE *Volcanos* 39 It [water] flashes instantly into steam with explosive violence. **1873** SYMONDS *Grk. Poets* vii. 189 Athens.. flashed.. into the full consciousness of her own greatness. **1875** *Harper's Mag.* Aug. 415/1 One day she flashed out upon Tom Saymour 'Vote!—why should I?' **1877** A. H. GREEN *Phys. Geol.* 219 The imprisoned steam flashes forth in repeated explosions. **1883** STEVENSON *Treasure Isl.* III. xiv, At this poor Tom flashed out like a hero. **1886** 'M. GRAY' *Silence of Dean Maitland* I. v, 'The whole village looking on and not lifting a finger—the cowards!' Lilian flashed out. **1907** *Munsey's Mag.* Nov. 169 'I intend to see Varani—alone,' she flashed.

b. ***to flash up***: to burst into sudden passion or anger.

1822 SCOTT *Fam. Let.* 25 June (1894) II. xviii. 143 Though we do not flash up in an instant like Paddy, our resentments are much more enduring.

11. a. *trans.* To cause to flash; to kindle with a flash; to draw or wave (a sword) so as to make it flash.

1632 LITHGOW *Trav.* VIII. 375 We eyther shot off a Harquebuse, or else flashed some powder in the Ayre. **1709** *Brit. Apollo* II. No. 7. 2/2 They will flash off the Gunpowder. **1801** SOUTHEY *Thalaba* v. xxxvi, Forth he flash'd his scymetar. **1816** KEATINGE *Trav.* (1817) I. 155 The oil.. is.. usually flashed; a few drops of water make it deflagrate. **1850** KINGSLEY *Alt. Locke* v. (1876) 60 Turning round I had a lantern flashed in my face. **1880** *Encycl. Brit.* XI. 325/2 Sometimes a small portion [of gunpowder] is roughly granulated, and 'flashed' on plates of glass.

†**b.** To illuminate intermittently; *transf.*, to make resplendent with bright colours. *Obs.* or *arch.*

1607 BREWER *Lingua* I. i, Limming and flashing it with various Dyes. **1861** BUCKLE *Civiliz.* II. 189 The darkened sky flashed by frequent lightning. **1894** E. H. BARKER *Two Summers in Guyenne* 71 The turf was flashed with splendid flowers of the purple orchis.

12. a. To express, utter, or communicate by a flash or flashes; *esp.* in modern use, to send (a message) along the wires of a telegraph.

1789 COWPER *Ann. Mirab.* 55 Then suddenly regain the prize And flash thanksgivings to the skies! **1813** SHELLEY *Q. Mab* v. 119 The proud rich man's eye Flashing command. **1847** TENNYSON *Princ.* Prol. 78 Thro' twenty posts of telegraph They flash'd a saucy message to and fro. **1858** FROUDE *Hist. Eng.* III. xvii. 459 The cannon.. flashed their

welcome through the darkness. **1888** BURGON *Lives 12 Gd. Men* II. v. 69 The intelligence was flashed next day all over England.

b. *Cinemat. trans.* and *intr.* To show abruptly on the screen; *intr.*, to change abruptly *to* (another scene).

1913 E. W. SARGENT *Technique of Photoplay* (ed. 2) ii. 15 A one word leader flashed on the screen that said 'Later'. **1935** H. G. WELLS *Things to Come* x. 93 Flash the date A.D. 2054. **1936** —— *Man who could work Miracles* (film ed.) VII. 43 Flash to a brief bright scene in a San Francisco hospital.

13. a. *intr.* To make a flash or display, cut a figure, show off. Also, *to flash it* (*about* or *away*). Now *colloq.* or *slang*.

1607 SHAKS. *Timon* II. i. 32 A naked gull Which flashes now a Phœnix. **1652** C. B. STAPYLTON *Herodian* 115 While they with Plaies and Sports doe squib and flash. **1697** COLLIER *Ess. Mor. Subj.* I. iii. 130 Methinks 'tis fine..to Flash in the Face of Danger. **1780** MRS. THRALE in Mad. D'Arblay *Diary & Lett.* 29 June (1842) I. 409 My master..jokes Peggy Owen for her want of power to flash. **1798** O'KEEFE *Fontainbleau* III. i, Spunging upon my customers, and flashing it away in their old clothes. **1798** *Geraldina* I. 46, I nod to him..whilst he is flashing the gentleman amongst the girls. **1877** *Five Years' Penal Serv.* iii. 220 He flashed it about a good deal for a long time..Sometimes he was a lord, at others an earl.

b. *slang.* To make a great display of, exhibit ostentatiously, show off, 'sport'.

1785 GROSE *Dict. Vulg. Tong.*, *Flash*..to shew ostentatiously; to flash one's ivory, to laugh and shew one's teeth. **1819** MOORE *Tom Crib's Mem.* (ed. 3) 2 His Lordship, as usual..is flashing his gab. **1832** *Examiner* 845/1 It was known that the deceased had money, in consequence of flashing his purse about. **1864** *Reader* 23 Jan. 96 Ladies go to church to exhibit their bonnets, and young gentlemen to flash their diamond rings.

c. *trans.* (also *refl.*). *slang.* Of a man: to exhibit or expose (part of one's body, esp. the genitals) briefly and indecently. Also *intr.*

1846 [see ROOT *sb.*[1] 4d]. **1893** FARMER & HENLEY *Slang* III. 11/2 *To flash it*,..to expose the person. **1968** [implied at FLASHING *vbl. sb.*[1] 5]. **1969** M. PUGH *Last Place Left* xv. 108 He has a great faith in people like me. He would flash himself to the Sovereign before he searched my house. **1978** G. VIDAL *Kalki* iv. 104 Men stared at me. Some leered. None, thank God, flashed.

14. In certain technical uses.

a. *Glass-making. intr.* Of a blown globe of glass: To spread *out* or expand into a sheet. Also *trans.* (*a*) To cause (a globe of glass) to expand into a sheet; (*b*) To cover (colourless glass) with a film of coloured glass; to melt (the film) *on* or *over* a sheet of colourless glass.

1839 URE *Dict. Arts* 581 s.v. *Glass-making* Few tools are needed for blowing and flashing crown-glass. **1846** W. JOHNSTON *Beckmann's Invent.* (ed. 4) I. 135 Plain glass flashed or coated with a very thin layer of [rose-coloured] glass. *Ibid.* 133 Glass-makers used to flash a thin layer of red over a substratum of plain glass. **1876** BARFF *Glass & Silicates* 82 Until at last the softened mass instantaneously flashes out into a circular sheet. **1883** PROCTOR in *19th Cent.* Nov. 882 Not merely flashed with a violet tint, but the glass itself so tinted.

b. *Electric lighting.* To make (a carbon filament) uniform in thickness, by plunging it when heated into a heavy hydro-carbon gas.

1888 *Pall Mall G.* 19 July 2/2 We have carried the manufacture of our filaments to such perfection that although we do not flash them there are absolutely no inequalities discoverable.

c. *Photogr.* To cover *over* with a very thin layer.

1903 *Nature* 29 Jan. 301/2 The so-formed negative is sprung from the wax, cleaned and polished, and flashed over with a very thin layer of nickel in a nickel bath.

Hence **flashed** *ppl. a.*

1876 BARFF *Glass & Silicates* 96 Glass made in this way is called 'coated' and sometimes 'flashed' glass. **1890** URQUHART *Electric Light* ix. (ed. 3) 284 'Flashed' Filaments.

flash (flæʃ), *v.*[2] [f. FLASH *sb.*[4]]

1884 *Cheshire Gloss.*, *Flash*, to put small sheets of lead under the slates of a house..to prevent the rain from running into the joint. **1957** *N.Z. Timber Jrnl.* Mar. 52/1 To flash means to make a watertight joint with sheet lead and other metal known as flashings, at the intersection, e.g. between chimney and roof. **1964** J. S. SCOTT *Dict. Building* 130 *Flash*, to make a weathertight joint, called a flashing.

'flashback, *sb.* [f. the verbal phr. **to flash back.*]

1. (See quots. and cf. FLASH *v.*[1] 9c.)

1903 *Motoring Ann.* 306 The highly inflammable vapour of petrol, and a 'flash-back', resulted in the total destruction of the car. **1963** *Times* 27 Feb. 4/5 Three electricians were taken to hospital with burns after a flashback and fire in the power house at the Premier Flour Mills, Silvertown, E.

2. *Cinemat.* A scene which is a return to a previous action in the film, a CUT-BACK; hence, a revival of the memory of past events, as in a pictorial or written presentation. (See FLASH *sb.*[2] 1e, and *v.*[1] 12b.)

1916 *Variety* 13 Oct. 28/4 In other words the whole thing is a flash-back of the episodes leading up to her marriage. **1928** J. GALLISHAW *Only Two Ways to write Story* I. vii. 177 With *Sunk* the method of presentation was chronological... In the case of *Paradise Island* the method is reversed. The order instead of being chronological is anti-chronological: it is the flash-back method. **1934** H. G. WELLS *Exper. Autobiogr.* II. vii. 487 When goddesses and Sea Ladies vanish and a flash back to the ancestral chimpanzee abolishes the magic caverns of Venus, human beings arrive. **1947** *Times* 1 Nov. 6/4 The film relates, in a prolonged flash-back, how the innocent Indian became corrupted by bewildering contact with those supposed to be his superiors in civilization. **1957** *Times Lit. Suppl.* 26 July 453/2 In his new novel..[he] uses with enviable ease a complicated system of flash-backs.

'flash-board. [f. FLASH *v.*[1] + BOARD *sb.*] **a.** (See quot. 1768.) **b.** A board set up on edge upon a mill-dam, when the water is low, to throw a larger quantity of water into the mill-race.

1768–74 TUCKER *Lt. Nat.* (1852) I. 32 The miller of an overshot mill..has shoots lying over every one of his wheels, stopped by flash-boards, at their upper ends. *Ibid.* Should an eel wriggle under any of the flash-boards, this might give the water a passage without any act of the miller. **1860** BARTLETT *Dict. Amer.*, *Flash Board.* **1868** PEARD *Water-Farm.* xv. 158 When..the connecting canals have been cut, and the flash-boards erected.

fig. **1822** T. L. PEACOCK *Maid Marian* iv, He pulled up all the flash-boards at once and gave loose to the full torrent of his indignation.

flasher ('flæʃə(r)). [f. FLASH *v.*[1] + -ER.] One who or that which flashes.

†**1.** One who splashes water. *Obs.*

1611 COTGR., *Gascheur*..also, a flasher or dasher of water. **1736** AINSWORTH, A flasher of water, *aspersor*.

2. a. Something which emits flashes of light.

1686 GOAD *Celest. Bodies* II. iv. 198 They were Spit-Fires, Thunderers and Flashers.

b. An automatic device for alternately lighting and extinguishing incandescent lamps, as in advertising and warning signs; such a sign or signal itself.

1909 *Install. News* III. 127 The effectiveness of the fixed pattern is greatly enhanced by the addition of a 'flasher'. **1928** *Publisher's Weekly* 30 June, Inset, Electric flashers 7 × 11" (loaned for special displays). **1932** *Flight* 1 July 613/2 A flasher is incorporated in the L.T. circuit and the beacon is usually operated on a flashing code sequence. **1944** *Times* 23 Aug. 5/4 A new technical term..comes from the Underground, where there are to be more thermal flashers..[i.e.] illuminated signs urging passengers to pass along the platform. **1958** *Observer* 17 Aug. 15/6 Triggers under the steering-wheel work the self-cancelling indicators and the headlamp flasher. **1966** T. WISDOM *High-Performance Driving* ix. 97 Never take for granted..that the car..with turn-indicator flashing left is actually proposing to turn left. The driver may well have left his 'flasher' on many corners ago. **1971** *Gloss. Electrotechnical, Power Terms* (*B.S.I.*) I. iii. 16 *Flasher relay*, relay in which the contact units make and break with a self-determined periodicity. **1971** K. ROYCE *Concrete Boot* iii. 36 The police closed in. They did it well. Plain cars and vans; no sirens or flashers.

†**3.** One of the attendants on a gaming table (see quot.). *Obs.*

1731 in Malcolm *Manners & Cust. Lond.* (1808) 166 A Flasher, to swear how often the bank has been stripped. **1756** W. TOLDERVY *Hist. Two Orphans* I. 68 [He] had often sate a flasher at M..d..g..n's. **1797** *Sporting Mag.* X. 312.

†**4.** A person of brilliant appearance or accomplishment.

1755 JOHNSON (citing *Dict.*), *Flasher*, a man of more appearance of wit than reality. **1779** MAD. D'ARBLAY *Diary* Oct. I. 260 They are reckoned the flashers of the place, yet everybody laughs at them for their airs. **1780** *Ibid.* May I. 333 Sir John Harrington..one of the gayest writers and flashers of her reign.

5. The workman who 'flashes' glass (see quot.).

1839 URE *Dict. Arts* 582 s.v. *Glass-making* He next hands it to the flasher, who..wheels it rapidly round opposite to a powerful flame, till it assumes..finally [the figure] of a flat circular table.

6. (See quot.)

1874 KNIGHT *Dict. Mech.* I. 876/2 *Flasher*..a form of steam-boiler in which small bodies of water are injected into a heated boiler and flashed into steam.

7. a. 'A name of the lesser butcher-bird: see *Flusher*' (Ogilvie 1882).

b. A fish (*Lobotes surinamensis*).

1882 JORDAN & GILBERT *Fishes N. Amer.* 555.

8. *Cricket.* (See quot. 1936.)

1936 *Daily Herald* 24 Dec. 15/6 The latter is a left-hand batsman, but is inclined to be a 'flasher' (one apt to chase balls outside the off-stump). **1956** R. ALSTON *Test Commentary* 14 If the regular opening batsmen fail, I'd try Benaud, he's no more of a 'flasher' than Trumper.

9. *slang.* One who 'flashes' or exposes himself indecently. See FLASH *v.*[1] 13c.

[**1896** FARMER & HENLEY *Slang* IV. 297/2 *Meat-flashing*, ..exposure of the person. Hence *meat-flasher* = a public offender in this line.] **1974** *Kingston* (Ontario) *News* 10 Jan. 2/6 A middle aged man indecently exposed himself to a female student... There were several reports of a so-called 'phantom flasher' in the University..area. **1976** A. POWELL *To keep Ball Rolling* I. iii. 44 He was apparently a 'flasher', who had just exposed himself.

flashful ('flæʃfʊl), *a. rare.* [f. FLASH *sb.* + -FUL.] Full of flashes.

1890 W. C. RUSSELL *Ocean Trag.* III. xxxi. 154 The sky..flashful in places with a view of the cross of the southern hemisphere. **1891** *Illustr. Lond. News* 13 June 774/3 A strange, gloomy huddle of discoloured countenances flashful with eyes.

flash-house. [f. FLASH *a.*[3] + HOUSE.] A house frequented by 'flash' persons (see FLASH *a.*[3] 5); a resort of thieves; also, a brothel.

1816 *Rep. Committee on Police Metrop.* 209 Is the flash-house an assistance to the officer? **1828** MACAULAY *Ess.*, *Hallam* (1843) I. 192 The humours of a gang of footpads, revelling with their favourite beauties at a flash-house. **1922** JOYCE *Ulysses* 434 You won't get a virgin in the flash houses.

flashily ('flæʃɪlɪ), *adv.* [f. FLASHY + -LY[2].] In a flashy manner; gaudily, showily. Also, like or as a flash.

1730–6 BAILEY (folio), *Flashily*, vainly, frothily. **1863** SPEKE *Discov. Nile* 154 (Farmer) Flashily dressed in coloured cloths and a turban. **1864** MISS BRADDON *H. Dunbar* v, He chose no gaudy colours or flashily-cut vestments. **1888** BRYCE *Amer. Commw.* III. xcix. 392 An ill-omened looking man, flashily dressed, and rude in demeanour.

flashiness ('flæʃɪnɪs). [f. as prec. + -NESS.] The quality of being flashy.

†**1.** Want of flavour, insipidity. *Obs.*

1626 BACON *Sylva* § 461 When you would take away either their [Artichokes, etc.] Flashiness or Bitterness. **1655** MOUFET & BENNET *Health's Improv.* (1746) 345 What is Fish ..before Salt correcteth the Flashiness thereof?

fig. *a* **1603** T. CARTWRIGHT *Confut. Rhem. N.T.* (1618) 481 The flashinesse and unsavourinesse of the allegories. **1769** *Public Advertiser* 8 June 4/2 The Insipidity and Flashiness of Quality-prattle.

2. a. Of speech: Superficial brilliance. **b.** Of dress: Gaudiness, showiness.

1709 *Brit. Apollo* II. No. 9. 2/2 The Flashyness of his Discourse. **1854** HAWTHORNE *Eng. Note-bks.* (1879) I. 163 With some little touch of sailor-like flashiness.

flashing ('flæʃɪŋ), *vbl. sb.*[1] [f. FLASH *v.*[1] + -ING[1].] The action of the vb. in various senses.

1. A splashing (of water).

1611 COTGR., *Gaschement*..a flashing, dashing, or plashing, as of water in rowing. **1727** BAILEY vol. II., *Flashing*..dashing or spurting as Water, a Spurting.

2. The process of letting down a flash of water to carry a boat over the shallows of a river.

1791 *Rep. Navig. Thames & Isis* 11 By removing the shallows, and continuing the use of Flashing.

3. The bursting out or sending forth of flame or light.

1573 BARET *Alv.* F 617 The Flashing of fire, or lightning, *coruscatio*. **1652** F. KIRKMAN *Clerio & Lozia* 81 They began their Flashings and Musique until all were gone out. **1748** FRANKLIN *Lett.* Wks. 1840 V. 218 The sphere of electrical attraction is far beyond the distance of flashing. **1880** BROWNING *Dram. Idylls*, Ser. II. *Echetlos* 8 A flashing came and went.

transf. and *fig.* **1613** PURCHAS *Pilgrimage* I. v. (1614) 26 So much the greater is their sinne, that seeke to flash out these flashings. **1641** MILTON *Ch. Govt.* I. (1851) 12 Rome, from whence was to be expected the furious flashing of Excommunications. **1676** R. DIXON *Nat. Two Test.* 282 Mingled with Poetical flashings and ginglings.

4. A rapid movement resembling or producing a flash of light; the drawing or waving of a sword with a flash.

1865 LECKY *Ration.* (1878) I. 43 The coruscations of the Aurora are said to have been attributed to the flashings of their wings. **1886** SHELDON tr. *Flaubert's Salammbo* 19 Excited by the flashing of the naked swords.

5. *slang.* = *indecent exposure* s.v. EXPOSURE 1f.

[**1896**: see FLASHER 9.] **1968** J. LOCK *Lady Policeman* ii. 11 City parks also have their share of 'flashing'. **1971** R. BUSBY *Deadlock* vi. 84 He's got two previous for indecent assault and one for flashing on his form sheet. **1977** E. J. TRIMMER et al. *Visual Dict. Sex* (1978) xxii. 246 The commonest of the indecent offences before the courts is *indecent exposure*, sometimes called 'flashing'.

6. *techn.* **a.** *Glass-making.* (See FLASH *v.* 14*a*.)

1832 BABBAGE *Econ. Manuf.* iv. (ed. 3) 35 The process for making window glass, termed flashing. **1839** *Sat. Mag.* 23 Feb. 66/1 Flashing, that is, uniting a thin layer of coloured glass with another layer which is colourless.

b. *Electric lighting.* (see quot. and FLASH *v.* 14b.)

1892 *Gloss. Electr. Terms* in *Lightning* 3 Mar. Suppl., *Flashing*, (*a*) Of a dynamo machine. Abnormally long sparks sometimes seen at the commutator of a dynamo. (*b*) A process for rendering the filaments of incandescent lamps of uniform resistance throughout.

7. *attrib.* and *Comb.*, as *flashing-furnace*; **flashing-board**, a sloping board at the bottom of a door or casement to keep off the rain; **flashing-point**, the temperature at which the vapour given off from an oil or hydrocarbon will 'flash' or ignite.

1852 BURN *Nav. & Mil. Techn. Dict.* II. Eng.-Fr., Flashing board, *reverseau*. **1839** URE *Dict. Arts* 580 (*Glass-making*) There are..several subsidiary furnaces to a crown-house..3. a flashing furnace, and bottoming hole for communicating a softening heat. **1878** *Ure's Dict. Arts* IV. 570 The flashing-point was proved to have been abnormally high.

flashing ('flæʃɪŋ), *vbl. sb.*[2] [f. FLASH *v.*[2]; cf. FLASH *sb.*[4]] *concr.* (See quot. 1874.)

1782 *Phil. Trans.* LXXII. 359 At its junction with the wall a flashing of lead is carried along horizontally. **1842** in GWILT *Encycl. Archit.* §2214. **1874** KNIGHT *Dict. Mech.* I. 876/2 *Flashing*, (*a*) A lap-joint used in sheet-metal roofing, where the edges of the sheets meet on a projecting edge. (*b*) A strip of lead leading the drip of a wall into a gutter.

flashing ('flæʃɪŋ), *ppl. a.* [f. FLASH *v.*[1] + -ING[2].]

1. a. That flashes, in various senses of the vb.

1548 UDALL, etc. *Erasm. Par. Jas.* iii. 5 Wherof cometh that horrible and broade flasshing flame of fyre? **1616** J. LANE *Cont. Sqr's. T.* xi. 330 His horse was of a sangine color redd, so weare his flasshinge plumes aloft his head. **1727–46** THOMSON *Summer* 382 Fast, fast they plunge amid the flashing wave. **1835** LYTTON *Rienzi* I. iii, Before the flashing eye and menacing gesture of the cavalier.

b. *transf.* and *fig.*

1613 HIERON *Triall of Adopt.* Wks. 1624 I. 315 Imagination and fancy may breed a certaine flashing ioy, but there is no perpetuity, no setlednesse of reioycing. **1654** Z. COKE *Logick* Ded. (1657) A v b, Scorched with flashing zeal. **1826** DISRAELI *Viv. Grey* v. xii, Her lovely face was crimsoned with her flashing blood. **1875** JOWETT *Plato* (ed. 2) II. 93 Again and again she beholds the flashing beauty of the beloved.

c. ***flashing light*** (in a lighthouse, etc.). ***flashing signals***, signals made with flashes of light. Hence, applied to a direction indicator on a motor vehicle which signals with flashes of light.

1858 *Merc. Marine Mag.* V. 30 Flashing Light on Hogsten .. It is Fixed, with a Flash once every three minutes. **1863** COLOMB in *Jrnl. R. United Service Instit.* VII. 386 We then agreed that .. a system of flashing signals was practicable. **1932** *Daily Express* 20 Sept. 3 Everyone's talking about the new flashing Direction Indicator which only Morris cars carry. This device gives safer signalling. **1959** '*Motor*' *Man.* (ed. 36) vi. 183 Another change since the war has been the progressive displacement of the semaphore-type of direction indicator by flashing light signals, and this latter system is now nearly universal on modern cars... Flashing turn indicators are operated either by a switch of the self-cancelling type mounted on the steering column, or by an independent switch mounted within easy reach of the driver.

2. *Comb.* as ***flashing-eyed*** adj.

1880 MISS BROUGHTON *Sec. Th.* III. iv, 'You are ruining the child!' cries Gillian, still flashing-eyed and panting.

Hence **ˈflashingly** *adv.*, in a flashing manner.

1891 *Illustr. Lond. News* 21 Nov. 658/3 They rain flashingly, a visible brilliance.

ˈflashless, *a.* Emitting or producing no flash, *esp.* of gunpowder which ignites without flashing; without a flash (various senses).

1908 *Westm. Gaz.* 2 Mar. 6/2 The latest American artillery wonder is .. a 'noiseless, smokeless, flashless, colourless, fumeless gun', which, it is claimed, can throw two million bullets an hour. **1922** [see *flash-spotting* s.v. FLASH *sb.*[2] 14 b]. **1929** R. GRAVES *Good-bye to All That* xi. 123 Before the war there were the two line battalions and the depot; the affiliated and flash-less territorials. **1945** *Times* 10 Oct. 3/4 General Marshall, however, gives the Germans two points: their triple-purpose 88 mm. gun and their powder, flashless as well as smokeless.

flashly *adv.*: see FLASH *a.*[3]

flash-man. (Also as two words.) [FLASH *a.*[3]]

a. One who is 'flash' or knowing; a companion of thieves; a bully, a 'fancy-man'. **b.** A sporting man; a patron of the 'ring'; a 'swell'.

a. **1789** G. PARKER *Life's Painter* 141 A flash-man is a fellow that lives upon the hackneyed prostitution of an unfortunate woman of the town. **1833** MARRYAT *P. Simple* (1863) 235 A large mob .. vowing vengeance on us for our treatment of their flash man. **1859** H. KINGSLEY *G. Hamlyn* v, 'You're playing a dangerous game, my flash man.'

b. **1812** *Sporting Mag.* XXXIX. 21 The display of flash-men, from the Peer on the coach-box, to the most gentlemanly-looking pick-pocket, was very complete. **1819** MOORE *Tom Crib's Mem.* 55 Shouts and yells From Trojan Flash-men and Sicilian Swells Fill'd the wide heav'n.

ˈflashmonger. [f. as prec. + MONGER.] One who uses the 'flash' language.

1825 C. M. WESTMACOTT *Eng. Spy* I. 395 A little crib, as the flashmongers would call it.

flashness (ˈflæʃnɪs). [f. FLASH *a.*[2] and [3] + -NESS.] The quality or state of being flash.

†**1. a.** Of the stomach: Weakness. **b.** Of reasoning: Insipid, flavourless character; superficiality.

1562 TURNER *Baths* 8 b, They are good for the lousnes and flashnes of the stomack. **1604** T. WRIGHT *Passions* v. iv. 184 The acutenesse in the other [plausible persuasions] will allay their flashnesse and render them pleasant.

2. a. Gaudiness. **b.** Affectation of 'flash' ways. See FLASH *a.*[3] 1.

1885 RUNCIMAN *Skippers & Sh.* 260 All the tawdry flashness of the place. **1888** BOLDREWOOD *Robbery under Arms* xvi. (1890) 109 'Through Starlight's cussed flashness and carryin's on in fine company.'

ˈflash-over. Also flashover. [f. verbal phr. *to flash over* (see FLASH *v.*[1] 5).] An accidental arc discharge from a conductor when its voltage is greater than that which the insulation can withstand.

1892 S. P. THOMPSON *Dyn.-Electr. Mach.* (ed. 4) 88 Commutators of the ordinary sort with thin mica insulation between the bars .. are easily short-circuited by the flash-over. **1931** *Nature* 21 Feb. 290 It was .. found out that flashovers occurred in the strings of suspended insulators in industrial areas. **1950** *Engineering* 20 Jan. 79/2 Lightning currents which flowed to earth after the tower or earth wire had been struck, did not build up .. high voltages .. and so cause flashover. **1962** H. C. WESTON *Sight, Light & Work* (ed. 2) ix. 253 Similar radiation is emitted when a 'flash over' occurs between electricity conductors other than welding electrodes.

flashy (ˈflæʃɪ), *a.* [f. FLASH *sb.*[2] and *v.* + -Y[1]. Association with FLASH *a.*[2] and [3] has probably affected some of the senses.]

†**1.** Throwing up water, splashing. *Obs.*

1583 STANYHURST *Aeneis* II. (Arb.) 59 Not so great a ruffling the riuer strong flasshye reteyneth. **1611** COTGR., *Gascheux*, flashie, plashie, washie, dashing, bespatling.

2. †**a.** Over-moist, watery, frothy. †**b.** Insipid, tasteless, vapid.

1625 BACON *Ess., Studies* (Arb.) 11 Distilled Bookes, are like common distilled Waters, Flashy things. **1658** EVELYN *Fr. Gard.* 198 The other [turnips] being soft, flashy, and insipid. **1669** WORLIDGE *Syst. Agric.* (1681) 41 The taste of them is more sweet and flashy than Groats made of common Oats. **1702** W. J. *Bruyn's Voy. Levant* xxi. 94 They [artichokes] eat not so flashy as when they are Boyled after our Way. **1743** *Lond. & Country Brew.* IV. (ed. 2) 329 It is not the first flashy, frothy Yeast. **1771** *Ann. Reg.* 107/1 The young grass which springs in consequence of a flood, is of so flashy a nature that it occasions this common complaint. **1847** HALLIWELL, *Flashy* .. loose, unstable, as unsound grass; insipid.

†**c.** *fig.* Of persons and immaterial things: Trifling, destitute of solidity or purpose; void of meaning, trashy. *Obs.*

1597–8 BP. HALL *Sat.* Postscr., It can yeeld nothing but a flashy and loose conceyt to the judgement. **1637** MILTON *Lycidas* 122 Their lean and flashie songs. **1647** TRAPP *Comm. Epistles* 146 Their mirth is frothy and flashy, such as smooths the brow, but fils not the brest. **1679** SHADWELL *True Widow* 31 They are a company of flashy, frothy Fellows. **1745** J. MASON *Self-Knowl.* III. vi. (1853) 202 To read Froth and Trifles all our Life, is the way always to retain a flashy and juvenile Turn.

3. Giving off flashes, shining by flashes; glittering, sparkling, brilliant. *lit.* and *fig.* Also, lasting only for a flash, transitory, momentary.

1609 HOLLAND *Amm. Marcell.* XXIII. xii. 239 Flashie lightenings. **1630** PRYNNE *God No Impostor* 13 Reprobates haue oft times many sodaine, transitory, and flashy ioyes. **1682** *New News from Bedlam* 28 My Gallick Tongue, and my rare flashy Wit, Shall make the Whigs and all the Tories split Themselves with laughing. *a* **1711** KEN *Hymnotheo* Poet. Wks. 1721 III. 119, I soon felt my flashy Goodness fade. **1741** RICHARDSON *Pamela* (1742) III. 343 So flashy and transient a Glare. **1780** MAD. D'ARBLAY *Diary* Apr., She was very flashy, and talked away all the evening. **1784** C. BURNEY *Let.* 16 Jan. in F. Burney *Early Diary* (1889) II. 317, I had a good flashey evening. **1819** H. BUSK *Vestriad* IV. 35 One ruby glitter'd like the flashy Mars. **1826** SCOTT *Jrnl.* 29 Mar., A fine, flashy, disagreeable day; snow-clouds sweeping past among sunshine. **1840** MACAULAY *Life & Lett.* (1883) II. 81, I will try to make as interesting an article, though I fear not so flashy, as that on Clive. **1884** *Manch. Exam.* 11 Sept. 5/1 He looks beyond the momentary triumphs of a flashy and adventurous policy.

b. In depreciative sense, chiefly of speech, a speaker, or writer: Superficially bright; brilliant, but shallow; cheaply attractive.

a **1690** G. FOX *Jrnl. Life*, etc. I. 108 An high Notionist, and a flashy Man. **1739** CIBBER *Apol.* v. 107 The false, flashy Pretender to Wit. **1823** DE QUINCEY *Lett. Educ.* v. (1860) 97 The secondhand report of a flashy rhetorician. **1835** BROWNING *Paracelsus* 129 Patient merit Obscured awhile by flashy tricks. **1883** *Century Mag.* XXVI. 295/1 As stories, these were cheap and flashy.

†**4.** Excited, impulsive, eager. *Obs.*

1632 VICARS *Virgil* XI. 366 The ladie .. With light-heel'd flashy haste the horse o'retook. **1767** BUSH *Hibernia Cur.* (1769) 22 By that time he has discharged his five or six bottles, he will get a little flashy, perhaps. **1781** P. BECKFORD *Hunting* xix. 244, I have seen hounds so flashy, that they would break away from the huntsman as soon as they saw a cover.

5. Showy, fine-looking; gaudy, glaring.

1801 GABRIELLI *Myst. Husb.* III. 255 They then got into their carriage, a mighty flashy one, to my mind. **1805** WELLINGTON in Gurw. *Disp.* 14 Jan., The equipment which I propose .. although not so flashy, would be more useful. **1829** CUNNINGHAM *Brit. Paint.* I. 31 People naturally fond of flashy colours. **1856** LEVER *Martins of Cro' M.* 315 The splendour of a very flashy silk waistcoat.

6. Of persons: Given to show, fond of cutting a dash, 'swellish'; also, vain and conceited.

1687 CONGREVE *Old Bach.* I. iv, Young termagant flashy sinners. *a* **1704** T. BROWN *Pleas. Epist.* Wks. 1730 I. 109 Those flashy fellows, your Covent Garden poets. **1787** G. COLMAN *Inkle & Yarico* II. i, A young flashy Englishman will sometimes carry a whole fortune on his back. **1850** HAWTHORNE *Amer. Note-bks.* (1883) 375 Veteran topers, flashy young men, visitors from the country.

7. *Comb.*, as ***flashy-looking*** adj.

1852 EARP *Gold Col. Australia* 72 That flashy-looking man in a tandem was transported for bank robbery. **1880** MARG. LONSDALE *Sister Dora* viii. 209 A flashy-looking man, with conspicuous rings and watch-chain.

†**flask**, *sb.*[1] *Obs.* [var. of FLASH *sb.*[1]] = FLASH *sb.*[1] 1.

a **1300** *E.E. Psalter* cxlii[i]. 7 Noght turne þou þi face fra me, And to falland in flask like sal I be. **1472** *Mem. Ripon* (Surtees) III. 242 Set respondet de 2s. de annuo reddito exeunte de uno clauso vocato Flask infra territorium de Northstanley.

flask (flɑːsk, -æ-), *sb.*[2] Forms: 1 flasce, flaxe, 6–7 flaske, 7 flasque, 6– flask. [A word found in nearly all the Teut. and Rom. langs.; whether adopted from late L. into Teut., or conversely, is undetermined. The earliest known examples are in Latin; three different declensional forms appear in med.L., and all of them are represented in the Rom. langs. (1) In Gregory's *Dialogues c* 600 (II. xviii; cf. I. ix) the form *flascō*, *flascōnem* (whence It. *fiascone*, F. *flacon*: see FLAGON) denotes a wooden vessel, apparently a small keg intended to be carried by pedestrians and to contain a supply of wine to be consumed on a journey; it is there stated to be a word belonging to the vulgar speech. In later use the word appears as a synonym of *butticula*, BOTTLE, and applied to a vessel either of wood, leather, metal, earthenware or glass. The Greek transl. of Gregory's *Dialogues*, believed to be of the 8th c., has φλασκίον, which is frequent in Byzantine writers of the 10th c. (2) In the 7th c. Isidore (*Etym.* XX. vi. §2) gives the form *flasca*, which he regards as a derivative of Gr. φιάλη, stating that *flascæ* were originally made for carrying and storing *phialæ* (? shallow drinking cups), though afterwards used to contain wine; the form survives in It. *fiasca*, OF. *flache*, *flasche*, *flaske*, *flasque* (the last of these survived till 16th c., and in the sense 'powder-flask' to a later period). (3) The form *flascus* is given in Du Cange, but is prob. only a latinized form of It. *fiasco*, which may represent med.L. *flasco* (nom.); equivalent forms are Sp. *flasco*, *frasco*, Pg. *frasco*.

The word occurs in all the Teut. langs. exc. Goth., and always as wk. fem.: OE. *flasce*, more usually *flaxe*, OHG. *flasca* (MHG. *vlasche*, also *vlesche* with the vowel change normal in some dialects before *sch*; mod.Ger. *flasche*), MDu. *flassche*, *flessche* (mod.Du. *flesch*); ON. *flaska* is doubtful, as it has only been found in the nicknames *flǫsku-skegg*, *flǫsku-bakr*, explained by Vigf. as 'bottle-beard', 'bottle-back'; Icel., Sw. *flaska*, Da. *flaske* may be from Ger. In the mod. continental Teut. langs. it is the ordinary word for bottle; in OHG. it had the same wider sense as in OE. (see 1 below).

The OE. word, which would normally have become **flash* in mod.E., appears not to have survived into ME. In 16th c. the F. *flasque* was adopted in the sense powder-flask (the wider sense being then already antiquated in Fr.). The older Fr. sense, a bottle, first appears in Eng. about 1700; whence it was adopted is not clear, but as the word is chiefly associated with Italian wine and oil, it may most naturally be regarded as from the It. *fiasco*, the etymological identity of which with the already existing Eng. word would be readily perceived.

Scholars who regard the word as of Rom. origin usually accept the view of Diez, that *flasco* is for **vlasco*, a metathesis of **vasclo*, from L. *vasculum*. This is satisfactory with regard to meaning (St. Gregory describes as *vascula lignea* what he says were vulgarly called *flascones*), and involves no insuperable difficulty with regard to form, though the phonetic process supposed has no precise parallel in any known instance; for approximately similar phenomena, such as *flaba* from *fābula*, see Diez. The early occurrence of the types *flascam*, *flascōnem*, and the absence of the type *flascum* in early use, are somewhat unfavourable to this hypothesis. The assumption that the word is of Teut. origin is chronologically legitimate, and presents no difficulty exc. the absence of any satisfactory etymology. A connexion with FLAT *a.* would be phonetically probable, but there is no evidence that the sb. originally meant a flat vessel. From Teut. the word has been adopted into many other langs.: Lapp *flasko*, *lasko*, Hung. *palaczk*, Polish *flasza*, Czech *flaše*.]

†**1.** In OE.: A vessel of wood, skin, or other material, for carrying liquor. *Obs.*

Prob. not widely current in OE.; it occurs chiefly as a rendering of the cognate L. word, which in some glossaries is rendered by *butruc*.

a **900** WERFERTH *Gregory's Dial.* II. xviii, Twa treowene fatu wines fulle ðа syndon on folcisc flaxan ȝehatene [orig. *quæ vulgo flascones vocantur*]. *c* **1000** *Ags. Gosp.* Mark xiv. 14 Sum man berende sume wæterflaxan [Vulg. *lagenam aquæ*]. *c* **1000** ÆLFRIC *Colloq.* in Wr.-Wülcker 97 Ic bicȝe hyda and fell .. and wyrce of him .. flaxan.

2. a. A case of leather or metal (formerly often of horn) carried by soldiers or sportsmen to hold gunpowder. Now usually *powder-flask*.

[The fig. quot. from Donne is referred by Latham to a supposed sense 'quiver'. The *Cent. Dict.* omits the quot., but gives the sense 'a quiver, a set of arrows in a quiver', quoting (prob. from Nares) a misprinted version of a passage from Fairfax, q.v. in FLASH *sb.*[3]]

1549 *Privy Council Acts* (1890) II. 348 Flaskes, cviij; touche boxes, c. **1598** BARRET *Theor. Warres* III. i. 34 To charge his peece, either with his flask or bandelier. **1630** *R. Johnson's Kingd. & Commw.* 217 Every souldier is able to make .. his owne Flaske and Touch-box. **1634** T. JOHNSON *Parey's Chirurg.* II. (1678) 273 His Guard had his Flasque full of Gunpowder set on fire. **1865** DOUGALL *Shooting* (ed. 2) 66 The most pleasant flask to handle is that covered with leather.

fig. **1612–5** BP. HALL *Contempl. O.T.* XX. ix, This sulphurous flaske [Rabshakeh], therefore, dyes in his own smoke. *a* **1631** DONNE *St. Lucie's Day* Wks. (Grosart) II. 203 The sun is spent, and now his flasks Send forth light squibbs, no constant rayes.

b. (See quot.) ? *Obs.*

1769 FALCONER *Dict. Marine* (1789) F iij, Powder-flasks, or flasks charged with gun-powder and fitted with a fuse, are .. provided .. to be thrown upon the enemy's deck.

3. a. A bottle, usually of glass, of spheroidal or bulbous shape, with a long narrow neck; applied *esp.* to the bottles of this form, protected by a covering of wicker-work or plaited grass, etc. in which wines and olive oil are exported from Italy (also more fully ***Florence flask***); a similar vessel for use in a laboratory. In verse

sometimes used loosely for 'bottle'. Also, the contents or capacity of a flask.
1693 SOUTHERNE *Maid's Last Prayer* II. i, A drop of oil left in a flask of wine. 1697 DAMPIER *Voy.* I. 535 A Flask of Wine which holds 3 quarts will cost 18 Stivers. 1701 DE FOE *True-born Eng.* II. 60 They toss the flask. 1705-30 S. GALE in *Bibl. Topog. Brit.* III. 33 We..were entertained with several flasks of excellent Florence. 1708 W. KING *Cookery* iv, Then for the Bourdeaux you may freely ask; But the Champaigne is to each man his flask. 1816 J. SMITH *Panorama Sc. & Art* II. 12 Having fitted a brass cap..to the mouth of a thin bottle, or Florence flask. 1841 W. SPALDING *Italy & It. Isl.* II. 42 In many graves earthen flasks. 1842 TENNYSON *Audley Crt.* 26 A flask of cider from his father's vats. 1878 HUXLEY *Physiogr.* 40 To boil water in a glass vessel, such as a Florence flask. 1882 OUIDA *Maremma* I. 191 Had some black bread and a flask of water.

†**b.** A definite quantity of liquid (see quot.).
a1700 B. E. *Dict. Cant. Crew, Flasque*..also a Pottle or five Pints and half, that quantity, formerly of Florence, now of any Wine.

c. A bottle of glass or metal, somewhat flat in shape and of size suitable to be carried in the pocket, intended to contain a supply of wine or other beverage for use on a journey; usually furnished with a screw-top, and (when made of glass) encased in leather for protection.
1814 SCOTT *Wav.* xlv, 'You shall have it', answered.. Waverley..giving him some drink from his flask. 1860 TYNDALL *Glac.* I. xi. 80 Our brandy flasks were also nearly exhausted. 1861 DICKENS *Gt. Expect.* xx, A pocket-flask of sherry.

d. (See quot.)
1872 RAYMOND *Statist. Mines & Mining* 16 Which claimed to have a capacity for delivering 4,000 flasks per month. 1881 —— *Mining Gloss., Flask*, an iron bottle in which quick-silver is sent to market. It contains 76½ pounds.

4. a. *Founding.* A frame or box used to hold a portion of the mould for casting. [Perh. a distinct word.]
1697 EVELYN *Numism.* vi. 214 Medals..counterfeited by casting off in the Flask. a1700 B. E. *Dict. Cant. Crew, Flasque*, a Bottle of Sand, bound about with Iron, into which the melted Metal is by Coyners and others poured. 1852-61 *Archit. Publ. Soc. Dict.* s.v., *Flask*, a term used by ironfounders to express the iron or wood frame intended to receive the sand which forms the upper or the movable part of the mould.

b. *Dentistry.* A sectional metal container for holding a denture during vulcanization.
1859 *Brit. Jrnl. Dental Sci.* Apr. 463/1 In 1846, the necessity became imperative for what are now called in America 'Putnam's vulcanizing flasks'. 1860 J. RICHARDSON *Pract. Treat. Mech. Dentistry* xv. 362 In forming the matrix, a vulcanizing flask is used. *Ibid.* 364 On separating the flask, the teeth, with the wax and temporary plate, will be found attached to the section of the matrix last formed. 1911 G. H. WILSON *Man. Dental Prosthetics* vi. 258 The edges of the denture as it comes from the flask are rough and irregular from the extension of excess vulcanite. 1963 J. OSBORNE *Dental Mechanics* (ed. 5) xix. 378 Whilst ordinary denture flasks may be used for acrylic teeth, small flasks are easier to handle and less wasteful in plaster.

5. *s.w. dial.* A kind of basket (see quot.).
[In Welsh *ffasg*; cf. FLASKET (Welsh *ffasged*), from which this may possibly be a back-formation. Cf. however the use of OF. *flache* for a certain measure of capacity for peas, etc.]
1888 ELWORTHY *W. Somerset Word-bk., Flask*, the large oval basket used for linen by all washerwomen. 1891 *Daily News* 15 May 7/2 A 'flask' containing either a turkey or a goose.

6. *attrib.* and *Comb.*, as ***flask-case, -glass, -shaped***; also, **flask-leather**, a fastening for a powder-flask; **flask-shell**, a mollusc whose shell is flask-shaped.
1709 *Lond. Gaz.* No. 4572/4 Her Majesty hath been graciously pleased..to Grant unto Jane Tasker..the sole working and making of *Flask-Cases, and covering and casing with Flags, Rushes and Straw, *Flask glasses now used in England, in imitation of those which come from Florence, during the space of fourteen Years. 1598 BARRET *Theor. Warres* III. i. 34 With his..*Flask-leather upon the right thigh. 1835-6 TODD *Cycl. Anat.* I. 43/2 The cirrigrada have..a large *flask-shaped stomach. 1868 WOOD *Homes without H.* v. 105 A common British species, the *Flask Shell (*Gastrochæna modiolina*) is notable for its habit of boring through various shells.

†**flask**, *sb.*[3] *Obs.* Also 7 **flasque**. [ad. Fr. *flasque* one of the cheeks of a gun-carriage, var. of *flaque* plank, beam, perh. of Teut. origin; cf. Ger. *flach* level, flat. In 16th c. *flanque* (app. = 'side piece,' f. *flanc* FLANK *sb.*[1]) occurs in the same sense.] The bed in a gun-carriage.
1578 *Inv. R. Wardrobe & Jewel-ho.* (1815) 258 Ane flask of elme for ane moyane. a1700 B. E. *Dict. Cant. Crew, Flasque*..a Carriage for Ordinance. 1721-1800 BAILEY, *Flask*, a Bed in the Carriage of a Piece of Ordnance.

†**flask**, *v.*[1] *Obs.* In 3 **flaskien, vlasken.** [See FLASH *v.*]
1. *trans.* To splash, sprinkle; = FLASH *v.* 2.
a1225 *Ancr. R.* 314 Heo vlaskeð water þeron. *Ibid.*, And ȝif dust of lihte þouhtes windeð up to swuðe, flaskie teares on ham.
2. To cause to wave or flutter, to flap.
1565 GOLDING *Ovid's Met.* II. 14 The weather flaskt and whisked vp her garmentes being slacke. *Ibid.* VI. 886 Boreas gan To flaske his wings, with wauing of the which he raysed than So great a gale.

flask (flɑːsk, -æ-), *v.*[2] [f. FLASK *sb.*[2]] *trans.*
†**a.** To protect as a flask is protected. **b.** To put into a flask.
1707 *Curios. in Husb. & Gard.* 212, I put at the bottom of a Vessel the Ozier that flask'd a Glass Bottle. 1855 BROWNING *Popularity* xii, There's the extract, flasked and fine.
c. *spec.* in *Dentistry*, to place (a denture) in a flask and surround with plaster ready for vulcanizing. So **flasked** *ppl. a.*, **'flasking** *vbl. sb.* and *ppl. a.*
1873 O. COLES *Man. Dental Mech.* x. 194 The teeth and bands having been properly adjusted to the model, and to each other, the case is ready for flasking. *Ibid.* 199 When sinking a repair in the flask cover everything but the portion that will require packing, and instead of flasking in the lower portion use the upper section. 1916 J. H. PROTHERO *Prosthetic Dentistry* (ed. 2) xiii. 194 The flasked case..will then present three separate openings, leading from the base of the crucible to the matrix. 1927 D. M. SHAW *Dental Prosthetic Mech.* vi. 75 The first portion of the flasking plaster is brought up on the gum nearly to the necks of the teeth. 1963 J. OSBORNE *Dental Mechanics* (ed. 5) xix. 379 Porcelain patterns must be flasked so that they are half-way into the flasking plaster and may thus be removed easily after flasking is completed.

†**'flasker**, *sb. Obs.*[−1] [f. as prec. + -ER[1].] (See quot.)
1816 *Chron.* in *Ann. Reg.* 133 The smugglers, or, as they are styled from the manner of conveying the whisky, Flaskers..They entered a house and deposited their laden flasks.

†**flasker** ('flæskə(r)), *v. Obs.* exc. *dial.* [Onomatopœic, with frequentative suffix common in vbs. expressing agitated motion; cf. FLASK *v.*[1]]
1. *intr.* To flap about (as a fish); to flutter (as a bird); to flounder.
1681 CHETHAM *Angler's Vade-m.* vii. §5 (1689) 76 Hale him not too near the top of the Water, lest by flaskering he break your Line. c1746 J. COLLIER (Tim Bobbin) *Lanc. Dialect* Wks. (1775) 29 Deawn coom I..i'th Wetur..on flaskert int' eh geete how'd on o Sawgh. 1888 *Sheffield Gloss., Flasker*, to struggle, to flutter as a bird does its wings.
2. *trans.* To smother, stifle; also, to bewilder.
1818 R. WILBRAHAM *Cheshire Gloss., Flasker*, to choke, or stifle; a person lying in the mud and unable to extricate himself, is said to be flaskered. 1884 *Cheshire Gloss.*, 'For goodness sake, childer, howd yer din, aw'm fair flaskert wi' th' nize.'

flasket ('flɑːskɪt, -æ-). Also 5-7 **flaskett**, 6 **-it**. [a. OF. *flasquet* (northern form of *flachet*), dim. of *flasque, flache*, FLASK *sb.*[2]
Sense 1 appears to be unknown in Fr.; Welsh has *ffasged* in same sense, doubtless adopted from Eng. (cf. FLASK *sb.*[2] 5). In sense 2 the earlier form is FLACKET.]
1. 'A long shallow basket' (J.).
1460-65 *Churchw. Acc. St. Andrew's, Eastcheap* in *Brit. Mag.* XXXI. 395 Item for a baskett to put in the Juellys.. and for iij Flasketts. 1596 SPENSER *Prothal.* 26 They gathered flowers to fill their flasket. 1664 EVELYN *Sylva* (1776) 254 The Osier likewise yields more limber and flexible twigs for baskets, flaskets, &c. 1700 PARNELL *Battle Frogs & Mice* I. 54 In vain the circled Loaves attempt to lie Conceal'd in Flaskets. 1770 *Poetry* in *Ann. Reg.* 220 The Fauns thro' ev'ry furrow shoot To load their flaskets with the fruit. a1849 J. C. MANGAN *Poems* (1859) 66 A fisher with his teeming flasket. 1881 MISS YONGE *Lads & Lasses Langley* iv. 147 There was a great flasket, which they carried between them, each holding one handle.
transf. 1756-66 AMORY *J. Buncle* (1825) III. 79 His belly as a vast flasket of garbage projected monstrously before.
b. A similar article made of metal.
1610 G. FLETCHER *Christ's Vict. in Heaven* 85 Bring, bring, ye Graces, all your silver flaskets. 1715 tr. *Mad. D'Ano's Wks.* 416 Precious Stones, Laces, Ribbands, all in large Flaskets of Filagreen Gold. 1725 POPE *Odyss.* x. 420 The silver stands with golden flaskets grac'd.
c. So much as is contained in a flasket.
1540 *Act 32 Hen. VIII*, c. 14 For a flasket of sope. iiii. *d.*
d. *dial.* 'A shallow washing tub' (Halliwell).
1814 PEGGE *Suppl. to Grose, Flasket*, an oval tub with two handles, used in washing. *York.* 1888 *Sheffield Gloss., Flasket*, an oblong or oval-shaped tub used in washing clothes.
2. A small flask.
1577 FENTON *Gold. Epist.* 30 Dauid was a theefe when he conueyed the..flasket of water from the beds head of Saule. 1583 *Wills & Inv. N.C.* (Surtees 1860) 74 Thre glasse flasketts 3/. 1634 *Malory's Arthur* VIII. xxiv, They..saw a little flasket [1485 flacked] of gold stand by them. 1891 A. LANG in *Longm. Mag.* Aug. 444 And then he takes his flasket out, And drinks a rousing cup.

†**'flaskisable**, *a. Obs.* [ad. OF. *flechisable* (also spelt *flacisable*), f. *flechir* to bend.] Pliable, inconstant, changeable.
1430 LYDG. *Chron. Troy* I. vi. (1513) D iv b, They be so flaskysable Who trusteth them shal fynde them ful vnstable. 1430 —— *Bochas* IV. xv. (1554) 116 Fortune of kynd is so flaskisable.

flasklet ('flɑːsklɪt, -æ-). *rare.* A little flask.
1862 T. A. TROLLOPE *Marietta* II. xv. 272 Flasklets.. ensconced in a..cupboard.

†**'flasky**, *a. Obs. rare*[−1]. [? f. FLASK *sb.*[1] + -Y[1].] ? Belonging to a 'flask' or muddy pool.
1575 R. B. *Appius & Virginia* E, Then flasky feends of Limbo Lake his ghoste do so turmoyle That he have neede of Carons helpe, for all his filthy toyle.

flasque (flɑːsk, -æ-). *Her.* [a. F. *flasque.*] A bearing similar to a flanch, but occupying a smaller part of the field (see FLANCH *sb.*[1]).
The heraldic use is not recorded in F., but in the sense 'cheek of a gun-carriage' (see FLASK *sb.*[3]) it was a synonym of *flanque*, which had also a heraldic sense = FLANCH *sb.*[1]
1562 LEIGH *Armory* 121 The fielde Or, ij. Flasques Azure. 1610 GUILLIM *Heraldry* II. vi. (1611) 63 A flasque is an ordinary consisting of one arch line drawne somewhat distant from the corners of the chiefe and meanely swelling by degrees until you come towards the middest of the Escocheon, and from thence again decreasing with a like comely discent unto the sinister base points. 1721-1800 in BAILEY, *Flask.* 1864 BOUTELL *Heraldry Hist. & Pop.* vii. 32 Flasques or Voiders..are formed by two curved lines, and are always borne in pairs. 1872 RUSKIN *Eagle's N.* §235 The Flasque, a space of colour terminated by a curved line on each flank of the shield.

flasqued (flɑːskt, -æ-), *a. Her.* [f. FLASQUE + -ED[2].] Having flasques.
1881 in R. S. FERGUSON *Church Plate Carlisle Dioc.* (1882) 52 Small Roman n in a shaped escutcheon, the sides flanched, or flasqued.

†**flat**, *sb.*[1] *Obs.* [a. OF. *flat.*] A blow, buffet.
c1320 *Sir Beues* 3432 Þe king of Scotlonde, wiþ is bat A ȝaf him swiche a sori flat Vpon þe helm. c1330 *Arth. & Merl.* 4910 Ther com the king Gvinbat, And gaf Gueheres swiche a flat.

flat (flæt), *sb.*[2] [Alteration of FLET, influenced by FLAT *a.* and *sb.*[3] The word was until recently peculiar to Scotland, where the original form survived into the present century.]
1. A floor or storey in a house.
1801 A. RANKEN *Hist. France* I. 442 The houses consisted of several flats or stories. 1827 *Ann. Reg.* 143 A tenement, consisting of three flats. 1861 *Morning Post* 27 Nov., The numerous family..in the fourth flat. 1887 *Times* 27 Aug. 11/3 A fire broke out in a flat of the mill.
2. A suite of rooms on one floor, forming a complete residence. ***first, second,*** etc. ***flat***: a suite on the first, second, etc. floor. In recent use, not necessarily a suite or a complete residence: also used even of one room with shared access to others.
1824 SCOTT *Redgauntlet* v, We chose to imitate some of the conveniences..of an English dwelling-house, instead of living piled up above each other in flats. 1845 MRS. JOHNSTONE *Edin. Tales* I. 267/2 That comfortable, airy, roomy, first-flat, consisting of dining-room, parlour, three bed-rooms. 1887 MISS BRADDON *Like & Unlike* II. iv., The rents of these flats seem to be extortionate.
3. *attrib.* and *Comb.*, as ***flatdom, -house, -land, -law, -lord*** [after LANDLORD *sb.* 1], ***-mate; flat-builder, -dweller, -holder; flat-breaking, -dwelling, -hunting, -letting, -warming.***
1936 J. CURTIS *Gilt Kid* xxx. 289 These crimes of housebreaking and *flatbreaking are far too common. 1889 *Pall Mall G.* 21 May 6/3 The cunning way in which the flats are planned deserves study by all *flat-builders. 1926 *Glasgow Herald* 2 Mar. 9 The centre of aristocratic *flatdom has also the reputation of being the abiding place of all that is best in dogdom. 1894 *Daily News* 4 Jan. 4/7 *Flat-dwellers and Hygiene. 1911 *Tariff Reform League: Rep. Labour & Soc. Cond. Germany* III. 173 In the attics of these '*flat' dwellings there is a store for each tenant. 1937 *Sunday Dispatch* 24 Jan. 2/1 So we resigned ourselves to flat-dwelling for ever. 1971 *News of World* 26 Sept. 8/7 Cats with access to gardens like to dose themselves regularly. It is hard on the flat dwelling cat when he cannot do so. 1894 *Westm. Gaz.* 10 Feb. 2/2 The defencelessness of the *flat-holder has been found out. 1884 *Times* (weekly ed.) 12 Sept. 14/1 Enormous '*flat' houses. 1920 J. JOYCE *Let.* 11 Oct. (1966) III. 24 Am very busy *flat hunting. 1924 A. CHRISTIE *Poirot Investigates* iii. 73 A horrid thing to do..but you know what flat-hunting is. 1889 E. DOWSON *Let.* 16 Nov. (1967) 117, I shall be spending the next 40 hours or so in *Flatland. 1901 *Daily News* 20 Apr. 4/5 An interesting study in flat-land was provided yesterday at the Royal Courts of Justice, when the owner of a block of flats sued a tenant for a quarter's rent. 1971 *Rand Daily Mail* 3 Apr. 1/8 Within three years Johannesburg's congested flatland will have gained nearly 6500 new flats. 1894 *Westm. Gaz.* 10 Feb. 2/2 She will settle a question of *flat-law. 1906 *Westm. Gaz.* 8 Feb. 5/1 Another firm of estate agents..stated that the outlook in the *flat-letting business was anything but cheerful. 1909 *Ibid.* 2 June 2/1 Its pious pretence is to warn simple *flatlords against non-payers of rent. 1960 *Woman* 5 Mar. 71/1 All the colourful tales your *flat-mates tell you. 1965 K. GILES *Some Beasts no More* i. 18 One day he doesn't come home and his little flatmate eventually gets round to telling the coppers. 1942 *Penguin New Writing* XV. 70 Felix was giving a flat-warming.

flat (flæt), *a.*, *adv.*, and *sb.*[3] Forms: 5-7 **flatte**, (9 *dial.*) **flatt**, 4- **flat**. [a. ON. *flatr* (Sw. *flat*, Da. *flad*) = OHG. *flaz*:—OTeut. **flato-*. Cf. FLET.
No certain cognates are known; connexion with OAryan **plat-, plath-* (Gr. πλατύς, Skr. *pṛthú*, broad) is plausible with regard to the sense (cf. F. *plat* flat, believed to be ultimately from πλατύς), but the representation of OAryan *t* or *th* by Teut. *t* (exc. when reduced from *tt* after a long vowel) is anomalous. The synonymous Ger. *flach* is unconnected.]
A. *adj.*
I. Literal senses.
1. a. Horizontally level; without inclination. Of a seam of coal: Lying in its original plane of deposition; not tilted.
c1400 *Destr. Troy* 7326 He felle to þe flat erthe. c1440 *Prom. Parv.* 164/1 Flatt, *bassus vel planus*. 1605 SHAKS. *Lear* III. ii. 7 Thou all-shaking Thunder, Strike flat the thicke Rotundity o' th' world. 1634 SIR T. HERBERT *Trav.* 35 Houses..flat a-top. 1634 MILTON *Comus* 375 Though sun

and moon Were in the flat sea sunk. 1669 STURMY *Mariner's Mag.* VII. v. 6 As the common flat Mariners Compass doth divide the Horizon. 1805 FORSYTH *Beauties Scotl.* I. 268 The strata near the Esk are termed flat seams of coal. 1842–76 GWILT *Archit.* §1903 g, In India..all buildings of any importance have flat roofs. 1860 TYNDALL *Glac.* I. ix. 62, I reached the flat summit of the rock. 1879 HARLAN *Eyesight* ix. 133 A flat desk promotes a stooping position.

b. *Arch.* ***flat arch*** (see quots.).

1715 LEONI *Palladio's Archit.* I. xxiv, Arches..flat (those are call'd so, which are but a Section of a Circle). *Ibid.* I. xxv, Certain Arches are turn'd over the Cornices of Doors and Windows, which Workmen call Flat-Arches, to prevent the Doors and Windows from being press'd with too much weight. 1762 H. WALPOLE *Vertue's Anecd. Paint.* (1765) I. v. 114 This Saxon style begins to be defined by flat and round arches. 1872 SHIPLEY *Gloss. Eccles. Terms, Flat arch.* An arch in which the sides of the voussoirs are cut so as to support each other, but their ends form a straight line top and bottom.

2. Spread out, stretched or lying at full length (*esp.* on the ground); *rare*, exc. in predicative use (often quasi-advb.) with *fall, fling, lay, lie*, etc.

a. Chiefly of a person: Prostrate; with the body at full length. †Also in phr. ***a flat fall***.

c1320 *Sir Beues* 1040 A felde him flat to grounde. 1399 LANGL. *Rich. Redeles* II. 183 [The birds] ffell with her ffetheris fflat vppon þe erthe..and mercy be-souȝte. c1440 *Jacob's Well* 23 Sche..flatt on þe ground cryed: 'god..haue mercy on me!' c1450 HOLLAND *Howlat* 838 The folk..Flang him flat in the fyre. 1535 COVERDALE *Isa.* xlix. 23 They shal fall before the with their faces flat vpon the earth. 1610 SHAKS. *Temp.* II. ii. 16, I'le fall flat, Perchance he will not minde me. 1621 LADY M. WROTH *Urania* 138 None parting from him without flat falles, or apparant losse of honour. 1657 J. SMITH *Myst. Rhet.* 56 Thus a great wound is called a scratch; a flat fall, a foile. 1719 DE FOE *Crusoe* (1840) II. xiv. 293 He laid me flat on the ground. 1726 *Adv. Capt. R. Boyle* 290, I order'd every Man..to lye flat upon their Bellies till we had received the Fire of the Enemy. 1856 KANE *Arct. Expl.* I. xxx. 411 The hunter is flat and motionless. 1860–1 FLO. NIGHTINGALE *Nursing* 33, I have seen a patient fall flat on the ground who was standing when his nurse came into the room. 1891 R. KIPLING *Tales from Hills* 186 That night a big wind blew..the tents flat.

b. Of a building or city: Level with the ground; also, levelled, overthrown.

1560 BIBLE (Genev.) *Josh.* vi. 20 The wall fell downe flat. 1607 SHAKS. *Cor.* III. i. 204 This is the way to lay the Citie flat. 1666 SOUTH *Serm. Consecr. Bp. Rochester* Serm. (1737) I. v. 166 That Christ-Church stands so high above ground, and that the church of Westminster lies not flat upon it, is [etc.]. 1671 MILTON *P.R.* IV. 363 What ruins kingdoms, and lays cities flat.

fig. 1611 SHAKS. *Cymb.* I. iv. 23 To fortifie her iudgement, which else an easie battery might lay flat.

c. Of things usually more or less erect or elevated.

1671 MILTON *P.R.* II. 223 Cease to admire, and all her Plumes Fall flat.

fig. 1671 MILTON *Samson* 596, I feel..My hopes all flat. 1684 T. HOCKIN *God's Decrees* 333 To raise our expectations of happiness high, and then to have them fall flat and low.

†d. Of a plant: Creeping, trailing on the ground.

1578 LYTE *Dodoens* I. lxxxvi. 127 *Verbenaca supina*..in English Base or flat Veruayne.

e. Lying in close apposition; with its whole length or surface in contact irrespectively of position. *Naut.* Of a sail: ***flat aback*** or ***aft*** (see quot. 1815): said also of the vessel.

1559 W. CUNNINGHAM *Cosmogr. Glasse* 86 Placing my Instrument flat on th' earth. 1581 MAPLET *Diall Destinie* 66 In theyr coursing they [Hares] apply their eares fast and flat to their backes. 1684 R. H. *School Recreat.* 138 Spreading your Net on the Ground smooth and flat. 1715 DESAGULIERS *Fires Impr.* 131 When it is open, it may be flat to the Chimney. 1769 FALCONER *Dict. Marine* (1789) s.v. *Aback*, Lay all flat Aback. 1796 WITHERING *Brit. Plants* IV. 76 Saucers dark green, lying flat on the leaves. 1815 *Falconer's Dict. Marine* (ed. Burney), *Flat aft* is the situation of the sails when their surfaces are pressed aft against the mast by the force of the wind. 1840 R. H. DANA *Bef. Mast* vi, We found the vessel hove flat aback. 1885 H. J. STONOR in *Law Times* LXXX. 119/1 The ladder was standing flat against the side wall.

f. *Paper-making.* Packed without folding.

1890 JACOBI *Printing* xxxi. 249 A ream may be either 'flat', 'folded', or 'lapped'.

g. Of the hand: Extended, not clenched.

1847 TENNYSON *Princ.* II. 345 The child Push'd her flat hand against his face and laugh'd. 1859 —— *Enid* 1565 The brute Earl..unknightly, with flat hand, However lightly, smote her on the cheek.

h. Of relatively small curvature or inclination. *spec.* Of a golf-club: having the head at a very obtuse angle to the shaft; of a swing of the club: not upright, oblique.

1857 H. B. FARNIE *Golfer's Man.* (1947) v. 27 Regarding the lie of a club for effecting distance, whether it should be flat or upright, little can be said..the rule being, the longer the club, the flatter the lie. 1887 *Jamieson's Scot. Dict.* Suppl., *Flat*, adj. A term in golfing, applied to a club of which the head is at a very obtuse angle to the shaft. 1888 *Lockwood's Dict. Mech. Engin.*, *Flat sweep*, a flat sweep or curve signifies one that is relatively of less curvature than others with which it may be compared. 1909 P. A. VAILE *Mod. Golf* i. 17 [One who plays an upright swing] will keep longer in the line of the ball's flight to the hole, and in the plane of its flight, than one who stands away from the ball and uses a flat swing. *Ibid.* iii. 32 A club with a lie which is too flat.

3. Without curvature or projection of surface.

a. Of land, the face of the country: Plain, level; not hilly or undulating.

c1440 [see I]. 1553 BRENDE *Q. Curtius* IV. 49, A Nacion..inhabiting vpon a flat shore. 1610 SHAKS. *Temp.* IV. i. 63 Thy ..flat Medes thetchd with Stouer, them [Sheepe] to keepe. 1673 TEMPLE *Observ. United Prov.* Wks. 1731 I. 44 The whole Province of Holland is generally flat. 1748 *Relat. Earthq. Lima* 2 This Town was built on a low flat Point of Land. 1838 *Murray's Hand-bk. N. Germ.* 71 High dykes.. protect the flat country from inundations. 1859 JEPHSON *Brittany* xii. 202 The country became more and more flat.

b. Of a surface: Without curvature, indentation, or protuberance; plane, level.

1551 T. WILSON *Logike* (1580) 37 When thei se the ground beaten flat round about. 1559 CUNNINGHAM *Cosmogr. Glasse* 47 As touchyng your opinion, that th' Earth is flat, I will prove it to be rounde. 1585 T. WASHINGTON tr. *Nicholay's Voy.* IV. xxxvi. 159 b, Not any carved images of saints..but on flat pictures painted. 1632 LITHGOW *Trav.* VI. 262 The flat face of the Rocke. 1703 MOXON *Mech. Exerc.* 268 That makes the Moulding flatter, this more circular. 1812–6 J. SMITH *Panorama Sc. & Art* I. 32 To grind one surface perfectly flat, it is..necessary to grind three at the same time. 1824 R. STUART *Hist. Steam Engine* 179 The flat face to which the blocks are ground. 1882 *Syd. Soc. Lex.*, *Chest, flat.* A chest which has lost its rounded front.

c. Of the face or nose.

c1400 *Ywaine & Gaw.* 259 His face was ful brade & flat. 1560 BIBLE (Genev.) *Lev.* xxi. 18 A man..that hath a flat nose. 1607 SHAKS. *Timon* IV. iii. 158 Downe with the Nose, Downe with it flat, take the Bridge quite away. 1697 DAMPIER *Voy.* I. 325 Their Faces are oval, their Foreheads flat. 1829 LYTTON *Devereux* II. iii, A very flat, ill-favoured countenance. 1836 W. IRVING *Astoria* II. 281 Their noses are broad and flat at top.

†d. ***flat numbers***: those corresponding to plane surfaces, i.e. numbers composed of two factors.

1557 RECORDE *Whetst.* C iij, Superficiall nombers, or Flatte nombers.

e. ***flat side*** (e.g. of a sword): opposed to the *edge*. Also ***to turn (a sword) flat***.

a1440 *Sir Eglam.* 1240 Syr Egyllamowre turnyd hys swerde flatt. 1727 W. SNELGRAVE *Guinea & Slave Trade* (1734) 236 Lifted up his broad Sword, and gave me a Blow on the Shoulder with the flat side of it. 1832 G. R. PORTER *Porcelain & Gl.* 226 The flat side..is to be turned towards the observer. 1835 LYTTON *Rienzi* I. iii, Touching the smith with the flat side of his sword.

f. Having little projection from the adjacent surface. Rarely const. *to*.

1728 POPE *Dunc.* II. 43 With pert flat eyes she windowed well its head. 1865 CARLYLE *Fredk. Gt.* V. XIV. v. 201 It can now be discovered..by any eyes, however flat to the head.

g. ***flat tyre*** (U.S. *tire*): (*a*) a deflated or punctured tyre; also *ellipt.* as ***flat***; (*b*) *U.S.* a dull and spiritless person. Also ***flat wheel***.

1923 WODEHOUSE *Inimitable Jeeves* xvi. 218 I'm bound to say it isn't very often I find my own existence getting a flat tyre. 1925 H. L. FOSTER *Trop. Tramp Tourists* xvi. 300 You think you're the berries, don't you? Well, you might have been once, but you're a flat-tire these days! You can't make the grade! 1927 *New Republic* 26 Jan. 277/2 He's a flat tire. 1929 'C. WALT' *Love in Chicago* xv. 211 Stopping at the crossroads to see if I had a flat. 1934 J. M. CAIN *Postman always rings Twice* i. 12, I was in the filling station, fixing flats. 1942 'N. SHUTE' *Pied Piper* 81 The driver wrestled to jack up the bus and get the flat wheel off.

h. Of the frequency response of an amplifier or other electronic device: uniform (over a certain range of frequencies); of a device: having such a response; amplifying, attenuating, or reproducing equally signals of all frequencies.

1926 *Encycl. Brit.* XXVI. 281/2 A properly designed system is 'flat', i.e., indiscriminatory, over a sufficiently wide auditory band. 1949 FRAYNE & WOLFE *Elem. Sound Recording* xxix. 604 With this machine a frequency response flat within 2 db is obtained from 30 to 15,000 cycles. 1958 J. TALL *Techn. Magn. Recording* vi. 86 A flat amplifier is one that amplifies all frequencies equally. 1970 J. EARL *Tuners & Amplifiers* ii. 57 Trimmers across the bass and treble tone controls..make it possible to balance them for a 'flat' response when the controls are at the centre setting.

4. *transf.* a. in *Painting*. Without appearance of relief or projection. ***flat tint***: one of uniform depth or shade.

1755 JOHNSON, *Flat*, without relief, without prominence of the figures. 1821 CRAIG *Lect. Drawing* ii. 95 Throwing every mass of shadow into a flat tint. *Ibid.* iii. 153 The pictures..were in their general appearance, flat, insipid, and uninteresting. 1859 GULLICK & TIMBS *Paint.* 18 The impossibility of spreading a flat tint on the vellum. 1879 *Cassell's Techn. Educ.* III. 186 Pictures..flat, and deficient in light and shade, or brilliance.

b. *Engraving.* Wanting in sharpness; applied to a pull or impression of a plate which has received only the flat impression of the press without the overlay used to develop light and shade.

1888 C. T. JACOBI *Printers' Voc.* 44 *Flat*, an expression used to indicate excessive flatness in an illustration owing to want of light and shade in overlaying. 1888 Flat pull [see sense 15]. 1897 SINGER & STRANG *Etching* 175 A 'flat' proof of a block as it comes from the photo-engraver generally shows itself to be in need of some touching up.

c. Of paint, lacquer, or varnish: lustreless, dull. (Cf. FLAT *a.*, etc. C. 12, FLAT *v.*² 8 a, FLATTED *ppl. a.* 5.)

1896 *N.E.D.* s.v. FLAT *v.*² 8 a, To cover (a surface) with flat, i.e. lustreless, paint. 1935 H. R. SIMONDS *Finishing Metal Products* xxv. 263 There may be gloss or flat paint, or an intermediate semigloss frequently known as egg-shell paint. 1940 R. C. MARTIN *Lacquer & Synthetic Enamel Finishes* xii. 370 Clear or flat lacquers may then be used to a finish. 1951 H. W. CHATFIELD *Gloss. Terms Paint Trades* 115 Flat varnishes, lacquers, enamels, etc. 1953, 1958 [see EGG-SHELL c]. 1971 *Sci. Amer.* Sept. 224/3 Coat the inside of the box with flat black paint.

d. *Photogr.* Wanting in contrast.

1901 G. E. BROWN *Finishing Negative* vii. 66 Increasing contrasts..gives a 'snap' to otherwise flat negatives which is often very welcome. 1923 *Kodak Mag.* Mar. 36 From the negative least developed we shall get a print flat and grey with little difference between high light and shadow. 1953 T. L. J. BENTLEY *Man. Miniat. Camera* (ed. 4) viii. 113 A negative may be so flat and deficient in printing density that straightforward printing will not yield an enlargement of acceptable quality.

5. a. With additional notion: Having a broad level surface and little thickness. Of a foot: Touching the ground with the whole surface; but little arched.

c1430 *Two Cookery-bks.* 29 Serue hem in almost flatte. 1530 PALSGR. 312/2 Flatte as a thyng is that is brode. 1577–87 HARRISON *England* III. iii. (1878) III. 224 Of fishes ..I find fiue sorts, the flat, [etc.]. 1597 GERARDE *Herbal* 58 Flat wheate is..bearded and bordered with very rough and sharpe ailes, wherein consisteth the difference. 1613–39 I. JONES in Leoni *Palladio's Archit.* (1742) II. 44 Those great Pilasters in the Angle of the inside of the Temple are too flat. 1632 LITHGOW *Trav.* VI. 247 They weare on their heads flat round Caps. 1697 DAMPIER *Voy.* I. 49 The Booby is a Water-fowl..her Feet are flat like a Ducks Feet. a1721 KEILL *Maupertuis' Diss.* (1734) 65 These conjectures concerning flat Stars..are rather the stronger. 1769 MRS. RAFFALD *Eng. Housekpr.* (1778) 303 To collar Flat Ribs of Beef. 1840 LARDNER *Geom.* 34 This ruler consists of a flat piece of wood with a straight edge. 1859–74 TENNYSON *Vivien* 348 May this hard earth cleave..and close again, and nip me flat, If I be such a traitress. 1888 *Lockwood's Dict. Mech. Eng.*, *Flat File*..is either a tapered or a parallel file. 1882 QUAIN *Anat.* (ed. 9) I. 8 Tabular or flat bones, like the scapula, ilium, and the bones forming the roof and sides of the skull.

†b. Of false dice: Broad and thin. *Obs.*

c1550 *Dice-Play* A j b, A bale of flatte synke deuxis..A bale of flat cater trees. 1711 PUCKLE *Club* 30 Flats. *Note*, Dice flatter than they are long, to throw Trays and Quaters.

c. Of a blade, as opposed to 'three-edged'.

d. Phrases: ***flat as a flawn, flounder, pancake*** (see those sbs.).

e. Of a vessel: Wide and shallow.

1471 *Bury Wills* (Camden) 242, I peluem laton voc' a flat basyn. 1492 *Ibid.* 75 My flatte gylte cuppe. 1533 *Will of C. Bedford* in Weaver *Wells Wills* 27 John Bys the yonger a flat cuppe of sylver. 1552 HULOET, Flatte bole for wine, *ecpatala*. 1611 BIBLE *Lev.* ii. 5 A meate offering baken in a panne [*marg.* on a flat plate].

II. Senses of figurative origin.

6. a. Unrelieved by conditions or qualifications; absolute, downright, unqualified, plain; peremptory. Now chiefly of a denial, contradiction, etc., and in Shaksperian phrases, ***flat blasphemy, burglary***.

1551 T. WILSON *Logike* (1567) 61 a, The aunswerer must still vse flatte deniyng. 1577 NORTHBROOKE *Dicing* (1843) 121 Whosoeuer taketh and keepeth the mony of another.. sheweth himself a flat theefe. 1586 B. YOUNG *Guazzo's Civ. Conv.* IV. 183 If I would tel you a flat lie, I wold say no. 1592 GREENE *Upst. Courtier* in *Harl. Misc.* (Malh.) II. 248 Why, Sir, to be flat with you, you liue by your legges. 1603 SHAKS. *Meas. for Meas.* II. ii. 131 That in the Captaine's but a chollericke word, Which in the souldier is flat blasphemie. 1611 BEAUM. & FL. *King & No King* IV. iii, This is my flat opinion, which I'll die in. 1614 BP. HALL *Recoll. Treat.* 864 Who knowes not, that S. Homer, and S. Virgil are flat for it? 1641 MILTON *Ch. Govt.* I. (1851) 23 His Son Constantius prov'd a flat Arian. 1685 BAXTER *Paraphr. N.T. 1 Cor.* vii. 12, 13, I bring you not this as a flat command of Christ, but as my best Advice. 1699 BENTLEY *Phal.* 304 A piece of flat Nonsense. 1713 SWIFT *Apollo outwitted* vi, She gave no flat denial. 1788 T. JEFFERSON *Writ.* (1859) II. 551 In flat contradiction to their Arret of December last. 1839 KEIGHTLEY *Hist. Eng.* I. 97 He claimed to be put in possession..but met with a flat refusal. 1871 MORLEY *Crit. Misc.* Ser. I. 163 A flat impostor. 1891 R. KIPLING *Tales from Hills* 212 It's flat, flagrant disobedience!

b. In the conclusive expression, ***that's flat*** (*a*) formerly = that's the absolute, undeniable truth; (*b*) a defiant expression of one's final resolve or determination.

1588 SHAKS. *L.L.L.* III. i. 102 The Boy hath seld him a bargaine, a Goose, that's flat. 1596 —— *1 Hen. IV*, IV. ii. 43. 1665 *Surv. Aff. Nethetl.* 120 Its the greatest Bogg of Europe ..that's flat. 1716 ADDISON *Drummer* I. i, I'll give Madam warning, that's flat. 1852 SMEDLEY *L. Arundel* i. 15 'I won't, then, that's flat', exclaimed Rachel.

c. Of a calm: Complete, 'dead'.

1651 HOWELL *Venice* 119 The wind..became..a flat calm. 1697 DAMPIER *Voy.* I. 415 It fell flat calm. 1880 LADY BRASSEY *Sunshine & Storm* 34 Half an hour later it was a flat calm.

d. Impecunious, penniless. *U.S. slang.* (Cf. ***flat broke*** s.v. FLAT *adv.* 2.)

1833 *Sk. & Eccentr. D. Crockett* (1834) 60 Retiring to bed, comfortably situated, he awoke next morning flat without a dollar. 1930 *Times Lit. Suppl.* 4 Sept. 698/2 Satisfying his desires freely when he can, starving when he is 'flat'.

e. ***to leave*** (a person) ***flat***, to 'drop' suddenly and completely; to go away from.

1902 G. V. HOBART *It's up to You* ii. 37 Then they both chuckled and left me flat. 1919 in *Saucy Stories* Aug. 83/2 She got up enough spunk to leave him flat on Broadway. Lost him in the crowd... Refused to see him when he showed up. 1930 WODEHOUSE *Very Good, Jeeves!* iii. 85 He buzzed off, leaving me flat. 1942 T. RATTIGAN *Flare Path* I. i. 121 You meant my Johnny's going to leave me flat the minute the war's over.

7. Wanting in points of attraction and interest; prosaic, dull, uninteresting, lifeless,

monotonous, insipid. Sometimes with allusion to sense 10.

a. of composition, discourse, a joke, etc. Also of a person with reference to his composition, conversation, etc.

1573 G. HARVEY *Letter-bk.* (Camden) 20 Mi over flat and homeli kind of writing. **1656** BP. HALL *Occas. Med.* (1851) 63 They have proved..poor and flat in all other subjects. **1662** PEPYS *Diary* 11 May, A dull, flat Presbiter preached. **1711** ADDISON *Spect.* No. 124 ¶2 We should complain of many flat Expressions. **1712** W. ROGERS *Voy.* Introd. 16 Such strange Stories, as make the Voyages of those who come after..to look flat and insipid. **1806–7** J. BERESFORD *Miseries Hum. Life* (1826) VII. xxx, The longest story of the flattest proser that ever droned. **1822** HAZLITT *Table-t.* Ser. II. x. (1869) 204 The flattest thing of yours they can find. **1861** M. PATTISON *Ess.* (1889) I. 31 A rather flat treatment of trite themes. **1866** G. MACDONALD *Ann. Q. Neighb.* xiii. (1878) 254 I am rather a flat teller of stories. **1889** *County* x. in *Cornhill Mag.* Mar., He is always appreciative of the flattest joke.

b. of one's circumstances, surroundings, etc.

1602 SHAKS. *Ham.* I. ii. 133 How weary, stale, flat, and vnprofitable Seemes to me all the vses of this world. **1706** ATTERBURY *Funeral Serm.* 8 All Earthly Satisfactions must needs..grow flat and unsavory. **1798** COLERIDGE *Fears in Solitude* 67 How flat and wearisome they feel their trade. **1848** MRS. GASKELL *M. Barton* xvii, It seems so flat to be left behind. **1884** Q. VICTORIA *More Leaves* 25 It seemed to strike me much less than when I first saw it, as all is flat now.

c. *to fall flat* (said of a composition, discourse, etc.): to prove unattractive, uninteresting, or ineffective; to fail in exciting applause or approval.

1841 MACAULAY *W. Hastings* (1880) 654 The best written defence must have fallen flat. **1860** DICKENS *Lett.* (1880) II. 125 All my news falls flat. **1885** C. L. PIRKIS *Lady Lovelace* II. xxv. 80 The haranguing..fell as flat as the reasoning.

8. Deficient in sense or mental vigour; stupid, dull, slow-witted.

1599 SHAKS. *Hen. V*, Prol. 9 Pardon, Gentles all: The flat vnraysed Spirits, that hath dar'd..to bring forth So great an Obiect. **1601** SIR J. OGLE *Parlie at Ostend* in Sir F. Vere *Comm.* 158 Nor do I believe that..any of you judge me so flat, or so stupid. *a* **1680** BUTLER *Rem.* (1759) I. 132 No dull Idolater was ere so flat In Things of deep and solid Weight. **1878** SEELEY *Stein* I. 312, I look for nothing from empty, slow, flat people.

9. a. Wanting in energy and spirit; lifeless, dull. Also, out of spirits, low, dejected, depressed.

1602 SHAKS. *Ham.* IV. vii. 31 You must not thinke That we are made of stuffe, so flat, and dull, That, [etc.]. **1642** DK. NEWCASTLE *Let.* in *Life* (1886) 330 The town will not admit of me..so I am very flat and out of countenance here. *c* **1680** BEVERIDGE *Serm.* (1729) I. 37 Lest he should grow flat in his devotions. **1801** *Med. Jrnl.* V. 324 Her spirits were dull and flat. **1805** LAMB *Lett.* (1888) I. 213, I am now calm, but sadly taken down and flat. **1844** ALB. SMITH *Adv. Mr. Ledbury* xxiii. (1886) 71 The audience..not witnessing any situation half so comic as the one they had just seen, were proportionately flat.

b. Of trade, etc.: Depressed, dull, inactive.

1831 *Lincoln Herald* 30 Dec. 1 The trade for barley is exceedingly flat. **1894** *Times* (weekly ed.) 9 Feb. 123/2 Tallow trade, flat, but prices unchanged. **1894** *Daily News* 1 June 3/5 A flat market for maize.

c. Of an electric battery: run down, (fully) discharged.

1951 *Autocar* 9 Nov. 1445/2 After five hundred miles of touring I found myself with a completely flat battery. **1961** *Which?* Apr. 89/1 If this discharging process goes on long enough, the battery will be left flat. **1969** N. FREELING *Tsing-Boum* ii. 17 The car battery is flat and I've got to charge it. **1984** B. FRANCIS *AA Car Duffer's Guide* 42/1 A bloke rings up saying he had a flat battery.

10. Of drink, etc.: That has lost its flavour or sharpness; dead, insipid, stale.

1607 HEYWOOD *Woman kilde* Epil., The wine..drunk too flat. **1626** BACON *Sylva* §367 Spirit of Wine burned..tasteth nothing so hot in the Mouth..but flat and dead. **1708** J. PHILIPS *Cyder* I. 49 Fruit..to the Tongue inelegant and flat. **1772** PRIESTLEY in *Phil. Trans.* LXII. 154 When..cyder is become flat or dead. **1861** GEO. ELIOT *Silas M.* 20 Tankards sending forth a scent of flat ale.

11. a. Of sound, a resonant instrument, a voice: Not clear and sharp; dead, dull. Also in *Combs.*, as ***flat-sounding***, ***-vowelled***.

1626 BACON *Sylva* §154 If..you stop the Holes of a Hawkes Bell, it will make no Ring, but a flat noise, or Rattle. *a* **1663** SANDERSON in *Treas. Dav.* Ps. cl. 5 The cymbal will be flat, it will have no life or spirit in it. **1718** PRIOR *Pleasure* 501 Too flat I thought this voice, and that too shrill. **1831** BREWSTER *Nat. Magic* ix. (1833) 217 The..variety of sounds ..produced by the report of his fowling-piece. Sometimes they are flat and prolonged, at other times short and sharp. **1920** 'K. MANSFIELD' *Lett.* (1928) II. 3 His *flat-sounding* voice. **1936** 'M. FRANKLIN' *All that Swagger* i. 10 The haw-haw, flat-vowelled Public School English.

b. *Music.* Of a note or singer: Relatively low in pitch; below the regular or true pitch. ***B, D, E,*** etc. ***flat***: a semitone lower than B, D, E, etc. Of an interval or scale: = MINOR.

1591 SHAKS. *Two Gent.* I. ii. 93 Now you are too flat; And marre the concord, with too harsh a descant. **1597** MORLEY *Introd. Mus.* 3, ♭..signifying the halfe note and flatt singing. **1609** DOULAND *Ornith. Microl.* 15 To sing *fa* in a flat Scale. **1613** DRUMM. OF HAWTH. *Poems* 144 Like Arions Harpe Now delicately flat, now sweetly sharp. **1674** PLAYFORD *Skill Mus.* II. 95 A flat Third lower, is C fa ut. **1678** PHILLIPS s.v. *Cliff*, The B-Cliff..being only to shew when Notes are to be sung flat. **1691** RAY *Creation* 204 Cartilages and Muscles to contract or dilate it [the windpipe] as we would have our Voice Flat or Sharp. **1773** BARRINGTON in *Phil. Trans.* LXIII. 270 The flat third is plaintive. **1874** HELPS *Soc. Press.* iii. 46 For the sixth time he hears C flat instead of C sharp played. **1875** OUSELEY *Harmony* v. 67 All the fifths in tuning keyed instruments, are tuned a little flatter than perfection.

c. quasi-*adv.*

Mod. She has a tendency to sing flat.

12. *Gram.* †**a.** Of an accent, a syllable: Unstressed.

1589 PUTTENHAM *Eng. Poesie* II. xiii. (Arb.) 135 [Re] being the first sillable, passing obscurely away with a flat accent is short. **1612** BRINSLEY *Pos. Parts* (1669) 94 Every Noun Substantive Commune increasing flat or short in the Genitive case, is the Masculine Gender. What mean you by this, to increase flat? *A.* To have the last syllable but one pressed down flat in the pronouncing.

b. *Phonetics.* Of a consonant: Voiced, i.e. uttered with vibration of the vocal chords, e.g. *b*, *d*, *v*, etc., as opposed to breath, e.g. *p*, *t*, *f*, etc. Of a vowel: (see quot. 1934[3]). Also, of a sound: characterized by the downward shift of higher frequencies.

1874 R. MORRIS *Hist. Eng. Gram.* §54 B and d, &c. are said to be soft or flat, while p and t, &c. are called hard or sharp consonants. **1901** H. SWEET in *Maître Phonétique* 145, if wij dis'tiŋgwiʃ bi'twijn 'mikst' pə'ziʃən ən 'flæt' ʃeip əv ðə tʌŋ, wij ʃəd nætʃərəli kɔːl ðə θrij njuw siəriz bæk-flæt bæk-mikst frʌnt-mikst. **1934** H. C. WYLD in *S.P.E. Tract* XXXIX. 607 Another long vowel [ʌ̄] (low-flat-tense). *Ibid.* 608 This vowel..is the mid-flat-tense. *Ibid.* 609 The tongue may be so used that neither back nor front predominates, but the whole tongue, which lies evenly in the mouth, is raised or lowered. Vowels so formed are called 'mixed' by Sweet, but I owe to him also the term 'flat' which I prefer as more descriptive. The vowel [ʌ̄] in *bird* is low-flat. **1952** R. JAKOBSON et al. *Prelim. Speech Analysis* 31 Flat vs. Plain... Flattening manifests itself by a downward shift of a set of formants.

c. *Gram.* Not distinguished by a characteristic ending, as an adverb which has the same form as an adjective or substantive, or a substantive used as an adjective.

Flat adverbs of modern English often go back to an Old English form ending in *-e*.

1871 J. EARLE *Philol. Eng. Tongue* 361 The Flat Adverb is simply a substantive or an adjective placed in an adverbial position. **1901** GREENOUGH & KITTREDGE *Words* (1902) 199 Not all of our 'flat adverbs' actually go back to such *-ë* forms. **1965** *English Studies* XLVI. 356 The 'flat-adverbs' (like e.g. *fast*).

13. a. *Stock-exchange* (*U.S.*) Stock is said to be borrowed *flat*, when the lender allows no interest on the money he takes as security for it (*Cent.* and *Standard Dicts.*).

1841 *N.Y. Standard* Jan. (Th.), *Flat*, without interest, in brokers' slang. **1870** *Congress. Globe* 25 Jan. 733/2 [Certificates] have been sold 'flat'..that is to say, without taking the interest into account. **1870** J. K. MEDBERY *Men & Myst. Wall St.* 61 Stock can almost always be obtained by borrowers, either flat, i.e. with no interest on either side, or with interest at market rates for the money advanced. **1885** *Harper's Mag.* Nov. 843/2 To lend 'flat' means without interest.

b. *Comm.* Unvarying, fixed, uniform; of a standard amount; not varying with changed conditions; without excess or diminution for particular cases. Also quasi-*adv.*

1898 *Engineering Mag.* XVI. 38 Three costs are kept,—the flat cost (including labor and material only), the factory cost (factory expense added to flat cost), and total cost (including all expenses of every kind). **1902** *Encycl. Brit.* XXXII. 163/2 The statistics as to the street railway earnings in America are based upon the universal practice there of charging a 'flat' 5 cent fare for the whole trip. **1903** *Westm. Gaz.* 30 July 10/2 The Tube Railway, on which there was what was known as a 'flat fare'—that was, a fare of twopence for the whole way. **1907** *N.Y. Even. Post* (semi-weekly ed.) 11 Feb. 4 A company..will take in exactly as much money if the whole lot pay fare at two cents flat. **1908** *Daily Chron.* 21 Feb. 2/6 They had found..that the 'flat' rate system—the fixed annual rate—was unsound. **1920** *Westm. Gaz.* 1 Apr. 4/2 There..ought not to be any flat rate for all classes of horse-drawn vehicles. **1928** *Britain's Industr. Future* (*Liberal Ind. Inq.*) III. xvi. 193 The majority of workers are paid at flat time-rates. **1950** T. H. MARSHALL *Citizenship & Social Class* 55 Flat-rate benefits do not reduce the gaps between different incomes. **1958** *Ann. Reg. 1957* 92 Labour offered a flat-rate reduction of £100 to every taxpayer. **1963** *Times* 24 May p. vii/3 The 'sixpenny tube', or to give it its correct name—the flat fare—if adopted by London Transport, would lead straight to bankruptcy.

14. *Comb.*

a. In parasynthetic adjs., as ***flat-backed***, ***-billed***, ***-breasted***, ***-browed***, ***-capped***, ***-chested***, ***coated*** (of animals), ***-crowned***, ***-cut***, ***-decked***, ***-edged***, ***-ended***, ***-faced***, ***-floored***, ***-handled***, ***-heeled***, ***-hoofed***, ***-leaved***, ***-mouthed***, ***-pearled***, ***-pointed***, ***-ribbed***, ***-roofed***, ***-soled***, ***-stemmed***, ***-surfaced***, ***-toothed***, ***-topped***, ***-visaged***.

1688 R. HOLME *Armoury* II. ix. 185/1 *Flat Backed, when it [Grey-Hound] is even between the neck, and spaces. **1646** SIR T. BROWNE *Pseud. Ep.* III. xix. 154 *Flat-bild birds. **1688** J. CLAYTON in *Phil. Trans.* XVII. 990 All Flat-bill'd Birds that groped for their Meat. **1667** N. FAIRFAX *ibid.* II. 548 This Woman was as *flat-breasted as a Man. **1838** DICKENS *O. Twist* viii, A snub-nosed, *flat-browed..boy. **1947** J. MULGAN *Report on Experience* 18 Tenement houses crowded with pale, *flat-capped working men. **1961** H. E. BATES *Now sleeps Crimson Petal* 25 A muscular flat-capped skittles player who drove a brewers' dray. **1771** SMOLLETT *H. Clinker* Wks. 1806 VI. 63 She is..awkward, *flat-chested, and stooping. **1929** Flat-chested [see CHEMICALIZE *v.*]. **1939** M. DICKENS *One Pair of Hands* vi. 97 It sounds so governessy and flat-chested. **1872** 'STONEHENGE' *Dogs Brit. Isl.* (ed. 2) 89 The *flat-coated or short-coated small St. John's or Labrador breed [of retriever]. **1902** C. J. CORNISH *Naturalist on Thames* 109 Our sheep..their wild ancestors, the active and flat-coated animals which still feed on the stony mountain-tops. **1948** C. L. B. HUBBARD *Dogs in Brit.* 227 Another of the lesser-known varieties is the Flat-coated Retriever. **1664** WOOD *Life* (Oxf. Hist. Soc.) II. 8 For a new hat *flat-croun'd 7*s.* 6*d.* **1922** JOYCE *Ulysses* 178 A *flatcut suit of herringbone tweed. **1884** J. COLBORNE *Hicks Pasha* 97 A *flat-decked vessel. **1923** D. H. LAWRENCE *Kangaroo* xiv. 311 They were walking home in a whirl of the coldest, most *flat-edged wind they had ever known. **1859** *Handbk. Turning* 97 A fine *flat-ended tool. **1859** HELPS *Friends in C.* Ser. II. II. viii. 143 The Sea..a melancholy *flat-faced thing. **1867** SMYTH *Sailor's Word-bk.* 304 *Flat-floored boats. **1676** *Lond. Gaz.* No. 1059/4 *Flat-handled Silver Spoons. **1725** DE FOE *Voy. round World* (1840) 267 Shoes *flat-heeled. **1890** KIPLING *Barrack-r. Ballads* (1892) 183 The hand of every honest man flat-heeled across your mouth. **1697** *Lond. Gaz.* No. 3301/4 A..punch Horse ..*flat Hoofed. **1926** D. H. LAWRENCE *Sun* i. 5 The *flat-leaved cactus called prickly pear. ? *a* **1400** *Morte Arth.* 1088 *Fflatt mowthede as a fluke. **1924** E. SITWELL *Sleeping Beauty* vi. 28 Upon the *flat-pearled and fantastic shore. **1710** J. HARRIS *Lex. Techn.* II, *Flat-pointed Nails. **1684** *Lond. Gaz.* No. 1908/4 One Dark brown Gelding..a little *flat Ribb'd. **1688** R. HOLME *Armoury* II. ix. 185/2 Flat Ribbed, is when the both side Ribbs [of a Grey-Hound] cling and are near to gather. **1598** HAKLUYT *Voy.* III. 391 Their houses are *flat-rooffed. **1847** DISRAELI *Tancred* IV. xii, Flat-roofed villages nestle amid groves of mulberry trees. **1662** J. DAVIES tr. *Olearius' Voy. Ambass.* 377 Their shooes are low and *flat-soal'd. **1849** JAMES *Woodman* ix, The..tread of the abbess in her flat-soled sandal. **1861** MISS PRATT *Flower. Pl.* VI. 89 *Flat-stemmed Meadow grass. **1794** SULLIVAN *View Nat.* I. 193 Place a *flat-surfaced bottle empty on its side. **1766** PENNANT *Zool.* (1769) III. 9 The fossil tooth of..some *flat-toothed fish. **1862** ANSTED *Channel Isl.* I. ii. (ed. 2) 32 The southern islet is..*flat-topped. **1774** CURTIS in *Phil. Trans.* LXIV. 383 They are *flat-visaged.

b. With pr. pple. forming adj., as ***flat-lying***.

1765 A. DICKSON *Treat. Agric.* (ed. 2) 284 Low flat-lying land. **1949** E. POUND *Pisan Cantos* lxxiv. 24 A nice little town in the Tyrol in a wide flat-lying valley. **1965** G. J. WILLIAMS *Econ. Geol. N.Z.* v. 55/2 (*caption*) Flat-lying lodes of the Golden Point group.

c. With *adjs.*, as ***flat-icy***, ***-sleek***.

1923 D. H. LAWRENCE *Kangaroo* xiv. 308 So, in the *flat-icy wind..they crouched. **1922** E. SITWELL *Façade* 11 And finer Their black hair seemed (*flat-sleek to see) Than the leaves of the springing Bohea.

15. Special comb., as **flat-arch** (see 1 b); **flat-back**, (*a*) (see quot. 1888); (*b*) *slang*, a bed bug (Farmer); (*c*) a book whose back is flat when the book is closed; (*d*) various other technical senses (see quots.); †**flat-bean**, a name for some species of *Lupinus*; **flat bed** [BED *sb.* 11], a bed or frame with a horizontal surface; *spec.* (freq. *attrib.* or as *adj.*): (*a*) a printing machine with a flat printing surface; (*b*) a trailer with no top or sides; (*c*) on a sewing machine, the flat surface on which the fabric rests; **flat-bedded** *a.* (*Geol.*), having a naturally plane cleavage; **flat-bill**, a name for certain birds having broad, flat bills, e.g. a bird of the genus *Platyrhynchus*; **flat-body** (*Entom.*), the name of a moth; **flat bug**, any of the family Aradidæ of bugs, which are very flat and live chiefly under the bark of trees; **flat candle**, a candle used in a flat-candlestick; **flat candlestick**, one with a broad stand and short stem; a bedroom-candlestick; **flat-car** (*U.S.*), 'a railroad-car consisting of a platform without sides or top; a platform-car' (*Cent. Dict.*); **flat chasing** (see quot. 1960); also **flat-chased** *ppl. a.* [CHASED *ppl. a.*[2]]; **flat chisel**, a smoothing chisel; **flat-coil**, a pond-snail of the genus *Planorbis*, having its shell coiled in a plane; so ***flat-coiled*** ppl. a.; **flat-compounded** *a.*, *Electr. Engin.* [COMPOUND *v.* 2 f] (see quot. 1940); **flat-crown** (*Arch.*) (*a*) = CORONA 4; (*b*) a popular name for two trees, *Albizzia gummifera* and *A. adianthifolia*, both found in southern Africa; **flat-earth** *a.*, of or pertaining to the theory that the earth is flat; so ***flat-earther***, ***flat-earth-man***; **flat-feet** (see quot.); **flat-fell seam** (see quot. 1964); **flat field** *Photogr.* (see quots. 1904 and 1918); **flat film** *Photogr.*, film on a card or sheet (opp. *roll film*); also *ellipt.* as ***flat***; **flat finish** (see quot. 1940); **flat-four** *a.*, of a four-cylinder engine in which two cylinders are placed on each side of the crankshaft and all the cylinders are parallel to the ground; **flat-hammer**, 'the hammer first used by the gold-beater in swaging out a pile of quartiers or pieces of gold ribbon' (Knight); †**flat-house**, ? a sheriff's office, a roofed shed for impounded animals; **flat impression** (*Printing*), see *flat-pull*; **flat joint**, (*a*) *Building* (see quot. 1904); (*b*) *U.S. slang* (see quot. 1914); **flat-knitting**, a knitting process in which the needles on which the yarn is spun are set in a straight line; so **flat-knit** *a.*, of a fabric made by flat-knitting; †**flat-lap**, a term describing a particular posture of the leaves of a plant (see quot.); **flat-lead**, sheet lead; **flat-minded** *a.* (see quot. 1928); **flat move** (*slang*: see quot.); **flat nail** (see quot.); **flat-orchil**, a kind of

lichen, *Roccella fusiformis*, used as a dye (Ogilvie 18..); **flat pea**: see PEA[1] 3; †**flat-piece**, a shallow drinking-cup; **flat pliers**, pliers having the holding part or jaws flat; **flat pointing** *Building* (see quot. 1940); hence ***flat-joint pointing***; **flat-pressing** (see quot.); **flat pull** *Printing* (see quot.); **flat race**, a race over clear and level ground, as opposed to hurdle-racing or steeple-chasing; whence ***flat-racer***, ***-racing***; **flat-rail**, 'a railroad rail consisting of a simple flat bar spiked to a longitudinal sleeper' (Knight); **flat-ring** *a.*, denoting an armature taking the form of a flat ring; **flat rod** (see quot.); **flat-rolled** *ppl. a.*, formed by rolling between smooth cylindrical rollers; **flat-roof** *v. trans.*, to cover with a flat roof; **flat rope** (see quots.); **flat-sawn** *a.* (see quot. 1957); **flat screen**, (*a*) a television screen that is flat rather than gently curved; usu. *attrib.* with hyphen; (*b*) a computer display that is thin in relation to its two visible dimensions; **flat seam** *Naut.* (see quot.); **flat-sheets** *pl.* (*a*) *Mining* (see quots.); (*b*) *Geol.* and *Mining*, 'thin beds, flat veins, or blanket veins or deposits of some mineral usually different from the adjacent layers; often contact-deposits' (*Standard Dict.*); **flat silver** *N. Amer.*, knives, forks, spoons, and other eating or serving utensils made of or plated with silver (Webster 1961); **flat-skein work** *Basket-making* (see quot. 1943 and SKEIN *sb.*[2] 1); **flat slab** *Building*, a concrete slab reinforced in two or more directions to enable it to be supported by columns, etc., without the use of beams or girders; also *attrib.*, as ***flat-slab construction***; **flat sour**, fermentation of tinned products by the action of micro-organisms which produce acid but not gas, and so do not cause distension of the tin; also (with hyphen) *attrib.*; **flat space**, Euclidean space; **flat spin** *Aeronaut.*, a spin in which an aircraft descends in tight circles while not departing greatly from a horizontal attitude; *fig.*, a frenzy of agitation, a worried confusion of mind; **flat spot** (see quot. 1940); **flat-square** *a.*, of a file: one whose section is a rectangle; **flat-tail mullet**, an Australian fish (*Liza argentea*); also ***flat-tailed mullet***; **flat-tool** (*a*) 'a turning chisel which cuts on both sides and on the end, which is square' (Knight); (*b*) an elongated conical tool used in seal-engraving for bringing ribbons or monograms to a flat surface (*Cent. Dict.*); **flat-top** (*a*) *U.S.*, a name for *Vernonia noveboracensis*; (*b*) *U.S. slang*, an aircraft-carrier; also ***baby flat-top***, a smaller (cargo, etc.) vessel converted into a carrier; (*c*) used *attrib.* of a style of hairdressing; **flat tuning** *Radio* [TUNING *vbl. sb.*] (see quot. 1940); **flat turn** *Aeronaut.* (see quot. 1935); **flat-ware**, (*a*) 'plates, dishes, saucers and the like, collectively, as distinguished from hollow-ware' (*Cent. Dict.*); (*b*) (esp. *U.S.*) domestic cutlery; **flat water** *local*, patches of oily water in the sea, indicating the presence of pilchards; **flat work**, (*a*) *Mining* (see quot. 1851); (*b*) a piece of material of any kind wrought into a flat shape; (*c*) *Laundry* (see quot. 1928); **flat-worm** (*Zool.*), an animal of the class *Platyhelmintha*. Also FLAT-BOAT, -BOTTOM, -CAP, -FISH, -FOOT, HEAD, etc.

1888 ADDY *Sheffield Gloss.*, **Flat-back*, a common knife with its back filed down after it is put together. **1904** GOODCHILD & TWENEY *Technol. & Sci. Dict.* 226/1 *Flat backs*, whole bound or half bound books whose backs have the leather firmly glued or pasted to them. **1940** *Chambers's Techn. Dict.* 339/1 *Flat-back* (*Moulding*), a pattern having a flat upper surface at the joint of the mould, so lying wholly within the drag or bottom half. **1957** MANKOWITZ & HAGGAR *Encycl. Eng. Pott. & Porc.* 53/1 Intended for display on the mantelpiece; often of a 'flat-back' type, modelled and decorated on one side only. **1963** C. R. COWELL et al. *Inlays, Crowns & Bridges* xii. 140 'Steele's' flatbacks—these are useful for patients with close bites. **1597** GERARDE *Herbal* 1042 Of the *flat Beane called Lupine. **1657** W. COLES *Adam in Eden* ccxii. 333 Some call them [Lupines] Flat-beans. **1875** J. SOUTHWARD *Dict. Typogr.* (ed. 2) 48 Hoe's Machines... The forme of type is locked-up in the bed by means of screws, by which the type is held as securely as in the ordinary manner upon a *flat bed. **1886–7** *Proc. Inst. Civil Engineers* LXXXIX. 247 In the second class is the single-cylinder machine—a cylinder impressing a forme of type on a flat bed, and printing one side only. **1892** J. SOUTHWARD *Princ. & Progr. Printg. Machin.* 108 The machine printed 3,145 sheets in the hour—a rate that is altogether unprecedented for a flat bed cylinder machine. **1906** F. H. HITCHCOCK *Building a Book* 121 In the latter part of 1812, the first flat-bed cylinder press was erected by them [*sc.* Koenig and Bauer] in Bensley's office. **1927** E. ST. JOHN *Pract. Hints Presswk.* p. xvi, For the general run of commercial work the two-revolution flat-bed cylinder press is preferred. **1932** C. C. KNIGHTS *Printing* 69 As the name implies the flat-bed machine has a flat surface or bed upon which the material to be printed is laid. **1959** *Times* 14 Jan. 12/4 The future will see photocomposition allied to letterpress printing, both flatbed and rotary, on an increasing scale. **1960** M. SPARK *Ballad of Peckham Rye* iv. 67 They are advertising for ten twin-needle flat-bed machinists. **1961** *Amer. Speech* XXXVI. 272 *Flat bed*, a truck, semitrailer, or trailer with no sides or top. **1970** *Which?* Aug. 237/2 All the [sewing] machines we tested this time had a flat bed. **1971** P. DRISCOLL *White Lie Assignment* x. 82 Two long flatbed trailers were parked with canvas-covered cylinders on them. **1793** SMEATON *Edystone L.* §221 No quarries affording *flat bedded stones having occurred. **1860** GOSSE *Rom. Nat. Hist.* 17 The *flat-bill uttered his plaintive wail. **1819** SAMOUELLE *Entomol. Compend.* 443 *Tinea applana*, the common *Flat-body. **1860** J. CURTIS *Farm Insects* 411 The..Flat-body Moth. **1895** J. H. & A. B. COMSTOCK *Man. Study of Insects* xiv. 139 The *flat-bugs.. are the flattest of all bugs, the body appearing as if it had been stepped upon. **1921** *Trans. Amer. Entom. Soc.* XLVII. 1 Every entomologist is in a general way familiar with the 'flatbugs' of the Hemipterous genus *Aradus*, which are often met with beneath the dead bark of trees, but no systematic treatment of the numerous..species has ever been attempted. **1923** W. E. BRITTON *Guide Insects Connecticut* IV. 11 It is believed the Aradidæ or 'flat bugs', are predatory on insects and other small animals. **1959** SOUTHWOOD & LESTON *Land & Water Bugs* ii. 13 *A. cinnamomeus* differs from other flatbugs whose habits are known in not being a fungus feeder, for it lives on pine sap. **1836–9** DICKENS *Sk. Boz, Scenes* xv. (1892) 125 The flaring *flat candle with the long snuff. **1493** *Bury Wills* (1850) 81 Another *flatt candelstyke of laton. **1859** DICKENS *Haunted Ho.* v. 22 A bedroom candlestick and candle, or a flat candlestick and candle—put it which way you like. **1881** *Chicago Times* 18 June, Demolishing a couple of *flat-cars. **1956** G. TAYLOR *Silver* iv. 73 *Flat-chased or embossed in such low relief as to be almost indistinguishable from flat-chasing. **1960** H. HAYWARD *Antique Coll.* 119/1 **Flat chasing*, surface decoration in low relief on precious metal, produced by hammering with small blunt tools. The characteristic feature of the process is that no metal is removed. **1688** R. HOLME *Armoury* III. viii. 359/1 The third is termed a Chissel, or a *Flat Chissel. **1881** YOUNG *Every man his own Mechanic* §568 The flat chisel..is used for smoothing the work, or taking off the remaining wood that was left by the gouge. **1901** E. STEP *Shell Life* xvii. 319 The next section of these Pond-snails comprises the *Flat-coils (*Planorbis*), made familiar by the typical species—the Ram's-horn or Trumpet-snail. **1926** A. E. ELLIS *Brit. Snails* II. 118 The snails of this family [*sc.* Planorbidæ] are popularly called Ram's-horns, Flat-coils, or Trumpet Snails. **1901** E. STEP *Shell Life* xiii. 234 The *Skenea planorbis*, whose reddish or tawny shell at first sight looks like one of the small fresh-water *Flat-coiled Shells (*Planorbis*), whence its specific name. **1915** R. LANKESTER *Divers. Nat.* xxxiv. 346 The flat-coiled pond-snail, Planorbis. **1909** WEBSTER I. 828/1 *Flat-compounded. **1940** *Chambers's Techn. Dict.* 339/1 *Flat-compounded*, said of a compound-wound generator the series winding of which has been so designed that the voltage remains constant at all loads between no-load and full-load. **1704** J. HARRIS *Lex. Techn.* I. s.v. *Corona*, The *Flat-Crown, is..a particular Member in the Dorick Gate..it hath six times more Breadth than Projecture. **1868** J. CHAPMAN *Trav. Int. S. Afr.* II. 451 The umbrella-like Flat-crown, common in the Berea-bush near D'Urban. **1887** C. A. MOLONEY *Sk. Forestry W. Afr.* 346 Flatcrown of Natal. **1897** 'MARK TWAIN' *More Tramps Abroad* lxviii, The 'flat-crown' (should be flat-roof)—half a dozen naked branches, full of elbows, slant upward like artificial supports, and fling a roof of delicate foliage out in a horizontal platform as flat as a floor. **1950** *Cape Argus* 18 Mar. (Mag. Section) 7/7 The Cape ebony, white stinkwood, flatcrown, essenhout and umzimbiti, trees that yield beautiful timber for furniture-making, grow in profusion in every kloof. **1905** *Westm. Gaz.* 25 Feb. 3/2 This *Flat-Earth Society. **1909** *Ibid.* 21 Sept. 4/1 A lifelong upholder of the flat-earth theory. **1922** A. S. EDDINGTON *Theory of Relativity* 26 Those who adhered to the flat-earth theory must hold that the flat map gives the true size of Greenland. **1934** *Punch* 21 Nov. 562/1 Without being a bigoted *flat-earther, he [*sc.* Mercator] perceived the nuisance..of fiddling about with globes..in order to discover the South Seas. **1963** *Times* 11 May 6/2 His treatment of appoggiaturas was that of a Flat Earther with spasmodic doubts. **1908** G. B. SHAW *Fabian Essays* p. xii, Fewer votes than one would have thought possible for any human candidate, were he even a *flat-earth-man. **1951** AUDEN *Nones* (1952) 47 Lovers of small numbers go benignly potty,..are Millerites, Baconians, Flat-Earth-Men. **1873** *Slang Dict.*, **Flat-feet*, the battalion companies in the Foot Guards. **1939** M. B. PICKEN *Lang. Fashion* 58/2 **Flat fell seam*, flat, sturdy seam. **1964** *McCall's Sewing* ii. 28/2 *Flat-fell*, seam used on shirts, slacks and other tailored garments in which one seam is trimmed and the other stitched over it. Gives a flat, finished seam on both sides of the garment. **1841** R. HUNT *Pop. Treat. Art of Photogr.* 80 A photographic camera should possess, according to Sir John Herschel, 'the three qualities of a *flat field, a sharp focus,..and a perfect achromaticity'. **1878** W. ABNEY *Treat. Photogr.* 205 Since the manufacture of non-distorting doublets giving a fairly flat field has been perfected. **1893** *Jrnl. Soc. Arts* XLI. 384/2 The efforts of opticians..are being continually put forth in the direction of the attainment of..as near approach as possible to a 'flat field'. **1904** GOODCHILD & TWENEY *Technol. & Sci. Dict.* 226/1 A lens is said to give a flat field when the image of a distant object is equally in focus, whatever part of the screen it occupies. **1918** *Photo-Miniature* Mar. 20 *Flat field*, applied to a lens which, when photographing a flat subject, e.g., a painting, gives equal definition in all parts of the plate. **1966** LACOUR & LATHROP *Photo Technol.* x. 115/1 Enlarging lenses are designed to produce an extremely flat field. **1950** *Rev. Documentation* XVII. 134 (*title*) The Microcopy on *flat film as an aid in documentation. **1958** *Engineering* 31 Jan. 155/1 The two basic types—roll-film and 'flats', the latter including micro-cards and micro-sheet (or micro-fiches). **1913** *Sat. Evening Post* 12 Apr. 43 (Advt.), The beautiful, modern *flat finish for interior walls and ceilings. **1940** *Chambers's Techn. Dict.* 339/1 *Flat finish*, a non-glossy finish, showing no brilliancy of surface. **1959** '*Motor*' *Man.* (ed. 36) 38 They [*sc.* each pair of cylinders] are at 180 degrees and the cylinders are parallel with the ground. This is known as the *flat-four type. **1961** *New Scientist* 19 Jan. 162/2 The main features of the Ferguson 'flat four' design are aimed at obtaining the utmost rigidity of the crankcase. **1698** S. SEWALL *Diary* 9 Mar. (1878) I. 472 Our Horses are broke out of themselves, or else are taken out of the stable.. Sent presently to their *flat-house, but hear nothing of them. **1706** *Ibid.* 25 Mar. (1879) II. 157 Surpris'd the Sheriff and his Men at the Flat-house. **1890** JACOBI *Printing* xxi. 185 Pull three or four good sound *flat impressions, with not too much ink. **1825** J. NICHOLSON *Oper. Mech.* 555 In one kind of pointing, the courses are simply marked with the end of a trowel, called **flat-joint pointing*. **1904** GOODCHILD & TWENEY *Technol. & Sci. Dict.* 126/1 *Flat joint*, a mortar joint flush with the face of the wall. **1914** JACKSON & HELLYER *Vocab. Criminal Slang* 34 *Flat joint.* Current amongst open-air sure-thing men who operate at circus gatherings, fairs, carnivals, any gaming establishment... The 'Shells'; 'three card monte'; the 'eight die case'..are all grafting flat joints. The term is derived from the essentiality in all of these crooked devices of a counter or other flat area across or upon which the swindle may be conducted. **1963** MENCKEN *Amer. Lang.* xi. 731 Carnival workers, and especially *strong-joint* or *flat-joint* operators, have a more or less secret argot. **1963** A. J. HALL *Textile Sci.* iii. 149 Large amounts of *flat-knit fabric are produced with straight bar knitting machines. **1969** *Sears Catal.* Spring/Summer 19 Seamless stretch tights knit of nylon... Flat knit heels and toes. **1939** M. B. PICKEN *Lang. Fashion* 58/2 **Flat knitting*, type of knitting done in flat form. **1671** GREW *Anat. Plants* I. iv. §16 Where the Leaves are not so thick set, as to stand in the Bow-Lap, there we have the Plicature, or the *Flat-Lap. **1885** G. MEREDITH *Diana of Crossways* I. i. 15 One is not astonished at her appearing an 'actress' to the *flat-minded. **1928** *Funk's Stand. Dict.* I. 937/3 *Flat-minded*, lacking mental power, imagination, or feeling; devoid of prominent characteristics. **1812** J. H. VAUX *Flash Dict.* s.v., Any attempt or project that miscarries, or any act of folly or mismanagement in human affairs is said to be a **flat move*. *c*1850 *Rudim. Navig.* (Weale) 135 **Flat nails* are small sharp-pointed nails, with flat thin heads. **1422–3** *Abingdon Acc.* (Camden) 92 Item j. *flatpece argenti. **1530** PALSGR. 220/2 Flatte pece, *tasse.* **1535** COVERDALE *1 Kings* vii. 50 Flat peces, charges, basens. **1881** YOUNG *Every man his own Mechanic* §275 A pair of *flat pliers, of the ordinary kind. **1891–3** *Dict. Techn. & Trade Terms of Arch. Design* 110/1 What is called '*flat pointing' is done by marking the joints of the brickwork with a flat trowel. **1900** *Eng. Dial. Dict.* II. 386/1 *Kentish.* In flat-pointing the mortar is smeared up against, and on to, the edges of each brick. **1940** *Chambers's Techn. Dict.* 339/2 *Flat pointing*, the method of pointing, used for uncovered internal wall surfaces, in which the stopping is formed into a smooth flat joint in the plane of the wall. **1881** *Porcelain Wks. Worcester* 21 The manufacture of plates and dishes is called *Flat Pressing. **1888** JACOBI *Printers' Voc.*, **Flat pull* (*or impression*), a simple proof without under or overlaying. **1848** THACKERAY *Bk. Snobs* xv, Sporting Snobs..who..rode *flat races. **1886** EARL OF SUFFOLK, etc. *Racing* (Badm. Libr.) i. 37 A few *flat-racers have come over [from Ireland] to us. *Ibid.*, *Steeple-chasing* ii. 289 As a rule, *flat-racing is a bad preparation for the jumper. **1890** *Daily News* 17 Feb. 3/5 When the flat-racing season begins. **1884** S. P. THOMPSON *Dyn.-Electr. Mach.* iii. 29 The *flat-ring armature may be said to present a distinct type from those in which the ring tends to the cylindrical form. **1893** HAWKINS & WALLIS *Dynamo* 122 A second magnet..can be presented to the other face of the flat-ring core. **1902** *Encycl. Brit.* XXVII. 577/2 The discoidal or flat-ring method. **1860** *Ure's Dict. Arts* (ed. 5) II. 226 **Flat rods* in mining, a series of rods for communicating motion from the engine, horizontally, to the pumps or other machinery in a distant shaft. **1935** H. L. CAMPBELL *Working of Steel* iii. 29 Steel is supplied in the form of strips, sheets, plates, and bars. The following definitions apply to these classes of *flat-rolled steel. **1962** *Times* 8 Feb. 3/1 Stainless flat-rolled products. **1717** TABOR in *Phil. Trans.* XXX. 562 The Græcians us'd to cover or *Flat-roof their Houses with these [tessellated] Pavements. **1874** KNIGHT *Dict. Mech.* I. 878/2 Some *flat ropes, for mining-shafts, are made by sewing together a number of ropes, making a wide, flat band. **1882** W. D. HAY *Brighter Britain* I. v. 120 Rough split sections of the great logs..fixed in the ground..so as to bring their *flat-sawn tops upon a uniform level. **1957** *N.Z. Timber Jrnl.* Mar. 52/1 *Flat sawn*, timber cut tangentially to the annual rings and giving flat grain. **1970** *New Scientist* 4 June 474/1 The development of *flat-screen television has been held back by the complexity of scanning systems for thin, flat cathode ray tubes. **1978** *Government Data Systems* July/Aug. 24/3 The displays of the future may well be electrochromic, cathodochromic, PLZT, gas plasma, flat-screen liquid crystals, or electroluminescent. **1983** *Austral. Personal Computer* Sept. 5/2 (*heading*) No rise for flat screen displays. **1986** *Times* 1 Feb. 11/1 Tomorrow's home entertainment—flat-screen, high quality television. **1867** SMYTH *Sailor's Word-bk.*, **Flat-seam*, the two edges or selvedges of canvas laid over each other and sewed down. **1869** R. B. SMYTH *Goldfields Victoria* 611 **Flat-sheets* , sheet iron flooring at the brace and in the plats and junction of drives to facilitate the turning and management of trucks. **1892** *Northumbld. Gloss.*, *Flat sheets*, smooth iron plates laid over an even floor at a pit bank, on which the tubs are run to be emptied or returned to the cage. **1928** E. POST *Etiquette* 626 The most complete list of *flat silver possible. **1968** *Canad. Antiques Coll.* June 10/3 Of what we call 'flat silver' there were of course spoons. **1912** T. OKEY *Introd. Basket-Making* xii. 143 Except for *Flat Skein work, a purely local industry, skeins are chiefly used by the ordinary basket-maker for handling, and for siding up light work. **1943** A. G. KNOCK *Willow Basketry* 25 What can be called Flat-Skein Work is being used, each stroke lying as nearly as possible flatly upon the one underneath. **1906** C. S. HILL in Buel & Hill *Reinforced Concrete Constr.* (ed. 2) II. vii. 175 (*heading*) *Flat slab construction. *Ibid.*, The arrangement of the reinforcement in flat-slab floors differs with the form of reinforcement used and with the form of slab arrangement. *Ibid.* 176 The accompanying drawings..show flat slab constructions with Columbian bars. **1960** K. BILLIG *Struct. Concrete* II. xiv. 537 Because of the absence of exposed corners, flat-slab construction is less vulnerable in case of fire than beam-and-girder construction. **1926** *Delineator* July 52 In the canning of greens, asparagus, peas, beans and corn, *flat sour seems to be responsible for more failures than any other one factor. **1943** J. G. BAUMGARTNER *Canned Foods* iv. 63 The facultative anaerobic group of 'flat-sour' organisms are so called because they attack carbohydrates with resultant acid..formation. *Ibid.* 64 Products containing sugar or starch are particularly liable to undergo severe spoilage by the 'flat-sour' organisms. [**1873** W. K.

CLIFFORD tr. Riemann in *Nature* 1 May 16/1 These manifoldnesses in which the square of the line-element may be expressed as the sum of the squares of complete differentials I will call *flat*.] **1883** *Encycl. Brit.* XV. 664/1 The space with which we are familiar..has been called *flat space or homaloidal space to distinguish it from other spaces in which the curvature is not zero. **1949** SYNGE & SCHILD *Tensor Calculus* viii. 295 A space in which the curvature tensor vanishes identically is called *flat*. **1953** B. SPAIN *Tensor Calculus* v. 56 In a flat space the property of parallelism is independent of the choice of a curve. **1917** 'CONTACT' *Airman's Outings* iv. 104 Suddenly the machine quivered, swung to the left, and nearly put itself in a *flat spin. **1919** W. H. DOWNING *Digger Dial.* 23 *Flat spin*, to be in difficulties. Only applied to an airman. 'On a flat spin', in a bad position. **1928** *Daily Mail* 7 May 6/4 When a person becomes excited or confused, aviators say 'He went into a flat spin'. **1930** *Punch* 30 Apr. 500 Getting into a flat spin over the perishing spelling. **1957** M. SPARK *Comforters* vi. 126 It is possible for a man matured in religion by half a century of punctilious observance..to go into a flat spin when faced with some trouble which does not come within a familiar category. **1967** D. PIGGOTT *Gliding* (ed. 2) xv. 90 Recovery from a flat spin is slow and unpredictable. **1935** C. G. BURGE *Compl. Bk. Aviation* 307/2 '**Flat spot*', a term applied to a particular form of hesitation when the throttle is opened from the slow running position. **1940** *Chambers's Techn. Dict.* 339/2 *Flat spot*, in a carburettor, a point during increase of air flow (resulting from increased throttle opening or speed) at which the air-fuel ratio becomes so weak as to prevent good acceleration. **1962** *Which?* Apr. (Suppl.) 74/1 Drivers complained repeatedly of a carburation 'flat spot'. **1831** J. HOLLAND *Manuf. Metal* I. 299 The files are *flat square. **1896** F. G. AFLALO *Nat. Hist. Austral.* 232 The *Flat-Tailed Mullet is also met with in estuaries. **1908** D. G. STEAD *Edible Fishes N.S.W.* 43 In form the Flat-tail Mullet is more compressed or slab-sided than the Sea Mullet. **1951** T. C. ROUGHLEY *Fish Austral.* 35 The flat-tail mullet is found in all states except Tasmania. **1853** O. BYRNE *Artisan's Handbk.* 28 *Flat tools for turning hard wood, ivory, and steel. **1859** BARTLETT *Dict. Amer.*, *Iron Weed*, a plant, called in the North-eastern States *Flat Top. **1943** F. PRATT *Navy has Wings* 190 'Scratch one flat top,' Commander Dixon's voice had shouted..through the ship's radio. **1943** *Time* 22 Nov. 26/3 That beats a previous high scorer: the escort carrier 'B'.., another 'baby flat-top'. **1955** C. S. FORESTER *Good Shepherd* 170 Escort vessels and destroyers and baby flat-tops were coming off the ways as fast as America and England and Canada could build them. **1956** L. S. TRUSTY *Art & Sci. Barbering* 93 The principal feature of the Flat Top style is the flat top... The top should be visualized as flat and smooth as the bristles of a brush and in length from 1 and ½ to ¾ of an inch. **1957** *N.Y. Times* 2 June vi. 26/1 A stiff version [of the crew cut] is the Flat Top Crew. **1933** 'R. STRANGER' *Dict. Wireless Terms* 72 **Flat tuning*. A receiver is said to possess flat tuning when a station can be heard over a wide range of movement of the condenser dial. **1940** *Chambers's Techn. Dict.* 339/2 *Flat tuning*, inability of a tuning system to discriminate sharply between signals having different frequencies. **1934** V. M. YEATES *Winged Victory* I. ix. 86 An Avro would do anything you wanted..even do a *flat turn just for fun if you kicked the rudder with decision. **1935** P. W. F. MILLS *Elem. Practical Flying* vi. 88 Turns made without any bank, or flat turns, as they are called. **1851** *Illustr. Catal. Gt. Exhib.* III. 719/1 Plates, dishes, saucers, &c., termed '*flat ware', are made from moulds which form the inside of the article, the exterior being given by 'profiles' of the required outline, made of fired clay, glazed. **1895** *Montgomery Ward Catal.* 188 Solid Sterling Flat Ware... Tea Spoons..Dessert Forks..Sugar Shells..Butter Knives. **1901** *N.Y. Even. Post* 7 May 4/5 A complete line of Rogers Flatware. **1914** G. ATHERTON *Perch of Devil* II. 241 A magnificent silver service, from many dozens of 'flat ware', to silver platters. **1952** M. MCCARTHY *Groves of Academe* (1953) ix. 198 She seemed to fix her eyes on the flatware and napery with the same hypnotised effort that dragged her fork to her lips and back again. **1927** *Glasgow Herald* 10 Sept. 4 We cruise back and forward watching for signs. The chief of these is '*flat' water, as the men call the smooth, oily patches that so puzzle landward folk. **1653** MANLOVE *Lead-Mines* 264 Roof-works, *Flat-works, Pipe-works. **1686** PLOT *Staffordsh.* ix. §7. 335 In hammering of this flat-work they beat the plates first one by one. **1851** TAPPING *Gloss. to Manlove*, *Flat Work*, a mining term descriptive of a species of lead mine, so called from its form, which is broad, spreading horizontally, not without inclination. [**1906** *Westm. Gaz.* 14 Nov. 9/1 Speaking generally, there has certainly been no rise during recent years, especially in what we call 'flat' articles—tablecloths, and such things.] **1921** *Electrician* 11 Mar. 304/2 In the United States..some women use their power wringer as a cold mangle for the smaller pieces of 'flat-work'. **1928** *Funk's Stand. Dict.* I. 937/3 *Flat work* (Laundry), articles that are not to be starched, as, sheets or pillow-cases, in distinction from starched articles, as, waists, collars, etc.

B. *adv.* (Cf. A. 2, in many examples of which the word admits of being taken as adv.)

†**1.** By horizontal measurement. *Obs.*

1663 GERBIER *Counsel* 82 Fret seelings..the workmanship only at five shillings a yard, measured flat.

2. Downright, absolutely, positively, plainly; entirely, fully, quite. Cf. DEAD *adv.* 2.

1577–87 HOLINSHED *Chron.* II. 33/2 As for Gerrot it differeth flat from Girald. *a* **1591** R. GREENHAM *Serm.* i. (1599) 98 They that are thus borne again..cannot fall flat away by sin. **1601** DENT *Pathw. Heaven* 246, I am flat of your minde. **1703** MOXON *Mech. Exerc.* 114 The Iron of a Plane is said to be set Rank, when its edge stands so flat below the Sole of the Plane, that..it will take off a thick shaving. **1770** JENNER *Placid Man* II. 117 Sir Harry contradicted him flat. **1784** BAGE *Barham Downs* II. 242 That wild thing, Peggy, told me, flat and plain, if I did so again, she would pull it off. **1838** DICKENS *Nickleby* lxiv. 621, I be not the mun to crow..so I tell 'ee flat. **1842** *Spirit of Times* 21 May 138/1 Every friend of Old Whitenose would have been flat broke! **1859** BARTLETT *Dict. Amer.*, *Flat broke*, utterly bankrupt, entirely out of money. **1933** W. S. MAUGHAM *Sheppey* (1952) II. 244 You haven't turned it [*sc.* the governor's invitation] down flat?

3. †**a.** Directly, exactly. With respect to the quarter of the heavens: Due. ***flat against***: *lit.* and *fig.* directly contrary to. Cf. DEAD *adv.* 3.

1531 TINDALE *Exp. John* (1537) 28 When the Sonne is flat sowth. **1538** LELAND *Itin.* IV. 54 Then Porte Crokerton flat Est. **1562** COOPER *Answ. Priv. Masse* 80 b, Christes wordes and institution is so flat agaynste you, as you [etc.]. **1653–4** WHITELOCKE *Jrnl. Swed. Emb.* (1772) I. 123 The wind continued flatt and high against Whitelocke's course.

b. Exactly, precisely, not exceeding the stated value: used of amounts, distances, and the like. orig. *U.S.*

1909 WEBSTER 827/3 *Flat*,..Without excess; exactly; due;—used chiefly of numbers or quantities; as, to run a hundred yards in ten seconds *flat*. **1945** *Sat. Rev.* 4 Aug. 22 This one, for instance,..all you fiendishly clever people will solve in no time flat. **1962** *Guardian* 5 July 1/5 In no time flat the very voice of Mrs Chichester..was on the horn. **1969** J. CLARKE *Foxon's Hole* viii. 49 It took her about two minutes flat to step into jeans and sweater.

4. *(to sit)* ***flat down***: plump on the ground.

1852 MRS. STOWE *Uncle Tom's C.* xxviii, Sitting flat down on the floor.

C. *absol.* and *sb.*[3]

1. *absol.* (quasi-*sb.*) That which is flat. ***on the flat***: on paper or canvas; on a smooth surface, as opposed to *in relief*. ***from the flat***: from a painting or drawing on paper, canvas, etc. (opposed to *from the round*).

1862 J. C. ROBINSON *Ital. Sculpt.* 60 Luca..simultaneously with his enamelled terra-cotta sculptures, also practised painting..on the flat. **1884** *Cassell's Fam. Mag.* Mar. 216/1 Occupied in shading in chalk from the flat. **1885** G. ALLEN *Babylon* v, To model a composition in relief from an engraving on the flat.

b. The flat surface or portion (of anything); *esp.* the broad surface (of a blade) as opposed to the edge; also, the inside of the open hand, etc.

Sometimes treated as a sb. admitting of a plural, as 'with the *flats* of their swords'; but *flat* is more usual.

c **1374** CHAUCER *Troylus* IV. 899 (927) Beth rather to hym cause of flat than egge. **1470–85** MALORY *Arthur* XVI. viii, Syre Bors..gafe hym grete strokes with the flatte of his swerd vpon the vysage. **1626** BACON *Sylva* §145 The Strings of a..Violl..doe giue a far greater Sound, by reason of the Knot, and Board, and Concaue vnderneath, than if there were nothing but onely the Flat of a Board. **1671** GREW *Anat. Plants* I. i. §16 This Cuticle is not only spread upon the Convex of the Lobes, but also on their Flats, where they are contiguous. **1719** DE FOE *Crusoe* (1840) I. iv. 69 On the flat of the green..I resolved to pitch my tent. **1727** W. SNELGRAVE *Guinea & Slave Trade* (1734) 258 He gave me a slight blow on the Shoulder, with the flat of his Cutlace. **1779** FORREST *Voy. N. Guinea* 77 An island..like the flat of a plate turned bottom up. **1816** KEATINGE *Trav.* (1817) II. 264 The breast, loins, flat of the neck. **1828** SCOTT *F.M. Perth* iii, Striking the flat of his hand against that which the armourer expanded towards him. **1833** *Regul. Instr. Cavalry* I. 47 The flat of the thigh to the saddle. **1861** DICKENS *Gt. Expect.* xlvi, Here's old Bill Barley on the flat of his back. **1885** *Manch. Exam.* 23 June 5/3 The military..cleared the piazza with the flats of their swords.

c. Level country. In *Horse-racing*: level ground without hedges or ditches; cf. *flat-race*; also, the level piece of turf at the end of some race-courses. Hence *gen.* The race-course.

1836 J. WILSON *Noct. Ambr.* Wks. 1855 I. 180 Sic a..body..could never hae been bred or born on the flat. **1847** G. H. H. OLIPHANT *Law conc. Horses, etc.* App. 278 A.F. Across the Flat 1 M. 2 Fur. 24 Yds. **1877** OUIDA *Puck* ix, Your young lordling spends all his..time on the 'flat'. **1886** EARL OF SUFFOLK, etc. *Racing* (Badm. Libr.) 273 In steeple-chases, hurdle races, and on the flat. **1892** J. KENT *Racing Life C. Bentinck* ii. 48 He will win..unless a crow flies down his throat as he comes across the flat.

2. a. A horizontal plane; a level as opposed to a slope. † ***on the flat of***: on the level or plane of. † ***of a flat***; ***on the same flat***: on the same level or plane.

1605 BACON *Adv. Learn.* I. v. §5. 24 No perfect discouerie can bee made vppon a flatte, or a leuell. **1607** CHAPMAN *Bussy d'Ambois* Plays 1873 II. 3 They move with equall feet on the same flat. **1626** BACON *Sylva* §805 It were good to trie that Exposing of Flesh or Fish both..some height aboue the Earth, and vpon the Flat of the Earth. **1636** MASSINGER *Bashf. Lover* III. i, It was not in The power of fortune to remove me from The flat I firmly stood on. **1650** TRAPP *Clavis* III. 17 The cloud levelled mountains, raised vallies, and laid all of a flat; that is..made all plain. **1791** BENTHAM *Panopt.* I. 155 A declivity is..preferable by far to a dead flat. **1822** T. STRANGEWAYS *Mosquito Shore* 28 This high eminence has a flat at top of about 1500 acres.

b. Sometimes opposed to *fall*.

1645 FULLER *Good Th. in Bad T.* (1841) 68 Either on the flat of an ordinary temper, or in the fall of an extraordinary temptation. **1887** RUSKIN *Præterita* II. ii. 60 Some three inches of fall to a foot of flat.

†**c.** A geometrical plane, irrespective of position; an even surface.

1624 WOTTON *Archit.* II. 83 It comes neere an Artificiall Miracle; to make diuerse distinct Eminences appeare vpon a Flat, by force of Shadowes. **1659** MOXON *Tutor Astron.* v. (1686) 137 A Plain in Dyalling is that Flat whereon a Dyal is Described. **1674** N. FAIRFAX *Bulk & Selv.* 69 Whatsoever moves as much in a flat as it can for the earths rim, we reckon [etc.].

†**d.** A plane figure. *Obs. rare.*

1674 JEAKE *Arith.* (1696) 175 Those Superficial Figures called Like Flats..are such..as bear a certain Proportion in their Sides unto each other.

e. A flat space or flattened surface; *spec.* a flat place on the tyre or wheel of a vehicle, or the flat space on a commutator caused by sparking or irregularity of rotation.

1873 J. H. BEADLE *Undevel. West* xxvii. 576 Up the cliffs, where caves open inward, flats have been worked upon the rock. **1883** HAWKINS & WALLIS *Dynamo* 391 Occasionally, one or two segments in a commutator wear down below the general cylindrical surface of the rest, and form what is known as a 'flat'. **1906** *Westm. Gaz.* 3 July 10/2 Flats on the wheels may to a great extent be avoided by skilful driving, but there is a potential 'flat' in every skid. **1906** GOODCHILD & TWENEY *Technol. & Sci. Dict.* 808/1 A violent application of the brakes may cause several pounds' worth of damage by grinding a 'flat' on the tyres. **1930** *Engineering* 30 May 708/2 It was suggested that flats in railway wheels could, with advantage, be restricted to a depth of 3 mm. (0·118 in.). **1966** H. SHEPPARD *Dict. Railway Slang* (ed. 2) 5 *Flat*, worn part on wheel tyre due to skidding, or, in London Transport, due to excessive braking.

f. In full ***optical flat***. A block or lamina (usually of glass) with one or more surfaces made accurately plane and smooth, any unevenness or departure from a perfect plane being small compared with the wavelength of light.

1897 *Astrophysical Jrnl.* V. 134 The second..requires two large optical flats, each about one and one-half times the aperture of the telescope itself. **1932** HARDY & PERRIN *Princ. Optics* xvi. 345 Round flats are edged exactly like lenses but rectangular ones are edged somewhat differently. **1957** R. S. LONGHURST *Geom. & Physical Optics* viii. 135 If an optical flat is placed in contact with a shallow convex spherical surface, a thin air film of varying thickness results. **1971** *Nature* 30 Apr. 575/1 Silver chloride sheet..was made as flat as possible by compression between glass optical flats.

3. *Building.* **a.** The horizontal part of a roof, usually covered with lead.

1842 BRANDE *Dict. Sc. etc.*, *Flat*, that part in the covering of a house, of lead or other metal which is laid horizontal. **1855** *Act 18–19 Vict.* c. 122 §17 Fifteen inches above the highest part of any flat or gutter.

†**b.** A landing on a stair-case; also, the 'tread' of a stair.

1730 A. GORDON *Maffei's Amphith.* 290 A Stair of 20 Steps, interrupted by a Flat. **1793** SMEATON *Edystone L.* §88 There was but one flat or tread of a step above the center of the house.

4. *Mining.* **a.** A horizontal bed or stratum of coal, stone, etc.; a horizontal vein of metal, or a lateral extension of a vein.

1747 HOOSON *Miner's Dict.*, The Flat always lies on that Side of the Vein which Faces the Water. **1793** SMEATON *Edystone L.* §108 The quarry-men..cross-cut the large flats, which are laid bare. **1881** RAYMOND *Mining Gloss.*, *Flat*, a horizontal vein or ore-deposit auxiliary to a main vein; also any horizontal portion of a vein elsewhere not horizontal. **1883** GRESLEY *Gloss. Coal Mining*, *Flats*, subterraneous beds or sheets of trap rock or whin. **1886** G. A. LEBOUR *Geol. Northumb. & Durh.* (ed. 2) 62 *Flat*, the lateral extension of a lead vein.

b. (See quots.)

1846 BROCKETT *N.C. Words* (ed. 3) *Flatt*, in a coal mine, the situation where the horses take the coal tubs from the putters. **1883** GRESLEY *Gloss. Coal Mining*, *Flat*, a district or set of stalls separated by faults, old workings, or barriers of solid coal. **1892** *Northumbld. Gloss.*, *Flat*, the part of a screen at a pit where the coals rest, and are cleaned before being put into the waggon.

5. a. A piece of level ground; a level expanse; a stretch of country without hills, a plain; the low ground through which a river flows.

1296 *Newminster Cartul.* (1878) 144 Stokwelflatte..Seruonreflatte. *c* **1340** *Gaw. & Gr. Knt.* 507 Fallez vpon fayre flat. ? *a* **1400** in *Cartul. Abb. de Seleby* (Yorks. Rec. Ser.) II. 42 Xij seliones jacentes in iiij locis sive flattes. **1510** in *Yorksh. Archæol. Jrnl.* VII. 59 *note*, One parcel of land called Peeston's flatt. **1602** SHAKS. *Ham.* v. i. 275 Till of this flat a Mountaine you haue made. **1695** BLACKMORE *Pr. Arth.* I. 200 Some range the Flats, and Scour the Champain Land. **1759** B. MARTIN *Nat. Hist. Eng.* I. 45 A large Flat of barren, heathy ground. **1765–75** P. POND in C. M. Gates *Five Fur Traders* (1933) 53 The wind took the Canew up in the Air—Leat hir fall on the frozen flat. **1811** J. FAREY *Gen. View Agric. Derbysh.* I. i. 133 Alluvial flat of loam or sandy loam has accumulated upon the Gravel. **1852** THACKERAY *Esmond* I. iii, A large pleasant green flat, where the village of Castlewood stood. **1857** R. B. PAUL *Lett. fr. Canterbury, N.Z.* iv. 68 The flat on which Mr. Gebbie's house stands. **1877** A. B. EDWARDS *Up Nile* viii. 199 The river widens away before us; the flats are green on either side. **1888** 'R. BOLDREWOOD' *Robbery under Arms* (1889) i. 6 Here it widened out into a large, well-grassed flat. **1944** *Living off Land* iii. 54 These mulga flats contain rocky boulders. **1968** K. WEATHERLY *Roo Shooter* 130 The doe usually fed on the plateau, but.., she sometimes came down on to the flats.

fig. **1685** DRYDEN *Pref. 2nd Misc.* Wks. 1800 III. 49 Milton's Paradise Lost is admirable; but am I..bound to maintain, that there are no flats amongst his elevations? **18**.. DE QUINCEY *Convers.* Wks. 1863 XIII. 176 Very often it [conversation] sinks into flats of insipidity through mere accident. **1878** MORLEY *Vauvenargues* Crit. Misc. 26 The mere bald and sterile flats of character.

b. A tract of low-lying marshy land; a swamp.

1610 SHAKS. *Temp.* II. ii. 2 All the infections that the Sunne suckes vp From Bogs, Fens, Flats. **1670** MILTON *Hist. Eng.* II. 53 Through bogs and dangerous flats. **1821** EARL DUDLEY *Lett.* 27 Nov. (1840) 294 The flats and swamps of Holland. **1859** *Autobiog. Beggar Boy* 99 The Cambridgeshire flats or marshes.

c. *Australian.* (See quot. 1869.)

1869 R. B. SMYTH *Goldfields Victoria* 611 *Flat*, a low even tract of land, generally occurring where creeks unite, over which are spread many strata of sand and gravel, with the usual rich auriferous drift immediately overlying the bed-rock. **1874** WALCH *Head over Heels* 79 Every man on the flat left his claim. **1879** D. M. WALLACE *Australas.* iv. 68 In the gold districts such deposits form 'flats'.

6. Chiefly *pl.* A nearly level tract, over which the tide flows, or which is covered by shallow water; a shallow, shoal.

1550 J. COKE *Eng. & Fr. Heralds* (1877) §155. 102 The sea is.. full of flattes. **1595** SHAKS. *John* v. vi. 40. **1628** DIGBY *Voy. Medit.* (1868) 94 Wee shaped our course to gett ouer the flattes into the riuer of Thames. **1678** R. L'ESTRANGE *Seneca's Mor.* (1702) 477 When we have scap'd so many Rocks and Flatts. **1772–84** COOK *Voy.* (1790) IV. 1408 We were insensibly drawn upon a large flat, upon which lay innumerable rocks of coral, below the surface of the sea. **1813** J. THOMSON *Lect. Inflam.* 621 The boat grounded on the flats a little to the east of the pier. **1867** SMYTH *Sailor's Word-bk., Flat*.. a shallow over which the tide flows.. If less than three fathoms, it is called shoal or shallow.

fig. **1644** MILTON *Educ.* 2 Those Grammatick flats & shallows where they stuck.

7. *Agric.* †**a.** One of the larger portions into which the common field was divided; a square furlong.

1523 FITZHERB. *Surv.* 2 If they [the acres] lye by great flattes or furlonges in the commyn feldes. **1641** BEST *Farm. Bks.* (Surtees) 43 In fower dayes the said dozen shearers finished the saide flatte, and there is in it 14 through landes and two gares. **1688** R. HOLME *Armoury* II. ii. §32, 3 Ridges, Butts, Flats. **1885** *Q. Rev.* CLIX. 325 Theoretically each flat was a square of 40 poles, containing 10 acres.

†**b.** A tract of arable land; a cornfield. *Obs.*

1513 DOUGLAS *Æneis* II. vii (vi). 13 The flate of cornys rank. *Ibid.* VII. xiii. 38 The 3allo corn flattis of Lyde.

c. *dial.* (See quots.)

1879 MISS JACKSON *Shropsh. Word-bk., Flats*, same as *Feerings*. **1884** *Chesh. Gloss., Flat*, a broad flat bed as distinguished from a narrow rounded butt. We speak of ploughing a field in *flats* when there is no indication of *reens*... A wide space covered by any particular crop is called a *flat*, as 'a flat o' taters'.

8. Something broad and thin.

a. A thin disc.

1732 BERKELEY *Alciphr.* IV. ix, Is it [a planet] not a round luminous Flat, no bigger than a Sixpence?

†**b.** Chiefly *pl.* Dice of a shape to fall unfairly when thrown. (Cf. A. 5 b.) *Obs.*

1545 ASCHAM *Toxoph.* (Arb.) 54 What false dise vse they? .. flattes, gourdes. **1664** J. WILSON *Cheats* IV. i. Dram. Wks. (1874) 67 Taught you the use of.. the fullam, the flat, the bristle. **1711** PUCKLE *Club* 21 *note*, At dice they have the doctors, the fulloms, loaded dice, flats.

c. *slang.* in *pl.* Playing-cards. Cf. BROAD *sb.* 6.

1812 J. H. VAUX *Flash Dict., Flats*, a cant name for playing cards. **1821** HAGGART *Life* 56 We played at flats in a budging-crib.

d. *Cotton-spinning.* (See quot. 1874.)

1851 L. D. B. GORDON in *Art Jrnl. Illustr. Catal.* p. iv**/2 The filaments, after emerging from the flats, lie in nearly parallel lines among the card teeth of the drum. **1874** KNIGHT *Dict. Mech.* I. 878/1 *Flat (Carding)*, a strip of wood clothed with bent teeth, and placed above the large cylinder of a carding-machine.

e. In a breech-loading gun: The piece of metal projecting from the breech to support the barrel.

1881 GREENER *Gun* 230 When the barrels are for breech-loaders, the flats are formed on the undersides of the breech-ends.

f. A flat strip of wood inserted under the inner edge of a picture-frame and projecting beyond it; usually gilded. Called also MAT.

1886 W. G. RAWLINSON in *19th Cent.* XIX. 400 Small drawings.. greatly injured by the very modern-looking deep gold flats brought close up to them.

g. In various uses (see quots.).

1688 R. HOLME *Armoury* II. 464/2 Women wear Hair.. in Falls or Flats when the hair hangs loose down about the shoulders. **1804** J. ROBERTS *Penn. Farmer* 55 It is made like a gate, with five bars or flats. **1847** HALLIWELL, *Flats*, small white fresh-water fish, as roach, etc. **1858** SIMMONDS *Dict. Trade, Flat*.. a rough piece of bone for a button mould. **1874** KNIGHT *Dict. Mech.* I. 878/1 *Flat*, a surface of size over gilding. **1888** *Lockwood's Dict. Mech. Engin., Flats*, Flat Bar Iron. **1891** *Century Mag.* Feb. 526/2 The Mexican system of crushing grain by hand on the *metate*, as the flat under the millstone of the Mexicans and native Californians is called. **1893** FARMER *Slang, Flats*, base money. **1962** A. NISBETT *Technique Sound Studio* 253 *Flat.* (*a*) On a stylus, this is a surface of wear which appears on the two sides of the tip after some period of use... (*b*) On the rubber tyre of an idler wheel, a 'flat' is an indentation which may form if the idler is left 'parked' in contact with the drive spindle, or other surface. **1967** E. CHAMBERS *Photolitho-Offset* 272 *Flat*, a number of negatives stripped-up or assembled in position for printing-down on to a single sheet of metal.

9. Something broad and shallow.

a. A broad, flat-bottomed boat.

1749 W. DOUGLASS *Summary* (1755) I. 461 A large scow or flat, to carry persons, cattle, and goods with a canoe-tender. **1801** NELSON in A. Duncan *Life* (1806) 194 The enemy's.. flats (lugger-rigged).. were.. anchored.. Three of the flats and a brig were sunk. **1867** SMYTH *Sailor's Word-bk., Flats* .. lighters used in river navigation, and very flat-floored boats for landing troops. **1879** F. POLLOK *Sport Brit. Burmah* I. 21, I.. went up in the first Government steamer and flat to Prome.

b. A broad, shallow basket used for packing produce for the market. Cf. A. 5 e.

1640 in ENTICK *London* II. 181 Packs, trusses, flats, or maunds. **1840** *New Monthly Mag.* LIX. 267 A basket.. resembling those which.. they call butter-flats. **1886** *Daily News* 4 Dec. 5/4 Watercress.. costs the hawker at the rate of from 16*s.* to 17*s.* a flat. **1889** A. T. PASK *Eyes Thames* 158 The Mimosa comes over in small flat hampers called 'flats'.

c. A shallow two-wheeled hand-cart.

1884 *Chamb. Jrnl.* 5 Jan. 9/1 Butchers' carts, costermongers' flats, and other light conveyances.

d. (See quots.)

1791 HAMILTON *Berthollet's Dyeing* II. II. I. ii. 32 Silk treated with these galls gained in the dye-bath or flat. **1804** CT. RUMFORD in *Phil. Trans.* XCIV. 178 The broad and shallow vessels (flats) in which brewers cool their wort.

e. *U.S.* = *flat-car*: see A. 15.

1864 in WEBSTER.

f. Applied to articles of dress. (*a*) A low shoe or sandal; (*b*) a low-crowned hat (U.S.).

1834 PLANCHÉ *Brit. Costume* 375 *Brogue-uirleaker*, that is flats made of untanned leather, graced their feet. **1859** BARTLETT *Dict. Amer., Flat*, a broad-brimmed, low-crowned, straw hat, worn by women. **1864** MISS WETHERELL *Old Helmet* II. xvi. 269 But you will not wear that flat there? **1938** *Times* 11 Mar. 19/4 With your suit, coloured shoes and bags are favourites. Particularly chic are the crocodile 'flats' in cornflower-blue, [etc.]. **1950** A. LOMAX *Mr. Jelly Roll* (1952) i. 19 They wore what they called the St. Louis Flats and the Chicago Flats, made with cork soles and without heels and with gambler designs on the toes.

10. *Ship-building.* **a.** (see quot. 1867.)

1815 *Falconer's Dict. Marine* (ed. Burney), *Flats*, in ship-building, the name given to all the timbers in midships. **1867** SMYTH *Sailor's Word-bk., Flats*, all the floor-timbers that have no bevellings in mid-ships, or pertaining to the dead-flat. **1869** SIR E. J. REED *Shipbuild.* v. 95 Horizontal flats extending between the bulkhead and a cast iron cellular stern-post.

b. The partial deck or floor of a particular compartment.

1869 SIR E. J. REED *Shipbuild.* ix. 177 Iron plates similar to those used in the flats of stoke-holes. **1893** *Daily News* 3 July 5/6 Tank room, capstan engine flat, and.. the patent fuel space.

11. *Theat.* A part of a scene mounted on a wooden frame which is pushed in horizontally or lowered on to the stage. Also phr., ***to join the flats***: to make into a consistent whole, to give unity.

[**1746** GARRICK *Let.* 11 Dec. in *Corresp.* (1831) I. 46 He had built up the stage, but as nobody came there, he shut in a flat scene to hide it.] **1795** F. REYNOLDS *Rage* II. ii. 27 An elegant Apartment leading to Lady Sarah's Dressing-Room —the Door in the Flat. **1807** *Director* II. 331 The entire assemblage of wings and drops and flat. **1836–9** DICKENS *Sk. Boz* (1850) 259/1 A strange jumble of flats, flies, wings [etc.]. **1901** *Daily Chron.* 21 Aug. 3/4 The 'flats' of her career, so to speak, are not quite joined. **1908** *Ibid.* 29 Apr. 3/3 The 'flats' of the new edition are not very well 'joined'. **1921** G. B. SHAW *Pen Portraits* (1932) 175 Really, Henry Arthur [Jones], you might at least join your flats. **1923** —— *Shaw on Theatre* (1958) 161 A pit without stalls, which jeered mercilessly when the flats would not join. **1932** E. V. LUCAS *Reading, Writing & Remembering* iii. 66 He [*sc.* Mr. Asquith] gave the reporters less work in making him grammatical and fluent than any other speaker. There was no need to join his flats. **1957** *Oxf. Compan. Theatre* (ed. 2) 264/1 The frame of an English flat consists of four 3 × 1 in. timbers, of which the two vertical side-pieces are the Stiles, and the others, the top and bottom Rails. *Ibid.* 265/1 In the mid-nineteenth century.. it was.. used in the phrase 'a pair of flats', and was confined to the two separate halves of a back scene... Farther back, the word is used only adjectivally, and the full term is Flat Scene.

12. *House-painting.* A surface painted without gloss, so as to appear dead: see DEAD *a.* 13 b. Also the pigment employed for this purpose. Cf. FLATTING. ***bastard flat*** (see quot.).

1823 *Mechanic's Mag.* No. 7. 108 The rooms.. were painted with Chinese Flat on walls. **1881** YOUNG *Every man his own Mechanic* §1591 *Bastard Flat* is thinned with turpentine and a little oil.. To procure a good flat, it is necessary to have a perfectly even glossy ground, and it should be of the same tint, but a little darker than the finishing flat.

13. *slang.* A person who is easily taken in, and is said to be 'only half sharp'; a duffer, simpleton. Cf. A. 8. ***a prime flat*** (see quot. 1812).

1762 GOLDSM. *Nash* Wks. (Globe) 546/2 If the flat has no money, the sailor cries, I have more money than any man in the fair. **1812** J. H. VAUX *Flash Dict., Flat*.. any person who is found an easy dupe to the designs of *the family* is said to be a *prime flat*. **1848** THACKERAY *Van. Fair* x, 'You wouldn't be such a flat as to let three thousand a year go out of the family.'

14. *Music.* **a.** A note lowered half a tone below the natural pitch. **b.** In musical notation, the sign ♭ which indicates this lowering of the note; a ***double flat*** ♭♭ indicates that it must be lowered by two semitones. **c.** ***sharps and flats***: the black keys of the keyboard of a piano.

1589 R. HARVEY *Pl. Perc.* (1590) 21 It can neuer be goode musicke, that stands all vpon sharpes, and neuer a flat. *a* **1634** RANDOLPH *Muses' Looking-Gl.* IV. v, The lutenist takes flats and sharps, And out of those so dissonant notes does strike A ravishing harmony. **1669** COKAINE *Fun. Elegy T. Pilkington* Poems 78 His Flats were all harmonious. **1674** PLAYFORD *Skill Mus.* I. iv. 15, I have seen some songs with four flats. **1694** *Phil. Trans.* XVIII. 72 Flats or Half-notes to other Keys. **1706** A. BEDFORD *Temple Mus.* iii. 57 Methods of altering their Tunes, by Flats and Sharps placed at the Beginning. **1806** CALLCOTT *Mus. Gram.* v. 57 The mark now used for the Flat was originally the letter B. **1834** MEDWIN *Angler in Wales* I. 215 Twelve lines in each, of hair and Indian hurl, alternately, like the flats and sharps of a piano. **1872** BANISTER *Music* 7 A Flat, ♭, indicates the lowering of the note to which it is prefixed, one semitone.

d. ***sharps and flats***: used punningly for (*a*) sharpers and their victims; (*b*) recourse to weapons.

(*a*) **1801** *Sporting Mag.* XVII. 37 There are sharps and flats in Paris as well as London. **1825** C. M. WESTMACOTT *Eng. Spy* I. 368 That emporium for sharps and flats, famed Tattersall's.

(*b*) **1818** SCOTT *Hrt. Midl.* xxx, He was somewhat hasty with his flats and sharps.

15. Short for *flat-racer*.

1811 *Sporting Mag.* XXXVIII. 168 He had one of the finest flats in the world in training.

16. U.S. colloq. ***to give the flat***: to give a flat refusal (to a suitor). (Cf. A. 6.)

1859 in BARTLETT *Dict. Amer.*

17. *attrib.* and *Comb.*, as ***flat-like*** adj.; **flat-catcher**, one who takes in simpletons; a swindler; also used of a horse; so ***flat-catching*** vbl. sb.

1821 MONCRIEFF *Tom & Jerry* I. vi. (1828) 22 Do you think we shall get the *flat-catcher [a horse] off to-day? **1841** *Blackw. Mag.* Aug. 202 Buttoners are those accomplices of thimbleriggers.. whose duty it is to act as flat-catchers or decoys, by personating flats. **1864** *Lond. Rev.* 18 June 643/2 'The Bobby' or chinked-back horse, is another favourite flat-catcher. **1821** EGAN *Tom & Jerry* 346 The no-pinned hero.. gave, as a toast, 'Success to *Flat-catching'. **1813** *Sporting Mag.* XLII. 24 It would appear degrading and *flat-like.

†**flat**, *v.*[1] *Obs.* Pa. t. 4 flat(te, flattide. [ad. OF. *flatir*, *flater* to dash, hurl, *intr.* to dash, be thrown down.]

1. *trans.* To cast suddenly, dash.

c **1330** *Arth. & Merl.* 9748 Arthour.. Wiþ his sextene, þat on hem plat, And euerich a paien to deþ flat. **1362** LANGL. *P. Pl.* A. v. 224 Til *vigilate* þe veil fette water at his ei3en, And flatte [*v.r* flat, flattide it] on his face. **1375** *Cantic. de Creatione* 221 in *Anglia* I. 303 etc., Doun she flat here face to grounde.

2. To smite or strike; in quots. *absol.*

c **1330** *Arth. & Merl.* 9562 Bothe on helmes and ysen hatten, The dintes of swordes flatten. **1362** LANGL. *P. Pl.* A. VII. 174 þenne Faytors.. flapten [*v.r.* flatte, flatten] on with fleiles from morwe til euen.

3. *intr.* To dash, rush; to dart *out*.

c **1300** *Arth. & Merl.* 5672 For the mouthe he [a dragon] had grininge And the tong out flattinge. *c* **1450** *Merlin* 275 The saisnes were so many that thei moste flat in to the foreste wolde thei or noon.

flat (flæt), *v.*[2] [f. FLAT *a.*]

†**1.** *trans.* To lay flat or level, raze, overthrow (a person or building). Const. *to*, *with* (the earth or ground). *Obs.*

1607 TOURNEUR *Rev. Trag.* II. ii, I durst vndertake.. With halfe those words to flat a Puritanes wife. **1611** SPEED *Hist. Gt. Brit.* IX. v. 447 Some few [Forts] wherof.. he flatted to the ground. **1627–77** FELTHAM *Resolves* I. iv. 5 She hath.. flatted their strongest Forts. **1637** HEYWOOD *Royal King* I. i, His bright sword.. Pierced the steel crests of barbarous infidels, And flatted them with earth.

2. *Naut.* **a.** To force (the sail) flat or close against the mast. Cf. FLAT *a.* 2 e. ***to flat in a sail*** (see quot. 1772); also *absol.*

a **1642** SIR W. MONSON *Naval Tracts* III. (1704) 329/2 He hears the Seamen cry.. flat a Sheet. **1667–70** DAVENANT & DRYDEN *Tempest* I. i, Flat, flat, flat in the fore-sheet there. **1726** *Adv. Capt. R. Boyle* 25 Who flatted their Sails and laid by till the Spanish Ship came up. **1769** FALCONER *Dict. Marine, Aback*, the situation of the sails when their surfaces are flatted against the masts by the force of the wind. **1772** J. H. MOORE *Pract. Navig.* (1810) 275 *To flat in*, to draw in the aftermost lower corner or clue of a sail towards the middle of a ship, to give the sail a greater power to turn the vessel. *To flat in forward*, to draw in the fore-sheet, jib-sheet [etc.], towards the middle of the ship.

†**b.** *intr.* Of a ship: To turn her head from the wind; to go round on her keel. *Obs.*

1622 R. HAWKINS *Voy. S. Sea* §34. 85 For in lesse then her length, shee flatted, and in all the Voyage but at that instant, she flatted with difficultie.

†**c.** Of the wind: To abate, drop. *Obs.*

1748 *Anson's Voy.* III. i. 297 The wind flatted to a calm.

3. *trans.* To make flat in shape. **a.** To reduce to a plane surface; to reduce or obliterate the convexity, projections, or protuberances of. **b.** To make broad and thin; to reduce the thickness or height of, *esp.* by pressure or percussion; to squeeze or beat flat. Also with *down*, *out*.

Now chiefly in technical use; ordinarily FLATTEN.

a. **1613** M. RIDLEY *Magn. Bodies* 5 Egge forme flatted at the bottome. **1626** BACON *Sylva* §477 Take two Twigs of seuerall Fruit Tres, and flat them on the Sides. **1684** R. WALLER *Nat. Exper.* 76 The Ball.. was flatted so, that it would stand upon the bottom. **1697** CREECH *Manilius* IV. 980 She.. Distends their swelling Lips, and flats their Nose. **1803** FESSENDEN *Terrible Tractoration* I. (ed. 2) 50 *note*, Suppose that the earth was flatted near the poles. **1857** *Fraser's Mag.* LVI. 608 The smooth crisp curves.. become cockled, flatted, and destroyed.

b. **1651** EVELYN *Mem.* (1857) I. 285 The bullet itself was flatted. **1658** EVELYN *Fr. Gard.* (1675) 279 In drying them [Abricots].. leave them whole.. only flatting them, that they may be equal in every part. **1741** *Compl. Fam.-Piece* I. ii. 163 Make them into Loaves, and flat them down a little. **1774** GOLDSM. *Nat. Hist.* VIII. 99 (*The Wasp*) The composition is at length flatted out until it becomes a small leaf. **1780** *Von Troil's Iceland* 356 Fishes.. which are to be found in slate, have been compressed or flatted. **1837** MARRYAT *Dog-Fiend* lv, Smallbones was flatted to a pancake. **1884** F. J. BRITTEN *Watch & Clockm.* 128 A suitable stone is selected and flatted to a proper thickness by holding it against a diamond mill which is kept wetted.

c. To spread or lay out flat.

1709 CONGREVE *Ovid's Art of Love*, A Face too long shou'd part and flat the Hair.

†**4.** **a.** *intr.* To become flattened. Of a swelling: To go down, lose its roundness. *Obs.*

1670 COTTON *Espernon* I. III. 143 A Harquebuss-shot.. that passing through one of his cheeks..flatted upon his Gorget. **1677** TEMPLE *Cure Gout* Wks. 1814 III. 260, I.. observed the skin about it to shrink, and the swelling to flat yet more than at first. **1725** HUXHAM *Small-pox* in *Phil. Trans.* XXXIII. 393 His Pox flatted and grew pale.

b. U.S. *to flat off*: to slope gradually to a level. *to flat out*: to become gradually thinner. Hence *fig.* to fail in business; to prove a failure, to collapse, etc.

1859 BARTLETT *Dict. Amer.*, *To Flat out*, to collapse, to prove a failure..as 'The meeting flatted out'. **1864** BUSHNELL *Work & Play, Growth of Law* 123 The great surge of numbers rolls up noisily and imposingly, but flats out on the shore and slides back into the mud of oblivion. **1865** THOREAU *Cape Cod.* ix. 166 The bank flatted off for the last ten miles. **1865** HOLLAND *Plain T.* iv. 129 Those who have failed in trade..or to use an expressive Yankee phrase, have 'flatted out' in a calling or profession. **1887** PROCTOR *Amer.* in *Knowledge* 1 June 184/1 *To flat out*, to diminish in value—a Western phrase suggested by the diminished productiveness of metallic layers as they grow thinner.

†**5.** ? To find the horizontal area of (land). *Obs.*

1770 *E. Heslerton Inclos. Act* 13 To flat, set out, and allot the lands.

†**6. a.** *trans.* To render (wine, etc.) insipid or vapid.

1626 [see FLATTED 4]. **1694** WESTMACOTT *Script. Herb.* 211 To demonstrate by what Principles Wines and Spirits are made, exalted, depressed, and flatted. **1703** *Art & Myst. Vintners* 11 The Genuine Spirits of the Wine also are much flatted and impaired.

†**b.** To make dull or spiritless; to make less lively or vivid; to deaden, depress. *Obs.*

1648 *Eikon Bas.* xvi. 141 Nor are constant Formes of Prayers more likely to flat and hinder the Spirit of prayer and devotion. **1692** BURNET *Past. Care* ix. 111 So great a length does..flat the Hearers, and tempt them to sleep. **1697** COLLIER *Ess. Mor. Subj.* II. (1709) 90 Any considerable Degrees of Sickness or Age flat the Senses. **1699** BURNET *39 Art.* x. (1700) 118 That Impression is worn out and flatted. **1710** NORRIS *Chr. Prud.* vi. 278 A multitude of words.. which serve only to flat and deaden out devotion.

†**c.** *intr.* To become dull, depressed or feeble; to droop, to slacken. *Obs.*

1654 FULLER *Ephemeris* Pref. 5 Their loyalty flatteth and deadeth by degrees. **1692** TEMPLE *Mem.* Wks. I. 448 The Hopes of those great Actions..began to flat. *a* **1718** PENN *Maxims* Wks. 1726 I. 819 Our Resolutions are apt to flat again upon fresh Temptations.

7. *Music.* To lower (a note) by one semitone.

1674 [see FLATTING *vbl. sb.* 3]. **1685** BOYLE *Effects of Mot.* vii. 88 A determinate note, which..was *Ce fa ut* a little flatted. (In some mod. Dicts.) **1868** *Harper's Mag.* Aug. 429/2 A bull..commenced to bellow, which awoke our friend, who..exclaimed—dreaming, of course, that some member of his class was exercising his vocal organ—'I say, you have flatted your A, and it won't do!' **1895** *North Amer. Rev.* July 11 When a person has a poor ear for music, he will flat and sharp right along. **1944** W. APEL *Harvard Dict. Mus.* 332/2 Variants in which some of the original tones are flatted.

8. a. To cover (a surface) with flat, i.e. lustreless, paint. **b.** *Carriage-building.* To remove the gloss from (a surface) preparatory to varnishing. **c.** To apply a finish of size to (gilding) as a protection.

a. 1842–76 GWILT *Archit.* §2290 The ceilings..to be painted..and flatted and picked in with..extra colours. **1858** *Skyring's Builders' Prices* 95 Moulded Skirtings..If flatted, add o½*d.* **1889** *Pall Mall G.* 15 May 1/2 Preferring to set it [a picture] on one side after it has been flatted in.

b. 1879 *Cassell's Techn. Educ.* IV. 222/1 Apply a second coat of black Japan, and flat again. The whole should then be varnished with hard drying varnish, flatted down and finished.

c. 1841 in MAUNDER *Sci. & Lit. Treas.*

9. *U.S. colloq.* To give a flat refusal to; to reject (a lover). Cf. FLAT *sb.* 16.

1859 BARTLETT *Dict. Amer.*, *To flat*, to reject a lover; as ..'She flatted him'.

10. *intr.* To fish from a FLAT (*sb.*³ 9 a).

1630 *Descr. Thames* (1758) 75 That every Hebberman shall fish by the Shore..and not to lie a Floating or Flatting for Smelts between two Anchors in the Midst of the Stream.

11. To saw lengthwise through the thickness of a plank, deal, or batten, so reducing the width.

1883 M. P. BALE *Saw-Mills* 333 *Flatting*, sawing through the flat or thinnest way of boards. **1945** J. W. BUSH in N. W. Kay *Pract. Carpenter & Joiner* iv. 68 This machine is most useful for..flatting, that is, resawing deals into scantlings.

†**flat**, *v.*³ *Obs. rare*⁻¹. In 7 flatt. [? f. L. *flāt-* ppl. stem of *flāre* to blow.] *trans.* ? To blow (a trumpet).

1675 TEONGE *Diary* 25 Dec. (1825) 127 Chrismas day wee keepe thus. At 4 in the morning our trumpeters all doe flatt their trumpetts, and begin at our Captain's cabin..playing a levite at each cabine doore.

†**flat**, *v.*⁴ *Obs.* [? ad. OF. *flat-er* to FLATTER; cf. however FLAITE *v.*¹] To flatter; in quot. *absol.*

1513 DOUGLAS *Æneis* IV. Prol. 240 Quhat slycht dissait quently to flat and fene.

'flat-boat. (Also as two words.)

1. A broad flat-bottomed boat, used for transport, *esp.* in shallow waters.

1660 F. BROOKE tr. *Le Blanc's Trav.* 209 Almost every inhabitant hath his Almady or flat boat, wherein they recreate upon the Lake. **1711** *Lond. Gaz.* No. 4919/2 They have a great number of flat Boats with them. **1801** NELSON in Nicolas *Disp.* 21 July IV. 427 A Flotilla..to consist of Gun-boats and Flat-boats. **1806** *Naval Chron.* XV. 90 He commanded a division of flat boats.

b. *U.S.* A large roughly-made boat formerly much used for floating goods, etc. down the Mississippi and other western rivers.

1837 HT. MARTINEAU *Soc. Amer.* II. 199 Notwithstanding the increase of steam-boats in the Mississippi, flat boats are still much in use. **1883** C. F. WOOLSON *For the Major* iv, African slaves poling their flat-boats along the Southern rivers.

2. *attrib.* and *Comb.*, as **flatboat-man**, 'a hand employed on a flat-boat' (Bartlett).

1837 HT. MARTINEAU *Soc. Amer.* II. 200, I felt a strong inclination for a flat-boat voyage down the vast and beautiful Mississippi. **1864** LOWELL *McClellan's Rep.* Prose Wks. 1890 V. 116 A country where a flatboatman may rise to the top, by virtue of mere manhood.

Hence **flat-boat** *v. trans.*, to transport in a flat-boat (*U.S. colloq.*).

1858 *Nat. Intelligencer* 29 July (Bartlett) Fruit, which he flat-boated from Wheeling to that point.

'flat-bottom, *sb.* A boat with a flat bottom. (Cf. prec. and BOTTOM *sb.* 7.)

1579–80 NORTH *Plutarch* (1676) 337 The Tarentines.. sent him great store of flat-bottoms, galleys, and of all sorts of passengers. **1660** F. BROOKE tr. *Le Blanc's Trav.* I. xviii. 58 They use flat-bottoms, which do great services upon the River. **1865** CARLYLE *Fredk. Gt.* XIX. v. 510 Admiral Conflans..Makes little of Rodney's havoc on the Flatbottoms at Havre.

'flat-'bottom, *a.* = FLAT-BOTTOMED.

1598 FLORIO, *Piatta*, a flat bottome boat or barge. **1660** F. BROOKE tr. *Le Blanc's Trav.* 70 Where they use flat-bottome boats. **1755** *Monitor* No. 16 (1756) I. 141 Frighted out of their senses with scarecrows, invasions, flat-bottom-boats, &c. **1884** *Pall Mall G.* 11 Sept. 11/1 A flat-bottom pontoon, divided into..watertight sections.

'flat-'bottomed, *a.* (Stress equal or variable.) Having a flat bottom: chiefly of a boat.

1582 N. LICHEFIELD tr. *Castenheda's Conq. E. Ind.* xiii. 33 b, They haue no quiell, but are flat bottomed. **1692** *Lond. Gaz.* No. 2797/3 Our Mortar-pieces are..put upon flat-bottom'd Boats. **1810** C. JAMES *Milit. Dict.*, Flat-bottomed boats..are made to swim in shallow water, and to carry a great number of troops, artillery, ammunition, etc. **1836** VIGNOLES 20 May in *Life* (1889) 200 Agreed with Mr. Gibbs to adopt my flat-bottomed form of rails for the Croydon line.

'flat-cap.

†**1.** A round cap with a low, flat crown, worn in the 16–17th c. by London citizens. *Obs.*

1598 B. JONSON *Ev. Man in Hum.* II. i, Mock me all over From my flat-cap, unto my shining shoes. **1615** J. STEPHENS *Satyr. Ess.* 292 With the same confidence that ignorant Painters make a broad face and a flat-cap to signifie King Harry the Eight. **1630** DEKKER *2nd Pt. Honest Wh.* I. Wks. 1873 II. 110 Flat caps as proper are to City Gownes As.. to kings their Crownes. **1688** R. HOLME *Armoury* III. i. 11/2. **1891** C. CREIGHTON *Hist. Epidemics Brit.* 483 The sight of a Londoner's flat-cap was dreadful to a lob.

2. One who wears a flat-cap; *esp.* a London citizen or 'prentice.

1600 HEYWOOD *1 Edw. IV*, I. Wks. 1874 I. 18 Flat-caps thou call'st vs. We scorne not the name. **1631** DEKKER *Match Mee* I. Wks. 1873 IV. 149 *King.* What's her Husband? *Lad.* A flatcap. **1719** D'URFEY *Pills* IV. 109 The Town of London, Where the Flat-caps call Men Cousins. **1822** SCOTT *Nigel* xv, The flatcaps of the city. **1922** JOYCE *Ulysses* 391 He..hankered about the coffee-houses and low taverns with crimps, ostlers, bookies, Paul's men, runners, flatcaps, waistcoateers, [etc.].

3. A size of writing-paper, usually 14 × 17 inches.

1875 in KNIGHT *Dict. Mech.*

†**'flatchet.** *Obs.* Also flachet. [Cf. MHG. *flatsche* broadsword.] A sword.

1577 STANYHURST *Descr. Irel.* in *Holinshed* VI. 14 They run like bedlam barretors into the streets with their naked flatchets. **1583** —— *Æneis* III. (Arb.) 77 In grasse theyre flachets and tergats warelye pitching.

†**flate,** *sb. Obs. rare*⁻¹. App. = FLATUS 2.

a **1644** QUARLES *Virg. Widow* v. i, There's a Malignant Hypocondriacall Flate within her, which fumes up, and disturbs her head.

†**flate,** *v. Obs.* [app. a dial. var. of WLATE, to feel disgust or nausea.] *intr.* To feel nausea. Hence †**'flatingness**, nausea.

1398 TREVISA *Barth. De P.R.* XVII. cxii. (1495) 676 Oyle drastes is not good to mete, For suche excytyth flatyngnesse & spewynge. *c* **1400** *Lanfranc's Cirurg.* 98 þat may be knowen..bi swetnes of þe mouþ, bi flating [*v.r.* wlattynge] whanne þat a man is fastynge.

flated ('fleɪtɪd), *a. Phonetics.* [formed as if pa. pple. of **flate v.*, f. FLAT-US.] Of consonant-sounds: Produced by *flatus*, i.e. by breath without any vibration of the vocal chords.

1887 ELLIS *Speech-sounds* in *Encycl. Brit.* XXII. 382 [The sounds produced by expelling air] are either *flated*..or *voiced*..or else *whispered*.

flateous, var. of FLATUOUS. *Obs.*

flat fish, 'flat-fish. A name for fish of the family *Pleuronectidæ*, which includes the sole, turbot, plaice, etc.

1710 *Lond. Gaz.* No. 4742/3 All sorts of Flat and fresh Fish. **1837** M. DONOVAN *Dom. Econ.* II. 167 Several flat-fish live many hours out of the water. **1870** YEATS *Nat. Hist. Comm.* 57 Turbot, soles, and other so-called flat fish.

'flat-foot.

1. a. (See quot. 1884.)

1870 HOLMES *Syst. Surg.* III. 693 A slight degree of flat-foot is common in girls. **1884** *Syd. Soc. Lex.*, *Flat-foot*, a condition of the foot in which the tarsus does not possess, or loses altogether, its usual arch.

b. A condition in draughthorses in which the hoof is large and very sloping, with a flat sole and large prominent frog.

1894 D. ROBERGE *Foot of Horse* 58 Thoroughbred horses are great sufferers from overgrowth of hoof, although the *form* of his foot is preferable to that of the flat foot or the convex form. **1903** *Dis. Horse* (U.S. Dept. Agric.) 372 Flatfoot is that condition in which the sole has little or no convexity. **1906** H. C. REEKS *Dis. Horse's Foot* 144 Flat-foot is undoubtedly a congenital defect, and is seen commonly in horses of a heavy, lymphatic type.

2. a. *U.S. slang.* (See quot.)

1887 PROCTOR *Amer.* in *Knowledge* 1 June 184/1 An American 'flat-foot' is a man who stands firmly for his party.

b. A foot-soldier, an infantryman. (Cf. *flat feet*, quot. 1873 s.v. FLAT *a.* 15.)

1889 BARRÈRE & LELAND *Dict. Slang* I. 348/2 *Flat-feet*, a foot-soldier; applied generally to the Foot-guards. **1903** *Westm. Gaz.* 13 Feb. 2/2 To increase the paper strength of the Army by..'flat-foots' who could not march. **1955** *Archivum Linguisticum* VII. 68 The flatfoot or infantrymen [*sic*].

c. A sailor. *slang.*

1897 *Daily News* 3 Sept. 5/6 When some marine reads it, he'll say, 'It's easy to see that a flat-foot has put that in the paper.' **1898** *Tit-Bits* 30 Apr. 81/3 The blue-jacket himself is a 'flatfoot'. **1904** KIPLING *Traffics & Discov.* 73 E's a flat-foot, a indigo-blue matlow. **1909** J. R. WARE *Passing Eng.* 134/1 *Flat-foot*, a young sailor less than twenty-one.

d. A policeman, a plain-clothes man. (Cf. FLATTY² 3.) *slang* (orig. *U.S.*).

1913 A. STRINGER *Shadow* ii. 48 By the time he had fought his way up to the office of Second Deputy he no longer resented being known as..a 'flat foot'. **1932** J. T. FARRELL *Studs Lonigan* (1936) iv. 73 He got sore as a boil and stepped up to the lousy flatfoot. **1933** E. C. VIVIAN *Ladies in Case* iii. 49 Spike laid out a flat-foot—pleeceman, I mean. **1938** J. CURTIS *They drive by Night* xxiii. 262, I don't like no flatfoots myself, but I'll help them get anyone of that sort. **1943** P. CHEYNEY *You can always Duck* iii. 52 This guy's a flatfoot—one of Mr. Hoover's little boys—a Special Agent of the Federal Bureau of Investigation. **1948** C. DAY LEWIS *Otterbury Incident* vii. 83 Suppose the flatfeet got to hear of it? **1959** I. & P. OPIE *Lore & Lang. Schoolch.* xvii. 369 His name is P. C. Wallace but we call him old Walrus. When he has gone round the corner we call names such as slob, natter knob, or flatfeet.

e. A person (with flat feet). *colloq.*

1922 JOYCE *Ulysses* 375 Some flatfoot tramp on it in the morning.

So **'flat-foot** *v. intr.*, to walk in a flat-footed manner.

1932 J. T. FARRELL *Young Lonigan* iv. 194 He flat-footed it back to the shade. **1966** *Listener* 27 Jan. 147/1 'Fit for an Alba..' he said, flat-footing round one of Europe's most extravagant palaces.

'flat-'footed, *a.* (Stress equal or variable.)

1. a. Having flat feet, i.e. feet with little or no hollow in the sole and a low instep. Of a horse: Having flat hoofs, with the soles near the ground.

1601 HOLLAND *Pliny* I. 351 There haue been now of late, Serpents knowne flat-footed like Geese. **1675** *Lond. Gaz.* No. 979/4 Stolen a Gelding..flat-footed before. **1688** R. HOLME *Armoury* II. ix. 185/2 [A Grey-Hound] Long, and Flat-footed. **1699** DAMPIER *Voy.* II. II. 70 Pelicans are large flat-footed Fowls, almost as big as Geese. **1860** MAYNE *Exp. Lex.*, *Leiopodes*, old term..applied by Galen..to those who were flat-footed.

b. *transf.* Of a rail = FLAT-BOTTOMED.

1889 G. FINDLAY *Eng. Railway* 42 The 'fish-bellied' rails were found troublesome to roll, and this led to the introduction of the flat-bottomed or 'flat-footed' section of rail.

2. a. *colloq.* (orig. *U.S.*) Downright, plain and positive; also, dead, insipid, maladroit. *to come out flat-footed (for)*: to make a bold or positive statement of one's opinion, or the like.

1828 A. ROYALL *Black Bk.* II. 114 He was one of your right down flat-footed ox-drivers. **1834** *Knickerbocker* III. 35, I haint got no shoes, tis true, but I stand flat-footed and damn the man who can move me one inch. **1846** *N.Y. Herald* 30 June (Bartlett), Mr. Pickens..has come out flat-footed for the administration. **1858** *Harper's Mag.* Sept. 563 His..bold, flat-footed way of saying things. **1863** GRAY *Lett.* II. 504, Complaining of Lyell that he does not come out 'flat-footed' as we say, as an advocate of natural-selection transmutation. **1899** *Westm. Gaz.* 6 Nov. 2/3 A flat-footed, commonplace scribbler of heroic verse. **1902** *Daily Chron.* 14 Jan. 3/2 His 'enigmatic smile' and his flat-footed compliments. **1923** *Times Lit. Suppl.* 4 Jan. 4/2 Histories of literature..in which the erudite..mind traverses with flat-footed thoroughness the country it has mapped out for itself. **1931** W. G. MCADOO *Crowded Years* 367 Germany came out flat-footed with the belligerent warning..that she would engage in unrestricted submarine warfare. **1957** R. CAMPBELL *Coll. Poems* II. 111 Weird blue-stockings with damp, flatfooted minds. **1962** *Daily Mail* 19 Jan. 3/8 It is time Associated-Rediffusion presented something less flat-footed and insipid.

b. *U.S.* Unready, not 'on one's toes'.

1912 in *Amer. Speech* (1951) XXVI. 31/1 (Baseball terminology) *Flat-footed*, unprepared, caught napping. **1928** *Funk's Stand. Dict.*, *Flat-footed* (slang). *Racing.* Standing still; unprepared: said of a horse when the jockey is not on the qui vive and expecting a start. **1940** *Topeka Jrnl.* 14 Nov. 1/4 (AP), The Italians were caught flat-footed ..and from that moment the story was one of deadly Greek

bayonet charges. **1955** H. Roth *Sleeper* ix. 68 A group of people who lie so shamelessly that they are constantly being caught flat-footed. **1963** J. Joesten *They call it Intelligence* I. v. 51 The C.I.A...was caught flatfooted by the military coup in Baghdad.

Hence ˌ**flat-ˈfootedly** *adv.*, ˌ**flat-ˈfootedness.**

1886 J. A. Logan *Gt. Conspiracy* 660 The old Rebel leaders..came out flat-footedly again with the 'demand that all Custom-house taxation shall be only for revenue'. **1890** *Daily News* 13 Sept. 3/1 The human foot is libelled by these dreadful coverings, in which many a good player flat-footedly dashes about. **1949** 'N. R. Nash' *Young & Fair* II. i. 50, I couldn't come out flatfootedly against the Vidge? **1963** *Times Lit. Suppl.* 18 Jan. 40/4 A flat-footedly dramatic definition of time and place. **1882** *Standard* 19 Sept. 5/1 Flat-footedness is due to..improperly-made shoes.

flath. *Irish Hist.* Also **flaith.** [Irish.] A lord (see quots.).

1873 Sullivan *Introd. O'Curry's Anc. Irish* I. 101 The first class [of *Aires*] were the true lords or *Flaths*, the *Hlaford* of the Anglo-Saxons. **1876** —— in *Encycl. Brit.* V. 799 An *aire* whose family held the same land for three generations was called a *flaith* or lord.

†**flathe, flath.** *Obs.* [Cf. OHG. *flado*, MHG. *flade* flat cake; an OE. **flaða* has not been found.]

1. = flathon, flawn.

c **1450** *Interl. Gloss. John de Garlande* in Wright *Voc.* 127 *Flaones fartos*, flathen ystuffyd.

2. A name for the ray or skate.

c **1440** *Promp. Parv.* 164/2 Flathe, or flathe [*sic*], fysche (flay, or flacch, fysch.) (*R*)*agadies*. **1466** *Mann. & Househ. Exp.* 334 Item, the same day my mastyr paid for a fflathe.. xiij. *d.* **1562** Turner *Herbal* II. 127 *a*, The fishe called in Latin *pastinaca marina*, whych is lyke vnto a flath. **1577** Harrison *Descr. Eng.* III. iii. in *Holinshed* (1587) I. 224 Our chaits, maidens, kingsons, flath and thornbacke. *c* **1601** J. Keymor *Dutch Fishing* (1664) 8 Soals, Thorneback, Floith [*sic*], Scate, Brett [etc.].

ˈ**flat-head.**

A. *sb.* **1. a.** One who has a flat head; *spec.* a member of a tribe of North American Indians named from their supposed practice of flattening their children's heads artificially.

The tribe now commonly known by this appellation is the Selish or Hopilpo; but 'they do not flatten the heads of their children, and appear never to have done so; the name Flathead being at first applied to them by mistake' (*Encycl. Amer.* 1886).

1837 Gen. P. Thompson *Exerc.* (1842) IV. 225 There are flat-heads there [Sierra Leone] as in other countries. **1837** W. Irving *Capt. Bonneville* I. 121 The Flathead levelled his piece, and brought the Blackfoot to the ground. **1841** Catlin *N. Amer. Ind.* (ed. 2) II. 110 The Chinooks.. correctly come under the name of Flat Heads, as they are almost the only people who strictly adhere to the custom of squeezing and flattening the head. **1862** D. Wilson *Preh. Man* (1876) II. xxi. 221 The strange practice of American Flatheads far to the north-east of the Altai chain.

b. A fool, simpleton. *dial.* and *slang.*

1862 C. C. Robinson *Dialect of Leeds* 50 Ah tell'd him 'at he hedn't t'sense 'at he wur born wi'—a big flathead. **1884** 'Mark Twain' *Huck. Finn* xxiii. 229 Greenhorns, flatheads! **1902** *Westm. Gaz.* 31 May 2/1 'G'n, ye little flathead,' he said admonishingly, 'folks don't get headaches here.' **1922** Wodehouse *Let.* 29 Dec. in *Performing Flea* (1953) 19 Your stuff is really too good for the ordinary magazine, so that when you don't have a plot which is all right for the flatheads anyway, editors are apt to turn you down. **1941** Baker *Austral. Slang* 29 Flathead, a simpleton or fool. **1966** *New Statesman* 6 May 654/2 Gobbledygook is the defence of the American intellectual aware of the hostile mockery of the surrounding flatheads.

2. *Australia.* The local name for a fish of the genus *Ceratodus*.

1832 Bischoff *Van Diemens Land* II. 32 The market of Hobart Town is supplied with small rock cod, flat-heads, and a fish called the perch. **1852** Mundy *Our Antipodes* viii. 195 A good basket of schnappers and flatheads.

3. *U.S.* 'A snake which flattens its head, as a species of Heterodon' (*Cent. Dict.*).

1888 Bergen in *Pop. Sci. Monthly* XXXIII. 660 The blow-snake of Illinois is variously known in other localities as hog-nose, flat-head, viper, and puff-adder.

4. *Arch.* An ornament of an archivolt with a flat uncarved surface.

1883 Mollett *Dict. Art & Archæol., Flat-heads*, an ornament peculiar to the Romano-Byzantine period, which decorates archivolts.

B. *attrib.* Having a flat head or top.

1874 Knight *Dict. Mech.* I. 878/1 *Flat-head Nail*, a forged nail with a round, flat head. **1891** *Scribner's Mag.* Sept. 311/1 The flat-head houses of Brooklyn.

ˈ**flat-ˈheaded,** *a.* (Stress equal or variable.)

a. Having a flat head or top. †**b.** Wearing a flat hat.

1652 Ld. Digby *Elvira* III. (1667) 36 A sharp-pointed Hat, (Now that you see the Gallants all Flat-headed) Appears not so ridiculous, as [etc.]. **1752** Sir J. Hill *Hist. Anim.* 103 The larger, smooth, and flat-headed Amphisbæna. **1853** Sir H. Douglas *Milit. Bridges* iv. 185 Flat-headed boats. **1880** G. Meredith *Trag. Com.* 242 I have not a spark of sense to distinguish me from a flat-headed Lapp, if she refuses. **1881** Freeman *Subj. Venice* 216 This doorway is flat-headed and has lost all mediæval character.

c. flat-headed borer *U.S.*, a larva of any beetle of the family Buprestidæ, which bores in the bark and sapwood of trees.

1882 M. Treat *Injurious Insects* 144 The Flat-Headed Apple-Tree Borer..may at once be recognized by it [*sic*] anterior ends being enormously enlarged and flattened. *Ibid.* 145 This Flat-headed borer is far more common with our Eastern brethren. **1926** E. O. Essig *Insects Western N. Amer.* xxiii. 395 The larvæ [of the family Buprestidæ] are known as flat-headed borers because of the greatly enlarged and flattened thoracic segments. **1968** *Gloss. Terms Timber Preservation* (*B.S.I.*) 13 *Buprestidae*, a family of beetles, often brightly coloured or of metallic brilliance, which bore in or under the bark or in the sapwood of dying trees or timber; called 'flat-headed borers' in the U.S.A.

†ˈ**flathon.** *Obs.* Also **flathoun.** [ad. med.L. *flatōn-em, fladōn-em*: see flawn.] = flawn.

c **1430** *Two Cookery Bks.* I. 56 Flathouns in lente. *c* **1450** *Ibid.* II. 73 Flathonys.

†ˈ**flatile,** *a. Obs.*$^{-0}$ [ad. L. *flātil-is* blown, f. *flāre* to blow.] (See quot.) So †**flaˈtility.**

1727 Bailey vol. II, *Flatile*, unconstant. **1656** Blount *Glossogr., Flatility*, inconstancy. **1721–1800** in Bailey.

†ˈ**flation.** *Obs. rare*$^{-1}$. [as if ad. L. *flātiōn-em*, f. *flāre* to blow.] Blowing or breathing.

1708 Dodwell *Mort. Humane Souls* 23 The πνοὴ, or Flatus, is by the Fathers supposed to continue so long, and no longer, than the Act of Spiration, or Flation, lasts.

ˈ**flat-iron,** *sb.*

1. a. An iron with a flat face for smoothing linen, etc.

1810 *Sporting Mag.* XXXV. 78 A certain flat iron, which she..held in her hand. **1845** Alb. Smith *Fort. Scatterg. Fam.* viii. (1887) 29 [She] attacked a small collar somewhat savagely with a flat-iron.

b. A kind of boat (see quot. 1961).

1886 *Outing* (U.S.) VIII. 58/1 There are..the 'pumpkin-seed', and the 'flat-iron' models. **1902** *Westm. Gaz.* 18 Aug. 5/2 Steaming down Southampton Water at half-past seven in the 'Albion', a craft which yachtsmen are fond of designating a 'flat-iron'. **1959** *Times* 16 Mar. (Suppl., Port of London) p. viii/3 At Battersea, a strange craft may be seen... This is a 'flat-iron', a coastal collier bringing fuel to the power stations and gasworks. **1961** F. H. Burgess *Dict. Sailing* 90 *Flat-iron.* Any vessel of shallow draft, abnormally wide in the beam, and with low upper-works.

2. *attrib.* and *Comb.* esp. applied to a building, from its triangular shape.

1862 H. Marryat *Year in Sweden* II. 370 Huge wooden triangular frames, like flat-iron stands. **1866** Larwood & Hotten *Hist. Signboards* xiv. 468 The house being wedgeshaped, has an entry at each side. Such a house in London is often called by the vulgar a 'Flat-iron'. **1874** Knight *Dict. Mech.* I. 878/2 *Flat-iron heater*, a stove specially adapted for heating smoothing-irons, a laundry-stove. **1893** Farmer & Henley *Slang* III. 16/2 *Flat-iron*, a corner public house. **1903** *Westm. Gaz.* 8 June 2/1 The Flatiron Building, it seems, did not exhaust all the possibilities of ingenuity in skyscraper construction. **1929** D. H. Lawrence *Pansies* 76 Then you will hit the Flat-iron Building and flatten it out. **1931** *Times Lit. Suppl.* 10 Sept. 677/3 A 'flat-iron' building is monotonous in a sense in which the Escorial is not.

Hence ˈ**flat-iron** *v.*, to smooth with a flat-iron; ˌ**flat-ˈironing** *vbl. sb.* (in quot. *fig.*).

1865 Mrs. Whitney *Gayworthys* xxxii. (1879) 314 Her features levelled themselves into a plane of benignity, as if they had been suddenly flatironed. **1879** E. Garrett *House by Works* I. 113 She is not the sort of woman to be put down by any of your flat-ironing processes.

†ˈ**flative,** *a. Obs. rare.* [ad. L. type **flātīv-us*, f. *flāre* to blow.] Engendering wind, flatulent.

1599 H. Buttes *Dyets drie Dinner* F vj b, Artichokes.. remove flative humours. **1607** Brewer *Lingua* v. xvii. M ij, Eate not too many of those Apples, they bee very flatiue.

flatland (ˈflætlənd, ˈflætlænd). Also **flat land.**

1. A region of flat land. orig. *U.S.*

1735 *Springfield Rec.* II. 505 In the Said Ledge Hill then over Rocky flatland we found a Small white marked & Renewed it. **1836** J. Hall *Statistics of West* 31 That [water] which overflows the flat lands, will be stagnant, or flow gently backward in eddies. **1892** A. E. Lee *Hist. Columbus, Ohio* I. 697 The rain poured down in sheets, inundating the flat-land. **1907** W. H. Koebel *Return of Joe* 167 A couple of thousand feet below us was spread the stretch of flatland. **1934** J. L. Myres in E. Eyre *Europ. Civilization* I. 89 Westward towards the Atlantic from the lofty core of Central Asia, the north-west quadrant of the Old World land-mass extends in three great belts, a Northern and a Southern Flatland, separated by a..Mountain-zone... The two flatlands consist of relatively steady blocks of old crust. **1959** *Times* 18 June (Suppl., Queen in Canada) p. vii/7 The flatlands of Prince Edward county. **1961** *Guardian* 25 March 6/4 Its rich wheat fields..do show what can be done in the Sardinian flatlands. **1970** *Guardian* 18 July 1/8 Newark sprawls across the industrial flatlands that lie across the Hudson River from New York.

2. (With capital initial.) An imaginary land in space of two dimensions (see quot. 1884).

1884 Abbott *Flatland* I. §1 (ed. 2) 3, I call our world Flatland..Imagine a vast sheet of paper on which straight Lines, Triangles, Squares, Pentagons, Hexagons, and other figures, instead of remaining fixed in their places, move freely about, on or in the surface, but without the power of rising above it or sinking below it. **1892** W. W. R. Ball *Math. Recr.* x. 191 We may picture the inhabitants of flatland as moving..on the surface of a plane or between two parallel and adjacent planes.

Hence ˈ**Flatlander**, an inhabitant of Flatland.

1884 Abbott *Flatland* (ed. 2) Pref.

flatlet (ˈflætlɪt). [f. flat *sb.*^{2} + -let.] A small flat, usu. of one or two rooms.

1925 *Glasgow Herald* 21 Mar. 7 There is a large scheme evolving by which big well-built houses..are adapted to provide one-two-roomed flatlets at a very moderate rental. **1931** W. Holtby *Poor Caroline* vi, The experimental pioneer life in a two-roomed flatlet at Haverstock Hill. **1935** *Times* 9 Oct. 1/7 Wanted. Flatlet houses in really good letting districts. **1950** L. A. G. Strong *Which I Never* 110 Full of tall houses which..were now let out in flats, flatlets and bed-sitting-rooms.

ˈ**flatling,** ˈ**flatlings,** *adv.* and *a. Obs.* exc. *arch.* or *dial.* [f. flat *a.* + -ling(s.]

A. *adv.*

1. In a prostrate position, at full length, flat. Often with *fall, lie*, etc.

1375 Barbour *Bruce* xvii. 369 Oft leddres, and men.. Thai gert fall flatlings to the ground. *c* **1450** *Mirour Saluacioun* 2501 The knyghtes upon the grounde laide than the crosse flatling. **1530** Lyndesay *Test. Papyngo* 184 Scho ..flatlyngis fell, and swappit in to swoun. *a* **1605** Montgomerie *Flyting w. Polwart* 111, I's fell thee like a fluike, flatlings on the flure. **1632** Lithgow *Trav.* I. 37 The halfe of his body and right arme fell flatlings in the fire. **1895** J. H. McCarthy *Lond. Leg.* III. 118 In a moment he had stumbled backwards and fallen flatlings into the ditch.

2. With the flat side.

1470–85 Malory *Arthur* viii. xxxii, Sire tristram..smote vpon hym fyue or sixe strokes flatlynge on the neck. **1578** Timme *Caluine on Gen.* 121 This shaking sword..was not always shaking with the edge towards Man, but sometimes flatling also. **1591** Harington *Orl. Fur.* xxx. liv, It [the blow] lighted flatling on him. **1820** Scott *Ivanhoe* xlii, [His] sword turned in his hand, so that the blade struck me flatlings. **1868** Morris *Earthly Par.* I. 321 He smote him flatling with his sheathed sword.

3. Of motion: On the level, horizontally.

1598 Sylvester *Du Bartas* II. ii. iv. Columnes 325 He doth not ride Flatling a-long, but vp the Sphears steep side.

4. *dial.* Plainly, peremptorily.

1847–78 in Halliwell, *Flatlins*, plainly, peremptory.

†**B.** *adj.* (In form *flatling* only.) Of a blow: Dealt with the flat side of a weapon. *Obs.*

1579–80 North *Plutarch, Alcibiades* 211 Flatling blowes. **1609** Heywood *Brit. Troy* xi. 91 A flatling blow that on his beauer glancst.

†ˈ**flatlong,** *adv. Obs.* Also 6 *Sc.* **flatlangis.** [f. flat *a.* + -long; an altered form of prec.]

1. In or into a prostrate position.

1570 *Henry's Wallace* v. 1110 Flatlangis [*MS.* thwortour]. **1600** F. Walker *Sp. Mandeville* 64 a, [They] let them selues fall flatlong downe to the earth. *a* **1632** in T. Taylor *God's Judgem.* I. I. xxix. 133.

2. With the flat side; also, with the flat sides in contact.

1580 Sidney *Arcadia* (1622) 304 The pittilesse sword.. did but hit flatlong. **1602** Carew *Cornwall* 34 a, They have a device of two sticks filled with corks, and crossed flatlong. **1610** Shaks. *Temp.* II. i. 181. *a* **1648** L. Herbert *Life* (1886) 141, I..clapt my left foot..flat-long to the left side.

flatly (ˈflætlɪ), *adv.* [f. flat *a.* + -ly^2.]

1. In a flat or prostrate position. ? *Obs.*

c **1425** Wyntoun *Cron.* viii. xxxviii. 69 He..ran And layd hym at þe erd flatly. **1592** Shaks. *Ven. & Ad.* 463 At his looke she flatly falleth downe.

2. a. With small curvature. **b.** As on a flat surface; without relief.

1797 Holcroft *Stolberg's Trav.* (ed. 2) II. l. 205 It was very flatly arched. **1883** C. C. Perkins *Ital. Sculpt.* 116 Plants, fruits, and flowers are..treated flatly, and not in the round.

3. a. In a plain, blunt, or decisive manner; without ambiguity, qualification, or hesitation; plainly, bluntly; decisively. **b.** In the unqualified sense of the statement; absolutely, completely.

a. 1562 Cooper *Answ. Priv. Masse* 38 If I should flatly deny, that the mynister receiued. **1578** *Chr. Prayers* in *Priv. Prayers* (1851) 541 To speak flatly, those only are the things, that are..hurtful unto us. *a* **1618** Raleigh *Prerog. Parl.* (1628) 9 He was flatly denied the Subsedy demanded. **1761–2** Hume *Hist. Eng.* (1806) IV. lxii. 641 The common council of London flatly refused to submit. **1809** Pinkney *Trav. France* 57 He..flatly told me, that I must either have that or none. **1879** McCarthy *Own Times* II. xxix. 389 He seldom expresses any opinion one day without flatly contradicting it the next.

b. 1577 tr. *Bullinger's Decades* (1592) 101 Mankind being flatly corrupted by sinne. **1583** Babington *Commandm.* i. (1615) 17 Such things as flatlie and directly are contrary to the loue of thee. **1641** Milton *Ch. Govt.* iv. 14 Flatly against Scripture. **1692** Bentley *Boyle Lect.* vii. 246 Which is flatly impossible. **1849** Ruskin *Sev. Lamps* ii. §1. 29 Of all sin there is..no one more flatly opposite to the Almighty. **1874** Micklethwaite *Mod. Par. Churches* 187 This is of course ..flatly impossible.

4. In a dull or spiritless manner; without zest; insipidly.

1644 Digby *Two Treat.* II. Concl. 461 We shall but flatly relish the most poinant meates. **1697** Dryden *Virg. Past.* Pref. (1721) I. 87 That famous Passage of Lucan..which Brabeuf has rendered so flatly. **1708** *Brit. Apollo* No. 45. 3/2 The Line [is] flatly Dull and Poor. **1865** Dickens *Mut. Fr.* III. vi, He did not appear to have hidden anything, so went off flatly. **1885** *Manch. Exam.* 22 July 3/1 It..simply says ineffectively and flatly what has been said effectively and brightly by a score of writers.

b. *Comm.* With little competition.

1887 *Daily News* 8 July 6/8 The more important parcels offered in public sale to-day went off flatly.

flatman (ˈflætmən). [f. flat *sb.*^{3} + man.]

One who navigates a flat. See flat *sb.*^{3} 9 a.

1883 *Manch. Guardian* 12 Oct. 5/2 Two flatmen have been ..charged with attempting to murder a woman. **1884** *L'pool Merc.* 14 Feb. 5/10 About 350 flatmen employed on the flats of the Bridgwater Navigation Company.

flatness ('flætnɪs). [f. FLAT *a.* + -NESS.]

1. The quality or condition of being flat or level; *esp.* of a country.

c **1440** *Promp. Parv.* 164/2 Flatnesse, *planicies.* **1601** HOLLAND *Pliny* II. lxv. 31 Wonderfull it remaineth..How it should become a Globe, considering so great flatnesse of Plaines and Seas. **1703** MOXON *Mech. Exerc.* 150 They try ..the flatness of the whole Frame of Flooring again. **1796** MORSE *Amer. Geog.* I. 725 The perfect flatness of the coasts. **1838** *Murray's Hand-bk. N. Germ.* 372 The wearisome flatness and monotony of their..country.

2. The quality or fact of having a small curvature; diminished convexity.

1683 RAY *Corr.* (1848) 134 The flatness of its bill. **1796** H. HUNTER tr. *St. Pierre's Stud. Nat.* (1799) I. p. iv, The flatness of the Earth at the Poles. **1816** J. SCOTT *Vis. Paris* (ed. 5) App. 324 To Neuilly, to view the bridge..celebrated for the flatness of its arches. **1870** WHYMPER in *Alpine Jrnl.* V. 6 The flatness of the curves of the *roches moutonnées.*

3. a. 'Want of relief or prominence' (J.). *spec.* in *Photogr.* Cf. FLAT *a.* 4 d.

1702 ADDISON *Dial. Medals* iii. 164 One would think the Coiner look'd on the flatness of a figure as one of the greatest beauties in Sculpture. **1885** A. MARY F. ROBINSON in *Mag. of Art* Sept. 478/2 The brilliant light in which the outline is lost, the solidity almost to flatness..all remind us of Hans Holbein. **1889** E. J. WALL *Dict. Photogr.* 71 *Flatness,* a want of vigour and contrast in the negative and resulting prints, due to under- or over-exposure, or to the use of too strong or too weak a developer.

b. ***flatness of field*** (see quots. and *flat field* s.v. FLAT *a.* 15).

1867 J. HOGG *Microsc.* I. ii. 72 Flatness of field..denotes the exact capability of an objective to show the peripheral or marginal portions of the field with the same sharpness as the central. **1878** W. ABNEY *Treat. Photogr.* 206 On the distance of the diaphragm from the lens is dependent the amount of distortion, as is also the size of the picture which the lens is capable of defining; whilst at the same time the flatness of the field is also in a great measure due to a large distance being maintained between them. **1884** *Encycl. Brit.* XVII. 805/2 To get tolerable definition and flatness of field a stop must be added. **1919** *Brit. Jrnl. Photogr. Alm.* 238 Flatness of field means the property of giving equal definition in all parts of the plate when photographing a flat subject with the lens pointed squarely to it.

4. The condition of having great breadth in proportion to the thickness.

1878 NEWCOMB *Pop. Astron.* III. iv. 344 The extreme thinness and flatness of the object.

5. a. Outspokenness, plainness (of speech).

1887 *Poor Nellie* (1888) 10 He feared he had contradicted the Archbishop with a flatness amounting to rudeness.

b. Absoluteness, unqualified condition.

1611 SHAKS. *Wint. T.* III. ii. 123 That he did but see The flatnesse of my miserie.

6. a. Want of incident or interest; monotony.

1882–3 H. S. HOLLAND in Schaff *Encycl. Relig. Knowl.* III. 2051 The prosy flatness of common life.

b. *Comm.* Dullness, lack of competition.

1812 G. CHALMERS *Dom. Econ. Gt. Brit.* 419 The flatness ..of the trade of Ireland. **1891** *Times* 10 Oct. 12/1 The flatness of the American market.

7. Deficiency in flavour; deadness, insipidity, vapidness.

1707 J. MORTIMER *Husb.* xx. 598 Deadness or Flatness in Cyder, which is often occasioned by the too free admission of Air into the Vessel. **1861** DELAMER *Kitch. Gard.* 93 A mixture of sorrel corrects the peculiar flatness of its flavour.

8. Of sound: Deadness.

1626 BACON *Sylva* § 157 That Flatnesse of Sound is ioyned with a Harshnesse of Sound. **1734** WATTS *Reliq. Juv.* (1789) 160 Long custom has induced a sort of flatness into these sounds.

9. Want of spirit or energy; apathetic condition, dejectedness; lack of mental acuteness or alertness; dulness of mind.

1641 J. SHUTE *Sarah & Hagar* (1649) 84 Jezebel.. reproached him with a flatness of spirit, as if he were not worthy to sway a Scepter. **1671** GLANVILL *Disc. M. Stubbe* Pref. A ij b, It would be look'd upon as flatness, or fear, if I should deal softly with such an Adversary. **1720** WELTON *Suffer. Son of God* I. xiii. 332 The disgust and Flattness of our Souls, in Relation to those never-fading Treasures. **1802** PALEY *Nat. Theol.* xxiii. (1803) 458 The flatness of being content with common reasons. **1810** KNOX & JEBB *Corr.* II. 5 A flatness of mind was gradually stealing upon me. **1876** GEO. ELIOT *Dan. Der.* III. xxxvi. 97 We should stamp every possible world with the flatness of our own inanity.

10. Of an author, literary style, conversation, etc.: Want of animation, brilliancy, or pointedness; prosaic dulness.

1649 MILTON *Eikon.* xvi, To help those many infirmities, [in prayer]..rudeness, impertinencie, flatness, and the like, we have a remedy of Gods finding out. **1715** POPE *Iliad* Pref., Some of his [Homer's] Translators having swell'd into Fustian..and others sunk into Flatness. **1741** WATTS *Improv. Mind* I. v. §10 For some scores of lines together there is a coldness and flatness. **1844** STANLEY *Arnold* (1858) II. 144 The flatnesses of most of those who have written on this subject.

'flat-nose, *sb.* and *a.*

A. *sb.* One who has a flat nose.

16.. *Old Round,* Call Philip flat-nose; straight he frets thereat. **1768–74** TUCKER *Lt. Nat.* (1852) I. 456 'You look at me so wistfully', says the flatnose. **1875** BROWNING *Aristoph. Apol.* 93, I and the Flat-nose..Oft make a pair.

B. *adj.* = FLAT-NOSED *a.*

1636 W. DURHAM in *Ann. Dubrensia* (1877) 8 The Flat-nose Satyres. **1650** BULWER *Anthropomet.* 12 Flat-nose Dogs which Ladies keep for pleasure. **1881** RAYMOND *Mining Gloss., Flat-nose shell,* a cylindrical tool with valve at bottom, for boring through soft clay.

'flat-nosed, *a.*

1. Having a flat nose.

1530 PALSGR. 312/2 Flatte nosed, *camus.* **1575** FLEMING *Virgil's Bucol.* x. 9 The litle flat nozde gotes Shall crop and nip the tender twige. **1581** PETTIE *Guazzo's Civ. Conv.* I. (1586) 37 If their beloved bee flat nosed, they tearme her amiable. **1677** HALE *Prim. Orig. Man.* II. vii. 200 The Ethiopian..flat-nosed and crisp-haired. **1853** HICKIE tr. *Aristoph.* (1872) II. 648 The..flat-nosed women shall sit by the side of the beautiful.

2. of a tool, as ***flat-nosed graver***.

1871 *Proc. Amer. Phil. Soc.* XII. 226 A flat-nosed graver would have left a smooth trough.

flat out, *advb. phr.* [Cf. FLAT *adv.* 2.]

1. Using or involving all one's (or its) strength or resources; at top speed; = ALL OUT *advb. phr.* 4. Also as *adj.*

Several of the quots. illustrate common Australian colloq. phrases.

1932 *Daily Dispatch* (Manch.) 25 July 6/4 Driving flat out. **1942** *We speak from Air* 51, I followed my bombs down until I was just above the ground again, and then I beat it, flat out, across the roof-tops of Nantes. *Ibid.,* We raced over the chimney-pots, our engines flat out. **1943** C. H. WARD-JACKSON *Piece of Cake* 29 *Flat out.* At full speed. Borrowed from motor-racing parlance early in the Great War, full speed being attained on the straight flat run of the track. **1944** J. DEVANNY *By Tropic Sea & Jungle* 227 The young [rat-kangaroo]..ran straight, as flat out as a lizard drinking. **1945** *Coast to Coast 1944* 157 I'm flat out!.. Flat out, like a lizard on a log. **1946** E. S. TOMPKINS *Speed Camera* 37 There is much more going on..than there is in straight flat-out running. **1957** *Economist* 16 Nov. 581/2 If the unions decide on war, they will have a strong incentive to choose the inexpensive guerrilla type rather than a flat-out effort. **1959** BAKER *Drum* 110 Ideas of lying flatly (on one's face, not one's back) and of travelling or working at great speed are recorded in the phrases 'flat out like a lizard drinking' and 'flat out like a lizard on a log'. **1962** *Listener* 29 Mar. 542/1 A flat-out strategic war. **1969** *Private Eye* 23 May 14 I've been flat out, like a lizard drinking, lugging your kiddies round the back paddock. **1969** *New Yorker* 14 June 44/2 Running flat out, Graebner hits a superb high backhand.

2. Phr. ***to be flat out for*** (something): to direct one's attention, energies, etc., towards securing, effecting, doing, etc. (something). (Emphatic form of *to be out for*: OUT *adv.*).

1930 *Morning Post* 7 Aug. 10/1 Everyone is 'flat out' for flying—my trouble is to persuade anyone to do anything else. **1943** C. H. WARD-JACKSON *Piece of Cake* 29 *Flat out for,* in favour of.

flat-out, *sb. U.S.* [f. verbal phr. *to flat out* (see FLAT *v.*[2] 4 b).] A failure, a fiasco.

a **1870** in D.A.E., *To flat out*..is heard also as a noun. 'It was a complete flat-out.' 'He made a flat-out.' —N[ew] E[ngland]. **1886** *Century Mag.* Mar. 727/1, I didn't know it was goin' to be s'ch a perfect flat-out.

†**flat'rise.** *Obs.*[−1] [var. of *flatery,* FLATTERY after the analogy of FAINTISE.] = FLATTERY.

c **1440** *Generydes* 4042 With his fayre wordes, full of flatrise.

flats, var. of FLOTESSE. *Obs.*

flatstone ('flætstəʊn). [f. FLAT *a.* + STONE *sb.*]

1. A kind of stone which cleaves into thin slabs.

1677 PLOT *Oxfordsh.* iv. §31. 77 The Houses are covered, for the most part in Oxfordshire (not with tiles) but flat-stone.

2. See quot. 1847.

1847 HALLIWELL, *Flat-stone,* a measure of iron-stone.

3. A horizontal grave-stone.

1855 *Parl. Papers 1854–5* XLI. I. 52 Flatstone, not exceeding 6 ft. 6 in. by 3 ft. *Ibid.* 53 Memorial, consisting of a flat stone over such grave, in remembrance of one person ..£1 10s.

flatted ('flætɪd), *ppl. a.* [f. FLAT *v.*[3] + -ED[1].]

1. Laid flat; levelled with the ground or surface. Of the sea: Made smooth or calm.

1681 W. ROBERTSON *Phraseol. Gen.* (1693) 611 Flatted or made flat, *æquatus.* **1700** DRYDEN *Fables, Ceyx & Alcyone* 131 Then frothy white appear the flatted seas. **1715–20** POPE *Iliad* v. 121 The yellow harvests..And flatted vineyards, one sad waste appear. **1730** THOMSON *Autumn* 337 The fields around Lie sunk, and flatted in the sordid wave.

2. Beaten or pressed out flat; flattened; deprived of convexity or rotundity; made broad and thin.

1578 BANISTER *Hist. Man.* I. 28 The inferiour part of Radius..is not onely at the end flatted, but also ample, large. **1650** T. B[AYLEY] *Worcester's Apoph.* 47 Turning the flatted bullet round with his finger. **1797** W. JOHNSTON tr. *Beckmann's Invent.* II. 232 Flatted metal wire began to be spun round linen or silk thread. **1812** J. SMYTH *Pract. Customs* (1821) 68 Coffee..is convex on one side, and flatted on the other, with a deep furrow, which runs along the flatted side. **1879** W. COLLINS *Rogue's Life* ix. 104 He turns out a tolerably neat article, from the simple flatted plates.

†**3.** Made of flat bars. *Obs.*

1805 R. W. DICKSON (1807) II. 161 The hurdles..are generally of two kinds, either flatted or rodded.

†**4.** Rendered vapid or insipid. *Obs.*

1626 BACON *Sylva* §377 An Orenge, Limon and Apple.. fresh in their Colour, But their Iuyce somewhat flatted.

5. Of pigments and painted surfaces: Dead, dull, without gloss.

1851 *Ord. & Regul. R. Engineers* xix. 89 Two rooms flatted or French grey. **1859** GULLICK & TIMBS *Paint.* 243 A 'flatted', dull, or unshining surface.

6. *Mus.* Of a note: lowered by one semitone. *U.S.*

1938 *Oxf. Compan. Mus.* 322 *Flat...* There is a slight difference of usage in the language of Britain and the United States—in the former 'to flatten' and 'flattened'; in the latter 'to flat' and 'flatted'. **1949** L. FEATHER *Inside Be-Bop* II. 50 The 'blue' (flatted) seventh was used incidentally. **1956** —— *Encycl. Jazz* 27 In California in 1940 Oscar Moore, guitarist with the King Cole trio, ended the group's first Decca record, *Sweet Lorraine,* on a ninth chord with a flatted fifth. **1958** A. JACOBS *New Dict. Mus.* 127 *Flattened seventh* (U.S., *flatted seventh*), the lowering of the seventh degree of the scale by a semitone.

flatted ('flætɪd), *a.*[2] [f. FLAT *sb.*[2] + -ED[2].]

Divided into, constructed as, or consisting partly of, flats.

1913 *Chamber's Etym. Dict.* Suppl., *Concierge,*..a door-keeper, esp. in a flatted house. **1921** *Glasgow Herald* 28 Jan. 10 English visitors..are sometimes astonished at our flatted houses. **1941** *When we build Again* (Bournville Village Trust) 107 Many of these numerous small factories are grouped in districts. From the planner's point of view this ..makes possible a consideration of the job in terms of units. The solution suggested here for this state of affairs is the 'flatted' factory. **1957** *Times* 22 Aug. 8/7 Some form of 'flatted factories' to cater for the smaller businesses which need more room. **1962** D. TENCH *Law for Consumers* vii. 106 The purchase and sale of flatted property has for a long time been a feature of Scottish life. **1970** D. CRAIG *Young Men may Die* xiv. 93 Opposite is another old flatted mansion.

†**'flatten,** *a. Obs. rare.* [? var. of FLOTTEN.]

1. Of milk: ? Skimmed (in quot. app. stale, sour; perh. associated with FLAT *a.*).

1593 PLAT *Jewell-ho.* II. 13 Soke..in broken beere, or flatten milk.

2. *fig.* = FLEETEN 2.

a **1625** FLETCHER *Hum. Lieutenant* III. v, What a flatten face he has now..How like an ass he looks!

flatten ('flæt(ə)n), *v.* [f. FLAT *a.* + -EN[5].]

†**1.** *trans.* To lay flat on the ground. *Obs. rare.*

1712 J. MORTIMER *Husb.* II. xii, If they [sheep] should lie in it [flax], and beat it down, or flatten it, it will rise again the next rain.

2. a. Naut. ***to flatten in*** (a sail): to extend it more nearly fore-and-aft of the vessel. Also *absol.* (Cf. FLAT *v.*[2] 2.)

1839 MARRYAT *Phant. Ship* x, Hard a-port! flatten in forward! **1856** R. H. DANA *Seamen's Friend* 51 Flatten in your jibsheets. **1867** SMYTH *Sailor's Word-bk., To flatten in,* the action of hauling in the aftmost clue of a sail to give it greater power of turning the vessel..hence *flatten in forward* ..to haul in the jib and foretopmast-staysail-sheets towards the middle of the ship, and haul forward the fore-bowline.

b. *intr.* Aeronautics. ***to flatten out***: to bring an aeroplane into a position parallel with the ground. Also, of the aeroplane: to assume such a position.

1913 *Aeroplane* 17 Apr. 453/1 Apparently he tried to flatten out too quickly. **1914** H. ROSHER *In R.N.A.S.* (1916) 37, I just managed to flatten out and straighten up a little as I hit the ground sideways. **1917** C. C. TURNER *Aircraft of To-Day* vii. 116 When the sea is calm the pilot often finds it anything but easy to see when to flatten out to 'land'. **1950** [see APPROACH *v.* 13].

3. = FLAT *v.*[2] 3, a and b.

a. *a* **1630** DONNE *Progr. Soule* xiv. Poems (1654) 298 As if for that time their round bodies flatned were. **1726** MONRO *Anat.* II. 201 The two superior of these four [superior *Dorsal vertebræ*]..are flatned..by the Action of the *Musculi longi colli.* **1755** JOHNSON, *Flatten,* to make even or level, without prominence or elevation. **1762** H. WALPOLE *Vertue's Anecd. Paint.* I. iv. 98 The superior honours paid to Michael Angelo, whose nose was flattened by the blow. **1802** PALEY *Nat. Theol.* iii. Wks. 1825 III. 20 Its muscular conformation ..is throughout calculated for flattening the eye. **1883** *Hardwick's Photogr. Chem.* (ed. Taylor) 214 A longer exposure in the Camera..invariably *flattens* the picture, destroying its rotundity and stereoscopic effect.

b. 1751 CHAMBERS *Cycl.* s.v. *Coining,* The bars or plates.. are passed several times through a mill, to flatten them further. **1794** SULLIVAN *View Nat.* I. 353 Beautiful crystallizations regularly flattened. **1871** L. STEPHEN *Playgr. Europe* ii. §1. 78 We were frequently flattened out against the rocks, like beasts of ill repute nailed to a barn. *fig.* **1884** ST. L. HERBERT in *Fortn. Rev.* Feb. 242 Reason ..snubbed and flattened out the emotion. **1889** BARRÈRE & LELAND *Slang, To flatten out* (American) 'I flattened him out' *i.e.,* I had the best of him, of the argument.

4. a. *intr.* for *refl.* To become flat, or more flat; to lose convexity or protuberance; to grow broad at the expense of thickness. Also *fig.* and with *down* or *out.*

a **1721** KEILL *Maupertuis' Diss.* (1734) 51 The Spheroid that continually flattens. **1734** WATTS *Reliq. Juv.* (1789) 85 Our real form grows cold and pale..it flattens, it withers into wrinkles. **1816** KEATINGE *Trav.* (1817) II. 97 On approaching the coast, the surface of the country flattens, and approaches water-level. **1828** STARK *Elem. Nat. Hist.* I. 149 The horn..flattens and turns inwards. **1884** H. JAMES *Little Tour* 109 (Cent. Dict.) As I proceeded it [the country] flattened out a good deal. **1885** L. WINGFIELD *Barbara Philpot* III. v. 132 A glittering doll in a shop-window causeth the noses of the bystanders to flatten. **1893** *Westm. Gaz.* 18 Mar. 8/1 The dip of the reef 'flattens'. **1924** *History* Oct. 209 The general average flattened down to a moderate thirteen shillings. **1971** *Guardian* 11 June 19/3 Furniture and silver prices have flattened out lately.

b. Of the wind or a storm: To decrease in force. Cf. FLAT *v.*[2] 2 c.

1748 ANSON *Voy.* I. viii. 79 The storm at length flattening to a calm. **1805** *Naval Chron.* XIII. 239 The Wind flattening..she missed stays.

5. a. *trans.* To make 'flat', vapid, or insipid. Also *fig.*

1631 SANDERSON *Serm.* II. 2 As if all use of rhethorical ornaments..did adulterate, corrupt, and flatten the sincere milk of the word. **1686** GOAD *Celest. Bodies* II. v. 221 The Celestial Bodies..do ferment or flatten the Air. **1755** JOHNSON, *Flatten*, to make vapid.

b. *intr.* to become insipid.

1692 R. L'ESTRANGE *Fables* clxi. 132 Satisfactions that.. flatten in the very tasting. **1702** *Eng. Theophrast.* 254 Without some tincture of Urbanity, good Humour flattens for want of Refreshment and Relief.

6. *trans.* To make dull, deprive of attraction, interest, or impressiveness; also ***to flatten down***.

1693 W. FREKE *Sel. Ess.* xxxiv. 210 When you gallop over a good Author, you..flatten him, and lose half his Life and Substance. **1710** STEELE *Tatler* No. 204 ¶5 It flattens the Narration, to say his Excellency in a Case which is common to all Men. *a* **1715** BURNET *Own Time* (1724) I. 162 The odiousness of the crime grew at last to be so much flatten'd by the frequent executions. **1820** LAMB *Lett.* (1888) II. 57 That I did not write..was simply that he was to come so soon, and that flattens letters. **1889** *Spectator* 14 Dec. 840 When the pilgrims..break out into verse, they..flatten down what had been far more effectively and imaginatively said in prose.

†**7. a.** To deprive of energy or 'fire'; to depress. Also with *away*. *Obs.*

1683 R. GROVE *Persuas. Communion* 22 Our Passions.. may be Charmed, or Raised, or Flattened. **1709** STEELE *Tatler* No. 47 ¶3 He was sunk and flattened to the lowest Degree. **1772** J. ADAMS *Diary* 23 Nov. Wks. 1850 II. 305, I find they are both cooled, both flattened away. **1796** BURKE *Corr.* IV. 362 So far from endeavouring to excite this spirit, nothing has been omitted to flatten and lower it.

b. To cause (a market) to become depressed.

1891 *Daily News* 12 Nov. 2/1 These two influences sufficed to flatten all the markets.

8. To lower (a musical note) in pitch; also *absol.*

1824 *Mirror* III. 105/2 Flattening and sharpening and rosining bows. **1825** DANNELEY *Dict. Mus.*, To *flatten*, to lower a note one or two half tones. **1872** BANISTER *Music* 55 That same note sharpened or flattened.

9. To paint (a surface) so that it shall have no gloss; to deprive (paint) of its lustre. Also *absol.*

1823 CRABB *Techn. Dict.*, To *flatten*, is to give a newly painted wall such a coat of colour as takes off its glossy appearance. **1874** W. CROOKES *Dyeing & Calico Print.* vii. 517 The colouring matter may also be flattened or deprived of its lustre.

10. *Tanning*: see quot.

1875 *Ure's Dict. Arts* III. 95 In some cases, as in the calf-skin, it is skived and then shaved, or, as it is called, flattened at right angles to the skiving.

flattened (ˈflæt(ə)nd), *ppl. a.* [f. prec. + -ED¹.] In senses of the verb.

1796 WITHERING *Brit. Plants* IV. 113 Long slender thread-shaped but flattened leaves. **1833** L. RITCHIE *Wand. by Loire* 39 The bridge is composed of fifteen flattened arches. **1863** LYELL *Antiq. Man* ii. 27 Its shape is that of a flattened cone. **1884** BOWER & SCOTT *De Bary's Phaner.* 290 Rings, of which the outer at least consist of broad flattened pieces. **1929** ST. JOHN ERVINE *First Mrs. Fraser* I. 9 Ninian ..has a conventional English public school accent; colourless, unvaried, with flattened vowels and elided consonants. **1948** *Penguin Music Mag.* Feb. 45 Its typical scale includes the flattened third and flattened seventh (over-flattened by any characteristic Blues singer). **1968** *Gloss. Terms Mechanized & Hand Sheet Metal Work (B.S.I.)* 28 *Flattened can*, a complete unflanged can body. **1969** [see BLUE *a.* 3 d].

fig. **1874** GEO. ELIOT *Coll. Breakf.-P.* 621 Is wisdom flattened sense and mere distaste?

flattener (ˈflæt(ə)nə(r)). [f. as prec. + -ER¹.] One who flattens; something used for flattening.

1741 [see FLATTER *sb.*² 1]. **1864** CARLYLE *Fredk. Gt.* IV. XVI. vi. 329 There followed a dryness between the divine Emilie and the Flattener of the Earth [*i.e.* Maupertuis, from his having proved the flattening of the earth at the poles.] **1875** *Plain Needle-work* 14 An old tooth brush handle, which..might be called the 'flattener'. **1879** J. PATON in *Encycl. Brit.* X. 661/2 The flattener, with a piece of charred wood, rubs it [the opened cylinder of glass] quite smooth.

ˈflattening, *vbl. sb.* [f. as prec. + -ING¹.]

1. The action or process of making flat. In *Glass-making*, the process of laying out (sheet-glass) flat.

1879 J. PATON in *Encycl. Brit.* X. 660/2 The opening, flattening, or spreading of the glass. *Ibid.* 661/1.

2. The process of becoming flat; the condition of being flattened.

1726 MONRO *Anat.* II. 199 This Flatning on their Sides.. is of good Use. **1854** W. K. KELLY tr. *Arago's Astron.* 131 The flattening at the poles [of the earth]. **1860** TYNDALL *Glac.* II. xxiv. 359 These disks [in ice] have been mistaken for bubbles..and their flattening has been ascribed to the pressure [etc.]. **1878** HUXLEY *Physiogr.* XIX. 325 The earth's flattening is very much less proportionally than that of the orange.

3. *attrib.* and *Comb.* (chiefly in *Glass-making*: see 1), as ***flattening arch, furnace, iron, kiln, oven, stone, tool.***

1879 J. PATON in *Encycl. Brit.* X. 661/2 The waggon then goes back to the *flattening arch. **1874** KNIGHT *Dict. Mech.* I. 878/2 **Flattening-furnace.* **1858** SIMMONDS *Dict. Trade*, **Flattening-iron*, a laundress's or workman's smoothing iron. **1872** W. R. GREG *Enigmas* 272 That..God will pass a flattening-iron over all..and smooth out every salient individuality. **1879** J. PATON in *Encycl. Brit.* X. 661/2 The *flattening kiln..consists of two chambers built together, the one for flattening the cylinders, the other for annealing the sheets..The cylinder, after being gradually reheated, is placed in the centre of the *flattening oven, upon a smooth stone. *Ibid.*, The *flattening stone or table, mounted on a movable waggon.

†**ˈflatter,** *sb.*¹ *Obs.* Forms: 4–5 **flatour, (vlatour),** 5 **flater,** 6 **flatter.** [a. OF. *flatere, flateour, flateur*, agent-n. f. *flater* to FLATTER.] = FLATTERER.

1340 *Ayenb.* 256 Ulatours and lyeȝeres byeþ to grat cheap ine hare cort. *c* **1400** *Cato's Morals* 8 in *Cursor M.* App. iv. 1669 Alle fals flaters. *a* **1450** *Knt. de la Tour* (1868) 123 Beter is the frende that prikithe thanne the flatour that oyntethe. **1559** *Mirr. Mag., Mowbray's Banishm.* xi, And whyle the rest prouyded for this thing, I flatter I..brake fayth and promise both.

flatter (ˈflætə(r)), *sb.*² [f. FLAT *v.* + -ER¹.]

1. A workman who makes something (e.g. a blank or planchet, a hide or skin, etc.) flat.

1714 MANDEVILLE *Fab. Bees* (1725) I. 249 The silver-spinner, the flatter, the wire-drawer..and the refiner. **1741** CHAMBERS *Cycl.*, *Flatter* or *Flattener*. See *Coining*. **1885** C. T. DAVIS *Manuf. Leather* xxix. 497 The sides next go to a flatter, who levels off the shanks..with a currier's knife.

2. A tool used in making things flat, e.g. a very broad-faced hammer used by smiths.

1874 KNIGHT *Dict. Mech.* I. 878/2 *Flatter* (Wire-drawing), a draw-plate with a flat orifice, to draw out flat strips, such as watch-springs, skirt-wire [etc.]. **1888** *Lockwood's Dict. Mech. Engin.*, *Flatter*, a species of hammer used by smiths. Its use is to finish over broad surfaces which have been brought to size by the sledge and set hammer.

†**ˈflatter,** *sb.*³ *Obs.* [f. FLATTER *v.*¹] Flattery.

1593–4 SYLVESTER *Profit Imprisonm.* 437 O that hee never had prefer'd the Serpents flatter Before th' eternall Law of all the Worlds Creator.

flatter (ˈflætə(r)), *sb.*⁴ [f. FLAT *sb.*³ 4 b + -ER¹.] One who couples and uncouples trucks at a flat in a coal-mine.

1894 *Times* 11 Oct. 4/6 After two years or so..the trapper is advanced to the rank of a flatter. His occupation then consists in coupling or uncoupling the trucks or wagons. **1921** *Dict. Occup. Terms* (1927) §043 *Flat keeper*, flat coupler-on; flatman, flatter; couples full and uncouples empty tubs at 'flat' or working face terminus of haulage system.

flatter (ˈflætə(r)), *v.*¹ Forms: α. 3 **flatteren,** 4–6 **flater(e(n,** (5 **flateryn**), 6 **flattir,** 6– **flatter.** β. 4 **vlaterien.** [Of somewhat doubtful etymology. In sense it represents OF. *flate-r* (mod.F. *flatter*), = Pr. *flatar*; the primary meaning of this word is believed to be 'to flatten down, smooth'; hence 'to stroke with the hand, caress' (a sense still current in Fr.); this sense, as well as that of OF. *flater, -ir* to dash to the ground, is plausibly accounted for by derivation from the Teut. word which we have as FLAT *a.* The normal form which *flat-er* should assume when adapted into E. is the rare Sc. FLAT *v.* As ME. did not adapt Fr. vbs. by addition of a suffix *-er* to the stem, or adopt them in their infinitive form, the Eng. *flatter* cannot be paralleled with Ger. *flattiren*, MDu. *'flatteren*, Sw. *flattera*, which are normally formed adaptations from the French; it might however have arisen by association of the vb. with its derivatives, OF. *flatere, -our* FLATTER *sb.*¹, and *flaterie* FLATTERY. More probably, however, the native FLATTER *v.*², an onomatopœia expressive of light repeated movement, may have developed a sense resembling the primary sense of the F. word, and hence have been accepted as its equivalent. Cf. ON. *flaðra*, MSw. *flakra, flikra*, to flatter, all prob. of onomatopœic origin. It may be significant that in the earliest instance of ME. *flatteren* it occurs as a various reading for *flakeren*, which corresponds precisely to MSw. *flakra* just cited.]

†**1. a.** *intr.* Of an animal, bird, etc.: To show delight or fondness (by wagging the tail, making a caressing sound, etc.). Const. *upon, with. Obs.*

c **1386** CHAUCER *Merch. T.* 815 Lyk to the scorpioun.. That flaterest with thin heed whan thou wilt stynge. **1387** TREVISA *Higden* (Rolls) II. 431 Þat foules at Diomedes temple springeþ water and flatereþ wiþ þe Grees. **1583** HOLLYBAND *Campo di Fior* 41 Here is a meery litle dogge: See how he flattereth with his tale. **1607** TOPSELL *Four-f. Beasts* 105 She [the Cat] hath one voice to beg and to complain..another among hir own kind, by flattring, by hissing, by puffing, by spitting. *Ibid.* 160 Dogges..who would fawne & gently flatter vpon all those which came chastly & religiously to worship there.

†**b.** *trans.* Rarely used in Fr. sense: To touch or stroke lightly and caressingly. *Obs.*

[**1580** BARET *Alv.* F 666 To feele and handle gently, to flatter, to dallie, and deceiue, *palpo*]. **1599** H. BUTTES *Dyets drie Dinner* M, Trout is a fish that loveth to be flattered and clawed in the water. **1650** [see FLATTERING *ppl. a.* 4]. **1725** BRADLEY *Fam. Dict.* s.v. *Bee*, The Bees that compose his Train..flatter him with their Trumps.

2. To try to please or win the favour of (a person) by obsequious speech or conduct; to court, fawn upon. †Also intr. ***to flatter with.***

1340 *Ayenb.* 61 Þe blondere defendeþ and excuseþ and wryeþ þe kueades and þe zennes of ham þet he wyle ulateri. *c* **1380** WYCLIF *Sel. Wks.* III. 344 Þes men..flateren hem, for þei hopen to haue wynnyng of hem. **1387** TREVISA *Higden* (Rolls) III. 315 ȝif þou woldest flatere wiþ Denys þe kyng, þou schuldest nouȝt wasche þese wortes. *c* **1440** *Promp. Parv.* 164 Flateryn, *adulor.* **1559** *Mirr. Mag., Worcester* ii, To frayne the truth, the living for to flatter. **1593** SHAKS. *Rich. II*, II. i. 88, I mocke my name (great King) to flatter thee. *a* **1744** POPE *Epitaph* xv, One poor Poet.. Who never flatter'd Folks like you. **1764** GOLDSM. *Trav.* 362 Yet think not..I mean to flatter kings, or court the great. **1830** TENNYSON *Mermaid* 43 The bold merry mermen.. would sue me, and woo me, and flatter me. **1842** LYTTON *Zanoni* I. i. 5 Yet was he thoroughly unsocial. He formed no friends, flattered no patrons.

absol. **1393** LANGL. *P. Pl.* C. IX. 147 Ancres and heremites þat eten bote at nones, And freres þat flateren not. **1413** *Pilgr. Sowle* (Caxton 1483) IV. xxxiii. 82 Them nedeth nought to glosen ne to flateren, for..hope of yeftes.

3. To praise or compliment unduly or insincerely. †Const. *of.* †Also in weaker sense, to gloss over, palliate (faults), speak too leniently to (an offender). †Formerly also intr. ***to flatter with.***

a **1225** *Ancr. R.* 222 (MS. Cleop. C. vi) Men..þet flattereð [*other texts* faltreð, flakereð] hire of freolac. **1535** COVERDALE *Prov.* xxviii. 23 He that rebuketh a man, shall fynde more fauoure at yᵉ last, then he that flatreth him. **1552** LATIMER *Serm.* 31 Jan., Here learne..not to flatter with any body when they do..wickedly, for Christ, perceauing his disciples to be vnbeleuers, flattered them not, but..rebuked them for their faultes. **1659** RAY *Corr.* (1848) 2, I would not be flattered, I am not so fond of my own conceits. **1738** POPE *Epil. Sat.* I. 86 Let..ev'ry Fool and Knave Be grac'd thro' Life, and flatter'd in his Grave. *Mod.* 'Your beautiful voice—' 'Ah! you are flattering me.'

absol. **1500–20** ? DUNBAR *Poems* (1893) 310 Wryte I of liberalitie..Than will thay say I flatter quyte. **1548** HALL *Chron. Edw. IV*, 198, I neither dare nor wil write..lest.. some men might thynke that I flattered a litle. **1782** COWPER *Table T.* 88 The lie that flatters I abhor the most.

4. To gratify the vanity or self-esteem of; to make self-complacent; to make (one) feel honoured or distinguished. Also, To tickle (a person's vanity).

c **1400** *Rom. Rose* 5941 Another shal have as moche..for right nought..If he can flater hir to hir pay. **1560** BIBLE (Genev.) *Ps.* xxxvi. 2 He flattereth himselfe in his owne eyes. **1601** SHAKS. *Jul. C.* II. i. 208 When I tell him, he hates Flatterers, He says, he does; being then most flattered. **1717** LADY M. W. MONTAGU *Let. to Abbé Conti* 1 Apr., It is the emperor's interest to flatter them. **1791** MRS. RADCLIFFE *Rom. Forest* viii, I am..flattered by the distinction you offer me. **1845** M. PATTISON *Ess.* (1889) I. 22 This was intended to flatter the bishop's vanity. *a* **1864** PRESCOTT (Webster), Others he flattered by asking their advice.

transf. **1864** TENNYSON *Aylmer's F.* 175 A splendid presence flattering the poor roofs.

5. To play upon the vanity or impressionableness of (a person); to beguile or persuade with artful blandishments; to coax, wheedle. Const. *from, into, to, out of.* †Also intr. ***to flatter with.***

1500–20 DUNBAR *Poems* xxx. 43 In me was falset with every wicht to flatter. **1537** MATTHEW *Judg.* xvi. 5 Flatter with hym [**1539** TAVERNER Flatter him] & se wherin hys great strenght lyeth. **1579** GOSSON *Sch. Abuse* (Arb.) 21 As waywarde children the more they bee flatered the worse they are. **1591** *Troub. Raigne K. John* II. (1611) 82 For Priests and women must be flattered. **1592** WARNER *Alb. Eng.* VII. xxxiv. (1612) 167 He flattered his Neeces from their mother. **1650** FULLER *Pisgah* II. i. §24. 65 Or did he hope..to flatter Heaven into a consent? **1667** MILTON *P.L.* x. 42 Man should be seduc't And flatter'd out of all, believing lies Against his Maker. **1706** PHILLIPS (ed. Kersey), *Flatter*, to coaks, soothe up or wheedle. **1833** ALISON *Hist. Europe* (1849) II. ix. §51. 276 You may easily flatter a tyrant: but to flatter twenty-five millions of people is as impossible as to flatter the Deity himself.

absol. **1611** BIBLE *1 Esdras* iv. 31 The King was faine to flatter, that she might be reconciled to him againe.

6. To beguile, charm away (sorrow, etc.); also, to beguile, charm to (tears). *arch.*

1580 SIDNEY *Arcadia* I. (1629) 52 A place for pleasantnesse, not vnfit to flatter solitarinesse. **1597** SHAKS. *Rich. III*, IV. iv. 245 Flatter my sorrows with report of it. **1820** KEATS *Eve. St. Agnes* iii, Music's golden tongue Flatter'd to tears this aged man. **1871** R. ELLIS tr. *Catullus* lxviii. 39 If nor books I send nor flatter sorrow to silence.

7. a. To encourage or cheer (a person) with hopeful or pleasing representations; to inspire with hope, usually on insufficient grounds. Also, To foster (hopes). †Formerly also intr. ***to flatter with.***

1377 LANGL. *P. Pl.* B. xx. 109 Fortune gan flateren..þo fewe..And byhight hem longe lyf. **1393** [see FLATTERING *ppl. a.* 2.] **1587** FLEMING *Contn. Holinshed* III. 1351/1 My lord, you are verie sicke, I will not flatter with you. **1592** SHAKS. *Ven. & Ad.* 989 Hope..doth flatter thee in thoughts vnlikely. **1597** —— *2 Hen. IV*, I. iii. 29 Flatt'ring himselfe with [*Qo.* in] Proiect of a power Much smaller, then the smallest of his Thoughts. **1601** —— *Twel. N.* I. v. 322 Desire him not to flatter with his Lord, Nor hold him up with hopes; I am not for him. **1730–1** *Swift's Lett.* (1766) II. 123 Now were you in vast hopes you should hear no more from me..but don't flatter yourself. **1762** H. WALPOLE *Vertue's Anecd. Paint.* (1765) I. vi. 137 The Carews..were flattered with the hopes of this match. **1794** PALEY *Evid.* II. v. (1817) 23 It was his business to have flattered the prevailing hopes. **1842** TENNYSON *Two Voices* 204 Wilt thou make everything a lie To flatter me that I may die? **1855** PRESCOTT *Philip II*, I. II. ix. 243 Men had flattered themsleves..with the expectation of some change for the better. **1890** *Daily News* 24 Nov. 3/5 The Irish filly never flattered her backers.

absol. **1593** SHAKS. *Lucr.* 172 Desire..sweetely flatters. **1913** *Field* 15 Nov. 1046/2 Two furlongs from home Maiden Erlegh looked most dangerous, but he flattered only to deceive. **1928** *Daily Express* 2 Aug. 12 Smirke..came

through well..to settle Goodwin and Dakota, who had flattered in the run home.

b. To please with the belief, idea, or suggestion *that*. Now chiefly *refl.*

1592 SHAKS. *Ven. & Ad.* 978 Reuiuing ioy bids her reioyce, And flatters her, it is Adonis voyce. **1711** ADDISON *Spect.* No. 165 ¶1 Their People might flatter themselves that Things are not so bad as they really are. **1753** HUME *Let.* 5 Jan. in Burton *Life & Corr.* (1846) I. 378 My friends flatter me..that I have succeeded. **1782** PRIESTLEY *Corrupt. Chr.* I. Pref. 13, I flatter myself..I have given reasonable satisfaction. *a* **1796** BURNS *'As I was a wandering'*, I flatter my fancy I may get anither. **1844** DISRAELI *Coningsby* V. iv, They flattered themselves it might be done. **1883** STEVENSON *Treasure Isl.* IV. xvi, We flattered ourselves we should be able to give a good account of a half-dozen.

8. To 'caress', gratify (the eye, ear, etc.).

Johnson describes this as 'a sense purely Gallick'; but it occurs in his own writings, and is now established.

1695 DRYDEN *Observ. Du Fresnoy's Art Paint.* 130 A Consort of Voices..pleasingly fills the Ears and flatters them. **1722** WOLLASTON *Relig. Nat.* ix. 206 He might..be flattered with some verdures and the smiles of a few daisies on the banks of the road. **1882** STEVENSON *New Arab. Nts.* (1884) 120 The beauty of the stone flattered the young clergyman's eyes.

absol. **1750** JOHNSON *Rambler* No. 80 ¶2 The Hill flatters with an extensive View.

9. a. To represent too favourably; to exaggerate the good points of. Said *esp.* of painters, or the like.

1581 PETTIE *Guazzo's Civ. Conv.* I. (1586) 4 But if I flatter not my selfe, I have a whole minde within my crasie bodie. **1591** SHAKS. *Two Gent.* IV. iv. 192 Yet the Painter flatter'd her a little. **1665** BOYLE *Occas. Refl.* VI. x. 222 If Art have not flatter'd Nature. **1765** H. WALPOLE *Vertue's Anecd. Paint.* IV. 18 Oliver..said to him 'Mr. Lely, I desire you would use all your skill to paint my picture truly like me, and not flatter me at all.' **1768** —— *Hist. Doubts* 95 How much the characters of princes are liable to be flattered or misrepresented. **1885** E. GARRETT *At any Cost* x. 169 My friends do not think that my portrait flatters me.

absol. **1634** PRYNNE *Documents agst. Prynne* (Camden) 25 A Queene, in whose prayse it is impossible for a poett to fayn, or orator to flatter. **1758** HOME *Agis* Ded., A grateful imagination adorns its benefactor with every virtue, and even flatters with sincerity.

b. To show to the best advantage, make effective, emphasize the good points of.

1904 *Westm. Gaz.* 11 Feb. 4/2 A dark blue velvet will flatter diamonds remarkably. *Ibid.* 27 Aug. 2/3 The wickets at Nottingham..flatter batsmen enormously. **1909** *Ibid.* 27 Feb. 15/1 A good white shoe worn with a white dress flatters the foot immensely.

10. With adverbs. ***to flatter in*** (nonce-use): to usher in or help forward with flattery. ***to flatter up***: †(*a*) to indulge unduly, pamper, 'coddle'; (*b*) to flatter extravagantly; to work (oneself) up into self-complacency; (*c*) *nonce-use*, to call up (a smile) by flattery.

1588 SHAKS. *L.L.L.* V. ii. 824 To flatter vp these powers of mine with rest. **1669** DRYDEN *Tyrannick Love* IV. i, I, like the Fiends, will flatter in his Doom. **1848** J. WATERWORTH *Canons & Decrees Trent* 38 No one ought to flatter himself up with faith alone. **1891** G. MEREDITH *One of our Conq.* III. xiii. 273 'We go', Victor said to Nataly, and flattered-up a smile about her lips.

Hence **'flattered** *ppl. a.*

c **1440** *Promp. Parv.* 164 Flateryd, *adulatus.* **1665** MANLEY *Grotius' Low C. Warres* 165 His Mind was so elevated into a flattered Conceit of himself. **1714** SHAFTESB. *Misc. Refl.* V. i, They become, like flatter'd Princes, impatient of Contradiction. **1725** YOUNG *Love Fame* i. 13 Flatter'd crimes of a licentious age, Reproach our silence. **1888** *Sat. Rev.* 23 June 773/2 The flattered monarch refused to interfere.

†**'flatter,** *v.*² *Obs.* [Onomatopœic; cf. *flacker, flutter, flitter*.] *intr.* To float, flutter.

c **1375** BARBOUR *Troy-bk.* II. 1752 He..Flatterand amange þe wawes wode With gret force of his armes gane swyme. ?*a* **1450** *Chaucer's Knt.'s T.* 1104 (Petworth MS.) Aboue her hede her dowues flateringe [*other texts* flikeringe]. *a* **1803** *Sir Patrick Spens* in Child *Ballads* III. lviii. 27/1 And mony was the feather-bed That flattered on the faem.

flatterable ('flætərəb(ə)l), *a. nonce-wd.* [f. FLATTER *v.*¹ + -ABLE.] That may be flattered, susceptible to flattery.

a **1734** NORTH *Lives* I. 124 He was the most flatterable creature that ever was known.

flatter-blind ('flætəblaınd), *v. nonce-wd.* [f. FLATTER *v.*¹ + BLIND *v.*] *trans.* To flatter so as to make blind; to blind with flattery.

1818 COLERIDGE *Let.* in *Lit. Rem.* (1836) II. 1 My next Friday's lecture will, if I do not grossly flatter-blind myself, be interesting.

flattercap ('flætəkæp). *Obs.* exc. *dial.* [f. as prec. + CAP *sb.*¹] A flatterer.

1681 W. ROBERTSON *Phraseol. Gen.* (1691) 613 Avaunt all flattercaps. **1855** ROBINSON *Whitby Gloss.*, *Flatch* or *Flattercap*, a flatterer; a term applied to wheedling children, when they try by flattery to gain their own little ends.

flatter-dock ('flætədɒk). [? f. FLATTER *v.*² + DOCK *sb.*¹] A provincial name given to several large-leaved aquatic plants ('docks'), probably from the floating leaf.

1820 WILBRAHAM *Chesh. Gloss.*, *Flatter Dock* or *Batter Dock*, pond weed or potamogeton. **1878–86** BRITTEN & HOLLAND *Plant-n.*, *Flatter Dock.*

flatterer ('flætərə(r)). [f. FLATTER *v.*¹ + -ER¹.]

1. One who flatters, in various senses of the vb.; *esp.* one who employs false praise to obtain favour or otherwise serve his own purposes.

a **1340** HAMPOLE *Psalter* xiv. 4 Flaterers & bakbiters ere fere fra þis life. **1413** *Pilgr. Sowle* (Caxton 1483) III. iii. 51 Ye that haue ben flaterours and traitours to youre frendes. **1526** *Pilgr. Perf.* (W. de W. 1531) 88, I had lever..be reproued..of euery persone, than to be praysed of a flaterer. *a* **1680** BUTLER *Rem.* (1759) II. 443 A Flatterer is a Dog, that fawns when he bites. **1727** GAY *Fables* I. i. 77 For beasts of prey, a servile train, Have been the flatt'rers of my reign. **1838** DICKENS *Nich. Nick.* xxviii, 'I am afraid Sir Mulberry is a flatterer, my lord', said Mrs. Wititterly. **1881** RITA *My Lady Coquette* xx, You are a sad flatterer, Rose.

2. *Comb.*, as ***flatterer-like*** adj.

1630 DRAYTON *Moses* I. 118 Three lab'ring months them flatterer-like beguiled.

'flatteress. *Obs.* [f. FLATTER *sb.*¹ + -ESS. Cf. OF. *flateresse.*] A female flatterer.

1483 CAXTON *G. de la Tour* G ij, In her companye she had a woman a flatteresse and a grete liar. **1569** J. SANFORD tr. *Agrippa's Van. Artes* 154 Wherefore Plato calleth this [Cookery] the flatteresse of Phisicke. **1658** HEXHAM, *Een Vleydersse*, a Flattresse, or a Flattering woman.

flattering ('flætərıŋ), *vbl. sb.* [f. FLATTER *v.*¹ + -ING¹.] The action of the vb. FLATTER, in its various senses. Now *rare* exc. in gerundial use.

a **1225** *Ancr. R.* 320 Vor fearlac, vor flatterunge. *a* **1340** HAMPOLE *Psalter* v. 11 Wiþ flaterynge þai deuoure wham swa þai may felaghe wiþ þaim. *c* **1430** *Syr Gener.* (Roxb.) 1977 Thurgh his fals flatering With the Sodon was he dwelling. **1563–87** FOXE *A. & M.* (1596) 951/2 The preachers..preached nothing but lies and flatterings. **1607** HIERON *Wks.* I. 430 Secret soothing and flattering of the heart. **1678** R. BARCLAY *Apol. Quakers* Ded., The flattering of court parasites.

'flattering, *ppl. a.* [f. as prec. + -ING².]

1. a. Of a person, his actions, utterances, etc.: That flatters or tries to please by praise, generally insincere; adulatory.

1484 CAXTON *Fables of Æsop* I. xv, The foole whiche herd the flaterynge wordes of the foxe beganne to open his bylle for to synge. **1550** CROWLEY *Epigr.* 839 Be ware of all flatterynge frendis. **1600** SHAKS. *A.Y.L.* IV. i. 188 That flattering tongue of yours wonne me. **1781** GIBBON *Decl. & F.* III. 115 The most flattering bard..would have hesitated to affirm, that he surpassed the measure of the demi-gods of antiquity.

†**b.** Coaxing, wheedling. *Obs.*

c **1386** CHAUCER *Friar's Prol.* 30, I schal him telle which a gret honour Is to ben a fals flateryng lymytour. **1697** DRYDEN *Virg. Georg.* III. 269 Thy flatt'ring Method on the Youth pursue.

2. a. Suggesting pleasurable (usually, delusive) anticipations or beliefs; pleasing to the imagination.

1393 GOWER *Conf.* III. 174, I shall..deceive and lie With flaterende prophecie. **1526** *Pilgr. Perf.* (W. de W. 1531) 57 Flee all yᵉ false flateryng promesses of yᵉ worlde. **1596** SHAKS. *Tam. Shr.* I. i. 44 Euen as a flatt'ring dreame. **1717** POPE *Epist. to Jervas* 23 What flatt'ring scenes our wand'ring fancy wrought! *a* **1859** MACAULAY *Hist. Eng.* V. 305 He had consulted by letter all the most eminent physicians..and, as he was apprehensive that they might return flattering answers if they knew who he was, he had [etc.]. **1871** R. HURLEY *Let.* in Raymond *Statist. Mines & Mining* (1872) 203 The prospects at this camp are very flattering.

b. Of the weather, the stars, etc.: Promising, (delusively) encouraging hope. Now *rare*.

1633 T. STAFFORD *Pac. Hib.* II. xxx. 278 Don Juan..hourely expecting a wind to bee gone, and finding a flattering gale went aboard. **1697** DAMPIER *Voy.* I. 413 Such flattering weather is commonly the forerunner of a Tempest. **1711** SWIFT *Jrnl. to Stella* 27 Oct., It has been a terrible rainy day, but so flattering in the morning, that I would needs go out in my new hat. **1847** EMERSON *Poems, Threnody* Wks. (Bohn) I. 490 For flattering planets seemed to say This child should ills of ages stay.

3. a. Gratifying to self-esteem; highly complimentary.

1757 BURKE *Abridgm. Eng. Hist.* Wks. 1842 II. 593 These opinions are flattering to national vanity. **1820** LAMB *Final Mem.* viii. To Mr. Rogers 277 It is not the flatteringest compliment..to an author to say, you have not read his book yet. **1831** SIR J. SINCLAIR *Corr.* II. 273 The very flattering terms in which he expressed himself. **1852** MRS. STOWE *Uncle Tom's C.* xxxvi, The dark beauty of the supposed little girl drew many flattering comments from the passengers.

b. ***flattering unction***: see UNCTION 5 b.

†**4.** Caressing, handling lightly. Cf. FLATTER *v.*¹ 1 b. *Obs.*

1650 FULLER *Pisgah* II. vi. 150 Their [Baal's priests'] flattering hands..did theatrically..let out some drops of wild bloud.

5. That represents too favourably; said *esp.* of a picture or the like.

1595 SHAKS. *John* II. i. 503 Till now, infixed I beheld my selfe, Drawne in the flattering table of her eie! **1718** PRIOR *Alma* III. 23 The flatt'ring Glass of Nature. **1774** GOLDSM. *Retal.* 63 A flattering painter, who made it his care To draw men as they ought to be, not as they are.

6. quasi-*adv.* = FLATTERINGLY *adv.*

1592 SHAKS. *Rom. & Jul.* II. ii. 141 All this is but a dreame, Too flattering sweet to be substantiall.

Hence **'flatteringness**, the quality of being flattering.

1894 *Temple Bar Mag.* CI. 195 She gently tempers its flatteringness by the remark.

flatteringly ('flætərıŋlı), *adv.* [f. prec. + -LY².] In a flattering manner.

1387 TREVISA *Higden* (Rolls) VII. 107 þey answerde ful falsely and flateryngly þat nay. **1548** HALL *Chron.* Introd. 7 The king flateringly and with great dissimulacion made proclamacion. **1661** COWLEY *Disc. Govt. O. Cromwell* Ess. (1669) 56 Pray Countryman (said he, very kindly and very flatteringly). **1719** LONDON & WISE *Compl. Gard.* 298 How flatteringly fair soever the weather appear. **1865** MRS. RIDDELL *Geo. Geith* II. vi. 56 Still hope whispered flatteringly that the girl might grow to love him.

†**'flatterous,** *a. Obs.* [f. FLATTER *sb.*¹ or FLATTER-Y + -OUS.] Of, pertaining to, or suitable for a flatterer; flattering.

1546 BALE *1st Exam. Anne Askewe* 18 b, Trust not to moche in the flatterouse faunynge of soche wylye foxes.

Hence **'flatterously** *adv.*, flatteringly.

1667 OLDENBURG *Let. to Boyle* 3 Dec. in *Boyle's Wks.* (1772) VI. 253 If he durst believe himself, who is flatterously given, he is much better than he was before.

flattery ('flætərı). Forms: 4 flaterie, (*south.* vlaterie), 4–6 flatery(e, (5 flatere, -eri, -irry, -urye, 6 flat(t)ry), 6–7 flatterie, 6– flattery. [ad. F. *flatterie* (OF. *flaterie* = Pr. *flataria*), f. *flatteur* (OF. *flatere*) a flatterer, f. *flatter* (OF. *flater*): see FLATTER *v.*¹ and -ERY 1 b.]

1. The action or practice of flattering; false or insincere praise; adulation; cajolery, blandishment.

c **1320** *Seuyn Sag.* (W.) 2155 For thou leuest wel flaterie. *c* **1386** CHAUCER *Pars. T.* ¶539 Flaterie is generally wrongful preysing. **1413** *Pilgr. Sowle* (Caxton 1483) IV. xxx. 78 How dar ther ony man deceyuen suche persone by fauour of flaterye. **1484** CAXTON *Fables of Æsop* I. ix, Ofte the good men lese theyr goodes by the decepcion and flaterye of the peruers and evylle folke. **1526** *Pilgr. Perf.* (W. de W. 1531) 111 Somtyme vnder the cloke of good maner, he bryngeth in adulacyon or flatery. **1646** J. BENBRIGGE *Vsura accommodata* 15 The flattery of deceitfull borrowers. **1710** STEELE *Tatler* No. 139 ¶1 That general Cause of all their [Women's] Follies, and our Misfortunes, their Love of Flattery. **1771** GOLDSM. *Hist. Eng.* II. 217 He was resolved to maintain himself in it..by tyranny over his inferiors, and flattery to the queen. **1826** DISRAELI *Viv. Grey* VI. i, Flattery is the destruction of all good fellowship.

2. *fig.* 'Gratifying deception, delusion' (Schmidt).

c **1600** SHAKS. *Sonn.* xlii. 14 My friend and I are one: Sweet flattery! then she loves but me alone. **1604** —— *Oth.* IV. i. 133.

3. With *a* and *pl.*

1593 SHAKS. *Rich. II*, III. ii. 216 He does me double wrong, that wounds me with the flatteries of his tongue. **1665** BOYLE *Occas. Refl.* Ded. 6 It is..Your Custome to look ev'n upon Smal Praises as Flatteries. **1700** DRYDEN *Fables* Pref., You never cool while you read Homer, even not in the Second Book (a graceful Flattery to his Countrymen).

flattie: see FLATTY².

flatting ('flætıŋ), *vbl. sb.* [f. FLAT *v.*² + -ING¹.]

1. a. The action or process of laying, pressing, or beating out flat; *spec.* the process of rolling metal into plates; also in *Glass-making*, the process of flattening a split glass cylinder.

1611 COTGR., *Emplatement*, a flatting; a laying flat vnto; a making broad or flat. **1687** TAUBMAN *London's Tri.* 6 In another apartment is..Flatting and Drawing of Gold..Wyre. **1799** G. SMITH *Laboratory* I. 318 A flatting-mill, such as those employed in the flatting of gold.

b. *concr.* A layer of mortar.

1829 J. HODGSON in J. Raine *Mem.* (1858) II. 161 The wall has been constructed in regular flattings, with layers of basaltic rumlar work between each flatting of the mortar.

†**2.** The process of becoming flat. Of wine: The process of becoming vapid or insipid.

1665 HOOKE *Microgr.* 30 The flatting of the Surface in the middle is from the abatement of the waters pressure outwards. **1675** W. CHARLETON *Two Disc.* II. 160 The Palling or Flatting of Wines.

3. *Music.* The lowering (of a note) by one semitone. Also *transf.*

1674 PLAYFORD *Skill Mus.* I. ii. 10 These two B Cliffs..are usually put to several Notes in the middle of any song or Lesson for the Flatting or Sharping of Notes. **1895** *N. Amer. Rev.* July 11 When a person has a poor ear for words, the result is a literary flatting and sharping; you perceive what he is intending to say, but you also perceive that he doesn't say it. **1956** JAKOBSON & HALLE in Saporta & Bastian *Psycholinguistics* (1961) 348/1 Secondary tonality features (flatting and/or sharping).

4. *Coal-mining.* (See quots., and see FLAT *sb.*³ 4.)

1883 GRESLEY *Gloss. Coal Mining*, *Flatting*, drawing or leading coals underground with horses and lads. **1891** *Labour Commission* Gloss., *Flatting*..is the stacking of coal by boys at the flat.

5. *Gilding* and *Housepainting*. The action of FLAT *v.*² 8. Also *concr.* The overlaid coat.

1823 P. NICHOLSON *Pract. Build.* 410 The Nottingham white-lead is the most esteemed for what is called flatting, or dead white. **1881** YOUNG *Every Man his own Mechanic* §1582 The finishing coat is to be 'flatting'.

6. *attrib.* and *Comb.*, as ***flatting furnace, hammer, hearth, stone, tool***, (chiefly in *Glass-making*: see 1); ***flatting coat, colour, white*** (sense 5); **flatting-mill**, a mill for flattening, *esp.* one for rolling metal into sheets and forming the ribbon from which the planchets are cut in coining.

1875 *Ure's Dict. Arts* II. 402 The *flatting colour should be incorporated with a large quantity of spirits of turpentine. **1810** James *Milit. Dict.*, *Flattoir*, a *flatting hammer. **1618** in *Lord's Debates* (Camd. 1870) 138 Twoe *flatting milnes. **1799** G. Smith *Laboratory* I. 318 A flatting-mill, such as silver-wire drawers use. **1823** P. Nicholson *Pract. Build.* 406 In the operation of making it [milled lead], a laminating-roller is used, or a flatting-mill. **1891** *Star* 24 Oct. 4/6 Jeweller's flatting mills.

flattish ('flætɪʃ), *a.* [f. flat *a.* + -ish.] Somewhat flat.

1611 Speed *Theat. Gt. Brit.* II. xi. §4 Where the hils settle any thing flattish. **1713** Derham *Phys.-Theol.* IV. xi. *note*, These worms..have large flattish Heads. **1840** *Evid. Hull Docks Com.* 9, It is a flattish shore. **1877** J. D. Chambers *Divine Worship* 253 The Chalices of the thirteenth century ..were round and wide-mouthed and flattish.

flatty ('flætɪ), *sb. slang.* [f. flat *sb.*³ + -y¹.] One who is ignorant of the methods of professional thieving; a flat; also comb.: **flatty-ken** (see quot.).

1851 Mayhew *Lond. Labour* (1861) I. 218 They betray to the 'flatties'..all their profits and proceedings. *Ibid.* (1851) I. 243 'Flatty-kens', that is, houses the landlord of which is not 'awake' or 'fly' to the 'moves' and dodges of the trade.

flatty² ('flætɪ). *colloq.* Also **flattie.** [f. flat *a.* + -y⁶.] **1.** A flatfish.

1892 O. Heslop *Northumberland Words* I. 291 *Flatty*, a flatfish. **1950** W. Holtby *South Riding* VI. iv. 384 They used to go spiking for flaties in the mud. **1971** *Angling Times* 10 June 25/4 A 2 lb 1¼ oz flounder was the best 'flattie' in Teignmouth SAS's first contest.

2. A flat-bottomed boat.

1892 *Otago Daily Times* 26 Mar., We..accepted the use of a flat-bottomed boat, of the species known in the district as 'flatties'. **1908** E. J. Banfield *Confessions of Beachcomber* I. ii. 60 A huge black beacon waddled along..followed by a roughly-built 'flatty'. **1937** Partridge *Dict. Slang*, *Flattie*, *flatty*, a small flat-bottomed sailing-boat: coll., esp. among boys: from ca. 1860. **1939** *Yachting* June 109 It's the ideal building material for rowboats, folding boats, kyaks and 'flatties'. **1946** K. Tennant *Lost Haven* (1947) ii. 31 Jamaica was breathing heavily with the effort of rowing the flattie against the tide. **1970** *Motor Boat & Yachting* 16 Oct. 38/3 To be successful a flattie should have a length/beam ratio of 4 to 5, the latter figure giving the faster boat. A typical American flattie of the 1800s was 20ft. in length with 5ft. beam at deck level and 4ft. 3in. at the bottom.

3. A policeman. Cf. flat-foot 2 d.

1899 'J. Flynt' *Tramping with Tramps* 393 *Flatty*, a policeman; synonymous with 'bull'. **1900** 'Flynt' & Walton *Powers that Prey* iv. 51 The 'flatties' in uniforms surrounded the place. **1911** *Sessions Papers* 13 Feb. 359 One of the men says, 'Look out, here comes a "flatty"' (meaning a policeman). **1922** Joyce *Ulysses* 487 The squeak is out. A split is gone for the flatties. **1928** E. Wallace *Gunner* xvii. 133 That is what you tell the flattie if there is any fuss. **1934** D. L. Sayers *Nine Tailors* 216 It's damned slack of you flatties not to have dug me out earlier. **1949** Wodehouse *Mating Season* xix. 166 'You know Dobbs?' 'The flatty?' 'Our village constable, yes.'

4. = flat *sb.*³ 9 f (a).

1937 *Amer. Speech* XII. 236/2 She was just a brown-haired kid who wore flatties and went barelegged. **1955** 'C. H. Rolph' *Women of Streets* vi. 77 I'm wearing flatties now to rest my feet. **1970** *Guardian* 2 May 1/2 Mary Wilson.. saying she liked to 'put on my flatties and head scarf and walk for miles'.

flatulence ('flætjʊləns). [a. F. *flatulence*, f. *flatulent*: see flatulent and -ence.]

1. *gen.* The condition of being charged with gas.

a **1816** Sheridan *Sch. Scand.* III. iii. Wks. 1821 I. 77 The Spa water..has all the pertness and flatulence of Champaigne, without the spirit or flavour.

2. *esp.* The state or condition of having the stomach or other portion of the alimentary canal charged with gas.

1858 Copland *Dict. Pract. Med.* I. 1044 When flatulence precedes or attends organic lesions of the stomach.

b. The tendency in various kinds of food to produce this state.

3. *fig.* Inflated or puffed-up condition, windiness, vanity; pomposity, pretentiousness.

1711 tr. *S. Werenfels' Dis. Logomachys* 229 Remember to distinguish between true Sublimity of Mind and Stile, and a vain flatulence of both. **1750** Johnson *Rambler* No. 75 ⁋10 Covert insults which serve to give vent to the flatulence of pride.

flatulency ('flætjʊlənsɪ). [f. next: see -ency.]

1. = flatulence 2. Also an instance of this.

1660 Lovell *Hist. Anim. & Min.* 159 They discussing their flatulency by garrulity. **1731** Arbuthnot *Aliments* v. (1735) 140 The most sure Sign of a deficient Perspiration is Flatulency, or Wind. **1757** A. Cooper *Distiller* II. viii. (1760) 135 Cinnamon..dispels Flatulencies, and is a pleasant Cardiac. **1806** *Med. Jrnl.* XV. 367 His disease originated from flatulency. **1858** Copland *Dict. Pract. Med.* I. 1043 *Flatulency*..an undue formation and accumulation of air in the stomach or intestines, with frequent rejection of it.

b. Tendency to cause flatulence.

1599 H. Buttes *Dyets drie Dinner* E viij, Other referre it to their [Beanes'] flatulencie, whereby they provoke to lechery.

2. = flatulence 3.

1662 Gurnall *Chr. in Arm.* (1669) 343/2 The flatulency of them which puffs up others into pride. *c* **1698** Locke *Cond. Underst.* xxii, Puffed up with a flatulency arising from a weak and narrow comprehension.

flatulent ('flætjʊlənt), *a.* Also 7 **flatilent.** [a. F. *flatulent*, ad. mod.L. *flātulent-us*, f. L. *flāt-us* a blowing, f. *flāre* to blow: see -ulent.]

†**1.** Of a windy nature, full of air or wind. Of a tumour: Turgid with air. *Obs.*

1600 Surflet *Countrie Farme* VI. xxii. 773 The vnprofitable and excrementous humour consumed, and the flatulent or windie parts thereof discussed. **1704** F. Fuller *Med. Gymn.* (1705) 70 The Contents of the Stomach are much rarefi'd and flatulent. *a* **1723** Quincy *Lex. Physico-Med.* (1730) *Flatulent Tumours* are such as easily yield to the Pressure of the Finger, but readily return, by their elasticity, to a tumid State again. **1745** Brownrigg in *Phil. Trans.* LV. 238 Those spirits of fountains are flatulent and elastic.

2. Liable to, or prolific in, windy blasts. *rare.*

1671 R. Bohun *Wind* 65 The Spring and Autumn..are the most Flatulent Seasons of the yeere. **1840** Barham *Ingol. Leg.*, *Bagman's Dog*, Those flatulent folks known in Classical story as Aquilo, Libs, Notus, Auster, and Boreas.

3. Generating or apt to generate gas in the alimentary canal; causing wind.

1599 H. Buttes *Dyets drie Dinner* C ij b, Peaches..Being soft, moist, and flatulent, they engender humours. **1674–81** Blount *Glossogr.* s.v., Pease and Beans are flatulent meat. **1731** Arbuthnot *Aliments* vi. (1735) 221 Vegetables abound more with aerial Particles, than animal Substances, and therefore are more flatulent. **1837** M. Donovan *Dom. Econ.* II. 321 Eaten in quantity it [beet-root] often proves flatulent.

4. a. Of a disease, etc.: Attended with or caused by the accumulation of gases in the alimentary canal. **b.** Of persons: Troubled with flatulence: see flatulence 2.

1655 Culpepper *Riverius* VII. i. 147 Whence comes a flatulent Asthma. **1732** Arbuthnot *Rules of Diet* 372 If they are not flatulent several have been cured by a Milk-Diet. **1844–57** G. Bird *Urin. Deposits* (ed. 5) 310 Being merely the subject of occasional attacks of indigestion, with flatulent eructations. **1847** Youatt *Horse* xiv. 300 Flatulent Colic. *absol.* **1858** Copland *Dict. Pract. Med.* III. I. 550 The dyspeptic, the flatulent, and the sedentary.

5. *fig.* Inflated or puffed-up, 'windy'; empty, vain, pretentious.

1658 Osborn *Adv. Son* (1673) 237 Religion grows flatulent and Hypocritical. **1697** Dryden *Æneis* Ded. e 4 How many of those flatulent Writers have I known. **1742** Young *Nt. Th.* vi. 239 Flatulent with fumes of self-applause. **1863** *N. & Q.* 3rd Ser. IV. 284 Much of the poetry is little more than very flatulent declamation. **1870** Swinburne *Ess. & Stud.* (1875) 261 A score or two of poems, each more feeble and more flatulent than the last.

Hence **'flatulently** *adv.*, in a flatulent manner; **'flatulentness**, the condition of being flatulent.

1563 T. Gale *Antidot.* II. 39 It..healeth flatulentnes of Hypochondria, etc. **1727** Bailey (vol. II), *Flatulentness*, Windiness, Flatulency. **1864** Webster, *Flatulently.*

†**'flatuling,** *vbl. sb. Obs. rare*⁻¹. [as if f. **flatule* vb., back-formation from flatulent.] Inflation (of the flesh); puffiness.

1634 T. Johnson *Parey's Chirurg.* xv. xii. 572 This half crude humor remaining there, raiseth much flatuling.

†**flatu'ose,** *a. Obs. rare.* [as if ad. L. **flātuōs-us*, f. *flātus* a blowing.] = flatuous.

1727 in Bailey vol. II.

†**flatuosity** (ˌflætjuː'ɒsɪtɪ). *Obs.* [ad. F. *flatuosité*, f. *flatueux*: see flatuous and -ity.] The state or condition of being 'flatuous'.

1. = flatulence 2.

1600 Surflet *Countrie Farme* VI. xxii. 777 It attenuateth ..crude and colde humours, and flatuosities abounding in flegmatike and melancholicke persons. **1675** J. Love *Clavis Med.* 45 Remove that flatuosity, which is the cause of thy Disease. **1727** Bradley *Fam. Dict.* s.v. *Apoplexes*, Caused either by..Phlegm, Melancholy, Flatuosity, or Choler. **1884** *Syd. Soc. Lex.*, *Flatuosity*, flatulence, the development of gas in the interior of the body.

b. Tendency to cause flatulence.

1708 *Brit. Apollo* No. 49. 2/1 It is..added to windy Aliments to correct their flatuosity.

2. *concr.* A quantity of wind, air, or gas.

1597 Lowe *Chirurg.* (1634) 108 Oedema, which is, the flatuosities dispersed in other parts musculous. **1601** Holland *Pliny* I. 21 If this flatuositie [L. *flatus*] or vapour doe struggle and wrestle within the cloud, from thence it commeth that thunderclaps be heard.

†**'flatuous,** *a. Obs.* Also 7 **flateous.** [ad. F. *flatueux*, as if ad. L. **flātuōs-us*, f. L. *flātus* a blowing: see -ous.]

1. Of a windy nature; full of wind or gas; = flatulent 1.

1580 G. Harvey *Three Proper Lett.* 12 Such feverous.. and flatuous spirits as lurke within. **1603** Holland *Plutarch's Mor.* 704 Like as in our bodies there..arise certeine flatuous tumors. **1653** Gauden *Hierasp.* 44 Their flatuous and unrefined Wines. **1710** *Death of T. Whigg* II. 45 Whose Blood being flatuous and foul.

2. a. Resulting from inflation. **b.** Resembling wind in its action.

1658 Sir T. Browne *Gard. Cyrus* iii. 134 Seeds, wherein at first may be discerned a flatuous distension of the husk. **1662** J. Chandler *Van Helmont's Oriat.* 78 It hath well pleased the Eternall, to place in the Stars, a flatuous, violent, motive force.

3. = flatulent 3.

1601 Holland *Pliny* II. 170 If a man eat them [mulberries] alone..they swell in the stomack and be very flatuous. **1603** Holland *Plutarch's Rom. Quest.* (1892) 64 So it is that pulse be flateous and windy. **1676** T. Glover in *Phil. Trans.* XI. 634 They use no correctives to take away the flatuous, nauseous, and other bad qualities of them.

4. = flatulent 4.

1600 W. Vaughan *Directions for Health* (1633) 55 The morphew, or else some flatuous windy humour. **1694** Westmacott *Script. Herb.* 20 The plaster seldom fails in cold flatuous pains. **1710** T. Fuller *Pharm. Extemp.* 118 It [i.e. the Electuary] is a notable experimented thing against ..flatuous Stitches in the Side.

5. *fig.* = flatulent 5.

1630 May *Lucan* Contn. I. 353 But swift as thoughts can flie..in a moment goe The flatuous dreames through th' aire. **1653** A. Wilson *Jas. I*, 291 Willing to be less than the least in the Times flatuous opinion. **1720** J. Johnson *Canons Ch. Eng.* Advt. to Reader §7 They were drawn in a very flatuous Style, and contain but very little Sense in many Lines.

Hence †**'flatuousness.**

1600 Surflet *Countrie Farme* VI. xxii. 797 Such [wines].. ingender a masse of many crudities, and much flatuousnes. **1620** Venner *Via Recta* vii. 113 In Feuers (by reason of their heat and flateousnes) they are not to be admitted. **1647** Ward *Simp. Cobler* 87, I can impute it to nothing, but to the flatuousnesse of our diet.

flatus ('fleɪtəs). Pl. **flatuses.** [a. L. *flātus* a blowing, f. *flāre* to blow.]

‖**1.** A blowing, a blast; a breath, a puff of wind. ***flatus vocis*** (the breath of the voice), a phrase used to describe the ultra-nominalist opinion attributed to Roscellinus (12th c.), that universals have no substantial or conceptual existence, but consist in nothing more than the mere sound of their names.

1692 Ray *Dissol. World* I. iii. (1693) 10 It might possibly be effected by the same Causes that Earthquakes are, viz. subterraneous Fires and Flatuses. **1706** S. Clarke *Let. to Dodwell* 31 You make the Soul, as being a mere *Flatus*, to have a more precarious subsistence even than mere Matter itself. **1875** Whitney *Life Lang.* iv. 64 Made by letting slip a bit of breath or *flatus*.

2. *Path.* An accumulation or development of wind in the stomach or bowels; wind.

1669 W. Simpson *Hydrol. Chym.* 85 From the antipathetical concourse of which two ariseth a secret incoercible flatus. **1728** Rutty in *Phil. Trans.* XXXV. 563 She said nevertheless, that Flatuses would sometimes be discharged from the Pudenda. **1858** Copland *Dict. Pract. Med.* I. 1043 To ascertain the source of the flatus which is often formed so abundantly in the digestive canal. **1872** F. G. Thomas *Dis. Women* 133 That a free escape of flatus might be unobstructed.

3. A morbid inflation or swelling. *lit.* and *fig.*

1702 *Eng. Theophrast.* 9 Blown up with a flatus of envy and vanity. **1730** Swift *Vind. Ld. Carteret* Wks. 1761 III. 189 An incensed political surgeon..will..lay open..the corruption of his heart, and spots and flatuses of his spleen.

4. *nonce-use.* = afflatus 2.

1719 D'Urfey *Pills* (1872) II. 201 But this is not it, That the flatus will fit, Or make the dull Reader grow merry.

flat-ways, -wise ('flætweɪz, -waɪz). Rarely **flat-way.** [f. flat *a.* + -ways, -wise.] With the flat side (instead of the edge) uppermost, foremost, or applied to another surface. Opposed to edge-ways, -wise.

1601 Holland *Pliny* XVIII. xviii. 578 The broad bit of the plough-share..lying flatwise. **1684** Boyle *Porousn. Anim. & Solid Bod.* vii. 108 These Plates..were laid on flat-wise. **1692** Rushworth *Hist. Coll.* (1721) V. 358 They drew their Swords, and laid on some of them Flatways. **1751** R. Paltock *P. Wilkins* (1884) I. xix. 195, I..leaped off flatwise with face towards the water. *c* **1790** Imison *Sch. Art* II. 11 Steep the print, flat way, in warm water. **1807** *Med. Jrnl.* XVII. 212 It [was] very difficult to get the handle of a spoon (flat-ways) between his teeth. **1870** E. J. Reed in *Macm. Mag.* Nov. 5/2 Such a raft will not float flatwise. **1879** F. W. Robinson *Coward Conscience* I. iii., He..fell flatwise upon the gravel.

flatwoods ('flætwʊdz). *U.S.* [f. flat *a.* + wood *sb.*¹] Low-lying timber land; applied especially to types of well-wooded land in Ohio, Alabama, and Florida.

1841 in *Amer. Speech* (1940) XV. 179/1 Running up under the foot of the ridge to a large span oak tree and a forked sugar standing in a flat woods. **1888** 'C. E. Craddock' *Keedon Bluffs* 169 The cattle.. had been..driven home to the farms in the 'flat-woods'. **1908** R. W. Chambers *Firing Line* ix, Where have you been for a week? In the flat-woods. *Ibid.* x, Those lemon-tinted butterflies which haunt the Florida flat-woods. **1946** G. Wilson *Fidelity Folks* 95 We got to see funny people from up the creek and out in the Flatwoods.

Flaubertian (fləʊ'bɜːtɪən), *a.* [f. the name of Gustave *Flaubert* (1821–1880), French novelist.] Of, pertaining to, or characteristic of Flaubert.

1926 *Glasgow Herald* 30 Sept. 5 The Flaubertian earnest and emotional intensity with which Conrad wrote his books. **1932** *Week-end Rev.* 13 Aug. 187/1 Flaubertian or Gauterian manifestos on art. **1959** *Listener* 1 Oct. 541/1 The novelist with the almost Flaubertian regard for form. **1963** *Punch* 27 Mar. 462/3 A Flaubertian sense of perfection in literature and in life.

flaughen ('flaxən). *Sc.* Also **flaughin, flauchin.** [Cognate with next; the precise formation is obscure.] A flake of fire or snow.

1649 Visct. Kenmure *Sp.* in *Select Biog.* (1845) I. 401 The sparks and flaughens of this love shall fly up. **1811** A. Scott *Poems* 43 (Jam.) As new fa'n snaw That, fleecy pure, in flaughins fa'.

flaught (flɔːt, *Sc.* flaxt), *sb.*¹ Chiefly *Sc.* Also 4–5 **flaght(e**, 8–9 **flaucht.** [ME. *flaȝt*, prob. repr.

either OE. *fleaht or ON. *flaht-r (Icel. *fláttr*, used only in the sense 'act of flaying': see Fritzner s.v.); the OTeut. type would be *flahtu-z, f. either of the parallel roots *flah-*, *flak-* (Aryan -*plak*, *plag*-), whence FLAKE *sb.*² and FLAW *sb.*², both which have senses identical with those of this word.]

1. = FLAKE *sb.*² 1 a. *Obs.* exc. *Sc.*

1483 *Cath. Angl.* 133 A flaghte of snawe, *floccus.* **1808** JAMIESON s.v. *Flaucht*, A flaucht of snaw.

b. A lock of hair or wool; = FLAKE *sb.*² 1 b; *spec.* (see quot. 1825).

1786 ROSS *Helenore* (1789) 55 In flaughts roove out her hair. **1806** R. JAMIESON *Pop. Ballads* I. 20 He's sent to you what ye lo'ed maist, A flaught o' his yellow hair. **1825** BROCKETT *Gloss. N.C. Words, Flaut, Flought* a roll of wool carded ready for spinning.

2. A flash; a flash of lightning; a 'tongue' of flame; = FLAKE *sb.*² 2. Cf. FIRE-FLAUGHT.

a **1300** *Cursor M.* 17372 (Cott.) His cher lik was flaght [*pr.* slaght] o fire. *a* **1724** *Vision* ii. in *Ramsay's Evergreen* (1824) I. 212 The Thunder crakt, and Flauchts did rift Frae the blak Vissart of the Lift. **1820** *Blackw. Mag.* Nov. 202 Naething but a flaucht o' fire every now and then, to keep the road by. **1876** *Mid-Yorksh. Gloss. Flaught* or *Fire-flaught* applied to the particle of 'live' gaseous coal which darts out of a fire. **1887** SWINBURNE *Locrine* IV. i. 159 When your eyes Wax red and dark, with flaughts of fire between, I fear them.

3. A sudden blast of wind (and rain); = FLAKE *sb.*⁵ b, FLAW *sb.*². *Sc.*

1802 SIBBALD *Chron. Sc. Poetry* IV. Gloss., *Flaggis, Flaughts*, sudden blasts of wind, or of wind and rain. *Mod. Sc.* The snaw is fleein by in flauchts.

4. A turf; also *collect.* turf. *Obs.* exc. *dial.* Cf. FLAG *sb.*², FLAKE *sb.*²

13.. *E.E. Allit. P.* A. 57, I felle vpon þat floury flaȝt. **1483** *Cath. Angl.* 133 A Flaghte..vbi a turfe. *c* **1746** J. COLLIER (Tim Bobbin) *View Lanc. Dial.* Wks. (1862) 47 Meh Heart as leet as o bit on o Flaight. *Ibid.* Gloss., *Flaight*, a light turf. **1876** *Whitby Gloss., Flaughts* pl. turves for the fire. In Whitby Abbey Rolls, 'flaghts.'

flaught (flaxt), *sb.*² *Sc.* [var. of FLOCHT.]

1. A spreading out, as of wings for flight; a fluttering or agitated movement; a commotion.

1821 GALT *Annals of Parish* vii. 75 Nothing was spared but what the servants in the first flaught gathered up in a hurry and ran with. **1822** *Sir A. Wylie* II. i. 5 Getting up wi a great flaught of his arms.

2. A flock of birds flying together; a flight.

1818 *Edin. Mag.* Aug. 155 As gin they had been a flaucht o' dows.

flaught, *sb.*³ *Sc.* [f. the vb.] In *pl.* 'Instruments used in preparing wool.' (Jam.)

1875 in *Ure's Dict. Arts* II. 402.

flaught (flaxt), *v.* *Sc.* and *north. dial.* Also flauch(t. [f. FLAUGHT *sb.*¹ (sense 1 b).] 'To card (wool) into thin flakes' (Jam. *Suppl.* 1825).

flaught (flɔːt, *Sc.* flaxt), *adv. Sc.* [Cf. FLAUGHT *sb.*²] With outspread wings; with great eagerness (Jam.). Cf. FLAUGHTBRED.

1806 TRAIN *Sparrow & H., Poet. Reveries* 80 Then flaught on Philip, wi' a rair, She flew, an' pluck't his bosom bare.

'flaughtbred, *adv. Sc.* [f. FLAUGHT *adv.* + *bred*, pa. pple. of BREDE *v.*² to spread out.] With the arms spread out like the wings of a flying bird; hence, eagerly.

1768 ROSS *Helenore* (1789) 14 Lindy..catcht a fa', Flaught-bred upon his face, and there he lay. *Ibid.* 82 Flaught-bred upon her, butt the house he sprang. **1785** *Poems Buchan Dial.* 4 The first man that..Came flaught-bred to the toulzie.

'flaughter, *sb. Sc.* Also 5–9 flauchter, (6 -tir), 9 flachter. [prob. a parallel formation to FLAUGHT *sb.*¹, with suffix -*tro-* instead of -*tu-*.] A paring of turf. Also *Comb.*, **flaughter-fail**, a turf cut with a **flaughter-spade**, i.e. a breast-plough used for this purpose.

1492 *Act. Dom. Conc.* (1839) 288 Twa hingand lokis, a flauchter sped, a cruk [etc.]. *a* **1550** *Christis Kirke Gr.* xxii, For faintness thae forfochtin fulis Fell doun lyk flauchtir fails. **1799** J. ROBERTSON *Agric. Perth* 247 The spade for paring ought to be similar to that used in Scotland for casting Turf, provincially the Flaughter-spade. **1818** *Edin. Mag.* Oct. 331 A sufficient quantity of flauchter-fail was pared from the eastern side of a hill. **1846** BROCKETT *Gloss. N.C. Words* (ed. 3), *Flaughter*, the thin turf turned up when ground is pared.

'flaughter, *v.*¹ *Sc.* Also 9 fla(u)chter. [f. prec.] 'To pare turf from the ground' (Jam.).

1721 *Gloss.* in *Ramsay's Wks.* I. 388.

flaughter ('flaxtər), *v.*² *Sc.* and *north. dial.* Also 8 flauchter, 8–9 **flawter**. [app. f. FLAUGHT *sb.*²; cf. FLICHTER, FLOGHTER *vbs.*]

1. *intr.* To make a fluttering motion; also of a light, to flicker.

1789 D. DAVIDSON *Seasons* 84 The wild duck..Fast flaughters, quacking to the farther shore. **1816** SCOTT *Antiq.* xxi, 'He wad hae seen a glance o' the light frae the door o' the cave, flaughtering against the hazels on the other bank.'

2. a. *intr.* To be in a flutter; to be angry or afraid. **b.** *trans.* To put into a flutter; to frighten, flurry.

1787 GROSE *Prov. Gloss., Flawter*, to be angry or afraid. N. **1847** *Whistlebinkie* (Sc. Songs) (1890) II. 238 His muckle thick skull she would flaughter. **1855** ROBINSON *Whitby Gloss.*, 'I was sair flowter'd.'

Hence **'flaughter** *sb.*, a fluttering motion, flutter.

1789 D. DAVIDSON *Seasons* 42 The swallows pop Wi lazy flaughter, on the gutter dub.

†**'flauging**, *ppl. a. Obs.* ? = FLOGGING.

1682 D'URFEY *Injured Princess* I. i. 6 Ask him if he knows where we may find a sound Wench: he's a flauging old Whipster, I warrant him.

†**flaumpaump.** [? Corruption of FLAMPOINT.]

1592 G. HARVEY *Pierce's Super.* 181, I have seldome.. tasted a more savoury flaumpaump of words..in any sluttish pamfletter.

flaumpeyn, var. of FLAMPOINT.

flaunching: see FLANCHING *vbl. sb.*

flaunt (flɔːnt), *sb.* Now *rare.* Also 6–7 **flant.** [f. FLAUNT *v.*]

1. The action or habit of flaunting, or making a display. Also † *in* or *upon the flaunt.*

a **1625** BOYS *Wks.* (1630) 403 The Flant and froth of a faire phrase without soundnesse of Argument. *a* **1625** FLETCHER *False One* II. iii, Dost thou come hither with thy flourishes, Thy flaunts, and faces, to abuse men's manners. *a* **1625** —— *Woman's Prize* II. i, Is this stern woman still upon the flaunt Of bold defiance? *Ibid.* II. vi, They are i' th' flaunt, sir. **1830** HOLMES *Our Yankee Girls* 19 Who heeds the silken tassel's flaunt Beside the golden corn?

†**2.** Something used to make a show; showy dress, finery. *Obs.*

1590 H. SMITH *Wedding Garment* 39 So the wedding Garment shall seeme better then all the flants of vanity. **1611** SHAKS. *Wint. T.* IV. iv. 23 In these my borrowed Flaunts.

flaunt (flɔːnt), *v.* Also 6–8 **flant.** [Of unknown origin.

The monosyllables of similar ending are (exc. perh. *gaunt*) all from Fr.; but no Fr. word is known which could be the source. Possibly the word may be an onomatopœia formed with a vague recollection of *fly, flout* and *vaunt*. Prof. Skeat compares mod. Sw. dial. *flankt* loosely, flutteringly (f. *flanka* to flutter, waver), also mod. Ger. (Bavarian) *flandern* to flutter, flaunt; but the late appearance of the word in Eng. makes it doubtful whether any connexion exists.]

1. *intr.* Of plumes, banners, etc.: To wave gaily or proudly. Of plants: To wave so as to display their beauty.

1576 GASCOIGNE *Steele Gl.* (Arb.) 63 [A soldier] Whose fethers flaunt, and flicker in the winde As though he were all onely to be markt. **1634** [see FLAUNTING *ppl. a.* 1.] **1717** E. FENTON tr. *Secundus' Bas.* ii. Poems 195 Where, flaunting in immortal Bloom, The Musk-Rose scents the verdant Gloom. **1789** MRS. PIOZZI *Journ. France* I. 59 Orange and lemon trees flaunt over the walls. **1814** SOUTHEY *Roderick* I. 36 Banners flaunting to the sun and breeze. **1844** HOOD *The Mary* ix. No pennons brave Flaunted upon the mast. **1859** W. S. COLEMAN *Woodlands* (1866) 149 Though woodbines flaunt and roses glow.

2. a. Of persons: To walk or move about so as to display one's finery; to display oneself in unbecomingly splendid or gaudy attire; to obtrude oneself boastfully, impudently, or defiantly on the public view. Often quasi-trans. *to flaunt it* (*away, out, forth*). **b.** Of things: To be extravagantly gaudy or glaringly conspicuous in appearance.

1566 DRANT *Hor. Sat.* I. ii. B, In suits of silkes to flaunte. **1583** STUBBES *Anat. Abus.* II. (1882) 108 That flaunt it out in their saten doblets. **1590** H. SMITH *Wedding Garment* Serm. (1592) 335 Else when our backs flant it like Courtiers, our soules shall strip like beggers. **1592** GREENE *Groatsw. Wit* (1617) 28 Lamilia came flaunting by, garnished with the iewels whereof shee beguiled him. **1652–62** HEYLIN *Cosmogr.* I. (1682) 124 The Wife of every Mechanick will flant it in her Silks and Taffaties. **1712** ARBUTHNOT *John Bull* I. iv, You loiter about alehouses..or flaunt about the streets in your new-gilt chariot. **1734** POPE *Ess. Man* IV. 196 One flaunts in rags, one flutters in brocade. **1748** RICHARDSON *Clarissa* Wks. 1883 VII. 312 They will flaunt it away in a chariot and six. **1820** W. IRVING *Sketch Bk.* (1821) II. 113 The Miss Lambs might now be seen flaunting along the street in French bonnets. **1840** THACKERAY *Bedford-Row Consp.* i. (1869) 270 He could not bear to see Sir George and my lady flaunting in their grand pew. **1847** TENNYSON *Princ.* Prol. 140 If our old halls could change their sex, and flaunt With prudes for proctors, dowagers for deans [etc.]. *fig.* **1581** SIDNEY *Astr. & Stella* iii. 3 Poems (Grosart 1877) I. 8 Let dainty wits crie on the Sisters nine..Or Pindares apes, flaunt they in phrases fine. **1624** GEE *Foot out of Snare* v. 39 Flanting with the vain, aeriall, fantastick bubble of an Episcopall Title.

3. *trans.* To display ostentatiously or obtrusively; to flourish, parade, show off.

1827 HOOD *Two Peacocks Bedfont* ii, The Summer air That flaunts their dewy robes. **1840** THACKERAY *Paris Sk.-bk.* (1872) 8 The haberdashers flaunt long strips of gaudy calicoes. **1871** R. ELLIS *Catullus* x. 17 Then supremely myself to flaunt before her. **1879** FROUDE *Cæsar* ix. 98 They [the pirates] flaunted their sails in front of Ostia itself. **1886** SIDGWICK *Outlines Hist. Ethics* ii. §4. 33 The eccentricities with which..Diogenes flaunted his fortitude and freedom.

Hence **'flaunting** *vbl. sb.*

1729 MRS. PENDARVES in *Mrs. Delany's Corr.* 230, I told him of your flauntings. **1876** MISS BRADDON *J. Haggard's Dau.* II. 59 'There'll be fine flaunting when she's a married woman and her own mistress.'

†**flaunt-a-flaunt**, *adv.* [f. FLAUNT *v.*; with onomatopœic reduplication expressive of the nodding movement of plumes: cf. *rub-a-dub, pit-a-pat*, and see AFLAUNT.] In a flaunting position; also quasi-*sb.* bragging display, swagger.

1576 GASCOIGNE *Steele Gl.* Epil. (Arb.) 83 With high copt hattes and fethers flaunt a flaunt. **1582** BRETON *Floorish vpon Fancie* (Grosart) 18 Thy Fethers flaunt a flaunte Are blowne awaie with winde. **1592** G. HARVEY *Pierce's Super.* (Grosart) II. 61 To shewe himselfe brauest in the flaunt-aflaunt of his courage.

flaunter ('flɔːntə(r)), *sb.* [f. FLAUNT *v.* + -ER¹.] One who flaunts.

1598 FLORIO, *Porta pennachij*, a tosse feather, a flanter, a swaggrer. **1681** T. JORDAN *London's Joy* 14 No Ranters or Vaunters or Chanters or Flaunters. **1719** D'URFEY *Pills* I. 5 St. James's Square, And Flaunters there. **1742** WARBURTON *Note on Pope's Ess. Man* IV. 194 (Jod.) The pride of heart is the same both in the flaunter, and the flutterer. **1877** MORLEY *Crit. Misc.* Ser. II. 400 The painted flaunter of the city. **1883** *Punch* 8 Sept. 120/2 Foolish flaunter caught By studied smile and calculated leer.

'flaunter, *v. intr.* **a.** *Sc.* To quiver; also *fig.* (see quot. 1808). **b.** *U.S.* ? To caper. Hence **'flauntering** *ppl. a.*

1768 ROSS *Helenore* II. 332 An' prest her flaunt'ring mou' upon her lips. **1808** JAMIESON, *Flanter*, 1. To waver, to be in some degree delirious. 2. To waver, to flinch, to faulter in evidence or narration. **1840** *P. Parley's Ann.* I. 215 Neddy ..flaunted and scampered again over the drying ground.

flaunting ('flɔːntɪŋ), *ppl. a.* That flaunts.

1. Waving gaily or proudly like a plume or a banner.

1623 MASSINGER *Bondman* II. i, For all your flaunting feathers. **1624** R. DAVENPORT *City Night-cap* III. i, My Taylor bringing home My last new gown, having made the sleeves too flanting. **1634** MILTON *Comus* 543 A bank With ivy canopied, and interwove With flaunting honeysuckle. **1681** *Moores Baffled* 24 In the Evening the Earl commanded a Squadron of Horse to fetch off the flanting Standard. **1809** W. IRVING *Knickerb.* (1861) 55 Mantled with the flaunting grape-vine. *a* **1839** PRAED *Poems* (1864) II. 394 Oh then I carried..casque with flaunting feather.

2. Making an obtrusive display; showy, gaudy.

1567 TURBERVILLE *To his friend that refused him, &c., Epitaphes*, etc. (1870) 203 Yeeld me thy flanting hood, shake off those belles of thine. **1577** STANYHURST *Descr. Irel.* in *Holinshed* VI. 47 A flaunting ostentation of a roisting kind of rhetorike. **1660** PEPYS *Diary* 29 June, He told me in what high flaunting terms Sir J. Grenville had caused his [preamble] to be done. **1758** JOHNSON *Idler* No. 28 ¶3 As flaunting as Mrs. Gingham, the deputy's wife. **1786** BURNS *To a Mountain Daisy*, The flaunting flow'rs our gardens yield. **1829** LYTTON *Disowned* 13 A flaunting carpet, green, red, and yellow, covered the floor. **1847** ALB. SMITH *Chr. Tadpole* xxix. (1879) 258 [A] dingy public-house.. completely thrown into obscurity by two flaunting gin-shops at the corner. **1868** MISS BRADDON *Dead Sea Fr.* I. xii. 254 Their serio-comic woes about recalcitrant butlers and flaunting housemaids. **1885** *Manch. Even. News* 10 Sept. 2/2 A strong effort was made to remove flaunting vice from the streets.

Hence **'flauntingly** *adv.*, in a flaunting manner.

1581 SIDNEY *Astr. & Stella* li. 2 Poems (Grosart 1877) I. 70 So may your tongue still flauntingly proceed. **1584** R. W. *Three Ladies Lond.* II. E ij, For I must to the wedding Both vauntingly and flauntingly, although I had no bidding. *a* **1693** URQUHART *Rabelais* III. viii. 71 The more flauntingly to gallantrize it. **1874** BURNAND *My Time* xviii. 157 Across the road..stood..a flauntingly dressed woman.

†**flaunt-tant.** *Obs. rare*⁻¹. [A reduplicated formation on FLAUNT. Cf. FLANTITANTING.] A showy array (of words).

1661 H. D. *Disc. Liturgies* 49 Not to be satisfied with a flaunt tant of high words.

flaunty ('flɔːntɪ), *a.* [f. FLAUNT *v.* + -Y¹.]

1. a. Of persons: Given to display or show, ostentatious, vain. **b.** Of things: Showy, gaudy.

1796 J. OWEN *Trav. Europe* II. 260 These flaunty caps are of no mean expence. **1825** HONE *Every-day Bk.* I. 585 A boy in female attire, indescribably flaunty and gaudy. **1833** MARRYAT *P. Simple* (1863) 272 'There's a flaunty sort of young woman at the poteen shop there.' **1843** LD. HOUGHTON *Let.* in T. W. Reid *Life* I. 292 His mind seems somewhat less flaunty. **1856** MRS. BROWNING *Aur. Leigh* I. 872 While your common men..dust the flaunty carpets of the world For kings to walk on.

2. *Sc.* 'Capricious, eccentric, unsteady.' (Jam.).

1821 GALT *Annals Parish* xx. 198 She was a flaunty woman and liked well to give a good-humoured jibe or jeer.

Hence **'flauntily** *adv.*, **'flauntiness.**

1830 *Examiner* 323/2 We like people to..air their gaudiest pretensions bravely and flauntily. **1851** D. JERROLD *St. Giles* iii. 24 A woman flauntily dressed..suddenly entered the shop. **1854** *Blackw. Mag.* LXXV. 434 Effeminacy of composition, and flauntiness of colouring.

flaur, obs. Sc. form of FLAVOUR.

‖**flautando** (flau'tando). *Mus.* [It.; pr. pple. of *flautare* to play the flute, f. *flauto* flute.] (See quot. 1876.)

1825 in DANNELEY *Encycl. Mus.* **1876** STAINER & BARRETT *Dict. Mus. Terms, Flautando, flautato* (It.), like a flute; a direction to produce the flageolet tones on the violin, &c.

‖**flautato** (flau'tato). *Mus.* [It.; lit. 'fluted'.] = FLAUTANDO.

1842 J. F. WARNER *Univ. Dict. Mus. Terms* p. xl/2 *Flageoletto*, when employed in relation to stringed instruments, denotes a particular way of making the strings sound, namely in such a manner as to elicit from them their natural accessory tones... The words *Flautino, Flautato, Flautando*..are used in the same sense. **1876** [see FLAUTANDO]. **1935** *Chambers's Encycl.* IV. 728/1 In violin music flautato or flautando is a direction to play harmonics, which have a flute-like quality of tone.

‖**flautino** (flau'tino). *Mus.* [It.; dim. of *flauto* flute.] **a.** A small flute, piccolo, or flageolet. **b.** A small accordion. **c.** = FLAUTANDO. **d.** An organ flute-stop.

1724 *Expl. Foreign Words Mus.* 31 *Flautino*, a little or small Flute..like what we call a Sixth Flute, or an Octave Flute. **1825** DANNELEY *Encycl. Mus.*, *Flautino*..also denotes a species of tone which is produced by a peculiar method of bowing on the violin or violoncello. **1852** SEIDEL *Organ* 97 Flautino..stands in the third manual of the new organ in St. Peter's, at Petersburg. **1876** STAINER & BARRETT *Dict. Mus. Terms*, *Flautino*, an instrument of the accordion kind.

flautist ('flɔːtɪst). *Mus.* [ad. It. *flautista*, f. *flauto* flute.] One who plays the flute, a flutist.

1860 HAWTHORNE *Marb. Faun* x. (1883) 109 The flautist poured his breath in quick puffs of jollity. **1879** STAINER *Music of Bible* 80 The attitude will not strike a modern flautist as being either comfortable or convenient.

‖**flauto** ('flauto). *Mus.* [It.: see FLUTE *sb.*] A flute; used also as a name for several organ-stops.

1724 *Expl. Foreign Words Mus.* 31 *Flauto* is a Flute. **1753** CHAMBERS *Cycl. Supp.*, *Flauto*..is used to denote a flute or the part to be played by that instrument. *Flauto trasverso*..a German flute. **1825** DANNELEY *Encycl. Mus.*, *Flauto dolce*, see *Flute à bec. Flauto piccolo*, an octave flute. *Flauto traverso*, a traverse, or German flute. **1876** STAINER & BARRETT *Dict. Mus. Terms*, *Flauto amabile*, an organ stop consisting of sweet-toned closed, or sometimes open, pipes. It is generally of 4 ft. pitch.

‖**flautone** (flau'tone). *Mus.* [It.; augmentative of *flauto* flute.] (See quot. 1825.)

1825 DANNELEY *Encycl. Mus.*, *Flautone*, an organ-stop of sixteen, and eight feet, stopt, and made of wood. **1876** in STAINER & BARRETT *Dict. Mus. Terms* s.v *Flute*.

flavaniline (fleɪ'vænɪlaɪn). *Chem.* [f. L. *flāv-us* yellow + ANILINE.] (See quot. 1889.)

1882 *Athenæum* No. 2859. 211 [Herren Fischer and Rudolph reported its discovery to the Berlin Chemical Society.] **1889** ROSCOE & SCHORLEMMER *Chem.* III. III. 238 When acetanilide is heated with zinc chloride for several hours to 250–260°, Flavaniline $C_6H_{14}N_2ClH$, a beautiful yellow colouring matter, is obtained.

flavanthrone (fleɪ'væn-, 'fleɪvænθrəʊn). *Chem.* Also -ene. [*flavanthrene* ad. G. *flavanthren*, f. FLAV(O- + ANTHR(A- + -ENE; *flavanthrone* f. *flavanthrene* after ANTHRONE (see -ONE).] An anthraquinone derivative, $C_{28}H_{12}N_2O_2$, isolated as yellowish brown needles and used as a yellow vat dye.

1902 in *Proc. R. Inst.* (1906) XVII. 107 Flavanthrene, a yellow dye-stuff, which has not yet left the laboratory of its inventor, has a blue leuco-compound. **1902** *Jrnl. Soc. Dyers & Colourists* XVIII. 188/1 The new colouring matter which was referred to by Prof. O. N. Witt in his recent lecture at the Royal Institution as *Flavanthrene*, does not appear to have come into the market yet. **1920** F. A. MASON tr. *Georgievics's Text-bk. Dye Chem.* (ed. 2) 452 Flavanthrone ..is sold as Indanthrene Yellow G (B.A.S.F.), Chloranthrene Yellow (B.D.L.), and Caledon Yellow G (Sol.). **1952** K. VENKATARAMAN *Chem. Synthetic Dyes* II. xxxii. 992 Flavanthrone..., which dyes orange-yellow shades from the blue vat, continues to be an important dye (partly because it is a nontenderer and has good light fastness). **1961** COCKETT & HILTON *Dyeing Cellulosic Fibres* i. 13 In 1901, the first anthraquinone vat dye, Indanthrone (Indanthrene Blue B), was discovered by Bohn... This was followed in the same year, and from the same chemist, by Flavanthrone (Indanthrene Yellow G) and many other variations.

†**flave**, *a. Obs. rare*⁻¹. [ad. L. *flāv-us*. Cf. OF. *flave* (Paré).] Yellow.

1657 TOMLINSON *Renou's Disp.* 504 The green..and flave part also of the flower.

flaver, obs. form of FLAVOUR *v.*

†'**flavescate**, *v. Obs. rare*⁻¹. [irreg. f. L. *flāvēsc-ĕre* (see next) + -ATE³.] *trans.* To make yellow.

1657 TOMLINSON *Renou's Disp.* 370 Art..flavescates the red, and changes many colours.

flavescent (fleɪ'vɛsənt), *a.* [ad. L. *flāvēscent-em*, pr. pple. of *flāvēscĕre* to become yellow, f. *flāv-us* yellow.] Turning a pale yellow, yellowish.

1853 in GRAY *Bot. Text-bk.* (ed. 4) cited in WORCESTER (1860). **1871** W. A. LEIGHTON *Lichen-Flora* 46 Spores.. colourless or flavescent.

Flavian ('fleɪvɪən), *a.* and *sb.* [ad. L. *Flaviānus.*] **A.** *adj.* Of or pertaining to the Roman gens Flavia. **B.** *sb.* A member of this gens.

1598 R. GRENEWEY tr. *Tacitus' Ann.* III. 123 The captaines also of the Flauian side helped. **1776** GIBBON *Decl. & F.* I. iii. 76 Such a prince [*sc.* Vespasian] consulted his true interest by the association of a son, whose more splendid..character might turn the public attention, from the obscure origin, to the future glories of the Flavian house. **1796** *Encycl. Brit.* XVI. 425/1 [Domitian] distributed great rewards; sitting as president himself, adorned with a purple robe and crown, with the priests of Jupiter and the college of Flavian priests about him. **1867** C. M. YONGE *Pupils of St. John* viii. 139 Beyond this colossus lay the great Flavian Amphitheatre, called from it the Colosseum. **1872** CHURCH & BRODRIBB *Pliny's Lett.* i. 4 With its close, which witnessed the establishment of the Flavian dynasty, began a more hopeful era. **1882** [see CLAUDIAN *a.* and *sb.*]. **1900** [see ANTONINE B. 2]. **1903** *Jewish Encycl.* V. 406/2 An early branch of the imperial Flavian house was at one time inclined toward Judaism and Christianity. **1956** M. HADAS *Hist. Rome* (1958) v. 93 (*heading*) Flavians and Antonines. **1956** M. J. COSTELLOE tr. *Hertling & Kirschbaum's Roman Catacombs* (1960) ii. 36 The domestic tragedy within the imperial household of the Flavians..reached its climax in the assassination of the emperor. **1959** *Chambers's Encycl.* XI. 787 Vespasian established the Flavian dynasty.

flavicant ('fleɪvɪkənt), *a.* [f. L. *flāv-us* yellow, after the analogy of ALBICANT.] Verging on yellow, yellowish.

1871 W. A. LEIGHTON *Lichen-Flora* 37 Thallus various in colour, white..flavicant. **1884** in *Syd. Soc. Lex.*

†**flavicomous**, *a. Obs.*⁻⁰ [f. L. *flāvicom-us* (f. *flāv-us* yellow + *coma* hair: see COMA²) + -OUS.] Having yellow hair.

1727 in BAILEY vol. II; whence in mod. Dicts.

flavid ('fleɪvɪd), *a.* [ad. L. *flāvid-us*, f. *flāvus* yellow.] Yellowish, tawny.

1762 FALCONER *Shipwr.* I. 169 No snowy breasts the flavid nymphs adorn.

flavido- ('fleɪvɪdəʊ), used as combining form of L. *flāvidus*; in Natural History descriptions occas. prefixed to other adjs. to indicate a yellowish tint.

1871 W. A. LEIGHTON *Lichen-Flora* 41 *C[alicium] trichiale*, Ach. flavido-cinerascent. *Ibid.* 88 *A[lectoria] cana*, Ach. pallido-canescent or pale flavido-rufescent.

flavin ('fleɪvɪn). *Chem.* Also **flavine.** [f. L. *flāv-us* yellow + -IN.] **1.** A yellow dye-stuff prepared from quercitron bark.

1853 NAPIER *Art Dyeing* 344 *Flavine*. **1864** WATTS *Dict. Chem.* II. 655 *Flavin*. **1886** *Encycl. Brit.* XX. 175/2 From 100 parts of quercitron about 85 of flavin are obtained, having a tinctorial power more than twice that of the original bark.

2. *Biochem.* [ad. G. *flavine* (R. Kuhn et al. 1933, in *Ber. d. Deut. Chem. Ges.* LXVI. B. 320).] Any of the derivatives of isoalloxazine, many of which are important biologically, esp. the cofactors flavin mononucleotide and flavin adenine dinucleotide. (See RIBOFLAVIN.)

1933 *Chem. Abstr.* XXVII. 2167 A water-sol. nitrogenous pigment having a yellow-green fluorescence can be isolated from natural sources of *vitamin* B_2... The group name flavin is proposed. **1967** J. P. LAMBOOY in R. C. Elderfield *Heterocyclic Compounds* IX. ii. 174 Since the majority of the flavins possess polyhydric side chains, there are some unique reactions which such functional groups undergo.

flavindin (fleɪ'vɪndɪn). *Chem.* [f. as prec. + INDIN.] (See quot.)

1854 THOMSON *Cycl. Chem.*, *Flavindine*. **1864** WATTS *Dict. Chem.* II. 655 *Flavindin*, a substance apparently isomeric with indin and indigo-blue.

flavine ('fleɪviːn). [f. L. *flāv-us* yellow + -INE⁵.] **1.** Var. FLAVIN 1 and 2.

2. *Pharm.* Any of an ill-defined series of yellow acridine derivatives used as antiseptics, esp. the chloride or other salt of 3,6-diamino-acridine. Cf. ACRIFLAVINE.

1917 C. H. BROWNING et al. in *Brit. Med. Jrnl.* 20 Jan. 75/2 On account of its trypanocidal action the compound was called trypaflavine, but, as its range of use promises to be much wider, we shall refer to it simply as flavine. **1951** A. GROLLMAN *Pharmacol. & Therapeutics* xxv. 520 These flavines or acridine dyes possess considerable antiseptic and bactericidal properties.

flavo- ('fleɪvəʊ), used as comb. form of L. *flāv-us* yellow, indicating the presence of a yellow tint.

1. *Bot.* and *Entom.* (Prefixed to other adjs.)

1816 KIRBY & SP. *Entomol.* (1828) II. xix. 125 *note*, The abdomen is covered with longish flavo-pallid hairs. **1847** J. HARDY in *Proc. Berw. Nat. Club* II. No. 5. 257 Legs dilute-flavo-testaceous. **1871** W. A. LEIGHTON *Lichen-Flora* 38 Thallus..yellow or flavo-virescent.

2. *Chem.* Used in the names of various compounds; as ***flavo-cobalt*** (whence ***flavo-cobaltic***), ***flavo-phenin***, ***flavo-purpurin***.

1879 WATTS *Dict. Chem.* 3rd Suppl. I. 111 *Flavopurpurin* is easily soluble in alcohol, and crystallises therefrom in golden-yellow needles. *Ibid.* 544 The so-called *flavocobalt*. **1889** ROSCOE & SCHORLEMMER *Chem.* II. II. 139 The Flavo-cobaltic Salts may be considered as roseo-cobalt compounds in which two-thirds of the acid radical is replaced by nitroxyl.

flavone ('fleɪ-, 'flævəʊn). *Chem.* [ad. G. *flavon* (von Kostanecki & Tambor 1895, in *Ber. d. Deut. Chem. Ges.* XXVIII. 2302), f. FLAV(O- + -ONE.] **a.** A colourless crystalline tricyclic compound, $C_{15}H_{10}O_2$; 2-phenylbenzo-1, 4-pyrone. **b.** Any of the derivatives of this compound, many of which are plant pigments; a flavonoid.

1897 *Jrnl. Chem. Soc.* LXXII. I. 425 Flavone, $C_{15}H_{10}O_2$, is formed by the condensation of ketocumaran with benzaldehyde, and separates in almost colourless crystals melting at 108°. **1938** G. H. RICHTER *Textbk. Org. Chem.* 664 The powder on the flower stalks, leaves, and seed capsules of many varieties of the primula is chiefly flavone. **1965** BELL & COOMBE tr. *Strasburger's Textbk. Bot.* (new ed.) 21 In many genera in which there are blue- or red-flowered species containing anthocyanins, other species have yellow flowers containing flavones.

flavonoid ('fleɪ-, 'flævənɔɪd). *Chem.* [f. FLAVON(E + -OID.] = FLAVONE b.

1949 *Jrnl. Pharmacol. & Exper. Therap.* XCV. 399 At a recent symposium on vitamin P it was suggested..that the generic term 'Flavonoids' be used to refer to the flavonols, flavanones and related compounds. **1962** *Lancet* 27 Jan. 194/1 A pharmacist who is a hæmophiliac had noted that by taking hesperidin chalcone (a flavonoid) he could ward off hæmorrhagic episodes. **1968** *New Scientist* 25 Jan. 188/1 Pigments found in higher plants include..the yellow, blue, or red flavonoids. **1970** *Watsonia* VIII. 168 Flavonoids may have important physiological functions and are not simply waste products of metabolism.

flavonol ('fleɪ-, 'flævənɒl). *Chem.* [a. G. *flavonol* (von Kostanecki & Tambor 1895, in *Ber. d. Deut. Chem. Ges.* XXVIII. 2303), f. FLAVON(E + -OL.] **a.** 3-Hydroxyflavone, $C_{15}H_{10}O_3$, a colourless crystalline flavone derivative. **b.** Any of the derivatives of this compound, many of which are yellow plant pigments.

1898 *Jrnl. Chem. Soc.* LXXIV. I. 327 Morin differs from quercetin and other flavonol derivatives in colour. **1922** *Encycl. Brit.* XXX. 478/1 A number of flavonol compounds has been found to exist in plants in the sugar free condition. **1949** [see FLAVONOID]. **1951** A. GROLLMAN *Pharmacol. & Therapeutics* xxvii. 611 The therapeutic value of rutin and other flavonols (hesperidin, eriodictin, citrin) is still disputed. **1959** E. H. RODD *Chem. Carbon Compounds* IVB. viii. 906 Many of the ubiquitous yellow colouring materials found in nature are derivatives of flavonol, 3-hydroxyflavone.

flavoprotein, flavo-protein (fleɪvəʊ'prəʊtiːn). *Biochem.* [f. FLAVO- + PROTEIN.] Any of a group of conjugated proteins having flavin mononucleotide or flavin adenine dinucleotide as cofactor and involved in oxidation-reduction reactions in the cell.

1934 *Chem. Abstr.* XXVIII. 3765 Flavins and flavo-proteins as vitamin B_2. **1954** *New Biol.* XVII. 63 For these reactions a series of catalysts is necessary (cytochromes, flavoproteins, cozymase, etc.) which appear to be common to all types of cell. **1966** D. KEILIN *Hist. Cell Respiration* xii. 287 With substrates other than succinate it appears that flavoprotein acts as the terminal oxidase.

flavorous ('fleɪvərəs), *a.* Also **flavourous.** [f. next + -OUS: cf. *humorous*.]

1. Full of flavour; pleasing to the taste and smell, savoury; 'fragrant, odorous' (J.).

1697 DRYDEN *Virg. Georg.* II. 326 Fruits, declin'd From their first flav'rous Taste. **1725** POPE *Odyss.* II. 386 Pure flav'rous wine. **1819** H. BUSK *Tea* 136 The flavorous drop Affection's hand instils. **1847** *Blackw. Mag.* LXII. 609 The addition to the daily stew of a bird or beast unusually flavorous.

fig. **1740** A. HILL *Let.* in A. L. Barbauld *Richardson's Life & Corr.* (1804) I. 50 Sheath the two contraries in a flavorous and spirited smoothness. **1888** P. CUSHING *Blacksmith of Voe* II. iv. 98 Women found something unusually flavorous in this piece of gossip.

2. *fig.* Having a flavour *of. rare*⁻¹.

1885 G. S. MERRIAM *Life S. Bowles* I. ii. 14 Ancient villages, flavorous of the olden time.

flavour, flavor ('fleɪvə(r)), *sb.* Forms: α. 4– flavor, 5 *Sc.* flewoure, 5– flavour. β. 6 *Sc.* fleoure, fleure, fleowre, fleware, -ere, 8 *Sc.* flaur. [app. an adoption of OF. *flaur, fleiur*, **flaor, fraor* smell. The euphonic *v* of the α forms cannot be proved to have existed in OF. (the OF. form *flaveur* alleged by Roquefort being unauthenticated); the analogy of OF. *emblaver* for earlier *emblaer, povoir* (mod. *pouvoir*) for earlier *pooir*, is open to question. Possibly the word may have undergone assimilation to *savour*.

The OF. forms cited above are treated by Godef. as variants of *flairor*:—vulgar L. **frāg(r)ōrem* (cf. It. *fragore*), f. *frāgrāre* (see FRAGRANT); but some scholars refer them to a Lat. type **flātōrem*, f. *flāt-* ppl. stem of *flāre* to blow.

With regard to the use of *-our* or *-or*, see FAVOUR.]

1. A smell, odour. In mod. use with more limited sense (cf. 2): A more or less subtle admixture or accompanying trace of a particular odour; an olfactory suggestion of the presence of some particular ingredient; an aroma.

13.. *E.E. Allit. P.* A. 87 So frech flauorez of frytez were, As fode hit con me fayre refete. *c* **1425** WYNTOUN *Chron.* IX. xxvi. 107 Of þat Rute þe kynd Flewoure, As Flouris havand, þat Sawoure He had. *c* **1450** HENRYSON *Mor. Fab.* 66 The Foxe the flewer of the fresh Herring feils. **1483** CAXTON *Gold. Leg.* 183/1 A flauour like a smoke of frankencense smellyng so swete. **1513** DOUGLAS *Æneis* VII. ii. 134 Ane strang flewir thrawis wp in the air. **1542** BOORDE *Dyetary* viii. (1870) 246 Stand or syt a good wayе of from the fyre, takyinge the flauour of it. **1568** SKEYNE *The Pest* (1860) 18 Fleure of stank or corrupt reueir. **1606** BIRNIE *Kirk-Buriall* (1833) 26 To avoyd the deads flewer, they were constrained to bury abroad. **1667** DRYDEN *State Innoc.* III. i, Myrtle,

Orange, and the blushing Rose.. Each seems to smell the flavor which the other blows. **1781** J. MOORE *View Soc. It.* (1790) I. xxiii. 266 The body..is said to emit a very agreeable..flavour. **1843** JAMES *Forest Days* ii, Spill a drop [of ale] on the floor, to give a new flavour to the room. **1870** DICKENS *E. Drood* iii, A..city, deriving an earthy flavour throughout from its cathedral crypt.

2. The element in the taste of a substance which depends on the co-operation of the sense of smell; a more or less subtle peculiarity of taste distinguishing a substance from others; a touch or slight admixture of a particular kind of taste; a savour.

Milton's use of *flavour* in the first quot., where he apparently distinguishes it both from *taste* and *smell*, has given rise to a conjecture that the sense is that of L. *flāvor* yellowness (a correctly formed word, though without classical authority.) Possibly a recollection of the text 'Ne intuearis vinum quando *flavescit*' (*Prov.* xxiii. 31) led Milton to use the word in what he may have imagined to be its etymological sense. But it is not certain that he did not mean it simply in sense 2.

[**1671** MILTON *Samson* 544 Desire of wine.. Thou couldst repress; nor did the dancing Rubie..the flavor, or the smell, Or taste.. Allure thee.] **1697** CONGREVE *Juvenal Sat.* xi. 32 If brought from far, it [Fish] very dear has cost, It has a Flavour then, which pleases most. **1712** ADDISON *Spect.* No. 409 ¶2 That Sensitive Taste, which gives us a Relish of every different Flavour that affects the Palate. **1745** P. THOMAS *Jrnl. Anson's Voy.* 331 White [Cape Wine]..if kept two years, has much the Flavor of Canary. **1789** MRS. PIOZZI *Journ. France* II. 372 Oak..smoke gives the peculiar flavour to that bacon. **1846** J. BAXTER *Libr. Pract. Agric.* (ed. 4) II. 419, I have seldom observed the wine to have any very sensible flavour,—meaning, by flavour, that compound sensation of smell and taste which characterises the finer kinds of wines.

3. *fig.* (of 1 and 2). †**a.** 'Fragrance' (of renown) (*obs.*). **b.** An undefinable characteristic quality instinctively apprehended. **c.** Piquancy, zest.

c **1449** PECOCK *Repr.* I. xvi. 90 He schulde thanne haue.. more noble flaouur of digne fame. **1699** POMFRET *Poems* (1724) 44 The soft Reflections..leave a grateful Flavour in my Breast. **1866** CARLYLE in *Glasg. Weekly Her.* 15 June (1883) 1/7 Happy is he (still more is she) who has got to know a Bad Book by the very flavour. **1874** MAHAFFY *Soc. Life Greece* viii. 244 A certain aristocratic flavour must have ever dwelt about the Athenian. **1875** JOWETT *Plato* (ed. 2) I. 338 They have lost the flavour of Socratic irony in the narrative of Xenophon. **1876** TREVELYAN *Macaulay* II. xiv. 399 The hospitality at Holly Lodge had about it a flavour of pleasant peculiarity.

d. ***flavour of the month*** (or ***week***) (orig. *U.S.*): an ice-cream flavour featured during a particular period; now freq. *fig.*, something that is currently fashionable.

1946 *Ice Cream Rev.* Sept. 72/2 Illinois Association of Ice Cream Manufacturers has set up a committee which will give serious study to a suggested flavor and flavor-of-the-month program for 1947. **1949** *Boston Daily Globe* 25 Aug. 22/1 (Advt.), Ice Cream Flavor of the Week special. Maple nut only. 25ᶜ pint. **1955** *Ice Cream Field* Mar. 77/2 (Advt.), Run any ripple flavor as your flavor of the month—every month of the year. **1968** *Dairy & Ice Cream Field* July 49/3 The routes will offer four standard flavors and special flavor-of-the-month ice cream. **1979** *Washington Post* 20 Sept. D2/1 Young Dan Quisenberry, the Royals' bullpen flavor of the month in their shattered relief corps, got five final outs in a row for a save. **1983** *Financial Times* 5 Nov. 28/6 The U.S. investment banks have been doing their bit—GEC is their flavour of the week. **1984** *Austral. Financial Rev.* 9 Nov. 17/2 This ranks Australia second only to Hawaii as the most popular holiday spot.. 'Australia is the flavour of the month,' as Mr Brian Walsh put it. **1986** *Times* 19 Feb. 19/1 Synergy is the flavour of the week.

4. = FLAVOURING 2.

1785 TRUSLER *Mod. Times* II. 82 Three fourths of the white wine drank in this kingdom are compositions put together here, and made palatable by a liquor they call *flavour*.

5. *Particle Physics.* [An arbitrary choice of name.] A quantized property of quarks which differentiates them into (at least) six varieties (called up and down, charmed and strange, top and bottom) and which can be changed by the weak interaction; an analogous property of leptons which differentiates the electron, the muon, the tau, and their respective neutrinos. Also, a quark or lepton of a particular flavour.

1975 *Sci. Amer.* Oct. 38/1 In the whimsical terminology that has evolved for the discussion of quarks they are said to come in four flavors, and each flavor is said to come in three colors. ('Flavor' and 'color' are, of course, arbitrary labels; they have no relation to the usual meanings of those words.) **1978** *Nature* 2 Feb. 406/2 The quarks in the proton and neutron are of two varieties (or flavours), 'up' (u) and 'down' (d). **1980** *Sci. Amer.* July 60/1 For almost 20 years it has been well established that there are at least two flavors, or kinds, of neutrino; one flavor can appear only in association with an electron and the other is always created together with a muon. **1981** M. GELL-MANN in J. H. Mulvey *Nature of Matter* viii. 176 The electromagnetic and weak forces are 'flavour forces': the electric charge of a particle depends on its flavour; weak forces are flavour exchange forces. **1981** [see CHARM *sb.*¹ 6]. **1982** [see UP *a.* 6]. **1985** *Sci. Amer.* Apr. 66/3 Like leptons, the quarks experience weak interactions that change one species, or flavor, into another.

flavour ('fleɪvə(r)), *v.* Also 6 **flaver**. [f. prec. sb.]

1. †**a.** *intr.* To be odorous, savour, smell. *Obs.*

c **1425** WYNTOUN *Cron.* VIII. viii. 16 Wyth Spycery welle savorand, And of kynd welle flaverand Ðat ilke Hart.. Scho bawmyd.

b. To have the flavour *of*, to savour.

1887 M. CORELLI *Thelma* I. xii, A strange sickening sense of unrest that flavoured of despair. **1897** *Westm. Gaz.* 4 Mar. 3/3 Though they flavour more of antiquity and the early Victorian era than of novelty.

2. To give flavour, taste, or scent to; to season; in first quot. †to make to 'smell' warm.

1542 BOORDE *Dyetary* viii. (1870) 248 Flauer the insyde of them [hosen] agaynst the fyre. **1730–6** in BAILEY (folio). **1830** M. DONOVAN *Dom. Econ.* I. 23 Some of their wines were flavoured with a kind of pitch. **1873** TRISTRAM *Moab* xiii. 241 The water only slightly flavoured our tea.

fig. **1883** S. C. HALL *Retrospect* I. 66 Oaths..flavoured every third sentence that was uttered on board ship.

3. To try the flavour of; to taste. *rare*⁻¹.

1823 LAMB *Lett.* (1888) II. 87 Yours is the delicatest.. melting piece I ever flavoured.

flavoured ('fleɪvəd), *ppl. a.* [f. FLAVOUR *sb.* and *v.* + -ED.] **a.** Mixed with some ingredient used to impart a flavour. **b.** Having flavour; chiefly, having a specified flavour, indicated by some defining word as ***ill-, well-, orange-, vanilla-***, etc. ***flavoured.***

1740 DYER *Ruins of Rome* 498 High testaceous Food And flavour'd Chian Wines. *a* **1764** DODSLEY *Agric.* II, Herbs, or flavour'd fruits. **1867** 'GUILA' *Invalid's Ck.* xli. (ed. 3) 23 Well-flavoured gravy [may be] poured over them. *Ibid.* xlv. 25 Any nicely-flavoured mince-meat. *Mod.* Vanilla-flavoured chocolate.

fig. **1789** GOUV. MORRIS in *Sparks Life & Writ.* (1832) I. 301 Her conversation is better flavored than her tea.

flavourer ('fleɪvərə(r)). [f. FLAVOUR *v.* + -ER¹.] Something used to impart flavour; a flavouring.

1884 P. BROWNE in *Girls' Own Paper* Jan. 155/3 Fill up the stock-pot..with half the original quantity of vegetables and flavourers. **1886** A. H. CHURCH *Food Grains Ind.* 174 Condiments, spices, and flavourers.

flavourful ('fleɪvəfʊl), *a.* [f. FLAVOUR *sb.* + -FUL.] Full of flavour.

1927 *Daily Express* 5 Oct. 5/2 One of the most nourishing and flavourful vegetables. **1968** *Globe & Mail* (Toronto) 17 Feb. 28 The oysters are beautifully succulent and flavorful. **1971** *Nat. Geogr.* May 715/2 Attracted partly by flavorful Norman ways, hordes of British vacationists crowd the [Channel] isles in July and August.

flavou'riferous, *a. nonce-wd.* [f. FLAVOUR *sb.* + -(I)FEROUS.] Bearing flavour; fragrant.

a **1774** FERGUSSON *Canongate Playhouse* 24 With flavouriferous sweets shall chace away The pestilential fumes of vulgar cits.

flavouring ('fleɪvərɪŋ), *vbl. sb.* [f. as prec. + -ING¹.]

1. The action of the vb. FLAVOUR (see FLAVOUR *v.* 2); also *attrib.*, as ***flavouring-essence, -purpose.***

1845 COOLEY *Cycl. Pract. Receipts* (ed. 2) s.v. *Essence of Soup Herbs*, A superior flavouring essence for soups, &c. **1867** 'GUILA' *Invalid's Ck.* i. (ed. 3) 2 Celery seeds..are a capital aid in flavouring. **1892** *Pall Mall G.* 5 Oct. 7/2 The liquor..which is to be used for flavouring purposes.

2. *concr.* Something used for giving flavour to food or drink.

1845 COOLEY *Cycl. Pract. Receipts* (ed. 2) s.v. *Essence*, The essences used as perfumes and flavouring. **1887** L. OLIPHANT *Episodes* 150 Sauces and flavourings.

fig. **1888** *Athenæum* 11 Aug. 181/3 The modern 'romantic ballad' too often produces the effect of having been made to order..with..an orthodox flavouring of ejaculatory irrelevance in italics.

flavourless ('fleɪvəlɪs), *a.* [f. FLAVOUR *sb.* + -LESS.] Without flavour.

1730–6 in BAILEY (folio). **1775** in ASH. **1871** M. COLLINS *Mrq. & Merch.* I. viii. 264 [He] sat disconsolately down to the..flavourless soup. **1883** *Century Mag.* XXVI. 813 Being flavorless in comparison with those grown in Europe.

b. *fig.* (cf. FLAVOUR *sb.* 3).

1861 HOLLAND *Less. Life* iii. 45 A life..by the side of which the life of childhood is as flavorless..as that of a fly. **1883** FROUDE *Short Stud.* Ser. IV. 184 To the many they seem flavourless and colourless.

Hence '**flavourlessness**, the state or condition of being without flavour; in quot *fig.*

1865 *Pall Mall G.* 23 Sept. 3/1 Something of flavourlessness..must mark a man who can represent a composite public opinion.

flavoursome ('fleɪvəsəm), *a.* [f. as prec. + -SOME.] Full of flavour.

1853 KANE *Grinnell Exp.* xvi. (1856) 130 These little Guillemots..are very..juicy..and flavorsome. **1863** *Pilgrimage over Prairies* II. 273 Whether..dog mutton ain't as flavoursome as hoss beef.

fig. **1866** *Ch. & State Rev.* 3 Aug. 488 Versification.. lacking..that flavoursome roughness which is the almost inevitable accompaniment of vigour.

'**flavoury.** *a.* [f. as prec. + -Y¹.] = prec.

1727 in BAILEY vol. II. **1892** *Daily News* 12 Dec. 7/6 Advt., Samples of..Tea..full and flavory in the cup.

flavous ('fleɪvəs), *a.* [f. L. *flāv-us* yellow + -OUS.] Yellow.

1666 J. SMITH *Old Age* (ed. 2) 219 The Membrane it self is somewhat of a flavous Colour. **1846** in BUCHANAN *Technol. Dict.* **1884** in *Syd. Soc. Lex.*

flaw (flɔː), *sb.*¹ Forms: 4 **flay**, 4–7 **flawe**, (6 **flaa**), 4– **flaw**. [Perh. a. ON. *flaga* wk. fem., recorded in sense 'slab of stone' (Sw. *flaga* flake, also flaw in a casting, etc.; Da. *flage* may correspond either to this word or to FLAKE *sb.*², q.v.). The ON. word may have been used in wider senses derived from the various applications of the Teut. root **flah-, flag-* parallel and synonymous with **flak-* whence FLAKE *sb.*²; the close resemblance in sense between *flaw* and *flake* is noteworthy. It is possible that an OE. **flaȝe*, **flaȝu* existed.]

I. A detached piece of something.

†**1.** A flake (of snow); a flake or spark (of fire). *Obs.* (Cf. FLAKE *sb.*² 1, 2.)

c **1325** *Gloss W. de Biblesw.* in Wright *Voc.* 160 La bouche me entra la aunf de neyf [*gloss* a flay of snow]. ? *a* **1400** *Morte Arth.* 2556 Þe flawes of fyre flawmes one theire helmes. *a* **1400–50** *Alexander* 1756 Riȝt as a flaw of fell snawe ware fallyn of a ryft. *c* **1425** WYNTOUN *Cron.* VI. i. 78 Sternys.. Wes sene, as flawys of fyre brynnand. **1483** *Cath. Angl.* 133/1 A flawe of fire. **1513** DOUGLAS *Æneis* VII. ii. 112 Hir crownell..Infyrit all of byrnand flawis schane. **1597** SHAKS. *2 Hen. IV*, IV. iv. 35 As sudden, As Flawes congealed in the Spring of day.

2. A fragment; *spec. Sc.* 'the point of a horsenail broken off by the smith after it has passed through the hoof' (Jam.). Hence in ***not worth a flaw.*** (Cf. FLAKE *sb.*² 3.) *Obs.* exc. *Sc.*

1605 SHAKS. *Lear* II. iv. 288 But this heart shal break into a hundred thousand flawes. **1607** TOPSELL *Four-f. Beasts* 415 It will ranckle worse, by reason of the flaw of yron remaining in the flesh. **1810** J. SIM *Deil & M'Ommie* in *Harp Perthsh.* (1893) 96 Your reasons are no worth a flaw.

3. (Cf. FLAKE *sb.*² 4, 5, and FLAG *sb.*² 1, 2.) **a.** A turf, or *collect.* turf. ***a flaw of peats***: the quantity got in a season.

1811 A. SCOTT *Poems* 161 (Jam.) A lusty whid About what flaws o' peats they've casten, and sae gude. **1836** RICHARDSON, Sods flayed or stripped from the top of the surface of the earth are in the North called 'flaws'.

†**b.** A slab or layer of stone. *Obs.*

1570–6 LAMBARDE *Peramb. Kent* (1826) 151 [An alleged Saxon *flostane*] signifieth a rocke, coast, or flaw of stone.

II. A breach, broken or faulty place.

4. A crack, breach, fissure, rent, rift.

1626 BACON *Sylva* §79 Though the Vessell were whole, without any Flaw. **1685** DRYDEN *Thren. August.* i. 31 If.. with a mighty Flaw the flaming wall, Shou'd gape immense. *a* **1700** B. E. *Dict. Cant. Crew, Flaw*, a water-flaw and a crack in Chrystals. **1712–4** POPE *Rape Lock* II. 106 Or some frail China-jar receive a Flaw. *a* **1745** SWIFT (J.), He that would keep his house in repair, must attend every little breach or flaw. **1764** BURN *Poor Laws* 236 Where a flaw is observed [in their apparel], a patch is provided for it. **1842** LONGF. *Sp. Stud.* III. vi, The merest flaw that dents the horizon's edge. **1860** TYNDALL *Glac.* II. xxiv. 355 On the closest examination no flaw is exhibited by the ice.

fig. **1606** SHAKS. *Ant. & Cl.* III. xii. 34 Obserue how Anthony becomes his flaw. **1615** WITHER *Sheph. Hunt* iii. Juvenilia (1633) 412 When to my minde griefe gives a flaw Best comforts doe but make my woes more fell. **1644** MILTON *Divorce* To Parl., He will soder up the shifting flaws of his unjust permissions. *a* **1862** BUCKLE *Civiliz.* (1869) III. v. 480 He has to be called in to alter the working of his own machine..to fill up its flaws.

†**b.** 'A disease in which the skin recedes from the nail' (*Cent. Dict.*). *Obs.*

The expression ***white flawe*** is one of the original forms of the word WHITLOW, q.v.

1579 LANGHAM *Gard. Health* (1633) 52 Rapes are good for white flawes, and such like diseases of the nailes. **1580** BARET *Alv.* F 669 A white flawe, *rediuia*.

5. A defect, imperfection, fault, blemish.

a. in material things.

1604 DEKKER *Honest Wh.* x. G iij a, I warrant they are sound pistols, and without flawes. *a* **1680** BUTLER *Rem.* (1759) I. 391 Thou hast a Crack, Flaw, soft Place in thy Skull. **1684** R. H. *Sch. Recreat.* 149 The best sound Cork without Flaws or Holes. **1713** STEELE *Guardian* No. 16 ¶5 The smallest blemish in it, like a flaw in a jewel, takes off the whole value of it. **1801** WOLCOTT (P. Pindar) *Tears & Smiles* Wks. 1812 V. 14 Grieve so fair a Diamond holds a flaw. **1869** J. J. RAVEN *Ch. Bells Camb.* (1881) 2 The bell was never good for anything, from the number of flaws in the casting. **1882** OUIDA *Maremma* I. 67 Grew..without a flaw anywhere, in feature, or limb, or body.

b. in immaterial things, and *fig.*

1586 A. DAY *Eng. Secretary* (1625) 75 There is..but one ..slender flaw in the touchstone of thy reputation. **1588** SHAKS. *L.L.L.* v. ii. 415 My loue to thee is sound sans cracke or flaw. **1625** BACON *Ess., Riches* (Arb.) 237 Vsury is the certainest Meanes of Gaine..But yet it hath Flawes. **1667** POOLE *Dial. betw. Protest. & Papist* (1735) 46 There is a Flaw in the very Foundation of your Argument. **1705** BERKELEY *Commonpl. Bk.* Wks. 1871 IV. 455 They discover flaws and imperfections in their faculties. **1772** PRIESTLEY *Inst. Relig.* (1782) II. 291 We should have thought [it] a considerable flaw in their characters. **1840** THIRLWALL *Greece* VII. lvi. 146 No flaw was ever detected in his reckonings. **1855** C. BRONTE *Villette* i. 2 He inherited..her health without a flaw.

c. *esp.* In a legal document or procedure, a pedigree, title, etc.: An invalidating defect or fault.

1616 R. C. *Times' Whistle* v. 2049 The lease, that hath noe flawe, For a whole hundred yeares is good in lawe. **1654** WHITLOCK *Zootomia* 448 Some flaw or other must be found in his Relations and Pedigree. *a* **1715** BURNET *Own Time* (1766) II. 194 A Prince who knew there was a flaw in his title would always govern well. **1848** DICKENS *Dombey* ii, There seemed to be no flaw in the title of Polly Toodle. **1883** SIR T. MARTIN *Ld. Lyndhurst* iv. 116 The evidence [was] clear, and a flaw in the indictment was the only chance of escape.

d. A failure in duty; a shortcoming in conduct, a fault.

1742 YOUNG *Nt. Th.* v. 142 Each salutation may slide in a sin Unthought before, or fix a former flaw. 1781 COWPER *Truth* 550 Life for obedience, death for every flaw. 1828 SCOTT *F.M. Perth* xxxvi, That will not only cure spiritual flaws, but make us friends with the Church again.

6. *Sc.* A 'fib', falsehood.

1724 RAMSAY *Gent. Sheph.* II. iii, I shall tell ye a' That ilk ane talks about you, but a flaw. 1788 E. PICKEN *Auld Harry's Elegy* 16 Poems 118 They taul sic flaws, An' wantet to mak' black o' white, Without a cause.

7. *Comb*, as ***flaw-seeking*** adj.

1844 LOWELL *Love* 25 Not with flaw-seeking eyes like needle-points.

flaw (flɔː), *sb.*^{2} [Not found until 16th c.; possibly:—OE. **flagu* = MDu. *vlāghe* (Du. *vlaag*), MLG. *vlage*, Sw. *flaga*, of same meaning; the primary sense may be 'stroke' (Aryan root **plak-*: see FLAY *v.*).]

1. A sudden burst or squall of wind; a sudden blast or gust, usually of short duration.

1513 DOUGLAS *Æneis* VII. Prol. 49 Flaggis of fyir, and mony felloun flawe. 1526 TINDALE *Acts* xxvii. 14 A flawe off wynde out of the northeste. 1585 T. WASHINGTON tr. *Nicholay's Voy.* I. xi. 13 Within a moment arose..a sodain Borasque or Flaa. 1628 DIGBY *Voy. Medit.* (1868) 51 Towardes night..wind..came vncertainely and by flawes. 1674 JOSSELYN *Voy. New Eng.* 54 We have upon our Coast in England a Michaelmas flaw, that seldom fails. 1725 DE FOE *Voy. round World* (1840) 128 It blew..not only by squalls and sudden flaws but a settled terrible tempest. 1809 W. IRVING *Knickerb.* VI. ix. (1849) 379 [He] was knocked overboard by the boom of a sloop in a flaw of wind. 1839 LONGF. *Wreck Hesperus* iii, He..watched how the veering flaw did blow The smoke, now West now South. 1881 *Scribner's Monthly* XXII. 530/1 The playful breeze freshens in flaws.

fig. 1567 TURBERV. *Louer to Cupid* Epitaphes (1867) 85 Dispaire that grewe by frowarde fortunes flawes. 1590 NASHE *Pasquil's Apol.* 7 The Church is ouertaken with such a flawe, that [etc.]. 1840 MARRYAT *Olla Podr.* III. 24 He would flounder and diverge away right and left, just as the flaws of ideas came into his head. 1863 MRS. C. CLARKE *Shaks. Char.* xv. 375 Flatterers who shroud themselves from the first flaw of adversity that rocks the structure.

b. A fall of rain or snow accompanied by gusty winds; a short spell of rough weather.

1791 *Statist. Acc. Scot.* I. 422 The falls of snow, which generally happen in March all over Great Britain, is in this neighbourhood called St. Causnan's Flaw. 1830 SCOTT *Jrnl.* 7 July, I rather like a flaw of weather. 1892 STEVENSON *Across the Plains* 209 The flaws of fine weather, which we pathetically call our summer. *Ibid.* 212 Scouring flaws of rain.

†**2.** *fig.* A sudden rush or onset; a burst of feeling or passion; a sudden uproar or tumult. *Obs.*

1596 SPENSER *F.Q.* V. v. 6 She at the first encounter on him ran..But he..from that first flaw him selfe right well defended. 1605 SHAKS. *Macb.* III. iv. 63 O, these flawes and starts..would well become A womans story. 1676 DRYDEN *Aurengz.* v. i, And deluges of armies from the town Came pouring in; I heard the mighty Flaw When first it broke.

¶**3.** Used as rendering of F. *fléau* scourge.

1481 CAXTON *Godfrey* 33 Suffred a grete flawe to come in to the contre, for to chastyse the peple.

4. *Comb.* as ***flaw-blown*** adj.; also, †**flaw-flower**, a name for *Anemone Pulsatilla*.

1820 KEATS *Eve St. Agnes* xxxvii, Quick pattereth the *flaw-blown sleet. 1597 GERARDE *Herbal* II. lxxiii. §3. 309 Passe flower is called..after the Latin name *Pulsatill*, or *Flawe flower.

†**flaw**, *a.* *Obs.*$^{-1}$ [? ad. L. *flāvus*.] ? Yellow. (So in glossaries, but the meaning is doubtful.)

c 1450 *Crt. of Love* 782 Lily forehede had this creature, With liveliche browes, flaw, of colour pure.

flaw (flɔː), *v.*^{1} [f. FLAW *sb.*^{1}]

1. *trans.* To make a flaw or crack in; to crack; to damage by a crack or fissure; to cause a defect in, mar.

1665 HOOKE *Microgr.* 34 The blunt end..seemed irregularly flawed with divers clefts. 1676 *Phil. Trans.* XI. 755 That stuns the Diamond and so flaws it. 1697 DRYDEN *Virg. Georg.* III. 558 The Brazen Cauldrons with the Frost are flaw'd. 1794 SULLIVAN *View Nat.* I. 362 [Glass] being reduced to powder, or otherwise flawed. 1800 HOWARD in *Phil. Trans.* XC. 208 The breech..was torn open and flawed in many directions. 1854 DICKENS *Hard T.* 131 They fell to pieces with such ease that you might suspect them of having been flawed before.

b. with immaterial object, or *fig.*

1613 SHAKS. *Hen. VIII*, I, i. 95 France hath flaw'd the League. *Ibid.* I. ii. 21 Which hath flaw'd the heart Of all their Loyalties. 1638 FORD *Lady's Trial* II. ii, He answer'd, My worship needed not to flaw his right. 1852 THACKERAY *Esmond* I. vii. (1869) 67 It must be owned..that she had a fault of character that flawed her perfections. 1887 SWINBURNE *Locrine* I. ii. 178 Have I not sinned already—flawed my faith?

†**c.** ***to flaw off***: to break off in 'flaws' or small pieces. *Obs.* Cf. *to flake off*.

1665 HOOKE *Microgr.* 98 By looking on the surface of a piece newly flaw'd off.

†**d.** *slang.* To make drunk. *Obs.*

1673 R. HEAD *Canting Acad.* 168 He that is flawed in the Company before the rest. *a* 1700 B. E. *Dict. Cant. Crew*, *Flaw'd*, drunk. 1725 in *New Cant. Dict.*

2. *intr.* To become cracked. †Also, to break *off* in flakes or small pieces (*obs.*).

1648 HERRICK *Hesper.* (1869) 68 This round Is no where found To flaw. 1665 HOOKE *Microgr.* 33 Those that flaw'd off in large pieces were prettily branched. 1691 T. H[ALE] *Acc. New Invent.* 103 It hath crack'd, flaw'd, and rose in ridges. 1774 *Projects* in *Ann. Reg.* 112/1 No less fit for the inside of buildings, than tenacious and incapable of cracking or flawing. 1831 LANDOR *Count Julian* Wks. 1846 II. 514 The original clay of coarse mortality Hardens and flaws around her. 1857 P. COLQUHOUN *Comp. Oarsman's Guide* 9 Elm is very apt to flaw and splinter short in the lans.

3. *Sc.* To lie or fib. Cf. FLAW *sb.*^{1} 6.

1724 RAMSAY *Gent. Sheph.* II. i, But dinna flaw, Tell o'er your news again, and swear till 't a'.

flaw (flɔː), *v.*^{2} [f. FLAW *sb.*^{2}] **a.** *intr.* Of the wind: To blow in gusts. **b.** *trans.* To ruffle as a flaw of wind does. *rare.*

1805 FLINDERS in *Phil. Trans.* XCVI. 245 The wind..flawing from one side and the other. 1891 STEVENSON *South Seas* II. xvi. in *Age* (Melbourne) 20 June 4/3 Long catspaws flawed the face of the lagoon.

flaw, obs. or dial. form of FLAY.

flawe(n, obs. pa. pple. of FLAY.

flawed (flɔːd), *ppl. a.* [f. FLAW *v.* + -ED^{1}.] In senses of the vb.: **a.** of material things; **b.** of immaterial things.

a. 1632 SHIRLEY *Ball* IV. iii, What wise gamester Will venture a hundred pounds to a flaw'd sixpence? 1665 HOOKE *Microgr.* 6 Appearing white, like flaw'd Horn or Glass. 1891 E. W. GOSSE *Gossip in Library* xvii. 219 [He] made his pictures of real life appear like scenes looked at through flawed glass.

b. 1605 SHAKS. *Lear* v. iii. 196 But his flaw'd heart..Twixt two extremes of passion, ioy and greefe, Burst smilingly. 1767 WARBURTON *Serm. 1 Cor.* xiii. 13 A flawed and faulty heart. 1851 THACKERAY *Eng. Hum.* v. (1876) 320 A hero with a flawed reputation.

†'**flawer.** *Obs.*$^{-1}$ [f. FLAW *v.*^{2} + -ER^{1}.] = FLAW *sb.*^{2}

1737 STACKHOUSE *Hist. Bible* (1767) VI. VIII. v. 417 *note*, Storms, commonly called Michaelmas flawers, at that time of the year make sailing..dangerous.

flawful ('flɔːfʊl), *a.* [f. FLAW *sb.* + -FUL.] Full of flaws or defects.

1881 FURNIVALL *Let.* 24 Nov., You American girls..insist on all us flawful men..being as good and flawless as you are. 1893 *Daily News* 29 Mar. 5/2 Few persons have left flawless poems, but Vaughan's are particularly flawful.

flawless ('flɔːlɪs), *a.* [f. as prec. + -LESS.] Free from flaws; without a crack, defect, or imperfection.

1648 BOYLE *Seraph. Love* iii. (1700) 20 Devotion is like a flawless Diamond. 1755 in JOHNSON. 1856 RUSKIN *Mod. Paint.* IV. v. viii. §18 The sea..is as unsullied as a flawless emerald. 1865 *Pall Mall G.* 22 Apr. 11 Reynolds was almost flawless. 1884 SYMONDS *Shaks. Predecessors* ix. 361 Flawless poetry.

Hence '**flawlessly** *adv.*, '**flawlessness**.

1884 *Princetown Rev.* July 78 We know her to be good and flawlessly pure. 1888 *Sat. Rev.* 22 Sept. 340/2 The strength and flawlessness of the reins. 1890 I. D. HARDY *New Othello* I. viii. 184 May was flawlessly fair.

flawn (flɔːn). *Obs.* exc. *arch.* Forms: 3–7, 9 flaun(e, (4 flaunne), 5–7 flawn(e, 8–9 flawn. [a. OF. *flaon* (Fr. *flan*) of same meaning:—early med.L. *fladōn-em* (It. *fiadone* honeycomb), a. OHG. *flado* flat cake (MHG. *vlade*, mod.Ger. *fladen*) = Du. *vlade*, *vla* pancake:—WGer. **flaþon-* (see FLATHE): by many scholars regarded as cognate with Gr. πλάθανον cake-mould, πλατύς broad.]

A kind of custard or cheese-cake, made in various ways. Also, a pancake. Prov. ***as flat as a flawn.***

c 1300 *Havelok* 644 Pastees and flaunes. ?*c* 1390 *Form of Cury* (1780) 74 Take hony clarified and flaunne. *c* 1400 *Rom. Rose* 7044 With tartes, or..With deynte flawnes, brode and flat. *c* 1440 *Anc. Cookery* in *Househ. Ord.* (1790) 452 A flaune of Almayne. 1576 TURBERV. *Venerie* 188 Master Raynard will be content with butter, cheese, creame, flaunes, and custardes. 1681 W. ROBERTSON *Phraseol. Gen.* (1693) 470, I love such dinners as Milkmeats, Flawns, Custards, Cheesecakes. 1721–1800 BAILEY *s.v.*, As flat as a Flawn. 1820 SCOTT *Abbot* xxxiii, He that is hanged in May will eat no flaunes in Midsummer. 1840 BARHAM *Ingol. Leg.*, *Jackd. Rheims*, The flawns and the custards had all disappear'd.

b. *transf.* of a flat cap.

1602 DEKKER *Satiro-mastix* H iv, Cast off that blew coate, away with that flawne.

flawy ('flɔːɪ), *a.* [f. FLAW *sb.*^{1} and ^{2} + -Y^{1}.]

1. Full of flaws or defects.

1712 W. DERHAM in *Phil. Trans.* XXVII. 479 Those Trees are become cracked, and very flawy within. 1755 in JOHNSON; and in mod. Dicts.

2. Coming in gusts; gusty.

1828 in WEBSTER. 1881 *Scribner's Monthly* XXII. 532/2 Pushing the yacht..is often required in light, flawy wind.

flawyn, obs. pa. pple. of FLAY.

flax (flæks), *sb.* Forms: 1 flæx, fleax, 1–5 flex, 4 *south.* vlexe, 4–6 flexe, 5–7 flaxe, (7 flacks), 4– flax. [Com. W.Ger.: OE. *fleax* = OFris. *flax*, OS. **flahs* (MDu., DU., LG. *vlas*), OHG. *flahs* (MHG. *vlahs*, mod.G. *flachs*):—OTeut. **flahso*^{m} str. neut.; commonly referred to the OTeut. root **fleh-*, *flah-* to plait:—OAryan **plek-*, *plok-*; cf. Ger. *flech-ten*, L. *plec-tere*, Gr. πλέκ-ειν. Some think however that the root is *flah-* (:—OAryan **plak-*) as in FLAY *v.*, the etymological notion being connected with the process of 'stripping', by which the fibre is prepared.]

I. The plant.

1. The plant *Linum usitatissimum* bearing blue flowers which are succeeded by pods containing the seeds commonly known as linseed. It is cultivated for its textile fibre and for its seeds.

c 1000 ÆLFRIC *Exod.* ix. 31 Witodlice eall hira flex and hira bernas wæron fordone. 1398 TREVISA *Barth. De P.R.* XVII. xcvii. (Tollem. MS.), Flexe groweþ in euen stalkes, and bereþ ȝelow floures or blewe. 1484 CAXTON *Fables of Æsop* I. xx. Whanne the flaxe was growen and pulled vp. 1562 TURNER *Herbal* II. 39 b, Flax..is called of the Northen men lynt. 1677 YARRANTON *Engl. Improv.* 47 The Land there for Flax is very good, being rich and dry. 1794 MARTYN *Rousseau's Bot.* xvii. 240 Flax has also a corolla of five petals. 1869 H. MACMILLAN *Bible Teach.* iii. (1870) 49 The flax extracting from the earth the materials of those fibres which are to be woven into garments for us.

2. a. With qualifying word prefixed, in the names of other species of *Linum* or of plants resembling the true flax, as ***dwarf-***, ***fairy-***, ***mountain-***, ***purging***, ***spurge-***, ***toad-***, ***wild flax***: see quots., and the different words.

a 1387 *Sinon. Barthol.* (Anecd. Oxon.) 28 *Linaria*, wilde flax. 1670 RAY *Catal. Plant.* 196 *Linum arvense*..Common wild Flax. 1863 PRIOR *Plant-n.* 81 Dwarf-, or Purging-, or Fairy-Flax, *Linum catharticum*. 1878–86 BRITTEN & HOLLAND *Plant-n.* 187 Mountain Flax, (1) *Linum catharticum*..(2) *Erythræa Centaurium*. *Ibid.*, Wild Flax, (1) *Linaria vulgaris*. (2) *Cuscuta Epilinum*.

b. New Zealand flax, *Phormium tenax* (also called ***flax bush***, ***-lily***, ***-plant***), a native of New Zealand, the leaves of which yield a textile fibre.

1832 A. EARLE *Narr. Res. N.Z.* (1966) 64 Their food is always eaten out of little baskets, rudely woven of green flax. 1846 LINDLEY *Veg. Kingd.* iv. 203 In New Zealand they [Lilyworts] are represented by the Phormium or Flaxbush. 1854 GOLDER *Pigeons' Parl.* Introd. 5, I had..to pass the night..under the shade of a flax-bush. 1870 BRAIM *New Homes* viii. 375 The native flax (*phormium tenax*) is found in all parts of New Zealand.

II. The fibre of flax.

3. a. The fibres of the plant whether dressed or undressed.

c 1325 *Gloss. W. de Biblesw.* in Wright *Voc.* 156 Pik thi flax. *c* 1386 CHAUCER *Prol.* 676 This pardoner hadde heer as yelwe as wex, But smothe it heng, as doth a strike of flex. *c* 1483 CAXTON *Vocab.* 18 The lynweuar, Weueth my lynnencloth Of threde of flaxe. 1530 PALSGR. 221/1 Flaxe redy to spynne, *fillace*. 1601 SHAKS. *Twel. N.* I. iii. 108 It [haire] hangs like flax on a distaffe. 1666 PEPYS *Diary* (1879) VI. 34 In the town did see an old man beating of flax. 1767 WARBURTON *Serm. 1 Cor.* xiii. 13 Human laws, like a thread of flax before a flame, vanish and disappear before popular commotions. 1825 J. NEAL *Bro. Jonathan* III. 323 You broke away from us like the Philistine from the un-twisted flax.

fig. 1533 MORE *Debell. Salem* v. Wks. 940/2 He spinneth that fyne lye with flex, fetchinge it out of his owne body as the spider spynneth her cobwebbe.

b. *pl.* Different sorts or qualities of flax.

1886 *Daily News* 6 Sept. 2/4 There is a brisk inquiry for tows, hemps, and flaxes.

†**4.** As a material of which a candle or lamp wick is made; the wick itself. *Obs.*

c 975 *Rushw. Gosp.* Matt. xii. 20 Flæx *vel* lin smikende ne adwæscet. *c* 1380 WYCLIF *Serm.* Sel. Wks. II. 189 Preestis of the chirche, þat smokiden bi pride as brent flex. 1529 MORE *Comf. agst. Trib.* II. Wks. 1200/1 It is a thing right hard..to put flexe vnto fyre, & yet kepe them [the fingers] fro burning. 1560 BIBLE (Genev.) *Isa.* xlii. 3 The smoking flax shall he not quench. 1593 SHAKS. *2 Hen. VI*, v. ii. 55 Beautie ..Shall to my flaming wrath, be Oyle and Flax. 1632 MASSINGER & FIELD *Fatal Dowry* IV. i, He has made me smell for all the world like a flax or a red-headed woman's chamber.

5. a. A material resembling the fibres of the flax-plant or used for a like purpose.

1553 EDEN *Treat. Newe Ind.* (Arb.) 19 The flaxe whiche is lefte, they spinne agayne. 1624 CAPT. SMITH *Virginia* VI. 216 A kinde..of Flax, wherewith they make Nets.

b. in the name of a variety of asbestos with flaxlike fibres, as EARTH-, FOSSIL-, MOUNTAIN-FLAX, q.v. For ***incombustible flax***, see ASBESTOS 2.

1860 WHITTIER *Double-h. Snake* 4 Whether he lurked in the Oldtown fen Or the gray earth-flax of the Devil's Den.

6. Cloth made of flax; linen.

c 897 K. ÆLFRED *Gregory's Past.* xiv. 87 Of ðære eorðan cymeð ðæt fleax, Ðæt bið hwites hiwes. 1340 *Ayenb.* 236 Chastete þet is be-tokned be þe huite ulexe. 1537 BARET *Alv.* F 643 That beareth or weareth flaxe or linnen. 1851 MRS. R. WILSON *New Zealand* 23 His robe of glossy flax which loosely flows. 1872 A. DOMETT *Ranolf* v. iii. 93 In flowing vest of silky flax, undyed.

III. *attrib.* and *Comb.*

7. a. simple *attrib.* General relations (with or without hyphen), as ***flax-blade***, †***-bolle*** (see BOLL *sb.*^{1}), ***fibre***, ***leaf***, ***plant***, ***stalk***, ***stem***, ***-stick***, ***straw***, †***top***, ***-swamp*** (N.Z.).

1872 A. DOMETT *Ranolf* I. v. 11 With *flax-blades binding to a tree the Maid. *c* 1325 *Gloss. W. de Biblesw.* in Wright *Voc.* 156 *note*, *Boceaus*, *flaxbolles [*printed* filaxlolles.] 1875 *Ure's Dict. Arts* 409 Attempts have been made to prepare *flax fibre without steeping. 1884 BRACKEN *Lays of Maori* 69 Zephyrs stirred the *flax leaves into tune. 1838 *Penny Cycl.* X. 305/1 The *flax plants are passed between these cylinders. 1875 *Ure's Dict. Arts* II. 409 The immersion of the *flax stems in water. 1871 C. L. MONEY *Knocking about in N.Z.* iv. 52 *Mogue*[s is the] Maori name for a raupo or *flax-stick raft. 1933 L. G. D. ACLAND in *Press*

(Christchurch) 14 Oct. 15/7 The dried reed stalks..are called f[lax]-sticks. **1860** *Ure's Dict. Arts* II. 228 The sheaves of *flax-straw are placed erect in crates. **1871** M. A. BARKER *Christmas Cake in Four Quarters* IV. i. 251 A view of downs rolling into a narrow gully, the *flax swamp of which formed a natural boundary to one bit of the kitchen garden. **1926** H. GUTHRIE-SMITH *Tutira* (ed. 2) 283 The destruction by fire of flax-swamps. **1382** WYCLIF *Ecclus* xxi. 10 A *flax top gedered togidere [Vulg. *stuppa collecta*] the synagoge of synneres.

b. Concerned with flax as a commercial product, as ***flax culture, -factory, -industry, -man, -merchant, -mill, -shop, -spindle, -tithe.***

1875 *Ure's Dict. Arts* II. 455 Lands..prepared for *flax culture. **1509** in *Mkt. Harborough Records* (1890) 232 Ric' Beale *Flaxman. **1799** A. YOUNG *Agric. Linc.* 197 Let it to flaxmen at £3 or £4 per acre. **1807** VANCOUVER *Agric. Devon* (1813) 207 The flaxman only finding seed, and agreeing to have the field cleared by a given time. **1835** URE *Philos. Manuf.* 221 The proprietors of many *flax-mills. **1600** *Sir John Oldcastle* I. iii, A man may make a *flax-shop in your chimnies, for any fire there is stirring. **1679** BEDLOE *Popish Plot* 27 A Gentle-woman that kept a Flax-shop in the Minories. **1875** *Ure's Dict. Arts* II. 456 The steam-driven *flax-spindle. **1692** ROKEBY *Diary* 18 Whether *Flax-tyth were small tythes or not.

c. Made of flax, as ***flax canvas, -sandal, -thread.***

1872 A. DOMETT *Ranolf* XXI. ii. 378 His feet—with green flax-sandals shod. **1882** CAULFEILD & SAWARD *Dict. Needlework* 210/1 Flax Canvas..may be procured in various degrees of fineness and make. **1891** *Daily News* 8 Dec. 5/8 Flax-thread and spun stuffs.

d. objective, as ***flax-dresser, -hackler, -spinner, †-swingler; flax-cutting, -dressing, -growing, raising, -spinning*** vbl. sbs.

1632 SHERWOOD, A *flax-dresser, *liniere*. **1894** H. SPEIGHT *Nidderdale* 304 As many as 800 flax-dressers. **1766** *Complete Farmer* s.v. *Flax* M 3/1 They laid out money for breeding apprentices to flax-raising and *flax-dressing. **1874** A. BATHGATE *Colonial Experiences* v. 52 Flax dressing is now a permanent industry. **1780** A. YOUNG *Tour Irel.* I. 164 They next send it to a *flax-hackler. **1766** *Flax-raising [see *flax-dressing* above]. **1856** *Farmer's Mag.* Nov. 379 The severe trial the *flaxspinners experienced. **1838** *Penny Cycl.* X. 305/2 *Flax-spinning is now carried on with most success in ..Yorkshire. **1663** *Canterbury Marriage Licences* (MS.), Charles Abbot..*flaxswingler.

e. Referring to the colour of the flower of the flax, as ***flax-blue, flax-flower blue.***

1899 *Daily News* 20 May 8/6 Flax-flower blue, a lovely shade that seems to reflect the summer sky itself. **1900** *Ibid.* 28 July 6/7 Flax-blue Irish linen.

8. a. Special comb.: **flax-bird**, (*a*) the North American goldfinch, *Chrysomitris tristis*; (*b*) *U.S.* 'a book-name of the scarlet tanager, *Piranga rubra*' (*Cent. Dict.*); (*c*) *dial.* the common Whitethroat, *Curruca cinerea*; **†flax-box**, a box to hold the flax or tow match for firing a caliver or matchlock; **flax-brake** (see quot.); **flax-breaker** = prec.; **flax-comb**, an instrument for cleansing and straightening flax fibres, a flax-hackle; **flax-cotton**, cottonized flax; **†flax-finch** ? some species of finch; **flax-hackle** (see quot.); **flax-honey** *N.Z.*, honey from bees feeding on flowers of *Phormium tenax*; **†flax-hoppe**, a head or seed-pod of flax; **flax-hurd**, the coarse parts of flax, tow; **flax-ripple** (see quot.); **flax-scutcher** (see SCUTCHER); so ***flax-scutching*** vbl. sb.; **flax-thrasher**, a machine for beating out the seeds from the bolls of the flax-plant; **flax-wench, -wife, -woman**, a female flax-worker.

1822 LATHAM *Hist. Birds* VI. 120 American Yellow Finch ..feeds on the seeds of flax, alder, &c., and is called in the back parts of Carolina, the *Flax Bird. **1576** *Lanc. Lieutenancy* I. 77 Six calliuers, fyve *flaxe boxes. **1688** R. HOLME *Armoury* III. iii. 48 A *Flax Brake is two pieces of Timber with Teeth made in them to bruse Flax stalks. **1889** ELVIN *Dict. Her.*, *Flax-breaker. **1611** COTGR., *Brosse*..a *flax-combe, or hatchell. **1755** JOHNSON, *Flax-comb*, the instrument with which the fibres of flax are cleansed from the brittle parts. **1851** LOWELL *Lett.* (1894) I. 192 The *flax-cotton is a great thing. **1639** HORN & ROB. *Gate Lang. Unl.* xiv. §153 The goldfinch, larke, nightingale..and *flax-finch are singing birds. **1825** J. NICHOLSON *Operat. Mechanic* 402 The *flax-hackle is an instrument or tool constructed for the purpose of hackling or straightening the fibres of the flax. **1950** G. DEMPSEY *Wind from Sea* ii. 20 There's plenty of *flax-honey..the season has been too dry for clover honey. **14..** *Voc.* in Wr.-Wülcker 584/3 *Folliculus*, a *flexhoppe. **1614** MARKHAM *Cheap Husb.* II. iv. 93 A little Rozen melted together with *Flaxehurds. **1673** *Phil. Trans.* VIII. 6067 Lap the joynted place about with a little hemp or flax-hurds. **1880** *Antrim & Down Gloss.*, *Flax-ripple, a comb with large iron teeth through which flax is drawn, to remove the bolls or seeds. **1846** J. BAXTER *Libr. Pract. Agric.* (ed. 4) I. 277 The first *flax-scutching mill. **1611** SHAKS. *Wint. T.* I. ii. 277 My Wife..deserues a Name As ranke as any *Flax-Wench. **1591** GREENE *Disc. Coosnage* (near end) How a *Flaxe wife [etc.]. **1611** COTGR., *Filandiere*, a *Flaxe-woman.

b. In the names of plants, as **flax-bush, -lily** (see sense 2 b); **flax-dodder**, *Cuscuta Epilinum*; **flax-tail**, a dialect name of the reed-mace, *Typha latifolia*; **flax-weed**, *Linaria vulgaris*, toad-flax; **flax-worts**, the name given by Lindley to the order *Linaceæ*.

1852 J. M. WILSON *Farmer's Dict. Agric.*, *Flax-dodder. **1861** MISS PRATT *Flower. Pl.* V. 313 The Reed-mace is in Kent often called *Flax-tail. **1597** GERARDE *Herbal* 445 Tode flaxe is called of the herbaristes of our time, Linaria, or *Flaxweede. **1846** LINDLEY *Veg. Kingd.* vii. 485 *Linaceæ*, *Flaxworts.

flax (flæks), *a. rare*⁻¹. [f. prec.] Having the colour of flax; flaxen.

1873 MISS BROUGHTON *Nancy* II. 241, I have my flax hair built in many strange and differing fashions.

flax (flæks), *v.* [f. prec. sb.]

1. *trans.* To wrap in fine linen. *rare*⁻¹.

1860 READE *Cloister & H.* IV. 368 And oh the sheets I lie in here..Dives was ne'er so flaxed as I.

2. *U.S.* **a.** *trans.* To beat; app. in allusion to the beating of flax. Cf. FLAXEN *v.* **b.** *intr.* ***to flax round***: to 'knock about,' bestir oneself.

1866 LOWELL *Biglow P.* Introd., I think..*to flax* for *to beat* [is American]. **1884** MISS L. W. BALDWIN *Yank. Sch. Teacher in Virginia* iv. 29 I'm goin' to make some dried-apple fritters f'r dinner, an' you must flax roun' an' give me a lift.

†flaxed, *ppl. a. Obs.* [f. FLAX *sb.* + -ED².] = FLAXEN.

1613-6 W. BROWNE *Brit. Past.* I. iv. 82 Her flaxed hair crown'd with an Anadem. *a* **1687** COTTON *Winter* 28 The Cup-bearer Ganimed Has capp'd his frizled flaxed head.

flaxen ('flæksən, 'flæks(ə)n), *a.* and *sb.* Forms: 6 **flaxan**, 6, 8 **flaxon**, 7 **flexen, -on**, 6– **flaxen**. [f. FLAX *sb.* + -EN⁴.]

A. *adj.*

1. Consisting or made of flax.

1521 *Bury Wills* (1850) 119 Item a flaxan shet. **1597** *1st Pt. Return fr. Parnass.* II. i. 700 He shall..lie in a good flaxon sheete. **1601** HOLLAND *Pliny* XIX. i. 3 The toile made of Cumes Flaxen cords, are so strong, that the wild Bore falling into it, will bee caught. **1660** BLOUNT *Boscobel* 41 His Majesty..put off his course shirt and put on a flexen one. **1739** SHARP *Surgery* Introd. 52 The best Materials for making Ligatures are the Flaxen Thread that Shoe-makers use. **1825** J. NICHOLSON *Operat. Mechanic* 405 A patent for spinning a flaxen thread. **1876** ROCK *Text. Fabr.* i. 6 Fine unmixed flaxen linen.

2. †a. ? Of the colour of the flax-flower; azure.

1603 *Tryall Chev.* III. iii. in Bullen *O. Pl.* (1884) III. 315 Like Eagles they shall cut the flaxen ayre.

b. Of the colour of dressed flax: chiefly in reference to the hair. ***†flaxen wheat*** (see quots.).

1523 FITZHERB. *Husb.* §34 Flaxen wheate hath a yelowe eare. **1602** SHAKS. *Ham.* IV. v. 196 All Flaxen was his Pole. **1616** SURFL. & MARKH. *Country Farme* 551 That kind of Wheat which amongst the English is called Flaxen-wheat, being as vvhite or vvhiter than the finest Flax. **1621** BURTON *Anat. Mel.* III. ii. II. ii. (1624) 376 Leland commends Guithera..for a faire flaxen haire. **1720** GAY *Poems* (1745) I. 179 Nor is the flaxen wig with safety worn. **1810** *Sporting Mag.* XXXVI. 182 He [the sick horse] had a white mouth and a flaxen tongue. **1862** MISS BRADDON *Lady Audley* i, That..drooping head, with its wealth of showering flaxen curls.

3. Of or pertaining to flax as a commercial product.

1707 *Lond. Gaz.* No. 4383/1 The Hempen and Flaxen Manufacture. **1757** DYER *Fleece* III. 369 Who tends the culture of the flaxen reed. **1875** *Ure's Dict. Arts* II. 405 The flaxen trades of the United Kingdom.

4. *attrib.* and *Comb.*, as ***flaxen-haired, -headed, -wigged*** adjs.; **flaxen-egg** (*dial.*), 'an abortive egg' (Halliwell).

1630 *R. Johnson's Kingd. & Commw.* 293 The people generally are..*flaxen haired. **1863** I. WILLIAMS *Baptistery* I. vii. (1874) 84 An Angel..Like a flaxen-hairèd child.

†B. *sb.* Material made of flax; linen; a linen-cloth. *Obs.*

1520 *Lanc. Wills* II. 8 A bordecloth of flaxen to be an alter cloth. **1599** *Nottingham Rec.* IV. 250 One diaper table cloathe; one of flaxen. **1672** J. LACY *Dumb Lady* II. Dram. Wks. (1875) 44 I'll see you byried in the flaxen your grandam spun herself. **1696** J. F. *Merchant's Ware-ho.* 16 Flaxens..made of the same Flax as the former.

flaxen ('flæksən), *v. dial.* [Cf. FLAX *v.* 2.] (See quot.).

1881 *Leicestersh. Gloss.*, *Flaxen*, to beat, thrash. 'Ah followed 'im up, an' flaxened him well.'

flaxenish ('flæksənɪʃ), *a. rare.* Also 7 **flexinish**. [f. FLAXEN *a.* + -ISH.] Somewhat flaxen.

1661 PEACHAM *Compl. Gent.* 167 A dark flexinish hair. **1662** J. BARGRAVE *Pope Alex. VII* (1867) 111 A hard-favoured, lean man, tall, with a thin-haired flaxenish beard.

'flax-seed, 'flaxseed.

1. a. The seed of flax, linseed.

1562 *Act 5 Eliz.* c. 5. §29 One Rood..is limited to be sown with Linseed otherwise Flaxseed or Hempseed. ?**16..** *L. Delaware* in Child *Ballads* VII. 314 I'll hie me To Lincolnshire, To sow hemp-seed and flax-seed. **1737** BERKELEY *Let.* Wks. 1871 IV. 248 It is hoped your flax-seed will come in time. **1858** SIMMONDS *Dict. Trade*, Flax-seed, the boll of flax, generally termed linseed.

b. The plant *Radiola Millegrana*, the seed-pods of which are similar to those of the flax plant; cf. ALLSEED c.

1848 C. A. JOHNS *Week at Lizard* 290 *Radiola Millegrana*, Flax-seed, grows in similar situations.

2. A name given to the pupa of the Hessian fly from its resemblance to a flax-seed. *U.S.*

1886 *Times* 18 Aug. 10/6 Pupæ..resembling small and rather elongated flax seeds. On this account they are called 'flax seeds' in America. **1888** *Riverside Nat. Hist.* II. 410 The larvæ [of the Hessian fly] assume the pupa state, called the flaxseed stage.

3. *attrib.* and *Comb.* (sense 1), as ***flax-seed mill, oil, tea.*** **flaxseed ore** = *dyestone ore*: see DYESTONE.

1831 J. DAVIES *Manual. Mat. Med.* 71 Flaxseed oil. **1874** KNIGHT *Dict. Mech.* I. 881/2 *Flax-seed Mill*, one for grinding flax-seed for the more ready abstraction of the oil. **1904** E. GLASGOW *Deliverance* 101 Polly makes her hot flaxseed tea every two hours. **1922** JOYCE *Ulysses* 89 Only measles. Flaxseed tea. Scarlatina influenza epidemics.

flaxy ('flæksɪ), *a.* [f. FLAX *sb.* + -Y¹.] Of the nature of or resembling flax; made of flax. Also *absol.*

1634 M. SANDYS *Prudence* 16 The Flaxie [colour] having whitenesse, appertaines to Temperance. **1659** TORRIANO, *Lineo*, flaxie, made of flax. **1835** URE *Philos. Manuf.* 20 The substance which attaches the flaxy filaments to the vegetable vessels and membranes.

flaxy, flaxie ('flæksɪ), *sb. N.Z.* [f. FLAX *sb.* + -Y⁶.] A worker in a flax-mill.

1927 J. DEVANNY *Old Savage* 51 They would..mingle with the 'flaxies' across the inlet. **1928** —— *Dawn Beloved* iii. 29 No one came by but a young flaxie.

flay (fleɪ), *sb. dial.* [f. FLAY *v.*] A part of a plough, for 'flaying' or paring off the surface of the ground.

1805 R. W. DICKSON *Pract. Agric.* I. 8 An iron earth-board firmly screwed to the coulter, which in some places is called a flay. **1879** MISS JACKSON *Shropsh. Word-bk.*, *Flay*, part of a plough; it goes before the coulter and pares off the surface of the ground, turning it under the furrow which the plough makes.

flay (fleɪ), *v.* Pa. t. and pa. pple. **flayed**. Forms: 1–3 **flean**, 3 **flan**, 3–4 **flen**, **flo**, 4 **flaȝe**, 4–5 **flyȝe**, **flyghe**, 5 **fla**, **fle**, 5–6, 8–9 *dial.* **flee**, 5–7, 9 *dial.* **fley**, 3–9 **flea**, 6–7 **flaye**, 6– **flay**. Also (see esp. sense 5) 6–7, 8–9 *dial.* **flaw(e**. *Pa. t.* 3 *south.* **vloȝ**, 3–4 **flow**, 4 **flouh**, 4–5 **flogh**, **flew**; 6 **fleyd(e**, **fleid**, 7–8 **flead**, 6– **flayed**. *Pa. pple.* 3 **ivlaȝen**, **flo**, 4 **vlaȝe**, **ylawe**, 4–7 **flain(e**, **flayn(e**, 5 **fleyn**, **fleyen**, 5–6 **flawe(n**, 6 **flene**, **fleine**, 6–7 **flean(e**; 5–6 **fleyed**, **fleyd**, 6–7 **flawed**, 6–8 **fleed**, **flead**, **flea'd**, 7–9 **fleaed**, 7 **fled**, **flaid**, **flaied**, 6– **flayed**. [A Com. Teut. str. vb.:—OE. *flēan* (pa. t. **flōȝ*, pl. **flōȝon*, pa. pple. **flaȝen*) = MDu. *vlaen*, *vlaeghen*, *vlaeden*, ON. *flá* (Sw. *flå*, Da. *flaae*):—OTeut. **flahan*, f. Aryan root **plăk-*, whence Gr. πλήσσειν to strike. Cf. FLAKE *sb.*², FLAW *sb.*¹ and ².]

1. *trans.* To strip or pull off the skin or hide of; to skin: **a.** with object a person: often in ***to flay alive*** (or ***†quick***).

a **800** *Corpus Gloss.* 659 *Deglobere*, flean. *c* **1205** LAY. 6418 Oðer he heom lette quic flan. *c* **1300** *Havelok* 612 He shal him hangen, or quik flo. **1430** LYDG. *Chron. Troy* I. iii, Out of his skynne he hath him stript and flawe. **1474** CAXTON *Chesse* 28 He dyd hym to be flayn al quyk. **1555** EDEN *Decades* 261 Whom the Barbarians fleyde alyue and slewe. **1687** CONGREVE *Old Bach.* II. i, No doubt, they would have flea'd me alive. **1709** PRIOR *Paulo Purganti*, They should be hang'd or starv'd, or flead. **1800** *Sporting Mag.* XV. 51 You must flea a Muscovite to make him feel. **1865** KINGSLEY *Herew.* v. 109 If I catch him, I will flay him alive.

b. with object an animal.

c **1302** *Pol. Songs* (Camden) 191 We shule flo the Conyng, ant make roste is loyne. *c* **1350** *Will. Palerne* 1682 Men.. that fast fonden alday to flen wilde bestes. *c* **1420** *Liber Cocorum* (1862) 50 Fyrst flyghe thyn elys. **1486** *Bk. St. Albans* E iij b, Now to speke of the bestes when thay be slayne How many be strypte and how many be flayne. **1558** WARDE tr. *Alexis Secr.* III. 73 b, Than kyll him [a young crow] and flawe him. **1681** CHETHAM *Angler's Vade-m.* xxxix. §12 (1689) 26 Take Eels, flea, gut and wipe them. **1741** *Compl. Fam. Piece* I. ii. 136 Flea your Hare, and lard it with Bacon. **1849** JAMES *Woodman* vii., Whole deer were often brought in to be broken and flayed.

absol. **1597** HOOKER *Eccl. Pol.* v. §65 (1632) 340 To them which thinke it alwayes imperfect reformation that doth but sheare and not flea.

2. To strip off or remove portions of the skin (or analogous membrane) from; to excoriate. Often *hyperbolically* (cf. *scarify*).

c **1250** *Meid Maregrete* xxxvi, Mit swopes ant mit scorges habbe ye me flo. **13..** *E.E. Allit. P.* A. 809 With boffetez watz hys face flayn. **1482** *Monk of Evesham* (Arb.) 73 Sum of hem had her fyngers f[l]ayne. **1565–73** COOPER *Thesaurus*, *Aduri*..to be flawed, to be scorched, as mens thies or legs be with fretting. **1596** COLSE *Penelope* (1880) 168 These fingers should have flead his face. **1610** B. JONSON *Alch.* IV. iii, You shall..Be curried, claw'd, and flaw'd, and taw'd, indeed. **1628** DONNE *Serm.* liv. 546 If thou flea thy selfe with haire cloathes and whips. **1659** LOVELACE *Poems* (1864) 233 Rayl, till your edged breath flea your raw throat. **1697** DRYDEN *Virg. Ess. Georg.* (1721) I. 200 The Goats and Oxen are almost flead with Cold. **1721** CIBBER *Rival Fools* 111, I' gad he wou'd have flea'd your Backside for you. **1748** *Relat. Earthq. Lima* iii. §3. 292 The Taste of it is so harsh, that it fleas the Tongues of such as are not used to it. **1840** MRS. CARLYLE *Let.* 5 Oct., In the ardour of my medical practice I flayed the whole neck of me with a blister. **1849** MACAULAY *Hist. Eng.* (1871) II. xv. 171 The prospect of dying in Newgate, with a back flayed and an eye knocked out.

3. *fig.* and *transf.*

a. To inflict acute pain or torture upon.

1782 COWPER *Progr. Err.* 583 Habits are soon assum'd; but when we strive To strip them off, 'tis being flay'd alive. **1884** L. J. JENNINGS *Croker Papers* II. xiv. 49 Macaulay has laid bare the entire process of flaying an author.

b. To divest (a person) of clothing; to 'strip', undress. *humorous nonce-use.*

1611 SHAKS. *Wint. T.* IV. iv. 655 Nay prethee dispatch: the Gentleman is halfe fled already.

c. To strip (a person) of his money or belongings by extortion or exaction; to pillage, plunder. Also, to do this by cheating; to 'clean out'. Cf. *fleece, shear.*

1584 POWEL *Lloyd's Cambria* 345 Officers were sent afresh to flea those who had beene shorne before. **1620** MELTON *Astrolog.* 3 A griping Lawyer.. will bee sure to fleece him, if hee do not flea him. **1620** *Frier Rush* 21, I haue beene among players at the Dice and Cardes, and I haue caused.. the one to flea the other. **1621** BURTON *Anat. Mel.* I. ii. IV. (1651) 157 They are.. so flead and fleeced by perpetuall exactions. **1665** TEMPLE *Let. to Ld. Arlington* Wks. 1731 II. 6 The Hollanders.. being.. flay'd with Taxes, distracted with Factions. **1879** FROUDE *Cæsar* xxii. 381 Plundering cities and temples and flaying the people with requisitions. **1893** FARMER *Slang, Flay*.. 2 (American) To clean out by unfair means.

d. To strip (a building, or the like) of its exterior ornament or covering.

1636 DAVENANT *Witts* V. v, How! flea monuments of their brazen skins! **1670** J. COVEL *Diary* (Hakl. 1893) 182 The ruins of an old castle that was here; it was all flead to build the Turkish moschs. **1687** BURNET *Trav.* iii. (1750) 169 The Outside.. is quite flay'd, if I may so speak, but on design to give it a rich Outside of Marble. **1847** TENNYSON *Princ.* V. 514 As comes a pillar of electric cloud, Flaying the roofs and sucking up the drains.

4. To strip or peel off (the skin). Also with *off*, †*up*.

c **1250** *Meid Maregrete* xxxiv, Al þet fel from þe fleisc gunnen ho to flo. **1382** WYCLIF *Micah* iii. 3 Whiche eeten fleshe of my peple and hildiden, or flewen, the skyn of hem fro aboue. *c* **1450** HENRYSON *Wolf & Wedder* 39 Poems (1865) 204 With that in hy the doggis skyn of he flew. **1587** MASCALL *Govt. Cattle, Hogges* 267 They doe vse to.. flea vp the skinne on both sides. *c* **1626** *Dick of Devon.* V. i. in Bullen *O. Pl.* II. 97 Flea the Divells skin over his eares. **1646** EVELYN *Diary* 23 Mar., As it snows often it perpetualy freezes, of which I was so sensible that it flaw'd the very skin of my face. **1651** H. MORE *Second Lash* in *Enthus. Triumph.* (1655) 168 Touchy, proud men.. as it were with their skins flean off. **1743** FIELDING *J. Wild* III. vii, The first man that offers to come in here, I will have his skin flea'd off. **1865** SWINBURNE *Atalanta* 58 And we will flay thy boarskin with male hands.

transf. and *fig.* **1607** DEKKER *Northw. Hoe* II. Wks. 1873 III. 28 Flea off your skins [*i.e.* take off your disguise]. **1654** WHITLOCK *Zootomia* 530 [The world's] out-side filme of contentednesse, which when flaid off, what appeareth but vanity, or vexation of Spirit.

†**b.** To tear off (a man's beard) together with the skin. *Obs.*

c **1330** R. BRUNNE *Chron. Wace* (Rolls) 12452 Fful manye kynges had he don slo, and flow þe berdes of alle þo. *c* **1450** *Merlin* 620, I shall.. make thy beerde be flayn, and draw from thy chyn boustously. **1470–85** MALORY *Arthur* I. xxvii, They gaf hym their berdys clene flayne of.

5. *transf.* (chiefly *dial.*) **a.** To strip the bark, rind, husk, or other integument from; to bark, peel. **b.** To remove or strip off (rind, bark, etc.) Also with *off*. (Chiefly in form *flaw*.)

a. 1574 R. SCOT *Hop Gard.* (1578) 59 To flawe the Poales .. is more than needeth to be done in thys behalfe. **1686** PLOT *Staffordsh.* 382 They flaw it [Timber] standing about the beginning or middle of May. **1713** DERHAM *Phys.-Theol.* IV. xi. 192 Birds, who have occasion to husk and flay the Grains they swallow. **1869** *Echo* 9 Oct., In Sussex.. a man was believed to earn from £40 to £45 in the year, including what he gets from flawing timber in the spring.

b. *c* **1320** *Cast. Love* 1308 As a mon þe rynde fleþ. **1577** B. GOOGE *Heresbach's Husb.* (1586) 74 Cutte it [a bud] round about, and flawe of the rinde. **1623** COCKERAM II, To Fley or pull off the rinde or skin, Deglubate. **1631** *MS. Acc. St. John's Hosp., Canterb.*, [Layd out] for flawinge the tanne iiijs. ixd. **1796** *Trans. Soc. Encourag. Arts* XIV. 234 From the largest of those arms, I flawed off slips of rind.

c. To pare or strip off thin slices of (turf). Also with *off, up*.

1634–5 BRERETON *Trav.* (1844) 96 They cutt and flea topturves with linge upon them. **1688** R. HOLME *Armoury* III. ix. 390/2 A Turf Spade.. is to cut and flea up the surface of any thing flat. **1724** SWIFT *Drap. Lett.* vii, That odious Custom.. of cutting Scraws.. which is flaying off the green Surface of the Ground, to cover their cabins. **1869** *Lonsdale Gloss., Flay*, to pare turf with a breast plough.

6. Phrases. *to flay a flint*: to be guilty of the worst meanness or extortion in order to get money. (cf. FLAY-FLINT). †*to flay the fox*: to vomit (translating F. slang *écorcher le renard*).

1653 URQUHART *Rabelais* I. xi. (1694) 42 He would flay the Fox. **1659** *Burton's Diary* (1828) IV. 398 Some of them were so strict that they would flea a flint. *a* **1700** B. E. *Dict. Cant. Crew*, s.v. *Flay*, He'll flay a Flint, of a meer Scrat or Miser.

†**7.** ? To clarify (oil). *Obs. rare*$^{-1}$. [Perh. a different word.]

1530 PALSGR. 551/1, I flaye oyle with water, whan it boyleth, to make it mete to frye fysshe with. *Je detaingz lhuyle.*

8. *Comb.* †**flaybreech**, a flogger.

1671 H. M. tr. *Colloq. Erasmus* 49 He is a more cruel flaybreech than even Orbilius.

Hence **flayed** (†*flayn*) *ppl. a.*

c **1440** *Promp. Parv.* 163/2 Flayne, or flawyn, *excoriatus.* **1585** LUPTON *Thous. Notable Th.* (1675) 10 A fleaed Mouse roasted. **1598** SYLVESTER *Du Bartas* II. i. III. *Furies* 467 The Dysentery.. Extorteth pure bloud from the flayéd veins. *a* **1613** OVERBURY *A Wife* (1638) 100 His jests are.. old flead Proverbs. *a* **1652** BROME *City Wit* V. Wks. 1873 I. 363 The fresh skin of a flea'd Cat. **1725** POPE *Odyss.* x. 635 Let the flea'd victims in the flames be cast. **1835** *Gentl. Mag.* Feb. 192/2 The loose flayed skin which belonged to the arms.

flay, var. of FLEY *v.* to frighten.

flayel, obs. form of FLAIL.

flayer ('fleɪə(r)). [f. FLAY *v.* + -ER[1].]

1. One who flays; also *fig.* one who 'fleeces' or practises extortion.

c **1440** *Promp. Parv.* 165/1 Flear of beest, *excoriator.* **1598** FLORIO *Scórticaporcélli*, a fleaer of hogs. **1613** PURCHAS *Pilgrimage* II. xiii. §1 Euery Fox must yeeld his owne skin and haires to the flayer. **1800** HURDIS *Fav. Village* 152 Her lamb By the bleak season slain, her welted coat Yields to the flayer. **1865** DICKENS *Mut. Fr.* III. i, Pubsby & Co. are regular flayers and grinders.

2. *Hist.* (transl. F. *écorcheur*). One of a number of French brigands in the 14th century, who 'flayed' or pillaged the people.

1832 tr. *Sismondi's Ital. Rep.* xiv. 310 The French.. had bands called flayers (*écorcheurs*). **1891** *Cornh. Mag.* Oct. 416 His whole life was spent in raids.. upon the Brabanters, late-comers, flayers, free companions [etc.].

'flay-flint. [See FLAY *v.* 6.] One who is guilty of the worst meanness or extortion for the sake of gain; a skin-flint.

1672 SHADWELL *Miser* I, A pox on this damn'd Flea-flint. **1719** D'URFEY *Pills* I. 141 The Flea-flints, the Germans strip 'em bare. **1842** TENNYSON *Walking to Mail*, There lived a flayflint near; we stole his fruit, His hens, his eggs.

flaying ('fleɪɪŋ), *vbl. sb.* [f. FLAY *v.* + -ING[1].]

1. The action of the vb. FLAY.

c **1440** *Promp. Parv.* 165/2 Fleynge of beestys, *excoriacio.* **1565** GOLDING *Ovid's Met.* Epist. (1593) 3 The fleaing off of piper Marsies skin. **1848** H. ROGERS *Ess.* I. vi. 321 The flaying and dissecting of a sophist at the hands of so dexterous an anatomist as Socrates.

2. *attrib.* and *Comb.*, as *flaying-knife, season, -shovel, -spade.*

1842 BROWNING *Waring* I. vi, Some Junius.. shall tuck His sleeve, and forth with *flaying-knife. **1794** J. BOYS *Agric. Surv. Kent* 97 The oaks are all cut in the *flawing season, for the bark of all sizes. **1887** *S. Chesh. Gloss.*, **Fleyin-shovel*, a sort of plough with a single long handle like a spade driven by the hand. **1573** *Richmond. Wills* (Surtees) 242, iij. peatspades, ij. *flainge spades. **1879** MISS JACKSON *Shropsh. Wordbk., Flaying-spade*, an implement for paring off the surface of rough grass land for burning.

'flaying, *ppl. a.* [f. FLAY + -ING[2].] That flays.

1663 BUTLER *Hud.* I. ii. 967 Could not the Whipping-Post prevail.. To keep from flaying Scourge thy Skin. **1728** GAY *Begg. Op.* II. i, Those fleaing Rascals the Surgeons.

flayl(le, obs. f. FLAIL.

flayn(e, obs. pa. pple. of FLAY.

flayre, obs. f. FLAIR[1] *sb.*

flayt, pa. t. of FLITE *v. Obs.* to scold.

fle(e, obs. f. of FLAY, FLEA, FLEY, FLY.

flea (fliː), *sb.* Forms: 1 **fléah, fléh, fléa, fléo,** 3–5 **fle,** 3–6 **flee,** 6 *Sc.* **fla,** 8 *Sc.* **flae,** *dial.* **fleigh,** 9 *Sc.* **flech,** *dial.* **fleck,** 6– **flea.** *Pl.* 1 **fléan,** 4–6 **fleen,** 5 **flen.** [Com. Teut.: OE. *fléah* str. (prob. masc.), *fléa* wk. masc. or fem.; corresponding to MDu., MLG. *vlô* (Du. *vloo*), OHG. *flôh, flôch* str. masc. (MHG. *vlôch* str. masc., pl. *flœhe, vlô* str. fem., mod.Ger. *floh* fem.), ON. *fló* str. fem. (pl. *flǿr*); repr. OTeut. **flauh-*, or more probably **plauh-* (cons.-stem) cogn. with FLEE *v.*]

1. a. A small wingless insect (or genus of insects, *Pulex*, the common flea being *P. irritans*), well known for its biting propensities and its agility in leaping; it feeds on the blood of man and of some other animals.

a **700** *Epinal Gloss.* 813 *Pulix*, fleah. *c* **1000** *Sax. Leechd.* I. 264 Heo [gorst] cwelð þa flean. *c* **1305** *Land Cokayne* 37 Nis þer flei, fle, no lowse. *c* **1386** CHAUCER *Manciple's Prol.* 17 Hast thou had fleen al night or artow dronke? **1547** BOORDE *Brev. Health* ccxcix. 98 Flees the whiche doth byte and stynge men in theyr beddes. **1626** BACON *Sylva* §696 Fleas breed principally of Straw or Mats. **1733** SWIFT *On Poetry* 353 So naturalists observe a flea Hath smaller fleas, that on him prey; And these have smaller still to bite 'em, And so proceed *ad infinitum.* **1791** BOSWELL *Johnson* (1831) II. 186 The counsel upon the circuit at Shrewsbury were much bitten by fleas. **1858** HAWTHORNE *Fr. & It. Jrnls.* I. 227 Fleas.. in Rome come home to everybody's business and bosom. **1874** WOOD *Insects Abr.* 771 The best-known foreign Flea, the Chigoe (*Pulex penetrans*).

b. As a type of anything small or contemptible.

1388 WYCLIF *1 Sam.* xxiv. 15 Thou pursuest a deed hound, and a quyk fle [1382 flyȝe]. *c* **1450** HENRYSON *Mor. Fab.* 195 For it is said in Proverb, But lawté All other vertewis ar nocht worth ane fle. **1501** DOUGLAS *Pal. Hon.* III. 660 Me thocht yu had nouther force.. nor will for till haue greiuit ane Fla. **1857** R. TOMES *Amer. in Japan* v. 126 These Lilliputian bumpers would not have floored a flea.

2. = *flea-beetle*: see 6 below.

1805 R. W. DICKSON *Pract. Agric.* II. 760 The hop-plant .. is liable to be wholly devoured.. by the ravages of the flea. **1842** JOHNSON *Farmer's Encycl., Fly in Turnips* (*Altica nemorum*).. It is sometimes called the black jack and sometimes the flea or black fly. **1860** CURTIS *Farm Insects* List Engravings, *Altica nemorum*, the Turnip fly or flea. *Altica concinna*, the Hop flea or beetle.

3. Applied, with defining word prefixed, to small crustaceans which leap like a flea: see SAND-FLEA, WATER-FLEA. *beach-flea* (U.S.) = *sand-flea.*

1888 *Riverside Nat. Hist.* II. 76 The 'beach-fleas' so common on the sandy beaches.

4. a. phr. *a flea in one's ear*: said of a stinging or mortifying reproof, rebuff, or repulse, which sends one away discomfited: chiefly in phr. *to go* (*send*, etc.) *away with a flea in one's ear.* †**b.** Formerly also = anything that surprises or alarms, matter for disquietude or agitation of spirit: after F. (*avoir* or *mettre*) *la puce à l'oreille.*

c **1430** *Pilgr. Lyf. Manhode* II. xxxix. (1869) 91 And manye oothere grete wundres [ye haue seyd] whiche ben fleen in myne eres [F. *puces es oreilles*]. **1577** tr. *De L'Isle's Legendarie* B vj b, Sending them away with fleas in their eares, vtterly disapointed of their purpose. **1577** DEE *Relat. Spir.* I. (1659) 423 [He] at length had such his answer, that he is gone to Rome with a flea in his eare, that disquieteth him. *a* **1625** BEAUM. & FL. *Love's Cure* III. iii, He went away with a flea in's ear, Like a poor cur. **1659** B. HARRIS *Parival's Iron Age* I. I. ix. 18 The Protestants.. have made Leagues to uphold themselves; and put a flea into the ear of France. **1712** ARBUTHNOT *John Bull* III. vi, We being stronger than they, sent them away with a flea in their ear. **1741** RICHARDSON *Pamela* I. xxii. 56, I was hurrying out with a Flea in my Ear, as the Saying is. **1838** C. K. SHARPE *Corr.* (1888) II. 510 [He] came off unvictorious with a flea in his ear. **1887** RIDER HAGGARD *Jess* xiii, I sent him off with a flea in his ear, I can tell you.

5. *Comb.*, as †*flea-catcher, -feeder, -skinning*; *flea-brown, -coloured* adjs.

1794 G. ADAMS *Nat. & Exp. Philos.* I. 538 The peroxide [of lead] may be precipitated of a brilliant *flea-brown colour. **1806** *Spirit Pub. Jrnls.* (1807) X. 221 Bug Destroyer to His Majesty, and *Flea Catcher in general. **1776** ANSTEY *Election Ball* (1808) 230 A new-fashioned *flea-coloured coat. **1603** BRETON *Wit's Priv. Wealth* (1639) B b, They that love their beds are great *Flea-feeders. **1860** SALA *Lady Chesterf.* v. 81 This.. pebble-peeling *flea-skinning principle.

6. a. Special comb.: **flea-bag** (*slang*), a bed; also, a soldier's sleeping-bag; also applied to a shabby building, place, etc.; **flea-beetle**, a small leaping beetle of the genus *Haltica*, the species of which ravage hops, grape-vines, turnips, and other plants; **flea-bug** *U.S.* = *flea-beetle*; **flea circus** orig. *U.S.*, a show of performing fleas; **flea collar**, a collar (for a dog or cat) impregnated with a substance that kills fleas; **flea-hopper** *U.S.*, any of various jumping species of bugs of the family Miridæ, esp. (*a*) the garden flea-hopper (genus *Halticus*), a small black bug that sucks sap from garden plants; (*b*) the cotton flea-hopper, *Psallus seriatus*, a small green sucking insect that attacks cotton; **flea-louse**, a leaping plant-louse of the family *Psyllidæ*; **flea-lugged** (*Sc.*), unsettled, harebrained (Jam.); **flea market** *colloq.* [cf. Fr. *marché aux puces*, in Paris], term applied jocularly to a street market; **flea pit** *colloq.*, an allegedly verminous place of public assembly, e.g. a cinema; **flea-powder**, a remedy against fleas; †**flea-trap**, in quot. an opprobrious epithet applied to a person.

1839 LEVER *H. Lorrequer* xxxix, I think the gentleman would be better if he went off to his *flea-bag himself. **1915** H. ROSHER *In R.N.A.S.* (1916) 41, I am going to invest in a Jaeger flea bag. **1930** R. PERTWEE *Pursuit* I. xi. 58 He snaked his feet into his flea bag. **1932** D. RUNYON *Guys & Dolls* v. 94 His room on the top of an old fleabag in Eighth Avenue. **1958** E. DUNDY *Dud Avocado* III. iv. 249 God, how I hated Paris! Paris was one big flea-bag. **1961** *John o' London's* 14 Sept. 296/4 Drab three-storey buildings that now serve as fleabag hotels. **1842** JOHNSON *Farmer's Encycl., Fly in Turnips* (*Altica nemorum*).. a species of *flea-beetle which attacks the turnip crop. **1877** *Rep. Vermont Board Agric.* IV. 158 It is very lively in its movements, and is sometimes called *flea-bug. **1928** *Amer. Mag.* May 67/1 Professor Heckler's Trained Fleas... Tiny golden carts rattled merrily across the strip of white blotting paper. The first act in the *flea circus was under way. **1932** *Screenland* Apr. 89/1 Shooting galleries, the flea circus, and ending the spree by having their pictures made. **1936** AUDEN & ISHERWOOD *Ascent of F6* (1937) II. iii, When I was at school, I tried to keep a flea circus. **1950** *Oxf. Jun. Encycl.* IX. 369/1 'Flea Circuses', which are still to be seen at fairs—the main attraction usually being a chariot race between fleas attached by wire to tiny aluminium chariots. **1953** Flea circus [see *Cheap Jack* s.v. CHEAP *a.* D]. **1953** *Pets & Pet Shop Management* Dec. 5/2 A new type of flea preventive is now being introduced—the Ace *Flea Collar for dogs... A Flea Collar for cats is said to be under way.., the collar now available is for dogs only. **1975** SCHNECK & NORRIS *Cat Care* §65 During the flea season.. the cat should wear a flea collar (available from pet shops). **1902** L. O. HOWARD *Insect Bk.* 301 *Halticus uhleri* Giard, known as the 'garden *flea-hopper', is common in gardens and is injurious to flowers and vegetables. **1920** *Jrnl. Agric. Res.* 15 Mar. 485 The cotton flea hopper, *Psallus seriatus* Reuter,.. has only recently become important as a cotton pest. **1926** *Jrnl. Econ. Ent.* Feb. 106 The natural hosts of the cotton flea-hopper are various species of Croton. **1959** SOUTHWOOD & LESTON *Land & Water Bugs Brit. Isles* ix. 244 The North American garden fleahopper *Halticus bracteatus* (Say), is often a serious pest of clovers or lucerne. **1724** RAMSAY *Tea-t. Misc.* (1733) I. 90 Wi *flae-lugged sharny-fac'd Lawrie. **1823** GALT *Entail* III. 70 Yon flea-luggit thing, Jamie. **1922** G. S. DOUGHERTY *In Europe* 130 It is called the '*Flea' Market because there are so many second hand articles sold of all kinds that they are believed to gather fleas. **1960** N. MITFORD *Don't tell Alfred* xx. 213 He must learn to clean and crate and pack the object as well as to discover it and

purchase it and resell it. From flea-market to Jayne Wrightsman's boudoir. **1970** *New Yorker* 15 Aug. 62/2 The preservation of the open-air flea market. **1937** *Daily Herald* 3 Feb. 12/4 Even the patrons of these palaces [*sc.* cinemas] referred to them as '*flea-pits'. *Ibid.*, A peaked service cap with the name of the flea pit written on the band in gold braid. **1971** *Ink* 12 June 14/4 He went to a fleapit cinema. **1699** *Poor Robin* A iv, Since Scoggin found out his *Flea-Powder. *a* **1616** BEAUM. & FL. *Bonduca* II. iii, 1 *Daughter.* Are they not our tormentors? *Car.* Tormentors? *flea-traps! **1681** OTWAY *Soldier's Fort.* v. i, Do you long to be ferking of Man's Flesh, Madam Flea-trap?

b. In various plant-names, as **flea-dock**, the butter-bur (*Petasites vulgaris*); **flea-grass, flea-sedge**, *Carex pulicaris*; †**flea-seed**, *Plantago Psyllium*; **flea-weed**, local name for *Galium verum*; **flea-wood** (see quot.).

1597 GERARDE *Herbal* App., *Fleadocke is *Petasites.* **1847** HALLIWELL, *Flea-dock*, the herb butter-burr. **1670** RAY *Catal. Plant. Angl.* 148 *Flea-grass. This was so denominated by Mr. Goodyer, because the seeds..do in shape and colour somewhat resemble Fleas. **1820** GREEN *Univ. Herbal* I. 252 *Carex Pulicaris* *Flea Sedge, or Flea Grass. **1562** TURNER *Herbal* II. 105 b, Psillium..may be well called *fleasede or fleawurt because yᵉ sede is very lyke vnto a fle. **1892** *Northumbld. Gloss.*, *Flea-wood*, the bog myrtle or sweet gale, *Myrica Gale.* A housewife's cure for fleas.

flea (fliː), *v.* Also *dial.* **fleck.** [f. prec. sb.] *trans.* To rid of fleas, remove fleas from.

a **1610** HEALEY *Theophrastus* (1636) 79 He sweepes the house and fleas the beds himselfe. **1700** CONGREVE *Way of World* IV. ix, Go flea dogs, and read romances! **1884** *Chesh. Gloss.* s.v. *Fleck*, 'Her father had gone up to fleck the bed.' **1920** T. S. ELIOT *Ara vos Prec* 15 Who clipped the lion's wings And flea'd his rump and pared his claws? **1930** E. WAUGH *Labels* 100 A pet monkey..fleaed its rump on the terrace. **1932** AUDEN *Orators* I. 21 The dog fleaing itself in the hot dust. **1937** *Sunday Times* 18 Apr. 8/4 She had the kind of vitality which is ready to start an open-air meeting at Hampstead with an audience of a policeman and a dog fleaing itself.

flea, obs. f. FLAY.

'flea-bane. [See BANE.] A name given to various plants: *esp.* **a.** A book-name for the genus *Inula* (or *Pulicaria*), esp. *Inula dysenterica* and *I. Pulicaria.*

1548 TURNER *Names of Herbes* (E.D.S.) 30 Coniza maye be called in englishe Flebayne. **1563** HYLL *Art Garden.* (1593) 35 The Gnats also be..chased away with the decoction of the herbe named Flebane, sprinckled on the beds. **1597** GERARDE *Herbal* II. cxxiv. 391 *Conyza* from time to time hath been called in English Fleabane. **1640** PARKINSON *Theat. Bot.* XIV. xv. 1232 *Conyza palustris major*, the greater Marsh or water Fleabane. **1794** MARTYN *Rousseau's Bot.* xxvi. 394 The Flea-banes middle (*dysenterica*) and less (*pulicaria*) are of this genus (*Inula*). **1854** S. THOMSON *Wild Fl.* III. (ed. 4) 243 The flea-banes (*Pulicaria*) noted for smoking off fleas.

b. A book-name for the genus *Erigeron*, esp. *E. acre* (called also ***blue fleabane***).

1813 SIR H. DAVY *Agric. Chem.* (1814) 364 The fleabane of Canada has only lately been found in Europe. **1820** GREEN *Univ. Herbal* I. 513 English botanists have named it [*Erigeron acre*] blue-flowered or purple flea bane. **1831** J. DAVIES *Manual Mat. Med.* 220 Philadelphia Flea Bane. Scabious. *Erigeron philadelphicum.* **1863** BARING-GOULD *Iceland* 190 The drier ground was starred with white and pink Alpine flea-bane (*Erigeron Alp.*).

c. Applied to *Plantago Psyllium* (from the appearance of the seed).

1578 LYTE *Dodoens* I. lxx. 104 This herbe is called in.. Latine *Psyllium* and *Herba Pulicaris*..in English Fleawurte and Fleabane. **1597** [see FLEAWORT].

†**flea-bit**, *a.* *rare* exc. *U.S.* = FLEA-BITTEN 2.

1696 *Lond. Gaz.* No. 3194/4 A flea-bit Mare. **1830** O. W. HOLMES *Poems* (1852) 181 The small-voiced pug-dog welcomes in the sun, And flea-bit mongrels..give answer all. **1917** E. POUND *Lustra* 195 Sheep! jabbing the wool upon their flea-bit backs.

'flea-bite. [f. FLEA *sb.* + BITE *sb.*]

1. The bite of a flea; the red spot caused by it.

1570 LEVINS *Manip.* 149/27 A Fleabit, *morsus culicis.* **1789** W. BUCHAN *Dom. Med.* (1790) 215 The small pox..begin to appear..At first they very nearly resemble flea-bites. **1801** SOUTHEY in Robberds *Mem. W. Taylor* I. 378, I am used to flea-bites, and never scratch a pimple to a sore. **1884** *Syd. Soc. Lex.* s.v., Flea-bites have been mistaken for..the rash of typhoid, and other appearances.

2. *fig.* Anything that causes only slight pain; a trifling inconvenience or discomfort; a hurt, loss, accident, etc. of very small consequence or importance; a mere trifle. (Cf. FLEA-BITING 2.)

[*c* **1440** HYLTON *Scala Perf.* (W. de W. 1494) I. xxxviii, The felynge of thyse temptacions fyleth the soule nomore than yf they herde an hounde berke, or a flee byte.] **1582** BRETON *Floorish vpon Fancie* (Grosart) 25/1 When all these pangues are but Flea-bytes to mine. **1630** J. TAYLOR (Water P.) *Brood Cormorants, Cutpurse* 12 If they doe lose by Pirates, tempests, rocks, 'Tis but a Fleabite to their wealthy stockes. *a* **1656** BP. HALL *Rem. Wks.* (1660) 2 The greatest bodily sicknesses were but Flea-bites to those scorpions. **1779** G. KEATE *Sketches Nat.* I. 64 The labours of Hercules were a flea-bite to it. **1862** SALA *Seven Sons* I. vii. 169 The money was a mere flea-bite, a miserable fifty.

3. A small reddish spot on a horse or dog, resembling the mark made by the bite of a flea. Cf. FLEA-BITTEN 2.

1681 *Lond. Gaz.* No. 1608/4 A middle-size White Spaniel Dog..with two reddish Ears full of little Fleabits. **1690** *Ibid.* No. 2571/4 A dapple-grey Mare..with red Flea-bites about her Head and Neck.

4. *attrib.*

1605 BRETON *Honour of Valour* xiii, When mortal wounds doe shew but flea-bite smarts.

Hence **flea-bite** *v. trans.* 'To cover with bites of fleas' (Hyde Clarke 1855). **flea-biter**, one who bites like a flea; in quot. *fig.*

1629 GAULE *Holy Madn.* 324 Wearish Wretch; so like a Flea-biter hee lookes.

†**'flea-biting**, *vbl. sb. Obs.* [f. as prec. + BITING *vbl. sb.*]

1. The biting of a flea; the spot caused by this.

1552 HULOET, Fleabitinge, *pulicina signa.* **1582** M. PHILIPS in Hakluyt *Voy.* (1600) III. 475 They..leaue behinde them a red spot somewhat bigger than a flea-biting. **1676** WISEMAN *Surgery, Lues Ven.* i. 5 The attendance of a Cancre is commonly a breaking out all over the body, like a fleabiting.

2. *fig.* A small hurt, damage, etc.; = FLEA-BITE 2.

1553 T. WILSON *Rhet.* 69 b, Al these are but fle bitynges in respect and comparison of that which I shal now showe you. **1593** NASHE *Christ's T.* 86 b, If wee..make a sport and flea-byting of his fearefull visitation. **1621** BURTON *Anat. Mel.* I. i. I. v. (1676) 8 That which is but a fleabiting to one causeth insufferable torment to another. **1711** R. COOPER *Country-Man's Proposal* (1712) 13 I will shew you that would be but a Flea-biting to the Nation.

3. = FLEA-BITE 3.

1598 FLORIO, *Liardo*, a horse marked with red or tannie spots or fleabitings.

flea-bitten, *a.* [f. as prec. + BITTEN *ppl. a.*]

1. Bitten by (or infested with) fleas.

1621 BURTON *Anat. Mel.* I. iii. III. (1676) 127 Redness of the face and itching, as if they were flea-bitten, or stung with Pis-mires. *c* **1626** *Dick of Devon* v. i. in Bullen *O. Pl.* (1883) II. 87 In my fleabitten Trundle bed. **1751** SMOLLETT *Per. Pic.* (1779) IV. lxxxvii. 36 You old flinty-faced, flea-bitten scrub. **1823** *Blackw. Mag.* XIV. 508 Snug and flea-bitten, in their own personal garrets.

2. Of the colour of a horse, dog, etc.: Having bay or sorrel spots or streaks, upon a lighter ground.

1570 *Will of Bartillmew* (Somerset Ho.), Geldinge flea-bitten colour. **1577** B. GOOGE *Heresbach's Husb.* II. (1586) 116 b, The fleabitten horse prooveth alwaies good in travell. **1685** *Lond. Gaz.* No. 2032/4 A Lusty strong well spread gray Gelding..beginning to be Flea-bitten about the Head and Neck. **1846** E. JESSE *Anecd. Dogs* 282 We now see them [pointers]..of a flea-bitten blue or grey. **1863** *Times* 21 May, A tall and very powerful flea-bitten gray.

3. Also *fig.*

1917 D. H. LAWRENCE *Look!* 89 As to whether you've found a fortune In me, or a flea-bitten fate. **1971** *Guardian* 3 July 11/1 Gwalior town itself is quite as seedy and flea-bitten as any other central Indian town.

Hence **'flea-bittenness.**

1837 *Fraser's Mag.* XVI. 532 The mares'-nests of its discovery were amply suited by the flea-bittenness of its style.

fleach, dial. var. of FLITCH.

flead: see FLEED.

fleagm, obs. form of PHLEGM.

†**fleak**, *sb.* [? A use of *fleak*, FLAKE *sb.*² 3.] A term of reproach used to a woman.

1636 DAVENANT *Witts* III. i, Scirvie Fleake! 'tis not for naught You boyle Eggs in your Gruell.

fleak(e, obs. or dial. form of FLAKE.

fleale, obs. form of FLAIL.

fleam, obs. and dial. var. of PHLEGM.

fleam (fliːm), *sb.*¹ Forms: 6 fleume, 7 flame, fleame, fleme, (8 fleem, flegme), 8, 9 *dial.* flem, (fleyam, vlem), 7– fleam. Also 8 phleam, 9 phleme. See also FLUE. [a. OF. *flieme* (Fr. *flamme*) = Pr. *flecme*, Sp. *fleme*, It. *fiama*, repr. med.L. *fletoma* (Wr.-Wülck. 400), *flēdomum* (Leiden Gloss. OET. 114), from late Lat. *flebotomum*, ad. Gr. φλεβοτόμον: see PHLEBOTOMY. From the med.L. forms were adopted OE. *flýtme*, OHG. *flietuma*, *fliedema* (MHG. *fliedeme*, *vliete(n*, *vliedene*, mod.Ger. *fliete*); cf. also MDu. *vlîme*, *vlieme*. The mod.F. use = sense 2 below.]

1. A surgical instrument for letting blood or for lancing the gums; a lancet. In Great Britain *Obs.* or *arch.*; the U.S. dicts. *c* 1897 treated it as still current for a gum-lancet.

[*a* **1000** *Aldhelm Gl.* in *Zeitschr. f. d. A.* IX. 453 *Flebotomo*, blodsexe *vel* flytman.] **1552** HULOET, Bloude lettynge..the instrumente wherwyth bloude is letten, called a fleume. **1611** COTGR., *Deschaussoir*, a Fleame; the toole wherewith Barbers diuide the gum from the tooth which they would draw out. **1688** R. HOLME *Armoury* III. xiii. 481/2 An.. Ancient Flegme, or Fleame. **1712** E. COOKE *Voy. S. Sea* 76 A little Fleem made of a Flint. **1790** J. WOLCOTT (P. Pindar) *Ep. to J. Bruce* 230 Wks. 1812 II. 166 Nor Scotch'd with fleams a sceptered Lady's hide. **1859** THACKERAY *Virgin.* xl, Get a fleam, Gumbo, and bleed him. **1865** TYLOR *Early Hist. Man.* viii. 219 The sharp stone with which the native phleme used to be armed. **1874** KNIGHT *Dict. Mech.* I. 881/2 *Fleam*, a gum-lancet.

2. A kind of lancet used for bleeding horses.

1616 SURFL. & MARKH. *Country Farme* I. xxviii. 123 The Farrier..must neuer be vnprouided..with tooles..as fleame to let bloud with [etc.]. **1748** tr. *Vegetius' Distemp. Horses* 46 You shall Strike into it a Fleam made of hard steel. **1769** *De Foe's Tour Gt. Brit.* III. 104 The principal Manufactures here [in Sheffield] are..Razors, Lancets, Phleams [etc.]. **1847** YOUATT *Horse* xi. 362 Bleeding..is performed with a fleam or a lancet.

3. *Comb.*, as ***fleam-shaped*** adj. Also **fleam-stick** (see quot. 1842); **fleam-tooth**, a fleam-shaped tooth of a saw.

1856 KANE *Arct. Expl.* I. xvii. 206 The *fleam-shaped tips of their lances were of unmistakable steel. **1842** AKERMAN *Gloss. Wilts*, **Flem-stick*, the small staff used to strike the flem into the vein. **1874** KNIGHT *Dict. Mech.* I. 881/2 **Fleam-tooth.*

fleam (fliːm) *sb.*² In 4–7 **fleme**, 4, 9 *dial.* **flem.** [App. a var. of FLUME (ME. *flum*), which has both senses; but the phonology is obscure; there may be some confusion with a Teut. word, OE. **fléam*:—**flaumo-* f. root of OHG. *flawen* to wash.]

†**1.** A stream, river. Chiefly in ***flem Jordan*** = L. *flumen Jordanis.* *Obs.*

c **1300** *St. Margarete* lviii, Ant let the folewen in holi fonston, Ase ihū christ was ymself y the flem iurdan. **13..** *E.E. Allit. P.* C. 309 þe grete flem of þy flod folded me vmbe. *c* **1430** *Syr Tryam.* 142 To fleme Jordon and to Bedlem. **1516** in *Myrr. our Ladye* (1873) p. l, The water of fleme Iordane was stopped ayenst the natural course.

2. An artificial channel, watercourse, mill-stream. Now only *dial.*

1523 FITZHERB. *Surv.* xi. (1539) 55 By a mylne fleme made with mens hande. **1686** PLOT *Staffordsh.* 356 Cutting a fleme or main carriage 18 foot broad. **1879** MISS JACKSON *Shropsh. Wordbk.*, *Flem*, a mill-stream i.e. the channel of water from the main-stream to the mill. **1881** *Leicester Gloss.*, *Fleam*, a 'mill-tail', the stream that flows from a watermill after having turned the wheel.

fleam (fliːm), *v.*¹ *Obs.* exc. *dial.* [f. prec. sb.²] *intr.* To flow, stream. Also, *transf.* to drift *away.*

c **1400** *Destr. Troy* xxv. 10004 Blode flemyt o fer in flattes aboute. *c* **1465** *Eng. Chron.* 92 His trew blode has flemed bothe be swerde and exyle. **1863** R. BUCHANAN *Undertones* 120 As the vapours fleam'd away, behold! I saw..A nymph.

†**fleam**, *v.*² *Obs. rare.* In 5 flym. [ad. OF. *flime-r*, *flieme-r*, f. *flieme* FLEAM *sb.*¹] *trans.* To cut with a lancet.

1483 CAXTON *Gold. Leg.* 434 b/1 Anone the same lytel whelke beganne to blede as one had flymed hit.

fleam, var. of FLEME *sb.* and *v.*

fleamy, obs. and dial. var. of PHLEGMY.

flean, obs. inf. and pa. pple. of FLAY.

flear, fleash, obs. ff. of FLEER, FLESH.

fleasome ('fliːsəm), *a. joc.* (in association with GLEESOME *a.*). [f. FLEA *sb.* + -SOME¹.] Full of fleas.

1853 J. PAYN *Poems* 79 (*On our Dog Jock*) A gleesome fleasome affectionate beast. **1886** KIPLING *Departmental Ditties* 38 Gentle *Bandar*, an Inscrutable Decree, Makes thee a gleesome fleasome Thou, and me a wretched Me. **1924** *Blackw. Mag.* Feb. 220/1 The still fleasome but now gleesome puppy.

fleat, var. of FLEET *v.*

fleawort ('fliːwɜːt). [OE. *fléawyrt*, f. FLEA sb. + -WORT.] A name given to various plants.

Amongst the plants that have been so called from their supposed virtues in destroying fleas are *Inula Conyza* and some species of *Cineraria* and *Erigeron.* Turner and many subsequent writers apply the name to *Plantago Psyllium*, the Lat. and Gr. names of which (*Pulicaria*, ψύλλιον) refer to the resemblance of the seeds to fleas.

c **1000** *Ags. Voc.* in Wr.-Wülcker 273/24 *Parirus* [? *papirus*], fleawyrt. **1548** TURNER *Names of Herbes* (1881) 65 It [Psyllium] may be called in English Flewurte. *c* **1550** LLOYD *Treas. Health* (1585) M vij b, A bath made of the decoction of flewort taketh away all goutes. **1597** GERARDE *Herbal* II. cxxiv. § 1. 390 *Conyza maior*, Great Fleawoort. **1601** HOLLAND *Pliny* II. 239 Psyllium, Fleawort, is good for the vlcers thereof. **1756** SIR J. HILL *Herbal* 159 Fleawort, *Psyllium*, the flower is composed of four small oval petals. **1820** GREEN *Univ. Herbal* I. 304 *Cineraria Integrifolia*, Mountain Cineraria or Fleawort. *Ibid.* I. 512 The old name of this plant [*Erigeron Viscosum*] is..great fleawort. **1825** J. E. SMITH *Eng. Flora* III. 443 *Cineraria palustris*, Marsh Flea-wort.

attrib. **1600** SURFLET *Countrie Farme* I. xii. 61 Putting thereto the muscilage of fleawort seede.

fleay ('fliːɪ), *a.* Also 7 fleaie, 9 *Sc.* flaeie, flechy. [f. FLEA *sb.* + -Y¹.] Full of fleas.

1611 COTGR., *Pulcier*, fleaie, of a flea, full of fleas. **1870** JAS. ORTON *Andes & Amazons* II. xxxvi. 487 After stopping at fleay Tiberias.

flebergebet, -gebit, -gibet, obs. forms of FLIBBERTIGIBBET *sb.*

†**'flebile**, *a. Obs.* [a. OF. *flebile*, ad. L. *flēbil-is* that is to be wept for, also tearful, plaintive: see FEEBLE.] Of style: Doleful, mournful, plaintive. Also *absol.*

a **1734** NORTH *Exam.* I. ii. § 37 (1740) 49 A flebile Style this upon a mournful Occasion. *Ibid.* II. v. § 94 (1740) 374 The more calm and moderate Style, not without a Tinct of the Flebile.

† **'fleble**, *v. Obs.* [var. of FEEBLE *v.*; cf. the OF. forms *fleible*, etc. of *feible* FEEBLE *a.*] *intr.* To grow weak.

c **1350** *Will. Palerne* 2660 Here men flebled fast & faileden of here mete.

flebotomy: see PHLE-.

† **flecche**, *v. Obs.* Forms: 4 flecchi, flechchi, (? *misprint*) fleeche, 3–5 flecche. See also FLINCH *v.* [ad. OF. *flechir* (mod.F. *fléchir* to bend), also *flechier* to bend, turn aside, flinch; of obscure etymology; connexion of some kind with L. *flectĕre* to bend, is commonly assumed, but the supposition has not been shown to be in accord with phonological laws.]

1. *intr.* To bend, flinch, give way; to waver, vacillate. *Obs.*

c **1300** *Beket* 951 Therfor he moste him wel bithenche and ne flecchi noȝt. *c* **1325** *Poem Times Edw. II*, 452 in *Pol. Songs* (Camden) 344 Hadde the clergie..noht flecched aboute nother hider ne thidere. **1340** *Ayenb.* 253 þet þou ne flechchi uor to leue to guod red. *c* **1350** *Will. Palerne* 763 He set his siȝt sadli to þat windowe euene, boute flecchinge or feyntise. **1387** TREVISA *Higden* (Rolls) V. 411 For þe staat of holy chirche in Engelond..schulde nouȝt fleeche [L. *vacillaret*]. **13..** *Minor Poems fr. Vernon MS.* 616/171 þe deuel.. flecchep fro godes spous. *a* **1420** HOCCLEVE *De Reg. Princ.* xli, Some man..Dampnable errour holdith, and can not flecche for no counseille ne rede.

2. *trans.* To turn out, drive away.

Perh. another word; cf. O.E. *flecȝan* (once) to drive away. *c* **1340** *Cursor M.* 994 (Trin.) Out is he put Adam þe wrecched Fro paradis fouly flecched.

flecchere, -our, var. of FLETCHER, *Obs.*

flech(e, var. of FLEECH.

‖ **flèche** (flɛʃ). Also 8 fletch. [Fr. *flèche*, primarily 'arrow'.]

1. *Fortif.* = ARROW 8.

1710 *Lond. Gaz.* No. 4755/2 We..attacked the two fleches. **1761** *Lond. Mag.* XXX. 460 Several small fletches that were thrown up along the front. **1804** WELLINGTON in Gurw. *Disp.*, *To Major Graham* 29 Mar., The best thing to do would be..to knock down that bad work in front of the gateway, and to make a good modern *flèche* in lieu thereof. **1827** SOUTHEY *Hist. Penins. War* II. 107 The suburb beyond the Ebro was defended by redoubts and flèches. **1851** J. S. MACAULAY *Field Fortif.* 101 The flèche..differs from a redan only in having no ditch.

2. *Arch.* A slender spire, *esp.* one placed over the intersection of the nave and transept.

1848 B. WEBB *Continent. Ecclesiol.* 160 A very elegant tall flèche for the sanct-bell. **1886** MRS. CADDY *Jeanne D'Arc* 83 Its high-pitched lead roof with many pinnacles and flèches.

3. One of the twenty-four points on a backgammon board; = POINT *sb.*[1] B. 3 g.

1863 G. F. PARDON *Hoyle's Games Modernized* 331 Backgammon is played..on a board divided into sections, and figured with twenty-four points or flèches, of different colours, placed alternately. **1867** *Bohn's Hand-bk. Games* 381 Backgammon is played..upon a quadrangular..board, on which are figured 24 points or *flèches*, of two colours, placed alternately. *Ibid.*, The points or flèches are numbered from 1 to 12 of each colour [*sc.* in a diagram]. **1897** R. F. FOSTER *Compl. Hoyle* 617 *Flèches*, the points upon a backgammon board.

4. *Fencing.* (See quot. 1961.)

1928 *Daily Tel.* 17 July 17/7 With the épée Walter met his most dangerous opponent..in the first round, and beat him with a rapid flèche attack on the body. **1930** *Morning Post* 14 July 15 In the concluding series Armstrong's pace embarrassed Mowlam into an ill-timed flèche. **1961** F. C. AVIS *Sportsman's Gloss.* 192/2 *Flèche*,..used in fencing to mean a running attack.

flecher, var. of FLETCHER, *Obs.*

fléchette (fle'ʃɛt). [Fr., dim. of *flèche* arrow.] A missile resembling a dart, dropped from aircraft. (*Disused.*)

1915 F. A. TALBOT *Aëroplanes & Dirigibles* 141 Another missile which has been introduced by the French airmen.. is the steel arrow, or 'fléchette' as it is called. **1915** GRAHAME-WHITE & HARPER *Aircraft in Gt. War* 247 The first use of 'flechettes' in the war was at the beginning of September.

fleck (flɛk), *sb.*[1] [Not found before 16th c.; though the related FLECK *v.* and FLECKED *ppl. a.* occur earlier; adopted from or cognate with ON. *flekkr* (Sw. *fläck*, MDa. *flække*), corresponding to MDu. *vlecke* fem. (Du. *vlek* fem., neut.), MLG. *vlecke* fem., *vlek* neut., OHG. *flec(ch*, *fleccho*, blow, mark of a blow, speck, spot, place (MHG. *vlec*, *vlecke*, mod.Ger. *fleck*, *flecken* speck, spot, hamlet):—OTeut. **flekko-*, *-kon-*. Cf. the derivative Ger. *flicken* to patch.

The ulterior affinities are somewhat obscure; some of the senses strongly suggest connexion with FLAKE *sb.*[1] and the OAryan root *plăg-* or *plāk-* to strike; but the root vowels seem to belong to different ablaut-series. Further, the sense 'patch', found in continental Teut., points to connexion with ON. *flík* patch, rag, the form of which implies *ī* (neither *e* nor *a*) as the root vowel. Possibly two distinct OTeut. words have coalesced.]

1. A mark in the skin; a blemish, freckle, spot; also, a sore or abrasion of the skin.

1598 FLORIO, *Varo*, a fleck, or freckle in ones face. **1601** HOLLAND *Pliny* II. 377 The greace of a swan is commended .. for to cleanse the skin of the face from all flecks and freckles. **1695** KENNETT *Par. Antiq.* s.v. *Flesche-Axe*, Fleck is..a sore in the flesh, from whence the skin is rubbed off. **1866** SWINBURNE *Poems & Ball.*, *Laus Ven.* 4 Her neck.. wears yet a purple speck..fairer for a fleck. **1889** *N.W. Linc. Gloss.* s.v., Them harvist-bugs hes maade big flecks cum oot all oher my airms.

fig. **1850** TENNYSON *In Mem.* lii, Fret not..That life is dash'd with flecks of sin. **1879** HESBA STRETTON *Needle's Eye* I. 196 There was not a fleck upon his reputation.

b. A patch, spot, or streak of colour, light, etc.

1804 NELSON in Nicolas *Disp.* (1846) VI. 120 They have been badly painted..as it is all run in flecks. **1849** LONGF. *Building Ship* 89 Shadows..broken by many a sunny fleck. **1863** *Macm. Mag.* Jan. 172 The universal blue from Earth to Heaven was filled with flecks of fire. **1863** BARING-GOULD *Iceland* 208 The red gable of Hlitharfyall..with a fleck of white on its apex. **1889** *N.W. Linc. Gloss.* s.v. *Fleck*, Black marble wi' yalla flecks in it.

2. A small particle; a flake, speck.

1750 WALPOLE in *Phil. Trans.* XLVII. 47, I never perceived, that I voided..any flecks of a stone. **1841–4** EMERSON *Ess. Circles* Wks. (Bohn) I. 125 As we see flecks and scraps of snow left in cold dells..in June. **1861** SIR T. MARTIN *Catullus, Lam. Ariadne* 202 And flecks of wool stick to their wither'd lips. **1875** H. C. WOOD *Therap.* (1879) 92 A fleck of rust on a bright surface of steel will steadily enlarge.

† **fleck**, *sb.*[2] *Obs. rare*⁻¹. [Origin unknown; the meaning is clear from Isidore *Etym.* XII. xxix, where the L. word is *vulpes*.] A fox.

1567 MAPLET *Gr. Forest* 86 The Fleck..saith Isidore..is naturally subtile, and hath many fetches to deceiue one.

† **fleck**, *sb.*[3] *Obs.* exc. *dial.* Also flick. = FLARE *sb.*[2]

1575 TURBERVILE *Falconrie* 364 Barrowes flicke or larde. **1591** PERCYVALL *Sp. Dict.*, *Enxúndia*, fat, flicke, sewet. **1630** J. TAYLOR (Water P.) *Gt. Eater Kent* Wks. I. 144/2 What say you to the Leafe or Flecke of a Brawne new kild..to be eaten hot out of the Bores belly raw? **1881** *I. of Wight Gloss.*, *Flick* or *Vlick*, the lard of the inside of a pig. **1883** *Hampsh. Gloss.*, *Fleck*, the fat of a pig before it is boiled down into lard.

† **fleck**, ? *proper name. Obs.* Used in proverbial phrase ***fleck and his make***, a contemptuous designation for a man and his paramour.

1529 MORE *Dyaloge* I. xvii. 22 b/1, I tell you nothyng now of..many a flekke and hys make that maketh theyre metyng at these holsum hallows. **1532** —— *Confut. Barnes* VIII. Wks. 780/2 What would the general counsail..haue sayed vnto that frere, and what vnto flecke hys make? **1546** J. HEYWOOD *Prov.* (1867) 57, I did..heere, How flek and his make, vse their secrete hauntyng.

fleck (flɛk), *v.*[1] Also 5 flek(k)e, 7 flecke. [f. FLECK *sb.*[1]; cf. ON. *flekka* (perh. the source), Da. *flække*, Sw. *fläcka*, Ger. *flecken*.] *trans.* To spot, streak or stripe; to dapple, variegate.

c **1430** LYDG. *Min. Poems* (Percy Soc.) 199 The whyght flekkyd with the brown. **1576** TURBERV. *Venerie* 10 Their legges streaked and flecked with redde and blacke. **1641** G. SANDYS *Paraphr. Song Sol.* IV. i, Vntill the Morning fleck the sky. **1697** DRYDEN *Virg. Past.* II. 55 Two Kids Both fleck'd with white. **1798** COLERIDGE *Anc. Mar.* iii. viii, The sun was flecked with bars. **1830** TENNYSON *Poems, Love & Sorrow*, The first green leaf With which the fearful springtide flecks the lea. **1872** BLACK *Adv. Phaeton* x. 139 Overhead the still blue is scarcely flecked by a cloud. **1873** SYMONDS *Grk. Poets* viii. 250 The feathers of the soaring bird were flecked with gold and crimson grain.

b. To force in flecks or patches *into. rare.*

1886 STEVENSON *Dr. Jekyll* viii, The wind..flecked the blood into the face.

Hence **'flecking** *vbl. sb.* Also *concr.*

1892 *Daily News* 3 May 2/4 In other materials this flecking with irregularly recurrent hints of colour is confined to stripes. **1893** *Westm. Gaz.* 9 Feb. 6/1 White spots and fleckings in the waistcoats.

† **fleck**, *v.*[2] *Obs.* exc. *dial.* [? var. of FLAG *v.*] *intr.* To fly low; to flit, flutter about.

1565 GOLDING *Ovid's Met.* VIII. (1593) 189 [She] flecketh neere the ground. **1621** MARKHAM *Prev. Hunger* (1655) 200 The old Cocke, the old Henne, and all their poots..flecke and runne together. **1621** G. SANDYS *Ovid's Met.* VIII. (1626) 156 They..fleck as lowe as earth, And lay their eggs in tufts. **1884** *Chesh. Gloss.*, *Fleck*, to fly.

transf. and *fig.* **1627–77** FELTHAM *Resolves* II. xiv. 188 He flecks from one Egg to another, so hatcheth nothing. **1648** EARL WESTMORELAND *Otia Sacra* (1879) 154 The Relict.. Doth voluntary fleck into Deaths armes. **1652** SHIRLEY *Sisters* Prol. 11 The Town will still be flecking, and a Play.. will starve the second day.

fleck (flɛk), *v.*[3] *dial.* and *U.S.* var. FLICK *v.*[2]

† **flecked**, *a. Her. Obs.* [? Misspelling of FLECT.] Arched, bent.

1661 MORGAN *Sph. Gentry* I. ii. 13 The Flecked, The Nubile, are of the nature of the Air. **1678–1706** PHILLIPS, *Flecked*, a term in Heraldry, arched like the Firmament. *fig.* **1661** MORGAN *Sph. Gentry* I. vii. 101 Devide not thy Coat among the deadly sins by..the Flecked and Waved line of pride.

flecked (flɛkt), *ppl. a.* [f. FLECK *sb.*[1] or *v.*[1] + -ED[1] or [2].] Having or marked with flecks; occas. preceded by some defining word as *foam-*, *pearl-flecked*, for which see those words.

1. Of animals, their feathers, skins, etc.: Dappled, pied, spotted.

1377 LANGL. *P. Pl.* B. XI. 321 Foules, With flekked fetheres. *c* **1386** CHAUCER *Merch. T.* 604 He was..ful of Iargon, as a flekked pye. **1548** *Will of R. North or Keling* (Somerset Ho.), Flecked cowe. **1601** HOLLAND *Pliny* II. 403 They [sheep] will proue flecked and of diuers colours. **1786** CULLEY *Live Stock* (ed. 4) 41 The generality are red and white mixed or what the breeders call flecked. **1881** *Leicestersh. Gloss.*, *Flecked*, spotted, mottled, speckled.

b. Of a person: Marked with spots; freckled.

1868 GEO. ELIOT *Sp. Gipsy* 54 Pepita, fair yet flecked.

† **c.** Of wood-work: Grained; marked. *Obs.*

1664 EVELYN *Sylva* viii. 27 The firme and close Timber ..[of the Wall-nut tree] is admirable for fleck'd and chambletted works. **1670** *Ibid.* xxvii. (ed. 2) 134 Curiously polish'd and fleck'd cups and boxes.

† **2.** Of persons, their faces or cheeks: Marked with patches of red; flushed. *Obs.*

1544 PHAER *Regim. Lyfe* (1560) Uvj, The face red in colour & flecked. *a* **1577** GASCOIGNE *Herbs* Wks. (1587) 103 His flecked cheekes Now chery red, now pale and green as leekes. **1621** BURTON *Anat. Mel.* II. v. I. vi. (1651) 396 If they drink a cup of wine or strong drink, they are as red and fleet ..as if they had been at a Majors feast. **1693** CONGREVE *Juvenal* xi. 317 What tho thy Wife..come reeking home, Fleck'd in her Face, and with disorder'd Hair.

3. Of darkness: Dappled with bright spots. Of the sky: Dappled with clouds. Of clouds: Cast like flecks over the sky; in quot. *fig.*

1597 SHAKS. *Rom. & Jul.* II. iii. 3 (Qo. 1) Flecked darkenes like a drunkard reeles, From forth daies path. *a* **1649** DRUMM. OF HAWTH. *Hist. Jas. V* Wks. (1711) 106 Many were groping through these flecked clouds of ignorance. **1810** SCOTT *Lady of L.* III. ii, Invisible in flecked sky, The lark sent down her revelry. **1866** T. EDMONDSTON *Shetl. & Ork. Dial.*, *Flecked*, applied to the bottom of the sea when it has bunches of seaweed growing upon it.

† **'flecken**, *v. Obs.* exc. *dial.* [f. FLECK *sb.* + -EN[5].] **a.** *intr.* To take a fleck or shade of colour; to colour, turn. **b.** *trans.* To mark with flecks. Hence **'fleckened** *ppl. a.*, flecked, grained, marked.

1641 BEST *Farm. Bks.* (Surtees) 50 When they [Oates] once beginne to shoote they will streightway after beginne to flecken. **1881** *Leicestersh. Gloss.*, You nivver see a prittier fleckened bit o' mapple-wood.

flecker, obs. form of FLICKER *v.*

flecker ('flɛkə(r)), *v.* [f. FLECK *v.* + -ER[5].] *trans.* **a.** To mark with flecks; to dapple. **b.** To scatter like flecks or flakes. (See next).

1828 STERLING *Ess. & Tales* (1848) II. 4 The wide and gleaming river..fleckered with a myriad of keels.

fleckered ('flɛkəd), *a.* Also 5 *Sc.* flekerit. [f. prec. + -ED[1].]

1. Marked with flecks or spots; dappled, streaked, variegated.

c **1450** *Golagros & Gaw.* 475 Ferly fayr wes the feild, flekerit and faw. **1792** R. CUMBERLAND *Calvary* v. 495 Morning..crimson'd all the flecker'd East. **1823** MOOR *Suff. Words*, *Flecker'd*, variegated, of two or more colours, descriptive of domestic poultry. **1861** GEO. ELIOT *Silas M.* 300 Silas and Eppie were seated..in the fleckered shade of the ash tree.

2. Scattered in flecks or patches.

1823 JOANNA BAILLIE *Poems* 292 Like spots of flecker'd snow. **1851** HELPS *Comp. Solit.* ii. (1874) 57 They arrange themselves like those fleckered clouds.

† **'flecket.** *Obs. rare*⁻¹. [f. FLECK *sb.* + -ET[1].] A small fleck or spot.

1684 *Lond. Gaz.* No. 1898/4 He is of a Liver colour with white Fleckets.

fleckled ('flɛk(ə)ld), *a.* [f. **fleckle*, dim. of FLECK *sb.* + -ED[2].] Marked with little flecks or spots; dappled; also of a person: freckled.

1592 SHAKS. *Rom. & Jul.* II. iii. 3 Fleckled darknesse like a drunkard reeles, From forth daies path. **1700** *Acc. Doctr. & Disc. R. Davis* 26 A woman..fleckled in her face. **1892** *Daily News* 17 Sept. 3/2 Tree trunks all fleckled and dappled by patches of quivering sunshine.

fleckless ('flɛklɪs), *a.* [f. FLECK *sb.*[1] + -LESS.] Without a fleck or spot; without blemish.

1847 TENNYSON *Princ.* II. 274, I fear My conscience will not count me fleckless. **1874** LISLE CARR *Jud. Gwynne* I. iv. 115, A..fleckless sky over-head.

Hence **'flecklessly** *adv.*

1891 MISS S. J. DUNCAN *Soc. Departure* 285 The passage was flecklessly whitewashed.

'flecky, *a.* [f. FLECK *sb.*[1] + -Y[1].] Full of flecks, i.e. spots or streaks; also, having a wavy appearance. (But in quot. 1694 *flecky* may be a variant of FLICKY.) Hence **'fleckiness**, the condition of being flecky.

1694 *Lond. Gaz.* No. 3004/4 One brown bay Mare, with a Flecky Tail. **1833** J. HOLLAND *Manuf. Metal* II. 69 A singular grain of fleckiness always observable on the surface [of real Damascus blades].

flecnode ('flɛknəʊd). *Math.* [f. *flec-* root of L. *flectĕre* to bend + *nod-us* knot, NODE.] (See quot.) Hence **'flecnodal** *a.*, pertaining to a flecnode, as ***flecnodal curve***.

1873 SALMON *Higher Plane Curves* vi. (1879) 217 Such a node may be considered as the union of an ordinary node with a point of inflexion..and the node may be termed a flecnode.

† **flect**, *v. Obs. rare.* In 6 flecte. [ad. L. *flect-ĕre* to bend.] *trans.* To bend, turn. *lit.* and *fig.*

1548 HALL *Chron.*, *Edw. IV*, 206 b, He with..faire wordes, did receive and intertain, to the intent to flecte and allure the hartes of other men. **1578** BANISTER *Hist. Man* I.

33 Those Muscles, by whose benefite..the thigh is outward flected.

†**flect**, *sb. Obs.* [ad. Ger. *fleck* hamlet, 'spot': see FLECK.] A hamlet, small village.
1637 R. MONRO *Exped.* II. 89 On this River of the Maine where the Townes and pleasant Flects lie by the water.. Their Dorpes and Flects walled about.

flect (flɛkt), *a. Her.* [Short for FLECTED.] = FLECTED *a.*
1830 [see FLECTED]. **1889** in ELVIN *Dict. Her.*

flectant (ˈflɛktænt), *a. Her.* = next.
1830 [see FLECTED]. **1889** in ELVIN *Dict. Her.*

flected (ˈflɛktɪd), *a. Her.* [f. FLECT *v.* + -ED¹.] Bent, bowed. ***flected and reflected*** (see quot. 1889).
1688 R. HOLME *Armoury* II. xviii. 466/1 Two Arms flected, or bowed. *Ibid.* II. xix. 474/1 Two Heart Leaves Pendant, their Stalks contrary flected and reflected. **1830** ROBSON *Brit. Herald* Gloss., *Flect, Flectant,* and *Flected,* any thing bowed or bent. **1889** ELVIN *Dict. Her., Flected and reflected,* bowed or bent in contrary directions or turns, in a serpentine form, like the letter S.

†ˈ**flectible**, *a. Obs. rare*⁻¹. [f. FLECT *v.* + -IBLE.] Capable of being bent.
1705 C. PURSHALL *Mech. Macrocosm* 227 Bodies that are ..Flectible and Yielding.

flection, -al, -less: see FLEX-.

flector (ˈflɛktə(r), -ɔː(r)). *Anat.* [f. FLECT *v.* + -OR.] = FLEXOR.
1666 J. SMITH *Old Age* (ed. 2) 65 The chief flector the Psoas. **1836** I. TAYLOR *Phys. Th. Another Life* xvii. 241 The muscles..of the arm..consisting only of flectors and deflectors.

fled (flɛd), *ppl. a.* [pa. pple. of FLEE *v.*] **1.** In senses of the vb.
1621 G. SANDYS *Ovid's Met.* II. 711 Fled Soules thou shalt restore to their aboads. *a* **1709** J. NIMMO *Narrative* (1889) 51 Ane honest fled Scotsman's hous. **1822** BYRON *Werner* III. iv. 100 The Fled Hungarian. **1884** TENNYSON *Becket* I. i, Bar the bird From following the fled summer.
2. Of pottery: liable to crack at a late stage of manufacture by a too rapid change of temperature during or after a firing. ***fled ware***, ware cracked after the bisque firing.
1904 in GOODCHILD & TWENEY *Technol. & Sci. Dict.*

†**flede**, *v. Obs.* [repr. OE. **flēdan*:—**flōdjan*, f. *flōd* FLOOD: cf. MDu. *vloeden*, MHG. *vluoten* (mod.Ger. *fluten*), ON. *flœða* (Sw. *flöda*).] *intr.* To flow.
c **1175** *Cott. Hom.* 209 Þine vif wunden, and þe eadi flod þet of ham fledde. *c* **1205** LAY. 22019 Whænne þa sæ vledeð. *a* **1225** *St. Marh.* 9 Þu steorest te sea stream þet it fleden ne mot fir þan þu markedest.

†**fledge**, *sb.*¹ *Obs.* Also 6 flege. App. the designation of some textile material. Also *attrib.*
1542 *Act 33 Hen. VIII*, c. 2 in *Stat. Irel.* (1621) 185 Hydes, fells, checkers, fleges, yarne, linnen, cloth, wooll and flockes. **1579** *Richmond Wills* (Surtees) 287 Vj cotton blankets, ij fledg blankets, ij caddow blankets.

fledge (flɛdʒ), *sb.*² [f. FLEDGE *v.* (sense 4).] A feather- or down-like covering.
1915 D. H. LAWRENCE *Rainbow* iv. 102 He now had a thick fledge on his upper lip, a black, finely-shaped line. **1923** —— *Birds, Beasts & Flowers* 44 The deep, soft fledge of Sicilian winter-green.

†**fledge**, *a. Obs.* exc. *dial.* Forms: 4–7 flegge, 6 fledg, 5–6 flygge, 6 flydge, 6–7 flidge, flig(ge, fleg, 6– fledge. [OE. **flycȝe* (in Kentish form **flecȝe*), not found exc. in the compound *unfliȝȝe*, rendering L. *inplumes* in *Avianus Glosses a* 1100 (see Napier in *Academy* 2 June 1894); corresponding to MDu. *vlugge* (Du. *vlug*), MHG. *vlücke*, OHG. *flucchi* (Ger. *flügge*, a LG. form for HG. *flücke*):—WGer. **fluggjo-*, f. **flug-* weak root of **fleugan* to FLY.]
1. Of young birds (rarely of the wings): Fit to fly; having the feathers fully developed, fledged.
1398 TREVISA *Barth. De P.R.* XII. iii. (1495) 411 They take fro them meete whan they ben flegge and rype. **14..** *Piers of Fullham* in Hartshorne *Metr. Rom.* 124 Which causeth them to be taake or they be flegge. **1526** *Pilgr. Perf.* (W. de W. 1531) 133 Byrdes full flygge. **1593** PEELE *Chron. Edw. I* 180 If his wings grow flig, they may be clipt. **1606** SYLVESTER *Du Bartas* II. iv. II. *Magnificence* 698 Some douny-clad, some (fledger) take a twig To pearch-upon. **1692** R. L'ESTRANGE *Fables* lxxii. 71 The Birds were not as yet Fledge enough to Shift for Themselves. **1706** in PHILLIPS (ed. Kersey), *Fledge* or *Fledged.* **1820** WILBRAHAM *Chesh. Gloss., Flig* or *Fligge.*
transf. and *fig.* **1566** DRANT *Horace* To Rdr. 2 Natheles such vices as were then flydge..he assaileth fearcely. **1623** T. SCOT *Highw. God* 64 As soone as he is fligge, and comes fresh out of the Vniuersitie. **1633** G. HERBERT *Temple, Death* iii, The shells of fledge souls left behinde. **1662** TUKE *Adv. 5 Hours* III. i, Your noble Love has Wings, And's ever Fledge.
2. Furnished for flight. Const. *with*. Also *fig.*
1631 MILTON in Birch *Life* Wks. 1738 I. 4 All the fond hopes, which forward Youth and Vanitie are fledge with. **1667** —— *P.L.* III. 627 His shoulders, fledge with wings. **1806** J. GRAHAME *Birds Scotl.* I. 4 Like an arrow-fledge he darts. **1814** CARY *Dante, Hell* XIII. 16 The huge belly fledge with wings.
3. *fig.* All in a flutter, high-spirited.
1461 M. PASTON in *Paston Lett.* I. 544 He and alle his olde felaweship..arn ryght flygge and mery. **1642** ROGERS *Naaman* 350 Haue not your recoveries made you more fledge and sawcy with God?
Hence †**fledgeness**. *Obs.*
c **1440** *Promp. Parv.* 167/1 Flygnesse, *maturitas.* **1530** PALSGR. 221/1 Flyggenesse of byrdes, *plumeuseté.*

fledge (flɛdʒ), *v.* Also 6–7 flidge, 9 *dial.* fleg, flig. [f. prec.]
1. *intr.* Of a young bird: To acquire feathers large enough for flight; to become fully plumed. Also *fig.*
1566 PAINTER *Pal. Pleas.* I. 72 When the wheate was ready to be ripped her yonge began to fledge. **1637** *Greene's Theeves falling out* Pref., In Westminster..doe they every day build their nests, every houre flidge. **1865** SWINBURNE *Poems & Ballads, Felise* 69 Birds quick to fledge and fly at call Are quick to fall.
2. *trans.* To bring up (a young bird) until its feathers are grown and it is able to fly. Also *fig.*
1589 *Pappe w. Hatchet* C b, They [the Martins] both breed in Churches, and hauing fledgde their young ones, leaue nothing behind them but durt. **1596** SHAKS. *Merch. V.* III. i. 32 Shylocke for his own part knew the bird was fledg'd. **1623** WEBSTER *Duchess Malfy* III. v, Your wiser buntings, Now they are fledg'd, are gone. **1659** D. PELL *Impr. Sea* Ded. A v b, This Book..was hatched and flidged in one of your ships. **1760** FAWKES *Anacreon* xxxiii. 15 Some, quite fledg'd and fully grown, Nurse the Younglings as their own.
3. To provide or furnish with feathers or plumage; to 'wing' for flight; also, to deck or adorn with feathers.
1614 C. BROOKE *Eglogues, To W. Browne* 21 Whose tender Pinions, scarcely fledg'd in show, Could make his way with whitest Swans in Poe. **1725** POPE *Odyss.* I. 125 The sandals of celestial mould, Fledged with ambrosial plumes. **1784** COWPER *Task* IV. 214 The world's time..has his pinions fledg'd With motley plumes.
fig. **1847** TENNYSON *Princ.* IV. 19 Lightlier move The minutes fledged with music.
4. To cover as with feathers or down; also, to form a feather-like covering for.
1597 SHAKS. *2 Hen. IV*, I. ii. 23 The Iuuenall (the Prince your Master) whose Chin is not yet fledg'd. **1773** *Poetry* in *Ann. Reg.* 235 Then talks of sport; how many wild ducks seen! What flocks of widgeon too hath fledg'd the green! **1784** COWPER *Task* v. 26 The bents And coarser grass..now ..fledged with icy feathers, nod superb. **1814** CARY *Dante, Paradise* IX. 96 The unripen'd down That fledged my cheek. **1820** KEATS *Ode to Psyche* 55 Far, far around shall those dark-cluster'd trees Fledge the wild-ridged mountains steep by steep. **1888** LOWELL *Recall* in *Heartsease & Rue* 91 Though snowflakes fledge the summer's nest.
5. To fit (an arrow) with a feather; to feather. Cf. FLETCH *v.*
1796 MORSE *Amer. Geog.* II. 596 Eagles' feathers to fledge arrows with. **1808** MOORE *Corruption* v. 96 Like a young eagle, who has lent his plume To fledge the shaft by which he meets his doom. **1871** ROSSETTI *Poems, Troy Town* xiii, Cupid took another dart, Fledged it for another heart.
Hence **fledged** *ppl. a., lit.* and *fig.*; sometimes in combinations as ***full-, half-, new-fledged***; ˈ**fledging** *vbl. sb.* and *ppl. a.*
1579 E. K. in *Spenser's Sheph. Cal.* Ep. Ded., You may perceiue he was..full fledged. *a* **1616** BEAUM. & FL. *Laws Candy* I. ii, That yong-man, who was not fledg'd nor skil'd In Martiall play. **1659** D. PELL *Impr. Sea* 98 This may pull down..your flidged plumes. **1774** WHITE in *Phil. Trans.* LXV. 268, I..found they had made very little progress towards a fledged state. **1806** J. GRAHAME *Birds Scotl.* 35 The parent's partial eye Shall view the fledging wing. **1833** WHEWELL *Astron. & Gen. Physics* i. 32 The..hatching, fledging, and flight of birds. **1865** SWINBURNE *Poems & Ball., Love at Sea* 17 Our seamen are fledged Loves. **1887** *Sat. Rev.* 12 Nov. 661 Such denials merely serve to mark the fact that thought is already fluttering, though it is not yet full fledged.

fledgeless (ˈflɛdʒlɪs), *a.* [f. FLEDGE *a.* + -LESS.] Unfledged.
1769 J. GERRARD in *Monthly Rev.* XLII. 185 For me his hand the fledgeless dove betray'd. **1806** J. GRAHAME *Birds Scotl.* 602 In seven days more expect the fledgeless young. **1859** LD. LYTTON *Wanderer* (ed. 2) 97 The fledgeless nurslings of Regret.

fledgeling, fledgling (ˈflɛdʒlɪŋ), *sb.* and *a.* [f. as prec. + -LING.]
1. A young bird just fledged.
1846 WORCESTER (citing *Monthly Rev.*). **1847** LONGF. *Ev.* I. i. 119 That wondrous stone which the swallow Brings from the shore of the sea to restore the sight of its fledglings. **1879** JEFFERIES *Wild Life in S. Co.* 239 The tiny fledglings swim at once if alarmed.
2. *fig.*; *esp.* A raw and inexperienced person, one just starting on his career.
1856 WHYTE MELVILLE *Kate Cov.* iii, Young fledglings pining madly for their enslavers. **1866** *Reader* 10 Feb. 148/2 The few ideas they have were hatched only yesterday; but the beauty and vitality of the fledglings they are so proud of, bear no proportion to their youth. **1877** OWEN *Wellesley's Desp.* p. xlvi, On emerging from the College, the fledgling should (as at Woolwich) take rank according to the impartial award of the educational authorities.
3. *attrib.* (*appositive*) or as *adj.*
1830 TENNYSON *Claribel* 17 The fledgling [*later edd.* callow] throstle lispeth. **1876** E. C. STEDMAN *Vict. Poets* xi. §3. 390 The style of fledgling poets. **1888** *Pall Mall G.* 3 Nov. 10/1 The little fledgling party which had hardly broken its shell..the Liberal Unionists.

fledgy (ˈflɛdʒɪ), *a.* [f. as prec. + -Y¹.]
†**1. a.** Of wings: Furnished with feathers, feathered. **b.** Of young bees: Ready to fly. *Obs.*
1583 STANYHURST *Aeneis* I. (Arb.) 27 Hee flitters swiftly with wynges ful fledgye beplumed. *Ibid.* 31 They [bees] do foorth carry theyre yoong swarme fledggie to gathring.
2. Covered with feathers, feathery.
1818 KEATS *Staffa* 41 Where a fledgy sea-bird choir Soars for ever! **1819** —— *Otho* II. ii. 102 The swan, soft leaning on her fledgy breast.

†ˈ**fledwite**. *Obs.* An alleged term of OE. law (see quot.).
[The explanation below is prob. a mere conjecture due to association with mod.Eng. *fled.* It has been suggested that the word may have arisen from a misreading of *ferdwite* (see FERD *sb.*¹).]
1579 *Rastall's Termes of the Lawe* 93 *Fledwite*, that is to bee quyte from amercements when an outlawed fugitive cometh to the Kinges peace. [Hence in many later Dicts.]

†**flee**, *sb. Obs.* [f. next vb.] Flight.
c **1560** A. SCOTT *Poems* (E.E.T.S.) 10 And all the feild cryd, fy on him! Sa cowartly tuk the fle for fer.

flee (fliː), *v.* Pa. t. and pa. pple. fled (flɛd). Forms: see below. [A Com. Teut. originally str. vb.: OE. *flēon* (*flēah, fluȝon, floȝen*) = OFris. *flīa*, OS. *fliohan* (MDu. *vlîen*, pa. t. *vlô*, later MDu. and mod.Du. *vlieden*, pa. t. *vlood*, pa. pple. *vloden*), OHG. *fliohan* (MHG. *vliehen*, mod.Ger. *fliehen*), ON. *flýa, flýja* (with *-jo-* suffix in pres. stem), str. pa. t. *fló, flugom*, more commonly inflected weak, pa. t. *flýða*, pa. pple. *flýiðr* (Sw. *fly*, pa. t. *flydde*, Da. *flye*, pa. t. *flyede*), Goth. *þliuhan*:—OTeut. **þleuhan* (inflected *þlauh, þlugum, þlogono-*). The root (pre-Teut. **tleuk-*) has not been found outside Teut. As the original initial *þ* has become *f* in all the Teut. langs. exc. Gothic, those forms of the vb. which according to Verner's law change *h* into *g* came to coincide with the corresponding forms of **fleugan* to FLY; hence in all these langs. the two vbs. have been more or less confused together.
In OE. the vb. was, so far as is known, always strong. The str. pa. t. and pa. pple. survived in occasional use down to the 15th c.; but in the 13th c. the weak pa. t. *fledde*, pa. pple. *fled(d* began to be used, and soon became more common than the earlier forms. Their origin is obscure: normally, they would imply an inf. *flede(n*, and one instance of *flede* inf., with the sense 'to flee', has been found in 15th c.; but little stress can be laid on this, on account of the late date, and the possibility that the form may have been invented by the writer for the sake of rime, on the analogy of the pa. t. *fledde* (for which Caxton has *fleded*). Identification with FLEDE to flow or flood seems impossible on account of the difference in sense. Some have compared *flede* with the Du. form *vlieden*; but the Du. practice of inserting a euphonic *d* in vbs. with roots ending in *h* (as in *belijden, wijden, vleiden*) is peculiar to that lang. (first appearing in late MDu.), and has no parallel in Eng.; further, the Du. vb., in spite of its alteration in form, is still conjugated strong; hence it seems probable that the resemblance between the Du. and Eng. forms is purely accidental. The resemblance of ME. *fledde* to Sw. *flydde* may possibly be more significant. In MSw. those vbs. which, in consequence of contraction, had their present stems ending in a long vowel, formed their past tense in *-dde* for the earlier *-þe*; the change, according to Noreen, dates, so far as the spelling is concerned, from about 1350; it may however have occurred much earlier in some East Scandinavian dialect. The supposition that ME. *fledde* may be of Scandinavian origin is supported by the fact that the earliest examples are chiefly from writers whose dialect is strongly marked by Scandinavian influence; on the other hand, it occurs as early as 1340 in the Kentish dialect of the Ayenbite.
The confusion between the vbs. *flee* and *fly* occurs already in OE. In northern dialects the form *flee* is the normal phonetic descendant both of OE. *flēon* to flee and of *flēoȝan* to fly. In mod.Eng. the association of the two vbs. has the curious result that the ordinary prose equivalent of L. *fugere* is *fly* with pa. t. and pa. pple. *fled* (the forms *flew, flown* have only the sense of L. *volare*), while *flee* has become archaic, being confined to more or less rhetorical or poetic diction. Even *fly* and *fled*, indeed, now belong rather to literary than to colloquial English: expressions like 'run away' being substituted in familiar speech.]
A. Forms.
1. Present stem. *α.* 1 *Inf.* (**ȝe**)**flēon**, **flīon**, (*north.* **flēa**); *pr. t. 1st pers.* **flēo**, (*Mercian* **flēom**), *2nd pers.* **flīhst**, *3rd pers.* **flīhð**, (*north.* **flīð**, **flēð**), *pl.* **flēoð**, (*north.* **flēað**); 3 *inf.* **flæen**, *pr. t. 3rd pers.* **flihþ**, **flicþ**, **fliȝt**, *imper.* **fli(h**, **fliȝ**, *south.* **vlih**, 3–4 **fléo-n**, (3 **flo**), **flei**, 3–5 **flee-n**, 4 *south.* **vle-n**, **vlee-n**, 3–6 **fle**, 6 **fley**, 3– **flee**.
c **888** K. ÆLFRED *Boeth.* xxxiii. §2 He..flihþ ða wædle. *a* **1000** *Boeth. Metr.* vii. 30 (Gr.) He sceal swiðe flion þisse woruld wlite. *a* **1225** *Ancr. R.* 162 Arseni, flih men. *Ibid.* 208 Vlih þer urommard, er þu beo iattred. *a* **1240** *Ureisun* in *Cott. Hom.* 203 Hwuder schal ich fleon hwon þe [etc.]. *a* **1250** *Owl & Night.* 176 Wel fiȝt that wel fliȝt. *a* **1300** *Cursor M.* 2818 (Cott.) Þe angls badd loth do him flee. *Ibid.* 4310 (Cott.) Þou do þe stallworthli to flei. *c* **1330** R. BRUNNE *Chron.* (1810) 39 Þei went egrely, & did þo kynges fle. **1340** *Ayenb.* 41 Oþer huanne me draȝþ þo out þet vleþ to holy cherche. *c* **1374** CHAUCER *Compl. Mars* 105 He..bad her fleen, lest Phebus her espye. *c* **1380** *Sir Ferumb.* 3901 He not wyder flene. **1393** LANGL. *P. Pl.* C. XXI. 346 Ich rede we fleo ..faste alle hennes. **1556** *Aurelio & Isab.* F v, It that you fley be the daye, you showe to desire it the nighte.
β. 5 **flede.**
c **1450** MYRC 1374 Wythowte werke or fleschly dede þy chastyte from þe doth flede.

2. Past tense. *α.* 1 **fléah, fléh,** 3 **fleah, flæh,** (*south.* 2 **vleh,** 4 **vleaȝ**), 4–5 **flagh(e,** (also rarely as *pl.*), 3–4 **flei, fleih, fleiȝ, fleigh** (rarely as *pl.*), **fley, fleȝ(h.**

c825 *Vesp. Psalter* cxiii [cxiv]. 3 Sae ȝeseah & fleh. a1000 *Boeth. Metr.* i. 20 (Gr.) Fleah casere mid þam æðelingum ut on Crecas. c1200 ORMIN 823 He flæh till wesste fra þe follc. a1225 *Leg. Kath.* 16 Wes Maxence ouercumen & fleah into Alixandre. a1225 *Ancr. R.* 160 He fleih his holi kun icoren of ure Louerde. c1250 *Gen. & Ex.* 430 Caym fro him [adam] fleȝ. 1340 *Ayenb.* 129 Þet hette agar þo hi uleaȝ uram hare lheuedi. c1340 *Cursor M.* 7592 (Trin.) Mony fley wiþ deþes wounde. 1382 WYCLIF *Ps.* cxiv. 3 The se saȝ and fleiȝ. 1387 TREVISA *Higden* (Rolls) I. 189 Þat prince sauede men þat fleigh to hym. a1400 *Octouian* 1149 Florentyn yaf hym swych a dent As he forth fleȝh, That [etc.]. c1400 *Destr. Troy* 6001 As þai flaghe in the filde.

β. 3 **fleu,** 3, 6 **flew(e,** 4 **flewgh.** [Common to this vb. with FLY; ? influenced by str. pa. t. of FLOW.]

1297 R. GLOUC. (1724) 18 Þe kyng with a fewe men hymself flew at the laste. *Ibid.* (1724) 258 He fleu [*printed* flen] wyþ muche wo. c1380 WYCLIF *Sel. Wks.* III. 412 Seynt Poule..flewȝh suche beggynge.

γ. plural. 1 **fluȝon, -un,** 2–4 **fluȝen,** (3 **fluȝhen,** *Orm.* **-enn, fluhen, flue**), 3 **flu(w)en,** *south.* **vluwen,** 3–5 **floȝen, floghen** (*hence* 5 **flogh** as *sing.*), 4 **floun,** 3–5 **flowe(n.**

c950 *Lindisf. Gosp.* Matt. xxvi. 56 Alle..ȝefluȝun. c1000 *Ags. Gosp.* Mark v. 14 Soþlice þa ðe hi heoldon fluȝon. c1200 ORMIN 893 Baþe fluȝhenn fra þe folc. c1205 LAY. 1845 Þa eatendes fluȝen [c1275 flowen]. c1225 *Ancr. R.* 106 His deore diciples fluen alle vrom him. *Ibid.* 392 His deciples..vluwen alle urom him. a1225 *Juliana* 52 Þat ter fluhen monie. c1250 *Gen. & Ex.* 861 On of hem, ðe floȝen a-wei. c1300 *Beket* 2144 His disciples flowe anon. 1382 WYCLIF *Isa.* xxxiii. 3 Fro the vois of the aungil floun puples. c1400 *Destr. Troy* 4732 The ffrigies floghen. *Ibid.* 11969 Ecuba..egerly flogh. c1425 *Seven Sag.* (P.) 822 As thay flowen toward the felde.

δ. 4–7 **fledd(e,** 4 *south.* **vledde,** 5 **fleded, fleede,** 6–7 **flet,** 7 *Sc.* **flaid,** 4– **fled.** *plural.* 3–4 ? **flededen,** 4–5 **fleden, fledden, -on.**

c1300 *K. Alis.* 2441 So heo ferden..And flodeden [? *read* flededen.] c1330 R. BRUNNE *Chron.* (1810) 88 Malcolme..fled for ferd. 1340 *Ayenb.* 206 He him uledde ase wys and hise uorlet. c1384 CHAUCER *H. Fame* I. 179 Iulo And eke askanius also ffleden. ? a1400 *Morte Arth.* 1431 Thane þe Bretons..fleede to þe foreste. c1400 *Destr. Troy* 1349 The Troiens..ffleddon in fere and þe filde leuyt. 1490 CAXTON *Eneydos* xxxi. 118 Dedalus fleded to Thetys for fere of the kynge Mynos of Crete. 1497 WRIOTHESLEY *Chron.* (1875) I. 3 Perkin Werbeck..fledd to Bowdley St. Marie. 1647 H. MORE *Song of Soul* I. III. lxvii, But what could well be sav'd to Simon flet.

3. *Pa. pple.* *α.* 1 **floȝen,** 2 **fluȝen,** 3 **ifloȝen,** *south.* **ivlowen,** 3–4 **yflowe(n,** 4–5 **flowe(n, -yn, iflowen,** (4 **flawen**).

c1205 LAY. 4764 Brennes wes awæi ifloȝen. a1225 *Ancr. R.* 168 Ȝe habbeð þene world ivlowen. 1297 R. GLOUC. (1724) 311 Of scaped he was & yflowe. c1320 *Cast. Love* 470 For-þi Ich am of londe i-flowen. 13.. *E.E. Allit. P.* C. 214 He watz flawen fro þe face of frelych dryȝtyn. c1340 *Cursor M.* 16743 (Laud) His appostils wern flowyn hym fro. ? a1400 *Arthur* 579 Mordred was flow. c1420 *Chron. Vilod.* 387 He nold not for þe crosse han flowe.

β. 4 **fledd, flede, -eed,** 5 **fledde,** 4– **fled.**

a1300 *Cursor M.* 17554 (Cott.) He..es vnto þe felles fledd. c1325 *Coer de L.* 2301 The emperour was fled away. c1380 WYCLIF *Wks.* (1880) 290 Fleed of men as disceyt of þe fend. ? a1400 *Morte Arth.* 2488 The dyre feemene are flede. c1440 *York Myst.* xxii. 188 Þis fende þat nowe is fledde. 1539 BIBLE (Great) *Acts* xvi. 27 Supposing that the presoners had bene fledde [1557 (Geneva), 1582 (Rheims) and 1611: fled].

B. Significations.

I. *intr.*

1. To run away from or as from danger; to take flight; to try to escape or seek safety by flight. Also, ***to flee away, out,*** and ***to flee for it.***

c825 [see A. 2]. c1000 *Ags. Gosp.* Matt. viii. 33 Ða hyrdas witodlice fluȝon. c1205 LAY. 5564, & swiðe monie þer fluwen & ferden to Rome. a1300 *Cursor M.* 2614 (Cott.) Sco was fain to fle a-wai. c1325 *Coer de L.* 2303 Flowen was that fals coward. c1340 *Cursor M.* 9213 (Trin.) Þe kyng fley out bi nyȝt. c1400 *Destr. Troy* 10077 The grekes flowen in fere & the feld leuyt. 1489 CAXTON *Faytes of A.* II. xxxvii. 155 They shall make as they dide flee. 1559 *Mirr. Mag., Mortimers* xx, For they flewe, I feared them the lesse. 1605 CAMDEN *Rem.* 216 One that had in his forehead a bounch of flesh, fledde away a great pase. 1709 STEELE *Tatler* No. 80 ¶3 My Confusion at last was so great, that without speaking, or being spoken to, I fled for it. 1847 JAMES *J. Marston Hall* ix, Some of them fled as fast as their legs would carry them. 1884 F. M. CRAWFORD *Rom. Singer* (1886) I. 90 A hundred women will tell you that they are ready to flee with you.

Proverb. a1250 *Owl & Night.* 176 'Wel fiȝt that wel fliȝt', seith the wise. 13.. *Prov. Hendyng* ix. in *Rel. Ant.* I. 111 'Wel fytht, that wel flyth' Quoth Hendyng.

b. Const. †*forth of, from, out of.*

c825 *Vesp. Psalter* lxvii[i]. 2 Feond his..flen from onsiene his. 1154 *O.E. Chron.* an. 1137 Sume fluȝen ut of lande. c1250 *Gen. & Ex.* 430 Caym fro him fleȝ. c1450 MYRC 1681 Ȝef he haue grace in herte to se How aungelus..From hym faste flen. 1550 CROWLEY *Last Trump* 29 When Elias fled away from Ahab. 1564 HAWARD *Eutropius* VII. 69 He [Nero] fled forthe of his palace. 1597 SHAKS. *2 Hen. IV*, II. iv. 248 The Rogue fled from me like Quick-siluer. 1611 BIBLE *Job* xx. 24 He shall flee from the iron weapon.

c. Conjugated with *be.*

c1250 *Gen. & Ex.* 3396 Ȝet sal ðe kinde of amalech Ben al fled dun in deades wrech. c1320 *Sir Tristr.* 2223 Tristrem was fled oway. 1480 CAXTON *Chron. Eng.* ccxxxii. 250 Whan pyers was fledde oute of spayn. 1535 STEWART *Cron. Scot.* II. 479 And mony freik out of the feild wes fled. 1671 H. M. tr. *Colloq. Erasmus* 543 He won by an assault a strong defenced Castle, whereinto the Lady great with child was fled.

†**d.** *refl.*; also quasi-*trans.*, ***to flee one's way.***

c1205 LAY. 16078 Ah flih flih þinne wæi. a1300 *Cursor M.* 5680 (Gött.) Moyses..fledd him into madian. c1340 *Ibid.* 7676 (Fairf.) He him fled to samuel. 1470–85 MALORY *Arthur* VIII. vii, Syr Marhaus..fledde his waye. 1535 COVERDALE *Judith* xv. 3 The Assirians..kept not them selues together, but fled their waye.

2. To hasten for safety or protection (*to*, †*on*).

Beowulf 764 (Gr.) Mynte se mæra, hwær he meahte..on weȝ þanon fleon on fenhopu. c825 *Vesp. Psalter* cxlii[i]. 9 Dryhten to ðe ic ȝefleh. c1205 LAY. 16080 Fleo þider þe þu fleo. a1300 *Cursor M.* 6675 (Cott.) Þof he to mine auter flei. 1393 LANGL. *P. Pl.* C. III. 220 Falsnesse for fere þo flegh to þe freres. 1535 COVERDALE *Zech.* xiv. 5 Ye shall fle vnto the valley of my hilles. 1678 TILLOTSON *Sermons* (ed. 3) I. 64 We can have..none in all the world to fle [ed. 1671 p. 64 flye] to, but Him. 1718 PRIOR *Solomon* III. 482 In vain for Life He to the Altar fled. 1849 MACAULAY *Hist. Eng.* I. 176 The Presbyterians..fled to the foot of the throne. 1858 M. PORTEOUS *Souter Johnny* 30 Or silly mortal blinks an ee To muckle Jupiter ye'll flee.

†**b.** *refl. Obs.*

a1300 *Cursor M.* 5680 (Gött.) Moises..fled him into madian. 1600 HOLLAND *Livy* XLIV. vi. (1609) 1174b, The king..fled himselfe to Pydna. 1610 HEALEY *St. Aug. Citie of God* (1620) 143 But those..either fled themselves into such places..or else were brought thither.

†**c.** To have recourse *to. Obs.*

1563 *Homilies* II. *Agst. Idolatry* III. (1859) 220 They..flee to this aunswere, that [etc.]. 1660 F. BROOKE tr. *Le Blanc's Trav.* 270 The servants and others fled to their swords.

3. To withdraw hastily, take oneself off, go away. Also with *away*. Const. *from, out of*. Also, To swerve *from* (a commandment); to keep free *from* (a practice).

c825 *Vesp. Psalter* cxxxviii[i]. 7 From onsiene ðinre hwider fleom ic. c1200 *Trin. Coll. Hom.* 127 On his ȝuweðe he fleh fro folke to weste. 1297 R. GLOUC. (1724) 501 Clerkes & lewede, that fram thi seruise wolle fle. c1340 *Cursor M.* 9816 (Trin.) His hert auȝte bettur breke in þre þen fro his biddyngis to fle. c1385 CHAUCER *L.G.W.* 1307 *Dido*, Ye wol nat fro your wyf thus foule fleene! c1440 *Partonope* 4881 Thys made me vtterly fro yow fleene. 1611 BIBLE *Gen.* xxxi. 27 Wherefore didst thou flee away secretly? 1717 POPE *Eloisa* 131 From the false world in early youth they fled. 1820 KEATS *St. Agnes* xlii, These lovers fled away into the storm. 1848 MRS. JAMESON *Sacr. & Leg. Art* (1850) 193 Two years later he fled from society.

†**b.** To depart this life.

a1300 *Cursor M.* 20260 (Gött.) Hu sal we liue quen þu will fle?

4. To make one's escape, get safely away.

a1300 *Cursor M.* 7755 (Cott.) Þar þai fell þat moght not fle. c1300 *Havelok* 1882 Late we nouth thise doges fle. 1382 WYCLIF *Acts* xvi. 27 Wenynge the boundyn men for to haue fled. c1430 LYDG. *Min. Poems* 186 He is a fole that..fled is fro prisoun. 1667 MILTON *P.L.* IV. 963 Flie thither whence thou [Satan] fledst. 1821 SHELLEY *Epips.* 272 As a hunted deer that could not flee, I..stood at bay.

5. To pass away quicky and suddenly; to disappear, vanish. Also with *away*.

c1200 *Trin. Coll. Hom.* 175 He is fleonde alse shadewe. a1300 *Cursor M.* 12075 (Cott.) And son þe spirit þat was fledd Again come in þat ilk stede. 1382 WYCLIF *Rev.* xvi. 20 And ech ijle fley awey and hilles ben not founde. c1450 HOLLAND *Howlat* 140 The Swallowe so swyft..is forthwart to fle. 1639 MASSINGER *Unnat. Combat* V. ii, Take not thy flight so soon immaculate spirit: 'Tis fled already. 1712–4 POPE *Rape Lock* I. 51 When Woman's transient breath is fled. 1776 GIBBON *Decl. & F.* I. vii. 199 The animating health and vigour were fled. 1818 SHELLEY *Rev. Islam* V. xliii. 6 As I approached, the morning's golden mist..fled. 1850 *Elder's House* 215 Pale flowers, Whose life and bloom are fled. 1886 A. WINCHELL *Walks & Talks in Geol. Field* 214 A million of years may flee away before one revolution is completed.

6. Occasionally used for FLY (= *volare*). (Often in Shelley.)

Examples of the present stem from dialect literature (Sc. and northern Eng.) are not given here, as in them *flee* is the regular form of FLY. In recent instances, the use of *flee* for *fly* is chiefly for the sake of rime, or to produce a sort of archaistic effect; in older writers it may be due variously to confusion between the two vbs., to adoption of dialectal phrases (esp. in 'to let flee'), or to a development from sense 5.

c1000 ÆLFRIC *Hom.* (Th.) I. 142 Culfran lufiað annysse, and fleoð him floccmælum. 1382 WYCLIF *Jer.* xlviii. 40 As an egle he shall fleen out. c1400 MAUNDEV. (1839) xxii. 238 The tronchouns flen in sprotes and peces. 1553 T. WILSON *Rhet.* (1580) 211 He let flee at hym like a Dragon. 1592 SHAKS. *Ven. & Ad.* 947 Loues golden arrow at him should haue fled. 1598 SYLVESTER *Du Bartas* II. ii. II. *Babylon* 221 Make fast this rope, and then they let it flee. 1612 J. DAVIES *Muse's Sacr.* Wks. (Grosart) II. 75/1 At which forthwith he [the Libard] flees, And piece-meal teares it. 1770 J. LOVE *Cricket* 5 The Youth cries Rub; O Flee, you Long'rer, Flee! 1815 SHELLEY *Alastor* 358 The boat fled on. 1821 —— *Ginevra* 211 The dark arrow fled In the noon.

II. *trans.*

7. To run away from, hasten away from; to quit abruptly, forsake (a person or place, etc.).

a1000 *Andreas* 1540 (Gr.) Wæs him ut myne fleon fealone stream. a1300 *Cursor M.* 14884 (Cott.) He folus þaim and þai him fle. 1386 *Rolls of Parlt.* III. 225/1 Some fledde the Citee for feere. 1548 HALL *Chron., Hen. VI*, 95 Straungers in great nombre fled the land. 1593 SHAKS. *3 Hen. VI*, II. i. 19 So fled his Enemies my Warlike Father. 1597 —— *2 Hen. IV*, I. i. 18 Yong Prince Iohn..fled the Field. 1598 SYLVESTER *Du Bartas* II. ii. I. *Ark* 43 The more he [a River] flees his source. 1634 SIR T. HERBERT *Trav.* 3 Upon better view he feared and fled us. 1647–8 COTTERELL *Davila's Hist. Fr.* (1678) 21 He was forced to flee his Country. 1726 *Adv. Capt. R. Boyle* 130 All his Attendants had fled his Presence. 1801 SOUTHEY *Thalaba* IX. xxxix, She fled the Place of Tombs.

fig. c1400 *Rom. Rose* 4786 If thou flee it, it shal flee thee; Folowe it, and folowen shal it thee. 1513 DOUGLAS *Æneis* VI. i. 132 Now, at the last, that fled ws euer moir, The forther cost Itaile haif we caucht. 1526 *Pilgr. Perf.* (W. de W. 1531) 291 All temptacyons fledde theyr holynesse. 1816 BYRON *Ch. Har.* III. xxxix, When Fortune fled her spoil'd and favourite child. 1882 STEVENSON *New Arab. Nts.* (1884) 130 Sleep continued to flee him.

8. In weaker sense: To avoid with dread or dislike; to eschew, shun. Occas. in passive; also †with *infin.* as *obj.*

a1000 *Boeth. Metr.* vii. 30 (Gr.) He sceal swiðe flion þisse worulde wlite. c1200 ORMIN 8056 Þa flæh I childess cosstess. c1200 *Trin. Coll. Hom.* 127 He fleȝ here ferrede. a1300 *Cursor M.* 1952 (Gött.) Fle falshed and theft. a1340 HAMPOLE *Psalter* i. 1 His verray lufers folous him fleand honur. c1386 CHAUCER *Monk's T.* 265 Fro hir childhod..sche fledde Office of wommen. ? a1400 *Cato's Morals* 55 in *Cursor M.* App. iv. 1670 Fle to take wife..bot ho be honest. c1400 *Lanfranc's Cirurg.* 59 A wood hound fleeþ mete & water. c1440 *Jacob's Well* xv. 100 An angry man..owyth to be fled as a raveynous dogge. 1550 CROWLEY *Epigr.* 667 Auoid and fle dice. 1563 *Homilies* II. *Agst. Idolatry* III. (1859) 230 Aungels flee to take vnto them by sacrelege the honoure dewe to God. 1766 FORDYCE *Serm. Yng. Wom.* (1767) II. xi. 159 Flee them, my fair pupils, flee them with horror. 1818 SHELLEY *Rosalind* 41, I would flee Thy tainting touch.

9. To contrive to avoid, save oneself from, escape from, evade. Now *rare*.

c1200 ORMIN 9803 Hu þeȝȝ mihhtenn fleon Drihhtiness irre. a1300 *Cursor M.* 3001 (Cott.) Your harm sa wend i best to fle. c1340 *Ibid.* 22503 (Fairf.) For to flee þe dai of awe. 1563–87 FOXE *A. & M.* (1596) 108/2, I..haue long fléene the hands of mine enemies. 1821 SHELLEY *Prometh. Unb.* I. 783 On Death's white and wingèd steed Which the fleetest cannot flee.

flee-boat: see FLY-BOAT.

fleece (fliːs), *sb.* Forms: 1 **fléos, flíes, flýs,** 3 **fleos,** 4–6 **flies, flyes,** 4–6 **flees, fles(e,** (4 **flus,** 5 **fleese, fleys, flesse,** 6 **fleise**), 5–6 *Sc.* **fleis(s,** 6 **flece,** *Sc.* **flesche,** 7 **fliece,** *Sc.* **fleesh,** 6– **fleece.** [Com. WGer. OE. *fléos* neut., corresponds to Du. *vlies*, MHG. *vlies* (Ger. *fliesz, vliesz*); there is also a form with umlaut, OE. *flíes, flýs* = MHG. *vlius* (Ger. *fleusz, flüsz*); the two types represent WGer. **fleusoz-, fliusiz-*; an ablaut variant **flûso-z* appears in MLG. and MHG. *vlûs* sheepskin, mod.Ger. *flaus* masc. woollen coat. Connexion with the root of L. *plūma* feather, PLUME, is probable.]

1. a. The woolly covering of a sheep or similar animal.

a1000 *Laws Ina* c. 69 Sceap sceal gongan mid his fliese oð midne sumor. c1000 *Ags. Ps.* lxxii. 6 And [he] astaȝ swe swe regn in fleos. a1225 *Ancr. R.* 66 Monie cumeð to ou ischrud mid lombes fleose, & beoð wode wulues. a1300 *E.E. Psalter* lxxii. 6 He sal com down als rain in flees soft. 1382 WYCLIF *Gen.* xxx. 35 Al the flok of o colour, that is, of whyet or of blak flese. c1450 HOLLAND *Howlat* 753 Thow joyuss fleiss of Gedion. 1501 DOUGLAS *Pal. Hon.* III. xxxvi, To win the fleis of gold. 1508 DUNBAR *Tua Mariit Wemen* 423 Cled in cair weid, As foxe in a lambis fleise fenȝe I my cheir. 1563 WINZET tr. *Vincent. Lirin.* xxxi. Wks. 1890 II. 65 Maid as certane fleisis of wow. 1637 T. MORTON *New Eng. Canaan* II. x. 98 These beasts are of the bignesse of a Cowe..their fleeces very usefull, being a kinde of wolle. 1725 POPE *Odyss.* I. 557 Stretch'd on the downy fleece, no rest he knows. 1804 J. GRAHAME *Sabbath* 456 Where lambs of whitest fleece sport on the hills. 1877 SIMMONDS *Anim. Products* 66 Its [the Alpaca's] fleece is superior to that of the sheep in length and softness.

b. *Her.* The figure of a sheepskin with its wool suspended by a ring. **c.** ***Order of the Golden Fleece***: an order of knighthood instituted at Bruges in 1430 by Philip the Good, duke of Burgundy.

The right of investiture in the order of the Golden Fleece belonged (after 1700) to the sovereigns of Austria and Spain.

1525 *Two Proph. Eng.* in Furniv., *Ballads from MSS.* I. 306 A king to were a flemyshe flece, all Sacksons shall hyt Rewe. 1539 *Inv. Habiliments, etc., Jas. V. Scot.* (1815) 49 Item the ordoure of the Empriour with the goldin fleis. 1548 HALL *Chron., Edw. IV*, 213 The kyng ware the golden Flees, and the duke ware the Garter. 1591 SHAKS. *1 Hen. VI*, IV. vii. 69 Knight of the Noble Order of S. George, Worthy S. Michael, and the Golden Fleece. 1842 LONGF. *Belfry Bruges* 22 Knights who bore the Fleece of Gold. 1849 DISRAELI *Corr. w. Sister* 11 Mar. (1886) 220 He [Guizot] had his red ribbon on and also his golden fleece.

2. a. The quantity of wool shorn from a sheep at one time.

c1460 FORTESCUE *Abs. & Lim. Mon.* xii. (1885) 140 The ixth fflese off thair wolles, and also the ixth Shef off þer graynes. 1672 PETTY *Pol. Anat.* (1691) 54 A Fleece of Wool in Ireland is about 2 *l.* weight. 1782 BURNS *Poor Mailie's Elegy* vi, A bonier fleesh ne'er cross'd the clips. 1829 SCOTT *Anne of G.* vi, Thou shalt have a necklace of jet at next shearing-feast, if our fleeces bear any price in the market. 1868 ROGERS *Pol. Econ.* xii. (1876) 11 The average weight of a fleece was not more than two pounds.

†**b.** *fig.* A share of booty. *Obs.*

In quot. 1703 *fleece* is apprehended as 'act of fleecing'.

1601 HOLLAND *Livy* VI. xv. (1609) 226 Thy selfe wouldest have a fliece with them [*in parte prædæ sis*]. 1603 BRETON *Packet Lett.* II. xxxix (Grosart) II. 43 When their wits goe a wool-gathering among shrewes that haue had fleeces. 1703 MRS. CENTLIVRE *Beau's Duel* II. ii, There's scarce a Match-maker in the whole Town, but has had a Fleece at his Purse.

3. In various transferred uses.

†**a.** A coating periodically shed or removed.

1603 Owen *Pembrokeshire* (1891) 74 The stonne Marle.. beinge cast on the lande, casteth yerely a ffleece of sande.

b. A crop of vegetation; also *fig.*

1513 Douglas *Æneis* xii. Prol. 80 So thik the plantis sprang in euery pece, The feyldis ferleis of thar fructuus flece. **1793** *Trans. Soc. Encourag. Arts* (ed. 2) V. 86 The land.. will produce little else but a fleece of weeds. **1793** *Ann. Agric., Suff.* XIX. 214 There was a very fine fleece of marl grass. **1831** Scott *Jrnl.* 5 May, A fleece of letters, which must be answered, I suppose. **1855** Browning *Two in Campagna* v, The champaign with its endless fleece Of feathery grasses everywhere.

c. A 'head' or mass of hair.

1577 B. Googe *Heresbach's Husb.* iv. (1586) 175 b, Others [Bees] cary water with their mouths, and droppes in their little fleeses. **1600** S. Nicholson *Acolastus* E ij b, Witnesse this snow-white fleece vpon my head. *c* **1600** Shaks. *Sonn.* lxviii, Ere beauties dead fleece made another gay. **1711** *Lond. Gaz.* No. 4841/4 Stolen.. a Mare.. with a white Fleece down the Face. **1831** Carlyle *Sart. Res.* i. v, The Aboriginal Savage, glaring fiercely from under his fleece of hair. **1859** Tennyson *Vivien* 839 The.. many-winter'd fleece of throat and chin. **1865** Swinburne *Poems & Ball., Faustine* 3 Back to the shoulder with its fleece Of locks.

d. Applied to anything resembling a sheep's fleece either in appearance or consistence; a white cloud, etc.; a quantity of falling snow, or of some light substance, as air, vapour, etc.

1671 R. Bohun *Wind* 40 Superincumbent Air; which I suppose to ly in severall fleeces or storys one above another. **1685** Goad *Celest. Bodies* i. ii. 4 Whenever it snows.. the greater is the Fleece, the warmer is the Air. **1692** Bentley *Boyle Lect.* i. 7 Certain thin fleeces of Atoms, that flow incessantly from the surfaces of Bodies. **1715–20** Pope *Iliad* iii. 284 Soft as the fleeces of descending snows. **1728** —— *Dunc.* ii. 362 Till show'rs of Sermons, Characters, Essays, In circling fleeces whiten all the ways. **1746–7** Hervey *Medit.* (1818) 83 Abundance of ruddy streaks tinge the fleeces of the firmament. **1834** H. Miller *Scenes & Leg.* xi. (1857) 167 A deep fleece of vapour rose from the surface. **1853** Kane *Grinnell Exp.* xxix. (1856) 246 The mackerel fleeces and mare's tails of our summer skies. **1865** Masson *Rec. Brit. Philos.* iii. 229 Beads or fleeces of oily substance hung in some gauze-work.

e. *spec.* The thin sheet of cotton or wool fibre that is taken from the breaking-card. Also, a textile fabric with a soft silky pile used for lining, etc.: cf. *fleece-lined* in 6.

1853 Ure *Dict. Arts* I. 510 One [card], called a breaker, which turns off the cotton in a broad fleece of extreme thinness. **1878** I. Watts in *Encycl. Brit.* VI. 493 The cotton is taken from the doffer in a very light fleece by means of a vibrating comb. **1957** M. B. Picken *Fashion Dict.* 133/1 *Fleece*, heavy erect-pile coat fabric of all wool or wool and hair of llama, alpaca, camel, vicuna or cashmere goat. **1964** *McCall's Sewing* iv. 57/1 *Fleece*, a heavy-weight woollen with very long nap used for coats. It is inclined to be bulky, and may be difficult to sew.

4. Used for a sheep, or *collect.* sheep.

1798 Wolcott (P. Pind.) *Tales of Hoy* Wks. 1812 IV. 427 And all the tribe of fleeces follow. ? *a* **1800** *Wowing of Jock & Jenny* viii, in Pinkerton *Sel. Scot. Ball.* (1783) II. 73 Fyve hundirth fleis now in a flok. **1855** Browning *Love among Ruins* ix, All our many-tinkling fleece.

5. *U.S.* The meat taken from the sides of the hump of the American bison.

1841 Catlin *N. Amer. Ind.* (1844) II. liv. 181 The fleece (hump) of a fat cow, was the luxury of luxuries. **1891** *Army & Navy Jrnl.* (N.Y.) 5 Sept. 30/1 The fleece [of a buffalo] is the meat lying on each side of the hump ribs and resting on the outside of the side ribs.

6. *Comb.*, as ***fleece-encumbered, -like, -lined*** adjs. Also †**fleece-feeder**, one who makes his profit out of fleeces (in quot. *fig.*); **fleece-merchant**, a dealer in wool; **fleece-picker** *N.Z.*, one who picks up fleeces in a shearing-shed; **fleece-wool**, that obtained from the living animal at the annual shearings.

1814 Wordsw. *Excursion* vii. 613 The *fleece-encumbered flock. **1549** Latimer *5th Serm. bef. Edw. VI.* (Arb.) 136 There are to many suche *flese feders. *a* **1729** Congreve *Impossible Thing* 128 That *fleece-like flow'r of fairy land. **1820** Shelley *Cloud* 47 The moon, Glides glimmering o'er my fleece-like floor. **1894** *Daily News* 26 Mar. 5/7 With the exception of *fleece-lined underwear. *a* **1774** Fergusson *Iron Kirk Bell* Poems (1845) 43 *Fleece-merchants may look bauld. **1861** H. W. Harper *Lett. fr. N.Z. 1857–1911* (1914) 20 July 54 Shearing, it happens, is in full swing, so there are a number of extra men, besides the shepherds of the station, shearers, *fleece-pickers, wool sorters, and 'rouse-abouts'. **1892** W. E. Swanton *Notes on N.Z.* ii. 96 There are the boys to pick up the fleeces, one fleece picker to every four or five shearers. **1945** Baker *Austral. Lang.* iii. 63 Woolshed workers include the fleece-picker or fleecy. **1954** E. C. Studholme *Te Waimate* (ed. 2) xv. 130 Fleece-pickers received 15s. a week, wool-rollers 25s. to 30s. [in 1882]. **1495** *Nottingham Rec.* III. 42 Centum stones de *flesse wolle. **1552** *Act 5–6 Edw. VI.* c. 6. §1 Mingling Fell-wool and Lambs-wool.. with Fleece-wool. **1769** *De Foe's Tour Gt. Brit.* I. 94 Fleece Wool, out of Lincolnshire. **1891** R. Wallace *Rural Econ. Austral. & N.Z.* xxix. 385 The years 1880, 1881, and 1882 were good years, when unsorted wool ranged between about 11*d.* and 1*s.* 0½*d.* per lb., and fleece wool rose to close upon 1*s.* 6*d.* per lb. **1921** *Daily Colonist* (Victoria, B.C.) 8 Oct. 15/2 The cost of putting an extremely good value in fleece wools has made it difficult for the puller to operate. **1951** L. Acland *Early Canterbury Runs* 378 *Fleece*.. The main part of a sheep's wool, which is picked up in one, skirted, and rolled. This is sold as fleece wool, as opposed to locks, bellies, and pieces.

fleece (fliːs), *v.* Also 6–7 fleese, (6 flece, fliese). [f. prec. sb.]

1. *trans.* To strip (a sheep) of the fleece; to clip off or strip the wool from; *lit.* and *fig.*

1628 Wither *Brit. Rememb.* viii. 1442 A Clergy, that shall more desire to fleece, Then feed the flock. **1652** *Season. Exp. Netherl.* 15 What signified the bleating of such of your Countreymen as they daily fleec'd? **1708** Ozell tr. *Boileau's Lutrin* v. 87 For Thee his Flocks are fleec'd. **1885** *Pall Mall G.* 6 Nov. 1/1 The impulsive eagerness of some owners to fleece their sheep rather more often than is good for them.

b. *transf.*

1667 Waterhouse *Fire Lond.* 171 Thrifty Oaks, though fleeced of under boughs, yet if not headed, may thrive.

2. To pluck or shear (the wool) *from* a sheep. Hence *fig.* to obtain by unjust or unfair means. Also, to take toll of, take pickings from. Now *rare.*

1537 Hen. VIII. in *State Papers* II. 423 To flece, from tyme to tyme, all that you may catche from Us. **1576** Turberv. *Venerie* 198 Men which fliese a fee From euerie widowes flocke: a capon or a chicke. **1593** Nashe *Four Lett. Confut.* Wks. (Grosart) II. 242 Many lockes fleec'd from Tullie. **1605** Verstegan *Dec. Intell.* v. (1628) 115 By fleesing from each of these two countrys a parte. **1613** Purchas *Pilgrimage* v. xiv. (1614) 519 Their wealth and substance being euery where so fleeced that [etc.] **1840** Carlyle *Heroes* iv. (1858) 293 To divide what they fleeced from these poor drudges.

absol. **1593** Nashe *Christ's T.* Wks. (Grosart) IV. 158 Much lesse are they to fleece or pluck from their Maister or Sheepheard. **1642** Rogers *Naaman* 317 Fleece not from God.

3. To strip (a person, city, country, etc.) of money, property, etc., as a sheep is stripped of its fleece; to make (any one) pay to the uttermost; to exact money from, or make exacting charges upon; to plunder, rob heartlessly; to victimize. Also with *of.*

1577–87 Holinshed *Chron.* III. 855/2 The cardinall knowing he was well prouided of monie, sought occasion to fleece him of part thereof. **1601** F. Godwin *Bps. of Eng.* 359 Alfred.. determined at his departure [from York] to fleece it. **1616** R. C. *Times' Whistle* vi. 2717 Many a gallant of his gold they fleece. **1691** Wood *Ath. Oxon.* I. 584 His father.. fleec'd the Church of Hereford to leave him an estate. **1719** D'Urfey *Pills* (1872) V. 99 When.. Lawyers forget a rich Client to fleece. **1772** Goldsm. *Stoops to Conq.* ii. Wks. (Globe) 650/2 In bad inns you are fleeced and starved. **1818** Jas. Mill *Brit. India* II. v. iv. 444 In this manner had Tanjore been humbled and fleeced. **1854** Hawthorne *Eng. Note-bks.* (1883) I. 463 A begging subscriptionist.. has just fleeced me to that amount. **1866** R. M. Ballantyne *Shift. Winds* xxvii. (1881) 310 A place.. where [seamen].. were soon fleeced of all their hardly-earned money.

absol. c **1572** Gascoigne *Fruites Warre* xcv. 1, I haue.. fleest in Flaunders eke among the rest.

4. a. To overspread as with a fleece. **b.** To dapple or fleck with fleece-like masses.

1730–46 Thomson *Autumn* 958 Meantime, light-shadowing all, a sober calm Fleeces unbounded ether. **1748** —— *Cast. Indol.* i. 394 Not Titian's pencil e'er could so array, So fleece with clouds, the pure etherial space. **1799** Wordsw. *Nutting*, One of those green stones That fleeced with moss, under the shady trees, Lay round me. **1855** Beecher *Star Papers* xxxii. (1873) 349 The trees are dressed with snow.. The bucket, the well-curb are fleeced over. **1888** Shairp in Knight *Shairp & Friends* 87 The sky was bright blue, fleeced with the whitest clouds.

Hence **fleeced** *ppl. a.*^{1}

a **1800** Cowper tr. *Andreini's Adam* Wks. 1835–7 X. 327 The lifeless skins Of fleeced animals. **1864** H. Spencer *Illust. Univ. Progr.* 99 The ill-educated children, the fleeced relatives, who have to suffer from it.

fleeceable (ˈfliːsəb(ə)l), *a.* [f. fleece *v.* + -able.] That may be fleeced, liable to be fleeced, cheatable.

1868 *Daily News* 24 Dec., The appearance.. of a member of the aristocracy.. paralyses their caution, and renders them the most fleeceable of mankind. **1892** *Punch* 5 Mar. 112/2 He had fleeced all that was fleeceable in Dansington.

fleeced (fliːst), *ppl. a.*^{2} [f. fleece *sb.* + -ed^{2}.] Furnished with a fleece: often preceded by some qualifying word as ***half-, rich-, well-fleeced.***

1580 C'tess Pembroke *Ps.* cxiv. 8 The fleezed rammes doe frisking bound. **1590** Spenser *F.Q.* i. ii. 16 As when two rams.. Fight for the rule of the rich fleeced flocke. **1610** Holland *Camden's Brit.* i. 663 A sow halfe fleeced with woole, was digged up. **1698** Fryer *Acc. E. India & P.* 34 Sheep.. fleeced rather with Hair than Wool. **1724** Swift *Drapier's Lett.* ii. Wks. 1755 V. ii. 27 If.. the grazier should bring me one single wether, fat and well fleec'd by way of pattern. **1892** *Daily News* 25 June 5/4 Who is reputed to have owed much of his great wealth to his fleeced flocks.

fleeceless (ˈfliːslɪs), *a.* [f. fleece *sb.* + -less.] Having no fleece.

1660 F. Brooke tr. *Le Blanc's Trav.* 183 The country abounds in fleecelesse sheep. **1846** in Worcester (citing Dr. Allen).

fleece-o, fleecy. = *fleece-picker. N.Z.*

1894 E. Wilson *In Land of Tui* xv. 244 Meanwhile the shorn fleeces are carried to a large table in the wool-shed by a man appropriately named 'Fleecy', and are spread out by four wool-pickers, who tear away the bad parts and fold the fleeces square, passing them to the classer. **1909** C. Owen *Philip Loveluck* 173 A young Maori boy acted as 'Fleece oh!'.. he flicked the fleece up in his arms when it was cut from the sheep, grasped it by its four ends, and flung it out for Loveluck to fold. **1933** 'E. Milton' *Waimana* iii. iv. 195 Two male Maori experts.. were engaged with the wife of Kuru.. to act as 'Fleeço'. **1956** G. Bowen *Wool Away!* (ed. 2) vii. 88 The 'fleece-o', whose work is to pick the fleece off the shearing board when shorn, to throw it on the wool-table, and also to keep the board swept clean.

fleecer (ˈfliːsə(r)). [f. fleece *v.* + -er^{1}.] One who fleeces (see the vb.).

1612 Adams *Pract. Wks.* (1862) I. 449 We have still fleecers enough. **1637** Prynne *Brev. Prel. Usurp.* 262 Not fleecers, but feeders. **1708** Motteux *Rabelais* v. *Prognostication* v. 163 Fleecers of Sheer'd-Asses. **1795** *Hull Advertiser* 5 Sept. 4/4. **1847** in Craig. **1884** Morris in *Pall Mall G.* 7 Oct. 8/1 Whereas if a labour employer, or fleecer, were to find himself possessed of no more to live on, his friends would.. hide his razors away.

fleech (fliːtʃ), *sb.*^{1} *Sc.* Also 7 fleaich. [f. next. vb.] Flattery; a piece of flattery.

a **1700** *Macqueen's Apol. Let.* in Maidment *Sc. Pasquils* (1868) 286 The compliments and fleaiches Which used to gain our Irish wenches. **1721** Kelly *Scot. Prov.* 105 Fair fall you and that's a Fleech.

†**fleech**, *sb.*^{2} *Obs. rare*$^{-1}$. App. a bout, spell.

1589 *Pappe w. Hatchet* (1844) 41 Martin, this is my last straine for this fleech of mirth.

fleech (fliːtʃ), *v. Sc.* and *north. dial.* Forms: 4–6, 9 flech(e, 4 fleeche, 4, 6 flesche, 6 fleache, 5–6 flei(s)che, 6 fleitsche, 7 fleitch, 7–8 fleetch, 9 *dial.* flaich, 6– fleech. [Of obscure origin; the identity of the senses with those of OTeut. **plaihan* and its derivatives (Goth. *ga-plaihan* to treat kindly, console, OHG. *flêhôn, flêhen* to fondle, flatter, beseech, MHG. *vlêhen*, mod.Ger. *flehen* to beseech, Du. *vleien* to flatter) suggests that the word may represent an OE. **flǽcean*:—OTeut. type **plaikjan*, related to **plaihan*, as OE. *tǽcean* teach *v.* to *téon*(:—**tîhan*).]

trans. To beguile, cajole, coax, wheedle; to entice, wheedle into going, *to* a place. Also, in good sense: To beseech, entreat. Also *absol.* and *intr.* (const. *on, with*), to speak coaxingly or beseechingly; to flatter, fawn.

1375 Barbour *Bruce* v. 619 Bot he, vith fals vordis flechand, Ves vith his sonnys ay cumand. *c* **1375** *Sc. Leg. Saints, Blasius* 179 Hyme cane flesche.. Fore to fore-sak crist his kynge. *c* **1425** Wyntoun *Cron.* viii. xi. 154 And wyth þe lang schankis þis Edwart Sayd flechand til þe Brws Robert, Ðat [etc.] **1535** Stewart *Cron. Scot.* II. 121 [He] louit men weill that culd fleche and le. **1580** Sir P. Hume *Promise Jas. VI* L'envoi 10 Thow dois but fleiche the King. **1603** *Philotus* ix, I can with fair anis fleitch and flatter. **1718** Ramsay *Christ's Kirk* iii. xxii, She fleech'd him fairly to his bed, Wi ca'ing him her burdy. **1792** Burns *Duncan Grey* ii, Duncan fleech'd, and Duncan pray'd. *a* **1810** Tannahill *Poems* (1815) 101 He fleichit her neatht that wudis dark glume, And revit hyr ther of lyffe. **1820** Scott *Abbot* xvi, The Papist.. fleeched us with pardons. **1834** M. Scott *Cruise Midge* i, Better flech with a madman than fecht with him. **1873** *Swaledale Gloss.*, *Flaich*, to flatter, to coax, to fawn. **1886** Stevenson *Kidnapped* xix, This lad that has.. seen the goodman fleeching like a suitor. **1894** Crockett *Raiders* 388 He would often fleech on me to take part in the exercises.

fleech, dial. var. of flitch *sb.*^{1}

fleecher (ˈfliːtʃə(r)). [f. fleech *v.* + -er^{1}.] One who coaxes or wheedles; a flatterer.

c **1425** Wyntoun *Cron.* vi. xvii. 77 A-mang þame wes fals Flechowris þan Ðat sayd [etc.]. *a* **1572** Knox *Hist. Ref.* Wks. 1846 I. 74 Fantastik fooles and feynȝeit fleacheris. *a* **1586** in Pinkerton *Anc. Scot. Poems* 259 Gif I dar the treuth declair, And nane me fleitschour call.

fleeching (ˈfliːtʃɪŋ), *vbl. sb. Sc.* [f. as prec. + -ing^{1}.] The action of coaxing or wheedling; also, a coaxing or wheedling speech.

c **1375** *Sc. Leg. Saints, Agatha* 66 Bot tuk bath ewine in a lyne þar harsknes and þare flechinge. *c* **1475** *Rauf Coilȝear* 902 Now faindis to haue fauour with thy fleichingis. **1535** Stewart *Cron. Scot.* II. 522 The plesand langage and the countenance, The fair flesching. **1824** Scott *Redgauntlet* let. xii, 'Hout wi' your fleeching', said Dame Martin. **1892** *Northumbld. Gloss.*, Aa wadna gan ti church wi' him for a' his fleechin.

fleeching (ˈfliːtʃɪŋ), *ppl. a. Sc.* [f. as prec. + -ing^{2}.] That fleeches; coaxing, wheedling.

1513 Douglas *Æneis* ii. iii. (ii.) 56 The fals flechand Vlixes. **1686** G. Stuart *Joco-ser. Disc.* 64 That fleetching knave. **1787** Burns *Ded. to G. Hamilton* i, Expect na, Sir,.. A fleechin, fleth'rin dedication. **1893** Stevenson *Catriona* vii, That long, false, fleeching beggar of a father of hers.

Hence ˈ**fleechingly** *adv.*

1688 Shields *Notes & Heads* 5 (Jam.) They be now speaking fair fleechingly and flatteringly to this generation.

fleechment (ˈfliːtʃmənt). *north. dial.*; in 9 flaitchment. [f. fleech *v.* + -ment.] Cajolery.

1886 Hall Caine *Son of Hagar* i. vii, And stuff her with all sorts of flaitchment and lies.

fleecing (ˈfliːsɪŋ), *vbl. sb.* [f. fleece *v.* + -ing.^{1}]

1. The action of the vb. fleece.

1593 Nashe *Christ's T.* 46 b, They [Vsurers] haue enforst him thereunto by their fleecing. **1641** Milton *Reform.* ii. 85 The whipping, fleecing, and fleaing us. **1783** Fox *Sp. E. India Bills* 18 Nov., The poor unhappy natives must undergo a second fleecing for the benefit of the proprietors.

2. *concr.* A fleecy streak.

1781 S. J. Pratt *Emma Corbett* II. 173 She is surrounded with sunbeams softened by tender fleecings of sky which form her chariot.

fleecy ('fliːsɪ), *a.* Also 6 fleesie, flycesie, 7 fleecie. [f. FLEECE *sb.* + -Y[1].]

1. Covered with a fleece or with wool; fleeced, wool-bearing. ***fleecy star*** = Aries.

1590 SPENSER *F.Q.* III. vi. 15 The gentle Shepheard swaynes, which sat Keeping their fleecy flockes, as they were hyr'd. **1612** DRAYTON *Poly-olb.* xiv. 263 The fleecie face. **1667** MILTON *P.L.* III. 558 The fleecie Starr that bears Andromeda. **1725** POPE *Odyss.* IX. 530 And first with stately step at evening hour Thy fleecy fellows usher to their bower. **1847** J. WILSON *Chr. North* (1857) I. 139 A collie.. compromises the affair with the fleecy nation.

b. Of a manufactured article: Having a fleece-like nap.

1790 W. BUCHAN (*title*) Letter to the Patentee, concerning the Medical Properties of the Fleecy Hosiery. **1881** RITA *My Lady Coquette* iv, A white thick fleecy shawl.

fig. **1826** HOOD *Irish Schoolm.* ix, Further down the naked red prevails Of his own naked fleecy hosierie.

2. Consisting of or derived from fleeces, woolly.

1567 DRANT *Horace' Epist.* xiii. E iv, Or drunken Pyrrhe beares her wool her flycesie filched gaine. **1634** MILTON *Comus* 504 The fleecy wealth That doth enrich these downs. **1638** COWLEY *Love's Riddle* ii, The gentle Lambs and Sheep ..which every Year pay him their fleecy Tribute. **1791** COWPER *Odyss.* XVI. 40 While on the variegated seats she spread Their fleecy covering.

3. Resembling a fleece in colour or conformation; woolly. Of the sky: Covered or flecked with fleece-like clouds.

1632 MILTON *Penseroso* 72 Stooping through a fleecy cloud. **1697** DRYDEN *Virg. Georg.* I. 417 When the Fleecy Skies new cloath the Wood. **1700** —— *Fables, Pythag. Philos.* 91 The fleecy snows In silence fell. **1788** COWPER *Negro's Compl.* 13 Fleecy locks and black complexion Cannot forfeit nature's claim. **1839** LONGF. *Wreck Hesper.* xviii, She struck where the white and fleecy waves Looked soft as carded wool. **1873** G. C. DAVIES *Mount. & Mere* xiii. 104 Beyond and above the bright fleecy blue.

4. *ellipt.* quasi-*sb.* (see quot.)

1855 in HYDE CLARKE *Dict.* **1882** CAULFEILD & SAWARD *Dict. Needlework, Fleecy*, sheep's wool prepared in loose threads, for Darning and Knitting.

5. *Comb.*, as ***fleecy-looking***, ***-winged*** adjs.

1803 *Edin. Rev.* II. 379 Mingled with the thick and fleecy-looking fog. **1822** SHELLEY *Chas. I*, iv. 11 That flock of fleecy-wingèd clouds Sailing athwart St. Margaret's.

Hence **'fleecily** *adv.*, in a fleecy manner.

1875 *Anderida* III. vi. 110 From rock with plumes of fern Shivering, fleecily falls the burn.

fleed (fliːd). *dial.* Also **flead**. The inside fat of a hog before it is melted into lard; = FLARE *sb.*[2]

1845 E. ACTON *Mod. Cookery* xi. 237 The leaf-fat, or fleed. *Ibid.* xvi. 347 Flead crust. *Ibid.* xxiii. 523 Fleed or flead cakes ..very much served as a tea-cake at the tables of the superior order of Kentish farmers. **1847** HALLIWELL, *Flead*, lard. Kent and Sussex. **1875** PARISH *Sussex Dial.*

fleed, obs. pa. pple. of FLAY.

fleegary, -erie: see FEGARY.

fleeing ('fliːɪŋ), *vbl. sb.* [f. FLEE *v.* + -ING[1].] The action of the vb. FLEE in various senses.

a **1300** *Cursor M.* 2615 (Cott.) Bot in hir fleing þar sco yode, An angel hir befor stode. *c* **1410** LOVE *Bonavent. Mirr.* x. (Gibbs MS.), Off the fleynge of oure lord Jhesu into Egypte. *c* **1440** *Gesta Rom.* xix. 336 (Harl. MS.) So shall he have fleyng to the paleys of holy chirche. **1559** ABP. HETHE in Strype *Ann. Ref.* I. App. vi. 8 This forsakinge and fleynge from the sea of Rome.

fleeing ('fliːɪŋ), *ppl. a.* [f. as prec. + -ING[2].] That flees, in various senses of the vb.

c **1374** CHAUCER *Boeth.* IV. pr. iii. 121 Yif he be dredeful and fleynge [L. *fugax*]. **1434** MISYN *Mending Life* 108 So þat þou sulde desire fleand þingis. *a* **1533** LD. BERNERS *Huon* liv. 181 Suche fleynge vacabondes. **1877** *Daily News* 5 Nov. 4/7 A large proportion of the fleeing troops would perish in the attempt.

fleem, obs. f. FLEAM *sb.*[1]

fleer ('fliːə(r)), *sb.*[1] Now *rare*. Also 4–6 **fleear**. [f. FLEE *v.* + -ER[1].] One who flees; **a.** one who runs away, a fugitive; **b.** one who withdraws from or shuns (const. *of*).

1375 BARBOUR *Bruce* III. 51 He reskewyt all the flearis. *c* **1470** HENRY *Wallace* x. 341 Sic a flear befor was neuir seyn. **1598** GRENEWEY *Tacitus' Ann.* xv. iv. 227 Which fear of the fleers away was no less ignominious, then if..they had turned their backs to the enemie. **1721** KELLY *Scot. Prov.* 47 A Fleer [*printed* Sleer] would ay have a Follower. **1829** J. GALT *Let.* in *Ann. Parish* Pref. 71 A refuge for the fleers from the calamities of the world. **1881** W. WILKINS *Songs of Study* 68 Shunner of sloth, and fleër of revels and feasts.

fleer (flɪə(r)), *sb.*[2] Also 7 **flear, fleere**. [f. FLEER *v.*]

1. A mocking look or speech; a sneer, a gibe; 'mockery expressed either in words or looks' (J.).

1604 SHAKS. *Oth.* IV. i. 83 Marke the Fleeres, the Gybes and notable Scornes That dwell in euery Region of his face. **1654** FULLER *Two Serm.* 4 The fleere and flout which their prophanenesse was pleased to bestow upon him. **1754** FOOTE *Knights* II. Wks. 1799 I. 84 None of your fleers! I am glad here's a husband coming that will take you down. **1886** MISS BROUGHTON *Dr. Cupid* II. i. 12 Perhaps there was some truth in Betty's fleer, of her never having known any better company than that of the village apothecary.

†**2.** 'A deceitful grin of civility' (J.). *Obs.*

1681 D'URFEY *Progr. Honesty* xiv. 62 A sly Phanatick fleer. **1688** SOUTH *Serm., Falshood* (1737) I. xii. 468 Such a sly, treacherous fleer upon their face. **1727** SWIFT *To Stella* 47 Flattery tipt with nauseous fleer.

b. *nonce-use.* In good sense: A cheerful look, a smile.

1866 CARLYLE *Remin.* (1881) I. 71 A tallish man of rugged countenance, which broke out oftenest into some innocent fleer of merriment, or readiness to be merry when you addressed him.

fleer (flɪə(r)), *v.* Forms: 4–6 **flery(e**, 5–7, 8–9 *dial.* **flyre, -er, flire**, 6 **flirre, flurre**, 6–8, 9 *dial.* **flear(e**, 6–7 **fle(e)re, flier(e**, 7–8 **fleir(e**, 6– **fleer**. [Perh. of Scandinavian origin, though not recorded in ON.; cf. Norw. and Sw. dial. *flira*, Da. dial. *flire* to grin, laugh unbecomingly.]

†**1.** *intr.* To make a wry face, distort the countenance; to grin, grimace. *Obs.*

? *a* **1400** [see FLEERING *ppl. a.*]. **1530** PALSGR. 551/2, I fleere, I make an yvell countenaunce with the mouthe by uncoveryng of the tethe. **1570** LEVINS *Manip.* 190 To flurre with the lippes, *labia promittere.* **1599** B. JONSON *Ev. Man out of Hum.* V. i, Let her fleere, and looke a scew. **1683** HICKERINGILL *Trimmer* i. Wks. 1716 I. 358 Treat a Monky seriously and correct him never so effectually, and he'll only flear at you. *a* **1715** PENNECUIK *Truth's Trav.* Wks. (1815) 395 Falset began to flier and greit. **1790** MORISON *Poems* 96 How then he'd stare wi' sour grimace..Syne flyre like some outlandish race, At wretched me.

2. To laugh in a coarse, impudent, or unbecoming manner.

1553 LATIMER *Serm.* (1562) 115/b, In some places they go with the corses girnyng and fleeryng, as though they went to a beare-baiting. **1603** H. CROSSE *Vertues Commw.* (1878) 141 For you shall neuer see a drunkard so wel-aduised..but either fleere and laugh it out, or be furious and quarrelsome. **1747** T. STORY *Life* 51 He whispered to me..'This is a Tythe-goose'; and then fleer'd. **1806** R. JAMIESON *Pop. Ballads* I. 348 He..flyret at me as I wad hae him. **1864** *Daily Tel.* 17 Mar., Impudent-looking wenches..leering and fleering and chuckling *con amore.*

†**3.** To laugh or smile flatteringly or fawningly. Const. *on, upon. Obs.*

15.. *Chester Pl.* (Shaks. Soc.) II. 51 Though he flyer, flatter, and flicker. **1549** CHALONER tr. *Ersasm. Moriæ Enc.* A iv, This next hir that fareth as if she flired upon you..is Adulacion. **1621** BURTON *Anat. Mel.* I. ii. III. xi, How popular and curteous, how they grinne and fliere vpon euery man they meet. **1673** F. KIRKMAN *Unlucky Citizen* 166, I found no alteration, she still fleir'd on me.

4. To laugh mockingly or scornfully; to smile or grin contemptuously; hence, to gibe, jeer, sneer. Const. *at*, †*upon*.

c **1440** *Bone Flor.* 1769 Tho two false..beganne to lagh and flerye. **1579** TOMSON *Calvin's Serm. Tim.* 1033/1 When they mocke all lessons that are giuen them and flyre at them. **1621** ELSING *Debates Ho. Lords* (Camden) 112 The affront of Sir J. B[ourchier] fleering into the L. Keeper's face. **1667** PEPYS *Diary* 8 Mar., All the people of the Hall did fleer and laugh upon him. **1732** GAY *Achilles* III. liv. Must you be fleering? Truce with your jeering. **1825** LAMB *Vision of Horns* Wks. (1875) 351 Instead of apology, he only grinned and fleered in my face. **1875** TENNYSON *Q. Mary* II. ii, I have heard One of your Council fleer and jeer at him.

5. *trans.* To laugh mockingly at, ridicule, deride.

1622 FLETCHER *Span. Curate* IV. vii, I blush to think how people fleer'd and scorn'd me. **1788** 'A. PASQUIN' *Childr. Thespis* I. (1792) 52 Their high born disdain if keen Satire should fleer 'em. **1871** DIXON *Tower* IV. vii. 73 That mimic fleered and mocked his [the King's] Chancellor.

Hence **fleered** *ppl. a.*

1632 LITHGOW *Trav.* III. 109 Nor ne'er ten miles was travell'd from his cradle Yet faine would sit the fleerd Pegasian sadle.

fleer, obs. var. FLARE *v.*

1761 MRS. F. SHERIDAN *Sidney Bidulph* (1767) V. 197 These little snug marriages, where Hymen comes as it were incog., without his tawdry saffron-coloured robe to fleer in people's eyes.

fleerer ('flɪərə(r)). [f. FLEER *v.* + -ER[1].] One who fleers; a mocker, †a 'fawner' (J.).

a **1625** FLETCHER *Nice Valour* V. i, Democritus, thou ancient Fleerer, How I miss thy laugh. **1676** D'URFEY *Mad. Fickle* III. i, This eternal fleerer will jear me to a Consumption. **1769** R. CUMBERLAND *Brothers* III. viii, A woman of your years shou'd have more sense than to mind what such idle young fleerers can say of you.

fleering ('flɪərɪŋ), *vbl. sb.* [f. FLEER *v.* + -ING[1].] The action of the vb. FLEER.

1533 MORE *Debell. Salem* Wks. 962/2 Haue they neuer so fayre a flering at the first face: yet..they bee..farre woorse than noughte. **1570** T. NORTON in *Udall's Royster D.* (1847) p. xli, Their fleering..their whisperings, shewed their hartes. **1669** PENN *No Cross* xvii. §5 What Laughing, what Fleering, what Mocking of their homely Fashion would there be? **1827** MACAULAY *Country Clergym. Trip* vi, No fleering! no distance! no scorn! **1892** G. S. LAYARD *C. Keene* viii. 176 He found little or no pleasure in..the fleering or flouting at a fellow-creature.

fig. **1840** BROWNING *Sordello* I. 277 He Partook the poppy's red effrontery, Till Autumn spoiled their fleering quite with rain.

fleering ('flɪərɪŋ), *ppl. a.* [f. as prec. + -ING[2].] That fleers; †grinning, grimacing; †smiling obsequiously; laughing coarsely or scornfully.

? *a* **1400** *Morte Arth.* 1088 Flatt mowthede as a fluke, with fleryande lyppys. *Ibid.* 2779 Thow flleryande wryche! *c* **1450** HOLLAND *Howlat* lxiv. 820 In come twa flyrand fulis with a fonde fair. *a* **1529** SKELTON *Poems agst. Garnesche* 152 Fleriing, flatyryng, fals, and fykkelle. **1576** FLEMING *Caius' Eng. Dogges* (1880) 37 This dogge exceedeth all other in.. his leering and fleering lookes. **1608** R. CAWDREY *Table Alph., Giglot*, strumpet, a fliering wench. **1673** DRYDEN *Amboyna* I. Wks. 1883 V. 18, I do not like these fleering Dutchmen, they overact their kindness. *a* **1712** W. KING *Hold Fast Below* 19 Says then the fleering spark, with courteous grin..'Nothing more easy'. **1833** MACAULAY *Walpole's Lett.* Ess. 1854 I. 272 His tone was light and fleering. **1879** HOWELLS *L. Aroostook* (1883) II. 26 His fleering, drunken laugh. **1890** H. M. STANLEY *Darkest Africa* II. 402 Jeering youths and fleering girls.

Hence **'fleeringly** *adv.*, in a fleering manner.

c **1613** ROWLANDS *Paire of Spy-Knaves* 3 A purblinde Momus fleeringly will looke, And spie no knaue but's selfe in all the Booke. **1728** MORGAN *Algiers* I. vi. 189 The Jerbin ..had looked fleeringly all the Time. **1887** STEVENSON *Merry Men* iv, He saw and recognized us with a toss of one hand fleeringly above his head.

fleerish ('flɪərɪʃ). *Sc.* Also **flourice, fleurish**. (Flint and) steel.

1825 JAMIESON Suppl., *Flourice.* **1871** W. ALEXANDER *Johnny Gibb* xi. 81 Parishioners..who cared not to carry 'fleerish and flint' in their 'Sunday claes'. **1880** SHIRLEY *Crookit Meg* xxii. in *Fraser's Mag.* May 651 A piece of tinder is ignited with the old-fashioned 'flint and fleerish'. **1892** *Blackw. Mag.* Oct. 486 In Buchan the steel was called the fleurish or fleerish.

fleet (fliːt), *sb.*[1] Forms: 1 **fléot**, 3 **fleote**, 4–6 **flete**, 6–7 **flete**, 6– **fleet**. [OE. *fléot* (? str. fem., as may be inferred from the early ME. form), recorded once in sense 'ship, vessel' (or *collect.* = means of sea-travel, boats or ships in general), f. *fléotan* FLEET *v.* Cf. OE. *flyte* (? or *flýte*) 'pontonium' (Ælfric *Gloss.*) from the same root.]

1. a. A sea force, or naval armament; in early use, a number of vessels carrying armed men, under a single command; in modern use, a number of ships armed and manned for war, each having its own commanding officer, under the orders of the admiral in chief, or of the flag-officer in command of a division. ***to go round*** or ***through the fleet***: to be flogged on board each vessel in the fleet. ***fleet in being***: a phrase first used by the Earl of Torrington after the engagement off Beachy Head in 1690 to describe a fleet which, though inferior to that of the enemy, is able to hamper his movements.

a **1000** *Prayers* (Gr.-Wülck.) iv. 100 Hwy ic ȝebycȝe þat on sæwe, fleot on faroðe. *c* **1205** LAY. 2155 Humber king & al his fleote, & his muchele scip ferde. *c* **1325** *Coer de L.* 1653 All redy they fonde ther her flete, Chargyd with armur. **1393** GOWER *Conf.* I. 197 That vessel..Which maister was of all the flete. *c* **1440** *Promp. Parv.* 166/2 Flete of schyppys yn þe see, *classis.* **1527** R. THORNE *His Booke* in Hakluyt *Voy.* (1589) 255 He armed a fleete. **1628** DIGBY *Voy. Medit.* (1868) 1 The straightes fleete..being gone 4 houres..when wee sett sayle. **1690** EARL OF TORRINGTON *Sp. to Ho. Comm.* (1710) 29 Most Men were in fear that the French wou'd invade; but I was always of another Opinion,..for I always said, that whilst we had a Fleet in being, they wou'd not dare to make an Attempt. **1718** *Freethinker* No. 60 ⁋7 They would not permit the Carthaginians to fit out any Fleets. **1841** MARRYAT *Poacher* xxxix, They..for the double offence, would go through the fleet. *Ibid.*, One of the marines..was to have gone round the fleet this morning. **1855** MILMAN *Lat. Chr.* (1864) II. IV. ix. 427 A formidable armament..embarked on board a great fleet. **1898** KIPLING (*title*) A Fleet in Being. **1899** *McClure's Mag.* Jan. 237/2 It is indeed as a threat to communications that the fleet in being is chiefly formidable. **1902** *Encycl. Brit.* XXXII. 501/1 Of late years controversy has raged round this phrase, 'a fleet in being' and the strategic principle which it expresses. **1964** D. MACINTYRE *Battle for Mediterranean* i. 31 A lack of desire on the part of the Italians to risk their fleet ..is..probable, a policy which accorded with the theory of maintenance of a 'fleet in being'.

b. *the fleet*: the navy.

1712 ADDISON *Spect.* No. 500 ⁋3 Whether it be in the army or in the fleet, in trade, or in any of the three learned professions. **1867** SMYTH *Sailor's Word-bk., Fleet*, a general name given to the royal navy.

c. In wider sense: A number of ships or boats sailing in company.

1697 DAMPIER *Voy.* I. 40 A Fleet of Pereagoes laden with Indian Corn..going to Cartagena. **1719** DE FOE *Crusoe* I. 338 The Brasil Ships come all in Fleets. **1777** ROBERTSON *Hist. Amer.* I. I. 45 He immediately equipped a fleet to carry a colony of Portuguese to these islands. **1840** DICKENS *Old C. Shop* v, A fleet of barges were coming lazily on. **1865** *Cornh. Mag.* Apr. 465 The whole 'fleet' [of colliers] as it is sometimes called, must anchor. **1884** *Stubbs' Mercantile Circular* 27 Feb. 194/1 The total catch of mackerel by the New England fleet was 226,685 barrels.

d. ***Fleet Air Arm***, the branch of the air force formed to operate with the fleet. (First formed 1923; came under the Admiralty's control in 1938.) Abbrev. *F.A.A.*

1923 *Rel. Navy & Air Force* 2 in *Parl. Papers* (Cmd. 1938) XV. 827, I. *Navy and Air Force.*..Naval officers belonging to the Fleet Air Arm are therefore to be attached to the Air Service on the nomination of the Admiralty. **1933** *Jrnl. R. Aeronaut. Soc.* XXXVII. 337 The references made..to the activities of the Fleet Air arm were fully justified... It was surprising how tiny a speck on the ocean an aircraft carrier could appear when one had to return to it after a sea reconnaissance. **1939** *Navy List* Sept. p. xiii, F.A.A.—Officers serving with or undergoing training in the Fleet Air Arm. **1940** E. C. SHEPHERD *Brit. Air Power* 27 But for the Fleet Air Arm, which is exclusively controlled by the Admiralty, the whole of British Air Power is thus under the direction of a single staff—the Air Staff—and is commanded by R.A.F. **1953** *Times* 21 May 8/2 The Admiralty has

decided to reintroduce the term 'Fleet Air Arm' after a lapse of seven years, during which the air forces of the Royal Navy have been known officially as 'Naval Aviation'.

2. *transf.* A number of persons, birds, or other objects moving or employed in company (now *rare*, exc. *dial.*); revived in the sense of: a number of vehicles or aircraft forming a definite group or 'unit'.

The dial. use (quot. 1884), which has passed into sporting lang., may be a northern pronunc. of FLIGHT.

a **1400–50** *Alexander* 1196 (Dublin) To founde forth with a flete [*Ashmole* flote] of fyfe hundreth knyghtez. **1649** BP. GUTHRIE *Mem.* (1702) 67 As soon as Episcopacy had been thrust out of this Church, there came..from Ireland a fleet of Scottish People. **1675** CROWNE *Country Wit* II. Dram. Wks. 1874 III. 53, I will convey you safe home with my fleet of lanthorns. **1810** *Sporting Mag.* XXXV. 311 A fleet of wild ducks had alighted. **1878** *Cumbld. Gloss.* s.v., 'Thou's cap't t'heall fleet o' them.' **1881** W. D. HAY *300 Years Hence* x. 248 The fleet of the Avengers sweeps onward through the air. **1884** *Chesh. Gloss.*, *Fleet*, an assemblage of birds when they come to their feeding ground or roosting quarters. **1889** *Kansas Times & Star* 7 May, A fleet of hacks was cruising around to take them to their..homes. **1905** *Daily Chron.* 11 Sept. 5/6 At five o'clock, when the motor fleet drew up. **1908** H. G. WELLS *War in Air* iii. §5, A fleet of airships. **1911** *Chambers's Jrnl.* 767/2 The vast sum of money..expended on..a single Dreadnought might better be devoted to creating a whole fleet of dirigibles and aeroplanes. **1915** W. J. LOCKE *Jaffery* iii, Barbara has gone away with the Daimler,..and as I don't keep a fleet of cars, I had to choose between this and the donkey-cart. **1924** F. J. HASKIN *Amer. Govt.* (rev. ed.) 433 Large fleets of trucks and automobiles. **1967** *Boston Sunday Globe* 23 Apr. 8/1 A separate electrically powered fleet [of trains] will be cutting the time between Manhattan and Washington, D.C. **1971** *Guardian* 22 Feb. 12/4 By accident I joined what drivers described as a company with one of the worst fleets of transport in the kingdom.

3. *Fisheries.* (See quots.)

1879 *Encycl. Brit.* IX. 251 They [nets in drift-fishing] are fastened together end to end, and thus form what is called a train, fleet, or drift of nets. **1887** *Kent. Gloss.* s.v., Every Folkestone herring-boat carries a fleet of nets, and sixty nets make a fleet. **1892** *Northumbld. Gloss.*, *Fleet*, a row of floating herring nets at sea attached to each other and to the fishing boat.

4. *attrib.*, as ***fleet-action***, ***engineer***, ***-man***, ***regatta***, ***surgeon***.

1901 J. BLAKE *How Sailors Fight* iv. 91 As the first phase of a *fleet action the captains of the various warships meet together on the admiral's flagship. **1910** *Daily Chron.* 17 Mar. 3/5 The fleet action of the future will..develop into an aggregation of duels between opposing battle units. **1901** J. BLAKE *How Sailors Fight* ii. 44 A *fleet engineer is always on duty in South Wales, and it is his business to recommend to the Government the coal they shall include in their contracts. **1904** *Daily Chron.* 1 Feb. 3/3 It will encourage straight shooting among the *fleetmen. **1905** *Ibid.* 19 July 5/6 The magic personality of British fleetmen. **1909** *London Mag.* Aug. 605/2 To cheer the fleetmen as they march through the streets. **1891** *Pall Mall G.* 18 Nov. 5/2 The annual *fleet regatta. **1892** *Ibid.* 30 Aug. 6/1 Dr. Irving was subsequently *fleet surgeon to Lord Wolseley in the Ashantee campaign.

fleet (fliːt), *sb.*[2] Now only *local.* Forms: 1 **fléot(e**, 5–9 **flete**, 6–7 **fleet(t)e**, 6 **flett**, 9 **flet**, 6– **fleet.** [OE. *fléot* str. masc. (also *fléote* wk. fem. or *fléota* wk. masc.), corresp. to OFr. *flêt*, MDu. *vliet* masc., neut. (mod.Du. *vliet* masc.), MLG. *vlêt*, MHG. *vliez* (early mod.Ger. *fliesz*) masc., ON. *fljót* neut.; f. OTeut. **fleut-an*: see FLEET *v.*[1]]

1. a. A place where water flows; an arm of the sea; a creek, inlet, run of water.

c **893** K. ÆLFRED *Oros.* I. i. §27 Ispania land is..eall mid fleote..ymbhæfd. *c* **1440** *Promp. Parv.* 166/2 Flete, there water cometh and goth, *fleta.* **1530** PALSGR. 221/1 Flete where water cometh, *breche.* **1622** DRAYTON *Poly-olb.* xxiii. 191 To the Sea..With Mosses, Fleets, and Fells, she showes most wild and rough. **1677** YARRANTON *Eng. Improv.* 108 Cloth..Fulled with our Mills by the open fleet. **1703** S. DALE in *Phil. Trans.* XXV. 1575/2 Certain remains of the old Channel, which the neighbouring Inhabitants still call Fleets. **1736** J. LEWIS *Hist. Isle of Tenet* (ed. 2) 78 A certain Flete..through which little Boats used to come to the aforesaid Town. **1827** *Sporting Mag.* XXI. 115 Nests formed amongst the reeds, by the side of the Fleets. **1891** A. J. FOSTER *Ouse* 214 Several narrow creeks running into the heart of the town [King's Lynn]..are called 'fleets'.

b. (from the use of creeks in drainage; see supra 1891): A drain, a sewer. *Obs.* exc. *dial.*

1583 *Sewers Inquisition* 8 (E.D.S.) A new and sufficient head like unto Stockwith new fleet shall [be] made and lade there. **1773** *Burstwick Inclos. Act* 22 The fleet or sewer. **1877** *N. W. Linc. Gloss.*, *Fleet*, a kind of drain.

c. *Comb.*: **fleet-dyke**, **-hole** (see quots.).

1839 STONEHOUSE *Axholme* 263 The west channel would then naturally warp up, and leave what is usually termed in such cases a fleet hole. **1858** SIMMONDS *Dict. Trade*, *Fleet-dyke*, an embankment for preventing inundation. **1877** *N. W. Linc. Gloss.*, *Fleet-hole*, a hole or hollow left by a drain having been diverted, or a bank having broken, and washed away the soil.

2. a. *the Fleet*: a run of water, flowing into the Thames between Ludgate Hill and Fleet Street, now a covered sewer; called also *Fleet ditch*; hence, the prison which stood near it.

1530 PALSGR. 201/1 Flete a prisone for gentylmen, *consergerie.* **1563–83** FOXE *A. & M.* 1191/2 Grafton was sent to the Fleet. **1613** *Letter* in Burn *Fleet Registers* (1833) 5 An ancyentt acquayntance of y^s and myne is yesterday maryed in the Fleete. **1712** ARBUTHNOT *John Bull* II. iv, Before the next [term] we shall have him in the Fleet. **1761** A. MURPHY (*title*), Ode to the Naiads of Fleet-ditch. **1837** DICKENS *Pickw.* xl, Mr. Pickwick alighted at the gate of the Fleet.

b. *attrib.*: ***Fleet books***, the records of the marriages celebrated in the Fleet Prison. ***Fleet chapel***, the place where the marriage ceremonies were performed. ***Fleet marriage***, one performed clandestinely by a Fleet parson in the Fleet; also ***Fleet-Street marriage***. ***Fleet parson***, one of a number of disreputable clergymen who were to be found in and about the Fleet ready to perform clandestine marriages. ***Fleet register*** = *Fleet book*. ***Fleet Street***, a street in London devoted largely to the production and publication of daily newspapers and periodical journals; hence *allusively*, the national newspapers generally, the journalistic press, journalism. So ***Fleet Streeter***.

1719 *Original Weekly Jrnl.* 26 Sept. in Burn *Fleet Registers* (1833) 7 Mrs. Ann Leigh..having been decoyed..and married at the Fleet Chapel. **1732** *Grub Street Jrnl.* 20 July (ibid.), A Fleet parson was convicted..of forty-three oaths. **1736** *Ibid.* 6 This advice cannot be taken by those that are concerned in ye Fleet marriages. *c* **1747** *Ibid.* (*title*), A Fleet Wedding. **1833** BURN *Fleet Registers* 5 The Fleet Registers ..commence about the period of the Order of the Ecclesiastical Commissioners. **1861** *Cornh. Mag.* June 688 A worthy woman whose daughter had been entrapped into a Fleet-Street marriage. **1882** C. PEBODY *Eng. Journalism* ii. 19 Fleet Street to-day, with its energy, enterprise, and intelligence, is a characteristic representation of the whole spirit of the English Press. **1893** FARMER & HENLEY *Slang* III. 19/2 *Fleet-Street*, the estate of journalism. *Ibid.*, *Fleet-Streeter*, a journalist of the baser sort. **1904** J. R. ROBINSON *50 Yrs. Fleet St.* 236 The passion for letter-writing to newspapers is recognised in Fleet Street as a distinct form of mental aberration. **1905** H. LEACH *Fleet St.* 87 A faculty for quick and perfect condensation is one of the most valuable possessions of the Fleet Street man. *Ibid.* 143 Fleet Street has its particular specialists for several of the courts of law. *Ibid.* 189 Their [*sc.* editors'] differences show how impossible it is for Fleet Street to tell what the morrow will bring forth for it. **1920** [see DOWNING STREET]. **1927** *Scots Observer* 12 Mar. 11/3 Shabbiness and flyblownness represent a Fleet Street tradition that has been broken. **1962** *John o'London's* 22 Feb. 177/3 The event is a natural for the copy-starved Fleet Streeters. **1969** *Times* 10 Dec. 11/4 The underminers in Fleet Street: *voilà l'ennemi.*

fleet, *sb.*[3]

1829 *Trial of J. Martin* 34, I saw the rope hanging from the window west of the Five Sisters window in the North transept. It was fastened to the fleet..the machine for cleaning the Minster.

fleet (fliːt), *sb.*[4] *Fishing.* [? f. FLEET *v.*[1] in sense 'to float'.] (See quots.) Cf. FLEET *sb.*[1] 3. Also, ***fleet-line***.

1880 *Antrim & Down Gloss.*, *Fleet-line* (float-line), a line used in a particular kind of sea-fishing; the hook floats midway between the surface and bottom. **1891** *Cent. Dict.*, *Fleet*, in fishing, a single line of 100 hooks: so called when the bultow was introduced in Newfoundland (1846).

fleet (fliːt), *a.*[1] Also 6 **flete.** Cf. FLIT *a.* [Not found before 16th c., but prob. much older; cogn. with or a. ON. *fliótr* swift; f. root of FLEET *v.*[1]]

1. Characterized by power of swift onward movement; swift, nimble. Said primarily of living beings, their limbs and movements; hence of things viewed as self-moving, thoughts, etc. Not in colloquial use.

a **1529** SKELTON *Replyc.* 50 Your tonges were to flete. **1579** LYLY *Euphues* (Arb.) 35 The fleetest fish swalloweth the delicatest bait. **1588** SHAKS. *L.L.L.* v. ii. 261 Their conceites haue winges, Fleeter than arrowes, bullets, wind, thought, swifter thinges. **1596** —— *Tam. Shr.* Induct. i. 26 If Eccho were as fleete, I would esteeme him worth a dozen such. **1671** MILTON *P.R.* III. 313 Thir horses..fleet and strong. **1752** CHESTERF. *Lett.* III. cclxxix. 281 In the situation of a man who should be very fleet of one leg, but very lame of the other. **1781** COWPER *A. Selkirk* 41 How fleet is a glance of the mind! **1810** SCOTT *Lady of L.* III. v, Fleet limbs that mocked at time. **1841** LANE *Arab. Nts.* I. 126 The antelope is supposed to be the fleetest quadruped on earth. **1869** FREEMAN *Norm. Conq.* (1876) III. xiv. 377 A messenger.. who had sped with a pace fleeter even than that of his own march.

2. Evanescent, shifting, passing away; not durable or lasting. *poet.*

1812 H. & J. SMITH *Rej. Addr.*, *Cui Bono* v, This goodly pile..Perchance than Holland's edifice more fleet. **1877** BRYANT *Poems*, *The Poet* iv, Seize the great thought..And bind, in words, the fleet emotion fast.

3. quasi-*adv.* Quickly, swiftly. *poet.*

1587 M. GROVE *Pelops & Hipp.* (1878) 82 When a man doth meete With such as stand more than his match, his winning goes to fleete. **1790** A. WILSON *Thunderstorm* Poet. Wks. (1846) 33 Fleet fled the shades of night. **1878** STEVENSON *Int. Voy.* 103 A thicket of willows..under which the river ran flush and fleet.

4. *attrib.* and *Comb.*, as ***fleet-feathered*** adj.; **fleet-foot** *a.*, *poet.* = next; : also *absol.*; **fleet-footed** *a.*, fleet of foot, swift in movement; also *fig.*; **fleet-hound**, ? a greyhound; in later use (see quot. 1888); **fleet-winged** *a.*, having fleet wings, swift of flight.

? **1862–63** G. M. HOPKINS *Poems* (1948) 177 Divinity of air, *fleet-feather'd gales. **1592** SHAKS. *Ven. & Ad.* 561 As the *fleet-foot Roe that's tyr'd with chasing. **1865** SWINBURNE *Atalanta* 6 Fleeter of foot than the fleet-foot kid. **1940** C. DAY LEWIS tr. *Virgil's Georg.* IV. 88 Arethusa the fleetfoot, her arrows at last laid by. *a* **1743** SAVAGE *To Bessy, C'Tess Rochford* Wks. 1775 II. 165 Tho' fate, *fleet-footed, scents thy languid son. **1791** COWPER *Odyss.* II. 13 His hounds Fleet-footed follow'd him. **1832** LONGF. *Coplas de Manrique* lii, Fleet-footed is the approach of woe. **1675** *Lond. Gaz.* No. 1037/4 An old white *fleet-hound Bitch. **1680** *Ibid.* No. 1550/4 A Brown spotted Foxhound Bitch.. a sharp long Red Head, like a Fleet Hound. **1888** H. DALZIEL *Brit. Dogs* (ed. 2) I. ii. 47 The Deerhound..is also named the Rough Greyhound, and the Northern, or Fleet-hound. **1593** SHAKS. *Lucr.* 1216 *Fleet-wing'd duetie with thoghts feathers flies. **1887** BOWEN *Virg. Æneid* IV. 180 Fleet-winged, speedy of foot, a colossal monster and dread.

fleet (fliːt), *a.*[2] Chiefly *dial.* Also 7 **flat**, 7–9 **flet**, (8 **flit**). [f. ME. *flet*, pa. pple. of FLEET *v.*[2] Cf. FLEETEN, FLATTEN, FLOTTEN.] Of milk: Skimmed. Also ***fleet cheese***, cheese made of skimmed milk.

1607 TOPSELL *Four-f. Beasts* (1658) 517 In Elsatia..they fat them [Hogs] with..Barly-meal wet with flat milk. **1688** R. HOLME *Armoury* III. 335/1 Dairy People..make..Flet and unflet Milk Cheese. **1741** *Compl. Fam. Piece* III. 498 Whey, flit Milk, Wash, Grains. **1807** VANCOUVER *Agric. Devon* (1813) 230 The milk..stands forty-eight hours before the flet-milk is run off. **1823** MOOR *Suff. Words*, s.v. *Flet*, Cheese made of this milk [flet-milk] is called Flet-cheese. **1882** *Lanc. Gloss.*, Flet-milk.

fleet (fliːt), *a.*[3] Now chiefly *dial.* and *Agric.* [Perh. repr. OE. **fléat*, corresponding to Du. *vloot* shallow (:—**flauto-*), f. root of FLEET *v.*[1]]

1. Having little depth; shallow.

1621 QUARLES *Argalus & P.* (1678) 9 Hazard no more To wrack your fortunes on so fleet a shore. **1647** TRAPP *Comm. Matt.* xv. 8 The deeper..the belly of the lute..is, the pleasanter is the sound; the fleeter, the more grating..in our ears. **1767** A. YOUNG *Farmer's Lett. to People* 120 Plough a very fleet furrow. **1802** W. TAYLOR in Robberds *Mem.* I. 407 The milk-trays..should be fleet. **1842** LONGF. *Sp. Stud.* III. vi, To pass through the dewy grass, And waters wide and fleet. **1882** *Blackw. Mag.* Jan. 104 Where the water is fleet and weedy.

b. (That is) at no great depth; near the surface; *esp.* quasi-*adv.* in ***to plough*** or ***sow fleet.***

1633 ROGERS *Treat. Sacraments* I. 160 The root is so.. fleet, that it will scarce furnish the tree with leaves. **1674** N. FAIRFAX *Bulk & Selv.* 185 Sometimes we find Gold..as fleet as the roots of shrubs in Peru. **1707** MORTIMER *Husb.* ii. 80 Those Lands must be ploughed fleet. **1803** SIR. J. SINCLAIR in *Annals Agric.* XL. 322 'Fallow deep, but sow fleet.' **1845** *Jrnl. R. Agric. Soc.* V. II. 326 The land is ploughed 'fleet', or about 3½ inches deep. **1876** *Surrey Gloss.* s.v., To plough fleet is to skim-plough land.

†**2.** Having little depth of soil; 'light, superficially fruitful' (J.). *Obs.*[−1]

1707 MORTIMER *Husb.* ii. 80 Marle Cope-ground, which is commonly a cold, stiff, wet Clay..unless..where it is very fleet for Pasture.

Hence **'fleetly** *adv.*, with little depth; shallowly.

1844 *Jrnl. R. Agric. Soc.* V. I. 19 Sown upon the surface or drilled fleetly.

fleet (fliːt), *v.*[1] Forms: *Infin.* 1 **fléotan**, (*3rd pers. pr. t.* **flýt**), 3–4 **fleoten**, (3 *south.* **vleoten**, **wleoten**), 3 **fleote**, 3–6 **flet(e(n**, 4–7 **fleete**, *Sc.* **fleit**, 4– **fleet.** *Pa. t.* 1 **fléat**, 3 *Orm.* **flæt**, 4 **fleet**, **flote**, 3–6 **flet**, *pl.* 1 **fluton**, 3 **fluten**, **floten**; weak forms 4 **fletide**, 4–6 **flette**, 6 *Sc.* **fletit**, **fletted**, 7 **fle(e)ted.** *Pa. pple.* 1, 4 **floten** (see FLOTTEN). [A Com. Teut. originally str. vb.; OE. *fléotan* (*fléat*, *fluton*, *floten*) to float, corresp. to OFris. *fliata*, OS. *fliotan* (MDu., Du. *vlieten*) to flow, OHG. *fliozzan* to float, flow (MHG. *vliezen*, mod.Ger. *fliesen* to flow), ON. *flióta* (Sw. *flyta*, Da. *flyde*) to float, flow (not recorded in Goth.):—OTeut. **fleutan* (*flaut*, *flutum*, *flotono-*), f. pre-Teut. root **pleud-*, *ploud-*, *plud-* (cf. Lettish *pludêt* to float, *pludi* flood, Lith. *plústi* to float away, *plūdis* float of a fishing-net), an extended form of the OAryan root **pleu-*, *plu-* (cf. Gr. πλέειν to sail, Skr. *plu*, *pru* to swim, float, flow, L. *pluĕre* to rain.]

I. To float.

1. *intr.* To rest upon the surface of a liquid; to be buoyed up; opposed to *sink*. *Obs.* exc. *dial.*

c **1000** ÆLFRIC *Hom.* (Th.) II. 564 Aʒeot ele uppon wæter oððe on oðrum wætan, se ele flyt bufon. *c* **1205** LAY. 21327 Heore scalen wleoteð, swulc gold-faȝe scelden. **13..** *E.E. Allit. P.* B. 1025 Lay þer-on [the Dead Sea] a lump of led & hit on loft fletez. **1398** TREVISA *Barth. De P.R.* XIII. xxi. (1495) 451 An egge fletyth in salte water and synkyth downe in fresshe water. **1460–70** *Bk. Quintessence* 9 A liquor of oyle fletynge aboue in maner of a skyn. *c* **1470** HARDING *Chron.* CCXVI. iv, The bodies flete amonge our shippes. **1578** LYTE *Dodoens* I. cci. 142 A water herbe which fleeteth upon the water. **1641** FRENCH *Distill.* v. (1651) 127 The Oil doth naturally fleet above. **1836** W. D. COOPER *Sussex Gloss.*, The tide comes in and the vessels fleet.

†**b.** *hyperbolically.* To 'swim' in blood, tears; to be 'bathed' in (happiness, etc.). *Obs.*

1297 R. GLOUC. (1724) 261 Heueden, (þat were of ysmyte,) Flete in blode. *a* **1500** *Chaucer's Dreme* 1962 Fleting they were in swich wele As folk that wolde in no wise Desire more perfit paradise. **1508** DUNBAR *Gold Targe* 70 Tullius, quhois lippis suete Off rethorike did in to termes flete. *a* **1605** MONTGOMERIE *Misc. P.* xxxv. 8 That..My pen in rhetoric may fleit. *c* **1611** CHAPMAN *Iliad* XIX. 204 My friend being dead..Lies in the entry of my tent, and in the tears doth fleet Of his associates.

†**c.** Of a vessel: To be or get afloat; to sail.

Beowulf (Th.) 3822 Sægenga for, Fleat famiȝheals forþ ofer yðe. *c* **1205** LAY. 32033 Alle þa scipen þa bi þare sæ fluten. *a* **1547** SURREY *Aeneid* IV. 525 Now fleetes the talowed kele. **1633** T. JAMES *Voy.* 82 Our Ship did not fleet.

†**2.** *intr.* To drift or be carried by the current or tide on the surface of the water. *Obs.*

c**897** ÆLFRED *Gregory's Past.* lviii. 445 Ðæt scip..sceal fleotan mid ðy streame. c**1250** *Gen. & Ex.* 3187 Moyses it [an gold gad] folwede ðider it flet. a**1305** *Life Pilate* 251 in *E.E.P.* (1862) 118 þat bodie flet vp and doun. **13..** *E.E. Allit. P.* B. 421 þe arc..flote forthe with þe flyt of þe felle wyndez. **1375** BARBOUR *Bruce* III. 630 The thingis that thar fletand war Thai tuk. **1501** DOUGLAS *Pal. Hon.* III 89 Part drownit, part to the Roche fleit or swam. **1590** MARLOWE *2nd. Pt. Tamburl.* I. i. Sailors..Shall meet those Christians, fleeting with the tide.

†**3.** *transf.* Of mists, clouds, spirits, an odour: To float (in air, etc.); to drift. *Obs.*

13.. *E.E. Allit. P.* A. 46 A fayre reflayr ȝet fro hit flot. **1528** LYNDESAY *Dreme* 223 Quhow that thay [spirits] lay, in to tha flammis fletyng. a**1623** W. PEMBLE *Zachary* (1629) 164 Thin Clouds, fleeting under the thicker and heavier. **1744** *J. Claridge's Sheph. Banbury's Rules* 9 Exhalations which while they fleet near the earth are stiled mists.

†**4.** To swim: said of fish, occas. of other animals and men. *Obs.*

Beowulf (Th.) 1089 No he fram me flodyðum feor fleotan meahte. c**1205** LAY. 22010 What letteð þene fisc to uleoten to þan oðere. **13..** *E.E. Allit. P.* B. 387 þe wylde of þe wode on þe water flette. **1377** LANGL. *P. Pl.* B. xx. 44 þe fisshe hath fyn to flete with. c**1470** HENRY *Wallace* VII. 847 The Irland folk..On craggis clam, and sum in wattir flett. a**1547** SURREY *Aeneid* II. 257 By the calme seas come fletyng adders twaine. a**1600** *Complaint* vi. in *Ramsay's Evergreen* I. 110 Leander on a stormy Nicht Diet fleitand on the Billous gray.

†**5.** Of a person: To be afloat (in a vessel); to journey or travel by water; to sail. Also with *in*. *Obs.*

c**1205** LAY. 28960 Forð flet mid vðe, folc vnimete. c**1320** *Sir Tristr.* 365 þe mariners flet on flode. c**1386** CHAUCER *Man of Law's T.* 365 Yeres and dayes flette this creature Thurghout the see of Grece. c**1460** *Towneley Myst.* (Surtees) 31 Apon this flood have we flett many day. **1563** B. GOOGE *Eglogs* viii. (Arb.) 66 Through the Chanell deepe..he fleets a pace. **1688** S. SEWALL *Diary* 14 Aug. (1882) I. 223 They..lay aground a pretty while before they could fleet in. **1725** DE FOE *Voy. round World* (1840) 319 They might fleet down this river.

†**6.** To move unsteadily, as a floating object; to shift or sway (*to and fro*, etc.); to fluctuate, waver. Both of material and immaterial things. *Obs.*

In 16–17th c. sometimes adopted to render the like-sounding L. *fluitare*.

c**1374** CHAUCER *Boeth.* I. pr. vi. 28 Wenest þou þat þise mutaciouns of fortune fleten wiþ outen gouernour. **15..** *Ragman Roll* 20 in Hazl. *E.P.P.* I. 70 She changyth euer, and fletyth to and fro. **1571** GOLDING *Calvin on Ps.* xxv. 15 Those that by fleeting to and fro forge sundry wayes to save themselves. **1597** LYLY *Euphues* (Arb.) 58 Can Euphues conuince me of fleeting, seeing for his sake I breake my fidelitie. **1581** SAVILE *Tacitus' Hist.* III. xxvii. (1591) 130 Those..who rowled down huge stones..forced the frame to stagger and fleete. **1638** SIR. T. HERBERT *Trav.* (ed. 2) 6 Shadowlesse when Sol is Zenith, from which point when it fleets either North or South [etc.].

II. To flow (and derived senses).

†**7.** Of liquid, *esp.* water, a river: To flow. *Obs.*

c**1200** ORMIN 18093 Se waterrstræm A33 fletteþþ forþ & erneþþ Towarrd te sæ. c**1400** *Destr. Troy* 1609 The water went vnder houses..And clensit by course all þe clene Cite Of filth and of feum, throughe fletyng by nethe. c**1425** *Festivals of the Church* 177 in *Leg. Rood* (1871) 261 Till fele teres gan flete. **1586** J. HOOKER *Girald. Irel.* in *Holinshed* II. 2/1 The riuer of the Surie..fleeteth by the citie of Waterford. **1595** SPENSER *Col. Clout* 596 Her words were like a streame of honny fleeting. **1610** W. FOLKINGHAM *Art of Survey* I. v. 10 Waters, which flit and fleete to and fro with wind-catches. c**1630** in Risdon *Surv. Devon* §225 (1810) 238 Still gliding forth, altho' it fleet full slow.

†**b.** *transf.* Of a multitude of persons: To 'stream'. *Obs.*

1596 DALRYMPLE tr. *Leslie's Hist. Scot.* x. 403 Cumis flowing and fleeting vnto thame troupis of the commoun peple. **1638** in Maidment *Sc. Pasquils* (1868) 29 Huge troups from quarters came fleeting.

†**8.** To overflow, abound. Const. *with.* (Cf. 'flowing with milk and honey'). *Obs.* [So ON. *fljóta*: see Fritzner *s.v.*]

c**1374** CHAUCER *Boeth.* I. metr. ii. 8 Who makeþ þat plenteuouse autumpne in fulle ȝeres fletiþ wiþ heuy grapes. *Ibid.* IV. pr. vii. 146 Ne hast [þou] nat comen to fleten wiþ delices. **1526** SKELTON *Magnyf.* 1093 With fantasyes my wyt dothe flete.

†**b.** *trans.* To overrun, flood, fill abundantly. *Obs. rare*$^{-1}$.

13.. *E.E. Allit. P.* B. 685 So folk schal falle fro, to flete alle þe worlde.

9. *intr.* †**a.** To dissolve or waste *away*; to become disintegrated, fall to pieces. *Obs.*

1382 WYCLIF *1 Macc.* ix. 7 Judas saw3 for his oost flette [1388 fleet (L. *defluxit*)] awey. c**1420** *Pallad. on Husb.* XII. 211 Yit pulle hem [plommes] rather then thai flete atwynne. **1583** STUBBES *Anat. Abus.* II. (1882) 36 Leather scarcely halfe tanned..within two or three daies wearing (especially if it come in any weat) wil..fleete and run abroad like a dish clout. **1598** W. PHILLIPS *Linschoten* (1864) 192 The bankes of sand doe fleet and vade away out of the Riuer. a**1661** FULLER *Worthies* (1840) II. 312 Leather, thus leisurely tanned..will prove serviceable, which otherwise will quickly fleet and rag out.

b. Of immaterial things: To fade or vanish, die out. Also with *away*. *Obs.* or *arch.* (blending with sense 10).

1576 NEWTON *Lemnie's Complex.* (1633) 192 No stampe, forme, or print, but such as presently fleeteth, and immediately vanisheth. **1596** SHAKS. *Merch. V.* III. ii. 108 How all the other passions fleet to ayre. **1616** B. JONSON *Poetaster* Apol., What they write 'gainst me Shall like a figure, drawn in water, fleet. **1787** MAD. D'ARBLAY *Diary* 26 Feb., Mr. Turbulent's compassion..fleeted away from the diversion of this recital. **1846** KEBLE *Lyra Innoc.* (1873) 59 The deeds we do, the words we say, Into still air they seem to fleet.

10. To glide away like a stream; to slip away, change position imperceptibly or stealthily; hence in wider sense, to flit, migrate, remove, vanish. Also with *away*. Now only *arch.* of immaterial things, and with mixture of sense 11.

c**1200** *Trin. Coll. Hom.* 177 Alle woreld þing ben fleted alse water erninde. c**1340** *Gaw. & Gr. Knt.* 714 Mony klyf he ouer-clambe in contrayez straunge, Fer floten fro his frendez fremedly he rydez. **1388** WYCLIF *Exod.* xxxix. 19 Lest tho [ryngis] weren loose and fletiden doun. **1563** GOLDING *Cæsar* IV. (1565) 95 b, The Sycambres had..fleeted out of theyr country. **1598** GRENEWEY *Tacitus' Ann.* VI. iii. (1622) 126 But Rubrius Fabatus..fleeting to the Parthians, and brought backe..by a Centurion, had keepers appointed him. **1667** MILTON *P.L.* III. 457 All th' unaccomplisht works of Natures hand,..Dissolv'd on earth, fleet hither. a**1730** FENTON *Poems* 14 The wand'ring ghosts..Fleet sullen to the shades. a**1839** PRAED *Poems* (1864) II. 48 The cares of boyhood fleet away. **1873** SYMONDS *Grk. Poets* iii. 75 The wealth that the gods give lasts, and fleets not away.

b. Of the soul: To pass away from the body; hence said of a dying man.

1590 MARLOWE *Edw. II*, IV. vi, Our souls are fleeting hence. **1622** FLETCHER *Span. Cur.* IV. v, *Bar.* I am sorry..To find ye in so week a state. *Die.* I am fleeting, Sir. **1713** STEELE *Guardian* No. 18 ¶5 You teach that souls..fleeting hence to other regions stray.

c. Of time: To pass rapidly and imperceptibly; to slip *away*. With mixture of the sense of FLEET *a.*[1]

a**1541** WYATT *Poet. Wks.* (1861) 11 My pleasant days they fleet and pass. **1621** MOLLE *Camerar. Liv. Libr.* III. i. 149 Six hundred yeares being fleeted away since. **1718** PRIOR *Poems* 297 The busie Moments..That fleet between the Cradle and the Grave. **1818** COLERIDGE *Method* in *Encycl. Metrop.* (1849) 5 He organizes the hours..the very essence of which is to fleet, and to have been. **1875** FARRAR *Silence & V.* xi. 195 Time may fleet, and youth may fade.

d. *trans.* To pass, while away (time); also, *to fleet it*. *rare.*

1600 SHAKS. *A.Y.L.* I. i. 124 Many yong Gentlemen..fleet the time carelesly. **1858** LEWES *Sea-side. Stud.* 396 Fleeting the quiet hour in observation of his pets. **1891** *Sat. Rev.* 8 Aug. 151/1 They read the Coinage Bill a third time, and so fleeted it goldenly..till one o'clock a.m.

11. *intr.* To move swiftly; to flit, fly. Also with *away*. Cf. FLEET *a.*[1]

c**1340** *Gaw. & Gr. Knt.* 1566 So felle flonez þer flete, when þe folk gedered. **1703** ROWE *Fair Penit.* v. i. 1885 Whether thro' the upper Air we fleet. **1801** *Lusignan* IV. 218 He fleeted across the plain. **1818** HOGG in *Blackw. Mag.* IV. 76 Yon little cloud..That..fleets away Beyond the very springs of day. **1836** T. HOOK *G. Gurney* III. 325 The thought had scarcely fleeted through my brain. **1856** STANLEY *Sinai & Pal.* i. (1858) 67 Sheets of sand fleeting along the surface of the Desert.

III. 12. *Naut. trans.* To change the position of, shift (a block, rope, etc.). Also *absol.* [Substituted for the earlier FLIT, owing prob. to association with sense 10 above.]

1769 FALCONER *Dict. Marine* (1789) Yb, To *fleet* or replace it, in a proper state of action..The man who performs this office..calls out, *fleet jigger*! **1859** F. A. GRIFFITHS *Artil. Man.* (1862) 107 To fleet blocks is to bring them as close together as possible. **1867** SMYTH *Sailor's Word-bk.*, *Fleeting*, the act of changing the situation of a tackle when the blocks are drawn together; also, changing the position of the dead-eyes, when the shrouds are become too long..*Fleet ho!* the order given at such times. *Ibid.*, *Fleet the messenger*, when about to weigh, to shift the eyes of the messenger past the capstan for the heavy heave. **1882** NARES *Seamanship* (ed. 6) 61 Fleet the purchase down to the water's edge.

Hence **'fleeted** *ppl. a.*

1810 SHELLEY *Zastrozzi* vii. Pr. Wks. 1888 I. 47 Matilda..succeeded in recalling to life Verezzi's fleeted faculties.

fleet (fliːt), *v.*[2] *Obs.* exc. *dial.* Forms: 5 fletyn, 6–7 flet(e, 6, 9 *dial.* flit, 6– fleet; *pa. pple.* 5 flet. [The precise formation is somewhat uncertain; prob. f. OE. *flét* cream, f. root of *fléotan* FLEET *v.*[1]; cf. Sw. dial. *flöta*, MDa. *flöde* (mod. *af-flöde*) of equivalent etymology. But as the Du. *vlieten* (= FLEET *v.*[1]) occurs in this sense, the Eng. vb. may possibly be a use of FLEET *v.*[1]]

1. *trans.* To take off that which floats upon the surface of a liquid; *esp.* to skim (milk, the cream from milk). Also with *compl.*

c**1440** *Promp. Parv.* 166/2 Flet, as mylke or oþer lyke, *despumatus*. *Ibid.* 167/1 Fletyn, or skomyn ale, or pottys, or oþer lycoure that hovythe, *despumo*. **1530** PALSGR. 551/2 Let us go flete this mylke agaynst she come to make her butter. **1577** B. GOOGE *Heresbach's Husb.* (1586) 146 b, The creame that swims aloft, is fletted off. **1601** HOLLAND *Pliny* II. 388 The fat which is fleeted or skimmed from the broth wherin dormice and rats be sodden. **1615** MARKHAM *Eng. Housew.* II. ii. (1668) 78 Boyl it..ever and anon fleeting it clean. **1725** BRADLEY *Fam. Dict.* s.v. *Milk*, You ought to fleet it [milk] by the Heat of warm Water. a**1796** VANCOUVER in A. Young *Ess. Agric.* (1813) II. 285 The milk of which cows..after standing 24 hours, is fleeted. **1836** W. D. COOPER *Sussex Gloss.*, *Fleet* or *Flit*, to skim milk.

b. *transf.* and *fig.*

1580 LYLY *Euphues* (Arb.) 336 It is he..that will fleete all the fat from thy beard. **1583** GOLDING *Calvin on Deut.* cxcvi. 1221 Wee shall not occupie the trade of marchandice by sea, we shall not flit off the fatte thereof. **1632** QUARLES *Div. Fancies* II. xxviii. (1660) 60 We Fleet the Mornings for our own design. a**1661** FULLER *Worthies* (1840) III. 4 Let us fleet the cream of a few of the primest libraries in all ages.

2. '*To Fleate.* To skim fresh water off the sea, as practised at the mouths of the Rhone, the Nile, &c.' (Smyth *Sailor's Word-bk.* 1867).

Hence **'fleeted** *ppl. a.*

1580 HOLLYBAND *Treas. Fr. Tong*, *Laict esburré*, fleeted milke. **1583** —— *Campo di Fior* 161 Upon fishe-dayes, fleeted milke. **1611** COTGR., *Escremé*, vncreamed, fleeted, as milk.

fleet (fliːt), *v.*[3] [? f. FLEET *sb.*[1] sense 3.] *intr.* ? To fish with a 'fleet'.

1630 in *Descr. Thames* (1758) 78 No Peter-man..shall fleet for Flounders with any Rug-Net in the Night-time.

fleet, dial. f. of FLIGHT; Sc. var. of FLUTE.

fleet(e, var. or dial. form of FLET *sb.* and *v.*

fleetch, obs. form of FLITCH *sb.*

'fleeten, *a.* *Obs.* [Altered form of FLOTTEN, assimilated to FLEET *v.*[2]]

1. (See FLOTTEN.)

2. Of the colour of skimmed milk. In quot. contemptuously of the face.

c**1618** FLETCHER *Q. Corinth* III. i, You know where you are you fleeten face.

3. quasi-*sb.* The *adj.* used *absol.* Skimmed milk.

1864 in WEBSTER.

†**'fleeter.**[1] *Obs. rare*$^{-1}$ [f. FLEET *v.*[1] + -ER[1].]

a. ? A shifty person (cf. FLEET *v.*[1] 6). **b.** A fugitive, deserter.

1581 MULCASTER *Positions* iii. (1887) 12 His countrey..pronounceth him to be but a fleeter, who so euer shall offer to force her that waye. **1598** FLORIO, *Profugo*, a fugitiue, a wandrer, a fleeter. **1609** J. DAVIES (Heref.) *Holy Roode* (Grosart) 9/1 Peter, Art thou for Christ his Church a fit foundation, That in Faith, from Faith, sans Faith, art a Fleeter?

fleeter[2] ('fliːtə(r)). [f. FLEET *sb.*[1] + -ER[1].] One who is engaged in 'fleeting' (see FLEETING *vbl. sb.*[3]). Also, a boat intended for 'fleeting'.

1888 *Scot. Leader* 11 July 7 The 'fleeters' do not always get free with smashes and cuts; one fleet alone loses 35 men on the average per year. **1893** *Ibid.* 15 Aug. 7 These vessels..differ from the ordinary trawlers in respect that while the latter return to port at least once a week, the fleeters remain at sea as long as their coals hold out.

fleetful ('fliːtfʊl). [f. FLEET *sb.*[1] + -FUL 2.] As many as would make a fleet; *transf.* a large number.

1899 *Westm. Gaz.* 21 Feb. 2/2 The public would have paid for a fleetful of ships. **1908** P. DINNEEN tr. *Keating's Hist. Irel.* II. 165 The king gave him a fleetful, that is, two thousand two hundred, and they put out to sea. **1923** S. GWYNN *Hist. Irel.* v. 45 The 'fleetfuls' of foreign students who came to attend surprisingly advanced teaching.

fleeting ('fliːtɪŋ), *vbl. sb.*[1] [f. FLEET *v.*[1] + -ING[1].] The action of the vb. in various senses.

1375 BARBOUR *Bruce* II. 588 To furthyr thaim off thar fleting. **1581** MULCASTER *Positions* xx. 84 It [walking] is good..for the iaundise, costifnesse, fleeting of the meat in the stomacke. **1587** GOLDING *De Mornay* xv. 229 The fleeting of soules out of one body into another. **1616** *Rich Cabinet* 95 b, The proudest confidence maketh our chiefest footing a changeable fleeting. **1871** TYLOR *Prim. Cult.* I. 127 One of the best known of English witch ordeals is the trial by 'fleeting' or swimming.

fleeting ('fliːtɪŋ), *vbl. sb.*[2] *Obs.* exc. *dial.* [f. FLEET *v.*[2] + -ING[1].]

1. The action of skimming a liquid, *esp.* milk.

c**1440** *Promp. Parv.* 167/1 Fletynge of lycowre, *spumacio, despumacio*. **1474** in *Househ. Ord.* (1790) 32 The maister cooke hath the fleetinge of the leade. **1615** MARKHAM *Eng. Housew.* ii. vi. (1668) 145 The fleeting or gathering of your Cream from the Milk.

b. *concr.* in *pl.* Skimmings, curds (see quots.).

1611 COTGR., *Sarrason*, *fleetings*, or hastie curds scumd from the whey of a new-milke cheese, then thickened [etc.]. **1845** H. WHITE in *Jrnl. R. Agric. Soc.* VI. I. 121 The last skimmings are termed fleetings, and are generally reserved for the use of the servants. **1873** E. SMITH *Foods* 329 When butter-milk is added to boiling whey..a soft curd is thrown down. This mixture is called fleetings in Wales.

2. *attrib.* and *Comb.*, as **fleeting-dish**, a dish used for skimming cream from milk; **fleeting-milk**, skim-milk; in quot. *fig.*

1736 BAILEY *Househ. Dict.* 181 Taking off the cream with a *fleeting dish. **1847** *Jrnl. R. Agric. Soc.* VIII. I. 75 This is..skimmed with a common fleeting-dish. a**1670** HACKET *Abp. Williams* I. (1692) 19 It was the *flitting milk of a poor Vicarage, the parsonage tithes being scumm'd from it.

fleeting ('fliːtɪŋ), *vbl. sb.*[3] [f. FLEET *sb.*[1] + -ING[1].] A particular kind of trawling (see quot.).

1884 *Daily News* 18 Sept. 5/2 The new 'fleeting' system, by which fishing boats are now kept at sea for a considerable time while fast steamers ply between them and the shore, carrying the fish as they are caught.

†**'fleeting**, *vbl. sb.*[4] *Obs.* [f. FLEET *sb.*[2]] Confinement in the Fleet Prison.

1589 SIR T. SMITH *Comm. Engl.* III. iv. 121 After they had..bin well disciplined as well by wordes, as by fleeting a while. **1592** G. HARVEY *Four Lett.* iii. Wks. (Grosart) I. 183 And that was all the Fleeting, that euer I felt.

fleeting (ˈfliːtɪŋ), *ppl. a.* [f. FLEET *v.*[1] + -ING[2].] That fleets, in senses of the vb.

†**1.** Floating; of a fish: Swimming. *Obs.*

a **1000** *Cædmon's Gen.* 1447 (Gr.) Se feond ʒespearn fleotende hreaw. **1340–70** *Alex. & Dind.* 491 þe fletinge fihs þat in þe fom lepen. **1578** LYTE *Dodoens* I. lxxi. 106 Amongst the fleeting herbes there is also a certayne herbe which some call Water Lyverworte.

†**2.** That moves constantly, shifting, unstable, wandering; hence of a person or his attributes: Changeable, fickle, inconstant, vacillating. *Obs.*

a **1225** *Ancr. R.* 76 Mid te fleotinde word, to fleoteð þe heorte. *c* **1374** CHAUCER *Boeth.* I. iii. (Camb. MS.) 6 Fleetynge Errour. **1413** *Pilgr. Sowle* (Caxton 1483) I. iii. 4 The fletyng ayer geuyth place to the flyght of byrdes. **1553** J. WILSON *Rhet.* (1580) 3 Preachers, must now and then plaie the fooles in the pulpit, to serve the tickle eares of their fletyng audience. **1592** GREENE *Groat's W. Wit* (1617) 15 If I finde thee firme, Lamilia will bee faithfull: if fleeting, she must..be infortunate. **1606** SHAKS. *Ant. & Cl.* v. ii. 240 The fleeting Moone No Planet is of mine. **1649** MILTON *Eikon.* ii. 17 Of such a variable and fleeting conscience what hold can be tak'n? **1650** FULLER *Pisgah* I. 424 Their wonder, that so firm a fabrick should stand on so fleeting a foundation.

†**3.** Flowing; fluid. ***fleeting sacrifices***: drink offerings. *Obs.*

c **1200** *Trin. Coll. Hom.* 177 Wat is folc bute fletende water. **1388** WYCLIF *Exod.* xxv. 29 Cuppis..in whiche fletynge sacrifices schulen be offrid. **1398** TREVISA *Barth. de P.R.* VI. xxii. (Tollem. MS.), Drynke is a fletynge substaunce nedful to þe fedynge of a beste. *c* **1420** *Liber Cocorum* (1862) 54 Take ryse and fletande fignade. **1567** TURBERV. *Epitaphes*, &c. (1870) 175 So stands the foole by fleeting floud. **1697** DRYDEN *Virg. Georg.* IV. 594 The slipp'ry God will..In fleeting Streams attempt to slide away.

4. Passing swiftly by. Chiefly of life or time.

c **1600** SHAKS. *Sonn.* xcvii, Thee, the pleasure of the fleeting yeare. *a* **1704** T. BROWN *Persius' Sat.* i. Wks. 1730 I. 53 Thy fleeting years of youth will soon be gone. **1811** W. R. SPENCER *Poems* 193 'Tis pain to part For e'en one fleeting night. **1862** STANLEY *Jew. Ch.* (1877) I. viii. 169 The fleeting generations of man.

5. Passing or gliding swiftly away.

1697 DRYDEN *Virg. Georg.* IV. 722 She said, and from his Eyes the fleeting Fair Retir'd like subtle Smoke dissolv'd in Air. *a* **1704** T. BROWN *On the Beauties* Wks. 1730 I. 44 Scarcely my breast my fleeting soul retains. **1797** MRS. RADCLIFFE *Italian* xvii. (1824) 619 He followed their fleeting figures. **1848** MRS. JAMESON *Sacr. & Leg. Art* 3 To catch the fleeting soul of the triumphant martyr.

6. Existing for a brief period; not permanent or enduring; transitory, passing, fading.

1563 B. GOOGE *Eglogs* (Arb.) 73 Beholde this fletyng world how al things fade. **1667** MILTON *P.L.* x. 741 O fleeting joyes Of Paradise. **1771** GRAY *Let.* 24 May, Poems (1775) 395, I have indeed a short one [journal]..that serves to recal and fix the fleeting images of these things. **1875** JOWETT *Plato* (ed. 2) IV. 30 Pleasure the most fleeting of all things.

Hence **ˈfleetingly** *adv.*, **ˈfleetingness.**

1709 BERKELEY *Th. Vision* §156 The perpetual mutability and fleetingness of those immediate objects of sight. **1842** MANNING *Serm. Faithf. Departed* (1848) I. 309 Poets were wont to bewail the fleetingness of life. **1883** M. K. MACMILLAN *Let.* 23 Oct., I have read, fleetingly, a very considerable section of his prose writings.

fleetly (ˈfliːtlɪ), *adv.* [f. FLEET *a.*[1] + -LY[2].] Swiftly, quickly; also *comb.*, as ***fleetly-mounted.***

1598 FLORIO, *Snellamente*, swiftlie, nimblie, fleetlie. **1814** SCOTT *Wav.* xviii, As fleetly as a roe. **1874** HOLLAND *Mistr. Manse* vii. 40 Full fleetly sped the morning hours. **1876–7** J. GRANT *Hist. India* I. xxiii. 122/1 Lightly-armed and fleetly-mounted horsemen.

fleetness (ˈfliːtnɪs). [f. as prec. + -NESS.] The quality of being fleet.

1. Swiftness.

1625 QUARLES *Sion's Sonn.* vii. 7 Behold the fleetnesse of his nimble feet. **1767** W. L. LEWIS *Statius' Thebaid* v. 1002 Fame..In Fleetness far outstrips the vig'rous Horse. **1856** STANLEY *Sinai & Pal.* viii. 321 The fleetness of foot, with which..he outran the chariot of Ahab.

2. Transitoriness.

1727 BAILEY, vol. II, *Fleetness*, fleeting Quality. **1863** I. WILLIAMS *Baptistery* II. xxiv. (1874) 95 All their notes..Are of our fleetness sighing, And singing of our dying.

fleety (ˈfliːtɪ), *a. rare.* [f. FLEET *a.*[1] + -Y[1].] = FLEET *a.*[1] I.

1841 *Tait's Mag.* VIII. 572 The rustle of thy fleety foot Upon my ear doth fall.

fleg (flɛg), *sb.*[1] *Sc.* [f. FLEG *v.*[1]] A fright, scare. Cf. FLEY *sb.*

1721 RAMSAY *Richy & Sandy* 9 Or has some Bogle-bo.. gi'en ye a fleg. **1818** SCOTT *Rob Roy* xviii, 'I got a fleg, and was ready to jump out o' my skin.'

fleg (flɛg), *sb.*[2] *Sc.* [Onomatopœic; cf. *fling*.] A random blow or kick, a stroke.

1722 HAMILTON *Wallace* III. i. (1822) 45 He..Syn at the loon a fearfull Fleg let flee, That from his Rumple shear'd away his Thigh. **1785** BURNS *Epist. to J. Lapraik* 21 Apr. ix, She's [Fortune's] gien me mony a jirt, an' fleg.

fleg (flɛg), *v.*[1] *Sc.* [The normal Sc. form of OE. *flecȝan* to put to flight, of which one example is known, if the reading of the MS. be correct. If not an error for *fléȝan* (see FLEY *v.*), it may perh. be a variant of that word, with abnormal doubled palatal and shortening of the vowel, as in *reckan* to reck, var. of *récan* (:—**rôkjan*).] *trans.* To frighten, scare.

1724 RAMSAY *Gent. Shep.* IV. i, We'll fleg him sae, he'll mint nae mair to gang A conjuring to do a lassie wrang. **1889** BARRIE *Wind. Thrums* xv. 141 'That was strong language', said Hendry, 'but he would be wantin' to fleg her?'

fleg (flɛg), *v.*[2] *Sc.* [? var. of FLAG *v.*, FLECK *v.*[2]] *intr.* To flee, run off; to fly away. Also with *off.*

1789 DAVIDSON *Seasons* 25 [The lambs] round a tammock wheel, an', fleggin, toss The moudy-hillan to the air in stoor. *Ibid.* 76 Nelly..aff wi' Gib the Mason Flegg'd fast, that day. **1893** STEVENSON *Catriona* 170 'The solan..flegged aff about the roundness of the craig.'

flegge, var. of FLEDGE *a. Obs.*

fleg(h), obs. pa. t. of FLEE *v.*; Sc. var. of FLEA.

flegm, var. of FLEAM.

flegm, flegm-: see PHLEGM, PHLEGM-.

fleiche, -sche, -tsche, var. ff. of FLEECH *v.*

fleicht, obs. f. of FLITE.

fleid, obs. pa. t. of FLAY.

fleigh, dial. f. of FLAKE, FLEA.

fleighter, var. of FLICHTER *v. Sc.*

fleih, obs. pa. t. of FLEE.

fleil(e, -yle, obs. ff. of FLAIL.

fleine, obs. pa. pple. of FLAY.

fleingall. [Prob. a spurious word, arising from a misprint in Topsell for *steingall*, the Ger. name of this bird; see STANIEL, STONEGALL.] An alleged name of the kestrel.

1607 TOPSELL *Serpents* 89 Those kind of Hawkes which are called Kaistrells or Fleingalls. **1611** COTGR., *Crecerelle*, a Kestrell, Fleingall. **1847** in HALLIWELL. **1885** SWAINSON *Prov. Names Birds* 140 *Fleingall*, i.e. Fly in gale.

fleir(e, obs. form of FLEER.

†**fleke**, *v. Obs. rare.* [? f. *fleke*, FLAKE *sb.*[1] hurdle.] *trans.* ? To cover with hurdles.

c **1330** R. BRUNNE *Chron.* (1810) 241 Botes he toke..þe sides togidere knytte..þei fleked þam ouerthuert..Ouer þe water..was so ordeynd a brigge.

fleke, obs. form of FLAKE.

flek(k)er, -ir, obs. ff. of FLICKER.

Flem (flɛm). An abbreviation of FLEMING[1].

1909 *Daily Chron.* 20 Aug. 3/3 Rubens..This exuberant, robust, vivacious Flem. **1925** *Contemp. Rev.* Mar. 312 The Flems outnumber the Walloons in Belgium.

flem(e, obs. var. of FLEAM.

†**fleme**, *sb.*[1] *Obs.* Forms: 1 flíema, fléma, flýma, 2–4 fleme, 3 flæme. [OE. *flíema* (:—earlier **fléamja*), f. *fléam*: see next.] A fugitive, exile, outlaw.

a **1000** *Cædmon's Gen.* 1020 (Gr.) þu flema scealt widlast wrecan. *c* **1000** ÆLFRIC *Gen.* iv. 12 þu..bist flyma ʒeond ealle eorþan. *c* **1175** *Lamb. Hom.* 157 We wunieð here alse fleme. *c* **1205** LAY. 5952 Alle þe flæmen þe iflowe buð of Rome. *c* **1305** *St. Dunstan* 101 in *E.E.P.* (1862) 37 He drof him out of Engelond: and let him grede fleme.

†**fleme**, *sb.*[2] *Obs.* Forms: 1 fléam, 3 flem, (vlem), fleom, (flæm, fleam), 3–4 fleme. [OE. *fléam* str. masc.:—OTeut. type **flauhmo-*, f. *flauh-* ablaut-var. of *fleuh-* to FLEE.] Flight; exile.

Beowulf 2889 (Gr.) Syððan æðelingas..ʒefricȝean fleam eowerne. *c* **1200** *Trin. Coll. Hom.* 149 We ben here alle on fleme. *c* **1205** LAY. 6407 He turnede to fleme. *Ibid.* 24070 Ofte he ulem makede. *c* **1300** *K. Alis.* 4341 So they hadde take fleme.

†**fleme**, *v. Obs.* From 16th c. chiefly *Sc.* Forms: 1 flíeman, fléman, flýman, 3 flæmen, fleman, -en, fleomen, *Orm.* flemmenn, *south.* vlemen, 4–5 flem, 4–7 fleeme, fleme, (4 flemme, flemon, 7 fleame). [OE. *flíeman* (:—earlier **fléamjan*), f. *fléam*: see prec. Cf. ON. *flǽma*.]

1. *trans.* To cause to flee, put to flight; to drive away, drive out, chase; hence, to banish, exile; *rarely*, to reject (a proposal). Also, ***to fleme away, out, to flight.*** **a.** simply.

a **1000** *Cædmon's Gen.* 2115 (Gr.) Ac hie god flymde. *c* **1200** ORMIN 8242 Augustuss..þatt flemmde himm ut. *a* **1300** *Cursor M.* 29022 (Cott.) Fasting flemes flexsli sakes. *c* **1330** R. BRUNNE *Chron.* (1810) 328 þo þat fled, þei flemed als þe kynges felons. *c* **1400** *Destr. Troy* 12377 And I..Thus am flemyt to flight thurgh his false caste. *c* **1425** *Festivals of Ch.* 183 in *Leg. Rood* (1871) 216 He will not flyte, But flemon all þi foos away. *a* **1450** *Le Morte Arth.* 2673 He were a fole ..So feyr forwardys for to fleme. **1496** *Dives & Paup.* (W. de W.) v. xiv. 215/1 God sayd to Caym..Thou shalt be wanderynge & flemed upon erth. **1553** KENNEDY *Comp. Tract.* in *Wodr. Soc. Misc.* (1844) 152 Geve the Kirk had the auld ancient libertie, than sulde all heresies be flemit. **1578** *Scot. Poems 16th C.* II. 171 They..flemit them full sair. **16..** *Merline* 1624 in Furniv. *Percy Folio* I. 472 The heyres that thou didst fleame With wrong out of the realme. **1814** SCOTT *Wav.* ix, 'He help'd Miss Rose when she was flemit with the Laird of Killancureit's new English bull.'

b. Const. *from, of* (= *out of*), *out of*; rarely with ellipsis of prep.

c **1200** *Trin. Coll. Hom.* 87 þis laȝe [circumcisio] flemeð þe fule gost ut of þe child. *c* **1205** LAY. 23447 þat he þa æð mihte wið Arðure uihte and ulemen of londe. **1352** MINOT *Halidon-Hyll* vi, The land that thai war flemid fra. *a* **1420** HOCCLEVE *De Reg. Princ.* 2788 Lawe is nye flemede out of this contree. **1494** FABYAN *Chron.* VI. ccxiii. 229 Algarus was accused by malyce, and flemyd the lande. **1513** DOUGLAS *Æneis* VIII. vi. 47 Banist and flemyt of my native land. **16..** *Marline* 426 in Furniv. *Percy Folio* I. 435 Many another doughtye Man that hee had fleemed out of the Land.

2. *intr.* To flee, run away. *rare*[−1].

c **1300** *K. Alis.* 3348 He is the furste with sweord that remith; Thou art the furste with hors that flemeth.

Hence **flemed** *ppl. a.*; **ˈfleming** *vbl. sb.* Also **ˈflemer**, one who puts to flight.

c **1205** LAY. 7733 Alle eowre flemede men. *a* **1300** *Cursor M.* 18626 (Gött.) Lang might adam thinc þe space Of fleming fra þat lauerd face. *c* **1374** CHAUCER *Troylus* III. 884 Dulcarnon clepid is 'flemyng of wrecchis'. *c* **1386** —— *Man of Law's T.* 362 Flemer of feendes. **13..** *Minor Poems fr. Vernon MS.* xxiii. 483 Went forþ A-pilgrimage And þe flemed visyted. **1496** *Dives & Paup.* (W. de W.) VII. vi. 284/1 He called them theues & outlawes & flemyd men. **15..** *Ragman Roll* 169 in Hazl. *E.P.P.* I. 76 Constant in vertu, flemer of malyce.

flemengo, obs. form of FLAMINGO.

ˈflemensfirth. [One of the many corrupt forms (see quots.) of OE. *flýmena fyrmð*, lit. 'entertainment of fugitives'.]

1. A term of OE. law, prob. meaning the offence of entertaining a banished person, and hence the king's right of exacting a penalty for this offence. The word was prob. not understood after the OE. period, but was preserved in formal enumerations of the rights pertaining to the king. The explanations in the quots. are the conjectures of legal antiquaries. A synonymous term *flýman feorm* (see FARM *sb.*[1]) occurs. in OE. laws, and is cited in various corrupt forms in law-books.

c **1020** *Secular Laws Cnut* c. 12 (Thorpe 1840) 164 Ðis syndon þa ʒerihta þe se cyning ah ofer eall men on Wessexan, þæt is..flymena-fyrmðe. *c* **1250** *Gloss. Law Terms* in *Rel. Ant.* I. 33 Fremenfremthe, *chatel de futif.* **1672** MANLEY *Cowell's Interpr.*, *Flemenes firinth*, But more truly Flymena frymthe..signifies the relieving of a Fugitive. This word is variously written in old Charters, as Flemeneferd, Flemenefrit, Flemenefremith, Flemanisflit, Flemenewurd, Fremenefenda, and Flemenesfricthe. *Ibid.*, *Flemenesfreme* and *Flemenesfrenthe* are said to be the Chattels of Fugitives.

¶**2.** Misused for: An asylum for outlaws.

1805 SCOTT *Last Minstr.* IV. xxiv, To make your towers a flemen's-firth.

Fleming[1] (ˈflɛmɪŋ). Also 5–6 flem(m)yng(e, 6–7 flemming(e, 7 flemin(e. [a. MDu. *Vlâming* (cf. ON. *Flǽmingr*, OHG. *Flaming*, med.L. *Flamingus*, Sp. *Flamenco*, Pg. *Flamengo*, Pr. *Flamenc*, Fr. *Flamand*), f. *Flâm-* (whence *Flanders*) + suffix -ING[3].]

1. A native or inhabitant of Flanders.

c **1430** LYDG. *Min. Poems* 105 Where Flemynges began on me for to cry, 'Master, what will you copen or by?' **1574** R. SCOT *Hop Gard.* (1578) 8 The more paynes you take..the nearer you resemble the trade of the Flemming. *c* **1645** HOWELL *Lett.* (1650) II. 30 Charles the Emperor..being a Flemin born. **1846** MCCULLOCH *Acc. Brit. Empire* (1854) 645 The Flemings, invited over..by Edward III., gave the first great impulse to the woollen manufacture.

†**2.** A Flemish vessel. *Obs.*

1595 DRAKE *Voy.* (Hakluyt Soc.) 7 We met with a small flemminge bounde for the streights.

3. *attrib.* quasi-*adj.* passing into *adj.*

1561 *Child Marriages* (E.E.T.S.) 70 A paire of Flemynge knyves. **1588** *Extracts Burgh Rec. Edin.* 8 May, The twa Flemyng wobsters dwelland within this burgh. **1656** BEN ISRAEL *Vind. Judæorum* 3 Some Flemine Christians.

†**ˈfleming**[2]. *Obs. rare.* Also 8 flemming. [Strictly only a use of prec., the continental names of the flamingo (Sp. *flamenco*, Fr. *flamant*) being popularly confused with the homophones = FLEMING[1], and hence rendered by the same word. (In quot. 1591 prob. FLEMING[1] was intended.)] = FLAMINGO.

[**1530** PALSGR., Flemmyng, *flammant.* **1591** PERCIVALL *Sp. Dict.*, *Flamenco*, a fleming, a kinde of birde like a shoueler.] **1708** MOTTEUX *Rabelais* IV. lix. (1737) 244 Flemmings, Cignets.

ˈfleming[3]. *dial.* In 7 flemminge. A local name of the soft clam (*Mya arenaria*).

1603 OWEN *Pembrokesh.* (1892) 126 Cockles, fflemminges, welkes. [Still in local use. (Editor's note).]

flemingin (flɛˈmɪndʒɪn). *Chem.* [f. mod.L. *Fleming-ia*, a genus of plants, f. the name of John *Fleming* (1747–1829), British physician and botanist + -IN[1].] A crystalline compound, $C_{12}H_{12}O_3$, obtained from *Flemingia* (= *Moghania*) *congesta* and used esp. as a yellow dye for silk.

1898 A. G. PERKIN in *Jrnl. Chem. Soc.* LXXIII. 661 *Flemingin*, which is the name proposed for the substance

thus obtained, is a dull, orange-red, crystalline powder, having a faint lustre. **1943** A. H. COOK tr. *Mayer's Chem. Natural Coloring Matters* iv. 258 Flemingin is obtained from waras.

†**Fleming-lauche.** *Obs. Sc.* [f. FLEMING[1] + *lauche*, Sc. form of LAW.] An old Scotch law which allowed the Flemings who settled in Scotland the practice of their own usages.

1629 in W. Robertson *Index Rec. Charters* (1798) 61 Carta to John Marr..una cum Lege Flemynga dicitur Fleming Lauche. **1807** G. CHALMERS *Caledonia* I. 735 The Flemings ..behaved so quietly, as to be allowed the practice of their own usages, by the name of Fleming-lauche, in the nature of a special custom.

Flemish ('flɛmɪʃ), *a.* Also 5 Flemis, 5–6 Flemys, 6–8 Flemmish(e. [ad. MDu. *Vlaemisch*, (Du. *Vlaamsch*): see FLEMING[1] and -ISH.]

1. Of or belonging to Flanders or its inhabitants. For ***Flemish ell, rider***: see the sbs.

1488 in *Ld. Treas. Acc. Scotl.* I. 79 Item, fyftene Flemis ridaris. **1540** *Act 32 Hen. VIII*, c. 14 A piece of flemmishe mony called an Englyshe. **1614** MARKHAM *Cheap Husb.* I. iii. (1668) 33 The best Stallion to beget horses for the Coach is the Flemish. **1703** MOXON *Mech. Exerc.* 240 The best sort of these are brought from Holland..and are called Flemmish Pan-Tiles. **1756–7** tr. *Keysler's Trav.* (1760) II. 385 Alexander duke of Parma, who signalized himself in the Flemish wars. **1865** MRS. PALLISER *Lace* vii. 99 The old Flemish laces are of great beauty.

b. *absol.* The Flemish language.

1727–41 CHAMBERS *Cycl.*, *Flemish*, or the Flemish tongue, is that which we otherwise call Low-Dutch. **1881** *Encycl. Brit.* XII. 85 Flemish or South Dutch.

2. Resembling a Fleming in habits and behaviour.

1598 SHAKS. *Merry W.* II. i. 23 This Flemish drunkard.

3. *Comb.*, **Flemish account**, an unsatisfactory account, one showing a deficit; **Flemish bond** (see BOND *sb.*[1] 13); **Flemish brick** (see quot. 1842); **Flemish coil** (see COIL *sb.*[3] 1); hence **Flemish-coil** *v.*, to lay up (a rope) in a Flemish coil; **Flemish eye**, *Naut.* (see quot. 1867); **Flemish fake**, *Naut.* (see quot.); **Flemish horse**, *Naut.* a foot-rope at the yard-arms of topsail yards; **Flemish point, stitch** (see quots.).

1785 GROSE *Dict. Vulg. Tongue*, **Flemish account*, a losing or bad account. **1790** HERBERT *Typogr. Antiq.* III. 1773, I am very much afraid my kind friend received but a Flemish account of his Caxtons. **1774** in *Archæol.* (1777) IV. 106 The *Flemish bond..is the strongest as well as the oldest regular bond used in building. **1890** RIMMER *Summer Rambles Manch.* 35 Red 'Dutch' bricks in 'Flemish bond'. **1727–41** CHAMBERS *Cycl.*, **Flemish Bricks*. **1842** GWILT *Encycl. Archit.* Gloss., *Flemish Bricks*, a species of brick used for paving..they were originally imported from Flanders, are of a yellowish colour and harder than common brick. **1841** R. H. DANA *Seaman's Man.* 106 This is called a *Flemish coil. **1878** W. C. RUSSELL *Wreck Grosvenor* ii. (1889) 11 Ordinary seamen, whom he had set to work to *flemish-coil the ropes along the deck. **1840** R. H. DANA *Bef. Mast* xxxv. 134 The knots, *Flemish eyes, splices. **1867** SMYTH *Sailor's Word-bk.*, *Flemish eye*, a kind of eye-splice in which the ends are scraped down, tapered, passed oppositely, marled, and served over with spun yarn. *Ibid.*, **Flemish Fake*, a method of coiling a rope that runs freely when let go..Each bend is slipped under the last, and the whole rendered flat and solid to walk on. **1841** R. H. DANA *Seaman's Man.* 105 **Flemish-horse*. **1882** CAULFEILD & SAWARD *Dict. Needlework*, **Flemish Point*, a Guipure Lace, also known as Point de Brabant. *Ibid.*, **Flemish Stitch*, one of the Fillings in Honiton Lace.

flemish ('flɛmɪʃ), *v.*[1] *Naut.* [f. prec.]

1. *trans.* To coil or lay up (a rope) in a Flemish coil (see prec. 3). Also ***to flemish down***.

1832 MARRYAT *N. Forster* xi, The ropes [had been] flemished down on deck. **1867** in SMYTH *Sailor's Word-bk.*

2. (See quot.)

1867 SMYTH *Sailor's Word-bk.*, *Flemishing*, a forcing or scoring of the planks.

flemish ('flɛmɪʃ), *v.*[2] *intr.* Of a hound: To make a quivering movement with the tail and body, while searching for the trail; to feather.

1857 KINGSLEY *Two Y. Ago* xviii, 'I thought they beauties starns weren't flemishing for nowt.' *Ibid.*, The hounds have overrun the scent, and are back again, flemishing about the plashed fence on the river brink.

flemy, flench, obs. ff. PHLEGMY, FLINCH.

flench, flinch, flense (flɛnʃ, flɪnʃ, flɛns), *v.* Also flence, flinse. [a. Da. *flense* of same meaning; the word with wider application is found in Norw. as *flinsa*, *flunsa* to flay, tear off.]

1. *trans.* To cut up and slice the fat from (a whale or flayed seal); to slice (the blubber) from the bones of the whale.

1814 SCOTT *To Dk. Buccleugh* 13 Aug. in *Lockhart*, The Islesmen of Sanda were..flinching..the blubber to boil. **1820** SCORESBY *Acc. Arctic Reg.* II. 292 Before a whale can be flensed, as the operation of taking off the fat and whale-bone is called. **1823** MANBY *Voy. Greenl.* 65 For the purpose of 'flinsing' or stripping it of its blubber. **1867** SMYTH *Sailor's Word-bk.*, *Flense*.

2. To flay or skin (a seal); to strip off (the skin of a seal).

1874 MARKHAM *Whaling Cruise* ii. 33 The marvellous rapidity..with which our men would skin, or as it is termed, 'flinch' the beast [seal]. **1875** CAPT. GRAY in Buckland *Log-bk.* 312 The [seal] skins are then flenched. **1881** LESLIE tr. *Nordenskiöld's Voy. Vega* iii. 114 The hunter lies to at an ice-floe to flense upon it a seal that has been shot.

Hence **'flenching, 'flensing** *vbl. sb.*; also **'flencher, 'flenser,** one who flenches or flenses whales.

1814 SCOTT *Diary* 11 Aug. in *Lockhart*, The crew..with their long flinching knives with which they cut up the whales. **1820** SCORESBY *Acc. Arctic Reg.* II. 299 The flensers commence with the belly and under jaw. *Ibid.* II. 301 During the progress of the flensing. **1874** MARKHAM *Whaling Cruise* iv. 50 The cutting up or 'flinching' of the fish.

'flench-gut, 'flens-gut. [f. prec. vb. + GUT.] The place on board, usually the hold, where the blubber of a whale, cut up in long slices, is stored before barrelling; also applied to the blubber itself.

1808 JAMIESON, *Flench-gut*, the blubber of a whale laid out in long slices, before being put into casks. **1820** SCORESBY *Acc. Arctic Reg.* II. 304 When the flens-gut is filled with blubber. **1867** in SMYTH *Sailor's Word-bk.*

flenders, obs. form of FLINDERS.

flene, obs. pa. pple. of FLAY.

fleng(e, flent, obs. ff. FLING, FLINT.

fleobotomie, obs. form of PHLEBOTOMY.

fleoure, -owre, obs. Sc. ff. FLAVOUR.

†**flerd.** *Obs.* Forms: 1 fleard, 3 flærd, flerd. [OE. *fleard*, app. cogn. with the synonymous ON. *flærð* str. fem., though the vowels do not regularly correspond.] Deceit, fraud, mockery.

c **1000** *Law Northumb. Priests* liv. (Thorpe 1840) 420 ȝif frið-ȝeard si on hwæs lande abuton stan oþþe treow, oþþe wille, oþþe swilces ænige fleard. *c* **1200** ORMIN 7334 Crist forrwerrpeþþ falls & flærd. *c* **1220** *Bestiary* 452 So was herodes fox and flerd.

flere, flerye, obs. ff. FLEER.

†**flerk,** *v. Obs.* Also 8 flirk. [Onomatopœic; cf. *flick, flirt, jerk.*] *intr.* To make a jerking movement. Hence **flerk** *sb.*, a jerk. **'flerking** *ppl. a.*, jerking, twitching.

1606 SYLVESTER *Du Bartas* II. iv. *Tropheis* 348 With sudden flerk the fatale hemp lets goe The humming Flint. *c* **1620** Z. BOYD *Zion's Flowers* (1855) 134 With sudden flerk the hempe I'le nowe let goe. **1710** *Lond. Gaz.* No. 4768/4 Stolen..Cart Mare..Saddle Backed, and a flirking Tail.

flerry ('flɛrɪ), *v. trans.* To split (slate). Also *intr.* for *refl.* of the slate itself. Hence **'flerrying** *vbl. sb.*

1865 J. T. F. TURNER *Slate Quarries* 13 The better the quality of the slate, the easier will it flerry, and also cleave. *Ibid.*, This peculiar operation is called 'flerrying'.

flert, obs. form of FLIRT.

flesh (flɛʃ), *sb.* Forms: 1 flǽsc, flǽc, (2 flec, flesce), 3 flæsce, flæs(h, flexs(s, fless(e, 4 *south.* vlesse, 3–4 fles, flei(e)s, fle(y)hs, 4–5 fleisch, 3–5 fle(c)che, flesch(e, 3 *south.* vlesche, (3 flashe, fleschs, 4 fleschsch), 3–6 flessh(e, (4 fleisshe), 4–6 fleshe, (6 fleash, flehsse, fleszhe, 9 *dial.* flash), 4– flesh. [Com. WGer. and Scandinavian: OE. *flǽsc* str. neut. corresponds to OFris. *flâsk*, OS. *flêsk* (Du. *vleesch*), OHG. *fleisc* (MHG. *vleisch*, mod.Ger. *fleisch*), of the same meaning, ON. *flesk* with shortened vowel (Sw. *fläsk*, Da. *flesk*), swine's flesh, pork, bacon:—OTeut. **flaiskoz-, -iz-* (or possibly *pl-*).

No satisfactory cognates have been discovered either in Teut. or in the related langs. Some have supposed that the specific Scandinavian sense, which exists in some Eng. dialects where ON. influence is out of the question (see, e.g., the *West Cornwall Glossary*), is the original meaning of the word, and that the occasional OE. form *flǽc* represents the primary word elsewhere replaced by a derivative with suffix *-sk-*. On this hypothesis the word might be related to OE. *flicce*, FLITCH. But general analogy rather indicates the priority of the wider sense found in Eng. and German; and it is most likely that the OE. *flǽc* is an inaccurate spelling, or at most a dialectal phonetic alteration, of the ordinary *flǽsc*. The shortening of the OE. long vowel before *s* followed by another cons. is normal.]

I. As a material substance.

1. a. The soft substance, *esp.* the muscular parts, of an animal body; that which covers the framework of bones and is enclosed by the skin. ***raw flesh***: that exposed by removal or fissure of the skin.

c **1000** ÆLFRIC *Gen.* ii. 23 Ðis ys nu ban of minum banum & flæsc of minum flæsce. *c* **1250** *Gen. & Ex.* 2089 Fugeles sulen ði fleis to-teren. **1398** TREVISA *Barth. de P.R.* V. i. (1495) 100 The heed hath lytill flessh and lytyll fatnesse. *c* **1400** *Lanfranc's Cirurg.* 218 If he be stronge & ful of fleisch. **1596** SHAKS. *Merch. V.* III. i. 54, I am sure if he forfaite, thou wilt not take his flesh. **1611** BIBLE *Lev.* xiii. 10 If..there be quicke raw flesh. *a* **1688** BUNYAN *Heavenly Footman* (1886) 164 His..sins, that stick as close to him as the flesh sticks to the bones. **1750** LADY LUXBOROUGH *Lett. to Shenstone* 13 May, One [wound] just above my knee..New flesh must grow there. **1819** SHELLEY *Cenci* III. i. 22 It..eats into my sinews, and dissolves My flesh to a pollution.

b. Often in connexion with or contrast to *bone*, *fell*, or *skin*.

c **1000** *Ags. Gosp.* Luke xxiv. 39 Gast næfþ flæsc & ban. *c* **1220** *Bestiary* 136 His fel he ðer leteð; his fles forð crepeð. *a* **1300** *Cursor M.* 17288 + 449 (Cott.) Spirit has nauther flesch ne bone. **1382** WYCLIF *Lev.* ix. 11 The flesh forsothe, and the skynne of it [calf]..he brent. *a* **1400** *Prymer* (1891) 79 With skyn and fleschsches thou clothedest me. *a* **1577** GASCOIGNE *Wks.* (1587) 36 To search between the fel and the flesh for fardings. **1611** BIBLE *Ezek.* xxxvii. 8 The sinews and the flesh came vp vpon them [bones], and the skin couered them aboue.

c. ***flesh and fell***: the whole substance of the body; hence as quasi-*advb.* phrase: entirely. (*to raise* or *rise*) ***in flesh and fell***, rarely ***in flesh and bone***: in bodily form. Cf. Fr. *en chair et en os.* (***fair***) ***of flesh and fell***: in form and complexion. *Obs.* exc. *arch.*

c **1000** ÆLFRIC *Exod.* xxix. 14 Þæs cealfes flæsc and fell ..þu bærnst. **1297** R. GLOUC. (1724) 287 He was..vayr of fless & felle. *a* **1300** *Cursor M.* 26564 (Cott.) To rise in flexss and ban. *c* **1375** *Lay Folks Mass Bk.* (MS. B.) 223 Vp he rose in flesshe & felle þo thryd day. *a* **1440** *Sir Eglam.* 29 Crystyabelle, A feyre thynge of flesche and felle. **1605** SHAKS. *Lear* v. iii. 24 The good yeares shall deuoure them, flesh and fell. **1840** BROWNING *Sordello* II. 300 Men burned Taurello's entire household, flesh and fell.

d. ***proud flesh***: the overgrowth of the granulations which spring upon a wound. Also *fig.*

1578 LYTE *Dodoens* VI. lxviii. 746 The same [oakgalls] doth..consume away superfluous and prowde fleshe. **1649** LOVELACE *Poems* 28 The anger of her eye, Had wrought some proud-flesh by it. **1686** W. HARRIS tr. *Lemery's Course Chym.* (ed. 2) 171 This Sublimate..eats proud flesh and cleanses old Ulcers. **1848** CARPENTER *Anim. Phys.* 302 The sprouting forth of a rapidly-growing tissue commonly known as proud-flesh.

e. phr. ***to make one's flesh creep***, etc. Also with *crawl* (cf. CRAWL *v.*[1] 6).

1727, 1840 [see CREEP *v.* 6]. **1725** RAMSAY *Gent. Sheph.* I. i, A..dream..That gars my flesh a' creep yet with the fright. **1834** MEDWIN *Angler in Wales* II. 252 A cold—a creeping of the flesh—like that. **1876** 'MARK TWAIN' *Tom Sawyer* 61 It makes my flesh crawl to hear you.

f. In, or with reference to, the Biblical phrase 'a heart of flesh', i.e. a heart capable of feeling, opposed to 'a heart of stone'.

1382 WYCLIF *Ezek.* xxxvi. 26, I shal take awey a stonen herte..and I shal ȝeue to ȝou an herte of fleshe. **1784** COWPER *Task* II. 8 There is no flesh in man's obdurate heart. **1814** SCOTT *Ld. of Isles* VI. xxix, Are your hearts of flesh or stone?

g. In euphemistic phrases with reference to sexual intercourse.

a **1300** *Cursor M.* 28475 (Cott.) Wit womman knaun and vnkend, I haue my fles wit þam blend. **1611** SHAKS. *Wint. T.* IV. iv. 285 She wold not exchange flesh with one that lou'd her. **1620** *Ballad 'As I was ridinge'* 18 in Furniv. *Percy Folio* (1867) App. 29.

h. ***to go after*** or ***follow strange flesh***: a Biblical expression referring to unnatural crime.

1382 WYCLIF *Jude* 7 Sodom and Gomor..goyng aftir other flesch. **1526** TINDALE *ibid.*, Folowed straunge flesshe [similarly in the later versions].

2. *transf.* The soft pulpy substance of fruit, or a plant; that part which is enclosed by the rind, and encloses the core or kernel, *esp.* when eatable. So Gr. σάρξ, L. *caro*, Fr. *chair*.

1573 BARET *Alv.* F 649 *Fleash*, the substance vnder the pille or rinde of herbs, &c. **1577** B. GOOGE *Heresbach's Husb.* II. (1586) 110 b, Reedes for the most parte have no fleshe at all. **1672** JOSSELYN *New Eng. Rarities* 57 The seeds are black, the flesh or pulpe exceeding juicy. **1779** MRS. BOSCAWEN in *Mrs. Delany's Life & Corr.* Ser. II. II. 489 The seeds are found in several parts of the flesh. **1846** *Proc. Berw. Nat. Club* II. No. 14. 174 (Agaric) Flesh thick, solid and firm. **1895** *Seed Catal.* (Potato) Flesh white, fine and floury.

3. Put for: Quantity or excess of flesh; hence, plumpness, good condition, embonpoint, *esp.* in phrases, ***to get***, (†***get oneself in***), ***lose flesh***; also (***to be***) ***in flesh***: in good condition, corpulent. Cf. Fr. *être en chair*.

1548 HALL *Chron.*, *Edw. IV*, 234 A beautefull Prince, beginninge a littel to growe in flesh. **1592** SHAKS. *Rom. & Jul.* V. i. 84 Buy food, and get thy selfe in flesh. **1608** BP. HALL *Char. Virtues & V.* 103 Hee is a slave to envie, and loseth flesh with fretting. **1677** HOLYOKE *Lat. Dict.*, To get flesh, *pinguesco*. **1684** R. H. *School Recreat.* 26 If he be low of Flesh..add a third part of clean old Beans. **1707** *Lond. Gaz.* No. 4350/4 A bay Gelding, well in Flesh. **1757** FRANKLIN *Lett.* Wks. 1887 II. 527, I..have not yet quite recovered my strength, flesh, or spirits. **1762** GOLDSM. *Cit. W.* lxxi, The widow, being a little in flesh, as warmly protested against walking. **1774** J. BRYANT *Mythol.* II. 452 Oxen that were in flesh and well fed. **1885** E. GARRETT *At Any Cost* ii. 27 Its [a face's] once noble outlines were blurred by too much flesh.

4. a. The muscular tissue, or the tissues generally, of animals, regarded as an article of food. Exc. when otherwise defined by the context, always understood as excluding *fish* (see FISH *sb.*[1]), and in recent use primarily suggesting 'butchers' meat', not poultry, etc. (cf. 'fish, flesh, and fowl'). Somewhat *arch.*, the current word being *meat* (it survives however in some northern dialects).

a **800** *Corpus Gloss.* 2135 *Viscera tosta*, ȝebreded flaesc. *a* **1154** *O.E. Chron.* an. 1137 Þa wæs corn dære & flec. *c* **1205** LAY. 19693 Neoþer flæs na no fisc no nanes cunnes drænc. *c* **1290** *S. Eng. Leg.* I. 12/374 To rosti ase men doht fersch flesch. *c* **1400** *Lanfranc's Cirurg.* 266 Sche schal drinke no wijn ne ete no fleisch. **1472** *Presentments Juries* in *Surtees Misc.* (1890) 23 We desyer a remedy of our buschers for

sellynge of thar flech. **1562-3** *Act 5 Eliz.* c. 5 §11 No maner of person shall eate any Fleshe on the same [Fishe] daye. **1599** NASHE *Lenten Stuffe* Wks. (Grosart) II. 273 The puffin that is halfe fish, halfe flesh. **1676** WOOD *Life* (Oxf. Hist. Soc.) II. 341 Not eat a bit of flesh from Shrove Tuesday till Easter Day. **1732** POPE *Hor. Sat.* II. ii. 70 The stomach (.. a tomb of boil'd and roast, and flesh and fish). **1772** JOHNSON *Lett. to Mrs. Thrale* 19 Oct., Flesh is likewise very dear. **1802** FOSBROOKE *Brit. Monachism* (1843) 70 Neither do they eat of fat or flesh.

b. With the name of the animal or other defining word attached; also †in *pl.* to signify what is derived from various animals.

c **825** *Vesp. Psalter* xlix. [l.] 13 Ah ic eotu flesc ferra. *c* **1250** *Gen. & Ex.* 1013 Bred, kalues fleis, and flures bred. *c* **1330** R. BRUNNE *Chron.* (1810) 175 þe comon of þe oste bouht þam hors flesch, Or mules or assis roste. **1486** *Bk. St. Albans* Cjb, Thees sayd fleshes bene goode to mewe an hawke. **1528** PAYNEL *Salerne Regim.* Eijb, Goottis fleshe .. oxe fleshe .. be melancolye fleshes. **1685** P. HENRY *Diaries & Lett.* (1882) 341, I am careful wt I eat, not Fishes & Fleshes. **1865** BARING GOULD *Were-wolves* xv. 264 When a wolf has once tasted human flesh, he desires to taste it again.

†**c.** phr. ***neither flesh nor fish***: neither one thing nor the other. Cf. FISH *sb.* 4c. *Obs.*

1528 ROY *Rede me* (Arb.) 117 Wone that is nether flesshe nor fisshe, At all tymes a commen lyer. **1661** BAXTER *Mor. Prognost.* I. xciii. 22 Men of no Zeal, neither Flesh nor Fish.

d. ***strange flesh***: unusual or loathsome food. *rare.*

Perh. an echo of the Biblical use *Jude* 7, though the meaning is different (see 1 h).

1606 SHAKS. *Ant. & Cl.* I. iv. 67 On the Alpes, It is reported thou did'st eate strange flesh. **1819** SHELLEY *Cenci* III. i. 48 Beatrice .. whom her father .. pens up naked in damp cells .. and starves her there, Till she will eat strange flesh.

†**e.** *collect.* Cattle intended for food. *Obs.*

16.. *Robin Hood & Butcher* 16 in Furniv. *Percy Folio* I. 20 A proud butcher Came driving flesh by the way. **1709** STRYPE *Ann. Ref.* I. xvi. 199 That no butcher should kill flesh, upon pain of a great fine.

†**f.** (See quot.) *Obs.*

1569 in J. Mackenzie *Gen. Grievances Orkney & Shetland* 17 Item, the Comptare charges him with the third of the flesh of the Bishoprick of Orknay. **1859** *Oppress. 16th C. in Orkney & Zetland* Gloss., *Flesh*, Rent paid in Cattle, generally estimated by Weight, 15 Meils = an ox, 10 Meils = a cow, 4 Meils = a sheep.

5. a. The visible surface of the body, with reference to its colour or appearance. Cf. FLESH-COLOUR.

1606 SHAKS. *Ant. & Cl.* I. ii. 17 *Sooth.* You shall be yet farre fairer then you are. *Char.* He meanes in flesh. **1657** *Lust's Dominion* I. ii. 9 Although my flesh be tawny, in my veines, Runs blood as red, as royal, as the best .. in Spain.

b. *ellipt.* for *flesh-colour.*

1852 *Meanderings of Mem.* I. 157 Air coloured, scarcely carnate, or a flesh. **1882** *Garden* 14 Oct. 341/1 The names of the best varieties .. are .. Perfection, flesh.

6. Short for *flesh-side* (of a skin); see 13.

1839 URE *Dict. Arts* 378 It [the leather] is then .. slicked upon the flesh with a broad smooth lump of glass. **1851** MAYHEW *Lond. Labour* I. 443 The skin is 'split' .. into two portions. That known as the 'grain' .. The other portion, the 'flesh'. **1870** *Eng. Mech.* 11 Feb. 534/2 Oil them [skins], flesh and grain.

II. Extended and figurative uses (chiefly of Biblical origin).

7. ***one's (own) flesh***: one's near kindred or descendants. Now *rare* exc. in FLESH AND BLOOD. Also, ***one flesh***: said (after *Gen.* ii. 24, *1 Cor.* vi. 16) of husband and wife to express the closeness of the relation created by marriage.

c **1000** ÆLFRIC *Gen.* xxxvii. 27 He ys ure broþor & ure flæsc. *c* **1300** *Harrow. Hell* 196 Mi leve moder wes Boren and shaped of thi fleyhs. **1382** WYCLIF *Isa.* lviii. 7 Thi flesh thou shalt not despise. **1553** T. WILSON *Rhet.* (1580) 71 Your grace, lackyng twoo suche portions of your owne fleshe [your two sons]. **1555** EDEN *Decades* Pref. to Rdr. (Arb.) 50 Owre brootherne, owre flesshe, & owre bones. **1694** CONGREVE *Double Dealer* II. i, Marriage makes man and wife one flesh. **1819** SHELLEY *Cenci* I. iii. 104 What, if we .. were his own flesh, His children and his wife?

8. That which has corporeal life. ***all flesh***, †***each flesh*** (*omnis caro*, Vulg. = Hebraistic Gr. πᾶσα σάρξ): all animals; in narrower sense, all mankind. So †***no flesh***: nobody on earth. †***a piece of flesh***: a human being, sample of humanity.

c **1000** *Ags. Ps.* cxxxv[i]. 26 He eac afedeð flæcsea æghwylc. *c* **1000** *Ags. Gosp.* Luke iii. 6 Ælc flæsc ȝesihð godes hæle. *c* **1250** *Gen. & Ex.* 591 Đo was ilc fleis on wer[l]de slaȝen. *a* **1300** *E.E. Psalter* cxliv. 21 Blisse sal alle flesche withal Unto hali name es hisse. *c* **1380** WYCLIF *Sel. Wks.* II. 400 But ȝif þes daies shulen be abreggid þer shulde not be saved ech fleish. *c* **1450** tr. *De Imitatione* III. lxii, þou art flesshe and non aungell. **1535** COVERDALE *Jer.* xvii. 5 Cursed be the man .. that taketh flesh for his arme. **1599** SHAKS. *Much Ado* IV. ii. 85 As pretty a peece of flesh as any in Messina. **1611** BIBLE *Dan.* ii. 11 The gods, whose dwelling is not with flesh. **1630** PRYNNE *Anti-Armin.* 124 What flesh, what person could be saued? *a* **1632** T. TAYLOR *God's Judgem.* I. ii. xli. (1642) 367 Julius Cesar, one of the most .. valiant pieces of flesh that ever was. **1662-3** PEPYS *Diary* 17 Feb., He had a great secret to tell me, such as no flesh knew but himself. **1774** J. BRYANT *Mythol.* II. 195 All flesh died. **1847** EMERSON *Repr. Men, Plato* Wks. (Bohn) I. 297 He .. visits worlds which flesh cannot enter.

9. a. The physical or material frame of man; the body. *Obs.* exc. in Biblical allusions. †***to be free of one's flesh***: to expose oneself boldly in battle.

In the 16th c. versions of the Apostles' Creed the earlier expression 'the resurrection of the *flesh*' (= *resurrectio carnis*) was changed to 'the resurrection of the *body*'.

Beowulf 4840 No þon lange wæs feorh æþelinges flæsce bewunden. *c* **1175** *Lamb. Hom.* 63 Gif .. to þe flesce scrud and clað. **12..** *Creed* in *Rel. Ant.* I. 282 Hie hleve in .. arysnesse of flesse & eche lif. *a* **1300** *Cursor M.* 22785 (Gött.) þat ilke flesh þat we haue nu, þan sal we haue. *c* **1400** *Prymer* (1891) 78 In my fleysch y schal se god my saueour. *c* **1500** *Melusine* xxxvi. 250 He deffended vygourously his flesshe. **1556** *Aurelio & Isab.* (1608) E viij, The grete colde penetrethe youre delicat fleshes. **1607** MARSTON *What you will* v, A true magnanimous spirit should .. with his own flesh dead his flesh. **1634** HABINGTON *Castara* (Arb.) 133 My frighted flesh trembles to dust. **1724** DE FOE *Mem. Cavalier* (1840) 132 They .. were as free of their flesh as we.

b. ***in (the) flesh***: in a bodily form, in a corporeal nature or state; also, in life, living. ***after the flesh***: in bodily appearance or likeness.

1382 WYCLIF *2 Cor.* v. 16 If we knowen Crist vp [**1388** aftir] the fleisch [TINDALE **1526** after the flehsse. Similarly in later versions]. **1382** —— *Phil.* i. 23 For to be with Crist, it is moche more bettere; forsoth for to dwelle in fleisch, it is nedeful for ȝou. *c* **1449** PECOCK *Repr.* I. xv. 83 That we schulen rise in fleisch aftir oure deeth. **1651** HOBBES *Leviath.* III. xlii. 273 To preach Christ come in the flesh. **1727** DE FOE *Hist. Appar.* i. (1840) 14 St. Paul .. did speak there of seeing Christ in the flesh. **1865** DICKENS *Mut. Fr.* IV. vi, The minutes passing on, and no Mrs. W. in the flesh appearing. **1874** MORLEY *Compromise* (1886) 162 We all know in the flesh liberal catholics and latitudinarian protestants, who [etc.].

c. The body (of Christ) regarded as spiritually 'eaten' by believers; also applied mystically to the bread in the sacrament of the Lord's Supper.

c **1000** *Ags. Gosp.* John vi. 55. *c* **1200** *Trin. Coll. Hom.* 97 þat husel þe ȝe understonden is his holi fleis and his blod. *a* **1300** *Cursor M.* 15234 (Gött.) Takes and ete of þis bredd, for flesse þan es it mine. *c* **1380** WYCLIF *Serm.* Sel. Wks. II. 110 ȝif ȝe eeten þe fleish of mannis sone, and drynke his blood. **1558** BP. WHITE *Serm.* in Strype *Eccl. Mem.* III. App. lxxxi. 279 Adore the same flesh in substance. **1651** C. CARTWRIGHT *Cert. Relig.* I. 59 Saint Remigius &c. affirme the flesh of Christ to be in the Sacrament. **1875** *Hymms A. & M.*, 'Now, my tongue' iv, True bread He maketh By His Word His Flesh to be.

†**d.** As a profane oath, ***God's flesh!*** Hence in 17–18th c. in ejaculations, as ***flesh! flesh and fire!*** Cf. ODDS-FLESH. *Obs.*

1362 LANGL. *P. Pl.* A. XI. 212 Godis flessh & his fet & hise fyue woundis Arn more in his mynde þan þe memorie of his foundours. **1695** CONGREVE *Love for L.* III. xv, Flesh, you don't think I'm false-hearted, like a Land-Man. **1701** CIBBER *Love Makes Man* II. i, Flesh and Fire! do but speak to her, Man. **1728** VANBR. & CIB. *Prov. Husb.* I. i. 29 Flesh! I thought we should never ha' got hither!

10. a. The animal or physical nature of man; human nature as subject to corporeal necessities and limitations.

c **1000** *Ags. Gosp.* Matt. xxvi. 41 Witudlice se gast in hræd, and þæt flæsc ys untrum. *a* **1225** *Ancr. R.* 132 Ine bitternesse of flesche, bereð Godes rode. *c* **1300** *Beket* 259 The here he dude next his liche, his flesches maister to beo. *c* **1384** CHAUCER *H. Fame* I. 49 But that our flessh ne hath no myght To understond hyt aryght. **1393** LANGL. *P. Pl.* C. IV. 59 Hit is bote frelete of flesch. **1526** *Pilgr. Perf.* (W. de W. 1531) 8b, They must despyse .. all delectacyons of the flesshe. **1559** *Mirr. Mag., Jack Cade* iv, Flesh is soft And yeldes it selfe to pleasure that it loueth. **1602** SHAKS. *Ham.* III. i. 63 The Heart-ake, and the thousand Naturall shockes That Flesh is heyre too. **1634** HABINGTON *Castara* (Arb.) 129 Flesh is loath By meditation to fore see How [etc.]. **1853** KINGSLEY *Hypatia* xxx, But though she had found trouble in the flesh, her spirit knew none. **1883** FROUDE *Short Stud.* IV. I. iii. 40 The archbishop retired to his see to afflict his flesh with public austerities.

b. In expressions relating to the Incarnation. ***the days of his flesh***: the period of his earthly life.

c **1000** *Ags. Gosp.* John i. 14 þæt word wæs flæsc ȝeworden. *c* **1200** ORMIN 19201, & Godess Word iss makedd flæsh. *a* **1250** *Orison our Lord* 6 in *O.E. Misc.* 139 þi goddede wes ihud in fleysse. *a* **1300** *Cursor M.* 14342 (Cott.), I haf tan flexs emang mine aun. **1382** WYCLIF *Heb.* v. 7 The which in the dayes of his fleisch offringe preieris and bisechingis to God. **1642** ROGERS *Naaman 2* Our Lord Jesus himselfe all the daies of his abasement and flesh endured them.

11. The sensual appetites and inclinations as antagonistic to the nobler elements of human nature. In theological language (after St. Paul's use of σάρξ) applied more widely to the depraved nature of man in its conflict with the promptings of the Spirit. ***sins of the flesh***: esp. those of unchastity.

c **1200** *Vices & Virtues* (1888) 23 And folȝeð hire flesches wille. *a* **1300** *Cursor M.* 10103 (Cott.) Ic am .. wit thrin fas bi-thrett, þis werld, my fleche, þe warlau als. **1382** WYCLIF *Rom.* viii. 8 Thei that ben in fleisch, mown not plese to God. *c* **1386** CHAUCER *Pars. T.* ¶279 If þat a man wiþstonde .. þe firste entisynges of his fleisshe. *c* **1500** *New Not-br. Mayd* 237 in Hazl. *E.P.P.* III. 11 The devyll, his flesshe, The worlde all fresshe, Provoke hym day and nyght. **1642** FULLER *Holy & Prof. St.* v. ix. 391, I know what Flesh will object. *a* **1729** CLARKE *Serm. 1 Cor.* xiii. 3 Wks. (1738) xlviii. 300 Disapproving the opinions of those whom a man sincerely thinks to be in the wrong, is not a work of the Flesh. **1823** SHELLEY *Hellas* 156 By .. conquering penance of the mutinous flesh. **1882** FARRAR *Early Chr.* II. 423 Things which tend to the gratification of the flesh.

III. *attrib.* and *Comb.*

12. General relations: **a.** simple attrib. (sense 1), as †***flesh-budget***, ***-bunch***, ***-burden***, ***-burst***, ***-case***, ***-creep***, ***-disguise***, ***-flower***, ***-frame***, ***-hotpot*** (nonce formation on FLESHPOT), ***-pimple***, ***-pistol*** (*fig.* of a person), ***-rind***, ***-rose***, ***-scape***, ***-scent***, ***-stuff***; (sense 4), as †***flesh-axe***, †***-broth***, ***-diet***, †***-kind***, †***-kit***, †***-market***, ***meal***, †***-pie***, ***-provision***, †***-stall***, ***-victual***; (sense 5), as ***flesh-tint***, ***tone***; (sense 9), as ***flesh-kinsman***; (sense 10, 11), as ***flesh-delight***, ***-lust***.

1424 in Kennett *Par. Antiq.* (1818) II. 255 Et in magna secure vocat. *fleschaxe xv. den. **1676** WISEMAN *Surgery* II. xii. 204 Her Leg being extreamly emaciated .. I advised the bathing it with *Flesh-broth. **1592** NASHE *P. Penilesse* Wks. (Grosart) II. 72 That surfit-swolne Churles .. might bee constrained to carrie their *flesh budgets from place to place on foote. **1841** BROWNING *Pippa* Introd. 90 Plump as the *flesh-bunch on some Turk bird's poll. **1605** SYLVESTER tr. *Nove's Profit Imprisonm.* 627 Here below this fraile *flesh-burden tyes him. **1876** G. M. HOPKINS *Wr. Deutschland* (1918) 60 How a lush-kept plush-capped sloe Will, mouthed to *flesh-burst, Gush! **1922** JOYCE *Ulysses* 189 For years in this *fleshcase a shesoul dwelt. **1904** *Daily Chron.* 17 Dec. 3/3 The fight between Tyler and the huge ape is worth the money, and Mr. Fritz Bergen's illustrations of it will throw in several extra *flesh-creeps. **1605** SYLVESTER tr. *Nove's Profit Imprisonm.* 218 Mid the *flesh-delights to rust in idle ease. **1731** ARBUTHNOT *Aliments* I. vi. vi. §5 Acidity in the Infant may be cur'd by a *Flesh-Diet in the Nurse. **1910** J. MASEFIELD *Ballads & Poems* 64 Arrayed in some new *flesh-disguise. **1862** G. M. HOPKINS *Vision of Mermaids* (1929) Diadem'd Like an Assyrian prince, with buds unsheath'd From *flesh-flowers of the rock. **1922** JOYCE *Ulysses* 560 Her sleeve, falling from gracing arms, reveals a white fleshflower of vaccination. **1839** BAILEY *Festus* xix. (1848) 210 Some, that Christ Received His *flesh-frame of the elements. **1860** FARRAR *Orig. Lang.* vi. 130 Language is the *flesh-garment of thought. **1922** JOYCE *Ulysses* 502 *Fleshhotpots of Egypt to hanker after. **1712** W. ROGERS *Voy.* 357 A good Quantity of Bread and Sweetmeats .. but little of *Flesh-kind. *c* **1300** *Cursor M.* 20068 (Edin.) Iohan þat was his *fles kinseman. **1575** *Richmond. Wills* (Surtees) 255, I *fleshe kytt, ijd. *a* **1300** *Cursor M.* 17227 (Gött.) Mi *fless lust to fulfill. **1535** COVERDALE *1 Cor.* x. 25 What soeuer is solde in the *fleshmarket that eate. **1766** WESLEY Jrnl. 13 June, I began preaching in the flesh-market. **1748** *Anson's Voy.* III. ii. 313 Instead of one reasonable *flesh-meal, they were now scarcely satisfied with three. **1616-61** HOLYDAY *Persius* 336 I'm pleas'd now Upon the people to bestow a doal Of oile and *flesh-pies. **1587** MASCALL *Govt. Cattell* I. (1653) 13 Barbes, which .. will grow and hang like *flesh-pimples under his tongue. **1608** MACHIN *Dumb Knight* III. in Hazl. *Dodsley* X. 164 My noble firelock of a *flesh pistol. **1795** BURKE *On Scarcity* Wks. VII. 411 Another cause .. tended to produce a scarcity in *flesh provision. **1593** NASHE *Christ's T.* Wks. (Grosart) IV. 173 It had stript his soule foorth of his *fleshe rinde. **1955** C. TOMLINSON *Necklace* 21 It moves with equal certainty Through a register of palm-greens and *flesh-rose. **1949** S. SPENDER *Edge of Being* 21 A *fleshscape woven of fiery fleece. **1923** D. H. LAWRENCE *Birds, Beasts & Flowers* 41 The *flesh-scent of this wicked tree. **14..** *Medulla* in *Cath. Angl.* 135 *note*, *Laniatorium*, a *fflessh stal. **1855** BROWNING *By the Fireside* xxiv, Your soul .. Piercing its fine *flesh-stuff. **1935** G. BARKER *Janus* 42 His face .. no more than a mounding of flesh-stuff. **1838** DICKENS *Nich. Nick.* x, A bright salmon *flesh-tint. **1967** E. SHORT *Embroidery & Fabric Collage* iv. 97 In figure work they depicted form with line rather than shading, and avoided naturalistic flesh tints. **1931** H. READ *Meaning of Art* II. 128 Flowers and the flower-like *flesh-tones of a woman's or a child's body. **1562-3** *Act 5 Eliz.* c. 5 §11 In sparing and encrease of *Fleshe Victuall of this Realme.

b. objective, as ***flesh-creeper***, ***-eater***, ***-former***, ***-maker***, ***-pleaser***, †***-tawer***, †***-vourer*** sbs.; ***flesh-pleasing*** vbl. sb.; ***flesh-amazing***, ***-consuming***, ***-creeping***, ***-devouring***, ***-eating***, ***-enraging***, ***-mangling***, ***-pleasing***, †***-tawing***, ***-transpiercing*** ppl. adjs.

1679 KEACH *Glorious Lover* II. v. 285 Hark! dost not hear that *flesh-amazing cry? **1603** J. DAVIES *Microcosmos* (Grosart) 63/1 Streight away they weare .. With *flesh-consuming fleshly fraile delight. **1887** H. BAUMANN *Londinismen* 56/1 **Flesh-creeper*, scherzhaft: Schauerroman Gruselgeschichte. **1932** T. S. ELIOT *Sel. Essays* 321 He is a little of the religious spell-binder .. the flesh-creeper, the sorcerer of emotional orgy. **1959** *Times* 14 Feb. 9/7 The moving *Funérailles* which he played simply as a flesh-creeper. **1896** *Westm. Gaz.* 17 Mar. 3/1 The *flesh-creeping announcement that our old friend Osman Digna, who has died so often, is advancing with a considerable force in the direction of Kassala. **1936** *Times Lit. Suppl.* 7 Mar. 195/3 Mr. Burke gets the right flesh-creeping quality into some of the scenes. **1609** J. DAVIES *Holy Roode* (Grosart) 22/1 The Monster *Flesh-deuouring Death. **1936** R. CAMPBELL *Mithraic Emblems* 28 The flesh-devouring bird of time. **1616** J. LANE *Contn. Sqr.'s T.* x. 433 Not Diomedes horse (*fleshe eatr of men) had e'ar th'obedience this atchiv'd o're them. **1862** H. SPENCER *First Princ.* II. xiv. §110 (1875) 315 Among animals the flesh-eaters cannot exist without the plant-eaters. **1592** NASHE *P. Penilesse* Wks. (Grosart) II. 73 We are such *flesh-eating Saracens. **1953** J. S. HUXLEY *Evol. in Action* iii. 72 One original tiny flesh-eating creature. *a* **1618** J. DAVIES *Wittes pilgrimage* (Grosart) 39/2 *Flesh-enraging Lust. **1873** E. SMITH *Foods* 6 The division of foods into the two great classes of *flesh-formers and heat-generators. **1550** BALE *Eng. Votaries* II. Eijb, Callynge bothe hym & his masmongers pulpifices, that is to saye, *fleshe-makers. **1813** SHELLEY *Q. Mab* VIII. 179 The *flesh-mangling scourge. **1586** WHETSTONE *Eng. Mirror* 63 One of these *fleshpleasers was the heretique Corinthius. **1647** TRAPP *Comm. Epist.* 176 His watchfull soul, displeased deeply with that *flesh-pleasing force. **1677** HORNECK *Gt. Law Consid.* iv. (1704) 128 He .. is enticed to idleness, to *flesh-pleasing. *c* **1050** *Suppl. Ælfric's Voc.* in Wr.-Wülcker 189 *Lanio, uel lanista, uel carnifex* .. flæctawere [*sic MS.*]. **1609** J. DAVIES *Holy Roode* (Grosart) 11/1 On his virgin skin .. *Flesh-tawing Whips engrosse the deeds of Hate! *Ibid.* 13/1 *Flesh-transpiercing Thornes. **1533** TINDALE *Supper of Lord* Cv, Thys carnall *fleshe vowerer and fleshly Jewe.

c. instrumental, etc., as ***flesh-bound, -clogged, -clouded, -freed, -gorged, -manured, -petalled, -smelling, -untrammelled, -winged.***

1877 G. M. HOPKINS *Poems* (1918) 31 Man's spirit will be *flesh-bound when found at best, But uncumbered. **1909** W. JAMES *Pluralistic Universe* vi. 252 Turn your face toward sensation, that flesh-bound thing which rationalism has always loaded with abuse. **1847** CRAIG, **Flesh-clogged.* **1869** W. P. MACKAY *Grace & Truth* 215 This will ever be..the longing of my flesh-clogged soul. **1647** H. MORE *Cupids Conflict* lx, Earthly minds..Discern not this *flesh-clouded Deity. *c* **1599** SYLVESTER *Epit. Death B. Nicolson* Wks. (Grosart) II. 339/1 Friends..Whose *flesh-freed Souls are henceforth free from sinning. **1878** BROWNING *La Saisiaz* 437 A touch..lifts his spirit where, flesh-freed, Knowledge shall be rightly named so. **1804** J. GRAHAME *Sabbath* (1808) 45 The croak of *flesh-gorged ravens. **1593** NASHE *Christ's T.* Wks. (Grosart) IV. 94 A newe storie of *flesh-manured earth haue they cast vpon it. **1949** S. SPENDER *Edge of Being* 36 This *flesh-petalled tree. **1627** MAY *Lucan* VI. (1635) K vij b, Their ashy garments, and *flesh-smelling coales. **1917** J. MASEFIELD *Lollingdon Downs* 57 Bodiless joy of *flesh-untrammelled mind. **1947** S. SPENDER *Poems of Dedication* 53 Legendary heroes..On *flesh-winged ships fluttered from their island.

d. similative, as ***flesh-fragrant, flesh-like, -rosy*** adjs.; ***flesh-pink, -red*** adj. and quasi-sb. Also FLESH-COLOURED *a.*

1923 D. H. LAWRENCE *Birds, Beasts & Flowers* 15 Gods.. half-sinisterly *flesh-fragrant As if with sweat. **1552** HULOET, *Fleshlike..*carnarius.* **1653** WALTON *Angler* 166 Carps have..a piece of flesh-like-fish in their mouth like a tongue. **1882** *Garden* 17 June 432/1 In colour it is a beautiful *flesh-pink. **1819** CHILDREN *Chem. Anal.* 380 A faint *flesh red colour. **1843** PORTLOCK *Geol.* 219 Crystals..of a yellowish-white or light flesh-red. **1957** L. DURRELL *Bitter Lemons* 102 There was a fine fire of *flesh-rosy carob wood.

13. Special comb.: **flesh-bag** (*slang*), a shirt; †**flesh-baste** *v.* (see quot. 1611); also (after BASTE *v.*³) to beat about the body; **flesh-beam** = *fleshing-beam*; **flesh-bird**, one that lives upon flesh; a carnivorous bird; †**flesh-board**, ? = *fleshing-board*; †**flesh-brand**, a mark burnt into the flesh; hence †**flesh-branded** *pa. pple.*; †**flesh-bred** *a.*, thoroughly trained (in crime); †**flesh-broker**, *slang* (see quots.); so †**flesh-brokery**; **flesh-brush**, a brush used for rubbing the surface of the body, in order to excite the circulation; †**flesh-company**, sexual intercourse; †**flesh-crook**, ? a kind of fork with hooked prongs; cf. FLESH-HOOK; **flesh-crow**, a dialect name for the carrion crow (*Corvus corone*); †**flesh-day**, a day on which flesh may be eaten; †**flesh-dresser**, ? applied to the beadle who flogged prostitutes; **flesh-fallen** *a.*, emaciated; †**flesh-father**, a father 'after the flesh', an earthly father; **flesh-flea**, the chigoe, *Sarcopsylla penetrans* (*Cent. Dict.*); †**flesh-fonding**, the act of gratifying fleshly appetites or desires; **flesh-fork**, a fork for removing meat from the pot; **flesh-germ**, a synonym of *Sarcophyte* (*Syd. Soc. Lex.* 1884); **flesh-glove**, a glove used to stimulate the circulation by rubbing the flesh; †**flesh-glue** = SARCOCOLLA; †**flesh-hold**, flesh enough to be held with the teeth; **flesh-juice**, 'the reddish, acid liquid which is contained in dead muscle' (*Syd. Soc. Lex.* 1884); **flesh-knife** = *fleshing-knife*; †**flesh-leech**, a physician for the body; †**flesh-marked** *pa. pple.*, having a mark on the body (cf. *flesh-branded*); **flesh-quake** [after the analogy of EARTHQUAKE], a trembling of the body; **flesh side**, the side of a skin that was nearest the flesh (see 6); 'the rough side of a leather belt' (Lockwood); †**flesh-spades** (*humorous*), the fingernails; **flesh-split**, that part of a split hide or skin which is nearest the flesh; †**flesh-string**, a muscle; †**flesh-tailor**, *humorously*, one who sews up wounds; a surgeon; **flesh-taster**, an officer appointed to test the wholesomeness of meat; †**fleshtimber**, corporeal matter; †**flesh-time**, a time when flesh may be eaten; **flesh-traffic**, 'the slave trade' (Adm. Smyth); **flesh-wound**, a wound that does not extend beyond the flesh.

1812 J. H. VAUX *Flash Dict.*, **Flesh-bag*, a shirt. **1820** *London Mag.* I. 29 They are often without a flesh-bag to their backs. **1611** COTGR., *Glacer*..to *flesh-bast, or stitch downe the lyning of a garment, thereby to keepe it from sagging. **1639** SHIRLEY *Maid's Rev.* IV. ii, We were going to flesh-baste one another. **1796** COLERIDGE *To Yng. Man of Fortune* Poems (1863) 263 O'er his uncoffined limbs The flocking *flesh-birds screamed. **1411** *Nottingham Rec.* II. 86, j. *fleschbord. **1646** GAULE *Cases Consc.* 105 Whether all Witches have Corporall Markes, or diabolicall *Flesh-brands. **1675** *Lond. Gaz.* No. 999/4 A Chesnut Sorrel Gelding..with I.S. *flesh branded on the Shoulder. **1513** MORE in Grafton *Chron.* (1568) II. 804 A felow *flesh bred in murther before time. *a* **1700** B. E. *Dict. Cant. Crew*, **Flesh-broker*, a Match-maker; also a Bawd. *Ibid.*, *Spiritual-flesh-broker*, a Parson. *a* **1643** W. CARTWRIGHT *Ordinary* V. iv. (1651) 86 She..that is So expert grown in this *flesh Brokery. **1704** F. FULLER *Med. Gymn.* (1718) 197 Chafing of the Skin, or..the Use of the *Flesh-Brush. **1884** *Cassell's Family Mag.* Feb. 143/2 Friction with rough towels and flesh-brush. **1522** *World & Child* in Hazl. *Dodsley* I. 273 The Son of God sickerly Took flesh and blood of the Virgin Mary, Without touching of man's *flesh-company. **1465** *Reg. Gild Corp. Chr. York* (1872) 295 Et j fustinula vocata *fleschcroke. **1576** E. JOHNSON in *Durham Depos.* (Surtees) 312 If ther were a hundrethe devils of hell..with fleshe croks in their hands..he wold run throughe them all to hir. **1885** SWAINSON *Prov. Names Brit. Birds* 82 Carrion Crow (*Corvus corone*), so called from the bird's habit of feeding on the flesh of dead animals; whence also..*Flesh crow. *c* **1440** *Anc. Cookery* in *Househ. Ord.* (1790) 429 Tempur hom, on fyssheday wyth wyn, and on *flesheday with broth of flesh. **1584-5** *Act 27 Eliz.* c. 11 §4 To utter and sell all maner of Sea Fish upon any Flesh Daye in the Weeke. **1674** JOSSELYN *Voy. New Eng.* 13 Three flesh dayes in the week. **1620** MELTON *Astrolog.* 32 Tom Todd and his fellow *flesh-dressers. **1876** TENNYSON *Harold* I. i, Am I not Work-wan, *flesh-fallen? **1876** *Whitby Gloss.*, *Flesh-fallen*, bodily pined. **13..** *Minor Poems fr. Vernon MS.* xxxii. 240 ȝe hedde boþe on *flesch-fadur. **1558** GRIMALDE *Cicero's Offices* Pref. to Rdr., In ryotting and banketing or in outragious *flesh-fondinges. **1662** SOUTH *Serm.* (1823) I. 109 To scour the *flesh-forks. **1879** MISS JACKSON *Shropsh. Word-bk.*, *Flesh-fork*, a long, two-pronged iron fork for getting up meat out of a pot or caldron. **1818** *Sporting Mag.* II. 225 Rubbing.. my body..with the mohair *flesh-glove. **1659** ROWBOTHAM *Gate Lang. Unl.* xi. §124 Frankincense, mastick, rosin, *flesh-glue are the juices and gums of certain trees. **1621** SANDERSON *12 Serm.* (1637) 369 There was *flesh-hould enough for the riming Satyrists..whereon to fasten the sorest and the strongest teeth they had. **1881** *Leicestersh. Gloss.*, **Flesh-knife*, the knife used by tanners to scrape or pare the flesh from the hide on the 'fleshing-beam'. *c* **1340** *Cursor M.* 27382 (Fairf.) Riȝt as *fleshe leche salle dele wiþ diuerse saluis to saris hele. **1682** *Lond. Gaz.* No. 1723/4 A large bay Nag..*Flesh-markt on the off Shoulder. **1631** B. JONSON *New Inne* To himselfe 6 They may, blood-shaken then, Feel such a *flesh-quake to possesse their powers, As they shall cry like ours. **1820** L. HUNT *Indicator* No. 26 (1822) I. 201 The fever of the soul..renders us liable to our most terrible 'flesh-quakes'. **1630** *Charter* in Maitland *Hist. Edin.* IV. (1753) 298 That none of the Trade presume to brock sheep-skins on the Rim or *Flesh-side. **1792** J. BELKNAP *Hist. New-Hampshire* III. 159 Skins..with the flesh sides together. **1749** FIELDING *Tom Jones* XI. viii, The injury, done to the beauty of her husband by the *flesh-spades of Mrs. Honour. **1897** C. T. DAVIS *Manuf. Leather* (ed. 2) 429 *Flesh splits are splits which are finished on the flesh side. The usual weight of the flesh splits is from 1½ to 3½ pounds. **1904** GOODCHILD & TWENEY *Technol. & Sci. Dict.* 37/2 s.v. *Bag hides*, The lower or Flesh Split is used for insoles and stiffeners in boots. **1587** GOLDING *De Mornay* xiv. 225 Wee see in mans body..a greate number of sinewes, *Fleshstrings, and knitters. **1633** FORD *'Tis Pity* III. vii, Here's a stitch fallen in my guts; oh for a *flesh-tailor quickly. **1766** ENTICK *London* IV. 403 Four aleconners, and four *flesh-tasters. **1860** W. WHITE *All round Wrekin* xx. (ed. 2) 195 The 'hardware village', as folk called it [Birmingham], with..an ale-taster and a flesh-taster among its functionaries. *a* **1225** *Leg. Kath.* 1188 Nes nawt iteiet to þe treo þer he deide upon, to drahen, buten *fleschtimber. *c* **1450** HOLLAND *Howlat* 696 In *flesche tyme, quhen the fische war away flemyt. **1611** COTGR., *Charnaut*, flesh-time. *a* **1674** CLARENDON *Hist. Reb.* XIV. (1704) III. 397 Poor Wogan..receiv'd upon a Party an ordinary *flesh wound. **1856** KANE *Arct. Expl.* I. xxix. 398, I hit..one of our dogs ..luckily a flesh-wound only.

flesh (flɛʃ), *v.* [f. prec. sb.]

1. *trans.* To reward (a hawk or hound) with a portion of the flesh of the game killed, in order to excite his eagerness in the chase. Hence in wider sense, to render (an animal) eager for prey by the taste of blood.

1530 PALSGR. 551/2 Flesshe, as we do an hounde, whan we gyve him any parte of a wylde beest to encourage hym to ronne wel. **1576** TURBERV. *Venerie* 131 Those rewardes.. will much better flesh and encourage the houndes. **1609** HOLLAND *Amm. Marcell.* XXVIII. xiii. 346 Ravening foules made more cruell and eagre with the tast of bloud that had so fleshed them. **1633** T. ADAMS *Exp. 2 Peter* ii. 4 An old bitten cur, that being fleshed to the game, will not be staved off. *a* **1743** SAVAGE *Valentine's Day* 7 No crocodile there flesh'd with prey appears. **1751** SMOLLETT *Per. Pic.* (1779) I. viii. 70 Before they had fleshed the hounds, he recollected himself.

2. *transf.* and *fig.* **a.** To initiate in or inure to bloodshed or warfare.

1530 PALSG. 416/2 He his fleshed and accustomed to kyll men lyke shepe. *a* **1611** FORMAN *Diary* 8 Simon would not shrink for a bluddi nose with any boye, for he was then thorowly fleshed. **1646** SIR J. TEMPLE *Irish Rebell.* 86 Flesht and blooded in the slaughter of many thousands of the English nation. **1704** J. BLAIR in W. S. Perry *Hist. Coll. Amer. Coll. Ch.* I. 110 Soldiers well fleshed in blood..can't endure to be reduced to private life again. **1826** E. IRVING *Babylon* I. II. 143 France..had been well fleshed in the work of blood by maiming and wounding herself. **1863** KINGLAKE *Crimea* (1877) II. iv. 41 He fleshed his troops by indulging them with enterprises against the enemy's posts.

†**b.** Hence, To initiate *in*, inure or habituate *to* any practice; to render inveterate, harden (in wrong doing). Also, to render (errors or vices) inveterate.

1581 SAVILE *Tacitus' Hist.* III. xv. (1591) 123 To the ende that the souldiers..might be enured and fleshed in ciuill spoile. **1597-8** BP. HALL *Sat.* IV. vi. 52 When he is once fleshed to the Presse..He sends forth thraues of Ballads to the sale. **1664** H. MORE *Myst. Iniq.* xii. 153 Were not this a mere method of fleshing men in leudness and wickedness. **1665** GLANVILL *Scepsis Sci.* x. 53 Yet others [Errors] are so flesht in us, that they maintain their interest upon the deceptibility of our decayed Nature. **1704** SWIFT *T. Tub* Wks. 1760 I. 53 Fleshed at these smaller sports, like young wolves, they grew up in time to be nimble.

c. To inflame the ardour, rage, or cupidity of (a person) by a foretaste of success or gratification (cf. *flush*); to incite, animate. ? *Obs.*

1573 G. HARVEY *Letter-bk.* (Camden) 28 Being flesshid and animatid as he was bi his tutors preamble. ? *c* **1600** *Distracted Emp.* V. i. in Bullen *O. Pl.* III. 242 There is no devyll in me..That could have flesht me to thy violent deathe. **1612-5** BP. HALL *Contempl.*, *O.T.* VIII. iv, The Israelites were so fleshed with their former victorie, that now they think no walls..can stand before them. **1660** T. M. *Hist. Independ.* IV. 56 The newes of this victory so fleshed our bloodhounds that they began to boast above measure. **1671** SHADWELL *Humourist* IV, This..Bully..was flesh'd, and would needs show his valour upon my shoulders. **1700** DRYDEN *Fables*, *Ajax & Ulysses* 137 Him, flesh'd with slaughter, and with conquest crown'd.

3. a. To plunge (a weapon, etc.) into the flesh. Also (originally with allusion to 1 or 2 a), ***to flesh one's (maiden, virgin) sword***: to use it for the first time upon flesh, to fight one's first battle.

1590 MARLOWE *2nd Pt. Tamburl.* IV. i, He..Beats down our foes, to flesh our taintless swords. **1597** SHAKS. *2 Hen. IV*, IV. v. 133 The wilde Dogge Shall flesh his tooth in euery Innocent. **1622** DEKKER *Virg. Martir* I. Wks. 1873 IV. 8 Antonius, so well hath flesh'd his maiden sword. **1725** POPE *Odyss.* xx. 461 Impatient strait to flesh his virgin-sword. **1866** *Cornh. Mag.* May 630 These rude retainers.. sometimes finish by fleshing their knives to the haft in each other. **1867** F. FRANCIS *Angling* iv. (1880) 113 The barbs of the hooks not being fleshed in them.

b. *transf.* and *fig.*

a **1592** GREENE *Selimus* Wks. 1881-3 XIV. 231 To see the brethren disinherited, To flesh their anger one vpon another. **1695** BLACKMORE *Pr. Arth.* IV. 575 [He] flesht his Courage first in Saxon Blood. **1814** BYRON *Corsair* II. i. 17 All..seek To flesh their glowing valour on the Greek. **1852** DICKENS *Bleak Ho.* i, Clerks have been in the habit of fleshing their wit upon it. **1870** LOWELL *Among my Bks.* Ser. I. (1873) 372 The poor youth, just fleshing his maiden pen in criticism.

c. To gratify (lust or destructive rage).

1601 SHAKS. *All's Well* IV. iii. 19 This night he fleshes his will in the spoyle of her honour. **1818** SCOTT *Hrt. Midl.* iii, He intended to..break into Butler's peaceful habitation, and flesh at once his appetite for plunder and revenge.

4. a. To clothe (a skeleton) with flesh; to embody in flesh. Also with *out, over*. Chiefly *fig.*

a **1661** FULLER *Worthies* i. (1662) 2 This bare Sceleton of Time, Place, and Person must be fleshed with some pleasant passages. **1862** *N. Brit. Rev.* May, 519 The strong imagination has difficulty enough to get fleshed..so as to dwell in common human forms. **1879** *Blackw. Mag.* Aug. 212 The making of man—a skeleton gradually fleshed over. **1886** G. ALLEN *Maimie's Sake* xi, A dainty bit of..word-painting, fleshed out and rendered thinkable.

b. To make fleshy; to fatten.

a **1682** SIR T. BROWNE *Tracts* 115 To restore and well Flesh them, they commonly gave them Hogs Flesh. **1682** *2nd Plea for Nonconformists* 16 The Rooks, the Informers,.. hope to flesh themselves by picking the bones of the Nonconformists. **1909** H. G. WELLS *Tono-Bungay* II. i. 103 We've fleshed ourselves a bit, eh? *a* **1909** *Century Mag.* (Webster), A rangy bay that ought to be fleshed for six months.

fig. *a* **1627** MIDDLETON *Spanish Gipsy* IV, Flesh me with gold, fat me with silver.

5. *Leather-manuf.* To remove the adhering flesh from (a skin or hide).

1777 [see FLESHING 2]. **1880** *Times* 27 Sept. 12/6 Unhairing, fleshing, and scudding all kinds of skins. **1885** A. WATT *Leather Manuf.* x. 120 After the hair is removed the hides are fleshed.

6. To paint flesh-colour.

1861 MAYHEW *Lond. Labour* III. 209/1 For colouring we [photographers] charge 3d more..We flesh the face..and blue the coat and colour the tablecloth.

flesh and blood.

1. Used as representing the material of which man's physical frame is composed; the body. ***in flesh and blood***: in a bodily form, or in a living form. ***to take flesh and blood***: to become incarnate.

a **1340** HAMPOLE *Psalter* xvii. 11 He maked his son to take fleisse and blode **1393** LANGL. *P. Pl.* C. II. 153 Whanne hit hadde of þe [folde] flesch and blod ytake. **1509** *Parl. Devylles* lxxii, I..toke flesshe and blode a mayde within. **1588** SHAKS. *L.L.L.* I. i. 186, I would see his own person in flesh and blood. **1874** BLACKIE *Self-Cult.* 39 A student ought to be.. careful about..the sound condition of his flesh and blood.

fig. **1861** O'CURRY *Lect. MS. Materials* 153 A skeleton, to be at some future time clothed with flesh and blood.

b. Mankind; an individual man or men. Also predicatively ***to be flesh and blood***: to be human, have human feelings or weaknesses.

c **1000** *Ags. Gosp.* Matt. xvi. 17 Hit þe ne onwreah flæsc ne blod. **1601** SHAKS. *All's Well* I. iii. 38 A wicked creature, as you and all flesh and blood are. **1636** MASSINGER *Gt. Dk. Florence* II. iii, I am flesh and blood, and have affections Like other men. **1694** CONGREVE *Double Dealer* I. i, Maskwell is flesh and blood at best. **1832** *Blackw. Mag.* July 61/2 British flesh and blood were sacrificed to the theories of cold-blooded political economists. **1874** L. STEPHEN *Hours in Library* (1892) I. x. 346 Our grand-fathers were human beings..in Walpole's pages they are still living flesh and blood.

c. Human nature with its emotions and infirmities.

c **1450** tr. *De Imitatione* III. xxx, My god, lete not fleshe and blode ouercome me. **1598** SYLVESTER *Du Bartas* II. i. II. *Imposture* 484 Heer I conceive that flesh and bloud will brangle. **1681** DRYDEN *Abs. & Achit.* 96 And what was harder yet to flesh and blood, Their gods disgraced. **1714** POPE *Epil. Rowe's Jane Shore* 47 A piece of failing flesh and blood. **1844** DICKENS *Mart. Chuz.* vii, There are certain things which flesh and blood cannot bear.

d. *attrib.* or *adj.* Having actual human existence.

1824 MISS FERRIER *Inher.* ix, A real flesh and blood living person. **1861** T. A. TROLLOPE *La Beata* I. i. 6 Those other flesh and blood visitors.

2. (One's) near kindred.

a **1300** *Cursor M.* 4129 (Cott.) He..es your aun fless and blod. **1393** Gower *Conf.* I. 149 He ne shulde his counseil hide From hir that..was so nigh flesshe and blod. **1563–87** Foxe *A. & M.* (1631) III. xi. 131/2 This sorrowfull sight of his owne flesh and bloud could nothing moue him. **1596** Shaks. *Merch. V.* ii. ii. 98. **1855** Milman *Lat. Chr.* v. vi, Athanasius..had not spared his own flesh and blood.

3. *slang.* Brandy and port in equal quantities.

1825 C. M. Westmacott *Eng. Spy* I. 294 Draughts composed of bishop and flesh and blood.

4. The plant *Potentilla Tormentilla*; also, the name of a kind of apple.

1853 G. Johnston *Nat. Hist. E. Bord.* 72 Tormentil.. The plant itself, under the name Flesh-and-Blood, is a popular astringent medicine for children. **1882** *Devonsh. Plant-n., Flesh and Blood*..a certain kind of Apple.

'flesh-colour. [f. flesh *sb.* + colour.] The colour of the flesh (of a 'white' human being) as seen through the skin; usually employed to denote a tint composed of 'a light pink with a little yellow' (O'Neill *Dyeing* 1862).

1611 Cotgr., *Baillet*, a pale red, or flesh colour. **1674** Josselyn *Voy. New Eng.* 74 The flesh of it [water-melon] is of a flesh colour. **1882** *Garden* 15 July 58/2 Flowers of fine substance and form..flesh colour, suffused with pink.

b. *attrib.* or *adj.* = next.

1711 Addison *Spect.* No. 13 ¶3 He once gave him a Ripp in his flesh-colour Doublet.

'flesh-coloured, *a.* Of the colour of flesh.

1703 tr. *H. van Oosten's Dutch Gardener* ii. lxix. 111 There are three sorts of common Pionies... Second, the Flesh Colour'd. **1752** Sir J. Hill *Hist. Anim.* 95 The little flesh-coloured actinia. **1774** Goldsm. *Hist. Earth* V. i. xi. 115 The head and neck are without feathers covered with a flesh-coloured skin on the upper part. **1840** J. Baxter *Libr. Pract. Agric.* (ed. 4) I. 177 The flesh-coloured clover. **1861** Miss Pratt *Flower Pl.* IV. 93 Flesh-coloured Speedwell. **1966** J. S. Cox *Illustr. Dict. Hairdressing* 58/2 Flesh-coloured hair net.

fleshed (flɛʃt), *ppl. a.* [f. flesh *sb.* and *v.* + -ed.]

1. Clothed or furnished with flesh: chiefly with some defining prefix. Also, ***fleshed and boned.***

1422 tr. *Secreta Secret., Priv. Priv.* (E.E.T.S.) 224 Lytill ..lymes of the body, and lene y flesshide. **1594** Carew *Huarte's Exam. Wits* (1616) 276 To be meanely fleshed, that is, neither ouermuch nor verie little. **1611** Bible *Gen.* xli. 2 There came vp out of the riuer seuen well fauoured kine, and fat fleshed. **1674** Josselyn *Voy. New Eng.* 99 The Partridge is larger than ours, white flesht. **1748** Richardson *Clarissa* Wks. 1883 VII. 287 His loose fleshed wabbling chaps, which hung on his shoulders. **1851** Ruskin *Mod. Paint.* II. ii. iii. iv. §16 Painters..who can set the supernatural form before us, fleshed and boned like ourselves. **1858** Hogg *Life Shelley* II. x. 316 My..hostess asked me..what I thought of the handsome, well-fleshed girl? **1869** *Daily News* 30 July, A very sleek, level-fleshed bull.

b. of fruit (with defining prefix).

1859 Jephson *Brittany* v. 63 The magnificent orange-fleshed melon. **1859** Darwin *Orig. Spec.* iv. (1873) 67 A yellow or purple fleshed fruit.

2. [Cf. F. *acharné*.] a. Inured to bloodshed, hardened. b. Eager for battle. c. Animated by relentless hatred, bent on the destruction or injury of a person. Const. *upon.*

a. **1594** Shaks. *Rich. III,* iv. iii. 6 They were flesht Villaines, bloody Dogges. *a* **1616** Beaum. & Fl. *Custom of Country* iv. i, A flesh'd ruffian.

b. **1591** Horsey *Trav.* (Hakluyt Soc.) 263 The Poll..with his..now fleshed armye, assaults..townes of the Muscovetts. **1719** D'Urfey *Pills* I. 355 The Jacks are fierce, and Williamites are flesh'd.

c. *c* **1620** *Trag. Barnavelt* iv. iii. in Bullen *Old Pl.* (1883) II. 277 There can be no attonement..Vandort is fleshd upon me. **1659** B. Harris *Parival's Iron Age* 176 They were so fleshed upon one another, that they aspired to nothing less then peace.

fleshen ('flɛʃ(ə)n). *a. rare.* [f. flesh *sb.* + -en^4. OE. had *flǽscen*.] Composed of flesh.

[*a* **1000** *Prudentius Glosses* in *Germania* XXIII. 394/2 *Carnulenta*, flæscene.] **1538** *Goodly Prymer* I ij, Gyue us a fleshen herte, a softe herte. **1879** Farrar *St. Paul* II. 103 Written..not on stonen tablets, but on fleshen tablets.

flesher^1 ('flɛʃə(r)). Chiefly *Sc.* Forms: 4–7 fles(c)har, -ir, -or, -(e)our, 7– flesher. [f. flesh *sb.* + -er. Cf. Ger. *fleischer*; also fleshhewer, of which this may be an alteration.]

1. A dealer in flesh, a butcher.

1369 *Mem. Ripon* (1882) I. 137 Joh. de Staynlay, Fleshour. **1483** *Cath. Angl.* 135/2 A Fleschour, *macellarius.* **1533** Bellenden *Livy* iii. (1822) 274 He pullit ane swerde fra ane flescheour. *a* **1651** Calderwood *Hist. Kirk* (1843) II. 121 A fleshiour, named Sandersone, had putt away his lawfull wife. **1826** J. Wilson *Noct. Ambr.* Wks. 1855 I. 186 A bit schachlin ewe-necked powney, coft frae a sporting flesher. **1853** Reade *Chr. Johnstone* 176 The baddish boy had obtained them [steaks]..at the flesher's.

transf. **1533** Bellenden *Livy* ii. (1822) 160 The pepill had na litill indignacioun that this Marcius suld rise sa haistelie to be thair new fleschour and skurgeare.

2. *U.S.* A tool for fleshing hides; a fleshing-knife.

1885 C. T. Davis *Manuf. Leather* 309 The saw-toothed flesher sometimes employed for dry hides.

Hence **'fleshery** (*Sc.*) 'The business of a butcher; now called *Fleshing*' (Jam. *Suppl.* 1825).

1483 [see fleshhewery]. **1541** *Aberdeen Reg.* V. 19 (Jam.), The counsale licent him to vse his craft of fleshary to outred his pennyworths.

†**'flesher**^{2}. *Obs.* [f. flesh *v.*] An encourager.

1646 Gaule *Cases Consc.* 87 To advise them to prudence ..in such a case; is to be reputed..a Favourer and a Flesher of Witches.

'flesh-fly.

1. A fly which deposits its eggs (or, if viviparous, its larvæ) in dead flesh; a blow-fly (as *Musca vomitoria* or *Sarcophaga carnaria*). Used by Wyclif to render L. *cynomyia.*

a **1300** *Cursor M.* 5956 Hungri flies..To fless-flies þai war likest. **1388** Wyclif *Ps.* lxxvii. 45 He sente a fleisch flie in to hem, and it eet hem. *c* **1440** Hylton *Scala Perf.* (W. de W. 1494) ii. xlii, There dare no flesshe flye rest vpon the pottes brynke. **1556** J. Heywood *Spider & F.* v. 9 A fleshe flie as big as a humble bee. **1658** Rowland *Moufet's Theat. Ins.* 934 The Flesh-fly..is the biggest of all other, he hath a reddish head, very greedy of flesh. **1789** G. White *Selborne* xvii. (1853) 70 The maggots which turn to flesh-flies. **1861** Hulme tr. *Moquin-Tandon* ii. iv. i. 237 The Flesh Fly.. produces a constant buzzing noise.

2. *fig.* of persons.

1532 More *Confut. Tindale* Wks. 715 Esaus, and reprobates, and very carnall fleshflyes. **1611** Speed *Hist. Gt. Brit.* viii. ii. §2. 378 Those flesh flies having once tasted the sweet, though often beaten off, would not long bee kept away. **1782** Cowper *Progr. Err.* 324 These flesh-flies of the land, Who fasten without mercy on the fair. **1825** Macaulay *Milton* Ess. (1854) 15/2 If there be anything unsound, these flesh-flies detect it with unerring instinct.

†**'fleshful,** *a. Obs.*$^{-0}$ [f. flesh *sb.* + -ful.] Full of flesh, fat, plump.

1552 in Huloet.

†**flesh-hewer.** *Obs.* In 4 flessehewer, flesch-hewere, fleschewar, 5 fleschewer, *Sc.* fleschowar. [Cf. Du. *vleeschhouwer*, MHG. *vleischhouwer*.] A butcher.

1335 *Nottingham Records* I. 431 Flesshewergate (Vicus Carnificum). **1379** *Poll Tax Returns for Sheffield* in *Sheffield Gloss.* (1888) s.v., Ricardus Stub & Emma vxor ejus, fflessehewer, vj d. *a* **1400** *Burgh Laws* lxiv. (*Sc. Stat.* I.) Gif þe fleschewer graythis ivil flesche he sal restor hym þe scathis þat aw þe bestys. **1444** *Aberdeen Reg.* 4 June, Item, that the fleschowaris dicht and mak clene the fleschous ilke ouke on Friday.

Hence †**fleshhewery**, a slaughter-house.

1483 *Cath. Angl.* 135 A Fleschewrye, *carnificium.*

'fleshhood, †**-head.** *arch.* [f. flesh *sb.* + -head, -hood.] a. Fleshly state or condition. b. The condition of being in the flesh, or becoming flesh; incarnation.

c **1440** Hylton *Scala Perf.* (W. de W. 1494) ii. xxx, The Soule myghte not that tyme for freelte of the flesshede suffre it soo. **1856** Mrs. Browning *Aur. Leigh* vii. 1030 God.. who hast thyself Endured this flesh-hood.

'flesh-hook.

1. A hook for removing meat from the pot.

c **1325** in *Rel. Ant.* I. 292 Summe notes..arn..kroken a-weyward als a fleshoke. *c* **1386** Chaucer *Sompn. T.* 22 Ful hard it is, with fleischhok or with oules To ben y-clawed. *c* **1440** *Promp. Parv.* 166/1 Flesche hooke, *creagra, fuscina.* **1514** Barclay *Cyt. & Uplondyshm.* Pref. (Percy Soc.) 50 The scullians..Came forth with whittles, some other with fleshhooks. **1611** Bible *2 Chron.* iv. 16 The pots also, and the shouels, and the fleshhookes.

fig. Brathwait *Descr. Death* in Farr *S.P. Jas. I.* (1848) 271 Earth-turned, mole-eied, flesh-hook, that puls us hence.

2. *dial.* (See quot.)

1881 *Leicestersh. Gloss., Flesh-hook*, an iron hook with a long 'stail,' used to pull hides out of the tan-pits.

3. A hook to hang meat upon; a 'pot-hook'.

1596 Nashe *Saffron Walden* Wks. (Grosart) III. 64 These roguish Arsemetrique gibbets or flesh-hookes, and cyphers, or round oos. **1874** in Knight *Dict. Mech.*

†**flesh house.** *Obs.* In 1 flǽschús, 5 fleshusse, 6 fleshows. A place where meat is killed or sold; a butcher's shop; shambles.

c **1000** Ælfric *Gloss.* in Wr.-Wülcker 184 *Carnale*, flæschus. **1435** *Nottingham Rec.* II. 357 Ye Comon Fleshouse in ye Setterday Merkeht. **1503** *Kalender of Sheph.* E iij, Oon dyrk plays ful [of] tablys et of stankys as oon fleshows.

'fleshify, *v. nonce-wd.* [f. flesh + -(i)fy.] *trans.* To turn into flesh. Hence **'fleshified** *ppl. a.*

1768 [See fishify.]

fleshiness ('flɛʃɪnɪs). Also 5 fleshnes. [f. fleshy *a.* + -ness.] The quality or state of being fleshy; fullness of flesh.

14.. tr. *Secreta Secret.* cxxxii. (E.E.T.S.) 117 With-oute gret fleshnes yn þe knees. **1533** Elyot *Cast. Helthe* i. (1541) 2/1 Carnositie or fleshynesse. **1581** Mulcaster *Positions* xxi. (1887) 90 Running..abateth the fleshinesse, and corpulence of the body. **1641** Milton *Ch. Govt.* ii. iii. (1851) 170 A diet puffing up the soul with a slimy fleshinesse. **1788** Baillie in *Phil. Trans.* LXXVIII. 358 [He] used his right hand in preference to his left..which was readily discovered by..the greater fleshiness of the arm. **1830** Lindley *Nat. Syst. Bot.* 72 Flowers, with no peculiar fleshiness in the anthers. **1883** G. Allen in *Longm. Mag.* July 311 (*Strawberries*), Suppose any ancestral potentilla ever to have shown any marked tendency towards fleshiness in the berry.

fig. **1644** Vaughan *Serm.* 8 A Wisdom of the flesh..a kind of flesh, and fleshines in the very mind and spirit.

b. *concr.* A fleshy substance or growth.

1616 Surfl. & Markh. *Country Farme* 83 The male hath no combe, as our Cockes, but in stead thereof a red fleshinesse.

fleshing ('flɛʃɪŋ), *vbl. sb.* [f. flesh *v.* and *sb.* + -ing^1.]

1. The action of inciting (hounds) to the chase by giving them a taste of flesh.

1576 Turberv. *Venerie* 213 Greyhoundes will requyre greater fleshyng and encouragement to a Wolfe than to any other chace. **1611** Cotgr., *Acharnement*, a fleshing.

2. *Leather-manuf.* The action or process of scraping off the pieces of flesh, etc., adhering to the flesh-side of a skin; also *pl.* that which is scraped off.

1777 Macbride in *Phil. Trans.* LXVIII. 114 The operation called fleshing..consists in a further scraping, with a particular kind of knife..and cutting away the jagged extremities and offal parts, such as the ears and nostrils. **1860** *Ure's Dict. Arts* (ed. 5) II. 676 The fleshings are pressed into cakes, and sold for making glue. **1885** A. Watt *Leather Manuf.* xxvi. 323 The unhairing and fleshing of calf skins.

3. (See quot., and cf. flesh *sb.* 6.)

1598 Florio *Andar in Carnafau*, to go a fleshing or a wenching.

4. *Sc.* 'The business of a butcher' (Jam. *Suppl.* 1825).

5. The distribution of the flesh on an animal.

1876 *Daily News* 5 Dec. 2/1 The dainty shapes, undeniable style, and even fleshing of Sir W. C. Trevelyan's beautiful white Irish and shorthorn cross.

6. *pl.* A close-fitting, flesh-coloured garment of a light material, usually of silk, worn upon the stage to represent the natural skin; also ***fleshing-tights.***

1838 D. Jerrold *Men of Character, J. Runnymede* v. Wks. 1864 III. 189 Mind and be very particular with the fleshings. **1851** Mayhew *Lond. Labour* (1861) III. 118/2 Then I'm dressed up in fleshing tights. **1856** Alb. Smith *Sketches of Day* Ser. i. ii. i. 9 Any lovely spirit, whose silk fleshings move in pliant grace. **1879** Geo. Eliot *Theo. Such* x. 178 Ophelia in fleshings.

7. *Comb.*, as **fleshing-beam** (see quot.); **fleshing-board** = prec.; **fleshing-iron** = next; **fleshing-knife** (see quot. 1839); **fleshing-shop**, the place where skins are fleshed; a beam-house.

1881 *Leicestersh. Gloss., Flesh-beam* or **Fleshing-beam*, a wooden instrument..on which is suspended the hide to be dressed, for the purpose of scraping off any remains of the flesh, &c. **1547** *Aberdeen Reg.* 17 Feb., Item, ane *flesching buird, with ane fuyt and ane *flesching jrne. **1839** Ure *Dict. Arts* 764 The *fleshing knife; a large two handled implement with a blunt edge, and bent to suit the curvature of the rounded beam of the wooden horse upon which the hide is scraped. **1885** A. Watt *Leather Manuf.* xxiv. 291 The goatskins, when ready for..fleshing, are removed to the *fleshing shop.

fleshless ('flɛʃlɪs), *a.* [f. flesh *sb.* + -less.]

1. Destitute of flesh.

1586 Marlowe *1st Pt. Tamburl.* v. ii, Death..is seated on my horsemen's spears, And on their points his fleshless body feeds. **1607** Dekker *Knt's Conjur.* (1842) 41 Fleshlesse shin-bones dig'd out of graues. **1786** tr. *Beckford's Vathek* (1868) 113 The fleshless forms of the Preadamite Kings. **1842** Barham *Ingol. Leg., Nell Cook*, A fleshless, sapless, skeleton lay in that horrid well.

†b. Without material substance; phantom-like.

a **1592** Greene *Alphonsus* iii. (Rtldg.) 235/2 When thou know'st the certainty thereof, By fleshless visions shew it.

2. Without superfluous flesh; emaciated, lean.

1598 Sylvester *Du Bartas* ii. i. iv. *Handy Crafts* 38 He chooseth one [horse]..With..Dry Sinewy shanks; strong, fleshless knees. **1809** Crabbe *Tales* 36 Sheep..fleshless, lank and lean. **1847** J. Wilson *Chr. North* (1857) I. 161 Racking pain was in her fleshless bones.

†3. Without meat. *Obs.*$^{-1}$

c **1394** *P. Pl. Crede* 787 Wortes flechles wroughte.

†**'fleshlihood.** Also fleshlihead. [f. fleshly + -head, -hood.] Fleshly state or condition, fleshliness, gratification of the flesh.

c **1440** Hylton *Scala Perf.* (W. de W. 1494) ii. xxxii, And the more it is departed fro flesshlyhede the sharper sighte it hath. *c* **1449** Pecock *Repr.* iii. vii. 319 Religiose men forsaking miche of worldlihode and of fleischlihode.

†**'fleshlily.** *rare.* [f. fleshly *a.* + -ly^2.] = fleshly *adv.*

1614 J. Robinson *Relig. Communion* 86 The most of them conceaving carnally or fleshlily of the Lords Covenant did glory in the flesh.

fleshliness ('flɛʃlɪnɪs). [OE. *flǽsclicness*, f. *flǽsclic*, fleshly + -ness.]

1. †a. In O.E.: Incarnate condition. b. Fleshly quality or state, carnality; 'carnal passions or appetites' (J.).

c **1000** Ælfric *Hom.* II. 278 Se ðe, æfter menniscum wisdome, wile smeagan ymbe ða ᵹerynu Christes flæsclicnysse. **1388** Wyclif *Deut.* xvii. 17 Ful many wyues ..drawen his [the King's] soule to ouer myche fleischlynesse. **1450–1530** *Myrr. our Ladye* 84 Thre maner of people..were called to oure Lordes soper, and came not, for pryde for worldlynesse and for flesshelynesse. **1658** *Whole Duty Man* xvi. 343 'Tis the carnality and fleshliness of our hearts that makes it seem so. **1859** I. Taylor *Logic in Theol.* 338 That extreme creed which satisfies a sensuous and sensual fleshliness.

†2. Fullness of flesh; fleshiness. *Obs.*$^{-0}$

1552 HULOET, Fleshlines, or abundaunce of flesh called carnositye, *carnositas.* **1580** BARET *Alv.* G 569 Grossenesse, or fleshlinesse, *corpulentia.* **1611** COTGR., *Carnosité,* fleshlinesse, fulnesse of flesh.

† '**fleshling.** *Obs. rare*⁻¹. [f. FLESH *sb.* + -LING. Cf. *worldling.*] A fleshly-minded person.

1548 *Confut. N. Shaxton* I v a, The justice of God..is to rewarde the spirituall..with the blessynges promised, & the fleshlynges, the reprobate, with the plages thretned.

fleshly ('flɛʃlɪ), *a.* and *adv.* [OE. *flǽsclic,* f. *flǽsc,* FLESH + *-lic,* -LY¹.]

A. *adj.*

I. Of or pertaining to the flesh, i.e. the body.

1. a. Of or pertaining to bodily appetites and indulgences; carnal, lascivious, sensual. Rarely of persons: Given up to bodily lusts; = CARNAL 3.

c **888** K. ÆLFRED *Boeth.* xxxi. §1 Hwæt godes maʒan we secʒan on þa flæsclican unþeawas. *c* **1000** ÆLFRIC *Hom.* II. 100 Unrihtlic bið þæt se cristena mann flæsclice lustas ʒefremme. *c* **1200** *Trin. Coll. Hom.* 63 Wiðtieð ȝiu fro flesliche lustes. *a* **1300** *Cursor M.* 26364 (Cott.) Flessely sin es lucheri. **1382** WYCLIF *1 Pet.* ii. 11 Fleschly desijris..fiȝten aȝens the soule. *c* **1440** HYLTON *Scala Perf.* (W. de W. 1494) II. viii, All the flesshly felynge of this synfull ymage. **1533** FRITH *Answ. Fisher* (1829) 194 Fleshly men..that follow their own lusts and appetites. *a* **1592** H. SMITH *Wks.* (1867) II. 410 The religion of Mahomet is fleshly, consisting in natural delights and corporal pleasures. **1602** MARSTON *Antonio's Rev.* IV. ii. Wks. 1856 I. 119 Shall justice sleepe In fleshly lethargie? **1714** POPE *Epil. Rowe's Jane Shore* 21 The godly dame, who fleshly failings damns. **1826** SCOTT *Woodst.* xxix, What he called a fleshly frailty..was in truth an attachment to strong liquors. **1872** R. BUCHANAN (*title*) The Fleshly School of Poetry and other Phenomena of the day. **1881** W. S. GILBERT *Patience, Dramatis Personae*..Reginald Bunthorne (a Fleshly Poet). **1882** [see ÆSTHETIC *a.* 4]. **1961** NEW ENGLISH BIBLE *John* i. 13 Not born of any human stock, or by the fleshly desire of a human father.

†**b.** Sexual; = CARNAL 3 b. *Obs.*

a **1300** *Cursor M.* 10874 (Cott.) Hu sal i brede, þat neuer hadd part of flessli dede of man? **1483** CAXTON *G. de la Tour* E vj b, [She] coueyted to haue his flesshely companye. **1485** *Act 1 Hen. VII,* c. 4 Advoutry, Fornication, Incest, or any other fleshly Incontinency.

†**2.** Connected by, or based upon, ties of flesh and blood; natural. = CARNAL 2. *Obs.*

c **900** *Bæda's Hist.* I. xvi. [xxvii.] (1890) 68 Ða goodan fædras ʒewuniað heora flæslecu bearn. *a* **1225** *Juliana* 5 Hire fleschliche feder wes affrican ihaten. *a* **1300** *Cursor M.* 20068 (Cott.) Saint iohan þat was his flexsli kinesman. **14..** *Prose Legends* in *Anglia* VIII. 117 This mayden was his fleschly cosyn. **1513** MORE in Grafton *Chron.* (1568) II. 760 Fleshly consanguinitie. **1578** *Gude & G. Ball.* (1868) 29 We our fleschely father dreid.

3. 'Natural', unredeemed, unregenerate; = CARNAL 5.

971 *Blickl. Hom.* 19 þa flæslican willan. *c* **1200** ORMIN 17276 To shæwenn himm whatt wise Flæshlike mann maȝȝ wurrþenn gast. **1526** TINDALE *Rom.* viii. 7 That the fleshly mynde is enmyte against God. **1550** CROWLEY *Epigr.* 1035 That wyth theyr fleshly fansey They may make it [Scripture] agre. **1871** RUSKIN *Fors Clav.* xxiv. (1872) 10 Avaricious..in an instinctive, fleshly way.

4. Of or pertaining to the material body, mortal; material as opposed to spiritual; human as opposed to divine. *the fleshly eye*: the bodily eye. Now *rare.* = CARNAL 1.

c **1200** ORMIN 12112 Ne mihhte he nohht þurrh flæshlic eȝhess sihhþe Seon þære [etc.]. *a* **1225** *Leg. Kath.* 914 Ðus he schrudde & hudde him..wið ure fleschliche schrud. **13..** *E.E. Allit. P.* A. 1081 An-vnder mone so gret merwayle No fleschly hert ne myȝt endeure. **1382** WYCLIF *2 Chron.* xxxii. 8 With hym is the fleschely arm; with us the Lord oure God. **1413** *Pilgr. Sowle* (Caxton) I. i. (1859) 1, I had made an ende and fully fynyshed my fleshely pylgremage. **1435** MISYN *Fire of Love* (E.E.T.S.) 61 With fflescly eyn bodily þingis ar seyn. **1590** SPENSER *F.Q.* II. x. 50 Th' eternall Lord in fleshly slime Enwombed was. **1607** ROWLANDS *Famous Hist.* 67 My golden Scepter, in a fleshly hand, Is taken from me by another King. **1732** BERKELEY *Alciphr.* IV. §14, I never imagined it could be pretended that we saw God with our fleshly eyes. **1874** BLACKIE *Self-Cult.* 10 The soul of a man underlies his features and his fleshly framework.

5. Pertaining to, concerned with, or influenced by the present life, and considerations connected with it; worldly. Now *rare.* = CARNAL 4.

c **1200** ORMIN 4852 All flæshliȝ care & serrȝhe. **1450–1530** *Myrr. our Ladye* 33 The hartes.. of fleshely people be harde. **1531** TINDALE *Exp. 1 John* (1537) 38 They preach hym falselye vnto theyr fleshly vauntage. *a* **1591** R. GREENHAM *Short forme Catechising* Wks. (1599) 418 Fleshly hatred of our enemies. **1648** CROMWELL *Let.* 25 Nov. in *Ann. Reg.* (1765) 52 Our fleshly reasonings ensnare us. **1798** *Missionary Mag.* No. 24. 217 Simplicity and godly sincerity, as opposed to fleshly wisdom, strongly marked his character. **1875** MANNING *Mission H. Ghost* i. 22 The man of flesh and blood, of fleshly reasons.

II. With reference to flesh (as a substance).

†**6.** Well furnished with flesh; fat, plump; = FLESHY 1. *Obs.*

c **1374** CHAUCER *Troylus* III. 1199 (1248) Her sidis longe, fleishely, smoothe, and white He gan to stroke. **1422** tr. *Secreta Secret., Priv. Priv.* (E.E.T.S.) 226 Men whyche haue fleshly theghes and not bony. **1562** TURNER *Baths* 8 b, They are good for them that are to fatt and fleshlye. **1651** *Life Father Sarpi* (1676) 97 Looking him in the face you would rather have thought it fleshly than otherwise. **1694** *Acc. Sev. Late Voy.* II. (1711) 92 They are very good Food..fleshly and fattish.

7. a. Consisting of flesh: = FLESHY 2. ? *Obs.*

1541 R. COPLAND *Guydon's Quest. Chirurg.* E iv a, Substaunce flesshely, bony, and cartilagynous. **1591** SPENSER *M. Hubberd* 1090 The Tygre, and the Bore..seeking to take occasion Upon his fleshly corpse to make invasion. **1654** VILVAIN *Epit. Ess.* v. lxxx. 116 b, Caling such Animals as liv on Land Flesh; and thos that dwel in Water Fish; yet in Nature the Bodies of both are Fleshly. **1853** KANE *Grinnell Exp.* xlvi. (1856) 423 A smiling country, like a smiling face, needs some provision of fleshly integuments.

b. *esp.* of the heart: Soft, as opposed to 'stony'; tender; = FLESHY 2 c.

1382 WYCLIF *2 Cor.* iii. 3 Not in stoony tablis, but in fleischly tablis of herte. **1541** BARNES *Wks.* (1573) 362/2 Then taketh hee awaye our stony hart, and geueth vs a fleshly hart. **1590** MARLOWE *2nd Pt. Tamburl.* II. ii, Can there be such..treason in the fleshly heart of man. **1856** MRS. BROWNING *Aur. Leigh* IV. 1192 Enough for me and for my fleshly heart To hearken the invocations of my kind.

†**c.** Of a leaf: = FLESHY 2 d. *Obs.*

1657 W. COLES *Adam in Eden* lxviii, The common Orpine riseth..with fat and fleshly Leaves.

†**8.** Of a hound: Fond of flesh. *Obs. rare.*

1576 TURBERV. *Venerie* 25 You should not feede haryers with fleshe..for if you do, they will become fleshly and gyuen to hunte great beastes of chace.

III. **9.** *Comb.*, as ***fleshly-minded*** adj., ***-mindedness.***

1528 TINDALE *Wicked Mammon* Wks. I. 105 Were altogether worldly and fleshly-minded. **1621** BURTON *Anat. Mel.* III. iv. II. i. (1651) 685 They are in a reprobate sense mere carnalists, fleshly minded men. **1840** HARE *Mission Comf.* iii. (1850) 77 In every man there is a root of carnal or fleshlymindedness.

†**B.** *adv. Obs.*

1. a. In bodily form, corporeally; as regards the body, 'in the flesh'; = CARNALLY *adv.* 1.

c **1230** *Hali Meid.* 19 þat ȝet þer he wuneð fleschliche on eorðe. *c* **1250** *Old Kentish Serm.* in *O.E. Misc.* 27 And offre we Gostliche to ure lorde, þet [h]i offrede flesliche. *c* **1440** *York Myst.* xlvi. 77 To rise flesshly, i-wis.

b. In a material or physical sense or manner; materially as opposed to spiritually.

c **1200** ORMIN 16257 Flæshlike follc, i flæshliȝ lif Flæshlike all unnderrstonndenn þe Laferrd Cristess word, tatt wass Gastlike tunnderrstanndenn. *c* **1386** CHAUCER *Pars. T.* ¶259 Of pilk adam..flesschly descendit be we alle. **1635** PAGITT *Christianogr.* I. iii. (1636) 196 If any man taketh it fleshly; it profiteth nothing.

2. a. Carnally, sensually.

a **1225** *Ancr. R.* 58 þu þæt dest eni þing hwarof þer mon is fleschliche ivonded of þe. *c* **1386** CHAUCER *Pars. T.* ¶128 Children that whylom loueden so fleshly euerich other. **1612** T. TAYLOR *Comm. Titus* ii. 4 Nature can loue naturally, that is, fleshly..but not holily.

b. In the way of sexual intercourse, sexually; = CARNALLY *adv.* 2.

c **1175** *Lamb. Hom.* 77 Na mon mine likame irineð ne mid me flesliche nefde to donne. **1303** R. BRUNNE *Handl. Synne* 2009 ȝyf þou euer þy wyfe lay by Yn tyme of penaunce, to seye flesshely..þou synnest gretly. **1494** FABYAN *Chron.* VI. cc. 224 He put her nat from his bedde, nor yet delte wᵗ her flesshely. **1585** T. WASHINGTON tr. *Nicholay's Voy.* IV. xxxiii. 155 b, If.. he was found not able to live with her so fleshly, as his youth required.

3. *Comb.*, as ***fleshly-wise*** adj.

1542 BECON *Pathw. Prayer* xviii. I j a, Seme it neuer so godly, vertuous and good in the syght of fleshly wyse men.

flesh-meat. Flesh (as opposed to fish and vegetables) as an article of food; also *pl.* various kinds of food consisting of flesh.

In some northern dialects applied to 'butchers' meat as opposed to bacon or pork'.

c **1020** *Laws Cnut* §47 ȝyt wyrse þæt man mid flæsc-mete hine sylfne afyle [riht fæsten-tide]. *a* **1154** *O.E. Chron.* an. 1131 þa scyrte ða flesc mete. *c* **1394** *P. Pl. Crede* 13 Wednes-day ich wyke wiþ-outen flech-mete. **1564** *Child Marriages* (E.E.T.S.) 200 They made an end of flesh meat that night for that weke. **1698** KEILL *Exam. Th. Earth* (1734) 213 Who seldom tast any Flesh-meats. **1848** *Secret Soc. Mid. Ages, Templars* 254 They had flesh-meat but three times a week, unless when festival-days occurred.

attrib. **1796** MORSE *Amer. Geog.* II. 419 His health requires a flesh-meat diet.

fleshment ('flɛʃmənt). *rare*⁻¹. [f. FLESH *v.* + -MENT.] The action of 'fleshing'; hence, the excitement resulting from a first success.

1605 SHAKS. *Lear* II. ii. 130 And in the fleshment of this dead exploit, [He] Drew on me here againe.

'**fleshmonger.** [see MONGER.] One who deals in flesh.

†**1.** A butcher. *Obs.*

c **1000** *Gloss.* in Wr.-Wülcker 438 *Lanio,* flæscmangere. *a* **1400** in *Eng. Gilds* (1870) 354 Euerych fleshemongere.. shal to þe kynge of custom fyue & twenty pans by þe ȝere. *c* **1515** *Cocke Lorell's B.* (Percy Soc.) 4 With slyngethryfte fleshemonger, Also fabyane flaterer. **1597** BRETON *Wits Trenchmour* Wks. (Grosart) II. 17/1 The Sonne of some Flesh-monger.

†**2.** A fornicator; a pander. *Obs.*

1603 SHAKS. *Meas. for M.* v. i. 337 Was the Duke a flesh-monger, a foole, and a coward, as you then reported him to be? **1624** HEYWOOD *Captives* II. ii. in Bullen *O. Pl.* IV, Inquire for us of wenshes? tush, wee fishe For no such perewinkles; farewell fleshmongeres.

3. A slave-dealer.

1845 F. DOUGLASS *Life* (1846) 4 Cruel as the deed may strike any one to be, for a man to sell his own children to human flesh-mongers, it is often the dictate of humanity for him to do so.

'**flesh-pot.** A pot in which flesh is boiled. Chiefly in phrase ***the flesh-pots of Egypt*** (see *Exod.* xvi. 3), or with allusion to that phrase: Luxuries or advantages regarded with regret or envy.

1535 COVERDALE *Exod.* xvi. 3 Whan we sat by yᵉ flesh pottes, and had bred ynough to eate. **1592** NASHE *P. Penilesse* Wks. (Grosart) II. 74 From the flesh-pots of Egipt, to the Prouant of the Lowe countreyes. **1632** LITHGOW *Trav.* VII. 299 Now well met Egypt..For we have appetite, for thy Flesh pots. **1710** SWIFT *Let. to Sterne* 17 Apr., I expect to hear the two ladies lamenting the fleshpots of Cavan-street. **1862** CARLYLE *Fredk. Gt.* (1865) III. x. ii. 213 Law, with..its high honours and deep flesh-pots. **1888** BRYCE *Amer. Commw.* III. lxxxviii. 177 The fleshpots of the city administration had therefore greater attractions for him.

attrib. **1876** RUSKIN *Fors Clav.* VI. lxiv. 112 Some flesh-pot comfort will always be needful for the education of such beasts as we are.

Hence **flesh-pottery** (*nonce-wd.*), high living, self-indulgence.

1876 G. MEREDITH *Beauch. Career* xxix, A band of dealers in flesh-pottery.

†**flesh-'shambles.** *Obs.* Also 5 **flesshchameles, -ylle, -shamels,** 6 **fleshamelles.** A place where meat is killed or sold.

a **1410** in *York Myst.* Introd. 24 *note,* All the folks of the salsemaker crafte..without the Flesshchameles. ? **1483** CAXTON *Vocab.* 5 Goo to the flesshshamels. **1546** *Mem. Ripon* (Surtees) III. 30 To the kinges majestie furth of one burgage in Fleshamelles xvjd. **1552** in HULOET.

b. A brothel.

1608 DAY *Hum. out of Br.* II. C iv, Venice..is counted the best flesh-shambles in Italie.

† '**fleshward,** *adv. Obs.* [f. FLESH *sb.* + -WARD.] Towards or in relation to humanity.

1674 N. FAIRFAX *Bulk & Selv.* vi. 184 The earths globe, or that of it that lyes fleshward.

flesh-worm. A worm that feeds on flesh. Also (see quot. 1884.)

c **1000** *Sax. Leechd.* II. 124 Wiþ flæsc wyrmum ʒenim monnes suran [etc.]. **1577–87** HOLINSHED *Chron.* II. 19/2 Nits, fleshwormes, bees, butterflies. **1586** J. HOOKER *Girald. Irel.* in *Holinshed* II. 91/1, I shall be able like a fleshworme to itch the bodie of his kingdome. **1795** SOUTHEY *Vis. Maid of Orleans* I. 136 Where thou seest the pamper'd flesh-worm trail, Once the white bosom heaved. **1884** *Syd. Soc. Lex.,* *Flesh worm,* the *Trichina spiralis.*

b. *transf.* A carnally-minded person.

1565 HARDING in Jewel *Def. Apol.* (1611) 317 Discoursing Parliament Machiauellists, and al other whatsoeuer fleshwormes, Merchants, idle artificers.

fleshy ('flɛʃɪ), *a.* [f. FLESH *sb.* + -Y¹. Cf. Ger. *fleischig.*]

1. Well furnished with flesh; fat, plump.

c **1369** CHAUCER *Dethe Blaunche* 954 Armes ever lith, Fattish, fleshy, nat great therewith. **14..** LYDG. & BURGH *Secrees* 2685 In knees..he that is ovir moche fflesshy. **1555** EDEN *Decades* 3 The other moste fleshy partes [of fattened children] they pouder for store. **1626** BACON *Sylva* §399 The Æthiopes..are Plumpe, and Fleshy. **1641** BEST *Farm. Bks.* (Surtees) 3 Sheepe that growe fleshy with foure teeth, will growe fatte with eight. **1793** LD. AUCKLAND *Corr.* III. 69 Colonel Pack..was shot through the fleshy part of the arm. **1820** W. IRVING *Sketch Bk., Country Ch.* (1865) 126 A fine, fleshy, comfortable dame. **1837** DICKENS *Pickw.* xxiii, His face..had expanded..and its bold fleshy curves had.. far extended beyond the limits originally assigned them.

fig. **1636** B. JONSON *Discov.* (Rtldg.) 759/1 It is a fleshy stile when there is much periphrasis, and circuit of words; and when with more than enough it grows fat and corpulent.

2. Of or pertaining to flesh; consisting of flesh; without bone.

c **1400** *Lanfranc's Cirurg.* 106 þe heed is maad of þre parties, of a fleischi partie, of a bony partie & a brawni partie. **1581** MULCASTER *Positions* xv. (1887) 69 Such fleshy partes as be about the ribbes. **1651** HOBBES *Leviath.* II. xxix. 173 The fleshy parts being congealed. **1700** DRYDEN *Pythag. Philos.* in *Fables* 508 If Men with fleshy Morsels must be fed [*ed.* 1721 *reads* fleshly, *and it is so cited by J.*]. **1792** BELKNAP *Hist. New-Hampshire* III. 215 Besides the fleshy parts of the cod, its liver is preserved in casks. **1807–26** COOPER *First Lines Surg.* 189 Every kind of fleshy tumour. **1828** STARK *Elem. Nat. Hist.* I. 335 No species of reptile is possessed of true fleshy lips.

b. Corporeal, bodily.

1624 MASSINGER *Renegado* III. ii, When it [the soul] grows weary Of this fleshy prison. *c* **1630** MILTON *Passion* 17 He, sovran priest..Poor fleshy tabernacle entered. **1814** BYRON *Lara* I. xviii, He..charged all faults upon the fleshy form She [Nature] gave to clog the soul. **1864** HAWTHORNE *S. Felton* (1883) 341 Fruits, milk, freshest butter, will make thy fleshy tabernacle youthful.

c. Of 'flesh', implying softness and tenderness. Cf. FLESH *sb.* 1 f.

1526 TINDALE *2 Cor.* iii. 3 The pistle of Christ..written.. not in tables of stone, but in flesshy tables of the herte. **1585** ABP. SANDYS *Serm.* Cant. ii. 15 §28 His wil is that stonie hearts be turned into fleshie. **1611** BIBLE *Ecclus.* xvii. 16 Neither could they make to themselues fleshie hearts for stonie.

d. Of a plant, leaf, fruit, etc.: Having a firm, or somewhat firm pulp; pulpy, not fibrous. Cf. FLESH *sb.* 2.

1577 B. GOOGE *Heresbach's Husb.* II. (1586) 110 b, The whole bodie of the Figge is fleshie. **1626** BACON *Sylva* §633 Those Juyces, that are so fleshy, as they cannot make Drinke by Expression..may make Drinke by Mixture of Water. **1672** JOSSELYN *New Eng. Rarities* 66 Vine, much differing in the Fruit, all of them very fleshy. **1712** tr. *Pomet's Hist. Drugs* I. 37 A round, fleshy Berry, like that of Myrtle. **1776** WITHERING *Brit. Plants* (1796) II. 428 Leaves opposite, egg-shaped, blunt, fleshy. **1807** J. E. SMITH *Phys. Bot.* 282

Drupa, a Stone-fruit, has a fleshy coat. **1854** HOOKER *Himal. Jrnls.* I. i. 16 The natives distil a kind of arrack from its fleshy flowers. **1870** H. MACMILLAN *Bible Teach.* xi. 211 They have..thick fleshy leaves.

†**3.** Of the 'flesh' as opposed to the 'spirit'; human as opposed to 'spiritual'; = FLESHLY 4.

a **1400** *Prymer* (1891) 78 Whethir þyn eyen be fleschchi, or thou seest as man schal se. **1535** COVERDALE *Job* x. 4 Hast thou fleszshy eyes then, or doest thou loke as man loketh?

†**b.** Carnal, sensual; = FLESHLY *a.* 1. *Obs.*

1604 T. WRIGHT *Passions* v. §4. 212 Fleshy concupiscence deserveth rather the name of Mercenarie Lust then Love. **1668** CULPEPPER & COLE *Barthol. Anat.* I. xvii. 45 Such as are given to fleshy desires, have larger Kidneys then ordinary.

4. Resembling flesh in its properties or qualities.

1555 EDEN *Decades* 233 They [Rubies]are..of a fleshye colour. **1665** SIR T. HERBERT *Trav.* (1677) 26 The Mannatee is the other fish..and from their using the shoar have a fleshie taste resembling Veal. **1762–71** H. WALPOLE *Vertue's Anecd. Paint.* (1786) I. 215 His colouring was good, and his figures fleshy and round. **1804** ABERNETHY *Surg. Obs.* 19 They agree in the external characters, those of an increase of bulk, and a fleshy feel.

†**flet**[1]. *Obs.* Forms: 1, 3–6, 8 flet, 3 *south.* vlet, 4–5 flett(e, (6 fleete, fleit, flelt), 7–8 flett. [OE. *flęt(t* = OFris. *flet*, OS. *flet*, *fletti*, OHG. *flazi*, *flezi* (MHG. *vletze*, Ger. dial. *fletz*), ON. *flet* str. neut.:—OTeut. **flatjoᵐ*, f. **flato-* FLAT *a.*]

1. The floor or ground under one's feet.

Beowulf 1568 (Gr.) Heo on flet ȝecrong. *a* **1000** *Canons Powerful Men* ii. (Thorpe, 1840) 414 & ne cume on bedde ac licȝe on flette. *a* **1300** *E.E. Psalter* cxviii. [cxix] 25 Clived mi saule to þi flet. *c* **1340** *Gaw. & Gr. Knt.* 568 A tule tapit tyȝt ouer þe flet. *a* **1420** *Pallad. on Husb.* I. 473 Thi berne also be playne, and harde the flette. *c* **1450** MYRC 273 Knelynge doun upon the flette.

b. ? A place, spot, field (of battle).

c **1205** LAY. 26023 þat he com to þan ulette þer þe feond lai and slæpte. *c* **1300** *K. Alis.* 2378 They broughte heom out of the flette.

2. A dwelling, house, 'hall'.

Beowulf 1025 (Gr.) Beowulf ȝeþah ful on flette. *a* **1000** *Laws Hlothhære & Eadric* xi. (Thorpe 1840) 14 Ȝif man mannan an oðres flette man-swara hateð..scilling aȝelde þam þe þæt flet aȝe. *a* **1300** *Siriz* 273 So ich evere brouke hous other flet. *c* **1325** *Poem Times Edw. II* 309 in *Pol. Songs* (Camden) 337 An hep of girles sittende aboute the flet. *c* **1460** *Towneley Myst.* (Surtees) 26, I shal not in thi det Flyt of this flett!

b. *Sc.* The inner part of a house.

a **1400** *Burgh Laws* xxiii. (*Sc. Stat.* I.) Þe inner halfe of þe hous þat is callyt þe flett. *c* **1450** HOLLAND *Howlat* lxiv. 830 The fulis fonde in the flet And mony mowis at mete On the flure maid. **1508** DUNBAR *Flyting* 242 Rank beggar, ostir dregar, foule fleggar, in the flet. **1598** FERGUSON *Sc. Prov.* 4 A fair fire makes a room flet. **1768** ROSS *Helenore* II. 588 That seven years have sitten i' the flet.

3. ***fire and flet*** (corruptly *fleet*): 'fire and house-room'; an expression often occurring in wills, etc.

Bp. Kennett (*a* 1728) quotes in *MS. Lansd.* 1033 fol. 132 an 'old northern song over a dead corps', containing the lines 'Fire and fleet and candle light, And Xᵗ receive thy sawle'. In Sir W. Scott's *Minstrelsy of Scot. Border* (1802) 232 the words appear as 'Fire and *sleet*', and the editor suggests that *sleet* 'seems to be corrupted from *selt*, or *salt*, a quantity of which is frequently placed on the breast of a corpse'!

1533 TRUBB in Weaver *Wells Wills* (1890) 129 To fynd the said wife..mete and drink, fyer and flelt. **1539** *Will of R. Morleyn* (Somerset Ho.) My wife to have..fyre & fleete in my haule & kechin. *c* **1570** *Durham Depos.* (Surtees) 207, I trobled..this house with a bedd roome and fier and fleit.

flet[2] (flɛt). *Sc.* Also fleat. [app. repr. ON. *flétta* plait, f. *flétta* = Ger. *flechten* to plait.] A mat of plaited straw placed on a pack-horse's back to prevent chafing or galling.

1794 W. SUTHERLAND in *Statist. Acc. Scotl.* X. 23 Straw creels..fixed over straw flets, on the horses backs, with a clubber and straw ropes. **1812** CAPT. HENDERSON *Agric. Surv. Sutherland* v. §5. 60 The horse being equipped with a fleat and clubbar on his back.

flet: see FLEET *v.*[1] and [2].

†**fletch**, ? *a.* (or *sb. attrib.*). [cf. FLIG, etc.]

1704 *Lond. Gaz.*, No. 4044/4 A..Mare about 14 hands and half..with..a long fletch Tail..and well in Case.

fletch (flɛtʃ), *v.* [Perh. a corruption (due to association with FLETCHER) of FLEDGE *v.* 4; though the latter has not been found earlier than 1796.] *trans.* To fit (an arrow) with a feather; to feather. *lit.* and *fig.*

1635–56 COWLEY *Davideis* II. 91 Thy Darts are..Soft as the Feathers that they're fletch'd withal. **1760** WARBURTON *Doctr. Grace* II. x, He dips his curses in the gall of irony; and ..fletches them with a prophane classical Parody. **1845** J. SAUNDERS *Pict. Eng. Life, Chaucer* 89 Arrows..fletched with the feathers of the goose. **1876** BANCROFT *Hist. U.S.* V. xliii. 25 They fletched their complaint by adding: 'America loved his brother'.

fletch, var. of FLITCH.

fletcher ('flɛtʃə(r)). Also 5 fleccher(e, flecher, flecchour; *Sc.* fle(d)ger. [ad. OF. *flecher*, *flechier* arrow-maker, f. *flèche* arrow: see FLÈCHE.]

1. One who makes or deals in arrows; occasionally, one who makes bows and arrows. *Obs.* exc. *Hist.* or *arch.*

c **1400** *Destr. Troy* 1593 Ferrers, flecchours, fele men of Crafte. **1457** *Sc. Acts Jas. II*, c. 65 (1814) II. 48/2 A bowar and a fleger. **1465** *Mann. & Househ. Exp.* 179 The flecher that..owyth hym ffor tymber, ixs. vjd. **1541** *Act 33 Hen. VIII*, c. 9 §1 The bowiers, fletchers, stringers and arrowe head makers of this your realme. **1616** SURFL. & MARKH. *Country Farme* 667 Which timber is of great..estimation amongst Fletchers, for it maketh the strongest and best arrow of any wood whatsoeuer. **1664** EVELYN *Sylva* (1776) 218 Our Fletchers commend it [the Quick-beam] for Bows next to Yew. **1733** P. LINDSAY *Interest Scot.* 56 Any other Corporation decayed and worn out, such as the Bowers, Fletchers, and several others in London are, as to their Business. **1854** H. MILLER *Sch. & Schm.* xxi. (1857) 460 As if some fletcher of the stone age had carried on his work on the spot. **1858** SIMMONDS *Dict. Trade*, *Fletchers' Company*, one of the minor livery companies of London.

attrib. **15..** *Kyng & Hermyt* 477 in Hazl. *E.P.P.* I. 32 Jake, seth thou can of flecher crafte, Thou may me es with a schafte.

†**2.** An archer, a bowman. *Obs.*

1529 MORE *Dyaloge* I. Wks. 143/1 Though one eye wer ynough for a fletcher.

Hence **'fletchery**, the wares or goods made or sold by a fletcher.

1594 *2nd Rep. Dr. Faustus* in Thoms *E.E. Prose Rom.* (1858) III. 411 They brought store of fletchery to them.

Fletcherian (flɛ'tʃɪərɪən), *a.* [f. the name of John *Fletcher* (1579–1625), English dramatist + -IAN.] Of, pertaining to, or characteristic of Fletcher or his works.

1850 *Gentl. Mag.* Aug. 119/2 Many passages were strongly marked with the favourite Fletcherian cadence. **1907** *Westm. Gaz.* 3 Apr. 4/1 It is curious..that FitzGerald should have made his translations of Calderon so strongly Fletcherian in style. **1921** *Spectator* 19 Feb. 236/2 We all know how this new flower flourished and ramped in the Fletcherian garden and was taken up by the poet's dramatic imitators. **1947** *Scrutiny* XIV. 318 Anxious to fit the play [sc. *Henry VIII*] in as the final goal of the Shakespearian progress..he is driven to explain away the limp 'Fletcherian' verse.

Fletcherism ('flɛtʃərɪz(ə)m). [f. the name of Horace *Fletcher* (1849–1919), American author + -ISM.] The practice of thorough mastication advocated by Fletcher. So **'Fletcherite**, a follower of Fletcher; **'fletcherize** *v. trans.*, to masticate thoroughly. Also *fig.*

1903 *Lit. Digest* 28 Nov. 739/1 It is now proposed to speak of the 'Fletcherizing' of food that is thoroughly chewed. **1904** *Daily Chron.* 31 Oct. 4/7 The Fletcherites preach the gospel of chewing. **1906** *Suburban Country Life* (Boston) Aug. 101/1 His investigation of what has been known as Fletcherism. **1907** *Practitioner* June 852 The Fletcherites, who, so far from not giving two bites to a cherry, insist on thirty-two to a mashed potato. **1909** H. JAMES in W. D. Orcutt *Quest Perf. Bk.* (1926) 88 It is impossible save in a long talk to make you understand how the blessed Fletcherism..lulled me, charmed me, beguiled me. **1910** 'O. HENRY' *Strictly Business* (1917) xvii. 182 Annette Fletcherized large numbers of romantic novels. **1922** WODEHOUSE *Adv. Sally* ii. 41 The raffish mongrel was apparently endeavouring to fletcherize a complete stranger of the Sealyham family. **1925** 'J. DOYLE' *Marmosite's Miscellany* 8 The rank spiny grass and the remotest flower.. I am garlanding together in a glorious wreath To fletcherise at leisure.

flether ('flɛðə(r)), *v. Sc.* Also flaither. [Cf. ON. *flaðra* to flatter.] *intr.* To flatter, use 'blarney'. Hence **'flethering** *ppl. a.* Also **'flethers**, flattering talk, blarney.

1786 BURNS *Ded. to G. Hamilton* 2 Expect na, Sir, in this narration, A fleechin, flethrin, dedication. **18..** *Donald & Flora* 13 (Jam.) *Lord.* Come now, my good fellow, and— *Wat.* Aye, flaither awa! Since I'll no do wi' foul play, try me wi' fair play. **1821** H. DUNCAN *Yng. S. Country Weaver* v. (ed. 2) 98 What! do you think to beguile me, wi' your fleeching and your flethers to do the devils' wark.

†**fle'tiferous**, *a. Obs.*⁻⁰ [f. L. *flētifer* (f. *flētus* weeping, f. *flēre* to weep + *ferre* to bear) + -OUS.] 'Causing weeping' (Bailey).

1656–81 BLOUNT *Glossogr.*, *Fletiferous* [**1656** ed. has *Flectiferous*]. **1721–66** in BAILEY.

†**'fletion.** *Obs. rare*⁻¹. [as if ad. L. **flētiōn-em*, n. of action f. *flēre*: see prec.] Weeping.

1716 M. DAVIES *Athen. Brit.* II. 254 The different degrees of Penitential Fletion, Audition, Substration and Consistence.

Fletton ('flɛtən). Also fletton. [The name of a town near Peterborough.] Used *attrib.* or *ellipt.* to designate a type of brick made by a semi-dry process, orig. from the Oxford clay found near Fletton.

1908 C. F. MITCHELL *Brickwork & Masonry* (ed. 2) xiv. 390 The average Fletton brick, when immersed in water for 24 hours, will absorb 20 per cent of its weight of water. **1927** *Daily Tel.* 24 May 3/3 The imported bricks cannot compete ..in our area with Fletton bricks. **1934** *Archit. Rev.* LXXVI. 122/2 The rear elevation has rustic flettons distempered. **1967** *Times* 9 Feb. 16/1 London Brick, the largest fletton producer in Britain. **1971** *Daily Tel.* (Colour Suppl.) 28 May 21/4 Nearly half the bricks made in Britain are 'flettons' from this bed of clay, and nearly half the flettons come from the Bedfordshire brickfield.

fleubothomye, obs. form of PHLEBOTOMY.

fleuk, obs. form of FLUKE.

fleum(e, obs. form of FLEAM, PHLEGM.

‖**fleur** (flœr). [F. *fleur*: see FLOWER.]

1. An ornamental flower.

1841 HAWKINS *Silver Coins* (1876) 178 Annulet enclosing pellet in place of the fleurs in the angles.

2. a. A kind of woollen stuff (see quot.).

1883 *Cassell's Fam. Mag.* Oct. 697/1 Fleur is..a serge ground on which are large patterns in a sort of weaving like a Brussels carpet, and of a numerous mixture of colours all deftly blending, so that no one tone prevails.

b. In names of artificial silk materials, as ***fleur de chine***, ***fleur de soie*** (also ***fleursoie***).

1927 *Daily Express* 5 Apr. 3 It is practically impossible to tell the newest material 'fleur de Chine' from crêpe de Chine. **1928** *Times* 9 May 10/4 A draped gown of parchment fleur de soie, trimmed with old lace. **1928** *Daily Express* 23 July 5/2 Fleursoie, a soft firm material rather like triple georgette.

3. fleur de coin (də kwɛ̃) *Numismatics*, mint or perfect condition.

1892, 1966 [see F.D.C. (s.v. F III. 3)]. **1931** *N. & Q.* 12 Dec. 430/2 The expression 'mint state' has passed on from our fraternity... The strange old French expression *fleur de coin* has generally been substituted for it, as expressing that exquisite gloss which characterizes virgin new-born specimens.

Hence **fleured** *ppl. a.* [+ -ED[2]], adorned or marked with a fleur or fleurs.

1841 HAWKINS *Silver Coins* (1876) 246 The arch on the king's breast is not fleured, but terminates in a crescent.

fleur-de-lis (flœr də liː, liːs), **flower-de-luce** (ˌflaʊə dɪ 'luːs). Forms: α. 4–6 flour(e-de-lys(e, -lice, -lyce, (*pl.* -lycis), 7 -lis, 5–7 -luce, *pl.* -luces, 6 floredelise, *Sc.* 5 flour(e-the-lis, -lys. β. 6–9 flower-, (6 flowre-)de-luce, (*pl.* -luces), 6–7 -lice, (*pl.* -lices), 6 -lyce, 8 -lys, 7–9 -lis. γ. 8–9 fleur-de-lys, 9 -lis, *pl.* 7 fleur-de-lysses, -lyzes, 9 fleurs-de-lis, -lys, -luce. [The prevailing form is a. mod.F. *fleur de lis* (flœr də lis), formerly *lys*; but this form is scarcely found in Eng. before the 19th c.; see above. The form *flower-de-luce* survives as a poetical archaism and in *U.S.* The Fr. is literally 'lily-flower' from *lis*, formerly *lys*, in OF. *liz* for *lils* lily, the *s* of the nom. sing. being retained in the oblique cases; the English spelling *de-lice*, *de-lyce*, was in its origin merely graphic (cf. *price*, *mice*, *syce*, etc.), but in the 16th c. was associated with a fanciful etymology *flos deliciæ*, and the form *deluce*, *de luce* apparently also leaned upon a fanciful derivation. Occasional English forms were *deluce*, *delyce flowre*.]

1. The flower of a plant of the genus *Iris* (esp. *I. pseudacorus*); the plant itself. Cf. FLAG *sb.*[1] 1.

13.. *E.E. Allit. P.* A. 752 Þy colour passez þe flour-de-lys. *a* **1400** *Hymn Virg.* vi. in Warton *Hist. Eng. Poetry* x. (1840) II. 110 Heil fairer then the flour de lys. *c* **1475** *Rauf Coilȝear* 670 Flowris with Flourdelycis formest in feir. **1500–20** DUNBAR *Thistle & Rose* 138 Lat no netill vyle..Hir fallow to the gudly flour delyce. **1590** SPENSER *F.Q.* II. vi. 16 The lilly, lady of the flowring field, The flowre-deluce, her lovely paramoure. **1699** BENTLEY *Phal.* Pref. 104 The Muses are invited to come under the shadow of Flower-de-luces. **1731–37** MILLER *Gard. Dict.* (ed. 3) s.v. *Iris*, *Iris purpurea*.. Common purple Fleur-de-Lys. **1837** CAMPBELL *Lines in La Perouse's Voy.* Poet. Wks. 298 When, rapt in fancy..I.. plucked the fleur-de-lys by Jesso's streams. **1866** LONGF. *Flower-de-luce* viii, O flower-de-luce, bloom on, and let the river linger to kiss thy feet!

b. *fig.*

1500–20 DUNBAR *Ballat Our Lady* 42 Haile, fair fresche flour-de-lyce!

2. The heraldic lily; a device supposed by some to have originally represented an iris, by others the top of a sceptre, of a battle-axe or other weapon. It is best known from having been borne upon the royal arms of France under the old monarchy.

c **1400** *Melayne* 94 Wende thy waye..To Charles that beris the flour delyce. **1488** in *Ld. Treas. Acc. Scotl.* I. 81 Item ane vche of gold like a flourethelis of diamantis. **1529** RASTELL *Pastyme* (1811) 75, .iii. floure delyse in a feld asure was sent to Kyng Clouys from hevyn for his armys. **1622** MALYNES *Anc. Law-Merch.* 189 The French Kings Tent with the three Flowerdeluces. **1709** ADDISON *Tatler* No. 161 ⁋9 A bloody Flag, embroidered with Flower-de Luces. **1843** LYTTON *Last Bar.* II. ii, A lofty head-gear, embroidered with fleur-de-lis. **1851** LAYARD *Pop. Acc. Discov. Nineveh* vii. 163 The first god wears the square horned cap, surmounted by a point, or fleur-de-lys.

b. The royal arms of France; hence also the French royal family, the French flag (before 1789), the French nation or government.

1352 MINOT *Poems* iv. 25 Than the riche floure de lice Wan thare ful litill prise, Fast he fled for ferde. **1494** FABYAN *Chron.* VII. 519 He, beyng of yᵉ naturall house of Fraunce, & one of yᵉ flouredelyce. **1523** LD. BERNERS *Froiss.* I. ccclxiv. 593 A great parte of the floure delyse and of the chiualry of Fraunce is within the towne. **1556** *Chron. Gr. Friars* (Camden) 4 By the wych qwene the flower de lyce came in to the armes of Yenglond, & the tyttyll of France. **1581** SIDNEY *Astr. & Stella* lxxv, He [Edw. IV] made the Flower-de-luce so fraid. *a* **1628** F. GREVILLE *Sidney* (1652) 65 To fly for protection to the Flower-de-Luce with whom they [the Netherlanders] join in continent. **1800** WEEMS *Washington* xi. (1810) 165 Blasting on every sea their sickly *fleurs-de-luce* of gallic piracy. **1865** PARKMAN *Huguenots* ii. (1875) 23 They ..saw the fleur-de-lis floating above the walls of Fort Coligny.

3. The representation or figure of a heraldic fleur-de-lis on any article, e.g. that used to mark the north on a compass. Also, (*Fr. Hist.*) a brand-mark on a criminal.

1475 *Bk. Noblesse* 4 To vapour, sprede out, according to the flour delice, and avaunce hem forthe. **1594** BLUNDEVIL *Exerc.* VII. xxiv. (ed. 7) 681 Of which lines, that which is marked with the Flower-deluce signifieth the North. **1676** B. W[ILLIS] *Man. Goldsm.* 100 Other sorts of weights.. Marked..with..the Dagger..a Flower-de-luce, and..a Vessel or Ewer. **1739** BEIGHTON in *Phil. Trans.* XLI. 754 Each Chart has a Flower de Lys on its North Edge. **1790** BURKE *Fr. Rev.* 124 The slanders of those who bring us their anecdotes with the attestation of the flower-de-luce on their shoulder. **1825** J. NICHOLSON *Operat. Mechanic* 491 As the ring turns round, the seconds upon it are shown by the top point of a fleur-de-lis C, engraved on the face of the dial-plate. *c* **1850** *Rudim. Navig.* (Weale) 5 In the compass, the northern extremity of the needle beneath is represented on the card..by the fleur-de-lis.

Hence **fleur-de-lis** *v.* (after F. *fleurdeliser*), to brand (a criminal) with the fleur-de-lis. **fleur-de-lised** *ppl. a.*, adorned with fleurs-de-lis.

1650 HOWELL *Cotgrave's Fr. Dict.* Ep. Ded., It was as much as if he had been flourdeliz'd, viz. burnt in the back or hand, or branded in his face. **1686** J. SERGEANT *Hist. Mon. Convent.* 104 A Cross Flower-de-lys'd. **1843** *Fraser's Mag.* XXVII. 418 The Count of Champagne..carried the fleur-de-lised banner.

fleuret[1] ('fluərɪt), ‖**fleurette** (flœ'rɛt). [ad. F. *fleurette*, dim. of *fleur* flower.] **a.** An ornament like a small flower. **b.** See quot. 1868.

1811 PINKERTON *Petral.* I. 428 The little fleurets, and other miniatures, which we admire in the tombs and buildings of that period. **1858** *Sat. Rev.* V. 425/2 The cymation, or wave-moulding, represented the sea;..the fleurette, the verdant plain. **1868** A. B. ALCOTT *Tablets* 22 The fruit..so arranged that the fleurets, or blossom ends, may look downwards. **1881** TERRIEN DE LA COUPERIE in *Numism. Chron.* Ser. III. I. 345 Bearing on the obverse eight fleurets.

fleuret[2]. *Fencing.* ? *Obs.* Also 7 fluret(t, floret. [a. F. *fleuret*, f. *fleur* flower = It. *fioretto*, dim. of *fiore* flower; so called because the button at the point was compared to a flower-bud.] A fencing-foil.

a **1648** LD. HERBERT *Life* (1886) 71 The good fencing-masters..when they present a foil or fleuret to their scholars, tell him it hath two parts. **1674** *Gov. Tongue* vii. §9. 141 In such fencings jest hath proved earnest, and florets have turn'd to swords. **1691** SIR W. HOPE *Compl. Fencing-master* (1697) 13 They see at every other Thrust their Flurett beat out of their Hand. **1885** E. CASTLE *Schools of Fence* xv. 246 The flexible fleuret could only be used when the play was restricted to the point.

†'**fleuret**[3]. *Obs.* [a. F. *fleuret* 'nom d'un ancien pas qui se composait d'un demicoupé et de deux pas marchés sur la pointe du pied' (Littré) = It. *fioretto*: cf. prec.] A step formerly used in dancing.

1677 SEDLEY *Ant. & Cl.* Prol., A brisk gallant..Does here and there in nimble fleurets pass.

fleurettée ('flɜːrɛteɪ). *Her.* Also 6–9 flurt(e, 9 florettée, -etty. [a. F. *fleuretté, -ée*, f. *fleurette*: cf. FLEURET[1].] = FLEURY.

1562 LEIGH *Armorie* (1597) 34 He beareth Azure, a crosse flurte Or. **1610** GUILLIM *Heraldry* VI. iv. 263 He beareth Gules, a Crosse flurte Or. **1706** PHILLIPS (ed. Kersey), *Fleurettee* (Fr. in Heraldry), flowered or set off with Flowers. **1830** E. HAWKINS *Anglo-Fr. Coinage* 121 A Greek cross, patée at the extremities, flurt. **1864** BOUTELL *Heraldry Hist. & Pop.* xv. 191 They substitute an orle of silver crescents for the field fleurettée [**1863** (ed. 1) florettée].

fleurish, var. of FLEERISH.

‖**fleuron** (flœrɔ̃). Also 4 floroun. [a. F. *fleuron*, OF. *floron*, f. *fleur* flower.]

1. A flower-shaped ornament, used *esp.* in architecture or printing, on coins, etc.

c **1385** CHAUCER *L.G.W.* Prol. 220 So were the florouns of her coroun whyte. *c* **1660** BP. COSIN in C. Walker *Ritual Reason Why* 43 *note*, In some MS. 'directions to the printer' ..he [Bp. Cosin] inserted after the Absolution 'Here set a fleuron'. **1830** E. HAWKINS *Anglo-Fr. Coinage* 73 Crown of eight lilies and four fleurons. **1833** ELLIS *Elgin Marb.* II. 169 The front is enriched with a fleuron. **1882** YULE in *Encycl. Brit.* XIV. 498 These latter [coins] bore (obverse) a Nepalese emblem surrounded by eight fleurons containing the eight sacred Buddhist jewels.

2. (See quot.)

1724–1800 BAILEY, *Fleurons* [in Cookery], fine Tarts or Puffs of Pastry Work for Garnishing. **1823** in CRABB.

†**3.** = FLORET. *Obs. rare*$^{-1}$.

1727 BRADLEY *Fam. Dict.* s.v. *Butter-Burr*, The Flower.. forms a Tuft with several Fleurons cut or divided into long Strings.

‖**fleuronée**, *a. Her.* [a. F. *fleuronné(e*, f. *fleuron*: see FLEURON.] Ornamented with fleurons: = BOTONÉ.

1614 SELDEN *Titles Hon.* 195 A Crown Fleuronee [*printed* Fleurnoee], only differing from what is now a Royall one, in that it was not arch't or close.

fleury ('fluərɪ), **flory** ('flɔːrɪ), *a. Her.* Also 5 flure, flourre, 5–6 flurri(e, 6 florie, 7 floury, 8 flore, florey, (flowery), 9 fleurie, flury, flurry. [ad. F. *fleuré, -ée*, OF. *floré, flouré*, f. *fleur*.] Decorated with fleurs-de-lis; *esp.* of a cross: Having its arms tipped with fleurs-de-lis. (Cf. also COUNTERFLEURY, -FLORY.)

c **1420** *Anturs of Arth.* xxxi, A tablet flourré [*Douce MS.* flure]. **1483** *Cath. Angl.* 136 Flory, *florulentus*. **1486** *Bk. St. Albans, Her.* C vij b, Hit is calde a cros flurri. **1572** BOSSEWELL *Armorie* II. 33 These Barrulettes are often founde Florie. **1612** DRAYTON *Poly-olb.* iv. Notes 69 Bearing..a Scepter fleury in his right. **1706** HEARNE *Collect.* 9 May, On ye other a Cross Flore. **1761** *Brit. Mag.* II. 251 A bordure, or, charged within a double tressure fleury. **1823** RUTTER *Fonthill* p. xxi, The Royal double tressure of Scotland, flory and counter flory of the first [gules]. **1864** BOUTELL *Heraldry Hist. & Pop.* xv. §1 (ed. 3) 182 The crosslets are drawn fleurie.

Fleuss (flɔɪs). The name of H. A. *Fleuss*, British inventor, used *attrib.* or in the possessive of apparatus designed by him.

1882 *Rep. Insp. Mines 1881* 463 Fleuss' breathing apparatus and lamp. **1883** *Encycl. Brit.* XVI. 467/1 Persons equipped with the Fleuss breathing apparatus can now enter mines after explosions. **1902** *Ibid.* XXXII. 190/1 The small Fleuss machine will produce about 1½ lb of ice in one operation of 20 minutes. **1904** GOODCHILD & TWENEY *Technol. & Sci. Dict.* s.v. *Air Pumps*, A great improvement in mechanical pumps has been made of recent years in what is called the Fleuss Pump. **1906** *Ibid.* s.v. *Tyres*, The Fleuss Tyre possesses no inner tube, but the edges of the cover overlap and fit together closely enough to retain the air. **1909** *Westm. Gaz.* 22 Feb. 8/1 'The Fleuss,' he added, 'is the prototype of all apparatus using compressed oxygen and caustic soda, and it has already proved its value in mine rescue-work.'

flew (fluː). [Of unknown origin.] Usually *pl.* The large chaps of a deep-mouthed hound (e.g. the bloodhound).

1575 TURBERV. *Faulconrie* 369 They..open his flew and jawes with a mannes hande. **1611** MARKHAM *Countr. Content.* I. i. (1668) 5 The flews of his [i.e. a hound's] upper lips almost two inches lower than his neither chaps. **1766–82** in BAILEY. **1818** HOGG *Hunt of Eildon* v. in *Brownie of Bodsbeck* II. 322 Their crukit tungis were dry for blood, An' the red lowe firled at their flews. **1883** STABLES *Friend Dog* vii. 60 *Flews*, the hanging lips, as in the Blood-hound.

flew, var. of FLUE.

flew, pa. t. of FLY *v.* and (*obs.*) of FLAY *v.*

fleware, -ere, -oure, obs. Sc. ff. FLAVOUR.

flewed (fluːd), *ppl. a.* [f. FLEW *sb.* + -ED[2].] Having flews (of a particular quality).

1590 SHAKS. *Mids. N.* IV. i. 125 My hounds are bred out of the Spartan kinde, So flew'd, so sanded. **1592** LYLY *Midas* IV. iii, A hound..fleet, faire flewde, and well hangd.

†'**flewen.** *Obs.* [a. Du. *fluwijn*, prob. a corruption of F. *fouine*.] A polecat.

1494 HALYBURTON *Ledger* (1867) 50 Item 100 rygis of flewenys, price 8½ gs.

flewen, obs. pa. pple. of FLAY.

flewet ('fluːɪt). *Obs.* exc. *Sc.* and *dial.* Also flewit, fluet. [Of unknown origin.] A smart blow or stroke, a buffet.

1563–83 FOXE *A. & M.* II. 1474 With his hand he..gaue Syr Thomas..a good flewet upon the vpper part of the neck. **1719** HAMILTON *Ep. to Ramsay* 24 July xiv, For an they winna had their blether, They's get a flewet. **1786** BURNS *What ails ye now* x, I'd rather suffer for my faut A hearty flewit. **1878** *Cumbrld. Gloss.* s.v., 'Hit him a fluet ower t' lug.'

flewk(e, obs. form of FLUKE.

flewm, flewm-: see PHLEGM, PHLEGM-.

†'**flewsey**, *a. Obs.* Also flusey. [f. *flew*, FLUE fluff.] Fluffy.

1711 PETIVER in *Phil. Trans.* XXVII. 382 Its flewsey Heads grow in round clusters, with elegant feathered Seed. **1713** *Ibid.* XXVIII. 62 Its blush Flowers stand in a round flusey Head, like our Haresfoot.

flex (flɛks), *v.* [f. L. *flex-* ppl. stem of *flectĕre* to bend.] *trans.* To bend. Now chiefly in *scientific* use, *esp.* with reference to the bending of a joint or limb by the action of the flexor muscles (opposed to EXTEND), and *Geol.* with reference to strata.

a **1521** *Helyas* in Thoms *Prose Rom.* (1828) III. 13 With his knees flexed he prostened him. **1560** ROLLAND *Crt. Venus* II. 943 Richt fair scho hes me flext. **1572** BOSSEWELL *Armorie* III. 20 b, This worme is here figured with the tayle flexed vnder his chinne. **1834** M'MURTRIE *Cuvier's Anim. Kingd.* 357 The tarsi..can only be flexed on the tibiæ. **1845** TODD & BOWMAN *Phys. Anat.* I. 169 A single muscle.. flexes the thigh. **1879** DANA *Man. Geol.* (ed. 3) 155 The whole series has been upturned and flexed, broken and displaced. **1912** L. J. VANCE *Destroying Angel* xiii. 160 Tensing and flexing his tired muscles while his eyes shifted quickly from one quarter to another. **1926** R. MACAULAY *Crewe Train* II. ix. 167 Flexed her toes against the rock's level face, and drew herself up. **1947** R. ALLEN *Home made Banners* iii. 16 It dedicated its soul to the war and flexed its muscles for the war, and then there was a pause.

flex (flɛks), *sb.*[1] *Math.* [f. L. *flexus*, f. *flectere* to bend.] A point of inflexion (see INFLEXION, INFLECTION 3).

1866 A. CAYLEY in *Q. Jrnl. Pure & Appl. Math.* VII. 213 The stationary ineunt, or cusp, considered as..a particular case of the double ineunt, is a spinode; to render this notation symmetrical, we require certain new terms, say link, as the correlative to node, and flex as the correlative to cusp... The ordinary singularities of a plane curve would thus be the node, the cusp, the link, and the flex. **1950** H. G. FORDER *Geometry* ix. 152 The line which joins two flexes of a cubic goes through a third flex.

flex (flɛks), *sb.*[2] [Abbrev. of FLEXIBLE *sb.*] Flexible low-current electric cable consisting of two or more stranded conductors separately insulated, used esp. for connections to electric lamps and portable domestic appliances.

1905 C. C. METCALFE *Pract. Electr. Wiring* vii. 104 Flexible cord, generally known in the wiring trade as 'Flex', consists of two flexible conductors laid together, each insulated from the other. **1907** *Install. News* July 10/2 A flat piece of vulcanite..provided with three holes, the bottom two being used to take the flex. **1922** *Daily Mail* 18 Dec. 1 Electric iron, complete with flex cord and adaptor. **1966** *Electricity at Work* Sept., In a 2 core flex there is no earth core. **1967** P. HONEY *Househ. Electr.* 65 Never run flexes under a carpet.

flex(e, obs. form of FLAX.

†**fle'xanimous**, *a. Obs.* [f. L. *flexanim-us* (f. *flex-* ppl. stem of *flectĕre* to bend + *anim-um* mind) + -OUS.]

1. Having power to bend or influence the mind; moving, affecting.

c **1621** S. WARD *Life Faith* (1627) 66 It stands not without doores as a Mendicant Flexanimous perswader. **1633** T. ADAMS *Exp. 2 Peter* ii. 5 He is that flexanimous Preacher whose pulpit is in heaven. **1672** *Life Jas. Arminius & Simon Episcopius* I. 8 There was in Beza beyond other mortals a flexanimous and perswasive eloquence.

2. (See quot.)

1656–81 BLOUNT *Glossogr.*, *Flexanimous*..that is of a minde easily bent or turned. **1721** in BAILEY.

Hence **fle'xanimousness**.

1727 BAILEY vol. II, *Flexanimousness*, flexibleness of Mind or Disposition.

flexed (flɛkst), *ppl. a.* [f. FLEX *v.* + -ED[1].]

a. Bent. Now only *Her.* and in scientific use. ***flexed and reflexed*** (Her.), having the two extremities curved in opposite directions, like the letter S.

1572 [see FLEX *v.*]. **1610** GUILLIM *Heraldry* III. xiii. (1611) 125 The proboscide Trunke..of an Elephant in pale Couped Flexed and reflexed after the forme of a roman S. **1632** LITHGOW *Trav.* VII. 334 Upon my flexed knees. **1828–40** BERRY *Encycl. Herald* I, *Flexed*, bent or bowed, somewhat circular. **1863** BOUTELL *Heraldry Hist. & Pop.* xi. §1. 59 Three Legs, armed, proper..flexed in a triangle. **1880** HUXLEY *Crayfish* iii. 99 When the abdomen is completely flexed.

b. *Archæol.* Of a corpse: buried with the legs drawn up under the chin. Hence also of a burial in which the corpse is in this position.

1915 A. KEITH *Antiquity of Man* vi. 117 The body had been laid on its back,..with knees, thighs, and elbows flexed. **1934** V. G. CHILDE *New Light Most Anc. East* ix. 274 The bodies had been interred extended or flexed. **1952** [see EXTENDED *ppl. a.* 1 b]. **1959** J. D. CLARK *Prehist. S. Afr.* ix. 249 The burial at Driekops Eiland was flexed, lying on its side and facing south.

flexen, obs. form of FLAXEN.

flexibility (flɛksɪ'bɪlɪtɪ). [a. F. *flexibilité*, ad. L. *flexibilitāt-em*, f. *flexibilis*: see FLEXIBLE and -ITY.] The quality of being flexible.

1. a. Capability of being bent; pliancy.

1616 BULLOKAR, *Flexibilitie*, aptnes to bend. **1656** RIDGLEY *Pract. Physick* 359 Smaller Tents must not be put in, because of their flexibility. **1796** BROUGHAM in *Phil. Trans.* LXXXVI. 234 The parts of light differ in flexibility. **1859–60** J. H. NEWMAN *Hist. Sk.* (1873) II. II. ii. 234 That strength and flexibility of limb..by which a man excels in manly games.

†**b.** The quality of yielding to pressure. *Obs.*

1677 HORNECK *Gt. Law Consid.* vi. (1704) 339 When this air yields to all gross bodies, and lets them pass without opposition..In that flexibility, thou mayest see the sinfulness of thy inexorable temper.

2. a. Susceptibility of modification or alteration; capacity for ready adaptation to various purposes or conditions; freedom from stiffness or rigidity.

1783 BLAIR *Lect. Rhet.* I. ix. 175 The flexibility of a Language, or its power of accommodation to different styles and manners. **1796** MORSE *Amer. Geog.* II. 54 It has not that softness and flexibility, which are found in other languages. **1838** THIRLWALL *Greece* II. xi. 46 The flexibility necessary for a continual adaptation to altered circumstances. **1865** M. ARNOLD *Ess. Crit.* ii. (1875) 57 Flexibility of intelligence. **1871** MARKBY *Elem. Law* §59 Its [judiciary law's] only advantage—that of flexibility or capacity of being adapted to any new combination of circumstances that may arise. **1875** HAMERTON *Intell. Life* x. v. 392 Men of exceptional power and exceptional flexibility. **1961** *Oxf. Univ. Gaz.* 19 Oct. 176/1 The principle of flexibility in fixing stipends within scales. **1962** *Listener* 29 Mar. 540/2 It follows then, doesn't it, that a civil defence programme is not meant primarily to add to the flexibility of American strategy?

b. Of the voice or fingers: Capacity for free, rapid, and varied execution or delivery. Also *pl.*

1795 MASON *Ch. Mus.* ii. 134 It required no flexibility of throat. **1807** tr. *Gœde's Trav.* II. 218 Mrs. Siddons possesses all the flexibilities of tone. **1848** RIMBAULT *First Bk. Piano* 43 When the fingers of the right hand have acquired some degree of flexibility. **1848** C. BRONTË *J. Eyre* xi. 102 A flexibility of voice and an appropriateness of gesture.

3. Readiness to yield to influence or persuasion, pliancy of mind or disposition. Const. *to*.

1647 CLARENDON *Hist. Reb.* VII. (1843) 426/1 The flexibility and instability of that gentleman's nature, not being then understood. **1751** JOHNSON *Rambler* No. 162 ¶6 Flexibility to his present humour. **1772** PRIESTLEY *Inst. Relig.* (1782) I. 151 The flexibility, as we may call it, of a child.

flexible (ˈflɛksɪb(ə)l), *a.* (*sb.*) Also 6 **flexable**, **-ibil(l**. [a. F. *flexible*, f. L. *flexibil-is*, f. *flex-* ppl. stem of *flectĕre* to bend.]

A. *adj.* **1. a.** Capable of being bent, admitting of change in figure without breaking; yielding to pressure, pliable, pliant.

1548 HALL *Chron., Edw. IV*, 212 Like a rede with every wind is agitable and flexible. **1562** BULLEYN *Bk. Sicke Men* 81 a, Feele also the pacient.. whither the partes be pained, or flexable, or haue loste their strength and are stiffe. **1606** SHAKS. *Tr. & Cr.* I. iii. 50 When the splitting winde Makes flexible the knees of knotted Oakes. **1626** BACON *Sylva* §796 And you shall finde.. the Stalke harder and less Flexible, than it was. **1664** POWER *Exp. Philos.* I. 42 It hath a Cartilaginous flexible Tube or Channel. **1731** ARBUTHNOT *Aliments* ii. (1735) 40 An Animal, in order to be moveable, must be flexible. **1802** BINGLEY *Anim. Biog.* (1813) II. 373 These parts, with the tail, are covered by a strong flexible skin. **1823** W. PHILLIPS *Introd. Min.* Introd. 9 A flexible granular quartz is found in Brazil. **1874** BOUTELL *Arms & Arm.* ii. 17 The long, flexible and pointless weapons that are described by the Roman historians.

b. In modern mechanical and electrical usage (see quots.).

1859 W. J. M. RANKINE *Man. Steam Engine* iv. 126 (*caption*) Flexible tube and diaphragm valves. *a* **1877** KNIGHT *Dict. Mech.* I. 882/1 Thirion's flexible coupling is used for conveying power from one shaft to another when they are not in line. **1888** *Lockwood's Dict. Mech. Engin.* 144 *Flexible crank shaft*, a crank shaft in which the strains due to the rigidity of an unyielding mass compelled to revolve under conditions of strain due to the want of alignment of its bearings, are reduced and minimised by the introduction of flexible joints in its length. **1909** *Install. News* II. 186/1 Flexible cord surface wiring. **1909** *Daily Chron.* 24 Aug. 7/5 Another advantage of the 'flexible' engine.. is the power it gives the driver to avoid accidents and collisions. **1918** E. S. FARROW *Dict. Mil. Terms*, *Flexible*, a term applied to a dirigible balloon in which a flexible gas container is held in shape only by the pressure of gas within and to which the load is hung. This characterizes the whole non-rigid system of airships. **1965** *Economist* 27 Mar. 1412/3 Flexible or 'black top' road design is also being studied. **1967** *Gloss. Sanitation Terms (B.S.I.)* 28 *Flexible joint*, a joint which permits some movement of the jointed parts out of their original alignment or which permits the jointing of parts which are not truly aligned. **1970** A. BYERS *Home Lighting* i. 22 Floor standards, table lamps,.. and permanent lighting may all be supplied from plugs and socket outlets using a flexible cord.

†**2.** Of a fluid: Not rigid, yielding. Of winds: Variable in direction, shifting. *Obs.*

1612 SPEED *Theat. Gt. Brit.* IV. v. 145 The quicke and flexible windes cooling the heat of Summer. **1612** BREREWOOD *Lang. & Relig.* 115 Water being.. heavy and flexible, will slide away at any inequalitie. **1692** LOCKE *Educ.* §1 A gentle application of the hand turns the flexible Waters into Channels.

3. † **a.** That can be 'bent', inclined, or rendered favourable *to* (*obs.*) **b.** Willing or disposed to yield to influence or persuasion; capable of being guided, easily led, impressionable, manageable, tractable.

a **1420** HOCCLEVE *De Reg. Princ.* 3358 To mercy were her hertes ay flexible. **1533** FRITH *Answ. Fisher* (1829) 189 Our judge, therefore, must not be partial, flexible, nor ignorant. **1548** HALL *Chron., Edw. IV*, 199 b, If he sawe hym flexible to his purpose. **1593** SHAKS. *3 Hen. VI*, I. iv. 141. **1611** SPEED *Hist. Gt. Brit.* VI. v. (1632) 38 They saw both heauen and earth flexible to their deliuerance. **1642** NEWCOMEN *Serm. bef. Ho. Com.* 5 Nov. (1643) 6 The tender and flexible age of her son. **1667** *Decay Chr. Piety* xvi. ¶2 The vulgar, who are commonly flexible to any new impression. **1727** *Philip Quarll* 139 Quarll.. was soon made flexible by her Tears. **1769** *Junius Lett.* xxxv. 160 Can you conceive that the people .. will long submit to be governed by so flexible a house of Commons? **1863** E. V. NEALE *Anal. Th. & Nat.* 99 A directing reason, easy to be entreated, and flexible.

absol. **1772** JOHNSON *Argt. Hastie* in *Boswell* App. II. (1848) 814/1 The flexible will be reformed by gentle discipline.

4. a. Susceptible of modification or adaptation to various purposes or uses; pliant, supple.

1643 SIR T. BROWNE *Relig. Med.* Pref., There are many things [in the book] to be taken in a soft and flexible sense. **1769** ROBERTSON *Chas. V*, III. 238 His flexible genius was capable of accommodating itself to every situation. **1837–9** HALLAM *Hist. Lit.* I. iii. I. §116. 227 In his Latin style.. he is less flexible and elegant. **1841** MYERS *Cath. Th.* III. §10. 38 To proclaim a more flexible rule of judgement. **1882** A. W. WARD *Dickens* iii. 55 Never was his inventive force more flexible and more at his command. **1886** LOWELL *Democr.* 226 A language at once so precise and so flexible as the Greek.

b. Of the voice: (see quot. 1825).

1712 HUGHES *Spect.* No. 541 ¶7 Sorrow and complaint demand a voice quite different, flexible, slow, interrupted. **1825** DANNELEY *Encycl. Mus.*, *Flexible*, a voice is said to be flexible when it can swell and diminish its tones, with such grace and power, as to give every shade of expression to the melody it executes. **1831** LYTTON *Godolph.* 30 His voice was so deep and flexible.

c. In depreciatory sense: Supple, complaisant.

1826 SYD. SMITH *Wks.* (1867) II. 118 But some have been selected for flexible politics.

d. *flexible response*: see quot. 1966. Cf. *controlled response* (CONTROLLED *ppl. a.* 2).

1963 *Time* (Internat. ed.) 26 July 15/3 Pentagon planning now puts relatively more emphasis than it did a few years ago on 'graduated' or 'flexible' responses. **1966** SCHWARZ & HADIK *Strategic Terminol.* 71 *Flexible response*, strategy based on the capability of reacting appropriately across the entire spectrum of possible challenge from atomic war to infiltration and subversion. **1967** *Punch* 26 Apr. 597/2 Both parties will have embarked on a policy of manufacturing anti-ballistic missiles on a scale which will cause defence costs to escalate out of all proportion, and possibly even to destroy the philosophy of flexible response, owing to the necessity to saturate enemy defences at the first stroke. **1968** *Economist* 10 Feb. 14/2 Last year Nato at long last adopted a strategy of flexible response in place of massive retaliation.

5. quasi-*adv.* = FLEXIBLY.

1833 *Regul. Instr. Cavalry* I. 115 The sword should be held flexible.

B. *ellipt.* as *sb.* = FLEX *sb.*[2]

1896 H. J. DOWSING *Griffin's Electr. Engin. Price-Bk.* (ed. 2) 254 In factories, mills, etc., where mechanical strength is of importance, a pendant fitting is made with iron armoured wire in place of the concentric flexible. **1907** *Install. News* May 11/1 Conductors (excepting flexibles) may be enclosed in steel conduits. **1925** *G.E.C. Publications: Wires & Cables* 77 Motor car ignition flexibles. **1942** MEARES & NEALE *Electr. Engin. Pract.* (ed. 5) II. xxii. 277 The flexible often gets caught as the sweeper is rolled along. **1971** *Engineering* Apr. 104/1 (Advt.), Braided flexibles.

flexibleness (ˈflɛksɪb(ə)lnɪs). [f. prec. + -NESS.] = FLEXIBILITY in various senses.

1612–15 BP. HALL *Contempl., O.T.* XIX. iii, If this son of Chenaanah had not had.. a heart of lead for flexiblenesse to humours and times. **1669** WOODHEAD *St. Teresa* II. App. I They.. perceive in the Superior such a flexibleness, as to pass by their faults. **1692** LOCKE *Educ.* §199. 255 The flexibleness of the former part of a Man's Age.

flexibly (ˈflɛksɪblɪ), *adv.* [f. as prec. + -LY[2].] In a flexible manner, with flexibility.

1607 TOPSELL *Four-f. Beasts* (1658) 149 They stand not stiffe, but bend flexibly. *Ibid.*, *Serpents* (1658) 705 Their bodies are leaner, flexibly turning to every side, according to the necessity of motion. **1861** GEO. ELIOT *Silas M.* 17 Two thick leather bags, which.. lent themselves flexibly to every corner. **1871** R. ELLIS *Catullus* lxiv. 183 O'er wide water his oars move flexibly fleeting.

flexicostate (flɛksɪˈkɒsteɪt). [f. *flexi-* combining form of L. *flex-us*, pa. pple of *flectĕre* to bend + COSTATE.] 'Having bent ribs' (1846 Smart). Hence in later Dicts.

flexile (ˈflɛksɪl), *a.* Now somewhat *rare.* Also 7 flexil. [ad. L. *flexil-em*, f. *flex-* ppl. stem of *flectĕre* to bend: see -ILE.]

1. Easily bending or bent, pliant, supple, flexible. Of the features: Mobile.

1633 T. ADAMS *Exp. 2 Peter* ii. 20 The serpent.. winds about it with his flexile and folding body. *a* **1734** NORTH *Lives* II. 202 From the box proceeds a flexile pipe with the tool at the end. **1774** *Westm. Mag.* II. 374 Hers is the humble eye, the flexile knee. **1814** WORDSW. *Excursion* VIII. 443 Whose flexile boughs.. conceal'd the stems and roots. **1834** LYTTON *Pompeii* 21 A Sicilian who with vehement gestures and flexile features was narrating.. a strange tale.

2. *transf.* and *fig.* **a.** Easily directed or swayed; yielding, tractable. **b.** Capable of varied adaptation, versatile.

1651 BIGGS *New Disp.* ¶291. 214 Their too flexile natures. **1738–46** THOMSON *Summer* 980 At sea, whose every flexile wave Obeys the blast. **1744** ARMSTRONG *Preserv. Health* ii. 383 Whose flexile genius sparkles in the gem, Grows firm in oak, and fugitive in wine. **1836** LYTTON *Athens* I. 111 The Ionians.. were susceptible, flexile [etc.]. **1842** TENNYSON *Amphion* viii. 59 Oh, nature first was fresh to men.. So youthful and so flexile then, You moved her at your pleasure.

Hence **fleˈxility** [+ -ITY], the quality or condition of being flexile.

1659 STANLEY *Hist. Philos.* (1701) 565/2 There are others which depend upon these; as Flexility, Tactility, Ductility, and others. **1815** W. TAYLOR in *Monthly Mag.* XL. 409 The flexility of the Samaritans.

† **fleˈxiloquent**, *a. Obs. rare.* [f. L. *flexiloquus* (f. *flexus*, pa. pple. of *flectĕre* to bend + *loquī* to speak): see -LOQUENT.] Speaking words of doubtful or double meaning.

1656–81 in BLOUNT *Glossogr.* **1692–1732** in COLES.

flexing (ˈflɛksɪŋ), *vbl. sb.* [f. FLEX *v.* + -ING[1].] The action of the verb FLEX. Also *transf.*

1902 *Westm. Gaz.* 9 May 10/1 Those earth movements which have resulted in the flexing and fracturing of strata. **1920** *Blackw. Mag.* July 71/1 Never a tremor of wing except just the flexing and twisting of the tips for balance. **1968** *Listener* 6 June 752/3 His critical flexings are limited to some he-man anecdotes and a lengthy interview.

flexinish, obs. form of FLAXENISH.

flexion, flection (ˈflɛkʃən). [ad. L. *flexiōn-em*, n. of action f. *flectĕre* (ppl. stem *flex-*) to bend. Cf. Fr. *flexion*, Sp. *flexion*, It. *flessione*. The etymological spelling *flexion* is the original in Eng.; *flection* (first in 18th c.) is due to the influence of such words as *affection*, *direction*, etc.]

1. The action of bending, curvature; bent condition; an instance of this.

1656 HOBBES *Six Less.* Wks. 1845 VII. 260 It is the quantity of that crookedness or flexion, by which a straight line is bent into an arch of a circle equal to it. **1659** PEARSON *Creed* vi. 562 Thus to sit doth not signifie any peculiar inclination or flexion. **1796** BROUGHAM in *Phil. Trans.* LXXXVI. 227 *Flexion*, or the bending of the rays [of light] in their passage by bodies. **1807** ROBINSON *Archæol. Græca* III. xx. 323 Eluding the stroke of the adversary by a flexion of the body. **1882** VINES *Sachs' Bot.* 692 The flexions.. of the stem and leaf-stalk produced by the wind.

attrib. **1869** BIGELOW (*title*) On the Mechanism of Dislocation and Fracture of the Hip. With the Reduction of the Dislocation by the Flexion Method.

b. *esp.* The bending of a limb or joint by the action of the flexor muscles. Cf. EXTENSION 2.

1615 CROOKE *Body of Man* 989 By this articulation both flexion and extention is made. **1644** BULWER *Chiron.* 121 Delicate flexions.. of the Fingers. **1799** *Med. Jrnl.* II. 166 It did not produce a perceptible flexion of the tibia. **1835–6** TODD *Cycl. Anat.* I. 256/1 When two segments of a limb.. can be brought to form an angle with each other, the motion is that of flexion. **1881** MIVART *Cat* 117 This ligament aids powerfully in preventing the flexion of the knee forwards.

c. A kneeling (in prayer), genuflexion. *rare.*

1862 *Lond. Rev.* 30 Aug., Next followed two prayer flections at the Tomb of Abraham.

† **d.** A turning of the eye in any direction. *Obs.*

1626 BACON *Sylva* §719 Pity causeth sometimes.. a Flexion or Cast of the Eye aside.

† **2.** Alteration, change, modification. *Obs.*

1603 HOLLAND *Plutarch's Mor.* 1251 In every one of them Sacadas made a certeine flexion.. called Strophe. **1644** BULWER *Chiron.* 123 Oratours.. (who hunted also after delicate flexions of words). **1655** FULLER *Ch. Hist.* III. v. §35 The Flexion of his condition (I mean, the altering of his occasions).

b. A modification of the sound or tone of the voice in singing or speaking; inflexion.

1758 JOHNSON *Idler* No. 25 ¶5 Variation of gesture, and flexion of voice, are to be obtained only by experience. **1846** GROTE *Greece* I. xxi. (1862) I. 530 Flexions and intonations of the voice.

3. *concr.* The bent part of anything; a bend, curve. Also, a joint.

1607 TOPSELL *Four-f. Beasts* 204 Being vnable to rise againe because of the short Nerues and no flexions in his Legs. **1626** BACON *Sylva* §222 Of a Sinuous Pipe, that may haue some foure Flexions, Triall would be made. **1726** LEONI *Alberti's Archit.* III. 20/1 There are like flexions in the boughs of trees. **1803** *Med. Jrnl.* X. 61 He put a blister .. below the flexion on the anterior part of the thigh. **1867** HOWELLS *Ital. Journ.* 56 A cavernous arcade which curves round the water with the flection of the shore.

4. *Gram.* Modification of the form of a word; *esp.* the change of ending in conjugation, declension, etc.; inflexion. Also, the modified form or ending of a word.

1605 CAMDEN *Rem.* (1657) 39 Neither are we loaden with those declensions, flexions, and variations which are incident to many other tongues. **1669** GALE *Crt. Gentiles* I. I. xi. 61 Those very words.. differ somewhat in the sound of the vowels and flexion. **1720** DE FOE *Duncan Campbell* (1841) 37 The flexion or conjugation of the verb. **1773** LD. MONBODDO *Lang.* I. III. xiv. 672 Proper terminations and flections. **1817** COLERIDGE *Biog. Lit.* 175 The common grammatic flexions of some tribe or province. **1875** WHITNEY *Life Lang.* xii. 241 An agglutinative dialect.. with no determinate flexion.

5. *Math.* = FLEXURE 6.

1704 HAYES *Treat. Fluxions* VI. 153 The Use of Fluxions in Investigating the Points of contrary Flexion and Retrogression of Curves. **1857** NICHOL *Cycl. Phys. Sc.* s.v., The mathematical theory of Flexion starts from the basis or datum of this Line of No-disturbance.

flexional, flectional (ˈflɛkʃənəl), *a.* [f. prec. + -AL[1].] Of, pertaining to, or of the nature of flexion, *esp.* in *Grammar*: see FLEXION 4. Also, of a language: Possessed of, or based upon flexions. Cf. INFLEXIONAL.

1833 J. C. HARE in *Philolog. Museum* II. 256 The meaning of a flexional termination. **1862** MARSH *Eng. Lang.* 347 An important advantage of a positional.. over a flectional syntax, is that [etc.]. **1869** FARRAR *Fam. Speech* iv. 119 *note*, A flexional language.. makes use of elements.. purely conventional and mechanical. **1874** SAYCE *Compar. Philol.* iv. 156 The clear flectional growth of the verb.

flexionless, flectionless (ˈflɛkʃənlɪs), *a.* [f. as prec. + -LESS.] Devoid of flexion or flexions: only in grammatical sense.

1860 FARRAR *Orig. Lang.* viii. 182 A language petrified in its first stage of flexionless and ungrammatical monosyllables. **1874** R. MORRIS *Hist. Eng. Gram.* ii. §ii. ¶22 Dialects.. almost as flexionless as modern English.

flexitime (ˈflɛksɪtaɪm). Also **flexi-time, flexi time**. [f. FLEXI(BLE *a.* + TIME *sb.*; cf. FLEXTIME.] An arrangement whereby employees, while working a contracted number of hours, are free to vary (within prescribed limits) their starting and finishing times.

1972 *Business Week* 7 Oct. 80/1 'Everybody told us flexitime was pie in the sky,' says Gösta Rehn. **1972** *N.Y. Post* 29 Dec. 21/1 Comments from workers and employers list multiple advantages of flexitime. **1973** *Monthly Labor Rev.* (U.S. Dept. Labor) Feb. 3/2 In Europe, the move has been toward flexible workweeks, or 'flexi-time', that change neither the total number of workdays nor the total hours required. **1973** *Sunday Sun* (Brisbane) 8 July 34/2 Flexitime —a new word meaning staggered work hours, work days and work weeks. **1975** *New Society* 14 Aug. 354/2 The 100,000 or so office workers who happen to be on 'flexi time'. **1978** *Jrnl. R. Soc. Arts* CXXVI. 424/2 In most cities, the relief which staggering—including the 'flexitime' system—can

afford is fairly limited. **1982** *Daily Tel.* 22 July 12/7 Solutions..are predictable but not easy to achieve: more flexi-time; shorter working weeks; leave-years for both parents of young children. **1985** *Observer* (Colour Suppl.) 14 Apr. 26/3 The involved and caring father who..works flexitime to ensure that he goes on being as positive a presence in the child's life as she is.

† **'flexity.** *Obs. rare.* [f. FLEX *v.* + -ITY.] The quality or condition of being bent from the straight line (said of rays of light).

1797 BROUGHAM in *Phil. Trans.* LXXXVII. 360 We may, therefore, say that the rays of light differ in degree of refrangity, reflexity, and flexity, comprehending inflexity and deflexity.

† **'flexive,** *a. Obs.* [f. L. *flex-* ppl. stem of *flectĕre* to bend + -IVE.] Tending to bend, flexible.

1629 DAVENANT *Albovine* III. Dram. Wks. 1872 I. 55 Be flexive in your smiles. **1647** R. STAPYLTON *Juvenal* XIV. 303 To cast his flexive body through a hoope. **1791** W. BARTRAM *Trav.* 329 These heavy spikes of flowers..bend the slender flexive stems to the ground.

Hence **'flexively** *adv.*

1651 *Fuller's Abel Rediv., Myconius* 141 His heart was alwayes flexively inclind To what was good.

flexography (flɛk'sɒgrəfɪ). [f. *flexo-* (f. L. *flexus*, f. *flectere* to bend) + -GRAPHY.] A rotary letterpress technique using rubber or plastic plates and aniline inks for printing on fabrics, plastics, metal foils, and other materials, as well as on paper; also called *aniline printing*. So **flexo'graphic** *a.*

1952 *Print* (U.S.) Nov. 51/1 An informal poll..indicated many drawbacks to the term *Aniline* printing... Three suggestions were presented: Flexographic Process, Permatone Process, or Rotopake Process. *Flexographic* was chosen as the new official description. **1954** *Penrose Ann.* XLVIII. 151 The process known as Flexography dates back to the time when the first rubber stamp was moulded. **1954** *Brit. Printer* LXVI. 36/1 The aniline process, or 'flexographic' printing, as it is now commonly termed in America, has its origins in the paper converting field rather than in the general printing industry. **1960** *News Chron.* 7 Sept. 8/3 Flexographic printing. Competent charge hand required by leading firm of film converters. **1966** *Print* (Wynkyn de Worde Soc.) iv. 55 To these three conventional processes may be added aniline or flexographic printing, which is a form of rotary letter-press, using a soft rubber plate and very thin inks, predominantly for printing packaging materials. **1970** *Brit. Printer* July 69/2 Screen process is now competing with offset-litho and flexography in some large packaging applications. *Ibid.* 85/1 Three models..are available in the new range of flexographic presses.

flexon, obs. f. FLAXEN.

flexor ('flɛksɔː(r)). Cf. FLECTOR. [a. mod.L. *flexor*, agent-n. f. *flectĕre* (ppl. stem *flex-*) to bend.]

1. A muscle whose function it is to produce flexion in any part of the body. Opposed to *extensor*.

1615 CROOKE *Body of Man* 743 The two Flexors and the two extensors. **1726** MONRO *Anat.* 331 The Flexors of the great toe. **1880** HUXLEY *Crayfish* iii. 99 The flexors of the abdomen.

2. *attrib.* in *flexor muscle, surface, tendon*.

1726 MONRO *Anat.* 328 This Bone is concave, for lodging the Flexor-muscles. *a* **1735** ARBUTHNOT *Mem. Scrib.* x. Wks. (1892) 345 Flatterers who have the flexor muscles so strong that they are always bowing and cringing. **1847** YOUATT *Horse* i. 14 Through the whole course of the flexor tendon. **1881** MIVART in *Nature* No. 615. 337 A spine which projects vertically from the inner, or flexor surface of each finger or toe.

Flexowriter ('flɛksəʊraɪtə(r)). Also **flexowriter**. The proprietary name of a kind of electric typewriter incorporating a tape-punch and a tape-reader.

1955 *Trade Marks Jrnl.* 21 Sept. 927/1 *Flexowriter.* Appliances consisting of a typewriter and a duplicator in one unit for office use. **1956** I. A. HERRMAN *Man. Office Reprod.* xiii. 142 A Flexowriter punches codes in the edge of cards or in tape, and reads edge-punched cards or punched tape for automatic operation. **1964** C. DENT *Quantity Surveying by Computer* iii. 31 If a computer has facilities for accepting eight-channel tape, then the additional expense of Flexowriter input and output with its greater flexibility may be justified. **1968** *Bodl. Libr. Rec.* VIII. 63 The entries were typed on the flexowriter at RSL on envelopes of a standard size.

† **'flexpeng.** *Obs.* ? A gudgeon.

c **1475** *Voc.* in Wr.-Wülcker 763 *Fundulus*, a flexpeng.

flexs(s, obs. form of FLESH.

flextime. Also **Flextime.** [f. FLEX(IBLE *a.* + TIME *sb.*; cf. G. *Gleitzeit*, lit. 'sliding time'.] = FLEXITIME.

Flextime is a proprietary term for a timing device used to record the number of hours worked by employees (*Trade Marks Jrnl.* (1972), 9 Feb. 251/2; *Official Gaz.* (U.S. Patent Off.) (1974), 8 Jan. 175/1).

1972 *Guardian* 15 Mar. 14/1 In Germany, 5 million workers..will..be operating Gleitzeit, or, as we call it, Flextime. **1972** *U.S. News & World Report* 19 June 100/1 Flextime also is showing up in the U.S. **1972** *Times* 25 Sept. 15/6 New working hours are based on the 'flextime' principle, with a 'core time' of three hours during the day when everyone must be at work. **1977** *Time* 10 Jan. 48/1 Flextime..is loosening the rigidity of the 9-to-5 day for a growing number of workers in the U.S... The basic idea is that employees can arrange their own work hours around a 'core' of time. **1980** *Nature* 29 May p. xxviii. (Advt.), Four weeks holiday. Luncheon Vouchers. Flextime. Salary according to experience.

flexuose (flɛksjuː'əʊs), *a.* Chiefly *Bot.* [ad. L. *flexuōs-us*, f. *flexu-s* sb. a bending (*u*-stem), f. *flectĕre* to bend.] Winding in and out, bending to and fro, serpentine, undulating, crooked.

1727 in BAILEY vol. II. **1794** MARTYN *Rousseau's Bot.* xxvi. 393 The stem is a little flexuose or winding. **1826** KIRBY & SP. *Entomol.* (1828) III. xxxv. 673 In Lygæus Pharaonis the posterior pair are flexuose. **1845** LINDLEY *Sch. Bot.* ix. (1858) 154 Stalk of sporangium curved, flexuose.

flexuosity (flɛksjuː'ɒsɪtɪ). [ad. F. *flexuosité*, ad. L. *flexuōsitāt-em*, n. of state f. *flexuōsus*: see prec. and -ITY.] The quality or condition of being flexuous; an instance of this; a winding.

1611 COTGR., *Flexuosite*, flexuositie; a most crooked or manifold turning. **1737** OZELL *Rabelais* III. iv. (1807) II. 261 By long ambages, circuits, and flexuosities. **1830** R. KNOX *Béclard's Anat.* 168 The flexuosity consists in a course alternately undulated above and below a straight line. **1853** PHILLIPS *Rivers Yorksh.* ix. 243 [Roads] which exhibit a negligent flexuosity.

flexuoso-, combining form of FLEXUOSE or FLEXUOUS, occas. prefixed to other adjs. to indicate a flexuous form or arrangement.

1846 DANA *Zooph.* (1848) 227 A[stræa] flexuoso-convex. *Ibid.* 327 Lobes carinato-angular, and flexuoso-divaricate. **1856** W. CLARK *Van der Hoeven's Zool.* I. 405 Antennæ in both sexes simple, flexuoso-clavate, with smooth apex.

flexuous ('flɛksjuːəs), *a.* [ad. L. *flexuōs-us*: see FLEXUOSE and -OUS.]

1. Full of bends or curves; winding, sinuous. Now chiefly in scientific use, said of animal or vegetable structures.

1605 BACON *Adv. Learn.* II. vi. §6. 28 Imitating the ordinarie flexuous courses of Nature. *a* **1661** FULLER *Worthies Barks.* (1662) 81 The flexuous River of Thames. **1828** STARK *Elem. Nat. Hist.* I. 420 Lateral line flexuous; tail slightly bilobate. **1860** O. W. HOLMES *Elsie V.* x, Her lithe body undulating with flexuous grace. **1874** T. HARDY *Madding Crowd* I. xxv. 282 About equal proportions of gnarled and flexuous forms, the former being the men, the latter the women.

2. Moving in bends or waves, undulating. *rare.*

1626 BACON *Sylva* §820 The Flexuous Burning of Flames doth shew the Aire beginneth to be vnquiet. **1872** DARWIN *Emotions* Introd. 11 Man cannot express love..by external signs, so plainly as does a dog, when with..flexuous body..he meets his beloved master.

Hence **'flexuously** *adv.*, in a flexuous manner.

1846 DANA *Zooph.* (1848) 382 Flexuously branched stems. **1872** H. C. WOOD *Fresh-W. Algæ* 34 Flexuously curved.

flexural ('flɛksjʊərəl), *a.* [f. next + -AL[1].] Of or relating to flexure.

1879 THOMSON & TAIT *Nat. Philos.* §591 The constants of flexural and torsional rigidity.

flexure ('flɛksjʊə(r)). [ad. L. *flexūra*, f. *flectĕre* to bend: see -URE.]

1. The action of flexing or bending; curvature; an instance of this.

1592 *Nobody & Someb.* 1062 in Simpson *Sch. Shaks.* (1878) I. 318 There's those are made For flexure, let them stoope. **1599** B. JONSON *Ev. Man out of Hum.* 'Grex' 26 The easie flexure of his supple hammes. *c* **1611** CHAPMAN *Iliad* XXIII. 409 Eumelus made most pace With his fleet mares, and he began the flexure as we thought. **1764** REID *Inquiry* v. §7 A new sensation, which accompanies the flexure of joints, and the swelling of muscles. **1775** JOHNSON *West. Isl.* Wks. X. 351 The way makes a flexure. **1827** FARADAY *Chem. Manip.* ii. 25 By flexure of the beam or change in the points of support. **1870** RUSKIN *Lect. Art* vi. 165 They give life by flexure of surface, not by quantity of detail.

fig. **1649** JER. TAYLOR *Gt. Exemp.* Ep. Ded. 1 That proposition which complies with..all the flexures of its temporall ends.

2. Flexed or bent condition; 'the form or direction in which anything is bent' (J.), bent figure or posture; bending, or winding form.

1628 EARLE *Microcosm.* xxx (1811) 86 No antick screws men's bodies into such strange flexures. **1658** EVELYN *Fr. Gard.* (1675) 15 Which..will oblige the trees to what flexure and forme you please. **1691** RAY *Creation* II. (1692) 5 The contrary flexure of the Joints of our Arms and Legs to that of Quadrupeds. **1794** G. ADAMS *Nat. & Exp. Philos.* I. v. 200 Muscles, by which he [man] can give..to his tongue, any kind of flexure he pleases. **1826** GOOD *Bk. Nat.* (1834) I. 1 The details..of planting the woods, of giving flexure to the rivers, [etc.]. **1875** BLACKMORE *Alice Lorraine* II. xxiii. 323 With classic flexure of luxuriant hair.

†**3.** A tendency to bend or be bent; a strain. *Obs.*

1652 ABP. SANCROFT *Mod. Pol.* in D'Oyly *Life* II. 254 There is no such equilibrious virtue, but has some flexure to one of the extremes. **1665** HOOKE *Microgr.* 42 The parts of the Glass are under a kind of tension or flexure.

†**4. a.** Power of bending. Const. *of.*

b. Capability of being bent; flexibility. *Obs.*

1651-3 JER. TAYLOR *Serm. for Year* (1850) 154 Stiff as icicles, and without flexure as the legs of elephants. **1779** *Phil. Trans.* LXIX. 10 He..had the perfect flexure and use of his fore arm. **1802** PALEY *Nat. Theol.* i. (1819) 2 A flexible chain artificially wrought for the sake of flexure.

5. *concr.* A thing of bent shape; the bent part of anything (e.g. a limb, river, road); a bend, curve, turn, winding.

1607 TOPSELL *Serpents* (1658) 674 An angle or flexure of sixteen ribs. **1652** F. KIRKMAN *Clerio & Lozia* 91 Her Coif ..with flexures in it for her hair to pass out most compleatly curled. *c* **1720** GIBSON *Farrier's Guide* I. v. (1738) 56 [They] lose their fleshy substance..as they approach the Flexure of the lower Jaw-bone. **1773** *Hist. Brit. Dom. N. Amer.* II. v. §2. 295 From the hook or flexure..vessels get out to sea with difficulty. **1800** *Med. Jrnl.* III. 23 The lowest part of the sigmoid flexure of the colon. **1814** CARY *Dante Purg.* xxv. 105 Now the last flexure of our way we reach'd. **1839** STONEHOUSE *Axholme* 152 The arched entrance to the north porch, which is richly ornamented by trefoil flexures. **1868** BROWNING *Ring & Bk.* IX. 57 Her babe—that flexure of soft limbs. **1874** COUES *Birds N.W.* 688 The wing from the flexure, differs..almost or quite an inch.

6. *Math.* The bending or curving of a line or surface. In the theory of elasticity, the bending of a surface or solid. ***flexure of a curve***: its bending towards or from a straight line. ***point of contrary flexure***: see CONTRARY A. 5 d.

1672 WALLIS in Rigaud *Corr. Sci. Men* (1841) II. 538 The figure of tangents applied to the arch stretched out into a straight line, hath no contrary flexure. **1831** BREWSTER *Optics* vi. 64 All the variety of caustics, with their cusps and points of contrary flexure. **1856** DENISON *Lect. Ch. Building* iii. 93 Hogarth's line of beauty..is..in mathematical language, a curve of contrary flexure. **1857** WHEWELL *Hist. Induct. Sc.* I. 79 This flexure is different at different angles. **1879** THOMSON & TAIT *Nat. Philos.* §141 Flexure stretches one side and condenses the other temporarily.

7. *Geol.* A bending of strata under pressure, chiefly from below.

1833 LYELL *Princ. Geol.* III. 316 The great flexure of the secondary and tertiary beds. **1845** DARWIN *Voy. Nat.* ix. (1879) 196 The quartz rock..underwent..remarkable flexures without being shattered. **1882** GEIKIE *Text-bk. Geol.* VII. 915 Various types of flexure may be noticed.

Hence **'flexured** *ppl. a.* [-ED[2]], having a flexure or flexures.

1881 BLACKMORE *Christowell* II. xiv. 276 The carven curves and flexured tracery of soft little ears.

fley, flay (fleɪ), *sb. Sc.* and *north. dial.* [f. next.] A fright; also in ***to get, take (a) fley***. Cf. FLEG *sb.*[1]

1804 TARRAS *Poems* 70, I watna, bit [but] I've gotten a fley. **1813** D. ANDERSON *Poems* 80 (Jam.) But bauldly then shook off their flay. *Ibid.* 121 Timorous fowk tak flay. **1892** *Northumbld. Gloss.*, *Flay*, a fright.

fley, flay (fleɪ), *v. Obs.* exc. *Sc.* and *north.* Forms: 3-9 **flay**, (5 **flaey**), 4-6 **fle**, (7 **flea**, 8 **flee**), 6 **flie**, 7-8 **fly**. See FLEG. [OE. **fliȝan*, **fléȝan* (found in the compound *á-flýȝan*: see AFLEY) = ON. *fleyja*, OHG. (*ar-*) *flaugen*, Goth. (*us-*) *flaugjan*:—OTeut. **flaugjan*, causative of *fleugan* to FLY.]

1. *trans.* To put to flight, frighten away. Also with *away*.

a **1225** *Leg. Kath.* 1602 An se swiðe swote smal com anan þrefter, þæt fleide awei þe fearlac. *c* **1325** *Metr. Hom.* 69 Many tyme Flayed he fendes fell fra hyme. *c* **1450** *Bk. Hawkyng* in *Rel. Ant.* I. 298 If thu handell thy hawke..with thi handes unwasch..thu fleyst thyn hawke..above all thyng. **1572** *Satir. Poems Reform.* xxxiii. 218 Quhair is ȝour wit..To fle away my husband Common-weill? *a* **1605** POLWART *Flyting w. Montgomerie* 211 And thinkes like fooles, to fley all faes With targets, tulȝies, and toome talk. **1871** C. GIBBON *Lack of Gold* xxi, 'Ye may fley the laird from the country.' **1876** *Whitby Gloss.*, *Flay*, to scare away.

2. To frighten, scare, terrify.

a **1300** *Cursor M.* 17288 + 359 (Cott.) Bot wymmen flayed vus foule with wordez þat þai saide. **1375** BARBOUR *Bruce* XVI. 217 Thai war so felly fleyit thar, That [etc.]. *c* **1450** *St. Cuthbert* (Surtees) 2374 þai flowe away as þai were flayde. **1563** DAVIDSON *Confut. Kennedy* in *Wodr. Soc. Misc.* (1844) 208 Thay walde faine fley us with the wynde of the worde of perturbatione. **1721** KELLY *Sc. Prov.* 391 You are more flay'd than hurt. **1785** BURNS *Death & Dr. Hornbook* ix, 'My name is Death But be na fley'd.' **1849** C. BRONTE *Shirley* v. 46 'Like as they're flayed wi' bogards.' **1889** NICHOLSON *Folk-speech E. Yorksh.* 33 Poor Billy was ommast flaid oot ov his wits.

3. *intr.* To be afraid or frightened.

1768 ROSS *Helenore* I. 378 Nory..had some farther gane, For Lindy fly'd. *a* **1776** in Herd *Collect.* II. 216 The feint a body was therein, ye need na fley'd for being seen.

4. *Comb.* **flay-crake, -crow,** a scarecrow.

1788 W. MARSHALL *Yorksh.* Gloss. (E.D.S.) **Flay-crake*, a scare-crow. **1883** *Longm. Mag.* June 166 Coming across a 'flaycrake' among the young wheat. **1824** *Craven Dial.* 74 **Flaycraw.* **1852** R. S. SURTEES *Sponge's Sp. Tour* xiv. 72 A hat that would disgrace anything but a flay-crow.

Hence **fleyed** *ppl. a.*, frightened; afraid; timorous. Const. *of.* Also **'fleyedly** (*flietlie*), *adv.*; **'fleyedness.**

c **1425** WYNTOUN *Cron.* VI. xviii. 1926 He..bad hyr noucht fleyd to be off that. *c* **1450** HENRYSON *Poems* (1865) 206 Quhill that the Wolf for fleidnes fylit the field. **1533** GAU *Richt Vay* (1888) 107 Zour fleyit conscience. **1563** WINȜET *Four Scoir Tre Quest.* Pref. Wks. 1888 I. 50 Of the silence and fleitnes of wtheris. **1596** DALRYMPLE tr. *Leslie's Hist. Scot.* IX. 215 Quhilk..waik throuch feir ouer flietlie stude abak. *a* **1605** POLWART *Flyting w. Montgomerie* 781 Fleyd foole, mad muile! **1674** RAY *N.C. Words* 26 A flaid Coxcomb, a fearful fellow. **1676** ROW *Suppl. Blair's Autobiog.*, (1848) xii. 539 Sharp who was as flyed as a fox. **1850** [MRS. LEAR] *Tales Kirkbeck* Ser. II. 121 'I'se flayed on't' Elky exclaimed.

fley(e, obs. forms of FLAY.

fleyen, obs. pa. pple. of FLAY.

fley(h)s, obs. form of FLESH.

fleying ('fleɪɪŋ), *vbl. sb. dial.* [f. FLEY *v.* + -ING¹.] The action of the vb. FLEY; an instance of this; hence, fright, fear. Also *concr.* Something that frightens; a hobgoblin.
1340 HAMPOLE *Pr. Consc.* 6112 Þe day of flaying and of af[r]ay. **1811** WILLAN in *Archæologia* XVII. 146 *Flaying*, an apparition or hobgoblin. **1869** *Lonsdale Gloss.*, *Flayin'*, a spectre, an apparition. **1876** *Whitby Gloss.*, 'I gat a sair flaying.'

fleyke, fleyl(e, fleys, obs. ff. of FLAKE, FLAIL, FLEECE.

fleysome, flaysome ('fleɪsəm), *a. dial.* [f. FLAY *sb.* + -SOME.] Frightful, dreadful.
1790 A. WILSON *Ep. to Picken* Poet. Wks. (1846) 106 He got on his fleesome cowl. **1848** E. BRONTE *Wuthering H.* xxxiii. 266 Yon flaysome graceless quean. **1891** ATKINSON *Last Giant-Killers* 150 Such flaysome, ghostlike beings.

fleyte, obs. form of FLITE.

fliar, obs. Sc. form of FLYER.

†**flibber gibber**, *a. Obs. rare*⁻¹. [Cf. next.] ? Glib-tongued.
1561 AWDELAY *Frat. Vacab.* (1575) B iv, This is a flibber gibber Knaue, that doth fayne tales.

flibbertigibbet ('flɪbətɪ'dʒɪbɪt), *sb.* Forms: 6 **flibbergib(be, flybbergybe, 7 flibber de' Jibb, 6-7 flebergebet, -gebit, -gibet, 6 flibber-gibbet, 7 fliberdigib(b)et, fliberdegibek, 9 flibberty-, flipperty-gibbet, 7- flibbertigibbet.** [App. an onomatopœic representation of unmeaning chatter. The earliest form in our quots., *flibbergib*, is prob. the original; the later expansions are of a kind commonly met with in imitative words. The ending may be due to association with *gibbet*.]
1. A chattering or gossiping person; a flighty or frivolous woman.
1549 LATIMER *2nd Serm. bef. Edw. VI*, D v, These.. flybbergybes an other daye shall come & clawe you by the backe and say [etc.]. **1611** COTGR., *Coquette*, a pratling, or proud gossip; a titifill, a flebergebit. **1640** BROME *Sparagus Gard.* I. iv, Good Mrs. Flibber de' Jibb with the French fly-flap o' your coxecombe. **1892** TRAVERS *Mona Maclean* I. 6 You.. are less of a flibbertigibbet than the world takes you to be.
2. †**a.** The name of a devil or fiend. *Obs.*
1603 HARSNET *Pop. Impost.* x. 49 Frateretto, Fliberdigibbet, Hoberdidance, Tocobatto were foure deuils of the round, or Morrice. **1605** SHAKS. *Lear* III. iv. 120 The foule Flibbertigibbet.. hurts the poore Creature of earth.
b. A person resembling the character so nicknamed in Scott's *Kenilworth*; an impish-looking, mischievous, and flighty urchin; a person of grotesque appearance and restless manners.
[**1821** SCOTT *Kenilw.* x, Dickie Sludge, or Flibbertigibbet, as he called the boy.] **1826** H. N. COLERIDGE *West Indies* 292 What with her dishevelled hair and young black Flibbertigibbet by her side, she looked like a real witch. **1861** F. METCALFE *Oxonian in Icel.* 305 A white-haired flibbertigibbet of a boy. **1878** STEVENSON *Inland Voy.* 63 He was a lean, nervous flibbertigibbet of a man.
Hence **'flibberty-'gibberty** *a.*, flighty, frivolous, senseless.
1879 MRS. WALFORD *Cousins* II. 146 The gentle, serious Jane was taken with the flibberty-gibberty fellow. **1888** in *Berksh. Gloss.*

'flibberti,gibbet, *v.* [f. FLIBBERTIGIBBET *sb.*] *intr.* To play the flibbertigibbet; to gad about frivolously.
1921 GALSWORTHY *To Let* I. i, His daughter *would* flibberty-gibbet all over the place like most young women since the War.

flibote: see FLY-BOAT.

†**flibrigo**, *sb. Obs. rare*⁻¹.
1762 *Lond. Mag.* XXXI. 612/2 Whoever desires to fatten and strengthen.. let him refrain from high-seasoned hodge-podge, French magma, and fish flibrigo.

flibustier, var. of FILIBUSTER *sb.*

‖**flic** (flik, flɪk). [Fr.] A French policeman.
1899 E. DOWSON *Let. c.* 13 June (1967) 413 The 'flics' are a joy for ever. Each one has a different face & each one is inevitably and transparently a policeman in plain clothes. **1918** C. B. JORDAN tr. *Ibañez's Four Horsemen Apocalypse* II. i. 168 He hated the *flics*, the Paris police. **1941** KOESTLER *Scum of Earth* II. i. 60 On the platform.. sat a row of *flics*, rifles between knees. **1964** WODEHOUSE *Frozen Assets* iii. 51 Just as I was about to strike him on the mazzard, this *flic* intervened, and his was the mazzard I struck.

flic(c)h(e, obs. forms of FLITCH.

‖**flicflac.** [Fr.; echoic of a succession of sharp sounds.] A kind of step in dancing.
1852 THACKERAY *Char. & Humour* Wks. 1886 XXIII. 321 He teaches pirouettes and flic-flacs. **1860** —— *Round. Papers, De Juventute* 77 The feet of five hundred nymphs were cutting flicflacs on the stage.

flicht, Sc. form of FLIGHT, FLITE.

flichter ('flɪxtə(r)), *sb. Sc.* [f. next vb.] = FLICKER *sb.*³
1826 J. WILSON *Noct. Ambr.* Wks. 1855 I. 240 In a flichter o' rainbow licht.

flichter, flighter ('flɪxtə(r)), *v.*¹ *Sc.* Also 6 **flichtir, flych-, flyghter,** 9 **fleighter.** [? f. *flicht*, FLIGHT *v.*; see -ER⁵. Cf. FLAUGHTER *v.*²]
1. *intr.* Of a bird: To beat its wings, fly irregularly or feebly, flutter. Of inanimate objects: To flutter, move quivering through the air.
1513 DOUGLAS *Æneis* v. ix. 33 The foul affrayit flichtiris on hir wingis. **1635** D. DICKSON *Pract. Wks.* (1845) I. 55 If ye will stir & flichter like a bird in a cage. **1790** A. WILSON *Rabby's Mistake* Poet. Wks. (1846) 101 Doos flighter't through amang the stacks. **1816** SCOTT *Antiq.* xxv, 'It's just a branch of ivy flightering awa frae the wa'.'
transf. **1871** WADDELL *Ps.* xc. 10 A gliff it gaes by an' we flichter hame.
2. To struggle; to tremble, quiver, throb.
1528 LYNDESAY *Dream* 303 Mony ane thousand Comoun peple laye flichtrand in the fyre. **1553** *Douglas' Æneis* v. viii. 115 The beist.. can ly.. flychterand in the dede thrawis [cf. FLICKER *v.* 3]. **1724** [see *ppl. a.*].
Hence **'flichtering** *vbl. sb.* and *ppl. a.*
1724 RAMSAY *Tea-t. Misc.* (1733) II. 162 My flighteren heart gangs pittie-pattie. **1768** ROSS *Helenore* I. 1738 Sleep.. for a wee her flightering breast did heal. **1785** BURNS *Cotter's Saturday Nt.* iii, Th'expectant wee-things, toddlin, stacher through To meet their Dad wi' flichterin noise and glee. **1820** SCOTT *Monast.* iii, 'Our leddy is half gane already, as ye may see by that fleightering of the ee-lid.'

†**'flichter, 'flighter**, *v.*² *Sc. Obs.* [? f. *flichter*, FLIGHTER, in the unrecorded sense of 'wing'; cf. *pinion* vb.] *trans.* To bind, pinion.
1680 in Wodrow *Hist. Suff. Ch. Scotl.* (1722) II. III. iv. § 5. 141 His Hands flightered with Ropes. **1703** WILLIAMSON *Serm. bef. Gen. Assembly* 48 Driven back to Lothian.. tied and flightered like thieves. **1768** ROSS *Helenore* 1229 His legs they loos'd, but flighter'd held his hands.

flichtered ('flɪxtəd), *ppl. a. Sc.* [f. FLICHTER *v.*¹ + -ED¹.] Thrown into a flutter: **a.** volatile, flighty; **b.** frightened.
1832-53 *Whistle-binkie* (Sc. Songs) Ser. III. 70, I canna say flichter'd an' foolish ye've been. **1889** BARRIE *Window in Thrums* 102 'They were juist as flichtered themsels.'

flick (flɪk), *sb.*¹ [Echoic; cf. F. *flicflac* the cracking of a whip.]
1. a. A light blow, *esp.* one given with something pliant, a whip, etc., or with the finger-nail.
1447 BOKENHAM *Seyntys* 85 Thy craft.. is not worth a flykke. **1591** PERCIVALL *Sp. Dict.*, *Cachete*, a flicke in the cheeke. **1749** FIELDING *Tom Jones* v. ii, 'If the parson had not his petticoats on, I should have lent un o flick.' **1859** BOYD *Recr. Country Parson* (1862) 74, I have sometimes given you an angry flick when you shied. **1886** D. C. MURRAY *First Person Sing.* xix. 146 With a dexterous flick of the towel he extinguished his own candle.
b. Any sudden movement; a jerk.
1866 *Reader* 6 Jan. 19/1 The peculiar flick of the brush in drawing the terminations of the foliage. **1867** F. FRANCIS *Angling* vii. (1880) 263 The slightest 'flick' or 'crack' [in throwing the line] will necessitate putting on a new fly.
c. quasi-*adv.* With a flick.
1862 H. KINGSLEY in *Macm. Mag.* July 225 The line came 'flick' home across his face.
d. *Cricket.* A quick turn of the batsman's or bowler's wrist in playing or delivering the ball; also, a turn of the ball. *Hockey.* A stroke played with such an action; so ***flick shot, stroke.***
1897 K. S. RANJITSINHJI *Jubilee Bk. Cricket* 73 There is a certain amount of 'flick' from the fingers, but this is quite different from the twist of the slow bowler. *Ibid.* 84 Spin imparted by wrist 'flick'. **1903** JEPHSON in H. G. Hutchinson *Cricket* 91 The varying 'flicks' or 'whips' of the wrist. *Ibid.* 112 Two or three long loose strides, two at a trot, and an arm swinging round like a flail, a good length, great pace, and on any wicket at times a considerable flick back from the off. **1957** *Encycl. Brit.* XI. s.v. *Hockey* (*caption*, facing p. 616) Start of flick stroke. **1959** *Times* 6 Mar. 16/2 Hodgetts.. placed his flick poorly. **1962** *Times* 10 Dec. 4/6 A flick shot.
e. A film; also in *pl.*, the cinema. *colloq.* (Cf. FLICKER *sb.*³ 3.)
1926 E. WALLACE *Square Emerald* xv, We'll occupy the afternoon with a 'flick'. I love the movies—especially the romantic ones. **1927** W. E. COLLINSON *Contemp. Eng.* 113 We all know the word movies, but still use pictures or cinema [si'nima] in preference to the American term... Mr. Titley adds the slang flicks or flickers, unknown to me. **1931** *Repertory* (Oxford) 18 Apr. 9/1 Hand in hand with the Muse of the Theatre departs the appropriate feminine deity who presides over the 'flicks'. **1936** *Times* 29 Feb. 13/4 The present flick-minded generation may see rather than read its Victorian classics. **1949** F. SWINNERTON *Doctor's Wife comes to Stay* 112 He would take her to the theatre, the ballet, the flicks. **1959** J. BRAINE *Vodi* xviii. 215 Where shall we go this afternoon anyway? Tanbury and tea at the Raynton, then a flick?
2. The sound produced by a light blow (see sense 1 a above); hence, any slight, sharp sound.
1844 ALB. SMITH *Adv. Mr. Ledbury* I. xix, The only evidences of sound.. being the creaking and straining of the wheels.. or the flick of the driver's whip. **1866** *Cornh. Mag.* Dec. 655 The flick of her cards falling upon the table was the music she loved best to hear. **1890** *Gloucestersh. Gloss.*, *Flick*, the hasty snap of a greyhound when he fails to secure the hare.
3. *concr.* Something thrown off with a jerk; a dash, splash. (Perh. influenced by FLECK *sb.*¹)
1848 THACKERAY *Van. Fair* xix, The flicks of yellow that the rushlight threw on the dreary darkened ceiling. **1891** *Pall Mall G.* 13 Nov. 7/2 Great flicks of spray and foam as big as a man's hand.
4. *Comb.* **flick-knife**, a weapon with the blade held in the handle by a catch which can be released with a flick of the finger; **flick roll** *Aeronaut.* (see quot. 1950); also as *vb.*
1957 *Times* 15 Nov. 13/1 Mr. Justice Streatfeild said at York Assizes yesterday: 'What an invention of the Devil is the "*flick" knife, which unhappily so often features in crimes of violence in this country, often committed by young people.' **1958** *New Statesman* 6 Sept. 261/2 Young thugs who have poured into the area carrying flick-knives, bicycle chains and petrol-bombs. **1967** *Spectator* 4 Aug. 138/3 There's only one flick knife on show; but the view of New York's educational system has seldom looked bleaker. **1928** O. STEWART *Aerobatics* 6 In the *flick roll the machine again turns over sideways but, instead of doing so gently and lazily, it does so quickly with a violent wriggle. *Ibid.* 9 Some aeroplanes require a good deal of firm handling before they can be induced to flick roll. **1950** *Gloss. Aeronaut. Terms* (*B.S.I.*) I. 9 *Flick roll*, a rapidly executed roll in which the autorotative tendency of the wings is aided to some extent by the rolling moment due to the use of rudder at high angles of incidence. **1956** D. BARNHAM *One Man's Window* 65, I have never seen flick rolls used in combat before.

flick (flɪk), *sb.*² [Origin unknown; perh. two distinct words.]
†**1.** *slang.* A thief. *Obs.*⁻⁰
1610 ROWLANDS *Martin Mark-all*, A Flicke [*printed* Afflicke], a Theefe.
2. *dial.* and *vulgar.* (See quots.)
1883 *Punch* 28 July 38/1 Last night, They'd a feet in these gardens, old flick. **1886** ELWORTHY *W. Somerset Word-bk.*, *Flick*, a very familiar epithet—as 'Come on, old flick'. **1920** 'SAPPER' *Bull-Dog Drummond* iii. 87 All that I have, dear old flick, is yours for the asking. **1930** G. MANNING-SANDERS *Burnt Man* xiv. 168 'Why, hullo Ambrose, old flick!' cried Joe.

flick, *sb.*³ *dial.* Also **fleck.** [var. of FLIX.] The fur of a hare or rabbit, etc.; hence *collect.* hares and rabbits. Cf. FEATHER *sb.* 4.
1812 *Sporting Mag.* XXXIX. 140 The black [cat] had lost a very large portion of his flick. **1840** SPURDENS *Supp. to Voc. E. Anglia*, *Flick*, hare's or rabbit's down. **1887** *Kent Gloss.*, *Fleck*, hares; rabbits; ground game. 'They killed over two hundred pheasants, but not but terr'ble little fleck.'

flick, *sb.*⁴ *dial.* See FLECK *sb.*³

flick (flɪk), *v.*¹ *Cant.* [prob. a dialectal variant of FLITCH *v.*] *trans.* To cut.
1677 COLES, *Flick*, to cut. **1750** *Apol. Life Bampfylde-M. Carew* 338 Flick me some panam and cassan; cut me some bread and cheese. **1785** GROSE *Dict. Vulg. Tongue*, *Flick* the peter, cut off the cloak bag, or portmanteau. **1815** SCOTT *Guy M.* xxviii, One of them.. desired one of the lads 'to hand in the black Peter, that they might flick it open'. **1837** DISRAELI *Venetia* xiv, Flick the bread, cut the bread.

flick (flɪk), *v.*² Also *dial.* and *U.S.* **fleck.** [f. FLICK *sb.*¹; app. not recorded before the 19th c.]
1. *trans.* To strike lightly with something flexible, as a whip.
1838 DICKENS *Nich. Nick.* xxiii, 'Many and many is the circuit this pony has gone,' said Mr. Crummles, flicking him skilfully on the eyelid. **1873** OUIDA *Pascarèl* II. xi. 247 Pascarèl flicking his mandoline into harmony with the lazzarone song which he was humming. **1875** A. R. HOPE *My Schoolboy Fr.* 149 Flicking each other with our towels. **1884** W. C. SMITH *Kildrostan* 61, O white-throat swallow flicking The loch with long wing-tips.
2. a. To remove (something) with a smart stroke of something flexible. Also with *away.*
1847 ALB. SMITH *Chr. Tadpole* ii. 30 [He] attempted to flick a fly from the horse's haunch. **1848** THACKERAY *Van. Fair* xxxviii, He would flick away.. the particles of dust with a graceful wave of his hand. **1887** MISS BRADDON *Like & Unlike* ii, Miss Deverill was flicking the chalk-marks off the cloth with her handkerchief. **1918** C. SANDBURG *Cornhuskers* 50 He lived flecking lint off coat lapels.
b. To throw (*off*, etc.) with a jerk; to jerk.
1816 T. L. PEACOCK *Headlong Hall* iv, Like so many spots of ink, flicked at random out of a pen. **1882** W. J. CUMMINS *Catalogue Fishing Tackle* 10 Don't attempt to throw against the wind, as you would be sure to 'flick' the fly off.
c. *Cricket.* (*a*) Of the batsman: to play (the ball) with a slight turn of the wrist.
1897 *Encycl. Sport* I. 223/2 The two wrists moving the bat with a sort of 'flicking' movement. **1903** P. F. WARNER in H. G. Hutchinson *Cricket* 62 Short and straight balls, if they do not get up to any height, may be flicked round on the on side by a quick turn of the wrist. **1927** M. A. NOBLE *Those 'Ashes'* 176 Gregory.. was all at sea to Larwood, whom he flicked three times dangerously through the slips.
(*b*) Of the bowler: to deliver (a ball) with a flicking movement of the wrist. Also *intr.*, said of the ball so delivered.
1903 JEPHSON in H. G. Hutchinson *Cricket* 110 Bowling with a long bouncing run, he can make the ball flick higher and faster than any other bowler. *Ibid.* 116 He 'flicks' the ball as we have all seen many a wrathful billiard-player do when returning the white from a most unexpected pocket. **1920** E. R. WILSON in P. F. Warner *Cricket* 102 He [*sc.* Simpson-Hayward, the underhand bowler] 'flicked' the cricket ball as if it were a billiard ball.
3. *intr.* To move with quick vibrations; (also, ***to flick it***). Of a bird: To flutter; in quot. with *out.* Of a wound: To palpitate, throb. Cf. FLICKER.

1853 KANE *Grinnell Exp.* xxxviii. (1856) 349 As it is, we are undoubtedly flicking it to the north again. **1866** BLACKMORE *Cradock Nowell* xxxi, The jar-bird flicked out from the ivy-drum. **1889** *N.W. Linc. Gloss.*, *Fleck*, to flutter, to throb. 'My thumb, I knew it was getherin', it fleck'd soä.' *a* **1890** R. F. BURTON in *Life* (1893) I. 90 They were flicking across the country at the rate of twelve miles an hour.

4. *trans.* To move or shake with a 'flick'; to make a light stroke or movement with (a whip, etc.).

1844 MRS. HOUSTON *Yacht Voy. Texas* II. 313 The ladies . . begin flicking about their fans. **1849** ALB. SMITH *Pottleton Leg.* xxxi. 357 The driver flicked his whip at her parasol. **1861** *Fraser's Mag.* Dec. 768 Our rotten old sail began to flick itself into shreds. **1877** C. KEENE *Let.* in G. S. Layard *Life* ix. (1892) 251, I was afraid of flicking my line into my host's eye. **1879** G. MEREDITH *Egoist* xxxii. (1889) 312 He stood . . flicking a wet towel at Crossjay. **1887** A. W. TOURGÉE *Button's Inn* 124 'You handle that as if there were eggs in it,' laughed the other, flecking the whip. **1886** STEVENSON *Pr. Otto* II. xii. 203 He flicked the order on the table.

absol. **1880** *Blackw. Mag.* Jan. 79/1 So, flicking first at one hind-leg, then at another, he succeeded . . in getting her to face him. **1889** 'C. E. CRADDOCK' *Despot of Broomsedge Cove* xxiii. 424 He experimented with some delicate flecking touches of the bow.

flick (flɪk), *v.*³ Chiefly *dial.* Also **fleck**. [f. FLICK *sb.*³]

1. *trans.* **a.** To cause the fur to fly from (a hare or rabbit); hence, to wound. **b.** Of a dog: To seize by the fur.

1843 J. T. HEWLETT *College Life* III. xxxiii. 299 They [the dogs] ran up to their hare . . flicked, and eventually killed her. **1876** *Surrey Provincialisms* (E.D.S.) s.v., 'You flicked him pretty much' means you shot him very hard. **1888** *Berksh. Gloss.* s.v. *Vleck*, 'I vlecked a rabbut zo's I thinks the dogs 'ull ketch un.'

2. To strip of fur. Hence, *fig.* To fleece, strip.

1823 MOOR *Suffolk Words*, 'I fleck't him of all his marbles.'

flick(ke, obs. form of FLITCH.

†**'flicker**, *sb.*¹ *Obs. rare*⁻¹. [cf. FLICK *sb.*²]

1598 FLORIO, *Guanciatore*, . . a pilferer, a flicker.

'flicker, *sb.*² *slang.* A drinking-glass. Hence **'flicker** *v.*, to drink (Farmer).

1677 in COLES. *a* **1700** in B. E. *Dict. Cant. Crew.* **1750** *Apol. Life Bampfylde-M. Carew* 338. **1785–1823** GROSE *Dict. Vulg. Tongue.*

flicker ('flɪkə(r)), *sb.*³ [f. FLICKER *v.*]

1. An act of flickering, a flickering movement.

1857 HUGHES *Tom Brown* II. iv, [The bird would] with an impudent flicker of his tail, dart into the depths of the quickset. **1861** WILSON & GEIKIE *Mem. E. Forbes* i. 35 The flicker of the leaves whose shadows mottle their waters.

2. a. A wavering unsteady light or flame.

1849 ALB. SMITH *Pottleton Leg.* vii. 36 After some delay, there was a flicker through the fanlight of the street door. **1856** KANE *Arct. Expl.* I. xxviii. 371 Writing by this miserable flicker of my pork-fat lamp. **1862** MISS BRADDON *Lady Audley* viii. 57 The pale sky, tinged with the last cold flicker of twilight.

fig. **1856** KANE *Arct. Expl.* I. v. 53 This little flicker of enthusiasm. **1865** CARLYLE *Fredk. Gt.* VII. XVII. vii. 75 His Enterprise was a final flicker of false hope. **1876** MAUDSLEY *Physiol. Mind* i. 25 The last flicker of departing life.

b. A rapid, rhythmic variation in the degree or quality of illumination which is perceptible to the eye; also, the visual sensation caused by this.

1892 E. S. FERRY in *Amer. Jrnl. Sci.* CXLIV. 195 A vibration of the lamp or of the diffraction-grating produces a flicker in the field of view that cannot be distinguished from the appearance produced by a too slow rotation of the sectored disc. **1912** *Phil. Mag.* 6th Ser. XXIV. 370 The fovea is more sensitive to red flicker, the periphery to blue. **1929** C. MURCHISON *Found. Exper. Psychol.* iv. 200 Chromatic flicker can be evoked by alternating, upon the same retinal area, two stimuli which differ in wave-length composition but which are photometrically equal. **1944** W. D. WRIGHT *Measurem. Colour* iv. 107 The sensation of flicker due to alternations in colour vanishes at a lower frequency of alternation than the flicker due to difference in brightness. **1962** H. C. WESTON *Sight, Light & Work* (ed. 2) v. 161 There is ordinarily no visible flicker from flourescent lamps, although sometimes it is apparent at their extremities as seen by peripheral vision.

c. *spec.* in *Cinemat.* and *Television*, a succession of sudden, abrupt changes in a picture, such as occurs when the number of frames per second is too small to produce persistence of vision.

1899 H. V. HOPWOOD *Living Pictures* vi. 208 A continual rattle impinging on the ear tends to intensify irritation caused to the eye by flicker on the screen. **1923** F. A. TALBOT *Moving Pictures* 7 The regularity of this recurring damping wave, described as 'flicker', set up severe eye-strain. **1933** *Discovery* May 157/1 The ultra-short waves enable images with much greater detail and almost complete absence of flicker to be transmitted. **1953** H. A. CHINN *Telev. Broadc.* i. 6 The minimum acceptable frame frequency is that required for the elimination of flicker. **1968** *Times* 18 Apr. 2/8 (*headline*) TV flicker led to death.

d. A rapid variation in the quality of a sound analogous to visual flicker (see 2 b above).

1922 *Physical Rev.* XX. 332 It has been found possible . . to make use of the perception of flicker in an alternation phonometer. Let two frequencies alternate in the ear at a suitable rate, [etc.]. **1934** C. MURCHISON *Handbk. Gen. Exper. Psychol.* xvi. 897 The former used a flicker method, the tones to be compared being presented to the ears alternately at the rate of about 25 alternations a second. **1953** C. E. OSGOOD *Method & Theory Exper. Psychol.* iv. 146 Simultaneous auditory flicker . . was found to increase the pronouncedness of visual flicker if it was already present.

3. *pl.* = FLICK *sb.*¹ 1 e. *colloq.*

1927 [see FLICK *sb.*¹ 1 e]. **1930** W. DE LA MARE *Desert Islands* 2 Some of the best of the 'flickers' or ' movies'. **1938** G. GREENE *Brighton Rock* I. iii. 43 What about you and me going across to the flickers? **1969** GISH & PINCHOT *L. Gish* iii. 31 Mother, guess who we saw acting in 'flickers'!

4. *attrib.*, as ***flicker frequency, method***; **flicker effect** *Electronics*, a relatively low-frequency random fluctuation in the current emitted by a cathode in a thermionic valve, caused by changes in the state of the emitting surface; also, a similar effect in transistors and other solid-state devices; **flicker fusion**, the apparent steadiness of a regularly varying source of light when the frequency of the variation is sufficiently great; so **flicker-fusion frequency**, the lowest rate of variation at which flicker is not perceptible; also called ***critical flicker*** (or ***fusion***) ***frequency***; **flicker noise** *Electronics*, noise due to the flicker effect; **flicker photometer**, an instrument for measuring the relative intensities of light from two different sources, esp. sources of different colours, by measuring the flicker or observing the absence of flicker when the field of view is illuminated alternately by the two sources of light; so **flicker photometry**.

1926 W. SCHOTTKY in *Physical Rev.* XXVIII. 77 If we had to do with emission of light instead of electrons, we would speak of a chaotic variation of light intensity taking place over the surface of the cathode, a phenomenon which we should describe by the word 'flicker'. If . . Johnson's explanation of the phenomenon is the correct one, then we may use the analogy and call the new effect the '*flicker effect'. **1907** *Nat. Electr. Light Assoc. 30th Convention* I. 337 The most sensitive *flicker frequency for small ranges of flicker was in the neighborhood of 2.5 cycles per second. **1922** *Jrnl. Optical Soc. Amer.* VI. 7 The substantial independence of critical flicker frequency upon chroma is . . the basis of the critical frequency method of heterochromatic photometry. **1936** *Jrnl. Gen. Physiol.* XIX. 514 *Flicker fusion depends upon the suppression of intensity discrimination. **1944** *Federation Proc.* III. 6 (*heading*) Changes in flicker fusion frequency (F.F.F.) under experimental stress. **1962** H. C. WESTON *Sight, Light & Work* (ed. 2) v. 161 The fluctuation in light output of electric lamps caused by a 50-cycle alternating current . . is faster than the usual 'flicker fusion frequency' for the bright-adapted eye. **1897** *Jrnl. Physiol.* XXII. 143 The most marked discrepancy between the band and *flicker methods was in the case of red. **1934** Flicker method [see 2 d above]. **1947** *Proc. Physical Soc.* LIX. 366 At low frequencies (< 10^3 to 10^4 c.p.s.) *flicker noise may be tens or even hundreds of times greater than Johnson or shot noise. **1960** D. A. BELL *Electr. Noise* xii. 274 When working with semiconductors there is always a risk of flicker noise being introduced at the electrode contacts. **1896** F. P. WHITMAN in *Physical Rev.* III. 241 (*heading*) On the photometry of differently colored lights and the '*flicker' photometer. **1955** J. W. WENTWORTH *Color Telev. Engin.* iii. 59 The best instrument for measuring the luminances of 'colored' surfaces is the flicker photometer. **1897** *Jrnl. Physiol.* XXI. 47 According to the rules of *flicker-photometry . . flicker should disappear from the whole surface of the disc at the same minimal speed.

flicker ('flɪkə(r)), *sb.*⁴ *U.S.* [Said to be echoic of the bird's note.] The popular name of various American species of woodpecker.

1849 THOREAU *Week Concord Riv.* Thursday 333 The flicker's cackle is heard in the clearing. **1870** LOWELL *Study Wind.* 19 The flicker makes good his claim to the title of pigeon-woodpecker. **1888** *Riverside Nat. Hist.* IV. Introd. 8 The two flickers are mainly characterized by the color of the under-surface of the wing and tail feathers, these being red in the red shafted (*Colaptes mexicanus*), gamboge yellow in the yellow-shafted flicker (*C. auratus*). *Ibid.* IV. 428 The Cape flicker (*C. chrysoides*), with red moustache.

†**flicker**, *a. Obs. rare*⁻¹. [f. FLICKER *v.*; cf. OE. *flacor* adj., mentioned under FLACKER *v.*] Unsteadfast, wavering.

c **1325** *Metr. Hom.* 36 Forthi asked Crist quether man him soht Als he war man of fliker thoht.

flicker ('flɪkə(r)), *v.* Forms: 1 flicerian, -orian, 3–5 flikeren, (4 flikkere), 4–5 fleker, -ir, 5–6 fly(c)ker, 6 flickar, *Sc.* flickir, flikker, 6– flicker. [OE. *flicorian*, an onomatopœic formation with frequentative suffix (see -ER⁵), expressing repeated quick movement similar to that expressed by FLACKER, but slighter or less noisy.]

1. *intr.* Of a bird: To flutter; to hover. occas. To flap the wings; to move by flapping the wings.

c **1000** ÆLFRIC *Hom.* II. 156 An blac þrostle flicorode ymbe his neb. *c* **1386** CHAUCER *Knt's. T.* 1104 Above hir heed hir dowves flikeringe. **1447** BOKENHAM *Seyntys* (Roxb.) 109 Ovyr hyr as she [a dove] dede hovyr flekerynge. **1581** MARBECK *Bk. of Notes* 348 *Estrich*, This bird . . cannot mount up to flie aloft, but flickereth in such wise as he cannot be overgone. **1616** SURFL. & MARKH. *Country Farme* 26 If the Duckes . . flicker with their wings often and a long time together. **1700** DRYDEN *Palamon & Arc.* III. 123 The tuneful lark . . flickering on her nest, made short essays to sing. **1801** C. SMITH *Solit. Wanderer* I. 255, I saw too . . the flying fish . . emerging from the waves on their wing-like fins, and flickering along the surface of the water. **1892** STEVENSON & OSBOURNE *Wrecker* xix. 304 The pinnacles . . were flickered about all day long by a multitude of wings.

fig. c **1374** CHAUCER *Troylus* IV. 1193 (1221) Her gost, that flikered aie a loft, Into her wofull herte ayen it went. **1583** STANYHURST *Aeneis* II. (Arb.) 64 From the fathers sermons shal such fond patcherye flicker?

†**2. a.** To make caressing or fondling movements with the wing; hence, to act in a fondling or coaxing manner; to dally, hanker, look longingly (*after*).

a **1225** *Ancr. R.* 290 Spit him amidde þe bearde . . þet flikereð so mit þe. *c* **1386** CHAUCER *Pars. T.* ¶783 Yit wol thay kisse, and flikkere, and besien hemself. **1530** PALSGR. 552/2, I flycker, I kysse togyther, *je baise.* **1556** J. HEYWOOD *Spider & F.* lxiii. 42 Where they may win ought . . they flickar, and flatter, in fauer to grow. **1621** BURTON *Anat. Mel.* III. iii. IV. ii, It is most odious, when an old acherontic dizzard that hath one foot in his grave . . shall flicker after a young wench. **1697** DRYDEN *Virgil* Life **iij b, Lavinia . . looks a little flickering after Turnus. **1806** R. JAMIESON *Pop. Ball.* I. 296 Dorothy . . flicker'd at Willie again.

b. *slang* and *dial.* (See quots.)

a **1700** B. E. *Dict. Cant. Crew*, *To flicker*, to grin or flout. **1785–1823** GROSE *Dict. Vulg. Tongue*, *Flickering*, grinning, or laughing in a man's face. **1868** ATKINSON *Cleveland Gloss.*, 'He flicker'd and flyred lahk a girning cat.'

3. a. To make a fluttering or vibratory movement; to wave to and fro; to flutter (in the air or wind); to quiver, vibrate, undulate. Of wind: To blow in light gusts.

c **1450** *Merlin* 324 Their baners . . flekered in the wynde. *a* **1577** GASCOIGNE *Wks.* (1587) 299, I see not one . . Whose feathers flant and flicker in the winds. **1601** HOLLAND *Pliny* I. XVIII. xxxv. 613 You shall marke the leaves of trees to move, flicker & play themselves. **1633** J. FISHER *True Trojans* II. v, Troopes, With gawdie pennons flickering in the aire. **1793** EARL BUCHAN *Ess.*, *Spring* (1812) 77 The darkest indigo blue was seen . . to flicker on the surface of this molten gold. **1832** TENNYSON *Dream Fair Wom.* 113 The high masts flicker'd as they lay afloat. **1850** —— *In Mem.* cx, Nor cared the serpent at thy side To flicker with his double tongue. **1873** MISS THACKERAY *Old Kensington* xi. 89 A wet foggy wind flickered in his face.

b. *trans.* (causatively.) (Cf. FLICK *v.*²)

1843 *Blackw. Mag.* LIV. 399/2 We mount beside the red-faced, much-becoated individual who is flickering his whip in idle listlessness on the box.

†**4.** To throb, palpitate, quiver. *Obs.*

c **1470** HENRY *Wallace* II. 268 His hart . . flykeryt to and fro. **1508** DUNBAR *Test. A. Kennedy* 43, I leif my hert . . That never mair wald flow nor flickir. **1513** DOUGLAS *Æneis* III. ix. 73 The hait flesch ondir his teth flikkerand. *Ibid.* v. viii. 115 Sprewland and flikkerand in the deid thrawis.

†**5.** *fig.* Of a person: To waver, vacillate. *Obs.*

c **1325** *Metr. Hom.* 92 This bischop flekerid in his thoht. *c* **1440** *Promp. Parv.* 165/2 Flekeryn, or waveryn yn vnstabylle herte, *nuto.*

6. a. To flash up and die away alternately. Of a flame: To burn fitfully or unsteadily; also with *compl.*, *out*, etc.

Now the prevailing sense, though scarcely found earlier than the 19th c.

1605, **1791** [see FLICKERING *ppl. a.* 5]. **1820** KEATS *St. Agnes* xl, A chain-droop'd lamp was flickering by each door. **1828** SCOTT *F.M. Perth* iv, Eying the firmament, in which no slight shades of grey were beginning to flicker. **1858** FROUDE *Hist. Eng.* III. xv. 305 Sheet lightning, flickering harmlessly in the distance. **1871** B. TAYLOR *Faust* (1875) II. v. iv. 285 The fire sinks down and flickers low. **1883** S. C. HALL *Retrospect* II. 197 The wasted flame soon afterwards flickered out.

b. *transf.* and *fig.*; also with *up.*

1833 LAMB *Elia* Ser. II. *Pop. Fallacies*, We love . . to watch . . a quirk . . flickering upon the lips some seconds before [it is spoken]. **1851** D. JERROLD *St. Giles* ix. 84 A faint smile flickered at his lips. **1862** MERIVALE *Rom. Emp.* (1865) VII. lix. 244 A gleam of hope still flickered in their bosoms. **1876** J. WEISS *Wit, Hum. & Shaks.* iii. 81 Dogberry flickers up into a kind of lukewarmness. **1892** *Speaker* 3 Sept. 276/2 Precious lives which have . . flickered out in the cruel storm.

7. *trans.* **a.** To cause to flash or burn unsteadily or fitfully.

1869 *Sat. Rev.* VIII. 70/2 The Supreme Pontiff . . flickers his lightnings over the prostrate rebels. **1882** T. MOZLEY *Remin.* II. Add. 428 The thought that the huge Alps all about us had been flickered like a candle.

b. To cause to move in a fitful and unsteady manner; to indicate by a flicker.

1903 R. LANGBRIDGE *Flame & Flood* viii, He watched her eye-lashes flicker dismissal. *Ibid.* xxii, There was yet a partial inhumanity which licked its lips . . which . . burned as fiercely on the side of justice as injustice, . . flickering an equal encouragement to 'I *can't* go!' and—'I must!' **1907** *Munsey's Mag.* Dec. 308/1 [They] entered the castle . .; the torches flickering weird shadows as they walked between them. **1923** D. H. LAWRENCE *Birds, Beasts & Flowers* 113 He lifted his head from his drinking . . And flickered his two-forked tongue from his lips.

8. *intr.* = BICKER. ? *Obs.*

1776 [see FLICKERING *vbl. sb.*]. **1809** J. ADAMS *Wks.* 1854 IX. 242 We flickered, disputed, and wrangled . . but always with a species of good humour.

flickered ('flɪkəd), *ppl. a.* [f. prec. + -ED¹.] Illuminated with flickering light.

1821 JOANNA BAILLIE *Met. Leg.*, *Columbus* vii, The flicker'd east.

'flickering, *vbl. sb.* [f. as prec. + -ING¹.] The action of the vb. FLICKER in various senses.

c **1440** *Promp. Parv.* 165/2 Flekerynge of byrdys, *volitacio.* Flekerynge, or wauerynge yn an vnstable hert, *vacillacio.* **1527** *Prose Life St. Brandan* (Percy Soc.) 40 He [the Byrde] with flykerynge of his wynges made a full mery noyse. **1776** J. ADAMS *Fam. Lett.* (1876) 175 The newspapers . . will inform you of public affairs, and the particular flickerings of

parties in this colony. **1816** Byron *Ch. Har.* III. xliv, A flame unfed, which runs to waste With its own flickering. **1875** Lanier *Poems, Symphony* 156 Fern-wavings and leaf-flickerings. **1883** *Gd. Words* July 469/1 What a flickering of mellowed sunlight comes over the eyes. **1968** *Times* 18 Apr. 2/8 A boy's susceptibility to the flickering of a television set led to his death.

flickering (ˈflɪkərɪŋ), *ppl. a.* [f. as prec. + -ING^2.] That flickers, in senses of the vb.

1. Of a bird: That flutters or hovers.
1531 Latimer *Let. Baynton* in Foxe *A. & M.* (1563) 1328/1 Howe manye Larkes for a penye, yf euerye Starre in the Elemente were a flyckeringe hobye. **1664** *Floddan F.* I. 5 Flickering fame that monstrous wight With hundred wings wapping was blown. **1807** Crabbe *Par. Reg.* III. Wks. 1834 II. 209 The bat shrill shrieking woo'd his flickering mate.

†**2.** Caressing, coaxing, seducing. *Obs.*
a **1536** *Calisto & Melib.* A iij b Theyre [women's] fals intents & flykkeryng smylyng. **1551** Robinson tr. *More's Utop.* (Arb.) 110 The peruerse and malicyous flickeringe inticementes of lewde and vnhoneste desyres. **1607** R. Niccols *Cuckoo* 198 Their chambring fortitude they did descrie By their soft maiden voice and flickeringe eie. *a* **1643** W. Cartwright *Ordinary* III. i. (1651) 36, I am not any flickering thing: I cannot boast of that slight-fading gift You men call beauty.

†**3.** Changeable, unreliable, unsteady, wavering.
1430 Lydg. *Chron. Troy* II. x, The enuious ordre of fortunat meuinge, In worldly thynge false and flikerynge. **1465** Marg. Paston in *Paston Lett.* No. 502 II. 183 Pyrs Waryn..whych ys a flykeryng felowe and a besy. **1586** in *Bibliographer* (1882) I. 75 All flickering wealth which flies in firmest hope. *a* **1619** Fotherby *Atheom.* I. x. §5 (1622) 109 A weake and a flickring opinion. *a* **1763** Shenstone *Price Equipage* 25 To keep a race of flickering knaves, He grows himself the worst of slaves.

4. Quivering, vibrating unsteadily.
1580 Sidney *Arcadia* II. (1638) 221 He..hopes the flickering wind with net to hold. **1594** Plat *Jewell-ho.* I. 66 Vnlesse the Wines happen to haue a flickering Lee. **1757** Dyer *Fleece* IV. 37 Rising o'er the flick'ring wave. **1852** Mrs. Stowe *Uncle Tom's C.* xx, A keen and furtive glance of her flickering eyes. **1871** B. Taylor *Faust* (1875) I. ii. 44 The lark sends down his flickering lay. **1887** Baring-Gould *Gaverocks* x. in *Cornh. Mag.* Mar. 229, I have seen a gilder blow the flickering sheet into the air.

5. That shines with, or is illuminated by, an unsteady or wavering light.
1605 Shaks. *Lear* (1st Q° 1608) II. ii. 114 Whose influence like the wreath of radient fire In flitkering [**1623** flicking] Phœbus front. **1791** Earl Buchan *Ess., Lett. Imitation Ancients* (1812) 99 The..flickering rays of the departing light. **1865** Swinburne *Atalanta* 1894, I see..Flushed pillars down the flickering vestibule. **1870** Morris *Earthly Par.* I. II. 623 In the chamber burned The flickering candles.

Hence ˈ**flickeringly** *adv.*, in a flickering manner.
1840 *Tait's Mag.* VII. 714 One moment, flickeringly, it shone. **1878** H. S. Wilson *Alp. Ascents* i. 12 The ruddy light glistening flickeringly upon the black rock.

flickerless (ˈflɪkəlɪs), *a.* [f. FLICKER *sb.*^{3} + -LESS.] Without flickers, producing no flicker.
1922 M. J. Wrigley *Film* 117 Mr. Martin Harper..has the credit to his name of producing the 'Extralite' flickerless shutter.

†ˈ**flickermouse.** *Obs.* [Altered form of FLITTERMOUSE.] A bat.
1630 B. Jonson *New Inn* III. i, Come, I will see the flicker mouse. **1708** Motteux *Rabelais* (1737) V. 234 The Flickermise flying through the Translucidity of the corner'd Gate.

flickery (ˈflɪkərɪ), *a.* [f. FLICKER *v.* or *sb.*^{3} + -Y.] = FLICKERING *ppl. a.*
1893 in *Funk's Stand. Dict.* **1922** *Daily Mail* 21 Nov. 10 A flickery resemblance of his old self. **1950** F. Stark *Traveller's Prelude* 197 One wonders if he will live through the night, his pulse is so flickery. **1953** R. Bradbury *Fahrenheit 451* (1954) 133 Running like an ancient flickery Keystone Comedy.

†**flicket-a-flacket,** *adv. Obs.* A representation of the sound made by something flapping. Cf. CRICKET-A-WICKET.
1719 D'Urfey *Pills* II. 20 Their Sleeves went Flicket-a-flacket.

†ˈ**flicketing,** *a. Obs. rare*$^{-1}$. [Cf. prec. and FLICKERING.] = FLICKERING 3.
1674 N. Fairfax *Bulk & Selv.* 135 To think how such a flicketing skipjackly thing as that [*i.e.* motion] is..should be bound to the behaviour of such a grave stayd thing as time is.

†ˈ**flickle.** *Obs. rare*$^{-1}$. App. an arbitrary extension of *flick*, FLITCH (for rime).
1546 J. Heywood *Prov.* (1562) I ij, Littell and littell the cat eateth the flickell.

†ˈ**flicky,** *a.*^{1} *Obs. rare*$^{-1}$. [Cf. FLIG, FLIGGY, FLETCH.]
1690 *Lond. Gaz.* No. 2559/4 A dark grey Mare about 14 hands..a rough Mane, and flicky Tayl.

flicky (ˈflɪkɪ), *a.*^{2} [f. FLICK *sb.*^{1} + -Y^1.] Of or pertaining to a flick, jerky.
1897 K. S. Ranjitsinhji *Jubilee Bk. Cricket* 127 There is something distinctly jerky and flicky in this projection of the elbow and straightening of the arm.

flidder (ˈflɪdə(r)). Also **flither, flitter**. A local name for the limpet.
1766 Pennant *Zool.* (1769) III. 195 The next baits in esteem are..limpets (called here [Scarborough] Flidders). **1867** M. S. Lovell *Edible Molluscs* 120 In the Isle of Man ..they [limpets] are known by the name of 'flitters'. **1876** *Whitby Gloss.*, s.v. 'He sticks like a flither.'

flidge, fliech, obs. ff. FLEDGE, FLITCH *sb.*

flied, obs. pa. t. of FLY *v.*

flier: alternative form of FLYER.

flier(e, obs. form of FLEER.

†**flig,** *a. Obs.* [Cf. FLICKY, FLIGGY, FLETCH.]
1677 *Lond. Gaz.* No. 1192/4 An Iron gray Gelding 5 years old..flig tailed. **1683** *Ibid.* No. 1798/4 One bright bay Mare ..with a black short Tail..and a black flig Main. **1723** *Ibid.* No. 6222/6 A black Gelding..with..a flig Tail.

flig(ge, var. of FLEDGE *a. Obs.*

†ˈ**fliggy,** *a. Obs.* [f. FLIG *a.* + -Y^1.] = FLIG *a.*
1711 *Lond. Gaz.* No. 4921/4 A black Gelding..with a fliggie Tail.

fligh, obs. form of FLY *v.*

flight (flaɪt), *sb.*^{1} Forms: 1 **fliht, flyht, flyð**, 2–3 **fluht(ü)**, *south.* **vluht**, 3–4 **fliȝt, (fliht, flith)**, 3, 5 **flygt**, 4–6 **flyght(e, (6 fleight, flighte)**, 5 **flyte**, 6 *Sc.* **flicht**, 3– **flight**. [OE. *flyht* masc. = OS. *fluht* fem. (MDu., Du. *vlucht* fem.):—OTeut. **fluhti-*, f. **flug-* weak root of **fleug-an* to FLY.]

1. a. The action or manner of flying or moving through the air with or as with wings. Also in phrases, *to take* (*make, wing*, etc.) *a* or *one's flight*: to fly. *lit.* and *fig.*
a **900** *Martyrology Fragm.* 8 in *O.E. Texts* 177 þa hi bæron to heofonum mid hiora fiðra flyhte. *c* **1000** Ælfric *Deut.* xxxii. 11 Swa earn his briddas spænþ to flihte. *c* **1175** *Lamb. Hom.* 81 Mid þisse fluhte he fleh in to houene. *c* **1220** *Bestiary* 59 Siðen his fliȝt is al unstrong. *c* **1250** *Gen. & Ex.* 277 'Min fliȝt' he seide, 'ic wile up-taken'. **1340** Hampole *Pr. Consc.* 543 He says, man es born to travaile right Als a foul es to þe flight. *c* **1435** *Torr. Portugal* 547 To the chyld he [the dragon] toke a flyght. **1605** Shaks. *Macb.* III. ii. 41 Ere the bat hath flown His cloister'd flight. **1632** Lithgow *Trav.* v. 203 The flights and arrivals of which [Pigeons] I have often seene..in Aleppo. **1697** Dryden *Georg.* III. 14 New ways I must attempt..To..wing my flight to fame. **1748** *Anson's Voy.* III. ii. 416 They could scarce fly further than an hundred yards at a flight. **1857** H. Reed *Lect. Eng. Poets* viii. 270 Undying words which wing their flight over each generation as it..passes away. **1871** E. Spender *Restored* I. vi. 115 Crowds of chaffinches went flitting along with their quick dancing flight.

†**b.** Power of flying. Also in *fig.* phrase, *to fond one's flight*, i.e. to make trial of one's powers.
a **1225** *Ancr. R.* 132 þe heuinesse of hire flesche & flesches unðeawes binimeð hire hire vluht. *c* **1425** *Seven Sag.* (P.) 1487 Al that day scho fonded hyre flygt, How scho myght.. Fonden a tale al newe, The childe deth for to brewe.

c. *Falconry.* Pursuit of game, etc. by a hawk; also, the quarry flown at.
1530 Palsgr. 221/1 Flyght of a hauke, *uol.* **1548** Hall *Chron., Edw. IV*, 199 b, That king Edward should be destitute of one of his best Hawkes, when he had moste nede to make a flight. **1603** Breton *Packet Mad Lett.* (Grosart) 21/1 If your Falcons be in tune, I shal be glad to see a flight. **1798** Sotheby tr. *Wieland's Oberon* (1826) I. 17 The boy.. gives his falcon flight. **1828** Sebright *Hawking* 51 The goshawk..if much used to these easier flights, will not even attempt to fly partridges. **1855** Salvin & Brodrick *Falconry* iv. 66 The Norfolk plover seldom takes the air, and makes an easy flight.
fig. **1654** Whitlock *Zootomia* 22 This steddy praise, is the flight and aime of truly noble soules.

†**d.** The time when the young birds first fly.
1600 Surflet *Countrie Farme* I. xxii. 120 There are some farmers which sell at euery flight, two hundred, & three hundred paire vnto the vittailers.

e. Of birds or insects: A migration or issuing forth in bodies.
1823 Moor *Suffolk Words, Flight*, the second or third migration from a bee-hive. The first only is called a Swarm. **1832** Lyell *Princ. Geol.* II. 114 A similar flight [of butterflies] at the end of the last century is recorded by M. Louch.

f. The action or technique of travelling through the air or space in an aircraft or spacecraft or in a balloon; the movement through air or space of such a machine.
1784 *Universal Mag.* Sept. 358 We again took our flight [in a balloon], and ascended to near 1200 feet. **1879** *Encycl. Brit.* IX. 308/1 It is not necessary to enter upon a history of artificial flight. **1909** *Daily Chron.* 19 Mar. 4/5 Lilienthal.. shares with Pilcher..and Le Bris, the honour of being the pioneer of modern experiments in gliding flight. **1916** H. Barber *Aeroplane Speaks* 1 The Elementary Principles of Flight. **1935** C. G. Burge *Compl. Bk. Aviation* 312/2 It [*sc.* the tail plane] will be set at such an angle of attack that it carries no load in normal flight. **1951** A. C. Clarke *Exploration of Space* ii. 9 The first difficulty one encounters in trying to envisage inter-planetary flight is that of scale. **1955** *Oxf. Jun. Encycl.* IV. 35/1 The modern balloon dates from 1783, when two kinds of lighter-than-air methods of flight were introduced almost at once. **1971** P. J. McMahon *Aircraft Propulsion* xiii. 350 Reference to any textbook on principles of flight will show that the induced drag is related to the lift of a wing.

g. An instance of flight (sense f above); a (usu.) numbered regularly timed journey by air-line from place to place; a journey through the air or through space; a voyage by an aircraft, balloon, or spacecraft through the air or through space.
1785 [See FLIGHT *sb.*^{1} 2]. **1835** *Nautical Mag.* Oct. 613 It is related that the aërial ship took her first flight in a waggon. **1842** *Household Words* IV. 98/2 Exertions he had undergone in preparing for the flight. **1868** *Aeronaut. Soc. Catal.* 8 Flying machine—which being attached to the body, enables a person to take short flights. **1904** *Pall Mall Mag.* Jan. 19/2 Nor is it an easy task to calculate an airship's speed. On these flights up and down the Mediterranean coast, [etc.]. **1909** *Aero* 25 May 14/1 Mr. J. T. C. Moore-Brabazon has made several short flights with the *Bird of Passage* at Shellness. **1912** *Aeroplane* 26 Dec. 637/2 Their Yuletide present takes the form of a ticket for a passenger flight at Hendon. **1922** *Encycl. Brit.* XXX. 57/1 The longest flight by an N.S. airship was 101 hours. **1928** *Times* 22 Mar., [The King of Afghanistan's] first flight in any civil aircraft, and his only flight since he visited Europe. **1940** Crump & Maul *Our Airliners* ii. 28 Transcontinental and Western Air announces that 'Flight 10..will arrive in three minutes at Gate Number 11'. **1951** N. Balchin *Way through Wood* viii. 108 We..happened just to catch a flight, and were at Heathrow by seven. **1962** F. I. Ordway et al. *Basic Astronautics* xiii. 547 During the 32-hr flight Dr. Simons wore a full-pressure suit and remained seated in the tiny gondola. *Ibid.* 550 Manned balloon flights. **1968** *Times* 10 Dec. 6/7 The Surveyor flights which soft-landed on the moon. **1969** *Listener* 20 Feb. 232/2 The pictures you brought back from the Moon were not as good as those taken on an unmanned flight——the American Lunar Orbiter flight.

h. A Royal Air Force unit consisting of about five or six machines; the members of such a unit.
1914 H. Rosher *In R.N.A.S.* (1916) 25 We shall not get our squadron together until the end of January... We may, however, go over in pieces, a flight at a time. **1915** *War Illustr.* 27 Nov. 345 This branch of the Army is organized in what are called wings, divided into squadrons, and subdivided into flights. **1917** *Blackw. Mag.* July 121/1 Twelve officers flew to France with the flight to which I belonged. **1932** W. S. Churchill *Thoughts & Advent.* 181 The art of flying was in its childhood [1911–15]... Even the nomenclature had to be invented, and I may claim myself to have added the words 'seaplane' and 'flight' (of aeroplanes) to the dictionary. *a* **1935** T. E. Lawrence *Mint* (1950) II. i. 101 The flight staggers off parade to drop bonelessly into bed. **1959** *Chambers's Encycl.* I. 189/1 The main formations of the R.A.F. are the flight, the squadron, the wing and the group. There are three flights to a squadron.

2. a. Swift movement in general; *esp.* of a projectile, etc. through the air. Of the heavenly bodies: Swift and regular course. Phr. *to take a* or *one's flight.*
c **1250** *Gen. & Ex.* 137 Ðe seuene he bad on fliȝte faren, And toknes ben. **1545** Ascham *Toxoph.* II. (Arb.) 152 A perfyte archer must firste learne to know the sure flyghte of his shaftes. **1662** Dryden *Astræa Redux* 270 Winds, that tempests brew, When through Arabian groves they take their flight..lose their spite. **1684** R. H. *School Recreat.* 85 The Racket strikes..And so the Ball takes Flight. **1715–20** Pope *Iliad* XV. 320 Skill'd to direct the Javelin's distant Flight. **1785** Burns *To W. Simpson* xxix, Some 'auld-light' herds..Are mind't, in things they ca' balloons To tak a flight. **1801** T. Roberts *Eng. Bowman* x. 237 By comparing the flight of..sharp and blunt-piled arrows. **1818** Shelley *Hymn Castor* 8 Ships, whose flight is swift along the wave. **1846** Greener *Sc. Gunnery* 328 If a high velocity be given to them to ensure a horizontal flight, the quantity of powder exploded must be in proportion. **1886** Ruskin *Præterita* I. 325 Watching the flight of the clouds.

†**b.** (*arrows*) *of the same flight*: having the same power of flight; of equal size and weight.
1545 Ascham *Toxoph.* II. (Arb.) 131 You must haue diuerse shaftes of one flight, fethered with diuerse winges, for diuerse windes. **1596** Shaks. *Merch. V.* I. i. 141 When I had lost one shaft I shot his fellow of the selfesame flight.. To finde the other forth.

c. Swift passage (of time).
1647 H. Vaughan *Son-Dayes* i, The rich, And full redemption of the whole weeks flight! **1667** Milton *P.L.* II. 221 Besides what hope the never-ending flight Of future days may bring. **1742** Young *Nt. Th.* i. 147 The flight of threescore years. **1820** Shelley *Good Night* 6 How can I call the lone night good, Though thy sweet wishes wing its flight?

3. *fig.* **a.** A mounting or soaring out of the regular course or beyond ordinary bounds; an excursion or sally (of the imagination, wit, intellect, ambition, etc.).
1668 Denham *On Cowley* 47 Old Pindar's flights by him are reacht. *a* **1674** Clarendon *Hist. Reb.* XIV. (1704) III. 414 Any other Man than himself, who was accustom'd to extraordinary flights in the Air. **1692** Wagstaffe *Vind. Carol.* ii. 34 That happy Flight of Sir Richard Fanshawe. **1732** Law *Serious C.* v. (ed. 2) 77 These are not speculative flights. **1760** C. Johnston *Chrysal* (1822) III. 10 A silence more expressive of his soul than all the flights of eloquence. **1781** Cowper *Ep. Lady Austen* 16 The world, who knows No flights above the pitch of prose. **1850** Hannay *Singleton Fontenoy* I. viii, Temple..had some thoughts of trying opium, which he believed a higher flight, but Singleton dissuaded him. **1868** Max Müller *Chips* (1880) III. v. 107 Drinking songs..do not belong to the highest flights of poetry.

†**b.** A fit or burst of unreasonable humour, caprice, or the like; also, flightiness, caprice.
1712–14 Pope *Rape of Lock* v. 32 Good humour can prevail, When airs, and flights, and screams, and scolding fail. **1754** Richardson *Grandison* I. vii. 33 But is not this wish of yours..a very singular one? A flight! a mere flight! *Ibid.* (1781) VII. l. 254, I am, at times, said she, too sensible of running into flight and absurdity.

†**4.** A state of flutter or agitation; a trembling, fright. Cf. FLAUGHT *sb.*^{2} 1, FLOCHT, and FLIGHT *v. a flight, in flight*: in a state of perturbation.

(The examples of *a flight*, placed under AFFLICT *ppl. a.*, possibly belong here.) *Obs.*

1513 MORE *Rich. III*, Wks. (1557) 42/2 Ye quene in gret flight & heuines, bewailing her childes rain. **1529** —— *Comf. agst. Trib.* I. Introd. Wks. (1557) 1141/2, I waxed..sodeinly sumwhat a flyghte. **1535** COVERDALE *1 Sam.* xiv. 15 There came a fearfulnes and flight in the hoost vpon the felde.

5. †**a.** A wing (*obs.*). **b.** In later use *collect.* the flight feathers, or those used in flying.

c **1205** LAY. 2885 Þe wind him com on wiðere weoðeleden his fluhtes. **1735** J. MOORE *Columbarium* 39 If the three Colours run thro' the Feathers of the Flight and Tail. **1765** *Treat. Dom. Pigeons* 74 The bald-pated tumblers..with a clean white head..white flight and white tail.

6. a. The distance which a bird can or does fly. †*capon's flight* (see quot.).

1600 SURFLET *Countrie Farme* I. xxii. 121 Let it [the douehouse] be distant a flight or two from any water. **1667** MILTON *P.L.* VII. 4 Above the flight of Pegasean wing. **1730–6** in BAILEY (folio) s.v. *Capon's flight*, a compass of ground, such as a capon might fly over, due to the eldest of several brothers in dividing the father's effects, when there is no principal manour in a lordship. *c* **1820** S. ROGERS *Italy, Meillerie* 28 Within an eagle's flight.

fig. **1667** MILTON *P.L.* VIII. 199 From this high pitch let us descend A lower flight. **1856** LD. COCKBURN *Mem.* ii. (1874) 116 His constitutional animation never failed to carry him a flight beyond ordinary mortals.

b. The distance to which a missile may be shot. Cf. Fr. *volée*.

1608 *Yorksh. Trag.* I. viii, Within a flight o' the town. **1801** SOUTHEY *Thalaba* IV. xv, Because the Hern soars upward in the sky Above the arrow's flight.

c. *flight of a shot* (see quot.).

1867 SMYTH *Sailor's Word-bk.*, *Flight of a shot*, the trajectory formed between the muzzle of the gun and the first graze.

d. *Cricket.* The trajectory and pace of the ball in its flight before pitching; also, the art of controlling these. (Cf. FLIGHT *v.* 7.)

[**1897** K. S. RANJITSINHJI *Jubilee Bk. Cricket* iii. 64 The bowler must learn to manipulate and deliver the ball in such a way that, after pitching, it deviates from its original line of flight.] **1903** JEPHSON in H. G. Hutchinson *Cricket* 88 He.. possesses a wonderful command of length,..a considerable variation of flight. **1911** P. F. WARNER *Bk. Cricket* 74 Every slow left-hander should cultivate 'flight'. **1924** N. CARDUS *Days in Sun* 48 Even the changeful flight of a Lohmann could not hold back our Haywards and our Frys from mastery. **1963** A. ROSS *Australia 63* v. 113 His..control of flight..had rescued a match that seemed to be drifting far out of England's reach.

7. a. The series of stairs between any two landings; hence a series of steps, terraces, etc., ascending without change of direction. [So F. *volée*.]

1703 T. N. *City & C. Purchaser* 249 From this second Half-pace the Stairs fly directly back again, parallel to the first flight. **1780** MAD. D'ARBLAY *Diary* 4 June I. 366 Miss Burney, better go up another flight (pointing upstairs)..for there's no room anywhere else. **1820** W. IRVING *Sketch-bk.* I. 171 A great flight of steps leads to the interior. **1855** MACAULAY *Hist. Eng.* IV. 243 On the slope..were constructed flights of terraces. **1859** W. COLLINS *Q. of Hearts* (1875) 21 She was away up the second flight before he could say any more.

b. A series of locks on a canal, rising like steps one above the other.

1861 SMILES *Engineers* II. 146 The canal..descending from the hill-tops by a flight of locks.

c. A set of rails or hurdles. [Possibly a distinct word, repr. OE. *fleohta*, = Ger. *flechte* hurdle.]

1852 R. S. SURTEES *Sponge's Sp. Tour* lxviii, Eyeing Mr. Sponge clearing a stiff flight of rails. **1865** *Pall Mall G.* 9 Feb. 3 Some..would as lief have led a forlorn-hope as put a horse at a flight of hurdles. **1894** *Daily News* 14 Dec. 8/1 Rylstone started in strong demand for the Handicap Hurdle, but he died away at the last flight.

8. A collection or flock of beings or things flying in or passing through the air together: **a.** of birds or insects. Also the special term for a company of doves, swallows, and various other birds.

c **1250** *Gen. & Ex.* 3012 Moyses bad meðe here on, And ðis fleȝes fliȝt vt is don. *c* **1430** LYDG. *Hors, Shepe & G.* (1822) 31 A flight of goshawkes A flight of douves A flight of cormerants. **1486** *Bk. St. Albans* F vj b, A Flight of swalowes. **1556** J. HEYWOOD *Spider & F.* lii. 2 Herewith.. Cam such a flight of flies in scattred ray, As shadowed the sonne. **1588** SHAKS. *Tit. A.* v. iii. 68 You sad fac'd men.. By vprores seuer'd like a flight of Fowle. **1605** SYLVESTER *Du Bartas* II. iii. I. *Vocation* 871 Like to a Cast of Falcons that pursue A flight of Pigeons. **1710** ADDISON *Tatler* No. 161 ¶8 Storks, that came thither in great Flights. **1875** 'STONEHENGE' *Brit. Sports* I. ix. 118 A 'flight' or 'rush' of dunbirds.

transf. **1850** L. HUNT *Autobiog.* II. xvii. 296 The rest of the heaven covered with large flights of..white clouds.

b. A company of angels.

1602 SHAKS. *Ham.* v. ii. 371 Goodnight..And flights of Angels sing thee to thy rest. **1671** MILTON *P.R.* II. 385, I can ..call swift flights of Angels. **1860** HAWTHORNE *Marb. Faun* (1879) II. xiii. 129 Around their lofty cornices hover flights of sculptured angels.

c. A volley of missiles, *esp.* arrows.

1535 STEWART *Cron. Scot.* II. 605 Fra bowmen bald and wicht, Of fedderit flanis flew ane felloun flicht Amang the Danis. **1591** GARRARD *Art Warre* 2 A whole flight of arrowes. **1640** T. HABINGTON *Edw. IV*, 17 In this trouble the Southerne men shot another flight. **1726** SWIFT *Gulliver* I. i, They shot another flight into the air, as we do bombs. **1864** TENNYSON *Aylmer's F.* 94 A flight of fairy arrows. **1869** BOUTELL *Arms & Arm.* viii. 131 The English archers ..poured upon them their deadly arrows in flights thick as hail.

d. colloq. *in the first flight*: in the van, taking a leading place.

1852 SMEDLEY *L. Arundel* xxxix, Fellows..that you're safe to find in the first flight. **1893** SIR G. CHESNEY *Lesters* III. II. xxi. 15 While his sisters..had all been in the first flight, he had come up with the ruck.

9. The young birds that take wing at one time, e.g. the *March flight* or the *May flight* of pigeons.

1577 B. GOOGE *Heresbach's Husb.* I. (1586) 10 b, For my Dovehouse.—The great flyghtes of this house must neede fyll the maisters purse, and serve the Kitchen well. **1600** SURFLET *Countrie Farme* I. xxii. 125 At this time, they [pigeons] affoord you a flight..called the March flight. **1829** SOUTHEY *Corresp. with C. Bowles* (1881) 177 The flight of summer birds are off, also, or on the wing.

transf. **1751** JOHNSON *Rambler* No. 175 ¶6 Every season brings a new flight of beauties into the world.

10. a. A flight-arrow (see 15).

1464 *Mann. & Househ. Exp.* 248 Item, in fflytys ffor my mastyr the sayd day, viij.d. **1540** *Act 33 Hen. VIII*, c. 9 With any prick shafte or fleight. **1599** B. JONSON *Cynthia's Rev.* v. x, Here be [arrowes] of all sorts, flights, rouers, and butt-shafts. *a* **1616** BEAUM. & FL. *Bonduca* I. i, Not a flight drawn home..ere made that haste that they have. **1801** T. ROBERTS *Eng. Bowman* vi. 151 For very small and light flights, deal seems to be the most eligible [wood].

b. = FLIGHT-SHOOTING.

1557 in *Vicary's Anat.* (1888) App. iii. 178 For the best game of the flight, he shall haue a flight of golde of the value of x *s.* **1599** SHAKS. *Much Ado* I. i. 40 He set vp his bils here in Messina, and challeng'd Cupid at the Flight.

c. The tail of a dart.

1938 A. & G. D'EGVILLE *Darts* 61 The flights, or tails, may be of paper, linen, tin, cardboard or feathers. **1950** *Oxf. Jun. Encycl.* IX. 176 There are many variations in the darts themselves, from heavy brass darts with paper or plastic flights, to light, sometimes unweighted, wooden darts with feather flights. **1968** N. E. WILLIAMSON *Darts* i. 15 Several friends of mine, all good dart players, will swear by the canes and paper flights, but used with brass barrels. *Ibid.* iii. 26 It is also advisable to make sure that you have a suitable box or container in which to place your darts when not in use in order to preserve the flights.

11. The husk or glume of oats, oat-chaff. Also, the outer covering of the coffee-berry.

1831 LOUDON *Encycl. Agric.* Gloss. (ed. 2) 1243 Oat flights are the glumes of the oat. **1855** *Morton's Cycl. Agric.* II. 722 *Flights*, oat chaff.

12. *Naut.* **a.** = FLY-BOAT, a Dutch flat-bottomed boat. [? A distinct word = *floyt*, FLUTE *sb.*[2]] **b.** (see quot. 1850).

1769 FALCONER *Dict. Marine* (1776), *Fly-boat* or *Flight*. *c* **1850** *Rudim. Navig.* (Weale) 118 *Flight*, a sudden rising, or a greater curve than sheer, as the cheeks, cat-heads, &c. *Flight of the transoms*, as the ends or arms of the transoms.. become more narrow as they approach the keel, the general figure or curve which they thus describe..is called the Flight of the Transoms. **1867** SMYTH *Sailor's Word-bk.*, *Flight*, a Dutch vessel or passage-boat on canals. **1879** *Cassell's Techn. Educ.* IV. 190/1 Special care is needed in fixing the lower cant-timbers at their proper heights and 'flights' or deviations from the transverse lines.

13. In various technical uses.

a. *Lead-smelting.* A light, volatile substance, given off during the melting of lead-ore.

1668 GLANVILL in *Phil. Trans.* II. 771 There is a flight in the smoak, which falling upon the Grass, poysons those Cattel that eat of it. **1710** J. HARRIS *Lex. Techn.* II. s.v., In melting the Lead-Oar in the Works at Mendip, there is a Substance flies away in the Smoak which they call the Flight. **1823** in CRABB *Techn. Dict.*

b. *Angling.* The set of fish-hooks in a spinning-trace.

1865 H. C. PENNELL *Bk. Pike* x. 136 The bait..[being] placed on the flight, and..hanging about 2 yards from the top of the rod. **1867** in F. FRANCIS *Angling* iv. (1880) 106.

c. *Campanology.* The lower part or tail of the clapper of a bell.

1872 ELLACOMBE *Ch. Bells Devon* ii. 25 Bells are sometimes chimed by..hitching the rope round the flight or tail of the clapper. **1874** BECKETT *Clocks, Watches & Bells* (ed. 6) 345 The tail F, called the flight, is almost always requisite to make the clapper fly properly.

d. *Machinery.* (see quots.)

1813 *Niles' Weekly Register* V. Add. A. 6/2 It was extended with flights to draw the meal towards the Hopper. **1874** KNIGHT *Dict. Mech.* I. 882 *Flight*, the slope or inclination of the arm of a crane. *Ibid.*, *Flight*, a spiral wing or vane on a shaft, acting as a propeller or conveyor.

14. a. *attrib.* and *Comb.* as *flight bag*, *flight-pond*, *-season*, *shed*, *-time*, *way*; *flight-performing* ppl. adj.

1943 REDDING & LEYSHON *Skyways to Berlin* 95 A *flight bag and a musette lay beside the foot locker. **1965** *Family Circle* Oct. 31/2 Get a handy, colorful flight bag. **1784** COWPER *Task* VI. 427 Noblest of the train That wait on man, the *flight-performing horse. **1801** DANIEL *Rural Sports* II. 475 A decoy for Dun Birds is called a *flight pond. **1886** *Daily News* 12 Oct. 3/1 We are just now in the *flight season. **1934** 'E. CAMBRIDGE' *Sycamore Tree* IV. vi. 260 Howell was gazetted..to an aerodrome..where the *flight sheds looked no longer than hen houses on the wide green plain. **1881** *Blackw. Mag.* Dec. 749 All repairs..must be carried on after *flight-time. **1959** F. D. ADAMS *Aeronaut. Dict.* 76 *Flight time*, time spent in flight or in flying operations, measured, when exactness is required, between specified instances, as between the commencement of the take-off run and the end of the landing run. **1971** *Guardian* 3 June 5/8 The flight time of 65 minutes allowed some..of the economy-class passengers to climb..to the first class lounge. **1933** *Jrnl. R. Aeronaut. Soc.* XXXVII. 3 It will become necessary clearly to mark *flightways to be used even on an 'all way' field. **1963** *Times* 28 Feb. 13/5 The Battle of Britain fighter station at Hornchurch, Essex, was sold yesterday for £517,000 by public auction... The last lot, comprising 38 acres of open grassland and flight-ways, was sold to a gravel company for £61,000.

b. In titles of officers of various ranks in the Royal Air Force. Also *ellipt.* = *flight sergeant*.

1914 *Times* 19 Nov. 3/4 Royal Naval Air Service. Flight Lieuts...reappointed as Acting Flight Commanders. **1916** H. BARBER *Aeroplane Speaks* 27 The Flight-Sergeant is awaiting the Pilot's orders. **1917** *Blackw. Mag.* Mar. 380/2 'Good-night, you chaps,' said one of the flight-commanders. *Ibid.* May 800/1 The good work of my pilot had brought him a flight commandership. **1922** *Man. Seamanship* (*H.M.S.O.*) I. 11 Distinction lace worn by officers of the Royal Air Force... R.A.F. Flight Lieutenant. R.N. Lieutenant. **1928** C. F. S. GAMBLE *N. Sea Air Station* iv. 75 Flight Commander (relative rank of Lieutenant, R.N.). Flight Lieutenant (relative rank of Lieutenant, R.N.). Flight Sub-Lieutenant (relative rank of Sub-Lieutenant, R.N.). **1943** C. H. WARD-JACKSON *Piece of Cake* 30 *Flight*, flight sergeant. **1959** *Chambers's Encycl.* XI. 519 Army and Royal Marines, Captain. Royal Air Force, Flight Lieutenant (Flight Officer, W.R.A.F.). *Ibid.*, Army and Royal Marines, Colour Sergeant. Royal Air Force, Flight-Sergeant. **1960** T. RATTIGAN *Ross* I. ii, We'd nearly finished fatigue, Flight.

15. Special comb., as **flight-arrow**, a light and well-feathered arrow for long-distance shooting; **flight attendant**, a person employed to serve passengers on an aircraft; an airline steward or stewardess; **flight call**, (*a*) the call made by a bird during flight; (*b*) an announcement at an airport to passengers for a particular flight, informing them that they may board the aircraft; **flight control** (see quot. 1959); **flight crew** (see quot. 1965); **flight deck**, (*a*) of an aircraft-carrier: the deck on which aircraft take off and land; (*b*) of an aeroplane: the part accommodating the pilot, navigator, etc.; **flight engineer** (see quot. 1965); **flight envelope** *Aeronaut.*, the set of limiting combinations of speed and altitude, or speed and range, etc., possible for a particular kind of aircraft or aero-engine; **flight-feather**, one of the wing-feathers on which a bird depends for its power of flight; †**flight-head**, 'a wild-headed person' (Nares); **flight-line**, (*a*) the direction of flight by birds, esp. during migration; (*b*) *Aeronaut.* (see quot. 1956); **flight-muscle**, one of the muscles by which the wings are worked in flight; **flight net**, a net used for the capture of birds; so *flight-netter*, *-netting*; **flight note** = *flight call* (a); **flight-number**, the identifying number of a flight (cf. 1 g above); **flight path** (see quot. 1919); the planned course of an aircraft or space vehicle from point to point; also *transf.*; **flight plan** *Aeronaut.*, the prearranged scheme for a particular flight; so **flight-plan** *v. intr.*, **flight-planning** *vbl. sb.*; **flight recorder**, a device in an aircraft which records the relevant technical details of each flight, in order to assist investigation in the event of an accident; hence *flight recording* vbl. sb.; **flight refuelling**, refuelling of an aircraft whilst in flight; so **flight-refuel** *v. trans.*; †**flight-ripe** *a.*, fit to fly; **flight-shaft** = *flight-arrow*; **flight simulator**, an apparatus designed to simulate the actual conditions of flight, used esp. by airline pilots in training; **flight-test** *v. trans.*, to test an aircraft, missile, etc., during flight; so **flight-testing** *vbl. sb.* Also FLIGHT-SHOOTING, SHOT.

1801 T. ROBERTS *Eng. Bowman* vi. 153 Roving arrows are much heavier, and *flight arrows much lighter, than others. **1881** GREENER *Gun* 6 The longest well-authenticated distance for shooting with flight-arrows is about 600 yards. **1947** W. L. GROSSMAN *Air Passenger Traffic* xii. 176 By picking up..the flight coupons, with the passengers' names on them, after the passengers are seated, a *flight attendant knows where, say, Mrs. Johnson is located and can address her by name. **1957** *Occupational Outlook Handbk.* (U.S. Dept. Labor) 561/1 Stewardesses or stewards (sometimes called flight attendants) are aboard almost all passenger planes operated by the commercial airlines. **1976** *Globe & Mail* (Toronto) 16 Feb. 9/1 Air Canada flight attendant Mary Dohey today will become the third and only living recipient of Canada's highest award for bravery, the Cross of Valor. **1982** *Sci. Amer.* Nov. 19/3 It is nice to see 'stewardess' and 'steward' gradually being replaced by the general term 'flight attendant'. **1937** *Brit. Birds* XXXI. 98 When disturbed, they flew up without travelling far, producing a whinnying and metallic *flight-call. **1959** BANNERMAN *Birds Brit. Isles* VIII. 63 Birds flying about the island..calling with a soft squeaky note..not unlike the flight call of the stormy petrel. **1969** 'J. MUNRO' *Innocent Bystanders* vi. 86 They were in the departure lounge, waiting for their flight call. **1937** *Discovery* Oct. 277/2 Since the reaction thrust, acting from the extreme rear of the plane, is in no way different from the pull of the aero engine in its nose, and remains in fixed relation to the aeroplane axis, stability and *flight-control are not interfered with. **1959** F. D. ADAMS *Aeronaut. Dict.* 75/1 *Flight control*, 1. *In plural.* Controls for guiding or trimming an aircraft, missile, [etc.]. 2. A general if somewhat loose term applied to any activity or organization that directs and controls the movement of aircraft. **1969** *Sunday Times* 13 July 13/2 *Flight Control System*, a system that serves to maintain stability and control during the flight. **1951** *Philippine Air Lines Timetable* 15 May 2 P.A.L.'s experienced *flight crews, with skilled American pilots and trained cabin attendants, are your assurance of a perfect trip. **1958** 'N. SHUTE' *Rainbow & Rose* i. 14 The flight crew were getting

ready to take off the freighter. **1965** *Gloss. Aeronaut. Terms (B.S.I.)* §16 *Flight crew* (operating crew), those members of the aircrew whose primary concern is the operation and navigation of the aircraft and its safety in flight. **1924** *Sci. Amer.* Oct. 248/2 On the *flight deck there are various devices for checking the speed of landing airplanes. **1936** *Meccano Mag.* June 325 The members of the flight deck party are rushing out to seize the machine as she comes to a standstill. **1949** *Aeronautics* Nov. 44/1 As one might expect, the Brabazon's flight deck is spacious and well laid out. **1958** *Oxf. Mail* 19 July 1/2 Rebel snipers fired on one of the planes..and hit it twice. One shot went through the flight deck. **1964** D. MACINTYRE *Battle for Mediterranean* iii. 47 But for her armoured flight deck which absorbed the shock of some of the hits, the *Illustrious* must have been sunk. **1971** *Guardian* 29 June 6/4 Airlines have been warned to review flight deck procedure after an air miss..between a BOAC VC10 and an El Al Boeing. **1938** *Flight* 21 July 67/2 Opposite the captain's desk are the *flight engineer's quarters. **1939** *Meccano Mag.* Oct. 570/3 The radio operator occupies a position behind them, and a little farther aft is the flight engineer, both on the port side of the cabin. **1958** 'N. SHUTE' *Rainbow & Rose* vi. 226, I was talking to Dick Scott, my new flight engineer. **1965** *Gloss. Aeronaut. Terms (B.S.I.)* §16 *Flight engineer*, a member of the flight crew responsible for engineering duties. **1944** *Jrnl. R. Aeronaut. Soc.* XLVIII. 488 The best known of the envelope cases is the '*flight envelope', which is in general use in this country and in the United States... The 'flight envelope' covers all probable conditions of symmetrical manœuvring flight instead of the few isolated points specified in the previous system. **1966** *McGraw-Hill Encycl. Sci. & Technol.* I. 177 (*caption*) Airplane flight envelope, speed and range, medium altitude. **1966** D. STINTON *Anat. of Aeroplane* ii. 10 The operational environment of an aircraft lies within a boundary, drawn on a basis of speed and height, called the flight-envelope... The outline marks the limit of performance in one particular configuration. **1735** J. MOORE *Columbarium* 35 The nine *flight Feathers of the Wing. **1890** COUES *Field Ornith.* II. iii. 164 The Remiges, or Flight-Feathers, give the wing its general character. **1605** in *Court & Times Jas. I* (1848) I. 38 Some Popish *flight-heads thinking to do wonders. **1933** *Brit. Birds* XXVI. 366 The migratory *flight-line of the others appears to lie well off the shores of west Wales. **1956** W. A. HEFLIN *U.S.A.F. Dict.* 210/2 *Flight line*, on an airfield, a general area including the hangars and the ramps and other grounds between and surrounding the hangars where aircraft are parked, serviced, etc. **1958** BANNERMAN *Birds Brit. Isles* VII. 147 The majority of the large flocks..travel by two main flight-lines. **1971** *Country Life* 25 Feb. 407/2 In America, the native geese regularly move on well-plotted flight lines. **1890** W. P. BALL *Effects Use & Disuse* 64 The shortening of the sternum in pigeons is attributed to disuse of the *flight muscles attached to it. **1889** *Leisure Hour* 675/2 The birds caught in the *flight nets are sold to a dealer. **1960** E. ENNION *House on Shore* vi. 78 The flight-net has been reintroduced recently..to 'control' oystercatchers in Morecambe Bay. **1897** *Pearson's Mag.* 216/2 The birds when captured are packed into large bags, and are carried in this way to the *flight-netter's home. **1897** *Pearson's Mag.* Feb. 213 (*heading*) *Flight-netting for wildfowl. **1937** *Discovery* Feb. 47/2 He [*sc.* an owl] has..a loud *flight-note..like the quacking of a duck. **1961** BANNERMAN *Birds Brit. Isles* IX. 77 J. T. Nichols, who considers this the 'flight note' of the transient bird. **1949** *Internat. Air Transport Assoc. Bull.* Dec. 136 **Flight number*, which is equivalent to the term line number, means the numerical designation of a flight. **1953** C. DAY LEWIS *Italian Visit* i. 21 We have Ten minutes until our flight-number is called. **1955** E. BOWEN *World of Love* xi. 204, *I* don't even know where he's coming from... Harris will have the flight-number. **1911** *Chambers's Jrnl.* I. 55/2 Instruments which will exhibit the angle of the *flight-path. **1919** W. B. FARADAY *Gloss. Aeronaut. Terms* 52 *Flight path*, the path of the centre of gravity of an aircraft with reference to the air. **1967** *Sunday Mail Mag.* (Brisbane) 1 Oct. 5/1 The peregrine flew towards it... Every bird in her flightpath froze to the ground. **1969** *Times* 19 Feb. 13/6 Another experiment..will measure the mass and distance of Mars simply by tracking the spacecraft and measuring the effect the planet exerts on its flight path. *Ibid.* 10 Mar. 10/1 Fortunately none of the flight paths used by the birds crosses the airport. **1936** M. B. GARBER *Mod. Mil. Dict.* 135 **Flight plan*, a plan for an aerial flight, setting forth the probable time of departure, direction of flight.., with estimated time of arrival. **1940** *Meccano Mag.* July 322/3 These flight plans cannot be standardised like a railway timetable, because of the great effect changes in weather have on the aircraft. **1945** *Aeroplane* 30 Nov. 638/2 Aircraft ex-Baltimore could always 'flight-plan' for Stephenville. **1971** *Guardian* 3 July 1/7 The pilot filed a flight plan for Trinidad with the airport tower. **1959** *Listener* 26 Feb. 372/1 Good *flight planning—to use a term already long in use in terrestrial air navigation—is going to be of the highest value [in space navigation]. **1971** *Flying* Apr. S5/1 Not enough pilots seem ready to lay out hard cash for weather and flight-planning information. **1948** *Shell Aviation News* cxv. 5/1 The Civil Aeronautics Board is now requiring all U.S. certified airlines to install *flight recorders on their aircraft by 30th June, 1948. **1964** Flight recorder [see *black box* (BLACK *a.* 19)]. **1971** *Times* 4 Oct. 1/3 Vital clues to the cause of the crash..were gained yesterday when the flight recorder was decoded. **1962** *Flight Internat.* LXXXI. 945/1 The relatively new art of *flight recording. **1963** *Economist* 23 Nov. 733/1 TSR 2 can be *flight-refuelled. **1939** *Air Ann. Brit. Emp.* 50 *Flight refuelling..is likely to become a prominent means of allowing flight at very high wing loadings. **1947** *Shell Aviation News* CXIII. 14/1 It is fairly generally known that a series of flight-refuelling trials has recently taken place, in conjunction with British South American Airways. **1398** TREVISA *Barth. De P.R.* XII. i. (Tollem. MS.), Whan hire [the eagle's] briddes beth *flyȝte-ripe sche puttep hem oute of hire neste. **1597** DANIEL *Civ. Wars* VIII. xv, Brave Falconbridge..assigned The archers their *flight-shafts, to shoot away. **1840** HANSARD *Archery* xi. 407 Barely within the range of his lightest flight-shaft. **1947** *Electronics* June 154/1 Installation of Teheran receiver in cockpit of *flight simulator brings this air navigation aid to the second of three..steps in its development. **1950** *Jrnl. R. Aeronaut. Soc.* LIV. 600/1 One recent development which should help both to raise the standard of training and reduce the time and cost of non-revenue flying involved in crew training is the 'flight simulator'. This ground equipment is designed to reproduce exactly the control cabin of the selected aircraft type, with all instruments and controls. **1961** *Engineering* 12 May 677/1 Control of an aircraft in bad flying conditions can now be tested on the ground by a machine..known as a 'rocking cockpit' or..flight simulator. **1931** C. SPRIGG *Airship* xiv. 210 Before the rigid airship can be used on a commercial service it must be thoroughly *flight-tested under every variety of conditions. **1958** *Observer* 9 Nov. 1/8 This is a new solid fuel rocket that had been flight-tested only once before. **1969** *Times* 3 June (Suppl.) p. iii/5 He [*sc.* Neil Armstrong] became a Nasa research pilot in 1955 and flight-tested the X-15 rocket plane. **1943** *Sci. News Let.* 30 Jan. 73/3 (*heading*) *Flight testing advances win award for MacClain. **1961** *Shell Aviation News* Dec. 2/2 With the coming of auto-observers and telemetry, 'test flying' has been gradually and unobtrusively ousted by 'flight testing'.

flight (flaɪt), *sb.*[2] Forms: 3 fluht, fliht, *Orm.* flihht, vliht, 4 fliȝt, (fluiȝt, flyight, flyȝt), 4–6 flyght, *Sc.* flicht, flycht, (6 flyette), 4– flight. [OE. **flyht* = OS. *fluht* (Du. *vlucht*), OHG. *fluht* (MHG. *vlucht*, mod.Ger. *flucht*) str. fem.:—OTeut. **pluhti-z* f. weak grade of root **pleuh-* to FLEE. A parallel form, differing in declension, is ON. *flótte*, the OTeut. type of which would be **plohton-*; the Sw. *flykt*, Da. *flygt* are adopted from Ger.]

1. a. The action of fleeing or running away from, or as from, danger, etc.; hasty departure or retreat, also, an absconding.

c **1200** ORMIN 19683 Forr þatt he wollde þurrh hiss flihht Uss mikell þing bitacnenn. *c* **1275** LAY. 21405 Ne mihte he fliht makie in neuere one side. *a* **1375** *Joseph Arim.* 506 þat luyte miȝte faren him fro and to fluiȝt founden. *c* **1425** WYNTOUN *Cron.* VIII. xlii. 143 In fycht is mensk, and schame in flycht. **1526** TINDALE *Matt.* xxiv. 20 Praye that youre flyght be not in the winther. **1591** SHAKS. *Two Gent.* IV. iv. 173 'Twas Ariadne, passioning For Thesus periury, and vniust flight. **1760–72** tr. *Juan & Ulloa's Voy.* (ed. 3) II. 344 It was..after eleven when the Delivrance thus began to seek her safety in flight. **1769** BLACKSTONE *Comm.* IV. 380 For the very flight is an offence, carrying with it a strong presumption of guilt. **1855** 'STONEHENGE' *Rur. Sports* I. I. x. (1856) 83 The direction of the Deer's flight is almost always up-wind. **1882** J. H. BLUNT *Ref. Ch. Eng.* II. 367 Many benefices had become vacant through the flight of the Marian clergy.

†**b.** Abhorrence or avoidance *of*; shrinking *from*.

1398 TREVISA *Barth. De P.R.* III. vi. (1495) 53 In the Irascibil is flyghte of contrarye and of euyll. **1626** BACON *Sylva* §766 The emission..of the Breath by a flight from Titillation. **1651** tr. *Bacon's Life & Death* 57 They contract themselves partly by their flight of Vacuum. **1665** HOOKE *Microgr.* 16 The antipathy or flight of others from each other.

c. A means of fleeing, way of escape. *rare*$^{-1}$.

1819 SHELLEY *Cyclops* 438 How secure a flight [I have] From your hard servitude.

d. *curve of flight*: a correlative term to *curve of pursuit*: see CURVE *sb.* 1.

1867 THOMSON & TAIT *Nat. Phil.* I. I. §40 The remainder of the curve satisfies a modified form of statement of the original question, and is called the Curve of Flight.

†**e.** *sure flight* (jocularly): ? one who is able to run away safely. *Obs.*

1599 NASHE *Lenten Stuffe* 11 Such..as were sure flights, (sauing a reuerence of their manhoods) ran crying and complayning to King Henry the Second.

f. *Economics.* The selling of a particular currency by foreign holders, e.g. in anticipation of a fall in its value; the withdrawal of investments from a particular country.

1923 *Ann. Reg. 1922* II. 88 The instability of money caused a continuous flight from the mark in Germany, the normal consequence of inflation. **1930** *Economist* 27 Sept. 554/1 For a few days at the beginning of the week there was an incipient flight from the mark, the French withdrawing funds. **1938** *Times* 18 Feb. 21/2 The ease with which ..'flight' money is prepared to exchange its refuge—either from one currency to another, or from currencies into gold or from gold into currencies. **1948** G. CROWTHER *Outl. Money* (ed. 2) vii. 205 There is..no less money [in London] as the result of a 'flight of foreign capital'. All that has happened is that..a smaller proportion..of the total of British money belongs to foreigners. **1967** *Times* 4 Aug. 19/8 It is a fallacy to conclude that such sales [by London banks] must represent a flight from the pound by UK residents.

2. Phrases: ***to take flight***, † ***to take*** (***on oneself***) ***the flight, to betake*** or †***smite oneself to flight, to take to flight***, † ***to set oneself in flight***: to flee. † ***to bring*** or ***do on*** (usually ***a, o***) ***flight, to put to*** (†***the***) ***flight*** (or †***upon the flight***): to cause to flee. ***to turn to*** or †***into flight***: to cause to flee, in early use also *intr.* to flee.

a **1225** *Ancr. R.* 248 Etstondeð one aȝean þe ueonde & he deð him o fluhte. *Ibid.* Herdi bileaue bringeð þene deouel a vlihte anon-rihtes. *a* **1225** *Juliana* 45, I þat ilke time we biginneð to fleon & turneð to fluhte. **1375** BARBOUR *Bruce* II. 267 For it suld be full mekill mycht, That now suld put thaim to the flycht. *c* **1489** CAXTON *Sonnes of Aymon* ix. 243 Whan they..sawe Reynawde come they smote theym selfe to flyghte. *c* **1500** *Lancelot* 3014 Ȝhone folk sal tak one them the flycht. **1526** TINDALE *Heb.* xi. 34 Which..wexed valient in fyght, turned to flyght the armees of the alients. **1625–6** PURCHAS *Pilgrims* II. 1128 They presently set themselves in flight. *a* **1639** SPOTTISWOOD *Hist. Ch. Scot.* III. (1655) 145 The French..took the flight and retired to the Town. **1745** P. THOMAS *Jrnl. Anson's Voy.* 207 It was his wisest Course to..betake himself to flight. **1816** J. MARRIOTT *Hymn*, '*Thou, Whose Almighty word*' i, Chaos and darkness..took their flight. **1817** SHELLEY *Rev. Islam* VI. xiv. 1 That onset turned the foes to flight almost. **1840** F. D. BENNET *Whaling Voy.* I. 258 The remainder..took to flight when their companions were harpooned. **1849** GROTE *Greece* II. lxxiii. (1862) VI. 422 The Persians were put to flight.

3. *Comb.*, as **flight-given**, inclined to flee.

c **1611** CHAPMAN *Iliad* II. 158 What prince.. He found *flight-giv'n, he would restrain with words of gentlest blame.

†**flight**, *sb.*[3] *Obs.* [var. of FLAUGHT *sb.*[1] (? OE. **fliht*:—**flahti-z*).] = FLAUGHT *sb.*[1] **a.** A flake of snow. **b.** A violent storm (of snow). **c.** A turf.

1483 *Cath. Angl.* 135/2 A Flyghte of snawe, *floccus niueus*. **1685** SEWALL *Diary* 9 Nov. (1882) I. 103 Flight of snow. **1780** in T. HUTCHINSON *Diary* II. 349 The trees..covered with snow this morning; afterwards several flights of snow. **1811** W. J. HOOKER *Iceland* (1813) II. 116 A flight of snow had recently fallen. **1847** HALLIWELL, *Flights*, turf or peat, cut into square pieces for fuel.

†**flight**, *a.* *Obs.* [f. FLIGHT *sb.*[1] Cf. FLEET *a.*]

1. Swift, fleet, fast-moving.

1581 B. R. tr. *Herodotus* 69 The most flight and swifte creature that liveth on the earth. **1596** COPLEY *Fig for Fort.* 21 So flight is Melancholie to darke disgrace And deadly drowsie to a bright good morrow. **1609** HOLLAND *Amm. Marcell.* XXVII. x. 321 This man, a certain twofold fortune.. carrying with her flight-wings [L. *præpetibus pinnis*] shewed [etc.]. **1642** H. MORE *Song of Soul* II. III. III. lix, That courses of unlike extension..in like time shall be run By the flight starres.

b. used as *sb.*: A swift runner. ? *nonce-use*.

1579–80 NORTH *Plutarch* (1657) 28 Young men called Celeres, as we would say, flights, for their swiftnesse and speed in executing of his commandements.

2. Of oats: Light. (Cf. FLIGHT sb.[1] 11).

1797 A. YOUNG *Agric. Suffolk* 56 The light, called also *flight* oats, are known only on the poorest sands, and in the fen district.

flight (flaɪt), *v.* Also 6 *Sc.* flicht. [f. FLIGHT *sb.*[1] and [2].]

1. *trans.* To put to flight, rout; hence, to frighten, scare. *Obs.* exc. *dial.*

1571 CAMPION *Hist. Irel.* II. i. (1633) 63 But Griffin.. flighted the Kyrneghes, and slew Ororick. **1579–80** NORTH *Plutarch* (1657) 245 Mount Ptoum..from whence the wild Bore came of a sudden that flighted her. **1583** GOLDING *Calvin on Deut.* vii. 41 Else..they should haue bene flighted with the wildernesse which was verie dreadfull. **1603** HARSNET *Pop. Impost.* 16 To Flight the Deviles from Fulmer. **1848** E. BRONTE *Wuthering Heights* (1858) 29 'And at the end of it to be flighted to death!' he said.

fig. **1676** GLANVILL *Ess.* iv. 34 Therefore [philosophy] is to be flighted [? *mispr. for* slighted], and exploded among Christians.

†**2.** *intr.* To fluctuate, change. *Obs. Sc.*

1500–20 DUNBAR *Poems* xxiv. 6 This warld evir dois flicht and wary.

3. †**a.** To migrate; = FLIT, FLEET (*obs.*). **b.** Of wild fowl: To fly in flights.

1604 MIDDLETON *Witch* III. iii, Prepare to flight then: I'll over-take you swiftly. [But *flight* may here be the *sb.*[2]] **1752** *Scotland's Glory* 5 The followers of John divine In Scotland when they flighted, And published here the Gospel news. **1873** *Young Englishwoman* Nov. 531/1 The habit of the wild fowl is this... At evening they 'flight' to the uplands. **1879** R. LUBBOCK *Fauna of Norfolk* 117 If undisturbed..they [snipe] merely flight for a few minutes morning and evening. **1891** LD. HOUGHTON *Stray Verses, In Winter* 11 The wildfowl flighting from the lake Wheel high.

4. *trans.* To set flying, start in flight. ***to flight off***: to start off in flights, send away in flights.

1823 *New Monthly Mag.* VII. 123 The superabundant population may be flighted off to the lunar region. **1892** *Northumbld. Gloss.*, 'Aa'll flight ye pigeons for a shillin'.'

5. To shoot (wildfowl) in flight.

1892 *Cornh. Mag.* Aug. 155 Wildfowlers know this habit well, and 'flighting', or shooting them as they go and come, is a favourite method of procuring wild ducks.

6. To feather (an arrow).

1869 BOUTELL *Arms & Arm.* ii. 34 The arrows, which had iron tips, were flighted with feathers. **1890** C. DIXON *Stray Feathers* ii. 20 The stiff quill feathers..are used by savages to flight their arrows.

7. *Cricket.* To vary the trajectory and pace of (the ball) in its flight before pitching. Also *intr.*

1912 P. F. WARNER *Eng. v. Austral.* iv. 33 Woolley kept an excellent length, and 'flighted' the ball. **1925** *Country Life* 18 July 95/1 This power of varying the trajectory of the ball and its pace is known as 'flighting' the ball. **1955** *Times* 16 Aug. 3/3 He flighted and turned from leg just enough on what had previously seemed to be an easy paced surface. **1961** *Times* 16 May 4 Cowper had been bowling slow flighted off-breaks.

flight, var. of FLITE.

flighted (ˈflaɪtɪd), *ppl. a.* [f. FLIGHT *sb.*[1] + -ED[2].]

1. Having a certain flight or speed.

1634 MILTON *Comus* 553 The drousy-flighted steeds, That draw the litter of close-curtain'd sleep. **1906** *Westm. Gaz.* 5 Jan. 4/2 Short-winged and feeble-flighted little birds.

2. Provided with feathers, feathered.

1735 J. MOORE *Columbarium* 35 The nine flight Feathers of the Wing ought to be White, otherwise he [the Powter] is said to be foul flighted. **1889** ELVIN *Dict. Her.*, *Flighted* applied to an arrow denotes that it is feathered.

3. Of steps: arranged in flights.

1929 A. CLARKE *Later Poems* (1961) 19 There Are flighted steps to climb.

flighter (ˈflaɪtə(r)). *Brewing.* [? f. FLIGHT + -ER[1]. ? Orig. = 'wing'; cf. FLICHTER *v.*[2]] (See quot.)

1825 JAMIESON *Suppl.*, *Flichters*, that part of the Fanners which raises the wind. **1874** KNIGHT *Dict. Mech.* I. 882 *Flighter*, a horizontal vane revolving over the surface of wort in a cooler, to produce a circular current in the liquor.

†ˈ**flightful**, *a.* *Obs.* [f. FLIGHT *sb.* + -FUL.]

1. Fleeting, transitory, fugitive.

1571 GOLDING *Calvin on Ps.* xxx. 7 His owne flightfull and tottering felicitie. **1587** —— *De Mornay* xxvii. (1617) 479 A light and flightfull ioy.

2. Producing flight; cowardly.

1621 G. SANDYS *Ovid's Met.* XIII. (1626) 254 Vlysses.. Whose flightfull feare did Hector's flames abhor.

3. Well-adapted for flight.

1580 SIDNEY *Ps.* CXXXIX. v, O Sun.. Suppose thy lightfull, flightfull wings Thou lend to me.

flightily (ˈflaɪtɪlɪ), *adv.* [f. FLIGHTY + -LY[2].] In a flighty manner.

1780 MAD. D'ARBLAY *Diary* 8 June I. 394 She seemed flightily gay. **1874** GREEN *Short Hist.* ix. §3. 627 Buckingham talked flightily about bringing the army to London.

flightiness (ˈflaɪtɪnɪs). [f. as prec. + -NESS.] The quality or state of being flighty; giddy capriciousness, fickleness or whimsicalness.

1748 RICHARDSON *Clarissa* (1811) II. i. 9 If my manner does not divert you, as my flightiness used to do. **1857** MAURICE *Ep. St. John* xiv. 216 There is a flightiness about our talk as if we disdained the earth.

flighting (ˈflaɪtɪŋ), *vbl. sb.* [f. FLIGHT *v.* + -ING[1].] The action of the vb. FLIGHT; in quots. = FLIGHT-SHOOTING.

1815 COL. HAWKER *Diary* (1893) I. 132 Warren Farm has excellent flighting when the wind is from S. to W. **1882** SIR R. PAYNE GALLWEY *Fowler in Irel.* 30 Admirable early flighting may be enjoyed on the inland ponds.

flightless (ˈflaɪtlɪs), *a.* [f. FLIGHT *sb.*[1] + -LESS.] Incapable of flying. Also *fig.*

1875 tr. *Schmidt's Desc. & Darw.* 186 The scanty but wide-spread remains of the order of flightless birds. **1889** A. R. WALLACE *Darwinism* 145 The origin of so many flightless and rather bulky birds in oceanic islands. **1953** E. SITWELL *Gardeners & Astronomers* 1 The entity of primal, flightless, winged Stupidity. **1967** M. E. HALE *Biol. Lichens* vii. 101 Large flightless weevils in the mossy forests of New Guinea. **1971** *Nature* 23 Apr. 482/1 BOAC this week found no difficulty in cramming the passengers from a flightless 747 into a conventional jet aircraft, with plenty of room to spare.

ˈ**flight-shooting**, *vbl. sb.* [f. FLIGHT *sb.*[1] + SHOOTING *vbl. sb.*]

1. *Archery.* Distance-shooting with flight-arrows.

1801 T. ROBERTS *Eng. Bowman* x. 237 *Flight-shooting* takes its appellation from the *flight*, or light arrows used in this game: which is shot without regard to mark, or fixed distance.. The greatest possible distance is the only object. **1875** SHARPE in *Encycl. Brit.* II. 377/2 'Flight' and 'clout' shooting has ceased.

2. Shooting wildfowl as they fly over.

1840 BLAINE *Encycl. Rural Sports* VII. iv. §2750 Flight-shooting. **1859** FOLKARD *Wild-Fowler* liii. 276 The term 'flight-shooting' signifies shooting wild-fowl at evening twilight as they fly overland from the sea [etc.].

attrib. **1859** FOLKARD *Wild-Fowler* liii. 279 A flight-shooting excursion.

So ˈ**flight-shooter**.

1859 FOLKARD *Wild-Fowler* liii. 276 The flight-shooter waits in ambush behind an embankment.

ˈ**flight-shot**. Also 6–7 **flight-shoot**. [f. FLIGHT *sb.*[1] + SHOT *sb.*]

1. The distance to which a flight-arrow is shot, a bow-shot.

1455 *Paston Lett.* No. 257 I. 351 And so he dede till he was a flyte shote or more from his place. **1538** LELAND *Itin.* (1744) IV. 41 The passage into it at ful Se is a flite Shot over, as much as the Tamise is above the Bridge. **1615** G. SANDYS *Trav.* 23 This hill lyeth South of the ruines.. and about three flight-shots remoued. **1625** J. TAYLOR (Water P.) *Thiefe* Wks. (1630) II. 119/2 Some two flight-shoot to th' Alehouse he did wag. *a* **1697** AUBREY *Nat. Hist. Surrey* (1719) I. 46 A Brook.. riseth four Mile off in a Cellar; and a Flight-shot off drives a Mill. **1852** HAWTHORNE *Blithedale Rom.* xviii, Far as her flight-shot was, those arrows hit the mark.

fig. **1647** WARD *Simp. Cobler* 29 Such as.. follow fashions .. a flight shot or two off. **1704** SWIFT *T. Tub* vi. 86 Jack was already gone a flight-shot beyond his patience.

2. A shot taken at wildfowl in flight.

1887 RYE *Norfolk Broads* 100 In the hope of getting a flight shot at duck or plover.

flighty (ˈflaɪtɪ), *a.* [f. FLIGHT *sb.*[1] + -Y[1].]

1. Swift, quick, fleet. *rare.*

1552 HULOET, Flighty, *pernix*. **1605** SHAKS. *Macb.* IV. i. 145 The flighty purpose neuer is o're-tooke Vnlesse the deed go with it. **1856** LOWELL *Lett.* (1894) I. 257 My journey thither was sudden and flighty.

b. ? *nonce-use.* = Fleeting.

1850 BROWNING *Christmas Eve* vi. 26 Another rainbow rose.. flushier and flightier.

2. Given to flights of imagination, humour, caprice, etc.; guided by whim or fancy rather than by judgement or settled purpose; fickle, frivolous, inconstant.

1768–74 TUCKER *Lt. Nat.* (1852) I. 592 The flighty gambols of chance are objects of no science, nor grounds of any dependence whatever. *a* **1774** GOLDSM. *New Simile* 20 With wit that's flighty. **1801** MAR. EDGEWORTH *Angelina* ii. (1832) 17, I believe by her flighty airs, she is upon no good errand. **1848** MILL *Pol. Econ.* I. vii. §5 The effect.. of flighty, unsteady habits upon the energy and continuity of their work. **1878** MRS. H. WOOD *Pomeroy Ab.* I. 88 Her own maid, a flighty, gossiping damsel.

b. Of a horse: Skittish.

1828 *Sporting Mag.* XXIII. 106 The management of a Flighty Horse in his exercise or sweat.

3. Of weak or disordered intellect, crazy, light-headed. Also *absol.*

1802 BEDDOES *Hygeia* III. 15 To protect the insane or flighty against their [relations'] rapacity. **1820** W. IRVING *Sketch-bk.* (1859) 34 This was one point on which he always remained flighty. **1845** DARWIN *Voy. Nat.* iv. (1879) 74 The poor flighty gentleman looked quite dolorous.

fligm(e, obs. form of PHLEGM.

flim[1]. *nonce-wd.* [Cf. FLIM-FLAM *sb.* and *a.*] = FLAM *sb.*[1] 3.

1825 J. WILSON *Noct. Ambr.* Wks. 1855 I. 5 The rest is a sham And all that comes after a flim and a flam.

flim[2] (flɪm). *slang.* [abbrev. of FLIMSY *sb.* 1.] A £5 note.

1870 *Chambers's Jrnl.* 9 July 448/1 'What would it be worth?' 'A flim, Sam.' **1954** 'N. BLAKE' *Whisper in Gloom* I. ii. 28 They.. offer Bert.. a flim for his boat.

flim-flam (ˈflɪmflæm), *sb.* and *a.* Also 6 ? **flym flawe.** [One of the many onomatopœic reduplications expressive of contempt; cf. *fidfad*, *skimble-skamble*, *whimwham*. Possibly based on a Scandinavian word which may have existed in some Eng. dialects; cf. ON. *flim* a lampoon, *flimska* mockery, *flimta* to flout.]

A. *sb.*

1. A piece of nonsense or idle talk; a trifle, a conceit. Cf. FLAM *sb.*[1] 2.

1546 J. HEYWOOD *Prov.* (1867) 19 She maketh earnest matters of euery flymflam. **1589** *Pappe w. Hatchet* E ij b, Trusse vp thy packet of flim flams, & roage to some countrey Faire, or read it among boyes in the belfrie. *a* **1634** RANDOLPH *Poems, To Mem. Brother-in-Law* (1681) B iv b, Such jig-like flim-flams being got to make The Rabble laugh. **1885** *L'pool Daily Post* 11 May 8/7 Grossmith.. crowds his picture with all kinds of flim-flams of the drawing-room.

2. A paltry attempt at deception; a contemptible trick or pretence; a piece of humbug. Cf. FLAM *sb.*[1] 3.

c **1538** in *State Papers* (1834) II. iii. 552 He and his fellawes were sent hither.. but for a flim flawe to stoppe the ymagination of the Kynge and Counsaile in that behalf. **1573** G. HARVEY *Letter-bk.* (Camden) 14 He gave me this flim flam, that I had persuadid him sumwhat. **1600** HOLLAND *Livy* VI. XVI. (1609) 227 The Dictatour commanded him to leave off these foolish flimflams & trifling shifts. **1673** COWLEY *Cutter Coleman St.* IV. iv, I'll ha' none of his Flim-flams, and his May-be's. **1805** D'ISRAELI (*title*), Flim-Flams, or the Life and Errors of my Uncle. **1880** DISRAELI *Endym.* xci, All these habitual flim-flams are, in general, the airy creatures of inaccuracy and exaggeration.

3. *collect.* Nonsense, rubbish; humbug, deception.

c **1570** *Marr. Wit & Science* II. i, A longe tale of a man in the moone, With such a circumstaunce and such flym-flam. **1749** FIELDING *Tom Jones* XVIII. xii, I tell thee 'tis all flimflam. **1890** W. A. WALLACE *Only a Sister* xxxi, They may be the wanderings of his dotage, and flim-flam after all.

4. The action of 'flim-flamming'; in quot. *attrib.*

1894 *Boston* (Mass.) *Jrnl.* 2 May 9/7 She notified the police, but the flim-flam artist was far away. *Ibid.* 17 Nov. 9/7 His success in the 'flim-flam' game.

B. *adj.* [Developed from an attrib. use of the sb.; cf. FANCY *a.*] Frivolous, idle, vain, nonsensical; also, deceptive, fictitious, sham.

1577–87 HOLINSHED *Chron.* II. 14/1 His slanderous reports are vnderpropt with flim-flam surmises. **1631** MABBE *Celestina* I. 12 She will tell you a thousand flim-flam tales. **1685** CROWNE *Sir C. Nice* III. Dram. Wks. 1874 III. 300 Do you think I regard your flimflam story o' the church? **1886** ELWORTHY *W. Somerset Word-bk.*, Don't thee tell up no such flim-flam stuff, else nobody ont never harky to thee.

flim-flam (ˈflɪmflæm), *v.* [f. prec. sb.] *trans.* **a.** To humbug, to beguile *into* (something). **b.** *U.S.* To cheat (a person) *out of* (money) 'while he is making change for a bill, by distracting or confusing him, so that he pays out more than the proper sum' (*Stand. Dict.*).

1660 FISHER *Rustick's Alarm* Wks. (1679) 307 None but Fools will by thy flood of Words be flim-flam'd into thy Faith. **1890** *Columbus* (Ohio) *Dispatch* 26 July, Sent [to jail] .. for flimflaming a.. saloon-keeper out of some money. **1903** O. KILDARE *My Mamie Rose* 72 'Flim-flamming'.. Doubling a bill in a number of them and counting each end of it as one separate bill. **1904** E. ROBINS *Magnetic North* II. 144 But I didn't know *you'd* get flim-flammed out o' your boots. **1911** H. QUICK *Yellowstone Nights* xi. 290 Financial ingenuity has found a way to flim flam the devil himself. **1929** D. HAMMETT *Dain Curse* (1930) xii. 127 His success in flimflamming his followers had gone to his head. **1934** J. M. CAIN *Postman always rings Twice* x. 117 We've been flim-flammed, Cora. **1963** *Punch* 1 May 620/1 Marketing practices that smacked of flimflamming the public. **1971** *Publishers' Weekly* 22 Mar. 33 One expects somehow to be flim-flammed on a vacuum cleaner.

Hence **flim-flammer** *U.S.* So **flim-flammery.**

1881 *Nat. Police Gaz.* 12 Nov. 10/2 Among the numberless small swindles of the metropolis there is none more curious than that of the flim-flammer. **1894** *Columbus* (Ohio) *Dispatch* 31 Jan., The New York flim-flammers and green goods men.. are still out of the clutches of the United Secret Service. **1898** W. J. LOCKE *Idols* xiv. 201 Sick of your flim-flammeries of philosophy. **1960** *Observer* 17 Jan. 12/6, I got a taste of his flimflammery the first time I met him. **1968** *Sat. Rev.* 27 Apr. 62/1 Peddlers, guides, flim-flammers and other friends of the tourist are forbidden there.

flim-flam-flirt. [Cf. FLIM-FLAM and FLAM-FLIRT.] A nonsensical speech, a gibe.

1573 TWYNE *Æneid* x. Dd iij, Flimflam flirts [thou] out throwst at them that nothing care.

†ˈ**flimmer**, *sb.* *Obs.* [? f. FLIM-(FLAM) *sb.* or *v.* + -ER[1].] ? A chatter-box, gossip.

1515 BARCLAY *Egloges* III. 145 Rural flimmers, and other of our sort.. They chat, they bable.

flimmer (ˈflɪmə(r)), *v.* *rare.* [Onomatopœic; cf. *glimmer*, *flicker* and Ger. *flimmern*.] *intr.* To burn unsteadily; to flicker. Also *transf.*

1880 WEBB *Goethe's Faust* IV. xix, Upwards the lamp's eternal light doth flimmer. **1918** C. SANDBURG *Cornhuskers* 17 Canada thistle blue and flimmering larkspur blue. *Ibid.* 114 The shafts across her bed are flimmering.

flimp (flɪmp), *v.* *slang.* [Cf. WFlem. *flimpe* knock, slap in the face.] *trans.* To rob in a certain manner (see quot.).

1839 BRANDON *Poverty, Mendicity & Crime* 111 (Farmer) To take a man's watch is to flimp him, it can only be done in a crowd, one gets behind and pushes him in the back, while the other in front is robbing him. **1862** *Cornh. Mag.* Nov. 651 We are going a flimping, buzzing, cracking [etc.].

Hence **flimp** *sb.* (see quot. 1857); ˈ**flimping** *vbl. sb.* Also ˈ**flimper**, one who flimps.

1857 'DUCANGE ANGLICUS' *Vulg. Tongue* 8 Putting on the flimp. Garotte robbery. **1862** H. KINGSLEY *Ravenshoe* III. xi. 180 What with flimping, and with cly-faking.. 'Flimping' is a style of theft which I have never practised.

flimsify (ˈflɪmzɪfaɪ), *v.* *nonce-wd.* [f. FLIMSY *a.* + -FY.] *trans.* To render flimsy.

1838 *Blackw. Mag.* XLIV. 533 Mysticism, which flimsifies religion.. into transcendental sentimentalities.

flimsily (ˈflɪmzɪlɪ), *adv.* [f. FLIMSY + -LY[2].] In a flimsy manner.

1787 *Minor* 159 How flimsily the contractor.. had executed his plans. *a* **1797** WALPOLE *Mem. Geo. II* (1847) II. ii. 54 Then ensued a variety of the different manners of speaking ill. Potter flimsily [etc.]. **1863** E. FITZ GERALD *Lett.* (1889) I. 292 Certainly I looked very flimsily at all. **1888** *Harper's Mag.* July 215 The work was done cheaply and flimsily.

flimsiness (ˈflɪmzɪnɪs). [f. FLIMSY *a.* + -NESS.] The quality of being flimsy.

1727 in BAILEY vol. II. *a* **1763** SHENSTONE *Ess. Writing & Bks.* Wks. (1764) 173 A certain flimziness of poetry. **1816** KEATINGE *Trav.* (1817) II. 81 Certainly the materials are spun out almost to flimziness. **1883** *Law Times* 29 Sept. 362/1 The courts.. were run up with a speed and flimsiness of construction which would do credit to a speculative suburban builder.

concr. **1871** R. ELLIS *Catullus* lxviii. 51 The spider, aloft her silk-slight flimsiness hanging.

flimsy (ˈflɪmzɪ), *a.* and *sb.* Also 8 **flimsey, -zy.** [First recorded in 18th c.; possibly (as Todd conjectured) an onomatopœic formation suggested by FILM. For the ending cf. *tipsy*, *bumpsy*; also *limpsy*, given by Webster as a U.S. synonym of *flimsy*.]

A. *adj.* **1.** In physical sense: Destitute of strength or solidity; easily destroyed; slight, frail, unsubstantial.

1702 in KERSEY. **1706** PHILLIPS (ed. Kersey), *Flimsy*, limber, slight. **1728** MORGAN *Algiers* I. iv. 141 The flesh [of the ostrich] is hard, black, and flimsy. **1780** COWPER *Progr. Err.* 495 Spun as fine As bloated spiders draw the flimsy line. **1813** SHELLEY *Q. Mab* v. 28 To screen With flimsy veil of justice.. Its unattractive lineaments. **1852** THACKERAY *Esmond* II. iv, There comes a day when the roused public indignation kicks their flimsy edifice down. **1874** L. STEPHEN *Hours in Library* (1892) I. iii. 109 The jewels have remained after the flimsy embroidery.. has fallen into decay.

†**b.** Of persons or their constitutions: Frail, 'delicate'. *Obs.*

1741–2 H. WALPOLE *Lett. H. Mann* (1834) I. xviii. 61, I have a very flimsy constitution. **1753** CHESTERF. *Lett.* IV. 195, I have not yet quite got over my last violent attack, and am weak and flimsy.

2. In immaterial sense: Destitute of solid value, slight, trivial, paltry.

[**1735** POPE *Prol. Sat.* 94 Proud of a vast extent of flimsy lines!] **1756–82** J. WARTON *Ess. Pope* (ed. 4) I. iii. 203 Walsh was in general a flimsy and frigid writer. **1765** BLACKSTONE *Comm.* I. 201 However flimsey this title.. may appear at this distance to us. **1830** HERSCHEL *Stud. Nat. Phil.* 109 The perverse and flimsy style of verbal disputation which had infected all learning. **1845** M. PATTISON *Ess.* (1889) I. 21 This flimsy hypocrisy, by which he.. sought to pass himself off as the victim of others' injustice. **1880** L. STEPHEN *Pope* vii. 171 A flimsy hypothesis learnt from Bolingbroke.

absol. **1794** GODWIN *Cal. Williams* 35 Choosing the flimsy before the substantial.

b. With reference to mental or moral attributes: Frivolous, trifling, superficial.

1827 SCOTT *Surg. Dau.* xii, But it was thine, flimsy villain, to execute the device which a bolder genius planned. **1847** L. HUNT *Men, Women & B.* II. ix. 195 Poor, flimsy, witty, wise, foolish.. Horace Walpole. **1853** LYNCH *Self-Improv.* iii. 66 The flimsy individual who has read fifty novels in a year, but nothing else.

B. *sb.*

1. *slang.* A bank-note; also, paper-money.

1824 P. EGAN *Boxiana* IV. 443 Martin produced some 'flimsies'; and said he would fight on Tuesday next. **1842** BARHAM *Ingol. Leg., Merch. Venice*, English Exchequer-bills .. the right sort of 'flimsy', all signed by Monteagle. **1845** ALB. SMITH *Fort. Scatterg. Fam.* xxxii. (1887) 108 I'll stand a five pun' flimsy for the piece.

2. A flimsy or thin kind of paper: *esp.* that used by reporters for the purpose of multiplying copies; hence, reporters' 'copy'. Also, a sheet of thin paper, esp. that used on a typewriter for taking carbon copies; a document on thin paper. Also *attrib.*

1857 J. E. RITCHIE *Night Side London* 202 The reporters —or, rather, the penny-a-liners—who write on 'flimsey', and leave 'copy' on spec. at all the daily paper offices. **1859** SALA *Tw. round Clock* (1861) 30 Sub-editors are now hard at work cutting down 'flimsy'. **1872** BESANT & RICE *Ready Money Mortiboy* xxiii, I'm afraid I shan't have enough flimsy. **1888** C. T. JACOBI *Printers' Vocab.* 44 *Flimsy*, thin paper, such as.. telegraph forms. **1892** *Pall Mall G.* 13 Apr. 6/3 The Post Office telegraph 'flimsy' messages.. are now to be multiplied by means of the typewriter. **1909** *Daily Chron.* 10 Mar. 7/6 He had sent to the defendants 'flimsies' of the original reports. **1916** J. BUCHAN *Greenmantle* i. 1, I had just finished breakfast.. when I got Bullivant's telegram... I flung him the flimsy with the blue strip pasted down on it. **1929** F. C. BOWEN *Sea Slang* 50 *Flimsy*, an officer's report at the end of a commission or when leaving a man-of-war. **1930** D. L. SAYERS *Strong Poison* xiv. 175 She dragged the cover off the typewriter.. shook the top sheet, carbons, and flimsies together as a terrier shakes a rat. **1952** M. TRIPP *Faith is Windsock* vi. 95 Craig scrambled among his flimsies and maps. *Ibid.* xi. 163 Wafer-like sheets of paper with transparent celluloid covering, known as flimsies, were distributed by the bombing leader. **1958** M. DICKENS *Man Overboard* xiii. 193 The character references supplied by the Flimsies of his Confidential Reports. **1960** 'N. SHUTE' *Trustee from Toolroom* iii. 47 'I told you that I had an answer to that cable...' He passed the flimsy to Keith.

Hence **'flimsy** *v. trans.*, to write on 'flimsy'.

1886 *Daily News* 17 July, Had the questions to be copied out?—Yes; and the answers to be flimsied.

flinch (flɪnʃ), *v.*[1] Also 7 flench. [app. a. OF. *flenchir, flainchir*, usually regarded as a variant of the synonymous *flechir*: see FLECCHE.]

1. *intr.* To give way, draw back, yield ground in a combat; to draw back or turn aside *from* a course of action, a duty or enterprise. In later use influenced by sense 3: To draw back through failure in courage, endurance, or resolve; to shrink *from* something as dangerous, painful, or difficult.

1579 LYLY *Euphues* (Arb.) 91 If thou wast minded.. to loue me, why dost thou flinch at the last? **1587** *Mirr. Mag., Humber* v, Pitch'd our fielde In hope to make them flinche, flye, fall or yeelde. **1611** BARRY *Ram-Alley* III. i, I shall catch him in a narrow room, Where neither of us can flinch. **1649** BP. GUTHRIE *Mem.* (1702) 65 Drawing them to his Tent, upon assurance, and afterwards flinching from it. **1712** ARBUTHNOT *John Bull* IV. xi, O the ingratitude and injustice .. that John Bull.. should flinch at last. **1826** E. IRVING *Babylon* II. 437 If you flinch not, like Jonah, from fulfilling your commission. **1840** ALISON *Hist. Europe* (1849–50) VIII. liv. §4. 464 The peasants withstood without flinching several attacks in front. **1873** H. ROGERS *Orig. Bible* vi. (1875) 220 Faintheartedness.. had often made him flinch in sudden temptation.

†**b.** *to flinch out*: to swerve, deviate, be deflected. *Obs. rare*⁻¹.

1642 H. MORE *Song of Soul* II. III. III. lxxi, Why Venus flincheth out More then Mercurius.

†**2.** To slink, sneak off. Also with *away, off.*

1563 in Strype *Ann. Ref.* I. xxxvi. 413 For the preventing of any of these dispensed Persons from flinching off from them, or falling from this Correspondence. **1605** CAMDEN *Rem.* 235 Which when they have beene well and kindely entertained flinch away never giving thankes. **1611** FLORIO, *Spicchiáre*, to sneake or flinch secretly out of sight. **1622** MABBE tr. *Aleman's Guzman d'Alf.* II. 131 They went flinching away, and got them home through bye-lanes.

3. To shrink under pain; to wince.

a **1677** BARROW *Serm.* Wks. 1716 II. 38 Doth not every man flinch at any trouble? **1692** LOCKE *Educ.* §115 A child .. may.. be accustom'd to bear very.. rough usage without flinching or complaining. **1791** BOSWELL *Johnson* 7 May an. 1773 *note*, He never flinched; but after reiterated blows, remained seemingly unmoved. **1879** BROWNING *Ivan Ivanovitch* 224 Gnaw through me, through and through: flat thus I lie nor flinch.

b. To blench: see BLENCH *v.*[1] 2 and 6.

1883 tr. *Stepniak's Undergr. Russia* Introd. II. iii. 43 He.. can die without flinching. **1884** W. C. SMITH *Kildrostan* 93 Serpents.. charm you with a gaze that will not flinch.

4. quasi-*trans.* To withdraw from, lose (one's ground). Also, *to flinch the flagon*: to let the bottle pass. *to flinch one's glass*: to avoid emptying it. †*to flinch* (*back*) *one's hand*: to draw it back; in quot. *fig.* to intermit one's activity.

1674 N. FAIRFAX *Bulk & Selv.* 75 If Nature should but flinch back her hand, or the world that is round about it should but be pluckt away from it. **1712** ARBUTHNOT *John Bull* III. vi, Lewis.. either by the strength of his brain, or flinching his glass, kept himself sober as a judge. **1790** BURNS *Election Ball.* xiv, Welsh who ne'er yet flinch'd his ground. **1838** JAMES *Robber* i, You flinched the flagon.

Hence **'flinching** *vbl. sb.*

1600 HOLLAND *Livy* XLII. 1127 This flinching of his and absenting himselfe. **1845** HOOD *True Story* xiv, A recollection strong enough To cause a very serious flinching. **1879** FROUDE *Cæsar* xvii. 277 There was no flinching and no cowardice.

†**flinch**, *v.*[2] *Obs.* [Cf. FLIP, FLIRT.] (See quot.) Hence **'flinching** *vbl. sb.*

1727–36 BAILEY, *Flinching*.. also a flirting the Nail of the Middle-finger slapped from the Thumb. **1735** DYCHE & PARDON, *Flinch*.. also to strike or cut the Flesh by a Stroke with the Nail of the middle Finger.

flinch (flɪnʃ), *v.*[3] *Naut.* [possibly identical in etymology with FLINCH *v.*[1]; cf. FLANCH.] *trans.* To bevel; = SNAPE *v.*

1867 in SMYTH *Sailor's Word-bk.* s.v. *Snape.*

flinch, var. of FLENCH *v.*

flinch (flɪnʃ), *sb.* [f. FLINCH *v.*[1]] The action of flinching.

1817 W. TAYLOR in *Monthly Rev.* LXXXIII. 498 That unwelcome flinch which the touch of egotism gives to benevolence. **1832** J. P. KENNEDY *Swallow Barn* I. xx. 205 Thar's no flinch in me, you may depend upon it. **1862** in A. E. Lee *Hist. Columbus* (1892) I. 741 Mr. Rarey.. leaped over its head, laid [*sic*] down upon it, and within its legs, all without a start or a flinch. **1922** A. S. M. HUTCHINSON *This Freedom* II. ii. 91 But she came back bravely from her flinch. **1930** AUDEN *Poems* 25 Nowise withdrawn by doubting flinch Nor joined to any by belief's firm flange.

flincher ('flɪnʃə(r)). [f. FLINCH *v.*[1] + -ER[1].]

1. One who hangs back or gives way, *esp.* at a crisis or in time of danger, etc.; one who shrinks *from* (an undertaking, etc.).

1598 FLORIO, *Taccognatore*.. a conycatcher, a micher, a flincher, a paltrer. **1609** BP. W. BARLOW *Answ. Nameless Cath.* 272 All the flinchers that forsooke him. **1664** H. MORE *Ep. 7 Churches* iv. (1669) 51 That sharp reprehension of Flinchers from the Faith. **1760** C. JOHNSTON *Chrysal* II. II. xiv, I am no flincher; I never say aye when I mean no. *a* **1834** LAMB *Final Mem.* ix. Wks. (1865) 295 In society, as in politics, he was no flincher.

transf. **1631** *Celestina* XVIII. 180 Gold and Silver will not tarry with mee; they are flinchers.

2. One who passes the bottle; one who abstains from drinking.

1549 COVERDALE, etc. *Erasm. Par. Jas.* i. 27 He is counted a flyncher that foloweth sobrietie. *a* **1668** DAVENANT *Siege* v. Dram. Wks. 1873 IV. 427 What! a flincher? Quaff it off, Mulciber. *a* **1748** C. PITT *Ep. to Mr. Spence* 94 The sot.. Swears at the flinchers who refuse their glass. **1826** DISRAELI *Viv. Grey* v. iv, A German student is no flincher at the bottle.

flinching ('flɪnʃɪŋ), *ppl. a.* [f. FLINCH *v.*[1] + -ING[2].] That flinches. Hence **'flinchingly** *adv.*

1847 in CRAIG. **1883** FENN *Middy & Ensign* xvii. 105 It held out one long thin black hand, flinchingly, as if expecting to be teased.

flinchless ('flɪnʃlɪs), *a.* or *adv. nonce-wd.* [f. FLINCH *sb.* + -LESS.] Without a flinch.

1847 J. HALLIDAY *Rustic Bard* 177 She flinchless views the gathering shower.

'flinder, *sb. Obs.* exc. *dial.* In 4 vlindre. [= mod.Du. *vlinder*.] A moth or butterfly.

1340 *Ayenb.* 206 Zuo long uliȝþ þe ulindre aboute the candle: þet hi bernþ. **1736** PEGGE *Kenticisms, Flinder*, a butterfly. **1887** in *Kent Gloss.*

flinder ('flɪndə(r)), *v.*[1] *Sc. rare*⁻¹. [f. FLINDER(S *sb.*] *trans.* To break into flinders or pieces.

1871 P. H. WADDELL *Ps.* x. 15 Flinder ye the arm o' the ill-doers. *Ibid.* xlvi. 9 He flinders the bow.

'flinder, *v.*[2] *Sc.* [Cf. Flemish *vlinderen*, LG. *flindern* to flutter, fly away.] (See quot.)

1808–80 JAMIESON, *To Flinder*, to flirt, to run about in a fluttering manner; also applied to cattle, when they break through inclosures, and scamper through the fields.

flinder-mouse ('flɪndəmaʊs). *Obs.* exc. *dial.* [f. FLINDER *sb.* or *v.*[2] + MOUSE.] A bat. Cf. FLICKER-, FLITTER-MOUSE.

1481 CAXTON *Reynard* (Arb.) 112 The flyndermows [Du. *die vledermuys*] and the wezel. **1565** B. GOOGE *Zodiac of Life* IX. HH iiij b, Large wings on him did growe, Framde like the wings of Flinder-mice. **1592** CHETTLE *Kind-Harts Dr.* (1841) 21 Blinde flinder-mise. **1624** BARGRAVE *Serm.* 6 An eunuch strooke a flinder-mouse in an elder tree. **1736** PEGGE *Kenticisms, Flindermouse*, a bat. **1875** in *Sussex Gloss.*

flinders[1] ('flɪndəz), *sb. pl.* rarely *sing.* Forms: 5–6 *Sc.* flend(e)ris, -ers, 9 *Sc.* (*sing.* and *pl.*) flinner(s, 8– flinders. [cf. mod.Norw. *flindra* thin chip or splinter, Du. *flenter* fragment.]

a. Fragments, pieces, splinters. Chiefly in phrases, as *to break* or *fly in*(*to*) *flinders*. Cf. FLITTERS.

c **1450** *Golagros & Gaw.* 915 Thair speris in the feild in flendris gart ga. *a* **1550** *Christis Kirke Gr.* ix, The bow in flenders flew. **1776** C. KEITH *Farmer's Ha'* in Chambers *Pop. Poems Scotl.* (1862) 32 He'll their doors to flinders toss. **1808** J. MAYNE *Siller Gun* II. 129 At length she [his gun] bounced out-ower a tree, In mony a flinner. **1840** BROWNING *Sordello* VI. 437 Flinders enrich the strand, and veins the rock. **1847** KINGSLEY *Poems, New Forest Ballad* 30 The metal good and the walnut wood Did soon in flinders flee. **1949** E. POUND *Pisan Cantos* lxxx. 86 And the Osservanza is broken And the best de la Robbia busted to flinders. **1971** W. BURROUGHS *Speed* 42 About noon the transmission went all to flinders.

fig. **1786** BURNS *On a Scotch Bard* v, 'Twill mak her poor auld heart.. In flinders flee. **1878** MRS. STOWE *Poganuc P.* iii. 27 Parson Cushing could knock that air [discourse] all to flinders.

b. *transf.* Pieces, scraps.

1869 GREENWOOD *Seven Curses* ii. 19 Her draggletail flinders of lace and ribbon.

Flinders[2] ('flɪndəz). The name of Captain Matthew *Flinders* (1774–1814), English navigator and explorer, used *attrib.* in **Flinders bar(s)**, a soft iron bar or bundle of rods, placed vertically near a ship's compass to correct deviation due to magnetic induction and to lessen the heeling-error.

1881 W. THOMSON in *Jrnl. R. United Serv. Inst.* XXIV. 408 The Flinders bar essentially corrects.. the constituent of the heeling error, which has its maximum values on the east and west courses. **1895** F. J. EVANS *Elem. Man. Deviations Compass in Iron Ships* (ed. 9) xi. 119 Sir W. Thomson in his patent compass has adopted a malleable iron bar.. which he has called a 'Flinders' bar' after its accomplished inventor. **1902** *Encycl. Brit.* XXVII. 181/2 A method of correcting deviation by means of a bar of vertical iron so placed as to correct the deviation nearly in all latitudes. This bar, now known as a 'Flinders bar', is still in general use. **1924** R. CLEMENTS *Gipsy of Horn* (1925) 217 The binnacle was useless.. for the Flinders-bars had gone with the sky-light. **1959** *Chambers's Encycl.* VIII. 822/1 A 'flinders' bar, a soft iron bar mounted vertically on the binnacle, will.. correct that part of the deviation that is due to the induced vertical fields.

flindosa (flɪn'dəʊzə). *Austral.* Also **flindosy**. [Corruption of *Flindersia*, a genus of trees, f. the name of Captain Matthew *Flinders*: see prec.] An Australian hardwood rain-forest tree, *Flindersia australis*, also known as Australian teak.

1862 *Internat. Exhib. Catal. Prod. N.S. Wales* 28/2 Flindersia Australis. *Cedrelaceæ*. A large-sized tree... Timber valuable for staves... Ash, Beech, and Flindosa. *Ibid.* 30/1 Flindersia Australis var. *Cedrelaceæ*... Timber used for house building, and occasionally for staves... Flindosa. **1884** A. NILSON *Timber Trees N.S.W.* 47 *C*[*ryptocarya*] *obovata*.—Sycamore; Flindosa. *Ibid.* 80 *F*[*lindersia*] *australis*.—Ash; Cugerie; Bulboro; Flindosa. **1907** J. H. MAIDEN *Forest Flora N.S.W.* II. 151, I have also seen it [sc. *Flindersia australis*] labelled 'Flindosa', a name more strictly applied to *F. Schottiana*. **1908** *Ibid.* III. 112 *Cryptocarya sp.* Called Flindosa at Brisbane Water. **1913** *Ibid.* V. 101, I have received it [sc. *Litsæa reticulata*] under the name of 'Flindosa'. **1929** W. D. FRANCIS *Austral. Rain-Forest Trees* 157 Flindersia australis R. Br. Crow's Ash, Teak, Flindosy, Flindersia. **1965** *Austral. Encycl.* IV. 111 *F*[*lindersia*] *australis* is a large tree.. known generally throughout Queensland as crow's ash, but in some places as 'flindosy' or 'flindowzee'.

fline, obs. var. of *flown*: see FLY.

fling (flɪŋ), *sb.* [f. next vb.]

1. An act of flinging or throwing; a cast, throw.

1589 R. HARVEY *Pl. Perc.* 10 Why may not we haue one cast in his Orchard, and a fling at his Medlar tree? **1856** KANE *Arct. Expl.* I. xxix. 391 In spite of the powerful flings which they were subjected to in the fight, not a dog suffers seriously.

2. *fig.* (Chiefly in phrase *to have a fling at.*)

a. A passing attempt at or attack upon something. **b.** A sarcastic remark thrown out in passing; a gibe, scoff.

1550 BALE *Apol.* 142/1 Not one kynge hath bene in Englande.. but they [monks] haue.. had theyr false flynges at him. *a* **1592** GREENE *Selimus* Wks. 1881–3 XIV. 290 Wee'll have a fling at the Ægyptian crowne. **1601** HOLLAND *Pliny* II. XXXVII. iii. 609, I meane.. to haue a fling at Magicians for their abhominable lies. **1659** D. PELL *Impr. Sea* 174 Will you not have one fling at Spain.. before you dye? **1727** A. HAMILTON *New Acc. E. Ind.* I. xiii. 148 He left his Estate to two Grandsons.. But the Court had a Fling at them, and got above a Million Sterl. of their Estate. **1741** RICHARDSON *Pamela* (1824) I. 117 He has had a taste of your satirical flings. **1760** C. JOHNSTON *Chrysal* (1822) II. 10 A fling at the clergy never fails to raise a laugh. **1878** SPURGEON *Serm.* XXIV. 356 These also have their fling against the Gospel.

3. A hasty, reckless, or wanton movement, a rush. *lit.* and *fig.* *at one fling*: at one movement or impulse. *full fling*: with haste or force, impetuously, violently. *Now rare.*

1556 J. HEYWOOD *Spider & F.* i. 33 In at a lattes hole.. Euen at a fling, fast flew there in a flie. **1575** GASCOIGNE *Pr. Pleas. Kenilw.* II. v, My willing feete, which fet these hastie frisking flings. *c* **1590** *Secr. Mem. Earl Leicester* (1706) 114 With many other Fetches Flings and Friskes besides. **1614** T. ADAMS *Diuells Banket* iv. 183 A man that hath taken his careere, and runnes full fling to a place, cannot recoile himselfe. **1621** FLETCHER *Wild Goose Chase* IV. i, Now ye see what your flings are, and your fancies. **1641** BROME *Jovial Crew* II. i, Shall we make a fling to London? **1650** B. *Discolliminium* 35 She would start from Newcastle to Michaels mount at one fling.

4. A flinging about of the body or limbs.

a. A dance in which the arms and legs are moved with great vigour, esp. in *the Highland fling* (also *fig.*)

1806 P. NEILL *Tour* i, We saw the Highlanders.. dancing the fling to the music of the bagpipe. **1824** SCOTT *St. Ronan's* vi, Dancing the highest Highland fling. **1845** HOOD *Last Man* xxiii, He.. danced me a saucy fling. **1866** 'MARK TWAIN' *Lett. fr. Hawaii* (1967) 32 Mrs. Jones.. felt

something grab her cheek; she dropped the sponge and out popped a scorpion... Well, she just got up and danced the Highland Fling for two hours and a half.

b. A violent movement, a plunge; of a horse: A kicking or throwing out the hind legs. Also *Sc. fig.* of persons: ***to take the fling***(*s*: 'to become unmanageable' (Jam.), to become fitful or ill-humoured.

a **1568** FLEMING *Ball. evill Wyffis* viii. in *Bannatyne Poems* (1770) 227 Quhen his wyfe taks the fling. **1719** HAMILTON *Ep. to Ramsay* 24 Aug. vii., Gin we ettle anes to taunt her, And dinna cawmly thole her banter, She'll tak the flings. **1826** H. N. COLERIDGE *West Indies* 126 The furious jerks and flings which he [the shark] made. **1852** MRS. STOWE *Uncle Tom's C.* vi, 'If dat ar gen'lman's crittur [a horse] should gib a fling.'

c. *fig.* Freedom from constraint in one's bearing; 'dash'.

1871 GEO. ELIOT *Middlem.* I. II. xiii. 218 About his ordinary bearing there was a certain fling, a fearless expectation of success, a confidence in his own powers.

5. A fit or spell of unrestrained indulgence of one's impulses. ***to have one's fling***: usually, to abandon oneself to pleasure until the impulse is satisfied.

1827 BARRINGTON *Pers. Sk.* II. 435 They took care previously to have their fling. **1840** E. HOWARD *Jack Ashore* III. iii, From this morning may Jack's fling of extravagance be dated. **1849** THACKERAY *Pendennis* xxxix, I should like to have my fling out before I marry. **1857** HUGHES *Tom Brown* II. ii. (1871) 230 During this hour or hour-and-a-half he used to take his fling. **1864** TENNYSON *Aylmer's F.* 399 Give me my fling, and let me say my say.

6. In various uses.

a. The length of netting which may be made on the mesh-pin at a time.

1780 A. YOUNG *Tour Irel.* I. 153 Weaving the nets 1*d.* a yard for one fling, or 63 meshes deep.

b. A number (of oxbirds) flying in company.

1859 FOLKARD *Wild-fowling* lx. 316 The whole fling [of ox-birds] every now and then presents the identical appearance of a beautiful silver cloud. **1875** 'STONEHENGE' *Brit. Sports* I. i. §1 A 'fling' of oxbirds.

†**c.** used to express: A thing of no importance.

a **1661** FULLER *Worthies, Barke-Shire* (1662) 84 England were but a fling, Save for the crooked stick and the gray-goose-wing.

7. *attrib.* and *Comb.*, as ***fling period*** (sense 5); †**fling-brain**, a person of flighty and hasty character; so †**fling-brained** *a.*

1554 in Foxe *A. & M.* (1583) II. 1459/1 A sort of flyng-braines and light heads, which were neuer constant in any one thyng. **1576** NEWTON *Lemnie's Complex.* (1633) 159 Their fickle heads, and flingbrained wits be easily allured and drawne into folly. **1885** *Athenæum* 24 Jan. 117/1 Chopin ..came when the fling period was drawing to an end.

fling (flɪŋ), *v.* Pa. t. and pa. pple. flung (flʌŋ). Forms: *Inf.* 4–6 **flyng(e**, 5 **flenge**, 4– **fling**. *Pa. t.* 4–8 (9 *dial.*) **flang**, 4–7 **flong**, (4 **flonc**), 6 **floong**, 4– **flung**. *Pa. pple.* 6–7 **flong**, 7 **flang**, 7– **flung**. [app. closely related to ON. *flengja*, MSw. *flängia*, MDa. *flænge* to flog (mod.Icel. *flengja*, Sw. *flänga*, Da. *flänge*, also *intr.* to move impetuously). As the E. verb is recorded only as strong, it is difficult to regard it as adopted from the Scand. wk. vb.; it may represent a prehistoric ON. **flinga*, of which *flengja* is a derivative.]

I. *intr.*

1. To move with haste or violence from or towards an object; to go or run violently or hastily; to dash, rush.

1300 *K. Alis.* 1165 Messangeris conne flyng, Into the halle byfore the kyng. *c* **1330** *Arth. & Merl.* 3916 Þe hors of baundoun lete þai frem & come flingand wiþ al her men. *c* **1435** *Torr. Portugal* 378 He fled a wey, ase he were wod, Flyngyng ase a fynd. **1556** J. HEYWOOD *Spider & F.* iv. 15 Full furiouslie he flang Towarde the flie. **1579** LYLY *Euphues* (Arb.) 88 There staying his words, he flang out of the dores. **1579–80** NORTH *Plutarch* (1676) 541 Posts came flinging to him from the Realm of Pontus. **1599** SANDYS *Europæ Spec.* (1637) 218 Unnaturall and rebellious Children, who have flung out of the Church. **1725** POPE *Odyss.* XXII. 334 Confus'd, distracted, thro' the rooms they fling. **1796** STEDMAN *Surinam* I. i. 20, I..angrily flung into the apartment. **1830** GALT *Laurie T.* VI. i. (1849) 253 He flung from me like a whirlwind. **1855** MOTLEY *Dutch Rep.* II. ii. (1866) 146 Granville..flung from the council-chamber. **1894** HALL CAINE *Manxman* I. i. 3 His son had flung out of the room.

b. with adverbs, as *away*, *forth*, *off*, *out*, etc.

c **1300** *K. Alis.* 1111 Alisaundres folk forth gon flyng, Fyve hundred in a rynge. *Ibid.* 5892 [They] Breken there the wal adoun; And in flunge in litel stounde. **1588** GREENE *Pandosto* (1887) 25 With that he flung away from his sonne in a rage. **1620** SHELTON *Quixote* I. III. iv. 142 Don Quixote ..did fling up and down among the sheep. **1633** BP. HALL *Hard Texts* 256 Do not venture to fling out from him as in a fury. **1712** ARBUTHNOT *John Bull* I. ix, Signior flang away out of the house in great disorder. **1836** IRVING *Astoria* 66 He concluded by flinging off from the party. **1849** MACAULAY *Hist. Eng.* viii, The Chancellor..flung away in a rage.

c. Of a missile or weapon: To be sent or driven forcibly or swiftly.

c **1300** *K. Alis.* 2749 Thorugh the heorte the launce flang. **1632** *Women's Rights* 333 They [the keys] flang out at the chamber window. **1856** MRS. BROWNING *Aurora Leigh* IX. 934, I flung closer to his breast, As sword that, after battle, flings to sheath.

†**2.** To make an onset or attack. *Obs.*

a. ***to fling together***: to close in fight; to engage in hand-to-hand contest.

c **1300** *K. Alis.* 6084 Bothe perty flang togedre. *c* **1380** *Sir Ferumb.* 674 Wiþ þe strokes þat þis frekes slente flyngande to-gader in fiȝte, Hur helmes & haberions þay to-rente. **1470–85** MALORY *Arthur* IX. vi. 347 They..drewe theire swerdes and flange to gyders as wood men.

b. To aim a stroke or blow (*at*); to hit *out*.

c **1380** *Sir Ferumb.* 583 So þikke he smot to Olyuer as he miȝte flynge. *c* **1400** *Rowland & O.* 830 Kyng Clariell.. flynges owte full fersely. *c* **1400** *Destr. Troy* 5253 He..flang at hym fuersly with a fyne swerde.

3. Of a horse or other animal: To kick and plunge violently, 'to fly into violent and irregular motions' (J.), to be unruly or restive. Also with *about*, *out*.

1375 BARBOUR *Bruce* VI. 143 He stekit the hors, and he can flyng. **1523** LD. BERNERS *Froiss.* I. clxii. 198 The horses whan they felt yᵉ sharpe arowes..flang and toke on so feersly, that many of them fell on their maisters. **1579** GOSSON *Sch. Abuse* (Arb.) 44 A Colt, giue him the bridle, he flinges about; raine him hard, and you may rule him. **1605** SHAKS. *Macb.* II. iv. 16 Duncans Horses..Turn'd wilde in nature, broke their stalls, flong out, Contending 'gainst Obedience. **1694** R. L'ESTRANGE *Fables* ccxxxvii, The same Humour of Kicking and Flinging at the Servant, took him again next Morning. **1815** SCOTT *Ld. of Isles* V. xxxi, The startling horses plunged and flung. **1862** in A. E. Lee *Hist. Columbus* I. 742 A good-natured..slap, at which the animal 'flung out' like a trip-hammer.

b. similarly of persons. Also, ***to fling out***: to break out into angry invective or complaint.

1531 ELYOT *Gov.* I. ii, Where they [the communes].. refuse to be brydled, they flynge and plunge: and if they ones throwe downe theyr gouernour [etc.]. **1575** J. STILL *Gamm. Gurton* IV. ii, There is the thing, That Hodge is so offended, that makes him starte and flyng. *a* **1605** MONTGOMERIE *Misc. Poems* vii. 20 The mair thou flings, the faster is the net. *a* **1694** TILLOTSON *Serm. 2 Pet.* iii. 3 Wks. 1735 I. 29 Their consciences are galled..this makes them winch and fling as if they had some mettle. *a* **1701** SEDLEY *Poems* Wks. 1722 I. 19 She like a wounded Otter flings and Rails. **1886** PAYN *Luck of Darrells* vii, I had rather she had flung out at me, as many a woman would do, than taken it as she did.

4. *Sc.* To caper, dance. (Cf. FLING *sb.* 4.)

1528 LYNDESAY *Dreme* Epist. 12 Sumtyme, in dansing, feiralie I flang. *a* **1572** KNOX *Hist. Ref.* IV. (1644) 374 They would have wished their Sonnes and Daughters rather..to have been exercised in flinging upon a Floore..then [etc.]. **1790** BURNS *Tam o' Shanter* 161 Rigwoodie hags wad spean a foal, Louping an' flinging on a crummock.

II. *trans.*

5. To throw, cast, toss, hurl. Frequently with adverbs, as *about*, *aside*, *away*, *by*, *out*, *up*, etc.

1375 BARBOUR *Bruce* XVI. 651 He evin apon his bak hym flang And with hym till the bat can gang. *c* **1420** *Pallad. on Husb.* I. 550 Fitches flynge Afore hem ofte. **1565** GOLDING *Ovid's Met.* VIII. (1593) 195 The bore..grunting flang his fome about. **1577** STANYHURST *Desc. Irel.* in Holinshed *Chron.* VI. 43 He floong them all in the fire. **1587** FLEMING *Contn. Holinshed* III. 1290/1 The boy there vpon flang vp his garland. **1593** SHAKS. *2 Hen. VI*, IV. viii. 15 Who loues the King..Fling vp his cap. **1607** —— *Cor.* II. i. 279 Matrons flong Gloues..Vpon him. *a* **1608** SIR F. VERE *Comm.* 8 They flang away their arms. **1647** C. HARVEY *School of Heart* xxxiv. 44 The door's flung off the hooks, the floor's unlay'd. *c* **1665** MRS. HUTCHINSON *Mem. Col. Hutchinson* (1846) 243 Which, when the governor read over, he flung by. **1711** BUDGELL *Spect.* No. 77 ¶9 He writes a Letter, and flings the Sand into the Ink-bottle. **1816** KEATINGE *Trav.* (1817) I. 237 He was dressed in long robes of white..muslin, one end of which was flung over his head. **1842** TENNYSON *Lady Clare* 40 Pull off, pull off, the brooch of gold, And fling the diamond necklace by. **1887** BOWEN *Virg. Æneid* II. 147 The King Bids them..aside his manacles fling.

b. To throw with violence or hostile intent; to hurl as a missile. ***to fling down***: to throw to the ground.

1375 BARBOUR *Bruce* XVII. 645 Ledderis to the ground thai flang. *c* **1500** *Maid Emlyn* in *Anc. Poet. Tracts* (Percy Soc.) 15 And if her husbande said ought, Loke what she sonest caught, At his heed she wolde it flynge. **1558** PHAER *Æneid* VI. Rij, Ioue almighty than, a firy dart on him down flang. **1593** SHAKS. *3 Hen. VI*, V. i. 51, I had rather chop this Hand off at a blow, And with the other, fling it at thy face. **1622** DRAYTON *Poly-olb.* xxii. (1748) 350 His approved men.. flang out such a flight Of shafts. **1700** S. L. tr. *Fryke's Voy. E. Ind.* 159, I..flung him upon his back. **1706** E. WARD *Hud. Rediv.* I. II. 11 Fling dirt enough, and some will stick. **1825** J. NEAL *Bro. Jonathan* I. 263 He tore off his jacket.. went up to Carter, and flung it in his face. **1879** FROUDE *Cæsar* xvii. 280 They..flung darts carrying lighted straw over the ramparts.

fig. **1713** ADDISON *Cato* I. i, I know thy generous Temper well; Fling but th' Appearance of Dishonour on it, It strait takes Fire. **1781** COWPER *Convers.* 153 Their nimble nonsense..Flings at your head conviction in a lump. **1840** CARLYLE *Heroes* ii. (1858) 234 These thoughts of his, flung-out unshaped. **1883** *Manch. Exam.* 29 Nov. 5/2 We are..not prepared to fling harsh words at any who do not at this moment agree with us.

c. *absol.* To throw or aim a missile *at*.

1635 QUARLES *Embl.* I. vii. 5 While death, that flings at all, Stands arm'd to strike thee down. *a* **1721** PRIOR *Cloe Hunting* 20, I and my Cloe take a nobler Aim: At human Hearts we fling, nor ever miss the Game. **1726** SHELVOCKE *Voy. round World* (1757) 132 They say they are sure of anything they fling at [with a lasso].

d. said of the sea, waves, wind, etc.

1684 BURNET *Th. Earth* I. vi. 75 Suppose a..heap of Rocks to fall..these would expel the waters out of their places with such a..violence as to fling them among the highest Clouds. **1781** COWPER *Expostulation* 273 The waves that..fling their foam against thy chalky shore. **1796** MORSE *Amer. Geog.* II. 146 This spring..is found to fling out about twenty-one tons of water in a minute. **1887** BOWEN *Virg. Ecl.* VII. 42 More cheap than the seaweed flung on the shore.

e. To throw (dice) from the box. Also *absol.*

1654 WHITLOCK *Zootomia* 423 Whole Armies then as truly having their lives played, as ever any private Souldier had, when condemned to fling for his. *a* **1700** DRYDEN (J.) 'Tis fate that flings the dice. **1712** ADDISON *Spect.* No. 543 ¶4 If one should always fling the same number with ten thousand dice. **1766** GOLDSM. *Vic. W.* ii, I only wanted to fling a quatre and yet I threw deuce-ace five times.

6. *refl.* To throw oneself; = sense 1.

1700 S. L. tr. *Fryke's Voy. E. Ind.* 321 A steep Rock; whence..the late King of Sittawack's Wife and Daughter flung themselves down headlong. **1812** J. WILSON *Isle of Palms* II. 75 He flings himself down on his rocky tomb. **1829** LYTTON *Devereux* I. iii, I flung myself into his arms and wept. **1874** GREEN *Short Hist.* ii. §6. 87 William flung himself..into the first boat he found.

b. *fig.* ***to fling oneself, one's energies,*** etc. ***into*** or ***upon***: to enter upon vigorously, take up with impetuous energy, abandon oneself to. Also, ***to fling oneself upon*** (a person): to confide oneself unreservedly to.

1842 MISS MITFORD in L'Estrange *Life* III. ix. 144 If they [Whigs] had flung themselves upon the people heartily and honestly, they might have set the Tories at defiance. **1865** CARLYLE *Fredk. Gt.* IX. xx. vii. 130 Goltz..honestly flings himself upon his task. **1874** GREEN *Short Hist.* ii. §7. 100 [He] returned to fling himself into the life of the young nobles of the time. **1880** MᶜCARTHY *Own Times* III. xxxv. 111 She had flung all her energies into the rebellion.

7. To extend (one's arms) with a sudden movement; *transf.* of a plant, etc. Also, to kick *up* (one's heels), etc.

1657 J. SMITH *Myst. Rhet.* 248 When in shew of disdainful contempt of a person or thing we fling up our nose. **1810** SCOTT *Lady of L.* I. xii, The pine-tree hung His shattered trunk, and..flung His boughs athwart the narrowed sky. *c* **1820** SHELLEY *Question* i, A shelving bank of turf, which.. hardly dared to fling Its green arms round the bosom of the stream. **1822** —— *Triumph of Life* 149 Maidens and youths fling their wild arms in air. **1884** TENNYSON *Becket* 23 The young colt..flung up her heels.

8. To cast scornfully (one's eyes, a glance) in a certain direction.

1654 WHITLOCK *Zootomia* 209 How many fling their Eyes off a Book, having but spied the name? **1821** CLARE *Vill. Minstr.* I. 121 One careless look on me she flung.

9. To emit, send forth, give out, diffuse (light, a sound, odour, etc.); to throw or cause to fall (light or shade) *on* or *over* an object. Also, ***to fling in*** (quot. 1704).

1632 MILTON *Penseroso* 131 When the sun begins to fling His flaring beams. **1634** —— *Comus* 989 West winds, with musky wing, About the cedarn allies fling Nard and casia's balmy smells. **1704** ADDISON *Italy* (1705) 217 The Entry at both Ends [of a subterraneous passage] is higher than the middle Parts of it, and sinks by degrees, to fling in more Light upon the rest. **1712–4** POPE *Rape Lock* II. 67 Ev'ry beam new transient colours flings. **1755** YOUNG *Centaur* v. Wks. 1757 IV. 231 This flings light on a part of Scripture, which has a cloud on it in some eyes. *c* **1800** K. WHITE *Poems* (1837) 141 No gale around its coolness flings. **1876** GREEN *Stray Stud.* 3 The huge beeches that fling their cool shade over the grass.

10. a. To put (any one) suddenly or violently *into* prison, confinement, or the like; 'to force into another condition, properly into a worse' (J.); also, †***to fling to death*** (obs.).

c **1400** *Destr. Troy* 8843 Alphenor the fuerse flung he to dethe. **1591** SPENSER *Teares Muses* 543 Squallid Fortune, into basenes flong, Doth scorne the pride of wonted ornaments. **1601** WEEVER *Mirr. Mart.* E vi, They were attacht, and into prison flong. **1762** H. WALPOLE *Vertue's Anecd. Paint.* (1765) I. iii. 53 Mabuse; whose excesses.. occasioned his being flung into prison. **1776** *Trial of Nundocomar* 66/1, I was, after the battle, flung into confinement. **1849** MACAULAY *Hist. Eng.* I. 98 Laud was flung into the Tower.

b. To bring up or dispatch (a body of troops) by a sudden or rapid movement; to cause (troops) to fall *on* (the enemy).

1707 FREIND *Peterborow's Cond. Sp.* 55 His Lordship found Methods to fling 500 Men into the Town. **1893** SAYCE *Higher Criticism* (1894) 426 He had flung his army on the western conspirators.

11. †**a.** Of an animal: To cast or shed (its coat) (*obs.*). **b.** To throw away, cast aside (as useless or burdensome). *rare.*

a **1547** SURREY *Descr. Spring, Songes & Sonn.* (1585) 2 b, The Bucke in brake his winter coate he flinges. **1847** TENNYSON *Princess* II. 48 You likewise will do well, Ladies, in entering here, to cast and fling The tricks, which make us toys of men.

12. To throw down, throw on the ground; *spec.* in wrestling. Of a horse: To throw (his rider) off his back.

1767 COWPER *Let.* 13 July, Poor Mr. Unwin, being flung from his horse as he was going to his Church. **1783** AINSWORTH *Lat. Dict.* (Morell) IV. s.v. *Aleii Campi*, Where Bellerophon wandered when flung by Pegasus. *a* **1797** H. WALPOLE (Webster) His horse started, flung him, and fell upon him. **1825** J. NEAL *Bro. Jonathan* I. 257 If he 'flung' Carter, he would have to fight him afterwards. **1863** TENNYSON *Grandmother* iii, Never a man could fling him; for Willy stood like a rock.

b. *fig.* To give a fall to, cause to fall, overthrow. Also *Sc.*, to jilt.

1790 MORISON *Poems* 152 (Girl speaks) Had I that maxim kept I'd ne'er been flung. **1808** JAMIESON *Fling*, to baffle, to deceive. **1828** WEBSTER *Fling* v. 6 To baffle; to defeat; as, to fling a party in litigation. **1889** *Tablet* 7 Dec. 897 An opportunity to fling the Ministry.

13. *slang.* To get the better of, cheat, swindle, 'do'; to cheat *out of* (money, etc.).

1749 GOADBY *Carew* 146 One of the Gentlemen proffered to lay a Wager he could not fling Dr. Glanfield. **1760** C. JOHNSTON *Chrysal* (1767) IV. I. xii. 77 He finds..that he cannot fling his worthy associate out of the whole spoil. *Ibid.*, To try if there was any possibility for him to *fling* his ..mistress, and get the whole fortune himself. **1806** SURR *Winter in Lond.* (ed. 3) II. 63 If I had not been..monstrous lucky..we should have been flung. **1830** LYTTON *P. Clifford* xxxi, Bob..cries, 'Flung the governor out of a guinea!'

14. Used in many phrases and idiomatic expressions merely as a variant (more emphatic or expressive of greater violence) of *throw* or *cast* (see *esp.* CAST *v.* XIII); such are ***to fling aside***, to disregard, reject; ***to fling away***, to discard, dismiss; to throw away, squander, ruin; ***to fling down***, to throw on the ground, overthrow, demolish; ***to fling off***, to abandon, disown; to baffle in the chase, throw off the scent; ***to fling up***, to throw up (an earthwork); to give up, relinquish, abandon; also (*dial.*) to 'rake up' and utter as a reproach. ***to fling (anything) in one's teeth***: see CAST *v.* 65. ***to fling open***, to open suddenly or violently (also, ***to fling wide***); similarly, ***to fling to***, to shut suddenly or forcibly.

1610 SHAKS. *Temp.* II. i. 116 He trod the water Whose enmity he flung aside. **1874** GREEN *Short Hist.* vi. §4. 298 This resolve of Colet to fling aside the traditional dogmas of his day.

1613 SHAKS. *Hen. VIII*, III. ii. 441 Cromwel, I charge thee, fling away Ambition. **1849** MACAULAY *Hist. Eng.* I. 4 Of the western provinces..she was the last that was conquered, and the first that was flung away. **1865** DICKENS *Mut. Fr.* I. vi, Don't fling yourself away, my girl. **1873** BLACK *Pr. Thule* xxii. 371 Don't fancy I am flinging away a fortune out of generosity.

1587 *Mirr. Mag., Sir N. Burdet* lxiii, On euery syde full fast wee flang the French men downe. **1695** WOODWARD *Nat. Hist. Earth* II. (1723) 124 These are so far from raising Mountains, that they overturn and fling down some of those which were before standing.

1619 FLETCHER & MASSINGER *False One* IV. ii, You flung me off, before the court disgrac'd me. **1711–4** ADDISON *Spect.* (J.) These men are too well acquainted with the chace to be flung off by any false steps or doubles. **1848** THACKERAY *Van. Fair* xxv, He has flung us off; and leaves us to poverty.

1649 BP. REYNOLDS *Serm. Hosea* iv. 88 To goe from his word, and fling up his bargaine. **1654** WHITLOCK *Zootomia* 94 Should there be any occasion of flinging up new works about the lines of communication. **1661** PEPYS *Diary* 15 Sept., If she will not be ruled, I shall fling up my executorship. **1743** FIELDING *Wedding-day* II. vi, If you stay one moment longer, I'll fling up the affair. **1884** *Punch* 29 Nov. 263/2 I've had enough of this game and will fling up politics.

1858 LYTTON *What will he do* II. xii, You wrote to fling my churlish favours in my teeth. **1892** *Speaker* 29 Oct. 528/2 The elderly maxim about brevity being the soul of wit may be flung in my teeth.

1595 SHAKS. *John* II. i. 449 The mouth of passage shall we fling wide ope, And giue you entrance. **1711** ADDISON *Spect.* No. 110 ¶5 The Knight..ordered all the Apartments to be flung open. **1847** TENNYSON *Princess* VI. 314 Fling our doors wide! **1862** MRS. H. WOOD *Mrs. Hallib.* I. xxi, The young lady..flung-to the door and departed. **1885** MABEL COLLINS *Prettiest Woman* xii, When the dawn broke he flung open his window.

b. similarly with adj. as *compl. rare.*

1865 CARLYLE *Fredk. Gt.* IX. xxi. 268 There are a great many hands flung idle in the present downbreak of finance.

III. 15. *Comb.* (the verb-stem used attrib.), as **fling-brand** (*attrib.*), that kindles strife or makes mischief; **fling-dust**, **-stink**, a contemptuous name for a harlot.

1616 T. ADAMS *Sacrif. Thank.* 23 It would a little Coole the preternaturall heate of the fling-brand fraternitie, as one wittily calleth them. **1621** FLETCHER *Wild Goose Chase* IV. i, She is an English whore, a kind of fling-dust, One of your London light-o'-loves. **1679** T. TICKLEFOOT *Trial Wakeman* 7 That he was not President of the Benedictines, his Lordship affirmed from the Testimony of three Flingstinks.

flingee (flɪŋ'iː). *nonce-wd.* [f. FLING *v.* + -EE.] One at whom anything is flung.

1879 *Daily News* 5 July 4/6 The person roughly called to account by the schoolmaster was not the flinger but the flingee.

flinger ('flɪŋə(r)). [f. FLING *v.* + -ER¹.] One who flings, in various senses of the verb.

a. in *intr.* senses: A dancer; also, one who rushes *out of*. Of a horse: A kicker.

1500–20 DUNBAR *Poems* lxiii. 10 Musicianis, menstralis.. callandaris, and flingaris. **1519** HORMAN *Vulg.* xix. 170 This is a great kykar or a flyngar: and therfore I wyll nat come on his backe. **1599** SANDYS *Europæ Spec.* (1632) 219 Hæretickes and Schismatickes, flingers out of the Church. **1822** SCOTT *Pirate* ix, 'I suld hae minded you was a flinger and a fiddler yourself.'

b. *trans.* One who throws or casts. ***flinger out***: one who casts or drives out; an expeller.

1598 FLORIO, *Piombatore*..a violent flinger, a hurler. **1600** J. MELVILL *Diary* (1842) 52 *Episcoporum exactor*, the flinger out of bishops. **1673** F. KIRKMAN *Unlucky Citizen* Pref. A iij, I ought not to look on the stone, but the hand of the flinger. **1851** MRS. BROWNING *Casa Guidi Windows* I. 1015 Were it good For any pope on earth to be a flinger Of stones against these high-niched counterfeits?

flinging ('flɪŋɪŋ), *vbl. sb.* [f. FLING *v.* + -ING¹.]

1. The action of the vb. FLING in various senses.

1375 BARBOUR *Bruce* VIII. 324 The hors..ruschit the folk in thair flynging. **1570–6** LAMBARDE *Peramb. Kent* (1826) 415 King Henry the fourth..kept the Saddle in all this leaping and flinging. **1631** WEEVER *Anc. Fun. Mon.* 443 Himselfe..by the flinging of his horse was cast out of his sadle. **1727** BAILEY vol. II, *Flinging* is the fiery, unruly Action of an unruly Horse, or a kicking with the Hind-legs.

2. *concr.* The thing thrown, a missile.

1618 BOLTON *Florus* (1636) 315 Plying them what with darts, and all sorts of flingings..scattred them all.

3. *Comb.*, as **flinging-tree**: (*a*) the striking part of the flail; (*b*) 'a piece of timber hung by way of partition between two horses in a stable' (*Burns' Poems* 1800, Gloss.).

1785 BURNS *Vision* I. ii, The thresher's weary flingin-tree The lee-lang day had tired me.

flinging ('flɪŋɪŋ), *ppl. a.* [f. FLING *v.* + -ING².] That flings: **a.** Of a horse: That kicks, unruly. †**b.** Of the Fiend: Raging, rampant, turbulent (cf. quot. *c* 1435 in FLING *v.* 1). †**c.** *fig.* Of a fault: Fatal, damning.

a. *a* **1533** LD. BERNERS *Gold. Bk. M. Aurel.* (1546) F viij, A lusty horse fyerse and flingyng. **1585** HIGINS *Junius' Nomenclator* 47/2 *Equus calcitro*, A flinging or kicking horse.

b. *a* **1529** SKELTON *Howe the douty Duke of Albany* Poems II. 317, I render the, fals rebelle, To the flingande fende of helle. **1560** INGELEND *Disob. Child* F ij b, The flyinge and [? = flingand] fiende go with my wyfe.

c. *a* **1577** GASCOIGNE *Dan Barth.* x, Wks. (1587) 67 At last (alas) she was vntrue, Whych flinging fault, because it is not new..I maruell not.

flingy ('flɪŋɪ), *a. nonce-wd.* [f. FLING *sb.* + -Y¹.] Inclined to fling or move abruptly; jerky.

1838 *Fraser's Mag.* XVII. 689 There was..nothing springy nor flingy in her movements.

flink (flɪŋk). *U.S.* [? alteration of FLINCH.] *intr.* To behave in a cowardly manner.

1893 E. B. CUSTER *Tenting on Plains* xix. 388 All the boys done bully, but Corporal Johnson—he flinked.

flinkite ('flɪŋkaɪt). *Min.* [ad. G. *flinkit* (A. Hamberg 1889, in *Geol. Fören. Förhandl.* XI. 213), f. the name of Gustav *Flink* (1849–1931), Swedish mineralogist + -ITE¹.] A basic arsenate of manganese known only as greenish-brown crystals from Sweden.

1891 *Jrnl. Chem. Soc.* LX. I. 20 Flinkite, a hydrated manganese arsenate, occurs in the Harstigen mine, Pajsberg, Wermland. **1967** *Amer. Mineralogist* LII. 1603 Flinkite, Mn_2^{2} + Mn^{3} + $(OH_4)(AsO_4)$. *Ibid.* 1604 Both retzian and flinkite have formulae suggesting isotypy.

flint (flɪnt), *sb.* Forms: 1–2 **flint**, 3–4 *south.* **vlint**, **-ynt**, (4 **flent**, 5 **flynd**), 4–6 **flynt(e**, 3– **flint**. [OE. *flint* str. masc. = MDu. *vlint*, related to OHG. *flins* (MHG. *vlins*, mod.Ger. dial. *flins*), Da. *flint* str. masc., Sw. *flinta* wk. fem.; usually regarded as cogn. with Gr. πλίνθος tile.]

I. 1. a. A kind of hard stone, most commonly of a steely gray colour, found in roundish nodules of varying size, usually covered with a white incrustation. In early and poetic use often put for hard stone in general.

Chemically, it is one of the purest native forms of silica, and by modern mineralogists is classed among the chalcedonic varieties of that mineral.

a **1000** *Crist* 6 (Gr.) þæt þu..ʒesomniʒe side weallas fæste ʒefoʒe, flint unbræcne. *c* **1000** ÆLFRIC *Num.* xx. 11 He..sloh..þone flint, and þær fleow sona of þam flinte wæter. *c* **1175** *Lamb. Hom.* 129 þurh þisse tacne Moyses werp ut þet welle weter of þan herda flinte. **1377** LANGL. *P. Pl.* B. XIV. 64 And oute of þe flynte spronge þe flode þat folke & bestes dronke. *a* **1400–50** *Alexander* 4447 þat modire ws cried þat fourmed þe flode & þe flynt & þe faire lyndis. **1594** SPENSER *Amoretti* xviii, The firmest flint doth in continuance weare. **1758** JOHNSON *Idler* No. 96 ¶1 A pillar of flint in the rocks of Hanga. **1832** G. R. PORTER *Porcelain & Gl.* 28 Flint is silica in a state nearly approaching to purity. **1855** LONGF. *Hiaw.* IV. 163 Arrow-heads of flint.

b. As a type of anything hard or unyielding.

c **1320** *Sir Tristr.* 1451 þe deuel dragouns hide Was hard so ani flint. **1590** SPENSER *F.Q.* I. ii. 26 Hart of flint would rew The undeserved woes and sorrowes, which ye shew. **1606** SHAKS. *Ant. & Cl.* IV. ix. 16 Throw my heart Against the flint and hardnesse of my fault. **1814** SCOTT *Wav.* xlvi, Callum, flint to other considerations, was penetrable to superstition. **1853** C. BRONTE *Villette* xix, He struck on the flint of what firmness I owned.

2. a. This stone, or a fragment of it, with reference to its property of giving off sparks when struck with iron or steel. ***flint and steel***: an apparatus consisting of a piece of each of these substances used for procuring fire by the ignition of tinder, touchwood, etc.

a **700** *Epinal Gloss.* 805 *Petrafocaria*, flint. *c* **1050** *Gloss.* in Wr.-Wülcker 469 *Petra focaria*, fyrstan, flint. *c* **1330** *Amis & Amil.* 1321 Sir Amiloun, as fer of flint, With wrethe anon to him he wint. *c* **1450** *Golagros & Gaw.* 758 As fyre that fleis fra the flynt. **1589** R. HARVEY *Pl. Perc.* (1590) 20 When the steele and the flint be knockde togither, a man may light his match by the sparkle. **1606** SHAKS. *Tr. & Cr.* III. iii. 257. **1665** HOOKE *Microg.* 46 Sparks struck from a Flint and a Steel. **1794** MRS. RADCLIFFE *Myst. Udolpho* xxxi, Ugo found a flint, and the torch was lighted. **1814** SCOTT *Ld. of Isles* II. xxvi, As from the flint the fire, Flash'd forth at once his generous ire. **1833** L. RITCHIE *Wand. by Loire* 81 The flint and steel, which a French peasant carries for the service of his pipe.

fig. **1659** B. HARRIS *Parival's Iron Age* 35 His offers were as flints, out of which they drew fire. **1677** HORNECK *Gt. Law Consid.* vii. (1704) 422 My heart is all flint, but when.. struck sufficiently, it will then send forth holy fire.

b. A fragment of this stone used to kindle the powder in a FLINT-LOCK. Also, a piece of metal (usu. an alloy of misch metal with a base metal such as iron) used to produce a spark for the ignition of the fuel in a cigarette-lighter.

1660 BOYLE *New Exp. Phys. Mech.* xiv. 100 We..caus'd a piece of Steel to be made of the form and bigness of the Flint, in whose place we put it. **1679** LEVINZ in *Trial of White, & other Jesuits* 10 The Flint of the Pistol failed. **1752** J. B. MACCOLL in *Scots Mag.* Aug. (1753) 401/2 The..gun had an old wore flint in it. **1808** WELLINGTON in Gurw. *Desp.* IV. 49 Each soldier will have with him three good flints. **1811** BYRON *Hints from Hor.* 555 Dogs blink their covey, flints withhold the spark. **1833** *Regul. Instr. Cavalry* I. 30 In fixing the flint of Carbines..the flat side of it must be placed upwards or downwards. **1929** *Sears, Roebuck Catal.* Spring-Summer 471 Extra flints. For all lighters using a round flint. **1944** *N. & Q.* 30 Dec. 294/1 The *flint* used in petrol lighters is a cerium-iron alloy, and has very questionably taken over the name given..to lumps of silicon oxide found in chalk. **1971** *Grattan's Catal., Autumn/Winter 1971–2* 615 Ronson 'Comet VC40' Gas Lighter... Flick-top design for easy access to flints.

3. A nodule or pebble of flint. In early and poetic use often applied to any hard piece of stone.

c **1300** *Havelok* 2667 So that with alþer-lest dint Were al to-shiuered a flint. **1523** LD. BERNERS *Froiss.* I. xvii. 18 A ryuer ful of flynt and great stones. *c* **1611** CHAPMAN *Iliad* VI. 541 The flints he trod upon Sparkled with lustre of his arms. **1634** SIR T. HERBERT *Trav.* 3 They shaved their heads with flints and other stones. **1662** J. DAVIES tr. *Mandelslo's Trav.* 276 They use in their buildings, the flints, which they find by the Sea-side. **1740** DYER *Ruins Rome* 281 Those ancient roads, o'er whose broad flints Such crowds have roll'd. **1816** W. SMITH *Strata Ident.* 7 Knotty and irregular Flints. **1876** PAGE *Adv. Text-bk. Geol.* xviii. 340 Flints and other nodular concretions.

4. Phrases. ***as true as flint***, used to express firmness in allegiance. ***to get*** or ***wring water from a flint***, used to express extreme difficulty in doing something. ***to skin a flint***: a hyperbolical exemplification of avarice. (***to set one's face) like a flint***: firmly, steadfastly.

1382 WYCLIF *Ezek.* iii. 9 Y ȝaue thi face as an adamaunt, and as a flynt. *a* **1592** GREENE *George a Greene* Dram. Wks. II. 189 Faith, I see, it is as hard to get water out of a flint, as to get him to have a bout with me. **1597** *1st Pt. Return fr. Parnass.* I. i. 141 Hoping to wringe some water from a flinte. **1655** FULLER *Ch. Hist.* III. vi. §37 They would, in a manner, make pottage of a flint. **1847** MARRYAT *Childr. N. Forest* xi, As true as flint was Jacob Armitage. **1859** KINGSLEY *Misc.* (1860) I. 321 Set his face like a flint. **1884** BESANT *Childr. Gibeon* II. xxxi, Just as the toper squeezes the empty bottle and the miser skins the flint.

II. Transferred senses.

5. A flint-like substance.

a. (see quot. 1892). **b.** (see quot. 1847.) **c.** short for *flint-hide* (see 10).

a. **1709** BLAIR in *Phil. Trans.* XXVII. 102 They [horns].. have a Protuberance arising from it [the Scull], and filling up their Capacity, if cavous, commonly call'd the Flint. **1892** *Northumbld. Gloss.*, *Flint*, the core of an animal's horn.. The term is likewise applied to the hard excrescence formed on a cow's head where a horn has been knocked off.

b. **1847** HALLIWELL, *Flints*, refuse barley in making malt.

c. **1885** C. T. DAVIS *Leather* I. i. 54 Dry flint is a thoroughly dry hide that has not been salted.

6. An avaricious person, a miser, skin-flint. *rare.*

1840 DICKENS *Old C. Shop* vii, The money which the old flint—rot him—first taught me to expect that I should share with her at his death.

7. *slang.* (See quots.)

1764 *Chron.* in *Ann. Reg.* 66/2 Journeymen taylors..who, refusing to comply with the masters terms, and the regulations of the magistrate, call themselves Flints, in contradistinction to those who submit, and are in derision stiled by the first Dungs. **1778** FOOTE *Tailors* II. v, Shall the Flints, like them [Dungs], e'er sink to slaves? **1820** SCOTT *Ivanhoe* xliii, To see whether the heroes of the day are, in the heroic language of insurgent tailors, flints or dunghills. **1859** *Slang Dict.* s.v., *Flint*, an operative who works for a 'society' master—full wages.

III. *attrib.* and *Comb.*

8. a. *simple attrib.* (or *adj.*): Of flint.

c **1175** *Lamb. Hom.* 81 Me sculde in þe ehtuþe dei þet knaue child embsniþen mid ane ulint sexe. **1552** HULOET, Flynt, or of flynte, *siliceus.* **1711** HEARNE *Collect.* (Oxf. Hist. Soc.) III. 163 A Flint Weapon and divers other Antiquities. **1851** D. WILSON *Preh. Ann.* (1863) II. III. iii. 87 Flint arrows and other primitive weapons. **1884** DAWSON in *Leisure H.* Aug. 490/2 Flint knives were used for sacrificial and surgical purposes.

b. ellipt. for FLINT-GLASS.

1755 *Oppenheim's Patent Specif.* No. 707 The compounds of the flint contain two parts of lead, one part sand, and one part of saltpetre or borax. **1816** J. SMITH *Panorama Sc. & Art* II. 211 French glass..is found to produce the greatest quantity of electricity next to English flint.

c. ellipt. for *flint corn* (see 10).

1802 J. DRAYTON *View South-Carolina* 137 The flint is more hard and nourishing. **1857** *Trans. Ill. Agric. Soc.* III. 63, I plant the white flint. It is rather on the gourd seed order. **1883** *Encycl. Brit.* XV. 309/2 The 'Flint' varieties are most common east of Lake Erie and north of Maryland. **1909** [see DENT *ppl. a.* 3]. **1947** *Ann. Missouri Bot. Garden* Feb. 17 There is as yet little exact evidence as to how

completely the gene combinations introduced from the northern flints have been broken up in modern dent corns.

9. General comb.: **a.** simple attrib., as ***flint-fragment***, ***-nodule***, ***-rock***, ***-tile***. **b.** objective, as ***flint-chipper***, ***digger***, ***-worker***; ***flint-using*** adj. **c.** instrumental, as ***flint-headed***, ***-wrapped*** adjs. **d.** parasynthetic and similative, as †***flint-edged***, ***-eyed***, †***-grey***, ***-hard***, †***-hardy*** adjs.

1872 *Amer. Naturalist* VI. 208 Unfinished specimens suggest that variety was continually aimed at by the '*flint chipper'. **1809** *Sporting Mag.* XXXIII. 263 A *flint-digger on the new Brighton road. **1665** DRYDEN *Ind. Emperor* III. iii, Lay your *flint-edged weapon by. **1898** *Westm. Gaz.* 30 Mar. 1/3 A tall, solemn, shy, *flint-eyed young man. *a* **1000** *Riddles* iv. 19 (Gr.) *Flintgræȝne flod. **1933** W. DE LA MARE *Fleeting* 51 A still quiet challenge Fills her dark, her *flint-grey eyes. **1951** S. SPENDER *World within World* 126 The sun-bathers [were] lying in profusion on the flint-grey grass. **1594** J. DICKENSON *Arisbas* (1878) 77 Heart more *flint-hard then beating waues haue wrought On sea-washt rockes. **1606** N. BAXTER *Man Created* in Farr *S.P. Jas. I* (1848) 238 The braine.. Both maters, and the *flint-hardie scull. **1843** 'R. CARLTON' *New Purchase* I. 2 Shadows of branching antlers and *flint-headed arrows caused many a darkness in his path. **1884** DAWSON in *Leisure H.* Aug. 490/2 They used flint-headed arrows for shooting birds. **1879** SIR G. G. SCOTT *Lect. Archit.* I. 220 The Romans.. were successful in employing.. the *flint nodules of Kent. **1871** PALGRAVE *Lyr. Poems* 77 As honey from the *flint-rock shed. **1428** in Heath *Grocers' Comp.* (1869) 6 Chalke, *flint-tyles and estriche boarde. **1894** *Academy* 18 Aug. 120/3 The old *flint-using folk. **1876** D. WILSON *Preh. Man* iii. (ed. 3) 79 The whole region.. is rich in remains of the old *flint-workers. **1646** G. DANIEL *Poems* Wks. 1878 I. 12, I stood A verie Statua.. Not *Flint-wrapt Niobe, more stone did rise.

10. Special comb.: **flint-coal** (see quot.); **flint-core** (see quot. and CORE *sb.*^{1} 5); **flint corn**, the name of certain varieties of maize, esp. *Zea mays* var. *indurata*, having very hard kernels; **flint-find**, a discovery of flint implements; **flint-flake**, a 'flake' or chip of flint used in prehistoric times as a cutting instrument; **flint-folk**, people who, in prehistoric times, used flint implements; **flint-gravel**, gravel containing flints; **flint-gun**, a gun with a flint-lock; **flint-head**, an arrow-head made of flint; †**flint-heart** *a.* = next; **flint-hearted** *a.*, hard-hearted; **flint-hide** (see quot.); **flint-knacker** = next; **flint-knapper**, one who fashions flints to any desired shape; so **flint-knapping**, fashioning flints (for gun-locks, etc.); **flint-man**, one of the 'flint-folk'; **flint-mill**, (*a*) *Pottery*, a mill in which calcined flints are ground to powder for mixing with clay to form slip for porcelain; (*b*) *Mining*, 'a mode formerly adopted for lighting mines, in which flints studded on the surface of a wheel were made to strike against a steel and give a quick succession of sparks to light the miner at his work' (Knight); †**flint-moving** *a.*, that would move a heart of flint; **flint paper** (see quot. 1962); also *ellipt.*; **flint-paring** = *flint-skinning*; **flint-pit**, a pit from which flint has been taken; **flint-rope**, the stem of the sponge *Hyalonema Sieboldii* (Cass.); **flint-skinning**, *fig.* the action of 'skinning a flint', parsimonious saving; **flint-soot** (see quot.); **flint-sponge**, the sponge *Hyalonema mirabilis* (*Cent. Dict.*); **flint-wall**, 'a wall made of broken flints set in mortar, and with quoins of masonry' (Knight); **flint-ware**, U.S. name for STONE-WARE, q.v.; **flint-wheat** (see quot.); **flintwood**, a name in New South Wales for *Eucalyptus pilularis*; †**flint-wort**, a name for aconite, suggested by Pliny's statement that it grows on bare rocks (*nudis cautibus*).

1841 HARTSHORNE *Salopia Antiqua* 427 **Flint Coal* a coal measure so called, partly from its hardness, and partly from reposing upon a siliceous rock. **1865** *Athenæum* 7 Jan. 23/2 Small arrow-heads and *flint-cores, from which such articles had been flaked, were found. **1705** R. BEVERLEY *Virginia* (1722) 126 The one [grain] looks as smooth, and as full as the early ripe Corn, and this they call **Flint-Corn*. **1838** H. COLMAN *Rep. Agric. Mass.* 20 The best kinds of flint corn weigh 60 lbs. to the bushel. **1872** E. EGGLESTON *End of World* viii. 60 The relative merits of 'gourd-seed' and 'flint' corn. **1950** *New Biol.* VIII. 37 Flint corns (type of maize) have hard flinty kernels with a little soft starch inside. **1865** LUBBOCK *Preh. Times* iv. (1890) 111 '*Flint-finds'.. resembling in many respects these Danish 'coast-finds', are not.. unknown in this country. **1851** D. WILSON *Preh. Ann.* (1863) I. 175 Rude and unshapely fragments of flint, known by the name of *Flint-Flakes. **1879** LUBBOCK *Sci. Lect.* v. 155 The simplest flint-flake forms a capital knife. **1874** CARPENTER *Ment. Phys.* I. ii. §88 Races of men, which (like the old '*flint-folk') had made but a very slight advance in the arts of life. **1865** LUBBOCK *Preh. Times* xii. (1869) 408 All the *flint gravels in the South East of England have been produced by the destruction of chalk. **1837** W. IRVING *Capt. Bonneville* (1895) II. 133 Their *flint guns were at fault, and missed fire. **1849** E. E. NAPIER *Excurs. S. Africa* II. 161 This inconvenience—with a flint gun—is generally to be remedied without firing off the piece. **1796** MORSE *Amer. Geog.* II. 151 The *flint-heads of arrows made use of by the Caledonians. **1827** G. HIGGINS *Celtic Druids* 226 The Celts and flint-heads prove nothing. **1596** *Edw. III*, II. i. 14 Make a *flint-heart Scythian pitiful. **1560** BECON *Flower Godly Prayers* Pref. *Wks.* II. 166 b, No man, excepte he be *flint hearted, can rede the history.. without most large teares. **1632** MASSINGER & FIELD *Fatal Dowry* IV. iv, You prove ungrateful, Flint-hearted Charalois. **1885** A. WATT *Leather Manuf.* iii. 30 Dried Hides.. are sometimes called '*flint' hides, from their excessive hardness. **1879** *Encycl. Brit.* IX. 325/2 In 1876 there were 21 *flint knappers in Brandon. **1887** *Illustr. Lond. News* 15 Oct. 468 The.. almost extinct trade of *flint-knapping. **1872** BAGEHOT *Physics & Pol.* (1876) 100 We are dealing with people capable of history.. not with pre-historic *flint-men. **1757** BRINDLEY in Smiles *Engineers* (1874) I. 146 A new *flint mill [in the Potteries]. *a* **1852** MOORE *Sylph's Ball* viii. 29 Musical flint-mills—swiftly played By elfin hands—that.. Gave out, at once, both light and sound. **1600** S. NICHOLSON *Acolastus* (1876) 36 And as I story my *flint-mouing wrong, Weepe thou. **1916** H. A. MADDOX *Paper* x. 137 *Flint papers and box enamels are burnished in the friction glazer. **1920** R. W. SINDALL *Paper Technol.* (ed. 3) xviii. 295 *Flint.*—Papers, usually coated, to which an extra polish has been imparted by friction with a long flat stone moving quickly to and fro across the surface of the paper. **1962** F. T. DAY *Introd. to Paper* 115/1 *Flint papers*, a base paper coated one side with a colour and afterwards hard burnished or flint glazed to produce a high gloss, water-proof surface. **1967** E. G. LOEBER *Suppl. Labarre's Dict. Paper* 25 *Flint*, also called *flint (glazed) paper*. *Ibid.*, *Flint paper*,.. an abrasive paper.. coated with ground flint-stone. **1860** MOTLEY *Netherl.* I. vi. 323 During this tedious *flint-paring, Antwerp.. was falling into the hands of Philip. **1891** D. WILSON *Right Hand* 62 A number of *flint-pits.. near Brandon. **1873** MISS BRADDON *Str. & Pilgr.* I. viii. 92 Her small economies, her domestic cheese-paring and *flint-skinning. **1577** B. GOOGE *Heresbach's Husb.* III. (1578) 137 Take *Flint soote, that is hard dryed vpon a Post or roofe, and beate it into powder. **1741** CHAMBERS *Cycl.* s.v. *Wall*, *Flint, or Boulder-Walls, are frequently used in divers parts for fence-walls. **1782** J. SCOTT *Ep. 1 Garden* 16 Where.. rough flint-walls are deck'd with shells and ores. **1859** *All Year Round* No. 32. 126 Turkish *flint-wheat is one of those recommended as 'a hardy, full variety, with.. a long, flinty, light-coloured berry'. **1884** A. NILSON *Timber Trees N.S.W.* 135 **Flintwood*, Eucalyptus pilularis. **1565** GOLDING *Ovid's Met.* VII. (1587) 94 a, A goblet ready filld With juice of *flint-woort venomous.

flint (flɪnt), *v.* [f. prec. sb.] *trans.* **a.** To fit (a gun) with a flint; to furnish or provide (a person) with a flint or flints. **b.** To pave (ground) with flints; in quot. *fig.*

1803 WELLINGTON in Gurw. *Desp.* II. 292 These parties will parade.. and then be completed to thirty-six rounds and well flinted. **1816** COL. HAWKER *Diary* (1893) I. 146 The same gun.. which was neither cleaned afresh nor even new flinted. **1834** LANDOR *Exam. Shaks.* Wks. 1846 II. 276/1 The groundwork and religious duty not being well rammer-beaten and flinted. **1848** J. GRANT *Adv. Aide-de-C.* xxv, Most carefully flinted and loaded.

†**flinted** ('flɪntɪd), *ppl. a. Obs.* [f. FLINT *sb.* + -ED^{2}; cf. MDa. *flinted* in sense 2.]

1. Of or consisting of flint.

1568 T. HOWELL *Arb. Amitie* (1879) 32 Then flinted stones and barked tree.. Shall waile my wofull hap by thee.

2. Hard, cruel, unfeeling.

1583 STANYHURST *Aeneis* III. (Arb.) 79 We the byrth place detest of flinted Vlisses. **1587** M. GROVE *Pelops & Hipp.* (1878) 35 Would it not moue a frozen heart yea flinted for to bowe.

†'**flintered**, *ppl. a. Obs. rare*$^{-1}$. [? for *flint-eared*; or f. FLINT + -ER^{5} + -ED^{1}.] (See quot.)

1523 FITZHERB. *Husb.* §34 Peeke wheate hath a red eare.. and oft tymes it is flyntered, that is to saye, small corne wrynkeled and dryed.

'**flintful**, *a. nonce-wd.* [f. FLINT *sb.* + -FUL.] = FLINTY *a.*

1576 R. L[INCHE] *Diella* (1877) 65 Thinking.. shee by his absence might at length intenerate her flintfull hart.

flint-glass. **1.** A pure lustrous glass, now made from a composition of lead oxide, sand, and alkali; originally made with ground flint or pebble as the siliceous ingredient.

1683 WORLIDGE in Houghton *Lett.* II. 42 A Pipe made of Chrystal, or Flint-Glass. **1799** G. SMITH *Laboratory* I. 171 Flint Glass is of the same general kind with that which in other places is called crystal glass. **1832** G. R. PORTER *Porcelain & Gl.* 138 The manufacture of flint glass was first begun in England in the year 1557. **1867** J. HOGG *Microsc.* II. i. 19 A lens of crown-glass will have a longer focus than a similar one of flint-glass.

†**2.** (with *a* and *pl.*) A vessel or other article made of this glass. *Obs.*

1675 *Sloane MSS.* 857. 18 Sept., Permission to Ravenscroft to export flint glasses.. to Ireland. **1708** *Brit. Apollo* No. 57. 2/1 Two Gentlemen sitting in a Tavern.. heard.. a flint Glass Crack. **1766** ENTICK *London* IV. 280 A glass-house for making flint-glasses.

3. *attrib.*

1683 WORLIDGE in Houghton *Lett.* I. 166 A Syphon.. made of a Crystal or Flint-glass Pipe. **1784** WATT in *Phil. Trans.* LXXIV. 343 A flint-glass retort. **1831** BREWSTER *Optics* ix. 82 The focal length.. of the concave flint-glass lens. **1871** tr. *Schellen's Spectr. Anal.* xix. 67 The flint-glass prism is replaced by one of bisulphide of carbon.

flintify ('flɪntɪfaɪ), *v.* [f. FLINT *sb.* + -(I)FY.] To turn to flint. Hence '**flintified** *ppl. a.*, '**flintifying** *vbl. sb.* or *ppl. a.*

1799 KIRWAN *Geol. Ep.* 447 There is no partial impregnation nor any gradation of the flintyfying operation. **1880** BLACKMORE *Mary Anerley* III. iv. 62 Rugged and flintified knobs and edges [of oysters].

flintless ('flɪntlɪs), *a.* [f. FLINT *sb.* + -LESS.] Without a flint or flints.

1810 *Sporting Mag.* XXXVI. 273 One of Forsyth's gun-locks, which, flintless, goes off by percussion. **1865** *Reader* 22 Apr. 461/1 A bed of comparatively flintless chalk overlies one with many flints.

'**flint-lock.** [See LOCK.] **a.** A gun-lock in which a flint, screwed to the cock, is struck against the hammer and produces sparks which ignite the priming in the flash-pan. Also *attrib.*, as ***flint-lock gun***, ***musket***. **b.** A gun fitted with this lock.

1683 SIR JAS. TURNER *Pallas Armata* 176 It were therefore good, that for the half of the Muskets (if not for them all) flint-locks were made. **1833** J. HOLLAND *Manuf. Metal* II. 89 The soldiers of that duchy [Brunswick] first obtained, in 1687, flint-locks, instead of matchlocks. **1887** *Whitaker's Almanack* 541 The old flint-lock musket became famous in the Peninsular War under the name of 'Brown Bess'.

Hence **flint-locked** *a.*, fitted with a flint-lock.

1885 *Century Mag.* XXIX. 684 The long flint-locked rifle.

'**flintstone.** [f. FLINT *sb.* + STONE.]

1. = FLINT *sb.* 1.

c **1340** *Cursor M.* 20897 (Fairf.) Soroufully þen fel he doun In liknes of flint-stane. **1375** *Cantic. de Creatione* 983 in *Anglia* I, Out of þe flynt ston Moyses dede ywis water out rennen. **1535** COVERDALE *Ps.* cxiii[i]. 8 The God of Iacob.. turned.. the flynt stone in to a sprynginge well. **1855** LONGF. *Hiaw.* XXI. 64 And the earth became as flint-stone.

2. = FLINT *sb.* 2, 3.

c **1400** MAUNDEV. (1839) v. 50 Men kutten the Braunches with a scharp Flyntston. *c* **1475** *Pict. Voc.* in Wr.-Wülcker 768/19 *Silex*, a flyntstone. **1535** COVERDALE *Isa.* l. 7, I haue hardened my face like a flynt stone. **1585** T. WASHINGTON tr. *Nicholay's Voy.* IV. xxix. 151 Prometheus.. was.. the firste that stroke fire out of the flint stone. **1638** SANDERSON *Serm.* II. 111 You may as soon squeeze water out of a flintstone. **1871** R. ELLIS tr. *Catullus* xxiii. 4 Each for penury fit to tooth a flint-stone.

flinty ('flɪntɪ), *a.* [f. FLINT *sb.* + -Y^{1}.]

1. Of or consisting of flint; derived from flint.

1591 SHAKS. *1 Hen. VI*, II. i. 27 Let vs resolue to scale their flinty bulwarkes. **1714** GAY *Trivia* I. 12 Earth from her Womb a flinty Tribute pays. **1799** KIRWAN *Geol. Ess.* 447 Pieces of fossil wood have been found penetrated with flinty matters. **1810** SCOTT *Lady of L.* I. xi, Each purple peak, each flinty spire, Was bathed in floods of living fire. **1891** T. HARDY *Tess* viii, Sometimes.. flinty sparks from the horse's hoofs outshone the daylight.

b. Full of flint-stones.

1626 BACON *Sylva* §599 The gathering up of Flints in Flinty Ground.. is no good Husbandry. **1802** PLAYFAIR *Illustr. Hutton. Th.* 108 Such a body of flinty gravel as is found about Kensington.

2. Resembling flint; **a.** in texture or in colour.

1641 BEST *Farm. Bks.* (Surtees) 99 Flinty wheate; that is, if yow bite a corne asunder with your teeth, yow shall see that the meale of it is of a darkish, bley, and flinty colour. **1779** J. MOORE *View Soc. Fr.* II. lv. 57 Black stones of a flinty texture. **1853** KANE *Grinnell Exp.* xxx. (1856) 258 We had to quarry out the blocks [of ice] in flinty, glassy lumps. **1859** [See *flint-wheat*, FLINT *sb.* 10].

b. Having the characteristic qualities of flint; hard, impenetrable, rugged.

1542 R. COPLAND *Galyen's Terap.* A. iij, The cause.. that before made the vlceres harde and flynty. **1602** MARSTON *Ant. & Mel.* I. Wks. 1856 I. 17 The flintie rocks groand at his plaints. **1697** DRYDEN *Virg. Georg.* III. 357 Rough upon the flinty Rock he lyes. **1847** EMERSON *Poems, Monadnoc* Wks. (Bohn) I. 435 The country's flinty face, Like wax, their fashioning skill betrays. **1871** BAKER *Nile Tribut.* xii. 202 The mare.. scattering the rounded pebbles.. from her flinty hoofs. **1884** *York Herald* 19 Aug. 7/2 All the new grain comes to hand in a flinty condition.

3. *fig.* Of a person or his heart: Obdurate, unfeeling, hard-hearted. (Cf. *stony*.)

1536 LATIMER *Let. to Cromwell* in *Serm. & Rem.* (1845) 372 If his heart be so stony, so flinty. **1601** SHAKS. *All's Well* IV. iv. 7 Gratitude Through flintie Tartars bosome would peepe forth. **1795** BURKE *Th. Scarcity* Wks. 1842 II. 250 The flinty heart and griping hand of base self-interest. **1829** CARLYLE *Misc.* (1857) I. 272 We ourselves have known the flintiest men, who professed to have wept over them. **1878** MISS BRADDON *Open Verd.* I. ii. 29 'Fathers have flinty hearts', retorted Kenrick lightly.

quasi-*adv.* **1580** LUPTON *Sivqila* 72 Their stonny hartes are so flintie harde.

b. Of immaterial things: Hard; harsh.

1613 *Uncasing of Machivils Instr.* 14 This is the flinty course of this our age. **1643** MILTON *Divorce* II. xvi. (1851) 103 The gracious.. not ruthlesse and flinty ordinance of mariage. **1888** *Star* 28 Nov. 2/5 Mr. George struck out sharp, strong, flinty sentences.

4. *attrib.* and *Comb.*, as ***flinty-looking*** adj.; **flinty-hearted** *a.*, (*a*) of a person: Hard-hearted; (*b*) Having a hard or flint-like core.

1626 MASSINGER *Rom. Actor* III. ii, If he were not A flinty-hearted slave, he could not use One of his form so harshly. **1845** LD. CAMPBELL *Chancellors* (1857) V. cxi. 192 The flinty-hearted father asked what settlement was to be made upon his daughter. **1860** *All Year Round* No. 48. 515 Three flinty-hearted potatoes. **1890** *Pall Mall G.* 29 Aug. 7/2 A dark flinty-looking grain rebounds from your face.

Hence '**flintily** *adv.*, in a flinty manner; '**flintiness**, the quality of being flinty.

1607 HIERON *Wks.* I. 362 When there is an vniuersall flintinesse in mens hearts. **1840** DICKENS *Old C. Shop* xi, Some people would have been all flintiness and granite. **1871** PROCTOR *Light Sc.* 290 The peculiar grittiness and flintiness of its structure. **1879** *Tinsley's Mag.* XXIV. 35 Her aunt was a flintily just woman.

flip (flɪp), *sb.*^{1} [? f. FLIP *v.*, with the sense of 'whipping up' into froth. Cf. mod.Norman patois *flip*, *phlippe*, cider mixed with brandy and spices (Moisy *Dict. du Patois Normand*), which

is probably of English origin. See Skeat in *Phil. Soc. Trans.* 1889.]

†**1.** The slimy scum rising to the surface of salt-pans. *Obs.*

1682 J. COLLINS *Making of Salt in Eng.* 31 The shallow Pans..are left open.. to carry away the Flip, or Slime in Currents.

2. A mixture of beer and spirit sweetened with sugar and heated with a hot iron. (Cf. *egg flip.*)

1695 CONGREVE *Love for L.* III. iv, Thus we live at sea; eat biscuit, and drink flip. **1709** *Brit. Apollo* II. No. 22. 3/1 The Gypsie With Flip and Geneve got most Damnably Typsie. **1755** *Mem. Capt. P. Drake* I. xiii. 99 The Sailors were plentifully supplied with their favourite Liquor Flip. **1820** L. HUNT *Indicator* No. 23 (1822) I. 180 With oceans of flip and grog. **1872** C. D. WARNER *Backlog Stud.* 16 In those good old days it was thought best to heat the poker red hot before plunging it into the mugs of flip.

3. *Comb.*: **flip-dog** (see quot. 1836); **flip-iron** *U.S.* = *flip-dog*.

1836 SMART, *Flip-dog, an iron heated to warm flip. **1851** S. JUDD *Margaret* II. xi. 164 Warm your nose with Porter's flip-dog. **1869** MRS. STOWE *Oldtown Folks* xxxvii. 480 Draw the *flip-iron from the fire and stir the foaming bowl. **1947** F. D. DOWNEY *Our Lusty Forefathers* 7 Shaking flip-irons in each other's face, as the saying went, 'at loggerheads'.

flip (flɪp), *sb.*[2] Also 7 phlip. [f. FLIP *v.*]

1. A smart stroke or blow, a fillip. Also *fig.*

1692 LOCKE *Toleration* III. iv. 105 A Phlip on the Forehead..may be Penalty enough. **1818** *Sporting Mag.* III. 29 Newton by a smart left-handed flip, drew the claret in profusion from his mouth. **1884** BESANT *Dorothy Forster* II. xiv. 64 The rubs and flips which we poor women have to endure from harsh masters.

2. a. A sudden jerk or movement; a flash or flicker of light.

1821 HAGGART *Life* (ed. 2) 23 Turning towards the prad [i.e. horse] Barney made a very unceremonious flip at the bit. **1867** F. FRANCIS *Angling* vi (1880) 225 This sometimes will require seven or eight 'flips'..to effect. **1873** G. C. DAVIES *Mount. & Mere* xiii. 98 A derisive flip of their white tails. **1881** BLACKMORE *Christowell* xli, Flips of reflected lightning here, there, and everywhere, shone upon the roadway.

fig. **1888** G. MOORE in *Fortn. Rev.* Feb. 249 Madame Bovary, with the little pessimistic flip at the end of every paragraph, is the most personal of books.

b. *Gunnery.* The springing of the barrel of a gun at the moment of discharge.

1896 W. W. GREENER *Gun* (ed. 6) xxiii. 546 Recoil ..'Jump' and 'flip' are secondary movements—vertical and lateral respectively. *Ibid.* 564 *Flip* is a term used to denote the lateral deflection of a rifle barrel due to the same or similar causes as the vertical deflection termed 'jump'. **1903** *Kynoch Jrnl.* June-July 101/2 The flip, or springing of the barrel may entirely counteract the increase in jump. **1904** *Ibid.* Jan.-Mar. 63 The flip was evidently not entirely vertical since the direction varied as well as the elevation. **1905** *Ibid.* Apr.-June 80 There is the probability that the 'jump' or 'flip' of the rifles will not be quite the same. **1925** G. BURRARD *Notes on Sporting Rifles* (ed. 2) 75 They do not take into account the effect of jump or flip. This varies in every individual rifle and barrel. **1960** *Times* 5 Mar. 9/5 A recoil carriage which allows full recoil of the gun, even at the pressures used, and permits 'flip'.

3. = FILLIP *sb.* 3.

1881 BLACKMORE *Christowell* xlvii, I must have a flip to my system.

4. A short flight in an aircraft; also, a trip in another form of conveyance; a quick tour on foot. *colloq.*

1914 H. ROSHER *In R.N.A.S.* (1916) 28 It was much too foggy for my trip to Hartlepool yesterday afternoon, but I went for a short flip around. **1920** *Blackw. Mag.* Feb. 167/2 The *Moewe* arrived, untouched, on 4th March, after a two months' 'flip'. **1929** *Daily Express* 7 Nov. 2/1, I went to Croydon and went up again for a short 'flip'. **1943** HUNT & PRINGLE *Service Slang* 32 *Flip*, a trip in an aeroplane or in a car. **1958** *Times* 16 June 12/4 He..promised her a flip in his five-metre yacht. **1959** *Vogue* Oct. 120 A quick flip around Fenwicks always delights us.

5. Applied to a person (see quots.). *slang.*

1942 BERREY & VAN DEN BARK *Amer. Thes. Slang* §398.3 *Impudent person,*..flip. *Ibid.* §410.3 *Flip*, a forward or flippant person. **1955** N. SHAPIRO *Hear me talkin' to Ya* 347 He's not a flip as far as business is concerned. **1958** *New Statesman* 6 Sept. 294/3 If you are not cool, you can be put down; you have lost your will and confidence. You are a flip and you are beat. **1961** 'I. ROSS' *Old Students never Die* (1963) iv. 60 'She's a flip... Nuts,' he translated, 'Loony. Off her rocker.'

6. Abbrev. of *flip side.*

1960 *Melody Maker* 31 Dec. 6/1 The same can be said of the flip, also featured in the film.

7. *Comb.* **flip jump**, a toe jump in figure skating; **flip side**, the reverse, or less important, side of a gramophone record; also *transf.*

1940 S. HENIE *Wings on my Feet* 163 A *flip jump..is done by placing the right toe-point to the right back outside edge at the finish of a left three. In this case, the left foot swings around, but on a close arc to the right, and you land as in a Salchow. **1960** M. V. OWEN *Fun Figure Skating* vii. 138 If you do add the half-turn, you will be doing a full 'flip jump', which lands on the ROB edge in the exact way that the waltz jump landed. **1964** 'J. NOEL' *Figure Skating for Beginners* ix. 92 The flip jump itself used to be known as the toe salchow or spot salchow. **1968** *Daily Tel.* 6 Dec. 15/6 She fell after attempting a double flip jump, but otherwise was always elegant and technically correct. **1949** *Down Beat* 11 Mar. 14 The *flip side (*South*) will be a shade slower but with the same general routine. **1962** *Spectator* 14 Dec. 945 A slice off the flipside. **1968** *Times Lit. Suppl.* 11 Apr. 377/1 The actual readings are on the flip side. **1971** *Guardian* 25 Mar. 14/4 A dogged courage..is the flip side of Mr Heath's best known vice. **1971** *Sunday Times* (Johannesburg) 28 Mar. 7/2 The manoeuvring, the muscling, the promoting and the hustling which is the flip-side of showbiz.

flip (flɪp), *a.*[1] orig. *dial.* and *U.S.* [f. FLIP *v.* (sense 5).] **a.** *s.w. dial.* (see quots.). Hence in standard use: glib, flippant. **b.** *U.S.* Voluble.

1847 HALLIWELL, *Flip*..(3) Nimble; flippant. *Devon.* **1863** W. BARNES *Dorset Dial.* 55 *Flip*, very kindly or friendly in talking. **1888** ELWORTHY *W. Somerset Wordbk.*, *Flip*, pliant, flexible, same as *Limber*. **1893** *Columbus* (Ohio) *Disp.* 13 Apr., She was disposed to be flip with her tongue. **1924** *Drama Mag.* (Chicago) Feb. 177/2 Doris is flip, exaggerated, and stagey—off the stage. **1935** *Time* 24 June 38/2 He is entirely too flip and smart-alecky. **1944** AUDEN *For Time Being* (1945) 110 Every martyrdom an occasion for flip cracks and sententious oratory. **1947** 'N. SHUTE' *Chequer Board* x. 290 He coloured hotly, and wished desperately for eloquence that he might make some flip and smart rejoinder, but no inspiration came. **1958** R. WILLIAMS in N. Mackenzie *Conviction* 78 How can anyone..use these new flip words for any attachment to learning or the arts? **1963** *Listener* 21 Mar. 529/2, I find it difficult to reconcile the authorship of the flip, alert opening scenes with the awful feyness of what followed. **1969** N. COHN *AWopBopaLooBop* (1970) xii. 104 The musicians fitted themselves sensibly to the situation—they kept things light and flip and sexy. **1970** *Times* 9 May 9/5 The word 'schizophrenia' is flung about today with flip facility.

†**flip**, *a.*[2] [? f. the vb.; cf. FLICKY, FLIG, FLIGGY, FLISK, FLETCH.]

1723 *Lond. Gaz.* No. 6181/4 Stolen..a..Gelding..with ..what is called a Flip Tail.

flip (flɪp), *v.* [Prob. onomatopœic; cf. FILLIP *v.* Not in Johnson, Todd, or Webster 1864.]

1. *trans.* To put into motion with a flip or fillip, to 'shoot'; to toss (a coin) with a flip. Also absol. *to flip* (*up*) (? U.S.): to toss up.

1616 W. BROWNE *Brit. Past.* II. iii. 200 As when your little ones Doe twixt their fingers flip their Cherry-stones. **1665** GLANVILL *Scepsis Sci.* xix. 122 When it's under question, 'twere as good flip cross and pile, as to dispute for't. **1839** THACKERAY *Major Gahagan* i, She..would flip the rice into her mouth with her fingers. **1861** THORNBURY *Turner* II. 123 Making a pellet of it, and flipping it into his eye. **1867** F. FRANCIS *Angling* iii. (1880) 81 Flip a few bits of ground-bait in. **1879** *N.Y. Tribune* 4 Oct., (Cent.) The two great men could flip up to see which should have the second place. **1885** 'HUGH CONWAY' *Family Affair* I. xii. 229 Flipping the ash from his cigarette. **1945** J. STEINBECK *Cannery Row* xxvii. 118 They had to flip for who would go to the party first. **1971** 'A. BLAISDELL' *Practice to Deceive* x. 146 You want to flip for who does the report?

2. = FILLIP *v.* 2.

1594 LYLY *Moth. Bomb.* V. iii, Like ivie he her fast does hold..And flips her too. **1676** D'URFEY *Mad. Fickle* V. ii, Sirra, you shall be hufft and cufft, and flip'd and kick'd, Sirra, if you talk of private Rooms. *a* **1695** WOOD *Life* (1848) 188 Then the scholars made some resistance by flipping them on the cheek.

3. *intr.* To make a flip or fillip with the fingers. Also quasi-*trans.* To give a flip with (the finger).

1852 DICKENS *Bleak Ho.* xxv, He revenges himself by flipping at their ears. **1859** LANG *Wand. India* 34 'My heart is as hard as this rock,' she said, flipping her finger against the granite.

4. *trans.* To move or throw about with a flip or sudden jerk.

1712 STEELE *Spect.* No. 376 ¶2 To twirl, flip or flirt a Fan. **1867** F. FRANCIS *Angling* vi. (1880) 225 You must..flip your fly to and fro to shake the water out and so dry it for another cast. **1884** *Leeds Mercury* Wkly. Supp. 15 Nov. 1/6 The carriole-driver..is seated so low that the tail is constantly flipped over the reins.

5. *intr.* To move with a flip or jerk; to step lightly and nimbly.

1863 KINGSLEY *Water Bab.* 105 He..began flirting and flipping up and down and singing. **1881** BLACKMORE *Christowell* iv, Still there were lapses in the vigilance of the brook, where a lady, with her skirts up, might flip through. **1886** *Science* VII. 263 When the water had disappeared, eight mackerel were found flipping about the deck.

6. a. *trans.* To strike smartly and lightly (with a whip, or the like); to flick.

1861 PYCROFT *Agony Point* II. iv. 45 Minnie laughed and flipped her old friend with her glove. **1863** W. BARNES *Dorset Dial.* 55 *Flick* or *Flip*, to snap lightly with a whip. **1866** R. M. BALLANTYNE *Shifting Winds* viii. (1881) 76 Taking up his whip..and flipping the toe of his boot with it.

b. *intr.* To make a sharp stroke *at.*

1893 S. GRAND *Heavenly Twins* (1894) 332 Viciously flipping at the flowers, as he passed, with the stick he carried.

7. *slang.* To shoot with a pistol, etc.

1812 J. H. VAUX *Flash Dict.*, *Flip*, to shoot. **1834** H. AINSWORTH *Rookwood* IV. iii, 'Flip him, Dick—fire or I'm taken,' cried King.

8. To fly in an aircraft. *colloq.* or *slang.*

1915 H. ROSHER *In R.N.A.S.* (1916) 41, I crashed into the atmosphere first thing this morning and flipped around for 55 minutes.

9. In full *to flip one's lid*, *wig*. To be or become wildly excited or enthusiastic; to go wild, lose one's head. *slang* (orig. *U.S.*).

1950 *Neurotica* Autumn 44 If I'm not right back don't flip. **1951** *Jrnl.* (Ithaca) 30 Jan. 6/6 Present war emergencies.. have been too much for local government officials. I fear they have flipped their lids. **1951** *N.Y. Times Bk. Rev.* 2 Dec. 50/2 The funniest book of the lot is enough to make a reader 'flip' or 'flip his lid'. **1952** C. BROSSARD *Who walk in Darkness* viii. 53 He flipped his wig when it was finished and they took him to a sanatorium. **1961** R. BLOCH *Blood runs Cold* (1963) 156 Mitch and his crowd didn't flip for jazz, but he'd come on strong with the bingos. **1960** B. CRUMP *Good Keen Man* 183 As he spoke one of the dogs sank his teeth into a tender part and the bull flipped his lid completely. **1960** *Time & Tide* 24 Dec. 1599/1 Does he make me flip my wig! **1967** *Boston Globe* 18 May 18/1 (Advt.), Our food and service are great. Our decor's delightful. Your club treasurer will flip over our low rates. **1969** 'R. MACDONALD' *Goodbye Look* iii. 23 She's a phoney blonde... I can't understand why he would flip over her.

10. The vb-stem in comb., as **flip chart** orig. *U.S.*, (a sheet of paper on) a display pad, erected on a stand and bound so that each page (usu. containing prepared information) can be turned over at the top to show the next.

1956 *Time* 25 June 31/2 Through demonstrations, *flip charts, radio talks and movies narrated in Quechua,.. 100,000 *campesinos* have learned the uses of chemical fertilizers. **1963** *Sci. News Let.* 18 May 320/3 *Automatic flip chart*, useful to advertisers, salesmen and teachers, automatically flips display charts, talks and show products. By plugging in the device the speaker can stand, sit or walk anywhere in the room and flip the pages automatically by pressing a button. **1985** *Computer Bull.* Mar. 21/2, I remember people being horrified when the first thing I had in my office in Number Ten was a flipchart.

flipe (flaɪp), *sb. north.* Also 6 flepe, 6–9 flype. [cf. Du. *fleb, flep*, a forehead-cloth worn by women, Da. *flip* lap, protruding piece (of a shirt, etc.), lip of a wound, mod.Icel. *flipi* a horse's lip; cf. also next vb., from which the senses in 2 are derived.]

1. A fold or flap; the flap or brim of a hat.

1530 PALSGR. 552/2, I tourne up the flepe of a cap. **1571** *Wills & Inv. N. Counties* (Surtees) I. 361, Vj cappes wth flypes in y[e] neke iiij *s.* *a* **1689** W. CLELAND *Poems* (1697) 12 With good blew Bonnets on their Heads; Which on the one side had a flipe, Adorn'd with a Tobacco pipe. **1796** W. MARSHALL *Yorksh.* (ed. 2) II. 319 *Flipe* (of a hat); the brim. **1828** BEWICK *Mem.* (1862) 38 In what king's reign his hat had been made was only to be guessed at, but the flipes of it were very large. **1868** ATKINSON *Cleveland Gloss.*, *Flipe*, the brim of a hat.

2. *dial.* (See quots.)

1847 HALLIWELL, *Flipe*, a flake of snow. **1892** *Northumbld. Gloss.*, *Flipe, Flype*, a thin piece, a piece of skin torn off. To take off in flypes, is to take off in thin pieces.

Hence **flip(p)ed** *ppl. a.*, having a flap.

1886 *Pall Mall G.* 4 June 11/1 A Jew, in a flipped hat of mottled straw.

flipe (flaɪp), *v.* Chiefly *Sc.* Also **flype, flip.** [? f. prec. sb. (which however is not recorded so early); cf. MDa. *flippe* to skin.]

1. *trans.* To strip off (the skin, etc.); to peel, flay. Also, † *to flipe off.* *Obs.* exc. *dial.*

c **1400** *Destr. Troy* 954 He..fflypit of the ffese. **1724** RAMSAY *Gent. Sheph.* IV. i, And ten sharp nails..Can flype the skin o' ye'r cheeks out o'er your chin. **1813** W. LESLIE *Agric. Surv. Nairn* Gloss., To *Flyp*, to ruffle back the skin. **1827** TENNANT *Papistry Storm'd* 210 Great faulds o' capper aff were flypit. **1892** *Northumbld. Gloss.* s.v., 'Aa flyped him' figuratively used, means 'I robbed or stripped him'.

†**2.** To turn up or down, to fold back; also, to turn inside out. Also with *up*. *Obs.*

1530 PALSGR. 552/2 I flype up my sleves, as one dothe that intendeth to do some thynge. *c* **1538** LYNDESAY *Supplic.* 97 Thair faldingis flappis about thair feit, Thair laithlie lyning furthward flypit. **1637–50** Row *Hist. Kirk* (1842) 451, I used often to flype up the lids of my eyes. **1788** E. PICKEN *Poems* Gloss., *Flype*, to turn outside in. **1847** HALLIWELL, *Flip up*, to turn up one's sleeves.

3. *Comb.*, **flipe-wool** *dial.* (Hawick): = *skin-wool.*

Hence **fliped** *ppl. a.*, of a fleece: Torn off bodily.

1888 *Daily News* 10 Sept. 2/6 Wool..fliped fleeces, 8½*d.*

†'**fliperous**, *a. Obs. rare.*

1611 COTGR. s.v. *Coquette*, A pratling or proud gossip; a fisking, or fliperous minx.

flip-flap ('flɪpflæp), *adv.*, *sb.* and *a.* [onomatopœic reduplication of FLAP, expressive of repeated oscillating movement.]

A. *adv.* With a repeated flapping movement.

1583 STUBBES *Anat. Abus.* I. (1879) 51 Then they goe flip-flap in the winde. **1775** in ASH. **1894** CROCKETT *Raiders* 35 Flounders fried in oatmeal..with their tails jerking Flip, flap, in the frizzle of the pan.

B. *sb.*

†**1.** Something that 'goes flip-flap' (see A.), e.g. a hanging piece of cloth, a fan, a fly-flapper. *Obs.*

1529 SKELTON *Elynour Rummyng* 514 Couer thy shap Wyth sum flyp flap. **1598** FLORIO, *Ventaglio*..a flip flap or any thing to make wind with. **1600** DEKKER *Old Fortunatus* in Dodsl. *O. Pl.* (1816) III. 127–8 If I hear any gingling but of the purse-strings that go flip, flap..would I were turn'd into a flip-flap and sold to the butchers. **1611** COTGR., *Esventoir*, a fanne, flip-flap.

†**2.** A frivolous woman: = FLAP *sb.* 9. *Obs.*[−1]

1702 VANBRUGH *False Friend* I, The light airy flipflap, she kills him with her motions.

3. *slang.* **a.** 'A kind of somersault in which the performer throws himself over on his hands and feet alternately'; also, 'a peculiar rollicking dance indulged in by costers' (*Slang Dict.* 1864). **b.** In sailors' use: 'The arm' (Barrère & Leland 1889). Cf. FLIPPER *sb.*[2] 2. **c.** A kind of firework, a cracker.

a. **1676** *Character Quack Doctor* 5 He danc'd a Saraband with Flip flaps, and Sommersets. **1727** GAY *Fables* xl. 31 The tumbler whirles the flip-flap round, With sommersets

he shakes the ground. **1764** GARRICK in G. Colman, Jun. *Posth. Lett.* (1820) 256 Flip flaps, and great changes without meaning. **1851** D. JERROLD *St. Giles* xxxi. 324 This.. iniquitous world—a world of flip-flaps and sumersets.

c. 1885 *Pall Mall G.* 5 Nov. 4/1 To-night..the sound of the obtrusive and saltatory flip-flap will be heard in the streets of Great Britain.

d. In a place of amusement or the amusement section of an exhibition, etc., a machine with long moving arms by which passengers are raised on platforms (see quot. 1908).

1908 *Daily Chron.* 3 Apr. 7/2 The..huge steel arms [are] 150 ft. in length, much like the main shaft of a crane, greatly magnified... These arms will be slowly raised until their extremities cross in the air, 150 ft. above the level, and then each will complete the semi-circle. Suspended from..the hand of each steel arm will be a car containing passengers... The flip-flap is built on the cantilever principle with heavy counter weights. **1922** C. SIDGWICK *Victorian* xxii, He is going to have millions of Japanese lanterns and a Flip-Flap and an open air café like at Earl's Court. **1937** *Evening News* 2 Feb. 8/6 Those who were young enough..for such delights thirty years ago must have been surprised to learn that the Flip-Flap of Franco-British Exhibition fame is still in existence.

4. *U.S.* 'A kind of tea-cake' (Farmer).

1876 BESANT & RICE *Gold. Butterfly* xviii, As we sat over her dough-nuts and flipflaps.

C. *adj.* That 'goes flip-flap' (see A.).

1841 *Blackw. Mag.* L. 635 Music..with..butterfly flip-flap flights, and die-away cadences. **1888** *Spectator* 7 July 934 That easy imitation of French flip-flap brush work which is so fashionable at the present time.

Hence **ˈflip-flap** *v.*

1599 NASHE *Lenten Stuffe* Wks. (Grosart) V. 255 The sly sheepe-biter..summer setted & flipt flapt it twenty times aboue ground. **1894** HALL CAINE *Manxman* IV. xii. 245 Nancy Joe went flip-flapping upstairs.

flip-flop (ˈflɪpflɒp), *sb.* [onomatopœic reduplication; cf. FLIP-FLAP *adv.*, *sb.* and *a.* and FLOP.] **a.** The 'flap' of the ear. **b.** The sound of a regular footfall. *nonce-uses.*

1661 K. W. *Conf. Charac., Informer* (1860) 47 We will stop the mishapen hols widdowed of their flip-flops..least there..still he retaine also too much of the faculty of enterance. **1889** J. K. JEROME *Three Men in Boat* 168 When he heard the regulation flip-flop approaching.

c. A somersault. Cf. FLIP-FLAP *sb.* 3 a. *U.S.*

1902 G. H. LORIMER *Lett. Merchant* xvii. 245 And when a fellow's turning flip-flops up among the clouds, he's naturally going to have the farmers gaping at him. **1929** *Liberty* 30 Nov. 43/1 Turning hand-springs and flip-flops all over the sawdust covered floor. **1946** *Gunnison* (Colo.) *News-Champion* 2 May 1/2 The convertible Ford coupe.. missed a narrow bridge..turned a flip-flop in the air and came to a stop right side up in waist-deep waters. **1969** *New Yorker* 12 Apr. 100/2 Every time Lind or any other astronaut opens his mouth, the entire space industry turns flip-flops.

d. As advb.

1904 H. G. WELLS *Food of Gods* II. i. 145 She..passed, flip-flop, within three yards of them.

e. *Electronics.* Either of two types of electronic switching circuit: (*a*) one that passes from a stable to an unstable state and back again in response to a triggering pulse; (*b*) one that has two stable states and makes a single transition from one to the other in response to a triggering pulse.

1935 *Wireless Engineer* XII. 606/2 The earliest accounts of the device, which is sometimes called the 'flip-flop', are by Eccles and Jordan. **1946** *Math. Tables & other Aids to Computation* II. 100 The basic electronic memory device of the ENIAC is the flip-flop or trigger. **1964** F. L. WESTWATER *Electronic Computers* ii. 27 If a pulse is supplied to the lowest flip-flop in the counter the number 1 will be registered. **1966** *New Scientist* 3 Nov. 242/3 The cell contains its own version of an electronic 'flip-flop' circuit, a two-tube circuit which is stable when either tube is conducting, but not when both are. **1971** *New Scientist* 11 Mar. 551/3 Flip-flops are widely used in computers.

f. A plastic or rubber sandal consisting of a flat sole and straps. Also *attrib.*

1970 *Observer* 15 Mar. 6/3 Milligan has a beard and wears flip-flops with jeans. **1971** M. POLLAND *Package to Spain* xii. 152 'She had flip-flops with white daisies on the front of them.' 'Flip-flops?'..'Sandals. Beach sandals all made of plastic.' **1971** W. J. BURLEY *Guilt Edged* i. 18 She wore.. blue jeans and flip-flop sandals.

Hence **flip-flop** *v. intr.*, to go, proceed, act, etc., with a flapping sound; also *trans.*, to turn (something) *over*. So **flip-flopping** *vbl. sb.*

1897 *Outing* (U.S.) XXX. 176/1, I could hear a vigorous flip-flopping going on beyond the weeds, and I knew the captive was a trout. **1924** W. DEEPING *Three Rooms* xxxv. 313 He [*sc.* a person distempering a wall] grew quite jaunty and confident, flip-flopping with considerable dexterity. **1940** F. D. DAVISON in B. James *Austral. Short Stories* (1963) 59 Wallabies flip-flopped out of your way as you rode. **1968** J. D. WATSON *Double Helix* xxvi. 197 Both pairs could be flipflopped over and still have their glycosidic bonds facing in the same direction.

flippancy (ˈflɪpənsɪ). [f. FLIPPANT: see -ANCY.] The quality of being flippant; *esp.* disposition to trifle, frivolity; occas. in earlier use, Volubility.

1746 H. WALPOLE *Lett. H. Mann* (1834) II. clxix. 176 The famous orator Henley is taken up for treasonable flippancies. **1789** MRS. PIOZZI *Journ. France* I. 8 It filled up my notions of French flippancy agreeably enough. **1807** tr. *Goede's Trav.* II. 183 A continued flippancy of chit-chat in the boxes. **1808** *Med. Jrnl.* XIX. 15 He..with asperity and flippancy adverted to a remarkable case I had written on nearly two years back. **1874** L. STEPHEN *Hours in Library* (1892) I. vii. 268 Effeminate prejudices and mere flippancies draped in elaborate rhetoric. **1882** MISS BRADDON *Mt. Royal* I. ii. 64 Why, Jessie, you are generally the very essence of flippancy.

flippant (ˈflɪpənt), *a.* Also 7 **flippent**. [app. f. FLIP *v.* (sense 5). Cf. FLIP *a.* used *dial.* in senses 1 and 2 below; an ablaut-var. of the root, with related meaning, occurs in ON. *fleipr* babble, *fleipa* (Sw. dial. *flepa*) to talk foolishly.

The suffix may possibly be an alteration of the ME. ppl. ending *-inde* -ING[2], or the word may have been formed in 16th c. on the analogy of ppl. adjs. in -ANT, such as the heraldic *trippant*.]

†**1.** Nimble, moving lightly or alertly; easily moved or managed, light to the hand; pliant, flexible, limber. *Obs.*

1622 MABBE tr. *Aleman's Guzman D' Alf.* I. 73 It is a bird of the flippantst wing, which as it moueth with most nimblenesse, so it doth the greatest mischiefe. **1677** EARL ORRERY *Art of War* 26 Targets, though very flippent ones, have not only resisted the Push of the Pikes, but also [etc.]. *Ibid.* 27 The Pike..is carried tapering, to poise it the better, and thereby renders it the more flippent for those who use it. **1895** *Windsor Mag.* July 21 'She weer flippant on 'er feet that night..an' tored hoff as fast as a wind-hover.'

†**2.** Of the tongue: 'Nimble', voluble. Hence of persons: Ready in the use of words, speaking freely, fluent, talkative, voluble. Of conversation or discourse: Fluent, sparkling. *Obs.*

1605 CHAPMAN *All Fooles* V. i, As for your mother, she was wise, a most flippant tongue she had. *a* **1677** BARROW *Serm.* I. 157 It becoming them not..to be dumpish..but.. pleasantly flippant and free in their speech. **1677** MIEGE *Eng.-Fr. Dict.*, A flippant discourse, *un discours coulant.* **1711** ADDISON *Spect.* No. 247 ¶9 An excellent Anatomist has promised me to dissect a Woman's Tongue, and to examine whether there may not be in it certain Juices, which render it so wonderfully voluble or flippant. *a* **1784** JOHNSON in *Boswell* an. 1765, She [Mrs. Thrale] is more flippant; but he has ten times her learning. **1794** GOUV. MORRIS in Sparks *Life & Writ.* (1832) I. 427 The wines are good and the conversation flippant.

†**b.** In bad sense: Impertinently voluble. (Cf. 4.)

1677 MIEGE *Eng.-Fr. Dict.*, A flippant and forward woman, *une coquete une libertine.* **1727** GAY *Fables* xii. 18 The husband's sullen, dogged, shy, The wife grows flippant in reply.

†**3.** Sportive, playful. *Obs.*

1711 STEELE *Spect.* No. 260 ¶1, I am now as..flippant if I see a pretty Woman, as when in my Youth. **1719** D'URFEY *Pills* (1872) VI. 156 Like Love's sprightly Goddess she's flippant and gay. **1784** COWPER *Task* VI. 315 The squirrel, flippant, pert, and full of play.

4. Displaying unbecoming levity in the consideration of serious subjects or in behaviour to persons entitled to respect.

1724 WATERLAND *Farther Vind.* Wks. IV. 12 It very ill becomes this gentleman..to grow so exceeding flippant. **1781** MAD. D'ARBLAY *Diary* 26 June, I was reading Sherlock's flippant but entertaining letters. **1836** H. ROGERS *J. Howe* i. (1863) 14 That..peculiarity, which a flippant and superficial philosophy has sometimes charged upon the Scriptures as a blemish. **1838** DICKENS *Nich. Nick.* xix, The flippant contempt with which the guests regarded her uncle. **1877** MRS. FORRESTER *Mignon* I. 251 The flippant way in which she has treated his attentions.

5. *absol.* passing into sb. A flippant person.

In first quot. Richardson seems to have thought the word was of It. origin, and fabricates a pseudo-It. plural.

[**1748** RICHARDSON *Clarissa* VI. lxxviii. 291 It concerns me, however, not a little, to find our affair so generally known among the *Flippanti* of both sexes.] **1791** COWPER *Judgm. Poets* 22 They gentle called, and kind and soft, The flippant and the scold. **1835** *Fraser's Mag.* XII. 269 The flippants and pragmatics who infest all the highways of society. **1850** TENNYSON *In Mem.* cx, The stern were mild when thou wert by, The flippant put himself to school And heard thee.

Hence **ˈflippantly** *adv.*, in a flippant manner; **ˈflippantness**, the quality of being flippant.

1727 BAILEY vol. II, *Flippantness.* **1758** H. WALPOLE *Lett. H. Mann* (1834) III. cccxxii. 268 It is time for me to check my pen that asks so flippantly. **1791** BOSWELL *Johnson* an. 1774 (1816) II. 298 *note*, Mrs. Thrale asked him somewhat flippantly, 'Why do you put him up in the counting-house?' **1817** J. GILCHRIST *Intellect. Patrim.* 84 The flippantness of French philosophers. **1880** G. MEREDITH *Trag. Com.* (1881) 49 Flippantly tapping at the doors of thought.

†**ˈflipper**, *sb.*[1] *Obs. rare*$^{-1}$. In 4 **fliper**. [f. FLIP *v.* + -ER[1].] A flippant and unreliable person.

c **1400** *Cato's Morals* in *Cursor M.* App. iv. 7. 1669 For-soþ flipers and alle fals flaters I rede sore þou fle.

flipper (ˈflɪpə(r)), *sb.*[2] [f. FLIP *v.* + -ER[1].] **1. a.** A limb used to swim with; e.g. any limb in a turtle; in a seal or walrus, *esp.* the fore-limb; the fore-limb of a cetacean; the wing of a penguin; the fin of a fish.

1822 MANBY *Voy. Greenland* 39 The fore paws or flippers [of the seal]. **1868** *Nat. Encycl.* I. 955 Their [penguins'] wings are true flippers. **1885** WOOD in *Longm. Mag.* V. 408 The fore limbs of the whale are technically named flippers.

b. A rubber attachment to the foot used for underwater swimming, esp. by frogmen.

1945 *Newsweek* 17 Sept. 113 (Advt.), He'd organized a spear-fishing party, and this is the proper regalia—glass-front mask, flipper shoes, and a..spear. **1953** *New Yorker* 29 Aug. 17/2 Such paraphernalia..as flippers,..Aqua-Lungs, and snorkels. **1959** *Spectator* 28 Aug. 251/1 He pulled on rubber flippers to join his wife in the water. **1970** *New Yorker* 19 Sept. 104/2 Clumping around in frogman flippers.

2. *transf.* The hand.

1832 MARRYAT *N. Forster* xlii, I like to touch the flipper of one who has helped to shame the enemy. **1840** BARHAM *Ingol. Leg.*, *St. Gengulphus* xx, They cut off his 'flippers', As the Clerk, very flippantly, term'd his fists. **1867** SMYTH *Sailor's Word-bk.* s.v., The boatswain's mate exulted in having 'taken a lord by the flipper'.

3. *Theat.* 'Part of a scene, hinged and painted on both sides, used in trick changes' (Farmer).

1928 A. E. KROWS *Equipm. Stage Prod.* iii. 40 The wing-piece for an exterior setting is usually..hinged in two parts. .. If it is very tall, a small extra section..called a 'flipper', is hinged to one of the larger parts.

4. *U.S.* = FLAPJACK (*Cent. Dict.*).

5. *Cricket colloq.* (See quot. 1967.)

1959 J. FINGLETON *Four Chukkas to Australia* 36 He [*sc.* Benaud] varied his attack with a leg-break..a well-disguised bosie and an excellent flipper. **1967** PARTRIDGE *Dict. Slang* Suppl., *Flipper*, a top-spinner delivered by the bowler with an extra flip of the fingers.

6. *Comb.*, as ***flipper-like*** adj.

1889 P. H. EMERSON *Eng. Idylls* 133 Holding their shaking sides with their brawny flipper-like hands.

flipper, *v.* [f. FLIPPER *sb.*[2]] *intr.* To move by means of flippers.

1955 A. ROSS *Australia 55* ix. 122, I saw green turtles surfacing sadly in pairs, soon flippering away as if in disappointment at the weather. **1969** *Look & Learn* 15 Mar. 35/1 Knowing that his harpoon gun was useless against two such killers, Frankie flippered for the raft.

ˈflipper-de-flapper. *Obs.* exc. *dial.* [Echoic.] (See quot. 1847).

1640 *King & poore North. Man* 36 in Hazl. *E.P.P.* IV. 307, I nere saw such a flipper de flapper before. **1847** HALLIWELL, *Flipper-de-flapper*, noise and confusion caused by show. *Sussex.*

flipperty-flopperty (ˈflɪpətɪˈflɒpətɪ), *a.* That 'goes flip-flop'; loose, dangling.

1859 SALA *Tw. round Clock* (1861) 83 She is a gaunt, awkward girl, in a 'flibberty-flobberty' hat. **1869** TROLLOPE *He knew*, etc., xii, He had..one of those flipperty-flopperty things on his head, that the butcher-boys wear.

flippery (ˈflɪpərɪ). *rare.*

†**1.** = FRIPPERY.

a **1616** BEAUM. & FL. *Wit without M.* II. v, If I be brought ..to carry..any gentle Lady of the Laundry..behinde my gelding, with all her Streamers, Knapsacks, Glasses, Gugawes, as if I were a running flippery.

2. Flippancy.

1819 *Metropolis* III. 86 He had a flippery in writing, *et voila tout.* **1863** OUIDA *Held in Bondage* I. vi. 131 'Mustn't she be a horrid, heartless, little bit of flippery?'

†**ˈflippet.** *Obs. rare.* [f. FLIP; cf. FLAPPET.] A narrow streamer.

1640 PARKINSON *Theat. Bot.* 291 With a long peece or flippet as it were, at one side of the top.

flipping (ˈflɪpɪŋ), *adv.* and *ppl. a. slang.* [FLIP *v.*] Used as a substitute for a strong expletive. Usually derog. (Cf. BLINKING *ppl. a.* 4.)

1911 D. H. LAWRENCE *White Peacock* II. ix. 347 'Ain't it flippin' 'ot?' drawled Creswell. **1948** C. DAY LEWIS *Otterbury Incident* i. 2 Flipping heroes, ain't we all? **1954** A. HECKSTALL-SMITH *Eighteen Months* xii. 145, I suggested that..he might take up the game professionally. He shook his head. 'Too much flippin' trainin',' he sneered. **1959** *Spectator* 20 Nov. 713/3 While terms of approval..change rapidly with the fashion, terms of disapproval (blinking.. flippin' awful..) show very little alteration. **1971** *Guardian* 24 Aug. 5/1 They wax indignant about pornography but when it comes to doing anything about it they are bone flipping lazy.

ˈflip-top, *a.* [f. FLIP *v.* + TOP *sb.*[1]] orig. *U.S.*

1. Of a package, etc.: that has a top which can be flipped open, usu. by pulling the lid or tab upwards and back.

1955 *Sales Management* 1 Apr. 93/1 (*heading*) New Marlboro bids for smokers with crush-proof, flip-top package. **1970** *New Yorker* 24 Oct. 58 (*caption*) They open flip-top can Diet Pepsi. **1976** *Evening Post* (Nottingham) 17 Dec. 9/3 (Advt.), Half recommended price Addis flip-top kitchen bin. **1982** S. B. FLEXNER *Listening to Amer.* 151 By 1953..a new 'crush proof, flip-top box' was being talked about.

2. Of a table: having a top with additional sections at either end that can be drawn or folded outwards to increase the surface area.

1956 *House Beautiful* Jan. 55 Flip-top table... When needed to serve a buffet or dinner for two, its folded top swings open to make a 70" surface. **1973** *Washington Post* 13 Jan. E14/2 Flip top, cocktail and end tables are also available in this collection. **1974** J. KEATS *Of Time & Island* i. 8 The bookcase, the three flip-top tables..all were dark brown.

flird, *sb. Sc.* [Possibly repr. OE. *fleard* trifle: see FLERD. But cf. Du. *flarden* splinters, shivers.] 'Anything that is thin and insufficient, as a thin piece of cake, board, etc.'; 'any thing viewed as a gaudy toy'; in *plural*, 'worn-out clothes', 'vain finery' (Jam.).

1788 E. PICKEN *Poems* 62 Thae flirds o' silk, brought owre the seas.

†**flird**, *v.* *Sc. Obs.* Also 6 flyrd. [Of obscure origin; cf. FLEER *v.*] *intr.* ? To sneer, gibe.

Jamieson has the senses 'to bounce, brag, also to flirt' as current in modern Sc. use.

1500–20 DUNBAR *Poems* lvii. 9 Sum flyrdis; sum feynȝeis; and sum flattiris.

†'**flirdom.** *Obs.* *Sc.* In 6 flyr-, 7 flirdom(e. [? Connected with prec.] Bounce, bluster, pretence; also, a braggart.

c **1450** HENRYSON *Poems* (1865) 142 Schir Tod, tak ye the flyrdome, and the fon, I haif respite ane yeir. *c* **1500** *Auchinleck Chron.* (1819) 15 þan þaj come with a flyrdome & said þat þaj come for na Ill of him ne his childer. **1508** KENNEDIE *Flyting w. Dunbar* 494 A myten, full of flyting, [the] flyrdom lyke. *a* **1605** MONTGOMERIE *Flyting w. Polwart* 90 Foule flirdome wanfucked, tersell of a taide!

flire, flirr(**e**, obs. ff. FLEER *v.*

flirt (flɜːt), *sb.* Also 6 flirte, flyrt, 7 flert, 6–8 flurt, (7 flurte). [f. next.]

†**1.** A smart tap or blow, a rap, fillip. (Also *fig.*). *Obs.* exc. *dial.*

1577 BRETON *Flourish upon Fancy* (Grosart) 18/1 Thus euerie one would haue a flyrt, ere I could get out free. **1621** FLETCHER *Pilgrim* III. iii, One flurt at him, and then I am for the voyage. *c* **1691** *Bagford Ball.* (1878) App., I'll give you a good flurt on the Ear. **1855** E. WAUGH *Lanc. Life* (1857) 29 Aw caren't a flirt abeawt it. **1888** *Sheffield Gloss.*, *Flirt*, a slight blow or fillip with the thumb and finger.

2. A sudden jerk or movement, a quick throw or cast, a darting motion. Of wind: A gust.

c **1590** GREENE *Fr. Bacon* vii. 119 Out with your blades.. Haue a flurt and a crash. **1666** SPURSTOWE *Spir. Chym.* (1668) 116 As weak as the Grashoppers who give only a small flirt upwards, and then fall down to the Earth again. **1699** DAMPIER *Voy.* II. III. 15 There may be some-times some small flurts of a Westerly Wind on these Coasts. **1711** ADDISON *Spect.* No. 102 ¶5 The next Motion is that of unfurling the Fan, in which are comprehended several little Flirts and Vibrations. **1789** G. WHITE *Selborne* xl. (1853) 140 Hedge-sparrows have a remarkable flirt with their wings. **1830** N. S. WHEATON *Jrnl.* 205 He.. tosses out his arm with a flirt and a flourish. **1860** HUGHES *Tom Brown at Oxf.* in *Macm. Mag.* II. 58 With a joyful squeak and flirt of his hind-quarters in the air.

†**3.** A smart stroke of wit, a joke, a jest; a gibe, jeer, scoff. *Obs.*

1549 COVERDALE, etc. *Erasm. Par. Eph.* v. 4 Vayne flirtes and iestes. **1613** SIR E. HOBY *Counter-snarle* 21 His next flurte is at my witt. *a* **1655** in *Anecd. & Trad.* (Camden) 24 She had a flurt at them presently. *a* **1713** ELLWOOD *Autobiog.* 101 He would sometimes.. cast out a jesting Flurt at me. **1726** SWIFT *Lett.* Wks. 1841 II. 584 Open reproaches, jesting flirts and contumelious terms.

†**b.** Of a person: One who mocks or finds fault.

1602 W. BAS *Sword & Buckler* xlv, The prescise flirts of eu'ry trades-mans stall Whose busie tongues.. defiles Our honest sort with vomited reviles.

†**4.** A fickle, inconstant person.

1577 BRETON *Flourish upon Fancy* (Grosart) 8/1 Fie on thee Fancie, flatteryng flyrt. **1689** T. PLUNKET *Char. Gd. Commander* 2 Nor is he one that's Valiant at a spurt; No, no, he's far from being such a flurt.

†**5.** A woman of a giddy, flighty character; 'a pert young hussey' (J.).

1562 PHAER *Æneid* IX. Cc ij, Your study chief is daunse in pampryng feasts with giglet flirts. **1621** BURTON *Anat. Mel.* I. ii. IV. i. (1651) 143 A peevish drunken flurt, a waspish cholerick slut. **1623** B. JONSON *Time Vind.* Wks. (Rtldg.) 636/1 To salute the Skirts Of her, to whom all Ladies else are Flirts. **1751** JOHNSON *Rambler* No. 84 ¶3 My aunt told me she was a forward flirt. **1774** W. WHITEHEAD *Song for Ranelagh, Plays & Poems* II. 224 Ye belles, and ye flirts, and ye pert little things, Who trip in this frolicsome round.

†**b.** A woman of loose character.

1600 BRETON *Pasquil's Fool's-cap* 22/2 Call'd a Foolish flirt.. When all the world is witnesse to her shame. **1676** ETHEREDGE *Man of Mode* II. i. (1684) 17 An idle Town Flurt, with a painted Face. **1703** THORESBY in *Ray's Lett.* (1718) 328 A Flurt, a light House-wife.

6. One who flirts, or plays at courtship. **a.** Said of a woman.

1748 RICHARDSON *Clarissa* I. ii. 8 She was not one of those flirts.. who would give pain to a person that deserved to be well-treated. **1782** WOLCOTT (P. Pindar) *Odes to R. Academicians* v. Wks. 1812 I. 24 How else could he have caught that handsome flirt? **1796** JANE AUSTEN *Pride & Prej.* viii. (1813) 202 A flirt too, in the worst and meanest degree of flirtation. **1880** WEBB *Goethe's Faust* III. viii, To bend the dainty little flirt To be conformable to your commands.

b. Said of a man.

a **1732** GAY *Distress'd Wife* II. Wks. (1772) 293 A flirt, One who gives himself all the airs of making love in public. **1863** OUIDA *Held in Bondage* I. xii. 274 Sabretasche had an universal reputation as a most unscrupulous flirt.

c. A person to flirt with.

1779 *Gentl. Mag.* XLIX. 357 The General [Howe] has found another Desdemona at Philadelphia.. who is now his Excellency's flirt. *a* **1817** JANE AUSTEN *Lady Susan* vii. (1879) 217 When I have inspired him with greater respect for me.. he may be an agreeable flirt. **1848** THACKERAY *Van. Fair* xxv, General Tufto is a great flirt of mine.

7. *Watch-making.* 'A lever or other device for causing sudden movement of mechanism' (Britten).

1786 *Trans. Soc. Encourag. Arts* IV. 175 The usual way of discharging the chime is by a flirt. **1884** F. J. BRITTEN *Watch & Clockm.* 124 The independent seconds hand is generally discharged by a flirt taking into a pinion.

8. *Comb.*, as **flirt-wort** (see quot.).

1882 FRIEND *Devon Plant-n.*, *Flirtwort*, *Pyrethrum Parthenium*, a name apparently nearly died out, but which was common in South Devon some years ago as the designation of the Feverfew.

flirt (flɜːt), *v.* Also 6 flyrtt, 6–8 flurt, 7 flert. [Onomatopœic; cf. *flick*, *flip*, *flerk*, *spurt*, *squirt*.]

1. *trans.* To propel or throw with a jerk or sudden movement; often, to propel by a blow from the finger-nail released from the thumb. Also with *away*, *off*, *out*. Cf. FILLIP *v.* 1.

1583 STANYHURST *Aeneis* III. (Arb.) 84 Scylla.. lurcketh, Close and slilye spying, too flirt thee nauye to rock bane. **1602** DEKKER *Satiromastix* Wks. 1873 I. 235 Tis thy fashion to flirt inke in everie mans face. **1612** DRAYTON *Poly-olb.* vi. 88 A little wand That bended end to end, and flerted from the hand Farre off itself doth cast. **1710** SWIFT *Tatler* No. 238 ¶3 That Sprinkling which some careless Quean Flirts on you from her Mop. **1735** J. MOORE *Columbarium* 5 To keep 'em from flirting the Grain over on the Floor. **1812** G. COLMAN *Br. Grins, Lady of Wreck* I. xviii, Flirting his sweet and tiny shower Upon a milk-white April flower. **1875** DARWIN *Insectiv. Pl.* xvii. 406 Minute particles of glass.. disappeared so suddenly that I thought I had flirted them off. **1876** GEO. ELIOT *Dan. Der.* II. xviii, 'I don't care what you call it', said Mab, flirting away her thimble.

b. With immaterial *obj.*; *esp.* to blurt *out* (something spoken).

1641 *Vox Borealis* Dj, Then the Foole, he flirts out his folly. **1649** G. DANIEL *Trinarch.*, *Rich. II*, cccxli, The Arch-Bishop still Flirting Divinitie against the Throne. **1652** *News fr. Low-Countr.* 11 If carping Momes shall flurt in Podex's face A Flout, to blur his Matter with Disgrace. **1889** MARK TWAIN (Clemens) *Yankee Crt. K. Arthur* (Tauchn.) II. 51 Of course I whet up now and then and flirt out a minor prophecy.

†**2.** To give (a person) a sharp, sudden blow or knock; to rap, strike. Cf. FILLIP *v.* 2.

1563–87 FOXE *A. & M.* (1631) III. XII. 881/1 Flirting him vnder the chin, and on the eares. **1611** COTGR., *Nasarder*, to fillip; to rap, or flirt, on the nose. **1631** QUARLES *Samson* Poems (1717) 327 Some gibe and flout him.. Whilst others flurt him on the starting lips.

3. To give a brisk, sudden motion to; to flick. Also with *out*, *up*. *to flirt a fan*: to open and close it with a jerk, to wave it smartly.

1665 EARL DORSET *To all you Ladies* viii, Whilst you.. Perhaps permit some happier man To kiss your hand or flirt your fan. **1748** SMOLLETT *Rod. Rand.* I. 343 She.. flirted her fan with such a fury. **1761** MRS. F. SHERIDAN *Sidney Bidulph* II. 62 One of the windows was already up, and I flurted up the other. **1798** BLOOMFIELD *Farmer's Boy*, *Summer* 78 The small dust-colour'd beetle.. flirts his filmy wings, and looks around. **1834** R. MUDIE *Brit. Birds* (1841) I. 11 In those birds which have a habit of flirting up the tail. **1855** BROWNING *Lovers' Quarrel* x, Teach me to flirt a fan As the Spanish ladies can. **1855** SMEDLEY *H. Coverdale* iv. 20 Harry again impatiently flirted the whip over the ears of 'My Old Aunt Sally'. **1893** R. KIPLING *Many Invent.* 229 He flirted the dinghy round the big ship.

b. *absol.* or *intr.* Of a turkey-cock: To set up its feathers. *rare*$^{-1}$.

1654 GAYTON *Pleas. Notes* IV. iii. 186 If you had but rusht and flurted like a Turky cocke.

†**4. a.** *intr.* To turn up one's nose; hence, to sneer, gibe, scoff *at*. Also of the nostrils: To be turned up or dilated, as if sneering (the earliest recorded use). **b.** *trans.* To sneer or scoff at, flout (not clearly distinguishable from *fig.* use of 2). *Obs.*

a. **1553** EDEN *Treat. Newe Ind.* (Arb.) 23 They haue.. nosethrilles flyrtting vpwarde & wyde. **1603** FLORIO *Montaigne* I. l. 165 Diogenes.. in.. rowling of his tub, and flurting [Fr. *hochant du nez*] at Alexander. **1615** G. SANDYS *Trav.* 27 Derided, and flurted at by diuers of the baser people. *a* **1734** NORTH *Lives* (1826) I. 63 Mr. Jones.. could not forbear flirting at him, as—'Come, Mr. Deputy Attorney, what have you to say now'?

b. **1593** NASHE *4 Lett. Confut.* Wks. (Grosart) II. 211 Titius shall not vpbraid Caius.. nor Zoylus anie more flurt Homer. **1621** FLETCHER *Pilgrim* I. i, I'le not be foold nor flurted. **1686** *Catholic Representer* II. 73 You that fleer, and flurt, and blaspheme Everything you do not understand.

5. *intr.* To move with a jerk or spring; to spring, dart. Of a winged creature: To take short quick flights. Also with *about*, *away*, *up*.

1583 STANYHURST *Aeneis* I. (Arb.) 31 Lyke bees.. That flirt in soonbeams. **1601** HOLLAND *Pliny* II. xx. i. 35 It wil leape & flurt in the handling.. against their faces. **1680** *Tom & Will* 90 in *Roxb. Ball.*, Three or four.. did flirt away. **1697** DAMPIER *Voy.* I. 148 In flurting about (as all Fish will when first taken). *a* **1800** COWPER tr. *Milton's Damon* 144 The sparrow.. Flirts here and there, and late returns to rest. **1822** J. FLINT *Lett. Amer.* 234 The velocity of every plunge made her long loose hair flirt up as if [etc.]. **1841** R. B. PEAKE *Court & City* II. i. (Stage direction), As he approaches nearer, she flirts from him. **1887** STEVENSON *Treas. Franchard* vi, With the tails of his night-shirt flirting as he turned. **1890** *Gloucester Gloss.* s.v., 'The paper must have flirted into the fire.'

†**6.** *fig.* To flit inconstantly from one object to another. *Obs.*

1578 T. PROCTOR *Gorg. Gallery* (1814) 133 Did love you intrap?.. That now you be flurting, and will not abide. **1707** J. STEVENS tr. *Quevedo's Com. Wks.* (1709) 348 Do not flirt, or fly from one thing to another.

7. To play at courtship; to practise coquetry; to make love without serious intentions. Often, *to flirt with* (a person); also in indirect *passive*.

1777 GARRICK *Prol. Sheridan's Sch. Scand.*, If Mrs. B. will still continue flirting. **1793** EARL BUCHAN *Anon. & Fugit. Ess.*, (1812) 261 You see them.. flirting with the beauties of the day. **1859** GEO. ELIOT *A. Bede* 258 Every man likes to flirt with a pretty girl, and every pretty girl likes to be flirted with. **1863** OUIDA *Held in Bondage* I. viii. 192 Scores of military men, who flirted more desperately and meant less by it than any fellows in the room.

b. To play, toy, trifle *with* (something).

1859 DICKENS *T. Two Cities* II. v, Occasionally flirting with some lighter document. **1883** F. M. CRAWFORD *Dr. Claudius* ii, Claudius was flirting with his fancies, and drawing pretty pictures in the smoke.

c. *trans.* = *to flirt with*. *rare*$^{-1}$.

1801 MOORE *Wks. T. Little*, *To Rosa* iii. 9 Do you thus seek to flirt a number?

flirtable ('flɜːtəb(ə)l), *a.* [f. FLIRT *v.* + -ABLE.] That is ready to flirt or be flirted with.

1860 W. COLLINS *Wom. White* I. vi. 22 A flirtable, danceable, small-talkable creature of the male sex. **1888** *Pall Mall G.* 18 Feb. 5/2 One hundred and fifty ladies.. of whom seventy-five per cent. are 'flirtable'.

flirtation (flɜː'teɪʃən). [f. as prec. + -ATION.]

†**1.** 'A quick, sprightly motion. A cant word among women' (J.); in quot. *attrib.* *Obs.*$^{-1}$

1737 POPE *Let. in Style of Lady* Wks. 1886 X. 262 A muslin flounce, made very full, would give one a very agreeable Flirtation-air.

2. The action or behaviour of a flirt; †flighty or giddy behaviour, frivolity; the action of playing at courtship.

1718 CIBBER *Non-juror* II, You know I always loved a little flirtation. **1745–6** MRS. DELANY *Let. to Mrs. Dewes* in *Life & Corr.* 1 Feb. II. 418 The sobriety of my own dwelling is much pleasanter to me than all the flirtations of the world. **1814** JANE AUSTEN *Mansf. Park* I. xvii. 335 Becoming soon too busy with his play to have time for more than one flirtation. **1876** BESANT & RICE *Gold. Butterfly* vi, The great art of flirtation.

b. *transf.* and *fig.*

1792 DK. LEEDS *Pol. Mem.* (1884) 202 The flirtations were seriously renewed between Mr. Pitt and Ld. Loughborough. **1819** BYRON *Juan* I. ccv, Thou shalt not.. Commit—flirtation with the muse of Moore.

Hence **flir'tational** *a.*, pertaining to flirtation; **flir'tationless** *a.*, devoid of flirtation; having no opportunity of flirting.

1862 *Sat. Rev.* XIII. 327/2 The flirtational element and its kindred infinitesimal phases. **1880** OUIDA *Moths* vi. 66 Flirtationless, unenvied, unregarded.

flirtatious (flɜː'teɪʃəs), *a.* [f. FLIRTATION; see -OUS.]

a. Of persons: Given to flirtation, inclined to flirt.

1834 C'TESS MORLEY *Dacre* I. vi. 132 Match-making mothers, flirtatious daughters, and coquettish wives. **1886** W. E. NORRIS *Bachelor's Blunder* ii. (1887) 15, I believe he is rather a flirtatious young gentleman.

b. Of speech, etc.: Of or pertaining to flirtation; of the nature of flirtation.

1870 MISS BROUGHTON *Red as Rose* I. xii. 243 And yet their talk.. holds nothing obnoxiously fond or flirtatious. **1891** B. HARTE *1st Fam. Tasajara* I. 58 An audaciously flirtatious declaration.

Hence **flir'tatiously**, *adv.*; **flir'tatiousness.**

1863 HOLME LEE *A. Warleigh's Fortunes* II. 294 When young men and women are flirtatiously disposed. **1886** *Atlantic Monthly* Sept. 432/1 A North Carolina girl of ingenuous flirtatiousness.

flirted ('flɜːtɪd), *ppl. a.* [f. FLIRT *v.* + -ED^{1}.] In senses of the vb. Also with *with*; cf. FLIRT *v.* 7.

1624 FLETCHER *Rule a Wife* III. v, Is this the Fellow That had the patience to become a Fool, A flurted Fool. **1781** COWPER *Hope* 344 The flirted fan, the bridle and the toss. **1863** OUIDA *Held in Bondage* I. ix. 205 Curly.. was the.. most flirted with young Guardsman of his time.

flirtee (flɜː'tiː). *nonce-wd.* [f. FLIRT *v.* + -EE.] One who is flirted with.

1862 *Sat. Rev.* 14 June 676/2 Because the flirt is clever, or the flirtee silly. **1891** *Temple Bar Mag.* Jan. 91 Three generations of flirtees.

flirter ('flɜːtə(r)). [f. FLIRT *v.* + -ER^{1}.] One who flirts; a flirt.

1814 *Sporting Mag.* XLIV. 45 She dresses not so fine as many a flirter. **1837** T. HOOK *Jack Brag* viii, As far distant as possible from the flirters themselves.

†**flirt-gill** (-dʒɪl). *Obs.* Also flirt-gillian. [f. FLIRT *sb.* or *v.* + GILL nickname for *Juliana*.] A woman of light or loose behaviour. Cf. GILL-FLIRT.

1592 SHAKS. *Rom. & Jul.* II. iv. 162 Scurvie knaue, I am none of his flurt-gils. **1613** BEAUM. & FL. *Knt. Burning Pestle* IV. i, You heard him take me vp like a flirt Gill, and sing baudy songs upon me. **1618** FLETCHER *Chances* III. i, As I had been a Mawkin, a flurt Gillian.

flirthood ('flɜːthʊd). *nonce-wd.* [see -HOOD.] The state of being a flirt.

1862 *Sat. Rev.* XIV. 102/1 Young ladies, just budding into flirthood.

flirtigig, -gigs ('flɜːtɪgɪg(z). *dial.* [f. FLIRT + GIG: cf. *whirligig*.] A giddy, flighty girl.

1683 *York-shire Dialogue* 17 Thou and she, and all sike Flirtigiggs. **1787** GROSE *Prov. Gloss.*, *Flirtigigs*, a wanton, fond lass. **1886** ELWORTHY *W. Somerset Word-bk.*, *Flirtigig*.

flirting ('flɜːtɪŋ), *vbl. sb.* [f. FLIRT *v.* + -ING^{1}.] The action of the vb. FLIRT in various senses; *esp.* trifling or coquetting with the opposite sex, flirtation.

1593 NASHE *4 Lett. Confut.* Wks. (Grosart) II. 274 Thou ..keepst such a flurting and a flinging in euerie leafe. **1644**

BULWER *Chirol.* 54 The flirting out of the Back part of the Hand. **1684** *Contempl. State of Man* I. iv. (1699) 44 The flirting up and down of a little Sparrow. **1710** STEELE *Tatler* No. 9 ¶3 Miss with all her Flirting and Ogling. **1806–7** J. BERESFORD *Miseries Hum. Life* IV. xxxiii, The filthy flirtings of a well twirled mop. **1865** DICKENS *Mut. Fr.* I. ix, You can have as much flirting as you like.

attrib. **1644** BULWER *Chiron.* 81 The middle Finger strongly comprest by the Thumbe, and their collision producing a flurting sound.

flirting ('flɜːtɪŋ), *ppl. a.* [f. as prec. + -ING².] That flirts, in various senses of the vb.

1577 tr. *Bullinger's Decades* (1592) 224 The wife that gads not gigglotwise with euerie flirting gill. **1651** FULLER *Abel Rediv.* (1867) II. 322 Some.. have cast out flirting censures against this Catalogue. **1663** DRYDEN *Wild Gallant* v. iii, Nothing vexes me, but that this flirting gentlewoman should go before me. **1668** SEDLEY *Mulb. Gard.* I. i, But that flirting Hat there looks as 'twere made rather for your Wit than your Head. *a* **1734** NORTH *Exam.* III. vii. (1740) 509 He could not bear such a flirting Wit and Libertine. **1819** *Metropolis* I. 215 Did you.. observe how flirting and amatory a certain very great personage is?

Hence **'flirtingly** *adv.*, in a flirting manner.

1855 in OGILVIE Suppl.

flirtish ('flɜːtɪʃ), *a.* [f. FLIRT *sb.* + -ISH.] Somewhat of the nature of or betokening a flirt.

c **1665** MRS. HUTCHINSON *Mem. Col. Hutchinson* (1846) 260 A flirtish girl of sixteen. **1840** DICKENS *Barn. Rudge* xx, Miss Haredale took occasion to charge upon Dolly certain flirtish and inconstant propensities.

Hence **'flirtishness**.

1750 *Hist. Cornelia* 211 She had an air of tenderness, mixed with all the flirtishness of coquetry.

flirtling ('flɜːtlɪŋ). *nonce-wd.* [f. FLIRT *sb.* + -LING.] A little flirt.

1883 F. M. CRAWFORD *Dr. Claudius* xv, The pair of trim-built flirtlings, walking so daintily down the gravel path.

'flirtship. *nonce-wd.* [f. FLIRT *sb.* + -SHIP.] The personality of a flirt; in quot. a mock title.

1703 MRS. CENTLIVRE *Stolen Heiress* III. i, Call your Lady, —what does your Flurt-ship do here? I want your mistress.

flirty ('flɜːtɪ), *a.* [f. FLIRT *sb.* + -Y¹.] Of or pertaining to flirtation; characterized by or inclined to flirtation.

1840 LADY C. M. C. BURY *Hist. Flirt* i, A laughing and flirty dialogue succeeded. **1863** OUIDA *Held in Bondage* I. ix. 206 Such a bold flirty girl. **1870** *Public Opinion* 6 Aug. 169 Criticising the flirty ways of a fascinating widow.

†**flish,** *v. Obs.* In 4 **flysche**. [app. imitative of the sound of a blade waved through the air.] *trans.* To slash or cut. Hence **'flyschand** *ppl. a.*

? *a* **1400** *Morte Arth.* 2141 With flyschande speris. *Ibid.* 2769 Fulle butt in þe frounte he flysches hyme evene.

†**'flish-flash,** *v.* [? reduplication of prec.] *intr.* To make cuts and slashes with a sword.

1641 *Vox Borealis* B i j b, I can Fence bravely, and flish flash, with the best of them.

flisk (flɪsk), *sb. dial.* [f. next.]

1. A whim, a freak. *Sc.*

1818 SCOTT *Br. Lamm.* xxviii, There is something in Miss Ashton's change.. too sudden and too serious for a mere flisk of her own.

2. A fillip with the finger. *in a flisk*: 'in a jiffy' (*Whitby Gloss.* 1855).

1891 ATKINSON *Last of Giant-Killers* 86 So down his throat she goes in a flisk.

3. In various concrete senses: **a.** A 'whisk' made of twigs or horsehair for brushing away dust, flies, etc. (Halliwell 1847, *Berks. Gloss.* 1888). **b.** A large-toothed comb (Halliwell 1847, *W. Cornw. Gloss.* (1880). **c.** A syringe (*Whitby Gloss.* 1876).

flisk, *a.* ? *Obs.* [f. next. Cf. FLIG *a.*]

1680 *Lond. Gaz.* No. 1563/4 A Black Mare, about 15 hands with a flisk Tail, lame on the near foot before. **1721** *Ibid.* No. 6000/3 Stolen.. a black Mare.. with a Flisk Tail.

flisk (flɪsk), *v.* Now *dial.* [onomatopœia expressive of a sudden movement through the air; cf. *whisk.*]

1. *intr.* To move or dance about in a frolicsome way; to frisk. Of a horse: To be restive.

1596 GOSSON *Pleas. Quips* 110, Fannes.. To flit away the flisking flies. *a* **1689** W. CLELAND *Effigies Cleri* Poems (1697) 62 Which make some Brethren flisk and fling. **1786** BURNS *Auld Farmers New-Year Salut.* xii, Thou never braindg't an' fetch't, an' fliskit. **1887** *Mod. Scott. Poets* Ser. x. 58 The hungry honey bees That flisked and feasted there.

2. *trans.* To make restless and uneasy; to put out, displease.

1792 A. DOUGLAS *Poems* (1806) 71 But, Willie lad, tak' my advice, An' at it binna fliskit. **1862** HISLOP *Prov. Scot.* 60 Fashious fools are easiest flisket.

3. To flick, knock about. Also, to spurt, sprinkle.

1847 HALLIWELL, *Flisk*, to flick, as with a whip. *Linc.* **1876** *Whitby Gloss.*, *Flisk*, to squirt liquids. **1890** *Gloucester Gloss.* s.v., Don't get flisking that corn about.

'fliskmahoy. *Sc.* [f. FLISK *v.* Jamieson gives also *Fliskmahaigo* with similar sense; the unmeaning endings may have been suggested by the place-names *Dalmahoy* and *Lesmahago.*] A flighty girl; a woman who gives herself airs.

1816 SCOTT *Antiq.* xxxv, 'That silly fliskmahoy, Jenny Rintherout.' **1818** —— *Hrt. Midl.* l, 'Seeing I hae prought worthy Mrs. Putler sic a fliskmahoy.'

flisky ('flɪskɪ), *a.*¹ [f. FLISK *sb.* or *v.* + -Y¹.]

1. *Sc.* Flighty, frolicsome; of a horse: Skittish.

1807 HOGG *Auld Ettrick John* 8 Mount. Bard 195 Auld Johnie's flisky dame. **1856** G. HENDERSON *Pop. Rhymes Berwick.* 48 You're like Adam Black's pony, Flisky, pranky —and no very canny. **1880** *Antrim & Down Gloss.*, *Flisky*, skittish, specially applied to a mare which kicks when touched on the flank.

2. *south. dial.* (See quots.)

1866 BLACKMORE *Cradock Nowell* xxxi, First come fitful scuds of rain, 'flisky' rain they call it.

flit (flɪt), *sb.*¹ [f. next vb.] The action of flitting. **a.** A removal; spec. *do a flit*, to decamp. **b.** A light movement, as of a bird's wing; a flutter; a light touch.

a. 1835 N. P. WILLIS in L'Estrange *Friendships Miss Mitford* (1882) I. 289 A flit from London and a visit to Reading. **1855** ROBINSON *Whitby Gloss.* s.v. *Flit*, 'A moonlight flit', a decampment by night with the furniture, to cheat the landlord. **1952** M. TRIPP *Faith is Windsock* vii. 108 They'll say I got windy and did a flit. **1964** R. BRADDON *Year Angry Rabbit* (1967) ii. 16 A fourth [daughter].. had cunningly got herself pregnant by the one pathologist in the team who was too honourable to do a flit. **1970** *Sunday Truth* (Brisbane) 27 Dec. 16/3 They live on the generosity of the small country storekeeper, then do a flit.

b. 1873 MISS THACKERAY *Old Kensington* xii. 99 There was a vague flit and consternation in the darkness at the farther end of the room. **1877** BLACKMORE *Erema* III. liv. 242 A flit of fancy touched me. **1880** —— *Mary Anerley* xxvi. Kneading it firmly with some rapid flits of thumb.

c. (See quots. 1942.) Also *attrib.* or as *adj.* *U.S. slang.*

1942 BERREY & VAN DEN BARK *Amer. Thes. Slang* §405.2 *Effeminate man*,.. Fauntleroy, flit, fuddyduddy. *Ibid.* §508.4 *Male homosexual*,.. flit, four-letter man, fruit, fruiter. **1951** J. D. SALINGER *Catcher in Rye* xix. 170 Sometimes it was hard to believe, the people he said were flits and lesbians. **1964** E. LACY *Pity Honest* ii. 30 'Could he have been on the flit side?' 'Doubt that,.. not that I'm any authority on queers.'

Flit (flɪt), *sb.*² [f. the vb.] The proprietary name of an insecticide. *Flit gun*, a syringe intended for use in spraying insecticides.

1923 *Official Gaz. U.S. Pat. Office* 27 Nov. 723/1 Standard Oil Company (New Jersey).. *Flit.* Insecticide. Claims use since May 17, 1923. **1926** *Trade Marks Jrnl.* 17 Mar. 628 *Flit*, chemical substances used for Agricultural, Horticultural, Veterinary and Sanitary purposes. Standard Oil Company.. New Jersey. *Ibid.* 10 Nov. 2513 *Flit*, Sprayers, Squirt-guns and Atomizers.. Standard Oil Company.. New Jersey. **1927** *Blackw. Mag.* Sept. 310/2 She had had the foresight to buy a metal spray and a tin of insecticide called *Flit*. With Flit we had come scatheless through Persia. *Ibid.*, Even our Flit gun ceased to interest him. **1932** E. HEMINGWAY *Death in Afternoon* xvi. 186 You ought to spray him with flit. **1948** C. DAY LEWIS *Otterbury Incident* iv. 43 They had a pail of muddy water.. and one of those Flit guns loaded with it. **1958** *Times* 7 Aug. 3/4 They only had a Flit-gun, the sort of thing we used in India to keep the mosquitoes off.

†**flit,** *a. poet. Obs.* Also **flitt**. [var. of FLEET *a.*, the form being influenced by FLIT *v.* Cf. also FLIGHT *a.*] **a.** Swift, nimble, quickly-moving. **b.** Fleeting, shifting; light, airy, unsubstantial.

a. 1590 SPENSER *F.Q.* II. iv. 38 And in his hand two dartes exceeding flit, And deadly sharp, he held. *Ibid.* III. xi. 39 Now, like a stag; now, like a faulcon flit. **1600** FAIRFAX *Tasso* XIV. lxxii. 265 That flit birde that Ioues hot weapon beares.

b. 1590 SPENSER *F.Q.* III. x. 57 On the rockes he fell so flit and light, That he thereby receiv'd no hurt at all. *Ibid.* III. i. 56 Therewith a while she her flit fancy fedd. **1633** P. FLETCHER *Purple Isl.* VII. vii, Life it self's as flit as is the aire we breathe.

flit (flɪt), *v.* Forms: 3–4 **flitten**, *Orm.* **flittenn**, 3 **flut(t)en**, 3–6 **flytt(e**, 4–6 **flyt(e**, 4–9 **flitt(e**, (6 **fliet**), 4– **flit**. *Pa. t.* 3 **flutte**, 4 **flitt**, 5 **flette**, **flyt**, 6 **flit**. *Pa. pple.* 4 **yflit**, **iflut**, 7 **flit**, [ME. *flitten*, *flutten*, a. ON. *flytja* (Sw. *flytta*, Da. *flytte*), f. **flut-* weak grade of the root of *flióta*: see FLEET *v.*¹]

1. *trans.* To remove, transport, or take away to another place; to transfer from one position to another; to remove (a person) from his house or habitation. Now chiefly *Sc.* or *dial.*

c **1200** ORMIN 15648 To flittenn menn till heffness ærd Ut off þe defless walde. *c* **1250** *Gen. & Ex.* 1522 Ðat folk.. deden him flitten hise ostel. *c* **1374** CHAUCER *Troylus* v. 1544 As regnes shal ben flitted Fro folk to folk. *c* **1375** *Lay Folks Mass Bk.* (MS. B.) 155 þen þo prest flyttes his boke north to þat oþer auter noke. *c* **1425** WYNTOUN *Cron.* VII. v. 181 A Towne Wes flyttyd out of þat ilke plas Quhare it fowndyt and byggyt was. *c* **1450** *St. Cuthbert* (Surtees) 3442 In to þat my body flitt. **1558** in Balfour *Practicks* (1754) 106 Scho may not flit nor remove the tenentis, occupiaris of the samin. **1572** *Sempill Ball* xxix. (1872) 152 That sum of thame mon flit thair kist. *c* **1640** J. SMYTH *Lives Berkeleys* (1883) I. 155 This lord.. exchanged, removed, and flitted part of his Cattle.. from one manor to another. **1782** SIR J. SINCLAIR *Observ. Scot. Dial.* 84 *To Flit*, to remove any thing in general, particularly furniture. **1807** *Overseer's Acct.* in *Rutland Gloss.* (1891) s.v., For fliting sarah Hails 1*s.* 6*d.* **1861** DASENT *Burnt Njal* II. 40 They flitted home their goods and laid up the ship. **1863** BARING GOULD *Iceland* 257 One fine afternoon he flitted his guest out to the island.

b. *spec.* To shift (a tethered animal, occas. the tether) from one spot to another, when it has eaten all the grass within reach; hence, to tether. Also, to shift the position of (a sheep-fold).

1523 FITZHERB. *Husb.* §18 To flyte it [the shepefolde] euery mornynge or nyght. *Ibid.* §148 Flytte hym [thy horse] as oft as thou wylt. **1786** BURNS *Auld Farmer's New-Year Salut.* xviii, Wi' tentie care I'll flit thy tether, To some hain'd rig. **1816** SIR A. BOSWELL *Skeldon Haughs* 44 A Sow upon your land I'll tether.. But deil a man o' Kyle shall flit her. **1881** *Leicester Gloss.* s.v., The goot (goat) were flitted to the middle cloo'es-poost.

†**c.** Of a boat, etc.: To serve to transport. *Obs.*

a **1300** *Cursor M.* 25709 (Cott.) Penance is þat oþer bord, þat fletand flittes man ouer ford.. it schal him hauen of merci win. **1375** BARBOUR *Bruce* III. 420 It [the bate] sa litill wes, that It Mycht our the wattir bot thresum flyt.

d. *Naut.* (See quots., and FLEET *v.*¹ 12.)

1750 T. R. BLANCKLEY *Naval Expos.*, *Flitting*, altering or removing a dead Eye in the Low or Top-mast Shrouds and Backstays, either to lengthen or shorten them, is called Flitting. **1793** SMEATON *Edystone L.* §143 In this way we proceeded flitting the tackle and lowering till our anchor was grounded. *Ibid.* 158 Having so many times to stop, overhawl, and flit.. the work could not go on very speedily.

†**2.** To remove, get rid of (a thing); to drive *away* (an insect). *Obs.*

c **1350** *Will. Palerne* 623 Fele times haue ich fonded to flitte it fro þouȝt. *c* **1400** *Rom. Rose* 1812 So sore it stikid whan I was hit, That by no craft I might it flit. **1596** GOSSON *Pleas. Quips* 110 Fannes.. To flit away the flisking flies.

†**3.** To change the condition or direction of; to alter, cause to deviate or waver; to pervert (law). *Obs.*

c **1200** ORMIN 13414 Ȝe sen þatt icc am flittedd nu Fra dæþ to lif onn erþe. *c* **1375** *Sc. Leg. Saints, Lucia* 279 þar-with for to flit hyre thocht. **1393** GOWER *Conf.* III. 183 If he wolde flitte The lawe for the covetise. **14..** LYDG. *Temple of Glas* 1248 Late not ȝoure corage ne ȝoure force fail, Ne non assautes ȝov flitten or remeve.

†**4.** *refl.* To betake oneself, go, direct one's course. *Obs.*

c **1200** ORMIN 15853 Uss birrþ aȝȝ Uss flittenn towarrd Criste. *Ibid.* 18038 Swa þatt teȝȝ.. Wel sholldenn muȝhenn flitten hemm & ferrsenn fra þe defell. **13..** in Horstmann *Altengl. Leg.* II. 97 Bot þou flit þe ferr, For his sake þou sal far (þe) werr.

5. *intr.* To shift one's position, either in a material or immaterial sense; to be gone, depart, pass away, remove. Also with *away*, or const. *from*, †*of*, *out of*, *to*.

c **1200** ORMIN 12765 O þatt oþerr daȝȝ Toc Jesu Crist to flittenn Inntill þe land off Galile. *a* **1240** *Sawles Warde* in *Cott. Hom.* 251 Ferliche ha flutteð from þe heate in to þe chele. *a* **1300** *Cursor M.* 12487 (Cott.) þan flitted þai vntil a tun þat cleped was chaphar-naum. **1340** HAMPOLE *Pr. Consc.* 3762 When a man fra þis world sal flitte. *c* **1400** *Rom. Rose* 5359 Whan it [Richesse] failith, he [Love] wol flit. **1471** RIPLEY *Comp. Alch.* IV. vii. in Ashm. (1652) 145 Out of thy mynde let not thys lesson flyt. **1529** MORE *Comf. agst. Trib.* I. Wks. 1147/2 But yf our self flyt from hym. **1576** GOSSON *Speculum Hum.* in *Sch. Abuse* (Arb.) 76 His lyfe shall flit, when most he trustes the same. **1619** J. WELSH in *Wodr. Soc. Misc.* 562 To flit owt of this lyfe. **1642** H. MORE *Song of Soul* III. II. xliii, Nor is his masters knowledge from him flit Into his scholars head. **1695** WOODWARD *Nat. Hist. Earth* I. (1723) 38 The Sea frequently flitted and changed its place. **1790** BURNS *Tam o' Shanter* vii, Like the Borealis race, That flit ere you can point their place. **1858** FROUDE *Hist. Eng.* III. xiii. 100 Towards the fall of the summer, clergy from the southern counties had been flitting northward. **1868** HAWTHORNE *Amer. Note-bks.* (1879) II. 65 Our spirits must have flitted away unconsciously.

†**b.** To depart, deviate, swerve *from* a custom, justice, law, etc. *Obs.*

c **1200** ORMIN 13430 Ȝuw iss nu baþe god & ned.. To flittenn o þiss oþerr daȝȝ Fra defless & fra sinness. *a* **1420** HOCCLEVE *De Reg. Princ.* 2704 To suche a jugge with-drawe the hope Of money, and he fro justice flittethe. *c* **1450** *St. Cuthbert* (Surtees) 7903 Fra alde custome þai walde noȝt flytt. **1571** CAMPION *Hist. Irel.* XI. xi. (1633) 72 Vivian the legate.. doth.. excommunicate all those that flitte from the obeysance of the Kings of England.

†**c.** Of a horseman: To lose his seat and fall to the ground. *Obs.*

1430 LYDG. *Chron. Troy* I. ix, From his sadell.. he made him flytte Downe to the ground. **1458** in Turner *Dom. Archit.* III. 41 Som oute of her sadels flette to the grounde. *a* **1605** MONTGOMERIE *Misc. Poems* xli. 51 Some perforce flittis On grund.

†**d.** quasi-*trans.* To migrate from (a place); to change (places); to shift (one's camp, etc.).

c **1330** R. BRUNNE *Chron. Wace* (Rolls) 13654 Wyþ force he dide hem flitte þet stede. **1570** BUCHANAN *Chamæleon* Wks. (1892) 52 The moist part flittit camp and went to Lynlythquow. **1674** N. FAIRFAX *Bulk & Selv.* 139 Spirits change their Beings.. far otherwise than bodies do when they flit places. **1715** *Roxb. Ball.* VI. 620 While I have might, I will you fight, from Stirling flit your Den, Sir.

6. To remove from one habitation to another, change one's residence, 'move'. Chiefly *north.* or *Sc.* (In proverbial expressions often opposed to *sit.*)

1504 *Plumpton Corr.* 191, I will flitt at this next Mighelmas. *a* **1553** UDALL *Royster D.* II. iii. (Arb.) 36 Fast for to sitte and not oft to flitte. **1641** BEST *Farm. Bks.* (Surtees) 135 Theire desire.. is to goe to theire newe masters eyther on a Tewsday, or on a Thursday; for.. they say Munday flitte, Neaver sitte. **1721** KELLY *Scot. Prov.* 105 Fools are fain of flitting, and wise Men of sitting. **1871** C. GIBBON *For Lack of Gold* v, When you need to flit, there's a house of mine standing empty that you can take at any time.

†7. To change from one state, condition, or direction to another; to alter, shift about, give way.

c 1386 CHAUCER *Pars. T.* ¶295 God..that may not chaunge and flitte. c 1430 *How Wise Man taust Son* 116 in *Babees Bk.* (1868) 51 Neiþer hasti for to chaunge ne flitte. 1500–20 DUNBAR *Poems* lxvi. 95 Of this fals failʒeand warld I tyre, That ever more flytis lyk ane phane. 1590 SPENSER *F.Q.* I. iv. 5 On a sandie hill, that still did flitt And fall away, it [the Pallace] mounted was full hie. a 1605 MONTGOMERIE *Misc. Poems* xxxi. 58 If ʒe be constant, I sall neuer change; If ʒe be fickle, I am forc't to flitt. 1725 RAMSAY *Gent. Sheph.* II. iv. (1875) 33 Your thoughts may flit, and I may thole the wrang. 1816 COLERIDGE *Statesm. Man.* App. 35 The intellectual eyes of the Many flit, and are incapable of looking fixedly toward the God-like.

b. Of a flame: To die down.

1839 MARRYAT *Phant. Ship* xi, Like a candle burnt down to the socket, flitting and flaring alternately. 1887 SWINBURNE *Locrine* I. i. 261 Thy smile is as a flame that plays and flits.

8. To move along, pass, proceed; to pass lightly or softly and (usually) with rapidity or suddenness. Often with adverbs, as *about, away, by, to and fro*, etc. Said both of material and immaterial things.

c 1430 LYDG. *Bochas* II. vi. (1554) 42 b, Or that I any farther flitte..To diuines this matter I committe. c 1440 *York Myst.* xv. 34 Flitte faste ouere thees felles. 1613 PURCHAS *Pilgrimage* IV. viii. (1614) 386 Forced to flee to the mountaines where he liued three months..flitting vp and downe with ten or twelue followers. 1618 BOLTON *Florus* Pref., The varietie of matter makes the minde abruptly flit from one thing to another. 1642 H. MORE *Song of Soul* I. II. v, Sith my wandring Bark so far is gone, And flitten forth upon the Ocean main. 1781 COWPER *Retirem.* 192 The clouds that flit, or slowly float away. 1810 SCOTT *Lady of L.* III. xi, When flits this Cross from man to man. 1838 DICKENS *Nich. Nick.* xvi, Postmen..flit to and fro. 1851 HELPS *Comp. Solit.* xiii. (1874) 246, I seemed to see the various races who had occupied the spot flit by. 1864 TENNYSON *Aylmer's F.* 202 Unawares they flitted off, Busying them-selves about the flowerage.

b. *esp.* Of a bird or other winged creature: To fly lightly and swiftly; also, to make short and swift flights, to flutter.

1535 COVERDALE *2 Esdras* v. 6 And the foules shal flyt, and the Sodomitysh see shall cast out his fish. 1556 J. HEYWOOD *Spider & F.* liv. 34 Downe the flie againe flitth. 1590 SPENSER *F.Q.* III. xi. 42 Faire Pegasus that flitteth in the ayre. 1700 DRYDEN *Fables, Meleager & Atalanta* 401 With wings endu'd..and sent to flit in air. 1817 CAMPBELL *Poems, Reullura* 17 The bat flits to and fro. 1864 TENNYSON *En. Ard.* 269 Like the caged bird escaping suddenly, The little innocent soul flitted away.

c. Of time: To pass away.

1573 BARET *Alv.* F 706 Time flitted away quickly. 1583 STANYHURST *Aeneis* I. (Arb.) 26 Hee shal bee the regent, vntil yeers thirtye be flitted. 1868 MORRIS *Earthly Par.* I. 72 So smoothly o'er our heads the days did flit.

†9. To sustain existence, to live *by* (i.e. upon). *Obs.*

[Cf. ON. *flytja* to provide with necessaries (a fig. application of the original sense 'to ferry, help forward'), whence refl. *flytjask* to maintain oneself.]

a 1225 *Ancr. R.* 202 Al so ʒisceð a ʒissare þet moni þusunt muhten bi flutten [*printed* biflutten]. *Ibid.* 428 Non ancre seruant ne ouhte..uorto asken i-sette huire, bute mete & cloð þet heo mei vlutten bi.

Hence †**flit**, **'flitted**, †**'flitten** *ppl. a.*, that has gone away, departed.

1590 SPENSER *F.Q.* I. vii. 21 So hardly he the flitted life does win Unto her native prison to retourne. 1642 H. MORE *Song of Soul* II. ii. II. xxxviii, The..flitten or shrunk spright. *Ibid.* II. iii. I. xxix, All flit souls be not in the same taking.

flit, var. of FLEET *v.*², to skim.

flitch (flɪtʃ), *sb.*¹ Forms: α. 1 flicci, flicce, 5 flykke, 5–6 flik, flyk(e, (5 flickke, 6 flycke), 6–7 (8, 9 *dial.*) flick. β. 3–4 flic(c)he, (5 vlycch, 6 fli(e)ch), 5–6 flitche, flytche, (6 fleetch, 9 *dial.* fleech, fleach), 6– flitch. [OE. *flicce* ? str. neut., corresp. to MLG. *vlike, vlicke*, ON. *flikki* (MDa. *flykke*):—OTeut. **flikkjo*ᵐ, f. root **flīk*, found in ON. *flík* rag, and perh. in FLECK *sb.*]

1. a. The side of an animal, now only of a hog, salted and cured; a 'side' of bacon.

α. a 700 *Epinal Gloss.* 774 *Perna*, flicci. 805–31 *Charters* xxxvii. 18 in *O.E. Texts* 444 Tua flicca. 901–9 *Charter Eadweard* in *Cod. Dipl.* V. 164 Feor fliccu. c 1000 *Ags. Voc.* in Wr.-Wülcker *Voc.* 272/5 *Perna*, flicce. 1462 *Test. Ebor.* II. 261, iiij. bakon-fliks, ij. beffe-fliks. a 1529 SKELTON *Col. Cloute* 846 A bacon flycke. 1643 *Inv. Skipton Castle* in Whitaker *Craven* (1805) 302, 35 great large beefe flicks. c 1746 J. COLLIER (Tim Bobbin) *Lanc. Dialect.* Gloss., *Flick*, a flitch of bacon. 1859 GEO. ELIOT *A. Bede* iv, 'Thee lookst as white as a flick o' new bacon.'

β. c 1230 *Hali Meid.* 37 Seoð þe cat at þe fliche. 1481 CAXTON *Reynard* (Arb.) 26 There fonde he..many goed flytches of bacon. 1577 B. GOOGE *Heresbach's Husb.* III. (1586) 152 b, Cutting out the Head, the Gammon and the fleetches, pouder them with salt. 1597–8 BP. HALL *Sat.* IV. iv. 32 Dried fliches of some smoked beeue. 1710 SWIFT *Baucis & Philemon* 25 He from out the Chimney took A Flitch of Bacon off the Hook. 1859 JEPHSON *Brittany* v. 55 From..the ceiling hung a goodly row of..flitches of bacon.

transf. 1648 HERRICK *Hesper., Bacchus*, He..walks with dangling breeches..And shewes his naked flitches.

b. The 'flitch' presented yearly at Dunmow, in Essex, to any married couple who could prove that they had lived in conjugal harmony for a year and a day. (Also at Wichnor: see quot. a 1509.)

1362 [see FLITCHEN]. a 1509 in Dugdale *Baronage* (1676) II. 106/2 The said Sir Philip shall fynde..one Bacon flyke, hanging in his Halle at Whichenore..to be given [etc.]. 1615 *Hist. Robert Fitz-walter* 25 One Richard Wright..came and required of the Bacon of Dunmow..And there was deliuered vnto the said Richard, one fleech of Bacon. 1820 COMBE *Dr. Syntax, Consol.* I. (Chandos) 125 They might have claim'd or I'm mistaken With conscience clear the Flitch of Bacon.

2. a. A square piece of blubber from a whale. **b.** A steak cut from a halibut.

1787 HUNTER in *Phil. Trans.* LXXVII. 394 The adipose covering from all of the Whale kind that is brought home in square pieces, called flitches. 1884 [see FLITCH *v.*¹].

3. a. A slice cut lengthways from the trunk of a tree, usually having the natural surface as one of its sides.

1823 MOOR *Suffolk Wds., Fleeches*, the portions into which a tree or piece of timber is cut by the saw. 1867 SMYTH *Sailor's Word-bk., Flitch*, the outside cut or slab of a tree. 1873 J. RICHARDS *Wood-working Factories* 126 In America lumber is..not cut first into deals or flitches for transportation, and then sawed again to sizes, as in Europe. 1875 T. LASLETT *Timber* xxvi. 190 Those [trees] with faulty centres furnish..pieces unequally sided, called flitches.

b. *Carpentry.* (See quot.)

1874 KNIGHT *Dict. Mech.* I. 883/1 *Flitch, a.* One of several associated planks fastened side by side to form a compound beam, or built-beam. *b.* A bolt of planks, united by the stub-shot.

c. In full ***flitch-plate***. A strengthening plate added to a beam, girder, or any woodwork.

1888 *Lockwood's Dict. Mech. Engin., Flitch*, a plate of metal or of wood bolted to an otherwise weak and unstayed beam or structure in order to strengthen and support it. *Flitch Plate*, a broad thin plate or rolled bar used in building up flitch beams or plated work. 1912 *Motor Man.* (ed. 14) iii. 89 To build the frame up of stout section ash and bolt on steel 'flitch' plates to the sides. 1950 *Engineering* 6 Jan. 3/3 The engine is reinforced by a channel-section flitch over most of its length.

4. *Comb.*, as **flitch-beam**, **-ware** (see quots.).

1884 KNIGHT *Dict. Mech.* IV. 348/1 *Flitch Beam*, a beam made in layers of material pinned together. 1750 ELLIS *Mod. Husbandm.* VII. ii. 60 *Flitch-ware*, that which is turned out of the intire round part of the [beech] tree.

flitch (flɪtʃ), *sb.*² *rare.* [Onomatopœic; cf. *flick, switch, twitch*.] A flick or stroke.

1893 G. D. LESLIE *Lett. to Marco* xvi. 106 They give continually a little sort of jerky flitch with their wings.

flitch (flɪtʃ), *v.*¹ Also fletch. [f. FLITCH *sb.*¹] *trans.* **a.** To cut (a log) into flitches, also, to cut as a flitch is cut. **b.** To cut (halibut) into flitches or steaks. Hence **'flitching** *vbl. sb.*, in quot. *attrib.*

1875 T. LASLETT *Timber* xxvi. 193 Great care is..necessary in..flitching the log. *Ibid.* xxvi. 202 Planks..flitched from some of the hollow trees. 1883 *Fisheries Exhib. Catal.* 197 Finning and flitching knives. 1884 KNIGHT *Dict. Mech.* IV. 348 *Flitching Knife*, for slicing halibut into steaks or flitches.

flitch (flɪtʃ), *v.*² *dial.* [? var. of FLIT *a.* ON. *flytja.*] **a.** *refl.* = FLIT *v.* 4. **b.** *intr.* for *refl.* = FLIT *v.* 5.

1555 ABP. PARKER *Ps.* lv. 157, I would me flitche, From hence to wildernes. 1787 W. MARSHALL *Norfolk* (1795) II. Gloss., *Flitch*, to move from place to place; as from farm to farm. 1857 WRIGHT *Dict. Provinc., Flitch*, to move from place to place.

'flitchen. *Obs.* exc. *dial.* Also 4 flucchen, 7 flitchin. [f. FLITCH *sb.*¹ + -EN¹.] = FLITCH.

1362 LANGL. *P. Pl.* A. x. 189 þauʒ þei don hem to [donmowe..] To folewen aftur þe Flucchen, fecche þei hit neuere. 1658 *MS. Inv. of Goods* (Nares) Fower flitchins of bacon in the chimney. 1786 *Lond. Mag.* Mar. 158 Bacon As good as e'er cut off a flitchen. 1804 J. DUNCUMB *Hist. Hereford* I. 213/1 Gloss. 1879 in MISS JACKSON *Shropsh. Word-bk.*

flite, flyte (flaɪt), *sb.* Now *dial.* Forms: 1–3 flit, 3–4, 9 flite, flitt(e, 4–5 flyt, (5 floyt, 7 fleyte), 8 flight, 8– flyte. [OE. *flīt* str. neut., f. *flītan* (see next): cf. OFris. and OS. *flīt* (Du. *vlijt*), OHG. *flīz* (MHG. *vlīz*, Ger. *fleiss* diligence, zeal.)

The *flitt* of the *Cursor M.*, where spelling and rime indicate a short vowel, is prob. a parallel formation repr. OE. *ʒeflit*.]

†**1.** Contention, strife, a dispute; also, abuse, an abusive speech. *Obs.*

c 1000 *Ags. Ps.* xlix. [l.] 21 Toʒeanes sunu modor ðine ðu settest flit. c 1200 *Trin. Coll. Hom.* 43 Ech þat is weorldes frend is ure drihtenes fo, and halt flit wið him. a 1300 *Cursor M.* 24537 (Cott.) Quen i..thogh apon þat juus flitt, þe tere fell o min ei. c 1400 *Ywaine & Gaw.* 93 Na mar moves me thi flyt Than it war a flies byt. 1600 in Tytler *Hist. Scot.* (1864) IV. 281 Fleytes and pretty taunts.

†**b.** A contest, struggle. *Obs.*

13.. *E.E. Allit. P.* B. 421 þe arc..flote forthe with þe flyt of þe felle wyndez. 1494 FABYAN *Chron.* VII. 581 The duke of Bedforde..had a great floyt and batayll with dyuers carykkes of Ieane.

2. A scolding-match.

1768 ROSS *Fort. Sheph.* I. 111 We'll ablins get a flyte, an' ablins nane. 1816 SCOTT *Antiq.* xxxix, 'I think maybe a flyte wi' the auld housekeeper at Monkbarns..would do me some gude.' 1876 *Mid. Yorksh. Gloss.*, There's such a flite going on between them.

flite, flyte (flaɪt), *v.* Now *dial.* Forms: *Infin.* 1–2 flitan, 2–3 fliten, (5 flytin), 3–6, 9 flite, (3 flitte, 5–6 flight, 6 flicht, 9 fleicht, fleyte,) 4– flyte. *Pa. t.* 1 flát, pl. fliton, fleotun, 4 flytte, 4–5 flot(e, 5, 8 flet(t, 5 flayt, 6 flait, 9 *dial.* flate. *Pa. pple.* 1–3 fliten, 4 flytyn, 6 flyttyn. [A Com. WGer. str. vb.; OE. *flītan* = OHG. *flīzzan* to strive (MHG. *vlīzen* to be eager; cf. mod.Ger. *sich befleissen* str., to busy oneself).]

†**1.** *intr.* To contend, strive; also, to contend in words, chide, wrangle. Const. *against, on, with.*

Beowulf 916 (Gr.) Hwilum flitende fealwe stræte mearum mæton. c 900 tr. *Bæda's Hist.* III. xiv. [xix.] 212 Ða fliton him on þa wergan gastas. c 1200 *Trin. Coll. Hom.* 81 Swo mote we flite togenes ure fule lustes. a 1300 *Cursor M.* 7556 (Cott.) [Goliath] þus bigan on him [David] to flite. c 1350 *Will. Palerne* 2545 A noþer werkman..gan flite wiþ þat felþe þat formest hadde spoke. c 1440 *Gesta Rom.* lxxx. 400 (Add. MS.) Anothere [devil] hade..made hem to chide, ande to flyte, ande feghte. 1535 STEWART *Cron. Scot.* II. 720 Thocht mony fuill throw folie with him flyte. 1598 BERNARD *Terence* (1607) 89 He did flite or chide with him. 1725 RAMSAY *Gent. Sheph.* I. i, Sair, sair she flet wi' me 'tween ilka smack.

fig. 13.. *E.E. Allit. P.* B. 950 þe wyndez..wroþely vp-waite & wrastled togeder..flytande loude.

2. To scold. Const. *at.* Now only *Sc.* and *north.*

1500–20 DUNBAR *Poems* xxxiv. 81 The fische wyffis flett and swoir. a 1592 GREENE *Alphonsus* II. (Rtldg.) 230/1 Let me die if e'er I flight again. a 1605 POLWART *Flyting w. Montgomerie* 739 Why flait thou, foole? 1794 BURNS *O Steer her up*, Gin she take the thing amiss, E'en let her flyte her fill, jo. 1816 SCOTT *Old Mort.* xvii, 'Sudna ye hae come faster up yoursells, instead of flyting at huz?' 1853 READE *Chr. Johnstone* 70 The men fight..the women fleicht or scold.

b. *trans.* To chide, scold (a person). *Obs.* exc. *Sc.* and *north.*

14.. *Psalms Penit.* (ed. Ellis 1894) ci. 18 How he was for us falsly fleten [*rime-wds.* writen, wyten, smyten]. 1848 *Tales Kirkb.* 159 'Dinna flyte me, grandfather.' 1876 *Mid. Yorksh. Gloss.* s.v.,'He'll flite you if you do.'

3. *intr.* 'To debate, to dispute, although without scolding or violent language' (Jam.). *Obs.*

a 1225 *Leg. Kath.* 721 Me come & fatte hire to fliten wið þe fifti. 15.. *Declar.* in *Scot. Poems 16th C.* II. 267 Off mony thingis they did togedder flyte.

†**4.** 'To pray in the language of complaint, or remonstrance' (Jam.); to complain. *Obs.*

c 1400 *Melayne* 563 Bot forthe he wente, his handis he wrange, And flote with Marye euer amange. c 1470 HENRY *Wallace* v. 229 Flayt by him self to the Makar off buffe. 1585 JAS. I *Ess. Poesie* (Arb.) 17 Or when I like great Tragedies to tell: Or flyte, or murne my fate.

fliter, flyter ('flaɪtə(r)), *Obs.* exc. *dial.* Also 5 flytar, 6 flytter. [OE. *flītere*, f. *flītan* to FLITE.] In OE.: A disputer. In later use: One who scolds; a scold.

a 700 *Epinal Gloss.* 854 *Rabulus*, flitere. a 1000 *Mone B.* 2816 (Bosw.-Toller) Flitera, *schismaticorum*. c 1440 *Promp. Parv.* 106/2 Cukstoke, for flyterys, *turbuscetum*. a 1605 POLWART *Flyting w. Montgomerie* 733 Fond flytter! 1616 R. ROLLOCKE *Passion* l. 500 The Lord was not a flyter, a chyder. 1868 ATKINSON *Cleveland Gloss., Fliter*, a scold, a scolding or abusive person.

flitfold ('flɪtfəʊld). *Sc.* and *north. dial.* [f. FLIT *v.* + FOLD *sb.*] A fold that may be flitted or moved from place to place.

1743 R. MAXWELL *Sel. Trans.* 154 Flaiks, Flit-folds, or Hurdles, may be provided for laying them [Sheep] on the Summer-fallow. 1868 in ATKINSON *Cleveland Gloss.*

fliting, flyting ('flaɪtɪŋ), *vbl. sb.* Now *dial.* [f. FLITE *v.* + -ING¹.]

1. a. The action of the verb FLITE; contention, wrangling; scolding, rebuking; †a reproach.

c 1200 *Trin. Coll. Hom.* 13 Twifold speche and ilch fliting of worde. a 1300 *Cursor M.* 27742 (Cott. Galba) Wreth..it makes fliteing. 1435 MISYN *Fire of Love* 9 No man suld dar presume nor be pryde raise vp hym-self..for when flitynges to hym ar cast. 1500–20 DUNBAR *Poems* lxxxii. 11 May nane pas throw ʒour principall gaittis..For fensum flyttingis of defame. 1636 RUTHERFORD *Lett.* lxxiii. (1863) I. 189 My meek Lord..would not contend for the last word of flyting. 1816 SCOTT *Antiq.* xxxix, 'I..maun just take what ony Christian body will gie, wi' few words and nae flyting.'

b. orig. *Sc.* Poetical invective; originally, a kind of contest practised by the Scottish poets of the 16th c., in which two persons assailed each other alternately with tirades of abusive verse; also in extended use.

1508 DUNBAR *Poems* (*title*), The flyting of Dunbar and Kennedie. 1585 JAS. I *Ess. Poesie* (Arb.) 63 Let all zour verse be Literall..bot speciallie Tumbling verse for flyting. a 1605 MONTGOMERIE *Poems* (*title*), The Flyting betwixt Montgomery and Polwart. 1934 A. HUXLEY *Beyond Mexique Bay* 21 The proceedings ended with a 'flyting'. Three of the singers..proceeded to improvise stanzas of derision at one another's expense. 1948 *English Studies* XXIX. 166 The flyting between Unferth and Beowulf. 1959 A. G. BRODEUR *Art of Beowulf* 144 Flytings are either exchanges of rude wit, rough games, or invective preceding a fight. 1962 G. K. HUNTER *John Lyly* vi. 335 In the 'flytings' between Katherine and Petruchio the exchanges wear the guise of wit. 1968 *Listener* 25 Apr. 525/3 Beckett had anticipated the sequence in the flyting in *Waiting for Godot.*

2. *Comb.*: **fliting-free** *a.*, unrestricted in administering rebukes.

1637 RUTHERFORD *Lett.* clxxxi. (1863) I. 436 Christ is honest, and in that is flyting-free with sinners. **1721** KELLY *Scot. Prov.* 219, I am flyting free with you.

flitter (ˈflɪtə(r)), *sb.*¹ [f. FLIT *v.* + -ER¹.] One who or that which flits. **a.** One who changes his dwelling. **b.** A fleeting thing.

1554 BRADFORD in Coverdale *Lett. Mart.* (1564) 323 If we be flitters and not dwellers (as was Loth a flitter from Segor). **1623** tr. *Favine's Theat. Hon.* II. xiii. 203 Such..were admonished to make themselues much fairer by the goods of the soule; because those of the body were but flitters [orig. *ceux du Corps ne sont que passagers*].

flitter (ˈflɪtə(r)), *sb.*² [f. FLITTER *v.*]

1. A flittering motion.

1892 *Daily News* 17 May 5/5 The flitter of crows.

2. *Comb.*, as **flitter-winged** *a.*, having wings that flutter; also *fig.*

1820 KEATS *Lamia* I. 394 The flitter-winged verse must tell, For truth's sake what woe afterwards befel. **1861** LYTTON & FANE *Tannhäuser* 74 Wheel'd at will The flitter-winged bat round lonely towers.

flitter (ˈflɪtə(r)), *sb.*³ [a. Ger. *flitter.*] 'A minute square of thin metal, used in decoration; collectively, a quantity of such squares' (*Cent. Dict.*).

18.. *Beck's Jrnl. Dec. Art* Suppl. II. 40 (Cent. Dict.) Strong and brilliant colors are freely used, together with gilt flitter, in the representation of flowering plants, fountains, and other devices [for window-shades].

flitter (ˈflɪtə(r)), *v.* Also 5 fliter, (fleter), 5–6 flyt(t)er. [f. FLIT *v.* + -ER⁵.]

1. *intr.* Of birds, etc.: To flit about, to fly with low or short flights; to flutter. Also with *by*.

1563 B. GOOGE *Eglogs* (Arb.) 94 Euer when she rested had aboute she flyttered styll. **1600** F. WALKER *Sp. Mandeville* 153 a, Their sight is so sharpe and pearcing, that fluttering ouer the sea..they see the fish through the water. **1797** *Monthly Mag.* III. 230 To mark the quick bat flitter by. *transf.* **1483** *Liber Festivalis* (Caxton) Ej (Pentecost), In lykenesse of tonges brennyng not smertyng..lightenyng not fliteryng. **1544** PHAER *Regim. Lyfe* (1553) Bj a, The peyne is flyttering from one place to an other, without heuynes. **1583** GOLDING *Calvin on Deut.* xli. 245 A thought commeth vpon a man..sleeping, and it flittereth before him. *a* **1593** H. SMITH *Serm., Christians Practice* (1637) 252 Like unto a shittle, which flittereth from the hand of a childe. **1823** LAMB *Elia* (1860) 137 The stiff-wigged living figures that still flitter and chatter about that area. **1878** P. W. WYATT *Hardrada* 7 Where..flitter the pale ghosts.

†**b.** To move the wings ineffectually. In quot. *transf.*

1598 BARCKLEY *Felic. Man* (1631) 209 Hee began to flitter with his hands, in steede of wings..& fell downe head-long to the ground.

†**2. a.** Of a person: To shift about in mind; to waver. **b.** Of a flower: To fade, wither. *Obs.*

1542 RECORDE *Gr. Artes* Biiij, Many there be so vnconstant of mynde, that flytter and turne with euery winde. **1577** HARRISON *England* III. viii. (1878) II. 53 The sunne..would cause them [floures] to welke or flitter. **1847** HALLIWELL, *Flitter*, to hang or droop.

†**3.** To fly all about; to fly *to* or *into* dust, pieces, etc. Of the sea: To break up in foam. *Obs.*

1548 RECORDE *Urin. Physick* v. 18 Unequal [substance of urine] is..when it is thynner in one parte then in another, or flyttered out. **1557** *K. Arthur* (Copland) v. iv, Than the dragon..smote the bore al to powder both flesh and bones that it flyttered all abrode on the sea. **1583** STANYHURST *Æneis* I. (Arb.) 23 Cabbans, where seas doo flitter in arches. **1664** COTTON *Scarronides* 183 Bottle-Bear..bounces, foams, and froaths, and flitters. **1665** HOOKE *Microgr.* 126 Others flitter'd as 'twere, or flown all to pieces. *a* **1677** MANTON *Serm. Ps.* cxix. 80 A sooty matter, which flitters into dust as soon as touched.

4. *trans.* To make to flit; to move rapidly backwards and forwards; to shuffle (cards). *rare.*

1864 LOWELL *Fireside Trav.* 243 As a skilful juggler flitters the cards before you. **1893** LE GALLIENNE in *Westm. Gaz.* 16 Feb. 2/3 Many a silly thing That..perks his tiny tail ..And flitters little wing.

Hence †**ˈflittered** *ppl. a.*, dispersed, scattered; **ˈflittering** *ppl. a.*, flitting about, fluttering; trembling; †shifting, unstable, fleeting.

1549–62 STERNHOLD & H. *Ps.* cii. (1566) 250 The dayes wherin I passe my life are lyke the flittering shade. **1583** STANYHURST *Aeneis* III. (Arb.) 84 Neauer dooth she laboure to reuoke her flittered issue. *a* **1602** W. PERKINS *Cases Consc.* (1619) 59 These beginnings of grace..must not be flittering and fleeting, but constant and setled. **1634** MILTON *Comus* 214 Thou hovering [MS. flittering] angell girt with golden wings. **1650** FULLER *Pisgah* II. xiii. 270 Which..lightly pressed..becomes flittering dust. **1786** BURNS *Again rejoicing Nature* vi, When the lark..mounts and sings on flittering wings. **1867** A. SARTORIS *Week in Fr. Country-Ho.* 29 The poor flittering little nun.

flitter-mouse (ˈflɪtəmaʊs). Also 8 (9 *dial.*) flutter-. [f. FLITTER *v.* + MOUSE, in imitation of Ger. *fledermaus* (OHG. *fledermûs*, MHG. *vledermûs*) or Du. *vledermuis* (in Kilian *vledder-muys*), f. the vb. which appears in OHG. as *fledarôn* to flutter. Cf. FLICKER-, FLINDERMOUSE.] A bat.

1547 BOORDE *Brev. Health* lvi. 25 b, The bloude of a backe or flytter mouse. **1637** B. JONSON *Sad Sheph.* II. ii, Giddy flitter-mice with leather wings! **1725** SLOANE *Jamaica* II. 530 *Vespertilio*, the Batt or Flutter-mouse. **1870** SWINBURNE *Ess. & Stud.* (1875) 39 The dreadful daylight has come, the flitter-mouse is blind.

b. Used as a term of playful endearment.

1610 B. JONSON *Alch.* v. iv, My fine flitter-mouse, My bird o' the night.

ˈflittern. Also 9 *dial.* flittering. †**a.** A strip of the wood of a young oak tree (*obs.*). **b.** *dial.* A young oak.

1682 J. COLLINS *Making Salt* 21 These Trees to be bound together..with flitterns or pieces of Oak, or cross Bars. **1863** J. R. WISE *New Forest* xvi. 183 The tops of the oaks are termed, when lopped, the 'flitterings'. **1876** *Bill of Sale* in *Hampsh. Gloss.* (1883) s.v., Oak-trees and clean oak flitterns with their tops, lops, and bark.

Comb., as **flittern bark** (see quot.).

1858 SIMMONDS *Dict. Trade, Flittern Bark*, the bark of young oak-trees, as distinguished from that of old oak-trees which is called timber bark and is less valuable to tanners.

flitters (ˈflɪtəz), *sb. pl.* Now *dial.* [Altered form of FITTERS, associated with FLITTER *v.*] Fragments, torn pieces; splinters, tatters. Chiefly in phrases, as ***to dash, break*** or ***tear into, to flitters.***

1620 R. WALLER in *Lismore Papers* (1887) Ser. II. II. 247 They two are torne all to flitters. **1660** F. BROOKE tr. *Le Blanc's Trav.* 90 They..broak the ship to flitters. *a* **1734** NORTH *Exam.* I. ii. §123 (1740) 97 Dashed into Flitters at a Stroke. *c* **1817** HOGG *Tales & Sk.* V. 205 Flesh..that was hanging in dark flitters about the spine.

ˈflitter-ˌtripe, *sb. rare.* App. a rustic or jocular synonym for 'tripe'.

1822 T. MITCHELL *Aristoph.* II. 284 (*Wasps*), Your woofs of Ecbatane Resemble much the breed of flitter tripes. **1830** tr. *Aristophanes' Wasps* 158 At Ecbatana is the woof composed of flitter-tripe?

ˈflittery, *a. rare*⁻¹.

1839 COLERIDGE *Lit. Rem.* IV. 287 Can anything be more flittery and special pleading than Skelton's objections?

flitting (ˈflɪtɪŋ), *vbl. sb.* [f. FLIT *v.* + -ING¹.]

1. The action of the vb. FLIT, in various senses.

a **1300** *Cursor M.* 2015 (Cott.) Sua lang wit flitting he þam sloght, þat wine treis he þam wroght. **1529** MORE *Comf. agst. Trib.* II. Wks. 1177/2 Yet will he rather abide it and suffer, then by the flyttynge from it, fall in yᵉ dyspleasure of God. **1695** WOODWARD *Nat. Hist. Earth* I. (1723) 46 The Sea's continual flitting and shifting its Chanel. **1821** CLARE *Vill. Minstr.* II. 77 The flittings of the shrieking bat.

2. *esp.* The action of removing from one abode to another; a removal. Now chiefly *north.* and *Sc.* ***moonlight flitting***: removal by moonlight, i.e. by night or by stealth.

c **1200** ORMIN 10781 Forr Galileo bitacneþþ uss Flittinng onn Ennglissh spæche. *a* **1300** *Cursor M.* 12518 (Cott.) Þai ..to bethleem þair flitting made. **1623** LISLE *Ælfric on O. & N. Test.* 21 The people returned from Chaldea to Iury.. seventy yeeres after their flitting. **1721** KELLY *Scot. Prov.* 145 He has taken a Moon light flitting. **1787** GROSE *Prov. Gloss.* s.v. *Flit*, Two flittings are as bad as one fire. **1804** SCOTT *Let. to Ellis* 1 Aug. in *Lockhart*, I had to superintend a removal, or what we call a flitting.

b. *concr.* The goods, furniture, etc. removed from one place to another at 'a flitting'. Hence, Baggage, stores.

a **1300** *Cursor M.* 3919 (Cott.) Þai bi night þam stal away, Wijf and barn, wit flitting hale. *c* **1425** WYNTOUN *Cron.* VIII. xxxviii. 50 Ðe Schip-men sone..Twrsyt on twa Hors þare flyttyng. *c* **1470** HENRY *Wallace* I. 396 All this forsuth sall in our flytting ga. **1637** RUTHERFORD *Lett.* ccl. (1863) II. 158 Those who would take the world and all their flitting on their back, and run away from Christ. **1823** J. WILSON *Trial Marg. Lyndsay* ix. 68 'Aye, aye, here's the flitting..frae Braehead.'

†**3.** Sustenance, maintenance. Cf. FLIT *v.* 9.

a **1225** *St. Marher.* 22 I pine of prisun þer ha wes iput in, ich hire fluttunge fond ant fleschliche fode. *c* **1230** *Hali Meid.* 27 Me beheoueð his help to fluttunge & to fode.

flitting (ˈflɪtɪŋ), *ppl. a.* [f. FLIT *v.* + -ING².]

1. That moves from place to place; moving, roving, migratory. *Obs.* exc. *dial.*

c **1425** WYNTOUN *Cron.* VI. xviii. 379 Ðe flyttand Wod þai callyd ay Ðat lang tyme eftyr-hend þat day. **1613** PURCHAS *Pilgrimage* (1614) 702 In their flitting wanderings. **1764** HARMER *Observ.* IV. ii. 51 This flitting kind of life. **1829** J. R. BEST *Pers. & Lit. Mem.* 352 In the course of my moving, or, as they call it in Lincolnshire my flitting life.

†**2.** Shifting, unstable; variable, inconstant.

1413 *Pilgr. Sowle* (Caxton) IV. xxix. (1859) 61 Yf a gouernour be not stable, but varyaunt and flytting fro veray stedfastness. **1590** SPENSER *F.Q.* I. xi. 18 The yielding ayre, which nigh too feeble found Her flitting parts. **1669** WOODHEAD *St. Teresa* II. xi. 91 The Imagination..not flitting, but such, as in apprehending and fixing on a thing, there stays. **1697** DRYDEN *Æneid* x. 484 It [the spear] stop'd at once the Passage of his Wind, And the free Soul to flitting Air resign'd.

†**3.** Fleeting, transitory; evanescent, unsubstantial. *Obs.*

c **1374** CHAUCER *Boeth.* III. pr. vi. 78 How veyne and how flittyng a þing it is. *c* **1400** *Test. Love* II. Chaucer's Wks. (1532) 343 b, Howe passynge is the beautie of fleesshly bodyes? more flyttynge than mouable floures of sommer. *a* **1563** BECON *Jewel of Joy* Wks. 1563 II. 34 That oure ioye and reioysyng in the Lorde be not flittynge, transitorye, and of smal continuaunce. **1614** BP. HALL *Recoll. Treat.* 455 What is more flitting than time? **1725** POPE *Odyss.* x. 587 The rest are forms of empty Æther made, Impassive semblance and a flitting shade.

†**4.** Floating in water. *Obs.*⁻¹

c **1425** *Found. St. Bartholomew's* 43 Oone of them oonly cleuyd to the flittynge maste.

5. Making short rapid flights; darting lightly from point to point; gliding rapidly and softly; coming intermittently into momentary view.

1620 QUARLES *Feast for Wormes* 1207 Conuay'd with speed vpon the nimble wing Of flitting Fame. **1703** POPE *Thebais* 132 Swift as she pass'd, the flitting ghosts withdrew. **1746–7** HERVEY *Medit.* (1818) 223 The flitting birds and humming bees. **1794** MRS. RADCLIFFE *Myst. Udolpho* vii, The ocean's misty bed, With flitting sails. **1798–9** COLERIDGE *Love* vii, She listened with a flitting blush. **1862** MRS. H. WOOD *Mrs. Hallib.* III. xv, A flitting smile playing on his lips.

Hence **ˈflittingly** *adv.*; **ˈflittingness**.

1847 CRAIG, *Flittingly*. **1860** in WORCESTER (citing COLERIDGE). **1884** G. GISSING *Unclassed* III. v. ii. 22 A slight wrinkle might show itself flittingly here and there. *a* **1680** CHARNOCK *Attrib. God* Wks. 1684 I. 231 This flittingness in our Nature.

†**ˈflitty**, *a. Obs.* [f. FLIT *v.* + -Y¹.] Flitting, unstable, flighty.

1642 H. MORE *Song of Soul* II. i. I. xi, Busying their brains in the mysterious toyes Of flittie motion.

Hence **ˈflittiness**, instability, volatility.

1692 BP. HOPKINS *Expos. Lord's Prayer* etc. 314 This would fix that Volatileness and Flittiness of our Memories.

†**ˈflitwite.** *Obs. OE. Law.* [OE. **flítwíte*, f. *flít* FLITE *sb.*¹ + WITE.] A fine for brawling.

c **1340** HIGDEN *Polychr.* I. 96 [In a list of OE. law terms] Flitwite, id est, emenda proveniens pro contentione. **1687** SPELMAN *Gloss.*, Flitwite & Scotice Flichtwite significant, mulctam ob contentiones, rixas, et jurgia impositam.

flivver (ˈflɪvə(r)), *sb. slang* (orig. *U.S.*). [Of obscure origin.]

1. A cheap motor car or aeroplane. Also, 'a destroyer of 750 tons or less' (*Funk's Stand. Dict.* 1928).

1910 W. A. FRASER *Red Meekins* (1921) 22 You stick to me an' you'll be travellin' 'round the country in a flivver. **1919** F. HURST *Humoresque* 296 Was his little Sid fool enough to beat it all the way over here in a flivver for eight bucks the round trip? **1920** *Glasgow Herald* 21 July 9 May be I will disguise the Shamrock as a 'flivver' (as the Ford car is known here). **1924** 'DIGIT' *Confess. 20th Cent. Hobo* 11 *Flivver*, Ford automobile. **1924** W. M. RAINE *Troubled Waters* vi. 58 Rowan McCoy drove his new car—it was a flivver, though they did not call it that in those days. **1926** *Ladies' Home Jrnl.* Apr. 39 Won't it be amusing when we can..step into our little up-shooting flivvers at the back door? **1927** *Punch* 2 Feb. 135/1 He has successfully fought the villain Trust; his workmen all own 'flivvers'; there has never been a strike. **1936** *Beaver* Mar. 9/1 So-called 'flea' or 'flivver' types [of aeroplanes]. **1956** S. BELLOW *Seize Day* (1957) i. 22 He had driven a painted flivver.

2. A person or thing that has a damaging or deleterious influence; a failure.

1915 H. L. WILSON *Ruggles of Red Gap* (1917) xiii. 230 That Jackson lad has offered me about ten thousand of them vegetable cigarettes, but I'll have to throw him down. He's the human flivver. Put him in a car of dressed beef and he'd freeze it between here and Spokane. **1915** *Dialect Notes* IV. 233 *Flivver*, a hoax; also, a failure.

Hence **ˈflivver** *v. intr.*, (*a*) to fail, to come short of success; (*b*) to travel in a flivver.

1912 L. J. VANCE *Destroying Angel* vi. 74 If the production flivvers, I'll need that thirty cents. **1927** *Bulletin* 11 Apr. 14/1, I was finding the desert a bit flat when you flivvered in.

flix (flɪks). See also FLICK *sb.* [Of unknown origin: possibly connected with FLY *v.*] The fur of various quadrupeds; the down of a beaver.

1666 DRYDEN *Ann. Mirab.* cxxxii, His warm breath blows her flix up as she lies. **1757** DYER *Fleece* (1807) 80 The beaver's flix Gives kindliest warmth to weak enervate limbs. **1818** MILMAN *Samor* IX. 441 The gray flix of the wolf. *transf.* **1864** BROWNING *Dram. Pers., Gold Hair* xv, Hair, such a wonder of flix and floss.

flix, obs. form of FLUX.

flix-weed, now usu. fixweed, see FLUX *sb.* 13.

flizz (flɪz), *v. dial.* In 7 flizze. [onomatopœic; cf. *whiz.*] (See quot.) Hence **ˈflizzing** *vbl. sb.*

1674 RAY *N.C. Words* 18 *Flizze*, to Fly off. *Ibid.*, *Flizzing*, a Splinter. **1867** SMYTH *Sailor's Word-bk.*, *Flizzing*, the passage of a splinter.

†**flo.** *Obs.* Forms: 1 flá(a, 3 fla(a, 3–5 flo, (7 floe). *Pl.* 1 flán, (3 flan), 3–4 flon, (5 floon, flone). [OE. *flá* wk. fem.] An arrow.

c **893** K. ÆLFRED *Oros.* III. ix. §14 Ðær wearð Alexander þurhscoten mid anre flan. *c* **1205** LAY. 1844 Heo letten gliden heora flan. **1297** R. GLOUC. (1724) 394 Þat me ne myȝte noȝt yse bote harewen & flon. *c* **1305** *St. Christopher* 207 in *E.E.P.* (1862) 65 Hi schote him to stronge deþe wiþ wel kene flo. *c* **1400** *Gamelyn* 648 Yeldeth up ȝonge men ȝoure bowes & ȝoure flone. *c* **1450** *Robyn & Gandeleyn* v. in Child *Ballads* v. cxv. 12/2 Robyn bent his joly bowe, þer in he set a flo. **1623** COCKERAM, *Floe*, an Arrow.

flo, obs. form of FLAY *v.*

float (fləʊt), *sb.* Forms: 1 flot, 3–7 flote, (4–6 flot, 5 floote, floit, floyt(e, 7 flotte), 6–7 floate, 6– float. [Several distinct formations, ultimately from the Teut. root *fleut-*, *flaut-*, *flot-* (see FLEET *v.*), seem to have coalesced. 1. OE. *flot* str. neut. (dat. *flote*) action or state of floating; the formally equivalent ON. *flot* has also the sense 'scum, grease' (see FLOT). 2. OE. *flota* wk. masc. = ON. *flote* ship, boat, fleet. 3. In many of its

senses the sb. appears to have been a new formation on FLOAT *v.* 4. In some senses it may be an adoption of, or influenced by, the F. *flotte* (OF. *flote* and *flot*), verbal nouns f. *flotter* to FLOAT.

Cognate words, with senses corresponding to some of those of *float*, are OHG. *flôz* masc. (MHG. *vlôz* masc., mod.G. *floss* neut.) raft, buoy, fishing-net, also stream:—OTeut. **flauto-z*; and OHG. *flozza* (MHG. *vlozze*, mod.Ger. *flosse*) fem., fin, swimming-bladder, cork float:—OTeut. **flotā*; an OE. **flotu*, corresponding to the latter, may possibly be the source of sense 8.]

I. The action or state of floating or flowing.

1. a. The action of floating or †swimming. Now *rare.* †Formerly also, the condition of floating or of being on the water; *esp.* in phrase ***on*** (rarely ***at***) ***float*** = AFLOAT. †***upon the float***: floating on the stream; also *fig.* in an unsettled condition.

With *on* or *at float* cf. the synonymous ON. *á floti*, F. *à flot* (OF. *a flote*). For instances of *on flote* before 15th c., see AFLOAT.

a **1000** *Elene* 226 (Gr.) Ongan þa ofstlîce eorla mengu to flote fysan. *c* **1250** *Gen. & Ex.* 162 God..taȝte fuel on walkene his fliȝt, Ilc fis on water his flotes miȝt. **1497** *Ld. Treas. Accts. Scot.* (1877) I. 378 To ger hir [a ship] com on floit. **1570–6** LAMBARDE *Peramb. Kent* (1826) 117 A ship being on flote at the full sea. **1651** N. BACON *Disc. Govt. Eng.* II. xxiv. (1739) 110 When both Winds and Currents are uncertain, to ride at flote, till [etc.]. **1652** ASHMOLE *Theat. Chem.* Prol. 1 Past Ages have like Rivers conveied downe to us (upon the floate), the more light, and Sophisticall pieces of Learning. **1693** LUTTRELL *Brief Rel.* (1857) III. 241 The next spring tide two fourth rates will also be putt on float. **1761** *Chron.* in *Ann. Reg.* 68/1 The Richmond soon afterwards got on float. **1768–74** TUCKER *Lt. Nat.* II. xvi. 60 Our ideas being perpetually upon the float. **1817** KEATS *Calidore*, And now the sharp keel of his little boat Comes up with ripple and with easy float.

b. *transf.* Buoyant motion through the air.

1807 W. TAYLOR in *Ann. Rev.* V. 553 [He] must bid his pupil saw the air..and stamp the earth..if he means to produce the desirable float of arm, and radiation of leg.

c. *Finance.* An operation of floating a currency. Cf. FLOAT *v.* 1 d.

1971 *Daily Tel.* 10 May 14 Between the two German mark 'floats'—in Oct. 1969 and today—the international monetary scene has been comparatively calm. **1971** *Guardian* 18 Aug. 18/3 A float against the dollar by a unified European block might provide the necessary breathing space. **1971** *Economist* 4 Sept. 13/1 The Bank of Japan is operating energetically to prevent the float from being anything except a bogus one.

†**2.** The flux or flood of the tide. *lit.* and *fig.* ***at float, in float***: at high water; in quots. *fig.*

1594 *Gesta Grayorum* in Nichols *Progr. Q. Eliz.* (1807) III. 317 Cynthias rays, Whose drawing virtues govern and direct The flots and re-flots of the ocean. **1594** HOOKER *Eccl. Pol.* ix. §4 Our trust in the Almighty is that with us contentions are now at their highest float. **1622** BACON *Hen. VII*, 139 Hee being now in Float for Treasure. **1633** FORD *Love's Sacr.* II. iii, Though the float Of infinite desires swell to a tide. **1642** FULLER *Holy & Prof. St.* II. xxi. 141 Men of his profession have as well an ebbe of riot, as a flote of fortune. **1797** MRS. BENNETT *Beggar Girl* (1813) V. 182 With all her animal spirits in the fullest float of exhilaration.

†**3. a.** A wave, billow. *lit.* and *fig.* Also, the sea.

c **1477** CAXTON *Jason* 114 In trauersing the wawes and flotes of the see. **1603** KNOLLES *Hist. Turks* (1621) 1304 A man which did swimme continually in the flotes of inconstancie. **1610** SHAKS. *Temp.* I. ii. 234 The rest o' th' Fleet..are vpon the Mediterranian Flote Bound sadly home for Naples. **1655** JENNINGS tr. *Elise* 2 The mutinous flotes which beat the flanks of this great Bark.

†**b.** *fig.* Agitation of mind. *Obs.*

1579 TOMSON *Calvin's Serm. Tim.* 396/2 [They] haue not onely those flotes which the faithfull haue, when they feele themselues narrowly besette, but are hornemadde.

†**4. a.** An overflow from a river, etc.; a flood; *lit.* and *fig.* ***on (a) float***: in flood, flooded; = AFLOAT 3; also *fig. Obs.*

1577 HANMER *Anc. Eccl. Hist* (1619) 317 Where a little before men went on foote, all then was on flote. **1590** T. WATSON *Eglog. Walsingham* 46 Poems (Arb.) 153 That your Pægasean springs may leap their bound and from their floate maie seas of teares distill. **1627** MAY *Lucan* IV. 150 In their Nilus floats (*quum tenet omnia Nilus*). **1664** *Floddan F.* iii. 28 That every brook burst forth on float. **1749** FIELDING *Tom Jones* v. iii, A very trifling accident set all his passions again on float. **1763** WHITAKER *Serm.* 30 June (1767) 37 How soon may we expect to see..a float of vice and error overspread our Jerusalem?

transf. **1523** SKELTON *Garl. Laurel* 335 Closters engrosyd with his [Bacchus'] ruddy flotis.

†**b.** A side-stream or back-water.

1629 H. BURTON *Babel no Bethel* Ep. Ded. 4 A continuall current, that so merrily driues the Popish mills about, and sets ours in a back water or float.

†**II. 5.** The liquor in a dye-vat. *Obs.*

a **1500** *E.E. Misc.* (Warton Club) 88 When the madere is in flotte, breke hit smalle, that ther be no ballys. *Ibid.*, Tylle that the flote that is in the lede begynne to sethe.

III. A floating object.

6. A mass of weeds, ice, etc. floating on the surface of water.

1600 HAKLUYT *Voy.* III. 415 For the space of fifty leagues ..we alwayes found swimming on the sea certaine flotes of weedes of a ships length, and of the bredth of two ships. **1692** R. L'ESTRANGE *Fables* clxxxix. 158 They took it at first for a Ship..but it prov'd at last to be no more then a Float of Weeds and Rushes. **1827** HONE *Every-day Bk.* II. 108 The river..casting forth..floats of ice like millstones. **1845** STOCQUELER *Handbk. Brit. India* (1854) 412 The heads of the sedges, reeds, and other plants of the float are now cut off and laid upon its surface.

7. a. A raft or raft-like construction.

1535 COVERDALE *2 Chron.* ii. 16 And so wyll we hewe yᵉ tymber vpon Libanus..and wyll brynge it by flotes in the See vnto Iapho. **1697** DAMPIER *Voy.* I. 189 A little before the Bark blew up he saw a small Float on the Water, and as it appeared, a Man on it. **1844** *Hull Dock Act* 89 To remove any floats or rafts of timber.

b. A flat-bottomed boat. Also a boat-load. In quot. 1890 = *fire-float.* See also *fishing-float.*

1557 NORTH *Guevara's Diall Pr.* 260 a/1 The Flote that came oute of Cetin with salte, oyle, and honye. **1611** SPEED *Hist. Gt. Brit.* VI. liv. §10. 280 An of-spring of the Britaines embarked in Flotes. **1774** J. BRYANT *Mythol.* II. 197 The Patriarch and his family were inclosed in an ark, or covered float. **1776** G. SEMPLE *Building in Water* 34 We..filled up the Vacancy..by throwing in several Floats of Clay. **1882** SIR R. PAYNE-GALLWEY *Fowler in Irel.* 25 The punts, or 'floats' as they are there [Wexford] called, are about fifteen feet long. **1890** *Times* 25 Apr. 10/2 The four river floats were directed to be brought from their moorings to the fire.

8. A floating appliance for supporting something in the water.

a. The cork or quill used to support a baited line, showing by its movement when a fish bites.

a **1450** *Treat. Fysshynge* (1883) 16 Ye schall make ȝowr flotes in þys wise. *a* **1609** DENNYS *Secr. Angling* I. in Arb. *Garner* I. 153 Your rod, line, float and hook. **1867** F. FRANCIS *Angling* i. (1880) 9 The floats should be proportioned to the depth and strength of the stream.

b. A cork or other light substance used to support a fishing-net, etc. in the water.

1577 B. GOOGE *Heresbach's Husb.* II. (1586) 110 The Corke hath the thickeste barke..Of his barke, are made.. Floates for fishing nettes. **1883** *Fisheries Exhib. Catal.* 12 Herring-net Floats..Mackerel-net Floats.

c. A hollow or inflated part or organ that supports an animal in the water. Hence used in Florida as a name for the genus *Velella* of medusæ.

1832 LYELL *Princ. Geol.* II. 108 This 'common oceanic snail' derives its buoyancy from an admirably contrived float. **1888** *Riverside Nat. Hist.* I. 107 *Velella*..is commonly called in Florida, where it is sometimes very abundant, the 'float'.

d. In various other applications (see quots.).

1874 KNIGHT *Dict. Mech.* I. 883/2 *Float*..an inflated bag or pillow to sustain a person in the water. **1880** *Lumberman's Gaz.* 28 Jan., Cribs are formed of about 20 sticks of timber fastened between two logs called 'floats'. **1883** *Fisheries Exhib. Catal.* (ed. 4) 45 *Respirator*..a small nipple in the mouth with flexible tube supported by a float.

e. A structure fitted to the alighting gear of an aircraft to enable it to float on water.

1897 *Strand Mag.* June 717/1 The conical vessel in front is an empty float, whose use is to keep the whole from sinking if it should fall in the water. **1909** *Flight* 30 Jan. 63/1 Delagrange..has ordered a set of special floats for his aeroplane. **1913** *Aeroplane* 17 Apr. 453 Labouret..'stalled' the machine, fell over sideways, and smashed..the right float. *Ibid.* 455 The concertina floats on this machine are evidently a great success. **1928** C. F. S. GAMBLE *N. Sea Air Station* 13 Experiments with various types of floats and flotation bags for aeroplanes. **1941** W. NELSON *Airplane Lofting* i. 11 Float bottoms are designed to give small water resistance, and the float as a whole is shaped to give as little air drag as is consistent with its other functions. **1958** R. D. BLACKER *Basic Aeronaut. Sci.* viii. 130/2 The particular model..is amphibious, inasmuch as it has wheels which are retracted into the floats by the pilot for water landings.

9. a. A hollow metallic ball, a piece of whinstone, etc., used to regulate the water-level in a boiler or tank. Also, in a petrol engine, a device which floats on the petrol in the float-chamber of the carburettor and regulates the supply so that the level remains constant.

1752 SMEATON in *Phil. Trans.* (1754) XLVII. 436 What is peculiar to this engine is a float within the receiver, composed of a light ball of copper. **1856** J. BOURNE *Catech. Steam Engine* iv. (ed. 4) 154 The float is usually formed of stone or iron. **1901** *Motor-Car World* Mar. 42/1 The Float. **1902** A. C. HARMSWORTH et al. *Motors* vii. 112, F is a float with wire attached to indicate the height of the petrol. **1912** *Motor Man.* (ed. 14) 10 When the float sinks it opens a small valve and allows the petrol to flow in till a certain level is reached. The float then rises and closes the valve. **1967** K. ULLYETT *1100 Companion* viii. 122 Fuel in the float chamber is maintained at constant level by float and needle in the conventional way.

b. The small piece of ivory on the surface of the mercury in the cistern of a barometer.

1855 in Ogilvie *Suppl.*

10. *Theatr. pl.* The footlights; *collect. sing.* the row of footlights.

1829 J. R. PLANCHÉ *Paris & London* I. v. 24 A diagonal view of the stage of the Odeon is seen through the wings... At the end of the float a section of the audience and part of the theatre is visible. **1840** A. BUNN *Stage* I. 54 That mysterious line of light across the stage, (yclept in theatrical phraseology the float). **1862** DICKENS *Let.* 24 Jan. III. 212 Pauline trotting about in front of the float. **1871** *Cassell's Techn. Educ.* II. 291/1 Patent gas floats, for theatrical purposes. *Ibid.* 291/2 The range of Argand burners composing the float are arranged upside down. **1884** L. WINGFIELD in *Fortn. Rev.* Apr. 476 A marvel, because it moved behind the floats.

11. One of the boards of an undershot water-wheel or of a paddle-wheel; a float-board.

1611 FLORIO, *Ala*..the flot of a Water-mill-wheele. **1731** BEIGHTON in *Phil. Trans.* XXXVII. 10 The Force on the Floats 18 Ct. 40 lb. **1806** TREVITHICK *Let.* in *Life* (1872) I. 327, I wish to know the size of the floats on the wheel. **1856** J. BOURNE *Catech. Steam Engine* viii. (ed. 4) 323 The paddle floats are usually made either of elm or pine.

IV. Something broad, level, and shallow.

12. *Brewing.* A broad shallow vat used for cooling. ? *Obs.*

[Cf. Du. *vloot* fem. a broad shallow wooden vessel for creaming milk; also F. *flotte*, mentioned in 16th c. as part of a brewer's stock-in-trade (Littré).]

1413 *E.E. Wills* (1882) 22 Y be-quethe..I gravers, an a flot, an a planer. **1616** SURFL. MARKH. *Country Farme* 587 Other vesselles called flotes or coolers, and they be broad like vnto the fats, but only one foot deepe.

13. One of the wooden frames attached to the sides, front, or back of a wagon or cart to increase the carrying capacity.

1686 PLOT *Staffordsh.* 354 A Cart that had its floats supported, with standards erected upon the ends of the Axles. **1887** in *Kent Gloss.*

14. a. A low-bodied, crank-axled cart, used for carrying heavy articles, live stock, etc.

1866 *Daily Tel.* 23 Feb. 3/4 The pikes and handles were removed in a float in the presence of a large crowd. **1891** *Sheffield Gloss.* Suppl., *Float*, a deep cart..used for carrying pigs to market.

b. A platform on wheels, having a spectacular display arranged upon it, used in a procession.

1888 *Boston* (Mass.) *Jrnl.* 13 Sept. 2/4 A parade two miles long was composed of gay floats of all sorts of food-supplies. **1889** *Pall Mall G.* 3 Oct. 6/3 A series of Floats representative of the Seven Centuries of the Mayoralty of London.

c. ellipt. = *milk-float* (MILK *sb.* 10).

1971 *Daily Tel.* 19 Apr. 2/6 Postmen and milkmen should share deliveries from two-man floats.

†**15.** A unit of measurement for embanking work.

1707 MORTIMER *Husb.* xiv. 309 They [banks] are measured by the Float or Floor, which is eighteen foot square and one deep.

V. In various senses corresponding with senses of FLOAT *v.*

16. A tool for 'floating' or making level.

a. *Plastering.* A trowel or rule for giving a plane surface to the plaster. Also ***float-rule***.

1703 MOXON *Mech. Exerc.* 249 Floats, made of Wood, with handles to them. **1823** P. NICHOLSON *Pract. Build.* 380 It is then spread, or rather splashed, upon the wall by a float made of wood. **1853** *Dict. Arch.* (Arch. Publ. Soc.), *Float* or *Float Rule.* **1876** *Rivingtons' Notes Build. Constr.* II. 400 The surface is then gone over with a smaller hand float.

b. A file having parallel, but not diagonal, rows of teeth; a single-cut file.

1750 BLANCKNEY *Naval Expositor*, *Float* is an Instrument used by the Smiths to make their Work smooth, instead of a File. **1881** GREENER *Gun* 230 The two coils being joined.. the barrels are heated, and the surplus metal removed with a float.

c. A tool used by bowyers, represented in the arms of the Bowyers' Company. *Obs.* exc. *Her.*

It is pictured as a flat plate with teeth on the under side and a handle at the top.

1823 in CRABB *Techn. Dict.* **1828–40** BERRY *Encycl. Her.* I. Uj, Bowyers..Sa. on a chev. betw. three floats or, as many mullets of the first.

d. Various. (See quots.)

1874 KNIGHT *Dict. Mech.* I. 883/2 *Float*..10 a polishing-block used in marble-working. A *runner. Ibid.*, *Float*..6 the serrated plate used by shoemakers for rasping off the ends of the pegs inside the boot or shoe.

17. A dock or place where vessels may float.

1840 *Evid. Hull Docks Commiss.* 207 The old rivers at Bristol have been penned up, and they are now made floats. **1867** in SMYTH *Sailor's Word-bk.*

18. One of the trenches used in 'floating' land.

1785 W. MARSHALL *Midland Co.* (1790) I. 278 The floats are trenches, receiving, by the means of floodgates..the waters of a river, brook, or rivulet, and conveying it along the upper margin, and upon the tops of the..swells of the field of improvement.

19. *Tin-mining.* (See quot.)

1778 PRYCE *Mineral. Cornub.* 137 [The blast] smelts the Tin [and] forces it out..into a moorstone trough six feet and a half high, and one foot wide, called the Float.

20. *Geol.* and *Mining.*

a. Loose rock or isolated masses of ore brought down by the action of water from their original formation. Also short for *float-ore.* Chiefly *U.S.*

1814 BRACKENRIDGE *Louisiana* 146 That kind of ore called floats. **1880** L. WALLACE *Ben-Hur* VIII. v. 503 Through the rocky float in the hollows of the road the agate hoofs drummed. **1885** W. NALL in *Trans. Cumb. & Westm. Antiq. Soc.* VIII. 7 Lead ores were then classified by miners as float and shoad ore, or float and shoad.

b. (See quot.)

1883 GRESLEY *Gloss. Coal Mining*, *Float*, a clean rent or fissure in strata unaccompanied by dislocation.

21. *Weaving.* The passing of weft-threads over a portion of the warp without being interwoven with it; also the group or mass of thread so passed.

1863 J. WATSON *Art Weaving* 141 A contrivance that would..prevent Floats without any other drawback, would be a very good thing. **1882** MORRIS *Hopes & Fears Art* iv. 150 The latter eke out their gaudy feebleness with spots and ribs and long floats.

22. *U.S.* (See quot. 1837)

1837 HT. MARTINEAU *Soc. Amer.* II. 93 Who..whenever a good tract of land is ready for sale, cover it over with their *floats*, (warrants of the required habitation), and thus put down competition. **1948** E. N. DICK *Dixie Frontier* 74 Quantities of affidavits were printed and distributed to paid agents, who with the co-operation of ignorant or corrupt justices of the peace secured floats wholesale for speculators.

23. *U.S.* A voter open to bribery. Cf. FLOATER.

1885 *Pall Mall G.* 6 Nov. 2 Something like one-twelfth of the remaining voters are 'floats'—that is, men who are looking for money.

24. a. A sum of money in a shop, etc., used to provide change, small payments, etc., at the start of business; a shop till or its contents (*slang*); a small loan. Also *attrib.*

1902 W. H. CHANTREY *Theatre Accounts* ii. 24 There seems no necessity in a Theatre to have a Petty Cash Account, as each week the treasurer will reimburse all the small amounts which have been laid out by the various members of the staff, and if necessary a 'float' could be provided to meet this expenditure meanwhile. **1931** *Police Jrnl.* Oct. 503 The other day a thief..stole (knocked off) the contents of the till (the float). **1955** *Times* 8 July 6/7 Mrs. Foote produced £57 from the shop till, which she said was her 'float'. **1966** L. SOUTHWORTH *Felon in Disguise* xi. 159 Larceny of cash from the pub float of the 'Crosby Arms'. **1967** K. GILES *Death in Diamonds* ix. 170 The branch offices carry a float account because the salesmen get a portion of their commission the following morning after a sale. **1967** V. CANNING *Python Project* ii. 18 'That's a lot of money to keep around the flat.' 'My husband always said one should have a substantial cash float, just in case.' **1969** *Times* 1 Apr. 6/1 (Advt.), When you need a quick £10 float, at any time, you go to a branch with a cash dispenser in the wall.

b. The amount of money represented by cheques, etc., in transit. Chiefly *U.S.*

1915 H. P. WILLIS *Federal Reserve* xi. 228 There is, in short, a so-called 'float' which represents the volume of checks afloat in the mails at any time and not liquidated. **1924** W. O. SCROGGS *Cent. Banking Progress* 273 The amount of these checks continually in transit, the 'float', was estimated at about $300,000,000. **1930** *Economist* 18 Oct. 707/2 A..'float', that is, clearing house checks and exchanges in transit, the volume of which depends largely on stock market activity. **1931** T. E. GREGORY in W. Rose *Outl. Mod. Knowl.* xv. 652 As the volume of speculation grows, the 'float', *i.e.* the sums due at any moment, also increases.

VI. 25. *Comb.*, as **float-ball**, the ball of a ball-cock; **float-barrel**, ? a barrel used as a float for a fishing-net; **float-bladder** (see sense 8 c); **float-board**, one of the boards of an undershot water-wheel; one of the paddles of a paddle-wheel; **float-bridge**, a bridge of floats or rafts; **float-case**, = CAISSON 2 d; **float-chamber**, a small chamber in the carburettor of a petrol engine from which petrol, maintained at a constant level by the action of a float, is supplied to the jets; **float-copper** (see *float-mineral*); **float-cut** *a.*, (of a file) cut in the manner of a float (see sense 16 b); **float-feed**, a device for controlling the feed of a liquid by means of a float; also *attrib.*; **float-fescue**, a variety of fescue-grass (*Festuca*); **float-file**, a single-cut file; **float fish** (see quot.); **float-fishing**, fishing with a line and float (sense 8 a); **float-fox-tails**, a variety of *Alopecurus* or fox-tail grass; **float-gauge** (see quot.); **float glass**, glass manufactured by the *float process*; †**float-glassed** *a.*, mirrored in the waves; **float-gold** (see *float-mineral*); **float-light**, a light-ship; **float-line**, a perpendicular line drawn from a float on the surface of a fluid to a specified point below the surface; **float-mineral**, fragments of ore detached and carried away by the action of water or by erosion; also, fine particles of metal which are detached in the process of stamping and do not readily settle in water; **float needle**, a thin rod attached to a float (sense 9 a) which by passing into or out of the inlet to the float-chamber allows less or more petrol to enter it; **float-net**, a net supported by floats; †**float-ore**[1], a kind of seaweed; **float-ore**[2], **float-quartz** (see *float-mineral*); **float-plane** = *float-seaplane*; **float process**, a process for making flat glass in which the glass is drawn in a continuous sheet from the melting tank and made to float on the surface of molten metal in a controlled atmosphere while it hardens; **float road** *U.S.* (see quot. 1905); **float-seaplane**, a seaplane equipped with floats; **float-shooter**, one who goes shooting wild-fowl from a punt at night; **float-valve** (see quot.). Also FLOAT-BOAT, FLOAT-GRASS, FLOAT-STONE.

1824 R. STUART *Hist. Steam Engine* 156 Having a *float-ball *o*, which opens and shuts the valve *p*. **1891** BLACK *Donald Ross* I. 266 Lobster-creels and *float-barrels. **1866** HARTWIG *Sea & Wond.* xvii. (ed. 3) 354 A large *float-bladder. **1719** DESAGULIERS *Exp. Philos.* (1744) II. 425 It is no Advantage to have a great Number of *Float-Boards. **1858** LARDNER *Handbk. Nat. Phil.* 135 *Breast wheels.*—This class of water wheels resemble in their form and construction the undershot wheel—the float-boards, however, being closer together. **1692** *Siege Lymerick* 14 This day was chiefly spent in removing our *Float-Bridge nearer the Town. **1874** KNIGHT *Dict. Mech.* I. 883/2 **Float-case.* **1901** *Motor-Car World* Mar. 42/1 Should petrol run over at the jet when the pressure is on, give the spindle in the centre of the *float-chamber a few turns with a screwdriver to grind in the needle valve. When the engine is not running keep the spring on the float needle. **1967** K. ULLYETT *1100 Companion* viii. 125 It is a compact, dustproof carburetter, with concentric float chamber. **1881** RAYMOND *Mining Gloss.*, **Float-Copper*..fine scales of metallic copper.. which do not readily settle in water. **1888** *Lockwood's Dict. Mech. Engin.*, **Float-Cut*..a file having single lines of cutting teeth only. **1902** A. C. HARMSWORTH et al. *Motors* vii. 115 The method of supplying petrol to the carburetter is on the same principle.., *float feed. **1907** *Westm. Gaz.* 28 Nov. 4/1 The carburetter is of the float-feed type. *Ibid.* 5 Dec. 4/2 Carburetter..of the usual float-feed spray type. **1759** B. STILLINGFL. *Grasses* in *Misc. Tracts* (1762) 387 The grass..proved to be the *flote Fescue. **1834** *Brit. Husb.* I. xxxiii. 520 The flote fescue, flote fox-tails, and rough-stalked poa. **1794** W. HUTCHINSON *Hist. Cumberland* I. 27/1 *note*, After they have spawned they [Salmon] are called *float fish. **1883** *Fisheries Exhib. Catal.* p. xxxiv, Some apparatus for *float-fishing. **1816–20** T. GREEN *Univ. Herbal* I. 81 *Alopecurus Geniculatus*, *Flote Fox-tail Grass. **1834** [See *float-fescue* above.] **1888** *Lockwood's Dict. Mech. Engin.*, **Float Gauge*, a water gauge, where the height of water in a steam boiler is registered by means of a float. **1959** *Times* 21 Jan. 10/3 The advantages of *float glass..include its freedom from distortion. **1962** *Guardian* 25 June 4/6 Float glass is an entirely new glass which combines the best qualities of both plate and sheet glass. **1632** LITHGOW *Trav.* I. 5 Where *flot-glass'd Nymphs, the Circe fled, Greeks enstal. **1873** J. MILLER *Life amongst Modocs* xvi. 204 They had found only a few bars with *float gold. **1881** RAYMOND *Mining Gloss.*, *Float-gold*, Pac[ific]. **1890** *Pall Mall G.* 28 May 2/1 If, on the other hand, you crush too fine, you get 'float gold'. **1819** J. HODGSON in J. Raine *Mem.* (1857) I. 265 The *float-light in sight (a vessel anchored in the deeps). **1833** HERSCHEL *Astron.* iii. 155 The difference of the two *float lines gives the height in question. **1901** *Float needle [see *float-chamber* above]. **1965** *Punch* 8 Dec. 824/1 Bits of radio aerial, carburettor float needles, and an AA route from Leicester to Devizes. **1647** R. STAPYLTON *Juvenal* 31 A retiarius, or net-bearer, so named from a kind of *floate net, which he carryed in his hand. **1602** CAREW *Cornwall* 27 b, This *Floteore is now and then found naturally formed like rufs, combs, and such like. **1683** PETTUS *Fleta Min.* I. (1686) 6 Also all float or Easy-flowing oars. **1881** RAYMOND *Mining Gloss.*, *Float-ore*, water-worn particles of ore. **1922** *Flight* XIV. 126/2 Seaplanes include *Float Planes and Flying Boats, denoting, respectively, seaplanes fitted with floats or hull. **1939** *War Weekly* 24 Nov. 140/4 It is almost impossible to make a floatplane anything like as fast as a landplane. **1958** *Listener* 20 Nov. 818/2 Nothing can be more hazardous than landing a float-plane among sea ice. **1965** *New Scientist* 27 May 577/1 The Organization of the USSR State Committee on Aviation Technology has patented a device..for use on cargo floatplanes. **1959** *Economist* 24 Jan. 346/1 In the *float process, a continuous ribbon of molten glass is fed out of the furnace across the surface of a tank of molten metal in a controlled atmosphere, gradually being allowed to cool. **1964** *Guardian* 6 Aug. 11/8 The float process's main advantage is that it cuts costs considerably, uses less labour, and takes up less than half the space of a production line using the grinding polishing method. **1970** *Physics Bull.* Apr. 153/1 The development of the float process for the manufacture of a continuous ribbon of flat glass has provided a rich variety of novel technological and scientific problems. **1872** —— *Statist. Mines & Mining* 212 A section of country twenty miles long..is covered with *float quartz. **1901** F. A. MONTGOMERY *Reminisc. Mississippian* 115 Next morning I determined to follow an old *float road in which we found ourselves. **1905** *Terms Forestry & Logging* 37 *Float road*, a channel cleared in a swamp and used to float cypress logs from the woods to the boom at the river or mill. **1919** W. B. FARADAY *Gloss. Aeronaut. Terms* 72 **Float seaplane*, an aeroplane provided with floats for alighting on water. **1928** C. F. S. GAMBLE *N. Sea Air Station* xiii. 212 The flying-boat is not so fast, nor has it the same ceiling, as float-seaplanes. **1882** SIR R. PAYNE-GALLWEY *Fowler in Irel.* 27 Two *float-shooters, lying low in their boats on the look-out for fowl. **1874** KNIGHT *Dict. Mech.* I. 885/2 **Float-valve*, a valve actuated by a float so as to open or close the port, according to the level of the liquid.

float (fləʊt), *v.* *Pa. t.* and *pa. pple.* floated. Forms: 1 flotian, 3 floten, flotien, 4 flotie(n, 4–7 flote, (8 floate), 6– float. *Pa. t.* 4 flotte. *Pa. pple.* 7 flote. [OE. *flotian* = MDu. *vlôten*, ON. *flota*:—OTeut. **flotôjan*, f. **flot-* weak grade of root of **fleutan* to float or flow: see FLEET *v.* The development of sense in ME. was doubtless influenced by the synonymous OF. *floter* (mod.F. *flotter*), Sp. *flotar*, It. *fiottare*:—med.L. type **flottare*, f. OTeut. **flotto-* f. the same root as Eng. *float*.]

I. Intransitive senses.

1. a. To rest on the surface of any liquid; to be buoyed up; to be or become buoyant.

a **1100** *O.E. Chron.* an. 1031 (Parker MS.) Beo an scip flotiȝende swa neh þan lande swa hit nyxt mæge. *c* **1200** *Vices & Virt.* (1888) 33 Ele..wile flotten ouer alle wætes. **1483** CAXTON *Gold. Leg.* (1493) 131 b/1 Whan the tyme approched of the passyon of our lord thys tree..floted aboue the water. **1585** J. B. tr. *Viret's Sch. Beastes* D v b, Halcions ..builde their houses..the which may flote..uppon the Sea. **1646** SIR T. BROWNE *Pseud. Ep.* IV. vi. 193 Men being drowned and sunke, doe float the ninth day. **1782** COWPER *Royal George* 30 Her timbers yet are sound, And she may float again. **1878** HUXLEY *Physiogr.* iv. 57 Ice floats readily on water.

fig. **1773** GRAY *Let.* in *Corr.* (1843) 151 All that floated on the surface of my mind is faded away and gone.

b. Of a stranded vessel: To get off the ground, to get afloat.

1699 DAMPIER *Voy.* II. III. 98 Our ship did not float then, nor the next Tide neither.

c. fig. *to float in one's cups*: to be half drunk, 'half seas over'.

1630 WADSWORTH *Sp. Pilgr.* vi. 58 M. P. floting in his Cups, began a discourse.

d. *transf. Finance.* Of a currency: to fluctuate as regards its international exchange rate. Also *trans.*, to arrange for (a currency) so to fluctuate.

1965 *Guardian* 30 Sept. 1/8 The decision to let the mark float was forced on the German authorities by a sudden inflow of funds. **1965** J. L. HANSON *Dict. Economics & Commerce* 182/1 To permit the pound to 'float'..would..be a return to free exchange rates. **1970** *Daily Tel.* 2 June 20/7 Foreign exchange markets went into a flurry of activity as a result of the decision to float the Canadian dollar. **1971** *Ibid.* 10 May 14 If the mark floats high, sterling and the franc may face large inflows of foreign currency. **1971** *Economist* 4 Sept. 3/2 Japan nominally floats the yen, but really keeps it fixed.

2. a. To move quietly and gently on the surface of a liquid, participating in its motion.

a **1300** *Cursor M.* 24833 (Cott.) Forth þai floted on þat flod. **13..** *E.E. Allit. P.* C. 248 A wylde walterande whal.. bi þat bot flotte. **1570–6** LAMBARDE *Peramb. Kent* (1826) 325 The Corps now..floted up and down the River. **1653** H. COGAN tr. *Pinto's Trav.* lxvi. 268 Upon a very little raft, where we floated at the mercy of the waves. **1790** BURNS *Peg Nicholson*, Now she's floating down the Nith. **1836** W. IRVING *Astoria* I. 126 The boat floating near to him he seized hold of it.

fig. **1752** YOUNG *Brothers* IV. i, The vulgar float as passion drives. **1790** PALEY *Horæ Paul.* i. 3 To have floated down upon the stream of general tradition. **1832** *Examiner* 802/1 The new Parliament will float with the stream of public opinion. **1869** LECKY *Europ. Mor.* I. iii. 397 Christianity floated into the Roman Empire on the wave of credulity.

†**b.** *transf.* of a person: To move up and down; be conversant. *Obs.*

c **1315** SHOREHAM 21 Thaȝ he her were inne hys manhode Amanges ous to flotie.

c. quasi-*trans.* = to float upon.

1705 J. PHILIPS *Blenheim* 236 Upborne By frothy billows thousands float the stream In cumbrous mail. **1829** CLARE *Autumn* in *Anniver.* 76 Weeds, That float the water's brim.

d. *Electr.* Of a part of an electrical circuit: to be unconnected to a source of fixed potential.

1931 *Proc. R. Soc.* A. CXXXI. 688 The grid of the first valve floats at a potential just over 2 volts negative with respect to the negative end of the filament. **1945** R. C. WALKER *Electronic Equipment* iii. 54 A floating grid acquires a negative potential by collecting electrons from the cathode emission, and its final potential is in equilibrium with the cathode stream. **1947** F. G. SPREADBURY *Electronics* ii. 94 Instead of allowing the probe to float, a potential difference is maintained between it and either the cathode or anode. **1967** *Electronics* 6 Mar. 118/2 A floating input that can be operated up to 500 v above ground.

3. a. To be suspended *in* a liquid with freedom to move; also, to move freely beneath the surface. †Of a fish: To swim.

1596 SPENSER *F.Q.* VII. vii. 21 The fish, still floting, doe at random range. **1696** WHISTON *Th. Earth* III. (1722) 278 The Parts of the present upper Strata..floated in the Waters among one another uncertainly. **1727** SWIFT *Gulliver* II. viii. 165 My box..floated about five feet depth in water. **1882** VINES *Sachs' Bot.* 437 The mass of mother-cells..floats entirely free in the fluid that fills the sporangium.

b. To be drenched or flooded; to 'run', 'swim'. *rare*$^{-1}$. (Cf. 10.)

1725 POPE *Odyss.* XIII. 452 The pavements float with guilty gore.

†**4. a.** To move unsteadily to and fro like an object on the surface of a liquid; to oscillate, undulate; *fig.* to vacillate, waver. *Obs.*

1598 BACON *Sacr. Medit.* vi. (Arb.) 113 A state of minde, which in all doubtfull expectations is setled and floteth not. **1712** J. JAMES tr. *Le Blond's Gardening* 190 Let the instrument rest till the Water has done floating. **1716** COLLIER tr. *Nazianzen* 8 Their Mother..floated between Joy and Fear. **1763** SCRAFTON *Indostan* (1770) 71 Floating between his fears and wishes.

b. *nonce-use.* To spread in undulating form.

1667 MILTON *P.L.* IX. 503 His circling Spires..on the grass Floted redundant.

c. *Mil.* Of a column on the march: To present a wavy line; to be unsteady.

1796 *Instr. & Reg. Cavalry* (1813) 263 The march in line is uniformly steady, without opening, floating, or closing. **1810** [see FLOATING *vbl. sb.* 1 a].

5. a. To move freely and gently in or through the air, as if buoyed up or carried along by it.

1634 MILTON *Comus* 249 How sweetly did they flote upon the wings Of silence. **1667** DRYDEN *Ind. Emp.* I. ii, What Divine Monsters, O ye gods, were these That float in air and flye upon the Seas! **1725** POPE *Odyss.* VI. 358 To the ear Floats a strong shout along the waves of air. **1782** COWPER *Retirement* 192 The clouds that flit, or slowly float away. **1808** *Med. Jrnl.* XIX. 313 Dark spots floating constantly before the eye. **1888** BESANT *Inner House* xvi. 188 A long tent before which floated a great flag on a flagstaff.

b. *nonce-use.* of the air itself, or portions of it.

1667 MILTON *P.L.* VII. 432 The Aire Floats, as they pass, fann'd with unnumber'd plumes.

c. *fig. esp.* with sense: To move or hover dimly before the eye or in the mind; also of a rumour, etc.: To pass from mouth to mouth.

1775 SHERIDAN *Rivals* Pref., Faded ideas float in the fancy like half-forgotten dreams. **1826** DISRAELI *Viv. Grey* III. viii, Here floated the latest anecdote of Bolivar. **1857** LIVINGSTONE *Trav.* xii. 224 The remnants of serpent-worship floating in their minds. **1882** SHORTHOUSE *J. Inglesant* II. 225 He tried to read, but the page floated before his eyes.

d. To move or proceed, esp. in a leisurely or casual way; to wander from place to place. *slang* (orig. *U.S.*).

1901 'H. MCHUGH' *John Henry* 10 I'm sitting on the sofa ..when my lady friend floats into the arena. **1909** R. A. WASON *Happy Hawkins* 96 So I just floated, punchin' cows most o' the time but not runnin' very long over the same range. **1931** 'D. STIFF' *Milk & Honey Route* i. 15 The hobo really floats, which explains the name 'floater', by which he is often labelled. **1935** G. INGRAM *Cockney Cavalcade* 232 Come on. Let's float. **1936** J. CURTIS *Gilt Kid* v. 53, I floated because I got fed up and wanted her to turn in thanking me.

1959 I. & P. OPIE *Lore & Lang. Schoolch.* x. 192 Juvenile language is well stocked..with expressions inviting a person's departure,..flit, float away, [etc.]. **1970** *Globe Mag.* (Toronto) 26 Sept. 18/2 Some immigrants are bound to float on, but is Canada really doing very well for itself when a chartered accountant like Chris Mawhood gets turned off?

6. *Weaving.* Of a thread: To pass over or under several threads either of the warp or weft, instead of being interwoven with them. Of a figure: To have its threads lying in this manner.

1878 A. BARLOW *Weaving* 104 When either of the white or black threads disappear on one side of the cloth, they are not found floating underneath. **1883** T. R. ASHENHURST *Design in Textile Fabrics* vi. 159 Lappet figures..must 'float' the entire length of the figure.

7. *Comm.* **a.** Of an acceptance: To be in circulation, to be awaiting maturity. **b.** Of a commercial company, etc.: To meet with public support, get 'floated' (see 12).

1778 H. LAURENS in Sparks *Corr. Amer. Rev.* (1853) II. 234 Our bills..are now floating, in imminent danger of dishonor and disgrace. **1884** *Truth* 13 Mar. 385/2 If the Company floats, the promoter gets his money.

†**8.** To fish with a float (see FLOAT *sb.* 8 a).

1630 [see FLAT *v.* 10]. **1651** J. BARKER *Art of Angling* (1653) 8, I will shew my opinion of floating for Scale Fish in the River or Pond.

9. *Sporting.* To hunt by approaching the game with a boat or float at night. (See FLOAT *sb.* 7 b.)

1871 J. BURROUGHS *Wake-Robin* (1884) 106 Our guide proposed to conduct us to a lake..where we could float for deer. **1877** HALLOCK *Sportman's Gazetteer* 83 In jacking or floating, the shooter sits in the bow of a canoe just behind a lantern which throws a powerful light ahead. **1885** *Outing* (U.S.) Oct. VII. 80/2 'Kill any deer over there?' 'No,' said Carl, 'we floated two nights, but it was terrible foggy.'

II. Transitive senses.

10. To cover or flood with a liquid. **a.** To cover (land) with water, either naturally or artificially, *esp.* for agricultural or military purposes; to flood, inundate, irrigate. Also with *over.*

1649 BLITHE *Eng. Improv. Impr.* (1652) 16 The first Piece of improvement of floating or watering lands. *c* **1710** C. FIENNES *Diary* (1888) 70 They can by them [ditches] floate ye grounds for 3 miles round. **1794** *Trans. Soc. Encourag. Arts* XII. 245 The above land was floated over by salt water, every full and change of the moon. **1816** JANE AUSTEN *Emma* (1866) 158 He thought..I should find the near way floated by this rain. **1833** HT. MARTINEAU *Brooke Farm* xiii. 97 Can he float his meadows at the cost of five pounds an acre?

b. (chiefly *hyperbolical*) To overspread with fluid; to drench, inundate. Also, To saturate (a powder magazine) with water.

1729 SAVAGE *Wanderer* II. 228 A smoaking spring of gore Wells from the wound, and floats the crimson'd floor. **1758** PARRY in *Naval Chron.* VIII. 154 We had taken care to float our powder. **1818** JAS. MILL *Brit. India* I. III. iv. 624 The field was floated with blood. **1836** MARRYAT *Midsh. Easy* xxvi, The danger [from fire] had been so great that the fore magazine had been floated.

c. *transf.* and *fig.*

1586 J. HOOKER *Girald. Irel.* in *Holinshed* II. 84/1 The ladie Margaret began to take heart, hir naturall stoutnesse floted, as well by the remembrance of hir noble birth, as by [etc.]. **1603** J. DAVIES *Microcosmos* (Grosart) 71/1 Each sense in pleasure's seas flotes [Fancie] flotes. **1860** HAWTHORNE *Marb. Faun* (1879) I. xii. 115 A..military band..floating her [the city] with strains. **1865** M. ARNOLD *Ess. Crit.* i. (1875) 16 He [Burke] so lived by ideas..that he could float even an epoch of concentration and English Tory politics with them.

11. a. Of water, the tide, etc.: To lift up, or support on its surface (anything buoyant); to bear (anything buoyant) along by the force of the current; occas. with mixture of the two senses. Also with *off, out, up.*

1606 *Choice, Chance, etc.* 5 With a sodaine tempest man and horse ouerthrown vpon a Rock, and the goods all flote or drownd. **1699** DAMPIER *Voy.* II. III. 44 For want of Water to float them over some flats in the Lagunes. *Ibid.* 98 The Tide then rose so high, as to float her quite up. **1739** LABELYE *Short Acc. Piers Westm. Bridge* 34 The Tide had..risen so high as to endanger the Caisson..from being floated out of its true Place. **1856** KANE *Arct. Expl.* II. xiv. 149 They [masses of ice] are floated off to be lost in the temperatures of other regions. **1890** *Spectator* 20 Sept. 362/2 The Manchester Canal..will float the biggest ocean steamers.

fig. **1877** OWEN *Wellesley's Desp.* Introd. 19 The vehement tide of public opinion..floated out the good old nobleman who had first broken Tippoo's power.

b. To set afloat; *fig.* to buoy up, support.

1823 LAMB *Elia* Ser. II. *Poor Relation,* She has wherewithal in the end..to float him again upon the brilliant surface. **1885** *Law Rep.* 15 Q. Bench Div. 11 He expended more than 5000 *l.* in floating the ship.

c. To place (a sheet of paper, etc.) flat on the surface of a liquid. Chiefly *Photogr.*

1853 *Fam. Herald* 3 Dec. 510/2 You float on the surface of this a sheet of paper prepared as follows. **1882** ABNEY *Instr. Photogr.* (ed. 5) 199 If the paper is floated much longer..the albumen..is apt to dissolve the size.

12. a. To get (a company, scheme, etc.) afloat or fully started (see AFLOAT 6); to procure public support or acceptance for.

1833 HT. MARTINEAU *Vanderput & S.* vi. 102 The means by which a present neighbour of yours is floating a scheme. **1865** *Pall Mall G.* 18 Aug. 9/1 Manufacturing lists of directors for new companies, in order to get them 'floated'. **1872** YEATS *Growth Comm.* 311 Serves as a reservoir for floating loans in cases of emergency. **1872** GREG *Enigmas* 229 The sages..have falsified their creed, in order to float it.

b. To set (a rumour) afloat (see AFLOAT 8); to give currency to; to circulate.

1883 *St. James's Gaz.* 21 Dec. 3/1 Floating all manner of embarrassing rumours.

13. To guide or convey along the surface of water; to convey by water. Also with *off.*

1739 LABELYE *Short Acc. Piers Westm. Bridge* 35 The Sides of the Caisson were floated off over the Sides of the Pier. **1776** GIBBON *Decl. & F.* I. (1846) V. 8 The treasures of Africa were floated on rafts to the mouth of the Euphrates. **1853** SIR H. DOUGLAS *Milit. Bridges* (ed. 3) 385 The great tubes constituting the Conway Bridge were floated across the river.

14. To convey gently through the air or ether; to cause to move lightly in the air; to waft.

1823 F. CLISSOLD *Ascent Mt. Blanc* 22 A soft breath of wind spread its folds, and floated it gently in the air. **1836** EMERSON *Nature, Commodity* Wks. (Bohn) II. 143 Provision..for his support..on this green ball which floats him through the heavens. **1840** MRS. BROWNING *Drama of Exile* Poems 1850 I. 83 Floated on a minor fine Into the full chant divine, We will draw you smoothly.

15. In various technical applications of senses 10, 11. **a.** *Pigment-making.* To levigate (pigments) by causing them to float in a stream of water, rejecting the heavier particles that sink to the bottom. **b.** *Electrotyping* and *Stereotyping.* To cover (a forme, a page of type) with fluid plaster of Paris, either to fill up the spaces before electrotyping, or (in the almost obsolete plaster-process) to form a plaster mould. **c.** *to float up* (a tin can) (see quot. 1884).

1880 F. J. F. WILSON *Stereotyping & Electrotyping* 128 The page or pages must be floated in plaster-of-Paris. *Ibid.* 134 When low spaces are used and the form has not been floated prior to moulding. **1883** R. HALDANE *Workshop Receipts* Ser. II. 405 The powder is then levigated (floated), in order to obtain various degrees of fineness. **1884** KNIGHT *Dict. Mech.* IV. 348/2 'Floating up' tin cans, *i.e.* soldering the ends inside, the can standing upon the heated plate till the solder runs.

16. To render smooth or level. In various technical uses: **a.** *Plastering.* To level (the surface of plaster) with a 'float'; to spread the second coat of plaster on (a ceiling, wall, etc.). Also with *down.* **b.** *Farriery.* To file the teeth of (a horse). **c.** *Agric.* (See quots.) **d.** *Wool-spinning.* To take *off* (the carded wool) in an even layer.

a. *a* **1703** MOXON *Mech. Exerc.* 249 To float Seelings or Walls. **1741** in Willis & Clark *Cambridge* (1886) I. 36 The Ceilings..to be floated and finished in the best and workmanlike manner. **1748** B. LANGLEY *Lond. Prices* 329 Fronts of old Houses..are frequently floated down, the old decay'd Mortar raked out, and the Joints fresh pointed anew. **1839** *Pract. Builder* II. 187 The space between the screeds..must be floated with a hand-float.

b. 1886 *N. Y. Weekly Tribune* 28 Dec. (Cent.) Many an old horse will renew its life if its teeth are floated, as the process is called.

c. 1785 W. MARSHALL *Midland Co.* (1790) II. 437 *Float*..to pare off the surface of sward. **1888** *Sheffield Gloss., Float,* to pare stubble from land by means of a paring knife.

d. 1879 *Cassell's Techn. Educ.* IV. 341/1 The teeth move in the same direction as those on the workers and cylinder, so as to clean or 'float' off the wool.

17. *Weaving.* To form (a figure) with 'floating' threads (see 6).

1894 *Textile Manuf.* 15 Apr. 151 This method of reeding ..necessitates the figure being floated.

floatable ('fləʊtəb(ə)l), *a.* [f. FLOAT *v.* + -ABLE. Cf. Fr. *flottable.*]

1. Capable of floating; that may be set afloat.

1846 *Pope's Jrnl. Trade* 576 (Advt.) Floatable and buoyant in the water. **1883** MISS BROUGHTON *Belinda* I. I. ix. 164 Employed in dropping..anything floatable that comes handy—into the earth-reddened stream.

2. Of a river or stream: That can be floated on; capable of supporting floating objects. Chiefly *U.S.*

1826 KENT *Comm.* (1873) III. 414 The owners of the lands on rivers not navigable or floatable have the exclusive right of fishing therein. **1884** *Law Rep.* 9 App. Cases 393 They [the streams] were made navigable and floatable for timber during freshets.

3. *absol.* passing into *sb.* Something that floats or may be floated.

1864 *Laws of Michigan* 23 To allow the free passage of boats, vessels, craft, logs, timber, lumber, or other floatables along such waters.

Hence **floata'bility** [see -ITY], the quality of being floatable.

1884 *Law Rep.* 9 App. Cases 393 The right applies to all streams..whether floatability is the result of improvements or not.

floatage ('fləʊtɪdʒ). [f. FLOAT *sb.* + -AGE. Cf. Fr. *flottage.*]

1. The action or state of floating.

1626 in *4th Rep. Hist. MSS. Comm.* 11/1 [The ship 'being taken at floatage' by..a Dutch captain..was seized for the Lord High Admiral of England.] **1868** GLADSTONE *Juv. Mundi* xiii. 487 Ten days of floatage from the Bosphorus will give five hundred miles, or thereabouts, from that point.

2. *concr.* Anything that floats.

a. = FLOTSAM; also the right to appropriate flotsam.

1672 *Cowell's Interpr., Flotages*..are such things as swim on the top of the Sea, or other great Rivers. **1858** in W. White *Month in Yorksh.* xv. 138 Free fisheries, plantage, floatage..and other maritime franchises. **1867** SMYTH *Sailor's Word-bk., Floatage,* synonymous with *flotsam.*

b. *collect.* Vessels that float on or pass up and down a river.

1854 *Michigan Rep.* II. 524 All streams susceptible of any valuable floatage. **1881** *Echo* 8 Dec. 2/4 The Government recouped itself out of tolls taken on the floatage.

c. A floating mass (of weeds).

1891 J. WINSOR *Columbus* ix. 204 They found around the ships much green floatage of weeds.

3. Floating power, buoyancy.

1877 BLACKMORE *Erema* I. ix. 102 Behind it..came all the ruin of the mill that had any floatage. **1883** *Daily News* 5 July 3/1 The metal pontoons giving floatage.

attrib. **1881** W. C. RUSSELL *Sailor's Sweeth.* II. v. 240 Without imperilling the floatage power of the timber.

4. The part of a ship above the water-line.

1839 MARRYAT *Phant. Ship* xli, The whole of her floatage was above water. **1847** *Illustr. Lond. News* 24 July 59/1 Nine inches more of floatage are required.

floatation, flotation (fləʊ'teɪʃən). [f. FLOAT *v.* + -ATION = Fr. *flottaison.*

The spelling *flotation* is not etymologically justifiable, but is more common in use, prob. because it disguises the hybrid formation, so that the word appears more conformable to the general analogy of scientific terms.]

1. a. The action, fact, or process of floating, in various senses; the condition of keeping afloat. *attrib.* Applied to any device that gives buoyancy.

centre of floatation: the centre of gravity in a floating body. ***plane*** or ***line of floatation*** = Fr. *flottaison, ligne de flottaison,* the plane or line in which the horizontal surface of a fluid cuts a body floating in it. ***stable floatation***: the position of stable equilibrium in a floating body.

1806 GREGORY *Mechanics* I. 377 The plane of floatation is the horizontal surface of the fluid in which the vessel floats. *c* **1850** *Rudim. Navig.* (Weale) 158 Water Lines, or Lines of Flotation. **1853** KANE *Grinnell Exp.* xv. (1856) 115 These constantly shifting centres of flotation. **1853** SIR H. DOUGLAS *Milit. Bridges* (ed. 3) 53 Compared with the stability of the vessel and its power of floatation. **1867** W. PENGELLY *Devon Trans.* II. 264 It may be doubted whether [these reasons]..are capable of explaining the floatation of clouds. **1878** MARKHAM *Gt. Frozen Sea* ii. 25 They [icebergs] were of very deep flotation. **1884** SIR R. BAGGALLAY in *Law Rep.* 13 Q. Bench Div. 171 During this period of flotation and transit.

attrib. **1883** *Chamb. Jrnl.* 8 Dec. 771/1 Spherical buoys which..show half..their shape above the flotation line. **1928** [see FLOAT *sb.* 8 e]. **1940** *Chambers's Techn. Dict.* 343/1 *Flotation gear,* a system of air or gas bags, sometimes with hydrovanes, to enable a land plane, in an emergency, to land and remain afloat, on water. **1958** *Times* 1 Sept. 4/6 A..general-purpose missile..is being shown complete with parachutes and flotation bag; the latter inflates automatically when the missile falls into the sea. **1963** *Times* 17 May 14/1 Divers jumped from the helicopters and attached the flotation collar to the capsule. **1971** *Times* 17 July 5/4 Under your seat there is a floatation device.

b. The separation of particulate material, esp. pulverized ore, by utilizing the varying capacity for floating on a given liquid that results from differences in the surface properties of the particles (rather than from differences in density); freq. *attrib.* So **froth flotation,** flotation in which the separation is enhanced by using a liquid to which a frothing agent has been added and bubbling air through it, so forming a froth in which certain of the particles collect.

1908 *Westm. Gaz.* 1 Aug. 15/1, 11,775 tons of dump tailings were treated by the flotation process. **1925** *Jrnl. Iron & Steel Inst.* CXI. 471 The application of flotation-methods to existing coal-washery-plants, and the cost and working expenses of such appliances, are discussed. *Ibid.* 472 The article describes the application of froth-flotation processes to the recovery of coal from the sludge. **1927** *Daily Express* 15 July 10/1 The original ore is readily amenable to treatment by flotation. **1951** KIRK & OTHMER *Encycl. Chem. Technol.* VI. 595 Separations made by flotation include not only the concentration of base-metal ores but also widely divergent applications such as the separation of ink from repulped paper stock, of peas from pea pods, [etc.]. **1968** COULSON & RICHARDSON *Chem. Engin.* (ed. 2) II. xvii. 704 Froth flotation is widely used in the metallurgical industries where, generally, the ore is difficult to wet and the residual earth is readily wetted. **1970** *Materials & Technol.* III. ii. 117 Many flotation plants treat over 20,000 tonnes of ore per day.

2. The action of floating a company or enterprise.

1889 *Financial Times* 23 Jan. 1 The London Mexican Prospecting and Finance Company, Limited. Since its flotation it has [etc.]. **1893** *Westm. Gaz.* 1 May 6/1 The flotation of this mine..is now contemplated.

'floatative, *a.* [f. as prec. + -ATIVE.] Tending to or producing floatation.

1886 T. O' C. SLOANE in *Sci. Amer.* 4 Dec. 356 The slight floatative effect of the additional portion of the glass submerged.

'float-boat. [f. FLOAT *sb.* or *v.* + BOAT *sb.*]

†**1.** A ship's long-boat. *Obs.*

So called because it was not carried on board like the other boats, but towed astern.

1322 *Close Roll* 15 Ed. II. mem. 8 (= Calendar p. 453) Navicula sua que vocatur flotebate. *a* **1572** KNOX *Hist. Ref.* Wks. (1846) I. 120 Schortlie thare after the Admirall schot a flote boite, which..sounded the deipe, and so returned to hir schippe. **1659** TORRIANO, *Zàttara,* a Float-boat, or long boat to attend a great ship.

2. A raft.

1600 Holland *Livy* xxi. lvi. (1609) 425 The remnant.. passed Trebia with float-boats and flat barges. 1810 James *Mil. Dict.* (ed. 3) *Float-boat*, a raft upon which persons or things may be conveyed by water.

floated ('fləʊtɪd), *ppl. a.* [f. float *v.* + -ed.[1]] That floats or is floated.

1799 Cowper *Castaway* 27 The cask, the coop, the floated cord.

b. *esp.* Of a field, tract of country, etc.: Flooded, inundated, irrigated. Cf. flotten.

1675 Evelyn *Terra* (1729) 42 Which is the reason that floated and irriguous Grounds are so pregnant. 1735 Somerville *Chase* iv. 170 O'er floated Meads, o'er Plains with Flocks distain'd. 1799 T. Wright *Art Floating Meadows* 15 Floated meadows require no manure from the farm yard.

c. *Plastering.* (see float *v.* 16 a.)

1823 P. Nicholson *Pract. Build.* 373 A coat of plaster, which is pricked-up for the floated work. 1842 Gwilt *Encycl. Archit.* Gloss., *Floated lath and plaster*, plastering of three coats. *Ibid.*, *Floated Work*, plastering rendered perfectly plane by means of a Float.

floater ('fləʊtə(r)). [f. as prec. + -er.] One who or that which floats.

1. a. In intransitive senses of the vb.

1717 Eusden *Ovid's Met.* iv, Pity the floaters on th' Ionian seas. 1831 *Blackw. Mag.* XXX. 15 Halcyons all, fair floaters hung in the sunshine on waveless seas. 1882 Sir R. Payne-Gallwey *Fowler in Irel.* 27 They [ducks] get no chance of quiet from the floaters. 1885 H. Stopes *Malt* xi. 133 The proportion of floaters [= 'floating corns'] depends partly upon the quality of the grain.

spec. (*a*) A dead body found floating in water. *U.S. slang.*

1890 J. A. Riis *How Other Half Lives* xix. 230 'Floaters' come ashore every now and then with pockets turned inside out. 1963 J. Mitford *Amer. Way Death* iii. 53 Floaters.. are another matter; a person who has been in the Bay for a week or more.. will decompose more rapidly.

(*b*) A golf-ball capable of floating on water.

1897 *Westm. Gaz.* 30 Mar. 9/2 There are bournes from which no ball, not e'en a floater, returns. 1927 *Daily Express* 29 Sept. 9 Many leading American professionals ask that the 'floater' be adopted as the official standard ball.

(*c*) A mine adrift.

1916 'Taffrail' *Carry On* 54 Almost every day 'floaters', which have broken adrift from their moorings, are solemnly sunk by rifle fire.

(*d*) A piece of float-ore.

1921 *Chambers's Jrnl.* 508/1 The molybdenite-seeker next proceeds to work in earnest by breaking all the loose 'floaters' or detached boulders, and collecting all the flakes that are set free in bags. 1928 *Sunday Dispatch* 25 Nov. 3/5 The chance discovery.. of a large 'floater', or piece of gold-bearing quartz. 1950 K. S. Prichard *Winged Seeds* 21 But I reckon the lode these floaters came down from 's not far off.

(*e*) (See quot. 1933.) *Prison slang.*

1933 *Punch* 25 Oct. 456/1 A 'floater' is an old magazine, book 'or even a newspaper' which is smuggled irregularly from cell to cell. 1958 F. Norman *Bang to Rights* 97 It's [*sc.* a book] a floater so you can sling it if you think you are going to get a turn over.

b. transitive senses.

1783 *Useful Projects* in *Ann. Reg.* 95/1, I consulted my meadow floaters. 1868 Yates *Rock Ahead* ii. iii, Directors of banks, and the 'floaters' of 'concerns'. 1889 *Harper's Mag.* Feb. 432/2 The 'floater' has to wade out in the water.. to cut loose with his axe the logs which have stuck fast.

2. In various technical uses.

a. The floating diaphragm in Papin's steam-engine.

1824 R. Stuart *Hist. Steam Engine* 52 Elevating the piston or floater.

b. (See quot.).

1857 Nichol *Cycl. Phys. Sc.*, *Floater*, a contrivance indicating the height of level of a fluid in a vessel, whose depth we cannot at the time directly examine.

c. = float *sb.* 14.

1888 Elworthy *W. Somerset Word-bk.*, *Floater*, a cart having the axle 'cranked down' so that though the wheels are high the body is very near the ground.

d. *Stereotyping.* = *floating-plate.*

1882 Southward *Pract. Printing* 566 The 'floater', a plate of metal fitting on the inside of the 'dipping pan'.

3. a. *Stock Exchange.* A government stock certificate, a railway-bond, etc. accepted as a recognized security.

1871 *Temple Bar Mag.* Feb. 320 Floaters are exchequer bills and similar unfunded stock. 1883 *Pall Mall G.* 3 May 5/1 The chief use of floaters is.. as a means by which banks .. can raise money in the general market when they are short of funds.. To describe exactly what a floater is.. would be a matter of some difficulty. Some.. affect to consider that a Government bond to bearer, provided the Government be not in default, may be tendered as a floater; others draw the line at United States bonds.

b. *Insurance.* A policy in general terms, esp. covering portable goods. (Cf. floating *ppl. a.* 5 b.)

1900 *Policy-holder* 6 June 441/2 The Norwich Union is largely interested.. by specific amounts and by floaters... Messrs. John McNairn and Co. had a £20,000 floater from the North British.

4. orig. *U.S.* **a.** A voter who has not attached himself to any political party, orig. one whose vote may be purchased. In later U.K. use, without any suggestion of corrupt practice.

1847 *Knickerbocker* XXIX. 329 Early the next morning the 'floaters' were marched in single file with votes in hand, to the ballot box. 1883 H. George in *N. Amer. Rev.* Mar. 203 'How many of them floaters?'—*i.e.* merchantable voters —continued the candidate. 'Four hundred' was again the answer. 1888 *Pall Mall G.* 5 Nov. 7/2 Expressions indicating the intention to buy the Indiana 'floaters'. 1896 *Westm. Gaz.* 22 Feb. 5/2 The 'floaters' should be mostly credited to Mr. Morley. Many people at Montrose believe he is certain to have a majority of 1,500. 1959 *Spectator* 25 Sept. 394/1, I find it hard to believe that many floaters were impressed by the Conservatives' first TV broadcast. 1963 *Punch* 6 Feb. 194/1 A charming Tory supporter.. may well sway incalculable numbers of 'floaters' when polling day comes.

b. One who is perpetually changing his place of abode; a vagrant. Also, one who frequently changes his job; a temporary employee.

1859 T. S. Woodward *Reminisc.* (1939) 49 He was a floater.. but he located him a tract in the fork of Coosa and Tallapoosa. 1873 J. H. Beadle *Undevel. West* xxiii. 455 There are clerks, agents.. and perhaps fifty 'floaters', making up the American population. 1878 —— *Western Wilds* iii. 45 A man.. failed, lost hope, and sank into a 'floater'. 1883 W. H. Bishop in *Harper's Mag.* Oct. 718/2 They are irresponsible floaters. 1909 Webster, *Floater*, one who takes temporary employment; specif., a substitute teacher. *U.S.* 1923 J. D. Hackett in *Managem. Engin.* May, *Floater*, a person who habitually leaves one occupation and goes to another for the sake of variety. 1927 W. T. Root in C. Johnson *Negro in Amer. Civ.* (1931) 321 The larger number of unmarried 'floaters' drifting into the city. 1931 [see float *v.* 5 d]. 1931 G. Irwin *Amer. Tramp & Underworld Slang* 76 *Floater*, a migratory worker, one who moves from place to place, but who has some excuse for this in that he works occasionally. 1934 *Sun* (Baltimore) 11 Jan. 1/5 He denied that the order marked the establishment of a policy designed to prevent the employment of transient or 'floater' labor. 1967 L. Deighton *Expensive Place* xv. 104 'The murdered girl was working for us'.. 'A floater?'.. 'No. Permanent.' 1969 *Daily Tel.* 24 Oct. 16/5 There are only a score of vacancies to be filled, and these are of no interest to a number of young 'floaters' in and out of jobs as delivery boys, petrol pump attendants, car washers. 1971 H. C. Rae *Marksman* ii. vi. 149 [He's a] Detective Inspector; a floater, I think they call it. He circulates from department to department.

c. In Southern U.S.: A representative of several counties grouped together, and therefore not directly responsible to any one of them.

1853 *Texas State Gaz.* 16 July (Farmer) A candidate for floater in the district composed of the counties of Fayette, Bastrop, and Travis.

d. An official order to leave a town or district; a sentence suspended on condition that the offender leaves the area. *U.S. slang.*

1914 Jackson & Hellyer *Vocab. Criminal Slang* 34 *Floater*... A suspended sentence; a mandatory order to quit a community or locality. Example: 'The rap wasn't strong enough, so they took a floater.' 1926 J. Black *You can't Win* vi. 69, I was just after gettin' a six months' floater out of Denver. 1952 J. Steinbeck *East of Eden* 334 There's a permanent order in the Sheriff's office.. that if I.. admit I'm your wife I'll get a floater out of the county and out of the state.

5. A mistake, 'bloomer'. *slang.*

1913 A. Lunn *Harrovians* iv. 78 There is no phrase for a *faux pas* at Harrow... It is only when he reaches the university that he realizes that such banter is often a 'floater', and for this handy expression he has no parallel in school slang. 1925 A. Huxley *Those Barren Leaves* i. i. 8 What she called, in her jovial undergraduatish moments, a 'floater'. 1929 Wodehouse in H. Cotton *Legion Bk.* 110 It's just when our intentions are best that we always make the most poisonous floaters. 1938 E. Waugh *Scoop* i. ii. 33 Have a cigarette or—had he made a floater?—or do you prefer your churchwarden? 1967 A. Wilson *No Laughing Matter* iii. 312 I've as good as said that we don't want your money... Just the sort of floater I would make, babbling on.

'float-grass. Also 5 flotgrese, 6 floter-, 7–8 flot, 6–9 flote-grass. [f. float *sb.* or *v.*; cf. Du. *vlotgras.*] A name given to various species of grass sedge growing in marshy ground, swampy meadows, etc.; e.g. *Glyceria fluitans* and *Alopecurus geniculatus.*

c 1440 *Promp. Parv.* 168/1 Flot grese, *ulva.* 1597 Gerarde *Herbal* i. xi. §2. 13 The second [spiked Flote grasse] is called *Gramen fluuiatile spicatum*: likewise Flote grasse and Floter grasse, bicause they swim and flote in the water. 1640 Parkinson *Theat. Bot.* xiv. xl. 1276 10 *Gramen Fluviatile cornutum*, Horned Flote grasse. 1725 Bradley *Fam. Dict.* s.v. *Springs*, The Furrows and Water Tracts, where they usually stalk and paddle for.. Flotgrass, Roots, and the like Things, on which they feed. 1863 Prior *Plant-n.* 82 Float —or more properly Flote-Grass.. *Poa fluitans.*

† floathing. *Obs. rare.* A thin stratum.

1743 R. Maxwell *Sel. Trans. Soc. Improv. Agric. Scot.* 185, I first lay upon the Bars small Wood or Whins, then a Floathing of small Coals, then Stones.

floating ('fləʊtɪŋ), *vbl. sb.* [f. float *v.* + -ing[1].]

1. The action of the vb. float in various senses.

a. intransitive uses.

1562 J. Heywood *Prov. & Epigr.* (1867) 135 Flotyng and fleetyng agree not there meete. 1587 Golding *De Mornay* viii. 98 A floting of a Vessell, at the pleasure of the winde. 1654 Whitlock *Zootomia* 391 While we are at Sea in the Floatings of this world. 1810–17 M. Wilks *Hist. Sketches S. India* (1869) I. xxi. 479 Hyder.. observed a floating to take place along the whole mass [of cavalry]. 1837 Whewell *Hist. Induct. Sc.* (1857) I. 56 The falling and floating of bodies. 1894 M. Grant in *Century Mag.* Jan. 354/1 'Jacking' or 'floating' for moose is seldom practised.

b. transitive uses.

1669 Worlidge *Syst. Agric.* 270 Floating, or drowning, or watering of Meadows. 1883 R. Haldane *Workshop Receipts* Ser. ii. 406 The washed clay is dried.. and immediately ground to fine powder. The floating is done by hand or power. 1888 *Daily Tel.* 18 Oct., The successful floating of the Salt Union.

2. *concr.* in *Plastering.* (Cf. float *v.* 16 a.)

1823 P. Nicholson *Pract. Build.* 391 Floating, in plastering.—The second coat of three-coat work. 1873 Spon *Workshop Receipts* 122 The floating is of fine stuff with a little hair mixed in it.

3. *Comb.*, as ***floating-trench***; also **floating-rule** (= float *sb.* 16 a); **floating-screed** (see quot.).

1649 Blithe *Eng. Improv. Impr.* vi. (1653) 27 The one called a Flowing or Floating Trench, wherin I carry my water. 1785 W. Marshall *Midland Co.* (1790) II. 61 By means of floodgates and floating trenches. 1842 Gwilt *Archit.* Gloss., *Floating Screeds*, strips of plaster previously set out on the work, at convenient intervals, for the range of the floating-rule or float.

floating ('fləʊtɪŋ), *ppl. a.* [f. as prec. + -ing[2].]

1. a. That floats (in various senses of the vb.). ***floating leaf***: see quot. 1790.

1600 Hakluyt *Voy.* III. 415 We supposed that these floting weeds did grow vpon some rocke vnder the water. 1745 P. Thomas *Voy. S. Seas* 256 The River is crouded.. with a prodigious Number of Barks.. which.. make a Kind of floating City. 1781 Cowper *Anti-Thelyphthora* 73 When .. floating films envelop every thorn. 1790 Martyn *Lang. Bot.*, Floating leaf, *Folium natans*, lying flat on the surface of the water. 1819 P. Wakefield *Excurs. N. Amer.* (ed. 3) 25 There is one boat which, without exaggeration, may be denominated a floating palace. 1832 J. Lindley *Introd. Bot.* i. 84 Stomata are found.. in floating leaves upon the latter [*sc.* the upper side] only. 1837 Irving *Capt. Bonneville* II. 215 The ice became broken and floating. 1838 *Southern Lit. Messenger* IV. 26/1 The noise of steam, and the dissonant voices of the crowd subside, and give place to the regular thump of the floating hotel [*sc.* a steamer]. 1843 *Knickerbocker* XXII. 85 The Knickerbocker-Steamer, that floating palace of the Hudson. 1872 B. Jerrold *London* xxi. 187 Soothing a convict's last moments in the floating infirmary off Woolwich Dockyard. 1877 Bennett tr. *Thomé's Bot.* iii. 73 The floating primary root of *Trapa.* 1878 A. Barlow *Weaving* 104 In some kinds of figured weaving these floating threads are cut off. 1912 *Chambers's Jrnl.* 184/2 A floating factory means an old steamer of three to four thousand tons, a size which has annually been increased... By using the larger size of steamers the owners are able to fit them with plant not only for trying out the blubber.. but also with plant for turning the carcasses into oil and guano. 1933 *Discovery* July 213/1 In 1930 floating factory ships, with their consorts the whale-catchers, were to be found encircling three-quarters of the Antarctic continent. 1966 *Guardian* 14 Mar. 18/5 Two floating hotels .. to carry tourists upstream from Cairo to Aswan. 1966 *Economist* 22 Oct. 366/1 The Poles started out as specialists in modern trawlers, floating fish factories and base ships—with reinforced hulls for operation in Arctic waters—and they now rank second in this specialised field to Japan. 1967 C. D. Sculthorpe *Biol. Aquat. Vasc. Plants* iv. 72 Floating-leaved hydrophytes are generally unable to withstand severe winds and turbulent waters.

b. Of water: Overflowing, flooding; also, fluctuating, ebbing and flowing.

1578 Lyte *Dodoens* iii. vi. 321 This.. groweth.. in the brinkes of diches and floting waters. 1712–4 Pope *Rape Lock* ii. 48 The sun-beams trembling on the floating tides.

2. *Comm.* Of a cargo: At sea. Of trade, rates, etc.: Of or pertaining to cargoes at sea.

1848 Arnould *Mar. Insur.* (1866) I. i. iii. 106 When a floating cargo (i.e. a cargo at sea) is sold in London. 1883 *Daily News* 19 Sept. 6/6 Floating terms, at 44*s.* 6*d.* to 48*s.* 6*d.* 1887 *Ibid.* 21 Nov. 2/7 A quiet tone has prevailed throughout the floating trade to-day.

3. a. Having little, or comparatively no attachment; disconnected. ***floating ribs*** (see quot. 1860).

1806 *Med. Jrnl.* XV. 273 A number of torn floating membranes. 1831 R. Knox *Cloquet's Anat.* 31 Twelfth Rib. This rib.. has been called the floating rib. 1840 F. D. Bennett *Whaling Voy.* 175 Tentacles.. spread out loose and floating. 1860 Mayne *Expos. Lex.*, *Floating Ribs*, the last two of the false ribs, whose anterior extremities are not connected to the rest or to each other. 1889 J. M. Duncan *Lect. Dis. Women* xxxiii. (ed. 4) 273 There are achings in cases of what is called floating kidney.

b. (See quot.)

1888 *Lockwood's Dict. Mech. Engin.* s.v., When the lever of a weigh-bridge or of a testing machine is in equal balance it is said to be floating.

4. Not fixed or settled in a definite state or place; fluctuating, variable, unstable. Esp. in ***floating population.***

1594 T. B. *La Primaud. Fr. Acad.* ii. 388 Because our mindes are more floting & vnstable. 1678 *Life Edw. Black Pr.* in *Harl. Misc.* (1809) III. 151 Floating-bands.. 'The Companions, or Adventurers'. 1690 Locke *Hum. Und.* i. iv. (1695) 26 There is scarce any one so floating and superficial in his Understanding, who hath not some reverenced Propositions, which [etc.]. 1793 Burke *Cond. Minority* Wks. 1842 I. 625 That floating multitude which goes with events. 1835 *Niles' Register* 27 June 289/1 The remark of a distinguished politician.. in the convention of 1822, as to the power of what he called the 'Floating Population' over the result of elections. 1838 Prescott *Ferd. & Is.* (1846) III. xiv. 120 Many floating rumours. 1876 *Cassell's Techn. Educ.* IV. 302/1 The floating population of the city is very numerous. 1933 'G. Orwell' *Down & Out* i. 7 The lodgers were a floating population.. who used to turn up.. stay a week and then disappear again. 1962 *Lancet* 26 May 1119/1 More people come to London. There is a greater floating population. 1965 B. Sweet-Escott *Baker St. Irreg.* i. 35 Innumerable other departments were represented—.. Electra House,.. the B.B.C., and a floating population from the Ministry of Information.

5. *Finance.* **a.** Not fixed or permanently invested; unfunded. (See capital, B 3 c; debt 4 e.)

1816 KEATINGE *Trav.* (1817) II. 180 Manual labour..is at present the floating capital of France. **1845** McCULLOCH *Taxation* III. ii. (1852) 448 Variations in the amount of floating capital. **1856** EMERSON *Eng. Traits, Wealth* Wks. (Bohn) II. 71 A thousand million of pounds sterling are said to compose the floating money of commerce. **1893** *Daily News* 15 Mar. 6/3 It appears that all the floating debt is secured by collateral securities.

b. Of a marine insurance policy: (see quot. 1959).

1839 *Southern Lit. Messenger* V. 7/1 The packets, by their 'floating policies of insurance' offer another inducement to shippers. **1902** *Encycl. Brit.* XXIX. 527/2 As it frequently happens that merchants desire to have all their shipments covered, by whatever vessel they may come, they require insurance in general terms; such a policy is termed a *floating* policy. **1959** JOWITT *Dict. Eng. Law* I. 814/2 *Floating policy*, a marine insurance policy issued to cover all shipments of goods by the assured by any vessel between specified places.

c. Of a currency, or its exchange rate: fluctuating, not fixed. Cf. FLOAT *v.* 1 d.

1964 H. G. GRUBEL *World Monetary Reform* 442/2 Floating exchange rates. **1970** P. EINZIG (*title*) The case against floating exchanges. **1971** M. A. G. VAN MEERHAEGHE *Economics* xii. 419 After 1931 several monetary units became floating currencies. **1971** *Guardian* 17 Aug. 3/6 The cumulative effect of the floating mark (now tantamount to an upward revaluation of more than 8 per cent) and the 10 per cent import surcharge means that German exports there will be 18 per cent dearer.

6. a. In various technical combs., as **floating anchor** (see quot.); **floating axle**, a live axle in which the revolving part turns the wheels while the weight of the vehicle is carried on the ends of a fixed axle housing; **floating battery**, a vessel fitted up and used as a battery; **floating clough** (see quot.); **floating collimator** (see quot.); **floating crane**, a crane mounted on a pontoon; **floating derrick** (see DERRICK 2 d); **floating dock**, a large (usually rectangular) vessel made with water-tight compartments, and used as a graving-dock; **floating drydock** = *floating dock*; **floating floor** (see quot. 1963); **floating harbour** (see quot.); **floating lever** (see quot.); **floating meadow** (see quot.); **floating mill** *U.S.*, a mill so constructed as to float in a river and be worked by the current; also *attrib.*; **floating pier**, a landing-stage which rises and falls with the tide; **floating plate**, *Stereotyping* (see quot.); **floating point** *Computers*, designating a method of representing numbers by two sequences of digits, one sequence being the significant digits of the number and the other indicating the position of the radix point; usu. *attrib.*; **floating rail** = FLOAT *sb.* 13; **floating reef** *Austral.* (see quot.); **floating voter**, a voter who has not attached himself to any political party; in U.S. *spec.* = FLOATER 4 a; also **floating vote**, the vote of such a person; also *collect.*

1874 KNIGHT *Dict. Mech.* I. 884/1 **Floating Anchor*, a frame of spars and sails dragging overboard, to lessen the drift of a ship to leeward in a gale. **1907** *Westm. Gaz.* 26 Nov. 4/3 The famous '*floating' back axle. **1695** *Lond. Gaz.* No. 3073/2 They..have made also two *Floating Batteries with 20 Pieces of Cannon upon them. **1803** *Naval Chron.* IX. 495 She is fitting as a floating-battery. **1866** E. A. POLLARD *Southern Hist. War* I. 60 The floating battery dismounted two of the parapet guns [of Fort Sumter]. **1841** BREES *Gloss. Civ. Engin.*, **Floating Clough*, a moveable dam or machine, used for scouring out channels or inlets. **1833** HERSCHEL *Astron.* ii. 95 *The *floating collimator*..is..a small telescope ..fastened horizontally..on a flat iron float which is made to swim on mercury. **1903** *Work* 27 June 331/2 Another crane in use in Germany is called the *floating crane, and is built on a large, massive flat boat. **1969** *Jane's Freight Containers 1968–69* 216 (*caption*) Port of Copenhagen. Floating crane 'Herkules'. 180 tons capacity also used for containers. **1866** E. CLARK in *Proc. Inst. Civ. Eng.* XXV. 296 *Floating docks were originally built of timber. **1838** E. FLAGG *Far West* I. 135 Upon the river-bank..stands the '*Floating Dry Dock'. **1921** *Daily Colonist* (Victoria, B.C.) 8 Apr. 19/4 Extensive improvements have been made in the floating drydock, increasing its efficiency. **1970** *Encycl. Brit.* VII. 712/2 The floating dry dock is a barge-like structure that can be partially submerged so that a vessel can enter it. The dock is then raised in the water and pumped dry to permit work on the vessel. **1934** *Builder* CXLVII. 552/1 The patent 'Cullum' soundproofing system..has suitable insulating value. The standard thickness of this *floating floor is 3¾ in. **1963** *Gloss. Build. Terms* (*B.S.I.*) 18 *Floating floor*, the upper portion of a floor including the flooring, when this is supported on a resilient layer or mountings to provide insulation against sound or vibration. **1970** *New Yorker* 8 Aug. 46/3 What is particularly effective against noise is a so-called floating floor. This consists of a main concrete floor four centimeters thick on top of which lies a one-centimeter-thick layer of glass wool, with another four-centimeter layer of concrete. **1841** BREES *Gloss. Civ. Engin.*, **Floating Harbour*, a breakwater, composed of large masses of timber, anchored and chained together..which rise and fall with the tide. **1884** KNIGHT *Dict. Mech.* IV. 348/2 **Floating Lever* (Railway) a name applied to the horizontal brake-levers beneath the car-body. **1813** T. DAVIS *Agric. Wilts* Gloss., *Floating or flowing meadows—Those that are laid up in ridges, with water carriages on each ridge and drains between. **1796** A. ELLICOTT in C. V. Mathews *A. Ellicott* (1908) 138 These *floating mills are erected upon two, or more, large canoes or boats, and anchored out in a strong current. **1817** S. R. BROWN *Western Gaz.* 52 It has a post office, and a floating mill anchored abreast of the town. **1888** *Lockwood's Dict. Mech. Engin.* 145 *Floating Mill Wheel*, a water wheel, having its bearings in a boat moored in the stream of a rapidly flowing river, which turns the wheel and performs work for which it is suitable. **1948** E. N. DICK *Dixie Frontier* 250 Some of the first water-power mills were 'floating mills'. These were built on two large dugout canoes. An undershot wheel was placed between them. **1855** CLARKE *Dict.*, **Floating-pier*. **1839** URE *Dict. Arts* 1177 (s.v. *Stereotype Printing*) Each mould..is laid, with the impression downwards, upon a flat cast-iron plate, called the *floating-plate. **1948** *Math. Tables & Other Aids to Computation* III. 318 *Floating-point operation greatly reduces the need for scale factors, but complicates the operations of addition and subtraction. **1954** *Jrnl. Assoc. Computing Machinery* Oct. 194 The Type 704 is the first large-scale commercially available computer to employ fully automatic floating point arithmetic commands. **1964** F. L. WESTWATER *Electronic Computers* ix. 143 Sets of subroutines to be performed in 'floating-point' rather than the fixed-point mode arithmetic. **1892** *Melbourne Age* 31 Dec. 10/3 Horse and Spring Cart, *floating rail, and Harness. **1869** R. B. SMYTH *Goldf. Victoria* 611 *Floating Reef, applied often to masses of bed-rock which are found displaced and lying among the alluvial *detritus*. **1847** *Knickerbocker* XXIX. 328 Such constitute what in common parlance is called the '*floating vote'. **1856** *Cincinnati Enquirer* 7 May 4/1 Fremont, having been a successful explorer and trapper, can discover and trap a great many floating votes. **1935** H. NICOLSON *Let.* 13 Nov. (1966) I. 223 There is always the slender chance that the floating vote may swing away from Labour and that I shall creep in. **1971** *Daily Tel.* 19 July 2/2 He has been fighting a vigorous campaign to mop up any floating votes among the 77 delegates at the union's fortnight-long conference. **1905** D. G. PHILLIPS *Plum Tree* 14 Those stiff-armed men were the '*floating voters' of that ward of Pulaski. **1955** *Observer* 1 May 11 The floating voter is not a unique creature. **1958** *Economist* 13 Sept. 828/2 That now well-known and inoffensive favourite of the touchy floating voter, Mr. Aneurin Bevan.

b. In the names of various aquatic plants (see quots.). *U.S.*

1814 J. BIGELOW *Florula Bostoniensis, Alopecurus geniculatus*, floating foxtail grass. **1847** Floating glyceria [see *manna grass*, MANNA[1] 9]. **1934** *Nat. Geogr. Mag.* LXV. 598 The dainty white display of floating-heart nods over its own reflection in the water. **1940** N. C. FASSETT *Man. Aquat. Plants* 42 Floating Moss. *Ibid.* 55 Floating Brownleaf. Floating-leaf Pondweed.

floating bridge. [f. FLOATING *ppl. a.*] In various applications (see quots.).

1706 PHILLIPS (ed. Kersey), *Floating-bridge*, a Bridge made in form of a Work in Fortification call'd a Redoubt, consisting of Two Boats cover'd with Planks. **1727–41** CHAMBERS *Cycl.*, *Flying* or *Floating-Bridge*, is ordinarily made of two small bridges, laid one over the other, in such a manner, as that the uppermost stretches and runs out, by the help of certain cords running through pullies placed along the sides of the under-bridge. **1842** G. W. FRANCIS *Dict. Arts*, etc., *Floating Bridge*, a collection of beams of timber, of sufficient buoyancy to sustain itself on the surface of a river, and reaching across it. **1858** SIMMONDS *Dict. Trade*, *Floating-bridge*, a flat-bottomed ferry steam-boat in harbours or rivers, running on chains laid across the bottom, and constructed for the conveyance of passengers, goods, and vehicles. **1867** SMYTH *Sailor's Word-bk.*, *Floating-bridge*, a passage formed across a river or creek by means of bridges of boats. **1889** *Century Dict.* s.v. *Bridge*, *Floating-bridge*, a part of a bridge, supported by a caisson or pontoon, which can swing into and away from the line of roadway.

floating island. [f. FLOATING *ppl. a.*]

1. An island that floats.

1638 SIR T. HERBERT *Trav.* (ed. 2) 13 The Whales, the Seas Leviathan..like so many floating Ilands concomitating us. **1850** LYELL *2nd Visit U.S.* II. xxxi. 186 There is a floating island in it, well wooded.

2. *Cookery.* (*U.S.*) A custard with floating masses of whipped cream or white of eggs.

1771 FRANKLIN *Lett.* Wks. 1887 IV. 415 At dinner..we had a floating island. **1860** O. W. HOLMES *Elsie V.* vii. (1891) 110 The marvellous floating-island.

floating light. [f. FLOATING *ppl. a.* + LIGHT *sb.*] **a.** A lightship: called also more fully, ***floating-light-vessel***. **b.** A life-buoy with a lantern, for use when any one falls overboard at night.

1793 SMEATON *Edystone L.* §94 A vessel was then fitting out..as a temporary floating Light. *Ibid.* Till the determination in respect to the floating light-vessel was known. **1858** SIMMONDS *Dict. Trade*, *Floating-light*, a life-buoy carried at a ship's stern, with a light or lanthorn.

floatingly (ˈfləʊtɪŋlɪ), *adv.* [f. as prec. + -LY[2].] In a floating manner.

1660 W. SECKER *Nonsuch Prof.* 256 The tide that so floatingly brings in the ship, suddenly leaves her in the mud. **1829** *Blackw. Mag.* XXVI. 952 Blest..the breath that sighs it floatingly aside! **1857** *Chamb. Jrnl.* VII. 272 All lost in pearly mist, that floatingly Seems her gray garments trailing low.

floating-out. [f. vbl. phrase *to float out* (see FLOAT *v.* 11).] The action of floating a ship out of dock. Also *attrib.*

1896 *Daily News* 18 Sept. 6/7 The floating-out of dock of the battleship Illustrious at Chatham Dockyard. **1899** *Ibid.* 29 June 5/5 Her floating-out weight was 1,500 tons.

floatless (ˈfləʊtlɪs), *a.* [f. FLOAT *sb.* + -LESS.] Without a float.

1871 *Cassell's Mag.* 22 July 335/1 We wait patiently, fishing in this floatless floating manner, for our next bite.

float-man, floatman (ˈfləʊtmən). [f. FLOAT *sb.* + MAN.] A man who manages a float.

1882 SIR R. PAYNE-GALLWEY *Fowler in Irel.* 26 One of the oldest Wexford floatmen, once told me [etc.].

floatsam, -some, obs. or dial. f. FLOTSAM.

ˈ**float-stone.** [f. FLOAT *v.* + STONE.]

1. A bricklayer's rubbing-stone for smoothing the surfaces of bricks used in curved work.

1703 MOXON *Mech. Exerc.* 246 Some use a Float Stone, with which they rub the moulding of the Brick. **1812** J. SMITH *Panorama Sc. & Art* I. 196 The stone upon which bricks cut with curved surfaces are rubbed, is called a float-stone.

2. A stone so light as to float upon water, e.g. a spongy variety of opal.

1805 R. JAMESON *Min.* II. 552 Floatstone..is light yellowish grey. **1814** tr. *Klaproth's Trav.* 57 A range of float-stone hills. **1859** PAGE *Handbk. Geol. Terms*, *Float-Stone*, a variety of earthy silica..Being porous, it swims on water till saturated.

ˈ**float-ways,** *adv. rare.* [f. FLOAT *sb.* (sense 16 b) + -WAYS.] In the manner of a float (or single-cut file), like a float.

1773 *Gentl. Mag.* XLIII. 18 [Marbles] are chips of stone, which are put into an iron mill that goes in water. There are several partitions, with rasps within, cut floatways, not with teeth, so turn constantly round with great swiftness.

ˈ**float-whey.** *Sc.* and *north. dial.* [f. FLOAT *v.* + WHEY.] 'Those parts of the curd left in whey, which, when it is boiled, float on the top' (Jam.).

1549 *Compl. Scotl.* vi. 43 Thai maid grit cheir of..reym, flot quhaye, grene cheis. **1823** GALT *Entail* vii. 22 The float whey which in a large china punch-bowl graced the centre of the table. **1847** in HALLIWELL. *Northumb.*

floaty (ˈfləʊtɪ), *a.* Also 4, 7 flotie. [f. FLOAT *sb.* or *v.* + -Y[1].]

†**1.** Watery. *Obs.*

13.. *E.E. Allit. P.* A. 127 Þe fyrre I folȝed Þose floty valez.

2. Fitted to float, capable of floating, buoyant; hence, of a ship: Drawing little water.

a **1608** SIR F. VERE *Comm.* 28 Mine was a floaty ship and well appointed for that service. **1624** CAPT. SMITH *Virginia* (1629) 194 Some few buttes of beare being flotie they got. **1793** SMEATON *Edystone L.* §170 To render them very floaty and lively in a rough hollow sea. **1862** *Temple Bar Mag.* IV. 351 The floaty air-cases rising on the other [side], the boat recovers her proper position.

Hence ˈ**floatiness**, the quality or state of being floaty; buoyant emptiness.

1839–44 TUPPER *Proverb. Philos.* (1852) 478 The foolish floatiness of vanity, and solemn trumperies of pride.

flob (flɒb), *v.* [onomatopœic var. of FLOP *v.*, indicating a softer movement and duller sound (see FLABBY).] *intr.* To move heavily or clumsily, with a dull heavy sound.

1860 *Squires & Parsons* 196 Fine cock-pheasants, heavy with buck-wheat and maize flobbed up through the branches of the trees, were fired at and flobbed down again. **1882** A. S. GIBSON *Adv. Pig Fam.* xxx, How they flobb'd, and how they flopp'd And flounder'd all around!

†ˈ**flobbage.** *Sc. Obs.* ? 'Phlegm' (Jam.).

1535 LYNDESAY *Satyre* 4380 Sic flobbage sche layis fra hir, About the wallis.

†ˈ**flobber,** *v. Obs. rare*$^{-1}$. In 4 flober. [app. onomatopœic; cf. *slubber*. (The readings *flober* here, and *beflobered* in B. XIII. 401, are established by the alliteration.)] *trans.* To dirty, soil.

1377 LANGL. *P. Pl.* B. xiv. 15 Couthe I neuere..kepen it clene an houre..Þat I ne flober it foule fro morwe tyl eue.

Flobert (ˈfləʊbət, ‖flobɛr). The name of a French armourer, N. *Flobert* (1819–94), used *attrib.* and *ellipt.* to describe a cartridge or breech-loading rifle designed by him.

1890 WEBSTER, *Flobert*, a small cartridge designed for target shooting. *Ibid.*, *Flobert rifle*, a rifle adapted to the use of floberts. **1895** *Montgomery Ward Catal.* 461/2 Flobert Rifle, oiled walnut pistol grip stock. *Ibid.* 463/3 Flobert Rifle Parts... Flobert Hammers, Remington action... Flobert Breech Blocks. **1904** *Kynoch Jrnl.* Jan.–Mar. 33 The Flobert cartridge is notable as being an evolution of the percussion cap. **1918** E. S. FARROW *Dict. Mil. Terms* 237 *Flobert*, a small cartridge used in target shooting, sometimes called ball cap. *Ibid.*, *Flobert-Gras Rifle*, a breech-loading rifle, having several valuable improvements on the Chassepot, used in France 1874–1885. **1950** *Publ. Amer. Dial. Soc.* xiv. 29 *Flobert, flaubert* [flobət] *n.*, any small rifle, twenty-two caliber. Florence, S.C. Obsolescent? Once a popular make of rifle.

floc (flɒk). [f. FLOC(CULUS.] A flocculent mass of fine particles and colloidal material.

1921 H. P. EDDY in *Jrnl. Western Soc. Engin.* XXVI. 259 When sewage containing a suitable supply of dissolved oxygen is agitated..the fine suspended matter and the colloidal substances here gather into small aggregations called flocculi or floc. [*Note*] The word 'floc' as used herein, signifies a single sponge-like mass or an aggregation of such masses. **1947** H. E. BABBITT *Sewerage & Sewage Treatm.* (ed. 6) xix. 396 As the floc settles through the liquid it sweeps other settleable particles down with it. **1959** J. CLEGG *Freshwater Life* (ed. 2) xix. 324 The flocs in the activated sludge system perform the same function of purification as the zooglea layer on the percolating filter.

†ˈ**floccify,** *v. Obs.*$^{-0}$. [f. L. phrase *floccī facĕre*: see -FY. Cf. FLOCK *v.*[2] 2.] (See quots.)

1623 COCKERAM *Floccifie*, to set nought by. **1656** BLOUNT *Glossogr.*, *Floccify*, to set nought by, to esteem little.

floccillation (flɒksɪˈleɪʃən). [f. L. *_floccill-us_ dim. of _floccus_ FLOCK _sb._[2] + -ATION.] = CARPHOLOGY.

1842 BRANDE _Dict. Sc._, _Floccillation_, picking the bedclothes. This is an alarming symptom in many acute diseases. **1847** in CRAIG; and in mod. Dicts.

ˌflocciˌnauciˌnihiliˌpilifiˈcation. _humorous._ [f. L. _floccī, naucī, nihilī, pilī_ words signifying 'at a small price' or 'at nothing' enumerated in a well-known rule of the Eton Latin Grammar + -FICATION.] The action or habit of estimating as worthless.

1741 SHENSTONE _Let._ xxii. Wks. 1777 III. 49, I loved him for nothing so much as his flocci-nauci-nihili-pili-fication of money. **1816** SOUTHEY in _Q. Rev._ XIV. 334. **1829** SCOTT _Jrnl._ 18 Mar., They must be taken with an air of contempt, a floccipaucinihilipilification [_sic_, here and in two other places] of all that can gratify the outward man.

Also **flocciˈnaucical** _a._, inconsiderable, trifling. **flocciˈnaucity**, a matter of small consequence.

1826 SOUTHEY _Vind. Eccl. Angl._ 38 The Poet used them significantly, and never intended them to bear a flocci-naucical signification. **1829** —— in _Q. Rev._ XXXIX. 108 The flocci-naucities to which so much importance is attached.

floccipend (ˈflɒksɪpɛnd), _v. rare._ [ad. L. phrase _floccī pendĕre_ (_floccī_, see prec. + _pendĕre_ to weigh, esteem). Cf. _vilipend_.] _trans._ To regard as insignificant or of no account; to make no account of.

1548 HALL _Chron._ (1809) 444 Articles..whiche the eares of euery honest creature knowynge the duetie of the subiect to hys prynce, woulde abhorre and floccipend. **1882** W. THOMSON _Bacon & Shaks._ 12 A profession prone to floccipend odd locks of thought from woolly-headed thinkers.

floccose (flɒˈkəʊs), _a._ [ad. late L. _floccōs-us_, f. _floccus_: see -OSE.]

1. Furnished with a tuft (or tufts) of woolly hair. ? _Obs._

1752 SIR J. HILL _Hist. Anim._ 542 The tail [of the lion] is long, thick, and floccose.

2. _Bot._ Covered with or composed of flocci.

1830 LINDLEY _Nat. Syst. Bot._ 331 In the..foliaceous species [of Lichens], the medulla is distinctly floccose. **1874** COOKE _Fungi_ (1875) 74 The spores..nestling on the floccose mycelium.

Hence **floˈccosely** _adv._, in a floccose manner.

1840–68 PAXTON _Bot. Dict._, _Floccosely-tomentose_, down, disposed in little tufts. **1847** in CRAIG.

floccular (ˈflɒkjʊlə(r)), _a. Anat._ [f. FLOCCUL-US + -AR.] Of or pertaining to the flocculus of the cerebellum. _floccular process_: the flocculus.

1870 W. H. FLOWER _Osteol. Mammal._ x. 127 The small depression..is the nearly obliterated floccular fossa.

flocculate (ˈflɒkjʊlət), _a. Ent._ [f. FLOCCULUS + -ATE[2].] (See quot.)

1826 KIRBY & SP. _Entomol._ IV. 346 _Flocculate_, when the posterior coxæ are distinguished by a curling lock of hair.

flocculate (ˈflɒkjʊleɪt), _v._ [f. as prec. + -ATE[3].] _trans._ To aggregate into flocculent masses.

1877 LE CONTE _Elem. Geol._ (1879) 70 _note_, The property, possessed by lime..of flocculating and precipitating clay sediments.

Hence **floccuˈlation**, the process of flocculating.

1885 BREWER in _Amer. Jrnl. Sc._ Ser. III. XXIX. 4 The flocculation and precipitation of the suspended material is almost equally rapid. **1961** _Lancet_ 16 Sept. 631/1 Flocculation tests [were] negative.

floccule (ˈflɒkjuːl). [anglicized form of FLOCCUL-US.] A small portion of matter resembling a flock or tuft of wool.

1845–6 G. E. DAY tr. _Simon's Anim. Chem._ II. 93 Some floccules separated themselves, but no coagulation took place. **1882** C. A. YOUNG _Sun_ ix. 292 As to the form of the floccules, it would seem that the successive precipitation.. must result in clouds of great vertical extent.

flocculence (ˈflɒkjʊləns). [f. FLOCCULENT: see -ENCE.] The state or condition of being flocculent; the condition of containing flocci.

1847 in CRAIG. **1878** TYNDALL in _Pop. Sci. Monthly_ XIII. 287 If..the air above be chilled, we have descending streams—if the air below be warmed, we have ascending streams as the initial cause of atmospheric flocculence.

flocculency (ˈflɒkjʊlənsɪ). [f. as prec.: see -ENCY.] = prec.

1881 SPOTTISWOODE in _Nature_ No. 623. 551 This tube.. shows flake-like fluttering striæ, with a slight tendency to flocculency near the head of the column.

flocculent (ˈflɒkjʊlənt), _a._ [f. L. _flocc-us_ FLOCK _sb._[2] + -ULENT.]

1. Resembling flocks or tufts of wool; consisting of loose woolly masses.

1800 tr. _Lagrange's Chem._ I. 249 A flocculent precipitate of magnesia. **1804** ABERNETHY _Surg. Obs._ 65 A congeries of flocculent fibres. **1821** _Blackw. Mag._ X. 270 [He] succeeded in sending up some pretty light flocculent cirri. **1857** HENFREY _Bot._ §343 The mushroom is the large fleshy fruit arising from the flocculent mycelium, or 'spawn'.

2. Of the atmosphere: Holding particles of aqueous vapour in suspension: cf. FLOCCULUS 1.

1878 _Smithsonian Inst. Rep._ 510 A flocculent condition of the atmosphere, due to the varying density produced by the mingling of aqueous vapor.

3. Covered with a short woolly substance; downy.

1870 HOOKER _Stud. Flora_ 125 Leaves..more or less pubescent or flocculent below when young. **1874** COUES _Birds N.W._ 265 For the first two or three days they [the chicks] are only densely flocculent on the under parts.

Hence **ˈflocculently** _adv._

1885 _Manch. Weekly Times_ Suppl. 8/1 The petioles were flocculently woolly.

flocculose (ˌflɒkjʊˈləʊs), _a. Bot._ [f. as next + -OSE.] Composed of flocculi.

1830 LINDLEY _Nat. Syst. Bot._ 331 A nucleus, consisting of a flocculose-gelatinous substance.

flocculous (ˈflɒkjʊləs), _a._ [f. FLOCCUL-US + -OUS.] Resembling flocculi.

1816 KIRBY & SP. _Entomol._ (1843) I. 344 A very curious combing or rather curling instrument..with which they comb out the peculiar silky material as it issues from these mammulæ into that flocculous texture.

‖**flocculus** (ˈflɒkjʊləs). Pl. flocculi. [mod.L. _flocculus_, dim. of L. _floccus_ FLOCK _sb._[2]] A small flock or tuft.

1. A small quantity of loosely-aggregated matter resembling a flock of wool, held in suspension in, or precipitated from, a fluid.

1799 KIRWAN _Geol. Ess._ 116 The very little that was dissolved was soon precipitated again in the form of minute flocculi. **1862** H. SPENCER _First Princ._ II. ix. §76 (1867) 227 If we assume the first stage in nebular condensation to be the precipitation into flocculi of denser matter. **1872** COHEN _Dis. Throat_ 3 Small quantities of it having coagulated spontaneously into clots or flocculi.

2. _Anat._ A small lobe in the under surface of the cerebellum, immediately behind the middle peduncle; the subpeduncular lobe.

1840 G. V. ELLIS _Anat._ 49 The flocculus, or sub-peduncular lobe. **1872** MIVART _Elem. Anat._ ix. 367.

3. _Astr._ **a.** Applied to the wisps of luminosity in a nebula.

1826 HERSCHEL in _Mem. Astron. Soc. Lond._ II. 491 The flocculi [in the nebula of Orion], instead of being generally round, are drawn out into little wisps.

b. One of the small cloudy wisps or masses on the sun's surface, revealed when the sun is photographed with the spectroheliograph.

1903 G. E. HALE in _Publ. Yerkes Observ._ III. I. 5, I now propose the name _flocculi_ for the regions on the Sun's disk which are shown only on photographs made with the spectroheliograph. _Ibid._ 14 It is necessary to speak of calcium flocculi, hydrogen flocculi etc. as the..forms of the various vapors in the same part of the disk are not identical. **1915** —— _Ten Yrs. Wk. Mount. Observ._ 20 The spectroheliograph..discloses extensive clouds of calcium, hydrogen, iron, and other vapors, which..are recorded (as flocculi). **1930** R. H. BAKER _Astron._ vii. 291 In the calcium spectroheliograms the flocculi are generally bright, and they are especially conspicuous in the sun-spot zones. **1953** L. H. ALLER _Astrophysics_ ix. 341 Elsewhere on the disk are often seen large sinuous dark filaments or dark flocculi, prominences seen in projection. **1967** [see FINE STRUCTURE 2].

‖**floccus** (ˈflɒkəs). Pl. flocci. [Lat. _floccus_ FLOCK _sb._[2]] Something resembling a flock of wool.

a. _Bot._ A tuft of woolly hairs; also _pl._ the _hyphæ_, or thread-like cells, which form the mycelium of a fungus. **b.** _Zool._ (see quot. 1842). **c.** 'A tuft of feathers on the head of young birds' (Webster 1890). **d.** 'The down of unfledged birds' (Worcester 1889).

1842 BRANDE _Dict. Sc._, _Flocci_, in Botany, the woolly filaments that are found mixed with the sporules of many Gastromyci. _Ibid._, _Floccus_, in Mammalogy, the tuft of long flaccid hairs which terminate the tail. **1874** COOKE _Fungi_ 44 The structure of the flocci in a number of species.

†**flocht** (flɒxt). _Sc. Obs._ Also 6–7 **flought**. See also FLAUGHT _sb._[2] [app. repr. an OE. *_flohta_, parallel with the _-ti_ stem _flyht_, FLIGHT _sb._[1] 4.] A state of agitation or excitement. Chiefly in phrases _in, on flocht, in a flocht_, in a flutter. Cf. FLIGHT _sb._[1] 4.

1500–20 DUNBAR _Poems_ xxvii. 66 Thair hairtis wer baith on flocht. **1596** BUREL _Pass. Pilgrimer_ II. 27 Feir pat my hart in sick a flocht. **1641** R. BAILLIE _Lett. & Jrnls._ (1841) I. 392 These horrible designes breaking out, all the citie was in a flought.

b. 'Fluctuation, constant variation' (Jam.).

1500–20 DUNBAR _Poems_ xxiv. 2 This fals warld is ay on flocht, Quhair no thing ferme is nor degest.

flock (flɒk), _sb._[1] Forms: 1 flocc, 2–4 floc, _Orm._ flocc, 3 _south._ vloc, (3 floch), 3–6 flok(e, 4–5 flokk(e, 4–7 flocke, 3– flock. [OE. _flocc_ = ON. _flokkr_ (Sw. _flock_, Da. _flok_).

Not found in the other Teut. langs. The etymology is obscure. As both in OE. and ON. the word means only an assemblage of persons, it can hardly be connected with FLY _v._; the hypothesis that it is cognate with FOLK is satisfactory with regard to meaning, but its phonological admissibility is doubtful.]

1. a. A band, body, or company (of persons). Now only as _transf._ from 2 or 3.

O.E. Chron. an. 894 Hi [MS. him] mon mid oþrum floccum sohte. _c_ **1000** ÆLFRIC _Gen._ xxxii. 8 Gif Esau cymþ to anum flocce & þone ofslihþ, se oþer flocc byþ ȝehealden. _c_ **1175** _Lamb. Hom._ 3 Moni of þan floc manna þe earþon fulieden ure drihten. _a_ **1225** _Ancr. R._ 162 Ne þunche þe neuer god amonge monne floc. _c_ **1394** _P. Pl. Crede_ 536 Fynd foure freres in a flok, þat folweþ þat rewle. **1523** LD. BERNERS _Froiss._ I. clxiv. 203 They parceyued a flocke of men of armes commynge togyder. **1609** BIBLE (Douay) _1 Sam._ x. 5 Thou shalt meete there a flocke of prophetes. **1822** SHELLEY _Triumph Life_ 264 Whom from the flock of conquerors Fame singled out.

b. _pl._ used to indicate: Great numbers, 'swarms'.

1535 COVERDALE _2 Macc._ xiv. 14 The Heithen which fled out of Iewry from Iudas, came to Nicanor by flockes. **1632** LITHGOW _Trav._ x. 443 Whence springeth these Flockes of Studientes, that over-swarme the whole land.

2. a. A number of animals of one kind, feeding or travelling in company. Now chiefly applied to an assemblage of birds (_esp._ geese) or (as in sense 3) of sheep or goats; in other applications commonly superseded by _herd_, _swarm_, etc.

_c_ **1200** _Trin. Coll. Hom._ 39 Þe deules beden ure louerd ihesu crist þat he hem sende into floc of swin. _a_ **1300** _Cursor M._ 1964 (Gött.) Alsua ȝe ete of na fiss ellis, Bot þat in flock and herd duellis. **1480** CAXTON _Descr. Brit._ 41 Ther is a pole at Brecknock, Therin of fish is many a flok. **1596** SHAKS. _1 Hen. IV_, II. iv. 152 If I do not..driue all thy Subiects afore thee like a flocke of Wilde-geese. **1614** RALEIGH _Hist. World_ II. v. v. §8. 602 Sixteene Elephants together in one flocke. **1665** HOOKE _Microgr._ 205, I found whole flocks of the same kind [mites] running to and fro among the..green moss. **1690** _Moral Ess. Pres. Times_ iii. 48 A Flock of Lions. **1839** tr. _Lamartine's Trav. East_ 102/1 Glades, where we saw flocks of camels and goats browsing. **1875** C. F. WOOD _Yachting Cruise_ iv. 91 Flocks of pigeons and parrots were fluttering about.

b. _transf._

_a_ **1225** _Ancr. R._ 120 Her aȝeines wreððe monie kunnes remedies, & frouren a muche vloc. **1601** SHAKS. _Twel. N._ I. i. 36 The rich golden shaft Hath kill'd the flocke of all affections else That live in her. **1642** FULLER _Holy & Prof. St._ To Rdr., Some serious books, which dare flie abroad, are hooted at by a flock of Pamphlets. **1775** J. Q. ADAMS in _Fam. Lett._ (1876) 100 Fire, sword, pestilence, famine, often keep company and visit a country in a flock. **1805** WORDSW. _Prelude_ III. 33 Courts, cloisters, flocks of churches, gateways, towers.

3. _esp._ A number of domestic animals (chiefly, and now exclusively, of sheep or goats) kept together under the charge of one or more persons. Often used vaguely in _pl._ for (a person's) possessions in sheep; _esp._ in _flocks and herds_ = sheep and cattle.

_a_ **1300** _Cursor M._ 3820 (Cott.) Jacob..Faand quare thre floks o beistes lai, Be-side a well. **1340** HAMPOLE _Pr. Consc._ 5891, I sal aske my flok of shepe Of þe hird þat had þam undir his hand. _c_ **1440** _Promp. Parv._ 167/2 Floke of bestys. _c_ **1450** _Mirour Saluacioun_ 3529 The fonden shepe on his shuldres laid he & broght to flokke. **1600** SHAKS. _A.Y.L._ II. iv. 83 His Flockes, and bounds of feede Are now on sale. **1725** POPE _Odyss._ IX. 289 He..sitting down, to milk his flocks prepares. **1810** SCOTT _Lady of L._ III. viii, A goat, the patriarch of the flock. **1815** ELPHINSTONE _Acc. Caubul_ (1842) I. 305 The increase both of men and flocks soon occasions disputes.

transf. and _fig._ **1751** _Affect. Narr. Wager_ 141 The Crew.. he should have consider'd as a Flock, whereof he had undertaken the Care. **1820** SHELLEY _Witch Atl._ x, Every shepherdess of Ocean's flocks.

4. _fig._ **a.** In spiritual sense, of a body or the whole body of Christians, in relation to Christ as the 'Chief Shepherd', or of a congregation in relation to its pastor.

_a_ **1340** HAMPOLE _Psalter_ xxviii. 1 Apostils þat ware ledirs of godis floke. **1393** GOWER _Conf._ Prol. I. 16 Christes.. flocke without guide Deuour'd is on euery side. _c_ **1440** _York Myst._ xxvii. 146 The flokke schall be full fayne to flee. **1588** J. UDALL _Demonstr. Discip._ (Arb.) 26 The minister is a shepheard, and his charge a flocke. **1611** BIBLE _1 Pet._ v. 2 Feede the flocke of God which is among you. **1641** MILTON _Reform._ 4 He that..faithfully from that time forward feeds his parochial flock. **1797** MRS. RADCLIFFE _Italian_ x, The Father-director and his flock seemed perfectly to understand each other. **1865** MRS. GASKELL _Cousin Phillis_ 40 The minister..had been calling on the different members of his flock.

b. Occasionally applied to any body of persons under the charge or guidance of some one; e.g. to a family of children in relation to their parents.

5. _attrib._ and _Comb._ **a.** simple attrib., as _flock district_, _farm_; **b.** objective, as _flock-feeder_; **c.** instrumental, as _flock-fed_, _-nibbled_ adjs. Also, **flock-book**, a list of pedigrees of sheep; **flock-duck** (_U.S._), a scaup-duck; **flock-feeding**, the habit of feeding in flocks; **flock-man**, a shepherd (_Cent. Dict._); **flock-master**, an owner or overseer of a flock; a sheep-farmer; **flock pigeon**, an Australian species of pigeon, _Histriophaps histrionica_, usu. seen in large flocks; the harlequin bronzewing; **flock-rake** _Sc._ (see quot.).

1912 W. DEEPING _Sincerity_ xxvi. 195 Crabbe kept a complete register of his tenants..their ages, resources, infirmities, and characters, like the records of sheep in a '*flock-book'. **1950** _N.Z. Jrnl. Agric._ Feb. 144/1 Stud sheep which are entered in flock books. **1795** _Scots Mag._ LVII. 480/1 The recent loss of sheep, after shearing, in the *flock districts. **1846** J. BAXTER _Libr. Pract. Agric._ II. 238 Where lands of this description are attached to *flock farms. **1800** HURDIS _Fav. Village_ 2 The proud eminence, whose steep

For ever *flock-fed, shelters his loved elms. **1545** Joye *Exp. Dan.* v. Iiij b, To maintayne..ydle bisshops, preistis and monkis, the trewe *flokfeders neglected. **1893** G. D. Leslie *Lett. to Marco* iii. 19 This *flock-feeding saves a lot of time spent in looking out for danger. **1798** *Sporting Mag.* XI. 307 The *flock-masters of the South Downs. **1883** *Times* 19 May 5 Many of..the flockmasters..have upwards of 10,000 sheep. **1800** Hurdis *Fav. Village* 107 On each blade Of the *flock-nibbled field. **1887** G. J. Broinowski *Birds Austral.* III. Pl. 111, *Leucomelana Norfolciensis..White-headed Fruit-Pigeon...* This bird, more commonly known among settlers as the '*Flock' Pigeon, is found generally along the whole of the north-eastern sea-coast. **1959** *Observer* 17 May 8/4 The flock-pigeon, a plump bronze-wing formerly thought to be on the brink of extinction. **1966** N. W. Cayley *What Bird is That?* (ed. 4) 23 *Topknot pigeon...* Also called Flock Pigeon. Usually seen in flocks, frequenting brushes. **1813** Kerr *Agric. Surv. Berwicksh.* vi. §2. 179 Very large pastures, provincially termed *flock-rakes.

flock (flɒk), *sb.*^{2} Forms: 3–5 **flokke**, 3–6 **flocke**, 6– **flock**. [prob. a. OF. *floc* lock of wool, snowflake, etc.:—L. *floccus*.

Words of similar sound and meaning exist in other Teut. langs.: OHG. *floccho* wk. masc. (MHG. *vlocke*, mod.Ger. *flocke*), MDu. *vlocke* MLG. (mod.Du. *vlok*), MDa. *flok*, *flock* (mod.Da. *flok*), MSw. *flokker* (mod.Sw. *flock*, *flocka*). It is doubtful whether these words are adopted from Lat. or Rom., or genuinely Teut.; in the latter case they would prob. be related by ablaut to ON. *flóke* felt, hair, wool, and to FLAKE *sb.*^{2} If the Teut. words are not of L. origin, they must be altogether unconnected with L. *floccus*, unless it be supposed that the pre-Teut. word began with *ph*.]

1. A lock, tuft or particle (of wool, cotton, etc.). †As a type of something valueless or contemptible: see quot. 1592 and FLOCK *v.*^{2} 2.

c **1440** *Promp. Parv.* 167/2 Flokkys of wulle or oþer lyke, *floccus*. **1563** W. Fulke *Meteors* (1640) 48 They look white, like flocks of wooll. **1592** Lyly *Midas* iv. ii, I will never care three flocks for his ambition. **1705** Bosman *Guinea* 250 A sort of Hair as thick set as Flocks of Wool. **1756** P. Browne *Jamaica* 283 When the pods [of cotton] are..ripe, they burst, and expose their seeds wrapt up in their native flocks, to the sun. **1869** E. A. Parkes *Pract. Hygiene* (ed. 3) 96 Bronchitis, from the inhalation of fine particles of coal.. flocks of cotton.

2. *pl.* A material consisting of the coarse tufts and refuse of wool or cotton, or of cloth torn to pieces by machinery, used for quilting garments, and stuffing beds, cushions, mattresses, etc.

1277 *Munim. Gildh. Lond.* (Rolls) III. 433, xv capella nigra..falsi operis et mixti de lana et flokkes. *a* **1400** *Cov. Myst.* 241 Cadace wolle or flokkys..To stuffe withal thi dobbelet. **1494** in *Ld. Treas. Acc. Scotl.* I. 238 Item, gevin to Gildow to by flolkis to the harnes sadillis ijs. **1495** *Act 11 Hen. VII* c. 19 Federbeddes bolsters and pillows made of.. flokkis and feders togidre. **1589** *Pappe w. Hatchet* E b, Their fleece [is] for flockes, not cloath. **1664** Cotton *Scarronides* 69 A Cushion stuff't with Flocks. **1695** Congreve *Love for L.* I. i. Plays (1887) 205 Put more flocks in her bed. **1801** Wolcott (P. Pindar) *Tears & Smiles* Wks. 1812 V. 60 A bed, but not of flocks. **1858** W. White *Month in Yorksh.* xxvii. 292 The cylinder..ground it [rag] up into flocks of short, frizzly-looking fibre.

fig. **1603** H. Crosse *Vertues Commw.* (1878) 99 Swelling words, bumbasted out with the flocks of sundry languages.

b. *sing. collect*; e.g. in ***cotton-flock***.

1881 Young *Every Man his own Mechanic* §797 The stuffing..may be clean cotton flock.

3. *pl.* (in later use *collect. sing.*) Powdered wool or cloth, or cloth-shearings, used formerly for thickening cloth and now in making flock-paper.

1483 *Act 1 Rich. III* c. 8 Preamble, The Sellers of such course Clothes, being bare of Threde, usen for to powder and cast Flokkys of fynner Cloth upon the same. **1541** *Act 33 Hen. VIII* c. 18 Thei..shall [not]..make or stoppe any maner kerseies with flockes. *c* **1720** W. Gibson *Farrier's Dispens.* iv. (1734) 44 Flocks, or Shavings of Cloth..are chiefly used to spread over Plaisters. **1893** *Jrnl. Soc. Arts* XLI. 367 The flock—which is composed of the cuttings of woollen cloth, cut up in a mill to the necessary degree of fineness, and dyed,—is then sprinkled over the paper.

†**b.** Often in the spelling *flox*(*e* taken as *sing*.

1558–68 Warde tr. *Alexis' Secr.* 112 b, Take..of cloth-maker's floxe or shearing one part. **1683** Pettus *Fleta Min.* i. (1686) 155 Make each apart into Pouder..add to it so much flox of woollen cloth.

4. a. = FLOCK-BED. **b.** *pl.* = *flock-papers*.

a. 1783 Crabbe *Village* i. Wks. 1834 II. 85 Here on a matted flock, with dust o'erspread, The drooping wretch reclines his languid head.

b. 1881 Young *Every Man his own Mechanic* §1646 Papers for sitting-rooms may be procured at all prices, from 1*s*... satins..ranging from 3*s*. to 6*s*., and flocks being even more expensive. **1884** *Health. Exhib. Catal.* 86/1 Artistic Wall Papers of various kinds..Raised Flocks.

5. *pl.* Of chemical precipitates, etc.: Light and loose masses, resembling tufts of wool.

1592 Nashe *P. Penilesse* (ed. 2) 24 a, Not to leaue any flockes in the bottom of the cup. **1676** *Phil. Trans.* XI. 617 In the evaporation of all those waters, their terrestrial parts form'd themselves diversly; some into floting filmes, some into flocks. **1788** Keir *ibid.* LXXVIII. 327 The minute particles collected and fell to the bottom in form of white flocks. **1838** T. Thomson *Chem. Org. Bodies* 200 It.. precipitates again, as the liquid cools, in large deep-blue flocks.

6. *attrib.* and *Comb.* **a.** simple attrib. passing into adj. (= made of, or stuffed with, flock), as ***flock-bed***, ***hangings***, ***mattress***, ***-wool***; also ***flock-mill***, ***-work***. **b.** similative, etc., as ***flock-hair***, ***-headed***; ***flock-like*** adj. Also, **flock-paper**, 'paper prepared for walls by being sized in the first instance, either over the whole surface or over special parts, constituting the pattern only, and then powdering over it flock..which has been previously dyed' (Brande *Dict. Sc.* 1842); †**flock-pate**, a foolish or giddy person; whence ***flock-pated*** adj., foolish, giddy, stupid; **flock-powder** = sense 3; †**flock-pox**, some eruptive disease; **flock-printing**, the process of printing paper in size or varnish for ornamentation and dusting with flock while wet.

1327 *Lanc. & Chesh. Wills* (Chetham 1854) 37, I beqweth to my sonne Hugh doghter a *fflokbedd. **1732** Pope *Ep. Bathurst* 301 On once a flock-bed, but repair'd with straw, Great Villiers lies. **1835** Willis *Pencillings* I. xxxiv. 238 No furniture but a flock-bed in the corner. **1877** Spry *Cruise 'Challenger'* xiii. (1878) 215 The *flock hair was trained to grow at right angles from the head. **1649** G. Daniel *Trinarch., Rich. II*, xcvi, Soe in *Flocke Hangings, wth an Azure Nose, Are Kings sett forth. **1891** Cotes *2 Girls on Barge* 109 He..apostrophised his steed as a 'nasty *flock-headed besom'. **1796** Withering *Brit. Plants* IV. 339 Pileus ..brown, with *flock-like radiated scores. **1720** *Lond. Gaz.* No. 5837/4 The great Paper Mills, *Flock-Mills, and Corn Mill. **1869** E. A. Parkes *Pract. Hygiene* (ed. 3) 331 All *flock and woollen mattresses should be discarded. **1750** Mrs. Delany *Autobiog. & Corr.* (1861) II. 593, I have hung my dressing room..with a dove-colour *flock paper. **1862** R. H. Patterson *Ess. Hist. & Art* 29 An artist..whose drawing-room wall..has a flock-paper of deep green. **1681** W. Robertson *Phraseol. Gen.* (1693) 510 Very *flockpates, dullberds. ? **1640** *Roxb. Ball.* (Ball. Soc.) II. 168 He that would be a poet Must no wayes be *flocke-pated. **1549** Latimer *3rd Serm. bef. Edw. VI*, G iv, Thei cal it *floke pouther they do so in corporate it to the cloth, that it is wonderfull to consider. **1672** in *13th Rep. Hist. MSS. Comm.* vi. 272 My grandchild's..illness of the *flock pox. **1789** *Trans. Soc. Encourag. Arts* VII. 169, I have made use of Spanish and Norfolk *flock-wool mixed. **1552** *Inv. Ch. Surrey* (1869) 28 Item ij alter clothes of *fflock worke. **1720** *Lond. Gaz.* no. 5877/3 Raw and thrown Silk, Flock-Work.

flock (flɒk), *v.*^{1} [f. FLOCK *sb.*^{1}]

†**1.** *trans.* To gather (individuals) together into a company; to assemble, muster (troops). ***to flock in***: to bring in in crowds. *Obs.*

c **1275** Lay. 4729 Brenne..flockede his cnihtes alse hii solde to fihte. *c* **1440** *Promp. Parv.* 167/2 Flokkyn, or gadyr to-gedyr, *aggrego, congrego*. **1586** J. Hooker *Girald. Irel.* in *Holinshed* II. 9/2 So had he flocked in Englishmen to ouerrun his countrie.

†**2.** To lead *away* to another flock. *Obs.*

1599 Sandys *Europæ Spec.* (1629) 220 There were more danger of flocking away theyr people, if they should haue but a bare view of our Reformed Churches. **1672** *Toleration not to be abused* 28 You may possibly gather together a few stragling sheep out of other mens folds, but..there will not be wanting such, as may exercise your vigilancy, by undermining you, and endeavouring to flock them away from you.

3. *intr.* (rarely †*refl.*) To gather in a company or crowd, to congregate; to come or go in great numbers, to troop. Const. *about*, *after* (a person), †*in*, *into*, *to*, *upon* (a place). Also with advbs. *in*, *out*, *over*, *together*.

a **1300** *Cursor M.* 1781 (Cott.) Þe fowuls floked þam on hei. **13..** *E.E. Allit. P.* B. 386 Þer-on [mountaynez] flokked þe folke, for ferde of þe wrake. *c* **1340** *Cursor M.* 4709 (Trin.) To gider þei flocked in þat lond Bi hundrides. *c* **1420** *Anturs of Arth.* xxvi, His fayre folke in firthes, flokkes in fere. **1575** Churchyard *Chippes* (1817) 194 They floke so fast, that daily sought my bloode. **1600** Shaks. *A.Y.L.* i. i. 123 Many yong Gentlemen flocke to him euery day. **1682** Luttrell *Brief Rel.* (1857) I. 158 [The Morocco ambassador] Hath been..much flock't after to be seen. **1684** R. H. *School Recreat.* 160 The Fish will flock about it from all Parts. **1718** Lady M. W. Montagu *Let. to Abbé Conti* 31 July, Many of the women flocked in to see me. **1865** Kingsley *Herew.* xvi, All the fowl of heaven were flocking to the feast. **1874** Helps *Soc. Press.* ii. 16 On their holidays, the whole population flock out to some beautiful garden. **1892** S. R. Gardiner *Student's Hist. Eng.* 12 Traders continued to flock over from Gaul.

4. *trans.* **a.** To crowd upon, throng (a person). **b.** *nonce-use.* To fill or occupy as a flock does.

1609 J. Taylor (Water-P.) *Pennyl. Pilgr.* Wks. (1630) 122 Good fellowes trooping, flock'd me so. **1839** Bailey *Festus* (1854) 206 Since first they flocked creation's fold. **1943** L. Bennett *Jamaican Humour in Dialect* 21 But dose bwoys ovah dere Wi' flock we like dese gals flock De soljas ovah here.

flock (flɒk), *v.*^{2} [f. FLOCK *sb.*^{2}]

1. *trans.* **a.** To stuff with flocks. **b.** To cover (a prepared surface of cloth or paper) with flock or wool-dust (see FLOCK *sb.*^{2} 2–4).

1530 Palsgr. 552/2 Flocke your mattres for woll is dere. **1567** *Sc. Act Jas. VI* (1814) 41/2 Þat þe said clayth be na wyiss flokkit. **18..** *Manufacturer's Rev.* XX. 223 (Cent.) If the goods have been heavily flocked..there may be trouble in getting them evenly sheared.

†**2.** To treat with contempt, set at naught (after L. *flocci facere*); also *absol.* Cf. FLOCK *sb.*^{2} 1. *Obs.*

1545 Udall, etc. *Erasm. Par. Luke* xx. 47 Suche simple wedowes therefore do they easily flocke and loute. **1548** Geste *Pr. Masse* 132 What is to flocke and despyse God yf that be not? *a* **1575** Pilkington *Expos. Nehem.* Wks. (Parker Soc.) 390 They..flock and flout whosoever would have them to continue there.

Hence '**flocking** *vbl. sb.* (*attrib.*).

1874 Knight *Dict. Mech.* I. 886/1 *Flocking-machine*, one for distributing flock on a prepared surface of cloth or paper.

†**flockard.** *Obs.* [ad. OFr. *flocquart*, *floccard*, explained by Godef. as a flowing veil hanging from the kind of head-dress called 'hennin' (worn in 14–16th c.).] A veil, a lappet.

1465 *Mann. & Househ. Exp.* 485 Payd for ij. flokardes for mastres Ysbelle the same day, ij.s. **1481–90** *Howard Househ. Bks.* (Roxb.) 99 A peir of flokkardes for my Lady Barneis xij.s. viii.d.

flocked (flɒkt), *ppl. a.* [f. FLOCK *v.*^{2} and *sb.*^{2} + -ED.] **a.** Covered or thickened with flock. †**b.** Formed into woolly-looking masses (*obs.*). †**c.** Adorned with a tuft (Fr. †*floqué*) (*obs.*). **d.** ***flocked enamel*** (see quot. 1884).

1607 R. C. tr. *H. Estienne's World Wond.* 125 Flocked cloth. **1626** A. Speed *Adam out of E.* i. (1659) 9 French furze ..will grow very spacious and to great flockt bodies in few years. **1660** F. Brooke tr. *Le Blanc's Trav.* I. xiii. 38 The Prince wears a red turban flocked with white [F. *floqué de blanc*], from whence he is called Sophy, which signifies a red-flock't cap. **1884** Knight *Dict. Mech.* IV. 348/2 *Flocked Enamel*, enamel ornamentation on glass whose surface has been previously dulled by grinding, or acid.

flocker ('flɒkə(r)). [f. FLOCK *v.*^{1} + -ER^1.] In *pl.* Those who flock *to* (a person or place).

[**14..** *Voc.* in Wr.-Wülcker 587 *Gregarius*, a fflockere, *et est canis pastoris*.] *c* **1611** Chapman *Iliad* ii. 71 The earth was overlaid With flockers to them.

†'**flocket.** *Obs.* [? a. OF. *floquet* tuft, shaggy cloth.] 'A loose garment with long sleeves' (Strutt).

a **1529** Skelton *Elynour Rummyng* 53 She wyll iet..In her furred flocket, And gray russet rocket.

flocking ('flɒkɪŋ), *vbl. sb.* [f. FLOCK *v.*^{1} + -ING^1.] Gathering in crowds, congregating.

1604 T. Wright *Passions* i. ix. 35 For what ende hath Nature given this alteration or flocking of humours to the hearte? **1669** Woodhead *St. Teresa* ii. xxxiv. 226 Wher-ever we went, there was such flocking. **1894** *Westm. Gaz.* 13 June 5/1 What a flocking of interviewers to Cheyne-row!

flocking ('flɒkɪŋ), *ppl. a.* [f. as prec. + -ING^2.] Assembling in flocks or crowds.

1581 Mulcaster *Positions* xxxvii. (1887) 145 To cut of this flocking multitude. **1878** *Masque Poets* 217 The flocking gulls that came and fled.

Hence '**flockingly** *adv.*, in a flock.

14.. *MS. Egerton* 829 f. 94 (Halliw.) *Gregatim*, flokynglyche.

flockless ('flɒklɪs), *a.* [f. FLOCK *sb.*^{1} + -LESS.] Without a flock or flocks.

1598 Sylvester *Du Bartas* ii. i. iii. 809 Our fields are flock-less. **1843** Syd. Smith *Let. C'tess Grey* Mem. & Lett. 1855 II. 500 You must remove the flockless pastors, or the payment of the priesthood will be useless.

†'**flockling.** *Obs.* [See -LING.] One of a flock.

a **1652** Brome *Q. & Concubine* iv. iii. Wks. 1873 II. 85 Turpentine and Tarre to keep my Flocklings cleanly.

†'**flockly,** *adv. Obs.* [f. as prec. + -LY^2.]

1552 Huloet, Flocklye, or in a bushement, *confertim*. **1847** Craig, *Flockly*, in a body or flocks.

†'**flock-meal**, *adv. Obs.* Forms: 1 **floc(c)-mælum**, 4 **flocmele**, **flockmel**, 5–6 **flo(c)kmell**, **-mele**, 6–7 **flock(e)meale**. [OE. *floccmǽlum*, f. *flocc* FLOCK *sb*^{1} + *mǽlum*, dat. pl. of *mǽl* measure: cf. *piecemeal*, *stoundemele*.] By companies or troops (of persons), *rarely* by groups or heaps (of things). In later use sometimes preceded by *by* or *in*.

c **893** K. Ælfred *Oros.* ii. v. §2 Hie þonne hie floccmælum slogan. **1382** Wyclif *2 Macc.* xiv. 14 Than heithen men that fledden Judas fro Judee, flocmele ioynyden hem to Nychanore. **1482** *Monk of Evesham* (Arb.) 107 Theder came flockemele the multytude of tho blessyd sowlys. **1566** Drant *Wail. Hierim.* K vij b, The stones..Flock meale to corners of eche strete are scatered. **1583** Stanyhurst *Aeneis* iv. (Arb.) 109 In cluster you see thee coompanye swarming On the shoare in flockmeale. **1600** Holland *Livy* ii. xxviii. (1609) 62 All the younger sort of the Senatours, approched by flockmeale, hard almost to the Consuls seats. **1611** Speed *Hist. Gt. Brit.* ix. xviii. (1632) 903 Some Lords, Knights and Gentlemen..assembled in sundry Companies, and went flocke-meale in harnesse.

flock-wise ('flɒkwaɪz), *adv.* [f. FLOCK *sb.*^{1} + -WISE.] In flocks or in a flock or group.

1837 Longf. *Frithiof's Homestead* 12 The white-looking stray clouds, flock-wise, spread o'er the heavenly vault. **1855** —— *Hiaw.* xvi. 250 Hiawatha's mountain chickens flock-wise swept and wheeled about him.

flocky ('flɒkɪ), *a.* [f. FLOCK *sb.*^{2} + -Y^1.]

1. a. Resembling flock; flock-like. **b.** Abounding with flocks or locks of woolly matter; floccose.

1597 Gerarde *Herbal* i. lxxiv. §1. 107 The whole plant consisteth of a woollie or flockie matter. **1707** J. Stevens tr. *Quevedo's Com. Wks.* (1709) 469 Flocky Heads and clotted Hair. **1833** Herschel *Astron.* xii. 403 It [this nebula] is formed of little flocky masses, like wisps of cloud. **1838** T. Thomson *Chem. Org. Bodies* 96 Bicolorin..is usually in the state of a light flocky powder.

2. *Comb.*, as ***flocky-white*** adj.

c **1865** J. Wylde in *Circ. Sc.* I. 191/2 The zinc becomes oxidised, producing a flocky-white powder.

flocoon (flɒˈkuːn). [ad. F. *flocon* tuft of wool, flake of snow, etc., f. OF. *floc*:—L. *floccus* FLOCK *sb.*[2]] (See quot.).

1826 KIRBY & SP. *Entomol.* IV. xli. 135 Those flocoons that look like cotton, and cover the body of several.. Aphides, if closely examined will be found of the nature of wax.

flod, obs. form of FLOOD.

† **flod**, *v. Obs.* [? onomatopœic; cf. *plod.*] *intr.* ? To walk slowly.

1677 N. COX *Gentl. Recreat.* III. 14 There is no getting a shoot at them without a Stalking-horse.. who will.. walk up and down in the Water which way you please, flodding and eating on the Grass that grows therein.

flodd(e, flod(e, obs. forms of FLOOD.

† **ˈflodder**, *v. Sc. Obs.* [f. *flod* FLOOD *sb.* + -ER[2]. Cf. FLOTTER.] *trans.* To flood. **a.** To overflow. **b.** *transf.* To 'blubber' or disfigure (the face) by weeping.

1513 DOUGLAS *Æneis* VII. Prol. 52 The law vaille flodderit all wyth spait. *Ibid.* XI. ii. 80 With gret terys flodderit his face and ene.

flodge (flɒdʒ). *dial.* [var. of FLOSH; cf. SLUSH, SLUDGE, and see FLASH *sb.*[1]] A small pool, a puddle.

1696 A. DE LA PRYME *Diary* (Surtees) 81 He himself saw .. in all the gutters and rivelets of water in the streets and in the flodges, great quantities of little young jacks. **1870** E. PEACOCK *Ralf Skirl.* I. 195 Miniature lakes which Lincolnshire men call flodges stretched across the path.

floe (fləʊ). [perh. a. Norse *flo* layer, level piece (Ivar Aasen):—ON. *fló* fem. The usual Da. word for (ice-)floe is *flage* = FLAW *sb.*[1]]

1. A sheet of floating ice, of greater or less extent; a detached portion of a field of ice. Also *ice-floe*.

1817 SCORESBY in *Ann. Reg., Chron.* 531 Pieces of very large dimensions, but smaller than fields, are called floes. **1823** —— *North. Whale Fishery* 71 We came to the edge of a heavy floe, 8 or 10 miles in diameter. **1857** E. PARRY *Mem. Sir W. E. Parry* 76 One of the whalers.. was crushed between two moving floes. **1878** MARKHAM *Gt. Frozen Sea* i. 2 They were destined to grapple and fight with the heavy and unyielding ice floes of the Polar Ocean.

transf. **1886** HALL CAINE *Son of Hagar* II. xiii, The moon might fly behind the cloud floes.

2. *attrib.* and *Comb.*, as *floe-edge*; **floeberg**, a berg composed of floe-ice; **floe-flat**, a seal = *floe rat*; **floe-ice** (see quot. 1882); **floe-rat**, a sealer's name for the small ringed seal (*Phoca hispida*).

1878 E. L. MOSS *Shores Polar Sea* Descr. Plate xii, The great stratified masses of salt ice.. are.. fragments broken from the edges of the perennial floes. We called them *floe-bergs in order to distinguish them from, and express their kinship to, icebergs. **1856** KANE *Arct. Expl.* I. vii. 72 We perceived that they were at some distance from the *floe-edge. **1883** *Fisheries Exhib. Catal.* (ed. 4) 173 Harbour Ranger or *Floe Flat. **1853** KANE *Grinnell Exp.* vii. (1856) 52 A vast plain of undulating ice.. This was the *floe ice. **1880** *Standard* 20 May 3 Of the '*floe-rat' the Greenlanders kill every year about fifty-one thousand.

floe, var. of FLOW *sb.*[2]

‖ **floetz** (flɛts), *a. Geol.* [attrib. use of Ger. *flötz* a layer, dialectal var. of *fletz*: see FLET.] (See quot. 1865.) Also in *Comb.*, as *floetz-trap*.

1811 PINKERTON *Petral.* I. 99 It belongs to the floetz-trap rocks. **1865** PAGE *Handbk. Geol. Terms, Flötz*.. a term applied by Werner to the Secondary strata, because they were flötz or flat-lying, compared with the Primary and Transition rocks.

flog (flɒg), *v.* [Mentioned in 1676 as a cant word. Presumably of onomatopœic formation; cf. FLACK, FLAP; if it originated in school slang, it may have been suggested by L. *flagellare*.]

1. a. *trans.* To beat, whip; to chastise with repeated blows of a rod or whip.

1676 COLES, *Flog*, to whip [marked as a cant word]. **1740** *Christm. Entertainm.* ii. (1883) 10 Then I was as certainly flogged. **1784** COWPER *Tiroc.* 329 How he was flogged, or had the luck to escape. **1809** BYRON *Let. to Hodgson* 25 June, The women are flogged at the cart's tail. **1830** MARRYAT *King's Own* i, A man sentenced to be flogged round the fleet receives an equal part of the whole number of lashes awarded alongside each ship composing that fleet. **1852** MRS. STOWE *Uncle Tom's C.* xxxiii, Tom shall have the pleasure of flogging her. **1881** BESANT & RICE *Chapl. Fleet* I. 49 Is it not barbarous to flog our soldiers and sailors for insubordination?

absol. **1727** SWIFT *Molly Mog* iv, The School-Master's joy is to flog. **1887** L. STEPHEN in *Dict. Nat. Biog.* XI. 303 Boyer flogged pitilessly.

b. Const. *into, out of, through.*

1830 *Gentl. Mag.* Jan. 56/2 Providence flogged him [Richter] into contentment. **1852** SMEDLEY *L. Arundel* i. 19, I have not forgotten the Greek and Latin flogged into us at Westminster. **1886** J. WESTBY-GIBSON in *Dict. Nat. Biog.* VI. 42/1 What he knew of mathematics he was 'flogged through'. **1887** HALL CAINE *Coleridge* i. 21 I'll flog your infidelity out of you!

c. To urge forward (a horse, etc.) by flogging. Also *fig.* (In early 19th c. to urge on by importunity, etc.) Also (freq. *intr.*) in slang use: (i) to proceed by violent or painful effort; (ii) to obtain, usu. by violent effort.

1793 *Spirit Pub. Jrnls.* (1799) I. 111 Two of the largest [turkeys].. were flogged up into the boot of a mail-coach. **1800** I. MILNER in *Life* xii. (1842) 220, I was flogged by good Richardson.. to let him have the *Life*. **1806–7** J. BERESFORD *Miseries Hum. Life* (1826) II. xvi, To flog yourself up into an inclination to work in your garden. **1841** JAMES *Brigand* iii, Take off the bridles of their horses, and flog them down the valley. **1925** FRASER & GIBBONS *Soldier & Sailor Words* 96 *To flog*,.. to walk; go on foot.—*e.g.*, 'There was no train so we flogged it.' **1936** *Geogr. Jrnl.* LXXXVII. 166 We had to flog our way through snow up to our waists. **1943** N. COWARD *Middle East Diary* 26 Aug. (1964) 64 Visualised himself flogging through the provinces in Shakespearian Rep. indefinitely. **1959** B. GOOLDEN *For Richer, for Poorer* viii. 121 A sports model out of which they could flog eighty with ease. **1964** *Times* 11 Feb. 11/6 [Lorry drivers] are being encouraged to 'flog on' even in bad weather.

d. *fig.* in phrases, ***to flog the glass*** (see quot.); ***to flog the clock***, to move the hands forward; ***to flog a dead horse***: see HORSE *sb.* 19.

1769 FALCONER *Dict. Marine* (1789), *Manger du sable*, to flog the glass, or cheat the glass; expressed of the steersman, who turns the watch-glasses before they have run out, in order to shorten the period of his watch. **1894** *Daily Chron.* 4 Aug. 3/5, I got suspicious that it [the clock] was being flogged—that is, altered—in the interest of making the time of those in the mate's watch shorter.

2. a. *slang.* To 'beat', excel. **b.** *dial.* in *pass.* To tire (*out.*) Cf. DEAD-BEAT A.

a **1841** T. HOOK (Ogilv.) Good cherry-bounce flogs all the foreign trash in the world. **1847** LE FANU *T. O'Brien* 253 Of all the brimstone spawn that I ever came across that same she-devil flogs them. **1875** *Sussex Gloss.* s.v., I was fairly flogged by the time I got home. **1883** E. A. FREEMAN in Stephens *Life & Lett.* (1895) II. 274, I think for position it flogs every place I know. **1924** KIPLING *Debits & Credits* (1926) 132, I went to bed; for I was fair flogged out.

c. *slang* (orig. *Mil.*). To sell or offer for sale, orig. illicitly.

1919 [Implied in FLOGGING *vbl. sb.* 2 d.]. **1925** FRASER & GIBBONS *Soldier & Sailor Words* 96 *To flog*, to sell something not the vendor's own to dispose of. **1951** G. HANLEY *Consul at Sunset* 125 He was dead... His kit was collected and flogged to those who would buy it in the mess. **1966** J. PORTER *Sour Cream* x. 134 Filching state property and flogging it to the eager populace is a common enough crime in the Soviet Union as it was with us during the war. **1967** M. DRABBLE *Jerusalem the Golden* v. 112 Let's go.. and look at the ghastly thing that Martin flogged us.

3. a. In general sense: To beat, lash, strike; also with *down. Fishing.* To cast the fly-line over (a stream) repeatedly; also *absol. Cricketing.* To 'punish' (bowling).

1801 WOLCOTT (P. Pind.), *Tears and Smiles* Wks. 1812 V. 44 As schoolboys flog a top. **1837** MARRYAT *Dog-fiend* v, The vessel so flogged by the waves. **1853** HERSCHEL *Pop. Lect. Sc.* I. §23 (1873) 17 Trees were seen to flog the ground with their branches. **1859** JEPHSON *Brittany* v. 56 Trout streams, which have not yet been flogged by cockneys. **1867** F. FRANCIS *Angling* ix. (1880) 327 A salmon bullied into rising by a customer who.. kept flogging on. **1884** I. BLYTH in *Lillywhite's Cricket Ann.* 8 Bonnor.. flogged the bowling to the extent of 54. **1892** WHYMPER *Great Andes* iii. 68 The only possible way of proceeding was to flog every yard of it [the snow] down.

b. *intr.* Of a sail: To beat or flap heavily.

1839 MARRYAT *Phant. Ship* xxii, The storm-staysail.. flogged and cracked with a noise louder than the gale.

4. *Comb.*, as **flog-master**, a prison flogger.

1702 T. BROWN *Lett. Dead to Living* Wks. 1760 II. 205 Busby was never a greater terror to a blockhead, or the Bridewell flog-master to a night-walking strumpet.

Hence **flogged**, **ˈflogging** *ppl. adjs.*

1682 [see FLAUGING]. **1836** GEN. P. THOMPSON *Exerc.* (1842) IV. 99 Keeping us what Mr. Cobbett denominated 'a flogged people'. **1884** *Athenæum* 19 July 75/3 He undergoes brutal treatment from a flogging master. **1891** *Sat. Rev.* 21 Mar. 343/2 The blood of flogged boys.

floˈggation. *nonce-wd.* [f. prec. + -ATION.] Flogging, a punishment by flogging.

1688–9 *Jeffrey's Last Will* in Ld. Campbell *Chancellors* (1846) III. cii. 579, I.. being in sound and perfect memory, of high commissions.. floggations, gibitations [etc.].

floggee (flɒˈgiː). [f. as prec. + -EE.] One who is flogged.

1836 MARRYAT *Midsh. Easy* (1863) 15 Why should there be a distinction between the flogger and the floggee? **1881** SALA in *Illustr. Ld. News* 7 May 443 The 'flogee' had received his twenty-five lashes.

flogger (ˈflɒgə(r)). [f. as prec. + -ER[1].]

1. One who flogs.

1708 MOTTEUX *Rabelais* IV. xxi. (1737) 93. **1713** *Doctor no Changeling* 13 Doctor Busby, the Famous Flogger of Westminster. **1844** LD. BROUGHAM *A. Lunel* II. vi. 145 The common gaol, where a public flogger attends. **1876** GRANT *Burgh Sch. Scotl.* II. v. 208 *note*, Dr. Parr was quite as distinguished a flogger as a scholar.

2. *slang.* A horse- or riding-whip.

1789 G. PARKER *Life's Painter* 173 Whip, flogger. **1795** POTTER *Dict. Cant* (ed. 2), *Flogger*, a whip. **18..** *Sporting Times* (Barrère), Compared with the light and elegant floggers of the present day, it is a heavy, common 'riding companion'.

3. A kind of tool (see quot.).

1884 KNIGHT *Dict. Mech.* IV. 348/2 *Flogger*, a bung-starter. An instrument for beating the bung stave of a cask to start the bung.

flogging (ˈflɒgɪŋ), *vbl. sb.* [f. as prec. + -ING[1].] The action of the vb. FLOG.

1. The practice or system of punishment by blows; an instance of it; a chastisement.

1758 SHENSTONE *Let. to Graves* 22 July, I have not only escaped a flogging [in the *Monthly Review*] but am treated with great civility. **1840** DICKENS *Barn. Rudge* xlvii, There's nothing like flogging to cure that disorder. **1851** HT. MARTINEAU *Hist. Peace* (1877) III. IV. xi. 92 The question of military flogging was brought forward year by year.

2. In various uses. **a.** The action of forcing up (a rent). **b.** The flapping (of a sail). **c.** *Fishing.* (See FLOG *v.* 3). **d.** Selling or offering for sale (see FLOG *v.* 2 c).

1835 MARRYAT *Pirate* iii, Keep the sheet fast.. or the flogging will frighten the lady. **1886** *Q. Rev.* CLXIII. 350 When a long day's flogging has been at last followed by a solitary rise. **1881** *Daily News* 9 Sept. 2/1 The tenants were really unable to stand any longer the flogging of rents which they had managed to pay for so many years. **1919** *War Terms* in *Athenæum* 1 Aug. 695/2 'Flogging', the illegal disposal of Army goods. **1935** 'D. HUME' *Gaol Gates are Open* 10 If a crook disposes of stolen property through a fence he is 'fencing', but if it is sold through any other channel it is 'flogging'.

3. *attrib.* and *Comb.*, as ***flogging-block***, ***-cove***, ***-stake***; **flogging-chisel**, a large cold chisel used in chipping castings; **flogging-hammer**, a small sledge-hammer used for striking a flogging-chisel.

1827 in Hansard *Parl. Debates* 12 Mar. XVI. 1126 Some of the men were brought out so frequently to be flogged, that they were known by the name of the *flogging-blocks. **1851** THACKERAY *Eng. Hum.* iii. (1876) 219 By good fortune [to] escape the flogging-block. **1874** KNIGHT *Dict. Mech.* I. 886/2 **Flogging-chisel.* **17..** B. E. *Dict. Cant. Crew*, **Flogging-cove*, the Beadle, or Whipper in Bridewell. **1874** KNIGHT *Dict. Mech.* I. 886/2 **Flogging-hammer.* **1785** GROSE *Dict. Vulg. Tongue*, **Flogging stake*, the whipping post.

Hence **ˈfloggingly** *adv.*

1840 *New Monthly Mag.* LVIII. 527 A frown from Mr. Innovate, floggingly put on, hastened his preparations.

flogh, obs. pa. t. of FLAY.

† **ˈfloghter**, *v. Obs.* [cf. FLOCHT and FLAUGHTER *v.*] *intr.* To waver. Hence **floghtering**, *ppl. a.*

1521 FISHER *Eng. Wks.* (1876) 313 That we floghter not in the catholike doctryne. *Ibid.* 334 Against all floghteryng doutfulnes.

flogster (ˈflɒgstə(r)). *rare.* [f. FLOG *v.*: see -STER.] 'One who is addicted to flogging' (*Cent. Dict.*).

† **floine.** *Obs.* Also 4 floyne, floygene. [a. OFr. *flouin* in same sense.] A kind of small ship.

13.. *Sege Jerus., MS. Cott. Calig.* A ii. f. 111 (Halliw.) Ther were floygenes on flote.. Cokkes and karekkes y-castelled alle. ? *a* **1400** *Morte Arth.* 743 In floynes and fercestez, and Flemesche schyppes. *a* **1400** *Octouian* 1485 Many galeys, schyppes, and floyne.

ˈfloister, *v.*

1569 J. SANFORD tr. *Agrippa's Van. Artes* 104 b *note*, Lawes enacted concerninge floisteringe beggers. **1847** HALLIWELL, *Floistering*, skittish, boyish.

floke, flokes, obs. ff. FLUKE, FLUX.

flok(k)ard: see FLOCKARD.

flom, obs. form of FLUME.

flomery, flommery, obs. ff. FLUMMERY.

flon, flone, vars. of FLANE *Obs.*, arrow.

flong (flɒŋ). *Stereotyping.* [anglicized pronunciation of Fr. *flan*: see FLAWN.] (See quots.)

1880 *Printing Times* 15 Feb. 30/1 The flong is really the substance made of several thicknesses of paper fastened together by the paste. **1888** JACOBI *Printer's Vocab., Flong*, the prepared paper used for making the moulds for casting stereo by the paper process.

flong, obs. pa. t. and pa. pple. of FLING *v.*

flood (flʌd), *sb.* Forms: 1 flód, 2–6 flod(e, 3 flodd, fludd, 3–4 *south.* vlod(e, 4–6 floode, flude, (5 flowede, flowyd, fluyd, floth), 5–7 flud, 6 flodde, floud(d)e, fludde, 6–7 floud, *Sc.* fluid, 4– flood. [Com. Teut.: OE. *flód* str. masc. and neut. = OFris. and OS. *flôd* masc., fem. and neut. (MDu. *vloet*, Du. *vloed*) = OHG. *fluot* fem. (MHG. *vluot* masc. and fem., Ger. *flut* fem.), ON. *flôð* neut., Goth. *flôdus* fem.:—OTeut. **flôðu(z*:—pre-Teut. *plōtús*, f. Aryan verbal stem **plō*, whence FLOW *v.* The primary sense, in accordance with the original function of the suffix *-tu*, is 'action of flowing', though the concrete uses are found in all Teut. langs.

For the abnormal development of the vowel in mod.Eng. cf. BLOOD.]

1. The flowing in of the tide. Often in phrases, ***ebb and flood***, † ***tide of flood***; also, ***young***, ***quarter***, ***half***, ***full flood***, ***top of flood***.

a **1000**, etc. [see EBB *sb.* 1]. *O.E. Chron.* an. 1031 Whenne þæt flod byþ ealra hehst & ealra fullost. *c* **1200** *Trin. Coll. Hom.* 177 For swiche flode, and for swich ebbinge þe prophete nemneð þis woreld se. **1297** R. GLOUC. (1724) 20 Heo.. wende uorþ with god wynd & wel dryuyng flode. *c* **1350** *Will. Palerne* 2745 At þe fulle flod þei gun to sayle. *c* **1425** WYNTOUN *Cron.* IX. iii. 47 For Swlway was at þare passyng All Eb, þat þai fand þan on Flud. **1523** LD. BERNERS

Froiss. I. xcii. 114 They cast anker and abode the fludde. **1627** CAPT. SMITH *Seaman's Gram.* x. 47 Flood is when the water beginneth to rise, which is young flood as we call it, then quarter flood, halfe flood, full Sea, still water, or high water. **1769** E. BANCROFT *Nat. Hist. Guiana* 323 The fish enter with the tide of flood. **1801** R. DONNELLY in *Naval Chron.* VI. 161 The young flood making close in shore. **1858** *Merc. Marine Mag.* V. 175 The flood runs 3 hours. **1867** SMYTH *Sailor's Word-bk.* s.v., Top of flood or high-water.

fig. **c1430** LYDG. *Min. Poems* 77 Ebbe after floode of al prosperite. **1559** FERRERS *Mirr. Mag., Dk. Glocester* xi, Whan Fortunes flud ran with full streame. **1601** SHAKS. *Jul. C.* IV. iii. 219 There is a Tide in the affayres of men, Which taken at the Flood, leades on to Fortune. **1647** R. STAPYLTON *Juvenal* Pref., The empire..was at the highest flood of humane prosperity. **1710** PALMER *Proverbs* 143 It seldom happens, but that a flood of words have an ebb of sense. **a1862** BUCKLE *Civiliz.* (1873) III. iii. 178 The flood of material prosperity had fairly set in.

2. A body of flowing water; a river, stream, usually, a large river. *Obs.* exc. *poet.* †*against the flood*: against the stream.

c825 *Vesp. Psalter* lxxix [lxxx]. 12 Ðu aðenedes..oð flod [Vulg. *flumen*] setene his. **c1000** ÆLFRIC *Gen.* ii. 10 þæt flod eode of stowe þære winsumnisse. **c1200** ORMIN 10612 O ȝonnd hallf flod wass Sannt Johan Bapptisste forr to fullhtnenn. **a1300** *Cursor M.* 5624 (Cott.) þe kings doghter plaiand yod And sagh þe vessel on þe flodd. **a1470** TIPTOFT *Cæsar* xii. (1530) 15 A flod called the Thames. **c1485** *Digby Myst.* v. 491, I wyll no more row a-geyn the fflode. **1562** TURNER *Baths* 3 b, The bathes of Baden..are betwene the famous flode the Rene and the black or martian wood. **1605** SPARKE *Brotherly Persw.* (1607) 59 The water of the flood Iordan. **1735** SOMERVILLE *Chase* IV. 407 Ev'ry..hollow Rock, that o'er the dimpling Flood Nods pendant. **1814** WORDSW. *Wh. Doe of Ryl.* II. 225 She will to her peaceful woods Return, and to her murmuring floods.

transf. and *fig.* **c1200** *Trin. Coll. Hom.* 111 He dranc of deðes flode. **1340** *Ayenb.* 247 Drinke of the ulode of þine zuetnesse.

3. In wider sense: Water as opposed to land, often contrasted with *field* and *fire*. Also *pl.*: cf. *waters*. Now *poet.* or *rhetorical*.

a1000 *Cædmon's Gen.* 204 (Gr.) Cynn, þa þe flod wecceð ..inc hyrað eall. **c1200** ORMIN 14816 Swa þatt te king wiþþ all hiss ferd Wass drunncnedd unnderr flodess. **a1300** *Cursor M.* 13323 (Cott.) 'Petre' he said, 'þou has ben god Fissar hiddir-til on flod'. **c1325** *Metr. Hom.* 135 Schip fletes on the flode. **c1450** *Golagros & Gaw.* 302 The roy..socht to the ciete of Criste, our the salt flude. **1590** SHAKS. *Mids. N.* II. i. 5 Through flood, through fire, I do wander euerie where. **a1668** DAVENANT *Distresses* Wks. (1673) 55 Those.. cold and slippery Creatures that Possess the restless Flood. **1788** COWPER *Morning Dream* 25 Thus swiftly dividing the flood, To a slave-cultured island we came. **1812** J. WILSON *Isle of Palms* I. 42 My spirit..Looks down on the far-off Flood. **1857** G. LAWRENCE *Guy Liv.* iv, The accidents of flood and field were discussed. [After SHAKS. *Oth.* I. iii. 135.]

fig. **a1711** KEN *Edmund* Poet. Wks. 1721 II. 167 The Floods of Joy celestial gently roll, Wave after Wave.

4. a. An overflowing or irruption of a great body of water over land not usually submerged; an inundation, a deluge. *in flood*, †*on a flood*: (of a river, etc.) overflowing its banks; (of land) in an inundated condition.

c1000 *Ags. Gosp.* Matt. vii. 25 þa com þær ren, & mycele flod. **1125** *O.E. Chron.* an. 1125 On ðes ilces ȝeares wearð swa micel flod..þæt feola tunes & men weorðan adrencte. **a1300** *Cursor M.* 1042 (Cott.) þis paradis es sett sua hei, þat moght neuer flod ani þar nei. **c1374** CHAUCER *Troylus* III. 591 Campsall MS. (640) Syn it ron, and al was on a flode. **1496** in *Ld. Treas. Acc. Scotl.* I. 283 For bering of the Kingis treis that the flude hed away. **1594** SHAKS. *Rich. III*, IV. iv. 512 By sudden Floods, and fall of Waters, Buckinghams Armie is dispers'd. **1673** RAY *Journ. Low C.* 8 Great Rivers, which..in times of Floods brought down with them abundance of Earth. **1781** COWPER *Charity* 282 Shipwreck ..fire, and flood, Are mighty mischiefs. **1855** MACAULAY *Hist. Eng.* III. xi. 78 On one occasion, when the floods were out, he exposed his life to imminent risk. **1874** FROUDE in *S. Afric. Notes* 13–19 Dec., The rivers in the colony are reported to be in flood.

transf. and *fig.* **a1225** *Ancr. R.* 74 Of a drope waxeð a muche flod..þet adreneð þe soule. **c1460** *Towneley Myst.* (Surtees) 149 Alas! my hart is alle on flood. **1611** SHAKS. *Cymb.* I. vi. 74 With his eyes in flood with laughter. **1864** TENNYSON *Aylmer's F.* 339 His passions all in flood And masters of his motion. **1883** MACFADYEN in *Congregational Year-bk.* 39 Floods of unbelief and carelessness have overspread the land.

b. *the flood*: the great deluge recorded in the book of Genesis as occurring in the time of Noah; hence often *Noah's flood*; also, *the great, general* or *universal flood*.

Beowulf 1689 (Gr.) Flod ofsloh..giganta cyn. **c1000** *Ags. Gosp.* Luke xvii. 27 Flod com and ealle forspilde. **c1175** *Lamb. Hom.* 93 Hit itimode efter noes flode. **1398** TREVISA *Barth. De P.R.* XIV. iv. (1495) 470 Therin [Ararat] Noes shyppe restyd after the flood. **c1450** tr. *De Imitatione* III. xxxvi, Euery flesshe had corrupte his wey, and þer fore folowed þe gret flode. **1533** ELYOT *Cast. Helthe* (1539) 32 b, The vniuersall deluge or floudde. **1571** CAMPION *Hist. Irel.* vii. (1633) 22 Three hundred yeares after the generall Floud. **1734** POPE *Ess. Man* IV. 212 If your ancient but ignoble blood Has crept through scoundrels ever since the flood. **a1839** PRAED *Poems* (1864) I. 199 You would have sworn.. He had fished in the flood with Ham and Shem!

c. *Deucalion's flood*: a great deluge said, in Greek mythology, to have occurred in Thessaly.

1653 WALTON *Angler* i. 12 Some say, it [Angling] is as ancient as Deucalions Floud.

5. a. A profuse and violent outpouring of water; a swollen stream, a torrent; a violent downpour of rain, threatening an inundation.

c1205 LAY. 3894 From heouene her com a sulcuð flod, þre dæȝes hit rinde blod. **1531** ELYOT *Gov.* II. xii. (1883) 138 A lande flode runnynge downe of a mountayne after a storme. **1611** BIBLE *Rev.* xii. 15 The serpent cast out of his mouth water as a flood. **1879** FROUDE *Cæsar* xxii. 369 The melting of the snows in the mountains brought a flood down the Segre. **1880** *W. Cornw. Gloss.* s.v., It's raining a flood.

b. *transf.* in various uses: Applied e.g. to a profuse burst of tears, a copious outpouring of flame or light, a torrent of lava, an overwhelming concourse or influx of persons.

1589 PUTTENHAM *Eng. Poesie* III. xxii. (Arb.) 263, I haue heard of the flouds of teares. **1607** SHAKS. *Timon* I. i. 42 You see this confluence, this great flood of visitors. **1711** POPE *Temp. Fame* 478 Tow'rs and temples sink in floods of fire. **1837** DICKENS *Pickwick* xxxvi, Miss Bolo..went straight home, in a flood of tears, and a sedan chair. **1860** TYNDALL *Glac.* I. ii. 12 Floods of golden light were poured down the sides of the mountain.

c. *fig.* in various applications.

1340 *Ayenb.* 247 Huanne god ssel do come ope his urendes ane ulod of pays. **c1450** *Mirour Saluacioun* 4856 What flodes thurgh thyn hert ran of trewest sorow and wepyng. **1589** PUTTENHAM *Eng. Poesie* III. xxii. (Arb.) 263, I haue heard of ..the flouds of eloquence, or of any thing that may resemble the nature of a water-course. **1601** SHAKS. *Jul. C.* III. ii. 215 Let me not stirre you vp To such a sodaine Flood of Mutiny. **1719** DE FOE *Crusoe* (1840) I. xviii. 327 The flood of joy in my breast. **1877** MRS. OLIPHANT *Makers Flor.* x. 241 A preacher who..poured forth what was in him in floods of fiery words. **1894** GIBBS *Colloq. Currency* 73 How do we know that there will be a flood of silver rather than of gold?

†**6.** *pl.* = FLOODING 2.

1666 G. HARVEY *Morb. Angl.* xxxii. (1672) 97 Others that have the good fortune of..being delivered, escape by means of their Floods. **1755** in JOHNSON; and in mod. Dicts.

7. Usu. in pl., colloq. abbrev. of *flood-lamp, -light*.

1930 *Punch* 19 Feb. 198/2 Spool is the dramatic society's honorary electrician. His conversation was full of floods, floats, spots, battens, and dimmers. **1933** P. GODFREY *Back-Stage* i. 14 The up-stage O.P. flood isn't properly masked. **1967** *Punch* 16 Aug. 242/3 For *Figaro* and Verdi's *Macbeth* at the first [Edinburgh] festival twenty-one years ago, John Christie had to bring in a lighting bridge and sixty floods and perches from Glyndebourne.

8. *attrib.* and *Comb.* (sense 1), as ***flood-stream, -wave***; (sense 2), as †***flood crab***, †***gravel***; (sense 3), as ***flood-bickerer***; (sense 4), as ***flood-bank, control, -dam, -discharge, -sluice, -water***; (sense 4 b), as ***flood-tradition***. Also ***flood-beat, -compelling, -like*** adjs.

1928 *Manch. Guardian Weekly* 31 Aug. 178/3 The building of *floodbanks, or levees, along the river banks. **1945** *Finito! Po Valley Campaign* 23 A battalion fought its way to the near floodbank. **a1593** MARLOWE *Ovid's Eleg.* ii. xvii, *Flood-beat Cythera. **1599** NASHE *Lenten Stuffe* 32 A ..hoast of vnfatigable *flud bickerers and foame-curbers. **1735** THOMSON *Liberty* v. 473 The *flood-compelling Arch. **1943** J. S. HUXLEY *TVA* iii. 22 Power as a by-product of *flood control. **1957** G. E. HUTCHINSON *Treat. Limnol.* I. i. 116 The whole system has recently been modified by flood-control works. **c1420** *Pallad. on Husb.* I. 862 *Floode crabbes here & ther to crucifie He seth, is goode. **1879** *Lumberman's Gaz.* 11 June 5 They plan to build a *flood-dam. **1878** *Macm. Mag.* Jan. 245/1 The *flood discharge of the Polar River. **c1420** *Pallad. on Husb.* I. 368 *Floode gravel is goode for coveryng. **1855** CLARKE *Dict.*, *Flood-like. **1791** W. JESSOP *Rep. Riv. Witham* 14 *Flood-sluices. **1858** *Merc. Marine Mag.* V. 366 The *flood stream..sets E. by N. **1865** TYLOR *Early Hist. Man.* xi. 324 The *flood-traditions of remote regions of the world. **1791** W. JESSOP *Rep. Riv. Witham* 11 Regulate the passage of *Flood waters. **1893** G. D. LESLIE *Lett. to Marco* xxii. 144 The gulls.. settled on the meadow by the flood-water. **1892** E. REEVES *Homeward Bound* 157 Driving the water against both banks like a *flood wave.

9. Special comb., as **flood-anchor**, 'that which the ship rides by during the flood-tide' (Adm. Smyth); **flood-arch**, an arch of a bridge under which the water flows in time of flood; **flood-boards**, boards fitted together so as to keep out a flood; **flood-bridge**, a bridge for use in flood-time; **flood-drift**, sticks, etc. brought down by a flood; **flood-flanking** (see quot.); **flood-lamp** = *flood-light*; **flood-land**, land covered by water in time of flood; **flood-light**, a light providing a beam of intense illumination; the illumination so provided; also *attrib.* and *fig.*; hence as *v. trans.*, to illuminate by means of flood-lights; **flood-lighting** *vbl. sb.*, the action of illuminating with flood-lights; also, flood-lights collectively; so **flood-lit** *ppl. a.*; **flood-loam** = ALLUVIUM; **flood-mark**, the high-water mark; **flood-plain** (see quot.); **flood-way**, (*a*) a piece of flooded road or path; (*b*) a channel constructed for the purpose of taking the flood-waters of a river; **flood-wheel**, a water wheel; † **flood-womb**, the river bed; **flood-wood**, pieces of wood brought down by a flood; also *transf.* and *fig.* Also FLOOD-GATE, FLOOD-TIDE.

1844 *Dict. Trade* s.v. *Anchor*, The *flood anchor. **1891** A. J. FOSTER *Ouse* 135 The bridge..with its long line of *flood arches crossing the meadows. **1869** BLACKMORE *Lorna D.* i, His place it is to stand at the gate, attending to the *flood-boards grooved into one another. **1741** *N. Riding Rec.* VIII. 237 The repairs of the *flood-bridge. **1869** BLACKMORE *Lorna D.* viii, I lay down..with..some *flood-drift combing over me. **1874** KNIGHT *Dict. Mech.* I. 886/2 **Flood-flanking* (Hydraulic Engin.), a mode of embanking with stiff moist clay. **1916** *Amer. Year Bk.* 563 The line of demarcation between search-lamps and so-called '*flood lamps' is a narrow one. **1933** P. GODFREY *Back-Stage* iv. 43 Lighting towers..each capable of carrying a dozen 1000-watt flood lamps to supplement the battens overhead in lighting the scene. **1957** *Economist* 21 Sept. 912/2 The officious display of security, the floodlamps and police dogs that surrounded the campaign train might have been better avoided. **a1881** ROSSETTI *Spring*, The drained *flood-lands flaunt their marigold. **1924** J. F. HOBART *Tulley's Handbk.* (ed. 7) III. 814 Another means of illumination is by *floodlights which are mounted at a distance from the space to be lighted. **1925** A. E. NEWTON *Greatest Bk. in World* 82 From either side of the proscenium arch two flood-lights played upon the actors. **1925** CADY & DATES *Illum. Engin.* 410 The light may be projected from flood-light projectors. **1928** *Daily Tel.* 29 May 10/5 From thirty flood-light projectors the Royal Pavilion was bathed in amber, red, and green. **1930** *Aberdeen Press & Jrnl.* 29 Mar. 7/1 It would be useless to turn a 'flood-light' on to any article which cannot stand this searching test. **1930** Flood light [see APPROACH *sb.* 13]. **1923** M. LUCKIESH *Light & Color* 256 Tall or isolated buildings are particularly attractive when *flood-lighted. **1928** C. F. S. GAMBLE *N. Sea Air Station* ix. 131 By flood-lighting the sky with flares placed on the tops of balloons. **1917** *Electr. News* 26, 48 A Resumé of *Flood-lighting. **1923** J. W. T. WALSH *Elem. Princ. Lighting* 188 The illumination of open spaces..may often be carried out satisfactorily by a floodlighting equipment. **1927** M. BORDEN *Flamingo* II. ii, It was, of course, most beautiful at night against the dark, when Peter's flood-lighting streamed over it to make it translucent as ice. **1955** *Times* 2 June 3/4 In view of the need to conserve fuel in the emergency, the Ministry of Works have discontinued the floodlighting of public buildings in London. **1928** *Daily Express* 6 Aug. 15/1 Its walls, brilliantly *flood-lit,..are made almost entirely of sheets of glass. **1934** H. NICOLSON *Curzon: Last Phase* 40 The flood-lit self-righteousness, the timid imprecisions, the appalling amateurishness of democratic diplomacy. **1958** W. T. O'DEA *Social Hist. Lighting* vii. 175 The floodlit office building or factory is an advertisement. **1880** J. GEIKIE *Preh. Europe* 22 The ancient löss or *flood-loam of the Meuse. **1622** MALYNES *Anc. Law-Merch.* 167 Things found vpon the Seas, or within the *flood-mark. **1808** SCOTT *Marm.* II. ix, The tide did now its flood-mark gain. **1873** J. H. BEADLE *Undevel. West* xxx. 656 West of the 'Buckskin' was a singular *flood plain some six miles wide. **1882** GEIKIE *Text-Bk. Geol.* III. II. xi. §3. 383 The level tracts or flood-plain over which a river spreads in flood. **1957** G. E. HUTCHINSON *Treat. Limnol.* I. i. 104 The local rise in the water table intensified solution and so produced in the flood plain very striking karstic forms. **1971** *Nat. Geogr.* Sept. 407 These are but puddles compared to the deluges that once ripped across the lower Missouri's flood-plain. **1889** F. E. GRETTON *Memory's Hardback* 108 Near Tewkesbury and Upton there was a nasty bit of *flood-way. **1915** E. POUND *Cathay* 25 The heart turns to travel so that he then thinks On flood-ways to be far departing. **1928** *Manch. Guardian Weekly* 31 Aug. 178/3 The construction of a 'floodway' leaving the main stream [of the Mississippi] at Bird Point, near Cairo. **1515** in Rogers *Agric & Prices* (1866) III. 564/1, 1 pr. *flode wheels 7/. **1382** WYCLIF *Isa.* xix. 7 Nakened shal be the *flod wombe, and the ryueres fro ther welle. **1839** MARRYAT *Diary Amer.* Ser. I. I. 229 The major part of the men were what they call here '**flood-wood*, that is, of all sizes and heights. **1869** BLACKMORE *Lorna D.* x, Between two bars, where a fog was of rushes, and flood-wood.

flood (flʌd), *v.* [f. prec. sb. Cf. earlier FLEDE.]

1. a. *trans.* To cover with a flood; to inundate.

1663 WOOD *Life* (Oxf. Hist. Soc.) I. 479 The streets in Oxon were all flouded with water. **1748** *Relat. Earthq. Lima* 2 It floods the Out-Skirts of the Town. **1841** ELPHINSTONE *Hist. Ind.* II. 451 The rainy season set in; the whole plain was flooded.

transf. and *fig.* **1841** L. HUNT *Seer* (1864) 1 The sunshine floods the sky and ocean. **1855** STANLEY *Mem. Canterb.* iii. (1857) 120 Flooding the hedgeless plains..the army..rolled along. **1882** J. H. BLUNT *Ref. Ch. Eng.* II. 484 The bookstalls were flooded with Puritan pamphlets. **1894** GIBBS *Colloq. Currency* 72 We shall be flooded with silver and all gold will go out of circulation. **1936** *Discovery* Oct. 320/2 Foreign pins still continued to flood the English market. **1944** *Ann. Reg. 1943* 265 The presence of large armies.. flooded the country with money. **1951** E. PAUL *Springtime in Paris* iv. 75 Where shall I be when rationing ends, and beef begins flooding the market?

†**b.** To duck (a person) in the river. *rare.*

?**14..** *Symmie & his Bruther* xi. in Laing *E.P.P.* (1822) All þe laddes cryd with a lairrum To flud him & to flyr him.

2. To cover or fill with water; to irrigate (grass land); to deluge (a burning house, mine, etc.) with water. Also of rain, etc.: To fill (a river) to overflowing.

1831 LOUDON *Encycl. Agric.* §2207 Flooding and warping are modes of irrigation, the former for manuring grass lands. **1841** W. SPALDING *Italy & It. Isl.* I. 364 On the arena of the circus or amphitheatre temporarily flooded. **1855** BAIN *Senses & Int.* III. iii. §14 A violent storm has flooded the rivers. **1883** *Manch. Exam.* 24 Oct. 4/6 It was decided yesterday..to flood the..Colliery.

3. a. To pour (*away, back, out*) in a flood. In quots. *fig. rare.*

1829 FONBLANQUE *England under Seven Administr.* (1837) I. 232 He floods away his sorrows in private. **1862** MERIVALE *Rom. Emp.* (1871) V. xl. 60 The lifeblood of the provinces is flooded back upon Paris. **1888** LIGHTHALL *Yng. Seigneur* 28 The merry girl left me to flood out her spirits on a friend.

b. To drive *out* by floods.

1910 *Westm. Gaz.* 21 June 8/3 The flooded-out attendants.

4. *intr.* **a.** Of rain: To fall in 'torrents', *rare.* **b.** To come in 'floods' or great quantities; also with *in. lit.* and *fig.* **c.** Of a river: To overflow.

1755 L. EVANS *Mid. Brit. Colonies* 30 If it floods early, it scarce retires within its Banks in a Month. **1813** BYRON *Giaour* xi, Though raves the gust, and floods the rain. **1829** I. TAYLOR *Enthus.* x. 268 Discourses, and reports, and tracts, that are..flooding from the religious press. **a1861** CLOUGH *Misc. Poems, Say not the Struggle* 12 Far back, through creeks and inlets making, Comes silent, flooding in, the main. **1886** J. K. JEROME *Idle Thoughts* 18 Thoughts.. flood in upon us.

d. To become flooded.

1908 *Daily Report* 24 Aug. 9/1 A carburettor which persistently floods is not uncommon. **1912** *Motor Man.* 13 A persistant tendency to flood..due to a punctured float.

5. To suffer from uterine hæmorrhage.

1770 Hewson in *Phil. Trans.* LX. 404 To give women, who are flooding, considerable quantities of port wine.

Hence **'flooding** *ppl. a.* Also **'flooder.**

1627–61 Feltham *Resolves* I. liii. 95 They..pour a plenty on the general world..Surely, we nickname this same floodding man, when we call him by the name of Brave. **1833** Mrs. Browning *Prometh. Bound* Poems (1850) I. 179 By the flow Of flooding Nile. **1871** *Daily News* 30 June, They flooded the constituency with money..and the result was that the honourable flooder was sent to what is called another place. **1891** Galabin *Midwifery* (ed. 2) 731 Certain women have a constitutional proclivity to flooding..and have been described as 'flooders'.

floodable ('flʌdəb(ə)l), *a.* [f. flood *v.* + -able.] Liable to be flooded, subject to inundation.

1872 *Daily News* 21 May, The late rains have flooded all floodable parts of the country.

floodage ('flʌdɪdʒ). [f. flood *sb.* + -age.] A flooded state, inundation.

1864 Carlyle *Fredk. Gt.* IV. xii. vi. 164 This place..had many accidents by floodage and by fire. **1870** *Law Rep. Com. Pleas* V. 667 The effect of the milldam..is to cause back water, or as it is called, floodage on the land above.

flooded, *ppl. a.* **1.** In the senses of the verb.

1834 M. Scott *Cruise Midge* (1859) 429 From the flooded floor the water was soaking through the seams. **1854** J. S. C. Abbott *Napoleon* (1855) II. iv. 76 'Pardon', she exclaimed with..flooded eyes. **1881** Mrs. C. Praed *Policy & P.* I. 130 Madox had..saved Cathcart's life in a flooded creek.

2. flooded gum *Austral.*, any of several eucalypts growing in damp soil.

1847 F. W. L. Leichhardt *Jrnl. Overland Exped. Austral.* x. 324 The latter part of the stage was again over a large box-flat, intersected by shallow grassy depressions, timbered with flooded-gum. **1884** A. Nilson *Timber Trees N.S.W.* 136 *Flooded gum*, Eucalyptus rostrata, saligna, viminalis, resinifera. **1933** D. G. Stead *Tree Bk.* 24 A splendid tree is the Sydney Blue Gum, also called Flooded Gum. This tree grows to more than 150 feet high in the eastern forests of New South Wales and southern Queensland. **1965** *Austral. Encycl.* III 405/1 Large Sydney blue gums or flooded gums (*E. saligna*) at Tamborine Mountain.

'flood-ˌgate, 'floodˌgate.

1. *sing.* and *pl.* A gate or gates that may be opened or closed, to admit or exclude water, *esp.* the water of a flood; *spec.* the lower gates of a lock.

c **1440** *Promp. Parv.* 167/2 Flodegate of a mylle, *sinoglocitorium.* **1519** *Churchw. Acc. St. Giles, Reading* 3 For a tent next the fflode gatis in the North side of the said mill lane. **1677** Plot *Oxfordsh.* 233 There are placed a great pair of Folding doors, or Flood-gates of Timber cross the river. **1769** Falconer *Dict. Marine* (1789), *Basin of a dock*, a place where the water is confined by double flood-gates. **1781** *Chambers's Cycl.* s.v. *Lock or Weir*, Lock is..a kind of canal inclosed between two gates; the upper called by workmen the sluice-gate, and the lower called the flood-gate. **1858** Lardner *Hydrost. etc.* iv. 66 The water in the higher level is confined by a floodgate.

b. *transf.* and *fig.* chiefly in expressions relating to rain or tears.

a **1225** *Ancr. R.* 72 Hwon ȝe nede moten speken a lutewiht, leseð up ower muðes flodȝeten, ase me deð et ter mulne, and leted adun sone. **1548** Hall *Chron., Hen. VI*, 158 b, To set open the fludde gates of these devises, it was thought necessary, to cause some great comocion and rysyng of people. **1592** Shaks. *Ven. & Ad.* 959 Through the floodgates breaks the siluer rain. **1607** Hieron *Wks.* I. 89 It setteth open the very floudgate of Gods wrath. *a* **1656** Bp. Hall *Rem. Wks.* (1660) 109 Let no Antinomian stop the floodgates of our eyes. **1663** Cowley *Disc. O. Cromwell* (1669) 67 It is God that breaks up the Flood-Gates of so general a Deluge. **1781** Cowper *Convers.* 264 When wine has..forced the flood-gates of licentious mirth! **1848** Thackeray *Van. Fair* xxvi, The floodgates were opened, and mother and daughter wept.

2. a. A sluice. **b.** *dial.* (see quot. 1886).

1559 A. Andrison in W. Boys *Sandwich* (1792) 739 Wheales..for the drawenge up of the fludgates. **1870** Spurgeon *Treas. Dav.* Ps. v. 3 It is idle to pull up the flood-gates of a dry brook, and then hope to see the wheel revolve. **1886** Elworthy *W. Somerset Word-bk.*, *Flood-gate*, a gate hung upon a pole across a stream, so that in flood-time it rises and falls by floating on the water. Its purpose is..to prevent cattle passing when the water is low.

†**3.** The stream that is closed by or passes through a flood-gate; a strong stream, a torrent. Also *transf.* and *fig.* *Obs.*

1388 Wyclif *Job* xxxvi. 27 Which..schedith out reynes at the licnesse of floodȝatis. **1533** *Act 25 Hen. VIII*, c. 7 Take ..in fludgate, salmon-pipe, or at the tayle of any mylle or were..the young fry..of..salmon. **1590** Spenser *F.Q.* ii. i. 43 Of her gored wound..He..did the floudgate stop With his faire garment. **1651** C. Cartwright *Cert. Relig.* i. 22 My Lord, you let a flood-gate of Arguments out.

b. *attrib.* passing into adj.

1604 Shaks. *Oth.* i. iii. 56 For my perticular griefe Is of so flood-gate, and ore-bearing Nature.

4. *Comb.*, as **flood-gate iron** (see quot. 1833).

1783 in Boswell *Johnson* (1848) 721/2 'Sir', said he, 'I am the great Twalmley, who invented the New Floodgate Iron'. **1833** J. Holland *Manuf. Metal* II. 253 The second [box-iron] is made hollow, for the reception of a heater; and with reference to the contrivance by which the heater is shut in, has been called the floodgate iron.

flood-hatch. [see hatch.] A framework of boards sliding in grooves, to be raised in time of flood; a sluice, floodgate. *lit.* and *fig.*

1587 Turberv. *Epit. & Sonn.* (1837) 299, I cannot liue if you doe stoppe, the floudhatch of your frendly brook. **1596** Fitz-Geffray *Sir F. Drake* (1881) 26 Let downe The flood-hatches of all spectators eies. **1806** Wolcott (P. Pindar) *Tristia* Wks. 1812 V. 340, I close the flood-hatch of your praise. **1807** Vancouver *Agric. Devon.* (1813) 319 At the end..another flood-hatch is fixed on a level with the bed of the river. **1880** in *W. Cornw. Gloss.*

flooding ('flʌdɪŋ), *vbl. sb.* [f. flood *v.* + -ing[1].]

1. The action of the vb. flood; an instance of it.

1799 J. Robertson *Agric. Perth* 166 Rivers, which, by their flooding, have..formed the richest and deepest mould.

b. *pl.* Floods. In quots. *fig.*: Fullness, superabundance.

1674 N. Fairfax *Bulk & Selv.* Ep. Ded., To..drown their sorrows for the jewel that was lost, in the floodings of their joy for the Cabinet that was left. **1854** Mrs. Browning *Drama of Exile* Poems 1850 I. 18 Thy body heaves Under the golden floodings of thine hair!

2. A popular term for uterine hæmorrhage, esp. in connexion with parturition.

1710 T. Fuller *Pharm. Extemp.* 299, I should by no means advise it to any..apt to Flouding. **1859** Waller in Hulme tr. *Moquin-Tandon* ii. iii. 162 Cases of hæmorrhage ..which from their severity are termed 'floodings'.

floodless ('flʌdlɪs), *a.* [f. flood *sb.* + -less.] Without water.

1605 Sylvester *Du Bartas* ii. iii. iii. *Lawe* 702 This flood-less Foord the Faithfull Legions pass. **1622** J. Taylor (Water P.) *Merry-Wherry-Ferry* B ij, We gat from Force-dikes floodles flood to Trent.

floodlet ('flʌdlɪt), [f. as prec. + -let.] A little flood.

1855 Bailey *Spirit Leg.* in *Mystic*, &c. 73 Where..sacred Sinde; Or Brahmapootra, fling o'er bordering meads Their annual floodlets fruitful.

floodometer (flʌ'dɒmɪtə(r)). [f. as prec. + -(o)meter.] An instrument for ascertaining the height of a flood.

1880 *Times* 17 Sept. 8/5 The floodometer at the county bridge registered 8 ft. of 'fresh' this noon, and, with falling rain, the water is still rising.

'flood-'tide. [f. flood *sb.* + tide.] The rising or inflowing tide: = flood *sb.* 1.

1719 De Foe *Crusoe* (1840) II. iv. 75 They had..the flood-tide with them. **1841** Marryat *Poacher* xxxviii, The flood-tide has made almost an hour, and we must sail at the first of the ebb.

fig. **1861** Trench *Comm. Ep. 7 Churches* 77 It seemed as if the flood-tides of a thankful love would never ebb. **1874** Morley *Compromise* (1886) 34 We have been..on a flood tide of high profits and a roaring trade.

floody ('flʌdɪ), *a.* Also 5 fludy, 6 floudy, fluddy. [f. flood *sb.* + -y[1].] Pertaining to the flood, *i.e.* to the river or to the sea.

c **1420** *Pallad. on Husb.* i. 372 Stone tiburtyne, or floody columbyne. **1483** *Cath. Angl.* 136/2 Fludy, *fluuialis.* **1599** Nashe *Lenten Stuffe* Wks. (Grosart) V. 232 To chaunt..an excelsitude of this monarchall fluddy Induperator [red herring]. **1818** Keats *Let.* 13 Mar. (1931) I. 119 Devonshire ..is a splashy, rainy, misty,..floody, muddy, slipshod County. **1964** *Penguin Bk. Austral. Ballads* 201 The creek was full and bloody floody.

flook: see fluke.

flookan, flooking. ('flʊkən, -ɪŋ). *Mining.* Also 9 fluc(c)an. [Of unknown origin; app. not Celtic.]

a. A cross-course or transverse vein composed of clay. **b.** (See quot. 1869.)

1728 Nicholls in *Phil. Trans* XXXV. 403 The Load is frequently intercepted by the crossing of a Vein of Earth, or Stone..This transient Load is by the Miners term'd a Flooking. **1807** Carne *ibid.* XCVII. 293 A flookan..was discovered..which cut the lode at an angle of 45°. **1869** R. B. Smyth *Goldf. Victoria* 611 *Flucan* or *Flookan*, a sort of clayey substance, often found against the walls of a quartz reef, and accompanying cross-spurs and slides.

floor (flɔə(r)), *sb.*[1] Forms: 1 flór, 3 flor, 4–7 flore, flour(e, 5–6, 9 *dial.* flur(e, 6 *Sc.* fluire, (6 floyyre), 6–7 floar(e, 6–8 flower, 7 floore, 7– floor. [OE. *flór* str. masc. and fem., corresponds to MDu., mod.Du. *vloer*, MHG. *vluor* masc. and fem. (mod.Ger. *flur* fem. field, plain, masc. floor), ON. *flór* floor of a cowstall:—OTeut. **floru-s*:—pre-Teut. **plāru-s* or **plōru-s*. Cf. OIr. *lár*, Welsh *llawr* of same meaning:—pre-Celtic **plār-*.]

I. In a house or other structure.

1. a. The layer of boards, brick, stone, etc. in an apartment, on which people tread; the under surface of the interior of a room. Phr. ***to mop*** or ***wipe the floor with***: see mop *v.*[2] 1 b, wipe *v.* 9 e.

Beowulf 725 (Gr.) On fagne flor feond treddode. *c* **888** K. Ælfred *Boeth.* i, He ȝefeoll niwol of dune on þa flor. *c* **1200** Ormin 15566, & all he warrp ut i þe flor þe bordess & te sillferr. **1297** R. Glouc. (1724) 288 þe flor to brac vnder hem. *a* **1400** *Isumbras* 653 The knyghtes..fande the golde right in the flore. **1528** Lyndesay *Dreme* 13 Sumtyme, playand fairsis on the flure. **1681** R. Knox *Hist. Ceylon* 116 They dig an hole in the floar of their house. **1718** *Freethinker* No. 17 ¶8 She..walks two or three Turns in a Fret over the Floor. **1828** Scott *F.M. Perth* xxiii, He threw his glove upon the floor of the church. **1860** Tyndall *Glac.* i. v. 40 The stone floor was dark with moisture.

b. In extended sense: The base of any cavity; the bottom of a lake, sea, etc. Also *fig.*: a minimum, esp. of prices or wages. Cf. ceiling *vbl. sb.* 6 d.

a **1000** *Satan* 318 (Gr.) Flor attre weol. *c* **1586** C'tess Pembroke *Ps.* lxxviii. vi, Where the deepe did show his sandy flore. **1844** Emerson *Lect. New Eng. Ref.* Wks. (Bohn) I. 268 They would know the worst, and tread the floor of hell. **1866** Tate *Brit. Mollusks* iii. 48 The tongue forms the floor of the mouth. **1869** Rawlinson *Anc. Hist.* 2 Found underneath the floors of caves. **1938** *Reader's Digest* Sept. 1 Even fair price ceilings and quality floors won't answer real needs unless an adequate supply of goods is made available. **1941** *Time* 21 July 70/3 Excuse for the silver-buying program and its artificial price floor..was to keep Western miners at work. **1949** *Economist* 24 Sept. 670/1 Price-floors were set for bituminous coal. **1959** *Ibid.* 11 Apr. 106/2 A floor of only £12 a week on the wages of British artists.

†**c.** *metonymically.* Those who sit on the floor, as opposed to those who occupy elevated seats in token of rank or dignity. *Obs.*

1655–62 Gurnall *Chr. in Arm.* (1669) 296/2 We are in their condition and rank, being of the floor and lowest of the people. **1683** R. North in *State Trials* (1811) IX. 193 Differences between him [the lord mayor] and the aldermen on the one side, and the floor or livery men on the other.

d. *spec.* The floor of a studio where films or television programmes are shot; hence used *allusively*: (*a*) a film or television studio; (*b*) in phr. ***on the floor***, of a film: in production.

1937 M. Robinson *Continuity Girl* v. 89 Rene was to be continuity. Mr. Kimmins asked me to come on the floor as her assistant. **1948** *Ann. Reg. 1947* 443 The inauguration of the modern Metro-Goldwyn-Mayer floors at Elstree. **1948** *Observer* 22 Feb. 5/1 At Elstree, only one film, the *Guinea Pig*, is on the floor. **1950** 'E. Crispin' *Freq. Hearses* i. 15 'How far has it [*sc.* a film] got?' 'It's not on the floor yet... I mean that they haven't actually started making it yet.' **1957** M. Kennedy *Heroes of Clone* i. i. 13 I'll make a shooting script... It'll be something you can go on the floor with. **1971** R. Busby *Deadlock* xiii. 200 [He's] down there on the floor. We're doing one for the can and then he goes out live.

2. a. The framework or structure of joists, etc. supporting the flooring of a room.

1703 Moxon *Mech. Exerc.* 160 Floor, in Carpentry, it is as well taken for the Fram'd work of Timber, as the Boarding over it. **1823** P. Nicholson *Pract. Build.* 220 *Bridging Floors*, floors in which bridging joists are used. **1858** Simmonds *Dict. Trade*, *Floor*, the timber, bricks &c. of the platform..on which the planks or flooring is laid.

b. Applied to the ceiling of a room, in its relation to the apartment above. Also *transf.* of the sky.

1596 Shaks. *Merch. V.* v. i. 58 Looke how the floore of heauen Is thick inlayed with pattens of bright gold. **1603** Holland *Plutarch's Mor.* 931 Sticking up a broch or spit.. to the floore over head. **1887** Bowen *Virg. Æneid* i. 287 Then Cæsar..Bounding his throne by Ocean, his fame by the firmament floor.

3. *Naut.* **a.** (see quot. 1867). †**b.** The deck. **c.** *pl.* = *floor-timbers.*

a **1618** Raleigh *Invent. Shipping* 18 We have given longer Floares to our Ships, then in elder times, and better bearing under Water. **1683** Hacke *Collect. Orig. Voy.* (1699) I. 37 We took up our Water Cask from out of the Main Hatch to the Floor, and cleared the Timbers amid-Ships. **1805** D. Steel *Naval Archit.* 378 In the Royal Navy..the floors are bolted through the keelson and keel. **1867** Smyth *Sailor's Word-bk.*, *Floor*, the bottom of a vessel on each side of the kelson; but strictly taken, it is only so much of her bottom as she rests upon when aground. *Ibid.*, *Floors* or *Floor-Timbers.*

4. a. In legislative assemblies, the part of the house where the members sit, and from which they speak.

Hence *fig.* The right of speaking; as ***to get*** or ***obtain the floor***. ***to take the floor***: to get up to address a meeting; to take part in a debate. Chiefly *U.S.*

1774 J. Q. Adams in *Fam. Lett.* (1876) 12 He came upon the floor, and asked a member, 'What state are you now in?' **1804** Pitt *Speeches* (1806) IV. 354 The right honourable gentleman on the floor. **1811** B. Rush in *J. Q. Adams' Wks.* (1854) IX. 638 *note*, It blazed forth..in the year 1776 upon the floor of Congress. **1816** Pickering *Voc.* s.v., *To get the floor*; that is, to obtain an opportunity of taking part in a debate. **1880** McCarthy *Own times* III. xlvi. 391 The Conservatives get what American politicians call 'the floor'. **1885** *Manch. Exam.* 15 May 6/1 Sauntering boldly up the floor of the House. **1886** *Lit. World* (U.S.) 11 Dec. 469/1 The President took the floor to second the above resolutions. **1888** Bryce *Amer. Commw.* I. xii. 157 The senator from Minnesota has the floor. *Ibid.* I. xiii. 177 The member who first 'obtains the floor'.

b. In Courts of Law (see quot.).

1867 Wharton *Law Lex.* (ed. 4), *Floor of the court*, the part of the court between the judges and the first row of counsel. Parties who appear in person stand there.

c. *from the floor*: of a question, speech, etc.: delivered by an individual (member, spectator, etc.), as opp. to the governing body, the 'platform'.

1966 *Rep. Comm. Inquiry Univ. Oxf.* I. 234 Resolutions moved not by Council, but from the floor.

5. A set of rooms and landings in a house on the same or nearly the same level; a story. See first-floor.

1585 Higins *Junius' Nomenclator* 181 *Trisiega*..an house of three sollers, floores, stories or lofts one ouer another.

1611 B. JONSON *Catiline* I. i, He that, building, stayes at one Floore or the second, hath erected none. **1751** JOHNSON *Rambler* No. 161 ¶5 The lodgers on the first floor had stipulated that [etc.]. **1830** TENNYSON *Mariana* vi, Old footsteps trod the upper floors. **1831** SIR J. SINCLAIR *Corr.* II. 330 Many buildings . . are let in floors to mechanics.

II. A level space or area.

6. a. An artificial platform, or levelled space, for the carrying on of some industry, *esp.* threshing. Cf. *threshing floor*. Also, a dance-floor; ***to take the floor***: to take part in a dance. †Rarely, a structure to walk over.

c **1000** *Ags. Gosp.* Luke iii. 17 He feormað his bernes flore. *c* **1300** *K. Alis.* 6104 Of hurdles of bruggen they made flores, And so they wente into the mores. *c* **1400** MAUNDEV. (Roxb.) xviii. 83 þan þai gader þe fruyt and . . layez it apon a flure til it becom blakk and runkled. **1573** BARET *Alv.* F 721 A floore where corne is threshed, *area*. **1702** in *Lond. Gaz.* No. 3790/4 Every Cistern . . Kiln, Floor, Room, or other Place . . made use of for the Wetting or Steeping of Corn. **1775** ROMANS *Hist. Florida* 166 One or two platforms . . called drying floors. **1839** W. CARLETON *Fardorougha* (1848) iv. 46 Answer Mrs. Fogarty, statin' fedher you'll take a month's larnin' on the flure. **1851** MAYNE REID *Scalp Hunt.* I. vii. 99 We returned to our seats again; and after refreshing . . again 'took the floor'. **1884** C. T. DAVIS *Bricks, Tiles, etc.* v. (1889) 128 The 'floors' . . the level places where the bricks are moulded. **1884** L. TROUBRIDGE *Life amongst Troubridges* (1966) 171 We all went to the New Club Ball . . such a floor, such music, and such a partner. **1888** *Lockwood's Dict. Mech. Engin.*, Floor, the sand bed of a foundry is termed the floor. **1938** [see CABARET[1] 2 b]. **1967** R. RENDELL *New Lease Death* viii. 82 'Hard to make conversation when you're dancing.' . . 'Like "Don't you think this is a good floor"?'

fig. **1782** COWPER *Expost.* 302 Where flails of oratory thresh the floor.

b. *transf.* The corn, etc. placed on a 'floor'. In *Malting*, A batch or quantity of grain laid at one time for steeping, a 'piece'.

1382 WYCLIF *Ruth* iii. 2 In this nyȝt he wynnewith the flore of his barli. **1832** W. CHAMPION *Maltster's Guide* 43 The turning of his floors or pieces, by which alone the proper form of the root can be acquired. **1876** WYLLIE in *Encycl. Brit.* IV. 268 Each steeping is called a 'floor' or piece, and must be laid in succession according to age.

7. a. A naturally level space or extended surface. Also = the ground (*obs.* exc. *dial.*).

?*a* **1400** *Morte Arth.* 3250 With þe drowghte of þe daye alle drye ware þe flores! **1555** EDEN *Decades* 234 The vpper crust or floure of the earth. **1637** MILTON *Lycidas* 167 Sunk though he be beneath the watery floor. **1692** RAY *Dissol. World* III. v. (1693) 302 Great Banks or Floors of Earth. **1697** DRYDEN *Virg. Past.* VI. 25 His rosie Wreath was . . Born by the tide of Wine, and floating on the Floor. **1820** SHELLEY *Cloud* 47 The moon Glides glimmering o'er my fleece-like floor. **1839** LONGF. *Celestial Pilot* 3 Down in the west upon the ocean floor. **1865** GARLAND in *Jrnl. Roy. Inst. Cornw.* Apr. 48 *Floor*, a grass meadow. **1871** L. STEPHEN *Playgr. Eur.* ix. (1894) 198 Forests of pine rise steeply from the meadow floor.

b. ***the floor*** (Cricket colloq.): the ground. So ***to put a catch on the floor***: to fail to hold it.

1903 *Strand Mag.* XXV. 624/2 A large majority of them [*sc.* catches] were 'put on the floor'. **1960** *Times* 14 June 16/1 With the field drawn tight around the bat and catches being snapped up off the floor.

†**8.** An area or region. *Obs.*$^{-1}$

1626 BACON *Sylva* §255 Both of them [visibles and audibles] spread themselves in Round, and fill a whole Floare or Orbe vnto certaine Limits.

†**9.** = BED *sb.* 8. *Obs. rare.* [Cf. MHG. *vluor* sown field.]

1600 SURFLET *Countrie Farme* II. iv. 206 Of the disposing or appointing of the floores of the kitchin garden.

III. 10. A surface on which something rests; a foundation.

1556 WITHALS *Dict.* (1566) 39 b/1 A flore, or foundacion, wherevpon buildynge is set. **1768** SMEATON *Reports* (1797) I. 330 The arches I would recommend are of 12 feet wide, and 6 feet from the floor to the springer. **1969** *Jane's Freight Containers 1968–69* 18/3 Freight Container Components. . . Floor. Component supporting the payload.

11. The stratum upon which a seam of coal, etc. immediately lies.

1869 R. B. SMYTH *Goldf. Victoria* 611 *Floor*, a false bottom, with washdirt lying on it. **1878** HUXLEY *Physiogr.* 235 Vegetable remains are also met with in rocks beneath the coal, forming what is called the floor. **1883** in GRESLEY *Gloss. Coal Mining* s.v.

IV. A layer = BED III.

12. A layer, a stratum; a horizontal course.

1692 RAY *Dissol. World* II. iv. (1732) 127 Many Beds or Floors of all kinds of Sea-Shells. **1778** PRYCE *Min. Cornub.* 321 A Floor is a bed of Ore in a Lode. **1851** RICHARDSON *Geol.* i. 7 In the case of tin it occasionally spreads out into a flat mass, technically called a floor.

13. A unit of measurement used for embankment work (see quots.).

1707 MORTIMER *Husb.* xv. 309 Banks are measured by the . . Floor, which is eighteen Foot square and one deep. **1797** *Trans. Soc. Encourag. Arts* XV. 148 A floor of earth is twenty feet square, and one foot deep. **1877** in *N.W. Linc. Gloss.* [= 400 cubic feet].

V. *attrib.* and *Comb.*

14. Simple attrib., as ***floor area***, ***-covering***, ***-joist***, ***level***, ***-slab***, ***-space***, ***-stone***, ***-tile***; ***floor-mounted*** adj.

1887 *Pall Mall G.* 9 Nov. 13/2 The . . *floor area of the large hall having been fully occupied. **1885** *List of Subscribers, Classified* (United Telephone Co.) (ed. 6) 122 *Corticine *Floor Covering Co., Limited*, 112 Queen Victoria Street, E.C. **1986** K. MOORE *Moving House* x. 121 She was also taking over the dull but still serviceable floor-covering of the flat which she meant to enliven by a couple of her favourite rugs. **1859** GEO. ELIOT *A. Bede* 183 A difficulty about a *floor-joist or a window-frame. **1874** MICKLETHWAITE *Mod. Par. Churches* 127 The steps and *floor levels. **1962** *Times* 25 May 18/5 The cranked, *floor-mounted gear lever. **1936** *Discovery* Feb. 56/1 The two principal *floor-slabs . . were of a specially hard kind of granite. **1963** *Gloss. Build. Terms* (*B.S.I.*) 18 *Floor slab*, a slab forming the continuous loadbearing structure of a floor and spanning between supports or laid on the ground. **1876** J. S. INGRAM *Centenn. Exposition* v. 150 It occupied about one-seventh of the entire *floor-space in that structure. **1930** *Times Educ. Suppl.* 23 Aug. 363/2 The small floor-space of the war museum. **1927** *Blackw. Mag.* Apr. 527 Little of the *floorstone remains. **1956** E. POUND tr. *Sophocles' Women of Trachis* 30 Seemed to corrode of itself. Ate itself up, there on the floor-stones. **1894** *Antiquary* Aug. 41 the *floor-tiles of these hearths . . have been burnt white.

15. Special comb., as **floor-arch** (see quot.); **floor-bank** (see quot. 1750); **floor-board**, a board used for flooring, also *attrib.*; hence as vb.: to press (the accelerator pedal of a motor vehicle) down until it reaches the floor; to accelerate, drive very fast; so **floor-boarding**; **floor-frame**, (*a*) the framework of the floor in a vessel; (*b*) *U.S.* the main frame of the body of a railway-carriage underneath the floor; **floor-guide**, **floor-hanger** (see quots.); **floor-head**, (*a*) the upper end of one of the floor-timbers in a vessel; (*b*) (see quot. 1867); **floor-hollow** (see quot.); **floor lamp**, one that stands on the floor; *U.S.*, a tall lamp designed to stand on the floor; **floor-layer**, *U.S.* a workman who lays down floors; **floor-laying**, the operation of laying down floors; **floor-leader** *U.S.*, a leader in debate, esp. in legislative assemblies; **floor-length** *a.*, reaching to the floor; **floor-light** (see quot.); **floor man**, one who helps to attract customers to a mock auction; **floor manager**, (*a*) *U.S.*, a 'master of ceremonies' at a dance; (*b*) orig. *U.S.*, a shop-walker; (*c*) *U.S.*, one who organizes support for a candidate in the hall of a political convention; (*d*) in television production: see quot. 1961; **floor pattern** (see quot. 1964); **floor-pipe**, a hot-air pipe laid along the floor of a conservatory; **floor-plan**, (*a*) *Shipbuilding* (see quot. 1867); (*b*) *Arch.* (see quot. 1874); **floor-plate**, (*a*) *Shipbuilding* (see quot. 1883); (*b*) *Mech. Engin.* = *foot-plate*; **floor polish**, a manufactured substance for rendering floors glossy; hence ***floor-polisher***; **floor-riband** (see quots.); **floor-rider** (see quot.); **floor show**, an entertainment presented on the floor of a restaurant, night-club, etc.; **floor-sweep** (see quot.); **floor-timber(s** (see quot. 1867); **floor-waiter**, a waiter who serves on one floor of a hotel; **floor-walker**, *U.S.* = SHOP-WALKER; **floorward** *a.*, directed towards the floor; **floor-ward(s** *adv.*, towards the floor.

1884 KNIGHT *Dict. Mech* IV. 349/1 **Floor Arch*, an arch with a flat extrados. **1750** ELLIS *Mod. Husbandm.* I. i. 93 What we call a *Flower-bank; that is, some earth that lies next the hedge, thrown over the roots with a spade . . so that with the first Original or first raised Flower-bank, the whole Rise of Earth is not above a foot. **1805** PRIEST in *Young's Ann. Agric.* XLIII. 586 The ditches will be filled up, so as to form what are called floor-banks. **1881** YOUNG *Every Man his own Mechanic* §146 *Floor boards are, or ought to be, an inch in thickness. **1884** *Health Exhib. Catal.* 83/2 Parts of a Solid Floor of fire-proof construction, with a floor-board surface. **1942** BERREY & VAN DEN BARK *Amer. Thes. Slang* §728/4 *Drive fast* . . floorboard, give 'er the gas. **1971** *Scope* (S. Afr.) 19 Mar. 59/2 (Advt.), You slice her into second gear—all clear ahead—and floorboard the pedal. **1971** *Islander* (Victoria, B.C.) 16 May 10/3 As he floor-boarded the throttle he noticed his quarry had turned a corner. **1807** HUTTON *Course Math.* II. 84 In *Floor-boarding, take the length of the room for one dimension, and the breadth for the other, [etc.]. **1948** MENCKEN *Amer. Lang.* (Suppl. II) xi. 719 Of the more original words and phrases of the truckmen I offer a few specimens:—floor-boarding. . . Running at high speed. **1775** FALCK *Day's Diving Vessel* 4 A *Floor frame of six beams athwart ship. **1855** OGLIVIE Suppl., **Floor-guide* in ship-building, a narrow flexible piece of timber placed between the floor-riband and the keel. **1884** KNIGHT *Dict. Mech.* IV. 349/1 **Floor Hanger*, a shaft bearing fastened to the floor. **1769** FALCONER *Dict. Marine* (1789), *Rung-heads* . . the upper ends of the floor-timbers, which are . . more properly called *floor-heads. **1856** R. H. DANA *Seamen's Friend* 5 When the ballast is iron, it is stowed up to the floor-heads. **1867** SMYTH *Sailor's Word-bk.*, *Floor-head*, the third diagonal, terminating the length of the floors near the bilge of the ship. *c* **1850** *Rudim. Navig.* (Weale) 118 **Floor hollow*, the inflected curve that terminates the floor next the keel, and to which the floor-hollow mould is made. **1892** *Daily News* 21 Nov. 2/6 The home demand for telescope *floor lamps is still growing. **1907** *Yesterday's Shopping* (1969) 255 Polished brass telescopic floor lamps. **1940** C. MCCULLERS *Heart is a Lonely Hunter* (1943) I. i. 5 He walked into a store one day and hauled out a floor lamp without paying for it. **1965** J. M. CAIN *Magician's Wife* (1966) ii. 18 He . . went into the living room, and without turning the floor lamps on, sat down in a chair by a window and stared out at the gathering dusk. **1863** *Boston* (Mass.) *Jrnl.* 10 May 4/6 The newly formed union of *floor-layers. **1884** *Health Exhib. Catal.* 83/1 Improved method of *Floor-laying without nails. **1899** *Congress. Rec.* 11 Feb. 1764/2 Congress has witnessed very few more successful *floor leaders. **1954** *Encounter* Mar. 59/1 Congressman John McCormack, Democratic floor-leader in the House. **1939** *Ottawa Jrnl.* 26 June 8/4 The bride wore a *floor-length gown of white chiffon over taffeta. **1967** E. SHORT *Embroidery & Fabric Collage* iii. 74 A round table in a bedroom or drawing-room may sometimes have a floor-length cover permanently in position. **1884** KNIGHT *Dict. Mech.* IV. 349/1 **Floor-light*, a frame with glass panes in a floor. **1928** *Daily Express* 3 Mar. 7 Meader and Solomons were what is known as '*floor men', or . . 'pitch gatherers'. **1887** *Harper's Mag.* May 967/1 Jerry, as one of the *floor-managers, was gorgeous. **1892** *Ibid.* Feb. 439/1 Like the floor-walkers in the stores, they're all floor or aisle managers now. **1913** J. LONDON *Valley of Moon* III. xiii, An' here's you making' rough-house at a dance, an' I'm the floor manager, an' I gotta put you out. **1924** W. S. HAYWARD *Retail Handbk.* 74 The floor manager is the first person to arrive in the department and the last to leave. **1930** J. B. PRIESTLEY *Angel Pavement* vi. 292 Tells me she's had some bother with the buyer or floor manager. **1953** *Manch. Guardian Weekly* 3 Sept. 3 The convention floor manager's hard-won knowledge. **1960** O. SKILBECK *ABC of Film & TV* 55 Floor manager. **1961** G. MILLERSON *Technique Telev. Production* 14 The floor-manager is the director's contact man on the studio floor, and checks staging, action and performers on his behalf. **1966** S. JACKMAN *Davidson Affair* i. 17, I . . saw the floor-manager's hand drop to cue me in . . and turned to face the camera. **1943** M. MAYO *Amer. Square Dance* 11 It is well also to picture clearly in the mind what the dance will look like and what the *floor pattern will be. **1958** J. WINEARLS *Mod. Dance* 130 (*caption*) Floor Pattern. **1964** W. G. RAFFÉ *Dict. Dance* 374/2 Floor pattern: the track, or footsteps, traced by the dancer on the stage. **1696** EVELYN *Kal. Hort.* (ed. 8) 162 The fresh Air . . circulating thorow the Orifice of the *Floor-pipe. **1867** SMYTH *Sailor's Word-bk.*, **Floor-plans*, longitudinal sections, whereon are represented the water-lines and ribband-lines. **1874** KNIGHT *Dict. Mech.* I. 889/1 *Floor-plan* . . (Architecture) a horizontal section, showing the thickness of the walls and partitions, the arrangement of the passages, apartments, and openings at the level of the principal, or receiving floor of the house. **1869** SIR E. J. REED *Shipbuild.* xix. 407 The *floor-plates are now required to extend to a perpendicular height up the bilges of twice the depth of the floors amidships. **1883** W. C. RUSSELL *Sailor's Lang.*, *Floorplates*, formerly plates in the bottom of an iron ship corresponding with the floor-timbers in wooden ones. **1888** *Lockwood's Dict. Mech. Engin.*, *Floor plates*, foot plates. **1907** *Yesterday's Shopping* (1969) 18/2 *Floor polish. **1926** *Daily Colonist* (Victoria, B.C.) 2 July 4/5 (Advt.), Floor polishes, you may say, are pretty much alike. But try 'Poliflor' just once and you will immediately realize what a vast difference there can be. **1895** *Army & Navy Co-op. Soc. Price List* 184/2 *Floor Polisher, extra large, with swivel joint, including handle. **1897** *Westm. Gaz.* 7 Dec. 10/2 One man only will be allowed on the premises—the floor-polisher. **1939–40** *Army & Navy Stores Catal.* 114/1 *Floor polisher*. . . Double sided. One side for applying wax. One side for polishing. *c* **1850** *Rudim. Navig.* (Weale) 118 **Floor riband*, the riband next below the floor-heads which supports the floors. **1867** SMYTH *Sailor's Word-bk.*, **Floor-riders*, knees brought in from side to side over the floor ceiling and kelson, to support the bottom, if bilged or weak, for heavy cargo. **1927** *Stage Year Bk.* 69 The opportunities and scope for employment [in vaudeville] of an artist are practically unlimited, apart from the large field in musical productions, cabaret *floor shows, etc. **1931** DURANTE & KEFOED *Night Clubs* 4 A floor show with six principals and no chorus. **1959** *Times* 2 Mar. 12/7 Snippets from a night-club floor-show of resplendent tattiness. *c* **1850** *Rudim. Navig.* (Weale) 119 **Floor-sweeps*, the radii that sweep the heads of the floors. **1627** CAPT. SMITH *Seaman's Gram.* ii. 2 They lay the Rungs, called *floore timbers . . thwart the keele. **1867** SMYTH *Sailor's Word-bk.*, *Floors* or *Floor-Timbers*, those parts of the ship's timbers which are placed immediately across the keel. **1930** A. BENNETT *Imperial Palace* xvii. 109 Once he had memorably discovered fourth-floor silver in the fifth-floor service-room . . which disconcerted all the *floor-waiters. **1967** G. GREENE *May we borrow your Husband?* 19 Peter's mislaid his tie. He thinks the floor-waiter has purloined it. **1876** *Scribner's Monthly* Feb. 599/2, I next went into a store a few doors further up Broadway. When I entered I approached the *floor-walker. **1884** *Milnor* (Dakota) *Teller* 30 July, These Boston merchants stationed their floor-walkers at the place appointed by the Philadelphia agent. **1942** E. PAUL *Narrow St.* iv. 32 The tenant of this room and bath was a floor-walker from the Samaritaine. **1887** *Pall Mall G.* 12 Mar. 12/1 A constantly repeated *floor-ward glance of bashfulness and modesty. **1863** *Reader* 31 Oct. 502 He is bundled down *floorwards.

floor, *sb.*[2] *colloq.* [f. FLOOR *v.*] Something that 'floors' or discomfits one; also, a fatal blunder (in a calculation, etc.).

1841 R. W. CHURCH *Let.* 21 Mar. in *Life & Lett.* (1894) 23 The Heads show that they feel it rather a floor for the present. **1846** *Ibid.* 64 We may be caught out in some 'floor'.

floor (flɔə(r)), *v.* [f. FLOOR *sb.*[1]]

1. a. *trans.* To cover or furnish with a floor or floors, in various senses of the word; to pave. Also with *over*.

c **1420** *Pallad. on Husb.* I. 334 Eke pave or floore it wele in somer tyde. *c* **1520** *Mem. Ripon* (Surtees) III. 201 Flowryng the lofte per v dies. **1581** MULCASTER *Positions* xxxi. (1887) 114 (He) must have his ground flowred so . . as in wrastling not hard to fall on. **1660** PEPYS *Diary* 4 Sept., Looking over the joiners, flooring my dining-room. **1698** FRYER *Acc. E. Ind. & P.* 226 [Persia] is floored with vast Sands pent in by the surrounding Sprouts of Taurus. **1782** COWPER *Expost.* 16 Fiery suns . . and oceans floored with ice. **1807** VANCOUVER *Agric. Devon* (1813) 473 The feeding and sleeping place floored with flat stones. **1823** *Examiner* 442/2 The pit was floored over to the height of the stage. **1857** B. TAYLOR *Northern Trav.* iii. (1858) 18 Thick fir forests, floored with bright-green moss.

b. To form, or serve as, the floor of.

1639 G. DANIEL *Ecclus.* i. 4 The Sands which floore the Sea. **1854** HOOKER *Himalayan Jrnls.* II. xviii. 44, 300 feet of deposit, which once floored its valleys.

2. a. To bring to the floor or ground; to knock down in boxing; to bring down (game). ***to be floored*** (of a horseman): to have a fall.

1642 *Lanc. Tracts.* (Chetham Soc.) 79 He commanded them all to shoote at once, and flore the enemie, if possible they could. **1812** *Sporting Mag.* XXXIX. 18 Crib..floored him with a blow of great strength. **1826** *Ibid.* New Ser. XVII. 270 My friend was floored, and Mr. Leader..rode over him. **1829** COL. HAWKER *Diary* (1893) II. 10 My wild swan, that I floored yesterday. **1866** SEEBOHM *Oxf. Reformers* iv. §4 Whereupon the poor boy was forthwith floored then and there, and flogged.

b. *slang.* (See quot.)

1812 J. H. VAUX *Flash Dict., Floor'd*, a person who is so drunk, as to be incapable of standing, is said to be floor'd.

3. In various figurative uses. *colloq.*

a. To confound, nonplus; to flabbergast, puzzle. In schoolboy slang, ***to be*** or ***get floored***: to grow confused, be at a loss, fail, break down.

1830 COLERIDGE *Table T.* 8 July (1884), The other day I was what you would call *floored* by a Jew. **1840** LD. BEACONSFIELD in *Corr. w. Sister* (1886) 158 My facts flabbergasted him, as well as..Hume, who was ludicrously floored. **1857** HUGHES *Tom Brown* II. iv, 'If you hadn't been floored yourself now at first lesson.' *Ibid.* II. v, 'He's never going to get floored.' **1886** RUSKIN *Præterita* I. 359 The consummate manner in which I had *floored* our tutor.

b. To overcome in any way; to beat, defeat, prove too much for. ***to floor the odds*** (see quot. 1893).

1827 LYTTON *Pelham* xxx, It is very singular that you who play so much better should not have *floored* him yesterday evening. **1834** J. H. NEWMAN in *Lett.* (1891) II. 22 I am floored as to the professorship. **1836** LD. BEACONSFIELD in *Corr. w. Sister* (1886) 50, I was the only man who could floor O'Connell. **1882** *Daily Tel.* 16 Nov. 3/5 The odds were, nevertheless, floored from an unexpected quarter. **1893** FARMER *Slang, Floor* (Racing), When a low-priced horse pulls off the event in the face of the betting, it is said *to floor the odds*.

c. To do thoroughly, get through (a piece of work) successfully. ***to floor a paper*** (*Univ. slang*): to answer every question in it.

1852 BRISTED 5 *Years in Eng. Univ.* I. 186 Our best classic had not time to floor the paper. **1861** HUGHES *Tom Brown at Oxf.* x. 83 I've nearly floored my little-go work.

d. To empty, finish (a bottle, etc.).

1836–48 B. D. WALSH *Aristoph. Acharnians* v. ii, I was the first man that floored his gallon. **1861** HUGHES *Tom Brown at Oxf.* xxiv. (1889) 228, I have a few bottles of old wine left; we may as well floor them.

e. *intr.* ? To commit a fatal blunder.

1835 J. H. NEWMAN *Lett* (1891) II. 97 We floored so miserably at the Reformation, that [etc.].

†**4.** *trans.* 'To bring forward in argument, to table' (Jam.). *Obs.*$^{-1}$

a **1687** M'WARD *Contendings* (1723) 177, I know not.. whom your Proposal..strikes against; save that you floor it, to fall on some, whom you mind to hit right or wrong.

5. To place *upon* (something) as a floor.

1871 TYLOR *Prim. Cult.* II. xiii. 68 The doctrine of a Heaven, floored upon a firmament, or placed in the upper air.

6. *Art slang.* To hang in the lowest row on the walls of a picture-gallery.

1884 *American* VIII. 376 One R.A. is 'skied' and another 'floored'.

floorage ('flɔːrɪdʒ). *rare*$^{-1}$. [f. as prec. + -AGE.] Floors collectively, amount of flooring.

1734 tr. *Rollin's Anc. Hist.* (1827) II. III. 147 All this floorage was contrived to keep the moisture of the mould from running away.

floor-cloth, 'floorcloth.

1. A fabric for covering floors; chiefly applied to substitutes for carpeting, as oilcloth, linoleum, etc.

1746 WATSON in *Phil. Trans.* XLIV. 716 A thick Carpet, instead of a Floor-cloth, is liable to prevent the Success of this Experiment. *a* **1818** MISS ROSE in G. Rose *Diaries* (1860) II. 75 The floor-cloth in the entrance-hall was taken up. **1836** DICKENS *Sk. Boz, Our Parish* vii, It was a neat, dull little house..with new, narrow floorcloth in the passage.

2. A cloth for washing floors.

1851 [See FILE *sb.*^{7}]. **1951** *Catal. of Exhibits, South Bank Exhib., Festival of Britain* 136/1 Dishcloths & floorcloths. **1960** M. SPARK *Bachelors* x. 154 Carrie, you have wiped the oven with the floor cloth.

Hence **'floor-cloth, 'floorcloth** *v.*, to cover with floorcloth. Also, **'floor-clothed** *ppl. a.*

1838 DICKENS *Nich. Nick.* xvi, He found himself in a little floor-clothed room. **1844** —— *Mart. Chuz.* ix, It was floor-clothed all over.

floored (flɔəd), *ppl. a.* [f. FLOOR *v.* + -ED.]

1. Provided with a floor.

1552 HULOET, Floored or dressed with bourdes, *contabulatus.* **1609** HOLLAND *Amm. Marcell.* 79 They passed over the river upon a floored bridge of ships. **1809** SOUTHEY in *Q. Rev.* II. 56 Till the natives live in floored houses.

2. Brought to the ground, overthrown; also *fig.* overpowered, done for.

1821 BYRON 12 Dec. in Moore *Life & Lett.* (1833) III. 301 The usual excuse of floored equestrians. **1857** DICKENS *Lett.* 7 Feb. (1880) II. 11 Wardour was in a floored condition.

floorer ('flɔərə(r)). [f. as prec. + -ER^1.] One who or that which floors.

1. a. One who or that which brings down to the floor or ground; *esp.* a knock-down blow.

1795 POTTER *Dict. Cant* (ed. 2), *Floorers*, fellows who throw persons down, after which their companions..rob them in the act of lifting them up. **1819** MOORE *Tom Crib's Mem.* (ed. 3) 59 Singling him from all her flash adorers, Shines in his hits, and thunders in his floorers. **1836–48** B. D. WALSH *Aristoph., Acharnians* II. ii. 33 Strike, O strike the precious rascal! He shall have a floorer dealt him!

b. In the game of skittles, a throw with the first of three balls which floors all the pins.

1881 *Cassell's Bk. Sports* 128 The only play that will secure a floorer is to throw the ball with a good round-handed swing, imparting to the ball what in billiards would be called a 'side', and so that the edge of the ball alights on the right-handed shoulder of the front pin. **1928** *Daily Express* 31 Mar. 3/4 A scroll on which are inscribed the names of members who have scored floorers. **1930** A. P. HERBERT *Water Gipsies* xxi, A stranger to the game could not have told how it happened, but in less than a second the frame was clear—not one pin standing—a 'floorer'. **1960** *Observer* 17 Jan. 3/5 A chap..said he had done nineteen floorers in a row.

2. Something which floors in a figurative sense (see FLOOR *v.* 3), *e.g.* unexpected news of an unpleasant nature, a decisive argument or retort, a question which utterly embarrasses one, a poser. Also in university slang, a question or paper too hard to be mastered.

1837 T. HOOK *Jack Brag* xxii,'Well', said Jack, 'that's a floorer, and no mistake'. **1867** J. HATTON *Tallants of B.* lviii, This case is a floorer to me. **1870** BREWER *Dict. Phrase & Fable, Floorer*, In the University we say, 'That paper or question was a floorer'. **1875** MISS BRADDON *Hostages to Fort.* xiv. 227, I didn't know the news would be such a floorer.

flooring ('flɔːrɪŋ), *vbl. sb.* [f. as prec. + -ING^1.] The action of the vb. FLOOR.

1. The action of flooring or laying down a floor.

1632 SHERWOOD, A flooring with plankes or boords, *planchage.* **1703** MOXON *Mech. Exerc.* 149 Of Flooring of Rooms. **1866** *Law Reports* Com. Pleas 163 The plaintiff is.. the patentee of certain buckle plates used for bridge flooring.

2. a. *concr.* The floor of a room, etc; also, the materials of which it is made.

1624 WOTTON *Archit.* in *Reliq. Wotton.* (1672) 63 Mosaique is..of most use in pavements and floorings. **1697** DRYDEN *Virg. Georg.* IV. 237 To pitch the waxen Flooring some contrive. **1754** LADY M. W. MONTAGU *Let. to C'tess. Bute* 23 June, The ceiling and flooring are in good repair. **1861** HUGHES *Tom Brown at Oxf.* iv, The Captain, Miller, and Blake who had many notions as to the flooring, lines, and keel of a racing boat. **1875** W. S. HAYWARD *Love agst. World* i, The polished oak flooring.

b. A natural floor; a stratum.

1697 DRYDEN *Vir. Georg.* I. 262 To smooth the Surface of th' unequal Ground; Lest crack'd with Summer Heats the flooring flies. **1804** C. B. BROWN tr. *Volney's View U.S.* 47 The flooring of the Miami and Clay Rivers. **1857** LIVINGSTONE *Trav.* xxii. 428 Sandstone rock..forms the flooring of the country.

3. *Malting.* The operation of spreading the grain on the malt-floor, and treating it there in the required manner.

1839 URE *Dict. Arts* 93 *Malting*..the couching, sweating, and flooring. **1885** H. STOPES *Malt* xix. 344 *Flooring*, this is also called spireing.

4. The action of knocking down or throwing to the ground.

1819 MOORE *Tom Crib's Mem.* Pref. (ed. 3) p. xii, Cross-buttocking..being as indispensable an ingredient, as nobbing, flooring, &c.

5. *attrib.* and *Comb.*, as ***flooring-beam, -board, -machine, -stone, -timber***; **flooring-clamp** (see quot.).

1847–8 H. MILLER *First Impr.* v. (1857) 81 *Flooring beams connect the walls of a skeleton building. **1733** W. ELLIS *Chiltern & Vale F.* vii. 95 So it will in *Flooring-boards, notwithstanding they are nailed down ever so fast. **1881** YOUNG *Every Man his own Mechanic* §173 Flooring boards 10s. per square. **1874** KNIGHT *Dict. Mech.* I. 889/1 **Flooring-clamp*, an implement for closing up the joints of flooring-boards. **1847** H. HOWE *Hist. Coll. Ohio* 372 There are now in operation within the corporate limits..2 *flooring machines. **1957** *N.Z. Timber Jrnl.* Mar. 52/1 *Flooring machine*, a machine for preparing floorboards. **1671** J. WEBSTER *Metallogr.* vii. 117 Quarries of Stone..where they get *flooring-stones for paving of houses.

floorish, obs. form of FLOURISH.

floorless ('flɔəlɪs), *a.* [f. FLOOR *sb.* + -LESS.] Having no floor, without a floor.

1847 in CRAIG. **1857** *Fraser's Mag.* LVI. 464 A roofless, floorless house.

†**floorth.** *Obs.* In 5–6 florthe. [f. FLOOR *sb.* + -TH^1.] = FLOOR *sb.*

1303 R. BRUNNE *Handl. Synne* 6184 Þys persone lay and lokede furþ Vn tyl a cofre yn þe florthe. **1494** FABYAN *Chron.* v. xcix. 73 Yᵉ sayd Goothis, by crafty & false meanes, caused yᵉ florthe of the sayd Chambre to falle. **1502** *Will of Amyas* (Somerset Ho.), A salt cote..wᵗ a salte florth. **1530** PALSGR. 169/2 This florthe is well leavelled.

floorwise ('flɔəwaɪz), *adv. rare*$^{-1}$. [f. FLOOR *sb.* + -WISE.] As on a floor.

1840 MRS. BROWNING *Drama of Exile* Wks. 1889 I. 29 While our feet struck glories..Which we stood on floorwise, Platformed in mid-air.

floose, var. FLUCE *sb.*

floosie, floozie, floozy ('fluːzɪ). *colloq.* [Orig. unkn., but cf. dial. *floosy* adj., fluffy, soft (f. *floose*, see FLOSS^2) and FLOSSY *a.*] A girl or woman, esp. one of disreputable character.

1911 C. B. CHRYSLER *White Slavery* iii. 30 Tell that floosie to cut out that yelping. **1911** *Dialect Notes* III. 543 John took his floozy to the baseball game. **1927** [see BABY *sb.* 1 c]. **1944** B. MARSHALL *All Glorious Within* xix. 144 In the bathroom scene..she has her bath and sings Ave Maria just to show she ain't no floosie. **1951** T. CAPOTE *Grass Harp* 39 He bought a red racy car and went skidding around..with every floozy in town; the only nice girls you ever saw in that car were his sisters. **1952** H. W. TILMAN *Nepal Himalaya* II. xv. 183 The men dallied with a Siren, in less classical language, a 'floozie' who sat on a roof combing her wonderfully straight black hair. **1958** B. NICHOLS *Sweet & Twenties* vii. 91 The usual anaemic floosies in pastel shades. **1959** B. GOOLDEN *For Richer, for Poorer* i. 11 Why the floozies? **1978** J. IRVING *World according to Garp* xviii. 383 Just think a minute... Suppose she's just a floozy. **1984** L. DEIGHTON *Mexico Set* vii. 107 Stinnes had reached that dangerous age when a man was only susceptible to an innocent cutie or to an experienced floozy.

flop (flɒp), *sb. colloq.* and *dial.* [See the vb., and cf. FLAP *sb.*]

1. a. The action of the vb. FLOP; the heavy dull sound produced by 'flopping'.

1823 MOOR *Suffolk Words* s.v., 'I'll gi yeow a flop.' **1854** L. LLOYD *Scandinavian Adv.* II. 271, I was startled by something descending, with a great flop, on to my hat. **1882** *Pall Mall G.* 11 Oct. 5 The flop of a water-rat or the whirr of the grey-hen.

b. A noise resembling this.

1836 T. HOOK *G. Gurney* III. 33 Stuffing his finger into his mouth and pulling it out suddenly, with what he..called a flop.

c. Something loose and pendulous; = FLAP *sb.* 4.

1900 in *Eng. Dial. Dict.* II. 419/1. **1902** *Westm. Gaz.* 11 Sept. 3/2 She achieves another immense flop with the back of the brim well pinned in position over the knob of hair which..flops on her neck. **1909** J. R. WARE *Passing Eng.* 134/2 *Flop*. When the lower classes of women adopted the 'cretin' or 'poodle' style of wearing the hair low down over the forehead, they gave it this name. **1933** V. WOOLF *Writer's Diary* 9 May (1953) 200 A little servant girl with honest eyes, hair brushed in a flop.

†**2.** = FLAP *sb.* 1 b. *Obs.*

1662 *Rump Songs* II. 3 To give us a Flop with a Fox-tail.

3. *dial.* A mass of thin mud. Also *transf.*

1844 W. BARNES *Poems Rural Life* Gloss. 304. **1852** C. FOX *Jrnl.* 23 Aug. (1882) 276 The oven where the fiery flop [molten metal] was shut up for six weeks to cool.

4. a. *U.S. college slang.* (see quot.)

1851 B. H. HALL *College Words*, s.v., Any 'cute' performance by which a man is sold [deceived] is a good flop.

b. A turn-round; a sudden change of policy or party. *U.S.*

1880 *N.Y. World* 22 Nov. 5/1 Mr. Skinner's apparent flop on the railroad question is injuring his chances in the Speakership struggle. **1904** *Springfield* (Mass.) *Weekly Republ.* 7 Oct. 2 That a flop by the most militant of the unionists is under contemplation has been denied. **1911** H. S. HARRISON *Queed* xviii. 230 So ran the editorial, which was offensively headed 'West's Fatal Flop'. **1929** *Collier's* 5 Jan. 41/1 It was basically a 'flop'.

c. A failure, collapse, or decline. Also, a person or enterprise (esp. a play, etc.) that is a failure. *slang.*

1893 FARMER *Slang, Flop.* 2... A sudden fall or 'flop' down. 3... A collapse or breakdown. **1899** *Westm. Gaz.* 28 Jan. 6/2 There has been a flop in Trunks, but Canadas have been good. **1927** *Sunday Express* 15 May 5/7 Nearly all the American turns prove a flop. Yet they think they can command the earth. **1930** *Publishers' Weekly* 18 Oct. 1851 These authors every once in a while write a flop. **1931** *Discovery* Nov. 372/2 Fokker's first invention was a 'flop'. **1934** *Times Lit. Suppl.* 7 June 406/3 She, too, is a common type—the Hollywood flop. **1936** *Amer. Speech* XI. 221 If it [*sc.* a play] just somehow doesn't click or register, it's doomed to be another flop. **1945** L. A. G. STRONG *Othello's Occupation* 121 He's pretty wobbly, professionally speaking. He's had two flops in the suburbs. **1957** *Economist* 5 Oct. 24/2 As a gesture of defiance Argentina's one-day general strike last week was a flop. **1969** *Times* 7 Nov. 3/1 Neil Simon..has had eight Broadway hits..and the question everyone is asking..is whether he's got a flop in him.

d. A 'flabby' or 'soft' person. *slang.*

1909 H. G. WELLS *Tono-Bungay* II. iv. 171 All the little, soft feminine hands, the nervous ugly males, the hands of the flops, and the hands of the snatchers! **1923** *Glasgow Herald* 12 Dec. 10 If that little flop..believes he can play fast and loose with the moral consciousness of this nation. **1936** 'F. O'CONNOR' *Bones of Contention* 70 She was a great flop of a woman.

e. *U.S. slang.* A bed; a place to rest or sleep; = *flop-house*.

1910 D. RANNEY *Autobiogr.* iv. 70 You can get a bed in a lodging-house for ten cents, or if you have only seven cents you can get a 'flop'. **1913** E. A. BROWN *Broke* iii. 28 Say, Jack, can you tell a fellow where he can find a free flop? **1916** *Amer. Mag.* May 14/1 She said to tell you this ain't no hobos' flop, neither. **1925** *Lit. Digest* 11 July 50/1 You better go around to one of the missions. There's a couple of 'em will give you a flop for nothing. **1930** J. DOS PASSOS *42nd Parallel* 75 They couldn't find any-place that looked as if it would give them a flop for thirty-five cents. **1955** *Publ. Amer. Dialect Soc.* XXIV. 120 So we go up to my flop.

5. *attrib.* and *Comb.*, in various words in which *flop* is a variant of *flap*; as ***flop-ear, -eared, -mouth.*** Also **flop-damper, flop-wing** (see quots.); **flop-house** *slang* (orig. *U.S.*), a doss-house.

1874 KNIGHT *Dict. Mech.* I. 889/1 **Flop-damper*, a stove or furnace damper which rests by its weight in open or shut position. **1879** *Cassell's Techn. Educ.* IV. 351/1 The old English hog with '*flop' ears. **1846** J. J. HOOPER *Adv. Simon Suggs* ii. 28 You..gnatty, *flop-eared varmint! **1880** MISS BRADDON *Just as I am* lii, A brace of flop-eared setters bounding before him. **1923** N. ANDERSON *Hobo* iii. 30

'*Flop-houses' are nearly all alike. Guests sleep on the floor or in bare, wooden bunks. The only privilege they buy is the privilege to lie down somewhere in a warm room. **1927** *Scots Observer* 26 Mar. 10/3 The lowest of the derelicts spent the night..in a 'flophouse' (which is worse than the lowest 'model'). **1930** *Harper's Mag.* July 133 The Welfare Council of New York had to charter an old barge..as an overflow flop house. **1941** WYNDHAM LEWIS *Let.* 3 Sept. (1963) 297 If I don't do something to break out of the net, I shall end my days in a Toronto flophouse. **1964** S. BELLOW *Herzog* (1965) 249 Get out! I leave you nothing!.. Croak in a flophouse. **1604** *Meeting of Gallants* 15, I love to heare tales when a merrie corpulent Host bandies them out of his *Flop-mouth. **1885** SWAINSON *Prov. Names Birds* 184 Lapwing (*Vanellus vulgaris*)..*Flopwing.

flop (flɒp), *adv.* and *int. colloq.* [The vb. stem so used.] With a flop, with a flopping noise. Also *fig.*

1728 VANBR. & CIB. *Prov. Husb.* I. i. 14 Dawn came I flop o' my Feace all along in the Channel. **1863** KINGSLEY *Water Bab.* iii, The beetles fell flop into the water. **1883** E. PENNELL-ELMHIRST *Cream Leicestersh.* 177 Reynard dashed out flop against the only hound on that side of the tree. *a* **1887** JEFFERIES *Field & Hedgerow* 177 'Dalled if he didn't fall into the pond, flop!' **1930** *Daily Express* 6 Sept. 4/2 Every one adopts a 'wait and see' policy, and business goes 'flop'.

flop (flɒp), *v. colloq.* and *dial.* [onomatopœic var. of FLAP *v.*, the change of vowel indicating a duller or heavier sound.]

1. *intr.* To swing or sway about heavily and loosely; = FLAP *v.* 5.

1602 MARSTON *Ant. & Mel.* v. Wks. 1856 I. 60 A husband ..with a bush of furs on the ridge of his chinne, readie still to flop into his foming chaps. **1838** HOLLOWAY *Provincialisms*, s.v., 'The sail flops against the mast.' **1883** K. W. HAMILTON in *Harper's Mag.* 845/1 One side [of a wet umbrella] flopped dejectedly.

2. a. To move clumsily or heavily; to move with a sudden bump or thud. Of a bird: To flap the wings heavily. Also with *away*, *down*, *over*, etc.

1692 [See FLOPPING]. **1827** CLARE *Sheph. Cal.* 4 They flop on heavy wings away. **1850** P. CROOK *War of Hats* 43 Then flopping on his seat..he sinks. **1859** MRS. CARLYLE *Lett.* III. 13 He flopped over on his side, quite stiff and unconscious. **1870** H. SMART *Race for Wife* x, She flopped down on her knees, and implored for mercy. **1879** BODDAM-WHETHAM *Roraima* 105 Tortoises flopped into the water. **1887** BESANT *The World went* i. 7 Blue water over your head, and the whales flopping around your grave. **1887** LADY BRASSEY in *Last Voy.* ix. 222 A..grey sea flopping up on our weather bow.

b. fig. *to flop* (*over*): to make a sudden change in one's attitude or behaviour. Also *trans.*, to cause to change sides; to bring over. *U.S.*

1884 *Puck* 6 Aug. 359/1 It is not the Independents who have 'flopped' this time. It is the Republican Party that has 'flopped' from honesty to dishonesty. **1892** *Nation* (N.Y.) 6 Oct. 268/3 His [Sardou's] characters..flop over and act in a way quite the reverse of what we had a right to expect. **1894** *Daily Ardmoreite* (Ardmore, Okla.) 18 Jan. 1/4 The purported change was..a fake to enable that canine barnacle, Soule, to flop his politics. **1904** *Omaha Bee* 3 Sept. 6 A number of New York newspapers have flopped to the support of Parker. **1904** *Springfield* (Mass.) *Weekly Republ.* 16 Dec. 8 Mr. Roche flopped the Boston Pilot to the support of the republican candidate. **1926** C. R. COOPER *Oklahoma* 123 Hurriedly lawmakers who had been opposed to it 'flopped' to the other side.

c. *spec.* To sleep. *slang* (orig. *U.S.*).

1907 J. LONDON *Road* (1914) 107 'Kip', 'doss', 'flop', 'pound your ear', all mean the same thing; namely, to sleep. **1926** J. BLACK *You can't Win* vi. 66 It was time to 'flop'. They took off their shoes and coats. **1936** W. A. GAPE *Half a Million Tramps* x. 301 Where the hell are you going to 'flop' tonight? **1959** N. MAILER *Advts. for Myself* (1961) 84 They're filthy..diseased..what's the town mean, why aren't they put in the coop where they belong, why should they be flopping so near our house in a meadow?

d. *fig.* To collapse, fail (cf. FLOP *sb.* 4 c). *slang.*

1919 WODEHOUSE *Damsel in Distress* viii, The summer-time number [in a theatre] flopped on the second night. **1928** *Observer* 15 July 15/1 If..the play 'flops' after a run of ..three or four nights. **1936** P. FLEMING *News from Tartary* 28 She published a book on that journey, which flopped. **1967** M. REYNOLDS *After Some Tomorrow* 61 Lenin supposedly tried to apply the teachings of Marx to Russia —and flopped.

3. *trans.* To throw suddenly, generally with the additional notion of making a bump or thud. Also with *down*, *in*, etc.

1823 MOOR *Suffolk Words* s.v., 'A floppt his affections' on such a one. **1836** MARRYAT *Midsh. Easy* xxxviii, She.. flopped herself into the standing bed-place. *a* **1845** HOOD *Agric. Distress* iii, In bolts our bacon-hog Atwixt the legs of Master Blogg, And flops him down in all the muck. **1854** BAKER *Northampton Gloss.* s.v., 'How you flop it in.' **1859** DICKENS *T. Two Cities* II. i, 'What do you mean by flopping yourself down and praying agin me?'

4. To move (wings, etc.) heavily and loosely up and down.

1859 TENNENT *Ceylon* II. vii. 254 Cawing and flopping his wings in the sky. **1891** *Camb. Rev.* 12 Mar. 264/2 One or two of them at least sat..feebly flopping their hands about.

5. To strike with a sudden blow. *to flop up* (the eyes): to bung up; = FLAP *v.* 1. *dial.*

1838 BYWATER *Sheffield* (ed. 3) 227 If thah gets drunk, an flops a watchman's een up. **1888** *Sporting Life* 15 Dec. 5/5 'E carnt flop a bloke.

6. *U.S. College slang* (see quot.).

1851 B. H. HALL *College Words*, s.v., 'A man writes cards during examination to feeze the profs..and he flops the examination if he gets a good mark by the means.' One usually flops his marks by feigning sickness.

Hence **'flopping** *ppl. a.*

1679 *Trial of Langhorn* 53 He had a gray Coat on, and plain Shooes, and a flopping Hat. **1692** R. L'ESTRANGE *Fables* ccccix. 384 A Huge Flopping Kyte. **1821** CLARE *Vill. Minstr.* I. 24 Jealous watch-dog..E'en rous'd by quawking of the flopping crows.

flopper ('flɒpə(r)). *U.S.* [f. FLOP *v.* 2 and 2 b.]

1. *Criminals' slang.* A perpetrator of any of several kinds of frauds.

1876 B. HARTE *G. Conroy* II. VI. ii. 312 It is worthy of a short-card sharp and a keno flopper. **1914** JACKSON & HELLYER *Vocab. Criminal Slang* 35 *Flopper*, in general use by money changers, switchers (substituters); flim-flammers. **1960** F. GIBNEY *Operators* v. 137 'Floppers' fall down on 'slippery' floors in..supermarkets, tumble deftly in front of slow-moving automobiles.... Then they submit their claims to the stores or the insurance companies.

2. One who deserts to the opposite side in politics.

1880 *Cleveland Leader* 8 June 1/7 On the twenty-fifth ballot the Florida flopper went to Sherman. **1904** *Courier Jrnl.* (Louisville, Ky.) 17 Aug. 4 There are always floppers. The mere circumstance that somebody deserts his party and goes over to the other proves nothing.

flopperoo (ˌflɒpəˈruː). *N. Amer. colloq.* Also floperoo. [f. FLOP *v.* 2 d; cf. -EROO.] A flop, failure.

1936 in *Amer. Speech* (1937) XII. 18/2 John Oliver in the Richmond *News-Leader* for Dec. 26, 1936, terms Georgia Tech the '*greatest flopperoo*' in football of the sports season. **1945** LOU SHELLY *Jive Talk Dict.* 11 Flopperoo,..a failure. **1951** M. MCLUHAN *Mech. Bride* (1967) 58/2 The intellectually creative men with whom the future of mankind always rests will be regarded only as floperoos. **1970** R. JEFFRIES *Dead Man's Bluff* xviii. 163 His case was a real floperoo.

floppy ('flɒpɪ), *a.* and *sb. colloq.* [f. FLOP *v.* + -Y¹.] **A.** *adj.* **1.** Inclined to flop, having a tendency to flop about. Also *fig.*

1858 GEO. ELIOT *Scenes Clerical Life*, *Amos Barton* ii, In those days even fashionable caps were large and floppy. **1890** *Pall Mall G.* 2 Sept. 7/1 A divided skirt..is the clumsiest, floppiest..article that a woman can put on. **1905** D. SLADEN *Playing Game* ix, She's such a young heifer— she's at the floppy sentimental age.

2. ***floppy disc*** (Computing): a small, flexible plastic disc with a magnetic coating used as an inexpensive light-weight storage device of moderate capacity (typically a megabyte or less); this together with its protective envelope.

1972 *Computer Design* May 132/1 Century Data Systems has introduced the CDS-100 'floppy disc' drive, a portable storage device that utilizes a single, removable, disc cartridge as the recording medium. **1977** *Sci. Amer.* June 57/2 The full system can include dual floppy disks, terminals, plotters, printers and tape cassettes. **1979** *Personal Computer World* Nov. 12 (Advt.), The basic Apple II Plus can be used on its own (with your TV) or as the basis of a most comprehensive business computer system by adding such items as floppy disc drives and printers. **1984** S. TOWNSEND *Growing Pains A. Mole* 180 Pandora went round to Brainbox Henderson's house to break the news, but he was out buying floppy discs, so she left a message on his word processor.

B. *ellipt.* as *sb. Computing.* A floppy disc.

1974 *Mod. Data* Dec. 38 The floppy disc has captured the DP industry's imagination since its introduction in 1970 as a loader on IBM's 3330 disc system. The floppy, however, was destined for a more visible fate. **1979** *Personal Computer World* Nov. 48 The review machine..was a 56K RAM, twin floppy system. **1982** *Which Computer?* June 83/3 Most systems sold with a Winchester disc have a floppy disc for back-up so that the floppies can be taken from the machine for safe-keeping and a permanent record of the data on the hard disc can be kept. **1983** *Guardian* 24 Nov. 25/4 Even better than floppies are hard or Winchester discs.

Hence **'floppily** *adv.*; **'floppiness.**

1884 *St. James's Gaz.* 11 Sept. 6/2 An aimless feeble old humbug, he sits floppily on the wrong side of his boat. **1892** *Daily News* 2 July 6/7 There is now a regrettable tendency to 'floppiness' of attire.

flopsy bunny ('flɒpsɪ 'bʌnɪ). [f. FLOP *v.* + -SY.] One of a group of rabbits in the children's stories of Beatrix Potter (1866–1943); hence, a sentimental designation of a rabbit. Also *transf.*

[**1902** B. POTTER *Tale of Peter Rabbit* 9 Once upon a time there were four little Rabbits, and their names were— Flopsy, Mopsy, Cotton-tail, and Peter.] **1909** —— (*title*) The tale of the Flopsy Bunnies. **1954** 'N. BLAKE' *Whisper in Gloom* ix. 128 A nauseating tale about some flopsy bunnies. **1960** *News Chron.* 30 June 6/4 Maybe a juxtaposition of Flopsy Bunny sentiment and harsh reality is just the kind of shock the human race needs. **1966** M. WADDELL *Otley* vii. 62 Her face looked pretty when she was asleep, like a sexy flopsy bunny. **1971** 'A. GILBERT' *Tenant for Tomb* vi. 96 All this Robin Redbreast malarky..it's all on a par with the Flopsy Bunnies in coloured hats and white pinnies.

flora ('flɔərə). Pl. **floræ**; also **floras**. [a. L. *Flōra* the goddess of flowers, f. *flōr-*, *flōs* flower.]

1. In Latin mythology, the goddess of flowers; hence, in modern poetical language, the personification of nature's power in producing flowers.

1508 DUNBAR *Goldyn Targe* 74 Thare saw I..The fresch Aurora, and lady Flora schene. **1667** MILTON *P.L.* v. 16 With voice Milde, as when Zephyrus or Flora breathes. **1762** FALCONER *Shipwr.* iii. 235 Indulgent Flora breathed perpetual May. **1812** CRABBE *Tales* x. 116 Here a grave Flora scarcely deigns to bloom. **1851** CARPENTER *Man Phys.* 65 The empire of Flora has no limit.

2. A descriptive catalogue of the plants of any geographical area, geological period, etc.

[From the use of the name *Flora* in Latin titles of works of this kind. The earliest known example is Simon Paulli's *Flora Danica* 1647; other early instances are Rupp's *Flora Jenensis* 1718, and Linnæus' *Flora Suecica* 1745.]

[**1665** RAY (*title*), Flora, seu de Florum Cultura. Or, a complete Florilege.] **1777** LIGHTFOOT *Flora Scotica* Pref. 17 It comprehends by far the greatest part, which is as much as the Flora of any country can pretend to. **1799** J. HULL (*title*), The British Flora. **1829** G. JOHNSTON (*title*), A Flora of Berwick-upon-Tweed. **1870** HOOKER *Stud. Flora* Pref. v, I have consulted the usual British and Continental Floras.

3. a. The plants or plant life of any particular region or epoch. Cf. FAUNA 1.

1778 G. WHITE *Let.* in *Selborne* (1877) I. 217 Chalks, clays, sands..woodlands, and champaign fields, cannot but furnish an ample Flora. **1830** LYELL *Princ. Geol.* I. 92 The flora of a country is peculiarly influenced by temperature. **1859** DARWIN *Orig. Spec.* xii. (1873) 329 The floras of distant continents would not by such means become mingled.

b. The plants or plant life of any particular type of environment.

1874 D. BRANDIS (*title*) The forest flora of North-West and Central India. **1880** A. R. WALLACE *Island Life* II. xxiv. 507 The discussion of a series of typical Insular Faunas and Floras with a view to explain the interesting phenomena they present. **1908** *Jrnl. Biol. Chem.* V. 285 The gas ratio is not an especially important characteristic in mixed fecal flora. *Ibid.* 296 The influence of these organisms upon the intestinal flora of mice. **1909** GROOM & BALFOUR tr. *Warming's Oecol. Plants* IX. lxvii. 257 In depressions lying within the subglacial tract where snow remains for a long time, one finds characteristic, greasy mud, which sustains a vegetation of its own—Öttli's snow-patch flora. **1939** A. HUXLEY *After Many a Summer* I. v. 65 He began to talk.. about fatty alcohols and the intestinal flora of carp. **1971** *Nature* 8 Jan. 120/1 The resident flora of the external auditory canal.

floral ('flɔərəl), *a.* [ad. L. *flōrāl-is* of or pertaining to *Flōra*: see FLORA and -AL¹. In sense 3 it may be regarded as a new formation on L. *flōr-*, *flōs* flower. Cf. F. *floral* in all the senses.]

1. *Hist.* Pertaining to or in honour of the goddess Flora. ***floral shows*** = L. *Floralia.*

1647 STAPYLTON *Juvenal* 270 The Florall showes were celebrated in the end of Aprill, in honour of the Goddesse of Flowers and gardens. **1718** PRIOR *Henry & Emma* 769 Let One great Day, To..Floral Play Be set aside. **1727–41** CHAMBERS *Cycl.*, *Florales Ludi*, Floral Games.

2. Pertaining to a flora or floras. ***floral zone***: one of the tracts into which the earth's surface may be divided with regard to the character of the vegetable life.

1870 YEATS *Nat. Hist. Comm.* 100 The floral zones are less irregular than the faunal.

3. Of or pertaining to a flower or flowers. ***floral clock*** (see quot. 1962). ***floral diagram***: a diagram exhibiting the relative position of the parts in the cross-section of a flower. ***floral envelope*** (see ENVELOPE *sb.* 3). ***floral leaf*** (see quot. 1753). ***floral tribute***: a gift of flowers at a funeral; a wreath.

1753 CHAMBERS *Cycl. Supp.* s.v. *Leaf*, *Floral Leaf* expresses one found near the flower, and which never appears but with the flower. **1793** MARTYN *Lang. Bot.*, *Floral bud*, containing the flowers. **1829** LOUDON *Encycl. Plants*, Gloss. 1099 *Floral envelopes*. **1845** *Florist's Jrnl.* 230 Floral Intelligence. **1861** BENTLEY *Bot.* (1870) 133 Floral leaves or bracts. **1876** HOOKER *Bot. Primer* 62 The outermost of the floral whorls, the calyx. **1879** *Cassell's Techn. Educ.* IV. 95/2 Another floral expedition. **1882** VINES *Sachs' Bot.* 601 The Floral Diagram is constructed differently according to the purpose it is intended to serve. **1887** *Nuneaton Chron. In Memoriam C. N. Newdegate* 13 Apr., Floral Tributes. Prior to the funeral, a large number of..wreaths were received. **1925** *Ward Lock's Pict. Guide Edin.* (ed. 8) 62 Below it, in summer, is a beautiful floral clock of rare design. **1962** E. BRUTON *Dict. Clocks* 74 *Floral clock*, large public clock set out in bedding plants on the ground. Some strike; a few are cuckoo clocks. **1963** *Listener* 14 Feb. 302/2 The road to the floral clock lay wide open. **1963** C. E. VULLIAMY (*title*) Floral tribute. *Ibid.* i. 17 Those pompous laurels and lilies, the floral tribute of a person or persons unknown. **1971** *Times* 31 July 2/2 Mrs. Meena Jayant Madhavani with her children..gratefully thank.. those who arranged floral tributes following the passing away of our Mr. Jayant in New Delhi.

Hence **'florally** *adv.*, in quot., like a flower.

1820 *Examiner* No. 631. 317/1 Profound in its depth of chiaroscuro, and florally blooming in its colour.

floral ('flɔərəl), *sb.* [f. the adj.] †**1.** A dancer at the Floralia, a Roman festival in honour of the goddess Flora. *Obs.*

a **1658** LOVELACE *Lucasta* (1659) 13 So Cato sometimes the nak'd Florals saw.

2. A fabric with a floral design.

1897 *Sears, Roebuck Catal.* 222/1 Persians, plaids, checks, brocades, dots, floral. **1953** A. UPFIELD *Murder must Wait* x. 91 The other women..wear dizzy florals. **1960** *Guardian* 8 Feb. 6/7 The initial designs..are all conventional florals.

floralize ('flɔərəlaɪz), *v.* [f. FLORAL + -IZE.] *trans.* To make floral; to adorn with flowers.

1890 *The Voice* (N.Y.) 10 Apr., How appropriate that all our cemeteries should be floralized and tree-shaded.

† **florameda.** *Obs. rare.* 'Probably a flowered or figured stuff' (Beck).

1640 *Charter* in Entick *London* II. 178 Stuffs.. Floramedas.

† **'floramour.** *Obs.* Forms: 6–7 flo(u)ramor(e, flor(e)amour, flower amo(u)r, ? florimer. [a. OF. **flor amour* (in Cotgr. *fleur d'amour*) lit. 'flower of love'. Cf. Ger. *floramor* (16th c.).

The suggestion that *amour* is a perversion of *amaranthus* seems not impossible, but is not supported by evidence.]

A name given to various cultivated species of *Amaranthus.*

1548 TURNER *Names of Herbes* (1881) 11 The other kynde [of Amarantus] is called here in Englande..flouramore. **1597** GERARDE *Herbal* II. xl. 255 In English flower Gentle, purple Veluet flower, Floramor. **1611** COTGR., *Fleur d'amour*, flower-gentle, flower-amour. **1665–76** RAY *Flora* 178 The great Floramour hath a thick and tall crested stalk, with many reddish large green leaves.

¶ Misused for: Love of flowers.

1873 L. WALLACE *Fair God* I. iv. 18 Ministering to the voluptuous floramour of the locality.

Floran ('flɔərən). *Min.* Also **Floran Tin.** (See quot. 1778.)

1778 PRYCE *Min. Cornub.* 321 *Floran* is an exceeding small grained Tin, scarce perceivable in the stone though perhaps very rich. Also any Tin which is stamped exceeding fine, and undersize, is called Floran Tin—quasi Flower Tin. **1881** RAYMOND *Mining Gloss.*, *Florantin*, tin ore scarely visible in the stone, or stamped very small.

florascope: see FLORISCOPE.

florche, obs. form of FLOURISH.

flore, obs. form of FLOOR.

floreal ('flɔəriːəl), *a.* [f. L. *flōre-us*, f. *flōr-*, *flōs* flower + -AL[1].] †**a.** = FLORAL 1 (*obs.*). **b.** = FLORAL 2.

1602 SEGAR *Hon. Mil. & Civ.* IV. iii. 213 In the Playes Floreall, and in the Pastoral Comedies. **1852** *Fraser's Mag.* XLV. 501 Ancient and universal has been the floreal homage paid to the floreal queen.

‖**Floreal** ('flɔəriːəl), *sb.* [Fr. *Floréal*, f. as prec.] The name adopted for the eighth month of the year in the calendar of the French Republic introduced in 1793; it extended from April 20 to May 19.

1802 C. WILMOT *Let.* 25 Apr. (1920) 56 Sunday 25th April, 1802, 5me Florial. **1827** SCOTT *Napoleon* iv. Wks. 1870 X. 62, 17th Floreal, (8th of May). **1838** NICOLAS *Chron. Hist.* 182 Floreal (Flowery Month).

floreat ('flɒriːæt). [L. *floreat* may he (it) flourish, 3rd sing. pres. subj. of *flōrēre* to flower, flourish.] Used in conjunction with a name to indicate the hope that the named person, institution, etc., may prosper; *spec.* in ***Floreat Etona***, the motto of Eton College.

1888 C. A. WILKINSON *Reminisc. Eton* xxxiv. 340 Join with one heart and voice in the old shout, 'Floreat Etona'. **1898** LADY BUTLER in W. Meynell *Life & Work Lady Butler* (*caption*, facing p. 1) Floreat Etona! **1899** L. CUST *Hist. Eton Coll.* xii. 294 When Robert Elwes rode to certain death against the Boer bullets at Laing's neck..his last words were 'Floreat Etona'. **1965** J. P. CARSTAIRS *Concrete Kimono* ii. 17 All decent fellow *Floreat Etona*, and all that jazz! **1967** 'J. ASHFORD' *Forget what you Saw* xiii. 109 My years at school weren't wasted. *Floreat Etona!* **1969** *Listener* 26 June 899/3 *Floreat* Barry Goldwater.

floreated, *ppl. a.*: see FLORIATED *ppl. a.*

floredelise, obs. form of FLEUR-DE-LIS.

floree: see FLOREY.

Florence[1] ('flɒrəns). [The name of the chief city of Tuscany (F. *Florence*, L. *Flōrentia*, early It. *Fiorenze*, now *Firenze*); used as the name of various things produced or originating there.]

† **1.** A gold florin. [In OF. *florence.*] *Obs.*

a **1400** *Octouian* 1910 Four outlawes..chepede me that chyld to sale For syxty florencys. ? *a* **1475** *Sqr. lowe Degre* 243 And offre there florences thre, In tokenyng of the trynyté. **1563** FOXE *A. & M.* (1570) 976/1 What money goeth out of Germany yearely to the Pope, mountyng to the summe of 3,000,000 Florences. **1598** STOW *Surv.* vii. (1603) 52 Edward III..commaunded Florences of gold to be made and coyned.

2. The name given to certain woven fabrics: †**a.** of wool. *Obs.* exc. *Hist.*

1483 *Act 1 Rich. III*, c. 8. §18 The making of any Clothes called Florences with Cremyll listes. **1583** *Rates Customho.* C j b, Florence wullen cloth the yarde. **1658** PHILLIPS, *Florences*, a kind of cloth brought over from Florence. **1721–1800** in BAILEY. **1846** in FAIRHOLT *Costume* Gloss.

b. of silk (see quot.). [So in Fr.]

1882 CAULFEILD & SAWARD *Dict. Needlework*, *Florence*. This dress stuff is also known as Florentine..a description of Corded Barége or Grenadine..There is also a thin description of Taffeta..which had its origin at Florence, and thence derived its name.

† **3.** A kind of wine brought from Florence. *Obs.*

1707 *Lond. Gaz.* No. 4343/7 A Parcel of extraordinary good Red Florence, at 6*s.* a Gallon. **1757** H. WALPOLE *Lett. to Mann* 20 Nov., The chest of Florence..proves to be Lord Hertford's drams.

4. *Comb.* **Florence-flask**, a flask of the kind used to contain Florence-oil (see FLASK *sb.*[2] 3); **Florence iris**, ? = *Florentine iris*; **Florence-leaf**, a fine yellow leaf-alloy; **Florence-oil**, a superior kind of olive oil.

1664 EVELYN *Kal. Hort.* (1729) 202 *Florence Iris.* **1762** FRANKLIN *Wks.* (1806) I. 345 Your experiment of the *Florence flask*, and boiling water is very curious. **1858** SIMMONDS *Dict. Trade*, *Florence-leaf*. *Ibid.*, *Florence-oil*, olive oil sold in flasks.

† **'Florence**[2]. *slang. Obs.* [? from the female Christian name.] (See quot.)

a **1700** B. E. *Dict. Cant. Crew*, *Florence*, a Wench that is touz'd and ruffled. **1785** in GROSE *Dict. Vulg. Tongue.*

florencite ('flɒrənsaɪt). *Min.* [f. the name of W. *Florence*, who made a preliminary examination of the mineral: see -ITE[1].] A basic phosphate of cerium (and sometimes other rare earths) and aluminium.

1899 *Nature* 30 Nov. 119/1 Dr. E. Hussak and Mr. G. T. Prior gave an account of a new Brazilian mineral, Florencite, a hydrated phosphate of aluminium and cerium earths. **1962** *Mineral. Mag.* XXXIII. 285 Florencite occurs at Kangankunde as pink rhombohedra about 0·01 cm long.

† **'florent**, *a. Obs.* [ad. L. *flōrent-em*, pr. pple. of *flōrēre* to FLOURISH.] **a.** Flourishing. **b.** Blooming, flowery.

1542 UDALL *Erasm. Apoph.* 68 b Sinopa..was a florent citee, and of greate power. **1719** D'URFEY *Pills* (1872) I. 340 Whose florent Spring now bears delightful bloom. **1721** —— *Two Queens of Brentford* II. in *New Opera's* 28 Scandal has our florent Glory spoil'd.

Florentine ('flɒrəntaɪn), *a.* and *sb.* Also (in sense B. 3) 7 florenden, 8 -ine. [ad. L. *Flōrentīn-us* of or pertaining to *Flōrentia* Florence.]

A. *adj.* Of or pertaining to Florence, the chief city of Tuscany.

1603 KNOLLES *Hist. Turks* (1638) 292 Francis the Florentine Cardinall. **1756–7** tr. *Keysler's Trav.* (1760) II. 305 Antonio del Pollajuolo, a Florentine painter, who died in 1498. **1877** NICOL in *Encycl. Brit.* VII. 166 The third [diamond] in weight is the Florentine or Grand Duke.

b. *esp.* in † **Florentine flower-de-luce** = *Florentine iris*; **Florentine fresco** (see quot.); **Florentine iris**, the white or pale-blue iris (*I. Florentina*); **Florentine lake** (see quot. 1854); **Florentine marble** (see quot.); **Florentine mosaic**, a kind of mosaic made by inlaying precious stones in marble or the like; **Florentine pie** = B. 3.

1597 GERARDE *Herbal* I. xxxv. 48 The white Flower-de-luce is like vnto the *Florentine Flower de-luce. **1854** FAIRHOLT *Dict. Terms Art*, **Florentine Fresco*, Like common fresco, the lime is used wet, but in this mode it can be moistened and kept damp, and fit for painting on. **1882** *Garden* 20 May 353/1 A large table bouquet..of tall white *Florentine Iris. **1822** IMISON *Sc. & Art* II. 411 *Florentine lake. **1854** FAIRHOLT *Dict. Terms Art*, *Florentine Lake*, a pigment prepared from cochineal. It is now obsolete. **1706** PHILLIPS (ed. Kersey) *Florentine or Landskip-Marble, a kind of Marble in which the Figures of Mountains, Rivers, Towers..and even whole Cities are naturally represented. **1854** FAIRHOLT *Dict. Terms Art*, **Florentine Mosaic.* **1823** GALT *Entail* III. 65 'A jigot o' mutton, a fine young poney cock, and a *florentine pye.'

B. *sb.*

1. A native or inhabitant of Florence. Also a Florentine ship.

1591 RALEIGH *Last Fight Rev.* (Arb.) 16 Their Nauy.. strengthened with Florentines and huge Hulkes of other countries. **1599** THYNNE *Animadv.* (1875) 45 The woorkemenne, beinge florentynes. **1601** SHAKS. *All's Well* I. ii. 1 The Florentines and Senoys are by th'eares. **1849** MACAULAY *Hist. Eng.* I. 353 London was, to the Londoner ..what Florence was to the Florentine of the fifteenth century.

2. A textile fabric of silk or †wool, used for wearing apparel. Cf. FLORENCE 2.

1545 *Rates Customho.* D iij b, Florentynes [*printed* -tyse] for a clothe. **1819** REES *Cycl.*, *Florentine*.. a species of satin or tweeled silk. **1882** CAULFEILD & SAWARD *Dict. Needlework*, *Florentine*..is a twilled silk, thicker than Florence, which latter is, however, sometimes called by the same name.

3. *Cookery.* A kind of pie or tart; *esp.* meat baked in a dish with a cover of paste.

1567–79 HAKE *Newes Powles Churchyarde* iv. (1872) D iij, With Custardes, Tarts, and Florentines, the bancquet to amende. *a* **1700** B. E. *Dict. Cant. Crew*, *Florentine*, a made Dish of Minced Meats, Currans, Spice, Eggs, &c., Bak'd. **1750** E. SMITH *Compleat Housewife* (ed. 14) 41 A Florendine of a kidney of Veal. **1870** RAMSAY *Remin.* v. (ed. 18) 126 A florentine (an excellent old Scottish dish composed of veal).

4. The Florentine dialect of Italian.

1855 MILMAN *Lat. Chr.* (1864) IX. XIV. v. 207 That exquisite all-admired Florentine..has secured its undying fame.

Hence **'Florentine** *v. trans.*, to cook or prepare in the manner of a florentine (B. 3).

1769 MRS. RAFFALD *Eng. Housekpr.* (1778) 137 To florendine Rabbits.

florentium (flə'rɛnʃɪəm). *Chem.* [a. It. *florentium* (also *florenzio*) (Rolla & Fernandes 1924: see *Gazz. chim. ital.* (1926) LVI. 862–4 and *Atti Accad. Lincei*: *Rend.* (*Sci. fisiche*, etc.) (1926) IV. 498–500), f. *Florentia*, ancient name of Florence, Italy + -IUM.] A disused name for the element PROMETHIUM.

1927 *Chem. Abstr.* XXI. 1209 The exact text of the original sealed note..shows that it contains..the proposal to name the new element *florentium* (*florenzio*), with the symbol Fr. **1939** *Nature* 9 Dec. 959/1 The existing data about No. 61, which is called illinium or florentium, are derived from X-ray spectral lines in the *L-* and *K-* series. **1962** COTTON & WILKINSON *Adv. Inorg. Chem.* xxxi. 871 As early as 1926, several groups of workers reported optical and X-ray evidence for the existence of element 61 in various lanthanide concentrates, and the names Illinium, Il, and Florentium, Fl, were proposed by workers at the Universities of Illinois and Florence.

† **'Florentizing**, *pa. pple.* or *ppl. a. Obs.* [f. L. *Flōrentia* Florence + -IZE.] ? *trans.* Making like Florence; or *intr.* Imitating Florence.

1591 SYLVESTER *Du Bartas* I. ii. 943 Strife-full Ambition, Florentizing States: Bribes..swaying Magistrates.

‖**flores**[1] ('flɔəriːz). *Obs.* [L. *flōres*, pl. of *flōs.*]

1. *Old Chem.* (See quot. 1706.)

1663 BOYLE *Usefuln. Nat. Philos.* I. II. 213 The same *Aurum fulminans* being calcin'd with..Flowers of Brimstone, till the *Flores* be burnt away. **1706** PHILLIPS (ed. Kersey), *Flores*..in Chymistry, the more subtil parts of a substance separated from the grosser by Sublimation.

2. *nonce use.* 'Flowers' of speech.

a **1734** NORTH *Exam.* I. iii. §94 One may also admire how the Author comes by these Flores of the Canaglia.

‖**flores**[2] ('flores). [Sp.; pl. of *flor* FLOWER. Cf. F. *indigo flore.*] (See quots.)

1858 SIMMONDS *Dict. Trade*, *Flores*, a commercial classification of indigo, the best quality of dye from Nos. 7 to 9. **1885** BALFOUR *Cycl. India* (ed. 3) II. 333 South American [indigo]..Its qualities are distinguished as follows:—1st, Flores; 2nd, Sobres; and 3rd, Cortes.

florescence (flɒ'rɛsəns). [ad. mod.L. *flōrescentia*, f. L. *flōrescent-em*: see next and -ENCE.] The process of producing flowers or bursting into flower; the period or state of flowering. Also *concr.* Flowers collectively.

1793 MARTYN *Lang. Bot.*, *Florescentia*, Florescence or the Flowering season. The time when vegetables usually expand their flowers. **1819** H. BUSK *Banquet* I. 16 The grass ..Fragrant with sweet florescence. **1853** G. JOHNSTON *Nat. Hist. E. Bord.* I. 124 All the Hieracia are erect throughout the process of florescence and semination.

florescent (flɒ'rɛsənt), *a.* [ad. L. *flōrescent-em*, pr. pple. of *flōrescĕre* to begin to blossom, inceptive of *flōrēre*: see FLOURISH.] Bursting into flower, flowering. *lit.* and *fig.*

1821 *Blackw. Mag.* IX. 201 [They] will..remain admired and florescent, when the essays of thy most witty emissary are superseded and forgotten.

floresche, floresshe, obs. forms of FLOURISH.

floret[1] ('flɔərɪt). [ad. OF. *florete*, F. *fleurette*, dim. of *fleur* flower.]

1. *Bot.* One of the little flowers that go to make up a composite flower or the spikelet in grasses. ***florets of the disk, of the ray*** (see quot. 1866).

1671 GREW *Anat. Plants* I. v. §18 (1682) 38 The outer Part of every Suit, is its Floret..a Floret is the Epitome of a Flower. **1785** MARTYN *Rousseau's Bot.* vi. 69 The choke..is an assemblage of florets which are beginning to be formed. **1807** J. E. SMITH *Phys. Bot.* 456 Florets of the disk furnished with stamens only. **1866** *Treas. Bot.*, The *florets of the disk* are those which occupy the centre of the head of a composite; while *florets of the ray* occupy the circumference. **1877** F. E. HULME *Wild Fl.* p. viii, Dandelion.—All the florets ligulate.

2. A small flower, a floweret.

1791 E. DARWIN *Bot. Gard.*, *Loves of Plants* II, He.. Crops the young floret and the bladed herb. **1865** RUSKIN *Sesame* (ed. 2) 192 These feeble florets are lying with all their fresh leaves torn, and their stems broken.

fig. **1786** MISS A. SEWARD *Lett.* (1811) I. 150, I may one day present you with my poetic florets. **1822** *Blackw. Mag.* XI. 424 Variegated by the florets of a superficial but ornate adulation.

† **'floret**[2]. *Obs.* [ad. OFr. *florete* (Fr. *fleuret*) floss-silk. Cf. FERRET *sb.*[2]] = FERRET *sb.*[2] Only *attrib.* as **floret-silk** = *floss-silk.*

1583 *Rates Customho.* E iv, Silk called Floret silk the pound contayning xvi. vnces. **1611** COTGR. *Fleuret*, course silke; floret silke. **1640** *Scavage Table* in Entick *London* (1766) II. 169 Ferret or Floret silk.

Hence † **'floreting.**

1775 ROMANS *Hist. Florida* 144 This mixture is carded and called *floretting.*

floret, obs. var. of FLEURET[2], fencing-foil.

floreted ('flɔərɪtɪd), *ppl. a.* [f. FLORET[1] + -ED[2].] Having florets, covered or ornamented with little flowers.

1856 RUSKIN *Mod. Paint.* IV. v. xix. §31 In bulging balconies, and floreted gratings of huge windows.

† **'floretry.** *Obs. rare.* In 7 floritry, flowretry. [? f. FLORET, FLOWERET + -RY.] Flowery ornament.

1615 G. SANDYS *Trav.* III. 161 The walls and arches.. garnished with floritry. **1650** FULLER *Pisgah* I. 367 The Cedar was..curiously carved with imagery of flowers..Nor was all this flowretry..lost labour.

florettée, -etty, vars. of FLEURETTÉE.

† **'florey, floree.** *Obs.* Forms: 6 floray, florrey, flurry, 6–7 florie, -y, 6–8 florey, 8 floree. [a. F. *florée*, var. of *fleurée* in same sense, f. *fleur* flower.] A blue pigment consisting of the scum collected from the vat in dyeing with woad or indigo.

1527 *MS. Acc. R. Gibson, Master of Revels* (Public Record Office), Boght..iiij *li* of dry flory, the *li* iij *s*. **1573** *Art of Limming* 4 Smalte or florrey being tempered in a shell with gumme water maketh a blewe. **1640** PARKINSON *Theat. Bot.* v. lxiii. 602 Florey..is the scumme of the dyfat, while the cloth is upon the dying a blew colour with Indico or Woade. **1721–1800** BAILEY, *Floree, Florey*. **1858** SIMMONDS *Dict. Trade*, *Floree*, powder blue or indigo.

attrib. **1606** PEACHAM *Art Drawing* 58 Take Florey Blew and grind it with a little fine Roset.

† **'floriage.** *Obs.* [badly f. L. *flōr-*, *flōs* flower, after *foliage*. Cf. Fr. *fleurage*.]

1. Bloom, blossom.

1782 J. SCOTT *Odes* xx. 26 And where the trees unfold their bloom, And where the banks their floriage bear.

2. 'The leaves of flowers' (Webster *Suppl.* 1880).

floriate ('flɔːrɪət), *ppl. a.* In quot. floreate. [f. L. *flōr(i)-* *flōs* + -ATE². See -ATE².] = next.

1894 *Sotheby & Co.'s Catal.* 11 July 124 The first page.. illuminated in floreate scrolls.

floriated ('flɔːrɪeɪtɪd), *ppl. a.* Also **floreated**. [f. as prec. + -ED¹.] Decorated or adorned with floral ornaments.

1845 *Ecclesiologist* IV. 17 The floriated Cross. **1857** WOOD *Com. Obj. Seashore* 25 A floriated coronet.

fig. **1892** *Sat. Rev.* 13 Aug. 183/2 The late mission to Fez, and the highly 'floriated' accounts of it.

floriation (flɔːrɪ'eɪʃən). [f. as prec. + -ATION.]

a. A floral decoration. **b.** A musical flourish.

1868 CUSSANS *Her.* iv. 60 A Cross Moline with its floriations more expanded. **1895** *Cent. Mag.* Aug. 575/2 He continued the tune, with his accustomed floriations.

floribunda (flɔːrɪ'bʌndə, flɒ-). [mod.L., f. *floribundus* flowering freely, f. L. *flōr(i)-*, *flōs* flower + *-bundus* (as in *moribundus*), influenced in meaning by *abundus* copious.] A plant bearing flowers in dense clusters, *esp.* a type of rose formerly described as a hybrid polyantha. Freq. *attrib.*

1898 *Daily News* 6 Dec. 5/3 Various primulas are making a pleasant show, especially the vivid little yellow floribunda. **1945** *Rose Ann.* 15 Fresh names have been found for the new group; in this country Hybrid Polyanthas, and in America Floribunda. **1956** B. PARK *Collins Guide to Roses* ix. 123 In recent years other species have been bred into this class of rose so that the term hybrid polyantha has been dropped, and floribunda has taken its place. **1959** *Times* 28 Mar., It is usually sufficient to cut these floribunda roses. **1969** E. B. LE GRICE *Rose Growing* vii. 91 Climbing sports of a perpetual flowering floribunda are not themselves necessarily perpetual. **1970** *Times* 28 Sept. 8/6 A hybrid tea or floribunda rose should have at least two shoots.

floricide ('flɔːrɪsaɪd). *nonce-wd.* [f. L. *flōr(i)-*, *flōs* flower + -CIDE 1.] One who destroys flowers.

1841 HOR. SMITH *Moneyed Man* II. viii. 263 I cannot like a floricide.

floricomous (flɒ'rɪkəməs), *a. rare.* [ad. late L. *flōricom-us* crowned with flowers, f. *flōr(i)-*, *flōs* flower + *coma* hair (see COMA²) + -OUS.]

† **1.** (See quot.) *Obs.*⁻⁰

1727 BAILEY vol. II, *Floricomous*, having the Top full of or adorn'd with Flowers.

2. *Zool.* The distinctive epithet of certain sponges, the rays of which end in a bunch of curved branches.

floricultural (flɒ-, flɔːrɪ'kʌltjʊərəl), *a.* [f. next + -AL¹.] Pertaining to floriculture.

1822 LOUDON *Encycl. Gard.* §1626 Floricultural Catalogue. **1845** *Florist's Jrnl.* 250 Royal South London Floricultural Society.

floriculture ('flɒ-, 'flɔːrɪkʌltjʊə(r)). [f. L. *flōr(i)-*, *flōs* flower + CULTURE: after *horticulture*.] The cultivation of flowers or flowering plants.

1822 LOUDON *Encycl. Gard.* §1559 Floriculture is obviously of limited interest..compared to horticulture. **1876** J. GRANT *One of the '600'* vi. 49 Displaying..some ignorance alike of botany and floriculture.

floriculturist (flɒrɪ'kʌltjʊərɪst). [f. prec. + -IST.] One who devotes himself to or is skilled in floriculture.

1869 *Athenæum* 6 Nov. 587 If you are a mere floriculturist ..the subject is exhausted.

florid ('flɒrɪd), *a.* [ad. (directly or through Fr. *floride*, Cotgr. in sense 6) L. *flōrid-us* (related to *flōrēre* to bloom: see -ID), f. *flōr-*, *flōs* flower.]

† **1. a.** Blooming with flowers; abounding in or covered with flowers; flowery. *Obs.*

1656 BLOUNT *Glossogr.*, *Florid*, garnished with flowers. **1667** MILTON *P.L.* VII. 90 The ambient Aire wide interfus'd Imbracing round this florid Earth.

† **b.** Consisting of flowers, floral.

1665 BOYLE *Occas. Refl.* III. iv. (1675) 151 Those, who are wont to make Fires..have generally displac'd the florid, and the verdent Ornaments of their Chimneys. **1678** VAUGHAN *Thalia Rediv.*, *Daphnis* 70 Bring here the florid glories of the Spring. *a* **1682** SIR T. BROWNE *Tracts* (1684) 91 Florid and purely ornamental Garlands..are of more free election.

2. *fig.* Profusely adorned as with flowers; elaborately or luxuriantly ornate. Often in somewhat disparaging sense: Excessively ornate. **a.** Of composition, speech, etc.: Abounding in ornaments or flowers of rhetoric; full of fine words and phrases; flowery.

1656 COWLEY *Pindar. Odes* Notes *Wks.* (1710) I. 238 Apollo is..the God of Poetry, and all kind of Florid Learning. **1658–9** *Burton's Diary* (1828) IV. 131 He made a very florid speech. **1712** ADDISON *Spect.* No. 321 ¶3 The Expressions are more florid and elaborate. **1782** V. KNOX *Ess.* (1819) II. lxi. 17 Several of the poems..are florid to excess. **1814** SCOTT *Wav.* xiv, He possessed that flow of natural, and somewhat florid eloquence, which, [etc.] **1878** MORLEY *Crit. Misc.*, *Vauvenargues* 6 The florid and declamatory style of youth.

b. Of a person or his attributes: Addicted to the use of flowery language or rhetorical ornament.

1671 GUMBLE *Life of Monck* Ep. Ded., This Subject required a..more florid Pen than mine. **1691** WOOD *Ath. Oxon.* I. 164 He took holy orders..and became a florid Preacher. **1735** POPE *Prol. Sat.* 317 In florid impotence he speaks. **1759** ROBERTSON *Hist. Scot.* (1817) 211 A copious and florid writer.

c. Of attire, manners, methods of procedure, etc.: Highly ornate; showy, ostentatious.

1816 J. SCOTT *Vis. Paris* (ed. 5) 172 Whole years of..florid and unnatural patronage. **1855** THACKERAY *Newcomes* I. 231 A florid apparel becomes some men, as simple raiment suits others. **1876** C. M. DAVIES *Unorth. Lond.* 89 The ritual is altogether of a more florid character.

3. *spec.* in technical use.

a. *Music.* (See quots. 1879, 1888.)

1708 [see FIGURATE *a.* 4.]. **1740** GRASSINEAU *Mus. Dict.* 77 Florid Descant and Counterpoint. **1774** BURNEY *Hist. Mus.* (1789) I. vi. 80 Our florid-song..is not always sufficiently subservient to poetry. **1875** OUSELEY *Mus. Form* ix. 49 Vary the accompaniments by introducing more florid figures. **1879** GROVE *Dict. Mus.*, *Florid*. Music in rapid figures, divisions, or passages, the stem of the simple melody bursting forth, as it were, into leaves and flowers. **1888** STAINER & BARRETT *Dict. Mus. Terms*, *Florid counterpoint*, a counterpoint not confined to any special species, but in which notes of various lengths are used.

b. *Arch.* Enriched with decorative details.

a **1704** EVELYN *Architects & Archit.*, *Misc. Writings* (1825) 422 How oddly would..the spruce and florid Corinthian [become] a Tuscan entablature. **1815** J. SMITH *Panorama Sc. & Art* I. 151 The next [style] is often called florid, as if it were richer in ornament. **1838** MURRAY *Hand-bk. N. Germ.* 111 The exterior, in the most elegant florid Gothic. **1886** WILLIS & CLARK *Cambridge* II. 526 A florid style of Jacobean architecture.

† **4.** Of blooming appearance; strikingly beautiful or attractive; brilliant. Of colour: Bright, resplendent. *Obs.*

1642 H. MORE *Song of Soul* II. ii. I. v, Slight proofs cannot well fit In so great cause, no phansies florid wile. **1664** BULTEEL *Birinthea* 133 The bewitching appearance of a florid beauty. **1677** PLOT *Oxfordsh.* 58 It gave the skin so florid a whiteness, that, [etc.] **1725** BUTLER *Serm.* vi. 113 Florid and gaudy Prospects and Expectations. **1770** H. WALPOLE *Vertue's Anecd. Paint.* (1771) IV. 140 The weeping-willow and every florid shrub..are new tints in the composition of our gardens.

5. a. Of the complexion (or the colour of a part of the body): Rosy or ruddy, flushed with red.

1650 JER. TAYLOR *Holy Living* ii. §4. 101 When it [our beauty] is most florid and gay, three fits of an ague can change it into yellowness. **1665** *Phil. Trans.* I. 118 Of a very florid clear Complexion. **1707** FLOYER *Physic. Pulse-Watch* 60 High florid Colour in the Cheeks. **1781** GIBBON *Decline & Fall* III. xlviii. 45 His complexion was fair and florid. **1800** *Med. Jrnl.* IV. 155 The gums..became florid on the third day. **1865** TROLLOPE *Belton Estate* iii. 26 A decidedly handsome man with a florid face.

† **b.** Of the blood: Bright red (i.e. arterial).

1650 tr. *Bacon's Life & Death* 64 The lively and floride bloud of the small Arteries. **1731** ARBUTHNOT *Aliments* 121 The Qualities of Blood in a healthy State are to be florid when let out of the Vessel. **1797** M. BAILLIE *Morb. Anat.* (1807) 40 A florid blood must have been always circulating between the lungs and the left side of the heart.

6. Flourishing, lively, vigorous; in the bloom of health. Now *rare.*

1656 *Artif. Handsom.* 76 Like snow in summer, falling on green and florid trees. **1669** W. SIMPSON *Hydrol. Chym.* 31 The circulation of the blood and humours become thereby more florid. **1713** STEELE *Guardian* No. 2. ¶1 I..attribute the florid old age I now enjoy, to my constant morning walks up Hedington-Hill. **1725** POPE *Odyss.* IV. 1096 With florid joy her heart dilating glows. **1748** HUME *Hum. Und.* i. 10 Bodies..endow'd with vigorous and florid Health. **1858** CARLYLE *Fredk. Gt.* II. VI. ix. 128 Wilhelmina, formerly almost too florid, is gone to a shadow.

Florida ('flɒrɪdə). The name of a State in the extreme south-east of the United States, used *attrib.* to designate things connected with it in origin or manufacture: as **Florida moss** = LONG-BEARD 2, *Spanish beard*; **Florida orange**, any of several varieties of orange grown in Florida; also *ellipt.*; **Florida water**, a perfume similar to eau-de-Cologne, largely used in the United States; **Florida wood**, a hard wood obtained from a species of dogwood, having close grain, and much used for inlaying-work by cabinet-makers (*Cent. Dict.*).

1840 *Picayune* (New Orleans) 28 July 4/1 Lavender and Florida waters; perfumed toilet and pearl powders. **1861** MRS. BEETON *Bk. Househ. Managem.* xxiii. 528 When the bird is roasted,..surround it with Florida oranges. **1883** *Fisheries Exhib. Catal.* (ed. 4) 160 Bahama and Florida sponges are about equal in texture and value. **1884** R. WHEATLEY in *Harper's Mag.* June 59/1 Merchandise such as Florida water. **1888** G. TRUMBULL *Names of Birds* 75 A large bunch of 'Florida moss'. **1892** S. HALE *Lett.* (1919) 270 Oranges are delicious... I think they must be Floridas. **1895** *Montgomery Ward Catal.* 259/2 Florida Water is either used as a perfume..or as a lotion. **1923** A. WARD *Encycl. Food* 360 The Florida orange is typically sweeter and less 'sprightly' than the California. *Ibid.*, The best Louisiana oranges are upheld by many as of equal rank with the Floridas. **1924** *Contemp. Rev.* Jan. 95 Giant trees hung with florida moss. **1967** J. MCPHEE *Oranges* i. 9 Californians say that if you want to eat a Florida orange you have to get into a bathtub first. **1970** *Harper's Bazaar* Oct. 120/2 A bottle of Florida water, 24s 6d.

Floridan ('flɒrɪdən), *a.* and *sb.* [f. FLORIDA + -AN.] = FLORIDIAN *a.* and *sb.*

1763 W. ROBERTS *First Discov. Florida* 3 The size, firmness,..and longevity of the Floridan Indians. **1763** T. ROBINSON *Let.* 6 June *Ibid.* 101 The Floridans are a manly well-shaped race. **1856** W. PHILLIPS *Conquest of Kansas* 320 Shortly after the sack of Lawrence, Colonel Titus, the Floridan, offered three hundred dollars for his head. **1900** *Proc. U.S. Nat. Mus.* XXIII. 287 Passing through the Suwanee Strait (now the neck of the Floridan peninsula).

floridean (flɒ'rɪdɪən), *a.* Also **Floridean.** [f. mod.L. *Florideæ* (f. L. *flōridus* FLORID) + -AN.] Of or pertaining to the Florideæ (cf. FLORIDEOUS *a.*) (now often considered a subclass of the Rhodophyceæ or red algæ); ***floridean starch***, a reserve polysaccharide found in many red algæ.

1902 *Encycl. Brit.* XXV. 272/1 The colourless granules of *Florideæ*..have been called floridean-starch. **1935** J. E. TILDEN *Algae* ii. 26 The empty shells of the Bryozoa contained large numbers of *Ph[ormidium] persinicum* of a Floridean (Rhodophycean) red color. **1956** *Nature* 25 Feb. 366/1 The purification of Floridean starch. **1970** G. O. ASPINALL *Polysaccharides* iv. 66 Floridean starch, which is found in granular form in various red seaweeds, notably *Dilsea edulis*, contains no amylose, and the branched polysaccharide has an average unit chain length of 18–19.

florideous (flɒ'rɪdɪəs), *a.* *Bot.* [f. mod.L. *Florideæ* (f. L. *flōridus* FLORID) + -OUS.] Belonging to the *Florideæ*, an order of Algæ, or having the characters of that group.

1884 [See FAVELLA].

Floridian (flɒ'rɪdɪən), *sb.* and *a.* [f. FLORIDA + -IAN.] **A.** *sb.* **a.** A Floridan Indian. *Obs.* exc. *Hist.* **b.** A native or inhabitant of Florida.

B. *adj.* Of, pertaining to, or associated with Florida.

1589 HAKLUYT *Princ. Navig.* 541 The Floridians haue pieces of Unicornes hornes, which they were about their necks. **1777** in C. F. Jenkins *B. Gwinnett* (1926) 218 The inroads & depradations of the Floridians. **1819** *Western Rev.* I. 307 In the basin of the St. Lawrence or even in the Floridian waters, a total difference of [fish] inhabitants may be detected. **1827** J. L. WILLIAMS *View W. Florida* 26 The barking..of a congregation of half starved whelps, is music to the ear of a native Floridian. **1859** D. G. BRINTON (*title*) Notes on the Floridian peninsula, its literary history, Indian tribes and antiquities. **1945** W. L. MCATEE *John & Joe* 14 There are..no fewer than 10 species and sub-species of birds in the Floridian region. **1957** G. E. HUTCHINSON *Treat. Limnol.* I. i. 102 The whole of the Floridian Peninsula ..is now covered with a considerable thickness of Tertiary sediments.

floridity (flɒ'rɪdɪtɪ). [f. FLORID *a.* + -ITY.] = FLORIDNESS.

1713 STEELE *Guardian* No. 42 ¶3 The Merit of his Wit was founded upon..the tossing up of a Pair of Rosie Jowles ..His Reputation..rose in proportion to his Floridity. **1759** DARWIN in *Phil. Trans.* LI. 527 That these hæmorrhages were from the pulmonary artery..appears from..the floridity. **1820** *Blackw. Mag.* VII. 312 There is nothing of this flutter and floridity in the poems of Mr. Anster. **1831** HOWITT *Seasons* 152 We soon perceive the floridity of nature merging into a verdant monotony. **1883** *Century Mag.* XXVI. 917/1 They were..dressed with a certain floridity.

floridly ('flɒrɪdlɪ), *adv.* [f. FLORID *a.* + -LY².] In a florid manner; *esp.* with respect to speech.

1667 H. STUBBE in *Phil. Trans.* II. 500 Their Spleen is Triangular..and floridly red. **1667** H. MORE *Div. Dial.* II. xiv. (1713) 131 You have apologized more floridly and rhetorically for me than [etc.]. **1739** CIBBER *Apol.* (1756) I. 40 By endeavouring to be floridly grateful I talk'd nonsense. **1881** *Macm. Mag.* XLIII. 386/2 A floridly sensational religious novel.

floridness ('flɒrɪdnɪs). [f. FLORID *a.* + -NESS.] The quality or condition of being florid; exuberant freshness or liveliness, brightness of ruddy hue; lavishness of ornamentation.

1661 FELTHAM *Resolves* II. lxx. 337 Some of the Ancient Grecians..deriving it [dancing] from the Amœnity and Floridness of the warm and spirited bloud. **1664** EVELYN *Sylva* (1776) 631 Allured it is likely by the..Floridness of the leaves. **1769** WESLEY *Jrnl.* 2 July, Her language is.. simple, without..affected floridness. **1776** PRIESTLEY in *Phil. Trans.* LXVI. 231 The floridness of the arterial blood. **1830** *Fraser's Mag.* I. 8 Refinement..tames down the floridness..of the imagination. **1842** *Ibid.* XXVI. 639 A clustering floridness sometimes conceals a flaw in the pillars.

1889 Bruce *Plant. Negro* 153 The man of ripe years has all the mental floridness of a boy.

floriferous (flɒˈrɪfərəs), *a.* [f. L. *flōrifer* (f. *flōr(i)-, flōs* + *-fer* bearing) + -ous.] Producing flowers. Hence **floˈriferousness**.

1656–81 Blount *Glossogr., Floriferous.* **1678** T. Jordan *Triumphs Lond.* 11, A Verdant Hill, which the Floriferous hand of Nature had Crown'd with [etc.]. **1727** Bailey, vol. II, *Floriferousness.* **1796** C. Marshall *Garden.* xix. (1813) 345 The dwarf sort..is not so floriferous as the large. **1881** *Pract. Gardener* 35 China Roses..none are more floriferous than these. **1882** *Garden* 25 Feb. 134/3 Its extreme floriferousness compared with that of any of the others.

fig. **1879** G. Meredith *Egoist* I. Prel. 5 This laughter of reason refreshed is floriferous.

florification (ˌflɔərɪfɪˈkeɪʃən). [a. Fr. *florification*, f. L. *flōr(i)-, flōs* flower + -fication.] The action of producing flowers; the process of flowering.

1796 H. Hunter tr. *St. Pierre's Stud. Nat.* (1799) II. 92 Without..enquiring what might be the particular use of the florification. **1828** in Webster.

floriform (ˈflɔərɪfɔːm), *a.* [f. L. *flōr(i)-, flōs* flower + -form.] Having the form of a flower.

1805–17 R. Jameson *Char. Min.* (ed. 3) 38 *Floriform.* **1835** Kirby *Hab. & Inst. Anim.* II. xiii. 14 The aperture being round in some [Crinoïdeans] and floriform in others.

florigen (ˈflɒrɪdʒən, ˈflɔə-). *Bot.* [f. L. *flōr(i)-, flōs* flower + -gen.] An unidentified hormone supposed to induce flowering in plants.

1936 M. Kh. Chaĭlakhyan in *Compt. Rend. Acad. Sci. URSS* XIII. 83 We may term this blossom forming or blossom hormone..florigen, meaning 'blossom-former'. **1966** *Austral. Jrnl. Sci.* XXIX. 427/1 Proposed bioassays for florigens cannot be tested because of the lack of isolated florigens.

† **floˈrigerous**, *a. Obs.*$^{-0}$ [f. L. *flōriger* flower-bearing (f. *flōr(i)-, flōs* flower + *-ger* bearing) + -ous.] Bearing flowers.

1727 in Bailey, vol. II. **1775** in Ash.

florikan, floriken (ˈflɔərɪkən). Also 9 florican, -ikan, -ikin. [Of unknown origin; cf. the synonym Flanderkin 2.] 'A name applied in India to two species of small bustard, the Bengal Florican (*Sypheotides bengalensis*, Gmelin) and the Lesser Florican (*S. auritus*, Latham)' (Yule).

1780 Munro *Narrative* (1789) 199 The floriken, a most delicious bird of the buzzard kind. **1863** Speke *Discov. Nile* 58, I shot a new variety of florikan.

† **ˈflorilege.** *Obs.* [a. Fr. *florilège*, or ad. mod.L. *flōrilegium*: see next.] = next.

a. **1665** Rea *(title)* Flora..or a Complete Florilege, furnished with all Requisites belonging to a Florist.

b. **1651** Biggs *New Disp.* ¶290 Which..have not bin sucked and elaborated (like the Bee) so much out of, either the poison of somes dotages and uncertain principles, or others Florilege and Analect. **1727–41** in Chambers *Cycl.*

florilegium (flɔərɪˈliːdʒɪəm). [mod.L., f. *flōrileg-us* flower-culling, f. *flōr(i)-, flōs* flower + *legĕre* to gather; a literal rendering of Gr. ἀνθολόγιον anthology, after the analogy of *spīcilegium*.] **a.** *lit.* A collection or selection of flowers; used *transf.* in the title of a book (see quot.). **b.** A collection of the flowers of literature, an anthology.

a. **1711** *Lond. Gaz.* No. 4901/4 A compleat Florilegium of all the choice Flowers cultivated.

b. **1647** C. Harvey *Synagogue* xxvi. 9 The florilegia of celestiall storyes. **1716** M. Davies *Athen. Brit.* iii. *Crit. Hist.* 4 Antonius Schorus's Ciceronian Florilegiums. **1815** Southey *Let.* 15 Aug. (1856) II. 423 Some [of Kirke White's poems]..must hold their place in our popular Florilegia as long as the English language endures. **1870** Lowell *Study Wind.* 373 We have made but a small florilegium from Mr. Hazlitt's remarkable volumes.

† Also in anglicized form **floˈrilegy.**

1621 Bp. Mountagu *Diatribæ* 29 Glossaries: Florilegies.

florimania (flɔərɪˈmeɪnɪə). [f. L. *flōr(i)-, flōs* flower + Gr. μανία madness (see mania).] A mania or 'rage' for flowers in general, or for one particular sort or species of flower.

1822 Loudon *Encycl. Gard.* §54 This florimania seems to have declined and given way to a taste for exotics.

So **florimanist** [see -ist], one possessed by florimania. (Cf. F. *florimane*.)

1822 Loudon *Encycl. Gard.* §44 The number of florimanists..was much more considerable towards the middle of the last century.

florin (ˈflɒrɪn). Forms: 4–9 floren(e, 4–7 florein, -eyne, 5 (floran), floryne, (floring), 4, 8– florin. [a. Fr. *florin* = Pr., Sp. *florin*, It. *fiorino*, f. *fiore*:—L. *flōr-em, flōs* flower, the coin originally so called having the figure of a lily stamped upon it.

Some of the early forms can hardly be distinguished from those of the synonymous florence; there is no direct etymological connexion between the two words, though the 'flower' from which the Florentine coin took its name may have been used with allusion to the name of the city.]

1. The English name of a gold coin weighing about 54 grs., first issued at Florence in 1252.

1303 R. Brunne *Handl. Synne* 6201 Þere þey fonde þe cofre ful..Of florens, and of goldrynges. *a* **1400** *Octouian* 396 A palmer..bad for that chyld so bold Well many floreyne. *c* **1470** Henry *Wallace* ix. 252 This blythis me mekill mor, Than off floryng [*v.r.* floringis] ye gaiff me sexty scor. *a* **1533** Ld. Berners *Huon* lxviii. 234 They left not in yᵉ abbey the valew of a floren. **1655** Fuller *Ch. Hist.* ii. i. §38 Yet in after-Ages the Arch-Bishop of Canterburie's Pall was sold for five thousand Florenes. **1765** Blackstone *Comm.* I. i. viii. 313 Edward the black prince..imposed a tax of a florin upon every hearth, in his French dominions. **1832** tr. *Sismondi's Ital. Rep.* iv. 85 The republic of Florence, in the year 1252, coined its golden florin, of 24 carats fine, and of the weight of one drachm.

2. An English gold coin of the value of six shillings or six and eightpence, issued by Edward III. *Obs.* exc. *Hist.*

1480 Caxton *Chron. Eng.* ccxxv. 231 The floreyne that was callid the noble pris of vj shillynges viij pens of sterlinges. **1568** Grafton *Chron.* II. 256 The king made a newe coyne of Golde and named it the Floreyn. **1697** Evelyn *Numism.* i. 4 Our golden Florens in the reign of Edward III. **1866** Crump *Banking* x. 222 Coinage of England..Edward III. Gold. Florin, half-florin.

3. The English name of various coins current at various times on the continent. **a.** Gold coins.

1611 Cotgr., *Florin*, a Florin, or Franc: an ancient coine of gold in France, worth ijs. sterl.: not currant at this day. **1811** P. Kelly *Univ. Cambist* I. 177 The gold florins are chiefly current in the countries on the banks of the Rhine, passing generally for 2 Rixdollars current.

b. Silver coins.

1716 Lady M. W. Montagu *Let. to Mrs. Thistlethwayte* 26 Sept., The laws of Austria confine a woman's portion not to exceed two thousand florins. **1727–41** Chambers *Cycl.* s.v. *Florin*, As to silver Florins..Those of Genoa, &c. were worth about 8½d. sterling. **1831** Sir J. Sinclair *Corr.* II. 299 He..pays no more than eight or ten florins Polish money, which is four or five shillings in England. **1873** Ouida *Pascarèl* I. 13 We only want a few florins.

4. An English silver coin of the value of two shillings, first minted in 1849.

1849 *Lond. Jrnl.* 12 May 149 The new two shilling coin is to be called a florin.

floriˈpondio. Also 8 floripendio, floripondy. [a. Sp. *floripondio*, ad. mod.L. *floripondium*, app. f. L. *flōr(i)-, flōs* flower + *pondus* weight.]

The Spanish name of two Peruvian species of datura or thorn-apple, *D. arborea* and *D. sanguinea*.

1604 E. G[rimston] tr. *Acosta's Nat. & Mor. Hist. Indies* iv. xxvii. 283 Flowers..of excellent scent, as those which growe vpon a tree termed by them Floripondio or carry flower [*orig. has only*: 'which some call Floripondio']. **1745** P. Thomas *Jrnl. Anson's Voy.* 92 The Floripendio is a tree which bears no fruit, but only Flowers like Bells. **1768** J. Byron *Narr. Patagonia* 218 Their gardens are full of noble orange-trees and flori-pondies. **1815** W. Bowles *Missionary* viii. 178 Above, The floripondio its rich trellis wove. **1866** *Treas. Bot.*, Floripondio, *Datura sanguinea.*

Florisbad (ˈflɒrɪsbæd). The name of a village near Bloemfontein, South Africa, applied *attrib.* to (the remains of) a primitive hominid discovered there.

1935 J. F. Dreyer in *Proc. Sect. Sci. Kon. Akad. Wetensch. Amsterdam* XXXVIII. 124 Until..the classification of the Hominidae is revised and modernised, the status of the Florisbad Man will be most suitably expressed by giving it the value of a sub-genus and calling it: Homo (Africanthropus) helmei. **1940** *Jrnl. R. Anthrop. Inst.* 18 The Florisbad skull. **1948** A. L. Kroeber *Anthropol.* (ed. 2) iii. 100 The fossil form nearest to Rhodesian man..is the Florisbad skull. *Ibid.* 107 The fragmentary Florisbad skull ..is probably the nearest to being Palaeoanthropic in type among the more recent South African skeletons. **1959** J. D. Clark *Prehist. S. Afr.* ii. 27 In 1932 Professor Dreyer found the Florisbad skull during excavations in the mineral spring there. *Ibid.* iv. 87 At the time that Florisbad Man was living at the site the vegetation must have been very like that of the Karoo and Middleveld today.

florische, florise, floris(s)h(e, florisse, obs. forms of flourish.

floriscope (ˈflɔərɪskəʊp). Less correctly florascope. [f. L. *flōr(i)-, flōs* flower + Gr. -σκόπος looker.] An optical instrument for inspecting flowers.

1847 Craig, *Florascope* [and so in later Dicts.]. **1889** *Catholic Househ.* 30 Nov. 6 A pocket microscope and Floriscope.

florist (ˈflɒ-, ˈflɔərɪst). [f. L. *flōr-, flōs* flower + -ist. Cf. Fr. *fleuriste*, It. *fiorista*.] One who cultivates flowers; one skilled in knowledge of flowering plants; also, one who raises flowers for sale, or who deals in flowers.

1623 Sir H. Wotton in *Reliq. Wotton.* 407 It hath given me acquaintance with some excellent Florists (as they are stiled). **1678** Vaughan *Thalia Rediv., To his Books* 47 Choice Flow'rs, all set and drest By old, sage florists. **1718** *Freethinker* No. 11 ¶7 She will watch..as a Florist does a Bed of Flowers in the Spring. **1808** Pike *Sources Mississ.* iii. 210 This father was a great naturalist or rather florist: he had large collections of flowers, plants, &c. **1871** Earle *Philol. Eng. Tongue* §251 They differ as the flowers of the florist differ from those of nature.

floristic (flɔˈrɪstɪk), *a.* and *sb.* [f. flora: see -istic.] **A.** *adj.* Of or pertaining to the study of plants with reference to their distribution. **B.** *sb. pl.* That branch of phytogeography which deals with the distribution and abundance of plants. So **floˈristically** *adv.*

1898 Pound & Clements *Phytogeogr. Nebraska* p. iii, The authors..directed the work of the Survey with a view to.. a report,.. in which the floral covering of the state should be treated from the phytogeographical stand-point, and a series of monographs dealing with it from a floristic standpoint. *Ibid.* v. 215 Phytogeography..dealing not only with floristic and distribution, but..with morphology, histology, and ecology as well. **1909** Groom & Balfour tr. *Warming's Oecol. Plants* 1 Floristic plant-geography is concerned with—1. The compilation of a 'Flora', that is, a list of species growing within a larger or smaller area... 2. The division of the earth's surface into natural floristic tracts..according to their affinities... 3. The sub-division of the larger natural floristic tracts—floristic kingdoms—into smaller natural tracts. *Ibid.* 145 Grassy surfaces lining a railway differ floristically according to the aspect. **1918** L. Huxley *Life J. D. Hooker* II. 414 This great floristic work was fitly rounded off by his completion of the 'Ceylon Flora'. **1928** V. G. Childe *Most Anc. East* iii. 50 To find a floristic and faunistic environment comparable to that encountered by the most ancient Egyptians one must travel far upstream into the monsoon zone. **1964** V. J. Chapman *Coastal Veget.* i. 9 On the Continent, another system of vegetation analysis is employed. This is based essentially on floristics. **1969** *Nature* 29 Nov. 846/2 The floristic and faunistic richness of old grasslands. **1970** *Watsonia* VIII. 99 Hundreds of plants of this fairly distinct species being scattered over a large area of otherwise floristically rather poor rock.

floristry (ˈflɒrɪstrɪ). [f. florist + -ry.] *collect.* The objects on which a florist exercises his skill; garden-flowers as a whole.

1822 Loudon *Encycl. Gard.* Index, Florists or floristry gardeners 2079. **1953** *John o' London's* 20 Mar. 255/4 Violet Stevenson, well known for her broadcasts on floristry and flower arrangement. **1969** *Oxford Times* 17 Oct. 30/5 (Advt.), Courses in Floristry.

florisugent (flɔərɪˈsjuːdʒənt), *a.* [f. L. *flōr(i)-, flōs* flower + *sūgent-em*, pr. pple. of *sūgĕre* to suck.] Sucking (honey from) flowers: applied to certain birds and insects.

1889 in *Cent. Dict.*

floritry: see floretry.

floroun: see fleuron.

‖ **floruit** (ˈflɔərjʊɪt). [L., 3rd sing. perf. indic. of *flōrēre* to flourish. Cf. *habitat*.] Occasionally used for: The period during which a person 'flourished'.

1843 Liddell & Scott *Greek-Eng. Lex.* Pref., The date of each Author's 'floruit' is added in the margin. **1882** Saintsbury *Hist. Fr. Lit.* Pref. 9 The Index will..be found to contain the date of the birth and death, or, if these be not obtainable, the *floruit* of every deceased author of any importance. **1890** H. W. Watkins *Bampton Lect.* ii. 100 Professor de Groot puts his life at a.d. 65–135, and his *floruit* in the reign of Trajan.

florula (ˈflɔərjʊlə). [as if L. **flōrula*, dim. of *flōra* (see flora).] A small flora or collection of plants.

1847 Gray *Lett.* (1893) 347 That makes a very homogeneous florula. **1853** Kane *Grinnell Exp.* vi. (1856) 46 My limited florula, gathered as I made a few hasty walks.

florule (ˈflɔərjʊl). Anglicized form of florula.

1894–5 *16th Ann. Rep. U.S. Geol. Surv.* i. 535 In view of the fact that in both countries [*sc.* Portugal and America] a number of distinct horizons showing the progressive change in the flora throughout that period have yielded fossil plants in such a way that, if the Portuguese beds were as fully developed as are the American ones, each of these florules might also be compared, the subject becomes rather fascinating.

florulent (ˈflɔə-, ˈflɒr(j)ʊlənt), *a.* [ad. L. *flōrulent-us*, f. *flōr-, flōs* flower.] **a.** Abounding in flowers, flowery. **b.** In decorative art: Consisting of depicted flowers.

a. **1592** R. D. *Hypnerotomachia* 91 Turning upon the florulent ground. **1670–81** in Blount *Glossogr.* **1869** A. Steele in W. S. Crockett *Minstrelsy Merse* (1893) 160 Nor name those balmy, spicy dells Though florulent they be.

b. **1859** H. S. Cuming in *Jrnl. Archæol. Assoc.* XV. 227 Florulent scrolls in relief upon a mat ground.

Hence **ˈflorulentness.**

1727 in Bailey vol. II.

† **ˈflory**, *sb.*[1] *Obs. rare.* Also flore. [? f. OF. *flor*, *fleur* flower; cf. OF. *floré* ppl. adj.]

1530 *Wills & Inv. N.C.* (Surtees 1835) 109 A fflorie of golde & a signet of golde. *Ibid.*, A flore of gold enameld with blew & j stone in it.

flory (ˈflɔərɪ), *a.* and *sb.*[2] *Sc.*

A. *adj.* Showy, vain.

1782 Sir J. Sinclair *Observ. Sc. Dial.* 102 *Flory*.. showey, vain. **1821** Scott *Redgauntlet* Let. xii, The words 'flory conceited chap'.

B. *sb.* A conceited, frothy fellow.

1757 H. I. *Player's Scourge* 5 A pedantic foolish flory.

flory, *a. Her.*: see fleury.

flory-boat. (See quot.)

1867 Smyth *Sailor's Word-bk., Flory-boat*, a local term for boats employed in carrying passengers to and fro from steamers which cannot get alongside of a quay at low-water.

florys(c)h(e, flor(y)schyn, floryse, floryss(h)e, obs. forms of flourish.

† **floscampy.** [a. med.L. *flōs campī* lit. 'flower of the field'.] (See quot. 1398.)

1398 TREVISA *Barth. De P.R.* XVII. xciii. (1495) 647 [*Flos campi* is a lytyll floure with a small stalke and the floure is red as blood]. *c* 1430 *Two Cookery-bks.* 31 Sette on euery pompe a flos campy flour. *c* 1440 *York Myst.* xli. 366 Haill! floscampy, and flower vyrgynall.

† **'floscle.** *Obs.* [ad. L. *flōsculus*: see FLOSCULE.] A flower.

1599 A. M. tr. *Gabelhouer's Bk. Physicke* 41/2 Infunde theron, of the beste oyle Olive, as much as wille cover the floscles. *Ibid.* (*at end*), Expos... wordes.. derived of the Latines, 'floscles, reade flowers'. *a* 1770 C. SMART *Hop Garden* I. 176 The hop.. began to hang Its folded floscles from the golden vine.

floscular ('flɒskjʊlə(r)), *a.* [f. L. *flōscul-us* little flower (see FLOSCULE) + -AR.]

1. Composed of floscules or flowerets.

1793 MARTYN *Lang. Bot.*, *Flosculosus flos*, a floscular flower. 1845 LINDLEY *Sch. Bot.* vi. (1858) 82 Flowers mostly floscular.

2. ? Flossy, fluffy.

1822 *New Monthly Mag.* IV. 6 An ample violet-coloured *chlaina* of floscular cotton.

† **floscu'lation.** *Obs. rare*$^{-1}$. [f. L. *flōscul-us* (see FLOSCULE) + -ATION.] A flower (of speech); an embellishment or ornament.

1651 FULLER *Abel Rediv.*, *Huss* 19 That.. with rhetoricall flusculations [*sic*] I should endevour to adorne his memoriall.

floscule ('flɒskju:l). [a. F. *floscule*, ad. L. *flōscul-us*, dim. of *flōs* flower.]

† 1. Something in the shape of a little flower.

1669 W. SIMPSON *Hydrol. Chym.* 53 What remained was a bright styriate floscule.

† b. An embellishment or ornament (of speech). *Obs.* Cf. Ger. *floskel.*

1669 *Sir K. Digby's Closet Open.* To Rdr., There needs no Rhetoricating Floscules to set it off.

2. *Bot.* A small blossom of a composite flower; a floret.

1785 MARTYN *Rousseau's Bot.* vi. 67 Giving the names of Floscules or Florets to the little component flowers. 1805 *Edin. Rev.* VI. 85 Each single anther will constitute a male floscule. 1828 in WEBSTER.

† **'flosculent,** *a. Obs.* [incorrectly f. as prec. + -ULENT. (Or is it a misprint for *florulent*?)] Of speech or a speaker: Flowery.

1646 J. HALL *Horæ Vac.* 104 But for private friendship, had it not onely allowance, but also praise, the Holy Spirit would not so oft have beene flosculent, when Hee touched here. 1652 —— *Height Eloquence* p. vi, Endeavouring either an exact flosculent or delightfully formed speech.

† **'flosculet.** *Obs. rare*$^{-1}$. [f. as prec. + -ET[1].] A little flower; in quot. *fig.* for an infant.

1648 HERRICK *Hesper.* (1869) I. 133 Your owne faire print was set Once in a virgin flosculet, Sweet as your selfe.

flosculose (ˌflɒskjʊ'ləʊs), *a.* [f. L. *flōscul-us* FLOSCULE + -OSE.]. = FLOSCULOUS.

1866 *Treas. Bot.*, *Flosculi* (adj. Flosculose). In mod. Dicts.

flosculous ('flɒskjʊləs), *a.* [f. as prec. + -OUS.]

† 1. Of, pertaining to, or of the nature of flowers; having the savour of flowers. *Obs.*

1646 SIR T. BROWNE *Pseud. Ep.* II. vi. 97 A dry and flosculous coat [of the nutmeg], commonly called Mace. *a* 1682 —— *Tracts* (1684) 25 Putting the dried Flowers of the Vine into new Wine to give it a.. flosculous race or spirit.

2. Abounding with flowers, flowery. *rare.*

1676 in COLES. 1824 PRICHARD *Welsh Minstr.* 13 Thou flosculous and fruitful fair one!

3. *Bot.* a. Composed of floscules or florets.

1785 MARTYN *Rousseau's Bot.* vi. 68 The Flosculous flowers, or such as are composed of florets. 1845 LINDLEY *Sch. Bot.* vi. (1858) 84 Flowers either flosculous or radiant.

b. Of a floret: Tubular.

1830 LINDLEY *Nat. Syst. Bot.* 198 *Corymbiferæ*, the florets of which are flosculous in the middle. 1870 BENTLEY *Bot.* (1887) 594 *Corymbiferæ*, the plants of which have either all tubular (flosculous) and perfect florets; or [etc.].

† **flose,** *v. Obs. rare*$^{-1}$. [Cf. FLOSS[2].] ? To be shaggy.

13.. *E.E. Allit. P.* B. 1689 Faxe fyltered, & felt flosed hym vmbe.

‖ **flos-ferri** ('flɒs'fɛraɪ). *Min.* [L.; = 'flower of iron'.] A coralloid variety of aragonite, often found with iron ore.

1748 SIR J. HILL *Hist. Fossils* 344 This species is.. called .. Flos Ferri. 1878 LAWRENCE tr. *Cotta's Rocks Class.* 51 Flos-ferri is formed in great perfection in the Styrian iron-mines.

flosh (flɒʃ), *sb.*[1] *Obs.* exc. *dial.* Also 3–4 flosche. [See FLASH *sb.*[1]; cf. also FLUSH *sb.*[2]]

1. A pool; sometimes, a stagnant pool overgrown with reeds, etc.; a swamp.

a 1300 *E.E. Psalter* lxxxvii[i]. 5 [4], I am wened, in ilka land To þas þat ere in flosche falland. 1789 D. DAVIDSON *Th. Seasons* 12 When.. powheads spartle in the oosy flosh. 1875 *Lanc. Gloss.*, *Flosh*, water, or a watery place.

b. *transf.* A pool (of blood).

a 1400–50 *Alexander* 2049 Sike scoures were of blude ..þat foles ferd in þe flosches to þe fetelakis.

2. *attrib.* (Cf. FLUSH *sb.*[2] 2 c.)

1847 HALLIWELL, *Flosh-hole*, a hole which receives the waste water from a mill-pond. 1875 in *Sussex Gloss.*

flosh (flɒʃ), *sb.*[2] (See quot.)

1874 KNIGHT *Dict. Mech.* I. 889/2 *Flosh* (*Metallurgy*), a hopper-shaped box in which ore is placed for the action of the stamps.

† **floshed,** *ppl. a. Obs. rare*$^{-1}$. [app. f. F. (*soie*) *floche* (see FLOSS[2]) + -ED.] Made to resemble floss-silk.

1548 HALL *Chron.* (1809) 517 Men appareiled like wilde men.. their bodies.. covered with grene Sylke flosshed.

floss[1] (flɒs). *dial.* In Orkney and Shetland: A collective term for reeds, rushes, etc.

1623 in Barry *Orkney Isl.* (1805) App. 467 That no persone shall.. pull floss.. before the first of Lammas. 1793 *Statist. Acc. Scotl.* VII. 524 The tenants paid in kind.. floss or reeds. 1866 EDMONDSTON *Shetl. & Orkn. Gloss.*, *Floss*, the common rush.

floss[2] (flɒs). Also 9 *dial.* floose. [Of doubtful origin. Possibly an adoption of some form of OF. *flosche* down, pile of velvet; also as adj. in *soye flosche* (mod.F. *soie floche*) floss-silk (= It. *seta floscia*). Possibly, however, there may have been a native Eng. or Scandinavian word *floss* cognate with FLEECE. Cf. mod.Icel. *flos* nap of cloth, Da. *flos* plush (recorded from 17th c.), and Cleveland dial. *floss-seave* the cotton-grass; also FLOSE *v.*]

1. The rough silk which envelopes the cocoon of the silk worm; also see quot. 1835.

1759 PULLEIN in *Phil. Trans.* LI. 56 The common silk-pod, with all its floss, weighs usually but three grains. 1835 URE *Philos. Manuf.* 3 Silk which occurs in entangled tufts, called floss, is spun like cotton.

b. *transf.* (see quot.).

1846 SMART, *Floss*, a downy substance in some plants. 1847 LONGF. *Evang.* I. iii, Hair, like the silken floss of the maize, hung over his shoulder.

2. Silk in fine filaments; = FLOSS-SILK.

1871 B. TAYLOR *Faust* (1875) II. I. iii. 22 Silken threads and silken flosses Here must play their parts. 1889 A. N. CARTER in *Century Mag.* Nov. 37/2 Old velvet embroidered with gold and floss.

3. A flossy surface; also, a quantity of flossy particles; fluff.

1784 HENLEY in *Beckford's Vathek* (1868) 160 *note*, The wrong side of tapestry will represent more truly the figures on the right, notwithstanding the floss that blurs them, than [etc.]. 1850 BAMFORD *Tim Bobbin's Wks.* Gloss., *Floose*, the flyings of wool or cotton. 1871 NAPHEYS *Prev. & Cure Dis.* I. iv. 121 When woven thick and with a floss, it is warm. 1891 *Labour Commission* Gloss., *Floss*, the small particles of fibre in the dust given off in the processes of the manufacture of textiles.

4. *attrib.* and *Comb.*, as ***floss line, thread, wig, yarn.*** Also FLOSS-SILK.

1894 *Daily News* 7 May 5/1 Men fish with a *floss line, and one, two, six, or more natural flies on a hook. 1872 MACELRATH *Dict. Commerce* (Webster 1879) **Floss-thread*, a kind of soft flaxen yarn or thread, used for embroidery. 1864 J. BROWN *Horæ Subsec.*, *J. Leech* (1882) 28 The coach-man's red face and *floss wig.

floss[3] (flɒs). *Metallurgy.* [a. Ger. *flosz* in same sense: see FLOAT *sb.*]

1. a. (See quot.) b. (See quot.) c. = *floss-hole* (see below).

a. 1839 URE *Dict. Arts* 509 *Floss* of the puddling furnace is the fluid glass floating upon the iron produced by the vitrification of the oxides and earths which are present.
b. 1839 URE *Dict. Arts* 711–2 White cast iron.. is employed.. for the manufacture of steel, and is then called steel floss, or lamellar floss.
c. 1839 URE *Dict. Arts* 702 The floss, or outlet of the slag from the furnace.

2. *Comb.*: **floss-hole**, (*a*) 'a hole at the back of a puddling-furnace, beneath the chimney, at which the slags of the iron pass out of the furnace; (*b*) the tap-hole of a melting furnace' (Knight).

1839 URE *Dict. Arts* 708 The excess of slag is allowed to run off by the chio or floss hole. 1881 RAYMOND *Mining Gloss.*, *Floss-hole*, a tap-hole.

floss[4] (flɒs). *rare*$^{-1}$. [Of doubtful genuineness. Ger. *flosz* has this sense; perh. the title of *The Mill on the Floss* (where *Floss* is a proper name) led Carlyle to think that the word existed in the same form in Eng. Cf. FLOUSE.] A stream.

1865 CARLYLE *Fredk. Gt.* V. XIV. iv. 472 There is one dirty stream or floss (*Hünerfliess*, Hen-Floss) which wanders dismally through those recesses.

flossifi'cation, erroneously for FLORIFICATION.
1828 WEBSTER cites *Med. Repos.*

floss silk. Also flox-, flosh-silk. [f. FLOSS[2], after F. *soie floche.*] a. The rough silk broken off in the winding of the cocoons. b. This rough silk carded like cotton or wool and used chiefly in the manufacture of common silk fabrics. c. Untwisted filaments of silk used in embroidery and crewel-work.

1759 PULLEIN in *Phil. Trans.* LI. 55 It was covered with some floss-silk. 1820 SCOTT *Ivanhoe* xiii, The flox-silk with which the billet was surrounded. *a* 1846 LANDOR *Imag. Conv.* Wks. 1846 II. 53 The truckle bed of Valour and Freedom is not wadded with flosh-silk. 1863 OUIDA *Held in Bondage* (1870) 89 Will you be kind enough to hold this skein of floss silk for me? 1884 J. PAYNE *Tales fr. Arabic* I. 17 He found himself upon a couch, stuffed all with floss-silk.

attrib. 1847 ALB. SMITH *Chr. Tadpole* v. (1879) 50 A bright blue stock, worked with floss silk sunflowers.

flossy ('flɒsɪ), *a.* [f. FLOSS *sb.*[2] + -Y[1].] Resembling floss or floss-silk; floss-like. Also (*N. Amer. colloq.*) *fig.* Saucy, impertinent, 'fresh'; fancy, showy.

1839 BAILEY *Festus* xx. (1848) 266 Flossy, tendrilled locks. 1874 T. HARDY *Madding Crowd* I. xxviii. 306 A thick flossy carpet of moss. 1884 *Daily News* 10 Nov. 3/1 Chenille embroideries brightened by.. the flossiest of silks. 1889 *Road* (Denver, Colo.) 28 Dec. 4/3 Phil, we have got it in for you if you don't quit being so flossy. 1895 W. C. GORE in *Inlander* Dec. 113 *Flossy*, beautiful, stylish. 1900 ADE *More Fables* (1902) 136 He'd show you if you could get Flossy with a Lady, even though she Works. 1903 A. H. LEWIS *Boss* 122 He's as flossy a proposition as ever came down the pike. 1922 H. TITUS *Timber* i. 14 Do you list that with your references? Your luck with these flossy young petticoats? 1958 *Fisherman* (Vancouver) 15 Aug. 2/3 The flossy propaganda issued by the CMA.

Hence **flossied up** *ppl. a.*, dressed up.

1943 *Penguin New Writing* XVIII. 63 There was a tremendous crowd going, all flossied up for a day out. 1946 F. SARGESON *That Summer* 57, I.. was all flossied up. 1957 I. MURDOCH *Sandcastle* i. 10, I suppose I'll have to dress. She's sure to be all flossied up.

flot[1] (flɒt). Now only *Sc.* [repr. OE. **flot* (in *flotsmeru* floating grease), or a. ON. *flot* (= Sw. *flott*), f. weak grade of root of FLEET *v.* Cf. FLOTESSE.] 'The scum of a pot of broth when it is boiling' (Jamieson).

13.. *E.E. Allit. P.* B. 1011 As a furnes ful of flot þat vpon fyr boyles.

flot[2] (flɒt), *Mining.* [? var. of FLOAT *sb.* (sense 20 a).] (See quot. 1881.)

1747 HOOSON *Miner's Dict.* Ij, Some of these Flots carry good Ore where never Vein was yet Discovered. 1881 DAKYNS in *Nature* No. 620. 473 The word 'flot' is a miner's term for ore lying between the beds, or at certain definite horizons in the strata. In text-books flots are generally called 'flats' or 'flattings'.

flot[3] (flɒt, ‖flo). [Fr., lit. 'wave'.] A trimming of lace or loops of ribbon, arranged in over-lapping rows.

1872 *Young Englishwoman* Nov. 595/2 A *flot* of mauve ribbon falling over the chignon. 1882 CAULFEILD & SAWARD *Dict. Needlework*, *Flôts*, a French term, used to signify successive loops of ribbon or lace arranged to lie over-lapping one another in rows, so as to resemble the flow of small waves.. What is called a Flôt-bow is made after the same style. 1902 *Daily Chron.* 12 Apr. 8/3 The long flots of frills.

flot, obs. form of FLOAT.

flota ('fləʊtə). [a. Sp. *flota* fleet.]

1. The name given to the Spanish fleet which used to cross the Atlantic and bring back to Spain the products of America and the West Indies. Also *gen.*

1690 CHILD *Disc. Trade* Pref. B. iv b, The arrival of the Spanish Flota. *a* 1763 SHENSTONE *Elegies* xiv, What envy'd flota bore so fair a freight? 1796 NELSON 28 Sept. in Nicolas *Disp.* II. 284, I believe I can destroy their Flota.

¶ 2. ? *erroneous use.* A floating barrier (see quot.).

1777 WATSON *Philip II*, II. XIX. 180 For the greater security of.. the work, a flota, one thousand two hundred feet long, was constructed of barks, bound together.. with .. beams pointed with iron, resembling a file of pikes.

flotage, flotation, flotative; see FLOAT-.

flotant ('fləʊtənt), *a. Her.* [ad. Fr. *flottant*, pres. pple. of *flotter* to float.] (See quot. 1828.)

1610 GUILLIM *Heraldry* III. xxvi. (1611) 183 He beareth azure an Harpey with her wings disclosed her Haire flotant. 1828–40 BERRY *Encycl. Her.* I, *Flotant*, a term used in blazon to express anything flying in the air, as a banner floatant, or displayed—it is likewise applicable to anything swimming. 1868 CUSSANS *Her.* vii. 105 Tied.. with ribbon, the ends flotant.

† **flotch.** *Obs. rare.* [Variant form of FLITCH.]

1623 FLETCHER & ROWLEY *Maid of Mill* III. i, He shall be hang'd in flotches: The dogs shall eat him in Lent.

† **flote,** *sb.*[1] *Obs.* Also 5–6 flot, 6 *Sc.* floit. [OE. *flota* wk. masc. = M.Du. *vlote*, ON. *flote*: see FLOAT *sb.* In sense 2 ad. Sp. *flota*: see FLOTA.]

1. A fleet or flotilla.

O.E. Chron. ann. 975 Næs se flota swa rang. *c* 1275 LAY. 2155 Humber king and his flote.. comen on Albanac his lond. 1375 BARBOUR *Bruce* III. 601 He had na ner socouris Then the kingis flote. *c* 1470 HENRY *Wallace* IX. 98 The lakest schip, that is his flot within. 1577 in Hakluyt *Voy.* (1599) I. 296 The good ship named the Primerose, shalbe Admirall of this flote.

2. = FLOTA 1.

1673 RAY *Journ. Low C.* 484 The Longha [in Sevil], where the Merchants meet about the affairs of the flote.

† **flote,** *sb.*[2] *Obs.* [a. OF. *flote* fem., company of persons, multitude = Sp. *flota*, Pg. *frota*:—pop. L. type **flotta*, prob. f. Teut. **flot-* weak grade

of the root of **fleutan* FLEET *v.* in the sense 'to flow'.

The Sp. and Pg. words also mean 'fleet of vessels', and in this meaning are prob. adoptions of the Teut. word appearing as ON. *flote*, OE. *flota* wk. masc., f. the same root in the sense 'to float'. The mod. sense of F. *flotte*, fleet, is believed to have been adopted from Sp. in the 16th c.; the older sense is still current in certain phrases, but there is popularly regarded as a transferred use. It. has *fiotta*, *frotta*, *flotta* in both senses, but their relation to the F. word is doubtful.]

A company, troop; also, a herd (of cattle), a shoal (of fish).

a **1300** *Cursor M.* 2444 (Cott.), O fee þai had a selly flot. *c* **1300** *Havelok* 738 Þere he made a litel cote To him and to hise flote. *a* **1375** *Joseph of Arim.* 28 Joseph ferde biforen and þe flote folewede. *a* **1400–50** *Alexander* 770 Aithire with a firs flote in þe fild metis. **1513** DOUGLAS *Æneis* XII. v. 191 Italians hurlis on him in a flote. **1603** HOLLAND *Plutarch's Mor.* 343 A great flote of dolphins. **1647** N. BACON *Hist. Disc. Govt. Eng.* I. v. 17 The Goths, Vandals.. and other flotes of people that about these times.. were weary of their own dwellings.

†**flote**, *v.*^{1} *Obs.* Also 7 float. [Of doubtful formation: either f. FLOT *sb.*^{1} or back formation from *floten*, FLOTTEN.] *trans.* To skim; = FLEET *v.*^{2} I.

1573 TUSSER *Husb.* xlix. (1878) 108 Gehezie his sicknes was whitish and drie, Such cheeses, good Cisley, ye floted too nie. **1669** WORLIDGE *Syst. Agric.* 270 Floating of a Cheese, is the separating the Whey from the Curd.

†**flote**, *v.*^{2} *Sc. Obs.* Also 5 floyt(e, flot. [Conjectured to be a variant of FLUTE *v.*] *trans.* ? To trim with 'fluting'. Hence '**floting** *vbl. sb.* (used *concr.* and *attrib.*).

1473 in *Ld. Treas. Acc. Scotl.* I. 16 To the sammyn ij. dowblatis ij½ elne of braid clath to flote thaim. **1474** *Ibid.* 23 To by stufe and floting for the Kingis doublat. **1491** *Ibid.* 188 Quhyt fustiane to floyt a dowblat of dwn sattin.

flote, flote-grass, obs. ff. FLOAT, FLOAT-GRASS.

floter, obs. form of FLUTTER.

†**flotesse.** *Obs.* Also 5 flotyce, -yse, 6 flotes, flattesse, flats. [Perh. the pl. of FLOT *sb.*^{1}, taken as sing. It may however represent an unrecorded F. derivative of *floter* to float.] Scum or grease floating on the surface of a liquid; *esp.* skimmed fat, dripping.

c **1440** *Promp. Parv.* 168/1 Flotyse or flotyce of a pott or other lyke, *spuma*. **1531** TINDALE *Exp. 1 John* v. 21 Doest thou make of God.. one that had lust to smell to burnt flotesse? **1536** *Lett. & Papers Hen. VIII*, X. 175, 4 stone of flattesse. **1548** RECORDE *Urin. Physick* v. 18 Be-syde these is there often tymes [in the urine] as it were a flotes or fattynes on the topp. **1585** *2nd Pt. good Huswifes Iewell* 12 Frie them with butter or flats.

†'**flother.** *Obs. rare*$^{-1}$. In 3 *pl.* floþre. [cf. OE. **flæðra* pl. flakes of snow (cited by Junius).] A flake (of snow).

c **1275** *XI Pains of Hell* 74 in *O.E. Misc.* (1872) 149 Mo saulen þolieþ þer sucche wowe þane be floþre in þe snowe.

flotilla (fləʊˈtɪlə). [a. Sp. *flotilla*, dim. of *flota* a fleet: see FLOTA.] A small fleet; a fleet of boats or small vessels.

1711 *Lond. Gaz.* No. 4890/1 The Flotilla.. was sail'd. **1739** *Let.* in *Descr. Windward Passage* (ed. 2) 3 They commonly dispatch a few Ships into Europe, who.. carry an Account of what is on Board the Galleons and Flota. The Ships are stiled the Flotilla. **1801** P. SOMERVILLE in A. Duncan *Nelson* (1806) 198 The enemy's flotilla in the bay of Boulogne. **1826** H. N. COLERIDGE *West Indies* 125 A flotilla of fishing or passage boats. **1858** CARLYLE *Fredk. Gt.* (1865) II. VI. iii. 155 Sailing.. in silken flotillas gayer than Cleopatra's, down the Elbe.

flotsam (ˈflɒtsəm). Forms: 7 floatsam, -son, flotsan, -sen, -zan, 7–8 flotzam, 7, 9 flotsom(e, 7–9 flotson, 9 flotsum, (dial.) floatsome, 8– flotsam. [ad. AF. *floteson* (= mod.F. *flottaison*):—late L. type **flottātiōnem*, f. **flottāre*, OF. *floter* to FLOAT.]

1. *Law.* Such part of the wreckage of a ship or its cargo as is found floating on the surface of the sea. Usually associated with JETSAM.

[*Liber Niger Admiralitatis* cxxxvi. (1871) I. 82 Pippe de vin flotants, balles de marchandises ou autre chose quelconque comme floteson.] **1607** COWELL *Interpr.*, Flotsen *alias* (Flotzam). *a* **1688** tr. *Blacke Bk. Admiralty* (1871) I. 83 Pipe of wine floating, bales of goods, or any other thing whatsoever, as ffloatson. **1708** J. CHAMBERLAYNE *St. Gt. Brit.* I. II. ix. (1743) 81 To the Lord High Admiral belongs .. a Share of all lawful prizes, Lagon, Flotson, and Jetson. **1814** SCOTT *Diary* 11 Aug. in *Lockhart*, The goods and chattles of the inhabitants are all said to savour of Flotsome and Jetsome. **1853** *Act 16–17 Vict.* c. 107 §76 All Goods derelict, jetsam, flotsam, and wreck brought or coming into the United Kingdom.

b. *transf.* and *fig.* Sometimes used jocularly for 'odds and ends'.

1861 *All Y. Round* 1 June 235 Turkey buzzards were searching for flotson and jetson in the shape of dead Irish deck hands. **1884** R. BUCHANAN in *Harper's Mag.* Sept. 603/1 A mania for buying all sorts of flotsam and jetsam.

2. *dial.* (See quot. 1804).

1804 DUNCUMB *Herefordsh.* I. 213 *Floatsome*, timber, etc. accidentally carried down a river by a flood. **1890** in *Gloucestersh. Gloss.* **1894** *Daily News* 23 Nov. 6/7 How far the water has gone down may be gathered from the flotsam caught in the willow boughs.

3. Newly ejected oyster-spawn.

1879 *Cassell's Techn. Educ.* IV. 154/1 Floatsome. **1882** *Standard* 18 Feb. 5/2 The spawn or 'flotsom' emitted from the bivalves.

†**flotte**, *ppl. a. Obs. rare.* [Cf. FLOTTEN and FLOTE *v.*^{1}] Skimmed.

1557 TUSSER *100 Points Husb.* lxxii, Their milk pannes so flotte, that their cheeses be lost.

flotte, obs. form of FLOAT *sb.*

†'**flotten**, *ppl. a. Obs.* Also floten. [pa. pple. of FLEET *v.*^{1} and ^{2}.]

1. Flooded with water.

1601 HOLLAND *Pliny* I. XVIII. xviii. 577 They were woont to cast their seed-corne upon the floten ground.

2. Skimmed. ***flotten milk***: skim milk.

1600 W. VAUGHAN *Direct. for Health* (1633) 72 Browne-bread crummed into.. flotten milke. **1608** ARMIN *Nest Ninn.* (1880) 48 Fed with the flottin milke of nicetie and wantonnesse. **1614** MARKHAM *Cheap Husb.* II. i. (1668) 71 Bring them [Calves] up upon the finger, with flotten milk. **1661** K. W. *Char. Coxcombs* (1860) 30 Flotten cheese. **1721** in BAILEY.

fig. **1632** QUARLES *Div. Fancies* II. xxviii. (1660) 60 We Fleet the Mornings for our own Design; Perchance the Flotten Afternoons are thine.

'**flotter**, *v. Sc.* [? freq. of FLOAT *v.* Cf. FLODDER.] *trans.* To overflow, wet. Hence **flottered, flottering**, *ppl. adjs.*

1513 DOUGLAS *Æneis* XI. i. 72 With flottyrit berd of teris all beweip. *Ibid.* XIII. iv. 14 Chekis wait of flotterand teris greite. **1827** TENNANT *Papistry Storm'd* 23 The flotter't table maist was steepit Wi' claret-dubs.

flotter, obs. f. FLUTTER.

flouck, floud(d(e, obs. ff. of FLUKE, FLOOD.

†**flought**, *v. Obs. rare*$^{-1}$. [perh. a dial. word, f. OE. **flohta* or ON. **flohte* (Icel. *flótti*) flight, f. root of FLEE *v.*] *intr.* To flee, take refuge.

1556 ABP. PARKER *Psalter* cxxxix. 7 From thee.. how can I fly: or whether shall I flought.

flought, var. form of FLOCHT.

flouh, obs. pa. t. FLAY.

flouke, obs. form of FLUKE.

floum, var. form of FLUME, river.

flounce (flaʊns), *sb.*^{1} Also 6 flownse, 7 flownce. [f. FLOUNCE *v.*^{1}]

1. A sudden fling or jerk of the body or a limb; a plunging or flopping movement.

1583 STANYHURST *Aeneis* II. (Arb.) 50 They [two serpents] doe frisk with flownse to the shoareward. **1802** M. MOORE *Lascelles* III. 36 The instrument was lodged in the shark's body, which, after several dreadful flounces, sunk. **1810** T. JEFFERSON *Writ.* (1830) IV. 144 A gripe of the paw, or flounce of the tail, may be our fortune. **1863** BARNES *Dorset Gloss.*, *Flounce*, a flying stroke.

b. A splash.

1622 MABBE tr. *Aleman's Guzman d'Alf.* II. 193 The Mariner.. as soone as he heard the flownce of the fall, presently cryde out *Hombre a la mar*.

2. A quick movement of the body, expressing impatience or disdain.

1751 JOHNSON *Rambler* No. 182 ¶12 He sometimes presumed to mention Marriage; but was always answered with a Hoot, and a Flounce. **1878** MRS. STOWE *Poganuc P.* i. 5 Nabby turned her batch of dough over with a final flounce, as if to emphasize the statement.

flounce (flaʊns), *sb.*^{2} [Alteration of earlier FROUNCE, prob. due to the influence of FLOUNCE *v.*^{1}

(The alleged AF. *flounce*, quoted in Skeat's *Etym. Dict.* (Suppl.), is a misprint for *founce* bottom (of a basin).)]

1. 'An ornamental appendage to the skirt of a lady's dress, consisting of a strip gathered and sewed on by its upper edge around the skirt, and left hanging and waving.' (W.)

1713 SWIFT *Cadenus & Vanessa* 45 From Fans, and Flounces, and Brocades. **1795** S. ROGERS *Words Mrs. Siddons* 59 The grey Dowager, in ancient flounces. **1862** MISS BRADDON *Lady Audley* iii. 27 She was shaking out the flounces of the silk dresses.

transf. **1799** J. ROBERTSON *Agric. Perth* 220 The tramp-ricks should also be.. well drawn all round close to the bottom.. not leaving the hay in a flounce at the skirts. **1891** BARING-GOULD *In Troubadour Land* x. 130 Two limestone blocks fallen from the precipices above, lying on the flounce of rubble near the bottom of the promontory.

2. *Mil.* The leather flap closing the holster-pipe.

1833 *Regul. Instr. Cavalry* I. 106 Take off the right-hand glove, unbutton the flounce, and push forward the cloak [etc.].

flounce (flaʊns), *v.*^{1} Also 6 flounse, 7 flownce. [Agrees in sense and form with Norw. *flunsa* to hurry, work briskly, Sw. dial. *flunsa* to fall with a splash; but as the Scand. words are not known earlier than the 18th c., and the Eng. word not till the 16th c., historical connexion cannot be proved.]

1. *intr.* To go with agitated, clumsy, or violent motion; to dash, flop, plunge, rush. Also with *away*, *out*, etc.

1542 UDALL *Erasm. Apophth.* 183 b, Alexander.. flounced me [*ethic dative*] into the flounde. **1639** FULLER *Holy War* II. xxviii. (1647) 80 He commanded them all at once to flownce into the river. **1736–7** MRS. A. GRANVILLE in *Mrs. Delany's Life & Corr.* 588 We flounced into great holes of ice and snow, enough to swallow up coach and horses. **1761** MRS. SHERIDAN *Sidney Bidulph* II. 128 She flounced off the chair to the other end of the room. **1784** tr. *Beckford's Vathek* (1868) 94 He flounced from the water like a carp. **1843** PAGET *Ward. Berkingholt* 233 So saying, Mrs. Carraway flounced off in a passion. **1865** CARLYLE *Fredk. Gt.* IX. XX. ix. 163 Upon which My Lady flounces out in a huff. **1876** T. HARDY *Ethelberta* xxxi, Picotee flounced away from him in indignation.

fig. *a* **1734** NORTH *Lives* II. 365 He thereupon resolved to flounce through. **1760** FOOTE *Minor* II. Wks. 1799 I. 260 One flower [of speech] flounced involuntarily from me that day.

b. ***to flounce down***; to flop down. ***to flounce over***: to turn over abruptly.

1786 MAD. D'ARBLAY *Diary* 25 Dec., I.. escape by mere miracle from flouncing down plump in all their faces! **1852** MRS. STOWE *Uncle Tom's C.* xxxvii, Tom flounced over,.. disarranging everything. **1855** THACKERAY *Newcomes* II. 299 Rosey's Mamma flouncing down on a chair.

2. *intr.* To make abrupt and jerky movements with the limbs or body; to throw the body about; to plunge, flounder, struggle. Also with *about*, *up*. Usually said of bulls, horses, or aquatic animals. ***to flounce it***, said of a woman dancing.

1609 HOLLAND *Amm. Marcell.* XVI. xii. 77 After his horse had flounced & floundered with his heeles in the soft and clammie mud. **1641** J. SHUTE *Sarah & Hagar* (1649) 109 When one hath struck a great fish, he plungeth and flounceth. **1704** J. TRAPP *Abra-Mulé* III. i. 1292 Whales.. Now flounc'd and panted on the slimy Beach. *c* **1710** C. FIENNES *Diary* (1888) 217 Giving him a good strap he fflounc'd up againe. **1728** MORGAN *Algiers* II. iii. 252 Laughing.. to behold them [infants] flounce about and struggle for Life in the Water. **1779** WESLEY *Wks.* (1872) IV. 163 One of them [his post-horses] began to kick and flounce, without any visible cause. **1841** CATLIN *N. Amer. Ind.* (1844) I. xvii. 120 Trinkets, and ribbons, in which they flounce and flirt about. **1851** MAYNE REID *Scalp Hunt.* vii. 53 Some of them [women] flounced it in polka jackets.

transf. and *fig.* **1655** FULLER *Ch. Hist.* XI. viii. §14 Waters long dammed up, oft-times flownce, and flie out too violently, when their sluces are pulled up. **1688** BUNYAN *Jerus. Sinner Saved* (1886) 60 Wood that is green will rather smother.. and crack, and flounce, than cast a brave light and a pleasant heat. *Ibid.* 90 It [despair] will make a man.. flounce and fling like a wild bull in a net.

3. †To express displeasure or ill-temper by agitated movements. *Obs.* Also ***to flounce into a temper***.

1702 STEELE *Funeral* II. ii, 'Tis in vain to flounce, and discompose your self. **1756** FOOTE *Eng. fr. Paris* II. Wks. 1799 I. 118 If you flounce, I fly. **1883** *Longm. Mag.* July 294 The little German gentleman flounced into a temper.

†**4.** *trans.* To dash or drive with violence; to fling with a flop or splash. *Obs.*

1583 STANYHURST *Aeneis* I. (Arb.) 38 What seas thee terribil hither Haue flounst? **1714** HEARNE *Duct. Hist.* (ed. 3) I. 184 At last it broke, and by the fall of large Pieces of it into the Abyss, flounc'd up the Water. **1719** A. SMITH *Lives of Highwaymen* II. 321 He is flounc'd thence into the Sea. **1794** MRS. BENNETT *Ellen* III. 107 She flounced the door in his face.

flounce (flaʊns). *v.*^{2} [Alteration of FROUNCE *v.*: cf. FLOUNCE *sb.*^{2}]

†**1.** *trans.* To curl, frizz, trim. *Obs.*

1672 WYCHERLEY *Love in Wood* III. iii, Let me Prune, and Flounce my Perruque a little.

2. To adorn or trim with a flounce or with flounces; also *transf.*

1711 ADDISON *Spect.* No. 129 ¶5 She was flounced and furbelowed from Head to Foot. **1737** POPE *Let. in Style Lady* Wks. 1824 VIII. 406 They have got into the.. fashion .. of flouncing the petticoat so very deep, that it looks like an entire coat of lutestring. **1749** H. WALPOLE *Lett.* (1857) II. 170 He has.. flounced himself with flowering shrubs. **1814** MISS MITFORD in L'Estrange *Life* (1870) I. 274 Striped muslin to flounce my gowns. **1818** *Blackw. Mag.* III. 403 It must take scores and scores of yards to flounce her. **1841** D'ISRAELI *Amen. Lit.* (1867) 523 The tarnished piece was drawn out of the theatrical wardrobe.. [and] flounced with new scenes. **1862** H. MARRYAT *Year in Sweden* II. 308 Its basement flounced round with trees.

absol. **1784** BAGE *Barham Downs* I. 171 They could trim, flounce, and furbelow to admiration.

flounce (flaʊns), *adv.* [The vb. stem so used.] With a flounce; with a sudden jerk or flop.

1583 STANYHURST *Aeneis* III. (Arb.) 89 Flounce to the stars towring thee fire, lyke a pellet, is hurled. **1604** *Meeting of Gallants* 21 He fell flounce into the saddle. **1707** FARQUHAR *Beaux' Stratagem* II. 1 Wks. 1892 II. 260 He comes flounce into bed.

flounced (flaʊnst), *ppl. a.* [f. FLOUNCE *v.* + -ED^1.] Adorned or trimmed with a flounce or with flounces.

1727 SWIFT *Baucis & Philemon* Wks. 1755 III. II. 36 Her petticoat.. Became black sattin flounc'd with lace. **1862** MISS YONGE *Countess Kate* ii. (1880) 13 They will do nothing all day long but try on flounced gowns.

flouncing ('flaʊnsɪŋ), *vbl. sb.*[1] [f. FLOUNCE *v.*[1] + -ING[1].] The action of the vb. FLOUNCE.

1601 DEACON & WALKER *Answ. to Darel* 190 The gallant ..keepes a flouncing and frisking about. **1679-80** SIR C. LYTTELTON in *Hatton Corr.* (1878) 213 What wth ye flounsing of ye hors and my own endeavors I soone was free. **1727** A. HAMILTON *New Acc. E. Ind.* II. xliv. 133 He turned Tail on us, and with great Flouncings, made towards the Shore. **1774** GOLDSM. *Nat. Hist.* (1776) VI. 245 To prevent his flouncing, they cut off the tail with an axe. **1874** BLACKIE *Self-Cult.* 10 A little floundering and flouncing in deep bottomless seas of speculation.

flouncing ('flaʊnsɪŋ), *vbl. sb.*[2] [f. FLOUNCE *v.*[2] + -ING[1].] **a.** The action of putting a flounce to a garment. **b.** *concr.* A flounce; also, the material of which flounces are made.

1766 GOLDSM. *Vic. W.* iv, I do not know whether such flouncing and shredding is becoming even in the rich. **1865** MRS. WHITNEY *Gayworthys* II. 53 The pink muslin was.. too dressy, perhaps, with its four little flouncings. **1873** —— *Other Girls* v. 97 She tossed a long flouncing over her sewing-table.

fig. **1891** *Month* LXXIII. 247 Those who merely dabble in good works may find time..to deck themselves out in such flouncings of vanity.

flouncing ('flaʊnsɪŋ), *ppl. a.* [f. FLOUNCE *v.* + -ING[2].] That flounces: said chiefly of animals, *esp.* aquatic animals; plunging, tossing.

1700 BLACKMORE *Job* 179 Canst thou stand angling on the banks of Nile..And thro the flood the flouncing monster draw? **1708** PRIOR *Epil. to Smith's Phædra & Hippol.* 15 Six flouncing Flanders mares. **1806-7** J. BERESFORD *Miseries Hum. Life* (1826) vi, Hearing the roof of a crazy coach groan ..beneath the flouncing weights of a dozen ponderous passengers. **1837** WHEELWRIGHT tr. *Aristophanes* I. 330 Why beatest thou the sea with flouncing oars?

fig. **1830** *Examiner* 790/1 The heroine of this flouncing trumpery, yclept a tragedy.

flouncy ('flaʊnsɪ), *a.* Also **-ey.** [f. FLOUNCE *sb.*[2] + -Y[1].] Having flounces, flounced.

1821 M. WILMOT *Let.* 17 Jan. (1935) 93 This gauzy, flowncy, furbelow, flybysky place. **1900** *Westm. Gaz.* 20 Sept. 3/2 A deep-kilted flouncy chiffon. **1906** *Daily Chron.* 31 Aug. 5/7 Floppy hats and skirts, all 'fluffy' and 'flouncy', have come into vogue again. **1909** H. G. WELLS *Tono-Bungay* I. i. 19 Shiny and flouncey clothing. **1927** *Sunday at Home* June 525/2 Flouncy petticoats..are giving way in Spain to modern styles.

flounder ('flaʊndə(r)), *sb.*[1] Also 5 floundre, flownder, -dre, flondyre, 7 flunder. [The phonology seems to show that the immediate source is AF. *floundre* (14th c., *Black Bk. Admir.* II. 102) = OF. *flondre* (still current in Normandy); app. of Scandinavian origin: cf. ON. *flyðra* (:— **flunþrjôn*-), MSw., Sw., Norw. *flundra*, Da. *flynder*; mod.Ger. has *flunder*, but this is given by Gesner in 16th c. as only an *English* name (Kluge).

The MHG. *vluoder* of the same meaning is related by ablaut to FLATHE, and cannot be directly connected with *flounder*; but the latter may possibly be from a nasalized form of the same root.]

1. A small flat-fish, *Pleuronectes Flesus*. In the U.S. applied to various other species of flat-fish. Prov. ***as flat as a flounder***.

a **1450** *Fysshynge wyth an angle* (1883) 30 The flounder is an holsom fisshe. **1513** *Bk. Keruynge* in *Babees Bk.* 282 Base, flounders, sole. **1622** PEACHAM *Compl. Gentl.* v. xxi. (1634) 254 The Eele and Flounder are two greedy Fish and bite at the redde worme. **1774** GOLDSM. *Nat. Hist.* (1776) VI. 174 Fish..that continually crawl at the bottom; such as the eel and the flounder. *a* **1845** HOOD *To Tom Woodgate* vi, Or are you where the flounders keep, Some dozen briny fathoms deep. **1856** KANE *Arct. Expl.* II. vii. 77 You came in upon four of us down as flat as flounders.

2. Something resembling this fish. **a.** *dial.* = FLUKE 2. **b.** See quot. 1874.

a. 1853 COOPER *Sussex Gloss.*, *Flounders*, animals found in the livers of rotten sheep, called in Somerset, *flooks*. S. **1883** in *Hampsh. Gloss.*

b. 1874 KNIGHT *Dict. Mech.* I. 889/2 *Flounder*, a slicking-tool whose edge is used to stretch leather for a boot front in a blocking or crimping board. **1875** *Ure's Dict. Arts* III. 100 After this, the fronts are regularly placed on a block, being forced into position by an instrument called the flounder, and tacked to their place.

3. *attrib.* and *Comb.*, as ***flounder-fishery***, ***flounder-like*** adj. Also **flounder-lantern**, a dial. name of the common flounder; **flounder-man**, a hawker of flounders; **flounder-mouth**, a mouth like a flounder's, a large mouth; whence ***flounder-mouthed*** adj.; **flounder's-head (whale)**, a bottle-nosed whale.

1884 *Pall Mall G.* 20 Sept. 2/1 The *flounder fishery is looking up again. **1630** MASSINGER *Renegado* III. i, To firke your belly vp *flounder like. **1700** CONGREVE *Way of World* v. 77 Hawkers, with Voices more Licentious than the loud *Flounder-man's. **1672-95** *Brickmaker's Lament.* in *Roxb. Ball.* II. 40 The cryer he bawl'd, And there with his *flounder-mouth loudly he yaul'd. **1663** COWLEY *Cutter of Colman St.* IV. vi, She..rails at me like a *Flounder-mouth'd Fish-woman. **1724** MRS. M. DAVYS *Reform'd Coquet* (1752) 110 You great Flounder-mouth'd Sea-calf. **1717** in S. Dale *Hist. Harwich* Tab. xiv, The Bottle-Head or *Flounders-Head-Whale.

flounder ('flaʊndə(r)), *sb.*[2] [f. next vb.] The action of the vb. FLOUNDER.

1867 F. FRANCIS *Angling* xiv (1880) 486 The fish gave one flounder. **1871** L. STEPHEN *Playgr. Eur.* IV. (1894) 105 With a graceful flounder I was presently landed in safety upon a ..ledge. **1887** SIR R. H. ROBERTS *In the Shires* ii. 33 His horse..after a severe flounder, regained his legs.

flounder ('flaʊndə(r)), *v.* Also 6-7 flunder. [Of obscure etymology.

Perh. an onomatopœic blending of the sound and sense of various earlier words; cf. FLOUNDER *v.* (OF. *fondrer*), BLUNDER, and the many vbs. with initial *fl-* expressing impetuous and clumsy movements. Wedgwood and Skeat compare Du. *flodderen*, to flounder in mire, to flop about: see the dialectal FLODDER *v.*, which may have affected the development of the present word.]

1. *intr.* In early use, to stumble (cf. FLOUNDER *v.*). Subsequently, to struggle violently and clumsily; to plunge, roll and tumble about in or as in mire; also (with *on*, *along*, etc.), to move on with clumsy or rolling gait, to struggle along with difficulty. Of a horse: To rear, plunge; †to 'shy' (*at* an object).

1592 WYRLEY *Armorie* 101 My foot did slide and.. Flundring, almost flat on earth I go. *a* **1625** FLETCHER *Woman's Prize* II. iii, If she flownder with you, Clap spurs on. **1687** DRYDEN *Hind & P.* III. 301 He champs the bit.. And starts a side, and flounders at the cross. **1735** SOMERVILLE *Chase* III. 135 Another in the treach'rous Bog Lies flound'ring. **1834** MEDWIN *Angler in Wales* I. 291 He lost his balance, and man and fish lay floundering together in the rapid. **1840** THACKERAY *Paris Sk.-bk.* (1872) 184 'You flounder in mud at every step.' **1861** HUGHES *Tom Brown at Oxf.* ii. (1889) 17 The four-oar floundered on ahead.

quasi-*trans.*

1694 CONGREVE *Double-Dealer* IV. v, You will but flounder yourself a-weary. **1816** CHALMERS *Let.* in *Life* II. 66 With the risk of floundering its uncertain way through [etc.].

b. *transf.* and *fig.*

1684 H. MORE *Answer* 299 The Remarker, in the very entrance, shuffles and flunders. **1728** POPE *Dunc.* I. 120 The Hero..wrote and flounder'd on in mere despair. **1807** W. IRVING *Salmag.* (1824) 202 He dashed off to a ball, time enough to flounder through a Cotillion. **1822** HAZLITT *Table-t.* Ser. II. v. (1869) 123 They flounder about between fustian in expression, and bathos in sentiment. **1865** CARLYLE *Fredk. Gt.* VII. XVIII. v. 178 The poor Prince's mind did flounder a good deal.

†**2.** *trans.* To cause to flounder: to confound, embarrass. *Obs.*

1654 GAYTON *Pleas. Notes* III. ii. 74 He..fell into Cocytus ..where floundred extreamly and uncouthly accoutred, yet he resolv'd to call for no helpe. **1685** H. MORE *Paralip. Proph.* 154. Those Interpreters..flunder and confound all.

†**3.** *to flounder up*: to choke up (a water-course). *Obs.* [Cf. FLODDER *v.*]

1576 in W. H. TURNER *Select. Rec. Oxford* 385 The streame behinde Oseney ys so floundred up that the water cannot passe.. The dyches..are so floundred up wth flaggs and fylth.

†**4.** *intr.* Of soil: To fall in. [Cf. OF. *fondrer* in same sense.] *Obs.*

1774 G. WHITE *Selborne* xx. (1789) 177 A soil..much too loose and mouldering, liable to flounder, and threatening to overwhelm them [Sand-martins] and their labours.

Hence '**flounderer**, one who flounders.

1836 HOR. SMITH *Tin Trump.* (1876) 345 Learn this ye flounderers in the traps Of insulated lines and scraps.

'**flounder-flat**, *v. nonce-wd. trans.* To make 'as flat as a flounder'.

1819 COLERIDGE in *Lit. Rem.* (1836) II. 119 Warburton could never have wooed by kisses and won, or he would not have flounder-flatted so just and humorous..an image into so profound a nihility.

floundering ('flaʊndərɪŋ), *vbl. sb.* [f. FLOUNDER *v.* + -ING[1].] The action of the verb FLOUNDER; a plunging, struggling, or stumbling; also *fig.*

1726 *Adv. Capt. R. Boyle* 351, I was..in danger of.. having my Brains dash'd out with his Hoofs in his Floundering. **1868** *Less. Mid. Age* 202 A little floundering for words..might add to the impression made by this speaker. **1883** *19th Cent.* Sept. 513 A floundering that may only plunge us deeper into the mire.

floundering ('flaʊndərɪŋ), *ppl. a.* [f. as prec. + -ING[2].] That flounders; plunging and tossing; stumbling. Also *fig.*

1592 NASH *Pierce Penilesse* E ij b, Report (which our moderners clippe flundring Fame). **1642** H. MORE *Song of Soul* I. I. xvii, Th' unruly flundring steeds wrought his confusion. **1852** MRS. STOWE *Uncle Tom's C.* viii, The swollen current and floundering masses of ice. **1887** T. A. TROLLOPE *What I remember* I. xvii. 346 The postboys.. dismounted from their floundering horses. **1887** SAINTSBURY *Hist. Elizab. Lit.* i. (1890) 12 There is nothing here of Wyatt's floundering prosody.

†'**Flounderkin.** *Obs.* [Comic perversion of FLANDERKIN, after FLOUNDER *sb.*[1] or *v.*] A contemptuous designation for a Dutchman.

a **1668** DAVENANT *News from Plymouth* III. Wks. (1673) 13/1 On our allegiance We must not suffer it, by your leave, Flounderkin. *Ibid.* v. 29/1.

flour (flaʊə(r)), *sb.* Forms: 3 flure, 5-6 floure, 5-7 flowre, 5-8 flower, 4- flour. [A specific use of FLOWER; cf. F. *fleur de farine* the 'flower' or finest part of the meal.

Johnson 1755 does not separate the words, nor does he recognize the spelling *flour*. But Cruden's *Concordance* 1738 recognizes the modern distinction.]

1. a. Originally, the 'flower' or finest quality of meal; hence, the finer portion of meal (whether from wheat or other grain) which is separated by bolting. Also, in modern use, the ordinary name for the meal or farina of wheat as opposed to that obtained from other grain.

c **1250** *Gen. & Ex.* 1013 Kalues fleis, and flures bred, And buttere. **1340** *Ayenb.* 210 Zuych difference ase þer is.. betuene bren and flour of huete. *c* **1400** *Lanfranc's Cirurg.* 46 Take mel roset..smal flour of barly & medle hem togidere. *c* **1420** *Liber Cocorum* (1862) 14 Floure of ryce þou grynd also. *c* **1440** *Promp. Parv.* 168/1 Flowre of mele, *farina, simila.* **1533** ELYOT *Cast. Helthe* II. xi. (1541) 28 b, Breade of fyne flowre of wheate..is slowe of digestion. **1691** TRYON *Wisd. Dictates* 21 Milk, Water, and Flower, seasoned with Salt..are rare Foods for them [Children]. **1769** MRS. RAFFALD *Eng. Housekpr.* (1778) 259 Rub a little of the butter into the flour. **1809** PINKNEY *Trav. France* 8 In a long voyage..flower will not keep. **1846** in BAXTER *Libr. Pract. Agric.* (ed. 4) II. 3 When perfectly ripe and ground into flour, it [Indian corn] is said [etc.]. **1872** YEATS *Techn. Hist. Comm.* 36 The art of obtaining flour from corn..was known to the Egyptians.

b. as type of whiteness.

1375 BARBOUR *Bruce* VIII. 232 Hawbrekis, that war quhit as flour. *a* **1440** *Sir Eglam.* 949 Kepe we thys lady whyte as flowre.

†**c.** In figurative phrase: ***to bolt all the flour***: to investigate a matter thoroughly. *Obs.*

1590 SPENSER *F.Q.* II. iv. 24 He now had boulted all the floure.

2. By extension. **a.** The fine soft powder obtained by grinding or triturating seeds, farinaceous roots, or other alimentary substances. **b.** Any finely-powdered dry substance.

a. 1660 F. BROOKE *Le Blanc's Trav.* 399 They make flower also of fish dryed in the Sun. **1836** MACGILLIVRAY tr. *Humboldt's Trav.* xxv. 378 The valuable plant Jatropha, of which the root..affords the flour of manioc. **1855** OGILVIE *Suppl.*, *Flour-of-mustard*, the seeds of mustard, dried, powdered, and sifted. **1879** *Encycl. Brit.* IX. 348/2 Dusting them [artificial flowers] with fine powdered glass or potato flour to represent the bloom. **1889** *Cent. Dict.* s.v. *Flour*, Flour of meat, a fine flour made of dried meat.

b. *c* **1400** *Lanfranc's Cirurg.* 99 Flour of bras brent. **1670** W. CLARKE *Nat. Hist. Nitre* 88 If it [gunpowder] should be in flour, or fine powder. **1880** W. H. WARDELL in *Encycl. Brit.* XI. 323 The crystallized saltpetre, having almost the appearance of snow, and technically called 'flour,' is raked into the 'washing-cistern.' **1894** *Nation* (N.Y.) 22 Mar. 209/3 The sulphur found in other parts of Italy..is..sold in 'flour,' in 'rolls,' or in 'cakes.'

3. *attrib.* and *Comb.*, as ***flour bag***, ***-barrel***, ***-dredge***, ***-dredger***, ***-grinder***, ***loaf***, ***man***, ***-mill***, ***miller***, ***milling***, ***-packer***, ***-paste***, ***-sack***, ***-shoot***; ***flour-like*** adj.

1806 S. MICKLE *Diary* 28 June in F. H. Stewart *Notes Old Glouc. County, N.J.* (1917) I. 181 Marked a number of my *flour bags with oil and lamp black. **1872** B. JERROLD *London* vii. 71 The whole scene, from thimble-rigger to the peer armed with flour-bags. **1950** *N.Z. Jrnl. Agric.* Jan. 27/3 For the domestic beekeeper an old flour bag makes an ideal strainer. **1809** W. IRVING *Knickerb.* (1850) VI. iii. 194 A cooper hooping a *flour-barrel. **1858** SIMMONDS *Dict. Trade*, **Flour-dredge*, a tin for sprinkling flour. **1867** 'T. LACKLAND' *Homespun* I. 125 Spoons, and knives, and rolling-pins, and *flour-dredgers. **1939-40** *Army & Navy Stores Catal.* 165/3 Flour dredgers. **1828** JAMES *Richelieu* xxxvii, Those dusty jackets, which have been the insignia of *flour-grinders from all generations. **1863** A. B. GROSART *Small Sins* (ed. 2) 84 You inevitably brush off its powdery *flour-like dust. **1828** A. SHERBURNE *Mem.* ii. 52 He withdrew and sent us in some *flour loaves. **1743** W. ELLIS *Mod. Husb.* IV. I. 7 The *Flour-men do not care to buy this Yellow Wheat in Summer. **1848** *Knickerbocker* XXXI. 221 The butcher's bill, the coal man's bill, the flour man's bill, the house rent, were all quickly settled. **1809** KENDALL *Trav.* II. lii. 213 Rivers..upon which are fulling, *flower and saw mills. **1825** J. NICHOLSON *Operat. Mechanic* 142 We have given a section of a double flour-mill. **1921** *Daily Colonist* (Victoria, B.C.) 26 Mar. 1/4 *Flour millers have asked for a compensatory duty on flour. **1888** BRYCE *Amer. Commw.* III. VI. cxiv. 643 Minneapolis..has become..the greatest *flour-milling centre in America. **1806** *Sporting Mag.* XXVIII. 212 Luting the interstices of the lid with *flour-paste. **1858** SIMMONDS *Dict. Trade*, **Flour-sack*, a coarse bag for flour. **1880** HARDY *Trumpet-Major* xxxii, The miller entered the mill as if he were simply staying up to grind. But he continually left the *flour-shoot to go outside and walk round.

4. Special comb., as **flour-ball**, a ball of flour; also a kind of potato which resembles a ball of flour when boiled; **flour-beetle**, a beetle which feeds on and is very destructive to flour (see quot.); **flour-bolt**, **-bolter**, a flour-sieve; **flour-box**, a tin box for dredging flour; **flour-bread**, wheaten bread; **flour-cake** *dial.* (see quot.); **flour-dresser** (see quot.); **flour-emery**, emery reduced to a fine powder; **flour-factor** (see quot. 1858); **flour-gold** (see quot.); **flour-meat** *dial.*, food made with flour; **flour-mite**, one of several mites or acarids which are found in flour; **flour-moth**, a moth which feeds on flour, esp. *Pyralis farinalis*; **flour-worm**, the larva of any one of the flour-beetles or flour-moths.

1877 W. JONES *Finger-ring Lore* 438 A wealthy German farmer..was making *flour-balls in 1871 for his cattle. **1877** *N.W. Linc. Gloss.*, *Flour-balls*, a kind of potato. **1888** POWLES tr. *Kick's Flour Manuf.* ix. 248 The *flour beetle (*Tenebrio molitor*) belongs to the family of *Melanosomata*, [and] is of a pitch black or brown colour. **1874** KNIGHT *Dict. Mech.* I. 889/2 **Flour-bolt.* **1888** POWLES tr. *Kick's Flour Manuf.* vi. 177 The *flour bolter in the old mills..was made of an open woven woollen cloth called bolting cloth. **1721** BAILEY *Dredger*, A *Flower Box. **17..** *Rose o' Malindie O'* iv. in Child *Ballads* I. No. 20 (1882) 224/1 Waur ye but mine,

I wald feed ye wi *flour-bread an wine. **1840** R. BREMNER *Excurs. Denmark, &c* II. 233 The many kinds of flour-bread. **1884** *Chesh. Gloss.*, **Flour-cakes*, a..cake..made from a small piece of ordinary bread dough rolled to the size of a plate, and about an inch thick, and then baked on both sides. **1858** SIMMONDS *Dict. Trade*, **Flour-dresser*, a cylinder for dressing flour, instead of passing it through bolting cloths. **1888** POWLES tr. *Kick's Flour Manuf.* vi. 176 The sieve is stretched on an inclined cylinder furnished with brushes on a spindle revolving inside..This variety is called the 'flour dresser', or wire and brush machine. **1884** F. J. BRITTEN *Watch & Clockm.* 101 *Flour Emery..used for smooth burnishers. **1815** *Gen. Hist.* in *Ann. Reg.* 53/2 They were chiefly mealmen and *flour factors. **1858** SIMMONDS *Dict. Trade, Flour-factor*, an agent for millers; one who sells flour to bakers. **1869** R. B. SMYTH *Goldfields Victoria* 611 *Flour-gold, the finest alluvial drift-gold. **1707** FLOYER *Physic. Pulse-Watch* 83 *Flower-meats, and cool Herbs, stop the Pulse. **1876** *Whitby Gloss., Flour-meat*, bread food; pastry. **1893** *Times* 15 May 7/1 The ravages of the *flour moth, and the damage it was doing in English mills. **1880** HARDY *Trumpet-Major* xvi, Such abundance of water that the old-established death-watches, wood-lice, and *flour-worms were all drowned.

flour (flaʊə(r)), *v.* [f. prec. sb.]

1. *trans.* To sprinkle with flour. Also *transf.* To powder (a wig).

1651-7 T. BARKER *Art of Angling* (1820) 14 Your fish being cut on the side and floured. **1725** BRADLEY *Fam. Dict., Sheeps-tongues*..after they have been flower'd and fry'd..may be soaked by degrees with Truffles and Mushrooms. **1732** E. FORREST *Hogarth's Tour* 5 We shaved, and had our wigs flowered. **1750** E. SMITH *Compl. Housew.* (ed. 14) 178 Flour some sheets of tin, and drop your biskets..and put them into the oven. **1887** BESANT *The World went* xxvi. 200 It was..one of the 'prentices flouring the Vicar's wig for Sunday.

2. *U.S.* To grind (grain) into flour.

1828 WEBSTER s.v., Great quantities of it [wheat] are floured in the interior countries. **1859** BARTLETT *Dict. Amer.* 156 The mill can flour two hundred barrels a day.

3. *intr. Mining.* Of mercury: To break up into dull particles coated with some sulphide and incapable of coalescing with other metals. Cf. FLOURING *vbl. sb.* Also *trans.*

1882 A. G. LOCKE *Gold* 21 The mercury employed for amalgamation..sickens or 'flours' when ground up with pyritous rocks. **1882** *Rep. Prec. Metals* (U.S.) 648 The action of pounding is likely..to flour the gold as well as the quicksilver.

flour, obs. form of FLOWER.

†**flour-dammes.** *Obs. rare*$^{-1}$. [f. OF. *flour* FLOWER + *damas* (explained by Godefroy as the auricula.] Some flower.

1513 DOUGLAS *Æneis* XII. Prol. 118 Flour-dammes, and columby blank and blew.

flour-de-lice, -lis, -luce, -lyce, -lys(e, obs. ff. FLEUR-DE-LIS.

floured (flaʊəd), *ppl. a.* [f. FLOUR *sb.* or *v.* + -ED.]

1. Sprinkled or covered with flour.

1814 SIR R. WILSON *Diary* II. 328 We are too old mice to be caught by a floured cat. **1849** *Sidonia Sorc.* I. 225 A miller ..was belabouring him stoutly with his floured fists. **1873** MISS BROUGHTON *Nancy* III. 184 Looking at me..from the highest summit of my floured head, to the point of my buckled shoes.

2. (See quot.)

1881 RAYMOND *Mining Gloss., Floured*, the finely granulated condition of quicksilver, produced to a greater or less extent by its agitation during the amalgamation process.

†**floure jonett.** *Obs.*$^{-1}$ [ad. OF. *flour* (Fr. *fleur*) flower and OF. *jaulnette* (Cotgr.), f. *jaulne* (Fr. *jaûne*) yellow.] ? The great St. John's wort.

1423 JAS. I. *Kingis Q.* xlvii, The plumys eke like to the floure-Ionettis.

†**flouren** ('flaʊərən), *a. Obs.* [f. FLOUR *sb.* + -EN[4].] Made of flour.

a **1300** *Land Cokayne* 57 in *E.E.P.* (1862) 157 Fluren cakes beþ þe scingles alle, Of..cloister, boure, and halle.

flouret, -ette, obs. ff. FLOWERET.

flouring ('flaʊərɪŋ), *vbl. sb.* [f. FLOUR *v.* + -ING[1].]

1. *U.S.* The action or process of grinding grain into flour: also *attrib.* in ***flouring-mill***, 'a mill for making flour, usually on a large scale; distinguished from grist-mill' (*Cent. Dict.*). Also ***flouring mill-stone***.

1797 *Southampton* (N.Y.) *Rec.* III. 353 John Jermain [shall] have privilege..of erecting a grist mill..for flouring or for packing. **1797** *N.Y. State Soc. Arts* I. 375 Possessing some flouring mills, I was naturally led to converse at times with my millers..on the economy of water in grinding. **1842** *Amer. Pioneer* I. 204 In the city and its vicinity are twenty-five pairs of flouring mill-stones. **1855** CLARKE *Dict., Flouring*, flour business. **1859** BARTLETT *Dict. Amer.* 156 *Flouring-Mill*, a grist-mill. **1888** *Amer. Anthropologist* Oct. I. No. 4. 307 The way from the mealing-stone to the flouring-mill is long. **1932** *Sun* (Baltimore) 19 Sept. 4/3 Fire destroyed the Alpine buckwheat flouring mill, which was to have resumed operations next week.

2. (See quot. 1869.)

1869 R. B. SMYTH *Goldfields Victoria* 611 'Flouring' is the forming of the mercury into small particles by the action of the reducing-machine and the subsequent coating of each particle by some sulphide, whereby the power of the particles to re-unite and to amalgamate with gold is lost. **1882** A. G. LOCKE *Gold* 21 The greater part of the flouring or sickening of the mercury used is due to the action of sulphate of iron.

flourish ('flʌrɪʃ), *sb.* Forms: 6 florishe, (*Sc.* flureise, -ss, fleureis, flurish), 6–7 florish, 7 floorish, 7–8 flowrish, 6– flourish. [f. next vb.]

1. The blossom or mass of flowers on a fruit-tree Also occas. in *pl.* Only *Sc.* and *north dial.*

a **1500** *Cokelbie Sow* Proem. 42 A fair flureiss fadit in a falty tre. **1548** *Compl. Scot.* vi. 38 The borial blastis..hed chaissit the fragrant flureise of euyrie frute tree far athourt the feildis. *a* **1605** MONTGOMERIE *Misc. Poems* xvii. 58 Beuties freshest florish. **1635** RUTHERFORD *Let.* 22 Apr., There shall be fair white flourishes again, with most pleasant fruits. **1868** ATKINSON *Cleveland Gloss., Flourish*, the blossom on fruit-trees. **1892** BOYD *25 Years St. Andrews* II. xxi. 139 Finding some very fine 'flourish' in a dirty back-court.

†**b.** *pl.* = *flowers* (see FLOWER *sb.* 2b).

1605 SYLVESTER *Du Bartas* II. iii. *Lawe* 85 Childe-great Women, or green Maydes (that misse Their Termes appointed for their flourishes).

†**2.** The state or condition of being in blossom, blossoming. Of vegetation: Luxuriant growth, luxuriance, greenness. *Obs.*

1594 J. DICKENSON *Arisbas* (1878) 75 The roote whose moisture fed their flourish. **1619** Z. BOYD *Battell Soul* (1629) 1101 The tree is first seene in the budde and then in the flourish, and after in the frute. **1719** DE FOE *Crusoe* I. 117 A constant Verdure, or Flourish of Spring. **1801** SOUTHEY *Thalaba* VIII. xvii, In the flourish of its [vine's] outwardness Wasting the sap and strength. **1818** SCOTT *Hrt. Midl.* xxxi, Fruit-trees, so many of which were at this time in flourish.

b. *fig.* Prosperity, vigour; the 'bloom' (of youth). Also, the highest degree of prosperity; perfection, prime. Now *rare.*

1597 J. PAYNE *Royal Exch.* 38 To be howld..wycked men to have the fayrest shew and greatest florishe. **1612** BREREWOOD *Lang. & Relig.* iii. 20 The Romans had generally (at least..in the flourish of the empire) great care to enlarge their tongue. **1665** *Life Earl Essex* in *Select Harl. Misc.* (1793) 157 The earl of Essex was then in the flourish of his youth. **1709** HEARNE *Collect.* 27 Aug., The Foundation & Increase & Flourish of [the University]. **1826** SCOTT *Woodst.* xi, The flourish of his powerful relative's fortunes had burst forth in the finery of his dress. **1848** THACKERAY *Bk. Snobs* iv, The *Court Circular* remains in full flourish.

†**3.** Ostentatious embellishment; gloss, varnish.

1588 SHAKS. *L.L.L.* IV. iii. 238 Lend me the flourish of all gentle tongues. *c* **1600** —— *Sonn.* lx, Time doth transfixe the florish set on youth. *c* **1632** CRASHAW *Epitaph Mr. Herrys*, The flourish of his sober youth, Was the pride of naked truth.

†**4.** A florid decoration; a piece of scroll-work, tracery, or the like. *Obs.*

1695 *Phil. Trans.* XIX. 154 An Octagonal Tower..beautified on the out-side with Florishes. **1721** BAILEY, A flourish [in Architecture] is a Flower Work. **1764** HARMER *Observ.* III. iv. 134 Cracknells are full of holes, being formed into a kind of flourish of lattice-work.

fig. **1675** TRAHERNE *Chr. Ethics* xxviii. 443 Mistake not these things for arbitrary flourishes of luxuriant fancy.

b. In *Penmanship*, a decoration about a letter or writing, consisting of flowing curves executed with a sweep of the pen.

1652 H. MORE *Antid. Ath.* II. vi. 68 They were intended onley for ludicrous ornaments of Nature, like the flourishes about a great letter that signify nothing. **1758** J. BLAKE *Plan Mar. Syst.* 8 In the middle of this sheet..let a flourish be printed, so that the sheet may be cut in two, indentwise. **1831** LAMB *Let. to Dyer* (1888) II. 268 By your flourishes, I should think you never learned to..flourish the governors' names in the writing-school. **1861** SALA *Dutch Pict.* 2 An original Rembrandt (with a flourish to the R).

5. Literary or rhetorical embellishment; ambitious copiousness or amplification; parade of fine words or phrases; a florid expression.

1603 HOLLAND *Plutarch's Mor.* 74 By a flourish of fine words, they devise shifts [and] evasions. **1673** *True Worship God* 56 Those pleasing Varieties and Flourishes in Pulpit Harangues. **1708** BERKELEY *Commonpl. Bk.* Wks. 1871 IV. 492, I abstain from all flourish and powers of words and figures. **1823** SCOTT *Peveril* xlvi, He commenced with a flourish about his sufferings for the Plot. **1867** FREEMAN *Norm. Conq.* (1876) I. App. 542 These unusual phrases are clearly mere flourishes.

†**b.** A boast, brag. *Obs.*

1586 A. DAY *Eng. Secretary* II. (1625) 44 All your..flourish made of your company, their reputation, your civilitie. **1706** PHILLIPS (ed. Kersey), *Flourish*..a Vaunt, Boast, or Brag.

6. An ostentatious waving about of a weapon or anything else held in the hand; a showy movement of the body or limbs.

1601 CORNWALLYES *Ess.* xii, Like seeming Fencers wee are meeter for a flourish, then defence. **1713** STEELE *Guardian* No. 50 ⁋2 Before he applied his weapon to my chin, he gave me a flourish with it. **1737** BRACKEN *Farriery Impr.* (1757) II. 167 It would splint him..if the Rider were to make his Flourishes upon his Back like a Rope-dancer. **1840** F. D. BENNETT *Whaling Voy.* I. 142 A few..musicians embellish their performance with a flourish of the fingers. **1859** DICKENS *T. Two Cities* I. v, The three customers pulled off their hats to Madame Defarge, with three flourishes.

fig. **1777** A. HAMILTON *Wks.* (1886) VII. 510 Their flourishes in the Jerseys, I believe, cannot have cost them less than six or seven hundred men.

b. *esp.* A graceful brandishing of the weapon by way of salute or display at the beginning of a fencing match. †Hence *fig.* a prolusion, ornamental preamble; a piece of compliment or display preliminary to serious business or discussion. (Cf. 7c.)

1552 HULOET, Florysh, *proludium.* **1571** GOLDING *Calvin on Ps.* xviii. 44 That was but a florish of the sovereintie promised to Christ. **1593** R. HARVEY *Philad.* 2 This is your florish, to no purpose, then to shew reading. *a* **1626** BACON *Ess., Fame* (Arb.) 579 This is a flourish: There follow excellent Parables. **1826** SCOTT *Woodst.* xxviii, Ere they had done more than salute each other, with the usual courteous flourish of their weapons.

7. *Music.* **a.** A fanfare (of horns, trumpets, etc.), *esp.* to announce the approach of a person of distinction.

1594 SHAKS. *Rich. III*, IV. iv. 148 A flourish, Trumpets! strike Alarum, Drummes! **1609** HEYWOOD *Lucrece* V. i, A flourish with drums and trumpets. **1712** PHILIPS *Distressed Mother* IV. i, A flourish of trumpets. **1788** CLARA REEVE *Exiles* II. 127 Two trumpeters..blew a flourish, and the herald gave his challenge. **1813** *Ann. Reg.* 52 The Duke of York gave the toast; it was announced from the head of the table by a flourish of trumpets. **1814** SCOTT *Wav.* xlv, When Waverley reached that part of the column which was filled by the clan of Mac-Ivor, they..received him with a triumphant flourish upon the bagpipes. **1868** *Regul. & Ord. Army* ⁋58 In corps not having a band, the bugles or trumpets will sound the flourish.

fig. **1884** J. A. H. MURRAY *13th Presid. Addr.* in *Trans. Philol. Soc.* 516 Friends, who..send..with a flourish of trumpets to *Notes and Queries*.

b. A florid passage; a florid style of composition; a decorative addition introduced by player or singer. Also, 'the execution of profuse but unmeaning ornamentation in music' (Stainer and Barrett).

1646 CRASHAW *Poems, Musick's Duell* 137 The Lute's light Genius now does proudly rise, Heav'd on the surges of swolne Rapsodyes. Whose flourish, (Meteor-like) doth curle the aire With flash of high-borne fancyes. **1724** RAMSAY *Tea-t. Misc.* (1733) I. p. v, Such are not judges of the fine flowrishes of new musick imported from Italy. **1823** CRABB *Technol. Dict., Flourish*..the decorative notes which a singer, or instrumental performer, adds sometimes to a passage.

c. A short extemporized sequence of notes sounded as a prelude at the beginning of a piece of music. Cf. 6b.

1706 A. BEDFORD *Temple Mus.* ix. 191 Each Side might begin with a different Flourish. **1876** STAINER & BARRETT *Dict. Mus. Terms, Flourish*..The preparatory cadenza for 'tuning the voice', in which singers formerly indulged just before commencing their song.

transf. **1850** W. IRVING *Knickerb.* IV. ii. 117 He preluded his address by a sonorous blast of the nose; a preliminary flourish much in vogue among public orators.

flourish ('flʌrɪʃ), *v. Pa. t.* and *pple.* flourished. Forms: 3–4 floris(e, (4 floryse, fluris), 4 florisse, 4–5 florysse, floresshe, florische, (4 flurshe, fluri(s)che, flors(c)he, 5 floresche, florche), 4–6 florisshe, -yssh(e, 4–7 florish(e, (6 floorish), 5–6 florys(c)h(e, 6 *Sc.* flures, -eis, -is, flwreis, 4–6 flourishe, (4 flouresshe), 5–6 flourysshe, (5 flowrysche, 6 flourys(c)h, 7 flowrish), 4– flourish. [a. OF. *floriss-* lengthened stem of *florir* (mod.F. *fleurir*) = Pr. *florir*, It. *fiorire*:—vulgar L. type **flōrīre*, f. *flōr-*, *flōs*, flower. The intr. senses represent those of L. *flōrēre*, which like many other vbs. in *-ēre* passed into the *-īre* conjugation in Romanic.]

I. *intr.* To blossom, thrive.

†**1.** Of a plant or tree: To blossom, flower. *Obs.*

a **1300** *Cursor M.* 21701 (Gött.) Þar florist ane [wand] als ȝe haue herd. *c* **1386** CHAUCER *Pars. T.* ⁋43 To smelle the sote savour of the vyne whanne it florissheth. **1485** CAXTON *Chas. Gt.* 36 The crowne began to florysshe & a meruayllous swete odour yssued out of the floures. **1578** LYTE *Dodoens* II. xx. 170 It beginneth to floure at the toppe of the stalke, and so goeth florishing downewarde.

b. To throw out leaves and shoots; to shoot forth; to grow vigorously and luxuriantly. Now only with mixture of sense 4.

1303 R. BRUNNE *Handl. Synne* 905 Here vynys florshede feyre and weyl. **1382** WYCLIF *Ezek.* xvii. 24 Y made the drye tree for to florisshe. **1577** B. GOOGE *Heresbach's Husb.* I. (1586) 25b, In hotte Countreys later, least they shoulde florishe before the Winter, and be..blasted. **1727** BROOME *Seat of War in Flanders* 157 Poems 76 Pallas with her Javelin smote the Ground, And peaceful Olives flourish'd from the Wound. **1784** COWPER *Task* III. 571 The spiry myrtle with unwithering leaf Shines there and flourishes. **1877** HUXLEY *Physiogr.* xiii. 212 As these trees do not grow in water, it is evident that the land on which they flourished has been depressed.

c. *fig.*

1340 HAMPOLE *Pr. Consc.* 725 Arely a man passes als þe gres, He floresshe and passes away. **1470–85** MALORY *Arthur* XVIII. xxv, Euery lusty herte that is in ony maner a louer spryngeth and floryssheth in lusty dedes. **1526** *Pilgr. Perf.* (W. de W. 1531) 74 Flourysshe the forenoone neuer so fresshe, at the last commeth the euentyde. *a* **1586** *Satir. Poems Reform.* xxxvii. 68 Bakbyttaris..flwreis sone, but forder fructe þai faill. **1611** BIBLE *Isa.* lxvi. 14 Your bones shall flourish like an herbe.

2. *gen.* To thrive. **a.** Of persons: To prosper, do well.

a **1340** HAMPOLE *Psalter* Cant. 518 Whare ere þai now all bicumyn þat florysst in þis warlde? **1572** FORREST *Theophilus* 697 in *Anglia* VII, Florishinge more then anye queene heere. **1670** R. COKE *Disc. Trade* 60 We flourish in the French Trade. **1704** NELSON *Compan. Festiv. & Fasts* xxiv.

255 Bad Men as frequently prosper and flourish. **1833** Ht. Martineau *Brooke Farm* iii. 31 Men who were starving on land of their own, are now flourishing on the wages I give them. **1874** L. Stephen *Hours in Libr.* (1892) I. vi. 233 Tartufe..flourishes and thrives.

b. Of things (e.g. art, science, an institution): To attain full development; to be prosperous or successful, be in vogue; to have many followers or patrons.

c **1400** *Rom. Rose* 6233 Men may in secular clothes see Florisshen holy religioun. **1504** Atkynson tr. *De Imitatione* I. xviii. 166 The holy sayntes..in whom florysshed the perfeccyon of all relygyon. **1571** Digges *Pantom., Math. Disc.* Pref. Tj, Where such sciences firste tooke their originall, and in what languages and countreys they chieflye florished. **1649** Bp. Reynolds *Hosea* v. 47 The way for the church to prosper and florish. **1754** Sherlock *Disc.* (1759) I. iv. 144 When Science flourished in the East. **1885** *Law Times* LXXIX. 130/1 The poor law system..has flourished for over three centuries.

†**3.** To thrive, display vigour *in, of, with* (something specified); also, to abound *in*, overflow *with*.

a **1300** *Cursor M.* 21222 (Cott.) Barnabas..In vertuz florisand sa fele. *c* **1380** Wyclif *Serm.* Sel. Wks. I. 96 Men þat shulden florishe in vertues. **1530** Lyndesay *Test. Papyngo* 795 Those dayis quhen so thay [the Prelatis] flurisit in fame. **1559** W. Cunningham *Cosmogr. Glasse* 175 Cambridge, a Universitie florishing with al kind of good letters. **1628** Hobbes *Thucyd.* (1822) 1 They flourished..in all manner of provision. **1660** F. Brooke tr. *Le Blanc's Trav.* Ded. Aij, An age that flourishes with Pens, and Criticks. **1726** Leoni *Alberti's Archit.* II. 4/1 Greece..flourishing in excellent geniusses.

4. To be at the height of fame or excellence; to be in one's bloom or prime. Also in weaker sense, used in pa. t. of a person to indicate that his life and activity belong to a specified period (cf. floruit).

1387 Trevisa *Higden* (Rolls) IV. 173 In his tyme Plautus Latinus..florischeþ at Rome. **1550** Veron *Godly Sayings* Aij, Origene..did florysshe in the yere of our lorde cc.lxi. **1661** Bramhall *Just Vind.* i. 3 His most renowned Ancestours..flourished whilest Popery was in its Zenith. **1700** Dryden *Pref. Fables* (Globe) 494 Spenser and Fairfax both flourished in the reign of Queen Elizabeth. **1820** W. Irving *Sketch Bk.* I. 189 James flourished nearly about the time of Chaucer and Gower. **1855** Tennyson *Brook* 11 In our schoolbooks we say, Of those that held their heads above the crowd, They flourish'd then or then.

II. To adorn.

†**5.** *trans.* To adorn with flowers or verdure; to cause to bloom or thrive.

a **1300** *Cursor M.* 16860 (Cott.) Þe rode it was wit leif and barc florist ful selcuthli. **1375** Barbour *Bruce* xvi. 69 Feldis florist ar with flowris. *c* **1430** Lydg. *Min. Poems* (Percy Soc.) 78 God..Hath florisshed the erthe on every side..Withe grete habundaunce of vyridite. **1500–20** Dunbar *Poems* xlvi. 21 Fresche Flora hes flurest every spray. **1716** Fenton *Ode to Ld. Gower* Poems (1717) 219 With shadowy verdure flourish'd high, A sudden youth the Groves enjoy.

fig. **1470–85** Malory *Arthur* xviii. xxv, Lete euery man of worship florysshe his herte in this world. *c* **1614** J. Davies *Scourge of Folly* To Earle Pembrooke, Wks. (Grosart) 52/1 But when the sonne of fauor shines on mee My May may then haue Might to flourish thee.

†**b.** *Cookery.* To ornament, garnish (a dish).

?*c* **1390** *Form of Cury* in Warner *Antiq. Culin.* 13 Take brede..Florish it with white coliandre in confyt. *c* **1430** *Two Cookery-bks.* i. 30 Florche it a-bouyn with Pome-garned. **1502** Arnolde *Chron.* (1811) 239 Storke roosted, pecoke florisshed, carpe in soppis.

†**6.** *gen.* To adorn, decorate, embellish, ornament. Also with *out, over, up. Obs.*

c **1325** *Coer de L.* 1842 Six stages ful of towrelles, Wel flourished with cornelles. ? *a* **1400** *Morte Arth.* 771 Hys feete ware floreschede alle in fyne sabylle. **1489–99** *Inscription Holloway Chapel, Widcome, nr. Bath* in Wood *Life* (O.H.S.) II. 409 Thys chapill floryschyd with formosyte spectabyll..prior Cantlow had edyfyd. **1581** Pettie *Guazzo's Civ. Conv.* iii. (1586) 125 Those which florish up themselves by arte. **1590** Greene *Never too late* Wks. (Grosart) VIII. 194 Her face full of chast colours: such as florish out the fronts of Dianas virgins. **1608** Topsell *Serpents* 738 Their skin seemeth to be flourished with certain pictures. **1611** Coryat *Crudities* 145 Sixe very precious sockets..flowrished ouer with a triple gilting. *a* **1716** South *Serm.* (1744) X. 56 This would make him begin to..try the foundation before he flourished the superstructure.

fig. **1377** Langl. *P. Pl.* B. xiv. 294 Þe fierthe [pouerte] is a fortune þat florissheth þe soule Wyth sobrete fram al synne. **1587** Fleming *Contn. Holinshed* III. 1323/1 Deceipt [sheweth] finest when he is cunninglie florished. **1603** Shaks. *Meas. for M.* iv. i. 75 The Iustice of your title to him Doth flourish the deceit.

b. To embellish or ornament (a book, writing, etc.) with 'flourishes' (see flourish *sb.* 4b). †In early use also: To illuminate; to adorn with colour or decorative designs of any kind. *Obs.*

c **1440** *Promp. Parv.* 167/2 Floryschen bokys, *floro*. **1573** *Art of Limming* 5 With this [turnesoll] you may flourishe redde letters, or vestures. **1679–88** *Secr. Serv. Money Chas. II & Jas. II* (Camden) 55 Gideon Roger, for writing and flourishing, partly in gold, a letter to the Emperor of Fez.

absol. **1660** *G. Tomlyn's Patent* No. 128 A way to text and flourish in velams and parchment.

†**7.** To embellish (a narration, etc.) with flowers of speech; to ornament or set off with fine words or phrases; to express in flowery language. *Obs.*

13.. *Minor P. fr. Vernon MS.* lii. 496 Þei3 þis tale beo florisshed with faire flour. **1494** Fabyan *Chron.* 3 So haue I nowe sette out this rude werke..That the lerned and the studyed clerke May..Flowrysshe it with Eloquence. **1540** Elyot *Image Gov.* Pref. (1556) 3 Desiryng more to make it playne to all readers, than to flourishe it with over muche eloquence. **1631** Shirley *Love in Maze* iii. iii, You have..Wanted no art to flourish your warm passion. **1678** Cudworth *Intell. Syst.* 63 Which Argument is further flourisht and descanted upon in this manner. **1691** G. D'Emilianne *Frauds Rom. Monks* 177 The Catechizer flourish'd his Discourse with Circumstances so extravagant [etc.].

b. *intr.* 'To use florid language; to speak with ambitious copiousness and elegance' (J.); to descant floridly *on* or *upon*. Also with *away*.

1700 T. Baker *Reflect. Learning* iv. (ed. 2) 32/2 Whilst he [Cicero] acts the part of the Rhetorician, he dilates and flourishes, and gives Example instead of Rule. **1725** Watts *Logic* iv. i. 518 They dilate sometimes, and flourish long upon little Incidents, and they skip over and but lightly touch the drier Part of their Theme. **1824** L. Murray *Eng. Gram.* (ed. 5) I. 435 They are often misled, by a desire of flourishing on the several properties of a metaphor. **1858** Gen. P. Thompson *Audi Alt.* II. lxxxi. 41 Another flourishes away upon the assertion that the French Emperor was chosen by the Ballot.

†**8.** *trans.* **a.** To lay (one tint) *upon* (another) by way of ornament; **b.** to work up ornamentally.

a **1592** Greene *Opharion* Wks. (Grosart) XII. 70 Touching the faultles mixture of vermillion flourisht vpon Iuory. *a* **1626** Bacon *War w. Spain* (1629) 3 Bottomes of threed close wound vp, which with a good needle..may be flourished into large workes.

III. To display ostentatiously.

9. To brandish (a weapon, etc.); to wave about by way of show or triumph. Also, to move (the limbs) vigorously.

1382 Wyclif *2 Macc.* xi. 8 An horsman apeeride goynge byfore hem..florishynge a shaft. **1388** —— *Ps.* vii. 13 If 3e ben not conuertid, he schal florische his swerd. **1592** Shaks. *Rom. & Jul.* i. i. 85 Old Mountague..flourishes his Blade in spight of me. **1646** Crashaw *Sospetto d'Herode* xxxiii, All the Powers of Hell in full applause Flourisht their snakes. **1820** Scott *Ivanhoe* II. iii. 45 Anon, balancing his expanded palms, he gently flourished them in time to the music. **1831** T. L. Peacock *Crotchet Castle* viii. 144 He began mechanically to flourish his bamboo. **1840** Dickens *Old C. Shop* xxi, Richard Swiveller..looking at the dwarf..as he flourished his arms and legs about.

†**b.** *absol. Obs.*

1588 Shaks. *Tit. A.* i. i. 311 Goe giue that changing peece, To him that flourisht for her with his sword. **1627–77** Feltham *Resolves* i. xxxviii. 63 Whosoever will jest, should be like him that flourishes at a show: he may turn his weapon any way. **1690** W. Walker *Idiomat. Anglo-Lat.*, To flourish is one thing, to fight another.

c. *intr.* Of a weapon (or the like): To be brandished or waved about.

1388 Wyclif *Job* xxxix. 23 A spere and scheeld schal florische. **1773** H. Luson in *Duncombe's Lett.* II. App. xlviii, All this while the cane kept flourishing over Jerry's head.

10. a. *trans.* To display, make a display or parade of. **b.** *intr.* 'To boast, brag' (J.); to talk big; to 'swagger', 'show off'; also with *about, off*. †**c.** To exhibit oneself conspicuously, make a flourish or parade. *Obs.*

a. *c* **1380** Wyclif *Sel. Wks.* III. 341 Summe florishen oþer names & seien þat he [the pope] is moost blissed fader. **1592** Greene *Disput.* 6 Your sugred words, that you florish rethorically like nettes to catch fooles. **1638** Sir T. Herbert *Trav.* (ed. 2) 93 He..florisht his colours in signe of victory, and as a call to Abdulchan to second him. **1755** Scott *Dict.*, To Flourish Colours [in military affairs] is to display them.

b. **1674** N. Fairfax *Bulk & Selv.* 159 If any man think to come flourishing off with this. **1699** Bentley *Phal.* Introd. 22 The Examiner, after he has cited this Scholiast on Aristophanes, thus flourishes. **1729** Swift *To Delany* Wks. 1755 III. ii. 233 To flourish o'er a cup of gin. **1816** J. Gilchrist *Philos. Etym.* p. xvii, Mr. Horne Tooke has flourished rather too much about Gothic and Saxon. **1866** Carlyle *Inaug. Addr.* 9 He goes flourishing about with them.

c. **1563** Foxe *A. & M.* 1710/1 All the other Ladies of the court florished in their brauerye. **1611** Bible *Song. Sol.* ii. 9 He looked forth at the window, shewing himself [*marg.* flourishing] through the lattice. **1750** Warburton *Julian* Wks. 1811 VIII. 192 A reverend Stole..came..into the possession of a notorious prostitute, who flourished with it on the public stage.

†**11. a.** *trans.* Of the sun: To shoot *out* (beams). **b.** *intr.* Of light. *Obs.*

1515 *Scot. Field* 427 in *Chetham Misc.* II, Phebus full faire florished out his beames. **1587** Golding *De Mornay* vi. 64 From thence there flourished a certeine holy brightnesse.

†**12.** *intr.* To move with a flourish; to make sweeping movements; 'to play in wanton and irregular motions' (J.). *Obs.*

1728 Pope *Dunc.* ii. 180 Impetuous spread The stream, and, smoaking, flourish'd o'er his head. **1735** Somerville *Chase* ii. 256 They're check'd—hold back with speed—on either Hand They flourish round.

†**13.** *Music* and *Fencing.* To give a short fanciful exhibition by way of exercise before the real performance. To play, with a flourish. Also quasi-*trans.* ***to flourish out*** (notes). *Obs.*

1552 Huloet, Florysh, as a maister of fence doth wt weapon, or a musitian in syngyng, *proludo*. **1718** *Freethinker* No. 15 ¶1 Musicians, before they begin to play, always flourish out some loose Notes. **1766** Goldsm. *Vic. W.* x, Instead..of finishing George's shirts, we now had them..flourishing upon catgut. **1810** James *Milit. Dict.*, To flourish..is to play some prelude or preparatory air without any settled rule.

b. Of trumpets: To sound a flourish or fanfare.

1588 Shaks. *Tit. A.* iv. ii. 49 Why do the Emperors trumpets flourish thus? **1706** Addison *Rosamond* i. iv, Trumpets flourish.

†**flourishable** ('flʌrɪʃəb(ə)l), *a. Obs.*$^{-1}$ [f. flourish *v.* + -able.] Adapted to flourish or make a display.

1614 T. Adams *Diuells Banket* iv. 141 Hee sets the countenance of continuance on them, which indeede are more fallible in their certaintie than flourishable in their brauerie.

flourished ('flʌrɪʃt), *ppl. a.* [f. flourish *v.* + -ed^{1}.]

†**1.** Adorned with flowers or verdure; *fig.* adorned with charms or virtues. *Obs.*

c **1350** *Will. Palerne* 2438 Þei..founden þan a fayr forest floriched ful þik. *c* **1400** Maundev. (Roxb.) xxxiii. 148 All þe tymes of þe 3ere er þaire gardynes flurisched and þaire mydews grene. *c* **1470** Harding *Chron.* xiv. vii, Bothe two dyed in their floreshed youthede. **1508** Dunbar *Tua mariit wemen* 27 Faceis..All full of flurist fairheid, as flouris in June. *a* **1605** Montgomerie *Misc. Poems* xix. 3 Gathring flours..Amidst the florisht meid.

†**b.** Of the brow: Adorned with clustering hair.

c **1400** *Rowland & O.* 82 With a florschede thonwange, Oure noble kynge þat es so strange, His doghety men I-melle.

c. *Her.* = fleury.

1486 *Bk. St. Albans, Her.* Ej a, They be calde florishit: for they be made bi ye maner of a flowre deluce. **1830** in Robson *Brit. Her.* III. Gloss., *Flourished*, the same as *fleury*.

†**2.** Of words: Of a flowery character; rhetorically arranged. *Obs.*

1303 R. Brunne *Handl. Synne* 3066 Flourshede wurdys..Are ful of pryde and trechery. *c* **1380** Wyclif *Wks.* (1880) 445 Þey [false freris] deprauen hem to þer parischens bi florizshid wordis þat þey bringen yn.

3. Decorated with flourishes or ornamental lines and tracery, or with figures in colours, embroidery, etc.; figured.

c **1400** *Rowland & O.* 281 Men..That wele kon feghte with floresched swerde [orig. *espee forbie*]. **1446–7** *Eton Coll. Acc.* in Willis & Clark *Cambridge* (1886) I. 394 Pro xxiiij pedibus vitri operati vocati florisshed glasse. **1563** *Homilies* ii. *Agst. Excess Apparel* (1859) 315 To see his wife in such painted and flourished visages. **1678** *Lond. Gaz.* No. 1265/4 One Silver Plate..marked with the Cipher E.G. flourished. **1758** Johnson *Idler* No. 13 ¶8 We have..three flourished quilts for every bed. **1792** Mrs. C. Smith *Desmond* II. 268 His wife put on..a fine flourished shawl. **1885** D. W. Kettle *Pens, Ink, & Paper* 65 The Flourished Printed headings to Deeds.

flourisher ('flʌrɪʃə(r)). [f. as prec. + -er^{1}.] One who or that which flourishes.

1387 Trevisa *Higden* (Rolls) I. 7 Faire florischers and hi3teres of wordes and of metre. **1435** Misyn *Fire of Love* 102 Florischars of þis warld, to qwhome temperall prosperite þou gyfs. **1491** in *York Myst.* Introd. 39 Luminers, turners, and florisschers. **1598** Florio, *Gladiatore*, a fencer or flourisher with his weapon. *c* **1611** Chapman *Iliad* xxiii. 689 Not our greatest flourisher can equall him in powre Of foote-strife, but Æacides. **1617** *Wardens' Acc.* in Heath *Grocers' Comp.* (1869) 429 John Bradshawe..and 18 fellow florishers with long swordes. **1624** Gataker *Transubst.* 233 So far is it from that which this flourisher affirmeth, that [etc.]. *a* **1734** North *Life F. North* (1742) 332 He was not an Orator, as commonly understood, that is a Flourisher. **1833** Marryat *P. Simple* xvii, Our..frigates have names as long as the main-top bowling..fine flourishers.

flourishing ('flʌrɪʃɪŋ), *vbl. sb.* [f. as prec. + -ing^{1}.]

1. The action of the vb. flourish in various senses.

1303 R. Brunne *Handl. Synne* 881 Every 3ere at þe florysyngge When þe vynys shulde sprynngge. **1387** Trevisa *Higden* (Rolls) I. 15 Nou3t sotilte of sentence, noþer faire florischynge of wordes. **1577** B. Googe *Heresbach's Husb.* ii. (1586) 83b, It must be digged before his florishing, or shooting out of his leaves. **1580** Hollyband *Treas. Fr. Tong., Regratement de vieilles choses*..the flourishing vp of old things. **1687** T. W. tr. *Hen. VIII's Assertio Septem Sacram.* (1688) 8 These two Chapters..are..but the flourishings or first essays of Luther, who now begins to murther and destroy the Sacraments. **1717** Berkeley *Tour Italy* Wks. 1871 IV. 531 Before the flourishing of arts in Rome. **1865** Trollope *Belton Est.* viii. 83 With some little flourishing at the commencement, Captain Aylmer made his speech.

2. In various *concr.* or quasi-*concr.* senses. †**a.** Blossom, also *fig.* **b.** A decoration, an embellishment; a flower-like design. **c.** *nonce-use.* An ornamental covering.

a. *a* **1300** *Cursor M.* 10726 (Gött) Þis wand suld florisching bere. **1500–20** Dunbar *Poems* lxxxv. 13 Haile, 3hyng, benyng, fresche flurising! [Virgin Mary; but perh. *ppl. a.*].

b. *c* **1384** Chaucer *H. Fame* iii. 211 Hit nedeth noght yow for to tellen..Of this yates florisshinges, Ne of compasses, ne of kervinges. **1611** Cotgr. s.v. *Draperie*, A flourishing with leaues, and flowers in wood, or stone, vsed especially on the heads of pillers. **1613** T. Godwin *Roman Antiq.* (1658) 28 Bestudded with flourishings of purple silk. **1665** Pepys *Diary* 26 Dec., Some fine writing-work and flourishing. **1847** C. Winston *Anc. Glass Paint.* I. 125 Many attempts were made to strengthen the shadows..in representations of architecture with a flourishing of thin lines.

c. **1633** P. Fletcher *Purple Isl.* ii. xviii, Cover'd..with silken flourishing, Which as it oft decaies, renews again.

3. = fumishing. *rare*$^{-1}$.

1726 *Dict. Rusticum* (ed. 3) s.v. *Hart-hunting*, He may observe his flourishings, which are in proportion to the Beast.

4. *attrib.* and *Comb.*, as ***flourishing hand***; **flourishing thread** (see quot.).

1713 STEELE *Guardian* No. 1 ¶1 Mr. Airs, that excellent penman..instructs the youth of this nation to arrive at a flourishing hand. **1882** CAULFIELD & SAWARD *Dict. Needlework, Flourishing Thread*, a flat, silky, linen thread specially adapted for mending Damask, Linen, [etc.].

flourishing ('flʌrɪʃɪŋ), *ppl. a.* [f. as prec. + -ING^2.] That flourishes.

1. Budding or blossoming; hence, that grows vigorously or luxuriantly. Of a landscape: Verdant.

c **1400** MAUNDEV. (1839) v. 54 The Gardyn is alweys grene and florisshing. **1535** COVERDALE *Ecclus.* xiv. 18 All flesh shal fade awaye..like a florishinge leaf in a grene tre. **1647** COWLEY *Mistress, Tree* i, The flourishingst Tree in all the Park. **1783** COWPER *Rose* ii, The buds it had left..On the flourishing bush where it grew. **1883** R. ZIMMERMANN in *Athenæum* 29 Dec. 847/2 Populous towns and flourishing landscapes.

2. Prosperous, thriving, conspicuous, eminent.

a **1340** HAMPOLE *Psalter* ix. 20 Thorgh him be þai put in tyll synn in þi syght, þof þai seme florischand bifor men. **1535** STEWART *Chron. Scot.* II. 156 Occa..Wyss into weir and fluresand in fame. **1697** DAMPIER *Voy.* I. 179 This is a flourishing City. **1741** MIDDLETON *Cicero* I. I. 18 Hortensius, the most florishing young Orator at the bar. **1855** MACAULAY *Hist. Eng.* III. 615 Belfast has become one of the greatest and most flourishing seats of industry in the British isles.

3. Vigorous; in the bloom of youth or health. Also in weakened or trivial use. †***flourishing age, years***: the prime of life.

1562 WINȜET *Cert. Tract.* iii. Wks. 1888 I. 23 That maist flurissand part of my aige, spent in the teching of the grammar scule. **1564** BULLEYN *Dial. agst. Pest.* To Rdr. (1888) 3 Some are preuented by death in their flourishyng yeres. *a* **1568** COVERDALE *Bk. Death* III. x. 296 The thirde [dieth] in his florishynge youth. **1600** W. VAUGHAN *Direct. Health* (1633) 23 It [Meath] will cause one to haue a flourishing colour. **1737** WHISTON *Josephus' Wars* VI. ix. §2 They slew the aged..but..those..in their flourishing age ..they drove them together into the temple. **1855** GEO. ELIOT *Let.* 7 May (1954) II. 201, I am extremely well and jolly..I hope you are all equally flourishing. **1942** N. BALCHIN *Darkness falls from Air* i. 9 He said, 'How's Marcia?'..I just said, 'Oh, flourishing.'

4. Of writing: Ornamented with flourishes.

1859 SALA *Gas-light & D.* iii. 37 As per flourishing gold letters on his door-jamb, he proposes to lend money.

5. Of style, etc.: Florid, highly embellished, grandiloquent, high sounding. Also of a writer: Addicted to floridness.

1538 LELAND *Itin.* I. p. xix, Men of Eloquence hath not enterprised to set them forthe yn a florisching style. **1592** G. HARVEY *Pierce's Super.* Wks. (Grosart) II. 252 An irrefragable Confutation of Beza, and our floorishingest New-writers. **1788** MAD. D'ARBLAY *Diary* June, He..spoke in flourishing terms of its contrast to former times.

6. Of persons and their actions: Boasting, swaggering, ostentatious.

1616 *Rich Cabinet* 57 All sorts of people thought it the greatest glory to liue in the florishingest shewe. **1688** WOOD *Life* 8 Dec. (O.H.S.) III. 287 A conceited flurishing coxcomb.

†**7.** Of a spear: Vibrating. *Obs.*

1388 WYCLIF *Job* xli. 20 He schal scorne a florischynge [1382 shakende] spere.

flourishingly ('flʌrɪʃɪŋlɪ), *adv.* [f. prec. + -LY^2.] In a flourishing manner. †**a.** In the shape of a flower (*obs.*). **b.** Vigorously, prosperously. †**c.** In flowery terms, floridly (*obs.*). †**d.** Ostentatiously, showily (*obs.*). **e.** With a flourish or flourishing movement.

a. 1486 *Bk. St. Albans, Her.* E j a, The forsayd letill barris ar othyrwyle made florishyngli.

b. 1609 W. M. *Man in Moone* (1849) 20 (Percy Soc.) Swaggering drunkards or swearing Jackes, which have thus flourishingly sprowted up by service. **1819** *Ann. Reg.* 36 We were going on flourishingly. **1879** STEVENSON *Trav. Cevennes* 196 Such as they have are hardy plants and thrive flourishingly.

c. 1580 BARET *Alv.* E 163 To vtter his mind eloquently, flourishingly, & finely. **1647** tr. *Malvezzi's Pourtract* 3 The Actions of Predecessours..require no more then to bee flourishingly related.

d. 1550 BALE *Image Both Ch.* II. xvii, She..is florishinglye decked with golde, preciouse stone, and pearles.

e. 1825 *Blackw. Mag.* XVII. 363 Round which the lash.. had so flourishingly played its..gambols. **1832** J. WILSON *ibid.* XXXI. 272, I came down waveringly..flourishingly, just as you have seen a lark from sky to furrow.

†'**flourishly**, *adv. Obs.* In 6 floryschelye. [f. FLOURISH *v.* + -LY^2.] In a flourishing manner, pre-eminently.

1558 FORREST *Grysilde Sec.* (1875) 146 Theis..sightes.. In Grisild weare seene florische floryschelye.

flourishment ('flʌrɪʃmənt). [f. FLOURISH + -MENT. OF. had *florissement.*] The state or condition of flourishing; prosperity, thriving.

1724 WELTON *Chr. Faith & Pract.* 375 The flourishment of a city. **1883** *Chicago Advance* 24 May, It cannot be claimed that..churches or schools had much flourishment.

flourishy ('flʌrɪʃɪ), *a.* [f. FLOURISH *sb.* + -Y^1.] Of or pertaining to flourishes or flourishing; of the nature of a flourish; abounding in flourishes.

1883 G. H. BOUGHTON in *Harper's Mag.* Feb. 392/2 When a windmilly town does flourish, it is (from a flourishy point of view) a thing to remember. **1884** *Ibid.* Sept. 523/2 There is a light, flourishy, courtly touch. **1891** *Longm. Mag.* Apr. 626 A big bill with a flourishy heading.

flourless ('flaʊəlɪs), *a.* [f. FLOUR *sb.* + -LESS.] Made without flour.

1880 VERN. LEE *Belcaro* iv. 79 Flourless bread.

floury ('flaʊərɪ), *a.* Also 6 flowry. [f. FLOUR *sb.* + -Y^1.] **a.** Of or pertaining to flour. †Of grain: Yielding flour. **b.** Covered or sprinkled with flour or powder. **c.** Resembling flour; flourlike, mealy, powdery.

a. 1591 SYLVESTER *Du Bartas* I. iv. 649 The stone which grinds the floury corns. **1870** MORRIS *Earthly Par.* IV. 296 A mill..whose floury duskiness Our hungry souls with many a hope did bless.

b. 1826 HOOD *Irish Schoolm.* xxix, Some dronish Dominie ..That wears a floury head. **1884** *Century Mag.* XXVIII. 88 There was blood upon her floury apron.

c. 1830 LINDLEY *Nat. Syst. Bot.* 171 Embryo surrounding floury albumen. **1865** MILTON & CHEADLE *N.W. Pass. by Land* 157 A sleigh, running along in the soft, floury powder at the sides. **1888** POWLES tr. *Kick's Flour Manuf.* App. §4. 283 Steam the peeled potatoes until they become quite floury ('mealy').

d. floury miller, *Abricta curvicosta*, an Australian cicada whose body is covered with white down.

1904 *Proc. Linn. Soc. N.S.W.* XXIX. 600 This is a common species in the neighbourhood of Sydney in mid-summer, and is known as the 'Floury Miller' on account of the quantity of silvery pubescence covering the body, which makes it look as though it had been dusted with flour. **1925** *Illustr. Austral. Encycl.* I. 269/1 Well-known species [of cicadas] are the Red-eye..and the Floury Miller.., both names well describing the insect's appearance. **1970** T. E. WOODWARD et al. in *Insects of Australia* (C.S.I.R.O.) xxvi. 413/1 Many striking cicadas occur in Australia... Among these are the 'double drummer', *Thopha saccata* (F.), the 'floury miller', *Abricta curvicosta* Germ., and the 'green Monday', *Cyclochila australasiae* (Don.).

flouse, floush (flaʊs, flaʊʃ), *v. dial.* [? onomatopœic; cf. FLUSH *v*^{2}]

1. To splash. *trans.* and *intr.*

1567 MAPLEY *Gr. Forest* 21 I haue seene it..when as this kinde of Mettall being molten in the pit, and but a sponefull of water being cast into, it hath floushed and leapt vp to the top of the house. **1838** HOLLOWAY *Dict. Provinc.*, *Floush*, to plash and beat water about with violence as boys frequently do when bathing. **1885** *N. & Q.* 26 Sept. Ser. VI. XII. 249.

2. *intr.* To come with a heavy splash.

1863 KINGSLEY *Water-bab.* 95 Out floushed a huge, old brown trout.

3. The verb stem used adverbially.

1819 MOORE *Tom Crib's Mem.* (ed. 3) 13 Old Georgy went floush, and his backers look'd shy.

Hence '**flousing** *ppl. a.*

1880 JEFFERIES *Gr. Ferne F.* 64 The flousing splash of the mill-race.

flout (flaʊt), *sb.*^{1} Also 6–7 floute. [f. FLOUT *v.*]

1. A mocking speech or action; a piece of mockery, jeer, scoff.

1570 in LEVINS *Manip.* 228. **1572–5** GASCOIGNE *Dan Bartholomew* Lenuoye iv, Remember that our sect Is sure to bee with floutes alwayes infect. **1678** BUTLER *Hud.* III. Heroic Ep. 356 She..read it out, With many a smile, and learing Flout. **1728** MORGAN *Algiers* I. Pref. 14 The Flouts and indifferent Reception I have met with. **1837** W. IRVING *Capt. Bonneville* III. 23 Blinking like an owl in daylight, when pestered by the flouts and peckings of mischievous birds. **1859** TENNYSON *Idylls, Enid* 1523 Who put your beauty to this flout and scorn By dressing it in rags.

†**2.** An object of flouting or mockery. *Obs.*

1708 tr. *Boileau's Lutrin* 52 Howlet will be the Word, a standing Jest, The Flout of Boys, and Mirth of Every Feast.

†**flout**, *sb.*^{2} *Obs. rare.* A truss (of straw.)

15.. *Kyng & Hermyt* 331 in Hazl. *E.E.P.* I. 25 Be syde my bed thou must goo And take up a floute of strowe, Als softly as thou may. **1847** in HALLIWELL.

†**flout**, *sb.*^{3} *Obs.* [? repr. OE. **flówet*, f. *flówan* to FLOW.] A watercourse.

14.. in *MS. Cantab. Ff.* v. 48 f. 106 (Halliw.) And at a window cast him owt, Riȝt into Temse flowt. **1583** *Inquisition in Lincolnsh.* (N.), One sewer in Scotterings at the ould flout shall be sufficiently diked.

flout (flaʊt), *v.* Also 6 floute, 6–7 flowte. [First recorded in 16th c.; possibly special use (preserved in some dialect) of *floute*, ME. form of FLUTE *v.* to play on the flute. Cf. a similar development of sense in Du. *fluiten* to play the flute, to mock, deride.]

1. *trans.* To mock, jeer, insult; to express contempt for, either in word or action. Also ***to flout*** (a person) ***out of*** (something).

1551 ROBINSON tr. *More's Utop.* (Arb.) 26 In moste spitefull maner mockynge..and flowtinge them. **1605** SHAKS. *Macb.* I. ii. 49 Where the Norweyan Banners flowt the Skie. **1607** HEYWOOD *Wom. Kilde* Wks. 1874 II. 116 Now will I flout her poverty. **1612–15** BP. HALL *Contempl. O.T.* I. v, Yet cannot they all flout Noah out of his faith. **1727** DE FOE *Syst. Magic* II. iv. 324 So the man was flouted on all hands. **1805** SCOTT *Last Minstr.* II. 4 The gay beams of lightsome day Gild, but to flout, the ruins gray. **1840** DICKENS *Old. C. Shop* xxxii, The genuine and only Jarley.. flouted by beadles. **1873** DIXON *Two Queens* I. II. ii. 80 One town grew jealous of another..Granada flouted Loga.

†**b.** To quote or recite with sarcastic purpose.

1599 SHAKS. *Much Ado* I. i. 290 Ere you flout old ends any further, examine your conscience.

2. *intr.* To behave with disdain or contumely, to mock, jeer, scoff; to express contempt either by action or speech. Also *dial.* to scold. Const. *at*; whence in *indirect passive*.

1575 R. B. *Appius & V.* B j b, What drake nosed driuell, begin you to floute. **1641** *Vind. Smectymnuus* 31 It never came into our thoughts..to flout, in so bold a manner. **1678** BARCLAY *Apol. Quakers* ii. § 1. 19 Some are apt to flout at it as ridiculous. **1726** *Adv. Capt. R. Boyle* 166 But I have the good Fortune not to be flouted at. **1844** BROWNING *Garden Fancies* I. vi, Ah, you may flout and turn up your faces. **1876** BESANT & RICE *Gold. Butterfly* iv, The women pointed and flouted at her.

¶**3.** ? *erroneous use* (or ? *another word*). To ruffle (a bird's feathers).

1875 MAYNE REID in *Chamb. Jrnl.* 7 Aug. 500 Not enough, breeze..to flout the long feathers in the tail of the..bird.

Hence '**flouted** *ppl. a.*

1855 SINGLETON *Æneid* VII. 602 Go now, to thankless jeopardy Expose thee, flouted [wight].

†'**floutage.** *Obs.* [f. FLOUT *v.* + -AGE.] The habit or practice of flouting; mockery, jeers.

1599 B. JONSON *Ev. Man out of Hum.* Dram. Pers., Puntarvolo, so palpably affected to his owne praise, that (for want of flatterers) he commends himselfe to the floutage of his owne family.

flouter ('flaʊtə(r)). [f. as prec. + -ER^1.] One who flouts or mocks.

1581 PETTIE *Guazzo's Civ. Conv.* I. (1586) 35 You..shew yourselfe a flatterer and a flouter. **1621** BURTON *Anat. Mel.* Democr. to Rdr. 64 Democritus that common flowter of folly. **1755** in JOHNSON. **1869** BLACKMORE *Lorna D.* xxvi, Perhaps she had cast me away altogether as a flouter.

flouting ('flaʊtɪŋ), *vbl. sb.* [f. as prec. + -ING^1.]

1. The action of the vb. FLOUT; an instance of this.

1574 WHITGIFT *Def. Aunsw.* II. i. §6. 91 What gybing and flouting would there be. **1621** MOLLE *Camerar. Liv. Libr.* v. xv. 382 A desperate impudencie, seconded with bloodie floutings, with terrible despightings, [etc.]. **1691** RAY *Creation* II. (1704) 453 Flouting, and Taunting, are to be censured as vicious Abuses of Speech. **1884** *Bath Herald* 25 Oct. 3/1 The second flouting of the popular will.

2. *Comb.* †**flouting-stock**, (*a*) a butt for flouting, an object of mockery; (*b*) = FLOUT *sb.* (perh. the use is a blunder ascribed to the Welsh speaker).

1592 G. HARVEY *Pierce's Super.* Wks. (Grosart) II. 309 Lesse peraduenture..thou be..made a notable flowting-stocke. **1598** SHAKS. *Merry W.* IV. v. 83 You are wise, and full of gibes, and vlouting-stocks. **1817** W. GODWIN *Mandeville* I. 263, I was..a flouting-stock and a make-game ..created for no other end than to be the scoff of my fellows.

flouting ('flaʊtɪŋ), *ppl. a.* [f. as prec. + -ING^2.] That flouts.

1581 PETTIE *Guazzo's Civ. Conv.* I. (1586) 30 b, Insinuating therby in flouting manner, that he might be his Fathers bastard sonne. **1597** FENTON *Let.* 23 May in Harington *Nugæ Ant.* (1779) II. 233 She would..out with all such ungracious flouting wenches. **1614** N. BRETON *I would & yet* cxxv, Then sure should I..Be followed with many a flowting-Iacke. **1727** DE FOE *Hist. Appar.* xiii. 329 A flouting atheistic man of wit. **1870** *Pall Mall G.* 23 Nov. 12 Less of..flouting ferocity than is usual in the epic tales of the Scandinavians.

Hence '**floutingly** *adv.* in a flouting manner.

1580 HOLLYBAND *Treas. Fr. Tong.*, *Par gaudisserie*, in iest, or floutingly. **1633** BP. HALL *Hard Texts, N.T.* 55 They floutingly put upon his head a wreath of thornes. **1858** CARLYLE *Fredk. Gt.* (1865) I. III. xiv. 228 'Goody Palsgrave' as her Mother floutingly called her.

flow (fləʊ), *sb.*^{1} [f. FLOW *v.*]

1. a. The action or fact of flowing; movement in a current or stream; an instance or mode of this. Orig. said of liquids, but extended in modern use to all fluids, as air, electricity, etc. †Phrase: *to set* (*the eyes*) *at flow*: to (cause to) weep. Also 'The course or direction of running waters' (Admiral Smyth).

a **1450** *Cov. Myst.* (Shaks. Soc.) 43 Thei xul not drede the flodys fflowe. **1607** SHAKS. *Timon* II. ii. 172 I haue..set mine eyes at flow. **1613** —— *Hen. VIII* I. i. 152 This top proud fellow, Whom from the flow of gall I name not. **1817** SHELLEY *Rev. Islam* XII. xxxvii. 5 In the flow Of sudden tears. **1856** MRS. CARLYLE *Lett.* II. 290 A gentle sound..like the flow of a brook. **1860** TYNDALL *Glac.* II. xxv. 362 The gentle flow of a current of air. **1885** WATSON & BURBURY *Math. Th. Electr. & Magn.* I. 208 A flow of positive electricity in the one direction along the wire.

b. *Physics.*

line of flow in *Hydrodynamics*, an imaginary curve so drawn within a liquid at any instant that at each point of the curve the instantaneous velocity of the liquid is along the tangent. In general a line of flow is not the path of a particle, but varies with the time. But when the motion is steady, i.e. not a function of the time, the lines of flow are fixed, and are paths of particles, being then called *stream-lines*. ***tube of flow*** in *Electricity* and *Hydrodynamics*, an imaginary tube bounded by surfaces across which there is no flow.

1881 MAXWELL *Electr. & Magn.* I. 378 Tube of Flow. **1882** MINCHIN *Unipl. Kinemat.* 150 We can in this way map out the whole region by drawing lines of flow.

c. The quantity that flows, volume of fluid. In *Hydrodynamics*, the volume of fluid which flows through a tube of any given section in a unit of time.

1807 *Med. Jrnl.* XXI. 378 Blood, which came out, with a jet, nearly equal to the flow of urine. **1851** CARPENTER *Man. Phys.* (ed. 2) 218 The flow of blood into them [Muscles] increases with the use that is made of them. **1877** W. H. BESANT *Hydromech.* (ed. 3) 238 The line-integral of the

tangential velocity along any line, lying entirely within the fluid, is called the flow along that line.

d. *concr.* That which flows; flowing water. Also, a mass of matter that moves or has moved in a stream.

1802 CAMPBELL *Hohenlinden* i, Dark as winter was the flow Of Iser, rolling rapidly. **1816** J. WILSON *City of Plague* I. i, The sunshine dances in its joy O'er the still flow of this majestic river. **1833** LYELL *Princ. Geol.* II. 240 Reiterated flows of lava. **1880** MISS BIRD *Japan* II. 152 The flows from the flank and summit craters of the Mauna Loa.

e. A gradual deformation of a solid (as rock or a metal) under stress in which it suffers a permanent change in shape without fracture or loss of cohesion between its parts.

1889 *Bull. U.S. Geol. Surv.* No. 55. 68 The elaborate and exhaustive series of experiments made by Henri Tresca on 'the Flow of Solids'. **1897** *Geol. Mag.* Nov. 513 Some Experiments on the Flow of Rocks. *Ibid.* 514 The conditions of pressure to which the marble is subjected are those in the 'zone of flow' of the earth's crust. **1932** F. F. GROUT *Petrography* VII. 402 The visible deformation of rocks near the surface of the earth is mostly by fracturing and only in very weak rocks, such as clays, by flow. **1959** A. G. GUY *Elem. Physical Metall.* (ed. 2) ix. 322 We might expect plastic flow to begin when the maximum shear stress reaches a certain value. **1965** A. HOLMES *Princ. Physical Geol.* (ed. 2) viii. 170 Slate is thus an example of a rock on which a new 'grain' has been impressed—partly by the mechanical effects of flow, partly by the growth of new minerals which have similarly accommodated themselves to the direction of flow. **1971** M. J. MANJOINE in H. Liebowitz *Fracture* III. iv. 275 In polycrystalline materials, the initiation and propagation of fracture are usually preceded or accompanied by plastic flow, even though this flow may be small.

2. Of dress, outlines, etc.: The manner of flowing.

1840 DICKENS *Barn. Rudge* xxxi, No dress but hers had such a flow as that. **1851** RUSKIN *Stones Ven.* (1874) I. App. 393 In the folds of the drapery..is a flow like that of waves.

3. a. *transf.* and *fig.* Any continuous movement resembling the even flow of a river and connoting a copious supply; an outpouring or stream; *esp.* of speech.

1641 J. JACKSON *True Evang. T.* III. 201 Without any flow of words to greaten it. **1733** POPE *Hor. Sat.* II. i. 128 The Feast of Reason and the Flow of Soul. **1775** PRATT *Liberal Opin.* (1783) I. 3 It is..hard to stop the pen, when the ideas are on the flow. **1782** T. A. MANN in *Lett. Lit. Men* (Camden) 420 The rupture with France..has thrown..a flow of Commerce into this Country. **1790** COWPER *On my Mother's Picture* 65 Thy constant flow of love, that knew no fall. **1796** JANE AUSTEN *Pride & Prej.* xxxi, They conversed with so much spirit and flow as to draw the attention of Lady Catherine. **1812** CHALMERS *Let.* in *Life* (1851) I. 296 We have had a flow of forenoon callers. **1832** HT. MARTINEAU *Hill & Valley* iv. 50 This vast flow of capital towards one point. **1873** BLACK *Pr. Thule* (1874) 22 This flow of talk. **1891** *Pall Mall G.* 18 Nov. 2/1 The cross flows of traffic.

b. = *honey-flow*.

1951 E. CRANE *Dict. Beekeeping Terms* 22 Main flow. Miellée principale. Haupttracht. **1952** H. MACE *Beekeeper's Man.* xvi. 87 In summers of continued drought, clover is soon over on light soil and the flow may not continue more than two or three weeks. **1953** R. GRAVES *Poems* 21 In the red West, Where bees come thronging to the apple flow.

4. The incoming or rise of the tide. Opposed to *ebb*; often in phrase *ebb and flow*; see EBB *sb.*[1]

1583 GREENE *Mamillia* Wks. (Grosart) II. 39 The greatest flowe hath the soonest ebbe. **1597** DANIEL *Civ. Wars* Wks. (1717) II. 41 The Ocean all at Discord with his Bounds, Reiterates his strange untimely Flows. **1618** BOLTON *Florus* II. viii. (1636) 118 A..sea having many ebbs & flowes. **1794** BURNS *Song,* '*Let not woman*' iii, Ocean's ebb, and ocean's flow. **1812** SOUTHEY *Omniana* I. 139 The flow drove him upon shore. **1886** RUSKIN *Præterita* I. vi. 177 The Thames tide, with its tossing wherries at the flow, and stranded barges at ebb.

fig. **1596** SHAKS. *1 Hen. IV*, I. ii. 43. **1627–77** FELTHAM *Resolves* I. xi. 16 We know not in the flows of our contentedness, what we ourselves are. **1758** S. HAWARD *Serm.* Introd. 9 The flows of affliction. **1865** FARRAR *Chapters on Lang.* 270 Great ebbs and flows in the tide of Jewish thought. **1870** [see EBB *sb.* 2.]

5. †**a.** A deluge, flood (*obs.*). **b.** An overflowing; applied *esp.* to the periodical overflow of the Nile, or similar phenomena.

a **1450** *Cov. Myst.* (Shaks. Soc.) 345, I am Abraham.. That reyned after Noes flowe. **1571** CAMPION *Hist. Irel.* II. x. (1633) 138 A flowe will shake your building. **1606** SHAKS. *Ant. & Cl.* II. vii. 20 They take the flow o' th' Nyle By certain scales i' th' Pyramid. **1725** POPE *Odyss.* IV. 100 Regions fatten'd with the flows of Nile. **1852** EARP *Gold Col. Australia* 48 The natives look to this periodical flow with as much anxiety as the Egyptians to that of the Nile.

6. ***flow of spirits***: **a.** in early use, a sudden access of cheerfulness or exhilaration; **b.** now chiefly (cf. sense 3) a habitual state of spontaneous cheerfulness.

1715–6 POPE *Let. to Blount* Wks. 1824 VIII. 359 As an unblemished conscience and inflexible resolution are above an accidental flow of spirits, or a sudden tide of blood. **1775** SHERIDAN *Duenna* II. ii, My joy..has given me such a flow of spirits. **18..** SCOTT *Let.*, No creature can be entitled to reckon upon such a flow of spirits and regular continuation of good health. **1834** *West Ind. Sketch-bk.* i. 252 A remarkable flow of animal spirits and activity.

7. *Porcelain Manufacture.* A flux for causing the colours to 'flow' or blend in firing.

1878 JEWITT *Ceramic Art* II. viii. 380 This effect was afterwards imitated..by means of what is technically called a 'flow'—that is, by introducing a little volatilising salt in the saggar in which the ware is placed and fired.

†**8.** A flowing or full-bottomed wig. *Obs.*

1755 *Connoisseur* No. 77 ¶5 Young counsellers..in a smart tye between a bob and a flow, contrived to cover a toupee. **1756** *Ibid.* No. 110 ¶2 In Queen Anne's reign..the nobility..wore large flaxen flows of thirty guineas price.

9. *attrib.* and *Comb.*, as ***flow pattern***, ***-rate***; **flow-blue**, a blue colour applied to pottery or porcelain which diffuses readily through the glaze; **flow chart**, a diagram showing the movement of goods, materials, or personnel in any complex system of activities (as an industrial plant) and the sequence of operations they perform or processes they undergo; also, a diagram in which conventional symbols show the sequence of actual or possible operations and decisions in a data-processing system or computer program, esp. one that is more detailed than a block diagram; hence ***flow(-)charting*** vbl. sb.; **flow diagram** = *flow chart*; **flow-dike**, an open channel to carry off surface water; **flow-function** = *velocity-function*; **flow** (*-off*) **-gate** (*Metallurgy*), an opening through which the molten metal is run out of the mould; **flow-line** (*a*) = *line of flow* (sense 1 b); (*b*) *pl.* [cf. F. *lignes d'écoulement*], the lines that appear on the surface of wrought metal when it is polished and etched, indicating the directions of flow and elongation of the metal during working; (*c*) (also *flowline*), any of the interrelated routes followed by goods, materials, etc., in passing through the various stages of manufacture or treatment; a route depicted on a flow chart; **flow(-line) production**, the continual passage of goods from one machine or piece of equipment to another in the successive stages of production; **flow-meadow**, one that may be flooded at will; **flow-meter**, an instrument for measuring rate of flow (of gas, liquid fuel, etc.); **flow-pipe**, the pipe by which hot water leaves the boiler in a system of heating (see also quot. 1967); **flow-sheet**, **flowsheet** = *flow chart*; hence ***flow-sheeting*** vbl. sb.; **flow-structure** *Geol.*, the structure in igneous rock produced by the flow of the molten mass before solidification.

1961 WEBSTER, *Flow-blue. **1962** K. SHAW *Ceramic Colours* iv. 42 Flow Blues depend for their formation on the volatilisation of chlorides which combine with the cobalt compound of the underglaze colour..during the glost firing. **1967** J. P. CUSHION *Eng. China Coll.* II. 71 The early prints tend to be of a rather dark and blurred blue, rather aptly named by the American collectors as 'flow-blue'. **1970** *Globe & Mail* (Toronto) 25 Sept. 37/4 (Advt.), Primitive scales, andirons, some flow blue china, glass. **1920** C. E. KNOEPPEL *Graphic Production Control* xii. 136 What should be considered in making up these *flow charts are [etc.]. **1949** G. R. TERRY *Office Managem.* xxviii. 637 The two types of procedure flow charts are paper distribution and paper correlation. **1966** *Digital Computer Needs* 156/2 A program..usually includes the preparation of a flow chart showing, diagrammatically, the desired sequence of discriminations and actions. **1968** *Brit. Med. Bull.* XXIV. 242/2 (*caption*) Flow chart showing scope of automation required in the treatment of a patient in a radiotherapy department. **1964** T. W. MCRAE *Impact of Computers on Accounting* i. 27 The technique of *flow charting is especially useful for pointing out improbable or unusual exceptions which have been omitted from the programme. **1943** *Industr. & Engin. Chem.* July 769/2 A simplified *flow diagram illustrating the first commercial design of a Fluid Catalyst cracking plant. **1947** GOLDSTINE & VON NEUMANN *Planning & Coding of Problems for Electronic Computing Instrument* vii. 3 We therefore propose to begin the planning of a coded sequence by laying out a schematic of the course of C [control] through that sequence.. This schematic is the flow diagram of C. **1949** D. R. HARTREE *Calculating Instruments & Machines* viii. 112 A method of indicating the structure of the sequence of operating instructions by means of a 'flow diagram' representing the control sequence. **1960** R. M. CURRIE *Work Study* 60 The flow diagram is a drawing, substantially to scale, of the working area, showing the location of the various activities identified by their numbered symbols. **1963** *Times Rev. Industry* May 83/1 A flow diagram..sets out every step of the calculation telling the computer exactly what to do wherever an alternative course presents itself. **1812** SOUTER *Agric. Surv. Banff. App.* 31 To construct *flow dikes. **1882** MINCHIN *Unipl. Kinemat.* 176 Is it possible to determine a velocity-potential function (or a *flow-function) of the form [etc.]? **1881** WYLIE *Iron Founding* 64 A violent bubbling takes place in the *flow-gates. **1889** *Pract. Iron Founding* iv. 57 In moulds of considerable area, risers or flow off gates are employed. **1882** MINCHIN *Unipl. Kinemat.* 248 The *flow-lines will then be lines of electro-static induction in the surrounding dielectric. **1912** P. A. AMOS *Processes Flour Manuf.* xxi. 171 Care in 'block-spacing'..before filling in the flow lines of the stock will keep the figures clear. **1913** G. H. GULLIVER *Metallic Alloys* (ed. 2) vii. 231 When the section is vigorously etched..the surface shows alternate dark and light striations called flow-lines. **1950** *Engineering* 3 Nov. 334/1 Flow-line production is a particular aspect of mass production. **1956** W. D. HARGREAVES in D. L. Linton *Sheffield* 294 An entirely new plant..provides for the continuous flow-line production of railway axles. **1959** B. CHALMERS *Physical Metallurgy* vii. 348 The strings of inclusions delineate the 'flow lines' of a forging, and indicate the directions and regions of weakness. **1960** *Times Rev. Industry* Apr. 48/1 A simultaneous attack on building layout, handling, flow lines, placing of equipment, and actual methods of construction is rarely carried out. **1834** *Brit. Husb.* I. 528 *Flow-meadows [*called also* flowing-meadows]. **1920** *Flight* XII. 353/1 A petrol *flowmeter should be fitted so that the engineer can see at a glance his fuel consumption. **1925** ODELL in E. F. Norton *Fight for Everest, 1924* 362 The..flow-meter..was connected up with the rubber tubing conveying the gas from the cylinders to the mouthpiece. **1952** *Electronic Engin.* XXIV. 162 The flowmeter to be described was designed for continuously recording the rate of flow of blood to the lungs of an animal. **1950** *Sci. News* XV. 141 Plate 13 shows a typical photograph of the *flow pattern in one of the planes of the model side-blown converter, showing particularly the flow of 'gases' above the 'steel' surface. **1955** *Times* 13 June 9/6 'Flow patterns' can be quickly calculated of air movements over the whole of north-western Europe, for interpreting millions of varied and detailed reports of meteorological observations from all over the Northern Hemisphere. **1904** GOODCHILD & TWENEY *Technol. & Sci. Dict.* 229/2 *Flow* or **flow pipe*, the pipe by which water leaves a boiler. **1967** *Gloss. Sanitation Terms (B.S.I.)* 34 *Flow pipe*, a pipe in a primary hot water circuit in which water moves away from the boiler, or a pipe in a secondary hot water circuit in which water moves away from the hot-water storage vessel. **1937** *Times* 13 Apr. p. xii/2 The layout of the Wolseley factory has been scientifically planned in accordance with modern *flow production methods. **1955** *Ibid.* 22 June 7/5 The common aim is to achieve in the building of ships a rhythm corresponding to the 'flow production' of, say, a motor-car factory. **1960** *Ibid.* 2 Dec. 17/2 Any significant leak leads to a reduction in *flow-rate at the place of the leak. **1962** *Lancet* 27 Jan. 182/2 The peak expiratory flow-rate was measured with a Wright's peak flow-meter. **1912** P. A. AMOS *Processes Flour Manuf.* xxi. 171 '*Flow-sheets', or diagrams, illustrating the course through which any material travels whilst undergoing treatment in manufacture. **1932** AUDEN *Orators* I. 22 Designs for the flow sheet of a mill. **1963** *Times Rev. Industry* May 83/2 He can..put the flowsheet information into machine code which entails a detailed time-consuming reproduction of the problem in computer language. **1964** M. GOWING *Britain & Atomic Energy* xii. 336 This involved much basic design work and *flowsheeting. **1890** *Flow-structure [see *fluxion-structure*]. **1893** Flow-structure [see FLUIDAL *a.*]. **1903** *Athenæum* 11 July 65/2 A flow-structure has been developed in the matrix. **1968** R. A. LYTTLETON *Myst. Solar Syst.* vi. 187 The solidified flow-structure within the tektite.

flow (fləʊ), *sb.*[2] Also 9 flo(w)e. [? a. ON. **flówe* (Icel. *flói*) of same meaning, related to *flóa* FLOW *v.*]

1. 'A watery moss, a morass' (Jam.).

16.. in Symson *Descr. Galloway* (1823) App. iv. 140 Moss Raploch, a great flow on the other side of Die. **1773** WALKER in *Phil. Trans.* LXII. 124 The Solway flow contains 1300 acres of very deep and tender moss. **1835** 'S. OLIVER' *Rambles Northumb.* 164 Dreading every instant that he will sink over head into the flow. **1852** *Jrnl. R. Agric. Soc.* XIII. II. 290 Dangerous 'flowes', or shaking bogs. **1895** CROCKETT *Moss-hags* xxxiii. Bog-wood dug from the flowes.

b. (See quots.)

1808–80 JAMIESON s.v., The term *flow* is applied to a low-lying piece of watery land rough and benty, which has not been broken up. **1886** LEBOUR *Geol. Northumb. & Durh.* 11 That part of it which thus dips away from the bog proper is aptly called the 'flow' of the bog.

2. A quicksand.

1818 SCOTT *Br. Lamm.* xvii, He shall stable his steed in the Kelpie's flow. **1882** STEVENSON *New Arab. Nts.* (1884) 210 The wind was driving the hat shoreward, and I ran round the border of the floe.

3. *attrib.*

1831 LOUDON *Agric.* (ed. 2) 1243 **Flow-bog* or flow moss, a peat bog, the surface of which is liable to rise and fall with every increase or diminution of water. *c* **1565** LINDESAY (Pitscottie) *Chron. Scot.* (1728) 130 He..ran his Horse into a *Flow-Moss. **1818** SCOTT *Rob Roy* xxviii, 'There wasna muckle flowmoss in the shaw.'

flow (fləʊ), *sb.*[3] *Sc.* [Of obscure origin; perh. f. root of FLAW *sb.* or FLY *v.*[1]] 'A jot, a particle, a small portion of any thing' (Jam.).

1804 TARRAS *Poems* 45 Wha on life's dainties nicely chow Yet left yir bard wi' fient a flowe. **1827** TENNANT *Papistry Storm'd* 69 Powther'd gay Wi' flows o' flour. **1840** WEBSTER in *Whistlebinkie* (Sc. Songs) Ser. II. (1890) I. 220 Tak hame a wee flow to your wife To help to be brose to your supper.

flow (fləʊ), *v. Pa. t.* and *pa. pple.* flowed (fləʊd). Forms: *Infin.* 1 flówan, 3 flohen, 3–5 flowen, (3 flouwen), *Orm.* flowenn, *south.* vlowen, 4 floȝe, flowyn, 5–7 flowe, 5– flow. *Pa. t.* 1 fléow, *pl.* fleowon, 3 fleaw, flew, *south.* vleau; weak forms: 3 fléowede, *Orm.* flowedd, 4 floȝed, flowede, 6 flowd, 6– flowed. *Pa. pple.* 1 flówen, 4–7 flowen, 7–8 flown; 6– flowed. [OE. *flówan*, a redupl. str. vb. occurring as such only in Eng. From the same root **flô-* are the wk. vbs. ON. *flóa* to flood, Du. *vloeijen* (= LG. *flojen*) to flow, and the Com. Teut. **flôdu-s* FLOOD *sb.* The wk. pa. t. and pa. pple. appear in early ME.; the original str. pa. t. appears not to have survived into the 14th c., but the str. pa. pple., though rare after 15th c., occurs down to the 18th c. (and still later as an archaism or a blunder, esp. in the compound *overflown*).

The Teut. **flô-*:—pre-Teut. **plō-* in Gr. πλώειν, to swim, float, πλωτός floating, navigable, L. *plōrāre* to weep. According to some scholars this is an ablaut-variant of **plē-* to fill, be full (cf. Gr. πληθύς fullness, L. *plēnus* full), perh. an extended form of **pel-*: see FULL *a.* Others regard. **plō-* as standing for **plōu-* lengthened grade of the root **pleu-*, *plou-*, *plu-* (Teut. **fleu-*, *flau-*, *flu-*), whence Skr. *plu* to swim, bathe, Gr. πλέειν to sail, πλύνειν to wash, L. *pluit* it rains, OHG. *flewen*, *flawen* (MHG. *vlöuwen*, *vlæn*) to rinse, ON, *flaumr* stream.

The sense-development of the vb. in Eng. shows traces of influence from the like-sounding but etymologically unconnected L. *fluĕre*, of which it is the usual translation.]

I. To glide along as a stream.

1. a. *intr.* Of fluids, a stream, etc.: To move on a gently inclined surface with a continual change of place among the particles or parts; to move along in a current; to stream, run; to spread *over* (a surface). Also with *along, down, on, out.*

a 1000 *Sal. & Sat.* 321 (Gr.) Siððan flowan mot yð ofer eal lond. *c* 1200 ORMIN 14567 & ta wass waterr wid & sid All oferr erþe flowedd. *a* 1250 *Owl & Night.* 918 An ydel wel, That..flohþ on idel thar a-dune. *c* 1325 *Body & Soul* in *Map's Poems* (Camden) 347 The thridde day shal flowe a flod that al this world shal hylen. *a* 1400-50 *Alexander* 2053 For bale to Blissh on blod þat on þe bent flowes. 1554 in Strype *Eccl. Mem.* III. App. xxiv. 67 Yf the water in Egypt called Nilus dyd not accustomably flow over Egypt. 1667 MILTON *P.L.* I. 11 Siloa's Brook that flow'd Fast by the Oracle of God. 1704 POPE *Winter* 13 Thames heard the numbers as he flow'd along. 1793 BURNS *Song, Wandering Willie* ii, O still flow between us, thou wide roaring main. 1854 RONALDS & RICHARDSON *Chem. Technol.* I. 363 The acid..is allowed to flow consecutively into the lower vessels. 1859 GULLICK & TIMBS *Paint.* 204 To admit of being discharged freely from the brush without flowing or spreading on the canvas.

b. Opposed to 'stand'. See FLOWING *ppl. a.*

1697 DRYDEN *Virg. Georg.* IV. 37 With Osier Floats the standing Water strow; Of massy stones make Bridges, if it flow.

c. Of the blood or other animal fluids: To pass along the vessels of the body; to circulate.

1603 SHAKS. *Meas. for M.* I. iii. 52 Lord Angelo..scarce confesses That his blood flowes. 1666 DRYDEN *Ann. Mirab.* ii, Trade, which like blood should circularly flow, Stopped in their channels. 1786 BURNS *Song, My Highland Lassie O* iii, While my crimson currents flow, I'll love my Highland lassie. 1817 SHELLEY *Rev. Islam* VII. xxi. 5 Our pulses [would] calmly flow and beat In response while we slept. 1845 BUDD *Dis. Liver* 276 Gall-stones are formed in numbers in the gall-bladder, only when the bile can flow into it through the cystic duct.

d. With advbs. *to flow over* = to overflow.

1526 TINDALE *2 Cor.* viii. 2 And howe that their povertie, though yt be depe, yet hath folowed [*sic*] over. 1606 SHAKS. *Ant. & Cl.* V. ii. 24 My Lord Who is so full of Grace, that it flowes ouer On all that neede.

e. quasi-*trans.* Of a river: To carry down (water) in its current.

1885 *Century Mag.* Sept. 747 It [a river] was flowing muddy water at the time.

†**2. a.** To become liquid; to stream *down*, melt; *lit.* and *fig.* *Obs.*

c 825 *Vesp. Psalter* lxvii[i]. 3 Swe floweð wex from onsiene fyres. *a* 1225 *Ancr. R.* 110 His moderes wop & þe oðres Maries, þæt fleoweden & melten al of teares. 1382 WYCLIF *Isa.* lxiv. 1 Fro thi face hillis shulden flowe doun. 1477 NORTON *Ord. Alch.* v in Ashm. (1652) 59 For nothinge maie be more contrary nowe Than to be fixt and unperfectly flowe. 1641 FRENCH *Distill.* iv. (1651) 105 This Oil of Tartar must bee made of salt of Tartar after it hath flowed in the fire. 1737 POPE *Hor. Epist.* II. i. 148 Yielding Metal flow'd to human form.

†**b.** *fig* To be unsteady, waver. *Obs.*

1434 MISYN *Mending Life* 112 Se þat þou flow nott with vayn þoghtis. 1500-20 DUNBAR *Poems* vi. 47 My hert that neuir wes sic[k]ir..That never mair wald flow nor flickir.

c. *Ceram.* To work or blend freely: said of a glaze. (*Cent. Dict.*)

d. Of a solid: to suffer a permanent (i.e. non-elastic) change in shape under stress without fracturing or rupturing.

1887 *Encycl. Brit.* XXII. 595/2 When the stress is sufficiently increased..the substance then assumes what may be called a completely plastic state; it flows under the applied stress like a viscous liquid. 1888 Flowing metal [see FLOWING *ppl. a.* 1]. 1894-5 VAN HISE in *16th Ann. Rep. U.S. Geol. Surv.* I. 594 Whether rocks flow or fracture is in many cases largely dependent on the rapidity of deformation. 1897 *Geol. Mag.* Nov. 514 The experiments therefore show that limestone..does possess a certain degree of plasticity, and can be made to 'flow'. 1901 *Phil. Trans. R. Soc.* A. CXCV. 398 Many limestones under pressure in the earth's crust flow precisely as metals do. 1914 RIES & WATSON *Engin. Geol.* iii. 192 When subjected to stresses of sufficient intensity, rocks are deformed either by fracturing or by flowing. 1932 F. F. GROUT *Petrography* VII. 402 At moderate and great depths in the crust, competent rocks yield elastically up to the elastic limit and then fracture; and weaker ones recrystallize and flow. 1971 M. J. MANJOINE in H. Liebowitz *Fracture* III. iv. 278 In this region, the material can flow more rapidly at a lower stress.

3. a. Of persons or animals: To come or go 'in a stream or streams.' Also with *in, together.*

1382 WYCLIF *Jer.* xxxi. 12 Thei shul..togidere flowen to the goodus of the Lord [1388 and thei schulen flowe togidere to the goodis of the Lord]. 1611 BIBLE *Jer.* li. 44 The nations shall not flow together any more vnto him. 1613 PURCHAS *Pilgrimage* II. x. (1614) 160 Thence they [Iewes] flowed into other parts. 1742 POPE *Dunc.* IV. 275 In flow'd at once a gay embroider'd race. 1817 SHELLEY *Rev. Islam* V. xli. 2 To hear the restless multitudes..Around the base of that great Altar flow. 1878 BOSW. SMITH *Carthage* 166 Men flowed in so plentifully that [etc.]. 1890 'R. BOLDREWOOD' *Col. Reformer* xix, He..confined himself to riding..round the cattle on the camp, preventing them from flowing out in unnecessary directions.

b. Of things material and immaterial: To move, pass as a stream. Also with *away, down, in, together.*

1382 WYCLIF *Ecclus.* li. 9 For the deth flowende doun I louly preȝede. 1548 HALL *Chron., Hen. VI,* 137 Thus the victory flowed some tyme on the one parte, and sometyme on the other. 1560 BIBLE (Genev.) *Job* xx. 28 The increase of his house shall go away; it shall flow away in the day of his wrath. 1607 HIERON *Wks.* I. 435 The euils of the precedent ages are flowne together into this. 1651 HOBBES *Leviath.* II. xxix. 173 The Treasure of the Common-wealth, flowing out of its due course. 1717 POPE *Elegy Unfort. Lady* 25 As into air the purer spirits flow. 1780 COXE *Russ. Disc.* 188 The final success which flowed in upon him. 1816 SHELLEY *Alastor* 533 As fast years flow away. 1833 HT. MARTINEAU *Berkeley the Banker* I. vii. 141 Gold flowed in. 1878 JEWITT *Ceramic Art.* II. viii. 350 Orders for the new kind of ware flowed in upon him.

4. Of composition or speech; in early use of a speaker or writer: To glide along smoothly, like a river.

1585 JAS. I *Ess. Poesie* (Arb.) 59 The first lyne flowis weil, and the vther nathing at all. 1643 DENHAM *Cooper's H.* 189 Could I flow like thee [Thames], and make thy streame My great example. 1737 POPE *Hor. Epist.* II. i. 266 Wit grew polite, and Numbers learn'd to flow. 1859 KINGSLEY *Misc.* (1860) I. 227 The most unmetrical..passages flow with a grace, a lightness [etc.]. 1870 E. PEACOCK *Ralf. Skirl.* III. 252 Conversation flowed freely.

5. Of a garment, hair, etc.: To 'stream'; to hang loose and waving; to lie in undulating curves. Also †of a person: ***to flow with*** (hair).

1606 B. JONSON *Hymenæi* Wks. (Rtldg.) 558 From the top of which [coronet] flow'd a transparent veile. 1608 —— *Masque Beauty* Splendour Wks. (Rtldg.) 549/1 Her bright hayre loose flowing. 1648 HERRICK *Hesper.* 29 A Cuffe neglectfull, and thereby Ribbands to flow confusedly. 1667 MILTON *P.L.* XI. 241 Over his lucid Armes A militarie Vest of purple flowd. 1697 DRYDEN *Virg. Georg.* III. 146 Grim Saturn..flow'd with such a Mane. 1712 CONGREVE *Ovid's Art Love* III. 376 Swell'd with the wanton wind, they [her coats] loosely flow. 1782 COWPER *Gilpin* xlvi, A wig that flowed behind. 1810 SCOTT *Lady of L.* II. xvi, Mark the gaudy streamers flow From their loud chanters down. *a* 1881 ROSSETTI *House of Life* vii, Across my breast the abandoned hair doth flow.

6. *Math.* To increase or diminish continuously by infinitesimal quantities: to 'vary' (in the Newtonian Calculus). See FLUENT.

1715 *Phil. Trans.* XXIX. 204 When the Letter *x* is put for a Quantity which flows uniformly, the symbol $\dot{x}$ is an Unit. 1758 I. LYONS *Fluxions* 4, *x* flows from $x-\frac{1}{2}\dot{x}$ to $x+\frac{1}{2}\dot{x}$. 1828 HUTTON *Course Math.* II. 304 To obtain the second fluxion it will suffice to make x^{n-1} flow.

†**7.** *trans.* (*causatively*). **a.** To make to flow, set flowing *in, out.* **b.** To make fluid. *Obs.*

1413 *Pilgr. Sowle* (Caxton 1483) v. i. 74 God must nedes contynuelly flowen oute his bounte. 1477 NORTON *Ord. Alch.* v. in Ashm. (1652) 79 Liquors helpeth to flux and to flowe Manie things. 1579 FULKE *Heskins' Parl.* 21 The Church is..verie wel compared vnto the sea, which floweth out waues from euery porch or entrie. 1635 BRATHWAIT *Arcad. Pr.* II. (1635) 175, I plenteously flowed in my afternoone's potation.

c. In *Founding*, to permit (the molten metal) to flow through the mould long enough to carry off all air and foreigh matter, in order to insure a casting free from bubbles and similar defects; to run through. (*Cent. Dict.*)

d. *Naut.* (See quot.)

1883 W. C. RUSSELL *Sailor's Lang.*, *Flow*, to let go the sheet of a head-sail.

II. To stream forth, issue in a stream.

8. a. To gush out, well forth, spring. Also with *down, forth, out, over.*

c 825 *Vesp. Psalter* lxxvii[i]. 20 Forðon sloȝ stan & fleowun weter. *c* 1000 *Ags. Gosp.* John xiv. 34 Hrædlice þar fleow blod ut & wæter. *c* 1250 *Gen. & Ex.* 3875 Ðo flew ðor water michil and strong. *a* 1400-50 *Alexander* 1350 Þar flowe out of fresh wynne flodez enowe. 1574 HYLL *Planting* 77 When the humour thereof is somewhat flowen. 1578 LYTE *Dodoens* III. xxi. 302 The sappe, when..first flowen out, is white. 1591 SPENSER *Ruins Time* 651 Streams of blood foorth flowed on the grass. *c* 1724 SWIFT *Fontinella* 4 Endless tears flow down in streams. 1813 J. THOMSON *Lect. Inflam.* 251 The blood will continue to flow..till the exhausted animal expires. 1828 SCOTT *F.M. Perth* xxix, His tears flowed plentifully and bitterly.

b. To issue or proceed *from*, †*of*, *out of*, something as a source.

c 1200 ORMIN 4783 War & wirrsenn toc anan Vt off hiss lic to flowenn. *a* 1240 *Lofsong* in *Cott. Hom.* 211 þet flod þet fleaw of þine wunden. 1535 COVERDALE *2 Esdras* i. 20 Dyd not I hew yᵉ hardstone & caused water ynough to flowe thereout? 1609 J. DAVIES *Holy Roode* (Grosart) 20/1 His Gore, That from his Blood-founts..flow'd before. 1824 R. STUART *Hist. Steam Engine* 62 Cold water is now allowed to flow from the reservoir.

transf. and *fig.* 1382 WYCLIF *Song Sol.* iv. 16 Bloȝ thurȝ my gardyn, and ther shul flowe swote spices of it. 1545 JOYE *Exp. Dan.* Text vii. 10 Longe fyery beames lyke a floude of fyer flouwing out of him. 1632 LITHGOW *Trav.* II. 75 This City was..the great Cisterne of Europe, whence flowed so many conduit pipes of learning. 1682 BURNET *Rights Princes* ii. 40 Some other reason that flowed not from him. 1713 STEELE *Englishman* No. 10. 66 His Behaviour does not flow from an Hardness in his Mind. 1794 BURNS *A Vision* vii, Frae his harp sic strains did flow. 1818 CRUISE *Digest* (ed. 2) II. 306 This rule flows..from the nature of a remainder. 1888 BRYCE *Amer. Commw.* II. xxxvii. 27 The Authority of the State Constitutions does not flow from Congress.

c. Of a person: To pour out one's feelings. Also with *out.*

1677 *Government Venice* Ep. Ded. 3, I perceive I am flown out insensibly in your praises. 1863 HAWTHORNE *Our Old Home, Recoll. Gifted Woman* (1884) 91 The interview lasted above an hour, during which she flowed out freely. 1864 TENNYSON *Aylmer's F.* 563 The mother flow'd in shallower acrimonies.

†**d.** *trans.* To pour forth in a stream. (Perh. reminiscent of the *trans.* use in 14 below).

1550 CRANMER *Def.* 77 b, The stone that floweth water. 1906 *Amer. Naturalist* June 446, I observed a tree which flowed little sap and continued flowing after the other trees had ceased.

9. Of the menstrual discharge. Said also of the person.

1754-64 [see CATAMENIA]. 1894 DUANE *Dict. Med.*, *Flow*, to menstruate; especially to menstruate profusely.

III. To run full; to be in flood.

10. Of the sea, a tidal river, etc.: To rise and advance; frequent in phrase ***to ebb and flow***: see EBB *v.* 1. ***to flow south, tide and half tide*** (see quots. 1627 and 1721). Cf. FLOOD *sb.* 1.

c 1050 *Byrhtferth's Handboc* in *Anglia* (1885) VIII. 327 Seo sæ symle feower prican oððe fif lator flowð. *c* 1200 *Trin. Coll. Hom.* 177 Eft son þe se flouweð. 13.. *E.E. Allit. P.* B. 397 Bi þat þe flod to her fete floȝed & waxed. *c* 1430 LYDG. *Min. Poems* 196 Watir..Now ebbithe, flowithe. 1568 GRAFTON *Chron.* II. 441 Thys yere the Thamys did flowe three times in one daye. 1624 HEYWOOD *Gunaik.* IV. 182 The waters..were flowed eighteene cubites above their woonted compasse. 1626 CAPT. SMITH *Accid. Yng. Seamen* 17 It flowes quarter floud. 1627 —— *Seaman's Gram.* (1653) 47 It flowes Tide and halfe Tide, that is, it will be halfe flood by the shore, before it begin to flow in the channell. 1691 SWIFT *Athenian Soc.* Wks. 1755 IV. I. 229 When the deluge first began to fall, That mighty ebb never to flow again. 1721-1800 in BAILEY, *It Flows South* [Sea Phrase] it is high Water when the Sun is at that Point at new or full Moon. 1739 LABELYE *Short Acc. Piers Westm. Bridge* 34 Before the Tide had flown or risen so high. 1816 BYRON *Prisoner Chillon* vi, The massy waters ebb and flow. 1830 LYELL *Princ. Geol.* I. 304 In the Thames..the tide requires about five hours to flow up. 1884 PAE *Eustace* 7 The tide was flowing.

fig. 1399 LANGL. *Rich. Redeles* III. 206 Vertue wolde fflowe whan vicis were ebbid. 1600 SHAKS. *A.Y.L.* II. vii. 72 Doth it [pride] not flow as hugely as the Sea? 1786 BURNS *Ded. to G. Hamilton* 111 When ebbing life nae mair shall flow. 1817 SHELLEY *Rev. Islam* V. li. 2 The throngs which ever ebbed and flowed. 1820 *Sporting Mag.* VII. 25 The tide of success that flowed to Vauxhall.

†**11. a.** To rise to a great height and overflow. In *fig.* phrases, ***to flow above the banks, to flow past shore***: to overflow. *Obs.*

1398 TREVISA *Barth. De P.R.* XIX. cxli. (1495) 945 The ryuer Nylus was flowen and arysen. *a* 1625 BEAUM. & FL. *False One* III. iv, Let Nylus flow, And perpetuall plenty show.

fig. 1590 SPENSER *F.Q.* II. ii. 36 In wine and meats she flowd aboue the bancke. 1606 SHAKS. *Tr. & Cr.* V. ii. 41 You flow to great distraction. 1615 CHAPMAN *Odyss.* III. 335 Grave Nestor..flows Past shore in all experience.

b. The obs. pa. pple. *flown*, orig. used of a stream with the sense 'swollen', 'in flood' (see quot. *c* 1510), was used *fig.* in 17th c. of persons, and survives in allusions to Milton's phrase. (It is doubtful whether the etymological sense was remembered in the 17th c.) Cf. HIGHFLOWN.

c 1510 *Sir R. Guilford's Pilgrimage* (Camden) 31 Cedron.. in wynter.. is meruaylously flowen with rage of water yᵗ commyth with grete vyolence thrugh the vale of Josophat. *a* 1656 USSHER *Ann.* VI. (1658) 250 Being somewhat high flowen with wine. 1667 MILTON *P.L.* I. 501 Then wander forth the Sons Of Belial, flown with insolence and wine. 1725 POPE *Odyss.* I. 292 Unseemly flown with insolence and wine. 1879 BUTCHER & LANG *Odyss.* 8 In such wise, flown with insolence, do they seem to me to revel.

†**12.** Of the eyes: To become overfull, to fill *of*, *with* (tears, etc.) *Obs.*

a 1225 *Ancr. R.* 64 Al þe leor schal ulowen o teares, he seið. *a* 1240 *Wohunge* in *Cott Hom.* 283 Nu min herte mai to breke, min ehne flowen al o water. *c* 1600 SHAKS. *Sonn.* xxx, Then can I drowne an eye (vn-vs'd to flow). *c* 1689 PRIOR *To Ld. Buckhurst* 19 Her eyes with tears no more will flow. 1710 STEELE *Tatler* No. 235 ¶3, I have often seen the old Man's Heart flow at his Eyes with joy.

13. Of wine, etc.: To be poured out without stint; also *fig.* †In early use of wealth, etc. (after L. *affluĕre*): To abound.

c 1000 *Ags. Ps.* lxi[i]. 11 [10] Þeah þe eow wealan to wearmum flowen. 1490 CAXTON *Eneydos* xxii. 85 Sorowes and heuynesses dyde flowe at her herte in grete haboundance. 1667 MILTON *P.L.* V. 633 Rubied nectar flows In pearl, in diamond, and massy gold. 1782 COWPER *Charity* 279 When thought is warm and fancy flows. 1817 SHELLEY *Rev. Islam* IX. xvii. 2 Gold was scattered thro' the streets, and wine Flowed at a hundred feasts.

14. ***to flow with*** (†*in*, †*of*): to abound in, to overflow with. Now rare exc. in Biblical phrase ***to flow with milk and honey*** (Wyclif and Mandeville, following a barbarism of the Vulgate, use the vb. in this phrase as transitive).

1382 WYCLIF *Exod.* iii. 8 A loond that flowith [1388 with] mylk and hony. 1388 —— *Eccl.* xi. 25 Who schal..flowe in delicis as Y dide? *c* 1400 MAUNDEV. (Roxb.) xxx. 137, I sall giffe to ȝow land flowande mylke and hony. 1539 TAVERNER *Erasm. Prov.* (1545) 53 Suche as flowe in worldly goodes. *a* 1592 H. SMITH *Three Serm.* (1624) 23 Christ so flowed now with Diciples, that [etc.]. 1678 CUDWORTH *Intell. Syst.* 877 The Unjust and Ungodly, often flow in all kind of Prosperity. 1781 GIBBON *Decl. & F.* III. lii. 269 A land flowing with milk and honey.

15. a. *trans.* To cover or fill with water; to flood.

1382 WYCLIF *Isa.* xxviii. 17 The proteccioun watris shul flowe. 1666 EVELYN *Mem.* 8 May (1819) I. 386 Here I flowed the drie moate. 1712 MORTIMER *Husb.* II. 232 Watering..is scarce practicable, unless you have a Stream at hand to flow the Ground. 1845 *Jrnl. R. Agric. Soc.* VI. II. 274 Care being taken not to flow the land in summer where sheep are kept.

b. To cover with any liquid, as varnish or glaze, by causing it to flow over the surface. Also, To allow (a film) to flow.

1864 J. TOWLER *Silver Sunbeam* 144 The glass is filed, cleaned, and flowed with collodion, as before directed. **1889** *Anthony's Photogr. Bull.* II. 257 As if a very attenuated film of milk and water had been flowed over its surface.

16. Of the tide: To overtake and surround (a person). *dial.* (See quots.)

1735 DYCHE & PARDON, *Flow*, to come upon a Person or Thing greatly or hastily, like the Motion of Water when the Tide is coming in. **1875** *Sussex Gloss.* s.v., 'If you doant mind you'll be flown in, one of these days.' **1876** *Whitby Gloss.* s.v., 'They got flow'd on.'

Hence **'flower** (fləʊə(r)), *Metallurgy*, a flow-gate (see FLOW *sb.*[1] 9).

1881 WYLIE *Iron-Founding* 50 The use of flo'ers or gates. *Ibid.* 66 According to the thickness of the part so should the size of the flow'er be.

flowage ('fləʊɪdʒ). [f. FLOW *v.* + -AGE.]

a. The act of flowing; the state of being flowed or flooded. In comb. ***flowage-line***.

1830 *Massachusetts Spy* 3 Feb. (Th.), The flowage, which would be occasioned by a dam to turn the water into the Feeder. **1846** WORCESTER cites WILKINS. **1884** J. G. PYLE in *Harper's Mag.* Sept. 621/1 Flowage line [of a reservoir]. **1936** *Sun* (Baltimore) 5 Oct. 4/6 Army engineers, faced with the task of completing the Maryland portion of the new waterway.., said today 633 acres [of land] would be purchased outright. Only flowage rights will be bought on 308 acres. **1971** *Capital Times* (Madison, Wis.) 28 Aug. 11/7 Campsites and picnic areas near the flowage..brought in more than $1 million of tourism to the Hayward area annually.

b. *Geol.* The flow (FLOW *sb.*[1] 1 e) of rock.

1894-5 VAN HISE in *16th Ann. Rep. U.S. Geol. Surv.* I. 594 Even in homogeneous rocks, the zone of fracture and the zone of flowage are not sharply separated from each other. **1921** *Science* 4 Mar. 196/2 While rock flowage and rock fracture constitute two distinct types of deformation, there is almost complete gradation between the two. **1965** G. J. WILLIAMS *Econ. Geol. N.Z.* xviii. 302/2 Upper seams tend to be lenticular and rarely of workable thickness, though local thickenings were found in areas of complex structure owing to flowage of the coal along structural lines.

flowe(n, obs. pa. t. and pa. ppl. of FLY.

flowede, obs. form of FLOOD.

flower (flaʊə(r), 'flaʊə(r)), *sb.* Forms: 3-4 **flur(e**, 3-7 **flour(e**, 4-7 **flowr(e**, (4 **flor**, **flowur**, 6 **flore**, *Sc.* **flouir**, 7 **floor**), 5- **flower**, (8, 9 *poet.* **flow'r**). See also FLOUR. [ME. *flour*, *flur*, a. OF. *flour*, *flur*, *flor* (Fr. *fleur*) = Pr. *flour*, *flor*, Sp., Pg., and OIt. *flor* (It. *fiore*):—L. *flōr-em*, *flōs*, f. Aryan root **bhlō-*: see BLOW *v.*[2]]

1. a. A complex organ in phenogamous plants, comprising a group of reproductive organs and its envelopes. In the popular use of the word, the characteristic feature of a *flower* is the 'coloured' (not green) envelope, and the term is not applied where this is absent, unless there is obvious resemblance in appearance to what is ordinarily so called. In botanical use, a flower consists normally of one or more stamens or pistils (or both), a corolla, and a calyx; but the two last are not universally present.

a **1225** *Ancr. R.* 340 Þe treou also, openeð ham & bringeð forð misliche flures. **1382** WYCLIF *Job* xiv. 2 As a flour goth out, and is totreden. **1500-20** DUNBAR *Poems* lxiv. 10 Leif nor flour fynd could I nane of rew. **1594** BARNFIELD *Affect. Sheph.* I. xxvi, Thou suckst the flowre till all the sweet be gone. **1672** W. HUGHES *Flower Garden* 31 Daffodils that have several Flowers on one Stalk. **1709** POPE *Ess. Crit.* 498 Like some fair flow'r the early spring supplies. **1820** BYRON *Mar. Fal.* III. ii, As faithless leaves drop from the o'erblown flower. **1845** LINDLEY *Sch. Bot.* i. (1858) 13 A flower, if complete in all its parts, consists of a *calyx*, a *corolla*, *stamens*, and a *pistil*. **1878** BROWNING *La Saisiaz* 20 Flower that's full-blown tempts the butterfly.

fig. *a* **1310** in Wright's *Lyric P.* 89 Thah thou be whyt ant bryth on ble, falewen shule thy floures. **1380** WYCLIF *Sel. Wks.* III. 30 Cristen men..Schal no flour schewe of virtu. *c* **1491** *Chast. Goddes Chyld.* 9 A foule blindnes whiche.. dystroyeth the floures and the frutes of al goostly vertues. **1592** SHAKS. *Rom. & Jul.* II. ii. 122 This bud of Loue..May proue a beautious Flower when next we meete. **1759** RUTTY *Spiritual Diary* (ed. 2) 140 An extract of some sweet flowers from the scriptures. **1841** TRENCH *Parables* xii. (1877) 241 Righteousness, both in its root of faith and its flower of charity.

b. In *Bryology*, extended to denote the growth comprising the reproductive organs in mosses.

2. *transf.* **a.** The down or feathery seeds of the dandelion and thistle. ? *Obs.*

1530 PALSGR. 221/2 Floure of a tasyll that flyeth about all rounde, *barbedieu*.

†**b.** *pl.* The menstrual discharge; the menses; = CATAMENIA. *Obs.* [After F. *fleurs*: but this is regarded by French scholars as a corruption of *flueurs*: see FLUOR.]

c **1400** *Rel. Ant.* I. 190 A woman schal in the harme blede For stoppyng of hure flowrys. **1527** ANDREW *Brunswyke's Distyll. Waters* A iij, The same water..causeth women to have her flowres, named menstruum. **1662** R. MATHEW *Unl. Alch.* §106 It helpeth the stopping of the Flowers. **1741** in CHAMBERS *Cycl.* **1859** TODD *Cycl. Anat.* V. 666/2 The French term 'fleurs' and the English 'flowers' are now fallen into disuse.

c. *Anc. Chem.* (*pl.*, earlier *sing.* also in form *flour*): The pulverulent form of any substance, *esp.* as the result of condensation after sublimation.

1398 TREVISA *Barth. De P.R.* XVI. lxxx. (1495) 579 Drieng and tempryng wyth vynegre it [leed] torneth in to whyte colour of floure of leed. **1641** FRENCH *Distill.* v. (1651) 164 Which whitenesse is partly the floures of the Nitre. **1730** SWIFT *Death & Daphne* 25 Flow'r of sulphur powder'd well. **1799** *Med. Jrnl.* I. 162 The benzoic acid, is sufficiently known by the name of *flowers of benzoine*. **1822** IMISON *Sc. & Art* II. 114 These [white flakes] have been called flowers of Zinc. **1834** GRIFFIN *Chem. Recreat.* (ed. 3) 117 Flowers of benjamin, a substance obtained by sublimation from gum benzoin. **1854** J. SCOFFERN in *Orr's Circ. Sc., Chem.* 337 Powdered sulphur is known in Commerce as flowers of sulphur.

d. Applied to various fungoid growths; a scum formed on wine, vinegar, etc. in fermentation. ***flowers of tan***: a fungus (*Fuligo*) growing on tan heaps.

1548 THOMAS *Ital. Gram.*, *Fiocchi*..flowers of wine. **1600** W. VAUGHAN *Direct. Health* (1633) 128 The Cholericke humour is hot and fiery, bitter, and like unto the flowre of wine. **1668** *Phil. Trans.* 21 Sept. 772 A somewhat moist and putrid matter..which ..is called..the Flower of this Substance [osteocolla]. **1675** CHARLETON *Myst. Vintners* 151 Reserving the Froth or Flower of it, and putting the same into small Casks. **1882** VINES *Sachs' Bot.* 263 The yellow plasmodia inside a tan-heap..come to the surface, and then coalesce into the large bodies which are known as 'flowers of tan'.

3. a. A blossom considered independently of the plant, and esp. in regard to its beauty or perfume. ***no flowers (by request)***: an intimation that flowers are not desired at a funeral; hence, no outward sign of mourning or regret.

c **1275** *Luue Ron* 151 in *O.E. Misc.* 97 Þu art swetture þane eny flur. *c* **1290** *S. Eng. Leg.* I. 214/491 A fair Medwe he saiȝ with swete floures. *a* **1300** *Floriz & Bl.* 434 Flures To strawen in þe maidenes bures. **1477** EARL RIVERS (Caxton) *Dictes* 86 As the bees loue the swetest of the floures. **1508** DUNBAR *Gold. Targe* 59 Als fresch as flouris that in May vp spredis. **1613** SHAKS. *Hen. VIII*, IV. ii. 169 Strew me ouer With Maiden Flowers. **1656** COWLEY *Anacreontiques, Another Epicure*, Beauteous Flowers, why do we spread, Upon the Mon'ments of the Dead? **1732** POPE *Ep. Cobham* 148 We..justly set the Gem above the Flower. **1900** C. HANBURY *Let.* 5 Aug. in *Autobiogr.* (1901) xv. 224 When the Home-going is, I want to say with more than common emphasis—'by desire'—no flowers; also no bell tolling. **1923** H. C. BAILEY *Mr. Fortune's Practice* iii. 84 No flowers, by request. Don't be an owl. **1928** E. WALLACE *Gunner* xxii, I shall..explain to the police why I shot you, and there will be no flowers from Scotland Yard. **1970** *Times* 17 Nov. 20/2 Cremation at 11.30 a.m. at Exeter Crematorium, Thursday 19th November. No flowers by request.

b. *fig.* (*esp.* as applied to a person.)

a **1225** *Ancr. R.* 340 Uertus beoð..swote smellinde flures ine Godes neose. *a* **1310** in Wright *Lyric P.* 93 Blessed be thou..suete flur of parays. **1500-20** DUNBAR *Poems* lxxxv. 10 Aue Maria..Haile, fresche flour femynyne! **1592** SHAKS. *Rom. & Jul.* I. iii. 77 Nay hee's a flower, in faith a very flower. **1741** RICHARDSON *Pamela* (1824) I. 217 My wife told me a good deal of the beauties of your person; but I did not think we had such a flower in our country. **1847** TENNYSON *Princess* v. 86 And they will beat my girl Remembering her mother: O my flower!

c. *pl.* The bloom of certain plants used in Medicine (formerly also in Cookery).

c **1430** *Two Cookery-bks.* 29 Take Flourys of Vyolet, boyle hem. **1586** W. BAILEY 2 *Treat. Eye-sight* (1633) 11 An ounce of the water of Rosemarie flowers. **1600** W. VAUGHAN *Direct. Health* (1633) 76 Halfe a handfull of the flowers of Camomill. **1652** Chamomel flowers [see CAMOMILE 2].

4. a. A flowering plant; a plant cultivated or esteemed for the sake of its blossoms.

1500-20 DUNBAR *Poems* x. 41 Now spring vp flouris fra the rute..Lay out ȝour levis lustely. **1593** SHAKS. *Lucr.* 870 Unwholesome weeds take root with precious flowers. **1667** MILTON *P.L.* XI. 273 O flours That never will in other climate grow. **1725** WATTS *Logic* I. vi. §3 (1822) 99 If the blossom be of most importance we call it [the plant] a flower. **1796** C. MARSHALL *Garden.* xviii. (1813) 289 Flowers..are classed into annuals, biennials and perennials.

b. In the names of various plants, as † **flower of Bristol**, † **flower (of) Constantinople**, the nonsuch, *Lychnis chalcedonica*; **flower of Jove** (see quot.); **flower of the night** (see quot. 1665); **flower of the sun** = SUNFLOWER.

1578 LYTE *Dodoens* II. viii. 157 *Flos Constantinopolitanus*, that is to say Floure Constantinople. **1597** GERARDE *Herbal* II. cxix. §5. 380 It is called..in English..of some Flower of Bristowe, and Nonesuch. *Ibid.* ccxlvii. 612 Of the flower of the Sunne, or the Marigolde of Peru. **1665** RAY *Flora* II. xvii. 195 The Mervail of Peru..These flowers..are to be seen late in evenings, or early in mornings, and therefore have been called the flowers of the night. **1672** W. HUGHES *Flower Garden* 33 Flowers of the Sun, do commonly flower about August. *Ibid.*, Flower of Bristol, Champion or Non-such. **1840** PAXTON *Bot. Dict.* 134 Flower of Jove, *Lychnis flos Jovis*.

5. The representation of a flower: **a.** in drawing, painting, and weaving.

c **1230** *Hali Meid.* 23 Þe flurs þat beoð idrahe þron [on a gerlaundesche]. *a* **1300** *Body & Soul* 14 in *Map's Poems* 334 Thi riche halles? I-peynted with so riche floures? **1303** R. BRUNNE *Handl. Synne* 1413 Some were..feyr peyntede wyth frute and floures. *c* **1400** *Rom. Rose* 891 Nought clad in silk was he But alle in floures. *a* **1400-50** *Alexander* 1539 A vestoure to vise on of violet floures. **1830** TENNYSON *Recoll. Arab. Nts.* xiv, Engarlanded and diaper'd With in-wrought flowers, a cloth of gold.

b. *Arch.*

1730-6 BAILEY (folio), Flowers [in Architecture], representations of some imaginary flowers, by way of crowning or finishing on the top of a dome. **1741** CHAMBERS *Cycl. Flower of the capital*, is an ornament..in form of a rose, in the middle of the sweep of the Corinthian abacus.

c. *Printing.* (See quot. 1871.)

1771 LUCKOMBE *Hist. & Art Print.* 287 Flowers were the first Ornaments which were used at the Head of..pages. **1779** FRANKLIN *Lett.* Wks. 1889 VI. 427 Did they take all the letters, flowers, etc., etc., except the five cases of money types which you say the Congress have? **1838** TIMPERLEY *Printers' Man.* 62 Flowers are used for borders. **1871** RINGWALT *Amer. Encycl. Printing* 172 *Flowers*, ornaments for embellishing chapter-headings, or forming tail-pieces to books. **1888** in JACOBI *Printers' Voc.*

d. = FLEUR-DE-LIS 2 and 3. ***flower of the winds***: see quot. 1867.

c **1314** *Guy Warw.* (A.) (1887) 462 He..hit him on þe helme so briȝt, That al þe floures fel doun riȝt. **1352** MINOT *Poems* IX. i, The flowres that faire war Er fallen in Fraunce. **1559** W. CUNNINGHAM *Cosmogr. Glasse* 162 If the flower of the nedle be righte Northe from it. **1849** ROCK *Ch. of Fathers* I. viii. 393 The favourite Anglo-Saxon kind of ornament, called the 'flower'. **1867** SMYTH *Sailors' Word-bk.*, *Flower of the Winds*, the mariner's compass on maps and charts.

e. †A flower-shaped branch or bowl of a candlestick. Also, a piece of iron shaped like a fleur-de-lis.

1521 *Test. Ebor.* (Surtees) V. 128, I will that there be maid for every flowre of the candlestike a tapur of wod. **1888** *Sheffield Gloss.*, *Flower*, the piece of iron which fastens a vice to a table or bench.

f. An artificial flower (as an ornament).

1881 *Illustr. Househ. Jrnl.* Sept. 121/3 The most popular flowers just now for bonnet trimmings..are made of velvet.

6. a. An adornment or ornament; a precious possession, a 'jewel'.

1542-5 BRINKLOW *Lament.* 9 London beyng one of the flowers of the worlde as touchinge worldlye riches. **1606** SHAKS. *Tr. & Cr.* I. ii. 203 That's Æneas..hee's one of the flowers of Troy. **1647** MAY *Hist. Parl.* II. iii. 40 The nomination of any persons to those places, he will reserve to himself, it being a principal and inseparable flower of his Crown. **1677** YARRANTON *Eng. Improv.* 63 The Dutch robbed of one of their greatest Flowers. **1783-94** BLAKE *Songs Innoc., Holy Thursday* 5 O what a multitude they seem'd, these flowers of London town. **1855** MACAULAY *Hist. Eng.* III. 219 The power of pardoning..a precious prerogative which..even the Whigs allowed to be a flower properly belonging to the Crown.

†**b.** phr. ***to bear, fang, have the flower (of)***: to gain the victory, to have preëminence (among).

c **1310** *Pol. Songs* (Camden) 248 Is Edward ded? Of Christendom he ber the flour! *a* **1400-50** *Alexander* 500 And þar þe floure in þe filde I fangid þurȝe himselfe. *Ibid.* 2603 For he þat folows hase þe floure · & he flees neuer. *c* **1435** *Torr. Portugal* 2595 Torent the floure away bare.

†**c.** Virginity. *Obs.*

a **1300** *Fall & Passion* 52 in *E.E.P.* (1862) 14 Maid bere heuen king.. þer for sso ne les noȝt hir flure. **1393** GOWER *Conf.* II. 334 O Pallas noble quene..Help, that I lese nought my flour.

d. An embellishment or ornament (of speech); a choice phrase. *rare* in *sing.*

1508 DUNBAR *Gold. Targe* 117 Thare was Mercurius, wise and eloquent, Of rethorike that fand the flouris faire. **1533** UDALL (*title*) Flovres for Latyne Spekynge, selected and gathered oute of Terence. **1665** BOYLE *Occas. Refl.* v. i. (1845) 298 Discourses not tricked up with Flowers of Rhetorick. **1779** SHERIDAN *Critic* I. i, Your occasional tropes and flowers suit the general coarseness of your style, as tambour sprigs would a ground of linsey-woolsey. **1819** MOORE *Tom Crib's Mem.* (ed. 3) 41 Bob's harangue, 'Twas deuced fine..All full of flowers. **1873** DIXON *Two Queens* III. XV. iii. 145 Ulrich von Hutten heard Italian orators smother them 'in flowers of speech'.

7. The choicest individual or individuals among a number of persons or things; 'the pick'.

flower of chivalry, etc., may belong to this sense or to 9, according as the accompanying sb. is taken as *abstr.* or *concr.*

c **1200** *Trin. Coll. Hom.* 257 Moder milde flur of alle. **1297** R. GLOUC. (1724) 433 Þe noble tour, þat of all þe tours of Engelond ys yholde flour. ? **1370** *Robt. Cicyle* 50 He was of chevalrye the floure. **1508** DUNBAR *Poems* iv. 50 The noble Chaucer, of makaris flouir. **1548** HALL *Chron.*, *Hen IV* (an. 1) 17 b, There wer slain the flower of all Loughdean. **1579** TOMSON *Calvin's Serm. Tim.* 1017/2 They were the flowre ..of the Elect. **1581** MULCASTER *Positions* xxxix. (1887) 197 Noblemen, which be the flowre of gentilitie. **1649** BP. HALL *Cases Consc.* 443 S. Ambrose, and S. Augustine (the flower of the Latine fathers)..doe bitterly oppose it. **1764** *Mem. G. Psalmanazar* 74 Yet I was always singled out as the flower of the flock. **1783** WATSON *Philip III* I. (1839) 49 They had consented to his selecting the flower of the English forces. **1800-24** CAMPBELL *Brave Roland* vi, Roland, the flower of chivalry. **1847** TENNYSON *Princess* v. 277, I take her for the flower of womankind. **1849** MACAULAY *Hist. Eng.* II. 348 The London clergy, then universally acknowledged to be the flower of their profession, held a meeting.

8. The best, choicest, most attractive or desirable part or product of anything, material or immaterial; the essence, quintessence; also 'the gist' (of a matter).

The earliest appearance of this sense in English is in the specific application now differentiated as FLOUR *sb.*, q.v.

1568 TILNEY *Disc. Mariage* A viij, Matromonie.. containeth the felicity of man's life, the Flower of Friendship. **1599** H. BUTTES *Dyets drie Dinner* N v, Creame ..Flos lactis. Rightly so tearmed by the Latines, for it is the very flower of milke, as also butter is the flower of Creame. **1630** *R. Johnson's Kingd. & Commw.* 351 The flower of gaine and emolument to this State. **1685** BAXTER *Paraph. N.T.*, *Phil.* iv. 4 That holy joy in the Lord is that Flower of Religion which all Christians should desire. *a* **1732** GAY *Fables, Man, Cat, Dog & Fly* 124, I sip the tea's delicious flower. **1837** CARLYLE *Fr. Rev.* III. III. v, The flower of the

matter is, that they are but nine; that they sit in secret. **1842** TENNYSON *E. Morris* 69 Thrice-happy days! The flower of each, those moments when we met. **1871** TYNDALL *Fragm. Sc.* (1879) II. ii. 27 Here we have the flower and outcome of Newton's induction.

9. The brightest and fairest example or embodiment of any quality. Cf. PINK.

1297 R. GLOUC. (1724) 213 Syre Wawein ys neueu, flour of corteysye. *c* **1386** CHAUCER *Monk's T.* 107 In his tyme of strengthe he [Hercules] was the flour. *c* **1450** *Crt. of Love* 3 The floure of porte in womanhede. **1508** DUNBAR *Poems* vii. 81 Prynce of fredom, and flour of gentilnes. **1581** SIDNEY *Astr. & Stella* xcix, Mornes messenger.. Cals each wight to salute the floure of blisse. **1592** SHAKS. *Rom. & Jul.* II. v. 44 He is not the flower of curtesie. **1611** CORYAT *Crudities* 353 Cicero, Hortensius, Caesar, and those other selected flowers of eloquence. **1859** TENNYSON *Elaine* 113 Lancelot, the flower of bravery.

10. a. The state or condition of being in bloom or blossom; in phrases ***in flower***, † ***in (their) flowers***.

1697 DRYDEN *Virg. Georg.* IV. 209 His Limes were first in Flow'rs. **1701** *Lond. Gaz.* No. 3697/4 Ranunculos's, and Tulips, in their Flowers. **1712** ADDISON *Spect.* No. 414 ⁋5 An Orchard in Flower looks.. more delightful than.. the most finished Parterre.

†**b.** *transf.* of birds. *Obs.*

1607 TOPSELL *Serpents* (1658) 654 Young birds.. are in their full flowre ere one be a ware. **1655** STANLEY *Hist. Philos.* I. (1701) 29/2 Cocks, Pheasants, and Peacocks.. are much more beautiful in their natural flower.

11. Of persons: The period or state of 'bloom', vigour, or prosperity. **a.** The prime (of life), the bloom (of youth); *esp.* in phrases, † ***in youth's flowers, in the flower of one's age***.

1508 DUNBAR *Twa mariit wemen* 170 A ȝoung man ryght ȝaip, bot nought in ȝouth[is] flouris. **1548** HALL *Chron., Hen. IV* (an. 13) 32 Taken prisoner and so remained in Englande.. till the flower of his age was passed or sore blemyshed. **1577** NORTHBROOKE *Dicing* (1843) 41 Let not the floure of life passe by us. **1647–8** COTTERELL *Davila's Hist. Fr.* (1678) 4 In the first flower of his age. **1733** POPE *Hor. Sat.* II. i. 102 In flow'r of age you perish for a song! **1827** SCOTT *Jrnl.* 4 Aug., He is a man in the flower of life, about thirty. **1830** TENNYSON *Lady Clara* ii, A simple maiden in her flower Is worth a hundred coats-of-arms. **1863** MARY HOWITT *F. Bremer's Greece* I. viii. 257 They were in the flower of youth and beauty.

†**b.** The state or condition of greatest eminence, fame, prosperity, etc. Chiefly phr. ***in one's flower(s***.

c **1380** WYCLIF *Serm.* Sel. Wks. I. 316 þe Emperour of Rome was þanne in his flouris. *c* **1386** CHAUCER *Knt's T.* 2190 A man hath most honour To dyen in his excellence and flour. ? *a* **1500** *Chester Pl.* (E.E.T.S.) 434 Alas! now fallen is my flower! **1547–64** BAULDWIN *Mor. Philos.* (Palfr.) 2 In which time Æsopus the orator was in his flower. **1550** COVERDALE *Bk. Death* I. xl. 158 Whyle a man is in his floures of health. **1665** J. WEBB *Stone-Heng* (1725) 207 Jeffery Monmouth was in his Flower Anno 1156.

†**c.** Bloom or beauty. *Obs.*

1608 SHAKS. *Per.* III. ii 96 See how she gins to blow Into life's flower again!

12. a. Simple attrib., as ***flower-bed, -bell, -border, -court, -garden, -garland, -jar, -plat, -plot, -root, -seed, -sheath, -shop, -show, -spike, -stand, -stick, -time, -tree***.

1873 LONGF. *Wayside Inn, Landlord's T., Sir Christopher* 41 A modest *flower-bed thickly sown with sweet alyssum. **1830** TENNYSON *Isabel* iii, The stem, which else had fallen quite With cluster'd *flower-bells. **1712** J. JAMES tr. *Le Blond's Gardening* 36 A *Flower-Border. **1824** MISS MITFORD *Village* Ser. I. (1863) 234 She was.. delving and digging in her flower-border. **1828** *Ibid.* Ser. III. (1863) 25 Behind the house is an ample kitchen-garden, and before, a neat *flower-court. **1672** W. HUGHES (*title*), The *Flower-Garden. **1841** LANE *Arab. Nts.* I. 96 The court resembled a flower-garden. **1303** R. BRUNNE *Handl. Synne* 997 Ȝyf þou euer.. Dedyst *floure gerlande or coroune To makë wommen to gadyr. **1835** *Southern Lit. Messenger* I. 239 Getting some water from a *flower jar, I sprinkled it over her face. **1863** B. TAYLOR *H. Thurston* ii. 35 Mrs. Babb.. had gathered.. the chrysanthemums.. and stuck them into an old glass flower-jar. **1796** *Plain Sense* II. 49 The little *flower plat put forth its beauties. **1854** HAWTHORNE *Eng. Note-bks.* (1870) II. 307 Suburban villas.. with fancifully ornamented flower-plats before them. **1644** J. SERGEANT in Digby *Nat. Bodies* (1645) *2 a, Yours is a *Flower-plot pav'd by Truth's rich Gold. **1838** THIRLWALL *Greece* III. xx. 140 A little flower-plot, the superfluous ornament of a rich man's estate. **1664** EVELYN *Kal. Hort.* (1729) 208 Such Plants and *Flower-Roots as endure not well out of the Ground. **1824** MISS MITFORD *Village* Ser. I. (1863) 241 Flower-roots, sundry boxes of books, a piano-forte. **1807** JANE AUSTEN *Let.* 20 Feb. (1932) I. 182 You are recommended to bring away some *flower-seeds. **1866** A. D. WHITNEY *L. Goldthwaite* vii, There were flower-seeds —bags labelled 'Petunia'. **1859** TENNYSON *Enid* 365 A blossom vermeil-white, That lightly breaks a faded *flower-sheath. **1867** *Amer. Naturalist* May. I. 154 Branches of this early gem may now be purchased.. at the *flower-shops of Boston. **1845** MRS. CARLYLE *Lett.* I. 316, I went.. to a *flower-show in the Botanical Gardens. **1845** *Florist's Jrnl.* 35 *Flower-spike from 2 to 3 feet long. **1838** LYTTON *Alice* 125 [She] busied herself with a *flower-stand in the recess. **1881** YOUNG *Ev. Man his own Mechanic* §708 *Flower-sticks may be square or round, according to the fancy of the maker. **1873** SYMONDS *Grk. Poets* v. 127 This was the *flower-time of the Aeolians, their brief and brilliant spring. *c* **1710** C. FIENNES *Diary* (1888) 142 All sort of Greens and *flower trees.

b. objective, as ***flower-gatherer, -maker, -painter, -vendor; flower-gathering, -making, painting***, vbl. sbs.; ***flower-bearing, -breeding, -infolding, -sucking*** adjs.

1870 HOOKER *Stud. Flora* 422 Gramineæ.. normally *flower-bearing (but sometimes also empty) glumes. **1891** *Daily News* 4 Feb. 5/7 Behind the hearse there was a body of flower-bearing mutes. **1767** G. S. CAREY *Hills of Hybla* 1 O'er.. *flower-breeding vales. **1611** SPEED *Theat. Gt. Brit.* xliv. 87/1 So the *flower gatherer of Westminster recordeth. **1933** R. TUVE *Seasons & Months* iv. 163 A *flower-gathering scene is similar in temper. **1821** SHELLEY *Prometh. Unb.* II. i, The *flower-infolding buds Burst on yon lightning-blasted almond-tree. **1809** HAN. MORE. *Cœlebs* (ed. 3) I. 145 The street where the poor *flower-maker lived. **1884** BECK *Draper's Dict.* 130 Dyed feathers when used in *flower-making are.. apt to fade. **1711** SHAFTESB. *Charac.* (1737) III. 349 The mere *flower-painter is.. oblig'd to study the form of festons. **1854** FAIRHOLT *Dict. Terms Art*, **Flower-painting*.. may be said to have asserted its proper place as an Art *sui generis* in the seventeenth century. **1621** G. SANDYS *Ovid's Met.* xv. (1626) 313 *Flowre-sucking Bees. **1861** *Crt. Life at Naples* I. 207 The beggars and *flower-vendors sought shady nooks.

c. instrumental, as ***flower-bespangled, -besprinkled, -crowned, -decked, -embroidered, -enamelled, -inwoven, -sprinkled, -strewn, -teeming*** adjs.

1883 STEVENSON *Silverado Sq.* (1886) 20 Thicket, still fragrant and still *flower-bespangled. **1851** LONGF. *Gold. Leg.* III. *Sq. in front Cathedral*, It looks like a *flower-besprinkled meadow. **1606** SYLVESTER *Du Bartas* II. iv. *Magnif.* 808 The *flowr-crown'd People, swarming on the Green. **1870** BRYANT *Iliad* I. VIII. 248 Bowls of wine flower-crowned. **1805** WORDSW. *Prelude* IV. (1888) 262/1, I had left a *flower-decked room. **1747** LD. G. LYTTELTON *Monody* v. 58 Sequester'd dales And *flower-embroider'd vales. **1603** DRAYTON *Bar. Wars* V. xviii, Along the *flow'r enamell'd vales The silver Trent.. doth slide. **1629** MILTON *Nativity* 187 With *flower-inwoven tresses torn The nymphs in twilight shade of tangled thickets mourn. **1859** GEO. ELIOT *A. Bede* 13 The scythe being whetted makes us cast more lingering looks at the *flower-sprinkled tresses of the meadows. **1847** MARY HOWITT *Ballads* etc. 363 The *flower-strewn earth is wondrous fair. **1838** MISS PARDOE *River & Desert* II. 43 A *flower-teeming land.

d. parasynthetic and similative, as ***flower-bright, -faced, -like, -shaped, -soft, -sweet, -wise*** adjs.; ***flower-like, -wise*** advs.

1906 *Daily Chron.* 11 Apr. 8/1 The.. *flower-bright stretches of the great park. **1952** C. DAY LEWIS tr. *Virgil's Aeneid* XII. 278 Led by the queen's daughter, who tore at her flower-bright tresses And rose-petal cheeks. **1881** RITA *My Lady Coquette* I. iii, He glances down at the slim, *flower-faced maiden. **1604** ROWLANDS *Looke to it* 47 *Flower-like they wither and decay. **1846** ELLIS *Elgin Marb.* I. 28 Surmounted by a flower-like ornament. **1836–7** TODD *Cycl. Anat.* II. 414/1 Tubes, ending in *flower-shaped capsules. **1606** SHAKS. *Ant. & Cl.* II. ii. 215 The Silken Tackle, Swell with the touches of those *Flower-soft hands. **1865** SWINBURNE *Chastelard* I. i, I love her for sweet eyes or brows or hair, For the smooth temples, where God touching her Made blue with sweeter veins the *flower-sweet white. **1908** HARDY *Dynasts* III. v. ii. 431 To put it so is flower-sweet of you. **1925** J. GREGORY *Bab of Backwoods* 34 Flower-sweet attributes of girlhood. **1865** SWINBURNE *Atlanta* 213 [Grief shall come] *Flower-wise upon the old root of tears brought forth.

13. a. Special comb.: **flower-animals**, a book-name for the Anthozoa; **flower arrangement**, the decorative arrangement of flowers; hence (as a back-formation) **flower-arrange** *v. intr.*; also **flower-arranger**, **flower-arranging** *vbl. sb.*; **flower-beetle** *U.S.*, a beetle which feeds upon flowers, esp. one belonging to the sub-family Cetoniinæ; **flower-book**, a book in which (*a*) drawings of flowers are made; (*b*) collected flowers are preserved; **flower-box**, a box in which flowers are grown, e.g. one placed outside a window, a window-box; **flower-bud**, an unopened flower, as distinguished from a leaf-bud; **flower-bug**, *U.S.*, the popular name of various small hemipterous insects which frequent the blossoms of flowering plants, as the species of *Anthocoris* (*Cent. Dict.*); **flower-cup**, (*a*) the calyx; (*b*) the cup-shaped receptacle formed by a flower; **flower decoration** = *flower arrangement*; **flower-fence**, the plant *Poinciana pulcherrima*; **flower-fly**, a dipterous insect which frequents flowers, esp. one belonging to the family Syrphidæ; **flower-girl**, a girl who sells flowers; **flower-head**, an inflorescence consisting of a close cluster of sessile florets; **flower-honey** (see quot.); **flower-knot**, a small flower-bed arranged in a pattern; **flower-leaf**, a petal; **flower-pecker**, (*a*) a name for birds of the family *Dicæidæ*; (*b*) 'an American honey-creeper or guitguit of the family *Cœrebidæ*' (*Cent. Dict.*); **flower-piece**, (*a*) a picture with flowers for its subject; (*b*) an arrangement of flowers; **flower-printed** *a.*, bearing a floral design; **flower room**, a work-room in which flowers are arranged; **flower-stalk**, the peduncle supporting the flower or flower-head; **flower-water**, distilled water containing the essential oil of flowers; **flower-work**, a representation of flowers in weaving, carving, etc.

1840 F. D. BENNETT *Whaling Voy.* I. 177 The elegant *flower-animal, *Diazoma*, is found on the barrier-reef. **1846** DANA *Zooph.* i. (1848) 7 The forms of life under consideration.. are appropriately styled flower-animals. **1900** G. JEKYLL *Home & Garden* xiii. 141 The elaborate system of *flower arrangement practised by the Japanese. **1933** A. L. SADLER *Art Flower Arrangem. Japan* iv. 54 The names of the three elements of a flower arrangement are taken from the three powers of nature, Heaven, Earth and Man. **1962** I. MURDOCH *Unofficial Rose* xxxv. 336 She noted .. which buds would be ready.. for her flower-arrangement at the Women's Institute. **1955** in *Amer. Speech* (1956) XXXI. 84 J—— is *flower-arranging. **1967** *Listener* 16 Mar. 357/3 It is no wonder that flower arranging is a difficult business. **1966** *Times* 17 Sept. 12/1 (*caption*) *Flower arrangers make great use of shrubs, both for their flowers and their foliage. **1842** T. W. HARRIS *Insects Injur. Veget.* 22 The tree-beetles.. during the same period of their lives, frequent flowers, and are called *flower-beetles. **1895** J. H. & A. COMSTOCK *Man. Stud. Insects* xxi. 564 The flower-beetles are so called because many of them are often seen feeding upon pollen and flying from flower to flower. **1955** BORROR & DELONG *Introd. Study Insects* xxii. 390 The flower beetles are principally pollen feeders. **1753–4** SHENSTONE *Poet. Wks.* (1854) 137 (*title*) Written in a *flower book of my own colouring. **1857** THOREAU *Maine W.* (1894) 277, I used some thin and delicate sheets of this bark.. in my flower-book. **1876** J. S. INGRAM *Centenn. Exposition* xii. 398 The general description of tiles made by this firm are here enumerated. Encaustic and tesselated tile pavement; .. *flower-boxes, etc. **1871** *Leisure Hour* 478/1 One kind [of caterpillar].. manages to enclose a young *flower-bud betwixt the leaves. **1756** P. BROWNE *Jamaica* 140 The *flower-cups are cut into four deep segments at the margin. **1860** TYAS *Wild Fl.* 41 The flower cup consists of two obtuse lips. **1907** G. JEKYLL (*title*) *Flower decoration in the house. **1937** C. SPRY *Flowers in House & Garden* 143 If one wants to achieve a facility with flower decorations there should be endless experiment of arranging them. **1967** *Everyman Encycl.* V. 338/1 Flower decoration. The arrangement of F[lower]s for interior adornment has achieved.. popularity. **1786** REES *Cycl.*, *Barbadoes *flower-fence, poinciana*.. is planted in hedges, to divide the lands in Barbadoes, from whence it had the title of flower-fence. **1882** J. SMITH *Dict. Econ. Plants*, *Flower-fence*, a name in India for *Cæsalpinia* (*Poinciana*) *pulcherrima*. **1842** T. W. HARRIS *Insects Injur. Veget.* 414 *Flower-flies.. are easily distinguished from the preceding flies.. by the smaller size of their winglets. **1951** C. N. COLYER *Flies Brit. Isles* xii. 154 (*heading*) *Syrphidae*, hover-flies, drone flies, flower flies. **1789** MRS. PIOZZI *Journ. France* I. 236 *Flower-girls with baskets. **1889** *Tablet* 3 Aug. 167 There are two classes of flower-girl—the day-sellers and the night-sellers. **1845** LINDLEY *Sch. Bot.* i. (1858) 12 The **flower-head*, when all the flowers are sessile upon a broad plate.. as in the Daisy. **1577** B. GOOGE *Heresbach's Husb.* IV. 184 There is three sortes of Hony, the best kinde is that which is called.. *flowre Hony, made in the springtime. **1601** HOLLAND *Pliny* I. 316 Floure-honey. **1770** ARMSTRONG *Misc.* II. 142 The sweet green.. is the predominant colour; while the gaudy flowers.. are carelessly interspersed. This is infinitely more pleasing and beautiful than.. a *flower-knot. **1893** *S.E. Worc. Gloss.*, *Flower-knot*, a small flower bed. **1727** BAILEY vol. II, *Dipetalous Flower* .. is that which has two *Flower Leaves. **1860** OLIVER *Less. Bot.* (1873) 4 Whether it be green, as are foliage-leaves, or coloured, as are flower-leaves. **1885** H. O. FORBES *Nat. Wand. E. Archip.* vi. 212 Little flocks of the small green *Flower-pecker (Zosterops). *a* **1784** JOHNSON *Wks.* (1816) I. 334 A room hung with *flower-pieces of her own painting. **1952** R. S. THOMAS *Acre of Land* 31 He cannot read the *flower-printed book Of nature. **1970** *Daily Tel.* 17 Apr. 17 Maxi dress with sash belt, in turquoise flower-printed cotton. **1873** *Young Englishwoman* Nov. 562 A *flower room. **1967** M. SUMMERTON *Memory of Darkness* vii. 95, I retired to the flower room in which Fenton had dumped enough ill-assorted blooms to stock a florist's. **1968** A. CHRISTIE *By Pricking of my Thumbs* vii. 85 'A flower room, I shouldn't wonder,' he said. 'Where people used to do the flowers. See?' **1789** PILKINGTON *View Derbysh.* I. 415 Three inches of its *flowerstalk may be seen above the surface. **1886** *U.S. Consular Rep.* No. lxviii. 581 *Flower waters are produced by ordinary distillation, in which the flowers are boiled with water in large alembics. **1601** HOLLAND *Pliny* I. 228 Robes .. wrought thick with *floure-worke, resembling poppies. **1848** RICKMAN *Archit.* 211 The benches.. present in their ends and fronts, combinations of panelling and flower-work. **1865** E. BURRITT *Walk to Land's End* 193 It is a pity.. such flower-work [lace] should be so poorly paid.

b. flower children, people, term applied to the adherents of a sub-group of hippies, so called from their habit of wearing or carrying flowers as symbols of peace and love. Also **flower power**, an expression used to describe the beliefs and conventions of this sub-group.

1967 *Times* 13 July 2/6 The term flower children has been given to devotees of mind-expanding drugs in California. **1967** *Guardian* 25 July 6/6 Beat-reared, Greenwich-nurtured teenagers are running away.. to be flower people. **1967** *Listener* 3 Aug. 131/3 A new world consisting very largely of the hippies, the flower-power generation. **1967** *Time* 25 Aug. 38 In came the beautiful people on four motorcycles, right into the ballroom, oozing with flower-power. **1969** N. COHN *AWopBopaLooBop* (1970) xxiv. 225 As fads go, Flower Power was less than impressive... London was content mostly to ape California. Everyone wore kaftans and beads and bells. Everyone spoke in hushed tones of San Francisco and Monterey, of acid and Love and the Maharishi. **1969** *Listener* 5 June 793/2 The political innocence of the Hornsey flower children. **1970** *Globe Mag.* (Toronto) 26 Sept. 14/1 The flower children.. arrive by the hundreds to find thousands like themselves sleeping in vacant lots. **1971** K. AMIS *Girl, 20* iv. 152 Just another fun thing and now thing, like these clothes they all wear and theatre in the nude and flower power and environmental art.

flower ('flaʊə(r)), *v.* Forms: 4–7 flour(e, 5–7 flowr, (5 flore), 6– flower. [f. prec. sb. Cf. OF. *florir* (mod.F. *fleurir*), L. *flōrēre*.]

1. a. *intr.* To bloom or blossom; to come into bloom, produce flowers. Of a flower: To expand, open.

13.. *K. Alis.* 2904 þe medes floureþ, þe foules syngeþ. **13..** *E.E. Allit. P.* A. 270 A rose, þat flowred and fayled as kynd hit gef. **1393** GOWER *Conf.* II. 266 A drie braunche..

which anon gan floure and bere. *c* **1440** *Promp. Parv.* 168/1 Flowryn. **1578** LYTE *Dodoens* v. lxxx. 651 The vine flowreth in high and base Germanie..about the beginning of June. **1672** GREW *Anat. Plants, Idea Philos. Hist.* (1682) §14 Plants, which flower all the Year. **1712** ADDISON *Spect.* No. 418 ¶8 His Rose-trees, Wood-bines and Jessamines may flower together. **1842** N. B. WARD *Closed Cases Pl.* iii. (1852) 51 All these [plants] flowered well. **1873** SYMONDS *Grk. Poets* v. 128 Olive-groves..where the cyclamen and violet flowered with feathery maiden-hair.

b. *fig.* Also with *out, into.* †*to flower off*: (of reflexions) to arise spontaneously in the treatment of a subject.

a **1225** *Ancr. R.* 340 Mi vlesch is iflured & bicumen al neowe. *c* **1374** CHAUCER *Anel. & Arc.* 306 Your chere floureth, but hit wol not sede. **1642** MORE *Song of Soul* III. III. xxxviii. 1 Whose drooping phansie never flowrd out. **1644** MILTON *Educ.* Wks. (1738) I. 135 If you can accept of these few Observations which have flowr'd off. **1846** LANDOR *Imag. Conv.* Wks. II. 34 The thorny and bitter aloe of dissension required less than a century to flower on the steps of your temple. **1859** HAWTHORNE *Marb. Faun* xxxiv. (1883) 358 The mediæval front of the cathedral, where the imagination of a Gothic architect had long ago flowered out indestructibly. **1865** M. C. HARRIS *Christine* xxxii, It seemed as if earth had suddenly flowered into a paradise. *Ibid.* xxxvi, The evil in him had flowered out into luxurious growth. **1885** CLODD *Myths & Dr.* II. i. 146 The germs of those capacities which..have flowered in the noblest and wisest of our race.

c. *trans.* (causatively). To cause (a plant) to bloom; to bring into blossom or flower.

1850 *Florist* Mar. 66 They winter better in the pots they were flowered in. **1887** BARING-GOULD *Gold. Feather* xii, Azaleas which were..put under glass and flowered.

†**2.** *transf.* Of beer and wine: **a.** To froth, mantle. *Obs.*

1382 WYCLIF *Prov.* xxiii. 31 Ne beholde..the win, whan it floureth. **1530** PALSGR. 552/2 This ale floureth better in a good drinkers eye. *a* **1592** GREENE & LODGE *Looking Glasse* Wks. (Rtldg.) 127/2 All Nineveh hath not such a cup of ale, it flowers in the cup. **1694** WESTMACOTT *Script. Herb.* 22 It makes beer to mantle, flower, and smile at you. **1750** W. ELLIS *Country Housewife's Fam. Comp.* 187 If a little wheat-bran is boiled in our ordinary beer, it will cause it to mantle or flower in the cup, when it is poured out.

†**b.** To become turbid. *Obs.*

1682 *Art & Myst. Vintners* IV. §17 Rack [sack] into another Cask, and it will not then flower nor be ill-conditioned.

†**c.** *trans.* To spice (wine). *Obs.*

1682 *Art & Myst. Vintners* I. §28 To flower a Butt of Muskadine.

†**3.** *intr.* To be in or attain the 'flower' or height of one's beauty, fame, or prosperity (also with *up*); to prosper, be distinguished; to thrive or be distinguished *in, of* or *with* (a specified thing); to abound; = FLOURISH *v.* 3, 4. *Obs.*

1340 *Ayenb.* 28 Ase ine yere þet wel floureþ ine guode. *c* **1374** CHAUCER *Boeth.* v. pr. v. 131 Forto dwellen in hys Citee and flouren of rychesses. *c* **1430** LYDG. *Bochas* I. viii. (1544) 12 b, While he floured in his worthines He toke a wyfe of excellent fayrenes. *Ibid.* I. iv. (1544) 8 Flouryng up in her tender age This sayd Isis so pleasaunt was and mete. **1494** FABYAN *Chron.* v. cxl. §125 In this tyme flowryd Hermafreditus. **1513** BRADSHAW *St. Werburge* I. 327 This Redwalde had .ii. sones flourynge in chyualrye. **1531** ELYOT *Gov.* I. xi, That noble clerke of Almaine, which late floured, called Agricola.

†**4.** *trans.* To adorn or cover with or as with flowers or a flower; to decorate; to serve as a decoration for. Also with *over. Obs.*

1577–8 HOLINSHED *Chron.* (1808) IV. 870 He..floured the top of the castell of Dublin with the archrebels head. **1630** *R. Johnson's Kingd. and Commw.* 290 The Chambers are flowred with coloured Marbles, and garnished. **1645** RUTHERFORD *Tryal & Tri. Faith* (1845) 11 Christ, who perfumeth and flowereth heaven with his royal presence. *c* **1650** *Robin Hood & Three Squires* 66 in Furniv. *Percy Folio* I. 18 Thou shalt be the first man shall flower this gallow tree. **1791** W. BARTRAM *Carolina* 161 Its thick foliage..is flowered over with large milk-white fragrant blossoms.

5. a. To embellish with figures of flowers or a floral design; to work flowers upon.

16.. *Young Tam Lane* iii. in Child *Ballads* II. (1884) 352/1 I'll away to Carterhaugh, And flower mysell the gown. **1699** DAMPIER *Voy* II. I. 61 The Pelongs and Gaws, are..either plain or flower'd. **1741** RICHARDSON *Pamela* (1824) I. xix. 30 Mrs. Jervis shewed my master the waistcoat I am flowering for him. **1838** MISS MITFORD in *Tait's Mag.* V. 165 The form of a heather sprig suggested an apron that she was flowering. **1857** MRS. CARLYLE *Lett.* II. 377 Ann flowered me a most lovely collar.

transf. and *fig.* **1853** M. ARNOLD *Poems, Sohrab & Rustum*, The frost flowers the whiten'd window-panes. **1882** BLACKMORE *Christowell* I. iv. 37 Many sweet beauties..flower the skirts of the desolate moor.

b. *intr.* Of silver alloyed for use as coin: To assume the appearance of being marked with figures of flowers. See FLOWERED *ppl. a.* 3 b.

1727 A. HAMILTON *New Acc. E. Ind.* II. xxxvi. 42 Rupee Silver..will bear twenty-eight per cent. of Copper-alloy..and if it flowers, it passes current.

flowerage ('flaʊərɪdʒ). [f. FLOWER *sb.* and *v.* + -AGE[1]. Cf. OF. *fleurage.*]

†**1.** (See quot.) Obs.

1688 R. HOLME *Armoury*, II. 115/2 Flowerage is the setting of sorts of Flower together, in husks, and so to hang them up with strings [Hence 1706 in PHILLIPS (ed. Kersey); and in later Dicts.].

2. a. Flowers collectively, blossom; a display or assemblage of flowers; floral ornament or decoration. *lit.* and *fig.* **b.** The process of flowering; the result of this process. *lit.* and *fig.*

1831 J. WILSON *Unimore* vi. 9 Never..the goats..On such profusion of wild flowerage browsed. **1840** CARLYLE *Heroes* iii. (1858) 261 This glorious Elizabethan Era with its Shakspeare, as the outcome and flowerage of all which had preceded it. **1864** TENNYSON *Aylmer's F.* 203 The flowerage That stood from out a rich brocade. **1880** SWINBURNE *Stud. in Song* 78 The zone of their flowerage [sea-weed] that knows not of sunshine and snow. **1887** W. PATER *Imag. Portraits* iv. 144 A wonderful flowerage of architectural fancy..passed over and beyond the earlier fabric.

flowered ('flaʊəd), *ppl. a.* [f. FLOWER *sb.* and *v.* + -ED[1], [2].]

1. Having flowers; covered with flowers or blossoms; adorned or decked with flowers.

c **1350** *Will. Palerne* 757 þat [appel] tre so fayre was floured & so ful leued. **1389** in *Eng. Gilds* (1870) 30 Yey..schullen offeren to floured candelys a-forn seynt Willyams toumbe. **1523** FITZHERB. *Husb.* §20 Hawdod hath..v. or syxe braunches, floured in the toppe. **1601** WEEVER *Mirr. Mart.* VI. ii. These Nimphs of Ashdon forrest neuer haunted Medways flour'd banks. **1832** TENNYSON *Miller's Dau.* 112 I came, and lay Upon the freshly-flower'd slope.

b. Bearing flowers (of a specified kind or number).

1592 BRETON *Pilgr. Parad.* xxxiii (Grosart) I. 8 He..faire flourd weedes, as poison foule refused. **1753** CHAMBERS *Cycl. Supp., Poinciana*..Purple-flowered *acacia*. **1776** WITHERING *Brit. Plants* (1796) II. 157 Calyx 6 or 8-flowered. **1842** TENNYSON *Godiva* 63 She saw The white-flower'd elder-thicket. **1877–84** F. E. HULME *Wild Fl.* p. v, Peduncle axillary, one or two-flowered.

†**2.** In flower or bloom. *Obs.*

1633 P. FLETCHER *Purple Isl.* VI. lxviii, The early Violet..spreading his flour'd purple to the skies. **1787** *Generous Attachm.* IV. 170 A bed of flowered asparagus.

3. Embellished with figures of flowers, or with flower-like patterns.

1592 SHAKS. *Rom. & Jul.* II. iv. 64 Why then is my Pump well flower'd. **1663** DRYDEN *Wild Gallant* III. ii, Your gown ..flowered satin. **1742** MRS. PENDARVES in Sydney *Eng. in 18 C.* I. 98 Very handsome flowered silks shaded like embroidery. **1796** MORSE *Amer. Geog.* II. 172 Polished stones, embossed and elegantly flowered. **1812–6** J. SMITH *Panorama Sc. & Art.* I. 151 Some of the later perpendicular buildings have much less flowered carvings. **1825** HONE *Every-day Bk.* I. 967 Flowered Indian gowns.

b. *flowered silver*: see quot. 1886.

1727 A. HAMILTON *New Acc. E. Ind.* II. xxxvi. 43 Tho' it [Silver] be not flower'd, it must go off in all his Payments, but from any Body else it may be refused if it is not flower'd. **1886** YULE & BURNELL *Gloss. Anglo-Ind., Flowered-Silver*, a term applied by Europeans in Burma to the standard quality of silver..The term is taken from the appearance of stars and radiating lines, which forms on the surface of this particular alloy, as it cools in the crucible.

c. *Her.* = FLEURY.

1739 J. COATS *Dict. Her.* (ed. 2) s.v. *Flory*, All Things Flower'd, or Flory, in Arms, respect only the French Lilly, or Fleur de Lys.

flowerer ('flaʊərə(r)). [f. FLOWER *v.* + -ER[1].] A person or thing that flowers.

1. A plant that flowers in some specified way or at some specified season.

1851 GLENNY *Handbk. Fl. Gard.* 194 These Chrysanthemums..being abundant flowerers. **1882** *Garden* 21 Jan. 34/1 Auriculas are spring flowerers.

2. (See quot.)

1865 E. METEYARD *Life J. Wedgwood* I. 234 Women, called flowerers, who..incised by faint lines flowers..or grotesque imitations of Chinese pagodas [etc.].

floweret ('flaʊərɪt). Chiefly *poet.* Also 4 flourette, 6–7 flouret, 7–8 flowret. [f. FLOWER *sb.* + -ET[1]. Cf. FLORET.] A small flower.

c **1400** *Rom. Rose* 891 For nought y-clad in silk was he, But al in floures and flourettes. **1590** SHAKS. *Mids. N.* IV. i. 60 That same dew..Stood now within the pretty flouriets eyes. **1667** MILTON *P.L.* v. 379 The Silvan Lodge..With flourets deck't. **1782** V. KNOX *Ess.* (1819) II. cxvii. 292 The charms of a tree or a flowret. **1838** LONGF. *Reaper & Flowers* iv, My Lord has need of these flowerets gay. **1873** GEIKIE *Gt. Ice Age* xxx. 423 In arctic regions the short summer brings into bloom a number of pretty flowerets.

fig. **1753–4** SHENSTONE *Poet. Wks.* (1854) 138 Let Art and Friendship's joint essay Diffuse their flowerets in her way.

flowerful ('flaʊəfʊl), *a.* [f. FLOWER *sb.* + -FUL.] Abounding in or filled with flowers.

1848 in CRAIG. **1865** SWINBURNE *Poems & Ball., A Match* 5 Blown fields and flowerful closes. **1887** MRS. COMPTON READE *Maid o' Mill* I. i. 2 A chestnut or two towering up straight and flowerful.

†'**flower-'gentle.** *Obs.* [f. FLOWER *sb.* + GENTLE *a.*; app. in imitation of the Fr. name *fleur noble.* No Fr. **fleur gentille* is known.] = FLORAMOUR.

1561 *Grant of Arms to Dr. Caius* in Willis & Clark *Cambridge* (1886) I. 179 Crest: a dove..with a flower gentle in his mouth. **1578** LYTE *Dodoens* I. xviii. 168 These pleasant ..floures are called..in English floure Gentill, Floramor, & Purple veluet floure. **1630** W. T. *Justif. Relig. Professed* v. 36 Of Flower-gentle whose beauty and colour doth not fade nor wither away. **1783** AINSWORTH *Lat. Dict.* (Morell) I, Flower gentle, or flower amour, **Amaranthus purpureus.*

'**flowering,** *vbl. sb.* [f. FLOWER *v.* + -ING[1].]

1. The action of the vb. FLOWER in various senses.

a. The putting forth of flowers or blossom; coming into flower, blooming.

1629 PARKINSON (*title*) Paradisus in Sole..or a choise Garden of..Flowers, with their Nature, place of Birth, time of flowring [etc.]. **1865** KINGSLEY *Herew.* xv. 185 She regretted the lengthening of the days and the flowering of the primroses. **1882** *Garden* 21 Jan. 34/1 Any dwarf growing annuals would also answer for a second flowering.

fig. **1865** M. ARNOLD *Ess. Crit.* iv. 119 She placed her whole joy in the flowering of this gifted nature.

b. The action of adorning with flowers, or with figures of flowers.

1739 J. COATS *Dict. Her.* (ed. 2) s.v. *Flory*, Fleury, Flory, Fleurty, Floretty..signify different Ways of Flowering. **1848** CRAIG, *Flowering*..the act of adorning with flowers.

2. *concr.* or quasi-*concr.* †**a.** *collect.* Blossoms. †**b.** Effervescence; frothiness. †**c.** Efflorescence or superficial growth. **d.** *pl.* Figures of flowers. **e.** (See quot. 1867).

a **1300** *Cursor M.* 10726 (Cott.) þis wand suld fluring bere þat suld o rote o iesse spring. **1626** BACON *Sylva* §312 The Spirits..become Dull, and the Drinke dead, which ought to haue a little Flouring. **1634** T. JOHNSON *Parry's Chirurg.* III. iii. 88 A certaine drie flouring, or production of the true skinne. **1864** CARLYLE *Fredk. Gt.* (1865) IV. XI. vii. 171 His dressing-gown, a grand yellow silky article with silver flowerings. **1867** SMYTH *Sailor's Word-bk., Flowering*, the phenomenon observed usually in connection with the spawning of fish, at the distance of four leagues from shore. The water appears to be saturated with a thick jelly, filled with the ova of fish.

3. *attrib.*

1377 LANGL. *P. Pl.* B. XVI. 31 þe flesshe is a fel wynde, and in flourynge-tyme þorw lykyng and lustes so loude he gynneth blowe. **1870** HOOKER *Stud. Flora* 300 Primula scotica..has three flowering seasons. **1879** O. W. HOLMES *Motley* i. 5 The..'flowering time of Authorship'.

flowering ('flaʊərɪŋ), *ppl. a.* [f. as prec. + -ING[2].] That flowers, in various senses.

1. a. That is in bloom; **b.** that bears flowers or blossoms.

a. 1592 WYRLEY *Armorie* 143 Worldly triumphs are like to flowering gras. **1697** DRYDEN *Virg. Georg.* I. 272 Mark well the flowring Almonds in the Wood.

b. 1745 BP. POCOCKE *Descr. East* (1889) II. 141 Clumps of evergreen and flowering plants. **1818** MISS MITFORD in L'Estrange *Life* II. xi. 30 The luxury of that fresh, growing, perfume, a flowering shrub in full bloom. **1872** OLIVER *Elem. Bot.* I. v. 53 Each flower [of Wheat] is enclosed between a flowering-glume and a pale. **1884** RITA *Vivienne* I. i, A broad white road..bordered..by flowering chestnuts.

c. Often in plant-names; as *flowering ash, box, currant, fern*, etc. (see the sbs.).

†**2.** Flourishing, vigorous; that is in one's bloom or prime. *flowering age, life, youth*: the bloom or prime of age, life, or youth. *Obs.*

c **1400** *Rom. Rose* 6259 The gode thought and the worching, That maketh religioun flowring. *a* **1450** *Fysshynge with Angle* (1883) 1 A glad spirit maket a flowryng age. **1558** PHAER *Æneid* VII. V ij b, The bodies twayne Of Almon, flouring lad, and good Galesus fouly slayne. **1586** WARNER *Alb. Eng.* II. x. 41 The one was in her flowring age, the other too too old. **1591** SHAKS. *1 Hen. VI*, II. v. 56 That cause..that..hath detayn'd me all my flowring Youth, Within a loathsome Dungeon. **1621** BURTON *Anat. Mel.* II. iii. III. (1651) 327 'Tis no dishonour..for a flouring man, City, or State to come to ruine.

3. Covered with or abounding in flowers or figures of flowers; = FLOWERY. Also, pertaining to or issuing from flowers.

1593 SHAKS. *2 Hen. VI*, III, i. 228 The Snake, roll'd in a flowring Banke. **1642** H. MORE *Song of Soul* I. I. lvii, This floting flouring changeable array. **1667** MILTON *P.L.* v. 293 Groves of Myrrhe, And flouring Odours. **1871** R. ELLIS *Catullus* lxi. 91 A flowering Garden, trimm'd for a lord's delight.

†'**flowerist.** *Obs.* [f. FLOWER *sb.* + -IST.] = FLORIST.

1694 WESTMACOTT *Script. Herb.* 181 Saffron..hath many kindred..which are propagated in the Gardens of curious Flowerists. **1708** *Lond. Gaz.* No. 4479/8 Charles Blackwell, Seedsman and Flow'rist. **1713** J. PETIVER in *Phil. Trans.* XXVIII. 206 A French Flowerist first communicated this to Cornutus.

flowerless ('flaʊəlɪs), *a.* [f. as prec. + -LESS.] Without flower or bloom; spec. in *Bot.*, *flowerless plant* = CRYPTOGAM.

a **1500** *Chaucer's Dreme* 1860 An herbe he brought, flourelesse, all greene. **1806** J. GRAHAME *Birds Scot.* 99 Lays his silvered head upon the flowerless bank. **1835** LINDLEY *Introd. Bot.* (1840) II. 88 The Antherids of Flowerless plants.

b. Unadorned with flowers.

1892 M. FIELD *Sight & Song* 86 Three virgins, flowerless, slow of step. **1895** *Pall Mall Mag.* Mar. 403 The room had a bleak flowerless look.

Hence '**flowerlessness**, the condition or quality of being flowerless.

1855 in OGILVIE *Supp.* **1895** A. AUSTIN in *Blackw. Mag.* Nov., 641/2 Another apologist for the flowerlessness of Irish peasant dwellings.

flower-pot, flowerpot ('flaʊəpɒt).

1. A vessel, most commonly of red earthenware and slightly tapering downwards, to contain soil in which flowers may be planted.

1598 FLORIO s.v. *Grasta*, Flowerpots or lillypots. **1692–3** *Queen's Coll. Acc.* in Willis & Clark *Cambridge* (1886) III. 385 A Blew flower-pott for the Parlour. **1780** COXE *Russ. Disc.* 223 An open gallery, adorned on both sides with flower-pots. **1856** MRS. CARLYLE *Lett.* II. 288, I brought two live plants in flower-pots.

2. (See quot.)
1842 FRANCIS *Dict. Arts, Flower Pot*, a particular kind of fire-work, that when ignited throws out a fountain of vivid spur-shaped sparks.

flowery (ˈflaʊərɪ), *a.* [f. FLOWER *sb.* + -Y¹.]
1. a. Abounding in or covered with flowers; producing flowers.
13.. *E.E. Allit. P.* A. 57, I felle vpon þat floury flaȝt. *c* **1374** CHAUCER *Boeth.* IV. metr. vi. 111 (Cambr. MS.) The floury ȝer [orig. *florifer annus*]. *c* **1586** C'TESS PEMBROKE *Ps.* xcii. iii, The wicked grow Like fraile, though flowry grasse. **1590** SHAKS. *Mids. N.* IV. i. 1 Come, sit thee downe vpon this flowry bed. **1630** MILTON *Song May Morn.*, The flowery May, who from her green lap throws The yellow cowslip. *a* **1751** DODDRIDGE *Hymns* (1758) 38 The flow'ry Spring at thy Command Embalms the Air. **1781** COWPER *Retirement* 179 The fruits that hang on pleasure's flowery stem. **1808** J. BARLOW *Columb.* I. 91 No more thy flowery vales I travel o'er.
b. In plant-names. †**flowery cole** = CAULIFLOWER.
1578 LYTE *Dodoens* IV. vi. 554 The thirde kinde is called ..in English, Flowrie Cole, or Cypres Colewurtes. **1853** G. JOHNSTON *Bot. E. Borders* 171 *Chenopodium bonus Henricus*, Flowery-Docken.
c. ***Flowery Empire, Kingdom, Land,*** or ***Nation*** [transl. Chinese *hwa kwo*]: China. ***Flowery Land*** also = Florida.
1847 R. FORTUNE *Three Years' Wand.* i. 2 Was this..the 'flowery land',..of which I had heard so much in England? **1859** MAYNE REID *Oçeola* i, The Flowery Land. **1862** *Once a Week* 26 July 138/1 Celestials of the 'flowery' empire. **1867** F. S. COZZENS *Sayings* i. 4 Silk, sir, came from the Flowery Nation. **1870** *Macm. Mag.* XXIII. 172/1 Nor has Christianity..ever been able to obtain a solid footing in the Flowery Land [*sc.* China]. **1901** *Daily Colonist* (Victoria, B.C.) 30 Oct. 8/4 Two of the big Chinese companies have had men at work at Ross Bay cemetery..exhuming the bodies of their dead countrymen for shipment home to China where all loyal citizens of the Flowery Kingdom wish to have their last resting place.
d. ***flowery dell***, rhyming slang for a prison cell. Also *ellipt.*
[**1859** HOTTEN *Dict. Mod. Slang* 40 *Flowery*, lodging, or house entertainment.] **1925** E. JERVIS *25 Yrs. in Six Prisons* i. 16, I talked to him of his 'flowery' ('flowery dell' rhymes with 'cell', hence 'flowery'). **1938** F. D. SHARPE *Sharpe of Flying Squad* xxiv. 248, I bangs and rattles on the door of the Flowery until the screw comes. **1970** T. CLAYTON *Men in Prison* vi. 128 Found aht on the Moor,..that if you have a new play to read weekends in the flowery..you can kid yourself you're having a Saturday night aht.
†**2.** Flourishing, vigorous. *Obs.*⁻¹
a **1420** HOCCLEVE *De Reg. Princ.* 877 Now age unorne away puttethe the favour, That floury youthe in his cesoun conquerde.
3. Composed of flowers; having the nature of flowers; proceeding from or characteristic of flowers.
1635-56 COWLEY *Davideis* I. 236 Neighbring Hermon sweated flowry dew. **1648** JOS. BEAUMONT *Psyche* XIX. ccxl, Herby and floury Gallantry combine Their fairest powers to make her [Earth's] mantle fine. **1712** POPE *Ep. Miss Blount* 65 As flow'ry bands in wantonness are worn. **1727-46** THOMSON *Summer* 212 The flowery race..their new-flushed bloom resign. **1791** MRS. RADCLIFFE *Rom. Forest* i, She viewed the flowery luxuriance of the turf. **1856** KANE *Arct. Expl.* I. xxi. 266 The first warm snows..enshrine the flowery growths.
4. *dial.* (See quot.)
1674-91 RAY *N.C. Words, Flowry*, florid, handsom, fair, of a good complexion. **1787-90** in GROSE *Provinc. Gloss.* **1838** in HOLLOWAY *Dict. Provinc.*
5. Ornamented with figures of flowers or floral designs.
1667 MILTON *P.L.* XI. 881 As a flourie verge, to binde The ..skirts of that same watrie Cloud. **1725** POPE *Odyss.* III. 596 O'er his fair limbs a flowery vest he threw. **1865** DICKENS *Mut. Fr.* I. v, There was a flowery carpet on the floor.
6. Abounding in flowers of speech; full of fine words and showy expressions, florid.
1603 SHAKS. *Meas. for M.* III. i. 83 Thinke you I can a resolution fetch From flowrie tendernesse? **1737** POPE *Hor. Ep.* II. i. 146 And every flowery courtier writ romance. **1767** SIR W. JONES *Seven Fount.* Poems (1777) 43 Bowers which oft in flowery lays..Arabian poets praise. **1784** BAGE *Barham Downs* I. 275 Certain flowery gentlemen, who told us, in very pretty language..that [etc.]. **1824** SYD. SMITH *Wks.* (1867) II. 191 The answer..was plain and practical; not flowery. **1879** DIXON *Windsor* II. xvi. 176 A man of flowery tongue.
7. *Her.* = FLEURY.
1681 T. JORDAN *London's Joy* 9 A Double Treasure flowry Counter flowry Mars. **1771** KIMBER & JOHNSON *Baronetage Eng.* III. 387 *Flowery*. This word signifies flowered, or adorned with the French lily.
8. *Comb.*, as ***flowery-kirtled, -mantled.***
1621 G. SANDYS *Ovid's Met.* II. (1626) 32 She..makes The flowry-mantled Earth her happy bed. **1634** MILTON *Comus* 254 Amidst the flowery-kirtled Naiades. **1810** *Associate Minstr.* 75 The flowery-mantled Spring.
Hence ˈ**flowerily** *adv.*, in a flowery manner. ˈ**floweriness**, the quality of being flowery.
1730-6 in BAILEY (folio), *Floweriness*. **1783** BLAIR *Lect.* I. xx. 422 That agreeable floweriness of fancy and style. **1821** *New Monthly Mag.* II. 176 The floweryness and green overgrowth of the past season. **1886** *Pall Mall G.* 31 Dec. 4/2 The critical judgment so flowerily expressed. **1890** *Temple Bar Mag.* July 440 All the neighbourhood, he remarked, flowerily, was talking..about Miss Arden's tulip-beds.

flowing (ˈfləʊɪŋ), *vbl. sb.* [f. FLOW *v.* + -ING¹.]
1. The action of the vb. FLOW in various senses.
c **950** *Lindisf. Gosp.* Matt. ix. 20 Wif ðiu blodes flouing ȝeðolade tuelf uinter. *c* **1440** *Promp. Parv.* 168/1 Flowynge of þe watur, *fluxus*. *c* **1489** CAXTON *Sonnes of Aymon* xxviii. 589 Soo grete a flowynge and gaderynge of the people. **1585** JAS. I. *Ess. Poesie* (Arb.) 54 They obseruit not Flovving, nor eschewit not Ryming in termes. **1642** HOWELL *For. Trav.* 42 We must have perpetuall ebbings and flowings of mirth and melancholy. **1704** SWIFT *T. Tub* v. (1709) 77 The happy turns and flowings of the author's wit. **1705** ADDISON *Italy* 513 The..Flowings in of the Holy Spirit. **1807** J. E. SMITH *Phys. Bot.* 63 This great motion, called the flowing, of the sap. **1853** SIR H. DOUGLAS *Milit. Bridges* 2 The flowing of water in a river.
2. *concr.* **a.** That which flows, that which streams *forth*, a stream, a wave; also *transf.* a 'stream' or herd of animals. Now *rare*.
1382 WYCLIF *Ps.* xcii[i]. 3 Flodis rereden vp ther flowingis. —— *Isa.* lx. 6 The flowyng of camalles shal couere thee. **1388** —— *Josh.* v. 1 The Lord hadden dried the flowyngis of Jordan bifor the sones of Israel. *a* **1679** T. GOODWIN *Wk. Holy Ghost* I. ix. Wks. 1704 V. 57 The Sun ..whose Emanations and flowings forth they are. **1844** UPTON *Physioglyphics* ii. 81 These rivers..were what I may term flowings, which may refer to any other fluid as well as water.
†**b.** An overflowing; a flood. *Obs.*
a **1340** HAMPOLE *Psalter* xxviii. 9 Lord þe flowynge makis into wone. **1382** WYCLIF *Isa.* xliv. 3, I shal heelden out.. flowingus vp on the drie. **1661** SIR E. TURNER *Sp. to King* in *Parl. Hist.* (1808) IV. 244 Your return into this nation.. resembles the flowing of the river Nilus. **1663** in Picton *L'pool Munic. Rec.* (1883) I. 328 For preserving of yᵉ same from yᵉ stormes and flowings of yᵉ sea.
3. *Naut.* (See quot.). Cf. FLOW *v.* 6 b.
1769-76 FALCONER *Dict. Marine, Flowing*, the position of the sheets, or lower corners of the principal sails, when they are loosened to the wind.
4. *attrib.*, as ***flowing-capacity.***
1895 *Westm. Gaz.* 4 June 3/3 The new aqueduct has a flowing capacity of 300,000,000 gallons a day.

flowing (ˈfləʊɪŋ), *ppl. a.* [f. as prec. + -ING².]
1. That flows, in various senses of the vb. ***flowing metal***: see quot. 1888.
a **1000** *Byrhtnoth* 65 (Gr.) þær com flowende flod æfter ebban. *a* **1300** *Cursor M.* 20882 (Gött.) Apon þe flouand see he ȝode. **1388** WYCLIF *Isa.* lxvi. 12 A flowynge streem. **1509** HAWES *Past. Pleas.* XXXIV. xxii, After an ebbe there commeth a flowyng tyde. **1698** FROGER *Voy.* 76 Where the Shallops ride at flowing Water. **1700** BLACKMORE *Job* 2 To pass the flowing hours in soft delight. **1825** A. CUNNINGHAM *Song*, A wet sheet and a flowing sea. **1841-4** EMERSON *Ess., Poet* Wks. (Bohn) I. 166 Plato defines a line to be a flowing point. **1867** *Ure's Dict. Arts* (ed. 6) III. 404 s.v. *Petroleum*, The first great flowing well at Ennis-killen. **1888** *Lockwood's Dict. Mech. Engin., Flowing Metals*, metals of the ductile class which..change their form, under impact, or tensile or compressive strain.
†**b.** *Math.* Continuously varying by infinitesimal quantities. (See FLUXION.) *Obs.*
1704 HAYES *Fluxions* i. 4 The respective flowing Quantities AP, PM, AM. **1758** J. LYONS *Fluxions* 4 If two flowing quantities *x* and *y* are to each other in a given ratio. **1807** HUTTON *Course Math.* II. 278 Variable or flowing quantities. **1842** FRANCIS *Dict. Arts, Fluent*, or *Flowing Quantity*.
†**2.** Fluctuating, unstable, inconstant. *Obs.*
1504 ATKYNSON tr. *De Imitatione* I. xxv. 176 His flowynge and vnstedfast mynde. **1536** BELLENDEN tr. *Boece* XVI. xv, For the mynd of commoun pepyll are euir flowand mair inconstant than wynd.
3. Of language, etc. Gliding easily and smoothly, fluent. Of a person: Having a flowing style (*arch.*).
1553 T. WILSON *Rhet.* (1580) 206 The flowyng stile. **1614** BP. HALL *Recoll. Treat.* 495 Resolute Hierome, or flowing Chrysostome. **1624** B. JONSON *Fortunate Isles*, In rime! fine tinckling rime! and flowand verse. **1627** HAKEWILL *Apol.* I. v. (1635) 62 A great wit, and flowing eloquence. **1718** PRIOR *Charity* 1 Did sweeter Sounds adorn my flowing Tongue, Than ever Man pronounc'd. **1782** COWPER *Table T.* 741 Flowing numbers and a flowery style. **1827** CARLYLE *Misc.* (1857) I. 20 Undoubtedly he has a flowing pen. **1832** L. HUNT *Sonnets* Poems 212 Flowing Garth.
quasi-*adv.* **1706** POPE *Let. Walsh* 22 Oct., In describing a gliding Stream, the Numbers shou'd run easy and flowing.
b. Of personal carriage and demeanour: Easy, graceful, smooth.
a **1611** BEAUM. & FL. *Maid's Trag.* IV. i, Thou art..A lady of..such a flowing carriage, that it cannot Chuse but inflame a kingdom. **1766** FORDYCE *Serm. Yng. Wom.* (1767) I. i. 23 A certain flowing urbanity is acquired. **1868** *Digby's Voy. Medit.* Pref. 20 A flowing courtesy and civility. **1870** DICKENS *E. Drood* iv, A certain gravely flowing action with his hands.
4. Of lines or curves, also of objects with reference to their contour: Smoothly continuous and free from rigidity or stiffness. ***flowing tracery*** (in *Arch.*: see quot. 1815).
1709 PRIOR *Ode to Howard*, Each flowing Line confirm'd his first Surprize. **1812-6** J. SMITH *Panorama Sc. & Art* I. 132 Tracery is..flowing, where the lines branch out into leaves, arches, &c. **1816** L. HUNT *Rimini* I. 203 The flowing back, firm chest, and fetlocks clean. **1853** TURNER *Dom. Archit.* III. II. vii. 315 The Chapel is Early English, with flowing windows inserted at the East and North. **1864** TENNYSON *Aylmer's F.* 654 Princely halls, and farms, and flowing lawns.
5. Of hair, garments, etc.: Swaying loosely and gracefully; waving, unconfined, streaming.
1606 B. JONSON *Hymenæi* Wks. (Rtldg.) 558 Beneath that, another flowing garment, of watchet cloth of silver. **1697** DRYDEN *Virg. Past.* VII. 88 With Hazle Phyllis crowns her flowing Hair. **1782** COWPER *Gilpin* 46 John..Seized fast the flowing mane. **1869** BOUTELL *Arms & Arm.* x. 193 The long and flowing surcoat.
b. *Naut.* ***flowing sail, sheet.*** (See quots. 1769, 1841, and cf. FLOWING *vbl. sb.* 3.)
1748 *Anson's Voy.* II. ii. 130 We were pleasingly surprized ..to see her open the N.W. point of the bay with a flowing sail. **1769** FALCONER *Dict. Marine* (1776) s.v., A ship is therefore said to have a flowing sheet when the wind crosses the line of her course nearly at right angles. **1825** H. B. GASCOIGNE *Nav. Fame* 91 With flowing sails..They seek their station on the western seas. **1841** DANA *Seaman's Man.* 105 *Flowing Sheet* when a vessel has the wind free, and the lee clews eased off.
fig. **1833** MARRYAT *P. Simple* xxxii, Didn't you say..that the captain had paid it [a bill] with a flowing sheet? **1861** GEN. P. THOMPSON *Audi Alt.* III. clxi. 174 To wait till the folly could be put down with a flowing sail.
6. Rising like the tide; full to overflowing, brimming, abundant, copious.
1526 *Pilgr. Perf.* (W. de W. 1531) 121 Sensualite with all her flowynge voluptuous desyres. **1613** SHAKS. *Hen. VIII*, II. iii. 62 The Kings Maiesty..Doe's purpose honour no lesse flowing Then Marchionesse of Pembrooke. **1644** MILTON *Educ.* (1738) 136 Fat contentions and flowing fees. **1702** ADDISON *Dial. Medals* ii. Wks. 1721 I. 474 Horace.. speaks of the moderation to be used in a flowing fortune. **1786** BURNS *Brigs Ayr* 221 All-cheering Plenty, with her flowing horn. **1871** SMILES *Charac.* ii. (1876) 49 She was full of joyous flowing mother-wit.
¶**7.** ***flowing hope***: mispron. of *forlorn hope*.
1867 SMYTH *Sailor's Wordbk., Flowing-hope*: see *Forlorn Hope*. **1889** in BARRÈRE & LELAND *Slang*.
Hence ˈ**flowingly** *adv.*, in a flowing manner; ˈ**flowingness**, the quality or state of being flowing.
a **1603** T. CARTWRIGHT *Confut. Rhem N.T.* (1618) 432 Not ..so flowingly by some, as by all the pipes of the Churches exercises. *a* **1712** W. NICHOLS *Def. Doct. Ch. Eng.* Introd. (1715) 118 The..flowingness of his easie Eloquence. **1804** SOUTHEY in Robberds *Mem. W. Taylor* I. 495 It more flowingly fills the sentence. **1852** H. SPENCER *Gracefulness* Ess. 1891 II. 384 A leading trait of grace is continuity, flowingness. **1880** G. MEREDITH *Trag. Com.* xi. (1892) 158 When the letters were unimportant, she wrote flowingly.

flowk, obs. Sc. form of FLUKE.

flown (fləʊn), *ppl. a.*¹ [pa. pple. of FLY *v.*¹]
a. Used adjectively in senses of the vb. Also with *out*, and with defining word prefixed, as ***far-flown, new-flown.***
1608 SYLVESTER *Du Bartas* II. iv. *Tropheis* 1049 Their far-flow'n wings. **1691** TAYLOR Behmen's *Theos. Phil., Three-fold Life* xiii. 309 The flown out Will hates that whence it sprung. **1813** T. BUSBY *Lucretius* i. 300 Hence new-flown birds the woods with music fill. **1865** SWINBURNE *Atalanta* 6 Swifter than dreams [follow] the white flown feet of sleep. **1877** BRYANT *Odyssey* v. 551 When he breathed again, And his flown senses had returned.
b. ***flown cover***, in *Philately*, an envelope or cover dispatched by airmail.
1930 *Times Educ. Suppl.* 16 Aug. p. iv/1 A new form of collecting is taking the imagination of those who are interested in flying. It is the collecting of what are called 'flown covers'. **1936** *Times* 3 Jan. 14/1 A collection of postage stamps and flown covers..are also on show. **1962** M. SAVILL tr. *Schenk's Romance Postage Stamps* III. 132 The expeditionary forces in Korea..sent their field post letters with their national airmail stamps, and so the Korean battles are..documented..by genuine flown covers.

†**flown** (fləʊn), *ppl. a.*² *Obs.* [str. pa. pple. of FLOW *v.*] Only in ***flown sheet***: see quot. 1653. Also *fig.* Cf. FLOWING *ppl. a.* 5 b.
1626 CAPT. SMITH *Accid. Yng. Sea-men* 28 A flown sheate. **1653** —— *Seaman's Gram.* 39 A flowne sheat, that is, when they are not haled home to the blocke..A flowne sheat is when she goes before the winde, or betwixt a paire of sheats, or all sailes drawing. **1697** DAMPIER *Voy.* I. 111 We could have sailed with a flown sheet to Ria Lexa. **1748** *Anson's Voy.* I. x. 98 The sheets being half flown.

flowretry: see FLORETRY.

†ˈ**flowsome**, *a. Obs. rare*⁻¹. [f. FLOW *sb.* or *v.* + -SOME.] Fluid.
1674 N. FAIRFAX *Bulk & Selv.* 73 An heavy body left to it self within a flowsom one that is lighter.

flowster, var. form of FLUSTER.

flowstone (ˈfləʊstəʊn). *Geol.* orig. *U.S.* [f. FLOW *v.* + STONE *sb.*] Rock, or a rock formation, deposited by water flowing in a thin sheet.
1925 *U.S. Geol. Surv. Bull.* 760 110 Deposits of calcium carbonate have also accumulated against the walls in many places where water trickles from the rock... To distinguish this material from that deposited by dripping water, it has been called 'flowstone'. *Ibid.* (Plate XXV, *caption*) Because of the resemblance of this material to ice, it is popularly known as flowstone. **1953** G. T. WARWICK in C. Cullingford *Brit. Caving* iv. 63 Very similar to these [dripstones] are those formed from thin films of water flowing over the surfaces of a cave, which are called flowstone deposits by the Americans. **1958** *Times Lit. Suppl.* 25 July 426/3 The reader who hardly knows what a pothole or a flowstone is. **1969** J. D. HANWELL in C. Cullingford *Man. Caving Techniques* xiii. 241 Massive barriers of stalagmite and flowstone can often block an obvious way on. **1971** *Islander* (Victoria, B.C.) 24 Jan. 5/2 Stalactites formed by water flowing along a wall or crack are flowstones.

flowyd, obs. form of FLOOD.

flox: see FLOCK.

†**floxe**, *v. Obs.*⁻¹ [Cf. Sw. *flaksa* to shake the wings.] *intr.* To 'leap'.

c **1200** *Trin. Coll. Hom.* 127 þat child on his blisse floxede and pleide to-genes hire.

floy, *a.* Alleged Americanism for: Dirty, foul.

1820 J. FLINT *Lett. Amer.* xxi. 264 These I must call Americanisms, and will subjoin some examples.. Floy = Dirty or foul.

floyne, var. form of FLOINE.

floyt(e, var. form of FLOTE, FLUTE.

flu, 'flu (fluː), *sb. colloq.* Also 9 **flue**. Short for INFLUENZA.

1839 SOUTHEY *Lett.* (1856) IV. 574, I have had a pretty fair share of the Flue. **1893** *Mod. Let.*, I've a bad attack of the flu. **1911** *Chambers's Jrnl.* Apr. 239/2 We naturally ask ourselves what season—the 'flu' season, or was it the festive season? **1935** G. BARKER *Janus* 151 She's in bed; she's got the 'flu. **1951** AUDEN *Nones* (1952) 28 Little birds with scarlet legs, Sitting on their speckled eggs, Eye each flu-infected city. **1957** *Times Lit. Suppl.* 15 Nov. p. ii/3 When the place is snowbound and the staff laid low with flu, the girls take over.

fluate ('fluːeɪt), *sb. Chem.* Also 8 **fluat**. [mod. f. FLU(ORIC) + -ATE.]

1. *Chem.* A name formerly given to the salts now called fluorides, which were supposed to result from the combination of fluoric acid with an oxide. ***fluate of lime*** = *Derbyshire spar*, or FLUOR SPAR.

1794 G. ADAMS *Nat. & Exp. Philos.* I. App. 546 Fluats.. when heated phosphoresce. **1806** DAVY in *Phil. Trans.* XCVII. 14, I made an experiment upon fluate of lime under like circumstances. **1849** MRS. SOMERVILLE *Connect. Phys. Sc.* xxv. 243 Limpid and colourless fluate of lime.

2. A hydrofluosilicate applied to building-stone with the view of rendering it harder and more durable. Hence **'fluate** *v. trans.*, to treat with fluate; **flu'ated** *ppl. a.*; **flu'ating** *vbl. sb.*; also **flu'atate** *v. trans.* and **flua'tation**.

1887 *Sci. Amer.* 28 May 344 *Fluatation.* The surface of the stone is covered.. with a solution of the fluate.. After the stone has been once fluated, it becomes [etc.].. After the stone has been once fluatated, it can [etc.]. **1893** *R.I.B.A. Jrnl.* 16 Mar. p. iii. The fluating will render it [Bath Stone] as durable as the most expensive stones.. Fluated Bath Stone.

fluavil ('fluːəvɪl). *Chem.* [ad. F. *fluavile* (Payen 1852, in *Compt. Rend.* XXXV. 118), f. L. *flu-ere* to flow + *fl-āv-us* yellow: see -IL, -ILE.] A yellow amorphous resin found in gutta-percha.

1864 WATTS *Dict. Chem.* II. 669 *Fluavil*, a constituent of gutta percha. **1910** *Encycl. Brit.* XII. 744/1 Albane $C_{10}H_{16}O$ and fluavil $C_{20}H_{32}O$.. can be separated from the pure gutta by the use of solvents. **1933** *Chem. Abstr.* XXXIII. 8447 Compns. which are suitable for sealing cans, etc., are produced substantially free from the balata hydrocarbon but comprising vulcanized rubber latex and fluavil substantially unchanged by interaction with S.

flub (flʌb), *v. U.S. colloq.* [Etym. unknown.] *trans.* To botch, bungle. Also *intr.* Hence as *sb.*, something badly or clumsily performed; a slip-up.

1924 P. MARKS *Plastic Age* xii. 122, I have the feeling.. that I have flubbed this talk. **1926** WODEHOUSE *Heart of Goof* iv. 142 The spectacle of a flubber flubbing ahead of us on the fairway inclines to make us flub as well. **1942** BERREY & VAN DEN BARK *Amer. Thes. Slang* §578.18 *Play inexpertly* [music],.. flub. *Ibid.* §711.8 Make a bad shot [golf].. flub. **1952** J. STEINBECK *East of Eden* 495 In my younger days I played tennis... A servant.. could pick up his master's flubs at doubles. **1952** S. KAUFFMANN *Philanderer* (1953) iv. 70 They'll bring someone else in for the other job if you flub it. **1959** N. MAILER *Advts. for Myself* (1961) 76 Al watched him flub balls all over the table. **1969** *TV Times* (Brisbane) 13 Aug. 8/3 Sullivan twitches. He mumbles. He flubs.

flubdub ('flʌbdʌb). Chiefly *U.S.* [Fanciful.] Bombastic or inept language.

1888 *Detroit Free Press* Aug. (Farmer), By swiping out the flub-dub and guff, I guess we'll have room to put in the points. **1902** KIPLING *Traffics & Discov.* (1904) 16 Any God's quantity of fuss and flubdub to bury a man. **1904** *Rochester Post-Express* 13 July 4 There is an immense amount of flubdub and nonsense and gush in this sort of talk. **1908** *Herald* (Buenos Aires) in *Daily Chron.* 30 June 4/7 All the oratory and political flub-dub that was ever mouthed or printed. **1928** *Daily Express* 6 Aug. 8/7 Psychic research.. whether mere 'flub-dub'—like some fortune-telling [etc.]. **1952** *Daily Mirror* (N.Y.) 8 July 11/4 Maybe Mike Todd or Berle should take over the management of the conventions... They would remove much of the amateur flub-dub.

fluc(c)an: see FLOOKAN.

‖**fluce, floose** (fluːs) *sb.* Also 6 **fluss**, 7 **flus(e)**, 9— **floos, fulus**. [Arab. *fulūs*, pl. of *fals* name of a small copper coin.] An old Persian coin; a small coin of north Africa, Arabia, India, and neighbouring countries.

1599 HAKLUYT *Voy.* II. 272 A sort of flusses of copper. **1625** in W. Foster *Eng. Factories India* (1909) III. 71 There money goeth by the caffala, of which 9½ maketh a doller and 60 fluse to a caffala. **1638** SIR T. HERBERT *Trav.* (ed. 2) 243 Cozbeg one halfe penny; Fluces are ten to a Cozbeg. **1698** FRYER *Acc. E. India & P.* 210, 5 Fluce is 1 Parrow. **1858** SIMMONDS *Dict. Trade, Floose*, the tenth part of a danim, a petty money of Bussorah and other parts of Arabia. **1877** *H. M. Elliot's Hist. India* VII. 345 They [*sc.* the Portuguese] also use bits of copper which they call *buzurg*, and four of these *buzurgs* pass for a *fulús*. **1906** *Daily Chron.* 2 May 7/6 To-day a well-dressed man, who sees a European passing in the street, extends his hand, and mutters something about 'flus'. **1907** *Daily Mail* 18 Jan. 6/4 Often have I bestowed upon him a *floos* for bread.

†**fluce**, *v. Obs. rare. intr.* ? To flounce, plunge.

1627 DRAYTON *Moone-Calfe* 1352 They [cattle].. backward fluce.. As though the Deuill in their heeles had bin.

fluck (flʌk). ? *nonce-wd.*

1885 H. O. FORBES *Nat. Wand. E. Archip.* 12 Not a sound to break the silence save the plunge of a porpoise or the fluck of the fishes in quest of their evening meal.

fluck, obs. and dial. form of FLUKE.

flucti-, comb. form of Lat. *fluctus* wave, in the following adjs. given by Blount and Bailey: **fluc'tiferous** [L. *-fer* bearing + -OUS], bearing or producing waves; **fluc'tifragous** [L. *fluctifrag-us*], wave-breaking; **fluc'tisonant** [L. *sonant-em*, pr. pple. of *sonāre* to sound], sounding with waves; **fluc'tisonous** [L. *fluctison-us*] = prec.; **fluc'tivagant** [L. *vagant-em*, pr. pple. of *vagārī* to wander], floating idly on the waves; **fluc'tivagous** [L. *fluctivag-us*] = prec.

fluctuable ('flʌktjuːəb(ə)l), *a. rare*⁻⁰. [as if ad. L. **fluctuābilis*, f. *fluctuāre* to FLUCTUATE: see -ABLE.] Capable of fluctuating. (Ogilvie 1882.)

Hence **fluctua'bility**, the quality of being fluctuable.

a **1786** WALPOLE *Lett. to Mann* (F. Hall). **1882** in OGILVIE.

†**'fluctuancy.** *rare*⁻¹. [f. next: see -ANCY.] Tendency to fluctuation.

1659 GAUDEN *Tears Ch.* II. xxvi. 222 However they may have their storms and tossings sometime.. by innate fluctuancy, as the rollings and tidings of the sea.

fluctuant ('flʌktjuːənt), *a.* [ad. L. *fluctuant-em*, pr. pple. of *fluctuāre*: see FLUCTUATE *v.* Cf. F. *fluctuant.*]

1. Moving like the waves; undulating. Chiefly *fig.*, unstable, wavering, changing.

1560 ROLLAND *Crt. Venus* III. 171 Howbeit of thame sum part be fluctuant. *a* **1640** JACKSON *Creed* x. xix. Wks. 1844 IX. 115 The other [sort] being of better birth, were fluctuant between virtue or civil honesty and base vices. *a* **1704** R. L'ESTRANGE (J.) How is it possible for any man to be at rest in this fluctuant wandering humour and opinion? **1862** MRS. BROWNING *Poems, Where's Agnes?* xxiv, None of these Fluctuant curves! but firs and pines. **1867** SWINBURNE *Song Italy* 23 In the long sound of fluctuant boughs of trees. **1870** —— *Ess. & Stud.* (1875) 260 His genius is fluctuant and moonstruck as the sea is. **1872** *Contemp. Rev.* XIX. 206 No shifting of positions, no fluctuant moods, no mobility of thought.

2. Floating on the waves.

1605 BACON *Adv. Learn.* II. iii. §1 The militant church, whether it be fluctuant as the ark of Noah, or [etc.]. **1849** J. STERLING in *Fraser's Mag.* XXXIX. 111 Where change has never urged its fluctuant bark.

†**'fluctuary**, *a. Obs.*⁻¹ [f. L. *fluctu-s* wave + -ARY.] Having the character of waves; fluctuating, uncertain.

1632 LITHGOW *Trav.* II. 71 The solid..man is not troubled with ..the fluctuary motions of the humerous multitude.

†**'fluctuate**, *a. Obs.* [ad. L. *fluctuāt-us*, pa. pple. of *fluctuāre*: see FLUCTUATE *v.*] Tossed on the waves; fickle as the waves, wavering.

1631 R. H. *Arraign. Whole Creature* x. §2. 86 The godly man hath his.. sure Anchor, when he seemes to be fluctuate. *Ibid.* xv. §4. 278 Ever vaine, and foolish, and fluctuate in all our wayes.

fluctuate ('flʌktjʊeɪt), *v.* [f. L. *fluctuāt-* ppl. stem of *fluctuāre* to undulate, f. *fluctus*, wave.]

1. *intr.* To move like a wave or waves, rise and fall in or as in waves; to be tossed up and down on the waves; *lit.* or with conscious metaphor. Now *rare*.

1656–81 in BLOUNT *Glossogr.* **1659** T. PECKE *Parnassi Puerp.* 75, I can't call him Rich, or Poor; whose Estate, Upon deluding Waters, fluctuate. **1698** FRYER *Acc. E. India & P.* 128 The.. Mists, which we could discern fluctuating against the impenetrable Promontories. **1711** W. KING *Ruffinus* 98 So sounds, so fluctuates, the troubled sea. **1712** ADDISON *Spect.* No. 549 ⁋2 The greatest part of my estate has been hitherto of an unsteddy and volatile nature, either tost upon seas or fluctuating in funds. *c* **1750** SHENSTONE *Ruined Abbey* 57 Sees the strong vessel fluctuate, less secure. **1754** WARBURTON *Wks.* (1811) X. xxxii. 270 Wanting those principles.. human knowledge only fluctuates in the head, but comes not near the heart. **1793** WORDSW. *Descr. Sk.* Poems (1888) 20/1 The traveller sees Thy [France's] three-striped banner fluctuate on the breeze. **1809** CAMPBELL *Gert. Wyom.* II. xvi, Wild-cane arch.. That fluctuates when the storms of El Dorado sound. **1849** BRYANT *Prairies* 13 The surface rolls and fluctuates to the eye.

2. *fig.* (Now chiefly without allusion to the literal sense.)

a. Of things, conditions, etc.: To vary irregularly, undergo alternating changes in level, position, form, constituent elements, etc.: to be unstable or unsettled.

1655 FULLER *Ch. Hist.* II. iv. §8 But not successive [Monarchs] and fixed in a Family, but fluctuating from one Kingdome to another. **1723** J. ATKINS *Voy. Guinea* Pref. (1735) 22 Our Bodies.. are continually fluctuating and changing while we live. **1769** BURKE *Late St. Nation* Wks. 1842 I. 83 Average estimates are never just but when the object fluctuates. **1779** J. JAY in Sparks *Corr. Amer. Rev.* (1853) II. 283 The Committee.. fluctuates, new members constantly coming in, and old ones going out. **1838** DICKENS *Nich. Nick.* i, Mr. Nickleby's income.. fluctuated between sixty and eighty pounds per annum. **1866** CRUMP *Banking* i. 20 Money fluctuates in price like any other article. **1874** *Deutsch's Rem.* 343 We see the text [of a Targum] fluctuating down to the middle of the 2nd century.

b. Of persons: To pass to and fro, from one opinion, sentiment, or course of conduct, to another; to vacillate, waver.

1634 in Row *Hist. Kirk* (1842) 378 His Majestie.. fluctuating by that occasion betuix love and feare. **1684** T. HOCKIN *God's Decrees* 248 Like silly Children.. fluctuating in our opinions. **1793** BURKE *Corr.* (1844) IV. 133 After fluctuating a long time without any system, we have adopted one that.. is completely ruinous. **1828** SCOTT *F.M. Perth* v, [His features] fluctuating between shamefacedness and apprehension of her displeasure. **1867** FREEMAN *Norm. Conq.* (1876) I. iv. 194 Lotharingia, the border land, ever fluctuating in its allegiance.

3. *trans.* **a.** To throw into fluctuation; to unsettle. **b.** To throw into a wave-like motion.

1788 MAD. D'ARBLAY *Diary* 28 July, The thought of guiding their mother.. flattered and fluctuated them. **1850** TENNYSON *In Mem.* xcv, A breeze began to.. fluctuate all the still perfume.

fluctuating ('flʌktjuːeɪtɪŋ), *ppl. a.* [f. prec. + -ING².] That fluctuates.

1. Moving as or in waves; irregularly rising and falling.

1712 BLACKMORE *Creation* I. 44 The fluctuating Fields of liquid Air. **1762** FALCONER *Shipwr.* III. (1790) 267 Hills of fluctuating fire. **1767** GOOCH *Treat. Wounds* I. 353 With some fluctuating motion of a fluid.

2. Irregularly varying; unsteady; unsettled, wavering.

1647 CLARENDON *Hist. Reb.* I. §49 So fluctuating and unsteady a testimony is the applause of popular councils. *a* **1679** T. GOODWIN *Just. Faith* II. viii, Driven about with the Whirlpools of a fluctuating Conscience. **1720** WELTON *Suffer. Son of God* II. xxxi. 799 They knew how Fluctuating the Opinion of the Mobb is. **1781** GIBBON *Decl. & F.* II. 113 The doubtful, fluctuating conduct of Vetranio. **1837** LYTTON *E. Maltrav.* 24 And copied out his poetry in a small, fluctuating hand. **1867** A. BARRY *Sir C. Barry* vii. 249 The fluctuating nature of the attendance.

absol. **1833** LAMB *Elia* Ser. II. *Pop. Fallacies*, Sharp distinctions of the fluctuating and the permanent.

fluctuation (flʌktjuː'eɪʃən). Also 5 **-acion**. [ad. (either directly or through Fr.) L. *fluctuātiōn-em*, n. of action f. *fluctuāre*: see FLUCTUATE *v.* and -ATION.] The action of fluctuating.

1. A motion like that of the waves, an alternate rise and fall. Now *rare* in physical sense.

1646 SIR T. BROWNE *Pseud. Ep.* VII. xvii. 377 In vaine wee expect a regularity in the waves of the Sea.. its Fluctuations are but motions subservient. **1774** GOLDSM. *Nat. Hist.* (1776) I. 259 This fluctuation of the sea. **1847** TENNYSON *Princess* VI. 335 Each base.. of those tall columns drown'd In silken fluctuation. **1850** —— *In Mem.* cxii, And world wide fluctuation sway'd In vassal tides that follow'd thought.

b. *Path.* The undulation of a fluid in any cavity or tumour of the body.

1620 VENNER *Via Recta* Introd. 8 They.. cause fluctuations, and flatuousnesse in the body. **1640** G. WATTS tr. *Bacon's Adv. Learn.* IV. i. 183 The fluctuation or pensility of the Bowells. **1754–64** SMELLIE *Midwif.* II. 149, I plainly felt a fluctuation of water. **1807–26** S. COOPER *First Lines Surg.* (ed. 5) 253 The inside of the thigh.. presented a kind of fluctuation. **1860** in FOWLER *Med. Voc.*

2. The action or condition of passing more or less rapidly and suddenly from one state to another; an instance of this; repeated variation, vicissitude. In *pl.* 'ups and downs'.

1609 BIBLE (Douay) *Ps.* liv. [lv]. 23 [22] He wil not geve fluctuation to the just for ever. *c* **1661** *Papers on Alter. Prayer-bk.* 82 The Moderatour of the Universe raised up such guides as were sufficient, in so great a fluctuation. **1712** BERKELEY *Pass. Obed.* §54 Wks. III. 138 In the various changes and fluctuations of government. **1753** (*title*), Travels and Adventures of Wm. Bingfield Esq. containing as surprizing a Fluctuation of Circumstances, both by Sea and Land, as ever befel one Man. **1841** D'ISRAELI *Amen. Lit.* (1867) 132 Every modern language has always existed in fluctuation and change.

b. An alternate rise and fall in amount or degree, price or value, temperature, etc.

1802 PALEY *Nat. Theol.* xxii. 430 Inconveniency from fluctuation of temperature and season. **1804** WELLINGTON in Gurw. *Desp.* III. 425 The expenses for the repairs.. are liable to fluctuation. **1878** HUXLEY *Physiogr.* 22 The height of the mercurial column is subject to.. fluctuation.

3. The condition of passing alternately from one opinion or sentiment to another; an instance of this; vacillation, wavering.

c **1450** tr. *De Imitatione* I. xxxv, He was comfortid.. & þe douteful fluctuacion cessid. **1608** D. T. *Ess. Pol. & Mor.* 42 Hee suffered not himselfe to be carried away with any such humourous fluctuation. **1717** L. HOWEL *Desiderius* (ed. 3) 99 Subject to no.. Fluctuations of the Mind. **1775** JOHNSON *Tax. no Tyr.* 54 The House of Commons was in a state of fluctuation. **1824** L. MURRAY *Eng. Gram.* (ed. 5) I. 205

During this inquiry, we should be plunged into a state of uncertainty and fluctuation. **1861** Geo. Eliot *Silas M.* 7 A strange fluctuation between an effort at an increased manifestation of regard and involuntary signs of shrinking and dislike.

fluctuational (flʌktjuːˈeɪʃənəl), *a.* [f. FLUCTUATION + -AL[1].] Of or pertaining to fluctuation.

1913 W. Bateson *Mendel's Princ. Heredity* 113 Negative results which suggest that these features are largely fluctuational.

† **fluctu'ose**, *a. Obs.*[−0] [ad. L. *fluctuōs-us*: see next and -OSE.] = FLUCTUOUS b.

1727 in Bailey vol. II.

fluctuous (ˈflʌktjuːəs), *a. Obs.* exc. *arch.* [ad. L. *fluctuōsus* full of waves f. *fluctus* wave: see -OUS.]

†**a.** Watery (*obs.*). **b.** Full of, or resembling waves, *lit.* and *fig.*

1599 A. M. tr. *Gabelhouer's Bk. Physicke* 61/2 An Excellent collyrion for tenebrous and fluctuous Eyes [orig. *für dunckele und flüssige Augen*]. **1599** Nashe *Lenten Stuffe* Wks. (Grosart) V. 212 All the fennie *Lerna* betwixt.. being ..fluctuous demeans or fee simple. **1627–77** Feltham *Resolves* I. xlviii. 76 How fluctuous are the salted waves. **1839** Bailey *Festus* (1854) 133 The base of the world's fluctuous lore.

Hence **fluctu'osity**.

1850 L. Hunt *Autobiog.* II. xvii. 278 Waves might be classed.. we ought to have waves, wavelets, billows, fluctuosities, etc., a marble sea, a sea weltering.

† **fludder** (ˈflʌθə(r)), *v. Sc. Obs.* Also **fluther**. *intr.* 'To exhibit the appearance of great regard for any one, to cajole' (Jam.).

c **1525** *Priests of Peebles* (1603) Dij, Than mony folk wil cum and with me fludder.

† **fludgs**, ?*int. Obs. rare.* [? cf. Ger. *flugs* int., quick!]

1611 Chapman *May Day* Plays 1873 II. 352 What, hee that sings, Maids in your smocks, hold open your locks, fludgs.

fludrocortisone (ˌfluːdrəʊˈkɔːtɪzəʊn). *Pharm.* [f. **flu(orohy)drocortisone*.] A synthetic derivative ($C_{21}H_{29}FO_5$) of hydrocortisone which causes retention of sodium and loss of potassium and which is given orally in the treatment of adrenocortical deficiency and to supplement cortisone in the treatment of Addison's disease; also *ellipt.* for the acetate, the form in which the drug is usu. given.

1958 *Clin. Sci.* XVII. 205 These compounds differed from hydrocortisone only by the presence of an additional halogen atom, and fludrocortisone (9α-fluorohydrocortisone acetate) has proved to be the most active of the series. **1961** *Lancet* 25 Mar. 632/1 In the adrenalectomised subjects, aldosterone by mouth had 1/25th to 1/30th the potency of fludrocortisone in the maintenance of sodium balance. **1965** Goodman & Gilman *Pharmacol. Basis Therapeutics* (ed. 3) lxxii. 1633 Fludrocortisone acetate.. is the most potent synthetic mineralocorticoid. **1969** R. George in J. A. Bevan *Essent. Pharmacol.* xxxiv. 361 Fludrocortisone is used extensively as an anti-inflammatory agent but only in topical preparations.

fludy, obs. form of FLOODY.

flue, flew (fluː), *sb.*[1] Also 4 flowe, 5 flw(e, 6 flewe. [cf. MDu. *vluwe* fishing-net (Du. *flouw* snipe-net), F. *flu fine nappe d'un tramail* (Boiste 1840: not in Littré), also *flucq* some kind of fishing apparatus (16th c. in Godef.); the mutual relation of the words is unknown.] A kind of fishing-net; **a.** a drag-net, **b.** a fixed net. Also *flue-net*.

1388–9 *Accts. Abingdon Abbey* (Camden) 57, J rete vocatum wade et j flowe. **1391** R. de Ryllynton in *Test. Ebor.* I. 157 Willo Broune servienti meo.. j flew, cum warrap et flot. *c* **1440** *Promp. Parv.* 168/1 Flwe, nette ..*tragum.* **1465** *Mann. & Househ. Exp.* 509 My master paid to Chelone fore knyttynge of a flew, xvj.*d.* **1569** in W. H. Turner *Select. Rec. Oxford* 329 Nor laye any flewe or other nett in any of the same waters. **1611** Bible *Hab.* i. 15 They ..gather them in their dragge [*marg.* flue-net]. **1630** in *Descr. Thames* (1758) 66 No Fisherman.. shall.. use or exercise any Flue, Trammel.. or hooped Net whatsoever. **1787** Best *Angling* (ed. 2) 5 Fishing with trammels, or flews in March or April. **1851** Newland *Erne* 75 It is generally caught by a flue, set between the openings of the weeds. **1882** *Three in Norway* vi. 44 Seven boats.. were out with a huge flue net.

flue (fluː), *sb.*[2] Also 6 floow, 7–9 flew. [of unknown origin; cf. mod.Flem. *vluwe* of same meaning (Franck s.v. *fluweel*) which, like the Du. *fluweel* and med.L. *fluetum* velvet, is believed to be derived from Fr. *velu* hairy, downy. But see FLUFF *sb.*[1]]

†**1.** A woolly or downy substance; down, nap. Also *pl.* bits of down. *Obs.*

1589 Fleming *Georg. Virg.* iv. 69 Towels with nap shorne off (The floow or roughnes shorne away for feare to hurt his handes). **1607** Topsell *Four-f. Beasts* (1658) 213 A bed filled with flew or wool of Hares. **1743** *Lond. & County Brew.* ii. (ed. 2) 100 They will be as big as Lice with Rags or Flews about them. **1823** in Crabb *Technol. Dict.*, *Flue*, The soft down from feathers, and the skins from rabbits, etc.

2. *esp.* The light flocculent substance formed by floating particles of cotton, down, etc.; fluff.

1796 Mrs. Glasse *Cookery* xxvii. 387 That will gather up all the flew and dust. **1814** Ware in *Trans. Med. & Chirurg. Soc.* 256 The flue that is swept from bedrooms. **1837** Howitt *Rur. Life* iii. iii. (1862) 242 Amid heat and dust and flue from the cotton. **1860** Dickens *Uncomm. Trav.* vi, Its old-established flue under its old-established four-post bedsteads. **1886** E. Hodder *Earl Shaftesbury* I. iii. 139 Parched and suffocated by the dust and flue.

b. *transf.* Any light floating particle. Cf. FLOW *sb.*[3]

c **1825** Beddoes *Poems, Torrismond* I. iii, It would not weigh a flue of melting snow In my opinion.

flue (fluː), *sb.*[3] [of unknown origin.

The exact primary sense is uncertain; assuming that it meant 'channel, passage', some have compared early mod.Du. *vloegh* flutings of a column (Kilian), and others would connect it with FLOW *v.* or FLUE *v.*[1] It is possible that the primary reference may be to the *fluing* (see FLUE *v.*[2]) of the sides of the chimney in houses of the 16th c. This view derives some support from sense 5.]

1. In early use = CHIMNEY; subsequently a smoke-duct in a chimney. Hence extended to denote a channel of various kinds for conveying heat, etc., *esp.* a hot-air passage in a wall; a pipe or tube for conveying heat to water in certain kinds of steam-boilers.

1582 in W. H. Turner *Select. Rec. Oxford* 424 All flewes and chymneys.. made of earth.. shalbe taken downe. **1654** Evelyn *Diary* 9 Aug., Ye chimney flues like so many smiths forges. **1715** Desaguliers *Fires Impr.* 12 Builders have.. carried the Flue or Funnel bending. **1757** W. Thompson *R.N. Advoc.* 33 Another notable Iron Invention, called a Flew, running through the Warehouses, fed with constant Fires to keep their dry Stores from being mouldy. **1811** A. T. Thomson *Lond. Disp.* (1818) 312 Stoves heated by means of flues. **1839** R. S. Robinson *Naut. Steam Eng.* 115 Each fire place has a flue, or gigantic pipe, which circulates from end to end of the boiler, making as many turns as the boiler will hold. **1863** Kingsley *Water-Bab.* (1878) 4 He had to climb the dark flues rubbing his poor knees and elbows raw.

¶ The following passage is usually quoted as the earliest example of the word, which is supposed to mean here the spiral cavity of a shell. But *flue* is prob. a misprint for *flute*.

1562 Phaer *Æneid* x. Ggjb, Wt whelkid shell Whose wrinckly wreathed flue, did fearful shril in seas outyell.

†**2.** *Coal-mining.* A sloping trough for conveying coal into a receptacle; a shoot. ? *Obs.*

1774 Pennant *Tour Scotl. in* 1772, 48 Galleries.. terminating in flues or hurries, placed sloping over the quay, and thro' these the coal is discharged.. into the holds of the ships.

3. *Organ-building.* The fissure or 'wind-way' characteristic of 'mouth-pipes' (hence also called flue-pipes: see 6) as opposed to 'reed-pipes'.

1879 Hopkins in Grove *Dict. Mus.* I. 535 All organ-stops in which the sound is produced by the wind passing through a fissure, *flue*, or wind-way.. belong to the Flue-work.

4. *slang.* The SPOUT in a pawnbroker's shop. *in flue*: in pawn. *up the flue*: (*a*) pawned, (*b*) dead, collapsed.

1821 Egan *Real Life in London* I. 566 *note*, *Up the spout* or *up the flue* are synonimous in their import. **1851** Mayhew *Lond. Labour* II. 250 I've had.. to leave half my stock in flue with a deputy for a night's rest.

5. *dial.* (See quot.) [Perh. a distinct word.]

1787 W. Marshall *Norfolk* (1795) II. 379 *Flue*, the coping of a gable or end-wall of a house.

6. *attrib.* and *Comb.*, as *flue-cleaner*, *-scraper*, *-tile*, *-tube*; *flue-like* adj.; also **flue-boiler** (see quot.); **flue-bridge**, a wall of fire-brick in a reverberatory furnace, between the hearth and the flue; **flue-brush** (see quot.); **flue-cinder** (see quot.); **flue-cure** *v. trans.*, to cure (tobacco) by using artificial heat introduced by flues; so *flue-cured* ppl. adj., *-curing* vbl. sb.; **flue-dust**, dust which collects in the flue of a furnace, *spec.* of a metallurgical furnace, and which contains valuable particles of metal, etc.; **flue-faker** *slang*, (*a*) a chimney sweep; (*b*) (see quot. 1860); **flue-full** *a.*, full to the flue, brimful; **flue-gas**, any mixture of gases from the flues of chemical or smelting factories; **flue-pipe**, an organ-pipe with a 'flue' (see 3), a mouth-pipe, as opposed to a reed-pipe; **flue-plate** (see quot.); **flue-register**, a register in an organ comprising a series of flue-pipes; **flue-salt** (see quot.); **flue-stop**, an organ stop controlling a flue-register; **flue-surface** (see quot.); **flue-work**, the flue-stops of an organ collectively, as distinguished from the reed-stops.

1859 *Trans. Ill. Agric. Soc.* III. 522 My boiling was not conducted under as favorable auspices.. as in the experiment previously alluded to with the *flue boiler. **1874** Knight *Dict. Mech.* I. 891/1 *Flue-boiler*, a steam-boiler whose water space is traversed by flues. **1881** Raymond *Mining Gloss.*, **Flue-bridge*. **1874** Knight *Dict. Mech.* I. 891/1 **Flue-brush*, a cylindrical brush of wire or steel strips used to clean the scale and soot from the interior of a flue. **1873** *Weale's Dict. Terms Archit.* etc. (ed. 4), **Flue cinder*, the cinder from an iron reheating furnace. **1874** Knight *Dict. Mech.* I. 891/1 *Flue-cleaner. **1909** *Cent. Dict.* Suppl., *Flue-cure. **1905** G. M. Odlum *Culture of Tobacco* 99 In case of the *flue-cured tobaccos, these barns would be too large to properly maintain the heat necessary. **1931** *Times* (Trade & Engin. Suppl.) 5 Sept. 535/4 The progress has been confined.. to the production of bright flue-cured tobacco, principally in Norfolk, Oxford, and Elgin counties in Ontario. **1966** *Times* 23 May 16/5 The flue-cured crop represents only a small fraction of the Malawi tobacco crop. **1886** C. G. W. Lock *Tobacco* iv. 220 We.. have no space to describe the different methods of 'curing' tobacco, as, for instance,.. '*flue-curing', 'open-fire-curing', &c. **1923** *Glasgow Herald* 23 June 10 Each of these growers has a flue-curing barn. **1857** R. S. Burn *Steam-Engine* (ed. 2) 77 Each chamber.. is also connected with the bottom of the boiler by a series of vertical flue passages,.. which.. allow the *flue-dust to precipitate into the spaces beneath. **1902** *Encycl. Brit.* XXV. 42/2 Both kinds of gas, when issuing from the burner, hold in mechanical suspension a considerable quantity of 'flue-dust'. **1917** *Nature* C. 92/1 The flue-dust of blast-furnaces. **1951** *Engineering* 20 July 75/2 Behaviour of aggregates of small particles such as.. boiler flue dusts. **1812** J. H. Vaux *Flash Dict.*, **Flue-faker*. **1860** *Slang Dict.* (ed. 2), *Flue fakers*.. low sporting characters, who are so termed from their chiefly betting on the *Great Sweeps*. **1703** Thoresby *Let. to Ray* 27 Apr., **Flue-full*, brim-full, flowing full. **1898** *Jrnl. Chem. Soc.* LXXIV. ii. 188 *Flue Gases in Relation to Furnace Efficiency. **1900** *Engineering Mag.* XIX. 760/1 The now easy process of flue-gas analysis. **1958** *Chambers's Techn. Dict.* Suppl. 980/1 *Flue gas temperature*, temperature of flue gases at the point in the flue where it leaves the furnace. **1908** *Westm. Gaz.* 9 Mar. 8/2 The bursting in of the door.. sent the flames up through the *flue-like staircase. **1852** Seidel *Organ* 27 The intonation of the *flue-pipes. **1874** Knight *Dict. Mech.* I. 891/1 **Flue-plate*, a plate into which the ends of the flue are set. **1852** Seidel *Organ* 27 Kaufmann, of Dresden.. made experiments with *flue-registers. **1884** *Chester Gloss.*, **Flue salt*.. the waste salt formed on the flues where the lumps are dried. **1855** Hopkins & Rimbault *Organ* xxi. 109 A *Flue-stop [is] a similar series of lip pipes. *a* **1877** Knight *Dict. Mech.* I. 891/1 **Flue-surface* (Steam-engine), the area of surface of the boiler which is exposed to the action of the flame and heated gases after they have left the fire-chamber or furnace. The heating surface of a boiler is made up of the fire-surface and flue-surface. **1859** *Archaeol. Cant.* II. p. xli, A very remarkable example of a Roman *flue-tile. **1878** *Design & Work* IV. 335/1 Smoke and soot were discharged in such abundance as speedily to choke the *flue-tubes. **1876** Hiles *Catech. Organ* ix. (1878) 57 All lip-stops belong to the *Flue-work.

flue (fluː), *sb.*[4] Also **flew**. [of obscure etymology; Sw. has *fly* in sense 2. It is not certain that senses 1 and 2 are of identical orgin.]

†**1.** 'The tip of a deer's [?] horn' (Halliwell s.v. *Flewed*). *Obs.*

1532–3 [app. implied in FLUED *ppl. a.*[2]].

2. *Naut.* The FLUKE of an anchor; also that of a harpoon.

c **1860** H. Stuart *Seaman's Catech.* 57 The fish-tackle is.. hooked to the inner flue. **1882** Nares *Seamanship* (ed. 6) 175 Ships which allow of the inner flues being got inboard.

flue, *sb.*[5] Obs. var. FLU.

flue (fluː), *sb.*[6] *Obs.* exc. *dial.* Also **flew**. [app. a corruption of *fleume*, obs. form of FLEAM.] A farrier's lancet, a fleam.

1790 W. Marshall *Midl. Counties* II. 437 *Flews*, phlemes, for bleeding cattle, etc. **1879** Miss Jackson *Shropsh. Word-bk.*, *Flues*, farriers' lancets.

flue, flew (fluː), *a.*[1] *Obs.* exc. *dial.* Also 6 **flewe**. [of obscure origin; possibly related to FLOW *v.*; cf. the relation of FLEET *a.* (= shallow) to FLEET *v.*]

1. Shallow.

c **1440** *Promp. Parv.* 167/1 Flew, or scholde, as vessell, *bassus.* **1552** Huloet, Flewe or not deape, but as one may wade, *breuia.* **1651** H. More *Enthus. Triumph.* (1656) 171, I hope you do not think, that I meant your skull was so flue and shallow that [etc.]. *Ibid.* 318. *a* **1825** Forby *Voc. E. Anglia*, *Flue*, shallow.

2. = FLAN *a.* (See quots., and FLUE *v.*[2])

1676 H. More *Remarks* 142 And the like experiment he makes.. of a heated Beer-glass with a more flew mouth. **1881** *Leicester Gloss.*, *Flew*, open, wide, expanded. 'Your bonnet is too flew'; 'a flew dish', i.e. one with wide spreading sides.

flue, flew (fluː), *a.*[2] *Obs.* exc. *dial.* [of uncertain origin; it corresponds in sense to OF. *flo*, *flou* (whence mod.F. *flou* in a specific sense relating to painting) and to Du. *flauw*, LG., mod.HG. *flau*; but the mutual relation of the words is disputed. See also FLUEY, *a.*

The initial *f* instead of *v* in Du. word is usually an indication of foreign origin (exc. in the case of onomatopœias); hence Kluge and Franck regard *flauw* as adopted, like the Eng. word, from Fr.; the ultimate source being OTeut. **hlēwo-* (Ger. *lau*, Eng. LEW) lukewarm. This is not very satisfactory. If Du. *flauw* were a native word, it might correspond to an OE. **fleowe* (:—**flawjo-*) related to OHG. *flewen* to rinse, wash; for the sense cf. *washy*.]

Weak, tender, sickly, delicate.

1613–16 W. Browne *Brit. Past.* iii. i. Wks. (Hazlitt) II. 149 She is flewe, and never will be fatter. **1679** *Lond. Gaz.* No. 1416/4 A flew Horse, and a star very remarkable in his forehead. **1736** Pegge *Kenticisms* (E.D.S.), *Flue*, tender, weak; of a horse or person. **1836** Cooper *Provincialisms Sussex* s.v., 'That horse is very flue'. **1889** in Hurst *Horsham* Sussex Gloss. s.v., 'My Fanny is ill again, poor dear, she is so flue'.

† **flue**, *v.*[1] *Obs. rare.* [ad. OF. *flue-r*, L. *flu-ĕre* to flow.] *intr.* To flow. Of parchment: To allow the ink to 'run'.

? **1483** Caxton *Vocab.* 22 b, Josse the parchemyn maker Solde me a skyn of parchemyn. That all fluede [Fr. *qui tout flua*]. **1483** *Cath. Angl.* 136/2 To Flue, *fluere.*

flue (flu:), *v.*[2] [App. f. FLUE *a.*[1] (sense 2). Cf. FLAN *v.* f. FLAN *a.*] *intr.* To expand; to splay. Hence **'fluing** *vbl. sb.*, the divergent lines of a splayed opening; **flued, 'fluing** *ppl. a.*

1778 W. PAIN *Carpenter's Repos.* Plate 51 A circular Soffit in a circular Wall, which is flewing on the Jambs. *Ibid.*, Draw the Flewing of the Jambs c. d. and e. f. to meet at the Point a. *Ibid.*, Figure A. is a circular Soffit on flewing Jambs. **1853** *Archit. Publ. Soc. Dict.*, *Flued*, this word is applied instead of *Splayed* to a circular or semi-circular splayed opening. **1893** *S.E. Worc. Gloss.*, *Flewed* (of a hoop) to be made larger on one side than on the other so that it may fit the taper shape of a cask.

flue, obs. pa. t. of FLY *v.*[1]

flued, *ppl. a.*[1] [f. FLUE *sb.*[3] + -ED[2].] Having a flue or duct. In comb., as ***double-flued*** adj.

1824 *Greenhouse Comp.* I. 114 All of them may be better grown and flowered in a flued pit. **1842** *Florist's Jrnl.* III. 87 In a green-house well raised, seed is produced better perhaps than even on the south side of a flued wall. **1895** *Daily News* 9 Jan. 10/2 Wanted Two..Lancashire Double-flued Boilers. **1963** *B.S.I. News* May 15/2 Flued convector heaters. **1969** *Sci. Jrnl.* Feb. 25/2 The burner works only in flued appliances where chimney draught can aspire the necessary air.

flued, *ppl. a.*[2] [f. FLUE *sb.*[4] + -ED[2].]

†**1.** Of a horn: Tipped. *Obs.*

1532-3 *Act 24 Hen. VIII*, c. 13 It shall be lefull for him to weare..a horne tipped or flewed with siluer.

2. Of an anchor, etc. Having a flue; fluked, barbed. Only in comb., as ***one-flued, two-flued***, adjs.

'flue-hammer. [f. FLUE *v.*[2]] A hammer used in flaring one edge of an iron hoop to make it fit the bulge of the cask.

1874 in KNIGHT *Dict. Mech.* I. 891/1.

flueless ('flu:lɪs), *a.* [f. FLUE *sb.*[3] + -LESS.] Without a flue.

1903 *Daily Chron.* 27 Jan. 3/7 Flueless fires. **1927** *Glasgow Herald* 25 Mar. 10 Flueless grates.

†**fluellin** (flu:'ɛlɪn). *Obs.* Also 6 fluellyn(g, 6–7 fluellen. [corruption of the Welsh name, *llysiau Llewelyn*, lit. 'Llewelyn's herbs'. Cf. the proper name *Fluellen* (= Llewelyn) in Shaks.]

1. A name given to several species of *Veronica* or Speedwell, esp. *V. officinalis.*

1548 TURNER *Names of Herbs* (E.D.S.) 88 Veronica..is called in englishe Fluellyng. **1597** GERARDE *Herbal* II. cxcvii. (1633) 629 In welch it is called Fluellen. **1646** SIR T. BROWNE *Pseud. Ep.* II. vi. 101 Betonica Pauli, or Pauls Betony..or Fluellen. **1756** WATSON in *Phil. Trans.* XLIX. 807 Male Speedwell, or Fluellin, or True Paul's Betony.

2. Misapplied to *Linaria elatine* and *L. spuria.*

1756 SIR J. HILL *Brit. Herbal* 113 Fluellin. Elatine. The flower is small; it consists of a single petal. **1816–20** GREEN *Univ. Herbal* I. 108 *Antirrhinum Elatine*, Sharp-pointed Toad-flax, or Fluellin.. *Antirrhinum Spurium*, Round-leaved Toad-flax or Fluellin. **1866** in *Treas. Bot.*

fluellite ('flu:əlaɪt). *Min.* [badly f. FLUORINE after *wavellite*.] A rare fluoride of aluminium, found in minute white crystals.

1824 *Ann. Phil.* VIII. 243 He [Wollaston] is..of opinion that these crystals belong to a distinct species [i.e. distinct from wavellite], for which he proposes the name of Fluellite. **1864** WATTS *Dict. Chem.* II. 669.

†**'fluence**[1]. *Obs.* [a. F. *fluence*, ad. L. *fluentia*, f. *fluentem*: see FLUENT.]

1. A flowing, a stream.

c **1611** CHAPMAN *Iliad* XVI. 224 That he first did cleanse With sulphur, then with fluences of sweetest water rense.

2. = FLUENCY 2, 3.

1607 HEYWOOD *Fayre Mayde Exch.* Wks. 1874 II. 56 The naturall fluence of my owne wit. **1691** WOOD *Ath. Oxon.* II. 547 He was esteemed a person..of a ready fluence in discourse.

fluence[2] ('flu:əns), aphæretic form of INFLUENCE *sb.*, occurring esp. in phr. ***to put the fluence on*** (a person), to apply mysterious, magical, or hypnotic power to (a person).

1909 J. R. WARE *Passing Eng.* 203/2 *Put on the flooence*, attract, subdue, overcome by mental force. **1923** WODEHOUSE *Inimitable Jeeves* iii. 31 She was always able to turn me inside out with a single glance, and I haven't come out from under the 'fluence yet. **1937** D. JONES *In Parenthesis* IV. 68 Put the fluence on..drownd the bastards on Christmass Day in the Morning. **1957** A. E. COPPARD *It's Me, O Lord!* ii. 21 It was avouched..that if you rubbed the juice of a lemon on the palm of your hand you were armoured against suffering..and as long as the 'fluence' lasted other canes broke too. **1958** M. PROCTER *Man in Ambush* vii. 82 If ever I saw a girl trying to put the 'fluence on a fellow it was Tess. **1965** E. BRUTON *Wicked Saint* viii. 105 Put the 'fluence on him and we'll be away.

fluency ('flu:ənsɪ). [ad. L. *fluentia*: see FLUENCE[1] and -ENCY.] The quality or state of flowing or being fluent.

†**1.** Affluence, copiousness, abundance. *Obs.*

a. 1623 MASSINGER *Bondman* II. iii, Thou, Gracculo, Hast fluency of courage. **1638** G. SANDYS *Paraphr. Job* xii. 16 Those who grow old in fluency and ease. **1657** HAWKE *Killing is M.* 20 Fluency in teares. **1658** OSBORN *Jas. I* Wks. (1673) 511 The Indies themselves would in time want fluency to feed so immense a prodigality. **1726** BRADLEY *Gardening* App. 23 This last operation [graffing] may be done when the sap is in its highest Fluencies.

2. a. A smooth and easy flow; readiness, smoothness; *esp.* with regard to speech. **b.** Absence of rigidity; ease.

1636 MASSINGER *Gt. Dk. Florence* V. ii, You are pleased to show, sir, The fluency of your language. **1727** POPE *Th. Var. Subj.* in *Swift's Wks.* (1755) II. I. 227 The common fluency of speech in many men. **1849** LYTTON *Caxtons* I. v, I had learned to write with some fluency. **1852** LD. COCKBURN *Jeffrey* I. 363 All his fluency of thought. **1878** J. W. EBSWORTH in *Braithwait's Strappado* Introd. 27 The genuine sweetness and musical fluency of his best lyrics.

3. Readiness of utterance, flow of words.

1654 EVELYN *Diary* 31 Aug., Dr. Collins, so..celebrated for his fluency in the Latin tongue. **1814** D'ISRAELI *Quarrels Auth.* (1867) 364 He indulged his satirical fluency on the scientific collectors. **1834** MACAULAY *Pitt* Ess. (1854) 293/1 The fluency and the personal advantages of the young orator.

fluent ('flu:ənt), *a.* and *sb.* Also 6–7 fluant. [ad. L. *fluent-em*, pr. pple. of *fluĕre* to flow.]

A. *adj.*

1. That flows, flowing.

1607 TOPSELL *Four-f. Beasts* 304 Whatsoeuer [water] is moueably fluent, is lesse subiect to poyson then that which standeth still. **1684** tr. *Bonet's Merc. Compit.* VIII. 272 Ligatures..seem to..impell the fluent bloud. **1719** D'URFEY *Pills* (1872) III. 97 Into a fluent stream she leapt. **1854** *Jrnl. R. Agric. Soc.* XV. II. 415 Streams which are permanent or fluent all the year. **1893** *Harper's Mag.* LXXXVI. 815/2 The metal..came fluent from the crucible.

b. *transf.* and *fig.*; esp. of things compared to a stream or to the tide.

1642 H. MORE *Song of Soul* II. ii. III. xxvi, Things that be fluent, As flitting time, by her be straight retent Unto one point. **1649** G. DANIEL *Trinarch., Hen. V*, ccxxviii, Yet Crouded Strength stifles the fluent Course Of many Glories. **1729** SAVAGE *Wanderer* III. 6 The sloping Sun To Ocean's Verge, his fluent Course has run. **1842** DE QUINCEY *Cicero* Wks. VI. 227 The fluent intercourse with this island. **1854** J. S. C. ABBOTT *Napoleon* (1855) II. xxvii. 502 Masses of cavalry, in fluent and refluent surges, trampled into the bloody mire the dying and the dead.

†**c.** Flowing readily as a consequence or inference. *Obs.*

1619 W. SCLATER *Expos. 1 Thess.* 244 In ancient Diuinitie the inference was fluent. *Ibid.* 567 See if from the fact of God, mentioned by the Apostle, it runnes not as fluent.

2. Having the property or capacity of flowing easily; ready to flow; fluid, liquid. Of a painter: Producing a fluid or liquid effect.

1601 R. JOHNSON *Kingd. & Commw.* (1611) 5 The people of the South haue their bloud thinne and fluent. *a* **1626** BACON *Physiol. Rem.* Wks. 1857 III. 83 When it is not malleable, but yet is not fluent, but stupified. **1686** W. HARRIS tr. *Lemery's Course Chym.* II. xiii. (ed. 3) 523 This fermentation subtilizes..the viscous parts..turns them into a thin fluent liquid. **1822** *Examiner* 347/2 Backhuysen is often heavy in his shadows, but admirably fluent in the representation of water and air. **1844** MRS. BROWNING *Drama of Exile* Poems 1850 I. 77 The broad, fluent strata of pure air. **1877** DIXON *Diana, Lady Lyle* I. III. iii. 190 A fairy pool of water lies, fluent and opalesque, under an amber slab.

b. *fig.* and of non-material things: Fluid, liable to change; not stable, fixed, or rigid.

1648 W. MOUNTAGUE *Devout Ess.* vi. §2. 57 While the matter of worldly goods remaineth fluent and transitory. **1691** RAY *Creation* 33 Motion being a fluent thing. **1814** WORDSW. *Excursion* IV. 733 His quick hand bestowed On fluent operations a fixed shape. **1851** HELPS *Comp. Solit.* x. 188 The general body of opinion is very fluent. **1872** M. COLLINS *Two Plunges for Pearl* I. 196 English society is curiously fluent.

3. *transf.* **a.** Of hair: Growing in abundant quantity and falling in graceful curves; flowing.

1607 TOPSELL *Four-f. Beasts* 566 Any one whose haires are too fluent and abundant. **1866** G. MEREDITH *Vittoria* i, A fluent black moustache ran with the curve of the upper lip. **1872** TENNYSON *Gareth & Lynette* 454 Broad brows and fair, a fluent hair and fine.

b. Moving easily or gracefully; not stiff or rigid.

1869 BLACKMORE *Lorna D.* x, I never had dreamed of such delicate motion, fluent and graceful.

†**4.** Flowing freely or abundantly. Also, abounding *in*. *Obs.*

1590 GREENE *Orl. Fur.* Wks. (Rtldg.) 98/1 Those fluent springs of your lamenting tears. **1611** SPEED *Hist. Gt. Brit.* VII. xii. §10. 222 Destitute of vertue and fluent in vice. **1639** DANIEL *Ecclus.* xliii. 53 A Cloud, swolne wth a fluent raine. *c* **1682** J. COLLINS *Making of Salt in Eng.* 2 At Namptwich they have one Pit within the Town, and two without, sufficient to serve the Fourth part of the Nation, the Bryne being so fluent.

b. Giving freely, generous. *Obs.* exc. *dial.*

1603 BRETON *Packet Mad Lett.* (Grosart.) 6/1 A sonne..bound..through the fluent bounty of a Father's loue. **1639** SALTMARSHE *Policy* 237 If you bee fluent in one kinde, bee sparing in another. **1887** *S. Chesh. Gloss.*, *Fluent*, liberal..as 'fluent i' givin'.

5. Of speech, style, etc.: Flowing easily and readily from the tongue or pen.

1625 BACON *Ess.*, *Youth & Age* (Arb.) 263 Such as is a fluent and Luxuriant Speech. **1660** WOOD *Life* (Oxf. Hist. Soc.) I. 360 Their fluent praying and preaching. **1670–1** NARBOROUGH *Jrnl.* in *Acc. Sev. Late Voy.* I. (1711) 70 Their Language is much in the Throat, and not very fluent, but uttered with good deliberation. **1728** POPE *Dunc.* III. 197 How fluent nonsense trickles from his tongue! **1828** D'ISRAELI *Chas. I*, I. ii. 21 The pain which conversation occasions him whose speech is not fluent. **1866** GEO. ELIOT *F. Holt* (1868) 63 A soft voice with a clear fluent utterance.

b. Of a speaker, etc.: Ready in the use of words, able to express oneself readily and easily in speech or writing.

1589 WARNER *Alb. Eng.* V. xxvii. 119 Rhetoricall I am not with a fluant tongue to ster. **1610** HEYWOOD *Gold. Age* I. i. Wks. (1874) III. 5 Fluent Mercury Speakes from my tongue. **1737** POPE *Hor. Epist.* II. i. 279 Fluent Shakespear scarce effac'd a line. **1784** COWPER *Task* IV. 19 His fluent quill. **1832** HT. MARTINEAU *Ireland* i. 6 Fluent story-tellers. **1882** FARRAR in *Contemp. Rev.* 807 As a speaker..Dean Stanley was by no means fluent.

6. *Math.* In the doctrine of fluxions: Continuously increasing or decreasing by an infinitesimal quantity.

1734 BERKELEY *Analyst* §45 Wks. 1871 III. 287 Each foregoing is a fluent quantity having the following one for its fluxion. **1807** HUTTON *Course Math.* II. 276 Suppose the right line *mn* to move..continually parallel to itself..so as to generate the fluent or flowing rectangle ABQP.

transf. **1844** GLADSTONE *Glean.* (1874) V. ii. 83 The Church..might be eliminated like a constant quantity from among those fluent materials with which history is conversant.

B. *sb.*

†**1.** A stream, a current of water. *Obs.*

[In the first two quots. strictly a distinct word ad. L. *fluent-um*.]

1598 YONG *Diana* 308 The fertill fields, which the great riuer Duerus with his cristalline fluents doth water. **1616** CHAPMAN *Homer's Hymn to Venus* 378 At the fluents of the Ocean Nere Earths extreame bounds. **1705** J. PHILIPS *Blenheim* 239 Their hands, that sed'lous strive To cut the outrageous fluent.

2. *Math.* The variable quantity in fluxions which is continually increasing or decreasing.

1706 W. JONES *Syn. Palmar. Matheseos* 226 Hence the Celerity of the Motion is..called Fluxion, and the Quantity generated Fluent. **1819** G. PEACOCK *View Fluxional Calculus* 23 Where the fluent or integral is expressed by an algebraic function. **1878** W. K. CLIFFORD *Dynamic* ii. 62.

3. *nonce-use.* Something fluent or liable to change.

1836 COLERIDGE *Lit. Rem.* II. 309 The guardian, as a fluent, is less than the permanent which he is to guard. He is the temporary and mutable mean.

†**'fluential**, *a. Math. Obs.* [f. prec. + -(I)AL. Cf. *exponential*.] Of or pertaining to fluents.

1784 WARING in *Phil. Trans.* LXXIV. 401 Whose sum *p* is either an algebraical, exponential, or fluential fluxion of *x*. **1807** HUTTON *Course Math.* II. 302 Being written for *c* in the general fluential equation.

fluently ('flu:əntlɪ), *adv.* [f. FLUENT *a.* + -LY[2].] In a fluent manner; *esp.* with easy and ready flow of words.

1613 TOURNEUR *P. Henry* 147 His aptnesse fluently appeares In ev'rie souldier's grief. **1621** W. SCLATER *Tythes* (1623) 169 Conclusions fluently deduced there from. **1648** W. MOUNTAGUE *Devout Ess.* xi. §2 133 When this humour of Medisance springeth in the head of the company, it runnes fluently into the lesse noble parts. *a* **1661** FULLER *Worthies* (1840) III. 205 He fluently could speak many..modern tongues. **1732** BERKELEY *Alciphr.* I. §2 Perceiving that Euphranor heard him with respect, he proceeded very fluently. **1839** *Fraser's Mag.* XX. 668 She [a ship] swims along calmly and fluently. **1874** GREEN *Short Hist.* vi. §4. 304 Elizabeth..spoke French and Italian as fluently as English. **1875** JOWETT *Plato* (ed. 2) III. 221 Thrasymachus made all these admissions, not fluently..but with extreme reluctance.

†**'fluentness.** *Obs. rare.* [f. as prec. + -NESS.] The quality of being fluent; fluency.

1652 COTTERELL *Cassandra* I. v. (1676) 469 The usual fluentnesse of his expression. **1654** W. MOUNTAGUE *Devout Ess.* v. §3. 96 The fluentness and consistencie of time has not this inconvenience, to deny us the taking a dimension of it. **1706** in PHILLIPS (ed. Kersey). **1721** in BAILEY.

fluey (flu:ɪ), *a.*[1] *Obs.* exc. *dial.* [prob. f. FLUE *a.*[2] (which however is later in our quots.) + -Y[1].] = FLUE *a.*[2]

1552 RAYNALDE *Birth Mankynde* I. viii. 13 a, The sede and sparme [of women is] weake, fluy, cold, and moyste, and of no greate fyrmytie. **1876** *Surrey Provincialisms* (E.D.S.), *Fluey*, of a weak delicate constitution..I have never heard the word applied except to animals.

fluey ('flu:ɪ), *a.*[2] [f. FLUE *sb.*[2] + -Y[1].] Covered with flue.

1861 DICKENS *Gt. Expect.* xxii, I went upon 'Change, and I saw fluey men sitting there under the bills about shipping. **1862** —— *Somebody's Luggage* 4/2, I had the Luggage out within a day or two..It was all very dusty and fluey.

fluff (flʌf), *sb.*[1] [app. connected with FLUE *sb.*[2]; perh. an onomatopœic modification of that word, imitating the action of puffing away some light substance; cf. FLUFF *sb.*[2] and *v.*[2] An OE. **fluȝ, fluh*, f. root of FLY *v.*[1], would, however, if it existed, account for both words; cf. LG. *flug, flog* flue. Not in Johnson or Todd.]

1. a. Light, feathery, flocculent stuff, such as the downy particles that separate from dressed wool.

1790 GROSE *Prov. Gloss.* (ed. 2), *Fluff*, down. The fluff of a peach. Kent. **1818** J. BROWN *Psyche* 171 Some fluff upon his cousin's cape. *a* **1825** FORBY *Voc. E. Anglia*, *Fluff*, any light, flying, downy, gossamer-like stuff. **1880** HOWELLS *Undisc. Country* xii. 173 A little fluff under the bed or a spot on the floor would have been a comfort to her.

b. The soft fur of a rabbit or other animal.

1883 F. C. GOULD in *Leisure Hour* 613/2 They sneaked back..with rabbits' fluff in their jaws.

c. ? Soft feathery material for dress.

1875 TENNYSON *Q. Mary* I. iv, If this Prince of fluff and feather come To woo you.

d. Usually ***bit of fluff*** (cf. BIT *sb.*[2] 4 h): a young woman. *colloq.*

1903 'MARJORIBANKS' *Fluff-hunters* 11 The guard was about to whistle, when a bit of fluff was blown up the platform, and, before Webster had had time to send up a petition for a safe journey, it (the fluff) had come to rest on the corner seat opposite him. **1919** W. DEEPING *Second Youth* xxiv. 207 Got a little party on, you know, two bits of fashionable fluff. **1937** W. S. MAUGHAM *Theatre* xiv. 120 It was strangely flattering for a woman to be treated as a little bit of fluff that you just tumbled on to a bed. **1962** WODEHOUSE *Service with Smile* ii. 39 His ball of fluff will be there.

2. a. A soft, downy mass or bunch.

1862 MRS. CARLYLE *Lett.* (1883) III. 127 Larks come with feathers all in a fluff. **1885** E. GARRETT *At any Cost* xv. 277 A young woman..with a fluff of golden hair about her face. **1891** T. HARDY *Tess* II. 27 All this fluff of muslin about you.

b. Something downy and feathery.

1870 LOWELL *Study Wind.* (1886) 46 Tiny fluffs of feathered life. **1883** T. GRAY in *Encycl. Brit.* XXIII. 129 Sometimes he [Edison] used what he describes as a fluff, that is, a little brush of silk fibre.

3. *slang.* **a.** On railways (see quots.).

1874 *Slang Dict.*, *Fluff*, railway ticket clerks' slang for short change given by them. The profits thus accruing are called 'fluffings', and the practice is known as 'fluffing'. **1890** *Star* 27 Jan. 2/4 Many porters on this line are but getting 15*s.* per week, and with regard to 'tips', or, as we say 'fluff'—well [etc.].

b. *Theatr.* '"Lines" half learned and imperfectly delivered' (Farmer). Also, a mistake made when broadcasting, playing music, etc.

1891 *World* 3 June 28/1 Even as seen through a veil of 'fluff', the burlesque is irresistibly amusing. **1937** *Variety Radio Directory 1937/38* 342 *Fluff*, missing a cue, or muffing a gag. **1962** A. NISBETT *Technique Sound Studio* 253 *Fluff*, a small accidental error in operational work or in speech. **1967** *Word Study* Oct. 2/2 The announcer's fluff: 'Kids, be sure Mother is stop*p*ed [stocked] u*p* with Kellogg's Pep.' **1970** *Daily Tel.* 28 Oct. 12/7 In spite of a surprising number of fluffs, there was some excellent playing.

c. A bungling of a stroke or movement in games; a mistake, a blunder.

1928 *Daily Express* 10 May 10/2 Walter Hagen..hit a [golf] ball no more than a couple of yards... There is nothing malicious in the way the mind fixes on that two-yard 'fluff'. **1960** *Times* 21 Mar. 3/3 In addition he achieved four astonishing place kicks, which made his costly fluff against France unbelievable. **1970** *Guardian* 5 Aug. 18/8 Naturally, the Manson defence lawyers leaped on the fluff as an outrage.

fluff (flʌf), *sb.*[2] *Sc.* and *north. dial.* [see FLUFF *v.*[2]] A puff; a quick, short blast, a whiff; a slight explosion. *lit.* and *fig.*

1819 RENNIE *St. Patrick* III. i. 31 I'm sure an ye warna a fish or something war, ye could never a' keepit ae fluff o' breath in the body o' ye in aneath the loch. **1871** C. GIBBON *Lack of Gold* x, You'll see how cozily we'll blaze together to a white ash, and go off at the same minute with a fluff of affection. *Ibid.* xviii, The nuts leapt off with a 'fluff'.

b. *Comb.*, as **fluff-gib**, a squib, 'explosion of gunpowder' (Jam.).

1818 SCOTT *Rob Roy* xxxi, Wi' fighting, and flashes, and fluff-gibs.

fluff (flʌf), *v.*[1] [f. FLUFF *sb.*[1]]

1. *trans. Leather-manuf.* (See quot.) Cf. BUFF *v.*

1882 PATON in *Encycl. Brit.* XIV. 387/1 The flesh side is whitened or fluffed.

2. To make into fluff, pick into oakum.

1892 *Pall Mall G.* 14 Mar. 2/2 Looking up from the rope I was fluffing.

3. To shake *out* or *up* into a soft mass like fluff. Also *refl.* (of a bird): To shake or puff out its feathers.

1875 L. TROUBRIDGE *Life amongst Troubridges* (1966) x. 103 Her black hair combed right down over her fore-head and fluffed out behind. **1885** LADY BRASSEY *The Trades* 137 The 'Johnny Crows'..fluff and plume and dust themselves without cessation. **1885** O. T. MILLER in *Harper's Mag.* Mar. 599 He [a bird] fluffs himself out into a ball. **1887** *Poor Nellie* (1888) 265 The young ladies showed off the silky satins..then fluffed them up into a kind of pyramid. **1893** S. GRAND *Heavenly Twins* (1894) 279 She..fluffed her hair out till her head seemed preposterously large.

4. *intr.* **a.** To move or float softly like fluff. **b.** To settle *down* like a ball or mass of fluff.

1872 O. W. HOLMES *Poet Breakf.-t.* iii. (1885) 60 She gave the music-stool a twirl or two and fluffed down on to it like a whirl of soapsuds in a hand-basin. **1888** W. C. RUSSELL *Death Ship* III. 221 'Twas a..fog..fluffing thick and soft as feathers about the ship.

5. *Slang.* **a.** ***fluff it!*** (see quot. 1859). **b.** (of railway booking-clerks) To give short change. **c.** To disconcert, 'floor' (a public speaker); (cf. FLUFF *v.*[2] 1 a). **d.** (*Theatr.*) To blunder one's part. Also, to make mistakes in broadcasting, playing music, etc.; to mispronounce, play wrongly (a phrase, note, etc.).

1859 *Slang. Dict.*, *Fluff it*, a term of disapprobation implying 'take it away, I don't want it'. **1884** G. MOORE *Mummer's Wife* xx. 286 Mortimer was drunk, did not know his words, and went 'fluffing' all over the shop. **1936** H. HERD *Press Days* i. 20, I had a good natural memory and could be relied upon [in reciting] not to fluff my lines. **1946** *Penguin Mus. Mag.* Dec. 71 But, if you are in his orchestra, don't fluff that phrase next morning. **1955** *Times* 11 May 15/1 He loomed nearer in a closeup to tell viewers (fluffing his lines a little) about the decision of the three Great Powers to invite Russia to join in four-Power talks. **1960** C. DAY LEWIS *Buried Day* ix. 186, I had kept fluffing when I practised them [*sc.* songs]. **1967** *Word Study* Oct. 3/1 Steve Allen fluffed one time in advertising Dunhills: 'They're *m*uch, *m*uch *w*ilder [milder].'

e. To bungle (esp. a stroke or movement in games); to make a mistake; to fail (an examination). (Cf. DUFF *v.*[2])

1902 *Westm. Gaz.* 30 Apr. 7/3 Blain played first, and topped his shot into the bunker. Hilton then played, half-fluffed his. **1909** *Ibid.* 10 June 12/3 He skied his second into the rough at the third, and then fluffed his approach. **1915** H. L. WILSON *Ruggles of Red Gap* (1917) xv. 264 If it proves that I have fluffed my catch, rely upon me to use extreme measures. **1944** 'N. SHUTE' *Pastoral* i. 18, I fluffed the twelfth and lost a ball. **1955** *Amer. Speech* XXX. 303 *Fluff*, flunk (an exam), or make a mistake of any kind. **1959** G. JENKINS *Twist of Sand* viii. 148 There's a new attack plan. I don't want it fluffed, like the other. **1971** *Daily Tel.* 6 Aug. 11/5 Many school-children..awaiting their summer exam results have now got this particular worry. Has mother fluffed hers—or has she got through? **1971** *Times* 17 Sept. 6/4 Palmer fluffed it because there was a hedge where his backswing should have gone.

f. *intr.* To bluff, to lie; also *trans.*, to falsify (accounts, etc.).

1902 E. NESBIT *Five Children & It* x. 268 We must pretend like mad. Like that game of cards where you pretend you've got aces when you haven't. Fluffing, they call it. **1941** M. ALLINGHAM *Traitor's Purse* xiv. 159 You're up to something you don't want me to know about... Don't fluff. **1955** M. GILBERT *Sky High* xv. 209 Watch him..he's fluffing... He's acting. Dangerous man. Don't relax. **1957** *Times Lit. Suppl.* 11 Oct. 603/2 If he had chosen to fluff the accounts, or to render none, he would not have exposed himself.

g. Of railway porters: (see quots.).

1923 in J. MANCHON *Le Slang* 127. **1926** *Westm. Gaz.* 7 Jan., 'Fluffing'—that is, unauthorized tip-hunting by railway men—must stop, by order of the National Union of Railwaymen. **1966** H. SHEPPARD *Dict. Railway Slang* (ed. 2) 5 *Fluffing*, selection of rich passengers by off duty employees.

fluff (flʌf), *v.*[2] *Sc.* [belongs to FLUFF *sb.*[2]; of onomatopœic origin.]

1. a. *trans.* To knock out of breath; to cause to pant. Only in *pass.* **b.** *intr.* To puff, pant. **c.** To make a fuss.

1790 SHIRREFS *Poems* 21 But yet, nae ferly gin I'm fluff'd. **1813** HOGG *Queen's Wake* 72 We borit the breiste of the bursting swale, Or fluffit i' the flotyng faem. **1889** MRS. LYNN LINTON *Thro' the Long Night* I. II. i. 310 She had often fluffed and fumed to Anne over that provision of her father's will.

2. *trans.* To make (gunpowder) ignite and go off. Also ***to fluff in the pan***. Cf. FLASH *v.* 5 c.

1825 JAMIESON, *To fluff powder*, to burn gunpowder; to make it fly off, S. **1855** OGILVIE *Suppl.*, *Fluffed i' the pan*, burned priming without firing the barrel of the gun or pistol [Scotch].

fluffed (flʌft), *ppl. a.* [f. FLUFF *sb.*[1] or *v.*[1] + -ED.]

a. Having or covered with fluff or soft hairs; puffed *out* like a ball of fluff. **b.** Of a bungled shot at golf (cf. FLUFF *v.*[1] 5 e). **c.** Of a badly-played piece of music (cf. FLUFF *v.*[1] 5 d).

1906 *Westm. Gaz.* 6 Jan. 14/1 A pair of little sedge-warblers busy feeding a fluffed-out young cuckoo. **1909** M. B. SAUNDERS *Litany Lane* I. xi, A dark-fluffed, dimple-fisted citizen [*sc.* a baby]. **1923** *Glasgow Herald* 25 June 9 There were fluffed strokes near the green. **1965** *New Statesman* 9 Apr. 586/2 The Mahler performance..had all the marks of under-rehearsal: changed character and contrast..and every now and again a fluffed entry.

fluffer (ˈflʌfə(r)). [f. FLUFF *sb.*[1] + -ER[1].] A worker on a railway system (*spec.* the London Underground) employed to clear the track of refuse (see also quot. 1964).

1956 in *Shorter Oxf. Dict.* Add. **1962** *Guardian* 19 Jan. 9/6 They call them fluffers..because their job is to remove the fluff and dust that gets..on to the rails. **1964** *Daily Mirror* 30 Jan. 18/5 Fluffers... That's the name given to the gangs of women employed to clean the walls of London Underground tunnels during the early hours of the morning.

fluffily (ˈflʌfɪlɪ), *adv.* [f. FLUFFY *a.* + -LY[2].] In a fluffy manner or condition, like fluff.

1906 W. CHURCHILL *Coniston* I. xiii. 166 Miss Cassandra was arrayed fluffily in cool, pink lawn. **1923** *Weekly Dispatch* 14 Jan. 15 Beautiful pink plumes..swing fluffily from the waist on either side. **1927** *Scots Observer* 30 Apr. 11/3 One was a fluffily pretty stranger. **1946** G. MILLAR *Horned Pigeon* xvi. 251 She was a blonde, fluffily pretty in grotesquely high wooden-soled shoes.

ˈfluffiness. [f. FLUFFY *a.* + -NESS.] The quality of being fluffy, in various senses.

1860 DICKENS *Uncomm. Trav.* vi, An air of mingled fluffiness and heeltaps. **1879** SALA *Paris herself again* (1880) II. x. 145 The old beaver hat, remarkable..for..its fluffiness of texture. **1886** *Fun* 4 Aug. 44/2 A..clerical-looking young man, charged with fluffiness in a public conveyance, said he was sober as a judge when taken into custody. **1893** FARMER *Slang*, *Fluffiness* 2 (theatrical), the trick, or habit, of forgetting words.

fluffing (ˈflʌfɪŋ), *vbl. sb.* [f. FLUFF *v.*[1] + -ING[1].] The action of the vb. FLUFF; *attrib.* in ***fluffing machine, wheel*** (see FLUFF *v.*[1] 1).

1885 C. T. DAVIS *Manuf. Leather* 550 Leather Fluffing and Grounding Machines. **1886** HARRIS *Techn. Dict. Fire Insurance*, *Fluffing Wheels*..fine skins have all roughnesses removed by being stretched against fine emery-cloth wheels, revolving at a high speed.

fluffment (ˈflʌfmənt). *dial.* and *U.S.* [f. FLUFF *sb.*[1] or *v.*[1] + -MENT.] Something having a light or loose texture (*lit.* and *fig.*).

1890 *Century Mag.* Apr. 817 That is but a fluffment of talk, my Lady... I never heard tell in my time of nurture being stronger than nature. **1899** DICKINSON & PREVOST *Gloss. Cumbld.*, *Fluffment*, light and loose talk, or material. [Ex.] Her dress o' fluffment an' leace. **1928** *Funk's Stand. Dict.*, *Fluffment*, a bustling manner or fussy style of dress.

fluffy (ˈflʌfɪ), *a.* [f. FLUFF *sb.*[1] + -Y.[1]]

1. a. Consisting of or resembling fluff; of soft, downy texture.

1825 JAMIESON, *Fluffy*, applied to any powdery substance that can be easily put in motion or blown away; as to ashes, hair-powder, meal &c. **1860** THACKERAY *Lovel* ii, A great hulking Bluecoat boy, with fluffy whiskers. **1863** MISS BRADDON *Eleanor's Vict.* I. v. 106 The fluffy worsted curtains were drawn. **1887** R. N. CAREY *Uncle Max* xiii. 103 [She] buried her face in a very fluffy little muff.

b. Of timber: (see quot.).

1888 *Lockwood's Dict. Mech. Engin.*, Timber is said to be fluffy when the sawdust is stringy, and moist and greasy instead of granular and sharp.

c. *fig.*, often with reference to personal character or intellect.

1898 *Westm. Gaz.* 16 Apr. 1/3 Celia is strong-minded. You would not think so to look at her: she is what I call a fluffy girl. **1904** E. F. BENSON *Challoners* xiv, Begin instantly without playing any fluffy arpeggios. **1927** A. P. HERBERT *Plain Jane* 10, I like them fluffy,..With downy soft eyebrows and artful blue eyes,..With fluffy complexions, like plums on a wall, And fluffy opinions, and no brains at all. **1964** *Punch* 23 Dec. 967/3 His fluffy wife prepared to help him by seducing the boss.

2. Of persons: Covered with fluff. Of plants and animals: Covered with down, soft hairs, feathers, or fur; downy.

1848 DICKENS *Dombey* lix, Fluffy and snuffy strangers. **1856** F. E. PAGET *Owlet Owlst.*, 110, That dreary-looking man, with a fluffy effect about his head, as though it were sprinkled with the contents of a pillow. **1862** H. MARRYAT *Year in Sweden* I. 75 The road-side bright with the fluffy blue anemone. **1863** FR. A. KEMBLE *Resid. in Georgia* 259 These poor little fluffy things [rabbits]. **1879** HESBA STRETTON *Needle's Eye* I. 145 The fluffy yellow chickens.

3. *slang.* **a.** Drunk and incapable (see quot. 1886 s.v. FLUFFINESS). **b.** *Theatr.* Liable to forget one's 'lines'.

1885 *Referee* 26 July 3/2 One or two others were..what actors call fluffy in their lines. **1893** *Pall Mall G.* 17 Jan. 7/2 After the chorus is perfect, the principals are 'fluffy', especially when the principals are fashionable amateurs.

4. quasi-*sb.* A fluffy animal.

1889 *Daily News* 23 Oct. 7/1 Strictly smooth haired creatures are at a disadvantage among the fluffies.

5. *Comb.*: ***fluffy-brained, -minded*** adjs.

1905 *Author* 1 Feb. 150 Has he thrown you over for *her*, the *fluffy-brained thing? **1902** *Westm. Gaz.* 23 Oct. 3/1 A *fluffy-minded woman. **1935** WODEHOUSE *Blandings Castle* i. 12 The ninth Earl of Emsworth was a fluffy-minded and amiable old gentleman with a fondness for new toys.

flügelhorn (ˈfluːg(ə)lhɔːn). Also flu-. [G., f. *flügel* wing + *horn* horn.] A brass wind instrument. Also *flugel* used *ellipt.*

1854 *Times* 20 Oct. 1/2 Henry Distin's Flugel Horn Union, at 9.15. **1878** STAINER & BARRETT *Dict. Mus. Terms* 171/2 *Flügel-horn*, a bugle. A valve-horn. **1926** WHITEMAN & MCBRIDE *Jazz* iv. 105 These extra ones included accordion, bass tuba, flugelhorns, euphonium, [etc.]. **1954** *Grove's Dict. Mus.* (ed. 5) III. 166/1 In English brass bands ..a 'flugel' (as it is usually called) is an essential constituent. **1958** R. VAUGHAN WILLIAMS in M. Kennedy *Works R.V.W.* (1964) 633 The usual symphony orchestra is used [in Vaughan Williams' ninth symphony], with the addition of three saxophones and flügel horn. This beautiful and neglected instrument is not usually allowed in the select circles of the orchestra and has been banished to the brass band, where it is allowed to indulge in the bad habit of vibrato to its heart's content. **1965** *Melody Maker* 10 July 12/5 Ian Carr swopped between muted trumpet and occasional flugelhorn.

flugelman, flught: see FUGLEMAN, FLUCHT.

fluȝen, -on, obs. pa. t. pl. of FLY.

fluht, obs. form of FLIGHT.

†**ˈfluible**, *a. Obs.* [ad. L. type **fluibil-is*, f. *fluĕre* to flow.] Capable of flowing, fluid.

1576 T. NEWTON tr. *Lemnie's Touchstone* I. iv. 26 b, Seede ..is..moyste, fluible and liquide. **1605** TIMME *Quersit.* I. xv. 70 The spiritual and fluible parts [of the body]. **1613** PURCHAS *Pilgrimage* V. xiii. 510 The sea being a liquid fluible bodie. **1683** PETTUS *Fleta Min.* I. II. xxxvii. 199 This Fluss or fluible Composition maketh the scoria's deft.

fluid (ˈfluːɪd), *a.* and *sb.* Also 7 fluide. [a. Fr. *fluide*, ad. L. *fluid-us*, f. *fluĕre* to flow; see -ID.]

A. *adj.*

1. a. Having the property of flowing; consisting of particles that move freely among themselves, so as to give way before the slightest pressure. (A general term including both

gaseous and *liquid* substances.) ***fluid extract*** (U.S.), a concentrated solution (usu. in alcohol) of the active principle of a vegetable drug prepared to a standard strength (see esp. quot. 1965); freq. as *fluidextract*.

1603 HOLLAND *Plutarch's Mor.* 1361 To..presse together that which of the owne nature is fluid and runneth out. **1638** WILKINS *New World* I. xii. (1640) 178 The appearance of the milky way dos not arise from some fluider parts of the heaven (as he supposes). **1667** MILTON *P.L.* VI. 349 Spirits ..Cannot..mortal wound Receive, no more then can the fluid air. **1711** POPE *Temp. Fame* 447 Thro' undulating air the sounds are sent, And spread o'er all the fluid element. **1756** C. LUCAS *Ess. Waters* III. 315 The salt fuses readily, and runs very fluid. **1845** DARWIN *Voy. Nat.* xxi. (1852) 493 Masses of lava have been shot through the air whilst fluid. **1851** WOOD & BACHE *Dispens. U.S.A.* (ed. 9) 991 Mix thoroughly with the resulting Fluid Extract the Tincture of Ginger. **1885** *Buck's Handbk. Med. Sci.* I. 783/1 The Aromatic Fluid Extract (*Extractum Aromaticum Fluidum*, U.S. Ph.). **1935** C. SOLOMON *Prescription Writing & Formulary* II. xi. 102 Fluidextracts (called liquidextracts in the B.P.) are liquid alcoholic preparations of drugs so prepared that 1 cc. contains 1 gram of the drug (or, 1 minim contains 1 grain). **1951** A. GROLLMAN *Pharmacol. & Therapeutics* i. 38 The tinctures and fluid extracts are the most commonly used liquid preparations. **1965** *Pharmacopeia U.S.A.* (ed. 17) 787/2 Fluidextracts are liquid preparations of vegetable drugs, containing alcohol as a solvent or as a preservative, or both, and so made that each ml. contains the therapeutic constituents of 1 Gm. of the standard drug that it represents.

b. *fig.* and of non-physical things: Flowing or moving readily; not solid or rigid; not fixed, firm, or stable.

1642 H. MORE *Song of Soul* I. II. iv, So fluid chance is set its certain bound. **1672** CAVE *Prim. Chr.* II. ii. (1673) 31 The fluid and transitory condition of man's life. **1719** DE FOE *Crusoe* II. i. 290 The French, whose Temper is allowed to be more volatile..and their Spirits more fluid than in other Nations. **1873** M. ARNOLD *Lit. & Dogma* (1876) p. xv, The language of the Bible is fluid, passing, and literary, not rigid, fixed, and scientific. **1885** *Academy* 6 June 400/1 A time when the Evangelical tradition was still fluid. **1949** KOESTLER *Promise & Fulfilment* xiv. 159 This phase of fluid guerilla fighting ended on April 2. **1956** A. HUXLEY *Let.* 10 Jan. (1969) 784 Fluid staging, as I remember, used to be all the rage in Germany and Belgium thirty-five years ago. **1959** *Times* 11 June 3/3 The position, as the scores suggest, is decidedly fluid.

2. Of speech, etc.: Flowing easily and clearly. †Of a speaker: Fluent.

1691 WOOD *Ath. Oxon.* (1815) II. 219 He [Edmund Bunney] was the most fluid preacher in the reign of qu. Elizabeth, for he seldom or never studied for what he was to deliver, but would preach and pray extempore. *c* **1789** GIBBON *Mem.* Misc. Wks. 1796 I. 159 Monsignor Stonor.. discovers much venom in the *fluid* and nervous style of Gibbon.

B. *sb.*

1. a. A substance whose particles move freely among themselves, so as to give way before the slightest pressure.

Fluids are divided into liquids, which are incompletely elastic, and gases, which are completely so.

1661 BOYLE *Spring of Air* I. iv. (1682) 10 The air being a fluid. *a* **1721** KEILL *Maupertuis' Diss.* iii. (1734) 19 Descartes to account for the Revolutions of the Planets around the Sun, supposes them imerged in a Fluid, which [etc.]. **1807** *Med. Jrnl.* XVII. 275 From the first he swallowed fluids with difficulty. **1813** SIR H. DAVY *Agric. Chem.* i. (1814) 13 Mr. Cavendish made the grand discovery that it [water] was composed of two elastic fluids or gases. **1882** MINCHIN *Unipl. Kinemat.* vi. *heading*, Kinematics of Fluids.

b. *spec.* Any liquid constituent or secretion of the body (or of a plant).

1704 F. FULLER *Med. Gymn.* Pref., Moderate exercise will enrich the Fluids. **1732** ARBUTHNOT *Rules of Diet* 259 They ..act strongly both on the Fluids and Solids. **1804** KNIGHT in *Phil. Trans.* 186 Gravitation will act on the fluid descending from the leaves. **1831** R. KNOX *Cloquet's Anat.* 3 The fluids constitute the greater part of the organs. **1844** HOBLYN *Dict. Med., Fluid of Cotunnius*, a thin gelatinous fluid, found in the bony cavities of the labyrinth of the ear. **1878** L. P. MEREDITH *Teeth* 49 They decay on account of the bad condition of the fluids of the mouth.

2. One of several subtle, imponderable, all-pervading substances, whose existence has been assumed to account for the phenomena of heat, magnetism, and electricity.

1750 FRANKLIN *Lett.* Wks. 1840 V. 246 The particles of the electrical fluid. **1832** *Nat. Philos., Magnetism* iv. §152. 36 (Useful Knowl. Soc.) The supposition, that its phenomena are occasioned by the agency of two magnetic fluids, residing in the particles of iron..They have been denominated respectively the Austral and Boreal fluids. **1881** MAXWELL *Electr. & Magn.* I. 39 In most expositions of this theory the two electricities are called 'Fluids'.

3. *Comb.* (also in sense of FLUIDIC *a.* 3) as ***fluid-containing*** adj.; also **fluid amplifier**, a fluidic device in which small changes in a low-energy flow of fluid produce corresponding changes in a much larger flow; **fluid circuit**, a system of tubes, nozzles, and cavities designed to perform a fluidic function in a way analogous to an electrical circuit; **fluid clutch** = *fluid drive*; **fluid compass, lens** (see quots.); **fluid compression**, compression of steel while in a fluid state; so ***fluid-compressed*** adj.; **fluid coupling**, a device that makes use of oil or some other liquid to transmit torque from one shaft to another; **fluid drive**, a transmission in a motor vehicle, etc., in which a fluid coupling is used to transmit the power from the engine to the gears; **fluid flywheel** = *fluid coupling*; **fluid logic**, the performance of logical operations by fluidic devices; fluidics; **fluid mechanics**, the branch of mechanics dealing with the flow of liquids and gases and the way they respond to and exert forces; **fluid pressure**, pressure of a fluid, or resembling that of a fluid, being equal in all directions about a point and acting perpendicularly to any surface.

1960 *Product Engin.* 14 Mar. 17/1 Oil or air circuits may soon compete for control applications previously thought suitable only for electronic and electrical controls. Reason: a simple new *fluid amplifier just unveiled at the Army's Diamond Ordnance Fuse Laboratories here. **1963** *S.A.E. Jrnl.* Aug. 38 Fluid amplifiers perform electronic-like functions. **1964** *Control Engin.* Sept. 92/2 (*heading*) Fabricating pure *fluid circuits. **1965** *New Scientist* 9 Dec. 719/1 Last year..an F-101B fighter was flown with stability against yaw under fluid-circuit control. **1966** *Ibid.* 24 Mar. 766/3 Fluid circuits. the gas or liquid analogues of electronic circuits, are much slower than their electronic counterparts. **1951** *Engineering* 26 Oct. 533/3 The transmission assembly ..incorporates a *fluid clutch. **1963** R. F. WEBB *Motorists' Dict.* 58 A fluid clutch is..operated by engine speeds through two propellers (turbos) facing each other in a fluid filled container. **1867** SMYTH *Sailor's Word-bk.*, **Fluid compass*, that in which the card revolves in its bowl floated by alcohol. **1888** *Lockwood's Dict. Mech. Engin.* 146 *Fluid Compressed Steel. **1884** W. H. GREENWOOD *Steel & Iron* xxii. 510 The moulds employed in Sir Joseph Whitworth's process of *fluid compression are of special construction. **1753** N. TORRIANO *Non-Naturals* 50 The *Fluid-containing Vessels. **1940** *Automobile Engin.* 50/3 An oil pump maintains pressure in the *fluid coupling. **1966** *McGraw-Hill Encycl. Sci. & Technol.* V. 335/1 Because the fluid flow cannot change abruptly, a fluid coupling absorbs rather than transmits shock loads. **1941** *Automobile Engin.* XXXI. 49/1 *Fluid drive is available as special equipment on Dodges with conventional transmission and clutch. **1968** *Jane's Surface Skimmer Systems 1967–68* 31/1 The two propulsion engines drive the propellers through a fluid drive system, a reversing gearbox and 1:1 ratio vee box. **1930** *Autocar* 5 Sept. 1 (Advt.), The Daimler transmission system, comprising the Daimler *fluid flywheel and a self-changing silent four-speed gear-box. **1967** E. RUDINGER *Consumer's Car Gloss.* (ed. 2) 44 The fluid flywheel was used originally in place of a clutch in cars with a pre-selector gearbox..and it is now used in some types of automatic transmission. **1874** KNIGHT *Dict. Mech.* I. 891/1 **Fluid-lens*, one in which a liquid is imprisoned between circular glass disks of the required curvatures. **1960** J. R. GREENWOOD *B.S. Thesis, Mass. Inst. Tech.* (*title*) The design and development of a *fluid logic element. **1963** *Trans. Soc. Instrument Technol.* XV. 123/2 Fluid devices..without movable parts originated much more recently and the interest in fluid logic is due mainly to these types of devices. **1965** *Times* 23 July 17/3 In a fluid logic system a switch is activated when a small jet of air impinges on another's path. **1937** A. H. JAMESON (*title*) An introduction to *fluid mechanics. **1937** O'BRIEN & HICKOX *Applied Fluid Mech.* p. ix, Fluid mechanics not only treats the external forces acting on a fluid but also recognizes the internal forces, such as those caused by viscosity, which may markedly affect the motion. **1967** CONDON & ODISHAW *Handbk. Physics* (ed. 2) III. i. 3/1 The entire subject falls into three parts, solid mechanics, fluid mechanics, and, for intermediate states, rheology. **1974** *Encycl. Brit. Macropædia* XI. 779/2 Fluid mechanics deals with the forces exerted on a fluid to hold it at rest, as well as with the interplay of forces between a fluid and boundaries that cause motion of the fluid. **1845** *Rep. Brit. Assoc. 1844* I. 348 To show how..each of the individual particles of water..shall unite in the production of an aggregate motion consistent with the continuity of mass and with the laws of *fluid pressure,—this is a problem which belongs to the mathematician. **1858** W. J. M. RANKINE *Man. Appl. Mech.* 100 The term fluid pressure is used to denote a thrust which is normal and equally intense in all directions round a point. **1910** *Encycl. Brit.* XIV. 117/1 This mechanical axiom of the normality of fluid pressure is the foundation of the mathematical theory of hydrostatics. **1940** J. D. JEVONS *Metallurgy of Deep Drawing & Pressing* ix. 311 With fluid-pressure actuation the applied pressure cannot rise above a value determined by a release valve.

fluid, obs. Sc. form of FLOOD.

fluidal (ˈfluːɪdəl), *a. Geol.* [f. FLUID *sb.* + -AL¹.] Of or resembling a fluid: (see quots.).

1879 DANA *Man. Geol.* (ed. 3) 65 Igneous rocks sometimes exhibit under the microscope a fluidal texture; that is, the material..shows wavy lines or bands, which are evidence of a former fluid state, and of movement or flowing when in that state. **1893** GEIKIE *Geol.* (ed. 3) 100 Streaked [structure] ..conspicuously shown by the lines of flow in vitreous rocks (flow-structure, fluxion-structure, fluidal-structure).

fluidible (ˈfluːɪdɪb(ə)l), *a.* [f. FLUID + -IBLE.] Capable of change of shape like a fluid under pressure.

1908 J. W. GREGORY *Geog.* 5 The shape of the earth depends on the fluidible nature of its interior. **1926** *Encycl. Brit.* II. 172 Under the influence of the intense heat and pressure, the material must at that depth be capable of flow into any cavities like a fluid, so that it has been described as elastico-rigid, or 'fluidible'.

fluidic (fluːˈɪdɪk), *a.* [f. as FLUIDAL *a.* + -IC. Cf. F. *fluidique* (sense 2).]

1. Of the nature of a fluid.

1883 WINCHELL *World-life* II. ii. §6. 242 The..older fluidic condition..impresses more important results on the life-history of satellites.

2. *Spiritualism.* Of or belonging to a supposed supersensible 'double' (of 'fluid' or ethereal consistence) possessed by every being.

1877 BLAVATSKY *Isis Unveiled* I. i. 12 The Astral Soul, or the inner, fluidic body. **1882** MABEL COLLINS *Cobwebs* II. 179 The fluidic atmosphere which passes from one human being to another. **1887** H. S. OLCOTT tr. *A. D'Assier's Posth. Humanity* iv. 103 Besides its exterior and organic form, the human body possesses an interior and fluidic form, moulded after the former.

3. [Back-formation from next.] Designed or operating in accordance with the principles and techniques of fluidics; of or pertaining to fluidics.

1960 [see FLUIDICS *sb. pl.*]. **1965** *Missiles & Rockets* 8 Feb. 18/3 In the first fluidic circuits..a fluid stream of relatively high energy was directed across a cavity. **1965** HUMPHREY & TARUMOTO *Fluidics* I. iii. 40/2 Fluidic systems often.. have few if any moving parts. **1968** *McGraw-Hill Yearbk. Sci. & Technol.* 12/2 Common to all of the many different types of fluidic devices is the principle that a stream of fluid flowing through a small channel..can be deflected from its initial path when hit by a smaller control jet. **1968** *Sci. Jrnl.* Dec. 53/1 The fluidic system uses a flow of fluid instead of a flow of electrons (electric current). **1969** *Nature* 20 Dec. 1193/1 When the control flows are provided by a feedback from the efflux of the power jet, a fluidic oscillator is set up.

So **fluˈidiform** *a.* [F. *fluidiforme.*]

1887 H. S. OLCOTT tr. *A. D'Assier's Posth. Humanity* ii. 68 The existence of a plexus of fluidiform capillaries connecting the phantom with the body from which it emanates.

fluidics (fluːˈɪdɪks), *sb. pl.* [f. FLUID *sb.* after *electronics*, *mathematics*, etc.] A field of technology concerned with using small interacting flows and jets of fluid in systems of tubes, nozzles, and cavities that have few or no moving parts, to carry out operations characteristic of electronics, such as amplification and switching.

Quot. 1960 represents a different sense.

[**1960** *Compressed Air & Hydraulics* Apr. 149/1 [Abstract of a paper by H. Masheder read at the 2nd European Fluid Power Conf., 28 Apr. 1960.] This paper examines future trends in automatic fluid power control in the light of the following factors: the reasons for the unique position occupied by fluidics; the stability of this position and whether it is likely to be threatened by competitive non-fluidic systems; [etc.]. *Ibid.* 171/2 One prominent engineer [*sc.* Masheder]..suggests 'fluidics' with which to designate all aspects of the behaviour of liquids and gases.] **1965** *Missiles & Rockets* 8 Feb. 18/1 In five short years, with an investment of some $30 million, the United States has brought into being a new technology—fluidics. *Ibid.* 18/2 The term 'fluidics' as used throughout this report refers to that field of technology that deals with the use of fluids, either gaseous or liquid, in motion to perform functions such as signal or power amplification, temperature or rate sensing, logic or computation, and control. Inherent in the term is the concept of achieving amplification or gain—and often, the absence of moving parts. **1965** HUMPHREY & TARUMOTO *Fluidics* III. xiv. 139 Fluidics will have significant applications in control valves; temperature, pressure and flow sensing and control systems;..and in small, low speed process computers. **1966** *Times* 6 Dec. 20/6 The technique of fluidics..is based on a method of controlling the flow of either gases or liquids just as electron flow is controlled and amplified in electronic circuits. **1967** *New Scientist* 19 Jan. 143/1 The analogy between fluidics and electronics has been taken one step further with the introduction of a planar turbulence amplifier. **1970** *Engineering* 13 Mar. 268 Moving-part fluidics using membrane elements is little practised in the West.

fluidify (fluːˈɪdɪfaɪ), *v.* [f. as FLUIDIC *a.* + -(I)FY.] *trans.* To make fluid.

1851–9 DARWIN in *Man. Sci. Enq.* 283 Granite rocks which have been fluidified. **1859** TODD *Cycl. Anat.* V. 280/2 This fluid condenses, fluidifies the respiratory gases *in transitu*.

Hence **fluˈidified** *ppl. a.*; also **fluidifiˈcation**, the action of making fluid; **fluˈidifier**, an agent that fluidifies.

1837 S. SMITH *Philos. Health* II. x. 161 It..needs no apparatus for the..fluidification of its food. **1842** DARWIN *Geol. Observ.* II. xiv. (1876) 500 The fluidified granite. **1876** BARTHOLOW *Mat. Med.* (1879) 235 The alvine dejections.. consist at first of fluidified faeces. **1876** GARROD *Treat. Gout* (ed. 3) 407 Bicarbonate of soda..causes a species of solution of the blood, and hence medicines of this class have been called fluidifiers.

fluidism (ˈfluːɪdɪz(ə)m). [f. as prec. + -ISM.]

1. The theory which refers all diseases to the state of the fluids in the body.

1835–6 TODD *Cycl. Anat.* I. 416/1 The less shall we feel inclined to admit the exclusive claims either of fluidism or solidism. **1860** WORCESTER, *Fluidism*, the doctrine of those who refer all diseases to alterations of the fluids of the body.

2. *Spiritualism.* The hypothesis of the existence of supersensible 'fluidic' bodies (see FLUIDIC 2).

So **ˈfluidist** [see -IST], one who supports the hypothesis of fluidism (in either sense).

1888 *Amer. Jrnl. Psychol.* I. 500 All such facts favor the fluidists.

fluidity (fluːˈɪdɪtɪ). [f. FLUID *a.* + -ITY. Cf. F. *fluidité.*]

1. The quality or condition of being fluid.

1605 TIMME *Quersit.* I. iv. Db, Sulphur..with his humidity, softnesse, and fluidity or passablenes. **1667** *Phil. Trans.* II. 491 A too great fluidity of the bloud..may cause death. **1744** BERKELEY *Siris* §60 Being good against too great fluidity as a balsamic. **1827** FARADAY *Chem. Manip.* xv. 359 The cement should be heated to fluidity. **1858** GREENER *Gunnery* 261 The immense resistance which the fluidity of

the air offered to projectiles. **1869** PHILLIPS *Vesuv.* iv. 107 A stream of lava of remarkable fluidity.

b. *fig.* and of non-physical things.

1824 GALT *Rothelan* II. IV. iii. 116 If Ralph Hanslap had any fluidity of mind. **1873** *Contemp. Rev.* XXII. 794 The remarkable diffusion and fluidity of these distinctively Semitic names of God. **1886** MRS. LYNN LINTON *Paston Carew* iii, He..ridiculed the fossilization of Toryism equally with the fluidity of Radicalism. **1892** *Speaker* 3 Sept. 294/2 The fluidity and informality of the Church's prime.

2. Of speech, literary composition, etc.: The quality of flowing easily and clearly.

1603 FLORIO *Montaigne* I. xxxvi. 115 First a blithe and ingenious fluiditie [F. *fluidité*], then a quaint-wittie and loftie conceit. **1822** *New Monthly Mag.* VI. 441 Singing with..sweetness and fluidity. **1880** SWINBURNE *Study Shaks.* ii. (ed. 2) 91 There is the same comparative tenuity and fluidity of verse. **1883** *Nation* (N.Y.) 29 Nov. 446/3 The letters [of Mme. de Rémusat]..have much grace, much fluidity of thought, and of expression.

fluidization (ˌfluːɪdaɪˈzeɪʃən). [f. FLUIDIZE *v.* + -ATION.] The process of fluidizing; the state of being fluidized. (In quot. 1932 = FLUIDITY 1 b.)

1932 *Private Let. J. Lonke* (G. & C. Merriam Co. files) 3 Feb., The correction of the present maldistribution and the restoration of the fluidization of the world's gold supply. **1947** *Chem. Engin. Progr.* XLIII. 429/2 If the gas velocity is relatively low the appearance of the column of solids will be like that of a boiling liquid, and the condition may be referred to as 'dense phase' fluidization. **1954** D. L. REYNOLDS in *Amer. Jrnl. Sci.* CCLII. 577 As a volcanic process fluidization is exemplified by the up-rushing gas phase at Vesuvius. **1955** *Science News* XXXVI. 74 Even and regular transport and feeding of the finest coal powder can be successfully brought about by fluidization. **1960** *Times Rev. Industry* Jan. 39/1 Compressed air is sometimes employed to discharge difficult material from storage bins by 'Fluidization'. **1962** E. M. SHOEMAKER et al. in A. E. J. Engel et al. *Petrologic Stud.* 344 Intricate mixing, rounding, and polishing of debris derived from depth..suggest fluidization.

fluidize (ˈfluːɪdaɪz), *v.* [f. FLUID + -IZE.]

1. *trans.* To convert into a fluid; to fluidify.

1855 in CLARKE *Dict.*

2. To cause (a mass of finely divided solid) to assume fluidity and other characteristics of a liquid by passing a current of gas, vapour, or liquid upwards through it.

1945 *Industr. & Engin. Chem.* Apr. 332/2 The density of the powder is related to the air rate necessary to fluidize it. **1950** *Petroleum Refiner* Sept. 191/1 Air serves to transfer catalyst to the regenerator and to fluidize the catalyst bed there. **1965** *Sci. Jrnl.* June 65/1 Powder is transferred by pipe..and is fluidized whenever it is necessary to lift it vertically. **1967** P. J. WYLLIE *Ultramafic & Related Rocks* viii. 241/1 In the Mesozoic, the massive kimberlite was invaded by an influx of gases, fluidized, and carried upwards at low temperatures. **1968** COULSON & RICHARDSON *Chem. Engin.* (ed. 2) II. vi. 196 Systems fluidised with a liquid do not tend to give rise to bubbles.

So **ˈfluidized** *ppl. a.*, esp. in *fluidized bed*; **ˈfluidizing** *ppl. a.* and *vbl. sb.* Also **ˈfluidizer**, an apparatus in which fluidization is carried out.

1943 *Industr. & Engin. Chem.* July 768/2 A fluidized mass can be circulated by application of the gas lift principle. **1947** *Chem. Engin. Progr.* XLIII. 435/1 Drop in pressure due to gas travel though a bed of solids is practically independent of its velocity when smooth, dense phase fluidizing action takes place. **1949** *Industr. & Engin. Chem.* June 1135/2 Heat transfer between the fluidized solid and the fluidizing gas. *Ibid.* 1227 (*heading*) Reaction of methane with copper oxide in a fluidized bed. **1954** D. L. REYNOLDS in *Amer. Jrnl. Sci.* CCLII. 580 The conduit of the volcano was eroded and widened by fluidized solid particles. **1955** *Science News* XXXVI. 69 (*caption*) Prototype of fluidizer. **1959** *Times Rev. Industry* June 55/1 The growing importance of fluidizing techniques for the movement of materials in bulk. **1963** *Jrnl. Pharm. Sci.* LII. 284 Fluidized bed drying of tablet granulations is at least 15 times faster than tray drying procedures. **1963** *Economist* 31 Aug. 760/2 Everything from fluidised-bed coating with plastics to electrophoretic deposition. **1964** *New Scientist* 24 Sept. 759/3 There are some interesting arguments in favour of the fluidiser as an auxiliary means of cooking. **1971** *Guardian* 4 June 9/4 Suspended in a fluidised bed like pingpong balls in a funfair.

ˈfluidly, *adv. rare.* [see -LY².] In a fluid manner.

1678 WOOD *Life* (Oxf. Hist. Soc.) II. 419 If they see a man talk seriously they talk fluidly nonsense. **1690** tr. *Plutarch's Mor.* III. VIII. 15 This being fluidly disposed did run into those places which were hollow. **1971** *Oxford Times* 5 Nov. 30 Movement is..confidently expressed by the additional use of fluidly handled wash.

†**ˈfluidness.** *Obs.* [see -NESS.] The state or quality of being fluid; fluidity. *lit.* and *fig.*

1626 DONNE *Serm.* lxxx. 817 The fluidnesse, the transitorinesse of all such temporall things. **1647** H. MORE *Song of Soul* Notes 388 The fluidnesse of the Planetary heavens is acknowledged. **1670** W. SIMPSON *Hydrol. Ess.* 137 The eucrasy & fluidness..of this balsamick ferment.

fluidra(ch)m, fluigram, contracted forms of *fluid dra(ch)m, fluid gram(me).*

1880 O. OLDBERG in *Med. Rec.* (N.Y.) 14 Aug. 178/2 We would have to learn *four* new units:..in fact, only two..are important. One is the Gram,..and the other the (cubic centimeter, which, as suggested by Mr. Alfred B. Taylor, should be called a) Fluigram, equal to about 15 minims, or ¼ fluid-drachm. **1889** *Buck's Handbk. Med. Sci.* VII. 731/2 In medicine and pharmacy the gram and the cubic centimeter are the most important metric units, and to express their close relationship the cubic centimeter has been very appropriately termed a 'Fluigram'. **1961** *Stedman's Med. Dict.* (ed. 21) 1827/1 The minim, fluidrachm, and fluidounce of the U.S. apothecaries' measure are slightly larger than the corresponding denominations in the Imperial (British) measure.

†**ˈfluish**, *a. Obs.* In 5 flewische. [f. FLUE *a.* + -ISH.] Somewhat weak or drooping. Of the countenance: Haggard, melancholy.

*c***1460** J. RUSSELL *Bk. Nurture* 777 With a flewische countenaunce. **1674** RAY *N.C. Words, Fluish*, fluid, wa[s]hy, tender, weak.

fluit, obs. form of FLUTE.

fluitant (ˈfluːɪtənt), *a. rare.* [ad. L. *fluitant-em*, pr. pple. of *fluitāre* freq. of *fluĕre* to flow.] Floating.

1676 H. MORE *Remarks* 54 That the fluitant parts of the Air in this more subtle fluid may yield to motion every way. **1889** *Cent. Dict., Fluitant*, in *bot.*, floating.

fluke (fluːk), *sb.*¹ Forms: 1–2 floc, flooc, 5–6 floke, (5 flewke,) 6–9 flook(e, 6–7 flouk(e, (6 *Sc.* fluike), 8–9 fleuk, flowk, (8 *dial.* fleak, fluck, 9 *dial.* fluik), 4– fluke. [OE. *flóc* str. (of uncertain gender), cognate with ON. *flóke* wk. masc.; related by ablaut to Ger. *flach* flat.]

1. A flat fish, *esp.* the common flounder, *Pleuronectes Flesus.*

*a***700** *Epinal Gloss.* 802 Platisa, flooc. *a* **1000** ÆLFRIC *Colloq.* in Wr.-Wülcker 94 Fage and floc and lopystran and fela swylces. **14..** *Nom.* ibid. 705 *Hic pelanius*, a flewke. **1478** BOTONER *Itin.* (Nasmith 1778) 291 Homines possunt piscare..de flokes. **1523** FITZHERB. *Husb.* §55 And thou cut the lyuer [of a rotten shepe] therin wylbe lytell quicknes lyke flokes. **1602** CAREW *Cornwall* 106 b, Wry-mouthed Flooke. **1744** PRESTON in *Phil. Trans.* XLIII. 61/2 In the Sea they catch..Flukes, Trouts, &c. **1790** MRS. A. WHEELER *Westmld. Dial.* 28 I'll gie the a Fleak and a Pot-ful a Saur Milk. **1819** SCOTT *Antiq.* xi, I'll bid you a shilling for the fluke and the cock-padle.

b. as a type of flatness.

?*a* **1400** *Morte Arth.* 1088 Flatt mowthede as a fluke. *a* **1605** MONTGOMERIE *Flyting w. Polwart* 111 I's fell thee like a fluike, flatlings on the flure. **1804** R. ANDERSON *Cumberld. Ball.* 106 Her feet flat and braid, as big fluiks.

c. *slang.* = FLAT *sb.*³ 13.

1804 *Sporting Mag.* XXIII. 201 The unguarded flukes, whom they can inveigle to play.

2. A parasitic trematoid worm, of several species, found *esp.* in the livers of sheep, so called from its resemblance to a fluke or flounder.

[Cf. quot. 1523 in sense 1]. **1668** WILKINS *Real Char.* II. v. §2. 123 Insects..whose shape doth somewhat resemble a Flounder, found..in..the liver of several of the Ruminant kind..Fluke. **1755** NICHOLLS in *Phil. Trans.* XLIX. 247 A small flat worm, resembling a sole..is found in the gall-duct, by the butchers term'd flooks. **1845** BUDD *Dis. Liver* 399 Fourteen flukes were found..in the duodenum of a Lascar. **1884** in *Chamb. Jrnl.* 3 May 278/2.

3. A variety of kidney potato, perh. so called from its shape.

1868 *N. & Q.* Ser. IV. I. 100. **1874** E. H. RUDDOCK *Text-bk. Mod. Med.* (1893) 38 The best sorts [of potatoes] are..the Forty-fold, and the Fluke. **1884** in *Chesh. Gloss.*

4. *attrib.* and *Comb.* **a.** simple attrib. (sense 2), as *fluke-disease, -worm*; **b.** instrumental (sense 2), as *fluke-infested* adj.; **c.** similative (sense 1), as *fluke-mouthed* adj. Also **fluke-rake**, a rake with triangular prongs used for taking flukes; **fluke-wort** (see quot. 1861).

1884 *Chamb. Jrnl.* 3 May 278/1 This disease—Liver-fluke, *Fluke Disease, Liver-rot, as it is variously termed. *Ibid.* 278/2 The bodies of *fluke-infested sheep. ?*a* **1400** *Morte Arth.* 2780 Thow wenes for to flay us, *ffloke-mouthed schrewe. **1766** BROOKES *Art Angling* 85 In the hot Months, there are great Quantities caught with the *Fluke-Rake. **1794–6** E. DARWIN *Zoon.* (1801) IV. 250 When the *fleuk-worm is preying on the substance of their livers. **1802** BINGLEY *Anim. Biog.* (1813) III. 395 Fluke-worms are oftentimes very numerous in the viscera of quadrupeds. **1597** GERARDE *Herbal.* II. cxliii. §3. 424 In Northfolke it [Water Pennywoort] is called *Flowkwoort. **1861** MRS. LANKESTER *Wild Flowers* 61 Marsh Pennywort..is also known as..Fluke-wort, and Sheep's bane. These..names it has obtained on account of its being supposed to produce the rot..in animals that feed upon it.

fluke (fluːk), *sb.*² Forms: 6–8 flook(e, 6 *Sc.* fluik, 7 flouke, (flouck), 8– fluke. [of uncertain origin; possibly a transferred use of FLUKE *sb.*¹, from resemblance of shape; cf. the inadmissible suggestion in the following quot.

1886 R. C. LESLIE *Sea-painter's Log* x. 200 The name 'fluke' or 'flowk' well expresses the shape of the flounder, which is that of the fluke of an old-fashioned anchor.

See also FLUE *sb.*³ 2.]

1. One of 'the broad triangular plates of iron on each arm of the anchor, inside the bills or extreme points, which, having entered the ground, hold the ship' (Admiral Smyth).

1561 EDEN *Arte Nauig.* A iij b, The Thirreni founde the vse of the anker of one graspe or flooke. **1600** HOLLAND *Livy* XXXVII. xxx. 962 Her owne anker, which by one of the floukes tooke fast hold. **1743** BULKELEY & CUMMINS *Voy. S. Seas* 115 All Hands haul'd..which weigh'd the Grapenel, but streighten'd one of the Flukes. **1864** TENNYSON *En. Ard.* 18 Among the waste and lumber of the shore..Anchors of rusty fluke.

b. The barbed head of a lance, arrow, etc. Cf. FLUKED 1629. Also *U.S.* 'one of the barbs of a harpoon or toggle-iron; a flue' (*Cent. Dict.*).

a **1605** MONTGOMERIE *Misc. Poems* xxviii. 58 And evry shaft..To haif als mony heeds, And evirie head als mony huikis, And evirie huik als mony fluiks. **1613** PURCHAS *Pilgrimage* v. xvii. (1614) 544 A great launce couered with gold and the fluke set with stones. **1841** CATLIN *N. Amer. Ind.* (1844) I. v. 33 The one [arrow] with long flukes or barbs.

c. A name for various instruments resembling the prec. in shape: see quots.

1841 HARTSHORNE *Salop. Ant.* Gloss., *Fluke*, a lancet used for letting blood from horses. **1849** WEALE *Dict. Terms, Fluke*, in mining, the head of a charger; an instrument used for cleansing the hole previous to blasting. **1878** *Cumbld. Gloss.* Supp., *Fleukk*, the web of the plough sock.

2. *pl.* 'The two parts which constitute the large triangular tail of the whale' (Adm. Smyth). *to turn* or *peak the flukes*: of a whale, to go under (see quot. 1839); hence *transf.* (*Naut. slang*) to go to bed, 'turn in'.

1725 DUDLEY in *Phil. Trans.* XXXIII. 256 While young, and carried by the Dam on the Flukes of their Tails. **1839** T. BEALE *Nat. Hist. Sperm Whale* 44 The flukes are then lifted high into the air, and the animal..descends perpendicularly..this act..is called by whalers 'peaking the flukes'. **1851** H. MELVILLE *Whale* iii. 21 It's getting dreadful late, you had better be turning flukes..it's a nice bed. **1860** HARTWIG *Sea & Wond.* vi. 79 The tail-fin, or 'flukes'.

3. *attrib.* and *Comb.*, as (*light*) *fluke plough*; **fluke-chain, -rope**, a chain or rope which is passed round the flukes of a whale to secure it when caught.

1851 H. MELVILLE *Whale* lxxxii. 399 The whale..was secured there by the stiffest *fluke-chains. **1775** G. WASHINGTON *Writ.* (1889) II. 461 Get 2 light *fluke Plows.

Hence **fluked** *a.*¹, having flukes.

1629 Z. BOYD *Last Battell* I. 14 Death..with its sting, like a flooked Dart, for to pierce thorow the heart of men. **1831** J. HOLLAND *Manuf. Metal* I. 96 Three or four fluked anchors are to be constructed.

fluke (fluːk), *sb.*³ *colloq.* [of unknown etymology. Possibly of Eng. dialectal origin; cf. '*fluke*, a guess' (*Whitby Gloss.* 1876).] In *Billiard-playing*, A successful stroke made by accident or chance. Hence *gen.* a lucky stroke, an unexpected success; a piece of good luck, *esp.* in phrase *by a fluke*. Also *attrib. a fluke of wind*: a chance breeze.

1857 *N. & Q.* Ser. II. IV. 208/1 In playing at billiards..Another term is, 'He made a flook (or fluke)'. **1861** H. KINGSLEY *Ravenshoe* v, That was rather a fluke, was it not? **1868** YATES *Rock Ahead* I. vi, The most unexpected fluke at trente et quarante. **1882** BAIN *J. S. Mill* 194 The transfer of power has gone on..by flukes and leaps in the dark. **1889** H. F. WOOD *Eng. of Rue Cain* x, Whose run-away horse he had stopped..by the merest fluke. **1906** 'Q' *Mayor of Troy* x. 139 The mass huddled together, rubbing flanks, swaying this way and that in the pressure of panic as corn is swayed by flukes of summer wind. **1909** *Daily Chron.* 12 Oct. 8/1 It was no fluke victory. **1955** *Times* 3 Aug. 4/5 Because of the calms and flukes of wind yesterday numbers of vessels retired from their respective events.

Hence **ˈflukeless** *a.*, without a fluke.

1895 *Westm. Gaz.* 5 Jan. 7/2 It was a faultless, flukeless performance on a standard table.

fluke (fluːk), *sb.*⁴ *dial.* [app. a. ON. *flóke* of same meaning: see FLOCK *sb.*²] (See quots.)

16.. T. MORE in *Ray's N.C. Words* (E.D.S.) note s.v. *Flukes*, locks of hair. Salop. **1847** HALLIWELL, *Fluke*, waste cotton. Lanc.

fluke (fluːk), *v.*¹ [f. FLUKE *sb.*²]

1. *intr.* Of a whale: To use the flukes, to 'peak the flukes': see FLUKE *sb.*² 2.

1840 F. D. BENNETT *Whaling Voy.* 6 *note*, There she blow-o-s! Th-e-r-e again! Flukes! **1892** R. KIPLING *Barrack-r. Ballads* 206 Where the scared whale flukes in flame!

b. *transf.* in phrase (*to go*) *fluking* or *all* (*-a-*) *fluking* (see quot. 1867).

1840 R. H. DANA *Bef. Mast* xxviii, We arrived on the following day, having gone 'all fluking'. **1867** SMYTH *Sailor's Word-bk.* s.v. *Flukes*, From the power of these [flukes of a whale] the phrase obtained among whalers of *fluking* or *all-a-fluking*, when running with a fresh free wind.

2. *trans.* In *Whaling.* **a.** To disable the flukes of (a whale) by spading. **b.** To fasten (a whale) by means of a chain or rope. (*Cent. Dict.*)

fluke (fluːk), *v.*² Also flook. [f. FLUKE *sb.*³]

1. trans. *Billiard-playing*: To hit or pocket (a ball) by a fluke; to make (a stroke) by a fluke.

1881 *Times* 14 Jan. 8/2 Bennett..tried for a cannon, but fluked the white, and..ran out the winner by 90 points. **1888** *Sportsm.* 20 Dec. 4/4 Fortune once more assisted Mitchell, who, in trying to make a red loser, fluked a cannon.

2. *transf.* To get (*in*) or obtain by a fluke. Also *intr.*

1885 *Pall Mall G.* 18 June 2 On the chance of crowding or fluking in one [picture] he will send the whole eight. **1889** *Ibid.* 2 May 7/3 It is very questionable whether the artist is really any better off for fluking £500 or £1000 now and again for a picture which is worth £50. **1892** *Ibid.* 25 Aug. 1/3 He wanted to fluke a last success. **1897** N. GOULD *Seeing him Through* xiii, Even if he managed to fluke home in this trial. **1904** *Daily Chron.* 5 May 7/2 Even if Mr. P. F. Warner's XI. were fluked out of the game. **1929** *Star* 21 Aug. 16/2 Marvellous handicap horses that may fluke the City and Suburban.

Hence ˈ**fluking** *vbl. sb.*, ˈ**fluking** *ppl. a.*, characterized by a fluke or flukes. ˈ**flukist**, one who succeeds rather by chance than by skill.

1865 *Daily Tel.* 21 Aug. 4 The sensation which was created last year by the Miner's fluking victory over Blair Athol. **1881** *Society* 23 July 24/1 Time..will show whether Mr. Beck is a lucky flukist or a really good shot. **1882** Miss Braddon *Mt. Royal* III. viii. 155 She would play that fluking game which she most affected at billiards. **1893** G. D. Leslie *Lett. Marco* xxi. 142 There is a lot of fluking in the art..when we once begin to try and make a good picture it is all up with it.

fluked (fluːkt), *a.*² [f. fluke *sb.*¹ + -ed².] Infested with flukes, fluky.

1855 [see fluky *a.*¹]. **1925** *Glasgow Herald* 20 June 4 Badly fluked sheep should be destroyed.

fluky (ˈfluːkɪ), *a.*¹ Also 9 **flukey**. [f. fluke *sb.*¹ + -y¹.] Infested with flukes; pertaining to an animal infested with flukes.

1855 Robinson *Whitby Gloss.*, *Fluked* or *Fluky*, worm-eaten, or rather when the worm holes channel or flow into each other. **1874** 'C. King' *Ion Duan* (Melbourne) lxv. 25 Regardless of flukey meat and damper.

ˈ**fluky**, *a.*² *rare*⁻¹. In 8 flooky. [f. fluke *sb.*² + -y¹.] Of an anchor: Having flukes.

1718 Rowe tr. *Lucan* 81 No loud-mouth'd Voices call.. To heave the flooky Anchors from the Sand.

fluky (ˈfluːkɪ), *a.*³ Also **flukey**. [f. fluke *sb.*³ + -y¹.]

1. Of the nature of a fluke or lucky chance; obtained by chance rather than by skill.

1867 *Australasian* 2 Mar. 268/1 Cosstick..playing a very flukey innings. **1879** *Sat. Rev.* 5 July 21 There was some flukey hitting off Mr. Steele. **1881** *Standard* 8 July 6/1 Lascelles scored a fluky two in the slips. **1886** G. B. Smith *Prime Ministers* 310 The ministry..sustained an actual but fluky defeat. **1893** *Pall Mall G.* 21 June 5/2 The result..is a capital example of the flukey nature of the game.

2. Uncertain; favouring unexpected results.

1880 *Daily Tel.* 7 Sept., There are the fluky days, when the best of the breeze brings all the stern boats up to you. **1882** *Sat. Rev.* LIV. 706 A very fluky etymology. **1894** *Times* 16 Apr. 10/3 The Britannia..beating Oretta and Valkyrie I. hull down in very fluky winds.

Hence ˈ**flukily** *adv.* ˈ**flukiness**.

1881 *Daily News* 22 June 2/7 He had played very flukily. **1888** *Ibid.* 7 July 6/5 When all has been said..as to the flukiness of cricket on wet wickets.

flumatic, see phlegmatic.

†**flumbarding**. *Obs. rare.* [app. f. OF. *flambard* torch.] 'A fiery character' (Weber).

c **1300** *K. Alis.* 1788 Hit is an hardy flumbardyng.

flume (fluːm), *sb.* Forms: 2–6 flum, 3 *Orm.* flumm, (3 flun), 3–4 flym, 3–5 flumme, 3–6 flom(e, 4–5 flomme, 5 floum, 8–9 floom, 4– flume. See also fleam. [a. OF. *flum*, *flun* = Pr. *flum*, It. *fiume*:—L. *flūmen* river, f. *fluĕre* to flow.]

†**1.** A stream, a river; also, water. *Obs.*

c **1175** *Lamb. Hom.* 141 Ine flum iordan. *a* **1300** *Cursor M.* 1035 Þis flummes four þat þar biginnes, thoru out all oþer contres rinnes. *a* **1300** *Magdalena* 427 in Horstmann *Alteng. Leg.* 158 To þe flym Jordan. *c* **1330** R. Brunne *Chron.* (1810) 186 At þat ilk flom Richard gaf bataile. *c* **1450** *Mirour Saluacioun* 1406 There bene baptismes thre Off ffvmme, of flavme, of blode. **1535** Stewart *Cron. Scot.* II. 450 All into that flume Tha drownit ilkone becaus tha culd not swym. **1652** Gaule *Magastrom.* 247 A deep flume, which was called the water of Juno.

2. A mill-tail. Cf. fleam *sb.*² 2.

1855 in Clarke *Dict.*

3. *U.S.*, etc. **a.** An artificial channel for a stream of water to be applied to some industrial use.

1784 J. Belknap *Tour to White Mts.* (1876) 17 One [stream] is so narrow as exactly to resemble a flume, and goes by that name. **1798** Root *Amer. Law Rep.* I. 359 Laid the bottom of the floom to the grist mill..about four feet lower than the saw mill. **1862** B. Taylor *Home & Abroad* Ser. II. ii. §6. 126 Wooden flumes, raised on tall tressels, brought water from some reservoir above to the diggings. **1882** *Harper's Mag.* Nov. 865 A curious V shaped wooden aqueduct or flume. **1940** *Chambers's Techn. Dict.* 343/2 *Flume*, a metal chute used for the distribution of concrete from a placing plant. **1957** *N.Z. Timber Jrnl.* Mar. 52/2 *Flume*, an inclined trough with running water for transporting logs. **1959** *B.S.I. News* Nov. 25 Notches, weirs and flumes for flow measurement.

b. A deep narrow channel or ravine with a stream running through it.

1792 J. Belknap *Hist. New Hampsh.* III. 52 Two streams ..one of which descends in a trench two feet wide, and is called the flume, from the near resemblance which it bears to an artificial flume. **1841** C. T. Jackson *Geol. New Hampsh.* 97 It is not practicable to walk in the bed of the flume. **1889** J. D. Whitney *United States* 222 Flume..as applied in the United States, and chiefly in the White Mountains, means a narrow passage or defile between nearly perpendicular rocks, through which runs a stream.

c. *U.S. slang. to go* or *be up the flume*: to 'come to grief', 'be done for'; to die.

1865 *Eastern Slope* (Washoe, Nev.) 23 Dec. 3/1 The great Stockholder..has in the classic language of the mines, 'gone up the flume'. **1882** Mark Twain [Clemens] *Stolen White Eleph.* etc. 97 Well, then, that idea's up the flume. **1888** *Longm. Mag.* XIII. 48 It's no good wishing—he's gone up the flume.

4. *Comb.*, as *flume-water*; **flume-car** (see quot.).

1884 Knight *Dict. Mech.* IV. 350/1 **Flume car*, a car to travel in a flume; wheels rest on the sides of the flume and the water runs a paddle wheel. **1897** B. Harraden *Hilda Strafford* 59, I wish I hadn't filled up my reservoir so full with *flume-water.

flume (fluːm), *v.* [f. prec. sb.]

1. *intr.* To build a flume or artificial channel for a water-course.

1855 in Clarke *Dict.* **1883** Burton & Cameron *Gold Coast* II. xvi. 116 The hydraulic system of sluicing and fluming.

2. *trans.* To convey (or bring *in*) down a flume.

1875 Miss Bird *Sandwich Isl.* (1880) 76 The cane is being flumed in with great rapidity.

3. (See quot.)

1876 Whitney in *Encycl. Brit.* IV. 701 The rivers..were 'flumed'—that is, the water was taken out of the natural channel by means of wooden flumes.

Hence ˈ**fluming** *vbl. sb.*; also *concr.* = material composing a flume.

1851 *San Francisco Picayune* 23 Sept. 2/5 There is another fluming company..that will commence operations this week. **1869** *Trans. N.Z. Inst.* II. 372 [The oldest drifts] can only be worked by bringing water to bear on them by a system of 'fluming'. **1879** Atcherley *Boerland* 173 The unsightly fluming and other erections which continually meet the eye.

†ˈ**fluminal**, *a. Obs.*⁻¹ [ad. L. *flūmināl-is* f. *flūmen* river.] Of or pertaining to a river.

1633 T. Adams *Exp. 2 Peter* ii. 8 Fluminall baptisme is a cold proofe of a mans Christendom, except this flaminall baptisme of fire..approve it. (Cf. *c* 1450 s.v. flume *sb.* 1.)

†**flumiˈnose**, *a. Obs.*⁻⁰ [as if ad. L. **flūminōs-us*, f. *flūmen*: see prec. and -ose.] 'Full of rivers' (Bailey vol. II. 1727).

†ˈ**fluminous**, *a. Obs.*⁻⁰ [f. as prec.: see -ous.] Full of rivers; of or pertaining to rivers.

1656 in Blount *Glossogr.* **1721–1800** in Bailey. Hence in mod. Dicts.

flummadiddle (ˈflʌmədɪd(ə)l). *U.S.* Also **flumme-**, **flummer-**, **flummy-**, **fuma-**. [prob. arbitrarily f. flummery.]

1. (See quot.)

1872 S. De Vere *Americanisms* 338 Flummadiddle.. consists of stale bread, pork-fat, molasses, cinnamon, allspice, [etc.]; by the aid of these materials a kind of mush is made, which is baked in the oven and brought to the table hot and brown. **1884** Sala *Illustr. Lond. News* 19 July 51/2.

2. *slang.* Nonsense, humbug; also, something trivial or ridiculous.

1850 in Wentworth *Amer. Dial. Dict.* s.v., Fuma-diddle, flummydiddle. **1854** M. J. Holmes *Tempest & Sunshine* iv. 51 What does she want of any more flummerdiddle notions? **1882** E. Cummings in *Chicago Advance* 21 Sept., Directions for..crocheting all sorts of flummediddles. **1882** *Century Mag.* Oct. 837 Well, see all that flummer-diddle he got off about it. **1941** *Sat. Even. Post* 25 Oct. 35/3 An' does you try any fuma-diddles, you is right away gwine happen to a catastrophe.

†**flummer** (ˈflʌmə(r)), *v. Obs.* [prob. two words: in sense 1 app. onomatopœic; in sense 2 back-formation from flummery.]

1. *trans.* To repeat indistinctly, mumble.

1533 Latimer in Foxe *A. & M.* (1563) 1310/2 As though the very worke & labour of flummering the Aue Marie is very acceptable to our Lady.

2. To deceive by flattery, to humbug.

1764 Foote *Mayor of G.* II. i. 37 No flummering me. I tell you, Matthew, 'twont do. **1777** F. Burney *Evelina* xvi, Do they spend all their time in flummering old women?

flummery (ˈflʌmərɪ). Also 7 **flommeri**, **flumery**, **thlummery**, 7–8 **flamery**. [a. Welsh *llymru*, of unknown etymology; the *fl-* and Herbert's *thl-* are attempts to render the sound of Welsh *ll-*; cf. fluellin.]

1. a. 'A kind of food made by coagulation of wheatflour or oatmeal' (J.). Cf. sowens.

1623 Markham *Eng. Housew.* vi. 222 From this small Oatmeale, by oft steeping it in water and clensing it, and then boyling it to a thicke and stiffe Ielly, is made that excellent dish of meat which is so esteemed in the West parts of this Kingdome, which they call Wash-brew, and in Cheshire and Lankasheire they call it Flamerie or Flumerie. **1634** Sir T. Herbert *Trav.* 150 The poore eat Rice sometimes, but most commonly Roots..and Fraize like to our Thlummery. **1760** Goldsm. *Cit. W.* lviii, A farmer..who used to sup upon wild ducks and flummery. **1821** *Blackw. Mag.* VIII. 541 Let Leigh Hunt sing of cabbages and flummery. **1839–73** Bywater *Sheffield Dial.* (1877) 257 Whoile he's had his throit scalded we heitin flummera.

b. *Modern Cookery.* A name given to various sweet dishes made with milk, flour, eggs, etc.

1747 Mrs. Glasse *Cookery* xvi. 146 To make Hartshorn Flummery. *Ibid.* 147 To make French Flummery. **1769** Mrs. Raffald *Eng. Housekpr.* (1778) 187 When you make a hen's or bird's nest, let part of your jelly be set in your bowl before you put on your flummery. **1877** *Cassell's Dict. Cookery*, *Flummery*—Boil two ounces of gelatine [etc.].

c. (See quot.)

1876 Crace-Calvert *Dyeing & Calico Print.* vi. 200 Flummery (the refuse product from wheaten starch manufactures).

2. a. *fig.* Mere flattery or empty compliment; nonsense, humbug, empty trifling.

1749 Lady Luxborough *Let. to Shenstone* 29 Nov. (1775) 143 This word flummery, you must know, Sir, means at London, flattery, and compliment. **1828** Scott *Jrnl.* 19 Feb., The proofs..are arrived..but I have had no time, saving to blot out some flummery. **1860** Thackeray *Round. Papers, Thorns in Cush.* (1876) 50 These petitioners..begin with a fine flummery about the..eminent genius of the person whom they are addressing. **1891** T. Hardy *Tess* II. xxvi. 66 Her father..is quite..opposed to such flummery.

attrib. **1802** Mrs. Parsons *Myst. Visit* IV. 39, I know you too well to be deceived by your fine flummery tales. **1858** Masson *Milton* (1874) I. 25 Flummery pictures representing the blind poet in a rapt attitude.

b. *dial.* and *U.S. collect.* Trifles, useless trappings or ornaments.

1879 *Dewsbre back at Mooin Olmenac* 5 (E.D.D.), For fear t'sun sud fade yor carpets and yor bits o' flummery. **1883** 'Mark Twain' *Life on Mississippi* 406 The bridal chamber whose pretentious flummery was overawing.

flummocky (ˈflʌməkɪ), *a. dial.* and *U.S. dial.* Also **-ucky**, **flommocky**, **-ucky**. [f. *flummock* sb. or vb.: see flummox *v.*] Confused, muddled; untidy, slovenly. (Cf. slummocky.)

1834 W. A. Carruthers *Kentuckian in N.Y.* II. 215 Hang me if I don't think he's a little flumucky altogether about the head. **1884–** in dial. glossaries (Cheshire, Shropshire, Warwick).

flummox (ˈflʌməks), *v. colloq.* or *vulgar*. Also **flummix**, **-ux**. [prob. of Eng. dialectal origin; cf. *flummocks* to maul, mangle (*Heref. Gloss.* 1839), *flummock* slovenly person, also hurry, bewilderment, *flummock* to make untidy, disorder, to confuse, bewilder (see various E.D.S. glossaries, Heref., Glouc., S. Cheshire, Sheffield). The formation seems to be onomatopœic, expressive of the notion of throwing down roughly and untidily; cf. *flump*, *hummock*, dial. *slommock* sloven.]

1. *trans.* To bring to confusion; to 'do for', cause to fail; to confound, bewilder, nonplus.

1837 Dickens *Pickw.* xxxiii, 'He'll be what the Italians call reg'larly flummoxed'. **1840** *Cambr. Univ. Mag.* I. in Whibley *In Cap & Gown* (1890) 169 So many of the men I know Were 'flummox'd' at the last great-go. *c* **1850** C. Kean in Barrère & Leland *Slang* s.v. 'Fool! fool! you distressed.. you—you flummuxed me!' **1892** *Pall Mall G.* 16 Feb. 2/1 The Unionists appear to be completely flummoxed by the failure of Mr. Balfour's Land Act.

2. U.S. *colloq.* To 'do up'.

1870 Talmage *Crumbs Swept up* 270 Brushes..with which heiresses..flumixed their hair.

3. *intr.* *U.S.* To give in, give up, collapse.

1839 D. P. Thompson *Green Mountain Boys* xxiv. 256 Well, if he should flummux at such a chance, I know of a chap..who'll agree to take his place. **1847** Field *Drama in Pokerville* 73 Pokerville didn't..finally 'flummix' right beneath him. **1849** *Oyster War of Accomac* iii. in *N.Y. Tribune* 25 Apr. 1/3 Men of mighty stomachs, Men that can't be made to flummux.

Hence ˈ**flummox** *sb.* (see quot.).

1851 B. H. Hall *College Words* s.v., Any failure is called a flummux. In some colleges the word is particularly applied to a poor recitation. At Williams College, a failure on the play-ground is called a flummux. **1857** in Ducange Anglicus *Vulg. Tongue* 8.

flump, *sb. colloq.* [f. next.] The action of 'flumping'; the heavy dull sound so produced.

1790 Grose *Prov. Gloss.* (ed. 2), *Flump*, a fall. **1832** J. H. Newman *Lett.* (1891) I. 288 The heavy flump, flump of the huge cloth which is meant to dry the deck. **1856** *Leisure Hour* V. 430/2 Broken now and then by..the flump of a dictionary on the leather-covered tables. **1891** Mrs. L. Adams *Bonnie Kate* II. vii. 196 Libbie sat down with a flump.

flump (flʌmp), *v. colloq.* [onomatopœic; cf. *dump*, *flop*, *plump*, *slump*. Not in Johnson, or Webster 1864.]

1. *intr.* To fall or move heavily with a dull noise.

1816 G. Colman *Br. Grins, Mr. Champernowne* viii, He.. thought it not unwise To join in flumping down. **1823** Moor *Suffolk Words*, A hawk flumps or flops on a bird. **1838** Thackeray *Yellowpl. Corr.* ii, She [Mrs. Shum] flumps past me. **1861** —— in *Cornh. Mag.* June 649 A little Skye-terrier dog..whines, runs, jumps, flumps up on him.

2. *trans.* To set or throw *down* with a dump.

1830 Miss Mitford *Village* Ser. IV. (1863) 182 Flumping himself down in the midst of a tuft of cowslips. **1840** Thackeray *Paris Sk. Bk.* (1872) 49 Chairs were flumped down on the floor. **1866** *St. James's Mag.* Oct. 345 She flumped herself down in the car.

b. To bump or strike (a saddle). In quot. *absol.*

1894 *Daily News* 20 June 6/4 This is a very different thing from jerking and flumping in the canter.

3. The vb. stem used advb. With a flump.

1790 Grose *Prov. Gloss.* (ed. 2) s.v., He came flump down. **1841** T. T. T. *Procelain Tower* 103 He cut it midway through—part fell down flump.

flunder, obs. form of flounder.

flung (flʌŋ), *ppl. a.* [pa. pple. of fling *v.*] In senses of the vb.

1880 G. Meredith *Trag. Com.* (1881) 170 Fish for the flung-away beauty, and hook your shadow of a Bottom's head! **1885** Lefroy *Echoes fr. Theocritus, etc.* II. xxviii, The flung ball takes one madding tortuous bound.

† **flunge**, *v. Obs.* [onomatopœic; cf. *fly* and *plunge*.] *intr.* ? To fly or be flung *out* with sudden impetus.

1583 STANYHURST *Æneis* I. (Arb.) 22 Now stoans and fyrebrands flundge owt.

flunk (flʌŋk), *sb. U.S.* [f. next vb.]

1. A backing out, a total failure, *esp.* in a college examination.

1846 *Yale Banger* 10 Nov. (B. H. Hall *College Wds.*) This O.. Tutor H—— said meant a perfect flunk. **1853** *Songs of Yale* (Bartlett) In moody meditation sunk, Reflecting on my future flunk. **1904** *N.Y. Even. Post* 6 Jan. 5 A sprinter and football player has received a flunk in one study and a condition in another. **1948** *Time* 16 Feb. 94/3 This time there were twice as many flunks.

2. (See quot.)

1893 FARMER *Slang*, *Flunk*, an idler, a loafer.

flunk (flʌŋk), *v. U.S.* [Cf. FLINK, FUNK.]

1. a. *intr.* To give up, back out, fail utterly. Also *to flunk out*. Also quasi-*trans.* To shirk (a recitation) (*Standard Dict.*).

1823 *Crayon* (Yale Coll.) (Bartlett), We must have at least as many subscribers as there are students in college or flunk out. *a* **1830** COL. HAY in *Humorous Poems* (ed. W. M. Rossetti) 474 He never flunked and he never lied. **1838** J. C. NEAL *Charcoal Sk., Rocky Smalt* 46 Why, little 'un, you must be cracked, if you flunk out before we begin. **1850** H. C. WATSON *Camp-fires Revol.* 414 They were, of course, exposed to the fire of the red-coats..but they didn't flunk a bit. **1894** P. L. FORD *Hon. Peter Stirling* (1898) 355 What will people say of me on November fourth, if my regiment flunks on September thirtieth? **1901** *Munsey's Mag.* XXV. 408/2 It looks pretty middling tough, and it won't do to try it and flunk. **1910** J. HART *Vigilante Girl* xxi. 294, I don't mean that he's flunking, for he's no coward. **1971** *Sunday Times* (Johannesburg) 28 Mar. 7/1 Sinatra himself said: 'I've flunked out with women more often than not. Like most men, I don't understand them.'

b. *College slang.* To fail utterly in an examination. Also *trans.*, to fail (an examination, etc.); *to flunk out*: to be dismissed from a school or university for failing examinations.

1848 *Yale Lit. Mag.* XIII. 322 Flunking so gloomily. **18..** *Amherst Indicator* I. 253 (Bartlett), A man who has flunked..is not in a state to appreciate joking. **1899** A. H. QUINN *Pennsylvania Stories* 166 He never attracted attention by his scholarship, but yet he drifted along somehow without flunking. **1920** F. SCOTT FITZGERALD *This Side of Paradise* (1921) 35 He'll fail his exams, tutor all summer..and flunk out in the middle of the freshman year. **1923** R. D. PAINE *Comr. Rolling Ocean* vi. 99 He tutored for Princeton and flunked in freshman year. **1924** P. MARKS *Plastic Age* xviii. 202, I don't..chase around with filthy bags or flunk my courses. **1936** L. C. DOUGLAS *White Banners* xvi. 342 He was working hard to take a calculus examination that he had flunked..two years ago. **1951** *Reader's Digest* May 12/1 He flunked out of various high schools, not because he was too stupid. **1968** *Listener* 27 June 841/1 The scene is..Columbia University, where a number of young Second World War vets and/or non-combatants are making gestures at working for degrees or just hanging around after flunking out. **1970** *Times* 12 Aug. 5/7, I was utterly, deeply, completely depressed and flunked my A levels.

2. *trans.* To cause to 'flunk'; to pluck.

1843 *Yale Lit. Mag.* IX. 61 That day poor Fullman was *flunked*, and was never again reinstated in the good graces of our officer. **1893** W. K. POST *Harvard Stories* 231 That was all very well for him, who..never got 'flunked'. **1899** A. H. QUINN *Pennsylvania Stories* 40 He..finally flunked him in his finals. **1910** *N.Y. Even. Post* 29 Nov. 8 Examining boards may 'flunk' an officer in his first examination. **1966** *Word Study* Feb. 2/2 For if English teachers had always based their grades in English on the moral probity of their students' private lives, they would have had to flunk such naughty boys as Christopher Marlowe, James Boswell, Dylan Thomas, and Baltimore's own Edgar Allan Poe.

Hence **'flunking** *ppl. a.*

1848 *Yale Gallinipper* Nov. (B. H. Hall *College Wds.*), See what a spot a flunking Soph'more made!

flunker ('flʌŋkə(r)). *U.S.* [f. FLUNK *v.* + -ER[1].]

a. One who fails in an examination. **b.** One who causes candidates to fail.

1895 W. C. GORE in *Inlander* Nov. 62 *Flunker*, one who habitually fails in recitations. **1910** O. JOHNSON *Varmint* i. 14 'What had he done to you?' said Jimmy, winking at Mr. Hopkins,..master of the Latin line and distinguished flunker of boys. **1948** *Chicago Daily News* 2 Nov. 10/5 College flunkers.

flunkey ('flʌŋkɪ). *sb.*[1] Also 8–9 **flunky**, *Sc.* **flunkie**, 9 **flanky**. [orig. Scotch: see quots. Possibly a diminutive corruption of FLANKER.]

1. a. A male servant in livery, *esp.* a footman, lackey; usually with implied contempt.

1782 SIR J. SINCLAIR *Observ. Scot. Dial.* in *Life* (1837) I. 48 Flunkie a footman; literally a sidesman or attendant at your flank. **1787** BURNS *Twa Dogs* 54 His flunkies answer at the bell. **1826** HOOD *Recipe for Civilization*, But play at dummy, like the monkeys, For fear mankind should make them flunkies. **1848** THACKERAY *Let.* 1 Aug. [They] did not see by my appearance that I was not a flunkey. **1876** J. SAUNDERS *Lion in Path* xx, The flunkey went off to seek Jemima the maid.

b. *Naut. slang.* A ship's steward.

1883 in W. C. RUSSELL *Sailors' Lang.*

c. (See quots.) *N. Amer.*

1906 *N.Y. Even. Post* 12 Sept. 7 'Flunkeys' in the Northwest do not wear uniforms; their work is to act as assistant cooks in mining and lumber camps. **1931** 'D. STIFF' *Milk & Honey Route* 205 *Flunky*, camp waiter. Always male. A woman is a *hasher*. **1956** J. S. GOWLAND *Sikanska Trail* 177 'You're a flunkey,' he said. 'Report to the cook.' **1970** *Islander* (Victoria, B.C.) 17 May 6/1 The first pay slips the waitresses received listed them as 'flunkies'. 'We didn't like this,' Mrs. Kusha says. 'The men employed in the cookhouse were flunkies, but we had been hired as waitresses.'

2. Applied contemptuously to a person who behaves obsequiously to persons above him in rank or position; a 'lackey', toady, snob.

1855 THACKERAY *Newcomes* II. v. 49 You young flunkeys of the aristocracy. **1856** OLMSTED *Slave States* 217 The miserable rabble of snobs and flunkies. **1884** LABOUCHERE in *Fortn. Rev.* Feb. 209 The rage and indignation of every flunkey in the kingdom.

3. *attrib.* and *Comb.*, as ***flunkey customer, species, work***; ***flunkey-flanked*** *a.*

1826 J. WILSON *Noct. Ambr.* Wks. 1855 I. 268 Rolling along in flunky-flanked eckipages. **1843** CARLYLE *Past & Pr.* I. v. 41 Certain of the flunkey species. **1858** DICKENS *Let.* 6 Sept., Such a schoolmaster..could not exist, unless he had flunkey customers by the dozen. **1887** FENN *Master Ceremonies* iv, It was beggarly work—flunkey work, and it disgusted me.

Hence many nonce-wds.: **'flunkey** *v. intr.*, to act like a flunkey. **'flunkeyage** [after *peerage* etc.], the class of flunkeys; a list of flunkeys. **'flunkeyal** *a.*, of, pertaining to, or characteristic of a flunkey. **'flunkeyfied** *ppl. a.*, imbued with flunkeyism. **'flunkeyhood**, the fact or state of being a flunkey. **flunkeyi'ana**, the sayings or characteristics of flunkeys. **'flunkeyish** *a.*, **flunkey'istic** *a.*, **'flunkeyite** *a.*, characteristic of or resembling a flunkey. **'flunkeyize** *v. trans.*, to imbue with the spirit of a flunkey.

1823 *Blackw. Mag.* XIV. 524 There is something flunkyish..in the whole passage. **1843** CARLYLE *Past & Pr.* II. vii. 102 All his flunkeyhood and horn-eyed dimness. **1848** THACKERAY *Bk. Snobs* xlii, That..inimitable, flunkefied pronunciation. **1848** (*title*) The Flunkey and the British Flunkeyage, a Companion to Burke's Peerage, by Birkenhare. **1854** *Punch* XXVI. 44 (*heading*), *Flunkeyiana*—a fact. *Flunkey* (*out of place*). 'There's just one question I should like to ask your Ladyship—Ham I engaged for Work, or ham I engaged for Ornament?' **1858** *Illustr. Times* 24 July, We do detest..the flunkeyite view of aristocracy. **1858** *Ibid.* 18 Dec. 407 A Titanic flunkey with the orthodox flunkeyistic calves. **1864** E. A. MURRAY *E. Norman* I. 253 By flunkeying after that set of rabble. **1864** *Times* 27 June 11/1 If he is anxious to proclaim his flunkial subserviency, let him do so. **1878** GOLDW. SMITH in *Echo* 19 Dec. 2 The attempt to flunkeyise the New World. **1879** T. P. O'CONNOR *Disraeli* 196 A very considerable amount of flunkeyish worship of the powerful. **1928** J. GORE in E. Eden *Semi-Attached Couple* p. xi, Miss Eden..could..draw..the characters of servants with brilliance of touch and a knowledge of flunkeiana which Thackeray might have envied.

flunkey ('flʌŋkɪ), *sb.*[2] *U.S.* [f. FLUNK *v.* or *sb.* + -Y]. One who 'flunks' or 'comes to grief'; in College slang, one who fails in an examination; in Stock Exchange language, an ignorant person who dabbles in financial speculation.

1841 *Week in Wall St.* 91 I'll help the bulls operate for a rise and draw in the flunkies. **1859** *Yale Lit. Mag.* (Farmer), I..Saved him from the flunkey's doom.

'flunkeydom. [f. FLUNKEY *sb.*[1] + -DOM.]

1. The domain of flunkeys; flunkeys collectively.

1849 *Fraser's Mag.* XL. 14 The finest 'marine parade', as flunkeydom terms it, in all England. **1884** *Punch* 29 Mar. 154/2 The whole of Flunkeydom will at once withdraw their Support.

2. The spirit or behaviour of a flunkey.

1850 KINGSLEY *Alt. Locke* xxv, Mackaye too, who, however he hated flunkeydom, never overlooked an act of discourtesy. **1879** *Contemp. Rev.* XXXVI. 291 Flunkeydom is much more insufferable..than swelldom itself.

flunkeyism ('flʌŋkɪɪz(ə)m). Also **flunkism.** [f. as prec. + -ISM.] The quality characteristic of a flunkey; the manners, speech, etc. of a flunkey.

1831 *Fraser's Mag.* IV. 312 A sinking journal, which its own inconsistencies and flunkism had irrevocably damned. **1843** CARLYLE *Past & Pr.* I. vi. (1872) 30 We, for our share, will put away all Flunkeyism from us. **1886** *Law Times* LXXX. 297/2 Flunkeyism and toadyism in legal proceedings have not been diminishing of late years.

fluo- ('fluːəʊ). *Chem.* and *Min.* Abbreviation of FLUOR, used as combining form in many names of compounds containing fluorine, as **ˌfluo'borate**, a salt of fluoboric acid. **ˌfluo'boric acid**, a name originally applied to the gas terfluoride of boron (BF_3), now applied to the compound ($H_2B_2O_4.6HF$) obtained by saturating water with this. **ˌfluo'cerine**, **ˌfluo-'cerite**, a native fluoride of cerium and the allied metals. **ˌfluo-'hydric** (acid) = *fluorhydric*. Also in the names of other acids of which fluorine is a component along with some other element as **ˌfluo'chromic, -si'licic, -tan'talic, -ti'tanic acid**, and in the names of salts as **ˌfluo-'carbonate, -'phosphate, -'silicate, -'tantalate, -'titanate, -'zirconate**.

1812 SIR H. DAVY *Chem. Philos.* 191 Fluoboric gas. **1819** CHILDREN *Chem. Anal.* §10. 7 Hydrochloric, fluoboric, fluosilicic, and hydriodic acids. **1821** URE *Dict. Chem.*, *Fluoborates*. **1854** THOMSON *Cycl. Chem.*, *Fluoboric Acid*.. Colourless incombustible gas, with acid reaction. *Ibid.* *Fluocerite*. *Ibid.* *Fluohydric Acid*. **1863** WATTS *Dict. Chem.* I. 834 A hydrated ceric oxyfluoride..occurs at Finbo as fluocerine. *Ibid.* The sesquifluoride Ce^2F^3..occurs native as fluocerite, in..six-sided prisms and plates..also massive. **1868** *Fownes' Chem.* (ed. 10) 259 The fluoniobates are known to be isomorphous with the fluosilicates and fluotitanates. **1873** *Ibid.* (ed. 11) 377 Double salts, called zircofluorides or fluozirconates. *Ibid.* 445 Stannic fluoride Sn F_4..unites with other metallic fluorides, forming crystalline fluostannates. **1894** MUIR & MORLEY *Watts' Dict. Chem.* IV. 639/2 *Fluotantalates*.

fluonomist (fluː'ɒnəmɪst). [f. FLU(E *sb.*[3] + -*onomist* as in *economist*.] (See quots.)

1947 *Christian Century* LXIV. 943 The 'fluonomist' is simply our old and much respected neighbor the chimney sweep. **1948** *Word Study* Oct. 11/1 [citing London *Times*] A sweep entitled himself 'fluonomist' and put up his prices. **1965** *N.Z. Woman's Weekly* 4 Oct. 103/1 Our chimney sweep calls himself a fluonomist!

fluor ('fluːɔː(r)), *sb.* Also 7 -our. [a. L. *fluor* flowing, f. *fluĕre* to flow. Cf. OF. *flueur*.]

†**1.** A flow or flowing; a flux, stream. Also = EFFLUVIUM 2b. *Obs.*

1644 DIGBY *Nat. Bodies* I. xxi. 189 These fluours do proceed out of the very substance and nature of the loadestone. **1664** POWER *Exp. Philos.* III. 156 Electrical fluors do presently recoil by short streight lines to their Bodies again. **1671** R. BOHUN *Wind* 54 They blow not in one constant fluor, or streame, but in gusts.

2. *spec.* in *Pathology*. †**a.** *pl.* = FLOWERS (*obs.*). ‖**b. fluor albus** = LEUCORRHŒA.

1621 AINSWORTH *Annot. Pentat.* Gen. xviii. 11 The custome (or manner) of women, for the ordinary and naturall course of the body, or fluors. **1662** TRAPP *Comm.* 2 Sam. xi. 4 Her monethly fluors. **1754–64** SMELLIE *Midwif.* I. 110 The *Fluor albus* is no other than this Mucus discharged in too great quantity.

†**3.** A fluid state, fluidity, esp. with regard to substances ordinarily solid; *concr.* something that is fluid, a fluid mass; in *pl.* the humours (of the body). *Obs.*

1665 G. HARVEY *Advice agst. Plague* 2 Pestilential Miasms, insinuating into the humoral..parts of the Body.. then corrupting the fluors. **1684** T. BURNET *Th. Earth* I. 210 A peculiar ferment that..dissolves the parts of the meat, and melts them into a fluor or pulp. **1686** GOAD *Celest. Bodies* I. ix. 31 Rarity is nothing but a Privation of Density ..Fluor of Solidity. **1704–21** NEWTON *Optics* III. (ed. 3) 371 Those agitations which keep Liquors in a Fluor.

4. *Min.* †**a.** The generic name for a class of minerals first defined by G. Agricola, and by him described (*Bermannus sive de Re Metallica* 1546) as resembling gems, but of less hardness, readily fusible, and useful as fluxes in smelting (*obs.*). **b.** After Scheele's discovery of hydrofluoric acid or 'Swedish air' in 1771 the name was applied *spec.* to such of these minerals as contain fluorine, chiefly (now exclusively) to calcium fluoride or FLUOR-SPAR.

Agricola's term *fluores* was a translation of the Ger. miners' name *flusse*—an apt designation, he remarks, for minerals formed 'ἐκ συρροης, i.e. confluxu in terra'.

1661 LOVELL *Hist. Anim. & Min.* Introd. E viij, Some [may be liquefied] by fire, as metallick fluores. **1676** J. BEAUMONT in *Phil. Trans.* XI. 728 This Stone is in substance a whitish opaque fluor. **1692** RAY *Dissol. World* 114 They..do shoot into that form, after the manner of Salts and Fluors. **1776** PRIESTLEY *Air* II. 187 A substance which the chymists distinguish by the name of fluor..which with us is called Derbyshire Spar. **1802** PLAYFAIR *Illustr. Hutton. Th.* 17 The strata are consolidated..by quartz, by fluor, by feltspar. **1823** H. J. BROOKE *Introd. Crystallogr.* 41 The octahedron of fluor, which we have just obtained. **1866** RUSKIN *Eth. Dust* 159 The fluor of Chamouni is rose-coloured..while the fluor of Weardale is green.

5. *attrib.* †**fluor acid**, hydrofluoric acid.

1791 TENNANT in *Phil. Trans.* LXXXI 184 A compound ..of fluor acid and calcareous earth. **1794** SULLIVAN *View Nat.* I. 230 Fluor acid air, or sparry air. **1828** WEBSTER, *Fluor-acid*, the acid of fluor.

fluor- ('fluːɔː(r)), used as comb. form of FLUORINE, before vowels. **fluor-apatite**, *Min.* (see quot.). **fluorhydric acid** [+ HYDR(-OGEN) + -IC], *Chem.*, hydrofluoric acid (HF).

1882 DANA *Min. & Lithol.* (ed. 4) 213 When chlorine is present in place of fluorine it is called *chlor-apatite*, and when the reverse fluor-apatite. **1864** WATTS *Dict. Chem.* II. 669 *Fluorhydric* or *Hydrofluoric acid.*

fluoranthene (fluːə'rænθiːn). *Chem.* [ad. G. *fluoranthen* (Fittig & Gebhard 1877, in *Ber. d. Deut. Chem. Ges.* X. 2143), f. FLUOR(ENE + PHEN)ANTH(R)ENE.] An aromatic hydrocarbon, $C_{16}H_{10}$, crystallizing as colourless needles or plates and found in coal tar; also, any of the derivatives of this compound.

1878 *Jrnl. Chem. Soc.* XXXIV. 431 (*heading*) Fluoranthrene [*sic*], a new coal-tar hydrocarbon. **1947** *Jrnl. Amer. Chem. Soc.* LXIX. 505/1 Pure synthetic fluoranthene is now readily available. *Ibid.* 507/1 The synthesis..of other compounds containing the fluoranthene nucleus is being investigated. **1952** *Chem. Rev.* I. 485 The solutions of many fluoranthenes fluoresce blue or blue-green in ultraviolet light.

fluorated ('fluːəreɪtɪd), *ppl. a.* [f. FLUOR- + -ATE + -ED[1].] Combined with hydrofluoric acid.

1796 KIRWAN *Elem. Min.* (ed. 2) I. 477 Fluorated soda. **1860** MAYNE *Expos. Lex.* s.v. *Fluoratus*, Hydrofluoric acid has been called *fluorated hydrogen*.

fluorene ('fluːəriːn). *Chem.* [f. FLUOR + -ENE.] A hydro-carbon extracted from coal tar ($C_{13}H_{10}$); when impure it is fluorescent, whence the name.

1883 *Athenæum* 10 Feb. 188/3 The fluorene was crystallized five or six times from alcohol.

fluoresce (fluːə'rɛs), *v.* [back formation from FLUORESCENCE.] To be or become fluorescent.

1874 *Lommel's Light* 184 A body capable of exhibiting fluorescence fluoresces by virtue of those rays which it absorbs. **1881** S. P. THOMPSON *Electr. & Magn.* iv. §292 Uranium glass..fluoresces with a fine green light.

fluorescein (fluːə'rɛsiːɪn). *Chem.* [f. FLUORESCE *v.* + -IN.] A chemical product fluorescent in solution obtained by heating phthalic anhydride with resorcin. Hence **fluore'sceic** (*acid*).

1876 CRACE CALVERT *Dyeing* viii. 251 Fluoresceïn..is a red crystalline powder..slightly soluble in alcohol. **1886** tr. *Benedikt's Coal-tar Colours* 161 The colouring matters known as eosins are derived from fluoresceïn. **1889** MUIR & MORLEY *Watts' Dict. Chem.* II. 557 *Fluoresceic acid.*

fluorescence (fluːə'rɛsəns). [f. FLUOR-(SPAR): see quot. 1852.] The coloured luminosity produced in some transparent bodies by the direct action of light, esp. of the violet and ultra-violet rays; the property, in certain substances, of rendering the ultra-violet rays visible, so as to produce this phenomenon. Also *attrib.*, as **fluorescence spectrum**, the spectrum of the light emitted by a substance when excited to fluorescence.

1852 PROF. STOKES in *Phil. Trans.* 479 *note*, I am almost inclined to coin a word and call the appearance *fluorescence*, from fluor-spar, as the analogous term *opalescence* is derived from the name of a mineral. **1867** *Ure's Dict. Arts* (ed. 6) III. 405 Pennsylvanian petroleum is dark-coloured, with a peculiar greenish lustre or fluorescence. **1885** J. & C. LASSELL tr. *Schellen's Spectrum Anal.* (ed. 2) lxi. 242 The visible part of the spectrum is then removed from sight, and the fluorescence spectrum alone occupies the field. **1962** R. E. DODD *Chem. Spectroscopy* ii. 80 The fluorescence spectrum appears at a characteristic wavelength and does not shift with the wavelength of the exciting light.

fluorescent (fluːə'rɛsənt), *a.* [f. FLUORESCE + -ENT.] **a.** Possessing the property of fluorescence. Of light: Proceeding from or having the nature of fluorescence.

1853 PROF. STOKES in *Phil. Trans.* 390 In those cases in which the fluorescent light is yellow. **1855** DR. GLADSTONE *Ibid.* 211 Other fluorescent Organic Substances. **1883-4** *Med. Ann.* 29/1 Both the acid and the alkaloid having fluorescent properties.

b. ***fluorescent lamp***, a lamp in which light is produced largely by fluorescence; *esp.* a tubular electric-discharge lamp containing mercury vapour, ultra-violet radiation from which causes the fluorescence of a coating of phosphor on the inside of the tube; also ***fluorescent light, lighting, tube***; ***fluorescent screen***, an opaque or transparent screen coated on one side with a fluorescent material and used for displaying images produced when it is struck by X-rays, electrons, or other ionizing radiation.

1896 T. A. EDISON *U.S. Pat. 865,367* (1907), Fluorescent Electric Lamp... The object I have in mind is to produce light by fluorescence... *Fluorescent lamps made in accordance with this invention may be operated singly or may be worked together in series. **1938** *Trans. Illum. Engin. Soc.* (London) III. 126/2 The tubluar fluorescent lamp. **1966** D. F. GALOUYE *Lost Perception* xiv. 147 He regained consciousness in the glare of *fluorescent lights strung along an acoustical tile ceiling. **1971** *Nature* 1 Jan. 46/1 The light intensity was 40Wm^{-2} from warm white fluorescent lights. **1942** C. L. AMICK **Fluorescent Lighting Man.* i. 2 From a lamp and fixture market that did not exist 4 years ago, fluorescent lighting has grown to an estimated $250,000,000 business for 1941. **1953** 'M. INNES' *Christmas at Candleshoe* i. 11 With a flicker and a ping a bar of fluorescent lighting has snapped on. **1961** L. MUMFORD *City in History* x. 298 The American super-market, with its ghastly fluorescent lighting. **1863** G. G. STOKES in *Phil. Trans. R. Soc.* CLII. 615 On forming an image of the spark between a sharp and a flat electrode..and receiving it on a *fluorescent screen, the flat electrode gave the brighter of the two images. **1901** F. H. WILLIAMS *Roentgen Rays* iii. 99 The X-ray examination by the photograph is better, as a rule, than that by the fluorescent screen for all parts of the body except the trunk. **1956** M. SLURZBERG et al. *Ess. Television* x. 361 The act of converging the beam of electrons to produce a pinpoint of light on the fluorescent screen is called focusing. **1938** *Trans. Illum. Engin. Soc.* (London) III. 126/2 The low-pressure mercury vapour *fluorescent tube..is singularly comparable with the sodium lamp.

fluorescer (fluːə'rɛsə(r)). [f. FLUORESCE *v.* + -ER[1].] A fluorescent substance.

1904 *Nature* 31 Mar. 523/1 The most powerful fluorescer towards the α radiations is Sidot's hexagonal blende, a crystallised form of zinc sulphide. **1959** *Guardian* 28 Sept. 3/5 A pair of pastel blue cotton sheets..had changed colour... The fluorescer added to synthetic detergents was the cause. **1967** M. DONBROW *Instrum. Meth. Analyt. Chem.* II. viii. 216 'Xanthene' dyes are usually good fluorescers.

fluorescing (fluːə'rɛsɪŋ), *ppl. a.* [f. FLUORESCE *v.* + -ING[2].] That fluoresces, fluorescent; that causes fluorescence.

1896 *Westm. Gaz.* 27 May 6/3 Mr. Edison by coating the interior surface of a Crookes' tube with crystals of a new fluorescing substance has succeeded in causing the X rays to change to light. **1924** *Discovery* June 97/2 A fluorescing screen. **1957** *Technology* July 168/4 Fluorescing agents, some of which, added to detergents, tend to intensify the colours..of cellulose fabrics such as cotton. **1966** *McGraw-Hill Encycl. Sci. & Technol.* V. 350/2 At very low fluorescent intensities, the intensity is almost directly proportional to the concentration of the fluorescing material.

fluorian ('fluːərɪən), *a. Min.* [f. FLUOR(INE + -IAN.] Of a mineral: having a (small) proportion of a constituent element replaced by fluorine.

1930 W. T. SCHALLER in *Amer. Mineralogist* XV. 571 The adjectival endings thus formed for the names of all the chemical elements are given below... Fluorine—fluorian. **1959** W. H. DENNEN *Princ. Mineral.* vii. 363 Chemical varieties [of phlogopite]: Fluorian, ferroan, manganoan.

fluoric (fluː'ɒrɪk), *a.* [ad. F. *fluorique*, f. *fluor*: see FLUOR and -IC.] Pertaining to or obtained from fluor or fluor-spar. Chiefly in †***fluoric acid***, the old name of hydrofluoric acid.

1790 KERR tr. *Lavoisier's Elem. Chem.* 210 The muriatic, fluoric, and boracic acids. **1854** F. C. BAKEWELL *Geol.* 12 Fluoric acid dissolves silex. **1860** HARTWIG *Sea & Wond.* i. 12 Wilson has pointed out fluoric combinations in sea water.

fluoridate ('fluːərɪdeɪt), *v.* [Back-formation from next.] *trans.* **a.** To add traces of a fluoride or other source of fluoride ions to (water, tooth-paste, food, etc.). Also *absol.* (Cf. FLUORIDATION 2 a.)

1949 *Bull. Amer. Assoc. Public Health Dentists* Aug. 12/1 Many cities throughout the nation..have taken or are taking steps to fluoridate their water supplies. **1951** *Jrnl. Amer. Water Works Assoc.* XLIII. 644/1 Some questions have been raised concerning the advisability of fluoridating a communal water supply because of the objection to so-called medication of water supplies. **1952** *Public Health Rep.* (U.S.) Jan. 41/1 It will take about 14 years after a community starts fluoridating before a two-thirds reduction can be made in the caries attack rate of all children. **1958** G. B. DENTON *Vocab. Dentistry & Oral Sci.* IV. 182 An opinion favoring the use of *fluoridate* was adopted by the *Journal of the American Dental Association* for its style in 1950, and the publicity given to it was probably largely responsible for establishing the use of that term to supersede *fluorinate*. **1964** GOOSE & HARTLES *Princ. Preventive Dentistry* vi. 93 Tablets containing about 1 mg of fluoride have been used.. as a means of fluoridating the daily water supply at home. **1969** *Brit. Dental Jrnl.* CXXVII. 605/1 There is no evidence of a general unwillingness on the part of water undertakings to fluoridate when asked to do so by the local health authorities.

b. To treat (teeth) with a preparation containing fluoride. (Cf. FLUORIDATION 2 b.)

1963 *Brit. Dental Jrnl.* CXIV. 219 If teeth are fluoridated topically with strong solutions, mostly protective fluorides are formed initially. **1966** *Helv. Odontol. Acta* X. 29 Investigations to study some aspects of the processes occurring at the enamel surface fluoridated topically under various conditions.

Hence **'fluoridated** *ppl. a.*

1950 *Amer. Mag.* May 46 (*heading*) They drink away their toothaches: fluoridated water. **1955** *Science News* XXXVIII. 41 The use of fluoridated toothpaste, tooth powders, mouthwashes, pastilles, and even chewing gum, has been canvassed. **1964** GOOSE & HARTLES *Princ. Preventive Dentistry* vi. 94 The effect of the consumption of fluoridated salt on the permanent teeth of children. **1965** *Helv. Odontol. Acta* IX. 148 The effect of the oral environment on the fluoride content of topically fluoridated enamel.

fluoridation (ˌfluːərɪ'deɪʃən). [f. FLUORIDE: see -ATION.] **1.** *Min.* The process by which a mineral absorbs fluorine.

1904 *Monogr. U.S. Geol. Surv.* XLVII. 206 Fluoridation is the addition of fluorine, forming fluorides. **1953** *Chem. & Engin. News* 4 May 1905/1 The earlier, geologic sense of 'fluoridation', namely, introduction of fluorine into a mineral, would seem to be more properly fluorination.

2. a. The addition of traces of a fluoride or other source of fluoride ions to drinking-water for the prevention or control of dental caries.

1949 *Jrnl. Amer. Water Works Assoc.* XLI. II. 576/1 The present demands for the fluoridation of water supplies are coming from the public and the press. **1955** *Sci. Amer.* Apr. 2/2, I believe that a big reason why fluoridation failed to win acceptance was the hasty and somewhat authoritarian way in which it had been introduced. **1958** *Spectator* 6 June 737/2 In Britain many leading dentists and physicians are opposing fluoridation. **1960** *Times* 10 Feb. 7/3 A Bill to introduce the compulsory fluoridation of water. **1966** MCKEOWN & LOWE *Introd. Social Med.* xiii. 139 In the British studies there was a sixty-six per cent reduction in caries among three year old children after the introduction of fluoridation. **1971** *Daily Tel.* 3 June 2/1 Fluoridation of water supplies..has been shown to prevent dental decay.

b. = FLUORIDIZATION b.

1963 *Brit. Dental Jrnl.* CXIV. 216 Topical fluoridation procedures shoud be discussed only as an alternative to water fluoridation if..a community cannot benefit from water fluoridation. **1965** *Helv. Odontol. Acta* IX. 150 The fluoride content of the outermost enamel layer immediately after topical fluoridation ranged between 1385 and 2800 ppm.

fluori'dationist. [-IST 3.] One who advocates the fluoridation of public water supplies.

1951 *Jrnl. Amer. Water Works Assoc.* XLIII. 1 'Medication', or even worse 'mass medication', has been plaguing fluoridationists almost ever since it was introduced innocently enough way back when. **1967** *Brit. Dental Jrnl.* CXXIII. 414/1 Dr. George Walbott, the well-known allergist and anti-fluoridationist is organising an international society for fluoride research.

fluoride ('fluːərɪd, -aɪd). *Chem.* Also **fluorid.** [f. FLUOR-INE + -IDE.] A binary compound of fluorine with another element.

1826 HENRY *Elem. Chem.* I. 283 Fluor spar, for example, may be either a fluate of lime, or a fluoride of calcium. **1849** DANA *Geol.* ii. (1850) 152 These fluorids are fluorids of calcium and magnesium. **1869** ROSCOE *Elem. Chem.* 123 Dry silver fluoride.

fluoridization (ˌfluːərɪdaɪ'zeɪʃən). [f. FLUORID(E + -IZATION.] **a.** = FLUORIDATION 2 a.

1939 *Jrnl. Amer. Water Wks. Assoc.* XXXI. 1929 Every use of water must be examined as well as current water treatment practices before fluoridization can be begun. **1947** *Amer. Jrnl. Public Health* XXXVII. 1156 Fluoridization of community water supplies. **1949** *Bull. Amer. Assoc. Public Health Dentists* Aug. 12/2 Investigators are agreed that the term 'fluorination' of water supplies is incorrect and that the proper term is 'fluoridization'. **1966** *Listener* 6 Oct. 499/3 The evidence upon which the Ministry of Health recommends the fluoridization of drinking water.

b. (See quot. 1963.)

1951 *Sci. News Let.* 19 May 310/3 Fluoridation for the water supply, fluoridization for the treatment procedure when the dentist puts a fluoride on the children's teeth. **1951** *Jrnl. Dental Res.* XXX. 181 In cases of rampant caries, fluoridization of the teeth would simply provide a delaying action. **1963** C. O. BOUCHER *Current Clinical Dental Terminol.* 151/2 *Fluoridization*, the topical application of a solution of a fluoride to teeth.

Hence **'fluoridize** *v. trans.*; **'fluoridized** *ppl. a.*

1951 *Sci. News Let.* 19 May 310/3 Your town may fluoridate your drinking water, but your dentist will fluoridize your children's teeth. **1951** *Jrnl. Dental Res.* XXX. 178 The normal enamel contained 126·5 ppm. F, while the fluoridized enamel contained 1,434·6 ppm F. *Ibid.* 251 They found increasingly more low lactobacillus counts among children from the city with artifically fluoridized water. **1952** *Public Health Rep.* (U.S.) Jan. 39/1 It is not necessary to continue the use of fluoridized water after the enamel has been calcified.

fluorimeter, var. FLUOROMETER 2.

fluorinate ('fluːərɪneɪt), *v. trans.* [f. FLUORIN(E + -ATE[3].] **1.** *Chem.* To introduce an atom of fluorine into (a molecule or compound).

1931 *Chem. Abstr.* XXV. 3643 The..unsatd. residues condense to compds. of higher mol. wt. and are also in part fluorinated by the [$PhIF_2$] still present. **1943** A. L. HENNE in H. Gilman *Org. Chem.* (ed. 2) I. xi. 946 Hydrocarbons can be fluorinated in the gaseous form over copper gauze by means of fluorine diluted by nitrogen. **1961** L. F. & M. FIESER *Adv. Org. Chem.* x. 356 A method in which hydrocarbons are fluorinated to saturated fluorocarbons by cobalt trifluoride was used on a small industrial scale during the war to produce fluorocarbon lubricants.

2. = FLUORIDATE *v.* a.

1945 *Fluorine in Dental Health* (N.Y. Inst. Clin. Oral Path.) 40 A method to control..dental caries—by fluorinating a communal water supply that is deficient in content of fluorine. **1958** [see FLUORIDATE *v.* a]. **1968** PASSMORE & ROBSON *Compan. Med. Studies* I. v. 9 Local authorities in Europe and America have fluorinated their water with a consequent improvement in the teeth of their children.

Hence **'fluorinated, 'fluorinating** *ppl. adjs.*

a. (sense 1.) **1932** *Industr. & Engin. Chem.* XXIV. 331/2 The series of fluorinated products, C_2F_6, C_2F_5Cl, and $C_2F_4Cl_2$. **1935** P. H. GROGGINS *Unit Processes in Org. Synthesis* iv. 180 Hydrofluoric acid, antimony trifluoride, and boron trifluoride are the fluorinating agents most frequently employed. **1966** COTTON & WILKINSON *Adv. Inorg. Chem.* (ed. 2) xiv. 388 Sulfur tetrafluoride is a particularly useful and selective fluorinating agent for organic oxygen compounds. **1969** H. B. HASS in S. A. Miller *Ethylene* x. 861 The production of fluorinated refrigerants and propellants for aerosol bombs consumes about 80 per cent of the carbon tetrachloride produced in the United States.

b. (sense 2.) **1945** *Fluorine in Dental Health* (N.Y. Inst. Clin. Oral Path.) 44 Will artificially fluorinated water produce in humans the results..caused by waters in which fluorine is found naturally? **1951** *Jrnl. Dental Res.* XXX. 380 Onset of use of fluorinated waters has to occur within the first six years of life in order to produce an appreciable protection against caries.

fluorination (ˌfluːərɪ'neɪʃən). [f. FLUORIN(E + -ATION.] **1.** *Chem.* The action or process of fluorinating a compound. (See FLUORINATE *v.* 1.)

1931 *Chem. Abstr.* XXV. 3642 (*heading*) Experiments on the fluorination of organic compounds. **1946** *Nature* 9 Nov. 673/1 Disproportionation occurs during the fluorination (whence the possiblity of preparing $(C_2H_5O)_2\ SiF_2$ from $(C_2H_5O)_3SiCl$). **1966** *McGraw-Hill Encycl. Sci. & Technol.* VI. 328/1 Fluorination reactions occur with enormous vigor.

2. = FLUORIDATION 2 a.

1943 *Jrnl. Amer. Water Wks. Assoc.* XXXV. 1179/1 Theoretically, the idea of fluorination of the domestic water supply for the reduction of dental caries prevalence appears sound. **1949** [see FLUORIDIZATION a]. **1950** *Lancet* 9 Dec. 779/2 Dr. A. P. Black..suggested that fluorination of drinking-water was 'the biggest step in public health in the last hundred years'. **1958** G. B. DENTON *Vocab. Dentistry & Oral Sci.* IV. 182 *Fluorinate* and *fluorination* were commonly employed for the addition of fluoride to drinking water from 1943–1949.

fluorine ('fluːərɪn, -aɪn). *Chem.* [f. FLUOR + -INE, after the analogy of BROMINE, CHLORINE, etc.] **1.** A non-metallic element (symbol F),

forming, with bromine, chlorine, and iodine, the halogen group.

1813 SIR H. DAVY in *Phil. Trans.* CIII. 278 It appears reasonable to conclude that there exists in the fluoric compounds a peculiar substance..it may be denominated fluorine, a name suggested to me by M. Ampère. **1869** ROSCOE *Elem. Chem.* 13 All the elements, with the single exception of fluorine, combine with oxygen to form oxides.

2. *attrib.*, as **fluorine dating, method, test,** etc., a method of determining the relative age of organic remains by measuring the amount of fluorine that has been absorbed from surrounding ground-water.

1949 OAKLEY & MONTAGU in *Bull. Brit. Mus.* (*N.H.*), *Geol.* I. II. 29 The authors..independently reached similar conclusions with regard to the probable dating of the [Galley Hill] skeleton and..prepared a joint report on their findings. One author (K.P.O.) has prepared the introductory sections, the account of the geology, and of the fluorine dating. **1959** J. D. CLARK *Prehist. S. Afr.* iv. 83 Fluorine and uranium tests have shown that the skull fragments are of the same age as the faunal remains found with them. **1968** R. G. WEST *Pleistocene Geol. & Biol.* ix. 160 The fluorine method is useful for the relative dating of animal skeletal remains found in sand and gravel.

fluorite (ˈfluːəraɪt). *Min.* [f. FLUOR + -ITE.] = FLUOR-SPAR.

1868 DANA *Min.* p. xxx, Fluor was written fluorite last century by Napione. **1887** —— *Min. & Petrogr.* 228 Massive fluorite receives a high polish.

fluoro- (fluːərəʊ). **1.** Used as comb. form of FLUORINE (rarely of FLUORIDE), chiefly in the names of chemical compounds, as **fluoroaˈcetamide**, $CH_2F{\cdot}CONH_2$, a stable, toxic, fluorinated derivative of acetamide with strong insecticidal properties; **ˈfluoroform** [ad. F. *fluoroforme* (Meslans 1890, in *Compt. Rend.* CX. 717): see CHLOROFORM], a gas (CHF_3) that is almost completely inert both chemically and physiologically and is the fluorine analogue of chloroform; **ˌfluorohydroˈcortisone** = FLUDROCORTISONE; **ˈfluorotype** *Photogr.* [-TYPE], an old positive process in which paper sensitized with sodium fluoride was used.

1909 *Jrnl. Chem. Soc.* XCVI. II. 297 The author has determined the heats of formation of the following compounds...*Fluoroacetamide, 249·55 cal. **1958** *Nature* 28 June 1810/2 Fluoroacetamide is as effective as the more dangerous sodium fluoracetate as a systemic insecticide. **1964** *New Statesman* 20 Mar. 438/3 Last month the government banned the sale of fluoroacetamide as an insect control. **1890** *Jrnl. Chem. Soc.* LVIII. II. 724 This gas is *fluoroform, CHF_3. **1950** N. V. SIDGWICK *Chem. Elements* II. vii. 1130 A guinea-pig put into a 50 per cent. air-fluoroform mixture..did not know that the gas was there. **1954** FRIED & SABO in *Jrnl. Amer. Chem. Soc.* LXXVI. 1455/2 9α-*Fluorohydrocortisone acetate..was obtained in about 50% yield. *Ibid.* 1456/1 Deacetylation of I [*sc.* 9α-fluorohydrocortisone acetate] with sodium methylate afforded 9α-fluorohydrocortisone. **1970** W. MODELL *Drugs of Choice 1970–71* xxxii. 511 All patients with Addison's disease now can be satisfactorily managed with oral therapy using 10 mg. of hydrocortisone 2 to 3 times a day, plus 0·1 mg. of 9-alpha-fluorohydrocortisone (fludrocortisone) a day or every other day. **1844** R. HUNT *Res. Light* 106 It has been found that the fluate of soda has the property of quickening the sensibility of bromidated papers to a very remarkable extent; and from this quality a new process, which I would distinguish by the name of the *Fluorotype, results. **1955** H. & A. GERNSHEIM *Hist. Photogr.* III. xi. 124 Fluorotype derives its name from the fluoride of sodium used in preparing the paper... The exposure was only half a minute and the picture was developed with protosulphate of iron.

2. Used as combining form of FLUORESCENCE, as in FLUOROMETER, etc.

fluorocarbon (ˌfluːərəʊˈkɑːbən). *Chem.* [f. FLUORO- + CARBON, after *hydrocarbon.*] Any of a large class of synthetic, chemically stable compounds of carbon and fluorine analogous to the hydrocarbons (see also quot. 1962).

1937 *Jrnl. Amer. Chem. Soc.* LIX. 1407/1 From a reaction mixture of carbon and fluorine..fluorocarbons have been isolated. **1950** J. H. SIMONS *Fluorine Chem.* I. xii. 402 Substances made from or protected by fluoro-carbons are free from decay and insect damage. **1951** *Sci. News Letter* 15 Sept. 165 The relatively new chemicals known as fluorocarbons when used as a cooling spray greatly increase the efficiency of electrical transformers. **1959** *Times* 27 Apr. (Rubber Industry Suppl.) p. vi/7 The newer fluoro-carbon polymers have valuable properties in heat and fluid resistance. **1962** A. J. RUDGE *Manuf. Fluorine* vii. 57 In the technical literature there has developed a tendency to use the term 'fluorocarbon' to include compounds containing elements additional to carbon and fluorine, e.g. CF_2Cl_2. This practice is confusing and is to be deprecated. **1964** R. E. BANKS *Fluorocarbons* v. 136 Like their aliphatic relatives, aromatic fluorocarbons are colourless. **1966** *New Scientist* 24 Nov. 456/2 Fluorocarbons such as polytetrafluoroethylene (PTFE) and related polymers.

fluoroid (ˈfluːərɔɪd). *Crystallogr.* [f. FLUOR + -OID.] A solid bounded by twenty-four triangular planes; occurring frequently in fluor-spar.

fluorometer (fluːəˈrɒmɪtə(r)). [f. FLUORO- + -METER.] **1.** A device used to aid in the fluoroscopic location of one object within another.

1897 *N.Y. Tribune* 9 Feb. 3/4 In a series of scientific experiments with the new fluorometer, invented by John Dennis of this city [*sc.* Rochester], Professor A. L. Arey demonstrated definitely the angles and direction of the Roentgen rays with regard to their source. **1898** *Sci. Amer.* 12 Feb. 101/1 It is the province of the 'fluorometer' to enable observers to form an exact and certain diagnosis of the presence of bullets, needles, calculi or any other substance which is comparatively more dense in its fluoroscopic shadow than the subject in which it is contained. **1899** D. WALSH *Röntgen Rays in Med. Work* (ed. 2) 97 In America the 'Dennis Fluorometer' is in vogue.

2. Also **fluorimeter**. Any apparatus or instrument for measuring the intensity of fluorescence or the duration of its afterglow. Hence **fluoro-, fluoriˈmetric** *adjs.*, of, pertaining to, or employing the fluorometer or fluorometry; **fluoro-, fluoriˈmetrically** *advs.*; **fluoˈro-, fluoˈrimetry**, the use of the fluorometer.

1913 *Chem. Abstr.* VII. 2905 The instrument described, termed a fluorometer. **1918** *Ibid.* XII. 450 (*heading*) New fluorometric apparatus for the determination of X-rays. **1920** *Ibid.* XIV. 2584 (*heading*) A fluorimeter. **1920** *Jrnl. Amer. Chem. Soc.* XLII. 1351 The natural term to designate the new method could be either 'fluorometry' or 'fluoremetry' [*sic*]. **1942** *Electronic Engin.* XV. 127 A supersonic cell fluorometer..for the measurement of the rise and decay of luminescence in phosphors. **1953** BOWEN & WOKES *Fluorescence of Solutions* viii. 58 The term 'fluorimeter'..is now generally accepted in Great Britain. Alternative terms such as 'fluorometer' and 'fluorophotometer' are in use in America. **1961** *Lancet* 7 Oct. 793/1 The urine was..estimated fluorimetrically. **1962** T. O. SIPPEL in A. Pirie *Lens Metabolism in Rel. Cataract* 368 The oxidized and reduced forms of diphospho- and triphosphopyridine nucleotide were measured fluorometrically. *Ibid.*, Readings were made on a photomultiplier fluorometer.

fluorophor, fluorophore (ˈfluːərəʊfɔə(r)). Also **fluorphor.** [a. G. *fluorophor* (R. E. Meyer 1897, in *Zeitschr. f. physiol. Chem.* XXIV. 508), f. FLUORO- + -PHORE.] **a.** An atomic group the presence of which in a molecule causes it to be fluorescent. **b.** A fluorescent substance.

1898 *Jrnl. Chem. Soc.* LXXIV. II. 105 In order..that the fluorescence may be developed, it is further necessary that the fluorphore be situated between two heavy atomic groups, usually benzene nuclei. **1939** RADLEY & GRANT *Fluorescence Anal. U.V. Light* (ed. 3) II. xiv. 290 Some fluorescent compounds of simple composition but containing no 'fluorophors' are known. **1962** S. UDENFRIEND *Fluorescence Assay* ii. 33 Nonfluorescent steroids are converted to fluorophores by dehydration in concentrated sulfuric acids. **1966** *McGraw-Hill Encycl. Sci. & Technol.* VII. 611/1 Other terms sometimes used synonymously with phosphor are luminophor..or fluorphor.

fluorophotometer (ˌfluːərəʊfəʊˈtɒmɪtə(r)). Also **ˌfluophoˈtometer, ˌfluorphoˈtometer.** [f. FLUORO- + PHOTOMETER.] A fluorometer (sense 2) incorporating a photometer. Hence **ˌfluorophotoˈmetric** *a.*, of, pertaining to, or employing a fluorophotometer or fluorophotometry; **ˌfluorophoˈtometry**, the use of the fluorophotometer.

1928 *Jrnl. Sci. Instrum.* V. 273 (*heading*) A simple ultra-violet fluorophotometer. **1946** *Nature* 28 Sept. 451/2 The result of the 'fluorimetry' or 'fluorphotometry' of samples will depend on their previous history as regards exposure to light. **1950** *Arch. Ind. Hyg. & Occup. Med.* II. 311 Fluorophotometric analysis for uranium. **1953** Fluoro-photometer [see FLUOROMETER 2]. **1969** G. W. EWING *Instrum. Meth. Chem. Analysis* (ed. 3) iv. 107 Instruments for the measurement of fluorescence are known as fluorimeters (sometimes fluorometers or fluophotometers).

fluoroscope (ˈfluːərəʊskəʊp). [f. FLUORO- + -SCOPE.] An apparatus which incorporates a fluorescent screen and is used in conjunction with an X-ray machine to produce a visible image of a body placed between the screen and the source of the rays. Hence **fluoroˈscopic** *a.*, formed or done by means of a fluoroscope or fluoroscopy; pertaining to the fluoroscope or fluoroscopy; **fluoroˈscopically** *adv.*; **fluoˈroscopy**, the use of the fluoroscope; an examination by means of a fluoroscope.

1896 *Lancaster* (Pa.) *New Era* 2 Apr. 2 He [*sc.* Edison] calls his instrument the Fluoroscope. **1896** *Boston Med. & Surg. Jrnl.* 1 Oct. 336/1 A fluoroscopic examination of the heart. *Ibid.* 335/1 The constant motion of the heart and diaphragm interfere with the use of radiography but renders fluoroscopy all the more valuable. **1897** *Chem. News* 24 Sept. 158/1 (*heading*) Photography of the fluoroscopic image. **1908** *Practitioner* Sept. 437 Fluoroscopic examination of the thorax was also negative. **1940** G. L. CLARK *Applied X-Rays* (ed. 3) ix. 166 A typical unit for continuous fluoroscopic inspection of..food products on the conveyor belt. **1959** *Medicamundi* V. 4 (*heading*) Fluoroscopically controlled cholangiography with the image intensifier. **1961** A. TAYLOR *X-Ray Metallogr.* iii. 32 The smaller castings made from light alloys are usually examined for major defects by fluoroscopic inspection. **1970** *Nature* 18 July 296/1 In many hospitals the records will be sufficiently accurate to determine the number of fluoroscopies per patient treated, as well as radiation dose per fluoroscopy.

fluorosis (fluːəˈrəʊsɪs). *Path.* [ad. F. *fluorose* (H. Christiani 1927, in *Compt. Rend. Sixième Congrès Chim. Ind.* 164/1), f. FLUOR- + -OSIS.] Poisoning by fluorine or a fluorine compound; any condition caused by such poisoning.

1927 *Chem. Abstr.* XXI. 3404 An investigation which resulted in characterizing a new disease, fluorosis. **1936** *Nature* 16 May 828/2 Fluorine from chemical works or resulting from volcanic activity can get into soil and pasture and cause fluorosis in cattle. **1958** *Spectator* 6 June 737/2 Crippling fluorosis in *natural* fluoride areas at or near the so-called safe concentration has been admitted by some of the top American proponents them-selves. **1971** *Daily Tel.* (Colour Suppl.) 28 May 21/4 Cattle nearby have in the past suffered from fluorosis, a condition not unlike rheumatoid arthritis in which the joints seize up.

†**ˈfluorous,** *a. Obs.* [f. FLUOR + -OUS.] Only in *fluorous acid*: (see quot. 1828: no such acid exists).

1790 KERR tr. *Lavoisier's Elem. Chem.* 185 (Table), Fluorous acid. **1828** WEBSTER s.v. (citing LAVOISIER), The fluorous acid is the acid of fluor in its first degree of oxygenation.

fluorphor, var. FLUOROPHOR.

fluor-spar (ˈfluːəspɑː(r)). *Min.* [f. FLUOR + SPAR.] Native fluoride of calcium (CaF_2); found abundantly in Derbyshire (where one variety is known as *Blue John*), and hence often called *Derbyshire spar.*

1794 KIRWAN *Min.* I. 127, 3d Family, Foliated or sparry, Fluor spar. **1812** SIR H. DAVY *Chem. Philos.* 465 A substance found abundantly in nature called *fluor spar*, it is usually either blue, green, yellow, or white, transparent, and crystallized in cubes. **1880** ANSTED *Minerals* 18 The crystal of fluor-spar has the striæ parallel all round the four sides.

†**ˈfluoruret.** *Chem. Obs.* [f. FLUOR + -URET, q.v.] = FLUORIDE.

1854 J. SCOFFERN in *Orr's Circ. Sc.* Chem. 397 Fluorides or fluorurets.

†**flur,** *sb.*[1] *Obs. rare. Bird-catching.* 'A moveable perch to which a bird is tied and which the bird-catcher can raise by means of a long string.' (Pennant). Also *attrib.*, as *flur-bird.*

1766 PENNANT *Zool.* (1768) II. 331 He hath, besides, what are called flur-birds, which are placed within the nets, are raised upon the flur and gently let down at the time the wild bird approaches them. **1797** P. WAKEFIELD *Mental Improv.* (1801) I. 57 The flur-birds are braced by a silken string.

flur (flɜː(r)), *sb.*[2] *Sc.* [? f. FLURR *v.*] Flue, fluff.

1845 *New Stat. Acc. Scot.* VI. 146 The dust and small flur separated from the cotton.

flur, obs. var. of FLOOR, FLURR.

flurdom, variant form of FLIRDOM.

fluren, obs. form of FLOUREN.

flures, flureis, fluris(che, obs. forms of FLOURISH.

flurn (flɜːn), *v. Obs.* exc. *dial.* [? alteration of *flurre*, FLEER, after *spurn* or *scorn.*] *intr.* To sneer (*at*).

1656 R. FLETCHER *Ex Otio Negotium* To Rdr., And for those abortive births slipp'd from my brain..give me leave to flurn at them, as the poor excrescencies of Nature. **1866** BROGDEN *Prov. Words Lincolnsh.* 72 Flurn, to show contempt by looks, to scorn.

flurr, *sb. rare.* [f. next vb.] Flutter, whirr.

1651 H. MORE *Enthus. Triumph.* (1656) 208 After the flur and farre flight of every partridge he let out of his basket.

flurr (flɜː(r)), *v.* [? onomatopœic.]

1. *trans.* To scatter, throw about; also with *up.*

1627–77 FELTHAM *Resolves* II. xxix. 218 Choler is as dust flur'd up into the eyes of Reason. **1813** HOGG *Queen's Wake* 39 The stately ship..flurred on high the slender spray.

2. *intr.* To fly up; to fly with whirring or fluttering wings.

1681 GLANVILL *Sadducismus* II. (ed. 2) 169 A Bird, that would flurr near to her face. **1824** *New Monthly Mag.* X. 322, I saw one [cuckoo]..flurr awkwardly away across the meadow. **1825** HOGG *Queen Hynde* 329 On the spray, that flurr'd and gleam'd A thousand little rainbows beam'd.

flurr(e, obs. f. FLEER.

†**flurred,** *a. Her. Obs.*[−1] [anglicized form of Fr. *fleuré, -ée*: see FLEURY.] Having flowerlike ornaments.

1655 M. CARTER *Hon. Rediv.* (1660) 86 A Coronet of gold flurred, the points and flowers of equall height.

flurri(e, obs. forms of FLEURY.

flurrifiˈcation. *nonce-wd.* [f. FLURRY + -FICATION.] The state of being flurried.

1822 MRS. NATHAN *Langreath* II. 327 To be put into such a flurrification.

flurrish, obs. form of FLOURISH.

flurry (ˈflʌrɪ), *sb.* [? onomatopœic, suggested by *flaw, hurry* etc.; cf. also FLURR *v.*]

1. a. A sudden agitation of the air, a gust or squall.

1698 FRYER *Acc. E. India & P.* 128 *marg.*, Flurries from the Hills carry Men and Oxen down the Precipice. **1726–7**

Swift *Gulliver* I. i. 22 The boat was overset by a sudden flurry from the north. **1831** Scott *Jrnl.* 18 Nov., Wind.. dies away in the morning, and blows in flurries rather contrary. **1890** *Pall Mall G.* 3 Dec. 1/3 You may watch 'catspaws' and 'flurries' on their rapid way.

fig. **1820** J. Q. Adams *Mem.* 2 June (1875) V. 137 His flurries of temper pass off as quickly as they rise.

b. Chiefly *U.S.* A sharp and sudden shower; a sudden rush (of birds).

1828 in Webster. **1836** W. Irving *Astoria* III. 91 Occasional flurries of snow. **1868** Lowell *First Snowfall* 15 The sudden flurries of snow-birds, Like brown leaves whirling by. **1892** Stevenson *Across the Plains* 223 Spat upon by flurries of rain.

2. a. A sudden commotion or excitement; perturbation, nervous agitation, flutter, hurry.

1710 Palmer *Proverbs* 82 A man is never more expos'd to temptation than in the flurry of his passions. **1768–74** Tucker *Lt. Nat.* (1852) II. 485 If we exert our endeavours, not in a fright and a flurry, but with a calm, steady determination, we [etc.]. **1836** W. Irving *Life & Lett.* (1866) III. 94, I cannot tell you how happy I was to.. leave behind me the hurry and worry and flurry of the city. **1882** *Mrs. Raven's Tempt.* II. 190 'That's sure to be the upshot of flurries and hurries and frights.'

transf. **1878** Browning *Poets Croisic* cxxxviii, Flurry of ruffles, flounce of wig-ties.

b. The death-throes of a dying whale.

1823 J. F. Cooper *Pilot* xvii, He's going into his flurry. **1882** *Illustr. Sport. & Dram. News* 18 Mar. 7/3 Unless you should be struck by the tail of a frantic cetacean during the 'flurry' or slaughter.

c. A sudden burst of activity (in the stock-market).

1876 *Fur, Fin & Feather* Sept. 129 The prospect of a flurry in stocks.. is sure to strip the island of visitors. **1889** *Kansas Times & Star* 2 Nov., The big flurry in the stock market yesterday should cause no particular alarm. **1907** E. S. Field *Six-Cylinder Courtship* 80 A column.. sandwiched in between The Latest Armenian Atrocities and the Unprecedented Flurry in Chewing Gum. **1971** *Daily Tel.* 25 Aug. 14 A flurry of speculative activity saw BSA 3 up at 26p.

3. *Comb.* as ***flurry-scurry***.

1888 *Pall Mall G.* 28 May 1/2 So utterly and hopelessly incomprehensible does your recent flurry-scurry appear to the enlightened foreigner.

flurry (ˈflʌrɪ), *v.* [f. prec. sb.]

1. *trans.* To bewilder or confuse as by haste or noise; to agitate, 'put out'.

a **1757** E. Moore *Envy & Fort.* 71 'Well may you wonder To see me thus flurry'd.' **1771** Mad. D'Arblay *Diary* July, This flurried me violently, insomuch that my memory failed me. **1832** Ht. Martineau *Hill & Valley* i. 11 How you flurry yourself for nothing. **1886** G. R. Sims *Ring o' Bells* xvi. 283 He.. flurried the other performers, and seemed only in a hurry to.. quit the stage.

2. *intr.* To flutter down in sudden or gusty showers. Also *transf.* and *fig.*

1883 H. H. Kane in *Harper's Mag.* Nov. 947/2 The music seemed.. to flurry, like snow-flakes, from the ceiling. **1884** Roe *Nat. Ser. Story* vii, The petals of the cherry were flurrying down like snow in every passing breeze. **1917** W. Owen *Let.* 13 Dec. (1967) 515, I was flurrying round like any Mrs. Smith de Smith when 'Company' is expected. **1920** D. Lindsay *Voy. Arcturus* xii. 145 The freezing wind, flurrying across the desert, drove the fine particles of sand painfully against their faces.

Hence ˈ**flurried** *ppl. a.*; ˈ**flurriedly** *adv.*, in a flurried manner.

1775 Mad. D'Arblay *Diary* May, She was so much flurried, that [etc.]. **1800** Mrs. Hervey *Mourtray Fam.* III. 235 To calm her flurried spirits. **1834** *Blackw. Mag.* XXXV. 137 Running flurriedly out. **1844** Alb. Smith *Adv. Mr. Ledbury* xxiv. (1886) 75 Titus immediately returned the salute with flurried courtesy. **1875** Jowett *Plato* (ed. 2) III. 208 What are you saying? he asked flurriedly.

flurshe, flurt, obs. ff. flourish, flirt.

flurt(e, var. form of fleurettée.

†ˈ**flurted,** *ppl. a. Obs.*⁻¹ [anglicized form of Fr. *fleureté*, fleurettée.] Flowered, figured.

13.. *E.E. Allit. P.* A. 208 Wyth flurted flowrez perfet vpon.

flus(e, var. floose.

flush (flʌʃ), *sb.*¹ [f. flush *v.*¹] A flight of birds suddenly started up. Also *transf.*

1596 Spenser *F.Q.* v. ii. 54 When a Falcon hath.. Flowne at a flush of ducks. **1668** H. More *Div. Dial.* ii. x. (1713) 118 When one shoots at a flock of Pigeons or a flush of Ducks. **1868** Kinglake *Crimea* (1877) III. i. 146 A body which might almost be called a mere flush of skirmishers.

flush (flʌʃ), *sb.*² [f. flush *v.*²]

†**1.** A pool or puddle. *Obs.*

1375 Barbour *Bruce* xiii. 20 The battale thair so felloune was And sua richt gret spilling of blud, That on the erd the fluss it stud. **1513** Douglas *Æneis* vii. Prol. 54 Every hieway Full of fluschis, doubbis, myre and clay.

2. a. A sudden increase in the volume of a stream; a rush of water coming down suddenly, or let down for a specific purpose.

1529 More *Dyaloge* iii. Wks. 245/2 It woulde happely be thought not a thyng metely to be aduentured to set all on a flushe at ones, and dashe rashelye out holye scrypture in euerye lewde felowes teeth. **1677** Yarranton *Engl. Improv.* 189 By making three Holds for water in the River.. to be let down as flushes in dry times. **1691** Ray *Creation* ii. (1704) 316 The pulsation of the heart, driving the blood through them in manner of a wave or flush. **1850** Netherway *Suggest. Drainage Lond.* 18 By a small reservoir, and letting it off by sluices.. a sufficient flush would be obtained. **1854** *Jrnl. R. Agric. Soc.* XV. i. 13 Cattle driven by a flush of water to some isolated spot of ground. **1870** *Illustr. Lond. News* 24 Sept. 319 Owing to.. the want of a good flush of water, few of them [trout] were taken.

b. A sudden plentiful increase or abundance of anything. Also, *rarely*, †the mass, great majority.

1592 G. Harvey *Four Lett.* Ep. Ded. Wks. (Grosart) I. 156 In such a flush of notable good fellowes. **1617** *Crt. & Times Jas. I* (1849) II. 7 When upon such a flush we are already come to so low an ebb. *a* **1626** Bacon *Certificate of Mint* Wks. 1740 I. App. 63 The great flush of gold that is come into the Mint since the proclamation. *a* **1679** T. Goodwin *Wks.* II. iii. 112 The shoal and the flush of Mankind. **1738** [G. Smith] *Curious Relat.* II. 311 When they had given their Folly a sudden Flush. **1823** *Blackw. Mag.* XIV. 507 The last flush of passengers is seen in the streets.

c. The stream from a mill-wheel.

a **1825** in Forby *Voc. E. Anglia.* **1892** *Longm. Mag.* Nov. 87 Nets so placed as to intercept them as they pass through mill flushes.

d. *Coal-mining.* (See quot.)

1883 Gresley *Gloss. Coal Mining, Flush*, a small quantity of ignited fire-damp.

3. A rush of emotion or passion; elation or excitement arising from this, or from success, victory, etc. Phr. ***in the (first, full) flush***.

1614 Raleigh *Hist. World* iii. 17 Unreasonable flushes of proud and vaine joy. **1692** R. L'Estrange *Fables* ccccxliii, Never had any Man such a Loss.. cries a Widdower, in the Flush of his Extravagancies for a Dead Wife. **1829** Lytton *Devereux* ii. vii, In the full flush of his.. restless schemes. **1843** Lever *J. Hinton* xxii, A momentary flush of passionate indignation. **1850** Merivale *Rom. Emp.* (1865) I. i. 40 The plunder of all Italy.. was too tempting to be relinquished in the first flush of victory. **1867** Parkman *Jesuits N. Amer.* xvii. (1875) 241 The Confederates at this time were in a flush of unparalleled audacity.

4. A sudden shooting up; a fresh growth (of grass, leaves, or flowers). Also ***in full flush***.

1773 Steevens in *Shaks. Wks.* Note on *Lear* iv. vi. 124 A horse.. turned out in the spring to take the first flush of grass. **1803** *Trans. Soc. Encourag. Arts* XXI. 120 The showers in July.. bringing up a new flush of annuals. **1844** *Jrnl. R. Agric. Soc.* V. i. 49 The general flush of grass.. comes on generally late in April. **1882** *Garden* 11 Mar. 169/2 Avoid producing a too vigorous flush of vine. **1893** *Cornh. Mag.* Nov. 534 Brown coolies are picking the young shoots, now in full 'flush' after a heavy shower.

5. The act of cleansing (a drain) by flushing.

1883 *Pall Mall G.* 21 Nov. 4/2 The quantity for a flush is two gallons.

6. a. A glow of light or colour, *esp.* the reddening in the face caused by a rush of blood; also, the rush of blood itself.

1630 J. Taylor (Water P.) *Praise Cleane Linnen* Wks. ii. 169I When bright Phœbus.. roabes the welkin with a purple flush. **1706** Phillips (ed. Kersey), *Flush*, a Red Colour in the Face. **1803** *Med. Jrnl.* X. 552 Periodical hectic flushes. **1832** Ht. Martineau *Hill & Valley* iv. 55 I see a fiery flush.. which I suppose comes from some iron-work near. **1860** Tyndall *Glac.* i. xviii. 131 A warm flush ran through me. **1865** Dickens *Mut. Fr.* iv. xvi. 299 'It belongs to me', returned the little creature, with a quick flush of her face and neck. **1873** Black *Pr. Thule* xxiv. 405 Along the west.. lay a great flush of gold.

fig. **1851** Carlyle *Sterling* i. iii. (1872) 13 Sudden flights to Dublin, to London, whithersoever any flush of bright outlook.. allured him.

b. A hot fit in a fever.

1858 O. W. Holmes *Aut. Breakf.-t.* x. 99 The throbbing flushes of the poetical intermittent. **1869** *Lonsdale Gloss., Flush*, the hot stage of a fever.

7. Glow, freshness, vigour (of beauty, health, life).

1735 Somerville *Chase* iii. 449 The Flush of Beauty in their Cheeks. **1826** Disraeli *Viv. Grey* v. x, Meeting death in the very flush of life. **1856** Masson *Ess.* v. 166 Swift.. in the full flush of his new popularity.. visited England. **1874** Miss Braddon *Taken at Flood* ii, It was in the very flush of summer.

8. a. *Comb.*, as ***flush-box, -pot, -tank, -vent***; **flush-wheel** (see quot. 1874).

1884 Knight *Dict. Mech.* IV. 350/2 *Flush Box, a cistern for especial use in dwellings where the supply of water is intermittent. **1884** G. E. Waring in *Century Mag.* Dec. 264/2 The outlet of the *flush-pot is closed with a plug. *Ibid.* 255/1 House drainage.. begins at the sewer, or *flush-tank. **1884** *Health Exhib. Catal.* 60/2 Owen's Patent Single *Flushvent. **1874** Knight *Dict. Mech.* I. 892/1 **Flush-wheel*, a wheel used in raising water for draining.

b. Of a lavatory, its plumbing, etc., as ***flush toilet***. Also occas. *ellipt.* Cf. flush *v.*² 3, ***flush-box, -tank***.

1908 *Sears, Roebuck Catal.* 604/1 The closet.. is furnished with a positive flush valve. *Ibid.* 605/3 China push button flush in front of tank. **1950** *Ann. Rep. Smithsonian Inst. 1949* 220 Flush toilets, bathing and laundry, street cleaning, and fire protection require an average of about 40 to 75 gallons per day per capita. **1961** L. Mumford *City in Hist.* viii. 216 Flush toilets both wasted potential fertilizer and polluted the streams. **1965** G. McInnes *Road to Gundagai* iii. 38 We were lucky to have arrived after the installation of 'the flush'. **1967** *Guardian* 28 Apr. 4/6 A notable change from chemical to flush lavatories, both inside and outside caravans. **1967** *Gloss. Sanitation Terms (B.S.I.)* 60 *Flush valve* (flushing valve), a valve, for controlling the flushing of a W.C. pan.

flush (flʌʃ), *sb.*³ *Cards.* [proximate source uncertain; F. has *flux, flus* from 15th c., Sp. *flux* (prob. from F., as the native form would be *fluxo*, mod. *flujo*), Flem. (16th c.) *fluys* (from Fr.); Florio 1611 gives It. *flusso* in the same sense (now obs.).

The F. and It. words appear to be merely special uses of the words in those langs. repr. L. *fluxus* flow, flux (for the sense in cardplaying cf. *run*). The Eng. word prob. owes its form to association with flush *sb.*²]

1. A hand consisting of cards all of one suit, or including a prescribed number all of one suit.

a **1529** Skelton *Sp. Parrot* 424 He facithe owte at a fflusshe, with, shewe, take all! **1599** Minsheu *Span. Dial.* 38/2 The Queene of Diamonds with which I made the last flush. *a* **1618** J. Davies *Wittes Pilgr.* Wks. (Grosart) 31/1 Your Prim's far inferior to their Flush. **1785** in *Archæologia* VIII. 132 If they [cards] are all of the same colour, he wins the flush. **1836–9** Dickens *Sk. Boz* (1850) 187/1 A flush! —that's good for four. **1891** *Punch* 26 Dec. 305/1, I guess there's a straight flush against me.

†**2.** A certain game at cards. *Obs.*⁻⁰

1598 Florio, *Flussata*, a play at cardes called Flush.

flush (flʌʃ), *a.*¹ [? f. flush *v.*¹]

1. a. Abundantly full. In later use chiefly of a stream, etc.: Full to overflowing, swollen, in flood.

1607 Shaks. *Timon* v. iv. 8 Now the time is flush. **1647** H. More *Poems* 333 Her [the Moon's] hollow horns fill'd up with flusher light. **1697** Dampier *Voy.* I. 393 Small Brooks of fresh Water, that run flush into the Sea for 10 months in the year. **1826** Disraeli *Viv. Grey* iii. vi, In the flush moment of joy. **1841** Hartshorne *Salop. Antiq.* Gloss. s.v., 'The Sivirn's pretty flush'. **1872** Browning *Fifine* lxxxviii, Unchoked, the channel's flush.

†**b.** ? 'Up to the mark', perfect, faultless. *Obs.*

c **1550** Wever *Lusty Juventus* ciij, I could so beare the busshe That al shuld be flusshe. That euer I dyd.

2. Full of life or spirit, lively, lusty, vigorous. Hence, Self-confident, self-conceited. Now *rare*.

1604 Shaks. *Ham.* (Qo. 2) iii. iii. 81 A tooke my father.. With all his crimes broad blowne, as flush [*Ff.* fresh] as May. **1606** —— *Ant. & Cl.* i. iv. 52 Many hot inrodes They make in Italy, the Borders Maritime Lacke blood to thinke on't, and flush youth reuolt. **1611** *Coryat's Crudities* Panegyricke Verses C iv b, He had a kind of simple blush That kept him still from being flush, When Ladies did him woe. *a* **1680** Charnock *Attrib. God* (1834) II. 569 Not as flush and gay .. as others. *a* **1690** E. Hopkins *Exp. Lord's Prayer*, etc. (1692) 297 The practice of some flush Notionists. **1767** H. Brooke *Fool of Qual.* (1792) I. iv. 143 Both appeared quite flush and confident of victory. **1826** J. Wilson *Noct. Ambr.* Wks. I. 5 The flush maiden, the rosy elf. **1894** Hardy *Life's Little Ironies, Trag. Two Ambitions* 84 Her bright eyes, brown hair.. and flush beauty.

3. a. Plentifully supplied (*esp.* with money). Const. *of*, († *in*, †*with*.) Of money: Abundant, plentiful.

1603 Dekker *Batch. Banq.* viii. G ij a, Some dames.. are more flush in crownes then her good man. **1637** Heywood *King & Loyal Subject* iii. Wks. 1874 VI. 45 So flush of money, and so bare in clothes. **1662** Dryden *Wild Gallant* ii. i, Since you are so flush, Sir, you shall give me a Locket of Diamonds. **1667** Waterhouse *Fire Lond.* 28 Monies being not so flush with them. **1712** Arbuthnot *John Bull* i. iii, He was not flush in ready, either to go to law, or clear old debts. **1727** *Philip Quarll* 81 Ill Language, of which they generally are flush, when Money is scant. **1767** S. Paterson *Another Trav.* I. 235 While they were flush with money. **1793** T. Jefferson *Writ.* (1830) IV. 482 Money being so flush, the six per cents run up to twenty-one, and twenty-two shillings. **1838** Dickens *Nich. Nick.* xiv, The first floor lodgers, being flush of furniture, kept an old mahogany table .. on the landing-place outside. **1871** M. Collins *Mrq. & Merch.* II. ix. 269 Tom.. is always very flush or very hard up.

b. *dial.* Lavish, profuse.

1703 Thoresby *Let. to Ray* (E.D.S.), *Flush*, full-handed, prodigal, wasteful. **1859** Geo. Eliot *A. Bede* 6 'When y'are six-an'-forty.. ye wonna be so flush o' working for nought.' **1884** *Chesh. Gloss., Flush*, lavish.

c. Of times: Prosperous.

1840 W. Irving *Life & Lett.* (1866) III. 153 If times ever again come smooth and flush with me. **1847** Disraeli *Tancred* iii. vi, Everything being thus in a state of flush and affluent prosperity. **1888** *Daily News* 17 Dec. 2/8 The output probably is greater now than it was during the best of the 'flush' times which preceded the long depression.

4. Of a high colour; blushing, ruddy; flushed.

1594 Drayton *Idea* 107 Thy Cheeke, now flush with Roses. **1817** Keats *Let.* Nov., Wks. 1889 III. 97 Jane looked very flush when I first looked in, but was much better when I left. **1821** —— *Isabel* xxvii, Sick and wan The brothers' faces.. did seem, Lorenzo's flush with love.

5. a. Even, level, in the same plane (whether horizontal or vertical) *with* (dial. *by*). [? Orig. of a river or stream running full (cf. sense 1), and so level with its banks: see quot. 1877. Cf. float.]

1791 Bentham *Panopt.* i. 172 Why.. place it [the building] in a recess, rather than close to the road, and flush with the surrounding wall? **1831** Brewster *Nat. Magic* xi. (1833) 285 He observed the edge of a pin flush with the edge of the receptacle. **1874** Moggridge *Ants & Spiders* ii. 91 The entire door does not shut flush with the surface. **1877** *N.W. Linc. Gloss.* s.v., 'Watter was flush by th' bank top.'

b. Even or level with the adjacent surface. Also *absol.*

bead and flush work, etc. (see quot. 1846). ***flush work***: (*a*) *Jewellery*: work in which the stones are level or nearly level with the setting. (*b*) *Bookbinding*: work in which the edges of the binding and leaves are cut level.

1799 A. Young *Agric. Lincoln.* 30 Two inch six-panel bead and flush. **1823** P. Nicholson *Pract. Build.* 160 The parallel faces of both are made flush, and.. appear almost like one single piece. **1842** Gwilt *Archit.* §2131 The panels are surrounded with a bead formed on the edge of the

framing, and the work is called bead and flush. **1846** BUCHANAN *Techn. Dict.*, *Bead and flush work*, a piece of framed work with beads run on each edge of the inclined panel. *Bead, flush, and square work*, framing with bead and flush on one side, and square on the other. **1850** *Chubb's Locks & Keys* 32 The bellies of the tumblers in Mr. Chubb's lock were always flush, or in the same plane. **1869** SIR E. J. REED *Shipbuild.* x. 180 The edges of the strakes of plating were fitted against one another, and the flush-joints thus formed were covered by internal edge-strips. **1883** W. C. RUSSELL *Sailors' Lang.*, *Flush-up*, said of a cargo that comes up to a level with the hatches. **1884** *B'ham Daily Post* 23 Feb. 3/4 Jeweller's Setter.—Wanted, a good Hand, used to flush work. **1885** *Spons' Mech. Own Bk.* 379 When it [*sc.* a piece of copebead stuff] lies close in the cheek, and also close at the mitres, it receives a little glue, and is nailed on with ⅝-in. fine brads, 3 or 4 to each. These are punched below the flush. **1885** J. GRANT *Royal Highlanders* iii. 32 The original castle..starts flush from the edge of the rock. **1892** *Pall Mall G.* 13 Jan. 2/3 Flush work, which is the elementary work of our trade [bookbinding]. **1937** [see BEAD *sb.* 6 a].

c. Of a vessel's deck: Continued on one level from stem to stern. Also ***flush fore and aft***.

1626 CAPT. SMITH *Accid. Yng. Sea-men* 11 A flush decke. **1772–84** COOK *Voy.* (1790) VI. 2216 The decks, fore and aft, being finished flush, had no covering for men or officers. **1840** R. H. DANA *Bef. Mast.* xxii. 66 Her decks were..flush fore and aft. **1933** *Jane's Fighting Ships* 527 Note raised C.T. [conning tower] and flush deck forward. **1940** *Illustr. London News* CXCVII. 359 (*caption*) The structure of an American 'flush-deck' destroyer, typical of the 50 transferred to Great Britain.

d. Of a vessel: Having no erection above the flush deck.

1800 *Naval Chron.* III. 294 The Danae is a flush vessel; the Captain's cabin is therefore below. **1833** MARRYAT *P. Simple* (1863) 261, I recollect faring harder than this through one cruise, in a flush vessel.

e. *Typogr.* Not indented or protruding.

1900 H. HART *Cent. Typogr.* 139/2 The ascending letters are cut flush at the top of the body. **1961** T. LANDAU *Encycl. Librarianship* (ed. 2) 144/1 *Flush*, 'even with', *i.e.* the left margin.

6. *Pugilism.* Of a blow: Direct, full on the mark, 'straight from the shoulder'.

1812 *Sporting Mag.* XXXIX. 18 He planted some dextrous flush hits. **1826** H. N. COLERIDGE *West Indies* 161 Audain..knocked him down with a flush hit on the nose.

7. *Comb.*, in parasynthetic adjs. as (sense 1 b) ***flush-coloured***; (sense 4 c), ***flush-decked***, ***-jointed***, ***-plated***. **flush-binder**, one who cuts the pages of a book flush with the cover; so ***flush hand***; **flush-decker**, a flush-decked ship; **flush ring** (see quot. 1967[1]).

1881 *Instr. Census Clerks* (1885) Index, *Flush binder. **1902** *Daily Chron.* 28 Apr. 11/4 Flush Binders wanted, used to piece work. **1921** *Dict. Occup. Terms* (1927) §532 *Binder, flush*; glues up books and affixes boards;..cuts book flush with edge of cover at top, bottom and fore-edge, by hand or power-operated guillotine. **1748** RICHARDSON *Clarissa* (1811) VI. xlii. 159 Lying upon a couch..bloated and *flush-coloured. **1883** J. D. J. KELLY in *Harper's Mag.* Aug. 450/2 The *flush-decked..well-ventilated deep boat. **1937** *Jane's Fighting Ships* 505 *United States*..boats by various yards (*Flush Deckers). **1957** *Ibid.* 285 In 1953–54 were modernised by Canada for submarine warfare and converted to flush-deckers. **1904** *Daily Chron.* 12 Jan. 10/6 *Flush Hands wanted. **1869** SIR E. J. REED *Shipbuild.* x. 180 In all succeeding arrangements, the butts of the plates were *flush-jointed. *Ibid.*, x. 185 The unprotected parts of the later iron-clads above the armour-belts are *flush-plated. **1961** WEBSTER, *Flush ring. **1967** *Gloss. Terms Builders' Hardware* (*B.S.I.*) IV. 13 *Flush ring*, a flush handle consisting of a metal ring lying in a circular recess in a mounting plate. *Ibid.* III. 8 *Flush ring catch* (showcase catch), a flush fitting catch having a spring bolt withdrawn by lifting a ring shaped handle from a recess in the body of the catch.

flush (flʌʃ), *a.*[2] *Cards.* [f. FLUSH *sb.*[3]]

1. †**a.** Of a player: Holding a flush, i.e. cards all of the same colour or suit (*obs.*). **b.** Of a hand or sequence: Forming or including a flush.

a. 1591 FLORIO *Sec. Fruites* 71, I was neither flush nor fiue and fiftie yet. *a* **1612** HARINGTON *Epigr.* II. 99 Crassus stopt a Club and so was flush.

b. 1883 *Longm. Mag.* Sept. 499 A flush sequence..a sequence of high cards all of the same suit.

2. *transf.* (*nonce-use*). Of corresponding quality throughout.

a **1658** CLEVELAND *Young Man to Old Woman* 33, I love to wear Clothes that are flush, Not prefacing old Rags with Plush.

flush (flʌʃ), *a.*[3] *Obs.* exc. *dial.* [Of obscure etymology; perh. an altered form of **fludge*, a possible dialectal representative of OE. *flycȝe* FLEDGE *a.* (cf. *cudgel* from OE. *cycȝel*; the form may be due to the influence of next vb.] = FLEDGE *a.*

1561 HOBY tr. *Castiglione's Courtyer* (1577) X viij b, Such as come to this loue are like yong Birdes almost flushe. **1599** A. M. tr. *Gabelhouer's Bk. Physicke* 80/2 When as they [swollowes] are fetherede, and allmost flushe. **1622** MABBE tr. *Aleman's Guzman D'Alf.* I. III. ii. 196 Then are they..like birds that are flush, to forsake the nest. **1825** BRITTON *Beaut. Wiltsh.* III. 373 *Flush*, fledged.

flush (flʌʃ), *v.*[1] [perh. onomatopœic; with initial *fl-* suggested by *fly*, *flutter*, etc., and an ending imitative of the sound of a swift sudden flight; cf. *rush*. (Some dialects have *flusk*: see FLUSKER *v.*)]

1. a. *intr.* To fly up quickly and suddenly; to start up and fly away. †Also, to flutter, to fly with fluttering wings. *transf.* Of a door: to fly open.

a **1300** *K. Horn* 1080 Horn the wyket puste, That hit open fluste. *a* **1300** *Floriz & Bl.* 473 Þer fliste ut a buterfliȝe. **1399** LANGL. *Rich. Redeles* II. 166 Þe blernyed boynard..Made þe ffawcon to ffloter and *ffussh ffor anger. **1558** PHAER *Æneid.* V. Miv, Flushing loud she flappes her winges. **1583** STANYHURST *Aeneis* I. (Arb.) 30 Se wel yoonder swans twelue in coompany flusshing. **1626** B. JONSON *Masque of Owls*, I make 'em to flush Each owl out of his bush. **1773** *Poetry* in *Ann. Reg.* 233 Another bird, just flushing at the sound, Scarce tops the fence. **1876** *Forest & Stream* 13 July 376/1 The spot from which the first [a woodcock] had flushed.

†**b.** *trans.* To flutter (the wings). *Obs.*

1558 PHAER *Æneid.* V. N iv, Of the stroke the bird afraied, Did flickring flush her winges.

2. a. *trans.* To cause to fly or take wing; to put up, start; also with *up*.

1450 *Bk. Hawkyng* in *Rel. Ant.* I. 297 Lete the spanyell flusch up the covey. ? **1645** C. MORTON *Enquiry* in *Harl. Misc.* (1810) V. 503 When they are flushed, or raised to the wing. **1772** BARRINGTON in *Phil. Trans.* LXII. 309 Whenever a woodcock..is flushed, he is roused from his sleep by the spaniel or sportsman. **1872** C. INNES *Lect. Sc. Legal Antiq.* ii. 65 A mirror for flushing larks as still used in Italy. *absol.* **1888** *Times* 15 Nov. 11/3 Pat Regan's hay and oats were thrown down because his sons flushed for Sir H. Burke.

b. *transf.* and *fig.* To reveal; to bring into the open; to drive *out*.

1950 [see EARTH *sb.*[1] 4]. **1958** *Spectator* 1 Aug. 176/1 After being flushed from his rural retreat in England by an unfortunate affair with a literary horsewoman, he [etc.]. **1971** *Scope* (S. Afr.) 19 Mar. 22/1 When we flushed them out of the old city of Jerusalem..we really knew fear.

†**3.** *intr.* Of persons: To rush like birds on the wing; to flock, swarm; also with *in*, *out*. *Obs.*

c **1450** *Merlin* xx. 330 All the x wardes of the kynge leodogan were flusshed to the standerd. **1581** J. BELL *Haddon's Answ. Osor.* 32 After them whole flockes of interpretours flusht in. *Ibid.* 292 b, Neyther had..so many swarmes of Heretickes flusht abroad. **1642** H. MORE *Song of Soul* II. i. ii. They straight flush out and her drad voice obey: Each shape, each life doth leapen out full light.

Hence **'flushing** *vbl. sb.*, a fluttering of the wings; a rustling rushing noise.

1398 TREVISA *Barth. De P.R.* XVIII. i. (1495) 741 Fisshe hereth..for they fle and voyde flusshynge and noyse. *c* **1420** *Pallad on Husb.* I. 628 A shuddering, a flusshing and affray He maketh thenne. **1583** STANYHURST *Aeneis* III. (Arb.) 77 With a suddeyn flushing thee gulligut harpeys From mountayns flitter.

flush (flʌʃ), *v.*[2] [Of uncertain etymology.

Perh. orig. identical with prec., the notion of 'sudden movement' being common to the two vbs. But the development of meaning appears to have been influenced by phonetic association with FLASH *v.*[2] (nearly all the senses of which have passed over to this vb., either unchanged or with modifications traceable to the echoism of the differing vowel), while the senses relating to colour have been affected by association with *blush*. It is doubtful whether there has been any influence from F. *flux* (see FLUX) or *fluiss-*, *fluir* to flow (whence the Du. *fluissen* to flow violently).]

I. Expressing sudden movement, *esp.* of a liquid.

1. *intr.* To rush out suddenly or copiously, to spurt; to flow with force or violence; also with *forth*, *out*, *over*, *up*. Said *esp.* of liquids, a river, etc., but also of immaterial things and *fig.*

1548 HALL *Chron.*, *Hen. IV* (an. 1) 18 b, A..furious storme sodainely flusshed and drowned .xii. of his great shippes. **1567** DRANT *Horace's Epist.* xv. E vj, Wine..that will flushe into my mynde, and vaines. **1581** J. BELL *Haddon's Answ. Osor.* 221 From hence flush out all these fluddes of complaints. **1624** H. MASON *Art of Lying* ii. 35 The..Well-head, whence first flushed forth this muddy Nylus. *a* **1625** FLETCHER *Nice Valour* III. ii, O your crush'd nostrils slakes your opilation And makes your pent powers flush to wholsome sneezes. **1678** BP. NICHOLSON *Exp. Catech.* Ep. Ded. 5 More will flush over and be lost, than poured into the Vessel. **1691** RAY *Creation* (1714) 45 Milk..being heated to such a degree doth suddenly..flush up and run over the vessel. **1707** MORTIMER *Husb.* 574 It [Beer] flushes violently out of the Cock for about a Quart. **1855** SINGLETON *Virgil* I. 237 It flushes through nine mouths, a broken sea.

2. a. To cause (water) to flow; to draw off; to draw off water from (a pond).

1594 NASHE *Vnfort. Trav.* 57 If those ponds were so full they need to be flust or let out. **1815** *Pocklington Canal Act* 35 If any person shall..cause to be flushed or drawn off any water.

†**b.** To burst *out* with, pour out suddenly.

1601 DENT *Pathw. Heaven* 142 Hee will flush out some of these [oathes] in his ordinarie speech. **1642** R. BAKER tr. *Malvezzi's Disc. Tacitus* 166 He after makes his greedinesse of blood appeare the more, by flushing it out all at once.

3. a. To cleanse (a drain, etc.); to drive *away* (an obstacle) by means of a rush of water.

1789 *Trans. Soc. Encourag. Arts* VII. 59 Paddles..are drawn up by screws, to flush away any obstacle. **1862** M. HOPKINS *Hawaii* 32 Rains..play their part in flushing streets. **1871** NAPHEYS *Prev. & Cure Dis.* I. v. 141 Sewer pipes should be flushed from time to time.

absol. **1850** NETHERWAY *Suggest. Drainage Lond.* 4 This would entirely dispense with the necessity of flushing.

transf. and *fig.* **1861** WYNTER *Soc. Bees* 277 The hot-air bath flushes the external sewers of the body. **1880** BEALE *Slight Ailm.* 173 The alimentary canal is thoroughly flushed in every part. **1884** HENLEY & STEVENSON *Adm. Guinea* I. viii, Flush out your sins with tears.

b. To inundate (a meadow).

1861 HUGHES *Tom Brown at Oxf.* xxxvi, Another considerable body of water..had been carried off..to flush the water-meadows.

4. *intr.* Of a plant: To send out shoots; to shoot. Also *trans.* in causative sense.

1810 [see FLUSHING *vbl. sb.* 1 c]. **1877** *N.W. Linc. Gloss.*, *Flush*, to make to grow. 'This sup o' rain hes flush't th' gress nistly.' **1893** *Cornh. Mag.* Nov. 543 The frequent showers ..'flush' the tea about every fortnight. **1893** *Chamb. Jrnl.* 7 Oct. 629/2 The [tea] plants flush, or throw out fresh shoots, all the year round.

5. *intr.* 'To become fluxed or fluid' (*Cent. Dict.*).

1885 FARROW *Milit. Encycl.* s.v. *Brazing* The solder flushes or becomes liquid enough to permeate the joint or crevice.

II. With reference to light or colour.

6. *intr.* †**a.** To emit light or sparks suddenly. **b.** To glow with sudden brilliance. Cf. FLASH *v.*[2] 5 and 7.

1646 SIR T. BROWNE *Pseud. Ep.* II. v. 90 Camphire though it flame well, yet will not flush so lively. *Ibid.* Thus in the preparation of Crocus Metallorum, the matter kindleth and flusheth like Gunpowder.

b. 1809 CAMPBELL *Gertr. Wyom.* II. xxv, Here and there, a solitary star Flush'd in the darkening firmament of June. **1842** TENNYSON *Locksley Hall* 26 A colour and a light, As I have seen the rosy red flushing in the northern night. **1868** FARRAR *Silence & V.* II. (1875) 46 The sunrise of its first day flushed over the manger.

7. Of the blood, etc.: To come with a rush, producing a heightened colour. Cf. sense 2 and FLASH *v.*[2] 9.

1667 MILTON *P.L.* IX. 886 In her Cheek distemper flushing glowd. **1677** DRYDEN *State Innoc.* v. i. 30 What means..That blood, which flushes guilty in your face? **1708** ROWE *Royal Convert* IV. i, A burning Purple flushes o'er my Face. **1813** BYRON *Br. Abydos* I. xiii, What fever in thy veins is flushing? **1845** CLOUGH *Early Poems* xvii. 15 The mantling blood to her cheek Flushed up. **1852** MRS. STOWE *Uncle Tom's C.* xiii, The blood flushed in Eliza's pale face.

8. Of the face, etc.: To become suffused with warm colour; to become suddenly red or hot; to 'colour up', redden, blush. Also with *up* or with adj. as complement.

1709 STEELE *Tatler* No. 33 ¶7 My Lord passes by; I flushed in a flame. **1789** W. BUCHAN *Dom. Med.* (1790) 177 The face generally flushes after eating. **1851** D. JERROLD *St. Giles* x. 102 His face flushed red as flame. **1869** DIXON *Tower* I. x. 96 Henry flushed into rage. **1890** BESANT *Demoniac* iv. 45 George flushed up; but he restrained himself.

quasi-*trans.* **1730–46** THOMSON *Autumn* 262 Her rising beauties flush'd a higher bloom.

9. a. *trans.* To make red or ruddy; to cause to blush or glow.

1697 DRYDEN *Virg. Past.* x. 33 Thy own Apollo came. Flush'd were his Cheeks. **1731** A. HILL *Adv. Poets* i, The Low Muse who lends Her feeble Fire, To flush pale Spleen. **1784** COWPER *Tiroc.* 833 Flushed with drunkenness. **1834** MEDWIN *Angler in Wales* I. 138 I had left my home young ..flushed with health. **1873** BLACK *Pr. Thule* xvii. 277 A face flushed with shame.

b. In wider sense: To suffuse or adorn with glowing colour.

1746–7 HERVEY *Refl. Flower-Garden* 62 They [tulips] flush the Parterre with one of the gayest Dresses that blooming Nature wears. **1821** CLARE *Vill. Minstr.* II. 69 Straying beams..In copper-coloured patches flush the sky. **1889** LOWELL *Latest Lit. Ess.* (1892) 83 A meadow flushed with primroses.

10. To inflame with pride or passion; to animate, encourage; also with *up*; *rarely*, †to initiate *in*. Cf. FLESH *v.*[1], which has influenced the sense.

1633 T. ADAMS *Exp. 2 Peter* ii. 6 This so flesheth and flusheth her, that she thinks no more of God. **1667** DRYDEN *Maiden Queen* I. i, But once or twice only, 'till I am a little flush'd in my Acquaintance with other Ladies, and have learn'd to prey for my self. *a* **1716** SOUTH *Serm.* (1737) IV. 141 This [success] flushes him up. **1713** ADDISON *Cato* I. ii, Armies flush'd with conquest. **1742** JOHNSON *Debates in Parl.* II. 94 They..who have flushed their new authority by a motion which [etc.]. **1790** BURKE *Fr. Rev.* Wks. V. 276 Flushed with the insolence of their first inglorious victories. **1867** FREEMAN *Norm. Conq.* (1876) I. iv. 183 Flushed with success they entered the Norman duchy.

11. *trans.* To fatten *up* (sheep); to stimulate (ewes) with generous diet at the breeding season.

1764 *Museum Rust.* III. xxxiii. 148, I had a fine piece of turneps, with which I intended to flush up five score sheep. **1886** C. SCOTT *Sheep-farming* 74 Nor is this the only evil of 'flushing' the ewes when they are put to the rams. From actual test we are convinced that ewes which have been flushed one year are never so prolific the next. **1923** *Discovery* Sept. 243/2 Many flockmasters..practised the methods of 'flushing' or artificially stimulating their ewes by means of an extra supply of special food at the approach of the 'tupping'..season.

flush (flʌʃ), *v.*[3] [f. FLUSH *a.*[1] 5.]

1. *trans.* To make flush or level; to fill in (a joint) level with the surface; to 'point'. Also with *up*.

1842 GWILT *Encycl. Archit.* Gloss., *Flush*..to leave no vacant space where the stones or bricks do not nicely fit in their places. **1883** H. S. DRINKER *Tunnelling* in Eissler *Mod. High Explosives* (1884) 238 In driving a heading, particular care should be taken that unnecessary cost in flushing the clear profile does not arise. **1883** *Specif. Alnwick & Cornhill*

Rlwy. 3 The whole of the work is to be flushed up with mortar or cement.

2. *Weaving.* **a.** *trans.* To throw (a thread) on the surface over several threads without intersecting. **b.** *intr.* To float over several threads without intersection. (See quots.).

1878 A. BARLOW *Weaving* 175 The threads [in tissue-weaving]..float or flush upon the surface of the cloth rather than form a component part of its substance. *Ibid.* 176 Two methods..for flushing or throwing the thread to form the tissue figure.

Hence **ˈflushing** *vbl. sb.*, the action of the vb. (sense 1); also *concr.* (sense 2), see quot.

1853 *Archit. Publ. Soc. Dict., Flushing*..the operation of filling in the joints of brickwork or masonry with mortar. **1878** A. BARLOW *Weaving* Index, *Flushing*, threads not required in the body of the cloth, and left loose on the surface.

flush (flʌʃ), *v.*^{4} [? var. of FRUSH.] *trans.* and *intr.* (See quots.) Hence **ˈflushing** *vbl. sb.*

1739 LABELYE *Short Acc. Piers Westm. Bridge* 77 Chamfering the Joints hinders the flushing or breaking of the Edges of the Stones. **1853** *Archit. Publ. Soc. Dict.* s.v., Masons..say that a stone has flushed, where more or less of its arrised edge has broken away in consequence of that edge being more loaded than the rest of the bed.

flush (flʌʃ), *adv.* [f. FLUSH *a.*^{1}] †**a.** Directly, straight. **b.** *Pugilism.* With direct force or with full effect.

1700 FARQUHAR *Constant Couple* v. i, This girl is just come flush from reading the *Rival Queens*! **1812** *Sporting Mag.* XXXIX. 139 Thorn..hitting his antagonist flush on the head right and left. **1888** *Sporting Leader* 15 Dec., Wilson.. leading off, and getting the left flush on the face.

flushed (flʌʃt), *ppl. a.* [f. FLUSH *v.*^{2} + -ED^1.]

1. Suffused with red or ruddy colour.

1690 *Lond. Gaz.* No. 2576/4 A Maid-Servant..extremely red and flushed, round her Mouth. **1793** BEDDOES *Lett. to Darwin* 53 A medical friend..was much struck with the flushed appearance of my countenance. **1849** RUSKIN *Sev. Lamps* iv. §39. 129 Flushed and melting spaces of colour. **1882** MISS BRADDON *Mt. Royal* i, I knew what the flushed cheek..and the short cough meant.

2. Heated, excited.

1749 SMOLLETT *Regicide* III. viii, Their flush'd intemperance will yield Occasion undisturbed. **1893** *Critic* (Boston) 25 Mar. 184/1 The solitary caprice of a flushed fantasy.

flusher^1 (ˈflʌʃə(r)). [f. as prec. + -ER^1.] One who is employed to flush sewers.

1882 *Pall Mall G.* 12 June 1/2 Superintendent of flushers.

Hence **ˈflusherman**, a sewer-flusher.

1851 MAYHEW *Lond. Labour* I. 28 The policeman on duty there wears huge..flushermen's boots. *Ibid.* II. 151.

flusher^2 (ˈflʌʃə(r)). *dial.* Also **flasher**. [of uncertain origin; by some regarded as a corruption of FLESHER (cf. the synonym *butcher-bird*); by others referred to FLUSH *v.*^{2}, the name being supposed to refer to the red colour. Cf. also FLUSH *v.*^{1}] The Red-backed Shrike, *Lanius collurio*.

1674 RAY *Eng. Words* 83 The lesser Butcher-bird, called in Yorkshire, Flusher, *Lanius tertius*. **1885** SWAINSON *Prov. Names Brit. Birds* 48 Red-backed Shrike (*Lanius collurio*).. Flasher or Flusher (Cornwall).

†**ˈflush-flash**, *v. Obs. rare*$^{-1}$. [Cf. FLISH-FLASH.] *intr.* To flash repeatedly.

1583 STANYHURST *Aeneis* I. (Arb.) 20 Thee lightnings riflye doe flush flash.

flushing (ˈflʌʃɪŋ), *sb.* [f. *Flushing* (Du. *Vlissingen*) a port in Holland.] A kind of rough and thick woollen cloth, so called from the place where it was first manufactured.

1833 MARRYAT *P. Simple* x, Pea jackets..made of.. Flushing. **1879** *Unif. Reg.* in *Navy List* July (1882) 496/2 To be of flushing, with seven buttons..on each side.

attrib. **1832** DARWIN in *Life & Lett.* (1887) I. 242 A.. flushing jacket. **1837** MARRYAT *Dog-fiend* iii, Wrapped up in Flushing garments [he] looked..like a bear.

ˈflushing, *vbl. sb.* [f. FLUSH *v.*^{2} + -ING^1.]

1. The action of the verb FLUSH in various senses.

†**a.** A rushing or splashing (of water). *Obs.*

1573 TWYNNE *Æneid.* x. D d iv b, His monstrous saluage lims through froth, through fome with flushing launch.

b. The cleansing (of a sewer, etc.) by a rush of water.

1853 *Archit. Publ. Soc. Dict., Flushing.* **1884** *Times* (weekly ed.) 14 Nov. 12/2 The flushing of sewers is..a most important part, of the rapid removal of refuse.

c. Of a plant: The sending out of new shoots.

1810 SCOTT *Lady of Lake* III. xvi, Our flower was in flushing, When blighting was nearest. **1894** *Times* 6 Apr. 4/6 [Tea] plants exhibiting great difference in form and luxuriance of growth and flushing.

2. A sudden flowing (of blood to the face); a wave (of heat); hence, reddening, redness.

1589 R. HARVEY *Pl. Perc.* 22 Walke about, and coole this flushing in the face. **1602** SHAKS. *Ham.* I. ii. 155. **1677** *Lond. Gaz.* No. 1180/4 A tall slender Man, with a great flushing in his face. **1731** ARBUTHNOT *Aliments* i. §2. 9 The Signs of the Functions of the Stomach being deprav'd, are..a Flushing in the Countenance [etc.]. **1803** *Med. Jrnl.* X. 11 Its approaches are marked by head-ach..flushings of heat. **1875** H. C. WOOD *Therap.* (1879) 348 Local flushings caused by small doses of the poison.

3. A flush or wave (of emotion, success, etc.).

a **1679** T. GOODWIN *Wks.* V. II. 163 It was not properly a Passion, which is a subitaneous flushing. **1711** ADDISON *Spect.* No. 351 ⁋15 The transient Flushings of Guilt and Joy, which the Poet represents in our first Parents upon their eating the forbidden Fruit. **1775** S. J. PRATT *Liberal Opin.* (1783) IV. 78 This strange mortal..was so truly elevated by the present flushings of his prosperity, that he said and did [etc.].

4. *attrib.* and *Comb.*: as ***flushing cistern, gate, machine***; also **flushing-rim** (*House-plumbing*), 'a hollow rim pierced with holes surrounding a basin, through which water can be turned into the basin to flush it out' (*Cent. Dict.*); **flushing-wheel** = *flush-wheel*.

1894 *Daily News* 9 Oct. 5/2 To raise the capacity of *flushing cisterns from two to three gallons. **1856** *Proc. Inst. Civ. Eng.* XVI. 43 *Flushing Machines, for cleansing house drains and sewers. **1884** G. E. WARING in *Century Mag.* Dec. 263/1 The closet is supplied with water through an ordinary *flushing-rim. **1884** *Health Exhib. Catal.* 98/2 Automatic *Flushing Wheel for utilizing waste water from Baths.

flushing (ˈflʌʃɪŋ), *ppl. a.* [f. as prec. + -ING^2.]

1. That flows quickly; rushing.

1550 BALE *Image both Ch.* III. xix. C c iij b, It sounded..as it hadde bene the flushynge noyse of manye waters. **1596** SPENSER *F.Q.* IV. vi. 29 The swift recourse of flushing blood.

2. Exhibiting or producing a sudden glow.

1728–46 THOMSON *Spring* 95 Array'd In all the colours of the flushing year. **1793** SOUTHEY *Tri. Woman* 307 No flushing fear that cheek o'erspread. **1820** SHELLEY *Sensitive Pl.* II. 14 Her tremulous breath and her flushing face.

Flushinger (ˈflʌʃɪŋə(r)). [f. *Flushing* (name of a Dutch port) + -ER^1.] A Flushing vessel or sailor.

1689 *Lond. Gaz.* No. 2553/2 The English Vessel..was the next day retaken by a Flushinger. **1865** *Athenæum* No. 1967. 43/1 Boarded by the Flushingers.

ˈFlushingize, *v. nonce-wd.* [f. as prec. + -IZE.] *trans.* To make like an inhabitant of Flushing.

1602 J. DAVIES *Mirum in modum* Wks. (Grosart) 10/2 Since our English (ah) were Flusheniz'd, Against good manners, and good men they kicke, As Beasts they were.

ˈflushness. [f. FLUSH *a.*^{1}] The quality of condition of being flush in various senses.

1661 GAUDEN *Life Hooker* 37 Those..whose interest it is, like Hernshaws, to hide the meagerness of their bodies, by the flushness of their feathers. **1868** SEYD *Bullion* 52 An over-issue of Paper Money in a country may apparently create a momentary flushness. **1878** SIR G. G. SCOTT *Lect. Archit.* I. 279 Windows in which the glass was flush with the exterior, and all the splay put inside..This excessive flushness is less frequent as the style advances.

flushy (ˈflʌʃɪ), *a.* [f. FLUSH *a.*^{1}, *sb.* or *v.* + -Y^1.] Somewhat flushed, or inclined to flush; reddish.

1706 in *14th Rep. Hist. MSS. Comm.* III. 28 Aug., A middle-sized man, of a flushy complexion. **1850** BROWNING *Christmas Eve* 177 Another rainbow rose—a mightier, Fainter, flushier, and flightier. **1876** *Mid. Yorksh. Gloss.*, *Flushy* is commonly applied to any red colour.

flusker (ˈflʌskə(r)), *v. Obs.* exc. *dial.* [freq. of *flusk* 'to fly at, as two cocks' ('Tim Bobbin' *Lanc. Dial.*), 'to startle a bird out of a bush' (*Almondbury Gloss.*, E.D.S.). Cf. FLUSH *v.*^{1}, FLASKER *v.*]

1. a. *intr.* To flutter or fly irregularly.

1660–1794 [see FLUSKERING *vbl. sb.* and *ppl. a.*]. **1820** CLARE *Rural Life* (ed. 3) 150 A blackbird, or thrush, That, started from sleep, flusker'd out of the bush. **1821** —— *Vill. Minstr.* I. 94 The crowing pheasant..fluskers up. **1877** LEIGH *Chesh. Gloss.*, *Flusker*..to fly irregularly, as nestlings taking their first purposeless flight.

2. *trans.* To fluster, confuse. Only in *pass.*

1841 HARTSHORNE *Salop. Antiq.* 429 'Meetily flusker'd'. **1854** BAKER *Northamptonsh. Gloss.* I. 248, 'I was so fluskered, I could not tell what to do'.

Hence **ˈfluskering** *vbl. sb.* and *ppl. a.*

1660 H. MORE *Myst. Godl.* VI. vi. 228 The offers and fluskerings, as I may so say, of the Faculties of the Soul of man. **1668** —— *Div. Dial.* II. 48 What strange..fluskering conceits flie up into the youthful imagination of Hylobares. **1794** GISBORNE *Walks Forest* (1796) 69 Then with fluskering wings Broke forth. **1821** CLARE *Vill. Minstr.* I. 72 The fluskering pheasant took to wing.

†**fluss.** *Obs. rare.* [a. Ger. *flusz*, f. root of *fliezen* to flow, FLEET.] = FLUX *sb.* 11.

1683 PETTUS *Fleta Min.* I. 199 Fluss is made by taking Litharge, Glass-gall, and melted Salt..and filed Iron, and ..graind Lead. *Ibid.* II. s.v., *Flus*..sometimes..is called Lead-Glass, which being put into dissolvible metal, it gives expedition to their Dissolutions.

fluss, obs. (Sc.) f. FLUSH *sb.*^{2}.

†**fluste.** *Obs. rare.*

1570 LEVINS *Manip.* 194 A Fluste, *flustrum*.

fluster (ˈflʌstə(r)), *sb.* [see next vb.]

1. †**a.** Excitement proceeding from intoxication (*obs.*). **b.** A confused or agitated state of mind; a flurry, flutter.

1710 *Tatler* No. 252 ⁋4 When Caska adds to his natural Impudence the Fluster of a Bottle. **1728** VANBR. & CIB. *Prov. Husb.* III. i, He has been in such a Fluster here. **1848** LOWELL *Biglow P.* Poems 1890 II. 85 In the Tower Victory sets, all of a fluster. **1863** MRS. C. CLARKE *Shaks. Char.* viii. 209 All this fluster may have arisen from a horror of the steward.

†**2.** ? Pomp, splendour. Cf. FLUSTER *v.* 3 c, d. *Obs.*

1676 MARVELL *Mr. Smirke* Wks. (Grosart) IV. 12 His wit consisting wholly in his dresse, he would..have it all about him; as to the end that being huff'd up in all his ecclesiastical fluster, he might appear more formidable. *a* **1716** SOUTH *Serm.* (1737) VI. vi. 235 Let no present fluster of fortune.. transport the man himself with confidence.

fluster (ˈflʌstə(r)), *v.* Also ? 5 **flostre**, 9 *dial.* **flowster.** [This and the related sb. closely resemble in sense the mod.Icel. *flaustr* hurry, bustle, *flaustra* to bustle. Cf. BLUSTER *v.*]

†**1.** ? *trans.* ? To excite, stimulate. *Obs.*

1422 [see FLUSTERING *vbl. sb.*].

2. *trans.* To flush or excite with drink, make half-tipsy.

1604 SHAKS. *Oth.* II. iii. 60 Three else of Cyprus..Haue I to night fluster'd with flowing Cups. **1731** FIELDING *Lett. Writers* II. v, My nephew..hath taken me to the Tavern, and..almost flustered me. **1851** THACKERAY *Eng. Hum.* iii. (1876) 233 His head is flustered with burgundy.

3. *intr.* To be excited or eager; to move with agitation or confusion; to bustle.

1613 F. ROBARTS *Rev. Gospel* 136 Who will not fluster to be one? **1636** *Div. Trag. lately Acted* 27 A blacke ball..flew into the bell free..then it flustered about the Church. **1808** JAMIESON, *Fluster*, to be in a state of bustle. **1865** G. MEREDITH *R. Fleming* xliii. (1890) 369 He broke out upon Mrs. Sumfit..which caused her to fluster guiltily. **1879** *Cornh. Mag.* June 699 They flustered out, abashed like poultry who have been played upon with garden hose. **1893** R. KIPLING *Many Invent.* 16 The Dutch gunboat came flustering up.

†**b.** Of seed: To shoot up quickly; to push.

1650 T. BAYLY *Herba Parietis* 123 Both were exceeding glad to see the corne so fluster upon the ground that was sown by their hands.

c. To bluster, swagger. **d.** *dial.* See quot.

1661 [see FLUSTERING *ppl. a.*]. **1876** *Whitby Gloss.*, *Flowster* or *fluster*, to flourish or flutter, in showy colours.

4. *trans.* To flurry, confuse.

1724 R. FALCONER *Voy.* (1769) 267 My scattered Thoughts, that were flustered upon that Occasion. **1760** A. MURPHY *Way to Keep Him* I. ii, Madam, If I was as you, I would not fluster myself about it. **1816** SCOTT *Antiq.* xxxiv, The aged housekeeper was no less flustered and hurried in obeying the numerous..commands of her mistress. **1870** SPURGEON *Treas. Dav.* Ps. lii. 9 Men must not too much fluster us.

Hence **ˈflustering** *vbl. sb.* and *ppl. a.* Also **ˈflusterment**, the state of being flustered.

1422 tr. *Secreta Secret., Priv. Priv.* (E.E.T.S.) 129 The flostyrynge of the losengers that the[e] Plesyn, thou sholdyst gretly drede. **1661–98** SOUTH *Serm.* III. 263 The Flustring Vain-glorious Greeks. **1804** BEWICK *Brit. Birds* II. 135 When it is very closely pursued, and compelled to rise, it [the coot] does this with much flustering and apparent difficulty. **1895** *Expositor* Apr. 296 Palpitations, flusterments, hesitancies seem to turn our message into farce.

†**ˈfluster-ˌbluster.** *nonce-wd.* [comic reduplication of BLUSTER.] A 'blustering' wind. So **fluster-blusterer**, a blusterer.

1696 *Monthly Mercury* VII. 85 The French..are.. seeking an early Atonement of the French Fluster Blusterer. **1708** MOTTEUX *Rabelais* V. vi, Unless you are resolv'd to encounter..Æolus and his Flusterblusters.

flustered (ˈflʌstəd), *ppl. a.* [f. FLUSTER *v.*]

1. Half-drunk, fuddled.

1615 SIR E. HOBY *Curry-combe* i. 11 Yet as flustred as hee was..hee could text her with *Labia Sacerdotis custodiunt sapientiam*. **1710** STEELE *Tatler* No. 3 ⁋1 A Young Nobleman who came flustered into the Box last Night. **1824** LAMB *Elia* Ser. II. *Capt. Jackson*, You got flustered without knowing whence; tipsy upon words. **1824** SCOTT *Redgauntlet* xiii, Becoming early what *bon vivants* term flustered. **1889** BARRÈRE & LELAND *Slang*, *Flustered* (common) intoxicated.

2. Confused, disconcerted, flurried.

1743 FIELDING *J. Wild* II. v, Heartfree..was..too much flustered to examine the woman with sufficient art. **1797** MRS. RADCLIFFE *Italian* xxx. (1824) 699 My lord..seemed very much flustered. **1863** MRS. C. CLARKE *Shaks. Char.* xv. 377 A vivid picture of a flustered man.

3. *dial.* (See quot.)

1876 *Whitby Gloss.*, *Fluster'd*, reddened or irritated..said of the feet.

flusterer (ˈflʌstərə(r)). *U.S.* [f. FLUSTER *v.* + -ER^1 (see quot. 1808).] The common American coot, *Fulica americana*.

1709 LAWSON *Carolina* 149 Black Flusterers..Some call these the great bald Coot. **1808–14** A. WILSON *Amer. Orinth.* IX. 62 *note*, In Carolina they are called flusterers from the noise they make in flying over the surface of the water.

flustery (ˈflʌstərɪ) *a.* [f. FLUSTER *sb.* or *v.* + -Y^1. Cf. BLUSTERY.] Full of fluster; confused.

1865 CARLYLE *Fredk. Gt.* (1873) V. XIV. iv. 188 A flustery singed condition.

flustra (ˈflʌstrə). *Pl.* **flustræ, -as.** [a. mod.L. *flustra.*] The typical genus of polyzoa or bryozoa of the family *Flustridæ*; the sea-mat.

The name was first used by Linnæus (*Fauna Suec.* ed. 2. 1761), who says that he has substituted it for the older name

Eschara, because the latter was 'homonymous with the name of a disease'; but he does not give the etymology.

1825 Hamilton *Handbk. Terms, Flustra*, the sea-mat. **1855** Kingsley *Glaucus* (1878) 73 Here are Flustræ, or sea-mats. **1860** Maury *Phys. Geog. Sea* xiii. §560 The leaf-like flustras and escharas.

flustrate ('flʌstreɪt). *v. vulgar* or *jocular*. Also **flusterate**. [f. FLUSTER *v.* + -ATE[3].] = FLUSTER *v.*[2] and [4].

1712 Steele *Spect.* No. 493 ¶4 We were coming down Essex Street one Night a little flustrated. **1797** Mrs. A. M. Bennett *Beggar Girl* (1813) I. 106 She was, she confessed, quite flusterated at the idea. **1876** Mrs. Oliphant *Curate in Charge* (ed. 5) II. iv. 100 The head of the college was slightly flustrated, if such a vulgar word can be used of such a sublime person.

flustration (flʌ'streɪʃən). *vulgar* or *jocular*. Also **flusteration**. [f. FLUSTER *v.* + -ATION.] The condition of being flustered; 'fluster', agitation.

1748 Richardson *Clarissa* (1811) II. xxxiii. 204 How soon these fine young ladies will be put into flusterations. **1812** G. Colman *Br. Grins, Two Parsons* lxxii, A kind of shocking, pleasing, queer flustration. **1868** Yates *Rock Ahead* I. i, Miles came out..in a state of 'flustration'.

†'**flutal**, *a. Obs. rare.* [f. FLUTE *sb.*[1] + -AL[1].] Pertaining to, or of the nature of, a flute.

1794 G. Adams *Nat. & Exp. Philos.* I. vi. 239 The organs of the human voice are partly flutal, and partly chordal.

flute (flu:t), *sb.*[1] Forms: 4–5 flowte, 5 flo(y)te, 6–7 fluit(e, 6– flute. [ME. a. OF. *fleüte, flaüte, flahute* (also written *flahuste*), mod.F. *flûte* = Pr. *flauta* fem., of unknown origin; the Sp. *flauta*, It. *flauto* are prob. adopted from Fr. or Pr. From Fr. are MHG. *floite* (mod.Ger. *flöte*), Da. *fluit* (whence possibly the ME. forms).

Diez's suggestion, that the Rom. *flauta, flauto* was f. the vb. *flautare*, and that this was a metathesis of L. *flātuāre*, is phonologically impossible. Ascoli's proposal to refer the vb. to a L. type **flāvitāre* is also inadmissable.]

1. a. A musical wind instrument, consisting of a hollow cylinder or pipe, with holes along its length, stopped by the fingers, or by keys which are opened by the fingers.

The flute of the ancients, whether single or double, was blown through a mouthpiece at the end. About the middle of the 18th cent. this was entirely superseded by the ***transverse*** or ***German flute***, which is blown through an orifice at the side near the upper end.

c **1384** Chaucer *H. Fame* III. 133 And many flowte and liltyng horne. **1483** Caxton *Gold. Leg.* 95/1 The mayde remembred the wordes and threwe doun her pype or floyte. **1555** Eden *Decades* 27 They harde the noyse of the flutes, shalmes, and drummes. **1625** Purchas *Pilgrims* IV. 1533 Indians met vs on the way, playing vpon Flutes; which is a token that they come in peace. **1718** Prior *Pleasure* 77 The trumpet's sound Provok'd the Dorian flute. **1756** T. Amory *Buncle* (1825) I. 5 My relaxation after study was my german-flute. *a* **1822** Shelley *Unf. Drama* 180, I nursed the plant, and on the double flute Played to it..Soft melodies. **1853** Kingsley *Hypatia* xxii, A single flute within the curtain began to send forth luscious strains. **1879** Stainer *Music of Bible* 80 A quartet was played by four flutes, treble, alto, tenor, and bass.

†**b.** phr. *to* (*go and*) ***blow one's flute***: to 'whistle' for something. *Obs.*

a **1529** Skelton *Vox Populi* vii. 9 When thei have any sute, Thei maye goo blowe theire flute.

c. A flute-player.

1542 *Privy Purse Exps. P'cess Mary* (1831) 104 The Welshe mynstrels iijs. ixd. The Flutes xs. **1630** J. Taylor (Water P.) *Trav. Twelvepence* Wks. I. 71/1 To Church-wardens, Cryers, To Fluits, Horse coursers, Sellers, and to Buyers. **1765** *Meretriciad* 48 Then, solus, hops, a dull Orchestran flute. **1837** Dickens *Sk. Boz, Tales* ix, Two flutes and a violoncello had pleaded severe colds.

2. An organ-stop having a flute-like tone. Also ***flute-stop*** (see 7).

There are various kinds of flute-stops known by special designations, as the ***clear, harmonic, oboe, snake flute***.

1613 *Organ Specif. Worcester Cathedral*, 1 flute of wood. **1776** Sir J. Hawkins *Hist. Musick* IV. I. x. 147 The simple stops are the..Flute..and some others. **1855** Hopkins *Organ* xxii. 118 As a Pedal stop, the Flute has not yet been much used in this country.

3. Applied to objects resembling a flute in shape.

a. A tall, slender wine-glass, used especially for sparkling wines. Called also ***flute-glass***.

1649 Lovelace *Lucasta* 99 Elles of Beere, Flutes of Canary, That well did washe downe pasties-mary. **1924** *Glasgow Herald* 6 Oct. 8 'Sect', or German champagne is to be drunk only from French-fashioned flutes or tall glasses. **1959** *House & Garden* Dec./Jan. 36/3 Deep wine goblets or tall champagne flutes. **1964** *Observer* 14 June 33/5 A champagne 'flute', tall enough for a quarter or a fifth of a bottle.

b. A shuttle used in tapestry-weaving.

1727–41 Chambers *Cycl.* s.v. *Tapestry*, The flute does the office of the weaver's shuttle.

c. *Cookery*, etc. (See quots.) Perh. only Fr.

1855 Clarke *Dict., Flute*..gaufer. **1858** Simmonds *Dict. Trade, Flute*..a long thin French roll eaten at breakfast.

4. *Arch.* A channel or furrow in a pillar, resembling the half of a flute split longitudinally, with the concave side outwards.

1660 Bloome *Archit.* A/1 *Stria*, the flat lying between the Flutes. **1728** R. Morris *Ess. Anc. Archit.* 81 The Column is divided into twenty-four Flutes, and..each Side contains three Flutes. **1879** Sir G. G. Scott *Lect. Archit.* II. 126 Vast round columns..having their shafts decorated with spiral, zig-zag, intersecting, and vertical flutes.

5. A similar groove or channel in any material. In *Botany*: see quot. 1727–41.

1727–41 Chambers *Cycl., Flutes* or *Flutings* are also used in botany, to denote the stems and fruits of certain plants, which have furrows analogous to those of columns. **1776** Withering *Brit. Plants* (1796) III. 98 The style..has 5 grooves or flutes to receive the 5 seeds with their appendages. **1842** Bischoff *Woollen Manuf.* II. 393 These, instead of being wound round a roller, fall into the flutes of a fluted cylinder. **1855** Ogilvie Suppl., *Flute*, a channel in the muslin of a lady's ruffle, similar to that in a column or pillar. **1865** Mrs. Palliser *Lace* xvi. 208 A cap of fine linen plaited in small flutes. **1878** Garnett in *Encycl. Brit.* VIII. 728 When it lies within the mean, or spheroidal, surface so as to form a 'flute', less surface is exposed by it. **1935** *Jrnl. Geol.* XLIII. 729 Swiftly moving sand or silt-laden water currents sometimes abrade grooves, elongated in the direction of flow, in stream boulders and in the bedrock of the stream channel... In this article the grooves are termed 'flutes', and the process of their formation is called 'stream fluting'. **1963** D. W. & E. E. Humphries tr. *Termier's Erosion & Sedimentation* 408 The *lapies* of karst scenery where small ridges or flutes of limestone are dissected and isolated by a surficial flow of water.

6. *slang.* **a.** (See quot. 1700.) **b.** A pistol.

a **1700** B. E. *Dict. Cant. Crew, Flute*, the Recorder of London, or of any other Town. **1842** S. Lover *Handy Andy* iii, 'I'll give it him in the pistol-arm or so'. 'Very well, Ned. Where are the flutes?'

7. *attrib.* and *Comb.*, as ***flute-girl, -maker, -music, -note; flute-playing*** vbl. sb.; ***flute-like*** adj. Also **flute-bird** (*Australia*), the piping crow (*Gymnorhina tibicen*); **flute-bit** (see quot.); **flute-glass**, see 3 above; **flute-mouth**, a fish of the family *Fistulariidæ*; **flute-organ** (see quot. 1828); **flute-player**, (*a*) one who plays the flute; (*b*) a South American wren of the genus *Cyphorinus*; **flute-stop** = sense 2 above; **flute-tool** (cf. *flute-bit*); **flute-work** (see quot. 1879).

1862 Kendall *Poems* 53 The *flute-bird's mellow tone. **1874** Knight *Dict. Mech.* I. 893/2 **Flute-bit*, a wood-boring tool..used in boring..hard woods. **1853** Hickie tr. *Aristoph.* (1887) I. 22 Chaplets, sprats, *flute-girls and black eyes. **1667** Dryden *Sir M. Mar-all* v. i, Bring two *Flute-glasses and some Stools. **1729** Savage *Wanderer* v, The bullfinch whistles soft his *flute-like notes. **1849** Marryat *Valerie* xi, Some *flute-music. **1887** *Encycl. Brit.* XXII. 548 *Flute Mouths (*Fistulariidæ*). **1833** Tennyson *Blackbird* 18 Now thy *flute-notes are changed to coarse. **1828** Busby *Music. Man.*, **Flute Organ*, a little barrel-organ, the compass and tone of the notes of which render it imitative of the German flute. **1633** Prynne *Histrio-Mastix* I. vii. iii. 652 A *flute-player, a fidler, a harper. **1875** Longf. *Pandora* vi, Hear how sweetly overhead the feathered flute-players pipe their songs of love. **1831** Macaulay in *Life & Lett.* (1880) I. 211 We had *flute-playing by the first flute-player in England. **1819** Rees *Cycl.*, **Flute-stop on an Organ*. **1887** *Pall Mall G.* 1 July 5/2 Chisels, modelling tools, files, *flute tools [etc.]. **1879** Hopkins in Grove *Dict. Mus.* I. 538 **Flute-work*, under this head are grouped all the flue-stops of whatever kind, shape, or tone, that are not classed as Principal-work, or Gedact-work.

flute (flu:t), *sb.*[2] *Naut.* Also 6 fluite, 7 fluyt(e. [a. Fr. *flûte*, a. Du. *fluit* (whence the Eng. forms *fluyt(e, fluit)*, perh. a transferred use of *fluit* = prec.]

1. (See quots.)

1567 Maplet *Gr. Forest* 91 The best..are those that be called Flutæ, in Greke Plootai, good saylers or fluites. **1698** Froger *Voy.* 107 A Portuguese Flute, that carried Negros to All-Saints Bay. **1727–41** Chambers *Cycl., Flute* or *Fluyt*, a kind of long vessel, with flat ribs or floor timbers; round behind, and swelled in the middle. **1867** Smyth *Sailor's Word-bk., Flute* or *Fluyt*, a pink-rigged fly-boat, the after-part of which is round-ribbed.

2. A vessel of war, carying only part of her armament, to serve as a transport.

1666 *Lond. Gaz.* No. 77/2 Two Men of War..with three Flutes of 18 or 20 Guns. **1799** Sir Sid. Smith 6 Feb. in Nicolas *Nelson's Disp.* III. 281 *note*, Captain Hood's list reported them to be eight in addition to two Flutes. **1876** J. Grant *Hist. India* I. xlvi. 231/2 Twenty-six sail, including eleven line-of-battle ships..six flutes and transports.

b. Hence ***armed en flute*** (Fr. *armé en flûte*) said of such a vessel.

1799 *Naval Chron.* I. 258 The Sceptre, 64 guns, armed *en flute*. **1832** Marryat *N. Forster* xxxvi.

flute (flu:t), *v.* [f. FLUTE *sb.*[1], or ad. OF. *fleüter*, mod.F. *flûter*.]

1. a. *intr.* To play upon a flute or pipe.

c **1386** Chaucer *Prol.* 91 Syngynge he was or flowtynge al the day. **1485** Caxton *Paris & V.* 89 Thys is he that so swetely songe and floyted. **1775** Sheridan *Duenna* I. i, Fiddling, fluting, rhyming, ranting. **1842** Tennyson *To E.L. on Trav.* vi, To him who sat upon the rocks, And fluted to the morning sea. **1875** Miss Braddon *Strange World* i, Corydon fluting sweetly on his tuneful pipe.

quasi-*trans.* **1867** M. Arnold *Poems, Thyrsis* ix, And flute his friend, like Orpheus from the dead.

b. To whistle or sing in flute-like tones.

1800 Hurdis *Fav. Village* 206 And ouzle fluting with melodious pipe. **1848** Kingsley *Saint's Trag.* IV. iv, Fluting like woodlarks, tender and low. **1859** G. Meredith *R. Feverel* xiv, The blackbird fluted, calling to her with thrice mellow note.

2. *trans.* To play (an air, etc.) on a flute; to sing in flute-like notes.

1842 Tennyson *Morte D'Arth.* 269 Some..swan..fluting a wild carol ere her death. **1847** —— *Princess* IV. 111 Men that lute and flute fantastic tenderness. **1847** Emerson *Poems, May Day* 59 The redwing flutes his o-ka-lee.

3. a. To form flutes (FLUTE *sb.*[1] 4, 5) in; to furnish with flutings; to arrange a dress, etc. in flutes.

1578 Lyte *Dodoens* IV. xiv. 468 Bockwheate hath round stalkes chanellured and fluted (or forowed and crested). **1665** Hooke *Microgr.* 148 The whole outward Superficies..is curiously adorned or fluted with little channels. **1723** Chambers tr. *Le Clerc's Treat. Archit.* I. 79 It had been better..to have fluted the upper part. **1853** Lindley *Veg. Kingd.* 601 The trunk appears as if fluted. **1862** M. T. Morrall *Hist. Needle Making* 37 He also took out a patent for grooving or fluting the sides of sail needles. **1862** Tyndall *Mountaineer.* ii. 12 Planing and fluting and scoring the rocks. **1865** Dickens *Mut. Fr.* II. x, A hatband of wholesale capacity—which was fluted behind.

b. *intr.* To hang or jut *out* in flutings.

1896 *Sun* 11 Dec. 1/7 Arranged with the usual side-pieces, which flute out gracefully to the lower edge. **1908** M. & J. Findlater *Crossriggs* xxxi, Her skirts fluted out about her like the ruffled petals of a flower.

‖**flûte-à-bec** (flytabɛk). [Fr., lit. 'flute with beak'.] An old form of flute, also called English flute, having a mouthpiece with a fipple; now, a recorder.

1797 *Encycl. Brit.* VII. 310/1 This [*sc.* the flute] is a very ancient instrument. It was at first called the flute *à bec*. **1825** [see FLAUTO]. **1876** Stainer & Barrett *Dict. Mus. Terms* 171 The *flûte à bec* was used so commonly in England that it was called on the continent *flûte d'Angleterre*. **1879** *Encycl. Brit.* IX. 351/1 The flageolet is a smaller variety of the old *flute-à-bec*. **1930** *Daily Express* 8 Sept. 6/3 The half-forgotten flute-a-becs, bassethorns..and oboes d'amore. **1959** *Collins' Music Encycl.* 250/1 *Flûte à bec, flûte douce*, recorder. **1959** A. Rowland-Jones *Recorder Technique* iii. 30 The wind-way of a recorder is formed by the insertion of an incised plug..into the blown end of the tube, which is generally made beak-shaped (whence 'Flûte à bec') to fit between the lips.

fluted ('flu:tɪd), *ppl. a.* [f. FLUTE *sb.*[1] and *v.* + -ED.]

1. Having, furnished, or ornamented with flutes, channels, or grooves. ***fluted-scale*** (*Entomol.*) = *cushion-scale*. ***fluted spectrum***, one in which the spectrum lines appear to be grouped in flutes.

1611 Cotgr., *Canelé*, channelled, fluted, furrowed, straked. **1717** Berkeley *Tour in Italy* Wks. 1871 IV. 531 Four noble fluted pillars. **1801** Southey *Thalaba* VI. xx, And fluted cypresses rear'd up Their living obelisks. **1835** Ure *Philos. Manuf.* 121 United on one fluted portion of the rollers. **1881** N. Lockyer in *Nature* No. 614. 318 Iodine vapour..gives us this fluted spectrum. **1882** Caulfeild & Saward *Dict. Needlework, Fluted Ruche*..is composed of single Box-pleats stitched to a certain depth inwards so as to leave the edges of the pleats loose.

2. *Music.* (See quot. 1828.)

1787 Beckford *Italy* II. 240 All the nauseous sweetness of a fluted falsetto. **1828** Busby *Music. Man.* s.v., When the upper notes of a soprano voice are of a thin and flute-like tone, they are said to be Fluted. **1879** E. Arnold *Lt. Asia* VI. xxvi, The koil's fluted song, the bulbul's hymn.

‖**flûte d'amour** (flyt damu:r). [Fr., lit. 'flute of love'.] An old form of flute with a pitch a third below that of the flute in D.

1876 Stainer & Barrett *Dict. Mus. Terms* 173/2 *Flûte d'amour*, a low-toned flute, an A flute, sounding a minor third below the notes actually written. It is now obsolete. **1961** J. A. Macgillivray in A. Baines *Mus. Instruments* x. 249 The..*flûte d'amour* in A seems to have been used mainly for variety in flute recitals.

‖**flute-douce** (flytdus). Also 7 *erron* -doux. [Fr. *flûte douce* lit. 'sweet flute'.]

†**1.** The highest-pitched variety of the old flute with a mouthpiece.

1676 Etheredge *Man of Mode* II. i, Nothing But Flute doux, and French Hoboys. **1679** Evelyn *Diary* 20 Nov., There was also a flute douce, now in much request for accompanying the voice. **1747** Lady M. W. Montagu *Let. to C'tess Bute* 24 July, They are all violins, lutes, mandolins, and flutes doux.

2. An organ-stop so named.

1876 Stainer & Barrett *Dict. Mus. Terms*.

†'**flutenist.** *Obs.* [f. FLUTE *sb.*[1]; cf. Ger. *flötenist*, Eng. *lutenist*.] A flute-player, a flutist.

1647 R. Stapylton *Juvenal* III. 42 These sometimes Flutenistes, Beare office now. **1687** tr. *Heliodorus* I. 24 You have heard of Arsinoe, the Flutenist. **1718** *Free-thinker* No. 37 ¶6 An excellent Flutenist.

fluter ('flu:tə(r)). [f. FLUTE *v.* + -ER[1]. Cf. OF. *fleuteur*.]

1. One who plays on the flute; a flute-player. Now *rare*; replaced by FLUTIST or FLAUTIST.

c **1400** *Rom. Rose* 763 These floutours, Minstrales and eek Iogelours. **1570** Levins *Manip.* 73 A Fluter, *aulœdus*. **1666** Pepys *Diary* 21 June, I saw..a picture of a fluter playing on his flute. **1796** W. Taylor in *Monthly Rev.* XXI. 499 Not a single fluter was to be found in the temple. **1856** Masson *Ess., Th. of Poetry* 440 You, fluter, with your silver flute!

2. One who makes flutings or grooves.

1858 Simmonds *Dict. Trade, Fluter*, one who grooves or channels metals;..a person who goffers or plaits.

Hence †'**fluteress** a female flute-player.

1611 Cotgr., *Fleuteuse*, a fluteresse; a woman that playes on a flute.

flutey, var. FLUTY *a.*

flutina (fluːˈtiːnə). [f. FLUTE *sb.*[1] with fem. ending -INA: cf. CONCERTINA *sb.*] A kind of accordion resembling the concertina.

1859 SALA *Gas-light & D.* xxiv. 274 Accordions, concertinas, and flutinas.

fluting (ˈfluːtɪŋ), *vbl. sb.* [f. FLUTE *v.* + -ING[1].] The action of the vb. FLUTE in various senses.

1. The action of playing on the flute or singing in flute-like tones; an instance of this.

1481 CAXTON *Reynard* (Arb.) 110 Thou losest thy flateryng and swete floytyng. **1858** CARLYLE *Fredk. Gt.* II. vi. vii. 108 Fritz's love of music, expecially of fluting. **1874** L. MORRIS *Poems, To a Lost Love* i, The earliest flutings of the lark. **1882** GOSSE in *Grosart's Spenser* III. p. xxxix, The delicious flutings of Herrick.

2. The action of making flutes in columns, or in frills, ruffles, etc.; ornamentation with flutes; the result of this action, fluted work. Also *attrib.* in names of appliances for fluting, as ***fluting-cylinder, -iron, -lathe, -machine, -plane,*** etc.

1728 R. MORRIS *Ess. Anc. Archit.* 81, I must just explain ..the foregoing Plate concerning Fluting or Grooving. **1860** TYNDALL *Glac.* I. xix. 99 Granite, on which the flutings and groovings are magnificently preserved. **1864** WEBSTER, *Fluting-plane* (*Carp.*), a plane with curved face, used in grooving flutes. **1878** BELL *Gegenbaur's Comp. Anat.* 104 Provided with various sculpturings, flutings, spines, ridges, and so on. **1879** SIR G. G. SCOTT *Lect. Archit.* I. 87 Singular ornamentation..by means of fluting.

3. = FLUTE *sb.*[1] 4, 5. Also *collect.*

1611 COTGR., *Caneleure*, a fluting, channelling, straking, furrowing. **1613–1639** I. JONES in Leoni *Palladio's Archit.* (1742) II. 50 The fluting in front are deep half Circles. **1723** CHAMBERS tr. *Le Clerc's Treat. Archit.* I. 31 The Flutings of this Column ought not to exceed twenty. **1725** BRADLEY *Fam. Dict.*, s.v. *Mushroom*, A..Cap or Head, garnished sometimes underneath with several Flutings. **1823** P. NICHOLSON *Pract. Build.* 308 Sometimes flutings of the semi-ellipsis shape, with fillets, were adopted. **1851** RICHARDSON *Geol.* (1855) 445 The trees..now appear completely decorticated, and present various flutings. **1869** BOUTELL *Arms & Arm.* v. 76 The corslet and cuirass.. sometimes show no other decoration than the bold flutings at their base. **1872** C. KING *Mountain. Sierra Nev.* iii. 70 Every fluting of the great valley was in itself a considerable cañon. **1880** BARING-GOULD *Mehalah* II. vi. 105 She ran her fingers through the flutings of her frills.

fluting (ˈfluːtɪŋ), *ppl. a.* [f. as prec. + -ING[2].] That flutes, in senses of the vb.

1794 D'ISRAELI *Cur. Lit.* (1848) I. 85 The genius which thus could form a clock in time formed a fluting automaton. **1852** SEIDEL *Organ* 78 The tone of the organ is at one time full and round, at another..fluting and whispering.

flutist (ˈfluːtɪst). [f. FLUTE *sb.*[1] + -IST. Cf. Fr. *flûtiste.*] A player on the flute.

1603 FLORIO *Montaigne* I. xxxix. 125 When some commended him to be an excellent Flutist. **1775** J. COLLIER *Musical Trav.* 45 That great flutist and warrior the King of Prussia. **1862** MERIVALE *Rom. Emp.* (1865) VII. lv. 37 He drove in pomp through the city..with the flutist Diodorus by his side.

flut(t)e, obs. form of FLIT *v.*

flutter (ˈflʌtə(r)), *sb.* [f. next vb.]

1. a. A fluttering; the action or condition of fluttering (whether in a trans. or intr. sense).

1641 MILTON *Animadv.* 19 Lest their various and jangling opinions put their leavs into a flutter. **1711** ADDISON *Spect.* No. 102 ¶10 There is an infinite Variety of Motions to be made use of in the flutter of a Fan. **1794** MRS. RADCLIFFE *Myst. Udolpho* iii, The drowsy murmur of the breeze..and its light flutter as it blew freshly into the carriage. **1848** DICKENS *Dombey* (C.D. ed.) v. 32 The flutter of her beating heart. **1875** MCLAREN *Serm.* Ser. II. viii. 138 Nor any least flutter of trembling love towards Him.

b. A 'run', a 'burst'. *colloq.*

1857 C. KEENE *Let.* in G. S. Layard *Life* iii. (1892) 62, I had a brief flutter down to the coast of Devon. **1883** E. PENNELL-ELMHIRST *Cream Leicestersh.* 376 The same fox.. had given us a first flutter across the country.

c. *Med.* Abnormal contractions of a muscular organ that are very rapid but regular.

1910 *Heart* II. 177 (*heading*) Auricular flutter & fibrillation. *Ibid.* 182 We cannot say how long the rapid auricular flutter lasted at that time. **1920** T. LEWIS *Mechanism & Graph. Repres. of Heart Beat* xxii. 263 We may divide the simple paroxysm from the attack of flutter arbitrarily by defining the latter as a new rhythm whose rate surpasses 200 and may reach 350 per minute. **1936** *Jrnl. Amer. Med. Assoc.* 21 Mar. 992/1 (*heading*) Diaphragmatic flutter with symptoms of angina pectoris. **1957** *Encycl. Brit.* XI. 311/2 Auricular flutter and auricular fibrillation are close cousins. **1966** DUNLOP & ALSTEAD *Textbk. Med. Treatm.* (ed. 10) 625 If flutter recurs, a second course of digitalis may succeed in establishing normal rhythm. **1969** CROFTON & DOUGLAS *Respiratory Dis.* xxxvi. 637/1 The rapid contraction of the diaphragm (up to 100/min or more) known as diaphragmatic tic may be a feature of encephalitis but more commonly is a hysterical phenomenon... When the rate is faster the term diaphragmatic flutter is used.

d. Abnormal oscillation of a wing or other part of an aircraft.

1911 H. T. WRIGHT in Grahame-White & Harper *Aeroplane* 258 Another experiment was tried recently to illustrate 'Propeller flutter'. **1916** H. BARBER *Aeroplane Speaks* 123 Propeller 'flutter' or vibration, may be due to faulty pitch angle, balance, camber, or surface area. **1927** *Aeronaut. Research Committee Rep. & Mem.* 1041 (1925) 1 Since its commencement the investigation of flutter and vibration in aeroplanes has proved to be a much more complex problem than was at first realised. **1930** *Flight* 3 Jan. 28/1 It is certain that wing flutter would have occurred. **1933** *Jrnl. R. Aeronaut. Soc.* XXXVII. 497 It speaks volumes for the reliability and safety of the wooden airscrew that it is not called upon to undergo any endurance test, and only very occasionally a spinning tower test when flutter is suspected. **1937** *Ibid.* XLI. 233 Later appeared a statement that the design criterion for cantilever wings, which determined flutter speed and critical reversal speed, was the torque stiffness. **1960** *Aeroplane* XCVIII. 192/1 Blades can self-excite in much the same way as aircraft wings flutter. 'Choking flutter' can occur at the high axial velocities obtaining at the back end of the compressor.

e. Rapid tonguing in playing wind instruments. Usu. *attrib.* and *Comb.*, as ***flutter-tongue, -tongued*** ppl. adj., ***-tonguing*** vbl. sb.

1926 WHITEMAN & MCBRIDE *Jazz* iv. 110 A flutter-tongued, drunken whoop of an introduction that had the audience rocking. *Ibid.* ix. 201 The flutter tongue in the brasses is rather like a covey of quail flying out from ambush. *Ibid.* 205 Schoenberg is also the father of the flutter on the trombone—that is, very rapid tonguing on the same note. **1944** W. APEL *Harvard Dict. Mus.* (1960) 754/1 A special type of tonguing, called *Flatter-zunge* or flutter-tonguing, has been introduced by R. Strauss. It calls for a rolling movement of the tongue, as if pronouncing d-r-r-r. **1962** N. DEL MAR *R. Strauss* v. 159 The whistling of the wind is given by harp glissandi and flutes fluttertonguing with the addition of a Wind Machine. **1967** *Spectator* 22 Dec. 787/3 His slow glissandos, his 'fluttertongue' effects (familiar enough as a flautist's device).

f. A rapid fluctuation in the pitch or loudness of a sound (in sound reproduction usu. the former).

1931 A. NADELL *Projecting Sound Pict.* ii. 43 Any condition that allows the film to be pulled past the sound aperture with the least trace of intermittent motion will cause flutter. **1933** C. W. GLOVER *Pract. Acoustics for Constructor* x. 126 The reflection of sound between parallel walls gives rise to a characteristic phenomenon known as flutter. **1946** *Electronic Engin.* XVIII. 311 Records of a combined playing of a violin and piano—the most exacting test for 'wow' and 'flutter'. **1948** P. M. MORSE *Vibration & Sound* (ed. 2) vi. 262 Proper auditorium design is aimed, in part, at the elimination of flutter echoes. **1955** *Gloss. Acoust. Terms* (*B.S.I.*) 36 *Flutter echo*, a rapid multiple echo of even rate. **1962** A. NISBETT *Technique Sound Studio* iv. 92 Once wow or flutter have actually been recorded on to a tape or disc, I know of no means of curing it. **1967** *Reader's Digest Pocket Compan.* 74 An annoying flutter, caused by bad acoustics in the..concert hall, was covered up by adding reverberation.

2. a. An agitated condition, a state of tremulous excitement. *Esp.* in phrases, ***to be in, fall, put,*** etc. ***into a flutter, all of a flutter.***

1742 RICHARDSON *Pamela* III. xxvii. 154 Mr. B. kept me in Suspense a good while and put me in great Flutters, before he let me into the Matter. **1748** —— *Clarissa* (1811) I. xvi. 107 No emotions, child! no flutters! **1768** J. BENTHAM *Let.* 16 Aug. (1968) I. 130, I will treat you with a Letter, but it must be but a short one being as usual like the french prints, all of a flutter. **1780** MAD. D'ARBLAY *Diary* May, A strain of delight..that put her into a flutter of spirits. **1818** J. W. CROKER in *Croker Papers* (1884) Sept., The flutter of her nerves..makes her very miserable. **1840** DICKENS *Old C. Shop* xxi, He immediately..fell into a great flutter. **1887** *Poor Nellie* (1888) 99 No wonder poor Adela's pulse was all in a flutter. **1981** *Christian Science Monitor* 25 Feb. 2 I've just heard Prince Charles is getting married and I'm all of a flutter.

b. A disordered or untidy state.

c **1825** MRS. SHERWOOD *Houlston Tracts* II. xxxi. 9 Let me never see this room in a flutter.

†**3.** Ostentatious display, fuss, sensation, show, stir. *Esp.* in phr. ***to make a*** (or ***their***) ***flutter***: to make a noise in the world. *Obs.*

1667 PEPYS *Diary* 30 Aug., I never knew people in my life that make their flutter, that do things so meanly. **1692** BENTLEY *Boyle Lect.* 58 They would..make a mighty flutter and triumph. *c* **1700** POPE *Artemisia* 24 A stately, worthless animal..All flutter, pride, and talk. **1812** *Examiner* 12 Oct. 652/2 The fanfarronade and flutter of the favourite Hussars. **1822** HAZLITT *Table-t.* Ser. II. xviii. (1869) 369 Why then all this flutter.

4. *slang.* An attempt or 'shy' at anything; an exciting venture at betting or cards. Now usu. used of speculation or betting on a small scale.

1874 *Slang Dict.* s.v., 'I'll have a flutter for it' means I'll have a good try for it. **1880** PAYN *Confid. Agent* I. 134, I am not funky of you at any game, and I want a 'flutter'. **1883** *Echo* 26 Feb. 4/2 (Farmer), I fancy the animal named will at any rate afford backers a flutter for their money. **1900** J. ROBINSON *Life Time S. Afr.* 366 The opportunities of the share market were open to the humblest operator. Men and youths, women and maidens, all could have a 'flutter'. **1930** *Cambridge Daily News* 24 Sept. 7/6 The shares ought to be worth a mild flutter at round 8s. 6d. **1967** *Listener* 13 Apr. 479/1 Money-raising efforts..like selling charity Christmas cards, a rake-off from football pools, and other flutters of various kinds.

5. *attrib.* and *Comb.*, as ***flutter-headed*** adj.; **flutter-mill** *U.S.*, a mill worked by a flutter-wheel; **flutter-pate**, a flighty or light-headed person; **flutter-wheel** (see quot. 1874).

1892 LD. LYTTON *King Poppy* Prol. 248 The snowy-vested *flutter-headed flower. **1866** C. H. SMITH *Bill Arp* 85 The Choctaw children built their *flutter mills. **1938** M. K. RAWLINGS *Yearling* i. 5 His knife was snug in his pocket;.. he had planned as long ago as Christmas, to make himself a flutter-mill. **1894** *Yellow Bk.* Apr. 65 Only fools and *flutterpates do not seek reverently for what is charming in their own day. **1817** *Index of Patents* (1874) 559 *Flutter-wheels, letting water on. **1858** SIMMONDS *Dict. Trade, Flutter-wheel.* **1874** KNIGHT *Dict. Mech.* I. 894 *Flutter wheel*, a water-wheel of moderate diameter placed at the bottom of a chute so as to receive the impact of the head of water in the chute and penstock.

flutter (ˈflʌtə(r)), *v.* Forms: 1 flot(e)orian, 3–4 flot(t)eren, -in, -yn, (4 flooter,) 4–6 floter, -tre, 4–7, 9 *Sc.* flotter, 6– flutter. [OE. *flotorian*, a frequentative formation on *flot-* weak-grade of root of *fléotan* FLEET *v.*]

†**1.** *intr.* To be borne or lie tossing on the waves; to float to and fro. *Obs.*

a **1000** *Gloss. Prudentius* (Record) 150 Flotorode, *fertur fluctibus.* *c* **1290** *S. Eng. Leg.* I. 304/153 And so to floteri in þe grete se! *c* **1400** *Destr. Troy* 12524 All the freikes in the flode floterand aboue. *c* **1470** HENRY *Wallace* VII. 1210 Vij thousand large at anys flottryt in Forth. **1506** GUYLFORDE *Pilgr.* (Camden) 67 We..laye and flotred in the see right werely by reason of the sayd tedyous calme. *a* **1800** *Sir P. Spence* xv. in Jamieson *Ballads* (1806) I. 160 Mony was the feather bed That flotter'd on the faem.

fig. *c* **1000** ÆLFRIC *Hom.* II. 392 Ðin heorte floterað on ðissere worulde ȝytsunge. *c* **1374** CHAUCER *Boeth.* III. pr. xi. (Camb. MS.) 78 Either alle thinges ben referred and browht to nowht and floteryn with owte gouernour..or [etc.]. **1513** DOUGLAS *Æneis* IV. Prol. 164 Thow ald hasart lychour.. That flotteris furth euermair in sluggardry.

2. a. Of birds, etc.: To move or flap the wings rapidly without flying or with short flights; to move up and down or to and fro in quick irregular motions, or hang upon wing in the air.

a **1000** *Gloss. Prudentius* (Record) 150 Flotorodon, *prævolant.* *c* **1340** *Cursor M.* 1781 (Trin.) þe foules flotered þo on heȝe. **1535** COVERDALE *Isa.* xxxi. 5 Like as byrdes flotre aboute their nestes. **1602** MARSTON *Ant. & Mel.* IV. Wks. 1856 I. 45 Troopes of pide butterflies, that flutter still In greatnesse summer. **1719** DE FOE *Crusoe* (1840) I. xv. 252 The parrot..had fluttered a good way off. **1824** BYRON *Juan* XV. xxvii, March, my Muse! If you cannot fly, yet flutter. **1850** MCCOSH *Div. Govt.* III. ii. (1874) 345 Like the moth fluttering about the light which is to consume it. **1870** MORRIS *Earthly Par.* III. IV. 204 The belfry..Fluttered about..By chattering daws.

transf. and *fig.* *c* **1449** PECOCK *Repr.* I. xvi. 91 He floteretħ not so ofte aboute the eeris of the lay peple. **1591** SIDNEY *Astr. & Stella* cviii, My yong soule flutters to thee his nest. *a* **1680** BUTLER *Rem.* (1759) II. 80 He flutters up and down like a Butterfly in a Garden. **1876** GEO. ELIOT *Dan. Der.* IV. lxi. 212 Hans's talk naturally fluttered towards mischief.

b. To move with a light quivering motion through the air.

1853 C. BRONTE *Villette* iii, An etching..happened to flutter to the floor. **1866** GEO. ELIOT *F. Holt* (1868) 10 Here and there a leaf fluttered down. **1873** OUIDA *Pascarel* I. 19 Paper money fluttered to her feet.

c. quasi-*trans.* with *adv.* or *prep.*, expressing the result of a 'fluttering' movement.

1600 F. WALKER *Sp. Mandeville* 152 a, They choppe downe into the Snowe, fluttering the same ouer them with theyr winges. **1789** WOLCOT (P. Pindar) *Ep. to falling Minis.* Wks. 1812 II. 125 So they, like Moths, may flutter life away. **1793** COWPER *Beau's Reply* 15 When your linnet..Had fluttered all his strength away. **1844** ALB. SMITH *Adv. Mr. Ledbury* I. xiv. 103 Seeds, which the bird had fluttered from his cage.

3. *transf.* To move about aimlessly, restlessly, sportively, or ostentatiously; to flit, hover.

1694 tr. *Milton's Lett. State* (1851) 372 Now he resides at Paris, or rather flutters unpunish'd about the City. **1734** POPE *Ess. Man* IV. 196 One flaunts in rags, one flutters in brocade. **1779** JOHNSON *Let. to Mrs. Thrale* 25 Oct., I hope Mr. Thrale..at night flutters about the rooms. **1877** BLACK *Green Past.* xliv. (1878) 354 She had kept fluttering about the hall, bothering the patient clerks with inquiries.

4. a. To move about or to and fro with quick vibrations or undulations; to quiver. Of the heart or pulse: To beat rapidly and irregularly.

1561 BECON *Sicke Mannes Salve* Wks. 1564 II. 220 My toung fluttereth in my mouth, my hands tremble & shake for payne. *a* **1661** FULLER *Worthies* (1840) III. 513 The weight [of a cloak] is diffused in several parts, and, fluttering above, all of them are supported by the clouds. **1712–4** POPE *Rape Lock* I. 90 Teach..little hearts to flutter at a Beau. **1815** SHELLEY *Alastor* 659 The pulse yet lingered in his heart. It paused—it fluttered. **1820** KEATS *Eve St. Agnes* xl, The arras ..Flutter'd in the besieging wind's uproar. **1859** KINGSLEY *Misc.* (1860) II. 289 A few rags of sail fluttered from her main and mizen.

b. Of wind or flame: To blow or flicker lightly and intermittently. Of water: To ripple.

1638 N. ROWE in *Lismore Papers* Ser. II. (1888) IV. 3 Once the winde fluttered a little, whereuppon wee went to sea. **1811** PINKERTON *Petral.* II. 554 A light, accompanied by a flame, fluttering from time to time on the surface. **1821** CLARE *Vill. Minstr.* I. 46 Down the rock the shallow water falls, Wild fluttering through the stones in feeble whimpering brawls. **1878** BROWNING *Poets Croisic* vi, Anyhow there they [tongues of flame] flutter.

fig. **1844** MRS. BROWNING *Drama of Exile* Poems 1850 I. 32 Its meaning flutters in me like a flame.

†**c.** *Music.* (See quot. 1819.) *Obs.*

1759 R. SMITH *Harmonics* (ed. 2) 97 They do not beat at all, like imperfect consonances, but only flutter, at a slower or quicker rate according to the pitch of the sounds. **1819** REES *Cycl.*, *Flutter in Music*, is a term applied by Dr. Robert Smith..to the fluttering roughness in the sound of two notes which are discords to each other.

5. To tremble with excitement; to be excited with hope, apprehension, or pleasure, etc.

1668 H. MORE *Div. Dial.* III. xxxiv. (1713) 273 O how do I flutter to be acquainted with this kind of People. **1754** RICHARDSON *Grandison* (1781) II. v. 73, I fluttered like a fool. **1848** THACKERAY *Van. Fair* lv, Fluttering with her own audacity. **1865** MERIVALE *Rom. Emp.* VIII. lxv. 162 All the tribes of the far East were fluttering with the anticipation of his descent upon them.

6. *trans.* (*causatively*).

a. To cause to flutter; to move (a thing) in quick irregular motions; to agitate, ruffle. Also

† *to flutter* (a thing) *into* rags, *to* pieces, etc. *to flutter out*: to wear out by 'fluttering'. *to flutter the ribbands of* (*a coach*) (slang): to drive.

1621 MARKHAM *Fowling* 32 If they [wild fowl] be flutterd or fleikt into any Riuer. **1644** MANWAYRING *Sea-man's Dict.* s.v. *Floane*, The gust hath fluttred all the saile to peeces. **1667** MILTON *P.L.* II. 933 All unawares, Fluttering his pennons vain. **1746-7** HERVEY *Medit.* (1818) 168 The gay butterfly flutters her painted wings. **1771** HULL *Sir W. Harrington* I. 216, I have already fluttered out all the cloaths I made up for first mourning, and must buy more. **1845** POE *Raven* Poems (1859) 48 Not a feather then he fluttered. **1864** *Eton Sch. Days* i. 11, I used to flutter the ribbands of the London Croydon and South Coast coach. **1893** MCCARTHY *Red Diamonds* II. 20 Shining spaces of water fluttered by the passing oar.

b. *fig.* To throw (a person) into confusion, agitation, or tremulous excitement. *to flutter the dove-cot(e)s*: to alarm, or cause excited discussion among, quiet people (cf. quot. 1664).

1664 *Shakspere's Cor.* (F. 3) v. vi. 116 Like an Eagle in a Dove-coat, I Flutter'd your Volcians in Coriolus. **1748** RICHARDSON *Clarissa* (1811) III. 39 You flutter one so! **1784** E. HAZARD in *Belknap Papers* (1877) I. 382, I am so fatigued and fluttered with my walk. **1853** LYTTON *My Novel* III. IX. xiii. 69 Nor did the great Roman general more nervously 'flutter the dove-cots in Corioli', than did the advance of the supposed X.Y. agitate the bosoms of Lord Spendquick and his sympathising friends. **1864** FROUDE *Short Stud., Sc. Hist.* (1867) 2 A work which..fluttered the dove-cotes of the Imperial Academy of St. Petersburg. **1875** JOWETT *Plato* (ed. 2) II. 45 If I thought that your nerves could be fluttered at a small party of friends. **1940** C. P. SNOW *Strangers & Brothers* ii. 24 'How are they taking it?' said George. 'It's fluttered the dove-cotes.'

7. *intr.* (*slang*). To 'toss' *for* anything.

1874 in *Slang Dict.* **1895** *Westm. Gaz.* 31 July 3/1 The three American girls..were seen..'fluttering' for the upper berth in their cabin.

flutterable ('flʌtərəb(ə)l), *a.* [f. FLUTTER *v.* + -ABLE.] That may be fluttered.

1891 *Sat. Rev.* 5 Sept. 264/2 The matter has fluttered the always rather easily flutterable dovecotes of Vienna.

flutte'ration. *rare.* [see -ATION.] The action of fluttering; the state of being fluttered.

1754 RICHARDSON *Grandison* III. vii. 50 Such a Love as.. she had in her days of *flutteration*, as she whimsically calls them. **1771** HULL *Sir W. Harrington* IV. 172 Even I, who am so much less concerned, am in a violent *flutteration* about it. **1805** in *Spirit Public Jrnls.* (1806) IX. 265 The names of Colonel, Major, and Captain scarce occasion the smallest flutteration. **1896** J. C. HARRIS *Sister Jane* 220, I heard a big flutteration at the top, and out came a pair of wood-peckers.

fluttered ('flʌtəd), *ppl. a.* [f. FLUTTER *v.* + -ED[1].] In senses of the vb. both *trans.* and *intr.* (In quot. 1589 perh. used for *fittered.*)

1589 NASHE *Anat. Absurd.* Wks. (Grosart) I. 29 That those..shoulde preferre their fluttered sutes before other mens glittering gorgious array. **1773** GRAVES *Euphrosyne* (1776) I. 18 The emblem of a flutter'd mind. **1813** SCOTT *Rokeby* IV. xxix, A fluttered hope his accents shook, A fluttered joy was in his look. **1878** BROWNING *Poets Croisic* 33 His fluttered faculties came back to roost.

flutterer ('flʌtərə(r)). [f. as prec. + -ER[1].]

†**1.** ? A vagrant. *Obs. rare.*

c **1450** MYRC 845 Of scoler, of flotterer, or of passyngere.

2. One who or that which flutters, *lit.* and *fig.*; †a flirt. Rarely in *trans.* sense.

c **1726** MRS. DELANY in *Life & Corr.* I. 133, I looked upon him as a flutterer, and was at a loss to know what his intentions were. **1748** RICHARDSON *Clarissa* (1811) I. iii. 13 A man of morals, was worth a thousand of such gay flutterers. **1838** DICKENS *Nich. Nick.* xiv, Dingy, ill-plumed drowsy flutterers. **1882** *Harper's Mag.* LXV. 588 She watched the boat until the handkerchief flutterer was no longer seen.

fluttering ('flʌtərɪŋ), *vbl. sb.* [f. as prec. + -ING[1].] The action of the vb. FLUTTER in various senses; an instance of the same.

1382 WYCLIF *Ps.* liv [lv]. 23 [22] He shal not ȝiue in to with oute ende flotering [Vulg. *fluctuationem*] to the riȝt-wise. **14..** *Prose Legends* in *Anglia* VIII. 185 Drowned in þe floteryngis of þis lyfe. **1627-61** FELTHAM *Resolves* I. xi. 200 The Bates and Flutterings of a Conscience within. **1719** DE FOE *Crusoe* (1840) I. xix. 341 It is impossible to express the flutterings of my..heart. **1759** R. SMITH *Harmonics* (ed. 2) 97 The flutterings and the beats of a tempered consonance. **1830** TENNYSON *Miller's Dau.* 153, I watch'd the little flutterings, The doubt my mother would not see. **1832** LYTTON *Eugene A.* II. iv, No fluttering of manner betrayed that he [etc.].

fluttering ('flʌtərɪŋ), *ppl. a.* [f. as prec. + -ING[2].] That flutters, in various senses of the vb.

c **1374** CHAUCER *Boeth.* III. metr. ix. 68 (Camb. MS.) To compowne werk of floterynge matere. **1590** SPENSER *F.Q.* II. iii. 10 Vain-glorious man, when fluttering wind does blow In his light winges, is lifted up to skie. **1625** GILL *Sacr. Philos.* iv. 43 That fluttering distinction..will not helpe. **1762** FALCONER *Shipwr.* II. 198 The fluttering sails expand. **1834** MEDWIN *Angler in Wales* II. 315 The thick-heaved breath And..fluttering pulse of death. **1863** GEO. ELIOT *Romola* II. i, A large..mulberry-tree..was now sending its last fluttering leaves in at the open doorways.

b. Untidy. (Cf. FLUTTER *sb.* 2 b.)

c **1830** MRS. SHERWOOD *Houlston Tracts* III. lxvii. 8 She would idle..and was very fluttering with her things.

Hence **'flutteringly** *adv.*, in a fluttering manner.

1819 WIFFEN *Aonian Hours* (1820) 33 O'er her young more flutteringly to brood. **1859** MASSON *Brit. Novelists* iv. 278 Of old it came flutteringly through prophets. **1861** G. MEREDITH *E. Harrington* II. xi. 197 Mrs. Hawkshaw began flutteringly to apologise.

flutterless ('flʌtəlɛs), *a.* [f. FLUTTER *sb.* + -LESS.] Not making a flutter, drooping.

1873 *Daily News* 21 Aug., The clinging, flutterless pennons of the lances.

fluttermouse, dial. form of FLITTERMOUSE.

fluttersome ('flʌtəsəm), *a.* [f. FLUTTER *v.* + -SOME.] Inclined to flutter.

1895 *Century Mag.* Feb. 540 Beribboned, belaced, and very fluttersome.

fluttery ('flʌtərɪ), *a.* In 4 **flotery**. [f. FLUTTER *v.* + -Y.] Apt to flutter, fluttering. Also *fig.*

c **1386** CHAUCER *Knt.'s T.* 2025 With flotery berd, and ruggy asshy heres. **1823** *New Monthly Mag.* VII. 569 His patchy, fluttery, and undecided mode of handling. **1855** J. HEWITT *Anc. Armour* I. 341 A light fluttery material. **1875** BROWNING *Aristoph. Apol.* 337 The fluttery tree-top.

fluty ('flu:tɪ), *a.* Also **flutey**. [f. FLUTE *sb.*[1] + -Y[1].] Resembling a flute in tone, flute-like; soft and clear.

1823 *New Monthly Mag.* VIII. 39 As on the wind its fluty music floats. **1845** ALB. SMITH *Fort. Scatterg. Fam.* xxiii, A delicate fluty voice. **1929** E. BOWEN *Joining Charles* 7 The blackbirds with a wild flutey note. **1938** E. WAUGH *Scoop* III. ii. 274 Mr. Salter's voice sounded curiously flutey and querulous.

fluvial ('flu:vɪəl). [a. F. *fluvial*, ad L. *fluviāl-is*, f. *fluvius* river.] Of or pertaining to a river or rivers; found or living in a river.

1398 TREVISA *Barth. De P.R.* XIX. lxv. (1495) 901 Yf fluuyall stones ben hette fyry hote and thenne quenchyd therin. **1599** A. M. tr. *Gabelhouer's Bk. Physicke* 33/2, Iij pintes of fluvial water. **1775** ROMANS *Florida* 316 This fluvial expedition. **1867** J. B. ROSE tr. *Virgil's Æneid* 190 The fluvial nymphs. **1875** *Wond. Phys. World* I. i. 39 The descent of fluvial ice frequently causes great disasters.

fluvialist ('flu:vɪəlɪst). [f. prec. + -IST.] One who explains certain phenomena in geology or physical geography by the action of existing streams.

1829 *Proc. Geol. Soc.* I. 145 He [W. D. Conybeare] first offers some introductory remarks on the opposite theories of the fluvialist and diluvialist.

'fluviated, *a.* [f. L. *fluviāt-us* soaked in a river, (f. *fluvius* river) + -ED[1].] Overflowed by a river, marshy.

1807 G. CHALMERS *Caledonia* I. I. iv. 129 A bank overlooking the low fluviated ground of the river.

fluviatic (flu:vɪ'ætɪk), *a.* [ad. L. *fluviātic-us*, f. *fluvius* river.] Growing or living in streams.

1727 BAILEY vol. II, *Fluviatick*. **1828** in WEBSTER.

fluviatile ('flu:vɪətɪl), *a.* [a. F. *fluviatile*, ad. L. *fluviātilis*, f. *fluvius* river.] Of or pertaining to a river or rivers; found, growing, or living in rivers; formed or produced by the action of rivers.

1599 A. M. tr. *Gabelhouer's Bk. Physicke* 48/1 Madefye a little linnen cloth in Fluviatile water. **1681** CHETHAM *Angler's Vade-m.* xi. § 1 (1689) 110 Fishes, whether Marine Fluviatile or Lakish. **1774** STRANGE in *Phil. Trans.* LXV. 45 It [buccinum] is of the fluviatile kind. **1823** W. BUCKLAND *Reliq. Diluv.* 164 The mud..is evidently fluviatile and not diluvian. **1878** HUXLEY *Physiog.* 134 The river is, itself, a powerful agent of direct denudation—fluviatile denudation as it is sometimes termed.

†**fluvi'ation.** *Obs. rare*[−1]. [as if ad. L. **fluviātiōn-em*, f. *fluviātus*, FLUVIATED.] The process of steeping (flax) in water.

a **1682** SIR T. BROWNE *Tracts* 54 This was the first preparation of Flax, and before fluviation or rotting.

fluvicoline (flu:'vɪkəlɪn, -aɪn), *a.* [f. mod.L. *fluvicol-a* (f. *fluvius* river + *colĕre* to inhabit) + -INE.] = FLUVIAL, FLUVIATILE.

In some mod. Dicts.

fluvio- ('flu:vɪəʊ), used as combining form of L. *fluvius* river, as in ˌ**fluvio-'glacial** *a.*, pertaining to or produced by the action of streams which have their source in glacial ice, or the combined action of rivers and glaciers; ˌ**fluviola'custrine** *a.*, pertaining to or produced by the action of both rivers and lakes; **fluviology** (flu:vɪ'ɒlədʒɪ), potamology; the facts and conditions relating to a river or river-system; **'fluvio-marine** *a.*, an epithet applied to deposits formed by river-currents at the bottom of the sea; also quasi-*sb.*; **fluvi'ometer**, an instrument for measuring the rise and fall of rivers; ˌ**fluvio-te'rrestrial** *a.*, pertaining to the land-surface of the globe and its rivers.

1894 *Geol. Mag.* Jan. 30 The younger *fluvio-glacial gravel deposits of the Limmat valley. **1970** R. J. SMALL *Study of Landforms* xi. 389 A number of different fluvio-glacial features are found at or very close to the margins of an ice-sheet. The best known of these are karnes, karne-terraces and eskers. **1864** *Q. Jrnl. Geol. Soc. London* XX. 383 The *fluvio-lacustrine series, consisting of deposits from lakes fed by mountain-rivers. **1963** D. W. & E. E. HUMPHRIES tr. *Termier's Erosion & Sedimentation* ix. 180 It [*sc.* tangue] is a fluvio-lacustrine silt, which has been reworked by the sea. **1904** *Amer. Geol.* Jan. 43 The modern science of *fluviology. **1924** *Glasgow Herald* 13 Dec. 8 An unexpected addition to the fluviology of Glasgow. **1848** CRAIG, **Fluvio-marine*. **1852** E. FORBES in Wilson & Geikie *Mem.* xiv. (1861) 505 The fluvio-marine portion of them [the Eocenes]. *Ibid.* 509 The whole series of fluvio-marines. **1863** LYELL *Antiq. Man* xi. (ed. 3) 204 The fluvio-marine bed of Abbeville. **1865** LIVINGSTONE *Zambesi* iii. 70 The only *fluviometer at Tette..was set up at our suggestion. **1885** GILL in *Proc. Biol. Soc.* II. 30 (Cent.) The marine realms..are entirely independent of the *fluvio-terrestrial.

†**fluvi'ose**, *a.* *Obs.*[−0] [as if ad. L. **fluviōs-us*, f. *fluvius* river: see -OSE.] (See quot.)

1727 BAILEY vol. II, *Fluviose*, flowing much.

†**'fluvious**, *a.* *Obs.*[−0] [f. as prec.: see -OUS.] (See quot.)

1656 BLOUNT *Glossogr.*, *Fluvious*, flowing much.

flux (flʌks), *sb.* Forms: α. (sense 1 only) 4-7 **flix(e**, **flyx(e**, (6 **flyckes**); β. 5-7 **fluxe**, (5 **flokes**), 4- **flux**. [a. Fr. *flux*, = Pr. *flux*, Sp. *fluxo* (now *flujo* in senses 1 and 4, *flux* from Fr.), It. *flusso*:—L. *fluxus* (*u* stem), f. *fluĕre* (Lat. root **flugv*-) to flow. The early form *flix* proceeds from the Fr. pronunciation with (y).] A flowing, flow.

I. *spec.* in physiological sense.

1. a. An abnormally copious flowing of blood, excrement, etc. from the bowels or other organs; a morbid or excessive discharge. *spec.* An early name for dysentery; also †*red flux*, †*flux of blood*, *bloody flux* (cf. BLOODY C. 2).

α. **1382** WYCLIF *Matt.* ix. 20 A womman that suffride the [**1388** blodi] flix, or rennynge, of blood twelue ȝeer. **1447** BOKENHAM *Seyntys* (Roxb.) 32 The reed flyx..Sodeynly dede Austyn so sore oppresse. **1577** B. GOOGE *Heresbach's Husb.* IV. (1586) 187 They [Bees] feed so greedilie, as they fall into a Flix. **1600** HOLLAND *Livy* III. xiii. (1609) 1367 *note*, Hee [Trajan]..died..of a flixe of blood. **1665** MANLEY *Grotius' Low C. Warres* 317 Both of them bred a sad Disease among them, with a great Flix.

β. **1377** LANGL. *P. Pl.* B. xx. 80 Kynd conscience..sent forth his foreioures, feures & fluxes. *c* **1450** *St. Cuthbert* (Surtees) 3548 He was lange seke in þe flokes. **1597** GERARDE *Herbal* (1636) 713 Agrimony boiled in wine and drunke helpes..hepaticke fluxes in old people. **1708** SWIFT *Predictions 1708* Wks. 1755 II. I. 153 It [his death] seems to be an effect of the gout in his stomach, followed by a flux. **1777** WATSON *Philip II.* (1839) 103 Rendered unfit for action by a bloody flux. **1807** VANCOUVER *Agric. Devon* (1813) 337 A flux or scowering is the complaint to which these animals are by far the most liable. **1854** JONES & SIEV. *Pathol. Anat.* (1874) 65 Fluxes will be active or passive, according to the kind of hyperæmia which occasions them.

b. *transf.* A 'running' from the eyes or mouth.

1377 LANGL. *P. Pl.* B. v. 179 Whan I drynke wyn at eue, I haue a fluxe of a foule mouthe, wel fyue dayes after. **1711** STEELE *Spect.* No. 95 ¶ 3 This Flux of the Eyes, this Faculty of Weeping.

2. a. A flowing out, issue, discharge (of humours, etc.).

1447 BOKENHAM *Seyntys* (Roxb.) 9 The margaryte, if of blood descende Gret flux, is good it to amende. **1563** T. GALE *Antidot.* I. i. 2 Compoundes..whiche doe..staye the fluxe of humours. **1650** BULWER *Anthropomet.* Pref., Here Females..do by Art that monethly Flux prevent. **1754-64** SMELLIE *Midwif.* I. 106 Several ingenious theories have been erected to account for the flux of the Menses. **1877** F. ROBERTS *Handbk. Med.* I. 27 The same condition leads to a watery flux.

†**b.** That which flows or is discharged. *Obs.*

1382 WYCLIF *Ezek.* xxiii. 20 As fluxis, or rennyngis, of horsis [ben] the fluxis of hem. **1600** SHAKS. *A.Y.L.* III. ii. 70 Ciuet is of a baser birth than Tarre, the verie vncleanly fluxe of a Cat. **1654** TRAPP *Comm. Job* v. 10 Raine is the flux of a moist cloud.

II. *gen.*

3. The action of flowing. Now *rare* in lit. sense.

c **1600** NORDEN *Spec. Brit.*, *Cornw.* (1728) 64 At the heade of this baye..is a poole of fresh water, notwithstanding the often fluxe of the sea into it. **1638** SIR T. HERBERT *Trav.* (ed. 2) 68 The river Ravee..after a stately flux of three thousand English miles..flowes into Indus. **1748** *Relat. Earthq. Lima* 93 Fire to subsist requires a Flux of Air. **1862** TYNDALL *Mountaineer.* iii. 24 If one portion of the universe be hotter than another, a flux instantly sets in to equalise the temperature.

transf. and *fig.* **1650-3** tr. *Hales' Dissert. de Pace* in *Phenix* (1708) II. 379 Which Consequence doth also flow by a fatal and inevitable Flux from that Doctrine of Fate. *a* **1711** KEN *Div. Love* Wks. (1838) 230, I love, and admire..the perpetual flux of thy goodness on every creature. **1865-6** H. PHILLIPS *Amer. Paper Curr.* II. 174 A flux of specie took place into the United States.

4. The flowing in of the tide. Often in phrase *flux and reflux.*

1612 in *Law Times' Rep.* LXV. 567/2 Lands within the flux and reflux of the sea. **1771** *Act 11 Geo. III*, c. 45 § 35 Any Barge..that shall not be navigated beyond the Flux of the Tide. *c* **1800** K. WHITE *Lett.* (1837) 265 Without any means of getting ashore till the flux or flood. **1854** TOMLINSON *Arago's Astron.* 157 The sea..undergoes a flux and reflux as often as the moon passes the meridian.

transf. and *fig.* **1722** DE FOE *Moll Flanders* (1840) 321 A.. flux and reflux of fears and hopes. **1799** VINCE *Elem. Astron.* xvii. (1810) 159 The alternate flux and reflux of the liquid igneous matter. **1835** THIRLWALL *Greece* I. iii. 71 The flux and reflux of the nations which fought and wandered in the countries adjacent.

5. a. A flowing stream, a flood.

1637 HEYWOOD *Dialogues, Jupiter & Io* Wks. 1874 VI. 258 Their waters keep a smooth and gentle course Not mov'd to

fury..When loud fluxes fall to swell their bounds. **1769** *De Foe's Tour Gt. Brit.* III. 40 The Syfer Spring is the most noted, having now four Fluxes of Water.

fig. **1855** THACKERAY *Newcomes* II. 264 The mouth from which issued that cool and limpid flux.

b. *transf.* A continuous stream (of people).

1600 SHAKS. *A.Y.L.* II. i. 52 Thus miserie doth part The Fluxe of companie. **1665** SIR T. HERBERT *Trav.* (1677) 327 At the keeping of this Feast we beheld..such a flux of Men, Women, Boyes and Girls.

c. *fig.* A copious flow, flood (*esp.* of talk, etc.).

1678 R. L'ESTRANGE *Seneca's Mor.* (1702) 376 No Man takes Satisfaction in a Flux of Words, without Choice. **1722** DE FOE *Plague* (1754) 22 The Court brought with them a great Flux of Pride, and new Fashions. **1817** SOUTHEY *Lett.* (1856) III. 60 If I had my old flux of the Muse. **1855** M. ARNOLD *New Sirens* 195 This flux of guesses. **1875** F. HALL in *Lippincott's Mag.* XV. 338/1 Neglecting the flux of verbiage that engulfed it.

6. The passing away (of life, time or a portion of time). Also, a passing period. *Obs.*

1612 J. DAVIES *Muses Sacrifice* Wks. (Grosart) II. 47/2 Age to Death is but the Gally-slaue, that on a moments fluxe, whafts life to death. **1641** SMECTYMNUUS *Vind. Answ.* vi. 78 That which Hierome speakes in the present tense, as true in all the moments and fluxes of time. **1727–46** THOMSON *Summer* 35 Thus to remain, Amid the flux of many thousand years. **1759** JOHNSON *Rasselas* iv, The moon by more than twenty changes admonished me of the flux of life.

7. A continuous succession of changes of condition, composition or substance.

1625 BACON *Ess., Viciss. of Things* (Arb.) 569 The Matter is in a Perpetuall Flux. **1691** LOCKE *Lowering Interest* Wks. 1714 II. 31 What the stated rate of Interest should be, in the constant change of Affairs, and flux of Money, is hard to determine. **1726–7** SWIFT *Gulliver* III. x, The language of this country being always upon the flux. **1736** BUTLER *Anal.* I. i. 27 The bodies of all animals are in a constant flux. **1862** MERIVALE *Rom. Emp.* (1865) III. xxvii. 240 The perpetual flux of property from hand to hand. **1878** SULLY in *Encycl. Brit.* VIII. 755 Heraclitus conceives of the incessant process of flux in which all things are involved as consisting of two sides or moments—generation and decay. **1885** CLODD *Myths & Dr.* I. iii. 23 The languages of savages are in a constant state of flux.

8. *Math.* **a.** A continued motion (of a point).

[**1597** HOOKER *Eccl. Pol.* v. lxix. §2 Time considered in it selfe, is but the flux of that very instant, wherein the Motion of the Heauen began.] **1656** tr. *Hobbes' Elem. Philos.* (1839) 508 Rough and smooth..are not perceived but by the flux of a point, that is to say, we have no sense of them without time. *a* **1696** SCARBURGH *Euclid* (1705) 3 Not that hereby a Line is A Flux of a Point, as some define It. **1796** HUTTON *Math. Dict.* I. 484 s.v. *Fluxion*, A line considered as generated by the flux or motion of a point, or a surface generated by the flux of a line.

b. = FLUXION 5.

1878 CLIFFORD *Dynamics* ii. 63 This rate of change of a fluent quantity is called its fluxion, or sometimes, more shortly, its flux.

9. *Physics.* **a.** The rate of flow of any fluid across a given area; the amount which crosses an area in a given time; it is thus a vector referred to unit area. Also used with reference to other forms of matter and energy that can be regarded as flowing, such as radiant energy, particles, etc. ***line of flux***, see quot. 1881. ***flux of force***, see quot. 1885.

1863 TYNDALL *Heat* vii. §268 The line of flux..was parallel to the fibre. **1881** MAXWELL *Electr. & Magn.* (1892) I. 11 The flux of heat in any direction at any point of a solid body may be defined as the quantity of heat which crosses a small area drawn perpendicular to that direction divided by that area and by the time. *Ibid.* 13 If two of these surfaces intersect, their line of intersection is a line of flux. **1882** MINCHIN *Unipl. Kinemat.* 159 The flux across each end of the tube would be zero. **1885** WATSON & BURBURY *Math. Th. Electr. & Magn.* I. 102 Flux of Force..This product, from its analogy to the flux of a fluid flowing through a small tube with velocity $u = F$, is called the flux of force across d S. **1911** *Encycl. Brit.* XXI. 525/2 Across this surface there will pass a definite amount of radiant energy, in other words a definite total luminous flux. **1947** *Science* 9 May 491/1 A graphite uranium pile, a 'hot' laboratory.., still another pile with 100 times the neutron flux of the first, [etc.]. **1957** *New Scientist* 23 May 32/2 The thermal neutron flux in such a reactor will be on the average about 2×10^{13} neutrons per square centimetre per second. **1963** R. W. DITCHBURN *Light* (ed. 2) x. 397 A flux of one watt of radiation of this wavelength constitutes a luminous flux of 692 lumens. **1964** C. J. MAIDEN in LeGalley & McKee *Space Explor.* ix. 242 Recently spacecraft have become available to make direct measurements of the flux of micrometeorites in space. **1967** CONDON & ODISHAW *Handbk. Physics* (ed. 2) ix. 280 A definite flux of $(1{\cdot}5 \pm 0{\cdot}8) \times 10^{-4}$ per cm² per sec for γ rays of a few hundred MeV has been reported..from the direction of the constellation Cygnus. **1971** *Nature* 7 May 11/1 The flux of hydrogen atoms in the solar wind.

b. *Electricity* and *Magnetism.* (The number of) lines of magnetic induction (***magnetic flux***) or electric displacement (***electric flux***); the quantity of flux through any surface is equal to the integral of the normal component of the induction or displacement over the surface.

1873 J. C. MAXWELL *Treat. Electr. & Magn.* I. 11 Electric and magnetic induction, and electric currents, belong to the second class, being defined with reference to areas. When we wish to indicate this fact, we shall refer to them as Fluxes. **1898** J. A. FLEMING *Magnets & Electr. Curr.* iii. 65 If..a disc of iron is placed in a uniform field of magnetic force, the flux concentrates itself in the iron. **1911** W. F. MAGIE *Princ. Physics* xix. 452 The theorems concerning electric flux are similar to those concerning magnetic flux. **1933** E. MALLETT *Vectors for Engineers* iv. 52 The e.m.f. produced by the alternating flux in the primary coil. **1957** B. I. & B. BLEANEY *Electr. & Magn.* vi. 147 If the two coils are closely wound.. then the ratio of the two fluxes N_1 and N_2 will just be equal to the ratio of the number of turns n_1, n_2 on the two coils. **1969** L. YOUNG *Syst. Units Electr. & Magn.* iv. 42 The flux 'lines' spread out over space to produce a certain electric flux density or electric displacement.

III. A state or means of fusion.

†**10.** Liquefaction or fusion. In phr. ***in (the) flux.***

1684 tr. *Bonet's Merc. Compit.* VI. 199 The morbifick matter..while it is in flux, is most destructive. **1799** G. SMITH *Laborat.* I. 107 Let it stand a little in the flux.

11. *Metall.* **a.** Any substance that is mixed with a metal etc. to facilitate its fusion; also a substance used to render colours fusible in enamelling and in the colouring of porcelain and glass. Cf. FLUSS *sb.*[2]

For ***black, crude, white flux***: see quots.

1704 W. NICHOLSON *Dict. Chem.*, Crude flux is a mixture of nitre and tartar. **1763** W. LEWIS *Philos. Commerce Arts* 68 Borax..is one of the best fluxes for gold. **1826** HENRY *Elem. Chem.* II. xiv. 586 The black flux is formed, by setting fire to a mixture of one part of nitrate of potassa, and two of bitartrate of potassa..White flux is obtained by projecting into a red-hot crucible equal parts of the same salts. **1832** G. R. PORTER *Porcelain & Gl.* 76 Fluxes which are necessary to render these [colours] fusible. **1875** FORTNUM *Majolica* i. 8 Lead has been found in some of the blue coloured glazes of Babylonia, and..probably employed as a flux.

b. *collect.* Substances used as fluxes.

1890 *Kapunda Herald* 26 July 2/6 The Trade in Flux. The following are the quantities of flux dispatched from the Kapunda Railway-station.

IV. 12. = FLUSH *sb.*[4] [So F. *flux.*]

1798 *Sporting Mag.* XII. 142 The flux [in game of Ambigu] is four cards in the same suit.

V. 13. *attrib.* and *Comb.*, as ***flux-linkage, -turn***; **flux ale**, ale likely to cause diarrhœa; **flux density**, the quantity of flux passing through unit area in a plane normal to the direction of the flux; *esp.* magnetic induction; **flux(-)gate, fluxgate (magnetometer)**, a kind of magnetometer used esp. in aerial surveys which consists essentially of one or more soft magnetic cores each surrounded by primary and secondary windings, the signal produced in the latter representing in phase and magnitude the direction and magnitude of the external magnetic field; **flux(-)gate compass**, an aeronautical compass incorporating a gyroscopically controlled flux-gate; **flux line**, (*a*) one of the lines conceived of as representing by their direction and density the direction and strength of either magnetic induction or electric displacement; (*b*) (see quot. 1962); **fluxmeter, flux meter** [ad. F. *fluxmètre* (M.E. Grassot 1904, in *Jrnl. de Physique* 4me Sér. III. 696)], an instrument for measuring changes in magnetic flux; **flux-powder** (see quot. 1704); **flux root**, 'the *Asclepias tuberosa* from its use in dysentery and catarrhs' (*Syd. Soc. Lex.*, 1884); **flux-spoon** (see quot. 1874); **flux-** or **flix-weed**, the plant *Sisymbrium Sophia*, formerly a supposed remedy for the flux or dysentery.

1742 *Lond. & Country Brew.* I. (ed. 4) 53 Brewers Servants, who formerly scorned what they then called *Flux Ale. **1898** J. A. FLEMING *Magnets & Electr. Curr.* iii. 63 When an iron circuit is strongly magnetised it may have across its section a magnetic *flux density as great as.. 20,000 lines or units of induction per square centimetre. **1934** *Discovery* Oct. 301/2 The 2-in. speech coil attached to the 11-in. cone works in a flux density of 11,500. **1967** CONDON & ODISHAW *Handbk. Physics* (ed. 2) vi. 48 The luminous intensity of a source of light in any given direction is the solid angular luminous flux density in the direction in question. **1947** *Canadian Jrnl. Res.* A. XXV. 125 (*heading*) *Flux-gate magnetometers. **1962** F. I. ORDWAY et al. *Basic Astronautics* iv. 156 A later satellite, Explorer 6, carried search coil and flux gate magnetometers. **1967** *New Scientist* 27 Apr. 217/3 The fluxgate is an electronic device that normally measures variations in field strength. **1946** M. DAVIDSON *Gyroscope* III. iv. 218 The gyro used to stabilise the *Flux-gate compass unit..consists of a capacitor type split-phase four-pole induction motor. **1898** J. A. FLEMING *Magnets & Electr. Curr.* iii. 62 Where the flux density is large the *flux lines are closely packed. **1925** HODKIN & COUSEN *Textbk. Glass Technol.* xxiii. 306 Fireclay blocks, intended for use as 'flux-line' blocks, should be made of the same clay mixture as pots. **1962** *Gloss. Terms Glass Industry* (*B.S.I.*) 19 *Fluxline*, 1. The level of the molten glass surface in a tank. 2. The boundary line between unmelted batch and clear glass in a tank. **1933** E. MALLETT *Vectors for Electrical Engineers* iv. 52 The *flux linkages..through the primary coil are made up of two parts,..due to the current in the primary, and..due to the current in the secondary. **1904** *Sci. Abstr.* B. VII. 741 (*heading*) Grassot *fluxmeter. **1933** *Proc. R. Soc.* CXXXIX. 619 The field was explored by means of a large search coil..connected to a fluxmeter. **1960** JERRARD & MCNEILL *Theoretic. & Exper. Physics* xv. 461 The Grassot fluxmeter..is a robust form of moving-coil ballistic galvanometer used for measuring magnetic flux. **1704** J. HARRIS *Lex. Techn.*, **Flux-powders*..are Powders prepared to facilitate the Fusion of the harder Metals. **1874** KNIGHT *Dict. Mech.* I. 894/2 **Flux-spoon*, a small ladle for dipping out a sample of molten metal to be tested. **1932** E. B. MOULLIN *Princ. Electromagn.* iii. 122 The scale of the flux meter can be engraved to read directly in *flux turns. **1578** LYTE *Dodoens* I. lxxix. 117 The seede of *Flixeweede or Sophia..stoppeth the bloudy flixe. **1878** BRITTEN & HOLLAND *Plant-n.*, *Flixweed* or *Flixwort.*

†**flux** (flʌks), *a. Obs.* [ad. L. *fluxus*, ppl. adj. f. *fluĕre* to flow.] That is in a state of flux; ever-changing, fluctuating, inconstant, variable.

a **1677** BARROW *Serm.* Wks. 1716 III. 61 Considering.. the flux nature of all things here. *a* **1735** POPE & ARBUTHNOT *Mart. Scribl.* I. xiii. (1741) 44 A Corporation..is..a flux body. **1768** BLACKSTONE *Comm.* III. xxi. 318 The record.. was more serviceable..in a dead and immutable language than in any flux or living one. **1797** SIR G. STAUNTON *Acc. Ld. Macartney's Embassy* (1798) III. 420 The form of those characters has not been so flux as the sound of words.

flux (flʌks), *v.* [f. FLUX *sb.*]

I. In medicine.

†**1.** *trans.* To treat medically by subjecting to a flux; *esp.* to salivate. Also, of food or drink: To produce a flux in (a person); to purge. *Obs.*

1666 W. BOGHURST *Loimographia* (1894) 40 Many people being fluxed with quicksilver for the Pox. **1684** tr. *Bonet's Merc. Compit.* XVII. 592 The Bone must be taken out..the Ulcer cleansed and the Body fluxed. **1711** SWIFT *Jrnl. to Stella* 15 Feb., She'll be fluxed in two months. **1756** NUGENT *Gr. Tour* IV. 21 Their small wines..will certainly flux you, if you drink too plentifully of them. **1768** FOOTE *Devil 2 Sticks* III. Wks. 1799 II. 275 Full power..to pill.. flux..and poultice all persons. **1785** GROSE *Dict. Vulg. Tongue, Flux*, to salivate.

†**b.** *fig.*; also to clear *of. Obs.*

1651 R. WARING *To W. Cartwright* 38 in *Cartwright's Comedies* *6 b, To cure the Itch, or flux the Pen. **1660** *Charac. Italy* 12 Praying for the Dead, which doth so flux the pocket. **1664** BUTLER *Hud.* II. I. 362 Twas he that gave our Senate purges, And fluxt the House of many a Burgess. *a* **1688** VILLIERS (Dk. Buckhm.) *Poems* (1775) 140 E'en gentle George (flux'd both in tongue and purse) Shunning one snare, yet fell into a worse.

†**c.** *jocosely.* (See quots.) *Obs.*

a **1763** BYROM *Black Bob Wig* xli, But what can Salivation do? It [a wig] has been fluxt and refluxt too. **1785** GROSE *Dict. Vulg. Tongue* s.v., To flux a wig, to put it up in curl, and bake it.

†**d.** *intr.* To submit to treatment by fluxing. *Obs.*

1693 SHADWELL *Volunteers* IV. i, Would not flux because times were unsettled. **1707** J. STEVENS tr. *Quevedo's Com. Wks.* (1709) 326 A young Wench fluxing for the Falling-sickness. **1755** LADY M. W. MONTAGU *Let. to C'tess Bute* 22 Sept., His natural spirits gave him..cheerfulness when he was fluxing in a garret.

fig. **1733** *Revolution Politicks* v. 3 This place [Purgatory] of late Years Priests have found, For sinning Souls to flux in till they're sound.

2. *dial.* and *slang* (*obs.*). (See quots.)

1785 GROSE *Dict. Vulg. Tongue, Flux*, to cheat, cozen, or overreach. **1875** *Sussex Gloss, Flux*, to snatch at anything.

II. In etymological sense.

3. *intr.* †**a.** Of a person: To bleed copiously (*obs.*[−1]); **b.** To issue in a flux, flow copiously.

1638 A. READ *Chirurg.* xxvi. 192 The wounded party doth flux to death most commonly before any Chirurgeon can come to stay the bleeding. **1823** LAMB *Let. B. Barton* 21 Nov., Once fix the seat of your disorder, and your fancies flux into it like so many bad humours. **1869** BLACKMORE *Lorna D.* i, The invading waters..fluxing along the wall.

III. In *ancient Chemistry* and *Metallurgy.*

4. *trans.* To make fluid, fuse, melt.

1477 NORTON *Ord. Alch.* v. in Ashm. (1652) 79 Liquors helpeth to flux and to flowe Manie things. **1666** BOYLE *Orig. Formes & Qual.* 260 Sea salt..if it be distill'd alone..is apt to be fluxt by the heat of the fire. **1762** *Gentl. Mag.* 102 An intense equal heat..fluxes the oar. **1883** NASMYTH *Autobiog.* vi. 105 The walls under the intense heat, were fluxed and melted into a sort of glass.

fig. **1754** SHEBBEARE *Matrimony* (1766) I. 79 The Alloy, which was fluxed out of him, left so little of the Original remaining, that [etc.]. **1860** EMERSON *Cond. Life* i. (1861) 29 Every solid in the universe is ready to become fluid on the approach of the mind, and the power to flux it is the measure of the mind.

5. To treat with a flux (see FLUX *sb.* 11); to heat in combination with a flux.

1781 *Dict. Chem.* in J. T. Dillon *Trav. Spain* 233 *note*, If ..cobalt..be fluxed like other metallic calxes, it will be reduced to a semi-metal. *c* **1790** IMISON *Sch. Art.* II. 151 To melt the copper as fluid as possible, and flux it with the black flux. **1802** *Ann. Reg.* 780 The highest finished ware..is.. returned to the enamel kiln, where the colours are fluxed six or seven times.

absol. **1872** W. S. SYMONDS *Rec. Rocks* ix. 306 These lower limestone beds are used for fluxing.

6. *intr.* To become fluid; to melt.

1669 W. SIMPSON *Hydrol. Chym.* 14 Firing [it] strongly in a crucible until it flux. **1789** G. WHITE *Selborne* iv. (1853) 21 The sand..fluxes and runs by the intense heat.

Hence **'fluxing** *ppl. a.*

1702 DE FOE *Reform. Manners* I. 190 From the fluxing Bagnio just dismist. **1711** E. WARD *Quix.* I. 71 As Fluxing Patients..Suck Broaths and Cordials thro' a Quill.

†**flu'xation.** *Obs.* [f. FLUX *v.* + -ATION.]

1. Treatment by fluxing: see FLUX *v.* 1.

1656 S. HOLLAND *Zara* (1719) 140 A drawl'd Prostitute, fitting her self for Fluxation.

2. Flowing or passing on.

1710 LESLIE *Vind. Short Meth. with Deists* Wks. 1721 I. 121 They [the Siamese] believe no God, but a continual fluxation and transmigration of Souls from eternity.

†**fluxed,** *ppl. a. Obs.* [f. as prec. + -ED[1].]

1. Caused to flow; flowing, weeping.

1627–77 FELTHAM *Resolves* I. lxxxix. 137 That God is merciful, that will admit offences to be expiated by the sigh, and fluxed eyes.

2. Salivated.

a **1679** EARL ORRERY tr. *Guzman* i, I spit Verses faster than a flux'd Wencher does his Rheum. **1730** SWIFT *Death & Daphne* xxxvii, No new-fluxt Rake shew'd fairer Skin.

fluxible ('flʌksɪb(ə)l), *a.* *Obs.* or *arch.* Also 5 fluxyble, 7 fluxable. [a. OF. *fluxible*, ad. late L. *fluxibilis*, f. *flux-* ppl. stem of *fluĕre* to flow.]

1. Apt to flow; fluid.

1551 RECORDE *Cast. Knowl.* (1556) 141 The water beynge a lyquide and fluxible bodye, can not be stayed by his owne partes. **1605** TIMME *Quersit.* II. i. 105 Salt, by the vehemencie of the heat of fire, is to be dissolued, moulten, and made fluxible. **1726** LEONI tr. *Alberti's Archit.* I. 45/2 Stones..are created by Nature..of a liquid and fluxible substance.

fig. **1660** MILTON *Free Commw.* 437 Good Education.. ought to correct the fluxible fault..of our watry situation.

b. Of a watery consistence; hence, pliable, supple.

1607 TOPSELL *Four-f. Beasts* (1658) 408 Not a fluxible or loose fat like the fat of Lambs, but a solid fat, like the fat of Hogs. **1618** M. BARET *Horsemanship* I. 9 The ends of the flint was rather to be hard and firme then soft and fluxable. **1684** tr. *Bonet's Merc. Compit.* x. 366/2 At that Age all things are fluxible..especially the Bones and Nerves.

2. Capable of being melted; fusible; liquefiable.

1471 RIPLEY *Comp. Alch.* I. vi. in Ashm. (1652) 130 We make Calxes unctious both Whyte and Red..Fluxyble as Wex. **1607** TOPSELL *Four-f. Beasts* (1658) 289 In them doth abound fluxible moisture, apt to be dissolved with every little heat. **1750** tr. *Leonardus' Mirr. Stones* 17 Minerals are of two sorts, some fluxible or liquifiable and others not.

quasi-*sb.* **1750** tr. *Leonardus' Mirr. Stones* 17 Dismissing the first Fluxibles, such as Gold.

3. Liable to flux or change; fluctuating, not permanent, variable.

1561 EDEN *Arte Nauig.* III. ii. 56 This is fluxible, wauering, and moueable. **1610** GUILLIM *Heraldry* III. v. (1660) 120 Meteors..be of nature fluxible, and nothing permanent. **1677** GALE *Crt. Gentiles* IV. 517 Is there not a natural leuitie and vanitie in every creature which renders it fluxible, variable, and inconstant?

Hence '**fluxibly** *adv.* **fluxi'bility**, '**fluxibleness**, the quality of being fluxible.

1471 RIPLEY *Comp. Alch.* VI. ix. in Ashm. (1652) 163 Every parte all fyre for to endure, Fluxybly fyxe and stabull in tyncture. **1574** NEWTON *Health Mag.* 38 It..stoppeth over much thinnesse and fluxibilitie of bloude. **1651** HAMMOND *Answ. Ld. Falkland* vii. Wks. 1684 II. 693 The Fluxibility of humane Nature is so great, that it is no wonder if errours should have crept in. **1727** BAILEY vol. II, Fluxibleness. **1750** tr. *Leonardus' Mirr. Stones* 20 Such humidity is disproportioned by the fluxibility..and therefore it resides more in one part than in another.

fluxile ('flʌksɪl), *a.* *Obs.* or *arch.* [ad. late L. *fluxil-is*, f. *flux-*: see prec. and -ILE.]

1. = FLUXIBLE 1.

1605 TIMME *Quersit.* II. iii. 115 The which water, albeit it alwayes remaineth fluxile and liquid. **1641** FRENCH *Distill.* v. (1651) 161, I extracted a good quantity of nitrous salt, which was almost fluxile. **1702** R. MEAD *Poisons* 114 The Mercurial Globules..dissolve the Preter-natural Cohæsions of all the Liquors..making them more Fluxile and Thin.

2. = FLUXIBLE 3.

a **1654** SELDEN *Engl. Epin.* x. §16 The fluxile nature of this deceitful prince [King John]. **1858** BUSHNELL *Serm. New Life* 212 Opinions..are in a fluxile shifting state.

Hence **flu'xility** [see -ITY], the quality or condition of being fluxile.

1660 BOYLE *New. Exp. Phys. Mech.* xxxiii. 249 The Weight and Fluidity, or, at least, Fluxility of the Bodies here below. **1707** FLOYER *Physic. Pulse-Watch* 37 The Fluxility, or thin consistence of the Blood. **1721** N. HODGES *Hist. Acc. Plague* 115 Salt adds to the Fluxility of Fluids.

fluxing ('flʌksɪŋ), *vbl. sb.* [f. FLUX *v.* + -ING[1].]

1. The action of the vb. FLUX in various senses.

1659 HEYLIN *Animadv.* in *Fuller's App. Inj. Innoc.* (1840) 313 An ordinary purge being sufficient for the one, whereas the foul body of the other doth require a fluxing. *a* **1734** NORTH *Lives* (1826) 353 A certain cure [for the mange].. was fluxing with mercury. **1777** WATSON in *Phil. Trans.* LXVIII. 875 The roasting or fluxing of an ore.

b. *concr.* = FLUX *sb.* 11.

1880 LOMAS *Alkali Trade* 127 The amount of 'fluxings' should be kept as small as possible.

2. *attrib.* as *fluxing-material*; **fluxing-bed**, in the manufacture of soda, one of the two parts into which the sole of the furnace is divided.

1832 G. R. PORTER *Porcelain & Gl.* 264 Other descriptions..do not contain an equal abundance of fluxing materials.

fluxion ('flʌkʃən). Also, 6 fluxione, -yon. [a. Fr. *fluxion*, ad. L. *fluxiōn-em*, f. *flux-* ppl. stem of *fluĕre* to flow; see -ION[1].]

1. The action of flowing; a flowing or issuing forth (of water, vapour, etc.). Also, continuous or progressive motion; continual change. Now *rare*.

1599 HAKLUYT *Voy.* II. II. 333 Whirlepooles, and fluxions are caused..in the middest of the sea. **1603** HOLLAND *Plutarch's Mor.* 962 The fluxion of the odour comming from the beast. **1606** J. DAVIES *Sel. Sec. Husb. &c.* Wks. (Grosart) II. 14 If the fluxion of this instant Now Effect not That, noght wil, that Time doth know. **1635** SWAN *Spec. M.* v. §2 (1643) 165 That [water]..which..hath some certain beginning of fluxion. **1656** T. STANLEY *Hist. Philos.* v. 10 In Sensibles neither magnitude nor quality is permanent, but in continuall fluxion and mutation. **1660** *Ibid.* IX. 550/1 The point by fluxion makes a Line. **1880** BLACKMORE *M. Anerley* I. viii. 92 Their bodies continually going up and down upon perpetual fluxion.

fig. **1829** GEN. P. THOMPSON *Exerc.* (1842) I. 31 The Catholics know that the fluxion of public opinion is in their favour.

†**b.** = EFFLUVIUM 2 a. *Obs.*

1603 HOLLAND *Plutarch's Mor.* 725 Those fluxions which rest upon waters, looking-glasses, or any such mirrors. **1655** STANLEY *Hist. Philos.* II. (1701) 65/1 Falling Stars are not fluxions of the æther extinguisht in the Air almost as soon as lighted. **1748** HARTLEY *Observ. Man.* I. iii. 352 The Rays of Light may be considered as a kind of Fluxions in respect of the biggest component Particles of Matter.

2. An excessive flow of blood, 'humour,' serum, etc. to any organ or part of the body. Also *concr.*, the matter which flows.

1541 R. COPLAND *Galyen's Terap.* 2 Bj, Yf the flux or rennynge wyll nat stop with salues, seke the cause of the sayde fluxyon. *c* **1550** LLOYD *Treas. Health* (1585) A iij, Horsnesse, and continuall fluxion of snevill in old men. **1601** HOLLAND *Pliny* II. 559 It is the better for to represse the fluxion of humors into the eies. **1612** WOODALL *Surg. Mate* Wks. (1653) 75 Galles..cure fluxions of the gums. **1746** LADY M. W. MONTAGU *Let. to W. Montagu* 23 Aug., I had so bad a fluxion on my eyes, I was really afraid of losing them. **1874** ROOSA *Dis. Ear* 75 A fluxion towards the labyrinth with serous exudation in the nerve structure.

fig. **1796** BURNEY *Metastasio* II. 351 To attempt the cure of the eloquent fluxion to which he is subject.

3. = FLUX *sb.* 1.

1563 W. FULKE *Meteors* (1640) 53 b, The common dew drunke of cattell..bringing them to a fluxion. **1599** A. M. tr. *Gabelhouer's Bk. Physicke* 217/2 It præventeth also.. superfluous fluxione [of the menstrualles]. **1657** TOMLINSON *Renou's Disp.* 165* This cures eroding fluxions. **1760–72** tr. *Juan & Ulloa's Voy.* (ed. 3) II. 67 At Lima it occasioned constipations and fluxions.

†**4.** = FUSION. *Obs.*

1731 BAILEY, *Fluxion* (among Chymists), signifies the running of Metals or any other Bodies, into a Fluid, by Fire or otherwise. **1848** in CRAIG.

5. *Math.* In the Newtonian form of the infinitesimal calculus: 'The rate or proportion at which a flowing or varying quantity increases its magnitude' (Hutton *Math. Dict.*).

This is Newton's own use of the word; but the 18th c. writers on the Newtonian calculus used *fluxion* for what Newton called the 'moment' of a fluent, and modern analysts call the 'differential'.

corresponding fluxions, rates at which two interdependent quantities may change simultaneously. ***second fluxion***, the rate of change of the fluxion of a variable quantity; the second differential coefficient with respect to the time.

1704 [see DIFFERENTIAL B 1]. **1706** W. JONES *Syn. Palmar. Matheseos* 174 Let $\dot{x}$ be a Ratiuncula, or Fluxion of the Ratio of 1 to 1 + x. **1806** HUTTON *Course Math.* II. 287 Rules.. for finding the fluxions of all sorts of quantities. **1828** *Ibid.* II. 323 The fluxion found from a given fluent is always perfect and complete.

b. Hence (***the method*** or †***doctrine of***) ***fluxions*** is used as a name for the Newtonian calculus.

The *direct* and *inverse* method of fluxions are (apart from differences of notation) essentially identical with the differential and the integral calculus respectively.

1702 [see DIFFERENTIAL A 3.]. **1741** WATTS *Improv. Mind* I. xx. 327 A Penetration into the abstruse Difficulties and Depths of modern Algebra and Fluxions. **1812** CRESSWELL *Max. & Min.* II. ii. 197 Its [quantity's] increase and decrease by motion, which is the foundation of the doctrine of Fluxions. **1830** HERSCHEL *Stud. Nat. Phil.* III. iii. (1851) 271 The method of fluxions, or, as it is now more generally called, the differential calculus. **1874** GREEN *Short Hist.* ix. §1. 599 Newton..facilitated the calculation of planetary movements by his theory of Fluxions.

¶ **c.** *loosely.* An infinitesimal quantity.

1846 DE QUINCEY *Christianity* Wks. XII. 234 The hour-hand of a watch—who can detect the separate fluxions of its advance?

6. *Comb.*: **fluxion-structure** (see quot. 1890).

1882 GEIKIE *Text-bk. Geol.* II. II. iv. 104 This is well shown by what is termed the fluxion-structure. **1890** —— *Class-bk. Geol.* (ed. 2) 146 *Flow-structure, Fluxion-structure*, an arrangement of the crystallites, crystals, or particles of a rock in streaky lines..indicative of the internal movement of the mass previous to its consolidation.

fluxional ('flʌkʃənal), *a.* [f. prec. + -AL[1].]

1. *Math.* Of the nature of or pertaining to a fluxion or the method of fluxions.

1748 HARTLEY *Observ. Man* I. iii. 357 The Justness of an arithmetical..or fluxional Operation. **1823** MITCHELL *Dict. Math. & Phys. Sc.*, *Fluxional Analysis* is the analysis of fluxions and flowing quantities, distinguishable from the differential calculus both by its metaphysics and notation. **1828** HUTTON *Course Math.* II. 321 Multiply every term by the fluxional letter.

2. Pertaining to, resulting from, or subject to 'fluxion' or flowing.

1827 COLERIDGE *Rem.* (1836) I. 215 How are we to explain the reaction of this fluxional body on the animal? **1842–3** GROVE *Corr. Phys. Forces* (1874) 134 The instability, or fluxional state, of all nature. **1862** F. HALL *Hindu Philos. Syst.* 36 Other effects besides the fluxional creation of the world are referred to.

fluxionary ('flʌkʃənərɪ), *a.* [see -ARY.]

1. = FLUXIONAL 1.

1734 BERKELEY *Analyst* §10 The great Author of the Fluxionary Method. **1763** W. EMERSON *Meth. Increm.* vii, Some fluxionary quantities have no fluents, but what are expressed by series. **1831** BREWSTER *Newton* (1855) I. ii. 35 We find him occupied with his fluxionary calculus.

2. Of the nature of, or subject to 'fluxion' or continuous change, fluctuating.

1748 *Lond. Mag.* June 255/2 The general ferment..in matter, whereby all bodies are..disposed to undergo those fluxionary changes necessary to their generation, growth and corruption. **1826** DE QUINCEY in *Blackw. Mag.* XX. 738 Appearances..which, by their very essence, are fluxionary, become unnatural when fixed and petrified. **1841** *Blackw. Mag.* XLIX. 416 All other wealth was fluxionary.

fluxionist ('flʌkʃənɪst). [see -IST.] One who uses or is skilled in mathematical fluxions.

1734 BERKELEY *Analyst Qu.* 43 Whether an Algebraist, Fluxionist..or Demonstrator of any kind can expect indulgence for obscure Principles? **1816** tr. *La Croix's Diff. & Int. Calc.* 620 The best argument of its utter insufficiency ..is derived from the practices of the fluxionists themselves.

† '**fluxive**, *a.* *Obs.* [as if ad. L. *fluxīvus*, f. *flux-* ppl. stem of *fluĕre* to flow: see -IVE.] That has the quality of flowing, apt to flow, fluid; *lit.* and *fig.* Also, fluctuating, variable.

1597 SHAKS. *Lover's Compl.* 50 These often bath'd she in her fluxive eyes. **1605** DRAYTON *Man in Moone* 311 In fluxive humour, which is ever found, As I doe wane, or wax up to my round. **1668** CULPEPPER & COLE *Barthol. Anat.* III. viii. 148 Thin and fluxive like water. *a* **1670** HACKET *Cent. Serm.* (1675) 532, I look not upon that which is fluxive and changeable. **1716** M. DAVIES *Athen. Brit.* II. 352 The Fluxive Disposition, or the great Pox.

† **fluxure** ('flʌksjʊə(r)). *Obs.* [ad. L. *fluxūra*, f. *flux-* ppl. stem of *fluĕre* to flow.] **a.** The quality of being fluid; fluidity. **b.** *concr.* That which flows; a quantity of fluid matter; sap.

a. **1599** B. JONSON *Ev. Man out of Hum.* Induct., Why, Humor..in it selfe holds these two properties, Moisture and Fluxure.

b. **1596** DRAYTON *Leg.* IV. 930 As in the Corne, the Fluxure when we see Fills but the Straw, when it should feede the Eare. **1603** —— *Bar. Wars* II. xvi, The swolne fluxure of the Clouds. **1622** —— *Poly-olb.* xxvii. 375 Those Tree-geese..which like a Ielly first To the beholder seeme, then by the fluxure nurst, Still great and greater thriue.

fluy, obs. var. of FLUEY *a.*

fluyd, flwe, obs. forms of FLOOD, FLUE.

flwreis, obs. Sc. form of FLOURISH.

fly (flaɪ), *sb.*[1] Pl. flies (flaɪz). Forms: **fléoȝe** (in comb. **fléoȝ-, fléoh-**), **flýȝe**, *Northumb.* **fléȝe**, 2–4 **fliȝe**, *south.* **vliȝe**, 3 **fleoȝe, flye**, *south.* **vlie**, 3–4 **fleȝe**, *south.* **vleȝe, fleih**, *south.* **vleih**, 3–7, 8 *Sc.* **flie**, 4– *north.* and *Sc.* **flee**, 4–5 **flegh**, (4 **fleeȝe, fleh, flei(ghe, fley(e, flij**), 5–7 **flye**, 7– **fly**. [OE. *fléoȝe, flýȝe*, wk. fem. (Northumb. *fléȝe* ? str. masc.) = MDu. *vlieghe* (mod.Du. *vlieg*, OHG. *flioga, fliuga* (MHG. *vliege*, mod.Ger. *fliege*):—OTeut. **fleugôn-*, f. root of **fleugan* to fly. From the weak grade of the same root comes the equivalent Scandinavian word, ON., Sw. *fluga*, Da. *flue*.

The plural form in *-s* appears in 13th c., but the original plural ending *-n* was not wholly obsolete in the 15th c.]

1. †**a.** Any winged insect; as the bee, gnat, locust, moth, etc. *Obs.* Cf. 2, 3, 4 below, and BUTTERFLY *sb.*

c **950** *Lindisf. Gosp.* Matt. xxiii. 24 Latuas blindo ȝie worðias ðone fleȝe. **1340** *Ayenb.* 136 He is ase þe smale uleȝe þet makeþ þet hony. **1563** HYLL *Art. Garden.* (1593) 36 Flies (with the long hinder legges). **1599** T. MOUFET (*title*) Silkewormes and their flies. **1608** TOPSELL *Serpents* (1658) 653 The black Flies called Beetles. **1649** JER. TAYLOR *Gt. Exemp.* I. viii. 113 Eating Flyes and wilde honey. **1694** *Acc. Sev. Late Voy.* II. (1711) 207 Here are divers sorts of Flies, as Butter-flies, Butchers-flies, Horse-flies. **1774** GOLDSM. *Nat. Hist.* (1796) VIII. 149 The cold weather frequently comes on before the worm is transformed into a fly.

b. A dipterous or two-winged insect, *esp.* of the family *Muscidæ*.

c **1000** ÆLFRIC *Exod.* viii. 29 For ðe ic ȝebidde and ðeos fleoȝe færþ fram ðe. *c* **1200** *Vices & Virtues* (1888) 89 Al dai ðar cumeð to þohtes, al swo doð fliȝen to sare. *c* **1220** *Bestiary* 473 Til ðat ðer fleȝes faren and fallen ðer-inne. *a* **1300** *Cursor M.* 5990 (Cott.) To-morn þe fleies sal be you fra. **1398** TREVISA *Barth. De P.R.* v. xxiii. (1495) 130 Bees and flyes haue no voys, but make a voys in fleenge. **1477** EARL RIVERS (Caxton) *Dictes* 72 The flye that setteth her vpon corrupt thinges. **1513** DOUGLAS *Æneis* XII. Prol. 172 To knit hyr nettis..Tharwith to caucht the myghe and littill fle. **1615** G. SANDYS *Trav.* 203 The infinite swarmes of flies that do shine like glow-wormes. **1841–4** EMERSON *Ess.*, *Prudence* Wks. (Bohn) I. 94 Do what we can, summer will have its flies.

c. *fig.*

a **1225** *Ancr. R.* 290 [þes] dogge of helle..mid his blodie vlien of stinkinde þouhtes. *c* **1325** *Coer de L.* 2917 In whyt schetys they gunne hem wryen For the bytyng of his flyen. **1607** DEKKER *Hist. Sir T. Wyatt* I. Wks. 1873 III. 84 The Fly is angrie, but hee wants a sting.

d. A type of something insignificant.

1297 R. GLOUC. (1724) 428 Wat was þy strengþe worþ?.. ywys noȝt worþ a flye. *c* **1386** CHAUCER *Reeve's T.* 272 Aleyn answerde I count hym nat a flye. **1529** MORE *Comf. agst. Trib.* I. ii. Wks. 1123/1 Without which..all the spiritual coumfort that any man maye speake of can neuer auaile a flye. **1794** BURNS '*O Philly, happy be that day*' x, I care nae wealth a single flie. *a* **1830** HAZLITT *Convers. Authors*, He would not hurt a fly.

e. Phr.: ***fly in amber***: see AMBER 5. ***a fly in the ointment*** [after Eccl. x. 1]: some small or trifling circumstance which spoils the enjoyment of a thing, or detracts from its agreeableness. ***fly on the (coach-)wheel*** (see quot. 1870). ***to send***

away with a fly in one's ear: cf. FLEA 4. ***to break, crush, a fly upon the wheel*** (*fig.*): to spend a great deal of energy and labour upon something not worth it. ***let that fly stick in*** (or *to*) ***the wall*** (*Sc.*): say nothing more on that subject. ***don't let flies stick to your heels***: be quick. (*to*) ***drink with the flies*** (Austral. and N.Z. colloq.): see quot. 1943.

1606 *Rel. Proc. agst. late Traitors* Zz 4 b, The princes.. sent away your second Mercury with a flie in his eare. **1695** WOODWARD *Nat. Hist. Earth* II. (1723) 82 Flyes..that I have yet seen inclos'd in Amber. **1814** SCOTT *Wav.* lxxi, 'O whist, Colonel, for the love o' God! let that flee stick i' the wa'.' **1833** LAMB *Elia* 2nd Ser. (1840) 3 A Poor Relation—is the most irrelevant thing in nature,—..a lion in your path,—a frog in your chamber,—a fly in your ointment. **1836** *Going to Service* iv. 44 Don't let flies stick to your heels, and don't let ten minutes get the start of you. **1840** LYTTON *Money* v. iii, I have the greatest respect.. for the worthy and intelligent flies upon both sides the wheel. *a* **1859** DE QUINCEY *Incognito* Wks. XI. 2 To apply any more elaborate criticism to them, would be 'to break a fly upon the wheel'. **1870** BREWER *Dict. Phrase & Fable, Fly on the coach wheel*, one who fancies himself of mighty importance, but who is in reality of none at all. **1914** *Scotsman* 10 Sept. 9/1 The present situation is not without its 'fly in the ointment' for those motorists who have patriotically lent the assistance of their cars to the military authorities. **1928** *Daily Express* 11 May 10/7 The insurance of school fees has now become so general that it is as well to point out to parents that there is a rather large fly in the ointment. **1936** A. HUXLEY *Olive Tree* 5 There is only one fly in the ointment offered by commercial propagandists; they want your money. **1940** *Bulletin* (Sydney) 3 Jan. 35/3 He never needs to buy whisky, either, though a natural antipathy to drinking with the flies saves the officer's supply. **1943** BAKER *Dict. Austral. Slang* (ed. 3) 28 *Drink with the flies*: a drink consumed without the company of others. Also, to drink alone.

f. *Proverbs.*

a **1420** HOCCLEVE *De Reg. Princ.* 110 A flye folowethe the hony. *a* **1529** SKELTON *Replyc.* 752 The blynde eteth many a flye. **1546** J. HEYWOOD *Prov.* (1867) 75 Hungry flies byte sore.

g. ***there are no flies on***: (*a*) there is no lack of activity or astuteness in (a person); there is no fault to be found with, there are no blemishes in; (*b*) there is nothing dishonest or 'shady' about (a transaction). So ***to have no flies on***, etc. *slang* (orig. *Austral.* or *U.S.*).

The earliest examples indicate that the phrase was prob. orig. applied to cattle that are so active that flies do not settle on them.

1848 H. W. HAYGARTH *Recoll. Bush Life Austral.* ix. 101 'It's lucky we got them,' said Amos; 'there were "no flies" about that black bull.' *Note.* This expression is very common in Australia... Anything particularly good is said by the class of men we are here describing to have 'no flies' about it. **1868** J. DIPROSE *St. Clement Danes* 99 To this celebrated pugilist [*sc.* Deaf Burke] is attributed the old story of the 'flies in the gin-and-water', and hence the term 'no flies' became prevalent. [The story follows.] **1888** *Missouri Republ.* 24 Feb. (Farmer *Amer.*), Persons who are capable of descending to New York and Boston English are fully justified in saying that there are no flies on St. Louis or the St. Louis delegation either. **1888** *Detroit Free Press* 25 Aug. (Farmer & Henley), There ain't no flies on him, signifies, that he is not quiet long enough for moss to grow on his heels, that he is wide awake. **1893** FARMER & HENLEY *Slang* s.v. *Flies, There are no flies on me, on him*, etc.,.. 'I am dealing honestly with you'; 'he is genuine, and is not humbugging'. In America, the expression is used of (1) a man of quick parts..(2) a person of superior breeding or descent. **1897** R. M. STUART *Simpkinsville* i. 18 They wasn't no flies on his shape, nor his rig, nor his manners neither. **1898** *Strand Mag.* May 516, I kin put you in the way of making your pile, I kin. This is a *bona-fide* offer. No flies on *my* business. **1900** G. BONNER *Hard-Pan* iii. 83 There are no flies on your little sister. **1928** GALSWORTHY *Swan Song* II. vi. 156 There are no flies on your uncle. **1948** C. DAY LEWIS *Otterbury Incident* iv. 43 There are no flies on Rickie. I'm pretty sure he'd spotted how his own shoes got dirty. **1961** *Observer* 23 Apr. 18/2 There are no flies on Benaud. If England start bowling their overs slowly, no one will have to draw his attention to it.

h. ***like flies***: in large numbers or huge quantities.

[**1595** SHAKES. *3 Hen. VI* II. vi. 8 The common people swarme like summer flies.] **1934** A. HYDER *Black-Girl, White-Lady* xxi. 309 'Yo' kills niggers?' 'Like flies,' Charley assured her. **1958** R. LIDDELL *Morea* III. ii. 245 Now, at the end of 1955, people were marrying like flies; it is unlucky to marry in a leap year.

i. ***fly on the wall***: (*a*) an unperceived observer; one who is able to overhear discussions, etc., without being observed or involved; (*b*) *Cinemat.*, a film-making technique in which events are presented realistically by observing rather than by directing the action; freq. *attrib.*; cf. CINÉMA-VÉRITÉ.

1949 N. MITFORD *Love in Cold Climate* I. vi. 61, I had been throwing an occasional glance in their direction, wondering what it could all be about and wishing I could be a fly on the wall to hear them. **1971** A. SAMPSON *New Anat. Brit.* xii. 239, I spent a week inside the department, overhearing committees and meetings as a fly on the wall. **1983** *Listener* 10 Feb. 8/3 The 'fly-on-the-wall' technique, so successful elsewhere, would not overcome this problem. **1985** M. R. D. MEEK *Split Second* vi. 38 'What did you wheedle out of Maggie?' 'Well..she was no fly on the wall, but there have to be letters, documents, papers to be typed.' **1986** *City Limits* 12 June 23 This is a film that has tried hard not to impinge its identity on its subject, using a fly on the wall approach.

2. With defining word as *blow-*, *flesh-*, *horse-*, *house-*, *sheep-fly*, etc.: see those words. **black fly**, *U.S.* (see quot.). **Hessian fly** (*Cecidomyia Destructor*), an insect that infests wheat, said to have been introduced into America with the Hessian troops, during the War of Independence. **Spanish fly** = CANTHARIDES. **tsetse-fly** (*Glossina morsitans*), an African fly which carries disease (esp. sleeping sickness) and transmits it to humans and animals by biting.

a **1605** MONTGOMERIE *Flyting w. Polwart* 314 The feavers, the fearcie, with the speinȝie flees. **1661** LOVELL *Hist. Anim. & Min.* Pref., The pilularie beetle and spanish flies. **1799** G. WASHINGTON *Let.* Writ. 1893 XIV. 196 Letter relative to the loss of his crop, by the Hessian fly. **1812** J. SMYTH *Pract. Customs* (1821) 59 Cantharides, commonly called Spanish Flies. **1877** T. BAINES *Gold Regions S.E. Africa* 109 A considerable portion of this step is infested with the Tsetse fly. **1889** *Century Dict.* s.v. *Fly, Black Fly*, any one of the species of the genus *Simulium*, some of which are extraordinarily abundant in the northern woods of America, and cause great suffering by their bites.

3. a. In farmers' and gardeners' language, often used without defining prefix for the insect parasite chiefly injurious to the particular crop or animal indicated by the context; the hop-fly, potato-fly, turnip-fly, sheep-fly, etc. Chiefly *collect.* in *sing.* as the name of the disease consisting in or caused by the ravages of these insects.

a **1704** LOCKE *Wks.* (1714) III. 436 Before they come to think of the Fly in their Sheep, or the Tares in their Corn. **1707** MORTIMER *Husb.* 122 To prevent the Fly [in turnips] some propose to sow Ashes with the Seed. **1799** *Trans. Soc. Encourag. Arts* XVII. 47 An easy and efficacious method of destroying the Fly on Hops. **1819** REES *Cycl.*, *Fly*..a disease incident to sheep, in consequence of their being stricken by a fly, which produces a sort of maggot, that eats into, and remains in the flesh. **1842** JOHNSON *Farmer's Encycl.*, *Fly in Turnips* (*Altica nemorum*) the vulgar name of a species of flea-beetle, which attacks the turnip-crop in the cotyledon or seed leaf, as soon as it appears. **1846** J. BAXTER *Libr. Pract. Agric.* (ed. 4) II. 281 The marks left on the skin by the blows of the fly. **1888** *Times* 26 June 12/1 In some (hop) gardens a good deal of fly exists.

b. *ellipt.* The tsetse fly. *S. Afr.*

1856 C. J. ANDERSSON *Lake Ngami* 488 The natives, who are well acquainted with localities frequented by the fly. **1864** T. BAINES *Explor. S.W. Afr.* [424] They have lost all their oxen by the fly. **1877** —— *Gold Regions S.E. Afr.* 57 Keeping a sharp look out upon our own and each others horses to see that no 'fly' settled on them.

4. *Angling.* **a.** An insect attached to a hook as a lure in the mode of angling called fly-fishing. **b.** An artificial fly, i.e. a fish-hook dressed with feathers, silk, etc., so as to imitate some insect.

Often *collect.* in the phrase *to fish with fly*.

1589 *Pappe w. Hatchet* 3, I doo but yet angle with a silken flye, to see whether Martins will nibble. **1653** WALTON *Angler* iv. 93 Or with a Flie, either a natural or an artificial Flie. *Ibid.* iv. 111 Your gold, or what materials soever you make your Fly of. *a* **1740** TICKELL *Ep. to Lady bef. Marriage* 39 Here let me..lure the trout with well-dissembled flies. **1881** C. GIBBON *Heart's Problem* x. 154 He..tossed it [fish] into his basket, and cast his fly again.

fig. **1624** FLETCHER *Rule a Wife* I. i, Sit close Don Perez, or your Worship's caught. I fear a Flye.

†**5. a.** A familiar demon (from the notion that devils were accustomed to assume the form of flies). **b.** *transf.*, and with allusion to the insect's finding its way into the most private places: A spy (cf. F. *mouche*). **c.** A parasite, flatterer (cf. L. *musca*). *Obs.*

1584 R. SCOT *Discov. Witchcr.* III. xv. 51 A flie, otherwise called a divell or familiar. **1610** B. JONSON *Alch.* I. ii, A rifling flye: none o' your great familiars. **1622** BACON *Hen. VII* 241 There was this..Good in his employing of these Flies and Familiars; that..the..Suspition of them kept..many Conspiracies from beeing attempted. *a* **1643** W. CARTWRIGHT *Ordinary* II. iv, He hath a Fly only to win good cloaths. **1649** BP. HALL *Cases Consc.* 179 These mercenary Flies, whether of State, or of Religion, are justly hatefull.

6. *Printing.* **a.** A 'printer's devil' (cf. 5 a). **b.** The person who takes the sheets from the press, the 'taker-off'; also, that part of a printing machine which usually performs that office now. (Cf. FLYER.)

a. 1683 MOXON *Printing* 373 *Devil*..the Workmen do Jocosely call them Devils; and sometimes Spirits, and sometimes Flies. **1841** SAVAGE *Dict. Printing*, s.v., These boys are not now called devils, as in the time of Moxon, but Flies, or Fly Boys.

b. 1732 in HONE *Every-day Bk.* (1825–7) II. 1240 The inferior order among us, called flies, employed in taking newspapers off the press. **1838** TIMPERLEY *Printer's Man.* 113 *Fly*, the person that takes off the sheet from the press in cases of expedition. **1871** *Amer. Encycl. Printing*, *Fly*, an invention for taking off or delivering the sheets from a power-press.

†**7. a.** A 'patch' for the face. [tr. F. *mouche*.]). *Obs.*

1658 WHITE tr. *A late Discourse* 102 The patches and flies which she put upon her face.

†**b.** Some kind of head-dress. Cf. *fly-cap* (in 11 below). *Obs.*

1773 *History of Lord Ainsworth* I. 139 Her beautiful tresses were..fasten'd behind with a diamond comb; over which was plac'd a small French fly, ornamented with large sprigs set with brilliants. **1774** *Westm. Mag.* II. 259 Ladies ..still wear their hair low before..Small flys, the wings very wide apart at the top, and very small and short lappets.

†**8.** With reference to a festival formerly observed by the Oxford cooks. *Obs.*

On Whit-Tuesday the cooks 'marched in silken doublets on horseback to Bartholomews or Bullingdon Green *to fetch the fly*', and 'on Michaelmas Day they rode thither again *to carry the fly away*'. See Aubrey *Rem. Gentilisme* (1881) 202 (written in 1686); Aubrey supposed the sense to be that of 5 a above.

c **1602** in *Narcissus* (ed. M. L. Lee 1893) App. ii. 32 They [the cooks] have sett a little porch before so great an house, and have called their show the flye. **1654** GAYTON *Pleas. Notes* III. v. 99 The man that preaches the Cooks Sermon at Oxford, when that plump Society rides upon their Governours Horses to fetch in the Enemie, the Flie. **1661–6** WOOD *Antiq. Oxford* (O.H.S.) II. 515 *note*, Many people resorted here [St. Bartholomew's Hospital]; as the cooks bringing in of the fly.

9. *slang.* A policeman. Cf. BLUE-BOTTLE 2.

1857 R. L. SNOWDEN *Magistr. Assist.* (ed. 3) 446 A policeman, a fly.

10. *attrib.* and *Comb.*

a. simple attributive, as ***fly-blight***, ***-bottle*** [tr. G. *fliegenglas*], ***-kind***, ***-maggot***, ***-screen***, ***state***, ***-wing***; (sense 2) (***tsetse-***)***fly-belt***, ***-country***; (sense 4) as ***fly-tackle***; (sense 6 b) as ***fly-pulley***.

1894 *Westm. Gaz.* 17 Nov. 5/1 The Beira line had now completely spanned the '*fly' belt. **1887** *Daily News* 28 June 2/5 The plantations in these districts being most affected by the *'fly blight'. **1953** G. E. M. ANSCOMBE tr. *Wittgenstein's Philos. Investig.* §309 What is your aim in philosophy?—To shew the fly the way out of the *fly-bottle. **1967** *Philos. Q.* XVII. 363, I would like an illustration of a flybottle, which people describe variously. **1969** *Proc. Arist. Soc.* Suppl. Vol. XLIII. 108 If the exit from the fly-bottle is an entry into too restrictive a cupboard, it seems necessary to find a way out of the cupboard as well. **1864** T. BAINES *Explor. S.W. Afr.* iv. 68 Treachery of guides purposely sent by the chiefs to lead him into the *fly country. **1891** *Pall Mall G.* 8 Dec. 1/3 When the railway..has crossed the fly country. **1691** RAY *Creation* 6 The *Fly-kind, if under that name we comprehend all other flying insects. **1692** *Ibid.* II. 123 The *fly maggots. **1875** SOUTHWARD *Dict. Typogr.* s.v. *Setting the Fly*, Let it run down the fly so that it is barely held by the *fly pulleys. **1903** *Work* 1 Aug. 412/3 Inside this lining will be laid a thin coating of tinfoil, on which will be placed what will look like a strong netting or *fly-screen, except that the wires of which it is composed will be carefully joined and highly polished. **1952** 'N. SHUTE' *Far Country* 18 She went and rang the dinner bell outside the flyscreen door. **1971** *Sunday Times* (Johannesburg) (Business Sect.) 28 Mar. 5/2 Adjustable aluminium louvres..may also be fitted with flyscreens. **1791** W. BARTRAM *Carolina* 83 When they appear in the *fly state. **1834** MEDWIN *Angler in Wales* II. 113, I was half sorry that I had no *fly-tackle, and soon tired. *c* **1460** *Towneley Myst.* 192 He settes not a *fle wyng bi Sir Cesar fulle even.

b. objective (sense 1 b) as ***fly-breeder***, ***-fancier***, ***-hunter***, ***-killer***, ***-scarer***, †***-way-driver***, ***-whipper***; ***fly-catching*** vbl. sb. and ppl. adj., ***-hunting*** vbl. sb.; ***fly-proof*** adj.; (sense 4) as ***fly-caster***, ***-maker***, ***-taker***; ***fly-dressing***, ***-making*** vbl. sbs.; ***fly-taking*** ppl. adj.

1751 SMOLLETT *Per. Pic.* (1779) IV. xciv. 144 'I never dispute..with the son of a cucumber,' said the *fly-breeder. **1897** *Outing* (U.S.) XXX. 221/2 It is not every *fly-caster who can properly manipulate a live or dead minnow, a crawfish, or a spoon. **1926** *Daily Colonist* (Victoria, B.C.) 9 July 16/1 Earl C. McFarland..nationally known fly-caster and sportsman, died..today. **1702** C. MATHER *Magn. Chr.* IV. (1853) II. 105 A certain soaring and serious greatness of soul, which rendered *fly-catching too low a business for him. **1890** WEBSTER, *Fly-catching* (Zoöl.), having the habit of catching insects on the wing. **1886** J. H. KEENE *Fish. Tackle* 202 There is no royal road to *fly-dressing however. **1751** SMOLLETT *Per. Pic.* (1779) IV. xciv. 145 The *fly-fancier..accused the mathematician. **1895** C. C. ABBOTT *Birds about us* iv. 113 They are fly-catchers, not *fly-hunters. **1838** DICKENS *Mem. Grimaldi* ii, He had been *fly-hunting with his friend. **1658** ROWLAND *Moufet's Theat. Ins.* 951 He was afterwards called by the name of Muscarius or *Fly-killer. **1787** BEST *Angling* (ed. 2) 77 Every man his own *fly-maker. **1653** WALTON *Angler* iv. 113 The Art of *flie-making. **1801–3** DANIEL *Rural Sports* II. 296 Hackles are a very important article in Fly-making. **1817** *Niles' Reg.* XII. 284/1, I found several of the other kinds of wheat.. growing on some farms in the same field with the *fly-proof or Lawler wheat. **1944** *Living off Land* ii. 34 Keep the smokehouse fly-proof by covering the top. **1638** SIR T. HERBERT *Trav.* (ed. 2) 68 On the left hand, Rajea Bousing *fly-skarer. **1889** *Century Dict.*, **Fly-taker*, in angling, any fish that will take the fly. **1840** TICKELL in *Jrnl. Asiat. Soc. Bengal* IX. 705 The little *fly-taking Cyprinus, miscalled 'trout' in Upper India. **1658** ROWLAND *Moufet's Theat. Ins.* 951 Jupiter, called ἀπομύιος, or the *Fly-way-driver. **1872** BAKER *Nile Tribut.* viii. 134 The long tails of the giraffes are admirable *fly-whippers.

c. instrumental, as ***fly-angling***, †***-biting*** vbl. sbs.; ***fly-bit***, ***-stuck***, ***-swarmed*** adjs.

1653 WALTON *Angler* iv. 110 These and the May-fly are the ground of all *fly-Angling. **1821** CLARE *Vill. Minstr.* I. 203 Their *fly-bit hides. **1659** D. PELL *Impr. Sea* 417 It is comparatively but a..meer *fly-biting to what they undergo. **1877** T. BAINES *Gold Regions S.E. Africa* 151 A *fly-stuck ox. **1879** E. ARNOLD *Lt. Asia* 69 The *fly-swarmed sweetmeat shops.

11. a. Special comb.: **fly-bat**, a species of fly found in Barbados; **fly-bird**, a humming-bird (cf. F. *oiseau-mouche*); **fly-blister**, a plaster made of *Cantharides*; **fly-book**, a case in the form of a book, in which anglers keep artificial flies; **fly-brush**, a brush for driving away flies; **fly-cage**, a contrivance for catching flies; †**fly-cap**, a kind of head-dress (see quot. 1762); **fly-case**, the covering of an insect; *spec.* the anterior wing of beetles, elytron; **fly-dope** *N. Amer.*, a

liniment used as a protection against flies; **fly-duster** = *fly-brush*; **fly-eater**, an eater of flies, *spec.* any of several small Australian fly-catchers of the genus *Gerygone*; **fly-fan**, a fly-flick, or a motor-driven fan for driving away flies; **fly-flick**, an instrument for killing or driving away flies; † **fly-fringe** (see quot.); **fly-fungus**, (*a*) the fly-agaric, *Amanita muscaria*; (*b*) the house-fly fungus, *Entomophthora muscæ*; **fly-hook**, a hook baited with a fly; **fly-line**, a line for fly-fishing; **fly-mould** = *fly-fungus* (*b*); **fly-paper**, (*a*) a sheet of paper prepared to catch or poison flies; (*b*) ***Flypaper Act*** (slang), the Prevention of Crimes Act, 1909; so ***to be on the flypaper***, to be subject to this Act, to be a criminal known to the police; **fly-powder**, a powder used to kill flies; **fly-rod**, a rod for fly-fishing; **fly-slicer**, *slang* (see quot.); **fly-snapper**, *U.S.*, a name of certain fly-catching birds: (*a*) the genus *Myiagra*; (*b*) *Phainopepla nitens*; **fly-speck, -spot**, (*a*) a stain produced by the excrement of an insect; also *fig.*; (*b*) a plant disease, esp. of apples and pears, caused by the fungus *Leptothyrium pomi*; also *attrib.*; **fly-specked, -speckled** *a.*, marked with fly-specks; **fly-strike**, a skin disease of sheep, caused by the maggots of blow-flies, esp. those of the genera *Lucilia* and *Calliphora*; hence **fly-struck** *a.*; **fly-swat, -swatter** = SWATTER; **fly-swish** = *fly-whisk*; **fly-tier, -tyer**, a maker of artificial flies; so ***fly-tying*** vbl. sb.; **fly-time**, the time when flies are to be met with or are troublesome; **fly-tip, -top**, a top-joint used for fly-fishing; **fly-water**, (*a*) an infusion or decoction of flies; (*b*) (see quot. 1855); **fly-weevil**, *U.S.*, the common grain-moth (*Gelechia cerealella*) (*Cent. Dict.*); **fly-weight** *Boxing*, a weight of 8 stone or less; a pugilist of such a weight; also *transf.*; **fly-whisk**, an instrument for driving away flies; **fly-wire**, screening to exclude flies, esp. ***fly-wire door***. Also FLY-BANE, -BITTEN, -BLOW, -BLOWN, -CATCHER, -FISH, etc.

1750 G. HUGHES *Barbadoes* 211 The *Fly-bats come from their lurking holes. **1782-3** W. F. MARTYN *Geog. Mag.* II. 468 The *fly-bird is esteemed one of the most beautiful. **1842** HOOD *Elm Tree* III. xxiii, The Fly-bird flutters up and down, To catch its tiny prey. **1869** 'MARK TWAIN' *Innoc. Abr.* xvii. 169 A Venus with a *fly-blister on her breast. **1848** KINGSLEY *Yeast* xi, I put it in the squire's *fly-book. **1841** G. CATLIN *Indians* I. 113 The Indian's *fly brush was made of the buffalo tail. **1888** J. L. ALLEN in *Century Mag.* Apr. 946 The abandoned fly-brush lay full across his face. **1838** DICKENS *O. Twist* xxxvii, A paper *fly-cage dangled from the ceiling. **1753** *Gentl. Mag.* XXIII. 123/2 The ladies.. should not sacrifice the vigor of health..to a *fly cap. **1762** *Lond. Chronicle* 16–18 Feb. 167/3 The Fly Cap..is fixed upon the forehead, forming the figure of an over-grown butterfly..with outstretched wings. **1826** MISS MITFORD *Village* Ser. II. (1863) 353 With powdered hair and fly-caps and lappets. **1897** *Outing* (U.S.) XXX. 377/1 The *fly-dope, or preventive against the attacks of insects. **1903** S. E. WHITE *Forest* ix. 106 Each and every man..heralds the particular merits of his own fly-dope. **1860** *Merc. Marine Mag.* VII. 270 The kahili is made of black feathers, fastened on a pole, much resembling a *fly-duster. **1895** W. O. LEGGE in *Rep. Australasian Assoc. Adv. Sci.* VI. 447 [The habits and habitats of the genus as] applied to *Gerygone* suggested the term *Fly-eater, as distinguished from Fly-catcher. **1906** *Westm. Gaz.* 30 May 12/1 Starlings [are] great fly-eaters. **1930** W. DE LA MARE *Desert Islands* 212 Owl, kingfisher, robin, fly-eater. **1958** P. C. MORRISON *Austral. Bird Bk.* 143 *Brown warbler*, flyeater, G[erygone] richmondii. **1891** A. H. KEANE tr. *Junker's Trav. Afr.* II. viii. 276 His hand also grasped, not a warlike assegai, but a peaceful *fly-fan! *a* **1911** D. G. PHILLIPS *Susan Lenox* (1917) I. xvii. 300 They went into a large restaurant with fly fans speeding. **1914** D. FRASER *Winning Prim. People* iv. 45 He carried nothing in his hand but a *fly-flick. **1860** FAIRHOLT *Costume*, *Fly-fringe*, a peculiar edging for ladies' sleeves and dresses; much worn in the early part of the reign of George III. **1822** *Mem. Wernerian Soc. Edinb.* IV. 343 The plant commonly known by the name of the *fly-fungus (from its property of destroying flies when steeped in milk), has made some noise of late on the Continent. **1910** *Encycl. Brit.* I. 780/1 *Amanita muscaria*, the fly fungus, formerly known as *Agaricus muscarius*. **1912** L. O. HOWARD *House Fly* ii. 64 With the common house fly fungus (*Empusa muscae*) a slight change in the amount of atmospheric moisture is sufficient to bring about germination. **1952** C. J. ALEXOPOULOS *Introd. Mycol.* vii. 177 The most familiar of the Entomophthorales is *Entomophthora muscae*, commonly called the fly fungus. **1706** R. H[OWLETT] *Angler's Sure Guide* 88 A middle-siz'd *Flie-Hook. *Ibid.* 97 The *Flie-Line should be made very taper. **1854** BADHAM *Halieut.* ii. 19 Neither fly-rods, fly-lines, reels..nor landing-net. **1908** *Westm. Gaz.* 8 Aug. 16/3 Flies..may be seen..lying about in odd corners covered with a mouldy grey fur, which is called *fly-mould. **1851** MAYHEW *Lond. Labour* I. 435 *Fly-papers came..into street-traffic..in the summer of 1848. **1910** F. MARTYN *Burglar in Baulk* 8 *On the flypaper*, subject to the Crimes Prevention Act. **1933** C. E. LEACH *On Top of Underworld* x. 139 *Flypaper Act*..Prevention of Crimes Act. **1936** J. CURTIS *Gilt Kid* ii. 23 He gets nicked for suspect and being on the flypaper, he gets a stretch in the Ville. **1941** *Coast to Coast 1941* 76 A spiral fly paper hung from the ceiling. **1971** *Islander* (Victoria, B.C.) 22 Aug. 3/1 From the ..ceiling hung a few well encrusted fly papers. **1839** URE *Dict. Arts*, *Fly powder, the black coloured powder obtained by the spontaneous oxidizement of metallic arsenic in the air. **1684** R. H. *School Recreat.* 149 The Line..for the *Fly-Rod..must be stronger than the first. **1843** ATKINSON in *Zoologist* I. 294, I tapped it with the end of my fly-rod. **1785** GROSE *Dict. Vulg. Tongue*, *Fly slicers, life guard men, from their sitting on horse-back, under an arch, where they are frequently observed to drive away flies with their swords. **1895** C. C. ABBOTT *Birds about us* ii. 75 Well..did the *flysnapper only make believe to launch out after insects? **1855** OGILVIE, *Fly-speck*. **1865** MRS. STOWE *House & Home Papers* 290, I would shut my eyes on fly-specks, and open them on the beauties of Nature. **1907** *Westm. Gaz.* 15 July 2/1 Even your Caesar Borgia is but a fly-speck in the infinite. **1909** R. A. WASON *Happy Hawkins* 113 Lookin' like a fly-speck on a new tablecloth. **1939** H. WORMALD *Dis. Fruits & Hops* v. 103 Frequently associated with Sooty Blotch, but sometimes occurring alone, are groups of black, circular dots which from their size and appearance are known as Fly Specks. **1943** BAKER *Dict. Austral. Slang* (ed. 3) 75 *The speck*, Tasmania. Also, 'the Fly Speck'. **1952** E. RAMSDEN tr. *Gram & Weber's Plant Dis.* 126/2 The fly speck fungus produces groups of round black dots on apples and sometimes on pears and plums. **1961** *Trans. Brit. Mycol. Soc.* XLIV. 304 The Micropeltaceae or 'fly-speck' fungi are treated by Prof. Batista as one of the seven families of the Microthyriales. **1872** 'MARK TWAIN' *Roughing It* 43 Only one cruet left..a stopperless, *fly-specked, broken-necked thing. **1883** *Harper's Mag.* Mar. 528/1 A fly-specked old engraving. **1881** MISS LAFFAN in *Macm. Mag.* XLIV. 388 Pictures, yellowed by turf smoke and well *fly-speckled. **1851** D. JERROLD *St. Giles* v. 47 There are a thousand cracks and flaws and *fly-spots upon everything about us. [**1890** J. H. STEEL *Treat. Dis. Sheep* x. 325 Even a dog is able to tell when sheep have been struck by the fly. **1937** A. FRASER *Sheep Farming* xv. 143 When the weather favours strike.. the maggot fly may cause hundreds of pounds worth of damage.] **1950** H. G. BELSCHNER *Sheep Managem.* vi. 178 The treatment of *fly-strike in sheep should be undertaken as soon as possible. **1965** C. R. W. SPEDDING *Sheep Prod.* viii. 210 When the eggs hatch, the maggots burrow under the skin and this is described as 'fly strike'. **1922** C. R. EDMONDS *Dis. Anim. S. Afr.* II. 310 This trouble [*sc.* sheep blowfly] is usually designated as 'fly-blown sheep' or '*fly-struck sheep'. **1934** *Bulletin* (Sydney) 18 Apr. 28/1 A fresh paddock will work wonders even if the flock is in includes fly-struck sheep. **1950** H. G. BELSCHNER *Sheep Managem.* vi. 178 The only equipment necessary to dress a fly-struck sheep is a pair of shears, a suitable dressing, and a small horsehair brush. **1937** A. N. LYONS *Tom, Dick & Harriet* xxvi. 225 He carried a *fly-swat..and flourished this..in a menacing manner. **1917** *Blackw. Mag.* May 753/1 Fly-papers and *fly-swatters proved illusive. **1937** *Sunday Express* 30 May 17/3 Then he took to 'fly-swatters' and things for protecting food from the fly menace. **1922** *Blackw. Mag.* Apr. 462/1 An old *fly-swish made of palm-leaves. **1927** *World Dominion* Oct. 318 His inevitable fly-swish under his arm. **1947** J. STEVENSON-HAMILTON *Wild Life S. Afr.* iv. 42 The trunk is indeed everything to the elephant..Furnished with a good large bunch of long grass it makes a better fly-swish than do most animals' own tails. **1881** *Echo* 11 Apr. 3/6 The..cleverest *fly-tier in England. **1706** R. H[OWLETT] *Angler's Sure Guide* 86 This is their [Fishes'] constant Course all *Flie-time. **1757** DYER *Fleece* I. 366 In teizing fly-time. **1706** R. H[OWLETT] *Angler's Sure Guide* 79 The Stock [of the Rod] bored no wider than to carry a Ground-top therein, or a *Flie-top. **1887** H. CHOLMONDELEY-PENNELL *Mod. Impr. Fish. Tackle* 23 This branch of *fly-tying. **1815** KIRBY & SP. *Entomol.* I. 306, I should have recommended..*fly-water for disorders in the eyes. **1855** OGILVIE Suppl., *Fly-water*, a solution of arsenic, or decoction of quassia-bark, for killing flies. **1789** L. CARTER in *Trans. Amer. Soc.* I. 274 (*title*), Observations concerning the *Fly-weevil that destroys the Wheat. **1911** *Boxing* 9 Sept. 454/3 Kleber reigns over the *fly-wt championship. **1913** J. G. B. LYNCH *Comp. Amat. Boxer* 234 Championships. Standard Weights. Fly Weight, 8 stone and under. **1914** —— *Promin. Pugilists* 158 He [*sc.* Jimmy Wilde] is far below the fly-weight limit. **1944** AUDEN *For Time Being* (1945) 12 A fly-weight hermit in a dream Of gardens. **1955** *Times* 12 May 4/3 They fell behind again when Gnr. Lloyd was beaten in one round by the opposing flyweight. **1841** LANE *Arab. Nts.* I. 132 A kind of *fly-whisk made of palm-leaves. **1930** E. WAUGH *Labels* iii. 65 He lunged out with a spanner and rapped an old man on the knuckles who was trying to sell us a fly-whisk. **1953** DYLAN THOMAS *Under Milk Wood* (1954) 52 Mrs. Ogmore-Pritchard belches in a teeny hanky and chases the sunlight with a flywhisk. **1963** W. SOYINKA *Lion & Jewel* 25 Fly-whisk and whisky. **1952** 'N. SHUTE' *Far Country* v. 140 The house itself had deep verandas on two sides and *fly-wire doors. **1969** *Southerly* XXIX. 305, I..pushed open the fly-wire door then walked into the kitchen.

b. In various plant-names, as **fly-agaric**, *Agaricus muscarius* = FLY-BANE 1 c; **fly-dod**, ragwort (*Senecio Jacobæa*); **fly-flower** (see quot. 1878); **fly-honeysuckle**, (*a*) a variety of honeysuckle (*Lonicera Xylosteum*); (*b*) a species of Halleria; **fly-orchid, -orchis**, a name for *Ophrys muscifera*; **fly-poison, fly-wort**, (see quots.).

1788 J. BOLTON *Hist. Fung.* I. 27 *Fly Agaric... The root is large, and bulb-shaped. **1866** *Treas. Bot.*, *Fly-agaric*. **1826** WILBRAHAM *Chesh. Gloss.*, *Fly-dod..is usually covered with a dusky yellow fly. **1640** PARKINSON *Theat. Bot.* 1351 *Orchis Myodes minor*, the lesser *Flye flower. **1878** BRITTEN & HOLLAND *Plant-n.*, *Fly Flowers*, (1) All species of *Orchis* except *O. mascula*—Glou... (2) *Prunella vulgaris*—Glou. **1819** REES *Cycl.*, *Fly-honeysuckle. **1861** MRS. LANKESTER *Wild Flowers* 71 Lonicera Xylosteum, the Fly or Upright Honey-suckle. **1578** LYTE *Dodoens* II. lvi. 222 We may call it in English properly *flie Orchis, bycause al the kindes of Serapias Orchis, haue in all their floures the.. likenesse of one kinde of flie or other. **1841** MAUNDER *Sci. & Lit. Treas.*, *Fly-orchis*, in botany, the *Orchis muscifera*. **1866** *Treas. Bot.*, *Fly-poison, *Amianthium muscætoxicum*. **1753** CHAMBERS *Cycl.* Suppl. App., *Fly-wort, in botany, a name by which some call the *lychnis* of authors. **1866** *Treas. Bot.*, *Fly-wort*, a name applied to those species of *Catasetum* formerly called *Myanthus*.

fly (flaɪ), *sb.*[2] Pl. **flies**; in sense 3 b usually **flys**. [f. FLY *v.*[1]; many of the senses have no mutual connexion, being separate formations on the vb. OE. had *flyᵹe* str. masc., action of flying = OHG. *flug* (MHG. *vluc*, mod.Ger. *flug*), ON. *flugr* (mod.Icel. *flug* neut.):—OTeut. **flugi-z*, f. weak grade of **fleugan* to FLY; but it is doubtful whether this survived the OE. period.]

I. The action of flying.

1. a. †The action or manner of flying, flight (*obs.*). In recent use, an act of flying.

a **1000** *Crist* 645 (Gr.) Se fæla fuᵹel flyᵹes cunnode. *a* **1000** *Satan* 112 (Gr.) Ic sceal on flyᵹe..earda neosan. *c* **1425** *Fest. Ch.* xxx. in *Leg. Rood* (1871) 221 Þe Egle is frikest fowle in flye. *c* **1650** *Earl Westmorland* in Furniv. *Percy Folio* I. 300 On Bramaball more shee caused my flye. **1786** NELSON in Nicolas *Disp.* (1845) I. 178 Indignity offered under the fly of his Flag. **1828** DISRAELI *Infernal Marriage* III. iii. Novels (1881) 345 'Twas an easy fly; the chariot [a car borne by owls] soon descended upon the crest of a hill. **1887** *Sporting Life* 22 June 2/6 A two miles pigeon fly.

b. A flying visit. *rare.*

1833 MRS. CARLYLE *Let.* 28 July, We have had..no other visitors except..my mother..for a fly.

c. *slang.* A trick, dodge.

1861 [F. W. ROBINSON] *No Church* I. ix. 192 Who's put you up to that fly?

d. Phr. ***to give*** (it) ***a fly***, to make an attempt, to have a go. Also, ***to have a fly at*** (1941 Baker, *Dict. Austral. Slang* 29). *Austral.*

1919 DOWNING *Digger Dial.* 24 *To give it a fly*, to make an attempt. **1926** K. S. PRICHARD *Working Bullocks* xiv. 129 'They say you're going to race him at Blue Flowers, Red?' 'Might give him a fly,' Red admitted. **1931** V. PALMER *Separate Lives* 114 Righto! I'm willing to give it a fly if that's settled. **1934** T. WOOD *Cobbers* ii. 19 They come in for miles ..to give it [*sc.* betting at trots] a fly.

e. *Football.* = *fly-half*.

1921 E. H. D. SEWELL *Rugby Football* 195 L. A. Phillips was a combination half, who was really equally at home as scrum or fly.

2. ***on the fly***: orig. on the wing, flying; hence, in motion, moving up and down.

a. *gen.* Also *slang* = 'on the spree'.

1851 MAYHEW *Lond. Labour* II. 51 Taking them on the fly; which means meeting the gentry on their walks, and beseeching or at times menacing them till something is given. **1855** [BURN] *Autobiog. Beggar Boy* 6 My father had been on the fly in that town for nine or ten days. **1868** *Temple Bar Mag.* XXIV. 538, I prigged an old woman's poke on the fly. **1892** *Nation* (N.Y.) 4 Aug. 91/3 To borrow the language of the sportsman, he may be said to have caught the Melanesian people 'on the fly'.

b. *Baseball* and (U.S. only) *Cricket*: The course of a ball that has been struck, until it touches the ground. Also in *Football* and *Hockey*. ***foul fly*** (see quot. 1874).

1856 *Spirit of Times* 8 Nov. 165/1 Several fine catches.. made on the fly. **1868** [see CATCH *sb.*[1] 1 c]. **1872** O. W. HOLMES *Poet Breakf.-t.* v. (1885) 119 Catching a ball on the fly. **1874** CHADWICK *Base Ball Man.* 41 Ketchum..was caught on the fly. *Ibid.* 58 Any high foul ball, held on the fly, is called a foul fly. **1882** *Philad. Press* 12 Aug. 8 That usually reliable fielder muffed the fly. **1887** DR. IRVINE in G. A. Hutchison *Football* iii. 91 If he throws forward, his opponent may make his mark, if he manages to catch the ball on the fly. **1960** T. MCLEAN *Kings of Rugby* xiii. 173 One such run..led to Dawson putting a hefty boot to the ball on the fly. **1961** J. S. SALAK *Dict. Amer. Sports* 226 *Hitting on the fly* (field hockey), hitting an oncoming ball without first stopping or fielding it.

II. Something that flies, in various senses.

3. A quick-travelling carriage.

a. 'A stage-coach, distinguished by this name, in order to impress a belief of its extraordinary quickness in travelling' (J.). *Obs.* exc. *Hist.*

1708 in *Mem. J. Hall* 21 Fly, a Waggon, i.e. Country Cart. **1759** GRAY *Lett.* Wks. 1884 III. 21 The parcel will come by one of the flies. **1774** BURKE *Corr.* (1844) I. 449 A letter.. sent on Tuesday night by the Grantham fly. **1816** SCOTT *Antiq.* i, The Queensferry Diligence or Hawes Fly. **1888** BURGON *Lives 12 Gd. Men* I. IV. 386 He had travelled up from Northamptonshire in a fly.

b. The name of a light vehicle, introduced at Brighton in 1816, and originally drawn or pushed by men; but a horse being soon employed, the name was gradually extended to any one-horse covered carriage, as a cab or hansom, let out on hire. Perh. short for FLY-BY-NIGHT, q.v. *Obs.* exc. *Hist.*

Local usage of the word varied; in some places *fly* was confined to a 'four-wheeler'; but it was generally applied to a vehicle hired from a livery-stable, and not plying for hire.

1818 C. WRIGHT *Brighton Ambulator* 170 A nouvelle kind of four-wheel vehicles, drawn by a man and an assistant, are very accommodating to visitors..They are denominated Flys. **1828** SCOTT *Jrnl.* (1890) II. 185 We then took a fly, as they call the light carriages, and drove as far as the Devil's Ditch. **1830** T. HOOK *Maxwell* II. ii. 53 One of the Brighton boatmen..bid him [a boy] go and get a fly..he heard an additional direction..not to bring a horse-fly. **1839** MRS. CARLYLE *Lett.* I. 114 A fly (a little chaise with one horse), furnished us from a livery-stable hard by. **1844** DISRAELI *Coningsby* IV. ii, Get a fly at the station. **1881** LADY HERBERT *Edith* 118 Soon after breakfast a fly at the door, to catch the 10.50 train.

4. Something attached by the edge. Cf. FLAP *sb.*[4]

a. A strip or lap on a garment, to contain or cover the button-holes; hence something used to cover or connect (see quot. 1884). *spec.* (freq. *pl.*) the piece of cloth that hides the fastening at the front of a pair of trousers; also, the fastening itself.

1844 *Regul. & Ord. Army* 154 [Trousers] Open in front, with a Fly and Five Buttons. **1884** KNIGHT *Dict. Mech.* IV. 351/1 *Fly*, the fore flap of a bootee. A strip of leather which overwraps the front vamp and receives the strings or other fastening. **1941** I. BAIRD *He rides the Sky* 234 A pair of tennis shorts with zipper fly. **1942** E. PAUL *Narrow St.* i. 6 The professor..turned toward the *pissoir*, unbuttoning his fly en route. **1952** 'VIGILANS' *Chamber of Horrors* 27 The words *button one's fly* are offensive only to the prurient. **1953** M. DICKENS *No More Meadows* i. 49 Champ, your flies are undone again. That boy! He'll be arrested yet. **1959** R. FULLER *Ruined Boys* II. viii. 128 'Your flies are undone,' said Matley primly.

b. In a tent: 'The sloping or roof part of the canvas' (Yule); also, the flap at the entrance, forming a door.

1810 WILLIAMSON *E. India Vade M.* II. 452 The main part of the operation of pitching the tent, consisting of raising the flies. **1840** E. E. NAPIER *Scenes & Sports Foreign Lands* II. iii. 55 The fly and white walls of our tent. (*Note.* The roof or top part of the tent). **1882** *Century Mag.* XXV. 195 Two or three Indians..peered through the fly, and then came in.

c. Of a flag: (*a*) The breadth from the staff to the end; (*b*) the part farthest from the staff.

1841 R. H. DANA *Seaman's Man.* 105 *Fly*, that part of a flag which extends from the Union to the extreme end. **1864** BOUTELL *Heraldry Hist. & Pop.* xviii. 286 The Pennon was small in size, pointed or swallow-tailed at the Fly.

d. *Theat.* in *pl.* The space over the proscenium, including the upper mechanism and the galleries on each side from which it is worked.

1805 *European Mag.* XLVII. 447 A large portion of scenery from the top (called the flies) fell upon the stage. **1859** SMILES *Self-Help* v. (1860) 126 First working under the stage, then behind the flies, then upon the stage itself. **1887** *Daily Tel.* 27 May 3 Sparks fell from the flies upon the stage.

5. In various technical uses.

a. *Naut.* A compass card: see quot. 1610 and CARD *sb.*² 4. Hence, on a terrestrial globe: The set of rhumbs drawn from a selected point on the surface (? *obs.*). Also, on a vane: see quot. 1773.

1571 DIGGES *Pantom.* I. xxix. I ij b, It is also requisite, that within Theodelitus you haue a needle or fly so rectified, that [etc.]. **1610** W. FOLKINGHAM *Art of Survey* II. vi. 56 The Flie is a Card diuided into eight, sixteene, thirty two equall parts in the Limbe with competent extention to shew the Meridian and Coastages of the Plot. **1690** LEYBOURN *Curs. Math.* 611 Upon the top of the Box wherein the Fly and Needle is fastned. **1773** JOHNSON (ed. 4), *Fly* 3, that part of a vane which points how the wind blows. **1789–96** J. MORSE *Am. Un. Geog.* I. 49 Observe..what rhumb of the nearest fly runs mostly parallel to the edge of the quadrant. **1867** SMYTH *Sailor's Word-bk.*, *Fly* or Compass-Card.

b. A speed-regulating device, usually consisting of vanes upon a rotating shaft, chiefly used in musical boxes and the striking parts of clock-machinery.

1599 T. M[OUFET] *Silkwormes* 35 Thy Springs, thy Scrues, thy rowells, and thy flie. **1812–6** J. SMITH *Panorama Sc. & Art* I. 380 This fly strikes the air with so large a surface, that the resistance it experiences prevents the train of wheels from going too fast. **1884** F. J. BRITTEN *Watch & Clockm.* 105 When the striking train is discharged it would run with increasing speed but for the fly.

c. A fly wheel, a pair of weighted arms, or other device involving the same principle, used to regulate the speed of machinery.

1648 WILKINS *Math. Magick* I. xiii. 87 A single hair fastned unto the fly or ballance of the Jack. **1703** MOXON *Mech. Exerc.* 49 The Fly is made sometimes with two, sometimes with four Arms from the Center. **1825** J. NICHOLSON *Operat. Mechanic* 51 A fly is sometimes..employed as a collector of power. **1874** KNIGHT *Dict. Mech.* I. 895/1 *Fly* 11, the swinging weighted arm of some kinds of presses.

d. = FANNER 2.

1807 VANCOUVER *Agric. Devon* (1813) 127 Few winnowing-machines, saving a common whisk or fly, are used in this county. **1836** *Penny Cycl.* V. 307 A winnowing machine with a fly and sieves is the only additional instrument.

e. One of the cylinders of a carding machine.

1842 *Encycl. Brit.* (ed. 7) XXI. 932/1 The worker next the doffers is called the fly, from its great velocity. **1888** R. BEAUMONT *Woollen Manuf.* ii. 56 The doffer removes the fibres brought on to the surface of the swift by the fly.

f. *In Knitting* (*machine*), *Spinning, Weaving* (see quots.). Also in *Hand-spinning*: the spindle.

1851 L. D. B. GORDON *Art Jrnl. Illust. Catal.* 1**/2 Drawing out the fibre from the rock, and supplying it regularly to the fly, which is caused to turn rapidly and twist it into a thread or yarn. **1874** KNIGHT *Dict. Mech.* I 895/1 *Fly* 3 (Knitting-machine), another name for the Latch. *Ibid.*, *Fly* 4 (Spinning), the arms which revolve around the bobbin in a spinning-frame, to twist the roving or yarn which is wound on the bobbin. *Ibid.*, *Fly* 6 (Weaving), a shuttle driven through the shed by a blow or jerk.

g. In the pianoforte (see quots.).

1876 STAINER & BARRETT *Dict. Mus. Terms*, *Fly*, a hinged board which covers the keys of the pianoforte or organ when not in use. **1879** A. J. HIPKINS in Grove *Dict. Mus.* I. 619/2 A screw perforating the jack, tongue, or fly as it is variously called, of the grasshopper [in a pianoforte].

h. In a screw-log (see quot.).

1882 CAPT. MORIARTY in *Encycl. Brit.* XIV. 770/2 The 'fly' [of a screw-log] consists of a hollow copper cylinder about 9 or 10 inches long with four fins or blades placed at a given angle, causing it to rotate once in a certain distance.

i. *Metal-working.* An apparatus worked by the horizontal swinging of a weighted lever, for cutting out with a die pieces of metal of a required shape from a bar or sheet.

1831 J. HOLLAND *Manuf. Metal* I. 211 With a fly..nails of almost any size or shape might..be cut out of rolled metal.

6. Waste cotton. Cf. FLUE *sb.*², FLUFF.

1879 *Cassell's Techn. Educ.* IV. 274/1 Fly or short staple cotton, which has gathered below the machine. **1893** *Labour Commission* Gloss., *Fly*, loose down.

III. *attrib.* and *Comb.* (In many of these the first element may be really the verb-stem.)

7. a. Simple attributive, as (sense 3b) ***fly-horse, -proprietor***, (sense 4a) ***fly-button, -front***, (sense 4d) ***fly-gallery***, (sense 5b) ***fly-pinion***, (sense 5c) ***fly-piston, -screw***.

1895 *Montgomery Ward Catal.* 86/1 Metal Snap *Fly Buttons. **1933** J. E. LIBERTY *Pract. Tailoring* vi. 87 The fly buttons..should be carefully marked first by laying the fly edge along the catch seam and marking over from the holes on to the button catch. **1961** A. WILSON *Old Men at Zoo* ii. 81 You've been state nursed from the cradle, without ever learning to do your own flybuttons up. **1893** *Times* 8 July 12/2 This coat has a *fly front buttoning underneath. **1897** *Sears, Roebuck Catal.* 175/2 Men's fancy fly front corduroy vests will be all the style for the coming season. **1961** *Sunday Express* 12 Mar. 16/7 Simple trench coat..fly-front. **1888** KOBBÉ in *Scribner's Mag.* IV. 437 The *fly-galleries on either side, from the lowest of which the drop-scenes and borders are worked. **1891** C. T. C. JAMES *Rom. Rigmarole* 134 That moribund *fly-horse. **1884** F. J. BRITTEN *Watch & Clockm.* 106 [The] *Fly Pinion..[is] the pinion in a clock which carries the fly. **1831** J. HOLLAND *Manuf. Metal* I. 48 In which [cylinder] works a weighted, or what is called a *fly-piston. **1845** *P.O. Directory 6 Home Counties* 631/1 Box John, *fly proprietor. **1831** J. HOLLAND *Manuf. Metal* II. 152 In the production of boxes for *fly-screws and others having several worms.

b. objective, as (sense 3b) ***fly-driver***, (sense 5g) ***fly-finisher***; ***fly-finishing*** vbl. sb.

1847 ALB. SMITH *Chr. Tadpole* v. (1879) 59 Prejudices, which..had somewhat operated against the *fly-drivers on the part of the family coachmen.

c. instrumental, as (sense 4a) ***fly-fronted*** adj.

1901 in C. W. Cunnington *Eng. Women's Clothing* (1952) ii. 43 A *fly-fronted coat. **1929** *Evening News* 18 Nov. 6/5 Look at the above Overcoat, the Fly-fronted Chester, which is a specially dignified style, and is much worn by business and professional men.

8. Special Comb., as **fly ash**, ash resulting from the burning of pulverized coal; **fly-ball** (*Baseball*), a ball that may be caught 'on the fly'; **fly-bill**, a handbill to be scattered broadcast, also *attrib.*; **fly-block** (*Naut.*), 'the block spliced into the topsail-tye' (Adm. Smyth); **fly boy** *U.S. slang*, a member of the Air Force, esp. a pilot; **fly-bridge** = FLYING BRIDGE; **fly camp**, a temporary camp; **fly-catch** (*Baseball*), a catch 'on the fly'; **fly-clock**, a clock regulated by a fly, before the introduction of pendulums; **fly-coach** = FLY *sb.*² 3a; **fly-cruise**, a holiday involving an air journey to the place where a sea-cruise begins; also *attrib.*; **fly-cutter**, a cutting tool driven at a high rate of speed; **fly-door** (*Mining*), a door opening either way; **fly-drill** (see quot.); **fly-frame**, (*a*) *Cotton-spinning* = *flyer frame*; (*b*) a machine used in the polishing and grinding of glass; **fly-governor** (see quot.) = FLY *sb.*² 5c; **fly-half** *Rugby Football*, the half-back who stands off from the scrum-half; = *stand-off half*; **fly-kick**, a kick (esp. in Rugby football) made while moving at rapid speed; so **fly-kick** *v. trans.* and *intr.*; **fly-line**, the line of flight taken by a bird in its regular migrations; **fly-nut**, a screw nut having wings or projections which enable it to be tightened by hand; **fly-page**, the side of a fly-leaf (see FLY-LEAF); **fly-penning** (see quot.); **fly-piston** (see quot.); **fly-pole**, = *giant-stride*; **fly-post** *v. trans.* and *intr.*, to display (posters) rapidly in unauthorized places; *trans.*, to cover with bills so posted; so ***fly-posting*** vbl. sb.; **fly-press**, a screw press worked by a fly (see 5c); **fly-pulley**, a pulley that may be shifted along the length of a shaft; **fly-punching press**, **fly-rail** (see quots.); **fly-reed** (*Weaving*), the reed of a fly-shuttle loom; **fly-rope** (see quot.); **fly-sail** (*Naut.*), ? = *flying* JIB; **fly-shuttle** (*Weaving*) (see quot. 1874); **fly-spring** (see quot.); **fly stitch** (see quots.); **fly-table**, a table with flaps that may be let down; **fly-tail**, *U.S.*, a small gill-net without sinkers formerly used for catching perch, etc. (*Cent. Dict.*); **fly-tent**, ? a tent having a fly (sense 4b); **fly-tip**, **fly-title**, **fly-tool**, **fly-up** (*Naut.*) (see quots.); **fly-wagon** = FLY *sb.*² 3a.

1931 *Electr. World* 23 May 961/1 The solution of the *fly-ash problem lies in reducing the amount of ash that is discharged to the atmosphere to the point where it is no longer objectionable. **1937** *Jrnl. Amer. Concrete Inst.* VIII. 578 The residue from the burning of powdered coal is commonly designated as 'fly ash'. **1956** *Science News* XL. 83 Fly-ash produced in boilers fired by pulverized fuel can be used in making building materials. **1967** *New Scientist* 15 June 650/1 Many schemes have been proposed for using up the millions of tons of 'fly-ash', a dust-like residue produced by coal-burning plant. **1874** CHADWICK *Base Ball Man.* 29 They should be..excellent judges of *fly-balls. **1891** *Daily News* 28 Sept. 7/1 A *fly-bill poster. **1841** R. H. DANA *Seaman's Man.* 46 Then..reeve the other end through the *fly-block for a fall. **1946** *Amer. Speech* XXI. 248 Airforce flying personnel are sometimes labelled bird-men or *flyboys. **1948** *Life* 1 Nov. 87/2 The generals are no full-throttle 'fly-boys'. **1954** BERREY & VAN DEN BARK *Amer. Thes. Slang* §756/2 Cloud hopper, eagle, eagle chaser, fly-boy, manbird, sky chauffeur. **1614** SYLVESTER *Bethulia's Rescue* III. 110 Th' Engineer..Brings here his *Fly-Bridge, there his batt'ring Crow. **1939** *Amer. Speech* XIV. 236, I heard the branch camps attached to one of our mountain divisions of the CCC referred to as *fly camps. **1959** *Tararua* (N.Z.) XIII. 49 Fly-camp for a small, subsidiary, temporary camp..suggests a camp with merely a fly as shelter. **1964** *Imperial Oil Review* (Toronto) Dec. 5/2 Outside on the river bank..Hughes moved one helicopter..off to the nearest fly camp, 35 miles southwest. **1874** CHADWICK *Base Ball Man.* 30 Chances for *fly-catches from short, high balls. **1830** HERSCHEL *Stud. Nat. Phil.* II. vi. (1851) 178 By clocks he [Lord Bacon] could not have meant pendulum clocks, which were not then known..but *fly-clocks. **1818** SCOTT *Hrt. Midl.* i, The slow and safe motion of the ancient *Fly-coaches. **1968** *Times* 14 Sept. 24/3 Sorting through the information I had gathered on '*fly-cruise' holidays, I came upon what was for me a new aspect of the regulations. **1970** *Daily Tel.* 19 Sept. 11 Flying to join a ship for a couple of weeks' cruising holiday in the Mediterranean had gradually won popularity... This year several firms are offering Caribbean fly-cruises. **1971** *Sunday Times* 3 Jan. 72/1 The increasingly popular fly-cruise holidays. **1884** F. J. BRITTEN *Watch & Clockm.* 105 Latterly *fly cutters are often made double. **1851** GREENWELL *Coal-trade Terms Northumb. & Durh.*, *Fly doors* or *swing doors.* **1874** KNIGHT *Dict. Mech.* I. 895 **Fly-drill*, one having a reciprocating fly-wheel which gives it a steady momentum. **1835** *Fly frame [see ROVING *vbl. sb.*³ 3a]. **1890** W. J. GORDON *Foundry* 131 The huge sheets of glass are..ground with sand under a heavy iron 'fly-frame', said to have been invented by James Watt. **1940** *Chambers's Techn. Dict.* 344/2 *Fly frames*, a series of machines used to attenuate roving in preparation for the spinning frame. **1874** KNIGHT *Dict. Mech.* I. 895 **Fly-governor*, one which regulates speed by the impact of vanes upon the air. **1918** J. E. RAPHAEL *Mod. Rugby Footb.* 127 It is the business of the three-quarters not to force the *fly half forward, but to stand back also. **1921** E. H. D. SEWELL *Rugby Football* 60 He [*sc.* the scrum half] knows by the signal which way his fly-half is going to run. **1955** *Times* 1 Aug. 3/3 Scrum half Williams and Morgan at fly-half. **1906** GALLAHER & STEAD *Compl. Rugby Footballer* 208 Ninety-nine successful *fly-kicks do not atone for one failure. **1921** E. H. D. SEWELL *Rugby Football* 92 Whether by punt, drop, or 'field' or fly-kick does not matter. **1930** *Daily Express* 6 Nov. 17/7 Hunt suddenly turned defence into attack by fly-kicking. **1959** *Observer* 28 June 29/3 A pass which Dawson fly-kicked some 30 or 40 yards down the field. **1884** H. SEEBOHM *Brit. Birds* II. 506 One of the *'fly-lines' of this species crosses the Bermuda Islands. **1825** J. NICHOLSON *Oper. Mech.* 454 The small binding screw with a *fly-nut. **1896** *Palmer Tyres* 22 Fly nut for opening valve. **1953** FLOOD & WEST *Dict. Sci. & Techn. Words* (ed. 2) 138/2 *Fly-nut*, nut with wings so that it can be screwed on by hand. **1892** J. CAVE-BROWNE *Hist. Boxley*, A parish-register..often contains on its *fly-pages, chance notes and memoranda. **1858** SIMMONDS *Dict. Trade*, **Fly-penning*, a mode of manuring land practised in England and in the colonies by folding cattle or sheep in rotation over different parts of it. **1884** J. J. POPE *Number One* iv. 101 A *'fly-pole' and a swing should be in every playground. **1903** *Daily Mail* 25 Feb. 3/7 A young advance agent for a theatrical company who went out '*fly-posting' in the dead of night and pasted bills on private property. **1906** *Daily Chron.* 21 July 6/6 A staff of men..to fly-post the constituency during the night with Tariff Reform literature. **1961** *Times* 21 June 13/6 The special triumph of what was known as 'fly posting' was to obliterate some rival announcement. **1970** *Daily Tel.* (Colour Suppl.) 11 Dec. 28/4 Intricate Art Nouveau offerings which he once used to help to fly-post stealthily all over London. **1819** REES *Cycl.*, The coining press or *fly-press. **1874** KNIGHT *Dict. Mech.* I. 896/2 *Fly-press*, a screw-press in which the power is derived from a weighted arm, swinging in a horizontal plane, as in embossing and die presses. **1884** *Health Exhib. Catal.* p. lvii/1 Crank-shaft which carries *fly-pulley for transmitting the power by means of a strap. **1874** KNIGHT *Dict. Mech.* I. 896 **Fly-punching press*, a press for cutting teeth on saws and for other purposes. **1855** OGILVIE Suppl., **Fly-rail*, that part of a table which turns out to support the leaf. **1863** J. WATSON *Art Weaving* 126 When Mr. Bullough introduced his Loom with the *Fly Reed. **1892** *Lockwood's Dict. Mech. Engin.* App., **Fly Rope*, a term often used to denote a rope of cotton or hemp used for telodynamic transmission of power. **1819** J. H. VAUX *Mem.* I. 65 With only a storm jib, and *fly-sail set. **1795** J. AIKIN *Manchester* 300 With the use of the *fly shuttle. **1874** KNIGHT *Dict. Mech.* I. 896 *Fly-shuttle*, a shuttle driven by a picker in contradistinction to one thrown by hand. **1884** F. J. BRITTEN *Watch & Clockm.* 106 [The] *Fly Spring..causes the outer cover of a watch case to fly open. **1934** M. THOMAS *Dict. Embroidery Stitches* 101 *Fly stitch is..a kind of open detached chain stitch. **1960** G. LEWIS *Handbk. Crafts* 32 Fly stitch or Y stitch... The needle comes up at the top of the left arm of the V part of the stitch. It is inserted at the top of the right arm of the V and comes out at the base of the V over the loop of the working thread. The tail of the Y can be as long or short as desired. **1785** COWPER *Let. to J. Newton* 19 Mar., The *fly-table was too slight and too small. **1816** KEATINGE *Trav.* (1817) II. 8 Three *fly-tents, with mattresses laid on the ground, accommodate six Europeans. **1874** CHADWICK *Base Ball Man.* 58 **Fly Tip.* This is a foul ball held by the catcher, sharp from the bat. **1888** JACOBI *Printer's Voc.*, **Fly-title*, the half-title in front of the general title, or which divides sections of a work. **1819** REES Cycl., **Fly-tool* is a very light narrow wooden spade shod with iron, which the navigators of a canal use for cutting or throwing out any soft clay..or the like. **1867** SMYTH *Sailor's Word-bk.*, **Fly-up*, a sudden deviation upwards from a sheer line. **1827** HOOD in Hone *Every-day Bk.* II. 1547 The ponderous *fly-waggon passed me.

fly (flaɪ), *a. slang.* [prob. f. FLY *v.*¹, though the etymological notion is doubtful.]

1. Knowing, wide-awake, sharp. ***fly to*** (anything): 'up' to, well acquainted with, clever at.

1811 *Lexicon Balatronicum* s.v. *Fly*.. The rattling cove is fly; the coachman knows what we are about. **1825** C. M. Westmacott *Eng. Spy* II. 5 You are fly to cant. **1851** Mayhew *Lond. Labour* II. 109 We're rather 'fly to a dodge'. **1852** Dickens *Bleak House* xvi, 'I am fly', says Jo.

2. Of the fingers: Dexterous, nimble, skilful.

1834 H. Ainsworth *Rookwood* III. v, No dummy hunter had forks so fly. **1839** Reynolds *Pickw. abroad* 224 We'll knap a fogle with fingers fly.

3. *Comb.* as **fly cop** *slang* (see quots. 1859 and 1962); *U.S.*, a detective, a plain-clothes policeman; **fly-flat** (see quots.); **fly-pitch** *slang*, a street pitch; hence **fly-pitcher**, one who operates a fly-pitch, a street-trader.

1859 Matsell *Vocabulum* 34 **Fly-cop*, sharp officer; .. an officer that understands his business. **1872** *Chicago Tribune* 27 Dec. 8/3 Blacklegs, gamblers, 'fly cops', and sports. **1889** Barrère & Leland *Dict. Slang* I. 376/1 *Fly-cop* (thieves'), a sharp policeman. **1900** Fly cop [see chair *sb.*[1] 1 d]. *a* **1906** 'O. Henry' *Trimmed Lamp* (1916) 227 It was purely the still panic produced by the sound of the ax of the fly cop, Conscience, hammering at the gambling-house doors of the Heart. **1929** Wodehouse *Gentleman of Leisure* xviii. 149 'A detective?' 'Dat's right. A fly cop.' **1962** *John o' London's* 25 Jan. 82/2 A motorised police officer is.. a *fly cop*. **1864** *Revelations Lady Detective* 126, I have an appointment with a *fly flat (*i.e.* a clever fool). **1889** Barrère & Leland *Dict. Slang*, *Fly-flat* (Turf), one who really knows little or nothing about racing, but fancies him-self thoroughly initiated in all its mysteries. **1907** *Daily Chron.* 1 Apr. 4/4 The criminal classes.. always speak of fools who think they are wise as 'fly-flats'. **1938** J. Cary *Castle Corner* x. 559 'I don't see why we should consider the speculators.' 'A lot of fly-flats who thought they could beat us at the game.' **1934** *Evening News* 9 July 11/2 There are the '*fly pitches', spots.. where the cheap-jacks take their stand... The most famous is at the foot of the Irving statue at the side of the National Portrait Gallery. Whenever you see a really big crowd collected at this spot you can be sure that one or other of the familiar *fly-pitchers of London is doing his stuff. It may be the coloured Prince of Tipsters, proving vehemently that he.. holds the secret of making money out of racing. **1939** J. B. Priestley *Let People Sing* x. 256 'Bin workin' a fly pitch in the Sat'day gaff,' said Micky Barnet. **1965** *Sun* 26 Oct. 7/6 Charlie Byass.. is one of the two dozen or so licensed chestnut men in London. There are others, called 'fly pitchers', who sell without a licence.

fly (flaɪ), *v.*[1] Pa. t. flew (fluː); pa. pple. flown (fləʊn). Forms: *Infin.* 1 **fléoȝ-an** (*Mercian* **fléȝ-an**, *north.* **fléȝa**, *Kent.* **flioȝan**), 2–3 **fleo(n**, **flon**, (3 **fleoin**, *south.* **vleoin**), **fli(en**, 3 **fleȝ(h)en**, *Orm.* **fleȝhenn**, 3–4 **flei(e**, **fliȝe(n**, **flihen**, **flyhen**, *south.* **vliȝen**, **vlien**, 4–6 **fley(e**, (4 **fleeȝ**, **fleighe**, **fleiȝ**, 5 **flegh**), 3–5 **fleen**, 3–6 **fle**, (4 *south.* **vle**), 4–7 **flie**, **flye**, (4 *south.* **vlie**, **vly**, 5 **flyyn**), 4– (now only *Sc.*) **flee**, 5– **fly**. *Pa. t.* α. *sing.* 1 **fléaȝ**, **fléah**, **fléȝ**, 2–3 **fleh**, 3 **fleah**, **flæh**, 3–4 **flagh(e**, **flaȝe**, 4–6 **flaw(e**, 3–5 **flegh(e**, **fleȝ(e**, **flei(g)h**, **fleyghe**, **fleiȝ**, **fligh**, **fly**. β. *pl.* 1 **fluȝon**, 2–3 **floȝe(n**, **fluȝen**, 3 **fluwen**, 3–4 **flow(e)n**. γ. *sing.* 3–5 **flough(e**, 4–5 **flou**, **flow**, 5 **floȝe**, **floy**. δ. *sing.* and *pl.* 5–6 **flewe**, (6 **flue**), 5– **flew**. *Pa. pple.* 1 **floȝen**, 3 **floȝen**, 4–6 **flowe(n**, (5 **flone**, **floon**, 6 **fleen**, **flighen**), 6–7 **fline**, **flyen**, **flowne**, (7–8 **flew**), 6– **flown**. Also weak *pa. t.* (rare and chiefly for rime): 4 **flyghed**, 5, 7 **flyde**, 7 **flide**, **flied**, **flyed**. [A com. Teut. str. vb. OE. *fléoȝan*, *flíoȝan* = OFris. *fliaga*, OS. **fliogan* (MDu. *vlieghen*, Du. *vliegen*) = OHG. *fliogan* (MHG. *vliegen*, Ger. *fliegen*), ON. *fljúga* (Sw. *flyga*, Da. *flyve*), Goth. **fliugan* (inferred from (*us*)*flaugjan* to lead forth in flight):—OTeut. **fleugan* (*flaug*, *flugum*, *flogono*-):—pre-Teut. **pleugh*-, *plough*-, *plugh*-. Not etymologically cognate with flee *v.*

The α. forms of pa. t. normally represent, according to period and dialect, the OE. *fléaȝ*, *fléah*, and the β. forms the OE. pl. *fluȝon*. The γ. forms are transferred to the sing. from the pl. and the pa. pple. The origin of the δ. form *flew(e*, which now alone survives, is more difficult to account for; possibly it arose from a confusion with flow (OE. pa. t. *fléow*), with which this vb. had in the 15th c. come to coincide in the pa. pple; cf. however the somewhat similar phenomenon in the vb. *slay*, pa. t. *slew*, for which no parallel explanation can be given.

With regard to the confusion between the verbs *fly* and *flee*, see flee.]

I. 1. a. *intr.* To move through the air with wings. Also with adverbs, as *about*, *away*, *forth*, *off*, *out*, etc. ***as the crow flies***: see crow *sb.*[1] 3 c.

Beowulf 2273 (Gr.) Nacod nið-draca, nihtes fleoȝeð fyre befangen. *a* **1000** *Judith* 209 (Gr.) Ac him fleah on laste earn ætes ȝeorn. *c* **1175** *Lamb. Hom.* 129 Alle þe fuȝelas þe fluȝen bi þam lufte. *c* **1200** Ormin 5991 Forr ærn maȝȝ heȝhe fleȝhenn. *c* **1205** Lay. 3901 Her comen blake fleȝen and fluȝen in mone eȝene. **1297** R. Glouc. (1724) 29 Beter hym hadde ybe Haue bi leued ther doune, than ylerned for to fle. *a* **1300** *Cursor M.* 13449 (Gött.) Nane þat mai fli sua hei [als þe arn]. *c* **1330** R. Brunne *Chron.* (1810) 305 Als fleihes doun þei fleih, ten þousand at ones. **1382** Wyclif *Isa.* vi. 6 Ther fleiȝ to me oon of the serafyn. *c* **1430** Lydg. *Min. Poems* 186 From their lyme-twygges I will flee fer asyde. *c* **1430** *Pilgr. Lyf Manhode* II. lii. (1869) 95, I fly aboue þe skyes heyere þan eyþer heroun or egret. *c* **1440** *Gesta Rom.* xix. 335 (Add. MS.) The bridde.. flew [*Camb. MS.* fly] forthe. **1500–20** Dunbar *Poems* xxii. 105 O gentle egill!.. That of all fowlis dois heest fle. **1533** *Anne Boleyn's Coronat.* in Furniv. *Ballads from MSS.* I. 380 She hathe fleen long, Vncertain where to light. *a* **1649** Drumm. of Hawth. *Poems* Wks. (1711) 13 The feathered troops that flee, and sweetly sing. **1711** Addison *Spect.* No. 159 ¶8, I wished for the Wings of an Eagle, that I might fly away to those happy seats. **1796** H. Hunter tr. *St. Pierre's Stud. Nat.* (1799) I. 580 On my approaching him, he [a butterfly] flew off. **1822** Shelley *Calderon* I. 46 Would that my feet were wings, So would I fly to Livia.

b. *fig.*; *esp.* of fame, a report, etc. ***to fly high*** (or ***a high pitch***): to aim at or reach a high pitch of action, feeling, etc. (cf. flight *sb.* 3). Also ***to fly low***: to avoid notoriety. ***to fly short of***: to fail in mounting to the level of.

c **1200** *Trin. Coll. Hom.* 165 Alse þe fugeles.. swo doð þis mannisse flieð fram iuele to werse. *a* **1225** *Ancr. R.* 152 Bi nihte beo fleoinde ant sechinde ouwer soule heouenliche uode. *c* **1384** Chaucer *H. Fame* III. 1028 Wenged wondres faste fleen. *c* **1489** Caxton *Sonnes of Aymon* i. 39 The renomme therof floughe vnto the duke. **1548** Udall, etc. *Erasm. Par. Luke* iv. 55 The fame which had to fore.. flighen abrode. **1571** Hanmer *Chron. Irel.* (1633) 125 The prosperous successes of Earle Richard, were no sooner effected, but fame flyed abroad. *a* **1592** H. Smith *Serm.* (1866) II. 14 Try every piece of gold, when many Flemish angels fly abroad. **1608** Topsell *Serpents* (1658) 706 A Dragon, whereof their flyeth this tale. **1611** Shaks. *Cymb.* III. v. 61 Wing'd with feruour of her loue, she's flowne To her desir'd Posthumus. **1611** Bible *Ps.* xc. 10 Their strength .. is soone cut off, and we flie away. **1646** Sir T. Browne *Pseud. Ep.* I. x. 40 How short they flew of that spirit.. their weaknesse sufficiently declared. **1655** Fuller *Ch. Hist.* IX. vii. §9 Matters flying thus high, the Arch-Bishop.. conceived it the safest way to [etc.]. **1705** Hickeringill *Priest-cr.* II. iv. 41 They fly High in their high-flown Divinity. **1709** Steele *Tatler* No. 194 ¶2 When the Fame, says he, of this celebrated Beauty first flew Abroad. **1716** Bp. of Bristol *Charge* 19 Where a Mean is commendable, He must neither fly too High, nor creep too Low. **1827** Southey *Penins. War* II. 752 Those brethren whose piety flies the highest pitch. **1837** Carlyle *Fr. Rev.* III. II. iv. 117 As for the elder Egalité he flies low at this time. **1847** Tennyson *Princ.* v. 271 She flies too high. **1859** —— *Elaine* 1188 When did not rumours fly?

c. quasi-*trans.* with cognate object.

1605 Shaks. *Macb.* III. ii. 40 Ere the Bat hath flowne His Cloyster'd flight. **1609** A. Craig *Poet. Recreat.* 7 Want.. makes my Muse so lowe a course to flee.

d. In a few expressions, as ***the bird is*** or ***has flown*** (chiefly *fig.*), ***to let*** (a bird) ***fly***, the simple vb. is used = 'fly away'.

1480 Caxton *Chron. Eng.* xcv. 75 They.. bonde it to the sparwes fete, and afterward lete hem flee. **1847** Tennyson *Princess* iv. 90 O tell her, Swallow, that thy brood is flown. **1855** —— *Maud* I. xxii. 2 The black bat, night, has flown. *a* **1881** Rossetti *House of Life* viii, Thank his wings to-day that he is flown.

e. Of birds: To migrate or issue forth in a body. Cf. flight *sb.*[1] 1 e.

1766 Pennant *Zool.* (1768) II. 330 The wild birds fly (as the bird-catchers term it) during the month of October.

f. Of fish: To spring from the water. Also in more literal sense said of flying-fish.

1579 T. Stevens *Lett. from Goa* in Hakluyt *Voy.* (1589) 160 There is another kind of fish as big almost as a herring, which hath wings and flieth. **1734** Mortimer in *Phil. Trans.* XXXVIII. 316 The Wings with which it flies in the Air are only a Pair of very large Finns. **1867** F. Francis *Angling* ix. (1880) 336 Seeing the small fry flying from the water as though a pike were after them.

g. To travel by aircraft. Also *trans.*, to cover, traverse, or perform by aircraft (also said of the machine). Also, *to fly in*, *out*, to arrive, depart, by air.

[**1826** W. Hone *Every-Day Bk.* I. 1462 He had purposed, by a pair of patent wings,.. to fly from one of the Dover cliffs down into the town of Calais.] **1884** *Illustr. London News* 26 Jan. 91/3 Many successful and unsuccessful attempts have been made to fly the Channel. **1909** *Flight* 20 Feb. 100/2 To bring together other would-be aviators who, like himself, are primarily anxious to learn to fly. **1909** *Punch* 4 Aug. 73/1 On the spot where the first man to fly the Channel alighted from his aeroplane. **1909** *Captain* Nov. p. xii (Advt.), Model of the Machine which flew the Channel. **1911** Grahame-White & Harper *Aeroplane* 265 As their skill and confidence increased, they began to fly in breezes. **1916** H. Barber *Aeroplane Speaks* 44 If he were flying over the shortest route to his destination. *Ibid.* 45 The Pilot and Observer fly on and on. **1917** *Brit. Dominions Year Bk.* 242 We who still regard flying the Straits of Dover as something of a feat. **1931** *Times* 2 Mar., The Sahara route which is now being flown by the French. **1958** 'N. Shute' *Rainbow & Rose* i. 4 He was flying a courier service. **1966** *Listener* 21 July 103/3 An expert who had flown in from Venezuela to do the job. **1967** *Daily Tel.* 14 Mar. 20/7 An Indian, aged 100, .. applied.. for a ticket home to Delhi on the 'Fly Now Pay Later' plan. **1968** *Globe & Mail* (Toronto) 17 Feb. B5/5 The [a]erial surveys flown by Texas Gulf in 1960. **1970** *Observer* 20 Sept. 26/1 The pilot [is] determined to fly no more World War Two bombing missions.

h. Of an aircraft or spacecraft: to travel through the air or through space.

1848 *Chambers's Edin. Jrnl.* 6 May 302/2 To construct a machine to fly by mechanical powers alone. **1902** *Aeronaut. World* (U.S.) I. 65/2 S. Byerley says he has been working on a novel flying machine, which, he is confident will fly when finished. **1959** *Chambers's Encycl.* I. 112/1 The faster a given aeroplane flies, the less is the power required to produced its lift. **1971** *Daily Tel.* (Colour Suppl.) 12 Nov. 8/1 Everything depends on three robot spacecraft.. which have been flying towards Mars for the past 22 weeks.

i. Of pigeons: to fly from (a certain place).

1898 *Daily News* 21 Nov. 7/1 There were also young birds that had, to use the technical term, 'flown Berwick'. **1907** E. Chamberlain *Homing Pigeon* 178 The best birds in the Barrowford lofts have all flown Nantes as yearlings, and subsequently flown Nantes and Marennes again and again.

2. *trans.* (*causatively*). To set (birds) flying one against the other. Const. *with*. Also with *away*: To send flying away; to let fly.

1607 Heywood *Woman killed w. Kindn.* II. Wks. (1874) II. 96 Meet me to morrow At Cheuy-chase, Ile flie my Hawke with yours. **1845** Carlyle *Cromwell* (1871) V. 58 (Sp. xiii) Ordered to fly-away their game-cocks. **1883** C. J. Wills *Mod. Persia* 94 The pigeons are flown twice a day.

3. *Hawking.* **a.** Of the hawk: To gain by flying a position of attack. Const. *at*. ***to fly on head***, ***to fly gross***: see quots.

1674 N. Cox *Gentl. Recreat.* II. (1677) 164 Fly on head is missing her Quarry and betaking her self to the next Check, as Crows [etc.]. *Ibid.* 203 It is less difficult to teach a Hawk to fly at Fowl than.. to.. love the Lure. **1677** Coles, *Fly gross* when hawks fly at great Birds, as Cranes. **1684** R. H. *School Recreat.* 78 Gerfaulcon Will fly at the Hern. Saker, at the Crane or Bittern. **1774** Goldsm. *Nat. Hist.* (1776) V. 131 They have been indeed taught to fly at game. **1826** Sir J. S. Sebright *Observ. Hawking* (1828) 57, I will suppose that hawks are to fly three days in the week.

fig. **1830** Sir J. Barrington *Pers. Sketches* (ed. 2) II. 186 He had occasionally flown at higher game in the regions of poesy. **1847** Marryat *Childr. N. Forest* vii, Deerstalking is all very well, but I fly at higher game.

b. *causatively.* Of the falconer: To cause (a hawk) to attack by flying. Also *absol.* and ***to fly with*** (a hawk). Const. *at*.

1591 Florio *Sec. Fruites* 37, I loue to flie at the Partridge and at the Fesant. **1593** Shaks. *2 Hen. VI*, II. i. 1 For flying at the Brooke, I saw not better sport these seuen yeeres day. **1638** Sir T. Herbert *Trav.* (ed. 2) 233 Their best Falcons are out of Russia.. they fly them at choise game. **1674** N. Cox *Gentl. Recreat.* (1677) 187 At first fly with her at young Pheasant or Partridge. *Ibid.* 213 They are flown at Field or Brook. *a* **1711** Ken *Edmund* Poet. Wks. 1721 II. 66 His Hawks he oft at Game Aerial flew. **1865** Kingsley *Herew.* xxi. He flew his hawks at a covey of partridges. **1879** Radcliffe in *Encycl. Brit.* IX. 9/1 Falcons or long-winged hawks are either 'flown out of the hood' *i.e.* unhooded and slipped when the quarry is in sight, or [etc.].

fig. **1643** Digby *Observ. Sir T. Browne's Relig. Med.* 10 Much lesse can it be expected that an excellent Physitian.. should.. flye his thoughts at so towring a Game.

c. To chase with a hawk. Also of the hawk: To attack by flying. ***to fly the river***: to chase water-fowl. ***to fly to the mark***: see quot. 1891.

c **1590** Greene *Fr. Bacon* xii, We'll fly the partridge, or go rouse the deer. *a* **1654** Selden *Table-t.* (Arb.) 80 A Hawk that flyes a covey of Partridges. **1674** N. Cox *Gentl. Recreat.* II. (1677) 209 These Hawks do not fly the River. *Ibid.* 225 When she hath flown a Partridge to the Mark, she will not away until [etc.]. **1710** *Apparition* 30 So wary Hawks do fearful Pidgeons fly. **1879** Radcliffe in *Encycl. Brit.* IX. 9/2 Rooks are flown in the same manner as herons. **1891** Harting *Biblioth. Accipitraria* Gloss. 226 Mark, to fly at, *v.* generally said of a Goshawk, when, having 'put in' a covey of partridges, she takes stand, marking the spot where they disappeared from view until the falconer arrives to put them out to her.

fig. **1632** B. Jonson *Magn. Lady* Induct., Fly everything you see to the mark, and censure it freely. **1691** Dryden *K. Arthur* III. ii, Oh, still thou think'st to fly a fool to mark.

4. *intr.* **a.** To pass or rise quickly in or through the air. Also with *about*, *away*, *forth*, *off*, *out*, *up*, etc. ***to fly compass***: see compass C. 3 b.

a **1000** *Elene* 140 (Gr.) Daroð-æsc fluȝon, hildenædran. *c* **1175** *Lamb. Hom.* 85 þet smal chef þet flid ford mid þe winde. *c* **1290** *S. Eng. Leg.* I. 45/377 Ore leuedi made þe soule a-non to þe bodi aȝen fleo. *c* **1340** *Cursor M.* 6381 (Fairf.) Hit [*sc.* the manna] flagh til ham als hit ware flour. **1551** T. Wilson *Logike* (1580) 43 Bullettes of Leade.. flie not into the Aire by their owne power. **1601** Shaks. *All's Well* III. ii. 113 You leaden messengers.. Fly with false ayme. **1633** Shirley *Yng. Admiral* I. i, Arrows that fly compass Arrive with.. happiness to the mark. **1665** Hooke *Microgr.* 203 The spirit of Wine would immediately fly away. **1697** Dryden *Virg. Georg.* II. 464 Golden Stars flew up to Light the Skies. **1732** Berkeley *Alciphr.* VI. §14 That the volatile salt or spirit may fly off. **1779–81** Johnson *Life Drake* Wks. IV. 448 They.. let the smoak fly out at the door. **1785** Burns *To W. Simpson* xiii, Blinding drifts wild-furious flee Dark'ning the day. **1807** Hutton *Course Math.* II. 264 Sound flies.. at the rate of about 1142 feet in 1 second. **1819** Byron *Juan* II. xi, The dashing spray Flies in one's face. **1820** Scoresby *Acc. Arctic Reg.* I. 106 Fragments of ice flying in all directions. **1860** Tyndall *Glac.* I. xv. 100 Fleecy clouds flew over the heavens.

b. To leap or spring lightly, or vault *over*. ***to fly the garter***: see fly-the-garter.

1719 De Foe *Crusoe* I. 273 Friday.. flew over my outer Wall or Fence. **1791** G. Gambado *Ann. Horsem.* vi. (1809) 94 When your horse has flown over a gate or stile. **1837** Dickens *Pickw.* xxxviii, Who.. will ever employ a professional man, when they see his boy.. flying the garter in the horse-road? *Mod.* He flew over two backs at once.

c. Of stairs: To descend or ascend without change of direction. Cf. flight *sb.*[1] 7.

1685 Temple *Gardening* Wks. 1731 I. 187 Many Steps flying on each Side of a Grotto. **1703** T. N. *City & C. Purchaser* 248 Straight Stairs.. are such as always fly, and never Wind. **1703** Moxon *Mech. Exerc.* 145 The stairs sometimes wind, and sometimes fly off from that winding.

5. *trans.* (*causatively*). **a.** To cause (a kite) to rise and maintain its position in the air. Also colloq. or slang, ***to fly a kite***: to raise money by an accommodation bill; also, to try something out; to act in an exploratory manner; hence ***to fly a bill***; colloq. (chiefly *U.S.*), ***go fly a kite*** = 'go away', 'be off'.

1739 Chesterf. *Lett.* (1792) I. xxxi. 108 If you were to fly your kite. **1808** *Sporting Mag.* XXXII. 181 In Ireland flying the kite is used as a cant phrase for raising money on accommodation bills. **1833** Marryat *P. Simple* II. ii. 23 One of the amusements of the prisoners was flying kites.

1848 *Punch* 27 May 226/1 He never does 'a little discounting' nor lends his hand to 'flying a kite'. 1860 TROLLOPE *Framley P.* xxvii, Fly a bill, and let Tozer have it to get cash on it in the city! 1875 TENNYSON *Q. Mary* I. v, O Madam, You fly your thoughts like kites. 1928 *Sat. Even. Post* 7 Jan. 21/2 Now would you like for mamma to go on reading to you about this Polark soldier and his girl friend, or would you like to go fly a kite. 1937 PARTRIDGE *Dict. Slang* 291/2 *Fly a, the, kite*,.. to test public opinion by tentative measures. 1942 'H. PENTECOST' *I'll sing at your Funeral* (1945) vii. 64 'He suggested,' said Bradley, with a sigh, 'that I go fly a kite!' 1951 C. P. SNOW *Masters* xv. 137 At the beginning Brown had, as he used to say, 'flown a kite' for compromise, now Chrystal joined him. 1961 *Lebende Sprachen* VI. 99/2 Go jump in the lake,.. go fly a kite; DDT (drop dead twice). 1971 *Nature* 26 Feb. 584/1 The solution, the committee suggests—and it is plainly flying a kite and not laying down policy—may be a more selective way of choosing the departments to which studentships will be allocated.

b. To convey through the air. Also, to conduct or pilot (an aircraft).

1864 SALA in *Daily Tel.* 23 Dec., The first wires were flown across by means of a kite. 1902 *Young Engineer* I. 265/1 He, in his indignation, undertook to fly his 'Illustrissimo', as he termed his balloon, with the whole of the Holy Office. 1911 GRAHAME-WHITE & HARPER *Aeroplane* 264 A machine that.. will require no more skill and nerve to fly it than does the driving of a car. 1917 *Brit. Dominions Year Bk.* 243 It calls for considerable courage.. to fly heavy sea-planes a hundred miles or so inland. 1920 *Act 10 & 11 Geo. V* c. 80 § 10 (1), Where an aircraft is flown in such a manner as to be the cause of unnecessary danger. 1928 *Manch. Guardian Weekly* 21 Sept. 224/3 Señor Juan de la Cierva, the inventor,.. flew one of these machines to Paris from Croydon on Tuesday. 1968 MILLER & SAWERS *Techn. Devel. Mod. Aviation* iv. 99 The prototype DC-1 was flown.

c. *slang.* ***to fly the mags***: see quots. ***to fly a tile***, to knock off a man's hat.

1812 J. H. VAUX *Flash Dict.*, *Fly the mags*, to gamble, by tossing up halfpence. 1825 C. M. WESTMACOTT *Eng. Spy* II. 158 Another point of amusement is *flying a tile*, or *slating* a man, as the phrases of the Stock Exchange describe it. 1838 H. AINSWORTH *Rookwood* III. xiii, 'Fly the mags',.. replied Rust; 'if heads, we scrag him.'

d. *colloq.* To send (a letter) hastily.

1846 DARWIN in *Life & Lett.* (1887) I. 351 Immediately that I hear I will fly you a line. 1859 *Ibid.* (1887) II. 160.

e. To convey by aircraft.

1928 *Daily Express* 18 May 2/6 More than £26,000,000 worth of gold coin and bullion has been flown in and out ot Croydon during the past three years. 1930 C. R. SAMSON *Fights & Flights* 209 You will fly me to Calais, and I will repair 1241. 1958 'N. SHUTE' *Rainbow & Rose* i. 17 You come to fly him out? 1971 *Daily Tel.* 9 Nov. 15/8 Cremation is taking place in Australia today. The ashes will be flown back to England.

6. a. *intr.* Of something attached by one edge or end, *esp.* of a flag, hair, a garment, etc.: To float loosely; to flutter, wave. Cf. FLYING *colours*.

1659 D. PELL *Impr. Sea* 271 The Antient-staff, about which the ships-colours do fly. 1659 B. HARRIS *Parival's Iron Age* 309 To.. march with drums beating and colours flying. 1725 POPE *Odyss.* XIII. 273 Around her shoulders flew the waving vest. 1782 COWPER *Gilpin* 101 The wind did blow, the cloak did fly. 1794 *Rigging & Seamanship* I. 214 Royals are set flying. 1797 NELSON 28 Nov. in Nicolas *Disp.* II. 455 A Captain was appointed to the Ship in which my Pendant flew. 1810 SCOTT *Lady of L.* II. xxi, Loose on the breeze their tresses flew. 1880 TENNYSON *Def. Lucknow* i, Banner of England.. Flying at top of the roofs in the ghastly siege of Lucknow.

b. *trans.* To set (a flag) flying; to carry at the mast-head; to hoist; occas. with *out*. Also, To set (a sail) loosely: see quots.

1655 M. CARTER *Hon. Rediv.* (1660) 187 From which time ever since they flye that Crosse in their Banners. 1794 *Rigging & Seamanship* I. 166 *Flying of Sails*, setting them in a loose manner; as royal sails without lifts. 1863 *Lond. Rev.* 10 Jan. 37 To sink, burn, and destroy everything that flew the ensign of the so-called United States of America. 1885 *Law Times* 23 May 63/1 The steamship.. flying signals of distress. 1887 KINGLAKE *Crimea* VIII. 300 She flew out the signal—'Farewell!' 1887 BESANT *World went* i, If they do fly the black flag, it is only [etc.].

7. a. *intr.* To move or travel swiftly, pass rapidly, rush along. Also with *about, along, away, back*, etc. Of a fox: to break covert.

a 1300 *Cursor M.* 21280 (Cott.) And [þe quil] fleis wit-vten blin. 1513 DOUGLAS *Æneis* III. ii. 110 We.. with swift cours flaw throw the salt see. 1563 W. FULKE *Meteors* (1640) 33 b, A whirlewind.. breaking forth, flyeth round like a great cart-wheele. *a* 1575 GASCOIGNE *Pr. Pleas. Kenilw.* A vj, The fierie flames, which through the waues so flue. *c* 1611 CHAPMAN *Iliad* XVIII. 191 So fear'd The fair man'd horses that they flew back. *a* 1667 JER. TAYLOR *Contempl. State Man.* I. v. (1699) 54 A corrupt Humour.. which flies into the Heart. 1703 ROWE *Ulyss.* II. i. 582 A Troop of Nymphs Flew lightly by us. 1756 C. LUCAS *Ess. Waters* I. 187 The pains.. wander, shoot, and fly about, sometimes with astonishing swiftness. 1782 COWPER *Gilpin* 234 Six Gentlemen upon the road, Thus seeing Gilpin fly. 1842 TENNYSON *Day-dream, Arrival* iii, The colour flies into his cheeks. 1849 MACAULAY *Hist. Eng.* I. 386 We fly from York.. to London by the light of a single winter's day. 1860 TYNDALL *Glac.* II. i. 223 The velocity with which the earth flies through space. 1883 E. PENNELL-ELMHIRST *Cream Leicestersh.* 132 He had never seen hounds fly along as they did now. 1897 *Encycl. Sport* I. 546/1 They force the fox through the cover in such a determined fashion as will make him 'fly or die'. 1902 *Daily Chron.* 14 Nov. 8/5 The pack had to wait some time before they could get their fox to fly.

b. *esp.* of time. [With mixture of senses 1 and 11; cf. *fugit invida ætas*.]

1597 SHAKS. *Lover's Compl.* 60 That.. had let go by The swiftest hours, observed as they flew. 1712 POPE *Messiah* 21 Swift fly the years, and rise th' expected morn! 1800–24 CAMPBELL *Poems, Song* ii, Time.. Flies like a courser nigh the goal. 1847 L. HUNT *Jar Honey* xii. (1848) 154 Time flies, and friends must part.

†**c.** Of a stage-coach: To 'run'. *Obs.*

1748 *St. James's Even. Post* No. 6039 Dover, and Deal Stage-Coaches, will continue Flying till the First Day of October.

†**d.** quasi-*trans.* To run over hurriedly. *Obs.*$^{-1}$

1589 *Hay any Work* 41 Your.. purciuantes flye citie & countrie to seeke for Waldegraue.

†**e.** ***fly (a)round*** (*U.S.* colloq.): to bustle about, bestir oneself.

1831 S. SMITH *Life & Writings J. Downing* 151, I flew round and washed my face and hands. 1833 J. HALL *Legends of West* 88 She flew around among the folks mighty peart. 1839 C. M. KIRKLAND *New Home* ii. 16 Come, gals! fly round, and let's git some supper. 1851 HOOPER *Night at Ugly Man's* in *Wdw. Rugby's Husb.* 44 Old 'ooman, fly around, git somethin' for the Squire and Dick to eat. 1871 MRS. STOWE *Oldtown Fires. Stories* 63 He flew round like a parched pea on a shovel.

f. ***to fly the coop***: to escape or elope; to leave suddenly; ***to fly the track***: to turn from the usual or expected course. *U.S. colloq.*

1847 *Congress. Globe* 4 Feb. 322/2, I had been accused of flying the track on the creed of the Democratic party. 1901 'B. BURGUNDY' *Toothsome Tales* (1902) 68 Chester.. used to.. toast her until she was on the edge of hysterics, then he'd fly the coop in quest of a new cargo of thirst-erasers. 1906 'O. HENRY' *Four Million* (1916) 123 She'll never regret flyin' the coop with Chunk McGowan. 1909 —— *Options* (1916) 157 One of them.. 'roller-coasters' flew the track and killed a man. 1966 H. KEMELMAN *Saturday the Rabbi went Hungry* (1967) xxi. 206 This man.. ran off, flew the coop, beat it.

8. a. Of persons and animals: To move with a start or rush; to spring, start, hasten, rush. ***to fly to arms***: to take up arms on a sudden. ***to fly in the face of***: see FACE *sb.* 4 b.

1590 SPENSER *F.Q.* I. ii. 17 The Sarazin.. Snatcheth his sword, and fiercely to him flies. 1768 STERNE *Sent. Journ.* (1778) I. 118 The bidet flew from one side of the road to the other. 1782 COWPER *Gilpin* 163 The calender.. flew to the gate. 1824 SCOTT *Redgauntlet* let. xi, The nag began to spring, and flee, and stend. 1826 DISRAELI *Viv. Grey* II. vi, In this dilemma he flew to his father. 1847 MRS. A. KERR *Hist. Servia* 185 In a violent commotion, they had flown to arms. 1854 MISS MANNING *Old Chelsea Bun-ho.* vii. (1855) 116 She flew up-stairs, without at all regarding the trouble. 1881 GARDINER & MULLINGER *Study Eng. Hist.* I. ii. 37 Danes and English were especially ready to fly apart.

b. ***to fly at, on, upon***: to spring with violence upon, attack with fury, rush upon; *lit.* and *fig.* Also (*rarely*) *transf.* of inanimate objects.

1549 COVERDALE etc. *Erasm. Par. 1 John* iii. 15 He hath not thrust his sword in him.. he hath not flowen upon him. 1583 RICH *Phylotus & Emelia* (1835) 17 He seemed, as though he would haue fline vpon her in the streate. 1586 WARNER *Alb. Eng.* I. vi, Whom Cerberus forsaking then at Hercules he flide. 1611 BIBLE *1 Sam.* xv. 19 Wherefore then didst thou.. flie vpon the spoile. 1692 SOUTH *Serm., 1 John* iii. 21 (1737) II. xii. 464 When an enraged conscience shall fly at him, and take him by the throat. 1748 *Anson's Voy.* III. ix. 393 One of them flew on the fellow who had the sword. 1782 MISS BURNEY *Cecilia* VI. xi, You.. never fly at your servants. 1807–8 SYD. SMITH *Plymley's Lett.* Wks. 1859 II. 160/1 If you have.. worried a mastiff dog for years.. he flies at you whenever he sees you. 1834 DARWIN in *Life & Lett.* (1887) I. 250 My hammer has flown with redoubled force on the devoted blocks. *c* 1860 MISS YONGE *Strayed Falcon* in *Hist. Dramas* No. 3 (Groombridge) 46 People came out of the dining-room, and Katie flew upon them. 1861 DICKENS *Gt. Expect.* ix, My sister with an exclamation of impatience was going to fly at me.

c. ***to fly in*** or ***into*** (a passion, rapture, etc.): to pass suddenly into (such a state).

1683 HACKE *Collect. Voy.* I. (1699) 32 Which made the other fly into a Passion with him. 1797 SCOTT *Let. to Mrs. Scott* in Lockhart *Life* viii, Without flying into raptures.. I may safely assure you, that [etc.]. 1819 BYRON *Juan* I. liv, She flew in a rage. 1887 R. N. CAREY *Uncle Max* xxii. 176, I only flew into a passion, and asked her how [etc.].

d. ***to fly off***: *lit.* to start away; 'to revolt' (J.); *fig.* to take another course; to break away (from an agreement or engagement).

1667 MILTON *P.L.* VI. 614 Strait they changd thir minds, Flew off and into strange vagaries fell. 1713 ADDISON *Cato* IV. 54 The traytor Syphax.. Flew off at once with his Numidian Horse. 1785 MAD. D'ARBLAY *Diary* 16 Dec., I was.. ready to fly off if any one knocked at the street-door. 1816 *Sporting Mag.* XLVIII. 173 From this agreement he flew off. 1864 H. AINSWORTH *John Law* III. ii. Were I to ask for time, [Nicomède] would inevitably fly off, and the affair would come to an end.

e. ***to fly out***: (*a*) to spring out, come out suddenly; to rush out; (*b*) to 'explode' or burst out into extravagance in conduct, language, or temper. Const. *against, at, upon* (an object); *into* (action, language, feeling, etc.).

(*a*) *c* 1400 MAUNDEV. (1839) iv. 27 There fleigh out an Eddere right hidous to see. 1607 SHAKS. *Cor.* I. x. 19 My valor.. for him Shall flye out of it selfe. 1653 H. COGAN tr. *Pinto's Trav.* xiv. 43 Eighty Mahometans came flying out from under their hatches. 1726 SHELVOCKE *Voy. round World* (1757) 163 Without flying out of the bounds they had prescribed to themselves.

(*b*) 1638 SIR T. HERBERT *Trav.* (ed. 2) 84 Upon his.. oath never more to fly out, is pardoned. 1649 BP. HALL *Cases Consc.* 498 Impatient.. of their conjugall disappointments, fly out into open contestations. 1667 PEPYS *Diary* (1877) V. 394, I was troubled.. to hear my Lord fly out against their great pretence of merit from the King. 1681 W. ROBERTSON *Phraseol. Gen.* (1693) 616 To fly out or squander his estate. 1779 MAD. D'ARBLAY *Diary* Nov., He constrained himself from flying out as long as he was able. 1865 *Cornh. Mag.* Oct. 390, I beg your pardon for flying out upon you so. 1868 G. DUFF *Pol. Surv.* 130 Another friend.. has flown out to me at the action of the Radicals. 1884 CHURCH *Bacon* iii. 62 She thought of the possibility of his flying out unexpectedly.. and attempting to serve her interests, not in her way, but in his own.

9. a. Of things: To be forced or driven off suddenly or with a jerk; to start. Of a limb: To be parted suddenly from the body. Const. *from, out of*. Also ***to send flying***.

c 1340 *Gaw. & Gr. Knt.* 459 Þat þe fyr of þe flynt flaȝe fro fole houes. 1375 BARBOUR *Bruce* III. 115 He raucht till him sic a dynt, That arme and schuldyr flaw him fra. *c* 1440 *Generydes* 2670 Mi swerd out of myn hond fligh. 1533 LD. BERNERS *Huon* xlvi. 153 His hede flewe fro hys sholders. 1593 SHAKS. *Lucr.* 177 From the could stone sparkes of fire doe flie. 1659 D. PELL *Impr. Sea* 427 Then flyes in his face all his whoring, swearing, lying. 1683 WALLER *Invas. Turks* 23 He Bassas' heads, to save his own, made fly. 1796 MRS. GLASSE *Cookery* xxi. 321 Let it stand an hour before you open it, lest it fly in your face. 1847 PORTER *Big Bear* etc. 132 Thar, they've got him agin, and now the fur flies. 1852 MRS. STOWE *Uncle Tom's C.* xx, 'Oughter see how old Mas'r made the flesh fly.' 1879 F. POLLOK *Sport Brit. Burmah* II. 149 Up would go the elephant's hind leg, sending the pig flying. 1885 *Spectator* 30 May 698/2 The engine minder who goes to the parish doctor because a spark has flown in his eye.

b. *fig.* Of money: To be rapidly spent.

1632 ROWLEY *Woman never vext* 11, Marry her, and let her estate fly. 1635 N. R. *Camden's Hist. Eliz.* an. 5. I. 48 Edward Earle of Oxford (who set his Patrimony flying). 1665 SIR T. HERBERT *Trav.* (1677) 97 In this resolve she lets her Treasure fly. 1840 LADY C. BURY *Hist. Flirt* iv, I shall certainly make his money fly.

c. With various advbs., *about, back, off, out, up*, etc. †***to fly off***: (of cannon) to be fired.

c 1340 *Cursor M.* 1769 (Fairf.) þe fire flaghe out with þonder and raine. *c* 1430 *Syr. Gener.* (Roxb.) 5934 Of his sheld floy of a grete cantel. *c* 1460 *Launfal* 473 The erl of Chestere.. smot hym the helm on hegh That the crest adoun flegh. 1590 SPENSER *F.Q.* I. v. 7 From their shields forth flyeth firie light. 1613 SHAKS. *Hen. VIII*, V. i. 111 My Chaffe and Corne shall flye asunder. 1650 HOWELL *Giraffi's Rev. Naples* I. (1664) 117 The Vice-roy.. caus'd all the ordnance to flie off. 1653 H. COGAN tr. *Pinto's Trav.* xvi. 55 The dog struck her over the head with his hatchet till her brains flew out. 1665 HOOKE *Microgr.* 15 They.. cannot agree together, but fly back from each other. 1684 R. H. *School Recreat.* 41 Which.. by spouting out, will make the Water fly about. 1703 MOXON *Mech. Exerc.* 169 The Tool will.. fly off where a Knot.. comes to the Tool. 1712 W. ROGERS *Voy.* 107 Lowering her Main-Yard: the Tack flew up. 1713 BERKELEY *Guardian* No. 126 ¶2 The earth.. without flying off in a tangent line, constantly rolls about the sun. 1820 SCORESBY *Acc. Arctic Reg.* II. 349 The ice shivering with the violence of the strain.. the anchor flew out.

d. *causative* and quasi-*trans.*

1676 WORLIDGE *Cyder* (1691) 146 The Liquor were better fly the Cork than break the Bottle. 1876 G. MEREDITH *Beauch. Career* II. vi. 108 The ship in the Arabian tale coming within the zone of the magnetic mountain, flies all its bolts and bars and becomes sheer timbers.

e. *intr.* Of a door or window: To be thrown suddenly *open, to, up*, etc. Rarely *trans.* (slang), to throw up (a window).

1625 MASSINGER *New Way* II. iii, I.. To whom great countesses' doors have oft flew open. 1782 COWPER *Gilpin* 110 Up flew the windows all. 1847 EMERSON *Poems* (1857) 116 At unawares, Self-moved, fly-to the doors. 1857 R. L. SNOWDEN *Magistr. Assist.* (ed. 3) 447 To lift a window, to fly a window. 1870 THORNBURY *Tour Eng.* I. ii. 36 The dark prison doors flew open at the first chink of the gold. 1885 STEVENSON *Dynamiter* ii. 10 The door flew back emitting clouds of smoke.

f. ***to fly in pieces***, or simply ***to fly***: to break up suddenly, shiver, split up. †***to fly on fire***: to burst into flames.

c 1470 HENRY *Wallace* II. 50 Bayn and brayn he gert in peces fle. 1624 MASSINGER *Renegado* II. iii, This pure metal.. rather Than hold one drop that's venomous, of itself It flies in pieces. 1692 RAY *Dissol. World* III. iv. (1732) 327 All the moisture will at length be drawn out and the world fly on fire. 1697 DRYDEN *Virg. Georg.* I. 262 Lest crack'd with Summer Heats the flooring flies. 1726 SHELVOCKE *Voy. round World* (1757) 245 It rent and split, and flew like glass. 1766 GOLDSM. *Hermit* xiv, The crackling faggot flies. 1881 YOUNG *Ev. Man his own Mechanic* § 1461 If.. the first time of using the heat is raised rapidly, they are certain to crack or 'fly'.

g. *Naut.* Of the wind: To shift or veer suddenly. Also with *about, off*. Of a ship, her head: ***to fly to, up in, into the wind*** (see quots.).

1699 DAMPIER *Voy.* II. III. 25 The Winds fly in a moment quite round the Compass. *Ibid.* 27 About Mid-day they fly off 2, 3 or 4 Points further from the Land. 1855 OGILVIE Suppl., *Fly*, To fly about. Among seamen, the wind is said to fly about, when it changes frequently during a short space of time. 1867 SMYTH *Sailor's Word-bk.* s.v. *Fly-up*, *To fly up in the wind*, is when a ship's head comes suddenly to windward, by carelessness of the helmsman. *Ibid.*, *Flying-to* is when a vessel.. is coming to the wind rapidly, the warning is given to the helmsman, 'Look out, she is flying-to'. 1882 NARES *Seamanship* (ed. 6) 232 The ship is sure to fly up into the wind.

h. *Baseball.* To hit a fly-ball (FLY *sb.*[2] 8). Chiefly with *out*. (Pa. t. usu. **flied**.)

1893 *Chicago Tribune* 3 July 7/3 Kittridge flied out to Brodie. 1904 *St. Louis Globe-Democrat* 4 July 12/3 Wallace flew to Lush for the third out. 1912 C. MATHEWSON *Pitching in a Pinch* ix. 202 Sheckard flied out to Seymour, Kling being held on second base. 1948 *Durant* (Okla.) *Daily Democrat* 2 July 4/4 Baker then flied to center and neither runner was able to advance.

10. to let fly. a. To discharge (missiles).

a 1000 *Judith* 220 (Gr.) Hie þa fromlice leton forð fleoȝan flana scuras. *c* 1250 *Gen. & Ex.* 479 An lamech droȝe is arwe ner, And letet fleȝen of ðe streng. 1664 BUTLER *Hud.* II. ii. 815 At that an egg let fly, Hit him directly o'er the eye. 1832

HT. MARTINEAU *Life in Wilds* v. 58 He let fly one of his precious arrows.

b. *absol.* To fire, shoot; also said occas. of a gun. Also, to make an attack (with any weapon).

1611 COTGR. s.v. *Pied, Jouër a quattre pieds contre*, to kicke, winse, or let fly at with all foure. **1624** CAPT. SMITH *Virginia* III. vi. 62 We let fly amongst them so that they fled. **1686** J. SERGEANT *Monast. Conventions* 185 Then..the Cannon of the Castle let fly. *a* **1735** GRANVILLE *Ess. Unnat. Flights in Poetry* 55 The noisy culverin, o'ercharg'd, lets fly. **1879** F. POLLOK *Sport Brit. Burmah* II. 41, I let fly again, and this time killed it.

c. *fig.* (*trans.* and *absol.*).

1590 SPENSER *F.Q.* III. ix. 52 Many fair belgardes let fly. **1654** H. L'ESTRANGE *Chas. I* (1655) 24 A Member of the House of Commons let fly this reply. **1678** *Trans. Crt. Spain* 180 And to take all pretext from those who by ignorance or malice let flye against me. **1859** *Punch* 6 Aug. 54/1 Lord Lyndhurst, at whom it pleased Mr. Bright to scoff..let fly at that respected Quaker. **1887** BESANT *The World went* xvi. 135 He let fly a round dozen or so of sailors' oaths.

d. *Naut.* To allow (a sail or sheet) to fly loose; rarely to set (a sail), to carry, hoist (colours).

1627 CAPT. SMITH *Seaman's Gram.* ix. 39 When we say, let fly the sheats, then they let go amaine, which commonly is in some gust. **1659** D. PELL *Impr. Sea* 297 If they finde them unwilling to bee spoke with all, Frigots let flye all the sails that ever they can make. **1699** DAMPIER *Voy.* II. I. 48 It is the custom of our Countrymen abroad, to let fly their Colours on Sundays. **1805** SIR E. BERRY in Nicolas *Nelson's Disp.* VII. 118, I then let fly the top-gallant sheets.

II. In senses of FLEE. (Now in pres.-stem only: see the remarks under FLEE *v.*)

11. a. = FLEE 1, 1 b, and 1 d. Also quasi-*trans.*

a **1000** *Byrhtnoth* 275 (Gr.) þæt he nolde fleoȝan fotmæl landes. **1523** LD. BERNERS *Froiss.* I. ccxxxvi. 334 For to dye in the place they wyll nat flye one fote. **1548** HALL *Chron., Edw. IV*, (an. 8) 204 b, Syr Robert was exhortyng..hys men ..which were..redy to flye. **1594** H. WILLOBIE in *Shaks. C. Praise* 10 Nor flye the field though she deny. *a* **1625** B. JONSON, etc. *Widow* I. i, I'll make him fly the land. **1662** WOOD *Life* (Oxf. Hist. Soc.) I. 462 Flying the realme at the king's returne. **1678** BUTLER *Hud.* III. iii. 243 Those that fly may fight again. *a* **1703** BURKITT *On N.T.* Mark ii. 2 Honour flies from them that pursue it. **1715–20** POPE *Iliad* I. 35 Hence on thy Life, and fly these hostile Plains. **1839** THIRLWALL *Greece* VI. l. 224 Sisygambis refused to fly. **1855** THACKERAY *Rose & Ring* xi, You must fly the country for a while.

b. = FLEE 2 and 2 c. Const. *into, to*, †*unto*.

a **1300** *Cursor M.* 6675 (Gött.) If he to min auter fly. **1584** POWEL *Lloyd's Cambria* 5 Being in the Battle..and Flieng to the wood. **1653** H. COGAN tr. *Pinto's Trav.* xxi. 76 Unless upon..the new Moons, one fly into the Ports for shelter. *a* **1711** KEN *Anodynes* Poet. Wks. 1721 III. 409 When Pangs ..disturb my Sleep, To various Anodynes I fly. **1818** JAS. MILL *Brit. India* III. v. viii. 641 It was to the English he must have flown for protection.

c. = FLEE 3 and 4.

1581 PETTIE tr. *Guazzo's Civ. Conv.* I. (1586) 4 Delightes, from which a great manie men flie. **1634** SIR T. HERBERT *Trav.* 48 All [*sc.* the inhabitants]..flie away in Summer to avoid the intolerable heat. **1725** POPE *Odyss.* v. 60 He [Hermes] grasps the wand that causes sleep to fly. **1817** SHELLEY *Rev. Islam.* XI. vii. 6, I cannot reach thee! whither dost thou fly? **1875** JOWETT *Plato* (ed. 2) V. 73 He grows like evil men, and is compelled to fly from the company of the good.

d. = FLEE 5. (Said of a shadow, colour, etc.)

1535 COVERDALE *Job* xiv. 2 He [man] flyeth as it were a shadowe. **1598** SHAKS. *Merry W.* II. ii. 215 Loue like a shadow flies, when substance Loue pursues. **1821** SHELLEY *Adonais* lii, Heaven's light for ever shines, Earth's shadows fly. *a* **1861** MRS. BROWNING *My Heart & I* ii, As if such colors could not fly.

e. *trans.* = FLEE 7 and 8. †*to fly the heels* (see quot. 1727).

1552 LATIMER *Serm. Third Sond. Epiph.* Fruitful Serm. (1584) 312 b, Haue an earnest desire to leaue sinne, and to flye the same. **1583** BABINGTON *Commandm.* ix. (1637) 87 Flye to heare as thou wouldest flye to speake what tendeth vnto slaunder. **1635** A. STAFFORD *Fem. Glory* (1869) 54 Though he be ambitious of Dignities..he seems to flie them. **1727** BAILEY vol. II. *s.v.*, To Fly the Heels..a Term used of a Horse, when he obeys the Spur. **1754** CHATHAM *Lett. Nephew* iv. 27 Fly with abhorrence and contempt superstition and enthusiasm. *a* **1839** PRAED *Poems* (1864) II. 241 True pity..flies the rich, it flies the vain.

†**f.** To escape the notice of. Cf. FLEE 9. *Obs.*$^{-1}$

c **1611** CHAPMAN *Iliad* XVI. Comm., It flies all his translators and interpreters.

fly (flaɪ), *v.*^{2} Pa. t. and pa. pple. flied, flyed. [f. FLY *sb.*^{1} and ^{2}.]

1. a. *intr.* To travel by a fly. **b.** *trans.* To convey in a fly.

1836 SOUTHEY *Let. to Miss. K. Southey* 25 Nov. (1856) IV. 476 We *flied*..over Quantock to Stowey. *Ibid.* 478 Poole *flied* us all the way to Sir T. Acland's Somersetshire seat.

2. *Printing.* To do the office of a fly (see FLY *sb.*^{1} 6) or fly-boy to. *to fly the frisket* (see quot.). *to fly the sheet*: to lift it, by holding it at one end, into the printing machine; as opposed to stroking it in. Also, in *U.S.* (see quot.).

1871 *Amer. Encycl. Print, Fly the Frisket*, to turn down the frisket and tympan by the same motion. *Ibid.* s.v. *Fly-boy*, When..it is requisite that boys should assist in taking the printed sheets, one by one, from the form or the press, this operation is called flying the sheets.

3. In the Hardware trades: To stamp or cut out by means of a fly (FLY *sb.*^{2} 5 i). Also with *out.*

fly, obs. form of FLAY, FLEY.

flyable (ˈflaɪəb(ə)l), *a.* [f. FLY *v.*^{1} + -ABLE.]

1. *Hunting colloq.* That can be flown or leapt over.

1893 *Field* 11 Feb. 188/3 An Irish bank is not 'flyable'.

2. Of weather: suitable for flying. Of goods: transportable by air. Of an aircraft: that is capable of flying or of being flown.

1936 J. GRIERSON *High Failure* xii. 271 McNab arranged ..to take me out to Robert Bruce [name of aeroplane], provided the weather should be flyable. **1945** *Times* 3 Aug. 5/6 Forecasters who are amazingly expert at assessing how long the weather will remain flyable at night at any particular airfield in the country. **1960** R. W. MARKS *Dymaxion World of B. Fuller* 151/4 The more ephemeralization advances the more flyable becomes any one cargo. **1963** *Economist* 30 Nov. 928/3 A real flyable aeroplane. **1970** *Daily Tel.* (Colour Suppl.) 9 Oct. 61/1 A corrugated silver Ford Tri-Motor in flyable condition.

fly-about, *a. nonce-wd.* **a.** Given to 'flying about.'

1799 MRS. J. WEST *Tale of Times* I. 298 Your good sense will keep you from running wild, as many of our young fly-about travellers do.

b. Of horses: skittish.

1889 F. E. GRETTON *Memory's Harkback* 110 Two little blood-chestnuts..very fly-about, and disposed to bolt.

fly-away, *a.* and *sb.* [f. vbl. phr. see FLY *v.*^{1}]

A. *adj.* Ready or apt to fly away. **a.** Of articles of dress: Streaming, loose, négligé. **b.** Of persons: Flighty, extravagant, volatile.

fly-away grass (*U.S.*), the *Agrostis scaba*, a common grass of North America, with a very loose light panicle. Also called *hair-grass* (*Cent. Dict.*).

1775 S. J. PRATT *Liberal Opin.* (1783) II. 230 His reducing the fly-away farmer's daughters to a proper sense of their condition. **1844** DICKENS *Mart. Chuz.* v, Drest in such a free and fly-away fashion, that the long ends of his loose red neckcloth were streaming out behind him. **1848** —— *Dombey* xl, It was not easy to put her into a fly-away bonnet now. **1856** *Rep. Mass. Board Agric.* I. 29 Hair Grass, or Fly Away Grass,..is another species belonging to the genus. **1871** M. COLLINS *Mrq. & Merch.* III. v. 136 Servant-girls with flyaway caps on their heads. **1891** *Pall Mall G.* 21 May 2/2 They have brought it home to the most flyaway supporter of the A.P.S.

B. *sb.* **a.** One that flies away. Cf. *runaway*.

1804 M. WILMOT *Let.* 24 Jan. (1934) I. 78 She was not amongst the fly aways but return'd for the Ball. **1838** EMERSON *Nat., Lit. Ethics* Wks. (Bohn) II. 212 Truth is such a flyaway, such a slyboots.

b. *Naut.* A delusive appearance, of land, a mirage. Also *quasi*-proper name, *Cape Flyaway*.

1867 in SMYTH *Sailor's Word-bk.* **1883** in W. C. RUSSELL *Sailor's Lang.*

'fly-back. [f. verbal phr. *to fly back* (see FLY *v.*^{1} 9 c).] **1.** In a stop-watch or chronograph, the return of the hands to zero. Usu. *attrib.*

1888 *Phil. Mag.* 5th Ser. XXV. 263 The fly-back chronograph enables time to be measured to $\frac{1}{5}$th second, without taking the eye for one moment off the object to be watched. **1903** F. J. GARRARD *Watch Repairing* xix. 200 (*caption*) Fly-back work of chronograph. **1923** W. I. MILHAM *Time & Timekeepers* xv. 250 A double split-second fly back stop watch..gets out of order quite easily. **1929** G. H. BAILLIE *Watches* x. 233 A watch with fly-back minute hand, which..flies back to 0 as soon as it reaches 60. **1953** W. J. GAZELEY *Watch & Clock Making & Repairing* xiv. 315 Another arrangement met with in some stop watches..is where a separate push-piece is used for the fly-back action.

2. a. The return of the scanning spot in a cathode-ray tube to the starting point after the end of a line or frame. Freq. *attrib.* **b.** The portion of each cycle of a saw-tooth wave-form in which the signal diminishes.

1934 *Jrnl. Inst. Electr. Engin.* LXXV. 66/1 The arrangement..constitutes a time base which provides a scanning sweep..and a rapid fly-back. **1948** T. SOLLER et al. *Cathode Ray Tube Displays* iv. 133 The flat portion [of the waveform] is the 'quiescent' voltage and the portion that follows the rise is the 'return' or 'flyback'. **1950** *Electronic Engin.* XXII. 55 The flyback time in these tests was about one-seventh of the sweep time. **1957** AMOS & BIRKINSHAW *Television Engin.* I. i. 15 During the time occupied by each horizontal traverse and fly-back the beam moves downwards.

fly-bane. [f. FLY *sb.*^{1} + BANE.]

1. The popular name of various plants: (*a*) = CATCHFLY; (*b*) the ploughman's spikenard (*Inula Conyza*); (*c*) (see quot. 1863).

1597 GERARDE *Herbal* Table Eng. names, Fliebane and his kinds, see catch Flie. **1819** REES *Cycl., Fly-bane*, in Botany, see *Silene*. **1861** MISS PRATT *Flower. Pl.* III. 300 *Inula Conyza* (Ploughman's Spikenard)..possesses..a valuable oil..which is said to destroy insects; hence the plant is sometimes called Fly-bane. **1863** PRIOR *Plant-n., Flybane*, from being used mixed with milk to kill flies. *Agaricus muscarius* L.

2. Poison for flies; in quot. the venom of spiders.

1704 SWIFT *Batt. Bks.* 247 An over-weening Pride [in the Spider]..turns all into Excrement and Venom; producing nothing at last, but Fly-bane and a Cobweb.

'fly-bitten, *ppl. a.* [f. as prec. + BITTEN.]

1. Bitten by flies; loosely used for: †**a.** Fly-specked; †**b.** FLY-BLOWN; **c.** Stung by flies.

1597 SHAKS. *2 Hen. IV*, II. i. 159 These Fly-bitten Tapistries. **1598** FLORIO, *Alida*..flie-bitten meate. **1884** A. GREGORY in *Fortn. Rev.* Mar. 378 Their [Baggara Arabs'] wealth consists of herds of lean fly-bitten cattle.

†**2.** = FLEA-BITTEN 2. *Obs.*

1639 DE GRAY *Compl. Horsem.* 22.

'fly-blow, *sb.* [f. FLY *sb.*^{1} + BLOW *sb.*^{2}]

1. The egg deposited by a fly in the flesh of an animal, or the maggot proceeding therefrom. Also *collect.* Rarely the action of depositing the egg.

1556 J. HEYWOOD *Spider & F.* xliv. 229 This flie hath blown fliblowe in mine eare a pecke. **1688** R. HOLME *Armoury* II. 467/1 Little long eggs called Fly blowes. **1713** WARDER *True Amazons* (ed. 2) 18 The Eggs..are.. something bigger than the common Fly-blow. **1757** DYER *Fleece* I. 579 Lest touch of busy fly-blows wound their skin. **1825** *On Bull Baiting* I. Houlston Tracts I. xxvii. 8 Its poor wounds were all full of fly-blows.

fig. *a* **1680** BUTLER *Rem.* (1759) I. 425 He is.. produced out of..the Flyblows of the Rabble.

attrib. **1606** [see FLY-BLOWN 1. *fig.* 1602]. **1856** MRS. BROWNING *Aur. Leigh* IX. 378 No fly-blow gossip ever specked my life.

2. = BY-BLOW 3.

1875 OUIDA *Signa* I. viii. 140.

'fly-blow, *v.* [f. FLY *sb.*^{1} + BLOW *v.*^{1}; after next.]

1. *trans.* Of the fly: To deposit eggs in (meat, etc.); hence, to corrupt secretly, taint. Chiefly *fig.* So **fly-blowing** *vbl. sb.*

1603 B. JONSON *Sejanus* v. x, Is not he blest That..Can claw his subtle elbow, or with a buzze Fly-blow his eares. **1610** ROWLANDS *Martin Mark-all* 13 If it were not for us, much good meate would be in danger of Fly-blowing. **1678** B. R. *Let. Pop. Friends* 7 If we cannot wound the Government mortally, lets Fly-blow it with Scandals and Suspicions. **1795** SOUTHEY *Joan of Arc* x. 77 Court vermin that..fly-blow the king's ear, and make him waste..his people's wealth. **1813** T. MOORE *Let.* in *Mem.* (1853) I. 349 A whole swarm of imitators..will completely fly-blow all the novelty of my subject. **1891** R. WALLACE *Rural Econ. Austral. & N.Z.* ii. 42 Sheep do not require to be dipped in this district, as there are no ticks, no foot-rot, and little fly-blowing.

2. *intr.* (or *absol.*) Of flies: To deposit their eggs.

1735 POPE *Ep. Lady* 28 So morning Insects..Shine, buzz, and fly-blow in the setting-sun.

fly-blown (ˈflaɪbləʊn), *ppl. a.* [f. FLY *sb.*^{1} + BLOWN *ppl. a.*]

1. Full of fly-blows; tainted, putrid, impure.

1573 G. HARVEY *Letter-bk.* (Camden) 138 Flyblowen fleshe comm not in my messe. **1612** WEBSTER *White Devil* v. iii, A dead fly-blown dog. **1692** BENTLEY *Boyle Lect.* iv. 137 The Manna was fly-blown. **1781** COWPER *Convers.* 676 Fly-blown flesh, whereon the maggot feeds.

fig. *a* **1529** SKELTON *Replyc.* Wks. 1862 II. 234 Agaynst whiche..flyblowen opynions..I purpose for to reply. **1602** *2nd Pt. Return fr. Pernass.* III. iv. 1412 His fliblowne [ed. 1606 (Arb. p. 46) fliblow] sonnettes. **1692** E. WALKER *Epictetus' Mor.* (1737) xxxi, By each Fly-blown Fool cares'd. **1860** THACKERAY *Lovel* i, Wherever fly-blown reputations were assembled.

2. *slang.* **a.** Intoxicated, drunk. **b.** *Austral.* and *N.Z.* 'Cleaned-out'; without a penny.

1853 C. R. READ *What I heard, saw & did at Austral. Gold Fields* 51 Being 'fly-blown' is a Colonial term for being 'done up'. **1864** C. R. THATCHER *Songs of War* 20 When they know you're *fly-blown*, You're then left alone By the damsels inside the Bazaar. **1877** *Judy* 18 May 236 (Farmer) The officer..hinted that he was slightly 'flyblown'. **1889** *Star* 3 Jan. (Farmer), Our diggers..get on the spree and come back fly-blown. **1921** H. FOSTON *At Front* vii. 56 [The men] usually returned to the works fly-blown.

fly-boat (ˈflaɪbəʊt). Forms: 6 flie-bote, flee-boate, flibote, 7 fly(e)boate(e, 7– fly-boat. [app. ad. Du. *vlieboot*, originally denoting one of the small boats used on the *Vlie* or channel leading out of the Zuyder Zee, afterwards applied in ridicule to the small vessels used against the Spaniards by the *Gueux de mer* (1572); the word has passed into several European langs.: F. *flibot*, Sp. *flibote*, Ger. *flieboot*. But in Eng. it was very early associated with FLY *v.*^{1}, and this is prob. the source of sense 4. Sense 3, belonging esp. to Shetland, may be a distinct word, representing ON. *fley*; cf. ONorthumb. *flœge*, perh. adopted from ON.]

†**1.** A fast-sailing vessel used chiefly in the sixteenth and seventeenth centuries: **a.** for rapid transport of goods, etc., *esp.* in the coasting trade; *Obs.* exc. *spec.* a Dutch flat-bottomed boat; = FLIGHT 12 a.

1577 DEE *Relat. Spir.* I. (1659) 33 Our Fisher-boat his sayl-yard and sayl was entangled on the Maynyard of the Fly-boat. **1588** *Wills Inv. N.C.* (Surtees 1860) II. 182 Paid to the fliebote, for freight of cxxx last of rye. **1698** FROGER *Voy.* 140 A small Fly-boat of forty Tunn..laden with Tobacco, Bacon, and Meal for Barbadoes. **1733** P. LINDSAY *Interest Scot.* 133 Our merchants might build..large Hag-boats and Fly-boats from 3 to 600 Tons, for the bulky trade. **1769** FALCONER *Dict. Marine* (1776) *Fly-boat*, or *Flight*, a large flat-bottom'd Dutch vessel, whose burthen is generally from four to six hundred tons.

fig. **1602** MARSTON *Ant. & Mel.* I. v, Here's such a companie of flibotes, hulling about this galleasse of greatnesse, that there's no boarding him. **1664** J. WILSON *Cheats* IV. iv. Dram. Wks. (1874) 79 She's [landlady] a pretty fly-boat; two men won't sink her!

†**b.** for warlike purposes, voyages of discovery, etc.; a kind of frigate. *Obs.* exc. *Hist.*

1590 NASHE *Pasquil's Apol.* I 1 He was built but for a Flieboate, to take and leaue, when the skyrmish is too hote for him to tarrie. **1673** *Lond. Gaz.* No. 758/4 This Caper is a Flyboat of two tire of Guns, carrying in all, as we suppose, 32. **1752** CARTE *Hist. Eng.* III. 539 The Flushingers..put a number of Fly-boats to sea and seized all ships coming from Spain. **1868** ST. JOHN *Life Raleigh* I. 257.

†**2.** A small boat, *esp.* a ship's boat. *Obs.*

1598 FLORIO, *Fusta*, a pinace or Fliebote. **1688** LUTTRELL *Brief Rel.* (1857) I. 473 Some of our ships, since the passing by the Dutch fleet, have pickt up a small fly boat or two belonging to them. **1820** SCOTT *Monast.* xxix, While the humble fly-boat carries to shore those friends.

†**3.** A fishing boat used in Shetland, a buss. *Obs.*

1614 T. GENTLEMAN *Eng. Way to Wealth* in *Harl. Misc.* (Malh.) III. 239 Fly-boats..ride at anchor all the season at Shetland. **1622** MALYNES *Anc. Law-Merch.* 24 Another fleete of Fisher-men (called Flyboats). **1794** *Rigging & Seamanship* I. 242 *plate*, Herring Buss or Fly Boat.

4. a. A swift passage boat used on canals. **b.** See quot. 1893.

1841 S. C. HALL *Ireland* (1843) III. 275 Voyaging part of the way in one of the 'Fly-boats'. **1841–56** S. C. BREES *Gloss. Civ. Engin.* s.v. *Canal*, Slow boats 2½ miles per hour..Fly boats 4 miles. **1893** *Labour Commission* Gloss. s.v. *Boats, Fly-Boats*..barges of unusual length and of a narrow construction, drawing a very small amount of water.

5. *Comb.*, as ***fly-boat-built*** adj.

1688 CLAYTON *Virginia* i. in *Phil. Trans.* XVII. 782 We Sail'd in the Ship Judith..'twas Fly-boat built, about 200 or 250 Tuns.

'fly-boy. [f. FLY *sb.*¹ and ² + BOY.]

1. *Printing* = FLY *sb.*¹ 6.

1841 [see FLY *sb.*¹ 6 a]. **1871** *Amer. Encycl. Print., Fly-Boy*, a boy who takes off the sheet from the tympan as the pressman turns it up.

2. A boy who sells fly-papers.

1851 MAYHEW *Lond. Labour* (1861) III. 28 I'm the only reg'lar fly-boy.

fly-by ('flaɪbaɪ). [f. verbal phr. *to fly by* (see FLY *v.*¹ 1).] **a.** = FLY-PAST. orig. *U.S.*

1953 *Tandemeer* 11 Dec. 2 On each day of the show there will be spectacular aerial flybys of jet planes. **1970** *Courier-Mail* (Brisbane) 29 Apr. 2/8 As for the fly-by, it was now surmised that having once passed overhead, the same planes had flown out of sight, circled and returned again and again.

b. In space flights: a close approach to a celestial body for the purpose of observation; a spacecraft that makes such an approach.

1960 *Missiles & Rockets* 31 Oct. 15/2 First *Mariner* mission will be a fly-by of Venus in 1962. **1961** *Ibid.* 2 Jan. 14/1 One of the major questions in the fly-by program is money. **1961** *Flight* 26 Oct. 653/2 Additional manœuvres carried out near to the target could reduce the dispersions still further so that it might be possible to accomplish close fly-bys, orbiters, or soft landings. **1962** F. I. ORDWAY et al. *Basic Astronautics* v. 235 Fly-bys would be equipped with magnetometers to detect the general interplanetary field and Jupiter's field. **1967** *Listener* 15 June 792/2 The surface [of Mars] was photographed [in 1965] at close range by the United States fly-by probe Mariner 4. **1969** *New Scientist* 27 Feb. 439/1 The first of a pair of *Mariner* spacecraft should now be on its way to carry out an observation fly-by of Mars.

'fly-by-night. [f. the vbl. phrase.]

1. One who flies by night; one addicted to nocturnal excursions (see also quot. 1796. Also *slang*, one who defrauds his landlord or creditors by decamping in the night.

1796 GROSE *Dict. Vulg. Tongue* (ed. 3) s.v., You old fly-by-night; an ancient term of reproach to an old woman, signifying that she was a witch. **1822** T. L. PEACOCK *Maid Marian* iii. 191 Would you have her married to a wild fly-by-night that accident made an earl and nature a deer-stealer? **1823** 'JON BEE' *Slang, Fly-by-night*, runaways who leave empty houses. **1894** *Daily News* 23 Oct. 4/7 The majority of the race [of moths] are fly-by-nights. **1903** G. S. WASSON *Cap'n Simeon's Store* 72 Blowed ef 't wa'n't downright horrid the works them two ole fly-by-nights was into them days! **1925** A. HUXLEY *Those Barren Leaves* II. v. 151 When the next full moon invites New bugaboos and fly-by-nights. *attrib.* **1810** W. COMBE *Devil upon Two Sticks* (1817) VI. 73 'The Fly by Night Club', whose symbol is an owl. **1914** J. LONDON *Let.* 25 June (1966) 425, I have no patience with fly-by-night philosophers such as Bergson. **1938** 'N. SHUTE' *Ruined City* (ed. 2) i. 5 We've come to you rather than to one of them fly-by-night financial houses because we're prudent business folk. **1958** E. DUNDY *Dud Avocado* I. vi. 96 This is no fly-by-night proposition. **1971** *Guardian* 12 July 7/3 It is not all heart in the mini-cab world. Far too many are fly-by-night hustlers.

2. a. = FLY *sb.*² 3 b. **b.** *Naut.* (See quot.)

1818 *Sporting Mag.* II. 6 A species of carriage, which in Gloucestershire, goes by the name of 'Fly-by-Night'. **1867** SMYTH *Sailor's Word-bk., Fly-by-night*, a sort of square-sail, like a studding-sail, used in sloops when running before the wind.

'fly-catcher. [f. FLY *sb.*¹ + CATCHER.]

1. a. One who catches flies. **b.** A contrivance for catching flies.

a. 1600 CORNWALLYES *Ess.* xix, To be of Domitians sect, a Fly-catcher. **1692** R. L'ESTRANGE *Fables* cclviii. 225 The Swallow was a Fly-Catcher as well as the Spider. **1887** *Pall Mall G.* 5 Nov. 2/2 'The fly-catcher', as he [Darwin] was known to the crew, was a prime favourite.

fig. **1708** MOTTEUX *Rabelais* v. xv. (1737) 61 Ye scurvy Fly-catchers you! [*i.e.* lawyers]. **1889** *Daily News* 5 Feb. 5/3 The quidnuncs and flycatchers.

b. 1848 HARDY in *Proc. Berw. Nat. Club* II. No. 6. 321 This implement is much used in Cornwall, where it is called the 'fly-catcher'. **1855** ANNE MANNING *Old Chelsea Bun-ho.* vi. 91 After Tea..my Mother began to snip a Fly-catcher.

2. A bird that catches flies; in England, usually one of the genus *Muscicapa*, esp. *M. grisola*; in America, usually one of the genus *Tyrannus*, *T. Carolinensis* or *T. pipiri.*

1678 RAY *Ornith.* 158 *Muscicapa*, the flycatcher. **1777** G. FORSTER *Voy. round World* II. 358 Several sorts of pigeons, parroquets, and fly-catchers. **1833** SELBY in *Proc. Berw. Nat. Club* I. No. 1. 20 The spotted flycatcher (*Muscicapa grisola*). **1845** DARWIN *Voy. Nat.* x. (1852) 137 The plaintive note of a white-tufted tyrant-flycatcher. **1869** W. P. TURNBULL *Birds E. Pennsylv.* 21 Least Flycatcher, *Empidonax minimus.* **1882** HARDY in *Proc. Berw. Nat. Club* IX. No. 3. 440 The rare pied flycatcher (*Muscicapa atricapilla*).

3. a. A spider that catches flies. **b.** A plant that catches flies; = FLY-TRAP 2.

1750 G. HUGHES *Barbadoes* 91 The Fly-Catcher..is of the Spider-kind. **1863** KINGSLEY *Water-Bab.* 13 A spring..which soaks up..in the bog, among red fly-catchers. *c* **1865** LD. BROUGHAM in *Circ. Sc.* I. Introd. Disc. 22 The *Muscipula, Fly-trap*, or *Fly-catcher*..has small prickles in the inside of two leaves.

4. In the war of 1914–18, a fast type of aeroplane. *colloq.*

1924 *Glasgow Herald* 28 July 9 The royal yacht had three 'fly-catchers'. **1925** FRASER & GIBBONS *Soldier & Sailor Words, Fly-catchers*, a fast type of aeroplane, officially rated as 'Fleet Fighters'. **1928** *Times* 23 Mar. 19/2 They were engaged in turn by the 'Flycatchers' from the Furious.

flydge, obs. form of FLEDGE *a.*

'fly-dung, *sb.* [f. FLY *sb.*¹ + DUNG *sb.*] The excrement of the fly, usually of the house-fly.

1855 CLARKE *Dict., Fly-dirt*, flydung.

'fly-dung, *v. Dyeing.* [f. FLY *sb.*¹ + DUNG *v.*] *trans.* In the process of dyeing with madder: To subject for the first time to the process of 'dunging': see DUNG *v.* Also *Comb.* as ***fly-dung bath, cistern.*** Hence **'fly-dunging** *vbl. sb.*

The name is said to be due to the fact that the object of the first dunging is to get rid of the 'flies' or irregularities in the dyeing.

1860 HIGGIN in Ure *Dict. Arts* (ed. 5) I. 531 The first [dunging process] is called *fly-dunging*. *Ibid.*, The fly-dung cistern. **1876** PATON in *Encycl. Brit.* IV. 687/2 Immediately after the fly-dunging the goods are washed and submitted to a second dunging. **1883** *Bleaching, Dyeing & Calico-Print.* iii. 73 The fly-dung bath.

flyer, flier ('flaɪə(r)). Forms: 5 flyare, 6 *Sc.* fliear, 9 *dial.* fleer, 5– flier, 6– flyer. [f. FLY *v.*¹ + -ER¹. The forms *flyer, flier* are both in good mod. use; in our recent quots. *flyer* is more common, notwithstanding the analogy of *crier, drier, trier.*]

1. a. A living thing (e.g. a bird or insect) that propels itself with wings; often preceded by some qualifying adj., as *high*, etc.

c **1440** *Promp. Parv.* 167/1 Flyare, *volator.* **1556** J. HEYWOOD *Spider & F.* lx. 35 A creper with spiders, and a flier with flise. **1686** W. DE BRITAINE *Hum. Prud.* vi. 27 Those of the Weakest Wing are commonly the highest Flyers. **1732** LAW *Serious C.* xi. 168 Suppose a man..studying night and day how to fly..where-ever you see an ambitious man, there you see this vain and senseless Flyer. **1775** WHITE in *Phil. Trans.* LXV. 260 In a day or two more they become flyers. **1816** KIRBY & SP. *Entomol.* (1828) II. xxiii. 355 There are three classes of fliers in this order. **1859** DARWIN *Orig. Spec.* i. (1873) 17 Birds breeding on precipices, and good fliers, are unlikely to be exterminated.

fig. **1601** CORNWALLYES *Ess.* x, I am now come from conversing with Princes, great spirits, and high fliers. **1667** PEPYS *Diary* 27 Feb., He is not so high a flyer as Mr. Chichley.

b. Something that flies or is carried by the air. †(*a*) A volatile spirit (*obs.*). (*b*) The petals of hops when they become detached.

1471 RIPLEY *Compl. Alch.* Ep. Edw. IV, xxix. in Ashm. (1652) 116 Till the same of the fixed by the same of the flier be over-gone. **1881** WHITEHEAD *Hops* ii. 14 They [hops] soon 'go off', and the petals of the flower cones become disintegrated, or 'flyers' in the pickers' parlance.

c. An aviator.

[**1679** tr. *R. Hooke's Philos. Coll.* I. 17 A Tail will help both to support, and also to steer or guide the Flyer.] **1934** WEBSTER, *Flier, flyer*, an airman. **1936** F. CLUNE *Roaming round Darling* ix. 79 In the dining-room were two lady fliers, dressed in blue. **1953** C. DAY LEWIS *Italian Visit* ii. 31 Recall how flyers from a raid returning, Lightened of one death, were elected for another.

d. A flying machine.

1880 *15th Rep. Aeronaut. Soc.* 21 June 22 If you will leave the balloon to me I will not trespass on your flyers. **1903** M. WRIGHT in M. W. McFarland *Wright Pap.* (1953) I. 393, I spend the day largely in getting typewriter copies of the description of the Wright flyer. **1908** H. G. WELLS *War in Air* viii. 254 Next only to the Butteridge machine these were certainly the most efficient heavier-than-air fliers that had ever appeared. **1964** *Listener* 14 May 780/1 Ordinary motorists will not mind, because about this time they will all possess small private flyers.

2. a. One who or that which moves with exceptional speed, e.g. a fish, horse, ship, etc.

1795 NELSON in Nicolas *Disp.* (1845) II. 50 Our flyers were able to get near them, but not nearer than half gun-shot. **1842** *Spirit of Times* 4 June 163 We hope the Rocket of our old friend Dr. W. may be such another 'flyer'; he certainly 'goes off' well. **1861** WHYTE MELVILLE *Mkt. Harb.* x. (ed. 12) 76 Grooms with led horses are overtaken by their masters, and we recognize many a well-known flyer. **1867** F. Francis *Angling* ix. (1880) 314 He [a fish] was a regular flier..He took out clear, without stopping for a second, over one hundred yards of line. **1877** *Coursing Calendar 1876* 79 Mr. Brocklebank's Bombard..although not a flyer, he will turn out a useful dog. **1887** TUER & FAGAN *1st Year Silken Reign* vii. 129 The..coach, achieved for itself an enviable reputation as a 'flyer' of the first order. **1888** *St. Louis Globe Democrat* 2 Mar. (Farmer), In spite of the strike, passenger trains excepting what are known as the flyers, are running with reasonable regularity. **1919** F. HURST *Humoresque* 131 You ought to see the flier a friend of mine has got. A Mercury Six [motor-car] with a limousine top like a grand-opera box. **1922** E. WALLACE *Flying Fifty-Five* xi. 67 Fifty-Five is a flyer... He did the five furlongs in fifty-eight and a fifth seconds. **1948** C. L. B. HUBBARD *Dogs in Brit.* 35 Heredity and environment count a great deal in whether a puppy will be a 'flyer' or a 'bad-doer'. **1971** *Daily Tel.* 21 July 11/2 The normal carburettor-fed 2002 is one of the fastest cars in its class: with the new Kugelfischer fuel injection system it is a real flyer.

b. A fast kangaroo. *Austral. colloq.*

1848 H. W. HAYGARTH *Recoll. Bush Life Austral.* xi. 118 At first starting, a young male or female kangaroo, called in the colony 'a flyer', can leave both horse and hound far behind. **1861** T. MCCOMBIE *Austral. Sks.* 172 The settlers designate the old kangaroos as 'old men' and 'old women', the full-grown animals are named 'Flyers'. **1968** K. WEATHERLY *Roo Shooter* 16 Two young fliers had got through the fence surrounding the 'turkey nest' tank.

c. *fig.* A person exceptional in some (specified) way.

1930 T. THURSTON *Man in Black Hat* xvi. 278 We had an extraordinarily pretty girl here in the bar. Real flier, she was. **1936** WODEHOUSE *Laughing Gas* iii. 30, I am no flier in the way of looks. **1939** J. CARY *Mister Johnson* 140 He's not a flier at the accounts.

d. *Cricket.* A ball pitched short that flies up sharply; a 'bouncer'.

1913 *Cricket* 305 Every bowler pitches short sometimes, and when he does so, the resultant rib-roaster..flier..call it what you will, is no more than an ordinary risk. **1954** J. H. FINGLETON *Ashes crown Year* 58 May ducked a flier from Archer and was hit on the back. **1962** *Times* 1 May 4/2 Nobody was the victim of a flyer.

3. Applied to mechanical contrivances that have a quick revolution.

a. An appliance for regulating the motion of a roasting-jack.

1674 FAIRFAX *Bulk & Selv.* 125 A Jack, by being only wown up, without thripping the..flyer. **1706** SWIFT *Baucis & Philemon* 71 The Flyer..Turn'd round so quick, you scarce cou'd see't. **1806–7** J. BERESFORD *Miseries Hum. Life* (1826) XVI. 95 Spinning like the flyer of a jack.

†**b.** One of the vanes used in an early form of ship's log. *Obs.* Cf. FLY *sb.*² 5 h.

1729 H. DE SAUMAREZ in *Phil. Trans.* XXXVI. 47 The four Iron Fins, or Flyers..These Flyers are so contrived as to have full Play in any Motion of the Boat.

†**c.** = FLY-WHEEL. *Obs.*

1781 WATT *Patent* in Muirhead *Mech. Invent. Watt* III. 52 In order that the said motion may be more regular, I fix to or upon the shaft or axis FML..a heavy wheel or flyer.

d. A sail of a windmill; also *pl.* 'the fan-wheel on the vane of a windmill cap which rotates the latter as the wind veers' (Knight).

1790 MRS. WHEELER *Westmld. Dial.* (1821) 97 Paur man wur ath fleers, en raund it went. *a* **1848** MRS. MARCET *Seasons* (ed. 5) IV. ii. 35 That mill with the great fliers, that the wind pushes round.

e. That part of a spinning machine which twists the thread as it conducts it to and winds it upon the bobbin. Cf. FLY *sb.*² 5 f. Also *attrib.*, as ***flyer frame.***

1825 J. NICHOLSON *Oper. Mech.* 383 A roving-frame of a different construction has received more general adoption..; it is called the bobbin and flier roving-frame. **1831** G. R. PORTER *Silk Manuf.* 201 At each extremity of the flyer an eye is formed..The thread from the bobbin is passed through both these eyes. **1879** *Cassell's Techn. Educ.* IV. 356/2 The flyer..winds it upon the bobbin. **1957** *Encycl. Brit.* VI. 562/1 Following on the last head of drawframes the process becomes one principally of attenuation. To this end the material is passed through one, two, three or four passages of machines collectively known as flyer frames.

f. The winder of a balling machine.

1869 J. H. WEBSTER in *Eng. Mech.* 31 Dec. 387/2 The 'flyer'..winds the string on to the mandrel.

4. In various uses, related to senses of the vb.

†**a.** *pl.* ? The fringe or tassels of a curtain. *Obs.*

1577 *Wills & Inv. N.C.* (Surtees 1836) 414, Iij payer of courtings withe the flyers of saye. **1580** *Ibid.* One payer of say hingers with fleers.

b. *pl.* Steps forming a straight flight; opposed to *winders.*

1667 PRIMATT *City & C. Build.* 66 *Flyers and winders*..are plain, and triangular Steps without any Landing place. **1703** T. N. *City & C. Purchaser* 248 Straight Stairs..always fly, and never Wind, and therefore are by some call'd *Flyers.* **1879** *Cassell's Techn. Educ.* I. 329/2 Straight stairs are called *flyers.*

c. *Printing.* (See quot.) Also *pl.*

1874 KNIGHT *Dict. Mech.* I. 895/2 *Flyer*, a vibratory rod with fingers which take the sheet of paper from the tapes and carry it to the delivery table, the sheet resting flatly against the flyer-fingers by the resistance of the air. **1888** *Encycl. Brit.* XXIII. 706.

d. *U.S.* A small handbill or fly-sheet; *spec.* one issued by the police (see also quot. 1952).

1889 *Lit. World* (U.S.) 21 Dec. 485/2 Inserting gaily-colored advertising fliers in the body of the magazine. **1952** BERREY & VAN DEN BARK *Amer. Thes. Slang* (ed. 2) §477.4 *Flyer*,..a warrant for arrest. **1955** D. W. MAURER in *Publ. Amer. Dial. Soc.* XXIV. 149 Is there a *flyer* out for this man? This is a police circular carrying photographs, fingerprints. **1962** K. ORVIS *Damned & Destroyed* xiv. 94 Boards covered

with tacked-up police flyers. **1965** E. McBain *Doll* (1966) iii. 38 Leslie offered him the agency flyer on Tinha, the composite that went to all photographers, advertising agency art directors, and prospective clients. **1966** D. Shannon *With a Vengeance* (1968) i. 13 They had also an unidentified corpse, and all the paperwork on that: the flyers sent out with the description. **1966** *Word Study* Feb. 6/2 This sentence from a recent advertising flier of *Fortune*.

e. A flying buttress.

1912 F. Bond *Cathedrals* 73 A second set of fliers was built above the aisle roof.

5. a. A flying jump or leap; a flight. In quot. *fig.*

1883 R. Grant White *W. Adams* 51 Haven't we taken rather a flyer? What has all this to do with Mrs. Trollope?

b. Hence, *U.S.* 'A speculative investment: applied to a purchase of stock by one not a regular buyer, in hope of immediate profit' (*Cent. Dict.*).

1846 *Spirit of Times* 11 July 229/3 Lend me a quarter.. just for a flyer. **1848** W. Armstrong *Stocks* 37 A. B. Neilson occasionally sells fifty or a hundred shares of stock by way of a flyer. **1870** J. K. Medbery *Men & Myst. Wall St.* 136 A 'flyer', is a small side operation, not employing one's whole capital. It is nearly equivalent to what is ordinarily known as a venture. **1886** *Pall Mall G.* 26 Aug. 11/1 He..turned to the Wall-street news to see how much he had already made on his flyer. **1888** *New Princeton Rev.* V. 328 The temptation to take a flyer in the market. **1966** *Newsweek* 2 May 64/1 More and more 'Aunt Janes' are deciding to take a flyer, growing impatient with their slow-moving quality stocks as they see high-flyers double and triple in value.

6. *slang.* (See quots.)

a **1700** B. E. *Dict. Cant. Crew*, *Flyers*, Shoes. **1851** Mayhew *Lond. Labour* (1861) II. 34 A 'flyer', that is, a shoe soled without having been welted.

7. One who runs away; a fugitive; = fleer. †Also, one who flies or shuns; an avoider of.

c **1460** *Towneley Myst.* (Surtees) 308 Here is a bag fulle, lokys..Of flytars, of flyars, and renderars of reffys. **1535** Stewart *Cron. Scot.* III. 440 As hapnis oft..ane greit braggar to be fund a fliear. *a* **1633** Lennard tr. *Charron's Wisd.* I. xxxvi. §1 (1670) 111 Timon that hater and flyer of the company of men. **1648** *Eikon Bas.* (1662) 127 Now the Fliers from..their Places carry the Parliamentary power along with them. **1751** R. Paltock *P. Wilkins* (1884) II. xxi. 254, I..let the flyers know I should soon give fire. **1871** Freeman *Norm. Conq.* (1876) IV. xviii. 117 The Norman horsemen followed on the fliers, slaying and taking captives.

flyer, obs. f. fleer.

'fly-fish, *v.* [A back-formation from fly-fishing *vbl. sb.*] *intr.* To fish with a fly (natural or artificial) as bait.

1755 Johnson *s.v.*, To Flyfish. v.n., to angle with a hook baited with a fly. **1869** S. Wilberforce *Diary* Sept. in *Life* (1882) III. 303 Fly-fished with Bishop of Rochester. **1881** Miss Braddon *One Thing Needful* xviii, [He] had passed them..wandering with his rod, fly-fishing.

Hence **'fly-fishing** *ppl. a.* So **'fly-fisher**, one who practises fly-fishing. Also **fly-'fisherman.**

1787 Best (*title*), The Complete Fly-Fisher. **1834** Medwin *Angler in Wales* I. 39 Amongst the most expert fly-fishers, no one was perfectly satisfied. **1858** *Sat. Rev.* V. 393/2 A fly-fishing, horse-loving..man.

'fly-fishing, *vbl. sb.* [f. fly *sb.*[1]] Fishing with a fly (whether natural or artificial).

1653 Walton *Angler* iv. 115, I promised to tell you more of the Flie-fishing for a Trout. **1741** *Compl. Fam. Piece* II. ii. 335 In Fly-fishing observe to have always the Wind on your Back. **1818** Scott *Hrt. Midl.* xxxii, There was nought to be done wi' fly-fishing. **1887** Miss Braddon *Like & Unlike* i, You must be fond of fly-fishing.

attrib. **1834** Medwin *Angler in Wales* II. 147 When the fly-fishing season is over.

'fly-flap. Also 7 -flop. [f. fly *sb.*[1] + flap *sb.*]

1. An instrument for driving away flies.

c **1440** *Promp. Parv.* 167/1 Fly flappe..*muscarium*. **1562** J. Heywood *Prov. & Epigr.* (1867) 153 Thy toung is a flie flap. **1632** Randolph *Jealous Lovers* II. iii. Wks. (1875) 94, I said ..that you had a brow Hung o'er your eyes like fly-flaps. **1772–84** Cook *Voy.* (1790) V. 2044 Both sexes make use of the fan, or fly-flap. **1837** Wheelwright tr. *Aristophanes* I. 297 Erect Holding his leather fly-flap.

fig. **1607** Tourneur *Rev. Trag.* v. i. Wks. 1878 II. 129 Ah, the fly-flop of vengeance beate 'em to peeces! *a* **1683** Oldham *Wks.* (1686) 55 How Fly-Flap of Church-Censure Houses rid Of Insects.

†2. A stroke with a fly-flap; (in quot.) *fig.*, an adroit manœuvre, a cunning prank. *Obs.*

a **1735** Arbuthnot *Misc. Wks.* (1751) I. 67 Not to forget the Quibbles and Fly-flaps he played against his Adversaries.

¶The alleged sense = flip-flap 3 a (see quot. 1676 there) is based on a mistake of Strutt (*Sports & Past.* III. v. 175).

'fly-flap, *v.* [f. prec.]

1. *trans.* To strike with a fly-flap; to beat, whip.

1620 Shelton *Quix.* II. lx. 405 I giue you my word to beat my selfe and fly-flappe mee when I haue a disposition to it. **1627** *Lisander & Cal.* VII. 123, I must call my husband to fly-flap you. **1707** J. Stevens tr. *Quevedo's Com. Wks.* (1709) 209, I was Fly-flap'd. **1796** Grose *Dict. Vulg. Tongue* (ed. 3), *Flyflapped*, whipt in the stocks, or at the cart's tail.

2. *intr.* To drive away flies with a fly-flap.

Hence **'fly-flapping** *vbl. sb.* and *ppl. a.*

1797 *Edin. Mag.* May 344 Beelzebub, or the Lord of Flies ..whom I must renounce with all his works, even that of fly flapping. **1881** Miss Braddon *Asph.* III. 204 There seemed to be nobody about save the fly-flapping boys.

'fly-flapper. [f. prec. vb. + -er[1].]

1. One who drives away flies with a fly-flap.

a **1661** Fuller *Worthies* (1840) II. 503 Jupiter the flie-flapper. **1829** Marryat *F. Mildmay* xvi, That fellow is only fit for fly-flapper at a pork shop! **1891** Hall Caine *Scapegoat* xxiv, Beside him walked the fly-flappers.

fig. **1810** James *Mil. Dict.* (ed. 3) Suppl., *Fly-flapper*, a figurative term alluding to any person who being in the confidence of another, keeps off impertinent intruders.

2. = fly-flap 1.

1749 Bp. Lavington *Enthus. Method. & Papists* (1754) I. 90 If a Fly-flapper be held up to blow it off. **1859** Darwin *Orig. Spec.* vi. (1878) 133 The tail of a giraffe, which serves as a fly-flapper.

fig. **1843** Cobden *Speeches* 19 Oct. (1870) I. 103 The men of Manchester, who, by these fly-flappers, have managed to rouse them into a little activity.

flygge, obs. form of fledge *a.*

flyghe, -ȝe, obs. forms of flay.

fly-in ('flaɪɪn). [f. verbal phr. *to fly in* (see fly *v.*[1] 1).] **a.** The action or an act of delivering troops, goods, etc., by air to a specified place. **b.** A service, entertainment, etc., provided for persons who have arrived by air. Also *attrib.*

1943 W. S. Churchill 6 Dec. in *Second World War* (1952) V. 368 Medium bombers should be..posted in Cyrenaica for 'softening' action against enemy airfields and shipping and to cover the fly-in of the British fighter squadrons. **1952** *N.Y. Times* 9 Mar. 2/7 Not eligible for this prize are small planes landing at a combination drive-in and fly-in. **1956** W. Slim *Defeat into Victory* 220 The fly-in of the 26th Division to Indaw. *Ibid.*, Wingate was dissatisfied with the rate of fly-in. **1960** in *Lebende Sprachen* (1963) VIII. 33/2 There are also fly-in banks at airports (a teller meets your helicopter or plane right on the runway) and sail-in banks for people in boats. **1966** *Times* 28 Feb. (Canada Suppl.) p. xii/5 He saw a column of smoke rising from a clearing, and recognized it as a beef barbecue 'fly-in' of Western Club pilots.

flying ('flaɪɪŋ), *vbl. sb.* [f. fly *v.*[1] + -ing[1].]

1. a. The action of the vb. fly, in various senses.

1548 Hall *Chron., Edw. IV*, (an. 9) 209 b, The fame was spred of kynge Edwardes flyenge. *c* **1565** Lindesay (Pitscottie) *Chron. Scot.* (1728) 113 Great slaughter was made..in the flyings of the timber. **1605** Shaks. *Lear* II. iv. 91 The images of reuolt and flying off. *a* **1679** T. Goodwin *Obj. Justifying Faith* II. ii. Wks. 1697 IV. II. 76 A flying to him that is gracious. **1703** Moxon *Mech. Exerc.* 147 The flying off, or else winding of these Steps will vary. **1801** Strutt *Sports & Past.* I. ii. 23 The training and flying of hawks became one of the essentials in the education of a young man of rank.

b. The action of guiding or piloting an aircraft or spacecraft, or of travelling in one.

1834 *Amer. Railroad Jrnl.* III. 791/1 Such is my plan for flying. **1864** *R. Chambers' Bk. Days* II. 722/1 This extraordinary aërial locomotive is perhaps one of the most curious of these apparatuses for the purpose of flying. **1909** *Flight* 27 Feb. 113/1 In the present stage of flight the art of learning how is almost as great as that of the art of flying itself. *Ibid.* 23 Oct. 668/2 As a result of the good flying on Saturday afternoon, a large attendance was attracted to the racecourse on Monday after-noon. **1916** H. Barber *Aeroplane Speaks* 48 When..involuntary descents [were] often a part of 'cross-country flying. **1930** P. White *How to fly Airplane* xxiii. 306 Cross-country flying includes all flights over land..more than a mile or two away from the home field. **1947** D. J. Ingells *They tamed Sky* i. 2 This is push-button flying, automatic flight. **1960** C. H. Gibbs-Smith *Aeroplane* 1 Flying has never appeared to its devotees as a mere method of transportation. **1962** J. Glenn in *Into Orbit* 5 There is nothing spooky or supernatural about flying in space. **1967** *Drive* Spring 106 He loathes flying, endures sea travel, is happy in a car only when at the wheel.

2. *concr.* in *pl.* (see quot. 1893).

1888 R. Beaumont *Woollen & Worsted Cloth Manuf.* 57 Otherwise they cast off a lot of loose fibres as 'flyings'. **1893** *Labour Commission* Gloss., *Flyings*, short fibres thrown out from the wool on to the sides of the carding machine.

3. *attrib.* as ***flying boot***, ***circus*** (see circus 2 d), ***coat***, ***ground***, ***meeting***, ***school***, ***squadron***, ***suit***, ***time***, ***velocity***, ***week***; **flying bedstead**, an experimental aircraft, shaped like a bedstead, for testing methods of vertical take-off; **flying boat**, (*a*) an experimental flying machine built by J. P. Blanchard; (*b*) a boat-shaped car on a merry-go-round; (*c*) a form of seaplane having a boat-like fuselage; **flying bomb**, a pilotless jet-propelled aeroplane with an explosive warhead, first used by the Germans against England in June 1944; **flying boxcar**, a bomber or a large freight-carrying aircraft; **flying corps**, a unit of aircraft for military or naval purposes; the Royal Flying Corps was the precursor of the Royal Air Force; **flying country**, **county** (*Hunting*), one that affords opportunity for long unbroken runs; **flying deck** = *flight deck* (a); **flying doctor**, a doctor who habitually uses an aeroplane for visiting patients in areas remote from his headquarters; also *attrib.*, as ***flying doctor service***, etc.; **flying fence**, one that must be taken at a flying leap; **flying field** = airfield; **flying hour** (see quot. 1956); **flying machine**, a machine or contrivance capable of being flown in the air; usu. restricted to a heavier-than-air machine dependent on its motors for maintenance and progression in the air (see also flying *ppl. a.* 4 b); **flying officer**, a rank in the Royal Air Force; **flying saucer**, the fanciful name given to various unidentified disc- or saucer-shaped objects reported as appearing in the sky; **flying speed**, the speed of an aircraft at take-off or in normal level flight; **flying test bed, bench**, an aircraft fitted with apparatus for measuring its performance in the air; **flying time**, (*a*) the time when a hawk is in condition to be flown; (*b*) the time during which an aircraft, etc., is in flight (see also quot. 1956); **flying wing** (see quots.). (Some of these collocations could with equal or greater justification be listed under the *ppl. a.*: for convenience they are all grouped here, since all of them fall within or appertain to the subject of aviation. Cf. sense 1 b above.)

1955 *Sci. News Let.* 4 June 357/2 Rolls-Royce, in Britain, has designed a model dubbed the '*flying bed-stead'. It is thrust into the air vertically by two jet nozzles pointed downward in the front and rear. **1957** *Times* 29 Nov. 10/6 The 'flying bedstead' is..a tubular structure on which two 5,000 lb. thrust Rolls-Royce Nene turbo-jet engines are mounted. **1784** *Universal Mag.* LXXV. 221/1 Mr. Blanchard..during the late war, formed a *flying boat, which he intended for carrying the dispatches from Brest to Paris, but as this did not answer his expectations, he was obliged to relinquish the idea of elevating himself above the clouds. **1854** A. C. Mowatt *Autobiogr. Actress* 108 In a single night, the booths, the fairy houses, the circus, flying boats, cars, horses disappear. **1903** O. Chanute *Let.* 13 Mar. in M. W. McFarland *Wright Pap.* (1953) I. 301 Today I spent with Wm. Kress who experimented with a flying boat last year. **1913** *Aeroplane* 24 Apr. 470/1 The death of Louis Gaudart showed what a deathtrap the ordinary type of flying-boat is. **1917** C. C. Turner *Aircraft of To-day* xix. 277 The twin-engined Curtiss flying-boat 'America'. **1928** *Manch. Guardian Weekly* 31 Aug. 178/3 A flying-boat service between Sydney and Wellington. **1934** 'R. Crompton' *William—the Gangster* iii. 49 Riding upon merry-go-rounds, flying in flying-boats, sliding down helter-skelters. **1958** *Times* 18 July 6/5 Britain's only remaining air line using flying-boats, Aquila Air-ways, are to cease operations on October 1. **1971** *Daily Tel.* (Colour Suppl.) 16 July 5/3 One of the Sunderland flying boats between Cairo and India: a yacht of the sky, landing on the sea or inland lakes as it hopped from point to point. **1944** *Times* 3 July 4/5 Strong measures to counter the *flying bombs have been continued throughout the week-end. *Ibid.* 5 July 4/5 The Prime Minister intended to make a statement on Thursday on the flying-bomb attack. **1946** Flying bomb [see buzz *sb.*[1] 5]. **1935** *Times* 9 Oct. 9/4 They are also showing *flying boots for women lined in sheepskin and covered in willow calf and crêpe rubber. **1944** G. Netherwood *Desert Squadron* vi. 49 An airman wearing a badge in the form of a silver flying boot..the insignia of the famous 'Late Arrivals' Club, a club formed from airmen who..after having been posted as missing, returned safely to their units. **1932** *Beaver* Mar. 393 The new Junkers freight plane 'JU-52', '*flying box-car'. **1941** *Amer. Speech* XVI. 165/2 *Flying boxcar*, a bomber. **1958** *Oxf. Mail* 19 July 1/2 A fleet of 'flying boxcars' bringing jeeps, bazookas and.. rifles. **1931** *Chambers's Jrnl.* Sept. 545/1 Outside the squadron office was gathered a small group of pilots, in their sheepskin thigh-boots and heavy leather *flying-coats. **1913** *Flying Corps [see *flying officer*]. **1914** *Scotsman* 15 Sept. 5/7 The success attained by the Royal Flying Corps. **1926** T. E. Lawrence *Seven Pillars* (1935) II. xxi. 134 It was decided to lay out on the beach by the aerodrome a small position, capable of being held..by the..Flying Corps. **1883** *Standard* 19 May 3/3 Viscount looked fitted for a *flying country. **1856** Whyte Melville *Kate Cov.* xii, Leicestershire, Northamptonshire, and other so-called '*flying counties'. **1931** *Jrnl. R. Aeronaut. Soc.* XXV. 373 The 'Vindex'..was the first ship to be fitted with a forward hangar and *flying deck. **1954** P. K. Kemp *Fleet Air Arm* 86 The first carrier..was fitted with a flying deck forward. **1926** *Lancet* 17 Apr. 824/1 (*heading*) *Flying Doctors. **1932** *Ibid.* 24 Dec. 1396/2 In May 1928 Dr. K. St. Vincent Welch, the first 'flying doctor', set up practice at Cloncurry in Queensland. **1944** F. Clune *Red Heart* 7 There are six Flying Doctor Bases in Arid Australia. **1966** *Daily Tel.* 27 Sept. 13/3 Dr. Anne Spoerry, of the East African Flying Doctor Service. **1971** *Ibid.* 19 Jan. 10/5 The Falkland Islands Government maintains a 'flying doctor' service. **1883** E. Pennell-Elmhirst *Cream Leicestersh.* 110 Honest *flying fences, big enough to extend a good hunter. **1927** J. M. Saunders *Wings* (1928) ii. 91 The giant searchlights from the tower played over the dark corners of the *flying field. **1958** P. Kemp *No Colours or Crest* ix. 183 A disused flying field pitted with craters. **1909** *Westm. Gaz.* 23 Oct. 2/1 Those who, in spite of the half-gale which was blowing, went to the *flying-ground. **1918** F. H. Colvin *Aircraft Mech. Handbk.* xxii. 305 To keep all the available machines of one squadron in commission for 800 *flying hours. **1956** W. A. Heflin *U.S.A.F. Dict.* 214/1 *Flying hour*, an hour spent in flight (which includes takeoff and landing) by a person, aircraft, or piece of equipment. **1736** *Gentl. Mag.* Oct. 617/1 One James Todd..at the Theatre in Covent-Garden, fell from the upper Stage, in a *flying Machine, the Wires breaking. **1769** *Oxf. Mag.* Sept. 108 (*caption*) A New Flying Machine upon Dr. Musgrave's Plan, that moves with y[e] same Rapidity as Mr. Moore's Machine without Horses. **1797** *Encycl. Brit.* I. 198/2 In the year 1709..as we were informed by a letter published in France in 1784, a Portuguese projector, Friar Gusman, applied to the king for encouragement to his invention of a flying machine. **1808** G. Cayley *Aeronaut. & Misc. Note-Bk.* (1933) 3 Apr. 63 It obliges the centre of gravity of flying machines to be much forwarder of the centre of bulk than could be supposed a priori. **1834** *Amer. Railroad Jrnl.* III. 790/1 (*caption*) Travelling Balloon, or Flying Machine. **1865** *Reader* 1 Apr. 375/3 Until the time shall arrive when an aerostat or flying machine can be introduced with something like success. **1881** L. Wagner *Pantomimes* 57 The manipulation of flying machines, or other contrivances whereby [etc.]. **1895** *Nature* 1 Aug. 321/2 A large party of scientific men..to witness a trial of the celebrated flying machine. **1908** H. G. Wells *War in Air* VIII. §2 It was not in their airships, but..

in their flying-machines proper, that the strength of the Asiatics lay. **1909** *Westm. Gaz.* 11 Jan. 9/1 The regulation of flying-machine races. **1959** *Times* 2 Apr. 4/6 The challenge of the missile does not mean that the flying machine is outdated. On the contrary, there will always be great need for the work of the manned aircraft, which it alone can perform. **1970** *Daily Tel.* 30 Oct. 11/2, I was at school when I saw my first real flying machine. **1909** *Flight* 20 Nov. 749/1 A *flying meeting to be held on the Napoule aerodrome. **1913** *Aeroplane* 17 Apr. 446 Royal Flying Corps, Military Wing.—To be *flying officers and to be seconded. **1922** *Man. Seamanship* (H.M.S.O.) I. i. 11 Distinctive Lace worn by members of the Royal Air Force. .. Flying Officer, Observation Officer. **1947** *Times* 8 July 4/4 During the past fortnight reports that dish-like objects, nicknamed '*flying saucers', have been seen travelling through the air at great speed.. have come from the United States and Canada. **1948** *Jrnl. Brit. Interplanetary Soc.* VII. 199, I haven't examined the details carefully, but the 'flying saucers' bear all the hall-marks of mass-suggestion. **1953** LESLIE & ADAMSKI *Flying Saucers have Landed* i. 13 Ever since the cliché 'flying saucer' was coined, the greatest and most exciting mystery of our age has been automatically reduced to the level of a music hall joke. **1965** *New Society* 9 Sept. 14/2 When Kenneth Arnold saw something from his airplane near Mount Rainier in June 1947, he gave them the happy name of flying saucers. **1894** *Proc. Internat. Conf. Aerial Navig. 1893* 307 Just as the rider and swimmer go to a school for their instruction, so we must go to a *flying school for ours. **1920** *Act 10 & 11 Geo. V* c. 80 §7 (I), Any aerodrome, flying school, or landing ground. **1917** 'CONTACT' *Airman's Outings* 39 The throttle was again opened full out as the bus raced into the wind until *flying speed had been attained, when it skimmed gently from the ground. **1785** H. WALPOLE *Let.* 24 June (1905) XIII. 278 France has conceived hopes of annihilating our Pyrenees by these *flying squadrons [*sc.* balloons]. **1917** 'CONTACT' *Airman's Outings* p. xii, A record for the casualties of any one flying squadron during any three months since the war began. **1935** D. PILLEY *Climbing Days* iii. 52 My brother John, looking magnificent in a Teddy Bear Jaeger *flying-suit. **1936** *Discovery* Sept. 285/1 Upper atmosphere flights employing.. special flying suits have actually been made. **1947** *Shell Aviation News* CXII. 11/1 This year the development of turbine installations in *flying test beds has been taken a step further. **1949** *Jrnl. R. Aeronaut. Soc.* LIII. 135/1 Neither the turbo-propeller nor the turbo-reaction engine had actually flown so far. A flying test bench was being prepared, which would take either engine. This test bench was a four-engined machine which had been fitted with a nacelle above the fuselage. **1966** *Times* 10 Sept. 1/5 A Vulcan V-bomber, modified to act as a 'flying test bed' for the Anglo-French Concord's.. engine, made a maiden flight yesterday. **1615** LATHAM *Falconry* (1633) 40 You cease and leaue off from all those.. obseruations of the *flying time. **1946** *Mod. Lang. Notes* Nov. 442 Travel time, flying time, running time. **1956** W. A. HEFLIN *U.S.A.F. Dict.* 214/2 *Flying time*, the elapsed time spent in flight or in associated actions by aircraft.. or by persons. **1918** E. S. FARROW *Dict. Mil. Terms*, **Flying velocity*, the speed requisite to raise an aëroplane from the ground. **1909** *Flight* 20 Nov. 749/2 The *flying week to be held there by the Aero Club of France. **1937** *Jrnl. R. Aeronaut. Soc.* XLI. 162 The final logical result.. is.. the *flying wing with the engines, passengers or military load housed inside... There are still certain difficulties which will prevent us from achieving.. a mere flying wing. **1948** *Science News* VII (*caption* to pl. 44) The Flying Wing... An aircraft without fuselage or tailplane.

flying ('flaɪɪŋ), *ppl. a.* [f. FLY *v.*[1] + -ING[2].] That flies, in senses of the vb. (See note at FLYING *vbl. sb.* 3.)

1. a. That moves through the air with wings. Sometimes with modifying word prefixed, as HIGH-FLYING.

c **1000** ÆLFRIC *Gram.* ix. (Z.) 44 *Uolucer*, fleoȝende. **1398** TREVISA *Barth. De P.R.* v. liv. (1495) 171 The popyniay and the pellycan amonge fleeng fowles fede theimself with the fote. *a* **1577** GASCOIGNE *Dan Barth.* xviii, The highest flying hauke will stoupe at laste. **1611** BIBLE *Isa.* xiv. 29 His fruite shall be a fierie flying serpent. **1667** MILTON *P.L.* II. 643 So seem'd Farr off the flying Fiend. **1732** POPE *Ep. Cobham* 96 In Man, the judgment shoots at flying game, A bird of passage! **1886** A. WINCHELL *Walks Geol. Field* 10 A menagerie of curious beasts, and crawling and creeping and flying things.

b. In names of insects, as ***flying-buck-beetle***, ***-glow-worm***. Also of fish, reptiles, quadrupeds, etc., which by means of special appendages are able to make movements resembling flight; as ***flying-frog***, ***-gecko***, ***-gurnard***, ***-herring***, ***-lemur***, ***-lizard***, ***-marmot***, ***-phalanger***, ***-squid***. Also **flying coachman**, the regent honey-eater, *Zanthomiza phrygia*; **flying-dog**, a kind of vampire-bat; **flying hart, stag** = Fr. *cerf-volant*, a stag-beetle; **flying mouse**, the smallest gliding marsupial, *Acrobates pygmæus*, of the family Phalangeridæ. Also FLYING-FISH, -FOX, -SQUIRREL.

1626 BACON *Sylva* §712 Lucciole.. may be the Flying-Glo-worm. **1676** *Phil. Trans.* XI. 652 A kind of large flying Beetle.. with a huge pair of horns.. Our people in Virginia .. calling it a Flying Hart. **1688** CLAYTON *ibid.* XVIII. 126 Another little green Frog, that will leap prodigiously, which they therefore call the Flying Frog. **1711** *Ibid.* XXVII. 350 Another strange one, which they call Ololo, and comes next to our *Cervus* [read *Cervus*] *volans*, or Flying Buckbeetle. **1765** H. TIMBERLAKE *Mem.* 46 Of insects, the flying stag is almost the only one worthy of notice. **1796** STEDMAN *Surinam* II. xxii. 142 The vampire.. of Guiana.. is also called the flying-dog of New Spain. **1840** F. D. BENNETT *Whaling Voy.* I. 269 The flying-squid rose from the sea in large flocks. **1854** OWEN in *Circ. Sc.* (1865) II. 62/2 The flying lizard (*Draco volans*). **1879** *Encycl. Brit.* IX. 352 The other (*Exocœtus*) has been called Flying Herring. **1883** FLOWER *ibid.* XV. 401 *Galeopithecus volans*.. The Flying Lemur of Linnæus. **1884** *Longm. Mag.* Mar. 523 Flying gurnards. **1918** J. A. LEACH *Austral. Bird Bk.* (ed. 4) 170 Regent Honey-eater (Warty-faced), [or] Turkey-Bird (Mock Regent), [or] Flying Coachman.. one of the most beautiful of birds. **1934** *Bulletin* (Sydney) 16 May 20/4 The .. flying-mouse is common in the wide belt of scrub which stretches across S.A. and Western Vic.

c. *fig.* †***flying pension*** (see quot.).

c **1770** H. WALPOLE *Mem. Geo. III* (1845) I. xxiv. 337 In the meantime Sandwich obtained what was called a flying pension, that is, it was to commence if he lost his place.

d. ***flying horse, mare***, a certain throw in wrestling.

1713 SIR T. PARKYNS *Inn-Play* (1714) 41 Flying Horse. [Described at length.] **1754** FOOTE *Knights* I. Wks. 1799 I. 67 We don't wrestle after your fashion.. we all go upon close hugs or the flying mare. **1823** in 'JON BEE' *Slang*.

2. a. That passes (*usually*, that passes quickly) through the air.

1535 COVERDALE *Job* xiii. 25 Wilt thou be so cruell and extreme unto a flyenge leaf. **1563** W. FULKE *Meteors* (1640) 7 b, A flying, shuting, or falling star. **1632** LITHGOW *Trav.* II. 61 A backe-sounding eccho of fiery flying shots. **1656** COWLEY in *Roxb. Ball.* VII. 449 Martha took the flying Ball. **1789** *Trans. Soc. Encourag. Arts* VII. 54 A very flat, loose, flying, sandy coast. **1811** W. J. HOOKER *Iceland* (1813) II. 187 The flying sands from the eastern country.

†**b.** *Old Chem.* = VOLATILE. *Obs.*

1471 RIPLEY *Compl. Alch.* VI. in Ashm. (1652) 161 Spyrits whych fleyng are.

3. a. Floating loosely, fluttering, waving. Hence in wider sense, Attached so as to have freedom of movement, hanging loose. ***flying jib***, 'a light sail set before the jib, on the *flying jib-boom*'; also ***flying-boom***, ***-iron***; ***flying deck***, 'a deck supported at the side by railings, stanchions, or the like' (Webster 1934); ***flying-kites***, see KITE *sb.* 5; ***flying ring***, each of a number of rings suspended in pairs or rows by swinging ropes used in acrobatics and gymnastics; ***flying trapeze***, = TRAPEZE 1.

1607 MARKHAM *Caval.* II. 54 This flying Trench is to be made in all proportion like a plain full english Snaffle. **1697** DRYDEN *Virg. Georg.* I. 347 To spread the flying Canvass for the Fleet. **1794** *Rigging & Seamanship* I. 239 They carry.. a flying topsail. **1832** MARRYAT *N. Forster* xli, Their flying jib-booms were.. pointed over the taffrails of their predecessors. **1849** CURZON *Visits Monast.* 4 A red cap, a jacket with flying sleeves. **1859** GULLICK & TIMBS *Paint.* 201 To give lightness to 'flying drapery'. **1864** P. PATERSON *Glimpses Real Life* xiii. 130 If the bounding youth be swinging to and fro on the flying trapeze. **1883** *Man. Seamanship for Boys* 24 The given diameter of a flying-boom is at the boom-iron. *Ibid.* 23 The extreme end [of the jib-boom] is eight-square and an iron hoop driven on to receive the flying iron. **1896** *Daily News* 17 Dec. 6/1 The boats are relegated to a flying deck overhead. **1901** *Ibid.* 20 Feb. 6/7 Flying-ring performers, a troupe consisting of two men and a girl. **1919** C. MACKENZIE *Sylvia & Michael* iii. 77 A fellow with a moustache like a flying trapeze. **1934** W. SAROYAN (*title*) The Daring Young Man on the Flying Trapeze & Other Stories. **1953** *Britannica Bk. Year* 639/2 *Flying boom*, a system used to refuel aircraft in flight. **1965** E. BRUTON *Wicked Saint* iii. 35 Heidi's mother continued in a ground job with the circus.. but for ever hankered after the flying trapeze.

b. In *fig.* phrase, (*to come off, out of it*) ***with flying colours***: with outward signs of success and victory. Cf. COLOUR *sb.* 7 d, and COME *v.* 61 f.

1706–7 FARQUHAR *Beaux' Strat.* I. i, We came off with flying colours. **1887** JESSOP *Arcady* ii. 63 The tenant farmers .. do they come out of it with any flying colours?

†**c.** ***under*** or ***with a flying seal*** (= F. *sous cachet volant*): said of a letter with a seal attached but not closed, so that it may be read by a person who is requested to forward it to its destination.

1638 W. PERKINS in *Lismore Papers* Ser. II. (1888) IV. 15 He.. prayeth yt your lordship would be pleased to send yt your order vp to him, with a flyinge seale. **1811** WELLINGTON in Gurw. *Desp.* VII. 540, I enclose the letter which I have written to the Prince Regent under a flying seal.

4. a. That passes or travels swiftly, that passes by rapidly or rushes along; rapid. ***flying leap***: a running jump. ***flying handicap, mile***: one in which the starting-post is passed at full speed. ***flying jump***, = flying leap. ***flying start***: in a race, (*a*) a start in which the competitors pass the starting-point at full speed; (*b*) a start by one competitor prior to the starting signal being given; (*c*) *transf.* and *fig.*

1658 tr. *Bergerac's Satyr. Char.* ix. 30 He got to the flying River side. **1697** DRYDEN *Virg. Georg.* III. 316 O'er th' Elean Plains, thy well-breath'd Horse Impels the flying Carr. **1701** ROWE *Amb. Step-Moth.* IV. i. 1794 Each minute of the flying Hours is precious. **1704** POPE *Windsor For.* 158 Earth rolls back beneath the flying steed. **1807** CRABBE *Par. Reg.* III. (1810) 31 Of men And manners treating with a flying pen. **1851** *Fraser's Mag.* XLIII. 658/2 A flying start being the rule. **1871** L. STEPHEN *Playgr. Eur.* viii. (1894) 187 A large crevasse.. forcing us to take a flying leap. *a* **1893** *Westm. Gaz.* 13 Oct. 5/3 Windle has done the 'flying' mile in 1 min. 56 4–5 secs. **1893** KIPLING *Many Invent.* 35 You know how you take a flying jump on to a fellow's head at school, when he snores in the dormitory. **1894** *Daily News* 21 May 7/1 The Flying Handicap I shall leave to Moonflower. **1899** *Harmsworth Mag.* July 531/2 The cycle is next best with a flying start record of 1 m. 35⅗ sec. **1921** E. H. D. SEWELL *Rugby Football* 61 The easiest way to make an opening is to steal a march on your opposing outside half by getting a flying start. **1924** G. LAMBTON *Men & Horses* 233 In the Knowsley Nursery, at Liverpool,.. thanks to a flying start, she was only just caught close home. **1928** *Daily Mail* 7 Aug. 15/5 [He] set up a new record for the mile (flying start) with a speed of 40 miles per hour. **1933** L. A. G. STRONG *Sea Wall* 245 How are the likes of you and me to get a good flying start with nothing to kick off from? **1958** *Spectator* 31 Jan. 137/2 It got him off to a flying start; in it were the seeds of his future Christian life. **1962** *Listener* 7 June 983/1 He climbed slowly in Elizabeth's reign, despite his flying start as the son of a Lord Keeper.

b. *esp.* in ***flying post***, a post travelling by relays of horses, an express. Also (17–18th c.) in ***flying coach*** (also ***machine, carriage***, etc.), the ordinary designation for a swift stage coach; ***flying packet***, a packet sent by 'flying post' (all *obs.*). ***Flying Scotchman*** (***Scotsman***): see SCOTCHMAN b.

1548 HALL *Chron., Hen. VI*, (an. 38) 177 Richarde Duke of Yorke.. by.. flieng postes, was advertised of the great victorie. **1669** WOOD *Life* (Oxf. Hist. Soc.) II. 153, 1669 Apr. 5—M(onday) flying coaches set up. **1685** *Lond. Gaz.* No. 2009/1 Last Night.. a Flying Pacquet.. brought us the .. News of the Death of our Late Gracious Soveraign. **1705** HEARNE *Collect.* 29 Sept., On the 19th came by a Flying Post a Pacquet from Court. **1741** RICHARDSON *Pamela* (1824) I. 222 She had set out in the flying-coach. **1764** *Ipswich Jrnl.* 18 Feb. 4/3 A new Flying Machine, to accommodate Passengers by.. the nearest Way for London, will set out.. on Mondays, Wednesdays, and Fridays. **1769** *Public Advertiser* 25 Sept. 4/2 One of the flying Machines from this City to London. **1849** MACAULAY *Hist. Eng.* I. 378 At the close of the reign of Charles II, flying carriages ran thrice a week from London to all the chief towns.

c. Passing, flitting; hasty, transient; *esp.* of a trip or visit. Also, Rapidly constructed, temporary.

1763 *Phil. Trans.* LIII. 259 This indeed was a flying observation, or taken, as the French would say, *en passant*. **1797** R. M. ROCHE *Childr. of Abbey* II. iv. 52 Amanda supposed, as usual, she only came to pay a flying visit. **1806** T. JEFFERSON *Writ.* (1830) IV. 52 Mr. Beckley then supposed he should take a flying trip to London. **1825** H. WILSON *Mem.* II. 175 He paid me a flying visit. **1844** J. W. CROKER in *C. Papers* 7 July, I shall probably pay a flying visit to town.. before the session is over. **1857** C'TESS CANNING in Hare *Two Noble Lives* (1893) II. 332 The superintendent of telegraphs.. goes to lay down a flying line to Lucknow if possible. **1878** BOSW. SMITH *Carthage* 286 A Carthaginian army.. made flying expeditions to other parts. **1879** B. TAYLOR *Stud. Germ. Lit.* 168 It is impossible.. now, to give even a flying explanation.

d. *Mil.* and *Naval.* (Sometimes with mixture of sense 5; all the expressions are from Fr.) Said of a body of troops, or a squadron of ships, designed and organized for rapid movement, as in ***flying*** †***army***, ***brigade***, ***column***, †***fleet***, ***hospital***, ***party***, ***squadron***. ***flying artillery***: a corps trained to rapid evolutions. ***flying camp***: see CAMP 2 b. ***flying sap*** (see quot. 1876). Also FLYING-BRIDGE.

1665 MANLEY *Grotius' Low C. Warres* 391 With a flying Brigade marching out of Antwerp. **1667** PEPYS *Diary* 28 Feb., We do intend to keep but a flying fleete this year. **1667** *Lond. Gaz.* No. 181/3 The Flying Army that has been so long designed, will be speedily formed. **1702** ROWE *Tamerl.* I. i. 116 He.. like a Storm swept with his flying Squadrons all the Plain. **1710** *Lond. Gaz.* No. 4690/2 A flying Party will encamp in the Neighbourhood. **1809** WELLINGTON in Gurw. *Desp.* V. 90 The stores belonging to the Flying Artillery. **1869** E. A. PARKES *Pract. Hygiene* (ed. 3) 624 The flying columns which go out from Aldershot. *Ibid.* 636 For moving columns.. flying hospitals are organized. **1876** VOYLE *Mil. Dict.*, *Flying sap*, a sap formed by placing and filling several gabions at the same time.. Also applied to the usual formation of the second parallel in the attack.

transf. **1872** *Daily News* 22 Aug., A 'flying brigade'.. has been formed to examine tickets at unexpected stations.

e. (*a*) ***flying squadron***: transf. and fig. applied to any body of persons organized for rapid movement or action.

1670 G. H. *Hist. Cardinals* II. II. 161 He manag'd himself so with his flying Squadron, that it gave no little disgust to the Crowns. **1875** *Temple Bar* June 197 A constant system of espionage carried on by the beautiful demoiselles of her Court, whom Brantôme has immortalised under the term of the Queen-Mother's 'flying squadron'. **1901** *Girls' Realm* 930/2 Flying Squadron Race.

(*b*) ***flying squad***: a detachment of a police force organized for rapid movement. Also = *flying squadron* transf. and fig.

1927 *Daily Tel.* 10 May 6 Fatally injured by being knocked down by a motor-van of the Flying Squad. **1929** J. B. PRIESTLEY *Good Companions* II. iv. 347 What with photographs and finger-prints and telegraphs and wireless and flying squads!.. Not a dog's chance! **1938** *Lancet* 109/2 A 'Flying Squad' in London... Islington is shortly to have the first maternity emergency unit to be established in London. **1939** T. S. ELIOT *Old Possum's Pract. Cats* 33 He's the bafflement of Scotland Yard, the Flying Squad's despair. **1961** *Daily Tel.* 1 Mar. 24/1 To speed justice, more frequent assizes, continuous quarter sessions and a 'flying squad' of judges to hear cases during the Long Vacation are recommended to-day. **1966** *Guardian* 13 Dec. 5/4 In 1920.. he [*sc.* W. Hambrook] was put in charge of a team of three inspectors, four sergeants, and four detective constables, together with two drivers... Within a few days the team had been named the Flying Squad.

f. ***flying flock***, ***flying*** (***ewe***) ***stock*** (see quot. 1886); opp. *running stock* (RUNNING *ppl. a.* 17 d). Also ***flying stock*** (in Austral. and N.Z.) (see quots. 1891). So ***flying herd*** (of cows).

1837 W. YOUATT *Sheep* xv. 519 In a breeding stock this [examination of ewes and lambs] is absolutely necessary, but in a flying stock, or that in which the ewes and the lambs are usually sold before the termination of the year, this may be dispensed with. **1844** H. STEPHENS *Bk. Farm* III. 1105 The ewes are sold in autumn to be fed on turnips, and the lambs

are disposed of, after being weaned, to rearers of sheep who breed none. Such a one is called a flying-flock... Flying-stock require no drafting. **1886** C. SCOTT *Sheep-farming* 29 A flying ewe stock is one where the ewes are bought in annually, and sold out again after bringing a lamb. **1891** R. WALLACE *Rural Econ. Austral. & N.Z.* xviii. 255 Walhallow Estate [Australia]..is largely used for fattening purposes, and a 'flying' stock is maintained in addition to the regular and permanent station flock. *Ibid.* 259 [On Edendale Estate, Southland, N.Z.] The sheep kept are largely a 'flying' or bought-in stock for fattening and marketing. **1950** J. G. DAVIS *Dict. Dairying* 437 Other herds are replenished by purchasing newly calved cows. These are called 'flying herds'.

g. *Football.* (*a*) ***flying man***, in the Eton field game (see quot. 1898); (*b*) ***flying half***, ***man***, earlier terms for ***fly-half*** (see FLY *sb.*^{2} 8).

1864 B. HEMYNG *Eton School Days* xxiii. 255 He was a little too heavy for 'flying man'. **1898** *Encycl. Sport* II. 143/1 In eleven a-side games the bully is formed of four players... Immediately behind is 'flying man', usually the most skilful forward on the side. **1906** GALLAHER & STEAD *Compl. Rugby Footballer* iv. 64 Two half backs, one being delegated to attention to the scrum, and the other being by way of a flying half. *a* **1914** J. E. RAPHAEL *Mod. Rugby Football* (1918) 127 With the flying man standing as far back as the scrum half can throw the ball full pitch, it is extremely difficult to bottle him.

h. ***flying shear***, a device for shearing a long, continuous length of metal into short pieces without arresting its forward motion; so ***flying-sheared*** adj.

1902 *Trans. Amer. Soc. Mech. Engin.* XXIII. 468 The success or failure of the whole equipment was entirely dependent on something so little demonstrated..as the Flying Shear. **1958** *Jrnl. Iron & Steel Inst.* CLXXXVIII. 30/2 The flying shear limits the finishing speed and reduces output. *Ibid.*, Flying-sheared sheets must be cooled quickly.

i. ***flying spot***: a small spot of light that is made to move rapidly over an object, the reflected or transmitted light from successive parts of it being converted by a photo-electric tube or cell into an electrical signal that can be made to reproduce an image of the object. Usu. *attrib.*, as ***flying-spot scanner***, ***scanning***.

1933 *Television* Oct. 342/1 The transmitter utilises the principle of indirect or 'flying spot' scanning by means of an aperture disc. **1960** *How TV Works* vi. 34/2 For many purposes..reproduction of higher quality is achieved by means of a 'flying spot' machine in which each frame of an ordinary positive film is rapidly scanned by a flying spot of light. **1965** *Math. in Biol. & Med.* (*Med. Res. Council*) iv. 192 The focus and intensity controls and high-voltage supplies are associated with the 1·5-mil-spot cathode ray tube that produces the short-persistence flying spot, with a sweep diameter of 10 cm. **1968** *Brit. Med. Bull.* XXIV. 191/2 They are scanned line by line (television-wise) by a 'flying-spot scanner'.

j. ***flying picket*** [PICKET *sb.*^{1} 5], a group of striking workers who picket premises or organizations other than those at which they are employed, esp. one which travels from another area to a striking site or sites in order to reinforce local pickets; a member of such a picket; cf. SECONDARY *a.* 3 q.

1974 *Socialist Worker* 9 Nov. 12/1, I first met the IS comrades in Swansea during the recent nurses' dispute. The nurses' *flying picket to the pits arose from the ideas and the hard work of the IS comrades. **1984** *Times* 16 Mar. 1/3, 138 pits are on strike or are 'picketed out' by flying pickets from..militant coalfields.

5. That flies about.

a. Of a tale, rumour, etc.: Circulating without definite authority. ***flying sheet***: a leaflet printed for distribution broadcast.

1425 *Paston Lett.* No. 5 I. 20, I..never hadde tydinges of this matier, but by seyd lettres and other fleyng tales. **1582** N. LICHEFIELD tr. *Castanheda's Conq. E. Ind.* lxxiii. 150 This was but a fleeing newes. **1630** LD. DUNGARVAN in *Lismore Papers* Ser. II. (1888) III. 157 There was a flying report heere that [etc.]. **1682** BUNYAN *Holy War* 40, I hope they are but flying stories. **1769** BURKE *Late St. Nat.* Wks. II. 10 The light squadrons of occasional pamphlets and flying sheets. **1855** MACAULAY *Hist. Eng.* IV. 374 There had been flying rumours that a Lord Keeper..would soon be appointed. **1888** BRYCE *Amer. Commw.* II. liii. 322 One must trust to a variety of flying and floating sources.

†**b.** Of a person's mind: Volatile, unsettled.

1509 BARCLAY *Shyp of Folys* (1874) I. 177 Wytles men of fleynge mynde.

†**c.** Of a hound: Apt to 'fly about'; not steady.

1684 R. H. *School Recreat.* 13 Bring them abroad with the ..best Hunting Hounds: (all babling and flying Curs being left at home).

d. Of pains: Passing irregularly from one part of the body to another; migratory.

1805 W. SAUNDERS *Min. Waters* 199 The internal use of Bath water in flying pains and weaknesses of the limbs.

e. Itinerant. ***flying stationer*** (slang): see quot.

1796 GROSE *Dict. Vulg. Tongue* (ed. 3), *Flying Stationers*, ballad-singers and hawkers of penny histories.

f. ***flying reed*** (Mining): see quot.

1798 J. KEIR *Min. Staffordsh.* in S. Shaw *Hist. Staff.* Gen. Hist. 119 These two beds [of coal]..when thus separated acquire the name of the Flying Reed. **1839** MURCHISON *Silur. Syst.* I. xxxv. 470.

6. = FLEEING *ppl. a.*

1594 ? GREENE *Selimus* Wks. 1881–3 XIV. 287 Ding downe the flying Persians with their swords. **1697** DRYDEN *Virg. Georg.* I. 416 To persecute from far the flying Doe. **1781** GIBBON *Decl. & F.* III. 116 The massacre of many thousands of the flying Bastarnæ. **1855** MACAULAY *Hist. Eng.* III. 641 Flying foot soldiers..were constantly coming in.

7. Building. ***flying façade***, a façade that rises above the level of the roof of a building; ***flying shore***, a horizontal shore used to provide temporary support between two walls.

1894 J. P. ALLEN *Pract. Building Construct.* xxii. 355 End houses which cannot be strutted from another building, are dealt with by means of flying shores. **1936** P. E. THOMAS *Mod. Building Pract.* II. 167 A 'flying shore' is horizontal, and incapable of taking any vertical load, its function being to keep the wall plumb. **1961** S. SITWELL *Golden Wall & Mirador* viii. 161 *Espesaña* denotes a bell-wall or flying facade, rising above and often doubling or trebling the height of the building. **1962** A. E. BRIDGWOOD *Newnes Carpentry & Joining* III. 5 The elevation of one of a series of flying shores offering support to the walls of four floors is shown.

'flying 'bridge. [f. FLYING *ppl. a.*] †**a.** Used by Caxton to render Fr. *pont-levis* (draw-bridge). †**b.** (See quot. 1727 s.v. FLOATING-BRIDGE). **c.** A temporary bridge for military purposes, *esp.* (see quot. 1876).

1489 CAXTON *Faytes of A.* II. xxxv. K ij, Pount leveiz that be made faste therto whiche are called flyghyng brygges. **1675** *Lond. Gaz.* No. 1043/3 The Munster Troops..have repassed the Weser..over a Flying-bridge above this City. **1726** CAVALLIER *Mem.* IV. 340, I had but just cross'd the River upon a flying Bridge. **1876** VOYLE *Mil. Dict.*, *Flying Bridge*, consists of one or more barges moored by a long cable to a point in the centre of the stream. When the barge is properly steered in a current sufficiently strong, it is swept by it from one bank to the other.

'flying 'buttress. A prop or stay (usually carried by a segment of an arch), springing from a pier or other support, and abutting against a structure, for the purpose of resisting thrust. = ARC-BOUTANT, *arch-buttress* (ARCH *sb.* III).

1669 SIR C. WREN in C. Wren *Parentalia* (1750) 304 The Ailes, from whence arise Bows or Flying Buttresses to the Walls of the *Navis*. **1828** SCOTT *F.M. Perth* iv, One of the flying buttresses of the chapel. **1874** PARKER *Goth. Archit.* I. iv. 150 The Flying Buttress..is often found in Norman work, but concealed under the roof of the triforium.

'flying 'fish. [f. FLYING *ppl. a.* + FISH.] A name given to two kinds of fish (*Dactylopterus* and *Exocœtus*), which are able to rise into the air by means of enlarged wing-like pectoral fins.

c **1511** *1st Eng. Bk. Amer.* (Arb.) Introd. 28/1 There by be many w[h]alefysshes and flyinge fysshes. **1624** CAPT. SMITH *Virginia* v. 182 On the eleuenth day..two flying fishes fals in his boat. **1821** SHELLEY *Prometh. Unb.* IV. i. 86 As the flying fish leap From the Indian deep.

b. A constellation of the Southern Hemisphere.

1868 LOCKYER *Guillemin's Heavens* (ed. 3) 335.

'flying 'fox. [f. FLYING *ppl. a.* + FOX.] **1.** A member of the genus *Pteropus* of fruit-eating bats, found in India, Madagascar, south-east Asia, and Australia.

1759 HIRST in *Duncombe's Lett.* (1773) III. 95 They have heads like foxes, and..are covered with hair of a reddish hue; for which reason they are generally called 'flying foxes'. **1827** P. CUNNINGHAM *2 Years N.S. Wales* (1828) I. 294 Our flying fox is an immense bat. **1859** TENNENT *Ceylon* (1860) I. 135 The Roussette of Ceylon (the Flying-Fox as it is usually called by Europeans). **1877** W. S. DALLAS in *Cassell's Nat. Hist.* I. 268 The Flying Fox drinks by lapping. **1910** *Encycl. Brit.* X. 586/1 The flying-foxes are the largest of the bats. **1965** D. MORRIS *Mammals* 98 The largest bats of this group are the Flying Foxes of the Pacific region. **1969** E. C. ROLLS *They all ran Wild* xvii. 390 The party shot fifty-five flying-foxes.

2. A carrier operated by cables across a gorge, etc. *Austral.* and *N.Z.*

1936 F. CLUNE *Roaming round Darling* vii. 64 The mountain-sides near by are vast stores of black marble which is quarried out and brought down by flying foxes (buckets run on overhead wires). **1948** PARTRIDGE *Dict. Forces' Slang*, *Flying Fox*, a device used by the Australians in the Pacific to speed up the advance by slinging heavy equipment across rivers and other obstacles by ropes. **1965** G. J. WILLIAMS *Econ. Geol. N.Z.* x. 157/1 A certain amount of serpentinous rather than nephritic material had been brought down by flying-fox and cut into slabs. **1969** *Landfall* XXIII. 59 Adam had rigged up two flying-foxes —two long wires across the valleys on which he sent the hay flying across to the ferny slopes on the other side where they fed the cattle.

'flyingly, *adv. rare.* With flying colours.

1741 RICHARDSON *Pamela* IV. 296 Studying what to say, that she may come off as flyingly as she can.

'flying 'squirrel. [f. FLYING *ppl. a.*] A name given to two genera (*Pteromys* and *Sciuropterus*) of *Sciuridæ*, which can float through the air by means of an extension of skin connecting their fore and hind limbs.

1624 CAPT. SMITH *Virginia* II. 27 A small beast they have they call Assapanick, but we call them flying Squirrels. **1726** *Adv. Capt. R. Boyle* 362 The Flying-Squirrel, with Wings like those of a Bat. **1849** *Sk. Nat. Hist.*, *Mammalia* IV. 14 It is in the possession of a lateral fold of skin, forming, when extended, a parachute..that the flying squirrels are distinguishable from the ordinary group.

'fly-leaf. [f. FLY *sb.*^{2} + LEAF.] A blank leaf at the beginning or end, but *esp.* at the beginning, of a book; the blank leaf of a circular, etc.

1832 J. CONSTABLE *Let.* 28 Mar. (1966) IV. 371, I have bothered Sparrow out of a fly leaf, & I like it very well, preserving the original title. **1850** CLOUGH *Dipsychus* IX. 160 The fly-leaves..in the family Bible. **1869** ROGERS in *Adam Smith's W.N.* I. Pref. 19 It contains a characteristic note by the author on the flyleaf. **1888** BURGON *Lives 12 Gd. Men* I. I. 26 On the fly-leaf of the first volume..is found the following memorandum.

flyless ('flaɪlɪs), *a.* [f. FLY *sb.*^{1} + -LESS.] Without flies. Hence **'flylessness.**

1904 *Daily Chron.* 28 July 4/7 You leave Brindisi..in a perfectly fly-less ship. **1906** *Ibid.* 2 Oct. 4/7 The window-panes of a hitherto flyless house. **1918** W. HUTCHINSON *Doctor in War* (1919) xviii. 254 This miracle of flylessness was achieved..even in most of the Ospedali da Campo and Ospedaletti da Campo in the..camps just behind the Front.

'flyman. [f. FLY *sb.*^{2} + MAN *sb.*]

1. One who drives a fly (*sb.*^{2} sense 3 b).

1845 *P.O. Directory 6 Home Co.* 631/2 Bull Henry, fly-man. **1879** F. W. ROBINSON *Coward Consc.* I. iv, Two flymen..did not solicit him as a fare.

2. *Theatr.* A man stationed in the 'flies' to work the ropes, etc.

1883 H. IRVING in *Lond. Figaro* 6 Jan. 15/3 The flyman may be said to carry some of the destiny of the performance in the hollow of his hand.

flyness ('flaɪnɪs). [f. FLY *a.* + -NESS.] The quality or fact of being 'fly'; wide-awakeness.

1888 *Inter-Ocean* (Chicago) 8 Mar. (Farmer *Amer.*). Each conviction is a lesson to the youthful politician that flyness and smartness cannot be pleaded in mitigation of contempt of honor. **1925** *United Free Ch. Mission Rec.* June 247 Free from any of that holy flyness, with which, justly or not, ecclesiastics are sometimes credited.

'fly-net. [f. FLY *sb.*^{1} OE. had *fléohnet*.]

1. A net to keep away flies.

a **1000** *Judith* 47 (Gr.) þær wæs eallgylden fleohnet. **1874** KNIGHT *Dict. Mech.* I. 896 *Fly-net* 1..a net of meshes or a fringe of leather strips, to protect a horse from flies. 2. A net in an open window to prevent entrance of flies.

†**2.** = *butterfly-net*. *Obs.*

1737 P. COLLINSON in Darlington *Mem.* (1849) 90 Pray take one or two, with the fly-nets, in a bag by thy side.

fly-off ('flaɪɒf). [f. verbal phr. *to fly off* (see FLY *v.*^{1} 9 c).] The action of flying off. Also *attrib.* or as *adj.*, designating a brake in a motor vehicle that requires a manual operation to put it on or off but not to keep it on.

1901 H. G. WELLS *First Men in Moon* xx. 180, I had reckoned that..the tangential 'fly off' of the moon's spin would be at least twenty-eight times less than the earth's. **1959** *Motor* 19 Aug. 7/1 Good features of the control include ..a central fly-off handbrake. **1970** *Motoring Which?* Apr. 47/2 Drivers liked the DB5's fly-off design. You pressed the button only if you wanted to set the brake on, not to release it.

fly-over ('flaɪəʊvə(r)). [f. verbal phr. *to fly over* (see FLY *v.*^{1} 9 c).] **1.** A railway or road bridge over another (e.g. a local over a main) line or road. Also *fig.* Similarly **fly-under**, a line or road under another. Both words also *attrib.*

1901 *Daily News* 5 Jan. 6/5 The junction for the Aldershot branch..is being..rearranged on the 'fly-over' system, that is, the down line..remains as it was, but a new one..is being brought over the top of the main line by means of a skew bridge... This 'fly-over'..will abolish a fruitful source of delay. **1930** *Engineering* 7 Nov. 596/1 At Cogload Junction a fly-over bridge..will be built. **1937** *Daily Express* 7 Apr. 8/4 Whitehall's idea now is that great motoring highways be driven across the parks from one end to the other. They would meet at fly-overs, where one road would be built over the other. **1937** *Archit. Rev.* LXXXI. 158 (*caption*) Fly-over [road] crossing. **1938** *Times* 26 Jan. 14/4 The council also approved schemes for the construction of a fly-over junction on the Sutton by-pass road at its junction with the Merton-Belmont road. *Ibid.* 8 Nov. 11/6 The scheme has involved the construction of a 'fly-under' bridge under the present electric lines near North Acton. **1961** *Daily Tel.* 30 Aug. 15/3 'Fly-under' on old railway. *Ibid.*, A stretch of abandoned railway line is to be converted into a 'fly-under' junction. **1962** W. NOWOTTNY *Lang. Poets Use* viii. 183 This kind of symbolic language can use vocabulary that is apparently very simple..but conceals a tracery of fly-overs from literal to metaphorical terrain. **1963** [see ELEVATED *ppl. a.* 1]. **1970** *Courier-Mail* (Brisbane) 15 May 2/3 The fly-over freeway leading from Tokyo International Airport to the centre of the world's biggest city.

2. = FLY-PAST; the passage of an aircraft over (an area).

1931 *Times* 5 Sept. 10/7 The fly-over, though robbed of the excitement of a race, should nevertheless afford a fine spectacle. **1953** *Time* 30 Mar. 25/1 On his way to England, four other Britons had been killed during a 60-plane 'flyover' staged at Gibraltar. **1971** *Daily Tel.* 24 Apr. 2/6 Concorde's approach and fly-over noise was less than that of the..Boeing 707.

fly-past ('flaɪ'pɑːst, -pæst). [f. verbal phr. *to fly past* (see FLY *v.*^{1} 1 g), after *march past*.] The action of flying past, or forming part of a procession of aircraft; also, a fly-by (sense b).

1914 *Flight* 24 July 791 The machines which took part in the 'fly past' were three of the big 160 h.p. Gnome-Short machines. **1928** *Daily Express* 12 Oct. 1 At the end of the display when a fly-past of five different types of bombers was taking place. **1956** *Times* 8 May 9/5 From the balcony of Buckingham Palace, the Queen will take the salute at a fly-

past of RAF aircraft. **1967** *Times* 19 Oct. 11/2 The American fly-past [of Venus]..cannot compete in results with the Russian soft landing. **1971** *Daily Tel.* 21 Aug. 4/5 A 21-gun salute and a fly past by South African air force jets completed his send-off.

flyre, dial. form of FLEER.

Flysch (flɪʃ). *Geol.* [Swiss dial.] A series of tertiary strata occurring in the Alps, consisting of slates, marls, and fucoidal sandstones.

[**1827** B. STUDER in *Leonhard's Ztschr. f. Mineral.* I. 39 (*translated*) The prevailing slaty alterations are in the country called *Flysch*, a name which we may suitably extend to the entire formation.] **1853** LYELL *Princ. Geol.* (ed. 9) 124 The nummulitic limestone, together with the overlying fucoidal grit and shale, called 'Flysch', in the Alps, belongs to the..Eocene group. **1875** CROLL *Climate and Time* xvii. 280.

ˈfly-sheet. [f. FLY *v.*[1]] **1.** = *flying-sheet*: see FLYING *ppl. a.* 5 a.

1833 W. C. MACREADY *Diary* 23 July (1912) I. 51 Received letter from Serle, written on the fly-sheet of a circular from the Society of Dramatic Authors. **1875** SOUTHWARD *Dict. Typogr.*, *Fly-sheet*, a description of handbill or two or four-page tract. **1889** WORCESTER Suppl., *Fly-sheet*, an advance sheet announcing a newspaper; a prospectus.

2. A canvas cover pitched outside and over a tent to provide protection against the weather.

1926–7 *Army & Navy Stores Catal.* 1000/2 Ridge tents.. fitted with outer fly sheet forming double roof. **1946** J. E. Q. BARFORD *Climbing in Brit.* ii. 33 A fly-sheet is desirable in heavy rain, but none have so far been designed which will stand up to a strong wind.

ˈfly-slow, *a. rare*[−1]. That flies slowly.

1632 *Shaks. Rich. II*, I. iii. 150 (2nd folio), The flye-slow houres. [A plausible but doubtful conjecture; the other folios and the quartos read *slie* (or *slye*) *slow*.]

flyte: see FLITE.

ˌfly-the-ˈgarter. [f. the vbl. phrase *to fly the garter*.] A game in which the players leap from one side of a 'garter' or line of stones over the back of one of their number.

1818 KEATS *Lett.* Wks. (1889) III. 153, I must..make Wordsworth and Coleman play at leap-frog, or keep one of them down a whole half-holiday at fly-the-garter. **1862** MISS BRADDON *Ralph Bailiff, Happy Xmas* 161 Prisoner's base and fly-the-garter in the great bare playground.

flyting, var. FLITING *vbl. sb.*

ˈfly-trap. [f. FLY *sb.*[1] + TRAP.]

1. a. A trap to catch flies.

1855 in OGILVIE Suppl. **1859** LANG *Wand. India* 382 A fly-trap which he had that morning invented.

b. *fig.*

1909 'O. HENRY' *Options* (1916) 62 Old Jerome was lingering long after breakfast..before setting forth to his down town fly-trap. **1925** W. DEEPING *Sorrell & Son* iv, The 'Cubby Hole' of the Angel Inn was a pivot, a fly-trap, a cave into which all sorts of male things crowded, and drank.

2. A fly-catching plant, esp. *Apocynum androsæmifolium*. ***Venus's fly-trap*** = *Dionæa muscipula*.

1774 GOLDSM. *Hist. Earth* VIII. v. viii. 162 The flower, which goes by the name of the fly-trap. **1776** LEE *Bot.* 276 *Dionæa*, Venus's flytrap. **1841** in MAUNDER *Sci. & Lit. Treasury*.

3. *slang.* The mouth.

c **1795** M. G. LEWIS in *Spirit Pub. Jrnls.* (1798) I. 323 The bride shuts her fly trap; the stranger complies.

fly-under: see FLY-OVER I.

fly-up-the-creek. *U.S.* [f. vbl. phrase.]

1. A popular name of the small green heron, *Butorides virescens*. Hence used as a nickname for an inhabitant of Florida.

1857 BÜCHMANN in Herrig's *Archiv.* XXI. 166 Fly-up-the-creek 1) Ein in Florida häufiger Sumpfvogel. 2) Spitzname der Einwohner von Florida. **1869** TURNBULL *Birds E. Pennsylv.* 37 Green Heron..Fly-up-the-Creek.

2. A giddy, capricious person (*colloq.*) (*Cent. Dict.*).

flyway. [f. FLY *v.*[1] + WAY *sb.*[1] 7.] The route taken by birds during migration; also in extended use (see quot. 1948[2]).

1891 *Outing* (U.S.) Dec. 222 But a few years ago San Diego Bay was gay with life as we rowed across it to the mouth of the Spanish Bight, which was then a favorite 'fly way' of this bird. **1948** *Brit. Birds* XLI. 279 The Yukon delta described as perhaps the richest breeding ground and migration flyway of arctic birds ever discovered. **1948** *Conservation in Action* V. 8/1 The term 'flyway' denotes a vast geographic region that is occupied by definite bird populations and contains both breeding and wintering grounds, connected by..migration routes. **1962** *Times* 26 Feb. (Canada Suppl.) p. xv/6 Wildfowl are abundant in the prairie provinces, on the central flyway. **1971** *Country Life* 25 Feb. 435/2 It [*sc.* Ireland] is indeed the terminus of two wildfowl flyways.

ˈfly-ˈwheel. [f. FLY *sb.*[2] + WHEEL.] A wheel with a heavy rim, attached to a revolving shaft, in order either to regulate the motion of the machinery, or to accumulate power. (Cf. FLY *sb.*[2] 5 c.) Also *attrib.* and *Comb.*

[**1782** WATT *Patent* in Muirhead *Mech. Invent. Watt* III. 71 The heavy fly *xx* is put in motion by means of a pinion or smaller wheel *y* fixed upon its axis.] **1784** *Ibid.* 105 The rod E..turns the fly wheel M M. **1809** *Edin. Rev.* Jan. 321 This engine had no fly-wheel, and went sluggishly and irregularly. **1862** SMILES *Engineers* III. 89 The engine was provided with..a flywheel working at one side to carry the crank over the dead points. **1896** *Daily News* 18 Nov. 7/7 The great problem was to get the required fly-wheel effect without too great a weight. **1909** *Westm. Gaz.* 30 Nov. 5/2 The flywheel effect is increased owing to the kinetic energy of the mass of the revolving liquid medium. **1963** BIRD & HUTTON-STOTT *Veteran Motor Car* 123 The flywheel-fed splash lubrication. **1971** *Flying* Apr. 72/2 The weight of the fuel at the wingtips created a 'flywheel effect'.

fig. **1876** T. HARDY *Hand Ethelb.* (1890) 106 A steadying power..a flywheel, in short, to the concern.

†**fnast**, *sb. Obs.* [OE. *fnæst* str. masc., f. root of ON. *fnasa, fnása* to snort, breathe hard.]

Breath.

c **1000** *Sax. Leechd.* III. 100 Hyt bring[ð] forð þane fnæst. *a* **1250** *Owl & Night.* 44 Wel neȝ hire fnast at-schet.

†**fnast**, *v. Obs. rare.* [OE. **fnæstian*, f. prec.; cf. OHG. *fnâstôn*.] *intr.* To breathe hard, pant; also quasi-*trans.* to breathe *out* (fire).

c **1000** *Sax. Leechd.* II. 242 Fnæstiað swiðe. *c* **1300** *Havelok* 548 He [ne] mouthe speke, ne fnaste, Hwere he wolde him bere or lede. *c* **1340** *Gaw. & Gr. Knt.* 1702 His felaȝes fallen hym to, þat fnasted ful þike. *c* **1400** *Destr. Troy* 878 Þe orible oxin..þat fyre out fnast.

Hence **ˈfnasting** *vbl. sb.*, breathing, snorting.

1382 WYCLIF *Jer.* viii. 16 Fro Dan is herd the fnesting of his hors. *c* **1400** *Destr. Troy* 171 These balfull bestes were.. ffull flaumond of fyre with fnastyng of logh.

†**fnese**, *v. Obs.* [OE. **fnéosan* (whence *fnéosung* 'sternutatio' (Wr.-Wülck. 162), *fnora* 'sternutatio' (*Corp. Gloss.*), *ȝe-fnésan* to sneeze (see below), cognate with Du. *fniezen*, ON. *fnýsa* (Da. *fnyse*, Sw. *fnysa* to snort).

The wk.-grade of the root **fneus-* (? cogn. with Gr. πνέ-ειν, root **pneu-* to breathe) is represented in OE. *fnora* sneezing (Corp. Gloss.). Closely parallel in sound and sense, though belonging to a different ablaut series, are ON. *fnasa* (see FNAST *sb.*) and *fnœsa* (:—**fnōs-ja*) to snort.]

intr. To sneeze; also, to puff, snort. Hence **ˈfnesing** *vbl. sb.*

c **1000** ÆLFRIC *Gloss.* in Wr.-Wülcker 162 *Sternutatio*.. snytingc, *uel* fneosung. *c* **1386** CHAUCER *Manciple's Prol.* 62 He spekeþ in his nose And fneseth faste. **1398** TREVISA *Barth. De P.R.* VII. xi. (1495) 230 Constantyne sayth that fnesynge is a vyolent meuynge of yᵉ brayne to putte out superfluytees of fumositees therof. *c* **1400** *Beryn* 42 And þere-with she gan to fnese.

fo, obs. form of FEW *a.*, FOE, FOH *int.*

foa, foan, obs. forms of FOE sing. and pl.

foad, var. of FODE *v. Obs.*, to beguile.

foal (fəʊl), *sb.* Forms: 1–2 fola, 3–7 fole, (4 fol, fowle), 4–6 foil(e, foole, (5 fool, folle, foyl(l)e, 6 foule,) 5–7 foale, (7 phoale,) 6– foal. [Com. Teut., OE. *fola* wk. masc. = OFris. *folla* (for **fola*) (MDu. *volen, veulen*, Du. *veulen*), OHG. *folo* (MHG. *vol, vole*, Ger. *fohlen* neut.), ON. *fole* (Da. *fole*, Sw. *fåle*), Goth. *fula*:—OTeut. **folon-*, cognate with Gr. πῶλος, L. *pullus*.]

1. The young of the equine genus of quadrupeds; *properly*, one of the male sex, a colt; but also used where the sex is not specified, a colt or filly.

c **950** *Lindisf. Gosp.* Mark xi. 4 And foerdon onfundon fola ȝebunden. **971** *Blickl. Hom.* 69 Þonne ȝemete ȝyt þær eoselan ȝesælede & hire folan. *c* **1200** *Trin. Coll. Hom.* 89 Hie funden an asse mid fole. **1382** WYCLIF *Zech.* ix. 9 A fole, sone of the she asse. **1484** CAXTON *Fables of Æsop* v. x, He sawe a mare and her yong foole with her. **1535** *Act 27 Hen. VIII*, c. 6. §2 Two mares..apte and able to beare folis. **1697** DRYDEN *Æneid* IV. 746 The Priestess..cuts the Forehead of a new-born Fole. **1794** COLERIDGE *To Yng. Ass* 1 Poor little foal of an oppressed race! **1859** DARWIN *Orig. Spec.* v. (1873) 128 The spinal stripe is much commoner in the foal than in the full-grown animal.

Proverb. **1546** J. HEYWOOD *Prov.* (1867) 27 How can the fole amble, if the hors and mare trot?

b. Phrases. ***in foal, with foal***, (of a mare): pregnant. †***tattered as a*** (***feltered*** or ***tattered***) ***foal***, of a person: ragged; also, rough, shaggy.

1340 HAMPOLE *Pr. Consc.* 1537 Som gas tatird als tatird foles. **1377** LANGL. *P. Pl.* B. XI. 335 Bothe horse and houndes and alle other bestes Medled nouȝte wyth here makes þat with fole were. *a* **1400** [see BAGGED]. *c* **1460** *Towneley Myst.* (Surtees) 4 Now ar we..tatyrd as a foylle. **1523** FITZHERB. *Husb.* §68 They [mares] mayе not be rydden ..whan they be with foole. **1727** SWIFT *Modest Proposal* Wks. 1755 II. II. 66 Their mears in foal. **1835** W. IRVING *Tour Prairies* 226 A fine black mare far gone with foal.

c. Applied to the young of the elephant or camel.

1398 TREVISA *Barth. De P.R.* XVIII. xlii. (1495) 803 Elyphauntes goo wyth foole two yeres. **1607** TOPSELL *Four-f. Beasts* (1658) 163 An Indian, who had brought up from a foal a white Elephant.

†**2.** A horse. *Obs.*

a **1300** *K. Horn* 589 Horne ȝede to stable: þar he tok his gode fole. *c* **1340** *Gaw. & Gr. Knt.* 173 Þe fole þat he ferkkes on. *a* **1400–50** *Alexander* 5588 Fare wele, my faire foole þou failid me neuire. **1513** DOUGLAS *Æneis* x. xiv. 89 O moist forcy steyd, my lovyt foill.

3. *Coal-mining.* (See quots.)

1770–4 A. HUNTER *Georg. Ess.* (1804) II. 158 What are termed lads or foals; supplying the inferior place at a machine called a tram. **1835** S. OLIVER *Ramb. Northumb.* i. 41 Where a youth is too weak to put the tram by him-self, he engages a junior assistant, who is called the foal.

4. *attrib.* and *Comb.*, as ***foal fair***, (objective) **-getter**; also **foal-bit** (see quots.); **foal-teeth**, the first teeth of a horse.

1706 PHILLIPS (ed. Kersey), **Fole-bit* and *Fole-foot*, two sorts of Herbs. **1755** JOHNSON, *Foalbit, Foalfoot*, plants. **1880** *Daily News* 18 Sept. 6/6 A public dinner held after the Holbeach *foal fair. **1809** *Spirit Publ. Jrnls.* (1810) XIII. 61 He is a sure *foal-getter. **1696** SIR W. HOPE tr. *Solleysel's Compl. Horsem.* v. 19 A little before a Horse hath attained to the Age of thiry Months..he hath twelve *Foal-teeth in the fore part of his mouth. **1855** *Farmer's Dict.* (Wilson) I. 21 The foal's nippers..technically called..foal teeth—are easily distinguished.

foal (fəʊl), *v.* [f. prec. sb.; cf. mod.Ger. *fohlen*.]

1. *trans.* To bear or bring forth (a foal); said of a mare, she-ass, etc.

c **1386** CHAUCER *Friar's T.* 247 The fend..yow fech body and bones, As ferforthly as ever wer ye folid! **1398** TREVISA *Barth. De P.R.* XVIII. viii. (1495) 756 The asse foolyth selde two coltes. **1638** BAKER tr. *Balzac's Lett.* I. 71 His Mare.. had foaled a Colt. **1727** BRADLEY *Fam. Dict.* s.v. *Colt*, When your Colts are foalen you may let them run with their Dams till about Michaelmas. **1887** MISS BRADDON *Like & Unlike* i, He would buy the maddest devil that was ever foaled if he fancied the..paces of the beast.

2. *absol.* or *intr.* To give birth to a foal.

1521 *Test. Ebor.* (Surtees) V. 129, I have yᵉ mares wᵗ foole, and, when they folyn, I gif the bettur [etc.]. **1607** TOPSELL *Four-f. Beasts* (1658) 18 They [Asses] will not Fole in the sight of man. **1707** MORTIMER *Husb.* 151 About September they take their Mares into the house again where they keep them till they foal.

b. Of a ewe: To yean. ? *U.S.* only.

1883 P. E. GIBBONS in *Harper's Mag.* Apr. 652/2 The ewes are..kept until they have foaled.

3. To get (a mare) in foal. *rare.*

1891 T. H. WEBSTER *Let. to Chaplin* in *Times* 9 Nov. 10/5 The horse..had foaled his mares well.

†**ˈfoalage.** *Obs. rare.* [f. FOAL *sb.* + -AGE: cf. COLTAGE.] = FOALHOOD.

1607 MARKHAM *Caval.*, I. i. 2 Both in their foleage, best strength, and old age. **1720** W. GIBSON *Diet. Horses* v. (1731) 71 He has been used from his folage to the eating of this or that sort.

foalfoot (ˈfəʊlfʊt). Also foal's-foot. Forms: see FOAL, FOOT. [Named from the shape of the leaves.]

1. = COLTSFOOT I.

a **1400** in *Archæologia* XXX. 407/1 Folesfoth..& yᵉ smale clote is all on. **1578** LYTE *Dodoens* I. xii. 20 This [Tussilago] is called in English Fole foote. **1877** in *N.W. Linc. Gloss.*, Foal-foot.

attrib. **1881** *Leicestersh. Gloss.* s.v., Home-made foal-foot wine used to be common in Leicestershire.

2. = ASARABACCA.

1538 TURNER *Libellus*, Folfot, *Asarum*. **1615** T. THOMAS *Lat. Dict.*, *Vulgago*..folefoote, or Asarabacca.

3. Applied to other plants resembling the preceding, as **sea foalfoot**, *Convolvulus Soldanella*.

1548 TURNER *Names of Herbs* (E.D.S.) 20 *Brassica marina* ..may be called in english seafolfote. **1597** GERARDE *Herbal* 690 Soldanella is called..in English..of some Sea Foalfoote. **1713** J. PETIVER in *Phil. Trans.* XXVIII. 184 White Canada Folesfoot.

foalhood (ˈfəʊlhʊd). [f. FOAL *sb.* + -HOOD.] The state or time of being a foal.

1892 *Edin. Rev.* 7 Jan. 44 A mare which has been well cared for during foalhood.

foaling (ˈfəʊlɪŋ), *vbl. sb.* [f. FOAL *v.* + -ING[1].] The bringing forth of a foal or of young.

1398 TREVISA *Barth. De P.R.* x. vi. (1495) 377 A mere in traueylle of folyng. **1607** TOPSELL *Four-f. Beasts* (1658) 258 It is mortal to their [Camels'] young ones to tast the dams milk for two dayes after their foaling. **1870** *Daily News* 14 Apr., This early time of foaling is prejudicial to the strength ..of foals.

ˈfoaling, *ppl. a.* [f. as prec. + -ING[2].] = next.

1885 *Bell's Life* 15 June 1/3 Foaling mares.

foaly (ˈfəʊlɪ), *a.* Of a mare: In foal.

1853 SURTEES *Sponge's Tour* xxiii. 122 Farmer Stubble, on the foaly mare.

foam (fəʊm), *sb.* Forms: 1 fám, faam, (3 fam), 3–6 fame, 4–8 fome, (5 foome,) 7 foame, 7–9 *Sc.* faem(e, fame, faim, feim, feame, 6– foam. [OE. *fám* str. (? masc. or neut.) = OHG. *feim* (MHG. *veim*, Ger. *feim*) masc.:—WGer. **faimo-*:—pre-Teut. **poimo-* or **phoimo-*. A parallel form with suffix *-no-* instead of *-mo-* appears in OSlav. *pěna*, Skr. *phena*, foam.

Joh. Schmidt regards the *-mo-* and *-no-* forms as divergent representations of an original with *-mn-* suffix, and considers the Lat. *spūma* (:—**spoimā*) foam, *pūmex* pumice-stone, Zend *paēman-*, Lith. *pēnas* milk, to be also cognate]

1. a. The aggregation of minute bubbles formed in water or other liquids by agitation, fermentation, effervescence, ebullition, etc.

Being the proper word for the product of the agitation of the waves, *foam* is more dignified than the synonymous *froth*, and usually implies more copious production.

a **700** *Epinal Gloss.* 426 *Famfaluca*: leasung *vel* faam. **1393** GOWER *Conf.* II. 261 She nome Both of the water and of the fome. *a* **1440** *Sir Degrev.* 546 Whyegh as the seys ffame. **1513** DOUGLAS *Æneis* I. viii. 76 The bittir blastis.. Throw.. salt fame, and wilsum wayis.. can ws drive. **1611** BIBLE *Hos.* x. 7 Her King is cut off as the fome vpon the water. **1652** FRENCH *Yorksh. Spa* iv. 50 That water is best for outward uses which will bear sope best, and make the greatest fome therewith. *c* **1720** W. GIBSON *Farrier's Dispens.* II. I. (1734) 32 Eggs.. when beat into a Fome with Alum. **1786** BURNS *Scotch Drink* ii, Guid auld Scotch Drink! Whether.. thou.. ream o'er the brink, In glorious faem. **1878** HUXLEY *Physiogr.* iv. 64 The foam of the sea becomes opaque white, by the light being scattered from the particles of water into which a wave is broken.

transf. and *fig.* *a* **1300** *Cursor M.* 26693 (Cott.) Quat es mans lijf bot fam. *a* **1310** in Wright *Lyric P.* 102 Mon is mad of feble fom. **1858** CARLYLE *Fredk. Gt.* (1865) II. VI. iii. 155 The foam of mankind.. the idle moneyed populations from all countries. **1866** B. TAYLOR *Poems, Test* 414 The meadows tossed their foam of flowers.

b. *spec.* The foaming saliva issuing from the mouth, e.g. in epilepsy, rabies, etc. Also, the froth of perspiration which gathers on the coat of a horse or other animal from intense exertion.

c **900** *Bæda's Hist.* III. ix. [xi]. (1890) 184 þa faam of his muðe ut eode. *c* **1290** *S. Eng. Leg.* I. 231/409 Brenninde fom out of is mouth.. he caste. *c* **1320** *Seuyn Sag.* (W.) 913 Thourgh the mouht the fom was wight. **1388** WYCLIF *Luke* ix. 39 A spirit takith hym, and sudenli he.. hurtlith doun, and to drawith hym with fome. **1612** DRAYTON *Poly-olb.* xii. 202 Two Boares.. with their gnashing teeth their angry foame doe bite. **1735** SOMERVILLE *Chase* IV. 312 The pois'nous Foam Through the deep wound instil'd. **1875** W. S. HAYWARD *Love agst. World* 237 Her horse was covered with foam.

fig. **1555** BP. BONNER *Profitable Doctrine* Sig. N iiij b, Baptysme.. doeth.. so weaken.. ye fome, or rage of concupiscence in vs.. that [etc.]. **1577–87** HOLINSHED *Chron.* III. 872/1 King Henrie.. is reported.. to cast out his fome against Luther. **1597** HOOKER *Eccl. Pol.* v. xix. §11 Our Churches, in the foame of that good spirit which directeth such fierie tongues, they terme spitefully the temples of Baal.

†**c.** ***foam of lead*** = LITHARGE. ***foam of nitre*** = APHRONITRE. ***foam of oil*** = LEES. ***foam of copperas*** = COLCOTHAR. *Obs.*

1538 ELYOT *Dict.*, *Amurca*, the mother or fome of all oyles. *Ibid.*, *Molybditis*, the spume or fome of leade. **1601** HOLLAND *Pliny* II. 421 The fome of nitre.. is commended as the best of all. **1623** COCKERAM II, The Foame that riseth from Lead tryed, *litargie*. **1631** WIDDOWES *Nat. Philos.* 24 Red vitrioll, or the fome of Copperasse.

d. A mass or layer of foam used in fire-fighting, produced by adding a foaming agent to a flow of water or by other means; also, a foaming agent so used. Also *attrib.*, as ***foam carpet***, ***extinguisher***, ***generator***.

1906 A. G. LAURENT *Brit. Pat. No. 18,357* 15 Aug., The invention has for its object a hand fire extinguishing apparatus.. that.. sprays foam instead of liquid. **1933** *Meccano Mag.* Feb. 99/3 A fire engine in use at Dagenham carries practically all the equipment likely to be required by a fire brigade. This includes a chemical 'foam' generator. **1934** WEBSTER, *Foam extinguisher*, a fire extinguisher discharging a frothy substance which covers and extinguishes by excluding air from the burning surface. **1957** *Encycl. Brit.* IX. 271/1 Foam is also used in the fire service in the form of a dry powder which employs a foam generator to mix the powder with water being discharged by the fire pump. **1960** *Daily Tel.* 12 Aug. 18/4 'Foam carpet' for runway... A device for carpeting a runway with foam has been developed by the Engineering Flight at the R.A.F. Station, Waddington, Lincs. **1966** *McGraw-Hill Encycl. Sci. & Technol.* V 279/1 On oil fires water is effective only as a foam, or in some cases as a fog. **1970** *Oxford Mail* 3 Aug. 1/7 The pilot was reported to have turned down the RAF offer, which would have given him a foam cushion to land on. *Ibid.*, The cost of laying an anti-fire foam carpet on the runway.

e. Rubber or plastic in the form of a cellular mass similar to foam in structure. Usu. *attrib.*, as ***foam mattress***, ***plastic***, ***rubber***, ***sheet***. Also **foamed** *ppl. a.*, made or existing in this form.

1937 *Jrnl. R. Aeronaut. Soc.* XLI. 1090 Some foam plastics are mentioned for the isolation against noise and the protection against cold. **1943** *Air News* 15 July 8/4 (*caption*) New uses for foamed rubber. **1945** *Life* 1 Oct. 129/1 Foam rubber.. will soon be used to soften millions of U.S. beds and chairs. **1948** *Daily Mail* 30 Aug. 3/6 The chief new outlet in the rubber industry is in 'foam' rubber. **1951** *Good Housek. Home Encycl.* 108/2 Latex foam padding. **1955** *Americana Ann.* 125/2 Addition of water to the resin during processing causes elimination of carbon dioxide with the production of a foamed plastic. **1959** *B.S.I. News* Apr. 4/2 To work economically, this method of heating requires really efficient thermal insulation, and this is to be provided by extensive use of plastics foam sheets. **1959** *Economist* 6 June 940/2 Protected by space suits and foam mattresses. **1959** *Observer* 27 Sept. 4/3 'Expanded neoprene' (a kind of foamed rubber). **1961** *B.S.I. News* Aug. 19/2 The B.S.I. recently drew the attention of the Board of Trade to a flock-filled pillow which was described as being made of 'foam'. **1962** *Which?* July 198/1 The fifth type (of life-jacket).. used non-absorbent foam plastic to provide buoyancy. **1966** *McGraw-Hill Encycl. Sci. & Technol.* X. 494a/2 The rigid foams are employed as the core in structural laminates, such as in airplane wings. **1971** *Brit. Med. Bull.* XXVII. 75/2 Alternative materials for insulation, such as.. foam plastics and cork.

2. Foaming water, the sea; (in early use occas. *pl.*) also ***salt***, ***sea***, ***water foam***. *arch.* (*poet.*).

a **1000** *Riddles* iii. 4 (Gr.) ðifen bið ȝewreȝed.. fam ȝewealcen. *c* **1290** *S. Eng. Leg.* I. 476/508 Huy gonne to seili swiþe in þat salte fom. *c* **1340** *Cursor M.* 14409 (Trin.) Moyses.. ladde þem þourȝe þe see fome. *c* **1440** *Bone Flor.* 137 Over fomes they flett withowtyn fayle. **1549** *Compl. Scot.* vi. 40, I sat doune to see the flouyng of the fame. **1613** J. D[ENNIS] *Angling* I. xxx, Long ere Phœbus set in Westerne fome.

3. *Min.* = APHRITE.

†**4.** [from the vb.] The action of foaming.

1573 BARET *Alv.* F 823 The fome, or sprinckling vp of new wine, in ale we call it working.

5. *attrib.* and *Comb.*

a. General comb.: (*a*) simple attrib., as ***foam bath***, ***-bell***, ***-flake***, ***-fleck***, ***-fleece***, ***-flower*** (see also 5 b), ***-froth***, ***-globe***, ***-wake***, ***-whirl***, ***-wreath***; (*b*) objective, as ***foam curber***; (*c*) instrumental and originative, as ***foam-backed***, ***-beat***, ***-bedappled***, †***-bespawled***, ***-born*** (also quasi-*sb.*), ***-crested***, ***-filled***, ***-flecked***, ***-flowered***, ***-girt***, ***-lit***, ***-painted***, ***-upholstered***, ***-white***, ***-wrought*** adjs.; also ***foam-like*** adj. and adv.; ***foam-cold***, ***-pale*** adjs.

1963 *Punch* 10 Apr. p. xiv, Men's wear.. includes *foam-backed car coats. **1938** L. MACNEICE *I Crossed Minch* II. xvi. 232 She says that you're using astringents and taking *foam baths. **1969** A. LASKI *Dominant Fifth* v. 181 She wanted.. to go home, take off her shoes, soak in a foam bath. **1777** WARTON *Poems, Ode* VIII. vi, Banks.. Fenc'd by the *foam-beat pier. **1633** [J. FISHER] *True Trojans* IV. i, Hyperions Sonne Shall couch in West his *fome-bedappled iades. **1813** HOGG *Queen's Wake* 307 Light as the.. *foam-bells floating on the brine. **1612** DRAYTON *Poly-olb.* II. Notes 33 Old Proteus hath been knowne.. to spunge his *foame-bespawled beard. **1862** E. ARNOLD in *Fraser's Mag.* July 114 The *'Foam-Born's' beauty. **1884** W. C. SMITH *Kildrostan* 85 Still reigned the foam-born Aphrodite. **1929** BLUNDEN *Near & Far* 39 This *foam-cold vale. *a* **1795** BURNS *Lament* 5 Ye *foam-crested billows, allow me to wail. **1599** NASHE *Lenten Stuffe* (1871) 51 A Lepanto like host of unfatigable flood-bickerers, and *foam-curbers. **1959** *Sunday Times* 21 June 19/4 A chair that folds into a neat parcel... *Foam-filled cushion and back. **1833** TENNYSON *Dream Fair Wom.* x, Crisp *foam-flakes scud along the level sand. **1895** M. PEMBERTON *Impregnable City* iv. 23 The *foam-flecks breaking upon the face. **1842** SIR A. DE VERE *Song of Faith* 253 *Foam-flecked waves. **1876** G. M. HOPKINS *Wr. Deutschland* (1918) 16 The cobbled *foam-fleece. **1928** BLUNDEN *Retreat* 56 Where befouled the foam-fleece stays. **1866** SWINBURNE *Poems & Ballads* 61 And the sea moving saw before it move One moon-flower making all the *foam-flowers fair. **1878** *Ibid.* 2nd Ser. 29 Look forth from the flowers to the sea; For the foam-flowers endure when the rose-blossoms wither. **1951** W. DE LA MARE *Winged Chariot* 31 The foam-flowers of sea-wilderness. **1876** SWINBURNE *Erechth.* (ed. 2) 448 The *foam-flowered sea. **1583** STANYHURST *Aeneis* I. (Arb.) 21 In *foam froth picturs, wyth Troian treasur, ar vpborne. **1817** SHELLEY *Rev. Islam* XI. x, On a *foam-girt crag. **1813** SCOTT *Rokeby* II. vii, *Foam-globes on her eddies ride. **1871** PALGRAVE *Lyr. Poems* 117 Pennons toss'd *foam-like o'er the fray. **1876** T. HARDY *Hand Ethelb.* (1890) 34 Ladies in their foam-like dresses. **1793** WORDSW. *Descr. Sk.* 249 They cross the chasmy torrent's *foam-lit bed. **1593** NASHE *Christ's T.* (1613) 62 Her Alablaster wals were all furred and *fome-painted. **1895** W. B. YEATS *Poems* 41 From the *foam-pale distance. **1961** *Housewife* Apr. 67/1 Chairs have *foam-upholstered seats. **1876** MORRIS *Sigurd* III. 210 They see.. a *foam-wake as the wet oars toss on high. **1841** in S. C. Hall *Ireland* (1843) III. 175 O'er the *foam-white waves. **1817** SHELLEY *Rev. Islam* I. xvii, The *foam-wreaths which the faint tide wove. *Ibid.* VI. iv, Like *foam-wrought waterfalls.

b. Special comb.: **foam-back**, **foamback** (see quot. 1963); **foam-bow**, a bow, similar to a rainbow, formed by sunlight upon foam or spray; **foam-cock** (see quot.); **foam-dock**, ? soapwort (*Saponaria officinalis*); **foam flower**, a member of the genus *Tiarella*, esp. *T. cordifolia*, a small perennial herb native to North America; = *false mitre-wort* (MITRE-WORT); **foam glass** (see quot. 1962); **foam-omelet**, **-sauce** (*Cookery*), a dish so called from its frothy appearance; **foam-spar**, **foam-stone**, see APHRITE and APHRODITE.

1961 *Drapery & Fashion Weekly* 2 Mar. 1 *Foambacks will change the trade's whole way of life. **1963** A. J. HALL *Textile Sci.* iii. 157 Foam-back fabrics. A new development in the manufacture of fabric is to apply to the back of a woven or knitted fabric a very thin layer of synthetic foam sheeting... The presence of the foam layer confers great warmth and induces the garment to retain its shape better during wear. **1830** TENNYSON *Œnone* 60 The *foambow brightens When the wind blows the foam. **1874** KNIGHT *Dict. Mech.* I. 897/1 **Foam-cock* (Steam-engine), a cock at the water-level to blow off scum. *c* **1500** *Gloss. Harl.* 3388 in *Sax. Leechd.* III. 327/1 *Fome dok. **1895** W. ROBINSON *Eng. Flower Garden* (ed. 4) II. 788/1 Some real treasures, for no apparent reason, are overlooked. Such has been the fate of the lovely little *Foam Flower, a hardy plant of rapid increase. **1908** *Suburban Country Life* July 20/2 The foam flower, the clintonia, [etc.].. make a carpet in a certain bit of woods. **1962** *Amat. Gardening* 27 Jan. 4 Tiarella cordifolia and the taller T. Wherryi are good weed suppressors.. their feathery appearance has earned them the name Foam Flower. **1948** *Archit. Rev.* CIV. 268 Insulation for walls, floors and ceilings is 6 in. cork, and for the roof it is *foam glass and composition. **1962** *Gloss. Terms Glass Ind.* (*B.S.I.*) 33 *Foam glass*, a rigid multi-cellular insulating block fabricated from glass of high durability and comprising a homogeneous mass of closed cells. **1892–4** *Encycl. Cookery* (Garrett) II. 21/1 *Foam Omelet. *Ibid.* II. 400/1 *Foam Sauce.

foam (fəʊm), *v.* Forms. *α.* 1 **fǽman**, 3 **femin**, **feamen**, *south.* **vemen**, 4 **feme**; *β.* 4–7 **fome** (4 *south.* **vome**, 5 **fomyn**,) 5 **fame**, 7 **foame**, 6– **foam**. [OE. *fǽman* = OHG. *feiman* (MHG. *veimen*, G. *feimen*:—WGer. **faimjan*, f. **faim-* FOAM *sb.* In 14th c. the OE. word was superseded by a new formation on the sb. (without umlaut).]

1. *intr.* To emit foam; *esp.* to froth at the mouth; also with *out*. Often as a hyperbolical description of vehement rage or wrath. Also of a horse, etc.: To be covered with foam (of perspiration). Cf. FOAM *sb.* 1 b.

c **950** *Lindisf. Gosp.* Mark ix. 18 *Spumat*, fæmeð. *a* **1225** *Juliana* 68 As an burst bar, þat grunde his tuskes ant feng on to femin. *a* **1350** *Life Jesus* 223 Bete and bite it wolde.. And grenny with is teth and feme. **1430** LYDG. *Chron. Troy* II. xii, Mine hors.. Fomyng full whyte vpon euery syde. *c* **1440** *Jacob's Well* 99 þe man.. fomyd out at his mowth. *a* **1529** SKELTON *Elynour Rummyng* 341 Her mouth fomyd. **1601** SHAKS. *Jul. C.* I. ii. 255 He [Caesar].. foam'd at mouth, and was speechlesse. **1735** SOMERVILLE *Chase* III. 113 He snorts, he foams. **1807–8** W. IRVING *Salmag.* (1824) 349, I expected every moment to see them fall down in convulsions [and] foam at the mouth. **1852** MRS. STOWE *Uncle Tom's C.* xl, Legree, foaming with rage, smote his victim to the ground.

fig. **1817** D'ISRAELI *Cur. Lit.* III. 303 A tedious invective, foaming at the mouth of its text with quotations and authorities. **1870** SWINBURNE *Ess. & Stud.* (1875) 248 He [Byron].. foams at things and creatures not worth a glance.

b. Const. †*of*, †*on*, *with* (blood).

c **1400** *Destr. Troy* 7261 The fas in the fell hast femyt on blode. *c* **1425** *Seven Sag.* (P.) 959 Hys mouthe famed of blode. **1573** BARET *Alv.* F 821 He fometh with bloud at the mouth.

†**2.** To come forth in foam. *Obs.*

c **1340** *Gaw. & Gr. Knt.* 1572 þe froþe femed at his mouth vnfayre. **1398** TREVISA *Barth. De P.R.* VII. xxx. (1495) 244 The blood fomith wyth cough and traueyle and ache.

3. Of water or other liquid: To froth, gather foam. Also, to run foaming *along*, *down*, *over*, etc. Also *fig.* ***to foam off***, ***foam itself away***: to pass away in foam.

1398 TREVISA *Barth. De P.R.* XIII. xxv. (1495) 456 For lightnesse of ayre that is closid water fomyth. *c* **1440** *Promp. Parv.* 169/2 Fomyn, *spumo*. **1535** COVERDALE *Isa.* lvii. 20 The raginge see.. whose water fometh with ye myre. **1576** in W. H. Turner *Select. Rec. Oxford* 386 In wynter the water fomyth over. **1606** SHAKS. *Ant. & Cl.* II. vi. 21 My Nauie. At whose burthen, The anger'd Ocean fomes. **1728** YOUNG *Odes to King* Wks. (1757) I. 173 The torrent roar'd, and foam'd along. **1820** W. IRVING *Sketch Bk.* I. 76 A mountain stream was now foaming down it. **1826** SCOTT *Woodst.* x, Enthusiasm is a stream that may foam off in its own time. **1852** TENNYSON *Death Dk. Wellington* 126 Their surging charges foam'd themselves away.

b. Of a steam-boiler: To become filled with foam (Webster 1864).

4. a. *intr.* Of a drinking vessel: To be filled with foaming liquor. **b.** *trans.* To fill or brim with foaming liquor.

1725 POPE *Odyss.* xv. 341 Few can with me.. contend.. To.. foam the goblet with a purple stream. **1822** SHELLEY *Hellas* 939 The cup is foaming with a nation's blood. **1855** M. ARNOLD *Mycerinus* 97 Flush'd guests, and golden goblets foam'd with wine.

5. *trans.* To send forth or emit in or like foam; to pour *out* with rage and violence. Chiefly *fig.*

1388 WYCLIF *Jude* 13 These ben.. wawis of the woode see, fomynge [**1382** frothinge] out her confusiouns. *a* **1535** MORE *Wks.* (1557) 579/1 Tindall.. fometh oute hys hyghe spirituall sentence in thys fashion. **1601** WEEVER *Mirr. Mart.* E viij b, Two fyrie coursers foming clottred blood. **1784** COWPER *Task* VI. 898 They roam the earth.. foaming out their own disgrace. **1864** TENNYSON *Aylmer's F.* 342 Leolin.. foam'd away his heart at Averill's ear.

†**6.** To cover with or as with foam. *Obs. rare.*

c **1400** *Destr. Troy* 10219 With þaire fawchons fell, femyt of blode. **1556** J. HEYWOOD *Spider & F.* lx. 5 The head spider (with wheat tuskes fomde like a bore).

7. *nonce-use.* To draw (a chariot) *along* with the accompaniment of foam.

1820 KEATS *Hyperion* II. 234 Have ye beheld the young God of the Seas?.. Have ye beheld his chariot, foam'd along By noble winged creatures he hath made?

Hence '**foamer**, one who foams.

1607 TOPSELL *Four-f. Beasts* (1658) 577 [Epithets applied to wolves].. bloud-sucker, foamer.

foamed (fəʊmd). *ppl. a.* [f. prec. + -ED[1].]

1. Covered with or as with foam.

1820 KEATS *Hyperion* II. 172 The far-foamed sands.

2. Having or made to have a cellular structure like that of foam.

1943, etc. [see FOAM *sb.* 1 e]. **1959** *Engineering* 6 Feb. 183/3 (*heading*) Foamed glass insulation.

b. ***foamed slag***, the product of blast-furnace slag subjected to a special treatment.

1937 *Discovery* Feb. 58/2 An example in this country of the use of foamed slag concrete blocks is to be found in the Fire Testing Station at Elstree. **1956** *Gloss. Terms Concrete* (*B.S.I.*) 5 *Foamed slag*, a lightweight cellular material [aggregate].. manufactured by treating molten blastfurnace slag with water or other suitable medium to produce a cellular dry product.

foaming ('fəʊmɪŋ), *vbl. sb.* [f. FOAM *v.* + -ING[1].] The action of the vb. FOAM.

1382 WYCLIF *Num.* xi. 20 To the tyme that it [flesh].. be turnyd into fomynge. **1573** BARET *Alv.* F 821 A foming, *spumatus*. **1709** STEELE *Tatler* No. 141 ¶11 He will fall into Ravings and Foamings, ill-becoming the Meekness of his Office. **1772** PRIESTLEY *Inst. Relig.* (1782) I. 367 The heathen diviners had.. foamings at the mouth.

foaming ('fəʊmɪŋ), *ppl. a.* [f. as prec. + -ING[2].]

That foams.

?*a* **1400** *Morte Arth.* 780 A blake bustous bere..wyth fomaunde lyppez. *a* **1400–50** *Alexander* 1133 With þat þe femand flode flasshed in hys eghen. **1590** SPENSER *F.Q.* I. i. 1 His angry steede did chide his foming bitt. **1604** SHAKS. *Oth.* II. i. 11 Do but stand vpon the Foaming Shore. **1667** MILTON *P.L.* x. 301 Over the foaming deep. **1717** BERKELEY *Tour Italy* Wks. 1871 IV. 580 Like the foaming priestesses ..among the ancients. **1725** POPE *Odyss.* III. 506 To Pallas high the foaming bowl he crown'd. **1850** TENNYSON *In Mem.* cxxxi. 92 The foaming grape of eastern France. **1868** FREEMAN *Norm. Conq.* (1876) II. viii. 253 William was still urging on his foaming horse.

Hence **'foamingly** *adv.*

1611 COTGR., *Baveusement*, foamingly. **1801** SOUTHEY *Thalaba* III. xix, The winter torrent rolls Down the deep-channell'd rain-course, foamingly. **1885** S. TROMHOLT *Aur. Bor.* II. 223 The river rushing foamingly downwards.

foamless ('fəʊmlɪs), *a.* [f. FOAM *sb.* + -LESS.] Without foam; free from foam.

1821 SHELLEY *Epipsych.* 412 The halcyons brood around the foamless isles. *a* **1881** ROSSETTI *House Life* xii. The blue line of a foamless sea.

foamy ('fəʊmɪ), *a.* Forms: 1 fámiȝ, fǽmiȝ, 4–7 fomy, -ie, 6 fomey, *Sc.* famy, 7- foamy. [OE. *fámiȝ, fǽmiȝ*; f. *fám*, FOAM.]

1. Covered with foam, full of foam, frothy.

a **1000** *Riddles* iv. 19 (Gr.) Famiȝ winneð wæȝ wið wealle. *c* **1385** CHAUCER *L.G.W.* 1208 *Dido*, The fomy brydil with the bit of gold Governyth he. **1513** DOUGLAS *Æneis* XII. vi. 151 The fomy mowthis of the haisty stedis. **1697** DRYDEN *Virg. Georg.* IV. 589 The slipp'ry God..With foamy Tusks will seem a bristly Boar. **1748** WARTON *Enthusiast* 30 Whence a foamy stream, Like Anio, tumbling roars. **1816** W. TAYLOR in *Monthly Mag.* XLI. 331 They drain the foamy mug. **1821** MOIR in *Blackw. Mag.* X. 642 The wild waves curl their bleak and foamy heads.

2. Consisting of, or of the nature of, foam; of, pertaining to, or resembling foam.

1398 TREVISA *Barth. De P.R.* IV. vi. (1495) 89 By medlynge of colera blood semyth redde..by flewme it semyth watry and fomy. **1601** HOLLAND *Pliny* II. 397 The foamie moisture that shel-snails yeeld. **1784** COWPER *Task* VI. 155 The foamy surf That the wind severs from the broken wave. **1878** GILDER *Poet & Master* 14 The foamy whitening Of the water below the mill. **1881** MALLOCK *Rom. 19th Cent.* II. 196 A cloud of foamy lilac-blossom.

Hence **'foaminess.**

1887 FENN *Devon Boys* xviii. 184 The waves lost their fierce foaminess.

foangen, foard, obs. ff. FANG *v.* and FORD *sb.*[1]

fob (fɒb), *sb.*[1] [Of obscure origin. Cf. FOB *v.*[1] Can it be a corruption of OF. *forbe* (mod. *fourbe*) masc. rogue, fem. cunning trick? But this suggestion does not explain the apparent connexion of *fob* sb. and v. with *fop* sb. and v., and Ger. *foppen*.]

†**1.** A cheat, impostor. *Obs. rare*⁻¹.

The association with *faitour* seems to require this active sense rather than the passive one of 'dupe, fool' (= 15th c. sense of *fop*). Cf. Ger. slang *fopper*, in 16th c. a malingerer esp. one who counterfeits madness (see Kluge *Etym. Wb.* ed. 5), which is much the sense of *faitour*.

1393 LANGL. *P. Pl.* C. III. 193 Makeþ of lyer a lang cart to lede alle þese oþere, As fobbes and faitours.

2. A trick, an artifice. Now only slang, *to come the fob on* (U.S.): to impose upon, cheat, trick.

1622 MABBE tr. *Aleman's Guzman d' Alf.* II. 243 Many men would deale more honestly..if these fobs and giggs were not put into their heads by others. **1654** tr. *Scudery's Curia Pol.* 49 Such fobbs and cheats are more tollerable..in persons of mean fortunes. *a* **1700** B. E. *Dict. Cant. Crew*, *Fob*, a cheat, trick. **1852** JUDSON *Myst. N. York* I. vii. 62 'He come ze fob on some of ze nobilitie.'

3. *Comb.*: †**fob-action**, a sham action (at law).

1673 F. KIRKMAN *Unlucky Cit.* 203 They should then arrest you in a Fobb-action at his Suit. **1697** LUTTRELL *Brief. Rel.* (1857) IV. 257 Endeavouring to steal a young lady..by the help of bailifs, who arrested her..in a fob action. **1730–6** BAILEY (folio) s.v., A Fob (or sham) action.

fob (fɒb), *sb.*[2] Also 7, 9 *Sc.* fab, 8 fobb. [of unknown origin; cf. HG. dial. *fuppe* pocket, *fuppen*, *einfuppen* to pocket stealthily; a Ger. word *fupsack* is cited by Skinner.

If the word meant originally a secret pocket, it may be connected with FOB *v.*]

1. A small pocket formerly made in the waistband of the breeches and used for carrying a watch, money, or other valuables.

1653 BROME *Crt. Beggar* II. i. Wks. 1873 I. i. 212 My Fob has been fubd to day of six pieces. **1667** *St. Papers, Dom.* CXCI. No. 63. II, The right side pockett..and the small pockett or fobb. **1711** ADDISON *Spectator* No. 77 ¶1, I saw him..squirt away his watch..into the Thames, and put up the Pebble, he had before found, in his Fob. **1751** SMOLLETT *Per. Pic.* (1779) III. lxxxiii. 294 The..young gentleman, with an hand in each fob, stood whistling an opera-tune. **1819** MOORE *Tom Crib's Mem.* 6 Whether diddling your subjects, and gutting their fobs. **1838** DICKENS *Nich. Nick.* iii, Mr. Nickleby replaced his watch in his fob.

b. *nonce-use.* The contents of the fob, 'cash'.

?*c* **1680** *Royal Resolutions* in *Marvell's Wks.* (Grosart) I. 431 When plate was at pawn, and fob at an ebb.

2. *U.S.* = *fob-chain.*

1889 M HATTON-RIPLEY *From Flag to Flag* xxiv. 211 The tempting fob that hung from his pocket. **1893** FARMER *Slang*, *Fob*..a watch chain or ribbon, with buckle and seals, worn hanging from the fob.

3. A trimming resembling a fob-chain.

1894 *Daily News* 22 June 6/6 Skirt trimmed on the hips with fobs of bright rose-pink velvet, two on either side.

4. *attrib.*, as *fob-pocket*, *-watch*; **fob-chain**, the chain attached to a watch carried in the fob.

1885 H. C. MCCOOK *Tenants Old Farm* 121 Beneath it [his waistcoat] a goodly *fobchain protrudes. **1837** DICKENS *Pickw.* xxviii, With..a gold watch in his *fob pocket. **1884** DOWELL *Tax. in Eng.* III. III. iii. §11 (1888) 273 A *fob watch is in existence that belonged to Oliver Cromwell.

fob (fɒb), *sb.*[3] **a.** Froth, foam; *dial.* **b.** *dial.* (See quot. 1890.)

1838 in HOLLOWAY *Provinc.* **1886** in ELWORTHY *W. Somerset Word-bk.* **1890** *Gloucestersh. Gloss.*, *Fob*, a little bunch or tuft, as of wool, etc.

c. *Soap-making.* The scum or froth which rises to the top of the semi-liquid soap during a certain process of manufacture.

1857 W. MILLER *Elem. Chem.* III. vi. §1. 373 The fob is skimmed off, and the semi-solid pasty mass of soap is transferred to the frames. **1860** *Ure's Dict. Arts* (ed. 5) III. 714. **1884** A. WATT *Soap-Making* v. 47 A black foam or 'fob' appears on the surface, which only ceases when the materials are completely saturated with alkali. **1904** GOODCHILD & TWENEY *Technol. & Sci. Dict.* s.v. *Fitting*, A solid crust or Fob of frothy soap.

Hence **fob** *v.*[3], to froth or foam. **'fobbing** *vbl. sb.*

1838 HOLLOWAY *Provinc.*, *Fob*, to froth as beer does when poured out quickly. *E. Sussex.* **1883** *Hampsh. Gloss.*, *Fob*, to froth as beer. **1898** G. H. HURST *Soaps* 229 The material may rise up in the form of froth very considerably, this proceeding being known to soap-makers as fobbing... It is this liability to fob that renders it undesirable that a soap pan should be fully charged to start with. **1938** *Thorpe's Dict. Appl. Chem.* (ed. 4) II. 95/2 Some brewers add only a small proportion of the hops as the copper is filling up—they help to prevent 'fobbing'.

fob (fɒb), *v.*[1] Also 6–7 fub, fobb(e. See also FOP *v.* [First recorded late in 16th c.; cogn. with or f. FOB *sb.*[1] 1. Cf. Ger. *foppen* to deceive, befool.]

1. *trans.* To cheat, deceive, delude, trick, impose upon, 'take in'; also with *up*. Also, *to fob* (a person) *of* or *out of* (something). *colloq.*

1583 GREENE *Mamillia* Wks. (Grosart) II. 102, I will not ..fobbe you with fayre wordes, and foule deedes. **1593** *Tell-Troth's N.Y. Gift* 25 He..would fobbe him vppe with a thousand vntruthes. **1647** CARTWRIGHT *Ordinary* IV. iv, I won't be fubb'd, ensure your self. **1731** FIELDING *Grub St. Op.* I. v, While every one else he is fobbing, He still may be honest to me. **1843** *Punch* V. 152/2 Kings and ministers have fobbed us of our renown. **1854** *Ibid.* XXVII. 232/1 Noodles who complain..of being fobbed..out of various sums from £25 to £90. **1861** *Standard* 4 Nov., They think themselves fobbed by our dextrous policy.

2. To bring or put *into*, or bestow *upon*, by jobbery or trickery; to palm or pass off *upon*. Also, to get up, procure, or promote by trickery; also with *up*. *to fob in*: to introduce in an underhand way. ? *Obs.*

1653 A. WILSON *Jas. I.* 68 Another young Gentlewoman, that had lesse offended, was fobbed into the place. *Ibid.* 241 These things were fobb'd in by several Popes..to serve their own turns. **1678** R. L'ESTRANGE *Seneca's Mor.* (1702) 522 Here's..the same Thing Fobb'd upon the World over again. **1704** J. LOGAN in *Pa. Hist. Soc. Mem.* IX. 311 Which place was..fobbed upon him. **1715** M. DAVIES *Athen. Brit.* I. 280 That Legendary Triumvirate found ways..to fob into Tinmouth's Gold-finding Legendary their own production of Winefred's Life. **1741** RICHARDSON *Pamela* (1824) I. xxxiii. 330 Don't fob upon us your girl with the Pagan name for Lady Jenny. **1792** WOLCOT (P. Pindar) *Ep. to Ld. Macartney* Wks. 1812 III. 126 No Janus he, with selfish views to fob. **1805** *Morning Chron.* 31 Aug. in *Spirit Pub. Jrnls.* (1806) IX. 208 So now it was time..To fob up an excuse for my sudden retreat. **1825** *Westm. Rev.* IV. 401 We find him with much point, pleasantry, and earnestness, fobbing an ale licence.

3. fob off.

a. To put off deceitfully; to attempt to satisfy with an excuse or pretence; to baffle, cajole; to put off (a person) *with* (something of inferior quality or something less than he has been led to expect).

1597 SHAKS. *2 Hen. IV*, II. i. 37, I haue..bin fub'd off, and fub'd-off, from this day to that day. **1602** ROWLANDS *Greene's Ghost* 8 Fubbing them off with these slender wasted blacke pots. **1650** COWLEY *Guardian* v. vii, I must not be fob'd off thus about my daughter. **1767** B. THORNTON tr. *Plautus* I. 318 The butchers..Will..fob you off With ram for weather mutton. **1842** BARHAM *Ingol. Leg.* Ser. II. *Row in Omnibus*, To exact such a sum For..stalls and pit, And then fob us off with a Fal-de-ral-tit. **1892** *Daily News* 21 Jan. 5/5 Able-bodied paupers have been fobbed off with..broth 'no better than hot water'.

†**b.** To put or shift off (a thing) by deceit or pretence; to get rid of, or set aside by a trick.

1607 SHAKS. *Cor.* I. i. 97 You must not thinke To fobbe off our disgrace with a tale. **1641** MILTON *Reform.* I. (1851) 16 It was not of old that a Conspiracie of Bishops could frustrate and fob off the right of the people.

c. To palm off *upon* (a person); cf. 2.

1894 *Times* 25 July 10/1 If a..novel cannot be fobbed off upon the..people of London..it is rusticated.

Hence **'fobbing** *vbl. sb.*

a **1619** BEAUM. & FL. *Wit at Sev. Weapons* IV. i, Now you talk of fobbing, I wonder the Lady sends not for me according to promise?

fob (fɒb), *v.*[2] [f. FOB *sb.*[2]] *trans.* To put into one's fob, to pocket; also with *up*.

1818 MOORE *Fudge Fam. Paris* vi. 160 The rogue but counts how many guineas He's fobbed. **1821** CLARE *Vill. Minstr.* I. 35 The sailor..styles them 'gentlemen', And fobs his money up. **1840** HOOD *Up Rhine* 4 When the qualm is over [he] quietly fobs the Timepiece. **1842** S. LOVER *Handy Andy* iv, The gentlemen in black silk stockings..have been fobbing fees for three weeks.

'fobbery. *nonce-wd.* [f. FOB *sb.*[1] + -ERY.] Something of the nature of a pretence; a sham.

1688 R. HOLME *Armoury* III. 177/1 These [rules] with a 100 more Fobberies and Foollaries are further set down.

'fobby, *a. Obs.* exc. *dial.* ? = FOGGY.

a **1535** MORE *Wks.* 99 Glotony..maketh..the body fat & fobby. **1895** RYE *E. Angl. Gloss.*, *Fobby*, soft, no substance.

†**'focage.** *Obs.* [ad. mod.L. *focagium*, f. L. *focus*, F. *feu*: see FEUAGE.] = FEUAGE.

1706 in PHILLIPS (ed. Kersey). **1721–82** in BAILEY.

focal ('fəʊkəl), *a.* [ad. mod.L. *focālis*, f. FOCUS: see -AL[1]. Cf. F. *focal*.]

1. Of or pertaining to a focus; collected or situated at a focus. *focal point* = FOCUS 2.

1713 DERHAM *Phys. Theol.* IV. iii. 126 *note*, Whether the Convexity or Concavity of the Drum collects those Rays into a focal Point, or scatters them. **1794** G. ADAMS *Nat. & Exp. Philos.* II. xv. 174 You may, by means of the focal rays from this glass, char or burn a piece of wood. **1808** J. WEBSTER *Nat. Phil.* 185 The rays..will..converge to the focal point. **1855** H. SPENCER *Princ. Psychol.* (1872) I. III. viii. 357 Perfect vision implies a focal adjustment of the eyes. **1862** G. P. SCROPE *Volcanos* 264 The *residuum* of..lava..in what may be called its focal reservoir.

fig. **1755** YOUNG *Centaur* v. Wks. 1757 IV. 239 Human thought, whose scattered rays must be collected, as it were, to a focal point, in order duly to warm our devotion. **1855** MACAULAY *Hist. Eng.* IV. 175 Titus, in order to be near the focal point of political intrigue and faction, had taken a house within the precinct of Whitehall.

2. *Math. focal axis* (in a conic): the axis which passes through the real foci. *focal conic* (i.e. ellipse or hyperbola): in the modular method of generating quadrics, a locus of the modular foci. *focal curve*: the locus of foci of a surface. *focal distance*, (*a*) of the parabola: the distance between the focus and the vertex; (*b*) of the ellipse and hyperbola: the distance between the foci and the centre. *focal lines*: in a quadric cone, the degenerate focal hyperbola. *focal property*: any property of a geometrical locus involving the intersections of the locus with the absolute. †*focal tangent*: a tangent from which the position of the foci of a central conic may be determined. *umbilical focal conic*, in the umbilical method of generating quadrics, the locus of the focus.

1706 W. JONES *Syn. Palmar. Matheseos* 250 If *c h* meet the Focal Tangent in *r*. **1807** HUTTON *Course Math.* II. 118 *A F* the focal distance. **1885** LEUDESDORF *Cremona's Proj. Geom.* 255 The point in which a directrix cuts the focal axis. **1886** P. FROST *Solid Geom.* (ed. 3) 147 The fixed point is called an umbilical focus..and the locus of the focus the umbilical focal conic.

3. *Optics. focal aperture, capacity*: see quots. *focal distance* or *length* (of a lens or mirror): the distance between the centre and the focus. *focal plane*: the locus of the foci of different systems of parallel rays refracted through a lens. Also often attrib., as *focal plane shutter*, a roller-blind shutter with a wide slit that moves across the front of the plate or film. *focal point*: the intersection of a focal plane with the axis of the lens.

1693 E. HALLEY in *Phil. Trans.* No. 205. 960 The focal distance sought. **1753** *Phil. Trans.* XLVIII. 170 An object-lens whose focal length is a little less. **1879** HARLAN *Eyesight* vi. 81 A double concave glass of twelve inches focal distance. **1895** R. S. HEATH *Geom. Optics* (ed. 2) 82 An incident system of parallel rays will then converge to a point on the common focal plane. *Ibid.* 83 It is clear that *F* is the first focal point of the combined system. **1905** *Westm. Gaz.* 21 Oct. 18/2 In photographing rapidly moving objects the focal-plane shutter does give unmistakable distortion. **1906** *Ibid.* 8 Sept. 14/2 In a piece of apparatus so complex as the focal-plane reflecting camera. **1918** *Photo-Miniature* XV. Mar. (Gloss.), *Focal aperture* (relative aperture), a term expressing the speed of a lens... *Focal capacity*, an item in the specification of a camera denoting the greatest focal length of lens which can be used. *Ibid.*, *Focal-plane shutter*, an exposure shutter of the roller-blind or curtain type, placed as nearly in contact with plate or film as possible. **1921** H. G. PONTING *Gt. White South* 58 To make focal-plane photographic exposures. **1950** [see *between-lens shutter* s.v. BETWEEN *adv.* 4].

fig. **1847** EMERSON *Repr. Men, Swedenborg* Wks. (Bohn) I. 315 A colossal soul, he lies vast abroad on his times.. requires a long focal distance to be seen. **1860** PATMORE *Faithf. for Ever* 214 Love requires the focal space Of recollection or of hope, Ere it can measure its own scope.

4. *Path.* Localized or centrally localized, as *focal disease, hæmorrhage*, etc.

1890 in GOULD *Med. Dict.*

Hence **'focally** *adv.*, at a focus.

1839 DE QUINCEY *War* Wks. 1863 IV. 280 The force of European opinion, focally converged upon the subject.

focalize ('fəʊkəlaɪz), *v.* [f. FOCAL *a.* + -IZE.]

1. *trans.* To bring (rays of light, heat, etc.) to a focal point (or focus); to focus.

1845 DE QUINCEY *Nat. Temp. Movem.* Wks. 1863 XI. 170 Light is focalised in the eye, sound in the ear. *c* **1865** J. WYLDE in *Circ. Sc.* I. 29/2 The rays of heat may be collected and focalised.

fig. **1860** T. MARTIN *Horace* Introd. 26 The mirror which focalizes for their old age the gathered wisdom of a lifetime. **1865** *Lond. Rev.* 9 Dec. 609/1 At the various central offices, the information..can be focalized.

2. To adjust or arrange the focus of (the eye); also *absol.* and *refl.* (of the eye).

1878 tr. *Ziemssen's Cycl. Pract. Med.* XVII. 668 The supposed amaurosis of many observers..is the result of the loss of the power of focalizing. **1886** W. F. WARREN in *Homilet. Rev.* (U.S.) Jan. 54 Gradually focalizing our eyes for remoter objects. *Ibid.*, Your eye, even if rightly directed, is focalizing itself upon the wrong object.

3. *Med.* To confine to a certain focus (FOCUS *sb.* 4). Also *intr.* for *pass.*

1906 *Practitioner* Nov. 589 The severer disturbances of the liver, those in which the intoxication..focalises in the liver.

Hence **'focalizing** *vbl. sb.* and *ppl. a.*; **'focalized** *ppl. a.* Also **focali'zation**, the action of focalizing.

1871 MORLEY *Voltaire* iii. (1872) 119 Voltaire does not use these focalising words and turns of composition. **1883** J. MILLINGTON *Are we to read backwards?* 71 Spectacles.. restoring to the eye its former focalizing power. **1887** *Sci. Amer.* 23 Apr. 261/2 Focalization in the eye was accomplished by a most wonderful condition, that of flexibility in the crystalline lens. **1893** *Chicago Advance* 24 Aug., Such a focalization of all-around information on any one subject has rarely ever been witnessed. **1906** [see DETOXICATE *v.*]. **1914** V. HORSLEY in S. Paget *Sir V. Horsley* (1919) II. 196 Every case of focalised epilepsy. **1937** G. W. ALLPORT *Personality* xi. 295 We are left with a concept of trait as a generalized and focalized neuropsychic system (peculiar to the individual). **1951** H. A. MURRAY in Parsons & Shils *Toward Gen. Theory Action* 452 The focalizations and reëvaluations that occur in the mind of a hungry man. **1959** S ARIETI *Amer. Handbk. Psychiatry* I. I. iv. 103 A need is a general disposition which commonly becomes associated (through 'focalization', or 'canalization', as Murphy would say) with a number of specific entities.

focaloid ('fəʊkəlɔɪd). *Math.* [f. as prec. + -OID.] A shell, in general indefinitely thin, bounded by two confocal ellipsoidal surfaces.

1879 THOMSON & TAIT *Nat. Phil.* §494 The attraction of a homogeneous solid ellipsoid is the same through all external space as the attraction of a homogeneous focaloid of equal mass coinciding with its surface.

† **'focary.** *Obs.*$^{-1}$ [ad. L. *focāri-us*, f. *focus*: see FOCUS *sb.* and -ARY.] One who tends the hearth or fire.

?*c* **1500** in *Myrr. Our Lady* (1873) Introd. xxi. *note*, In the order & degre of a lay brother or ffocary.

foc(c)he, obs. form of FETCH *v.*

focer, var. FORCER, *Obs.*, a chest or coffer.

fochesave, obs. form of VOUCHSAFE.

fochtyn, *Sc.* form of *fought*, p. p. of FIGHT *v.*

† **'focile.** *Anat. Obs.* Forms: 5 fosile, 6 faucylle, focyll, focil, 6–8 focile. [ad. med.Lat. *focile*. Cf. Pr. *focil*, Fr. *focile*, Pg. and It. *focile*.

The med.Lat. word was a transferred use of *focīle* steel for striking fire (see FUSIL). The Arabian anatomists applied the word *zand*, one of a pair of sticks for producing fire by friction (dual *zandān*), to these bones on account of their shape; the Lat. translators rendered this by *focile* as being the word most nearly equivalent in literal sense.]

One of the bones of the fore-arm or of the leg. ***greater focile***, the ulna or tibia. ***lesser*** (or ***over***) ***focile***, the radius or fibula.

c **1400** *Lanfranc's Cirurg.* 157 þe þombe..conteyneþ his firste boon wiþ þe extremite of þe ouer fosile. **1541** R. COPLAND *Guydon's Quest. Chirurg.* D ij b, The faucylles or forke bones. **1543** TRAHERON *Vigo's Chirurg.* (1586) 281 The great focile is that which susteineth the arme. **1638** A. READ *Treat. Chirurg.* ii. 15 [A] Taylor..fractured both the focils of the legge, a little below the knee. **1721** NAISH in *Phil. Trans.* XXXI. 228 The Ligament that ties the Fociles together.

attrib. **1541** R. COPLAND *Guydon's Quest. Chirurg.* K iv b, Of what shape are yᵉ two focyl bones? **1548–77** VICARY *Anat.* vii. (1888) 49 Of the two Focel bones..the lesse goeth from the Elbowe to the Thombe. **1706** PHILLIPS (ed. Kersey), *Focil-bone.*

† **'focillate**, *v. Obs.*$^{-0}$ [f. L. *focillāt-* ppl. stem of *focillā-re* to revive or refresh, f. FOCUS: see FOCUS *sb.* and -ATE.] (See quots.)

1676 in COLES. **1681** BLOUNT *Glossogr.*, *Focillate*..to nourish, comfort, or refresh. **1721–90** in BAILEY.

Hence † **'focillated** *ppl. a.* Also † **foci'llation.**

1727 BAILEY vol. II, *Focillated.* **1658** PHILLIPS, *Focillation.* **1721–90** BAILEY, *Focillation.*

focimeter (fəʊ'sɪmɪtə(r)). *Photogr.* Also focometer. [f. FOC-US + -METER.] An instrument for finding the chemical focus of a lens which has not been properly achromatized.

1853 R. HUNT *Man. Photogr.* II. iv. 159 M. Claudet has also devised a very ingenious instrument for focusing, which he calls his Focimeter. **1891** S. P. THOMPSON in *Proc. R. Soc.* XLIX. 227 These principles are embodied in an instrument described in the paper, and called a focometer.

focimetry (fəʊ'sɪmɪtrɪ). Also **focometry.** [f. as prec. + Gr. -μετρία measurement.] Measurement of focal distance.

1881 G. R. PIGGOTT in *Nature* No. 622. 515 If now an over-corrected lens were substituted, the diffraction rings.. and the nebulosity..exactly changed positions as regards focimetry. **1891** S. P. THOMPSON in *Proc. R. Soc.* XLIX. 225 The accepted methods of focometry.

focke, obs. Sc. form of FOLK.

focoid ('fəʊkɔɪd). [f. FOC-US + -OID.] One of the points in which every circle in a given plane meets the line at infinity in that plane.

1881 C. TAYLOR *Geom. Conics* 308 The two focoids or circular points at infinity.

fo'c'sle: see FORECASTLE.

focus ('fəʊkəs), *sb. Pl.* foci; also focuses, in the U.K. often written irregularly focusses. [a. L. *focus* hearth, fireplace, in various modern uses.

The Lat. word was first used in sense 1 by Kepler (*Astron. pars optica* iv. 4, written in 1604); his reason for the choice of the name is not stated, but it is conjectured that the optical sense 2, 'burning point of a lens or mirror' (which is easily derived from the lit. sense) must have been already in existence; this would account for Kepler's use, as the 'burning point' or 'focus' of a parabolic mirror is situate at the geometrical 'focus' of its curvature. Sense 4 is from medical Latin. In all senses cf. Fr. *foyer*:—L. **focārium* f. *focus*.]

1. *Geom.* **a.** In plane geometry: One of the points from which the distances to any point of a given curve are connected by a linear relation.

Also defined as a point from which a pair of isotropic tangents can be drawn to a curve; or as the intersection of tangents from the points in which the line at infinity meets a co-planar circle. (For definitions specially relating to the focus of a conic, see quots. 1881 and 1893.)

1656 HOBBES *Six Lessons* Wks. 1845 VII. 317 The focus of an hyperbole, is in the axis. **1703** MOXON *Mech. Exerc.* 272 Which two points are called the Focusses, or burning points. **1734** tr. *Maupertuis' Diss.* 19 in *Keill's Exam.* (ed. 2), The Orbits of the Planets are..Ellipses, in whose Focus the Sun is. **1807** HUTTON *Course Math.* II. 96 The ellipse and hyperbola have each two foci; but the parabola only one. **1851** NICHOL *Archit. Heav.* 199 The second star being in the focus and not the centre of the ellipse. **1881** C. TAYLOR *Geom. Conics* 1 A conic is a curve traced by a point which moves in a plane containing a fixed point and a fixed straight line in such a way that its distance from the fixed point is in a constant ratio to its perpendicular distance from the fixed straight line. The fixed point is called a focus. **1893** J. W. RUSSELL *Pure Geom.* vii. 67 A focus of a conic is a point at which every two conjugate lines are perpendicular.

b. In solid geometry (see quot.).

1874 G. SALMON *Analytic Geom.* (ed. 3) 109 A point through which can be drawn two lines, each touching the surface and the imaginary circle at infinity and such that the tangent plane to the surface through either also touches the circle at infinity.

2. a. *Optics, Heat*, etc. The point at which rays meet after being reflected or refracted; also, the point from which the rays appear to proceed (= *virtual focus*: see 2 b).

1685 BOYLE *Effects Motion* ii. 13 Sunbeams refracted or reflected by a burning-glass to a focus. **1704** NEWTON *Opticks* I. vi. 7 The point from which rays diverge, or to which they converge, may be called their focus. **1831** BREWSTER *Optics* i. 11 The points that were formerly the radiant points being now the foci. **1853** HERSCHEL *Pop. Lect. Sc.* ii. §24 (1873) 65 A far greater heat than can be produced in the focus of any burning-glass. **1865** LIVINGSTONE *Zambesi* ii. 59 This deep trough-like shape caused the sun's rays to converge as into a focus.

b. With various defining words.

conjugate foci: see CONJUGATE *a* 6 b; ***principal focus***, the point at which parallel rays meet after passing through a convergent lens; ***solar focus*** = prec.; ***virtual focus***, a point at which diverging rays would meet if their directions were reversed; ***actinic*** or ***chemical focus*** (of a lens), the point to which the actinic rays converge.

1706 PHILLIPS (ed. Kersey), *Virtual Focus*, or *Point of Divergence* (in Dioptricks). **1812–16** J. SMITH *Panorama Sc. & Art* I. 426 When parallel rays fall upon a double-convex glass, KG, they will..meet..in a point or principal focus at F. **1874** *Lommel's Light* 90 The lenses of the second group have virtual foci. **1890** WOODBURY *Encycl. Photogr.* 293 Unless the lens be rendered achromatic, the actinic or chemical focus does not coincide with the visual focus.

c. *transf.* and *fig.*

1762 GOLDSM. *Cit. W.* lxxi, A box where they might see and be seen; one, as they expressed it, in the very focus of public view. **1781** COWPER *Conversation* 239 Centering in a focus round and neat, Let all your rays of information meet. **1824** CARLYLE in Froude *Life* (1882) I. 260, I am meditating ..on the great focus of all purposes—the arranging of my future life. **1874** MICKLETHWAITE *Mod. Par. Churches* 106 If it [a picture] be placed over the altar, it is in the very focus of the building.

† **d.** *Theatr.* The best-illuminated part of the stage. *Obs.*

1881 *Era Almanack* 97 He tried to keep me out of the focus! **1885** *Eng. Illustr. Mag.* 647/1 Every body tried to get into what was called the focus—the 'blaze of publicity' furnished by the 'float' or footlights.

e. That point or position at which an object must be situated, in order that the image produced by the lens may be clear and well-defined. Hence *in*, or *out of focus*, lit. and fig. ***depth of focus*** (of a lens): the power of giving a 'sharp' image of objects not in the same plane; now usu. expressed as a distance, and (*a*) used as a synonym of *depth of field* (see FIELD *sb.* 16 c); (*b*) distinguished from this and used with the sense: the distance between the two extreme axial points behind a lens at which an image is judged to be in focus.

1713 DERHAM *Phys.-Theol.* IV. ii. 89 *note*, If the paper..be ..in the focus of the glass, [the image will be] distinct. **1727** SWIFT *Petit. Colliers &c.* Wks. 1755 III. I. 129 To know the due distances of the said focus's. **1799** *Med. Jrnl.* II. 228 At the nearest focus of distinct vision. **1840** DICKENS *Barn. Rudge* i, John gradually concentrated the whole power of his eyes into one focus. **1858** *A B C of Photogr.* (ed. 10) 48 The focus of a portrait lens is very limited in depth. **1860** C. WALDACK *Treat. Photogr.* ii. 22 The most essential conditions required in a portrait tube, are, rapidity of action, sharpness, and depth of focus... It is for want of depth of focus, that in so many portraits the hands..are out of shape. **1890** WOODBURY *Encycl. Photogr.* 295 After a certain distance all objects will be in focus. **1894** H. DRUMMOND *Ascent of Man* vi, Evolution was given to the modern world out of focus. **1911**, **1939** [see *depth of field* s.v. FIELD *sb.* 16 c]. **1940** MORTIMER & SOWERBY *Wall's Dict. Photogr.* (ed. 15) 183 Depth of focus. Synonyms: Depth of Field, Depth of Definition. **1948** A. L. M. SOWERBY *Dict. Photogr.* (ed. 17) 179 Depth of focus, strictly, means range of movement of lens that is permissible before image of object focused upon becomes noticeably unsharp. More usually applied to range of distances over which an object can move without becoming noticeably unsharp... In this sense..synonyms are 'Depth of Field' and 'Depth of Definition'. **1958** M. L. HALL *Newnes Compl. Amat. Photogr.* 48 Another type of depth of focus scale is engraved upon the lens barrel. **1961** G. MILLERSON *Technique Telev. Prod.* iii. 35 The near and far distances..give us the depth of field (often erroneously called depth of focus—a different matter entirely). **1966** *McGraw-Hill Encycl. Sci. & Technol.* II. 431/1 There may be some latitude in focusing in which there is no apparent change in sharpness. This distance is known as the depth of focus.

f. ***to bring***, etc., ***in, into, to a focus***; *lit.* and *fig.*

1788 FRANKLIN *Autobiog.* Wks. 1840 I. 122 The bringing all these scattered counsels into a focus. **1860** TYNDALL *Glac.* II. xxiv. 354 The place where the rays were brought to a focus behind the lens. **1875** JEVONS *Money* (1878) 252 The transactions of many different individuals..are brought to a focus.

g. The focal length (of a lens); also, the adjustment (of the eye, or an eyeglass) necessary to produce a clear image.

1693 E. HALLEY in *Phil. Trans.* No. 205. 960 This dioptric problem, is that of finding the focus of any sort of lens. **1757** ELLIS *ibid.* L. 287 A lens of about one inch and half focus. **1837** BREWSTER *Magnet.* 332 The focus of the lens being suited to the distance of the needle. **1861** PALGRAVE *Gold. Treas.* Pref., Rapid alteration of the eye's focus in looking at the landscape. **1871** TYNDALL *Fragm. Sc.* (1879) I. ii. 50 The focus was attained, first by the pupil and afterwards by the retina.

3. Similarly in *Acoustics*. The point or space towards which the sound waves converge.

1644 EVELYN *Diary* 8 Feb., Standing at one of the focuses, which is under a tree..the voice seems to descend from the clouds. **1843** J. MARTINEAU *Chr. Life* xliii. (1876) 499 Could we only find the focus of those stray tones. **1857** THOREAU *Maine W.* (1894) 362 We were exactly in the focus of many echoes.

4. Of a disease: The principal seat (in the body); also, a point where its activity is manifest.

1684 tr. *Bonet's Merc. Compit.* VI. 183 That the focus of burning fevers is in the Head Hippocrates seems to assert. **1796** H. HUNTER tr. *St. Pierre's Stud. Nat.* (1799) III. 231 She informed me that the focus of my disorder was in the nerves. **1854** JONES & SIEV. *Pathol. Anat.* (1874) 304 Sclerosis of particular regions or isolated foci occurs in the Cord as in the brain.

5. a. The centre of activity, or area of greatest energy, of a storm, volcanic eruption, etc.

1796 H. HUNTER tr. *St. Pierre's Stud. Nat.* (1799) I. p. lx, The focus of the tides is removing farther and farther from our coasts. **1804** C. B. BROWN tr. *Volney's View* 98 One of the great layers of the country, where earthquakes have their principal focus. **1832** LYELL *Princ. Geol.* II. 127 The original isle was the primitive focus, or centre, of a certain type of vegetation. **1862** SCROPE *Volcanos* 266 Any..focus or reservoir of lava from which an eruption has proceeded. **1869** PHILLIPS *Vesuv.* ii. 13 Vesuvius was seen to be the focus of the eruption. **1875** BEDFORD *Sailor's Pocket-bk.* iv. (ed. 2) 78 The centre or focus of the West Indian hurricanes.

b. *fig.* A centre or 'hotbed' (of intrigue, sedition, etc.); a centre of activity or energy.

1808 WELLINGTON in Gurw. *Desp.* II. 440 Poonah is the focus of his intrigues. **1830** R. KNOX *Béclard's Anat.* Life 8 Central Schools..had been established in the departments as so many foci of knowledge. **1837** W. IRVING *Capt. Bonneville* (1849) p. xv, New-York, the great focus of American enterprise. **1870** HUXLEY *Lay Serm.* i. (ed. 5) 5 The principal focus of scientific activity.

6. *nonce-uses.* **a.** In Lat. sense: A fireplace or furnace; in quot. *fig.* **b.** A centre of radiant heat.

1779 J. MOORE *View Soc. Fr.* I. xx. 175, I consider these men as the enemies of their country, and that place as a focus for consuming freedom. **1794** J. HUTTON *Philos. Light, etc.* 174 Surrounding particles receiving that addition of heat from the focus, are made to burn; and in burning, these coals return that heating species of light to the focus, for the increase of its burning.

7. *attrib.*, as ***focus point, error.***

1891 *Pall Mall G.* 31 Aug. 2/1 That all railway servants shall have..not more than an agreed amount of focus error.

focus ('fəʊkəs), *v.* Pples. focused, -ing; in the U.K. commonly, but irregularly, written focussed, -ing. [f. prec. sb.]

1. *trans.* To draw to a focus; to cause to converge to or as to a focus.

1875 BEDFORD *Sailor's Pocket-bk.* v. (ed. 2) 132 The catoptric system..requiring less delicacy in putting up and focussing the light. **1881** A. G. BELL *Sound by Radiant Energy* 2 A beam of sunlight was focussed into one end of an open tube. **1895** *Jrnl. R. Inst. Brit. Archit.* 28 Mar. 353 Focussing and concentrating the sound in one or more points in his building.

b. *fig.*

1807 *Uti Possidetis* xxx, All the Talent of the Nation Focuss'd in Cab'net concentration. **1862** W. M. ROSSETTI in *Fraser's Mag.* Aug. 195 Focussing our observation to a single point. **1863** J. BROWN *Horæ Subs.* (ed. 3) 80 Inferior to my father..in power of—so to speak—focussing himself. **1888** BURGON *Lives 12 Gd. Men* I. iii. 331 He could.. instantly focus his thoughts.

c. *intr.* for *refl.* To converge to or as to a focus.

1863 THORNBURY *True as Steel* I. 148 Light flashing and focussing on armour. **1888** *Harper's Mag.* Apr. 764 The eyes..flamed as if the life of the man had centralized and focussed within them.

2. To adjust the focus of (the eye, a lens, etc.).

1814 W. TAYLOR in *Monthly Mag.* XXXVIII. 214 Accordingly as the eye is supposed to be focussed for seeing the foreground of the distance. *c* **1865** J. WYLDE in *Circ. Sc.* I. 66/2 Arrangements..for focussing the lenses. **1881** TYLOR *Anthropol.* ii. 47 The eagle's eyes are focussed to see small objects far beyond man's range. **1885** *Illustr. Lond. News* 9 May 491/3 Austell focussed his eye-glass on his wife.

absol. **1853** *Hand-bk. Photogr.* 13 It is well in focusing to make the first adjustment by placing the lens midway. **1890** WOODBURY *Encycl. Photogr.* 294 Focus upon some distinct object about 150 or 200 yards away.

3. To bring into focus; to bring (the image, etc.) to the proper focus.

1775 S. J. PRATT *Lib. Opin.* (1783) III. 8 Sir Charles Crazy *focuss'd* her through an opera-glass. **1858** *A B C of Photogr.* (ed. 10) 57 Having focussed the right-hand view, half of the sensitive plate is first impressed. *c* **1865** J. WYLDE in *Circ. Sc.* I. 143/1 The image..is focussed..by..adjusting the lens. **1879** *Cassell's Techn. Educ.* III. 97 Unless the picture be accurately focussed it will appear blurred.

focusable ('fəʊkəsəb(ə)l), *a.* [f. prec. + -ABLE.] That may be focused.

1889 H. BLAND *Fab. Ess. Socialism* (ed. Shaw) 218 Thus far the outlook has been clear and focusable enough.

focused ('fəʊkəst), *ppl. a.* [f. FOCUS *v.* and *sb.* + -ED.]

1. a. In senses of the vb.; brought to or into a focus.

1864 *Daily Tel.* 12 Apr., Photographers alone has he shunned..and if ever he runs away from anything, it will be from a focussed lens. **1890** WOODBURY *Encycl. Photogr.* 294 Make the focussed image fall on one of these lines.

b. *transf.* and *fig.*

1892 J. D. HOOD *Waterspouts Yorksh. Wolds* 25 The force of the focussed body of water made a triple rent down the slope of the hill. **1909** *Milton Memorial Lect.* 99 The beautiful, but not strictly focussed scenery of 'Lycidas'. **1934** H. G. WELLS *Exper. Autobiogr.* I. iii. §2. 95 Yet impossible as it is to get any focussed clearness and exactitude here, it is equally impossible to ignore this phase of completed puerility.

2. Having a focus (of a specified length); used only in comb., as ***short focused***.

1858 L. PRICE *Man. Photogr. Manip.* ii. 69 'Short-focused' lenses are employed for children.

focuser ('fəʊkəsə(r)). [f. FOCUS *v.* + -ER^{1}.]

1. A focusing-glass.

1890 WOODBURY *Encycl. Photogr.* s.v. *Focussing Glass.*

2. An electrostatic or magnetic device for focusing particles.

1954 *Physical Rev.* 2nd Ser. XCV. 284/1 Some selection of rotational states could be effected by such a focuser. Similarly, a focuser using magnetic fields would allow spectroscopy of atoms. **1958** *Sci. News* L. 60 The stream of molecules..passes through the focuser, which consists of four cylindrical electrodes... Those in the higher of the two energy states are deflected toward the axis of the focuser. **1963** G. TROUP *Masers & Lasers* (ed. 2) viii. 120 An electrostatic focuser and state separator..was used to provide a beam of excited molecules.

'focusing, *vbl. sb.* [f. as prec. + -ING^{1}.]

1. The action of the vb. FOCUS (*gerundially*).

1851 RUSKIN *Mod. Paint.* II. III. i. v. §18 The right gradation or focusing of light and colour. **1881** MIVART *Cat* 295 The focussing of rays coming from points varying in remoteness. **1883** A. BARRATT *Phys. Metempiric* 217 Thought is the focussing of phenomena into a universe.

2. *attrib.* and *Comb.*, chiefly in names of appliances used by photographers, as ***focusing screen, tube***; **focusing cloth** (see quot. 1890); **focusing-glass** (see quot. 1858).

1853 in *Jrnl. Photogr. Soc.* I. No. 3. 39/2 A *focusing cloth. **1890** WOODBURY *Encycl. Photogr., Focussing Cloth*, a black cloth used for covering over the head and back portion of the camera to exclude all extraneous light. **1853** in *Jrnl. Photogr. Soc.* I. No. 3. 39/2 The *Focusing glass. **1858** T. SUTTON *Dict. Photogr., Focussing Glass*..a magnifier used for the purpose of magnifying the image on the ground glass, and enabling the operator to get it into better focus. *Ibid.* 56 The real image formed by a convex lens is received on a *focussing screen.

focusless ('fəʊkəslɪs), *a.* [f. FOCUS *sb.* + -LESS.] Without focus.

1879 G. MACDONALD *Sir Gibbie* III. xv. 241 Something like a flash of cold moonlight on wintred water gleamed over ..his poor focusless eyes.

focyll, fodar, obs. forms of FOCILE, FOTHER.

†**'fodden,** *v. Obs.* [? repr. OE. **fódnian*, f. *fódan-* FOOD.] ? *intr.* To be produced.

? *a* **1400** *Morte Arth.* 3247 Alle froytez foddenid was þat floreschede in erthe.

fodder ('fɒdə(r)), *sb.* Forms: 1 fód(d)or, fód(d)er, fóddur, 2 fodre, 3 *south.* vodder, 4 foddre, 4–7 foder, 5 foddur, *south.* voddur, fo(o)dyr, 6 footer, 6–8 fother, 3– fodder. [OE. *fōdor* str. neut. = MDu. and Du. *voeder*, OHG. *fuotar* (MHG. *vuoter*, Ger. *futter*), ON. *fóðr* (Sw., Da. *foder*) :—OTeut. **fôðrom*:—pre-Teut. **pāt-ró-m*, f. root *pāt-* to feed: see FOOD.

The homophonous word in all Teut. langs., with the sense of 'sheath, case,' is distinct both in root and suffix, as it represents OAryan **pō-tróm*.]

†**1.** Food in general. *Obs.*

c **1000** *Canons Edgar* §15 in Thorpe *Anc. Laws* II. 283 Gif ..þam þe þæs beþurfe..fyr & foddor. *c* **1205** LAY. 27031 Heo weoren ifaren into þan londe, fodder to biwinnen. *c* **1374** CHAUCER *Boeth.* IV. metr. vii. 115 (Camb. MS.) He.. hath put an vnmeke lorde foddre to his crwel hors. **1634** J. TAYLOR (Water P.) *Gt. Eater Kent* 12 Let any come in the shape of fodder or eating-stuffe, it is welcome.

2. Food for cattle. Now in a more restricted sense: Dried food, as hay, straw, etc., for stall-feeding.

c **1000** ÆLFRIC *Gen.* xlii. 27 þa undyde hira an his sacc & wolde syllan his assan foddur. *c* **1100** *Voc.* in Wr.-Wülcker 501 *Sagina*, fodre. *a* **1225** *Ancr. R.* 416 þeonne mot heo þenchen of þe kues foddre. *a* **1300** *Cursor M.* 3317 (Cott.) Fodder and hai þou sal find bun. *c* **1386** CHAUCER *Reeve's Prol.* 14 Gras-tyme is doon, my fodder is now forage. *c* **1440** *Promp. Parv.* 168/2 Foddur, bestys mete, or forage. **1562** TURNER *Herbal* II. 74 Som nationes make fother for Cattel of Dates. **1697** DRYDEN *Virg. Georg.* III. 331 The youthful Bull must..in the Stall..his Fodder find. **1765** T. HUTCHINSON *Hist. Mass.* I. 207 The hay..serves for fodder for their cattle. **1816** J. SMITH *Panorama Sc. & Art* II. 634 Bean-straw makes good fodder, when cut to chaff. **1883** S. C. HALL *Retrospect* II. 323 There was fodder running to waste on the slopes of every mountain.

transf. **1890** A. J. WAUTERS *Stanley's Emin Pasha Exped.* ix. 167 For fodder all they [locomotives] want is wood.

†**3.** Child, offspring. *Obs. rare*$^{-1}$. Cf. FOOD *sb.* 6.

13.. *K. Alis.* 645 Kyng Phelip saide to the modur, 'Thou hast born a sori foder!'

4. *attrib.* and *Comb.*, as ***fodder-crop, -cutter, grass, house, passage, plant, -rack, -stack***; **fodder-cheese** (see quot. 1884); **fodder-corn**, a supply of fodder for the horses of a feudal lord, or an equivalent in money; also the right of exacting this; also *U.S.*, maize used as fodder.

1784 TWAMLEY *Dairying* 25 As the quantity of..*Fodder Cheese sent to London Markets clearly shews. **1884** *Chesh. Gloss., Fodder cheese*, cheese made..when they [cows] are being foddered on hay. **1655** DUGDALE *Monast. Angl.* I. 297 a, Redditus qui dicuntur Hidagium & *Foddercorn. **1856** in *D.A.* s.v., Hauled up two loads wood & 1 of fodder corn. **1947** *Reader's Digest* Jan. 59/2 Barns and stable-loft bulging with hay, grain and fodder corn. **1850** *Rep. U.S. Comm. Patents 1849: Agric.* 158 It is..a *fodder-crop and an improver of the land. **1867** *Rep. Mass. Board Agric.* I. 297 Hay and *fodder cutters have become quite indispensable. **1830** LINDLEY *Nat. Syst. Bot.* 304 The best *fodder-Grasses of Europe are usually dwarf species. **1807** P. GASS *Jrnl.* 209 This lodge is built much after the form of the Virginia *fodder houses. **1882** OGILVIE, **Fodder passage*, the passage in a cattle-shed along which the food is carried for cattle. **1848** *Rep. U.S. Comm. Patents 1847* 229 The perfection which has been obtained in the root culture and of the *fodder-plants. **1894** *Daily News* 25 June 6/6 A new *fodder plant, known as the Siberian knot-grass. **1902** *Daily Chron.* 9 Sept. 3/1 When he [*sc.* a horse] happens to be confronted with an overhead *fodder-rack..he raises his head to snatch a mouthful and then lowers it to the pendent position. **1961** *Countryman* LVIII. 464, I doubt if a single Corsican flock knows the luxury of fodder-racks for the night. *a* **1738** W. BYRD *Hist. Dividing Line* (1929) 305 When it rain'd, or was colder than Ordinary, the whole Family took refuge in a *Fodder Stack (not far from their roofless house). **1835** A. B. LONGSTREET *Georgia Scenes* (1871) 24 He commanded all the corn-cribs and fodder-stacks in Georgia. **1890** *Century Mag.* Dec. 284 The fodder stacks..might conceal dozens of guerrillas.

fodder ('fɒdə(r)), *v.* Forms: 3 foþer, 4 foddre, 5–6 foder, 7–8 fother, 6– fodder. [f. prec. sb.; cf. MDu. and Du. *voederen*, OHG. *fuotiren* (MHG. *vuotern, vüetern*, Ger. *füttern*), ON. *fóðra.*] *trans.* To give fodder to (cattle); to feed *with* (something) as fodder. †In early use *gen.* To feed.

a **1300** *E.E. Psalter* xxx[i]. 3 For þi name me lede and foþer [*printed* froþer: Vulg. *enutries*] þou sal. **1382** [see FODDERED *ppl. a.*]. *c* **1460** *Towneley Myst.* (Surtees) 89 Let us go foder our mompyns. **1523** FITZHERB. *Husb.* §70 Horses and shepe, maye not be fodered togyder in wynter. **1641** BEST *Farm. Bks.* (Surtees) 73 Yow are neaver to..fother sheepe soe longe as they can gette any thing on the grownde. **1707** MORTIMER *Husb.* 172 Straw will do well enough to Fodder them with. **1773** BARKER in *Phil. Trans.* LXIII. 222 There was so little grass..that many were forced to fodder their cattle. **1832** MISS MITFORD *Village* Ser. v. (1863) 328 A lad ..had gone thither for hay to fodder his cattle. **1876** *Whitby Gloss.* s.v. *Fodder*, 'Fodder'd up', fed and bedded, as the stalled animals.

transf. and *fig.* **1659** H. MORE *Immort. Soul* III. xviii. §12 This notion of foddering the Stars with the thick foggs of the Earth. **1742** YOUNG *Nt. Th.* VII. 42 This foreign field, Where nature fodders him [man] with other food. **1891** *Daily News* 26 Jan. 6/3 They..fodder their souls on all kinds of stale and withered doctrinal herbage.

†**b.** To give cattle fodder upon (ground). Also *to fodder on* (ground), in *indirect passive. Obs.*

1655 [see FODDERING 1]. **1664** EVELYN *Kal. Hort.* May 56 A place that has been well fother'd on. **1693** [see FODDERED *ppl. a.*].

Hence **'foddered** *ppl. a.*

1382 WYCLIF *1 Sam.* xxviii. 24 A foddred [**1388** fat] calf. **1692** DRYDEN *Cleomenes* III. ii, Accursed be thou, grass-eating foddered god! **1693** EVELYN *De la Quint. Compl. Gard.* Gloss., *Fotherd Grounds*, ground upon which Cattel are fed in Winter, with Hay, &c., to better it. **1713** YOUNG *Last Day* II. 256 The fodder'd beast. **1864** *Ret. Agric. Soc. Maine* 52 It will require the attraction of provender..to bring them [*sc.* sheep] back to their foddered rack.

fodder, obs. form of FOTHER.

fodderer ('fɒdərə(r)). [f. FODDER *v.* + -ER^{1}.] One who fodders or feeds (cattle).

1623 MINSHEU, *Cruero*, a fodderer of cattle. **1691** J. P. *Quakers Unmasked* 16 Cattle..that kick against their Fodderers. **1755** in JOHNSON; and in mod. Dicts.

'foddering, *vbl. sb.* [f. FODDER *v.* + -ING^{1}.]

1. The action of the vb. FODDER.

c **1570** *Pride & Lowl.* (1841) 54 Farthest..from skil, But yf it be in fodderyng of a beast. **1655** HARTLIB *Legacy* (ed. 3) 249 This way of pasturing of Clover will be a kind of foddering of the land, and rather improve then impair it. **1727** BRADLEY *Fam. Dict.* s.v. *Barn*, Barns..for..the more convenient Foddering of Cattle with the Straw.

2. *concr.* An allowance of fodder.

1601 HOLLAND *Pliny* I. 401 Ten pound of it is a sufficient foddering for an horse. **1808** CURWEN *Econ. Feeding Stock* 55 A foddering of straw from six to eight pounds.

fig. **1622** MABBE tr. *Aleman's Guzman d'Alf.* II. 46 Then did she reduce vnto her remembrance..what drie fodderings he did giue her. **1662** *Rump Songs* (1874) I. 161 A foddering of Prayer four hours by the Clock. **1843** CARLYLE *Misc.* (1857) IV. 267 Heavy fodderings of Jesuit theology.

3. *attrib.* and *Comb.*, as ***foddering band, boy, cord, ground, herb, place, rack,*** † ***stead, time.***

1837 *Boston Advert.* 17 Jan. 2/2 One fork and one *foddering band. **1827** CLARE *Sheph. Cal.* 21 Nor ling'ring wait the *foddering-boy. **1890** *Gloucestersh. Gloss.*, **Foddering cord*, a hair and hemp cord used for binding up hay to take out to beasts. **1789** W. MARSHALL *Gloucester* I. 230 A small dry grass inclosure, (near the homestall)—provincially a '*foddering ground'—where they have their fill of hay. **1816** F. VANDERSTRAETEN *Impr. Agric.* 8 Roots and *foddering herbs for cattle. **1587** MASCALL *Govt. Cattle* (1627) 203 The Shepheard..shall often cleanse the *foddering places of his sheepe. **1697** DRYDEN *Virg. Georg.* III. 606 Salt Herbage for the *fodd'ring Rack provide. **1619** *N. Riding Rec.* IV. 153 A messuage and land with one *fotheringe stead. **1641** BEST *Farm. Bks.* (Surtees) 10 As soon as *fotheringe time is past..remoove them.

fodderless ('fɒdəlɪs), *a.* [f. FODDER *sb.* + -LESS.] Without fodder.

1852 *Tait's Mag.* XIX. 760 Fodderless cattle.

†**'fodding.** *Obs.*$^{-1}$ [? for *fadyng*:—OE. *fadung* apportionment.] ? A division.

13.. *K. Alis.* 48 Wyse men fond also there, xij foddyng to thes yere..Thes furste was cleped Mars, That othir Averil [etc.].

†**fode,** *sb. Obs. rare*$^{-1}$. ? One who beguiles with fair words (see the verb).

a **1529** SKELTON *Manerly Margery* 10 Strawe, Jamys foder, ye play the fode, I am no hakney for your rode.

†**fode,** *v. Obs.* Forms: α. 6 foad, foude, foode, 7 foord, 4–6 fode. β. 6 foder, fowder, foadre. [Of obscure etymology.

Commonly regarded as a fig. use of FOOD *v.* The occasional use of *to fede forth* instead of *to fode forth* (see FEED *v.* 2 b) seems to show that the word was sometimes so interpreted in 15–16th c.; but the spelling *foade*, and the late survival of *fode*, prove that the vowel sound was not that which represented OE. *ó*, but that which represented OE. *á* or OE. *o* in open syllables. No certain connexions are known; Grimm gives several examples of an early mod.Ger. *fot* sb., app. meaning 'guile, deceit.']

1. *trans.* To beguile with show of kindness or fair words; to entertain with delusive expectations; to encourage or confirm in a foolish purpose or opinion, soothe in fancied security; to give countenance to (a delusion).

α. *c* **1350** *Will. Palerne* 1646 Foule þow me fodest wiþ þi faire wordes. *Ibid.* 57 þe cherl..foded it [þe barn] wiþ floures & wiþ faire by-hest. **1526** SKELTON *Magnyf.* 1719, I am not wont to fode Them that dare put theyr truste in me. **1565** CALFHILL *Answ. Treat. Crosse* (1846) 3 Least..you your selues be fooded in your folly. **1565** GOLDING *Ovid's Met.* VII. (1587) 99 b, The morning foading this my feare, to further my deceit, my shape..had altered with a trice. **1571** —— *Calvin on Ps.* xxxii. 1 The frowarde reckelessenesse of the flesh fodeth many.

β. **1545** *State Papers Hen. VIII*, X. 297 Thempereur myndeth..to fowder His Highnes with woordes of pleasure, until he may [etc.]. **1571** *Mirr. Mag., Rivers* xxxii, And as they foadred [**1563** foaded] these and diuers other With like deceit they vsed the King my brother.

2. *to fode forth*, (occas. ***forward, off, on, out***): **a.** To lead on (a person, etc.) by raising delusive expectations; to 'fob off' with excuses or evasive devices for gaining time.

α. **1479** SIR J. PASTON in *Paston Lett.* No. 840 III. 255, I hopyd to have borowyd some off Tounesend and he hath ffoodyd me fforthe evyrsynys. **1525** LD. BERNERS *Froiss.* II. cxxviii [cxxiv]. 365 The duke alwayes foded hym forthe and made semblant that he had great affection to treate for this mariage. **1556** J. HEYWOOD *Spider & F.* i. 30 A booke I tooke in hand Some thinge to reade, to fode foorth fantasie. **1573** BARET *Alv.* F 827 He was fooded foorth in vaine with long talke. **1591** HARINGTON *Orl. Fur.* IX. lix, In this meane time with words he foded out The worthy Earle. **1603** KNOLLES *Hist. Turks* 114 Feeding him vp with faire words, and foording him on from time to time with delaies. **1616** HIERON *Wks.* II. 42 Hee feeds and foades vs off with vaine words.

β. **1545** *State Pap. Hen. VIII*, X. 297 If he shall still foder Us furth with fayre wordes.

b. To waste (time), delay or postpone (a matter) by evasive excuses. Also *absol.*

1525 LD. BERNERS *Froiss.* II. xlii. 129 Syr Othes..foded forth the tyme as he that wyst not what to do. **1529** MORE *Comf. agst. Trib.* II. Wks. 1163/2 The Wolfe would not come to confession tyl..Palme sondaye:..and then foded yet forth farther, on tyl good Fryday. **1544** *State Pap. Hen. VIII*, IX. 653 They seke..to fode the matier forwarde, until [etc.]. **1577** tr. *Bullinger's Decades* (1592) 237 Whatsoeuer is ..foaded off till a longer time then it ought to be.

fode, -er, -yr, obs. ff. FOOD, FODDER, FOTHER.

foderate ('fɒdəreɪt), *a. Numism. rare.* [ad. med.Lat. *foderāt-us*, f. Rom. *fodero (It. *fodero*, OF. *fuerre*), a. Teut. **fôdr-* sheath, case (see note s.v. FODDER). The etymologically equivalent F. *fourré* is used in the same sense.] Of a coin: Coated or sheathed.

1854 BADHAM *Halieut.* 287 *note*, Foderate coins..consist of an interior or *anima* of copper laminated on both sides with an apparently continuous coating of the purest silver.

†**fodge,** *v. Obs.*$^{-1}$ = FADGE *v.* 6.

1591 LYLY *Endym.* IV. ii, My fancies began to fodge.

fodgel ('fɒdʒəl), *a. Sc.* [f. *fodge*, var. of FADGE *sb.*^{3} + -EL^2.] 'Fat, squat and plump' (Jam.).

1724 RAMSAY *Tea-t. Misc.* (1733) I. 23, I am a fine fodgel lass. **1789** BURNS *Grose's Peregrin.* ii, If..ye chance to light Upon a fine, fat, fodgel wight. **1858** M. PORTEOUS *Souter Johnny* 11 He was a gash wee fodgel body.

fodient ('fəʊdɪənt), *a.* and *sb.* [ad. L. *fodient-em*, pr. pple. of *fodĕre* to dig.]

A. *adj.* Digging; (of certain animals) burrowing.

1676 COLES, *Fodient*, digging. **1721** in BAILEY. **1881** *Nature* XXIV. 209 Such are its fodient powers..that [etc.].

B. *sb.* A burrowing animal.

1879 E. W. WHITE in *Proc. Zool. Soc.* (1880) 9 As a fodient ..it perhaps excels all other burrowing animals. **1888** *Riverside Nat. Hist.* V. 61 As a family the Fodients are entitled Orycteropodidæ.

†'**fodme,** *sb. Obs.* [f. root of FOOD.] ? Product.

c **1250** *Gen. & Ex.* 124 Ðe ðridde dai was al ðis wroȝt, And erðes fodme on werldes broȝt.

†'**fodme,** *v. Obs.*$^{-1}$ In 4 fodeme. [f. as prec. Cf. FODDEN *v.*] *trans.* To produce.

c **1400** *Pistil of Susan* 92 Þe fyge and þe filbert were fodemed so fayre.

†'**fodneth.** [? OE. **fódnoð* (Somner), f. root of *fóda*, FOOD. Cf. FODDEN, *v.*] Sustenance.

c **1175** *Lamb. Hom.* 137 Swulche monne þe he ahte mid rihte helpe to fodneðe and to scrude.

fodyr, obs. form of FODDER, FOTHER.

foe, obs. form of FEW.

foe (fəʊ), *a.* and *sb.* Forms: *adj.* 1 fáh, fáȝ, 2–7 (see forms of the sb.); *sb. sing.* 1 ȝefá, 2–3 ifa, ifo, ivo, 2–6 fa(a, 3 *south.* va, (4 fau), 3–6 fo(o, 3 *south.* vo, (3 foa), 4–5 *Sc.* fai, fay, 8–9 *Sc.* fae, 5– foe. *pl.* *a.* weak forms: 1 ȝefán, 2–3 ifan, ifon, ivon, 3 fan, foan, *south.* voan, (feon), 4–7 fon(e, foon(e, 4 *south.* von, 6 foen, 5–6 foyn. *β.* strong forms: 4–5 fa(a)s, faes, fais, fase, 4–6 fois, foo(e)s, 5 fos(e, (5 fosse, 6 fowys, *Sc.* feys), 8–9 *Sc.* faes, 4– foes. [repr. two distinct. OE. words: (1) the simple *fáh, fáȝ* adj. (:—OTeut. **faiho-*); (2) the compound *ȝefá* sb. (wk. masc.), originally an absolute use of **ȝefáh* adj. (not recorded as such) = OHG. *gifêh* at feud, odious (MHG. *gevêch, gevê*):—OTeut. **ga-faiho-*, where the prefix imports the notion of 'mutually' (see Y-). As in many other sbs., the prefix *ȝe-, i-*, fell away in early ME., so that the compound sb. and the absolute use of the simple adj. became coincident.

The Teut. adj. **faiho-* (represented only in W.Ger.) is referred to the Aryan root **peiq- poiq- piq-*, whence OIrish *oech* enemy (:—*poiqos*, Gr. πικρός bitter, Lith. *pikta-s* angry. The current statement that the word is etymologically akin to FIEND depends on the doubtful hypothesis that the root **peiq-* is an extension of **pei-* to hate.]

†**A.** *adj. Obs.* (In 16–17th c., the adjectival use is to be regarded as a new development from the sb., not as a continuation of the OE. adj.)

1. At feud *with*; hostile, inimical (*to*).

Beowulf 811 He wæs faȝ wið god. *a* **1175** *Cott. Hom.* 231 Frend oðer fend, hold oðer fá. *c* **1425** WYNTOUN *Cron.* VIII. xxxvii. 164 Fortown forsyd hyr to be Fa. *a* **1568** ASCHAM *Scholem.* II. (Arb.) 91 So fast to frende, so foe to few, so good to euery wight. **1603** FLORIO *Montaigne* I. xlvii. 154 An enemie-country and foe-land.

2. Hindering progress, rough, rugged.

c **1340** *Gaw. & Gr. Knt.* 1430 Bitwene a flosche in þat fryth & a foo cragge.

B. *sb.* (Now somewhat *rhetorical*; superseded in general use by ENEMY.)

1. In early use, an adversary in deadly feud or mortal combat; now in wider sense, one who hates and seeks to injure another; a personal enemy.

a **1000** *Laws Ælfred* II. (Thorpe) xlii, Gif he mæȝnes hæbbe þæt he his ȝefan beride. *c* **1175** *Lamb. Hom.* 87 God heom aredde wið heore ifan and heom fordude. *c* **1200** *Trin. Coll. Hom.* 219 Nu is euerihc man ifo þare he solde fren be. *a* **1225** *Ancr. R.* 274 Þauh þi foa hurte þe oðe vet. *a* **1250** *Owl & Night.* 1714 Moni man..Thurh belde worde..Deth his ivo for arehwe swete. *a* **1300** *Cursor M.* 1593 (Cott.) Hijs faas to bring al o lijf. **1340** *Ayenb.* 255 He ualþ liȝtliche ine þe honden of his uon. **1375** BARBOUR *Bruce* II. 208 Robert the bruce, that wes his fa. *c* **1460** *Towneley Myst.* (Surtees) 223 And freyndes fynde I foyn. **1526** TINDALE *Matt.* x. 36 A mannes fooes shalbe they of his owne housholde. **1625** MILTON *On Death fair Infant* 66 To slake his wrath whom sin hath made our foe. **1728** POPE *Dunc.* III. 177 Embrace, embrace, my sons! be foes no more! **1787** BURNS *Tam Samson's Elegy* vii, Your mortal fae is now awa', Tam Samson's dead! **1823** BYRON *Juan* VIII. lxx, He..could crack His jest alike in face of friend or foe. **1859** TENNYSON *Elaine* 1083 He makes no friend who never made a foe.

b. *our foe, the arch foe*: the Devil; = ENEMY 1 b.

a **1225** *Ancr. R.* 62 Vre vo, þe weorreur of helle. *c* **1366** CHAUCER *A B C* 84 Lat not our alder foo make his bobance. **1667** MILTON *P.L.* VI. 259 The arch foe subdu'd Or Captive drag'd in Chains.

c. In a weaker sense: An adversary, antagonist, opponent.

1697 DRYDEN *Virg. Georg.* II. 776 The Groom..watches with a Trip his Foe to foil. **1870** MORRIS *Earthly Par.* I. 133 Made happy that the foe the prize hath won.

d. *transf.* and *fig.* (*a*) One who feels unfriendly or acts in opposition or prejudicially *to* (some thing), an ill-wisher; (*b*) Anything that harms or is likely to injure.

(*a*) **1607** SHAKS. *Cor.* III. i. 176 A Foe to' th' publike Weale. **1742** POPE *Dunc.* IV. 460 A gloomy Clerk, Sworn foe to Myst'ry, yet divinely dark. **1813** SHELLEY *Q. Mab* IX. 176 Death is no foe to virtue. **1859** TENNYSON *Guinevere* 508, I hold that man the worst of public foes Who [etc.].

(*b*) *c* **1200** *Trin. Coll. Hom.* 33 Crist him hadde warned togenes þre fon, synne..sor and deað. **1413** *Pilgr. Sowle* (Caxton 1483) IV. xx. 65 Myrthe is to me become a very foo. **1607** SHAKS. *Timon* II. ii. 241 That thought is Bounties Foe. **1807** CRABBE *Village* II. 192 Grief is a foe, expel him then thy soul.

2. One belonging to a hostile army or nation, an enemy in battle or war.

c **1205** LAY. 215 Inne þane fehte his feon heo him binomen. **1375** BARBOUR *Bruce* XVIII. 228 Deliuerit of sic felloune a faa. *c* **1470** HENRY *Wallace* I. 54 Foly it was.. Succour to sek of thar alde mortale fa. **1591** SPENSER *Vis. Bellay* 66 A barbarous troupe of clownish fone. **1667** MILTON *P.L.* I. 437 Before the Spear Of despicable foes. **1704** ADDISON *Poems, Campaign*, Give thy brave foes their due. **1838** THIRLWALL *Greece* III. 251 Abundant opportunities of annoying their hereditary foes in the land of their fathers. **1887** BOWEN *Virg. Æneid* II. 71 Trojans eye me in wrath, and demand my life as a foe!

3. *collect.* A hostile force; = ENEMY 3.

1593 SHAKS. *3 Hen. VI*, I. iv. 3 All my followers, to the eager foe Turne back, and flye. **1633** MASSINGER *Guardian* I. i, For a flying foe, Discreet and provident conquerors build up A bridge of gold. **1794** BURNS *On the Seas & Far Away*, He's on the seas to meet the foe. **1816** BYRON *Ch. Har.* III. xxv, Whispering with white lips—'The foe! they come! they come!' **1861** M. PATTISON *Ess.* (1889) I. 47 Long after London had ceased to fear a foreign foe.

4. *attrib.* and *Comb.*, as ***foe-god; foe-reaped, -subduing*** adjs.; ***foe-like***, adj. and adv.; also †**foe-hearted** *a.*, having the heart of a foe, hostile; †**foe-Troy** *a.* (*nonce-wd.*), hostile to Troy.

1870 ROSSETTI *Eden-Bower* 53 Is not the *foe-God weak as the foeman When love grows hate in the heart of a woman? **1598** ROWLANDS *Betraying Christ* 6 Now *foe-harted, trecherous of intent. **1556** J. HEYWOOD *Spider & F.* lxiii. 57 These *folike freendes. **1638** G. SANDYS *Paraphr. Lament.* ii. 13 He..Foe-like hath bent his Bow. **1812** BYRON *Curse Minerva* 301 The rifled mansion, and the *foe-reap'd field. **1590** T. WATSON *Eclog. Death Sir F. Walsingham* 300 Poems (Arb.) 169 Where arms are vsd by *foe-subduing powers. **1615** CHAPMAN *Odyss.* XIV. 332 Till the Thunderer drew Our Forces out in his *foe-Troy decrees.

†**foe,** *v. Obs.* [f. prec. sb.] *trans.* **a.** To set at enmity. **b.** To make or treat as a foe or enemy.

c **1200** *Trin. Coll. Hom.* 209 þe deuel..fode þe forme man wið god. **1596** SPENSER *F.Q.* VI. xi. 6 Sith in his powre she was to foe or frend. **1602** WARNER *Alb. Eng.* x. lv. (1612) 245 So far was she from fooing her that sought her life and Rayne.

†**fœde,** *a. Obs.*$^{-1}$ [ad. L. *fœdus* foul.] Foul.

1657 TOMLINSON *Renou's Disp.* 319 No King..was ever correpted with such a fœde disease.

fœderal, fœderally, fœdity: see FED-.

foehn, var. FÖHN.

†'**foehood.** *Obs.* [f. FOE + -HOOD; app. an alteration of *food*, earlier form of FEUD *sb.*^{2}] Enmity, hatred; a state of mutual hostility.

1575 LANEHAM *Let.* (1871) 17 At vtter deadly fohod. **1606** WARNER *Alb. Eng.* XV. xcvi. (1612) 382 And faith with vs not to be held, but foehood euermore. **1625** JACKSON *Christ's Answ.* §57. Wks. 1844 VI. 417 These strange reconciliations and composals of these inbred fohoods.

†'**foeish,** *a. Obs. rare.* [f. FOE *sb.* + -ISH.] Of, pertaining to, or characteristic of a foe.

1566 DRANT *Wail. Hierem.* Kjb, Fell into foyshe hande. *Ibid.* Kiij b, He bent his bowe in foyshe guyse.

'**foeless,** *a.* [f. FOE *sb.* + -LESS.] Having no foe.

1865 S. EVANS *Bro. Fabian* 102 Nickar the soulless..Sits ..Friendless and foeless.

foeman ('fəʊmən). *arch.* and *poet.* Forms: see FOE. [OE. *fáhman*, f. *fah*, FOE *a.* + MAN.] An enemy in war, an adversary.

a **1000** *Polit. Laws Ælfred* v, Gif hie fah-mon ȝeierne. *a* **1175** *Cott. Hom.* 241 Ne nanman ne fiht buton wið his ifómenn. *a* **1225** *Ancr. R.* 404 Mon worpeð Grickischs fur upon his fomen, & so me ouerkumeð ham. **1375** BARBOUR *Bruce* VI. 648 He of his famen four has slayn. **14..** *Sir Beues* 244 (MS. M.) Dame, why haste thou my fader betrayde And wyll be wedyd to his foman? **1579** SPENSER *Sheph. Cal.* Feb. 21 Ne euer was to Fortune foeman. **1620** QUARLES *Jonah* (1717) 48 To save us harmless from our Fo-mans jaws. **1810** SCOTT *Lady of L.* V. x, Foemen worthy of their steel. **1864** A. MCKAY *Hist. Kilmarnock* 12 Every movement of the advancing foeman.

†'**foemate.** *Obs. rare.* [f. FOE *sb.* + MATE.] ? One matched against another in battle; an enemy.

1592 WYRLEY *Armorie, Ld. Chandos* 92 His folks assaild, the foemate was too strong.

fœnugreek, var. of FENUGREEK.

foeship ('fəʊʃɪp). [f. FOE *sb.* + -SHIP.]

†**1.** Enmity, hatred. *Obs.*

c **1200** *Trin. Coll. Hom.* 45 Þanne is here foshipe turnd al to frendship. **13..** *E.E. Allit. P.* B. 919 No foschip oure fader hatz þe schewed. **1556** *Aurelio & Isabel* Fiij, The foshippe that you beare me.

2. The relation of foes. *nonce-use.*

1883 H. STEVENS in *Athenæum* 6 Oct. 433/3 His friendships and foeships.

fœtal, fetal ('fiːtəl), *a.* [f. FŒT-US + -AL^1.] Of or pertaining to or of the nature of a fœtus; in the condition of a fœtus.

1811 B. WATERHOUSE *Botanist* ii. 26 A glutinous substance, laid up for the nourishment of the fœtal animal. **1834** J. FORBES *Laennec's Dis. Chest* (ed. 4) 663 The action of the fœtal heart. **1858** J. H. BENNET *Nutrition* i. 1 During fœtal life the materials of nutrition are..supplied by the mother. **1859** DARWIN *Orig. Spec.* xiv. 397 The presence of teeth in fœtal whales.

fig. **1820** COLERIDGE *Lett.* (1836) I. 88 Meteorology, a science so misnamed, which so far from being in its infancy is not yet in its fetal state. **1890** J. H. STIRLING *Gifford Lect.* v. 88 Their life was as yet fœtal in the State, their mother.

fœtalization, fetalization (ˌfiːtəlaɪ'zeɪʃən). [ad. G. *fetalisation* (L. Bolk *Das Problem der Menschwerdung* (1926) 25).] (See quot. 1957.) So '**fœtalized, fetalized** *a.*

1930 G. R. DE BEER *Embryol. & Evol.* viii. 59 The principle here described..is that to which Bolk has applied the term *foetalization*. **1937** *Nature* 2 Jan. 37/1 The Bushman..shows features, in which it [*sc.* the skull] resembles the juvenile skull. It is here suggested that this 'fœtalization'..is not due to an adult retention of juvenile features, but is a precocious assumption of the adult. **1940** AUDEN in *I Believe* 19 The distinguishing mark of man as an animal is his plastic, unspecialized 'foetalized' nature. **1957** L. EISELEY *Immense Journey* 130 'Foetalization' or 'pedomorphism', as it is termed, means simply the retention, into adult life, of bodily characters which at some earlier stage of evolutionary history were actually only infantile. *Ibid.* 133 It [*sc.* man] is not..the most foetalized race nor the largest brained.

†'**fœtant,** *a. Obs.*$^{-1}$ *erron.* -ent. [ad. L. *fētant-em*, pr. pple. of *fētare*: see next.] Fruitful.

1678 R. R[USSELL] *Geber* I. 19 Our Stone is no other than a Foetent (or fruitful) Spirit and Living Water.

fœ'tation, fe'tation. [agent-n. f. L. *fētāre* to produce offspring, f. root of *fētus* FŒTUS.] The formation of a fœtus or embryo.

1669 WORLIDGE *Syst. Agric.* (1681) 3 The fruitful Fœtation and Progeny of Animals. **1677** HALES *Prim. Orig. Man.* III. vi. 280 The Eggs of Silkworms..being ripen'd to fœtation by the heat of the Sun. **1851** F. H. RAMSBOTHAM *Obstet. Med.* (ed. 3) 631 Extra-uterine fœtation.

fœticide, feticide ('fiːtɪsaɪd). [f. FŒT-US + -(I)CIDE: see -CIDE 2.] The action of destroying a fœtus or causing abortion. Also *attrib.*

1844 in HOBLYN *Dict. Med.* **1862** M. HOPKINS *Hawaii* 365 Foeticide and abortion are meant..to be included under.. infant murder. **1889** J. M. DUNCAN *Lect. Dis. Women* viii. (ed. 4) 49 The value of fœticide treatment.

Hence **fœti'cidal** *a.*, of or pertaining to fœticide.

In some mod. Dicts.

fœtid, fœtor, var. forms of FETID, FETOR.

fœtiferous, fetiferous (fiː'tɪfərəs), *a.* [f. L. *fētifer* (f. *fēt-us* offspring + *-fer* producing) + -OUS.] Producing offspring.

1656–81 in BLOUNT *Glossogr.* **1775** in ASH. **1859** TODD *Cycl. Anat.* V. 587/2 An 'undisputed case of purely ovarian fœtiferous ovum'.

Similarly **fœ'tific** *a.* [see -FIC], making fruitful (Bailey 1727, vol. II). **fœtifi'cation** [see -FICATION], a bringing forth fruit (Bailey 1727, vol. II). **fœ'tiparous** *a.* [+ L. *-parus* producing (*parĕre* to produce) + -OUS]. (see quot.).

1884 *Syd. Soc. Lex.*, *Fœtiparous*, producing premature offspring, such as occurs in *Marsupialia*.

†'**fœture.** *Obs.* Also 5–7 feture, 6–7 feature. [ad. L. *fētūra*, f. **fē-*: see FŒTUS.]

1. The action or process of bearing young.

c **1420** *Pallad. on Husb.* IV. 731 Luke water best helpeth thaire feture [*note* calvyng]. **1657** TOMLINSON *Renou's Disp.* 447 [The Hen] exhibits most commodious fœture.

2. *concr.* **a.** The embryo; the fœtus. **b.** The matured offspring; the product. Also *collect.*

1545 RAYNOLD *Byrth Mankynde* (1564) 27 b, A continuall course of blood..redy to..norysh the feature, so sone as it shalbe conceiued. **1658** ROWLAND *Moufet's Theat. Ins.* 984 The..feture is so tender, that with the least touch it is bruised to pieces.

fig. **1584** tr. *Latimer's Serm. Luke* xvi. in *Fruitf. Serm.* 12 Some of them ingendred one, some other such features. **1605** B. JONSON *Volpone* Ded., Because in some mens abortiue features..it is ouer-true.

fœtus, fetus (ˈfiːtəs). [a. L. *fētus* (*u* stem) offspring (incorrectly written *fœtus*), f. root **fē-* to produce offspring:—Aryan **bhwē-*, an extension of root **bheu-*, *bhu-*, to grow, come into being: see BE *v.*]

The etymologically preferable spelling with *e* in this word and its cognates is adopted as the standard form in some recent Dicts., but in actual use is almost unknown. (N.E.D.)

The young of viviparous animals in the womb, and of oviparous animals in the egg, when fully developed.

1398 TREVISA *Barth. De P.R.* v. xlix. (1495) 167 The chylde that is conceyued in the moder hyght Fetus in latyn. **1594** T. B. *La Primaud. Fr. Acad.* II. 397 At this time the burthen is called Fœtus of the Latines, and Embryon of the Greekes. **1660** BOYLE *New Exp. Phys. Mech.* Digress. 373 The Fœtus respires in the Womb. **1796** DE SERRA in *Phil. Trans.* LXXXVI. 500 The gems as correspondent to living born fœtuses. **1847–71** T. R. JONES *Anim. Kingd.* (ed. 4) 867 We have yet to learn how the fœtus is matured after the exhaustion of this supply.

transf. **1692** BENTLEY *Boyle Lect.* 142 The soil, pregnant and big with fœtus's of all imaginable..structures of body.

fog (fɒg), *sb.*^{1} Also 4, 6–7, 9 **fogg(e**, 6 *Sc.* **foge**, 7, 9 **feg**, 8 *Sc.* **fouge**, **fug**. [of unknown origin; the Welsh *ffwg* 'dry grass' (O. Pughe), often given as the source, is from Eng.]

1. a. The grass which springs up immediately after the hay-crop has been taken off, aftermath. **b.** The long grass left standing in the fields during winter; rank grass. (*to leave*) *under fog*: with the long grass standing.

13.. *E.E. Allit. P.* B. 1683 He fares forth on alle faure, fogge watz his mete. *c* **1400** *Sowdone Bab.* 2865 And fille oure somers withe fog and haye. **1500–20** DUNBAR *Poems* lxi. 34 Great court horss puttis me fra the staw, To fang the fog be firthe and fald. **1570** LEVINS *Manip.* 157 Fogge, *postfœnium.* **1641** BEST *Farm. Bks.* (Surtees) 130 I haue knowne the fogge of this close letten from Michael-masse till Lady-day for 33*s.* 4*d.* **1674** N. COX *Gentl. Recreat.* III. (1677) 40 These Partridges..do lodge in the dead Grass or Fog under Hedges. **1789** *Trans. Soc. Encourag. Arts* VII. 39 The fog, or after-grass, was ploughed in. **1807** VANCOUVER *Agric. Devon* (1813) 226 The last year's fog is pared down as close and even as possible. **1834** *Brit. Husb.* I. 484 The precaution of leaving a portion under fog forms a sure resource against a scarcity of summer feed. **1876** *World* V. No. 115. 13 To be let, the eatage of fog on thirteen acres of old grass-land.

†**c.** ? A growth of this grass. *Obs.*$^{-1}$

1661 LOVELL *Hist. Anim. & Min.* 158 They..make their nests in foggs.

d. ? A tangled mass.

1869 BLACKMORE *Lorna D.* x, Where a fog was of rushes, and floodwood, and wild celery-haulm.

2. *Sc.* and *north.* = MOSS.

c **1450** HENRYSON *Mor. Fab.* 9 It was a sober wane, Of foge and farne full febillie way made. **1494** in *Ld. Treas. Acc. Scotl.* I. 249 Item gyffyne for fog to the barge iij*s.* **1724** RAMSAY *Tea-t. Misc.* (1733) I. 66 Between hands..we'll..sport upon the velvet fog. **1750** in Ramsay *Sc. Prov.* 12 A rowing stane gathers nae fog. **1788** E. PICKEN *Elegy on Yon Place* Poems 181 Green fug, mantlan' owre the sclates, Held out the air. **1805** FORSYTH *Beauties Scotl.* II. 458 Lime is the mortal enemy of all sorts of fog or moss. **1853** G. JOHNSTON *Nat. Hist. E. Bord.* 261 The term 'fog' comprehends many species of Hypna.

3. *attrib.* and *Comb.*, as *fog grass*, *-harrow*, *-land*, *-moss*. Also, **fog-cheese** = *eddish-cheese*; **fog-earth**, peat; **fog-fruit** (see quot.); **fog-house** (see quot.).

1822 NARES, **Fog-cheeses* in Yorkshire, are such as are made from this latter grass. **1886** ELWORTHY *W. Somerset Word-bk.*, **Fog-earth*, peat, bog-earth. **1866** *Treas. Bot.*, **Fog-fruit*, an American name for *Lippia nodiflora.* **1886** ELWORTHY *W. Somerset Word-bk.*, **Fog-grass*, coarse sedgy grass, such as grows in wet places. **1880** *Antrim & Down Gloss.*, **Fog-harrow*, a harrow to clear moss away. **1842** C. W. JOHNSON *Farmer's Encycl.* 494 A *fog-house means a house built or lined with moss. **1829** J. HODGSON in J. Raine *Mem.* (1858) II. 158 The corn and *foglands. **1805** FORSYTH *Beauties Scotl.* II. 257 Yellowish, or *fogg-moss, is much less compact than [black moss].

fog (fɒg), *sb.*^{2} Also 6–7 **fogge**. [prob. a back-formation from FOGGY *a.*]

†**I. 1.** Flabby substance (in the body), unwholesome fat; 'waste flesh' (cf. quot. from Palsgrave s.v. FOGGY 3). *Obs.* [Cf. FOGGY *a.* 3.]

1586 BRIGHT *Melanch.* xxi. 124 In stead of firme substance the bodie is ouercharged with a counterfette kind of fatte, and hydropical fogge, which beareth shewe of good habite.

II. [Cf. FOGGY *a.* 4.]

2. a. Thick mist or watery vapour suspended in the atmosphere at or near the earth's surface; an obscured condition of the atmosphere due to the presence of dense vapour.

1544 *Late Exped. Scotl.* C iij a, The sonne brake out, the fogge went awaye. **1578** T. ELLIS in Hakluyt *Voy.* III. 41 A hidious fogge and mist, that continued till the nineteenth. **1590** SHAKS. *Mids. N.* III. ii. 357 The starrie Welkin couer thou anon With drooping fogge as blacke as Acheron. **1634** MILTON *Comus* 433 No evil thing that walks by night, In fog, or fire. **1670** EVELYN *Diary* 15 Dec., The thickest and darkest fogg on the Thames that was ever known. **1758** JOHNSON *Idler* No. 49 ¶8 Hills obscured by fogs. **1833** HT. MARTINEAU *Loom & Lugger* I. iii. 28 A dense fog hung so low that there was no use in keeping watch. **1860** TYNDALL *Glac.* I. x. 66 His guides had lost their way in the fog. **1887** ASHBY-STERRY *Lazy Minstr.* (1892) 141 'Tis sometimes yellow, sometimes brown, A London Fog!

b. *fig.* *in a fog*: at a loss to know what to do.

1602 MARSTON *Antonio's Rev.* III. i. Wks. 1856 I. 105 Stoop and beat downe this rising fog of shame. **1612** DRAYTON *Poly-olb.* To Rdr., The thicke fogges and mists of ignorance. **1792** WOLCOTT (P. Pindar) *Ode to Ld. Lonsdale* Wks. 1812 III. 45 The people's brains are losing their old fogs. **1874** MICKLETHWAITE *Mod. Par. Churches* 326 Our sculptors are still blinded by the pseudo-Greek fog. **1888** M. ROBERTSON *Lombard St. Myst.* xxii, I confess that, until it came to light, I was in a fog.

3. *transf.* **a.** Any abnormal darkened state of the atmosphere. **b.** Any substance diffused through the atmosphere, so as to cause darkness; a dark mass (of smoke). Also *slang* = SMOKE.

1601 SHAKS. *Twel. N.* IV. ii. 48 Ignorance, in which thou art more puzel'd then the Ægyptians in their fogge. **1699** GARTH *Dispens.* III. 30 Smouldring Fogs of smoke benight the Fire. *c* **1700** *Street Robberies Consider'd*, *Fog*, smoke. **1854** KELLY & TOMLINSON tr. *Arago's Astron.* (ed. 5) 133 The fog of 1783..extended from the north of Africa to Sweden..It rose above the loftiest mountains.

4. *Photogr.* A cloud or coating obscuring a developed plate.

1858 SUTTON *Dict. Photogr.* s.v., A frequent cause of fog is [etc.]. **1873** SPON *Workshop Rec.* I. 254 A deposit of red fog will take place.

5. Short for FOG-SIGNAL 2.

1883 F. S. WILLIAMS *Our Iron Roads* ix. (ed. 4) 295 As long as the distance-signal stands at 'danger' he is to keep two 'fogs' on the rail.

6. *attrib.* and *Comb.* **a.** attrib., as *fog-cloud*, *-land*, *-smoke*.

1846 WHITTIER *Exiles* lii, No *fog-cloud veiled the deep. **1886** *Gentl. Mag.* Apr. 411 We..step into the luminc *fog-land of poetry. **1808** SCOTT *Marm.* II. Introd. ix, Ris , the *fog-smoke white as snow.

b. *esp.* in the names of instruments used for giving warning in foggy weather, as *fog-alarm*, *-bell*, *-detonator*, *-gong*, *-gun*, *-horn*, *-lamp*, *-light*, *-trumpet*, *-whistle*. Also FOG-SIGNAL.

1841 LONGF. *Wreck Hesp.*, 'Tis a *fog-bell on a rock-bound coast. **1892** *Pall Mall G.* 17 Oct. 4/3 The cap of a *fog-detonator. **1883** *Fisheries Exhib. Catal.* 32 A..Bell Metal Chinese *Fog Gong. **1858** in *Merc. Marine Mag.* V. 363 A gong and *fog-horn is..sounded in foggy weather. **1937** *Times* 13 Apr. p. xxii/4 In contributing to safety on the road by day or night, the makers of direction indicators and *fog and anti-dazzle lamps have played a notable part. **1962** *Fog-light [see ACCESSORY B. *sb.* 1]. **1859** *First Impressions New World* i. 3 We had a good deal of fog when off Newfoundland, which obliged us to use the *fog-whistle frequently.

c. instrumental and originative, as *fog-born*, *-bound*, *-bred*, *-hidden*, *-ridden*, adjs.

1818 KEATS *Endymion* II. 278 The *fog-born elf. **1855** CLARKE *Dict.*, **Fog-bound*, detained by fog. **1848** KINGSLEY *Saint's Trag.* I. iii, This *fog-bred mushroom-spawn of brain-sick wits. **1893** *Catholic News* 21 Jan. 5/1 That *fog-hidden day. **1887** *All Year Round* 26 Feb. 135 Our chilly *fog-ridden towns.

d. Special comb.: **fog-bow**, a phenomenon similar to the rainbow, produced by the action of light on the particles of fog; **fog-buoy** (see quots.); **fog-circle** = *fog-bow*; **fog-dog** (see DOG *sb.*^{1} 10); **fog-drift**, a drifting mass of fog; **fog-eater** (see quot.); **fog-horn** *v. intr.*, to speak with a loud, penetrating voice; **fog-logged** *a.*, stopped by fog; **fog-man** = FOGGER^3; †**fog-pate**, a stupid muddle-headed person; **fog-ring** (see quot.).

1831 BREWSTER *Optics* xxxii. 268 A *fog-bow, which resembled a nebulous arch, in which the colours were invisible. **1899** F. T. BULLEN *Way Navy* 31 A *fog-buoy—a barrel towed at the end of a rope at the distance each ship should keep astern of the other. **1939** *War Illustr.* 29 Dec. 532/2 In foggy weather..every ship tows from the stern on the end of a long line a brightly-painted wooden cask, which is known as a fog-buoy. **1890** E. GOSSE *Life P. H. Gosse* 62 The rare Arctic appearance known as the fog-bow, or *fog-circle. **1853** *Ecclesiologist* XIV. 390 *Fog-drifts drove rapidly over the bleak crags. **1867** SMYTH *Sailor's Word-bk.*, **Fog-eater*, a synonym of *fog-dog and fog-bow. **1923** A. HUXLEY *Antic Hay* i. 4 The Reverend Pelvey, M.A., *foghorning away from behind the imperial bird. **1846** *P. Parley's Ann.* VII. 5 The Prince Regent..proceeding towards Hatfield got *'fog-logged', as it was called, and could not proceed. **1883** F. S. WILLIAMS *Our Iron Roads* ix. (ed. 4) 294 In that cottage lives a *'fog-man' and he was wanted for his duties. **1732** *Hyp-Doctor* 2 May 1/1 Reasoning with these eternal *Fog-pates. **1852** BRANDE Suppl., **Fog-rings*, banks of fog arranged in a circular or ring form.

†**fog**, *a.* *Obs. rare.* [Shortened from FOGGY *a.*] Gross, bloated. Cf. FOGGY *a.*^{3}

1583 STANYHURST *Aeneis* III. (Arb.) 92 Polyphem..A fowle fog monster.

fog (fɒg), *v.*^{1} [f. FOG *sb.*^{1}]

1. *intr.* To become overgrown with moss. *Sc.*

1715 PENNECUIK *Tweeddale* 31 About this town [Peebles]..fruit and forest trees..are seldom seen either to fog or be bark-bound. **1805** FORSYTH *Beauties Scotl.* I. 525 The hedges fog at the stem. **1810** G. CHALMERS *Caledonia* II. iii. 204 St. Bothan's well..neither fogs nor freezes.

2. *Agric.* (*trans.*) **a.** To leave land 'under fog': see FOG *sb.*^{1} 1 and FOGGING *vbl. sb.* **b.** To feed (cattle) on fog.

1814 DAVIES *Agric. S. Wales* I. 545 We saw a piece that had been fogged successively during sixteen years, and..was improving annually. **1828** CARR *Craven Gloss.* s.v., When farmers take the cattle out of their pastures in autumn; they say 'they are boun to fog them'. **1855** OGILVIE Suppl., *Fog*, in agriculture, to feed off the fog or pasture in winter, as cattle. **1893** *Wilts Gloss.*, *Fog*, to give fodder to cattle.

fog (fɒg), *v.*^{2} [f. FOG *sb.*^{2} Cf. *befog.*]

1. *trans.* To envelope with or as with fog; to stifle with fog. Also *fig.*

1599 *Soliman & P.* I. C ij, Fog not thy glory with so fowle eclipse. **1601** BP. BARLOW *Defence* 19 Somtimes by clouds it [the sun] is enueloped, and by mists fogged. *a* **1684** LEIGHTON *Comm. 1st Pet.* i. 10–12 That the light of divine truth may..not be fogged and misted with filthy vapours. **1811** BYRON *Let. to Mrs. Byron* 14 Jan., I might have stayed, smoked in your towns, or fogged in your country, a century. **1881** W. C. RUSSELL *Ocean Free Lance* I. vi. 296 The hurricanes which..fogged her decks with flying spume.

2. *fig.* To put (a person) in a 'fog'; to bewilder utterly, mystify, perplex; to render (ideas, etc.) misty or confused.

1818 KEATS *Lett.* Wks. 1889 III. 124, I must fog your memories about them [*viz.* books he had borrowed]. **1888** *Illustr. Lond. News* Xmas No. 11/1 These folks fog me..I can't talk their lingo. **1890** B. SHARPE in *Nature* 30 Oct. 634 To merge many species under the genus Picus tends to fog and confuse the ideas of geographical distribution.

3. *intr.* **a.** To become covered or filled with fog. (In mod. Dicts.) **b.** *to fog off*: to perish from damp, to damp off.

1849 *Florist* Aug. 221 Watch carefully that decayed leaves do not cause the cuttings to fog off. **1880** *N. & Q.* 20 Nov. 406 A gardener speaks of his cuttings from bedding plants which have not taken root as having 'fogged off'.

4. *Photogr.* (*trans.*) To cloud or cover with an obscuring coating. Also *to fog over*.

1854 *Jrnl. Photogr. Soc.* 21 Jan. 163/2 The relative values of acid or alkaline baths with respect to 'fogging over' the impressions taken on collodion. **1865** *Reader* No. 116. 320/1 The negative was slightly fogged. **1893** SIR R. BALL *Story of Sun* 210 The flash of sunlight fogged the plate.

5. *Railway slang.* (*intr.*) To place fog-signals on the line in foggy weather.

1886 *Lloyd's Weekly* 26 Dec. 1/5 Engaged in the duty of 'fogging'. **1891** *Star* 21 Feb. 3/1 While he was fogging on the south side of Charing-cross-bridge.

Hence **fogged** *ppl. a.*; ˈ**fogging** *ppl. a.*

1617 HIERON *Wks.* (1619–20) II. 191 In some sicknesses, you shall see a man forget himselfe a little by some fogging sleepe. **1661** FELTHAM *Resolves* II. *Lusoria* xxviii, The Sun, before man's damning Fall Threw a fogg'd guilt upon this All. **1849** *Florist* Dec. 321 To remove any fogged foliage. **1886** STEVENSON *Dr. Jekyll* 20 Under the face of the fogged city moon. **1890** WOODBURY *Encycl. Photogr.* 300 Fogged plates will be produced if [etc.].

†**fog**, *v.*^{3} *Obs. rare.* [? Back formation from FOGGER^1.] *intr.* To act in a 'pettifogging' manner; to adopt underhand or unworthy means to secure gain. Hence ˈ**fogging** *ppl. a.*

1588 M. KYFFIN *Terence's Andria* v. iv, Hah fogging knaue. **1628** R. S. *Counter Scuffle* lxix, Wert not for vs, thou Swad, quoth hee, Where would'st thou fog to get a fee? **1641** MILTON *Reform.* II. (1851) 65 The fogging proctorage of money.

fogage, obs. form of FOGGAGE.

fogan (ˈfəʊgən). *dial.* Also **foggin**, **fogon**. [? cf. OE. *foca* loaf baked under the ashes (Ælfric *Gen.* xviii. 6).] (See quots.)

1810 *Monthly Mag.* June 436 *Fogan, fogon*..In some parts of Cornwall..a cake made of the fat of pork and barley-meal. **1848** C. A. JOHNS *Week at Lizard* 228 The latter, which they called 'foggin', consisting of cakes made of wheaten flour and currants.

fog-bank. [f. FOG *sb.*^{2} + BANK *sb.*^{1}] (See quot. 1867.) Also *fig.*

1659 D. PELL *Impr. Sea* 499 *note*, Quoth the Ship-master, It is but a fog-bank, there is no danger. **1769** HIRST in *Phil. Trans.* LIX. 230 A dark cloud, or rather fog-bank. **1819** BYRON *Juan* II. xcvi, The frequent fog-banks gave them cause to doubt. **1865** MERIVALE *Rom. Emp.* VIII. lxviii. 366 The clouds and fogbanks of Plotinus..were replaced by the enduring fabric of the doctrine of the Christian Trinity. **1867** SMYTH *Sailor's Word-bk.*, *Fog-bank*, a dense haze, presenting the appearance of a thick cloud resting upon the horizon.

fogdom (ˈfɒgdəm). *nonce-wd.* [f. FOG *sb.*^{2} + -DOM.] The state of fog, foggy condition.

1890 *Longm. Mag.* Mar. 488 The fogdom dun and brown Of thy streets, O London Town.

†**foge.**^{1} *Obs.* [? cf. FEAUGES.] ? Some ailment.

1483 *Cath. Angl.* 137 Foge, *reuma*, *vnemia* [sic MS.; ? read *anemia*].

foge^2 (fəʊdʒ). *Min.* [Of obscure origin: perh. local pronunciation of FORGE.] (See quot. 1778.)

1778 W. PRYCE *Min. Cornub.* 321 *Foge* (Cornish), a forge or blowing-house for smelting of Tin. **1808** POLWHELE *Cornish-Eng. Voc.*, *Foge*, a blowing house.

fogey: see FOGY.

foggage ('fɒgɪdʒ). *Sc.* Also 7-8 fogage, (7 foggadge). [ad. Sc. Law-Lat. (14th c. *fogagium*) prob. f. FOG *sb.*[1]]

1. a. *Law.* The pasturing of cattle on 'fog'; the privilege of doing this.

? *a* **1500** tr. *Leges Forestarum* xv. in *Sc. Acts* (1844) I. 690 Gif þe king will set gers be þe tym of fogage þe quhilk is fra þe fest of all hallowys quhil þe fest of Sanct Patrik in lentryn ilk beest sal pay viij d. for fogage [Orig. *per tempus fogagii ..pro fogagio*]. **1593** *Sc. Acts Jas. VI* (1597) §161 That the saidis glebes be designed with freedome of foggage, pastourage, fewall, faill, diffat, loning, frie ischue and entrie. **1872** C. INNES *Lect. Scot. Legal Antiq.* vi. 252 The foggage of the Bishop's forest of Birss.

b. = FOG *sb.*[1] 1.

1775 J. WATSON *Hist. Halifax* 538 *Fog*, the Grass which grows in meadows after mowing... It is otherwise called Feg, or Fogage. **1834** W. YOUATT *Cattle* 118 Highland stots ..are turned out on the foggage. **1844** H. STEPHENS *Bk. Farm* III. 841 A foggage field. **1886** C. SCOTT *Sheep-farming* 169 Lambs..will do very well..if they have the run of a good aftermath or foggage. **1909** *Daily Chron.* 28 Jan. 4/7 Devonshire did not recognise what Yorkshire meant by 'fog'—the second crop of grass, the aftermath, known also as 'foggage' and 'eddish'.

2. Moss; = FOG *sb.*[1] 2.

1786 BURNS *To a Mouse* iv, An' naething, now, to big a new ane O' foggage green!

fogged (fɒgd), *ppl. a.* [f. FOG *v.*[1] + -ED[1].]

1. *Sc.* Covered with moss; hence *fig.* (well) furnished or provided.

1743 MAXWELL *Sel. Trans. Soc. Improv. Agric. Scot.* 100 The grass..is become very sour, full of sprets, and in many places fogged. **1790** SHIRREFS *Poems* 332 In case auld lucky be well fogget. *a* **1800** JAMIESON *Pop. Ball.* I. 293 For noucht but a house-wife was wantin' To plenish his weel-foggit byke.

2. Left 'under fog': see FOG *sb.*[1] 1.

1834 *Brit. Husb.* I. 484 The practice of putting cattle from fogged-fields into the straw yard at night.

fogger[1] ('fɒgə(r)). [Of somewhat obscure history; but prob. derived from *Fugger*, the surname of a renowned family of merchants and financiers of Augsburg in the 15th and 16th c.

The name passed as an appellative into several European langs. In German *fugger, fucker, focker* (see Grimm) has had the senses 'monopolist, engrosser', 'usurer', 'man of great wealth', 'great merchant', and, in certain dialects (doubtless originally through ironical use), 'huckster, pedlar.' Kilian 1598 has Flem. *focker* 'monopolist, universal dealer' (*monopola, pantopola*), giving *fuggerus* and *fuccardus* as popular mod.L. equivalents; and in mod.Du. *rijke fokker* is an avaricious rich man. Walloon *foukeur* and Sp. *fúcar* are contemptuous designations for a man of great wealth. A 'petty Fugger' would mean one who on a small scale practises the dishonourable devices for gain poularly attributed to great financiers; it seems possible that the phrase 'petty fogger of the law', applied in this sense to some notorious person, may have caught the popular fancy, and so have given rise to the specialized use in sense 1. Sense 2 was already developed in Ger. dialects (see Grimm), though the channel by which it came to England is unknown. Cf. FOOKER.]

†**1.** A person given to underhand practices for the sake of gain; chiefly, a contemptuous designation for a lawyer of a low class. Usually preceded by *petty* (see PETTIFOGGER). *Obs.*

1576 FLEMING *Panopl. Epist.* 320 As for this pettie fogger, this false fellowe that is in no credite or countenance. **1577** HARRISON *England* II. ix. (1877) I. 206 Brokers betweene the pettie foggers of the lawe and the common people. **1588** M. KYFFIN *Terence's Andria* IV. v, I should be exclaimed vpon to bee a beggerly fogger, greedily hunting after heritage. *c* **1600** NORDEN *Spec. Brit., Cornw.* (1728) 27 The baser sorte of people [are]..verie litigious..by meanes wherof the Fogers and Petie Lawiers..gett vnto themselues..great advauntage.

2. *dial.* 'A huckster; a petty chapman carrying small wares from village to village' (Forby *Voc. E. Anglia*, *a* 1825).

1800 LARWOOD *Norf. Dialogue* in Skeat *Nine Spec. Eng. Dialects* (E.D.S.) 119 The fogger [in the 'translation' rendered 'the man at the chandler's shop']. **1805** W. TAYLOR in *Ann. Rev.* III. 60 All hawkers, foggers, and pedlars.

3. A middleman in the nail and chain trade.

1868 *Morn. Star* 10 Mar., Down with the 'foggers', says I. **1871** *Gd. Words* 610 Where, as is often the case, the 'fogger' keeps a public-house, the truck system is so worked as to foster drunkenness. **1888** *Times* 29 Nov. 9/5 The nailers.. are at the mercy of 'foggers' or factors.

fogger[2] ('fɒgə(r)). *dial.* [perh. f. FOG *v.*[1] + -ER[1]; the word has a curious resemblance to Du. *fokker* breeder of cattle, f. *fokken* vb.] An agricultural labourer chiefly engaged in feeding and attending to cattle.

1851 in *Berksh. Gloss.* **1858** HUGHES *Scouring White Horse* 75, I found Joe with his fogger..looking at some calves. **1879** JEFFERIES *Amateur Poacher* (1889) 223 A fogger going to fodder his cattle came across a pheasant lying dead on the path.

fogger[3] ('fɒgə(r)). [f. FOG *v.*[2] + -ER[1].] One who 'fogs' on a railway, a fog-signalman.

1881 *Echo* 5 Nov. 1/5 The 'foggers' place their signals on the line at some little distance from the signal-post.

foggie ('fɒgɪ). *Sc.* Also fogie. [prob. a use of FOGGY *a.*, either because the insect inhabits mossy places (Jam.), or because it is clothed with a moss-like covering.] A kind of humble-bee; = CARDER 1 b. Also *foggie-bee.*

1819 *Blackw. Mag.* Sept. 677 Humble bees, of that brown irritable sort called foggies. **1853** *N. & Q.* 1st Ser. VIII. 64/1 Its name among the Scotch peasantry is the fogie-bee. **1856** T. AIRD *Poet. Wks.* 130 The mower in the meadow ruffles up The foggie's nest.

foggily ('fɒgɪlɪ), *adv.* [f. FOGGY *a.* + -LY[2].] In a foggy manner.

1599 MINSHEU, *Grossamente*, grossely, rudely, foggily, bungarly. **1730–6** BAILEY (folio), *Foggily*, heavily. **1755** JOHNSON *Foggily*, mistily, darkly, cloudily. **1891** C. DUNSTAN *Quita* II. II. v. 115 It was damply, foggily cold.

fogginess ('fɒgɪnɪs). [f. FOGGY *a.* + -NESS.]

†**1.** Flabbiness, grossness. *Obs.*

1547 BOORDE *Brev. Health* cclxxx. 93 In Englyshe it is named fatnes or fogyenes or such lyke. **1609** W. M. *Man in Moone* (1857) 125 Keeping them from foggineesse, grosnesse, and fiery faces. **1720** W. GIBSON *Diet Horses* xi. (ed. 3) 170 All fogginess..proceeds from an over great Relaxation of the Canals and Vessels.

2. A foggy or misty condition.

1660 INGELO *Bentiv. & Urania* (1682) I. 75 By reason of the natural fogginess of the air. **1674** N. FAIRFAX *Bulk & Selv.* 128 Whence new moisture or fogginess presses in. **1764** REID *Inquiry* vi. §22. 451 The clearness or fogginess of the air. **1859** *Photogr. News* 9 Sept. 7 The pictures..are likely to be affected with fogginess.

fig. **1893** *Ch. Times* 3 Mar. 221/1 There would be much less fogginess..and much more common sense.

fogging ('fɒgɪŋ), *vbl. sb.*[1] [f. FOG *v.*[1] + -ING[1].] The action of the vb.: *spec.* (see quot. 1804).

1804 A. YOUNG *Farmer's Calendar* 325 *Fogging*..consists in keeping the whole growth of grass in upland meadows.. free from either scythe or stock..and eating it in the following winter. **1834** *Brit. Husb.* I. 484 There is an ancient practice respecting grass lands in some of the Welch counties, called fogging,—or keeping the land without stock from May or June to December. **1883** *N. & Q.* 10 Nov. 377 Cattle turned out in the winter season to find a precarious subsistence in the fields are said to 'go a-fogging'.

fogging ('fɒgɪŋ), *vbl. sb.*[2] [f. FOG *v.*[2] + -ING[1].]

1. The action of the vb. in various senses. Also used *attrib.* (= fog-signalling), as *fogging duty*, *post.*

1854 *Jrnl. Photogr. Soc.* 21 Jan. 163/2 Another secondary cause of 'fogging'..is the diffused light reflected from the top, bottom and sides of the camera. **1878** BESANT & RICE *Celia's Arb.* vii. (1887) 56 Some strange fogging of his enthusiastic brain. **1883** *Gd. Words* Nov. 722/1 Without dust 'fogging' is impossible. **1889** ACWORTH *Railways Eng.* vii. 320 Again, 'fogging' is never resorted to merely to protect goods trains. **1898** *Daily News* 5 Jan. 2 A platelayer ..proceeding to his post on 'fogging' duty, was knocked down. **1902** *Westm. Gaz.* 5 Nov. 12/1 At the different fogging posts on their system. **1907** *Ibid.* 29 Oct. 9/1 The light of the home signal was out when he arrived at his fogging post.

2. *Theatr.* (See quot.)

1889 BARRÈRE & LELAND *Slang*, *Fogging*, getting through one's part anyhow, like a man lost in a fog.

fogging ('fɒgɪŋ), *vbl. sb.*[3] *Nail trade.* [Cf. FOGGER *sb.*[1] 3.] (See quot.)

1892 *Labour Commission* Gloss., *Fogging*, the system by which small employers in the nail and chain trade..make their profits by paying their workpeople less than the recognised price, and by selling their work..to the larger employers.

†'**foggish**, *a.*[1] *Obs. rare.* [f. FOG *a.* + -ISH.] Somewhat bloated or fat.

1570 LEVINS *Manip.* 145 Foggish, *pinguis.* **1573** BARET *Alv.* F 766 Foggishe or fatte bodie.

†'**foggish**, *a.*[2] *Obs.* [f. FOG *sb.*[2] + -ISH.] Somewhat foggy or misty.

1686 GOAD *Celest. Bodies* II. x. 294 Foggish and misling.

foggy ('fɒgɪ), *a.* Also (in sense 1 feggy) *Sc.* fuggie. [f. FOG *sb.*[1] + -Y[1].

The identity of the word in its various senses is somewhat doubtful, but the development of meaning suggested below seems plausible.]

1. a. Resembling, consisting of, or covered with 'fog' or coarse grass. **b.** *Sc.* Covered with moss, mossy.

1635 *Tom a Lincolne* II. in Thoms *Prose Rom.* (1858) II. 332 Toads croaking in foggy grasse. **1747** R. MAXWELL *Sel. Trans. Soc. Improv. Agric. Scot.* 18 It may be laid down with Grass seeds..so to ly, unless it turn sour or foggy. **1790** A. WILSON *Disconsolate Wren* Poet. Wks. (1846) 96, I spied a bonny wee bit Wren, Lone on a fuggy stane. **1806** A. DOUGLAS *Poems* 87 Yonder foggy mountain. *a* **1810** TANNAHILL *Poems* (1846) 75 He liked to stray, By fuggie rocks, or castle gray. **1875** 'STONEHENGE' *Brit. Sports* I. I. v. §5. 92 A field of good feggy grass.

†**2.** Boggy, marshy. *Obs.*

a **1568** COVERDALE *Bk. Death* I. xl. 160 He that is fallen into a depe foggy wel and sticketh fast in it. **1577** B. GOOGE *Heresbach's Husb.* (1586) 78 In the loamie and leane ground, as in the fatte and foggie. [Cf. sense 3.] **1651** R. CHILD in *Hartlib's Legacy* (1655) 11 Low, moist, foggy ground. *a* **1661** FULLER *Worthies, Bedfordsh.* I. (1662) 114 The foggy fens in the next County.

†**3. a.** Of flesh, etc.: Flabby or spongy in consistency; not solid; = BOGGY *a.* **b.** Hence of persons or animals: Unwholesomely bloated, swollen with flabby and unhealthy corpulence, puffy. Also quasi-*adv.* in *foggy fat. Obs.*

a **1529** SKELTON *Elynour Rummyng* 483 All foggy fat she was. **1530** PALSGR. 313/1 Foggy to full of waste flesshe. **1562** BULLEYN *Dial. Soarnes & Chir.* 29 b, In case the fleshe appere foggie and fattishe. **1565** GOLDING *Ovid's Met.* xv. (1567) 189 b, Then greene, and voyd of strength, and lush, and foggye, is the blade. **1603** KNOLLES *Hist. Turks* (1621) 530 Which [horses] being foggie fat, and delicately brought up. **1618** CHAPMAN *Hesiod* II. 24 And with a leane hand, stroke a foggie foot. **1657** S. PURCHAS *Pol. Flying-Ins.* 40 They return to feed, and that alwayes of the purest honey, whereby they may become so foggy, that [etc.]. *a* **1704** T. BROWN *Praise Poverty* Wks. 1730 I. 100 Drowned in foggy quagmires of fat and dropsy. **1741** *Compl. Fam. Piece* II. I. 300 Being very fat and foggy by means of their gross Food. **1817** *Sporting Mag.* L. 26 How foggy, unwieldly..and helpless are such crazy mortals. **1828** CARR *Craven Gloss.*, *Foggy*, fat, gross.

†**b.** Of food: Apt to puff up the body. *Obs.*

1657 S. PURCHAS *Pol. Flying-Ins.* I. xv. 93 Woad, which affords a foggy food that over-lades the Bees. **1761** EARL PEMBROKE *Milit. Equit.* (1778) 123 All sorts of grains are foggy feeding, and though they plump up the body, they do not give a wholesome and sound fat.

†**c.** Of ale, etc.: Full of floating particles, thick. *Obs.* Cf. FAT *a.* 7 a.

1619 *Pasquil's Palin.* (1877) 155 The Draymans Beere is not so cleere, and foggy Ale is thicker. **1764** *Low Life* 67 In search of..thick foggy Beer and Ale.

4. a. Of air, mist, cloud, etc.: Thick, murky. Hence (through FOG *sb.*[2], which appears to be a back-formation from this sense): Of the nature of, or resembling, fog or thick mist; full of, or abounding in, fog.

[For the development of this sense from 3, cf. FAT *a.* 7 c, and Lat. *pinguis aer, pingue cælum.* But some of the quotations suggest allusion to sense 2.]

1544 *Late Exped. Scotl.* C ij b, That mornynge being very mystie and foggie. **1548** UDALL, etc. *Erasm. Par. Luke* xviii. 34 With muche foggie derkenesse. **1570** TURBERV. *Penitent Louer* Epitaphes, etc. 112 With errors foggie mist at first, that Reason gaue no light. **1600** SHAKS. *A.Y.L.* III. v. 50 Like foggy South, puffing with winde and raine. **1624** WOTTON *Archit.* 3 That it [the Aire] be not..subiect to any foggy noysomenesse from Fenns or Marshes neere adioyning. **1627** MAY *Lucan* v. (1635) Iij b, The thicke aire was..clogg'd with foggy stormes. **1733–4** BERKELEY *Let. to Prior* 22 Jan. Wks. 1871 IV. 212, I myself have gotten a cold this sharp foggy weather. **1797** NELSON in A. Duncan *Life* (1806) 44 The action happening on a foggy day. **1812** COL. HAWKER *Diary* (1893) I. 63 The..foggy asthmatic town of Glasgow. **1859** MRS. CARLYLE *Lett.* III. 15 On a foggy October morning. **1877** M. M. GRANT *Sun-Maid* i, He pointed across the foggy valley. **1885** *L'pool. Daily Post* 1 May 4/9 Days of foggy drizzle.

b. *fig.* Obscure, dull, bemuddled, confused.

In some of the earlier quots. the sense may be 3, which in fig. use coincides nearly with this sense.

1603 HAYWARD *Answ. to Doleman* ii. 35 Your course, foggie, drowsie conceite, that there are few or none simple monarchies in the world. **1637** POCKLINGTON *Altare Chr.* xxiv. 172 A dull device of a foggie braine and willing blunderer. **1737** OZELL *Rabelais* I. 365 His Understanding must be very foggy. **1771** FOOTE *Maid of B.* I. Wks. 1799 II. 214 Your rival is a fusty, foggy, lumbering log! **1888** BURGON *Lives 12 Gd. Men* I. III. 358 Making merry over some extremely foggy production.

5. a. Of the eye: Beclouded, dim. **b.** Not clear to one's mind, etc., dim, indistinct. Used negatively in superl., with ellipsis of *idea, notion.*

1840 DICKENS *Barn. Rudge* (1849) 90/2 A dull and foggy sort of idea that Mrs. Varden wasn't fond of him. **1847** ALB. SMITH *Chr. Tadpole* xix. (1879) 177 The cold foggy grey eyes of the old lady looked after him. **1883** F. M. CRAWFORD *Dr. Claudius* i. 7 All this uncertain saturation of foggy visions and contradictory speculations. **1917** *Punch* 22 Aug. 145 *Uncle.* '..Wonder who she is.' *Niece.* 'Haven't the foggiest. Must be pre-war.' **1933** D. L. SAYERS *Murder must Advertise* viii. 147 'Who was the benefactor?' 'I don't know. Do you, Mr. Bredon?' 'Haven't the foggiest.' **1951** J. B. PRIESTLEY *Festival at Farbridge* II. iii. 375 'Is that a good idea?' asked Laura. 'My dear, I haven't the foggiest.' **1966** I. JEFFERIES *House Surgeon* iii. 27 'D'you know where he's to be found at this time?' 'Haven't the foggiest.' **1967** P. MCGERR *Murder is Absurd* i. 14 'Then you've no idea what his play's about?' 'Not the foggiest,' she said cheerfully.

6. *Photogr.* Fogged, indistinct. Cf. FOG *sb.*[2] 4.

1859 *Photogr. News* 9 Sept. 7 A greater tendency to give foggy pictures. **1873** SPON *Workshop Rec.* I. 292/2 Many weak thin foggy negatives.

7. *slang.* Not quite sober.

1823 MOOR *Suffolk Words, Foggy*, a quaint term for one 'somewhat bemused in beer'; not very clear-headed. **1867** in SMYTH *Sailor's Word-bk.*

8. *Comb.*, as *foggy-brained.*

1594 NASHE *Terrors Nt.* Wks. (Grosart) III. 232 Feeding on foggie-braind melancholly.

fogh, obs. var. of FAUGH *int.*

1681 OTWAY *Soldiers Fort.* I. i. Wks. 1728 I. 340 Fogh! let's leave the nasty Sows to Fools and Diseases.

fogh, foghil, obs. ff. FAW *a.* and FOWL.

†**foȝ**, *Obs. rare*[−1]. [repr. OE. **fóȝ* = MHG. *vuoc*, mod.Ger. *fug*; cf. OE. *ȝe-fóȝ*, and the derivative *féȝan*, FAY *v.*] Fitness; in phr. = Ger. *mit fug und recht.*

a **1250** *Owl & Night.* 184 We muȝe..Plaidi mid foȝe and mid riȝte.

fogie, var. FOGY.

fogle ('fəʊg(ə)l). *slang.* A handkerchief or neckerchief, usually of silk.

1811 *Lexicon Balatron.*, *Fogle*, a silk handkerchief. **1834** W. H. AINSWORTH *Rookwood* III. v, Fogles and fawnies soon

went their way. **1840** Barham *Ingol. Leg.*, *Tragedy* vii, The 'fogle' that caused all this breeze.

b. *Comb.*, as **fogle-hunter**, a pick-pocket; **fogle-drawing**, **-hunting** *vbl. sbs.*, picking pockets.

1823 *Grose's Dict. Vulg. Tongue* (ed. Egan), Fogle Hunter, a pickpocket. *Cant.* **1823** 'Jon Bee' *Slang* s.v. *Fogle*, 'He's out a fogle-hunting.' Sometimes 'tis said.. 'fogle-drawing.' **1838** Dickens *O. Twist* xi, A young fogle-hunter.

fogless (ˈfɒglɪs), *a.* [f. fog *sb.*² + -less.] Without fog, not foggy, clear.

1853 Kane *Grinnell Exp.* iv. (1856) 31 It has been a long day, but.. so clear and fogless. **1894** *Brit. Jrnl. Photogr.* XLI. 17 The second fogless one.

‖**foglietto** (foʎˈʎetto). *Mus.* [It.; dim. of *foglio* sheet of paper.] (See quot.)

1876–88 Stainer & Barrett *Dict. Mus. Terms*, *Foglietto*, a first violin part; the leader's part, which contains cues, &c., used by a conductor in the absence of a full score.

fogo (ˈfəʊgəʊ). [? Arbitrarily formed on the suggestion of *foh* int., or fog *sb.*² Cf. hogo.] A disagreeable smell, stench.

1823 'Jon Bee' *Slang*, *Fogo*, the same with a stench. **1837–40** Haliburton *Clockm.* (1862) 381 That word.. smelt so strong in his nose he had to take out his handkerchief, all scented with musk to get clear of the fogo of it.

fogou (ˈfəʊguː). [ad. Cornish *fogo*, *fougo* a cave, underground chamber. Cf. vogal, vug.] A Cornish souterrain or earth-house.

1889 *Chambers's Encycl.* III. 490 Cornwall abounds in.. menhirs, cromlechs, artificial caves or fogous, cairns and barrows. **1891** J. H. Pearce *Esther Pentreath* iv. ix. 299 He do know the owld adits and fogous.. p'raps he's shiltrin' in wan o' they somewhere. **1932** *Times Lit. Suppl.* 11 Aug. 565/1 The fogous, or covered tunnels, are unknown in the rest of South Britain or on the Continent. **1962** *Listener* 5 Apr. 591/1 If.. you visit the enclosure which contains the fogou, the underground structure, that is, which is called Carn Euny. **1963** *Field Archæol.* (Ordnance Survey) (ed. 4) 65 *Earth-houses*... The other part of Britain where similar underground structures are found is Cornwall. Here they are known as fogous... Several Cornish forts.. have a fogou which acts as a kind of narrow postern giving access to the ditch from inside the defences. **1970** N. Chadwick *Celts* v. 126 The *souterrain*, sometimes referred to in Cornwall as a *fogou*.

†**fog-race.** *Obs. jocular.* = progress.

1689 Calverley *Note-bk.* 20 May in *Yorksh. Diaries* (Surtees) II. 45, I went the college fog-race with Mr. Lancaster, Mr. Smith, and my tutor. The first day we went to Salsbury, the next to Gilsig.

fogram (ˈfəʊgrəm), *a.* and *sb.* Also **fogrum**.

†**A.** *adj.* Antiquated, old-fashioned, out of date.

1772 Mad. D'Arblay *Early Diary*, 3 Feb., His taste is terribly fogrum and old-fashioned. **1778** Foote *Trip Calais* I. Wks. 1799 II. 331 A couple of fogrum old fools. **1832** *Country Houses* I. i. 143 You really are growing quite old and fogram, I fear.

B. *sb.* **1.** An antiquated or old-fashioned person, a fogy.

1775 Crisp in *Mad. D'Arblay's Early Diary* (1889) II. 136 A parcel of old Fograms. **1776** Anstey *Election Ball.* Poet. Wks. (1808) 223, I very much fear that she thought me a fogram. **1840** Mrs. F. Trollope *Widow Married* xiv, I suppose I may think them fogrums and quizzes, if I choose? **1883** L. Wingfield *A. Rowe* II. ii. 34 Some dowagers and fograms were invited to meet the Princess.

2. *Naut. slang.* (See quot.)

1867 Smyth *Sailor's Word-bk.*, *Fogram*, wine, beer or spirits of indifferent quality; in fact, any kind of liquor.

So ˈ**fogramite**, a fogy; foˈ**gramity**, an antiquated thing; also, a fogy.

1796 Miss Burney *Camilla* I. ii. v. 250 Nobody's civil now, you know; 'tis a fogramity quite out. **1823** 'Jon Bee' *Slang*, The *fogramites*, a supposed club of imbeciles. **1832** *Country Houses* I. i. 3 The Christmas parties, of old fogramities, collected in this house.

fog-signal. [f. fog *sb.*² + signal *sb.*]

1. *Naut.* (See quot. 1867.)

1759 A. Holmes in *Naval Chron.* XXIV. 123 Came to an anchor with the fog signal on English Bank. **1867** Smyth *Sailor's Word-bk.*, *Fog-signals*, the naval code established by guns to keep a fleet together, to tack, wear, and perform sundry evolutions.. also, certain sounds made in fogs as warnings to other vessels.

2. *Railways.* A detonator placed on the metals in foggy weather to guide drivers of trains.

1856 *Engineer* 536/1 The detonating fog signal.

So **fog-signalling** *vbl. sb.*; **fog-signaller**, **fog-signalman**, a man with fog-signals.

1883 F. S. Williams *Our Iron Roads* ix. (ed. 4) 295 The duty now devolving upon the fog-signalman is this. **1889** G. Findlay *Eng. Railway* 164 A system of what is called 'fog-signalling' has been devised. **1893** *Westm. Gaz.* 14 Nov. 6/3 Fog-signallers were placed along the railway lines.

fogue, obs. var. of ‖fougue.

fogus (ˈfəʊgəs). *slang.* [? a pseudo-L. formation suggested by fog *sb.*² in sense 'smoke'.] Tobacco.

1673 R. Head *Canting Acad.* 10 Store of booz and fogus ..[was] brought them. *a***1700** in B. E. *Dict. Cant. Crew.* **1834** W. H. Ainsworth *Rookwood* iii. v, In the mean time tip me a gage of fogus, Jerry.

fogy, fogey (ˈfəʊgɪ). Forms: 8–9 **fogey, fogie,** 9 **fogy,** *Sc.* **foggie.** [Possibly a subst. use of foggy *a.* in sense 3, fat, bloated, or in sense 2, moss-grown. Cf. foggie and fogram.]

1. *Sc.* An invalid or garrison soldier.

1785 Grose *Dict. Vulg. Tongue*, *Fogey*, old fogey, a nick name for an invalid soldier. **1808** in Jamieson. **1867** in Smyth *Sailor's Word-bk.*

2. (Orig. *Sc.*) A disrespectful appellation for a man advanced in life; *esp.* one with antiquated notions, an old-fashioned fellow, one 'behind the times'. Usually preceded by *old*. See also young fogey.

1780 J. Mayne *Siller Gun* i. (1808) 117 Foggies the zig-zag followers sped, But scarce had power To keep some.. Frae stoit'rin ower. **1790** *Scots Songs* II. 56 Now ilka lad has got a lass, Save yon auld doited fogie. **1821** Galt *Ayrsh. Legatees* 217 They're just a whin auld fogies that Mr. Andrew describes. **1848** Thackeray *Bk. Snobs* xxxvii, The honest rosy old fogies. **1857** Kingsley *Two Y. Ago* (1877) 262 Jesting at him about his old fogies.

transf. **1862** Shirley *Nugæ Crit.* xi. 483 The classic 'old fogies' on my shelves began to look very dingy to me.

3. *U.S. colloq.* [Cf. sense 1.] (See quot.)

1881 Hamersley *Naval Encycl.*, *Fogy*, an increase of pay due to length of service.

4. *attrib.* use of *sb.* passing into *adj.*

1852 *Democr. Rev.* XXX. 207 The fogy atmosphere of Washington makes cowards of you all. **1865** *Trans. Ill. Agric. Soc.* 1862–4 V. 691 We flaunt our labor-saving farm machinery in the faces of slow and fogy Germany. **1887** T. A. Trollope *What I remember* I. ii. 51 The younger generation.. ridicules much the old fogey narrowness. **1892** *Daily News* 8 June 2/3 With a smile which the old fogiest of curmudgeons could not resist.

¶ See also *old-fogyish*, *-fogyism* s.v. old *a.* E. 2.

fogydom, fogeydom (ˈfəʊgɪdəm). [f. prec. + -dom.] The state or condition of a fogy; the disposition and bearing of a fogy; fogies as a class.

1859 *Eminent Men & Pop. Bks.* 158 The pleasures of Fogeydom. **1861** *Cornh. Mag.* Sept. 327 Mr. Brown is now sinking, into the foggy depths of fogeydom. **1890** *Pall Mall G.* 29 Aug. 3/1 The gentlemanlike fogeydom of Mr. Carteret.

fogyish (ˈfəʊgɪɪʃ), *a.* [f. as prec. + -ish.] Partaking of the nature of a fogy; somewhat antiquated or old-fashioned.

1873 Miss Braddon *Strangers & Pilgr.* v, The fogy-ish element in the party. **1876** Besant & Rice *Gold. Butterfly* i, Their club.. now past its prime and a little fogyish.

fogyism (ˈfəʊgɪɪz(ə)m). [f. as prec. + -ism.] The state of being a fogy; the characteristic behaviour of fogies.

1859 Holland *Gold F.* xviii. 219 The 'fogyism' and 'hunkerism' of politics. **1862** Sala *Seven Sins* III. iv. 72 When he reaches middle age, or approaches fogeyism.

foh, var. of faugh. Hence ˈ**fohing** *vbl. sb.*, the action of crying *foh!*

1685 Crowne *Sir C. Nice* iv. 39 Foh! what's this fohing at? **1712** Arbuthnot *John Bull* iii. viii, Foh, say they, to see a handsome, brisk, genteel, young fellow, so much governed by a doating old woman! **1840** Dickens *Barn. Rudge* xxiii, Foh!.. The very atmosphere.. seems tainted.

foh, var. of faw *a. Obs.*

‖**föhn** (føːn). Also **fön**. [Ger.; according to Grimm a. Rumansch *favugn*:—L. *Favōnius*.]

1. A warm dry south wind which blows down the valleys on the north side of the Alps.

1861 A. Catlow *Sketching Rambles* I. ii. 57 The most violent tempests are raised by the Föhn, or south wind. **1865** Page *Geol. Terms*, Föhn, the name given in Switzerland to the hot southerly winds of summer (the sirocco). **1883** Ouida *Wanda* I. 77 The fohn was blowing fiercely all the time. **1883** *Guardian* 14 Mar. 392 Builders.. had to guard against the *föhn* and other Swiss winds.

2. Also **foehn**. A warm dry katabatic wind developing on the lee side of a mountain range in response to air moving across the range. Also *föhn wind*.

1889 W. Ferrel *Pop. Treat. Winds* vi. 333 Temporary foehns are produced whenever there is a cyclone so situated as to draw a current of air over a high mountain range. **1910** *Encycl. Brit.* VI. 523/2 Greenland föhn winds.. blow down warm and dry, raising the temperature even 30° or 40° above the winter mean, and melting the snow. **1951** F. Defant in T. F. Malone *Compend. Meteorol.* 667/1 In North America the foehn, known as the chinook, has a climatic influence on a very wide belt east of the Rocky Mountains. **1957** J. K. Charlesworth *Quaternary Era* II. xxxi. 678 Foehn winds, varying in strength, duration and range as in modern Greenland.. probably blew throughout the year.

foi, var. form of foy.

foible (ˈfɔɪb(ə)l), *a.* and *sb.* [a. Fr. *foible*, obs. f. of *faible*; see feeble.]

†**A.** *adj.* Weak. *Obs.*

1716 M. Davies *Athen. Brit.* i. Pref. 53 In case the Spell of English Musical Poetry prove too foible for the Serpentin Venom of that Italick Insect. **1727–41** Chambers *Cycl.*, *Foible*, a French term, frequently used also in our language .. applied to the body of animals, and the parts therof: As, foible reins, foible sight, &c.

B. *sb.*

1. A weak point; a failing or weakness of character. Cf. feeble *sb.* 3.

1673 Dryden *Marr. à la Mode* iii. i, I fear they have found my foible, and will turn me into ridicule. **1691** Beverley *Thous. Years Kingd. Christ* 1 The Smaller Foiblees [*sic*] or Faylures of speech.. signifie little in the main Pursuit of Truth. **1742** Fielding *J. Andrews* Pref. (1815) 7 The accidental consequences of some human frailty or foible. **1852** Thackeray *Esmond* ii. xiii. A foible of Mr. Holt's.. was omniscience. **1883** J. Hawthorne *Dust* I. 72 It has always been my foible to speak before I look.

2. *Fencing.* = feeble *sb.* 4.

*a***1648** Ld. Herbert *Life* (1764) 46 A Foyle.. hath two Parts, one of which he calleth the Fort or strong, and the other the Foyble or weak. **1755** *Dict. Arts & Sciences* IV. 3073 Fencing-masters divide the sword into.. the fort, middle, and foible. **1833** *Reg. Instr. Cavalry* i. 115 The 'forte' ought always to gain the 'foible' of the opponent's weapon. **1879** *Encycl. Brit.* IX. 70 The wrist must be suddenly raised, so as to bring the 'forte' of one's sword to the 'foible' of the adversary's.

‖**foiblesse.** ? *Obs.* [a. Fr. *foiblesse*, obs. spelling of *faiblesse*, f. *faible* feeble.] **a.** A characteristic weakness; a failing. **b.** A liking or 'weakness' *for* (something).

1685 Crowne *Sir C. Nice* iv. 38 Besides, i've another humour, but that's a *Foibless* will ridicule me. **1755** T. H. Croker *Orl. Fur.* I. Pref. 5, I.. must acknowledge my own *foiblesse* in conception of a sensible pleasure, when [etc.]. **1813** Jeffrey in *Edin. Rev.* XXI. 294 A mere *foiblesse*. **1834** *Ibid.* LIX. 153 Our own *foiblesse* for such speculations might tempt us to select a few more samples.

‖**foie gras, foie-gras** (fwagra). *colloq.* Short for *pâté de foie gras*: see pâté 1.

1818 T. Moore *Fudge Fam. Paris* 23 The liver of the unfortunate goose is enlarged, in order to produce that richest of all dainties, the *foie gras*. **1865** 'Ouida' *Strathmore* I. i. 5 The host and the guests.. lounged;.. peeling an apricot, or cutting into a foie gras. **1913** H. Caradoc *City of Plain* iii, Sussex here helped himself to two *foie-gras* sandwiches. **1946** G. Millar *Horned Pigeon* xx. 307 They were *foie gras* sandwiches. **1958** L. van der Post *Lost World of Kalahari* i. 15 The nocturnal hippopotamus whose sweet lard meant more to him than foie-gras to any gourmet. **1970** *New Yorker* 3 Oct. 43/2 Mothers perennially sending caviar and foie gras to their sons on duty.

foil (fɔɪl), *sb.*¹ Forms: 4–7 **foil(l)e**, 4–8 **foyl(l)e**, (5 **fole**, 7 **fyle**), 5– **foil**. [a. OF. *foil*, *fuil*, *fueil* masc. (= Pr. *folh*, *fuoill*, It. *foglio*:—L. *folium* leaf, cogn. with Gr. φύλλον), and OF. *foille*, *fueille* fem. (mod.F. *feuille*, = Pr. *folha*. *foilla*, Sp. *hoja*, It. *foglia*:—L. *folia*, pl. of *folium*). The fem. sb., originally collective, has superseded the masc. in all mod.Rom. langs., except that It. *foglio* remains in the sense 'leaf of a book'.]

†**1. a.** A leaf (of a plant). *Obs.*

14.. Lydg. *Balade of our Ladie* vi, Fructified oliue of foiles faire and thicke. *c* **1420** *Pallad. on Husb.* v. 144 Take Of violette, not but oonly the foil. *c* **1450** *Two Cookery-bks.* ii. 102 Wete faire foiles of parcely in vinegre.

†**b.** With allusion to the annual fall of the leaf: A year. Cf. Fr. *vin de deux, trois feuilles*. *Obs.*⁻¹

1481 Caxton *Tully's Friendsh.* iv, For the more foylles that the wyne is of the more plesaunt it is in drynkyng.

2. The representation of a leaf. **a.** *Her.*

1562 Leigh *Armorie* (1597) 95 This though it be termed a foyle, yet is it a flower by the name of the primrose.

b. *Arch.* One of the small arcs or spaces between the cusps of a window. *foil arch* (see quot. 1891).

1835 R. Willis *Archit. Mid. Ages* 195 Multifoils, with the foils alternately round and angular. **1849** Freeman *Archit.* 344 Foil arches are doubtless one of the Arabian features of the style. **1891** *Adeline's Art Dict.*, *Foil Arch*.. is an arch made of our several smaller arches or foils.

†**3.** By analogy: Anything flat and thin. *Obs.*

a. A thin layer (of any material), a leaf, paring.

?*c* **1390** *Form of Cury* in Warner *Antiq. Culin.* (1791) 18 Take a thynne foyle of dowh, and Kerve it in pieces. *c* **1450** *Two Cookery-bks.* ii. 96 Cast there-on.. foyles of tried ginger pared. **1601** Holland *Pliny* I. 493 The mast-Holme also may be cut into fine thin foile or leaues like plates.

b. A leaf (of paper).

1528 *Will of J. Parke* (Somerset Ho.), Paper conteynyng vj foyles or leves.

c. A counterfoil.

a **1483** *Liber Niger* in *Househ. Ord.* (1790) 69 To recorde the foylles of provision weekely. **1511–2** *Act 3 Hen. VIII*, c. 23 §3 The same Barons.. [shall] cause the Chamberleyn.. to joyne the said tailes.. to their foile or foiles. **1601** F. Tate *Househ. Ord. Edw. II* §40 (1876) 23 He shal receve and write the foilles of the tallies. **1738** *Hist. Crt. Excheq.* v. 9 They shewed him their Tallies of Payment below, the Foils of which were likewise entred.

4. a. As a substance (without *pl.*): Metal hammered or rolled into a thin sheet; often with the name of a metal prefixed; as, *gold-*, *silver-*, *tin-foil*.

1398 Trevisa *Barth. de P.R.* xvi. iv. (Tollem. MS.) Golde .. bitwene þe anfelde and þe hamoure with oute breakynge .. strecchep in to golde foyle. *c* **1430** *Two Cookery-bks.* i. 27 When þou dressyst forth, plante it with foyle of Syluer. **1519** Horman *Vulg.* 236 b, Makers and leyers of golde foyle occupie a boris tothe. **1598** Stow *Surv.* vii. (1603) 53 Fine siluer, such as was then made into foyle. **1685** Cole *Let. to Ray* in *Ray's Lett.* (1718) 197 Some.. covered with a superficies as thin, and exactly of the Colour of silver Foil. **1794** N. E. Kindersley *Hindoo Lit.*, *Hist. Nella-Rajah* 117 The wings, generally of a mixed green and yellow, have the appearance of foil. **1838** T. Thomson *Chem. Org. Bodies* 373 When heated on platinum foil it gives a beautiful purple

smoke. **1871** TYNDALL *Fragm. Sc.* I. ii. 47 Blackened zinc foil..is instantly caused to blaze.

fig. **1610** G. FLETCHER *Christ's Vict., On Earth* 18 That aged Syre could tip his tongue With golden foyle of eloquence.

b. A sheet of the same (in modern use an amalgam of tin and quicksilver) placed behind the glass of a mirror, to produce a reflexion.

a **1583** W. BOURNE *Prop. Glasses* i. in *Rara Math.* (1838) 35 Lookinge Glasses..are those sortes of Glasses, that have a ffoyle, layde on the backe syde thereof. **1625** B. JONSON *Staple of N.* v. i, I now begin to see my vanity, Shine in this Glasse, reflected by the foile! **1662** J. BARGRAVE *Pope Alex. VII* (1867) 131 The isinglass having a foyle of quicksilver and pewter put behind it, like a lookingglass. **1832** G. R. PORTER *Porcelain & Gl.* 210 The art of properly effecting this deposit of the glass upon the foil.

c. In wider sense: A backing.

1684 R. WALLER *Nat. Exper.* 42 The Air..serving as a Foile to the lower Superficies of a Lens of Glass. **1859** GULLICK & TIMBS *Paint.* 13 Silver..served as a foil over which yellow and other colours ground with oil were glazed. **1879** *Cassell's Techn. Educ.* IV. 403/1 The foundation colour should form a foil for that which is inlaid on it.

d. Used as a wrapping, container, etc., for food.

1946 *Steelways* Sept. 30 Aluminum foil is the star in frozen foods packaging. **1959** *Woman* 30 May 3/4 The little foil trays in which tarts are sold are useful afterwards for placing beneath medicine bottles. **1961** *Harrods Food News* 3 Cover the pan with two or three layers of foil. **1969** *Daily Tel.* 27 Mar. 17/4 Cut and trim the toast bread and set it in table position (tightly foil-wrapped to keep it perfectly moist) with the butter.

5. a. A thin leaf of some metal placed under a precious stone to increase its brilliancy or under some transparent substance to give it the appearance of a precious stone.

c **1592** MARLOWE *Jew of Malta* II. ii, What sparkle does it [the diamond] give without a foil? *a* **1661** FULLER *Worthies* (1840) I. 300 They [Cornish diamonds]..set with a good foil ..may at the first sight deceive no unskilful lapidary. **1767** GRAY *Let. to Mason* 19 July, In gems that want colour and perfection, a foil is put under them to add to their lustre. In others, as in diamonds, the foil is black; and in this sense, when a pretty woman chooses to appear in public with a homely one, we say she uses her as a foil. **1875** in *Ure's Dict. Arts* II. 465.

†**b.** The setting (of a jewel). *Obs.*

1587 TURBERV. *Trag. T.* (1837) 19, I frame the foyle, I graue the golde, I fashion up the ring. **1611** BIBLE *Song Sol.* v. 12 *marg.* Set as a precious stone in the foile of a ring.

fig. **1593** SHAKS. *Rich. II*, I. iii. 266 A foyle wherein thou art to set The precious Iewell of thy home returne. **1650** W. BROUGH *Sacr. Princ.* (1659) 506 O Bright Diamond of Heaven..Set in the Foil of Flesh, for a Time.

6. Anything that serves by contrast of colour or quality to adorn another thing or set it off to advantage.

1581 J. BELL tr. *Haddon's Answ. Osor.* 145b, He practizeth to make his defence carry a certeine shewe of truth, paintyng it out with a deceavable foyle. **1639** MAYNE *City Match* II. ii, I need no foile, nor shall I think I me white only between two Moores. **1711** ADDISON *Spect.* No. 112 ¶4 His Friends observe these little Singularities as Foils that rather set off than blemish his good Qualities. **1791** WOLCOTT (P. Pindar) *Ode to my Ass* Wks. 1812 II..466 Lady Mount her Majesty's fine foil. **1822** HAZLITT *Table-t.* I. xvi. 378 Real excellence does not seek for a foil in inferiority. **1871** TYNDALL *Fragm. Sc.* (1879) I. vi. 202 They formed a bright foil to the sombre mass.

7. *attrib.* and *Comb.*, as *foil-ground*, *-paper*, *-spangle*; also **foil-alum**, alum in foils or laminæ; **foil-stone** (see quot. 1858).

1453 in Heath *Grocers' Comp.* (1829) 322 Alum, *foyle or rooch, ye bale..iiij*d.* **1859** GULLICK & TIMBS *Paint.* 13 Gold and silver, glazed or lacquered *foil-grounds. **1859** SALA *Gas-light & D.* ii. 20 *Foil-paper, spangles and Dutch Metal. **1851** R. F. BURTON *Goa* 133 A pair of slippers adorned with *foil spangles. **1858** SIMMONDS *Dict. Trade, Foil-stone*, an imitation jewel.

foil (fɔɪl), *sb.*[2] Forms: 5–7 foyle, 6–7 foile, 7 *Sc.* foillie, 6– foil. [f. FOIL *v.*[1] 4.]

†**1.** *Wrestling.* The fact of being almost thrown; a throw not resulting in a flat fall; also in phrase *to give (a person) the foil*. *Obs.* Cf. FALL *sb.* 13.

1553 [see FALL *sb.* 13]. **1567** *Trial Treasure* Bij, In wrestling with me he gaue me the foyle. **1622** BRETON *Strange Newes* (Grosart) 6/1 Chiefly wrestling, when they haue more foiles then faire falls. **1687** *Answ. to Representer's 8th Ch.* 4 Two Foils makes a Fall. **1706** PHILLIPS (ed. Kersey), *Foil*, a Fall in Wrestling, that is not clearly given. **1721–90** in BAILEY.

2. A repulse, defeat in an onset or enterprise; a baffling check. *arch.* †In early use often in phrases: *to give a* or *the foil*; *to have, receive, take a (the, one's) foil*; *to put to (a, the) foil*.

c **1478** in *Eng. Gilds* 304 Myndynge not to take the foyle, stande to defende theyre cause. **1548** UDALL, etc. *Erasm. Par.* Pref. 11 Could neuer yet fynde how to geue him any foile. **1573** G. HARVEY *Letter-bk.* (Camden) 13 Considering what a foul shame and foil it had alreddi bene unto me. **1603** HOLLAND *Plutarch's Mor.* 427 Chabrias..having put to foile and defaited some few Thebans. **1609** HUME *Admon.* in Wodr. Soc. *Misc.* (1844) 582 And receaved the foillie. **1615** G. SANDYS *Trav.* III. 145 The alternate changes of foiles and victories. **1647** N. BACON *Disc. Govt. Eng.* I. lxiv. (1739) 132 The Lords received the first blow, and gave the first foil. *a* **1716** SOUTH *Serm.* (1744) XI. 24 It may give a man many a..foil and many a disheartening blow. **1738** tr. *Johnson's ad Urbanum* in *Gentl. Mag.* May, Whom no base calumny can put to foil. **1814** SOUTHEY *Roderick* XVIII. 358 When Africa received her final foil. **1821** JOANNA BAILLIE *Met. Leg.*, *Wallace* lv. Ashamed and wroth at such unseemly foil. **1870** MORRIS *Earthly Par.* III. IV. 232 He thinks No more of yesterday's disgrace and foil.

†**b.** With mixture of the sense of FOIL *v.*[1] 6: A disgrace, stigma. *Obs.*

1599 PORTER *Angry Wom. Abingd.* (Percy Soc.) 26 It hath set a foyle upon thy fame. **1616** BRETON *Good & Badde* 5/2 He [an Vnworthy king] is the foyle of a crowne.

†**3.** The cause of (one's) defeat or failure. *Obs.*

a **1683** OLDHAM *Ode to Vice* Poet. Wks. (1686) 106 Thou ..Whom baffled Hell esteems its greatest Foyl. *a* **1704** T. BROWN *Sat. agst. Woman* Wks. 1730 I. 55 Oh! gawdy source of all mens hopes and fears, Foil of their youth.

† **foil**, *sb.*[3] *Obs.* In 6 foill. Also *Sc.* fulyie. [f. FOIL *v.*] What is trampled under foot; hence, Manure, dung.

1565 *Wills & Inv. N.C.* (Surtees 1835) 244 Raffe Vasye of lumlye castell oweth me for all my foill or muke that I left at my fermhold at crook.

foil (fɔɪl), *sb.*[4] Forms: 6 *pl.* ? foyelles (perh. mispr. for *foylles*), 6–7 foyl(e, 7– foil. [f. FOIL *v.*[1] (sense 2); cf. OF. *foulis*, Cotgr. *foulée*, *foulement* in same sense, f. *fouler* FOIL *v.*[1]] The track of a hunted animal.

1576 TURBERV. *Venerie* 77 Marking all his tokens as well by the slot as by the entries, foyelles, and such like. **1674** N. COX *Gentl. Recreat.* I. (1677) 72 The Dew will be beaten off, the Foil fresh, or the ground broken. *a* **1734** NORTH *Lives* II. 353 Fellows..have lain down upon the foil to prove whether the dogs followed the track or not. **1810** *Sporting Mag.* XXXV. 206 Having rounded the hill he crossed the foil. **1894** *Scotsman* 27 Aug. 11/2 Mr. Davidson decided to lay the hounds on the foil of the otter first found.

fig. **1682** OTWAY *Venice Preserved* III, What, hunt A wife on the dull foil! **1684** SOUTHERNE *Disappointment* I, Fleeting pleasure leaves me on the foyle. **1749** FIELDING *Tom Jones* VII. iv, Here's another b—— follows me upon the foil. **1790** WOLCOT (P. Pindar) *Ode to Bruce* iii, O Bruce, thou treadest Abyssinian grounds; Nor can our British noses hunt thy foil.

b. Phrases. *to run* (or †*take*) *the foil*, *to run upon the foil*: to run over the same track a second time (with the effect of baffling the hounds). *to break her foil*: to run out of the track after having doubled.

1601 in Farr *S. P. Eliz.* (1845) II. 431 The chafed deare doth take the foyle. **1650** FULLER *Pisgah* IV. iii. 44 No Hare, when hardly put to it..and running foile, makes moe doublings. **1781** P. BECKFORD *Hunting* xi. 151 You must..try to hit her off where she breaks her foil. **1798** *Sporting Mag.* XI. 87 The ground so stained by running the foil that the scent lay with no certainty. **1828** CARR *Craven Gloss.* s.v., To run the foil.

transf. and *fig.* **1658** J. HARRINGTON *Prerog. Pop. Govt.* I. x. (1700) 289 To affirm that..is to run upon the foil. **1666** J. SMITH *Old Age* 233 From whence it [the blood] is recommitted into the right ventricle of the Heart, to be chased the Foyl. **1878** *Cumbld. Gloss.* Suppl. s.v., 'Runnin' oald foils', following former courses.

foil (fɔɪl), *sb.*[5] Forms; 6–7 foile, foyle, 8 file, 7– foil. [Of obscure origin.

Usually regarded as f. FOIL *v.*[1], and as denoting etymologically 'a sword with the point *foiled* or blunted.' But the vb. does not appear to have meant 'to blunt': the reading of the quarto in *Oth.* I. iii. 270, even if genuine, does not admit of this interpretation. Another suggestion is that the phrase *at foils* originally belonged to FOIL *sb.*[2] in the sense of parrying, and that the name of the instrument was evolved from the phrase. It is noteworthy that FOIN *sb.* occurs in 17th c. in the sense of *foil*; possible (in spite of the want of evidence) this goes back to the 16th c, so that *foil* might be an etymologizing alteration of *foin*, after FOIL *v.*[1] That the word is, by some far-fetched association, a transferred use of FOIL *sb.*[1] a leaf (cf. F. *fleuret* fencing foil, lit. 'floweret', the button being compared to a bud) is a possibility for which at present there is no evidence.]

1. A light weapon used in fencing; a kind of small-sword with a blunt edge and a button at the point.

1594 NASHE *Unfort. Trav.* 21 Iacke Leiden..had..a peece of a rustie sword..by his side..it was but a foyle neither, and he wore it, to shewe that he should haue the foyle of his Enemies. **1606** DRUMM. OF HAWTH. *Let.* 6 Aug. Wks. (1711) 233 They would have most willingly taken the buttons off the foils. **1703** MRS. CENTLIVRE *Beau's Duel* III. i. I hope to see it as much a fashion to fight with files, as 'tis to fence with them. **1729** *Art of Fencing* 3 The Sword (or File, in imitation of the Sword). **1852** THACKERAY *Esmond* I. xiv, I can use the foils..indifferently well.

2. *pl.* The exercise of fencing with foils, *esp.* in phrase *at foils*.

1600 NASHE *Summers Last Will* (Grosart) 130 It makes him..fight..as though hee were but a foyles amongst his fellows. *a* **1643** W. CARTWRIGHT *Ordinary* II. v, *Credulous.* Where's your cloak? *Andrew.* Going to foiles ev'n now, I put it off. **1841–44** EMERSON *Ess., Prudence* Wks. (Bohn) I. 100 Entire self-possession may make a battle very little more dangerous to life than a match at foils.

3. *attrib.*, as *foil-button*.

1599 MARSTON *Sco. Villanie* III. xi. 226 This bumbast foile-button..For want of talke-stuffe, fals to foinery, Out goes his Rapier.

foil (fɔɪl), *v.*[1] Forms: 4–6 foile, foyle, 7 foyl, 6– foil. See also FOUL *v.* and *Sc.* FULYIE *v.* [irreg. repr. of OF. *fuler*, *foler*, *fouler* (mod.F. *fouler*), to full cloth, to tread, trample down, press hard upon, crush, oppress; corresponding to Pr. *folar*, Sp. *hollar*, It. *follare* in similar senses:—popular Lat. **fullāre* originally to full cloth, f. *fullō* a fuller: cf. FULL *v.*

The Eng. forms *foyle, foil*, and Sc. *fulȝe, fulyie*, would normally represent not OF. *foler, fouler*, but *fouillier* (mod.F. *fouiller*), which has the quite different senses 'to dig, grub up, root (as a swine), search'. The cause of the irregularity has not been discovered: a suggestion is that the sb. *foulis, foleïz* = FOIL *sb.*[3] may have been confused with *fouillis* the 'rooting' of a swine, a mass of dirt and rubbish, and that this led to a confusion in the verb; but it is doubtful whether this would account for the facts.]

I. In sense of Fr. *fouler*.

†**1.** *trans.* To tread under foot, trample down.

13.. *K. Alis.* 2712 Mony gentil cors, Was y-foiled undur fet of hors. *c* **1330** *Arth. & Merl.* 9440 Pinogras he feld of hors, And foiled al his cursed cors. **1502** *Ord. Crysten Men* (W. de W. 1506) v. ii. 363 They shall foyle and threste all the dampned togyder. **1577–87** HOLINSHED *Chron.* (1808) IV. 877 The more they contended to suppresse him, the more (like the camomill being foiled and troden) his vertues rose vp. **1596** DANETT tr. *Comines* IV. iii. 124 But the third [man] the Beare tooke and ouerthrew, and foiled vnder hir feete. **1603** KNOLLES *Hist. Turks* (1621) 69 King Richard..caused the ensignes of Leopold..to be puld downe, and foiled vnder foot.

fig. *c* **1400** *Apol. Loll.* 44 In veyn þu foilist þi flesch wiþ abstinens. *c* **1440** *Gesta Rom.* xxxvii. 151 (Harl. MS.) A synner..enterithe in to holy chirche, and foylithe the comaundementes of god. **1470–85** MALORY *Arthur* XVIII. xxv, Worshyp in armes may neuer be foyled.

2. Of animals: To trample or tread down; to tread into mud; *esp.* in *Hunting*, to run over or cross (the ground, scent, or track) with the effect of baffling the hounds. Also *absol.* of a deer (see quot. 1886); †*refl.* of a hound: To spoil his own scent.

1649 BLITHE *Eng. Improv. Impr.* (1653) 25 Soak not thy Land too much, that Cattell treading, or Grazing upon it, foyl it not. **1651** DAVENANT *Gondibert* II. xlv, Their [Doggs'] scent no North-east winde could e're deceave..nor Flocks that foyle the Ground. **1672–3** MARVELL *Reh. Transp.* 72 A ..dog having foil'd himself..with everything he meets. **1735** SOMERVILLE *Chase* II. 174 In the same Round Persisting still, she'll foil the beaten Track. **1781** P. BECKFORD *Hunting* (1802) 279 If you suffer all your hounds to hunt on the line of him, they will foil the ground. **1828** CARR *Craven Gloss., Foil*, to trample, as meadow grass is said to be foiled when trampled or trodden down by hares. **1886** ELWORTHY *W. Somerset Word-bk., Foil*..the scent, or the ground, are said to be foiled when other deer than the hunted one have crossed the scent. *Ibid., Foil*..a deer is said to foil when he retraces his steps over the same track.

fig. *a* **1719** ADDISON (J.), I..put up such a variety of odd creatures..that they foil the scent of one another.

†**3.** To press hard upon, oppress. *Obs. rare*$^{-1}$.

This sense, common in OF., appears to be required by the context, though the other texts read *fylus, fylen*.

a **1300** *Cursor M.* 10104 (Cott.) Þis world, my flesh, the fend als þat folus [*Laud MS.* foylyn] me wiþ fondyng fals to make me falle in fylthis fele.

II. To overthrow, defeat, baffle.

4. To overthrow, defeat (an antagonist); to beat off, repulse, discomfit (an assailant or an attack). †In *Wrestling*: To throw, to inflict a 'foil' upon: see FOIL *sb.*[2] 1. Also *fig.*

1548 HALL *Chron., Edw. IV.* (an. 23) If they lacke actiuitie, euery creature be he neuer so base of birthe, shall foyle and ouerthrowe them. **1600** SHAKS. *A.Y.L.* II. ii. 14 The Wrastler That did but lately foile the synowie Charles. **1610** GUILLIM *Heraldry* III. ii. (1660) 102 To chase away and foil all passionate perturbations of the mind. **1648** BP. HALL *Breathings Devout Soul* (1851) 175, I strive..but, sometimes, I am foiled; and go halting out of the field. **1667** MILTON *P.L.* I. 273 Leader of those Armies bright, Which but th' Omnipotent none could have foyld. **1697** DRYDEN *Virg. Georg.* II. 776 The Groom..watches with a Trip his Foe to foil. **1725** POPE *Odyss.* xx. 25 Not fiercer woes they fortitude could foil. **1736** WEST *Let.* in *Gray's Poems* (1775) 10 You have foiled him..at his own weapon. **1737** BURKE *Abridgm. Eng. Hist.* Wks. 1842 II. 572 Suits..in every one of which he was sure to be foiled. **1808** J. BARLOW *Columb.* IV. 247 Howard..foils the force of Spain. **1875** JOWETT *Plato* (ed. 2) I. 344 Meletus, who is easily foiled and mastered in the hands of the great dialectician.

b. To outdo, surpass.

a **1687** WALLER *Of a tree cut in paper* 7 Fair hand!.. Strange, that your fingers should the pencil foil. **1786** BURNS *Lass o' Ballochmyle* iii, Woman, Nature's darling child!.. Ev'n there her other works are foil'd. **1812** H. & J. SMITH *Rej. Addr.* No. 10 Not chusing her charms should be foil'd By Lady Elizabeth Mugg.

†**c.** *intr.* To suffer discomfiture. *Obs.*

1591 GREENE *Maiden's Dreame* xlix, His toil He took, lest that the English state might foil. **1639** VERGER tr. *Camus' Admir. Events* To Rdr. a vj, There be mindes which foyle in reading a history of great length, humane patience being not of any great extent.

5. To frustrate, render nugatory (an attempt or purpose); to parry (a blow); to baulk, disappoint (hopes, etc.); to baffle, frustrate the efforts of (a person).

App. developed from sense 4 with some influence of the notion of 'foiling a scent': see 2.

a **1564** BECON *Jewel of Joy* in *Catechism, &c.* (1844) 426 Paul..had so many years been foiled with the..elvish expositions of certain doting doctors. **1600** HAKLUYT *Voy.* III. 160 Lest his credite, foyled in his first attempt, in a second should be vtterly disgraced. **1612** T. TAYLOR *Comm. Titus* i. 2 Faith shall be easily shaken, hope quickly foyled. **1621** MARQ. BUCKINGHAM in *Fortesc. Papers* 172 That whole businesse will be foyled. **1676** WISEMAN *Surgery* V. v. 363 He had been foiled in the Cure, and had left it to Nature. **1784** COWPER *Task* III. 4 Having long in miry ways been foiled. **1823** SCOTT *Peveril* xxxi, To be foiled in a gallant intrigue was to subject himself to the ridicule of his gay court. **1841** BORROW *Zincali* I. iv. II. 301 He foiled the stroke

of Chaléco. **1853** KANE *Grinnell Exp.* xxviii. (1856) 227 The project..was foiled for a time. **1871** DIXON *Tower* III. xii. 123 But here their wits were foiled. **1871** R. H. HUTTON *Ess.* (1877) I. 19 The narrow anxiety..is apt to foil its own end.

III. Influenced by FOUL *a.* and *v.*; cf. *defoil*, DEFOUL *v.* and FILE *v.*

6. To foul, defile, pollute. In material or immaterial sense. *Obs.* exc. *dial.* (In some mod. dialects perh. a pronunciation of FILE.)

Quot. 1440 may belong to sense 3 or 4.

c **1380** WYCLIF *Serm.* Sel. Wks. II. 86 þei preche not to profit of þe folk but..to foile [*v.r.* foulen] hem wiþ many synnes. *c* **1440** HYLTON *Scala Perf.* (W. de W. 1494) I. xxxiv, A man that hath be moche foyled wyth worldly or flesshely synnes. *a* **1553** UDALL *Royster D.* v. vi. (Arb.) 85 A man hath no honour to foile his handes on a woman. **1633** P. FLETCHER *Purple Isl.* xi. 33 Ranc'rous enemies, that hourely toil Thy humble votarie with loathsome spot to foil. **1878** *Cumbld. Gloss.*, *Foil*, to defile.

†**7.** To dishonour; *esp.* to deflower (a woman), to violate (chastity).

c **1440** *Gesta Rom.* xxxvi. 143 (Harl. Ms.) Hast thowe foylid my dowter. *a* **1577** GASCOIGNE *Wks.* (1587) 300 Rather chose to die..Than filthie men should foile their chastitie. *a* **1592** GREENE *Mamillia* Wks. (Grosart) II. 153 Hast thou..no more regard to thy solemne othe than to foile it with periurie?

†**8.** To cause filth, drop excrement; = FILE *v.*[2] 1 d.

1599 HAYWARD *1st Pt. Hen. IV*, 77 They did nothing but feede and foyle in the summer of her sweete sun shine. **1616** —— *Sanct. Troub. Soul* I. §13 (1620) 285 Swine..doe nothing else but feede and foile.

Hence **foiled** *ppl. a.*, in senses of vb.; also of a horse: Injured. Also **'foiler**, one who foils.

1607 TOPSELL *Four-f. Beasts* 425 If he [a horse] be foiled on his forefeet by foundering or otherwise. **1700** PARKER *Six Philosoph. Ess.* 2 O thou..divine Burnet! thou foiler of all Philosophers. **1810** SCOTT *Lady of L.* II. xxx, Till the foiled King..Shall bootless turn him home agen. **1869** *Lonsdale Gloss.*, *Folied-girse*, grass much trodden.

foil (fɔɪl), *v.*[2] [f. FOIL *sb.*[5]] *intr.* To make a thrust *at* with a foil. In quot. *transf.*

1600 ROWLANDS *Let. Humours Blood* ix, In single cumbat, being hurt..As he was closely foyling at a Wench.

†**foil**, *v.*[3] *Obs.* [perh. ad. F. *fouiller* to grub up; cf. F. *fouilleuse* (Boiste), *fouilleur* (Littré), a kind of light plough.]

trans. To subject (land) to the third of the series of ploughing; formerly prescribed for preparing it for sowing. Hence **'foiling** *vbl. sb.*

1616 SURFL. & MARKHAM *Country Farme* 555 At August you shall giue it the third ardor or earing, vvhich is called foyling..this ardor is..one of the best, especially for the destroying of weeds. **1620** MARKHAM *Farew. Husb.* Pref. to Rdr., Sixe seuerall plowings, as fallowing in Ianuary and February, Stirring in Aprill and May, Foiling in Iuly and August [etc.]. **1669** WORLIDGE *Syst. Agric.* (1681) 326 To Foyl, that is, to fallow Land in the summer or autumn.

foil (fɔɪl), *v.*[4] [f. FOIL *sb.*[1]]

1. *trans.* To apply foil or a foil to.

†**a.** To spread *over* with a thin sheet of metal or other substance. See FOIL *sb.*[1] 4. In quot. *fig.*

1611 SPEED *Hist. Gt. Brit.* v. iii. §16 Foiling them [tales] ouer with a new colour of the Latine tongue.

†**b.** To apply an amalgam of tinfoil and mercury to (glass, a mirror). See FOIL *sb.*[1] 4 b. *Obs.*

1714 *Fr. Bk. of Rates* 83 Tin..to Foile Looking-Glasses. **1787** *Gentl. Mag.* Suppl. 1166/2 He could..foil mirrors. *c* **1790** IMISON *Sch. Art* II. 6 When this amalgam is used for foiling or silvering, let it first be strained through a linen rag. **1818** *Blackw. Mag.* III. 615/2 The difficulty of foiling glass to the various forms necessary.

c. To back (a crystal) with a foil (FOIL *sb.*[1] 5).

1887 *Archæologia* L. 110 A crystal (?) foiled to resemble sapphire.

2. To set off by contrast. See FOIL *sb.*[1] 6.

1856 RUSKIN *Mod. Paint.* III. IV. iii. §14 Beauty..must be foiled by inferiority before its own power can be developed.

3. *Arch.* To ornament with foils.

1835 R. WILLIS *Archit. Mid. Ages* v. 41 At the same time there came in the practice of *Foiling* arches; that is, of uniting a series of three or more by their bases, so as to form one. **1849** [see FOILING *vbl. sb.*[2] b].

Hence **'foiler**, one who foils.

1612 WOODALL *Surg. Mate* Wks. (1653) 171 Foilers of looking-glasses.

foil, obs. form of FOAL.

foilable ('fɔɪləb(ə)l), *a.* [f. FOIL *v.*[1] + -ABLE.] That may be foiled or defeated.

1611 COTGR., *Rebutable*, reiectable, refusable; foylable. **1848** in CRAIG; and in mod. Dicts.

foilage, obs. form of FOLIAGE.

'foil-borne, foilborne, *a.* [BORNE *ppl. a.* 2 b.] Of a craft: raised out of the water by lift provided by hydrofoils. Of the motion, etc., of a craft: taking place while it is so supported.

1961 *Hovering Craft & Hydrofoil* Oct. 6/2 The foils will be lowered, the main engine started, and the craft can proceed foilborne at 60 knots. *Ibid.*, Driftwood and other floating debris has little effect on foilborne boats. **1964** *Weekly News* (Auckland) 8 July 31 (*caption*) The Manu-wai ..settles heavily as her foil-borne hull re-enters the water. **1967** *Jane's Surface Skimmer Systems 1967–68* 95/1 An automatic control system is installed that utilises craft motion and height inputs to maintain foilborne flight. *Ibid.* 91/2 Foilborne propulsion. **1968** *New Scientist* 17 Oct. 138/2 One civil application would be to inject additive round the hull of a hydrofoil while it was accelerating to become foil-borne.

foile, obs. form of FILE *sb.*[5]

foiled (fɔɪld), *ppl. a.* [f. FOIL *v.*[4] + -ED[1] and FOIL *sb.*[1] + -ED[2].]

1. †**a.** Coated on one side, or backed with foil (*obs.*). **b.** Produced by a coating of foil.

1662 J. BARGRAVE *Pope Alex. VII* (1867) 131 Two cylinders..the one of steel..the other of foyled isinglass. **1703** T. N. *City & C. Purchaser* 153 Looking-glasses foil'd being in vogue for Ornaments. **1864** *Realm* 24 Feb. 8 If we are content with painted and foiled glitter.

2. *Arch.* Ornamented with foils; resembling foils. ***foiled arch*** = *foil-arch*. See FOIL *sb.*[1] 2 b.

1835 R. WILLIS *Archit. Mid. Ages* 194 This is the Saracen mode of treating foiled arches. **1840** PARKER *Gloss. Archit.* 93 *Foiled Arch*, an arch in the form of a trefoil, cinquefoil, or multifoil. **1848** J. G. WILKINSON *Dalmatia, etc.* I. 255 A foiled corbel table. **1849** RUSKIN *Sev. Lamps* iii. §20. 86 Holes cut into foiled shapes.

†**'foilery.** *Obs.* In 6 **folery**, *Sc.* **fulȝery.** [f. FOIL *sb.*[1] 2 + -ERY: there may have been an OF. **fueillerie*.] Ornamentation resembling foliage.

1501 DOUGLAS *Pal. Hon.* III. xvii, Skarsment, reprise, corbell, and battellingis, Fulȝery, bordouris of mony precious stone. **1527** PRIOR MOORE in Noake *Worcester Monastery* (1866) 157 The gest chamber..hanged with peynted clothes of folery, with bests, fulks, etc.

foiling ('fɔɪlɪŋ), *vbl. sb.*[1] [f. FOIL *v.*[1] + -ING[1].]

1. The action of the vb. FOIL in various senses.

a **1533** LD. BERNERS *Gold Bk. M. Aurel.* (1559) Z, There was neuer mortall man..that could scape fro the ..foilyng of hir [Enuie's] feete. **1683** tr. *Erasm. Moriæ Enc.* 90 The foiling of them in an irresistible battle.

2. *esp.* The treading of a deer or other animal. Hence the slot or trail; = FOIL *sb.*[4]

1576 TURBERV. *Venerie* 237 We cal it the foyling of a deare if it be on grasse where the print of the foote cannot well be seene. **1617** MARKHAM *Caval.* VIII. 36 How a Horses nose is able to direct him when hee comes..to the foylings of other Cattle.

foiling ('fɔɪlɪŋ), *vbl. sb.*[2] [f. FOIL *v.*[4] + -ING[1].]

a. The action or process of backing (glass) with foil. **b.** *Arch.* Ornamentation by foils; a foil ornament. See FOIL *sb.*[1] 2 b.

a **1583** W. BOURNE *Prop. Glasses* in *Rara Math.* (1838) No. I. 34 According vnto the several formes, facyons, and makyngs of them, and allso the foylinges of them. **1703** T. N. *City & C. Purchaser* 153 The..Foiling of these Glasses. **1849** RUSKIN *Sev. Lamps* iii. §20. 86 Where the wall was thick, and the foilings were large.

foilist ('fɔɪlɪst). [f. FOIL *sb.*[5] + -IST.] One who fences with a foil.

1907 *Times* 2 Apr., I implore you..to withdraw the word 'foilist' from circulation before the authority of *The Times* has given it..currency. **1932** *Times Lit. Suppl.* 24 Mar. 220/2 The beginner..should be able to develop into a more than competent foilist. **1958** *Oxf. Mag.* 13 Mar. 377/1 The foilists..defeated the strong Cambridge foil team.

†**foin**, *sb.*[1] *Obs.* Forms: 4–7 **foyn(e**, 5 **fooyne, fune**, *Sc.* **fonȝe, founȝe, foynȝe(e, funȝe**, 6 **fowyng, fouoyne**, 6–8 **foin(e.** [a. OF. *foine* (Fr. *fouine*), altered form (after OF. *fou*:—L. *fāgum* beech) of *faîne*:—late L. *fāgīna*, f. *fāg-um*; the animal was so named from its feeding on beech-mast.]

1. An animal of the polecat or weasel kind; the beech-marten (*Mustela foina*).

1423 JAS. I. *Kingis Q.* clvii, There sawe I..The martrik sable; the foynzee, and mony mo. **1550** J. COKE *Eng. & Fr. Heralds* §213 (1877) 118 We have marterns, foynes.. squerelles, etc. **1619** MIDDLETON *Triumphs Love & Antiq.* Wks. V. 289 The names of those beasts bearing fur.. Ermine, foine, sables, martin [etc.].

2. The fur of this animal; in *plural*, trimmings or garments made of the fur.

c **1394** *P. Pl. Crede* 295 A cote haþ he furred, Wiþ foyns, or wiþ fitchewes. **1399** LANGL. *Rich. Redeles* III. 150 Ffurris of ffoyne and oþer ffelle-ware. **1493** in *Halyburton's Ledger* (1867) 30 Item 100 rygis of fownȝes. **1562** in Heath *Grocers' Comp.* (1869) 426 *note*, Anye kind of furs in their gownes, but onlye foynes and budge. **1641** *Triumph Chas. I* in *Harl. Misc.* (Malh.) V. 96 About eighty comely and grave citizens, in foins and liveries. **1718** OZELL *Tournefort's Voy.* II. 376 The French Foines are much in esteem there.

3. *attrib.* and *Comb.*, as *foin(s-back, -skin, -tail*, etc.; **foins-bachelor**, one of a company dressed in gowns trimmed with foins, who took part in London civic processions (see BACHELOR 2); **foins-gown**, one trimmed with foins.

1561 in *Vicary's Anat.* (1888) App. vi. 189 My gowne.. faced with *foyne backes. **1612** *Sc. Bk. Customs* in *Halyburton's Ledger* (1867) 306 Furres called..Foynes— backes..tailes..powtes. **1681** T. JORDAN *Lond. Joy* 1 A youthful number of *Foyns Batchellors. **1692** *Lond. Gaz.* No. 2812/4 Also *Foins Gowns, and Scarlet Hoods for Rich Batchelors. **1718** OZELL *Tournefort's Voy.* II. 376 These *Foine-Skins.

foin (fɔɪn), *sb.*[2] Forms: see vb. [f. FOIN *v.*]

1. A thrust or push with a pointed weapon. ***to cast a foin at***: to make a thrust at. *Obs.* or *arch.*

c **1450** *Fencing w. two handed Sword* in *Rel. Ant.* I. 309 Thy quarters abowte, Thy stoppis, thy foynys. **1558** PHAER *Æneid* VII. U iv, They..fight with foyne of pointed speare. **1565** GOLDING *Ovid's Met.* XII. (1593) 284 Sir Dryant with a stake..did cast at him a foine, And thrust him through. *c* **1570** *Marr. Wit & Science* v. iv, Kepe at the foyne; come not wythin his reache. **1638** HEYWOOD *Wise Woman* IV. Wks. 1874 V. 330, I had my wards, and foynes, and quarter-blowes. **1814** SOUTHEY *Roderick* xxv. 400 Many a foin and thrust Aimed, and rebated.

fig. **1589** *Pappe w. Hatchet* B ij, I thought that hee which thrust at the bodie in game, would one day cast a foyne at the soule in earnest. *c* **1610** J. DAVIES *Scourge Folly* (Grosart) 10/2 They with foynes of wit, The foes of their vpholders home do hit.

†**b.** A wound made by such a stroke. *Obs.*

1543 TRAHERON *Vigo's Chirurg.* III. I. xv. 107 This playstre..is convenient at the begynnyng of a foyne. **1576** BAKER *Jewell of Health* 66 a, The water..healeth all maner of woundes..foynes or cuttes.

†**2.** = FOIL *sb.*[5] *Obs.*

[**1631** GOUGE *God's Arrows* 206 Such recreations as.. playing at wasters and foines.] **1656** OSBORN *Adv. Son* 22 The vast difference between a Foyn and a Sword. **1701** COLLIER *M. Aurel.* Life p. 1, Ordering the [Gladiators] to fight with Foins, or Buttons upon their Swords.

foin (fɔɪn), *v.* Forms: 4–7 **foyn(e(n**, (4 **foygne**, *Sc.* **funȝe**), 6–7 **foine**, 5– **foin.** [app. f. OFr. *foine, foisne, fouisne* (Fr. *fouine*), a three-pronged fish-spear:—L. *fuscina* in same sense.

This etymology involves some difficulties, as there is no evidence of the adoption of the sb. in Eng., nor of the existence of any OF. verb **foisnier, foinier*.]

1. *intr.* To make a thrust with a pointed weapon, or with the point of a weapon; to lunge, push. Often *to foin at* (a person) or *with* (a weapon). *arch.*

1375 BARBOUR *Bruce* VIII. 307 Thai..Fwnȝeit and fawcht all sturdely. ? *a* **1400** *Morte Arth.* 1494 They..ffoynes faste att þe fore breste with flawmande swerdez. *a* **1440** *Sir Degrev.* 274 With speres ferisly they foynede. **1565** JEWEL *Def. Apol.* (1611) 571 Ye foine only at your owne shadow, and hit nothing. **1635** N. R. *Camden's Hist. Eliz.* III. 353 That deadly manner of foyning with the rapier. **1700** DRYDEN *Palamon & Arc.* II. 196 They lash, they foin, they pass, they strive to bore Their Corslets. **1826** SCOTT *Woodst.* xviii, The fellow foins well. **1855** KINGSLEY *Westw. Ho!* (1861) 49 Foining with his point.

transf. and *fig.* *a* **1562** G. CAVENDISH *Wolsey* in Wordsworth *Eccl. Biog.* (1839) I. 527 The boare continually foining at him with his great tuskes. **1567** MAPLET *Gr. Forest* 101 He whetteth his Horne..and in his fight wardeth and foyneth at the Elephant his bellye. **1677** HALE *Prim. Orig. Man.* II. ix. 211 Heat, and..Cold, are always persecuting and foyning at the weaker..parts of Nature.

†**2.** *trans.* To thrust at, stab, pierce, prick.

c **1380** *Sir Ferumb.* 5640 Foygnede hym with þat knyf. **1520** *Caxton's Chron. Eng.* VII. 118/2 They..foyned theym with theyr swerdes and speres thrugh theyr bodyes. **1548** PATTEN *Exped. Scot.* I iiij b, Lashe at þe legges of þe horse, or foyne him in þe belly.

transf. *c* **1340** *Gaw. & Gr. Knt.* 428 þat fele hit [a head] foyned wyth her fete.

Hence **'foining** *vbl. sb.* and *ppl. a.*; **'foiningly** *adv.*

c **1400** *Destr. Troy* 10287 Fell was the fight foynyng of speires. **1523** LD. BERNERS *Froiss.* I. ccclxxiii. 617 With their foyninge the Englyssheman was ouerthrowen to the erthe. **1558** PHAER *Æneid* VII, Borespeares longe they whirle, or foynyng forks. **1599** SHAKS. *Much Ado* v. i. 84 Sir boy, ile whip you from your foyning fence. **1618** FLETCHER *Loyal Subj.* I. iv, Are you afraid of foining? **1620** THOMAS *Lat. Dict.*, *Punctim*..foiningly, pointingly. **1628** WITHER *Brit. Rememb.* III. 945 The capring Dancer, and the foining Fencer.

†**'foinery.** *Obs. rare.* [f. FOIN *v.* + -ERY.] Thrusting with the foil, fencing with the point.

1599 MARSTON *Sco. Villanie* III. xi. 22 [He] fals to foinery, Out goes his Rapier.

foir-: see FORE-[1].

fois, obs. pl. of FOE.

foison ('fɔɪz(ə)n), *sb.* Forms: 3 **fouss-, fusun**, 3–4 **fuisum, -un**, 4–6 **fusiou(n)n(e, -on, fuysion, -on**, 7 **fouson, fuzzen**, 4–7 **foyson**, 5 **-un**, 6 **-en**, 4 **fosoun**, 4–5 **foi-, foysoun(e**, 6–7 **foi-, foyzon(e**, 7 **-zen, -eson**, 5 **fysoun**, 7–8 **fizon**, 9 **fizzen**, 4– **foison.** [a. OF. *foison, foyson, fuison, fuson* = Pr. *foison*:—popular L. **fūsiōn-em*, for L. *fūsiōn-em* a pouring, n. of action f. *fundĕre* to pour.]

1. Plenty, abundance, a plentiful supply; a great quantity or number (of persons or things). *arch.*

13.. *K. Alis.* 1030 Alle the innes of the town Haddyn litel foisoun. **1303** R. BRUNNE *Handl. Synne* 5808 Gode shal ȝyue þe hys blessyng And foysyn yn alle þyng. **1375** BARBOUR *Bruce* XIX. 482 Fyres in gret foysoune thai maid. **1489** CAXTON *Faytes of A.* II. xxxix. 163 They muste haue grete foyson of arowes with brode hedes. **1545** RAYNOLD *Byrth Mankynde* I. ii. (1634) 20 The greater foyson of fat that there is betweene the two skinnes, the lesse be the vaines. **1652** ASHMOLE *Theatr. Chem. Brit.* 217 Of al deyntes plente and foyson. **1810** LAMB *Farew. to Tobacco*, Africa, that brags her foison, Breeds no such prodigious poison. **1848** LOWELL *Fable for Critics* Poet. Wks. 1890 III. 70 He has a perennial foison of sappiness.

b. Plentiful crop or harvest.

1587 GOLDING *De Mornay* xxxiv. 549 If it [the grayne] spring not vp, it yeldeth no foyson. **1610** SHAKS. *Temp.* IV. i. 110 Earths increase, foyzon plentie, Barnes and Garners neuer empty. **1845** R. W. HAMILTON *Pop. Educ.* x. 330 We anticipate the foison of an unknown husbandry.

c. quasi-*adv.* In abundance. So OF. *foison*.

13.. *K. Alis.* 1012 Heo..was deliverid liversoon, Skarschliche and nought foisoun [*MS. Laud* 622 nouȝth a foyson].

2. Inherent vigour or vitality; power, strength, capacity. *pl.* Resources. Now chiefly *Sc.*

a **1300** *Cursor M.* 8516 (Cott.) Gains him his fas had na fusun. *Ibid.* 13499 (Gött.) He bliscid siþen þe fisses tuine, And sett his fuisum þaim widine. ? *a* **1400** *Arthur* 476 He, for alle hys grete Renoun, Aȝenst Arthour hadde no fusoun. *c* **1550** BALE *K. Johan* (Camden) 77, I wyll gyve Kynge Iohan thys poyson, So makynge hym sure that he shall never have foyson. *a* **1592** H. SMITH *Serm.* (1866) II. 114 Such a foison hath your alms that..it increases, like the widows meal. **1605** SHAKS. *Macb.* IV. iii. 88 Scotland hath Foysons to fill vp your will Of your meere Owne. **1808** JAMIESON, *Foison* 2, Pith, ability; used to express..bodily strength. **1825** *Ibid.*, 'He has nae foison in him'; he has no understanding, or mental energy. *Loth.*

b. Nourishing power; hence, nourishment, *lit.* and *fig.* Now *dial.* and *Sc.*

c **1430** LYDG. in *Lay Folks Mass-bk.* (1879) Notes 368 Quat man here messe or he dyne..Hys mete xal han þe more fysoun. **1607** WALKINGTON *Opt. Glasse* i. B3b, Them two are poyson to men though foison to birds. *Ibid.*, v. F1a, Like the foieson or oile of the lampe, wherewith it continewes burning. *Ibid.* xii. K4a, The foison of our best phantasies. **1624** GEE *Foot out of Snare* v. 41 The Liturgie ..is but dry meat, and hath no foison in it. **1674** RAY *S. & E.C. Words* 66 *Foison* or *Fizon*, the natural juice or moisture of the Grass or other herbs. **1787** GROSE *Prov. Gloss.* Suppl., *Foison* or *Fizon*. *a* **1825** FORBY *Voc. E. Anglia*, s.v., There is no foison in this hay. **1825** JAMIESON s.v., 'Ye'll tak a' the fizzen out o't [meat].'

foison ('fɔız(ə)n), *v. Obs.* exc. *arch.* [ad. OFr. *foisonner*, f. *foison*: see prec.] *trans.* **a.** To supply plentifully. **b.** To nourish.

1393 GOWER *Conf.* III. 341 Where all good him was foisoned. *c* **1485** *Digby Myst.* II. 513 Yt fedyth and foysonnes. **1891** E. ARNOLD *Lt. World* 190 Earth To fill and foison with His Father's will.

†'**foisonable**, *a. Obs.* [f. FOISON *sb.* or *v.*] Capable of yielding a crop, productive.

1613 F. ROBARTS *Rev. Gospel* 91 A ground which..was vtterly vnprofitable, nor could be made foysonable without great expence. **1627** [see BATTLESOME *a.*[2]].

foisonless ('fɔız(ə)nlıs), *a.* Chiefly *Sc.* Also fison-, fishion-, fissen-, fiz(z)en-, fusion-, fushionless. [f. FOISON *sb.* + -LESS.] Wanting substance, strength, or 'sap'; weak, ineffective, both in a material and immaterial sense. Of grass: Wanting in succulence or nourishing properties.

1721 KELLY *Sc. Prov.* 104 Fair Folk is ay Fisonless. *a* **1796** BURNS '*The Deuk's dang o'er my Daddie*', An' he is but a fusionless carlie. *c* **1817** HOGG *Tales & Sk.* I. 328 Old rusty and fizenless sword. **1824** SCOTT *St. Ronan's* xxxii, And puir thin fusionless skink it was. **1837** CARLYLE *Misc.* (1857) IV. 3 Our very Biographies, how stiff-starched, foisonless, hollow. **1864** *Athenæum* No. 1921. 234/2 The fusionless bog hay. **1870** *Pall Mall G.* 27 Sept. 11 These fusionless idlers who never derange themselves for anything. **1888** R. F. D. PALGRAVE in *Eng. Hist. Rev.* Oct. 745 The 'wild-fire' proved a very fizzenless mixture.

†'**foisonous**, *a. Obs. rare.* [f. as prec. + -OUS.] Full of energy; fruitful.

1570 LEVINS *Manip.* 226 Foysonouse, *foecundus.* **1602** WARNER *Alb. Eng.* XIII. lxxviii. (1612) 324 Union, in breefe, is foysonous, and discorde works decay.

†**foist, fust**, *sb.*[1] *Obs.* Forms: 5–7 fuste, (6 fuyst), 6–7 foiste, foyst(e, 6–8, 9 *Hist.* foist, (7 foise). [a. OF. *fuste*, ad. It. *fusta* fem. originally log, piece of timber, f. L. *fustis* cudgel.]

1. A light galley; a vessel propelled both by sails and oars. Cf. FELUCCA.

1485 CAXTON *Paris & V.* 80 By adventure they fonde a fuste. **1558–80** WARDE tr. *Alexis' Secr.* I. I. 17b, Wee were set vpon by fiue foystes of Pirates. **1603** KNOLLES *Hist. Turks* (1621) 430 Peeces of great ordinance placed in fusts and gallies. **1777** HOOLE *Comenius' Vis. World* (ed. 12) 111 A ship furnished with oars is a barge, or a foyst.

fig. **1569** *Shippe of Safegarde* (N.) Nor taking heede his fleshly foyst to guide. *a* **1625** FLETCHER *Woman's Prize* II. vi. This Pinck, this painted Foyst, this Cockle-boat.

2. A barge, a small boat used on the river.

1533 WRIOTHESLEY *Chron.* (1875) I. 18 A barge..rytchlie behanged with cloath of golde and a foyste to wayte on her. **1616** B. JONSON *Epigr.* cxxxiii. *Voy.* 100 That is when it is the Lord Maiors foist.

foist, *sb.*[2] [a. OF. *fust* (mod.F. *fût*) cask, primarily log, tree-trunk:—L. *fustem* cudgel.]

†**1.** A cask for wine; in phrase *to savour of the foist*: to be 'fusty', *Obs.*

a **1533** LD. BERNERS *Gold. Bk. M. Aurel.* (1546) Qb, Good wyne sometyme sauoureth of the foyst.

2. Hence, Fustiness. [F. *fust* (Cotgr.).]

1819 REES *Cycl.*, *Foist*, used to signify a musty sort of smell among hay, straw, grain, and other farm products. **1876** *Whitby Gloss.*, *Foist*, the mildew'd scent of a cellar.

foist, *sb.*[3] *Obs.* exc. *dial.* [dial. var. of FIST *sb.*[2]]

a. = FIST *sb.*[2] 1. **b.** *dial.* = FIST *sb.*[2] 2. **c.** *Comb.* = *fist-ball.*

1593 NASHE *Lett. Confut.* Wks. (Grosart) II. 204 A fatall foyst. **1640** [see FIST *sb.*[2] 4]. *a* **1700** B. E. *Dict. Cant. Crew*, *Foyst*..a close strong Stink, without Noise or Report. **1847** HALLIWELL, *Foist*, a toad-stool, *Suffolk.*

d. *U.S.* = FICE, FIST *sb.*[2] 3.

1851 T. A. BURKE *Polly Peablossom's Wedding* 18 [The sounding of the horn] was sufficient invitation to every hound, foist, and 'cur of low degree' to join in the chorus.

†**foist**, *sb.*[4] *Obs.* [f. FOIST *v.*[1]]

1. A cheat, a rogue; a pick-pocket.

1591 GREENE *Disc. Coosnage* Pref. 3 The Foist, the picke-pockets (sir reuerence, I meane). **1611** MIDDLETON & DEKKER *Roaring Girle* v. M.'s Wks. (Bullen) IV. 134 *Mol.* This braue fellow is no better then a foyst. *Omnes.* Foyst, what's that? *Mol.* A..picke-pocket. **1659** *Lady Alimony* v. iii, You shall play no more the sharking foist with me. *a* **1700** B. E. *Dict. Cant. Crew*, *Foyst*, a Cheat or Rogue.

2. A piece of roguery, trick.

1605 B. JONSON *Volpone* III. ix, Put not your foist's vpon me, I shall sent 'hem. **1641** 'SMECTYMNUUS' *Vind. Answ.* vi. 83 Which if you call a foyst, all your owne side are as guilty as our selves. **1654** R. VILVAIN *Theorem. Theol.* iii. 115 What fine foists and brazen bolts are thes to bolster a bad caus? **1677** in COLES *Eng.-Lat. Dict.*

3. Something foisted in.

a **1734** NORTH *Exam.* III. vi. §101 (1740) 495 The Author gives the following Speech of May 28, by Way of Foist in the Place of that before of the 23[d] of May.

foist, *sb.*[5] *rare.* [f. next.] A fogy.

1820 *Blackwood's Mag.* VIII. 105 The reins were continually slipping out of the fingers of the ancient foists ['the old drivers of the periodical Heavies'].

foist (fɔıst), *a. dial.* [? f. FOIST *sb.*[2]] Fusty.

1691 RAY *N.C. Words*, *Foist*, Fusty. **1721–92** in BAILEY. **1842** JOHNSON *Farmer's Encycl.*, *Foist* or *Foust*, a provincial word signifying mouldy or rusty. **1868** ATKINSON *Cleveland Gloss.*, *Foist, foisty.*

foist (fɔıst), *v.*[1] [prob. ad. Du. dial. *vuisten* to take in the hand, f. *vuist* fist; cf. Ger. dial. *fäusten.*

The Du. word now means to play at a game in which one player holds some coins in his hand, and the others guess at their number (Prof. Gallée).]

†**1.** *trans.* (*Dicing*). To palm (a 'flat' or false die) so as to be able to introduce it when required. Also *intr.* to cheat by this means (in quot. 1545 app. used loosely). *to foist in*: to introduce (the flat) surreptitiously when palmed. *Obs.*

1545 ASCHAM *Toxoph.* (Arb.) 54 If they be trew dise, what shyfte wil they make to set the one of them with slyding, with cogging, with foysting, with coytinge, as they call it. *c* **1550** *Dice-Play* Cjb, *R.* What shift haue they to bring the flat in & out? *M.* A ioly fine shifte, y[t] properly is called foysting, & it is..a sleight to cary easely within the hand as often as the foister list. So y[t] when either he or his partener shall cast y[e] dice, the flat comes not abrod til he haue made a great hande, and won as much as him list. *Ibid.* Cij, If.. this young scholler haue not so redy..an eye, to deserne the flat at euery time that hee is foysted in. **1565** HARDING in Jewel *Def. Apol.* (1611) 127 Through Foisting and Cogging their Die, and other false play.

†**2.** *intr.* To practise roguery, to cheat. *Obs.* Cf. COG *v.*[3]

1584 R. WILSON *Three Ladies Lond.* I. Aiijb, Thou doest nothing but cog, lie, and foist with hypocrisie. **1611** MIDDLETON & DEKKER *Roaring Girl* v. i. M.'s Wks. (Bullen) IV. 134 A pickpocket; all his train study the figging law, that's to say, cutting of purses and foisting.

†**b.** *trans.* To cheat (a person) *out of*. *Obs.* Cf. COG *v.*[3] 3b.

1622 FLETCHER *Sea Voy.* I. iii, If I be foysted and jeer'd out of my goods!

†**3.** To put forth or allege fraudulently. *Obs.* Cf. COG *v.* 6.

a **1640** W. FENNER *Sacrif. Faithf.* (1648) 35 Men must take heed that they foyst not the name of Christ: that they foyst not a ticket to say that Christ sent them. **1678** MARVELL *Growth Popery* Wks. I. 450 Some..by foisting a counterfeit donation of Constantine..advanced themselves.

b. To introduce surreptitiously or unwarrantably *into*; also with *in* adv.

1563–87 FOXE *A. & M.* (1596) 776/2 Unlesse..by some fraudulent misdealing of mine enemies, there be any thing foysted into them. **1570** T. NORTON tr. *Nowel's Catech.* (1853) 173 They..desire to shift and foist in the Bishop of Rome to be head of the church in earth, in the stead of Christ. **1641** SHUTE *Sarah & Hagar* (1649) 76 A rude.. familiarity..with the name of God (foisting it up and down in common communication and oathes). **1676** W. ROW *Contin. Blair's Autobiog.* xii. (1848) 372 A general and ambiguous clause was foisted into the Oath of Allegiance. **1704** SWIFT *T. Tub* xi (1709) 127 A passage..(whether foisted in by the Transcriber is not known). **1836** LYTTON *Athens* I. 275 The..interpolations..supposed to be foisted into the Odyssey. **1861** BERESF. HOPE *Eng. Cathedr. 19th C.* 73 The zeal of San Carlo Borromeo has foisted in subsidiary altars, to the detriment of the grand simplicity of its first plan. **1889** JESSOPP *Coming of Friars* iii. 156 [He] was eventually foisted into the see of Durham.

c. To palm or put off; to fasten or fix stealthily or unwarrantably *on* or *upon*; occas. to father (a composition) upon: rarely with *off*.

1599 MARSTON *Sco. Villanie* I. iii. 182 When Tegeran Brags that hee foysts his rotten Curtezan Vpon his heire. **1633** MASSINGER *Guardian* III. vi, Am I grown So weak.. that these gross tricks May be foisted on me? **1641** MILTON *Prel. Episc.* (1851) 79 The unskilfull fraud of him that foisted this Epistle upon Ignatius. **1772–84** COOK *Voy.* (1790) VI. 1971 The ignorant assertions foisted on the public by editors. **1841** S. WARREN *Ten Thous. a Year* III. i. 18 To attempt to foist himself upon a borough with which he had no connexion. **1849** C. BRONTE *Shirley* I. vii. 157 Each lady-contributor takes it in her turn..to foist off its contents on a shrinking male public. **1879** SALA *Paris herself again* (1880) II. iii. 34 You have inferior articles foisted on you while being charged for the best.

†**d.** To remove surreptitiously *out of*. *Obs.*[−1]

1658 BRAMHALL *Consecr. Bps.* 163 There is rather something foisted out of the former Edition, then foisted in.

†**4.** To put (a person) off *with* something inferior.

1602 *Life T. Cromwell* I. iii. 85 Where he had wont to give a thousand crowns Doth he now foist me with a portague?

†**5.** *intr.* for *refl.* To intrude oneself *into*. With *away*: To slip off, vanish. *Obs.*

1603 H. CROSSE *Vertues Commw.* (1878) 66 These beg no place, nor foist into office, but if it come, they vnwillingly hold it. **1664** COTTON *Scarron.* I. (1776) 34 But she was gone for when she list, She foist away could in a Mist.

6. *intr. slang.* (See quot.)

1585 FLEETWOOD in Ellis *Orig. Lett.* Ser. I. II. 303 Note that *ffoyste* is to cutt a pockett, *nyppe* is to cutt a purse, *lyft* is to robbe a shoppe. **1785** GROSE *Dict. Vulg. Tongue*, *Foyst*, to pick a pocket.

Hence '**foisted** *ppl. a.*; '**foisting** *vbl. sb.* and *ppl. a.*

1586 NEWTON tr. *Daneau's Diceplay* vi, As many foysting coseners..use to do. **1587** GOLDING *De Mornay* xxiv. 364 If it be possible for a booke to bee preserued from falsifying and foisting what booke shal y[t] be but the Byble? **1611** SPEED *Hist. Gt. Brit.* IX. xv. §21 This foisted and falsely termed fundamentall law Salique. **1628** R. S. *Counter Scuffle* lviii, Thou cogging Base foysting Lawyer. **1631** *Celestina* IX. 105 You well enough perceive her foystings and her flatteries. **1641** *Vind. Smectymnuus* v. 70 The bold foysting in of a Parenthesis. *a* **1687** COTTON *Poet. Wks.* (1765) 18 Make no more such Foisting here.

foist (fɔıst), *v.*[2] *Obs.* exc. *dial.* See also FUST *v.* [f. FOIST *sb.*[2]] *intr.* To smell or grow musty.

1583 GOLDING *Calvin on Deut.* cxix. 735 And what becomes of the Corne in the meanewhyle? It foysteth and rotteth. **1641** BEST *Farm. Bks.* (Surtees) 103 Corne..will foyst with lyinge long in the garner. **1869** *Lonsdale Gloss.*, *Foist*, to smell fusty.

Hence '**foisted** *ppl. a.*, musty.

1688 R. HOLME *Armoury* III. 317/1 Musty, Fusty, Foisted, Puft Corn. **1720** STRYPE *Stow's Surv.* (1754) II. v. xi. 289/2 They brewed foisted Beer and corrupt Beer again. **1876** *Whitby Gloss.*, *Foisted*..musty, as a mouldy cask.

†**foist**, *v.*[3] *Obs.* [var. of FIST *v.*[2]] *intr.* To break wind silently.

1594 NASHE *Unfort. Trav.* 18 If at anie time hee should foyst. **1604** DEKKER *Honest Whore* I. ix. Wks. 1873 II. 52 Spurne your hounds when they foiste. **1694** *Urquhart's Rabelais* II. xv. 102 [ed. 1653 has *fist*].

Hence '**foisting** *ppl. a.*, usually in ***foisting cur, hound***, etc.; cf. FISTING *ppl. a.*; also '**foister**, one who foists.

c **1611** CHAPMAN *Iliad* Pref. (1857) 65 The barkings of puppies, or foisting hounds. **1656** DAVENANT *Siege Rhodes* III. Dram. Wks. 1873 IV. 395 D'ye snarl, ye foisting mongrels? **1674** N. COX *Gentl. Recreat.* I. (1677) 24. **1677** MIEGE, *Vesseur*, a foister, or a fizzler.

†**foister** ('fɔıstə(r)). *Obs.* [f. FOIST *v.*[1] + -ER[1].] One who foists, in senses of the vb. **a.** One who 'foists' dice. **b.** One who interpolates spurious words or passages, etc. **c.** A cheat, sharper. **d.** A pickpocket.

c **1550** [see FOIST *v.*[1] 1]. **1566** T. STAPLETON *Ret. Untr. Jewel* IV. 36 A Forger, a Foyster or a Cogger. **1585** FLEETWOOD in Ellis *Orig. Lett.* Ser. I. II. 298 A publique ffoyster..Nota that a ffoister is a Pick-pockett. **1610** HOLLAND *Camden's Brit.* I. 10 Some craftie foister and jugling deceiver. **1823** *Leigh's New Pict. Lond.* 104 His proficiency was rewarded by styling him a nypper and a foyster.

foisty ('fɔıstı), *a.* See also FUSTY. [f. FOIST *sb.*[2] + -Y.[1]] Fusty, musty, mouldy. *lit.* and *fig.*

1519 HORMAN *Vulg.* 151b, Lest suche placis waxe filthy and foysty. **1566** DRANT *Horace's Sat.* iv. H, As if..thou shouldst..sauce thy meate with foystie oyles. **1619** FAVOUR *Antiq. Tri. over Novelty* xiii. 334 The foisty and fenowed Festiuall. **1669** WORLIDGE *Syst. Agric.* (1681) 285 Thrash not Wheat to keep untill March, lest it prove foisty. *c* **1750** J. COLLIER (Tim Bobbin) *Misc. Wks.* (1812) 19 Well boh we'n had enough o this foisty matter; lets tawk o' summot elze. **1859** H. T. ELLIS *Hong Kong to Manilla* 219 Pure Indians, and pure Chinese (if such a term can be applied to so 'foisty' a race as the latter). **1876** *Whitby Gloss.* s.v., 'As foisty as an old York church.'

Hence '**foisty** *v. intr.*, to become foisty or musty; implied in '**foistied** *ppl. a.*, '**foistiness**, the quality or condition of being foisty.

1572 HULOET, Foistied, mustied or vinoed, *mucidus.* **1576** BAKER *Jewell of Health* 38 Least..there may remayne some smatch of rottennesse or foystynes in the lycour dystilled. **1595** LUPTON *Thous. Notable Th.* II. 36 So the Wyne wyll be preserued from foystines and euyll sauor.

†'**foiterer.** *Obs.* [erron. f. *faiterer*, FAITOUR.]

[**1528** ROY *Rede me* (Arb.) 55 Thou makest hym then a trayter? I recken hym a falce fayterer.] **1616** BULLOKAR, *Foiterers*, vagabonds. **1623** COKERAM II, A Vagabond, *foyterer.* **1677** in COLES. **1848** in WHARTON *Law Lex.*

fok, fok(k)e, obs. forms of FOLK.

†'**fokel**, *a. Obs. rare.* [? altered form of *foken*, FAKEN; or perh. miswritten for *fekel*, FICKLE.] Treacherous. (In quots. *absol.* and quasi-*adv.*)

a **1275** *Prov. Ælfred* 255 in *O.E. Misc.* 119 Ofte mon on faire fokel chesed. *Ibid.* 349 in *O.E. Misc.* 123 Seiet him faire bi-foren, fokel at henden.

†'**foken**, *v.* [f. *foken*, FAKEN *sb.*; cf. OHG. *feihnôn.*] *intr.* To play false.

a **1275** *Prov. Ælfred* 485 in *O.E. Misc.* 132 For ofte sibbie men foken hem bitwenen.

Fokker ('fɒkə(r)). [Name of A. H. G. *Fokker* (1890–1939), a Dutch engineer, the inventor.] Orig. a German tractor monoplane characterized by its speed and climbing power. Later used *attrib.* to designate aircraft manufactured by the Fokker company in the Netherlands and elsewhere.

1913 *Aeroplane* 23 Jan. 78/1 The..successful flying of the Rumpler 'Taube', the 'Albatros', and the 'Fokker' in Germany. **1917** 'CONTACT' *Airman's Outings* 41 An aerodrome just east of the wood was the home of the Fokker star, Boelcke. **1930** C. R. SAMSON *Fights & Flights* 324 A German Fokker, which..was more than a match for a slow old Short with only a Lewis gun. **1941** W. S. CHURCHILL *Secret Session Speeches* (1946) 27 Air attack upon our Western Approaches by means of long-range Fokker Wulf machines. **1966** *Times* 9 Aug. 13/6 This company of 5,000 employees has an international reputation, based primarily on the popularity of the F27, the Fokker Friendship.

fol, obs. form of FOOL, FULL.

†**folability**. *Obs. rare*$^{-1}$. [f. *fol.* FOOL; see -ABLE and -ITY.] Folly.

a **1529** SKELTON *Agst. ven. Tongues* viii. 10 Ye are so full of vertibilite, And of frenetyke folabilite.

folacin ('fəʊləsɪn, 'fɒləsɪn). *Biochem.* Also **-ine**. [f. FOL(IC *ac*(*id* + -IN^1.] = *folic acid* (pteroylmonoglutamic acid).

1949 *Jrnl. Laboratory & Clinical Med.* XXXIV. 501 Evidence indicating rapid metabolic liberation of folacin (folic acid, pteroylglutamic acid) from teropterin (pteroyltriglumic acid). **1955** *Chem. & Engin. News* 6 June 2433/1 The pteroylglutamic acids may be designated generically as folic acids. The pure substance hitherto known as folic acid, folacine, or vitamin B_c shall be named pteroylmonoglutamic acid.

folargesse, var. of FOOL-LARGESSE, *Obs.*

folboat, var. *fold boat* (FOLD *sb.*^{3} 7).

folc(k, obs. form of FOLK.

†**fold**, *sb.*^{1} *Obs.* Forms: 1 folde, 3–5 folde, (3 *south.* volde, 4 foulde), 4– fold. [OE. *folde* wk. fem. = OLG. *folda*, ON. *fold*:—OTeut. **foldôn-*, **foldâ*, prob. related to **felþu* FIELD *sb.*]

1. a. The surface of the earth; the ground. **b.** Dry land; the earth, as the dwelling-place of man. ***in, on, upon fold***: on the earth; often as a mere expletive.

Beowulf 1137 (Gr.) þa wæs winter scacen, Fæȝer foldan bearm. *c* **1000** *Judith* 281 (Gr.) He..ȝefeoll..to foldan. *c* **1205** LAY. 1922 Al þe feond to-barst ær he to folde come. *Ibid.* 15730 Nat ic on folde What his fader weoren. *c* **1320** *Sir Tristr.* 643 Formest þo in fold He lete him in þring. *c* **1340** *Gaw. & Gr. Knt.* 422 Þe kay fote on þe folde he be-fore sette. *c* **1350** *Will. Palerne* 5382 A kastel ful nobul, þe fairest vpon fold. *c* **1400** *Rowland & O.* 418 Then sayde thies Damesels fre one folde. *a* **1400–50** *Alexander* 2087 Fey falne to þe fold many fers erlis. *c* **1440** *Bone Flor.* 342 Many other waturs come thorow the town, That fresche are upon folde. *c* **1450** HENRYSON *Poems* (1865) 24, I was..Ane freik on fold, as fair..as ye. *c* **1470** HENRY *Wallace* III. 385 Felle frekis on fold war fallyt wndyr feit.

2. A country, district, land.

a **1000** *Cædmon's Gen.* 1969 (Gr.) þa wæs guðhergum be Jordane wera eðelland wide ȝeondsended, folde feondum. *c* **1340** *Gaw. & Gr. Knt.* 25 Mo ferlyes on þis folde han fallen here oft þen in any oþer þat I wot.

3. *Comb.*, as **foldsitter**, of the hare: one who sits on the ground.

a **1325** *Names Hare* in *Rel. Ant.* I. 133 The fitelfot, the foldsittere.

fold (fəʊld), *sb.*^{2} Forms: 1 falæd, falod, falud, 1–2 fald, 3–5 fald(e, (3 *south.* vold), 4–6 fo(u)ld(e, (5 foolde), 5–6 *Sc.* fald, 5–9 *Sc.* fauld, 9 *dial.* faud, fowd, fowt. [OE. *falæd, falod, falud, fald*, str. masc., app. corresp. to MLG. *vālt*, mod.LG. *falt*, Du. *vaalt*, EFris. *folt* enclosed space, dunghill.]

1. A pen or enclosure for domestic animals, *esp.* sheep.

a **700** *Epinal Gloss.* 959 *Stabulum*, falaed. *a* **800** *Corpus Gloss.* 310 *Bofellum*, falud. *c* **1000** *Ags. Gosp.* John x. 1 Se þe ne gæð æt þam gete into sceapa falde..he is þeof. *a* **1100** *Gerefa* in *Anglia* (1886) IX. 260 Ge on felda, ȝe on falde. *c* **1200** ORMIN 3339 Till hirdess þær þær þeȝȝ þat nihht Biwokenn þeȝȝre faldess. *a* **1300** *Cursor M.* 3671 (Cott.) Jacob went vn to þe fald And broght þe bestes. **1382** WYCLIF *John* x. 1 In to the fold of the scheep. *c* **1470** HENRY *Wallace* v. 177 Twa scheipe thai tuk besid thaim of a fauld. **1523** FITZHERB. *Husb.* §6 To be set in a folde all nyghte without meate. **1697** DRYDEN *Virg. Georg.* III. 530 Oft the Flocks,..Nor Folds, nor hospitable Harbour know. **1788** BURNS *My Hoggie* ii, The lee-lang night we watch'd the fauld, Me and my faithfu' doggie. **1800** WORDSW. *Pet Lamb* 48 Our house shall be thy fold.

b. *fig.*, *esp* in a spiritual sense.

1340 HAMPOLE *Pr. Consc.* 4640 In haly kirkes falde. **1541** BARNES *Wks.* (1573) 247 You come into the fold of Christ without him. **1548** HALL *Chron., Edw. IV* (an. 14) 232 To kepe the wolfe from the folde, that is the Frenche kynge from your Castels and dominions. **1821** SHELLEY *Death Napoleon* 5 The last of the flock of the starry fold. **1868** G. DUFF *Pol. Surv.* 182 Although South America is nominally Catholic, there are few parts of the fold which give more anxiety at Rome.

c. The sheep contained in a fold. Also †the movable fold, and the sheep penned in it.

1669 WORLIDGE *Syst. Agric.* (1681) 219 To run the Fold over it, and well settle it. **1697** DRYDEN *Virg. Past.* VII. 73 The bleating Fold. **1742** COLLINS *Eclog.* III. 14 Till late at silent eve she penn'd the fold.

d. *transf.* An enclosure of any kind; a dwelling. † ***in fere and fold***: in prison together.

c **1435** *Torr. Portugal* 309 In a dongon..Fowyre good erylles sonnys..Ys fet in fere and fold. **1513** DOUGLAS *Æneis* IX. x. 18 Inclositt amyd ane fald of stakis. **1552** HULOET, Folde, or packe, or pownde to pinne distress, *caula.* **1847** TENNYSON *Princ.* v. 380 Far off from men I built a fold for them.

2. An enclosed piece of ground forming part of a farm, as a farm-yard.

c **1450** HENRYSON *Poems* (1865) 6 Be firth, forrest, or fauld. **1500–20** DUNBAR *Thistle & Rose* 68 That no schouris..Effray suld flouris or fowlis on the fold. **1802** R. ANDERSON *Cumberld. Ball.* 49 Auld Marget in the fauld she sits.

b. *transf.* The 'yard' belonging to a mill, etc.; a cluster of houses standing in such a yard.

1863 *Lancash. Fents, New Shirt* 3 A pretty weaver lass..had taken her sewing up the 'fowt'. **1882** *Lanc. Gloss., Fold, Fowd*, or *Fowt*, a cluster of houses. **1889** BARING-GOULD *Pennycomequicks* (1890) 58 The houses in the 'folds' were deserted.

3. *attrib.* and *Comb.*, as ***fold-manure***, ***-stake***, ***-stead***; also **fold-garth**, **-yard**, farm-yard; **fold-mucked** *a.*, (ground) manured by folding sheep upon it; **fold-pitcher**, an iron crowbar used in pitching or setting up hurdles; **fold-shore** (see quot. 1813); **fold-tread** *v.* = FOLD *v.*^{2} 2; **foldwards** *adv.*, towards the fold.

1788 W. MARSHALL *E. Yorksh.* Gloss., **Foldgarth*, farm-yard. **1876** *Whitby Gloss., Faud-garth*, the fold-yard. **1829** *Bone Manure, Rep. Doncast. Commission* 5 Forty or fifty cart loads of *fold manure. **1641** BEST *Farm. Bks.* (Surtees) 17 Wee can neaver gette above one Demaine-flatte *fold-mucked in a whole summer. **1832** *Q. Jrnl. Agric.* III. 648 Setting hurdles is most expeditiously done by the aid of a ..*fold pitcher. **1813** T. DAVIS *Agric. Wilts.* 63 *Fossels*, or **Fold-shores*, the stakes to which the hurdles are fastened with a loose twig-wreath at the top. **1878** JACKSON in *Wilts. Archæol. Mag.* XVII. 304 The fold-shores. *c* **1475** *Pict. Voc.* in Wr.-Wülcker 814 *Hic palus*, a *foldstake. **1663** *MS. Indenture* (Barlby, Yorks.), 2 gardens and 2 *fold-steads. **1854** *Jrnl. R. Agric. Soc.* XV. II. 420 [He] also *fold-treads his turnip-land before the seed is drilled. **1870** MORRIS *Earthly Par.* I. II. 462 Who stood awhile..Then slowly gat him *foldwards. **1800** *Gentl. Mag.* II. 1291 He..had been feeding him in the *fold yard. **1839** SELBY in *Proc. Berw. Nat. Club* I. No. 7. 192 The..Finch tribe..found..food..in the stack and fold-yards.

fold (fəʊld), *sb.*^{3} Forms: 4–5 falde, 4–6 folde, 4 felde, (6 folte), 6–7 foulde, 3– fold. [ME. *fald*, f. *fald-en*, FOLD *v.*^{1}; cf. MDu. *voude* (Du. *vouw*), OHG. *falt* masc. (MHG. *valte*, mod.Ger. *falte* fem.), ON. *fald-r* masc., *falda* fem. (Sw. *fåll*, Da. *fold*).

OE. had *fyld*, **field*:—WGer. **faldi-z* of equivalent formation, but it did not survive into ME.]

1. a. A bend or ply, such as is produced when any more or less flexible object is folded; one of the parts, or both of them together, which are brought together in folding; *spec.* (see quot. 1882). †In early poetic use, ***in fold, of rich fold***, is a formula often introduced with little meaning in descriptions of costly garments.

a **1300** *Cursor M.* 23452 (Cott.) In clething cled o riche fald. *c* **1325** *Metr. Hom.* 113 Uestement of riche fold. *a* **1400** *Sir Perc.* 32 He gaffe his sister hym tille..With robes in folde. ?*c* **1475** *Sqr. Lowe Degre* 835 Your curtaines of camaca, all in folde. **1513** DOUGLAS *Æneis* VIII. viii. 94 Thai byd display thair banaris out of faldis. **1689** *Lond. Gaz.* No. 2470/4 Several Pieces of Guilix and Gentish Hollands in the Long Fold. **1741** CHAMBERS *Cycl.* s.v. *Drapery*, The folds ..should be so managed that you may easily perceive what it is that they cover. **1814** SCOTT *Ld. of Isles* IV. xxvi, The monarch's mantle too he bore, And drew the fold his visage o'er. **1852** SEIDEL *Organ* 36 When blown, these bellows form two, three, or more folds. **1874** KNIGHT *Dict. Mech.* I. 105/1 s.v. *Angle-joint*, *g* has a fold to each plate; these lock upon each other. **1882** CAULFEILD & SAWARD *Dict. Needlework, Folds*, the draping produced by Pleating or Gathering at the waist of a skirt; or the flat plaits on any part of a skirt, bodice or sleeve, secured at each end to the dress to keep them in place.

fig. **1605** SHAKS. *Lear* I. i 221 A thing so monstrous, to dismantle So many folds of fauour! **1683** DRYSEN *Life Plutarch* 113 The folds and doubles of Sylla's disposition. **1742** YOUNG *Nt. Th.* IV. 733 My heart is thine; Deep in its inmost folds, Live thou. **1820** SHELLEY *Sensit. Plant* I. 31 Till, fold after fold, to the fainting air The soul of her beauty and love lay bare. **1873** MAX MÜLLER *Sc. Relig.* I The flowing folds of language.

b. A similar configuration in animal and vegetable structures.

a **1250** *Owl & Night.* 602 A mong þe folde of harde rinde. **1562** BULLEYN *Bk. Sicke Men* 50a, Masticke..will..not suffre Scamonie, to cliue to the foltes [**1579** foldes] of the stomacke. **1651** *Life Father Sarpi* 30 Those inward shuts or folds that are within the veines. **1731** ARBUTHNOT *Aliments* VI. viii. 217 The inward Coat of a Lion's Stomach has stronger Folds than a Human. **1841–71** T. R. JONES *Anim. Kingd.* 522 A fold of the alimentary canal. **1854** OWEN *Teeth* in *Orr's Circ. Sc., Organ. Nat.* I. 283 The folds of enamel that penetrate the substance of the tooth. **1888** ROLLESTON & JACKSON *Forms Anim. Life* 294 Two 'mantle' folds, one dorsal, the other ventral, line the corresponding valves... A 'brachial' groove bounded on its inner side by a prominent fold or lip. *Ibid.* 692 They [*sc.* the valves of Coelomate Metazoa] are lined by two mantle folds or extensions of the body walls. **1895** *Cambr. Nat. Hist.* III. 264 The folds or plaits on the columella, which are often characteristic of the genus or even family (*e.g.* Fasciolariidae, Mitridae, Turbinellidae) are not merely external, but continue down the whole spire. **1942** L. H. HYMAN *Compar. Vertebr. Anat.* (ed. 2) xi. 289 The tonsillar fossa is bounded in front and behind by low folds. **1949** A. S. ROMER *Vertebr. Body* x. 294 In jawed fishes, amphibians and reptiles, the lips are in general small and unimportant skin folds. **1964** W. W. BALLARD *Compar. Anat. & Embryol.* xi. 193 The amnion is usually formed through the agency of two crescentic amniotic folds.

c. A winding or sinuosity; *spec.* an undulation or gentle curve of the ground; a slight hill or hollow; the general grouping of heights and hollows.

a **1250** *Owl & Night.* 696 ȝif he ne con his wit atholde Ne fint he red in one folde. **1555** EDEN *Decades* 178 The fouldes or indented places of the mountaynes. **1601** HOLLAND *Pliny* II. 113 That towne..stood as it were in a fold, or plait, or nouke thereof [*i.e.* of the gulf]. **1832** W. IRVING *Alhambra* II. 231 The folds of the mountains. **1869** G. M. HOPKINS *Jrnl.* 27 June (1959) 191 Br. Sidgreaves has heard the high ridges of a field called *folds* and the hollow between the *drip.* **1887** BOWEN *Virg. Æneid* II. 748 The winding folds of the glen. **1901** *Daily News* 19 Jan. 5/3 Four companies of the Rifle Brigade were concealed behind a fold of ground. **1904** A. E. FLETCHER *Gainsborough* 88 The fold of the fields and the grouping of trees. **1930** *Morning Post* 17 June 20/5 Delightful house in a fold of the Downs.

d. A layer or 'thickness' (of cloth, etc.); a coat (of an onion). †With numerals, *sing.* in *pl.* sense.

1527 ANDREW *Brunswyke's Distyll. Waters* D j b, Two or iii folde of clowte wet in the same water. **1626** BACON *Sylva* §771 The Ancient Ægyptian Mummies were shrowded in a Number of Folds of Linnen. **1675** HOBBES *Odyssey* (1677) 232 The fold of a dry onion. **1697** DRYDEN *Æneid* v. 538 With sev'n distinguish'd folds Of tough Bull Hides. **1804** *Med. Jrnl.* XII. 64 Wrapping up the part in several folds of flannel. **1838** T. THOMSON *Chem. Org. Bodies* 116 It must be ..dried between folds of blotting paper.

e. In a serpent's body: A coil.

1592 SHAKS. *Ven. & Ad.* 879 An adder Wreath'd vp in fatall folds. **1667** MILTON *P.L.* IX. 498–9 Circular base of rising foulds, that tour'd Fould above fould a surging Maze. **1697** CREECH *Manilius* I. 14 Secure from meeting they're distinctly roll'd, Nor leave their Seats, and pass the dreadfull fold [of the constellation *Draco*]. **1884** W. C. SMITH *Kildrostan* 93 Serpents..clasp you in their folds.

f. A length (of string) between two bends.

1839 G. BIRD *Nat. Philos.* 69 Each fold of string sustains a share of the weight.

g. *Building.* (See quot.)

1842 GWILT *Encycl. Arch.* §2172 Floors..which are folded, that is when the boards are laid in divisions, whose side vertical joints are not continuous, but in bays of three, four, five, or more boards in a bay or fold.

h. *Geol.* A bend in rock strata, esp. one having a wave-like form.

1863 J. D. DANA *Man. Geol.* 104 One fold or flexure in the rocks may succeed to another, or they may form interrupted series. **1885** C. LYELL *Elem. Geol.* (ed. 4) 61 Stratified rocks have their strata usually bent into parallel folds forming anticlinal and synclinal curves. **1937** [see FAN *sb.*^{1} 10 f]. **1965** A. HOLMES *Princ. Physical Geol.* (ed. 2) ix. 212 Folds range in intensity from broad and gentle undulations to tightly compressed plications in which the dips of the beds are almost parallel, except near the hinge-lines.

2. Something that is or may be folded; a leaf of a book, a sheet of paper, one of the leaves of a folding-door.

c **1315** SHOREHAM 91 Ase hyt hys in holye boke I-wryten ine many a felde [? *read* fealde; the rimes are y-halde, tealde, ealde]. **1624** MASSINGER *Parl. Love* III. ii, As I, in this fold —this—receive her favours. **1667** MILTON *P.L.* I. 724 The dores Op'ning thir brazen foulds. **1808** J. BARLOW *Columb.* III. 683 The wide gates receive their rapid flight. The folds are barr'd.

†**3.** ? A wrapping, covering. *Obs.*

1497 *Will of Sympson* (Somerset Ho.), A folde and a standard of Mayle. **1633** FORD *Broken Heart* III. v, That remedy Must be a winding-sheet, a fold of lead, And some untrod-on corner in the earth.

4. The action of folding; †a clasp or embrace.

1606 SHAKS. *Tr. & Cr.* III. iii. 223 Weake wanton Cupid Shall from your necke vnloose his amorous fould. **1885** CRANE *Bookbinding* iv. 33 Still another fold gives a '32mo'.

5. The line or mark made by folding.

1840 LARDNER *Geom.* 18 Both coincide with the fold of the paper.

6. The words *manifold*, *threefold*, etc. (see -FOLD *suffix*) have occasionally been viewed (erroneously) as syntactical combinations of the adjs. with the present sb. Hence the following uses:

†**a.** ***many a fold*** = many times, with many repetitions. *Obs.*

c **1400** *Melayne* 445 Thay caste one it full many a folde. *c* **1420** *Chron. Vilod.* 306 And þonkede þefore God mony a ffolde. **1503** HAWES *Examp. Virt.* lxxxii. (Arb.) 22 Set with dyamondes many a fold.

†**b.** ***by many a fold***: in manifold proportion, many times over. So ***by foldes seven***. *Obs.*

c **1450** *Mirour Saluacioun* 4300 Clerere than is the sonne shalle be, be faldes seven. *c* **1460** *Towneley Myst.* (Surtees) 20 More bi foldes seven then I can welle expres. **1577** HARRISON *England* II. iii. (1877) I. 73 The towne of Cambridge..exceedeth that of Oxford..by manie a fold.

c. One portion of a 'manifold' thing.

1826 E. IRVING *Babylon* I. ii. 77 Which fourfold chain of evidence, upon any single fold of which I am willing [etc.]. **1839** R. PHILIP *Life W. Milne* I. 22 It stopped his basket-

making before he got through two folds of the 'Fourfould State'.

7. *attrib.* **fold boat** = FALTBOAT; also in contracted form *folboat*; **fold(-)mountain**, a mountain formed directly by folding, or one in which the strata are extensively folded; so *fold ridge*.

1938 *Times Lit. Suppl.* 24 Sept. 616/2 With his wife he made a journey in a *fold-boat.. down the Danube. **1946** R. CAPELL *Simiomata* I. 19 The Marines entered the harbour in their little collapsible Folboats, attached explosive charges to two destroyers and two cargo boats, and retired. **1955** 'N. SHUTE' *Requiem for Wren* 128 An M.T.B... with a folboat on board, a sort of kayak built of waterproof canvas on a wooden frame. **1969** *Publ. Amer. Dial. Soc.* LI. 6 *Fold boat*, kayak made of skeleton frame covered with a skin of rubberized cloth. It folds into a small package. **1908** J. W. GREGORY *Geogr.* 34 *Fold-mountains arise from the crumpling of bands of the earth's crust by lateral pressure. Such fold-mountains resemble the wrinkles formed when a table-cloth is pushed across a table. **1965** A. HOLMES *Princ. Physical Geol.* (ed. 2) xxx. 1111 The axes of the major structures of a range of fold mountains.. are generally roughly parallel to the trend of the range. **1936** *Discovery* Jan. 20/1 The late Miocene-Pliocene *fold ridge which extended to New Caledonia, and in the other direction formed the Himalayas and the European Alps.

†**fold**, *sb.*[4] *Obs. rare.* Also foold(e. ? The mountain-ash (app. rendering L. *ornus*).

c **1420** *Pallad. on Husb.* I. 1021 Ook, fold, and birche. *Ibid.* III. 770 Foolde, ashes, quynce.

fold (fəʊld), *v.*[1] *Pa. t.* and *pa. pple.* folded (ˈfəʊldɪd). Forms: *Infin.* 1 fealdan, *Northumb.* (ȝe)falda, 3–5 fald(e(n, 3–6 folden, (5 -yn), 4 felde, *south.* viealde, 4–6 *south.* volde, 5–7 fould, 6–9 *Sc.* fald, fauld, 9 *dial.* faud, 5– fold. *Pa. t. str.* 1 féold, 4–5 feld(e, 6 fald. *wk.* 4–5 foldid. (5 -et, -it), 6– folded. *Pa. pple., str.* 1 fealden, 3–7 fold(e(n, (4–6 -in, -un, -yn, 7 foulden), 3 *south.* volden, 3–4 fald(e(n, (6 fauden), 5 y-falt, folte, (6 falt), fould. *wk.* 4 foldid, 6–7 foldit, (6 folted), 7 foulded, 4– folded. [Com. Teut. reduplicating strong vb.: OE. *fealdan* = MDu. *vouden* (Du. *vouwen*), OHG. *faldan, faltan* (MHG. *valten*, Ger. *falten*), ON. *falda* (pa. t. *félt*), Goth. *falþan* (pa. t. *faifalþ*):—OTeut. **falþan*, f. **falþ*:—pre-Teut. **plt-*, found in Lith. *pleta* I plait, Gr. δί-παλτος, also δι-πλάσιος (:—**-pltiyos*) double; according to Brugmann an extended form of the root *pl-* (in Gr. ἁ-πλό-ος, simple, lit. 'one-fold') of which another extension appears in Gr. πλέκ-ειν, L. *plicāre* to plait, fold. In OE. and early ME. the forms are those of a strong vb.; from 15th c. onwards weak forms were developed, and the vb. is now conjugated entirely as weak; cf. Da. *folde.*]

1. a. *trans.* To arrange (a piece of cloth, a surface, etc.), so that one portion lies reversed over or alongside another; to double or bend over upon itself. Also with *in, over, together*. Often contextually implying repeated action of this kind. *to fold up*: to close or bring into a more compact form by repeated folding.

c **888** K. ÆLFRED *Boeth.* xli. §3 God scipstyra ongit micelne wind hreose ær ær hit weorþe, and hæt fealdan þæt segl. *a* **1000** *Riddles* xxvii. 7 (Gr.) Mec [a parchment] fingras feoldon. *a* **1250** *Owl & Night.* 1324 On ape mai a boc bi-halde, An leves wenden, and eft folde. **13..** *Coer de L.* 3497 Whenne they hadde eeten, the cloth was folde. **1480** CAXTON *Chron. Eng.* ccxxi. 213 He opened the letter that he had folden afore to geder. **1535** COVERDALE *Ezek.* xli. 23 Euery dore had two litle wickettes which were folden in one vpon another on euery syde two. **1621** AINSWORTH *Annot. Pentat.* Exod. xiii. 9 These foure sections.. written on parchment, folden up they.. tyed to the forehead. **1707** *Curios. in Husb. & Gard.* 87 During.. the Night, they join and fold in their Leaves. **1712** ADDISON *Spect.* No. 305 ¶9 To open a Letter, to fold it up again. **1840** LARDNER *Geom.* 44 If the triangle be conceived to be folded over. **1878** BROWNING *Poets Croisic* 41 Our René folds his paper.

transf. and *fig.* **1633** EARL MANCH. *Al Mondo* (1636) 122 When death hath foulded up thy dayes, all opportunity is past. **1642** FULLER *Holy & Prof. St.* II. x. 26 So handsomely folding up her discourse, that his virtues are shown outwards, and his vices wrapped up in silence. **1677** CROWNE *Destr. Jerusalem* I. IV. i, Every night their Bodies were not worn, But gently lapt and folded up till morn. **1820** SHELLEY *Let. Gisborne* 245 Let his page.. Fold itself up for the serener clime Of years to come.

Prov. **1622** MALYNES *Anc. Law-Merch.* 90 Hee that buyeth Lawne before he can fold it, will repent before he hath sold it.

b. *Geol.* To double up (strata). Also *intr.* for *refl.* To become doubled up.

1857 LIVINGSTONE *Trav.* xxviii. 570 Making the strata fold over them on each side. **1872** C. KING *Mountain. Sierra Nev.* ix. 185 When the Sierra Nevada and Wahsatch mountains were folded. **1885** BECKER in *Amer. Jrnl. Sc.* Ser. III. xxx. 208 The result of a tendency to fold carried beyond the limit of elasticity of the rock.

c. To bend or turn *back* or *down* (a portion of something). †*to fold off*: to bend back and break off.

c **1420** *Pallad. on Husb.* III. 774 Or me sette him [a graft] in the tree The tendron and the leves of thou folde.

d. *Building.* (See quot. s.v. FOLD *sb.*[3] 1 g.)

e. *intr.* To yield to pressure, so as to become folded; to be capable of being folded. Now esp. with *up*.

1398 TREVISA *Barth. De P.R.* XVII. xxvii. (1495) 620 That cassia is best that brekyth not soone but bendyth and foldeth. **1793** SMEATON *Edystone L.* 194 Having a joint in the middle, it folds. **1914** *Daily Mail* 21 Feb. 10/1 One of the little seats that folded up when they were not required. **1939–40** *Army & Navy Stores Catal.* 759/1 This roll-up chair.. folds up small enough to go in a large pocket.

†**f.** *trans.* To roll up, as a scroll. *Obs.*

1382 WYCLIF *Luke* iv. 20 Whanne he hadde closid [*v.r.* folded, or closed] the book. *c* **1400** *St. Alexius* (Laud 622) 932 A book in his honde he halt Swiþe fast, & narewe yfalt. **1561** DAUS tr. *Bullinger on Apoc.* (1573) 283 Heauen fled backe, and was folden vp lyke a scrolle.

2. a. *trans.* To place in a spiral or sinuous form; to coil, wind. Now only with const. *about, round*, or the like. Also *intr.* for *refl.*

1579 TOMSON *Calvin's Serm. Tim.* 346/2 The deceiuers double and folde in themselues like serpents. *c* **1650** *Merline* 1465 in Furniv. *Percy Folio* I. 467 Beneathe the stones under the Mold tow dragons Lyen there fould. **1816** J. WILSON *City of Plague* II. iv, Thus I fold one arm Round thy blest neck. **1833** TENNYSON *Poems* 6, I dare not fold My arms about thee. **1842** —— *Talking Oak* 148 When I feel about my feet The berried briony fold. **1842** —— *Day-dream, Departure* i, On her lover's arm she leant, And round her waist she felt it fold.

†**b.** *intr.* Of a stream: To take a winding course.

c **1420** *Pallad. on Husb.* III. 557 So that the towne water doune folde Streght hem amonge.

†**3.** *trans.* To cause to bend; hence, to throw down, overthrow; also, to overcome. (Cf. mod. *double up.*) *fig.* To prevail upon by entreaty.

c **1205** LAY. 20077 Feollen þa uæie uolden to grunde. *c* **1330** *King of Tars* 1118 The feendes strengthe to folde. *c* **1430** *Syr Tryam.* 326 Fourti Syr Roger downe can folde.

†**4. a.** To bend, bow (oneself, the body, or limbs).

a **1300** *Cursor M.* 8965 (Cott.) To þe tre sco can hir fald. *c* **1380** *Sir Ferumb.* 841 Is bodi a-side he felde. **1571** HANMER *Chron. Irel.* (1633) 17 A red Lyon Rampant, with his taile folden towards his backe. *a* **1605** MONTGOMERIE *Misc. Poems* li. 35 Befoir Europe.. he his feit did fauld.

fig. **1578** *Ps.* lxxvii. in *Scot. Poems 16th C.* II. 109 They.. hes vs left all foldit into cair.

†**b.** *intr.* for *refl.* Of the body or limbs: To bend, crook, double up, yield. Also, of a person: To bow, bend down, crouch, drop down. *Obs.*

13.. *Maximon* iv. in *Rel. Ant.* I. 120 Care and kunde of elde Maketh mi body felde, That y ne mai stonde upright. **1382** WYCLIF *Matt.* xvii. 14 A man cam to hym, foldid on knees byfore hym, seyinge. **1393** LANGL. *P. Pl.* C. xx. 120 The fyngres þat freo beo to folden and to clycchen. *c* **1460** *Towneley Myst.* (Surtees) 98 My legys thay fold, my fyngers ar chappyed.

5. a. *intr.* To give way, collapse; to fail, falter. Esp. with *up*.

a **1250** *Owl & Night.* 37 And falt mi tonge. *a* **1300** *Cursor M.* 24348 (Cott.) In suime al falden dun i fell. *c* **1325** *Song of Mercy* 136 in *E.E.P.* (1862) 122 Vr feiþ is frele to flecche and folde. *c* **1430** *Hymns Virg.* (1867) 73 My lymes foulden þat weren fast. **1596** SPENSER *Hymn Heavenly Beautie* 7, I.. feele my wits to faile, and tongue to fold. **1911** A. BENNETT *Honeymoon* I. 15 *Cedric*: The mater folded up like that? *Flora*: ..Naturally she folded up. She only needs proper treatment. **1928** J. P. MCEVOY *Showgirl* 199 The Main Stem hears under cover that 'Get Your Girl' may fold up soon for lack of suitable house. **1936** *Variety* 24 June 66/1 First tour of the Draegermen.. proved a box office flop, and folded here. **1937** N. COWARD *Present Indicative* V. vi. 191 In spite of excellent press notices.. the play folded up at the end of eight weeks. **1939** E. B. WHITE *Quo Vadimus?* I. 47 *Nutshell* folded up, because, an expert said, the name was too long; but half a dozen others sprang up to take its place. **1942** *Penguin New Writing* XV. 12 Yes, but when he gets outside he'll fold up. **1958** I. MURDOCH *Bell* xxvi. 315 He was sorry.. to hear that Imber was folding up. **1965** G. MELLY *Owning-Up* vi. 71 The band folded in December 1961. **1971** *Guardian* 21 Jan. 1/1 (*headline*) Skyways folds up. **1971** *Sunday Times* (Colour Suppl.) 24 Oct. 31/1 This generous subsidy could not go on for ever and when it was withdrawn the magazine folded.

†**b.** To succumb, yield ground. *Obs.*

c **1400** *Rowland & O.* 1250 Charlles me thynke that thou scholdeste folde. **1535** STEWART *Cron. Scot.* II. 84 Thir barbour bodeis.. Docht nocht of force than for to gar ws fald. *a* **1625** A. GARDEN *Theat. Scot. Kings* (Abbotsf. Club.) 14 Thou forced for to fald Such as deboir'd from thy Obedience darre.

†**c.** To swerve or turn aside (from truth, etc.).

c **1380** WYCLIF *Serm.* Sel. Wks. II. 126 He shulde teche þes worldly men.. to drede to folde fro treuþe as Pilat dide. **1450** HENRYSON *Mor. Fab.* 42 For prayer or price trow yee that they wald fald.

6. a. *trans.* To lay (the arms, etc.) together, so as to overlap; to clasp (one's hands) together. Also *intr.* for *refl.* In mod. use freq. with *together*.

c **1000** ÆLFRIC *Gen.* xlix. 32 He feold his fet [Vulg. *collegit pedes suos*] uppan his bedd. *c* **1374** CHAUCER *Troylus* IV. 331 (359) With his armes folden. **1535** COVERDALE *Prov.* vi. 10 Yee.. folde thine handes together yet a litle, that thou mayest slepe. **1632** LITHGOW *Trav.* v. 205 They.. sit downe on the ground, folding their feete vnder them. **1697** COLLIER *Ess. Mor. Subj.* II. (1703) 114 Envy.. folds its arms in despair. **1732** BERKELEY *Alciphr.* I. §5 Alciphron stood.. with his arms folded across. **1771** H. MACKENZIE *Man Feel.* 223 He folded his hands together. **1821** SHELLEY *Prometh. Unb.* I. 222 My wings are folded o'er mine ears. **1849** C. BRONTE *Shirley* x. 142 Her head drooped, her hands folded. **1853** KINGSLEY *Hypatia* x, Her hands folded together before her. **1865** DICKENS *Mut. Fr.* I. ii, She folds her hands in the manner of a supplicating child. **1894** B. HARRADEN *Varying Moods* 60 She folded her hands together on the buckle of her waist-belt.

b. ? *absol.* = To fold the hands (app. given as an uneducated use).

1865 DICKENS *Mut. Fr.* II. xiv, 'I'd far sooner be.. tiring of myself out, than a-sitting folding and folding by the fire.'

†**7. a.** To plait; to mat (hair). *Obs.*

1382 WYCLIF *Matt.* xxvii. 29 Thei foldynge a crowne of thornis. **1535** COVERDALE *Song Sol.* vii. 5 The hayre of thy heade is like the kynges purple folden vp in plates. **1555** EDEN *Decades* 43 Images of gossampine cotton foulded or wrethed. **1563–87** FOXE *A. & M.* (1596) 936/2 He remained so long manicled that his haire was folded togither.

†**b.** *fig.* To attach, plight (faith). *Obs.*

c **1340** *Gaw. & Gr. Knt.* 1783 Bot if ȝe haf a lemman, a leuer, þat yow lyke better, & folden fayth to þat fre, festned so harde þat you lausen ne lyst.

†**c.** *intr.* To be suitable or accordant. *Obs.*

c **1340** *Gaw. & Gr. Knt.* 359 Syþen þis note is so nys, þat noȝt hit yow falles, & I haue frayned hit at yow fyrst, foldez hit to me. *Ibid.* 499 þe forme to þe fynisment foldez ful selden.

8. a. To enclose in or as in a fold or folds; to cover or wrap up; to swathe, envelop. Const. *in*; formerly const. *with*, and *simply*; also const. certain advs. and prepositions.

13.. *E.E. Allit. P.* A. 434 Knelande to grounde [ho] folde vp hyr face. *c* **1394** *P. Pl. Crede* 126 Seynt Fraunces him-self schall folden the in his cope. *c* **1400** *Lanfranc's Cirurg.* 168 þer ben manye maner causis whi þat guttis ben folde with nerves. **1530** *Comedy Beauties Women* C j, I thynk he be xxiiii. yeres of age, I saw hym born and holpe for to fold hym. **1594** MARLOWE & NASHE *Dido* I. ii, The rest, we fear, are folded in the floods. **1697** DRYDEN *Æneid* VII. 496 With his circling volumes folds her hairs. **1707** *Curios. in Husb. & Gard.* 333 The Seed is the Plant folded and wrapt up. **1854** B. TAYLOR *Poems Orient, On the Sea* (1866) 162 The mountain isles.. Folded in shadows gray. **1906** K. TRASK *Night & Morn.* 34 Take me, Leonidas, to thy strong arms —.. fold me from the whole wide world.

fig. **1590** GREENE *Orl. Fur.* Wks. (Rtldg.) 92/1 Folding their wraths in cinders of fair Troy. **1593** SHAKS. *Lucr.* 1073, I will not.. fold my fault in cleanly coin'd excuses. **1649** W. BRADFORD *Plymouth Plant.* II. (1856) 276 These businesses were not.. well understood of a longe time, but foulded up in obscuritie. **1878** GILDER *Poet & Master* 36 Then must I.. In myself fold me. **1891** [see ENEMY *sb.* and *a.* B. 2]. **1915** H. MACKAY *London, One Nov.* 46 The mystery of things the twilights fold away.

b. Of the surrounding medium: To serve as a wrapping for. *poet.*

1592 SHAKS. *Ven. & Ad.* 822 So did the.. night, Fold in the obiect that did feed her sight. **1793** SOUTHEY *Tri. Woman* 389 The purple robe of state thy form shall fold. **1815** W. H. IRELAND *Scribbleomania* 15 Paper.. purchas'd, brown sugar to fold. **1830** TENNYSON *Dirge* i, Shadows of the silver birk Sweep the green that folds thy grave.

†**c.** Of a hostile army: To surround, beleaguer.

c **1400** *Destr. Troy* 11263 ȝour cité is set all aboute With ȝour fomen fuerse foldyn with in.

†**d.** To wrap or entangle in a snare. *Obs.*

a **1592** GREENE *Fr. Bacon* (1630) 2 In her tresses she doth fold the lookes Of such as gaze vpon her golden haire. **1614** RALEIGH *Hist. World* II. §3. 418 Those perills: within which they were so speedily folded vp.

e. *Cookery.* Const. *in*. To add an ingredient gently by lifting a mixture with a spoon, etc., so as to enclose it without stirring or beating.

1915 D. C. PEEL *Learning to Cook* xiv. 172 Add the whipped whites last, and.. fold them in lightly. **1933** W. G. R. FRANCILLON *Good Cookery* xv. 316 Fold in the slightly warmed flour. **1958** *Listener* 20 Nov. 855/2 Add the yolks and cheese to the mixture, then stiffly beat the whites of the eggs and fold in gently.

9. To clasp (*in one's arms, to one's breast*); to embrace.

a **1300** *Cursor M.* 24491 (Cott.) Quen i him had in armes fald. *c* **1400** *Ywaine & Gaw.* 1425 He hir in armes hent, And ful fair he gan hir falde. **1593** SHAKS. *Rich. II*, I. iii. 54 We will descend and fold him in our armes. **1621** LADY M. WROTH *Urania* 353 [They] together fold in each others armes, sate downe. **1794** BURNS *Lassie wi' the lint-white locks* iv, I'll fauld thee to my faithfu' breast. **1821** SHELLEY *Death Napoleon* 21 To my bosom I fold All my sons when their knell is knolled. **1859** TENNYSON *Idylls, Geraint* 99 Not to be folded more in these dear arms.

10. *Comb.*: the vb. stem in comb. with a sb., in sense 'that can or will fold'; as *fold-net, -skirt*. Also **foldaway** *a.*, adapted to be folded away; **fold-out** *sb.*, an oversize page in a book, magazine, etc., which has to be unfolded by the reader; also as *adj.*; **fold-up** *a.*, adapted to be folded-up.

1960 *Farmer & Stockbreeder* Suppl. 26 Jan. 4/1 A wash boiler with all refinements except a pump but with a *fold-away hand wringer. **1967** *Gloss. Caravan Terms* (*B.S.I.*) 3 *Foldaway bed*, a bed designed to be lowered from and retract into a cupboard or wall or to fold on itself to make an upright furniture unit. **1969** *Jane's Freight Containers 1968–69* 577/3 Foldaway guides to aid truck location. **1971** *Guardian* 24 Aug. 7/3 An 84-year-old woman.. was trapped in her foldaway bed for 13 hours. **1706** PHILLIPS (ed. Kersey), **Fold-net*, a sort of Net with which small Birds are taken in the Night. **1961** WEBSTER, *Foldout. **1963** *Amer. Speech* XXXVIII. 125 It might be well to include a fold-out map at the end of each volume. **1967** *Time* 17 Mar. 7 The prurient appeal of an overripe foldout is no worse than the peekaboo enticement of gossip about 'People'. **1968** *Listener* 30 May 705/1 A coffee-table book, with Topolski drawings, wide margins and a fold-out frontispiece. **1855** BROWNING *Men & Wom., Saul* 21 The tent was unlooped.. I groped my way on Till I felt where the *foldskirts fly open. **1894** WILKINS & VIVIAN *Green Bay-tree* I. 23 The famous Harrow *fold-up bed.

fold (fəʊld), *v.*² Also 5 fooldyn, 6 folde, 8 *Sc.* fauld, 9 *dial.* faud. [f. FOLD *sb.*²]

1. *trans.* To shut up (sheep, etc.) in a fold, to pen; *occas.* with *up*; also *absol.* Of hurdles: To serve for penning. (In OE. once *intr.* to make or set up sheepfolds.)

a **1100** *Gerefa* in *Anglia* (1886) IX. 261 Faldian, fiscwer and mylne macian. *c* **1440** *Promp. Parv.* 168/2 Fooldyn, or put beestys in a folde, *caulo.* **1565** COOPER *Thesaurus* s.v. *Claudo*, To folde with hurdels. **1590** NASHE *Pasquil's Apol.* I. D iv, God commaunded his people to be folded vp, and to stand within the barres. **1600** SURFLET *Countrie Farme* I. xxvi. 165 By folding them [goats] vpon..fallowes in the summer time. **1634** MILTON *Comus* 93 The star that bids the shepherd fold Now the top of Heav'n doth hold. **1661** WEBSTER & ROWLEY *Thracian Wonder* I. B iij, Let's make haste to fold up our flocks. **1765** A. DICKSON *Treat. Agric.* III. (ed. 2) 380 It is a custom, in some places, to fold sheep and cattle, for the sake of their dung. **1822** ROGERS *Italy, Monte Cassino* 32 Counts, as he folds, five hundred of his sheep. **1842** JOHNSON *Farmer's Encycl.*, s.v. *Hurdle*, A dozen and a half hurdles will fold 30 sheep. **1842** BISCHOFF *Woollen Manuf.* II. 137 We never fold our merino or other sheep, the land is too wet. **1894** *Times* 6 Mar. 4/1 Flock masters are folding on it [rye] early.

b. *fig.*; *esp.* in spiritual sense. Cf. FEED *v.* 2.

1826 MACAULAY *Dies Iræ* 51 Fold me with the sheep that stand..at thy right hand. **1871** MACDUFF *Mem. Patmos* xiv. 192 The Lamb..shall..guide them, fold them. **1887** *Pall Mall G.* 18 Oct. 1/2 These hitherto wandering sheep are in process of being folded into the comprehensive pastures of the national religion.

2. To place sheep in a fold or folds upon (a piece of ground), for the purpose of manuring it. *to fold off*: to use (a crop) as pasture for folded sheep.

1671 *St. Foine Improved* 3 The Men of the Vale might.. desire that those of the Hill-country might not Fold, or Dung their Ground, or Sow any Corn. **1759** tr. *Duhamel's Husb.* II. i. (1762) 127 Two contiguous pieces of ground.. had been folded. **1794** J. BOYS *Agric. Kent* 37 The clover being again folded off. **1846** J. BAXTER *Libr. Pract. Agric.* II. 61 When his grass fields have been partially folded with sheep.

Hence **'folded** *ppl. a.* Also **'folder**, one who folds sheep; a shepherd.

1571 W. ELDERTON *Epit. on Jewel* in Farr *S. P. Eliz.* (1845) II. 512 Alas! is Juell dead, the folder of the flocke? **1579** SPENSER *Sheph. Cal.* Epil., From the falsers fraud his folded flocke to keepe. **1607** TOPSELL *Four-f. Beasts* 74 Among folded beasts. **1725** POPE *Odyss.* IX. 257 The folded flocks. **1801** J. BREE *Derwent Water* iii, What time the folder hears the mandrake's moan.

fold, var. form of FOUD.

-fold, *suffix* (OE. *-feald*, Northumb. *-fald*, ME. *-fald*, *-fold*), corresponds to OFris., OS *-fald* (Du. *-voud*), OHG. *-falt* (MHG. *-valt*, mod.Ger. *-falt*), ON. *-faldr* (Sw. *-fald*, Da. *-fold*), Goth. *-falþs*; cognate with FOLD *v.*¹, and with the equivalent Gr. -παλτος, -πλασιος, also, more remotely, with Gr. -πλο- in ἁπλός single, διπλός double (= L. *duplus*), and probably with the L. (*sim-*, *du-*, *tri-*) *plex*. Like the Gr. and L. equivalents, the Teut. suffix is appended to cardinal numerals (and adjs. meaning 'many'), forming adjs. of which the primary sense is 'folded in two, three, four, etc.,' or 'plaited of two, three, four, etc. strands' (cf. 'a threefold cord'), but which serve also and chiefly as arithmetical multiplicatives. The OE. forms, *twi-*, *twio-*, *twiefeald*, *ðrifeald*, *fyðerfeald*, which retain the combining form of the cardinal inherited from OTeut., were superseded in early ME. by new formations on the analogy of *fivefold*, etc., where the cardinal has the normal form.

The adjs. were already in OE. used absol. in the neut. (e.g. *ðrifeald* threefold, three times as much and as advbs. (= doubly, triply, etc.), and these uses still continue. In OE. the adverbial notion was also expressed by phrases like *be fiffealdum*, *be manizfealdum*, in late Eng. †*by fivefold*, *by manifold*. The introduction of the Romanic synonyms *double* and *treble* or *triple*, to which were afterwards added the adapted Latin *quadruple*, *quintuple*, etc., has considerably narrowed the use of the derivatives in *-fold*; indeed the latter seem to be (in many dialects) no longer current among illiterate people. In educated use the strictly multiplicative sense survives chiefly in the adv. and quasi-sb., and with reference to somewhat large numbers ('He has repaid me tenfold'; 'that is a thousandfold worse'); the adjs. express rather a plurality of things more or less different, than mere quantitative multiplication: cf. 'a double charm' with 'a two-fold charm'.

In ME. a few new and unanalogical compounds were formed with the suffix, as *thick-fold* (= frequent, -ly), *double-fold*; but these did not survive into the modern period. Of the nonce-combinations, formed by attaching *-fold* to indefinite numerals, interrogatives, and the like, the following quots. afford examples.

1695 ALINGHAM *Geom. Epit.* 63 The quantitie of proportion is more generally defined by *how much fold* rather than by *how many times* the consequent is contained in the antecedent. **1833** N. ARNOTT *Physics* (ed. 5) II. 78 The effect was found to be several fold greater than of steam from the same quantity of fuel. **1879** H. GEORGE *Progr. & Pov.* II. iii. (1881) 115 All of the things which furnish man's subsistence have the power to multiply many fold.

foldable ('fəʊldəb(ə)l), *a.* [f. FOLD *v.*¹ + -ABLE.] That may be folded.

1893 *Nat. Observ.* 13 May 645/2 All foldable tissues.. will own their sway.

†**foldage**¹ ('fəʊldɪdʒ). *Obs.* [f. FOLD *sb.*² + -AGE. Cf. FALDAGE.] **a.** = FALDAGE. **b.** The practice of feeding sheep in movable folds.

1533-4 *Act 25 Hen. VIII.* c. 13 §7 Euerie personne.. which..shal haue..libertie of foldage. **1628** COKE *On Litt.* II. x. §170 To haue..Franke foldage..a man may make a Title by vsage. **1657** SIR H. GRIMSTONE in *Croke's Rep.* I. 475 Land which was..made good by foldage, or other industrious means.

foldage² ('fəʊldɪdʒ). *Her.* [f. FOLD *sb.*³ or *v.*¹ + -AGE.] (See quot. 1688.)

1688 R. HOLME *Armoury* II. xvii. 396 Foldage when these kind of Leaves have several foldings and turnings, one from another: as in mantles. Some call them Festune heads. **1703** in *Jrnl. Derbysh. Archæol. Soc.* III. 33 Runing of foldage in the margent of the pannels.

'fold-,course. [f. FOLD *sb.*² + COURSE.] Land to which pertained the right of foldage; the right itself; hence, a sheepwalk.

1538 FITZHERB. *Just. Peas* 127 b, Theyr owne demeane landes, pastures, and foldcourses. **1677** COLES, *Fold course*, as *Faldage*. **1726** *Dict. Rust.* (ed. 3) s.v. *Faldage*, This Faldage in some places is call'd a Fold-course or Free-hold. **1848** WHARTON *Law Lex.*, *Foldage* and *Foldcourse*.

'fold-,dike. *Sc.* [f. FOLD *sb.*² + DIKE *sb.*¹; prob. alteration of *fail-dike*: see FAIL *sb.*] A wall of turf surrounding a fold.

1437 *Merches of Bp. Brynnes* in *Cart. Aberd.* F. 14 (Jam.) Fra that wele ascended up an ald fald dyk to the hill. **1513-75** *Diurnal Occurrents* (1833) 130 Ane narrow passage in fauld dykkis. **1816** SCOTT *Old Mort.* ix, One of the.. whig dogs shot at me from behind a fauld-dike.

folded ('fəʊldɪd), *ppl. a.* [f. FOLD *v.* + -ED¹.] In various senses of the vb.; bent, closed, coiled, doubled, twisted.

1570 *Satir. Poems Reform.* xxii. 60 With fauldit neif. **1629** MILTON *Christ's Nativ.* 172 The scaly Horrour of his foulded tail. **1646** BUCK *Rich. III*, II. 58 Otherwise he might sit downe with folded hands. **1748** COWPER *Task* I. 331 The folded gates would bar my progress now. **1801** SOUTHEY *Thalaba* IV. v, With folded arms..he sate. **1850** MRS. BROWNING *Poems* II. 150 Folded eyes see brighter colours than the open ever do. **1855** BROWNING *Any Wife* viii, The book I opened keeps a folded leaf.

fig. **1593** A. BACON in *Bacon's Wks.* (1862) VIII. 245 His enigmatical folded writing. **1649** JER. TAYLOR *Gt. Exemp.* II. §12. 56 An implicit and folded duty. **1707** TATE in Southey *Comm.-pl. Bk.* Ser. II (1849) 337 Untie your folded thoughts, And let them dangle loose as a bride's hair. **1832** TENNYSON *Dr. Fair Wom.* 263 The white dawn's creeping beams..dissolved the mystery Of folded sleep.

b. Of a mantle: Arranged in folds.

1831 CARLYLE *Sart. Res.* I. v, In folded mantles.

c. *folded angle-joint* (see quot.); †*folded table*, ? a table with flaps.

1504 *Bury Wills* (Camden) 101 The hall tabyll and trystells in the hall, parlurrs, and chamburs, except falt tabells. **1554** *Ibid.* 146 A goblet..and a folted table wᵗ iron. **1874** KNIGHT *Dict. Mech.* I. 105/1, *h* is a riveted joint, one plate being bent to lap upon the other. This joint is called the folded angle.

Hence **'foldedly** *adv.*, in a folded manner.

1613 CHAPMAN *Maske Inns of Court* Plays 1873 III. 94 A pentacle of siluered stuffe about her shoulders, hanging foldedly downe both before and behind.

folden ('fəʊldən), *ppl. a. Obs.* exc. *arch.* [str. pa. pple. of FOLD *v.*¹] = FOLDED.

1435 MISYN *Fire of Love* 74 Bolnyd with foldyn Argumentis. **1512** *Nottingham Rec.* III. 114 Unam tabulam vocatam 'a folden borde' cum tribus foliis. **1513** DOUGLAS *Æneis* X. i. 11 The faldin ȝettis baith vp warpit brayd. **1572** *Wills & Inv. N.C.* (Surtess 1835) I. 348 One lyttle fauden table. **1611** SPEED *Theat. Gt. Brit.* IV. i. §18. 138/2 Foulden wreathes of fine linnen. **1702** W. J. *Bruyn's Voy. Levant* liv. 211 A wooden Chest of Drawers, which opens with Folden Doors. **1857** *Blackw. Mag.* LXXXI. 337 He sang, and drew ..Angels down, on folden wings.

folder ('fəʊldə(r)), *sb.* [f. FOLD *v.*¹ + -ER¹.] One who or that which folds.

a. *gen.* Also *folder up.*

1552 HULOET, Folder, *rugator*, Folder vp of clothes or garmentes, *vestiplicus.* **1837** HT. MARTINEAU *Soc. Amer.* III. 148 Women are employed..as compositors, as well as folders and stitchers. **1885** CRANE *Bookbinding* iv. 30 With.. the 'head' on top of the pages farthest from the folder. **1891** *Econ. Jrnl.* I. 641 Folders up: Men, 17*s.* 5*d.*; Women, 10*s.* 9*d.*

b. An instrument for folding paper, etc.

1846 in WORCESTER. **1886** *N.Y. Herald* 27 Oct. 6/3 The press is a new Hoe perfecting machine, with a folder attached.

c. (See quot. 1867.) **d.** (See quot. 1874.) **e.** *U.S.* A sheet or leaf (e.g. a map or time-table) which can be folded up. **f.** (See quot. 1884.) **g.** An insect that folds leaves, a leaf-folder. (*Cent. Dict.*)

1867 SMYTH *Sailor's Word-bk.*, *Folder*, the movable sight of a fire-arm. **1874** KNIGHT *Dict. Mech.* I. 899 *Folder*..2. a form of spectacles in which the lenses fold together for the pocket. **1884** *Ibid.* IV. 353 *Folder* (Sheet Metal Working), a machine for turning locks or tapping edges of cans. **1889** *Scribner's Mag.* Aug. 219/1 The time table sheets or folders, which every company must keep on hand at its stations.

h. A folding case or cover for loose papers.

1911 H. S. HARRISON *Queed* 329 West went to a filing cabinet..pulled out a large folder marked, Reformatory. **1922** *Brit. Stationer* 11 Dec. 66 Folders for name and number system. **1930** A. PALMER *Company Secretarial Pract.* 182 To file the copies in a folder. **1950** E. BOWEN *Coll. Impressions* p. vi, These are impressions..which, by force of continuing to be written and of having been kept in a folder, have collected themselves.

†**'folder**, *v. Obs.*⁻¹ [variant form of FALTER *v.*]

1617 MARKHAM *Caval.* VII. xlix. 67 The Horsse wil in his going reele and folder.

folderol, *v.*: see FALDERAL *v.* Hence **fol-de-rolling** *vbl. sb.*

a **1847** ELIZA COOK *Happy Mind* vii, Some rough native harp Strikes up With English fol-de-rolling.

†**fold-gabel.** *Obs. rare.* [f. FOLD *sb.*² + GABEL tax.] Rent paid for a fold.

1384-5 *Abingdon Acc.* (1892) 143 Of faldgabul nothing, because no fold.

folding ('fəʊldɪŋ), *vbl. sb.*¹ [f. FOLD *v.*¹ + -ING¹.]

1. a. The action of the vb. FOLD in its various senses; a doubling together, rolling up, etc.; the result of such action. *spec.* (see quot. 1874).

1375 BARBOUR *Bruce* XIII. 632 Lo! quhat falding in fortoune is. *c* **1440** *Promp. Parv.* 168/2 Foldynge of cloþys ..*plicacio.* **1560** BIBLE (Genev.) *Prov.* vi. 10 A little folding of the handes to sleepe. **1561** T. NORTON *Calvin's Inst.* I. xiii. (1634) 44 With such folding and crooked winding these slippery snakes doe slide away. **1642** JER. TAYLOR *Episc.* (1647) 98 To summe up this digest of their acts and ordinations in those generall foldings us'd by the Fathers. **1671** GREW *Anat. Plants* I. iv. §17 (1682) 32 According to the Form and Foulding of every Leaf..is its protection order'd. **1691** G. D'EMILIANNE *Frauds Romish Monks* 263 Of a Candid and Open Spirit, without any foldings or deceit. **1712** BUDGELL *Spect.* No. 539 ¶1 The many Foldings..and Doublings which I make. **1789** G. WHITE *Selborne* iii. 7 The curious foldings of the suture the one into the other. **1874** KNIGHT *Dict. Mech.* I. 899 *Folding*, the process by which printed sheets are so doubled up as to bring the pages into consecutiveness for gathering and binding.

†**b.** A clasping, an embrace. *lit.* and *fig. Obs.*

1685 EARL HALIFAX *Death Chas. II* Wks. (1715) 5 When round his Trunk the Vine Does in soft Wreaths and amorous Foldings twine. **1713** C'TESS WINCHELSEA *Misc. Poems* 381 The gentle foldings of my Love. **1781** *Emma Corbett* II. 172 Replace brother in the embraces of brother, and friend in the foldings of friend.

c. *Geol.* The doubling up of strata; the result of this.

1849 MURCHISON *Siluria* viii. 154 Illustrating the foldings ..of the Silurian series. **1884** GEIKIE in *Nature* 13 Nov. 30/1 The general trend of all these foldings and ruptures is from north-north-east to south-south-west.

2. quasi-*concr.* and *concr.*

a. The point or region of folding; the bend or depression of a limb; a sinuous part or curve of a range of hills, the winding of a valley. Cf. FOLD *sb.*³ 1 c.

c **1400** *Lanfranc's Cirurg.* 109 A smal seem in foldynge of þe forheed. *Ibid.* 159 In þe foldynge of þe myddil of þe arm. **1818** SHELLEY *Let. to Mrs. Shelley* 20 Aug., The foldings of the Vale of Arno. **1886** T. WESTWOOD *Quest of the Sancgreall*, From the far folding of the hills.

b. A fold of a garment, etc., of flesh, skin, etc.; †a lock or plait of hair; †*pl.* the leaves of a folding-door; also, †a coil or wreath of flame.

1552 HULOET, Folding of a womans heere, *trica.* **1558** PHAER *Æneid* III. 584 With..flames in foldings round. **1603** KNOLLES *Hist. Turks.* (1638) 37 Many pleits and foldings. **1669** W. SIMPSON *Hydrol. Chym.* 347 The tunicles and fouldings of the Stomach. **1756-7** tr. *Keysler's Trav.* (1760) II. 256 [This door] is made of brass, with two foldings. **1808** SCOTT *Marm.* III. xxvii, The foldings of his mantle green. **1808** BARLOW *Columb.* III. 370 The lightning's glancing fires ..Bend their long forky foldings o'er the world.

transf. and *fig.* **1719** YOUNG *Revenge* IV. i, Deep in the secret foldings of my heart, She liv'd. **1853** TALFOURD *Castilian* III. ii, The parted foldings of the mist.

3. *attrib.* and *Comb.*, as *folding-machine*, *-place*, *-room*; **folding-stick** (*Bookbinding*) = FOLDER b.; **folding strength**, the strength of paper when subjected to continuous alternate creasing.

1858 SIMMONDS *Dict. Trade*, **Folding-machine*, a machine which delivers newspapers or printed book-work folded. **1874** KNIGHT *Dict. Mech.* I. 900 *Folding-machine*..2 (Metal.), one which bends pans and tin-ware to form. **1884** *Ibid.* IV. 353 *Folding Machine* (Printing), a folder attached to a perfecting printing machine. (Bookbinding), a machine for folding sheets, signatures or quires. **1715** DESAGULIERS *Fires Impr.* 160 The prick'd Lines represent the *folding Places where the Plates must be bent. **1892** *Pall Mall G.* 23 Mar. 4/2 The *folding-room in a sub-basement of the south wing. **1880** ZAEHNSDORF *Bookbinding* 1 Holding a *folding-stick in the right hand. **1936** *Discovery* May 156/2 The percentage decrease in the *folding-strength of a paper after it has been heated for 72 hours at 105°C. is taken as a measure of its permanence on ageing. **1963** R. R. A. HIGHAM *Handbk. Papermaking* iii. 79 The folding strength of a paper is dependent on the fibre length and flexibility of the sheet.

folding ('fəʊldɪŋ), *vbl. sb.*² [f. FOLD *v.*²]

1. The action of folding sheep; an instance of this. Also *concr.* Manure dropped in the fold.

c **1440** *Promp. Parv.* 168/2 Foldynge or puttynge in felde *incaulacio.* **1626** BACON *Sylva* §599 We see againe that Foldings of Sheepe helpe Ground..by their Compost. **1794** BURNS *Hark! the Mavis*, Then a faulding let us gang. **1855** BROWNING *Love among the Ruins* v, The quiet-coloured eve

Smiles to leave To their folding, all our many-tinkling fleece.

2. *attrib.* and *Comb.*, as *folding-hour, -time*; also **folding-slap** (*Sc.*), the gate of the fold; **folding-star**, a star rising at folding-time, an evening-star.

1803 LEYDEN *Scenes of Inf.* I. 291 When evening brings the merry *folding hours. **1786** BURNS *And Maun I still*, The sheep-herd steeks his *faulding slap. **1746–7** COLLINS *Ode to Evening* Poems (1771) 72 When thy *folding-star arising shows His paly circlet. **1822** SHELLEY *Hellas* 221 The powers of earth and air Fled from the folding star of Bethlehem. **1876** *Whitby Gloss.*, *Fauding-time, the time when the cattle are housed or folded.

folding ('fəʊldɪŋ), *ppl. a.* [f. FOLD *v.*[1] + -ING[2].]

1. a. That folds; that is or can be folded.

1611 BIBLE *1 Kings* vi. 34 The two leaues of the one doore were folding. **1701** ROWE *Amb. Step-Moth.* III. ii. 1178 The circle of my folding arms. **1863** T. WRIGHT in *Macm. Mag.* Jan. 173 Written on folding sheets of vellum. **1871** R. ELLIS *Catullus* lxiv. 307 Round them a folding robe their weak limbs aguish hiding.

b. *folding money*: paper money. *colloq.* (chiefly *U.S.*).

1930– in WENTWORTH *Amer. Dial. Dict.* (1944) 225/1 *Foldin' money*, paper money, bills;—humorous. W.Va. & general. **1940** J. O'HARA *Pal Joey* 162 Any time the socialites go out they leave there [*sic*] folding money at home. **1968** L. DEIGHTON *Only when I Larf* iv. 47 I'd walked straight out of the bank carrying a bag full of folding money. **1970** *Daily Tel.* (Colour Suppl.) 15 May 10/2 They used to ask me to prepare the cars and then work, say, in the pits at Le Mans. This gave me a bit of folding money.

2. *esp.* in the names of various articles of furniture, appliances, etc. as ***folding-bed, -board, -boat, -chair, -chase, -joint, -net, -screen, -spoon, -stool, -table***. Often hyphened. Also FOLDING-DOOR.

1771 SMOLLETT *Humphry Clinker*, Wks. 1806 VI. 179 When the *folding-bed is down, there is just room sufficient to pass between it and the fire. **1422–3** *Abingdon Acc.* (1892) 98 In Aula: j tabula vocata *voldyngbord. **1874** KNIGHT *Dict. Mech.* I. 899 **Folding-boat*, one whose frame is collapsible for compact stowage. **1677** *Govt. Venice* 316 The Parasol, the *Folding-Chair, the Cushions. **1884** F. M. CRAWFORD *Rom. Singer* I. 24 They bring strange little folding chairs. **1875** SOUTHWARD *Dict. Typogr.*, **Folding chases*, two or more chases, constructed in such a manner that when laid together they form one large chase. **1842** GWILT *Encycl. Arch.* Gloss., **Folding Joint*, a joint made like a rule-joint or the joint of a hinge. **1874** KNIGHT *Dict. Mech.* I. 900 **Folding-net*, a bird-net shutting upon its prey. **1858** SIMMONDS *Dict. Trade*, **Folding-screen*, an upright portable screen, in several leaves or parts, which shuts up. **1480** *Will Don* Somerset Ho., A *folding spone of siluer. **1340** *Ayenb.* 239 Ane *uyealdinde stole. **1705** HICKERINGILL *Priest-cr.* II. iii. 29 One of them.. flung a little folding Stool, whereon she sat, at the Dean's Head. **1502** *Bury Wills* (Camden) 93 The beste *faldyng table. **1532** *Inv.* in Noakes *Worc. Mon. & Cathedr.* (1866) 157 A voldyng table with two leves.

'folding 'door. [f. FOLDING *ppl. a.* + DOOR.] A door consisting of two parts hung on opposite jambs, so that their edges come into contact when the door is closed. Now usually *pl.* in same sense.

In the mod. sense of the adj. the name is more appropriate when, as is often the case, each of the parts of the door consists of two or more leaves, hinged so as to fold up when the door is open. 'Folding doors' are often used to form a removable partition between two adjacent rooms; hence the term is sometimes loosely applied to a partition used for the same purpose, but opened by lateral sliding of its parts.

1611 COTGR. s.v. *Batant*, A foulding, or two leaued doore. **1723** CHAMBERS tr. *Le Clerc's Treat. Archit.* I. 102 In one of the Folding-doors is usually a Wicket. **1794** MRS. RADCLIFFE *Myst. Udolpho* xix, Through a folding-door she passed from the great hall to the ramparts. **1829** *University Instr.* in Willis & Clark *Cambridge* (1886) III. 103 The four Schools.. are.. to communicate with each other.. by large double folding doors. **1838** LYTTON *Calderon* i, The folding-doors were thrown open. **1882** OUIDA *Maremma* I. 125 A double or, as it is commonly termed, folding-door.

So **folding gates**.

1824 SCOTT *Redgauntlet* Let. xi, 'They rode.. through the muckle faulding yetts.' **1870** BRYANT *Iliad* I. XII. 397 The beams that strengthened the tall folding-gates.

foldless ('fəʊldlɪs), *a.*[1] [f. FOLD *sb.*[2] + -LESS.] Having no fold or pen.

1822 MILMAN *Martyr of Antioch* 38 Who shall lead The foldless sheep to life's eternal pastures When their good shepherd's gone? **1895** W. WATSON *Purple East* vi, Christ's foldless flock, shorn of their fleece.

foldless ('fəʊldlɪs), *a.*[2] [f. FOLD *sb.*[3] + -LESS.] Without a fold or crease.

1845 MRS. NORTON *Child Isl.* (1846) 131 One foldless mantle. **1850** BROWNING *Xmas Eve & Easter Day* 217 To have it [a curtain] go Foldless and flat along the wall.

foldure ('fəʊldjʊə(r)). *rare*[−1]. [f. FOLD *v.*[1] + -URE.] The action of process of folding.

1823 LAMB *Lett.* (1888) II. 72 My letters are generally charged as double at the Post Office, from their inveterate clumsiness of foldure.

foldy ('fəʊldɪ), *a.* [f. FOLD *sb.*[3] + -Y[1].] Full of folds, hanging in folds.

a **1851** JOANNA BAILLIE (Ogilv.), Those limbs beneath their foldy vestments moving.

fole, obs. form of FOAL, FOIL, FOOL.

†**foleant**, *pple. Obs.*[−1] [ad. OF. *foliant, foleiant*, pr. pple. of *folier, foleier*, to FOOL.] Playing the fool.

1340 *Ayenb.* 244 Huet y-zyxt þou foleant uor to zeche diuerse guodes to þine zaule and to þine bodye.

†**folebayrie.** *Obs.*[−1] [a. OF. *fole baerie* (*fole*, fem. of *fol* foolish + *baërie* lit. 'gaping', whence eagerness, f. *baer* to gape).]

1340 *Ayenb.* 17 Folebayrie þet we clepieþ ambicion.

folet: see FOLT. *Obs.*

†**fo'leye**, *v. Obs.* [ad. OF. *foleier, folier, foloier*, f. *fol* foolish.] *intr.* To act foolishly, play the fool.

c **1374** CHAUCER *Boeth.* III. pr. ii. 67 And foleyen swyche folk þanne, þat wenen þat [etc.]. *c* **1420** HOCCLEVE *To Richard Dk. of York* xlv, If that I in my wrytynge foleye, As I do oft. ? *a* **1500** *Ragman Roll* 60 in Hazl. *E.P.P.* I. 72 That with your bodé foleyed han ye.

folghthe, var. f. FULLOUGHT *Obs.*, baptism.

‖**folia**[1] ('fəʊlɪə), *sb. pl.* [pl. of L. *folium* leaf.]

1. *Bot.* In Latin sense: Leaves (of a plant).

1730–6 BAILEY (folio), *Folia* [in Botany], the leaves of plants and flowers, but more properly of plants. **1861** J. R. GREENE *Man. Anim. Kingd., Cœlent.* 191 Many species spread out in broad leaves or folia.

2. Laminæ or thin layers.

1796 KIRWAN *Elem. Min.* I. 155 Fracture, undulatingly foliated, or the folia exceedingly thin. **1854** HOOKER *Himal. Jrnls.* I. xvii. 408 Zigzag folia of quartz. **1882** GEIKIE *Text-bk. Geol.* II. II. §3. 88 Wavy layers or folia.

‖**folia**[2] (fo'lia). [Sp.; lit. 'folly', a. F. *folie.*] A Spanish dance similar to the fandango. Also, music for such a dance.

1772–84 COOK *Voy.* (1790) II. 413 The dances practised here are sarabands and folias.

foliaceous (fəʊlɪ'eɪʃəs), *a.* Also 7 foleaceous, 8–9 foliacious. [f. L. *foliāce-us* leafy, f. *folium* leaf: see -ACEOUS. Cf. Fr. *foliacé.*]

1. a. Having the appearance or nature of a leaf; leaf-like. Of certain cryptogamous plants: Having organs resembling leaves. †Of a flower: Having petals.

1658 SIR T. BROWNE *Gard. Cyrus* iii. 134 Seeds themselves in their rudimentall discoveries, appear in foliaceous surcles. **1668** WILKINS *Real Char.* 70 Herbs.. Not flowring; (i.) not having any foliaceous flower. **1756** P. BROWNE *Jamaica* (1789) 128 The largest foliaceous Cyperus. **1806** J. GALPINE *Brit. Bot.* 335 Teeth of the calyx foliaceous. **1861** H. MACMILLAN *Footn. Page Nat.* 23 Mosses belong to the foliaceous.. division of flowerless plants. **1877** DARWIN *Forms of Fl.* iii. 116 The foliaceous stigma is more expanded.

b. Bearing leaves, leafy; having an abundance of foliage. *rare.*

1677 COLES, *Foliaceous*, leavy. **1800** W. TAYLOR in *Monthly Mag.* X. 318 Some withering words would drop from the foliaceous tree of our language.

c. Of or pertaining to a leaf or leaves, consisting of leaves.

1816 KIRBY & SP. *Entomol.* xii. 378 A foliaceous or farinaceous diet. **1870** H. MACMILLAN *Bible Teach.* vii. 134 The study of plants in which it [the stem] departs from the normal form, will clearly indicate its foliaceous origin.

2. Consisting of, or having the character of, thin leaf-like plates or laminæ.

1728 WOODWARD *Fossils* I. I. 163 A blue talky foliaceous spar. **1766** *Phil. Trans.* LVI. 37 The metal is.. found.. in a foliaceous manner issuing out of the quartz. **1770–4** A. HUNTER *Georg. Ess.* (1803) I. 231 Flakes of foliaceous talc. **1861** HULME tr. *Moquin-Tandon* II. III. ii. 86 The shell [of the Oyster] is attached.. foliaceous, rough.

3. *Zool.* and *Ent.* Shaped or arranged like leaves.

1828 STARK *Elem. Nat. Hist.* II. 170 A foliaceous appendage at the origin of the feet which surround the mouth. **1854** WOODWARD *Mollusca* (1856) 276 Valves foliaceous, the upper smallest. **1879** WRIGHT *Anim. Life* 59 The bats of this family have.. foliaceous cutaneous appendages surrounding the nasal apertures.

Hence **foli'aceousness**, the condition or quality of being foliaceous.

1727 in BAILEY vol. II.

foliage ('fəʊlɪɪdʒ), *sb.* Forms: 6–7 foillage, 7 folliage, fuellage, (9 *dial.* foilage), 7– foliage. [An altered form (after L. *folium* leaf, or its Eng. derivatives) of *foillage*, a. F. *feuillage* (earlier *fueillage, foillage*) f. *feuille* leaf: see FOIL *sb.*[1] and -AGE.]

1. The leaves (of a plant or tree) collectively; leafage.

1601 HOLLAND *Pliny* II. 25 There is not an hearbe.. that taketh vp greater compasse with fuellage than doth the Beet. **1708** PHILIPS *Cyder* I. 384 Swelling Buds their od'rous Foliage shed. **1784** COWPER *Task* VI. 144 These naked shoots.. Shall put their graceful foliage on again. **1858** GLENNY *Gard. Every-day Bk.* 175/1 Bulbs are too frequently attacked by vermin when allowed to remain in the ground after the foliage has died down. **1867** MISS BRADDON *Aur. Floyd* i. 5 Labouring men's cottages, gleaming white from the surrounding foliage.

transf. and *fig.* **1747** GOULD *Eng. Ants* 53 You will.. observe on each Side of its Breast a small white Foliage of Wings. **1850** HAWTHORNE *Scarlet L.* xiii. (1883) 197 The light and graceful foliage of her character.

2. In *Art*: The representation of leaves, etc. used for decoration or ornament.

1598 FLORIO, *Fogliami*.. foillage, or branched worke. **1664** EVELYN tr. *Freart's Archit.* xxxiv. 80 The foliage which domineers in the Freeze. **1762–71** H. WALPOLE *Vertue's Anecd. Paint.* (1786) III. 150 The simplicity of the carver's foliage at once sets off.. the glare of Verrio's paintings. **1874** PARKER *Goth. Archit.* I. iv. 119 Foliage is by no means an essential feature of the Early English style. **1879** SIR G. G. SCOTT *Lect. Archit.* I. 80 Foliage.. most beautifully carved.

b. A representation of a cluster of leaves, sprays, or branches. ? *Obs.*

1699 GARTH *Dispens.* 66 A Foliage of dissembl'd Senna leaves Grav'd round its Brim. **1730** A. GORDON *Maffei's Amphith.* 371 Foliages, or Branch-work. **1801** COXE *Tour Monmouthsh.* I. 74 A semicircular arch, ornamented with a foliage of twisted branches.

3. *attrib.* and *Comb.*, as ***foliage-border, -stem, -trimming***; ***foliage-bound*** adj. Also, **foliage crop** (see quot. 1831); **foliage leaf**, a leaf in the restricted sense of the word, excluding petals and other modified leaves; **foliage plant**, one cultivated for its foliage and not for its blossom.

1891 *Daily News* 2 July 6/1 A Louis XVI octagonal gold box, *foliage borders and amber-coloured panels. **1805** SCOTT *Last Minstr.* VI. xxiii, Shone every pillar *foliage-bound. **1831** LOUDON *Encycl. Agric.* 1243/2 **Foliage crops*, plants cultivated for their leaves to be used green, and which will not make into hay, as the cabbage tribe. **1872** OLIVER *Elem. Bot.* I. i. 4, I use the term *foliage-leaves at present simply in order to avoid confusion with the leaves of which flowers are composed. **1882** VINES *Sachs' Bot.* 634 The cotyledons remain thin like shortly stalked foliage-leaves. **1862** *Times* 10 Apr., *Foliage plants.. produce the effect required of them throughout the whole period of their growth. **1884** BOWER & SCOTT *De Bary's Phaner.* 122 The rhizome and *foliage-stem may be similar or dissimilar. **1818** *La Belle Assemblée* XVII. 36/6 A *foliage trimming of pale blue satin.

foliage ('fəʊlɪɪdʒ), *v.* [f. prec. sb.] *trans.* To adorn with foliage or with a representation of leaves and flowers.

1836 in SMART. **1846** *P. Parley's Ann.* VII. 64 The tombs.. are inlaid with wreaths of flowers, and foliaged in their natural colours.

foliaged ('fəʊlɪɪdʒd), *ppl. a.* [f. FOLIAGE *sb.* and *v.* + -ED.]

1. Decorated or ornamented with the representation of foliage.

1754 A. DRUMMOND *Trav.* ii. 58 An huge composite foliaged column. *a* **1763** SHENSTONE *Economy* III. 40 Replete with dust The foliag'd velvet. **1831** *Fraser's Mag.* IV. 282 The foliaged frieze re-echoing.. the idea of the capital.

2. Covered or furnished with (natural) foliage.

1815 SHELLEY *Alastor* 464 Some inconstant star Between one foliaged lattice twinkling fair. **1859** CORNWALLIS *New World* I. 175 The trunks were charred, but their foliaged tops had escaped the fiery element.

foliageous (fəʊlɪ'eɪdʒəs), *a.* [f. FOLIAGE *sb.* + -OUS.] Containing representations of foliage.

1882 *Athenæum* 3 June 704/1 The scroll-work upon them [Northumbrian stone crosses] is foliageous. *c* **1890** J. R. ALLEN *Notes Monum. Wilts.* 2 Foliageous terminations are introduced.

folial ('fəʊlɪəl), *a.* [f. L. *foli-um* leaf + -AL[1].] = next.

1878 G. D. BOARDMAN *Creative Week* 314 (Cent. Dict.), Wolff in 1759.. asserted the community of structure in the folial and the floral leaves. **1884** *Syd. Soc. Lex.*, *Folial Cycle*, the mode of arrangement of leaves on an axis.

foliar ('fəʊlɪə(r)), *a.* [ad. mod.L. *foliāris*, f. L. *folium* leaf. Cf. Fr. *foliaire.*] Of, pertaining to, or of the nature of a leaf.

1875 DARWIN *Insectiv. Pl.* xv. 358 In innumerable instances foliar organs move when excited. **1880** GRAY *Struct. Bot.* iii. §3. 54 Whatever subtends a lateral axis or branch may be taken for a leaf or foliar production. **1884** BOWER & SCOTT *De Bary's Phaner.* 284 In many Ferns the original axile bundle widens out.. into a tube, which.. has.. a relatively small slit or foliar gap.. from the margin of which one or several bundles pass into the leaf.

foliate ('fəʊlɪət), *a.* [ad. L. *foliāt-us* leaved, f. *folium* leaf: see -ATE.]

†**1.** Beaten out into a thin sheet or foil. *foliate gold* = *leaf-gold*. *Obs.*

1626 BACON *Sylva* §293 Gold Foliate, or any Metall Foliate, cleaveth. **1646** SIR T. BROWNE *Pseud. Ep.* II. iv. 79 This attraction have wee tried.. in gold and silver foliate. **1819** H. BUSK *Vestriad* I. 452 On foliate gold his aching head was laid.

†**b.** ? Consisting of laminæ. *Obs.*

1683 SALMON *Doron Med.* I. xxvii. 334 The which is called the foliate Earth.

2. Resembling a leaf; leaf-life.

1658 SIR T. BROWNE *Gard. Cyrus* ii. 40 The leaves and foliate works are commonly thus contrived. **1846** DANA *Zooph.* 433 Coalescing into a solid plate, without branches above (foliate).

b. *Geom. foliate curve*; also *foliate* quasi-*sb.*: see quot. 1796.

1715 A. DE MOIVRE in *Phil. Trans.* XXIX. 330 The Foliate is exactly quadrable, the whole Leaf thereof being but one third of the Square of AB. **1796** HUTTON *Math. Dict.* (1815) I. 533 *Foliate*, a curve of the 2[d] order.. consisting of two infinite legs crossing each other, forming a kind of leaf.

3. *Bot.* **a.** Furnished with leaves.

1677 COLES, *Foliate*, leaved. 1721–90 BAILEY, *Foliate*, Leaved, or having Leaves, as, a foliate stalk. 1866 *Treas. Bot.*, *Foliate*, clothed with leaves.

b. Having (a specified number of) leaflets.

1840 PAXTON *Bot. Dict.*, *Foliate*, when a leaf is divided into leaflets, it is called 1, 2, 3, 5, or 10-foliate, according to the number of leaflets.

foliate (ˈfəʊlɪeɪt), *v.* [f. L. *foli-um* + -ATE.]

†**1.** *trans.* To beat (metal) to a leaf or foil.

1704–21 NEWTON *Optics* (ed. 3) 140 If Gold be foliated and held between your Eye and the Light, the Light looks blue.

b. *intr.* To split into leaves or laminæ.

1798 GREVILLE in *Phil. Trans.* LXXXVIII. 414 Other parts appear to foliate. 1836 CALDCLEUGH in *Foreign Q. Rev.* XVII. 15 [It] foliates at its surface..and becomes a friable and very light kind of stone.

2. *trans.* To foil (glass); to silver.

1665 HOOKE *Microgr.* 83 If you foliate that part of a Glass-ball that is to reflect an Iris. 1818 *Blackw. Mag.* III. 614 The lens..a peculiar part of which he intended to foliate.

3. *intr.* To put forth leaves.

1775 ROMANS *Nat. Hist. Florida* 7 This tardy tree budded, foliated, blossomed. 1893 Q. [COUCH] *Delect. Duchy* 162 The ash was foliating on the 29th of April.

4. *trans.* To decorate with foils (see FOIL *sb.*[1] 2 b).

1812–6 J. SMITH *Panorama Sc. & Art* I. 136 There seems to have been little if any attempt at feathering or foliating the heads of Norman doors. 1835 WILLIS *Arch. Mid. Ages* 45 There is a manifest distinction between foiling an arch and foliating it. [He explains that a 'foiled arch' is one indented into a number of small arches; a 'foliated arch' is a plain arch with a foiled arch placed below it. But his distinction is seldom recognised.] 1851 RUSKIN *Stones Ven.* (1874) I. i. 13 The Arabs pointed and foliated the arch.

5. *trans.* To mark the folios or leaves of (a volume, etc.) with consecutive numbers.

1846–7 MASKELL *Mon. Rit.* I. p. cxix, It is regularly foliated to the end, from i. to c. iiij. 1848 HALLIWELL *Acc. Vernon MS.* 3 It numbers ff. 412 and 8 ab init.; ff. 311–318, 403–412, not foliated.

Hence ˈ**foliating** *ppl. a.*

1835 WILLIS *Arch. Mid. Ages* 45 This foliating arch continued..to be treated as an independent order.

foliated (ˈfəʊlɪeɪtɪd), *ppl. a.* [f. prec. + -ED[1].]

†**1.** = FOLIATE *a.* 1. *Obs.*

1666 BOYLE *Orig. Formes & Qual.* II. v. 334 Spirit of Salt ..being heated..would readily enough dissolve foliated Gold.

b. Covered with foil, silvered.

1665 HOOKE *Microgr.* 214 A convex Looking-glass, or foliated Glass-ball.

2. Composed of thin leaf-like layers or laminæ. Chiefly *Geol.* and *Min.* ***foliated earth of tartar***, an old name of potassium acetate.

1650 ASHMOLE *Arcanum* 205 This Earth is white and foliated, wherein Philosophers doe sow their gold. 1794 SULLIVAN *View Nat.* II. 332 Crystals and gems are found to be of a foliated structure. 1833 LYELL *Princ. Geol.* III. 11 Crystalline precipitates..with a foliated and stratified structure. 1854 THOMSON *Cycl. Chem.*, *Foliated Tellurium*, Red Telluride of Lead. 1866–7 LIVINGSTONE *Last Jrnls.* (1873) I. iv. 85 Near the Lake..mica schist and gneiss foliated.

3. Chiefly *Zool.* and *Conchol.* Shaped like a leaf or leaves; in leaf-like forms. See also quot. 1859.

1846 PATTERSON *Zool.* 28 Some of these ['sea-mats']..present a foliated appearance. 1846 DANA *Zooph.* iv. 83 By growth laterally, the explanate or oblique foliated species originate. 1854 WOODWARD *Mollusca* (1856) 91 Sutures angulated, or lobed and foliated. 1859 PAGE *Handbk. Geol. Terms* s.v. *Foliated*, Certain shells are said to be foliated, when their surfaces are covered with leaf-like projections, as the rose-bush murex.

4. *Arch.*, etc. **a.** Ornamented with foils. ***foliated arch*** (see quot. 1840). **b.** Consisting of or ornamented with leaf-work or foliage.

1840 PARKER *Gloss. Archit.* (ed. 3), *Foliated Arch*, an arch with a trefoil, cinquefoil, or multifoil under it. 1849 BRANDON *Goth. Archit.* I. 25 Small shafts with delicately carved foliated caps. 1851 E. SHARPE *Seven Periods* 25 The earlier Windows exhibit tracery which consists almost exclusively of plain foliated circles. 1886 RUSKIN *Præterita* I. v. 163 Our parlour table loaded with foliated silver.

5. Furnished with or consisting of leaves. *spec.* in *Her.*

1721–90 BAILEY, *Foliated*, Leaved or having Leaves. 1756 P. BROWNE *Jamaica* (1789) 128 This plant..bears a large foliated top. 1828–40 BERRY *Encycl. Her.* I, *Foliated*, leaved.

6. *Mus.* (See quot.)

1876 STAINER & BARRETT *Dict. Mus. Terms*, *Foliated*, a melody or portion of plain-song is said to be foliated when slurred notes have been added above or below those of which it originally consisted.

7. *Carpentry.* Rabbeted.

1874 KNIGHT *Dict. Mech.* I. 900/2 *Foliated-joint* (Carpentry), a rabbeted joint, where one part overlies another.

foliation (fəʊlɪˈeɪʃən). Also 7 -acion. [f. FOLIATE *a.*: see -ATION and cf. Fr. *foliation.*]

1. The leafing (of a plant); the process of bursting into leaf; the state of being in leaf.

1623 COCKERAM, *Foliacion*, budding of the leaues. 1779 MASON *Eng. Gard.* III. 221 Plants..rul'd by Foliation's different law. 1795 *Gentl. Mag.* 540/1 Between total denudation and perfect foliation the rind..of various trees exhibits various tints. 1864 in WEBSTER.

b. *concr.* †(*a*) Something resembling a leaf; (*b*) a leaf-like process.

1658 SIR T. BROWNE *Gard. Cyrus* iii. 48 Thus are also disposed the triangular foliations, in the conicall fruit of the firre tree. 1875 BLAKE *Zool.* 55 Variously shaped and grotesque membranous foliations.

2. *Bot.* †**a.** The assemblage of leaves or petals forming the corolla of a flower. *Obs.*

1671 [see ATTIRE *sb.* 8]. 1746–7 HERVEY *Medit.* (1818) 116 Thou wilt not find a rival in the feathers of a peacock, or the foliation of a tulip.

b. The formation or arrangement of leaves in the bud; = VERNATION.

1794 MARTYN *Rousseau's Bot.* xxxi. 485 The foliation, or different folding of the leaves, before they are expanded. 1835 in LINDLEY *Introd. Bot.* (1848) I. 176. 1845 —— *Sch. Bot.* iv. (1858) 25 Flowers regular, with.. gyrate foliation.

3. The action or process of beating (metal) into foil.

1755 JOHNSON, *Foliation*, the act of beating into thin leaves. 1828 in WEBSTER; and in mod. Dicts.

4. *Geol.* The process and the property of splitting up into leaf-like layers; also the laminæ or plates into which crystalline rocks are divided.

1851–9 DARWIN in *Man. Sci. Enq.* 283 The foliation of the metamorphic schists..is intimately connected with the cleavage of homogeneous slaty rocks. 1876 PAGE *Advd. Text-Bk. Geol.* viii. 159 Contortions and foliations among the gneiss and mica-schists.

5. *Arch.* Ornamentation with foils; tracery consisting chiefly of small arcs or foils.

1816 [see FEATHERING *vbl. sb.* 2 b]. 1849 FREEMAN *Archit.* 280 Foliations hanging free like lace-work. 1853 RUSKIN *Stones Ven.* II. vi, Foliation..is..the easiest method of decoration which Gothic architecture possesses.

b. An arrangement of foliage.

1875 POLLEN *Anc. & Mod. Furn.* 85 Figured sculpture.. in the form of..acanthus foliations.

6. The consecutive numbering of the folios (or leaves) of a book or MS.

1846–7 MASKELL *Mon. Rit.* II. p. xxiii, These..beginning with fresh signatures, and foliation, may be mistaken for perfect books. 1885 C. PLUMMER Introd. to *Fortescue's Abs. & Lim. Mon.* 88 Monarchia occupies ff. 172–194 according to the old foliation.

7. The action or process of applying foil to glass.

1828 in WEBSTER; and in mod. Dicts.

foli'ato-, combining form of L. *foliātus* FOLIATE, in sense 'formed like a leaf'.

1846 DANA *Zooph.* (1848) 497 Foliato-explanate at base.

foliator (ˈfəʊlɪeɪtə(r)). [f. FOLIATE *v.* + -OR.] One who foliates or numbers the leaves of a book.

1848 HALLIWELL *Acc. Vernon MS.* 3 Ff. 337–60, 369–72 interchanged by the foliator, but rightly bound.

foliature (ˈfəʊlɪətjʊə(r)). [ad. late L. *foliātūra*, f. *foliātus* FOLIATE.]

1. a. A cluster of leaves; foliage. **b.** Leaf-ornamentation.

1676 GREW *Anat. Plants* IV. v. §2 (1682) 171 Those Plants which have no Flower or Foliature, are yet some way or other Attir'd. 1753 SHUCKFORD *Creation* xi. 203 They wreathed together a Foliature of the Fig-tree. 1815 SOUTHEY *Roderick* XVIII. 130 The crosier richly wrought With silver foliature.

2. 'The state of being hammered into leaves' (J.).

folic (ˈfəʊlɪk, ˈfɒlɪk), *a.* *Biochem.* [f. L. *fol-ium* leaf + -IC.] ***folic acid***: pteroyl(mono)glutamic acid, a vitamin of the B group found in a wide variety of organisms, the deficiency of which in man is associated with anæmia; also, any of the other pteroylglutamic acids.

1941 K. MITCHELL et al. in *Jrnl. Amer. Chem. Soc.* LXIII. 2284/1 Using *Streptococcus lactis R* as a test organism, we have obtained..an acid nutrilite... It is especially abundant in green leaves... Because of this fact, and since we have obtained what appears to be a nearly pure chemical entity, we suggest the name folic acid. 1949 H. W. FLOREY et al. *Antibiotics* II. xlvii. 1448 The synthesis of pteroylglutamic acid (folic acid). 1960 A. HUXLEY *Let.* 23 June (1969) 892 She is doing very well on the B12 + Folic Acid which I prescribed..as a cure for her dizzy spells. 1961 W. J. E. JESSOP *Fearon's Introd. Biochem.* (ed. 4) xiii. 201 All the folic acids are effective in the treatment of..non pernicious anæmias. 1961 *Lancet* 26 Aug. 483/1 The complex relation between vitamin B12 and folic acid is still far from being completely understood.

†**folie**, *v.* *Obs.*$^{-1}$ = FOLIATE *v.* 5, FOLIO *v.*

1697 *Sec. Narrat. Proc. Turners Hall* 36 *Errata*, That sheet is wrong Folied, which correct thus, p. 17, 18, 19.

‖**folie** (fɔli), *sb.* [Fr.; see FOLLY.] Madness, insanity, mania. Chiefly in various pathological terms (see quots.).

1803 *Edin. Rev.* II. 163 The maniac appears perfectly composed, makes the best and most correct answers to the questions put to him; but, if set at liberty, immediately becomes furious. This kind of derangement..is what is vulgarly called *folie raisonnante.* 1880 *Encycl. Brit.* XIII. 109/2 To this condition foreign authorities have applied the term *folie circulaire*... After intervals of comparative sanity, the patient manifests symptoms which run their course through the prodromal, the acute, and the demented stages, on again to recovery. 1890 BILLINGS *Med. Dict.*, *Folie du doute*, doubting insanity. *Ibid.*, *Folie des grandeurs*, delirium of grandeur. 1913 DORLAND *Med. Dict.* (ed. 7), *Folie à deux*, communicated insanity. 1914 W. J. LOCKE *Jaffery* viii, This is absurd. It's megalomania—*la folie des grandeurs.* 1915 A. HUXLEY *Let.* Oct. (1969) 80 A new growing country, swelled with its own pride, filled by its growing pains with an immense folie de grandeur. 1923 —— *On Margin* 181 The baroque *folie de grandeur.* 1960 *Guardian* 8 July 13/6 Friedrich Grunwald..denied having 'folie de grandeur'—being a big head who has gone round the bend. 1961 *Listener* 24 Aug. 290/2 You..are afflicted with *folie de doute* (was it really 10,000,000 cells per minute, or 10,000, and if so, why?). 1962 *Sci. Amer.* Aug. 66/3 In twins, as in other pairs of individuals who are emotionally close to each other, the condition known as *folie à deux* has been commonly observed. The two partners tend to develop shared delusions and symptoms. 1962 *John o' London's* 27 Sept. 307/4 A brilliantly observed clinical study of the *folie à deux* indulged in by a pair of chronic fantasists.

folie, obs. form of FOLLY.

†**folier.** *Obs. rare.* [Of doubtful genuineness; the author was a German; cf. G. *folie* = FOIL *sb.*[1]] A foil to put under a precious stone.

1671 SCHROTER in Birch *Hist. Royal Soc.* II. 489–493 *passim.* 1818 in TODD; and in mod. Dicts.

foliicolous (ˌfəʊlɪˈɪkələs), *a.* [f. L. *folii-* combining form of *foli-um* leaf + *col-* (stem of *colĕre* to inhabit + -OUS.] Growing parasitically on leaves.

1874 COOKE *Fungi* 287 Foliicolous species.

foliiferous (ˌfəʊlɪˈɪfərəs), *a.* Also *erron.* foliferous. [f. as prec. + -FEROUS.] Bearing leaves or leaf-like appendages. ***foliiferous staff***: a pastoral staff decorated with figures of buds or leaves.

1828 WEBSTER, *Foliferous*, producing leaves. 1857 BERKELEY *Cryptog. Bot.* §34. 48 A true embryo, with the radicular end pointing one way, and the foliiferous end another. 1876 AXEL BLYTT *Norwegian Flora* 54 The tender foliferous trees in the Danish forest bogs.

foliiform (ˈfəʊlɪˌfɔːm), *a.* [f. as prec. + -FORM.] Having the form of a leaf, leaf-like.

1880 GRAY *Struct. Bot.* iii. §3. 65 Special foliiform Branches.

foliiparous (ˌfəʊlɪˈɪpərəs), *a.* [f. as prec. + *-par-us* producing (*parĕre* to produce) + -OUS.] 'Producing leaves only' (*Treas. Bot.* 1866).

folily: see FOLLILY *adv. Obs.*

folimot, folimort, obs. forms of FILEMOT.

1622 PEACHAM *Compl. Gentl.* (1661) 157 Folimot colour signifieth Withered. *c* 1640 [SHIRLEY] *Capt. Underwit* II. ii. in Bullen *O. Pl.* II. 345 Shall I decipher my Colours to you now?.. Folimort is withered, [etc.].

folinic (fəʊˈlɪnɪk, fɒl-), *a.* *Biochem.* [f. FOL(IC *a.* + -IN + -IC.] ***folinic acid***: a derivative of folic acid, believed to be the form in which the latter acts as a coenzyme.

1949 T. J. BOND et al. in *Jrnl. Amer. Chem. Soc.* LXXI. 3852/2 On the basis of structure and functional relationship to folic acid, this active principle has been termed folinic acid. 1962 *New Scientist* 17 May 364/3 To counter-act the damaging effects of the methotrexate that spilled over into the general circulation, a biological antagonist, folinic acid (leucovorin), was injected intramuscularly. 1966 E. S. WEST et al. *Textbk. Biochem.* (ed. 4) xviii. 814 Folinic acid, citrovorum factor (CF), and leucovorin are names for a naturally occurring derivative of folic acid... It is N^5-formyl-5,6,7,8-tetrahydropteroylglutamic acid.

folio (ˈfəʊlɪəʊ), *sb.* and *a.* Also 7 follio. [a. L. *foliō*, abl. of *folium* leaf. Branch I proceeds from the med.L. use of the ablative in references, though in sense 2 the word may be a. It. *foglio.* In branch II the phrase *in folio* is either a. Lat. or a refashioning of the Italian *in foglio.* Cf. the use of *in folio* in Fr. both in sense 5 b and as *sb.* = sense 7.]

A. *sb.*

I. With reference to pagination.

1. A leaf of paper, parchment, etc. (either loose as one of a series, or in a bound volume) which is numbered only on the front.

In the early instances the word may have been regarded as Latin. The front and back of the leaf were referred to as (*folio*) *recto* and *verso*; these words became Eng. as sbs.

1533 T. MORE *Debell. Salem* Wks. 958/2 The .xlv. Chapiter of mine Apology beginnyng, Folio .243. 1548 STAUNFORD *Kinges Prerog.* ix. (1567) 35 a, There it appeares folio .285. allso. 1585 WASHINGTON tr. *Nicholay's Voy. Turkie*, Table, The first number signifieth the chapter, the second the folio. 1669 STURMY *Mariner's Mag.* II. xvii. *marg.*, Place this between folio 202. and folio 203.

2. In *Bookkeeping*, The two opposite pages of a ledger or other account-book in which these are used concurrently; hence used for a page of a ledger in which one page serves for both sides of an account, and sometimes for a page of an account book generally.

1588 MELLIS *Briefe Instruct.* C v, The number of the leafe or folio of your Creditor. 1622 MALYNES *Anc. Law-Merch.* 364 The Leaves or Folio of the Leidger. 1849 FREESE *Comm. Class-bk.* 109 A narrow column, for the figures which denote the Folio, where each account will be found in the Ledger.

3. The page-number of a printed book.

1683 MOXON *Mech. Exerc.* II. 376 The Corrector and Compositer..examine..how the Folio's of those Pages properly and numerically follow and succeed one another.

1841 SAVAGE *Dict. Print.*, When there is a running title, the folios are placed at the outside corners of the pages.

4. *Law.* A certain number of words (in Gt. Britain and Ireland 72 or 90, in U.S. generally 100) taken as a unit in reckoning the length of a document.

Many legal documents of 16th c. are found to be written in pages of 12–15 lines, each containing 6 words. This is doubtless the origin of the above sense.

1836 SIR H. TAYLOR *Statesman* xxiii. 169 Paying persons in the rank of life of law-stationers and their hired writers at the rate of so much per folio. **1848** WHARTON *Law Lex.*, *Folio*, a certain number of words; in conveyances, &c., amounting to seventy-two, and in Chancery proceedings to ninety.

II. With reference to size.

5. *in folio*, a phrase signifying 'in the form of a full-sized sheet folded once'. Orig. apprehended as a Latin phrase, used appositively or attributively; afterwards as consisting of an English prep. and sb.

1582 PARSONS *Def. of Censure* 148, I haue two editions in greeke: the one of learned Pagnine *in folio*, the other of Plantyne *in octavo*. **1588** SHAKS. *L.L.L.* I. ii. 192 Deuise Wit, write Pen, for I am for whole volumes in folio. **1644** EVELYN *Mem.* (1857) I. 89 That rare book in a large folio. **1679** BP. HEREFORD *Coll. Jesuits* 4 Divinity Books..in Folio and Quarto. **1763** MASSEY *Orig. of Lett.* II. 59 All the curious hands..engraved on 28 brass plates in folio. **1819** *Blackw. Mag.* Oct. 29, I asked her if she would have it in folio, with marginal notes? **1837–9** HALLAM *Hist. Lit.* I. iii. I. §148. 250 The more usual form of books printed in the 15th century is in folio.

b. *transf.* and *fig.*; *spec.* in a full and loose dress. *Obs.* exc. *dial.*

1590 GREENE *Neuer too late* (1600) 96 His lippes were of the largest sise in folio, able to furnish a Coblers shoppe with clowting leather. *a* **1613** OVERBURY *A Wife &c.* (1638) 133 Many ride poast to Chandlers and Tobacco shops in folio. *a* **1625** FLETCHER *Love's Cure* II. ii, I had rather walke In folio again, loose, like a woman. **1630** J. TAYLOR (Water P.) *Jack-a-Lent* 114/1 When a mans stomacke is in Folio, and knowes not where to haue a dinner in *Decimo sexto*. **1651** LILLY *Chas. I* (1774) 244 The scorns..he saw now returned upon himself in folio. **1670** LASSELS *Voy. Italy* II. 7 It [Rome] hath its Hospitals..and many of those are Hospitals in folio. **1698** VANBRUGH *Prov. Wife* v. (1710) 95 Cuckoldom in Folio, is newly printed: and Matrimony in Quarto, is just going into the Press. **1828** *Craven Gloss.* (ed. 2) s.v., 'In full folio', in full dress.

6. A sheet of paper when folded once. Also, †such a sheet used for a specific purpose.

1616 BULLOKAR, *Folio*, a sheete or large leafe of paper. **1691** EVELYN *Diary* 16 Apr., Severall folios of dried plants. **1710** ADDISON *Tatler* No. 216 ⁋5 To his Daughter..I bequeath..my large Folio of Indian Cabbage. **1876** J. GOULD *Letter-press Printer* 40 Folio denotes a sheet of paper folded into two leaves.

7. A volume made up of sheets of paper folded once; a volume of the largest size.

1628 EARLE *Microcosm. Sergeant* (Arb.) 57 He swels them [Bookes] into Folio's with his Comments. **1713** SWIFT *Frenzy J. Dennis* Wks. 1821 XIII. 211 The gentleman..let drive at us with a vast folio. **1826** SCOTT *Woodst.* iii, Tomkins began to turn the leaves of a folio, which lay open on the reading-desk. **1867** STUBBS *Benedict's Chron.* I. Pref. 24 The other manuscript..is a small folio.

transf. and *fig.* **1659** D. PELL *Impr. Sea* 286 The little decimo sextos..the small fish..as well as..the great folios of the Whale, and Elephant. **1813** BYRON *Jrnl.* 16 Nov. in Moore *Life* (1833) I. 541 This same lady writes octavos, and talks folios. **1885** *Pall Mall G.* 25 July 3/2 The London police—those folios in dark blue, lettered, and uniform.

b. *attrib.* and *Comb.*

1712 ADDISON *Spect.* No. 529 ⁋1, I have seen a folio writer place himself in an elbow chair, when [etc.]. **1849** SIR J. STEPHEN *Eccl. Biog.* (1850) II. 37 They lower, in the sullen majority of the folio age, over the pigmies of this duodecimo generation. **1879** DOWDEN *Southey* iii. 78 He received from his Lisbon collection precious boxes folio-crammed.

B. *adj.*

1. Formed of sheets or a sheet folded once; of the largest size; folio-sized. Often following the sb.; cf. A. 5.

1597–8 BP. HALL *Sat.* II. i. 29 With folio volumes, two to an oxe hide. **1642** FULLER *Holy & Prof. St.* v. xi. 404 Small Pocket-Bibles, and a great Folio-Alchoran. **1680** EVELYN *Diary* (1850) II. 147 A folio MS. of good thickness. **1683** MOXON *Mech. Exerc.* II. 231 If it be a large Folio Page ..he ..has Tyed up. **1728** POPE *Dunc.* I. 139 A folio Common-place Founds the whole pyle, of all his works the base. **1802** DIBDIN *Introd. Classics* 26 There are some Folio editions of this beautiful work. **1808** SCOTT *Autobiog.* in Lockhart *Life* i, I remember writing upwards of 120 folio pages with no interval either for food or rest. **1870** DICKENS *E. Drood* ii, The folio music-books on the stand. *Mod.* A history in ten volumes folio.

fig. **1622** J. TAYLOR (Water P.) *Water-cormorant, Separatist* 21 These fellowes with their ample folio graces. *a* **1839** PRAED *Poems* (1864) I. 366 A minute will supply To thought a folio history Of blighted hopes.

2. *Printing* and *Stationery.* (See quots.)

1871 *Amer. Encycl. Print.*, *Folio Post*, a flat writing-paper, usually 17 by 22 inches. **1888** JACOBI *Printers' Voc.*, *Folio chase*, a chase with one bar only. **1890** —— *Printing* ii. 32 In the wooden kinds we have slip, octavo, quarto, and folio galleys. *Ibid.* 42 These chases are often divided or subdivided into folio or quarto by means of cross-bars.

folio (fəʊlɪəʊ), *v.* [f. prec. sb.] = FOLIATE *v.* 5.

In mod. Dicts.

Hence **'folioing** *vbl. sb.*

1858 SIMMONDS *Dict. Trade*, *Folioing*, the operation of paging or marking a book. **1895** CONWAY *Paine's Rights of Man* (*fly-leaf*), It has been thought advisable to preserve in this volume the folioing of the complete edition of the work.

foliolar ('fəʊlɪələ(r)), *a.* [f. FOLIOLE + -AR. Cf. F. *foliolaire.*] 'Like to or connected with a leaflet' (*Syd. Soc. Lex.* 1884).

foliolate ('fəʊlɪəleɪt), *a. Bot.* [a. L. **foliolātus*: see FOLIOLE and -ATE.] Of, pertaining to, or consisting of folioles or leaflets; chiefly in comb. with numerical prefix (usually written with Arabic figure) used instead of the Latin *uni-*, *bi-*, *tri-*. Cf. BIFOLIOLATE *a.*

1866 in *Treas. Bot.*; and in mod. Dicts. **1870** HOOKER *Stud. Flora* 86 Leaves 3-foliolate in seedling plants.. Minute 1-foliolate leaves.

foliole ('fəʊlɪəʊl). [a. F. *foliole*, ad. L. *foliolum*, dim. of *folium* leaf.]

1. *Bot.* One of the divisions of a compound leaf; a leaflet.

1794 MARTYN *Rousseau's Bot.* ii. 28 Pieces, which we must call leaves, leaflets, or folioles. **1830** LINDLEY *Nat. Syst. Bot.* 31 Compound leaves reduced to a single foliole. **1852** TH. ROSS *Humboldt's Trav.* III. xxix. 177 A..palm-tree.. having a free thread between the interstices of the folioles.

2. *Zool.* A small leaf-like appendage.

1849–52 TODD *Cycl. Anat.* IV. 1205/1 In *Boltenia reniformis* the stomach is destitute of any internal folioles or lacunæ. **1888** *Riverside Nat. Hist.* II. 221 A series of flat transparent leaflets..Similar folioles also arise from the basal joint of the antennæ.

Hence ˌ**folio'liferous** *a.* [see -(I)-FEROUS], bearing folioles or small leaf-like appendages (*Cent. Dict.*). ˌ**folio'lose** *a.* [see -OSE], having leaves composed of folioles (*Syd. Soc. Lex.*).

foliomort, obs. form of FILEMOT.

foliophagous (fəʊlɪˈɒfəgəs), *a. nonce-wd.* [f. FOLIO + Gr. -φαγ-ος eating + -OUS.] *fig.* That devours folios.

1829 SOUTHEY *Sir T. More* II. 353 Call to mind..my foliophagous friend, what was the extent of Michael Montagne's library.

foliose (fəʊlɪˈəʊs), *a.* [ad. L. *foliōs-us*, f. *folium* leaf: see -OSE.] Having, or abounding in, leaves; leafy, folious.

1727 BAILEY vol. II, *Foliose*, full of Leaves. **1758** *Phil. Trans.* L. 677 Linnæus has observed..a foliose lichen of this order. **1882** VINES *Sachs' Bot.* 343 The foliose Jungermannieæ.

b. = FOLIOUS *a.*² b.

1864 in WEBSTER.

foliosity (fəʊlɪˈɒsɪtɪ). [f. FOLIOSE + -ITY.] The state or condition of being foliose; abundance of foliage; in quot. with jocular allusion to FOLIO.

1847 DE QUINCEY *Schlosser's Lit. Hist.* Wks. VIII. 44 It is because he does not shoot into German foliosity that Schlosser finds him 'intolerable'.

'foliot. [? a. OF. *foliot*.

The OF. word is recorded only as meaning watch-spring; but according to Hatz.-Darm. it is derived from the vb. *folier* to play the fool, to dance about, and so may have had other meanings related to this vb. Cf. the surname Foliot, known from 12th c. in Eng. How Burton obtained the word there is nothing to show; he evidently connects it with It. *folletto*, = F. (*esprit*) *follet*, hobgoblin, properly a dim. of *fol* foolish. Can it be a misprint for *follet?*]

†**1.** ? Foolish matter. *Obs. rare.*

a **1250** *Owl & Night.* 866 Ne singe ih hom no foliot.

†**2.** A kind of goblin. *Obs. rare.*

1621 BURTON *Anat. Mel.* I. ii. I. ii, Another sort of these [devils] there are, which frequent forlorn houses, which the Italians call foliots. [He refers to Cardano *De rerum var.* XVI. (1581) 1123 Dæmon est familiaris, uocant folletos.]

3. [Fr., 14th cent.: see etym. note.] A type of clock escapement consisting of a bar with adjustable weights on the ends. (*Disused.*)

1899 F. J. BRITTEN *Old Clocks & Watches* 23 Froissart has left a descriptive eulogium of a clock, written in 1370... In this the controlling medium is referred to as a 'foliot', which was doubtless the straight armed balance with weights. **1948** A. L. KROEBER *Anthropol.* (ed. 2) xi. 453 The first clock escapements, large and heavy, were of the type called 'foliot balance and verge escape'. **1958** *New Scientist* 11 Dec. 1481/1 (*caption*) The Dover Castle clock, showing the verge-and-foliot escapement. **1962** E. BRUTON *Dict. Clocks* 152 Many years ago it had been converted to pendulum. In 1956 it was restored to foliot..and set going again inside the cathedral.

†**'folious,** *a.*¹ *rare.* Also 5 folyus. [ad. OF. *folieus*, *folieux*, f. *folie* FOLLY.] Foolish. Hence **'foliously** *adv.*

a **1450** *Knt. de la Tour* (1868) 58 For the whiche folyus dede, there is falle so moche sorw. *Ibid.* 83 Thorughe the said folious loue he toke her unto his wiff. **1481** CAXTON *Tulle of Old Age* G iv/1 The yong man hopeth foliously, if by cause of his yong age he wenith to live long.

folious ('fəʊlɪəs), *a.*² [ad. L. *foliōs-us*, f. *folium* leaf: see -OUS.] Abounding in, or of the nature of, leaves; leafy, foliose.

1658 SIR T. BROWNE *Gard. Cyrus* iii. 51 The folious and stalky emission distinguisheth herbs and trees. **1682** —— *Chr. Mor.* II. iii, To obtrude them [assertions] as Sibyls leaves, which after considerations may find to be but folious apparences, and not the central and vital interiours of Truth.

b. (See quot.)

1828 WEBSTER, *Folious*, having leaves intermixed with flowers.

†**'folity.** *Obs.* In 5 folite. [ad. OF. *folité*, *follité*, f. *fol*, *fou*, masc., *folle* fem. foolish.] Foolishness.

a **1400–50** *Alexander* 5366 ȝe fare bot with folite: quare ere ȝoure fyue wittis?

‖**folium** ('fəʊlɪəm). [L. *folium* leaf.]

1. = FOLIO 6.

1886 *Statem. Land Laws Incorp. Law Soc.* 26 Certificates ..each constituting a distinct folium consisting of two or more pages.

2. *Geom.* **a.** A finite loop of a nodal curve terminated at both ends by the same node. **b.** *Folium of Descartes*, a plane nodal cubic curve with real nodal tangents, and one real inflexion at infinity.

1848 B. PRICE *Diff. Calculus* (1852) 319 To determine the nature of the point at the origin of the Folium of Descartes.

c. Used with prefixes *uni-*, *bi-*, etc. to indicate a curve with one, two, etc. indentations.

1873 SALMON *Higher Plane Curves* vi. (1879) 221 Zeuthen confines the name oval to a branch having no real bitangent or inflexions, one with a single real bitangent he calls a unifolium, one with 2, 3, or 4 such bitangents, a bifolium, trifolium or quadrifolium.

folk (fəʊk). Forms: 1–2 folc (*pl.* folc), 2 folche, *Orm.* follc, follk, 3 folck, *south.* volck, 3–4 folc, *south.* volc, volk, 3–6 folke, 3–8 fok(e, (5 fokke), 6 folck(e, 8 *Sc.* fouk, 3– folk. Also 3–4 *wk. gen.* folken(e. [OE. *folc* str. neut. = OFris. *folk*, OS. *folc* (Du. *volk*), OHG. *folc* neut., masc. (MHG. *volc* neut., masc., mod.Ger. *volk* neut.), ON. *folk* neut., people, army, detachment (Sw., Da. *folk*):—OTeut. **folkom*. The original sense is perh. best preserved in ON.; cf. OSl. *plŭkŭ* (Russ. *polk*) division of an army, Lith. *pulkas* crowd, which are believed to be early adoptions from Teut.

The view of some scholars, that the Teut. word and the L. *vulgus* both descend from a common type **qolgos*, is very doubtful.]

1. a. A people, nation, race, tribe. *Obs.* exc. *arch.*

Beowulf 1582 (Gr.) He..sloh..folces Deniȝea fyftyne men. *c* **1000** ÆLFRIC *Gen.* xxv. 23 Twa folc beoþ todæled on þe, & þæt folc oferswið þæt oþer folc. **1297** R. GLOUC. (1724) 3 Brytones were þe firste folc þat to Engelond come. **1388** WYCLIF *John* xi. 48 Romayns schulen come, and schulen take our place and oure folk. **1535** COVERDALE *2 Esdras* v. 26 Amonge all yᵉ multitudes of folkes thou hast gotten the one people. **1850** NEALE *Med. Hymns* (1867) 24 Met Thee with Palms in their hands that day the folk of the Hebrews.

b. *transf.* of animals. (After the Vulg. and Heb.)

1382 WYCLIF *Prov.* xxx. 26 A litil hare, a folc vnmyȝti. **1535** COVERDALE *ibid.*, The conyes are but a feble folke [so **1611** and **1885** (R.V.)].

2. a. An aggregation of people in relation to a superior, *e.g.* God, a king or priest; the great mass as opposed to an individual; the people; the vulgar. *Obs* exc. *arch.*

c **888** K. ÆLFRED *Boeth.* xxx. §1 Forþæm is ðæs folces hlisa ælcum men for nauht to habbenne. **971** *Blickl. Hom.* 35 Swa swa ȝeara beboden wæs Godes folce. *c* **1250** *Gen. & Ex.* 2785 Ic haue min folkes pine soȝen. *a* **1300** *Cursor M.* 12838 (Cott.) Ion..said þat all þaa fok moght here, þis es [etc.]. *c* **1375** *Lay Folks Mass Bk.* (MS. B) 43 Til alle þo folk he [preste] shryues him þare of alle his synnes. **1483** CAXTON *G. de la Tour* E vii b, The said hoost of the Hebreux..were al folke of god. **1549–62** STERNHOLD & H. *Ps.* c. 247 We are his folke, he doth vs feede. **1863** LONGF. *Wayside Inn, Olaf* VII, Choose ye between two things, my folk. **1886** *Academy* 7 Aug. 85/2 It..did not hold back the Bible from the folk.

†**b.** (also *pl.*) Retainers, followers; servants, workpeople. *Obs.*

c **1205** LAY. 433 þa lette he riden vnirimed folc. *a* **1400–50** *Alexander* 3053 Dary..seȝis his foke faile. **1568** GRAFTON *Chron.* II. 377 He founde it kept by the Erle of Darbyes folkes. **1577** B. GOOGE *Heresbach's Husb.* (1586) II. 71 b, Least my folkes labouring in some of them should come into the rest, contrarie to my pleasure. **1581** G. PETTIE tr. *Guazzo's Civ. Conv.* (1586) III. 170 The maister of the house ..ought..to shewe himselfe more seuere towards his owne folke, then towards others. **1632** J. HAYWARD tr. *Biondi's Eromena* 68 Wherein (wanting so many of your folke) you could not have defended your selfe.

3. a. Men, people indefinitely. Also, people of a particular class, which is indicated by an adj. or some attributive phrase.

From 14th c. onward the pl. has been used in the same sense, and since 17th c. is the ordinary form, the sing. being *arch.* or *dial.* The word is now chiefly *colloq.*, being superseded in more formal use by *people*.

O.E. Chron. an. 999 þa elkede man fram dæȝe to dæȝe, & swencte þæt earme folc þe on ðam scipon lagon. *a* **1225** *Ancr. R.* 156 Vor te biweopen isleien uolc—þet is, mest al þe world. **1340** *Ayenb.* 139 þe benes and þe oreysons of guode uolke. **1377** LANGL. *P. Pl.* B. xv. 360 Now faileth þe folke of þe flode And of þe londe bothe. *c* **1386** CHAUCER *Knt.'s T.* 2035 Upon the steedes, that weren grete and white, Ther seeten folk. **1413** *Pilgr. Sowle* (Caxton) II. xlv. (1859) 51 Now beholde, and see with goode auysement vpon these folkes. *c* **1430** *Diatorie* in *Babees Bk.* 58 With .iij. maner of folk be not at debate: First with þi bettir. **1450–1530** *Myrr. our Ladye* 311 The masse crede is to be sayd when folcke lye a dyenge. *a* **1500** *Gregory's Chron.* (Camd. Soc.) 155 Summys of v c men of armys or of folke of schotte [orig. *gens de trait*, i.e. archers]. **1565** T. STAPLETON *Fortr. Faith.* 126 Howseling of Christen folcke before deathe. **1619** *Crt. & Times Jas. I* (1849) II. 186 They played three pieces glick, as ordinary folks use to play twopenny glick. **1710** SWIFT *Lett.* (1767) III. 71, I have heard wise folks say, An ill tongue may

do much. **1727** A. Hamilton *New Acc. E. Ind.* I. xxiv. 297 There were Folks killed in 1723. **1756** Mrs. Calderwood *Jrnl.* (1884) 83, I could not speak to the folks and ask questions. **1774** A. Adams in *J. Q. Adams' Fam. Lett.* (1876) 49 Some folks say I grow very fat. **1774** Franklin *Wks.* 1887 V. 414 It was the *ton* with the ministerial folks to abuse them. **1775** Johnson *Let. to Mrs. Thrale* 11 June, Folks want me to go to Italy. **1845** S. Austin *Ranke's Hist. Ref.* II. 29 He is unkind to the poor folk. **1870** Rossetti *Poems* 100 A decree..Whereby all banished folk might win Free pardon. **1871** Smiles *Charac.* i. (1876) 25 The character of a nation is not to be learnt from its fine folks. **1879** Browning *Martin Relph* 119 It was hard to get at the folks in power. **1882** Ouida *Maremma* I. 23 The hearts of the folk in Grosseto were sad for his fate.

b. Individual persons; individuals.

c **1450** *Bk. Curtasye* 546 in *Babees Bk.*, Thes thre folke and no mo. **1504** *Burv Wills* (Camden) 97 Substancyall folkys of the seid parych. **1641** Best *Farm. Bks.* (Surtees) 35 Three folkes, viz. two men and a wooman. **1833** Ht. Martineau *Berkeley the Banker* I. ii. 31 To think it prudent for these young folks to settle.

c. ***folk of peace*** [mistranslation of Gael. *daoine sídhe*, lit. people of the fairy hill (cf. Ir. *bean sídhe* BANSHEE), by confusion with *síthe*, gen. of *síth* peace]: fairy folk, fairies. *Sc.*

[**1691** R. Kirk *Secret Commonwealth* (1815) 30 The Seers avouch, that severalls who go to the *Siths*, (or People at Rest, and, in respect of us, in Peace,) before the natural Period of their Lyfe expyre, do frequently appear to them. **1841** H. Miller *Old Red Sandstone* xi. 215 'Not of the race of Adam,' said the creature, turning for a moment in its saddle: 'the People of Peace shall never more be seen in Scotland.' **1900** J. G. Campbell *Superstitions Highlands & Islands Scotland* i. 1 The Fairy or Elfin people, or, as they are called both in Irish and Scottish Gaelic, the *sith* people, that is, 'the people of peace', the 'still folk', or 'silently-moving' people.] **1875** *Encycl. Brit.* II. 203/2 The Highlanders call them the folk of peace. **1893** R. L. Stevenson *Catriona* I. i, I am nameless, like the Folk of Peace.

4. a. *pl.* (exc. *dial.*) The people of one's family, parents, children, relatives.

1715 *Pattern to true love* in Halliwell *Yorksh. Anthol.* (1851) 414 Our folks will angry be I fear. **1776** J. Q. Adams in *Fam. Lett.* (1876) 203 All that I could learn of you and my little folks. **1828** Carr *Craven Gloss.*, (ed. 2) *Folk*, family. 'How's yower folk'. **1833** Ht. Martineau *Loom & Lugger* I. i. 15 Your young folks are flourishing, I hope.

b. *dial.* Friends, intimates.

1854 Baker *Northampt. Words*, s.v., 'We're not folks now.' **1881** *Leicestersh. Gloss.*, s.v., 'They'd use to be such folks.'

5. a. *attrib.* and *Comb.*, as †***folk-king***, †***-need***.

Beowulf 2873 (Gr.) Nealles *folc-cyning fyrdȝesteallum gylpan þorfte. *c* **1205** Lay. 9501 Fareð swide aȝe, to þan folc-kinge. *c* **1000** *Ags. Ps.* lxxvii[i]. 14 Him ealle niht, oðer beacen, fyres leoma, *folc nede heold.

b. *esp.* in numerous mod. Combs. (formed after Ger. precedent) with the sense 'of, pertaining to, current or existing among, the people; traditional, of the common (local) people, esp. opp. sophisticated, cosmopolitan'; as ***folk-art***, ***-artist***, ***-belief***, ***-comedy***, ***-culture***, ***-custom***, ***-drama***, ***-epic***, ***-hero***, ***-legend***, ***-life***, ***-literature***, ***-medicine***, ***-mind***, ***-museum***, ***-name***, ***-poem***, ***-poetry***, ***-rhyme***, ***-speech***, ***-tale***, ***-tradition***, etc.

1921 *Art & Archæol.* XI. 185 (*title*) *Folk art. **1938** *Encycl. Brit. Bk. of Yr.* 476/2 A quiet growth of more spontaneous painting, some of it idyllic and reminiscent of folk art. **1967** E. Short *Embroidery & Fabric Collage* ii. 41 A more recent tradition in dress which could be classed as folk art is that of the pearly kings and queens. **1934** *Hound & Horn* July–Sept. 589 The spirit of a folk school of music so excites the *folk artist that [etc.]. **1959** *Times* 11 Dec. 16/2 He [*sc.* Barrie] remains a folk-artist. **1892** G. L. Gomme *Ethnol. in Folklore* v. 123 These ghastly ceremonies throw much light on the old *folk-belief as to the dead. **1922** W. B. Yeats *Trembling of Veil* 243 Folk-belief, tales of the fairies. **1933** E. K. Chambers *Eng. Folk-Play* 216 A folk-belief may ..explain the singular passage..in which the Fool.. beholds his own face. **1952** D. Hoffman *Paul Bunyan* iv. 73 The authors..can dramatize *folk comedy by contrasting it with the standards of cultivated society. **1936** *Discovery* Mar. 95/2 The volume is an important contribution to the study of European *folk-culture. **1963** Auden *Dyer's Hand* 300 The beast in it [*sc.* fable] may be a folk-culture hero whose qualities of courage or cunning are to be imitated. **1964** Gould & Kolb *Dict. Social Sci.* 272/1 A folk culture ..is a culture in which behaviour is highly conventionalized, personal, based on kinship, and controlled informally, traditionally, and through the 'sacred'. **1917** W. B. Yeats in *Lett. J. Joyce* (1966) II. 405 We do not play the *folk drama very well. **1961** *Times* 23 May 15/1 Ballad and folk-drama. **1904** C. G. Child *Beowulf* p. v, Great indeed would have been our loss, if..the only remaining *folk-epic of the Germanic peoples, had perished in doing menial service to grocer or soap-seller. **1950** *John o' London's* 24 Nov. 629/1 A great folk-epic about the Cid Campeador. **1850** *N. & Q.* 1st Ser. II. 99/2, I believe that one item of *folk-faith is that farm-yard odours are healthy. **1899** *Folk-lore* X. iv. 407 The *folk-heroes Hari Chand and Raja Amba. **1927** J. L. Brooks (*title of unpubl. thesis*) Paul Bunyan: American Folk Hero. **1932** Q. D. Leavis *Fiction & Reading Public* ii. i. 92 The traditional folk-heroes like Crispine and Crispianus, Simon Eyre, and the Six Worthy Yeomen of the West. **1960** *20th Cent.* Dec. 557 Blues-singers..sanctified by white jazz intellectuals into folk-heroes. **1971** P. Driscoll *White Lie Assignment* xiii. 103 A guerilla in the new folk-hero style. **1909** A. Herbert *Isle of Man* vii. 101 Around..the golden plover..is hung one of the prettiest of the *folk-legends abounding in the isle. **1864** *Reader* 1 Oct. 407 The minute notices concerning medicine [etc.]..that are scattered through the pages of our mediaeval biographers will increase our knowledge of the *folk-life of the past. **1923** W. B. Yeats *Plays & Controversies* 210 We thought we could bring the old folk-life to Dublin. **1955** A. Lomax *Mister Jelly Roll* (ed. 3) p. xv, It is within the folklife of these Creoles that the emotional character of hot jazz is to be found. **1966** G. E. Evans *Pattern under Plough* 21 Folk-life implies a holistic approach whose main definition is not in method but in the field of study. **1893** W. B. Yeats *Celtic Twilight* 201 Irish *folk-literature. **1898** E. Clodd *Tom Tit Tot* vi. 61 *Folk-medicine, the wide world through, is full of prescriptions based on sympathetic or antipathetic magic. **1931** *Times Lit. Suppl.* 6 Aug. 605/1 In this book an attempt is made to resuscitate and standardize much forgotten folk medicine. **1968** *Times* 3 Dec. 10/7 Yet another piece of folk medicine seems to have been vindicated in the laboratory. **1899** *Folk-Lore* X. iv. 385 The surest way therefore of projecting oneself into the *folk-mind..is..to take up the various points as they have seemed to grow one out of the other in folk-logic and processes of thought. **1924** P. C. Buck *Scope of Music* ix. 116 The composer, if it is the work of one man, or the folk-mind, if it is the result of the friction of use, knew better. **1957** *Times Lit. Suppl.* 1 Nov. 656/3 It is hard..to think of Loki as other than fundamentally malignant, and very hard to think of the folk-mind, even over centuries, turning him into a *sympathetic* comic figure. **1936** M. Allis *Eng. Prelude* xxiv. 258 In Strangers' Hall and Suckling House Norwich offers the most complete, if not the only, *folk museums in England. **1966** P. V. Price *France* 126 Collections of objects connected with wine and food..are frequently found in folk museums. **1924** Mawer & Stenton *Introd. Surv. Eng. Place-Names* iii. 50 These names are important as a link between the *folk-names and place-names restricted to some particular spot. **1960** P. H. Reaney *Orig. Eng. Place-Names* vi. 99 The earliest place-names created by the Anglo-Saxons were not originally place-names in the strict sense of the word; they were folk-names. **1940** *Horizon* Mar. 170 A real *folk-poem, it was in its way a work of art. **1963** *Times* 18 July 5/3 A suite of old folk-poems about Charity as exemplified in the tale of Dives and Lazarus. **1892** S. A. Brooke *Hist. Early Eng. Lit.* I. 90 As to the spears singing..that is a common phrase in ancient *folk-poetry. **1903** L. F. Anderson *Anglo-Saxon Scop* 10 Mone..states his belief that we have in the..passage a reference to Germanic folk-poetry. **1923** A. Huxley *On Margin* 54 The Folk Poetry of 1920 may best be classified according to subject-matter. **1965** G. McInnes *Road to Gundagai* xvi. 280 The earthy folk-poetry of C. J. Dennis. **1889** *Chambers's Jrnl.* VI. 670/1 English *folk-rhymes are very numerous and curious. **1959** I. & P. Opie *Lore & Lang. Schoolch.* xv. 333 The future is worked out with the aid of an old folk rhyme. **1891** *Athenæum* 10 Oct. 486/3 Those who believe in the origin of *folk-tales from the cultured. **1935** R. Girvan *Beowulf & 7th Cent.* 82 In *Beowulf* the folk-tale *is* the story: all the rest is incidental. **1950** M. J. C. Hodgart *Ballads* v. 110 There were poets of taste who were close enough to *folk-tradition to be able to adapt it without making it look literary. **1971** *Guardian* 3 July 8/5 We [*sc.* Londoners] 've got so much more folk tradition than most places. **1880** J. Geikie *Prehist. Europe* 9 One of those great *folk-waves which have successively swept over Europe.

6. a. Special comb.: **folk-blues** [BLUES], the original 'blues' of the Negroes of the southern U.S., as opposed to composed imitations; so ***folk-jazz***; **folk-dance**, a dance of popular origin; the music for such a dance; also **folk-dance** *v. intr.*, **folk-dancer**; **folk-dancing** *vbl. sb.*; **folk-etymology**, usually, the popular perversion of the form of words in order to render it apparently significant; **folkfest** chiefly *N. Amer.* [FEST], a festival of folk songs and other elements of folk culture; **folk-free** *a.*, having the rights of a freeman; **folk high school** [tr. Da. *folkehøjskole*], a school of adult education, originating in Denmark, now also in other Scandinavian countries; **folk-law** (usu. in *pl.*), a customary law of the people, applied esp. to the *Leges Barbarorum*, the laws of the Germanic peoples; **folk-leasing** (OE. *Law*), public lying, slander; **folk-memory**, recollection of the past persisting among a people or group; **folk-music**, music of popular origin; hence **folk-musician**; so ***folk-tune***; **'folknik** [after *beatnik*], a devotee of folk-music; also *attrib.*; **folk-play**, a traditional type of play; so ***folk-player***; **folk-psychology** [tr. G. *völkerpsychologie*] = ETHNOPSYCHOLOGY; so ***folk-psychologist***; **folk-singer**, a singer of folk-songs; so **folk-singing**; **folk-stead** (see quot. 1876); **folkway** (usu. in *pl.*), the traditional behaviour of a people or group; **folk weave, folkweave** (see quot. 1960); also *attrib.*

1926 A. Niles in W. C. Handy *Blues* 3 Some *folk-blues were love songs. **1959** 'F. Newton' *Jazz Scene* vi. 99 The anonymity and impersonal grandeur of the folk-blues. **1909** E. Burchenal (*title*) *Folk-dances and singing games. **1912** C. J. Sharp *Folk Dancing in Schools* 4 The three main types of folk-dance found in England are:—(1) The Morris Dance. (2) The Sword Dance. (3) The Country Dance. **1927** *Observer* 2 Oct. 19/4 He defied anyone who folk-danced to be unhappy. **1954** M. Ewer *Heart Untouched* v. 77 Do they folk-dance? Do they make ghastly things in raffia? **1967** Chujoy & Manchester *Dance Encycl.* 370/2 In N.Y. alone there are enough folk dance sessions to offer anyone an opportunity to join in folk-dancing almost every day of the week. **1936** *Discovery* Dec. 396/2 The Portuguese folk-singers, folk-players, and *folk-dancers go through their traditional performances with a complete lack of self consciousness. **1907** *Folk-dancing [see *folk-singing*]. **1908** *Amer. Physical Educ. Rev.* Oct. 375 The place of folk dancing. **1927** *Observer* 2 Oct. 19/4 If there was more singing of the old songs and more folk-dancing. **1883** G. Stephens *S. Bugge's Stud. on N. Mythol.* 28 It does not mend the matter, if, when we have no better argument, we call it *folk-etymology. **1963** *Variety* 7 Aug. 2/4 (*heading*) Newport *Folk Fest's P[ublic] D[omain] & Civil Rights overtones stir Attorney John Clark. **1968** *Guardian* 8 Apr. 1/3 The Mayors have set a curfew..and there are no theatres,..banquets, dances, and folkfests. **1975** *Daily Colonist* (Victoria, B.C.) 24 June 18/2 Folkfest is part of July 1 events.. Songs and dances from around the world will be performed. *a* **1000** *Laws Withræd* §8 Gif man his mæn an wiofode freols ȝefe, se sie *folcfry. **1820** Scott *Ivanhoe* xxxii, Folkfree and Sacless art thou in town and from town. **1914** *U.S. Bureau of Education Bull.* no. xxii. 1914 (*title*) The Danish *Folk High Schools. **1949** E. L. Allen *Bishop Grundtvig* vii. 82 A large proportion of the heads of folk high-schools to-day are men with a theological training. **1966** D. Jenkins *Educated Society* iii. 125 The Folk High School movement obviously has achieved a great success in the predominantly agrarian communities of Scandinavia. **1950** A. Lomax *Mister Jelly Roll* (1952) 185 Linking the *folk-jazz half-world to the super-respectable and stuffy world of the music business. **1884** *Academy* 23 Feb. 126/1 *Folk-law is astonishingly conservative. **1898** E. Jenks *Law & Politics Middle Ages* ii. 32 While France and Germany have their feudal laws..England is still in the twilight of the folk-laws. **1962** H. R. Loyn *Anglo-Saxon England* iv. 175 It is not a mere quibble..to question a sharp cleavage between ideas of royal law and folk-law. *a* **1000** *Laws Ælf.* §32 Gif mon *folc-leasunge ȝewyrce..him mon aceorfe þa tungan. **1771** Burke *Powers of Juries in Prosecutions* Wks. X. 114 An offence of this species, called Folk-leasing. **1908** W. Johnson (*title*) *Folk-memory; or, The continuity of British archæology. **1939** R. G. Collingwood *Autobiogr.* xi. 143 'Folk-memory'..the transmission by example and precept of certain ways of thinking and acting from generation to generation. **1960** K. M. Kenyon *Archæol. in Holy Land* viii. 208 The length of folk memory, though it may be reasonably accurate as to the occurrence of important events, is short as regards chronological exactitude. **1889** G. B. Shaw *London Music 1888–89* (1937) 79 All good '*folk music' is as international as the story of Jack the Giant Killer. **1907** C. J. Sharp *Eng. Folk-Song* p. ix, It is impossible to say how far the folk-music that has survived in a county like Somerset is ..truly representative of English folk-song as a whole. **1971** *Guardian* 3 July 8/1 Cecil Sharp deliberately looked for English folk music in other countries, especially America. **1907** C. J. Sharp *Eng. Folk-Song* 34 The *folk-musician.. is under no such temptation [to make music for the sake of making it]. **1941** L. MacNeice *Poetry of Yeats* viii. 165 A poet of the folk-musician type. **1958** in *Amer. Speech* (1966) XLI. 139 In Greenwich Village..lies the Folklore Center.. near the door is the lettering 'Israel G. Young'... Invariably, *folkniks (to quote Izzy) are present, for this den is the meeting place..for New York's up and coming folksingers and hangers on. **1961** *McLean's* 25 Mar. 18/1 He is exhibiting with increasing frequency in the circle of Toronto restaurants and coffee houses known locally as folknik spots. **1963** *Observer* 8 Sept. 12/6 Folkniks..are the adherents, mostly teenaged, of the new-style folk-song movement—an austere group who prefer their songs unaccompanied... In the spreading folknik clubs, amplifiers are forbidden. **1905** *Westm. Gaz.* 7 Apr. 12/1 This pageant, which takes the form of a *folk-play specially written and invented by Mr. Louis N. Parker, deals with the chief events in the history of the town. **1933** E. K. Chambers (*title*) The English folk play. **1969** in Halpert & Story *Christmas Mumming in Newfoundland* 59 An attempt to write the detailed history of the folk play must await the results of current investigations. **1936** *Folk-player [see *folk-dancer*]. **1889** *Cent. Dict.*, *Folk-psychology. **1918** R. S. Woodworth *Dynamic Psychol.* i. 12 In the sixties, there was even published for several years in Germany a journal of 'folk psychology'. *Ibid.* 13 The methods and presuppositions of the older folk psychologists have not stood the test of time. **1957** J. S. Huxley *Relig. without Revelation* v. 108 Explanations of the origin of religion in terms of animism or magic or folk psychology. **1898** *Folk-lore* IX. i. 49 The sagas..died out because there were no *folk-singers qualified to present them. **1927** *Observer* 12 June 13/2 Altogether more than fifty folk-singers and craft workers hailing from all parts of French Canada were gathered together. **1961** *Guardian* 9 May 7/2 The white folk-singers of the southern back-woods. **1907** C. J. Sharp *Eng. Folk-Song* p. viii, Only those, perhaps, who have been brought into close contact with the old folk-singers of to-day, can fully realize how intimately *folk-singing and folk-dancing have..been bound up with the social life of the English village. **1931** *Times Lit. Suppl.* 30 Apr. 344/4 The free rhythm and florid ornament..characteristic of Greek folk-singing. **1934** W. B. Yeats *King of Gt. Clock Tower* 18 Her method was 'folk-singing' or allied to it. **1971** *Guardian* 3 July 8/2 Purists..regard the folk-singing..as being 'impure'. *a* **1000** *Beowulf* 76 þa ic wide ȝefrægn..manigre mæȝþe..*folcstede frætwian. **1876** *Mid-Yorks. Gloss.*, *Folkstead*, an out-door place of assembly for general purposes. 'The chapel wouldn't hold them all, so they made a folkstead of the garth.' **1907** C. J. Sharp *Eng. Folk-Song* p. x, The *folk-tune presents many problems of absorbing interest to the musical theorist. **1914** —— *Folk Singing in Schools* 5 The folk-tunes which have recently been collected from the English peasantry. **1957** Manvell & Huntley *Technique Film Music* ii. 51 A glimpse of a folk-tune is sometimes heard on French horns. **1907** W. G. Sumner *Folkways* p. iii, I formed the word '*folkways' on the analogy of words already in use in sociology.... Folkways are habits of the individual and customs of the society which arise from efforts to satisfy needs... Then they become regulative for succeeding generations and take on the character of a social force. **1925** W. P. Montague *Ways of Knowing* v. 142 There are cases when a 'folkway' or social habit becomes actively evil. **1959** G. D. Mitchell *Sociol.* v. 78 Customs may be differentiated into folkways and mores. **1964** Gould & Kolb *Dict. Social Sci.* 273/2 *Folkways* are the learned shared behaviour common to a people. **1971** E. Fenwick *Impeccable People* iii. 17 He had learned to swallow the folkways of Parsons Point. **1938** *Decorative Art* 50 The gaily striped *folk-weaves on sofas. **1939** *Soft Furnishing in Workroom* 10 Brown/Beige Folkweave Fabric..for Loose Cover. **1949** E. Coxhead *Wind in West* v. 123 Her three-piece leatherette suite, her beige and orange folk-weave curtains. **1960** *Textile Terms & Defs.* (ed. 4) 70 *Folk weave*, *n.* or *adj.*, a term applied to any construction which, when used in loosely woven fabrics made from coarse yarns, gives a rough and irregular surface effect.

b. Short for *folk-music*. So ***folk-rock***, folk-music with a strong beat; ***folk club***, etc.

1963 *Observer* 8 Sept. 12/7 MacColl learnt folk at his mother's knee, felt people should know their own music. **1965** *New Society* 20 May 26/3 There are..as many as 300

folk clubs..all over Britain..most of them grouped around a resident singer or group. **1966** *Time* 1 July 50 The folk-rock movement. **1966** *Guardian* 22 Dec. 4/7 In the pop/folk field the best new release is by The Incredible String Band. **1969** *Down Beat* 17 Apr. 24/2 The lyrics are characterized by the self-consciously whimsical or ironic or nouveau-romantic trends of folk-rock at its worst. **1971** *Melody Maker* 18 Sept. 36/1 The Crown is one of the foremost folk clubs in Edinburgh. *Ibid.* 36/3 It's still one of the best places in the country for folk in terms of performance and audience reaction.

folkie ('fəʊkɪ), *sb.* [f. FOLK + -IE.] A folk-musician or folk-singer; a devotee of folk-music.

1966 *Times* 12 Jan. 13/7 'Pop' singers, disc jockeys, rock 'n rollers, bands, folkies, balladists, and others will give free concerts in the open air. **1970** *Sun* 9 Oct. 13/3 She..plays a bulky guitar with rich technique that any folkie would envy. **1977** *N.Y. Times* 23 Jan. 1/47/3 Mr. Rush is a folkie who emerged in the early 1960's in Cambridge, Mass... He is still a most engaging performer, singing a wide variety of folk music and blues in a comfortable commanding manner. **1987** *New Yorker* 12 Jan. 5/1 Music for many kinds of people, including unreconstructed folkies,..and rock-and-roll fundamentalists.

folkish ('fəʊkɪʃ), *a.* [f. FOLK + -ISH.] Of the common people; traditional, unsophisticated.

1938 D. DAVIDSON *Attack on Leviathan* 226 Semi-literary but folkish creations like Leatherstocking, Rip Van Winkle, Huck Finn. **1951** M. COOPER *Russian Opera* iv. 40 Most striking is the warm, folkish lyricism [of the opera]. **1962** *Listener* 25 Oct. 695/1 The generally folkish vein of much of the vocal melody. **1968** *Vogue* 15 Apr. 23/1 Covent Garden's production..is folkish, parochial in style.

† **'folkland.** *Obs.* exc. *Hist.* A term of OE. law, designating land held by a certain kind of tenure; opposed to BOOKLAND.

As to the nature of the antithesis between folkland and bookland there have been many conjectures. Since the publication of Allen's *Inquiry into the Growth of the Royal Prerogative*, 1830, the prevailing view has been that *folkland* was land belonging to the state, which the king or the witan might grant to a person for his life, but which did not descend to heirs, while *bookland* was land held by charter or deed. But in the *Eng. Hist. Rev.* VIII. (1893) Prof. Vinogradoff has forcibly argued that *folkland* was simply land heritable by *folkright* or common law, while the estate in *bookland* was conferred by charter or deed, and could be alienated freely.

a **1000** *Laws Edgar* §2 Oþþe on boc-lande oþþe on folclande. **1641** *Termes de la Ley* 54 This land was held with more easie and commodious conditions than Folkeland. **1767** BLACKSTONE *Comm.* II. 91 Fold-land..was held by no assurance in writing, but distributed among the common folk or people at the pleasure of the lord. **1830** J. ALLEN *R. Prerog.* (1849) 135 Folcland, as the word imports, was the land of the folk or people. It was the property of the community. It might be occupied in common, or possessed in severalty; and, in the latter case, it was probably parcelled out to individuals in the folcgemôt. But while it continued to be folcland, it could not be alienated in perpetuity; and therefore, on the expiration of the term for which it had been granted, it reverted to the community, and was again distributed by the same authority. **1871** FREEMAN *Norm. Conq.* (1876) IV. xvii. 24 The folkland, the common land of the nation, was now [1066–7] changed, fully and for ever, into *terra Regis*, the land of the King.

folklore ('fəʊklɔə(r)). Also **folk-lore.** [f. FOLK + LORE.] **a.** The traditional beliefs, legends, and customs, current among the common people; the study of these.

1846 AMBROSE MERTON [W. J. Thoms] in *Athenæum* 22 Aug. 862/3 What we in England designate as Popular Antiquities, or Popular Literature (though..it..would be most aptly described by a good Saxon compound, Folk-Lore,—the Lore of the People). **1862** *Ecclesiologist* XXIII. 279 Mr. Lee gives us a piece of folks-lore. **1863** MAX MÜLLER *Chips* (1880) II. xxi. 206 A healing virtue is ascribed in German folk-lore to the mistletoe. **1884** A. LANG *Custom & Myth* 11 Properly speaking, folklore is only concerned with the legends, customs, beliefs, of the folk—of the people.

b. Recently in extended use: popular fantasy or belief.

1954 *Economist* 11 Sept. 8/1 Some scientists..add to the store of folk lore by asking whether the occasional flying saucer is not a Russian technician who has missed his bearings on the return to earth. **1959** J. BRAINE *Vodi* xvii. 211 She was always the Little Woman, almost the Pretty Little Nursie of masculine folklore. **1959** *Listener* 5 Nov. 763/1 Finland..has a special niche in American folklore, under the caption: 'Brave little Finland'. **1971** *Nature* 29 Jan. 293/2 The Santa Barbara oil spill..may not be entirely worthy of its place in contemporary ecological folklore.

Hence **'folklorism**, a piece of folk-lore; **'folklorist**, a student of folk-lore; **folklo'ristic** *a.*

1876 *N. & Q.* 5th Ser. VI. 12/2 Success to the Folk-Lore Society! An Old Folk-Lorist. **1886** *Sat. Rev.* 28 Aug. 306 The Revue..contains divers 'folklorisms'. **1888** BULLEN *Peele's Wks.* I. Introd. 11 The Ghost of Jack ought to be an object of interest to folklorists. **1888** *Science* XII. 132 Some interesting philological and folk-loristic information.

'folkloric, *a.* [f. FOLK-LOR(E + -IC.] Of or pertaining to folklore.

1883 C. S. BURNE *Shrops. Folk-Lore* xxxviii. 618 Thus two independent lines of research, philological and folkloric, combine to support the historic evidence. **1952** G. SARTON *Hist. Science* I. iv. 106 The intimate knowledge of Aegean culture that we owe primarily to a great variety of monuments is confirmed..by folkloric remains in the Aegean area. **1969** *Daily Tel.* (Colour Suppl.) 10 Jan. 32/3 A folkloric dance group from a mining town.

'folklorish, *a.* [f. FOLK-LOR(E + -ISH.] Resembling folklore.

1926 *Sat. Rev.* 10 July 914 This..piece of humor..is, on the surface, anything but folk-lorish. **1944** BLUNDEN *Cricket Country* 164 Bowlers who insist on being symbolical or folk-lorish will not be given a second over. **1964** F. WHITE *West of Rhone* xiii. 125 The Langue d'Oc..dwindled to a *patois*... Latterly there has been a folklorish revival of the patois, with..poetry competitions at the *jeux floraux*.

folkloristics (fəʊklɔ'rɪstɪks), *sb. pl.* (const. *sing.*). [ad. Russ. *fol'kloristika* (1926, Yu. M. Sokolov in *Khudozhestvennyĭ Fol'klor* I. 7), f. FOLKLORISTIC *a.*: see -IC 2.] The study of folklore; folklore as a discipline or subject of research.

1950 tr. *Yu. M. Sokolov's Russian Folklore* 3 At the present time, in accordance with the practice of European and Soviet scholars, the term 'folklore' is used to designate the material of study; to indicate the science which deals with this material, the term 'folkloristics' is employed. **1959** U. WEINREICH *Yiddish Lang. & Folklore* 46 (*heading*) History of Yiddish folkloristics. **1978** *Canad. Jrnl. Linguistics* 1977 XXII. 219 The complete title of the book may be taken to include, or at least intersect, those fields commonly known as 'text linguistics', 'folkloristics' and 'narratology'. **1985** *Jrnl. Amer. Folklore* XCVIII. 331 The following contribution to the folkloristics controversy is intended to shift the discussion..away from a condemnation of the term toward a consideration of terminology.

† **'folkmoot, folkmote.** *Obs.* exc. *Hist.* Forms: 1 folcmót, -ȝemót, 5 folkesmot, 6 folckmote, 6–7 folkemote, (7 *erron.* falkmoth, 9 folkmuth), 9 folkemote, folcmoot, 6–9 folkmote, 5–9 folkmoot. [OE. *folc-mót, -ȝemót*, f. *folc*, FOLK + *mót, ȝemót* meeting.] A general assembly of the people of a town, city, or shire.

a **1000** *Laws Athelst.* (Thorpe) §12 On þara ȝerefena ȝewitnesse on folcȝemote [*v.r.* on folcmote]. **1494** FABYAN *Chron.* VII. 340 He anone sent Johnne Mancell, one of his iustycys, vnto London; and there..callyd at Pawlys crosse a folkmoot. **1529** RASTELL *Pastyme, Hist. Brit.* (1811) 184 Place of sittyng..appoynted at the Folkmote at Poules crosse. **1596** SPENSER *F.Q.* IV. iv. 6 To which folke-mote they all with one consent..Agreed to travell, and their fortunes try. **1642** *Antid. to prevent Civ. Wars* 9 Commanders of the Militia in every County were elected.. in a full Falkmoth. **1750** CARTE *Hist. Eng.* II. 112 *note*, He ..directed a folkmote or common hall to be held on Sunday the 27th of that month. **1848** LYTTON *Harold* IV. v, I will ask the King's leave to go to my East Anglians, and hold a folkmuth. **1892** TENNYSON *Foresters* I. iii, How should we cope with John? The London folkmote Has made him all but king.

Hence † **'folk-mooter**, ? a parochial politician.

1645 MILTON *Colast.* Wks. (1847) 228/1 These matters are not for pragmatics and folkmooters to babble in.

† **'folkright.** *Obs.* exc. *Hist.* [OE. *folcriht* f. *folc* FOLK + *riht* RIGHT.] 'Common law, public right, the understood compact by which every freeman enjoys his rights as a freeman' (Bosw.).

a **1000** *Laws Cnut* §1 Heonan-forð læte manna ȝehwylcne, ȝe earmne ȝe eadiȝne, folc-rihtes wyrðe. **1849** KEMBLE *Saxons* II. vi. 205 New laws which were to be added to the existing folcriht. [**1876** *Whitby Gloss.*, *Fooakreeght*, public right.]

folksay ('fəʊkseɪ). *U.S.* Also **folk-say.** [f. FOLK + SAY *sb.*[4] 2.] Folk-speech; the traditional speech or proverbs of an ethnic or regional group; an instance of this.

1929 B. A. BOTKIN in *Oklahoma Folk-Lore Soc.* June 5 (*title*) Folk-say, a regional miscellany. **1936** H. PREECE in A. Dundes *Mother Wit* (1973) 35/1 Negro spirituals and folksay. **1950** PATTERSON & CONRAD *Scottsboro Boy* II. iii. 100 It's an old Negro folksay, if a mud turtle catches hold of your finger it will hold until it thunders. **1976** A. MURRAY *Stomping Blues* vi. 79 For all the apt phrases, insightful folksay, and striking imagery that blues singers have added to the national lore, the definitive element of a blues statement is not verbal.

folk-song ('fəʊksɒŋ). Earlier **folk's song.** [f. FOLK + SONG *sb.*, after G. *volkslied.*] A song originating from the common people; also, a modern imitation of such a song; also *collect. sing.*

1847 *Howitt's Jrnl.* 17 Apr. 212/1 The Three Little Roses. A German Folk's song. Translated by Mary Howitt. **1870** W. E. A. AXON (*title*) Folk-Song & Folk-Speech of Lancashire. **1871** *Cornh. Mag.* Nov. 573 In a large collection of folk-songs from all the chief Dravidian languages, not one may be called immoral, not one cheerful. **1875** *Encycl. Brit.* III. 283/1 It was not till the publication of Allan Ramsay's *Ever-green* and *Tea Table Miscellany*, and of Bishop Percy's *Reliques*, that a serious effort was made to recover Scotch and English folk-songs from the recitation of the old people who still knew them by heart. **1883** *Grove's Dict. Mus.* III. 584/2 In some countries of Europe the development of the Song can be followed from the primitive form of folk-song to the highest type of artistic composition. **1907** C. J. SHARP (*title*) English Folk-Song. **1964** GOULD & KOLB *Dict. Social Sci.* 272/2 Folklore or folksong..belong to such small, scattered, isolated groups. **1965** M. MORSE *Unattached* v. 180 Folk-song concerts. **1966** *Listener* 18 Aug. 236/2 That passage from Ecclesiastes which Pete Seeger has turned into a beautiful folk song.

Hence **'folk-songish, -songy** *adjs.*, resembling or relating to folk-song.

1925 P. A. SCHOLES *2nd Bk. Gramophone Rec.* 154 The dignity of Jupiter in a fine folk-songish strain. **1934** C. LAMBERT *Music Ho!* iii. 151 Vaughan Williams..whose style..without necessarily being folk-songy in the picturesque way, is intimately connected with the inflections and mood of English folk music. **1959** *Times* 11 May 3/7 I'm sure that the folk-songy sounds, the flattened leading notes and so on, are as artificial as a Tudor Tea Shoppe.

folksy ('fəʊksɪ), *a.* orig. *U.S.* [f. *folks*, pl. of FOLK + -Y[1].] **1.** Sociable; also, unpretentiously companionable; informal, casual.

1852 L. CLAPPE *Let. from Calif.* 15 Mar. (1922) 199 'They ain't kinder like *eour* folks', or, as that universal Aunt Somebody used so expressively to observe, 'Somehow, they ain't *folksy*!' **1868** A. D. WHITNEY *P. Strong's Outings* 178 So pleasant and folksy. **1890** *Harper's Mag.* Dec. 138/2 I'd kind o' thought 'twould be folksy an'..cheerful. **1892** R. T. COOKE *Huckleberries* 331 I'm real folksy; grasshoppers ain't no neighbours to me. **1942** D. POWELL *Time to be Born* (1943) v. 117 The public really doesn't like its idols to be folksy. **1953** *John o' London's* 23 Jan. 76/4 A homesy, folksy, knowing account of a small town boy called Jason.

2. Having the characteristics of folk-art, culture, etc.; *esp.* ostensibly or artificially folkish.

1947 A. EINSTEIN *Mus. Romantic Era* vi. 55 Mozart is not 'folksy': he is always himself. **1949** *New Statesman* 15 Oct. 422/1 A chorus of youths and maidens, wearing a specially designed fancy dress of folksy cut. **1958** *Manch. Guardian* 20 Sept. 4/6 There lingers around the island of Lundy..an agreeable aura of folksy romance, eminently conducive to fables and premonitions. **1964** M. ANDERSON *Saint at Stake* xx. 174 Even the least 'folksy' modern doctors admit that in such cases 'magic' is sometimes effective.

Hence **'folksiness**, the state or quality of being 'folksy' (in either sense). orig. *U.S.*

1931 P. W. SLOSSON *Gt. Crusade* viii. 227 The democratic geniality and 'folksiness' which Michigan..ranked as the chief of human virtues. **1956** *Ess. Divers Hands* XXVIII. 80 There is a smack of folk-lore about them, but no earnest, bespectacled folksiness. **1961** *Times* 9 Feb. 3/1 The folksiness of choruses and peasant dances recalls *Der Freischütz*.

folky ('fəʊkɪ), *a.* [f. FOLK + -Y[1].] Characteristic of the common people; = FOLKSY *a.* 2. Hence **'folkiness**, the state or quality of being folky.

1914 A. H. SIDGWICK *Prom. Ticket* 41 Schubert could have written..folk-songs, much better and much folkier than anything collected from embarrassed rustics. **1936** *Scrutiny* V. 151 One admits the futility and sentimentality, at this date, of the folky composer. **1938** L. MACNEICE *I Crossed Minch* i. 8 That more blatant surface-charm or glamour—that sugared folkiness—which we are led to expect in out-of-the-way places. **1940** *Archit. Rev.* LXXXVII. 87/2 What must be avoided at all costs is folky architecture. **1964** *Listener* 20 Feb. 330/3 Conventional Slav folkiness. **1970** E. LEE *Music of People* x. 197 The Seekers were beginning to gain a success with a 'Folky Pop' style.

folle, follery, obs. ff. of FOAL, FOOLERY.

† **'follial,** *a. Obs.*[−1] [f. FOLLY + -AL[1]; cf. OF. *folial* (perh. the source).] Foolish.

1602 WARNER *Alb. Eng.* x. lv. 245 Whereto these folliall Traytors did themselues and Senses fit.

follicle ('fɒlɪk(ə)l). Also 7–8 folliacle, 8–9 FOLLICULE. [ad. L. *folliculus* little bag, dim. of *follis* bellows.]

1. **a.** *Anat.* A small sac. Chiefly, 'a simple lymphatic gland, consisting of lymphoid tissue arranged in the form of a sac' (*Syd. Soc. Lex.*).

1646 SIR T. BROWNE *Pseud. Ep.* III. ii. 108 Although there be no eminent and circular follicle, no round bagge or vesicle which long containeth this humor. **1748** HARTLEY *Observ. Man* I. ii. 117 Gall-bladder, Follicles, and Ducts of the Glands. **1830** R. KNOX *Béclard's Anat.* 38 The membranous stomach, furnished with numerous secreting follicles. **1842** PRICHARD *Nat. Hist. Man* 95 The hair issues from follicles, by a club-shaped root or bulb.

b. = COD *sb.*[1] 4 b.

1646 SIR T. BROWNE *Pseud. Ep.* III. iv. 113 These cods or follicles are found in both sexes. [**1812** J. SMYTH *Pract. Customs* (1821) 64 Castor.—This is a substance secreted in a follicle situated near the anus of the beaver, perhaps the inguinal gland.]

2. **a.** *Bot.* 'A kind of fruit, consisting of a single carpel, dehiscing by the ventral suture only (Lindley); formerly used for any kind of capsular fruit.

a **1706** EVELYN *Sylva* xi. (1729) 65 They [the Maples] are all produced of Seeds contained in the Folliacles and Keys, or Birds-Tongues. **1785** MARTYN *Rousseau's Bot.* xvi. 219 In most of the genera these fruits are follicles. **1877** HULME *Wild Fl.* p. x, Fruit a follicle of two elongated capsules.

b. *Bot.* A small bag or vesicle distended with air.

1793 MARTYN *Lang. Bot.* s.v. *Folliculus*, Follicles..are vessels distended with air: as at the root in Utricularia, and on the leaves in Aldrovanda. **1816–20** GREEN *Herbal* II. 784 Two-celled follicles in whorls, in order to support the scape in the water. **1863** BERKELEY *Brit. Mosses* Gloss. 312 *Follicle*, a little bladder on the leaves, as in *Pottia cavifolia*.

3. *Entom.* A cocoon; the covering made by a larva for its protection during the pupa state.

1856–8 W. CLARK *Van der Hoeven's Zool.* I. 397 Pupa included in a thin follicle.

4. Comb. ***follicle-stimulating*** adj. (see quot. 1956).

1948 *Biol. Abstr.* XXII. 2389/1 In the ♀ only the follicle-stimulating hormone can exert its effect. **1956** *New Gould Med. Dict.* 559/1 *Follicle-stimulating hormone*, an adenohypophyseal hormone which stimulates follicular growth in the ovary, and spermatogenesis in the testis... Abbreviated FSH.

follicular (fɒˈlɪkjʊlə(r)), *a.* [ad. L. *folliculār-is*, f. *folliculus*: see FOLLICLE and -AR[1].]

1. Of the nature of, or resembling, a follicle; composed or consisting of follicles; also, provided with follicles.

1677 PLOT *Oxfordsh.* 305 Many other strong scented Animals..have follicular Repositories or Bags. **1750** *Phil. Trans.* XLVII. 99 Vascular and follicular minute membranes. **1830** LINDLEY *Nat. Syst. Bot.* 6 Fruit.. follicular with one or two valves. **1835-6** TODD *Cycl. Anat.* I. 23 The follicular structure of the glands. **1870** HOOKER *Stud. Flora* p. xiii, Crassulaceæ.. Fruit follicular.

2. a. Of or pertaining to a follicle or follicles.

1877 COUES *Fur Anim.* i. 14 An enormous reservoir.. containing a considerable quantity of the follicular product.

b. *Path.* Of a disease: Affecting the follicles of a particular organ.

1859 J. TOMES *Dental Surg.* 508 Follicular stomatitis. **1877** ROBERTS *Handbk. Med.* (ed. 3) I. 209 Follicular pharyngitis is often associated with stomach-disorders.

c. *follicular hormone*, a natural œstrogenic hormone, now usually called œstrone.

1923 *Jrnl. Amer. Med. Assoc.* LXXXI. 821/1 The conclusion seems justified that this follicular hormone is the cause of estrual or mating instincts. **1947** A. T. CAMERON *Recent Adv. Endocrinol.* vi. 181 Oestrone (follicular hormone)..has marked oestrogenic properties.

3. In etymol. sense: Of or pertaining to bellows; performed by means of bellows. *nonce-use.*

1676 SHADWELL *Virtuoso* II. Wks. 1720 I. 343 An animal may be preserved without respiration..by follicular impulsion of air.

folliculated (fɒˈlɪkjʊˌleɪtɛd), *ppl. a.* Also **folliculate** (*Cent. Dict.*). [as if f. *folliculate vb. (f. FOLLICULE + -ATE) + -ED[1].]

1. *Anat.* and *Bot.* Provided with a follicle or follicles.

1775 ASH, *Folliculated* (adj. in botany) having seed vessels. **1787** HUNTER in *Phil. Trans.* LXXVII. 418 Ending below the thyroid, which is folliculated on its inner surface. **1839-47** TODD *Cycl. Anat.* III. 572/1 The integuments.. are..highly folliculated.

2. *Entom.* Contained in a follicle or cocoon.

1856-8 W. CLARK *Van der Hoeven's Zool.* I. 404 Pupa smooth, in some folliculated.

follicule (ˈfɒlɪkjuːl). Variant of FOLLICLE.

1774 GOLDSM. *Nat. Hist.* II. ii. 37 The follicules, or the membrane covering the eggs contained in the ovary. **1848** LINDLEY *Introd. Bot.* (ed. 4) II. 19 The fruit of these plants is better understood to be a union of several follicules within a single flower.

† **folliculiferous**, *a. Obs.* -[1] [f. L. *folliculus* + -(I)FEROUS.] Bearing a follicle or follicles.

1693 *Phil. Trans.* XVII. 621 Two sorts of Folliculiferous Willows from Barbados.

folliculitis (fɒˌlɪkjuːˈlaɪtɪs). *Path.* [f. L. *folliculus* FOLLICLE + -ITIS.] Inflammation of a follicle or follicles.

1860 FOWLER *Med. Voc.*, *Folliculitis*, follicular inflammation. **1874** VAN BUREN *Dis. Genit. Org.* 77 Folliculitis sometimes appears along the urethra.

folliculose (fɒˌlɪkjuːˈləʊs), *a.* [ad. L. *folliculōsus*, f. *folliculus*: see FOLLICLE and -OSE.] **a.** Full of or containing follicles. **b.** Of the nature or appearance of a follicle.

1802 HOOPER *Quincy's Lex.-Med.*, *Folliculose gland*, one of the most simple species of gland, consisting merely of a hollow vascular membrane or follicle and an excretory duct. **18..** *Bull. Ill. State Laboratory Nat. Hist.* II. 30 (Cent. Dict.) Antheridia in folliculose bodies on the surface of separate thalli.

folliculous (fɒˈlɪkjʊləs), *a.* [f. L. *follicul-us* + -OUS.] = prec.

1828 STARK *Elem. Nat. Hist.* I. 10 Other membranes are called mucous or folliculous, because they secrete a viscid fluid. **1884** *Syd. Soc. Lex.*, *Folliculous*, having, or consisting of, follicles. Same as *Follicular.*

† **folliful**, *a. Obs.* Also 6 foliful. [f. FOLLY *sb.* + -FUL.] Full of folly or foolishness.

1549 *Compl. Scot.* xv. 87 Foliful affectionis vil be ther auen confusione quhen god pleysis. **1683** E. HOOKER *Pref. Ep. Pordage's Mystic Div.* 82 O vain, wild, pittifull, follifull, vile man! a **1763** SHENSTONE *Ess.* Wks. (1764) II. 279 The common people call wit, mirth; and fancy, folly; fanciful and folliful, they use indiscriminately.

† **follily**, *adv. Obs.* Forms: 3-5 folili, 4-6 folyly, 4-7 folily, (4 foleli), 4-5 folilich(e, 4 folyliche, 5 folilyche, 6 follilie. [ME. *foliliche*, f. *foli*, FOLLY *a.* foolish + -*liche* -LY[2].] Foolishly.

a **1300** *Cursor M.* 23326 (Cott.) þai þe sorfuller sal þat losen folili has þat le. **1393** LANGL. *P. Pl.* C. XVII. 234 To teche..how þat folke folyliche here fif wittes myspenden. c **1449** PECOCK *Repr.* II. vi. 171 Thei wolen seie sturdili and folili. **1535** STEWART *Cron. Scot.* I. 600 To quhome the Britis follilie gaif feild. **1598** STOW *Surv.* xxviii. (1603) 243 From loosing of time follilie in lust.

b. Lewdly, unchastely.

13.. [see FELTER *v.* 3 b]. c **1386** CHAUCER *Merch. T.* 159, I have my body folily dispended.

follis (ˈfɒlɪs). Pl. **folles** (-eɪz). [L.] A bronze or copper coin introduced by Diocletian in 296 A.D. and again used in Byzantine currency c 800 A.D.

1885 H. A. GRUEBER in S. Lane-Poole *Coins & Medals* iii. 60 In copper two new pieces were issued, called the follis and the denarius. **1908** W. WROTH *Imperial Byzantine Coins* I. p. lxxviii, The chief denominations are marked *M* (the follis), *K*, *I*, *E*, being pieces of 40, 20, 10, and 5 nummia. **1962** R. A. G. CARSON *Coins* 176 For both Augusti and Caesars the mints in Britain and Gaul and the Eastern mints continued to issue folles with the Genio reverse. *Ibid.* 211 Theophilus also replaced the old 40 nummia coin by a new bronze coinage of follis and half-pieces with types. **1971** *Ashmolean Mus. Rep. of Visitors 1970* 46 The Byzantine coins from the same source include a 'consular' follis of Heraclius and his father.